Y0-CGK-446

6m

SAN FRANCISCO
PUBLIC LIBRARY

REFERENCE BOOK

Not to be taken from the Library

THE UNIVERSAL REFERENCE SYSTEM

Administrative Management:
Public and Private Bureaucracy

Volume IV of the

POLITICAL SCIENCE, GOVERNMENT, AND

PUBLIC POLICY SERIES

Included in this series:

POLITICAL SCIENCE, GOVERNMENT, & PUBLIC POLICY SERIES

Volume IV

Administrative Management: Public and Private Bureaucracy

An annotated and intensively indexed compilation of significant
books, pamphlets, and articles, selected and processed by
The UNIVERSAL REFERENCE SYSTEM—a computerized
information retrieval service in the social and behavioral sciences.

Prepared under the direction of

ALFRED DE GRAZIA, GENERAL EDITOR
Professor of Social Theory in Government, New York University,
and Founder, *The American Behavioral Scientist*

CARL E. MARTINSON, MANAGING EDITOR

and

JOHN B. SIMEONE, CONSULTANT

Published by
PRINCETON RESEARCH PUBLISHING COMPANY
Princeton, New Jersey

Copyright © 1967, 1968, 1969, Princeton Information Technology,
A Division of IFI/Plenum Data Corporation

All rights in this book are reserved. No part of this book,
including the index classification system, may be used
or reproduced in any manner whatsoever without
written permission except in the case of brief
quotations embodied in critical articles and reviews.

For information, address:

UNIVERSAL REFERENCE SYSTEM
32 Nassau Street, Princeton, N.J. 08540

. . . and see the subscription information contained
on the last page of this volume.

*16.3
Un34
V.4

69 97

Standard Book No. 87635-004-X
Library of Congress Catalog Card No. 68-57820

Printed and Bound in the U.S.A. by
KINGSPORT PRESS, INC., KINGSPORT, TENN.

SAN FRANCISCO PUBLIC LIBRARY

Contents

Advisory Committee* for the UNIVERSAL REFERENCE SYSTEM

CHAIRMAN: Alfred de Grazia, *New York University*

Kenneth J. Arrow, *Stanford University*
Peter Bock, *Brooklyn College*
Kenneth E. Boulding, *University of Michigan*
Hadley Cantril, *The Institute for International Social Research, Princeton*
Bernard C. Cohen, *The University of Wisconsin*
Richard M. Cyert, *Carnegie Institute of Technology*
Karl W. Deutsch, *Harvard University*
Ward Edwards, *University of Michigan*
Luther H. Evans, *Director of International and Legal Collections, Columbia University Law Library*
Helen Fairbanks, *Woodrow Wilson School of Public and International Affairs*
Richard F. Fenno, Jr., *University of Rochester*
William J. Gore, *Indiana University*
E. de Grolier, *International Social Science Council, Paris*
Stanley Hoffmann, *Harvard University*
Thomas Hovet, *University of Oregon*
Morton A. Kaplan, *University of Chicago*
Harold D. Lasswell, *Yale University Law School*
Wayne Leys, *University of Southern Illinois*
Charles A. McClelland, *School of International Relations, University of Southern California*
Hans J. Morgenthau, *City University of New York*
Stuart S. Nagel, *University of Illinois*
Robert C. North, *Stanford University*
A. F. K. Organski, *University of Michigan*
Robert Pages, *Chef du Laboratoire de Psychologie Sociale a la Sorbonne*
E. Raymond Platig, *Director, External Research Division, U. S. Department of State*
James A. Robinson, *Ohio State University*
Stein Rokkan, *Bergen, Norway, and Chairman, International Committee on Documentation in the Social Sciences*
James N. Rosenau, *Douglass College, Rutgers University*
Giovanni Sartori, *University of Florence*
John R. Schmidhauser, *University of Iowa*
Glendon A. Schubert, Jr., *York University*
Martin Shubik, *Yale University*
David L. Sills, *The Population Council*
Herbert A. Simon, *Carnegie Institute of Technology*
J. David Singer, *Mental Health Research Institute, University of Michigan*
Richard C. Snyder, *University of California at Irvine*
Richard N. Swift, *New York University*
Joseph Tanenhaus, *University of Iowa*
S. Sidney Ulmer, *University of Kentucky*
Quincy Wright, *University of Virginia*

*Not all members advise in all areas.

Introduction to the CODEX of Administrative Management: Public and Private Bureaucracy

Books, articles, reports, and other documents that are designated to the field of *Administrative Management: Public and Private Bureaucracy* deal with the study of goal-directed organization. The Catalog of the CODEX describes 2,311 documents, and the Index contains approximately 29,000 entries.

A balance between theoretical (pure) and applied materials is intended, as well as between public (that is, state-oriented or -directed) and non-governmental organizations. The UNIVERSAL REFERENCE SYSTEM is interested here in screening and analyzing the better works that discuss human behavior under management, without regard to the substance of the tasks; the focus is upon the development of the science of administration. Formal or structural studies are not slighted, but sheerly descriptive works of passing interest are avoided. The distinctions between public and private bureaucracy, never fully persuasive, are to be made by using the Index to segregate, for example, administrative activity of any given level of government and of any type of industry. Both the external and the internal behaviors of administered groups are treated.

In contemporary capitalist societies, nearly half of the activities of industry and commerce are directly affected by public agencies; furthermore, the size of non-governmental organizations is growing to match that of the governmental agencies, and the behavior of the two is similar in many important respects. Most political scientists engaged in the study of administration find a considerable proportion of their reference material in the literature of private company management.

Exchange of ideas and practices is common, and there is a large area of mutual concern, where both governmental and non-governmental executives have to know the same concepts, laws, rules, and subject matter. For example, banking is a highly intertwined public-private business; knowledge and practice in this area are shared with little attempt to distinguish what should be known by a governmental official and what by a private banker. The behavior of the Federal Communications Commission is usually observed by students of government, but the managers of television networks must be careful to study it, too.

Indeed, if it were not for the fact that the field of public administration grew out of public law and political science, whereas business administration evolved from economics as firms grew larger and more bureaucratic, the two might well be taught and studied together rather than in distinct departments and schools of modern universities.

According to Professor Dwight Waldo, writing in the *International Encyclopedia of the Social Sciences*, public administration not only overlaps the areas of general and business administration, but also there is a "tendency to merge its activities and interests with related activities and interests under the broader term *public affairs.*" This occurs because of a reaction against the sheer descriptive detail to which conventional public administration reduces itself, and from the realization that public administration cannot clearly be separated from politics. As the activities of government have expanded in scope and power, a great many important decisions have been given over to the authority of public officials of career status. Consequently, the literature of public administration is incomplete without a complement of studies dealing with governmental decisions on the highest levels. In private corporations, too, the "managerial revolution" has merged the owners and executives of business, so that the top decisions of business become the appropriate concerns of management and therefore of the literature of management. No less than 186 of the works indexed in this CODEX deal with top executives, as the Dictionary of Descriptors reveals.

It should be noted, too, that the bibliography of administrative management covers the administration of labor unions, religious organizations, interest groups, and other so-called voluntary associations. At least 110 documents fall into this category.

It is hoped that this CODEX IV will help the interdisciplinary development of the several sciences dealing with administrative behavior and move them all toward a synthesis on the general level of policy formation.

How To Use This CODEX
(Hypothetical Example is Used)

1. Frame your need as specifically as possible. (Example: "I want articles written in 1968 that deal with the activities of labor leaders and small business owners in city politics in America.")
2. Scan the Dictionary of Descriptors in this Volume, page xv and following, for URS terms that match your subject. (Example: for cities you find MUNIC and LOC/G; for labor, LABOR; for small companies, SML/CO.) Find the number of titles each Descriptor carries. For rapidity select terms having few entries; for comprehensiveness, select terms having many entries.
3. Having identified terms that match your subject, enter the Index at one of them, say SML/CO, which heads a list of works on small business. For rapid identification of highly relevant titles, search the narrow right-hand column, which contains the Critical Descriptors; these index the primary facets of a work. Even if you read every title under a Descriptor, the critical column will help you identify works of high probable value. Titles are arranged by year of publication and within each year by format: books (B), long articles (L), short articles (S), and chapters (C). The designation "N" covers serials and titles lacking dates or published over several years. The Index entry carries author, title, secondary Descriptors (which index secondary facets of the work), page of the Catalog containing full citation and annotation, and Catalog accession number. Secondary Descriptors are always arranged in the order of the Topical and Methodological Index.
4. Listings of the document would be found in fourteen

SAMPLE CATALOG LISTING

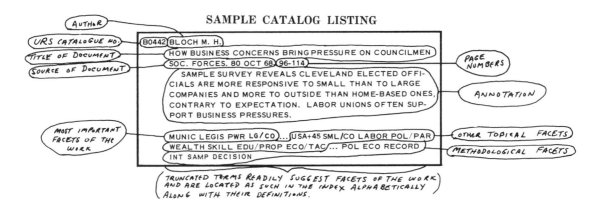

places in the Index, that is, under each of its numerous significant facets. One of them could be located in a search of "the small company in politics" as follows:

SAMPLE INDEX LISTING

5. Jot down the page numbers and the accession numbers of items that interest you and look them up in the Catalog. There you will find the full citation and a brief annotation of each work.
6. You may locate information on methods authors employ, as well as topics they discuss. Survey the methodological Descriptors in the Grazian Index, pp. xiii-xiv, and locate the relevant Descriptors in the Index of Documents. (Example: if you wished to discover whether any studies of urban business politics had employed recorded interviews, you would look up the term INT [interviews]).
7. Read the Topical and Methodological classification of terms (Grazian Index System) once or twice to grasp the ways in which ideas and groups of related ideas are compressed. The truncated Descriptors, though obvious, are defined in the dictionary of the Index.
8. Although the Catalog is arranged alphabetically by author (except for Volumes II and III), accession numbers have been retained. The major exception to alphabetical arrangement is the group of journals and unsigned articles that begin the Catalog.
9. The Catalogs of Volumes I, IV, V, VI, VII, VIII, IX, and X do not carry Descriptors.
10. The Directory of Publishers pertains to all ten CODEXes.

Concerning the
UNIVERSAL REFERENCE SYSTEM
in General

The UNIVERSAL REFERENCE SYSTEM is a computerized documentation and information retrieval system employing citations of material above a modest level of quality, appearing in all social and behavioral sciences, annotated. It is indexed by author and employs a set of Standard Descriptors that are arranged according to a master system of topics and methodological techniques, plus various Unique Descriptors.

The flow chart on page x, entitled "The Universal Reference System," shows the numerous steps taken to process documents which come from the intellectual community until they cycle back into the same community as delivered instruments of improved scholarship.

Background of the Work

The many fields of social sciences have suffered for a long time from inadequate searching systems and information storage. The rate of development of periodical and book literature is well known to be far beyond the capacities of the existing book-form document retrieval services. Thousands of new books appear each year, dealing with society and man. Thousands of journals pour forth articles. Hundreds of periodicals are founded each year.

Countries outside of the United States have gone into the social sciences, so that the need for making available foreign publications in intelligible form is ever greater. If there is a light year's distance between present capabilities and the best available service in the social sciences, there is an even greater distance to be traversed in bringing into use the material being published in languages other than English.

A vicious economic cycle is at work in the matter of information retrieval, too: Scholars and students give up research because there are no tools to search with, and therefore their demand for searching tools decreases because they have learned to get along without the materials. Thus, the standards of all the social sciences are lowered because of an anticipated lack of success in handling the problem of information retrieval. The economic risk, therefore, of an information retrieval service has to be taken into account: Many professionals are like the Bengal peasant who cannot aid in his own economic development because he cannot conceive of the nature of the problem and has learned to live as a victim outside of it.

A study in the June, 1964, issue of *The American Behavioral Scientist* magazine showed what the need is today, even before the full capabilities of new systems are appreciated. One-half of a sample of social and behavioral scientists reported that, due to inadequate bibliographic aids, they had discovered significant information on some research too late to use it, and that this information would have significantly affected the scope and nature of their research. In a number of cases, the problem of the researcher was reported to be inadequate access to pre-existing materials, and in other cases was said to be insufficient means of addressing oneself to current material.

So the current ways of information retrieval, or lack thereof, are deficient with respect both to retrospective searching and to current material, not to mention the alarming problem of access to prospective material, in the form of current research project activities and current news of scientific development in relevant categories.

The international scholarly associations centered mainly in Paris have endeavored, with help of UNESCO and other sources of aid, to bring out bibliographies and abstracting services. These services are not fully used, because of their format, their incompleteness, their lack of selectivity, their formulation in traditional and conventional terms of the social sciences (slighting the so-called inter-disciplinary subject matters in methodology), and the simple indexing that they employ. Continuous efforts are being made to solve such problems. Lately, such solutions have been sought via computerized systems. The American Council of Learned Societies, for example, has funded projects at New York University to which the computer is integral.

The Universal Reference System is endeavoring to take an immediately practical view of the literature-access problem, while designing the system so that it will remain open to advances and permit a number of alterations. One must contemplate projects leading to automatic reading and indexing; retrieval of information in the form of propositions, historical dates, and other factual materials; encyclopedic information-providing services; movement into other scientific fields joining social and natural science materials; automatized printing and reproduction of a large variety of materials in quantities ranging from individual to thousands of copies, and provision for televised or other rapid-fire communication services from information retrieval centers.

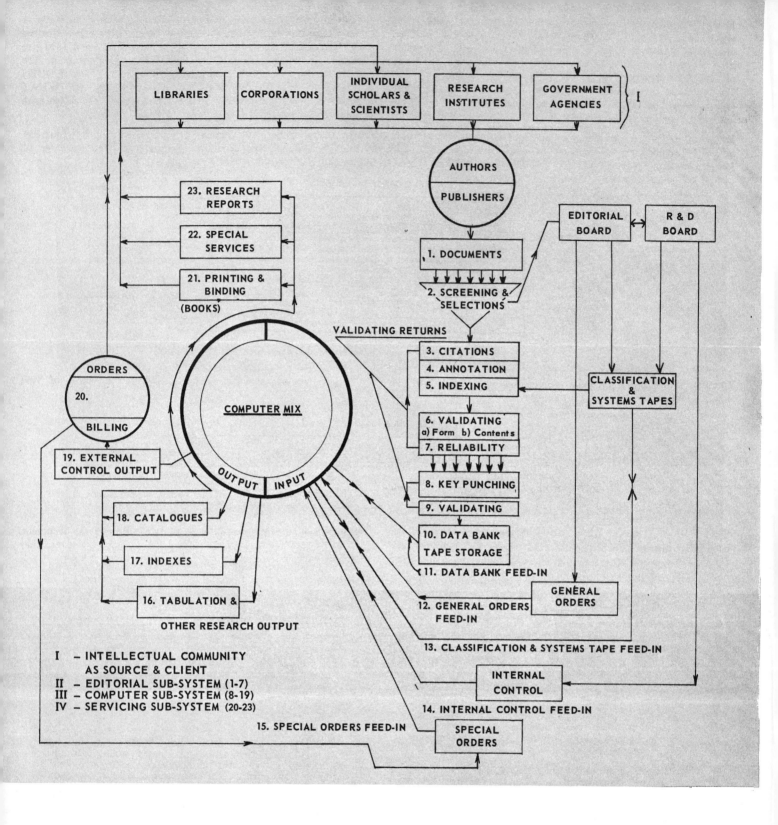

UNIVERSAL REFERENCE SYSTEM

A diagrammatic representation of the numerous steps taken to process documents which come from the intellectual community until they cycle back to the same community as pinpointed sources of information.

The Grazian Classification and Indexing System

The theory behind the URS Classification System is operational. It asks the question: "Who says, 'Who does what with whom, where and when, by what means, why' and how does he know so?" This question leads to the general categories and subcategories of the system, which is presented in its logical form on pages xii-xiv, along with the truncated terms used in the computerized Index of Documents. The advantage of reading the logical classification is that one will learn in a few minutes the general meaning of the truncated terms and can usually go directly and rapidly to the proper terms in the Index.

The Grazian classification cuts across various disciplines of social science to call attention to the methodological aspects of works which would appear to be important to scholars in the behavioral, instrumental, positivistic tradition of philosophy and science.

The constant recourse to method also serves as a screening device for eliminating numerous documents that are purely evaluative, journalistic, nonempirical, or of an intuitive type. The Grazian index contains some 351 Standard Descriptor categories at the present time. To them are added Unique Descriptors as they occur. Some additional categories logically subtending from the existing ones will be added as time goes on. These will be expanded as part of the original coding as the need is shown. (Several categories may be altered, too, on the same grounds.) From two to four of the Standard and Unique Descriptors are selected as most important facets of the work and are indicated as Critical Descriptors. These are printed apart in the Index of Documents.

The possibilities of utilizing cross-categories are immediate. Cross-categories can be used (both by the searcher and by the creator of the index) to provide a more specialized bibliography. This Cross-Faceting can permit adjusting to changes in the interests of scientists. An almost infinite number of cross-categories is possible, of course. The user of the system will find it set up beyond any existing system to facilitate this. In the future, and upon request, complicated cross-category or multi-faceted searches will be performed by the Universal Reference System's machinery. The ultimate instrumental goal is Controlled Faceting—contractible or expansible according to need and logic.

In practice, the Standard Descriptors, the Unique Descriptors, the Critical Descriptors, the Multiple Faceting, and the Cross-Faceting are interlaced in the operations of documentary analysis and control. Thus, to allow for gaps in the system, to go along with conventional practice, to employ more specialized terms, and to carry important proper nouns, the indexing rules permit the documentary analyst to add Unique Descriptors to the Standard Descriptors already taken from the master list. There are 63 of these in the *Codex of Legislative Process, Representation, and Decision-Making*. The total number of descriptors finally averaged 13 per item.

Some persons have inquired whether it might be useful to print out the whole descriptor rather than a truncated term. Several reasons arbitrate against this procedure, at least for the present. In most cases there is really no single term for which the printed-out truncated descriptor is the symbol. Most Standard Descriptors stand for several synonymous words and related ideas. Printing out the full descriptor *word* would be deluding in many cases, leading searchers to believe a word has only its face meaning.

Moreover, if all truncated descriptors were spelled out, the search time (after the first few searches) would be extended greatly since the eye would have to cover much more lettering and space. Furthermore, the size of the CODEX would be at least tripled, for the space provided for permuting would have to be open enough to carry the longest, not the average, words. There are other technical difficulties.

The repetition of numerous descriptors following each entry in the Index of Documents serves the purpose of targeting the search precisely. The richness of descriptors also postpones the moment of returning to the catalogue and thus enlarges the marginal utility of the first resort to the catalogue.

The intensive indexing of each document, which ranges from 10 to 20 entries, serves a purpose. Intensive indexing permits a document to exhibit all of its important facets to the searcher. The ratio of index carriage to title carriage is here termed the "carriage ratio." The carriage ratio of the URS is much higher than that of most bibliographies. The magnitude of the difference shows the meaning of high intensity indexing. Under other systems, unlike the URS CODEX, a topic is understated in the index. And, less obviously, topics other than the one carried as a flag in the title are sunk into oblivion; thus "Relations Between France and Indochina," which may be a valuable work on questions of economic development, would probably not be indexed on that question at all.

To sum up, the URS, when used as in this CODEX, thoroughly exposes the facets of a listed document. It makes the document thoroughly *retrievable*.

Also under consideration are suggestions to eliminate (or suppress) more of the descriptors. What is the optimal number? It is difficult to say, *a priori*. Experience and experiment will tell, over time. Meanwhile, the Critical Descriptors offer a researcher the "fast search," if he pleases. The more numerous group of descriptors in the final column offers a more complete faceting.

The search time of a researcher should be an important concern of a bibliographer. Search time begins to run, of course, with the knowledge of and access to a work that probably covers a searcher's need. It runs, too, with the ingenuity of the searcher's phrasing of his need. Then it runs with the presence of the works needed in the list searched; a missing document can be translated into lost time. An index saves time, too, when the term searched is the term under which a document is indexed; the need to compromise between detailed vocabularies and generalized ones is evident: it can reasonably be argued that more time is lost in research in social science in getting on the same semantic beam than in solving substantive problems of the "real world." Finally, the structure of an index should lessen search time while permitting a rich search.

Research and experimentation are in order, and it is hoped that a by-product of the initial publications of the Universal Reference System will be an increased stimulation of research into research procedures with respect to the URS' problems and to those of other reference systems.

Topical and Methodological Index (Grazian Index System)

The truncated descriptors (left of each column) and their expanded definitions (right of each column) that follow were employed in systematically computerizing the topics and methods of the Social and Behavioral Sciences. Truncated descriptors that are underscored in the listing that follows have not been carried in the left-hand index entry column of this CODEX; several others (denoted by a double underscore) have been entirely eliminated from this CODEX. Fuller definitions are included in the Index of Documents. So are proper names, place names, organization names, and incidents.

I. TOPICS

1. TIME—SPACE—CULTURE INDEX: Cultural-temporal location of subject.

   Centuries covered (e.g., -4; 14-19; 20)

PREHIST	Prehistoric.
MEDIT-7	Mediterranean and Near East, pre-Islamic.
PRE/AMER	Pre-European Americas.
CHRIST-17C	Christendom to 1700.
AFR	Sub-Sahara Africa.
ASIA	China, Japan, Korea.
S/ASIA	India, Southeast Asia, Oceania, except European settlements.
ISLAM	Islamic world.
MOD/EUR	Europe, 1700 to 1918, including European settlements.
USA-45	USA, 1700 to 1945.
WOR-45	Worldwide to 1945.
L/A+17C	Latin America since 1700.
EUR+WWI	Europe, 1918 to present, including colonies, but excluding Communist countries.
COM	Communist countries.
USA+45	USA since 1945.
WOR+45	Worldwide since 1945.
FUT	Future.
SPACE	Outer space.
UNIV	Free of historical position.
SEA	Locale of activity is aquatic.
AIR	Locale of activity is aerial.

   (Nations are readily identifiable.)

2. INSTITUTIONAL INDEX: (or subject treated).

   A. General

SOCIETY	Society as a whole.
CULTURE	Cultural patterns.
STRUCT	Social structure.
CONSTN	Constitution. Basic group structure.
LAW	Sanctioned practices, enforced ethics in a community.
ELITES	A power-holding group.
INTELL	Intelligentsia.
SOC/INTEG	Social integration.
STRATA	Social strata.
CLIENT	Clients.

   B. Economic type

ECO/UNDEV	Developing countries.
ECO/DEV	Developed countries.

   C. Economic function

AGRI	Agriculture, including hunting.
R+D	Research and development organization.
FINAN	Financial services.
INDUS	All or most industry.
COM/IND	Communications industry.
CONSTRUC	Construction and building.
DIST/IND	Distributive system: Includes transportation, warehousing.
EXTR/IND	Extractive industry.
MARKET	Marketing system.
PROC/MFG	Processing or manufacturing.
SERV/IND	Service industry.

   D. Organizations

SML/CO	Small company: 50 employees or less.
LG/CO	Company of more than 50 employees.
LABOR	Labor unions.
PROF/ORG	Professional organizations, including guilds.
PUB/INST	Habitational institutions: hospitals, prisons, sanitariums, etc.
POL/PAR	Political party.
SCHOOL	School (except University).
ACADEM	Higher learning.
PERF/ART	Performing arts groupings.

SECT	Church, sect, religious group.
FAM	Family.
KIN	Kinship groups.
NEIGH	Neighborhood.
LOC/G	Local governments.
MUNIC	Cities, villages, towns.
PROVS	State or province.
NAT/G	National governments.
FACE/GP	Acquaintance group: face-to-face association.
VOL/ASSN	Voluntary association.
INT/ORG	International organizations.

3. ORGANIC OR INTERNAL STRUCTURE INDEX: Sub-groupings or substructures treated.

CONSULT	Consultants.
FORCES	Armed forces and police.
DELIB/GP	Conferences, committees, boards, cabinets.
LEGIS	Legislatures.
CT/SYS	Court systems.
EX/STRUC	Formal executive establishment.
TOP/EX	Individuals holding executive positions.
CHIEF	Chief officer of a government.
WORKER	Workers and work conditions.

4. PROCESSES AND PRACTICES: Procedures or tactics used by subject or discussed as subject.

   A. Creating and Sciencing

CREATE	Creative and innovative processes.
ACT/RES	Combined research and social action.
COMPUTER	Computer techniques.
INSPECT	Inspecting quality, output, legality.
OP/RES	Operations research.
PLAN	Planning.
PROB/SOLV	Problem-solving and decision-making.
TEC/DEV	Development and change of technology.

   B. Economizing

ACCT	Accounting, bookkeeping.
BAL/PWR	Balance of power.
BARGAIN	Bargaining, trade.
BUDGET	Budgeting, fiscal planning.
CAP/ISM	Enterprise, entrepreneurship.
DIPLOM	Diplomacy.
ECO/TAC	Economic measures or tactics.
FOR/AID	Foreign aid.
INT/TRADE	International trade.
RATION	Rationing, official control of goods or costs.
RENT	Renting.
TARIFFS	Tariffs.
TAX	Taxation.

   C. Awarding

GIVE	Giving, philanthropy.
LICENSE	Legal permit.
PAY	Paying.
RECEIVE	Receiving of welfare.
REPAR	Reparations.
TRIBUTE	Payments to dominant by minor power, racketeering.
WORSHIP	Worship, ritual.

   D. Symbolizing

DOMIN	Domination.
EDU/PROP	Education or propaganda.
LEGIT	Legitimacy.
PRESS	Printed media.
RUMOR	Rumor, gossip.
TV	Television.
WRITING	Writing.

   E. Evaluating

CONFER	Group consultation.
DEBATE	Organized collective arguments.

ETIQUET	Etiquette, fashion, manners.
PRICE	Pricing.
SENIOR	Seniority.

F. Determining

ADJUD	Judicial behavior and personality.
ADMIN	Behavior of non-top executive personnel (except armed forces).
AGREE	Agreements, treaties, compacts.
AUTOMAT	Automation.
COLONIAL	Colonialism.
CONTROL	Specific ability of power to determine achievement.
EXEC	Executive, regularized management.
FEEDBACK	Feedback phenomena.
GAMBLE	Speculative activity.
LEAD	Leading.
LOBBY	Lobbying.
NEUTRAL	Neutralism, neutrality.
PARL/PROC	Parliamentary procedures (legislative).
PARTIC	Participation: civic apathy or activity.
REGION	Regionalism.
RISK	Risk, uncertainty, certainty.
ROUTINE	Procedural and work systems.
SANCTION	Sanctions of law and social law.
TASK	A specific operation within a work setting.
TIME	Timing, time-factor.

G. Forcing

ARMS/CONT	Arms control and disarmament.
COERCE	Force and violence.
CRIME	Criminal behavior.
CROWD	Mass behavior.
DEATH	Death-related behavior.
DETER	Military deterrence.
GUERRILLA	Guerrilla warfare.
MURDER	Murder, assassination.
NUC/PWR	All uses of nuclear energy.
REV	Revolution.
SUICIDE	Suicide.
WAR	War.
WEAPON	Conventional military weapons.

H. Choosing

APPORT	Apportionment of assemblies.
CHOOSE	Choice, election.
REPRESENT	Representation.
SUFF	Suffrage.

I. Consuming

DREAM	Dreaming.
LEISURE	Unobligated time expenditures.
SLEEP	Sleep-related behavior.
EATING	Eating, cuisine.

5. RELATIONS INDEX: Relationship of individuals and/or group under discussion.

CIVMIL/REL	Civil-military relation.
GOV/REL	Relations between local or state governments and governmental agencies.
GP/REL	Relations among groups, except nations.
INT/REL	Relations among sovereign states.
INGP/REL	Relations within groups.
PERS/REL	Relations between persons; interpersonal communication.
RACE/REL	Race relations.

6. CONDITIONS AND MEASURES (of activities being discussed).

ADJUST	Social adjustment, socialization.
BAL/PAY	Balance of payments.
CENTRAL	Centralization.
CONSEN	Consensus.
COST	Costs.
DEMAND	In economic sense, a demand.
DISCRIM	Social differentiation in support of inequalities.
EFFICIENCY	Effectiveness, measures.
EQUILIB	Equilibrium (technical).
FEDERAL	Federalism.
HAPPINESS	Satisfaction and unhappiness.
ILLEGIT	Bastardy.
INCOME	Income distribution, shares, earnings.
ISOLAT	Isolation and community.
LITERACY	Ability to read and write.
MAJORITY	Behavior of major parts of grouping.
MARRIAGE	Legal wedlock.

NAT/LISM	Nationalism.
OPTIMAL	Optimality in its economic usages.
OWN	Ownership.
PEACE	Freedom from conflict or termination of hostilities.
PRIVIL	Privilege, parliamentary.
PRODUC	Productivity.
PROFIT	Profit in economic sense.
RATIONAL	Instrumental rationality.
STRANGE	Estrangement or outsiders.
TOTALISM	Totalitarianism.
UTIL	Utility as in economics.
UTOPIA	Envisioned general social conditions.

7. PERSONALITY INDEX: Behavior of actors to their actions.

HABITAT	Ecology.
HEREDITY	Genetic influences on personality.
DRIVE	Drive, morale, or antithesis.
PERCEPT	Perception.
PERSON	Personality and human nature.
ROLE	Role, reference group feelings, cross-pressures.
AGE	Age factors in general.
AGE/C	Infants and children.
AGE/Y	Youth, adolescence.
AGE/A	Adults.
AGE/O	Old.
SEX	Sexual behavior.
SUPEGO	Conscience, superego, and responsibility.
RIGID/FLEX	Rigidity/flexibility; exclusive/inclusive.
ATTIT	Attitudes, opinions, ideology.
DISPL	Displacement and projection.
AUTHORIT	Authoritarianism, as personal behavior.
BIO/SOC	Bio-social processes: drugs, psychosomatic phenomena, etc.
ANOMIE	Alienation, anomie, generalized personal anxiety.

8. VALUES INDEX: Basically desired (or nondesired) conditions held or believed in by subjects.

HEALTH	Well-being, bodily and psychic integrity (sickness).
KNOWL	Enlightenment (ignorance).
LOVE	Affection, friendship (hatred).
MORAL	Rectitude, morality (immorality), goodness.
PWR	Power, participation in decision-making (impotence).
RESPECT	Respect, social class attitudes (contempt, disrespect).
SKILL	Skill, practical competence (incompetence).
WEALTH	Wealth, access to goods and services (poverty).
ALL/VALS	All, or six or more of above.
ORD/FREE	Security, order, restraint (change, experience, freedom).
SOVEREIGN	Sovereignty; home-rule.

9. IDEOLOGICAL TOPIC: Ideology discussed in work.

CATHISM	Roman Catholicism.
CONSERVE	Traditionalism.
FASCISM	Fascism.
LAISSEZ	Laissez-faire-ism (old liberal).
MARXISM	Marxism.
MYSTICISM	Mysticism.
NEW/LIB	New Liberalism (welfare state).
OBJECTIVE	Value-free thought.
PACIFISM	Pacifism.
PLURISM	Socio-political order of autonomous groups.
POPULISM	Majoritarianism.
RELATISM	Relativism.
SOCISM	Socialism.
TECHRACY	Socio-political order dominated by technicians.
ALL/IDEOS	Three or more of above.

II. METHODOLOGY (What techniques are dealt with by the author and what techniques the document employs or describes).

10. ETHICAL STANDARDS APPLIED BY AUTHOR

ETHIC	Personal ethics (private and professional).
LAW/ETHIC	Ethics of laws and court processes.

POLICY Treats ethics of public policies.

11. IDEOLOGY OF AUTHOR (where clear).

ANARCH	Anarchism.
CATH	Roman Catholic.
CONVNTL	Conventional: unsystematic acceptance of values in common currency.
FASCIST	Totalitarian with nonworker, upper class, or leader cult.
MAJORIT	Majoritarian, consensual.
MARXIST	Marxist Communist in viewpoint.
MYSTIC	Otherworldly, mystical.
OLD/LIB	Old liberal, laissez-faire.
PACIFIST	Pacifist
PLURIST	Pluralist.
REALPOL	Realpolitik, Machiavellism.
RELATIV	Relativist.
SOCIALIST	Socialist (except Communist).
TECHNIC	Technocratic.
TRADIT	Traditional or aristocratic.
WELF/ST	Welfare state advocate.

12. FIELD INDEX: Fields, discipline, or methodological approach of document.

ART/METH	Fine Arts, Graphics, Performing Arts, Aesthetics.
CRIMLGY	Criminology.
DECISION	Decision-making and gaming (game theory).
ECO	Economics and economic enterprise.
ECOMETRIC	Econometrics, mathematical economics.
EPIST	Epistemology, sociology of knowledge.
GEOG	Demography and geography.
HEAL	Health sciences.
HIST	History (including current events).
HUM	Methods of the "Humanities." Literary analysis.
INT/LAW	International law. Uses legal approach.
JURID	Uses legal approach. Concerns largely the laws.
MGT	Administrative management.
PHIL/SCI	Scientific method and Philosophy of Science.
POL	Deals with political and power process.
PSY	Psychology.
SOC	Sociology.
SOC/WK	Social services.

13. CONCEPTS: Document is noteworthy for systematic and/or basic treatment of:

CONCPT	Subject-matter abstract concepts.
METH/CNCPT	Methodological concepts.
MYTH	Treats assumptions unconsciously accepted, fictions.
NEW/IDEA	Word inventions, new concepts and ideas.

14. LOGIC, MATHEMATICS, AND LANGUAGE

LOG	Logic: syntax, semantics, pragmatics.
MATH	Mathematics.
STAT	Statistics.
AVERAGE	Mean, average behaviors.
PROBABIL	Probability, chance.
MODAL	Modal types, fashions.
CORREL	Correlations (statistical).
REGRESS	Regression analysis.
QUANT	Nature and limits of quantification.
CLASSIF	Classification, typology, set theory.
INDICATOR	Numerical indicator, index weights.
LING	Linguistics.
STYLE	The styles and terminology of scientific communications.

15. DIRECT OBSERVATION

OBS	Trained or participant observation.
SELF/OBS	Self-observation, psycho-drama.
OBS/ENVIR	Social milieu of and resistances to observation.
CONT/OBS	Controlled direct observation.
RECORD	Recording direct observations. (But not content analysis, q.v.)

16. INTERVIEWS

INT	Interviews, short or long, in general.
STAND/INT	Standardized interviews.
DEEP/INT	Depth interviews.
UNPLAN/INT	Impromptu interview.
RESIST/INT	Social resistance to interviewing.
REC/INT	Recording, systematizing, and analyzing of interviews.

17. QUESTIONNAIRES

QU	Questionnaires in general, short or long.
DEEP/QU	Depth questionnaires, including projective or probing.
QU/SEMANT	Semantic and social problems of questionnaires.
SYS/QU	Systematizing and analyzing questionnaires.

18. TESTS AND SCALES

TESTS	Theory and uses of tests and scales.
APT/TEST	Aptitude tests.
KNO/TEST	Tests for factual knowledge, beliefs, or abilities.
PERS/TEST	Personality tests.
PROJ/TEST	Projective tests.

19. UNIVERSES AND SAMPLING

CENSUS	Census.
SAMP	Sample survey in general.
SAMP/SIZ	Sizes and techniques of sampling.
NET/THEORY	Systematic group-member connections analysis.

20. ANALYSIS OF TEMPORAL SEQUENCES

BIOG	Biography, personality development, and psychoanalysis.
HIST/WRIT	Historiography.
TIME/SEQ	Chronology and genetic series of men, institutions, processes, etc.
TREND	Projection of trends, individual and social.
PREDICT	Prediction of future events.

21. COMMUNICATION CONTENT ANALYSIS

CON/ANAL	Quantitative content analysis.
DOC/ANAL	Conventional analysis of records or documents.

22. INFORMATION STORAGE AND RETRIEVAL

OLD/STOR	Conventional libraries, books, records, tape, film.
THING/STOR	Artifacts and material evidence.
COMPUT/IR	Mechanical and electronic information retrieval.

23. GRAPHICS AND AUDIO-VISUAL TECHNIQUES: Used in the research and/or in the presentation.

AUD/VIS	Film and sound, photographs.
CHARTS	Graphs, charts, diagrams, maps.
EXHIBIT	Exhibits.
PROG/TEAC	Programmed instruction.

24. COMPARATIVE ANALYSIS INDEX

METH/COMP	Of methods, approaches, styles.
IDEA/COMP	Of ideas, methods, ideologies.
PERS/COMP	Of persons.
GP/COMP	Of groups.
GOV/COMP	Of governments.
NAT/COMP	Of nations.

25. EXPERIMENTATION

LAB/EXP	Laboratory or strictly controlled groups.
SOC/EXP	"Social" experimentation.
HYPO/EXP	Hypothetical, intellectual constructs.

26. MODELS: Intellectual representations of objects or processes.

SIMUL	Scientific models.
ORG/CHARTS	Blueprints and organization charts.
STERTYP	Stereotypes, ideologies, utopias.
GAME	Game or Decision Theory models.

27. GENERAL THEORY

GEN/LAWS	Systems based on substantive relations, such as idealism, economic determinism.
GEN/METH	Systems based on methodology, such as cycles, pragmatism, sociometry.

28. SPECIAL FORMATS

ANTHOL	Anthology, symposium, collection.
BIBLIOG	Bibliography over fifty items, or of rare utility.
BIBLIOG/A	Contains bibliography over fifty items or of rare utility, annotated.
DICTIONARY	Dictionary.
INDEX	List of names or subjects.
METH	Document heavily emphasizes methodology (Part II) rather than topics (Part I).
T	Textbook.

Dictionary of Descriptors in this Volume

(Incorporating List of Frequency of Descriptors in Index)

This Dictionary contains all Descriptors employed in this volume, and thus enables you to identify in a few minutes every Descriptor that may pertain to your subject. The frequency list calls your attention to the number of works carried under each Descriptor and assists you in determining the term at which you may most advantageously begin your search in the Index. A modest system of cross-references may be found in the Dictionary that appears in the Index.

CATALOGUE OF DOCUMENTS

0001 AMERICAN POLITICAL SCIENCE REVIEW.
WASHINGTON: AMER POL SCI ASSOC.
QUARTERLY JOURNAL SINCE 1906 WHICH DEALS WITH GOVERNMENT, POLITICS, LAW, AND INTERNATIONAL RELATIONS. CONTAINS EXTENSIVE BOOK REVIEW SECTION AND BIBLIOGRAPHIES OF BOOKS, SERIALS, GOVERNMENT DOCUMENTS, PAMPHLETS, AND DOCTORAL DISSERTATIONS. CLASSIFIED IN FIVE CATEGORIES: POLITICAL THEORY, AMERICAN POLITICS, COMPARATIVE PUBLIC ADMINISTRATION, COMPARATIVE GOVERNMENT, AND INTERNATIONAL POLITICS.

0002 CONGRESSIONAL MONITOR.
WASHINGTON: US GOVERNMENT.
DAILY PROGRAM OF CONGRESS. LISTS SCHEDULED ACTION IN BOTH HOUSES, SPEAKERS, COMMITTEE MEETINGS. CONTAINS INDEX OF ACTIVE LEGISLATION AND CHARTS WHICH FOLLOW COURSE OF MEASURES THROUGH CONGRESS AND PRESIDENT'S APPROVAL. ACTIVE LEGISLATION LISTED ALPHABETICALLY BY TOPIC.

0003 INTERNATIONAL BIBLIOGRAPHY OF ECONOMICS.
LONDON: TAVISTOCK.
ANNUAL PUBLICATION, BEGUN IN 1925, WHICH LISTS WORLDWIDE PUBLICATIONS PERTAINING TO ECONOMICS. ENTRIES CLASSIFIED BY SUBJECT; CONTAINS BOOKS, ARTICLES, REPORTS, AND ALL TYPES OF SOURCES EXCEPT UNPUBLISHED MATERIALS. AUTHOR INDEX. TOPICS INCLUDE ECONOMIC HISTORY AND THOUGHT, MONEY AND FINANCE, PUBLIC ECONOMY, INCOME AND INCOME DISTRIBUTION, SOCIAL ECONOMICS AND POLICY, AND PRODUCTION.

0004 INTERNATIONAL REVIEW OF ADMINISTRATIVE SCIENCES.
BRUSSELS: INTL INST OF ADMIN SCI.
QUARTERLY PUBLICATION, BEGUN IN 1928. CONTAINS SECTION REVIEWING BOOKS AND SERIALS. BIBLIOGRAPHIC SECTION DIVIDED INTO ONE REVIEWING BOOKS RELATING TO PROBLEMS AND ASPECTS OF ADMINISTRATION, AND ONE CONTAINING LIST OF PERIODICAL ARTICLES CLOSELY RELATED TO INTERNATIONAL RELATIONS. LIST IS ALPHABETICAL BY AUTHOR. INCLUDES WESTERN-LANGUAGE SOURCES.

0005 JOURNAL OF POLITICS.
NEW YORK: SOUTHERN POL SCI ASSN.
QUARTERLY PUBLICATION, BEGUN IN 1939, WHICH DEALS WITH POLITICS, GOVERNMENT, AND LAW PRIMARILY IN US. INCLUDES FOREIGN COUNTRIES. CONTAINS BOOK REVIEW SECTION.

0006 REVIEW OF POLITICS.
SOUTH BEND: U OF NOTRE DAME.
QUARTERLY PUBLICATION WITH BOOK REVIEWS. FIRST PUBLISHED 1939, IT DEALS WITH POLITICS, GOVERNMENT, AND FOREIGN AFFAIRS.

0007 THE AMERICAN CITY.
NEW YORK: BUTTENHEIM PUB. CORP.
A MONTHLY MAGAZINE OF MUNICIPAL MANAGEMENT AND ENGINEERING FIRST ISSUED IN 1885. EACH ISSUE CONTAINS A BIBLIOGRAPHY OF MUNICIPAL AND CIVIC PUBLICATIONS TOPICALLY ARRANGED. BOTH CRITICALLY AND DESCRIPTIVELY ANNOTATED.

0008 BIBLIO, CATALOGUE DES OUVRAGES PARUS EN LANGUE FRANCAISE DANS LE MONDE ENTIER.
LONDON: FABER AND FABER.
MONTHLY CATALOGUE OF FRENCH PUBLICATIONS ON VARIOUS SUBJECTS. ITEMS CROSS-REFERENCED BY TITLE, AUTHOR, AND SUBJECT.

0009 WHITAKER'S CUMULATIVE BOOKLIST.
LONDON: J WHITAKER & SONS, LTD.
COMPLETE LIST OF ALL BOOKS PUBLISHED IN UNITED KINGDOM FOR EACH YEAR, LISTING ALPHABETICAL DETAILS ON AUTHOR, TITLE, SUB-TITLE, SIZE, NUMBER OF PAGES, PRICE, DATE, CLASSIFICATION, AND PUBLISHER. IN ADDITION CONTAINS SPECIAL CLASSIFIED LIST GIVING DETAILS OF EACH BOOK UNDER AUTHOR IN SEPARATE CLASSIFICATIONS. FIRST PUBLISHED IN 1924.

0010 BULLETIN OF THE PUBLIC AFFAIRS INFORMATION SERVICE.
NEW YORK: H W WILSON.
BEGAN 1915 AND ISSUED WEEKLY; ALSO FIVE CUMULATED ISSUES AND AN ANNUAL COMPILATION. SUBJECT INDEX TO CURRENT LITERATURE IN POLITICAL SCIENCE, GOVERNMENT, ECONOMICS, AND SOCIAL SCIENCES. INDEXES BOOK, PAMPHLETS, DOCUMENTS, AND ARTICLES FROM OVER 1,000 ENGLISH-LANGUAGE PERIODICALS.

0011 CIVIL SERVICE JOURNAL.
WASHINGTON: US GOVERNMENT.
QUARTERLY FIRST PUBLISHED BY THE US CIVIL SERVICE COMMISSION IN 1960. EACH ISSUE CONTAINS FIVE TO EIGHT OF INTEREST TO THE CIVIL SERVICE WORKING PUBLIC, AND SECTIONS ON LEGAL DECISIONS AND LEGISLATION. EACH ISSUE INCLUDES A ONE OR TWO PAGE ANNOTATED BIBLIOGRAPHY OF PRIMARILY GOVERNMENT-PUBLISHED MATERIALS ON EMPLOYEE TRAINING, PERSONNEL MANAGEMENT, AND RELATED TOPICS.

0012 CUMULATIVE BOOK INDEX.
NEW YORK: H W WILSON.
ISSUED MONTHLY, CUMULATED BIANNUALLY, ANNUALLY, BIENNIALLY, AND EVERY FOUR TO FIVE YEARS. BEGAN PUBLICATION IN 1898 TO SUPPLEMENT "US CATALOG." CONTAINS SOCIETY PUBLICATIONS, WORKS OF PERSONAL AUTHORS, AND GOVERNMENT DOCUMENTS. SINCE 1925, THE INDEX HAS INCLUDED BOOKS IN THE ENGLISH LANGUAGE PUBLISHED OUTSIDE THE US.

0013 DEUTSCHE BIBLIOGRAPHIE, HALBJAHRESVERZEICHNIS.
FRANKFURT: BUCHHANDLER VEREIN.
SEMIANNUAL COMPILATION OF "DEUTSCHE BIBLIOGRAPHIE" IN ALPHABETICAL LISTING BY AUTHOR AND SUBJECT. PUBLISHED SINCE 1951.

0014 HANDBOOK OF LATIN AMERICAN STUDIES.
GAINESVILLE: U OF FLA PR.
ANNOTATED ANNUAL GUIDE LISTING ABOUT 4,000 BOOKS AND ARTICLES ON ALL SUBJECTS. ITEMS ARRANGED BY SUBJECT AND BY COUNTRY. FIRST PUBLISHED 1935.

0015 JOURNAL OF PUBLIC ADMINISTRATION: JOURNAL OF THE ROYAL INSTITUTE OF PUBLIC ADMINISTRATION.
LONDON: ROYAL INST OF PUB ADMIN.
QUARTERLY JOURNAL FIRST PUBLISHED IN 1923. CONTAINS A FAIRLY EXTENSIVE CRITICAL BOOK REVIEW SECTION AND A QUARTERLY REVIEW OF RECENT PUBLICATIONS WITH DESCRIPTIVE ANNOTATIONS. THIS LATTER SECTION LISTS 30 RECENT WORKS. INCLUDES ALSO A LISTING OF NEW GOVERNMENT PUBLICATIONS IN THE FIELD. ALTHOUGH WORKS ARE IN ENGLISH THEY HAVE AN INTERNATIONAL SCOPE.

0016 LOCAL GOVERNMENT SERVICE.
LONDON: NATL ASSN LOC GOVT OFFS.
OFFICIAL JOURNAL OF THE NATIONAL ASSOCIATION OF LOCAL GOVERNMENT OFFICERS, FIRST PUBLISHED IN 1920. ISSUED MONTHLY WITH A BRIEF ANNOTATED BIBLIOGRAPHY OF WORKS IN GOVERNMENT AND SOCIOLOGY.

0017 THE MANAGEMENT REVIEW.
NEW YORK: AMER MANAGEMENT ASSN.
MONTHLY PUBLICATION, FIRST PUT OUT BY AMERICAN MANAGEMENT ASSOCIATION IN 1914. INCLUDES SURVEY OF BOOKS FOR EXECUTIVES, CRITICAL REVIEWS OF 10-22 RECENT WORKS, AND A LISTING OF RECENT PUBLICATIONS RECEIVED FROM PUBLISHERS. BOOKS COVER TOPICS ON LABOR RELATIONS AND HUMAN RELATIONS, ARBITRATION OF LABOR DISPUTES, UNION-MANAGEMENT RELATIONS, ETC.

0018 MARKETING INFORMATION GUIDE.
WASHINGTON: US BUS + DEF SERV.
MONTHLY PUBLICATION LISTING CURRENT US GOVERNMENT AND NONGOVERNMENTAL BOOKS, PAMPHLETS, REPORTS, AND ARTICLES ON MARKETING AND DISTRIBUTION. ENTRIES ARRANGED BY SUBJECT AND ANNOTATED. INCLUDES CUMULATIVE INDEX TWICE A YEAR. FIRST PUBLISHED 1954.

0019 PUBLIC ADMINISTRATION ABSTRACTS AND INDEX OF ARTICLES.
NEW DELHI: INDIAN INST PUB ADMIN.
MONTHLY PUBLICATION, FIRST ISSUED 1957, INDEXING ARTICLES FROM SELECTED ENGLISH-LANGUAGE JOURNALS PERTAINING TO PUBLIC ADMINISTRATION. PRIMARY EMPHASIS ON UNDERDEVELOPED AREAS.

0020 PUBLISHERS' TRADE LIST ANNUAL.
NEW YORK: RR BOWKER.
ANNUAL COMPILATION OF CATALOGS OF MOST US PUBLISHERS AND SOME CANADIAN. FIRST PUBLISHED 1873.

0021 READERS GUIDE TO PERIODICAL LITERATURE.
NEW YORK: H W WILSON.
AUTHOR, TITLE, AND SUBJECT INDEXING OF GENERAL AND POPULAR MAGAZINES IN DICTIONARY CATALOGUING. COVERS PUBLICATIONS SINCE 1900 WITH MANY CROSS REFERENCES. ANNUAL PUBLICATION SINCE 1905. INDEXES ARTICLES FROM OVER 100 PERIODICALS.

0022 REVUE FRANCAISE DE SCIENCE POLITIQUE.
PARIS: PR UNIV DE FRANCE.
FRENCH QUARTERLY FIRST PUBLISHED IN 1951, CONTAINS SECTION DEVOTED TO CRITICAL REVIEWS OF RECENT IMPORTANT PUBLICATIONS IN POLITICAL SCIENCE AND SECTION LISTING RECENT PUBLICATIONS RECEIVED BY JOURNAL. CONTAINS ALSO LISTING OF BRITISH COMMONWEALTH POLITICAL SCIENCE REFERENCE WORKS AND JOURNALS.

0023 SUBJECT GUIDE TO BOOKS IN PRINT: AN INDEX TO THE PUBLISHERS' TRADE LIST ANNUAL.
NEW YORK: RR BOWKER.
ARRANGED ALPHABETICALLY BY SUBJECT. BASICALLY FOLLOWS THE SUBJECT HEADINGS SET UP BY THE LIBRARY OF CONGRESS, WITH EXTENSIVE CROSS REFERENCES. ANNUAL PUBLICATION.

0024 SUMMARIES OF SELECTED JAPANESE MAGAZINES.
WASHINGTON: US GOVERNMENT.
ISSUED BY US EMBASSY. WEEKLY TRANSLATIONS AND SUMMARIES OF ARTICLES FROM LEADING JAPANESE MAGAZINES ON ALL SUBJECTS. FIRST PUBLISHED IN 1964.

0025 THE JAPAN SCIENCE REVIEW: LAW AND POLITICS: LIST OF BOOKS AND ARTICLES ON LAW AND POLITICS.
TOKYO: UNION JAP SOC LAWS + POL.
DESIGNED TO INTRODUCE FOREIGN SCHOLARS TO CURRENT WORKS IN JAPANESE LAW AND POLITICS. FIRST PUBLISHED IN 1956 AND PUBLISHED ANNUALLY THROUGH 1960. SECTIONS ON LEGAL HISTORY AND PHILOSOPHY; COMPARATIVE LAW; CONSTITUTION; ADMINISTRA-

TIVE AND INTERNATIONAL LAW; CIVIL LAW; COMMERCIAL AND CRIM-
INAL LAW; POLITICS AND INTERNATIONAL POLITICS; SOCIOLOGY
OF LAW.

0026 ECONOMIC LIBRARY SELECTIONS.
BALTIMORE: JOHNS HOPKINS PRESS.
QUARTERLY ANNOTATED LISTING OF ECONOMICS BOOKS PUBLISHED
IN ENGLISH. FIRST ISSUED IN 1957, SELECTIONS LIST ABOUT 160
NEW PUBLICATIONS IN EACH ISSUE. TOPICALLY CLASSIFIED.

0027 NEUE POLITISCHE LITERATUR; BERICHTE UBER DAS INTERNATIONALE
SCHRIFTTUM ZUR POLITIK.
FRANKFURT: EUROPAISCHE VERLAGS, 1956.
MONTHLY GERMAN PERIODICAL TREATING ALL ASPECTS OF NATION-
AL AND INTERNATIONAL POLITICS. CONTAINS EXTENSIVE BOOK RE-
VIEW SECTION OF LATEST BOOKS PUBLISHED IN WESTERN WORLD.

0028 PERSONNEL ADMINISTRATION: THE JOURNAL OF THE SOCIETY FOR
PERSONNEL ADMINISTRATION.
WASHINGTON: PERSONNEL ADMIN.
DESIGNED TO PROVIDE INFORMATION ABOUT RESEARCH ON HUMAN
BEHAVIOR IN WORK SITUATION AND VIEWPOINTS ON MAJOR ISSUES
IN PERSONNEL MANAGEMENT. CRITICAL BOOK REVIEW SECTION IN
ADDITION TO EXTENSIVELY ANNOTATED SELECTION OF RECENT PUBLI-
CATIONS. FIRST PUBLISHED IN 1938; BIMONTHLY PUBLICATION.

0029 SUBJECT GUIDE TO BOOKS IN PRINT; AN INDEX TO THE PUBLISHERS'
TRADE LIST ANNUAL.
NEW YORK: RR BOWKER.
ANNUAL PUBLICATION SINCE 1957 LISTING BOOKS-IN-PRINT FOR
CURRENT YEAR. ITEMS ARRANGED BY SUBJECT WITH EXTENSIVE
CROSS REFERENCES.

0030 PERSONNEL.
NEW YORK: AMER MANAGEMENT ASSN.
BIMONTHLY PERIODICAL CONCERNED WITH MANAGEMENT OF PEOPLE
AT WORK. INCLUDES BOOK REVIEW SECTION OF CURRENT PUBLI-
CATIONS.

0031 BUSINESS LITERATURE.
NEWARK: NEWARK PUBLIC LIB.
DESCRIPTIVE ANNOTATIONS OF BUSINESS LITERATURE. ISSUED
TEN TIMES YEARLY, WITH A SINGLE SPECIFIC TOPIC COVERED IN
EACH ISSUE.

0032 FINANCIAL INDEX.
NEW YORK: FINANCIAL INDEX CO.
ISSUED WEEKLY, WITH QUARTERLY CUMULATIONS, BEGINNING MAY,
1960. INDEXES ARTICLES FROM MAJOR BUSINESS, FINANCIAL, AND
TRADE MAGAZINES, NEWSPAPERS, ANALYTIC REPORTS, AND SPEECHES.
COVERS US, UK, CANADA, AND OTHERS. ARRANGED BY SUBJECT.
ABSORBED 1963 BY "FUNK AND SCOTT INDEX OF CORPORATIONS AND
INDUSTRIES."

0033 THE GOVERNMENT OF SOUTH AFRICA (VOL. II)
CAPETOWN: CENTRAL NEWS AGENCY, 1908, 423 PP.
COMPARATIVE ANALYSIS OF GOVERNMENT AGENCIES IN SOUTH AF-
RICAN COLONIES. INCLUDES MINING LAWS, COMPARISON OF COURTS,
CENSUS, RAILWAY ORGANIZATION AND FINANCES, POST OFFICE
ACCOUNTS AND ORGANIZATION, HARBOR FINANCES, DISTRIBUTION OF
GOVERNMENT FUNCTIONS, REVENUE SOURCES, EXPENDITURE COMPARI-
SONS, CIVIL SERVICE DIAGRAMS, CONSTITUTIONAL PROVISIONS FOR
HOUSES AND GOVERNOR, AND VOTING QUALIFICATION.

0034 INTERNATIONAL BIBLIOGRAPHY OF POLITICAL SCIENCE.
CHICAGO: ALDINE PUBLISHING CO, 1954.
ANNUAL LISTING SINCE 1954 OF ARTICLES, BOOKS, SERIALS,
GOVERNMENT DOCUMENTS COVERING FIELD OF POLITICAL SCIENCE AS
A WHOLE. SURVEYS OVER 1,000 JOURNALS IN ABOUT 20 LANGUAGES.
TITLES TRANSLATED INTO ENGLISH. ITEMS GROUPED INTO SIX TOP-
ICS: POLITICAL SCIENCE, POLITICAL THOUGHT, GOVERNMENT AND
PUBLIC ADMINISTRATION, GOVERNMENTAL PROCESS, INTERNATIONAL
RELATIONS, AND AREA STUDIES. 4,000 TO 5,000 ENTRIES.

0035 BIBLIOGRAFIIA DISSERTATSII: DOKTORSKIE DISSERTATSII ZA 1941-
1944 (2 VOLS.)
MOSCOW: UDARSTVENNA BIBL LENINA, 1946.
LIST OF DISSERTATIONS IN RUSSIAN UNIVERSITIES ON ALL
SUBJECTS. ARRANGED BY SUBJECT. ALSO CONTAINS AUTHOR AND
INSTITUTION INDEXES.

0036 A BIBLIOGRAPHY AND SUBJECT INDEX OF PUBLICATIONS OF FLORIDA
STATE AGENCIES.
GAINESVILLE: U OF FLORIDA LIB, 1953, 376 PP.
COVERS THE PERIOD JANUARY, 1942-DECEMBER, 1951.
LISTING IS BY AGENCIES, WITH TITLES ALPHABETIZED AND
NUMBERED CONSECUTIVELY. SUBJECT INDEX INCLUDED.

0037 LIST OF PUBLICATIONS (PERIODICAL OR AD HOC) ISSUED BY VAR-
IOUS MINISTRIES OF THE GOVERNMENT OF INDIA (3RD ED.)
NEW DELHI: LOK SABHA SECRETARIAT, 1958, 282 PP.
LISTING OF PUBLICATIONS OF ALL MINISTRIES UNDER MINIS-
TRY ISSUING MATERIAL. EVERY EFFORT IS MADE TO KEEP VOLUME
UP-TO-DATE BY ISSUING ADDENDA AND CORRIGENDA TO VOLUME
FROM TIME TO TIME. MATERIAL IS LISTED IN TABLE FORM
WITHOUT INDEXES.

0038 "A BIBLIOGRAPHICAL ESSAY ON DECISION MAKING."
ADMINISTRATIVE SCI. Q., 4 (JUNE 59), 97-121.
ESSAY DEALS WITH VARIOUS APPROACHES TO ADMINISTRATIVE
THEORY. INCLUDES REFERENCES TO OVER 100 PUBLICATIONS ON
VARIOUS FACETS OF DECISION-MAKING. CONCERNED WITH ORGANISMIC
APPROACH, ORGANIZATIONAL RELATIONSHIPS, CONTEXT OF DECISION-
MAKING, AND MANAGEMENT OF SCIENCE ORIENTATION.

0039 "THE EMERGING COMMON MARKETS IN LATIN AMERICA."
FED. RES. BANK N.Y. MON. REV., 42 (SEPT. 60), 154-60.
DISCUSSES ECONOMIC INTEGRATION PROGRAM IN LATIN AMERICA.
ANALYZES AGREEMENT TO ELIMINATE BARRIERS. APPRAISES STEPS
TAKEN TO COORDINATE INDUSTRIAL DEVELOPMENT. CONSIDERS
SIGNIFICANCE OF MONTEVIDEO TREATY IN DEVELOPMENT OF LATIN
AMERICAN COMMON MARKET. PREDICTS INCREASE IN INVESTMENTS
IN LATIN AMERICA.

0040 RECENT PUBLICATIONS ON GOVERNMENTAL PROBLEMS.
CHICAGO: JOINT REFERENCE LIBRARY, 1964.
A WEEKLY PERIODICAL CATALOGING THE MOST RECENT PUBLI-
CATIONS ON GOVERNMENTAL PROBLEMS. PUBLISHED SINCE 1932.

0041 THE SPECIAL COMMONWEALTH AFRICAN ASSISTANCE PLAN.
LONDON: COMMONWEALTH ECO COMM, 1964, 75 PP.
REPORTS THREE YEARS' OPERATIONS OF SPECIAL COMMONWEALTH
AFRICAN ASSISTANCE PLAN. NOTES BROADENING BASIS OF UK
ASSISTANCE. SHOWS TREND TOWARD INCREASE OF HELP IN
DEVELOPING NATIONS, PARTICULARLY IN AFRICA.

0042 "FURTHER READING."
SEMINAR, (AUG. 65), 3-56.
BIBLIOGRAPHY ON INCREASING EFFICIENCY IN INDIA'S
ECONOMY. INCLUDES MANAGEMENT, PERSONNEL, PERFORMANCE,
FINANCES, ETC.

0043 "FURTHER READING."
SEMINAR, (JULY 65), 39-41.
BIBLIOGRAPHY ON PRIMARY AND SECONDARY EDUCATION IN INDIA.

0044 "FURTHER READING."
SEMINAR, (MAY 65), 41-42.
BIBLIOGRAPHY "ON THE MANY FACETS OF... GOA'S CRISIS OF
TRANSITION."

0045 "FURTHER READING."
SEMINAR, (MAR. 66), 42-44.
BIBLIOGRAPHY ON URBAN DEVELOPMENT IN INDIA.

0046 "A PROPOS DES INCITATIONS FINANCIERES AUX GROUPEMENTS DES
COMMUNES: ESSAI D'INTERPRETATION."
REV. DROIT PUBLIC ET SCI. POL., (MAR.-APR. 67), 245-287.
ANALYZES NEW LEGISLATION IN FRANCE WHICH TENDED TO
FINANCIALLY ENCOURAGE THE REGROUPING OF TRADITIONAL LOCAL
POLITICAL SUBDIVISIONS. INTERPRETS THE MOTIVES, FORCES, AND
RESULTS OF THIS LEGISLATION.

0047 "RESTRICTIVE SOVEREIGN IMMUNITY, THE STATE DEPARTMENT, AND
THE COURTS."
NORTHWESTERN U. LAW REVIEW, 62 (JULY-AUG.67), 397-427.
DISCUSSES 20TH-CENTURY APPLICATION OF DOCTRINES OF IM-
MUNITY. EXAMINES INTERRLLATIONSHIP BETWEEN COURTS AND EXECU-
TIVE DEPARTMENT IN FIELD OF SOVEREIGN IMMUNITY, SHOWING EX-
TENT OF EXECUTIVE CONTROL OVER JUDICIARY. SEEKS TO DETERMINE
WHETHER JUDICIAL DEFERENCE IS CONSONANT WITH ORIGINAL DOC-
TRINES, PRESENT CONCEPTS, OR RIGHTS OF AMERICANS. SUGGESTS
SOVEREIGN IMMUNITY IS AN OUTDATED CONCEPT.

0048 JUNZ A.J. ED.
PRESENT TRENDS IN AMERICAN NATIONAL GOVERNMENT.
LONDON: HANSARD SOCIETY, 1960, 232 PP.
STUDIES BY AMERICAN SCHOLARS ON DEVELOPMENTS IN AMERICAN
GOVERNMENT IN THE FIFTIES. ESSAYS OF AMERICAN POLITICAL
THOUGHT, ELECTION AND PARTY TRENDS, THE SUPREME COURT,
CIVIL LIBERTIES, CONGRESS AND THE PRESIDENCY INCLUDED.

0049 AARON T.J.
THE CONTROL OF POLICE DISCRETION: THE DANISH EXPERIENCE.
SPRINGFIELD: THOMAS, 1966, 107 PP., LC#66-24622.
DISCUSSES INSTITUTION OF DANISH OMBUDSMAN AS REPRESENTA-
TIVE OF PEOPLE TO PRESENT THEIR COMPLAINTS, IN THIS CASE,
ABOUT POLICE BEHAVIOR. CONSIDERS APPLICABILITY TO AMERICAN
POLICE SYSTEM.

0050 ABBOT F.C.
THE CAMBRIDGE CITY MANAGER (PAMPHLET)
INDIANAPOLIS: BOBBS-MERRILL, 1951, 48 PP.
STUDY OF RELATIONS BETWEEN CITY MANAGER AND CITY COUNCIL
OF CAMBRIDGE, MASS. EXAMINES PROBLEMS STEMMING FROM DIVISION
OF AUTHORITY WITHIN THE ADMINISTRATION, 1941-49.

0051 ABEL T.
"THE ELEMENT OF DECISION IN THE PATTERN OF WAR."
AMER. SOCIOL. REV., 6 (1941), 853-859.
THE DECISION TO GO TO WAR IS NOT A SUDDEN ONE BUT MAY
OFTEN BE DECIDED YEARS BEFORE OPEN CONFLICT ACTUALLY BEGINS.
CRISIS MERELY INAUGURATES THE PHYSICAL CONFRONTATION ALREADY

KNOWN TO BE PENDING. BELIEVES SUCH FOREKNOWLEDGE COULD BE
USED TO PREVENT WARS AS WELL.

0052 ABELS J.
THE TRUMAN SCANDALS.
CHICAGO: HENRY REGNERY CO, 1956, 329 PP., LC#56-8261.
ASSERTS THAT TRUMAN ADMINISTRATION WAS THE MOST
CORRUPT IN AMERICAN HISTORY. REPORTS ON RECORDS OF COURTS
AND CONGRESSIONAL INVESTIGATIONS. DISCUSSES TAX FIXING
IN EXCHANGE FOR CAMPAIGN CONTRIBUTIONS, AND BILLIONS IN
GOVERNMENT CONTRACTS AND SURPLUS PROPERTY LADLED OUT TO
POLITICAL FRIENDS AND HACKS.

0053 ABERLE D.F.
"CHAHAR AND DAGOR MONGOL BUREAUCRATIC ADMINISTRATION: 1962-
1945."
NEW HAVEN: HRAF, 1962, 117 PP., $3.25.
PAPER.
ADAPTATION OF MONGOL GROUPS TO THE STATES OF WHICH THEY
WERE PART. ALSO COMMENTS ON NATIONALIST ATTITUDES AND
STRATIFICATION SYSTEMS IN THE TWO AREAS AS WELL AS DIS-
CUSSION ON THE BUREAUCRACIES THEMSELVES.

0054 ABERNATHY B.R.
SOME PERSISTING QUESTIONS CONCERNING THE CONSTITUTIONAL
STATE EXECUTIVE (PAMPHLET)
LAWRENCE: U KANS, GOVTL RES CTR, 1960, 94 PP.
DISCUSSES PROBLEMS OF CONSTITUTIONAL EXECUTIVE IN STATE
GOVERNMENTS OF US CAUSED BY CHANGE. QUESTIONS ABILITY OF
GOVERNMENT TO SOLVE NEW PROBLEMS AND MEET NEEDS OF CITIZENS
IN CHANGING SOCIETY. CONCERNS ROLE OF GOVERNOR, LIEUTENANT
GOVERNOR, AND ATTORNEY GENERAL AND THEIR SUPPORTING ADMINIS-
TRATIVE DEPARTMENTS.

0055 ABLARD C.D.
"EX PARTE CONTACTS WITH FEDERAL ADMINISTRATIVE AGENCIES."
AMER BAR ASSN., 47 (MAY 61), 473-476.
REPORT ON THE STATUS OF LEGISLATION PROPOSED BY THE ABA
TO RESTRICT "EX PARTE" COMMUNICATIONS IN ADMINISTRATIVE
ADJUDICATORY PROCEEDINGS. HOLDS THAT SUCH COMMUNICATIONS
HINDER DEMOCRATIC, REPRESENTATIVE PROCESSES BY GIVING UNFAIR
ADVANTAGE TO THOSE GROUPS INDULGING IN SUCH PRACTICES.

0056 ACKOFF R.L., RIVETT P.
A MANAGER'S GUIDE TO OPERATIONS RESEARCH.
NEW YORK: JOHN WILEY, 1963, 107 PP., LC#63-14115.
ACQUAINTS INDUSTRIAL EXECUTIVE WITH TASK OF OPERATIONS
RESEARCH, ITS METHODS, AND PROCESS OF ESTABLISHING
OPERATIONS RESEARCH DEPARTMENT. EXPLAINS FORM AND CONTENT
OF PROBLEMS DISCUSSED UNDER OPERATIONS RESEARCH AND ITS
RELATION TO OTHER MANAGEMENT SERVICES.

0057 ADAMS J.C., BARILE P.
THE GOVERNMENT OF REPUBLICAN ITALY (2ND ED.)
BOSTON: HOUGHTON MIFFLIN, 1966, 251 PP.
STUDIES ITALIAN FASCISM AND ITS EFFECT UPON PRESENT GOV-
ERNMENTAL POLICIES. DISCUSSES MANY ASPECTS OF STRUCTURE
OF GOVERNMENT TODAY. DEALS WITH THE CONSTITUTION, PARLIA-
MENT, PRESIDENT AND MINISTERS, ADMINISTRATION, LOCAL GOV-
ERNMENT, JUDICAL SYSTEM, PARTY SYSTEM, ECONOMY, AND LABOR
MOVEMENT. DISCUSSES IN DETAIL ITALY'S PROBLEMS IN ATTAINING
LIBERAL DEMOCRACY.

0058 ADAMS V.
THE PEACE CORPS IN ACTION.
CHICAGO: FOLLETT PUBLISHING CO, 1964, 318 PP., LC#64-23606.
OBJECTIVE REPORT OF ORIGIN, ORGANIZATION, AND DEVELOPMENT
OF PEACE CORPS. EMPHASIZES TYPE OF PEOPLE INVOLVED, THEIR
GOALS, VALUES, ETC. INCLUDES CRITICISM AND NEGATIVE ASPECTS
OF CORPS, BUT FEELS IT IS WORTHY TOOL OF FOREIGN POLICY.

0059 ADMINISTRATIVE STAFF COLLEGE
THE ACCOUNTABILITY OF GOVERNMENT DEPARTMENTS (PAMPHLET)
(REV. ED.)
HENLEY-ON-THAMES: ADMIN STAFF C, 1966, 49 PP.
DISCUSSES CONCEPT OF ACCOUNTABILITY OR PROCEDURE OF
MINISTER'S BEING CALLED UPON BY PARLIAMENT TO JUSTIFY HIS
ACTIONS OR ADVICE. INCLUDES PERSONS ACCOUNTABLE AND PROCESS
AS IT HAS DEVELOPED IN DIFFERENT DEPARTMENTS.

0060 ADRIAN C.R.
STATE AND LOCAL GOVERNMENTS: A STUDY IN THE POLITICAL
NEW YORK: MCGRAW HILL, 1960, 531 PP., LC#59-15042.
RELATES STATE AND LOCAL GOVERNMENTS TO TOTAL POLITICAL
PROCESS. EXAMINES SOCIAL AND ECONOMIC ENVIRONMENT IN WHICH
IT EXISTS. PROVIDES NECESSARY BASIC INSIGHTS INTO
AMERICAN GOVERNMENT.

0061 ADRIAN C.R.
GOVERNING OVER FIFTY STATES AND THEIR COMMUNITIES.
NEW YORK: MCGRAW HILL, 1963, 130 PP., LC#63-13132.
DISCUSSION OF STATE AND LOCAL GOVERNMENT, RELATIONS TO
FEDERAL GOVERNMENT AND COMPARISON OF SYSTEMS INCLUDING
FUNCTIONS AND STRUCTURE OF COURTS, POLITICS, LEGISLATURES,
AND EXECUTIVES.

0062 ADU A.L.
THE CIVIL SERVICE IN NEW AFRICAN STATES.
NEW YORK: FREDERICK PRAEGER, 1965, 242 PP., LC#65-12315.
DESCRIBES PROBLEMS AND PRINCIPLES RELATING TO GROWTH AND
DEVELOPMENT OF CIVIL SERVICES IN FORMER BRITISH COLONIAL
TERRITORIES. DRAWS ON EXPERIENCES IN GHANA AND OTHER STATES
OF WEST AND EAST AFRICA. DESCRIBES STRUCTURE, FUNCTION,
AND POLICY OF ADMINISTRATIVE MACHINERY.

0063 AFRICAN BIBLIOGRAPHIC CENTER
"A CURRENT VIEW OF AFRICANA: A SELECT AND ANNOTATED BIBLIO-
GRAPHICAL PUBLISHING GUIDE, 1965-1966."
AFR. BIBLIOG. CTR., SPEC. SERIES, 4 (JULY 66), 1-17.
ANNOTATED BIBLIOGRAPHICAL COLLECTION INTENDED TO COLLATE
A WIDE RANGE OF TITLES PUBLISHED BY US AND FOREIGN PUBLISH-
ING HOUSES OVER TWO-YEAR PERIOD, 1965-66, IN FIELD OF AFRI-
CAN STUDIES. COLLECTION OF 73 ENTRIES ARRANGED BY PUBLISHER,
AUTHOR INDEX, TITLE, AND SUBJECT INDEX. COMPLETE BIBLIOGRA-
PHICAL INFORMATION PLUS DESCRIPTIVE ANNOTATIONS.

0064 AGARWAL R.C.
STATE ENTERPRISE IN INDIA.
ALLAHABAD: CHAITANYA PUBL HSE, 1961, 271 PP.
ANALYZES PROBLEMS RELATING TO PUBLIC ASPECTS OF INDIA'S
CORPORATIONS, THEIR GROWTH AND OPERATIONS SINCE 1948. FEELS
PUBLIC ENTERPRISE IS PERMANENT INSTITUTION IN INDIA, BUT
CRITICIZES PROGRAM OF TOO RAPID INDUSTRIALIZATION. USES RR
AND UTILITIES INDUSTRIES TO POINT OUT GAPS AND FLAWS IN DEV-
ELOPMENT. BIBLIOGRAPHY OF SPECIFIC WORKS ON SUBJECT IN INDIA
AND UK.

0065 AHMAD M.
THE CIVIL SERVANT IN PAKISTAN.
LONDON: OXFORD U PR, 1964, 288 PP.
SOCIOLOGICAL STUDY OF PUBLIC SERVANTS IN PAKISTAN. SEEKS
TO FIND FROM WHICH SOCIAL CLASSES PUBLIC SERVANTS ARE MAINLY
DRAWN. ATTEMPTS TO ASCERTAIN ATTITUDE OF PUBLIC SERVANTS.
INVESTIGATES IN-SERVICE RELATIONS, STUDYING RELATIONSHIP
BETWEEN SUPERIOR AND SUBORDINATE AT VARIOUS LEVELS.

0066 AIKEN C.
"THE BRITISH BUREAUCRACY AND THE ORIGINS OF PARLIAMENTARY
DEMOCRACY"
AM. POL. SCI. REV., 33 (FEB. 39), 26-46.
A STUDY "OF THE FACTORS THAT ARE AT WORK IN THE DETERMI-
NATION OF BRITISH LEGISLATIVE POLICY." THE WORK OF A MINIS-
TER AS AN INDIVIDUAL IS CONSIDERED, AS WELL AS THE FUNCTION-
ING OF CABINET MINISTERS IN THEIR QUASI-CORPORATE CAPACITY
AND THE ORGANIZATION AND FUNCTIONS OF THE CIVIL SERVICE.
SERVICE.

0067 AIYAR S.P., SRINIVASAN R.
STUDIES IN INDIAN DEMOCRACY.
NEW DELHI: ALLIED PUBLISHERS, 1965, 779 PP.
COLLECTION OF DESCRIPTIVE AND ANALYTICAL ESSAYS ON PO-
LITICAL, SOCIOLOGICAL, ECONOMIC, AND CULTURAL ASPECTS OF IN-
DIAN DEMOCRACY. INTRODUCTION PROVIDES BRIEF HISTORY OF
INDIA SINCE INDEPENDENCE. CHAPTERS CLASSIFY TOPICS
INTO HISTORICAL, INSTITUTIONAL AND SOCIOLOGICAL CATE-
GORIES, WITH ESSAYS ON PUBLIC OPINION, PRESSURE GROUPS, AND
POLITICAL PARTIES.

0068 ALBI F.
TRATADO DE LOS MODOS DE GESTION DE LAS CORPORACIONES LOCALES
MADRID: AGUILAR, 1960, 771 PP.
EXAMINES MUNICIPAL PUBLIC ADMINISTRATION IN SPAIN IN ITS
LEGAL AND FUNCTIONAL ASPECTS. DISCUSSES RESPONSIBILITIES OF
MUNICIPAL GOVERNMENT AS OPPOSED TO NATIONAL GOVERNMENT,
EXPLAINING FINANCIAL AND POLITICAL OBLIGATION OF URBAN
GOVERNMENT TO MEET NEEDS OF LOCAL POPULATION. COVERS PROCESS
OF INCORPORATION AND MANAGEMENT.

0069 ALBONETTI A.
"IL SECONDO PROGRAMMA QUINQUENNALE 1963-67 ED IL BILANCIO
RICERCHE ED INVESTIMENTI PER IL 1963 DELL'ERATOM."
DR. ECON. NUCL., 4 (NO.2, 62), 163-78.
HISTORICAL APPROACH TO QUESTION OF DEVELOPMENT OF RE-
SEARCH INSTITUTE. DEALS WITH NEW PROGRAM PLANS AND RELATES
THEM TO ITALIAN ECONOMY. POINTS OUT OTHER NATIONS' NUCLEAR
POWER POLITICS.

0070 ALDERFER H.F.
NEW YORK: MCGRAW-HILL, 1964, 251 PP., $8.50.
AN OVERVIEW OF EVOLVING STRUCTURES ON A COUNTRY-BY-
COUNTRY BASIS, AND A SURVEY OF FUNCTIONS AND PROBLEMS,
WITH POLICY SUGGESTIONS.

0071 ALDERSON W.
DYNAMIC MARKETING BEHAVIOR.
HOMEWOOD: RICHARD IRWIN, 1965, 383 PP., LC#65-27839.
DISCUSSES FLOW OF INFORMATION, NEGOTIATED PRICES AND MAR-
KET DETERMINED PRICES, ADVERTISING POLICIES, CONSUMER BEHAV-
IOR, RETAILING, COOPERATION AND CONFLICT IN MARKETING CHAN-
NELS, TECHNOLOGICAL CHANGES, AND GENERAL METHODS IN MANAGE-
MENT SCIENCE.

0072 ALEXANDER R.S., CROSS J.S., CUNNINGHAM R.M.
INDUSTRIAL MARKETING.
HOMEWOOD: RICHARD IRWIN, 1956, 590 PP.
DISCUSSES PROBLEMS OF MARKETING INDUSTRIAL GOODS, INCLUD-
ING PLANNING OF PRODUCTS AND MARKETS, OUTLETS AND STRATEGY,
PRICING, DISTRIBUTION AND MARKET FINANCING, SELLING GOODS,
MANAGERIAL CONTROL, AND RELATIONS WITH GOVERNMENT.

0073 ALEXANDER T.
"SYNECTICS: INVENTING BY THE MADNESS METHOD."
FORTUNE, 72 (AUG. 65), 165-167, 190-194.
DESCRIBES WORK OF WILLIAM GORDON AND HIS CONSULTING FIRM
IN THE DEVELOPMENT OF CREATIVITY IN EXECUTIVES AND SCIEN-
TISTS THROUGH ANALOGICAL AND ASSOCIATIVE METHODS. GIVES
EXAMPLES OF METHODS USED FOR CERTAIN PROJECTS.

0074 ALEXANDER Y.
INTERNATIONAL TECHNICAL ASSISTANCE EXPERTS* A CASE STUDY OF
THE U.N. EXPERIENCE.
NEW YORK: FREDERICK PRAEGER, 1966, 223 PP., LC#66-21767.
STUDY OF THE FUNCTIONS AND CHARACTERISTICS OF TECHNICAL
ASSISTANCE AGENCIES, PROGRAMS AND PERSONNEL. FOCUS ON OBJEC-
TIVES, FINANCING, MACHINERY, AND PLANNING OF UN PROGRAMS FOR
TECHNICAL CO-OPERATION. FURTHER ANALYSIS OF PROBLEMS OF DE-
TERMINING QUALIFICATIONS FOR ASSISTANCE PERSONNEL AND THEIR
RECRUITMENT. INTERVIEWS WITHIN UN PERSONNEL, ND UN DOCUMENTS
USED; DATA REPORTED IN APPENDICES.

0075 ALGER C.F.
"NON-RESOLUTION CONSEQUENCES OF THE UNITED NATIONS AND
THEIR EFFECT ON INTERNATIONAL CONFLICT."
J. CONFL. RESOLUT., 5 (JUNE 61), 128-46.
ANALYZES CHARACTERISTICS OF GENERAL ASSEMBLY. AIMS TO
PROVIDE DIRECTION FOR RESEARCH ON THE EFFECT OF THE UN
AND OTHER INTERNATIONAL ORGANIZATIONS ON INTERNATIONAL
RELATIONS.

0076 ALGER C.F.
"THE EXTERNAL BUREAUCRACY IN UNITED STATES FOREIGN AFFAIRS."
ADMIN. SCI. QUART., 7 (JUNE 62), 50-78.
ANALYSIS CONCLUDES THAT BASIC FUNCTION OF BUREAUCRATS IS
COMMUNICATION OF INFORMATION AND PERSPECTIVES FROM COUNTRY
OF PLACEMENT TO BUREAUCRATIC CENTER AND VICE VERSA.

0077 ALI S., JONES G.N.
PLANNING, DEVELOPMENT AND CHANGE: AN ANNOTATED BIBLIOGRAPHY
ON DEVELOPMENTAL ADMINISTRATION.
BALTIMORE: J HOPKINS SCHOOL HYG, 1966, 217 PP.
ANNOTATED BIBLIOGRAPHY OF 655 BOOKS, JOURNAL ARTICLES,
AND GOVERNMENT PUBLICATIONS IN ENGLISH ON TOPICS OF PLANNING
AND DEVELOPMENT IN EMERGING NATIONS, AND PROCESS OF CHANGE
IN ALL SOCIETIES. ARRANGED ACCORDING TO TOPICS OF RESEARCH
METHODOLOGY AND TYPES OF PLANNING; ECONOMIC, SOCIAL,
POLITICAL, AND ADMINISTRATIVE DEVELOPMENT; AND
ORGANIZATIONAL THEORY AND BEHAVIOR.

0078 ALLPORT G.W.
THE NATURE OF PREJUDICE.
BOSTON: 1954, 536 PP.
ANALYZES CAUSES AND FORMS OF PREJUDICE AND DISCRIMINA-
TION. CONCENTRATES ON USA BUT INCLUDES CROSS-CULTURAL
COMPARISON. ATTEMPTS TO SHOW HOW GROWING KNOWLEDGE OF SOCIAL
SCIENCES CAN BE USED TO REDUCE GROUP TENSIONS. INCLUDES
QUESTIONNAIRES, ANALYSIS OF STEREOTYPES, INTERVIEWS,
COMPARATIVE STUDIES OF SITUATIONAL FACTORS.

0079 ALMOND G.A.
"COMPARATIVE STUDY OF INTEREST GROUPS."
AM. POL. SCI. REV., 52 (MAR. 58), 270-282.
REPORTS AND CONCLUSIONS OF WORK GROUPS OF FIRST RESEARCH
PLANNING SESSION OF SSRC COMMITTEE ON COMPARATIVE POLITICS.

0080 ALPANDER G.G.
"ENTREPRENEURS AND PRIVATE ENTERPRISE IN TURKEY."
BUSINESS TOPICS, 15 (SPRING 67), 59-68.
DISCUSSES DEVELOPMENT OF PRIVATE ENTERPRISE IN TURKEY,
WHERE PRIVATE CORPORATE ENTERPRISE HAS HAD LITTLE
RECEPTIVITY; EXAMINES REASONS WHY. FOCUSES ON FIRMS THAT DO
EXIST AND TREATS GROWTH PATTERNS, GEOGRAPHICAL DISTRIBUTION,
PUBLIC POLICY, WHOLESALING, AND RETAILING. ANALYZES
SOCIOLOGICAL AND BEHAVIORAL CHARACTERISTICS OF
ENTREPRENEURS.

0081 AMER ENTERPRISE INST PUB POL
CONGRESS: THE FIRST BRANCH OF GOVERNMENT.
WASHINGTON: AMER ENTERPRISE INST, 1966, 515 PP., LC#66-14193
TWELVE STUDIES OF THE ORGANIZATION OF CONGRESS. THE
AUTHORS PROPOSE A SERIES OF REFORMS IN ORDER TO INCREASE
THE EFFICIENCY AND EFFECTIVENESS OF LEGISLATIVE CONTROL IN
AN AGE IN WHICH THE COMPLEXITY OF GOVERNMENT OPERATIONS HAS
BEEN USED TO JUSTIFY THE INCREASE OF POWER EXERCISED BY THE
EXECUTIVE BRANCH. COORDINATED BY ALFRED DE GRAZIA.

0082 AMERICAN ASSEMBLY COLUMBIA U
THE FEDERAL GOVERNMENT SERVICE.
ENGLEWOOD CLIFFS: PRENTICE HALL, 1965, 245 PP., LC#65-20600.
COLLECTION OF ESSAYS ON EVOLUTION, FUNCTION, AND PROBLEMS
OF US GOVERNMENT SERVICE. DISCUSSES ISSUES ARISING FROM
PROBLEMS OF ACCOUNTABILITY AND SUPERVISION, POLITICAL PA-
TRONAGE, AND PERSONNEL MANAGEMENT. INCLUDES DISCUSSION OF
INTERNAL STRUCTURE.

0083 AMERICAN ECONOMIC ASSOCIATION
INDEX OF ECONOMIC JOURNALS 1886-1965 (7 VOLS.)
HOMEWOOD: RICHARD IRWIN, 1965, 2200 PP.
INDEX COVERING ENGLISH-LANGUAGE ARTICLES IN MAJOR ECO-
NOMIC JOURNALS PUBLISHED BETWEEN 1886 AND 1965. INCLUDES
CLASSIFIED INDEX IN WHICH MATERIAL IS ARRANGED BY SUBJECT;
CONTAINS AN AUTHOR INDEX.

0084 AMERICAN ECONOMIC REVIEW
"SIXTY-THIRD LIST OF DOCTORAL DISSERTATIONS IN POLITICAL
ECONOMY IN AMERICAN UNIVERSITIES AND COLLEGES."
AMER. ECO. REVIEW, 56 (SEPT. 66), 1024-1062.
THE ANNOTATED LIST SPECIFIES DOCTORAL DEGREES CONFERRED
DURING THE ACADEMIC YEAR TERMINATING JUNE, 1966. ABSTRACTS
OF MANY OF THE DISSERTATIONS ARE SUPPLIED. LIST EXCLUDES
THESES UNDERTAKEN IN THE SAME PERIOD.

0085 AMERICAN FRIENDS SERVICE COMM
IN PLACE OF WAR.
NEW YORK: GROSSMAN PUBL, 1967, 115 PP., LC#67-21234.
DEVOTED TO STRATEGY OF NONVIOLENT DEFENSE. BEGINS WITH
SHORT HISTORY OF THE POLICY AND OUTLINES EFFECTIVENESS AND
DIFFERENT KINDS OF NONVIOLENCE, ORGANIZATION OF THE
GOVERNMENT, PREPARATION OF THE NATION, AND FORMS PROTEST
SHOULD TAKE IN EVENT OF INVASION.

0086 AMERICAN MANAGEMENT ASSN
SUPERIOR-SUBORDINATE COMMUNICATION IN MANAGEMENT.
NEW YORK: AMER MANAGEMENT ASSN, 1961, 96 PP., LC#61-18463.
ESSAYS ANALYZING PROBLEM OF COMMUNICATION BETWEEN SUPERI-
ORS AND SUBORDINATES IN A BUSINESS SITUATION. SUGGESTS
POSSIBLE WAYS OF OVERCOMING BARRIERS. ITEMS SELECTED
FROM WORKS OF PSYCHOLOGIST, LINGUIST, EXECUTIVE, AND
PERSONNEL DIRECTOR.

0087 AMERICAN POLITICAL SCI ASSN
TOWARD A MORE RESPONSIBLE TWO-PARTY SYSTEM.
NEW YORK: RINEHART, 1950, 99 PP.
REPORT ON PRESENT STATE OF POLITICAL PARTIES IN AMERICA
INCLUDES NEED FOR GREATER PARTY RESPONSIBILITY, PROPOSALS
FOR PARTY RESPONSIBILITY, AND PROSPECT FOR ACTION.

0088 AMERICAN SOCIETY PUBLIC ADMIN
STRENGTHENING MANAGEMENT FOR DEMOCRATIC GOVERNMENT.
WASHINGTON: AM SOC PUBLIC ADMIN, 1958, 159 PP., LC#59-11123.
PRESENTS REPORTS ON DISCUSSIONS AT AMERICAN SOCIETY FOR
PUBLIC ADMINISTRATION'S 1958 CONFERENCE. FOCUSES ON
EXECUTIVE PROCESSES, SUCH AS PROGRAM PLANNING, STAFF
DELEGATION, AND PERFORMANCE MEASUREMENT AND ON LARGE-SCALE
ADMINISTRATIVE STRATEGY AND ORGANIZATION OF SEVERAL
SYSTEMS, SUCH AS COURTS.

0089 AMERICAN SOCIETY PUBLIC ADMIN
PUBLIC ADMINISTRATION AND THE WAR ON POVERTY (PAMPHLET)
WASHINGTON: AM SOC PUBLIC ADMIN, 1966, 28 PP.
REPORT OF 1965 REGIONAL CONFERENCE OF AMERICAN SOCIETY
FOR PUBLIC ADMINISTRATION. THEME OF CONFERENCE WAS NEW
PUBLIC PROGRAM, WAR ON POVERTY. EXAMINES ROLE OF FEDERAL
GOVERNMENT, COMMUNITY PROGRAMS, RESOURCES, AND ECONOMIC
SUPPORT.

0090 AMLUND C.A.
"EXECUTIVE-LEGISLATIVE IMBALANCE: TRUMAN TO KENNEDY."
WESTERN POLIT. QUART., 18 (SEPT. 65), 640-645.
QUESTIONS THE PROPOSITION THAT IN THE 20TH CENTURY THE
EXECUTIVE BRANCH HAS ACQUIRED A PREPONDERANT ROLE IN DECIS-
ION-MAKING IN THE NATIONAL GOVERNMENT. POLICY INITIATION HAS
FALLEN INCREASINGLY TO THE PRESIDENT. BUT CONGRESS HAS THE
EQUALLY IMPORTANT TASK OF ACCOMMODATING INITIATED POLICIES
TO THE DIVERSITIES OF THE COUNTRY'S SPECIFIC NEEDS AND IN-
TERESTS. THIS APPLIES ALSO TO FOREIGN POLICY.

0091 ANDERSON C.W.
POLITICS AND ECONOMIC CHANGE IN LATIN AMERICA.
PRINCETON: VAN NOSTRAND, 1967, 388 PP.
ANALYSIS OF ECONOMIC CHANGE IN LATIN AMERICA THROUGH ITS
RELATIONSHIP WITH POLITICAL ELEMENTS. ATTEMPTS TO SEE A
SYSTEMATIC IMPACT OF POLITICAL FORCES ON DEVELOPMENT POLICY
AND THUS CREATE OVER-ALL THEORETICAL STATEMENT ON DEVELOP-
MENTAL POLICY-MAKING IN LATIN AMERICA. DEMONSTRATES THAT
"PRUDENCE MODEL" HAS BEEN APPROACH SINCE 1945 AND SUGGESTS,
IN CONCLUSION, A CONSISTENT APPROACH TO DEVELOPMENT POLICY.

0092 ANDERSON D.L. ED.
MUNICIPAL PUBLIC RELATIONS (1ST ED.)
CHICAGO: INT CITY MANAGER'S ASSN, 1966, 273 PP., LC#66-20874
DISCUSSES PUBLIC RELATIONS INFORMATION FROM
VIEWPOINTS OF CITY COUNCILS, POLICE, PUBLIC, AND REPORTERS
FOR MASS MEDIA. PROVIDES PERSPECTIVE FOR PUBLIC RELATIONS IN
SOCIETY, GOVERNMENT, AND ADMINISTRATION. DEALS WITH PROGRAMS

AND POLICY, CONVENTIONAL PUBLIC INFORMATION TECHNIQUES, AND
PUBLIC RELATIONS IN ADMINISTRATIVE ORGANIZATION.

0093 ANDERSON J.
THE ORGANIZATION OF ECONOMIC STUDIES IN RELATION TO THE
PROBLEMS OF GOVERNMENT (PAMPHLET)
LONDON: OXFORD U PR, 1947, 25 PP.
EXAMINES PROGRESS MADE IN APPLICATION OF ECONOMIC THEORY
TO PRACTICAL PROBLEMS DURING LAST 30 YEARS IN ENGLAND.
PROPOSES THERE BE INCLUDED IN MACHINERY OF GOVERNMENT A CEN-
TRAL ECONOMIC ORGANIZATION IN WHICH ALL DEPARTMENTS CON-
CERNED WITH ECONOMIC PROBLEMS COULD COLLABORATE EFFECTIVELY.

0094 ANDERSON L.G.
"ADMINISTERING A GOVERNMENT SOCIAL SERVICE"
NEW ZEALAND J. OF PUBLIC ADMIN., 29 (MAR. 67), 32-46.
COMMENTS ON ADMINISTRATION OF CHILD WELFARE DIVISION OF
NEW ZEALAND SOCIAL SERVICE. ONE TASK OF ADMINISTRATION IS
TO CURB SOCIAL-REFORM IMPULSES OF WORKERS AND DIRECT THEM TO
WORK WITH INDIVIDUALS. OTHERS ARE TO EXPLOIT SKILLS OF HIS
STAFF, DIRECT ANCILLARY SERVICE, PROVIDE LIAISON BETWEEN HIS
SERVICE AND THE GOVERNMENT, AND TO FOSTER STAFF MORALE.

0095 ANDERSON M.
"THE FRENCH PARLIAMENT."
PARLIAMENTARIAN, 48 (APR. 67), 65-69.
COMPARISON OF FIFTH REPUBLIC WITH THIRD AND FOURTH TO
SHOW HOW MUCH THE CURRENT 5TH HAS CHANGED FROM TRADITION.
SUPREMACY OF PARLIAMENT HAS GONE AND ITS POWER HAS BEEN RE-
DUCED AS WELL AS ITS PRESTIGE. ARTICLE SHOWS HOW ITS POWER
HAS DECLINED, ITS MALFUNCTIONING, THE SUPREME ROLE OF DE-
GAULLE, CABINET STRUCTURE, ALTERED BALANCE, AND DECLINE IN
IMPORTANCE OF INTRIGUE.

0096 ANDERSON S.V.
CANADIAN OMBUDSMAN PROPOSALS.
BERKELEY: U CAL, INST GOVT STUD, 1966, 168 PP.
REVIEW OF PROPOSALS SINCE 1960 FOR CREATION OF
PARLIAMENTARY GRIEVANCE COMMISSIONERS MODELED ON
SCANDINAVIAN OMBUDSMAN. PROPOSALS HAVE BEEN PUT FORWARD BY
MINORITY PARTIES, THEN PLACED IN LIMBO BY MAJORITY. PRESENTS
CHRONOLOGY OF EVENTS AND DEBATE, ANALYZES PROPOSALS, AND
APPRAISES CANADA'S NEED FOR AN OMBUDSMAN.

0097 ANDERSON T.J.
"PRESSURE GROUPS AND INTERGOVERNMENTAL RELATIONS."
ANN. ACAD. POL. SOC. SCI., 359 (MAY 65), 116-126.
ADMINISTRATIVE AGENCIES REPRESENT PRIVATE INTERESTS TO
BUILD THEIR OWN POWER BASE: THIS GIVES PRIVATE INTERESTS A
DIRECT AND INTIMATE CONNECTION WITH THE GOVERNMENT.

0098 ANDERSON W.
THE UNITS OF GOVERNMENT IN THE UNITED STATES (PAMPHLET)
CHICAGO: PUBLIC ADMIN SERVICE, 1942, 47 PP.
STUDIES NUMBER, CLASSES, AND CHARACTERISTICS OF UNITS OF
GOVERNMENT IN US. DISCUSSES DIMENSIONS OF UNITS IN MATTERS
SUCH AS AREA AND POPULATION SERVED, AND ANALYZES TRENDS IN
INCREASES AND DECREASES IN NUMBER OF UNITS. CONSIDERS
ADEQUACY OF GOVERNMENTAL UNITS FOR FUNCTION THEY MUST
PERFORM.

0099 ANDERSON W. ED.
LOCAL GOVERNMENT IN EUROPE.
NEW YORK: APPLETON, 1939, 453 PP.
DESCRIBES LOCAL GOVERNMENT OF FRANCE, ENGLAND, GERMANY,
ITALY, AND THE SOVIET UNION. ANALYZES CENTRAL-LOCAL
RELATIONS. INCLUDES PRINCIPAL LOCAL LAW OF COUNTRIES
DISCUSSED.

0100 ANDERSON W., WEIDNER E.W.
STATE AND LOCAL GOVERNMENT IN THE UNITED STATES.
NEW YORK: HOLT RINEHART WINSTON, 1951, 744 PP.
TEXTBOOK ON STATE AND LOCAL GOVERNMENT FROM STRUCTURAL
AND FUNCTIONAL APPROACH COVERING RELATIONS AMONG LEVELS OF
GOVERNMENT, STATE, LOCAL, AND URBAN GOVERNMENTAL ORGANIZA-
TIONS, PUBLIC SERVICES, PERSONNEL AND FINANCE, AND VOTERS'
PLACE IN SYSTEM.

0101 ANDERSON W., PENNIMAN C., WEIDNER E.W.
GOVERNMENT IN THE FIFTY STATES.
NEW YORK: HOLT RINEHART WINSTON, 1951, 509 PP., LC#60-9131.
REVISED EDITION OF "STATE AND LOCAL GOVERNMENT IN THE
UNITED STATES" BY ANDERSON, EMPHASIZING STATE GOVERNMENT.

0102 ANDREN N.
GOVERNMENT AND POLITICS IN THE NORDIC COUNTRIES: DENMARK,
FINLAND, ICELAND, NORWAY, SWEDEN.
STOCKHOLM: ALMQUIST & WIKSELL, 1964, 240 PP.
EXAMINES NORDIC HERITAGE AND WESTERN TRADITION, AND THE
IMPACT OF ECONOMIC AND SOCIAL CHANGE. STUDIES EACH COUNTRY
IN TERMS OF ITS CONSTITUTIONAL DEVELOPMENT, POPULAR REPRE-
SENTATION, EXECUTIVE AND ADMINISTRATIVE SYSTEM, AND PARLIA-
MENTARY ORGANIZATION. CONCLUDES BY DISCUSSING NATIONAL AND
NORDIC TRAITS, LOCAL SELF-GOVERNMENT, COOPERATION AND INTE-
GRATION OF THESE NATIONS, AND POLITICAL PARTY STRENGTH.

0103 ANDREWS K.R.
THE EFFECTIVENESS OF UNIVERSITY MANAGEMENT DEVELOPMENT
PROGRAMS.
CAMBRIDGE: HARVARD BUS SCHOOL, 1966, 340 PP., LC#66-22596.
STUDY OF UNIVERSITY-SPONSORED PROGRAMS FOR TRAINING OF
EXECUTIVES. EXPLAINS PURPOSES AND METHODS, EXPERIENCE AND
EXPECTATIONS OF EXECUTIVE STUDENT, REACTIONS TO PROGRAMS,
AND IMPACT AND CONSEQUENCES OF PROGRAMS WITH IMPLICATIONS
FOR BOTH COMPANY AND UNIVERSITY ACTION.

0104 ANDREWS W.G.
EUROPEAN POLITICAL INSTITUTIONS.
PRINCETON: VAN NOSTRAND, 1962, 387 PP.
DISCUSSES GOVERNMENTAL SYSTEMS (POLITICAL PARTIES, ELEC-
TION PROCESSES, LEGISLATURES, EXECUTIVE ESTABLISHMENTS) OF
UK, FRANCE, GERMANY, AND USSR.

0105 ANDREWS W.G.
FRENCH POLITICS AND ALGERIA: THE PROCESS OF POLICY FORMATION
1954-1962.
NEW YORK: APPLETON, 1962, 217 PP., LC#62-15310.
COMPARATIVE CASE STUDY OF TWO FRENCH REGIMES DEALING WITH
SAME PROBLEM. DIFFERENCES AND SIMILARITIES IN OPERATIONS
OF FRENCH ADMINISTRATIONS VIS-A-VIS ALGERIA.

0106 ANDRIOT J.L.
GUIDE TO POPULAR GOVERNMENT PUBLICATIONS.
ARLINGTON: DOCUMENTS INDEX, 1960, 125 PP., LC#60-9768.
REFERENCES, PUBLICATIONS, MAPS, AND AUDIO-VISUAL AIDS
ISSUED BY GOVERNMENT AGENCIES. INCLUDES ONLY ITEMS PRESENTLY
AVAILABLE, AS WELL AS SIZE, COST, MEANS OF OBTAINING, ETC.
FIRST SECTION ARRANGED BY AGENCIES AND THEIR PUBLICATIONS;
SECOND SECTION ARRANGED BY SUBJECT AND INCLUDES 2,000 ITEMS
OF POPULAR PUBLICATIONS IN PRINT.

0107 ANDRIOT J.L.
GUIDE TO US GOVERNMENT SERIALS AND PERIODICALS (VOL. IV)
ARLINGTON: DOCUMENTS INDEX, 1967, 352 PP.
UPDATES PRIOR THREE VOLUMES TO DECEMBER 31, 1965. IN-
CLUDES AN AGENCY INDEX, SUBJECT INDEX, AND TITLE INDEX
CONSOLIDATED FOR THE OVER 4,200 ENTRIES CONTAINED IN THE
FOUR VOLUMES. COMPLETE SET FORMS A COMPREHENSIVE GUIDE TO
AVAILABLE GOVERNMENT PUBLICATIONS.

0108 ANGEL D.D.
ROMNEY.
NEW YORK: EXPOSITION PRESS, 1967, 266 PP., LC#67-26387.
RELATES ROMNEY'S CHILDHOOD, BUSINESS, AND POLITICAL
CAREER. DISCUSSES HIM IN RELATION TO BIG BUSINESS, LABOR,
RACE RELATIONS, AND CIVIL RIGHTS. ANALYZES HIS RECORD AS
GOVERNOR, ROLE OF MORMON CHURCH IN HIS LIFE, AND HIS YEARS
WITH AMERICAN MOTORS. ASSESSES ROMNEY'S CHANCE FOR THE
PRESIDENCY AND HIS PERSONAL ATTRIBUTES. EMPHASIZES HIS PO-
SITION ON VIETNAM.

0109 ANGELL N.
THE PUBLIC MIND.
NEW YORK: DUTTON, 1927, 232 PP.
ASSERTS THAT PUBLIC IS NOT QUALIFIED TO JUDGE IMPORTANT
POLICY QUESTIONS AS IT'S NOT PREDISPOSED TO APPLY INTELLIG-
ENCE IN EVALUATING CURRENT AFFAIRS. 'ATROCITY' IN POLITICS,
ECONOMIC INTERESTS AND VIEWS OF SOCIETY ARE FALSE BASES OF
PUBLIC ATTITUDES. ONLY DEMOCRACY POSSIBLE IS RECOGNITION OF
PUBLIC WILL AS BASIS OF GOVERNMENT ACTION. PUBLIC NEEDS 1)
TO RECOGNIZE LIMITS OF DECISION AND 2) EDUCATIONAL REFORM.

0110 ANGELL R.
"GOVERNMENTS AND PEOPLES AS FOCI FOR PEACE-ORIENTED
RESEARCH."
J. SOC. ISSUES, 11 (1955), 36-41.
APPRAISES EFFECTIVENESS OF SOCIOLOGY-ORIENTED STUDIES IN
INTERNATIONAL RELATIONS. CONSIDERS HISTORICAL ANALOGIES,
FUNCTIONING OF GOVERNMENT LEADERS AND INTERGOVERNMENTAL
BODIES AS VALID FOR STUDY, AS MEANS TO SOCIAL INTEGRATION,
CULTURAL LIKENESSES AND DIFFERENCES, SOCIAL TENSIONS AND
POSSIBLE INTER-CULTURAL BRIDGES SHOULD BE RECOGNIZED.

0111 ANGERS F.A.
ESSAI SUR LA CENTRALISATION: ANALYSE DES PRINCIPES ET
PERSPECTIVES CANADIENNES.
MONTREAL: PR L'ECOLE ETUD COMM, 1960, 331 PP.
EXAMINES GENERAL ASPECTS OF PROBLEM OF CENTRALIZATION IN
CANADA: OVER-ALL ECONOMIC AND SOCIOLOGICAL PRINCIPLES THAT
PROMPT ADMINISTRATION AND POLITICS. FIRST SECTION DEALS WITH
WHOLE OF QUESTION AND ITS SOCIOLOGICAL, ECONOMIC, POLITICAL,
AND ADMINISTRATIVE BASES. SECOND DEALS WITH CONTROL AND
ECONOMIC STABILITY IN RELATION TO CENTRALIZATION. SPECIAL
INTEREST IN THEORIES FROM 1945-55.

0112 ANGLIN D.
"UNITED STATES OPPOSITION TO CANADIAN MEMBERSHIP IN THE
PAN AMERICAN UNION: A CANADIAN VIEW."
INT. ORGAN., 15 (WINTER 61), 1-20.
HISTORY OF DEBATES OVER CANADA'S ADMISSION TO THE UNION.
ALSO DISCUSSED ARE CANADA'S MEMBERSHIP IN THE COMMONWEALTH,
AND U.S. AND LATIN AMERICAN ATTITUDES TOWARDS CANADA'S STAND

ON SOME MAJOR ISSUES. A POLICY INDEPENDENT OF BOTH LONDON AND WASHINGTON IS RECOMMENDED.

0113 ANTHON C.G.
"THE END OF THE ADENAUER ERA."
CURR. HIST., 44 (APRIL 63), 193-201.
FOCUSES ON STABILITY OF WEST GERMAN POLITICAL SYSTEM AND ACHIEVEMENTS OF KONRAD ADENAUER. GREATEST MIRACLE IS THAT OVERWHELMING MAJORITY OF GERMANS TODAY IDENTIFY THEMSELVES WITH DEMOCRATIC INSTITUTIONS AND POLICIES OF REPUBLIC.

0114 ANTHONY R.N.
PLANNING AND CONTROL SYSTEMS.
CAMBRIDGE: HARVARD U, DIV OF RES, 1965, 180 PP., LC#65-18724
A BRIEF INQUIRY INTO THE NATURE AND FUNCTION OF CONTROL SYSTEMS. EMPHASIZES SELECTION OF A FRAMEWORK UNDER WHICH SUCH TOPICS AS STRATEGIC PLANNING, MANAGEMENT CONTROL, AND OPERATIONAL CONTROL ARE DISCUSSED IN SYSTEMATIC DETAIL. AN APPENDIX ON TERMINOLOGY IS INCLUDED.

0115 APPLEBY P.H.
BIG DEMOCRACY.
NEW YORK: ALFRED KNOPF, 1945, 197 PP.
GENERAL TREATISE ON BUREAUCRACY IN THE UNITED STATES. HOLDS THAT THE BUREAUCRACY OPERATES AS A BASIC TOOL OF DEMOCRACY, AND THAT IT TRADITIONALLY HAS DEFENDED AND REPRESENTED THE GENERAL PUBLIC AGAINST THE PRESSURES EXERTED BY SPECIFIC ECONOMIC AND POLITICAL INTEREST GROUPS.

0116 APPLEBY P.H.
POLICY AND ADMINISTRATION.
UNIVERSITY: U ALABAMA PR, 1949, 173 PP.
SERIES OF LECTURES ON THE THEME THAT THE ADMINISTRATIVE BRANCH OF GOVERNMENT MAKES POLICY AS WELL AS CARRIES OUT POLICY. HOLDS THAT ADMINISTRATIVE AGENCIES, ESPECIALLY THOSE WITH NARROW RANGE OF FUNCTIONS, TEND TO REPRESENT THEIR SPECIFIC CLIENTELE, OFTEN TO THE DETRIMENT OF THE PUBLIC INTEREST.

0117 APPLEBY P.H.
MORALITY AND ADMINISTRATION IN DEMOCRATIC GOVERNMENT.
BATON ROUGE: LOUISIANA ST U PR, 1952, 261 PP.
GENERAL DESCRIPTION OF FUNCTIONS OF BUREAUCRACY, WHOM IT REPRESENTS AND HOW. CONSIDERS IMPACT OF PRESSURE GROUPS, PUBLIC OPINION, THE COURTS, AND CONGRESS ON THE PRESIDENT, EXECUTIVE DEPARTMENTS, AND REGULATORY AGENCIES.

0118 APPLEBY P.H.
PUBLIC ADMINISTRATION IN INDIA: REPORT OF A SURVEY.
NEW DELHI: MANAGER OF PUBLICATIONS, 1953, 65 PP.
FORD FOUNDATION STUDY WITH RECOMMENDATIONS FOR IMPROVE-MENT OF THE SYSTEM OF PUBLIC ADMINISTRATION IN INDIA. CRIT-ICIZES BUREAUCRATIC OPERATIONS IN VARIOUS DEPARTMENTS AND POINTS OUT POSSIBLE IMPROVEMENT. THOROUGH SURVEY OF INDIAN PUBLIC ADMINISTRATION.

0119 APPLEBY P.H.
"BUREAUCRACY AND THE FUTURE."
ANN. ACAD. POL. SOC. SCI., (MAR. 54), 136-151.
AMERICA'S DEDICATION TO PLURALISM STRAINS DEMOCRATIC PROCESSES IN ADMINISTRATION BY PERMITTING TOO MANY PRIVATE INTEREST PRESSURES. ADDITIONAL INTEGRATION AND CONSOLIDATION OF THE BUREAUCRACY IS NEEDED.

0120 APTER D.E.
THE GOLD COAST IN TRANSITION.
PRINCETON: U. PR., 1955, 355 PP.
CASE STUDY OF POLITICAL INSTITUTIONAL TRANSFER OF GOLD COAST FROM TRIBAL DEPENDANCY TO PARLIAMENTARY DEMOCRACY. EX-AMINES HISTORICAL BACKGROUND, INCLUDING ETHNIC ORIGINS, TRADITIONAL SYSTEM OF LIFE AND INTRODUCTION OF WESTERN RULE. PRESENT AND FUTURE OF GOLD COAST DEMOCRACY EXAMINED.

0121 APTER D.E.
"THE ROLE OF TRADITIONALISM IN THE POLITICAL MODERNIZATION OF GHANA AND UGANDA" (BMR)"
WORLD POLITICS, 12 (OCT. 60), 45-68.
EXAMINES THE TRADITIONAL SYSTEMS OF GHANA AND UGANDA WITH RESPECT TO THE PROBLEMS THEY POSE FOR POLITICAL MODERNIZA-TION. CONTENDS THAT CENTRAL PROBLEM OF BUILDING NATIONAL PO-LITICAL INSTITUTIONS IS TO CREATE GOVERNMENTAL FORMS THAT BRIDGE OLDER PAROCHIALISMS. COMPARES RECENT EVENTS IN GHANA AND UGANDA TO SHOW HOW THEY HAVE BEEN SHAPED BY THEIR TWO DIFFERENT KINDS OF TRADITIONALISM.

0122 APTER D.E. ED.
IDEOLOGY AND DISCONTENT.
NEW YORK: FREE PRESS, 1964, 342 PP., $9.95.
A COMPARATIVE TREATMENT OF IDEOLOGIES AS 'FRAMEWORKS OF CONSCIOUSNESS' DESIGNED TO INTERPRET THE WORLD FOR PURPOSES OF ACTING IN IT. ESSAYS ON THE STRUGGLE FOR CONSENSUS IN NEW INDEPENDENT NATIONS, JAPAN AND THE GROWTH OF WESTERN INFLU-ENCE, THE FOUNDATIONS OF ARAB NATIONALISM, SOCIALISM AND DEMOCRACY IN AFRICA, AND THE AMERICAN RADICAL RIGHT. BIB-LIOGRAPHY INCLUDED.

0123 ARASTEH R.
"THE ROLE OF INTELLECTUALS IN ADMINISTRATIVE DEVELOPMENT AND SOCIAL CHANGE IN MODERN IRAN."
INT. REV. EDUC., 9 (63), 326-39.
EXAMINES ROLE OF INTELLECTUALS AGAINST BACKGROUND OF PERSIAN SOCIAL STRUCTURE. THE WESTERN-TRAINED ELITE EXHIBIT DISHARMONIES OF A PSYCHOLOGICAL, MORAL, SOCIAL AND POLITICAL NATURE. DISHARMONIES ARE ROOTED IN PROLONGED EXPOSURE TO EUROPEAN CONCEPTS WHICH CONFLICT WITH BASIC ASSUMPTIONS OF PERSIAN LIFE AND EXPERIENCE.

0124 ARCIENEGAS G., GOODALL M.C. ET AL.
"POST-WAR SOVIET FOREIGN POLICY: A WORLD PERSPECTIVE."
J. INT. AFF., 8 (JAN. 54), 5-113.
PRESENTS METHODS EMPLOYED AND POLICIES FOLLOWED BY USSR IN RESPONSE TO CONDITIONS IN VARIOUS AREAS OF WORLD. CALLS FOR BETTER UNDERSTANDING OF PROBLEMS FACING AMERICAN POLICY MAKERS. OUTLINES POSSIBILITIES FOR RUSSIAN FOREIGN POLICY IN THE 'TWO WORLDS' CONFLICT.

0125 ARCO EDITORIAL BOARD
PUBLIC MANAGEMENT AND ADMINISTRATION.
NEW YORK: ARCO PUBL CO, 1962, 368 PP., LC#57-14731.
PREPARATION FOR CIVIL SERVICE TESTS TO GAIN ADMINIS-TRATIVE AND MANAGERIAL POSITIONS. INCLUDES BASIC THEORY, ROUTINE, AND SAMPLE TESTS, GIVING IDEA OF WHAT TO EXPECT IN TESTS, SALARY OFFERINGS, AND POSITIONS.

0126 ARGAL R.
MUNICIPAL GOVERNMENT IN INDIA.
ALLAHABAD: AGARWAL PRESS, 1960, 245 PP.
TRACES DEVELOPMENT OF MUNICIPAL GOVERNMENT IN INDIA. EXAMINES WORK OF COUNCILS, FUNCTIONS AND POWERS OF MUNICIPAL EXECUTIVE, SUPERVISION OF MUNICIPAL COUNCIL, AND FISCAL ADMINISTRATION PROCEDURES.

0127 ARGYRIS C.
EXECUTIVE LEADERSHIP: AN APPRAISAL OF A MANAGER IN ACTION.
NEW YORK: HARPER & ROW, 1953, 139 PP., LC#67-14500.
PORTRAYS CHARACTERISTIC FEATURES THAT DISTINGUISH AN EXECUTIVE AS A LEADER. DESCRIBES EFFECTS A GOOD LEADER HAS ON HIS SUBORDINATES AND SUPERIORS. ANALYZES SUBORDINATES' BEHAVIOR WHEN LEADER IS ABSENT. EXAMINES SUBORDINATES' ATTEMPTS TO ADAPT TO LEADER. OFFERS COMMENTS AND SUGGESTIONS FOR SMOOTHING SUBORDINATE-LEADER RELATIONSHIPS.

0128 ARGYRIS C.
"THE INDIVIDUAL AND ORGANIZATION: SOME PROBLEMS OF MUTUAL ADJUSTMENT" (BMR)"
ADMINISTRATIVE SCI. Q., 2 (JUNE 57), 1-24.
STUDIES IMPACT OF FORMAL STRUCTURE AND INDIVIDUALS, CONTINUOUSLY INTERACTING AND TRANSACTING, UPON EACH OTHER. OUTLINES BEGINNINGS OF SYSTEMATIC FRAMEWORK TO ANALYZE NATURE OF RELATIONSHIP BETWEEN TWO, AND DERIVES SPECIFIC HYPOTHESES REGARDING THEIR MUTUAL IMPACT.

0129 ARGYRIS C.
"SOME PROBLEMS IN CONCEPTUALIZING ORGANIZATIONAL CLIMATE: A CASE STUDY OF A BANK" (BMR)"
ADMINISTRATIVE SCI. Q., 2 (MAR. 58), 501-520.
CONCERNED WITH WAY OF ORDERING COMPLEX OF VARIABLES COMPRISING ORGANIZATIONS. USES MODEL OF A BANK TO STUDY INTERPERSONAL RELATIONS. FINDS THREE SYSTEMS OF VARIABLES: POLICIES, PROCEDURES, AND POSITIONS; PERSONALITY FACTORS SUCH AS INDIVIDUAL'S NEEDS, VALUES, AND ABILITIES; AND INDIVIDUAL'S EFFORTS TO ACCOMMODATE HIS OWN EFFORTS TO THE ORGANIZATION'S.

0130 ARGYRIS C.
UNDERSTANDING ORGANIZATIONAL BEHAVIOR.
HOMEWOOD: DORSEY, 1960, 179 PP.
THEORETICAL MODEL FOR DEFINING AND STUDYING VARIABLES IN PERSONALITY AND ORGANIZATIONS AND THEIR INTERACTION. STUDIES ACTIVITIES, ORGANIZATION, AND BEHAVIOR OF INDIVIDUAL WITHIN ORGANIZATIONAL FRAMEWORK. USES INTERVIEWS WITH MANAGEMENT AS FEEDBACK.

0131 ARGYRIS C., HARRISON R.
INTERPERSONAL COMPETENCE AND ORGANIZATIONAL EFFECTIVENESS.
HOMEWOOD: DORSEY, 1962, 290 PP., LC#62-11287.
INTERPERSONAL RELATIONS AND THEIR EFFECT ON EFFICIENCY ARE EVALUATED BY CONSULTANTS TO INCREASE PRODUCTIVITY. BEGINS WITH EXECUTIVE STRUCTURE, GOING DOWN ORGANIZATIONAL LADDER. LABORATORY EDUCATION DISCUSSED TO PROMOTE EFFECTIVENESS.

0132 ARGYRIS C.
INTEGRATING THE INDIVIDUAL AND THE ORGANIZATION.
NEW YORK: JOHN WILEY, 1964, 330 PP., LC#64-13209.
DESCRIBES THE DILEMMA OF ORGANIZATION AS A RATIONAL YET GOING, LIVING SYSTEM, INCLUDING WORKER SELF-RESPONSIBILITY AND SELF-CONTROL. CITING EMPIRICAL STUDIES, APPROACHING REPRESENTATION FROM THE POINT OF NEEDS, OPPORTUNITIES, MENTAL HEALTH, AND ADAPTIVE MECHANISMS, SUCH AS PROBLEM SOLVING AND ADEQUATE LEADERSHIP AS WELL AS PROPER USE OF SANCTIONS.

0134 ARMSTRONG J.A.
AN ESSAY ON SOURCES FOR THE STUDY OF THE COMMUNIST PARTY OF
THE SOVIET UNION, 1934-1960 (EXTERNAL RESEARCH PAPER 137)
WASHINGTON: DEPT OF STATE, 1961.
BIBLIOGRAPHICAL ESSAY OF 20TH-CENTURY BOOKS AND ARTICLES
PUBLISHED IN ENGLISH AND RUSSIAN.

0135 ARNOW K.
SELF-INSURANCE IN THE TREASURY (PAMPHLET)
INDIANAPOLIS: BOBBS-MERRILL, 1952, 52 PP.
CASE STUDY OF TWO "LOW TENSION" ADMINISTRATIVE PROBLEMS
IN THE US TREASURY DEPARTMENT. COMPARES TWO INSTANCES OF
ADMINISTERING TRANSFER OF SHIPPING METHODS TO A SELF-
INSURANCE BASIS. ILLUMINATES NEED FOR REFORM IN BUREAUCRATIC
PROCEDURE.

0136 ARON R. ED.
FRANCE DEFEATS EDC.
NEW YORK: PRAEGER, 1957, 225 PP.
HISTORICAL DEVELOPMENT AND ANALYSIS OF DEBATE IN FRANCE
REGARDING HER DECISION NOT TO PARTICIPATE IN A EUROPEAN
DEFENSE COMMUNITY. PROBLEMS FACING FRANCE IN JOINING A
SUPRA-NATIONAL ARMY ARE OBSERVED. PERIOD DISCUSSED IS 1950
TO 1954.

0137 ARROW K.J. ED., KARLIN S. ED., SUPPES P. ED.
MATHEMATICAL METHODS IN THE SOCIAL SCIENCES, 1959.
STANFORD: STANFORD U PRESS, 1960.
23 PAPERS OF STANFORD SYMPOSIUM ON MATHEMATICAL METHODS
IN THE SOCIAL SCIENCES - JUNE 1959 - ON ECONOMICS (STABIL-
ITY, CAPITAL ACCUMULATION, CONSUMER BEHAVIOR AND TECHNOLOG-
ICAL CHANGE); MANAGEMENT SCIENCE (A PROBLEM IN QUEUING THEO-
RY AND INVENTORY PROBLEMS); AND ON PSYCHOLOGY (UTILITY, STO-
CHASTIC MODELS FOR INTELLIGENCE TEST SCORES, CHOICE BEHAV-
IOR, RESPONSE LATENCY, ETC).

0138 ARTHUR D LITTLE INC
SAN FRANCISCO COMMUNITY RENEWAL PROGRAM.
SAN FRANCISCO: COMM RENEWAL PROG, 1965, 173 PP.
REPORT TO CITY PLANNING COMMISSION ON SAN FRANCISCO
PROGRAM. PRESENTS FIVE BASIC OBJECTIVES OF PROGRAM AND THE
ADMINISTRATIVE AND ORGANIZATIONAL PROCEDURES NECESSARY TO
ACHIEVE THEM. CONTENDS THAT MAINTAINING LIVABLE AND
PROSPERING COMMUNITY FOR PEOPLE OF ALL INCOME LEVELS IS
PUBLIC AND PRIVATE OBLIGATION.

0139 ASHER R.E.
THE UNITED NATIONS AND THE PROMOTION OF THE GENERAL
WELFARE.
WASHINGTON: BROOKINGS INST., 1957, 1216 PP.
DEALS WITH NON-POLITICAL ORGANS OF UNITED NATIONS. FIRST
SECTION OF VOLUME OUTLINES EVOLUTION OF THE UN AND REMAINING
CHAPTERS ASSESS THE ROLES, FUNCTIONS, SUCCESSES AND FAILURES
OF THE UN IN NON-POLITICAL FIELD.

0140 ASHFORD D.E.
"BUREAUCRATS AND CITIZENS."
ANN. ACAD. POL. SOC. SCI., 358 (MAR. 65), 89-100.
DISCUSSION OF THE ROLE OF, AND EFFECTS ON, THE
BUREAUCRACY OF THE PROCESS OF MODERNIZATION OF TUNISIA,
MOROCCO, AND PAKISTAN.

0141 ASHRAF A.
THE CITY GOVERNMENT OF CALCUTTA: A STUDY OF INERTIA.
NEW YORK: ASIA PUBL HOUSE, 1966, 126 PP.
EXAMINES NEED FOR REORGANIZATION OF URBAN GOVERNMENT TO
SUIT REQUIREMENTS OF GOVERNMENT PROGRAM OF PLANNED
DEVELOPMENT. APPRAISES CALCUTTA'S CITY GOVERNMENT, RELATING
IT TO ENVIRONMENT. MAINTAINS GREATEST NEED OF MUNICIPAL
ORGANIZATION IS DYNAMIC EXECUTIVE LEADERSHIP.

0142 ASPINALL A.
POLITICS AND THE PRESS 1780-1850.
LONDON: HOME & VAN THAL, 1949, 511 PP.
STORY OF HOW ENGLISH PRESS CONTRIVED TO EMANCIPATE ITSELF
FROM CONTROL WHICH POLITICIANS AND GOVERNMENT HAD LONG HELD
UPON IT. SHOWS WAYS IN WHICH GOVERNMENT DIRECTLY AND INDI-
RECTLY SUBSIDIZED NEWSPAPERS; CONCENTRATES LARGELY ON PRESS
IN METROPOLITAN AREAS.

0143 ASPREMONT-LYNDEN H.
RAPPORT SUR L'ADMINISTRATION BELGE DU RUANDA-URUNDI PENDANT
L'ANNEE 1959.
BRUSSELS: IMPR VAN MUYSEWINKEL, 1960, 494 PP.
DOCUMENTS AND SUMMARIZES BELGIAN COLONIAL ADMINISTRATION
OF RUANDA-URUNDI FOR 1959. INCLUDES DESCRIPTIVE DATA
INDICATING GEOGRAPHY AND DEMOGRAPHY OF THE AREA; INDICATES
LEGAL STATUS OF THE INHABITANTS; DESCRIBES EXTENT AND SCOPE
OF COLONIAL COOPERATION WITH INTERNATIONAL AND REGIONAL
AGENCIES; STRESSES SOCIAL, ECONOMIC, AND POLITICAL PROGRESS
OF THE REGION.

0144 ATKIN J.M.
"THE FEDERAL GOVERNMENT, BIG BUSINESS, AND COLLEGES OF EDU-
CATION."
EDUCATIONAL FORUM, 31 (MAY 67), 391-402.

A CRITIQUE OF THE ROLE OF THE FEDERAL GOVERNMENT AND OF
BIG BUSINESS IN EDUCATION. THE BACKGROUND OF THIS INVOLVE-
MENT, SOME OF ITS FEATURES, AND THE PROBLEMS IT HAS AND IS
CREATING ARE EXPLORED. MAJOR ISSUES ARE THAT PROFESSIONALLY
TRAINED EDUCATORS HAVE NOT BEEN SUFFICIENTLY INVOLVED IN THE
PROGRAMS, AND THAT TECHNIQUES AND APPROACHES OF BUSINESS AND
GOVERNMENT ARE SOMETIMES INAPPROPRIATELY USED IN EDUCATION.

0145 ATOMIC INDUSTRIAL FORUM
MANAGEMENT AND ATOMIC ENERGY.
NEW YORK: ATOMIC INDUS FORUM, 1958, 460 PP.
PROCEEDINGS OF ATOMIC ENERGY MANAGEMENT CONFERENCE ON
STATUS AND GROWTH OF ATOMIC INDUSTRY. CONSIDERS POLICY,
HEALTH AND SAFETY, ASSESSMENT OF US POWER REACTOR PROGRAM,
FEASIBILITY OF SMALL REACTORS, SALE OF NUCLEAR PRODUCTS
OUTSIDE US, AMENDMENTS TO ATOMIC ENERGY ACT, NUCLEAR SHIPS,
REDUCTION OF COST, INTERNATIONAL ACTIVITIES, PEACEFUL USES,
INDEMNIFICATION LAW, AND RESEARCH DEVELOPMENTS.

0146 AUERBACH C.A., GARRISON L.K. ET AL.
THE LEGAL PROCESS.
SAN FRANCISCO: CHANDLER, 1961, 915 PP., LC#61-12972.
DISCUSSES METHODS AND PROCESSES OF LEGAL DECISION-MAKING
BY JUDICIAL, LEGISLATIVE, EXECUTIVE, AND ADMINISTRATIVE
AGENCIES. EXAMINES LAW-MAKING FUNCTION OF JUDGE AND REVIEW
OF LEGISLATION AND ADMINISTRATIVE DECISIONS. STUDIES IN DE-
TAIL LEGISLATIVE PROCESS.

0147 AUMANN F.R.
"THE INSTRUMENTALITIES OF JUSTICE: THEIR FORMS, FUNCTIONS,
AND LIMITATIONS."
COLUMBUS: OHIO STATE U PR, 1956.
EXAMINATION OF PROBLEMS OF LEGAL ADMINISTRATION FROM A
POLITICAL SCIENCE VIEWPOINT. ANALYZES PROBLEM OF SYSTEMATIZ-
ING JUSTICE THROUGH LAW WITH ATTENTION DIRECTED TO THE
EMERGENCE OF LAW FROM THE INFLUENCES OF ENGLISH COMMON LAW
AND ROMAN CIVIL LAW. DISCUSSES MACHINERY OF JUSTICE AND SOME
POPULAR ATTITUDES ON JUSTICE AND LAW. UNANNOTATED BIBLIOGRA-
PHY OF WORKS IN ENGLISH, TOPICALLY ARRANGED.

0148 AUSLAND J.C., RICHARDSON H.F.
"CRISIS MANAGEMENT* BERLIN, CYPRUS, LAOS."
FOREIGN AFFAIRS, 44 (JAN. 66), 291-303.
ANALYSIS OF KENNEDY'S ATTEMPTS TO GAIN DECISION TIME
THROUGH ORGANIZATIONAL INNOVATIONS IN CRISIS MANAGEMENT. THE
SUCCESS OF DIFFERENT TYPES OF PRE-PLANNING AND ORGANIZATIONS
IS COMPARED IN THREE SPECIFIC CASES. COORDINATION OF FULL
RANGE OF PLANS IS MAIN PROBLEM DISCOVERED.

0149 AUSTRALIAN NATIONAL RES COUN
AUSTRALIAN SOCIAL SCIENCE ABSTRACTS.
MELBOURNE: AUSTRAL NAT RESEARCH.
A PUBLICATION OF ABSTRACTS IN THE SOCIAL SCIENCES INTEN-
DED TO PROVIDE A SURVEY OF MATERIAL PUBLISHED IN OR RELATED
TO AUSTRALIA, NEW ZEALAND, AND TERRITORIES. DEALING WITH
THE VARIOUS SOCIAL SCIENCES. PUBLISHED BIANNUALLY SINCE
MARCH, 1946. "ABSTRACTS" OFFERS A PRECISE OF EACH WORK
COVERED AND CLASSIFIES MATERIAL ACCORDING TO DIVISIONS
WITHIN THE SOCIAL SCIENCE DISCIPLINES.

0150 AVASTHI A. ED., VARMA S.N. ED.
ASPECTS OF ADMINISTRATION.
NEW DELHI: ALLIED PUBLISHERS, 1964, 450 PP.
ESSAYS ON PUBLIC ADMINISTRATION AND POLITICS IN INDIA.
DISCUSSES PUBLIC SERVICE, FINANCIAL COMMITTEES, WELFARE
ADMINISTRATION, FREEDOM OF EXPRESSION AND PARLIAMENTARY
PRIVILEGES, TEACHING OF POLITICAL SCIENCE IN UNIVERSITIES,
ETC. INCLUDES ESSAYS ON SCIENTIFIC RESEARCH AND
ADMINISTRATION IN US AND UK.

0151 AVERY M.W.
GOVERNMENT OF WASHINGTON STATE.
SEATTLE: U OF WASHINGTON PR, 1961, 320 PP., LC#61-8211.
PRESENTS ACCOUNT OF PRESENT STRUCTURE OF STATE AND LOCAL
GOVERNMENT IN WASHINGTON. SHOWS POWERS AND DUTIES OF EACH
OFFICE AND ITS RELATIONS WITH OTHER AGENCIES. TRACES EVOLU-
TION OF OFFICES AND OFFERS SUGGESTIONS FOR GREATER EFFICIEN-
CY IN THEIR OPERATION. STATES MAIN PROBLEMS CONFRONTING LEG-
ISLATURE AND COURTS. STRESSES ROLE OF CITIZEN IN WORKING EF-
FECTIVELY FOR GOOD GOVERNMENT.

0152 AYEARST M.
THE BRITISH WEST INDIES: THE SEARCH FOR SELF-GOVERNMENT.
LONDON: ALLEN & UNWIN, 1960, 258 PP., LC#60-6636.
SURVEYS DEVELOPMENT OF GOVERNMENT IN WEST INDIES. TREATS
PERIODS OF OLD REPRESENTATIVE AND CROWN COLONY SYSTEMS.
DISCUSSES CONSTITUTIONAL AND POLITICAL DEVELOPMENTS IN THE
ISLANDS AND MAINLAND COLONIES, AND BRITISH COLONIAL
POLICIES AND THEIR IMPLEMENTATION. DESCRIBES PRESENT
LEGISLATIVE AND EXECUTIVE BODIES, LOCAL GOVERNMENT,
POLITICAL PARTIES. ASSESSES FUTURE OF FEDERATION.

0153 AYLMER G.
THE KING'S SERVANTS.
NEW YORK: COLUMBIA U PRESS, 1961, 488 PP.
DESCRIBES ADMINISTRATIVE PROCEDURES, OFFICES, AND STRUC-

TURES UNDER CHARLES I, 1625-42. RELATES TYPE OF BUREAUCRACY
TO OVERTHROW BY CROMWELL, NOTING TYPES OF CHANGES AND
INNOVATIONS.

0154 BABCOCK R.S.
STATE & LOCAL GOVERNMENT AND POLITICS.
NEW YORK: RANDOM HOUSE, INC, 1957, 430 PP., LC#57-12777.
TEXTBOOK DEALS WITH LOBBIES, POLITICAL PARTIES,
ELECTIONS, STATE JUDICIARY, LEGISLATURE AND EXECUTIVE,
STATE SERVICES, ORGANIZATION, AND FINANCES.

0155 BACHELDER G.L. ED., SHAW P.C. ED.
THE LITERATURE OF FEDERALISM: A SELECTED BIBLIOGRAPHY (REV
ED) (A PAMPHLET)
E LANSING: MSU COMM DEV & SERV, 1966, 18 PP.
BIBLIOGRAPHICAL LISTING OF 192 SOURCES PERTAINING TO
FEDERALISM. ENTRIES DIVIDED INTO: AMERICAN FEDERALISM,
GENERAL WORKS, FEDERALISM IN OTHER NATIONS, AND GOVERNMENTAL
UBLICATIONS. ITEMS CITED INCLUDE ENGLISH-LANGUAGE PERIODICAL
ARTICLES AND BOOKS PUBLISHED 1863 THROUGH 1965.

0156 BACHRACH P., BARATZ M.S.
"DECISIONS AND NONDECISIONS: AN ANALYTICAL FRAMEWORK."
AMER. POLIT. SCI. REV., 57 (SEPT. 63), 632-642.
ATTEMPT TO CLARIFY KEY CONCEPTS FOR STUDY OF SUBJECT AND
TO SHOW HOW THOSE CONCEPTS CAN BE UTILIZED SYSTEMATICALLY
IN CASE STUDIES.

0157 BADI J.
THE GOVERNMENT OF THE STATE OF ISRAEL: A CRITICAL ACCOUNT OF
ITS PARLIAMENT, EXECUTIVE, AND JUDICIARY.
NEW YORK: TWAYNE, 1963, 307 PP., LC#63-17404.
STUDIES DEVELOPMENT OF ISRAEL'S GOVERNMENTAL STRUCTURE,
DELINEATING NATURE AND FUNCTION OF BODIES OF GOVERNMENT AND
POLITICAL PARTIES. ANALYZES VARIOUS ASSEMBLIES AND CABINETS
THAT HAVE DIRECTED POLICY SINCE INDEPENDENCE. STATES THAT
ISRAEL'S FUTURE DEPENDS ON HER ABILITY TO SOLVE THREE PROB-
LEMS: ACHIEVEMENT OF ECONOMIC INDEPENDENCE, INTEGRATION OF
IMMIGRANTS, AND PEACE WITH ARABS.

0158 BAERWALD F.
FUNDAMENTALS OF LABOR ECONOMICS.
NEW YORK: MC MULLEN BOOKS, INC, 1947, 464 PP.
STUDIES LABOR ECONOMICS, EMPHASIZING INTERRELATION OF
CENTRAL TOPICS. STRESSES NEED FOR RECONCILING ADVANCING
TECHNOLOGY WITH FULL EMPLOYMENT AND FOR BALANCING PRODUCTIVE
POTENTIAL AND CONSUMER INCOME. DISCUSSES PROBLEM OF FREE
SOCIETY FIGHTING TOTALITARIANISM OUTSIDE AND BUSINESS
CONCENTRATION INSIDE. EXPLORES WAGE THEORIES, LABOR MARKET,
EMPLOYMENT, SOCIAL SECURITY, AND LABOR RELATIONS.

0159 BAERWALD F.
ECONOMIC SYSTEM ANALYSIS: CONCEPTS AND PERSPECTIVES.
NEW YORK: FORDHAM U PR, 1960, 113 PP., LC#60-13937.
STUDY OF SCOPE AND PURPOSE OF SYSTEM ANALYSIS. PRESENTA-
TION OF GROWTH ON MACRO-ECONOMIC SCALE; SPONTANEOUS ECONOMIC
DEVELOPMENT; GROWTH-RATE; CONSUMER, INVESTMENT, AND PUBLIC
SECTOR; ECONOMIC GROWTH AND PRICE STABILITY. PROPOSES, IN
WIDER CONTEXT, THAT SYSTEM ANALYSIS CAN ACT AS DEFLATOR OF
IDEOLOGICAL COMPONENTS IN ECONOMIC THOUGHT AND ANALYSIS.

0160 BAGEHOT W.
THE ENGLISH CONSTITUTION AND OTHER POLITICAL ESSAYS.
LONDON: CHAPMAN AND HALL, 1924, 468 PP.
DISCUSSION OF FUNDAMENTAL PRINCIPLES AND STRUCTURES OF
BRITISH GOVERNMENT AND ITS PRACTICAL OPERATION. PRESENTS
ANALYSES OF CABINET, MONARCHY, HOUSES OF LORDS AND COMMONS,
CHANGES OF MINISTRY, CHECKS AND BALANCES, AND EXECUTIVE
PECULIARITIES AND THEIR HISTORICAL DETERMINANTS.

0161 BAILEY S.D.
"THE FUTURE COMPOSITION OF THE TRUSTEESHIP COUNCIL."
INT. ORG., 13 (SUMMER 59), 412-421.
DISCUSSES THE THREAT TO WORKABILITY OF THE COUNCIL CRE-
ATED BY THE RAPID DISAPPEARANCE OF THE TRUST TERRITORIES.
POINTS OUT THE PROBLEM OF HAVING MAJORITY OF COLONIAL AND
FORMER COLONIAL NATIONS ON THE PERMANENT TRUSTEESHIP COUNCIL
BECAUSE OF THEIR MEMBERSHIP ON THE SECURITY COUNCIL. A NUM-
BER OF POSSIBLE SOLUTIONS ARE SUGGESTED.

0162 BAILEY S.D.
THE SECRETARIAT OF THE UNITED NATIONS.
NEW YORK: CARNEGIE ENDOWMENT, 1962, 113 PP.
DISCUSSES EVOLUTION, ORGANIZATIONAL WORK, AND GROWING
STRENGTH OF THE SECRETARIAT AND OF THE SECRETARY-GENERAL.
PRESENTS MAJOR HISTORICAL EVENTS IN WHICH THE UN DECISIONS
PLAYED IMPORTANT ROLE.

0163 BAILEY S.D.
"THE TROIKA AND THE FUTURE OF THE UN."
INT. CONCIL., 538 (MAY 62), 3-64.
SEES THE TROIKA AS A DEVICE WHICH WOULD CONFINE THE UN
TO A DIPLOMATIC FORUM AND WOULD BRING MAJOR OPERATIONAL
ACTIVITIES TO A HALT. EMPHASIZES THAT IT IS NOT MERELY AN
ADMINISTRATIVE ADJUSTMENT, BUT A METHOD OF BRINGING THE VETO
INTO SECRETARIAT. GENERAL AND BRIEF DISCUSSION OF UN, INTER-

NATIONAL CIVIL SERVICE AND SECRETARY-GENERAL.

0164 BAILEY S.K., SIMON H.A. ET AL.
RESEARCH FRONTIERS IN POLITICS AND GOVERNMENT.
WASHINGTON: BROOKINGS INST, 1955, 240 PP.
REVIEWS NEW RESEARCH IN POLITICAL SCIENCE AND NEW
TECHNIQUES FOR FURTHER STUDY. EXAMINES RESEARCH AREAS OPEN
TO LEGISLATORS AND ADMINISTRATORS, NEW ADVANCES IN
ORGANIZATION THEORY, AND USE OF CONCEPTS OF HIERARCHY AND
BARGAINING. DISCUSSES USE OF GAME THEORY IN POLITICAL
BEHAVIOR ANALYSES AND RESEARCH ON NOMINATIONS AND ELECTIONS,
IMPACT OF REVOLUTIONS, AND COMPARATIVE POLITICS.

0165 BAINS J.S. ED.
STUDIES IN POLITICAL SCIENCE.
NEW YORK: ASIA PUBL HOUSE, 1961, 450 PP.
DEALS WITH INTERNATIONAL LAW AND RELATIONS INCLUDING JUR-
ISDICTION AND THEORY; POLITICAL RESEARCH AND THEORY; AND
PUBLIC ADMINISTRATION. CONCENTRATES ON WORK IN INDIA AND BY
INDIANS, BUT TOPICS ARE WORLD-WIDE.

0166 BAKER G.
THE COUNTY AGENT.
CHICAGO: U OF CHICAGO PRESS, 1939, 225 PP.
STUDIES COUNTY AGENT AS A SEMI-ADMINISTRATIVE AND
GOVERNMENTAL OFFICER WHO NOT ONLY REPRESENTS EDUCATIONAL-
SERVICE ASPECTS OF GOVERNMENT, BUT ALSO SERVES AS AN
EFFECTIVE CO-ORDINATOR OF DIFFERENT GOVERNMENTAL LEVELS AND
OF VARIED AGRICULTURAL PROGRAMS. ATTEMPTS TO ANALYZE
DEVELOPMENT AND FUNCTIONS OF COUNTY AGRICULTURAL AGENT
MOVEMENT FROM INCEPTION THROUGH NEW DEAL PERIOD.

0167 BAKER H.
PROBLEMS OF REEMPLOYMENT AND RETRAINING OF MANPOWER DURING
THE TRANSITION FROM WAR TO PEACE.
PRINCETON: PRIN U INDUS REL CTR, 1945, 45 PP.
APPROXIMATELY 275 ENTRIES INCLUDING BOOKS, GOVERNMENT
PUBLICATIONS, AND ARTICLES FROM TECHNICAL JOURNALS DEALING
WITH PROBLEMS OF RETRAINING VETERANS AND ENACTING MEASURES
TO ABSORB VETERANS INTO NORMAL, GAINFUL EMPLOYMENT. ALL EN-
TRIES ARE IN ENGLISH AND WERE PUBLISHED 1943-45. ARRANGED
BY SUBJECT AND ALPHABETICALLY BY AUTHOR.

0168 BAKER R.J.
"DISCUSSION AND DECISION-MAKING IN THE CIVIL SERVICE."
PUBLIC ADMINISTRATION, 41 (WINTER 63), 345-356.
INFORMAL ORAL COMMUNICATION IS BASIS FOR DECISION-MAKING
IN BRITISH POSTAL ADMINISTRATION; THIS MAKES IT DIFFICULT
FOR ANY INDIVIDUAL TO BE HELD RESPONSIBLE FOR A DECISION.
IN GENERAL, BRITISH ADMINISTRATIVE DEPARTMENTS ARE RESPON-
SIVE TO PARLIAMENTARY DIRECTIVES.

0169 BAKKE E.W.
BONDS OF ORGANIZATION (2ND ED.)
HAMDEN, CONN: ARCHON BOOKS, 1950, 239 PP., LC#66-14603.
STUDY OF THE "FUNCTIONAL INTERDEPENDENCE" OF SUCH AS-
PECTS OF ORGANIZATIONAL ACTIVITY AS FINANCE, LEADERSHIP PRO-
CESS, AND DEVELOPMENT OF BASIC RESOURCES. EMPIRICAL
STUDY OF HUMAN RELATIONS IN TWO ORGANIZATIONS.

0170 BAKKE E.W.
MUTUAL SURVIVAL; THE GOAL OF UNION AND MANAGEMENT (2ND ED.)
HAMDEN, CONN: ARCHON BOOKS, 1966, 116 PP.
ANALYSIS OF UNION-MANAGEMENT RELATIONS IN 1946 AND 1966,
COMPARING STRUCTURE OF EACH AND THEIR SIGNIFICANCE TO US
ECONOMY. INCLUDES ATTITUDES OF UNIONS AND MANAGEMENT TOWARD
OTHER.

0171 BALDWIN D.A.
"CONGRESSIONAL INITIATIVE IN FOREIGN POLICY."
J. OF POLITICS, 28 (NOV. 66), 54-773.
BY USE OF CASE STUDIES, THE CREATION OF THE INTERNATIONAL
DEVELOPMENT ASSOCIATION AND THE DEVELOPMENT LOAN FUND,
BALDWIN TAKES THE POSITION THAT CONGRESS DID NOT USE
INITIATIVE IN FOREIGN POLICY FORMATION. INSTEAD, VETO AND
THREAT OF VETO FORCED THE ADMINISTRATION TO PROPOSE ONLY
POLITICALLY ACCEPTABLE PROGRAMS.

0172 BALDWIN D.A.
FOREIGN AID AND AMERICAN FOREIGN POLICY; A DOCUMENTARY
ANALYSIS.
NEW YORK: FREDERICK PRAEGER, 1966, 261 PP., LC#66-18888.
BALDWIN CONSIDERS FOREIGN AID TO BE AN INTEGRAL COMPONENT
OF AMERICAN FOREIGN POLICY. WORK IS STRUCTURED TO PROVIDE
AN INDEPENDENT LEARNING EXPERIENCE FOR THE STUDENT-READER.
PRESENTS ALTERNATIVE FOREIGN-AID-POLICY THEORIES, STRUCTURES
AND CAVEATS; FOLLOWS WITH EXTENSIVE 1945-1965 STATISTICS;
PRESENTS BULK OF WORK, A CHRONOLOGICAL AND TOPICAL ORGANI-
ZATION, WITH DOCUMENTS, REPORTS, RESOLUTIONS, STATEMENTS.

0173 BALDWIN G.B.
PLANNING AND DEVELOPMENT IN IRAN.
BALTIMORE: JOHNS HOPKINS PRESS, 1967, 213 PP., LC#67-18377.
DESCRIBES SUCCESS AND FAILURE OF IRANIAN DEVELOPMENT PLAN
1962-67. SHOWS HOW PLAN WAS FORMULATED AND HOW IRAN CONTIN-
UES TO PROFIT FROM ORIGINAL PLANNING EFFORT, THOUGH NATION-

AL DEVELOPMENT AGENCY FAILED IN 1957. RECONCILES ECONOMIC
THEORY WITH POLITICAL, ECONOMIC, CULTURAL, AND INSTITUTIONAL
PROBLEMS OF PLANNING IN DEVELOPING COUNTRY. POINTS OUT THAT
PLANNING AND DEVELOPMENT DO NOT NECESSARILY GO HAND-IN-HAND.

0174 BALDWIN H.
"SLOW-DOWN IN THE PENTAGON."
FOREIGN AFFAIRS, 43 (JAN. 65), 262-280.
   A CRITIQUE OF THE BUREAUCRATIZATION AND OVER-CENTRALIZA-
TION OF THE DEPARTMENT OF DEFENSE, WHICH BALDWIN BELIEVES
HAS LED TO A DANGEROUS SLOW DOWN IN WEAPONS RESEARCH, AND
IMPLEMENTATION. CORROBORATIVE CASES AND SOURCES CITED.

0175 BALDWIN R.N., RANDALL C.B.
CIVIL LIBERTIES AND INDUSTRIAL CONFLICT.
CAMBRIDGE: HARVARD U PR, 1938, 137 PP.
   ESSAYS BY MEMBER OF AMERICAN CIVIL LIBERTIES UNION AND
EXECUTIVE OF A MAJOR STEEL COMPANY. DISCUSS PLACE OF
ORGANIZED LABOR IN A POLITICAL DEMOCRACY, PUBLIC OPINION
REGARDING LABOR-INDUSTRY TROUBLES, AND ROLE OF MANAGEMENT
IN DEALING WITH MASS ACTIVITIES OF LABOR FORCE. ANALYZES
CAUSES AND NATURE OF "PLIGHT" OF THE WORKER.

0176 BANFIELD E.C.
"THE POLITICAL IMPLICATIONS OF METROPOLITAN GROWTH" (BMR)"
DAEDALUS, 90 (WINTER 60), 61-78.
   EXAMINES EFFECTS OF RAPID POPULATION GROWTH ON POLITICAL
STRUCTURE AND OUTLINES TASKS OF METROPOLITAN GOVERNMENT
IN TWO CONTRASTING SYSTEMS, US AND UK. DISCUSSES RELATION OF
CITIZEN TO GOVERNMENT, ADMINISTRATIVE STRUCTURES OF LOCAL
GOVERNMENTS, AND PROBLEMS OF CHANGE. FEELS TASKS GOVERNMENT
MUST PERFORM IN SUPPLYING GOODS AND SERVICES HAVE NO
NECESSARY RELATION TO POLITICAL MATTERS.

0177 BANFIELD E.C. ED.
URBAN GOVERNMENT; A READER IN POLITICS AND ADMINISTRATION.
NEW YORK: FREE PRESS OF GLENCOE, 1961, 593 PP.
   PLANNERS, REFORMERS, AND SOCIAL SCIENTISTS GIVE THEIR
VIEWS ON URBAN GOVERNMENT AS IT IS ACTUALLY PRACTICED.

0178 BANFIELD E.C., WILSON J.Q.
CITY POLITICS.
CAMBRIDGE: HARVARD U PR, 1963, 362 PP.
   A "POLITICAL" ANALYSIS OF THE WAY CITIES FUNCTION WHICH
IS BASED ON THE VIEW THAT CITY GOVERNMENT CAN BE BEST UNDER-
STOOD BY LOOKING AT THE CONFLICT OF OPINIONS AND INTEREST
THAT DEVELOP IN URBAN AREAS, THE ISSUES WHICH ARISE AS A
RESULT OF THIS CONFLICT, AND THE WAY INSTITUTIONS TRY TO
RESOLVE THE ISSUES. UNLIKE PAST WORKS, THIS STUDY DOES NOT
SEE LOCAL POLITICS IN TERMS OF "ADMINISTRATIVE" ISSUES.

0179 BANFIELD E.C.
BIG CITY POLITICS.
NEW YORK: RANDOM HOUSE, INC, 1965, 149 PP., LC#65-13765.
   COMPARATIVE GUIDE TO POLITICAL SYSTEMS OF ATLANTA, MIAMI,
BOSTON, DETROIT, EL PASO, LOS ANGELES, PHILADELPHIA, ST.
LOUIS, AND SEATTLE. DESCRIBES TYPICAL, NORMAL ASPECTS OF
EACH CITY'S POLITICS. GIVES FACTS ABOUT CITY, PRESENTS
FORMAL ORGANIZATION OF ITS CITY GOVERNMENT, TELLS HOW
INFORMAL OPERATION WORKS, EXPLAINS ELECTORAL SYSTEM, STUDIES
INTEREST GROUPS, AND DESCRIBES INTERCONNECTIONS OF SYSTEM.

0180 BANFIELD J.
"FEDERATION IN EAST-AFRICA."
INT. J., 18 (SPRING 63), 181-194.
   EXAMINES EAST-AFRICAN EXPERIENCE WITH FEDERATION FROM THE
EARLY PERIOD OF COLONIAL RULE TO THE PRESENT WITH REFERENCE
TO RECENT UPSURGE OF INTEREST BY KENYA, TANGANYIKA AND
UGANDA IN FEDERATION AS A REGIONAL ALTERNATIVE TO NATIONAL
DEVELOPMENT. SURVEYS ACCOMPLISHMENT AND AREAS OF CONFLICT
THAT REMAIN. GREATEST OBSTACLE TO EAST-AFRICAN UNITY IS
ABSENCE OF 'PRINCIPLES OF COHESION'.

0181 BANTON M.
THE POLICEMAN IN THE COMMUNITY.
LONDON: TAVISTOCK, 1964, 276 PP.
   SOCIOLOGICAL APPROACH TO ROLE OF THE POLICEMAN IN THE
COMMUNITY. EMPHASIZES OCCUPATIONAL DEMANDS AND NORMS.
DISCUSSES POLICE ORGANIZATION IN US AND UK. CASE STUDIES
OF POLICE WORK IN SCOTTISH AND AMERICAN CITIES.

0182 BARBASH J.
THE PRACTICE OF UNIONISM.
NEW YORK: HARPER & ROW, 1956, 465 PP., LC#56-9325.
   A WELL-WRITTEN BOOK ON THE INTERNAL AND EXTERNAL ASPECTS
OF UNIONS, THEIR GOVERNANCE, ADMINISTRATION, AND RIVALRY
BETWEEN THE AFL AND CIO FOR REPRESENTATION, AS WELL AS
THE MACHINERY OF COLLECTIVE BARGAINING, STRIKES, THE UNION
AS A LOBBY. SPECIFIC PROBLEMS SUCH AS RACKETEERING
INFLUENCE IN UNIONS AND COMMUNISM ARE DISCUSSED.

0183 BARBER W.F., RONNING C.N.
INTERNAL SECURITY AND MILITARY POWER* COUNTERINSURGENCY AND
CIVIC ACTION IN LATIN AMERICA.
COLUMBUS: OHIO STATE U PR, 1966, 338 PP., LC#66-11608.
   THE PROMOTION OF THE POLICY OF MILITARY CIVIC ACTION BY
THE US AS A MEANS OF STAVING OFF INSURGENCY IN LATIN AMERICA
IS EXAMINED AND QUESTIONED BY THE AUTHORS. ORGANIZATIONS
AND PROGRAMS INVOLVED IN CIVIC ACTION DEMONSTRATE DILEMMA
OF HAVING MILITARY ENGAGED IN DOMESTIC ACTIVITY IN COMPETI-
TION WITH CIVILIANS. WELL DOCUMENTED, LENGTHY BIBLIOGRAPHY.

0184 BARISH N.N. ED., VERHULST M. ED.
MANAGEMENT SCIENCES IN THE EMERGING COUNTRIES.
NEW YORK: PERGAMON PRESS, 1965, 261 PP., LC#63-18929.
   EXPLORES WAYS IN WHICH MANAGEMENT TOOLS DEVELOPED FOR USE
IN MORE ADVANCED ECONOMIES MAY BE APPLIED TO NEWLY EMERGING
COUNTRIES. SURVEYS SIGNIFICANT ENVIRONMENTAL DIFFERENCES
BETWEEN THESE ECONOMIES TO AVOID ILL-ADVISED APPLICATIONS
OF OPERATIONS RESEARCH AND MANAGEMENT SCIENCE TECHNIQUES.
SOME PAPERS PRESENTED IN FRENCH.

0185 BARKER E.
THE DEVELOPMENT OF PUBLIC SERVICES IN WESTERN EUROPE:
1660-1930.
LONDON: OXFORD U PR, 1944, 93 PP.
   HISTORY OF THE DEVELOPMENT OF PUBLIC ADMINISTRATION IN
ENGLAND, FRANCE, AND PRUSSIA, WITH COMPARISONS OF STRUCTURES
AND FUNCTIONS. CONCENTRATES ON MILITARY CONSCRIPTION,
TAXATION, SOCIAL WELFARE, AND EDUCATION.

0187 BARNARD C.I.
THE FUNCTIONS OF THE EXECUTIVE.
CAMBRIDGE: HARVARD U. PR., 1947, 334 PP.
   CONCERNS ESSENTIALLY THE PHYSICAL, PERSONAL, AND SOCIAL
FACTORS THAT UNDERLIE THE THEORY OF EXECUTIVE COOPERATION
AND ORGANIZATION AND A STUDY OF THE FUNCTIONS AND METHODS OF
EXECUTIVE OPERATIONS.

0188 BARNES W., MORGAN J.
THE FOREIGN SERVICE OF THE UNITED STATES.
WASHINGTON: DEPT/STATE, 1961, 430 PP., $3.50.
   ACCOUNT OF ORIGINS AND DEVELOPMENT OF FOREIGN SERVICE, AS
WELL AS A DESCRIPTION OF ITS PRESENT STATUS.

0189 BARNETT V.M. JR. ED.
THE REPRESENTATION OF THE UNITED STATES ABROAD* REVISED
EDITION.
NEW YORK: FREDERICK PRAEGER, 1965, 251 PP., LC#65-15651.
   7 PAPERS ANALYZING PROBLEMS OF REPRESENTATION IN A WORLD
OF "COMPETITIVE COEXISTENCE." CONCERNED WITH= "CHANGING AS-
PECTS, GROWTH OF AMERICAN REPRESENTATION, ECONOMIC REPRE-
SENTATION, INFORMATION AND CULTURAL REPRESENTATION, MILITARY
REPRESENTATION, REPRESENTATION TO INTERNATIONAL AND MULTI-
LATERAL ORGANIZATIONS, AND THE COORDINATION OF OVERSEAS
REPRESENTATION.

0190 BARRASH J.
LABOR'S GRASS ROOTS; A STUDY OF THE LOCAL UNION.
NEW YORK: HARPER & ROW, 1961, 250 PP., LC#61-14839.
   STUDIES LOCAL US LABOR UNIONS IN RELATION TO NATIONAL
LABOR MOVEMENT. DISCUSSES UNION GOVERNMENT, LEADERSHIP,
INTERNAL CONFLICT, DEMOCRATIC OPERATION, AND CROSS SECTION
OF LOCAL MEMBERSHIP.

0191 BARTLEY H.J.
"COMMAND EXPERIENCE."
MIL. REV., 41 (NOV. 61), 9-14.
   THE PUBLIC CONCEPTION OF THE ARMY LEADER HAS CHANGED
SINCE 1945. 'THE ARMY - FOR BETTER OR FOR WORSE - HAS BEEN
SO SUCCESSFUL IN PUTTING ACROSS ITS CORPORATE IMAGE THAT THE
PUBLIC THINKS OF AN ARMY LEADER THAN AS A COMMANDER.
ACCEPTANCE OF THIS IMAGE WITHIN THE ARMY COULD MEAN A CHANGE
IN ATTITUDE TOWARD COMMAND EXPERIENCE.' ARMY MUST EMPHASIZE
THAT MOLDING-EXPERIENCES ARE OFFICER'S OWN RESPONSIBILITY.

0192 BARZANSKI S.
"REGIONAL UNDERDEVELOPMENT IN THE EUROPEAN ECONOMIC
COMMUNITY."
ORBIS, 7 (SPRING 63), 105-119.
   EXAMINES UNBALANCED ECONOMIC GROWTH WITHIN EEC AND THREAT
POSED TO EUROPEAN POLITICAL AND ECONOMIC UNION. CONFLICTING
NATIONAL INTERESTS LIMIT EFFECTIVENESS OF NATIONAL PROGRAMS
AS LONG-TERM SOLUTION. CONCLUDES THAT UNIFIED EUROPE DEPENDS
ON PLANNED ECONOMY ACCORDING TO NEEDS OF WHOLE COMMUNITY
UNDER A FORM OF CENTRALIZED CONTROL.

0193 BASS B.M.
LEADERSHIP, PSYCHOLOGY, AND ORGANIZATIONAL BEHAVIOR.
NEW YORK: HARPER & ROW, 1960, 548 PP.
   A SOCIO-PSYCHOLOGICAL STUDY OF GROUP LEADERSHIP. DEFINES
TYPES OF LEADERS (SELF-ORIENTED, TASK-ORIENTED, AND INTER-
ACTION-ORIENTED) AND ANALYZES PSYCHOLOGICAL TRAITS OF EACH.
MEASURES LEADERSHIP IN TERMS OF GROUP EFFECTIVENESS, ORGAN-
IZATION, AND INTERACTION.

0194 BASS M.E., MARTIN E.D.
SELECTIVE BIBLIOGRAPHY ON MUNICIPAL GOVERNMENT FROM THE
FILES OF THE MUNICIPAL TECHNICAL ADVISORY SERVICE.
KNOXVILLE: U TENN MUNIC TECH ADV, 1963, 40 PP.
   BIBLIOGRAPHIC LISTING OF PUBLICATIONS PERTAINING TO EVERY
AREA OF MUNICIPAL ADMINISTRATION. MATERIAL LISTED COVERS

SPECIFIC TOPICS WITHIN BROADER FIELDS OF FINANCE, PUBLIC
SERVICES, ADMINISTRATION, AND PLANNING.

0195 BASTID M.
"ORIGINES ET DEVELOPMENT DE LA REVOLUTION CULTURELLE."
POLITIQUE ETRANGERE, 32 (1967), 68-86.
WITNESS OF BEGINNINGS OF CHINESE CULTURAL REVOLUTION AND
COMMENTS ON SERIES OF EVENTS UP TO SEPTEMBER 16, 1966.
DIVIDES EVENTS INTO TWO PERIODS: SOCIALIST CULTURAL REVOLU-
TION AND GREAT PROLETARIAN CULTURAL REVOLUTION. PARTICULAR
EMPHASIS ON ROLE OF UNIVERSITIES. ARGUES THAT CULTURAL REVO-
LUTION WAS NOT EFFECT OF PRECONCEIVED PLAN AND WAS IN SOME
SENSES ACCIDENTAL, BASED ON A LOGIC OF CHANCE AND UTILITY.

0196 BAUER R.A.
"BRAINWASHING: PSYCHOLOGY OR DEMONOLOGY."
J. SOC. ISSUES, 13 (NO.3, 57), 41-47.
A PAPER FROM A SYMPOSIUM ON BRAINWASHING CONCLUDES THAT
NO POSITIVE EVIDENCE THAT BRAINWASHING BASED ON UNNATURAL
INFLUENCES AND THAT SOVIET METHODS ARE ORDINARY PSYCHOLOGI-
CAL TECHNIQUES OF COERCION AND PERSUASION.

0197 BAUM R.D.
"IDEOLOGY REDIVIVUS."
PROBLEMS OF COMMUNISM, 16 (MAY-JUNE 67), 1-11.
TRACES THE DEVELOPMENT OF CHINA'S CULTURAL REVOLUTION,
BEGINNING IN 1963-64, FROM ATTACKS ON BUREAUCRACY AND SIMPLE
APOLITICISM TO THE IDEOLOGICAL "REVIVALISM" OF 1966-67. ONE
EXPLANATION OFFERED IS THAT OF REACTION AGAINST AN ERODING
OF REVOLUTIONARY SPIRIT, USUAL WHEN REVOLUTIONARY CONDITIONS
PASS. MAO'S VISION OF THE GOOD SOCIETY MAY PROVE IRRECONCIL-
ABLE WITH THE NECESSITIES OF A MODERN SOCIETY.

0198 BAUMGARTEL H.
"LEADERSHIP STYLE AS A VARIABLE IN RESEARCH ADMINISTRATION."
ADMINISTRATIVE SCI. Q., 2 (DEC. 57), 344-360.
REPORT ON THE RELATIONSHIP BETWEEN LEADERSHIP STYLES OF
LABORATORY DIRECTORS IN A GOVERNMENT RESEARCH ORGANIZATION
AND CERTAIN ATTITUDES AND MOTIVATIONS OF THE SCIENTISTS
WITHIN THOSE LABORATORIES. SAYS THAT SCIENTISTS WORK BEST
WHEN THEY FEEL REPRESENTED IN MANAGEMENT'S DECISION-MAKING.

0199 BAVELAS A.
"LEADERSHIP: MAN AND FUNCTION."
ADMINISTRATIVE SCI. Q., 4 (MAR. 60), 491-498.
DISCUSSES LEADERSHIP FROM FUNCTIONAL AND PERSONAL STAND-
POINT, CLAIMING THAT FUNCTIONAL ASPECT IS INCREASING WHILE
PERSONAL ELEMENT IN LEADERSHIP DECLINES AS BUREAUCRACIES
FLOURISH. CALLS FOR RECONSIDERATION OF BUREAUCRACY AS IDEAL
FORM FOR ORGANIZATION.

0200 BEAL J.R.
JOHN FOSTER DULLES, A BIOGRAPHY.
NEW YORK: HARPER, 1957, 331 PP.
THE STORY OF THE LIFE OF THE LATE US SECRETARY OF STATE
WHICH ASSERTS HE WAS 'ONE MAN WHO WAS NEVER DECEIVED ABOUT
THE NATURE OF THE SOVIET MENACE.'

0201 BEASLEY K.E.
STATE SUPERVISION OF MUNICIPAL DEBT IN KANSAS - A CASE STUDY
LAWRENCE: U KANSAS, GOV RES CTR, 1961, 220 PP.
TRACES DEVELOPMENT OF REGULATION OF MUNICIPAL DEBT IN
KANSAS. FOCUSES ON LEGISLATIVE JUDICIAL, AND ADMINISTRA-
TIVE SUPERVISION. INCLUDES STATISTICAL DATA AND TABLE OF
CASES.

0202 BEASLEY W.G.
"POLITICS AND THE SAMURAI CLASS STRUCTURE IN SATSUMA, 1858-
1868."
MODERN ASIAN STUDIES, 1 (JAN. 67), 47-57.
ANALYZES SOCIAL AND ECONOMIC BACKGROUND OF SATSUMA SAMUR-
AI DURING CRUCIAL DECADE TO FIND OUT WHAT POLITICAL AND SOC-
IAL OUTLETS MEMBERS OF THIS CLASS HAD. COMPARISON WITH SIM-
ILAR STUDY OF TOSA ELITES. ANALYSIS ACCORDING TO RANK, STA-
TUS, AGE, BACKGROUND, AND MEANS. CONCLUDES THAT TRADITIONAL
INSTITUTIONS WERE VERY STRONG IN SATSUMA AND CITES REASONS
WHY INTERNAL REBELLION WAS SO EASILY QUELLED.

0203 BEAUFRE A.
NATO AND EUROPE.
NEW YORK: VINTAGE BOOKS, 1966, 170 PP., LC#66-28867.
ANALYSIS OF DEVELOPMENT OF NATO AND STATUS OF EUROPEAN
UNITY. DISCUSSES STRUCTURE AND STRATEGY OF NATO DEFENSE AND
RECENT CHANGES IN ATTITUDE AND ORGANIZATION.

0204 BECHHOEFER B.G.
"UNITED NATIONS PROCEDURES IN CASE OF VIOLATIONS OF DISARM-
AMENT AGREEMENTS."
J. ARMS CONTR., 1 (JULY 63), 191-202.
DISCUSSES UN'S STRUCTURE AND PAST HISTORY IN ORDER TO
ASSESS UN'S EFFECTIVENESS AND AVAILIBILITY IN MATTERS CON-
CERNING DISARMAMENT VIOLATIONS. UN MILITARY FORCE AND INTER-
NATIONAL COURT OF JUSTICE ARE REJECTED AS POTENTIAL ORGANS
OF CONTROL. RECOMMENDS SECURITY COUNCIL AND GENERAL ASSEM-
BLY AS POTENTIAL VEHICLES FOR EFFECTING SANCTIONS.

0205 BECKMAN T.N., DAVIDSON W.R.
MARKETING (7TH ED.)
NEW YORK: RONALD PRESS, 1962, 873 PP., LC#62-09764.
DISCUSSES PROBLEMS OF MARKETING INDUSTRY, INCLUDING FUN-
DAMENTALS, CONSUMER BEHAVIOR, OUR RETAIL SYSTEM, WHOLESALING
PRODUCTS, FUNCTIONAL ANALYSIS OF MARKETING, MARKETING POLI-
CIES, AND MARKETING IN RELATION TO GOVERNMENT.

0206 BEGUIN H.
"ASPECTS GEOGRAPHIQUES DE LA POLARISATION."
TIERS-MONDE, 4 (NO. 16, 63), 559-608.
DEALS WITH FIRST STAGES OF DEVELOPMENT OF THIRD WORLD
COUNTRIES. RELATES PATTERN OF THEIR DEVELOPMENT TO
GEOGRAPHIC ENVIRONMENT. CALLS FOR INCREASED KNOWLEDGE OF
GEOGRAPHIC FACTORS INFLUENCING POLARIZATION PROCESS.

0207 BEISEL A.R.
CONTROL OVER ILLEGAL ENFORCEMENT OF THE CRIMINAL LAW: ROLE
OF THE SUPREME COURT.
BOSTON: BOSTON U PR, 1955, 112 PP., LC#55-9910.
STUDY OF PROBLEMS ARISING WHEN ILLEGAL METHODS ARE USED
BY POLICE TO ENFORCE CRIMINAL LAW AND ROLE OF SUPREME COURT
IN DEALING WITH AND CONTROLLING THESE OCCURRENCES. CONSIDERS
STANDARDS OF LEGALITY FOR SEARCHES AND SEIZURES, WIRE TAP-
PING, INVASIONS OF PRIVACY AND OTHER PREVALENT EXAMPLES OF
ABUSE OF GOVERNMENTAL POWER BY POLICE. STRESSES NECESSITY OF
LAWS TO PROTECT INDIVIDUAL PRIVACY.

0208 BELL J.
THE SPLENDID MISERY: THE STORY OF THE PRESIDENCY AND POWER
POLITICS AT CLOSE RANGE.
GARDEN CITY: DOUBLEDAY, 1960, 474 PP., LC#60-0858.
REVIVING MEMORIES OF A DOZEN NATIONAL ADMINISTRATIONS,
AUTHOR TRACES RUNNING BATTLE BETWEEN EXECUTIVE AND LEGIS-
LATIVE BRANCHES TO CAPTURE LEADERSHIP OF NATION; SKETCHES
THE PATTERN BY WHICH DAILY FUNCTIONS OF PRESIDENCY ARE
CARRIED OUT, IF NOT ALWAYS BY PRESIDENT.

0209 BELSHAW D.G.R.
"PUBLIC INVESTMENT IN AGRICULTURE AND ECONOMIC DEVELOPMENT
OF UGANDA"
J. OF EAST AFRICAN ECONOMIC REV., 9 (DEC. 62), 69-94.
CRITICISM OF 1960 ECONOMIC SURVEY MISSION OF WORLD BANK.
SUGGESTS CENTRALIZED ECONOMIC PLANNING, APPLIED RESEARCH,
AND A FLEXIBLE SYSTEM FOR REVIEWING PUBLIC EXPENDITURE.

0210 BENDIX R.
"INDUSTRIALIZATION, IDEOLOGIES, AND SOCIAL STRUCTURE" (BMR)"
AMER. SOCIOLOGICAL REV., 24 (OCT. 59), 613-623.
ILLUSTRATES BASIC DIFFERENCE BETWEEN MANAGERIAL IDEOLOGY
IN ENGLAND AND RUSSIA, AND RELATES IT TO STRUCTURAL
DIFFERENCES IN BUREAUCRACY. STUDIES EFFECTIVENESS OF
IDEOLOGY PRESUPPOSING SELF-RELIANCE AND GOOD FAITH.

0211 BENJAMIN H.C.
EMPLOYMENT TESTS IN INDUSTRY AND BUSINESS.
PRINCETON: PRIN U INDUS REL CTR, 1945, 46 PP.
APPROXIMATELY 250 ENTRIES CONSISTING OF BOOKS AND ARTI-
CLES FROM SCHOLARLY AND TECHNICAL JOURNALS AND BIBLIOGRA-
PHIES, DISCUSSING SEVERAL TYPES OF TESTS USED IN SELECTING
NEW EMPLOYEES IN BUSINESS AND INDUSTRY. ALL ENTRIES ARE IN
ENGLISH; PUBLICATIONS DATED 1930-45 ARRANGED BY SUBJECT
AND ALPHABETICALLY BY AUTHOR.

0212 BENNETT H.A.
THE COMMISSION AND THE COMMON LAW: A STUDY IN
ADMINISTRATIVE ADJUDICATION.
NEW YORK: EXPOSITION PRESS, 1964, 127 PP., LC#64-25097.
A STUDY OF PROBLEMS IN ADMINISTRATIVE ADJUDICATION,
CARRIED ON THROUGH STUDYING ICC DECISIONS ON FREIGHT
FORWARDING. IS PARTICULARLY CONCERNED WITH UNNECESSARY
DEPARTURES FROM PRINCIPLES OF COMMON LAW. CONCLUDES THAT
ICC RECORD IS ONE OF "EXPEDIENCY AND MANIPULATION," THAT
CORRECT DECISIONS HAVE OFTEN BEEN INCORRECTLY REACHED, AND
THAT ICC ERRORS HAVE HAD TO BE - AND ARE - REDRESSED.

0213 BENNETT J.W.
HUTTERIAN BRETHREN: THE AGRICULTURAL ECONOMY AND SOCIAL
ORGANIZATION OF A COMMUNAL PEOPLE.
STANFORD: STANFORD U PRESS, 1967, 228 PP.
EXAMINES SIX COLONIES OF HUTTERIAN SECT TO SHOW HOW
COMMUNAL FARMS WERE ESTABLISHED AND RELATIONS WERE FORMED
WITH OTHER LOCAL PEOPLE. DISCUSSES FAMILY AND KINSHIP,
AGRICULTURAL MANAGEMENT AND DECISION-MAKING, METHODS OF
PRODUCTION, AND CHANGES IN HUTTERIAN SOCIETY AND TECHNOLOGY
TO DETERMINE CAUSES OF COMMUNES' SUCCESS. COMPARES COLONY
WITH ISRAELI KIBBUTZ.

0214 BENNIS W.G.
"LEADERSHIP THEORY AND ADMINISTRATIVE BEHAVIOR: THE PROBLEM
OF AUTHORITY."
ADMINISTRATIVE SCI. Q., 4 (1959), 259-301.
A THOROUGH STUDY OF CONTEMPORARY AND PAST THEORIES OF
LEADERSHIP, AND PREVIOUS ATTEMPTS TOWARD A UNIFIED APPROACH.
TWO MAJOR APPROACHES, THE HUMAN-RELATIONS AND THE
RATIONALIST, ARE NOTEWORTHY. CONSIDERS THE BASIC COMPONENTS

ESSENTIAL TO LEADERSHIP EFFICIENCY AND EFFECTIVENESS.

0215 BENNIS W.G.
"REVISIONIST THEORY OF LEADERSHIP"
HARVARD BUSINESS REV., 39 (1961), 26-36, 146-150.
CITES NEED OF DEVELOPING A MORE RELIABLE AND SATISFACTORY
APPROACH TO THE STUDY AND DESIGNATION OF THE THEORY OF
LEADERSHIP, AND PRESENTS ALTERNATIVES DESCRIBED BY
MCMURRY, ARGYRIS, AND MCGREGOR.

0216 BENNIS W.G.
"A NEW ROLE FOR THE BEHAVIORAL SCIENCES: EFFECTING ORGAN-
IZATIONAL CHANGE."
ADMINISTRATIVE SCI. Q., 8 (SEPT. 63), 125-165.
ARTICLE IDENTIFIES A NEWLY EMERGING FUNCTION FOR THE BE-
HAVIORAL SCIENTIST AND EXEMPLIFIES ITS ACTIVITIES BY DE-
SCRIBING AND ANALYZING SOME RECENT WORK IN THE ORGANIZATION-
CHANGE AREA. SOME TRADITIONAL STRATEGIES OF CHANGE ARE DIS-
DISCUSSED, FOLLOWED BY A DESCRIPTION AND ANALYSIS OF SOME OF
THE NEWER CHANGE PROGRAMS. LASTLY, THE ROLE STRAINS INHERENT
IN THIS NEW ACTION ROLE ARE DISCUSSED.

0217 BENOIT E.
EUROPE AT SIXES AND SEVENS: THE COMMON MARKET, THE FREE
TRADE ASSOCIATION AND THE UNITED STATES.
NEW YORK: COLUMBIA U. PR. 1961, 287 PP.
STATES THAT CREATION OF EUROPEAN COMMUNITY REPRESENTS
ATTEMPT TO FIND NEW WAYS OF ORDERING RELATIONS BETWEEN
STATES AUGMENTING MERE PROFESSIONS OF COOPERATION. EXAMINES
STRUGGLE FOR INTEGRATION, DOLLAR CRISIS AND AMERICAN COM-
PETITIVENESS. STUDIES BUSINESS OPPORTUNITIES IN A CONSOL-
DATED EUROPEAN COMMUNITY.

0218 BENSON E.T.
CROSS FIRE: THE EIGHT YEARS WITH EISENHOWER.
GARDEN CITY: DOUBLEDAY, 1962, 627 PP., LC#62-11368.
DETAILED ACCOUNT OF IKE'S CABINET MAN WHO SERVED BOTH
TERMS - HIS LIFE, PERSONALITY, CONSERVATIVE BELIEFS, AND
PEOPLE WHO INFLUENCED HIM AS HE FOUGHT CONGRESS AND PARTY
POLITICIANS FOR HIS POLICIES. ANALYZES TAFT AND DULLES AS
LAST TWO REPUBLICAN "GIANTS"; TREATS CHANGE IN NIXON UP TO
1960.

0220 BENTLEY A.F.
INQUIRY INTO INQUIRIES: ESSAYS IN SOCIAL THEORY.
BOSTON: BEACON PRESS, 1954, 365 PP., LC#54-6165.
EXAMINES BASIC PROBLEMS IN NATURAL AND SOCIAL SCI-
ENCES, AND IN THE THEORY OF KNOWING AND THE KNOWN. CONTAINS
ESSAYS BY BENTLEY, 1910-54. THEME IS THAT REAL BASIS OF
GOVERNMENT IS FOUND WITHIN LEGISLATIVE-ADMINISTRATIVE-
ADJUDICATIVE ACTIVITIES OF NATION AND CURRENTS OF ACTIVITY
THAT GATHER AMONG PEOPLE WITHIN THESE SPHERES.

0221 BERGER M.
BUREAUCRACY AND SOCIETY IN MODERN EGYPT; A STUDY OF THE
HIGHER CIVIL SERVICE.
PRINCETON: PRINCETON U PRESS, 1957, 231 PP., LC#57-5445.
STUDY, BASED ON QUESTIONNAIRE GIVEN TO CIVIL SERVANTS, OF
THEIR BACKGROUNDS, ATTITUDES TOWARD JOB, GOVERNMENT, PUBLIC,
ETC., AND ORIENTATION TOWARD WESTERN VALUES.

0222 BERGER R.
"ADMINISTRATIVE ARBITRARINESS* A SEQUEL."
MINN. LAW REV., 51 (MAR. 67), 601-654.
CONTINUES DEBATE WITH PROFESSOR KENNETH DAVID CONCERNING
JUDICIAL REVIEW OF ADMINISTRATIVE ARBITRARINESS. ACCUSES
DAVID OF DISTORTIONS AND MISREPRESENTATIONS IN ANALYSIS OF
CASE. DEFENDS OWN POSITION THAT ARBITRARINESS IS
REVIEWABLE.

0223 BERLINER J.S.
"RUSSIA'S BUREAUCRATS - WHY THEY'RE REACTIONARY."
TRANSACTIONS, 5 (DEC. 67), 53-58.
ANALYZES WHY SOVIET BUREAUCRACY TENDS TO TAKE ON A LIFE
OF ITS OWN AND PURSUE POLICIES THAT FURTHER ITS OWN INTER-
ESTS, EVEN WHEN THOSE INTERESTS CONFLICT WITH WHAT THE LEAD-
ERSHIP WANTS. AUTHOR SUGGESTS ONE REASON IS THAT BUREAUCRAT-
IC INNOVATIONS ARE NOT REWARDED. EMPHASIZES GOVERNMENT
IMPOSED RESTRICTIONS ON INNOVATIVE TECHNIQUES.

0224 BERNAYS E.L. ED.
THE ENGINEERING OF CONSENT.
NORMAN: U OF OKLAHOMA PR, 1955, 246 PP., LC#55-9621.
EXAMINATION OF PUBLIC RELATIONS FROM A BROAD VIEWPOINT
CONSIDERING WHAT IT IS, WHAT RELATION IT HAS TO SOCIETY,
HOW IT APPROACHES A PROBLEM, AND HOW THAT APPROACH IS MADE.
BERNAYS REVIEWS THE SUBJECT AS A WHOLE; SEVEN EXPERTS PRE-
SENT THEIR THINKING ON VARIOUS ASPECTS. INCLUDES SUBJECT
INDEX.

0225 BERNDT R.M. ED., BERNDT C.H. ED.
ABORIGINAL MAN IN AUSTRALIA.
LONDON; SYDNEY: ANGUS & ROBERTSN, 1965, 491 PP.
COLLECTION OF DETAILED ESSAYS ON ANTHROPOLOGICAL STUDIES
OF ABORIGINES IN AUSTRALIA INCLUDING ARCHEOLOGICAL EVIDENCES
OF CIVILIZATION, DISCUSSIONS OF SOCIETY AND CULTURE, MUSIC,

AND IMPACT OF CONTEMPORARY CIVILIZATION ON THEIR PATTERNS OF
CULTURE. ALSO CONTAINS CHAPTER ON A.P. ELKIN AND BIBLIOGRA-
PHY OF HIS WORKS.

0226 BERNE E.
THE STRUCTURE AND DYNAMICS OF ORGANIZATIONS AND GROUPS.
PHILADELPHIA: J B LIPPINCOTT, 1963, 260 PP.
A PSYCHIATRIST'S VIEW OF THE GROUP AS A WHOLE AND FROM
ITS MEMBERS POINT OF VIEW, CONSIDERS SYSTEMATIC ANALYSIS
OF GROUPS, GROUP PROCESS AND AUTHORITY (INCLUDING GROUP
"CANON" AND CULTURE), CLASSIFICATION OF GROUPS, INDIVI-
DUALS' DRIVES, AND MANAGEMENT OF ORGANIZATIONS. CONSIDERS
ALL GROUPS "AUTHORITARIAN," TO SOME EXTENT, SINCE MEMBERS
COMPLY WITH A "CANON."

0227 BERNSTEIN I.
THE LEAN YEARS.
BOSTON: HOUGHTON MIFFLIN, 1960, 577 PP., LC#60-9143.
HISTORY OF THE WORKER IN AMERICAN SOCIETY FROM 1920-33.
DISCUSSES WORKER BOTH WITHIN AND OUTSIDE ORGANIZATION, PAR-
TICULARLY DURING TIME PERIOD WHEN UNIONS AND COLLECTIVE BAR-
GAINING HAD LITTLE IMPACT. EMPHASIZES LEGAL STATUS, POLITI-
CAL BEHAVIOR, SOCIAL AND CULTURAL ACTIVITIES, AND TREATMENT
BY EMPLOYER AND STATE OF THE UNORGANIZED WORKER.

0228 BERNSTEIN M.H.
THE JOB OF THE FEDERAL EXECUTIVE.
WASHINGTON: BROOKINGS INST, 1958, 219 PP., LC#58-14472.
REPORT ON EXECUTIVE'S JOB IN GOVERNMENT. EXPLORES DIFFER-
ENCES IN WORK OF CAREER MAN AND EXECUTIVE. BASED ON VERBATIM
TRANSCRIPTS OF BROOKINGS INSTITUTION ROUND-TABLE CONFEREN-
CES.

0229 BERNTHAL W.F.
"VALUE PERSPECTIVES IN MANAGEMENT DECISIONS."
J. ABNORMAL SOC. PSYCH., 5 (1962), 190-96.
STUDIES THE CONFLICT BETWEEN THE GOALS OF THE FIRM AND
THE VALUES OF SOCIETY. BELIEVES MANAGEMENT DECISIONS MUST
RECOGNIZE SOCIAL VALUES, AND ARGUES THAT A VALUE SCALE
SHOULD BE SET UP TO BE USED AS A GUIDE FOR THE MANAGER.

0230 BERRODIN E.F.
"AT THE BARGAINING TABLE."
NATIONAL CIVIC REV., 56 (JULY 67), 392-397.
EXAMINES 1965 MICHIGAN LAW GIVING PUBLIC EMPLOYEES RIGHT
TO BARGAIN AND TO STRIKE. COMPARES IT WITH LAWS IN OTHER
STATES AND DESCRIBES REACTIONS OF EMPLOYERS TO IT. PROVIDES
SUGGESTIONS FOR MORE EFFECTIVE COLLECTIVE BARGAINING.

0231 BERTON P.A.
MANCHURIA: AN ANNOTATED BIBLIOGRAPHY.
WASHINGTON: US GOVERNMENT, 1951, 187 PP., LC#51-60031.
SELECTIVE COVERAGE (843 ITEMS) OF AVAILABLE LITERATURE
ON MANCHURIA. EMPHASIS IS ON ECONOMIC CONDITIONS AND DEVEL-
OPMENTS IN MANCHURIA. LARGEST CONCENTRATION IS ON JAPANESE
PUBLICATIONS, THOUGH CHINESE, ENGLISH, FRENCH, RUSSIAN, AND
OTHER EUROPEAN-LANGUAGE PUBLICATIONS ARE INCLUDED. PERIODI-
CAL LITERATURE ONLY OCCASIONALLY INCLUDED. MATERIAL IS
ARRANGED TOPICALLY WITH AUTHOR AND SUBJECT INDEX.

0232 BESCOBY I.
"A COLONIAL ADMINISTRATION* AN ANALYSIS OF ADMINISTRATION IN
BRITISH COLUMBIA 1869-1871."
CAN. PUBLIC ADMIN., 12 (MAR. 67), 48-104.
ASSESSMENT OF THE COLONIAL ADMINISTRATION OF GOVERNOR
MUSGRAVE WHOSE TASK WAS TO BRING ABOUT UNION WITH CANADA.
MUSGRAVE EXCELLED AS A POLITICAL STRATEGIST AND ADMINISTRA-
TOR. AUTHOR EVALUATES ROLE AND METHODS USED TO BRING ABOUT
SUCCESSFUL CONFEDERATION.

0233 BHALERAO C.N.
PUBLIC SERVICE COMMISSIONS OF INDIA: A STUDY.
LONDON: STERLING PUBL LTD, 1966, 271 PP.
TRACES HISTORY OF INDIAN PUBLIC SERVICE COMMISSION.
ANALYZES FUNCTION AND STRUCTURE OF VARIOUS AGENCIES
INCLUDING APPOINTMENT, REMOVAL, AND SUSPENSION OF COMMISSION
MEMBERS. NOTES PRINCIPLES AND PROCEDURES OF MEMBER
RECRUITMENT, EXAMINATIONS, AND INTERVIEWS. DISCUSSES
COMMISSIONS' ADVISORY FUNCTIONS IN GOVERNMENT, AND EXAMINES
RELATION BETWEEN COMMISSIONS AND GOVERNMENTS.

0234 BHAMBHRI C.P.
SUBSTANCE OF HINDU POLITY.
MEERUT: INTERNATIONAL PUBL H, 1959, 206 PP.
EXAMINES HINDU CONCEPT OF STATE AND "KINGSHIP" ALONG WITH
SPECIFIC FUNCTIONS OF GOVERNMENT AS OUTLINED IN VARIOUS RE-
LIGIOUS WRITINGS. DESCRIBES EARLY STATE REPUBLICS IN INDIA
INCLUDING TAXATION AND INTER-STATE RELATIONS. TRACES DEVEL-
OPMENT IN LITERATURE OF HINDU CONCEPTS OF JUSTICE, JUST
PUBLIC AUTHORITY AND COERCION, AND PHILOSOPHY OF POLITICAL
SCIENCE. DISCUSSES GREAT FIGURES IN HINDU LITERATURE.

0235 BHAMBHRI C.P.
PARLIAMENTARY CONTROL OVER STATE ENTERPRISE IN INDIA.
NEW DELHI: METROPOLITAN BOOK, 1960, 115 PP.
STUDIES METHODS OF PARLIAMENTARY CONTROL OVER PUBLIC EN-

TERPRISE INCLUDING MINISTERIAL, FINANCIAL, AND AUDIT CONTROL AND CONTROL THROUGH COMMITTEES. ALSO DISCUSSES GENERAL RELATIONSHIP OF GOVERNMENT AND STATE ENTERPRISES. CONCLUDES THAT INDIAN PARLIAMENT HAS NEEDED CONTROLS AT ITS DISPOSAL, BUT THEY ARE NOT BEING FULLY UTILIZED.

0236 BIENSTOCK G., SCHWARZ S.M., ZUGOW A.
MANAGEMENT IN RUSSIAN INDUSTRY AND AGRICULTURE.
NEW YORK: OXFORD U PR, 1944, 198 PP.
STUDY OF SOVIET ECONOMIC SYSTEM FOCUSING ON MANAGERS OF SMALL INDUSTRIAL PLANTS AND OFFICERS OF COLLECTIVE FARMS. DESCRIBES MACHINERY OF SOVIET MANAGEMENT; DISTRIBUTION OF FUNCTIONS AND POWERS; AND STATUS, INCENTIVES, AND IDEOLOGY OF MANAGERIAL PERSONNEL. INCLUDES DISCUSSION OF PRODUCTION PLANNING, PROFITS, ORGANIZATION OF FARM WORKERS, ACCOUNTING METHODS, AND PRIVATE VERSUS COLLECTIVE SYSTEMS.

0237 BIESANZ J.
MODERN SOCIETY: AN INTRODUCTION TO SOCIAL SCIENCE.
ENGLEWOOD CLIFFS: PRENTICE HALL, 1954, 718 PP., LC#54-989.
GENERAL, INTRODUCTORY DISCUSSION OF SOCIAL SCIENCEINTENDED AS GUIDE TO BASIC PROBLEMS OF MODERN SOCIETY. MAJOR SECTIONS DEVOTED TO CULTURE AND PERSONAL RELATIONS, ECONOMIC SYSTEMS AND WORKERS, AND BASIC PROCESSES OF GOVERNMENT AND POLITICS. APPROACH AND STYLE ARE UNTECHNICAL.

0238 BINANI G.D., RAMA RAO T.V.
INDIA AT A GLANCE (REV. ED.)
BOMBAY: ORIENT LONGMANS, 1954, 1756 PP.
A COMPREHENSIVE REFERENCE MANUAL ON INDIA THAT PROVIDES A CLASSIFIED SYSTEM OF INFORMATION ON 25 TOPICS OF GENERAL AND SPECIALIZED INTEREST. COORDINATES INFORMATION ON THE NATIONAL GOVERNMENT, FOREIGN POLICY, NATIONAL ECONOMY, COMMUNICATIONS, INDUSTRIAL FINANCE, PRODUCTION TRENDS, THE JUDICIAL SYSTEM, ETC. INCLUDES A GENERAL INDEX AND DETAILED TABLE OF CONTENTS.

0239 BINDER L.
IRAN: POLITICAL DEVELOPMENT IN A CHANGING SOCIETY.
BERKELEY: U OF CALIF PR, 1962, 362 PP., LC#62-14944.
ANALYTICAL, THEORETICAL, AND EMPIRICAL RECONSTRUCTION OF CHANGING POLITICAL SYSTEM IN IRAN. DEVELOPS A WORKING BASIS FOR FORMULATING POLITICAL THEORY IN TERMS OF SYSTEM AND FUNCTION. CONTENDS THAT CONCRETE POLITICAL SYSTEMS EXHIBIT A VARYING DEGREE OF UNITY OR INTEGRATION IN STRUCTURE AND FUNCTION. MAINTAINS FOCUS ON REAL STRUCTURES OF POWER RELATIONSHIPS, RATHER THAN ABSTRACTING THEIR NATURES.

0240 BINGHAM A.M.
THE TECHNIQUES OF DEMOCRACY.
NEW YORK: DUELL, SLOAN & PEARCE, 1942, 314 PP.
ANALYZES VARIOUS INSTITUTIONAL DEVICES AND METHODS OF GROUP ACTION, EMPHASIZING DEMOCRATIC PUBLIC ADMINISTRATION. DESCRIBES TRADITIONAL TECHNIQUES OF VOTING, FEDERALISM, AND CONSTITUTIONS. DISCUSSES FAILURE OF THESE AND RISE OF TOTALITARIAN TECHNIQUES OF DISCIPLINE AND CENTRALISM. STUDIES MODERN DEMOCRATIC TECHNIQUES OF PUBLIC MANAGEMENT AND FREEDOM.

0241 BIRKHEAD G.S. ED.
ADMINISTRATIVE PROBLEMS IN PAKISTAN.
SYRACUSE: SYRACUSE U PRESS, 1966, 223 PP., LC#66-25174.
DISCUSSES PROBLEMS IN PAKISTAN RELATING TO PUBLIC ADMINISTRATION INCLUDING ADMINISTRATION OF BASIC DEMOCRACIES, BUSINESS PARTICIPATION IN ADMINISTRATION, AGRICULTURE AND ADMINISTRATION, GOVERNMENT BY CORPORATIONS, AND ADMINISTRATIVE REFORM.

0242 BIRNBACH B.
NEO-FREUDIAN SOCIAL PHILOSOPHY.
STANFORD: STANFORD U PRESS, 1961, 283 PP.
SYNTHESIS OF NEO-FREUDIAN VIEWS ON "MAN IN OUR SOCIETY; HOW HE IS FORMED, AND EXPLANATION OF HIS BEHAVIOR IN POLITICAL ENVIRONMENT." INCLUDES BACKGROUND OF FREUD'S VIEWS, OTHER VIEWS AND THEORY OF POLITICAL SCIENCE AS PSYCHOPATHOLOGY. BIBLIOGRAPHY OF PRIMARY CASE STUDIES IN FIELD.

0243 BISHOP D.G.
THE ADMINISTRATION OF BRITISH FOREIGN RELATIONS.
SYRACUSE: U. PR., 1961, 410 PP.
A COMPREHENSIVE VIEW OF RELEVANT INSTITUTIONS, THEIR ORGANIZATION AND METHODS OF PROCEDURE. HISTORIC EXAMPLES OF DEVELOPMENT ARE PRESENTED. INCLUDES CRITICISM AND PROPOSALS FOR INSTITUTIONAL REFORM.

0244 BISHOP H.M. ED., HENDEL S. ED.
BASIC ISSUES OF AMERICAN DEMOCRACY.
NEW YORK: APPLETON, 1948, 323 PP.
READINGS ON A VARIETY OF TOPICS INCLUDING DEMOCRACY IN A CHANGING WORLD, CONSTITUTIONAL PRINCIPLES, POLITICAL POWER, AND FOREIGN POLICY. FIFTY-TWO SELECTIONS. BIBLIOGRAPHY OF 50 ENTRIES, IN ENGLISH, BOOKS AND ARTICLES, LISTED ALPHABETICALLY BY AUTHOR.

0245 BISHOP D.B. ED.

PUBLICATIONS OF THE GOVERNMENTS OF NOVA SCOTIA, PRINCE EDWARD ISLAND, NEW BRUNSWICK 1758-1952.
OTTAWA: NATL LIB OF CANADA, 1957, 237 PP.
INCLUDES ONLY THOSE PAMPHLETS OR BOOKS WHICH HAVE BEEN PRINTED "WITH THE IMPRINT OF, OR AT THE EXPENSE OF, OR BY AUTHORITY OF ANY ONE OF THE THREE GOVERNMENTS OF THE MARITIME PROVINCE." PAPERS, BROADSIDES, HANDBILLS, PROCLAMATIONS, AND MAPS HAVE BEEN OMITTED, AS HAVE WORKS DEALING WITH THE JUDICIAL AND MUNICIPAL ASPECTS OF GOVERNMENT.

0246 BLACHLY F.F., OATMAN M.E.
"THE GOVERNMENT AND ADMINISTRATION OF GERMANY."
BALTIMORE: JOHNS HOPKINS PRESS, 1920.
FIRST OF SERIES OF VOLUMES PUBLISHED BY THE INSTITUTE FOR GOVERNMENT RESEARCH CONCERNING ADMINISTRATIVE SYSTEMS OF CHIEF EUROPEAN NATIONS. EMPHASIS ON ADMINISTRATIVE AND GOVERNMENTAL SYSTEMS. UNDERLYING SOCIAL AND POLITICAL PHILOSOPHY, CONSTITUTIONAL STRUCTURE, AND POLITICAL ACTION. COVERS CENTRAL GOVERNMENT AS WELL AS SUBORDINATE UNITS. EXTENSIVE, PARTIALLY ANNOTATED, BIBLIOGRAPHY.

0247 BLACKSTOCK P.W.
THE STRATEGY OF SUBVERSION.
CHICAGO: QUADRANGLE BOOKS, INC, 1964, 349 PP., LC#64-19620.
EXAMINES PROBLEMS OF MANAGEMENT AND CONTROL IN COVERT ESPIONAGE OPERATIONS. STUDIES EFFECTS UPON US STATE DEPARTMENT, MILITARY ESTABLISHMENT, AND INTELLIGENCE COMMUNITY. USES CASE STUDIES AND HISTORICAL ANALYSIS.

0248 BLAIR L.
THE COMMONWEALTH PUBLIC SERVICE.
MELBOURNE: MELBOURNE UNIV PRESS, 1958, 78 PP.
STUDIES AUSTRALIAN PUBLIC SERVICE, ITS DEVELOPMENT, AND ASPECTS OF ITS PRESENT ORGANIZATION AND FUNCTIONS, SUCH AS STAFF, MANAGEMENT, EMPLOYER-EMPLOYEE RELATIONS, RESOLUTION OF INTERDEPARTMENTAL DISPUTES, AND PROBLEMS OF BUREAUCRACY.

0249 BLAISDELL D.C.
"PRESSURE GROUPS, FOREIGN POLICIES, AND INTERNATIONAL POLITICS."
ANN. AMER. ACAD. POLIT. SOC. SCI., 319 (SEPT. 58), 542-550.
DEMONSTRATES CONFLICT AND CO-ORDINATION OF GROUPS AND NATIONAL INTERESTS, POINTING OUT DOMINATING ROLE OF MILITARY INTERESTS IN AMERICAN DIPLOMACY. EVALUATES INTERNATIONAL NON-GOVERNMENTAL ORGANIZATIONS' PARTICIPATION IN BROAD POLICY DECISIONS.

0250 BLAKE R.R., SHEPARD H.A., MOUTON J.S.
MANAGING INTERGROUP CONFLICT IN INDUSTRY.
HOUSTON: GULF PUBL, 1964, 210 PP., LC#64-8696.
A WORKING MANUAL SUPPORTED BY ACTUAL CASE HISTORIES OF INDUSTRIAL CONFLICTS AND HOW THEY WERE SOLVED. SHOWS THAT THERE ARE 9 POSSIBLE METHODS FOR DEALING WITH CONFLICT, BUT THAT 8 HAVE INHERENT SIDE-EFFECTS WHICH ARE DETRIMENTAL TO OVERALL ORGANIZATIONAL OBJECTIVES AND GOALS. THE MOST COMMON OF THESE 8 IS THE WIN-LOOSE POWER STRUGGLE AMONG GROUPS. PRESENTS A PROBLEM-SOLVING METHOD THAT WORKS CREATIVELY.

0251 BLAU P.M.
THE DYNAMICS OF BUREAUCRACY: A STUDY OF INTERPERSONAL RELATIONS IN TWO GOVERNMENT AGENCIES.
BERKELEY: U OF CALIF PR, 1955, 269 PP., LC#55-5116.
STUDIES OF LOWER-LEVEL OFFICIALS IN A STATE EMPLOYMENT AGENCY AND A FEDERAL ENFORCEMENT AGENCY, AND THEIR ATTITUDES TOWARD BUREAUCRATIC CHANGE.

0252 BLAU P.M.
BUREAUCRACY IN MODERN SOCIETY.
NEW YORK: RANDOM HOUSE, INC, 1956, 127 PP., LC#56-7690.
ANALYSIS OF SOCIOLOGICAL IMPLICATIONS AND CONSEQUENCES OF LARGE-SCALE BUREAUCRACIES IN ORGANIZATIONAL STRUCTURES OF BUSINESS, GOVERNMENT, ARMED FORCES, EDUCATION, AND INDUSTRY. EMPHASIS IS ON UNPRECEDENTED GROWTH OF BUREAUCRACIES IN RECENT YEARS. DISCUSSES INTERRELATIONS BETWEEN BUREAUCRACY AND DEMOCRATIC GOVERNMENT AND USES CASE STUDIES TO ILLUSTRATE BASIC BUREAUCRATIC PROCESSES.

0253 BLAU P.M., SCOTT W.R.
"FORMAL ORGANIZATIONS."
SAN FRANCISCO: CHANDLER, 1962.
A SOCIOLOGICAL ANALYSIS OF SOME OF MAIN FACETS OF ORGANIZATIONAL LIFE. EXAMINES NATURE AND TYPES OF FORMAL ORGANIZATIONS, CONNECTIONS BETWEEN THEM AND LARGER SOCIAL CONTEXT OF WHICH THEY ARE PART, AND VARIOUS ASPECTS OF INTERNAL STRUCTURE, SUCH AS PEER GROUP RELATIONS, PROCESSES OF COMMUNICATION, MANAGEMENT, AND IMPERSONAL MECHANISMS OF CONTROL. EXTENSIVE BIBLIOGRAPHY OF RECENT WORKS IN ENGLISH.

0254 BOCK E.A. ED.
STATE AND LOCAL GOVERNMENT: A CASE BOOK.
UNIVERSITY: U ALABAMA PR, 1963, 670 PP., LC#59-11736.
SELECTED CASE STUDIES OF ADMINISTRATION ON STATE AND LOCAL LEVELS INCLUDE PROBLEMS OF COMMUNICATION WITH PUBLIC, THE GOVERNOR OR MAYOR AND HIS AIDES, AND BUDGET.

0255 BLONDEL J.

VOTERS, PARTIES, AND LEADERS.
BALTIMORE: PENGUIN BOOKS, 1963, 271 PP.
TREATMENT OF RELATION BETWEEN BRITISH CONTEMPORARY SOCI-
ETY AND POLITICS. DISCUSSES THE EFFECT OF ELITES AND STRATA
ON ALL FORMS OF GOVERNMENT AND THE RELATION OF PARTY TO
SOCIAL GROUP.

0256 BLOUGH R.
"THE ROLE OF THE ECONOMIST IN FEDERAL POLICY MAKING."
U. ILLINOIS BULL., 5 (NOV. 53), 26 PP.
COUNCIL OF ECONOMIC ADVISERS HAS A DEFINITE ROLE IN THE
FORMULATION OF FEDERAL POLICY. GIVES BRIEF ANALYSIS OF
FUNCTIONS, ATTITUDES, QUALIFICATIONS AND DUTIES OF THE ECON-
OMIST IN GOVERNMENT AFFAIRS.

0257 BLUM H.L., LEONARD A.R.
PUBLIC ADMINISTRATION - A PUBLIC HEALTH VIEWPOINT.
NEW YORK: MACMILLAN, 1963, 532 PP., LC#63-18796.
GENERAL TEXT FOR PUBLIC HEALTH ADMINISTRATORS: EMPHASIZES
THE ROLE OF THE ADMINISTRATOR AS A SERVANT OF THE GENERAL
PUBLIC RATHER THAN OF ANY SPECIAL INTEREST GROUPS.
OFFICIAL APPOINTMENTS SHOULD BE BASED ON TECHNICAL
COMPETENCE RATHER THAN POLITICS TO ENSURE THAT THE PUBLIC
INTEREST IS REPRESENTED.

0258 BLUM J.M., CATTON B. ET AL.
"THE NATIONAL EXPERIENCE."
NEW YORK: HARCOURT BRACE, 1963.
HISTORICAL SURVEY OF US FROM ITS DISCOVERY THROUGH THE
KENNEDY ADMINISTRATION. EMPHASIS ON QUESTIONS OF PUBLIC
POLICY. ORGANIZATIONAL STRUCTURE VARIES BETWEEN CHRONOLOGI-
CAL AND TOPICAL, DEPENDING ON MATERIAL UNDER DISCUSSION.
BRIEF BIBLIOGRAPHY OF SELECTED READINGS IN AMERICAN HISTORY
SUGGESTS BIBLIOGRAPHIES, CONTEMPORARY DOCUMENTS, AND PROBLEM
BOOKS. REFERENCES POSTDATE 1949.

0259 BLUMBERG A.S.
CRIMINAL JUSTICE.
CHICAGO: QUADRANGLE BOOKS, INC, 1967, 206 PP.
MAINTAINS THAT AMERICAN CRIMINAL COURTS DENY JUSTICE TO
ACCUSED UNDER VEIL OF BUREAUCRATIC "EFFICIENCY." STUDIES A
METROPOLITAN COURT AND FINDS IDEAL MODEL OF JUSTICE REPLACED
BY A "JUSTICE BY NEGOTIATION." TREATS TENDENCY OF JURIES TO
CONVICT, PROBLEM OF OVERCROWDED CALENDARS, AND "RATIONAL"
CHARACTER OF BUREAUCRACY ITSELF. FORESEES CONTINUATION OF
PRESENT SYSTEM.

0260 BLUMBERG A.S.
"THE PRACTICE OF LAW AS CONFIDENCE GAME: ORGANIZATIONAL
COOPTATION OF A PROFESSION."
LAW AND SOCIETY REVIEW, 1 (JUNE 67), 15-39.
DISCUSSES IMPACT OF THREE RECENT LANDMARK DECISIONS OF
US SUPREME COURT AFFECTING FUTURE OF CRIMINAL LAW
ADMINISTRATION AND ENFORCEMENT. QUESTIONS COMPATIBILITY OF
COURT'S CONCEPTION OF ROLE OF COUNSEL WITH SOCIAL REALITY.
ASSERTS THAT COURT DECISIONS OVERLOOK FORMAL ORGANIZATION OF
COURTS, RELATION BETWEEN LAWYER AND COURT, AND RELATION
BETWEEN LAWYER AND CLIENT.

0261 BOCK E. ED.
GOVERNMENT REGULATION OF BUSINESS.
ENGLEWOOD CLIFFS: PRENTICE HALL, 1965, 448 PP., LC#65-16944.
SEVEN CASE STUDIES DESCRIBE EVENTS AND FORCES AT WORK
WHEN GOVERNMENTAL AGENCIES INITIATE REGULATORY ACTIONS
IN BUSINESS. ANALYZES STRATEGY OF ONE OF THE MAJOR
PARTICIPANTS INVOLVED IN EACH OF THE CASES.

0262 BOCK E.A. ED., CAMPBELL A.K. ED.
CASE STUDIES IN AMERICAN GOVERNMENT.
ENGLEWOOD CLIFFS: PRENTICE HALL, 1962, 368 PP., LC#62-12624.
COLLECTION OF CASE STUDIES TO BE USED AS TEXTBOOK SUPPLE-
MENT IN UNDERGRADUATE CLASSES IN POLITICAL SCIENCE. MAIN
TOPIC HEADINGS INCLUDE: CONSTITUTION, COURTS AND CIVIL
RIGHTS, POLITICS, LEGISLATIVE PROCESS, PRESIDENCY, GOVERN-
MENT, SCIENCE, AND THE ECONOMY. BOOK IS PART OF INTER-UNI-
VERSITY CASE PROGRAM.

0263 BOCK E.A. ED.
STATE AND LOCAL GOVERNMENT: A CASE BOOK.
UNIVERSITY: U ALABAMA PR, 1963, 671 PP., LC#59-11736.
PART OF THE INTER-UNIVERSITY CASE PROGRAM SERIES, THIS
VOLUME PRESENTS CASES FOR CLASS USE AND CONCERNS ITSELF
MAINLY WITH STUDIES OF THE EVERYDAY AFFAIRS OF LOCAL AND
STATE ADMINISTRATION.

0264 BOGARDUS E.S.
"THE SOCIOLOGY OF A STRUCTURED PEACE."
SOCIOL. SOC. RES., 44 (MAY 1960), 352-357.
CONSIDERS ACHIEVEMENT OF WORLD PEACE THROUGH STRUCTURES
OF THE UN, AND USE OF UN ORGANS AS BASIS FOR INTERNATIONAL
LAW. ALSO SUGGESTS, AS A SOCIOLOGICAL APPROACH TO PEACE,
THE DEVELOPMENT OF A POINT OF VIEW, NATIONAL PHILOSOPHY AND
BEHAVIOR WHICH WOULD BE CONDUCIVE TO MUTUAL TRUST AMONG
NATIONS.

0265 BOGUSLAW R.
THE NEW UTOPIANS.
ENGLEWOOD CLIFFS: PRENTICE HALL, 1965, 213 PP., LC#65-19764.
STUDY OF SYSTEM DESIGN AND SOCIAL CHANGE EMPHASIZING
SIMILARITY BETWEEN INTELLECTUAL FOUNDATIONS OF MOD-
ERN SYSTEMS ANALYSIS AND THE FORMULATIONS OF SOCIAL THEOR-
ISTS IN THE UTOPIAN TRADITION. DISCUSSES CHARACTERISTICS OF
TECHNOLOGY AND SYSTEM DESIGN THAT SHAPE POSSIBILITIES FOR
SOCIAL CHANGE IN A GIVEN SOCIETY. COVERS FORMALIST, HEURIS-
TIC, OPERATING UNIT, AND AD HOC DESIGNS.

0266 BOHLKE R.H., WINETROUT K.
BUREAUCRATS AND INTELLECTUALS: A CRITIQUE OF C. WRIGHT MILLS
(PAMPHLET)
SPRINGFIELD: AMER INTERNATL COLL, 1963, 52 PP.
CRITIQUE OF MILLS' "WHITE COLLAR" AND SEVERAL OTHER
WORKS. MAINTAINS THAT MILLS HAS NOT SUBSTANTIATED HIS THESIS
AND THAT HE GOES BEYOND HIS OWN EVIDENCE. AUTHORS ARE
SYMPATHETIC TO MILLS' INTERPRETATION BUT INSIST THAT HIS
ASSERTIONS NEED MORE SYSTEMATIC ANALYSIS.

0267 BOISSIER P.
HISTOIRE DU COMITE INTERNATIONAL DE LA CROIX ROUGE.
PARIS: PLON, 1963, 512 PP.
TRACES DEVELOPMENT OF THE INTERNATIONAL RED CROSS IN THE
PERIOD FROM 1859 TO 1905. EMPHASIS ON ROLE OF THE SOCIETY IN
FOSTERING GENERAL RULES OF 'HUMANE WARFARE.'

0268 BULGAR V.
"THE PUBLIC INTEREST: A JURISPRUDENTIAL AND COMPARATIVE
OVERVIEW OF SYMPOSIUM ON FUNDAMENTAL CONCEPTS OF PUBLIC LAW"
JOURNAL OF PUBLIC LAW, 12 (JAN. 63), 13-52.
SURVEYS THEORIES THAT ARE SOURCES OF DELIMITATION OF
PRIVATE RIGHTS FROM PUBLIC INTERESTS AND DEMONSTRATES
EVOLUTION OF CONCEPT OF PUBLIC INTEREST. COMPARES ISSUES
INVOLVING LEGAL REGULATION, ESPECIALLY THOSE IN FIELD OF
ADMINISTRATIVE CONTRACTS, IN FRANCE, SWITZERLAND, GERMANY,
AND COMMUNIST COUNTRIES.

0269 BOLINGBROKE H. ST.J.
A DISSERTATION UPON PARTIES (1729)
LONDON: T. CADELL IN THE STRAND, 1786, 316 PP.
ARGUES THAT THE WORST THING TO HAPPEN TO ENGLAND WAS THE
APPEARANCE OF POLITICAL PARTIES, WHICH PROMOTE DISUNITY IN
THE COUNTRY AND DIVISION IN THE GOVERNMENT. MAINTAINS THAT
PEOPLE ARE BETTER SERVED WHEN THE COMMONS ACTS MERELY AS
ADVISER TO THE KING RATHER THAN AS LAWMAKER.

0270 BOLLENS J.C.
"THE PROBLEM OF GOVERNMENT IN THE SAN FRANCISCO BAY REGION."
BERKELEY: U OF CALIF PR, 1948.
SUMMARY AND ANALYSIS OF PROBLEMS OF METROPOLITAN GOV-
ERNMENT IN THE PERSPECTIVE OF THE SAN FRANCISCO BAY REGION.
ATTEMPTS TO UNIVERSALIZE METROPOLITAN PROBLEMS THROUGH EX-
TENSIVE STUDY OF A SINGLE AREA. REVIEWS GOVERNMENTAL PATTERN
OF THE REGION, RESULTING REGIONAL PROBLEMS, MAJOR EFFORTS
TO SOLVE REGIONAL PROBLEMS, SUCH AS ANNEXATION.
BIBLIOGRAPHY OF GOVERNMENT DOCUMENTS, PERIODICALS, ETC.

0271 BONAPARTE M.
MYTHS OF WAR.
LONDON: IMAGO, 1948, 161 PP.
PROPOSES STUDY OF GERMAN MYTHOLOGY AND ITS PHILO-
SOPHICAL BACKGROND. COMMENTS ON POLITICAL AND MORAL BEHAVIOR
OF WORLD WAR TWO VICTORS AND VANQUISHED. ANALYZES HISTOR-
ICAL, SOCIAL, AND ECONOMIC ASPECTS OF ANTI-SEMITISM.

0272 BONER H.A.
"HUNGRY GENERATIONS."
LONDON: OXFORD U PR, 1955.
HISTORY OF THE ACCEPTANCE AND EVENTUAL REJECTION OF MAL-
THUSIAN THEORY IN 19TH-CENTURY ENGLAND. ARGUES THAT THE
ENTIRE MALTHUSIAN THEORY, INCLUDING "ITS FALLACIOUS AND
SOCIALLY DISASTROUS" CONCLUSION THAT THE MAJOR CAUSE OF
POVERTY WAS THE RECKLESS OVERBREEDING OF THE POOR, WAS AN
INVIDIOUS INSTRUMENT FOR CONCEALING EXPLOITATION AND ECONOM-
IC INJUSTICE. BIBLIOGRAPHY OF WORKS PUBLISHED SINCE 1840.

0273 BONINI C.P.
SIMULATION OF INFORMATION AND DECISION SYSTEMS IN THE FIRM.
ENGLEWOOD CLIFFS: PRENTICE HALL, 1963, 152 PP., LC#63-16585.
DESCRIBES SIMULATION MODEL OF HYPOTHETICAL BUSINESS FIRM.
SYNTHESIS OF RELEVANT THEORY FROM DISCIPLINES OF ECONOMICS,
ACCOUNTING, ORGANIZATION THEORY, AND BEHAVIORAL SCIENCE
WITHIN SETTING OF TRADITIONAL CONCEPTS OF BUSINESS PRACTICE.
STUDIES EFFECTS OF INFORMATIONAL, ORGANIZATIONAL, AND ENVI-
RONMENTAL FACTORS UPON DECISIONS OF BUSINESS FIRM.

0274 BONNETT C.E.
LABOR-MANAGEMENT RELATIONS.
NEW YORK: EXPOSITION PRESS, 1959, 956 PP.
ANALYSIS OF BOTH SIDES OF THE UNION AND ASSOCIATION
PROBLEM FROM PUBLIC VIEWPOINT. EXTENSIVE USE OF VISUAL
AIDS IN FORM OF CARTOONS AND PICTURES FOUND IN LITERATURE OF
SUBJECT. COORDINATED WITH DISCUSSION OF CENTRAL LABOR-MAN-
AGEMENT RELATIONS PROBLEM - ITS SOCIAL IMPLICATIONS, ORGA-
NIZED FORCES, INTERRELATIONS, AND PROPAGANDA ACTIVITIES.

0275 BOOTH D.A., ADRIAN C.R.
"POWER STRUCTURE AND COMMUNITY CHANGE: A REPLICATION STUDY
OF COMMUNITY A."
MIDWEST J. OF POLI. SCI., 6 (AUG. 62), 277-296.
A REPLICATED STUDY, SEVEN YEARS LATER. TOP LEADERS OF
1954 CONTINUED TO DOMINATE DECISION-MAKING IN 1961, BUT
THEIR GROUP IS LESS MONOLITHIC. THERE IS INCREASED CONFLICT
BETWEEN BUSINESS AND LABOR SPOKESMEN IN COMMUNITY
DECISION-MAKING.

0276 BORBA DE MORAES R., BERRIEN W.
MANUAL BIBLIOGRAFICO DE ESTUDOS BRASILEIROS.
RIO DE JANEIRO: EDITORIAL SOUZA, 1949, 895 PP.
DETAILED BIBLIOGRAPHY OF BRAZILIAN RESEARCH.

0277 BORCHARD E.H., STUMBERG G.W.
GUIDE TO THE LAW AND LEGAL LITERATURE OF FRANCE.
WASHINGTON: LIBRARY OF CONGRESS, 1931, 242 PP., LC#30-26002.
BIBLIOGRAPHICAL ESSAY AND GUIDE DESIGNED TO FURNISH
PRACTICAL INFORMATION ON THE LEGAL INSTITUTIONS OF FRANCE;
METHODS BY WHICH IT HAS SOLVED ECONOMIC AND SOCIAL PROBLEMS
FACING IT IN AN INDUSTRIAL AGE; LEGAL METHOD, DOCTRINE, AND
PHILOSOPHY OF SCIENTIFIC INVESTIGATION UNDERLYING CONSTITU-
TIONAL INSTITUTIONS.

0278 BORCHARDT K.
"CONGRESSIONAL USE OF ADMINISTRATIVE ORGANIZATION AND
PROCEDURE FOR POLICY-MAKING PURPOSES."
G. WASH. LAW REV., 30 (MAR. 62), 429-46.
SIX CASE STUDIES WHICH LEAD TO CONCLUSION THAT "CONGRESS
DOES NOT LOOK WITH FAVOR UPON PROPOSALS TO GRANT BROAD
DISCRETION TO ADMINISTRATIVE AGENCIES TO CARRY OUT
SOCIAL OR ECONOMIC PROGRAMS; CONGRESS PREFERS TO RETAIN
CONTROL OF SUCH PROGRAMS."

0279 BORGESE G. ED.
COMMON CAUSE.
NEW YORK: COMM. FRAME WORLD CONST., 1947-51, 4 VOLS.
REPORT PUBLISHED TO CLARIFY THE ISSUES SURROUNDING THE
QUESTION OF WORLD GOVERNMENT BY CONTRIBUTORS FROM THE
SPECIALIZED-STUDY FIELDS OF PSYCHOLOGY, SOCIOLOGY,
ECONOMICS, POLITICS AND PHILOSOPHY.

0280 BOSWORTH K.A.
"THE POLITICS OF MANAGEMENT IMPROVEMENT IN THE STATES"
AM. POL. SCI. REV., 47 (MAR. 53), 84-99.
AUTHOR DESCRIBES THE WAVE OF STATE COMMISSIONS CONCERNED
WITH REORGANIZATION OF STATE EXECUTIVE BRANCHES. HE DISCUS-
SES THE RESPONSES OF LEGISLATURES TO THE RECOMMENDATIONS OF
THESE COMMISSIONS. DATA COVERS 30 STATES. IT REVEALS AMBI-
VALENCE OF LEGISLATORS TOWARD CENTRALIZATION OF MANAGEMENT
IN EXECUTIVE DEPARTMENTS.

0281 BOTTOMORE T.B.
ELITES AND SOCIETY.
ENGLEWOOD CLIFFS: PRENTICE HALL, 1964, 160 PP.
STUDIES ELITISTS - SOCIAL THEORISTS WHO HAVE EXAMINED
WORKINGS OF SOCIETY IN TERMS OF THEIR MINORITY ELITE GROUPS.
SURVEYS PRINCIPAL ELITIST THEORIES AND DISTINGUISHES BETWEEN
THEORETICAL AND IDEOLOGICAL ELEMENTS IN SUCH THEORIES.
REVIEWS SOME EXPERIMENTAL STUDIES OF ELITE GROUPS IN
ADVANCED AND UNDERDEVELOPED COUNTRIES.

0282 BOUDET P., BOURGEOIS R.
BIBLIOGRAPHIE DE L'INDOCHINE FRANCAISE.
HANOI: IMPRIM O'EXTREME ORIENT, 1929, 75 PP.
TWO-VOLUME BIBLIOGRAPHY OF FRENCH MATERIALS ON FRENCH
INDOCHINA. VOLUME I, PUBLISHED IN 1929, COVERS ISSUING DATES
1913-1926. VOLUME II, PUBLISHED IN 1943, COVERS PERIOD 1933-
1935. MATERIAL IN FORMER VOLUME IS ARRANGED BY SUBJECT AND
INCLUDES ALPHABETICAL AUTHOR INDEX. VOLUME II IS CLASSIFIED
ALPHABETICALLY BY AUTHOR.

0283 BOULDING K.E., SPIVEY W.A.
LINEAR PROGRAMMING AND THE THEORY OF THE FIRM.
NEW YORK: MACMILLAN, 1960.
REVIEW OF RECENT DEVELOPMENTS IN FIELD RELEVANT TO THE
THEORY OF THE FIRM. DISCUSSES PRESENT CONCEPT OF THEORY AND
ADAPTABILITY OF DATA TO LINEAR PROGRAMMING. PRESENTS STUDY
OF RELATION OF OPERATIONS RESEARCH TO ECONOMIC APPLICATION,
ESPECIALLY IN RELATION TO CYCLICAL CHANGES.

0284 BOUVIER-AJAM M.
MANUEL TECHNIQUE ET PRATIQUE DU MAIRE ET DES ELUS ET AGENTS
COMMUNAUX.
PARIS: EDITIONS SOCIALES, 1964, 254 PP.
GENERAL TEXT ON MUNICIPAL ORGANIZATION IN FRANCE, DUTIES
OF ELECTED OFFICIALS, AND MEANS FOR CARRYING OUT DUTIES.
RETRACES HISTORY OF "COMMUNAL" MOVEMENT IN FRANCE, SITUATES
"COMMUNE" IN ITS SOCIAL, JUDICIAL, AND POLITICAL FRAMEWORK,
DISCUSSES LAWS CONCERNING ELECTED OFFICIALS, ETC. INCLUDES
BIBLIOGRAPHY OF APPROXIMATELY 100 ITEMS LISTED BY SUBJECT.

0285 BOWEN W.G.
THE FEDERAL GOVERNMENT AND PRINCETON UNIVERSITY.
PRINCETON: PRINCETON U PRESS, 1962, 319 PP.

REPORT ON EFFECTS OF PRINCETON'S INVOLVEMENTS WITH FEDE-
RAL GOVERNMENT ON OPERATIONS OF THE UNIVERSITY, INCLUDING
PROCEDURES, FINANCIAL ASPECTS, RESEARCH, ORGANIZATION, AND
GENERAL IMPLICATIONS.

0286 BOWETT D.W.
THE LAW OF INTERNATIONAL INSTITUTIONS.
NEW YORK: PRAEGER, 1965, 347 PP.
PRESENTS A DETAILED DESCRIPTION OF INTERNATIONAL INSTI-
TUTIONS ARISING IN THE WAKE OF TWO WORLD WARS. BESIDES OUT-
LINING INSTITUTIONAL STRUCTURES, E.G. THE UNITED NATIONS OR
THE WARSAW TREATY ORGANIZATION, FOCUSES ATTENTION ON GENERAL
PROBLEMS OF INTERNATIONAL ORGANIZATIONS.

0287 BOWIE R.
"STRATEGY AND THE ATLANTIC ALLIANCE."
INT. ORGAN., 17 (SUMMER 63), 709-733.
SOURCES OF TENSION WITHIN NATO AND NATURE OF THE SOVIET
THREAT ARE CONTEMPLATED WITH REGARD TO NATO STRATEGY.
ATTENTION ALSO FOCUSED ON WEAPONS-CONTROL PREROGATIVES AND
DECISION-MAKING MACHINERY WITHIN THE ALLIANCE.

0288 BOWLES C.
THE COMING POLITICAL BREAKTHROUGH.
NEW YORK: HARPER & ROW, 1959, 209 PP., LC#59-13278.
CONTENDS THAT EXISTING AMERICAN POLITICAL AND ECONOMIC
POLICIES ARE NOT PROPERLY GEARED TO EMERGING PRESSURES AND
PROBLEMS ON DOMESTIC AND INTERNATIONAL SCENES. URGES REAS-
SERTION OF TRADITIONAL AMERICAN DEMOCRATIC BELIEF AND NEW
DEFINITION OF NATIONAL PURPOSE IN 20TH-CENTURY TERMS.
PREDICTS 1960 ELECTION TO BE MOST DECISIVE OF CENTURY WITH
WINNING PARTY REMAINING DOMINANT FOR MANY YEARS.

0290 BOXER C.R.
PORTUGUESE SOCIETY IN THE TROPICS - THE MUNICIPAL COUNCILS
OF GOA, MACAO, BAHIA, AND LUANDA, 1510-1800.
MADISON: U OF WISCONSIN PR, 1965, 244 PP., LC#65-18878.
STUDIES MUNICIPAL COUNCILS IN PORTUGUESE TROPICAL COLO-
NIES AND THE COMPOSITION OF MUNICIPALITIES. EXAMINES
FUNCTIONS OF COUNCILS, PEOPLE THEY DEAL WITH, AND ACTIONS
THEY TAKE IN TIMES OF CRISES.

0291 BOYD A.M., RIPS R.E.
UNITED STATES GOVERNMENT PUBLICATIONS (3RD ED.)
NEW YORK: H W WILSON, 1949, 627 PP.
EXTENSIVE, COMPREHENSIVE, AND WELL-INDEXED GUIDE TO US
GOVERNMENT PUBLICATIONS WITH DETAILED ANNOTATION AND INTRO-
DUCTORY MATERIAL DEALING WITH THE NATURE, HISTORY, PRINTING,
DISTRIBUTION, AND AVAILABILITY OF VARIOUS GOVERNMENT PUBLI-
CATIONS. LISTED BY AGENCY WITH APPENDIXES, INDEXES, AND A
KEY TO CHARTS, ILLUSTRATIVE MATERIALS, ETC.

0292 BOYD H.W. ED., IFFLAND C.P. ED., GIBSON D.M.T. ED.
MARKETING MANAGEMENT: CASES FROM EMERGING COUNTRIES.
READING, MASS: ADDISON-WESLEY, 1966, 424 PP., LC#66-25595.
COLLECTION OF FORTY-EIGHT CASE STUDIES OF EMERGING COUN-
RIES WITH CONSIDERATION OF MARKETING PROBLEMS THAT BUSINESS
AND GOVERNMENT EXECUTIVES CONFRONT IN EMERGING ECONOMIES.
CASES ORIGINATED IN SEVENTEEN COUNTRIES IN ARGENTINA, BRA-
ZIL, CHILE, TAIWAN, COLUMBIA, GHANA, INDIA, INDONESIA, IS-
RAEL, SOUTH KOREA, MALAYSIA, MEXICO, NICARAGUA, PERU, PHIL-
IPPINES, THAILAND, AND UAR.

0293 BOYER W.W.
"POLICY MAKING BY GOVERNMENT AGENCIES."
MID. EAST. J., 3 (AUG. 60), 267-88.
ATTEMPTS TO DEVISE A CONCEPTUAL FRAMEWORK AIDING ANALYSIS
OF GOVERNMENT POLICIES, PROCEDURES, AND AGENCIES. INCLUDES
STUDY OF PRIVATE INTEREST GROUPS.

0294 BOYER W.W.
BUREAUCRACY ON TRIAL: POLICY MAKING BY GOVERNMENT AGENCIES.
INDIANAPOLIS: BOBBS-MERRILL, 1964, 184 PP., LC#63-16942.
GENERAL DESCRIPTION AND ANALYSIS OF POLICY-MAKING IN
ADMINISTRATIVE AGENCIES WITH SPECIAL REFERENCE TO THE
EFFECTS OF SUCH POLICY-MAKING ON DEMOCRATIC GOVERNMENT.
EMPHASIZES THE IMPORTANCE OF PRESSURE GROUPS.

0295 BRADLEY A.W.
"CONSTITUTION-MAKING IN UGANDA."
TRANSITION, 7 (AUG. 67), 25-31.
ANALYZES UGANDA GOVERNMENT'S PROPOSALS FOR A NEW CONSTI-
TUTION. DISCUSSES FEATURES OF THE PROPOSED CONSTITUTION:
UGANDA IS TO BE A UNITARY REPUBLIC; THE KINGDOMS AND DIS-
TRICTS ARE TO DISAPPEAR AS CONSTITUTIONAL UNITS OF GOVERN-
MENT; CABINET GOVERNMENT WILL CHANGE TO PRESIDENTIAL EXECU-
TIVE FORM; AND GREATER POWERS WILL BE GIVEN THE GOVERNMENT.
DISCUSSES CABINET, PRESIDENT, AND NATIONAL ASSEMBLY.

0296 BRADY R.A.
ORGANIZATION, AUTOMATION, AND SOCIETY.
BERKELEY: U OF CALIF PR, 1961, 481 PP., LC#61-7535.
STUDY CONCENTRATES ON INDUSTRIAL TECHNOLOGY, WITH SPE-
CIAL ATTENTION TO THAT LEVEL OF DEVELOPMENT WHEREIN THE
CLEANING-UP OPERATIONS NECESSARY TO BRING PRACTICE FULLY
IN LINE WITH SCIENTIFIC THEORY ARE ALREADY WELL ADVANCED.

TRIES TO DECIDE BEST WAY TO ORGANIZE PRODUCTIVE RESOURCES
OF ECONOMY WHEN DECISION-MAKERS ARE PREPARED TO USE POTEN-
TIALITIES OF ADVANCED SCIENCE AND ENGINEERING.

0297 BRADY R.H.
"COMPUTERS IN TOP-LEVEL DECISION MAKING"
HARVARD BUSINESS REV., 45 (JULY 67), 67-76.
INQUIRES INTO IMPACT OF COMPUTER ON TOP-LEVEL MANAGEMENT
DECISION-MAKING. MAINTAINS THAT IMPACT HAS BEEN NEGLIGIBLE
WITH EFFECTS BEING FASTER DECISIONS, MORE THOROUGH ANLAYSES,
MORE TIME FOR EXECUTIVES TO MAKE DECISIONS, MORE CHOICES,
AND MORE INFORMATION. PREDICTS THAT BY 1975 MOST MANAGEMENT
DECISIONS WILL BE MADE WITH COMPUTERS.

0298 BRAIBANTI R.J.D.
"REFLECTIONS ON BUREAUCRATIC CORRUPTION."
PUBLIC ADMINISTRATION, 40 (WINTER 62), 357-372.
ALL GOVERNMENTS EXPERIENCE CORRUPTION, WHICH IS A VERY
COMPLEX PHENOMENON. AS A SOCIETY MATURES, GOVERNMENT TENDS
TO BE LESS CORRUPT AND HENCE BETTER FOR THE PUBLIC INTEREST.

0299 BRAIBANTI R.J.D.
RESEARCH ON THE BUREAUCRACY OF PAKISTAN.
DURHAM: DUKE U PR, 1966, 565 PP., LC#66-14888.
NARRATES PROBLEMS OF PAKISTANI GOVERNMENT IN 1947-65 SO
AS TO SET TO ORDER THE PUBLIC RECORD AND IDENTIFY, CLASSIFY,
AND EVALUATE SOURCE MATERIALS FOR STUDY OF PAKISTANI BUREAU-
CRACY. DEALS WITH HISTORY AND ORGANIZATION OF BUREAUCRACY
AT LOCAL AND NATIONAL LEVELS. NOTES EFFECTS OF NATIONAL
ENVIRONMENT ON GOVERNMENT OPERATION. TRACES REFORM EFFORTS.

0300 BRAIBANTI R.J.D., SPENGLER J.J.
ADMINISTRATION AND ECONOMIC DEVELOPMENT IN INDIA.
DURHAM: DUKE U. PR., 1963, 312 PP., $7.50.
INDIAN AND AMERICAN POLITICAL SCIENTISTS AND ECONOMISTS
DISCUSS THE RELATIONSHIP OF ECONOMIC DEVELOPMENT AND
ADMINISTRATION IN INDIA. ECONOMIC DEVELOPMENT 'HAS BEEN
BLOCKED TO A LARGE EXTENT PRECISELY BECAUSE ITS IMPLEMEN-
TATION DEPENDS ON A STRUCTURE AND DISPOSITION OF BUREAUC-
RACY, NEITHER OF WHICH CAN BE JARRED OUT OF THE LARGER
SOCIETAL WHOLE.'

0301 BRAUN K.
LABOR DISPUTES AND THEIR SETTLEMENT.
BALTIMORE: JOHNS HOPKINS PRESS, 1955, 393 PP., LC#55-8425.
TRACES HISTORY OF LABOR MANAGEMENT DISPUTES AND PRINCI-
PLES OF CURRENT SETTLEMENT PRACTICES. THESE PRACTICES ARE
CONCILIATION, ARBITRATION, AND LITIGATION. EACH IS ANALYZED
ACCORDING TO PURPOSE AND SUCCESS UNDER SPECIFIC CIRCUM-
STANCES. OPINIONS FOR AND AGAINST EACH ARE DISCUSSED, THOUGH
NO ATTEMPT IS MADE TO GIVE RECOMMENDATIONS FOR OR AGAINST
ANY SPECIFIC METHOD OF LABOR SETTLEMENT.

0302 BRAYMAN H.
CORPORATE MANAGEMENT IN A WORLD OF POLITICS.
NEW YORK: MCGRAW HILL, 1967, 272 PP., LC#67-13899.
DISCUSSES FORCE OF PUBLIC OPINION, RELATIONS BETWEEN
BUSINESS AND GOVERNMENT, CHANGING CHARACTER OF MARKETS AND
COMPETITION, TRADE ORGANIZATIONS, AND FOREIGN TRADE OF US
BUSINESS. MAINTAINS MODERN BUSINESSMEN NEED EXPERIENCE IN
POLITICS TO REDUCE FRICTION BETWEEN GOVERNMENT AND BUSINESS.

0303 BRECHT A.
FEDERALISM AND REGIONALISM IN GERMANY; THE DIVISION OF
PRUSSIA.
ITHACA: CORNELL U PRESS, 1945, 202 PP.
ANALYZES PROBLEMS OF GERMAN FEDERALISM AND REGIONALISM
FROM 1900-45, INCLUDING ADMINISTRATIVE QUESTIONS. DISCUSSES
POLITICAL FACTORS OF BOTH, FEDERALISM IN PRACTICE, AND
ATTEMPTS AT REFORM. EXAMINES DECENTRALIZATION, TOTALITARIAN
REGIONALISM UNDER HITLER, AND POSSIBLE STRUCTURE OF POSTWAR
GERMANY.

0304 BREGMAN A.
"WHITHER RUSSIA?"
PROBLEMS OF COMMUNISM, 16 (MAY-JUNE 67), 50-54.
DELINEATES THE EXTENT OF INTERDEPENDENCE BETWEEN USSR AND
EASTERN EUROPE AND OF POTENTIAL SOCIAL AND IDEOLOGICAL IN-
TERACTION. ARGUES THAT THE URGE OF YOUNG LIBERAL EAST EURO-
PEAN MARXISTS TO REFORM VESTED BUREAUCRATIC INTERESTS AND
CREATE A FREER SOCIETY MAY INFLUENCE USSR TO LIBERALIZE ITS
OWN SYSTEM. CALLS THE PROCESS "EVOLUTIONARY," PERHAPS AFTER
A FINNISH OR RUMANIAN MODEL.

0305 BRENNAN D.G.
"SETTING AND GOALS OF ARMS CONTROL."
DAEDALUS, 89 (WINTER 1960), 681-707.
ANALYZES THE STRATEGY ON WHICH ARMS CONTROL IS BASED,
INCLUDING A REVIEW OF THE CONTEMPORARY MILITARY GOALS OF
DETERRENCE, LIMITED WAR AND GENERAL WAR. ELABORATES ON
EFFECTS OF THERMONUCLEAR ACTIONS IN CONFINED AREAS AND
CONTENDS THEIR OCCURRENCE CAN BE AVOIDED BY ACHIEVING A
WORKABLE ARMAMENT AGREEMENT WITH THE SOVIET UNION BASED ON
COMMON OBJECTIVES AND ENFORCED BY INTERNATIONAL SANCTIONS.

0306 BRIEFS H.W.

PRICING POWER AND "ADMINISTRATIVE" INFLATION (PAMPHLET)
WASHINGTON: AMER ENTERPRISE INST, 1962, 63 PP., LC#62-21990.
ANALYSIS OF NATIONAL POLICY OF PRICE CONTROL AS MEANS TO
REGULATE INFLATION. DISCUSSES CONCEPT OF ADMINISTERED PRICE
AND OPINIONS ON ITS VALUE AND DEALS WITH STEEL INDUSTRY
FOR UNDERSTANDING OF PRACTICE.

0307 BRIGHT J.R.
AUTOMATION AND MANAGEMENT.
CAMBRIDGE: HARVARD BUS SCHOOL, 1958, 270 PP., LC#58-5968.
ANALYZES THE NATURE AND CHARACTERISTICS OF AUTOMATION,
SOME OF ITS BENEFITS AND DISADVANTAGES, SOME OF MAJOR
EFFECTS ON BUSINESS OPERATIONS, AND ITS IMPLICATIONS FOR
BUSINESS MANAGEMENT. CONCLUDES THAT AUTOMATION PLACES A
GREATER PREMIUM ON PLANNING IN ALL ASPECTS OF BUSINESS OPER-
ATION. CONTENDS ACCELERATED TECHNOLOGICAL DEVELOPMENTS MUST
BE ANTICIPATED IF BUSINESS IS TO ACHIEVE SOCIAL FUNCTION.

0308 BRIGHT J.R.
RESEARCH, DEVELOPMENT AND TECHNOLOGICAL INNOVATION.
HOMEWOOD: RICHARD IRWIN, 1964, 764 PP., LC#64-11711.
DISCUSSION OF TECHNOLOGICAL INNOVATION AND ITS PROBLEMS.
TYPICAL BUSINESS PROBLEMS ANALYZED IN ATTEMPT TO ILLUMINATE
METHODS OF HANDLING ISSUES CONCERNING IDENTIFICATION OF,
SUPPORT FOR, AND DEFENSE AGAINST RADICAL TECHNOLOGICAL CON-
CEPTS. CHANGE AND INNOVATION IN POPULATION, SOCIAL TRENDS,
NATURAL RESOURCE POSITIONS, ETC. ARE CONSIDERED.

0309 BRIMMER A.F.
"INITIATIVE AND INNOVATION IN CENTRAL BANKING."
BUSINESS TOPICS, 15 (SUMMER 67), 7-15.
REVIEWS RECORD OF MONETARY MANAGEMENT FOR 1966, ECONOMIC
POLICY, AND STABILIZATION EFFORTS. DISCUSSES EXCESS DEMAND,
DEBT MANAGEMENT, OPEN MARKET OPERATIONS, FEDERAL RESERVE
BOARD REQUIREMENTS, DISCOUNT RATE, SELECTIVE MEASURES, AND
LESSENING OF CREDIT RESTRAINT. CONCLUDES THAT OF THREE TYPES
OF ECONOMIC POLICIES, MONETARY DID BETTER THAN FISCAL AND
DEBT; NEED BETTER BALANCE OF STABILIZATION.

0310 BRIMMER B.
A GUIDE TO THE USE OF UNITED NATIONS DOCUMENTS.
NEW YORK: OCEANA PUBLISHING, 1962, 272 PP.
INCLUDES REFERENCES TO PUBLICATIONS OF ALL SPECIALIZED
AGENCIES OF THE UN AND SPECIAL UN BODIES.

0311 BRINTON C.
THE ANATOMY OF REVOLUTION.
NEW YORK: PRENTICE HALL, 1952, 324 PP.
TRACES THE UNIFORMITIES IN FOUR SUCCESSFUL REVOLUTIONS:
AMERICAN, FRENCH, COMMUNIST AND CROMWELL'S UPRISING IN
ENGLAND. IN ANALYZING THESE REBELLIONS, PROBES
ECONOMIC LEVEL OF SOCIETY, CLASS ANTAGONISMS, INFLUENCE OF
INTELLECTUALS AND STRUCTURE OF GOVERNMENTAL GROUPS.

0312 BRISTOL L.H. JR.
DEVELOPING THE CORPORATE IMAGE.
NEW YORK: CHAS SCRIBNER'S SONS, 1960, 298 PP., LC#60-06325.
MANAGEMENT GUIDE TO PUBLIC RELATIONS, INCLUDING THIRTY-
TWO ARTICLES BY PUBLIC RELATIONS PROFESSIONALS ON NEED FOR
CORPORATE IMAGE, ITS VARIOUS FACETS, TOOLS, TECHNIQUES AND
MEDIA, AND ON EVALUATING IMAGE.

0313 BROGAN D.W., VERNEY D.V.
POLITICAL PATTERNS IN TODAY'S WORLD.
NEW YORK: HARCOURT BRACE, 1963, 274 PP., LC#63-11413.
BRIEF COMPARATIVE INTRODUCTION TO POLITICAL SCIENCE.
COMPARES FOUR LIBERAL DEMOCRACIES IN THEIR COMMON TRADITION,
POLITICAL PROCESSES, ORGANIZATION, AND ROLE IN INTERNATIONAL
RELATIONS, TO THE COMMUNIST WORLD. DISCUSSES DECLINE AND
FAILURE OF DEMOCRACY'S LEADERSHIP IN FRANCE AND IN
TOTALITARIAN DICTATORSHIPS.

0314 BROMAGE A.W.
AMERICAN COUNTY GOVERNMENT.
NEW YORK: SEARS PUBL CO INC, 1933, 306 PP.
DISCUSSES THE HISTORY, ORGANIZATION, POWER, INFLUENCE,
AND COMPLEXITIES OF COUNTY, MUNICIPAL, AND RURAL GOVERN-
MENT AND DESCRIBES EFFORTS AT RECONSTRUCTION. OFFERS A
SELECTED BIBLIOGRAPHY LISTING REFERENCES, BIBLIOGRAPHIES,
BOOKS, ARTICLES, AND PAMPHLETS WHICH DEAL WITH COUNTY
GOVERNMENT AND COUNTY GOVERNMENT REFORM.

0315 BROMAGE A.W.
MANAGER PLAN ABANDONMENTS: WHY A FEW HAVE DROPPED COUNCIL-
MANAGER GOVERNMENT.
NEW YORK: NATL MUNICIPAL LEAGUE, 1964, 40 PP.
EXAMINES CITIES IN WHICH COUNCIL-MANAGER GOVERNMENT WAS
ABANDONED BY POPULAR VOTE. FINDS THAT RATE OF ABANDONMENT
HAS NOT INCREASED OVER TIME; IT IS LEAST EFFECTIVE IN CITIES
WITH POPULATION OVER 100,000; VOTER APATHY AIDS DEFEAT.
GIVES SEVERAL POLITICAL REASONS FOR DEFEAT AND ILLUSTRATES
THEM WITH SHORT CASE STUDIES.

0316 BROOKINGS INSTITUTION
"GOVERNMENT MECHANISM FOR CONDUCT OF US FOREIGN RELATIONS."
WASHINGTON: BROOKINGS INST., 1949, 56 PP.

SHOWS ORGANIZATION AND FUNCTIONING OF GOVERNMENT MECHA-
NISM. DISCUSSES ROLE AND POWERS OF EXECUTIVE AND LEGISLATIVE
BRANCHES AND OF PUBLIC OPINION.

0317 BROOKINGS INSTITUTION
UNITED STATES FOREIGN POLICY: STUDY NO 9: THE FORMULATION
AND ADMINISTRATION OF UNITED STATES FOREIGN POLICY.
WASHINGTON: BROOKINGS INST, 1960, 191 PP.
STUDY DONE FOR US SENATE COMMITTEE ON FOREIGN RELATIONS.
APPRAISES ENDS AND MEANS OF US FOREIGN POLICY IN RELATION TO
CHANGING WORLD CONDITIONS. COVERS CONGRESSIONAL AND EXECU-
TIVE PROCEDURE, ROLE OF MULTILATERAL ORGANIZATIONS, RELATION
WITH MILITARY ESTABLISHMENT, OUR AMBASSADORIAL SETUP, PER-
SONNEL MANAGEMENT, AND INTELLIGENCE AND INFORMATIONAL OPERA-
TIONS. MAKES MANY RECOMMENDATIONS.

0318 BROOKS R.R.
WHEN LABOR ORGANIZES.
NEW HAVEN: YALE U PR, 1937, 361 PP.
A SYSTEMATICL EXAMINATION OF UNIONS FROM ORGANIZATION,
STRIKES, FINANCES, ADMINISTRATION AND LEADERSHIP, BENEFIT
AND WELFARE POLICIES TO BROADER ISSUES OF POLITICAL ACTION,
ANTI-UNIONISM AND BUSINESS POLICIES OF LABOR, WITH A
HISTORICAL SECTION AND TRENDS FOR UNIONISM. REPRESENTATION,
EXTERNAL AN INTERNAL, IS DISCUSSED THROUGHOUT THE WORK.

0319 BROWN A.D.
LIST OF REFERENCES ON THE CIVIL SERVICE AND PERSONNEL ADMIN-
ISTRATION IN THE UNITED STATES (2ND MIMEOGRAPHED SUPPLEMENT)
WASHINGTON: LIBRARY OF CONGRESS, 1942.
UPDATES EARLIER EDITIONS DEALING WITH THE POLICIES AND
PROBLEMS OF PERSONNEL MANAGEMENT IN THE CIVIL SERVICE.
INCLUDES BOOKS, ARTICLES, PAMPHLETS, SPEECHES, ETC. 829
ITEMS IN ALL PLUS SUBJECT AND AUTHOR INDEXES.

0320 BROWN B.E.
NEW DIRECTIONS IN COMPARATIVE POLITICS.
LONDON: ASIA PUBL HOUSE, 1962, 91 PP.
EXAMINES NATURE AND TRENDS IN COMPARATIVE APPROACH TO
POLITICS AND APPLIES COMPARATIVE METHOD TO STUDY OF INTER-
ACTION BETWEEN PEOPLE AND GOVERNMENT THROUGH PARTIES, ROLE
OF ARMIES IN RIVALRY FOR POWER, AND SHIFTING BALANCE AMONG
PUBLIC POWERS. COMPARES POLITICS OF WEST AND NON-WEST IN
CONCLUSION.

0321 BROWN C.V.
GOVERNMENT AND BANKING IN WESTERN NIGERIA.
LONDON: OXFORD U PR, 1964, 141 PP.
ANALYZES IMPLEMENTATION OF WESTERN NIGERIAN GOVERNMENT'S
ECONOMIC POLICY OF AIDING INDIGENOUS BANKS. RELIES HEAVILY
ON INFORMATION AND QUOTATIONS FROM COKER COMMISSION OF IN-
QUIRY. SIGNIFICANT CASE STUDY MAY INDICATE TYPE OF RELATION-
SHIP EXISTING AMONG POLITICIANS, CIVIL SERVANTS, AND PUBLIC
CORPORATIONS IN WESTERN NIGERIA AND OTHER DEVELOPING AREAS.

0322 BROWN E.S.
MANUAL OF GOVERNMENT PUBLICATIONS.
NEW YORK: APPLETON, 1950, 121 PP.
ANNOTATED LISTING OF APPROXIMATELY 1,000 BOOKS, PERIODI-
CALS, ARTICLES, AND PAMPHLETS PUBLISHED BY US GOVERNMENT,
STATES, AND FOREIGN GOVERNMENTS. INCLUDES LAWS, CONSTITU-
TIONS, MUNICIPAL AND LOCAL GOVERNMENT, RECORDS OF LEGISLA-
TURES, AND INTERNATIONAL ORGANIZATIONS.

0323 BROWN L.C.
LATIN AMERICA, A BIBLIOGRAPHY.
KINSVILLE: TEX COL ARTS & INDUS, 1962, 80 PP.
LIST OF MATERIALS IN LIBRARY OF TEXAS A&I ON LATIN AMER-
ICA, WITH PARTICULAR EMPHASIS ON INTERNATIONAL RELATIONS,
POLITICS, AND GOVERNMENT. CONTAINS LIST OF ARTICLES ON LATIN
AMERICA.

0324 BROWN L.N., GARNER J.F.
FRENCH ADMINISTRATIVE LAW.
LONDON, WASH, DC: BUTTERWORTHS, 1967, 160 PP.
COMPARE FRENCH LAW WITH ANGLO-SAXON. EXPLAIN THE LEGAL
INSTITUTIONS OF FRANCE AND BRITAIN THAT EXERCISE CONTROL
OVER ACTS OF THE ADMINISTRATION. DELINEATE BASIC LEGAL
STRUCTURE OF BOTH NATIONS, AND DISCUSS MERITS AND DEFECTS
OF THE FRENCH SYSTEM. GIVE MANY SPECIFIC CASES.

0325 BROWN M.
"THE DEMISE OF STATE DEPARTMENT PUBLIC OPINION POLLS: A
STUDY IN LEGISLATIVE OVERSIGHT."
MIDWEST J. OF POLI. SCI., 5 (1961), 1-17.
DESCRIBES THE USE OF PUBLIC OPINION POLLS BY STATE DE-
PARTMENT. TELLS OF PROPAGANDIST LEANING OF UNPUBLISHED POLL
DATA ON FOREIGN AID SENTIMENT AND SUBSEQUENT CONGRESSIONAL
RESPONSE. AUTHOR RAISES QUESTIONS ABOUT ETHICAL USE OF POLL
DATA IN POLICY FORMATION.

0326 BROWN R.E.
JUDGMENT IN ADMINISTRATION.
NEW YORK: MCGRAW HILL, 1966, 225 PP., LC#65-25540.
STUDIES ART OF ADMINISTRATION BY INVESTIGATION OF FAIL-
URES OF GOOD ADMINISTRATIVE DECISION-MAKING, CAUSES AND

CURES.

0327 BROWN S.
"AN ALTERNATIVE TO THE GRAND DESIGN."
WORLD POLIT., 17 (JAN. 65), 232-242.
CRITICIZES GRAND DESIGN FOR ATLANTIC PARTNERSHIP (POLICY
TOWARD NATO, EEC AND REACTION TO FRENCH ASSERTIVENESS).
PROPOSES 'NORTH ATLANTIC CONCERT WITH ITS WEB OF SPECIAL
RELATIONSHIPS IN TRADE AND DEFENSE - DOMINATION AND
SUBORDINATION.' DOES NOT SUGGEST ABANDONMENT OF MULTI-
NATION COMMITMENTS AND ORGANIZATIONAL ARRANGEMENTS WHEN
FEASIBLE. CAN ADJUST TO GLOBAL TREND OF MULTI-POLARITY.

0328 BROWNE C.G. ED., COHN T.S. ED.
THE CONCEPT OF LEADERSHIP.
DANVILLE: INTERSTATE, 1958, 487 PP., $5.75.
ANALYSIS OF LEADERSHIP IN VIEW OF FUNCTION, RECOGNITION,
PERSONEL RELATIONS, AND TRAINING.

0329 BROWNE D.G.
THE RISE OF SCOTLAND YARD: A HISTORY OF THE METROPOLITAN PO-
LICE.
LONDON: GEORGE HARRAP & CO, 1956, 392 PP.
HISTORY OF SCOTLAND YARD, SHOWING HOW IT IS BOUND UP WITH
ATIONAL AND POLITICAL BACKGROWUND OF OVER 120 YEARS, AND HOW
IT IS CREATION AND SERVANT OF PARLIAMENT; EXAMINES CONSEQU-
ENCES OF SUCH CLOSE CONTROL.

0330 BRUEGEL J.W.
"DIE INTERNAZIONALE GEWERKSCHAFTSBEWEGUNG."
EUROPA ARCHIV., 7 (JAN. 52), 4663-70.
ANALYSIS OF INTERNATIONAL TRADE-UNION MOVEMENT AFTER WW 2
WITH EMPHASIS ON INTERNATIONAL FEDERATION OF FREE-TRADE
UNIONS. THOUGH MANY OF ITS AFFILIATED UNIONS ARE CONNECTED
WITH POLITICAL PARTIES, FEDERATION'S OBJECTIVE IS TO FURTHER
INTERESTS OF WORKERS. CITES ITS STAND AGAINST TOTALITARIAN
REGIMES AND ITS SUPPORT OF EUROPEAN INTEGRATION. DISCUSSES
INFLUENCE OF AMERICAN LABOR UNIONS ON THE FEDERATION.

0331 BRUNTON R.L., CARRELL J.J.
MANAGEMENT PRACTICES FOR SMALLER CITIES.
CHICAGO: INTL MANAGERS ASSOC, 1959, 59-8486 PP.
REFERENCE TEXT AND TRAINING MANUAL FOR ADMINISTRATORS OF
SMALL CITIES. PROVIDES OVERVIEW OF MAJOR OBJECTIVES, METH-
ODS, AND PROCEDURES IN EACH OF THE "LINE" ACTIVITIES. ALSO
PLACES EMPHASIS ON "STAFF" ASPECTS OF CHIEF ADMINIS-
TRATOR'S JOB: PLANNING, FINANCING, HANDLING PERSONNEL, ANA-
LYZING TRENDS AND PROBLEMS, REPORTING TO THE PUBLIC.

0332 BRYCE J.
MODERN DEMOCRACIES.
NEW YORK: MACMILLAN, 1921, 676 PP.
DESCRIBES WORKINGS OF MODERN DEMOCRACIES. DISCUSSES NORTH
AMERICAN MODEL AND ITS INFLUENCE ON AUSTRALIA AND NEW
ZEALAND. EXAMINES TRENDS IN DEMOCRATIC STATES, SUCH AS DE-
CLINE IN ROLE OF LEGISLATURES AND CHANGES IN JUDICIARY.

0333 BRZEZINSKI Z.K.
"DEVIATION CONTROL: A STUDY IN THE DYNAMICS OF
DOCTRINAL CONFLICT."
AMER. POLIT. SCI. REV., 56 (MARCH 62), 5-22.
CONSIDERS THE EXPERIENCES OF CATHOLICISM AND COMMUNISM
IN DEALING WITH DEVIATION FROM THE CENTER (BUT WITHIN COMMON
DOCTRINE) AND SUGGESTS THAT KNOWLEDGE DERIVED WILL LEAD TO
METHODS WHICH FURTHER DOCTRINAL EVOLUTION.

0334 BRZEZINSKI Z.K., HUNTINGTON S.P.
"CINCINNATUS AND THE APPARATCHIK."
WORLD POLIT., 16 (OCT. 63), 52-78.
DESCRIBES AND CONTRASTS PROFESSIONAL POLITICIANS IN USA
AND USSR AS TO QUALIFICATIONS, BACKGROUND AND RULES GOVERN-
ING ACTIONS. CONCLUDES BY STATING A NEED FOR GREATER PRO-
FESSIONAL LEADERSHIP IN THE UNITED STATES.

0335 BRZEZINSKI Z.K.
IDEOLOGY AND POWER IN SOVIET POLITICS.
NEW YORK: FREDERICK PRAEGER, 1967, 291 PP., LC#66-18893.
MAKES DISTINCTION BETWEEN IDEOLOGICAL AND POWER INFLUENCE
ON SOVIET FOREIGN POLICY, AND INDICATES LACK OF DISTINCTION
BECAUSE OF DEPENDENCE OF LEADERS UPON DOGMATIC IDEOLOGY FOR
DETERMINATION OF USAGE OF POWER. ANALYZES CONFLICTS IN SYS-
TEM CONSISTING OF THIS POWER-IDEOLOGY CONGLOMERATION. APPLI-
CATION OF THEORY TO CURRENT FOREIGN AFFAIRS PROBLEMS.

0336 BRZEZINSKI Z.K.
THE SOVIET BLOC: UNITY AND CONFLICT (2ND ED., REV.,
ENLARGED)
CAMBRIDGE: HARVARD U PR, 1967, 599 PP., LC#67-12531.
EXAMINES HOW SOVIET BLOC HAS CHANGED OVER THE YEARS,
WHAT PROBLEMS FACED AND CONTINUE TO FACE ITS LEADERS, AND
HOW LEADERS GO ABOUT SOLVING THESE IN TERMS OF THEIR
GENERAL IDEOLOGICAL ORIENTATION. ALSO SHOWS HOW INTERNAL
CHANGES IN USSR AFFECTED POLITICAL DEVELOPMENTS WITHIN
OTHER COMMUNIST STATES AND CHANGED THE PATTERN OF RELATIONS
AMONG THEM.

0337 BUDER S.
PULLMAN: AN EXPERIMENT IN INDUSTRIAL ORDER AND COMMUNITY
PLANNING, 1880-1930.
NEW YORK: OXFORD U PR, 1967, 263 PP., LC#67-25456.
CONCERNS MODEL TOWN PULLMAN CONSTRUCTED OUTSIDE CHICAGO
FOR PRODUCTION OF HIS RAILROAD CARS AND HOUSING OF WORKERS.
BEGINS WITH DEVELOPMENT OF PULLMAN'S INDUSTRY; EXAMINES
SOCIAL AND INDUSTRIAL PROBLEMS. COVERS PHYSICAL PLANNING
OF TOWN AND FACTORY, RELATIONS OF COMMUNITY AND COMPANY,
EMPLOYEE DISSATISFACTION, AND LABOR STRIFE AND STRIKE.
ENDS WITH SEPARATION OF FACTORY AND TOWN.

0338 BUECHNER J.C.
DIFFERENCES IN ROLE PERCEPTIONS IN COLORADO COUNCIL-MANAGER
CITIES.
BOULDER: U OF COLORADO PR, 1965, 62 PP.
STUDIES PERCEPTIONS OF ROLE OF CITY MANAGERS HELD BY
COLORADO CITY MANAGERS AND CITY COUNCILMEN USING INTERVIEWS
AND QUESTIONNAIRES. EXPLAINS ROLE ANALYSIS AND METHODOLOGY;
GIVES PROFILE OF CITIES, MANAGERS, AND COUNCILMEN INVOLVED;
COMPARES RESULTS AND ACCOUNTS FOR DIFFERENCES IN ROLE
PERCEPTION.

0339 BUELL R.
THE NATIVE PROBLEM IN AFRICA.
NEW YORK: MACMILLAN, 1928, 1045 PP.
COMPREHENSIVE STUDY OF POLITICAL, SOCIAL, AND ECONOMIC
SITUATION OF A NUMBER OF AFRICAN COUNTRIES AND TERRITORIES.
POINTS OUT MAIN PROBLEMS OF CONTINENT, FOCUSING ON THOSE
RESULTING FROM IMPACT OF INDUSTRIAL CIVILIZATION ON PRIMI-
TIVE PEOPLE.

0340 BUELL R.
INTERNATIONAL RELATIONS.
NEW YORK: HOLT, 1929, 758 PP.
A TEXTBOOK CASE STYLE STUDY, WELL-DOCUMENTED, OF THE
PROBLEMS ARISING HISTORICALLY AMONG STATES. ANALYSES ARE
MADE OF THE SOCIO-ECONOMIC BASES OF THESE DISPUTES AND THE
SETTLEMENTS ATTEMPTED OR ATTAINED IN THE PAST.

0341 BUENO M.
"ASPECTOS SOCIOLOGICOS DE LA EDUCACION."
REV. MEX. SOCIOL., 24 (NO. 3, 62), 751-62.
EXAMINES EDUCATIONAL, CULTURAL, PERSONALITY, AND BEHAVIOR
PATTERNS. DISCUSSES RELATIONSHIP OF SOCIETY TO THE
INDIVIDUAL. ANALYZES EDUCATIONAL TRENDS IN COLONIAL
COUNTRIES IN LIGHT OF IDEOLOGICAL AND POLITICAL PROBLEMS.

0342 BULLIS H.A.
MANIFESTO FOR AMERICANS.
NEW YORK: MCGRAW HILL, 1961, 213 PP., LC#61-15310.
AFFIRMATION OF POTENTIAL IN DEMOCRATIC SOCIETY THROUGH
PERSONAL ENTERPRISE. AUTHOR IS RELIGIOUSLY ORIENTED AND
POSITIVE IN ATTITUDES CONCERNING PRESENT DOMESTIC CONDITIONS
AND FUTURE OF AMERICA.

0343 BULMER-THOMAS I.
"THE PARTY SYSTEM IN GREAT BRITAIN."
LONDON: PHOENIX HOUSE LTD, 1953.
STUDY OF ORGANIZATION AND WORKING OF PARTY SYSTEM IN
PRACTICE. SKETCHES HISTORY OF PARTY ORGANIZATION BEFORE 1900
BUT EMPHASIZES DEVELOPMENT OF POLITICAL ALIGNMENTS IN 20TH
CENTURY. SELECTED BIBLIOGRAPHY ORGANIZED TOPICALLY WITH
MATERIAL RELATED TO SPECIFIC PARTY DEVELOPMENTS.

0344 BULPITT J.G.
PARTY POLITICS IN ENGLISH LOCAL GOVERNMENT.
LONDON: LONGMANS, GREEN & CO, 1967, 133 PP.
FOUR CASE STUDIES COMPARING TYPES OF LOCAL GOVERNMENTS.
ATTEMPTS TO ANALYZE LOCAL PARTY POLITICS AND RELATIONSHIP
BETWEEN IT AND THE COUNCIL.

0345 BUNZEL J.H.
"THE GENERAL IDEOLOGY OF AMERICAN SMALL BUSINESS"(BMR)"
POLIT. SCI. QUART., 70 (MAR. 55), 87-102.
DISCUSSES BELIEFS AND VALUES OF THE AMERICAN SMALL
BUSINESSMAN. ARGUES THAT IDEOLOGY OF SMALL BUSINESS PARTAKES
OF A GOOD DEAL OF WHAT WAS PREVALENT IN US PRIOR TO THE RISE
OF INDUSTRY. PLACES IDEOLOGY IN CONTEXT OF "AGRARIAN SPIRIT"
OF PRE-INDUSTRIAL AMERICA, SHOWING BELIEFS OF SMALL BUSINESS
AND PERSONALITY OF SMALL BUSINESSMAN THAT PERSIST TODAY.

0346 BURACK E.H.
"INDUSTRIAL MANAGEMENT IN ADVANCED PRODUCTION SYSTEMS: SOME
THEORETICAL CONCEPTS AND PRELIMINARY FINDINGS."
ADMINISTRATIVE SCI. Q., 12 (DEC. 67), 479-500.
DISCUSSES SOME OF THE EFFECTS OF TECHNOLOGICAL MODIFI-
CATIONS AND IMPROVEMENTS ON INDUSTRIAL MANAGEMENT IN TWO
TYPES OF ADVANCED MANUFACTURING SYSTEMS. INFORMATION OB-
TAINED THROUGH QUESTIONNAIRES, INTERVIEWS, RECORDS ANALY-
SIS, AND OBSERVATION. DETECTS UNDERLYING SHIFTS IN MANAGER-
IAL ORGANIZATION AND FUNCTIONS THAT ACCOMPANY TECHNICAL
INNOVATIONS.

0347 BURDETTE F.L., WILLMORE J.N., WITHERSPOON J.V.
POLITICAL SCIENCE: A SELECTED BIBLIOGRAPHY OF BOOKS IN
PRINT, WITH ANNOTATIONS (PAMPHLET)
COLLEGE PARK: U MD, BUR PUB ADM, 1961, 97 PP., LC#61-64130.
CONTAINS APPROXIMATELY 250 TITLES WITH EXTENSIVE THOUGH
NONCRITICAL ANNOTATIONS IN ALL FIELDS OF POLITICAL
SCIENCE: AMERICAN NATIONAL GOVERNMENT, COMPARATIVE GOVERN-
MENT, INTERNATIONAL POLITICS, POLITICAL PARTIES, PUBLIC
OPINION AND ELECTORAL PROCESS, POLITICAL THEORY, PUBLIC
ADMINISTRATION, PUBLIC LAW, AND LOCAL AND STATE GOVERNMENT.
DESIGNED FOR REFERENCE USERS.

0348 BURDETTE F.L.
"SELECTED ARTICLES AND DOCUMENTS ON AMERICAN GOVERNMENT AND
POLITICS."
AM. POL. SCI. REV., 60 (SEPT. 66), 728-737.
AN UNANNOTATED BIBLIOGRAPHY ON AMERICAN GOVERNMENT AND
POLITICS. ENGLISH-LANGUAGE MATERIALS, PUBLISHED IN 1966;
390 ENTRIES. TOPICAL HEADINGS: MILITARY, HEALTH, EDUCATION,
WELFARE, BUSINESS, LABOR, AGRICULTURE, NATIONAL ECONOMY,
POLITICS, PUBLIC ADMINISTRATION, CONSTITUTIONAL LAW, NATION-
AL, STATE, AND LOCAL GOVERNMENTS, AND INTERGOVERNMENTAL
RELATIONS.

0349 BUREAU GOVERNMENT RES AND SERV
COUNTY GOVERNMENT REORGANIZATION - A SELECTED ANNOTATED BIB-
LIOGRAPHY (PAPER)
SEATTLE: U OF WASH, BUR GOVT RES, 1967, 10 PP.
ANNOTATED COMPILATION OF 60 SOURCES ON COUNTY GOVERNMENT
STRUCTURE AND URBAN PROBLEMS IN THE US. INCLUDES BOOKS AND
GOVERNMENT PUBLICATIONS FROM 1948 THROUGH 1966. FIRST PART
CONSISTS OF GENERAL SOURCES; SECOND PART ON COUNTY CHARTER;
AND THIRD SECTION IS DIVIDED INTO STUDIES BY STATES.

0350 BUREAU OF NATIONAL AFFAIRS
A CURRENT LOOK AT: (1) THE NEGRO AND TITLE VII, (2) SEX AND
TITLE VII (PAMPHLET)
WASHINGTON: BUREAU NATL AFFAIRS, 1967, 23 PP.
DISCUSSES CONSEQUENCES OF TITLE VII OF THE CIVIL RIGHTS
ACT OF 1964 WHICH MAKES DISCRIMINATION IN EMPLOYMENT ILLE-
GAL. SAMPLES BOTH LARGE AND SMALL COMPANIES TO ASCERTAIN
BOTH NEGRO AND FEMALE MEMBERSHIP IN WORK FORCE, ANALYZING
REASONS FOR THEIR INCREASE. DISCUSSES TYPES OF JOBS MOST
COMMONLY HELD BY NEGROES AND WOMEN.

0351 BUREAU OF NATIONAL AFFAIRS
LABOR RELATIONS REFERENCE MANUAL VOL 1, 1935-1937.
WASHINGTON: BUREAU NATL AFFAIRS, 1937, 979 PP.
LISTS STATUTES ON LABOR RELATIONS, OPINIONS OF COURTS,
AND DECISIONS OF NATIONAL LABOR RELATIONS BOARD DURING FIRST
TWO YEARS.

0352 BURKE E.M.
"THE SEARCH FOR AUTHORITY IN PLANNING."
SOCIAL SERVICE REV., 41 (SEPT. 67), 250-260.
DISCUSSES CHANGE IN METHODOLOGY OF SOCIAL PLANNING.
NEW TECHNIQUES AND CONCEPTUALLY BASED MODELS FOR DECISION-
MAKING ARE REPLACING DECISION PROCESS BASED ON INDIVIDUAL
WHIM. ALSO DEALS WITH TYPES OF AUTHORITY THAT MAY BE
APPLIED TO SOCIAL PLANNING GOALS. CONSIDERS HOW TO FIT
PLANNING INTO THE SYSTEM WITHIN WHICH IT OPERATES. IS CON-
CERNED WITH PLANNING ON LOCAL LEVEL.

0353 BURNS A.C. ED.
PARLIAMENT AS AN EXPORT.
NEW YORK: BARNES AND NOBLE, 1966, 271 PP.
STUDIES ADOPTION OF PARLIAMENTARY SYSTEM BY FOREIGN COUN-
TRIES, PARTICULARLY MEMBERS OF COMMONWEALTH. EXAMINES OR-
GANIZATION AND PROCEDURES OF COMMONWEALTH PARLIAMENTS COVER-
ING POLITICAL PARTIES, ROLE OF MP, SECOND CHAMBER, AND
RELATIONSHIP TO EXECUTIVE, CIVIL SERVICE, AND COURTS.

0354 BURNS J.M.
CONGRESS ON TRIAL: THE LEGISLATIVE PROCESS AND THE ADMINIS-
TRATIVE STATE.
NEW YORK: HARPER & ROW, 1949, 224 PP.
STUDY OF CONGRESSMEN, REPRESENTATION, MISREPRESENTATION,
PARTY IMPOTENCE, AND THE REASONS FOR IMPENDING CONGRESSIONAL
CRISIS. FORECASTS REPEATED PERIODS OF CONGRESSIONAL-EXECU-
TIVE DEADLOCK IN POWER STRUGGLE, WITH INCREASING PRESIDEN-
TIAL AUTHORITY IN CRUCIAL TIMES, IF THE PARTIES FAIL TO ES-
TABLISH PARTY UNITY.

0355 BURRUS B.R.
INVESTIGATION AND DISCOVERY IN STATE ANTITRUST (PAMPHLET)
ANN ARBOR: U OF MICH LAW SCHOOL, 1967, 95 PP.
BEGINS WITH BACKGROUND INFORMATION ON ANTITRUST LAWS;
EXAMINES ENFORCEMENT PROCEDURES AND INVESTIGATIONS, STATE
PRETRIAL PROCEDURES, STATE PRECOMPLAINT INVESTIGATIVE
POWERS, AND CURRENT STATUS OF STATE. INCLUDES RIGHTS OF
DEFENDANTS, JUDICIAL VS. ADMINISTRATIVE PROCESS, STATE AND
FEDERAL LAWS, AND CRIMINAL AND CIVIL CASES. CONCLUDES WITH
BALANCING INTERESTS AND JUDICIAL SUPERINTENDENCE.

0356 BURRUS B.R.
ADMINISTRATIVE LAW AND LOCAL GOVERNMENT.
ANN ARBOR: U OF MICH LAW SCHOOL, 1963, 139 PP.
DISCUSSES CONSTITUTIONAL CONCEPTS OF LIMITATION, JUDICIAL

REVIEW, AND STATE ADMINISTRATIVE PROCEDURES. EMPHASIZES AD-
MINISTRATIVE FUNCTIONS ON LOCAL LEVELS, SUCH AS GRANTING OF
PERMITS, LICENSES, AND CERTIFICATES.

0357 BURSK E.C., CHAPMAN J.F.
NEW DECISION-MAKING TOOLS FOR MANAGERS.
CAMBRIDGE: HARVARD U PR, 1963.
PRESENTS MATHEMATICAL DECISION-MAKING AS A USEFUL AND
ESSENTIAL AID TO THE BUSINESS MANAGER. ATTEMPTS TO SHOW THE
SPECIFIC APPLICATIONS OF THE MATHEMATICAL APPROACH IN COL-
LECTION AND INTERPRETATION OF DATA. WARNS OF POSSIBILITY OF
SACRIFICING UTILITY IN PRESERVING TECHNIQUE.

0358 BURT F.A.
AMERICAN ADVERTISING AGENCIES.
NEW YORK: HARPER & ROW, 1940, 282 PP.
SURVEY OF GROWTH, FUNCTION, AND FUTURE OF AMERICAN
ADVERTISING AGENCIES. ALSO CONTAINS INFORMATION ON
PRACTICAL PROBLEMS OF SUCH FIRMS: COPY WRITING, FILING,
AND LAYOUT.

0359 BURTON M.E.
THE ASSEMBLY OF THE LEAGUE OF NATIONS.
CHICAGO: U. CHI. PR., 1941, 441 PP.
ORIGIN, HISTORY AND CHARACTER OF ASSEMBLY. PRESENTS EARLY
PROPOSALS AND DRAFTS FOR ASSEMBLY STRUCTURE. OUTLINES AND
EVALUATES COMMITTEES, RULES, AND DISPUTES. CONSIDERS EFFECTS
OF PUBLICITY. APPENDIX INCLUDES LEAGUE CONVENANT.

0360 BUSH V.
SCIENCE, THE ENDLESS FRONTIER.
WASHINGTON: G.P.O., 1945, 184 PP.
REPORT TO PRESIDENT BY DIRECTOR OF THE OFFICE OF SCIEN-
TIFIC RESEARCH AND DEVELOPMENT, AND SALVAGES WARTIME ENGEN-
DERED THINKING AND EXPERIENCES, IN GOVERNMENT SPONSORED RE-
SEARCH, FOR PEACETIME APPLICATION. PROPOSES ESTABLISHMENT OF
NATIONAL RESEARCH FOUNDATION AND POLICY FOR IMPROVING SCIEN-
TIFIC DEVELOPMENT AND THE TRAINING OF SCIENTISTS.

0361 BUSH V.
MODERN ARMS AND FREE MEN.
NEW YORK: SIMON SCHUSTER, 1949, 273 PP.
DISCUSSES IMPACT OF MODERN SCIENCE ON WAR, INTERNATIONAL
RELATIONS, AND ON CONCEPT OF DEMOCRACY. EXAMINES NEW TECH-
NIQUES: NUCLEAR MISSILES, SUBVERSION, COLD WAR, AND
UNLIMITED WAR. EXPLORES CHALLENGES OF TOTALITARIANISM TO
DEMOCRACY.

0362 CAHIER P.
"LE RECOURS EN CONSTATATION DE MANQUEMENTS DES ETATS MEMBRES
DEVANT LA COUR DES COMMUNAUTES EUROPEENNES."
CAHIERS DU DROIT EUR., 2 (1967), 123-163.
STUDIES FORMALITIES OBSERVED IN REACHING HIGH AUTHORITY'S
DECISION AND COMMISSION'S OPINION, AND PROBLEMS OF ADMIS-
SION AND PROCEDURE IN CONTEXT OF ARTICLES 88 AND 89 OF
ECSC'S CONSTITUTION. EXAMINES EFFECTS OF JUDGMENTS OF COURT
AND PROBLEMS OF POSSIBLE SANCTIONS.

0363 CAIRNCROSS A.K.
FACTORS IN ECONOMIC DEVELOPMENT.
NEW YORK: PRAEGER, 1962, 346 PP., $6.60.
AMONG THE FACTORS THAT INFLUENCE DEVELOPMENT ARE INVEST-
MENT AND TECHNICAL PROGRESS, ADMINISTRATION AND PLANNING,
AND THE GROWTH OF MARKETS. ALSO STRESSES EDUCATION.

0364 CALDWELL L.K.
"STRENGTHENING STATE LEGISLATURES"
AM. POL. SCI. REV., 41 (APR. 47), 281-289.
DISCUSSES THE PROPOSALS SUBMITTED TO THE COUNCIL OF STATE
GOVERNMENTS BY A COMMITTEE OF STATE OFFICIALS, AIMING AT
STRENGTHENING STATE LEGISLATURES. THE PROPOSALS DEAL WITH
SESSIONS, COMPENSATION, LEGISLATIVE EMPLOYEES, LEGISLATIVE
COMMITTEES, AND THE LEGISLATIVE PROCESS.

0365 CALDWELL L.K.
RESEARCH METHODS IN PUBLIC ADMINISTRATION; AN OUTLINE OF
TOPICS AND READINGS (PAMPHLET)
ALBANY: STATE U OF NY AT ALBANY, 1953, 35 PP.
A DESCRIPTIVELY ANNOTATED BIBLIOGRAPHY DESIGNED TO ASSIST
THE EFFECTIVE APPLICATION OF TOOLS AND TECHNIQUES OF SOCIAL
RESEARCH TO ADMINISTRATIVE PROBLEMS OF THE PUBLIC SERVICE.
ATTENTION GIVEN TO INTERPRETATION OF STATISTICS, PUNCH-CARD
METHODS OF PROCESSING DATA, BIBLIOGRAPHICAL RESEARCH, AND
THE DOCUMENTATION OF RESEARCH PAPERS. ENTRIES LISTED ALPHA-
BETICALLY BY AUTHOR WITHIN EACH TOPICAL DIVISION.

0366 CALDWELL L.K.
"THE GOVERNMENT AND ADMINISTRATION OF NEW YORK."
NEW YORK: THOMAS Y CROWELL, 1954.
DESCRIPTIVE STUDY OF GOVERNMENT AND PUBLIC ADMINISTRA-
TION IN NEW YORK STATE. SELECTED, PARTIALLY-ANNOTATED BIBLI-
OGRAPHY OF PUBLIC RECORDS AND DOCUMENTARY MATERIALS RELATING
TO NY STATE GOVERNMENT; LIMITED TO ESSENTIAL OFFICIAL AND
SEMI-OFFICIAL SOURCES AND TO THE MORE COMPREHENSIVE GENERAL
WORKS. MOST ENTRIES CONSIST OF ANNUAL PUBLICATIONS OR POST-
1949 WORKS.

0367 CALKINS E.E.
BUSINESS THE CIVILIZER.
BOSTON: LITTLE BROWN, 1928, 309 PP.
INFORMAL ACCOUNT OF THE COURSE OF BUSINESS PRACTICES
THROUGH NINETEENTH CENTURY. MAINTAINS THAT AGE OF "ROBBER
BARONS" IS PAST; BUSINESS PRACTICES TODAY ARE ETHICALLY
SOUND.

0368 CALKINS R.D.
"THE DECISION PROCESS IN ADMINISTRATION."
BUSINESS HORIZONS, 2 (FALL 59).
ANALYZES DECISION-MAKING PROCESS IN ORGANIZATIONS.
STUDIES PROBLEM IDENTIFICATION, GOAL DEFINITION, ALTERNATIVE
CHOICE SOLUTION AND CONSEQUENCE ANALYSIS AS PART OF THE
APPRAISAL-CHOICE SYNDROME. PROPOSES MORE SYSTEMATIC AP-
PROACHES TO PROMOTE INCREASED EFFICIENCY.

0369 CAMPBELL A.
"THE USES OF INTERVIEW SURVEYS IN FEDERAL ADMNISTRATION"
SOCIOLOGICAL INQUIRY, (MAY 46).
DESCRIPTION OF THE GROWING USE AND IMPORTANCE OF
INTERVIEW SURVEYS IN FEDERAL ADMINISTRATION. THESE LEAD TO
AN EXTENSION OF FACT-FINDING SERVICES, AND ARE IMPORTANT IN
ASSESSING PUBLIC OPINION. BECUSE OF THESE FACTORS, THESE
ARE OF GROWING IMPORTANCE IN DECISION-MAKING.

0370 CAMPBELL G.A.
THE CIVIL SERVICE IN BRITAIN (2ND ED.)
LONDON: DUCKWORTH, 1965, 255 PP.
ANALYZES GREAT BRITAIN'S CIVIL SERVICE ADMINISTRATION
DURING 19TH AND 20TH CENTURIES, INCLUDING REFORM, ORGANIZA-
TION, RECRUITMENT, AND OVERSEAS DEPARTMENTS. DISCUSSES
MINISTERIAL RESPONSIBILITY, STANDARDS, AND COMMON SERVICES.

0371 CAMPBELL R.W.
SOVIET ECONOMIC POWER.
CAMBRIDGE: HOUGHTON, 1960, 209 PP., $4.75.
EXAMINES FUNCTIONS AND OPERATIONS OF SOVIET ECONOMY.
EVALUATES GROWTH, EFFICIENCY, AND OUTPUT. EXPLORES PROBLEMS
IN COORDINATION AND OPTIMAL USE OF PLANNING PROCESS. CON-
CLUDES POTENTIAL PRODUCTIVITY OF SOVIET UNION POSES MAJOR
CHALLENGE TO USA LEADERSHIP.

0372 CANADA CIVIL SERV COMM
THE ANALYSIS OF ORGANIZATION IN THE GOVERNMENT OF CANADA
(PAMPHLET)
OTTAWA: ORG DIV CAN CIV SERV COM, 1964, 79 PP.
DISCUSSES ADMINISTRATIVE FUNCTIONS AND DIVISIONS OF AU-
THORITY WITHIN DEPARTMENTS OF CANADIAN GOVERNMENT. EXAMINES
IN DETAIL ROLE OF DEPUTY HEAD, AND ORGANIZATION OF SUPPORT
SERVICES.

0373 CANADA NATL JT COUN PUB SERV
THE CANADA NATIONAL JOINT COUNCIL OF THE PUBLIC SERVICE
1944-1964 (PAMPHLET)
OTTAWA: CAN NATL COUN PUB SERV, 1964, 29 PP.
STATEMENTS BY PRIME MINISTER PEARSON AND CHAIRMAN AND
VICE-CHAIRMAN OF NATIONAL JOINT COUNCIL. SUMMARIZES ACHIEVE-
MENTS OF COUNCIL; DESCRIBES MEMBERSHIP, CONSTITUTIONAL
CHANGES, AND AREAS DEALT WITH. COUNCIL WAS ESTABLISHED TO
PROVIDE EMPLOYER-EMPLOYEE CONSULTATIVE PROCEDURE FOR
GOVERNMENT EMPLOYEES.

0374 CAPLOW T.
PRINCIPLES OF ORGANIZATION.
NEW YORK: HARCOURT BRACE, 1964, 383 PP., LC#64-25626.
ARGUES THAT HUMAN ORGANIZATIONS ARE A CLASS OF NATURAL
PHENOMENA, THE ATTRIBUTES OF WHICH ARE NOT TIME OR CULTURE
BOUND, AND WHOSE WORKINGS ARE ORDERLY. DEMONSTRATES THAT
SINGLE THEORETICAL MODEL CAN BE USED TO ANALYZE
ORGANIZATIONS OF ANY TYPE OR STRUCTURE, REGARDLESS OF
CULTURAL OR HISTORICAL LOCATION.

0375 CARALEY D. ED.
PARTY POLITICS AND NATIONAL ELECTIONS.
BOSTON: LITTLE BROWN, 1966, 238 PP., LC#66-16643.
ANALYSIS OF US POLITICAL PARTIES IN RELATION TO NATIONAL
ELECTIONS. EXPLAINS DEVELOPMENT AND ORGANIZATION OF PARTIES
ON NATIONAL, STATE, AND LOCAL LEVELS. DISCUSSES NOMINATING
PROCESS, ELECTION CAMPAIGNS, AND BEHAVIOR OF ELECTORATE.

0376 CARDINALL AW
A BIBLIOGRAPHY OF THE GOLD COAST.
ACCRA: GOVT PRINTER, 1932, 384 PP., LC#32-24984.
BIBLIOGRAPHY OF EARLY PERIOD OF BRITISH ADMINISTRATION.

0377 CARIAS B.
"EL CONTROL DE LAS EMPRESAS PUBLICAS POR GRUPOS DE
INTERESES DE LA COMUNIDAD."
INT. REV. OF ADMIN. SCI., 33 (1967), 47-57.
DESCRIBES SYSTEM OF CONTROL OF PUBLIC ENTERPRISE IN
VENEZUELA. STATES THAT RECENT LAW GIVES WORKERS
REPRESENTATION IN PUBLIC ENTERPRISE. ALTHOUGH THIS HAPPENS
INFREQUENTLY. COMPARES VENEZUELAN SITUATION TO FRENCH AND
BRITISH. CLAIMS THAT WORKER REPRESENTATION IS NECESSARY IN
SOCIALIST STATE AND CAN BE FUNCTIONAL.

0378 CARLETON W.G.
"AMERICAN FOREIGN POLICY: MYTHS AND REALITIES."
VIRGINIA QUART. REV., 37 (SPRING 61), 177-97.
ANALYZES MYTH OF TOLERATING LIMITED WARS TO ASSURE PEACE.
REALISTIC NEW FOREIGN POLICIES SUGGEST BETTER UNDERSTANDING
OF ANTI-IMPERIALIST REVOLUTIONS. EXAMINES NEW DIMENSIONS
FOR US ECONOMIC AID TO UNDERDEVELOPED COUNTRIES.

0379 CARLETON UNIVERSITY LIBRARY
SELECTED LIST OF CURRENT MATERIALS ON CANADIAN PUBLIC
ADMINISTRATION.
OTTAWA: CARLETON U LIBRARY.
BIBLIOGRAPHY ISSUED TWICE A YEAR SINCE 1954 BY CARLETON
UNIVERSITY LIBRARY SCHOOL OF PUBLIC ADMINISTRATION. INCLUDES
ALL IMPORTANT CURRENT MATERIALS RELEVANT TO CANADIAN PUBLIC
ADMINISTRATION WITH EXCLUSION OF DEPARTMENTAL PUBLICATIONS
OTHER THAN PUBLIC ACCOUNTS, BUDGET SPEECHES, COLLECTED
STATUTES, AND PUBLIC SERVICES STUDIES. CLASSIFIED BY NATURE
OF STUDY. CUMULATIVE ISSUE RELEASED IN 1963.

0380 CARLISLE D.
"PARTY LOYALTY; THE ELECTION PROCESS IN SOUTH CAROLINA."
WASHINGTON: PUBLIC AFFAIRS PRESS, 1963.
DETAILED ANALYSIS OF ELECTION PROCESS IN SOUTH CAROLINA
CHARACTERIZES SOUTH CAROLINA AS A ONE-PARTY STATE WHOSE EM-
PHASIS THROUGHOUT THE ELECTION AND NOMINATION SYSTEM IS ON
PARTY LOYALTY. EXAMINES AND SURVEYS EARLY AND MODERN DEVEL-
OPMENT OF ELECTION PROCESS, SUFFRAGE, REGISTRATION AND EN-
ROLLMENT, POLITICAL PARTIES, GENERAL AND MUNICIPAL ELEC-
TIONS. UNANNOTATED BIBLIOGRAPHY OF REFERENCES CITED IN TEXT.

0381 CARLO A.M., MANTECON J.
ENSAYO DE UNA BIBLIOGRAFIA DE BIBLIOGRAFIAS MEXICANAS.
MEXICO CITY: DIR GEN ACCION SOC, 1943, 224 PP.
A BIBLIOGRAPHY OF BIBLIOGRAPHIES PUBLISHED IN AND ABOUT
MEXICO. ENTRIES CLASSIFIED BY SUBJECT. CONTAINS CATALOGUES,
DIRECTORIES OF BOOKS, PERIODICALS, AND LIBRARIES.

0382 CARMICHAEL D.M.
"FORTY YEARS OF WATER POLLUTION CONTROL IN WISCONSIN: A CASE
STUDY."
WISC. LAW REV., 67 (SPRING 67), 350-419.
HISTORY OF POLLUTION CONTROL EMPHASIZING PRESENT POLICY
AND ENFORCEMENT AND OF DEPARTMENT OF RESOURCE DEVELOPMENT
AND DRAINAGE BASIN HEARINGS.

0383 CARNEGIE ENDOWMENT INT. PEACE
"ADMINISTRATION AND BUDGET (ISSUES BEFORE THE NINETEENTH
GENERAL ASSEMBLY)."
INT. CONCIL., 550 (NOV. 64), 197-205.
DISCUSSES MONETARY AND ADMINISTRATIVE ISSUES WHICH WERE
RAISED DURING THE NINETEENTH SESSION.

0384 CARNEY D.E.
GOVERNMENT AND ECONOMY IN BRITISH WEST AFRICA.
NEW YORK: BOOKMAN ASSOCIATES, 1961, 343 PP., LC#61-09845.
STUDY OF 1947-55 ECONOMIC PRACTICES OF BRITISH ADMIN-
ISTRATORS IN PREPARING COLONIES IN AFRICA FOR INDEPENDENCE.
COMPARISON OF ECONOMIC TACTICS OF GOVERNMENT OWNERSHIP AND
PRIVATE INDUSTRY.

0385 CARPER E.T.
ILLINOIS GOES TO CONGRESS FOR ARMY LAND.
INDIANAPOLIS: BOBBS-MERRILL, 1962, 332 PP.
DESCRIBES SENATORS DOUGLAS'S AND DIRKSEN'S 2-YEAR
OCCUPATION WITH REQUESTS FROM SPORTSMEN AND A BUSINESS
SYNDICATE, EACH SEEKING SAME PIECE OF SURPLUS ARMY LAND.
CONGRESSIONAL LEGISLATION ULTIMATELY TRANSFERRED THE LAND,
IN LIEU OF FEDERAL AGENCY RESPONSIBLE, THE GENERAL
SERVICE ADMINISTRATION.

0386 CARROTHERS A.W.R.
LABOR ARBITRATION IN CANADA.
TORONTO: BUTTERWORTHS, 1961, 190 PP.
EVALUATES ARBITRATION AS METHOD OF SETTLING GRIEVANCES IN
LABOR DISPUTES. CONSIDERS RELEVANT SECTIONS OF ALL COLLEC-
TIVE BARGAINING STATUTES IN CANADA AND ARBITRATION STATUTES
OF COMMON LAW PROVINCES, WITH ILLUSTRATIVE CASE STUDIES IN
BASIC AREAS.

0387 CARSON P.
MATERIALS FOR WEST AFRICAN HISTORY IN THE ARCHIVES OF BEL-
GIUM AND HOLLAND.
LONDON: ATHLONE PRESS, 1962, 86 PP.
FIRST IN A SERIES OF VOLUMES COVERING EUROPEAN AR-
CHIVES. THIS BOOKS ARRANGES MATERIAL ACCORDING TO CITY AND
INSTITUTION WHERE FOUND; CATALOGUES LETTERS, RECEIPTS, MAPS,
CHARTS, SHIPS' RECORDS, AND MANY OTHER ITEMS. DOES NOT COVER
DIPLOMATIC RELATIONS AMONG EUROPEAN POWERS. 1,250 ENTRIES.

0388 CARTER B.E.
THE OFFICE OF THE PRIME MINISTER.
PRINCETON: PRINCETON U PRESS, 1956, 362 PP.
GENERAL WORK ON THE OFFICE OF THE PRIME MINISTER IN GREAT
BRITAIN; ITS ORGANIZATION, FUNCTIONS, POWERS, AND RELATIONS
WITH THE PUBLIC, THE CABINET, PARLIAMENT, AND THE CIVIL
SERVICE.

0389 CARTER G.M., BROWN W.O.
TRANSITION IN AFRICA; STUDIES IN POLITICAL ADAPTATION.
BOSTON: BOSTON U AFR RES PROG, 1958, 158 PP., LC#58-12220.
FOUR PAPERS PRESENTED AT AMERICAN POLITICAL SCIENCE
ASSOCIATION MEETINGS UNDER HEADING OF "PROBLEMS OF
POLITICAL INTEGRATION IN AFRICA." ANALYZES PROBLEMS OF
POLITICAL ADAPTATION WHICH ARISE DURING AND AFTER THE
TRANSFER OF POLITICAL POWER. AREA STUDIES COVER GHANA,
KENYA, NIGERIA, AND CENTRAL AFRICA.

0390 CARTER G.M.
THE GOVERNMENT OF THE SOVIET UNION.
NEW YORK: HARCOURT BRACE, 1962, 181 PP., LC#63-20430.
HISTORICAL ANALYSIS OF SOVIET UNION'S PEOPLE AND
POLITICAL STRUCTURE SINCE 1917. COVERS GOVERNMENT
STRUCTURE AND ADMINISTRATION IN DETAIL. INCLUDES PEOPLE'S
RELATIONSHIP TO GOVERNMENT, PARTY, AND METHODS FOR
IMPLEMENTING PARTY POLICY.

0391 CASE H.L.
"GORDON R. CLAPP: THE ROLE OF FAITH, PURPOSES AND PEOPLE IN
ADMINISTRATION."
PUBLIC ADMIN. REV., 24 (JUNE 64), 86-91.
BIOGRAPHICAL NOTES ON GORDON CLAPP, PERSONNEL DIRECTOR
FOR TVA. LAUDS CLAPP'S PROMOTION OF MAXIMUM PARTICIPATION IN
DECISION-MAKING, DECENTRALIZATION OF ADMINISTRATION.

0392 CATER D.
POWER IN WASHINGTON: A CRITICAL LOOK AT TODAY'S STRUGGLE TO
GOVERN IN THE NATION'S CAPITAL.
NEW YORK: RANDOM HOUSE, INC, 1964, 275 PP., LC#64-11984.
DISCUSSION OF THE ACTUAL GIVE AND TAKE OF PRESSURES
WITHIN AND UPON THE FEDERAL GOVERNMENT, GENERALLY FAVORABLE
TO THE ACTIONS OF ADMINISTRATIVE AGENCIES AND THE PRESIDENT.

0393 CATHERINE R. ED., THUILLIER G. ED.
LA REVUE ADMINISTRATIVE.
PARIS: REVUE ADMINISTRATIVE.
A BIMONTHLY REVIEW OF MODERN ADMINISTRATION FIRST ISSUED
IN 1948. EACH ISSUE CONTAINS ARTICLES CONCERNING THE BUSI-
NESS AND FINANCE WORLD AS WELL AS MATERIAL ON JUDICIAL AND
GOVERNMENTAL FUNCTIONING. ANNOTATED BIBLIOGRAPHY OF TRADE
LITERATURE AND SEVERAL BOOK REVIEWS APPEAR IN EACH ISSUE.

0394 CATHERINE R.
LE FONCTIONNAIRE FRANCAIS.
PARIS: MICHEL, EDITIONS ALBIN, 1961, 411 PP.
INTRODUCTORY STUDY OF FRENCH CIVIL SERVANTS. AUTHOR IS
PRIMARILY INTERESTED IN INTELLECTUAL AND MORAL ATTITUDES
OF CIVIL SERVANTS, AND THEIR RELATIONS WITH THE GOVERNMENT,
THEIR COLLEAGUES, AND CITIZENS.

0395 CAVERS D.F.
"ADMINISTRATIVE DECISION-MAKING IN NUCLEAR FACILITIES
LICENSING."
U. PENN. LAW REV., 110 (JAN. 62), 330-370.
AEC IS CHARGED WITH UPHOLDING PUBLIC INTEREST IN AREAS
OF SAFETY, EFFICIENCY, ETC., BUT HAS NOT DONE SO, SINCE MOST
OF ITS LICENSING ACTIONS ARE UNCONTESTED. IT OFTEN SERVES
MERELY AS A RUBBER STAMP FOR THE PLANS OF PRIVATE POWER
CORPORATIONS.

0396 CAVERS D.F.
THE CHOICE-OF-LAW PROCESS.
ANN ARBOR: U OF MICH PR, 1965, 336 PP., LC#65-21050.
PROVIDES ANALYTICAL FRAMEWORK FOR DISCUSSING THE JUDICIAL
CHOICE BETWEEN CONFLICTING LAWS WHICH MAY BE DETERMINATIVE
OF A PARTICULAR CONTROVERSY. SUMMARIZES COMPETING VIEWS OF
CHOICE-OF-LAW METHODOLOGY AND SUGGESTS REFORMS IN DOCTRINE
AND APPROACH.

0397 CECIL L.
ALBERT BALLIN; BUSINESS AND POLITICS IN IMPERIAL GERMANY
1888-1918.
PRINCETON: PRINCETON U PRESS, 1967, 388 PP., LC#66-21830.
STUDIES PLACE OF ALBERT BALLIN IN BUSINESS AND POLITICS
OF IMPERIAL GERMANY. DISCUSSES ANGLO-GERMAN RELATIONS AND
RIVALRY IN INTERNATIONAL SHIPPING AND NAVAL CONSTRUCTION AND
REACTIONARY POLITICAL AND SOCIAL SYSTEMS IN INDUSTRIALIZED
GERMANY. INCLUDES HYPOTHESIS THAT BUSINESS LEADERS SUCH AS
BALLIN OPPOSED REFORM BECAUSE OF FEAR OF SOCIALISM AND DE-
SIRE TO CONTROL GOVERNMENT.

0398 CENTRAL AFRICAN ARCHIVES
A GUIDE TO THE PUBLIC RECORDS OF SOUTHERN RHODESIA UNDER THE
REGIME OF THE BRITISH SOUTH AFRICA COMPANY, 1890-1923.
LONDON: LONGMANS, GREEN & CO, 1956, 282 PP.
CONSISTS OF GENERAL HISTORICAL INTRODUCTION, SUMMARY AND
DESCRIPTION OF RECORDS OF BRITISH SOUTH AFRICAN COMPANY'S
ADMINISTRATION, ADMINISTRATIVE HISTORY OF ALL DEPARTMENTS OF
SOUTHERN RHODESIAN GOVERNMENT, AND DETAILED INDEX.

0399 CENTRAL ASIAN RESEARCH CENTRE
BIBLIOGRAPHY OF RECENT SOVIET SOURCE MATERIAL ON SOVIET

CENTRAL ASIA AND THE BORDERLANDS.
LONDON: CENT ASIAN RES CENTRE, 1957.
ISSUED AS BIANNUAL SUPPLEMENT TO "CENTRAL ASIAN REVIEW."
CONTINUES THE BIBLIOGRAPHIES EMBODIED IN VOLUMES I-V OF THE
"REVIEW." A BRIEFLY ANNOTATED BIBLIOGRAPHY RELATING TO SOVI-
ET PERIODICALS AND BOOKS. HIGHLY TECHNICAL SOURCE MATERIAL
NOT INCLUDED. TITLES AND AUTHORS ARE TRANSLITERATED INTO
ROMAN LETTERS AND ANNOTATIONS OF LENGTH AND CONTENT GIVEN
IN ENGLISH. WITHIN THE TOPICS, ARRANGED BY COUNTRY.

0400 CHAMBERLAIN N.W.
"STRIKES IN CONTEMPORARY CONTEXT."
INDUST. LABOR REL. REV., 20 (JULY 67), 602-617.
EXAMINES ACTUAL NECESSITY FOR WORK STOPPAGES IN FUNCTION-
ING OF COLLECTIVE BARGAINING. DEFINES EMERGENCY CONDITIONS
UNDER WHICH GOVERNMENT INTERVENTION SHOULD OCCUR. EXPLAINS
"ARSENAL-OF-WEAPONS" LEGISLATIVE APPROACH, BENEFITS OF
COMPULSORY ARBITRATION, AND "NON-STOPPAGE STRIKE" OR
"STRIKE-WORK AGREEMENT" WHICH IMPOSES FINES ON BOTH WORKERS
AND MANAGEMENT DURING NEGOTIATIONS, WHILE WORK CONTINUES.

0401 CHAMBERLIN W. ED.
INDUSTRIAL RELATIONS IN GERMANY 1914-1939.
STANFORD: STANFORD U PRESS, 1942, 403 PP.
SELECTED BIBLIOGRAPHY OF MATERIALS ON INDUSTRIAL RELA-
TIONS IN GERMANY IN STANFORD UNIVERSITY LIBRARIES, ES-
PECIALLY IN HOOVER LIBRARY ON WAR, REVOLUTION AND PEACE.
THE TERM INDUSTRIAL RELATIONS IS CONSTRUED TO MEAN ANY
MATTER AFFECTING RELATIONSHIP BETWEEN EMPLOYERS AND
EMPLOYEES. ANNOTATED AND CONTAINS A BIBLIOGRAPHY OF
BIBLIOGRAPHIES.

0402 CHANDA A.
FEDERALISM IN INDIA.
NEW YORK: HILLARY HOUSE PUBL, 1965, 347 PP.
STUDY OF UNION-STATE RELATIONS IN INDIA WHICH TRACES PRO-
CESS OF INDIAN CONSOLIDATION AND POLITICAL UNIFICATION. CEN-
TERS ON EVOLUTION OF DEMOCRATIC GOVERNMENT IN INDIA AND CEN-
TRALIZATION AND CONCENTRATION OF POLITICAL AUTHORITY IN
HANDS OF SELECT FEW, WHICH WAS ESSENTIAL IN CONSOLIDATION
PROCESS.

0403 CHANDLER A.D.
STRATEGY AND STRUCTURE: CHAPTERS IN THE HISTORY OF THE
INDUSTRIAL ENTERPRISE.
CAMBRIDGE: M I T PRESS, 1962, 463 PP., LC#62-11990.
STUDY OF AMERICAN BIG BUSINESS: FINDS THAT DIFFERENT
ORGANIZATIONAL FORMS RESULT FROM DIFFERENT TYPES OF
GROWTH. MAINLY STUDIES DUPONT, GENERAL MOTORS, STANDARD OIL,
AND SEARS, THEIR CHANGING STRUCTURE AND THE STRATEGY WHICH
CREATES CHANGE.

0404 CHANDLER A.D. JR. ED.
GIANT ENTERPRISE: FORD, GENERAL MOTORS, AND THE AUTOMOBILE
INDUSTRY; SOURCES AND READINGS.
NEW YORK: HARCOURT BRACE, 1964, 342 PP., LC#64-12560.
DOCUMENTS PRESENTED ARE INTENDED TO SHOW HOW NEW
PATTERNS OF ECONOMIC ACTION OCCURRED AND HOW LABOR AND
MANAGEMENT FUNCTIONED AT DIFFERENT PERIODS OF HISTORY.

0405 CHANDRA S.
PARTIES AND POLITICS AT THE MUGHAL COURT: 1707-1740.
ALIGARH: ALIGARH MUSLIM UNIV., DEPT. HIST., 1957, 309 PP.
STUDY OF ROLE OF NOBILITY IN ORGANIZATION, GROWTH, ADMIN-
ISTRATIVE STRUCTURE, SOCIAL AND CULTURAL LIFE, AND DOWNFALL
OF MUGHAL EMPIRE IN MEDIEVAL PERIOD OF INDIAN HISTORY.
COVERS RISE AND STRUGGLE OF POLITICAL PARTIES AT MUGHAL
COURT.

0406 CHANG C.
THE INFLATIONARY SPIRAL: THE EXPERIENCE IN CHINA 1939-50.
NEW YORK: JOHN WILEY, 1958, 394 PP., LC#58-6083.
ANALYZES ECONOMIC COLLAPSE OF CHINA AND CURRENCY AS
RESULT OF POOR POLICY AND MISMANAGEMENT OF NATIONALISTS.
HOPES TO WARN AND PREVENT OTHER ASIAN NATIONS FROM SAME
ERRORS. DISCUSSES FAILURE OF NATIONALISTS TO HAVE SUPPLY
MEET DEMAND, ESPECIALLY IN WARTIME SITUATION. REVEALS BASIC
CONDITIONS THAT CAUSE INFLATIONARY SYMPTOMS AND SUGGESTS
POLICY ALTERNATIVES TO COMBAT THEM.

0407 CHAPIN F.S., TSOUDEROS J.E.
"FORMALIZATION OBSERVED IN TEN VOLUNTARY ORGANIZATIONS:
CONCEPTS, MORPHOLOGY, PROCESS."
SOCIAL FORCES, 33 (MAY 55), 306-309.
DESCRIBES PROCESS WHEREBY GROUPS CREATE RULES AND
PROCEDURES FOR REGULATION OF MEMBERS AND OPERATION.
EXPRESSES ALARM AT FORMALIZATION AND "LENGTHENED OSSIF-
ICATION" OF COMMUNICATIONS BETWEEN LEADERS AND FOLLOWERS
IN SMALL, AS WELL AS LARGE, ORGANIZATIONS. SETS UP FOUR
MORPHOLOGICAL TYPES OF GROUPS, INCLUDING THE REPRESENTATIVE-
ROLE GROUP, AND NOTES THEIR EVOLUTION.

0408 CHAPMAN B.
THE PREFECTS AND PROVINCIAL FRANCE.
NEW YORK: MACMILLAN, 1955, 246 PP.
TREATS ASPECTS OF FRENCH PREFECTORAL ADMINISTRATION.

SUMMARIZES ROLE PREFECTORAL CORPS HAS PLAYED IN HISTORY.
PRESENTS BACKGROUND TO POLITICAL AND ADMINISTRATIVE
STRUCTURE WITHIN CORPS TODAY. ANALYZES POWERS AND DUTIES OF
SUB-PREFECT, PREFECT, AND "CHEF DE CABINET."

0409 CHAPMAN B.
THE PROFESSION OF GOVERNMENT: THE PUBLIC SERVICE IN EUROPE.
NEW YORK: MACMILLAN, 1959, 352 PP.
STUDY OF MODERN PUBLIC ADMINISTRATION IN EUROPE BEGINNING
WITH A HISTORICAL INTRODUCTION. DISCUSSES COMPOSITION, CON-
DITIONS OF SERVICE, CONTROL, POLITICS, AND THE PUBLIC.

0410 CHAPMAN B.
"THE FRENCH CONSEIL D'ETAT."
PARLIAMENTARY AFFAIRS, 12 (SPRING 59), 164-173.
EXAMINES JURISDICTION, ADMINISTRATIVE OPERATIONS, AND
ADVISORY POWERS OF THE "CONSEIL D'ETAT" UNDER THE FIFTH
REPUBLIC. CRITICIZES THE GREAT DELAY BETWEEN COMMENCEMENT
OF A CASE AND THE FINAL VERDICT; CONTENDS THAT AN INCREASE
IN COUNCILLORS, ALTHOUGH AGAINST LAW, IS CHIEF SOLUTION TO
THIS DILEMMA. OBSERVES THAT CONTACT WITH PUBLIC SERVICES
GUARANTEES ADMINISTRATIVE ETHIC IN THE COURT.

0411 CHAPMAN B.
THE PROFESSION OF GOVERNMENT: THE PUBLIC SERVICE IN EUROPE.
LONDON: UNWIN UNIVERSITY BOOKS, 1966, 322 PP.
TEXTBOOK OF COMPARATIVE GOVERNMENT. UNANNOTATED BIBLIOG-
RAPHY APPENDED TO TEXT ORGANIZED ACCORDING TO THE MAIN
DIVISIONS OF THE BOOK - REFERENCE WORKS, REVIEWS, BOOKS,
ARTICLES TAKEN FROM ENGLISH, FRENCH, GERMAN, ITALIAN,
SCANDINAVIAN, DUTCH, AND SPANISH SOURCES. WITHIN SUBJECT
DIVISIONS, BIBLIOGRAPHY ORGANIZED GEOGRAPHICALLY.

0412 CHAPPLE E.D., SAYLES L.R.
THE MEASURE OF MANAGEMENT.
NEW YORK: MACMILLAN, 1961, 218 PP., LC#60-6654.
CONSIDERATION OF METHODS BY WHICH MANAGEMENT CAN EFFI-
CIENTLY UTILIZE HUMAN ORGANIZATIONAL RESOURCES, ADVOCATING
A CONSISTENT SCIENTIFIC SYSTEM OF MEASUREMENT. ARGUES THAT
MEASUREMENTS, PROVIDING CRITERIA FOR MANAGEMENT ACTION, ARE
BASIC TO ORGANIZATIONAL AND ADMINISTRATIVE DECISIONS, AND
THAT HUMAN BEHAVIOR IN THE ORGANIZATION IS QUANTIFIABLE. DE-
VELOPS AN ORGANIZATION OF WORK - TECHNOLOGY, METHOD, ETC.

0413 CHARLES R.
LA JUSTICE EN FRANCE.
PARIS: PR UNIV DE FRANCE, 1958, 127 PP.
DISCUSSES LEGAL STRUCTURE, BOTH CIVIL AND CRIMINAL, AS
WELL AS POLITICAL AND ADMINISTRATIVE JUSTICE IN MODERN
FRANCE. EXAMINES PROCEDURAL RULES AND SUBSTANTIVE CONTENT
OF FRENCH LEGAL SYSTEM.

0414 CHARLES S.
MINISTER OF RELIEF: HARRY HOPKINS AND THE DEPRESSION.
SYRACUSE: SYRACUSE U PRESS, 1963, 286 PP., LC#63-13889.
BIOGRAPHY OF HOPKINS AS DIRECTOR OF FEDERAL RELIEF DURING
THE DEPRESSION. FINDS THAT HOPKINS ESTABLISHED FRAMEWORK FOR
ADMINISTRATION OF OTHER PROGRAMS, AND THAT HIS MISTAKES WERE
USEFUL IN AVOIDING SIMILAR ERRORS LATER. THROUGH HIS BATTLES
WITH CONGRESS AND HIS PERSONAL CONTROL OVER THE RELIEF
AGENCY, HE BECAME THE FOUNDER OF PRESENT FEDERAL RELIEF
PROGRAMS.

0415 CHARLESWORTH J.C.
"ALLOCATION OF RESPONSIBILITIES AND RESOURCES AMONG THE
THREE LEVELS OF GOVERNMENT."
ANN. ACAD. POL. SOC. SCI., 359 (MAY 65), 71-80.
ARGUES THAT THE QUESTION OF OPTIMUM SERVICES ALLOCATION
CAN'T BE SEPARATED FROM AVAILABILITY OF TAX RESOURCES, THAT
THERE SHOULD BE AN EXTENSIVE PROGRAM OF FUNCTIONAL CONSOLI-
DATION OF LOCAL GOVERNMENTS, AND THAT THERE SHOULD BE AN
INCREASE IN CERTAIN STATE FUNCTIONS.

0416 CHEEK G.
ECONOMIC AND SOCIAL IMPLICATIONS OF AUTOMATION: A BIBLIO-
GRAPHIC REVIEW (PAMPHLET)
E LANSING: MSU LABOR & IND REL, 1958, 125 PP.
SOME 600 WELL-ANNOTATED BIBLIOGRAPHIES, BOOKS, ARTICLES,
CONFERENCE REPORTS, CASE STUDIES, AND SPEECHES ARRANGED TOP-
ICALLY AND PUBLISHED FROM 1948-57. SUBJECTS INCLUDE
MANPOWER, SOCIETY AND GOVERNMENT, HUMAN RELATIONS, COLLEC-
TIVE BARGAINING, AND MANAGEMENT ORGANIZATION. SUBJECT AND
AUTHOR INDEX.

0417 CHEN T.H.
THE CHINESE COMMUNIST REGIME: A DOCUMENTARY STUDY (2 VOLS.)
LOS ANGELES: U OF S CALIF PR, 1965, 238 PP.
CONSISTS OF DOCUMENTS DEALING WITH THE ORGANIZATION OF
THE CHINESE COMMUNIST GOVERNMENT AND THE CHINESE COMMUNIST
PARTY. EMPHASIS IS ON INTERNAL FEATURES OF THE REGIME,
INCLUDING ECONOMIC POLICY AND SOCIAL AND POLITICAL REFORM.

0418 CHERNICK J., INDIK B.P., CRAIG R.
THE SELECTION OF TRAINEES UNDER MDTA.
N BRUNSWICK: RUTGERS, INST MGT, 1962, 124 PP.
DISCUSSES PROVISIONS OF MANPOWER DEVELOPMENT AND TRAINING

ACT OF 1962 WHICH CHARGES THE SECRETARY OF LABOR WITH PROVIDING TRAINEE PROGRAM. EXAMINES SELECTION PROCESS FOR TRAINING AND DELINEATES CHARACTERISTICS OF PERSONS SELECTED OR REJECTED FOR GOVERNMENT POSITIONS.

0419 CHICAGO JOINT REFERENCE LIB
FEDERAL-STATE-LOCAL RELATIONS; A SELECTED BIBLIOGRAPHY.
CHICAGO: CHICAGO JOINT REF LIB, 1954, 37 PP.
SELECTED BIBLIOGRAPHY ON INTERGOVERNMENTAL RELATIONS PREPARED FOR AMERICAN MUNICIPAL ASSOCIATION AND COUNCIL OF STATE GOVERNMENTS. EMPHASIS ON RECENT PUBLICATIONS IN PRINCIPLE OF FEDERALISM, INTERGOVERNMENTAL FUNCTIONAL RELATIONS, STATE-LOCAL AND METROPOLITAN RELATIONS. ARRANGED BY TOPIC.

0420 CHICAGO U CTR PROG GOVT ADMIN
EDUCATION FOR INNOVATIVE BEHAVIOR IN EXECUTIVES.
CHICAGO: U CHI. PROG GOV ADMIN, 1962, 250 PP.
RESEARCH PROJECT TO INVESTIGATE CHARACTERISTICS OF INNOVATIVE BEHAVIOR PARTICULARLY IN EXECUTIVE POSITIONS AND APPLY THIS TO EDUCATIONAL PROCEDURES TO INCREASE INNOVATION. EXPERIMENTAL EDUCATIONAL APPROACH DEVELOPED AND EVALUATED.

0421 CHICAGO U LAW SCHOOL
CONFERENCE ON JUDICIAL ADMINISTRATION.
CHICAGO: U OF CHICAGO LAW SCHOOL, 1957.
ESSAYS DISCUSSING ADMINISTRATION OF COURT SYSTEMS, ROLE OF APPELLATE COURTS IN JUDICIAL ADMINISTRATION, AND OTHER PROBLEMS OF JUDICIAL ADMINISTRATION ON FEDERAL, STATE, AND MUNICIPAL LEVELS.

0422 CHILDS J.B. ED.
A GUIDE TO THE OFFICIAL PUBLICATIONS OF THE OTHER AMERICAN REPUBLICS: ARGENTINA.
WASHINGTON: LIBRARY OF CONGRESS, 1941, 124 PP.
GUIDE PREPARED TO FILL NEED FOR PRACTICAL REFERENCE WORK OF AMERICAN REPUBLICS. ATTEMPT IS MADE TO CENTER UPON CURRENT AGENCIES AND PUBLICATIONS STRESSING INFORMATIONAL POTENTIALITIES AND GIVING BRIEF DATA ABOUT EACH WHERE SPACE PERMITS. PRESENT ARGENTINA GOVERNMENT ORGANIZATION IS USED AS ARRANGEMENT OF VOLUME.

0423 CHILDS J.R.
AMERICAN FOREIGN SERVICE.
NEW YORK: HOLT RINEHART WINSTON, 1948, 261 PP.
STUDIES EVOLUTION OF US FOREIGN SERVICE AND DISCUSSES ITS NATURE AS A CAREER. SHOWS RELATIONS BETWEEN SERVICE AND DEPARTMENT OF STATE AND OTHER GOVERNMENT AGENCIES. ANALYZES PROFESSION AND PRACTICE OF DIPLOMACY, AND PORTRAYS AN EMBASSY AND AMBASSADOR IN ACTION. DESCRIBES EMBASSY'S POLITICAL, CONSULAR, ECONOMIC, INFORMATION, AND CULTURAL RELATIONS SECTIONS.

0424 CHILDS R.S.
"CITIZEN ORGANIZATION FOR CONTROL OF GOVERNMENT."
ANN. ACAD. POL. SOC. SCI., 292 (MAR. 54), 129-135.
GOVERNMENT, ESPECIALLY THE EXECUTIVE BRANCH, IS TOO COMPLICATED NOW TO BE CONTROLLED BY THE PEOPLE. SIMPLIFICATION OF THE ELECTORAL PROCESS IS NEEDED TO MAKE MORE GOVERNMENT OFFICES AND POLICIES DIRECTLY RESPONSIBLE TO THE PUBLIC.

0425 CHINA INSTITUTE OF AMERICA.
CHINA AND THE UNITED NATIONS.
NEW YORK: MANHATTAN PUBL., 1959, 285 PP.
STUDIES CHINESE PARTICIPATION IN AND ATTITUDES TOWARDS THE UN, VIEWING MEMBERSHIP AS FULFILLMENT OF HER AIM OF EQUALITY OF NATIONS. DEALS WITH POSITION OF CHINA AS ONE OF THE FOUNDERS AND ORGANIZERS OF THE WORLD ORGANIZATION, AS WELL AS HER POSITION IN IT TODAY. CONSIDERS CHINESE SUPPORT OF LEAGUE OF NATIONS, AS MEANS TOWARD COLLECTIVE SECURITY.

0426 CHOJNACKI S. ED., PANKHURST R. ED., SHACK W.A. ED.
REGISTER ON CURRENT RESEARCH ON ETHIOPIA AND THE HORN OF AFRICA.
ADDIS ABABA: INST ETHIOPIAN STUD, 1963, 44 PP.
AN UNANNOTATED BIBLIOGRAPHY LISTING 341 PROJECTS OF CURRENT RESEARCH ON ETHIOPIA BEING CONDUCTED BOTH IN ETHIOPIA AND ABROAD. PROVIDES INFORMATION ON THE STATE OF RESEARCH AS OF 1963: STARTING DATE, DATE OF COMPLETION, PUBLICATIONS, SCHOLARSHIPS INVOLVED, AND NAMES OF SUPERVISORS AND ASSISTANTS. CLASSIFIED INTO 23 SUBJECT CATEGORIES.

0427 CHOWDHURI R.N.
INTERNATIONAL MANDATES AND TRUSTEESHIP SYSTEMS.
GENEVA: NIJHOFF, 1955, 328 PP.
DISCUSSES HISTORY, OPERATION, AND FUNCTION OF INTERNATIONAL MANDATE SYSTEM, TRUSTEESHIP SYSTEM, AND OF AGENCIES ADMINISTERING THEM. PROVIDES EXAMPLES OF PROBLEMS FACING TRUSTEESHIP COUNCIL AND SOLUTIONS REACHED.

0428 CHRISTENSEN A.N. ED.
THE EVOLUTION OF LATIN AMERICAN GOVERNMENT: A BOOK OF READINGS.
NEW YORK: HOLT RINEHART WINSTON, 1951, 747 PP.
SELECTIONS DISCUSSING HISTORICAL FACTORS, CONSTITUTIONAL BASES, AND PRACTICAL ORGANIZATION OF LATIN AMERICAN GOVERNMENTS. EMPHASIZES DISPARITY BETWEEN CONSTITUTIONS AND ACTUAL FUNCTIONING OF GOVERNMENT. SECTIONS ON LATIN AMERICAN SOCIAL PROBLEMS AND INTERNATIONAL AFFAIRS.

0429 CHRISTENSON R.M.
THE BRANNAN PLAN: FARM POLITICS AND POLICY.
ANN ARBOR: U OF MICH PR, 1959, 207 PP., LC#59-5265.
STUDY OF HISTORY OF AGRICULTURAL POLICY UNDER THE SECRETARYSHIP OF CHARLES BRANNAN. DISCUSSES ROLE OF DEPARTMENT OF AGRICULTURE IN FORMATION OF PUBLIC POLICY. INCLUDES CRITICAL EXAMINATION OF MERITS OF THE BRANNAN PLAN.

0430 CLAPP G.R., DIMOCK M.E. ET AL.
NEW HORIZONS IN PUBLIC ADMINISTRATION: A SYMPOSIUM.
UNIVERSITY: U ALABAMA PR, 1945, 145 PP.
SIX LECTURES ON PROBLEMS OF PUBLIC ADMINISTRATION DEALING WITH NECESSITY TO FREE ADMINISTRATORS FROM TOO-DETAILED LEGISLATIVE CONTROL; PROBLEM OF BUREAUCRATIC INTERFERENCE WITH LIBERTY; ROLE OF EXECUTIVES; FIELD ORGANIZATION; AND SIMILARLY DIVERSE ISSUES.

0431 CLARK J.S.
THE SENATE ESTABLISHMENT.
NEW YORK: HILL AND WANG, 1963, 138 PP.
SENATOR CLARK'S SPEECH CRITICAL OF SENATE LEADERSHIP SYSTEM WITH RESPONSES BY SENATORS JAVITS, MANSFIELD, DOUGLAS, LONG, MCGOVERN, KEATING, PROXMIRE. REVELATORY OF ROLE AND METHODS OF COMMITTEE APPOINTMENTS, OF BIPARTISAN CONSERVATIVE COALITION ROOTED IN ONE-PARTY STATES. CALLS FOR MODERNIZATION AND REFORM OF SENATE, TO MAKE PROCEDURES MORE DEMOCRATIC.

0432 CLARK J.S.
CONGRESS: THE SAPLESS BRANCH.
NEW YORK: HARPER & ROW, 1964, 268 PP.
CRITIQUE OF CONGRESS TODAY, ESPECIALLY LACK OF PARTY DISCIPLINE AND LOYALTY TO PARTY PLATFORM. PROCEDURES FOR COMMITTEE ASSIGNMENTS, AND RULES. SUGGESTS REFORMS TO MAKE MORE EFFICIENT AND RESPONSIVE TO PUBLIC WILL.

0433 CLARKE M.P.
PARLIAMENTARY PRIVILEGE IN THE AMERICAN COLONIES.
NEW HAVEN: YALE U PR, 1943, 303 PP.
STUDY OF AMERICAN REPRESENTATIVE ASSEMBLIES 1619-1783 AND HOW THEY EXERCISED PARLIAMENTARY PRIVILEGE, BY WHICH THEY BECAME MORE AND MORE LIKE THEIR ENGLISH MODEL. RESULT WAS DEVELOPMENT OF SENSE OF POLITICAL INDEPENDENCE IN COLONIES.

0434 CLEGG R.K.
THE ADMINISTRATOR IN PUBLIC WELFARE.
SPRINGFIELD: THOMAS, 1966, 271 PP., LC#66-21421.
STUDY OF ADMINISTRATION OF PUBLIC WELFARE. DISCUSSES HISTORY AND DEVELOPMENT OF WELFARE, AND ROLE OF FEDERAL AND STATE GOVERNMENT. DESCRIBES HOW LOCAL WELFARE OFFICE IS ORGANIZED, HOW ITS BUDGET OPERATES, HOW IT RECRUITS AND MANAGES PERSONNEL. DESCRIBES PUBLIC RELATIONS AND INTEROFFICE COMMUNICATION. OUTLINES VARIOUS TYPES OF WELFARE PROGRAMS AND THEIR ADMINISTRATION.

0435 CLEMENTS R.V.
MANAGERS - A STUDY OF THEIR CAREERS IN INDUSTRY.
LONDON: ALLEN & UNWIN, 1958, 200 PP.
TRACES CAREERS OF VARIOUS TYPES OF BUSINESS EXECUTIVES. EXAMINES EXPERTLY TRAINED PERSONS PLUS THOSE RISING FROM BOTTOM WITHOUT INTENSIVE THEORETICAL TRAINING. DISCUSSES SOCIAL ORIGINS, MOBILITY, AND SPECIALIZATION OF SUCH PERSONNEL.

0436 CLEMHOUT S.
"PRODUCTION FUNCTION ANALYSIS APPLIED TO THE LEONTIEF SCARCE-FACTOR PARADOX OF INTERNATIONAL TRADE."
MANCHESTER ECON. SOC. STUD., 31 (MAY 63), 103-114.
CONCLUDES THAT A COUNTRY WHICH HAS AN ABSOLUTE (OR COMPARATIVE) ADVANTAGE IN PRODUCTIVITY HAS 'PREPONDERANCE IN THE OPPORTUNITY-COSTS OF PRODUCTION' BESIDES THOSE RESULTING FROM NATURAL ENDOWMENTS. THE NATION SUPERIOR IN PRODUCTIVITY WILL EXPORT IN THESE LINES OF PRODUCTION AND MIGHT WELL DO SO REGARDLESS OF FACTOR-PROPORTIONS.

0437 CLEVELAND H.
"THE EXECUTIVE AND THE PUBLIC INTEREST."
ANN. ACAD. POL. SOC. SCI., 307 (SEPT. 56), 237-254.
LOBBIES ARE EXTREMELY STRONG AND WORK FOR THEIR OWN ADVANTAGE WITHOUT REGARD TO THE PUBLIC INTEREST. THE PRESIDENT AND THE PEOPLE THEMSELVES MUST DEFEND THE PUBLIC INTEREST, AND THE EXTENT TO WHICH THIS IS DONE DEPENDS A GREAT DEAL UPON THE ATTITUDES OF THE PRESIDENCY TOWARD ACTIVE CONTROL OF THE ADMINISTRATION.

0438 CLIGNET R., FOSTER P.
"POTENTIAL ELITES IN GHANA AND THE IVORY COAST: A PRELIMINARY SURVEY."
AMER. J. SOCIOL., 70(NOV. 64), 349-62.
A COMPARATIVE STUDY OF EMERGING ELITE GROUPS IN TWO

NEWLY INDEPENDENT AFRICAN STATES. DISCUSSED TRIBAL LEADERS
AS A SOURCE OF NATIONAL ELITES.

0439 CLOKIE H.M., ROBINSON J.W.
ROYAL COMMISSIONS OF INQUIRY: THE SIGNIFICANCE OF
INVESTIGATIONS IN BRITISH POLITICS.
STANFORD: STANFORD U PRESS, 1937, 242 PP.
EXPLORES SIGNIFICANCE AND STATUS OF ROYAL COMMISSIONS OF
INQUIRY IN RELATION TO BRITISH POLITICS. TRACES DEVELOPMENT
OF COMMISSIONS, DESCRIBES THEIR PROCEDURE, AND EXAMINES
THEIR FUNCTION AS A COMBINATION FACT-FINDING AND POLICY-
MAKING ORGANIZATION. MAINTAINS THAT COMMISSIONS ARE
DECLINING IN IMPORTANCE, BEING REPLACED BY COMMITTEES AND
BOARDS, AND POLITICAL PARTY CONFERENCES.

0440 CLOUGH S.B., COLE C.W.
ECONOMIC HISTORY OF EUROPE.
BOSTON: HEATH, 1946, 841 PP.
TRACES THE ECONOMIC HISTORY OF EUROPE FROM 600 AD TO THE
BEGINNING OF THE SECOND WORLD WAR. SHOWS THE CONNECTION BE-
TWEEN ECONOMIC DEVELOPMENT AND SOCIAL CONDITIONS, POLITICAL
POWER, AND INTELLECTUAL LIFE.

0441 COCH L., FRENCH J.R.P. JR.
"OVERCOMING RESISTANCE TO CHANGE" (BMR)"
HUMAN RELATIONS, 1 (1948), 512-532.
REPORTS A RESEARCH PROGRAM CONDUCTED FOR THE BENEFIT OF
FACTORY MANAGEMENT IN ORDER TO DETERMINE: (1) WHY WORKERS
RESIST CHANGE SO STRONGLY AND (2) WHAT CAN BE DONE TO OVER-
COME THIS RESISTANCE. ON THE BASIS OF A PRELIMINARY THEORY
DEVISED BY THE RESEARCHERS TO ACCOUNT FOR THIS RESISTANCE,
A REAL LIFE ACTION EXPERIMENT WAS CONDUCTED WITHIN THE CON-
TEXT OF THE FACTORY SITUATION. THE RESULTS ARE INTERPRETED.

0442 COHEN E.W.
THE GROWTH OF THE BRITISH CIVIL SERVICE 1780-1939.
NEW YORK: W W NORTON, 1941, 221 PP.
DEVELOPMENT OF CIVIL SERVICE BUREAUCRACY, SINECURES, PEN-
SIONS, ADMINISTRATION PROCEDURES. ATTITUDES OF LOCAL OFFI-
CIALS AND EFFECT ON GOVERNMENT OF CENTRALIZATION. CONTAINS
BIBLIOGRAPHY CITING OFFICIAL STATE PAPERS, BOOKS, AND BIOG-
RAPHIES. ARRANGED BY NATURE OF SOURCE AND ALPHABETICALLY.
NO FOREIGN-LANGUAGE MATERIALS.

0443 COHEN H.
THE DEMONICS OF BUREAUCRACY: PROBLEMS OF CHANGE IN A
GOVERNMENT AGENCY.
AMES: IOWA STATE U PR, 1965, 276 PP., LC#65-10570.
STUDY OF A LOCAL OFFICE OF A FEDERAL EMPLOYMENT AGENCY.
COMPARES WITH SIMILAR STUDY BY PETER BLAU: "DYNAMICS OF
BUREAUCRACY." SAYS AGENCY PROCEDURES ARE AIMED TOWARD
EFFICIENCY WHEN FIRST SET UP, BUT ARE TRANSFORMED BY THE
BUREAUCRATIC HIERARCHY TO REPRESENT ITS OWN INTERESTS OF
PRESTIGE, POWER, AND PERSONAL SECURITY.

0444 COHEN K.J., RHENMAN E.
"THE ROLE OF MANAGEMENT GAMES IN EDUCATION AND RESEARCH."
MANAGEMENT SCIENCE, 7 (JAN. 61), 131-66.
STRESSES THAT, FOR TRAINING PURPOSES, MORE ATTENTION
SHOULD BE GIVEN IN GAMES TO FINANCIAL, LABOR, PUBLIC RELA-
TIONS ASPECTS. THEY MIGHT ALSO BE USED TO DISCOVER OPTIMAL
PATTERNS OF BUSINESS BEHAVIOR.

0445 COHEN M.
"THE DEMISE OF UNEF."
INT. J., 23 (WINTER 67), 18-51.
EVALUATES PERFORMANCE OF UN EMERGENCY FORCE IN TEN YEARS
OF ITS EXISTENCE. DISCUSSES ITS CONSTITUTIONAL, ADMINIS-
TRATIVE, AND HISTORICAL ASPECTS UP TO ITS WITHDRAWAL FROM
SINAI AND GAZA IN 1967. LINKS ITS PAST SUCCESSES TO HAMMAR-
SKJOLD'S WORK AND RELATES U THANT'S EXPERIENCE WITH IT.

0446 COHEN M.B., COHEN R.A.
"PERSONALITY AS A FACTOR IN ADMINISTRATIVE DECISIONS."
PSYCHOANALYTIC QUART., 14 (FEB. 51), 47-53.
FOUR CASE-STUDIES SHOWING HOW PERSONALITY STRUCTURE
AFFECTS ADMINISTRATION AND THE RANGE OF REPRESENTATION.
DISCUSSES DISTORTIONS BY LESS RATIONAL EMPLOYEES AND USE OF
DEFENSE MECHANISMS, BUT SHOWS, ALSO, THAT CERTAIN FEARS CAN
BE TURNED INTO AN EMPATHY USEFUL IN SOLVING COMMUNITY
PROJECT CONFLICT.

0447 COHEN R., MIDDLETON J.
COMPARATIVE POLITICAL SYSTEMS: STUDIES IN THE POLITICS OF
PRE-INDUSTRIAL SOCIETIES.
NEW YORK: AMER MUS NAT HIST PR, 1967, 512 PP.
BRINGS TOGETHER CLASSIC AND RECENT ANTHROPOLOGICAL WORKS
ON POLITICS OF NON-WESTERNIZED POLITICAL SYSTEMS. DISCUSSES
HUNTING AND GATHERING SOCIETIES, AND STATE SOCIETIES. SHOWS
LEADERSHIP PATTERNS, MARRIAGE CUSTOMS, AND SUBGROUP ORGAN-
IZATION. STUDIES PRESENT-DAY PRIMITIVE AND EXTINCT
SOCIETIES.

0448 COHN B.S.
DEVELOPMENT AND IMPACT OF BRITISH ADMINISTRATION IN INDIA:
A BIBLIOGRAPHIC ESSAY.

NEW DELHI: INDIAN INST PUB ADMIN, 1961, 88 PP.
DESCRIBES AND HIGHLIGHTS FACETS OF BRITISH ADMINISTRATION
IN INDIA THROUGH REFERENCES TO BOOKS, ARTICLES, AND PAMPH-
LETS RELATING TO BRITISH COLONIAL POLICY AND ADMINISTRA-
TION. ORGANIZES, ASSESSES, AND ANNOTATES WIDE RANGE OF
MATERIALS DEALING WITH THE BACKGROUND, ESTABLISHMENT,
DEVELOPMENT, FUNCTIONING, AND IMPACT OF BRITISH COLONIAL
ADMINISTRATION.

0449 COHN H.J.
THE GOVERNMENT OF THE RHINE PALATINATE IN THE FIFTEENTH
CENTURY.
LONDON: OXFORD U PR, 1965, 289 PP.
TRACES HISTORY OF RHINE PALATINATE FROM ISSUANCE OF
GOLDEN BULL IN 1356 TO END OF 15TH CENTURY. EXAMINES TERRI-
TORIAL EXPANSION, RIGHTS OF TERRITORIAL PRINCE, RELATIONS
WITH ROMAN CHURCH, AND ADMINISTRATIVE ASPECTS SUCH AS COURT
SYSTEM, FINANCIAL ADMINISTRATION, AND WORK OF COUNCILS AND
LOCAL ADMINISTRATIONS.

0450 COLE T.
"LESSONS FROM RECENT EUROPEAN EXPERIENCE."
ANN. ACAD. POL. SOC. SCI., 292 (MAR. 54), 55-75.
DISCUSSION OF POST-WAR DEVELOPMENTS IN CIVIL SERVICE IN
WESTERN EUROPE. CHANGES HAVE BENEFITED DEMOCRACY, AND AT
LEAST SOME SHOULD BE TRIED IN UNITED STATES.

0451 COLEGROVE K.W.
"THE ROLE OF CONGRESS AND PUBLIC OPINION IN FORMULATING
FOREIGN POLICY."
AM. POL. SCI. REV., 38 (DEC. 44), 956-969.
A DISCUSSION ON WHETHER THE PRESIDENTIAL SYSTEM IS WELL
ADAPTED TO THE PROMOTION OF COMPETENCE IN THE CONDUCT OF
FOREIGN RELATIONS. SOME DEFECTS IN THE DEMOCRATIC PROCESS
"STILL CAUSE AMERICAN DIRECTION OF FOREIGN POLICY TO REMAIN
LARGELY OUT OF CONTROL OF A MAJORITY OF PEOPLE." HOWEVER,
IMPROVEMENTS ALONG THIS LINE ARE NOTED AND SOME CONCRETE
FACTS DISCUSSED.

0452 COLEMAN J.S.
NIGERIA: BACKGROUND TO NATIONALISM.
BERKELEY: U. CALIF. PR., 1958, 510 PP.
A STUDY OF CONDITIONS STIMULATING RISE AND GROWTH OF
NATIONALISM IN NIGERIA. ALSO DESCRIBES CULTURAL AND HISTORI-
CAL BACKGROUND, AND IMPACT OF WESTERN ECONOMIC AND POLITICAL
FORCES.

0453 COLLINS B.E., GUETZKOW H.
A SOCIAL PSYCHOLOGY OF GROUP PROCESSES FOR DECISION-MAKING.
NEW YORK: JOHN WILEY, 1964, 247 PP.
FOUNDATIONAL MATERIAL ON SOCIAL PSYCHOLOGY AS RELEVANT TO
GROUP DECISION-MAKING IN GOVERNMENT AND INDUSTRY, BASED ON
EMPIRICAL DATA. PRESENTS INDUCTIVE THEORY OF FACE-TO-FACE
GROUPS.

0454 COM INTERNAT DES MOUVEMENTS
REPERTOIRE INTERNATIONAL DES SOURCES POUR L'ETUDE DES MOUVE-
MENTS SOCIAUX AUX XIXE ET XXE SIECLES (VOL. III)
PARIS: LIBRAIRIE ARMAND COLIN, 1963, 224 PP.
COMPILES, ANNOTATES, AND INDEXES 588 OFFICIAL ACTS
PUBLISHED BY NATIONAL ORGANIZATIONS UNDER THE AEGIS OF THE
FIRST INTERNATIONAL. INCLUDES AN INTRODUCTION. ITEMS ARE
ARRANGED BY COUNTRY AND DATE FROM 1864-1876. PREPARED UNDER
THE AUSPICES OF UNESCO AND THE INTERNATIONAL COUNCIL OF
PHILOSOPHY AND THE HUMAN SCIENCES.

0455 COMBS C.H. ED., THRALL R.M. ED., DAVIS R.L. ED.
DECISION PROCESSES.
NEW YORK: WILEY, 1954, 332 PP.
INDIVIDUAL PAPERS RANGING FROM PURE MATHEMATICS TO EXPER-
IMENTS IN GROUP DYNAMICS - ALL DIRECTED AT APPLYING MATHEMA-
TICS TO BEHAVIORAL SCIENCES IN GENERAL AND TO DECISION PRO-
CESSES IN PARTICULAR.

0456 COMISION DE HISTORIO
GUIA DE LOS DOCUMENTOS MICROFOTOGRAFIADOS POR LA UNIDAD
MOVIL DE LA UNESCO.
INST PANAMERICANO DE GEOGRAFIA, 1963, 317 PP.
LIST OF BOOKS, DOCUMENTS, AND MATERIALS IN THE ARCHIVES
OF SEVERAL LATIN AMERICAN NATIONS THAT HAVE BEEN MICROFILMED
BY UNESCO.

0457 COMMITTEE ECONOMIC DEVELOPMENT
IMPROVING EXECUTIVE MANAGEMENT IN THE FEDERAL GOVERNMENT.
NEW YORK: COMM FOR ECO DEV, 1964, 76 PP., LC#64-25240.
STATES POLICY FOR IMPROVING PRESIDENTS' STAFF. RECOMMENDS
SETTING UP TOP-LEVEL PERSONNEL RECRUITING AGENCY, REASSESS-
MENT OF PRESENT RECRUITING PROGRAM, ANNUAL PERFORMANCE
REVIEW FOR EXECUTIVES, AND LINKING PROMOTION TO PERFORMANCE,
RATHER THAN SENIORITY.

0458 COMMONS J.R.
THE ECONOMICS OF COLLECTIVE ACTION.
NEW YORK: MACMILLAN, 1950, 414 PP.
SUMMATION OF ECONOMIC THOUGHT OF LEADING AMERICAN ECONO-
MIST, INCLUDING DESCRIPTION OF ECONOMIC ACTIVITIES AND DEFI-

NITION OF ASSUMPTIONS, ECONOMIC RELATIVITIES, AND PUBLIC
ADMINISTRATION IN ECONOMIC AFFAIRS. CONTAINS BIBLIOGRAPHY
OF 450 ENTRIES, ARRANGED CHRONOLOGICALLY.

0459 CONAWAY O.B. ED.
DEMOCRACY IN FEDERAL ADMINISTRATION (PAMPHLET)
WASHINGTON: US GOVERNMENT, 1956, 73 PP.
LECTURES BEARING ON PUBLIC SERVICE, PUBLIC PARTICIPATION
IN FEDERAL PROGRAMS, ETHICS IN PUBLIC ADMINISTRATION, SPE-
CIALIZATION, AND GOVERNMENT COMMUNICATION WITH THE PUBLIC.
ALL ARE CRITICALLY FRANK ABOUT CONTEMPORARY FEDERAL ADMIN-
ISTRATION, AND SEVERAL MAKE CONCRETE SUGGESTIONS FOR FUTURE
CHANGES IN POLICIES, PRACTICES, AND ATTITUDES.

0460 CONF ON FUTURE OF COMMONWEALTH
THE FUTURE OF THE COMMONWEALTH.
LONDON: H M STATIONERY OFFICE, 1963, 51 PP.
GENERAL DISCUSSION OF ROLE OF BRITISH COMMONWEALTH IN
RACE RELATIONS, MUTUAL DEFENSE, ECONOMIC PROGRESS, AND PO-
LITICAL STABILITY. SUGGESTS TECHNICAL AID, TRAINING OF AD-
MINISTRATORS, COOPERATION IN AGRICULTURAL MATTERS, AND ED-
UCATION AS CHIEF MEASURES TO ACHIEVE ECONOMIC PROGRESS AND
POLITICAL COHESION.

0461 CONFREY E.A. ED.
ADMINISTRATION OF COMMUNITY HEALTH SERVICES.
CHICAGO: INT CITY MANAGER'S ASSN, 1961, 560 PP., LC#61-15342
ILLUMINATES PROBLEMS OF COMMUNITY HEALTH SERVICES.
COVERS SCOPE, ORGANIZATION, MANAGEMENT, AND SPECIFIC PROB-
LEMS OF CHILD CARE: REHABILITATION, VENEREAL DISEASE, MENTAL
AND DENTAL HEALTH.

0462 CONNECTICUT U INST PUBLIC SERV
SUMMARY OF CHARTER PROVISIONS IN CONNECTICUT LOCAL GOVERN-
MENT (PAMPHLET)
STORRS: U CONN INST PUBLIC SERV, 1964, 46 PP.
OUTLINES GOVERNMENTAL STRUCTURE OF EACH OF 41 CONNECTICUT
TOWNS AND CITIES THAT OPERATE UNDER COUNCIL-MANAGER,
SELECTMEN-CHIEF ADMINISTRATIVE OFFICER, AND MAYOR-COUNCIL
FORMS OF GOVERNMENT.

0463 CONOVER H.F.
MADAGASCAR: A SELECTED LIST OF REFERENCES.
WASHINGTON: LIBRARY OF CONGRESS, 1942, 22 PP.
AN ANNOTATED BIBLIOGRAPHY OF 199 BOOKS, PERIODICALS, AND
MONOGRAPHS ON MADAGASCAR. INDEX ACCORDING TO TOPIC:
GENERAL SURVEYS, SCIENCES, ETHNOLOGY, DESCRIPTION
ECONOMICS, GOVERNMENT, AND HISTORIES. SOURCES PRIMARILY IN
FRENCH AND ENGLISH, ALTHOUGH SOME GERMAN ARE INCLUDED.
CONTAINS BRIEF SECTION ON WORLD WAR II THROUGH 1942.

0464 CONOVER H.F. ED.
THE GOVERNMENTS OF THE MAJOR FOREIGN POWERS: A BIBLIOGRAPHY.
WASHINGTON: LIBRARY OF CONGRESS, 1945, 45 PP.
LISTINGS OF 428 ENGLISH WORKS AS SUPPLEMENT TO TEXTBOOK
ON FOREIGN GOVERNMENTS PUBLISHED BY US MILITARY ACADEMY AT
WEST POINT. CLASSIFICATIONS FOLLOW CHAPTER HEADINGS OF THAT
WORK. INCLUDES ASPECTS OF POLITICAL AND MILITARY ORGANIZA-
TION OF FRANCE, GREAT BRITAIN, ITALY, GERMANY, USSR, AND
JAPAN. AUTHOR INDEX. COMPILED FOR LIBRARY OF CONGRESS.

0465 CONOVER H.F. ED.
NON-SELF-GOVERNING AREAS.
WASHINGTON: LIBRARY OF CONGRESS, 1947, 467 PP.
ANNOTATED BIBLIOGRAPHY OF 3603 BOOKS AND ARTICLES FROM
ENGLISH, FRENCH, AND SPANISH SOURCES. ARRANGED IN
THREE MAIN SECTIONS: POLICIES AND PRACTICES OF COLONIAL GOV-
ERNMENT, MANDATES AND TRUSTEESHIPS, AND REGIONS. SOUR-
CES SELECTED FOR STATISTICAL AND TECHNICAL INFORMATION
RELATING TO ECONOMIC, SOCIAL, AND EDUCATIONAL CONDITIONS
IN NON-SELF-GOVERNING AREAS THROUGHOUT THE WORLD.

0466 CONOVER H.F. ED.
NIGERIAN OFFICIAL PUBLICATIONS, 1869-1959: A GUIDE.
WASHINGTON: LIBRARY OF CONGRESS, 1959, 153 PP., LC#59-60079.
LISTINGS ARRANGED INVERSELY IN TIME: 1946-1959; ESTAB-
LISHMENT OF LEGISLATIVE COUNCIL IN 1923; PART 3, 1861-1922.
LISTINGS REPRESENT COMPROMISE BETWEEN HISTORICAL NOTE AND
ALPHABETICAL LISTING. LIBRARY OF CONGRESS STYLE HAS PROVIDED
GENERAL MODEL FOR FORM OF ENTRY. INCLUDES 1204 LISTINGS OF
ENGLISH-LANGUAGE PUBLICATIONS WITH AN INDEX AND CROSS-
REFERENCING.

0467 CONRAD J.P.
CRIME AND ITS CORRECTION: AN INTERNATIONAL SURVEY OF ATTI-
TUDES AND PRACTICES.
LONDON: TAVISTOCK, 1965, 312 PP.
REPORT ON SURVEY WHICH SETS FORTH IN BROAD OUTLINES STA-
TUS AND DYNAMICS OF CORRECTIONAL EFFORTS IN NUMBER OF EURO-
PEAN COUNTRIES. SECTIONS ON THE STRUCTURE OF CORRECTIONS,
CORRECTIONAL PATTERNS IN US, UK, NETHERLANDS, SCANDINAVIA,
FRANCE, AND USSR. DISCUSSION OF ISSUES IN CORRECTION.

0468 CONSERVATIVE POLITICAL CENTRE
A WORLD SECURITY AUTHORITY?
LONDON: CONSERVATIVE POL CENTRE, 1958, 40 PP.

COLLECTED SHORT ESSAYS DISCUSS WORLD FORCE FOR POLICING,
INSPECTION, AND NATIONAL DISARMAMENT INCLUDING FUNCTIONS,
ESTABLISHMENT PROCESS, STRUCTURE, AUTHORITY, AND CONTROL
FROM CONSERVATIVE VIEWPOINT.

0469 CONWAY J.E.
"MAKING RESEARCH EFFECTIVE IN LEGISLATION."
WISC. LAW REV., 67 (WINTER 67), 252-266.
ASKS QUESTION IS THERE WAY OF ORGANIZING AND ADMINISTER-
ING RESEARCH PROJECT SO THAT LAWMAKERS MORE LIKELY TO ADOPT
LEGISLATION BASED ON RESEARCH. ARGUES THAT CERTAIN FUNCTIONS
MUST BE ORGANIZATIONALLY LOCATED IF RESEARCH IS TO BE BEST
POSSIBLE AND CHANCES OF ADOPTION MAXIMIZED. ADVOCATES ADVI-
SORY AND EXECUTIVE COMMITTEES TO CARRY OUT RESEARCH AND SEP-
ARATION OF EXECUTIVE DIRECTION FROM SPONSORING GROUP.

0470 CONWAY O.B. JR. ED.
LEGISLATIVE-EXECUTIVE RELATIONS IN THE GOVERNMENT OF THE
UNITED STATES (PAMPHLET)
WASHINGTON: US DEPT OF AGRI, 1954, 64 PP.
ANTHOLOGY ON LEGISLATIVE-EXECUTIVE RELATIONS BY MEMBERS
OF EACH BODY REGARDING FORMATION OF POLICY, BUDGETING, AND
ADMINISTRATION OF PROGRAMS.

0471 COOK P.W. JR. ED., VON PETERFRY G. ED.
PROBLEMS OF CORPORATE POWER.
HOMEWOOD: RICHARD IRWIN, 1966, 371 PP., LC#66-27457.
PRESENTS CASES DEALING WITH DEVELOPMENT AND USES OF
CORPORATE POWER. MOST INVOLVE SITUATIONS WHERE DECISIONS
WILL AFFECT WORLD OUTSIDE OF BUSINESS. MANY INVOLVE BARGAINS
OR NEGOTIATIONS WITH COMPETING INTERESTS. STUDIES PROBLEMS
THAT EXISTENCE OF ECONOMIC POWER PRESENTS TO SOCIETY.

0472 COOMBS C.H.
A THEORY OF DATA.
NEW YORK: JOHN WILEY, 1964, 585 PP., LC#63-20629.
CONSTRUCTS A COMPREHENSIVE SYSTEM FOR DISTINGUISHING AND
RELATING FOUR TYPES OF DATA WITH WHICH MEASUREMENT AND
SCALING THEORIES DEAL: PREFERENTIAL CHOICE DATA, SINGLE
STIMULUS DATA, STIMULI COMPARISON DATA, AND SIMILARITIES
DATA. CONCLUDES WITH ANALYSIS OF THE INTERRELATIONS AMONG
VARIOUS KINDS OF DATA AND FACTORS COMMON TO ALL. ANALYZ-
ES FOUNDATIONS OF PSYCHOLOGICAL MEASUREMENT AND SCALING.

0473 COOPER F.E.
THE LAWYER AND ADMINISTRATIVE AGENCIES.
ENGLEWOOD CLIFFS: PRENTICE HALL, 1957, 331 PP., LC#57-10617.
CONSIDERS PROBLEMS ATTORNEYS FACE IN REPRESENTING CLIENTS
BEFORE ADMINISTRATIVE TRIBUNALS. POINTS OUT SIGNIFICANT DIF-
FERENCES BETWEEN ADMINISTRATIVE AND JUDICIAL ADJUDICATION,
AND ROLE OF DISCRETIONARY POWER. TRACES PROCESSES IN DEALING
WITH CLIENT, PREPARING PLEADINGS, AND INTRODUCING EVIDENCE.
OUTLINES PROCEDURES TO BE FOLLOWED AT HEARINGS.

0474 COOPER F.E.
STATE ADMINISTRATIVE LAW (2 VOLS.)
INDIANAPOLIS: BOBBS-MERRILL, 1965, 951 PP., LC#65-20272.
EXAMINES STATUTORY AND CASE LAW OF STATES OF THE UNION
IN RELATION TO ADMINISTRATIVE PROCEDURE. DISCUSSES
PRINCIPLES OF DELEGATION, RULE-MAKING PROCEDURES,
CONCEPTS OF "RES JUDICATA" AND "STARE DECISIS," AND
JUDICIAL REVIEW OF ADMINISTRATIVE ACTION.

0475 COOPER L.
"ADMINISTRATIVE JUSTICE."
PUBLIC ADMINISTRATION, 32 (SUMMER 54), 165-171.
EXECUTIVE DECISIONS ARE ACTUALLY MADE WITHOUT REAL
CONTROL BY EITHER THE MINISTER OF PARLIAMENT, AND WITHOUT
DIRECT REFERENCE TO PUBLIC INTEREST. SUGGESTS COURTS BE
GIVEN ROLE OF MORE DIRECT INTERVENTION IN ADMINISTRATIVE
PROCEEDINGS.

0476 COPELAND M.A.
OUR FREE ENTERPRISE ECONOMY.
NEW YORK: MACMILLAN, 1965, 302 PP., LC#65-16562.
STUDIES ORGANIZATION BY INSTITUTIONS OF ECONOMIC ACTIVITY
IN A FREE-ENTERPRISE, INDUSTRIALIZED COUNTRY SUCH AS THE
US. FOCUSES ON PROBLEMS RELATING TO BUSINESS CYCLE AND
THE ECONOMY'S OPERATION AT LESS THAN CAPACITY, AND RELEVANT
PROBLEMS IN LABOR-MANAGEMENT RELATIONS.

0477 CORLEY R.N., BLACK R.L.
THE LEGAL ENVIRONMENT OF BUSINESS.
NEW YORK: MCGRAW HILL, 1963, 378 PP., LC#63-15890.
TREATS LEGAL ENVIRONMENT IN WHICH BUSINESS DECISIONS OF
TODAY ARE MADE. DISCUSSES GENERAL MEANING AND NATURE OF LAW
AND THE ENVIRONMENT OF BUSINESS AS IT RESULTS FROM LAW.
REVEALS ATTITUDE OF GOVERNMENT TOWARD BUSINESS AND PRESENTS
TODAY'S MAJOR ISSUES IN LAW AND BUSINESS.

0478 CORNWELL E.E. JR.
THE AMERICAN PRESIDENCY: VITAL CENTER.
GLENVIEW, ILL: SCOTT, FORESMAN, 1966, 172 PP.
GENERAL INTERPRETATION OF OFFICE OF PRESIDENT, INCLUDING
THEORY AND PRACTICE, AND RELATIONS WITH POLITICAL PARTIES,
ADMINISTRATION, CONGRESS, AND THE PUBLIC.

0479 CORRY J.A.
DEMOCRATIC GOVERNMENT AND POLITICS.
TORONTO: TORONTO UNIV PRESS, 1946, 468 PP.
GENERAL INTRODUCTION TO POLITICAL PROCESS IN MODERN
DEMOCRATIC SOCIETIES. DISCUSSES CENTRAL ORGANS AS JUDICIARY,
PARTIES, PRESSURE GROUPS, ETC., WITHIN FRAMEWORK OF CON-
TINUOUSLY EXPANDING RESPONSIBILITIES. CONCLUDES WITH A COM-
PARISON OF DEMOCRACY AND DICTATORSHIP.

0480 CORSON J.J.
EXECUTIVES FOR THE FEDERAL SERVICE.
NEW YORK: COLUMBIA U PRESS, 1952, 91 PP.
PLEA FOR MORE QUALIFIED EXECUTIVES TO BE TRAINED AND TO
ENTER FEDERAL GOVERNMENT SERVICE. AGENCY HEADS OFTEN APPOINT
ONLY PERSONAL FRIENDS TO IMPORTANT POSITIONS, AND PRESSURE
GROUPS OFTEN PREVENT MOST CAPABLE MEN FROM BEING APPOINTED
TO REGULATORY POSITIONS.

0481 CORSON J.J.
GOVERNANCE OF COLLEGES AND UNIVERSITIES.
NEW YORK: MCGRAW HILL, 1960, 202 PP., LC#60-12765.
AN APPRAISAL, BY A PROFESSIONAL MANAGEMENT CONSULTANT, OF
INSTITUTIONS OF HIGHER EDUCATION, THEIR FUNCTION, AND
ENVIRONMENT. DISCUSSES ROLE OF FACULTY, ACADEMIC OFFICERS,
AND UNIVERSITY-WIDE OFFICERS IN UNIVERSITY GOVERNANCE.
BIBLIOGRAPHY INCLUDED.

0482 CORSON J.J., HARRIS J.P.
PUBLIC ADMINISTRATION IN MODERN SOCIETY.
NEW YORK: MCGRAW HILL, 1963, 155 PP., LC#63-13135.
ANALYSIS OF CONTEMPORARY PUBLIC ADMINISTRATION AS TO ITS
POSITION IN SOCIETY, MANAGEMENT OF PUBLIC AGENCIES, AND
ORGANIZATION AND STRUCTURE OF PUBLIC SERVICE. SECOND PART
DEALS WITH US FEDERAL GOVERNMENT AND ITS FUNCTIONS REGARDING
NATIONAL DEFENSE, ECONOMY, AND REGULATION OF PRIVATE ENTER-
PRISE.

0483 CORWIN E.S.
THE PRESIDENT'S CONTROL OF FOREIGN RELATIONS.
PRINCETON: U. PR., 1917, 216 PP.
PRESIDENT IS MAIN DETERMINANT OF USA FOREIGN POLICY.
OBSERVES PART OF CONGRESS AND INFLUENCE OF HAMILTON
AND MADISON IN SHAPING PRESENT-DAY PRESIDENTIAL ROLE.

0484 CORWIN E.S.
"THE CONSTITUTION AND WORLD ORGANIZATION."
PRINCETON: U. PR., 1944, 64 PP.
CONTENT ANALYSIS OF CONSTITUTIONAL TERMS TO DETERMINE
WHETHER THEY BLOCK USA ENTRANCE INTO UN. PROBES FOLLOWING
TERMS AND CONCEPTUAL BASES: NATIONAL SOVEREIGNTY, DUAL
FEDERALISM, SEPARATION OF POWERS AND SENATE TREATY POWERS.

0485 CORWIN E.S.
"THE PRESIDENCY IN PERSPECTIVE."
J. OF POLITICS, 11 (FEB. 49), 7-13.
OVER THE YEARS, ESPECIALLY SINCE THEODORE ROOSEVELT'S
PRESIDENCY, THE OFFICE OF THE PRESIDENT HAS BECOME EXTREMELY
POWERFUL, AND THE OPERATIVE RESTRAINTS ON IT ARE NOT
SUFFICIENT TO MAINTAIN THE DEMOCRATIC BALANCE OF POWERS
ENVISAGED BY THE FOUNDING FATHERS.

0486 CORY R.H. JR.
"FORGING A PUBLIC INFORMATION POLICY FOR THE UNITED
NATIONS."
INT. ORG., 7 (MAY 53), 229-42.
ATTEMPTS TO CLARIFY WHAT ARE PROBLEMS FACING UN DELEGATES
DECIDING WAY IN WHICH INTERNATIONAL SECRETARIAT SHOULD
ATTEMPT TO INFLUENCE PUBLIC OPINION.

0487 COSTA RICA UNIVERSIDAD BIBL
LISTA DE TESIS DE GRADO DE LA UNIVERSIDAD DE COSTA RICA.
SAN JOSE: CIUDAD U, 1962, 131 PP.
BIBLIOGRAPHICAL LISTING OF THESES ACCEPTED AT THE UNIVER-
SITY OF COSTA RICA IN 1961. EACH ITEM INCLUDES AN ABSTRACT.
ENTRIES ARRANGED BY DEPARTMENT.

0488 COSTELLO T.W., ZALKIND S.S.
PSYCHOLOGY IN ADMINISTRATION: A RESEARCH ORIENTATION.
ENGLEWOOD CLIFFS: PRENTICE HALL, 1963, 500 PP., LC#63-19695.
ORIGINAL TEXT PLUS SELECTED READINGS DISCUSSING PSYCHO-
LOGICAL LAWS AND APPLYING THEM TO ORGANIZATIONAL PROBLEMS.
BASED ON RESEARCH, WITH AIM OF FACILITATING OPERATIONS OF
ADMINISTRATION.

0489 COTTER C.P., SMITH J.M.
"ADMINISTRATIVE ACCOUNTABILITY TO CONGRESS: THE CONCURRENT
RESOLUTION."
WESTERN POLIT. QUART., (DEC. 56), 955-966.
CONCURRENT RESOLUTIONS, SINCE THEY DO NOT REQUIRE
SIGNATURE OF THE PRESIDENT, ARE OFTEN USED TO APPROVE OR
REJECT ADMINISTRATIVE DECISIONS.

0490 COTTER C.P., SMITH J.M.
"ADMINISTRATIVE ACCOUNTABILITY: REPORTING TO CONGRESS."
WESTERN POLIT. QUART., 10 (JUNE 57), 405-415.
IN RECENT YEARS CONGRESS HAS EXPANDED THE PRACTICE OF

ASKING THE EXECUTIVE TO SUBMIT REPORTS ON THE USE OF DELE-
GATED POWERS. EXAMINES THE SEVERAL TYPES OF DEVICES ADOPTED
IN ORDER TO MAINTAIN ADMINSTRATIVE RESPONSIBILITY IN THE
EXECUTION OF THESE POWERS. CONCLUDES THAT THE EFFECTIVENESS
OF THESE DEVICES IS STILL OPEN TO QUESTION.

0491 COTTER C.P., HENNESSEY B.C.
POLITICS WITHOUT POWER: THE NATIONAL PARTY COMMITTEES.
NEW YORK: ATHERTON PRESS, 1964, 246 PP., LC#64-15752.
STUDY OF NATIONAL PARTY COMMITTEES. DEFINES THEM AND
DISCUSSES THEIR STATUS IN RELATION TO OTHER POLITICALLY
ORIENTED ORGANIZATIONS. DESCRIBES THEIR FUNCTION AND HOW
BETTER USE COULD BE MADE OF THEM. ARGUES THAT NATIONAL
PARTY COMMITTEES ARE AN IMPORTANT SOURCE IN FURTHERING
RESPONSIBILITY IN AMERICAN POLITICS.

0492 COTTER C.P., SMITH J.M.
"ADMINISTRATIVE RESPONSIBILITY: CONGRESSIONAL PRESCRIPTION
OF INTERAGENCY RELATIONSHIPS."
WESTERN POLIT. QUART., 10 (DEC. 57), 765-782.
SURVEY OF CONGRESSIONAL REGULATIONS AND BILLS ON
INTERAGENCY RELATIONS. IN GENERAL THE AUTHOR HOLDS THAT
SUCH REGULATION HAS INCREASED THE EFFECTIVENESS AND
EFFICIENCY OF THE AGENCIES INVOLVED.

0493 COTTRELL A.J., DOUGHERTY J.E.
THE POLITICS OF THE ATLANTIC ALLIANCE.
NEW YORK: PRAEGER, 1964, 248 PP.
ANALYZES MAJOR POLITICAL AND ECONOMIC ASPECTS OF NATO,
POINTING OUT PROBLEMS OF ACHIEVING AND MAINTAINING UNITY OF
THE WEST. CHALLENGES LEADERS TO SURMOUNT THE CRISES.

0494 COUNCIL OF STATE GOVERNMENTS
STATE GOVERNMENT: AN ANNOTATED BIBLIOGRAPHY (PAMPHLET)
CHICAGO: COUNCIL OF STATE GOVTS, 1959, 46 PP.
ANNOTATED TOPICAL LISTING OF PERIODICALLY REVISED SOURCES
OF COMPARATIVE DATA ON STATE GOVERNMENT. SOME 450 PERIODICAL
INDEXES AND DIGESTS, REPORTING SERVICES, DIRECTORIES, BOOKS,
PERIODICAL ARTICLES, PAMPHLETS, AND REPORTS OF SPECIFIC
STATE LEGAL PROVISIONS. EMPHASIS IS ON STATE LAWS, ADMIN-
ISTRATIVE REGULATIONS, CHARACTERISTICS OF STATE OPERATIONS,
AND ADMINISTRATIVE ORGANIZATION. PUBLICATIONS ARE CURRENT.

0495 COUNCIL OF STATE GOVERNORS
AMERICAN LEGISLATURES: STRUCTURE AND PROCEDURES. SUMMARY
AND TABULATIONS OF A 1959 SURVEY.
CHICAGO: COUNCIL OF STATE GOVTS, 1959, 62 PP.
COMPARATIVE SURVEY OF VARIETY OF LEGISLATIVE STRUCTURAL
PROVISIONS AND PRACTICES AMONG 50 STATES, PUERTO RICO, GUAM,
AND VIRGIN ISLANDS. DISCUSSES PROPOSALS INVOLVING LEGISLA-
TIVE TERMS, SESSIONS, AND DELEGATES' COMPENSATIONS. ALSO
COVERS RECENT ACTION ON REAPPORTIONMENT AND STANDING
COMMITTEES.

0496 COUNCIL STATE GOVERNMENTS
HANDBOOK FOR LEGISLATIVE COMMITTEES.
CHICAGO: COUNCIL OF STATE GOVTS, 1963, 79 PP., LC#63-62704.
COMPILATION OF RULES AND GUIDES THAT DETERMINE PROCEDURE
OF STATE LEGISLATURES. COVERS METHODS OF ORGANIZATION,
DUTIES AND RIGHTS OF MEMBERS, AND POWERS OF COMMITTEES IN
ALL 52 STATES.

0497 COUTY P.
"L'ASSISTANCE POUR LE DEVELOPPEMENT: POINTS DE VUE SCANDI-
NAVES."
TIERS-MONDE, 4 (NOS.13-14, 63), 278-84.
STUDIES FINANCIAL SITUATION OF FINLAND AND SWEDEN. SHOWS
THAT TRADITIONAL INDIFFERENCE TO PROBLEMS OF UNDERDE-
VELOPED COUNTRIES CHANGED TO INVOLVEMENT. RELATES THEIR NEW
INTEREST TO PLANS FOR WIDER COMMERCIAL ACTIVITY.

0498 COWAN L.G.
LOCAL GOVERNMENT IN WEST AFRICA.
NEW YORK: COLUMBIA U PRESS, 1958, 292 PP., LC#58-11900.
DEALS WITH BRITISH AND FRENCH ATTEMPTS TO CREATE FORMS
OF REPRESENTATIVE GOVERNMENT IN WEST AFRICAN COLONIES DURING
1950'S. FOCUSES ON PROBLEMS RAISED BY IMPOSITION OF WESTERN
FORMS ON COMMUNITIES WITH QUITE DIFFERENT INDIGENOUS POLITI-
CAL STRUCTURES, AND ON CONFLICT BETWEEN TRIBAL CHIEFS AND
ELECTED COUNCILS. COMPARES FRENCH AND BRITISH APPROACHES TO
AFRICAN LOCAL, REGIONAL, AND NATIONAL SELF-GOVERNMENT.

0499 COX R. ED., ALDERSON W. ED., SHAPIRO S.J. ED.
THEORY IN MARKETING.
HOMEWOOD: RICHARD IRWIN, 1964, 414 PP., LC#64-21023.
COLLECTION OF ARTICLES DISCUSSING PROBLEMS OF MARKETING,
INCLUDING DESIGN OF MARKETING THEORY, MARKETING AGENCIES AND
CHANNELS, CONSUMER BEHAVIOR, AND MARKETING THEORY AND
MANAGEMENT.

0500 CRAIG J. ED.
BIBLIOGRAPHY OF PUBLIC ADMINISTRATION IN AUSTRALIA.
SYDNEY: U SYDNEY, GOVT & PUB ADM, 1955, 183 PP.
CLASSIFICATION BY SUBJECT OF RELEVANT DOCUMENTS FOUND IN
PAPERS OF NEW SOUTH WALES PARLIAMENT FOR YEARS 1856-1947 AND
OF COMMONWEALTH OF AUSTRALIA PARLIAMENT, 1901-1947. RELEVANT

GENERAL PERIODICALS LISTED. ARRANGEMENT WITHIN SUBJECT CLAS-
SIFICATION IS ALPHABETICAL. SECTIONS ON ADMINISTRATIVE
MACHINERY OF GOVERNMENT DOMINATE CONTENT OF WORK.

0501 CRAIN R.L., ROSENTHAL D.B.
"STRUCTURE AND VALUES IN LOCAL POLITICAL SYSTEMS: THE CASE
OF FLUORIDATION DECISIONS."
J. OF POLITICS, 28 (FEB. 66), 169-195.
THIS STUDY FOUND THAT FLUORIDATION HAS A BETTER CHANCE
OF CONSIDERATION AND ADOPTION IN THE FOLLOWING CIRCUM-
STANCES: WHERE DECISION-MAKING IS CENTRALIZED IN A STRONG
EXECUTIVE; WHERE THE FORM OF GOVERNMENT INSULATES THE
EXECUTIVE FROM MINORITY GROUP PRESSURES; AND WHERE THE
POLITICAL SYSTEM IS CHARACTERIZED BY A LOW LEVEL OF
DIRECT CITIZEN PARTICIPATION.

0502 CRAMER J.F., BROWNE G.S.
CONTEMPORARY EDUCATION: A COMPARATIVE STUDY OF NATIONAL
SYSTEMS (2ND ED.)
NEW YORK: HARCOURT BRACE, 1965, 598 PP., LC#65-11365.
FOUR PART COMPARATIVE STUDY OF NATIONAL ATTITUDES AND
PRACTICES IN EDUCATION. SKETCHES BASIC INFLUENCES AND
BACKGROUND FACTORS DETERMINING CHARACTER OF NATIONAL
SYSTEMS. DESCRIBES ADMINISTRATION, CONTROL, AND FINANCING
IN SEVEN MAJOR NATIONS. DESCRIBES OPERATIONS OF SCHOOLS AND
UNIVERSITIES. DEALS WITH SPECIAL PROBLEMS OF SYSTEMS IN
INDIA, COMMUNIST CHINA, AND JAPAN.

0503 CRAUMER L.V. ED.
BUSINESS PERIODICALS INDEX (8VOLS.)
NEW YORK: H W WILSON, 1960, 6240 PP.
CUMULATIVE SUBJECT INDEX TO PERIODICALS IN FIELD OF
BUSINESS AND RELATED AREAS. COVERS ACCOUNTING, ADVERTISING,
FINANCE, BANKING, LABOR, INSURANCE, TAXATION, ETC. ARRANGED
ALPHABETICALLY BY TOPIC. COVERS 1958-66.

0504 CRAWFORD F.G.
"THE EXECUTIVE BUDGET DECISION IN NEW YORK."
AM. POL. SCI. REV., 24 (MAR. 30),403-408.
TRACES DEVELOPMENT OF THE EXECUTIVE BUDGET IN NEW YORK,
1910-29. THE STRUGGLE FOR CONTROL OF THE FISCAL POLICIES
BETWEEN THE GOVERNOR AND THE LEGISLATORS IS EXAMINED.

0505 CROCKER W.R.
ON GOVERNING COLONIES: BEING AN OUTLINE OF THE REAL ISSUES
AND A COMPARISON OF THE BRITISH, FRENCH, AND BELGIAN...
NEW YORK: MACMILLAN, 1947, 152 PP.
DISCUSSION OF COLONIAL POLICY IN AFRICA BASED ON PERSONAL
OBSERVATIONS OF OFFICER AND SOLDIER IN BRITISH COLONIAL
SERVICE. COMPARISON OF BRITISH, FRENCH, AND BELGIAN POLICIES
AND PRACTICES. FAVORS COLONIAL SYSTEM.

0506 CROCKETT D.G.
"THE MP AND HIS CONSTITUENTS."
PARLIMENTARY AFFAIRS, 20 (SUMMER 67), 281-284.
SURVEYS TYPES OF COMMUNICATION, AND THEIR VOLUME, WHICH
PASS BETWEEN A MEMBER OF PARLIAMENT AND HIS CONSTITUENTS.
CONSIDERS CONFLICT BETWEEN DUTIES TO CONSTITUENTS AND DUTY
TO NATION AS A WHOLE.

0507 CROCKETT W.H.
"EMERGENT LEADERSHIP IN SMALL DECISION MAKING GROUPS."
J. ABNORMAL SOC. PSYCH., 51 (NOV. 55), 378-383.
DEFINES THE EMERGENT LEADER, ANALYZES CONDITIONS RELEVANT
TO HIS PRESENCE AND HIS RELATIONSHIP WITH GROUP MEMBERS.
STUDIES MADE OF DECISION-MAKING CONFERENCES IN 72 BUSINESS
AND GOVERNMENT ORGANIZATIONS. METHOD AND RESULT DETAILED IN
VARIOUS TABLES.

0508 CRONBACK L.J., GLESER G.C.
PSYCHOLOGICAL TESTS AND PERSONNEL DECISIONS.
URBANA: U OF ILLINOIS PR, 1957, 156 PP., LC#57-06949.
APPLIES STATISTICAL DECISION THEORY TO PERSONNEL SELEC-
TION, ABANDONING VIEW OF APTITUDE TEST AS A QUANTITATIVE
MEASURE AND USING IT AS A QUALITATIVE ONE. SEEKS ANALYSIS
OF ABILITY AND OF ITS UTILITY AS A PARAMETER. ENTERS INTO
PROBLEMS OF BOTH THEORETICAL AND APPLICATIONAL DECISIONS.
CONTAINS EXTENSIVE MATHEMATICAL ANALYSIS AND DEVELOPMENT.

0509 CROTTY W.J. ED.
APPROACHES TO THE STUDY OF PARTY ORGANIZATION.
NEW YORK: ALLYN AND BACON, 1967, 352 PP.
INDIVIDUAL READINGS RELATE THE POLITICAL PARTY TO BROADER
SOCIAL CONCERNS, PROVIDE MEANINGFUL FOCUS FOR
INTERRELATIONSHIPS AND ACTIVITIES WITHIN PARTY ORGANIZATION,
AND EMPIRICALLY INVESTIGATE PROBLEM AREAS. INCLUDES
SELECTIONS ON THEORY AND STUDY OF POLITICAL PARTIES.
SUITABLE FOR UNDERGRADUATE COURSES IN PARTY ORGANIZATION.

0510 CROUCH W.W., DINERMAN B.
SOUTHERN CALIFORNIA METROPOLIS: A STUDY IN
DEVELOPMENT OF GOVERNMENT FOR A METROPOLITAN AREA.
BERKELEY: U OF CALIF PR, 1963, 443 PP., LC#63-21640.
STUDY OF LOS ANGELES METROPOLITAN AREA. FOCUSES ON
PROCESS BY WHICH ORGANIZED GROUPS HAVE SOUGHT TO IDENTIFY
PUBLIC ISSUES AND MAKE DECISIONS ON THEM. EMPHASIZES

IMPORTANCE OF REVISIONS IN CALIFORNIA POLITICAL SYSTEM
FASHIONED BY PROGRESSIVE MOVEMENT OF 1910-16 ERA.

0511 CROZIER B.
THE MORNING AFTER; A STUDY OF INDEPENDENCE.
NEW YORK: OXFORD U PR, 1963, 299 PP.
ANALYSIS OF INDEPENDENCE IN DEVELOPING NATIONS AND PROB-
LEMS OF ORGANIZATION AND ADMINISTRATION IN NEW STATUS. DIS-
CUSSES DIFFICULTIES IN CHANGING FROM COLONIAL RULE AND ROLE
OF NATIONAL LEADERS IN EARLY YEARS OF NEW NATIONS AND POSI-
TION OF THESE NATIONS IN COLD WAR.

0512 CULLINGWORTH J.B.
TOWN AND COUNTRY PLANNING IN ENGLAND AND WALES.
TORONTO: TORONTO UNIV PRESS, 1964, 301 PP.
STUDIES TOWN AND COUNTRY PLANNING, PAST PROGRAMS AND
THEIR PROBLEMS; ORGANIZATION OF PRESENT SYSTEM; QUESTIONS
OF CONTROLLED LAND VALUES, AMENITY, DERELICT LAND, LEISURE
PLANNING; RESTRAINT OF URBAN GROWTH; DEVELOPMENT OF NEW
TOWNS; URBAN RENEWAL; REGIONAL PLANNING; AND RELATIONSHIP
BETWEEN PLANNERS AND PEOPLE PLANNED FOR.

0513 CUSHMAN R.E.
LEADING CONSTITUTIONAL DECISIONS.
NEW YORK: APPLETON, 1955, 453 PP., LC#54-11851.
COLLECTION OF SUPREME COURT CASES FOR STUDENT OF AMERICAN
GOVERNMENT WITH HISTORICAL INTRODUCTORY NOTES. INCLUDES SEC-
TIONS ON AMENDMENTS, FEDERAL AND STATES RIGHTS, EXECUTIVE,
JUDICIAL, AND LEGISLATIVE POWER, COMMERCE, AND TAXATION.

0514 CUTLER R.
"THE DEVELOPMENT OF THE NATIONAL SECURITY COUNCIL."
FORTUNE, 34 (APR. 56), 441-458.
SUMMARIZES IMPORTANT ASPECTS OF NATIONAL SECURITY
COUNCIL. POINTS UP COUNCIL'S DIFFERENT USE UNDER TRUMAN
AND EISENHOWER. DISCUSSES PROPOSITION THAT COUNCIL INCLUDE
IN ITS REGULAR MEMBERSHIP A NUMBER OF QUALIFIED CIVILIANS,
AND ARGUES AGAINST SUCH A CHANGE.

0515 CUTLIP S.M.
A PUBLIC RELATIONS BIBLIOGRAPHY.
MADISON: U OF WISCONSIN PR, 1965, 305 PP., LC#65-16360.
A COMPLETE CATALOG OF PUBLISHED SOURCES IN THE FIELD OF
PUBLIC RELATIONS. CONTAINS 5,947 ANNOTATED ENTRIES COVERING
WRITINGS FROM THE EARLY 1900'S TO PRESENT. SOURCES OF INFOR-
MATION INCLUDE OTHER BIBLIOGRAPHIES, PERIODICAL AND BOOK
INDEXES, ORGANIZATIONS OF PUBLIC RELATIONS PRACTITIONERS,
AND PERIODICALS. TOPICS INCLUDE THEORY AND DEVELOPMENT OF
PUBLIC RELATIONS, COMMUNICATIONS, TOOLS, MASS MEDIA, ETC.

0516 CYERT R.M., DILL W.R., MARCH J.G.
"THE ROLE OF EXPECTATIONS IN BUSINESS DECISION-MAKING."
ADMINISTRATIVE SCI. Q., 3 (DEC. 58), 307-40.
STUDY OF FOUR MAJOR DECISIONS IN THREE FIRMS. ANALYZES
ROLE OF EXPECTATIONS IN DECISION-MAKING. QUESTIONS VALIDITY
OF STANDARD THEORY OF PRICE IN INVESTMENT AND INTERNAL RE-
SOURCE ALLOCATION DECISIONS.

0517 CYERT R.M., FEIGENBAUM E.A., MARCH J.G.
"MODELS IN A BEHAVIORAL THEORY OF THE FIRM."
BEHAVIORAL SCIENCE, 4 (APR. 59), 81-96.
PROPOSES A COMPLEX MODEL OF THE FIRM AS A DECISION-MAKING
ORGANIZATION WHICH CAN YIELD ECONOMICALLY RELEVANT AND TEST-
ABLE PREDICTIONS OF BUSINESS BEHAVIOR. EMPLOYS COMPUTER
SIMULATION TECHNIQUES.

0518 CYERT R.M., MARCH J.G., STARBUCK W.H.
"TWO EXPERIMENTS ON BIAS AND CONFLICT IN ORGANIZATIONAL
ESTIMATION."
MANAGEMENT SCIENCE, 7 (APR. 61), 254-264.
TWO EXPERIMENTS TESTING HYPOTHESES RELATING BIAS IN IN-
TERNAL COMMUNICATION TO FINAL DECISIONS. ONE TESTS HYPOTHE-
SIS THAT COST AND SALES ESTIMATIONS ARE MADE WITH IMPLICIT
ASSUMPTION THAT A PAY-OFF STRUCTURE EXISTS. SECOND EXPLICIT-
LY TESTS EFFECTS OF BIASED AND UNBIASED PAY-OFF STRUCTURES
ON ESTIMATION WITHIN AN ORGANIZATION. INVOLVES DESCRIPTIVE
STATISTICS. CONCLUSION: MICRO- BUT NO MACRO-LEVEL VARIATION.

0519 DAHL D.
SICKNESS BENEFITS AND GROUP PURCHASE OF MEDICAL CARE FOR IN-
DUSTRIAL EMPLOYEES.
PRINCETON: PRIN U INDUS REL CTR, 1944, 28 PP.
APPROXIMATELY 150 ENTRIES CONSISTING OF BOOKS AND ARTI-
CLES FROM SCHOLARLY AND TECHNICAL JOURNALS, AND PUBLICATIONS
OF PROFESSIONAL ORGANIZATIONS. DEALS WITH CASH BENEFITS, IN-
SURANCE PLANS, HOSPITALIZATION, AND MEDICAL CARE AVAILABLE
TO INDUSTRIAL EMPLOYEES AND WITH PLANS TO EXTEND THESE TYPES
OF PROGRAMS. ENTRIES ARE IN ENGLISH AND PUBLISHED FROM 1932
TO 1944. ARRANGED BY SUBJECT AND ALPHABETICALLY BY AUTHOR.

0520 DAHL R.A.
"A CRITIQUE OF THE RULING ELITE MODEL."
AMER. POLIT. SCI. REV., 52 (NO.2 4UNE 58), 463-69.
DEFINES RULING ELITE, I. E., A MINORITY OF INDIVIDUALS
WHOSE POLITICAL PREFERENCES USUALLY PREVAIL, AND SUGGESTS
TESTS TO DETERMINE IF THEY EXIST IN ANY USA COMMUNITY.

0521 DAHL R.A., HAIRE M., LAZARSFELD P.F.
"SOCIAL SCIENCE RESEARCH ON BUSINESS: PRODUCT AND POTENTIAL"
NEW YORK: COLUMBIA U PRESS, 1959.
    THREE INDEPENDENT ESSAYS CONCERNED WITH ANALYSIS OF INDI-
VIDUAL DECISIONS OF CONSUMERS AND BUSINESSMEN. EXAMINATION
OF STRUCTURAL ASPECTS OF BUSINESS AS ORDERS OR SYSTEMS,
DISCUSSION OF CONDITIONS OF EFFICIENCY IN BUSINESS ENTER-
PRISE. CONTAINS 233 REFERENCES TOPICALLY ARRANGED
AND ANNOTATED BIBLIOGRAPHY SELECTED SO AS TO GIVE
BROAD VIEW OF CONTRIBUTIONS OF SOCIAL SCIENCE TO BUSINESS.

0522 DAHLBERG J.S.
THE NEW YORK BUREAU OF MUNICIPAL RESEARCH: PIONEER IN
GOVERNMENT ADMINISTRATION.
NEW YORK: NEW YORK U PR, 1966, 258 PP., LC#66-22223.
    ANALYZES ROLE OF NY BUREAU IN DEVELOPMENT OF FIELD OF
PUBLIC ADMINISTRATION IN US. COVERS ACTIVITIES OF EVERY
DEPARTMENT, AND INNOVATIONS THAT HAVE GONE UNNOTICED.
CONCENTRATES ON ITS EARLY STAGES OF DEVELOPMENT, 1906-21, IN
PERIOD WHEN IT JOINED NATIONAL INSTITUTE OF PUBLIC
ADMINISTRATION. FIRST SYNTHESIS OF BUREAU DONE TO DATE.
INCLUDES BIBLIOGRAPHY OF BOOKS, REPORTS, ETC., IN FIELD.

0523 DAHRENDORF R.
CLASS AND CLASS CONFLICT IN INDUSTRIAL SOCIETY.
STANFORD: STANFORD U PRESS, 1959, 336 PP., LC#59-7425.
    PART TWO OF THIS BOOK, "TOWARD A SOCIOLOGICAL THEORY
OF CONFLICT IN INDUSTRIAL SOCIETY," DEALS WITH GROUP
THEORY RELEVANT TO REPRESENTATION, THE ROLE OF LATENT AND
MANIFEST INTERESTS OF GROUPS AND QUASI-GROUPS, AND THE
FUNCTIONS AND MEDIATION OF SOCIAL AND GROUP CONFT ARE

0524 DAKIN R.E.
"VARIATIONS IN POWER STRUCTURES AND ORGANIZING EFFICIENCY:
A COMPARATIVE STUDY OF FOUR AREAS."
SOCIOLOGICAL Q., 3 (JULY 62), 228-250.
    USING A COMPARATIVE APPROACH, THIS STUDY EXAMINED THE
RELATIONSHIP BETWEEN VARIATIONS IN COMMUNITY POWER
STRUCTURES AND THE EFFECTIVENESS WITH WHICH AREAS ARE
ORGANIZED TO DEAL WITH AREA-WIDE ISSUES. ONE FINDING WAS
THAT THE DEGREE OF CONCENTRATION OF POWER WAS NOT AN
IMPORTANT VARIABLE.

0525 DALAND R.T. ED.
PERSPECTIVES OF BRAZILIAN PUBLIC ADMINISTRATION (VOL. I)
LOS ANGELES: U OF S CAL, PUB ADM, 1963, 171 PP.
    PAPERS WRITTEN FOR BRAZILIAN SCHOOL OF PUBLIC ADMINIS-
TRATION. CONCERNED PRIMARILY WITH OVER-ALL VIEW OF BRAZILIAN
ADMINISTRATION IN NATIONAL GOVERNMENT, FOCUSING ON THE
ADMINISTRATION DEPARTMENT OF PUBLIC SERVICE, PERSONNEL SYS-
TEM, AND PLANNING.

0526 DALTON M.
"CONFLICTS BETWEEN STAFF AND LINE MANAGERIAL OFFICERS" (BMR)
AMER. SOCIOLOGICAL REV., 15 (JUNE 50), 342-351.
    RESEARCH IN THREE INDUSTRIAL PLANTS SHOWING CONFLICT
BETWEEN MANAGERIAL STAFF AND LINE GROUPS THAT HINDERED
ATTAINMENT OF ORGANIZATIONAL GOALS. EXAMINES CAUSES OF
CONFLICT AND PRESENTS POSSIBLE REMEDIAL MEASURES.

0527 DANELSKI D.J.
"CONFLICT AND ITS RESOLUTION IN THE SUPREME COURT."
J. OF CONFLICT RESOLUTION, 11 (MAR. 67), 71-86.
    DISTINGUISHES AMONG TYPES OF DISAGREEMENTS AND REPORTS
ON INSTANCES. DISCUSSES EFFECT OF VALUES HELD, CONFLICT BE-
TWEEN PERSONAL AND SOCIETAL VALUES, ROLES FILLED BY JUSTICES
AT VARIOUS TIMES. SPECIFIC REFERENCE TO CHIEF JUSTICE'S
JOB OF AVOIDING CONFLICTS AND RESOLVING ARGUMENTS BY USE OF
SPECIAL POWERS.

0528 DANGERFIELD R.
IN DEFENSE OF THE SENATE.
NORMAN: U. OKLAHOMA PR., 1933.
    EFFECT OF SENATE PARTICIPATION IN TREATY-RATIFICATION
SYSTEMATICALLY ANALYZED. FACTORS INFLUENCING SENATE ACTION,
INCLUDING ORGANIZATIONS, INSTITUTIONS, AND PERSONALITIES,
ARE EXAMINED. CONCLUDES THAT SENATE APPROVED MOST
TREATIES EXPEDIENTLY AND RECOMMENDS FORMATION OF
DELIBERATIVE ORGANS, E.G., A LEGISLATIVE-EXECUTIVE CABINET
AND/OR THE LIKE, TO ENSURE EFFECTIVE FOREIGN POLICY.

0529 DANIELSON L.E., MAIER N.R.F.
"SUPERVISORY PROBLEMS IN DECISION MAKING."
PERSONNEL PSYCHOLOGY, 10 (SUMMER 57), 169-180.
    ACCOUNT OF MULTIPLE ROLE-PLAYING GAME DESIGNED TO INVES-
TIGATE FOREMAN-WORKER INTERACTION. FINDS THAT JUDICIAL AP-
PROACH BY SUPERVISOR IN DEALING WITH INFRACTION OF WORK
RULES IS MOST COMMON BUT NOT MOST SATISFACTORY RESPONSE.

0530 DARRAH E.L., POLAND O.F.
FIFTY STATE GOVERNMENTS: A COMPILATION OF EXECUTIVE
ORGANIZATION CHARTS.
BERKELEY: U CALIF, BUR PUB ADMIN, 1961, 70 PP.
    PRESENTS EXECUTIVE ORGANIZATION CHARTS FROM EACH OF US
STATE GOVERNMENTS, MOST LIMITED TO EXECUTIVE BRANCH, THOUGH
SOME INCLUDE JUDICIAL AND LEGISLATIVE BRANCH. SHOWS MANY AND
VARIED ACTIVITIES OF STATE GOVERNMENTS, SIZE AND COMPLEXITY
OF AGENCIES. CHARTS POINT OUT TYPICALLY LIMITED POWER OF
GOVERNOR, SHOWING WHOM HE APPOINTS AND THOSE WHO ARE
RESPONSIBLE TO HIM.

0531 DAS M.N.
INDIA UNDER MORLEY AND MINTO.
LONDON: ALLEN & UNWIN, 1964, 279 PP.
    DISCUSSES AFFECTS OF MORLEY-MINTO ERA OF BRITISH RULE IN
INDIA (1905-1910) ON POLITICAL EVOLUTION OF MODERN INDIA.
FOCUSES ON REVOLUTION, REPRESSION, AND REFORMS IN BRITISH
AND INDIAN RELATIONS AND SIGNIFICANCE OF POLITICAL EVENTS
BEHIND THESE THREE ISSUES.

0532 DAVEE R.
"POUR UN FONDS DE DEVELOPPEMENT SOCIAL."
TIERS-MONDE, 4 (NOS.13-14, 63), 181-92.
    STATES THAT UN ECONOMIC AID PROGRAM PARTS REQUIRE COORDI-
NATION. EXAMINES PROGRAM OF TECHNICAL ASSISTANCE TO VARI-
OUS NATIONS. EXAMINES PROBLEM OF URGENT SOCIAL REFORMS.
INDICATES PATTERNS OF INTERNATIONAL COOPERATION.

0533 DAVENPORT J.
"ARMS AND THE WELFARE STATE."
YALE REV., 47 (SPR. 58), 335-346.
    BELIEVES THAT US NEEDS A STRONG AND EFFECTIVE GOVERNMENT
FOR NATIONAL DEFENSE, DIPLOMACY, SOUND MONEY, AND TO RESIST
MONOPOLY IN BUSINESS AND LABOR, BUT THIS DOES NOT HAVE TO
MEAN 'WELFARE STATE'. ARGUES FOR A NEW 'INTELLECTUAL COM-
MUNITY SYNTHESIS, WHICH WILL TAKE THE THREAT OF RUSSIAN
DANGER SERIOUSLY, WHILE KEEPING FREE SOCIETY AT HOME. ANSWER
TO TOBIN'S 'DEFENSE, DOLLARS AND DOCTINES' OF SAME ISSUE.

0534 DAVID P.T., POLLOCK R.
EXECUTIVES FOR THE GOVERNMENT: CENTRAL ISSUES OF FEDERAL
PERSONNEL ADMINISTRATION.
WASHINGTON: BROOKINGS INST, 1957, 196 PP., LC#57-13369.
    DISCUSSION OF HOOVER COMMISSION REPORT AND GENERAL
PROBLEM OF GETTING FEDERAL EXECUTIVES.

0535 DAVIDSON R.H., KOVENOCK D.M., O'LEARY M.K.
CONGRESS IN CRISIS: POLITICS AND CONGRESSIONAL REFORM.
NEW YORK: HAWTHORNE BOOKS, 1966, 208 PP., LC#66-23795.
    DISCUSSES NEED FOR REFORM IN CONGRESS AND POLITICAL PRES-
SURES WHICH IMPEL OR IMPEDE IT, INCLUDING CHARACTER AND EX-
TENT OF DISSENSION AMONG PUBLIC AND LEGISLATORS, AND GUIDE-
LINES FOR CHANGE STRATEGISTS.

0536 DAVIES E.
NATIONAL ENTERPRISE: THE DEVELOPMENT OF THE PUBLIC
CORPORATION.
LONDON: VICTOR GOLLANCZ, 1946, 173 PP.
    DISCUSSES ISSUES OF NATIONALIZATION OF BRITISH
INDUSTRY, AND PROBLEMS THAT HAVE ARISEN IN REGARD TO
ADMINISTRATION. ANALYZES THESE PROBLEMS IN RELATION TO
PUBLIC CORPORATIONS ALREADY OPERATING, AND THOSE IN COURSE
OF ESTABLISHMENT. ATTEMPTS TO DETERMINE GENERAL PRINCIPLES
THAT CAN BE APPLIED TO NATIONAL ENTERPRISE TO ENSURE
CONTINUED SUCCESS AND PUBLIC APPRECIATION OF ITS BENEFITS.

0537 DAVIS H.E.
PIONEERS IN WORLD ORDER.
NEW YORK: COLUMB. U. PR., 1944, 272 PP.
    COLLECTION OF ESSAYS EVALUATING THE WORK OF THE LEAGUE OF
NATIONS, COVERING THE ORGANIZATIONAL, ECONOMIC, POLITICAL,
AND SOCIAL ASPECTS.

0538 DAVIS J.A. ED., BAKER J.K. ED.
SOUTHERN AFRICA IN TRANSITION.
NEW YORK: AMER SOC AFR CULTURE, 1966, 427 PP., LC#65-13963.
    ARTICLES PUBLISHED FOR AMERICAN SOCIETY OF AFRICAN
CULTURE ON POLITICAL AND SOCIAL CONDITIONS IN SOUTHERN
AFRICA. TREAT HISTORY, LAND, RESOURCES, PEOPLES, AND
POLITICS OF NATIONS. EXAMINE NONVIOLENCE, NATIONALISM,
FORCE, PAN-AFRICANISM, INTERNATIONAL RELATIONS, INDEPENDENCE
AND RESULTING RACIAL ADJUSTMENTS, AND US POLICY. MAINTAINS
THAT TRANSITION WILL BE LONG AND HARD.

0539 DAVIS K.C.
ADMINISTRATIVE LAW.
MINNEAPOLIS: WEST PUBL CO, 1951, 1024 PP.
    DISCUSSES BASIC ADMINISTRATIVE PROCESSES AND REQUIREMENTS
OF HEARING, NOTICE, AND OTHER SAFEGUARDS. EXAMINES PRINCI-
PLES OF DELEGATION AND SEPARATION OF POWERS, AND PRESENTS
NATURE OF JUDICIAL REVIEW OF ADMINISTRATIVE ACTION.

0540 DAVIS K.C.
ADMINISTRATIVE LAW TREATISE (VOLS. I AND IV)
MINNEAPOLIS: WEST PUBL CO, 1958, 1310 PP.
    VOL. I DISCUSSES NATURE AND PROCESS OF ADMINISTRATIVE
LAW. EXAMINES CONCEPT OF DELEGATION OF POWER, RULE-MAKING
FUNCTION OF ADMINISTRATIVE AGENCIES, ADJUDICATIVE PROCEDURE,
AND SUBDELEGATION OF POWER. VOL. IV DISCUSSES NATURE OF UN-
REVIEWABLE ADMINISTRATIVE ACTION, SCOPE OF REVIEWABLE EVI-
DENCE, AND SCOPE OF REVIEW OF LEGAL CONCEPTS AS APPLIED TO
FACTS.

0541 DAVIS K.C.
ADMINISTRATIVE LAW: CASES, TEXT, PROBLEMS.
ST PAUL, MINN: WEST PUBL CO, 1958.
TREATISE ON LAW SEEKS TO PRESENT SYSTEMATIC TREATMENT OF
ADMINISTRATIVE LAW IN 1958. CRITICIZES SUPREME COURT FOR A
NUMBER OF ITS RECENT DECISIONS. LAW IS SURVEYED WITH
PERTINENT COMMENTS ON ARTICLES WHICH AUTHOR FEELS NEED
EXPLANATION. A FOUR-VOLUME SET.

0542 DAVIS K.C.
ADMINISTRATIVE LAW TEXT.
MINNEAPOLIS: WEST PUBL CO, 1959, 617 PP.
DISCUSSES ADMINISTRATIVE PROCESSES IN US. EXAMINES RULE-
MAKING POWER, ADJUDICATION PROCEDURES, INSTITUTIONAL DECI-
SIONS, AND JURISDICTION OF ADMINISTRATIVE AGENCIES. ANALYZES
IN DETAIL PROCEEDINGS FOR REVIEW OF ADMINISTRATIVE ACTION BY
FEDERAL COURTS. TEXT INTENDED FOR LAW STUDENTS.

0543 DAVIS K.C.
ADMINISTRATIVE LAW AND GOVERNMENT.
MINNEAPOLIS: WEST PUBL CO, 1960, 547 PP.
DISCUSSES FUNDAMENTAL PROBLEMS OF ADMINISTRATIVE PROCESS
IN US. EXAMINES CONCEPTS OF DELEGATION OF POWER, RULE-MAK-
ING, RES JUDICATA AND STARE DECISIS, AND REVIEW OF ADMINIS-
TRATIVE ACTION BY COURTS. EACH CHAPTER CONTAINS PROBLEM
SECTION.

0544 DAVIS R.G.
PLANNING HUMAN RESOURCE DEVELOPMENT, EDUCATIONAL MODELS AND
SCHEMATA.
SKOKIE: RAND MCNALLY & CO, 1966, LC#66-19441.
INTRODUCES SCIENTIFIC OPERATIONS ANALYSIS USING MODELS
FOR PURPOSE OF INCREASING PRODUCTIVITY, EFFICIENCY, AND RE-
DUCING COST WHEN DEALING WITH LABOR, MANPOWER, AND
EDUCATION.

0545 DAVISON W.P.
INTERNATIONAL POLITICAL COMMUNICATION.
NEW YORK: FREDERICK PRAEGER, 1965, 404 PP., LC#65-24723.
SEARCHES FOR WAYS US CAN UTILIZE PUBLIC COMMUNICATION
MORE EFFECTIVELY TO ADVANCE ITS FOREIGN POLICIES. ATTEMPTS
REALISTICALLY TO EVALUATE POLITICAL EFFECTS OF NEWSPAPERS,
RADIO, FILM, AND EXCHANGE OF PERSONS. SUGGESTS THAT
CORNERSTONE OF INTERNATIONAL COMMUNICATION POLICY SHOULD BE
TRADITION OF FREE PUBLIC DISCUSSION. GOVERNMENT PROGRAMS
SHOULD ADHERE TO STANDARDS OF OBJECTIVITY AND TRUTHFULNESS.

0546 DAY C.
A HISTORY OF COMMERCE.
LONDON: LONGMANS, 1938, 703 PP.
HISTORY OF TRADE AND COMMERCE AMONG NATIONS FROM ANCIENT
TIMES TO THE PERIOD AFTER WORLD WAR 2. STRESSES TRADE POLI-
CIES OF THE EUROPEAN NATIONS AND THE US. DISCUSSES FORMS OF
ECONOMIC ORGANIZATION AND PUBLIC FINANCE.

0547 DAY E.E.
EDUCATION FOR FREEDOM AND RESPONSIBILITY.
ITHACA: CORNELL U. PR., 1952.
DISCUSSES IMPACT OF PROFESSIONALISM AND TREND TOWARDS
SPECIALIZATION IN RESEARCH. ADVOCATES RE-ORIENTATION OF
LIBERAL EDUCATION REJECTING THE CONANT PLAN AS INFLEXIBLE.
IN WAKE OF COLD WAR SUGGESTS TRAINING OF LOYAL LEADERSHIP
AND EXPANSION OF EDUCATION IN GENERAL.

0548 DAY P.
CRISIS IN SOUTH AFRICA.
BALTIMORE: BALTIMORE SUN, 1948, 37 PP.
EXAMINATION OF EVENTS AND TRENDS IN BRITISH EMPIRE, CON-
CENTRATING UPON SOUTH AFRICA. INDICATES THAT BRITAIN IS
LOOSENING HER CONTROL. STUDIES PROBLEM OF INDIANS, DEFEAT
OF SMUTS, LAND SHORTAGE PROBLEM, RACIAL ISSUE DUE TO INFLUX
OF NATIVES INTO CITIES, UNION'S ECONOMIC LIFE, AND
IMMIGRATION POLICIES.

0549 DE ARAGAO J.G.
LA JURIDICTION ADMINISTRATIVE AU BRESIL.
RIO DE JAN: DEP DE IMPR NACIONAL, 1955, 255 PP.
REVIEWS DUAL ADMINISTRATIVE JURISDICTION, 1824-89, AND
SUBSEQUENT UNITY OF JURISDICTION, 1889-PRESENT. DUALITY WAS
DUE TO FACT THAT "CONSEIL D'ETAT" HAD DE JURE AUTHORITY,
BUT WAS A CONSULTATIVE BODY, WITH REAL AUTHORITY EXERCISED
BY OTHERS. IN 1889, REVOLUTION ESTABLISHED REPUBLICAN
FEDERATIVE GOVERNMENT WITH CLEAR DIVISION OF AUTHORITY.

0550 DE BLIJ H.J.
SYSTEMATIC POLITICAL GEOGRAPHY.
NEW YORK: JOHN WILEY, 1967, 618 PP., LC#66-28752.
PRESENTS INTRODUCTION TO FIELD OF POLITICAL GEOGRAPHY,
WITH PROFESSIONAL PAPERS AND CASE STUDIES. DISCUSSES RISE
OF NATION-STATE, ITS ELEMENTS, RESTRICTIONS, FUNCTIONS,
AND ROLE IN GEOPOLITICAL ACTIVITY, AND ITS INTERNAL
STRUCTURE. APPLIES STUDY TO COLONIALISM, SUPRA-NATIONALISM,
AND EMERGENT WORLD FORCES.

0551 DE CENIVAL P., FUNCK-BRETANO C., BOUSSER M.
BIBLIOGRAPHIE MAROCAINE: 1923-1933.

PARIS: LIBRAIRIE LA ROSE, 1934, 607 PP.
COLLECTS AND ARRANGES BIBLIOGRAPHIES DEALING WITH MOROCCO
WHICH APPEARED IN THE REVIEW "HESPERIS" BETWEEN 1923 AND
1933. INCLUDES BOOKS, ARTICLES, AND PAMPHLETS PUBLISHED IN
WESTERN LANGUAGES. ORGANIZED TOPICALLY: INCLUDES ANTHROPOL-
OGY, ARCHEOLOGY, LANGUAGE, BIBLIOGRAPHY, CARTOGRAPHY,
SCIENCE, ARTS, HISTORY, ETC.

0552 DE GRAZIA A.
HUMAN RELATIONS IN PUBLIC ADMINISTRATION.
CHICAGO: PUBLIC ADMIN SERVICE, 1949, 52 PP.
ANNOTATED BIBLIOGRAPHY OF 363 WORKS FROM FIELDS OF PSY-
CHOLOGY, SOCIOLOGY, ANTHROPOLOGY, AND POLITICAL SCIENCE
ON PROBLEMS OF PUBLIC ADMINISTRATION. ORGANIZED ALPHA-
BETICALLY IN FOUR CATEGORIES: GENERAL FRAMES OF REFERENCE,
ADMINISTRATIVE PROCESS, ORGANIZATION'S IMPACT ON SOCIETY AND
METHODS OF STUDYING ADMINISTRATION. SOME BIBLIOGRAPHIES IN-
CLUDED. FOREIGN TITLES KEPT TO MINIMUM. LIST OF PERIODICALS.

0553 DE GRAZIA A.
POLITICAL ORGANIZATION.
NEW YORK: CROWELL COLLIER, 1952, 306 PP., LC#62-19200.
SURVEYS LAWS, CONSTITUTIONS, LEGISLATURES, EXECUTIVES,
ADMINISTRATIVE AGENCIES, AND COURTS. EXPLAINS OPERATION OF
POLITICAL BEHAVIOR WITHIN THESE INSTITUTIONS. ASSAYS RECENT
DEVELOPMENTS IN POLITICAL SCIENCE.

0554 DE GRAZIA A. ED.
GRASS ROOTS PRIVATE WELFARE.
NEW YORK: NEW YORK U PR, 1957, 295 PP., LC#57-14539.
PRACTICAL IDEAS AND OBSERVATIONS ON COMMUNITY SOCIAL
PROBLEMS. DEALS WITH RECOGNITION OF PROBLEM, COMMUNITY
REACTION TO IT, HOW IT WAS SUCCESSFULLY DEALT WITH. NEW
METHODS AND PROGRAMS IN SOCIAL WELFARE ARE SUGGESTED.

0555 DE GRAZIA A.
"POLITICAL BEHAVIOR (REV. ED.)"
NEW YORK: FREE PRESS OF GLENCOE, 1962.
DESCRIPTION OF GREAT POLITICAL SCIENTISTS AND THEIR
IDEAS, METHODOLOGY OF POLITICAL SCIENCE, CONTENT, AND
MEANING FOR LAYMEN. INTRODUCTION TO BASIC CONCEPTS:
LEADERSHIP, POLITICAL GROUPINGS, PUBLIC OPINION, REPRESENTA-
TION, PARTY ORGANIZATION, ETC. INVESTIGATES NATURE OF PUB-
LIC POLICY AND HOW IT AFFECTS PRIVATE RIGHTS. SHORT BIBLI-
OGRAPHY INCLUDED.

0556 DE GRAZIA A.
REPUBLIC IN CRISIS: CONGRESS AGAINST THE EXECUTIVE FORCE.
NEW YORK: FEDERAL LEGAL PUBL, 1965, LC#65-28094.
ARGUES THAT CONGRESS AND THE EXECUTIVE REPRESENT TWO
OPPOSING FORCES OF LIBERTY AND ORDER. URGES RE-EVALUATION
OF THEIR RESPECTIVE ROLES AND POWERS WITHIN AMERICAN
CONSTITUTIONAL AND SOCIAL SYSTEM. CONCLUDES WITH BIBLIO-
GRAPHICAL NOTE ON METHODS AND SOURCES.

0557 DE GUZMAN R.P. ED.
PATTERNS IN DECISION-MAKING: CASE STUDIES IN PHILIPPINE
PUBLIC ADMINISTRATION.
QUEZON CITY: U OF PHILIPPINES, 1963, 569 PP.
REALISTIC ANALYSIS OF GOVERNMENTAL PROCESSES IN NEW
NATION BY STUDYING ACTUAL ON-JOB, IN-CONTEXT CASES.
FOCUSES ON DECISIONS FELT TO BE ESSENCE OF GOVERNMENT AND
KEY TO VALUE STRUCTURE UNDERLYING GOVERNMENT. STUDIES ONE
PROBLEM IN EACH CASE, PEOPLE INVOLVED, AND METHOD OR MOTIVE
FOR ARRIVING AT DECISIONS.

0558 DE NOIA J., CHILDS J.B., MCGEORGE H.
GUIDE TO OFFICIAL PUBLICATIONS OF THE OTHER AMERICAN RE-
PUBLICS: EL SALVADOR.
WASHINGTON: LIBRARY OF CONGRESS, 1947, 64 PP.
ANNOTATED BIBLIOGRAPHY AND GUIDE TO GOVERNMENT PUBLICA-
TIONS IN EL SALVADOR, ARRANGED BY AGENCY OR DEPARTMENT OF
ORIGIN AND INDEXED ALPHABETICALLY BY TITLE. ALSO INCLUDES
PREFATORY NOTE AND AN INTRODUCTION EXPLAINING GENERAL FACETS
OF STATE STRUCTURE TO FACILITATE THE USE OF GUIDE. COMPILED
FOR LIBRARY OF CONGRESS.

0559 DE NOIA J.
GUIDE TO OFFICIAL PUBLICATIONS OF THE OTHER AMERICAN REPUB-
LICS: NICARAGUA (VOL. XIV)
WASHINGTON: LIBRARY OF CONGRESS, 1947, 33 PP.
ANNOTATED AND INDEXED BIBLIOGRAPHY AND GUIDE TO THE HOLD-
INGS IN THE LIBRARY OF CONGRESS OF SERIES, SERIALS, MONO-
GRAPHS, AND OTHER STATE PUBLICATIONS ISSUED BY NICARAGUAN
REPUBLIC. ARRANGED BY DEPARTMENT OR AGENCY OF ISSUANCE.
INCLUDES GENERAL PUBLICATIONS AND OFFICIAL GAZETTES.
LISTS ALL MATERIAL SINCE 1821.

0560 DE NOIA J.
GUIDE TO OFFICIAL PUBLICATIONS OF THE OTHER AMERICAN REPUB-
LICS: PANAMA (VOL. XV)
WASHINGTON: LIBRARY OF CONGRESS, 1947, 34 PP.
INDEXED AND ANNOTATED BIBLIOGRAPHY AND GUIDE TO OFFICIAL
GOVERNMENT PUBLICATIONS AND DOCUMENTS OF PANAMA ARRANGED
BY AGENCY OR DEPARTMENT OF ISSUANCE. PART OF A LIBRARY OF
CONGRESS PROJECT BEGUN IN 1941 UNDER THE AEGIS OF THE

STATE DEPARTMENT'S INTERDEPARTMENTAL COMMITTEE ON SCIENTIFIC
AND CULTURAL COOPERATION. INCLUDES SERIALS, SERIES, AND
MONOGRAPHS PUBLISHED SINCE 1903.

0561 DE NOIA J.
GUIDE TO OFFICIAL PUBLICATIONS OF OTHER AMERICAN REPUBLICS:
PERU (VOL. XVII)
WASHINGTON: LIBRARY OF CONGRESS, 1948, 90 PP.
ANNOTATED CHECKLIST OF ALL OFFICIAL STATE PUBLICATIONS
ISSUED SINCE INDEPENDENCE IN 1826 BY THE PERUVIAN GOVERN-
MENT AND AVAILABLE IN THE LIBRARY OF CONGRESS. PART OF STATE
DEPARTMENT PROJECT. INCLUDES A SUBJECT-TITLE INDEX. DOCU-
MENTS ARE ARRANGED UNDER THE DEPARTMENT OR AGENCY OF
ISSUANCE.

0562 DE VRIES E. ED., ECHAVARRIA J.M. ED.
SOCIAL ASPECTS OF ECONOMIC DEVELOPMENT IN LATIN AMERICA.
PARIS: UNESCO, 1963, 401 PP., $5.00.
A COLLECTION OF PAPERS SUBMITTED TO EXPERT WORKING
GROUP ON SOCIAL ASPECTS OF ECONOMIC DEVELOPMENT IN LATIN
AMERICA IN DECEMBER 1960. VARIOUS SPECIALISTS IN ECONOM-
ICS, SOCIOLOGY, POLITICAL SCIENCE, SOCIAL PSYCHOLOGY, AND
PUBLIC ADMINISTRATION OFFER A MORE BALANCED VIEW OF
ECONOMIC DEVELOPMENT PROBLEMS IN LATIN AMERICA.

0563 DEAN A.L. ED.
FEDERAL AGENCY APPROACHES TO FIELD MANAGEMENT (PAMPHLET)
CHICAGO: AMER SOC FOR PUB ADMIN, 1963, 28 PP., LC#63-21421.
SYMPOSIUM DRAWN FROM PAPERS PRESENTED AT 1963 NATIONAL
CONFERENCE ON PUBLIC ADMINISTRATION. INCLUDES BRIEF NOTES
ON GENERAL AREA OF FEDERAL FIELD MANAGEMENT AND STUDIES OF
FIELD MANAGEMENT IN THE INTERNAL REVENUE SERVICE; POST
OFFICE DEPARTMENT; A MULTI-PURPOSE AGENCY (HEW); A RESEARCH
AND DEVELOPMENT AGENCY (NASA); AND AN INTEGRATED AGENCY
(FAA).

0564 DEAN A.W.
"SECOND GENEVA CONFERENCE OF THE LAW OF THE SEA: THE FIGHT
FOR FREEDOM OF THE SEAS."
AMER. J. INT. LAW, 54-55 (OCT.60 - JULY 61), 751-89, 675-80.
ATTEMPTS TO SETTLE CONTROVERSIES OVER WIDTH OF TERRITOR-
IAL SEA. SHOWS DANGERS TO FREEDOM OF NAVIGATION, FREE COM-
MERCE, AND COMMUNICATION INHERENT IN ANY EXTENSION. STUDIES
COMPROMISE BETWEEN USA PROPOSED SIX MILE LIMIT AND USSR PLAN
FOR TWELVE MILE EXTENSION OF RIGHTS. ALSO RECOUNTS PREVIOUS
AGREEMENTS OVER AIR SPACE AND RELATED ISSUES.

0565 DEAN B.V.
"APPLICATION OF OPERATIONS RESEARCH TO MANAGERIAL DECISION
MAKING"
ADMINISTRATIVE SCI. Q., 3 (1958), 412-428.
OUTLINES DECISION-MAKING PROCESS AND ROLE OF DECISION
MAKER IN THIS PROCESS. INDICATES UTILITY OF OPERATIONS
RESEARCH IN SOLVING DECISION-MAKING PROBLEMS. SHOWS HOW
ANALYTIC MODELS ARE CONSTRUCTED AND SOLVED, NOTES SOME
TOOLS AND TECHNIQUES FOR SOLVING SUCH MODELS, AND FORECASTS
POSSIBLE FUTURE DEVELOPMENTS OF OPERATIONS RESEARCH TECH-
NIQUES AND THEIR POSSIBLE EFFECTS ON DECISION-MAKING.

0566 DEBENKO E., KRISHNAN V.N.
RESEARCH SOURCES FOR SOUTH ASIAN STUDIES IN ECONOMIC DEVEL-
OPMENT: A SELECT BIBLIOGRAPHY OF SERIAL PUBLICATIONS.
E LANSING: ASIAN STUD CTR, MSU, 1966, 97 PP., LC#66-63953.
BIBLIOGRAPHICAL LISTING OF PERIODICALS, MONOGRAPHS IN
SERIES, PERIODICAL GOVERNMENT DOCUMENTS, AND ANNUALS ON NE-
PAL, INDIA, PAKISTAN, AND CEYLON. TREATS PLANNING, POLICIES,
AND PROCESSES. INCLUDES POLITICAL SCIENCE AND RELATED AREAS.
ENGLISH-LANGUAGE PUBLICATIONS. OVER 1,000 ENTRIES. (ASIAN
STUDIES CENTER OCCASIONAL PAPER NO. 4)

0567 DEBRAY P., SABRAN B.
LE PORTUGAL ENTRE DEUX REVOLUTIONS.
PARIS: AU FIL D'ARIANE, 1963, 112 PP.
ANALYSIS AND EVOLUTION OF THE PORTUGUESE GOVERNMENTAL AND
POLITICAL PROCESS; DECISION-MAKING IN PORTUGUESE POLITICS
AND ROLE OF THE PRIME MINISTER.

0568 DEES J.W. JR.
URBAN SOCIOLOGY AND THE EMERGING ATOMIC MEGALOPOLIS,
PART I.
ANN ARBOR: ANN ARBOR PUBL, 1950, 267 PP.
INTRODUCTORY TEXT AND CASEBOOK IN FIELD OF URBAN SOCIETY
AND SOCIAL PATHOLOGY. ATTEMPTS TO ENLARGE SCOPE OF URBANISM
INTO DEVELOPMENT OF EMERGING ATOMIC MEGALOPOLIS. FOCUSES ON
PROBLEMS OF FRINGE DEVELOPMENT, SOCIOLOGY OF WATER AND
SEWAGE, SCIENTIFIC MEASUREMENT OF CITIES, THEORIES OF URBAN
ECOLOGICAL EXPANSION, PLANS FOR PUBLIC HOUSING, AND
NEIGHBORHOODS.

0569 DEGRAS J. ED.
THE COMMUNIST INTERNATIONAL, 1919-1943: DOCUMENTS (3 VOLS.)
LONDON: OXFORD U PR, 1956.
DOCUMENTS INCLUDE PROGRAMMATIC AND THEORETICAL STATEMENT
OF COMMUNIST INTERNATIONAL FORMULATING GENERAL POLICY;
STATEMENTS ON CURRENT EVENTS; LETTERS TO AND RESOLUTIONS ON
NATIONAL COMMUNIST PARTIES; DOCUMENTS REFERRING TO PARTY'S

INTERNAL ORGANIZATION. INTRODUCTORY REMARKS GIVE BRIEFLY
THE CONTEXT OF DOCUMENT. CONCLUDES WITH LIST OF SOURCES.

0570 DEKAT A.D.A.
COLONIAL POLICY.
CHICAGO: U. CHI. PR., 1931, 674 PP.
ANALYZES HOW DUTCH AUTHORITY, BY CONTROLLING EAST INDIA
COMPANY, EXPANDED IN JAVA AND SURROUNDING ISLANDS. EVALUATES
DUTCH COLONIAL POLICY, REGARDING ADMINISTRATION, EDUCATION,
TAXATION, AND WAYS IN WHICH IT AFFECTED CONSTRUCTION OF THE
SOCIETY.

0571 DELANY V.T.H.
THE ADMINISTRATION OF JUSTICE IN IRELAND.
DUBLIN: INST PUBLIC ADMIN, 1962, 91 PP.
HISTORY OF IRISH JUDICIARY SINCE 1800 INCLUDING SOURCES
OF IRISH LAW, COURT SYSTEMS, CRIMINAL AND CIVIL JURISDIC-
TION, COURT PERSONNEL, AND LEGAL FINANCES.

0572 DELLIN L.A.D.
"BULGARIA UNDER SOVIET LEADERSHIP."
CURR. HIST., 44 (MAY 63), 281-287.
REVEALS EXCESSIVE SUBSERVIENCE TO USSR. DE-STALINIZATION
MORE NOMINAL THAN REAL. USA REMAINS PUBLIC ENEMY NO.1 OF
REGIME YET SOURCE OF HOPE TO PEOPLE. COUNTRY'S TENSIONS
FOUND IN ECONOMIC FIELD: CRISIS IN AGRICULTURE ACUTE.

0573 DENNING A.
FREEDOM UNDER THE LAW.
TORONTO: CARSWELL, 1949, 126 PP.
SUMMARIZES DEVELOPMENT OF ENGLISH LAW, DETAILING ITS
PROVISIONS ON PERSONAL FREEDOM, FREEDOM OF MIND AND CON-
SCIENCE, JUSTICE BETWEEN MAN AND STATE, AND POWERS OF
EXECUTIVE.

0574 DENNISON E.
THE SENATE FOREIGN RELATIONS COMMITTEE.
STANFORD: U. PR., 1942, 201 PP.
OUTLINES HISTORY, ORGANIZATION, PROCEDURES, AND INFLUENCE
OF SENATE FOREIGN RELATIONS COMMITTEE. ARGUES THAT MEMBER-
SHIP IS DETERMINED BY GEOGRAPHICAL BALANCE AND POLITICAL
EXPEDIENCY AND NOT BY ABILITY TO HANDLE SPECIALIZED PROBLEMS
OF WORLD POLITICS. PROPOSES MEASURES TO IMPROVE ITS LEVEL OF
COMPETENCY AND TO REGULARIZE MACHINERY NECESSARY TO PROMOTE
COOPERATION WITH THE EXECUTIVE BRANCH.

0575 DERGE D.R.
"METROPOLITAN AND OUTSTATE ALIGNMENTS IN ILLINOIS AND
MISSOURI LEGISLATIVE DELEGATIONS" (BMR)"
AM. POL. SCI. REV., 52 (DEC. 58), 1051-1065.
MAINTAINS THAT TRADITIONAL BITTER CONFLICT BETWEEN
METROPOLITAN AND NONMETROPOLITAN AREAS IN THESE STATE
LEGISLATURES DOES NOT EXIST. DIFFERENT TYPE OF CONFLICT
EXISTS THERE: POLITICAL FACTORS WITHIN METROPOLITAN
AREA ALONE DETERMINE FATE OF CITY LEGISLATION.

0576 DESMITH S.A.
JUDICIAL REVIEW OF ADMINISTRATIVE ACTION.
NEW YORK: OCEANA PUBLISHING, 1959, 486 PP., LC#59-12294.
DISCUSSES ROLE OF ENGLISH COURTS IN REVIEWING ACTS,
ORDERS, AND DECISIONS OF MINISTERS, LOCAL AUTHORITIES,
PUBLIC CORPORATIONS AND OFFICIALS, AND ADMINISTRATIVE
TRIBUNALS. EXAMINES SCOPE OF JUDICIAL REMEDIES,
CIRCUMSTANCES FOR RECOURSE TO COURTS, LEGAL STANDARDS TO
WHICH EXERCISE OF DISCRETIONARY POWERS MUST CONFORM, AND
TIMES WHEN ADMINISTRATION MUST EXPLAIN DECISIONS.

0577 DEUTSCH K.W., MADOW W.G.
"A NOTE ON THE APPEARANCE OF WISDOM IN LARGE BUREAUCRATIC
ORGANIZATIONS."
BEHAVIORAL SCIENCE, 6 (JAN. 61), 72-85.
STATISTICAL MODEL TO DETERMINE PROBABILITY FOR OFFICIALS
TO MAKE CORRECT DECISIONS WHEN DECISION-MAKERS OF COMPAR-
ABLE COMPETENCE HAVE FAILED. DISCUSSES APPLICABILITY OF RE-
SULTS TO POLITICAL AND ORGANIZATIONAL BEHAVIOR.

0578 DEUTSCHE BIBLIOTH FRANKF A M
DEUTSCHE BIBLIOGRAPHIE.
FRANKFURT: DEUT BIBLIOG FRANKFE.
WEEKLY REGISTER (JAN 1965-JULY 1967) LISTING BOOKS
PUBLISHED IN THE PRECEDING YEARS (1965 AND 1966). ARRANGED
BY SUBJECT AND HAS SUCH CLASSIFICATIONS AS PHILOSOPHY, LAW,
AND ADMINISTRATION, SOCIAL SCIENCES, POLITICS, DEFENSE, FINE
ARTS, ETC. HAS A SUBJECT-AUTHOR INDEX. FOREIGN PUBLICATIONS
INCLUDED.

0579 DEUTSCHE BUCHEREI
JAHRESVERZEICHNIS DER DEUTSCHEN HOCHSCHULSCHRIFTEN.
LEIPZIG: VEB VERL FUR BUCH BIBL.
ANNUAL BIBLIOGRAPHY OF DISSERTATIONS AND ACADEMIC
WRITINGS WITH APPROXIMATELY 10,000 LISTINGS PER YEAR.
ORGANIZED BY ACADEMIC INSTITUTION, FACULTY, AND PLACE OF
PUBLICATION. INDEXED BY SUBJECT AND AUTHOR WITH CROSS-REFER-
ENCES UNDER MAIN TOPIC. VOLUME 80 (1964) WAS FIRST ISSUE TO
APPEAR IN PAPERBACK.

0580 DEUTSCHE BUCHEREI
JAHRESVERZEICHNIS DES DEUTSCHEN SCHRIFTUMS.
LEIPZIG: VEB.VERL. FUR BUCH-BIBL.
ANNUAL BIBLIOGRAPHY OF BOOKS IN GERMAN PUBLISHED DURING
THE PERIOD UNDER CONSIDERATION IN GERMAN', AUSTRIA, SWITZ-
ERLAND, AND OTHER COUNTRIES. EACH VOLUME DIVIDED INTO TWO
SECTIONS: WORKS ORGANIZED BY AUTHOR; WORKS INDEXED UNDER
SUBJECT.

0581 DEUTSCHE BUCHEREI
DEUTSCHES BUCHERVERZEICHNIS.
LEIPZIG: VEB.VERL. FUR BUCH-BIBL.
ANNUAL LISTING OF PRIMARY PUBLICATIONS IN BOTH EAST AND
WEST GERMANY. ENTRIES ARRANGE ALPHABETICALLY BY AUTHOR WITH
A SUBJECT INDEX. FIRST PUBLISHED 1911.

0582 DEVINS J.H.
"THE INITIATIVE."
MIL. REV., 41 (NOV. 61), 79-85.
SPECULATES THAT 'LACK OF QUICK RESPONSIVENESS IN THE
SOVIET COMMAND STRUCTURE IS PROBABLY ITS GREATEST WEAKNESS.
MENTAL CONDITIONING OF OUR TROOP LEADERS MAKES THEM FAR MORE
ADAPTABLE TO A FLUID WAR OF MOVEMENT AND INITIATIVE THAN
COMMUNIST COUNTERPARTS, ACCUSTOMED TO THE RESTRICTIVE
ENVIRONMENT OF SOVIET LIFE.' POINTS OUT GAP BETWEEN RECOG-
NITION OF INITIATIVE AND ABILITY TO USE IT INTELLIGENTLY.

0563 DEVLIN P.
THE CRIMINAL PROSECUTION IN ENGLAND.
NEW HAVEN: YALE U PR, 1958, 150 PP., LC#58-11251.
STUDY OF GENERAL LEGAL PRINCIPLES AND PROCEDURES INVOLVED
IN ENGLISH SYSTEM OF PROSECUTION FOR CRIME. TRACES PROCESS
FROM TIME OF ARREST THROUGH TIME OF ARRAIGNMENT. DISCUSSES
RIGHTS AND DUTIES OF GOVERNMENT AND OF ACCUSED WHILE CASE IS
BEING PREPARED FOR TRIAL.

0584 DEXTER L.A.
"HAS THE PUBLIC OFFICIAL ON OBLIGATION TO RESTRICT HIS
FRIENDSHIPS?"
AMER. BEHAVIORAL SCIENTIST, (APR. 61), 25-28.
SHORT DISCUSSION OF EFFECTS OF PERSONAL FRIENDSHIPS ON
THE ATTITUDES AND DECISIONS OF PUBLIC OFFICIALS.

0585 DIAMANT A.
"A CASE STUDY OF ADMINISTRATIVE AUTONOMY: CONTROLS AND TEN-
SIONS IN FRENCH ADMINISTRATION."
POLITICAL STUDIES, 6 (JUNE 58), 147-165.
FRENCH ADMINISTRATIVE SYSTEM IS RATHER INSENSITIVE TO
POLITICAL AUTHORITY AND THE DEMOCRATIC PROCESS, BUT CAPABLE
OF OPERATING WITHOUT POLITICAL DIRECTION AND DEVELOPING ITS
OWN SUBSTANTIVE GOALS AND STANDARDS OF PERFORMANCE.

0586 DICKINSON J.
ADMINISTRATIVE JUSTICE AND THE SUPREMACY OF LAW IN THE
UNITED STATES.
CAMBRIDGE: HARVARD U PR, 1927, 403 PP., LC#27-14657.
EXAMINES RELATIONSHIP OF FEDERAL REGULATORY AGENCIES AND
LEGISLATED LAW IN HANDLING PROBLEMS OF GOVERNMENTAL REGULA-
TION. NECESSITY FOR WIDE APPLICABILITY OF LAW MEANS THAT
INTERPRETATION BECOMES NECESSARY. EVALUATES ADMINISTRATORS
VS. JUDGES AS POLICY-MAKERS IN ECONOMIC REGULATION. ALSO
CONSIDERS PROBLEM OF EDUCATING JUDGES TO BE CAPABLE OF DEAL-
ING WITH THESE PROBLEMS.

0587 DICKSON P.G.M.
THE FINANCIAL REVOLUTION IN ENGLAND.
NEW YORK: ST MARTIN'S PRESS, 1967, 580 PP., LC#67-12509.
CITES AND EXPLORES IMPORTANCE OF DEVELOPMENT OF PUBLIC
CREDIT SYSTEMS TO POLITICAL, SOCIAL, AND ECONOMIC HISTORY
OF 18TH CENTURY ENGLAND. NATIONAL DEBT, ADMINISTRATIVE PROB-
LEMS, PUBLIC CREDITORS, GOVERNMENT BORROWING, SECURITY MAR-
ETS, ARE ALL ANALYZED IN DEPTH. COMPREHENSIVE WORK INCLUDING
WIDE RANGE OF DISCIPLINES.

0588 DICKSON W.J., ROETHLISBERGER F.J.
COUNSELING IN AN ORGANIZATION: A SEQUEL TO THE HAWTHORNE
RESEARCHES.
CAMBRIDGE: HARVARD BUS SCHOOL, 1966, 480 PP., LC#66-28808.
STUDY OF EMPLOYEE COUNSELING PROJECT AT WESTERN ELECTRIC
COMPANY: AN OVERVIEW; RATIONALE OF PROGRAM, ORGANIZATION,
AND SPECIFIC CASES OF EMPLOYEES' PROBLEMS. EVALUATES CONTRI-
BUTIONS OF COUNSELING AND DISCUSSES INSTANCES OF AMBIGUITY.

0589 DIEBOLD J.
BEYOND AUTOMATION: MANAGERIAL PROBLEMS OF AN EXPLODING
TECHNOLOGY.
NEW YORK: MCGRAW HILL, 1964, 220 PP., LC#64-25598.
STRESSES THE IMPERATIVES OF ADJUSTING TO THE NEW
TECHNOLOGY, ONLY ONE OF WHOSE CHALLENGES IS INCREASE IN
EMPLOYMENT PROBLEMS, WHICH MUST BE UNDERSTOOD AGAINST THE
PROSPECT OF A RADICALLY TRANSFORMED SOCIETY. VOLUME IS BASED
ON PUBLIC ADDRESSES OF THE AUTHOR, WHO HAS ADVISED THE
SECRETARY OF LABOR.

0590 DIEBOLD J.
"COMPUTERS, PROGRAM MANAGEMENT AND FOREIGN AFFAIRS."
FOREIGN AFFAIRS, 45 (OCT. 66), 125-134.
OUTLINES INFORMATIONAL PROBLEMS INHERENT IN MANAGING US
FOREIGN AFFAIRS THROUGH STATE DEPARTMENT WHICH PROCESSES
SOME 2000 TELEGRAMS A DAY. SUGGESTS THAT WHILE DEPARTMENT OF
DEFENSE PROGRAM SYSTEM AND BUSINESS COMPUTER EXPERIENCE
PROVIDES TECHNOLOGICAL BASE FOR IMPROVEMENT, IT IS NO PANA-
CEA, AND MUST BE BASED ON THOROUGH INFORMATIONAL STRATEGY.

0591 DIEBOLD W. JR.
THE SCHUMAN PLAN: A STUDY IN ECONOMIC COOPERATION,
1950-1959.
NEW YORK: PRAEGER, 1959, 750 PP.
RECOUNTS THE ORIGINS OF THE SCHUMAN PLAN AND EVENTS WHICH
LED TO FORMATION OF THE EUROPEAN COAL AND STEEL COMMUNITY.
CONSIDERS THE COMMUNITY'S OPERATIONS, DEVELOPMENTS, PROS-
PECTS, AND IMPLICATIONS FOR AMERICAN FOREIGN POLICY. DIS-
CUSSES ITS RELATION TO PROSPECT OF EUROPEAN INTEGRATION.

0592 DIESNER H.J.
KIRCHE UND STAAT IM SPATROMISCHEN REICH.
ZURICH: EVANGELISCHER VERLAG, 1963, 167 PP.
DISCUSSES RELATIONSHIP OF CHURCH AND STATE IN ROMAN
EMPIRE BETWEEN A.D. 350 AND 500. ALSO EXAMINES SITUATION OF
NORTH AFRICAN PEOPLES IN RELATION TO EMPIRE.

0593 DILL W.R. ED. JACKSON J.R. ED. SWEENEY J.W. ED.
PROCEEDINGS OF THE CONFERENCE ON BUSINESS GAMES AS TEACHING
DEVICES.
NEW ORLEANS: TULANE U, SCH BUS, 1961, 138 PP.
REPORT ON CONFERENCE DISCUSSING EDUCATIONAL PURPOSES, DE-
SIGNS, AND EVALUATION OF BUSINESS GAMES USED AS METHOD TO
TEACH MANAGEMENT DECISION-MAKING.

0594 DILLEY M.R.
BRITISH POLICY IN KENYA COLONY (2ND ED.)
NEW YORK: BARNES AND NOBLE, 1966, 300 PP.
TREATS BRITISH COLONIAL POLICY IN KENYA FROM 1900-1965.
PROVIDES BACKGROUND INFORMATION ON REGION AND PRESENTS
DEVELOPMENT OF EUROPEAN COLONY AND ATTEMPTS BY COLONISTS
TO GAIN ELECTIVE REPRESENTATION IN PARLIAMENT, HOME-RULE,
AND FINANCIAL CONTROL. EXAMINES RELATIONS WITH INDIAN
SETTLERS AND STUDIES PROBLEMS OF TRUSTEESHIPS, LAND, LABOR,
AND TAXES.

0595 DIMOCK M.E.
FREE ENTERPRISE AND THE ADMINISTRATIVE STATE.
UNIVERSITY: U ALABAMA PR, 1951, 179 PP.
EXAMINES SYSTEM OF FREE ENTERPRISE FROM STANDPOINT OF
INSTITUTIONS, THEIR ORGANIZATION AND FUNCTION. DISCUSSES
ASPECTS OF MANAGEMENT, MONOPOLY, AND DECENTRALIZATION.
MAINTAINS THAT DECENTRALIZATION IS NECESSARY TO PRESERVE
SYSTEM.

0596 DIMOCK M.E., DIMOCK G.O.
PUBLIC ADMINISTRATION.
NEW YORK: RINEHART, 1953, 410 PP., LC#53-6880.
INTRODUCTORY TEXTBOOK EMPHASIZING PRACTICAL, OPERATIONAL
SIDE OF GOVERNMENT. EXAMINES DYNAMICS OF POLICY FORMATION,
ORGANIZATION, PERSONNEL, AND FINANCE OF ADMINISTRATION.
EVALUATES DEGREE OF DEMOCRATIC CONTROL OPERATIVE IN PUBLIC
ADMINISTRATION.

0597 DIMOCK M.E.
ADMINISTRATIVE VITALITY: THE CONFLICT WITH BUREAUCRACY.
LONDON: ROUTLEDGE & KEGAN PAUL, 1959, 298 PP.
THERE IS OFTEN A CONFLICT BETWEEN RESPONSIBILITY, WHICH
IMPLIES COMPLETE ADHERENCE TO REGULATIONS, AND
RESPONSIVENESS TO IMMEDIATE NEEDS OF THE PEOPLE. GOOD
PUBLIC SERVANTS WILL BE BOTH RESPONSIVE AND RESPONSIBLE.

0598 DIMOCK M.E.
THE NEW AMERICAN POLITICAL ECONOMY: A SYNTHESIS OF POLITICS
AND ECONOMICS.
NEW YORK: HARPER & ROW, 1962, 306 PP., LC#62-7315.
BUSINESS AND GOVERNMENT MUST WORK TOGETHER IF MEN'S BASIC
ASPIRATIONS ARE TO BE REACHED: POLICY MUST BE MADE BY BOTH
PRIVATE AND PUBLIC GROUPS; BUSINESS WILL NOT THRIVE UNLESS
GOVERNMENT IS ENTERPRISING; VALUES AND MORAL PHILOSOPHY ARE
VERY IMPORTANT. ON THESE ASSUMPTIONS AUTHOR PROPOSES MASSIVE
DECENTRALIZATION OF FEDERAL FUNCTIONS THAT COULD BE TURNED
BACK TO STATE AND LOCAL OR VOLUNTARY GROUPS.

0599 DIXON D.F.
"A SOCIAL SYSTEMS APPROACH TO MARKETING."
S.W. SOCIAL SCI. QUART., 48 (SEPT. 67), 164-173.
CONCERNED WITH MANNER IN WHICH PROCESS OF MARKETING
MANAGEMENT IN FIRM INTERACTS WITH COMPLEX NETWORK OF SOCIETY
AS WHOLE. STUDIES MARKETING AS SOCIAL SYSTEM. MAINTAINS THAT
GOALS OF MARKET MUST MEET THOSE OF SOCIETY, INPUT-OUTPUT
RELATIONS AND CONSTRAINTS MUST BE CONSIDERED, AND EFFICIENCY
MUST BE MAINTAINED OR SYSTEM WILL BE REPLACED.

0600 DJILAS M.
THE NEW CLASS: AN ANALYSIS OF THE COMMUNIST SYSTEM.
NEW YORK: PRAEGER, 1957, 214 PP., $3.95.
ANALYSIS OF CONTEMPORARY COMMUNISM BY YUGOSLAV COMMUNIST.

PRESENTS THESIS THAT, CONTRARY TO MARXIST THEORY, COMMUNIST
REVOLUTIONARIES HAVE CREATED A NEW SOCIAL CLASS, WHICH TO-
GETHER WITH THE COMMUNIST PARTY DOMINATES AND EXPLOITS THE
PEOPLE OF THE SOCIALIST STATES. THEORIZES ON EFFECT OF
MARXIST DOGMA UPON SOCIETY.

0601 DODDS H.W.
THE ACADEMIC PRESIDENT "EDUCATOR OR CARETAKER?
NEW YORK: MCGRAW HILL, 1962, 294 PP., LC#61-18625.
DEALS WITH MANY REPRESENTATIONAL ISSUES, SUCH AS THE
ADMINISTRATIVE COUNCIL, FACULTY PARTICIPATION IN ADMIN-
ISTRATION, BOARD OF TRUSTEES, FORMAL AND INFORMAL POWER
CENTERS, AND THE NATURE OF ACADEMIC LEADERSHIP. A COMPANION
VOLUME IS AN ANNOTATED BIBLIOGRAPHY (1961) PREPARED BY
W.C. EELLS AND E.V. HOLLIS.

0602 DODSON D.W.
"NEW FORCES OPERATING IN EDUCATIONAL DECISION-MAKING."
INTEGRATED EDUCATION, 5 (JUNE-JULY 67), 36-43.
DISCUSSES CHANGING RELATIONSHIPS IN EDUCATIONAL SYSTEMS
WHICH ARE OCCASIONED BY SHIFTING OF POWER RELATIONSHIPS IN
THE COMMUNITY. SHOWS HOW THESE CHANGES HAVE AFFECTED
DECISION-MAKING IN SCHOOL SYSTEMS. STATES THAT MORALITY IN
DECISION-MAKING WILL COME ONLY WHEN SUBORDINATES LEARN HOW
TO USE THEIR POWER AND DEVELOP A SENSE OF RESPONSIBILITY.

0603 DOERN G.B.
"THE ROYAL COMMISSIONS IN THE GENERAL POLICY PROCESS AND IN
FEDERAL-PROVINCIAL RELATIONS."
CAN. PUBLIC ADMIN., 10 (DEC. 67), 417-433.
STUDIES THE FUNCTIONS AND USEFULNESS OF CANADIAN ROYAL
COMMISSIONS, AD HOC BODIES APPOINTED BY THE GOVERNMENT IN
POWER FOR PURPOSE OF EXPERT STUDY OF SUCH PROBLEMS AS
TRANSPORTATION AND AGRICULTURE. CONCLUDES THAT SENATE COM-
MITTEES OR RESEARCH INSTITUTES AT UNIVERSITIES COULD BETTER
SERVE THE PURPOSE; THEY WOULD EXIST IN PERPETUITY AND HAVE
BETTER CHANCE OF IMPLEMENTING THEIR SUGGESTIONS.

0604 DOHERTY D.K. ED.
PRELIMINARY BIBLIOGRAPHY OF COLONIZATION AND SETTLEMENT IN
LATIN AMERICA AND ANGLO-AMERICA.
NEW YORK: INST HUMAN REL PRESS.
ISSUED IN ENGLISH, PORTUGUESE, AND SPANISH. EMPHASIZES
PERSON AND AGENCIES ATTEMPTING COLONIZATION AND DEVELOPMENT.

0605 DONHAM W.B.
ADMINISTRATION AND BLIND SPOTS.
CAMBRIDGE: HARVARD BUS SCHOOL, 1952, 95 PP.
LECTURES DELIVERED IN 1951, GIVES BACKGROUNDS OF ADMINI-
STRATORS, RELATIONSHIP OF ADMINISTRATION TO PUBLIC INTEREST.
SUGGESTS NEED FOR ADMINISTRATOR WITH BROAD VIEW OF RESPONSI-
BILITY TO SOCIETY.

0606 DONNELL J.C.
"PACIFICATION REASSESSED."
ASIAN SURVEY, 7 (AUG. 67), 567-576.
DISCUSSES ROLE OF REVOLUTIONARY DEVELOPMENT (RD) CADRE
GROUPS IN PACIFICATION EFFORTS IN RURAL SOUTH VIETNAM, ES-
PECIALLY THEIR EFFORTS TO PROVIDE PHYSICAL SECURITY AND
SOCIAL WELFARE. EXAMINES TRAINING PROGRAMS AND EFFORTS TO
INSTILL POLITICAL MOTIVATION. FOCUSES ON DEVELOPMENTS IN
RECENT YEARS (1965-67).

0607 DONNELLY D.
"THE POLITICS AND ADMINISTRATION OF PLANNING."
POLIT. QUART., 33 (OCT.-DEC. 62), 404-413.
HISTORY OF ECONOMIC AND SOCIAL WELFARE PLANNING IN UK,
AND HOW POOR LOCAL GOVERNMENT ORGANIZATION AND RESOURCES
HAVE HINDERED OPERATION OF PLANS.

0608 DORWART R.A.
"THE ADMINISTRATIVE REFORMS OF FREDRICK WILLIAM I OF PRUSSIA
CAMBRIDGE: HARVARD U PR, 1953.
PRESENTS A HISTORICAL DESCRIPTION OF THE EVOLUTION OF
INSTITUTIONS OF PUBLIC ADMINISTRATION IN THE CENTRAL GOVERN-
MENT OF BRANDENBURG-PRUSSIA. CONCENTRATES ON REFORMS IN AD-
MINISTRATION AND ADMINISTRATIVE ORGANIZATION INTRODUCED DUR-
ING THE REIGN OF FREDRICK WILLIAM I, 1713-40. EMPHASIS ON
ROLE PLAYED BY CENTRALIZED, ABSOLUTIST PUBLIC ADMINISTRA-
TION. BIBLIOGRAPHY OF GERMAN AND FRENCH WORKS.

0609 DOSSICK J.J.
DOCTORAL RESEARCH ON PUERTO RICO AND PUERTO RICANS.
NEW YORK: NEW YORK U PR, 1967, 34 PP.
LIST OF 320 DOCTORAL DISSERTATIONS ACCEPTED IN AMERICAN
UNIVERSITIES DURING THE PAST 66 YEARS. FIFTY PER CENT ARE
BY PUERTO RICANS. INCLUDES DISSERTATIONS ON POLITICAL SCI-
ENCE AND RELATED DISCIPLINES. MANY ARE ON THE RELATIONSHIP
TO THE US.

0610 DOTSON A.
PRODUCTION PLANNING IN THE PATENT OFFICE (PAMPHLET)
INDIANAPOLIS: BOBBS-MERRILL, 1952, 13 PP.
DESCRIBES 1945 TROUBLES OF US PATENT OFFICE REGARDING
DISTRIBUTION OF PATENT COPIES TO PUBLIC. ILLUSTRATES USE
OF SCIENTIFIC MANAGEMENT TO EXPEDITE GOVERNMENT CLERICAL

OPERATION.

0611 DOTSON A.
"FUNDAMENTAL APPROACHES TO RESPONSIBILITY."
WESTERN POLIT. QUART., 10 (JUNE 57), 701-727.
SAYS THAT THE CONTROL OF ADMINISTRATIVE POWER IS A
SERIOUS PROBLEM THAT IS GETTING HARDER TO SOLVE. IMPLIES
THAT ONLY REAL SOLUTION IS A MORE ACTIVE, BETTER EDUCATED
PUBLIC.

0612 DOUGLAS P.H.
"OCCUPATIONAL V PROPORTIONAL REPRESENTATION."
AMER. J. OF SOCIOLOGY, 29 (SEPT. 23), 129-157.
TREATS OF DIFFICULTIES IN THE USE OF OCCUPATIONAL REP-
RESENTATION IN THE US, SUCH AS CLASSIFICATION OF INDUSTRIAL
GROUPS AND A VOTER'S OCCUPATIONAL SITE, AS WELL AS THE
REPRESENTATION OF MINORITIES WITHIN THE OCCUPATIONAL GROUPS.
PREFERS PROPORTIONAL REPRESENTATION BASED ON COMMON
DESIRES AND INTERESTS.

0613 DOUGLASS H.R.
MODERN ADMINISTRATION OF SECONDARY SCHOOLS.
BOSTON: GINN AND CO, 1963, 636 PP., LC#63-8696.
THIS TEXT OFFERS INSIGHTS ON WHAT MIGHT BE CALLED
"VIRTUAL" REPRESENTATION IN SCHOOL ADMINISTRATION. DEALS
WITH DEMOCRATIC AND COOPERATIVE PRINCIPLES, THE INTERRELA-
TIONSHIPS OF ADMINISTRATORS, THE SUPERVISION, DIRECTION,
AND WORK ASSIGNMENTS OF THE STAFF. INCLUDES SECTIONS ON
USING STUDENTS IN GOVERNMENT, MANAGEMENT, AND PUBLIC
RELATIONS OF SCHOOLS.

0614 DOWD L.P.
PRINCIPLES OF WORLD BUSINESS.
NEW YORK: ALLYN AND BACON, 1965, 573 PP., LC#65-15936.
DISCUSSES SOURCES AND BASES FOR INTERNATIONAL TRADE,
PRINCIPLES OF FOREIGN EXCHANGE, GOVERNMENTAL CONTROLS,
MANAGEMENT OF INTERNATIONAL BUSINESS (MARKETING RESEARCH,
ADVERTISING, FINANCING, ETC., AND EXPORT PROCEDURES.

0615 DRAGNICH A.N.
MAJOR EUROPEAN GOVERNMENTS.
HOMEWOOD: DORSEY, 1961, 454 PP., LC#61-11608.
DISCUSSES POLITICAL INSTITUTIONS AND PROCESSES OF UK,
FRANCE, GERMANY, AND USSR. INCLUDES DISCUSSION OF HISTORI-
CAL DEVELOPMENT OF INSTITUTIONS, BUT CENTERS ON MODERN
CONDITIONS.

0616 DRAPER A.P.
"UNIONS AND THE WAR IN VIETNAM."
NEW POLITICS, 5 (1967), 7-12.
EXPOSES THE EFFORT OF MAJOR UNION LEADERS TO UNDERWRITE
THE GOVERNMENT VIETNAM POLICY AND TO STIFLE DISSENT. MAIN-
TAINS THAT UNDERLYING OFFICIAL UNION POLICY IS A LARGE
PACIFIST ELEMENT WITH NO OUTLET FOR ITS OPINIONS. CALLS FOR
THE FORMATION OF A TRADES UNION DIVISION OF SANE AS A
UNITED FRONT FOR WORKERS OPPOSED TO WAR. CITES CRITICS OF
ESCALATION AMONG UNIONISTS AS EVIDENCE.

0617 DRAPER T.
AMERICAN COMMUNISM AND SOVIET RUSSIA.
NEW YORK: VIKING, 1960, 558 PP.
TRACES ORIGINS OF AMERICAN COMMUNISM TO DUTCH LEFT-WING
THE LETTISH, RUSSIAN, JAPANESE AND IRISH EMIGREES. AS A
MOVEMENT, AMERICAN COMMUNISM DOMINATED BY SOVIET UNION
DURING 1920-30 PERIOD. FAILED TO BECOME INDIGENIOUS,
AND REMAINED OUTSIDE MAINSTREAM OF AMERICAN LIFE. DESCRIBES
LEADERSHIP AND ORGANIZATIONAL PROBLEMS OF POST-WW 1 ERA AND
REVEALS UTTER FAILURE OF AMERICAN COMMUNISTS TO OPERATE AS
EFFECTIVE UNIT WITHIN THE COMINTERN.

0618 DROR Y.
"POLICY ANALYSTS."
PUBLIC ADMIN. REV., 27 (SEPT. 67), 197-204.
DISCUSSES RISE OF SYSTEMS ANALYSIS WITH SPECIFIC APPLI-
CATION TO FEDERAL ADMINISTRATION. PROPOSES IT TO BE NEW
INTERDISCIPLINARY SPECIALIZATION IN POLITICAL SCIENCE.
ALSO TREATS BASIC PROBLEMS OF INCREMENTAL DECISION-MAKING
IN POLICY FORMATION, SUCH AS THE TENDENCY TO BECOME CON-
CERNED WITH TRIVIA AND LOSE SIGHT OF OBJECTIVES.

0619 DRUCKER P.F.
"THE EMPLOYEE SOCIETY."
AMER. J. OF SOCIOLOGY, 58 (JAN. 53), 358-363.
EXPLORES AMERICAN SOCIETY AS AN "EMPLOYEE SOCIETY" WHERE
THE BOSS HIMSELF IS USUALLY AN EMPLOYEE AND DEPENDS ON
STATUS (CF. MAINE'S THESIS). CALLS FOR RESEARCH INTO IMPLI-
CATIONS OF "MANAGEMENT" AND ITS ACCOUNTABILITY. THE
REALIZATION OF HOPES AND BELIEFS THROUGH EMPLOYEE SOCIETY,
RIGHTS AND DUTIES IN SUCH A SOCIETY RELATED TO POWER,
EFFICIENCY, AND REDISTRIBUTION.

0620 DRUCKER P.F.
"'MANAGEMENT SCIENCE' AND THE MANAGER."
MANAGEMENT SCIENCE, 1 (JAN. 55), 115-118.
LOOKS AT 'MANAGEMENT SCIENCE' FROM POINT OF VIEW OF MANA-
GER. FOCUSES ON DETERMINING METHODOLOGY, TOOLS, AND TECHNI-

QUES NECESSARY TO AN ORDERLY AND SYSTEMATIC JOB OF MANAGING.
CONCENTRATES ON DECISION-MAKING AND BUSINESS ENTERPRISE
AND ITS STRUCTURE.

0621 DRURY J.W.
THE GOVERNMENT OF KANSAS.
LAWRENCE: U OF KANSAS PR, 1961, 393 PP., LC#61-16950.
STUDIES STRUCTURE AND FUNCTION OF STATE GOVERNMENT IN
KANSAS, POINTING OUT PARTICULAR ACTIVITIES OF LEGISLATURE,
GOVERNOR, ADMINISTRATIVE OFFICES, AND COURTS. THOROUGHLY
COVERS PUBLIC HEALTH, EDUCATION, WELFARE, AND PLANNING.
SHOWS STATE'S ROLE IN REGULATION OF BUSINESS, MUNICIPAL GOV-
ERNMENT, AND INTERGOVERNMENTAL RELATIONS.

0622 DRYDEN S.
"LOCAL GOVERNMENT IN TANZANIA PART II"
J. OF ADMINISTRATION OVERSEAS, 6 (JULY 67), 165-178.
DETAILED DESCRIPTION OF PROGRESS IN METHODS OF LOCAL
GOVERNMENT IN TANZANIA. INCLUDES ROLE OF POLITICAL PARTIES,
AND METHODS OF REPRESENTATION. PROVIDES ALTERNATIVE TO
SYSTEM OF POWERFUL REGIONAL COMMISSIONER BY ESTABLISHING
A REGIONAL DEVELOPMENT BOARD TO ENLARGE LOCAL COUNCILS'
PARTICIPATION IN DECISIONS.

0623 DUBIN R. ED.
HUMAN RELATIONS IN ADMINISTRATION.
ENGLEWOOD CLIFFS: PRENTICE HALL, 1961, 635 PP., LC#61-9217.
INVESTIGATES HUMAN-RELATIONS ASPECTS OF ORGANIZATIONAL
ADMINISTRATION. INCLUDES SOCIAL SYSTEMS WITHIN BUSINESS AND
OTHER ORGANIZATIONS, MOTIVATION, ADMINISTRATIVE AND EXECU-
TIVE PERSONNEL, SPECIALISTS, WORK SUPERVISORS, BUREAUCRACY,
ORGANIZATIONAL POWER AND STATUS STRUCTURES, COMMUNICATIONS,
DECISION-MAKING, SUBORDINATION, AUTHORITY STRUCTURES, AND
INTERNAL AND EXTERNAL ORGANIZATIONAL ENVIRONMENTS.

0624 DUCKWORTH W.E.
A GUIDE TO OPERATIONAL RESEARCH.
LONDON: METHUEN, 1962, 145 PP.
DEFINES AND EXPLAINS OPERATIONAL RESEARCH AS IT APPLIES
TO THE STUDY OF ADMINISTRATIVE SYSTEMS. SUMMARIZES
TECHNIQUES OF APPLYING SCIENTIFIC METHODOLOGY TO STUDY
OF COMPLEX ORGANIZATIONS, THEIR FUNCTIONS AND PROCESSES.
INCLUDES: STATISTICS, LINEAR PROGRAMMING, QUEUEING, MONTE
CARLO AND SIMULATION, GAME THEORY, CYBERNETICS, AND
DECISION THEORY.

0625 DUCROS B.
"MOBILISATION DES RESSOURCES PRODUCTIVES ET DEVELOPPEMENT."
REV. ECON. FRANC., 14 (NO.2, 63), 216-41.
APPRAISES PATTERNS OF DEVELOPMENT IN UNDERDEVELOPED
COUNTRIES IN RELATION TO INVESTMENTS AND OTHER FACTORS OF
PRODUCTION. FOCUSES ON PROBLEM OF MOBILIZATION OF UNSKILLED
WORKERS. CRITICIZES IDEA OF ACCELERATED DEVELOPMENT.

0626 DUE J.F.
STATE SALES TAX ADMINISTRATION.
CHICAGO: PUBLIC ADMIN SERVICE, 1963, 259 PP., LC#63-20355.
REVIEW AND ANALYSIS OF SALES TAX STRUCTURE, ADMINIS-
TRATION, AND OPERATION IN 33 STATES. AREAS COVERED INCLUDE:
DEVELOPMENT, FORM, AND YIELDS; ADMINISTRATIVE AND PERSONNEL
PRACTICE; PROCESSING OF TAX RETURNS; CONTROL OF DELINQUENTS;
AUDIT; MEASURES OF LIABILITY AND TAX RATES; TREATMENT OF
SERVICES AND REAL PROPERTY; EXEMPTIONS; USES; INFORMATION,
COSTS, AND STUDIES; AND USE BY LOCAL GOVERNMENTS.

0627 DUFTY N.F., TAYLOR P.M.
"THE IMPLEMENTATION OF A DECISION."
ADMINISTRATIVE SCI. Q., 7 (1962), 110-119.
THE AUTHOR TRIES TO ANALYZE AN ORGANIZATIONAL DECISION OF
A LARGELY NONPROGRAMMED TYPE WITHIN A GIVEN FRAMEWORK. EVEN
IN SUCH A RELATIVELY MINOR DECISION AND SHORT TIME SPAN
THIS, THE HIERARCHICAL STRUCTURE OF PROGRAMS IS APPARENT.

0628 DUGGAR G.S.
RENEWAL OF TOWN AND VILLAGE I: A WORLD-WIDE SURVEY OF LOCAL
GOVERNMENT EXPERIENCE.
THE HAGUE: MARTINUS NIJHOFF, 1965, 95 PP.
COMPILATION AND ANALYSIS OF DATA RECEIVED IN ANSWER TO
QUESTIONNAIRES SENT TO 31 COUNTRIES. FACTS DEAL WITH ECO-
NOMIC, FINANCIAL, AND SOCIAL POLICIES OF URBAN RENEWAL,
DISTRICT RENEWAL AND TOWN AND REGIONAL PLANNING, AND
NATION'S GENERAL POLICY FOR RENEWAL ADMINISTRATION.

0629 DUGGAR J.W.
"THE DEVELOPMENT OF MONEY SUPPLY IN ETHIOPIA."
MIDDLE EAST J., 21 (SPRING 67), 255-261.
TRACES THE INCREASING INFLUENCE OF THE ETHIOPIAN NATIONAL
BANK AS A STABILIZING FORCE IN DOMESTIC ECONOMY, FROM ITS
FOUNDING IN 1931 THROUGH THE ITALIAN OCCUPATION TO ITS
REORGANIZATION IN 1959 AND 1964.

0630 DUN J.L. ED.
THE ESSENCE OF CHINESE CIVILIZATION.
PRINCETON: VAN NOSTRAND, 1967, 476 PP., LC#67-25328.
COLLECTION OF ABOUT 200 SKETCHES, OBSERVATIONS, LETTERS,
SHORT STORIES, AND ESSAYS PORTRAYING FULL RANGE OF TRA-

DITIONAL CHINESE CULTURE, THAT IS BEFORE IMPACT OF WESTERN
INFLUENCE. SUBJECT HEADINGS INCLUDE PHILOSOPHY AND RELIGION,
GOVERNMENT, ECONOMICS, AND FAMILY AND SOCIETY.

0631 DUNCOMBE H.S.
COUNTY GOVERNMENT IN AMERICA.
WASHINGTN: NAT ASSN COUNTIES RES, 1966, 288 PP., LC#66-26090
STUDIES CURRENT TRENDS AND STATUS OF ORGANIZATION, FUNC-
TIONS, FINANCING, AND INTERGOVERNMENTAL RELATIONS OF COUNTY
GOVERNMENT. DESCRIBES SERVICES AND FUNCTIONS OF COUNTIES
COMPARATIVELY, AND DISCUSSES SIGNIFICANT DIFFERENCES BETWEEN
THEM, STRESSING URBAN COUNTIES AND BREAKDOWN OF TRADITIONAL
FUNCTIONS WITH GROWING URBANIZATION.

0632 DUNN A.
SCIENTIFIC SELLING AND ADVERTISING.
NEW YORK: INDUSTRIAL PUBL CO, 1919, 119 PP.
PERSONAL ACCOUNT OF SALESMANSHIP BY CORPORATION PRES-
IDENT. CONTAINS METHODS OF SELLING INSURANCE, STOCKS, ADVER-
TISING. SUGGESTS PERSONAL CHARACTERISTICS OF SUCCESSFUL
SALESMAN.

0633 DUNNILL F.
THE CIVIL SERVICE.
NEW YORK: MACMILLAN, 1956, 226 PP.
STUDY OF CIVIL SERVANTS AS INDIVIDUALS, THEIR LIVES,
INFLUENCES, AND THE PRESSURES THEY FACE. CONSIDERED ARE
RECRUITMENT, DEPLOYMENT, CONDITIONING, METHODS, PERSONALITY,
RELATIONS WITH PARLIAMENT AND LAW.

0634 DUROSELLE J.B. ED., MEYRIAT J.
POLITIQUES NATIONALES ENVERS LES JEUNES ETATS.
PARIS: LIBRAIRIE ARMAND COLIN, 1964, 347 PP.
STUDY OF RELATIONS OF FORMER COLONIAL POWERS WITH NEW
NATIONS. DISCUSSES FORMER GREAT COLINIZERS SUCH AS FRANCE
AND GREAT BRITAIN; US AND USSR, WHO HAVE DISAPPROVED OF
COLONIALISM BUT HAVE PRACTICED OTHER FORMS OF DOMINATION;
AND YUGOSLAVIA AND ISRAEL, BOTH MORE DEVELOPED THAN MOST
FORMER COLONIALIZED STATES. CONSIDERS NEW PRESSURES THAT
GREAT POWERS EXERT UPON NEW NATIONS.

0635 DUVERGER M.
POLITICAL PARTIES: THEIR ORGANIZATION AND ACTIVITY IN
THE MODERN STATE.
NEW YORK: WILEY, 1954, 439 PP.
CONDUCTED ON BASIS OF SCIENTIFIC PRINCIPLES OF RESEARCH,
AUTHOR ANALYZES IN DETAIL THE QUESTIONS OF THE ORIGINS OF
PARTIES, PARTY ORGANIZATION, MEMBERSHIP AND LEADERSHIP.
DESCRIBING RELATIONSHIP OF PARTIES TO POLITICAL REGIMES,
AUTHOR FINDS THAT THE ORGANIZATION OF POLITICAL PARTIES
TENDS TO BE ANTI-DEMOCRATIC AND OLIGARCHIC.

0636 DUVERGER M.
LA CINQUIEME REPUBLIQUE.
PARIS: PR UNIV DE FRANCE, 1959, 323 PP.
STUDY OF FIFTH FRENCH REPUBLIC COVERING ITS ESTABLISHMENT
AND SUBSEQUENT CONSTITUTION AND GOVERNMENTAL STRUCTURE.
DISCUSSES POWERS OF PRESIDENT AND PARLIAMENT AND RELATIONS
BETWEEN THEM. DEALS WITH POLITICAL PARTIES AND PRESSURE
GROUPS OPERATING WITH FRENCH POLITICAL SYSTEM.

0637 DWARKADAS R.
ROLE OF HIGHER CIVIL SERVICE IN INDIA.
BOMBAY: POPULAR BOOK DEPOT, 1958, 260 PP.
TREATS PROBLEM OF DEFINING ROLE OF HIGHER CIVIL SERVICE
IN EMERGING, WELFARE-STATE ECONOMY OF INDIA. INITIAL PROBLEM
IS IN TRANSFORMING ESSENTIALLY REGULATORY AND POLICE
MECHANISM OF COLONIAL PERIOD INTO AN INSTRUMENT FOR PLANNING
AND EXECUTING ECONOMIC AND SOCIAL DEVELOPMENT. FURTHER,
DYNAMICS OF POLICY-MAKING AND OF ADMINISTRATIVE-LEGISLATIVE
RELATIONSHIP MUST BE FORMULATED.

0638 DWYER R.J.
"THE ADMINISTRATIVE ROLE IN DESEGREGATION."
SOCIOLOGY AND SOCIAL RESEARCH, 43 (JAN. 59), 183-188.
DESCRIBES PATTERNS OF ADMINISTRATIVE POLICY AND ROLE OF
ADMINISTRATOR IN PUBLIC SCHOOL DESEGREGATION IN MISSOURI
FROM 1955-56. DIRECTION OF DESEGREGATION WAS DETERMINED BY
EXTENT AND NATURE OF OPPOSITION AND TENDED TOWARD SEGMENTAL,
GRADUAL DESEGREGATION. DISCUSSES STATUS OF NEGRO STUDENTS
AND ATTITUDES OF ADMINISTRATORS TO INTEGRATION. MAINTAINS
THAT STRONG LEADERSHIP IS NECESSARY FOR SUCCESS.

0639 DYER F.C., DYER J.M.
BUREAUCRACY VS CREATIVITY.
CORAL GABLES: U OF MIAMI PR, 1965, 153 PP., LC#65-25638.
ANALYSIS ON PRESENT DAY BUREAUCRACY. DISCUSSES ACTIONS OF
BUREAUCRATIC SYSTEM IN COMPLETING ITS DUTY AND ATTAINING
GOALS. DESCRIBES BUREAUCRATIC CHARACTERISTICS, CHAIN OF COM-
MAND, CREATIVE ACTIVITY, MAINTAINING PERSPECTIVE OF PURPOSE.

0640 DYKMAN J.W.
"REVIEW ARTICLE* PLANNING AND DECISION THEORY."
J. OF AM. INST. OF PLANNERS, 27 (NOV. 61), 335-345.
"PLANNING IS ITSELF A KIND OF DECISION-MAKING," REQUIRING
GOALS OF EQUITY AND LEGALITY, SOCIAL ACCEPTABILITY AND EFFI-

CIENCY. ANALYZES HISTORICAL FOUNDATIONS OF DECISION THEORY FROM UTILITARIAN RATIONALITY TO NORMATIVE, QUALITATIVE THEORIES. PLANNERS MUST COMBINE THEORY EXTREMES, NORMATIVE TASKS, AND RATIONAL ACTION.

0641 EAKIN T.C., RICE R.R. ET AL.
"LEGISLATIVE POLITICS -- I AND II THE WESTERN STATES, 1958-1964" (SUPPLEMENT)"
WESTERN POLIT. QUART., 17 (SEPT. 64), 68-78, 88-96 .
     A SERIES OF 12 ARTICLES COVERING LEGISLATIVE POLITICS IN 12 WESTERN STATES INCLUDING ALASKA AND HAWAII. DEALS WITH PERSONAL CHARACTERISTICS OF LEGISLATURE, POLITICAL STRUCTURE, VOTING BEHAVIOR, LEGISLATIVE SESSIONS, POLITICAL PARTIES, AND LOBBYISTS. IN SOME INSTANCES DEALS WITH SPECIFIC INDIVIDUALS AND GROUPS WITHIN THE STATE.

0642 EAST J.P.
COUNCIL-MANAGER GOVERNMENT: THE POLITICAL THOUGHT OF ITS FOUNDER, RICHARD S. CHILDS.
CHAPEL HILL: U OF N CAR PR, 1965, 183 PP., LC#65-19386.
     STUDY IN DEPTH OF RICHARD S CHILDS, WHOSE GREATEST IMPORTANCE LIES IN DEVELOPMENT OF A MODEL AND SUPPORTING DOCTRINE OF COUNCIL-MANAGER GOVERNMENT. ANALYZES FOUNDATIONS OF CHILDS' PHILOSOPHY AND HIS MODEL OF MUNICIPAL GOVERNMENT, EVALUATING ESSENCE AND EFFECTS OF A CLOSED SYSTEM.

0643 EAST KENTUCKY REGIONAL PLAN
PROGRAM 60: A DECADE OF ACTION FOR PROGRESS IN EASTERN KENTUCKY (PAMPHLET)
FRANKFURT, KY: E KY ST PLAN COMN, 1960, 60 PP.
     REPORT OF PLANS FOR REGIONAL DEVELOPMENT OF EASTERN KENTUCKY--PROPOSALS FOR ADMINISTRATIVE AGENCIES, HIGHWAYS, AIR SERVICE, ZONING, WATER DEVELOPMENT; IDEAS FOR IMPROVEMENT OF AGRICULTURE, FORESTRY, TOURIST TRAVEL, INDUSTRY, EDUCATION, HEALTH, AND WELFARE.

0644 EAST KENTUCKY REGIONAL PLAN
PROGRAM 60 REPORT: ACTION FOR PORGRESS IN EASTERN KENTUCKY (PAMPHLET)
FRANKFURT, KY: E KY ST PLAN COMN, 1962, 15 PP.
     REPORT OUTLINING PROGRESS AND ACHIEVEMENTS OF KENTUCKY REGIONAL PLANNING COMMISSION IN FIRST QUARTER OF 1960 DECADE; INCLUDES KEY RECOMMENDATIONS FOR CONTINUING PROGRESS AND INDICATIONS OF OUTLOOK FOR NEAR FUTURE IN EASTERN KENTUCKY.

0645 EASTON S.C.
THE TWILIGHT OF EUROPEAN COLONIALISM.
NEW YORK: HOLT, 1960, 571 PP.
     A SYSTEMATIC ANALYSIS OF POLITICAL MEANS BY WHICH COLONIES OF WESTERN POWERS TRIUMPHED IN THEIR STRUGGLES FOR INDEPENDENCE. CONTAINS VALUABLE INFORMATION ON POLITICAL INSTITUTIONS DEVELOPED IN COLONIES AND THEIR RELATIONSHIP TO THE IMPERIAL LEGACIES LEFT BEHIND BY COLONIAL POWERS. TREATS AT LENGTH INDEPENDENT NATIONS' ABILITY TO SURVIVE AFTER DEPARTURE OF COLONIAL RULERS. PRESENTS GHANA AS LEADING EXAMPLE IN AFRICA.

0646 EATON H.
PRESIDENTIAL TIMBER: A HISTORY OF NOMINATING CONVENTIONS, 1868-1960.
NEW YORK: FREE PRESS OF GLENCOE, 1964, 528 PP., LC#64-16971.
     ACCOUNT OF HOW PRESIDENTIAL CANDIDATES HAVE BEEN NOMINATED, NATIONAL CONVENTIONS, AND POLITICAL EVENTS AND ISSUES AFFECTING PRESIDENTIAL NOMINATIONS FROM 1868-1960. RELIES ON ANECDOTAL MATERIAL IN DISCUSSING MAJOR CONVENTIONS. ATTEMPTS TO DESTROY MYTHS SURROUNDING CERTAIN PRESIDENTIAL NOMINATIONS. INCLUDES BIBLIOGRAPHY AND INDEX.

0647 EATON J.W.
STONE WALLS NOT A PRISON MAKE: THE ANATOMY OF PLANNED ADMINISTRATIVE CHANGE.
SPRINGFIELD: THOMAS, 1962, 212 PP.
     CASE STUDY OF THE REFORM OF THE CALIFORNIA PRISON SYSTEM. EMPHASIZES CORRECTIONAL IDEOLOGY, ADMINISTRATION, GROWTH, AND DEVELOPMENT OF A NEW PROFESSION OF CORRECTION.

0648 ECCLES H.E.
MILITARY CONCEPTS AND PHILOSOPHY.
NEW BRUNSWICK: RUTGERS U PR, 1965, 339 PP., LC#65-14457.
     OUTGROWTH OF LECTURES GIVEN BY REAR ADMIRAL ECCLES AT THE NAVAL WAR COLLEGE. ANALYZES CONCEPTS OF CONFLICT, STRATEGY, LOGISTICS, AND COMMAND IN RELATION TO POLITICO-ECONOMIC FACTORS, INTELLIGENCE, ORGANIZATION, ARMS CONTROL, DECISION-MAKING, COMMUNICATIONS, AND MORALE. SEES MORALE AND LEADERSHIP AS KEY VARIABLES IN CONFLICT SITUATION. CLAIMS US MILITARY PLANNING SUFFERS FROM LACK OF MODERN CONFLICT THEORY.

0649 ECKHOFF T., JACOBSEN K.D.
RATIONALITY AND RESPONSIBILITY IN ADMINISTRATIVE AND JUDICIAL DECISION-MAKING.
COPENHAGEN: MUNKSGAARD INTL, 1960, 45 PP.
     DISCUSSES ROLE OF THOSE LIABLE TO CRITICISM IN DECISION-MAKING PROCESS. FOCUSES ESPECIALLY ON CONNECTION BETWEEN RESPONSIBILITY AND REASONS, EXAMINING VARIOUS DECISION-

MODELS, INCLUDING MEANS-END MODELS AND OTHERS.

0650 ECOLE NATIONALE D'ADMIN.
RECRUITMENT AND TRAINING FOR THE HIGHER CIVIL SERVICE IN FRANCE.
PARIS: ECOLE NATIONALE D'ADMIN, 1956, 134 PP.
     CATALOGS COURSES AND REQUIREMENTS FOR ENTRANCE INTO END. SCHOOL FOR CIVIL SERVICE EXECUTIVES, DISCUSSING GOALS AND METHODS OF SCHOOL IN PREPARING MANAGEMENT PERSONNEL.

0651 ECOLE NATIONALE D'ADMIN
BIBLIOGRAPHIE SELECTIVE D'OUVRAGES DE LANGUE FRANCAISE TRAITANT DES PROBLEMES GOUVERNEMENTAUX ET ADMINISTRATIFS.
PARIS: ECOLE NATIONALE D'ADMIN, 1963.
     FRENCH-LANGUAGE BIBLIOGRAPHY OF 540 ITEMS DESIGNED FOR INSTITUTIONS IN FRENCH-SPEAKING AFRICA RESPONSIBLE FOR THE TRAINING OF ADMINISTRATORS. PREPARED UNDER AUSPICES OF DEVELOPMENT RESEARCH CENTER OF BOSTON UNIVERSITY. INCLUDES INDEX AND ADDRESSES OF PUBLISHING HOUSES CITED. BIBLIOGRAPHY GEARED TO TEACHING, INCLUDES TEXTBOOKS AND WORKS PUBLISHED AFTER WWII.

0652 EDELMAN M.
"GOVERNMENTAL ORGANIZATION AND PUBLIC POLICY."
PUBLIC ADMIN. REV., 12 (FALL 52), 276-283.
     SETS OF PROPOSITIONS CONCERNING RELATIONSHIP BETWEEN INTEREST GROUP INFLUENCE AND DISTRIBUTION OF FUNCTIONS BETWEEN ADMINISTRATIVE ORGANIZATIONS.

0653 EDELMAN M.
THE SYMBOLIC USES OF POWER.
URBANA: U OF ILLINOIS PR, 1964, 201 PP., LC#64-20654.
     GENERAL THEORETICAL TEXT. DISCUSSES REPRESENTATION IN ADMINISTRATIVE AGENCIES WITH REFERENCE TO THE MAINTENANCE AND DEVELOPMENT OF POWER OF AGENCY AND ITS PERSONNEL. HOLDS THAT AN AGENCY WILL HEED ONLY THE WISHES OF THOSE PERSONS OR ORGANIZATIONS WHICH CAN HARM THE AGENCY. IN GENERAL, AGENCIES REPRESENT THE GROUPS THEY ARE INTENDED TO REGULATE RATHER THAN THE PUBLIC INTEREST.

0654 EDELMAN M., FLEMING R.W.
THE POLITICS OF WAGE-PRICE DECISIONS.
URBANA: U OF ILLINOIS PR, 1965, 321 PP., LC#65-10077.
     ANALYSIS OF ATTEMPTS TO RESTRAIN PRICE AND WAGE LEVELS SINCE WWII. APPRAISES GAMUT OF INTERESTS, ORGANIZATIONAL AND POLITICAL PRESSURES THAT EXPLAIN WAGE-PRICE DECISION-MAKING IN POSTWAR EUROPE. EXAMINATION OF GOVERNMENTAL INSTITUTIONS AND PATTERNS OF INTERVENTION, PRIVATE AND PUBLIC ACTION, IDEOLOGIES, POLITICAL PARTIES, STRIKES, ETC.

0655 EDWARDS H.T.
"POWER STRUCTURE AND ITS COMMUNICATION IN SAN JOSE, COSTA RICA."
J. INTER-AMER. STUDIES, 10 (APR. 67), 236-247.
     ATTEMPTS TO SHOW METHODS OF DETERMINING MOST INFLUENTIAL MEMBERS OF STUDIED COMMUNITY AND TO SUGGEST THEIR MEANS OF INTERACTION AND INTERCOMMUNICATION. PROVES THROUGH INTERVIEWS THAT TWO GROUPS EXIST, BELONG TO OPPOSING POLITICAL PARTIES, AND REPRESENT AGRICULTURAL VERSUS PROFESSIONAL INTERESTS. ALSO INDICATES MUCH INTERCOMMUNICATION THROUGH DESIGNATED INTERMEDIARIES.

0656 EGLE W.P.
ECONOMIC STABILIZATION.
PRINCETON: U. PR., 1952, 264 PP.
     EXAMINES POSSIBILITIES OF ECONOMIC STABILIZATION WITHIN THE FRAMEWORK OF A PRIVATE ENTERPRISE SYSTEM. SUGGESTS THAT THIS CAN BE DONE THROUGH FIRM GOVERNMENTAL COMMITMENT TO ECONOMIC STABILIZATION, WHICH, AFTER YEARS OF ENFORCEMENT, WILL BECOME AN INCREASINGLY SELF-SUSTAINING ASPECT OF THE SYSTEM.

0657 EHRMANN H.W.
"FRENCH BUREAUCRACY AND ORGANIZED INTERESTS" (BMR)"
ADMINISTRATIVE SCI. Q., 5 (MAR. 61), 534-555.
     ON THE BASIS OF INTERVIEWS WITH FRENCH CIVIL SERVANTS, INVESTIGATES WHETHER EXTENSIVE ADMINISTRATIVE RULE-MAKING IN THE FOURTH REPUBLIC HAS LIMITED PRESSURE-GROUP INFLUENCE OR WHETHER DIRECT IMPACT OF THE GROUPS HAS IMPINGED ON ADMINISTRATIVE AUTONOMY. IT IS FOUND THAT CERTAIN ADMINISTRATIVE PATTERNS GENERALLY INCREASE THE ACCESS OF ORGANIZED INTERESTS TO AUTHORITATIVE DECISION-MAKING.

0658 EISENSTADT S.N.
"INTERNAL CONTRADICTIONS IN BUREAUCRATIC POLITICS."
COMP. STUD. SOC. AND HIST., 1 (OCT. 58), 58-75.
     THE CHARACTERISTICS AND PURPOSES OF THE RULING ELITES OF CONTRALIZED BUREAUCRATIC POLITICS IN A NUMBER OF PRE-MODERN HISTORICAL SOCIETIES.

0659 EISENSTADT S.N.
"BUREAUCRACY AND BUREAUCRATIZATION."
CURRENT SOCIOLOGY, 7 (1958), 99-164.
     SUMMARIZES THOSE ASPECTS OF BUREAUCRACY WHICH CONSTITUTE TOPICS FOR ANALYSIS IN THE SOCIOLOGICAL "CLASSICS," AND BRIEFLY SURVEYS MAJOR TRENDS IN SPECIALIZED RESEARCH FIELDS.

PROPOSES A SYSTEMATIC METHOD OF EXAMINING THE BUREAUCRACY-
BUREAUCRATIZATION RELATION AND SHOWS ITS RELATION TO STUDY
OF INTERNAL STRUCTURE, NATURE OF BUREAUCRATIC ROLE, AND EF-
FICIENCY OF PERFORMANCE. CLASSIFIED LISTING OF 608 WORKS.

0661 EISENSTADT S.N.
"POLITICAL STRUGGLE IN BUREAUCRATIC SOCIETIES"
WORLD POLITICS, 9 (OCT. 56), 15-36.
BUREAUCRATIC SYSTEMS IN ANCIENT EMPIRES - THE BYZANTINE,
THE CHINESE, AND THE OTTOMAN - AND IN EUROPEAN COUNTRIES IN
THE AGE OF ABSOLUTISM. EACH SYSTEM SAID TO DIFFER ACCORDING
TO THE SOCIOLOGICAL CONTEXT IN WHICH THE BUREAUCRACY
OPERATES.

0662 ELAZAR D.J.
INTERGOVERNMENTAL RELATIONS IN NINETEENTH CENTURY AMERICAN
FEDERALISM (DOCTORAL THESIS)
CHICAGO: U OF CHICAGO, POL DEPT, 1959, 506 PP.
STUDIES ADMINISTRATIVE ASPECTS OF FEDERAL-STATE-LOCAL
RELATIONSHIPS 1790-1900. CLAIMS 19TH-CENTURY GOVERNMENTAL
ACTIVITIES WERE COOPERATIVE ENDEAVORS OPERATING ON A MULTI-
LEVEL BASIS. INDICATES RELATIVELY LITTLE CHANGE IN PATTERN
OF RELATIONSHIPS OVER THE YEARS.

0663 ELDER R.E.
OVERSEAS REPRESENTATION AND SERVICES FOR FEDERAL DOMESTIC
AGENCIES.
NEW YORK: TAPLINGER PUBL CO, 1965, 106 PP., LC#64-24648.
SINCE WORLD WAR TWO THE NUMBER OF US GOVERNMENTAL AGEN-
CIES ENGAGING IN INTERNATIONAL ACTIVITIES HAS PROLIFERATED.
HERE THE HISTORY, STAFFING, CAREER AND PERSONNEL SYSTEMS,
AND PROBLEMS OF INTERAGENCY COORDINATION ARE DISCUSSED.

0664 ELDREDGE H.W.
THE SECOND AMERICAN REVOLUTION.
NEW YORK: WILLIAM MORROW, 1964, 403 PP., LC#64-15473.
EXAMINES PROBLEM OF ELITISM AND PROFESSIONAL GOVERNMENT
IN A DEMOCRATIC SOCIETY. TRACES TRANSITION OF SOCIETY FROM
IDEOLOGY OF LIMITED STATE TO MODERN SETTING IN WHICH SOCIAL,
POLITICAL, AND ECONOMIC INSTITUTIONS MUST BE ADAPTED TO MEET
TECHNOLOGICAL ADVANCES AND THREAT OF TOTALITARIANISM.

0665 ELIAS T.O.
THE NIGERIAN LEGAL SYSTEM.
NEW YORK: HUMANITIES PRESS, 1963, 386 PP.
HISTORICAL STUDY OF IMPACT OF BRITISH COMMON LAW ON
NIGERIAN LEGAL SYSTEM. STUDIES LEGAL PROFESSION, AND COURT
SYSTEMS AND PROCEDURES OF TODAY.

0666 ELKIN A.B.
"OEEC-ITS STRUCTURE AND POWERS."
EUROP. YRB., 4 (58), 96-149.
STUDIES POWER AND JURISDICTION OF OEEC VIS A VIS ITS
MEMBER GOVERNMENTS. COUNCIL IS MAIN ORGAN WITH SUBORDINATE
BODIES, SUCH AS STEERING BOARD FOR TRADE. ORIGINAL
RULE OF UNANIMOUS VOTE HAS CHANGED TO MAJORITY RULE IN
SUBORDINATE ORGANS.

0667 ELKOURI F., ELKOURI E.A.
HOW ARBITRATION WORKS (REV. ED.)
WASHINGTON: BUREAU NATL AFFAIRS, 1960, 498 PP., LC#60-11972.
THROUGH AN EXAMINATION OF ARBITRATION CASES, THE AUTHORS
ANALYZE PROCEDURAL AND SUBSTANTIVE ASPECTS OF THE ARBITRA-
TION PROCESS. DISCUSSION OF LEGAL STATUS, SCOPE, PRECEDENT,
AND CUSTOMS ASSOCIATED WITH LABOR ARBITRATION IN AMERICA.
EVALUATE ROLE OF ARBITRATION AS AN INDUSTRIAL INSTITUTION.

0668 ELLIOTT O.
MEN AT THE TOP.
LONDON: HARPER & ROW, 1959, 246 PP., LC#59-10579.
ANALYZES PUBLIC POLICY AND US INDUSTRIAL LEADERS WHO HAVE
BECOME NATIONAL LEADERS. INTERVIEWED 250 INDUSTRIAL
EXECUTIVES IN US CITIES. FEELS THAT PUBLICITY MISREPRESENTS
THEM; GIVES ACCOUNT OF THEIR RESPONSES TO VALUE JUDGMENTS,
ETC., AND STUDIES SUB-CULTURES IN WHICH THEY LIVE AND WORK.

0669 ELLIOTT S.D.
IMPROVING OUR COURTS.
NEW YORK: OCEANA PUBLISHING, 1959, 190 PP., LC#59-14271.
DISCUSSIONS OF JUDICIAL ADMINISTRATION AND OPERATION OF
US COURT SYSTEMS WHICH STRESS NEED FOR COORDINATION AND
UNIFICATION OF LEGAL SYSTEM. DISCUSSES GENERAL IMPROVEMENTS
MADE IN JUDICIAL ADMINISTRATION IN US 1906-56 AND PROVIDES
DETAILED DISCUSSIONS OF IMPROVEMENTS MADE 1952-58.

0670 ELLIOTT W.
UNITED STATES FOREIGN POLICY, ITS ORGANIZATION AND CON-
TROL.
NEW YORK: COLUMB. U. PR., 1952, 288 PP.
PROBLEMS ON SUBJECT ARISE FROM GOVERNMENT STRUCTURE AS
INFLUENCED BY CONSTITUTION, ECONOMICS, POLITICS AND THE MIL-
ITARY. CRITICISES PARTY DISCIPLINE AND FAULTY LEGISLATIVE-
EXECUTIVE RELATIONSHIP. URGES ASSESSMENT OF LONG-TERM IN-
TERESTS.

0671 EMERSON R.

"THE EROSION OF DEMOCRACY."
J. ASIAN STUD., 20 (NOV. 60), 1-8.
DESCRIBES CHARACTERISTICS IN SOCIETY NECESSARY FOR DEVEL-
OPMENT OF DEMOCRACY. TREATS DEMOCRATIC PRACTICES IN ASIA AND
AFRICA WITH REFERENCE TO THEIR INSTITUTIONS. COMPARES
SUCCESS AND FAILURE OF DEMOCRATIC SYSTEMS IN THE LIGHT OF
ASIAN ENVIRONMENT WITH PARTICULAR EMPHASIS ON ECONOMIC
CONDITIONS.

0672 EMERSON R.
"POLITICAL MODERNIZATION."
DENVER: U. PR. (SOC. SCI. FOUND.), 1963, 30 PP., $1.00.
DEALS SPECIFICALLY WITH THE ISSUES OF THE SINGLE PARTY
SYSTEM, OR THE MILITARY RULE THAT HAS BEEN IMPOSED IN
SEVERAL COUNTRIES, AND THE 'EVIDENT VIRTUES' OF SUCH
SYSTEMS FOR THE DEVELOPING NATION.

0673 EMMERICH H.
"COOPERATION AMONG ADMINISTRATIVE AGENCIES."
AMER. J. OF ECO. AND SOC., 15 (APR. 56), 237-244.
ADMINISTRATIVE AGENCIES ON ALL LEVELS ARE COOPERATING
MORE AND MORE WITH EACH OTHER TO SERVE THE PUBLIC INTEREST.
OFTEN THIS COOPERATION IS FACILITATED BY A NONGOVERNMENTAL
GROUP WHICH COORDINATES THE ACTIVITIES OF THE GOVERNMENT
AGENCIES.

0674 ENDACOTT G.B.
GOVERNMENT AND PEOPLE IN HONG KONG 1841-1962: A CONSTITU-
TIONAL HISTORY.
HONG KONG: HONG KONG UNIV PRESS, 1964, 263 PP.
HISTORY OF HONG KONG'S CONSTITUTIONAL GOVERNMENT. POINTS
OUT CITY'S DISTINCTIVENESS AMONG BRITISH COLONIES.
SHOWS APPLICATION OF BRITISH IDEAS OF GOVERNMENT TO AN OVER-
WHELMING CHINESE COMMUNITY, AND ATTEMPT TO ADAPT COLONIAL
INSTITUTIONS SET UP IN HONG KONG TO ADMINISTRATIVE
NEEDS OF BRITISH COMMUNITIES LIVING IN THE TREATY PORTS.

0675 ENKE S. ED.
DEFENSE MANAGEMENT.
ENGLEWOOD CLIFFS: PRENTICE HALL, 1967, 404 PP., LC#67-10540.
ESSAYS EXAMINING CHANGES IN DECISION-MAKING AT THE PENTA-
GON, APPLICATION OF COST-BENEFIT ANALYSIS TO SPECIFIC DE-
FENSE PROGRAMS, PROBLEMS IN RESEARCH AND DEVELOPMENT, AND
ECONOMIC IMPACT OF DEFENSE SPENDING. ALSO DISCUSS PROBLEMS
OTHER FEDERAL AGENCIES WILL FACE IN SHIFTING TO COST-EFFEC-
TIVENESS TECHNIQUES.

0676 ENSOR R.C.K.
COURTS AND JUDGES IN FRANCE, GERMANY, AND ENGLAND.
LONDON: OXFORD U PR, 1933, 144 PP.
A SHORT STUDY OF LEGAL ADMINISTRATION IN FRANCE AND
GERMANY AND A COMPARATIVE ANALYSIS OF BRITISH PRACTICE.
OUTLINES THE COMPOSITION OF THE TWO CONTINENTAL COURT
SYSTEMS. COMPARES METHODS OF FILLING JUDICIAL POSTS, COURT
PROCEDURES IN CRIMINAL AND CIVIL CASES, METHODS OF APPEAL,
AND ULTIMATE JUDICIAL AUTHORITY IN THE THREE COUNTRIES.

0677 EPSTEIN F.T.
EAST GERMANY: A SELECTED BIBLIOGRAPHY (PAMPHLET)
WASHINGTON: LIBRARY OF CONGRESS, 1959, 55 PP., LC#59-60084.
SOME 350 ANNOTATED US GOVERNMENT DOCUMENTS, BIBLIOGRA-
PHIES, STATISTICAL HANDBOOKS, WEST GERMAN DOCUMENTS, PER-
IODICALS, LEGISLATION, MONOGRAPHS, AND BOOKS ON EAST GERMANY
PUBLISHED 1947-58. ARRANGED TOPICALLY AND BY TYPE
OF SOURCE, WITH MOST IN GERMAN. SUBJECT INDEX.

0678 EPSTEIN F.T. ED., WHITTAKER C.H. ED.
THE AMERICAN BIBLIOGRAPHY OF RUSSIAN AND EAST EUROPEAN
STUDIES FOR 1964.
BLOOMINGTON: INDIANA U PR, 1966, 119 PP., LC#58-63499.
BIBLIOGRAPHICAL LISTING OF BOOKS AND ARTICLES PUBLISHED
IN ENGLISH IN THE US IN 1964. ALSO INCLUDES BOOKS PUBLISHED
IN ENGLISH THROUGHOUT THE WORLD WITH THE EXCEPTION OF RUSSIA
AND EAST EUROPE. TRANSLATIONS NOT INCLUDED. ITEMS GROUPED
BY SUBJECT AND COUNTRY. CONTAINS AUTHOR INDEX. 2,260 EN-
TRIES.

0679 EPSTEIN L.D.
"POLITICAL STERILIZATION OF CIVIL SERVANTS: THE UNITED
STATES AND GREAT BRITAIN."
PUBLIC ADMIN. REV., 10 (FALL 50), 281-290.
WARNS AGAINST USING BRITISH MODEL OF ADMINISTRATION AS
ALTERNATIVE TO HATCH ACT. POLITICAL ACTIVITY OF CIVIL
SERVANTS DIFFERS IN EACH SOCIETY. DIFFERENT LEVELS OF PUBLIC
SPIRIT, POLITICAL MATURITY, AND SOCIAL EQUANIMITY MUST BE
CONSIDERED.

0680 ERDMANN H.H. ED.
"ADMINISTRATIVE LAW AND FARM ECONOMICS."
JOURNAL OF FARM ECONOMICS, 44 (DEC. 62), 1627-1658.
ANTHOLOGY OF REPORTS AND DISCUSSIONS ON ADMINISTRATIVE
PROCESSES ON NATIONAL AND LOCAL LEVEL AND ROLE OF JUDICIAL
REVIEW IN ADMINISTRATIVE PROCESS. ALL REPORTS ARE RELATED TO
IMPACT ON AGRICULTURAL INDUSTRY.

0681 ESCUELA SUPERIOR DE ADMIN PUBL

INFORME DEL SEMINARIO SOBRE SERVICIO CIVIL O CARRERA
ADMINISTRATIVA.
SAN JOSE, CR: ESCUELA ADMIN PUBL, 1962, 358 PP.
REPORT OF SEMINAR ON PUBLIC ADMINISTRATION IN CENTRAL
AMERICA. DISCUSSES CIVIL SERVICE STRUCTURE, RECRUITMENT,
CIVIL SERVANT EVALUATION, JOB CLASSIFICATIONS, AND ETHICS
AND DISCIPLINE REQUIRED IN PUBLIC ADMINISTRATION.

0682 ETIENNE G.
"'LOIS OBJECTIVES' ET PROBLEMES DE DEVELOPPEMENT DANS LE
CONTEXTE CHINE-URSS."
TIERS-MONDE, 4 (NO.16, 63), 609-27.
DESCRIBES SEVERAL ASPECTS OF MOST RECENT CHINESE ECONOMIC
POLICY. SEEKS TO CLARIFY CONTENT OF WHAT RUSSIANS TERM
OBJECTIVE STRUCTURAL LAW. FOCUSES ON GEOGRAPHIC, DEMO-
GRAPHIC AND SOCIO-ECONOMIC DIFFERENCES CURRENTLY HINDERING
SINO-SOVIET RELATIONS.

0683 ETZIONI A.
COMPLEX ORGANIZATIONS: A SOCIOLOGICAL READER.
NEW YORK: HOLT RINEHART WINSTON, 1961, 497 PP., LC#61-7443.
ARTICLES ON "SOCIAL UNITS WHICH ARE PREDOMINANTLY
ORIENTED TO THE ATTAINMENT OF SPECIFIC GOALS," DEALING
WITH THEORY, CONCEPTUAL AND APPLIED, GOALS, STRUCTURES
(INCLUDING THOSE OF UNIONS, CHURCHES, HOSPITALS SCHOOLS),
AND ORGANIZATIONAL CHANGE, AS WELL AS THE POSITIONS OF
ORGANIZATIONS WITHIN THE FRAMEWORK OF SOCIETY AND METHODO-
LOGICAL DISCUSSIONS.

0684 ETZIONI A.
"A COMPARATIVE ANALYSIS OF COMPLEX ORGANIZATIONS: ON POWER,
INVOLVEMENT AND THEIR CORRELATES."
NEW YORK: FREE PRESS OF GLENCOE, 1961.
CONTRIBUTION TO FORMULATION OF MODELS FOR ANALYSIS OF
VARIOUS ORGANIZATIONAL TYPES THROUGH STUDY OF CONTROL AND
RELATED VARIABLES. USES NUMEROUS PUBLISHED AND UNPUBLISHED
STUDIES FOR DEVELOPMENT AND ILLUSTRATION OF PROPOSITIONS.
COMPLIANCE, POWER, AND INVOLVEMENT DEFINED AS CONCEPTS ES-
SENTIAL TO SOCIAL ORDER. INCLUDES CLASSIFICATION, TYPOLOGY
OF ORGANIZATIONS ON VARIABLES SCHEME. LARGE BIBLIOGRAPHY.

0685 ETZIONI A.
MODERN ORGANIZATIONS.
ENGLEWOOD CLIFFS: PRENTICE HALL, 1964, 120 PP., LC#64-17073.
DEALS WITH STRUCTURE AND VARIOUS THEORIES APPLICABLE
TO IT, WITH ORGANIZATIONAL CONTROL AND LEADERSHIP (INCLUD-
ING REPRESENTATIONAL ASPECTS OF INFORMAL LEADERS), THE
CONCEPT OF ADMINISTRATIVE AND PROFESSIONAL AUTHORITY, AS
WELL AS THE RELATION OF MODERN ORGANIZATIONS TO VARIOUS
PUBLICS AND CLIENT SYSTEMS AND NOTES RELATIVE LACK OF
CONSUMER REPRESENTATION.

0686 ETZIONI A.
POLITICAL UNIFICATION* A COMPARATIVE STUDY OF LEADERS AND
FORCES.
NEW YORK: HOLT RINEHART WINSTON, 1965, 346 PP., LC#65-14882.
DISCUSSES THE CONDITIONS UNDER WHICH NATIONS FORM POLITI-
CAL COMMUNITIES WHICH EVOLVE TOWARD MEMBERSHIP IN A WORLD
COMMUNITY. INCLUDES THE CONDITIONS THAT BLOCK SUCH EVOLU-
TION. ANALYSIS ATTEMPTS TO FORM REGIONAL COMMUNITIES IN
THE CARIBBEAN, WESTERN EUROPE, SCANDINAVIA, AND
THE MIDDLE EAST.

0687 EVAN W.M., ZELDITCH M., JR.
"A LABORATORY EXPERIMENT ON BUREAUCRATIC AUTHORITY"
AMER. SOCIOLOGICAL REV., 26 (DEC. 61), 883-893.
PURPOSE IS TO SEPARATE RATIONAL AND LEGAL COMPONENTS OF
WEBER'S THEORY OF BUREAUCRATIC AUTHORITY, AND TO VARY
DIMENSION OF AUTHORITY OF KNOWLEDGE WHILE HOLDING CONSTANT
AUTHORITY OF OFFICE. ORGANIZATION SIMULATED. TESTS WHETHER,
IF OFFICIAL LACKS KNOWLEDGE, SUBORDINATES WOULD QUESTION HIS
AUTHORITY AND REDUCE PERFORMANCE AND CONFORMITY TO RULES AND
COMMANDS. EXAMINES EFFECT OF DIFFERENCES OF TREATMENT.

0688 EVANS L.H.
"SOME MANAGEMENT PROBLEMS OF UNESCO."
INT. ORGAN., 17 (WINTER 63), 76-90.
PROBLEMS CONSIDERED ARE UNESCO'S FUNCTIONS, THE ORGANI-
ZATION OF ITS SECRETARIAT, RELATIONS OF DIRECTOR-GENERAL
WITH LEGISLATIVE ORGANS, AND PERSONNEL ADMINISTRATION.

0689 EVANS M.S.
THE FRINGE ON TOP.
NEW YORK: AMER FEATURE, 1962, 223 PP.
ANALYSIS OF POLITICAL POWER AND POLICIES OF RADICAL LEFT
IN AMERICAN GOVERNMENT. STRESSES DANGER OF INCREASED POWER
AND INFLUENCE OF LIBERAL EXTREMISM, AND CRITICIZES KENNEDY
ADMINISTRATION FOR ITS ALLEGED ENCOURAGEMENT OF THIS ELE-
MENT. FOCUSES ON RADICAL LEFT'S ATTEMPT TO IMPOSE POLITICAL
AND ECONOMIC CENTRALIZATION ON AMERICAN SOCIETY AND ITS POL-
ICY OF CONCILIATION TOWARD USSR.

0690 EVANS R.H.
COEXISTENCE: COMMUNISM AND ITS PRACTICE IN BOLOGNA,
1945-1965.
SOUTH BEND: U OF NOTRE DAME, 1967, 225 PP.
ANALYZES BOLOGNA AS PARADIGM OF PEACEFUL COEXISTENCE OF
COMMUNISM AND CAPITALISM. STUDIES MOTIVATION AND CONTENT OF
SPECIFIC LOCAL BRAND OF COMMUNISM, AND REACTION AND RESPONSE
TO IT BY SURROUNDING MIDDLE-CLASS MILIEU. EXAMINES STRENGTHS
AND WEAKNESSES OF COMMUNIST ADMINISTRATION. ANALYZES REASONS
FOR MODUS VIVENDI AND EXPOSTULATES ON FUTURE NEEDS.

0691 EVERETT R.O. ED., LEACH R.H. ED.
URBAN PROBLEMS AND PROSPECTS.
DURHAM, NC: DUKE U, SCH OF LAW, 1965, 221 PP.
COLLECTION OF ESSAYS ANALYZING PAST, PRESENT, AND FUTURE
CONCEPTS OF URBAN RENEWAL AND PROSPECTS FOR SPEEDIER AND
MORE EFFICIENT SOLUTION OF URBAN PROBLEMS. WRITERS AGREE
THAT URBAN RESIDENTS MUST BE MADE AWARE OF DIFFICULTIES
FACING THEM AND BE PERSUADED THAT LONG-TERM INTERESTS ARE
BEST SERVED BY ACTING NOW.

0692 EWING D.W.
THE MANAGERIAL MIND.
NEW YORK: FREE PRESS OF GLENCOE, 1964, 218 PP., LC#64-16957.
EXAMINES MANAGERIAL ENVIRONMENT IN RELATION TO CREATIVI-
TY, EFFICIENCY, NONCONFORMITY, LEVELS OF KNOWLEDGE, ETC.
DISCUSSES DEVELOPMENT OF MANAGERIAL MIND AND ITS IMPLICATION
FOR SOCIETY AT LARGE.

0693 FABAR R.
THE VISION AND THE NEED: LATE VICTORIAN IMPERIALIST AIMS.
NEW YORK: HUMANITIES PRESS, 1966, 150 PP.
EXPLORES INFLUENCE, NATURE, AND ACCURACY OF KIPLING'S
VIEWS ON BRITISH EMPIRE, TOGETHER WITH THOSE OF LATE 19TH-
CENTURY IMPERIALISTS. ATTEMPTS TO UNDERSTAND "LATE VICTORIAN
MOOD" AND SIMULTANEOUS ELEMENTS OF EXPANSION AND WITHDRAWAL
IN LATE BRITISH IMPERIALISTIC PERIOD.

0694 FABREGA J.
"ANTECEDENTES EXTRANJEROS EN LA CONSTITUCION PANAMENA."
CENTRO, 3 (FEB. 67), 25-29.
EXAMINES PANAMANIAN CONSTITUTION OF 1946 AND FOREIGN
INFLUENCES UPON ITS FINAL FORM. STUDIES COLOMBIAN
CONSTITUTION OF 1886, SOCIAL ASPECTS OF MEXICAN CONSTITUTION
OF 1917, AND CONSTITUTIONS OF CUBA AND URUGUAY IN 1940.

0695 FABRYCKY W.J., TORGERSEN P.E.
OPERATIONS ECONOMY INDUSTRIAL APPLICATIONS OF OPERATIONS
RESEARCH.
ENGLEWOOD CLIFFS: PRENTICE HALL, 1966, 486 PP., LC#66-19247.
EXPLAINS SIGNIFICANCE OF ANALYTICAL APPROACH TO DECISION-
MAKING AND HELPS MANAGERIAL STAFF TO BECOME PROFICIENT IN
APPLICATION OF QUANTITATIVE MODELS IN OPERATIONAL SYSTEMS.
DISCUSSES MODELS INVOLVING ECONOMY OF PRODUCTION, CONTROL
OF OPERATIONS, PROCUREMENT AND INVENTORY, WAITING
LINE, AND PROGRAMMING FOR ECONOMY OF OPERATIONS.

0696 FAHRNKOPF N. ED., LYNCH M.C. ED.
STATE AND LOCAL GOVERNMENT IN ILLINOIS (PAMPHLET)
URBANA: U OF ILLINOIS PR, 1965, 47 PP.
TOPICALLY ARRANGED, WORKS LISTED COVER 1954-64 IN FIELDS
OF STATE, LOCAL, AND INTERGOVERNMENTAL PROCESSES. FIRST TWO
SECTIONS INCLUDE CONSTITUTION, LEGISLATURE, COURT SYSTEMS,
ADMINISTRATION, SERVICES, VOTING, AND ECONOMY. LAST SECTION
LISTS WORKS IN INTERLOCAL, INTERSTATE, AND FEDERAL-STATE-
LOCAL RELATIONSHIPS.

0697 FAHS C.B.
"POLITICAL GROUPS IN THE JAPANESE HOUSE OF PEERS."
AM. POL. SCI. REV., 34 (OCT. 40), 896-919.
TRACES HISTORICAL DEVELOPMENT OF JAPANESE HOUSE OF PEERS,
AND NOTES FAILURE OF HOUSE TO DEVELOP ALONG NON-PARTISAN
LINES. CITES EVOLVEMENT OF SIX DISTINCT, ANTAGONISTIC
SPLINTER GROUPS.

0698 FAHS C.B.
"GOVERNMENT IN JAPAN."
NEW YORK: NYC COL, INST PAC REL, 1940.
PART OF THE DOCUMENTATION OF AN INQUIRY ORGANIZED BY THE
INSTITUTE OF PACIFIC RELATIONS INTO THE PROBLEMS ARISING
FROM THE CONFLICT IN THE FAR EAST. ITS PURPOSE WAS TO OFFER
AN IMPARTIAL AND CONSTRUCTIVE ANALYSIS OF THE SITUATION IN
FAR EAST WITH VIEW TO INDICATING MAJOR ISSUES TO BE CONSID-
ERED IN ADJUSTMENT OF INTERNATIONAL RELATIONS. ANALYSIS OF
ECONOMIC AND POLITICAL CONDITIONS. ANNOTATED BIBLIOGRAPHY.

0699 FAINSOD M.
"RECENT DEVELOPMENTS IN SOVIET PUBLIC ADMINISTRATION."
J. OF POLITICS, 11 (NOV. 49), 679-714.
DESCRIPTION OF THE ORGANIZATION AND CONTROL OF THE SOVIET
ADMINISTRATIVE SYSTEM. THE ADMINISTRATOR IS UNDER CONSTANT
SURVEILLANCE BY MANY PEOPLE AND ORGANIZATIONS TO INSURE
ABSOLUTE LOYALTY TO PARTY POLICY.

0700 FAINSOD M.
HOW RUSSIA IS RULED (REV. ED.)
CAMBRIDGE: HARVARD, CTR RUSS RES, 1964, 648 PP., LC#63-11418
FIRST SCHOLARLY STUDY OF SOVIET GOVERNMENT OF THE POST-
STALIN ERA TO 1962 TO LOOK INTO FORCES AND FACTORS THAT PRO-
DUCED BOLSHEVIK REVOLUTION AND LATER TRANSFORMED ITS CHAR-

ACTER, TO TRACE THE PARTY'S CHANGING ROLE, TO DESCRIBE PATTERNS AND INSTRUMENTS OF RULE, TO PORTRAY THE IMPACT OF STATE CONTROL OF FARM AND FACTORY, AND TO APPRAISE THE PROBLEMS AND PROSPECTS OF THE SOVIET POLITICAL SYSTEM.

0701 FAIRLIE J.A., KNEIR C.M.
COUNTY GOVERNMENT AND ADMINISTRATION.
NEW YORK: CENTURY CO, 1930, 585 PP., LC#30-1116.
EXPANSION OF AN EARLIER WORK ON SAME TOPIC. REVIEWS INCREASING IMPORTANCE OF COUNTY GOVERNMENT, BOTH IN SCOPE OF OLDER FUNCTIONS AND IN EXPANSION OF ACTIVITIES IN NEW DIRECTIONS. REVIEWS RELFECTION OF THIS DEVELOPMENT IN GREATER VOLUME OF STATUTORY LEGISLATON AND INCREASING NUMBER OF JUDICIAL OPINIONS BROUGHT BEFORE COURTS. ATTENTION GIVEN TO ADMINISTRATION AND OPERATION OF GOVERNMENTAL ACTIVITIES.

0702 FALK L.A., MUSHRUSH G.J., SKRIVANEK M.S.
ADMINISTRATIVE ASPECTS OF GROUP PRACTICE.
PITTSBURGH: UNIVERSITY PR, 1964, 100 PP., LC#64-16014.
LISTS 222 REFERENCES RELATED TO ADMINISTRATIVE ASPECTS OF GROUP HEALTH PLANS PAID FOR BY INSTALLMENTS THAT WERE PUBLISHED 1950-64. ENTRIES ARRANGED BY SUBJECT AND AUTHOR.

0703 FALL B.B.
"THE VIET-MINH REGIME."
ITHACA: CORNELL U, DEPT ASIAN ST, 1956.
STUDY OF VIET-MINH REGIME IN ORGANIZATIONAL AND ADMINISTRATIVE ASPECTS. INSTITUTIONAL ANALYSIS SUPPORTED BY CULTURAL RESEARCH. AUTHOR DISCUSSES PERSONALITY AND CHARACTER OF LEADERS, PARTICULARLY HO CHI MINH, IDEOLOGICAL FOUNDATIONS OF RULING PARTY, ECONOMIC DEVELOPMENT, ORGANIZATION OF ARMY. SELECTED BIBLIOGRAPHY CONFINED TO WORKS SPECIALIZING ON VIETMINH REGIME IN FRENCH, ENGLISH, AND RUSSIAN.

0704 FARBER W.O., GEARY T.C., CAPE W.H.
GOVERNMENT OF SOUTH DAKOTA.
SIOUX FALLS: MIDWEST BEACH CO, 1962, 211 PP.
CONCISE SURVEY OF STRUCTURE, ACTIVITIES, AND PROBLEMS OF SOUTH DAKOTA GOVERNMENT. INCLUDES DISCUSSION OF STATE CONSTITUTION; POLITICAL PARTIES; COMPOSITION AND PROCEDURE OF LEGISLATURE; GOVERNOR; THE COURTS; STATE FINANCE; PUBLIC HEALTH, EDUCATION, AND WELFARE. POINTS OUT THOSE AREAS IN WHICH CIVIC ACTION IS MOST URGENTLY NEEDED.

0705 FARNSWORTH B.
WILLIAM C. BULLITT AND THE SOVIET UNION.
BLOOMINGTON: INDIANA U PR, 1967, 244 PP., LC#67-13022.
ACCOUNT OF BULLITT'S DIPLOMATIC CONTRIBUTION TO RUSSIAN-AMERICAN POLICY DURING THE WILSON ADMINISTRATION AND AS ADVISER TO FDR ON SOVIET AFFAIRS. INCLUDES BULLITT'S WORK AT PARIS PEACE CONFERENCE, NEGOTIATIONS WITH LENIN, DENOUNCEMENT OF THE VERSAILLES TREATY, AND SERVICE AS AMBASSADOR TO USSR AND FRANCE. BIOGRAPHICAL IN NATURE, BOOK EMPHASIZES BULLITT'S DISILLUSIONMENTS WITH STALIN.

0706 FARRIS M.T. ED., MCELHINEY P.T. ED.
MODERN TRANSPORTATION: SELECTED READINGS.
BOSTON: HOUGHTON MIFFLIN, 1967, 416 PP.
VARIOUS VIEWPOINTS ON GENERAL PRINCIPLES OF TRANSPROTATION: ECONOMICS, MANAGEMENT, REGULATION, AND PUBLIC POLICY. READINGS SELECTED FROM ACADEMIC AND TRADE JOURNALS. DESIGNED FOR USE IN BASIC TRANSPORTATION COURSE.

0707 FATOUROS A.A., KELSON R N.
CANADA'S OVERSEAS AID.
TORONTO: CAN INST OF INTL AFF, 1964, 123 PP.
STUDY OF CANADIAN FOREIGN AID, 1950-62, BASED UPON CONFERENCE ON CANADIAN OVERSEAS AID, 1962. STUDIES TYPES, AIMS AND MOTIVES, DISTRIBUTION, AMOUNT AND FORMS, ADMINISTRATION OF AID. RECOMMENDS CONTINUED AID PROGRAM.

0708 FAUNT J.R. ED.
A CHECKLIST OF SOUTH CAROLINA STATE PUBLICATIONS.
COLUMBIA: S CAROLINA ARCH LIB.
ANNUAL SHORT-TITLE CHECKLIST OF PUBLICATIONS OF THE DEPARTMENTS, INSTITUTIONS, AND OTHER AGENCIES OF NORTH CAROLINA. FIRST PUBLISHED IN 1950. PUBLICATIONS LISTED ALPHABETICALLY ACCORDING TO NAMES OF ISSUING AGENTS. ADDITIONAL BIBLIOGRAPHIC INFORMATION GIVEN WHEN AVAILABLE.

0709 FAYERWEATHER J.
THE EXECUTIVE OVERSEAS: ADMINISTRATIVE ATTITUDES AND RELATIONSHIPS IN A FOREIGN CULTURE.
SYRACUSE: SYRACUSE U PRESS, 1959, 195 PP., LC#59-11259.
STUDIES RELATIONSHIPS BETWEEN US AND FOREIGN EXECUTIVES. SURVEYS OPINIONS ABOUT ADMINISTRATIVE RELATIONSHIPS IN MANY COUNTRIES AND OBSERVES SELECTED MANAGERIAL GROUPS IN MEXICO. DISCUSSES CULTURAL DIFFERENCES AND PROPOSES CONCEPTUAL PLAN TO ALLEVIATE DIFFICULTIES IN INTERNATIONAL BUSINESS TRANSACTIONS.

0710 FEERICK J.D.
FROM FAILING HANDS: THE STUDY OF PRESIDENTIAL SUCCESSION.
NEW YORK: FORDHAM U PR, 1965, 368 PP., LC#65-14917.
DISCUSSION OF HISTORY OF PRESIDENTIAL SUCCESSION FROM

COLONIAL GOVERNMENT TO PRESENT INCLUDING OCCASIONS WHEN SUCCESSION TOOK OR SHOULD HAVE TAKEN PLACE. OPENS WITH DISCUSSION OF KENNEDY'S ASSASSINATION AND JOHNSON'S SUCCESSION. LAST PORTION DEALS WITH SUGGESTED IMPROVEMENTS OF SYSTEM AND DEVELOPMENT OF OFFICE OF VICE-PRESIDENT.

0711 FENN DH J.R., GRUNEWALD D., KATZ R.N.
BUSINESS DECISION MAKING AND GOVERNMENT POLICY.
ENGLEWOOD CLIFFS: PRENTICE HALL, 1966, 386 PP.
CASEBOOK DEALS WITH AREAS OF COOPERATION BETWEEN CORPORATE GIANTS AND FEDERAL AGENCIES AND THE INDIVIDUAL AND HIS LOCAL PLANNING BOARD. ANALYZES CASES INVOLVING GOVERNMENTAL GRANTING OF LICENSES AND PROVISION OF SERVICES. DISCUSSES PROBLEMS OF ACCESS TO VARIOUS DIVISIONS AND LEVELS OF GOVERNMENT. CONTENDS THAT PARTICIPATION OF GOVERNMENT IN BUSINESS AFFAIRS IS EXPANDING.

0712 FERGUSON H.
"3-CITY CONSOLIDATION."
NATIONAL CIVIC REV., 56 (MAY 67), 255-259.
REPORT ON ATTEMPT TO CONSOLIDATE CITIES OF ROCK ISLAND, MORLINE, & EAST MORLINE UNDER CIVIC LEADERSHIP AND PRIVATE FINANCING. ARGUES THAT MUNICIPAL CONSOLIDATION IS IMPORTANT MEASURE IN MEETING METROPOLITAN PROBLEMS.

0713 FESLER J.W.
"ADMINISTRATIVE LITERATURE AND THE SECOND HOOVER COMMISSION REPORTS" (BMR)
AM. POL. SCI. REV., 51 (MAR. 57), 135-157.
ATTEMPTS TO PLACE HOOVER COMMISSION REPORTS IN CONTEXT OF OFFICIAL AND UNOFFICIAL EFFORTS IN PAST 25 YEARS TO GIVE ORDER AND MEANING TO STUDY OF PUBLIC ADMINISTRATION. ANALYZES CONTRIBUTION OF SUCH REPORTS TO KNOWLEDGE AND POLICY OF ORGANIZATION. STATES THAT HOOVER COMMISSION REPORTS WERE ALREADY OUTDATED BY THE TIME OF THEIR PUBLICATION.

0714 FESLER J.W.
"FRENCH FIELD ADMINISTRATION: THE BEGINNINGS."
COMP. STUD. SOC. HIST., 5 (OCT. 62), 76-111.
USES A DEVELOPMENTAL FOCUS TO EXAMINE IN DETAIL THE EARLY STAGES OF FRENCH FIELD ADMINISTRATION (LATE 12TH TO 14TH CENT.) AND ITS CONTRIBUTION TO THE DEVELOPMENT OF THE NATION-STATE.

0715 FESLER J.W. ED.
THE FIFTY STATES AND THEIR LOCAL GOVERNMENTS.
NEW YORK: ALFRED KNOPF, 1967, 603 PP., LC#66-12816.
ESSAYS ON VARIOUS ASPECTS OF STATE GOVERNMENT, INCLUDING A BRIEF HISTORY OF STATE GOVERNMENT TO 1950, FUNCTIONS OF STATE AND LOCAL GOVERNMENTS, INTERGOVERNMENTAL RELATIONS, ELECTIONS, POLICY-MAKING, COURT SYSTEMS, AND ADMINISTRATIVE ORGANIZATION. EMPHASIZE THE FUNCTIONS AND RELATIONSHIPS OF STATE AND LOCAL GOVERNMENTS. CONCLUDE WITH DISCUSSION OF FUTURE CHARACTER OF FEDERALISM.

0716 FIELD G.L.
THE SYNDICAL AND CORPORATIVE INSTITUTIONS OF ITALIAN FASCISM
NEW YORK: COLUMBIA U PRESS, 1938, 209 PP.
EXAMINES FASCISM IN ITALY BY CONSIDERING ITS THREE MAJOR INSTITUTIONS: DICTATORSHIP, SYNDICATE, AND CORPORATION. THE FIRST HAD THOROUGH LEGAL CONTROL, THE SECOND PROVIDED STATE CONTROL OF CAPITAL AND LABOR, AND THE THIRD HAD CONTROL OF VARIOUS ECONOMIC ACTIVITIES. WRITTEN AT PEAK OF FASCISM'S POPULARITY, WORK ATTEMPTS TO BE ANALYTIC.

0717 FIGANIERE J.C.
BIBLIOTHECA HISTORICA PORTUGUEZA.
LISBON: NA TIPOGRAFIA DO PANORAMA, 1850, 349 PP.
BIBLIOGRAPHY OF PORTUGUESE BOOKS AND DOCUMENTS ON PORTUGUESE POLITICAL, CIVIL, AND RELIGIOUS HISTORY. ALSO INCLUDES PORTUGUESE POSSESSIONS.

0718 FIKS M.
PUBLIC ADMINISTRATION IN ISRAEL (PAMPHLET)
NEW YORK: PERSONNEL RES ASSN, 1958, 29 PP.
ANALYSIS OF CIVIL SERVICE AND OTHER PUBLIC EMPLOYMENT IN ISRAEL, INCLUDING EDUCATIONAL SYSTEM. EXAMINES STRUCTURE AND PERSONNEL OF PUBLIC ADMINISTRATION AND BENEFITS OF PUBLIC EMPLOYMENT.

0719 FINCHER F.
THE GOVERNMENT OF THE UNITED STATES.
ENGLEWOOD CLIFFS: PRENTICE HALL, 1967, 310 PP., LC#67-10169.
DISCUSSES FRAMEWORK AND FUNCTION OF US GOVERNMENT. INCLUDES BASIC LEGISLATIVE AND POLITICAL PROCESSES, COURTS, LOBBYING, AND PRESSURE GROUPS. EXAMINES GOVERNMENTAL ACTIVITY IN VARIOUS CONTEXTS, INCLUDING CIVIL RIGHTS AND LIBERTIES, BUSINESS-LABOR RELATIONS, PEACE AND NATIONAL SECURITY, AND HEALTH, EDUCATION, AND WELFARE. EMPHASIZES CONTEMPORARY PROBLEMS AND POLITICAL PHILOSOPHIES.

0720 FINK M.
A SELECTIVE BIBLIOGRAPHY ON STATE CONSTITUTIONAL REVISION (PAMPHLET)
ALBUQUERQUE: U NEW MEX LAW SCH, 1966, 26 PP.

LIST OF SELECTED MATERIALS PUBLISHED SINCE JANUARY 1, 1963, DEALING WITH STATE CONSTITUTIONAL REVISION AND SUBSTANTIVE AREAS OF THE CONSTITUTIONAL SYSTEM. INDEX OF AUTHORS AND EDITORS. ABOUT 400 BOOKS, PERIODICAL ARTICLES, AND GOVERNMENT DOCUMENTS.

0721 FINNISH POLITICAL SCIENCE ASSN
SCANDINAVIAN POLITICAL STUDIES (VOL. I)
HELSINKI: FINNISH POL SCI ASSN, 1966, 341 PP.
YEARBOOK OF POLITICAL RESEARCH ON PARTIES, PRESSURES, AND IDEOLOGICAL STRUCTURES IN FINLAND AND FINNISH ELECTIONS. ANALYZES RECENT ELECTIONS, GIVES GENERAL BACKGROUND ON POLITICAL RESEARCH IN SCANDINAVIA, AND PRESENTS CLASSIFIED BIBLIOGRAPHY OF 850 BOOKS, ARTICLES, AND GOVERNMENT REPORTS FROM 1960-64 IN ENGLISH AND MODERN EUROPEAN LANGUAGES, ON POLITICAL THEORY, ADMINISTRATION, AND FOREIGN RELATIONS.

0722 FIRMALINO T.
THE DISTRICT SCHOOL SUPERVISOR VS. TEACHERS AND PARENTS: A PHILIPPINE CASE STUDY (PAMPHLET) (BMR)
INDIANAPOLIS: BOBBS-MERRILL, 1962, 18 PP.
RELATES UNSUCCESSFUL ATTEMPT OF PHILIPPINE DISTRICT SCHOOL SUPERVISOR TO INTRODUCE COMMUNITY SCHOOL SYSTEM IN RURAL AREA. RESISTANCE BY TEACHERS, PARENTS, AND TOWN OFFICIALS LED TO DEFEAT OF PLAN. CASE STUDY ILLUMINATES CONFLICTS.

0723 FISCHER F.C.
THE GOVERNMENT OF MICHIGAN.
NEW YORK: ALLYN AND BACON, 1965, 230 PP.
STUDY OF MICHIGAN STATE LEGISLATURE AND LAW-MAKING, ADMINISTRATIVE DEPARTMENTS, COURT STRUCTURE, LOCAL GOVERNMENT, AND STATE EDUCATION. DISCUSSES POLITICAL PARTIES, FINANCE OF GOVERNMENT, AND STATE INSTITUTIONS.

0724 FISHER M.J., STARRATT E.E.
"PARTIES AND POLITICS IN THE LOCAL COMMUNITY."
NEW YORK: NATL COUN SOC STUDIES, 1945.
STRESSES FUNCTIONING OF POLITICAL PARTIES IN LOCAL GOVERNMENT, THE OPERATION OF "INVISIBLE" GOVERNMENT IN THIS AREA. DEALS WITH STRUCTURE OF PARTY ORGANIZATION AND POLITICAL WORK PROCESSES, SUFFRAGE, REGISTRATION, AND ELECTIONS. DESIGNED AS RESOURCE AND TEACHING AID. BIBLIOGRAPHY OF BOOKS ON GOVERNMENT, PROBLEMS OF DEMOCRACY, AND RELATED SUBJECTS.

0725 FISHER S.N. ED.
THE MILITARY IN THE MIDDLE EAST: PROBLEMS IN SOCIETY AND GOVERNMENT.
COLUMBUS: OHIO STATE U. PR., 1963, 138 PP., $4.75.
DISCUSSION OF STATE DEPARTMENT POLICY-PLANNING IN MIDDLE EAST, ANALYSIS OF GENERAL TRENDS IN M.E. POLITICS AND OF SPECIFIC POLITICAL-MILITARY SITUATIONS IN INDIVIDUAL COUNTRIES.

0726 FISK E.K. ED.
NEW GUINEA ON THE THRESHOLD; ASPECTS OF SOCIAL, POLITICAL, AND ECONOMIC DEVELOPMENT.
LONDON: LONGMANS, GREEN & CO, 1966, 290 PP.
PAPERS ON ECONOMICS, SOCIAL PROBLEMS, AND POLITICS OF SITUATION IN PAPUA, NEW GUINEA, AT PRESENT AND DURING NEXT DECADE. COVERS HISTORICAL BACKGROUND, ECONOMIC STRUCTURE, RESOURCES, TRADE, DEMOGRAPHY, EDUCATION, LITERACY, SOCIAL CHANGE, ROLE OF WOMEN, EXPATRIATES, GROWTH OF TERRITORIAL ADMINISTRATION, AND ADVANCE TO RESPONSIBLE GOVERNMENT.

0727 FISK W.M.
ADMINISTRATIVE PROCEDURE IN A REGULATORY AGENCY: THE CAB AND THE NEW YORK-CHICAGO CASE (PAMPHLET)
INDIANAPOLIS: BOBBS-MERRILL, 1964.
STUDIES ECONOMIC REGULATION EXERCISED BY CIVIL AERONAUTICS BOARD OVER US AIR TRANSPORT INDUSTRY. EXAMINES CAB'S POWER IN DETERMINING AIR ROUTES, SERVICE POINTS, AND NATURE OF SERVICE. EMPHASIZES PROCEDURAL ASPECTS OF NEW YORK-CHICAGO CASE OF 1953 WHICH LED TO OVERHAUL OF STRUCTURE OF AIR ROUTES.

0728 FITZSIMMONS T., MALOF P. ET AL.
"USSR: ITS PEOPLE, ITS SOCIETY, ITS CULTURE."
NEW HAVEN: HUMAN REL AREA FILES, 1960.
ANALYSIS DEFINING DOMINANT SOCIOLOGICAL, POLITICAL, AND ECONOMIC ASPECTS OF FUNCTIONING SOCIETY, AND IDENTIFICATION OF PATTERNS OF CHARACTERISTIC BEHAVIOR. EMPHASIS ON SOCIAL ORGANIZATION, VALUES AND PATTERNS OF LIVING; INCLUDES MATERIAL ON POLITICAL AND ECONOMIC ORGANIZATION OF SOCIETY. CONTAINS EXTENSIVE SELECTED AND SOMEWHAT SPECIALIZED BIBLIOGRAPHY.

0729 FLORENCE P.S.
ECONOMICS AND SOCIOLOGY OF INDUSTRY; A REALISTIC ANALYSIS OF DEVELOPMENT.
NEW YORK: WATTS, 1964, 258 PP.
CONTAINS ANALYSIS OF INDUSTRIAL DEVELOPMENT AND RELATION OF SOCIOLOGY AND ECONOMICS TO ITS STUDY. EXAMINES INDUSTRY'S ECONOMIC AND SOCIAL MOBILITY, URBANIZATION AND INDUSTRIAL LOCATION, ORGANIZATIONAL SYSTEMS, INDUSTRIAL GOVERNMENT,

INDUSTRIALIZATION IN UNDERDEVELOPED COUNTRIES, SOCIAL LIMITS ON ECONOMIC DEVELOPMENT, AND SOCIAL RESEARCH.

0730 FLORES R.H.
CATALOGO DE TESIS DOCTORALES DE LAS FACULTADES DE LA UNIVERSIDAD DE EL SALVADOR.
EL SALVADOR: U DE EL SALVADOR, 1960, 620 PP.
CATALOG OF DOCTORAL THESES PRESENTED FROM 1878 TO 1960 AT UNIVERSITY OF EL SALVADOR. ENTRIES ARRANGED BY FACULTY AND CLASSIFIED BY DEWEY CLASSIFICATION SYSTEM.

0731 FLORINSKY M.T.
"TRENDS IN THE SOVIET ECONOMY."
CURR. HIST., 47 (NOV. 64), 266-271.
WHEN DEALING WITH USSR DIFFICULT TO RESIST TEMPTATION TO COMPARE WITH USA. POPULAR GROUND FOR COMPARISON IS RATE OF ECONOMIC GROWTH WHICH AUTHOR (AND OTHERS FAMILIAR WITH STATISTICAL METHODS) ASSERTS IS AN UNSOUND METHOD.

0732 FLYNN E.J.
YOU'RE THE BOSS.
NEW YORK: VIKING PRESS, 1947, 241 PP.
AUTOBIOGRAPHY OF BOSS FLYNN, NYC MACHINE BOSS, IN WHICH HE ATTEMPTS TO EXPLAIN WORKINGS OF A POLITICAL MACHINE. CLAIMS MACHINES ARE NECESSARY TO AMERICAN FORM OF GOVERNMENT, AND THAT REPRESENTATION IS AS EFFECTIVE THROUGH A MACHINE AS ANY OTHER WAY. DESCRIBES POLITICS IN NEW YORK IN 1930'S AND HIS RELATIONS WITH FDR.

0733 FOLSOM M.B., PRICE D.K., ROLL E.
BETTER MANAGEMENT OF THE PUBLIC'S BUSINESS (PAMPHLET)
NEW YORK: COMM FOR ECO DEV, 1964, 39 PP.
EXAMINES ADMINISTRATION OF GOVERNMENTAL AGENCIES, AREAS IN GREATEST NEED OF CHANGE, AND METHODS BY WHICH BUSINESSMEN MAY ACCOMPLISH THESE CHANGES. INCLUDES DISCUSSION OF COMMITTEE FOR ECONOMIC DEVELOPMENT AND ITS ROLE IN ACCOMPLISHING REFORMS IN GOVERNMENTAL ADMINISTRATION.

0734 FOLTZ W.J.
FROM FRENCH WEST AFRICA TO THE MALI FEDERATION.
NEW HAVEN: YALE U PR, 1965, 235 PP., LC#65-11178.
STUDIES WEST AFRICAN POLITICAL CONTEXT, 1956-60. CONCLUDES THAT THE CRUCIAL DETERMINANTS OF MALI'S FORMATION WERE THE POLITICAL LEADERS IN THE CONSTITUENT TERRITORIES WHO ATTEMPTED TO USE THE FEDERATION AS A MEANS OF GUARANTEEING AND INCREASING CONTROL OVER THEIR RESPECTIVE STATES' DOMESTIC POLITICAL PROCESSES. WHEN THE FEDERATION THREATENED THIS CONTROL THE LEADERS WITHDREW THEIR STATES.

0735 FONTENEAU J.
LE CONSEIL MUNICIPAL: LE MAIRE-LES ADJOINTS.
PARIS: EDITIONS OUVRIERES, 1964, 142 PP.
ANALYZES RESPONSIBILITIES OF TOWN COUNSELORS, DEPUTY MAYORS, AND MAYORS IN FRANCE. CONSIDERS ORIGINS, STRUCTURES, AND RESPONSIBILITIES OF "COMMUNES." DEFINES AND DISCUSSES ROLE OF TOWN COUNCIL, FINANCES, AND TOWN COUNCIL PROGRAMS.

0736 FORBES A.H. ED.
CURRENT RESEARCH IN BRITISH STUDIES.
MARQUETTE: NORTHERN MICH U PR, 1964, 88 PP.
LIST OF 700 US AND CANADIAN SCHOLARS ENGAGED IN RESEARCH IN BRITISH AND IMPERIAL HISTORY. SCHOLARS TOGETHER WITH RESEARCH INTERESTS ARE LISTED BY MAJOR HISTORICAL PERIODS AND BY SUBJECT. INCLUDES BIOGRAPHICAL STUDIES; PARLIAMENTARY GOVERNMENT; ADMINISTRATION;CONSTITUTIONAL AND LEGAL HISTORY; CULTURAL, LITERARY, AND RELIGIOUS HISTORY; AND EXTERNAL AFFAIRS.

0737 FORD A.G.
THE GOLD STANDARD 1880-1914: BRITAIN AND ARGENTINA.
LONDON: OXFORD U PR, 1962, 200 PP.
STUDIES OPERATIONS OF GOLD STANDARD IN EACH COUNTRY PRIOR TO WWI. EMPHASIZES STRUCTURE OF INTERNATIONAL ACCOUNTS AND SYSTEMS, POINTING OUT TRADE, ETC., BETWEEN THESE NATIONS AS AN EXAMPLE. THEORIZES FROM NEW APPROACH BALANCE OF PAYMENTS' PROBLEMS AND THEIR SOLUTIONS WHICH LED TO SUCCESS OF GOLD STANDARD IN ENGLAND AND ITS FAILURE IN ARGENTINA.

0739 FORD FOUNDATION
REPORT OF THE STUDY FOR THE FORD FOUNDATION ON POLICY AND PROGRAM.
DETROIT: FORD FOUND., 1949, 139 PP.
MAJOR OBJECTIVES ARE TO ARRIVE AT A CLEARER UNDERSTANDING OF THE MEANING OF HUMAN WELFARE AND TO CONSIDER THE WAYS IN WHICH IT IS MOST THWARTED AND THREATENED. PROPOSES PROGRAMS WHICH THE FOUNDATION MIGHT SPONSOR AND OUTLINES PROCEDURES.

0740 FORGAC A.A.
NEW DIPLOMACY AND THE UNITED NATIONS.
NEW YORK: PAGEANT PR, 1965, 173 PP., LC#65-24549.
TRACES EVOLUTION OF DIPLOMACY AND EXAMINES FUNCTIONS OF DIPLOMATS AND FOREIGN OFFICE. DESCRIBES CEREMONIALS, TITLES AND PRECEDENTS, AND ANALYZES DIPLOMATIC PRACTICES OF UK, GERMANY, USSR, AND FRANCE. EXAMINES IMPACT OF UN ON MODERN DIPLOMACY.

0741 FORRESTAL J. ED., KALBUS E.C. ET AL.
"THE NAVY: A STUDY IN ADMINISTRATION."
PUBLIC ADMIN. REV., (FALL 46), 1-64.
COLLECTION OF SHORT ARTICLES BY HIGH-RANKING NAVY
PERSONNEL ON VARIOUS TYPES OF NAVY DEPARTMENT ADMINISTRATIVE
ACTIVITY, SUCH AS SHIP-BUILDING, PROCUREMENT, PRODUCTION,
AND STATISTICAL CONTROLS. DISCUSSES BUREAU SYSTEM OF
ORGANIZATION AS MEANS OF RESTRICTING OUTSIDE INFLUENCE ON
NAVY DECISIONS. OUTSIDE GROUPS REPRESENTED IN NAVY AFFAIRS
ARE CONGRESS, BUREAU OF BUDGET, AND SOMETIMES WHITE HOUSE.

0742 FORTES A.B., WAGNER J.B.
HISTORIA ADMINISTRATIVA, JUDICIARIA E ECLESIASTICA DO RIO
GRANDE DO SUL.
PORTO ALEGRE: EDITORA GLOBO, 1963, 496 PP.
ANALYZES ADMINISTRATIVE, JUDICIAL, AND ECCLESIASTICAL
DEVELOPMENT OF IMPORTANT BRAZILIAN STATE OF RIO GRANDE DO
SUL. DISCUSSES MUNICIPAL AND PROVINCIAL ADMINISTRATION OF
STATE IN COLONIAL TIMES AND SINCE INDEPENDENCE. EXAMINES
FORMATION AND ACTION OF JUDICIARY IN POLITICAL PROCESS.
COVERS CATHOLIC CHURCH'S HIERARCHY AND STRUCTURE IN STATE
DURING SAME PERIOD.

0743 FOSS P.
POLITICS AND GRASS: THE ADMINISTRATION OF GRAZING ON THE
PUBLIC DOMAIN.
SEATTLE: U OF WASHINGTON PR, 1960, 236 PP., LC#60-11822.
"OUTLINE OF THE HISTORY OF THE PUBLIC DOMAIN....AND A
DETAILED EXAMINATION OF THE FORMATION AND ADMINISTRATION OF
PUBLIC POLICY FOR THE CONTROL AND REGULATION OF THE FEDERAL
RANGE UNDER THE TAYLOR GRAZING ACT."

0744 FOSS P.O.
REORGANIZATION AND REASSIGNMENT IN THE CALIFORNIA HIGHWAY
PATROL (PAMPHLET)
INDIANAPOLIS: BOBBS-MERRILL, 1962, 28 PP.
DESCRIBES REORGANIZATION PROCESS WITHIN QUASI - MILITARY
CALIFORNIA HIGHWAY PATROL IN 1959. OBJECTIVES WERE TO
EXPEDITE COMMUNICATION, DECENTRALIZE DECISION-MAKING, AND
IMPROVE TRAINING PROGRAM. WAS ACCOMPLISHED WITH MINIMAL
PERSONAL DISRUPTION AMONG PATROL MEMBERS.

0745 FOX G.H., FOINER C.A.
"PERCEPTIONS OF THE VIETNAMESE PUBLIC ADMINISTRATION SYSTEM"
ADMINISTRATIVE SCI. Q., 8 (MAR. 64), 443-481.
EXAMINATION OF CIVIL SERVANTS' ROLES IN POLITICAL SYSTEM,
RELATIONS WITH OTHER BUREAUCRATS, ROLES OF POLITICAL ELITE,
AND STUDY OF HOW CIVIL SERVANTS VIEW THEIR OWN POSITION.

0746 FOX K.A., SENGUPTA J.K., THORBECKE E.
THE THEORY OF QUANTITATIVE ECONOMIC POLICY WITH APPLICATIONS
TO ECONOMIC GROWTH AND STABILIZATION.
NEW YORK: SIGNET BOOKS, 1966, 514 PP.
IN TEXTBOOK FORM PRESENTS BASIC THEORY OF QUANTITATIVE
ECONOMIC POLICY AND SUPPLIES MOTIVATIONAL AND EMPIRICAL
CONTENT FOR THEORY. DISCUSSES PARTICULAR ECONOMETRIC OR
STABILIZATION MODELS FROM PERSPECTIVE OF POLICY-MAKING.
SHOWS HOW THEORY MAY BE EXTENDED INTO REGIONAL SUBDIVISIONS
OF A NATIONAL ECONOMY. DISCUSSES MODELS OF ECONOMIC GROWTH
AND DEVELOPMENT PLANNING.

0747 FOX R.G.
"FAMILY, CASTE, AND COMMERCE IN A NORTH INDIAN MARKET TOWN."
ECO. DEV. AND CULTURAL CHANGE, 15 (APR. 67), 297-314.
ANALYZES HOW THE SOCIAL STRUCTURE OF TEZIBAZAR, A NORTH
INDIAN MARKET TOWN, CREATES A COMMERCIAL CASTE, THE BANI-
YAS, WHO DETERMINE THE STYLE OF COMMERCIAL ACTIVITY. THE
STEREOTYPED IMAGE OF THE BANIYAS INCLUDES MISERLINESS, PAS-
SIVITY, ANONYMITY, AND ISOLATION, ATTITUDES REINFORCED BY
THE CONTEMPT OF NON-BANIYAN CASTES TOWARD BUSINESS. SHOWS
HOW PREJUDICES DELEGATE ECONOMIC CONTROL TO AN OUTGROUP.

0748 FRANCIS R.G., STONE R.C.
SERVICE AND PROCEDURE IN BUREAUCRACY.
MINNEAPOLIS: U OF MINN PR, 1956, 201 PP., LC#56-9876.
CASE STUDY OF A LOCAL OFFICE OF THE LOUISIANA DIVISION OF
THE FEDERAL EMPLOYMENT SECURITY SYSTEM. STUDIES CONTENT OF
OFFICIAL DOCUMENTS, RELATIONS BETWEEN MEMBERS OF THE
ORGANIZATION, AND ATTITUDES TOWARD CLIENTELE.

0749 FRANK T.
A HISTORY OF ROME.
NEW YORK: HOLT, 1923, 613 PP.
COMPREHENSIVE SURVEY OF 'POLITICAL AND CULTURAL FORTUNES
OF THE ANCIENT REPUBLIC WHICH IN SO MANY RESPECTS DID
PIONEER WORK IN DEMOCRATIC GOVERNMENT.' TOPICS INCLUDE:
PUNIC WARS BETWEEN ROME AND CARTHAGE, SOCIETY IN DAYS OF
CATO, ROMAN CONSTITUTION, GRACCHAN REFORMS, THE FIRST
TRIUMVIRATE, THE CIVIL WAR, AUGUSTUS' EMPIRE, DOMITIAN, M.
AURELIUS, CONSTANTINE AND CAUSES OF ROME'S DECLINE.

0750 FRANKE W.
THE REFORM AND ABOLITION OF THE TRADITIONAL CHINESE EXAMINA-
TION SYSTEM.
CAMBRIDGE: HARV CTR ASIAN STUD, 1960, 100 PP.
STUDIES ONE ASPECT OF INSTITUTIONAL CHANGE - TRAINING OF
OFFICIALS AND CIVIL SERVICE EXAMINATIONS - AS EXAMPLE OF
GENERAL ADJUSTMENTS AS CHINA MOVED FROM TRADITIONAL AGRI-
CULTURAL NATION TO MODERN INDUSTRIALIZED ONE. BEGINS WITH
EARLY REFORM MOVEMENTS BEFORE 1900 AND TRACES THEM THROUGH
ABOLITION OF EXAMINATION SYSTEM IN 1905.

0751 FRANKEL S.H.
"ECONOMIC ASPECTS OF POLITICAL INDEPENDENCE IN AFRICA."
INT. AFF., 36 (OCT. 60), 440-446.
RAISES SERIOUS DOUBTS REGARDING EFFECTS OF POLITICAL IND-
EPENDENCE ON ECONOMY OF EMERGENT AFRICAN STATES. EXPLAINS
THEORY IN ECONOMIC TERMS OF ABSOLUTE INDEPENDENCE COUPLED
WITH ABSOLUTE ISOLATION. SHOWS HOW NEW AFRICA IS ESTABLISH-
ING ECONOMIC RELATIONSHIP WITH REST OF THE WORLD, BUT FEELS
PRESENT CONDITIONS IN AFRICA OFFER LITTLE INDUCEMENT FOR
CAPITAL AND SKILLED ASSISTANCE FROM ABROAD.

0752 FREEMAN J.L.
"THE BUREAUCRACY IN PRESSURE POLITICS."
ANN. ACAD. POL. SOC. SCI., 319 (SEPT. 58), 10-19.
ADMINISTRATIVE AGENCIES SERVE THEIR OWN AND OFTEN THEIR
CLIENTELE'S SPECIFIC INTEREST WITHOUT MUCH REGARD TO THE
PUBLIC WELFARE. THERE IS NOT SUFFICIENT CONTROL OF
ADMINISTRATIVE AGENCIES.

0753 FREUND G.
"ADENAUER AND THE FUTURE OF GERMANY."
INT. J., 18, (AUTUMN 63), 458-468.
ASSERTS THAT ADENAUER, AS OUTSTANDING GERMAN STATESMAN OF
TWENTIETH CENTURY, HAS HELPED GERMANY ACHIEVE MAJOR STATUS
IN WESTERN DEFENSE POLICY. HOWEVER, OTHERS WILL DETERMINE
GERMANYS FUTURE ROLE.

0754 FREYRE G.
THE PORTUGUESE AND THE TROPICS.
LISBON: INTL CONG HIST OF DISCOV, 1961, 296 PP.
DISCUSSES PORTUGUESE METHODS AND CONCEPTS OF INTEGRATING
INHABITANTS OF TROPIC AREAS INTO NEW COMPLEX CULTURAL AND
SOCIAL PATTERNS. EMPHASIZES VARIOUS ART FORMS RESULTING FROM
PROCESS OF INTEGRATING NON-EUROPEANS INTO EUROPEAN-BASED
CULTURE.

0755 FRIED R.C.
THE ITALIAN PREFECTS.
NEW HAVEN: YALE U PR, 1963, 343 PP., LC#63-13960.
STUDY ATTEMPTS TO OUTLINE MAIN STAGES OF ITALIAN FIELD
DEVELOPMENT, WHICH AUTHOR SITUATES WITHIN DEVELOPING
PREFECTORAL SYSTEM. PERHAPS FIRST ATTEMPT TO ANALYZE AND
DESCRIBE ANY PREFECTORAL SYSTEM OTHER THAN FRENCH.

0756 FRIEDLANDER W.A.
INDIVIDUALISM AND SOCIAL WELFARE.
NEW YORK: FREE PRESS OF GLENCOE, 1962, 251 PP., LC#61-62519.
ANALYSIS OF SYSTEM OF SOCIAL SECURITY AND SOCIAL WELFARE
IN FRANCE. HISTORY OF CHARITIES, CHILD WELFARE, PUBLIC AND
PRIVATE SOCIAL AGENCIES.

0757 FRIEDMAN L.
"DECISION MAKING IN COMPETITIVE SITUATIONS"
MANAGEMENT TECHNOLOGY, 1 (SEPT. 60), 85-93.
METHOD OF DECISION-MAKING IN COMPETITIVE SITUATIONS IS
DISCUSSED WHICH ATTEMPTS TO USE ANALYSIS IN MORE RATIONAL
MANNER THAN IN METHODS GIVEN BY MATHEMATICAL GAME THEORY.
METHOD BASED ON TWO CONTROVERSIAL PRINCIPLES: THERE IS ONLY
ONE OPTIMAL COURSE OF ACTION AND ONE OBJECTIVE FUNCTION IN
ANY COMPETITIVE SITUATION. THIS OBJECTIVE FUNCTION IS THE
MAXIMIZATION OF EXPECTED UTILITY.

0758 FRIEDMAN L. ED.
SOUTHERN JUSTICE.
NEW YORK: PANTHEON BOOKS, 1965, 306 PP., LC#65-14581.
ANTHOLOGY OF ARTICLES BY LAWYERS INVOLVED IN CIVIL
RIGHTS CASES IN THE SOUTH. ARTICLES DEAL WITH SPECIFIC
PHASE OF ADMINISTRATION OF JUSTICE IN SOUTH: HOW LEGAL
INSTITUTIONS HAVE BEEN USED AGAINST NEGRO STRUGGLE FOR
CIVIL RIGHTS AND WHAT HAS BEEN DONE TO END THIS LEGAL
ABUSE.

0759 FRIEDMANN W.
METHODS AND POLICIES OF PRINCIPAL DONOR COUNTRIES IN PUBLIC
INTERNATIONAL DEVELOPMENT FINANCING: PRELIMINARY APPRAISAL.
NEW YORK: COLUMBIA U LAW SCHOOL, 1962, 49 PP.
ANALYZES FOREIGN AID MACHINERY IN US, UK, WEST GERMANY,
AND FRANCE, AS WELL AS EEC, SHOWING THERE IS AGREEMENT ON
PRE-EMINENCE OF NEED FOR TECHNICAL ASSISTANCE, BUT
DISAGREEMENT ON CONCEPT AND PRINCIPLES OF CAPITAL AID FOR
DEVELOPING COUNTRIES. POINTS OUT NATURE OF OTHER ISSUES
UPON WHICH NATIONS AGREE AND DIFFER. SUGGESTS FURTHER
TASKS FOR MULTILATERAL COORDINATION.

0760 FRIEDMANN W.G. ED., KALMANOFF G. ED.
JOINT INTERNATIONAL BUSINESS VENTURES.
NEW YORK: COLUMB. U. PR., 1961, 558 PP.
EXAMINES PROBLEMS AND PROSPECTS OF PARTNERSHIP IN BUSI-
NESS ASSOCIATIONS BETWEEN DEVELOPED AND LESS DEVELOPED COUN-
TRIES. OUTLINES TYPES OF JOINT VENTURES, SURVEYS THEIR IM-

PORTANCE IN RELATION TO TOTAL FOREIGN INVESTMENTS, ANALYZES THEIR RESULTS IN INDIVIDUAL COUNTRIES, AND REVIEWS GOVERNMENTAL REGULATIONS AFFECTING THEM.

0761 FRYE R.J.
GOVERNMENT AND LABOR: THE ALABAMA PROGRAM.
UNIVERSITY: U ALA, BUR PUBL ADM, 1960, 157 PP.
ANALYZES ADMINISTRATION OF SPECIFIC PUBLIC FUNCTIONS BY ALABAMA'S STATE GOVERNMENT. CHAPTERS DEVOTED TO CHILD LABOR, WORKMEN'S COMPENSATION, SAFETY AND INSPECTION, MEDIATION, STATE EMPLOYMENT SERVICE, AND UNEMPLOYMENT COMPENSATION. DISCUSSES HISTORY, PROGRAM, AND ORGANIZATION AND MANAGEMENT OF EACH.

0762 FRYE R.J.
HOUSING AND URBAN RENEWAL IN ALABAMA.
UNIVERSITY: U ALA, BUR PUBL ADM, 1965, 103 PP.
DISCUSSES RELATIONSHIPS BETWEEN FEDERAL AND CITY GOVERNMENTS IN SPHERE OF URBAN RENEWAL, EMPHASIZING HISTORICAL AND LEGAL FRAMEWORK OF PROGRAM, ORGANIZATIONAL ARRANGEMENTS AT BOTH LEVELS FOR IMPLEMENTATION OF PROGRAMS, PROGRAM CONTENT, AND PROCESSES THROUGH WHICH INTERGOVERNMENTAL ASPECTS OF THE PROGRAMS MANIFEST THEMSELVES.

0763 FRYKENBURG R.E.
"STUDIES OF LAND CONTROL IN INDIAN HISTORY: REVIEW ARTICLE."
ECO. DEV. AND CULTURAL CHANGE, 15 (APR. 67), 347-353.
REVIEWS FOUR STUDIES OF THE RELATIONSHIPS OF SOCIAL STRUCTURE AND LAND CONTROL IN INDIA BY AUTHORS HABIB, GUPTA, KUMAR, AND MUKHERJEE. CRITICIZES ALL FOUR FOR THEIR POORLY DEFINED USE OF EUROPEAN TERMINOLOGY SUCH AS "PEASANT," "TENURE," "RIGHT," ETC., WHICH MAY NOT BE VALID IN CONTEXT OF INDIAN CULTURE. CITES KUMAR STUDY AS BEST ANALYSIS OF INTERLOCKED SOCIAL RIGIDITY AND ECONOMIC RESTRICTION.

0764 FUCHS R.F.
"FAIRNESS AND EFFECTIVENESS IN ADMINISTRATIVE AGENCY ORGANIZATION AND PROCEDURES."
INDIANA LAW J., 36 (FALL 60), 1-50.
REFORM OF ORGANIZATION AND PROCEDURES SHOULD BE MADE TO FURTHER PROTECT INDIVIDUAL RIGHTS AND THE PUBLIC INTEREST AND TO INCREASE EFFICIENCY. ON THE WHOLE, ADMINISTRATIVE AGENCIES HAVE GREATLY IMPROVED IN THESE AREAS IN RECENT YEARS.

0765 FULLER C.D.
TRAINING OF SPECIALISTS IN INTERNATIONAL RELATIONS.
WASHINGTON: AMER. COUNCIL EDUC., 1957, 136 PP.
BELIEVES MORE EMPHASIS ON ECONOMIC GEOGRAPHY AND BEHAVIORAL SCIENCES MUST BE MADE. URGES DEVELOPMENT OF SPECIALIZED SKILLS, OTHER THAN RESEARCH AND ANALYSIS, SUCH AS WRITTEN AND ORAL EXPRESSION. EVALUATION OF USA GRADUATE-SCHOOL PROGRAMS IN INTERNATIONAL RELATIONS.

0766 FURNISS E.S.
"WEAKNESSES IN FRENCH FOREIGN POLICY-MAKING."
PRINCETON: CENT. INT. STUD., 1954, 52 PP.
ATTEMPTS TO SHOW CONSEQUENCES WITHIN POLITICAL STRUCTURE OF FOURTH FRENCH REPUBLIC THAT HAVE FOLLOWED UPON FAILURE OF FRENCH TO UNITE BEHIND INSTITUTIONAL SYSTEM AFTER WORLD WAR TWO. RELATES THIS FAILURE TO WEAK FOREIGN POLICY AND REEXAMINATION OF EUROPEAN POLICY BY US.

0767 FURNISS E.S.
FRANCE, TROUBLED ALLY.
NEW YORK: HARPER, 1960, 512 PP.
FOCUSES ON POLICIES OF AND CONTINUITY BETWEEN FOURTH AND FIFTH REPUBLICS. ASSESSES DE GAULLE'S DOMESTIC AND FOREIGN PROGRAMS. STRESSES NEED TO STUDY FRENCH FOREIGN POLICY IN RELATION TO THE GALLIC SOCIAL AND ECONOMIC SITUATION IN WHICH IT WAS CREATED.

0768 FYFE H.
THE BRITISH LIBERAL PARTY.
LONDON: ALLEN & UNWIN, 1928, 272 PP.
SKETCHES DEVELOPMENT OF LIBERAL PARTY 1868-1925, DISCUSSING REASONS FOR ITS ORGANIZATION, ITS DEBT TO OTHER PARTIES, ITS INTERNAL STRUGGLES, ITS RISE TO POWER, AND ITS STATE IN 1927. ITS RELATION TO SOCIALISM, THE ANGLICAN CHURCH, AND THE CONSERVATIVE PARTY IS EXPLORED, ALONG WITH ITS SEARCH FOR SOLID LEADERSHIP.

0769 GABLE R.W.
"NAM: INFLUENTIAL LOBBY OR KISS OF DEATH?" (BMR)"
J. OF POLITICS, 15 (MAY 53), 254-273.
DISCUSSES CHARGES MADE BY SEVERAL CONGRESSMEN THAT THE NATIONAL ASSOCIATION OF MANUFACTURERS WROTE THE TAFT-HARTLEY PROPOSAL. EXAMINES QUESTION OF THE GROUP'S POLITICAL POWER AS A LOBBY. CONSTRUCTS FRAME OF REFERENCE FOR STUDY OF POLITICAL INFLUENCE, AND ANALYZES NAM'S PUBLIC RELATIONS, PROPAGANDA, ACCESS TO CONGRESS. SHOWS EXTENT OF GROUP'S SUCCESS IN INFLUENCING CONGRESSIONAL DECISIONS.

0770 GABLE R.W.
"CULTURE AND ADMINISTRATION IN IRAN."
MIDDLE EAST J., 13 (FALL 59), 407-421.

OBSERVATIONS ON IRANIAN INDIVIDUAL CHARACTERISTICS, RELIGION, SOCIETY, ETC., THAT HAVE BEARING ON THE IRANIAN SYSTEM OF ADMINISTRATION.

0771 GABRIEL P.P.
THE INTERNATIONAL TRANSFER OF CORPORATE SKILLS: MANAGEMENT CONTRACTS IN LESS DEVELOPED COUNTRIES.
CAMBRIDGE: HARVARD BUS SCHOOL, 1967, 230 PP., LC#66-28809.
AUTHOR ARGUES THAT SKILLS UNDERDEVELOPED NATIONS NEED TO IMPORT FROM THE ADVANCED ECONOMIES CANNOT BE DETACHED FROM THE FIRMS POSSESSING THEM, AND THAT FIRMS IN DEVELOPED AREAS SHOULD BE CONTRACTED TO MANAGE NEWLY ESTABLISHED FOREIGN INDUSTRIES. DISCUSSES DEPENDENCE OF UNDERDEVELOPED NATIONS ON THE WEST'S SKILLS WITHIN THE CONTEXT OF CONTRACTING MANAGEMENT TO SUPERVISE FOREIGN INDUSTRY.

0772 GAINES J.E., SKRABUT P.A.
"THE YOUTH COURT CONCEPT AND ITS IMPLEMENTATION IN TOMPKINS COUNTY, NEW YORK."
CORNELL LAW Q., 52 (SUMMER 67), 942-974.
DESCRIBES COURT SYSTEM WHERE YOUTHS CHARGED WITH MINOR OFFENSES MAY CHOOSE TRIAL BY OTHER TEENAGERS. IF FOUND GUILTY, THEY ARE SENTENCED TO PERFORM CERTAIN CONSTRUCTIVE TASKS. SHOWS HOW SYSTEM AIMS TO MAKE LAW A CODE OF CONDUCT WITH WHICH YOUTHS CAN IDENTIFY. DISCUSSES SYSTEM'S STRUCTURE AND SUGGESTS LEGISLATIVE ACTION TO ESTABLISH SIMILAR YOUTH COURTS IN ALL NEW YORK COUNTIES.

0773 GALBRAITH J.K.
"ECONOMIC DEVELOPMENT IN PERSPECTIVE."
CAMBRIDGE: HARVARD U. PR., 1962, 76 PP.
EXPLORES WAYS OF AIDING UNDER-DEVELOPED NATIONS ATTAIN THEIR GOALS, I.E. ECONOMIC ADVANCEMENT AND STABILITY. PREFERS THEIR USE OF FREE ENTERPRISE SYSTEM AS CONTRASTED TO A SYSTEM OF FOREIGN OWNERSHIP OF INDUSTRY. OUTLINES PROGRAM FOR GROWTH.

0774 GALBRAITH J.S.
RELUCTANT EMPIRE: BRITISH POLICY OF THE SOUTH AFRICAN FRONTIER, 1834-1854.
BERKELEY: U OF CALIF PR, 1963, 293 PP., LC#63-9801.
A NARRATIVE OF BRITISH IMPERIAL POLICY. CENTERS AROUND THESIS THAT THROUGHOUT PERIOD UNDER CONSIDERATION, ZEAL FOR RETRENCHMENT CONDITIONED BASIC DECISIONS OF IMPERIAL POLICY. EXAMINES POWER OF MISSIONARY SOCIETY IN RELATION TO OTHER INFLUENCES ON COLONIAL POLICY.

0775 GALENSON W. ED.
LABOR IN DEVELOPING COUNTRIES.
BERKELEY: U OF CALIF PR, 1962, 299 PP., LC#62-16108.
FIVE ESSAYS ON LABOR RELATIONS IN VARIOUS ENVIRONMENTAL SETTINGS. EXAMINE TRADE UNION POWER IN UNDERDEVELOPED NATIONS, THE INFLUENCE OF UNIONS IN POLITICS, COLLECTIVE BARGAINING, AND WAGE DIFFERENTIALS. ANALYZE PROBLEMS INVOLVED IN CONVERSION OF A BACKWARD PEASANTRY TO AN INDUSTRIAL WORK FORCE.

0776 GALLOWAY G.B.
AMERICAN PAMPHLET LITERATURE OF PUBLIC AFFAIRS (PAMPHLET)
WASHINGTON: NAT ECO SOCIAL PLAN, 1937, 16 PP.
ANNOTATED BIBLIOGRAPHICAL GUIDE TO PAMPHLETS ISSUED IN THE FIELDS OF ECONOMIC AND SOCIAL PLANNING FROM 1931-36. MATERIALS RANGE IN SCOPE FROM MUNICIPAL TO INTERNATIONAL. LISTS 13 MISCELLANEOUS AND 36 PUBLIC AFFAIRS PAMPHLET SERIES.

0777 GALLOWAY G.B.
CONGRESS AND PARLIAMENT: THEIR ORGANIZATION AND OPERATION IN THE US AND THE UK: PLANNING PAMPHLET NO. 93.
WASHINGTON: NATL PLANNING ASSN, 1955, 105 PP., LC#55-4850.
COMPARES ASPECTS OF CONTEMPORARY PARLIAMENTARY PRACTICE IN THE US CONGRESS AND THE BRITISH PARLIAMENT. TREATS PLANNING THE LEGISLATIVE PROGRAM, COMMITTEE STRUCTURE AND OPERATION, LEGISLATIVE INVESTIGATIONS, LEGISLATIVE LEADERSHIP, PARTY ORGANIZATION, CONTROL OF POLICY AND ADMINISTRATION, AND SECOND CHAMBERS.

0778 GALTUNG J.
"BALANCE OF POWER AND THE PROBLEM OF PERCEPTION, A LOGICAL ANALYSIS."
INQUIRY, 7 (FALL 64), 277-94.
ANALYSIS OF HOW STRUCTURAL AND PSYCHOLOGICAL DETERMINANTS OF PERCEPTION WILL OPERATE IN POWER SYSTEMS, HOW THEY CHANGE IN CRISIS, AND THE POSSIBILITY OF FINDING A POINT OF BALANCE. RELEVANT TO THE CONCEPT OF 'PREVENTIVE WAR' AND DISARMAMENT.

0779 GANGULY D.S.
PUBLIC CORPORATIONS IN A NATIONAL ECONOMY.
CALCUTTA: BOOKLAND PRIVATE, 1963, 410 PP.
ANALYZES PRINCIPLES AND OPERATIONS OF PUBLIC CORPORATIONS SET UP BY STATUTES, PRIMARILY IN INDIA. CONCENTRATES ON NATIONAL LEVEL OPERATIONS AND STUDIES PRINCIPLES BORROWED FROM UK AND OTHER WESTERN NATIONS. INDIA ALONE HAS INTRODUCED PUBLIC CORPORATIONS IN INDUSTRIAL AND COMMERCIAL SPHERES OF GOVERNMENT AS WELL AS UTILITIES AND SOCIAL

SERVICES.

0780 GARCIA E.
LA ADMINISTRACION ESPANOLA.
MADRID: INST DE ESTUDIOS POLIT, 1961, 239 PP.
STUDY OF CONTEMPORARY PUBLIC ADMINISTRATION IN SPAIN. EX-
AMINES EXISTING CONCEPTS OF ADMINISTRATIVE ORGANIZATION AND
PROBLEMS OF SPANISH SYSTEM ON LOCAL AND NATIONAL LEVELS.

0781 GARDNER R.N.
STERLING-DOLLAR DIPLOMACY.
NEW YORK: OXFORD U. PR., 1956, 423 PP.
STUDY OF INTERNATIONAL ECONOMIC POLICY FORMULATION AND
OF INSTITUTIONS FOR ITS IMPLEMENTATION. PLACES SPECIAL
EMPHASIS ON INTERACTION OF OFFICIAL POLICY AND PUBLIC
OPINION. DWELLS ON PROBLEM OF EXPLAINING COMPLEX ECONOMIC
POLICIES TO A DEMOCRATIC ELECTORATE.

0782 GARFIELD PJ   LOVEJOY WF
PUBLIC UTILITY ECONOMICS.
ENGLEWOOD CLIFFS: PRENTICE HALL, 1964, 503 PP., LC#64-10255.
TEXTBOOK DIFFERENTIATES PUBLIC OWNERSHIP, ADMINISTRATES
PRICING, AND FINANCING OF UTILITIES FROM PRIVATE. DISCUSSES
MARKETING AND DISTRIBUTION AS WELL AS LEGAL ASPECTS
OF PUBLIC OWNERSHIP.

0783 GARNER J.F.
ADMINISTRATIVE LAW.
LONDON, WASH, DC: BUTTERWORTHS, 1963, 408 PP.
DISCUSSES PROBLEMS FO LAW IN RELATION TO ADMINISTRATION,
INCLUDING POWERS OF CENTRAL GOVERNMENT, LEGISLATURE, REDRESS
OF GRIEVANCES, PUBLIC CORPORATIONS AND LOCAL AUTHORITIES.
BASED ON ENGLISH LAW.

0784 GARNICK D.H.
"ON THE ECONOMIC FEASIBILITY OF A MIDDLE EASTERN COMMON
MARKET."
MID. EAST. J., 14 (SUMMER 60), 265-276.
VIEWS PROSPECTS FOR FORMATION OF ECONOMIC UNION. ENUMER-
ATES THREE MAJOR OBSTACLES: LACK OF (1)POLITICAL LIAISONS,
(2)PARALLEL SYSTEMS OF ECONOMICS AND (3)SIMILAR LEVELS OF
ECONOMIC STABILITY. EQUAL DISTRIBUTION OF RESOURCES, GROWTH
POTENTIAL, REGIONAL COOPERATION AND STIMULATION OF TRADE
CITED AS AIDS TO EVENTUAL ECONOMIC UNION.

0785 GAUS J.M., WHITE L.D., DIMOCK M.E.
THE FRONTIERS OF PUBLIC ADMINISTRATION.
CHICAGO: U OF CHICAGO PRESS, 1936, 146 PP.
ESSAYS ON NATURE OF PUBLIC ADMINISTRATION, TECHNIQUES,
AND PROBLEMS OF GOVERNMENTAL ORGANIZATION, DISCUSSING SCOPE,
PRINCIPLES, RESPONSIBILITY, OBJECTIVES, AND POSITION OF
PUBLIC ADMINISTRATION IN US SOCIETY.

0786 GAUS J.M., WOLCOTT L.O., LEWIS V.B.
PUBLIC ADMINISTRATION AND THE UNITED STATES DEPARTMENT OF
AGRICULTURE.
CHICAGO: PUBLIC ADMIN SERVICE, 1940, 534 PP.
DESCRIBES EVOLUTION AND FUNCTION OF DEPARTMENT OF
AGRICULTURE. SHOWS HOW IT INFLUENCES PRODUCTION, LAND USE,
MARKETING AND DISTRIBUTION, RURAL LIFE, AND AGRICULTURAL
CREDIT. DISCUSSES OVER-ALL FUNCTION AND ADMINISTRATIVE
STRUCTURE OF DEPARTMENT, AND ANALYZES ITS POTENTIAL IN
SOLUTION OF PROBLEMS OF 1940'S.

0787 GAUS J.M.
REFLECTIONS ON PUBLIC ADMINISTRATION.
UNIVERSITY: U ALABAMA PR, 1947, 153 PP.
STUDY OF PUBLIC ADMINISTRATION AS TO FUNCTIONS OF GOVERN-
MENT, RELATION TO POLITICS, POLICY-MAKING AND ADMINISTRA-
TION, FEDERATION, AND PROCEDURES OF CONTROL.

0788 GELLHORN W.
FEDERAL ADMINISTRATIVE PROCEEDINGS.
BALTIMORE: JOHNS HOPKINS PRESS, 1941, 150 PP.
HOLDS THAT ADMINISTRATIVE ADJUDICATIVE PROCEDURES ARE
DEMOCRATIC, EFFICIENT, AND GENERALLY REPRESENT THE PUBLIC
INTEREST. INTEREST GROUPS ARE STRONGLY REPRESENTED IN
ADMINISTRATIVE PROCEEDINGS THROUGH INFORMAL RELATIONS
BETWEEN ADMINISTRATIVE OFFICERS AND INTEREST GROUP
REPRESENTATIVES.

0789 GELLHORN W.
OMBUDSMEN AND OTHERS: CITIZENS' PROTECTORS IN NINE COUNTRIES
CAMBRIDGE: HARVARD U PR, 1967, 448 PP., LC#66-23465.
STUDIES INSTITUTION OF OMBUDSMAN, REPRESENTATIVE OF PEO-
PLE IN CASES OF GOVERNMENTAL INJUSTICE. INCLUDES COUNTRIES
OF DENMARK, FINLAND, NEW ZEALAND, NORWAY, SWEDEN, YUGOSLA-
VIA, POLAND, USSR, AND JAPAN. APPLIES FINDINGS TO DEVELOP-
MENT OF SUCH AN INSTITUTION IN US.

0790 GEORGE P.
"MATERIAUX ET REFLEXIONS POUR UNE POLITIQUE URBAINE
RATIONNELLE DANS LES PAYS EN COURS DE DEVELOPPEMENT."
TIERS-MONDE, 3 (NO.11, 62), 337-59.
DISCUSSES QUESTION OF URBAN DEVELOPMENT PROJECTS IN NON-
INDUSTRIALIZED COUNTRIES. BASES ANALYSIS ON SEVERAL

REPRESENTATIVE EXAMPLES. MAKES RECOMMENDATIONS FOR URBAN
PLANNING.

0791 GERBERDING W.P.
UNITED STATES FOREIGN POLICY: PERSPECTIVES AND ANALYSIS.
NEW YORK: MCGRAW HILL, 1966, 383 PP., LC#65-28816.
TEXT ON THE FORMULATION AND OPERATION OF US FOREIGN
POLICY SINCE 1945. DISCUSSES FORMAL STRUCTURE IN INFORMAL
POWERS OF CONGRESS, ROLE OF PRESIDENT AS LEADER AND
COORDINATOR, AND HIS INFLUENCE ON THE STATE DEPARTMENT
AND OTHER POLICY-MAKING AGENCIES.

0792 GERTH H.
"THE NAZI PARTY: ITS LEADERSHIP AND COMPOSITION" (BMR)"
AMER. J. OF SOCIOLOGY, 45 (JAN. 40), 517-541.
EXPLAINS NAZI PARTY AS A FUSION OF TWO TYPES OF
DOMINATION: CHARISMATIC AND BUREAUCRATIC. STATES THAT THERE
IS NO PARTY DEMOCRACY BECAUSE ALL AUTHORITY EMANATES FROM
THE LEADER. FINDS GREAT PERCENTAGE OF MEMBERS ARE MIDDLE
CLASS AND/OR YOUNG. SHOWS THAT NEW BUREAUCRACY IS LESS RIGID
THAN OLD PRUSSIAN SYSTEM BECAUSE OF ARBITRARY CONDUCT OF THE
POLICE, JUDICIAL, AND ECONOMIC DEPARTMENTS.

0793 GERWIG R.
"PUBLIC AUTHORITIES IN THE UNITED STATES."
LAW AND CONTEMPORARY PROB., 26 (FALL 61), 591-618.
DISCUSSES THE DEFINITION OF PUBLIC AUTHORITIES, THEIR
HISTORICAL DEVELOPMENT, THEIR STRUCTURE, SOME LEGAL ASPECTS,
THE FUNDING, BOND ISSUING AND TAXING POWERS OF AUTHORITIES,
AND THEIR SOVEREIGN IMMUNITY AND TORT LIABILITY.

0794 GESELLSCHAFT RECHTSVERGLEICH
BIBLIOGRAPHIE DES DEUTSCHEN RECHTS (BIBLIOGRAPHY OF GERMAN
LAW, TRANS. BY COURTLAND PETERSON)
KARLSRUHE: VERLAG CF MULLER, 1964, 584 PP.
ANALYTIC AND THOROUGHLY CATEGORIZED BIBLIOGRAPHY OF
WORKS, DOCUMENTS, STUDIES, TEXTS, ETC., INVOLVING GERMAN
LAW. INCLUDES A LENGTHY INTRODUCTION BY PROFESSOR FRITZ BAUR
ELUCIDATING GERMAN LAW AND LEGAL PROCEDURES SINCE 1949.
BILINGUAL EDITION WITH ENGLISH AND GERMAN ANNOTATION.

0795 GHOSH P.K.
THE CONSTITUTION OF INDIA: HOW IT HAS BEEN FRAMED.
CALCUTTA: WORLD PRESS LTD, 1966, 427 PP.
PRESENTS HISTORICAL BACKGROUND OF INDIAN CONSTITUTION.
NARRATES CONTEMPORARY POLITICAL EVENTS, SHOWING HOW THEY
INFLUENCED DELIBERATIONS OF INDIAN CONSTITUENT ASSEMBLY.
DISCUSSES SEVERAL SUPREME AND HIGH COURT DECISIONS THAT
AMENDED CONSTITUTION, AND ANALYZES REGIONAL FORCES MAKING
AMENDMENTS NECESSARY.

0796 GIDWANI K.A., VALUNJKAR T.N., CHOWDRY K.
"LEADER BEHAVIOUR IN ELECTED AND NON-ELECTED GROUPS."
HUMAN ORGANIZATION, 21 (SPRING 62), 36-42.
TESTS THEORY THAT MEMBER OF SMALL GROUP WHO PROVIDES BEST
IDEAS AND GUIDANCE WILL NOT BE ELECTED LEADER, BUT RATHER
ONE WHO CAN BEST KEEP GROUP TOGETHER AND EMOTIONALLY SATIS-
FIED. FOUR GROUPS TESTED, TWO WITH ELECTED LEADERS. BALES
SYSTEM OF CATEGORIES USED IN INTERACTION ANALYSIS. CONCLUDES
SUPPORTING THEORY AND ITS COROLLARY THAT SECOND-ELECTED PER-
FORMS TASKS, NONELECTED GROUP LEADER DOES BOTH FUNCTIONS.

0797 GIFFORD P. ED., LOUIS W.R. ED.
BRITAIN AND GERMANY IN AFRICA.
NEW HAVEN: YALE U PR, 1967, 825 PP., LC#67-24500.
ESSAYS TREAT ANGLO-GERMAN COLONIAL RIVALRY AND FORMS OF
COLONIAL ADMINISTRATION AFTER OCCUPATION OF AFRICA. DEVOTE
SPECIAL ATTENTION TO WWI AND CONSIDER SIMILARITIES AND
DIFFERENCES OF BRITISH AND GERMAN COLONIAL RULE. EXAMINE
LEADERSHIP, ATTITUDES, RESISTANCE AND REBELLION, SOCIAL
DISCORD, TAXATION, AND BRITISH POLICY OF INDIRECT RULE.
CONCLUDE WITH HISTORIOGRAPHICAL ESSAY.

0798 GILBERT C.E., KAMPELMAN M.M.
"LEGISLATIVE CONTROL OF THE BUREAUCRACY."
ANN. ACAD. POL. SOC. SCI., 292 (MAR. 54), 76-87.
ARGUES THAT CONGRESS IS MOST REPRESENTATIVE ORGAN OF
GOVERNMENT AND SHOULD THEREFORE EXERCISE ACTIVE CONTROL
OVER THE BUREAUCRACY. OUTLINES METHODS OF CONGRESSIONAL
CONTROL OF THE ADMINISTRATION.

0799 GILBERT C.E.
"THE FRAMEWORK OF ADMINISTRATIVE RESPONSIBILITY."
J. OF POLITICS, 21 (AUG. 59), 373-407.
THEORETICAL DISCUSSION OF HOW ADMINISTRATIVE
RESPONSIBILITY SHOULD BE DEFINED AND INVESTIGATED. CITES
VARIOUS THEORIES FOR ACHIEVING RESPONSIBILITY THROUGH THE
COURTS, THE LEGISLATURE, ELECTIONS, ETC.

0800 GILBERT C.E.
"NATIONAL POLITICAL ALIGNMENTS AND THE POLITICS OF LARGE
CITIES."
POLIT. SCI. QUART., 79 (MAR. 64), 25-51.
A HISTORICAL AND COMPARATIVE ANALYSIS OF ELECTIONS IN
LARGE, NORTHERN, PARTISAN CITIES.

0801 GILMORE D.R.
DEVELOPING THE "LITTLE" ECONOMIES.
NEW YORK: COMM FOR ECO DEV, 1960, 200 PP., LC#60-11823.
DISCUSSES LOCAL ECONOMIC GROWTH IN US THROUGH PUBLICLY
AND PRIVATELY FINANCED PROGRAMS. EXAMINES ROLE OF STATE
PLANNING AGENCIES, LOCAL PLANNING ORGANIZATIONS, LOCAL
CHAMBERS OF COMMERCE, INDUSTRIAL DEVELOPMENT GROUPS, DEVEL-
OPMENT CREDIT CORPORATIONS, ETC.

0802 GINSBURG M. ED.
LAW AND OPINION IN ENGLAND.
BERKELEY: U OF CALIF PR, 1959, 405 PP.
RELATION OF DEVELOPMENTS IN ENGLISH LAW TO PUBLIC OPINION
DISCUSSED IN 17 LECTURES DELIVERED AT LONDON SCHOOL OF ECO-
NOMIC AND POLITICAL SCIENCE, 1957-58. COVERS PROPERTY, LA-
BOR, CRIME, ADMINISTRATION, AND HEALTH.

0803 GINZBERG E.
MANPOWER FOR GOVERNMENT (PAMPHLET)
CHICAGO: PUBLIC PERSONNEL ASSN, 1958, 31 PP.
ATTEMPTS 10-YEAR FORECAST OF MAJOR MANPOWER ISSUES FACING
GOVERNMENT. DIVIDED INTO THREE PARTS, IT DISCUSSES: BASIC
TRENDS, SUGGESTED ACTION TO SECURE RESOURCES, AND
CONSIDERATION OF HOW BEST TO USE RESOURCES AVAILABLE. LISTS
WAYS OF INDUCING YOUTHS TO JOIN GOVERNMENT SERVICE AND MEANS
OF IMPROVING PUBLIC RELATIONS.

0804 GITTELL M.
"METROPOLITAN MAYOR: DEAD END."
PUBLIC ADMIN. REV., 23 (MAR. 63), 20-24.
PRESENTS DATA SHOWING THAT THE OFFICE OF MAYOR IN LARGE
CITIES IS A POLITICAL DEAD-END AVOIDED BY OUR BEST
POTENTIAL NATIONAL LEADERS. THE NEW ALLIANCE BETWEEN THE
CITIES AND THE FEDERAL GOVERNMENT MAY BE THE BEST WAY OF
SALVAGING LOCAL GOVERNMENT AS A TRAINING GROUND FOR FUTURE
NATIONAL LEADERS.

0805 GITTELL M.
"PROFESSIONALISM AND PUBLIC PARTICIPATION IN EDUCATIONAL
POLICY MAKING."
PUBLIC ADMIN. REV., 27 (SEPT. 67), 237-251.
DISCUSSES DECISION-MAKING AND ANALYSES OF LOCAL POWER
STRUCTURE IN CITIES AS CONTRIBUTING FACTORS IN SCHOOL
PLANNING. STUDIES COMMUNITY GROUPS, POWER DISPERSION, AND
INCREASED ROLE OF BUREAUCRACY IN DECISION-MAKING.

0806 GITTELL M.
PARTICIPANTS AND PARTICIPATION: A STUDY OF SCHOOL POLICY IN
NEW YORK.
NEW YORK: FREDERICK PRAEGER, 1967, 230 PP.
DESCRIBES ROLE OF PARTICIPANTS IN DECISION-MAKING IN NEW
YORK CITY SCHOOL SYSTEM. EXAMINES HOW POLICY IS MADE IN
MATTERS OF BUDGETING, CURRICULUM, INTEGRATION, SELECTION
OF THE SUPERINTENDENT, AND TEACHERS' SALARIES. MAKES
RECOMMENDATIONS DESIGNED TO INCREASE PUBLIC PARTICIPATION
IN POLICY-MAKING BY DECENTRALIZING SCHOOL SYSTEM.

0807 GJUPANOVIC H., ADAMOVITCH A.
LEGAL SOURCES AND BIBLIOGRAPHY OF YUGOSLAVIA.
NEW YORK: FREDERICK PRAEGER, 1964, 353 PP., LC#64-15520.
TOPICALLY ARRANGES, ANNOTATES, AND THOROUGHLY INDEXES BY
SUBJECT AND AUTHOR 2,467 ITEMS IN EUROPEAN LANGUAGES
RELATING TO THE DEVELOPMENT AND SUBSTANCE OF YUGOSLAVIAN
LAW. COVERS THE FORMATION OF YUGOSLAVIA, THE KINGDOM, WORLD
WAR II, AND THE PRESENT POLITICAL AND LEGAL ORDER. MATERIALS
ARE VERY DIVERSIFIED: DOCUMENTS, SERIALS, MONOGRAPHS, REC-
ORDS, COURT DECISIONS, TREATIES, PERIODICALS, ETC.

0808 GLADDEN E.N.
CIVIL SERVICE OR BUREAUCRACY?
TUCKAHOE, NY: JOHN DE GRAFF, 1956, 224 PP.
STUDIES BRITISH CIVIL SERVICE, ITS HISTORICAL DEVELOPMENT
FROM 1850'S TO AUTOMATION IN 20TH CENTURY. CONFINES STUDY TO
ADMINISTRATIVE SECTORS, POINTING OUT PROBLEMS AS A UNITED
WORKING BODY. CRITICIZES PRESENT SYSTEM FOR COMPLACENCY AND
STATISM BASED ON PAST VIRTUES. GIVES SUGGESTIONS TO IMPROVE
FUTURE DEVELOPMENT.

0809 GLADDEN E.N.
BRITISH PUBLIC SERVICE ADMINISTRATION.
NEW YORK: STAPLES PRESS, 1961, 328 PP.
DETAILED HISTORICAL AND ANALYTICAL STUDY OF THE FUNC-
TIONS, STRUCTURE, AND ORGANIZATION OF ALL BRANCHES OF
BRITISH PUBLIC ADMINISTRATION: EMPHASIS IS ON EFFICIENCY
RATHER THAN RESPONSIBILITY.

0810 GLAZER M.
THE FEDERAL GOVERNMENT AND THE UNIVERSITY.
PRINCETON: PRIN U INDUS REL CTR, 1966, 4 PP.
CONTAINS MAGAZINE AND JOURNAL ARTICLES DEALING WITH
FEDERAL GOVERNMENT SUPPORT OF SOCIAL SCIENCE RESEARCH AND
IMPACT OF PROJECT CAMELOT. ALL ENTRIES ARE IN ENGLISH AND
WERE PUBLISHED 1960-66. ARRANGED ACCORDING TO FOLLOWING
TOPICS: GOVERNMENT-UNIVERSITY RELATIONS, GOVERNMENT SUPPORT
FOR SOCIAL SCIENCE RESEARCH, AND PROJECT CAMELOT.

0811 GLOVER J.D., HOWER R.M.
THE ADMINISTRATOR.
HOMEWOOD: RICHARD IRWIN, 1949, 833 PP., LC#63-10325.
CASES ON HUMAN RELATIONS AND BEHAVIOR. EMPHASIZED ARE
ADMINISTRATIVE SITUATIONS AND PROBLEMS RELATING TO ALL
LEVELS OF ORGANIZATIONAL STRUCTURE. GUIDE TO TRAINING OF
ADMINISTRATORS AND COMPANY TRAINING PROGRAMS.

0812 GLOVER J.D., LAWRENCE P.R.
A CASE STUDY OF HIGH LEVEL ADMINISTRATION IN A LARGE
ORGANIZATION.
CAMBRIDGE: HARVARD U. DIV OF RES, 1960, 117 PP., LC#60-53200
STUDY, CONDUCTED BY AIR FORCE, ON PUBLIC ADMINISTRATION
IN NATIONAL GOVERNMENT BASED ON INTENSIVE RESEARCH OF OFFICE
OF THE ASSISTANT SECRETARY. INTERESTED IN TYPES OF ADMINIS-
TRATION, ATTITUDES, AND BEHAVIOR THAT CONFIRM GOOD JUDG-
MENTS, BETTER PLANS OF ACTION, AND HEALTHY PERSONAL
RELATIONS.

0813 GOBER J.L.
"FEDERALISM AT WORK."
NATIONAL CIVIC REV., 56 (MAY 67), 260-264.
DISCUSSION OF PROBLEMS OF INTERAGENCY COOPERATION AS IL-
LUSTRATED IN JELLICO, TENNESSEE. CITES SUDDEN GROWTH OF PRO-
GRAMS AND FACILITIES AND REACTION OF MUNICIPAL GOVERNMENT IN
SEEKING STATE AID IN COORDINATING STATE AND FEDERAL AGEN-
CIES. DISCUSSES CONSTRICTIVE EFFORTS OF TVA AND STATE PLAN-
NING COMMISSION.

0814 GOLAY J.F.
"THE FOUNDING OF THE FEDERAL REPUBLIC OF GERMANY."
CHICAGO: U OF CHICAGO PRESS, 1958.
DISCUSSES PROCESS IN WHICH CONSTITUTIONAL FOUNDATIONS OF
THE GERMAN FEDERAL REPUBLIC ORIGINATED IN PREVIOUS GERMAN
CONSTITUTIONAL AND POLITICAL DEVELOPMENT. REVIEWS PRESENT
NEEDS AND INTERESTS OF WEST GERMAN PEOPLE AND INFLUENCES
BROUGHT TO BEAR BY WESTERN ALLIED GOVERNMENTS. PARTIALLY
ANNOTATED BIBLIOGRAPHY OF 19 GERMAN AND AMERICAN DOCUMENTS
AND VARIOUS BOOKS, PERIODICALS, AND NEWSPAPERS.

0815 GOLDEN C.S.
"NEW PATTERNS OF DEMOCRACY."
ANTIOCH REV., 3 (SEPT. 43), 391-404.
THE PROBLEM OF WORKER DEPENDENCE ON AN IMPERSONAL
MANAGEMENT IS STILL UNSOLVED; THE WAR PRODUCTION DRIVE
COMMITTEES, HOWEVER, BUILT NEW PATTERNS OF DEMOCRACY.
COOPERATION BASED ON PARTICIPATION IS HELD TO BE THE
BEST WAY TO INTEGRATE SOCIAL FORCES.

0816 GOULDNER A.W.
WILDCAT STRIKE.
YELLOW SPRINGS: ANTIOCH, 1954, 179 PP., LC#54-6176.
STUDY OF A "WILDCAT STRIKE" IN A GYPSUM COMPANY.
DESCRIBES IN DETAIL FACTS AND EVENTS WHICH TOOK PLACE,
FROM A SOCIOLOGICAL POINT OF VIEW. ATTEMPTS TO FORMULATE
A CONCEPTUAL CLARIFICATION TO DISTINGUISH BETWEEN A "WILD-
CAT" STRIKE AND OTHER STRIKES. ALSO DEVELOPS HYPOTHESES TO
AID IN ANALYZING OTHER INDUSTRIAL SOCIAL PROCESSES.

0817 GOLDSTEIN J.
THE GOVERNMENT OF BRITISH TRADE UNIONS.
LONDON: ALLEN & UNWIN, 1952, 300 PP.
DESCRIBES THE TRANSPORT AND GENERAL WORKERS UNION ON
THREE LEVELS - THEORETICAL, NATIONAL, AND BRANCH. GREATEST
EMPHASIS ON UNION ACTIVITY ON BRANCH LEVEL AND PROBLEMS OF
ELICITING ACTIVE PARTICIPATION.

0818 GOLDWIN R.A. ED.
POLITICAL PARTIES, USA.
SKOKIE: RAND MCNALLY & CO, 1964, 158 PP., LC#64-14112.
SUBJECTS INCLUDE: CRITICISMS AND WEAKNESSES, ESPECIALLY
SENSE OF CONFUSION AND CITIZEN DISSATISFACTION; STRENGTHS
AND SUGGESTED REFORMS IN SYSTEM; STRUCTURAL LIMITATIONS
CREATED BY CONSTITUTION; PARTY ADMINISTRATION AND PARTISAN-
SHIP; ORIGINS OF US PARTY SYSTEM; FEDERALISM AND HETERO-
GENEITY AS OBSTACLES; AND CONGRESSIONAL INVOLVEMENT.

0819 GOLEMBIEWSKI R.T.
MEN, MANAGEMENT, AND MORALITY; TOWARD A NEW ORGANIZATIONAL
ETHIC.
NEW YORK: MCGRAW HILL, 1965, 320 PP., LC#65-22106.
TREATS PROBLEMS OF ETHICAL CONSEQUENCE IN ORGANIZATION
OF WORK AND DESCRIBES STRUCTURAL INNOVATIONS AND MANAGERIAL
TECHNIQUES THAT MAY BE EFFECTIVE AND MORAL SOLUTIONS TO
ORGANIZATIONAL PROBLEMS. STUDIES ORGANIZATION THAT ALLOWS
INDIVIDUAL DEVELOPMENT, RELATION OF MAN TO ORGANIZATION,
INDIVIDUAL RESPONSIBILITY, AUTHORITARIANISM, DECENTRALIZING,
AND ORGANIZATION UNDER COMMUNISM, CAPITALISM, AND SOCIALISM.

0820 GOLIGHTLY H.O.
"THE AIRLINES: A CASE STUDY IN MANAGEMENT INNOVATION."
BUSINESS HORIZONS, 10 (FALL 67), 67-78.
EXAMINES ADVENT OF JET TRANSPORTATION AND ITS EFFECT ON
MANAGEMENT POLICY IN US AIRLINES. STUDIES ITS EFFECT ON
ORGANIZATION, PLANNING, INFORMATION SYSTEMS, AND MARKETING
APPROACH. GENERALIZES FROM SUCCESS OF AIRLINES TO MAKE

SUGGESTIONS FOR OTHER INDUSTRIES.

0821 GOODMAN W.
THE TWO-PARTY SYSTEM IN THE UNITED STATES.
PRINCETON: VAN NOSTRAND, 1964, 650 PP., LC#56-08395.
DISCUSSES US POLITICS FROM BIPARTISAN STANDPOINT WITH
ONLY OCCASIONAL REFERENCE TO THIRD PARTIES, STATING THAT
THEIR INSIGNIFICANCE IS MAJOR FLAW IN SYSTEM. EXAMINES
ORGANIZATION, BACKGROUND, REASONS FOR, AND REFORMS OF PARTY
SYSTEMS IN US. IS ESPECIALLY CRITICAL OF CAMPAIGN METHODS.

0822 GOODNOW F.J.
THE PRINCIPLES OF THE ADMINISTRATIVE LAW OF THE UNITED
STATES.
NEW YORK: G P PUTNAM'S SONS, 1905, 479 PP.
STUDIES THEORY AND APPLICATION OF SEPARATION OF POWERS IN
US GOVERNMENT. TREATS POWERS AND STRUCTURE OF CHIEF
EXECUTIVE AUTHORITY IN STATE AND NATION. DISCUSSES STRUCTURE
OF LOCAL RURAL AND MUNICIPAL ADMINISTRATION, AND OF CIVIL
SERVICE. DESCRIBES METHODS AND FORMS OF ADMINISTRATIVE
ACTION. ANALYZES JUDICIAL AND LEGISLATIVE CONTROL OVER
ADMINISTRATIVE OFFICES.

0823 GOODNOW F.J.
"AN EXECUTIVE AND THE COURTS: JUDICIAL REMEDIES AGAINST
ADMINISTRATIVE ACTION"
POLIT. SCI. QUART., 1 (DEC. 86), 533-559.
DEFINES PUBLIC LAW AS ONE PART CONSTITUTIONAL LAW AND ONE
PART ADMINISTRATIVE LAW. SPELLS OUT RULES GOVERNING RELATION
BETWEEN GOVERNMENT AND INDIVIDUAL CITIZEN OR ADMINISTRATIVE
LAW. ANALYZES ACCORDING TO KIND OF ADMINISTRATIVE ACTION
NECESSARY, THUS REMEDY GIVEN PERSON TO PROTECT HIS RIGHTS.
CITES SPECIFIC CASES IN US, FRANCE, AND ENGLAND.

0824 GOODNOW H.F.
THE CIVIL SERVICE OF PAKISTAN: BUREAUCRACY IN A NEW NATION.
NEW HAVEN: YALE U PR, 1964, 328 PP., LC#64-20918.
COVERS CONDITIONS PRIOR TO 1958 UNDER INDIAN CIVIL SER-
VICE OF ENGLAND. AFTER 1958 PERIOD OF MILITARY RULE LED TO
INDEPENDENT CIVIL SERVICE. DONE AS CASE STUDY OF BUREAUCRACY
IN UNDEVELOPED NATIONS. ANALYZES POLITICAL ORGANIZATION IN
ALL NEW STATES. APPENDIX OF FISCAL REPORTS AND GOVERNMENT
JOB TITLES. EXTENSIVE BIBLIOGRAPHY OF BOOKS AND ARTICLES ON
INDIA AND BUREAUCRACY DEVELOPMENT.

0825 GOODRICH L.
THE UNITED NATIONS.
NEW YORK: CROWELL, 1959, 419 PP.
EXAMINES HOW STRUCTURE, FUNCTIONS, AND PROCEDURES OF UN
ARE RELATED TO ITS PRINCIPLES. RELATES CONCESSIONS MADE IN
RECOGNITION OF POWER POLITICS AND NATIONAL INTEREST.

0826 GOODRICH L., HAMBRO E.
"CHARTER OF THE UNITED NATIONS: COMMENTARY AND DOCUMENTS."
BOSTON: WORLD PEACE FOUNDATION, 1946.
COMMENTARY ON CONSTITUTION INCLUDES DISCUSSION OF ITS
HISTORY AND ORIGINS, ORGANIZATION OF ORIGINATING CONFERENCE,
CONTENT OF CHARTER, ITS IMPLEMENTATION. HAS COMMENTARY ON
ARTICLES, LIST OF DOCUMENTS AND EXTENSIVE BIBLIOGRAPHY WHICH
CONTAINS REFERENCES TO MANY ORIGINAL SOURCES.

0827 GOODSELL C.T.
ADMINISTRATION OF A REVOLUTION.
CAMBRIDGE: HARVARD U PR, 1965, 254 PP., LC#65-16684.
DISCUSSES EXECUTIVE REFORM IN PUERTO RICO UNDER GOVERNOR
TUGWELL, 1941-46. ANALYZES THE ECONOMIC REVOLUTION DURING
WWII. DISCUSSES BUDGET PLANNING, THE LEGISLATURE, THE CIVIL
SERVICE, MUNICIPAL IMPROVEMENT, AND THE LEADERSHIP FOR ECO-
NOMIC REFORM THAT WAS GIVEN BY THE ADMINISTRATION.

0828 GOPAL S.
BRITISH POLICY IN INDIA 1858-1905.
CAMBRIDGE: CAMBRIDGE UNIV PRESS, 1965, 423 PP.
STUDY OF FIRST PHASE OF BRITISH RULE IN INDIA UNDER THE
CROWN. NOT PRIMARILY CONCERNED WITH INDIAN ATTITUDES AND
REACTIONS, BUT WITH IDEAS AND ASPIRATIONS OF BRITISH PARTIES
AND STATESMEN, THEIR WAYS AND METHODS OF IMPLEMENTING THEM,
AND THE CONSEQUENCES, ANTICIPATED AND UNINTENDED, OF THESE
EFFORTS.

0829 GORDENKER L.
THE UNITED NATIONS AND THE PEACEFUL UNIFICATION OF KOREA.
GENEVA: NIJHOFF, 1959, 306 PP.
DISCUSSES THE ROLE OF UN FIELD COMMISSIONS IN KOREA PRIOR
TO AND DURING THE OUTBREAK OF HOSTILITIES. EXAMINES THE
COMISSIONS' ACTIVITIES AND INSIGHTS THEY PROVIDED FOR UN
FIELD BODIES. CONCLUDES: FIELD COMMISSIONS WERE NOT THE BEST
POSSIBLE ORGAN FOR DELICATE KOREAN SITUATION BEFORE 1950.

0830 GORDON L.
"ECONOMIC REGIONALISM RECONSIDERED."
WORLD POLIT., 13 (JAN. 61), 231-253.
ANY REAPPRAISAL OF ECONOMIC REGIONALISM MUST START WITH
REVIEW OF PRESENT STRUCTURE OF WORLD ECONOMY. ANALYZES
INDUSTRIALIZED AND NON-INDUSTRIALIZED FREE COUNTRIES, DEVEL-
OPMENTAL REGIONALISM, INTERREGIONAL RELATIONS, AND AMERICAN

FOREIGN ECONOMIC POLICY.

0831 GORDON R.A.
BUSINESS LEADERSHIP IN THE LARGE CORPORATION.
BERKELEY: U OF CALIF PR, 1961, 364 PP., LC#61-1574.
DOCUMENTS IMPORTANCE OF LARGE BUSINESS CORPORATION IN
AMERICAN SOCIETY. INVESTIGATES WAYS IN WHICH LEADERSHIP
ACTIVITIES ARE CARRIED ON IN LARGE FIRM. EVALUATES
SOME OF ECONOMIC CONSEQUENCES OF ORGANIZATIONAL STRUCTURE
AND THE INCENTIVE SYSTEM, AND THE POLITICAL RELATIONSHIPS
CONDITIONING DECISION-MAKING PROCESS.

0832 GORDON W.J.J.
SYNECTICS: THE DEVELOPMENT OF CREATIVE CAPACITY.
NEW YORK: HARPER & ROW, 1961, 177 PP., LC#61-10237.
DATED ACCOUNT OF GORDON'S FIRM, ITS DEVELOPMENT, AND HIS
METHOD OF INSPIRING CREATIVITY. TRACES HISTORY OF RESEARCH
INTO DEVELOPMENT OF CREATIVITY, DESCRIBES HOW IT OPERATES,
AND DISCUSSES SOME OF ITS APPLICATIONS IN INDUSTRY. AIMED
AT TOP EXECUTIVES AND RESEARCHERS, THE PROGRAM ORIGINATED
AND UTILIZED MANY TECHNIQUES NOW CURRENT.

0833 GORE W.J.
"ADMINISTRATIVE DECISION-MAKING IN FEDERAL FIELD
OFFICES."
PUBLIC ADMIN. REV., 16 (1956), 281-291.
AN ATTEMPT TO EXPLAIN HOW AND, TO A LIMITED EXTENT, WHY
AN OFFICE DECIDES UPON ONE ALTERNATIVE INSTEAD OF ANOTHER.
THE STUDY IS BASED ON A SAMPLE OF DECISIONS OF FEDERAL FIELD
OFFICES LOCATED IN THE STATE OF WASHINGTON. FOUR PHASES OF
THE DECISION-MAKING PROCESS ARE DISCUSSED - PERCEPTION,
INTERPRETATION, STRUGGLE FOR POWER, AND FORMALIZATION.

0834 GORE W.J.
ADMINISTRATIVE DECISION-MAKING* A HEURISTIC MODEL.
NEW YORK: JOHN WILEY, 1964, 191 PP., LC#64-17139.
SYSTEMATICALLY REPRESENTS THE DYNAMICS OF AN ADMINISTRA-
TIVE SLICE OF LIFE- THE LAWRENCE KANSAS FIRE DEPARTMENT.
COLLECTS AND CONCEPTUALIZES DATA ON DECISION-MAKING. TOPICS*
GENERAL MODEL AND FUNCTIONS, DECISION-MAKING PROCESS, DECIS-
ION THEORY FRAGMENTS, AND ORGANIZATION THEORY UNDERLYING THE
DECISION CONCEPT.

0835 GORER G.
AFRICA DANCES: A BOOK ABOUT WEST AFRICAN NEGROES.
LONDON: FABER AND FABER, 1935, 363 PP., LC#35-16904.
DESCRIBES CUSTOMS OF WEST AFRICAN NEGROES. STUDIES THEIR
RELIGION, CULTIC PRACTICE, ATHLETIC AND DANCE PRACTICES,
AGRICULTURE, AND SOCIAL STRUCTURE. TREATS GOVERNMENT SYSTEM,
ADMINISTRATIVE CUSTOMS, TAXATION, MILITARY SERVICE, AND
NEGRO ATTITUDES TOWARD COLONIAL GOVERNMENT. SHOWS ROLE
OF MAGIC AND INFLUENCE OF CHRISTIANITY.

0836 GORHAM W.
"NOTES OF A PRACTITIONER."
PUBLIC INTEREST, 8 (SUMMER 67), 4-8.
COMMENTS ON NEW DECISION-MAKING PROGRAM OF LBJ. PLANNING-
PROGRAMMING-BUDGETING SYSTEM COMPARES SIMILAR FUNCTIONS OF
FEDERAL AGENCIES TOGETHER TO FIND THE OPTIMUM. DISCREDITS
IDEA THAT "COST-BENEFITERS" ARE CONTROLLING ALL DECISIONS
OF US GOVERNMENT.

0837 GORMAN W.
"ELLUL - A PROPHETIC VOICE."
CENTER MAGAZINE, 1 (OCT.-NOV. 67), 34-37.
DISCUSSES JACQUES ELLUL'S BOOK "POLITICAL ILLUSION,"
WHICH STATES THAT POLITICS IS NOW IN SERVITUDE TO TECHNICAL
NECESSITY. EFFICIENCY, NOT MORALITY, IS THE SUPREME GOOD.
FEELS RESISTANCE TO STATE IS REQUIRED TO CREATE TENSIONS
WHICH WILL LIMIT STATE'S AUTONOMY. GORMAN HAS RESERVATIONS
ON THIS.

0838 GORWALA A.D.
THE ADMINISTRATIVE JUNGLE (PAMPHLET)
PATNA, INDIA: PATNA U PRESS, 1957, 47 PP.
ESSAY ON PUBLIC ADMINISTRATION BRIEFLY DEALING WITH GOV-
ERNMENT RELATIONS, POLICY PLANNING, BUREAUCRATIC PROCESS AND
MAINTAINING WORKING RELATIONS BETWEEN LOCAL AND NATIONAL
GOVERNMENT.

0839 GOSNELL H.F.
"BRITISH ROYAL COMMISSIONS OF INQUIRY"
POLIT. SCI. QUART., 49 (MAR. 34), 84-118.
DISCUSSES ROYAL COMMISSIONS OF INQUIRY AS PART OF BRITISH
PARLIAMENTARY SYSTEM. PRESENTS METHODS OF DERIVING THEIR
COMPOSITION AND SYSTEM OF ORGANIZATION. DESCRIBES IMPORTANCE
PLACED ON THEIR REPORTS ON POLICY QUESTIONS AS EXPRESSED BY
PRESS RECEPTIONS. EXAMINES REPORTS' EFFECTS ON POLICY
DECISIONS.

0840 GOSNELL H.F.
MACHINE POLITICS: CHICAGO MODEL.
CHICAGO: U OF CHICAGO PRESS, 1937, 229 PP., LC#37-20974.
EXAMINES CHICAGO PARTY MACHINE AND CHARACTERISTICS OF
PARTY WORKERS; ANALYZES VOTING BEHAVIOR IN CANDIDATE AND
PROPOSITION ELECTIONS; PAST AND PRESENT ACTIVITIES OF PRE-

CINCT CAPTAINS AND WARD BOSSES; RELATION OF DAILY NEWSPAPERS
TO VOTING. AUTHOR BOTH CLOSE OBSERVER AND PARTICIPANT IN
URBAN POLITICS. USES MATHEMATICAL ANALYSIS.

0841 GOTLIEB A.
DISARMAMENT AND INTERNATIONAL LAW* A STUDY OF THE ROLE OF
LAW IN THE DISARMAMENT PROCESS.
TORONTO: CAN INST OF INTL AFF, 1965, 232 PP.
AUTHOR IS PROFESSOR OF INTERNATIONAL LAW, DEPUTY LEGAL
HEAD OF CANADIAN DEPARTMENT OF EXTERNAL AFFAIRS, AND WAS ONE
OF HER DELEGATES TO GENEVA DISARMAMENT CONFERENCES. DISCUS-
SES LEGAL PROBLEMS FOUND IN SOVIET AND AMERICAN PROPOSALS.
APPENDICES HAVE SOVIET AND AMERICAN OUTLINES AND REVISIONS
TRANSPOSED.

0842 GOULD W.B.
"THE STATUS OF UNAUTHORIZED AND 'WILDCAT' STRIKES UNDER THE
NATIONAL LABOR RELATIONS ACT."
CORNELL LAW Q., 52 (SPRING 67), 672-704.
EXAMINATION OF PROBLEMS THAT UNAUTHORIZED STRIKE PRESENTS
FOR MANAGEMENT AND RESPONSIBLE UNION LEADERSHIP. OUTLINES
PRESENT APPROACH TAKEN BY NATIONAL LABOR RELATIONS BOARD
AND CIRCUIT COURTS. CONTENDS PRESENT METHODS OF HANDLING
WORK STOPPAGES NEITHER WORKABLE NOR EFFECTIVE. SUGGESTS AP-
PROACH MORE CONDUCIVE TO SECURING INDUSTRIAL PEACE AND EM-
PLOYEE JUSTICE TO BE FOUND IN DECISION OF CONGRESS.

0843 GOULDNER A.W.
"PATTERNS OF INDUSTRIAL BUREAUCRACY."
NEW YORK: FREE PRESS OF GLENCOE, 1954.
STUDY OF BUREAUCRATIC ORGANIZATION DERIVED FROM DIRECT
SYSTEMATIC OBSERVATION OF MODERN FACTORY ADMINISTRATION. IN-
QUIRES INTO TENSIONS AND PROBLEMS EVOKED BY BUREAUCRATIZA-
TION UNDERMINING THE CONSENT OF THOSE GOVERNED. BIBLIOGRAPHY
OF BOOKS AND ARTICLES PUBLISHED IN FRENCH AND ENGLISH
BETWEEN 1921-51. ARRANGED IN ONE ALPHABETICAL LISTING.

0844 GOULDNER A.W.
PATTERNS OF INDUSTRIAL BUREAUCRACY.
NEW YORK: FREE PRESS OF GLENCOE, 1954, 282 PP.
STUDY OF BUREAUCRATIC ORGANIZATION DERIVED FROM DIRECT,
SYSTEMATIC OBSERVATION OF MODERN FACTORY ADMINISTRATION.
CONCERNED WITH CONFLICT, ACTION, AND RESISTANCE BY WHICH THE
GOVERNED YIELD OR REFUSE CONSENT TO THEIR GOVERNORS. CONCEN-
TRATES ON THOSE SITUATIONS IN WHICH ADVANCE OF BUREAUCRATI-
ZATION EFFECTIVELY RESISTED. INQUIRES INTO TENSIONS AND
PROBLEMS EVOKED BY BUREAUCRATIZATION'S UNDERMINING CONSENT.

0845 GOULDNER A.W. ED.
STUDIES IN LEADERSHIP.
NEW YORK: RUSSELL & RUSSELL, 1965, 736 PP., LC#64-66395.
A COLLECTION OF ESSAYS ON THE TYPOLOGY OF LEADERS,
THEIR RELATION TO VARIOUS TYPE OF GROUPS, AND THE
ETHICS AND TECHNIQUES OF LEADERSHIP, WITH SUMMARY REMARKS
SEARCHING FOR THEORIES OF LEADERSHIP.

0846 GOURNAY B.
PUBLIC ADMINISTRATION.
NEW YORK: CULTURAL CTR FRENCH EM, 1963, 207 PP.
ANNOTATED TOPICAL LISTING OF 1,000 BOOKS, COURSES, MAN-
UALS, ANTHOLOGIES, MAGAZINE ARTICLES, THESES, REPORTS OF
STUDY GROUPS, AND DOCUMENTS EMANATING FROM CENTRAL FRENCH
ADMINISTRATIONS. ALL ITEMS DEAL WITH PUBLIC ADMINISTRATIONS
IN METROPOLITAN FRANCE; ALL WERE PUBLISHED 1944-58 AND
MOST ARE IN FRENCH. CONCLUDING AUTHOR AND PUBLISHER INDEX.
TITLES AND ANNOTATIONS GIVEN IN ENGLISH.

0847 GOVERNORS CONF STATE PLANNING
STATE PLANNING: A POLICY STATEMENT (PAMPHLET)
CHICAGO: COUNCIL OF STATE GOVTS, 1962, 35 PP.
EMPHASIZES NEED FOR STATES TO ENGAGE IN COMPREHENSIVE,
STATE-WIDE PLANNING RELATING LOCAL NEEDS TO STATE POLI-
CIES. FEDERAL GOVERNMENT CAN THEN ENGAGE IN LONG-RANGE PLAN-
NING, BASED ON STATES' NEEDS TEMPERED BY NATIONAL INTEREST.

0848 GRABER D.
CRISIS DIPLOMACY.
WASHINGTON: PUBL. AFF. PR., 1959, 402 PP.
TRACES DEVELOPMENT OF PRINCIPLE OF NON-INTERVENTION IN
USA FOREIGN POLICY. POINTS OUT CONFLICT BETWEEN POLICY AND
PRACTICE. ARGUES THAT MILITARY INTERVENTION SHOULD BE USED
ONLY WHEN VITAL INTERESTS ARE AT STAKE AND NO OTHER MEANS
OF PROTECTION ARE AVAILABLE. OUTLINES NECESSITY FOR CLEAR
DEFINITION OF CIRCUMSTANCES FOR INTERVENTION TO AVOID SPLIT
BETWEEN LEGALISTIC IDEALS AND POLITICAL REALITIES.

0849 GRAHAM G.A.
AMERICA'S CAPACITY TO GOVERN: SOME PRELIMINARY THOUGHTS FOR
PROSPECTIVE ADMINISTRATORS.
UNIVERSITY: U ALABAMA PR, 1960, 159 PP., LC#60-8100.
EXAMINATION OF MAN AS A POLITICAL ANIMAL INCLUDES THE
VIABILITY OF DEMOCRACY, MEASUREMENT OF GOVERNING CAPACITY,
DISCUSSION OF AMERICA AS THE BEST POSSIBLE SOCIETY, AND
THE CAREER EXECUTIVE PROGRAM.

0850 GRAM H.A.

"BUSINESS ETHICS AND THE CORPORATION."
THE CRESSET, 31 (FEB. 68), 8-12.
DISCUSSES ETHICAL PROBLEMS OF MANAGEMENT STEMMING FROM
MANAGER'S ROLE AS ADMINISTRATOR OF GOALS, OBJECTIVES, POL-
ICIES, AND PLANS THAT OFTEN HE HAS HAD NO PART IN ESTAB-
LISHING. NOTES TWO DIMENSIONS OF ETHICS: APPLICATION OF IN-
DIVIDUAL PERSONAL ETHICS TO ALL ASPECTS OF HUMAN RELATION-
SHIPS, AND THE ETHICS OF BUSINESS-SOCIETY RELATIONSHIPS.
STRESSES IMPORTANCE OF RIGHT AND RESPONSIBLE USE OF POWER.

0851 GRANICK D.
THE RED EXECUTIVE.
NEW YORK: DOUBLEDAY, 1960, 334 PP.
SOVIET INDUSTRIAL SYSTEM RUN BY MANAGERIAL CLASS SIMILAR
TO AMERICAN COUNTERPART. AMERICAN AND RED EXECUTIVES POSSESS
SIMILAR EDUCATION AND EXPERIENTIAL BACKGROUNDS. RED EXECU-
TIVES ENJOYS GREATER STATUS AND WEALTH, BUT LACK DECISION
MAKING POWER AND PERSONAL SECURITY.

0852 GRANICK D.
THE EUROPEAN EXECUTIVE.
GARDEN CITY: DOUBLEDAY, 1962, 384 PP., LC#62-07635.
ANALYZES EUROPEAN ECONOMIC MANAGEMENT, ESPECIALLY IN
GREAT BRITAIN, BELGIUM, GERMANY, AND FRANCE. DISCUSSES THE
TECHNOCRAT, ENTREPRENEURSHIP, LABOR PRACTICES, MANAGEMENT
CONCEPTS, AND OWNER-MANAGER RELATIONS.

0853 GRANT D.R., NIXON H.C.
STATE AND LOCAL GOVERNMENT IN AMERICA.
NEW YORK: ALLYN AND BACON, 1963, 439 PP., LC#63-14890.
DISCUSSES ROLE AND FUNCTION OF STATE AND LOCAL
GOVERNMENTS IN US. EXAMINES POLICE POWER, CONSTITUTIONS,
VOTING, PARTY ORGANIZATION AND ELECTIONS, PUBLIC OPINION,
LEGISLATIVE PROCESSES, JUDICIARY, COUNTRY ADMINISTRATIONS,
URBAN AREAS, EDUCATION, AND PUBLIC WELFARE.

0854 GRASSMUCK G.L., SALIBI K.
"A MANUAL OF LEBANESE ADMINISTRATION."
BEIRUT: CATHOLIC PR, 1955.
A GENERAL MANUAL COVERING THE GOVERNMENTAL AND ADMINIS-
TRATIVE OPERATIONS OF LEBANON. PROVIDES BRIEF DESCRIPTIVE
HISTORY OF ADMINISTRATIVE DEVELOPMENT SINCE INDEPENDENCE.
DIAGRAMMATIC DESCRIPTION OF EACH MAJOR DIVISION IN PRESENT
ADMINISTRATION, BASED UPON LEGISLATIVE DECREES OF 1952-53;
ENDEAVORS TO SPECIFY AGENCIES, FUNCTIONS, AND DUTIES. PAR-
TIALLY ANNOTATED BIBLIOGRAPHY OF WORKS ON TOPIC SINCE WWI.

0855 GRAVES W.B.
AMERICAN STATE GOVERNMENT.
BOSTON: D C HEATH, 1936, 829 PP.
PROVIDES A BASIS FOR ASSESSING THE STRUCTURE, POLITICS,
LEGISLATURE, ADMINISTRATION, FINANCE, AND CONSTITUTION OF
STATE GOVERNMENTS. DESCRIBES INTERGOVERNMENTAL RELATIONS,
PROJECTS THE HISTORICAL TRENDS OF STATE GOVERNMENT, AND
PREDICTS FUTURE. INTENDED TO SUPPLEMENT AND UPDATE
OTHER TEXTS IN THIS FIELD. REGARDS STATE GOVERNMENTS AS
"GOING CONCERNS" RATHER THAN STATIC INSTITUTIONS.

0856 GRAVES W.B.
"LEGISLATIVE REFERENCE SYSTEM FOR THE CONGRESS OF THE
UNITED STATES."
AM. POL. SCI. REV., 41 (APR. 47), 289-293.
OUTLINES NATURE OF LEGISLATIVE REFERENCE SYSTEM AND
DESCRIBES CHARACTER OF SERVICES IT RENDERS. DISCUSSES
EXPANSION OF THE SERVICE.

0857 GRAVES W.B.
BASIC INFORMATION ON THE REORGANIZATION OF THE EXECUTIVE
BRANCH: 1912-1948.
WASHINGTON: LIBRARY OF CONGRESS, 1949, 425 PP.
PRESENTS PROGRESS OF EXECUTIVE REORGANIZATION FROM 1912
TO 1948 BY LISTING CHRONOLOGICALLY ALL EXECUTIVE AND LEGIS-
LATIVE ACTIONS ON SUBJECT, BY PRESENTING DOCUMENTARY HIS-
TORY OF REORGANIZATION EFFORTS, AND BY GIVING STATEMENTS OF
PRESIDENTS. CONCLUDING BIBLIOGRAPHY OF BOOKS AND ARTICLES
ON THE SUBJECT.

0858 GRAVES W.B.
PUBLIC ADMINISTRATION: A COMPREHENSIVE BIBLIOGRAPHY ON
PUBLIC ADMINISTRATION IN THE UNITED STATES (PAMPHLET)
WASHINGTON: LIBRARY OF CONGRESS, 1950, 388 PP.
SOME 5,500 UNANNOTATED BOOKS, ARTICLES, MONOGRAPHS, PUB-
LIC DOCUMENTS, AND BIBLIOGRAPHIES PUBLISHED 1924-49
AND ARRANGED TOPICALLY. TOPICS INCLUDE ADMINISTRATIVE STRUC-
TURE, PERSONNEL MANAGEMENT, FISCAL MANAGEMENT, INTERNAL AND
EXTERNAL MANAGEMENT.

0859 GRAVIER J.F.
AMENAGEMENT DU TERRITOIRE ET L'AVENIR DES REGIONS FRANCAISES
PARIS: FLAMMARION, 1964, 336 PP.
CONCERNS TOWN AND COUNTRY PLANNING, ESPECIALLY IN FRANCE.
DISCUSSES GEOGRAPHIC CONDITIONS AND HOW THEY AFFECT THE
ECONOMY, INDUSTRIALIZATION, REFORM IN CITY AND COUNTRY
PLANNING, REFORMS IN PARIS, ETC. AUTHOR BELIEVES REFORM
TO BE IMPEDED BY BUREAUCRACY.

0860 GRAY R.K.
EIGHTEEN ACRES UNDER GLASS.
GARDEN CITY: DOUBLEDAY, 1962, 372 PP., LC#61-12532.
ACCOUNT OF EISENHOWER ADMINISTRATION PROVIDING BASICALLY
NON-TECHNICAL AND NON-ANALYTICAL DESCRIPTION OF PRESIDENT,
HIS CABINET, HIS STAFF OF SPECIAL ASSISTANTS AND OTHER PER-
SONALITIES AND DIGNITARIES INVOLVED IN ACTIVITY CENTERING
AROUND WHITE HOUSE DURING EISENHOWER'S TERM OF OFFICE.

0861 GREAT BRITAIN DEPT TECH COOP
PUBLIC ADMINISTRATION: A SELECT BIBLIOGRAPHY (PAMPHLET)
LONDON: GT BRIT, DEPT TECH COOP, 1963, 119 PP.
ANNOTATED LISTING BY SUBJECT OF 1,000 BOOKS, GOVERNMENT
DOCUMENTS, CONFERENCE REPORTS, NATIONAL STUDIES, BIBLIOG-
RAPHIES, AND PERIODICALS ON ALL PHASES OF PUBLIC ADMIN-
ISTRATION. WORKS ARE IN ENGLISH AND PUBLISHED 1950-63.

0862 GREAT BRITAIN TREASURY
PUBLIC ADMINISTRATION: A BIBLIOGRAPHY FOR ORGANISATION AND
METHODS (PAMPHLET)
LONDON: GREAT BRITAIN TREASURY, 1950, 18 PP.
UNANNOTATED SUBJECT LISTING OF 300 BOOKS, REPORTS, AND
GOVERNMENT PUBLICATIONS FROM EITHER BRITAIN OR US ON
"MANAGEMENT OF PUBLIC BUSINESS." SPECIAL EMPHASIS ON CIVIL
SERVICE, ORGANIZATION, AND METHODS IN LISTING. PUBLICATIONS
FROM 1937-50.

0863 GREBLER L.
URBAN RENEWAL IN EUROPEAN COUNTRIES: ITS EMERGENCE AND
POTENTIALS.
PHILA: U OF PENN PR, 1964, 132 PP., LC#63-21714.
STUDY OF EUROPEAN EFFORTS, SUCCESSES, AND FAILURES AT
URBAN RENEWAL. POINTS OUT THAT RENEWAL OFTEN GOES ON INDE-
PENDENTLY OF NATIONAL PROGRAMS. ALSO SHOWS THAT BRITISH
EFFORTS HAVE BEEN FAR MORE SUSTAINED AND EFFECTIVE THAN
THOSE OF NATIONS ON CONTINENT.

0864 GREEN H.P., ROSENTHAL A.
GOVERNMENT OF THE ATOM.
NEW YORK: ATHERTON PRESS, 1963, 281 PP., LC#63-8916.
STUDY OF JOINT COMMITTEE ON ATOMIC ENERGY, FOCUSING ON
COMMITTEE'S POWER RELATIONS WITH EXECUTIVE BRANCH AND
CONGRESS. ANALYZES COMMITTEE'S SOURCES OF AUTHORITY AND
ITS TECHNIQUES AS LEGISLATOR AND POLICY-MAKER. STUDY IS
BASED ON THEORY THAT COMMITTEE'S BEHAVIOR RESEMBLES THAT OF
HIGHER ECHELONS IN EXECUTIVE BRANCH.

0865 GREENE K.R.C.
INSTITUTIONS AND INDIVIDUALS: AN ANNOTATED LIST OF
DIRECTORIES USEFUL IN INTERNATIONAL ADMINISTRATION.
CHICAGO: PUBLIC ADMIN CLEAR HSE, 1953.
GUIDE TO DIRECTORIES OF INSTITUTIONS AND INDIVIDUALS.
INCLUDES 220 WORKS ALL OF WHICH WERE PUBLISHED AFTER
1945. ANNOTATIONS INDICATE EXTENT TO WHICH BOOK FULFILLS
FUNCTIONS. ENTRIES ARE ARRANGED ALPHABETICALLY WITH
CROSS REFERENCES. MOST ENTRIES DESCRIBE PUBLICATIONS IN
FRENCH, ENGLISH, AND OTHER WEST EUROPEAN LANGUAGES.

0866 GREENE L.S., AVERY R.S.
GOVERNMENT IN TENNESSEE (2ND ED.)
KNOXVILLE: U OF TENN PR, 1966, 371 PP., LC#66-21194.
CONTAINS MATERIAL ON STRUCTURE, FUNCTION, AND ADMINISTRA-
TION OF TENNESSEE STATE GOVERNMENT. INCLUDES COPY OF STATE
CONSTITUTION; DEALS WITH STATE POLITICS AND COURTS; COUNTY
GOVERNMENT; BUSINESS AND INDUSTRY; PUBLIC HEALTH, EDUCA-
TION, AND WELFARE; TRANSPORT FACILITIES, STATE REVENUES, AND
STATE AND LOCAL PLANNING.

0867 GREENE L.S., PARTHEMOS G.S.
AMERICAN GOVERNMENT POLICIES AND FUNCTIONS.
NEW YORK: CHAS SCRIBNER'S SONS, 1967, 450 PP., LC#67-10455.
ANALYZES FUNCTIONS AND POLICIES OF US GOVERNMENT AND
PROCEDURES THROUGH WHICH DECISIONS ARE MADE REGARDING PUBLIC
POLICY. STUDIES THEORIES DEFINING PUBLIC POLICIES, POLITICAL
ADMINISTRATIVE PROCESS, CONTENT OF MAJOR POLICIES, AND
POLICY PROBLEMS.

0868 GREENEWALT C.H.
THE UNCOMMON MAN.
NEW YORK: MCGRAW HILL, 1959, 142 PP., LC#58-59777.
THESIS OF VOLUME IS THAT ALL ORGANIZATIONS, NATIONS,
CIVILIZATIONS, AND SOCIETIES WILL PROSPER AND ADVANCE ONLY
TO EXTENT THEY ENCOURAGE COMMON MEN TO PERFORM UNCOMMON
DEEDS. THIRD SERIES IN MCKINSEY FOUNDATION LECTURES AT
COLUMBIA UNIVERSITY HELD IN 1958.

0869 GREER S.
A BIBLIOGRAPHY OF PUBLIC ADMINISTRATION.
NY: COLUMBIA U, INST PUB ADMIN, 1933, 90 PP.
BIBLIOGRAPHY OF BIBLIOGRAPHIES, REFERENCES, GOVERNMENT
DOCUMENTS, AND CONSTITUTIONS INCLUDING FOREIGN-LANGUAGE
SOURCES. RANGE EXTENDS FROM NATIONAL GOVERNMENTS TO THE
LOCAL LEVEL, US AND ABROAD, AS WELL AS SECTIONS ON THEORY
OF ADMINISTRATION, AND MANAGEMENT. ARRANGED BY GENERAL
TOPIC, THEN BY COUNTRY OR LOCALITY. GREATEST ATTENTION TO
POST-1918 PERIOD.

0870 GREER S.
BIBLIOGRAPHY ON CIVIL SERVICE AND PERSONNEL ADMINISTRATION.
NEW YORK: MCGRAW HILL, 1935, 143 PP.
ANNOTATED BIBLIOGRAPHY PREPARED BY SOCIAL SCIENCE RE-
SEARCH COUNCIL TO INVESTIGATE MATERIALS TOUCHING UPON
"THE BROAD PROBLEM OF PERSONNEL IN THE ADMINISTRATIVE, EXEC-
UTIVE, AND TECHNICAL SERVICES OF NATIONAL, STATE, AND LOCAL
GOVERNMENT." COVERS MAJOR EUROPEAN COUNTRIES, DISCUSSES
PROMOTION, SALARY, TRAINING, APPOINTMENT, ETC.; HAS SECTIONS
ON WORLDWIDE CIVIL SERVICE. INDEXES AUTHORS.

0871 GREER S.
URBAN RENEWAL AND AMERICAN CITIES: THE DILEMMA OF
DEMOCRATIC INTERVENTION.
INDIANAPOLIS: BOBBS-MERRILL, 1965, 201 PP., LC#65-26544.
SOCIOLOGICAL STUDY BASED UPON OBSERVATIONS OF AMER-
ICAN CITIES AND INTERVIEWS WITH URBAN RENEWAL ADMINISTRA-
TORS. ANALYZES RENEWAL AS PART OF US CULTURE; ORGANIZATIONAL
ASPECTS, WITH EMPHASIS ON LOCAL PUBLIC AUTHORITY, STUDIES
MASSIVE AND INTERTWINED SOCIAL TRENDS IN US CITIES. PROPOSES
THAT GOVERNMENT SPEND MORE MONEY RESEARCHING NEEDS OF CITIES
BEFORE MONEY IS PUMPED INTO URBAN RENEWAL PROJECTS.

0872 GREGG J.L.
POLITICAL PARTIES AND PARTY SYSTEMS IN GUATEMALA, 1944-1963.
GAINESVILLE: U OF FLA PR, 1965, 173 PP.
IN CONTEXT OF PREVAILING POLITICAL SYSTEMS AND ENVIRON-
MENT, EXAMINES ORGANIZATION, LEADERSHIP, IDEOLOGY, AND AC-
TIVITY OF THE VARIOUS GROUPS PURPORTING TO HAVE CONSTITUTED
POLITICAL PARTIES OPERATING IN GUATEMALA, 1944-63. ASSESSES
DOMINANT FEATURES OF VARIOUS GUATEMALAN POLITICAL REGIMES.

0873 GRENIEWSKI H.
"INTENTION AND PERFORMANCE: A PRIMER OF CYBERNETICS OF PLAN-
NING."
MANAGEMENT SCIENCE, 11 (JULY 65), 263-282.
THE OBJECT OF A GOAL IS ALWAYS A RELATIVELY ISOLATED PRO-
SPECTIVE SYSTEM; THE GOAL IS A CERTAIN STATE OF THE OUTPUT;
THE MEANS ARE THE STATES OF THE CONTROLLED INPUTS. RELATIONS
AMONG GOALS, MEANS, AND CIRCUMSTANCES ARE ANALYZED; PLANNING
IS GIVEN A GAME THEORETICAL INTERPRETATION; THE IMPLEMENTA-
TION OF A PLAN IS A 2 PERSON GAME, THE PLANNER AND THE CIR-
CUMSTANCES BEING THE TWO PLAYERS.

0874 GRETHER E.T.
MARKETING AND PUBLIC POLICY.
ENGLEWOOD CLIFFS: PRENTICE HALL, 1966, 120 PP., LC#66-14745.
DISCUSSES PROBLEMS RELATING TO INDUSTRIAL MARKETING, IN-
CLUDING HISTORICAL BACKGROUND, GOVERNMENT REGULATION, DECI-
SION AND POLICY MAKING, PRODUCT PROMOTION AND PRICING POL-
ICIES, AND RELATION OF POLICY TO MARKETING SYSTEM.

0875 GRIFFIN A.P.C. ED.
LIST OF BOOKS ON THE CABINETS OF ENGLAND AND AMERICA
(PAMPHLET)
WASHINGTON: LIBRARY OF CONGRESS, 1903, 8 PP.
ANNOTATION OF ABOUT 30 ITEMS, ARRANGED ALPHABETICALLY BY
AUTHOR. INCLUDES COMPARATIVE TREATISES. ENGLISH-LANGUAGE MA-
TERIALS BY ENGLISH AND AMERICAN AUTHORS. DATE FROM MIDDLE OF
9TH CENTURY TO 1903. COVERS CONSTITUTIONAL GOVERNMENT, CABI-
NET STRUCTURE, COMPARISONS AND CONTRASTS. UNINDEXED.
COMPILED FOR LIBRARY OF CONGRESS.

0876 GRIFFIN G.G. ED.
A GUIDE TO MANUSCRIPTS RELATING TO AMERICAN HISTORY IN
BRITISH DEPOSITORIES.
WASHINGTON: LIBRARY OF CONGRESS, 1946, 313 PP.
NOT A COMPLETE LISTING OF DOCUMENTS RELATING TO US HIS-
TORY IN BRITISH DEPOSITORIES, BUT A GUIDE TO FACSIMILE
REPRODUCTIONS OF MANUSCRIPTS AVAILABLE IN THE LIBRARY OF
CONGRESS. SOURCES INCLUDE OFFICIAL ARCHIVES OF BRITAIN,
CANADA, SCOTLAND, WALES, IRELAND, AND VARIOUS PRIVATE
COLLECTIONS. MANUSCRIPTS ARE MOSTLY 18TH-CENTURY RECORDS
COVERING MANY DIVERSE TOPICS.

0877 GRIFFITH E.S.
"THE CHANGING PATTERN OF PUBLIC POLICY FORMATION."
AM. POL. SCI. REV., 38 (JUNE 44), 445-459.
CONSIDERS CHANGES IN OVER-ALL CULTURE OF WHICH PUBLIC
POLICY FORMATION IS A PART AND MORE PRECISE CHANGES IN
POLICY FORMATION.

0878 GRIFFITH E.S.
CONGRESS: ITS CONTEMPORARY ROLE.
NEW YORK: NEW YORK U PR, 1961, 244 PP., LC#61-70865.
TREATS CONGRESS IN ITS ENTIRETY INCLUDING MEMBERS,
LEADERS, INTERNAL ORGANIZATION, EXECUTIVE-LEGISLATIVE RELA-
TIONS APPROPRIATIONS, CONGRESSIONAL INVESTIGATIONS, CONGRESS
AND ADMINISTRATION, INTERNATIONAL POLICY, PRESSURE GROUPS,
ECONOMIC PLANNING, LOCALISM, POLITICAL PARTIES, CONGRESS
IN A CRISIS AND LEGISLATIVE RESPONSIBILITIES IN NATIONAL
DEFENSE.

0879 GRIFFITH J.A.G., STREET H.
PRINCIPLES OF ADMINISTRATIVE LAW (3RD ED.)
NEW YORK: PITMAN PUBLISHING, 1963, 339 PP., LC#63-24929.

DISCUSSES PROBLEMS OF LAW IN ITS RELATION TO ADMINISTRA-
TION, INCLUDING LEGISLATIVE POWERS OF ADMINISTRATION AND
THEIR CONTROL, ADMINISTRATIVE AND JUDICIAL POWERS AND
CONTROL, AND PUBLIC CORPORATIONS.

0880 GRIFFITH W.
THE PUBLIC SERVICE (PAMPHLET)
LONDON: BRITISH COUNCIL, 1957, 48 PP.
SURVEY OF PUBLIC SERVICE, ITS HISTORY, STRUCTURE, AND
RELATIONS WITH BRITISH GOVERNMENT. STUDY AIMED AT MAKING
VOTERS AWARE AND KNOWLEDGEABLE OF METHODS OF SELECTION AND
TRAINING FOR PUBLIC SERVICE. STRESSES NEED FOR HIGH QUALITY
PEOPLE IN GOVERNMENT.

0882 GRINYER P.H., KESSLER S.
"THE SYSTEMATIC EVALUATION OF METHODS OF WAGE PAYMENT."
J. MANAGEMENT STUDIES, 4 (OCT. 67), 309-320.
EXPLAINS METHOD OF DETERMINING EFFICIENCY OF INCENTIVE
PAYMENTS FOR PRODUCTION INCREASES. SYSTEM COMPOSED OF CON-
SIDERATIONS OF REWARD BASIS, PROCEDURE, NORMS AFFECTING
PRODUCTION, PAYMENT FREQUENCY, AND SIZE OF GROUP TO WHICH
PAYMENT IS MADE.

0883 GRODZINS M.
"AMERICAN POLITICAL PARTIES AND THE AMERICAN SYSTEM" (BMR)"
WESTERN POLIT. QUART., 13 (DEC. 60), 974-998.
PAPER COMMENTS ON FUNCTIONAL CONSEQUENCES OF UNIQUE US
PARTY SYSTEM FOR LARGER GOVERNMENTAL SYSTEM IN WHICH IT
OPERATES. AUTHOR ASKS HOW THE OPERATION OF PARTY SYSTEM
AFFECTS US GOVERNMENT. CONCLUDES THAT PARTIES FUNCTION
TO PRESERVE EXISTENCE AND FORM OF GOVERNMENTAL DECENTRAL-
IZATION. HE FOCUSES ATTENTION ON CLASSIC FEDERAL PROBLEM
OF THE DISTRIBUTION OF POWER.

0884 GROGAN V.
ADMINISTRATIVE TRIBUNALS IN THE PUBLIC SERVICE.
DUBLIN: INST PUBLIC ADMIN, 1962, 76 PP.
STUDIES GROUPS WHOSE FUNCTION IS TO JUDGE ISSUES ARISING
IN ADMINISTRATION OF JUDICIAL CONTROL OVER TRIBUNALS AND
ADMINISTRATIVE LAW. COMPARES IRISH AND ENGLISH ADMINISTRA-
TIVE SYSTEMS.

0885 GROSS B.M.
THE LEGISLATIVE STRUGGLE: A STUDY IN SOCIAL COMBAT.
NEW YORK: MCGRAW HILL, 1953, 459 PP., LC#52-11509.
ATTEMPTS TO DEVELOP A SYSTEMATIC METHOD OF DEALING WITH
LEGISLATION. EMPHASIZES PEOPLE IN ACTION AS ESSENCE OF
LEGISLATIVE ACTIVITY.

0886 GROSS B.M.
THE MANAGING OF ORGANIZATIONS (VOL. I)
NEW YORK: FREE PRESS OF GLENCOE, 1964, 463 PP., LC#64-20312.
STUDY OF ORGANIZATION MANAGEMENT, INCLUDING ADMINISTRA-
TIVE REVOLUTION, DEVELOPMENT OF ADMINISTRATIVE THOUGHT, IN-
TEGRATION OF MANAGEMENT, AND PEOPLE IN ORGANIZATIONS.

0887 GROSS B.M.
THE MANAGING OF ORGANIZATIONS (VOL. II)
NEW YORK: FREE PRESS OF GLENCOE, 1964, 508 PP., LC#64-20312.
STUDY OF ORGANIZATION MANAGEMENT, INCLUDING PURPOSES IN
MANAGEMENT, SATISFACTION OF INTERESTS, GOODS AND SERVICES,
OPERATIONS, EFFICIENCY, ADMINISTRATIVE PROCESSES, FUTURE OF
ADMINISTERED SOCIETY, AND EXPANSION OF ADMINISTRATIVE
EDUCATION.

0888 GROSS C.
A BIBLIOGRAPHY OF BRITISH MUNICIPAL HISTORY (2ND ED.)
LONDON: LEICESTER UNIV PRESS, 1966, 430 PP.
ANNOTATED BIBLIOGRAPHY OF 3,077 BOOKS, PAMPHLETS,
MAGAZINE ARTICLES, AND PAPERS IN ENGLISH, PUBLISHED FROM
1656 TO 1895 ON GOVERNMENTAL AND CONSTITUTIONAL HISTORY OF
BRITISH TOWNS. ENTRIES ARE ARRANGED BY TYPE OF ENTRY,
AUTHORITY OF HISTORY, AND PARTICULAR TOWN STUDIED. COVERS
HISTORY FROM 1066 TO 19TH CENTURY.

0889 GROSS H.
MAKE OR BUY.
ENGLEWOOD CLIFFS: PRENTICE HALL, 1966, 231 PP., LC#66-14071.
EXAMINES CONDITIONS WHICH CONTROL MAKE-OR-BUY DECISIONS
IN MODERN US BUSINESS. DISCUSSES ROLE OF ADMINISTRATIVE
STAFF, COST ACCOUNTING ANALYSIS, AND TECHNIQUES FOR PLANNING
IN MAKE-OR-BUY DECISIONS.

0890 GROSS J.A.
"WHITEHALL AND THE COMMONWEALTH."
J. COMMONWEALTH POLIT. STUD., 2 (NOV. 64), 189-206.
HISTORICAL DEVELOPMENT OF THE RISE AND FALL OF THE
COLONIAL OFFICE IN THE BRITISH EMPIRE STRUCTURE. ANALYZES
AND EVALUATES FORTHCOMING ABSORPTION OF COLONIAL OFFICE BY
THE COMMONWEALTH RELATIONS OFFICE IN LIGHT OF BRITAIN'S
CHANGING ROLE IN THE WORLD TODAY.

0891 GROSSMAN G.
"SOVIET GROWTH: ROUTINE, INERTIA, AND PRESSURE."
AMER. ECON. REV., 50 (MAY 60), 62-72.
STUDY SOURCE OF INITIATIVE IN SOVIET ECONOMIC GROWTH.

POLITICAL LEADERSHIP ACKNOWLEDGED PRIME MOVER. RESISTANCE OF
BUREAUCRACY TO NEW TECHNIQUES AND PRODUCTS IS SERIOUS OBSTA-
CLE IN RACE WITH CAPITALISM. CHAIN OF COMMAND TRANSMITS
PRESSURE FROM ABOVE, OVERCOMING OBSTACLES BY SANCTIONS AND
INCENTIVES.

0892 GROSSMAN G.
ECONOMIC SYSTEMS.
ENGLEWOOD CLIFFS: PRENTICE HALL, 1967, 120 PP., LC#67-10741.
COMPARES AND ANALYZES SYSTEMATIC APPROACHES TO BALANCING
NATIONAL ECONOMY UNDER CAPITALIST, SOCIALIST, AND MIXED
ECONOMIES. DISCUSSES THEORIES AND PRACTICE TODAY IN US,
USSR, AND YUGOSLAVIA AND IMPORTANCE OF WORKER, MANAGER, AND
CONSUMER IN EACH SYSTEM.

0893 GROSSMAN J.
BIBLIOGRAPHY ON PUBLIC ADMINISTRATION IN LATIN AMERICA.
WASHINGTON: PAN AMERICAN UNION, 1958, 198 PP.
LIST OF 3,392 TITLES OF BOOKS, PERIODICALS, AND OFFICIAL
DOCUMENTS INCLUDING FOREIGN LANGUAGES. ARRANGED TOPICALLY;
INCLUDES ECONOMIC DEVELOPMENT, BUDGETING, TAXATION AND STA-
TISTICS, ETC. BRIEF SECTION OF BIBLIOGRAPHY AND PERIODICALS
AT END.

0894 GROVE J.W.
GOVERNMENT AND INDUSTRY IN BRITAIN.
LONDON: LONGMANS, GREEN & CO, 1962, 514 PP.
REVIEWS, SYSTEMATICALLY AND COMPREHENSIVELY, THE SUBJECT
OF RELATIONS BETWEEN GOVERNMENT AND INDUSTRY. WRITTEN FROM
VIEWPOINT OF CENTRAL ADMINISTRATION. SHOWS HOW DEPARTMENTS
STAND IN CENTER OF "ENVIRONMENT" MADE UP OF VARIOUS AGENCIES
THROUGH WHICH DEPARTMENTS WORK. DESCRIBES GOVERNMENT AS
"REGULATOR, PROMOTER, ENTREPRENEUR, AND PLANNER."

0895 GRUBER H.
INTERNATIONAL COMMUNISM IN THE ERA OF LENIN.
NEW YORK: FAWCETT WORLD LIB, 1967, 512 PP., LC#67-20946.
DOCUMENTARY HISTORY OF EARLY YEARS OF THE COMMUNIST
MOVEMENT. INCLUDES SIGNIFICANT DOCTRINAL STATEMENTS, MANI-
FESTOES, ANALYSES, TACTICAL DECISIONS, AND POLEMICS. HIGH-
LIGHTS OUTSTANDING EVENTS OF PERIOD, TRACES DEVELOPMENTS,
CONFLICTS, AND SPLITS OF NATIONAL COMMUNIST PARTIES AGAINST
BACKGROUND OF GROWING AND CENTRALIZING COMMUNIST INTER-
NATIONAL.

0896 GRUNDLICH T.
DIE TECHNIK DER DIKTATUR.
RASTALT: S GROTESCHE V BUCHH, 1960, 177 PP.
TRANSLATION OF ARISTOTLE'S "TRADE OF TYRANTS." DISCUSSES
MEASURES OF POWER, DISTRIBUTION AND ADMINISTRATION OF POWER,
POWER AND WAR, OPPOSITION TO DICTATORSHIP, ETC.

0897 GRUNDY K.W., WEINSTEIN M.
"THE POLITICAL USES OF IMAGINATION."
TRANSITION, 6 (APR.-MAY 67), 20-24.
CRITICIZES MAZRUI'S VIEW("TRANSACTIONS" NO. 26) ON NKRUMAH
AS A LENINIST CZAR. SUGGESTS INSTEAD THAT NKRUMAH'S IDEOLOGY
WAS AFRICAN, NOT SOVIET, AND THAT NKRUMAH USED WHAT SANTAYA-
NA CALLED "DIRECTIVE IMAGINATION" TO CREATE A NEW SELF-IMAGE
FOR THE AFRICAN PSYCHE WHICH ENABLED THE GHANIANS TO REJECT
THE "COLONIAL MENTALITY."

0898 GRZYBOWSKI K.
THE SOCIALIST COMMONWEALTH OF NATIONS: ORGANIZATIONS AND
INSTITUTIONS.
NEW HAVEN: YALE U PR, 1964, 265 PP., LC#64-20919.
ANALYSIS OF LEGAL BASES AND PRACTICES OF THE SEVERAL
REGIONAL ORGANIZATIONS IN EASTERN EUROPE.

0899 GT BRIT ADMIN STAFF COLLEGE
THE ACCOUNTABILITY OF PUBLIC CORPORATIONS (REV. ED.)
HENLEY-ON-THAMES: ADMIN STAFF C, 1965, 97 PP.
DISCUSSES PARLIAMENTARY AND MINISTERIAL CONTROL OVER
FINANCIAL POLICIES OF PUBLIC CORPORATIONS IN GREAT BRITAIN.
EXAMINES FINANCIAL REQUIREMENTS CONCERNING STOCK, BORROWING,
PRICES, RESERVE FUNDS, ETC.

0900 GUAITA A.
BIBLIOGRAFIA ESPANOLA DE DERECHO ADMINISTRATIVO (PAMPHLET)
BARCELONA: INST DERECHO COMPAREDO, 1955, 113 PP.
BIBLIOGRAPHY OF ADMINISTRATIVE LAW WITH 80 PAGES OF EN-
TRIES, IN SPANISH, 1882-1953, LISTED TOPICALLY.

0901 GUETZKOW H. ED.
GROUPS, LEADERSHIP, AND MEN.
PITTSBURGH: CARNEGIE PR., 1951, 273 PP.
SERIES OF RESEARCH ARTICLES EMPHASIZING PRAGMATIC, IN-
DUCTIVE AND PSYCHOLOGICAL APPROACH TO GROUP-BEHAVIOR COMMUN-
ICATIONS, DECISIONS AND COMPONENTS. STUDIES OF LEADERSHIP IN
SMALL GROUPS, GROUP ACCEPTANCE AND IDENTIFICATION, EFFECT OF
MASS MEDIA AND SELECTIVE SCREENING PROCEDURES OF INDIVIDUAL
BEHAVIOR.

0902 GULICK C.A., OCKERT R.A., WALLACE R.J.
HISTORY AND THEORIES OF WORKING-CLASS MOVEMENTS: A
SELECT BIBLIOGRAPHY.

BERKELEY: U OF CALIF PR, 1955, 364 PP.
BIBLIOGRAPHY LIMITED TO ARTICLES, NOTES, AND OCCASIONAL
DOCUMENTS IN JOURNALS AND MAGAZINES IN ENGLISH. RESTRICTED
TO 250 ENTRIES ON AMERICAN MOVEMENTS. CONCERNED PRIMARILY
WITH BRITISH AND SECONDARILY WITH OTHER FOREIGN MOVE-
MENTS. ENTRIES LISTED ALPHABETICALLY BY AUTHOR UNDER
HEADINGS: TRADE UNIONISM; POLITICS; COOPERATIVES; CULTURE.
DESPITE SELECTIVITY AN EXTENSIVE AND IMPORTANT LIST.

0903 GULICK L. ED., URWICK L. ED.
PAPERS ON THE SCIENCE OF ADMINISTRATION.
NY: COLUMBIA U. INST PUB ADMIN, 1937, 195 PP., LC#37-25327.
DISCUSSES ADMINISTRATION FROM SCIENTIFIC ORIENTATION,
ATTEMPTING TO FORMULATE WHAT HAS COME TO BE KNOWN AS
OPERATIONAL RESEARCH. TREATS ADMINISTRATION AS A
TECHNICAL PROBLEM, CONTROL PROCESSES, STANDARDIZATION OF
NOMENCLATURE, ENVIRONMENTAL ASPECTS, AND BASIC
FUNCTIONALISM. GULICK ATTEMPTS INTEGRATION OF SCIENCE,
VALUES, AND ADMINISTRATION.

0904 GULICK L.
"METROPOLITAN ORGANIZATION."
ANN. ACAD. POL. SOC. SCI., 314 (NOV. 57), 57-65.
PAPER WHICH CONSIDERS THE COST PROBLEMS, THE MANAGEMENT
PROBLEMS, AND THE PROBLEMS OF DEMOCRACY FOR GOVERNMENT IN
METROPOLITAN AREAS. DISCUSSES THE METROPOLITAN COUNTY,
THE OPEN-ENDED METROPOLITAN COMMISSION, AND A NEW
METROPOLITAN LEGISLATIVE AND ADMINISTRATIVE COUNCIL.

0905 GUTTSMAN W.L.
THE BRITISH POLITICAL ELITE.
NEW YORK: BASIC, 1964, 398 PP., $7.50.
HISTORY OF THE BRITISH POLITICAL LEADERS FROM THE
OLIGARCHY OF THE EARLY 19TH CENTURY THROUGH THE PERIOD OF
MIDDLE AND WORKING CLASS CONTROL TO TODAY'S COMPLEX
BUREAUCRATIC FORMS OF GOVERNMENT. SOCIOLOGICAL ANALYSIS OF
PARTIES, LEADERSHIP, AND CAREER PATTERNS OF POLITICAL AND
GOVERNMENT OFFICE HOLDERS.

0906 GUYOT J.F.
"GOVERNMENT BUREAUCRATS ARE DIFFERENT."
PUBLIC ADMIN. REV., 22 (DEC. 62), 195-202.
STUDY OF ACHIEVEMENT, AFFILIATION, AND POWER AS
MOTIVATIONAL PERSONALITY FACTORS FOR MIDDLE-MANAGEMENT
GOVERNMENT AND BUSINESS BUREAUCRATS. FINDS GOVERNMENT
BUREAUCRATS MOST REPRESENTATIVE OF THE AMERICAN ETHIC.

0907 GUZZARDI W. JR.
"THE SECOND BATTLE OF BRITAIN."
FORTUNE, 77 (1968), 108-112, 210-217.
AUTHOR BELIEVES THAT DEVALUATION GIVES BRITAIN A CHANCE
TO START ON THE NEEDED REFORMATION OF ITS ECONOMY, BUT
FIRST IT MUST REGAIN SOLVENCY BY RETRENCHING ABROAD AND
AT HOME. DISCUSSES NECESSARY REFORMS FOR THE WORKING CLASS,
BRITISH MANAGEMENT'S DESIRE FOR A PURPOSE, LABOR'S NEED FOR
STRONG LEADERSHIP, AND THE NEED FOR EDUCATIONAL REFORM.

0908 HAAS E.B.
"REGIONAL INTEGRATION AND NATIONAL POLICY."
INT. CONCIL., 513 (MAY 57), 381-442.
ANALYZING THE EXISTING MULTI-PARTITE ALLIANCES,
EVALUATES MILITARY PACTS AS INSTRUMENTS OF NATIONAL POLICY
AND THEIR UTILITY IN STIMULATING ALLEGIANCES TO LARGER
COMMUNITIES. EXAMINES THE SHIFTING OBJECTIVES PROMPTING
ALLIANCES AND RELATIVE ABILITY OF RELATIONSHIPS TO ADJUST TO
CHANGING CIRCUMSTANCES. CONFLICTS BETWEEN REGIONAL
ASSOCIATIONS AND U.N. AIMS ARE SURVEYED.

0909 HAAS E.B.
"INTERNATIONAL INTEGRATION: THE EUROPEAN AND THE UNIVERSAL
PROCESS."
INT. ORGAN., 15 (SUMMER 61), 366-92.
EXAMINATION OF VARIOUS BLOCS OPERATING ON THE WORLD
SCENE: OEEC-EPU, COUNCIL OF EUROPE, NATO, ETC. 'THE GROWTH
OF FEWER AND LARGER POLITICAL COMMUNITIES WILL CONTRIBUTE TO
REGIONAL, BUT NOT TO UNIVERSAL PEACE.'

0910 HAAS E.B., SCHMITTER P.C.
"ECONOMICS AND DIFFERENTIAL PATTERNS OF POLITICAL INTEGRA-
TION: PROJECTIONS ABOUT UNITY IN LATIN AMERICA."
INT. ORGAN., 18 (AUTUMN 64), 705-37.
PRESENTS THESIS THAT 'UNDER MODERN CONDITIONS THE RELA-
TIONSHIP BETWEEN ECONOMIC AND POLITICAL UNION HAD BEST BE
TREATED AS A CONTINUUM.... POLITICAL IMPLICATIONS CAN BE
ASSOCIATED WITH MOST MOVEMENTS TOWARD ECONOMIC INTEGRATION
EVEN WHEN THE CHIEF ACTORS THEMSELVES DO NOT ENTERTAIN SUCH
NOTIONS AT THE TIME OF ADOPTING THEIR NEW CONSTUITIVE CHAR-
TER.' CITES LAFTA AS EXAMPLE.

0911 HAASE A.R.
INDEX OF ECONOMIC MATERIAL IN DOCUMENTS OF STATES OF THE
UNITED STATES (13 VOLS.)
WASHINGTON: CARNEGIE ENDOWMENT, 1907.
INDEX OF INFORMATION ON HISTORY OF US ECONOMY IN OFFICIAL
REPORTS AND DOCUMENTS. DEALS WITH 13 STATES.

0912 HADWEN J.G., KAUFMANN J.
HOW UNITED NATIONS DECISIONS ARE MADE.
LEYDEN: SYTHOFF, 1962, 179 PP., $3.75.
DESCRIBES MACHINERY OF UN FOR CONSIDERING ECONOMIC QUES-
TIONS AND INDICATES DETERMINANT FORCES AND PROCEDURES.
USE PERSONAL UN EXPERIENCE AS REFERENCE, ELUCIDATES UNWRIT-
TEN PROCEDURES OF NATIONAL DELEGATIONS.

0913 HADWIGER D.F., TALBOTT R.B.
PRESSURES AND PROTEST.
SAN FRANCISCO: CHANDLER, 1965, 336 PP., LC#64-8160.
DISCUSSES THE KENNEDY FARM PROGRAM AND THE WHEAT
REFERENDUM OF 1963 IN THE FORM OF A CASE STUDY. FARMER
COMMITTEE SYSTEMS OF THE DEPT. OF AGRICULTURE, FARMER
ORGANIZATIONS AND METHODS, AND THE DYNAMICS OF A FARM
REFERENDUM ARE EXAMINED.

0914 HADY T.F., HEIN C.J.
"CONGRESSIONAL TOWNSHIPS AS INCORPORATED MUNICIPALITIES."
MIDWEST J. OF POLI. SCI., 8 (NOV. 64), 408-424.
STUDY OF MUNICIPAL INCORPORATIONS IN THE MINNEAPOLIS-ST
PAUL METROPOLITAN AREA DESIGNED TO DETERMINE THE FORCES
BEHIND THE TREND TOWARD INCORPORATION OF GOVERNMENTS ON
THE URBAN FRINGE.

0915 HAIGHT D.E. ED., JOHNSTON L.P. ED.
THE PRESIDENT: ROLES AND POWERS.
NEW YORK: RAND MCNALLY & CO, 1965, 400 PP., LC#65-14098.
GENERAL INTRODUCTION TO PRESIDENCY. HISTORICAL DEVELOP-
MENTS OF OFFICE AS WELL AS PRESENT CHARACTERISTICS. DESIGNED
TO BRING OUT CONTROVERSIAL QUESTIONS ABOUT PRESIDENCY, AND
THEN LEAVE THEM UNRESOLVED. TREATS PRESIDENT AS PARTY LEADER
AS CHIEF EXECUTIVE AND ADMINISTRATOR, AND AS COMMANDER IN
CHIEF. SHOWS HIS RELATION TO HIS ADVISORS, CONGRESS, THE
PUBLIC, AND FOREIGN AFFAIRS.

0916 HAILEY
"THE FUTURE OF COLONIAL PEOPLES."
PRINCETON: U. PR., 1944, 62 PP.
PRESENTS BRITISH VIEW TOWARDS COLONIAL PEOPLE AND THEIR
FUTURE. CONTRASTS THE COLONIAL POLICIES OF VARIOUS
COUNTRIES. CONCLUDES LONG RANGE POLICY OF GREAT BRITAIN WILL
ACHIEVE SELF-GOVERNMENT IN ALL HER COLONIES.

0917 HAILEY
"TOMORROW IN AFRICA."
SUSSEX: AFRICA BUREAU, 1957, 12 PP.
DISCUSSES RACIAL PROBLEM IN AFRICA. GIVES SUMMARY OF
NATIVE STATUS IN ALL NATIONS SOUTH OF THE SAHARA.

0918 HAINES R.M.
THE ADMINISTRATION OF THE DIOCESE OF WORCESTER IN THE FIRST
HALF OF THE FOURTEENTH CENTURY.
LONDON: SOC PROM CHRIST KNOWL, 1965, 393 PP.
STUDIES ADMINISTRATION SYSTEM AT WORCESTER, INCLUDING
RECORDS AND SEALS, LOCAL AND CENTRAL ADMINISTRATION,
EXAMPLES OF TASKS PERFORMED BY EPISCOPAL ADMINISTRATION,
AND ROLE OF PRIOR AND CHAPTER.

0919 HAIRE M. ED.
MODERN ORGANIZATION THEORY.
NEW YORK: JOHN WILEY, 1961, 324 PP., LC#59-13426.
A COLLECTION OF PAPERS BY DIFFERENT AUTHORS FIRST READ AT
A SYMPOSIUM HELD BY THE FOUNDATION FOR RESEARCH ON HUMAN
BEHAVIOR AND DEALING WITH THE THEORY OF ORGANIZATION UNDER
DIFFERENT MODERN APPROACHES AND A DIVERSITY OF IDENTIFIED
PROBLEMS. THEY RANGE FROM DETAILED OBSERVATION TO
ABSTRACT MODELS. THERE IS LITTLE DISCUSSION OF THE ECONOMIC
CONTEXT OF POWER AND OF BUREAUCRACY OF ORGANIZATIONS.

0920 HAIRE M.
"MANAGING MANAGEMENT MANPOWER."
BUSINESS HORIZONS, 10 (WINTER 67), 23-28.
DEVELOPS MATRIX REPRESENTING PROBLEM OF MANAGERIAL CA-
REER DEVELOPMENT. INCLUDING PERSONNEL FLOW AS WELL AS PAY,
RECRUITMENT, TRAINING, ETC., TO PROVIDE GUIDE FOR MANAGE-
MENT TO DETERMINE PROBABILITIES OF MOVEMENT IN A FIRM AND
IN WHAT WAYS INPUT VARIABLES AFFECT PERSONNEL FLOW.

0921 HALDANE R.B.
BEFORE THE WAR.
NEW YORK: FUNK/WAGNALLS, 1920, 234 PP.
TRACES FOREIGN POLICY OF BRITISH GOVERNMENT IN PERIOD
FROM JANUARY 1906 TO AUGUST 1914. PLACES BLAME FOR THE OUT-
BREAK OF WORLD WAR ONE ON THE GERMANS.

0922 HALL B.
"THE PAINTER'S UNION: A PARTIAL VICTORY."
NEW POLITICS, 6 (WINTER 67), 62-66.
DESCRIBES EFFORT OF MEMBERS OF PAINTERS' DISTRICT COUNCIL
19 IN NEW YORK CITY TO END CORRUPT RULE OF MARTIN
RARBACK. DISCUSSES RESULTS OF ELECTION OF MEMBERS'
CANDIDATE, FRANK SCHONFIELD, AND HIS SUBSEQUENT COURTING
OF RARBACK AND HIS SUPPORTERS. URGES UNION MEMBERS TO
CONSIDER ORIGINAL OVERTHROW AS VICTORY AND TO CONTINUE FIGHT
AGAINST CORRUPTION.

0923 HALL B.
"THE COALITION AGAINST DISHWASHERS."
NEW POLITICS, 6 (WINTER 67), 23-32.
EXPLORES TRADE UNION BUREAUCRACIES AND THEIR EXTREME
POWER OVER RANK-AND-FILE MEMBERS. DISCUSSES LAWS OF UNIONS
PROHIBITING ELECTION OF WORKERS AS OFFICERS, LIMITING
CRITICISM OF OFFICERS BY MEMBERS, AND MAKING REMOVAL OF
UNION AS BARGAINING FORCE VERY DIFFICULT. MAINTAINS THAT
RADICALS MUST CHOOSE BETWEEN COALITION WITH ANT-DEMOCRATIC
BUREAUCRACY AND STRUGGLE AGAINST IT.

0924 HALL M., KNAPP J., WINSTEN C.
DISTRIBUTION IN GREAT BRITAIN AND NORTH AMERICA.
LONDON: OXFORD U PR, 1961, 231 PP.
STUDY OF INDUSTRIAL STRUCTURE AND PRODUCTIVITY, SURVEYING
DISTRIBUTION OF GOODS IN BRITAIN AND NORTH AMERICA, INCLUD-
ING EFFICIENCY, DISTRIBUTIVE INPUT AND OUTPUT, EFFECTS OF
RETAIL COMPETITION, CLOTHING AND FOOD TRADES, AND EFFECTS OF
ENVIRONMENT ON PRODUCTIVITY.

0925 HALL W.P.
EMPIRE TO COMMONWEALTH.
NEW YORK: HOLT, 1928, 526 PP.
APPRAISES 'THOSE FORCES WITHIN THE EMPIRE.... WHICH MAKE
FOR CLOSER UNION AND COHESION IN COMPARISON WITH THOSE WHICH
MAKE FOR DISINTEGRATION AND DECAY.' DEVOTES MUCH SPACE TO
A DISCUSSION OF THE BRITISH DOMINIONS.

0926 HALLER W.
DER SCHWEDISCHE JUSTITIEOMBUDSMAN.
ZURICH: POLYGRAPHISCHER VERLAG, 1964, 320 PP.
DISCUSSES BASIC FOUNDATIONS OF SWEDISH LAW, HISTORY OF
OFFICE OF PARLIAMENTARY COMMISSIONER FOR JUDICIAL AND CIVIL-
ADMINISTRATION, AND FUNCTIONS AND RESPONSIBILITIES OF COM-
MISSIONER (JUSTITIEOMBUDSMAN). COMPARES HIS FUNCTION TO
SIMILAR PRACTICES IN OTHER COUNTRIES.

0927 HALPERIN M.H.
"IS THE SENATE'S FOREIGN RELATIONS RESEARCH WORTHWHILE."
AMER. BEHAV. SCI., 4 (SEPT. 60), 21-24.
EXAMINES STUDIES ON MAJOR QUESTIONS OF AMERICAN FOREIGN
POLICY. ANALYZES PROBLEMS OF DEVELOPING AREAS, NATURE OF
SOVIET CHALLENGE, STRUCTURE NEEDED TO DEVELOP AND IMPLEMENT
POLICY.

0928 HALPERIN M.H.
"THE GAITHER COMMITTEE AND THE POLICY PROCESS."
WORLD POLIT., 13 (APR. 61), 360-84.
FIGHT OVER THE RELEASE OF THE REPORT REFLECTED ALMOST
EXACTLY THE LARGER DISPUTE ON DEFENSE SPENDING. WHILE THE
REPORT DID NOT SUBSTANTIALLY ALTER THE COURSE OF THE
STRUGGLE, IT HELPED TO BRING SOME OF THE ISSUES AND PRES-
SURES MORE SHARPLY INTO FOCUS.

0929 HALPIN A.W.
THEORY AND RESEARCH IN ADMINISTRATION.
NEW YORK: MACMILLAN, 1966, 352 PP., LC#66-11578.
TREATS THEORIES BEHIND RESEARCH ON EDUCATIONAL
ADMINISTRATION AND PRESENTS SUBSTANTIVE RESEARCH RESULTS.
STUDIES RELATIONSHIP BETWEEN VERBAL AND NONVERBAL BEHAVIOR
AND RESULTS OF DISCREPANCIES; REFLECTS ON NATURE OF
SCIENTIFIC INQUIRY AND ITS PERTINENCE FOR RESEARCH IN
EDUCATION.

0930 HAMBRIDGE G. ED.
DYNAMICS OF DEVELOPMENT.
NEW YORK: FREDERICK PRAEGER, 1964, 401 PP., LC#64-16678.
ARTICLES FROM INTERNATIONAL DEVELOPMENT REVIEW DEALING
WITH PROBLEMS OF AGRICULTURE, INDUSTRY, EDUCATION, LEADER-
SHIP, ADMINISTRATION OF AID, AND HEALTH IN DEVELOPING
NATIONS.

0931 HAMILTON A., MADISON J., JAY J.
THE FEDERALIST.
CLEVELAND: WORLD, 1961, 672 PP., $2.45.
ARTICLES ON THE POLITICAL PHILOSOPHY UNDERLYING THE CON-
STITUTION OF THE UNITED STATES. ANALYZE POWERS, MECHANICS,
CONTROLS AND IDEAS THAT ARE BUILT INTO U.S. CONSTITUTION IN
ATTEMPT TO HAVE IT RATIFIED BY NEW YORK.

0932 HAMILTON B.L.S.
PROBLEMS OF ADMINISTRATION IN AN EMERGENT NATION: CASE STUDY
OF JAMAICA.
NEW YORK: FREDERICK PRAEGER, 1964, 218 PP., LC#64-25595.
TREATS THEORY THAT EMERGING NATIONS OF BRITISH EMPIRE
HAVE PATTERNS FOR GOVERNMENT ADMINISTRATION AND CIVIL SER-
VICE OWING TO UNIQUE ENVIRONMENTS. STUDIES JAMAICA IN DE-
TAIL TO PROVE THEORY. INCLUDES BACKGROUND OF BRITISH METHOD
OF RULING AND BIBLIOGRAPHY FOR READINGS ON OTHER NATIONS.

0933 HAMILTON R.F.
"SKILL LEVEL AND POLITICS."
PUBLIC OPINION QUART., 29 (1965), 390-399.
ON BASIS OF SECONDARY ANALYSIS OF NATIONAL SURVEYS, THE
AUTHOR QUESTIONS SOME ASSUMPTIONS ABOUT THE RELATIONSHIP
OF SKILL LEVEL AND POLITICS. REJECTING BOTH ECONOMIC FACTORS

AND THE POSSIBILITY OF STATUS DEPRIVATIONS, THE EVIDENCE
POINTS TO SPECIAL RECRUITMENT PATTERNS AND THE STRUCTURING
OF GROUP INFLUENCES.

0934 HAMMOND A.
"COMPREHENSIVE VERSUS INCREMENTAL BUDGETING IN THE DEPART-
MENT OF AGRICULTURE"
ADMINISTRATIVE SCI. Q., 10 (JUNE-AUG. 65), 321-346.
DESCRIBES EXPERIMENT OF DEPARTMENT OF AGRICULTURE TO
EVALUATE ALL DEPARTMENTAL PROGRAMS, ESPECIALLY ADOPTION OF
"ZERO-BASE BUDGETING," WHICH ACCORDING TO AUTHOR ACHIEVED
FEW SPECIFIC CHANGES OR IMPROVEMENTS. SHOWS THAT "ZERO-BASE
BUDGETING" INSTEAD RESULTED IN "PSYCHIC BENEFITS" IN THAT
TOP OFFICIALS COULD SHOW THEIR EXPERTISE TO BUREAU
OFFICIALS.

0935 HAMMOND P.Y.
"FOREIGN POLICY-MAKING AND ADMINISTRATIVE POLITICS."
WORLD POLITICS, 17 (JULY 65), 656-671.
EXPLICIT DISCUSSION OF RELATION BETWEEN UNITARY (FOR
COMPREHENSIVE SOLUTIONS ON BASIS OF GENERAL VISION OF TRUTH)
AND PLURALISTIC (ASSERTS VALUE OF MANY APPROACHES AND DENIES
CERTAINTY OF ANY ONE) APPROACHES TO ANALYZING AND MAKING
FOREIGN POLICY. DISCUSSION IS CENTERED ON US FOREIGN POL-
ICY AND EMPIRICAL METHODS FOR STUDYING ADMINISTRATIVE POL-
ITICS.

0936 HANBURY H.G.
ENGLISH COURTS OF LAW.
LONDON: OXFORD U PR, 1960, 196 PP.
DISCUSSES HISTORY OF ENGLISH JUDICIAL SYSTEM FROM REIGN
OF HENRY II TO 20TH CENTURY. DISCUSSES ESTABLISHMENT AND
EVOLUTION OF COURTS OF COMMON LAW AND CHANCERY. EXAMINES
JUDICIAL SYSTEM IN RELATION TO OTHER BRANCHES OF GOVERNMENT
AND CONSIDERS ROLES OF JUDGES, BARRISTERS, AND SOLICITORS
IN CONSTITUTIONAL SYSTEM.

0937 HANKE L. ED.
HANDBOOK OF LATIN AMERICAN STUDIES.
GAINESVILLE: U OF FLA PR, 1966, 424 PP., LC#36-32633.
PUBLISHED ANNUALLY SINCE 1935, THE HANDBOOK IS A GUIDE
TO WORKS ON LATIN AMERICA IN THE HUMANITIES AND THE SOCIAL
SCIENCES. DIFFERENT FIELDS BEING SELECTED EACH YEAR.
INTRODUCTORY ARTICLES ARE INCLUDED. ANNOTATED.

0938 HANNA W.J. ED.
INDEPENDENT BLACK AFRICA: THE POLITICS OF FREEDOM.
SKOKIE: RAND MCNALLY & CO, 1964, 651 PP., LC#64-14113.
COLLECTION OF ESSAYS, MOST BY NON-AFRICANS, CONCERNED
WITH POLITICAL AND ADMINISTRATIVE PROBLEMS OF AFRICA, AND
FOCUSING ON THE "MODAL" POLITICAL SYSTEM AND FACTORS WHICH
HAVE CONTRIBUTED TO ITS DEVELOPMENT; ILLUMINATES PROBLEMS
ALL SHARE: DEEP SOCIAL DIVISIONS, FRAGILE GOVERNMENTS, AND
UNDERDEVELOPED ECONOMIES.

0939 HANSON A.H.
THE STRUCTURE AND CONTROL OF STATE ENTERPRISES IN TURKEY.
ANKARA: PUBLIC ADMIN INST, 1959, 24 PP.
ANALYZES SYSTEM OF STATE ENTERPRISES, DEFINES FEW MAIN
PROBLEMS, AND MAKES SUGGESTIONS FOR THEIR SOLUTIONS. EMPHA-
SIZES DEVELOPMENTS AND CHANGES IN SYSTEM TO 1959. STRESSES
AREAS OF ORGANIZATION AND STATE CONTROL OR RESPONSIBILITY.

0940 HANSON A.H.
MANAGERIAL PROBLEMS IN PUBLIC ENTERPRISE.
NEW YORK: ASIA PUBL HOUSE, 1962, 148 PP.
ANALYZES PROBLEMS OF MANAGEMENT IN PUBLIC ENTERPRISE SUCH
AS ORGANIZATIONAL FORMS, PARLIAMENTARY ACCOUNTABILITY, RE-
LATIONS WITH MINISTERS, EFFICIENCY, AND PRICE AND PROFIT
POLICIES. INCLUDES TYPES OF PUBLIC ENTERPRISE AND THEIR RE-
LATIONS WITH STATE. DISCUSSES EXPERIENCES AND SOLUTIONS OF
OTHER AREAS OF WORLD AS THEY APPLY TO PROBLEMS IN INDIA.

0941 HANSON A.H. ED.
NATIONALIZATION: A BOOK OF READINGS.
TORONTO: U OF TORONTO PRESS, 1963, 475 PP.
READINGS THAT PROVIDE BACKGROUND TO MANY CONTROVERSIES
ARISING FROM NATIONALIZATION OF INDUSTRY, AND COVER MANY SO-
LUTIONS ATTEMPTED OR PROPOSED FOR CONSTITUTIONAL, ORGANIZA-
TIONAL, AND ECONOMIC PROBLEMS OF THE PUBLIC SECTOR. EACH
CHAPTER GROUPS SELECTIONS RELATED TO ONE ASPECT (SUCH AS
PERSONNEL, FINANCE, ORGANIZATION) AND INCLUDES EXTENSIVE IN-
TRODUCTION TO THE ISSUES.

0942 HANSON A.H.
"PLANNING AND THE POLITICIANS* SOME REFLECTIONS ON ECONOMIC
PLANNING IN WESTERN EUROPE."
INT. REV. OF ADMIN. SCI., 32 (1966), 277-286.
AUTHOR CONTENDS THAT ECONOMIC PLANNING SHOULD BE A COMBI-
NATION OF ECONOMISTS, POLITICIANS, AND ADMINISTRATORS WORK-
ING TOGETHER JOINTLY. ADMINISTRATORS AND POLITICIANS ARE
NEEDED TO DEVISE THE MACHINERY AND FORMULATE RULES AND REGU-
LATIONS WHEREBY BROAD OBJECTIVES MAY BE TRANSLATED INTO DE-
TAILED AND CONSISTENT DECISIONS. COMPARES AND CONTRASTS WHAT
INDIVIDUAL COUNTRIES IN EUROPE ARE NOW DOING.

0943 HARARI M.
GOVERNMENT AND POLITICS OF THE MIDDLE EAST.
ENGLEWOOD CLIFFS: PRENTICE HALL, 1962, 179 PP., LC#62-16659.
CLAIMS US POLICY IS MILITARISTIC AND THAT ECONOMIC
ASSISTANCE MAY PROVE MORE USEFUL. ADVOCATES CONSISTENT
MIDDLE EAST POLICY RATHER THAN THE CONTINGENCY PLANNING OF
PAST. DISCUSSES ROLE OF ISLAM IN POLITICAL INSTITUTIONS AND
DOMESTIC AND FOREIGN POLICIES OF INDIVIDUAL GOVERNMENTS.

0944 HARDMAN J.B. ED.
AMERICAN LABOR DYNAMICS.
NEW YORK: HARCOURT BRACE, 1928, 432 PP.
THE RESULT OF A GROUP STUDY, IT EXAMINES VARIOUS EARLY
20TH CENTURY LABOR DEVELOPMENTS, A VIEW OF TRADE UNIONISM
AS CONTENDER FOR SOCIAL POWER, LABOR POLICIES AND THEIR
EFFECTIVENESS IN SELECTED TRADES, AS WELL AS A REVIEW OF
LABOR'S LOBBYING ACTIVITIES AND A LONG SECTION ON LABOR
IN-GROUP RELATIONSHIPS: ORGANIZATION, LEADERSHIP, MEMBER-
SHIP, FACTIONS, FOREIGN INFLUENCES ON AMERICAN LABOR.

0945 HARDMAN J.B.
THE HOUSE OF LABOR.
ENGLEWOOD CLIFFS: PRENTICE HALL, 1951, 555 PP.
A COMPREHENSIVE TREATMENT OF LABOR UNIONS AND THEIR
FUNCTIONING, WITH SECTION ON UNION GOVERNMENT, PARTICIPATION
IN THE COMMUNITY, UNION STAFF AND ADMINISTRATION, UNION
RESEARCH AND SOCIAL ENGINEERING, THE LABOR PRESS, AND
LOBBYING ACTIVITIES.

0946 HARGROVE M.M. ED., HARRISON I.H. ED., SWEARINGEN E.L. ED.
BUSINESS POLICY CASES-WITH BEHAVIORAL SCIENCE IMPLICATIONS.
HOMEWOOD: RICHARD IRWIN, 1963, 639 PP., LC#63-14227.
THIRTY-ONE VARIED BUSINESS POLICY CASES WITH BEHAVIORAL
SCIENCE IMPLICATIONS, PRIMARILY FOR A BUSINESS SCHOOL
COURSE INTEGRATING CORE COURSES. PROVIDES FRAMEWORK TO ANA1-
LYZE BUSINESS POLICY CASE IN TERMS OF THE PLANNING, ORGANIZ-
ING, EVALUATING, AND CONTROLLING FUNCTIONS OF MANAGEMENT.
ALSO, EACH CASE CAN BE ANALYZED IN TERMS OF CORE COURSES AND
IN TERMS OF BEHAVIORAL SCIENCE.

0947 HARLOW R.F.
PUBLIC RELATIONS IN WAR AND PEACE.
NEW YORK: HARPER & ROW, 1942, 220 PP.
DISCUSSION OF NATURE OF PUBLIC RELATIONS, INCLUDING ITS
FOUNDATIONS, VARIOUS TYPES, CONTENT, TOOLS, ROLE DURING
WARTIME, AND ITS FUTURE.

0948 HARLOW R.V.
THE HISTORY OF LEGISLATIVE METHODS IN THE PERIOD BEFORE 1825
NEW HAVEN: YALE U PR, 1917, 269 PP., LC#17-30135.
TRACES GROWTH OF COMMITTEE SYSTEMS IN LAWMAKING BODIES OF
COLONIES AND STATES FROM 1750 TO 1790, AND IN HOUSE OF REP-
RESENTATIVES FROM BEGINNING TO 1825. DISCUSSES BOTH FORMAL
ORGANIZATION, PROVIDED BY RULES, AND INFORMAL, SUPPLIED BY
POLITICAL PARTIES.

0949 HARMON R.B.
BIBLIOGRAPHY OF BIBLIOGRAPHIES IN POLITICAL SCIENCE
(MIMEOGRAPHED PAPER: LIMITED EDITION)
SAN JOSE: DIBCO PRESS, 1964, 16 PP.
AN UNANNOTATED LISTING OF GENERAL, CURRENT, AND RETRO-
SPECTIVE BIBLIOGRAPHIES DIVIDED INTO SEVEN SUBJECT AREAS.
MOST ENTRIES FROM 20TH CENTURY AND A FEW FROM LATTER 19TH OR
EARLIER. INCLUDES FOREIGN PUBLICATIONS THOUGH MAJORITY ARE
AMERICAN. A GOOD BASIC LIST WHICH THE AUTHOR EXPANDS IN SUB-
SEQUENT WORKS. SUBJECT AND AUTHOR INDEXES. BOOKS ONLY.
109 ENTRIES.

0950 HARMON R.B.
POLITICAL SCIENCE: A BIBLIOGRAPHICAL GUIDE TO THE LITERATURE
METUCHEN: SCARECROW PRESS, 1965, 388 PP., LC#65-13557.
UNANNOTATED COMPILATION OF 2,500 ENGLISH-LANGUAGE BOOKS
PUBLISHED 1859 THROUGH 1963. INCLUDES SEPARATE INDEXES FOR
JOURNALS, GOVERNMENT DOCUMENTS, AND AUTHORS. ENTRIES DIVID-
ED INTO TEN GENERAL CATEGORIES AND THEN SUBDIVIDED. INCLUDES
SECTION ON GENERAL REFERENCE WORKS AND BIBLIOGRAPHIES AND A
SECTION ON RESEARCH AND METHODOLOGY IN POLITICAL SCIENCE.
EXCELLENT AND THOROUGH COVERAGE OF POLITICAL SCIENCE.

0951 HARMON R.B.
SOURCES AND PROBLEMS OF BIBLIOGRAPHY IN POLITICAL SCIENCE
(PAMPHLET)
SAN JOSE: DIBCO PRESS, 1966, 73 PP., LC#66-18521.
A REVISED AND ENLARGED EDITION OF THE AUTHOR'S "BIBLIOG-
RAPHY OF BIBLIOGRAPHIES IN POLITICAL SCIENCE." MOST COMPRE-
HENSIVE LISTING OF BIBLIOGRAPHIES, CURRENT AND RETROSPEC-
TIVE, IN POLITICAL SCIENCE. INDEXED UNDER GENERAL TOPICS.
SEPARATE AUTHOR-TITLE INDEX AND SEPARATE LISTING OF BIBLIO-
GRAPHIC PERIODICALS. GOOD SECTION ON GENERAL BIBLIOGRAPHIES
OF VALUE TO POLITICAL SCIENCE. 244 ENTRIES.

0952 HARPER S.N.
THE GOVERNMENT OF THE SOVIET UNION.
PRINCETON: VAN NOSTRAND, 1938, 204 PP.
DISCUSSES SOVIET INSTITUTIONS, GOVERNMENTAL STRUCTURES,
AND METHODS OF GOVERNING IMMEDIATELY PRECEDING AND AFTER
BOLSHEVIK RISE TO POWER. INCLUDES ECONOMIC STRUCTURES AND
PLANS, PARTY POLICY, LAW-MAKING, PUBLIC ADMINISTRATION, AND
PUBLIC SERVICES. ALSO TREATS ROLE OF INDIVIDUAL IN A
COLLECTIVIZED STATE, INTERNATIONAL RELATIONSHIPS, GOAL OF
WORLD REVOLUTION, AND 1937-38 TREASON TRIALS.

0953 HARR J.E.
THE DEVELOPMENT OF CAREERS IN THE FOREIGN SERVICE.
NEW YORK: TAPLINGER PUBL CO, 1965, 104 PP., LC#64-24648.
FOREIGN SERVICE OFFICER CORPS IS THE MOST IMPORTANT GROUP
IN THE CONDUCT OF US FOREIGN AFFAIRS AND HAS BEEN AT THE
CENTER OF MOST PERSONNEL REFORMS IN FOREIGN AFFAIRS. HERE
THE INTERACTION OF THE DEPARTMENT OF STATE ADMINISTRATIVE
NEEDS AND FSO NEEDS ARE ANALYZED IN TERMS OF THE MANAGEMENT
OF A CAREER DEVELOPMENT PROGRAM. GOOD DATA.

0954 HARRIS J.P.
"LEGISLATIVE CONTROL OF ADMINISTRATION: SOME COMPARISONS OF
AMERICAN AND EUROPEAN PRACTICES."
WESTERN POLIT. QUART., 10 (JUNE 57), 465-468.
THE US CONGRESS HAS NOT EVOLVED PROCEDURES WHEREBY
EXECUTIVE OFFICERS ARE HELD RESPONSIBLE FOR ASMINISTRATION
UNDER THEIR DIRECTION. IN GREAT BRITAIN, ON THE CONTRARY,
MINISTERIAL RESPONSIBILITY IS A CARDINAL ASPECT OF
EXECUTIVE-LEGISLATIVE RELATIONS. IN FRANCE, SWITZERLAND,
WEST GERMANY, THE NETHERLANDS, AND SWEDEN THE SITUATION
IS SIMILAR TO THAT OF GREAT BRITAIN.

0955 HARRIS R.L., KEARNEY R.N.
"A COMPARATIVE ANALYSIS OF THE ADMINISTRATIVE SYSTEMS OF
CANADA AND CEYLON."
ADMIN. SCI. QUART., 8 (DEC. 63), 339-60.
ATTEMPTS TO IDENTIFY CULTURAL VARIABLES INFLUENCING
PUBLIC ADMINISTRATION IN AN INDUSTRIALLY WELL-DEVELOPED
WESTERN NATION AND A DEVELOPING NEW STATE. UTILIZES AN
ECOLOGICAL-ENVIRONMENTAL APPROACH, A NEW TECHNIQUE OF COM-
PARATIVE ANALYSIS FOR THE STUDY OF FOREIGN SYSTEMS OF
PUBLIC ADMINISTRATION.

0956 HARRISON S.
INDIA AND THE UNITED STATES.
NEW YORK: MACMILLAN, 1961, 244 PP.
CONFERENCE IN 1959 OF MAJOR ADMINISTRATORS REPRESENTING
BOTH COUNTRIES DEALT WITH ISSUES OF NEUTRALISM AND FOREIGN
ASSISTANCE. VARIOUS PROPOSALS ADVANCED TO ALLEVIATE INDIA'S
FOOD CRISES AND POPULATION-GROWTH PROBLEM.

0957 HART H.C.
ADMINISTRATIVE ASPECTS OF RIVER VALLEY DEVELOPMENT.
NEW YORK: ASIA PUBL HOUSE, 1961, 111 PP.
COMPARES AMERICAN AND INDIAN PROGRAMS OF RIVER VALLEY DE-
VELOPMENT SUCH AS TVA AND DAMODAR VALLEY CORPORATION AS TO
METHODS, ADMINISTRATION, AND EFFECTIVENESS.

0958 HART J.
AN INTRODUCTION TO ADMINISTRATIVE LAW, WITH SELECTED CASES.
NEW YORK: F S CROFTS & CO, 1940, 621 PP.
GENERAL INTRODUCTION TO US ADMINISTRATIVE LAW. DEFINES
ADMINISTRATIVE LAW, THEN DISCUSSES PUBLIC OFFICE AND
OFFICERS. CONSIDERS POWERS OF ADMINISTRATIVE AUTHORITIES AND
SCOPE AND LIMITS OF ADMINISTRATIVE POWERS. ENFORCEMENT OF
ADMINISTRATIVE DECISIONS AND REMEDIES AGAINST ADMINISTRATIVE
ACTION ARE TREATED. INCLUDES CRIMINAL, CONTRACTUAL, AND TORT
LIABILITIES OF PUBLIC ADMINISTRATIVE OFFICERS.

0959 HART J.
THE AMERICAN PRESIDENCY IN ACTION 1789: A STUDY IN
CONSTITUTIONAL HISTORY.
NEW YORK: MACMILLAN, 1948, 256 PP.
STUDY OF FIRST YEAR OF AMERICAN PRESIDENCY IN ACTION,
SHOWING HOW SEVERAL ASPECTS OF PRESIDENT'S ROLE HAD EMERGED
BY THEN: THE PRESIDENT AS CHIEF OF STATE, FOREIGN RELATIONS,
ARMED FORCES, GOVERNMENT, AND PARTY. VIEWS HISTORICAL
BEGINNINGS FROM POLITICAL SCIENTIST'S STANCE.

0960 HART J.
"ADMINISTRATION AND THE COURTS."
ANN. ACAD. POL. SOC. SCI., 292 (MAR. 54), 88-94.
COURTS HAVE A TRADITIONAL CONSTITUTIONAL ROLE TO CONTROL
AND CHECK ADMINISTRATION. BEST POSSIBLE POSITION OF COURTS
IS THAT TAKEN SO FAR: NEITHER TRYING TO RUN ADMINISTRATIVE
PROCESS NOR IGNORING IT.

0961 HART W.R.
COLLECTIVE BARGAINING IN THE FEDERAL CIVIL SERVICE.
NEW YORK: HARPER & ROW, 1961, 302 PP., LC#61-7926.
STUDY OF LABOR-MANAGEMENT RELATIONS IN THE FEDERAL CIVIL
SERVICE. CONSIDERS CRITICISMS AND DEFENSES OF REGULAR
GOVERNMENT POLICY PROHIBITING COLLECTIVE BARGAINING.
SUGGESTS COLLECTIVE BARGAINING BE TRIED, BUT SAYS IT ALONE
CANNOT SOLVE ALL LABOR-MANAGEMENT PROBLEMS OF THE FEDERAL
GOVERNMENT.

0962 HARTLAND P.C.
BALANCE OF INTERREGIONAL PAYMENTS OF NEW ENGLAND.
PROVIDENCE: BROWN U PRESS, 1950, 125 PP.

STUDY OF BALANCE-OF-PAYMENTS OF NEW ENGLAND WITH OTHER
REGIONS OF COUNTRY IN RELATION TO DETERMINING SIZE OF BANK
RESERVES. TREATS GOLD MOVEMENTS AND DEPOSITS IN NEW ENGLAND
AS INDICATOR OF FUNCTION OF FEDERAL RESERVE SYSTEM IN ONE
REGION AND ITS RELATION TO NATIONAL ECONOMY.

0963 HARVARD UNIVERSITY LAW LIBRARY
CATALOGUE OF THE LIBRARY OF THE LAW SCHOOL OF HARVARD
UNIVERSITY (3 VOLS.)
CAMBRIDGE: HARVARD U PR, 1909, 2462 PP.
CATALOGUE OF BOOKS ON AMERICAN AND ENGLISH COMMON LAW
CONTAINED IN THE HARVARD LAW LIBRARY. PUBLICATIONS AND CODES
COVER LEGAL HISTORY SINCE THE 14TH CENTURY. WORKS ENTERED
UNDER AUTHOR'S NAME ONLY.

0964 HARVEY M.F.
"THE PALESTINE REFUGEE PROBLEM: ELEMENTS OF A SOLUTION."
ORBIS, 3 (SUMMER 59), 193-207.
CONTENDS THAT THE REGULATED REPATRIATION OF ARAB REFUGEES
INTO ISRAEL IS THE LOGICAL SOLUTION TO THE DIFFICULT SITUAT-
ION IN THE MIDDLE-EAST.

0965 HASAN H.S.
PAKISTAN AND THE UN.
NEW YORK: MANHATTAN, 1961, 328 PP.
ASSUMES THAT ORGANIZATIONS SIGNIFICANCE AND FUNCTIONING
DEPENDS PRIMARILY UPON THE ATTITUDES AND POLICIES OF MEMBER
NATIONS. DEPICTS PAKISTANI POINTS OF VIEW, AS
OFFICIALLY STATED AND UNOFFICIALLY CONSIDERED, AND OBSERVES
THE WORKING OF CHARTER SYSTEM PRESCRIBES MODIFICATIONS AND
ASSESSES POSSIBILITY OF ACCOMPLISHING THIS.

0966 HASTINGS P.G.
THE MANAGEMENT OF BUSINESS FINANCE.
PRINCETON: VAN NOSTRAND, 1966, 527 PP.
INTRODUCTORY SURVEY OF MANAGEMENT TECHNIQUES FUNDAMENTAL
TO MAKING FINANCIAL DECISIONS IN BUSINESS. EMPHASIZES
RELATION BETWEEN FINANCIAL ASPECTS OF FIRM AND MANAGEMENT'S
POLICY-MAKING. WHICH DECISIONS MAKE MOST MONEY? COVERS ALL
ASPECTS OF INVESTING AND BORROWING. BIBLIOGRAPHY AFTER
EACH CHAPTER.

0967 HATHAWAY D.A.
GOVERNMENT AND AGRICULTURE: PUBLIC POLICY IN A DEMOCRATIC
SOCIETY.
NEW YORK: MACMILLAN, 1963, 412 PP., LC#61-11797.
DISCUSSION OF THE ROLE OF GOVERNMENT IN DETERMINING FARM
POLICY. SEES AGRICULTURAL POLICY AS PART OF A NATIONAL
ATTEMPT AT DEVELOPING A UNIFORMLY PROSPEROUS, STABLE,
CAPITALIST ECONOMY.

0968 HATTERY L.H. ED., MCCORMICK E.M. ED.
INFORMATION RETRIEVAL MANAGEMENT.
DETROIT: AMER DATA PROCESSING, 1962, 151 PP., LC#62-18060.
SERIES OF 18 PAPERS BY DIFFERENT AUTHORS CONCERNING
VARIOUS ASPECTS OF MANAGERIAL PROBLEMS IN SCIENCE
INFORMATION PROCESSES. SOME DEAL WITH HISTORICAL, SOCIAL,
AND CULTURAL BACKGROUNDS, OTHERS WITH QUESTIONS OF COST,
ACCEPTANCE, AND COMMUNICATIONS. GENERAL TECHNIQUES AND
SPECIFIC APPLICATION TO SCIENTIFIC AND INDUSTRIAL RESEARCH
ARE DISCUSSED, INCLUDING EXAMPLES OF ACTUAL OPERATIONS.

0969 HAUSER O.
PREUSSISCHE STAATSRASON UND NATIONALER GEDANKE.
NEUMUNSTER: KARL WACHHOLTZ VERL, 1960, 285 PP.
DISCUSSES ORIGINS OF PRUSSIAN ADMINISTRATION IN SCHLES-
WIG-HOLSTEIN, NATIONAL MOVEMENTS, AND ATTITUDE TOWARD LAN-
GUAGE PROBLEM IN NORTHERN SCHLESWIG. EXAMINES BROADER IMPLI-
CATIONS OF CULTURAL NATIONALISM IN SCHLESWIG-HOLSTEIN BE-
TWEEN 1860 AND 1920.

0970 HAUSMAN W.H. ED.
MANAGING ECONOMIC DEVELOPMENT IN AFRICA.
CAMBRIDGE: M I T PRESS, 1963, 253 PP., LC#63-16233.
ANTHOLOGY OF PAPERS ON MANAGEMENT OF AFRICAN ECONOMIC DE-
VELOPMENT COVERING PLANNING, MANPOWER, TECHNICAL ASSISTANCE,
CAPITAL, FOREIGN AID, LEGAL ASPECTS, AND US ROLE.

0971 HAVILAND H.F.
"FOREIGN AID AND THE POLICY PROCESS: 1957."
AMER. POLIT. SCI. REV., 52 (SEPT. 58), 689-724.
FACTIONS FOR AND AGAINST THE AID PROGRAM ARE CLASSIFIED.
INTERACTION BETWEEN THE EXECUTIVE AND TWO HOUSES EMPHASIZED.
INEFFECTIVE RELATIONSHIP FOUND BETWEEN THE SUBSTANTIVE AND
APPROPRIATION COMMITTEES OF CONGRESS.

0972 HAVILAND H.F.
"BUILDING A POLITICAL COMMUNITY."
INT. ORGAN., 17 (SUMMER 63), 733-53.
INDENTIFIES AND ANALYZES PRINCIPAL CONSIDERATIONS OF
ATLANTIC POLITICAL COMMUNITY. MILITARY PROBLEM GENERATES
STRONGEST PRESSURES FOR CLOSER POLITICAL RELATIONS. CON-
SIDERS MAJOR ECONOMIC PROBLEMS. PRESENTS ATTITUDES OF UNITED
KINGDOM, NEUTRALS AND UNDERDEVELOPED NATIONS TOWARDS ATLAN-
TIC COMMUNITY.

0973 HAWLEY C.E. ED., WEINTRAUB R.G. ED.
ADMINISTRATIVE QUESTIONS AND POLITICAL ANSWERS.
PRINCETON: VAN NOSTRAND, 1966, 601 PP.
COLLECTION OF ESSAYS ON PUBLIC ADMINISTRATION. DISCUSSES
THEORY AND POLITICAL SETTING OF ADMINISTRATION. STUDIES
ADMINISTRATIVE PRACTICE, PERSONNEL, AND COMPARATIVE
ADMINISTRATION. EXAMINES MODERN THEORY AND PRACTICE OF
ADMINISTRATIVE TRAINING AND EDUCATION. ESSAYS ARE RECENT
ADDITIONS TO STUDY OF ADMINISTRATION.

0974 VON HAYEK F.A.
THE CONSTITUTION OF LIBERTY.
CHICAGO: U OF CHICAGO PRESS, 1960, 570 PP., LC#59-11618.
DISCUSSES CONCEPT OF FREEDOM AND MEANS OF ACHIEVING IT.
EXAMINES FACTORS THAT DETERMINE GROWTH OF ALL CIVILIZATIONS
AND INSTITUTIONS THE WEST HAS DEVELOPED TO SECURE INDIVIDUAL
LIBERTY. TESTS PRINCIPLES OF FREEDOM AGAINST INSTITUTIONS
OF THE WELFARE STATE, SHOWING HOW OFTEN PURSUIT OF THE SAME
GOALS BY DIFFERENT METHODS MAY EITHER ENHANCE OR DESTROY
LIBERTY.

0975 HAYER T.
FRENCH AID.
LONDON: OVERSEAS DEVELOPMT INST, 1966, 230 PP.
DESCRIBES FRENCH AID IN CONTEXT BOTH OF FRANCE'S PAST
COLONIAL POLICY AND FRENCH INTEREST IN THE THIRD WORLD.
SIGNIFICANCE OF SIZE OF FRENCH PROGRAM IS FULLY DISCUSSED.
EXAMINES CLOSENESS OF FRANCO-AFRICAN RELATIONS AND CONSIDERS
ADVANTAGES AND DISADVANTAGES. STUDY IS ONE OF OVERSEAS
DEVELOPMENT INSTITUTE'S.

0976 HAYMAN D., STAHL O.G.
POLITICAL ACTIVITY RESTRICTION; AN ANALYSIS WITH
RECOMMENDATIONS (PAMPHLET)
CHICAGO: PUBLIC PERSONNEL ASSN, 1963, 19 PP.
SHORT REVIEW OF RESTRICTIONS PLACED ON THE POLITICAL
ACTIVITIES OF CIVIL SERVANTS, AND THE RELATION OF THESE
RESTRICTIONS TO DEMOCRACY.

0977 HAYNES G.H.
THE SENATE OF THE UNITED STATES: ITS HISTORY AND PRACTICE.
NEW YORK: RUSSELL & RUSSELL, 1960, 567 PP., LC#60-5280.
DETAILED COMPREHENSIVE ANALYSIS OF THE UNITED STATES SE-
NATE FROM ITS INCEPTION TO THE ADJOURNMENT OF THE 75TH CON-
GRESS. TREATS ELECTION OF SENATORS, SENATE OFFICERS AND OR-
GANIZATION, COMMITTEES, RULES AND PROCEDURES, DEBATE IN THE
SENATE, LEADERSHIP AND LOBBYING, SENATE INVESTIGATIONS AND
SENATE INFLUENCE IN FINANCIAL LEGISLATION.

0978 HAYTER W.
THE DIPLOMACY OF THE GREAT POWERS.
NEW YORK: MACMILLAN, 1961, 74 PP.
DISCUSSES DIPLOMACY OF US, USSR, GREAT BRITAIN, AND
FRANCE. EMPHASIS IS ON DIPLOMATIC METHODS AND GOVERNMENT
POLICIES THAT DETERMINE THEM. EACH COUNTRY IS DISCUSSED
SEPARATELY. ORIENTATION IS BASICALLY IMPRESSIONISTIC AND AP-
PROACH IS INFORMAL.

0979 HEADLAM-MORLEY
BIBLIOGRAPHY IN POLITICS FOR THE HONOUR SCHOOL OF PHILOSO-
PHY, POLITICS AND ECONOMICS (PAMPHLET)
LONDON: OXFORD U PR, 1949, 56 PP.
UNANNOTATED BIBLIOGRAPHY DESIGNED PRIMARILY FOR THOSE
WORKING FOR THE HONOUR SCHOOL; THUS IT IS NEITHER EXHAUSTIVE
NOR SELF-CONTAINED. ENTRIES ARRANGED INTO NINE TOPICAL CLAS-
SIFICATIONS COVERING HISTORY AND THEORY OF POLITICAL INSTI-
TUTIONS FROM HOBBES THROUGH 1948. LISTS BOTH 19TH AND 20TH
CENTURY WORKS, WITH EMPHASIS ON MORE RECENT PUBLICATIONS.

0980 HEADY F., PEALY R.H.
"THE MICHIGAN DEPARTMENT OF ADMINISTRATION; A CASE STUDY
IN THE POLITICS OF ADMINISTRATION" (BMR)"
PUBLIC ADMIN. REV., 16 (SPRING 56), 82-89.
ASSESSES POLITICAL RAMIFICATIONS OF MICHIGAN DEPARTMENT
OF ADMINISTRATION'S POLITICAL ACTIVITIES. SHOWS THAT
POLITICAL FORCES PRESIDED OVER BIRTH OF THE DEPARTMENT AND
"POLITICAL" LIFE HAS BEEN MOST SIGNIFICANT FEATURE OF ITS
HISTORY. DISCUSSES POLITICAL CONSIDERATIONS WHICH MADE
NECESSARY THE CLOSE AFFILIATION BETWEEN THE ADMINISTRATIVE
BOARD AND THE DEPARTMENT IT OVERSEES.

0981 HEADY F.
"RECENT LITERATURE ON COMPARATIVE PUBLIC ADMINISTRATION."
ADMINISTRATIVE SCI. Q., 5 (JUNE 60), 134-154.
SURVEY OF RECENT LITERATURE ON THEORY AND METHODOLOGY;
COMPARATIVE STUDIES OF WESTERN SOCIETIES; COMPARATIVE
STUDIES OF NON-WESTERN SOCIETIES; STUDIES ON INDIVIDUAL
COUNTRIES.

0982 HEADY F.
PUBLIC ADMINISTRATION: A COMPARATIVE PERSPECTIVE.
ENGLEWOOD CLIFFS: PRENTICE HALL, 1966, 115 PP., LC#66-17372.
A COMPREHENSIVE EFFORT TO ASSESS THE PRESENT STATE OF THE
COMPARATIVE STUDY OF PUBLIC ADMINISTRATION AND TO CHARACTER-
IZE ADMINISTRATIVE SYSTEMS IN A WIDE RANGE OF CONTEMPORARY
NATION-STATES. COLLATES ADMINISTRATIVE SYSTEMS OF WIDE

VARIATION; FOCUSES ON PUBLIC BUREAUCRACIES AS COMMON GOVERN-
MENTAL INSTITUTIONS AND PLACES EMPHASIS UPON RELATIONSHIPS
BETWEEN BUREAUCRACIES AND POLITICAL REGIME TYPES.

0983 HEAP D.
AN OUTLINE OF PLANNING LAW (3RD ED.)
LONDON: SWEET & MAXWELL, 1960, 213 PP.
   OUTLINES LEGAL FRAMEWORK OF TOWN PLANNING, ESPECIALLY
TOWN AND COUNTRY PLANNING ACTS OF 1947-59, AND EXAMINES EF-
FECT OF LAWS ON CENTRAL AND LOCAL ADMINISTRATION. STUDIES
PLANS FOR DEVELOPMENT, CONTROL OF DEVELOPMENT AND ADVERTISE-
MENTS, PRESERVATION OF BUILDINGS AND LAND, ENFORCEMENT OF
CONTROL, AND DEVELOPMENT OF NEW TOWNS.

0984 HEARLE E.F.R., MASON R.J.
A DATA PROCESSING SYSTEM FOR STATE AND LOCAL GOVERNMENTS.
ENGLEWOOD CLIFFS: PRENTICE HALL, 1963, 150 PP., LC#63-21039.
   EXAMINES NATURE OF DATA USED BY STATE AND LOCAL GOVERN-
MENTS AND DATA SYSTEM DESIGNS FOR LONG-RANGE NEEDS. FOCUSES
ON TOTAL COMPLEX OF FUNCTIONS PERFORMED BY STATE AND LOCAL
GOVERNMENTS RATHER THAN ON SPECIFIC AGENCIES. STUDY IS
CONCEPTUAL RATHER THAN PROCEDURAL IN NATURE.

0985 HEATH S.
CITADEL, MARKET, AND ALTAR; EMERGING SOCIETY.
BALTIMORE:SCIENCE OF SOCIETY FDN, 1957, 259 PP.
   OUTLINE OF SOCIONOMY, THE NEW NATURAL SCIENCE OF SOCI-
ETY, WHICH REORGANIZES SOCIAL INSTITUTIONS TO RELEASE OPTI-
MUM AMOUNT OF CREATIVITY, DEEPEST NEED OF MAN. BASED ON
STUDY OF BRITISH SOCIAL SYSTEM. AUTHOR FORECASTS A "MODEL
SYSTEM" INVOLVING OWNERSHIP, CONTRACT, EXCHANGE IN FREE EN-
TERPRISE FOR TRUE SOCIALIZATION.

0987 HECTOR L.J.
"GOVERNMENT BY ANONYMITY: WHO WRITES OUR REGULATORY
OPINIONS?"
AMER BAR ASSN., 45 (DEC. 59).
   COMMISSIONERS IN MOST FEDERAL AGENCIES DO NOT WRITE THEIR
OWN OPINIONS. SINCE KNOWING WHO MAKES DECISIONS IS ESSENTIAL
FOR THE PRESERVATION OF DEMOCRACY, COMMISSIONERS SHOULD BE
REQUIRED TO WRITE THEIR OWN OPINIONS.

0988 HELLMAN F.S. ED.
COUNTY GOVERNMENT IN THE UNITED STATES: A LIST OF RECENT
REFERENCES (PAMPHLET)
WASHINGTON: LIBRARY OF CONGRESS, 1940, 13 PP.
   146-ITEM BIBLIOGRAPHY INCLUDES SUMMARY ANNOTATIONS ON
BOOKS, ARTICLES, PAMPHLETS, ETC. PRINTED AFTER 1938. NO
INDEX. LISTS THREE OTHER REFERENCE BIBLIOGRAPHIES ON SAME
SUBJECT. COMPILED FOR LIBRARY OF CONGRESS.

0989 HELMER O.
"THE PROSPECTS OF A UNIFIED THEORY OF ORGANIZATIONS"
MANAGEMENT SCIENCE, 4 (1958), 172-176.
   CITES LACK OF UNIFIED CONCEPTUAL FRAMEWORK AND STANDARD
METHODOLOGY AS REASON FOR LITTLE PROGRESS IN FIELD OF
ORGANIZATIONAL THEORY. SUGGESTS INCORPORATION WITHIN GAME
THEORY FRAMEWORK AND EXPANSION TO INCLUDE OTHER FACTORS
BESIDES UTILITY PREFERENCES. ADVOCATES CONSTRUCTION OF
SCIENTIFIC MODELS.

0990 HENKIN L.
ARMS CONTROL AND INSPECTION IN AMERICAN LAW.
NEW YORK: COLUMB. U. PR., 1958, 289 PP.
   STUDIED FROM POINT OF VIEW OF LEGAL AND ADMINISTRATIVE
PROBLEMS INVOLVED IN ENFORCING AN INSPECTION SYSTEM IN USA.
WRITTEN PRIMARILY FOR THOSE INTERESTED IN DEVELOPMENT OF
INTERNATIONAL INSTITUTIONS. CONTENDS THAT THE PROVISIONS
OUTLINED MAKE NO OR FEW INROADS INTO ACCEPTED CONSTITU-
TIONAL LIMITATIONS.

0991 HENTOFF N. MUSTE A.J.
EDUCATION, INTERACTION, AND SOCIAL CHANGE.
ENGLEWOOD CLIFFS: PRENTICE HALL, 1967, 228 PP., LC#67-12932.
   TRIES TO EXPLAIN AND DESCRIBE THE WAY IN WHICH PEOPLE ARE
INFLUENCED BY THE SOCIAL SYSTEMS AROUND THEM. AUTHOR BE-
LIEVES THAT SOCIAL SYSTEMS ARE PEOPLE IN CONDITION OF CON-
TINUOUS AND RECIPROCAL INTERACTION. INFORMAL EDUCATIONAL
DEVICES SOCIALIZE YOUNG PEOPLE INTO PATTERNS CONTRADICTORY
TO PATTERNS ESPOUSED BY FORMAL EDUCATIONAL SYSTEMS.

0992 HERMAN H.
NEW YORK STATE AND THE METROPOLITAN PROBLEM.
PHILA: U OF PENN PR, 1963, 192 PP., LC#63-07856.
   EXAMINATION OF NEW YORK'S METROPOLITAN POLICY AS DERIVED
FROM AND APPLIED TO STATE PARTICIPATION IN SELECTED LOCAL
AND JOINT STATE-LOCAL ACTIVITIES. EVALUATES POLICY'S
IMPACT ON METROPOLITAN INTEGRATION.

0993 HERNDON J. ED., PRESS C. ED., WILLIAMS D.P. ED.
A SELECTED BIBLIOGRAPHY OF MATERIALS IN STATE GOVERNMENT AND
POLITICS (PAMPHLET)
LEXINGTON: U KY BUR GOVT RES, 1963, 143 PP.
   AN UNANNOTATED BIBLIOGRAPHY OF RECENT MATERIAL IN POLITI-
CAL SCIENCE, EMPHASIZING THE BEHAVIORAL APPROACH. STRESS IS
ANALYTICAL AND EMPIRICAL AND FOCUSES ON MATERIAL IN DECI-

SION-MAKING BY PUBLIC OFFICIALS. CLASSIFICATIONS DIVIDED IN-
TO BACKGROUND MATERIALS, POLITICAL ANALYSES, AND BIBLIOGRA-
PHIC STUDIES. ARRANGED ALPHABETICALLY BY STATE.

0994 HERRERA F.
"THE INTER-AMERICAN DEVELOPMENT BANK."
SOC. SCI., 16 (1960), 216-21.
   DISCUSSES MECHANISMS OF INTER-AMERICAN DEVELOPMENT BANK
AND HOW IT WORKS TO PROVIDE NEEDED EXTERNAL CAPITAL FOR
LATIN AMERICA, BY FURNISHING LOANS AND TECHNICAL ASSISTANCE.

0995 HERRING E.P.
PUBLIC ADMINISTRATION AND THE PUBLIC INTEREST.
NEW YORK: MCGRAW HILL, 1936, 416 PP.
   A STUDY OF THE FEDERAL ADMINISTRATIVE MACHINERY SHOWING
THE DIFFICULTIES OF FEDERAL OFFICIALS IN DEALING WITH
POLITICIANS AND SPECIAL INTEREST ORGANIZATIONS AND ANALYZING
THE RELATIONS BETWEEN PRESSURE GROUPS AND OFFICIALS AND
THE VARIOUS EFFORTS BEING MADE TO ADJUST THE BUREAUCRACY TO
ITS HEAVY RESPONSIBILITIES.

0996 HERSKOVITS M.J. ED., HARWITZ M. ED.
ECONOMIC TRANSITION IN AFRICA.
EVANSTON: NORTHWESTERN U PRESS, 1964, 444 PP.
   COLLECTION OF PAPERS ANALYZING ECONOMIC GROWTH OF SUB-
SAHARA AFRICA. DISCUSSES INDIGENOUS CHARACTER, DEVELOPMENT
PLANNING, AND PROBLEMS.

0997 HERZ J.H.
"EAST GERMANY: PROGRESS AND PROSPECTS."
SOC. RES., 27 (SUMMER 60), 139-156.
   CONTRASTS STALINISTIC DICTATORSHIP OF ULBRICHT REGIME
WITH OTHER SOVIET SATELLITES. STRICT CONTROLS HAVE CONSOL-
IDATED REGIME THEREBY REDUCING CHANCES OF GERMAN REUNIFICAT-
ION. BRINGS TO LIGHT SWEEPING MEASURES FOR COLLECTIVIZED
AGRICULTURE AND NATIONALIZATION OF COMMERCE AND INDUSTRY.
SHOWS CLOSER TIES OF EAST GERMANY WITH EASTERN BLOC ECONOMY
AS IMPORTANT STEP TOWARD ECONOMIC INTERGRATION.

0998 HESSLER I.M.O.
29 WAYS TO GOVERN A CITY.
CINCINNATI: UNIV OF CINCINNATI, 1966, 101 PP.
   COMPARATIVE ANALYSIS OF GOVERNMENTS OF 29 LARGEST US
CITIES. EMPHASIZES ADEQUACY OF MUNICIPAL SERVICES, RESPON-
SIVENESS OF GOVERNMENT TO PROBLEMS ON HAND, AND ROLE OF
CITIZENS IN DECISION-MAKING FOR CITY'S WELFARE. DIVIDES
CITIES BY STRONG MAYORS, WEAK MAYORS, MAYOR-ADMIN-
ISTRATORS, AND COUNCIL-MANAGERS. ANALYZES ELECTION SYSTEMS
IN DETAIL

0999 HETTINGER H.S.
A DECADE OF RADIO ADVERTISING.
CHICAGO: U OF CHICAGO PRESS, 1933, 354 PP.
   DESCRIBES ORIGINS OF RADIO ADVERTISING, ITS PSYCHOLOGICAL
AND ECONOMIC BASES, ITS USE BY ADVERTISERS, AND ITS CURRENT
PRACTICES. COVERS FIRST DECADE OF RADIO BROADCASTING,
1920-1930.

1000 HEUSSLER R.
YESTERDAY'S RULERS: THE MAKING OF THE BRITISH COLONIAL
SERVICE.
SYRACUSE: U. PR., 1963, 260 PP., $5.75.
   STUDY OF THE NATURE AND BACKGROUND OF THE MEMBERS OF
THE COLONIAL SERVICE, WHOSE SELECTION WAS DETERMINED BY
MURAL RATHER THAN SCIENTIFIC CONSIDERATIONS. TRACES THE
RISE AND FALL OF THE ELITIST, AUTHORITARIAN, PATERNALISTIC
SPIRIT OF ADMINISTRATION.

1001 HEWITT W.H. ED.
ADMINISTRATION OF CRIMINAL JUSTICE IN NEW YORK.
ROCHESTER: AQUEDUCT BOOKS, 1967, 397 PP., LC#67-20710.
   MANUAL FOR LAW ENFORCEMENT OFFICERS THAT DESCRIBES, BY
WAY OF TEXT AND ILLUSTRATION, ADMINISTRATION OF JUSTICE
IN NEW YORK STATE AS IT AFFECTS POLICE IN PARTICULAR.
DEALS ONLY WITH THE CONVENTIONAL AREA OF CRIMINAL
PROSECUTION.

1002 HEYEL C. ED.
THE ENCYCLOPEDIA OF MANAGEMENT.
NEW YORK:REINHOLD PUBLISHING CO., 1963, 1084 PP.
   EXTENSIVE ALPHABETIZED DESCRIPTIONS OF AREAS PERTAINING
TO MANAGEMENT. SEEKS TO SHOW CONCERNS OF TOP MANAGEMENT,
MARKETING, AND FINANCE; DEFINES PROBLEMS OF PRODUCTION AND
PLANT ENGINEERING AND ADVANCES IN NEW MANAGEMENT SCIENCES,
SUCH AS GAME THEORY, HUMAN ENGINEERING, AND APPLIED
PROBABILITY THEORY. CONTAINS 300 DEFINITIONS, EACH ENTRY
FOLLOWED BY SUGGESTED READINGS.

1003 HICKEY G.C.
VILLAGE IN VIETNAM.
NEW HAVEN: YALE U PR, 1964, 325 PP.
   DETAILED STUDY OF CULTURAL, SOCIAL, AND POLITICAL SIGNIF-
ICANCE OF VILLAGE IN VIETNAM. DISCUSSES SELF-CONTAINED,
HOMOGENEOUS, RELATIVELY AUTONOMOUS NATURE OF VIETNAMESE
VILLAGES AND IMPLICATIONS OF THEIR DISTRUST AND DISLIKE
OF OUTSIDE WORLD IN RELATION TO PRESENT AMERICAN EFFORTS IN

VIETNAM.

TICULAR AREA OF SPECIALIZATION IN THE FOREIGN POLICY FIELD.

1004 HICKMAN B.G. ED.
QUANTITATIVE PLANNING OF ECONOMIC POLICY.
WASHINGTON: BROOKINGS INST, 1965, 266 PP., LC#65-18314.
    SURVEY OF THEORETICAL AND EMPIRICAL DEVELOPMENTS IN
QUANTITATIVE PLANNING OF ECONOMIC POLICY. APPRAISAL OF TECH-
NIQUES OF QUANTITATIVE POLICY ANALYSIS AND OF SPECIFIC AP-
PLICATION IN NETHERLANDS, FRANCE, AND JAPAN. PROPOSALS FOR
FUTURE RESEARCH INCLUDE METHODS OF DETERMINING POLICY AL-
TERNATIVES, AND PRACTICAL EXAMINATION OF POLITICAL DECISION-
MAKING PROCESS. ECONOMETRIC MODELS INCLUDED.

1005 HICKMAN C.A., KUHN M.H.
INDIVIDUALS, GROUPS, AND ECONOMIC BEHAVIOR.
NEW YORK: THE DRYDEN PRESS, 1956, 216 PP.
    SEEKS TO DEMONSTRATE USEFULNESS OF APPLYING SOCIAL PSY-
CHOLOGY TO ECONOMIC PROBLEMS. EXPLORES THREE BASIC ISSUES
IN ECONOMICS: NATURE OF MANAGERIAL MOTIVATION, FEASIBILITY
OF MAKING INTERPERSONAL COMPARISONS, AND RECONCILIATION OF
PLANNING AND INDIVIDUAL FREEDOM.

1006 HICKS U.K.
DEVELOPMENT FROM BELOW.
LONDON: OXFORD U PR, 1961, 549 PP.
    COMPARATIVE STUDY OF DEVELOPMENT OF LOCAL GOVERNMENT
STRUCTURES AND FINANCIAL AND ECONOMIC SYSTEMS IN SEVERAL UN-
DERDEVELOPED COUNTRIES OF BRITISH COMMONWEALTH. ORIENTATION
IS SCHOLARLY AND TECHNICAL. CONSIDERS DEVELOPMENTS FROM BE-
GINNINGS OF COLONIAL ERA TO PRESENT.

1007 HIDAYATULLAH M.
DEMOCRACY IN INDIA AND THE JUDICIAL PROCESS.
NEW YORK: ASIA PUBL HOUSE, 1966, 89 PP.
    DISCUSSES FUNDAMENTAL PRINCIPLES OF DEMOCRACY AND EVOLU-
TION OF DEMOCRATIC GOVERNMENT IN INDIA. APPRAISES CAPACITY
OF DEMOCRACY IN INDIA TO WITHSTAND LOSS OF NEHRU. EXAMINES
INDIAN JUDICIAL PROCESS AND ITS RELATION TO PRESERVATION OF
DEMOCRATIC VALUES OF INDIAN PEOPLE.

1008 HIGA M.
POLITICS AND PARTIES IN POSTWAR OKINAWA.
VANCOUVER: UNIV. BRIT. COLUMBIA, 1963, 128 PP.
    DISCUSSES US ADMINISTRATIVE PROGRAMS WITHIN OKINAWA, AND
INTERNAL OKINAWAN POLITICS. EXPLORES THESE PROGRAMS WITHIN
THE FRAMEWORK OF THE POLITICAL PARTY MOVEMENT IN OKINAWA,
1945-62. THE HISTORICAL INTERNATIONAL POSITION OF OKINAWA IS
BRIEFLY TRACED AND THE DEVELOPMENT, CHARACTER, AND OPERATION
OF THE OKINAWAN PARTIES ARE EXAMINED. EMPHASIZES AMERICAN
IMPACT ON THE POLITICAL PARTY SYSTEM.

1009 HIGGINS R.
THE ADMINISTRATION OF UNITED KINGDOM FOREIGN POLICY THROUGH
THE UNITED NATIONS (PAMPHLET)
SYRACUSE: SYRACUSE U PRESS, 1966, 63 PP., LC#66-18648.
    STUDIES IMPACT OF UN ON ADMINISTRATION OF BRITISH FOREIGN
POLICY, AND ON TRADITIONAL DIPLOMACY, INCLUDING ADJUSTMENTS
WITHIN BRITISH GOVERNMENT TO CENTRAL FORUM PROVIDED BY UN.

1010 HILL F.G.
"VEBLEN, BERLE AND THE MODERN CORPORATION."
AMER. J. OF ECO. AND SOC., 26 (JULY 67), 279-296.
    CONCERNED WITH RECENT AND CURRENT THEORIZING ABOUT THE
"GOVERNMENTAL" CHARACTER OF HUGE, PUBLICLY HELD BUSINESS
CORPORATION. DISCUSSES VEBLEN'S VIEW OF CORPORATIONS (GENER-
ALLY HELD BEFORE 1930DS), OF DICHOTOMY BETWEEN BUSINESS
AND INDUSTRY. REVIEWS SHIFT IN VIEW, WITH BURNS, WHERE
DIVORCE OF OWNERSHIP FROM CONTROL IN TYPICAL CORPORATION IS
STRESSED.

1011 HILL N.
INTERNATIONAL ADMINISTRATION.
NEW YORK: MCGRAW HILL, 1931, 292 PP.
    AN ANALYSIS OF INTERNATIONAL ADMINISTRATIVE BODIES IN-
CLUDING COMMISSIONS, INFORMATIONAL BUREAUS, CONVENTIONS,
MANDATE SYSTEM SUPERVISED BY THE LEAGUE OF NATIONS, ETC. IN-
CLUDES APPENDIX OF RELATED DOCUMENTS.

1012 HILLS R.J.
"THE REPRESENTATIVE FUNCTION: NEGLECTED DIMENSION OF
LEADERSHIP BEHAVIOR"
ADMINISTRATIVE SCI. Q., 8 (JUNE 63), 83-101.
    RESULTS OF EMPIRICAL TEST OF THESIS THAT CONCEPT OF LEAD-
ERSHIP INCLUDES LEADER'S REPRESENTATION OF GROUP TO THOSE IN
HIGHER AUTHORITY AND TO CLIENTELE. "LEADER BEHAVIOR DES-
SCRIPTION" QUESTIONNAIRE DEVELOPED AND GIVEN TO ELEMENTARY
SCHOOL TEACHERS TO DESCRIBE LEADERSHIP OF PRINCIPALS.
HYPOTHESIS SUPPORTED.

1013 HILSMAN R.
"THE FOREIGN-POLICY CONSENSUS: AN INTERIM RESEARCH REPORT."
J. OF CONFLICT RESOLUTION, 3 (DEC. 59), 361-382.
    INTERNAL FOREIGN-POLICY-MAKING PROCESS IS COMPLEX PRO -
SIS BY CONFLICT AND CONSENSUS-BUILDING SIMILAR TO THAT OF
CONFLICT AND ACCOMMODATION IN INTERNAT'L RELATIONS. NOTES
INFLUENCE OF MOST GROUPS AND INDIVIDUALS CONFINED TO A PAR-

1014 HIMMELFARB G.
LORD ACTON: A STUDY IN CONSCIENCE AND POLITICS.
CHICAGO: U. CHI. PR., 1952, 260 PP.
    SUSPICION OF POWER, HIGH IDEALS AND MODEST EXPECTATIONS
IN POLITICS ARE CONTEMPLATED IN THIS BIOGRAPHY. EMPHASIS ON
HISTORICAL, POLITICAL AND RELIGIOUS INFLUENCES ON ACTON.
DENUNCIATIONS OF NATIONALISM, RACISM AND STATISM FOUND
APPLICABLE FOR LIBERALS TODAY.

1015 HINDERLING A.
DIE REFORMATORISCHE VERWALTUNGSGERICHTSBARKEIT.
WINTERTHUR: VERL H SCHELLENBERG, 1957, 101 PP.
    EXAMINES CONCEPTS OF JURIDICAL AND ADMINISTRATIVE ADJUDI-
CATION. DISCUSSES IN DETAIL NATURE AND EXTENT OF JUDICIAL
REVIEW OF ADMINISTRATIVE DECREES. STUDIES VARIOUS TYPES
OF REVIEW COURTS AND INQUIRES INTO PROBLEM OF SEPARATION OF
POWERS.

1016 HIRSCHMAN A.O.
DEVELOPMENT PROJECTS OBSERVED.
WASHINGTON: BROOKINGS INST, 1967, 197 PP., LC#67-27683.
    POLITICAL ECONOMIST STUDIES COMPARATIVE BEHAVIOR AND
STRUCTURAL CHARACTERISTICS OF DEVELOPMENT PROJECTS. USES 11
WORLD BANK PROJECTS IN 11 COUNTRIES AS BASIS. BELIEVES
EVEN BEST-RESEARCHED PROJECTS ARE SUBJECT TO UNFORESEEN
PROBLEMS AND WINDFALLS. DISCUSSES UNCERTAINTIES IN SUPPLY
OF TECHNOLOGY, ADMINISTRATION, FINANCE; AND IN DEMAND. EX-
AMINES PROJECT IMPLEMENTATION, DESIGN, AND APPRAISAL.

1017 HIRSHBERG H.S., MELINAT C.H.
SUBJECT GUIDE TO UNITED STATES GOVERNMENT PUBLICATIONS.
CHICAGO: AMER LIB ASSN, 1947, 228 PP.
    COMPILATION OF BOOKS, PAMPHLETS, SERIALS, DIRECTORIES,
BIBLIOGRAPHIES, AND HANDBOOKS.

1018 HISPANIC SOCIETY OF AMERICA
CATALOGUE (10 VOLS.)
BOSTON: HALL, 1965.
    BIBLIOGRAPHY OF BOOKS ON VARIOUS FACETS OF LATIN AMERICA
DURING THE COLONIAL PERIOD. INCLUDES MATERIAL ON SPAIN AND
PORTUGAL.

1019 HITCHNER D.G., HARBOLD W.H.
MODERN GOVERNMENT: A SURVEY OF POLITICAL SCIENCE.
NEW YORK: DODD, MEAD, 1962, 718 PP., LC#62-11690.
    DESCRIPTION OF DEMOCRATIC STATE IN MODERN WORLD.
CHARACTERIZES MAIN ELEMENTS OF MODERN STATES, SYSTEMS OF
PUBLIC LAW, POLITICS, INSTITUTIONS, PATTERNS OF PUBLIC
ADMINISTRATIONS, AND THEIR RELATIONS WITH ONE ANOTHER.
EXTENSIVE DISCUSSION OF THEORY AND METHOD OF POLITICAL
SCIENCE. INTRODUCTORY COLLEGE TEXT.

1020 HITLER A.
MEIN KAMPF.
NEW YORK: STACKPOLE, 1939, 669 PP.
    AUTOBIOGRAPHY INCLUDING HITLER'S IDEAS CONCERNING GERMAN
SOCIALISM, HIS VIEW ON THE STATE AND WORLD ORGANIZATION, AND
HIS PLANS TO ACHIEVE WORLD DOMINATION.

1021 HOBBS E.H.
EXECUTIVE REORGANIZATION IN THE NATIONAL GOVERNMENT.
AUSTIN: U OF TEXAS PR, 1953, 104 PP.
    DISCUSSES ADMINISTRATIVE REFORMS, ACTUAL AND PROPOSED,
IN THE MAJOR DEPARTMENTS OF THE FEDERAL EXECUTIVE BRANCH,
WITH AN EMPHASIS ON EFFICIENCY RATHER THAN REPRESENTATION.

1022 HOBBS E.H.
BEHIND THE PRESIDENT - A STUDY OF EXECUTIVE OFFICE AGENCIES.
WASHINGTON: PUBLIC AFFAIRS PRESS, 1954, 248 PP., LC#53-5789.
    EXAMINES OPERATION OF VARIOUS EXECUTIVE OFFICE AGENCIES
AND COUNCILS, SUCH AS BUREAU OF BUDGET, NATIONAL RESOURCES
PLANNING BOARD, NATIONAL SECURITY COUNCIL, COUNCIL OF
ECONOMIC ADVISERS, ETC.

1023 HODGETTS J.E.
"THE CIVIL SERVICE AND POLICY FORMATION."
CAN. J. OF ECO. AND POL. SCI., 23 (NOV. 57), 467-479.
    CANADIAN STUDIES IN THE FORMING OF POLICY AS VIEWED
FROM THE VANTAGE POINT OF THE CIVIL SERVANT. DISCUSSES THE
NEED FOR THE CIVIL SERVANT TO LOOK IN ALL DIRECTIONS BEFORE
FORMING POLICY.

1024 HODGETTS J.E., CORBETT D.C.
CANADIAN PUBLIC ADMINISTRATION.
TORONTO: MACMILLAN CO OF CANADA, 1960, 575 PP.
    DEFINITIVE TEXT CONSISTING OF READINGS IN PUBLIC
ADMINISTRATION THEORY, ORGANIZATION, EFFICIENCY, AND CONTROL
WITH SPECIAL REFERENCE TO SPECIFIC PRACTICES AND AGENCIES OF
THE CANADIAN GOVERNMENT.

1025 HODGETTS J.E.
ADMINISTERING THE ATOM FOR PEACE.
NEW YORK: ATHERTON PRESS, 1964, 193 PP., LC#64-11506.
    STUDY OF ADMINISTRATIVE PROBLEMS ASSOCIATED WITH PEACEFUL

APPLICATIONS OF NUCLEAR ENERGY. COMPARATIVE ANALYSIS OF IM-
PACT OF INSTITUTIONAL, ECONOMIC, AND TECHNOLOGICAL FEATURES
OF EACH COUNTRY ON ITS RESPECTIVE SOLUTIONS TO PROBLEMS
POSED BY EMERGENT USES OF ATOMIC ENERGY.

1026 HODGSON J.G.
THE OFFICIAL PUBLICATIONS OF AMERICAN COUNTIES: A UNION LIST
NEW YORK: COL U. INST WAR-PEACE, 1956.
    UNANNOTATED BIBLIOGRAPHY OF 5,243 OFFICIAL DOCUMENTS OF
AMERICAN COUNTIES, ARRANGED BY STATE AND COUNTY, THROUGH
1936. LISTS LOCATIONS OF ALL INDEXED DOCUMENTS. INDEX OF
SUBJECTS.

1027 HODGSON R.C., LEVINSON D.J., ZALEZNIK A.
THE EXECUTIVE ROLE CONSTELLATION: AN ANALYSIS OF PERSONALITY
AND ROLE RELATIONS IN MANAGEMENT.
CAMBRIDGE: HARVARD BUS SCHOOL, 1965, 509 PP., LC#65-23443.
    DISCUSSES ADMINISTRATION OF TOP EXECUTIVE ECHELON IN
MENTAL HOSPITAL. PRESENTS COMPREHENSIVE THEORETICAL PER-
SPECTIVE FOR ANALYSIS OF EXECUTIVE GROUPS IN GENERAL. TAKES
ANALYTIC APPROACH TO EXECUTIVE BEHAVIOR IN ORGANIZATIONS.

1028 HOFFHERR R.
"LE PROBLEME DE L'ENCADREMENT DANS LES JEUNES ETATS DE
LANGUE FRANCAISE EN AFRIQUE CENTRALE ET A MADAGASCAR."
TIERS-MONDE, 3 (NO.12, 62), 529-63.
    COMPARES ORGANIZATIONAL STRUCTURE OF NEW AFRICAN STATES
WITH OLD COLONIAL ADMINISTRATION. EMPHASIZES NECESSITY FOR
CHANGE. BASES EVALUATION ON ECONOMIC AND POLITICAL SITU-
ATION.

1029 HOFFMANN S.
"IMPLEMENTATION OF INTERNATIONAL INSTRUMENTS ON HUMAN
RIGHTS."
PROC. AMER. SOC. INT. LAW, (1959), 235-245.
    PRESENT WORLD SITUATION NECESSITATES ORIGINATING GUARAN-
TEES OF HUMAN RIGHTS AT THE NATIONAL RATHER THAN AT THE IN-
TERNATIONAL LEVEL. INTERNATIONAL SYSTEM MUST PRIMARILY CON-
CERN ITSELF WITH BASIC ISSUES OF COLD WAR.

1030 HOFMANN W.
"THE PUBLIC INTEREST PRESSURE GROUP: THE CASE OF THE
DEUTSCHE STADTETAG."
PUBLIC ADMINISTRATION, 45 (FALL 67), 245-260.
    TREATS DEUTSCHE STADTETAG (DST), GERMAN ASSOCIATION OF
CITIES AND TOWNS, AS INTEREST GROUP. DISCUSSES ITS ORIGINS
AND DEVELOPMENT FROM 1905-66. STUDIES ITS ORGANIZATION AND
GROUP STRUCTURE AND FUNCTIONS OF TIS THREE MAIN ORGANS.
DESCRIBES CHANGING PLACE OF LOCAL GOVERNMENT AS GERMANY
MOVED FROM CENTRALIIZING STATE TO FEDERAL REPUBLIC. EXPLORES
DST'S POLITICAL ACTIVITIES AS PRESSURE GROUP.

1031 HOLCOMBE A.
"OUR MORE PERFECT UNION."
CAMBRIDGE: HARVARD U PR, 1950.
    CRITICAL ESSAY ON US CONSTITUTION EMBODIES THESIS THAT
CONSTITUTION MUST BE REGARDED AS AN UNFINISHED EXPERIMENT IN
GOVERNMENT AND THAT FURTHER EXTENSION OF ITS PRINCIPLES IS
ESSENTIAL FOR MAINTENANCE OF SATISFACTORY POSITION OF AMERI-
CAN PEOPLE IN MODERN WORLD. ARGUES THAT CONSTITUTION HAS NOT
BEEN ADJUSTED TO REFLECT TREND OF GREATER DEMANDS ON THE NA-
TIONAL GOVERNMENT BY CITIZENS. NOTES CONTAIN BIBLIOGRAPHY.

1032 HOLCOMBE A.N.
STRENGTHENING THE UNITED NATIONS.
NEW YORK: HARPER, 1957, 276 PP.
    HAVING SURVEYED THE RECORD AND APPRAISED THE PROPOSALS
FROM VARIOUS QUARTERS, ADVANCES THREE RECOMMENDATIONS
IN ORDER TO REINFORCE THE WORLD ORGANIZATION. PROPOSES
CHANGES IN UN CHARTER, INNOVATIVE MODIFICATION OF EXISTING
PRACTICES IN UN STRUCTURE AND FUNCTION, AND ALTERATION OF
POLICIES OF USA.

1033 HOLDSWORTH W.S.
A HISTORY OF ENGLISH LAW: THE COMMON LAW AND ITS RIVALS
(VOL. V)
LONDON: METHUEN, 1924, 529 PP.
    CONCERNED WITH ENGLISH LAW IN 16TH AND EARLY 17TH
CENTURIES. BEGINS WITH DEVELOPMENTS OUTSIDE SPHERE OF COMMON
LAW AND INCLUDES MARITIME, INTERNATIONAL, AND COMMERCIAL
LAW. COVERS LAW ADMINISTERED BY STAR CHAMBER AND CHANCERY.
CONCLUDES WITH DEVELOPMENT OF COMMON LAW PROPER AND STUDIES
INFLUENCES ON ITS GROWTH SUCH AS CHANGING ROLE OF JUDGES,
POLITICAL AND RELIGIOUS CHANGES, AND IMPORTANT LITERATURE.

1034 HOLDSWORTH W.S.
A HISTORY OF ENGLISH LAW: THE COMMON LAW AND ITS RIVALS
(VOL. VI)
LONDON: METHUEN, 1924, 763 PP.
    CONCERNED WITH PUBLIC AND ENACTED LAW OF 17TH CENTURY.
BEGINS WITH LAW UNDER STUART KINGS AND DISCUSSES PERIOD OF
CIVIL WAR AND COMMONWEALTH. INCLUDES POLITICAL THEORIES,
PRINCIPLES OF PUBLIC LAW, ROYAL PROCLAMATIONS, AND LAWS ON
COMMERCE AND INDUSTRY, AGRICULTURE, PRESS, AND FRAUDS. ENDS
WITH PROFESSIONAL DEVELOPMENT OF LAW - GROWTH OF LEGAL
PROFESSION, LAWYERS, DIVISIONS, AND LITERATURE.

1035 HOLECOMBE A.N.
GOVERNMENT IN A PLANNED DEMOCRACY.
NEW YORK: W W NORTON, 1935, 173 PP.
    DISCUSSES NEED TO EXPERIMENT WITH VARIOUS FORMS OF
REPRESENTATIVE GOVERNMENT TO FIND MOST VIABLE SYSTEM. TRACES
GROWTH OF REPRESENTATION OF CAPITAL AND LABOR THROUGH
DEVELOPMENT OF PRESSURE GROUPS TO ESTABLISHMENT OF
ADMINISTRATIVE AGENCIES TO SERVE THEIR NEEDS.

1036 HOLSTI O.R.
"THE 1914 CASE."
AM. POL. SCI. REV., 59 (JUNE 65), 365-378.
    CONTENT ANALYSIS OF HIGH LEVEL STATEMENTS DURING THE 1914
CRISIS PERIOD IS USED TO TEST HYPOTHESES CONCERNING THE
PERCEPTION OF TIME, ONE'S OWN AND THE ADVERSARIES ALTERNA-
TIVES, AND THE SIZE AND PATTERN OF THE COMMUNICATIONS FLOW
DURING HIGH STRESS PERIODS. ANALYTIC METHOD, ASSUMPTIONS,
HYPOTHESES, DATA, AND CONCLUSIONS CAREFULLY PRESENTED.

1037 HOMANS G.C.
"THE WESTERN ELECTRIC RESEARCHES" IN S. HOSLETT, ED., HUMAN
FACTORS IN MANAGEMENT (BMR)"
NEW YORK: HARPER & ROW, 1951.
    A DISCUSSION OF THE PROGRAM OF MANAGEMENT RESEARCH AND
OF THE WORKER, CONDUCTED AT THE CHICAGO WORKS OF THE WESTERN
ELECTRIC COMPANY. EXAMINES A NUMBER OF EXPERIMENTS TESTING
THE HAPPINESS AND RESULTING PRODUCTIVITY OF THE WORKERS IN
THIS PLANT. ANALYZES THE FAILURE AND SUCCESS OF THESE
EXPERIMENTS.

1038 HONEY J.C.
"RESEARCH IN PUBLIC ADMINISTRATION: A FURTHER NOTE."
PUBLIC ADMIN. REV., 17 (1957), 238.
    REMARKS ON VARIETIES OF, AND MEANS OF FOSTERING,
RESEARCH.

1039 HONORD S.
PUBLIC RELATIONS IN ADMINISTRATION.
BRUSSELS: INTL INST OF ADMIN SCI, 1963, 83 PP.
    BRIEF DESCRIPTION OF THE METHODS OF PUBLICATION AND
DISTRIBUTION OF PUBLIC DOCUMENTS IN MORE THAN 30 COUNTRIES.
DISCUSSES VARIOUS KINDS OF OFFICIAL PUBLICATIONS AS WELL
AS PROBLEMS RELATING TO COPYRIGHT AND REPRODUCTION. APPENDED
IS A LIST OF NATIONAL REPORTS AND A BIBLIOGRAPHY CITING
PRIMARY SOURCES OF CURRENT BIBLIOGRAPHIES OF OFFICIAL PUB-
LICATIONS.

1040 HOOK S.
"SECOND THOUGHTS ON BERKELEY"
TECHNOLOGY REV., 67 (OCT. 65), 32-62.
    DISCUSSES STUDENT-FACULTY RELATIONS, PROBLEMS OF STUDENT
RIGHTS, AND RESPONSIBILITIES OF FACULTY. INCLUDES EFFECTS
OF REBELLING STUDENTS ON ADMINISTRATION. ATTACKS FSM AS
"OBVIOUSLY (OUT) TO BRING THE UNIVERSITY TO A HALT NOT IN
THE INTERESTS OF FREE SPEECH BUT FOR OTHER REASONS."

1041 HOOVER E.M.
THE LOCATION OF ECONOMIC ACTIVITY.
NEW YORK: MCGRAW HILL, 1948, 310 PP.
    PRESENTS PROBLEMS OF SPATIAL RELATIONS OF ECONOMIC
ACTIVITIES. TREATS FACTORS DETERMINING ADVANTAGES OF
LOCATION, ACCESS TO SUPPLIERS AND MARKET AND PRODUCTION
COST. DISCUSSES URBAN SITES AND ROLE OF ACCESSIBILITY IN
DETERMINING LOCATION. ANALYZES CAUSES OF LOCATIONAL CHANGE,
AND EFFECTS OF POLITICAL BOUNDARIES ON TRADE, LABOR, AND
ADMINISTRATION. EXAMINES AIMS OF PUBLIC LOCATIONAL POLICY.

1042 HORECKY P.L.
"LIBRARY OF CONGRESS PUBLICATIONS IN AID OF USSR AND EAST
EUROPEAN RESEARCH."
SLAVIC REVIEW, 23 (JAN. 64), 309-327.
    AN ANNOTATED BIBLIOGRAPHY OF RESEARCH AIDS PUBLISHED BY
THE LIBRARY OF CONGRESS TO ASSIST IN RESEARCHING USSR AND
EAST EUROPEAN MATERIAL IN THE LIBRARY OF CONGRESS. CONTAINS
ENTRIES IN ENGLISH, RANGING FROM 1929-1963.

1043 HOROWITZ I.L. ED.
THE RISE AND FALL OF PROJECT CAMELOT: STUDIES IN THE
RELATIONSHIP BETWEEN SOCIAL SCIENCE AND PRACTICAL POLITICS.
CAMBRIDGE: M I T PRESS, 1967, 385 PP., LC#67-14204.
    EXAMINES EXTENT TO WHICH SOCIAL SCIENCE COMMUNITY SHOULD
ASSIST IN GOVERNMENTAL STUDIES AND COMMENT UPON MATTERS
RELEVANT TO MILITARY SCIENCE AND TECHNOLOGY. OUTLINES AIMS,
FEASIBILITY, ETHICS, METHODS, AND OPERATIONS OF PROJECT
CAMELOT, A STUDY IN POLITICAL ASPECTS OF SOCIAL CHANGE IN
ALL NATIONS. GIVES REPRESENTATIVE RESEARCH FINDINGS. NOTES
REASONS OF CONFLICT AND POLITICS LEADING TO END OF PROJECT.

1044 HOROWITZ M.
INCENTIVE WAGE SYSTEMS.
PRINCETON: PRIN U INDUS REL CTR, 1955, 24 PP.
    APPROXIMATELY 150 ENTRIES INCLUDING BOOKS, GOVERNMENT
PUBLICATIONS, AND JOURNAL ARTICLES DISCUSSING SELECTION, IN-
STALLATION, AND MANAGEMENT OF INCENTIVE SYSTEMS. ENTRIES ARE
IN ENGLISH AND BULK WERE PUBLISHED FROM MID-1940'S
TO 1955. ARRANGED BY SUBJECT AND ALPHABETICALLY BY AUTHOR.

1045 HORVATH B.
THE CHARACTERISTICS OF YUGOSLAV ECONOMIC DEVELOPMENT.
SOCIALIST THOUGHT AND PRACTICE, (NO.1, 61), 83-97.
ANALYZES IN DETAIL FACTORS CONTRIBUTING TO HIGH RATE OF
ECONOMIC GROWTH IN POSTWAR YUGOSLAVIA, EMPHASIZING REASONS
FOR GROWTH AND FUTURE CAPABILITIES. THEORIZES AS TO PROJECT-
ED PRODUCTIVITY OF LABOR AND CAPITAL INVESTMENT.

1046 HOSCH L.G.
"PUBLIC ADMINISTRATION ON THE INTERNATIONAL FRONTIER."
PUB. PERSON. REV., 25 (JULY 64), 165-70.
SINCE EARLY IN ITS EXISTENCE, THE UN HAS BEEN HELPING
GOVERNMENTS EAGER TO IMPROVE ADMINISTRATIVE PRACTICES.
EXAMINES THE WORLD-WIDE INTEREST IN THIS AREA AND WHAT
INTERNATIONAL AGENCIES ARE DOING TO SPUR ITS GROWTH.

1047 HOUGHTELING J.L. JR., PIERCE G.G.
THE LEGAL ENVIRONMENT OF BUSINESS.
NEW YORK: HARCOURT BRACE, 1963, 901 PP., LC#63-11409.
CONSIDERS NATURE OF LAWS AND PROCESSES OF ADJUDICATION
AND LAWMAKING. ECPLORES SEVEN FIELDS OF LAW OF SPECIAL
INTEREST TO BUSINESSMEN: CONTRACTS, SALES, NEGOTIABLE
INSTRUMENTS, AGENCY, PARTNERSHIPS, CORPORATIONS, AND
GOVERNMENT REGULATION OF BUSINESS. ILLUSTRATES EACH AREA
WITH PERTINENT CASE STUDIES.

1048 HOUN F.W.
TO CHANGE A NATION; PROPAGANDA AND INDOCTRINATION IN
COMMUNIST CHINA.
NEW YORK: FREE PRESS OF GLENCOE, 1961, 250 PP.
STUDY OF THE AIMS AND METHODS OF CHINESE COMMUNIST
ATTEMPTS TO CREATE A COMMON SOCIAL CONSCIOUSNESS AND LOYALTY
TO COMMUNIST GOALS. ANALYZES THEIR FAILURE TO DEVELOP NECES-
SARY INTELLECTUAL LEADERSHIP BY CHANNELING COMMUNICATION
ONE WAY - FROM THE TOP DOWN. CONCLUDES THAT THE REVOLUTION-
ARY INSTABILITY OF MODERN CHINA LEADS TO USING THE COMMUNI-
CATION CHANNELS TO DIRECT, NOT DISCUSS, SOCIAL ACTION.

1049 HOVING W.
THE DISTRIBUTION REVOLUTION.
NEW YORK: IVES WASHBURN, INC, 1960, 150 PP., LC#60-14598.
DISCUSSES PROBLEMS RELATED TO DISTRIBUTION OF GOODS, IN-
CLUDING NATURE OF MASS DISTRIBUTION, EFFECTS OF COMPETITION,
SALESMANSHIP, AND MASS TRANSPORTATION. ARGUES THAT MANY
ECONOMIC PROBLEMS MIGHT BE SOLVED THROUGH NEGLECTED FIELD
OF DISTRIBUTION, RATHER THAN OVEREMPHASIZED FIELD OF
PRODUCTION.

1050 HOWARD L.V.
TULANE STUDIES IN POLITICAL SCIENCE: CIVIL SERVICE DEVELOP-
MENT IN LOUISIANA VOLUME 3.
NEW ORLEANS: TULANE U PR, 1956, 190 PP.
ANALYSIS OF REFORM IN CIVIL SERVICE FROM QUANTITY-
SPOILS SYSTEM TO MODERN MERIT SYSTEM OF QUALITY. REVIEWS
LEGISLATING DONE FOR REFORM AS WELL AS INDIVIDUALS
INVOLVED. EMPHASIS ON STUDYING POLITICS AND HISTORY OF
REFORM AND EVALUATING CHANGES. TABLES OF STATISTICS AND
CIVIL SERVICE DOCUMENTS.

1051 HOWE R.
THE STORY OF SCOTLAND YARD: A HISTORY OF THE CID FROM THE
EARLIEST TIMES TO THE PRESENT DAY.
NEW YORK: HORIZON PRESS, 1965, 176 PP., LC#66-16299.
HISTORY OF SCOTLAND YARD BY FORMER HEAD OF CRIMINAL
INVESTIGATION DEPARTMENT, DWELLING UPON CID AND ITS
DEVELOPMENT FROM FIRST DETECTIVES OF 1830'S TO TODAY'S
ELEVEN DEPARTMENTS OF SCIENTIFIC CRIMINAL INVESTIGATION.

1052 HOWER R.M., ORTH C.D.
MANAGERS AND SCIENTISTS.
CAMBRIDGE: HARVARD U, DIV OF RES, 1963, 310 PP., LC#63-10191
STUDY INTO PERSONAL RELATIONS BETWEEN SCIENTISTS AND
MANAGEMENT, INTERNAL TO RESEARCH ORGANIZATIONS. FOCUSES
ON HUMAN RELATIONS, STATUS, COMMUNICATION, MOTIVATION,
MORALE, MANAGER DEVELOPMENT, ETC. DESCRIPTION AND ANALYSIS
OF CASE SITUATIONS IN TWO COMPANIES.

1053 HSIAO K.C.
"POLITICAL PLURALISM."
NEW YORK: HARCOURT BRACE, 1927.
CONSIDERS THE VALIDITY OF PLURALISTIC CRITICISMS OF TRA-
DITIONAL POLITICAL THEORY AND THE INTRINSIC VALUE OF POLITI-
CAL PLURALISM AS A THEORY IN ITSELF. UNANNOTATED BIBLIOGRA-
PHY OF SOURCES AND REFERENCES IN FRENCH, ENGLISH, AND LATIN.
WRITINGS OF PLURALISTS LISTED UNDER SOURCES; EXPOSITIONS AND
CRITICISMS OF PLURALISTIC THEORY LISTED UNDER REFERENCES;
SUPPLEMENTARY LIST CONTAINS WORKS OF MAJOR MONISTIC WRITERS.

1054 HSUEH C.T.
"THE CULTURAL REVOLUTION AND LEADERSHIP CRISIS IN COMMUNIST
CHINA."
POLIT. SCI. QUART., 82 (JUNE 67), 169-190.
DISCUSSES THE FACTORS LEADING UP TO AND RESULTS OF THE
CULTURAL REVOLUTION WHICH BEGAN IN 1965, NURTURED BY RAMPAGE
BY RED GUARDS IN 1966, AND INTENSIFIED BY REVOLUTIONARY REB-
ELS' SEIZURE OF POWER IN 1967. IT IS MOST EXTENSIVE CAMPAIGN

AND PURGE EVER OCCURRING IN CHINESE COMMUNIST REGIME AND HAS
SPLIT TOP LEADERSHIP, CAUSED DISUNITY IN PARTY RULE, AND
PLUNGED COUNTRY INTO INTERNAL STRIFE.

1055 HSUEH S.-.S.
GOVERNMENT AND ADMINISTRATION OF HONG KONG.
HONG KONG: U BOOK STORE, 1962, 99 PP.
SHORT, NON-TECHNICAL STUDY OF STRUCTURE AND FUNCTION OF
GOVERNMENT OF HONG KONG. DESCRIBES IMPORTANT FUNCTION OF
COLONIAL OFFICE, AND ANALYZES STRUCTURES OF OFFICE OF GOVER-
NOR, EXECUTIVE COUNCIL, LEGISLATIVE COUNCIL, URBAN COUNCIL,
GOVERNMENT DEPARTMENTS, THE PUBLIC SERVICE, JUDICIARY, AND
ADMINISTRATION OF NEW TERRITORIES.

1056 HUDDLESTON J.
"TRADE UNIONS IN THE GERMAN FEDERAL REPUBLIC."
POLIT. QUART., 38 (APR.-JUNE 67), 165-176.
TRACES DEVELOPMENT OF POST-1945 TRADE UNIONS AND THEIR
EDUCATIONAL RECONSTRUCTION. BELIEVES THEIR ACHIEVEMENT IS
IMPRESSIVE. SOME OF OUTSTANDING FEATURES OF MOVEMENT ARE:
BELIEF IN VALUE OF BODY OF HIGHLY TRAINED OFFICIALS, WILL-
INGNESS TO EXPERIMENT IN MATTERS RELATED TO INDUSTRIAL
MANAGEMENT, AND ADHERENCE TO IDEA OF STRONG CENTRAL DIREC-
TION OF UNION AFFAIRS. COMPARES BRITISH TO GERMAN UNIONS.

1057 HUDSON G.F.
"SOVIET FEARS OF THE WEST."
CURR. HIST., 42 (MAY 62), 291-295.
COMMUNIST PARTY ABSOLUTELY NEEDS THE WORLD OF VIOLENT
CONFLICT WHICH ITS THEORY PRESUPPOSES...INTERNATIONAL
TENSIONS MUST BE MAINTAINED (RELAXATION OF WHICH IS A GOOD
PROPAGANDA SLOGAN).' RUSSIAN HOPES OF EXPANSION AND FEAR OF
BEING ATTACKED SERIOUSLY MODIFIED BY PROPAGATION OF PEACE-
FUL CO-EXISTENCE. POINTS OUT HOW STALIN'S 'TOUGH-POLICIES'
(BERLIN BLOCKADE AND KOREA) UNITED WEST (NATO).

1058 HUELIN D.
"ECONOMIC INTEGRATION IN LATIN AMERICAN: PROGRESS AND
PROBLEMS."
INT. AFF., 40 (JULY 64), 430-439.
LATIN AMERICA'S ECONOMIC AND SOCIAL PROBLEMS RELATED TO
FAILURE OF REGION TO MAINTAIN SHARE IN WORLD TRADE. LATIN
AMERICAN FREE TRADE ASSOCIATION REALIZES FUTURE OF ECONOMIC
INTEGRATION LIES IN SIGNIFICANTLY EXPANDING MARKET OF
MANUFACTURED GOODS.

1059 HUGHES J.M.
EDUCATION IN AMERICA (2ND ED.)
NEW YORK: HARPER & ROW, 1965, 570 PP., LC#65-11136.
PROGRESS THAT HAS BEEN MADE IN AMERICAN EDUCATION ANA-
LYZED. TEACHER'S POSITION AND ROLE, IDEAS THAT HAVE BEEN IN-
FLUENTIAL, AND SCHOOL SYSTEM ARE DISCUSSED. SUGGESTS MEANS
OF STIMULATING AND DIRECTING GROWTH AND DEVELOPMENT.

1060 HUGON P.
"BLOCAGES ET DESEQUILIBRES DE LA CROISSANCE ECONOMIQUE EN
AFRIQUE NOIRE."
TABLE RONDE, (APR. 67), 42-63.
DISCUSSES SOCIAL AND POLITICAL FACTORS THAT HAVE STIFLED
AFRICA'S GROWTH: TRIBALISM, WHICH HAS BLOCKED THE DEVELOP-
MENT OF A VIABLE STATE* DEPENDENCE ON FOREIGN TRADE WHICH
HAS HINDERED DECOLONIALIZATION* LACK OF ECONOMIC INTEGRA-
TION. SHOWS THE REVOLUTIONIZING FORCES OF POPULATION AND SO-
CIAL CHANGES. STRESSES RESPONSIBILITY OF EUROPE TO ASSIST
IN AFRICA'S ECONOMIC DEVELOPMENT.

1061 HUITT R.K.
"THE MORSE COMMITTEE ASSIGNMENT CONTROVERSY: A STUDY IN
SENATE NORMS."
AM. POL. SCI. REV., 51 (JUNE 57), 313-329.
STUDY RESTS ON THE ASSUMPTION THAT PARTICULAR CONFLICT
SITUATIONS MAY FURNISH CLUES ABOUT THE NORMS THAT AFFECT
BEHAVIOR AND THEIR RELATIVE STRENGTH AMONG DIFFERENT MEMBERS
OF THE GROUP. IN THE SENATE, THE CASE OF SENATOR MORSE
CONFIRMS THAT BOLTING THE PARTY TICKET IN A PRESIDENTIAL
ELECTION DOES NOT IMPLY LOSS OF RANK OR COMMITTEE MEMBER-
SHIP. PARTY LOYALTY IS EXPECTED IN THE SENATE ORGANIZATION.

1062 HULL C.
THE MEMOIRS OF CORDELL HULL (VOLUME ONE).
NEW YORK: MACMILLAN, 1948, 916 PP.
COVERS LIFE OF THIS SECRETARY OF STATE UP TO 1941, AND
EMPHASIZES THE INEVITABILITY OF AMERICAN INVOLVEMENT IN
WORLD WAR TWO.

1063 HUMPHREY H.H.
"A MORE PERFECT UNION."
NATIONAL CIVIC REV., 56 (JUNE 67), 322-328.
ARGUES THAT PARAMOUNT GOAL AND ACHIEVEMENT OF JOHNSON AD-
MINISTRATION HAS BEEN EFFECTIVE COOPERATION AMONG LEVELS OF
GOVERNMENT. CALLS FOR STATE RESPONSIBILITY IN ADMINISTERING
GRANT-IN-AID PROGRAMS, DRIVE FOR BETTER COMMUNICATIONS,
IMPROVED COORDINATION AND CONSOLIDATION, AND MEANINGFUL
DECENTRALIZATION.

1064 HUMPHREY H.H.

"THE SENATE ON TRIAL."
AM. POL. SCI. REV., 44 (SEPT. 50), 650-660.
A SENATOR REVIEWS THE RECORD AND PONDERS THE PERFORMANCE OF THE SENATE SINCE 1949. THE VOTERS MUST REMEMBER THAT THE EYES OF THE WORLD ARE CONTINUALLY ON SENATE ACTION, AND THE SENATE ITSELF, BEING RESPONSIBLE FOR ITS INTERNAL METHODS, MUST SHAPE ITS PROCEDURES SO THAT ITS PUBLIC ESTEEM AND PRESTIGE WILL BE INCREASED. INSISTS ON THE NEED FOR PARTY RESPONSIBILITY.

1065 HUNTINGTON S.P.
THE SOLDIER AND THE STATE: THE THEORY AND POLITICS OF CIVIL-MILITARY RELATIONS.
CAMBRIDGE: HARVARD U. PR., 1957, 534 PP.
OUTLINING THE TENSION THAT EXISTS BETWEEN ARMED FORCES AND CIVILIANS, PROPOSES FRAME-WORK FOR MORE EFFECTIVE CIVIL-MILITARY RELATIONSHIP IN USA. DEFINES MAJOR ISSUES INVOLVED AND EVALUATES CURRENT THOUGHTS PERTAINING TO NATIONAL SECURITY IN A DEMOCRATIC SOCIETY.

1066 HUNTINGTON S.P.
"STRATEGIC PLANNING AND THE POLITICAL PROCESS."
FOR. AFF., 38 (JAN. 60), 285-89.
CRITICIZES LEGISLATIVE LEADERSHIP AND SCOPE OF THE STRATEGIC CONSENSUS IN THE EXECUTIVE BRANCH AS WEAK AND LIMITED AND SUGGESTS BOTH BE CLARIFIED TO IMPROVE THE CONTENT OF MILITARY DECISIONS. URGES THE ADMINISTRATION ABANDON ITS DEFENSIVE ROLE REGARDING STRATEGIC PROGRAMS AND PERMIT THEIR BROADER AND EARLIER PUBLIC DISCUSSION TO ASCERTAIN ACCURATELY WHAT THE PEOPLE WILL SUPPORT.

1067 HUNTINGTON S.P.
"CONGRESSIONAL RESPONSES TO THE TWENTIETH CENTURY IN D. TRUMAN, ED. THE CONGRESS AND AMERICA'S FUTURE."
ENGLEWOOD CLIFFS: PRENTICE HALL, 1965.
SUBMITS FIGURES TO SHOW THAT SINCE THE BEGINNING OF THE CENTURY THERE HAS BEEN A GROWING INSULATION OF CONGRESS FROM OTHER SOCIAL GROUPS AND POLITICAL INSTITUTIONS. AT THE SAME TIME CENTRAL LEADERSHIP BOTH IN THE SENATE AND THE HOUSE HAS BEEN WEAKENED AND POWER DISPERSED TO COMMITTEES. AS A RESULT CONGRESS HAS LOST INITIATIVE IN THE ENACTMENT OF LEGISLA-TION AND PLAYS THE ROLE OF OVERSEER OF THE ADMINISTRATION.

1068 HUTCHINSON C.E.
"AN INSTITUTE FOR NATIONAL SECURITY AFFAIRS."
AMER. BEHAV. SCI., 4 (SEPT. 60), 31-35.
NATIONAL SECURITY POLICY DEPENDENT UPON QUESTIONS OF TIMING PROCESS AND AVAILABLE RESOURCES PREDICTION. COMMUN-ICATION AND TECHNICAL UTILIZATION REQUIRE RESEARCH AND DE-VELOPMENT, AND PROFESSIONAL ADVISORS FOR NATIONAL LEADERS.

1069 HUZAR E.
"LEGISLATIVE CONTROL OVER ADMINISTRATION: CONGRESS AND WPA"
AM. POL. SCI. REV., 36 (FEB. 42), 51.
USING THE WPA AS A CASE STUDY, THE AUTHOR DEALS WITH RE-LATIONS BETWEEN THE LEGISLATURE AND A PARTICULAR AGENCY. EXAMINES THE MACHINERY OF CONTROL AND THE PROBLEMS INVOLVED. CONCLUDES THAT MOST OF THE FRICTION BETWEEN CONGRESS AND WPA HAS BEEN THE RESULT OF DEFECTIVE LEGISLATION WHICH IMPOSED NEGATIVE PROHIBITIONS RATHER THAN AFFIRMATIVE MANDATES.

1070 HYDE L.K.G.
THE US AND THE UN.
NEW YORK: MANHATTAN, 1960, 249 PP.
ATTEMPTS TO GIVE THE READER SOME IDEA OF ACTION TAKEN BY USA DURING THE DECADE 1945-55 TO ADVANCE AMERICAN FOREIGN POLICY OBJECTIVES IN SOCIAL AND ECONOMIC FIELDS. EXPLORES THE REFUGEE PROBLEM, AND THE EFFORTS FOR ACHIEVING A FI-NANCIAL AID PLAN.

1071 HYNEMAN C.S.
BUREAUCRACY IN A DEMOCRACY.
NEW YORK: HARPER & ROW, 1950, 579 PP.
DEFINES BUREAUCRACY AND ITS PLACE IN STRUCTURE OF DEMO-CRATIC GOVERNMENT. CHALLENGES CURRENT AMERICAN MYTHS ON THIS SUBJECT. INCLUDES IN DISCUSSION ANALYSIS OF BUREAUCRATIC BEHAVIOR, MORALITY, FORMATION AND COORDINATION OF POLICY, AND PROBLEMS OF INEFFICIENCY AND RED TAPE.

1072 IANNACCONE L.
POLITICS IN EDUCATION.
NEW YORK: CTR APPLIED RES EDUC, 1967, 112 PP., LC#67-28052.
THEORETICAL STUDY OF INFLUENCE OF POLITICAL FORCES ON EDUCATION. DEVELOPS MODEL TO EXAMINE POLITICAL ACTS IN EDUCATION. CATEGORIZES POLITICAL ACTIONS OF EDUCATIONISTS AT STATE LEVEL AND SKETCHES MODES AND DIRECTIONS OF CHANGE IN STATE EDUCATION POLITICS. ALSO INVESTIGATES LOCAL POLITICS AND EDUCATION. DESCRIBES POWER STRUGGLE IN NEA AND DYSFUNCTIONS OF OLD BUREAUCRATIC EDUCATIONAL AGENCIES.

1073 IBERO-AMERICAN INSTITUTES
IBEROAMERICANA.
STOCKHOLM: IBERO-AMER INST, 1964.
BIBLIOGRAPHIC COMPILATION OF BOOKS AND PAMPHLETS IN THE LIBRARIES OF THE IBERO-AMERICAN INSTITUTES OF STOCKHOLM AND GOTHENBURG. ITEMS ARRANGED BY AUTHOR, COUNTRY, AND SUBJECT.

1074 IDENBURG P.J.
"POLITICAL STRUCTURAL DEVELOPMENT IN TROPICAL AFRICA."
ORBIS, 11 (SPRING 67), 256-270.
EXAMINES DEVELOPMENT OF STATE STRUCTURES IN AFRICA IN TERMS OF DISCERNIBLE TRENDS. NOTES THAT MANY TRADITIONAL CHIEFS HAVE CONSIDERABLE POWER, SOME COMBINING BOTH TRIBAL AND STATE AUTHORITY, SOME FORMING PROFESSIONAL GROUPS. FINDS THAT FORMER BRITISH COLONIES TEND TO RETAIN COLONIAL STRUCTURE, AND THAT MANY STATES ARE CONSTITUTIONAL DEMOC-RACIES IN THEORY IF NOT YET IN PRACTICE.

1075 IKE N.
JAPANESE POLITICS.
NEW YORK: ALFRED KNOPF, 1957, 300 PP., LC#57-5065.
INTRODUCTORY SURVEY OF JAPANESE POLITICS IN TERMS OF SETTING, DOMINANT POLITICAL FORCES, AND BASIC POLIT-ICAL PROCESSES. ESTABLISHES A GENERAL FRAMEWORK FOR ANALYZ-ING JAPANESE POLITICS IN ITS TOTALITY. BIBLIOGRAPHY OF WORKS CONSULTED: NEWSPAPERS, BOOKS, AND ARTICLES IN BOTH ENGLISH AND JAPANESE.

1076 IKLE F.C., LEITES N.
"POLITICAL NEGOTIATION AS A PROCESS OF MODIFYING UTILITIES."
J. CONFL. RESOLUT., 6 (MAR. 62), 17-28.
PRESENTS THEORETICAL MODEL FOR ANALYZING NEGOTIATIONS. POINTS OUT THAT BASIC ASPECT OF NEGOTIATIONS IS THAT IT DOES NOT RECOGNIZE KNOWN OR STABLE UTILITIES. RECOMMENDS EXTEN-SIVE ANALYSIS OF POLITICAL NEGOTIATIONS AS PREREQUISITE TO RELATING IT TO CURRENT BARGAINING THEORY.

1077 ILLINOIS COMMISSION
IMPROVING THE STATE LEGISLATURE.
URBANA: U OF ILLINOIS PR, 1967, 146 PP.
A REPORT OF THE ILLINOIS COMMISSION ON THE ORGANIZATION OF THE GENERAL ASSEMBLY, STRESSING THE NEED TO REVITALIZE THE LEGISLATIVE BRANCH OF GOVERNMENT AT THE STATE LEVEL. PRESENTS SYSTEMATIC INQUIRY INTO PROBLEMS AND RECOMMENDS SPECIFIC MEASURES FOR IMPROVEMENT. INCLUDES CONSTITUTION, LEGISLATIVE PROCEDURES AND TECHNIQUES, PUBLICATIONS, COMMIT-TEES AND COMMISSIONS, AND THE APPROPRIATIONS PROCESS.

1078 INAYATULLAH
BUREAUCRACY AND DEVELOPMENT IN PAKISTAN.
PESHAWAR: PAKIS. ACAD. RURAL DEV., 1962, 450 PP.
PAPERS READ AT SEMINAR OF PAKISTAN ACADEMY FOR RURAL DE-VELOPMENT DEALING WITH PROBLEMS OF BUREAUCRACY IN DEVELOPING COUNTRY, STRUCTURE OF PAKISTAN'S GOVERNMENT AND BUREAUCRACY, LOCAL GOVERNMENT AND RURAL DEVELOPMENT, AND TRAINING OF BU-REAUCRATS TO FURTHER SOCIO-ECONOMIC PROGRESS.

1079 INDIAN COMM PREVENTION CORRUPT
REPORT, 1964.
NEW DELHI: MINISTRY HOME AFFAIRS, 1964, 299 PP.
PROCEDURES OF DEALING WITH BRIBERY AND CORRUPTION IN LO-CAL GOVERNMENT. REGULATIONS, MEASURES, SPECIAL POLICE ESTAB-LISHMENT, SOCIAL CLIMATE. RESULTS, CONCLUSIONS, AND RECOMMENDATIONS.

1080 INDIAN INST OF PUBLIC ADMIN
IMPROVING CITY GOVERNMENT.
NEW DELHI: INDIAN INST PUB ADMIN, 1958, 208 PP.
PAPERS FROM SEMINAR ON PROBLEMS OF LOCAL GOVERNMENT IN INDIA. DISCUSSES RELATIONS BETWEEN DELIBERATIVE AND EXECU-TIVE AGENCIES IN CITY GOVERNMENT, TRENDS IN MUNICIPAL FINANCES, DEVELOPMENT AND REDEVELOPMENT OF CITIES. EXAMINES ASPECTS AND PROBLEMS OF PARTICIPATION OF CITIZENS IN MUNICI-PAL GOVERNMENT.

1081 INDIAN INST OF PUBLIC ADMIN
STATE UNDERTAKINGS: REPORT OF A CONFERENCE, DECEMBER 19-20, 1959 (PAMPHLET)
NEW DELHI: INDRAPRASTHA ESTATE, 1960, 14 PP.
DISCUSSION OF TWO FOLLOWING TOPICS REGARDING DEVELOPMENT OF PUBLIC ADMINISTRATION IN INDIA IN PAST TWO YEARS. UNDER QUESTION OF ACCOUNTABILITY OF PUBLIC ENTERPRISES TO PARLIAMENT, TOPIC ONE IS BOARD OF MANAGEMENT FOR PUBLIC ENTERPRISES, INCLUDING CONSTITUTION, FUNCTIONS, ETC. TOPIC TWO IS FORMATION OF A STANDING SELECT COMMITTEE ON PUBLIC ENTERPRISES TO ANSWER TO PARLIAMENT.

1082 INDIAN INSTITUTE PUBLIC ADMIN
MORALE IN THE PUBLIC SERVICES: REPORT OF A CONFERENCE JAN., 3-4, 1959.
NEW DELHI: INDIAN INST PUB ADMIN, 1959, 118 PP.
ANALYSIS OF NEED FOR HIGH MORALE AND UNITY OF PURPOSE IN INDIA SINCE BECOMING INDEPENDENT. CHOICE OF SOCIALISTIC STATE MEANS EXPANSION OF CIVIL SERVICE WITH COMMON PURPOSE TO ACHIEVE THEIR NEW PLANNED ECONOMY. MORALE IS KEY TO EFFICIENCY AND SUGGESTIONS ARE LEFT FOR EVERY DEPARTMENT TO BOOST MORALE. INCLUDES SECTION OF IMPORTANT PAPERS ON SUBJECT BY PARTICIPANTS.

1083 INDIAN INSTITUTE PUBLIC ADMIN
CASES IN INDIAN ADMINISTRATION.

NEW DELHI: INDIAN INST PUB ADMIN, 1963, 261 PP.
CASE STUDIES OF VARIED INDIAN PUBLIC PROGRAMS INTEND-
ED TO ILLUSTRATE ADMINISTRATIVE DECISION-MAKING AND VARIOUS
OTHER FACETS OF ADMINISTRATIVE PROCESS.

1084 INDUSTRIAL RELATIONS RES ASSN
RESEARCH IN INDUSTRIAL HUMAN RELATIONS.
NEW YORK: HARPER & ROW, 1957, 213 PP., LC#59-9087.
ANALYSIS OF THE CONTROVERSIES SURROUNDING HUMAN RELATIONS
RESEARCH AND ITS APPLICATION IN INDUSTRY. THIRTEEN ESSAYS
WRITTEN BY DIFFERENT AUTHORS REPRESENT CRITICAL AND SELEC-
TIVE REPORTING OF ILLUSTRATIVE FINDINGS. CONCENTRATES ON
NONECONOMIC ASPECTS OF ORGANIZATION OF WORK: WORK AND LEI-
SURE, NATURE OF AUTHORITY, LABOR UNIONS, ETC.

1085 INGHAM K.
A HISTORY OF EAST AFRICA.
LONDON: LONGMANS, GREEN & CO, 1962, 458 PP.
HISTORY OF EAST AFRICA FROM ANCIENT TIMES TO MODERN
CONSTITUTIONAL DEVELOPMENT AND EMERGENCE OF AFRICAN NA-
TIONALISM. INCLUDES CHAPTERS ON EAST AFRICA, INTERNATIONAL
DIPLOMACY, COLONIAL ADMINISTRATION, THE SECOND WORLD WAR,
AND POLITICS AND ADMINISTRATION FROM 1919-1939. CHARTS,
MAPS, AND SELECT BIBLIOGRAPHY IN ENGLISH AND FRENCH.

1086 INKELES A.
"UNDERSTANDING A FOREIGN SOCIETY: A SOCIOLOGIST'S VIEW."
WORLD POLIT. 3, (JAN. 51), 269-280.
A PAPER SEEKING TO POINT OUT SOME GENERAL FEATURES OF THE
SOCIOLOGIST'S ORIENTATION WHICH SUIT HIM TO THE TASK OF
CONTRIBUTING TO THE UNDERSTANDING OF SOCIAL SYSTEMS. BESIDES
THE TYPICALLY SOCIOLOGICAL, RELATED INTERESTS IN OTHER
DISCIPLINARY AREAS AND STRUCTURAL-FUNCTIONAL ANALYSIS OF
THESE AREAS ARE CONSIDERED.

1087 INST D'ETUDE POL L'U GRENOBLE
ADMINISTRATION TRADITIONELLE ET PLANIFICATION REGIONALE.
PARIS: COLIN (LIB ARMAND), 1964, 306 PP.
STUDY OF TRADITIONAL FRENCH ADMINISTRATION, WHICH CANNOT
MEET MODERN PROBLEMS OF CITY PLANNING. ANALYZES NEW PLANNING
EFFORTS, THEIR FUNCTIONAL CHARACTERISTICS, AND THEIR
POLITICAL DIMENSIONS. ANALYZES IN DETAIL STEPS OF NEW
PLANNING. BIBLIOGRAPHY OF 394 ITEMS.

1088 INST INTL DES CIVILISATION DIF
THE CONSTITUTIONS AND ADMINISTRATIVE INSTITUTIONS OF THE
NEW STATES.
BRUSSELS: INTL INST DIFF CIVILIZ, 1965, 886 PP.
EXAMINES LEGAL, ECONOMIC, POLITICAL, AND SOCIAL ASPECTS
OF CONSTITUTIONS IN NEW STATES AND ADMINISTRATIVE ASPECTS OF
THEM. ATTEMPTS DETERMINATION OF EFFECTIVENESS IN VARIOUS
COUNTRIES.

1089 INST TRAINING MUNICIPAL ADMIN
MUNICIPAL FINANCE ADMINISTRATION (6TH ED.)
CHICAGO: INT CITY MANAGER'S ASSN, 1962, 519 PP.
ONE OF SERIES OF 11 VOLUMES, EACH A COMPLETE AND SEPARATE
TRAINING AND REFERENCE MANUAL DEALING WITH ONE FIELD OF
MUNICIPAL ADMINISTRATION. THIS VOLUME APPROACHES MUNICIPAL
FINANCE FROM ADMINISTRATIVE POINT OF VIEW, AND APPRAISES
SIGNIFICANCE AND USEFULNESS OF FISCAL MECHANISMS.

1090 INSTITUTE JUDICIAL ADMIN
JUDGES: THEIR TEMPORARY APPOINTMENT, ASSIGNMENT AND TRANS-
FER: SURVEY OF FED AND STATE CONSTN'S STATUTES, ROLES OF CT.
NEW YORK: INST OF JUDICIAL ADMIN, 1962, 116 PP.
STUDY OF JUDGES, CONCENTRATING ON PERSON OR COURT HAVING
POWER OF APPOINTMENT OF JUDGES AND GIVING SPECIFIC POLICY
OF EACH STATE; ARRANGED BY STATE.

1091 INSTITUTE OF PUBLIC ADMIN
A SHORT HISTORY OF THE PUBLIC SERVICE IN IRELAND.
DUBLIN: INST PUBLIC ADMIN, 1962, 48 PP.
ATTEMPTS TO TRACE HISTORY OF IRISH CIVIL SERVICE FROM
BEGINNING IN 1215 A.D., SHOWING COMPLEX AND SOMEWHAT IL-
LOGICAL DEPARTMENTAL DIVISIONS - THE RESULT OF YEARS OF DE-
VELOPMENT THROUGH BRITISH AND IRISH ADMINISTRATION.

1092 INT. BANK RECONSTR. DEVELOP.
ECONOMIC DEVELOPMENT OF KUWAIT.
BALTIMORE: JOHNS HOPKINS PR., 1965, 194 PP.
KUWAIT IS FOURTH LARGEST OIL PRODUCER IN WORLD AND
SECOND ONLY TO VENEZUELA AS AN OIL EXPORTER. SUMMARIZES
RESULTS OF FINDINGS AND RECOMMENDATIONS OF TWO 'ECONOMIC
MISSIONS' TO COUNTRY. DOMESTIC NEEDS AND INVESTMENT
OPPORTUNITIES ARE EMPHASIZED WITH REVALUATION OF TARIFFS
AND IMPORT RESTRICTIONS.

1093 INTERAMERICAN CULTURAL COUN
LISTA DE LIBROS REPRESENTAVOS DE AMERICA.
WASHINGTON: PAN AMERICAN UNION, 1959, 364 PP.
ANNOTATED BIBLIOGRAPHY OF THE MOST SIGNIFICANT PUBLICA-
TIONS IN THE SOCIAL SCIENCES. ENTRIES ARRANGED BY COUNTRY.

1094 INTERNAT CONGRESS OF JURISTS
EXECUTIVE ACTION AND THE RULE OF RULE: REPORTION PROCEEDINGS
OF INT'T CONGRESS OF JURISTS,-RIO DE JANEIRO, BRAZIL.
RIO DE JANEIR: INTL CONG JURISTS, 1962, 187 PP.
CONGRESS RECOGNIZES ONE GREAT MODERN DILEMMA IS POWER OF
EXECUTIVE VS RIGHTS OF INDIVIDUAL. EXAMINES ROLE OF
JUDGES, LAWYERS, AND TEACHERS OF LAW IN STRIKING BALANCE BE-
TWEEN THE TWO, THUS ADJUSTING RULE OF LAW TO NEEDS OF
SOCIAL AND ECONOMIC DEVELOPMENT.

1095 INTERNATIONAL AFRICAN INST
SELECT ANNOTATED BIBLIOGRAPHY OF TROPICAL AFRICA.
LONDON: INTERNATL AFRICAN INST, 1956.
GENERAL BIBLIOGRAPHY OF WORKS LISTED UNDER SEVEN MAJOR
SUBJECT HEADINGS: GEOGRAPHY, ETHNOGRAPHY, SOCIOLOGY,
LINGUISTICS, GOVERNMENT AND ADMINISTRATION, ECONOMICS,
EDUCATION, MISSIONS, AND HEALTH. ANNOTATED WITH
INTRODUCTIONS TO MAJOR SECTIONS.

1096 INTERNATIONAL CITY MGRS ASSN
POST-ENTRY TRAINING IN THE LOCAL PUBLIC SERVICE (PAMPHLET)
CHICAGO: INT CITY MANAGER'S ASSN, 1963, 82 PP.
ANALYZES PROGRAMS AND METHODS FOR TRAINING AND DEVELOPING
PUBLIC SERVICE PERSONNEL IN VARIOUS US CITIES. EVALUATES AND
COMPARES THEM WITH PRIVATE INDUSTRY PERSONNEL. COVERS
TRAINING FACILITIES AVAILABLE BY COLLEGES, ETC., IN
VARIOUS CITIES. EMPHASIZES ON-JOB TRAINING, AND COURSE-
TAKING TRAINING AND METHODS TO MOBILIZE OTHER COMMUNITY
RESOURCES FOR FUTURE TRAINING.

1097 INTERNATIONAL CITY MGRS ASSN
COUNCIL-MANAGER GOVERNMENT, 1940-64: AN ANNOTATED
BIBLIOGRAPHY.
CHICAGO: INT CITY MANAGER'S ASSN, 1965, 38 PP.
ANNOTATED BIBLIOGRAPHY OF 340 REFERENCES TO BOOKS, ARTI-
CLES, AND GOVERNMENT PUBLICATIONS IN ENGLISH OR ENGLISH
TRANSLATIONS; ARRANGED UNDER TOPICS OF HISTORY OF COUNCIL-
MANAGER GOVERNMENT, INITIATION OF PLAN, CITY MANAGER, BASIC
COUNCIL-MANAGER PLAN AND INTERGOVERNMENTAL RELATIONS.

1098 INTERNATIONAL LABOUR OFFICE
WORKERS' MANAGEMENT IN YUGOSLAVIA.
GENEVA: INTL LABOUR OFFICE, 1962, 320 PP.
DESCRIBES AIMS AND FUNCTIONING OF SYSTEM OF WORKERS'
MANAGEMENT OF INDUSTRY IN YUGOSLAVIA AND ANALYZES ITS CHAR-
ACTERISTICS AND RESULTS. INCLUDES BACKGROUND ON YUGOSLAVIAN
ECONOMIC AND POLITICAL STRUCTURE, LEGAL STATUS AND ADMINIS-
TRATION OF WORKERS' MANAGEMENT BODIES, AND POWERS, FINAN-
CIAL FUNCTIONS, LABOR RELATIONS, DISTRIBUTION OF INCOME, AND
CONTROL OVER WORKING CONDITIONS AND WELFARE.

1099 INTERPARLIAMENTARY UNION
PARLIAMENTS: COMPARATIVE STUDY ON STRUCTURE AND FUNCTIONING
OF REPRESENTATIVE INSTITUTIONS IN FIFTY-FIVE COUNTRIES.
LONDON: CASSELL & CO LTD, 1966, 346 PP.
COMPARES STRUCTURE, ORGANIZATION, FUNCTION, AND POWERS
OF PARLIAMENTS IN DIFFERENT COUNTRIES, AND HOW THESE ARE
DETERMINED BY VARYING CONDITIONS AND ATTITUDES. SPECIAL
DISCUSSION OF PARLIAMENTS' GROWING CONTROL OVER EXECUTIVE.

1100 INTL INST ADMIN SCIENCES
EDUCATION IN PUBLIC ADMINISTRATION: A SYMPOSIUM ON TEACHING
METHODS AND MATERIALS.
BRUSSELS: INTL INST OF ADMIN SCI, 1963, 196 PP.
MAIN DOCUMENTS DISCUSSED AT SPECIAL MEETINGS OF REPRE-
SENTATIVES OF PUBLIC ADMINISTRATION EDUCATION. COMPARES
TEACHING METHODS OF SEVERAL COUNTRIES AND EXAMINES CASE
STUDIES. TREATS TRAINING PROBLEMS AND NEEDS, DEVICES AND
MATERIALS, AND RELEVANT FEDERAL LEGISLATION SINCE 1957.

1101 INTL UNION LOCAL AUTHORITIES
LOCAL GOVERNMENT IN THE USA.
THE HAGUE: MARTINUS NIJHOFF, 1961, 133 PP.
GENERAL DISCUSSIONS OF NEW DEVELOPMENTS IN LOCAL GOVERN-
MENTS OF US IN 1960-61. COVERS NEW METHODS AND TECHNIQUES OF
CARRYING OUT LOCAL GOVERNMENT'S FUNCTIONS IN AREAS OF PUBLIC
RELATIONS, PERSONNEL, ETC., BOTH IN CITIES AND TOWNS.
COVERS DEVELOPMENT OF MECHANIZATION IN GOVERNMENT.

1102 IOVTCHOUK M.T., OSSIPOV G.
"ON SOME THEORETICAL PRINCIPLES AND METHODS OF SOCIOLOGICAL
INVESTIGATIONS (IN RUSSIAN)."
VOP. FILOZOF., 16 (NO.12, 62), 23-34.
ANALYZES AND COMPARES ECONOMIC ADVANCE OF SOVIET UNION
AND USA. DISCUSSES FUTURE PROBLEMS THAT MAY ARISE OUT OF
CONFLICT BETWEEN COMMUNIST AND CAPITALIST ECONOMIC SYSTEMS.
SUPPORTS THESIS OF SUPERIORITY OF MARXIST SYSTEM.

1103 IPSEN H.P.
HAMBURGISCHES STAATS- UND VERWALTUNGSRECHT.
HAMBURG: LUDWIG APPEL VERLAG, 1959, 80 PP.
DISCUSSES DEVELOPMENT AND STRUCTURE OF CONSTITUTIONAL AND
ADMINISTRATIVE SYSTEM OF CITY-STATE HAMBURG. EXAMINES SENATE
AND ADMINISTRATION OF LOCAL SUBDIVISIONS, PLUS BUDGETARY
AND FINANCIAL MEASURES. CONTAINS EXTENSIVE DOCUMENTARY
APPENDIX ON CONSTITUTIONAL COURT, POLICE ADMINISTRATION,
ELECTIONS, ETC.

1104 IRIKURA J.K.
SOUTHEAST ASIA: SELECTED ANNOTATED BIBLIOGRAPHY OF
JAPANESE PUBLICATIONS.
NEW HAVEN: HUMAN REL AREA FILES, 1956, 544 PP., LC#56-71519.
CONTAINS 965 EXTENSIVELY ANNOTATED ITEMS ON HISTORY,
GOVERNMENT, ECONOMY, FOREIGN RELATIONS, FOREIGN TRADE,
HEALTH, WELFARE AND EDUCATION, AND MINORITIES OF AREA.
PARTICULAR EMPHASIS ON JAPAN-SOUTHEAST ASIAN RELATIONS.
WORKS ON BURMA, INDOCHINA, INDONESIA, MALAYA, PHILIPPINES,
AND THAILAND.

1105 ISLAM R.
INTERNATIONAL ECONOMIC COOPERATION AND THE UNITED NATIONS.
NEW YORK: UNITED NATIONS, 1958, 129 PP.
DISCUSSES DEVELOPMENTS IN SEVERAL AREAS OF INTERNATIONAL
ECONOMIC AID OCCURRING UNDER AUSPICES OF LEAGUE OF NATIONS
AND UN. GREATER EMPHASIS IS ON UN ACTIVITIES, SPECIFICALLY
ON FORMATION OF SPECIALIZED UN AGENCIES FOR MAINTAINING VAR-
IOUS INTERNATIONAL SERVICES AND ECONOMIC PLANS. STRESSES NE-
CESSITY OF FULL-FLEDGED ECONOMIC COOPERATION IN WORLD COM-
MUNITY UNDER UN REGULATION.

1106 JACKSON E.
"CONSTITUTIONAL DEVELOPMENTS OF THE UNITED NATIONS: THE
GROWTH OF ITS EXECUTIVE CAPACITY."
PROC. AMER. SOC. INT. LAW., 55 (APR. 61), 138-49.
SURVEYS EXPERIENCE OF UN SINCE FOUNDING. SUGGESTS THAT
PROCEDURE AND PRACTICE OF GENERAL ASSEMBLY NEED MODIFICATION
FOR MORE EFFECTIVE PARLIAMENTARY DIPLOMACY.

1107 JACKSON H.M. ED.
THE SECRETARY OF STATE AND THE AMBASSADOR* JACKSON SUBCOM-
MITTEE PAPERS ON THE CONDUCT OF AMERICAN FOREIGN POLICY.
NEW YORK: FREDERICK PRAEGER, 1964, 203 PP., LC#64-8342.
SIX PAPERS AND SENATOR JACKSON'S INTRODUCTION AND ANALYSIS
OF PROBLEM AREAS WHICH TEND TO LOOSEN PRESIDENTIAL RESPON-
SIBLE CONTROL OF FOREIGN POLICY. CONCENTRATES ON THE DIFFI-
CULTIES INHERENT IN THE SECRETARY OF STATE'S COMPETING ROLES
AS PRESIDENTIAL ADVISOR, PLANNING COORDINATOR, LEGISLATIVE
LIAISON AND CHIEF BUREAUCRAT. SIMILAR PROBLEMS OF THE AMBAS-
SADOR AND COUNTRY TEAM ALSO DISCUSSED.

1108 JACKSON R.G.A.
THE CASE FOR AN INTERNATIONAL DEVELOPMENT AUTHORITY
(PAMPHLET)
SYRACUSE: SYRACUSE U PRESS, 1959, 67 PP., LC#59-9104.
LECTURES IN FAVOR OF THE ESTABLISHMENT OF A COOPERATING
INTERNATIONAL ORGANIZATION WHICH WOULD CHANNEL FOREIGN AID
OF ALL COUNTRIES TO ALL UNDERDEVELOPED AREAS. MEMBERSHIP
WOULD BE OPEN TO ALL, INCLUDING COMMUNIST COUNTRIES THOUGH
THEY WOULD BE IN MINORITY, AND VOTING WOULD BE WEIGHED IN
RELATION TO CONTRIBUTION. THIS BODY WOULD FACILITATE
ADMINISTRATION OF FOREIGN AID AND MAKE IT MORE EQUITABLE.

1109 JACKSON R.M.
THE MACHINERY OF JUSTICE IN ENGLAND.
NEW YORK: CAMBRIDGE U PRESS, 1964, 455 PP.
DISCUSSES ENGLISH SYSTEM OF LAW AND COURTS AND ADMINI-
STRATIVE DETAILS LIKE PERSONNEL AND COSTS. GIVES HISTORICAL
INTRODUCTION AND EXAMINES CIVIL AND CRIMINAL JURISDICTION.

1110 JACKSON W.V.
LIBRARY GUIDE FOR BRAZILIAN STUDIES.
PITTSBURGH: U OF PITT BOOK CTRS., 1964, 197 PP., LC#64-66279
BIBLIOGRAPHY OF RESEARCH COLLECTIONS ON BRAZIL IN 74
AMERICAN UNIVERSITIES.

1111 JACOB H.
GERMAN ADMINISTRATION SINCE BISMARCK: CENTRAL AUTHORITY
VERSUS LOCAL AUTONOMY.
NEW HAVEN: YALE U PR, 1963, 324 PP., LC#63-7937.
ANALYZES AND COMPARES SECOND REICH, WEIMAR REPUBLIC,
THIRD REICH, AND GERMAN FEDERAL REPUBLIC IN HISTORICAL
PERSPECTIVE. STUDIES INSTITUTIONS AND ADMINISTRATIVE
POLICIES. EXAMINES DEVELOPMENT OF CONTROLS, LEGALISTIC
PERSPECTIVES, PARTY INFILTRATION, AND LARGE-SCALE PERSONNEL
CHANGES. INCLUDES GERMAN CIVIL SERVICE, QUEST FOR
RESPONSIVENESS, AND ADAPTIVE CHARACTERISTICS.

1112 JACOB H.
"DIMENSIONS OF STATE POLITICS HEARD A. ED. STATE LEGISLA.
TURES IN AMERICAN POLITICS."
ENGLEWOOD CLIFFS: PRENTICE HALL, 1966.
EXAMINES STATE LEGISLATURES IN TERMS OF THE CONCEPT OF
POLITICAL SYSTEMS AS DEVELOPED BY DAVID EASTON. CONSIDERS
AND RANKS FORCES, SUCH AS PHYSICAL, SOCIAL, AND CULTURAL EN-
VIRONMENT OF LEGISLATORS, WHICH AFFECT LEGISLATIVE DECIS-
IONS. ALSO EXAMINES GROUPS WHICH COMMUNICATE DEMANDS AND
GIVE SUPPORT TO THE LEGISLATORS.

1113 JACOBS J.
THE DEATH AND LIFE OF GREAT AMERICAN CITIES.
NEW YORK: RANDOM HOUSE, INC, 1961, 458 PP., LC#61-6262.
ATTACKS PRACTICE, PRINCIPLES, AND AIMS OF CURRENT URBAN
PLANNING AND RENEWAL. SEEKS TO DETERMINE BASIS OF CITY
SOCIETY, AND ASSERTS THAT CITIES REQUIRE AN INTRICATE

COMPLEX OF DIVERSE BUT MUTUALLY SUPPORTIVE ACTIVITIES.
EXAMINES ASPECTS OF URBAN DECAY, AND SUGGESTS CHANGES IN
HOUSING, TRAFFIC, DESIGN, PLANNING, AND ADMINISTRATIVE
PRACTICES. BASIC PROBLEM IS PROPERLY TO ORGANIZE COMPLEXITY.

1114 JACOBS P.
"RE-RADICALIZING THE DE-RADICALIZED."
NEW POLITICS, 5 (FALL 66), 14-21.
DISCUSSES FORMATION OF ANTI-POVERTY PROGRAM AND SHIFT BY
MANY EX-RADICALS TO SUPPORT OF IT. MAINTAINS PROGRAM'S LACK
OF REAL IMPACT IS RESULT OF NEED TO COMPROMISE FOR POLITICAL
PURPOSES, INSUFFICIENT FUNDS, ADMINISTRATIVE INEFFICIENCY,
AND MAINLY, INVALID BASIC ASSUMPTIONS. POVERTY IS VIEWED AS
NATURAL PART OF SOCIAL SCENE, NOT A DYSFUNCTION. MUST FIND
RADICAL PROGRAMS TO SOLVE DOMESTIC CRISES.

1115 JACOBSON H.K.
"THE UNITED NATIONS AND COLONIALISM: A TENTATIVE APPRAISAL."
INT. ORGAN., 16 (WINTER 62), 137-56.
SHOWS DECREASING ROLE OF UN IN COLONIAL AFFAIRS AS MORE
COLONIES ACHIEVE INDEPENDENCE. NOTES LACK OF SOVIET AFFECT
ON COLONIAL AFFAIRS, BUT CITES US INVOLVEMENT IN STRUGGLE
BETWEEN COLONIAL AND ANTI-COLONIAL POWERS. ASSESSES UN CON-
TRIBUTION TO COLONIAL REVOLUTION AS MODEST, BUT TO STABILITY
AND DEVELOPMENT AS SIGNIFICANT.

1116 JACOBSON J.
"COALITIONISM: FROM PROTEST TO POLITICKING"
NEW POLITICS, 5 (FALL 66), 47-65.
MAINTAINS CIVIL RIGHTS MOVEMENT IS FAILING TO BREAK US
RACIAL BARRIERS BECAUSE OF WARRING CAMPS WITHIN MOVEMENT:
BLACK POWER VS. COALITION POLITICS. COALITIONISTS FIND TRADE
UNION MOVEMENT NEGRO'S ALLY. EXAMINES LABOR SIDE OF NEGRO-
LABOR ALLIANCE AND SUPPORTS RADICALS' PARTICIPATION TO BREAK
LABOR'S BUREAUCRACY AND CORRUPTION. COALITIONISTS CRIPPLED
BY PRIMARY ALLEGIANCE TO THEIR DOGMA AND UNION PATRONS.

1117 JACOBY S.B.
"THE 89TH CONGRESS AND GOVERNMENT LITIGATION."
COLUMBIA LAW REV., 77 (NOV. 67), 1212-1240.
DESCRIBES FOUR STATUTES ENACTED IN 89TH CONGRESS TREATING
GOVERNMENT LITIGATION, WHICH INCREASE ADMINISTRATIVE
SETTLEMENT OF TORT CLAIMS AGAINST GOVERNMENT, LIMIT CLAIMS
OF GOVERNMENT, AND MAKE GOVERNMENT RESPONSIBLE FOR SOME
COSTS OF LITIGATION. DISCUSSES INTERPRETATIONS OF THESE LAWS
AND EXTENT OF THEIR APPLICATION. BELIEVES THAT GOVERNMENT'S
UNFAIR ADVANTAGE THROUGH SOVEREIGN IMMUNITY WILL BE REDUCED.

1118 JAIN R.K.
MANAGEMENT OF STATE ENTERPRISES.
BOMBAY: MANAKTALAS, 1967, 532 PP.
EXAMINES OBJECTIVELY PROBLEMS FACING THE PUBLIC SECTOR
IN INDIA WITH A VIEW TO FINDING A WAY FORWARD DURING TRANSI-
TIONAL STAGE OF SOCIAL TRANSFORMATION. SEEKS WAYS TO ESTAB-
LISH AND STRENGTHEN POWER OF DEMOCRATIC INSTITUTIONS WITHIN
SOCIETY WHERE PUBLIC SECTOR CONTROLS INDUSTRIES. ANALYZES
INTERNAL AND FINANCIAL ORGANIZATION OF SUCH INDUSTRIES, AS
WELL AS PERSONNEL MANAGEMENT.

1119 JAKUBAUSKAS E.B. ED., BAUMEL C.P. ED.
HUMAN RESOURCES DEVELOPMENT.
AMES: IOWA STATE U PR, 1967, 162 PP., LC#67-26062.
COLLECTS ESSAYS ON HUMAN RESOURCES DEVELOPMENT BY MEMBERS
OF FEDERAL, STATE, AND PRIVATE ORGANIZATIONS INVOLVED IN
MANPOWER AND HUMAN RESOURCE DEVELOPMENT PROGRAMS. DISCUSSES
CONCEPT AND PROBLEMS OF DEVELOPMENT, TRENDS IN SERVICE
SECTOR EMPLOYMENT, AND TRENDS RELATED TO AGRICULTURAL AND
MANUFACTURING EMPLOYMENT. STUDIES RACIAL BARRIERS IN
APPRENTICE TRAINING PROGRAMS AND AREAS OF NEEDED RESEARCH.

1120 JANOWITZ M., DELANEY W.
"THE BUREAUCRAT AND THE PUBLIC: A STUDY OF INFORMATIONAL
PERSPECTIVES."
ADMINISTRATIVE SCI. Q., 2 (SEPT. 57), 141-162.
STUDY OF DIFFERENCE IN CONTACT WITH PUBLIC BETWEEN HIGH-
AND LOW LEVEL BUREAUCRATS IN THREE DETROIT AGENCIES. FOUND
LOW-LEVEL BUREAUCRATS HAVE MORE CONTACT WITH PUBLIC, BUT
BUREAUCRACY IN GENERAL NOT RESPONSIVE TO PUBLIC FEELINGS.

1121 JANOWITZ M.
SOCIOLOGY AND THE MILITARY ESTABLISHMENT.
NEW YORK: RUSSELL SAGE FOUNDATION, 1959, 112 PP.
THE COMPLEXITY OF THE MODERN SOCIAL STRUCTURE WITH ITS
EMPHASIS ON THE TECHNOLOGICAL, POLITICAL, AND EDUCATIONAL
ASPECTS OF SOCIETY HAS PRODUCED A NEW MILITARY ORGANIZATION.
THE CHANGING NATURE OF THE MILITARY ORGANIZATION MAKES IT
NECESSARY TO VIEW THE ARMED FORCES AS A MODERN COMPLEX
STRUCTURE AND NOT SIMPLY AS A FIGHTING MACHINE.

1122 JANOWITZ M.
"CHANGING PATTERNS OF ORGANIZATIONAL AUTHORITY: THE MILITARY
ESTABLISHMENT" (BMR)
ADMINISTRATIVE SCI. Q., 3 (MAR. 59), 473-493.
ANALYZES BASES AND MANIFESTATIONS OF TREND IN MILITARY
ESTABLISHMENT TOWARD LESS DIRECT, ARBITRARY, AND AUTHORI-
TARIAN BUREAUCRACY. SHOWS CHANGE IS FROM AN AUTHORITY SYSTEM

BASED UPON DOMINATION TO ONE BASED UPON TECHNIQUES OF MANIP-
ULATION BROUGHT ABOUT BY NEW WEAPONS, AUTOMATION OF WAR-
FARE, DEMANDS OF TECHNICAL EXPERTISE, AND EMPHASIS UPON
INDIVIDUAL INITIATIVE.

1123 JANOWITZ M. ED.
COMMUNITY POLITICAL SYSTEMS.
NEW YORK: FREE PRESS OF GLENCOE, 1961, 259 PP., LC#59-13864.
A STUDY OF COMMUNITY ORGANIZATION APPROACHED FROM THE BE-
HAVIORAL POINT OF VIEW. ANALYZES LEADERSHIP AND POWER
STRUCTURES, THE EFFECT OF INDUSTRIALIZATION, METHODOLOGICAL
PROBLEMS IN SOCIOLOGICAL RESEARCH, AND STUDIES OF SAMPLE
CITIES.

1124 JANSE R.S.
SOVIET TRANSPORTATION AND COMMUNICATIONS: A BIBLIOGRAPHY.
WASHINGTON: US GOVERNMENT, 1952, 330 PP., LC#52-60024.
COMPREHENSIVE, PARTIALLY ANNOTATED LIST OF RUSSIAN AND
NON-RUSSIAN SOURCES DEALING WITH MAJOR FORMS OF TRANSPORTA-
TION AND COMMUNICATIONS IN USSR, AND TO CERTAIN EXTENT
INFORMATION ON RELATED SUBJECTS SUCH AS ENGINEERING PROBLEMS
AND RELEVANT LEGISLATIVE AND ADMINISTRATIVE MEASURES. EMPHA-
SIS ON MATERIAL PUBLISHED SINCE 1930. CONTAINS 4,951 ITEMS
AND AUTHOR INDEX.

1125 JAPAN MINISTRY OF JUSTICE
CRIMINAL JUSTICE IN JAPAN.
TOKYO: JAPAN MINISTRY OF JUSTICE, 1958, 37 PP.
ATTEMPTS TO PRESENT CONCISE PICTURE OF ADMINISTRATION OF
CRIMINAL JUSTICE IN POSTWAR JAPAN. DISCUSSES POLICE ACTIVI-
TIES AND ORGANIZATION, CRIMINAL PROCEDURE, CONSTITUTIONAL
GUARANTEES, CORRECTIONAL SERVICES AND REHABILITATION OF OF-
FENDERS. BRIEFLY EXAMINES JAPANESE LAWYERS.

1126 JAPAN MOMBUSHO DAIGAKU GAKIYUT
BIBLIOGRAPHY OF THE STUDIES ON LAW AND POLITICS (PAMPHLET)
TOKYO: JAPAN MINISTRY EDUCATION, 1955, 83 PP.
UNANNOTATED BIBLIOGRAPHY OF 918 WORKS IN FIELDS OF
LAW AND POLITICS THAT APPEARED IN VARIOUS JAPANESE SCHOLARLY
BOOKS, JOURNALS, BULLETINS ETC., IN 1952. AUTHOR, TITLE,
AND JOURNAL GIVEN IN BOTH ROMAN SCRIPT AND CHARACTERS. WORKS
ARRANGED ALPHABETICALLY BY AUTHOR WITHIN 16 SUBJECT CLASSI-
FICATIONS, AND INDEXED BY AUTHOR. LIST OF ALL PERIODICALS
MENTIONED IS APPENDED TO TEXT.

1127 JAVITS J.K.
"THE USE OF AMERICAN PLURALISM."
COLORADO QUARTERLY, 16 (FALL 67), 119-126.
DISCUSSES "NEW DEAL THINKING" WHICH HOLDS THAT FEDERAL
GOVERNMENT IS ONLY INSTRUMENT FOR DEFINING, DEVELOPING,
DMINISTERING, AND FINANCING SOLUTIONS TO US PROBLEMS. FEELS
PEOPLE OF US ARE GRADUALLY LOSING CONFIDENCE IN THIS THESIS
AND BECOMING DISENCHANTED WITH DEPERSONALIZATION OF
POLITICS. PROPOSES NEW PHILOSOPHY WHICH WILL MAKE USE OF
PLURALISM THAT HAS PROVIDED AMERICAN FREEDOM AND WEALTH.

1128 JENCKS C.E.
"SOCIAL STATUS OF COAL MINERS IN BRITAIN SINCE NATIONALIZA-
TION."
AMER.J. OF COMPARATIVE LAW, 26(JULY 67), 301-312.
FINDS COAL MINERS' WAGES, WORKING CONDITIONS, FRINGE BEN-
EFITS, LABOR-MANAGEMENT REALTIONS, HOUSING, AND GENERAL WEL-
FARE HAVE IMPROVED SINCE NATIONALIZATION. DISCUSSES MIN-
ERS' ATTITUDES TOWARD THEIR "LOW" SOCIAL POSITION, AND SHOWS
HOW THESE ATTITUDES AFFECT INDUSTRIAL RELATIONS.

1129 JENKINS W.S.
COLLECTED PUBLIC DOCUMENTS OF THE STATES: A CHECK LIST.
BOSTON: NATL ASSN OF STATE LIB, 1947, 87 PP.
A SIMPLE LISTING BY YEAR AND VOLUME OF ALL SERIALLY
ISSUED STATE DOCUMENTS. ITEMIZED INDIVIDUALLY BY STATE WITH
NO DESCRIPTIVE MATERIAL.

1130 JENKINS W.S.
A GUIDE TO THE MICROFILM COLLECTION OF EARLY STATE RECORDS.
WASHINGTON: LIBRARY OF CONGRESS, 1950, 761 PP., LC#50-62956.
A COMPREHENSIVE GUIDE TO 160,000 FEET OF FILM REPRESENT-
ING 2,500,000 PAGES OF PRIMARY SOURCE MATERIAL. CLASSIFICA-
TION ARRANGED BY STATE, SUBJECT, AND CHRONOLOGY, RESPECTIVE-
LY. DESIGNED TO SERVE DUAL PURPOSE OF SUPPLYING USER WITH
INFORMATION ON THE LOCATION OF BOTH THE ORIGINAL AND FILM OF
EACH DOCUMENT, AND PROVIDING CATALOG FROM WHICH ORDERS FOR
REPRODUCTIONS MAY BE FILLED. A MECHANIZED BIBLIOGRAPHY.

1131 JENNINGS E.E.
THE EXECUTIVE: AUTOCRAT, BUREAUCRAT, DEMOCRAT.
NEW YORK: HARPER & ROW, 1962, 272 PP., LC#62-13248.
THE AUTHOR DISCUSSES THE EXECUTIVE IMAGE, DUALITY,
CALISTHENICS, ETC., IN TERMS OF ANXIETY AND HOSTILE COMPETI-
TIVE FEELINGS AND THE NEED TO MAKE PRODUCTIVE USE OF THESE
EMOTIONS IN ORDER TO AVOID BEING OVERWHELMED BY THEM.

1132 JENNINGS I.
THE QUEEN'S GOVERNMENT.
BALTIMORE: PENGUIN BOOKS, 1954, 158 PP.
BRIEF INTRODUCTION TO INSTITUTIONS OF BRITISH GOVERNMENT,
WITH PARTICULAR EMPHASIS ON HISTORY AND DEVELOPMENT OF
BRITISH CONSTITUTION. SURVEYS THE PERSONAL AND POLITICAL
ROLE OF THE MONARCH; THE PARTY SYSTEM; THE NATURE, FUNCTION,
AND ORGANIZATION OF PARLIAMENT; GOVERNMENTAL ADMINISTRATION;
PRIME MINISTER AND CABINET; AND THE JUDICIAL SYSTEM.

1133 JENNINGS I.
PARLIAMENT.
WORCESTER: CLARK U PRESS, 1957, 574 PP., LC#57-14459.
ANALYZES THE BRITISH PARLIAMENT. TREATS THE MEMBERS, THE
POLITICAL PARTIES AND THE OFFICIALS, THE ART OF MANAGEMENT,
THE TECHNIQUE OF OPPOSITION, WHO MAKES THE LAWS, THE PROCESS
OF LEGISLATION, FINANCIAL CONTROL, NATIONALIZED INDUSTRIES,
HOUSE OF LORDS, PRIVATE BILL LEGISLATION, DELEGATED LEGISLA-
TION AND PARLIAMENTARY DEMOCRACY.

1134 JENNINGS M.K.
"PUBLIC ADMINISTRATORS AND COMMUNITY DECISION-MAKING."
ADMINISTRATIVE SCI. Q., 8 (JUNE 63), 18-43.
THIS STUDY OF TWO SOUTHERN COMMUNITIES FOUND THAT
ADMINISTRATORS WERE MODERATELY TO HIGHLY INVOLVED IN,
AND INFLUENTIAL OVER, COMMUNITY DECISION-MAKING.

1135 JENNINGS W.I.
PARLIAMENT.
LONDON: CAMBRIDGE UNIV PRESS, 1939, 540 PP.
DESCRIBES AND ANALYZES WORKING OF PARLIAMENTARY PORTION
OF MACHINERY OF GOVERNMENT. DISCUSSES COMPOSITION OF
PARLIAMENT, MEMBERS AND THEIR INTERESTS, PARTIES AND
OFFICIALS OF HOUSES. DESCRIBES FRAMEWORK OF ORATORY, ART
OF MANAGEMENT, AND TECHNIQUE OF OPPOSITION. TREATS PROCESS
OF LEGISLATION, FINANCIAL CONTROL, HOUSE OF LORDS, PRIVATE
LEGISLATION, AND HOUSE OF COMMONS.

1136 JENNINGS W.I.
THE APPROACH TO SELF-GOVERNMENT.
CAMBRIDGE, ENGLAND: U. PR., 1956, 204 PP.
A SERIES OF BROADCAST LECTURES DISCUSSING THE CONSTITU-
TIONAL PROBLEMS FACED BY COLONIAL NATIONS APPROACHING INDE-
PENDENCE. SHOWS ADAPTATION OF BRITISH CONSTITUTIONAL TRADI-
TION IN CEYLON, INDIA AND PAKISTAN.

1137 JENNINGS W.I.
CABINET GOVERNMENT (3RD ED.)
LONDON: CAMBRIDGE UNIV PRESS, 1959, 586 PP.
DESCRIBES WORKING OF CABINET FORM OF GOVERNMENT IN
BRITAIN. COLLECTS PRECEDENTS REGULATING CONVENTIONS OF
CABINET GOVERNMENT. DISCUSSES CONSTITUTION, CHOICE OF
PRIME MINISTER, ADMINISTRATIVE STRUCTURE, FUNCTION OF
MINISTERS, AND INTERDEPARTMENTAL RELATIONS. STUDIES
TREASURY CONTROL, STRUCTURE AND FUNCTION OF CABINET.

1138 JEWELL M.E.
SENATORIAL POLITICS AND FOREIGN POLICY.
LEXINGTON: U. KENTUCKY PR., 1963, 214 PP.
STUDIES POLITICAL PROCESSES OF US SENATE THROUGH AN
EXAMINATION OF ITS FOREIGN POLICY PROGRAM DURING YEARS 1947
THROUGH 1960. STRESSES INFLUENCE OF BOTH PRESIDENT AND PUB-
LIC OPINION UPON BODY'S LEGISLATION. CONCLUDES THAT POLIT-
ICAL PARTIES 'CAN CONTRIBUTE A GREATER MEASURE OF RATIONAL-
ITY AND RESPONSIBILITY TO THE POLICYMAKING PROCESS....'

1139 JEWELL M.E.
"THE SENATE REPUBLICAN POLICY COMMITTEE AND FOREIGN POLICY."
WESTERN POLIT. QUART., 12 (DEC. 59), 966-980.
REVIEWS ROLE AND ACTIONS OF COMMITTEE SINCE 1947 AND
SUGGESTS ITS INEFFECTIVENESS HAS BEEN DUE TO POOR LEADERSHIP
AND INFLEXIBILITY. IT MUST UNITE AND BECOME AN AGENT OF
COMMUNICATION WITH WHITE HOUSE DURING REPUBLICAN ADMINIS-
TRATION AND POLICY-FORMING BODY DURING DEMOCRATIC.

1140 JHANGIANI M.A.
JANA SANGH AND SWATANTRA: A PROFILE OF THE RIGHTIST PARTIES
IN INDIA.
BOMBAY: MANAKTALAS, 1967, 223 PP.
STUDIES TWO NEW "RIGHTIST" PARTIES IN INDIA. JANA SANGH
CLAIMS "LEFTISTS" ARE TOO WESTERN AND DERIVES INSPIRATION
FROM VALUES OF BHARATIYA CULTURE. SWATANTRA OPPOSES
SOCIALISM AND SEEKS TO MAINTAIN STATUS QUO OF FREE
ENTERPRISE. DISCUSSES DEVELOPMENT, STRUCTURE, ORGANIZATION,
AND IDEOLOGY OF TWO PARTIES, PLUS THEIR RESULTS IN
ELECTIONS.

1141 JOELSON M.R.
"THE DISMISSAL OF CIVIL SERVANTS IN THE INTERESTS OF
NATIONAL SECURITY."
PUB. LAW, (SPRING 63), 51-75.
A COMPARISON OF PROCEDURES AND EFFECTIVENESS OF SECURTY
PROGRAMS IN THE U.S., FRANCE, AND BRITAIN.

1142 JOHNS R.
CONFRONTING ORGANIZATIONAL CHANGE.
NEW YORK: ASSOCIATION PRESS, 1963, 158 PP., LC#63-17418.
EXPLORATION OF PROCESS OF PLANNED ORGANIZATIONAL CHANGE,
PARTICULARLY IN COMMUNITY SERVICE ORGANIZATIONS. GIVES BRIEF
OUTLINES ON NEED FOR LEADERSHIP IN CHANGE, THE APPLICATION

OF LEWIN'S "FIELD OF FORCES." THE IMPORTANCE OF TIME
SCHEDULES, GOALS, ILLUSTRATED WITH CASE STUDIES.

1143 JOHNSON H.
"CANADA IN A CHANGING WORLD."
INT. J., 18 (WINTER 62-63), 17-28.
MAINTAINS CANADA NEEDS DRASTIC CHANGES IN DOMESTIC AND
INTERNATIONAL POLICY. FIVE-YEAR ECONOMIC STAGNATION DUE TO
RESTRICTED MONETARY SYSTEM AND HIGH TARIFFS. SUGGESTS RETURN
TO FLOATING EXCHANGE RATE AND SPECIALIZED PRODUCTION. EXA-
MINES CANADA IN RELATION TO BRITAIN, USA, AND COMMON MARKET.

1144 JOHNSON K.F.
"CAUSAL FACTORS IN LATIN AMERICAN POLITICAL INSTABILITY."
WEST. POLIT. QUART., 17 (SEPT. 64), 432-446.
APPLYING THE 'POLITICAL CULTURE' CONCEPT OF ALMOND AND
VERBA, THE AUTHOR SEEKS TO FORMULATE A SYSTEMATIC THEORY
OF INSTABILITY IN LATIN AMERICA AS AN INTERACTION SET
WHICH CAN BE EITHER OPERATIONALIZED EMPIRICALLY OR INVOKED
THEORETICALLY. TENTATIVE HYPOTHESES AMENABLE TO PRECISION
TESTING WITH A RIGOROUS METHODOLOGY ARE ALSO SUGGESTED.

1145 JOHNSON L.B.
"BULLETS DO NOT DISCRIMINATE-LANDLORDS DO."
CRISIS, 74 (MAR. 67), 61-67, 95-101.
MESSAGE TO CONGRESS ON CIVIL RIGHTS. CALLS FOR EQUAL
HOUSING OPPORTUNITY, NONDISCRIMINATE JURY SELECTION, FEDERAL
PROTECTION FOR PURSUANCE OF CONSTITUTIONAL RIGHTS, INCREASED
APPROPRIATIONS FOR COMMUNITY RELATIONS SERVICE, EMPOWERING
EQUAL EMPLOYMENT OPPORTUNITY COMMISSION TO TAKE STRONGER
ACTION, AND EXTENSION OF CIVIL RIGHTS COMMISSION.

1146 JOHNSON N.
"PARLIAMENTARY QUESTIONS AND THE CONDUCT OF ADMINISTRATION."
PUBLIC ADMINISTRATION, 39 (SUMMER 61), 131-148.
DESCRIPTION OF PARLIAMENTARY SYSTEM OF QUESTIONING
THE GOVERNMENT AS A MEANS OF CONTROLLING THE ADMINISTRATION
OF GREAT BRITAIN.

1147 JOHNSON N.
PARLIAMENT AND ADMINISTRATION: THE ESTIMATES COMMITTEE
1945-65.
NEW YORK: AUGUSTUS M. KELLEY, 1966, 187 PP.
ANALYZES ORGANIZATION AND FUNCTIONS OF MAJOR COMMITTEE
OF HOUSE OF COMMONS. CLASSIFIES AND SUMMARIZES MATERIAL
PRODUCED BY COMMITTEE TO DISPROVE THAT "VEIL OF SECRECY"
COVERS ALL IMPORTANT ACTIONS OF PARLIAMENT. TAKES THREE
MAJOR COMMITTEE REPORTS AS DETAILED CASE STUDIES OF WAY
COMMITTEE WORKS. INCLUDES STUDY OF 1965 PROPOSALS THAT
MIGHT AFFECT FUTURE OF COMMITTEE.

1148 JONAS F.H.
"BIBLIOGRAPHY ON WESTERN POLITICS."
WESTERN POLIT. QUART., 11 (DEC. 58), 1-165.
AN ANNOTATED BIBLIOGRAPHY ON WESTERN POLITICS. DIVIDED
INTO TWELVE HEADINGS: ONE OVER-ALL CHAPTER ON WESTERN POLI-
TICS AND THE OTHER ELEVEN EACH DEVOTED TO ONE WESTERN STATE.
2250 ENGLISH-LANGUAGE ENTRIES. MATERIAL RANGES FROM 1890
TO 1957.

1149 JONES A.G.
THE EVOLUTION OF PERSONNEL SYSTEMS FOR US FOREIGN AFFAIRS*
A HISTORY OF REFORM EFFORTS.
NEW YORK: TAPLINGER PUBL CO, 1965, 136 PP., LC#64-24648.
HISTORICAL ANALYSIS OF US EFFORTS TO DEVELOP AND IMPROVE
ITS PROFESSIONAL FOREIGN SERVICE. DEALS WITH DRIVE FOR A
UNITARY SERVICE CULMINATING IN ROGERS ACT OF 1924, AND THE
SEVERAL POSTWAR REFORM EFFORTS INCLUDING THE HOOVER COMMIS-
SION, THE WRISTON COMMITTEE, AND BROOKINGS STUDIES. PRESENTS
SOME OF THEIR DATA AND EVALUATES THEIR SUCCESSES.

1150 JONES G.S.
"STRATEGIC PLANNING."
MILITARY REV., 47 (SEPT. 67), 14-19.
ANALYZES ROLE OF JOINT CHIEFS OF STAFF IN POLICY FORMA-
TION IN AREA OF SECURITY. DISCUSSES RELATIONSHIP OF JCS
TO PRESIDENT AND DEVELOPMENT OF THE JOINT STRATEGIC OBJEC-
TIVES PLAN, STARTING POINT IN PREPARING MILITARY BUDGET.

1151 JONES V.
METROPOLITAN GOVERNMENT.
CHICAGO: U OF CHICAGO PRESS, 1942, 364 PP.
SHOWS THE DISINTEGRATING EFFECTS OF SWELLING POPULATION
ON METROPOLITAN AREAS. ARGUES THAT SUBURBAN GOVERNMENTS
SHOULD BE INTEGRATED WITH THE CENTRAL CITY SO THAT PUBLIC
SERVICES WILL BE MORE EFFICIENT. ADVOCATES A TECHNOCRATIC
STRUCTURING OF CITY GOVERNMENT SO THAT PEOPLE WILL BE
BETTER SERVED.

1152 JONES V., HUDSON B., JOHNSTON L.D.
METROPOLITAN COMMUNITIES: A BIBLIOGRAPHY WITH SPECIAL
EMPHASIS UPON GOVERNMENT AND POLITICS, 1955-1957.
CHICAGO: PUBLIC ADMIN SERVICE, 1960, 229 PP., LC#56-13382.
SUPPLEMENT TO BASIC BIBLIOGRAPHY OF GOVERNMENT AFFAIRS
FOUNDATION ON METROPOLITAN COMMUNITIES. COVERS PERIOD JULY,
1955 THROUGH DECEMBER, 1957. FOCUSES ON GOVERNMENT AND POLI-

TICS BUT INCLUDES REFERENCES TO ITEMS CONCERNING SOCIO-
ECONOMIC CHARACTERISTICS AND DEVELOPMENT OF URBAN CENTERS.
CONTAINS LIMITED ANNOTATIONS; CROSS REFERENCES; SUBJECT,
AUTHOR, AND PLACE INDEXES; LISTING OF INFORMATION SOURCES.

1153 JORDAN A.
"MILITARY ASSISTANCE AND NATIONAL POLICY."
ORBIS, 2 (SUMMER 58), 236-53.
PRESENTS HISTORY OF MILITARY AID AND RESULTS OF AID TO
ALLIES AND 'FRIENDLY' UNDERDEVELOPED NATIONS. SUGGESTS THAT
INADEQUATE AID TO CHINA RESULTED IN COMMUNIST VICTORY.
MAKES RECOMMENDATIONS FOR ALTERNATIVE AID POLICY.

1154 JOSEPHSON E.
"IRRATIONAL LEADERSHIP IN FORMAL ORGANIZATIONS."
SOCIAL FORCES, 31 (DEC. 52), 109-117.
SEARCHES THE LIMITS OF RATIONALITY IN ADMINISTRATIVE
ORGANIZATION, DISCUSSING MUTUAL IMPACT OF PERSONALITY AND
OFFICE, TYPES OF PERSONALITY AND AUTHORITY, LEADERS AND
SUBORDINATES, EXECUTIVE STRUCTURE AND OPERATIONAL MORALE
AND STABILITY.

1155 JOYCE J.A.
RED CROSS INTERNATIONAL AND THE STRATEGY OF PEACE.
NEW YORK: OCEANA, 1959, 270 PP.
TRACES DEVELOPMENT OF RED CROSS UNDER HENRI DUNANT,
REVIEWING AIMS AND LAWS OF THAT INTERNATIONAL ORGANIZATION.
BASIC CONTENTION IS THAT PEACE CAN ONLY BE ESTABLISHED
THROUGH HUMANISTIC EFFORTS OF WORLD-CITIZENRY.

1156 JUVILER P.H.
"INTERPARLIAMENTARY CONTACTS IN SOVIET FOREIGN POLICY."
AMER. SLAV. EASTEUROPE. REV., 20 (FEB. 61), 25-39.
BRIEF HISTORY OF THE INTERNATIONAL PARLIAMENTARY UNION
FROM ITS FOUNDATION IN 1889 TO THE PRESENT. DESCRIBES STRUC-
TURE AND PURPOSE OF THE PARLIAMENTARY GROUP RECENTLY ORIGI-
NATED AROUND THE USSR, AND EXPECTS IT TO BECOME A USEFUL
CHANNEL OF CONTACT WITH THE WEST.

1157 KAACK H.
DIE PARTEIEN IN DER VERFASSUNGSWIRKLICHKEIT DER BUNDES-
REPUBLIK.
FLANDERS, N.J.: O'HARE BOOKS, 1964, 128 PP.
INTRODUCTION TO THE HISTORY AND STRUCTURE OF THE POLITI-
CAL PARTIES OF THE GERMAN FEDERAL REPUBLIC. DISCUSSES THE
ELECTIONS ON NATIONAL AND STATE LEVEL AND SOME OF THE PRO-
GRAMMATIC CHANGES THAT HAVE OCCURRED SINCE 1945.

1158 KAAS L.
DIE GEISTLICHE GERICHTSBARKEIT DER KATHOLISCHEN KIRCHE IN
PREUSSEN (2 VOLS.)
AMSTERDAM: VERLAG P SCHIPPERS, 1965, 962 PP.
EXAMINES JURISDICTION OF CATHOLIC CHURCH IN PRUSSIA FROM
REFORMATION TO PRESENT. DISCUSSES DISPUTES WITH STATE AS
WELL AS STRUCTURE AND PROCESSES OF ECCLESIASTICAL COURTS.

1159 KAESTNER K.
GESAMTWIRTSCHAFTLICHE PLANUNG IN EINER GEMISCHTEN WIRT-
SCHAFTSORDNUNG (WIRTSCHAFTSPOLITISCHE STUDIEN 5)
GOTTINGEN: VAN DEN HOECK UND RUPRECHT, 1966, 140 PP.
PRESENTS CONCEPTS AND METHODS OF TOTAL ECONOMIC PLANNING;
DISCUSSES SCOPE OF PLANNING (PUBLIC SECTOR, MANAGEMENT POL-
ICY, PRIVATE SECTOR), TREATS PLANNING OF PRODUCTION IN THE
PRIVATE SECTOR; CONSIDERS POSSIBILITIES OF TOTAL ECONOMIC
PLANNING IN A MIXED ECONOMY. BIBLIOGRAPHY LISTS 146 BOOKS
AND ARTICLES IN GERMAN, FRENCH, ENGLISH, 1883-1965.

1160 KAHNG T.J.
LAW, POLITICS, AND THE SECURITY COUNCIL* AN INQUIRY INTO THE
HANDLING OF LEGAL QUESTIONS.
LONDON: LONGMANS, GREEN & CO, 1964, 252 PP.
ANALYSIS OF PATTERN OF SECURITY COUNCIL'S HANDLING OF LE-
GAL QUESTIONS BY COMPARING ITS BEHAVIOR IN A WEALTH OF CASES
AGAINST BEHAVIOR PRESCRIBED BY CHARTER. QUESTIONS OF COMPE-
TENCE, PROCEDURES, AND NATIONAL RIGHTS AND DUTIES TREATED.
FINDS THAT COUNCIL IS CONCERNED WITH LEGALITY BUT PREFERS TO
DECIDE FOR ITSELF AND NOT SUBMIT QUESTIONS TO CHARTER-AU-
THORIZED BODIES.

1161 KAMMERER G.M.
CITY MANAGERS IN POLITICS: AN ANALYSIS OF MANAGER TENURE
AND TERMINATION.
GAINESVILLE: U FLA PUB ADM CLEAR, 1962, 93 PP.
A STUDY OF MANAGER TENURE OVER A 15-YEAR SPAN WHICH
ATTEMPTS TO RELATE TENURE TO INSTITUTIONAL-STRUCTURAL
VARIABLES, PERSONAL CHARACTERISTICS VARIABLES, WITH NONPOL-
ITICAL AND WITH POLITICAL VARIABLES.

1162 KAMMERER G.M., FARRIS C.D. ET AL.
THE URBAN POLITICAL COMMUNITY: PROFILES IN TOWN POLITICS.
BOSTON: HOUGHTON MIFFLIN, 1963, 216 PP.
THIS WORK EXAMINES THE RELATIONSHIP BETWEEN CITY MANAGER
TENURE AND TURNOVER AND THE POWER STRUCTURES AND PROCESSES
IN EIGHT FLORIDA COMMUNITIES.

1163 KAMMERER G.M.

"ROLE DIVERSITY OF CITY MANAGERS."
ADMINISTRATIVE SCI. Q., 8 (MAR. 64), 421-442.
AN ATTEMPT TO PROVIDE PRECISE DESCRIPTIONS OF ROLE
BEHAVIOR AND TO FIND A POSITIVE RELATIONSHIP BETWEEN
LIMITATIONS IN RANGE OF DISCRETION ACCORDED CITY MANAGERS
AND ELECTED MAYORS.

1164 KAMMERER G.M., DEGROVE J.M.
"URBAN LEADERSHIP DURING CHANGE."
ANN. ACAD. POL. SOC. SCI., 353 (MAY 64), 95-106.
TYPES OF LEADERSHIP IN FLORIDA COMMUNITIES, WHICH ARE
CHARACTERIZED BY MONOPOLISTIC OR COMPETITIVE POWER
STRUCTURES, ARE EXAMINED. EACH OF THE STRUCTURES TENDS TO
PRODUCE DISTINCTIVE POLITICAL STYLES IN THE LOCAL LEADER-
SHIP. THE INFLUENCE OF MAYORS AND CITY MANAGERS IN THESE
SETTINGS IS DISCUSSED.

1165 KAMPELMAN M.M.
"CONGRESSIONAL CONTROL VS EXECUTIVE FLEXIBILITY."
PUBLIC ADMIN. REV., 18 (SUMMER 58), 185-188.
DISCUSSION OF EISENHOWER'S PLAN TO REORGANIZE AND
CONSOLIDATE THE MILITARY, WHICH THE AUTHOR SAYS WILL MAKE IT
MORE DIFFICULT FOR CONGRESS TO CONTROL THE MILITARY.

1166 KAPLAN H.
URBAN POLITICAL SYSTEMS: A FUNCTIONAL ANALYSIS OF METRO
TORONTO.
NEW YORK: COLUMBIA U PRESS, 1967, 320 PP., LC#67-29577.
PRESENTS HISTORY AND ANALYSIS OF TORONTO'S EXPERIENCE
AS FIRST WORKING NORTH EXAMPLE OF "METROPOLITAN
FEDERATION PLAN." EXPLORES USES AND LIMITS OF STRUCTURAL-
FUNCTIONAL ANALYSIS IN THE STUDY OF URBAN POLITICAL SYSTEMS.

1167 KAPLAN H.E.
THE LAW OF CIVIL SERVICE.
ALBANY & NY: MATTHEW BENDER & CO, 1958, 440 PP.
SURVEYS FIELD OF CIVIL SERVICE LITIGATION DISCUSSING CON-
STITUTIONALITY OF CIVIL SERVICE LAW, ITS ADOPTION AND SCOPE,
MEANS OF HANDLING CASES, PUNISHMENTS, JUDICIAL REVIEW,
VETEREN PREFERENCES, AND LIMITATIONS ON EMPLOYEES POLITICAL
ACTIVITIES.

1168 KAPLAN M.A.
SYSTEM AND PROCESS OF INTERNATIONAL POLITICS.
NEW YORK: WILEY, 1957, 283 PP.
A STUDY OF THE HISTORY OF INTERNATIONAL RELATIONS IS
NECESSARY IN ORDER TO DISCERN WHICH FACTORS ARE REALLY
ESSENTIAL TO AN UNDERSTANDING OF THIS FIELD. AN EXAMINATION
OF THE REGULATORY PROCESSES, VALUES, AND STRATEGY AS THEY
APPLY TO INTERNATIONAL RELATIONS IS ALSO REQUIRED.

1169 KAPLAN N.
"RESEARCH ADMINISTRATION AND THE ADMINISTRATOR: USSR AND
US."
ADMIN. SCI. 2 (JUNE 64), 57-72.
SOVIET ADMINISTRATION IS RESTRICTED TO 'PURE EXECUTION
OF POLICY.' HAS LESS PRESTIGE AND FEWER SCIENTISTS. USSR
STAFFS ARE LESS COMPLEX.

1170 KAPP E.
THE MERGER OF THE EXECUTIVES OF THE EUROPEAN COMMUNITIES.
BRUGES: DE TEMPEL, 1964, 114 PP.
FURTHER ECONOMIC INTEGRATION IN EUROPE IS BURDENED BY THE
FACT THAT THE EUROPEAN ECONOMIC COMMUNITY, EURATON, AND
THE EUROPEAN COAL AND STEEL COMMUNITY WERE ALL ESTABLISHED
WITH SEPARATE TREATIES, HAVE SEPARATE EXECUTIVES, AND YET
HANDLE OVERLAPPING PROBLEMS. HERE A PLAN IS PRESENTED IN
DETAIL FOR MERGING THE EXECUTIVES INTO ONE BODY.

1171 KAPP W.K.
HINDU CULTURE: ECONOMIC DEVELOPMENT AND ECONOMIC
PLANNING IN INDIA.
NEW YORK: ASIA PUBL., 1963, 228 PP.
ANALYZES ECONOMIC DEVELOPMENT AND PLANNING IN TERMS OF
'HINDUISM, AS A RELIGION AND AS A SOCIAL SYSTEM...IN AN
EFFORT TO DETERMINE THE EXTENT TO WHICH HINDU CULTURE
SERVES OR CONTRADICTS THE SOCIAL PURPOSES OF INDIA'S DEVEL-
OPMENT EFFORT. CONCLUDES THAT CERTAIN ASPECTS OF HINDU
CULTURE, TOGETHER WITH THE RELATED ADMINISTRATIVE DEFECTS,
HAVE RETARDED ECONOMIC GROWTH IN INDIA IN THE PAST AND ARE
LIKELY TO FRUSTRATE THE AIMS OF ECONOMIC DEVELOPMENT IN
THE FUTURE.'

1172 KARDOUCHE G.K.
THE UAR IN DEVELOPMENT.
NEW YORK: FREDERICK PRAEGER, 1967, 170 PP., LC#67-14184.
COMPREHENSIVE COVERAGE OF EGYPTIAN ECONOMIC DEVELOPMENT,
INCLUDING FOREIGN TRADE, BANKING, DEVELOPMENT, AND ALSO
MONETARY DEVELOPMENT, INCLUDING FOREIGN ASSETS, CREDIT,
BANKING CONTROL. DISCUSSES EFFECTS OF GOVERNMENT POLICY.
WRITTEN FOR OTHER RESEARCHERS AS WELL AS ECONOMISTS.

1173 KARIEL H.S.
IN SEARCH OF AUTHORITY: TWENTIETH-CENTURY POLITICAL THOUGHT.
NEW YORK: FREE PRESS OF GLENCOE, 1964, 258 PP., LC#64-21205.
DISCUSSION OF CURRENT STATE OF POLITICAL PHILOSOPHY

THROUGH ANALYSES OF POLITICAL WRITINGS OF NIETZSCHE, FREUD,
MANNHEIM, SOREL, MICHAEL OAKESHOTT, ERICH FROMM, MAYO,
LENIN, WEBER, CAMUS, NIEBUHR, MARITAIN, DEWEY. ORGANIZED
AROUND CONCEPTS OF CONSTITUTIONALISM, ORGANIZATION AS
AN END, DOCTRINES OF QUIETISM AND ACTIVISM.

1174 KARL B.D.
EXECUTIVE REORGANIZATION AND REFORM IN THE NEW DEAL.
CAMBRIDGE: HARVARD U PR, 1963, 292 PP., LC#63-13813.
VOLUME BORDERS ON BIOGRAPHY YET WITHOUT PRETENDING TO BE
SUCH IN RIGOROUS SENSE. CHARLES MERRIAM, LOUIS BROWNLOW,
LUTHER GULICK, AND REORGANIZATION OF THE PRESIDENCY ARE
DISCUSSED.

1175 KARLEN D.
THE CITIZEN IN COURT.
NEW YORK: HOLT RINEHART WINSTON, 1964, 211 PP., LC#64-18754.
NONTECHNICAL EXPLANATION OF COURT SYSTEMS, PROCEDURE,
RELATIONS AND APPEALS, AND EFFECT ON OTHER BRANCHES OF GOV-
ERNMENT. USES CASE STUDIES TO ILLUSTRATE COURT PROCESS.

1176 KARNJAHAPRAKORN C.
MUNICIPAL GOVERNMENT IN THAILAND AS AN INSTITUTION AND PRO-
CESS OF SELF-GOVERNMENT.
BANGKOK: THAMMASAT U. PUB. ADMIN., 1962, 249 PP.
ANALYZES DEVELOPMENT OF PHILOSOPHY AND PRACTICE OF
MUNICIPAL SELF-GOVERNMENT. FINDS THAT THAILAND CAN
ACCEPT FORM OF SELF-GOVERNMENT USED IN WESTERN DEMOCRACIES
BUT NOT ITS PHILOSOPHY. DISCUSSES PROBLEM OF KEEPING
MUNICIPAL GOVERNMENT IN THAILAND AND SUGGESTS WAYS TO GAIN
ACCEPTANCE FOR IT.

1177 KASER M.
COMECON* INTEGRATION PROBLEMS OF THE PLANNED ECONOMIES.
LONDON: OXFORD U PR, 1965, 215 PP.
THE LACK OF AUTOMATIC REGULATION THROUGH THE PRICE MECH-
ANISM HAS MADE TRADE A DIFFICULT PROBLEM WITHIN THE REGIONAL
ECONOMIC ORGANIZATION OF THE EUROPEAN COMMUNIST STATES. IN-
STITUTIONAL HISTORY OF COMECON SHOWS INTERPLAY BETWEEN PO-
LITICAL FACTORS LIKE NATIONALISM AND ECONOMIC PLANNING PARA-
DOXES SUCH AS PROFITS. INTEGRATION PROBLEMS COMPARED TO
THOSE FACING EEC.

1178 KASSOF A.
"THE ADMINISTERED SOCIETY: TOTALITARIANISM WITHOUT TERROR."
WORLD POLIT., 16 (JULY 64), 558-75.
PROPOSES THE CONCEPT OF THE ADMINISTERED SOCIETY AS A
TOOL TO SUMMARIZE AND EVALUATE RECENT CHANGES IN THE
SOVIET SYSTEM AND TO IDENTIFY CURRENT TRENDS. ASSERTS
THAT SOVIET SOCIETY IS BEING SUBJECTED TO NEW AND MORE
SUBTLE FORMS OF TOTALISM -TOTALISM WITHOUT TERROR. THE
STALINIST PAST IS BEING ADAPTED RATHER THAN REJECTED.

1179 NATL ADVANCED-TECH MGT CONF
SCIENCE, TECHNOLOGY, AND MANAGEMENT.
NEW YORK: MCGRAW HILL, 1963, 368 PP., LC#63-11852.
PROCEEDINGS OF 1962 NATIONAL ADVANCED-TECHNOLOGY
MANAGEMENT CONFERENCE ON PROBLEMS OF MANAGING VERY LARGE
PROGRAMS USING LATEST TECHNOLOGICAL DEVELOPMENTS. SHOWS
PROGRESS IN SOLVING PROBLEMS AND AREAS THAT NEED FURTHER
IMPOVEMENT. SEEKS TO DEVELOP MANAGERIAL SCIENCE TO DEAL
WITH TECHNICAL PROGRAMS, SUCH AS DEFENSE, NASA, AND NUCLEAR
POWER PROGRAMS.

1180 KATZ J., GOLDSTEIN J. ET AL.
PSYCHOANALYSIS, PSYCHIATRY, AND LAW.
NEW YORK: MACMILLAN, 1967, 846 PP.
FIRST PART OF VOLUME PRESENTS DETAILED STUDY OF PSYCHO-
ANALYSIS AND LAW; SECOND PART, LAW AND PHYCHIATRY. DETAILED
STUDY OF THEORY GIVEN AND RELEVANCE TO FUNDAMENTAL LEGAL
ISSUES IS EXPLORED. ALSO INCLUDED IS THE ROLE OF THE
LAWYER AND THE PROCESS OF INVOKING, ADMINISTERING, AND AP-
PRAISING MENTAL HEALTH LAWS. MANY CASES ARE INCORPORATED IN-
TO THE TEXT.

1181 KAUFMAN H.
"EMERGING CONFLICTS IN THE DOCTRINES OF PUBLIC
ADMINISTRATION" (BMR)"
AM. POL. SCI. REV., 50 (DEC. 56), 1057-1073.
ANALYZES SOURCES AND SIGNIFICANCE OF GROWING DISCORD
AMONG STUDENTS OF PUBLIC ADMINISTRATION. CONTENDS THAT
EXAMINATION OF AMERICAN ADMINISTRATIVE INSTITUTIONS SUGGESTS
THAT THEY HAVE BEEN ORGANIZED AND OPERATED IN PURSUIT OF
THREE VALUES: REPRESENTATIVENESS, NEUTRAL COMPETENCE, AND
EXECUTIVE LEADERSHIP. IDENTIFIES SHIFT FROM ONE TO ANOTHER
OF THESE VALUES WITH HISTORICAL AND POLITICAL TRENDS.

1182 KAUFMANN W.W. ED.
MILITARY POLICY AND NATIONAL SECURITY.
PRINCETON: U. PR., 1956, 266 PP.
ASSESSES ABILITY OF USA STRATEGISTS TO MAINTAIN SECURITY
IN VIEW OF CONTINUED COMMUNIST AGGRESSIVENESS AND PROLIFER-
ATION OF NUCLEAR WEAPONS. ASSUMING THAT MILITARY PLANNING
SHOULD BE SERVANT NOT MASTER OF POLICY GOALS, EVALUATES
THE MERITS OF AVAILABLE CHOICES IN TERMS OF COURSES OF
ACTION OPEN TO THE COMMUNISTS WITH REFERENCE TO EXISTING

TECHNOLOGICAL AND POLITICAL CONDITIONS IN USA.

1183 KAUNDA K.
ZAMBIA: INDEPENDENCE AND BEYOND: THE SPEECHES OF KENNETH
KAUNDA.
LONDON: THOMAS NELSON & SONS, 1966, 265 PP.
COLLECTION OF SPEECHES BY PRESIDENT OF ZAMBIA. DISCUSSES
END OF COLONIALISM AND THE TRANSITION TO INDEPENDENCE.
DESCRIBES BIRTH OF COUNTRY, PROBLEMS IT HAS ENCOUNTERED,
AND HOPES FOR THE FUTURE. PICTURES STRUCTURE AND
ADMINISTRATION, METHODS USED TO SOLVE PROBLEMS OF RACE
RELATIONS, AND STRATEGIES OF ECONOMIC DEVELOPMENT.

1184 KAUTSKY J.H.
"THE NEW STRATEGY OF INTERNATIONAL COMMUNISM."
AMER. POLIT. SCI. REV., 49 (JUNE 55), 478-485.
NEW RUSSIAN STRATEGY INVOLVES A RADICAL DEPARTURE FROM
MARXISM. MAINTAINS THIS IS ONLY A LOGICAL DEVELOPMENT
OF LENINISM. IN ORDER TO ELUCIDATE THE IMPLICATIONS OF
LENINISM, DOCTRINES OF MAO TSE TUNG ARE REVIEWED.

1185 KAYSEN C.
"DATA BANKS AND DOSSIERS."
PUBLIC INTEREST, 7 (SPRING 67), 52-60.
GIVES BACKGROUND ON CONCEPTION OF NATIONAL DATA CENTER.
SUGGESTS PROBLEMS RAISED BY INTENSIVE CENTRALIZATION OF
INFORMATION BUT ARGUES THAT CENTRALIZATION NECESSARY TO
COUNTER INEFFICIENCIES OF OVER DECENTRALIZED STATISTICAL
SYSTEM. PROPOSES CHECKS TO DANGERS TO PRIVACY IN DISTIN-
GUISHING BETWEEN "DOSSIER" & "STATISTICAL DATA FILE."

1186 KEE R.
REFUGEE WORLD.
LONDON: OXFORD U PR, 1961, 153 PP.
DESCRIPTIVE PICTURE OF CONDITIONS OF STARVATION AND
POVERTY AMONG REFUGEES, CONCENTRATING ON GERMANY AND
AUSTRIA. SHOWS HORROR OF LIVING IN REFUGEE CAMPS, AND
SUGGESTS WHAT IS NEEDED TO ALLEVIATE PROBLEMS: MORE MONEY,
A FRESH APPROACH TO RESPONSIBILITY ON THE PART OF ALL
BUREAUCRACIES CONCERNED, AND BETTER AND MORE READILY
AVAILABLE HOUSING.

1187 KEEFE W.J., OGUL M.S.
THE AMERICAN LEGISLATIVE PROCESS: CONGRESS AND THE STATES.
ENGLEWOOD CLIFFS: PRENTICE HALL, 1964, 498 PP., LC#64-15466.
DESCRIBES AND ANALYZES THE AMERICAN LEGISLATIVE PROCESS.
MAINTAINS THAT LEGISLATIVE INSTITUTIONS MUST BE VIEWED IN
RELATION TO LARGER ENVIRONMENTS AND INCLUSIVE POLITICAL
SYSTEMS. HENCE, GIVES AS MUCH ATTENTION TO THE "OUTSIDERS"
SUCH AS PARTIES, INTEREST GROUPS, EXECUTIVES, AND COURTS, AS
TO THE LEGISLATURES THEMSELVES. DEALS BOTH WITH CONGRESS AND
WITH STATE LEGISLATURES.

1188 KEFAUVER E.
"THE NEED FOR BETTER EXECUTIVE-LEGISLATIVE TEAMWORK IN THE
NATIONAL GOVERNMENT."
AM. POL. SCI. REV., 38 (APR. 44), 317-325.
ON THE ASSUMPTION THAT THE US MUST BE THE WORLD LEADER,
THE THEN REPRESENTATIVE FROM TENNESSEE ADVOCATES BETTER
TEAMWORK BETWEEN THE EXECUTIVE AND LEGISLATIVE BRANCHES.
PARTICULARLY USEFUL WOULD BE A BILL PROPOSED BY HIM TO PRO-
VIDE A QUESTION PERIOD DURING WHICH HEADS OF EXECUTIVE DE-
PARTMENTS WOULD BE ASKED TO APPEAR, REPORT, AND ANSWER
QUESTIONS.

1189 KEFAUVER E., LEVIN J.
A TWENTIETH-CENTURY CONGRESS.
NEW YORK: DUELL, SLOAN & PEARCE, 1947, 236 PP., LC#47-3751.
A CRITICISM OF THE WORKINGS OF CONGRESS BY ITS MEMBERS.
DISCUSSES WHY MUCH LEGISLATION IS STALLED IN COMMITTEE, AND
WHY MANY LEGISLATORES BECOME SO DISCOURAGED. RELATES ENOR-
MITY OF THE BURDENS OF CONGRESSMEN AND THE CLUMSY TOOLS
THEY HAVE TO WORK WITH, AND SUGGESTS HOW TO IMPROVE THE
LEGISLATIVE PROCESS.

1190 KEISER N.F.
"PUBLIC RESPONSIBILITY AND FEDERAL ADVISORY GROUPS: A CASE
STUDY."
WESTERN POLIT. QUART., 11 (JUNE 58), 251-264.
STUDY OF THE BUSINESS ADVISORY COUNCIL OF DEPARTMENT OF
COMMERCE. BAC IS TYPICAL OF MANY PRIVATE GROUPS WHICH ARE
OFFICIAL DUTIES AND PRIVILEGES OFTEN MASK A SPECIFIC
INTEREST AT THE EXPENSE OF THE PUBLIC INTEREST.

1191 KELLEY E.J.
MARKETING: STRATEGY AND FUNCTIONS.
ENGLEWOOD CLIFFS: PRENTICE HALL, 1965, 120 PP., LC#65-20227.
DISCUSSES PROBLEMS RELATED TO MARKETING POLICY AND ROU-
TINE, INCLUDING CHANGE AND FUNCTIONS OF MARKETING, MANAGE-
MENT AND MARKETING, PRICE POLICIES, AND PROMOTION AND DIS-
TRIBUTION POLICIES.

1192 KENNAN G.F.
"POLYCENTRISM AND WESTERN POLICY."
FOR. AFF., 42 (JAN. 64), 171-183.
EVALUATES CONSEQUENCES OF INDEPENDENT CENTERS OF

POLITICAL AUTHORITY WITHIN THE COMMUNIST BLOC. SEES A
MULTIPLICITY OF POLICY ALTERNATIVES FOR THE WEST IF THE
SINO-SOVIET RIFT ENDURES. THE FUNDAMENTAL ISSUE IS WHETHER
OR NOT TO EXAGGERATE RUSSO-CHINESE TENSIONS.

1193 KENNEDY J.F.
TO TURN THE TIDE.
NEW YORK: HARPER & ROW, 1962, 235 PP., LC#61-12221.
SELECTION OF PRESIDENT KENNEDY'S SPEECHES AND WRITINGS
FROM HIS ELECTION THROUGH 1961 ADJOURNMENT OF CONGRESS.
GREATEST EMPHASIS IS ON IMPORTANT INTERNATIONAL ISSUES BUT
ALSO INCLUDES DISCUSSION OF DOMESTIC ECONOMIC SITUATION,
SPACE PROGRAM, CIVIL RIGHTS, AND OTHER INTERNAL AFFAIRS.

1194 KENT F.R.
THE GREAT GAME OF POLITICS.
GARDEN CITY: DOUBLEDAY, 1924, 322 PP., LC#23-17524.
DESCRIBES THE AMERICAN POLITICAL MACHINE FROM LOCAL
PRECINCT TO NATIONAL GOVERNMENT. SHOWS HOW IT WORKS, ITS
PRACTICAL AND HUMAN SIDE, GOOD AND BAD ASPECTS OF ITS
OPERATION, AND ITS FINANCIAL STRUCTURE. POINTS OUT AREAS
WHERE IMPROVEMENTS COULD BE MADE, SHOWING THAT INTELLIGENT
REGULAR VOTING WOULD ELIMINATE MANY POLITICAL PROBLEMS.

1195 KENT S.
STRATEGIC INTELLIGENCE FOR AMERICAN WORLD POLICY.
PRINCETON: U. PR., 1949, 226 PP.
DISCUSSES CONTENT AND USES OF STRATEGIC INTELLIGENCE IN
ITS DESCRIPTIVE, REPORTORIAL AND EVALUATIVE ASPECTS. ORGAN-
IZATION AND ADMINISTRATIVE PROBLEMS OF USA INTELLIGENCE
SERVICES ARE DESCRIBED AND SUGGESTIONS FOR IMPROVEMENT
OFFERED. ANALYSIS OF INFORMATION-GATHERING PROCESSES IN
PEACE AND WARTIME.

1196 KENTUCKY STATE ARCHIVES
CHECKLIST OF KENTUCKY STATE PUBLICATIONS AND STATE DIRECTORY
FRANKFORT: KENTUCKY ST ARCHIVES.
AN ANNOTATED CHECKLIST OF APPROXIMATELY 500 DOCUMENTS
ISSUED ANNUALLY. ORGANIZED ACCORDING TO A HIERARCHICAL AR-
RANGEMENT: EXECUTIVE, LEGISLATIVE, AND JUDICIAL; CONSTITU-
TIONAL ADMINISTRATIVE DEPARTMENTS; STATUTORY ADMINISTRATIVE
DEPARTMENTS; STATE BOARDS, COMMISSIONS, AND INDEPENDENT
AGENCIES; AND HIGHER EDUCATION. INCLUDES DIRECTORY OF STATE
OFFICIALS.

1197 KERR C., ET A.L.
INDUSTRIALISM AND INDUSTRIAL MAN.
CAMBRIDGE: HARVARD U PR, 1960, 331 PP., LC#60-15239.
EXAMINES PROCESS OF INDUSTRIALIZATION AND ITS EFFECT ON
WORKERS AND SOCIETY IN VARIOUS COUNTRIES. APPROACH IS AB-
STRACT RATHER THAN FACTUAL, AND AN ATTEMPT IS MADE TO FOR-
MULATE PARADIGMS FOR PREDICTING OUTCOME OF INDUSTRIALIZA-
TION ON SOCIETY AND ON MANKIND.

1198 KERSELL J.E.
PARLIAMENTARY SUPERVISION OF DELEGATED LEGISLATION.
LONDON: STEVENS, 1960, 178 PP.
STUDY DEALING WITH LEGISLATIVE TECHNIQUES OF CONTROLLING
GOVERNMENT. ASSUMES THE MOST APPROPRIATE INSTITUTION TO
SUPERVISE USE OF DELEGATED LEGISLATIVE POWERS IS PARLIAMENT.
IF EXECUTIVE OFFICIALS EXERCISE THESE POWERS EFFECTIVELY,
SOUND TECHNIQUES OF CONTROL MUST RESULT.

1199 KERTESZ S.D. ED.
AMERICAN DIPLOMACY IN A NEW ERA.
NOTRE DAME: U OF NOTRE DAME, 1961, 601 PP., LC#61-8466.
VOLUME ENDEAVORS TO CLARIFY COURSE OF AMERICAN FOREIGN
POLICY SINCE 1945, ITS MAJOR OBJECTIVES, AND PROBLEMS OF
FORMULATING AND IMPLEMENTING THEM. EXAMINES MAJOR FOREIGN
POLICY ISSUES TOGETHER WITH DIPLOMACY. DEALS WITH POLICY-
MAKING AND ORGANIZATIONAL PROBLEMS.

1200 KESSELMAN L.C.
THE SOCIAL POLITICS OF THE FEPC.
CHAPEL HILL: U OF N CAR PR, 1948, 253 PP.
EXAMINES EFFORT TO INFLUENCE PUBLIC POLICY INTO SUPPORT
OF FAIR EMPLOYMENT PRACTICES COMMISSION AS MEANS TO ABOLISH
DISCRIMINATION IN INDUSTRY. WORK DEALS WITH DISCRIMINATION
IN EMPLOYMENT, IMPORTANCE OF SOCIAL COHESION AND IDEOLOGICAL
OPPOSITION TO IT, AND USE OF COMMUNICATIONS MEDIA TO SECURE
SUPPORT.

1201 KHAMA T.
"POLITICAL CHANGE IN AFRICAN SOCIETY."
SUSSEX: AFRICA BUREAU, 1956, 16 PP.
STUDIES THE DEVELOPMENT OF REPRESENTATIVE GOVERNMENT
FROM THE TIME OF THE FIRST WHITE COLONIZATION. CONCLUDES
THERE IS A NEED FOR CLOSE COOPERATION BETWEEN TRIBAL CHIEFS
AND NEWLY RISING POLITICAL STATESMEN.

1202 KHAN M.Z.
"THE PRESIDENT OF THE GENERAL ASSEMBLY."
INT. ORGAN., 18 (SPRING 64), 231-40.
CITES EVOLUTION AND DESIGNATION OF THE OFFICE UNDER UN
CHARTER USING COMPARISONS WITH US AND BRITISH LEGISLATURES
TO CLARIFY ROLE. AS AN EX-PRESIDENT, POINTS OUT SPECIFIC

CHARACTERISTICS OF POSITION AS IT RELATES TO THE GENERAL
ASSEMBLY, REGIONALISM, AND EFFECTIVENESS AND STRENGTH OF
LEADER.

1203 KIESER P.J.
THE COST OF ADMINISTRATION, SUPERVISION AND SERVICES IN
URBAN BANTU TOWNSHIPS.
PRETORIA: S AFR COUN SCI IND RES, 1964, 148 PP.
AN EMPIRICAL STUDY OF THE EXPENDITURES FOR ADMINISTRATION
AND SUCH SERVICES AS REFUSE REMOVAL, SANITATION, PROVISION
OF WATER, ETC., IN 21 TOWNSHIPS. INCLUDES STATISTICAL TABLES
AND A COPY OF THE QUESTIONNAIRE USED.

1204 KEITH-LUCAS A.
DECISIONS ABOUT PEOPLE IN NEED, A STUDY OF ADMINISTRATIVE
RESPONSIVENESS IN PUBLIC ASSISTANCE.
CHAPEL HILL: U OF N CAR PR, 1957, 318 PP.
ANALYZES DECISION-MAKING SETTINGS AND PROCESSES IN PUB-
LIC WELFARE ADMINISTRATION INCLUDING SOCIAL, MORAL, AND POL-
ITICAL FACTORS. DISCUSSES IMPORTANT IMPLICATIONS OF AGENCY-
RECIPIENT RELATIONSHIP AND PROPOSES FORCES AND IDEAS TO
WHICH AGENCY ADMINISTRATION SHOULD BE RESPONSIVE. OUTLINES
STUDY OF AID TO DEPENDENT CHILDREN PROGRAM IN TWO STATES,
USED TO ANALYZES DECISION-MAKING PROCEDURES AND EFFECTS.

1205 KILPATRICK F.P., CUMMINGS M.C., JENNINGS M.K.
SOURCE BOOK OF OCCUPATIONAL VALUES AND THE IMAGE OF THE
FEDERAL SERVICE.
WASHINGTON: BROOKINGS INST, 1964, 681 PP., LC#64-13906.
REPORTS BASIC DATA OF STUDY ON PUBLIC ATTITUDE TOWARD
CIVIL SERVICE AND ITS EFFECT ON WORKER PRCRUITMENT. INTER-
VIEWS COMPARE METHODS OF RECRUITING IN PRIVATE INDUSTRY AND
GOVERNMENT

1206 KILPATRICK F.P., CUMMINGS M.C., JENNINGS M.K.
THE IMAGE OF THE FEDERAL SERVICE.
WASHINGTON: BROOKINGS INST, 1964, 303 PP., LC#64-13789.
STUDIES PUBLIC ATTITUDE TOWARD CIVIL SERVICE AND ITS
EFFECT ON WORKER RECRUITMENT. COMPARES METHODS OF RECRUIT-
ING IN PRIVATE AND PUBLIC ADMINISTRATION, DISCUSSING DIFFER-
ENCES IN JOB SATISFACTION, EXPECTATIONS AND PROGRESS. INTER-
PRETS MATERIAL FOR IMPROVING PUBLIC RELATIONS.

1207 KIMBROUGH R.B.
POLITICAL POWER AND EDUCATIONAL DECISION-MAKING.
SKOKIE: RAND MCNALLY & CO, 1964, 307 PP., LC#64-17635.
CITES LACK OF EMPIRICAL RESEARCH ON THE DECISION-MAKING
PROCESS AS IT EXISTS IN AMERICAN PUBLIC SCHOOLS ON THE STATE
AND LOCAL LEVELS. NOTES NEED FOR INCREASING KNOWLEDGE IN
FIELD TO BETTER EQUIP ADMINISTRATORS FOR THEIR HANDLING OF
MAJOR POLICY DECISIONS IN PROGRAM DEVELOPMENT, FISCAL PLAN-
NING, AND IN DEVELOPING RELATIONSHIP WITH THE POLITICAL
LEADERS.

1208 KINGSLEY J.D.
REPRESENTATIVE BUREAUCRACY.
YELLOW SPRINGS: ANTIOCH, 1944, 324 PP.
INTERPRETATION OF THE BRITISH CIVIL SERVICE. SAYS THAT IT
IS REPRESENTATIVE AND HAS PRESERVED POPULAR GOVERNMENT
AGAINST THE ANTI-DEMOCRATIC PRESSURES OF THE MANAGERIAL
REVOLUTION.

1209 KINGSTON-MCCLOUG E.
DEFENSE: POLICY AND STRATEGY.
NEW YORK: FREDERICK PRAEGER, 1960, 272 PP., LC#60-7662.
KINGSTON-MCCLOUGHTY EXPLAINS PROBLEMS INVOLVED IN
EVOLUTION OF DEFENSE POLICY AND IN DEVELOPMENT OF
INTERNATIONAL FRAMEWORK OF PLANNING. EMPHASIZES INCREASED
IMPORTANCE OF POLITICAL LEADER IN MAKING DEFENSE POLICY
AND STRATEGIC DECISIONS. DISCUSSES VARIOUS TYPES OF
DEFENSE SYSTEMS AND THEIR ORGANIZATION.

1210 KINNEAR J.B.
PRINCIPLES OF CIVIL GOVERNMENT.
LONDON: SMITH, ELDER & CO, 1887, 237 PP.
DESCRIBES SCIENCE AND NATURE OF GOVERNMENT; ITS OBJECTS,
REPRESENTATIVE GOVERNMENT, CONDITIONS OF NATIONAL UNITY,
CONSTITUTIONS, LOCAL GOVERNMENT, AND NATIONAL OBLIGATIONS.

1211 KINTNER W.R.
ORGANIZING FOR CONFLICT: A PROPOSAL.
ORBIS, 2 (SUMMER 58), 155-74.
DISCUSSION OF ROLE OF EXECUTIVE IN THE FORMULATION AND
EXECUTION OF US NATIONAL SECURITY POLICY. ANALYZES AGENCIES
RESPONSIBLY FOR SUCH POLICY AND COMPARES THEM WITH SOVIET
STRUCTURES, AND MAKES PROPOSALS FOR GREATER COORDINATION
BETWEEN PLANS AND PROGRAMS.

1213 KIRDAR U.
THE STRUCTURE OF UNITED NATIONS ECONOMIC AID TO UNDERDEVEL-
OPED COUNTRIES.
THE HAGUE: MARTINUS NIJHOFF, 1966, 361 PP., LC#66-54220.
DETAILED STUDY OF VARIOUS FORMS OF FINANCIAL AND TECHNI-
CAL ASSISTANCE TO UNDERDEVELOPED COUNTRIES, EMPHASIZING AID
PROGRAMS THAT ARE MEDIATED AND ADMINISTERED BY UN AND OTHER
INTERNATIONAL BODIES. STRESSES INTERNATIONAL NATURE OF ECO-

NOMIC AID PROGRAMS IN RELATION TO BOTH ORGANIZATIONAL
STRUCTURE AND POLITICAL IMPLICATIONS.

1214 KIRK G.
THE CHANGING ENVIRONMENT OF INTERNATIONAL RELATIONS.
WASHINGTON: BROOKINGS INST., 1956, 158 PP.
STUDIES RELATIONSHIP OF MODERN FORCES AND AMERICAN
FOREIGN POLICY. FORESEES DIVERGENT NATIONAL FORMS AND
CHANGES IN POWER LOCUS. CALLS UNIVERSAL ACCEPTANCE OF MUTUAL
SECURITY CONCEPT PREREQUISITE FOR WORLD ORDER.

1215 KISER M.
"ORGANIZATION OF AMERICAN STATES."
WASHINGTON: PAN AMER. UNION, 1955, 74 PP.
A HANDBOOK ABOUT ORGANIZATION DESCRIBING WHAT IT IS, HOW
IT IS ORGANIZED, WHAT IT DOES, AND THE INTER-AMERICAN
AGENCIES.

1216 KISSINGER H.A.
"THE POLICYMAKER AND THE INTELLECTUAL."
REPORTER, 20 (MAR. 59), 30-35.
CONCERNED WITH PROBLEM OF POLICY-MAKING BY THOSE WHO SEE
ONLY A SERIES OF TECHNICAL ADMINISTRATIVE DECISIONS. FEELS
THE INTELLECTUAL IS UTILIZED AS AN EXPERT, BUT SERVES ONLY
AS A COG IN THE DECISION-MAKING PROCESS WHEREAS HIS TRUE
VALUE SHOULD BE AS A POTENTIAL INNOVATOR WHO CAN
CONCEPTUALIZE PROBLEMS AND THINK IN TERMS OF THE ULTIMATE
GOALS OF POLICY.

1217 KLEIN F.J.
JUDICIAL ADMINISTRATION AND THE LEGAL PROFESSION.
NEW YORK: OCEANA PUBLISHING, 1963, 650 PP., LC#62-12025.
LIST OF 6,654 ITEMS IN ENGLISH ARRANGED BY SUBJECT ON
COURT SYSTEMS AND PROCEDURES. PUBLICATION DATES OF
LISTINGS, 1940-1962.

1218 KLESMENT J., KRIVICKAS D. ET AL.
LEGAL SOURCES AND BIBLIOGRAPHY OF THE BALTIC STATES (ESTON-
IA, LATVIA, LITHUANIA)
NEW YORK: FREDERICK PRAEGER, 1963, 197 PP., LC#63-15981.
PART OF A SERIES PREPARED BY THE MID-EUROPEAN LAW PROJECT
AND PUBLISHED BY THE MID-EUROPEAN STUDIES CENTER. PART I
COVERS PERIOD PRIOR TO 1918; PART II IS CONCERNED WITH THE
CONTINUITY OF LAW, EFFORTS TOWARD UNIFICATION OF LAW, ETC.;
PART III COVERS EACH COUNTRY SEPARATELY, BOTH TRADITIONAL
AND SPECIFIC TOPICS; PART IV CONCERNS POST-SOVIET ERA. 1207
ITEMS IN EUROPEAN LANGUAGES; INDEXED; ANNOTATED.

1219 KNEIER C.M.
CITY GOVERNMENT IN THE UNITED STATES (3RD ED.)
NEW YORK: HARPER & ROW, 1957, 611 PP.
SURVEYS CITY GOVERNMENTS AND THEIR RELATION TO STATE AND
NATIONAL AUTHORITIES, AND CONSIDERS EFFECT OF URBANIZATION
ON POLITICS IN US. MAJOR PROBLEM DISCUSSED IS REAPPORTION-
MENT AND CONTROL OF MUNICIPALITIES BY POLITICAL MACHINES.
EXPOUNDS ADVANTAGES OF COUNCIL-MANAGER SYSTEM FOR CITIES OF
UP TO 500,000 INHABITANTS.

1220 KNICKERBOCKER I.
"LEADERSHIP: A CONCEPTION AND SOME IMPLICATIONS."
J. SOCIAL ISSUES, 4 (SUMMER 48), 23-40.
ARE THE CONCEPTS OF SYMBOLIC AND FUNCTIONAL LEADERSHIP
OFTEN FUSED? SEARCHING FOR AN ANSWER, THE AUTHOR POSES
HYPOTHETICAL QUESTIONS ON THE MEANING OF GROUP DIRECTION,
WHY AND HOW LEADERS ARISE, WHY LEADERS LEAD, THE
CLASSIFICATIONS OF LEADERS, AND METHODS LEADERS USE FOR
DIRECTING OTHER PEOPLE.

1221 KNOX V.H.
PUBLIC FINANCE: INFORMATION SOURCES.
DETROIT: GALE RESEARCH CO, 1964, 142 PP., LC#64-16503.
BIBLIOGRAPHY IN FIELDS OF PUBLIC FINANCE AND TAXATION.
STRESSES NEW STUDIES IN FIELDS; MOST OF THE MATERIAL COVERS
PERIOD OF 1960'S. ANNOTATIONS ARE INCLUDED WHERE TITLES ARE
UNCLEAR. INCLUDES ITEMS ON GENERAL FIELD AS WELL AS MATERI-
ALS ON REVENUES, PUBLIC EXPENDITURES, PUBLIC DEBT, FISCAL
POLICY AND ADMINISTRATION, AND INTERNATIONAL PUBLIC FINANCE.
CONTAINS AUTHOR AND SUBJECT INDEXES; IN ENGLISH.

1222 KOENIG L.W.
OFFICIAL MAKERS OF PUBLIC POLICY: CONGRESS AND THE
PRESIDENT.
CHICAGO: SCOTT, FORESMAN & CO, 1965, 197 PP., LC#65-26230.
STUDY OF THE EXECUTIVE AND THE LEGISLATURE AS INTEGRAL
PARTS OF PLURALISTIC GOVERNMENT. PRESIDENCY HAS DECLINED IN
RELATIVE POWER IN RECENT YEARS IN CERTAIN RESPECTS.

1223 KOENIG L.W.
THE SALE OF THE TANKERS.
WASHINGTON: COMM ON PUBLIC ADMIN, 1950, 184 PP.
STUDY RELATES 1947-48 US GOVERNMENT SALE OF 83 TANKERS TO
13 FOREIGN NATIONS. EXAMINES ENSUING DIFFICULTIES AMONG
PUBLIC AND PRIVATE GROUPS IN AMERICAN POLITICAL AND ADMINIS-
TRATIVE LIFE. REVIEWS ATTITUDES AND ACTIONS OF ALL INVOLVED
PARTIES.

1224 KOENIG L.W.
THE TRUMAN ADMINISTRATION: ITS PRINCIPLES AND PRACTICE.
NEW YORK: NEW YORK U PR, 1956, 394 PP., LC#56-7425.
ANALYZES COMPLEX PROBLEMS TRUMAN FACED ASSUMING POWER IN
MIDDLE OF WORLD WAR AND IN FOUR MONTHS COPING WITH PROBLEM
OF DEMOBILIZING NATION GEARED FOR WAR FOR THREE YEARS.
INCLUDES PROBLEM OF USING BOMB AND POLITICAL SCENE AT
POTSDAM, WHICH INITIATED COLD WAR. FOLLOWS HIM THROUGH IKE'S
ELECTION.

1225 KOENIG L.W.
OFFICIAL MAKERS OF PUBLIC POLICY: CONGRESS AND THE PRESIDENT
GLENVIEW, ILL: SCOTT, FORESMAN, 1965, 204 PP.
DISCUSSION OF RESPECTIVE ROLES OF CONGRESS AND THE
PRESIDENT, TOGETHER WITH ADMINISTRATION IN THE FORMULATION
OF POLICY. INCLUDES CASE STUDIES.

1226 KOESTLER A.
THE LOTUS AND THE ROBOT.
NEW YORK: MACMILLAN, 1961, 296 PP.
DRAWS CERTAIN COMPARISONS BETWEEN INDIA AND JAPAN, THE
MOST TRADITIONAL AND THE MOST MODERN AMONG THE COUNTRIES OF
ASIA, AND EXAMINES THE DECLINE OF MYSTIC ENLIGHTENMENT AND
SPIRITUAL GUIDANCE IN ASIA. CONCLUDES THAT OUR HABIT OF CON-
TRASTING THE CONTEMPLATIVE AND SPIRITUAL EAST WITH THE CRUDE
MATERIALISM OF THE WEST IS BASED ON FALLACY, AS THE DIFFER-
ENCE IS BETWEEN TWO BASICALLY UNLIKE PHILOSOPHIES.

1227 KOGAN N.
THE POLITICS OF ITALIAN FOREIGN POLICY.
NEW YORK: PRAEGER, 1963, 178 PP.
BROAD INVESTIGATION OF ITALIAN POLITICAL SYSTEM, ORIENTED
TOWARDS QUESTIONS OF FOREIGN POLICY. ANALYZES METHODS BY
WHICH POLITICAL DECISIONS AFFECTING FOREIGN POLICY ARE MADE,
KINDS OF DECISIONS MADE, AND FORCES OPERATING TO INFLUENCE
THEM.

1228 KONCZACKI Z.A.
PUBLIC FINANCE AND ECONOMIC DEVELOPMENT OF NATAL 1893-1910.
DURHAM: DUKE U PR, 1967, 224 PP., LC#67-23301.
STUDIES ECONOMIC HISTORY AND PUBLIC FINANCE OF NATAL AS
COLONY OF BRITAIN UNTIL 1893, AND TRACES VARIATIONS IN
GOVERNMENT REVENUE AND EXPENDITURES AND PUBLIC FINANCE FROM
INDEPENDENCE IN 1893 TO FEDERATION WITH UNION OF SOUTH
AFRICA IN 1910. EMPHASIZES IMPACT OF PUBLIC FINANCE ON
ECONOMIC DEVELOPMENT.

1229 KORNHAUSER W.
SCIENTISTS IN INDUSTRY: CONFLICT AND ACCOMMODATION.
BERKELEY: U OF CALIF PR, 1963, 230 PP., LC#62-8491.
STUDIES SCIENTISTS AND ENGINEERS WHO CONDUCT RESEARCH FOR
INDUSTRY. PRIMARY SOURCE OF DATA IS SERIES OF INTERVIEWS
WITH RESEARCH SCIENTISTS, ENGINEERS, AND MANAGERS.
IDENTIFIES MAJOR PROBLEMS AND VARIABLES OF PROFESSIONAL
RELATIONS IN ORGANIZATIONS. DISCUSSES PROFESSIONAL GOALS,
STRAINS BETWEEN PROFESSIONS AND ORGANIZATIONS, CONTROLS,
ADAPTATIONS, AND PROFESSIONAL INFLUENCE IN INDUSTRY.

1230 KOUSOULAS D.G.
REVOLUTION AND DEFEAT; THE STORY OF THE GREEK COMMUNIST
PARTY.
LONDON: OXFORD U PR, 1965, 306 PP.
ANALYSIS OF DEVELOPMENT OF GREEK COMMUNIST PARTY FROM
START IN 1918 THROUGH ITS AFFILIATION WITH COMINTERN AND ITS
PARTICIPATION IN GREEK POLITICS AND LEGISLATIVE PROCESS.
COVERS PARTY STRUCTURE AND POLICIES IN DIFFERENT PERIODS OF
ACTIVITY, INCLUDING ITS REVOLUTIONARY MOVEMENT AND AFTERMATH
OF DEFEAT.

1231 KRACKE E.A. JR.
"CIVIL SERVICE IN EARLY SUNG CHINA, 960-1067."
CAMBRIDGE: HARVARD U PR, 1953.
DISCUSSION OF EARLY SUNG CIVIL SERVICE WITH PARTICULAR
EMPHASIS ON THE DEVELOPMENT OF CONTROLLED SPONSORSHIP TO
FOSTER ADMINISTRATIVE RESPONSIBILITY. ANNOTATED BIBLIOGRAPHY
APPENDED TO TEXT.

1232 KRAINES O.
CONGRESS AND THE CHALLENGE OF BIG GOVERNMENT.
NEW YORK: BOOKMAN ASSOC. RECORD PR.,1958,129 PP.,LC#59-3301.
CREATION, PROCEDURES, FINDINGS, AND PROPOSALS OF THE
COCKRELL COMMITTEE FROM 1885-87, AND OF THE DOCKERY-
COCKRELL COMMISSION, 1893-95. A HISTORY OF THE FIRST TWO
COMPREHENSIVE CONGRESSIONAL INVESTIGATIONS INTO ADMINISTRA-
TION, AND SUGGESTIONS AS TO FUTURE ACTIONS.

1233 KRAMER R., MARCUSE H.
"EXECUTIVE PRIVILEGE - A STUDY OF THE PERIOD 1953-1960."
G. WASH. LAW REV., 29 (APR.-MAY 61), 623-717, 827-916.
"EXECUTIVE PRIVILEGE IS DERIVED DIRECTLY FROM THE
CONSTITUTION...THE PRESIDENT HAS THE POWER TO WITHHOLD
INFORMATION WHENEVER THIS IS NECESSARY FOR THE EFFECTIVE
PERFORMANCE OF HIS FUNCTIONS."

1234 KRARUP O.
"JUDICIAL REVIEW OF ADMINISTRATIVE ACTION IN DENMARK."
INT. REV. OF ADMIN. SCI., 33 (JAN. 67), 9-16.
SURVEY OF DEVELOPMENT OF CONCEPT OF JUDICIAL REVIEW IN
DENMARK. BASIS FOR DECISION-MAKING IS "FREE DISCRETION" AND
PROBLEMS RELATING TO THIS METHOD ARE DISCUSSED. STATES THAT
FIXED THEORY OF JUDICIAL REVIEW BASED ON DISCRETION MAKES
GIVING NEW LEGAL DEVELOPMENTS ADEQUATE THEORETICAL FORM VERY
DIFFICULT.

1235 KRIESBERG M.
CANCELLATION OF THE RATION STAMPS (PAMPHLET)
INDIANAPOLIS: BOBBS-MERRILL, 1952, 13 PP.
STUDY OF PROBLEMS RELATING TO ADMINISTRATIVE DECISION-
MAKING AND PUBLIC RELATIONS IN SPECIFIC CASE OF FOOD RATION
STAMPS CANCELLATION, 1944-45. INVOLVED QUESTION OF WHETHER
OR NOT TO CANCEL RATIONING IN LIGHT OF SUDDEN FOOD CRISIS.

1236 KRIESBERG M.
"WHAT CONGRESSMEN AND ADMINISTRATORS THINK OF THE POLLS."
PUBLIC OPINION QUART., 9 (FALL 45), 333-337.
BY INTERVIEWS AND QUESTIONNAIRES INVOLVING 52 CONGRESSMEN
AND 36 ADMINISTRATIVE OFFICIALS, FOUND THAT CONGRESSMEN ARE
LESS FAVORABLE TO PUBLIC OPINION POLLS. HOSTILITY OR INDIF-
FERENCE OF CONGRESSMEN RESULTS FROM FEELING THAT POLLS CHAL-
LENGE THEIR PREROGATIVES AS INTERPRETORS OF PUBLIC WILL,
FROM UNFAMILIARITY WITH POLLS AND DISTRUST OF ACCURACY,
AND FROM DISLIKE OF BEING TIED TO INFLUENTIAL CONSTITUENTS.

1237 KRIESBERG M. ED.
PUBLIC ADMINISTRATION IN DEVELOPING COUNTRIES: PROCEEDINGS
OF AN INTERNATIONAL CONFERENCE HELD IN BOGOTA, COLUMBIA,1963
WASHINGTON: BROOKINGS INST, 1965, 198 PP., LC#65-24220.
TOPICS CENTER ON INFLUENCES ON PUBLIC ADMINISTRATION IN
NEW NATIONS; PUBLIC ADMINISTRATION AND DEVELOPMENT; AND
ESTABLISHING A CAREER SERVICE AND CIVIL SERVICE. AUTHORS
INCLUDE M. DUVERGER, F. TANNENBAUM, D.C. STONE, G.A. GRAHAM,
E.E. KAPLAN, AND MARCEAU LONG.

1238 KRISLOV S.
THE NEGRO IN FEDERAL EMPLOYMENT.
MINNEAPOLIS: U OF MINN PR, 1967, 157 PP., LC#67-22017.
SURVEYS THE HISTORY OF NEGRO EMPLOYMENT IN THE FEDERAL
CIVIL SERVICE, THE EFFECTS OF WWI AND WWII ON EMPLOYMENT
OPPORTUNITY, FEDERAL ORGANIZATIONAL ARRANGEMENTS FOR PRO-
MOTING NEGRO EMPLOYMENT, THE RECORD OF SEVERAL OF THE
PRINCIPAL FEDERAL DEPARTMENTS IN EMPLOYING NEGROES, AND THE
PRESENT SITUATION AND PROBLEMS IN NEGRO EMPLOYMENT UNDER
CIVIL SERVICE. BASED ON INTERVIEWS.

1239 KRUPP S.
PATTERN IN ORGANIZATIONAL ANALYSIS: A CRITICAL EXAMINATION.
NEW YORK: CHILTON BOOKS, 1961, 185 PP., LC#61-11614.
CONCERNED WITH METHODOLOGICAL AND PHILOSOPHICAL ISSUES
OF ORGANIZATION THEORY. THE LATTER HAS EXCLUDED, UNDULY,
PHENOMENA OF POWER, CONFLICT, RESOURCE ALLOCATION, INCOME
DISTRIBUTION AND FOLLETT'S "LAW OF THE SITUATION," AND
HAS OBSCURED THE FACT THAT STRUCTURE OF AUTHORITY CAN BE AN
OBJECT OF CONCERTED PARTICIPANT CONTEST.

1240 KUHN T.E.
PUBLIC ENTERPRISES, PROJECT PLANNING AND ECONOMIC
DEVELOPMENT (PAMPHLET)
HONDURAS: STANFORD RESEARCH INSTITUTE, 1962, 55 PP.
COMPREHENSIVE ECONOMIC THEORY OF PUBLIC ENTERPRISE,
ORGANIZATIONS WHOSE POLICIES AND MANAGEMENT ACTIONS ARE
DIRECTLY OR INDIRECTLY DETERMINED BY PUBLIC DECISIONS.
(INCLUDES PUBLIC UTILITIES OF US.) ANALYZES THESE CORPORA-
TIONS IN TERMS OF THEIR IMPORTANCE TO ECONOMICALLY DEVELOP-
ING NATIONS. TRIES TO ESTABLISH METHOD FOR PLANNING PROJECTS
UNDER PUBLIC MANAGEMENT.

1241 KUIC V.
"THEORY AND PRACTICE OF THE AMERICAN PRESIDENCY."
REV. OF POLITICS, 23 (JULY 61), 307-322.
DISCUSSION OF THEORIES OF THE EXECUTIVE, CONCENTRATING
ON THEORIES OF THE AMERICAN PRESIDENCY. SAYS THAT AMERICAN
PRESIDENT HAS BECOME MORE POWERFUL IN RESPONSE TO PRAGMATIC
POLITICAL NEED AND NOT BECAUSE OF ANY THEORY.

1242 KULZ H.R. ED.
STAATSBURGER UND STAATSGEWALT (2 VOLS.)
KARLSRUHE: VERL C F MULLER, 1963, 1120 PP.
COLLECTION OF ESSAYS ON ASPECTS OF ADMINISTRATIVE LAW AND
ADJUDICATION IN GERMANY AND ABROAD (SWITZERLAND, ENGLAND,
US, USSR, SCANDINAVIA). EXAMINES IN DETAIL GERMAN ADMINI-
STRATIVE COURTS.

1243 KURAKOV I.G.
SCIENCE, TECHNOLOGY AND COMMUNISM; SOME QUESTIONS OF
DEVELOPMENT (TRANS. BY CARIN DEDIJER)
NEW YORK: PERGAMON PRESS, 1966, 126 PP., LC#66-12657.
IN LIGHT OF MARXIST SOCIAL THEORY AND METHODS OF MARXIST
ECONOMICS, TREATS PROBLEMS OF ECONOMICS, RESEARCH POLICY,
AND INDUSTRIAL MANAGEMENT. EMPHASIZES ACCOUNTING FOR
RESEARCH WORK INPUTS IN COST BENEFIT ANALYSES. CRITICIZES
SOVIET RESEARCH PLANNING AND USE OF MATERIAL INCENTIVES.
SHOWS ROLE OF SCIENCE AND TECHNOLOGY IN SOVIET PRODUCTION

AND EXPLAINS DIRECTION OF THEIR DEVELOPMENT.

1244 KURON J., MODZELEWSKI
"AN OPEN LETTER TO THE PARTY."
NEW POLITICS, 5 (1967), 5-46.
    FIRST PRINTING OF THE "OPEN LETTER" OF TWO LECTURERS FROM
WARSAW UNIVERSITY. IN IT THEY ACCUSED THE POLISH PARTY OF
BETRAYING ITS DEMOCRATIC AND SOCIALIST PRINCIPLES, OF FOS-
TERING AN "EASTERN CENTRAL POLITICAL BUREAUCRACY." A VERY
ASTUTE PRESENTATION OF EVIDENCE SHOWS THAT THIS BUREAUCRATIC
ELITE WAS PARTIALLY RESPONSIBLE FOR POLISH ECONOMIC ILLS.
THE TWO AUTHORS WERE SENTENCED TO PRISON.

1245 KUWAIT   ARABIA
KUWAIT FUND FOR ARAB ECONOMIC DEVELOPMENT (PAMPHLET)
KUWAIT: GOVERNMENT PRINTING PR, 1963, 17 PP.
    LAW ESTABLISHING KUWAIT FUND, THE PURPOSE OF WHICH IS TO
ASSIST ARAB STATES IN DEVELOPING THEIR ECONOMIES AND
PROVIDE THEM WITH LOANS NECESSARY FOR THE EXECUTION OF
THEIR PROGRAMS OF DEVELOPMENT. ALSO CONTAINS KUWAIT
FUND'S CHARTER OUTLINING ADMINISTRATION, OPERATIONS, AND
GENERAL PROVISIONS.

1246 KWEDER J.B.
THE ROLES OF THE MANAGER, MAYOR, AND COUNCILMEN IN POLICY-
MAKING.
CHAPEL HILL: U OF N CAR INST GOV, 1965, 138 PP.
    STUDY DESCRIBES ROLES OF MANAGERS, MAYORS, AND COUNCILMEN
IN NORTH CAROLINA CITIES AND RELATES THESE ROLES TO
STRUCTURAL CHARACTERISTICS OF THE GOVERNMENTS STUDIED.
FINDINGS ARE COMPARED WITH SIMILAR STUDIES DONE ELSEWHERE.

1247 KYRIAK T.E. ED.
EAST EUROPE: BIBLIOGRAPHY--INDEX TO US JPRS RESEARCH TRANS-
LATIONS.
ANNAPOLIS: RES MICROFILM PUBL.
    A PERIODICAL PUBLISHED MONTHLY INDEXING ALL JOINT PUB-
LICATIONS RESEARCH SERVICE MATERIALS TRANSLATED IN THE MONTH
COVERED. FOREIGN DOCUMENTS, SCHOLARLY WORKS, AND OTHER MA-
TERIALS NOT AVAILABLE IN ENGLISH ARE INDEXED BY SUBJECT AND
CROSS-REFERENCED WITH THE OTHER THREE AREA BIBLIOGRAPHIES
IN THIS SERIES. MOST ITEMS ARE IN SOCIAL SCIENCES WITH ABOUT
110 ITEMS PER PERIODICAL. INCLUDES INDEX TO MICROFILM.

1248 LA PALOMBARA J.G.
ALTERNATIVE STRATEGIES FOR DEVELOPING ADMINISTRATIVE
CAPABILITIES IN EMERGING NATIONS (PAMPHLET)
BLOOMINGTON: INDIANA U, INTL DEV, 1965, 43 PP.
    PROPOSES THAT CRISIS MANAGEMENT IN EMERGING NATIONS IS
MOST EFFECTIVE IF IT DOES NOT DEVIATE FROM PLURALISTIC-
BUREAUCRATIC ARRANGEMENT. CRITICIZES MOST OF THE LITERATURE
IN FIELD AS THEORETICAL AND LACKING REFERENCE TO
APPLICATION. CLAIMS ONE-PARTY SYSTEM IS NOT EFFECTIVE IN
SOLVING PROBLEMS OF NEW NATIONS.

1249 LA PORTE T.
"DIFFUSION AND DISCONTINUITY IN SCIENCE, TECHNOLOGY AND PUB-
LIC AFFAIRS: RESULTS OF A SEARCH IN THE FIELD."
AMER. BEHAVIORAL SCIENTIST, 10 (MAY 67), 23-29.
    IN AN EXTENSIVE SERIES OF INTERVIEWS WITH INDIVIDUAL
SCHOLARS AND FEDERAL ADMINISTRATORS, AUTHOR FOUND A
"DISTRESSING" DISCONTINUITY BETWEEN SCHOLAR AND RESEARCHER.
SUGGESTS THE TWO BEGIN ACCOMMODATION PROCESS.

1250 LAHAYE R.
LES ENTREPRISES PUBLIQUES AU MAROC.
PARIS: LIBRAIRIE DE MEDICIS, 1961, 340 PP.
    ANALYSIS OF STATE OWNERSHIP AND PARTICIPATION IN PUBLIC
SERVICES AND INDUSTRY IN MOROCCO. DESCRIBES ENTERPRISES,
ANALYZES THEIR STRUCTURE, AND DISCUSSES THEIR ECONOMIC AND
ADMINISTRATIVE EVOLUTION. STATE PARTNERSHIP IN PRIVATE IN-
DUSTRY IS IMPORTANT TO ECONOMIC DEVELOPMENT, AS WELL AS
STATE OWNERSHIP WHERE INDUSTRY HAS NOT DEVELOPED SUCCESS-
FULLY. DISCUSSES GROWTH OF ADMINISTRATIVE JURISPRUDENCE.

1251 LALL B.G.
"GAPS IN THE ABM DEBATE."
BUL. ATOMIC SCIENTISTS, 23 (APR. 67), 45-46.
    POINTS OUT THAT US OFFICIALS IN DISCUSSING HOPES FOR AN
AGREEMENT WITH THE USSR AGAINST BUILDING AN ANTI-BALLISTIC
MISSILE SYSTEM FAIL TO POINT OUT ESTABLISHED SOVIET DISIN-
TEREST IN SUCH A MOVE WHEN UNACCOMPANIED BY REDUCTIONS IN
OFFENSIVE STRENGTH. ALSO NOTES LACK OF COUNTER-PRESSURE IN
US EXECUTIVE ESTABLISHMENT TO MILITARY DESIRES.

1252 LAMBIRI I.
SOCIAL CHANGE IN A GREEK COUNTRY TOWN.
WASHINGTON: CTR PLAN ECO RES, 1965, 165 PP.
    STUDY OF CULTURAL AND SOCIAL PROBLEMS CREATED IN GREEK
TOWN BY RAPID INDUSTRIALIZATION AND UNAVOIDABLE INCREASED
PARTICIPARTION OF WOMEN IN INDUSTRIAL EMPLOYMENT.

1253 LANCASTER L.W.
"GOVERNMENT IN RURAL AMERICA."
PRINCETON: VAN NOSTRAND, 1952.
    DESCRIBES GOVERNMENT AND ADMINISTRATION OF RURAL COUN-
TY, TOWNSHIP, AND SCHOOL DISTRICT IN US. REVIEWS AREA AND
STRUCTURE OF TOWN, COUNTY, TOWNSHIP; LEGAL ASPECTS OF RUR-
AL GOVERNMENT; PATTERN OF FISCAL RELATIONS; POLICE AND JU-
DICIAL ADMINISTRATION; PUBLIC HIGHWAYS, EDUCATION, WELFARE
AND HEALTH. BIBLIOGRAPHY CONTAINS RELATED BIBLIOGRAPHICAL
AIDS, STATISTICAL COMPILATIONS, STUDIES, AND PERIODICALS.

1254 LANDAU J.M.
"PARLIAMENTS AND PARTIES IN EGYPT."
NEW YORK: FREDERICK PRAEGER, 1954.
    TRACES DEVELOPMENT OF PARLIAMENTARY INSTITUTIONS AND PO-
LITICAL PARTIES IN EGYPT. EXAMINES EXTENT OF EUROPEAN INFLU-
ENCE ON INCEPTION, EVOLUTION, AND DISRUPTION. BASED ON
ARABIC AND EUROPEAN SOURCES, WITH GREATEST SIGNIFICANCE
GIVEN TO PRIMARY SOURCE-MATERIAL FOR THE POLITICAL-CONSTITU-
TIONAL HISTORY OF EGYPT SINCE 1860. BIBLIOGRAPHY OF 139 MAN-
USCRIPTS, ARCHIVAL, AND SOURCE MATERIALS.

1255 LANDES W.M.
"THE EFFECT OF STATE FAIR EMPLOYMENT LAWS ON THE ECONOMIC
POSITION OF NONWHITES."
AMER. ECO. REVIEW, 57 (MAY 67), 578-590.
    AUTHOR INVESTIGATES EFFECTS OF FAIR EMPLOYMENT LAW TO DE-
TERMINE WHETHER OR NOT SUCH LEGISLATION HAS IMPROVED ECONOM-
IC POSITION OF RACIAL & RELIGIOUS MINORITIES IN REALITY. HE
FIRST DEVELOPS A THEORETICAL MODEL TO ANALYZE IMPACT OF FAIR
EMPLOYMENT LAWS, AND THEN TESTS HYPOTHESIS HE FINDS AGAINST
EMPIRICAL EVIDENCE ON EFFECT OF STATE LAWS ON RATIO OF
NONWHITE TO WHITE EARNINGS AND MARKET DISCRIMINATION.

1256 LANE E.
"INTEREST GROUPS AND BUREAUCRACY."
ANN. ACAD. POL. SOC. SCI., (MAR. 54), 104-110.
    INTEREST GROUPS ARE DIRECTLY AND STRONGLY REPRESENTED IN
ADMINISTRATIVE AND REGULATORY AGENCIES, AND THIS IS OFTEN
DETRIMENTAL TO THE PUBLIC INTEREST.

1257 LANFALUSSY A.
"EUROPE'S PROGRESS: DUE TO COMMON MARKET."
LLOYD BANK REV., 62 (OCT. 61), 1-16.
    REVIEWS DATA SHOWING THAT COMMON MARKET HAD NOT CAUSED
GREAT ADVANCES. WARNS AGAINST LIMITS OF HIS FIGURES BE-
CAUSE OF IMPONDERABLES OF MORALE AND POSSIBLE GROWING EFFECT
NOT YET TOO APPARENT.

1258 LANGE O., TAYLOR F.Y.
ON THE ECONOMIC THEORY OF SOCIALISM.
MINNEAPOLIS: U. MINN. PR., 1938, 143 PP.
    ANALYZES THE PROBLEM OF GOVERNMENT CONTROL OF ECONOMY.
STUDIES REGULATION OF PRODUCTION IN SOCIALIST STATE. NOTES
GENERAL APPLICATION OF TRIAL AND ERROR PROCEDURE. ALSO
STUDIES DETERMINATION OF EQUILIBRIUM IN COMPETITIVE MARKET.

1259 LANGROD G.
THE INTERNATIONAL CIVIL SERVICE: ITS ORIGINS, ITS NATURE,
ITS EVALUATION.
DOBBS FERRY: SYTHOFF/OCEANA, 1963, 358 PP., $13.00.
    EXAMINES ITS DEVELOPMENT IN THE LEAGUE OF NATIONS AND
THE I.L.O.. SHOWS THE INFLUENCE EXERCISED BY SUCCESSIVE
LEADING PERSONALITIES. CONCLUDES WITH A DETAILED ANALYSIS
OF THE SECRETARIAT OF THE U.N., DEMONSTRATING THE
ROLES OF THE SECRETARIES-GENERAL, INTERNAL CRISES, AND
INTERNATIONAL TENSIONS IN THE MOLDING OF THE INTERNATIONAL
CIVIL SERVICE AS IT EXISTS TODAY, AND AS IT IS LIKELY TO
DEVELOP.

1260 LAPIERRE R.T.
A THEORY OF SOCIAL CONTROL.
NEW YORK: MCGRAW HILL, 1954, 567 PP., LC#54-6724.
    AN ATTEMPT TOWARD A THEORY OF SOCIAL CONTROL WHICH
MEDIATES BETWEEN PERSONALITY AND SPECIFIC SITUATIONS.
CONTROL IS USUALLY EXERCISED IN SMALL GROUPS, USING DESIRE
FOR STATUS AS A KEY LEVERAGE. CLASSIFIES STATUS GROUPS (I.E.
ASSOCIATIONAL GROUPS), DISCUSSES GROUP LAW, TOLERANCE,
VALUES, NORMS, SANCTIONS, POWER STRUCTURE AND GROUP RULE,
PERSUASION, AND OTHER PHENOMENA RELEVANT TO REPRESENTATION.

1261 LAQUEUR W.Z. ED.
THE MIDDLE EAST IN TRANSITION.
NEW YORK: PRAEGER, 1958, 513 PP.
    THIRTY-SIX ESSAYS COVER SOCIAL AND POLITICAL CHANGE. FO-
CUSES ON POLITICAL IDEOLOGY, COMMUNISM, SOVIET STRATEGY IN
MIDDLE EAST. STUDIES TRENDS OF INDIVIDUAL COUNTRIES AND RE-
GION AS WHOLE.

1262 LARSEN K.
NATIONAL BIBLIOGRAPHIC SERVICES: THEIR CREATION AND
OPERATION.
PARIS: UNESCO, 1953, 146 PP.
    DEFINES PURPOSE, SCOPE, AND TECHNIQUES FOR ESTABLISHING
A BIBLIOGRAPHIC CENTER UNDER THE AUSPICES OF UNESCO; OUT-
LINES ITS FUNCTIONS, STRESSES ITS IMPORTANCE, AND SPECIFIES
TECHNIQUES. DESCRIBES THE MEANS FOR PROCURING, PRODUCING,
AND PROMOTING MATERIALS; DEALS WITH THE UNION CATALOGUE,
DIRECTORIES, INFORMATION SERVICE, ADMINISTRATION OF THE
CENTER, ETC.

1263 LARSON R.L.
"HOW TO DEFINE ADMINISTRATIVE PROBLEMS."
HARVARD BUSINESS REV., 40 (JAN. 62), 68-80.
DISCUSSES METHODS BY WHICH EXECUTIVES CAN ACHIEVE MORE
PRECISE DEFINITION OF ADMINISTRATIVE PROBLEMS. THE AUTHOR
SUGGESTS THAT SPECIFIC PROBLEMS SHOULD BE CONSIDERED IN
RELATION TO MORE GENERAL PROBLEMS; ALTERNATIVE STRATEGIES
SHOULD BE DEVISED TO FULFILL OBJECTIVES; AND THE CONSEQUENCE
OF SPECIFIC CHOICES UPON BUSINESS POLICY SHOULD BE CAREFULLY
EXPLORED.

1265 LASLETT J.H.M.
"SOCIALISM AND THE AMERICAN LABOR MOVEMENT* SOME NEW REFLEC-
TIONS."
LABOR HISTORY, 8 (SPRING 67), 136-155.
DRAWS CONCLUSION FROM STUDY OF AFL IN POST-1900 ERA THAT
SOCIALIST POLICIES FAILED TO ACHIEVE AS MUCH FOR LABOR AS
MORE CONSERVATIVE PHILOSOPHIES DID. CITES FACTORS SUCH AS
WORKING WITHIN THE MAJOR-PARTY SYSTEM, WHICH MAY BE MOST
IMPORTANT, AND EXTENT OF CENTRALIZATION OF POWER. SPECIFIC
REFERENCE MADE TO NUMEROUS UNIONS OF THIS PERIOD.

1266 LASSWELL H.D., SERENO R.
"GOVERNMENTAL AND PARTY LEADERS IN FASCIST ITALY."
AM. POL. SCI. REV., 31 (MAY 37), 914-929.
EXAMINES GOVERNMENT MEMBERSHIP FROM STANDPOINT OF CLASS
ORIGIN, PARTY AFFILIATION BEFORE 1923, AND OCCUPATIONAL
SKILLS. FINDS THAT THE RISING AGENCIES (CABINET AND PRE-
FECTORS) ARE STAFFED BY MEN FROM THE LOWER CLASSES, WHILE
THE ARISTOCRACY IS ALLOWED TO STAFF DECLINING AGENCIES
SUCH AS THE SENATE. CONCLUDES THAT EARLY PARTY AFFILIATION
AND USE OF VIOLENCE LED TO PRESENT LEADERSHIP.

1267 LASSWELL H.D.
THE ANALYSIS OF POLITICAL BEHAVIOUR: AN EMPIRICAL
APPROACH.
NEW YORK: OXFORD U. PR., 1947, 314 PP.
ARTICLES AND ESSAYS DIVIDED INTO THREE MAJOR FIELDS OF
INQUIRY: HOW TO INTEGRATE SCIENCE, MORALS AND POLITICS, HOW
TO ANALYZE POLITICS AND HOW TO OBSERVE AND RECORD POLITICS.
INCLUDES CRITIQUE OF LEGAL EDUCATION, MILITARY STATE, THE
FASCIST STATE AND DESCRIBES VARIOUS SCIENTIFIC TECHNIQUES
FOR POLITICAL SCIENCE RESEARCH.

1268 LASSWELL H.D.
NATIONAL SECURITY AND INDIVIDUAL FREEDOM.
NEW YORK: MCGRAW HILL, 1950, 259 PP.
MAINTAINS THAT THROUGH THE COMMITTEE SYSTEM INDIVIDUAL
FREEDOM IS EXERCISED AND PROVIDES A MEANS BY WHICH ALL
SECTORS OF AMERICA CAN EFFECT NATIONAL SECURITY.

1269 LASSWELL H.D.
THE POLITICAL WRITINGS OF HAROLD D LASSWELL.
NEW YORK: FREE PRESS OF GLENCOE, 1951, 525 PP.
CONTAINS THREE VOLUMES OF LASSWELL'S WORKS ON POLITICAL
SCIENCE: "PSYCHOPATHOLOGY AND POLITICS," "POLITICS: WHO GETS
WHAT, WHEN, HOW," AND "DEMOCRATIC CHARACTER." THESE INCLUDE
LASSWELL'S CLASSIC WORK ON THE PSYCHOLOGICAL BASES OF POLIT-
ICAL ACTIVITY, STUDY OF POLITICS AS THE SHAPING AND SHARING
OF VALUES, AND ANALYSIS OF THE INTERRELATIONSHIP OF PERSONAL
"CHARACTER" AND HISTORICAL FORCES.

1270 LASSWELL H.D., LERNER D., ROTHWELL G.E.
"THE COMPARATIVE STUDY OF ELITES: AN INTRODUCTION AND
BIBLIOGRAPHY."
STANFORD: STANFORD U PRESS, 1952.
INTRODUCTORY MONOGRAPH TO ELITE STUDIES IN WHICH ELITE
CONCEPT IS ELABORATED, AND VARIOUS HYPOTHESES ARE SUGGESTED
TO EXPLAIN CHANGES OF ELITE STRUCTURE DISCERNED IN SOCIETY.
EXPLAINS SCOPE OF SERIES AND CONCEPTUAL FRAMEWORK WITHIN
WHICH INDIVIDUAL STUDIES ARE DEVELOPED, METHODS USED.
EXTENSIVE BIBLIOGRAPHY SUGGESTS GENERALIZED AND SPECIAL
WORKS IN RELEVANT LANGUAGES AND FIELDS THROUGHOUT HISTORY.

1271 LASSWELL H.D.
"UNIVERSALITY IN PERSPECTIVE."
PROC. AMER. SOC. INT. LAW. (1959), 1-9.
IT IS NECESSARY TO CREATE A STRONGER AND MORE DECISIVE
SYSTEM OF INTERNATIONAL ORDER IF MAN IS TO SURVIVE. THE
UNIVERSAL SYSTEM OF PUBLIC ORDER CAN BE IMPLEMENTED WITHOUT
RESORTING TO TOTALITARIANISM.

1272 LASSWELL H.D.
PSYCOPATHOLOGY AND POLITICS.
NEW YORK: COMPASS, 1961, $1.65.
DEFENDS PSYCHIATRIC LIFE-HISTORIES AS MEANS OF PENETRAT-
ING PERSONALITY SYSTEMS OF PEOPLE CONCERNED WITH POLITICS.
FREE-FANTASY METHOD AN ALTERNATIVE TO TRADITIONAL SYSTEMS OF
RATIONAL INQUIRY INTO POLITICAL SCIENCE ISSUES. DEVELOPS SET
OF CRITERIA OF POLITICAL TYPES, SUCH AS AGITATORS, ADMIN-
ISTRATORS, AND THEORISTS.

1273 LASSWELL H.D.
"THE POLICY SCIENCES OF DEVELOPMENT."
WORLD POLIT., 17 (JAN. 65), 286-309.
'SELF-SUSTAINING LEVEL OF CREATIVE CONCERN WITH THE POWER

VALUE AND ITS DIVERSE MODES OF INSTITUTIONAL EXPRESSION...
CAN PROVIDE AN INCLUSIVE FRAME OF REFERENCE FOR THE
DECISION-MAKERS AND CHOOSERS INVOLVED IN GIVING OR
RECEIVING ASSISTANCE OR IN DIRECTING SELF-SUSTAINING
AND INTEGRATED GROWTH.'

1274 LATHAM E.
THE GROUP BASIS OF POLITICS: A STUDY IN BASING-POINT
LEGISLATION.
NEW YORK: OCTAGON PUBL CO, 1965, 244 PP., LC#65-16775.
STUDY OF THE STRUGGLE IN THE 80TH AND 81ST CONGRESS TO
ENACT LEGISLATION DEALING WITH THE BASING-POINT SYSTEM OF
QUOTING DELIVERED PRICES. COVERS GROUP CONFLICT AND THE
POLITICAL PROCESS, THE CEMENT CASE OF 1948, THE EVOLUTION OF
THE MEYERS BILL, THE O'MAHONEY BILL, TRUMAN'S DEFEAT IN 1950
CONGRESS, AND THE VOTING HISTORY OF THE STRUGGLE.

1275 LATIMER E.W.
EUROPE IN AFRICA IN THE NINETEENTH CENTURY.
CHICAGO: MCCLURE & CO, 1895, 451 PP.
HISTORY OF COLONIAL RIVALRIES, EUROPEAN ECONOMIC EMPIRES
(RHODES AND OTHERS), AND EUROPEAN SETTLERS IN AFRICA.
PROBLEMS AND CONFLICTS WITH NATIVES TREATED.

1276 LAW COMMISSION OF INDIA
REFORM OF JUDICIAL ADMINISTRATION.
NEW DELHI: INDIA, MIN OF LAW, 1958, 1326 PP.
FOURTEENTH REPORT ON JUDICIAL REFORM IN INDIA, BY COMMIS-
SION ESTABLISHED BY MINISTRY OF LAW. CRITICAL OF CLASS
AND ETHNIC HOMOGENEITY OF HIGH COURT JUDGES. NEW TRIAL
METHODS TO EXPEDITE FLOW OF LITIGATION SUGGESTED.

1277 LAWSON R.
INTERNATIONAL REGIONAL ORGANIZATIONS.
NEW YORK: PRAEGER, 1962, 387 PP.
DISCUSSES POSTWAR PROLIFERATION OF REGIONAL ORGANIZATIONS
UNDER UN AND MEANS DEVISED TO EFFECT FUNCTIONS. LISTS
SERIES OF DOCUMENTS PRINTED BY VARIOUS REGIONAL ORGANIZA-
TIONS.

1278 LEACH R.H.
GOVERNING THE AMERICAN NATION.
NEW YORK: ALLYN AND BACON, 1967, 723 PP.
PROPOSES TO GIVE GENERAL KNOWLEDGE ABOUT AMERICAN
GOVERNMENT AND HOW IT OPERATES. ITS DEMOCRATIC CHARACTER IS
EMPHASIZED. THE TEXT IS INTENDED TO BE A POINT OF DEPARTURE
FOR THE COLLEGE CLASSROOM. THE AUTHOR INTENDS THE STYLE TO
BE INFORMAL AND AS NEARLY LIKE LECTURES AS POSSIBLE,
STRESSING THE MAIN PRINCIPLES AND PROCEDURES OF DEMOCRATIC
GOVERNMENT.

1279 LEE L.T.
VIENNA CONVENTION ON CONSULAR RELATIONS.
DURHAM: RULE OF LAW PRESS, 1966, 315 PP., LC#66-25083.
DESCRIBES AND ANALYZES FEATURES OF VIENNA CONVENTION ON
CONSULAR RELATIONS ADOPTED AT 1963 VIENNA CONFERENCE.
DISCUSSES CONSULAR RELATIONS IN GENERAL, FUNCTION OF
CONSULS, PRIVILEGES AND IMMUNITIES, AND RELATIONSHIP OF
CONSULS AND DIPLOMATS. MAINTAINS THAT AGREEMENT HAS
FURTHERED INTERNATIONAL UNDERSTANDING AND UNITY OF LAW.

1280 LEE R.R., FLEISCHER G.A., ROGGEVEEN V.J.
ENGINEERING-ECONOMIC PLANNING MISCELLANEOUS SUBJECTS: A
SELECTED BIBLIOGRAPHY (MIMEOGRAPHED)
STANFORD: STAN U PROJ ENG & ECO, 1961, 53 PP.
SELECTION OF REFERENCES TO CITY AND REGIONAL PLANNING.
SPECIAL EMPHASIS ON ADMINISTRATIVE, ECONOMIC, LEGISLATIVE,
AND POLITICAL ASPECTS. INCLUDES SECTIONS ON ENGINEERING
ECONOMY THEORY, INVESTMENT DECISION-MAKING, LAND AND NATURAL
RESOURCES, PUBLIC FINANCE, AND URBAN RENEWAL. INCLUDES BRIEF
DESCRIPTIONS OF MANY BOOKS AND ARTICLES LISTED. STUDIES ARE
BOTH GENERAL AND OF SPECIFIC TOPICS.

1281 LEES J.P.
"LEGISLATIVE REVIEW AND BUREAUCRATIC RESPONSIBILITY."
PUBLIC ADMINISTRATION, 45 (WINTER 67), 369-386.
ILLUSTRATES NATURE OF COMMUNICATION BETWEEN MEMBERS
AND STAFF OF THE APPROPRIATIONS COMMITTEES AND MEMBERS OF
EXECUTIVE DEPARTMENTS CONCERNING LEGISLATIVE REVIEW OF
FUNDS APPROPRIATED TO EXECUTIVE DEPARTMENTS. DISCUSSES
IMPACT ON THE AMERICAN FEDERAL ADMINISTRATION OF FISCAL
SUPERVISION BY CONGRESS.

1282 LEGISLATIVE REFERENCE SERVICE
PROBLEMS OF LEGISLATIVE APPORTIONMENT ON BOTH FEDERAL AND
STATE LEVELS: SELECTED REFERENCES (PAMPHLET)
WASHINGTON: LIBRARY OF CONGRESS, 1952, 7 PP.
SHORT BIBLIOGRAPHY OF GOVERNMENT PUBLICATIONS, BOTH
STATE AND FEDERAL, AND ARTICLES ON ISSUE OF REPRESENTATION
AND APPORTIONMENT. ARRANGEMENT IS ALPHABETICAL BY
AUTHOR. ITEMS COVER 20TH CENTURY.

1283 LEISERSON A.
ADMINISTRATIVE REGULATION: A STUDY IN REPRESENTATION OF
INTERESTS.
CHICAGO: U OF CHICAGO PRESS, 1942, 292 PP., LC#42-18098.

STUDY OF PROCESS OF INTEGRATING CONFLICTS OF ECONOMIC
GROUPS WITH THE EXERCISE OF PUBLIC AUTHORITY. OBSERVES OPER-
ATION OF LEGISLATIVE PROVISIONS AND ADMINISTRATIVE ORGANIZA-
TIONS. STUDIES INTEREST REPRESENTATION ON ADMINISTRATIVE
PROCEDURE AND BOARDS, GROUP INTERESTS AS SOURCES OF PUBLIC
POLICY, ADMINISTRATIVE FUNCTIONS OF INTEREST GROUPS, REPRE-
SENTATIVE ADVISORY COMMITTEES, AND LEGAL ASPECTS.

1284 LEITES N.
THE OPERATIONAL CODE OF THE POLITBURO.
NEW YORK: MCGRAW HILL, 1951, 100 PP.
STUDIES RULES OF POLITICAL CONDUCT FOR THE BOLSHEVIK
PARTY, AS DERIVED FROM WRITINGS OF LENIN AND STALIN. SUG-
GESTS SOME TENTATIVE CONCLUSIONS ON THE APPLICABILITY OF
SUCH RULES TO CURRENT POLITBURO BEHAVIOR.

1285 LEMARCHAND R.
"SOCIAL CHANGE AND POLITICAL MODERNISATION IN BURUNDI."
J. OF MOD. AFR. STUD., 4 (DEC. 66), 401-434.
EXPLORES INTERACTION OF SOCIAL CHANGE AND POLITICAL STA-
BILITY IN BURUNDI. RELATES CHANGES IN ELITES TO DECLINE OF
MONARCHIAL POWER. STUDIES GENERAL STRATIFICATION OF UPPER
ECHELONS IN BURUNDI'S POWER STRUCTURE.

1286 LEMAY G.H.
BRITISH SUPREMACY IN SOUTH AFRICA 1899-1907.
LONDON: OXFORD U PR, 1965, 229 PP.
ANALYSIS OF BRITISH ACTION IN SOUTH AFRICA THAT MAIN-
TAINED ITS DOMINATION OF REGION FROM 1899-1907. EXAMINES
POLICY TOWARD BOERS AND ADMINISTRATION OF SIR ALFRED MILNER,
AS WELL AS WAR ITSELF.

1287 LEMBERG E. ED., EDDING F.
DIE VERTRIEBENEN IN WESTDEUTSCHLAND (3 VOLS.)
KIEL: FERDINAND HIRT, 1959, 1940 PP.
COLLECTION OF ESSAYS ON REFUGEE PROBLEM IN WEST GERMANY.
EXAMINES DIFFICULTIES OF ASSIMILATION FROM CULTURAL, LEGAL,
AND ECONOMIC PERSPECTIVES. DISCUSSES PROBLEMS OF
ADMINISTRATION AND ANALYZES IN DETAIL IMPACT OF REFUGEES
ON VARIOUS SECTORS OF ECONOMY SUCH AS AGRICULTURE, TRADES,
ETC.

1288 LENCZOWSKI G.
OIL AND STATE IN THE MIDDLE EAST.
ITHACA: CORNELL U. PR., 1960, 360 PP.
BY EMPHASIZING AND EXPLAINING CERTAIN ASPECTS OF THE
MIDDLE-EASTERN OIL COMPANIES (LEGAL STATUS, CONCESSION
AGREEMENTS, METHOD OF HANDLING EMPLOYEES AND GOVERNMENT
OFFICIALS, AND GENERAL RELATIONSHIP TO HOST NATION) ATTEMPTS
TO PROJECT THEIR FUTURE POSITION IN THESE COUNTRIES.

1289 LENDVAI P.
"HUNGARY* CHANGE VS. IMMOBILISM."
PROBLEMS OF COMMUNISM, 16 (MAR.-APR. 67), 11-17.
THE NOVEMBER 1966 PARTY CONFERENCE IN COMMUNIST HUNGARY
CONFIRMED IMPRESSIONS THAT THE GOVERNMENT IS COMMITTING IT-
SELF TO SIGNIFICANT POLITICO-ECONOMIC REFORMS. THOUGH SPLITS
IN THE PARTY AND POPULAR DISTRUST WILL BE PROBLEMS, THERE IS
CERTAINLY MOVEMENT TOWARD ECONOMIC DE-CENTRALIZATION, ELECT-
TORAL REFORM, AND REJUVENATION OF TRADE UNIONS. CHANGE WILL
BE SLOW BUT MAY FINALLY LEAD TO A MORE PLURALISTIC SOCIETY.

1290 LENG S.C.
JUSTICE IN COMMUNIST CHINA: A SURVEY OF THE JUDICIAL SYSTEM
OF THE CHINESE PEOPLE'S REPUBLIC.
NEW YORK: OCEANA PUBLISHING, 1967, 196 PP., LC#67-14398.
INTRODUCTORY SURVEY OF DEVELOPMENT, ORGANIZATION, AND
FUNCTIONING OF JUDICIAL SYSTEM FOCUSES ON JUDICIAL PATTERN
RATHER THAN LAW; LAWS ARE TREATED ONLY WITHIN CONTEXT OF
ADMINISTRATION OF JUSTICE. CONCERNED PRIMARILY WITH HISTORY
OF "PEOPLE'S JUSTICE" SINCE 1920 AND WITH MACHINERY AND
PROCEDURES BY WHICH JUSTICE IS ADMINISTERED. INCLUDES COURT
SYSTEM, POLICE, LAWYERS, AND TRIAL SYSTEMS.

1291 LENGYEL P.
"SOME TRENDS IN THE INTERNATIONAL CIVIL SERVICE."
INT. ORGAN., 13 (AUTUMN 59), 520-537.
PROBLEMS OF PERSONNEL RECRUITMENT, PROMOTIONS, GRADING,
ASSIGNMENTS, TRAINING AND MORALE ARE DISCUSSED. THE ROLE OF
LEADERSHIP AND THE IMPORTANCE OF DYNAMISM AMONG EMPLOYEES IS
EMPHASIZED AS THE IMPORTANT ELEMENT OF EFFICIENT SERVICE.

1292 LENIN V.I.
WHAT IS TO BE DONE? (1902)
MOSCOW: FOREIGN LANG PUBL HOUSE, 1961, 183 PP.
DISCUSSES CHARACTER AND MAIN CONTENT OF POLITICAL AGITA-
TION, AS SEEN BY LENIN IN 1901. CONSIDERS ORGANIZATIONAL
TASKS OF THE PARTY, AND PLAN FOR BUILDING MILITANT, TO-
TALLY RUSSIAN ORGANIZATION. ATTACKS CURRENT ECONOMISTS FOR
SUPPORTING OPPRESSION AND PROCLAIMS WORKING CLASS TO BE
CAPABLE OF POWERFUL COLLECTIVE ACTION, PROPOSING USE OF
NEWSPAPER "ISKA" AS ITS ORGAN.

1293 LEONARD T.J.
THE FEDERAL SYSTEM OF INDIA.
TUCSON: ARIZONA ST U BUR GOV RES, 1963, 15 PP.

DISCUSSES DISTRIBUTION OF ADMINISTRATIVE AND POLITICAL
POWER IN FEDERAL SYSTEM OF INDIA. COMPARES METHODS AND TRA-
DITIONS WITH US PRACTICES.

1294 LEPAWSKY A.
ADMINISTRATION.
NEW YORK: ALFRED KNOPF, 1949, 675 PP.
DISCUSSES ADMINISTRATION AS ART, SCIENCE, AND VOCATION,
EMPHASIZING ROLE OF ADMINISTRATIVE MACHINERY IN SOCIAL,
ECONOMIC, AND POLITICAL AFFAIRS. ATTEMPTS TO DEVELOP
APPRECIATION OF SOUND AND TESTED ADMINISTRATIVE METHODS,
MANAGERIAL TECHNIQUES, AND ORGANIZATIONAL DEVICES, AND TO
AID RECOGNITION OF UNSOUND ADMINISTRATIVE PRACTICES.

1295 LERNER A.P.
THE ECONOMICS OF CONTROL.
NEW YORK: MACMILLAN, 1960, 428 PP.
STATES THAT PRINCIPAL PROBLEMS OF A CONTROLLED ECONOMY
ARE EMPLOYMENT, MONOPOLY, AND DISTRIBUTION OF INCOME. ANA-
LYZES BENEFITS OF BOTH CAPITALISTIC AND COLLECTIVIST ECONO-
MIES, AND WARNS AGAINST RIGHTIST OR LEFTIST POLITICAL DOGMA-
TISM.

1296 LERNER A.P.
"EMPLOYMENT THEORY AND EMPLOYMENT POLICY."
AMER. ECO. REVIEW, 57 (MAY 67), 1-18.
DISCUSSES DIFFERING ATTITUDES TOWARD EMPLOYMENT BASED ON
POSSIBLE INFLATION CAUSED BY "HIGH FULL EMPLOYMENT." CON-
CLUDES THAT HIGH FULL EMPLOYMENT IS NOT INCOMPATIBLE WITH
PRICE STABILITY IF VALID AND EFFECTIVE WAGE-PRICE GUIDEPOSTS
ARE USED. THIS WOULD INCREASE NATIONAL PRODUCT, CHALLENGE
THE MARXIAN BELIEF IN CAPITALIST DEPENDENCY ON UNEMPLOYMENT,
AND IMPROVE MORALE IN WORKING CLASS.

1297 LERNER D. ED., LASSWELL H.D. ED.
"THE POLICY SCIENCES: RECENT DEVELOPMENTS IN SCOPE AND
METHODS."
STANFORD: U. PR., 1951, 344 PP., $7.50.
SUGGESTS HOW SCIENTIFIC METHODS OF INVESTIGATION AND
MEASUREMENT CAN BE APPLIED TO PROBLEMS IN FIELD OF HUMAN
RELATIONS. DEMONSTRATES HOW COMBINED EFFORTS OF POLICY SCI-
ENTISTS WOULD BENEFIT BOTH NATIONAL AND INTERNATIONAL
POLICY-MAKERS.

1298 LESTER R.A.
ECONOMICS OF LABOR.
NEW YORK: MACMILLAN, 1941, 913 PP.
DEALS WITH ECONOMIC ASPECTS OF LABOR PROBLEMS, INCLUDING
WAGES, HOURS, AND UNEMPLOYMENT, THE GROWTH OF ORGANIZED
LABOR, INCLUDING UNIONS AND MANAGEMENT-UNION RELATIONS, AND
COLLECTIVE BARGAINING IN CERTAIN INDUSTRIES.

1299 LESTER R.A.
AS UNIONS MATURE.
PRINCETON: PRIN U INDUS REL CTR, 1958, 171 PP., LC#58-10048.
TRACES GROWTH OF US LABOR UNIONS, DEALING WITH MANAGEMENT
RELATIONS, CENTRALIZATION OF POWER IN NATIONAL UNIONS, AND
ECONOMIC ASPECTS OF UNIONISM. ALSO TREATS POLITICAL EFFECTS
OF UNIONS AND THEIR ROLE IN AFFECTING PUBLIC POLICY.
DISCUSSES TACTICS OF UNIONS IN HANDLING MANAGEMENT AND
RELATIVE SUCCESS OF EACH.

1300 LEVCIK B.
"WAGES AND EMPLOYMENT PROBLEMS IN THE NEW SYSTEM OF PLANNED
MANAGEMENT IN CZECHOSLOVAKIA."
INTERNATIONAL LABOR REVIEW, 95 (APR. 67), 299-314.
ECONOMIC REFORMS IN CZECHOSLOVAKIA HAVE RECENTLY GIVEN
MUCH GREATER INDIVIDUAL RESPONSIBILITY TO WORKERS WHILE
MAINTAINING THE PRINCIPLE OF CENTRAL PLANNING. AUTHOR VIEWS
THIS AS PROGRESSIVE PROGRAM OFFERING WIDER WAGE DIFFEREN-
TIALS, RAISING MORALE, AND INCREASING WORKER MOBILITY. EX-
PECTS THIS DIVERSIFIED APPROACH TO IMPROVE PRODUCTION AND
THE ECONOMY IN GENERAL.

1301 LEVIN M.R.
"PLANNERS AND METROPOLITAN PLANNING."
J. OF AM. INST. OF PLANNERS, 33 (MAR. 67), 78-89.
DISCUSSES METHODS TO IMPROVE METROPOLITAN PLANNING. AUTH-
OR CONTENDS THAT ADDITIONAL INFLUENCE AND PARTICIPATION OF
FEDERAL AND STATE GOVERNMENTS ARE NEEDED TO PROVIDE NEW
STRENGTH. AMONG 4 ALTERNATIVES AUTHOR REJECTS REVIEW AGENCY
WITH ADVISORY POWERS AS INADEQUATE TO PROVIDE SUFFICIENT
STRENGTH. HOPE LIES IN EITHER ONE OR ALL OF STATE,
METROPOLITAN, AND FEDERAL GOVERNMENTS.

1302 LEVY H.P.
A STUDY IN PUBLIC RELATIONS: CASE HISTORY OF THE RELATIONS
MAINTAINED BETWEEN A DEPT OF PUBLIC ASSISTANCE AND PEOPLE.
NEW YORK: RUSSELL SAGE FDN, 1943, 165 PP., LC#43-5517.
HOLDS PUBLIC RELATIONS AS AN ASSIGNMENT, WITH PROGRAM,
ORGANIZATION, AND INFORMATION CENTER WHICH MAINTAINS CONTACT
BETWEEN SOCIETY AND THE POOR.

1303 LEWIN E.
ROYAL EMPIRE SOCIETY BIBLIOGRAPHIES NO. 9: SUB-SAHARA
AFRICA.

LONDON: ROYAL COMMONWEALTH SOC, 1945, 104 PP.
INTENDED TO DEAL SPECIFICALLY WITH SOUTH AFRICA, DIVIDES SOURCES INTO FOUR CATEGORIES: ADMINISTRATIVE, POLITICAL, ECONOMIC, AND SOCIOLOGICAL.

1304 LEWIS J.W.
LEADERSHIP IN COMMUNIST CHINA.
ITHACA: CORNELL U. PR., 1963, 305 PP., $5.00.
EXAMINES THE GENERAL INTEGRATING PRINCIPLES AND RATIONALE WHICH UNDERLIE THE LEADERSHIP TECHNIQUES BY WHICH PARTY LEADERS HAVE ATTEMPTED TO INITIATE AND DIRECT AFFIRMATIVE RESPONSE OF THE GENERAL POPULATION. THE AUTHOR STUDIES THE LEADERSHIP THEORIES AND PRACTICES IN TERMS OF COMMUNE LEADERSHIP, AND DISCUSSES THE PROBLEM OF TRANSMITTING THE REVOLUTIONARY SYSTEM TO THE NEXT GENERATION OF THE ELITE. BASED ON DOCUMENTARY ANALYSIS AND REFUGEE INTERVIEWS. EXCELLENT TABLES AND CHARTS.

1305 LEWIS P.H.
"LEADERSHIP AND CONFLICT WITHIN FEBRERISTA PARTY OF PARAGUAY."
J. INTER-AMER. STUDIES, 10 (APR. 67), 283-295.
TRACES GROWTH OF FEBRERISTA PARTY FROM 1936 TO PRESENT AND INDICATES THAT IT FOLLOWS NEITHER MICHEL'S "IRON LAW OF OLIGARCHY" NOR LASSWELL-KAPLAN THEORY OF "STRATARCHY." OLD GUARD AND YOUNG ADHERENTS VIE FOR PARTY CONTROL. DEMOCRATIC TENETS AND THIS INTERNAL STRUGGLE DELAY OLIGARCHIZATION, BUT ASCENDANCY OF OLD GUARD AND 1962 CHARTER REDUCE INDIVIDUAL AUTONOMY AND SUGGEST EVENTUAL OLIGARCHIZATION.

1306 LEWIS P.R.
LITERATURE OF THE SOCIAL SCIENCES: AN INTRODUCTORY SURVEY AND GUIDE.
LONDON: LIBRARY ASSOC, 1960, 222 PP.
LISTS AND DISCUSSES MATERIALS PERTINENT TO SOCIAL SCIENCES DATING FROM THE 1800'S FOR THE INTEREST OF THE BRITISH READER. SURVEYS ECONOMIC THEORY AND HISTORY, ESPECIALLY IN THE UK; STATISTICS; COMMERCE AND INDUSTRY; POLITICAL SCIENCE, ADMINISTRATION, AND THEORY; LAW; INTERNATIONAL RELATIONS; AND SOCIOLOGY. INCLUDES AN INDEX AND SUGGESTIONS FOR MAKING USE OF RESEARCH SOURCES.

1307 LEWIS W.A.
DEVELOPMENT PLANNING; THE ESSENTIALS OF ECONOMIC POLICY.
NEW YORK: HARPER & ROW, 1966, 278 PP., LC#66-10655.
CONCERNED WITH TECHNIQUES AND ECONOMICS OF DEVELOPMENT PLANNING; EMPHASIZES POLICY. BEGINS WITH PATTERNS OF PLANNING, THEN EXAMINES STRATEGY. ARITHMETIC AND STATISTICAL FRAMEWORK OF A PLAN EXPLAINED IN DETAIL. CLOSES WITH PROCESS OF PLANNING. AREAS COVERED INCLUDE ADMINISTRATIVE STRUCTURE OF FEDERAL AND PRIVATE PLANNING AGENCIES AND COMMITTEES, FOREIGN TRADE AND AID, LINEAR PROGRAMMING, CAPITAL.

1308 LEWY G.
"SUPERIOR ORDERS, NUCLEAR WARFARE AND THE DICTATES OF CONSCIENCE: THE DILEMMA OF MILITARY OBEDIENCE IN THE ATOMIC AGE."
AMER. POLIT. SCI. REV., 55 (MARCH 61), 3-23.
DISCUSSES 3 ASPECTS OF INTERNATIONAL LAW: VALIDITY OF THE PLEA OF SUPERIOR ORDERS AS A DEFENSE IN WAR CRIME TRIALS, LEGALITY OF USE OF NUCLEAR WEAPONS, PRESENT AND FUTURE OF THE LAW OF WAR.

1309 LEYDER J.
BIBLIOGRAPHIE DE L'ENSEIGNEMENT SUPERIEUR ET DE LA RECHERCHE SCIENTIFIQUE EN AFRIQUE INTERTROPICALE (2 VOLS.)
BRUSSELS: CEN DOC ECO ET SOC AFR, 1960, 287 PP.
ANNOTATED BIBLIOGRAPHY OF 1,025 WORKS IN WESTERN LANGUAGES COVERING PERIOD 1940-59. MATERIAL IS CHRONOLOGICALLY ARRANGED AND PROVIDES ANALYTICAL ANNOTATIONS IN FRENCH TOGETHER WITH COMPLETE BIBLIOGRAPHICAL INFORMATION. MANY SOURCES GATHERED FROM DOCUMENTS OF OFFICIAL ORGANS AND SCIENTIFIC INSTITUTIONS. CONTAINS A COMPREHENSIVE ALPHABETICAL INDEX.

1310 LEYS C.T. ED., ROBSON P. ED.
FEDERATION IN EAST AFRICA.
LONDON: OXFORD U PR, 1965, 244 PP.
ANTHOLOGY OF PAPERS ON EAST AFRICAN FEDERATION DEALING WITH TRADE, ADMINISTRATION, FINANCE, LABOR, AGRICULTURE, TRANSPORTATION, LAW, AND COOPERATION IN REGION.

1311 LI C.M. ED.
INDUSTRIAL DEVELOPMENT IN COMMUNIST CHINA.
NEW YORK: PRAEGER, 1964, 205 PP., $5.00.
PRESENTS UP TO DATE INFORMATION AND CRITICAL ANALYSES ON CAPITAL FORMATION, WORK-INCENTIVE POLICY, ECONOMIC PLANNING, CHANGES IN THE STEEL INDUSTRY, HANDICRAFTS AND AGRICULTURE, SINO-SOVIET TRADE AND EXCHANGE RATES, AND THE DIFFICULTIES IN MEASURING CHINESE INDUSTRIAL OUTPUT.

1312 LIEBENOW J.G.
"LEGITIMACY OF ALIEN RELATIONSHIP: THE NYATURU OF TANGANYIKA" (BMR)"
WESTERN POLIT. QUART., 14 (MAR. 61), 64-86.
EXAMINES ATTEMPTS OF BRITISH TO ESTABLISH LEGITIMACY OF THEIR RULE IN NYATURU TRIBAL AREA OF CENTRAL TANGANYIKA. PAPER DISCUSSES CHANGES TAKING PLACE IN POLITICAL LIFE OF THIS AREA; ELEMENTS OF COERCION AND CONCEPT OF LEGITIMACY; CHIEFS AND THE ACCEPTANCE OF BRITISH OBJECTIVES; EUROPEAN VS. POPULAR SELECTION AND CONTROL. AUTHOR THEN ASSESSES SUCCESS OF BRITISH IN LEGITIMIZING THEIR RULE.

1313 LINDBERG L.
POLITICAL DYNAMICS OF EUROPEAN ECONOMIC INTEGRATION.
STANFORD: U. PR., 1963, 295 PP.
ATTEMPTS TO EXAMINE THE EEC AS AN INSTITUTIONAL SYSTEM AND ASSESS ITS IMPACT ON DECISION-MAKING PATTERNS OF THE COMMON MARKET COUNTRIES. RELATES THIS TO PROBLEM OF EUROPEAN INTEGRATION.

1314 LINDFORS G.V.
INTERCOLLEGIATE BIBLIOGRAPHY; CASES IN BUSINESS ADMINISTRATION (VOL. X)
BOSTON: INTERCOL CASE CLEAR HSE, 1966, 197 PP.
TEN-VOLUME BIBLIOGRAPHY CONTAINING 5,000 CASES IN BUSINESS ADMINISTRATION SUBMITTED BY 1,200 CONTRIBUTORS (AUTHORS AND SUPERVISORS) FROM 190 INSTITUTIONS, BOTH FOREIGN AND DOMESTIC. SPECIAL BIBLIOGRAPHIES FREQUENTLY ISSUED DOCUMENTING POPULAR CASES OR SPECIAL LISTINGS. ENTRIES ARE TOPICALLY ORGANIZED AND ARRANGED IN ONE COMPREHENSIVE TABLE WHICH PROVIDES A SUMMARY AND COMPLETE BIBLIOGRAPHICAL DATA.

1315 LINDSAY K.
EUROPEAN ASSEMBLIES: THE EXPERIMENTAL PERIOD 1949-1959.
NEW YORK: PRAEGER, 1960, 267 PP.
EXAMINES EXPERIMENTAL BEGINNINGS OF EUROPEAN ASSEMBLIES. OUTLINES RELATIONS WITH NATIONAL BODIES, INHERENT PROBLEMS AND POSSIBILITIES FOR FUTURE EVOLUTION.

1316 LINDVEIT E.N.
SCIENTISTS IN GOVERNMENT.
WASHINGTON: PUBLIC AFFAIRS PRESS, 1960, 84 PP., LC#59-15849.
STUDY OF PROBLEMS OF RETAINING SCIENTIFIC PERSONNEL IN US GOVERNMENT AND DEVELOPMENT OF GREATER NEED FOR THEM IN GOVERNMENT SINCE WWII. COVERS ALL FIELDS OF SCIENCE EXCEPT MEDICAL AND STRESSES RESPONSIBILITY OF GOVERNMENT TO KEEP QUALITY SCIENTISTS IN TECHNICAL AGE. BIBLIOGRAPHY OF WORKS CITED IN TEXT AND GOVERNMENT PUBLICATIONS ON SUBJECT SINCE 1945.

1317 LINEBERRY R.L., FOWLER E.P.
"REFORMISM AND PUBLIC POLICIES IN AMERICAN CITIES."
AM. POL. SCI. REV., 61 (SEPT. 67), 701-716.
TREATS TWO POLICY OUTPUTS, TAXATION AND EXPENDITURE LEVELS OF CITIES, AS VARIABLES. RELATES THESE TO SOCIO-ECONOMIC CHARACTERISTICS OF CITIES AND TO STRUCTURAL CHARACTERISTICS OF THEIR GOVERNMENT. EXAMINES IMPACT OF POLITICAL STRUCTURES, REFORMED AND UNREFORMED, ON POLICY-MAKING IN US CITIES.

1318 LIPPMANN W.
PREFACE TO POLITICS.
ANN ARBOR: U OF MICH PR, 1962, 238 PP.
FIRST PUBLISHED IN 1913, ESSAY CALLS UPON W. JAMES, BERGSON, SANTAYANA, H.G. WELLS, NIETZSCHE, AND G.K. CHESTERTON TO SUPPORT POINT THAT POLITICS MUST SATISFY BASIC HUMAN WANTS, NOT ABSTRACT POLITICAL RIGHTS OR CONCEPTS. DEMANDS CREATIVE LEADERSHIP AND CONDEMNS PUBLIC APATHY.

1319 LIPSET S.M.
"DEMOCRACY IN PRIVATE GOVERNMENT; (A CASE STUDY OF THE INTERNATIONAL TYPOGRAPHICAL UNION)" (BMR)"
BRIT. J. OF SOCIOLOGY, 3 (MAR. 52), 47-63.
OUTLINES AN EXCEPTION TO ROBERT MICHEL'S PREDICTION THAT STRUCTURAL FORCES ENDEMIC IN LARGE-SCALE ORGANIZATIONS MAKE CONTROL BY SELF-OPTING LEADERS OF A BUREAUCRATIC HIERARCHY INEVITABLE. EXAMINES THE INTERNAL STRUCTURE OF THE INTERNATIONAL TYPOGRAPHICAL UNION TO SHOW WHY IT DOES NOT FIT INTO A MICHELSIAN OLIGARCHIC PATTERN. HIS RESEARCH SUGGESTS A UNIQUE CLUSTER OF VARIABLES PROVIDING DEMOCRATIC PROCESSES.

1320 LIPSET S.M.
POLITICAL MAN.
NEW YORK: DOUBLEDAY, 1960, 432 PP.
EXAMINES POLITICAL PROCESS IN WESTERN DEMOCRACIES FOR MAIN INTEGRATING FACTOR. FACTORS CREATING SOCIAL INSTABILITY IN AFRO-ASIAN NATIONS MAY BAR ADVANCE TO LEVEL OF WEST.

1321 LIPSET S.M.
"SOCIOLOGY AND POLITICAL SCIENCE: A BIBLIOGRAPHICAL NOTE."
AMER. SOCIOLOGICAL REV., 29 (OCT. 64), 730-734.
AN ANNOTATED BIBLIOGRAPHY OF POLITICAL SCIENCE PUBLICATIONS WITH BEHAVIORAL APPROACHES. MATERIAL RANGES FROM 1945 TO 1964; ENGLISH LANGUAGE. THE AUTHOR POINTS TO THE INCREASING BEHAVIORAL PERSPECTIVE BEING USED IN STUDIES IN POLITICAL SCIENCE.

1322 LIPSET S.M. ED., WOLIN S.S. ED.
THE BERKELEY STUDENT REVOLT: FACTS AND INTERPRETATIONS.
GARDEN CITY: DOUBLEDAY, 1965, 585 PP., LC#65-20058.

COLLECTION OF ARTICLES, STATEMENTS, AND DOCUMENTS DEPICT-
ING EVENTS OF FALL, 1964, AND CONVEYING WHAT PARTICIPANTS
THOUGHT AND FELT; INCLUDES GENERAL ARTICLES ON PROBLEMS OF
STUDENTS AND POLITICS AND THE MULTIVERSITY; SPECIFIC STATE-
MENTS OF STUDENTS, FACULTY, AND ADMINISTRATION; AND PERSPEC-
TIVES OF EDITORS, FACULTY, OUTSIDERS, AND SOCIAL SCIEN-
TISTS.

1323 LISKA G.
THE NEW STATECRAFT.
CHICAGO: U. CHI. PR., 1960, 246 PP., $5.00.
FOREIGN AID IS AN INTEGRAL PART OF FOREIGN POLICY.
DEBUNKS IDEA THAT IT'S A SELF-SUFFICIENT ENTERPRISE IN
ITSELF. AID IS VIEWED FROM SUCH VANTAGE POINTS AS ITS PLACE
IN THE COLD WAR, ROLE IN INTERNATIONAL SECURITY, AND ITS
INFLUENCE ON RECIPIENT COUNTRY. WITH REGARD TO INDIVIDUAL
RECIPIENTS, DEMANDS THAT FOREIGN AID BE CONSISTENT
IF DONOR IS TO SECURE 'INTERNALLY COHERENT' FOREIGN POLICY.

1324 LITCHFIELD E.H.
"NOTES ON A GENERAL THEORY OF ADMINISTRATION."
ADMINISTRATIVE SCI. Q., 1 (JUNE 56), 3-29.
CRITICISM OF EXISTING THOUGHT AND THEORY IN FIELD OF AD-
MINISTRATION. SHOWS NEED FOR A WORKING THEORY AND SETS FORTH
A SERIES OF WORKING HYPOTHESES WHICH COULD PROVIDE A FRAME-
WORK FOR GENERAL THEORY OF ADMINISTRATIVE ACTION. HYPOTHESES
ATTEMPT TO RELATE THE PROCESS AND ADMINISTRATION TO LARGER
CONCEPTS OF ACTION SYSTEMS.

1325 LITTERER J.A.
ORGANIZATIONS: STRUCTURE AND BEHAVIOR.
NEW YORK: JOHN WILEY, 1963, 418 PP., LC#63-12285.
A COLLECTION OF PAPERS ON FORMAL AND INFORMAL
ORGANIZATIONS, WITH BASIC CONCEPTS, PROBLEMS AND ANATOMY,
AND THEIR INTERRELATIONS. INFORMAL LEADERSHIP, "STRATEGIC
LENIENCY," INTERNALIZED STANDARDS OF BUREAUCRACY AS SUB-
STITUTES FOR REPRESENTATION, COMPETITION OF STAFF AND LINE
FOR POWER, FORMAL-INFORMAL ORGANIZATION NEXUS, AND ORGAN-
IZATIONAL ADAPTATION ARE TREATED IN DETAIL.

1326 LITTLE I.M.D.
AID TO AFRICA.
NEW YORK: MACMILLAN, 1964, 76 PP., LC#64-22219.
STUDIES AID TO UNDERDEVELOPED COUNTRIES WITH PARTICULAR
REFERENCE TO BRITISH AID POLICY, ESPECIALLY THOSE IN SUB-SA-
HARAN AFRICA, EXCLUDING REPUBLIC OF SOUTH AFRICA. CONSIDERS
REASONS FOR GIVING AID, PROBLEM OF ADMINISTERING IT, ROLE
OF PRIVATE CAPITAL, AND IMPORTANCE OF TECHNICAL DEVELOPMENT
IN ASSISTING THESE COUNTRIES.

1327 LITTLE HOOVER COMM
HOW TO ACHIEVE GREATER EFFICIENCY AND ECONOMY IN MINNESOTA'S
GOVERNMENT (PAMPHLET)
ST PAUL: MINN EFFICIENCY IN GOVT, 1950, 175 PP.
COMPREHENSIVE DESCRIPTION OF STATE SERVICES AND OFFICES,
WITH SPECIFIC RECOMMENDATIONS FOR CONSOLIDATION OF
DEPARTMENTS AND EFFICIENCY PLANNING. PURPOSE IS TO PRESENT
A SET OF PROPOSALS DESIGNED TO MAKE STATE GOVERNMENT
LESS COSTLY, MORE EFFICIENT, AND MORE RESPONSIVE TO THE
PEOPLE. ADVOCATES GREATER POWER FOR GOVERNOR AND LONGER
TERM FOR HIM.

1328 LITTLEFIELD N.
METROPOLITAN AREA PROBLEMS AND MUNICIPAL HOME RULE.
ANN ARBOR: U OF MICH LAW SCHOOL, 1962, 83 PP.
EXAMINES LAW OF MUNICIPAL HOME RULE IN RELATION TO
METROPOLITAN AREA PROBLEMS. REEXAMINES JURISPRUDENCE OF
HOME RULE IN THE LIGHT OF INCREASING DOMINANCE OF AREA IN-
TERESTS. EXAMINES POWERS OF ANNEXATION, STATE ADMINISTRA-
TIVE CONTROL OVER LOCAL RULE, AND SOME MODEL HOME RULE
PROVISIONS.

1329 LIU K.C.
"DISINTEGRATION OF THE OLD ORDER."
CHICAGO TODAY, 4 (SPRING 67), 14-20.
THOROUGH STUDY OF CHINA'S 19TH-CENTURY INSTITUTIONS AND
INTELLECTUAL HISTORY. CHINA ENTERED 20TH CENTURY AND WESTERN
TECHNOLOGY WITH DEMOCRATIC SENTIMENT BUT AUTHORITARIAN
GOVERNMENT. TREATS IMPACT OF WESTERN WORLD ON REFORM
MOVEMENTS AND THEIR FAILURE TO CREATE POLITICAL CHANGE.
EMPHASIZES PROBLEMS OF SOCIAL TENSION, ADMINISTRATIVE
DISINTEGRATION, AND NATIONALISM VERSUS REGIONALISM.

1330 LIVERNASH E.R.
"THE RELATION OF POWER TO THE STRUCTURE AND PROCESS OF
COLLECTIVE BARGAINING."
J. OF LATIN AM. RES. REV., 6 (OCT. 63), 10-40.
A TENATIVE ANALYSIS OF COLLECTIVE BARGAINING, ITS
MULTI-EMPLOYER AND SINGLE EMPLOYER TYPES, DECENTRALIZATION
OF THE PROCESS AND ITS CAUSES, STRIKE FUNDS AND TACTICS,
THE RELATION OF STRIKES AND ORGANIZATIONAL STRUCTURE,
PROCESSES OF NEGOTATION AND CONSIDERATIONS OF PUBLIC
POLICY SUCH AS PARTIAL INJUNCTIONS AND PARTIAL OPERATION
DURING STRIKES AND THE QUESTION OF RESTRICTIVE PRACTICES.

1331 LIVINGSTON J.C., THOMPSON R.G.

THE CONSENT OF THE GOVERNED.
NEW YORK: MACMILLAN, 1966, 591 PP., LC#66-17386.
INTRODUCTORY STUDY OF AMERICAN GOVERNMENT AND POLITICS
BASED ON ANALYSIS OF DEMOCRATIC THEORY AND PROBLEMS OF MASS
DEMOCRACY. CONTENDS PRESENT POLITICAL SYSTEM IS ACTUALLY
AT ODDS WITH TRADITIONAL DEMOCRATIC IDEAS ON WHICH IT WAS
FOUNDED. EMPHASIZES NEED FOR ELIMINATION OF MANIPULATIVE
GOVERNMENT AND INCREASE IN POLITICAL PARTICIPATION ON PART
OF PUBLIC.

1332 LLOYD K.
"URBAN RACE RIOTS V EFFECTIVE ANTI-DISCRIMINATION
AGENCIES* AN END OR A BEGINNING?"
PUBLIC ADMINISTRATION, 45 (SPRING 67), 43-55.
SUGGESTS THE DEVELOPMENT OF LOCAL HUMAN RELATIONS COMMIS-
SIONS AS STOP-GAP PROGRAMS WHERE URBAN RACE RIOTS ARE LIKE-
LY. SUCH COMMISSIONS COULD ENLIST COMMUNITY GROUPS IN HUMAN
RELATIONS PROGRAMS AND DEVELOP SOCIAL RESEARCH AND AN EFFEC-
TIVE ADMINISTRATIVE STRUCTURE THROUGH WHICH RACIAL
DISCONTENT CAN BE EXPRESSED WITHOUT VIOLENCE.

1333 LOCKARD D.
"THE CITY MANAGER, ADMINISTRATIVE THEORY AND POLITICAL
POWER."
POLIT. QUART., 77 (JUNE 62), 224-236.
THE BASIC DISTINCTION MADE BETWEEN POLICY FORMULATION OR
POLTICS AND ADMINISTRATION UPON WHICH THE CITY MANAGER
PLAN WAS BASED IS NO LONGER ACCEPTED AS BEING REALISTIC.
YET IT IS IMPORTANT TO REMEMBER IN STUDY THE PLAN THAT
MANAGERS MAY STILL GUIDE THEIR ACTIONS BY THIS DISTINCTION.

1334 LOCKARD D.
THE POLITICS OF STATE AND LOCAL GOVERNMENT.
NEW YORK: MACMILLAN, 1963, LC#63-13569.
COMPREHENSIVE TEXT ON STATE AND LOCAL GOVERNMENT, EMPHA-
SIZING OPERATIONAL DETAILS AND POLITICAL DYNAMICS. CONTENDS
THAT THERE IS AN INTEGRAL RELATIONSHIP BETWEEN POLITICAL
PROCESS AND GOVERNMENTAL PROCESS; ANALYZES INTERRELA-
TIONSHIP OF THE TWO IN TERMS OF THE DYNAMICS OF POLITICAL
PRACTICE. UNANNOTATED BIBLIOGRAPHY OF POST-1950 MATERIAL IS
ARRANGED BY STATES AND CITIES.

1335 LOCKLIN D.P.
ECONOMICS OF TRANSPORTATION (4TH ED.)
HOMEWOOD: RICHARD IRWIN, 1954, 916 PP.
EXTENSIVE ANALYSIS OF ORGANIZATION OF TRANSPORTATION
SYSTEM IN US. BEGINS WITH OVER-ALL LOOK AT VARIOUS MODES OF
TRANSPORTATION; NOTES SIGNIFICANT DIFFERENCES IN THEIR
ORGANIZATION AND DEVELOPMENT. COVERS GOVERNMENTAL CONTROLS,
MAJOR PROBLEMS, FINANCING, AND SERVICES. MAJOR PORTION
DEVOTED TO RAILROADS; INCLUDES HIGHWAY, WATER, AND AIR
TRANSPORTATION. ENDS WITH TRANSPORT COMPETITION.

1336 LOEWENSTEIN K.
POLITICAL POWER AND THE GOVERNMENTAL PROCESS.
CHICAGO: U. CHI. PR., 1957, 442 PP.
DEALS WITH CONCEPT OF POLITICAL POWER IN THEORY AND IN
ACTUAL GOVERNMENTAL USAGE. BASICALLY, A STUDY IN COMPARATIVE
GOVERNMENT BUT COMPARISONS ARE BASED ON CONCEPTS AND
VARIATIONS IN APPLICATION OF THESE CONCEPTS. DISTINGUISHES
BETWEEN CONSTITUTIONALISM, SEPARATION OF POWERS, FEDERALISM,
PLURALISM AND INDIVIDUALISM.

1337 LOEWENSTEIN K.
VERFASSUNGSRECHT UND VERFASSUNGSPRAXIS DER VEREINIGTEN
STAATEN.
BERLIN: SPRINGER VERLAG, 1959, 656 PP.
TRACES US CONSTITUTIONAL HISTORY FROM COLONIAL BEGINNINGS
TO PRESENT AND EXAMINES ROLE OF POLITICAL PARTIES, CONGRESS,
EXECUTIVE, AND COURTS UNDER CONSTITUTION. DISCUSSES BASIC
FREEDOMS AS GUARANTEED BY CONSTITUTION AND BILL OF RIGHTS.

1338 LONG N.E.
"PUBLIC POLICY AND ADMINISTRATION: THE GOALS OF RATIONALITY
AND RESPONSIBILITY."
PUBLIC ADMIN. REV., 14 (WINTER 54), 22-31.
POLICY AND FACT-GATHERING ARE PART OF SAME PROCESS.
SUBORDINATES SHOULD PRESENT AS WIDE A RANGE OF CHOICES AS
POSSIBLE TO THE POLITICAL DECISION-MAKERS: THIS WILL
INCREASE CHANCES OF PUBLIC WILL BEING SERVED BY AN
ADMINISTRATIVE DECISION.

1339 LONG T.G.
"THE ADMINISTRATIVE PROCESS: AGONIZING REAPPRAISAL IN THE
FTC."
G. WASH. LAW REV., 33 (MAR. 65), 671-691.
COMMISSIONER ELMAN'S DRIVE TO MAKE CEASE AND DESIST
ORDERS MORE SPECIFIC HAS RESULTED IN MUCH MORE ACTIVE
INTERST GROUP PARTICIPATION IN FTC DECISION-MAKING.

1340 LOS ANGELES BD CIV SERV COMNRS
ANNUAL REPORT: LOS ANGELES CALIFORNIA: 1919-1936.
LOS ANGELES: L.A. BOARD CIVIL SERV. COMNRS.,1919, 500 PP.
REPORTS OF ACTIVITIES OF BOARD OF COMMISSIONERS TO MAYOR
OF CITY. INCLUDES STATISTICS ON EXAMS HELD, CHARTER
PROVISIONS, ETC.

1341 LOSCHELDER W.
AUSBILDUNG UND AUSLESE DER BEAMTEN.
BADEN-BADEN: VERLAG A LUTZEYER, 1961, 125 PP.
DISCUSSES TRAINING AND RECRUITMENT OF CIVIL SERVANTS IN
WEST GERMANY. EXAMINES CAREER PRINCIPLE, LEGAL REQUIRE-
MENTS, METHODS OF SELECTION, ETC.

1342 LOVEDAY A.
REFLECTIONS ON INTERNATIONAL ADMINISTRATION.
LONDON: OXFORD U. PR., 1956, 334 PP., $7.20.
A DETAILED ANALYSIS OF THE ORGANIZATION AND OPERATION OF
INTERNATIONAL AGENCIES. DISCUSSION OF PERSONNEL POLICY IN
TERMS OF NATURE OF WORK, STANDARDS, MORALE AND RECRUITMENT,
AND ADMINISTRATION FUNCTION IN RELATION TO PROBLEMS OF RE-
SEARCH, BUDGET, FINANCE CONTROL, AND COORDINATION IN ANY
DEALINGS WITH POLITICAL ORGANIZATIONS OF AN INTERNATIONAL
INSTITUTION.

1343 LOVEJOY D.S.
RHODE ISLAND POLITICS AND THE AMERICAN REVOLUTION 1760-1776.
PROVIDENCE: BROWN U PRESS, 1958, 256 PP., LC#58-10478.
ANALYSIS OF ATTITUDE AND POLITICS IN RHODE ISLAND AS ITS
BACKGROUND INFLUENCED REVOLUTIONARY ACTION IN OPPOSITION TO
BRITISH DOMINATION. EXAMINES ECONOMIC ASPECTS AND POLITICAL
STRUCTURE LEADING TO REVOLUTION.

1344 LOW D.A.
"LION RAMPANT."
J. COMMONWEALTH POLIT STUD., 2 (NOV. 64), 235-252.
OUTLINES FACTORS LEADING TO ESTABLISHMENT AND MAINTENANCE
OF BRITISH AUTHORITY OVER ASIAN AND AFRICAN PEOPLES, TRACING
METHODS USED TO PERPETUATE DOMINION.

1345 LOWI T.J. ED.
LEGISLATIVE POLITICS U.S.A.
BOSTON: LITTLE BROWN, 1962, 326 PP., LC#62-14043.
READINGS ON LEGISLATIVE POLITICS, INCLUDING NATURE OF
REPRESENTATIVE GOVERNMENT, USERICAN CONGRESS, POLITICAL PRO-
ESS IN CONGRESS, CONGRESS AS AN INSTRUMENT OF GOVERNMENT,
AND MEANING OF MODERN REPRESENTATIVE GOVERNMENT.

1346 LOWI T.J.
AT THE PLEASURE OF THE MAYOR.
NEW YORK: FREE PRESS OF GLENCOE, 1964, 272 PP., LC#64-11216.
ANALYSIS OF NEW YORK CITY POLITICAL STRUCTURE WITH EMPHA-
SIS ON INTRICACIES OF PATRONAGE. DISCUSSES MANY COMPETING
DEMANDS AND RESPONSIBILITIES MAYOR MUST FACE IN DEALING
WITH MANY HIGHLY ORGANIZED ELEMENTS WITHIN CITY. DISCUSSES
ROLE PLAYED BY INTEREST GROUPS IN POLITICAL APPOINTMENTS AND
DECISION-MAKING. NUMEROUS CHARTS, TABLES, AND DIAGRAMS.

1347 LUCE R.
CONGRESS: AN EXPLANATION.
CAMBRIDGE: HARVARD U PR, 1926, 154 PP.
IN EXAMINING THE ROLE OF CONGRESS IN THE ENACTMENT OF
LEGISLATION, POINTS OUT THAT CONGRESS IS NOT TO ANY MATERIAL
EXTENT AN ORIGINATING BODY. THE SOURCE OF LEGISLATION IS
USUALLY FOUND OUTSIDE CONGRESS, OUR REPRESENTATIVES BEING
MERELY CONDUITS. DEFENDS LAWMAKERS AGAINST CRITICISM LEVIED
UPON THEM.

1348 LUTZ V.
FRENCH PLANNING.
WASHINGTON: AMER ENTERPRISE INST, 1965, 105 PP., LC#65-22084
FINDS IMPOSSIBLE TO ASCERTAIN EFFECT OF FRENCH ECONOMIC
PLANNING ON POSTWAR ECONOMIC GROWTH OR TO DISCOVER WHETHER
PLAN WILL BECOME AN INSTRUMENT OF REGIMENTATION. DESCRIBES
PLAN AS IN AN UNSTABLE POSITION. DETAILS ITS ADMINISTRATIVE
MACHINERY, PREPARATION, OBJECTIVES, OPTIONS, INSTRUMENTS,
AND RECORD OF PAREDICTIVE SUCCESSES.

1349 LYNCH J.
ADMINISTRATION COLONIAL ESPANOLA 1782-1810.
BUENOS AIRES: ED U BUENOS AIRES, 1962, 311 PP.
STUDY OF SPANISH COLONIAL ADMINISTRATION IN ARGENTINE RIO
DE LA PLATA AREA. DEALS WITH GOVERNMENT STRUCTURES IN INDI-
VIDUAL PROVINCES AND SYSTEM USED BY CROWN TO MAINTAIN CON-
TROL OVER ACTIVITIES IN OVERSEAS COLONIES.

1350 LYONS G.M.
"THE NEW CIVIL-MILITARY RELATIONS."
AM. POL. SCI. REV., 55 (MAR. 61), 53-63.
DEFENSE ESTABLISHMENT HAS BECOME POLITICIZED AND MILITARY
TAKES ACTIVE INTEREST IN POLICY FORMULATION.

1351 LYONS G.M., MORTON L.
SCHOOLS FOR STRATEGY* EDUCATION AND RESEARCH IN NATIONAL
SECURITY AFFAIRS.
NEW YORK: FREDERICK PRAEGER, 1965, 356 PP., LC#65-14056.
HISTORY OF THE RESPONSE AMERICA'S EDUCATIONAL ESTABLISH-
MENT HAS MADE TOWARDS CREATING SKILLED CIVILIAN SCHOLARS,
PUBLIC OFFICIALS AND CITIZENRY IN THE FIELD OF NATIONAL SE-
CURITY AFFAIRS. NOTES THE INTERACTION OF GOVERNMENT, FOUNDA-
TIONS, UNIVERSITIES, AND BUSINESS IN FORMING INSTITUTIONS
LIKE RAND, "THE CAMBRIDGE COMPLEX," ET AL FOR THE STUDY OF
COLD WAR PROBLEMS. DESCRIBES PROGRAMS.

1352 ROBINSON R.D.
INTERNATIONAL MANAGEMENT.
NEW YORK: HOLT RINEHART WINSTON, 1967, 178 PP., LC#67-11817.
DESIGNED FOR BASIC MANAGEMENT COURSES, TO PROVIDE THEO-
RETICAL STRUCTURE, RELEVANT DETAILS, AND CASE MATERIAL FOR
FIELD OF INTERNATIONAL MANAGEMENT. CONCERNS STRATEGY AND
INTERRELATIONSHIPS OF MARKETING, SUPPLY LABOR, MANAGEMENT,
OWNERSHIP, FINANCE, LAW, AND CONTROL.

1353 MAASS A.
MUDDY WATERS: THE ARMY ENGINEERS AND THE NATIONS RIVERS.
CAMBRIDGE: HARVARD U PR, 1951, 306 PP.
CASE STUDY OF POWERFUL GROUP, ITS WORKINGS AND RELATIONS
TO EXECUTIVE, LEGISLATIVE ESTABLISHMENTS. ATTEMPTS TO ESTAB-
LISH CRITERIA WHICH WILL BE USEFUL IN DETERMINING EXTENT TO
WHICH ANY ADMINISTRATIVE AGENCY CONDUCTS ITSELF AS A RESPON-
SIBLE INSTRUMENT OF GOVERNMENT.

1354 MAASS A. ED.
AREA AND POWER: A THEORY OF LOCAL GOVERNMENT.
NEW YORK: FREE PRESS OF GLENCOE, 1959, 228 PP., LC#58-12850.
SEVEN ESSAYS ON POLITICAL THOUGHT AND THE DIVISION OF
POWERS. APPLIED AREAL ANALYSIS.

1355 MACDONALD D.
AFRICANA; OR, THE HEART OF HEATHEN AFRICA, VOL. II: MISSION
LIFE.
LONDON: SIMPKIN, MARSHALL, 1882, 371 PP.
HISTORY OF MISSIONARY EFFORT IN "DARKEST AFRICA," WRITTEN
BY A MISSIONARY OF LATE 19TH CENTURY. TRACES DEVELOPMENT
FROM LIVINGSTONE THROUGH BEGINNINGS OF CONTACT WITH SLAVERY.
DEVOTES LARGE PORTION TO PICTURE OF MISSION'S EVERYDAY
LIFE. APPENDIX OF NATIVE TALES.

1356 MACDONALD G.E.
CHECK LIST OF LEGISLATIVE JOURNALS OF THE STATES OF THE
UNITED STATES OF AMERICA.
BOSTON: NATL ASSN OF STATE LIB, 1938, 274 PP.
UNANNOTATED AND VERY BRIEFLY IDENTIFIED LIST OF LEGISLA-
TIVE JOURNALS, BOTH PUBLISHED AND IN MANUSCRIPT FORM, FROM
THE STATES' LEGISLATURES, DATING FROM PRE-ENTRY INTO THE
UNION. GEOGRAPHICALLY ARRANGED.

1357 MACDONALD G.J.F.
"SCIENCE AND SPACE POLICY* HOW DOES IT GET PLANNED?"
BUL. ATOMIC SCIENTISTS, 23 (MAY 67), 2-9.
A DISCUSSION OF THE STRUCTURE OF NASA, THE PROCEDURES
AND PRIORITIES IN PLANNING SPACE PROGRAMS AND FLIGHTS, AND
THE ROLE OF SCIENTISTS IN PLANNING. THE NECESSITY OF LONG-
RANGE PLANNING IS STRESSED, AS IS THE IMPORTANCE OF GREATER
SCIENTIFIC INFLUENCE IN THE SPACE AGENCY.

1358 MACDONALD R.W.
THE LEAGUE OF ARAB STATES: A STUDY IN THE DYNAMICS OF
REGIONAL ORGANIZATION.
PRINCETON: PRINCETON U PRESS, 1965, 407 PP., LC#65-10832.
ANALYZES STRUCTURAL AND OPERATIONAL ASPECTS OF ARAB
LEAGUE INCLUDING TREATIES, BALANCE OF POWER, AND AMERICAN
INVOLVEMENT. INCLUDES BIBLIOGRAPHY CITING DOCUMENTS, BOOKS,
ARTICLES, PERIODICALS, AND NEWSPAPERS CONTAINING MATERIAL ON
SUBJECT. ARRANGED BY NATURE OF SOURCE AND ALPHABETICALLY.
INCLUDES FOREIGN-LANGUAGE MATERIAL.

1359 MACFARQUHAR R. ED.
CHINA UNDER MAO: POLITICS TAKES COMMAND.
CAMBRIDGE: M I T PRESS, 1966, 525 PP., LC#66-25630.
ESSAYS FROM "CHINA QUARTERLY" SINCE 1960 DEAL WITH POLI-
TICS AND ORGANIZATION, ECONOMIC DEVELOPMENT, CULTURE, SO-
CIETY, FOREIGN RELATIONS, AND RECENT CHINESE HISTORY, WITH
ATTENTION TO ABIDING THEORIES AND PRACTICES OF CHINESE
COMMUNISM.

1360 MACHIAVELLI N.
THE ART OF WAR.
LONDON: NUTT, 1905, 249 PP.
CENTERS ATTENTION ON ORIGIN AND STRUCTURE OF ARMY. POINTS
TO NECESSITY OF FORMING NATIONAL ARMY BY CONSCRIPTION. CON-
SIDERS SYSTEM OF MERCENARY FORCES A WASTEFUL FAILURE. CRITI-
CIZES ITALY FOR SEPARATING CIVIL AND MILITARY LIFE.

1362 MACIVER R.M.
THE NATIONS AND THE UN.
NEW YORK: MANHATTAN, 1959, 186 PP.
INSIGHTS PROVIDED ON SUCH TOPICS AS: HOW NATIONAL
INTEREST IS SERVED, STATE POLICIES ARE AFFECTED AND THE
FUTURE OF WORLD ORGANIZATIONS. AUTHOR FEELS THE UNITED
NATIONS IS A NEW FORM OF DIPLOMACY AND ACTS AS THE
GUARDIAN OF DEVELOPING COUNTRIES.

1363 MACK R.T.
RAISING THE WORLDS STANDARD OF LIVING.
NEW YORK: CITADEL, 1953, 285 PP.
DEALS WITH FOREIGN AID PROGRAMS OF POST-WAR PERIOD. DE-
TAILS SEVERAL AID PROGRAMS SUCH AS POINT FOUR AND TECHNICAL
ASSISTANCE CONFERENCE OF THE UN. CITES IRAN AS EXAMPLE.

1364 MACKINTOSH J.M.
JUGGERNAUT.
NEW YORK: MACMILLAN, 1967, 352 PP.
   HISTORY OF THE SOVIET ARMY FROM ITS FOUNDATION IN CIVIL
WAR TO ITS PRESENT STATUS AS ONE OF THE MOST DOMINANT MILI-
TARY FORCES IN THE WORLD. DESCRIBES HOW ITS RECONSTRUCTION
FROM A WEAK ORGANIZATION OCCURRED AND AT WHAT COST. RECOUNTS
ITS BATTLES AND CAMPAIGNS OF WWII, AND DESCRIBES THE ARMY
UNDER THE REGIMES OF STALIN AND KHRUSHCHEV.

1365 MACKINTOSH J.P.
"NIGERIA'S EXTERNAL AFFAIRS."
J. COMMONWEALTH POLIT. STUD., 2 (NOV. 64), 189-206.
   UNDERTAKES A STUDY OF THE HISTORY OF NIGERIA'S RELATIVE
ISOLATIONISM, PRESENTING THE POLITICAL ISSUES FACING
NIGERIA TODAY IN ITS RELATIONS WITH AFRICA AND GREAT
BRITAIN. EVALUATES NIGERIA'S SMALL BUT INCREASING INTEREST
IN FOREIGN AFFAIRS.

1366 MACMAHON A.W.
FEDERAL ADMINISTRATORS: A BIOGRAPHICAL APPROACH TO THE
PROBLEM OF DEPARTMENTAL MANAGEMENT.
NEW YORK: COLUMBIA U PRESS, 1939, 524 PP.
   APPROACHES PROBLEM OF MANAGEMENT IN TERMS OF THE
INDIVIDUALS WHO HOLD HIGH POSITIONS IN NATIONAL DEPARTMENTS.
TREATS EXISTING PERSONNEL AT CENTERS OF THE DEPARTMENTS,
RELATING PERSONAL HISTORIES TO AN ANALYSIS OF UNDERLYING
NECESSITIES OF LEADERSHIP. TRACES OFFICES OF ASSISTANT AND
UNDER-SECRETARY FROM THEIR ESTABLISHMENT, AND SUMMARIZES
CAREERS OF ALL WHO HAVE FILLED THESE POSITIONS.

1367 MACMAHON A.W., MILLETT J.D., OGDEN G.
THE ADMINISTRATION OF FEDERAL WORK RELIEF.
CHICAGO: PUBLIC ADMIN SERVICE, 1941, 407 PP.
   REPORT APPRAISING STRUCTURE AND EFFECTIVENESS OF FEDERAL
WORK RELIEF. TRACES ORIGINS OF WORK PROGRAM, SHOWING HOW
ADMINISTRATIVE PATTERN WAS SET UP. DISCUSSES CENTRAL
MANAGEMENT OF WORKS PROGRAM, AND MANAGEMENT WITHIN THE
WPA. DESCRIBES COLLABORATIVE RELATIONSHIPS IN PROJECT,
EMPLOYMENT, AND FISCAL ADMINISTRATION.

1368 MACMAHON A.W.
"CONGRESSIONAL OVERSIGHT OF ADMINISTRATION: THE POWER OF
THE PURSE."
POLIT. SCI. QUART., 58 (JUNE-SEPT. 43), 161-190, 380-414 .
   STATES CONGRESSIONAL ATTITUDE, EFFECTIVENESS IN CURBING
ADMINISTRATIVE DISCRETION; HOW CONTINUOUS INTERVENTION IS
ESSAYED; COMMITTEE SYSTEM AND HOW SEPARATION OF LEGISLATION-
AUTHORIZATION FROM YEARLY APPROPRIATION HAS WORKED; HOW AP-
PROPRIATIONS SUBCOMMITTEES, STAFFS, HEARINGS, REPORTS, AND
INTERACTION WITH ADMINISTRATORS ARE ALL IMPORTANT. CONCLUDES
THAT APPROPRIATIONS COMMITTEE IS TOO FRACTIONALIZED.

1369 MACMAHON A.W.
ADMINISTRATION IN FOREIGN AFFAIRS.
UNIVERSITY, ALA: U. PR., 1953, 275 PP.
   DISCUSSES ADMINISTRATIVE PROCESS EMPLOYED BY US GOVERN-
MENT IN THE FORMULATION AND EXECUTION OF ITS FOREIGN POLICY.
ARGUES THAT ADMINISTRATION'S GOALS DETERMINE ITS STRUCTURE.
DEMONSTRATES THIS BY SHOWING POST-WAR STRUCTURAL CHANGES IN
THE STATE DEPARTMENT TO BE RELATED TO NEW FOREIGN POLICY
PROGRAM AIMS.

1370 MACMAHON A.W. ED.
FEDERALISM: MATURE AND EMERGENT.
GARDEN CITY: DOUBLEDAY, 1955, 557 PP.
   REVIEWS NATURE AND ROLE OF FEDERALISM IN THE MODERN ERA.
EXAMINES THE MECHANISMS PROVIDING FOR CONTROLS AND BALANCES
IN FEDERALIST SYSTEMS. PROBES THE COMPLEX INTERACTION AMONG
GOVERNMENTAL LEVELS IN TREATING NATIONAL PROBLEMS WITHIN
FEDERAL FRAMEWORK. NOTES THE APPLICABILITY OF FEDERALIST
PRINCIPLES TO FORMATIONS IN THE POLITICAL COMMUNITY OF
WESTERN EUROPE.

1371 MACMAHON A.W.
"WOODROW WILSON AS LEGISLATIVE LEADER AND ADMINISTRATOR."
AM. POL. SCI. REV., 50 (SEPT. 56), 641-675.
   PORTRAYAL OF WILSON'S LEGISLATIVE LEADERSHIP AND ADMIN-
ISTRATIVE METHODS BASED ON POSTHUMOUSLY PUBLISHED MEMOIRS.
EMPHASIZES DOMESTIC POLICY.

1372 MACMAHON A.W.
ADMINISTRATION AND FOREIGN POLICY (PAMPHLET)
URBANA: U OF ILL, INST OF GOVT, 1957, 24 PP.
   TREATS RELATIONSHIP BETWEEN ADMINISTRATIVE STRUCTURE AND
SUBSTANTIVE CONTENT OF FOREIGN POLICY. INCLUDES STRUCTURES
AND METHODS OF COORDINATION - NATIONAL SECURITY COUNCIL,
OPERATIONS COORDINATING BOARD.

1373 MACMAHON A.W.
DELEGATION AND AUTONOMY.
BOMBAY: ASIA PUBL HOUSE, 1961, 170 PP.
   DISCUSSES USES AND LIMITS OF AUTONOMOUS ELEMENTS IN MOD-
ERN ADMINISTRATION WITH EMPHASIS ON ECONOMIC REGULATION
AND COMPATIBILITY BETWEEN THESE ELEMENTS AND INTEGRATIVE
IDEALS OF PUBLIC ADMINISTRATION. CONSIDERS PROBLEMS OF

STRUCTURE AND RELATIONSHIPS ARISING FROM DIRECT CONTACT
BETWEEN GOVERNMENT AND MARKETPLACE.

1374 MACNEIL N.
FORGE OF DEMOCRACY: THE HOUSE OF REPRESENTATIVES.
NEW YORK: DAVID MCKAY, 1963, 496 PP., LC#63-11721.
   ATTEMPT TO DEFINE HOUSE OF REPRESENTATIVES. PORTRAYS IT
AS A LIVING POLITICAL ONSTITUTION. VIEWS HOUSE AS SUM TOTAL
OF ITS LEGAL POWERS, ITS 435 MEMBERS, AND ITS PAST AND TRA-
DITIONS. IN WRITING A HISTORY OF THE HOUSE, THE AUTHOR DRAWS
ON DIRECT OBSERVATION AS WELL AS PAST HISTORIES. CONCLUDES
THAT HOUSE HAS REMAINED THE REPRESENTATIVE OF THE PEOPLE,
DEPOSITORY OF THEIR POWER, AND THE IMAGE OF THEIR WISDOM.

1375 MACPHERSON C.
"TECHNICAL CHANGE AND POLITICAL DECISION."
INT. SOC. SCI. J., 12 (1960), 357-405.
   OUTLINES THE RATIONALIZATION OF METHODS AND MEANS OF
ACTION IN PUBLIC ADMINISTRATION, SHOWING EFFECTS OF TECH-
NICAL INNOVATIONS ON THE RELATIONSHIP BETWEEN CENTRAL AND
LOCAL AUTHORITIES. EVALUATES RECRUITMENT AND TRAINING OF
CIVIL SERVANTS.

1376 MACRIDIS R.C., BROWN B.E.
COMPARATIVE POLITICS: NOTES AND READINGS.
NEW YORK: PRENTICE HALL, 577 PP., $5.25.
   COMPENDIUM OF NOTES AND READINGS FROM COMPARATIVE, CROSS-
CULTURAL POINT OF VIEW. INDICATES PROGRESS MADE BY POLITICAL
SCIENCE TOWARDS CONCEPTUALIZING FIELD THAT WAS FOREIGN, NOT
COMPARATIVE GOVERNMENT. READINGS EMPHASIZE GENERAL THEORY
GROUPS, PARTIES, IDEOLOGIES, CONSTITUTIONS, DECISIONS, AD-
MINISTRATION, LEGITIMACY, REVOLUTION, AND STABILITY.

1377 MAHAR J.M.
INDIA: A CRITICAL BIBLIOGRAPHY.
TUCSON: U OF ARIZONA PR, 1964, 119 PP., LC#64-17992.
   LIST OF 2023 TITLES, MOSTLY BOOKS WITH FEW FOREIGN-LAN-
GUAGE SOURCES. ARRANGED BY TOPIC IN DETAIL; PUBLICA-
TIONS SINCE 1940 GIVEN GREATEST ATTENTION.

1378 MAHESHWARI B.
STUDIES IN PANCHAYATI RAJ.
NEW DELHI: METROPOLITAN BOOK, 1963, 196 PP.
   STUDY OF RURAL GOVERNMENT IN INDIA SINCE 1959 IN SYSTEM
OF DEMOCRATIC DECENTRALIZATION CALLED PANCHAYATI RAJ. EXAM-
INES EFFECTIVENESS OF LOCAL GOVERNMENT AND HOW IT FUNCTIONS.

1379 MAIER N.R.F.
PRINCIPLES OF HUMAN RELATIONS.
NEW YORK: WILEY, 1952, 474 PP.
   DISCUSSES PROBLEM OF OVERCOMING COMMUNICATION BARRIERS,
PREVENTING MISUNDERSTANDINGS AND DEVELOPING CONSTRUCTIVE
NATURE OF MAN IN THE FIELD OF HUMAN RELATIONS. PRESENTS
SPECIFIC EXAMPLES PERTAINING TO INDUSTRY, BUT APPLIES PRIN-
CIPLES TO ALL SITUATIONS CONCERNED WITH A LEADER-GROUP OR A
LEADER-INDIVIDUAL RELATIONSHIP.

1380 MAILICK S. ED., VAN NESS E.H. ED.
CONCEPTS AND ISSUES IN ADMINISTRATIVE BEHAVIOR.
ENGLEWOOD CLIFFS: PRENTICE HALL, 1962, 201 PP., LC#62-12845.
   COLLECTION OF PAPERS CONCENTRATING ON DECISION-MAKING AND
ROLES OF EXECUTIVES IN ADMINISTRATIVE ORGANIZATIONS.
DISCUSSES INTERPERSONAL AND STRUCTURAL FUNCTIONS WITHIN
BUSINESS, GOVERNMENT, EDUCATIONAL AND OTHER TYPES OF
ORGANIZATIONS.

1381 MAINZER L.C.
"INJUSTICE AND BUREAUCRACY."
YALE REV., 51 (SUMMER 62), 559-573.
   EXAMINES TWO QUESTIONS: IS INJUSTICE LIKELY WITHIN BU-
REAUCRACY? HOW CAN ONE RESPOND TO INJUSTICE WITHIN BUREAU-
CRACY? SEEN AS RELATIONSHIP BETWEEN RULER AND RULED. THE
SUBORDINATE IS ALWAYS SUBJECT TO DICTATE OF HIS SUPERIOR,
WHO MUST HIMSELF COMPLY TO RULES OF THE ORGANIZATION. THAT
INJUSTICE EXISTS IS ADMITTED. DIFFERENT FORMS OF RESIGNA-
TION TO THIS FACT ARE DISCUSSED.

1382 MAINZER L.C.
"HONOR IN THE BUREAUCRATIC LIFE."
REV. OF POLITICS, 26 (JAN. 67), 70-90.
   BUREAUCRATIC PROCEDURES AND ORGANIZATION GIVE MEN LITTLE
OPPORTUNITY TO ACHIEVE A SENSE OF HONOR, WHICH IS
NECESSARY FOR THE MAINTENANCE OF EFFICIENT, RESPONSIBLE
GOVERNMENT OPERATIONS.

1383 MAIR L.P.
"REPRESENTATIVE LOCAL GOVERNMENT AS A PROBLEM IN
SOCIAL CHANGE."
J. AFR. ADMIN., 10 (JAN. 58), 11-24.
   DISCUSSION OF PROBLEMS WHICH FACE THE DEVELOPMENT OF
REPRESENTATIVE GOVERNMENT IN NEWLY INDEPENDENT, ECONOMICALLY
UNDER-DEVELOPED NATIONS, ESPECIALLY THOSE IN AFRICA. AUTHOR
PARTICULARLY CONCERNED WITH NATURE OF THE TRADITIONAL RULING
CLASS AND THE FUNCTIONING OF EMERGENT POLITICAL ELITES.

1384 MAJUMDAR B.B. ED.

PROBLEMS OF PUBLIC ADMINISTRATION IN INDIA.
BANKIPORE: BHARATI BHAWAN, 1953, 310 PP.
   SCHOLARS' VIEWS ON ADMINISTRATION IN INDIA AND PUBLIC
PLANNING, PUBLIC CORPORATIONS AND GOVERNMENT CONTROL, EXEC-
UTIVES IN CIVIL SERVICE, JUDICIAL ADMINISTRATION, AND LOCAL
ADMINISTRATION AND FINANCE.

1385 MALINOWSKI W.R.
"CENTRALIZATION AND DE-CENTRALIZATION IN THE UNITED
NATIONS' ECONOMIC AND SOCIAL ACTIVITIES."
INT. ORGAN., 16 (SUMMER 62), 521-541.
   ALTHOUGH U.N. ORGANIZED AS CENTRALIZED UNIT, THE JOINING
TO THE PARENT GROUP OF REGIONAL SYSTEMS DEVOID OF
RESPONSIBILITY, SOON BROKE THIS DOWN. REGIONAL STAFFS OFTEN
ACT INDEPENDENTLY OF SECRETARY-GENERAL IN SPECIALIZED AREAS
WITH WHICH THEY ARE MOST FAMILIAR THEREBY CRIPPLING UTILITY.

1386 MANGIN G.
"LES ACCORDS DE COOPERATION EN MATIERE DE JUSTICE ENTRE LA
FRANCE ET LES ETATS AFRICAINS ET MALGACHE."
REV. JURID. POLIT. OUTREMER, 16 (JULY-SEPT. 62), 339-64.
   IDENTIFIES AGREEMENTS BETWEEN FRANCE AND AFRICAN STATES
ON PROBLEMS OF JUSTICE, TRANSITIONAL DISPOSITION OF JUDICIAL
PERSONNEL. TREATS FRENCH EFFECT ON AFRICAN EVOLUTION. IN-
CLUDES LIST OF ARTICLES DEALING WITH CIVIL AND CRIMINAL LAW.

1387 MANGIN G.
"L'ORGANIZATION JUDICIAIRE DES ETATS D'AFRIQUE ET DE
MADAGASCAR."
REV. JURID. POLIT. OUTREMER, 16 (JAN.-MARCH 62), 77-134.
   DESCRIBES JUDICIAL ORGANIZATION IN DEVELOPING AFRICAN
COUNTRIES, CLARIFYING DIFFERENCES AND COMMON FEATURES.
STUDIES STRUCTURE OF TRIBUNALS AND EXTENT OF POWER. CON-
CLUDES WITH STUDY OF SUPREME COURTS.

1388 MANGONE G.
"THE IDEA AND PRACTICE OF WORLD GOVERNMENT."
NEW YORK: COLUMB. U. PR., 1951, 278 PP.
   ENUMERATES VARIOUS FORMS PREFERABLE FOR WORLD GOV-
ERNMENT. DESCRIBES PROBABLE SUBSEQUENT ECONOMIC AND SPIRITU-
AL PROGRESS. DENOTES PLACE OF JUSTICE AND INTERNATIONAL LAW
IN NEW WORLD ORGANIZATION.

1389 MANGONE G.
A SHORT HISTORY OF INTERNATIONAL ORGANIZATION.
NEW YORK: MCGRAW-HILL, 1954, 326 PP.
   HISTORICALLY TRACES DEVELOPMENT OF INTERNATIONAL ORGANIZ-
ATIONS FROM NAPOLEONIC ERA TO THE UN. DISCUSSES INCEPTION
AND GROWTH OF INTERNATIONAL LAW.

1390 MANGONE G.
"THE UNITED NATIONS AND UNITED STATES FOREIGN POLICY."
TEXAS QUART., 6 (SPRING 63), 11-18.
   CRITICIZES CHANGING CHARACTER OF UN. SAYS UN HAS EXCEEDED
ORIGINAL POWERS AND HAS SPENT EXCESSIVE AMOUNTS. USA DE-
FENSE POLICY AND ECONOMIC ASSISTANCE PROGRAMS ARE INDEPEN-
DENT OF UN. REFUTES CHARGES OF UN IRRESPONSIBILITY. HOLDS UN
NOT COUNTER TO VITAL USA INTERESTS.

1391 MANGONE G.J.
UN ADMINISTRATION OF ECONOMIC AND AOCIAL PROGRAMS.
NEW YORK: COLUMBIA U PRESS, 1966, 291 PP., LC#66-20490.
   COLLECTION OF ESSAYS ON PROGRAMMING, IMPLEMENTATION, AND
ADMINISTRATION OF UN ECONOMIC AND SOCIAL ACTIVITIES. DIS-
CUSSES FUNCTION OF SECRETARIAT, BUDGETARY COORDINATION BY
GENERAL ASSEMBLY, FIELD ADMINISTRATION, AND TASK OF RE-
GIONAL COMMISSIONS.

1392 MANNE H.G.
"OUR TWO CORPORATION SYSTEMS* LAW AND ECONOMICS."
VIRGINIA LAW REV., 53 (MAR.67), 259-284.
   DEVELOPMENT OF AMERICAN CORPORATIONS IN 19TH CENTURY BE-
CAUSE ENTREPRENEURS NEEDED SOME DEVICE TO RAISE CAPITAL
FROM A RELATIVELY LARGE NUMBER OF INVESTORS. CONCEPT OF
LIMITED LIABILITY DISCUSSED. INTERRELATION BETWEEN LAW AND
BUSINESS TRACED AND DEVELOPED. MANAGEMENT OR "BOARD OF DI-
RECTORS" AND SHAREHOLDERS' RIGHTS AND DUTIES ARE DISCUSSED.
INTERESTS OF THE CLOSED CORPORATION ARE MAINLY UNCHALLENGED.

1393 MANNHEIM K.
FREEDOM, POWER, AND DEMOCRATIC PLANNING.
NEW YORK: OXFORD U. PR., 1950, 313 PP.
   OUTLINES PRINCIPLES OF A SOCIETY THAT IS PLANNED YET
DEMOCRATIC. END OF LAISSEZ-FAIRE ERA HAS SIGNALLED NEED FOR
REAL PLANNING CONSISTING OF THE CO-ORDINATION OF
INSTITUTIONS, EDUCATION, VALUATIONS AND PSYCHOLOGY.

1394 MANNONI D.O.
PROSPERO AND CALIBAN: THE PSYCHOLOGY OF COLONIZATION.
NEW YORK: PRAEGER, 1956, 218 PP.
   EXPLORES PSYCHOLOGICAL ATTITUDES OF MALAGASY NATIVES AS
MANIFESTED IN FAMILY, RELIGION, MORES, AND TRADITIONS. ANA-
LYZES REACTION TO EUROPEAN CULTURE AND TO INDEPENDENCE. ALSO
STUDIES EUROPEAN REACTION TO MALAGASY CULTURE.

1395 MANSFIELD E., WEIN H.H.
"A STUDY OF DECISION-MAKING WITHIN THE FIRM."
J. ABNORMAL SOC. PSYCH., 72 (NOV. 58), 515-536.
   AUTHOR EXPLAINS SOME DECISIONS OF A MANAGER AT AN INTER-
MEDIATE LEVEL IN A RAILROAD AND LINKS THESE DECISIONS TO THE
SHORT-RUN FLUCTUATIONS IN OUTPUT AND COST OF INDIVIDUAL
FREIGHT YARDS. CONTAINS INTRODUCTORY MATERIAL CONCERNING
FREIGHT YARDS, DESCRIPTION OF THE MODEL, AND TEST OF THE
MODEL.

1396 MANSFIELD E. ED.
MANAGERIAL ECONOMICS AND OPERATIONS RESEARCH; A
NONMATHEMATICAL INTRODUCTION.
NEW YORK: W W NORTON, 1966, 244 PP., LC#65-23036.
   ANALYZES THE DECISION-MAKING PROCESS IN INDUSTRIAL ORGAN-
IZATIONS, EMPHASIZING NECESSITY OF SCIENTIFIC METHODS.
INCLUDES STUDY OF CONCEPTS, TECHNIQUES, AND PROBLEMS IN MAN-
AGERIAL ECONOMICS, I.E., PROFITS, PRICE, DEMAND, CAPITAL,
AND FORECASTING. ALSO INTRODUCES TECHNIQUES OF OPERATIONS
RESEARCH, SUCH AS PROGRAM SCHEDULING, LINEAR PROGRAMMING,
GAME THEORY, AND ROLE OF COMPUTER IN INDUSTRIAL MANAGEMENT.

1397 MARCH J.G., SIMON H.A., GUETZKOW H.
ORGANIZATIONS.
NEW YORK: JOHN WILEY, 1958, 262 PP., LC#58-13464.
   STUDY OF THEORY OF ORGANIZATIONS AND ORGANIZATIONAL BE-
HAVIOR. INCLUDES MOTIVATIONAL RESTRAINTS IN INTRA-
ORGANIZATIONAL DECISIONS AND DECISIONS TO PARTICIPATE; CON-
FLICT IN ORGANIZATION; COGNITIVE LIMITS ON RATIONALITY;
PLANNING AND INNOVATION IN ORGANIZATIONS. EXTENSIVE SELECT-
ED BIBLIOGRAPHY.

1398 MARGOLIS J.
"ON MUNICIPAL LAND POLICY FOR FISCAL GAINS."
NATIONAL TAX J., 9 (SEPT. 56), 247-257.
   STATES THAT A RECENT LAND-USE POLICY OF CITIES HAS BEEN
THE ENCOURAGEMENT OF SPECIFIC USES IN ORDER TO IMPROVE
FISCAL CONDITION OF LOCAL GOVERNMENT. EVALUATES THIS PROGRAM
FROM ASPECT OF ITS GOALS, EFFECTIVENESS OF THE POLICY, AND
LEVEL OF SCIENTIFIC KNOWLEDGE AND MANAGERIAL ABILITIES
NECESSARY TO USE POLICIES EFFECTIVELY. EMPHASIZES PROBLEM OF
ALLOCATION OF PUBLIC COSTS AMONG TYPES OF LAND USES.

1399 MARKMANN C.L., SHERWIN M.
JOHN F. KENNEDY: A SENSE OF PURPOSE.
NEW YORK: ST MARTIN'S PRESS, 1961, 346 PP., LC#61-13380.
   ANALYSIS OF EVENTS, ACTIVITIES, AND PERSONALITIES
CONNECTED WITH JOHN KENNEDY BEFORE AND DURING HIS FIRST
YEAR IN OFFICE. AUTHORS WERE ENTHUSIASTIC ABOUT THE
POSSIBILITIES OF THE NEW, ENERGETIC PRESIDENT.

1400 MARKSHAK J.
"ECONOMIC PLANNING AND THE COST OF THINKING."
SOCIAL RESEARCH, 33 (SUMMER 66), 151-159.
   CENTRALIZATION, OR ECONOMIC PLANNING, HAS AN ADVANTAGE
OVER THE DECENTRALIZED MARKET SYSTEM, IN THAT ALL INFORMA-
TION AS TO NEEDS OF THE SOCIETY IS COLLECTED FROM ALL
SOURCES BEFORE PRODUCTION IS BEGUN. THE COST OF THIS CEN-
TRALIZATION IS, A LOSS OF LIBERTY, INCENTIVES, AND LOWERED
UTILITY TO ALMOST ALL CITIZENS.

1401 MARRIS P., REIN M.
DILEMMAS OF SOCIAL REFORM: POVERTY AND COMMUNITY ACTION IN
THE UNITED STATES.
NEW YORK: ATHERTON PRESS, 1967, 248 PP., LC#67-17146.
   DISCUSSION OF THE PROBLEMS SOCIAL REFORM FACES IN US.
PHASIS IS ON STRATEGIES OF REFORM, ADMINISTRATIVE-POLITICAL
CONFLICT, BUREAUCRATIC IMPEDIMENTS, AND EXISTENT POVERTY
PROGRAM. MOST STRESS IS ON PRACTICAL ASPECTS AND OVER-ALL
ACHIEVEMENTS OF OBJECTIVES. CONCLUDES THAT NO REFORM
MOVEMENT IN US CAN SUPPLANT CONFLICTS OF INTEREST FROM WHICH
POLICY EVOLVED.

1402 MARRIS R.
THE ECONOMIC THEORY OF "MANAGERIAL" CAPITALISM.
NEW YORK: FREE PRESS OF GLENCOE, 1964, 346 PP., LC#64-10371.
   STUDIES SEPARATION OF MANAGEMENT CONTROL FROM OWNERSHIP
IN FIRMS, INCLUDING INSTITUTIONAL FRAMEWORK, SUPPLY AND
DEMAND, AND BEHAVIOR AND EVIDENCE. BIBLIOGRAPHY OF ENGLISH
BOOKS AND ARTICLES, LISTED ALPHABETICALLY BY AUTHOR, 1932-
1962; 125 ENTRIES.

1403 MARS D.
SUGGESTED LIBRARY IN PUBLIC ADMINISTRATION.
LOS ANGELES: U OF S CAL, PUB ADM, 1962, 133 PP.
   INDEXED BIBLIOGRAPHY ON PUBLIC ADMINISTRATION AIMS AT
SELECTING MOST IMPORTANT WORKS IN THIS FIELD. ALSO INCLUDES
PERIODICALS DEALING WITH PUBLIC ADMINISTRATION AND MANAGE-
MENT. AN OUTGROWTH OF THE BERKELY BRAZIL PROJECT DESIGNED
PRIMARILY FOR OVERSEAS LIBRARIES.

1404 MARSH D.C.
THE FUTURE OF THE WELFARE STATE.
BALTIMORE: PENGUIN BOOKS, 1964, 140 PP.
   EXAMINES ASSUMPTIONS ON WHICH BRITISH SOCIAL POLICIES ARE
BASED, WAYS BRITAIN HAS ATTEMPTED TO ACHIEVE POST-WWII AIMS,
AND APPLICABILITY OF TITLE "WELFARE STATE." ARGUES THAT

WELFARE STATE MUST SERVE NEEDS OF CITIZENS AND THAT 20TH-
CENTURY CONCEPT HAS BEEN RESTRAINED BY 19TH-CENTURY SYSTEM
OF ADMINISTRATION. WARNS THAT LARGEST DANGER IS IN INERTIA
OF MACHINE ITSELF AND ADVOCATES REMODELING.

1405 MARSH J.F. JR.
THE FBI RETIREMENT BILL (PAMPHLET)
INDIANAPOLIS: BOBBS-MERRILL, 1949, 26 PP.
     CASE STUDY OF FBI RETIREMENT BILL. ILLUMINATES
CONTROVERSY BETWEEN FBI AND BUDGET BUREAU. CONTRASTS
SMOOTH FUNCTIONING OF EXECUTIVE-LEGISLATIVE RELATIONS WITH
DIFFICULTIES OF EXECUTIVE POLICY COORDINATION.

1406 MARSH R.M.
THE MANDARINS: THE CIRCULATION OF ELITES IN CHINA, 1600-1900
NEW YORK: FREE PRESS OF GLENCOE, 1961, 300 PP., LC#60-10899.
     STUDY OF "OPEN-CLASS" VALUES IN CH'ING PERIOD OF TRADI-
TIONAL CHINA TO DETERMINE EXTENT USED IN RECRUITMENT AND
PROMOTION OF OFFICIALS. ALSO EXPLAINS OFFICIALS' CAREER
PATTERNS BY SOCIOLOGICAL THEORY. BIBLIOGRAPHY LISTS ITEMS IN
BOTH CHINESE AND ENGLISH.

1407 MARSH R.M.
"FORMAL ORGANIZATION AND PROMOTION IN A PRE-INDUSTRIAL
SOCIETY" (BMR)"
AMER. SOCIOLOGICAL REV., 26 (AUG. 61), 547-556.
     AN ANALYSIS OF FORMAL ORGANIZATION IN HISTORICAL EMPIRES
AND STATES. FOCUSES ON PROBLEM OF DETERMINANTS OF
ADVANCEMENT IN 19TH-CENTURY CHINESE IMPERIAL BUREAUCRACY.
ANALYSIS IS BASED ON WEBER'S WORK AND ENLARGES HIS ANALYSIS.
AUTHOR CONTENDS THAT IN 19TH-CENTURY CHINA, ADVANCEMENT WAS
DETERMINED SOMEWHAT MORE BY EXTRA-BUREAUCRATIC THAN BY
BUREAUCRATIC FACTORS.

1408 MARSHALL A.H.
FINANCIAL ADMINISTRATION IN LOCAL GOVERNMENT.
LONDON: ALLEN & UNWIN, 1960, 391 PP.
     DISCUSSES INTERNAL ORGANIZATION AND PRINCIPLES OF FINAN-
CIAL ADMINISTRATION IN LOCAL GOVERNMENTS IN ENGLAND. EXAM-
INES BUDGETARY PROCEDURES, COLLECTION OF INCOME, ROLE OF
COUNTY, TOWN, OR DISTRICT COUNCIL CLERK, AND ROLE OF CHIEF
FINANCIAL OFFICER.

1409 MARSHALL G.
"POLICE RESPONSIBILITY."
PUBLIC ADMINISTRATION, 38 (FALL 60), 213-226.
     LOCAL POLICE OFFICIALS HAVE BOTH ADMINISTRATIVE AND
QUASI-JUDICIAL FUNCTIONS. TO PRESERVE REPRESENTATIVE
GOVERNMENT POLICE SHOULD BE FULLY RESPONSIBLE FOR
ADMINISTRATIVE FUNCTIONS TO AN ELECTED BODY.

1410 MARTIN L.W.
"POLITICAL SETTLEMENTS AND ARMS CONTROL."
CURR. HIST., 42 (MAY 62), 296-301.
     IF GENERAL DISARMAMENT REALIZED, THE COLD WAR AND REST OF
DISPUTES WOULD PERSIST: BELIEF IN COMPROMISE IS AN INTEL
LECTUAL HANGOVER. PEACEFUL CO-EXISTENCE IS MERELY NAME FOR
ANOTHER TYPE OF CONFLICT. POLITICAL SETTLEMENTS MAINTAINED
BETWEEN HOSTILE STATES BY BALANCE OF INTERESTS AND POWER.
QUESTIONS HOW EQUILIBRIUM CAN BE SUSTAINED BUT DOES
NOT MINIMIZE VALUE OF SETTLEMENT PROPOSALS.

1411 MARTIN L.W.
DIPLOMACY IN MODERN EUROPEAN HISTORY.
NEW YORK: MACMILLAN, 1966, 138 PP., LC#66-17387.
     ESSAYS DISCUSSING CENTRAL IMPORTANCE OF DIPLOMACY IN
WESTERN EUROPEAN POLITICAL RELATIONS FROM TIME OF ITS ORI-
GIN IN 15TH-CENTURY ITALY TO ITS MODIFICATIONS AND REFINE-
MENTS IN COLD WAR ERA. TOPICS ARE BROAD IN SCOPE AND ORIEN-
TATION IS SCHOLARLY AND TECHNICAL. EMPHASIS IS ON SOCIAL,
HISTORICAL, AND POLITICAL FACTORS.

1412 MARTIN R. ED.
PUBLIC ADMINISTRATION AND DEMOCRACY.
SYRACUSE: SYRACUSE U PRESS, 1965, 355 PP., LC#65-24509.
     COLLECTION OF ARTICLES DISCUSSING THE POTENTIAL OF
BUREAUCRATIC ORGANIZATIONS TO SERVE THE PUBLIC INTEREST.
TOPICS DISCUSSED ARE DECISION-MAKING, REPRESENTATION OF
INTEREST GROUPS AND THE PUBLIC, ORGANIZATION, CULTURAL
INFLUENCES.

1413 MARTIN R.C.
"ADMINISTRATIVE LEADERSHIP IN GOVERNMENT."
PUBLIC ADMINISTRATION, 33 (FALL 55), 277-285.
     DISCUSSION OF PERSONAL SKILLS AND QUALIFICATIONS NEEDED
ON ALL LEVELS OF FEDERAL SERVICE. FOR ADMINISTRATION TO
FURTHER DEMOCRACY, EXECUTIVES MUST BE CONSCIOUSLY COMMITTED
TO IT AS AN IDEOLOGY.

1414 MARTIN R.C.
GOVERNMENT AND THE SUBURBAN SCHOOL.
SYRACUSE: SYRACUSE U PRESS, 1962, 115 PP., LC#62-19365.
     STUDY OF SUBURBAN SCHOOL SYSTEM AND ITS PECULIARITIES OF
ENVIRONMENT, FINANCES, ADMINISTRATION. SPECIAL EMPHASIS ON
PROBLEM OF INDEPENDENCE AND ISOLATION OF ESSENTIALLY DEPEND-
ENT INSTITUTION, AND DIFFICULTIES OF FUTURE.

1415 MARTIN W.O. JR. ED.
STATE OF LOUISIANA OFFICIAL PUBLICATIONS.
BATON ROUGE: T G MORGAN'S SONS, INC.
     CHECKLIST OF OFFICIAL LITERATURE COMPILED AND PUBLISHED
SEMI-ANNUALLY SINCE 1948. MATERIAL PRIOR TO 1948 IS COVERED
IN "BIBLIOGRAPHY OF THE OFFICIAL PUBLICATIONS OF LOUISIANA,
1803-1934" AND A SUPPLEMENTARY BIBLIOGRAPHY FOR YEARS
1935-48. LIST IS ARRANGED ALPHABETICALLY BY DIRECT CORPOR-
ATE FORM OF ENTRY. EACH CUMULATION IS COMPILED AND EDITED
BY SEPARATE AUTHORS.

1416 MARVICK D. ED.
POLITICAL DECISION-MAKERS.
NEW YORK: FREE PRESS, 1961, 347 PP.
     SERIES OF ESSAYS DISCUSSING POLITICAL LEADERS OF FRANCE,
INDIA, BRITAIN, GERMANY AND AMERICA. ANALYZES THEIR SOCIAL,
ECONOMIC AND EDUCATIONAL BACKGROUNDS AS WELL AS MOTIVATING
INFLUENCES DETERMINING THEIR ENTRANCE INTO POLITICS. CON-
CLUDES WITH AN OVER-ALL SURVEY OF THE STUDY OF POLITICAL
ELITES AND A REVIEW OF THE PSYCHO-ANALYTIC METHOD OF THE
STUDY OF POLITICAL PERSONALITIES.

1417 MARX C.M.
"ADMINISTRATIVE ETHICS AND THE RULE OF LAW."
AM. POL. SCI. REV., 43 (DEC. 49), 1119-1144.
     EXPLORES INTERPLAY OF ADMINISTRATIVE ETHICS AND ADMINIS-
TRATIVE LAW TO UNDERSTAND DIFFERENCE IN OUTLOOK BETWEEN AN
OFFICIAL CHARGED WITH EXECUTION OF PUBLIC POLICY AND A JUDGE
ENFORCING LEGAL RESTRAINTS. REJECTS EFFICIENCY AS AN ETHICAL
NORM; SEES AS CRITERION THE CONFORMITY BETWEEN ADMINISTRA-
TION AND THE FUNDAMENTAL VALUES OF THE POLITICAL ORDER.

1418 MARX F.M.
"POLICY FORMULATION AND THE ADMINISTRATIVE PROCESS"
AM. POL. SCI. REV., 33 (FEB. 39), 55-60.
     CONSIDERATION OF PUBLIC PERSONNEL PROBLEMS AND ADMINIS-
TRATIVE LEADERSHIP WITHIN CIVIL SERVICE. DESIGNATES CERTAIN
GROUPS AS "POLICY-DETERMINING" AND, BY PLACING THEM UNDER
SEPARATE RULES, DIFFERENTIATES THEIR STATUS FROM THE BODY OF
CIVIL SERVANTS.

1419 MARX F.M.
THE PRESIDENT AND HIS STAFF SERVICES PUBLIC ADMINISTRATION
SERVICES NUMBER 98 (PAMPHLET)
CHICAGO: PUBLIC ADMIN SERVICE, 1947, 26 PP.
     DEFINES OFFICE OF PRESIDENT IN TERMS OF ITS
CONSTITUTIONAL STRUCTURE AND THE LEGISLATION WHICH HAS
EXPANDED ITS POWERS. DISCUSSES THE VARIOUS AGENCIES
DIRECTLY RESPONSIBLE TO THE PRESIDENT AND HOW THEY INCREASE
HIS POWER. IS DESIGNED TO ACQUAINT THE FOREIGN READER
WITH THE EXECUTIVE BRANCH.

1420 MARX F.M.
"SIGNIFICANCE FOR THE ADMINISTRATIVE PROCESS."
AM. POL. SCI. REV., 41 (AUG. 47), 733-743.
     DISCUSSES NEED FOR FACTS IN GOVERNMENTAL ACTION AND ROLE
OF INVESTIGATIVE FUNCTION IN MEETING THIS NEED, OPERATION OF
INVESTIGATIVE POWER IN RELATION TO ADMINISTRATIVE RESPON-
SIBILITY AND ITS OPERATION IN RELATION TO LEGISLATIVE RES-
PONSIBILITY.

1421 MARX K., ENGELS F.
THE COMMUNIST MANIFESTO.
IN (MENDEL A. ESSENTIAL WORKS OF MARXISM, NEW YORK: BANTAM.
BOOKS, 1961, CHAPTER 1, PAGES 13-44).
     SETS FORTH THE DOCTRINE OF CLASS STRUGGLE BETWEEN THE RU-
LING BOURGEOISIE AND THE PROLETARIAT, AND DESCRIBES HOW THE
LATTER WILL RISE UP AND CONQUER ITS OPPRESSORS. UNTIL THE
COMPLETE SUPPRESSION OF THE BOURGEOISIE, THE DICTATORSHIP OF
THE PROLETARIAT WOULD PREVAIL. EVENTUALLY, IT WOULD WITHER
AWAY, ALONG WITH THE STATE, A CLASSLESS SOCIETY EMERGING.

1422 MASLAND J.W.
"THE NATIONAL WAR COLLEGE AND THE ADMINISTRATION OF FOREIGN
AFFAIRS."
PUBLIC ADMIN. REV., 12 (FALL 52), 267-275.
     DESCRIBES THE ORGANIZATION AND FUNCTION OF THE COLLEGE.
IT APPEARS TO REPRESENT THE COMBINED VIEWS OF THE MILITARY
SERVICES AND TO WORK TOWARD INCREASING MILITARY
REPRESENTATION IN FOREIGN POLICY-MAKING PROCESS.

1423 MASON J.B. ED., PARISH H.C. ED.
THAILAND BIBLIOGRAPHY.
GAINESVILLE: U OF FLORIDA LIB, 1958, 245 PP.
     CONTAINS MORE THAN 2,300 ENTRIES, MANY ANNOTATED, TO
BOOKS, ARTICLES, AND DOCUMENTS IN NINE WESTERN LANGUAGES.
WORKS ON HISTORY, GOVERNMENT, INTERNATIONAL RELATIONS,
PUBLIC ADMINISTRATION, ECONOMICS, ARCHEOLOGY, GEOGRAPHY,
SOCIOLOGY, EDUCATION, ART, LANGUAGE STUDY, AND THE NATURAL
SCIENCES. HAS A LIST OF BIBLIOGRAPHIES.

1424 MASSART L.
"L'ORGANISATION DE LA RECHERCHE SCIENTIFIQUE EN EUROPE."
TABLE RONDE, 181 (FEB. 63), 23-30.
     ANALYZES STAGES OF EVOLUTION OF ORGANIZATION OF
SCIENTIFIC RESEARCH IN EUROPEAN COUNTRIES. DEFINES IDEA

OF SCIENTIFIC POLITICS, ITS PURPOSES AND ACTIVITIES.
EXAMINES PROBLEMS POSED BY THIS SCIENCE. DISCUSSES EUROPEAN
SCIENTIFIC RESEARCH UNDERTAKEN BY INTERNATIONAL ORGANIZA-
TIONS.

1425 MASTERS N.A.
COMMITTEE ASSIGNMENTS IN THE HOUSE OF REPRESENTATIVES
(BMR)
AM. POL. SCI. REV., 55 (JUNE 61), 345-357.
STUDIES FORMAL AND INFORMAL PROCESSES OF COMMITTEE
ASSIGNMENTS, SUCH AS GEOGRAPHICAL REPRESENTATION, COMMITTEE
STRUCTURE, POLITICAL AFFILIATION, ROLE OF PARTY LEADERS,
LEGISLATIVE RESPONSIBILITY, AND PERSONAL COMPETITION.
FINDS THAT PARTY LEADERS USE ASSIGNMENTS TO BARGAIN AND
THAT MOST IMPORTANT CONSIDERATION IS TO INSURE RE-ELECTION.

1426 MATHEWS J.M.
AMERICAN STATE GOVERNMENT.
NEW YORK: APPLETON, 1925, 660 PP.
SURVEYS AMERICAN SYSTEM OF STATE GOVERNMENT. DISCUSSES
POSITION OF STATES IN FEDERAL SYSTEM, STATE CONSTITUTIONS,
LEGISLATURES, COURTS, AND EXECUTIVES. EXAMINES STATE POWERS,
ADMINISTRATIVE ORGANIZATION, ELECTIONS AND POLITICS, AND
CONTROL OVER TAXES, FINANCE, BUSINESS, AND UNIONS. DESCRIBES
RELATIONSHIP BETWEEN STATE AND LOCAL GOVERNMENTS.

1427 MATRAS J.
SOCIAL CHANGE IN ISRAEL.
CHICAGO: ALDINE PUBLISHING CO, 1965, 211 PP., LC#65-22491.
ANALYSIS OF DIRECTIONS OF CHANGE IN SOCIAL
STRUCTURE IN ISRAEL. PRESENTS EMPIRICAL DATA TO FORM STATIS-
TICAL REPRESENTATIONS OF SOCIAL STRUCTURE AND SOCIAL CHANGE.
REVIEWS GROWTH AND SETTLEMENT OF JEWISH POPULATION
OF PALESTINE AND ISRAEL FROM 1880 THROUGH 1961 CENSUS.
EXAMINES CHANGE IN RELIGIOUS AND POLITICAL SPHERES, IN
EDUCATIONAL AND OCCUPATIONAL SPHERES, AND IN THE FAMILY.

1428 MATTHEWS D.G.
"A CURRENT BIBLIOGRAPHY ON ETHIOPIAN AFFAIRS: A SELECT
BIBLIOGRAPHY FROM 1950-1964."
AFR. BIBLIOG. CTR., SPEC. SERIES, 3 (MAR. 65), 1-46.
A PARTIALLY ANNOTATED BIBLIOGRAPHY OF 594 BOOKS, ARTI-
CLES, AND OFFICIAL DOCUMENTS PUBLISHED BETWEEN 1950-64 ON
ETHOPIA. EMPHASIS PLACED ON ENGLISH-LANGUAGE PUBLICATIONS,
BUT SOME SOURCES IN FRENCH, RUSSIAN, ITALIAN, AND GERMAN.
BRIEF DESCRIPTIVE ANNOTATIONS SUPPLIED WHEN TITLE INSUFFI-
CIENTLY CLEAR TO EXPLAIN CONTENTS OF A GIVEN PUBLICATION.
A SYSTEMATIC GUIDE FOR RESEARCH OR GENERAL USE.

1429 MATTHEWS D.G. ED.
"ETHIOPIAN OUTLINE: A BIBLIOGRAPHIC RESEARCH GUIDE."
AFR. BIBLIOG. CTR., SPEC. SERIES, 4 (FEB. 66), 1-17.
SUPPLEMENT TO "A CURRENT BIBLIOGRAPHY ON ETHIOPIAN AF-
FAIRS." PREPARED FOR INTERNATIONAL CONFERENCE OF ETHIOPIAN
STUDIES HELD APRIL 2-8, 1966. CONTAINS CHRONOLOGICAL AND RE-
SEARCH DATA LISTING NEW ETHIOPIAN CABINET AS OF APRIL 11,
1966. SUBJECT BIBLIOGRAPHY OF 93 UNANNOTATED ENTRIES PUB-
LISHED BETWEEN 1960-65; AUTHOR INDEX.

1430 MATTHEWS D.G. ED.
"PRELUDE-COUP D'ETAT-MILITARY GOVERNMENT: A BIBLIOGRAPHICAL
AND RESEARCH GUIDE TO NIGERIAN POL AND GOVT, JAN, 1965-66."
AFR. BIBLIOG. CTR., SPEC. SERIES, 4 (MAR. 66), 1-21.
FIRST ISSUE OF "BIBLIO-RESEARCH SERIES" DESIGNED TO
AUGMENT BIBLIOGRAPHICAL INFORMATION WITH CHRONOLOGICAL, BIO-
GRAPHICAL, AND RESEARCH DATA. CONTAINS CHRONOLOGY OF EVENTS
FROM 1965-66; LISTING OF MEMBERS OF NIGERIAN FEDERAL GOVERN-
MENT AS OF MARCH 31, 1965; LISTING OF OTHER MINISTERS AND
GOVERNORS; AND A BIBLIOGRAPHY OF GOVERNMENT MATERIALS FROM
1964-65 ARRANGED GEOGRAPHICALLY.

1431 MATTHEWS D.R.
THE SOCIAL BACKGROUND OF POLITICAL DECISION-MAKERS.
GARDEN CITY: DOUBLEDAY, 1954, 62 PP., LC#54-10200.
BRIEF ANALYSIS OF THEORETICAL WRITINGS AND FACTUAL STUD-
IES ABOUT SOCIAL AND PSYCHOLOGICAL BACKGROUNDS OF GOVERN-
MENT OFFICIALS. CONSIDERS POLITICS AND DECISION-MAKING,
RECRUITMENT OF DECISION-MAKERS, DECISION-MAKERS AND SOCIAL
CHANGE.

1432 MATTOD P.K.
A STUDY OF LOCAL SELF GOVERNMENT IN URBAN INDIA.
JULLUNDUR CITY: JAIN GENERAL H, 1960, 62 PP.
DISCUSSES CONSTITUTIONAL PROVISIONS, FUNCTIONS OF LOCAL
BODIES, LOCAL FINANCE; AND CONSTITUTIONAL, ADMINISTRATIVE,
AND FINANCIAL REFORMS IN LOCAL SELF-GOVERNMENT IN URBAN IN-
DIA. CONCLUDES WITH COMPARISON OF URBAN AND RURAL AREAS.

1433 MAYDA J. ED.
ATOMIC ENERGY AND LAW.
SAN JUAN: U OF PUERTO RICO, 1959, 254 PP.
CONSIDERS PROBLEMS OF BOTH TECHNICAL AND LEGAL ASPECTS
IN USE OF ATOMIC POWER IN UNDERDEVELOPED COUNTRIES. DIS-
CUSSES PRODUCTION, STORAGE, SALE, APPLICATION, AND DISPOSAL
IN ATTEMPTING TO SET NEW POLICY FOR SOUTH AMERICAN
GOVERNMENTS TO FOLLOW.

1434 MAYER C.S.
INTERVIEWING COSTS IN SURVEY RESEARCH.
ANN ARBOR: U MICH SCHOOL BUS ADM, 1964, 114 PP.
CONCLUDES THAT IT IS POSSIBLE TO CONSTRUCT A SIMULATION
MODEL OF THE FIELD INTERVIEWING PROCESS THAT BEHAVES IN
APPROXIMATELY THE SAME WAY AS THE REAL SYSTEM. SUCH A MODEL
CAN BE USED EFFECTIVELY BY THE MANAGER OF A FIELD FORCE TO
PRE-TEST THE COST IMPLICATIONS OF ALTERNATE PLANS OF SAMPLE
DESIGN AND FIELD PROCEDURE. OTHER ADVANTAGES OF SIMULATION
ARE DISCUSSED, INCLUDING VARIOUS INCREASE IN EFFECTIVENESS.

1435 MAYNE A.
DESIGNING AND ADMINISTERING A REGIONAL ECONOMIC DEVELOPMENT
PLAN WITH SPECIFIC REFERENCE TO PUERTO RICO (PAMPHLET)
PARIS: ORG FOR ECO COOP AND DEV, 1961, 62 PP.
STUDIES METHODS OF DESIGNING REGIONAL ECONOMIC
DEVELOPMENT PLANS STRESSING NEED TO EVALUATE POTENTIALS,
TRANSLATE OBJECTIVES INTO PROGRAMS, CHOOSE ALTERNATIVE
PROGRAMS, AND COORDINATE PLANS. MAINTAINS THAT ONE REASON
FOR PROGRAM FAILURES IS NEGLECT OF PUBLIC ADMINISTRATION
PROCEDURE AND GOVERNMENT DECISION-MAKING PROCESS. LOOKS AT
SOCIAL AND ECONOMIC DEVELOPMENT SINCE 1940.

1436 MAYNE R.
THE COMMUNITY OF EUROPE.
LONDON: GOLLANCZ, 1963, 192 PP.
BRIEF HISTORY OF EVOLVING ENTITY OF THE EUROPEAN COMMUN-
ITY, INCLUDING POLITICAL AND ECONOMIC BACKGROUND, POST-WAR
DEBATES, BRITISH 'DILEMMA,' AND EUROPE'S RELATION TO REST OF
WORLD. ALSO DISCUSSES VARIOUS EUROPEAN REGIONAL ORGANIZA-
TIONS.

1437 MAYNTZ R.
PARTEIGRUPPEN IN DER GROSSSTADT.
KOLN: WESTDEUTSCHER VERLAG, 1959, 159 PP.
DISCUSSES HISTORY, STRUCTURE, MEMBERSHIP, SELECTION OF
OFFICIALS, ADMINISTRATION, ETC., OF A MUNICIPAL BOROUGH. IN-
CLUDES EXAMINATION OF PARTY EFFORTS TO SHAPE PUBLIC OPINION
AND TO ENLARGE MEMBERSHIP.

1438 MAYO E.
THE SOCIAL PROBLEMS OF AN INDUSTRIAL CIVILIZATION.
CAMBRIDGE: HARVARD U PR, 1945, 150 PP.
DISCUSSES PROBLEMS OF EFFECTIVE COOPERATION IN 20TH CEN-
TURY INDUSTRIAL SOCIETY. DEALS WITH DEFECTS OF POLITICAL AS
WELL AS ECONOMIC THINKING IN OUR SOCIETY. CALLS ATTENTION
TO IMBALANCE IN SYSTEMATIC STUDIES; CONFLICT BETWEEN
TECHNICAL AND SCIENTIFIC; AND HUMAN AND SOCIAL. COMMENTS
ON THE HAWTHORNE EXPERIMENT.

1439 MAZZINI J.
THE DUTIES OF MAN.
NEW YORK: DUTTON, 1955, 336 PP.
'WHATEVER MEN HAVE SAID, MATERIAL INTERESTS HAVE NEVER
CAUSED, AND NEVER WILL CAUSE, A REVOLUTION. REVOLUTIONS HAVE
THEIR ORIGIN IN THE MIND, IN THE VERY ROOT OF LIFE: NOT IN
THE BODY, IN THE MATERIAL ORGANISM. A RELIGION OR A
PHILOSOPHY, LIES AT BASE OF EVERY REVOLUTION.' CONCEIVES
NATIONS 'NOT AS MONSTERS LIKE THE LEVIATHAN OF HOBBES BUT AS
SUBLIMATED INDIVIDUAL HUMAN BEINGS.'

1440 MCAUSLAN J.P.W., GHAI Y.P.
"CONSTITUTIONAL INNOVATION AND POLITICAL STABILITY IN TAN-
ZANIA: A PRELIMINARY ASSESSMENT."
J. OF MOD. AFR. STUD., (DEC. 66), 479-515.
EVALUATES PERFORMANCE OF TANZANIAN GOVERNMENT UP TO 1966,
CRITICIZING ITS INSTABILITY, EXCESSIVE POWER VESTED IN THE
PRESIDENT, LACK OF PROVISION FOR SUCCESSION. FEELS THAT OUT-
OUTLOOK IS FAIRLY HOPEFUL, AS LONG AS BUREAUCRACY DOES NOT
BECOME TOO RIGID OR PRESIDENT TOO POWERFUL.

1441 MCCAMY J.
THE ADMINISTRATION OF AMERICAN FOREIGN AFFAIRS.
NEW YORK: KNOPF, 1950, 364 PP.
DEALS WITH FOREIGN POLICIES IN TERMS OF ORGANIZATION OF
GOVERNMENT. CONSIDERS THE OBJECTS OF ADMINISTRATION, THEIR
COSTS AND EFFECTS IN POLITICAL ECONOMY. INCLUDES STUDIES OF
THE DEPARTMENT OF STATE, PRESSURE GROUPS AND CONGRESS.

1442 MCCAMY J.L.
GOVERNMENT PUBLICITY: ITS PRACTICE IN FEDERAL ADMINISTRATION
CHICAGO: U OF CHICAGO PRESS, 1939, 275 PP.
ANALYSIS OF USE OF PUBLICITY BY FEDERAL GOVERNMENT AS
PLANNED PROGRAM OF DISTRIBUTING INFORMATION TO PUBLIC. DEALS
WITH SELECTION, MEDIA, PERSONNEL, AND COORDINATION OF
PUBLICITY AS USED BY FEDERAL GOVERNMENT IN PERIOD 1937-38.

1443 MCCLEERY R.
"COMMUNICATION PATTERNS AS BASES OF SYSTEMS OF AUTHORITY AND
POWER" IN THEORETICAL STUDIES IN SOCIAL ORGAN. OF PRISON-BMR
SYDNEY: SOC SCI RES COUN AUSTRAL, 1960.
STUDIES ADMINISTRATION AND SOCIAL CHARACTERISTICS OF OLD
AUTHORITARIAN PRISON, CHANGES INTRODUCED AND ADMINISTRATIVE
AND SOCIAL CONSEQUENCES, AND PROCESSES OF RECONSTRUCTION IN
OFFICIAL AND INTIMATE GROUPS. DISCUSSES EXERCISE OF POWER,
ORGANIZATION AND COMMUNICATION, INMATE SOCIETY, AND LIBERAL

MANAGEMENT POLICIES.

1444 MCCLELLAND C.A.
"DECISIONAL OPPORTUNITY AND POLITICAL CONTROVERSY."
J. CONFL. RESOLUT., 6 (SEPT. 62), 201-213.
ASSESSES USA DECISIONS (LISTING PROBABLE-INFLUENCE
FACTORS) WITH REGARD TO 1958 QUEMOY ISLAND CRISIS. SUGGESTS
IMPLEMENTATION OF CRISIS-CONTROL TO PREVENT MOVING OVER
BRINK TO WAR-POSTURE. LEVEL OF USA JUDGMENT IS PATTERNED,
POINTING OUT WEAKNESSES. DEMANDS MORE THOUGHTFUL DEBATES
AMONG OPPOSITION AND CONTENDS DECISIONS LIMITED BY 'PLIGHT.'

1445 MCCLOSKEY J.F. ED., TREFETHEN F.N. ED.
OPERATIONS RESEARCH FOR MANAGEMENT.
BALTIMORE: JOHNS HOPKINS PRESS, 1954, 972 PP., LC#54-13114.
PAPERS COVER HISTORY, METHODOLOGY, EXPERIMENTAL ANALYSIS,
INFORMATION HANDLING, AND CASE HISTORIES IN OPERATIONS
RESEARCH FOR MANAGEMENT AND ARE PRODUCTS OF SEMINAR HELD AT
JOHN HOPKINS UNIVERSITY IN 1952.

1446 MCCONNELL G.
THE MODERN PRESIDENCY.
NEW YORK: ST MARTIN'S PRESS, 1967, 114 PP., LC#67-12242.
DETAILED DISCUSSION OF OFFICE OF PRESIDENCY. EXPLANATION
OF PROCESS OF CHOOSING CANDIDATES, ELECTIONS, RELATIONS WITH
CONGRESS, LEGISLATIVE PROGRAM, EXECUTIVE DEPARTMENTS AND
THEIR OPERATION. MEANT AS AN INTRODUCTION TO THE SUBJECT.
ANALYZES RECENT PRESIDENTS AND THEIR LEADERSHIP.

1447 MCDIARMID J.
"THE MOBILIZATION OF SOCIAL SCIENTISTS," IN L. WHITE'S CIVIL
CIVIL SERVICE IN WARTIME."
CHICAGO: U OF CHICAGO PRESS, 1945.
DISCUSSES PROCESS BY WHICH AMERICAN SOCIAL SCIENTISTS
WERE MOBILIZED FOR THEIR PART IN WWII. DESCRIBES CIVIL
SERVICE COMMISSION'S WAR-RECRUITING AND REPLACEMENT
PROGRAM, SHOWING METHODS OF DECENTRALIZATION AND DELEGATION
OF AUTHORITY.

1448 MCDONOUGH A.M.
INFORMATION ECONOMICS AND MANAGEMENT SYSTEMS.
NEW YORK: MCGRAW HILL, 1963, 321 PP., LC#63-15459.
EXAMINES STUDIES IN INFORMATION FIELD, ESTABLISHES
THEORETICAL FRAMEWORK UNDER WHICH VALUES PLACED ON
KNOWLEDGE AND INFORMATION ARE DISCUSSED, AND PROBES INTO
INFORMATION-RETRIEVAL SYSTEMS IN CONTEXT OF MANAGEMENT
SYSTEMS.

1449 MCGREGOR D.
THE HUMAN SIDE OF ENTERPRISE.
NEW YORK: MCGRAW HILL, 1960, 246 PP., LC#60-10608.
DISCUSSES WHETHER SUCCESSFUL MANAGERS ARE BORN OR MADE.
FINDS THAT MAKING OF MANAGERS IS ONLY SLIGHTLY THE RESULT
OF MANAGEMENT'S FORMAL EFFORTS IN MANAGEMENT DEVELOPMENT.
IT IS MORE THE RESULT OF MANAGEMENT'S CONCEPTION OF
NATURE OF ITS TASK AND OF ALL POLICIES AND PRACTICES
CONSTRUCTED TO IMPLEMENT THIS CONCEPTION. SUGGESTS MORE
ADEQUATE ASSUMPTIONS UPON WHICH TO BASE TRAINING.

1450 MCHENRY D.E.
HIS MAJESTY'S OPPOSITION: STRUCTURE AND PROBLEMS OF THE
BRITISH LABOUR PARTY 1931-1938.
BERKELEY: U OF CALIF PR, 1940, 320 PP.
SKETCHES BRIEFLY THE ORIGINS AND GROWTH OF THE LABOR
PARTY. DEALS MAINLY WITH EXAMINATION OF LABOR ORGANIZATION
AND ITS RECORD SINCE GENERAL ELECTIONS OF 1931. STUDY
CONFINED TO EXAMINING PARTY RESOURCES AND TRACING TRENDS
DURING THIS BRIEF PERIOD.

1451 MCHENRY D.E.
THE THIRD FORCE IN CANADA: THE COOPERATIVE COMMONWEALTH
FEDERATION 1932-1948.
BERKELEY: U OF CALIF PR, 1950, 351 PP.
STORY OF NEW CANADIAN POLITICAL PARTY, BUILT ON PATTERN
OF BRITISH LABOUR PARTY. ARGUES THAT CCF IS A MIDDLE WAY
BETWEEN REACTION AND REVOLUTION ANALYSIS OF PARTY
ORGANIZATION, POLICY, AND PROSPECTS.

1452 MCKENZIE J.L.
AUTHORITY IN THE CHURCH.
LONDON: GEOFFREY CHAPMAN, 1966, 184 PP.
FOLLOWING A PRESENTATION OF HISTORICAL AND DOCTRINAL
CONTEXT OF AUTHORITY IN THE ROMAN CATHOLIC CHURCH, THE
AUTHOR OFFERS VARIOUS REFLECTIONS ON PRESTIGE, LEADERSHIP,
ORGANIZATION AND THE TENSION BETWEEN FREEDOM AND AUTHORITY.
DECRIES THE IMPOSITION OF A MILITARY-IMPERSONAL FARM ON
AN ORGANIZATION THAT SHOULD PROMOTE PERSONAL AND FELLOWSHIP
RELATIONS, WITH SUPERIORS AS SERVANTS.

1453 MCKIE R.
MALAYSIA IN FOCUS.
SYDNEY: ROBERTSON, 1963, 235 PP.
TRACES DEVELOPMENT OF MALAYSIAN FEDERATION. ANALYZES ITS
PRESENT ECONOMIC AND SOCIAL PROBLEMS, INCLUDING DIFFICULTIES
WITH INDONESIA.

1454 MCKISACK M.
THE PARLIAMENTARY REPRESENTATION OF THE ENGLISH BOROUGHS
DURING THE MIDDLE AGES.
LONDON: OXFORD U PR, 1932, 180 PP.
ANALYSIS OF PARLIAMENTARY INSTITUTIONS IN MEDIEVAL
ENGLAND AND BOROUGH REPRESENTATION IN THE VARIOUS COUNCILS
CONVENED FOR JUDICIAL, LEGISLATIVE, AND ADMINISTRATIVE
PURPOSES. DISCUSSES METHODS OF ELECTION AND TAXATION AND
PROBLEMS OF ATTENDANCE AND PAYMENT OF PARLIAMENTARY
PERSONNEL. PRESENTS NEW INFORMATION FROM LOCAL ARCHIVES
ON MEMBERSHIP AND ADMINISTRATION OF THE VARIOUS COUNCILS.

1455 MCLEAN J.M.
THE PUBLIC SERVICE AND UNIVERSITY EDUCATION.
PRINCETON: PRINCETON U PRESS, 1949, 241 PP.
CONSIDERS BASIC ISSUES OF SOCIAL AND GOVERNMENTAL ORGAN-
IZATION, SOCIAL AND ADMINISTRATIVE VALUES, AND BASIC TRENDS
IN PUBLIC ADMINISTRATION. IS PRIMARILY CONCERNED WITH ROLE
OF UNIVERSITY IN TRAINING ABLE AND RESPONSIBLE ADMINISTRA-
TORS TO MEET GROWING NEED FOR QUALIFIED GOVERNMENT PERSON-
NEL. COMPARES AMERICAN AND BRITISH ATTEMPTS.

1456 MCNAMARA R.L.
"THE NEED FOR INNOVATIVENESS IN DEVELOPING SOCIETIES."
RURAL SOCIOLOGY, 32 (DEC. 67), 395-399.
EXAMINES COLOMBIA AS CASE OF DEVELOPING SOCIETY'S ATTEMPT
TO ASCERTAIN GENERAL SITUATIONAL FEATURES THAT REQUIRE
INNOVATION BY LEADERS, ADMINISTRATORS, AND OFFICIALS IN
DEALING WITH PROBLEMS. POINTS TO FAILURE OF CONVENTIONAL
SCHEMES TO HANDLE PROBLEMS SUCCESSFULLY, ILLUSTRATING
IDEAS WITH SELECT PROBLEMS.

1457 MCNAMEE B.J., PAYNE E.M.
"CONFLICT OF INTEREST: STATE GOVERNMENT EMPLOYEES."
VIRGINIA LAW REV., 47 (OCT. 61), 1034-1076.
REVIEW OF CONFLICT OF INTEREST LAWS AND PRACTICES.
SUCH LAWS ARE NECESSARY TO INSURE THAT STATE EMPLOYEES ACT
ONLY IN THE PUBLIC INTEREST.

1458 MCNULTY J.E.
SOME ECONOMIC ASPECTS OF BUSINESS ORGANIZATION.
PHILA: U OF PENN PR, 1964, 122 PP., LC#64-18620.
APPLIES ECONOMIC THEORY TO BUREAUCRATIC ORGANIZATION OF
BUSINESS. EXAMINES EVOLUTION OF THOUGHT AND RESEARCH IN
ECONOMICS CONCERNING NATURE AND SIGNIFICANCE OF ORGANIZED
FIRM. DISCUSSES TESTING PROCEDURES FOR HYPOTHESES USED IN
THESE THEORIES. FINDS THAT ADJUSTMENTS TO ORGANIZATIONAL
UTILITY FUNCTION ARE NECESSARY TO UNDERSTAND RELATIONSHIP.

1459 MEANS G.C.
THE CORPORATE REVOLUTION IN AMERICA: ECONOMIC REALITY VS.
ECONOMIC THEORY.
NEW YORK: CROWELL COLLIER, 1962, 191 PP., LC#62-15809.
COLLECTION OF ESSAYS ON SUBJECT OF BIG BUSINESS
AND ADMINISTERED PRICES; MOST OF MATERIAL WAS TESTIMONY BE-
FORE CONGRESSIONAL SUBCOMMITTEES. EACH ESSAY IS CONCERNED
WITH ASPECT OF PROBLEM CREATED BY BIG BUSINESS. SOME FOCUS
ON FACTS OF BIGNESS AND OF PRICE ADMINISTRATION. SOME DEAL
WITH IMPLICATIONS OF THESE FACTS FOR ECONOMIC POLICY, AND
SOME ARE CONCERNED WITH IMPLICATIONS FOR PUBLIC POLICY.

1460 MEDALIA N.Z., MASON W.S.
"POSITION AND PROSPECTS OF SOCIOLOGISTS IN FEDERAL
EMPLOYMENT."
AMER. SOCIOLOGICAL REV., 28 (APR. 63), 280-287.
DESCRIBES RANGE OF POSITIONS OCCUPIED BY SOCIOLOGISTS IN
FEDERAL GOVERNMENT, NOTING SPECIAL CONDITIONS FOR RECRUIT-
MENT, TENURE, AND ADVANCEMENT THAT CIVIL SERVICE ENTAILS
FOR PROFESSIONAL SOCIOLOGISTS, AND INCLUDING COMMENTS ON
FUTURE PROSPECTS.

1461 MEEHAN E.J.
THE BRITISH LEFT WING AND FOREIGN POLICY: A STUDY OF THE
INFLUENCE OF IDEOLOGY.
NEW BRUNSWICK: RUTGERS U. PR. 1960, 198 PP.
ATTEMPTS TO ILLUSTRATE MANNER IN WHICH IDEOLOGY INFLU-
ENCES HUMAN THOUGHT REGARDING FACTUAL DATA OF INTERNATIONAL
RELATIONS. CONTENDS IDEOLOGY IS SIMPLY A PATTERN OF BELIEFS
WHICH AN INDIVIDUAL OR GROUP ACCEPTS.

1462 MEEK C.K.
COLONIAL LAW: A BIBLIOGRAPHY WITH SPECIAL REFERENCE TO
NATIVE AFRICAN SYSTEMS OF LAW AND LAND TENURE.
LONDON: OXFORD U PR, 1948, 58 PP.
BIBLIOGRAPHY PREPARED FOR USE OF MEMBERS OF THE COLONIAL
SERVICE OR ANY OTHERS INTERESTED IN THE LAW AND ITS ADMINIS-
TRATION IN THE BRITISH COLONIAL TERRITORIES. EMPHASIZES IN-
DIGENOUS SYSTEMS OF AFRICAN LAW AND CUSTOM AS THEY ARE DE-
VELOPING UNDER NEW SOCIAL AND ECONOMIC CONDITIONS. LIST OF
813 PARTIALLY ANNOTATED ENTRIES COVERS POST-1900 MATERIAL ON
LEGAL THEORY AND HISTORY AND SOCIOLOGICAL JURISPRUDENCE.

1463 MEISEL J.H. ED.
PARETO & MOSCA.
ENGLEWOOD CLIFFS: PRENTICE HALL, 1965, 184 PP., LC#65-20601.
A COLLECTION OF 14 ESSAYS BY TALCOTT PARSONS, JOSEPH

SCHUMPETER, C. WRIGHT MILLS, AND OTHERS ON THE POLITICAL
WRITINGS OF VILFREDO PARETO AND GAETANO MOSCA. CONTAINS
DYNAMICS, TOGETHER WITH DISCUSSIONS ON POWER SOURCE AND
FLOW, MORPHOLOGY AND SOCIAL PSYCHOLOGY, AND TEH ITALIAN
POLITICAL CONTEXT.

1464 MELMAN S.
DECISION-MAKING AND PRODUCTIVITY.
NEW YORK: JOHN WILEY, 1958, 260 PP.
SHOWS THAT MAJOR ALTERNATIVES IN INDUSTRIAL DECISION-
MAKING EXIST AND HAVE EFFECTS ON PRODUCTIVITY. COVERS DECI-
SION-MAKING BY THE UNION AND BY MANAGEMENT AND EFFECTS ON
PRODUCTIVITY. COMPARES COST OF LABOR AND MACHINERY. PRODUC-
TIVITY IN DETROIT AND COVENTRY, ENGLAND. MANY TABLES.

1465 MELMANS S.
OUR DEPLETED SOCIETY.
NEW YORK: HOLT RINEHART WINSTON, 1965, 366 PP., LC#65-14453.
EFFECT OF COLD WAR MILITARY EXPENDITURES ON ECONOMIC
CONDITIONS OF US. DEFENSE RESEARCH AND DEVELOPMENT CON-
TRACTS; SPACE PROGRAM PRIORITIES AND ARMS SALE BUSINESS SEEN
AS DESTRUCTIVE TO THE SOCIAL WELFARE OF THE AMERICAN PEOPLE.

1466 MELTZER B.D.
"RUMINATIONS ABOUT IDEOLOGY, LAW, AND LABOR ARBITRATION."
UNIV. CHICAGO LAW REV., 34 (SPRING 67), 545-561.
INQUIRES INTO VULNERABILITY OF ARBITRATION SYSTEM TO
PRESSURES INCOMPATIBLE WITH FAIR DISPUTE-SETTLING MECHANISM.
DISCUSSES APPROPRIATE ROLE OF COURTS IN CHALLENGING AWARD AS
INCOMPATIBLE WITH GOVERNMENT AGREEMENT. EXPLAINS ROLE OF AR-
BITRATOR WITH RESPECT TO POLICY ISSUES CONCERNED WITH INTER-
PRETING COLLECTIVE BARGAINING AGREEMENT. DESIRES ARBITRATORS
TO SOLVE PROBLEM WITHIN REGULATORY FRAMEWORK.

1467 MENHENNET D., PALMER J.
PARLIAMENT IN PERSPECTIVE.
LONDON: THE BODLEY HEAD, 1967, 156 PP.
PRESENTS ACCOUNT OF CONTEMPORARY ROLE OF BRITISH
PARLIAMENT. DISCUSSES PARLIAMENTARY GOVERNMENT AND ITS
HISTORICAL DEVELOPMENT. DESCRIBES ACTUAL WORKINGS OF TWO
HOUSES AS PART OF DEMOCRATIC SYSTEM. CONSIDERS INFLUENCE OF
PARLIAMENTARY SYSTEM ON OTHER GOVERNMENTS, PARTICULARLY
THOSE OF DEVELOPING NATIONS.

1468 MENZEL J.M. ED.
THE CHINESE CIVIL SERVICE: CAREER OPEN TO TALENT?
BOSTON: D C HEATH, 1963, 110 PP., LC#63-12327.
STRUCTURE AND COMPOSITION OF CHINESE CIVIL SERVICE IN ITS
HISTORICAL DEVELOPMENT. EXAMINES BACKGROUND AND EDUCATIONAL
REQUIREMENTS AND MOBILITY IN GOVERNMENT.

1469 MERILLAT H.C.L. ED.
LEGAL ADVISERS AND FOREIGN AFFAIRS.
NEW YORK: OCEANA, 1964, 176 PP., $4.00.
DESCRIBES METHODS AND PROCEDURES BY WHICH STATES,
GOVERNMENTS AND FOREIGN OFFICES OBTAIN OR ORGANIZE THE
PROCURING OF LEGAL ADVICE FOR THE PURPOSE OF CONDUCTING
FOREIGN AFFAIRS. EVALUATES ROLE OF SUCH ADVICE IN THE POLICY
MAKING AND DECIDING PROCESS.

1470 MERON T.
"THE UN'S 'COMMON SYSTEM' OF SALARY, ALLOWANCE, AND
BENEFITS: CRITICAL APPR'SAL OF COORD IN PERSONNEL MATTERS."
INTL. ORGANIZATION, 21 (SPRING 67), 284-305.
ANALYZES SYSTEM OF AGREEMENTS MADE BETWEEN UN AND ITS
AGENCIES, IN 1945, TO PROVIDE SALARIES AND OTHER BENEFITS
FOR MEMBERS. FEELS AGREEMENTS SHOULD BE RE-EVALUATED AND
RE-JUSTIFIED AFTER 20 YEARS. SEES NEED FOR MORE STABLE,
COMPETENT SYSTEM. STUDIES AGREEMENTS THEMSELVES AND PROCESS
BY WHICH THEY WERE ESTABLISHED.

1471 MERRIAM C.E. ED., BARNES H.E. ED.
A HISTORY OF POLITICAL THEORIES - RECENT TIMES.
NEW YORK: MACMILLAN 1924, 597 PP.
MAKES EFFORTS TO DISCUSS POLITICAL THEORIES IN RELA-
TION TO PECULIAR CONDITIONS UNDER WHICH THEY HAVE DEVELOPED
AND TO TAKE NOTE OF THE INTIMATE CONNECTION BETWEEN PHILOSO-
PHY AND FACTS CONDITIONING IT.

1472 MERRIAM C.E.
CHICAGO: A MORE INTIMATE VIEW OF URBAN POLITICS.
NEW YORK: MACMILLAN, 1929, 304 PP.
EXAMINES THE AMERICAN CITY, THROUGH DETAILED STUDY OF
CHICAGO. GIVES BRIEF HISTORY OF ITS GROWTH; EXAMINES THE
"BIG FIX." I.E., VICE AND GRAFT; THEN SHIFTS TO URBAN
GOVERNMENT. ANALYZES CITY BUILDERS, NATURE OF THE CITY,
GOVERNING STRUCTURES, AND ACTUAL CITY LEADERS. CONCLUDES
WITH VIEW THAT URBAN POLITICS ARE CLOSELY TIED TO FUTURE
OF AMERICA.

1473 MEYER H.H.B. ED.
SELECT LIST OF REFERENCES ON COMMISSION GOVERNMENT FOR
CITIES (PAMPHLET)
WASHINGTON: LIBRARY OF CONGRESS, 1913, 70 PP., LC#12-35017.
CLASSIFIES 497 ITEMS UNDER HEADINGSOF GENERAL, FAVORABLE,
AND OPPOSED. REFERENCES TO PARTICULAR AUTHORS AND CITIES

MAY BE FOUND IN INDEXES. MOST REFERENCES ARE TO PERIODICAL
AND PAMPHLET LITERATURE.

1474 MEYER P. ET AL.
THE JEWS IN THE SOVIET SATELLITES.
SYRACUSE: U. PR., 1953, 637 PP.
STUDIES STATUS AND TREATMENT OF JEWS BEFORE, DURING AND
AFTER WW 2 IN CZECHOSLOVAKIA, POLAND, RUSSIA, HUNGARY, RU-
MANIA AND BULGARIA. ANALYZES RISE OF ANTI-SEMITISM IN SOVIET
BLOC IN REGARD TO CENTRAL EUROPEAN SOCIAL, POLITICAL AND
ETHNIC CHARACTERISTICS.

1475 MEYER P.
ADMINISTRATIVE ORGANIZATION: A COMPARATIVE STUDY OF THE
ORGANIZATION OF PUBLIC ADMINISTRATION.
LONDON: STEVENS, 1957, 323 PP.
ANALYZES THE PHENOMENA OCCURRING WITHIN PUBLIC ADMINIS-
TRATION. ATTEMPTS TO DISCOVER A COMPLEX OF PHENOMENA THAT
ARE COMMON TO ALL FORMS OF PUBLIC ADMINISTRATION, REGARDLESS
OF THEIR SOCIAL FUNCTIONS. DEFINES PUBLIC ADMINISTRATION AS
THE WORK THAT GOVERNMENT DOES TO GIVE EFFECT TO A LAW.
DISCUSSES ADMINISTRATIVE SCIENCE AND ADMINISTRATIVE DIVISION
OF WORK, AUTHORITY, HIERARCHY, AND DECENTRALIZATION.

1476 MEYERHOFF A.E.
THE STRATEGY OF PERSUASION.
NEW YORK: COWARD MCCANN, 1965, 191 PP., LC#64-25768.
INDUSTRIAL ADVERTISING PRESIDENT'S APPROACH TO US PRO-
PAGANDA EFFORTS. SUGGESTS USE OF ADVERTISING SKILLS
IN PROPAGANDA FORMULATION AND DISSEMINATION; CALLS FOR
CABINET-LEVEL DEPARTMENT OF EXTERNAL RELATIONS WITH FIELD
OFFICES IN ALL COUNTRIES.

1477 MEYNAUD J.
PLANIFICATION ET POLITIQUE.
LAUSANNE: ETUDES DE SCIENCE POL, 1963, 190 PP.
EXAMINES THE MOTIVATION OF ECONOMIC PLANNING, ITS VALUE,
AND CHARACTERISTICS INCLUDING JURISDICTION, TECHNIQUES, THE
POLITICS OF PLANNING AND ITS PROBLEMS.

1478 MEYRIAT J. ED.
LA SCIENCE POLITIQUE EN FRANCE, 1945-1958; BIBLIOGRAPHIES
FRANCAISES DE SCIENCES SOCIALES (VOL. I)
PARIS: FDN NAT DES SCIENCES POL, 1960, 134 PP.
ANNOTATED BIBLIOGRAPHY OF 603 ENTRIES REPRESENTING FRENCH
POLITICAL SCIENCE PUBLICATIONS SINCE 1945, WITH EMPHASIS ON
PERIOD OF 1950-58. MATERIAL SEPARATED INTO NINE CATEGORIES
REPRESENTING METHODOLOGICAL, HISTORICAL, THEORETICAL, INSTI-
TUTIONAL, INTERNATIONAL, AND NATIONAL STUDIES. SPECIAL
INDEXES TO SCHOLARLY PERIODICALS, AUTHORS, AND EDITORS.

1479 MILLARD E.L.
FREEDOM IN A FEDERAL WORLD.
NEW YORK: OCEANA, 1959, 206 PP.
PRESENTS THE VIEW THAT A WORLD LEVEL FEDERAL GOVERNMENT
IS NECESSARY TO INSURE BOTH PEACE AND FREEDOM IN THE FUTURE.
EXPLAINS WORLD LAW AND THE METHOD USED TO CREATE IT.

1480 MILLER E.
"LEGAL ASPECTS OF UN ACTION IN THE CONGO."
AMER. J. INT. LAW, 55 (JAN. 61), 1-28.
ATTEMPTS TO DEMONSTRATE THAT CONSIDERATIONS OF LAW AND
PRINCIPLE CAN PLAY A ROLE IN INTERNATIONAL ACTION, IN SPITE
OF POLITICAL CONFLICT AND TENSION.

1481 MILLER M.
THE JUDGES AND THE JUDGED.
GARDEN CITY: DOUBLEDAY, 1952, 220 PP., LC#52-05749.
PUBLISHED BY AMERICAN CIVIL LIBERTIES UNION TO EXPOSE
BLACKLISTING AND CONSEQUENT DEFAMATION OF ALLEGED LEFTISTS
IN RADIO AND TV INDUSTRY.

1482 MILLETT J.D.
THE PROCESS AND ORGANIZATION OF GOVERNMENT PLANNING.
NEW YORK: COLUMBIA U PRESS, 1947, 187 PP.
DISCUSSES PROCEDURES BY WHICH GOVERNMENTAL POLICY GOALS
ARE ACHIEVED. ANALYZES ACTIVITIES OF NATIONAL RESOURCES
PLANNING BOARD. INDICATES PROCESS OF FIXING GOALS,
MEASURING EXISTING SITUATION, AND DESIGNING POSITIVE ACTION.
DESCRIBES IMPORTANCE OF TIME FACTOR, GEOGRAPHICAL FACTOR,
AND RESEARCH.

1483 MILLETT J.D.
GOVERNMENT AND PUBLIC ADMINISTRATION; THE QUEST FOR
RESPONSIBLE PERFORMANCE.
NEW YORK: MCGRAW HILL, 1959, 484 PP., LC#58-13883.
DISCUSSES AMERICAN POLITICAL INSTITUTIONS AND MEHTODS
USED TO CREATE POLITICAL RESPONSIBILTY IN ADMINISTRATIVE
PROCESS. MAINTAINS THAT SEPARATE IDENTITY OF ORGANS OF PO-
LITICAL DECISION-MAKING AND ADMINISTRATIVE AGENCIES PLACES
FIRST IN POSITION OF POLITICAL SUPERIORITY OVER SECOND.
DESCRIBES BUREAUGRACY AND POWER STRUCTURE IN ALL THREE
BRANCHES OF GOVERNMENT.

1484 MILLIKAN M.F. ED.
INCOME STABILIZATION FOR A DEVELOPING DEMOCRACY.

NEW HAVEN: YALE U PR, 1953, 730 PP., LC#52-12073.
ESSAYS WRITTEN DURING POST WWII RECESSION AND POST-KOREAN INFLATION. AUTHORS AVOID COMMENT ON CURRENT SCENE BUT PRESENT RELEVANT ANALYSIS IN VARIOUS PROBLEM AREAS. SOME RETREAT TO FUNDAMENTAL PRINCIPLES WHILE OTHERS PRESENT ORIGINAL ANALYSES.

1485 MILLIS H.A., MONTGOMERY R.E.
ORGANIZED LABOR (FIRST ED.)
NEW YORK: MCGRAW HILL, 1945, 930 PP.
AN EXHAUSTIVE TREATMENT BY TWO ECONOMISTS OF AMERICAN UNIONISM. SECTIONS RELEVANT TO REPRESENTATION INCLUDE TRADE-UNION STRUCTURE, GOVERNMENT, GROUP RELATIONS, TRADE UNION POLICIES AND PRACTICES, EMPLOYEE-REPRESENTATION PLANS, AND UNIONS' USE OF COOPERATIVES. AN EXAMINATION OF THE RELATIONSHIP BETWEEN TRADE UNIONS, THE LAW, AND COURTS IS INCLUDED.

1486 MILLIS W.
"THE DEMILITARIZED WORLD."
SANTA BARBARA: CENTER STUDY DEMOC. INSTIT., 1964, 61 PP.
SEES STABILIZATION OF USA-SOVIET COLD WAR SINCE 1954, AND TREND TO NON-VIOLENT REGULATION OF POWER STRUGGLES. FORESEES CONSTITUTION FOR DEMILITARIZED WORLD BASED ON ASSUMPTION THAT MAJOR WARS OBSOLETE. OUTLINES SUPRA-NATIONAL AUTHORITY.

1487 MILLS C.W.
THE CAUSES OF WORLD WAR THREE.
NEW YORK: SIMON SCHUSTER, 1958, 172 PP.
STUDIES WHETHER HISTORY THE PRODUCT OF FATE OR DECISION. CONCLUDES IN FAVOR OF THE LATTER. OBSERVES TWO MEANS OF POWER IN OPERATION TODAY. CONDEMNING THE POWER ELITE, OFFERS PROGRAM FOR OVERCOMING OBSTACLES TO PEACE.

1488 MILNE R.S.
"CONTROL OF GOVERNMENT CORPORATIONS IN THE UNITED STATES."
PUBLIC ADMINISTRATION, 34 (WINTER 56), 355-364.
CONTROL OF ALL FORMS OF GOVERNMENT CORPORATIONS IS SHARED BY THE PRESIDENT AND VARIOUS CONGRESSIONAL COMMITTEES, WITH A VERY IMPORTANT ROLE BEING PLAYED BY THE GENERAL ACCOUNTING OFFICE.

1489 MILNE R.S.
GOVERNMENT AND POLITICS IN MALAYSIA.
BOSTON: HOUGHTON MIFFLIN, 1967, 259 PP.
TRACES HISTORY OF NATION AND DEVELOPMENT OF ITS POLITICAL INSTITUTIONS. EXAMINES STRUCTURE AND FUNCTION OF MALAYSIA'S POLITICAL SYSTEM. DEALS WITH DEVELOPMENTS IN 1966 WHEN IN-DONESIA ADOPTED MORE CONCILIATORY ATTITUDE TOWARD THE FED-ERATION, AND WITH PROSPECTS AND POLITICS OF SINGAPORE.

1490 MINISTERE DE L'EDUC NATIONALE
CATALOGUE DES THESES DE DOCTORAT SOUTENUES DEVANT LES UNIVERSITAIRES FRANCAISES.
PARIS: MIN DE L'EDUCATION NAT.
ANNUAL PUBLICATION SINCE 1884 LISTING DOCTORAL THESES IN FRENCH UNIVERSITIES. ITEMS ARRANGED BY UNIVERSITY AND FACULTY, THEN ALPHABETICALLY BY AUTHOR.

1491 MINTZ M.
BY PRESCRIPTION ONLY.
BOSTON: BEACON PRESS, 1967, 446 PP.
ANALYSIS OF COMMERCIAL PRODUCTION AND GOVERNMENTAL REGU-LATION OF PRESCRIPTION DRUGS IN US. EXAMINES SUCCESS AND DANGER OF DRUGS, THE FDA, THE DRUG INDUSTRY, THE DOCTOR'S ROLE AND PROFITS. STUDIES "MIND" DRUGS, THALIDOMIDE, AND ORAL CONTRACEPTIVES. CONCLUDES THAT WITH US INGENUITY AND TECHNOLOGY, THERE SHOULD ALSO BE THE INSIGHT TO TEST, ANA-LYZE, AND CONTROL DRUGS TO PROTECT THE PUBLIC.

1492 MITCHELL W.C.
"OCCUPATIONAL ROLE STRAINS: THE AMERICAN ELECTIVE PUBLIC OFFICIAL."
ADMINISTRATIVE SCI. Q., 3 (JAN. 58), 210-228.
USE OF ROLE ANALYSIS TO DEVELOP CONCEPTUAL SCHEME FOR ANALYZING ROLE STRAINS AMONG ELECTED POLITICAL OFFICIALS. SEVEN GENERAL SOURCES OF STRAIN ARE SUGGESTED AND TYPICAL REACTIONS OF POLITICIANS TO THEM ARE ANALYZED.

1493 MODELSKI G.
"AUSTRALIA AND SEATO."
INT. ORG., (SUMMER 60), 429-37.
DESCRIBES AUSTRALIAN INFLUENCE IN SOUTH EAST ASIA. DISCUSSES VALUABLE ROLE IT HAS COME TO PLAY WITHIN THE TREATY. DESCRIBES SEATO'S POLITICAL AND MILITARY FUNCTIONS. ANALYZES AMERICAN INTEREST IN AUSTRALIA.

1494 MODELSKI G.
A THEORY OF FOREIGN POLICY.
NEW YORK: PRAEGER, 1962, 152 PP., $5.00.
EXAMINES ROLE OF THEORY, OF POWER, AND OF PARTICULAR COMMUNITY AGENTS IN POLICY PLANNING. POINTS OUT NECESSITY FOR CONCRETE OBJECTIVES AND FOR FLEXIBILITY IN FORMULATING POLICY.

1495 MODELSKI G.

"STUDY OF ALLIANCES."
J. CONFL. RESOLUT., 7 (DEC. 63), 769-76.
REVIEWS RECENT BOOKS ON ALLIANCES. FAVORS FINER DIS-TINCTIONS BETWEEN TERMS.

1496 MOEN N.W.
THE GOVERNMENT OF SCOTLAND 1603 - 1625.
ANN ARBOR: U MICROFILMS, INC, 1958, 468 PP., LC#58-3551.
DISCUSSES POWERS OF CROWN, OPERATION OF PRIVY COUNCIL, AND ADMINISTRATION OF JUSTICE IN SCOTLAND FROM ACCESSION OF JAMES I TO 1625. EXAMINES IN DETAIL EXTENSION OF ROYAL PREROGATIVE AND CONTROL OVER SCOTTISH AFFAIRS THROUGH AB-SENTEE GOVERNMENT OF JAMES I.

1497 MOLEY R.
POLITICS AND CRIMINAL PROSECUTION.
NEW YORK: MINTON, BALCH & CO, 1929, 241 PP.
EXAMINES POLITICAL FACTORS THAT ENTER INTO CRIMINAL-LAW ADMINISTRATION IN THE US. EMPHASIZES ROLE OF THE PROSECUTOR AS DOMINANT OVER MAGISTRATE-JUDGE, SHERIFF, GRAND JURY, AND PETIT JURY. DESCRIBES PROSECUTOR'S POWER TO RESTRICT ACCESS TO RECORDS AND DROP CASES AND RELATES THESE PREROGATIVES TO THE POLITICAL EXIGENCIES OF THE OFFICE. ATTENTION IS FOCUSED ON MAJOR STATE OFFENSES RATHER THAN MISDEMEANORS.

1498 MOLLAU G.
INTERNATIONAL COMMUNISM AND WORLD REVOLUTION: HISTORY AND METHODS.
NEW YORK: PRAEGER, 1961, 357 PP.
TRACES INTERNATIONAL COMMUNIST MOVEMENT FROM 1848 TO PRESENT. INCLUDES DISCUSSION OF THE RUSSIAN REVOLUTION, THE SOVIET UNION, THE COMINTERN, THE COMINFORM AND THE METHODS USED TO ACHIEVE SOVIET GOALS.

1499 MONAS S.
THE THIRD SECTION: POLICE AND SOCIETY IN RUSSIA UNDER NICHOLAS I.
CAMBRIDGE: HARVARD U PR, 1961, 354 PP., LC#61-6350.
RECORDS DEVELOPMENT OF THE RUSSIAN POLITICAL POLICE BY NICHOLAS I AS THE "THIRD SECTION" OF THE IMPERIAL CHANCERY. DESIGNED ON PRUSSIAN MODELS AS AN ATTEMPT TO REGULATE SOCIAL AND POLITICAL UNREST UNDER A "BEAUTIFUL AUTOCRACY" OF PATER-NAL BENEVOLENCE, THE "THIRD SECTION" IS SHOWN HERE TO HAVE BEEN PLANNED AS A TEMPORARY INSTITUTION WHICH SURVIVED ITS CREATOR AND HIS IDEALISTIC VISION.

1500 MONEYPENNY P.
"UNIVERSITY PURPOSE, DISCIPLINE, AND DUE PROCESS."
NORTH DAKOTA LAW REVIEW, 43 (SUMMER 67), 739-752.
DISCUSSES ROLE OF UNIVERSITY IN SHAPING STUDENT FOR LIFE OF SELF-GOVERNMENT AND INDEPENDENT DECISION. FEELS UNIVER-SITY CONTROL OF NONCLASSROOM ACTIVITIES SHOULD BE MINIMAL; STUDENT SHOULD HAVE RIGHTS OF PRIVACY AND SELF-REGULATION. ARGUES THAT STUDENT MUST HAVE DUE PROCESS OF LAW IN CASES INVOLVING RULE INFRACTION.

1501 MONPIED E., ROUSCOS G., ZALESKI E.
BIBLIOGRAPHIE FEDERALISTE: ARTICLES ET DOCUMENTS PUBLIES DANS LES PERIODIQUES PARUS EN FRANCE NOV. 1945-OCT. 1950.
PARIS: UNION FEDER INTER-UNIV, 1950, 162 PP.
LISTS, ANNOTATES, AND INDEXES 1,227 ARTICLES APPEARING IN FRENCH PERIODICALS FROM 1945 TO 1950. DEALS WITH THEORIES AND DOCTRINES OF FEDERALISM; EUROPEAN FEDERATIONS; WORLD FEDERAL GOVERNMENT; FEDERALIST ACTIVITIES THROUGHOUT THE WORLD. COUNTRY-BY-COUNTRY GUIDE TO FEDERALISM WITH AN INTRODUCTION STATING FEDERALIST PRINCIPLES AND POLICIES.

1502 MONPIED E., ZALESKI E. ET AL.
BIBLIOGRAPHIE FEDERALISTE: OUVRAGES CHOISIS (VOL. I, MIMEOGRAPHED PAPER)
PARIS: UNION FEDER INTER-UNIV, 1950, 87 PP.
LISTS AND ANNOTATES 640 ITEMS PUBLISHED PRIOR TO, DURING, AND SINCE WORLD WAR I DEALING WITH FEDERALISM, EUROPEAN FEDERATION, OR WORLD GOVERNMENT. ARRANGED TOPICALLY AND CHRONOLOGICALLY.

1503 MONTEIRO J.B.
CORRUPTION: CONTROL OF MALADMINISTRATION.
BOMBAY: MANAKTALAS, 1966, 303 PP.
ANALYSIS OF POLITICAL CORRUPTION, ITS DIMENSIONS AND CAUSES WITH MAJOR EMPHASIS ON ORGANS OF DOMESTIC CONTROL AS CONGRESSIONAL INVESTIGATIONS, CONSEIL D'ETAT, AND TRIBUNALS INCLUDING THE OMBUDSMAN.

1504 MONTER W.
THE GOVERNMENT OF GENEVA, 1536-1605 (DOCTORAL THESIS)
PRINCETON: PRIN U, DEPT OF HIST, 1963, 299 PP.
CONCENTRATING ON POLITICS IN NARROW SENSE AND OMITTING ECCLESIASTICAL DEVELOPMENTS, AUTHOR PROVIDES GENERAL REIN-TERPRETATION OF GENEVA'S POLITICAL HISTORY 1536-1605. AT-TEMPTS TO SHED LIGHT ON ASPECTS OF CALVIN'S ROME. RELATES HISTORY OF GENEVAN PUBLIC FINANCE DURING FIRST 70 YEARS OF NDEPENDENCE. ALSO EXPLAINS ASPECTS OF ADMINISTRATION, EVOLU-TION OF RULING CLASS; ASSESSES CALVIN'S POLITICAL ROLE.

1505 MONTGOMERY H.

CRACKER PARTIES.
BATON ROUGE: LOUISIANA ST U PR, 1950, 278 PP.
EXAMINES EFFECT AND DEVELOPMENT OF HOWELL COBB ON GEORGIA
POLITICS, 1845-61. EXPLORES RELATION TO ANDREW JACKSON AND
JOHN CALHOUN. RELATES POLITICAL PARTY STRUCTURE.

1506 MONTGOMERY J.D.
CASES IN VIETNAMESE ADMINISTRATION.
SAIGON: NATL INST OF ADMIN, 1959, 481 PP.
SERIES OF CASE STUDIES ATTEMPTING TO SHOW HOW EFFECTIVE
LOCAL ADMINISTRATORS CAN BE. AVOIDS DISCUSSION OF POLITICAL
PROBLEMS INVOLVED.

1507 MONTGOMERY J.D. ED., SIFFIN W.J. ED.
APPROACHES TO DEVELOPMENT: POLITICS, ADMINISTRATION AND
CHANGE.
NEW YORK: MCGRAW HILL, 1966, 299 PP., LC#66-14536.
EXAMINES RELATIONSHIP BETWEEN ADMINISTRATIVE CONCEPTS
AND THEIR SOCIO-POLITICAL CONTEXT. INCLUDES STUDIES OF
POLITICAL DEVELOPMENT; POLITICS OF DEVELOPMENT ADMINI-
STRATION; RURAL GOVERNMENT AND STRATEGY OF AGRICULTURAL
DEVELOPMENT; STRATEGY AND TACTICS OF PUBLIC ADMINISTRATION;
TECHNICAL ASSISTANCE.

1508 MOODIE G.C.
"THE GOVERNMENT OF GREAT BRITAIN."
NEW YORK: THOMAS Y CROWELL, 1961.
INTRODUCTION TO BRITISH POLITICS AND GOVERNMENT WITH
EMPHASIS ON SOCIAL-ECONOMIC CONTEXT OF POLITICAL STRUCTURE.
FRAMEWORK OF STUDY IS LARGELY INSTITUTIONAL WITH SOME
REFERENCE TO APPROACHES BASED ON DECISION-MAKING AND
THEORIES OF GROUP INTERACTION. CONTAINS BIBLIOGRAPHICAL
GUIDE.

1509 MOOMAW I.W.
THE CHALLENGE OF HUNGER.
NEW YORK: FREDERICK PRAEGER, 1966, 222 PP., LC#66-13670.
DESCRIBES NEED FOR INCREASES IN FOREIGN AID AND PROGRAM
TO ACCOMPLISH IT. DISCUSSES PAST WASTEFULNESS IN PROGRAM
AND IMPORTANCE OF FOREIGN AID TO NATIONAL INTEREST AND
POSSIBLE ROLE OF PRIVATE INDUSTRY IN HELPING.

1510 MOON P.T.
IMPERIALISM AND WORLD POLITICS.
NEW YORK: MACMILLAN, 1926, 583 PP.
EUROPEAN AND USA IMPERIALISM IN ASIA, MIDDLE EAST AND
AFRICA FOMENTED NEW NATIONALISM IN THESE AREAS. NATIONALISM,
IN INTERDEPENDENT WORLD, POSES PROBLEMS OF ADJUSTMENT. MAN-
DATE SYSTEM FIRST STEP TO END OF IMPERIALISM.

1511 MOOR E.J.
"THE INTERNATIONAL IMPACT OF AUTOMATION."
LEX ET SCIENTIA, 4 (JAN.-MAR. 67), 10-14.
GIVES REPRESENTATIVE OPERATIONAL, ADMINISTRATIVE, AND
PLANNING EXAMPLES TO FORECAST AUTOMATION'S FUTURE IMPACT.
ADVOCATES RESPONSIVE RELATIONSHIP WITH DEVICES ADOPTED TO
AID OUR CONGNITIVE POWERS.

1512 MOORE B.
"SOVIET POLITICS - THE DILEMMA OF POWER: THE ROLE OF IDEAS
IN SOCIAL CHANGE."
CAMBRIDGE: HARVARD U PR, 1951.
SOVIET SOCIETY SERVES AS CASE STUDY FOR QUESTIONS: WHAT
IS ROLE OF IDEAS IN ACTION, PARTICULARLY POLITICAL, AND
TO WHAT EXTENT IS IT POSSIBLE TO CREATE A NEW SOCIAL ORDER.
ATTEMPTS TO PROVIDE ANSWERS TO PROBLEM OF INTERACTION BE-
TWEEN COMMUNIST IDEOLOGY AND CERTAIN SOVIET POLITICAL PRAC-
TICES. CONTAINS EXTENSIVE BIBLIOGRAPHY IN RUSSIAN AND
ENGLISH.

1513 MOORE C.H.
TUNISIA SINCE INDEPENDENCE.
BERKELEY: U OF CALIF PR, 1965, 230 PP., LC#65-12926.
ILLUSTRATES THE POLITICS OF MODERNIZATION OF A ONE-PARTY
SYSTEM. EXPLAINS HISTORICAL CONDITIONS THAT MAKE ONE-PARTY
RULE POSSIBLE. DISCUSSES TO WHAT EXTENT THE PARTY IS A POLI-
TICAL FORCE DISTINCT FROM ITS LEADER. ANALYZES THE INSTITU-
TIONAL RELATIONSHIPS BETWEEN PARTY AND THE STATE ADMINISTRA-
TION AT THE NATIONAL AND REGIONAL LEVELS.

1514 MOORE W.E. ED., FELDMAN A.S. ED.
LABOR COMMITMENT AND SOCIAL CHANGE IN DEVELOPING AREAS.
NEW YORK: SOCIAL SCI RES COUNCIL, 1960, 378 PP., LC#60-53440
ANALYTICAL STUDY OF NEWLY DEVELOPING AREAS, WITH PAR-
TICULAR EMPHASIS ON PROBLEM OF LABOR MOTIVATION IN UNFA-
MILIAR TASKS. EXAMINES COMMITMENT OF INDUSTRIAL LABOR
BOTH IN SHORT-RUN OBJECTIVE PERFORMANCE OF MODERN ECONOM-
IC ACTIVITY AND LONG-RUN AND DEEP-SEATED ACCEPTANCE OF
ATTITUDES AND BELIEFS APPROPRIATE TO A MODERNIZED ECONOMY.

1515 MOORE W.E.
MAN, TIME, AND SOCIETY.
NEW YORK: JOHN WILEY, 1963, 163 PP., LC#63-15999.
DISCUSSES EFFECTS OF CONCEPT OF TIME ON HUMAN ACTIONS AND
STRUCTURE OF SOCIETAL INSTITUTIONS. CONSIDERS TIME AS LIMIT
AS WELL AS MEASURE OF CHANGE.

1516 MOORE W.E.
THE IMPACT OF INDUSTRY.
ENGLEWOOD CLIFFS: PRENTICE HALL, 1965, 117 PP., LC#65-23228.
INTRODUCTION TO SERIES OF STUDIES ON "MODERNIZATION OF
TRADITIONAL SOCIETIES. "ATTEMPTS TO PRESENT OVER-ALL VIEW
OF INTERPLAY OF PROCESSES OF CHANGE. DISCUSSES WORLD INDUS-
TRIAL REVOLUTION; CREATION OF A COMMON CULTURE; CONDI-
TIONS FOR INDUSTRIALIZATION; INDUSTRIAL ORGANIZATION; AND
THE FUTURE OF INDUSTRIAL SOCIETY.

1517 MOOS M., ROURKE F.E.
THE CAMPUS AND THE STATE.
LONDON: OXFORD U PR, 1959, 414 PP., LC#59-10768.
ABOUT ADMINISTRATIVE CONTROLS OVER STATE-SUPPORTED
COLLEGES AND UNIVERSITIES. FRUITS OF A DISTINGUISHED
COMMITTEE ON GOVERNMENT AND HIGHER EDUCATION, BOOK PROBES
DANGERS TO THE "FREE" COLLEGE TRADITION EXAMINING THE
EFFECTS OF FINANCING AND THE ROLE OF "INDEPENDENT"LAY
BOARDS, LEGISLATIVE OVERSIGHT, THE APPLICABLE LAW, CIVIL
SERVICE PROBLEMS, AND THE EFFICIENCY OF "FREE INSTITUTIONS.

1518 MORA J.A.
"THE ORGANIZATION OF AMERICAN STATES."
INT. ORGAN., 14 (FALL 60), 514-523.
OUTLINES PRINCIPLES, RULES AND ORGANS THROUGH WHICH
MEMBER STATES SEEK TO ATTAIN SYSTEM'S OBJECTIVES. DISCUSSION
OF MAJOR ISSUE (ECONOMIC CO-OPERATION BETWEEN MEMBERS) AND
EXPRESSION OF ENCOURAGEMENT AT 'CURRENT VISION OF MEMBERS.'

1519 MORALES C.J.
"TRADE AND ECONOMIC INTEGRATION IN LATIN AMERICA."
SOC. SCI., 35 (OCT. 60), 231-37.
ILLUSTRATES ARRANGEMENTS FOR ECONOMIC INTEGRATION BY
LATIN AMERICAN COUNTRIES, BUT CONSIDERS ECONOMIC FOUNDATIONS
NOT FAVORABLE FOR SUCH PLANS AND INDUSTRIAL DEVELOPMENT NOT
SUFFICIENTLY ADVANCED. PROPOSES A TRADE FREE ZONE AS AN
ALTERNATIVE SCHEME. LAFTA COUNTRIES' PLANS TO ELIMINATE
TARIFFS AND OTHER TRADE BARRIERS MAY PROMOTE INTRA-REGIONAL
TRADE.

1520 MORE S.S.
REMODELLING OF DEMOCRACY FOR AFRO-ASIAN NATIONS.
NEW DELHI: ALLIED PUBLISHERS, 1962, 347 PP.
EXAMINES FAILURE OF TRADITIONAL PARLIAMENTARY DEMOCRACIES
IN DEVELOPING COUNTRIES IN ASIA AND AFRICA. SUGGESTS REFORMS
IN EXECUTIVE AND LEGISLATIVE PROCESSES, ELECTION PROCEDURES,
AND PUBLIC ADMINISTRATION. URGES REMODELING OF PRESENT
PATTERNS OF DEMOCRACY TO MEET CHALLENGE OF "NAKED
DICTATORSHIP."

1521 MOREL E.D.
AFFAIRS OF WEST AFRICA.
LONDON: HEINEMANN, 1902, 381 PP.
CONSIDERS THE RACIAL, POLITICAL, AND COMMERCIAL PROBLEMS,
AND THEIR YEARLY INCREASE IN MAGNITUDE, CONNECTED WITH THE
ADMINISTRATION OF WEST AFRICA BY GREAT BRITAIN AND OTHER
POWERS OF WESTERN EUROPE THAT PARTICIPATED IN THE SCRAMBLE
FOR AFRICAN TERRITORY. INCLUDES STUDIES OF TRIBES, PLANTA-
TIONS, TRADE, FINANCE, AND GOVERNMENT. HAS MANY INTERESTING
OLD PHOTOGRAPHS.

1522 MORGAN G.G.
"SOVIET ADMINISTRATIVE LEGALITY: THE ROLE OF THE ATTORNEY
GENERAL'S OFFICE."
STANFORD: STANFORD U PRESS, 1962.
STUDY OF "GENERAL SUPERVISION " FUNCTION OF USSR PROCUR-
ACY - ROLE OF EXERCISING SUPERVISION OVER LEGALITY OF SUBOR-
DINATE LEGISLATION, CERTAIN TYPES OF GOVERNMENT ENACTMENTS,
AND OFFICIAL ACTIONS OF VARIOUS GOVERNMENTAL OFFICERS.
BIBLIOGRAPHY IS, FOR MOST PART, IN RUSSIAN.

1523 MORGENTHAU H.J.
MORGENTHAU DIARY (CHINA) (2 VOLS.)
WASHINGTON: US GOVERNMENT, 1965, 1699 PP.
RECORD OF SECRETARY OF TREASURY MORGENTHAU'S ACTIVITIES
RELATING TO CHINA, FROM JANUARY, 1934 TO JULY, 1945. PRE-
PARED BY SUBCOMMITTEE TO INVESTIGATE ADMINISTRATION OF
INTERNAL SECURITY ACT AND OTHER SECURITY LAWS OF SENATE
COMMITTEE ON THE JUDICIARY.

1524 MORGENTHAU H.J.
"THE POLITICAL CONDITIONS FOR AN INTERNATIONAL POLICE
FORCE."
INT. ORGAN., 17 (SPRING 63), 393-403.
EFFECTIVENESS AND RELIABILITY OF INTERNATIONAL POLICE
FORCE DEPEND ON LEGAL ORDER AND MAINTENANCE OF POLITICAL
STATUS QUO. WOULD FUNCTION BEST IN TOTALLY DISARMED WORLD.

1525 MORISON E.E.
TURMOIL AND TRADITION: A STUDY OF THE LIFE AND TIMES OF
HENRY L. STIMSON.
BOSTON: HOUGHTON MIFFLIN, 1960, 565 PP.
BIOGRAPHY OF THE STATESMAN FROM 1867-1950. COVERS MOST
ASPECTS OF HIS PUBLIC LIFE, INCLUDING HIS SERVICE AS UNITED
STATES DISTRICT ATTORNEY, SECRETARY OF WAR UNDER PRESIDENT
TAFT, SECRETARY OF STATE UNDER PRESIDENT HOOVER, AND SECRE-

TARY OF WAR UNDER PRESIDENT FRANKLIN ROOSEVELT.

1526 MORLAN R.L.
"INTERGOVERNMENTAL RELATIONS IN EDUCATION."
MINNEAPOLIS: U OF MINN PR, 1950.
FOCUSES ON INTERGOVERNMENTAL RELATIONS RATHER THAN EDUCA-
TIONAL PROGRAMS IN MINNESOTA. DISCUSSES PUBLIC SCHOOL SYSTEM
IN TERMS OF STATE-LOCAL, INTERLOCAL, INTERSTATE RELATIONS;
VOCATIONAL EDUCATION IN SECONDARY AND HIGHER EDUCATION; EDU-
CATION OF INDIANS; LUNCH AND LIBRARY PROGRAMS; EDUCATION
OF VETERANS; AGRICULTURAL TRAINING; ETC. EXTENSIVE BIBLI-
OGRAPHY INCLUDED.

1527 MORRIS B.S.
"THE COMINFORM: A FIVE YEAR PERSPECTIVE."
WORLD POLIT., 5 (APRIL 53), 368-76.
PRESENTS THE FIVE YEAR HISTORY OF THE COMINFORM EXIS-
TANCE. CONCLUDES THAT COMINFORM HAS NOT FULFILLED ITS STATED
ECONOMIC AND POLITICAL GOALS, INSTEAD IT HAS BECOME ONE OF
THE PROPAGANDA TOOLS OF THE COMMUNIST ORGANIZATION.

1528 MORRIS H.C.
THE HISTORY OF COLONIZATION.
NEW YORK: MACMILLAN, 1900, 842 PP.
DISCUSSES ORIGINS, METHODS AND OBJECTIVES OF COLONIZA-
TION, AND CITES ADVANTAGES AND DISADVANTAGES OF SUCH A POL-
ICY. STUDIES THE CAUSES WHICH LEAD TO THE EVENTUAL SEVERANCE
OF COLONIAL TIES AND THE ESTABLISHMENT OF INDEPENDENT
STATES.

1529 MORRIS W.T.
ENGINEERING ECONOMY.
HOMEWOOD: RICHARD IRWIN, 1960, 506 PP., LC#60-12922.
A PRESENTATION OF ENGINEERING ECONOMY WITHIN THE LARGER
CONTEXT OF MANAGEMENT DECISION ANALYSIS. DISCUSSES FUNDAMEN-
TALS OF ENGINEERING DECISIONS IN TERMS OF APPROACHES, GOALS,
MODELS, AND CASES UNDER CERTAINTY, UNCERTAINTY, AND RISK.
EXAMINES SOURCES OF INFORMATION, PREDICTION AND JUDGMENT,
EVALUATION OF INTANGIBLES, REPLACEMENT POLICY, AND PROBABIL-
ITY THEORY. ANALYZES ECONOMICS OF AUTOMATION IN MANAGEMENT.

1530 MORSTEIN-MARX F.
THE ADMINISTRATIVE STATE: AN INTRODUCTION TO BUREAUCRACY.
CHICAGO: U. CHI. PR., 1957, 202 PP.
ATTRIBUTES RISE OF ADMINISTRATIVE STATE TO INCREASING
INDUSTRIALISM. EXPLORES ASSETS AND DEFECTS OF SYSTEM. EX-
AMINES ROLE OF ADMINISTRATOR AND QUALIFICATIONS FOR EXPERT
CIVIL SERVANTS.

1531 MORTON J.A.
"A SYSTEMS APPROACH TO THE INNOVATION PROCESS: ITS USE IN
THE BELL SYSTEM."
BUSINESS HORIZONS, 10 (SUMMER 67), 27-36.
AS A PROCESS, INNOVATION CAN BE STUDIED AND MANAGED FROM
SYSTEMS VIEWPOINT; IN LAB STAGE, SPECIALIZED FUNCTIONS
OF BASIC RESEARCH, APPLIED RESEARCH, AND DEVELOPMENT DESIGN
CAN BE PROVIDED WITH OVER-ALL GUIDANCE, JUDGMENTS, AND CA-
TALYSIS BY SYSTEMS ENGINEERING.

1532 MORTON L.
STRATEGY AND COMMAND: THE FIRST TWO YEARS.
WASHINGTON: US GOVERNMENT, 1962, 761 PP., LC#61-60001.
OFFICIAL HISTORY OF US ARMY IN PACIFIC IN WWII. THIS VO-
LUME COVERS FIRST TWO YEARS. INCLUDES ROAD TO WAR, PEARL
HARBOR TO MIDWAY, SEIZING INITIATIVE, AND EMERGING PAT-
TERNS, PLUS OFFICIAL DOCUMENTS AND MAPS.

1533 MOSK S.A.
INDUSTRIAL REVOLUTION IN MEXICO.
BERKELEY: U OF CALIF PR, 1954, 331 PP.
ANALYZES REVOLUTION IN MEXICAN ECONOMY SINCE 1940, BASIC
ATTITUDES OF INDUSTRIAL DRIVE, AND PERSPECTIVES OF
BUSINESS, GOVERNMENT, AND LABOR. DISCUSSES GOVERNMENTAL
POLICIES ENCOURAGING INDUSTRIAL DEVELOPMENT. SURVEYS
DEVELOPMENTS IN PRINCIPAL INDUSTRIAL FIELDS.

1534 MOTE M.E.
SOVIET LOCAL AND REPUBLIC ELECTIONS.
STANFORD: HOOVER INSTITUTE, 1965, 123 PP., LC#65-26268.
PAPER DESCRIBES 1963 ELECTIONS IN LENINGRAD BASED ON
OFFICIAL DOCUMENTS, PRESS ACCOUNTS, AND PRIVATE INTERVIEWS.
GENERAL FEATURES OF PAPER APPLY TO ALL OF USSR. PAPER COVERS
STEPS IN ELECTION PROCESS ONE-BY-ONE AS THEY OCCUR. TIME
INVOLVED IS SIX OR SEVEN WEEKS, FROM MID-JANUARY TO MARCH 3.

1535 MOWER A.G.
"THE OFFICIAL PRESSURE GROUP OF THE COUNCIL OF EUROPE'S
CONSULATIVE ASSEMBLY."
INT. ORGAN., 18 (SPRING 64), 292-306.
'THE UNIVERSAL AND REGIONAL INTERNATIONAL ORGANIZATIONS
...CONFRONT ONE BASIC QUESTION: HOW TO MOVE SUCCESSFULLY
FROM INTERNATIONAL RECOMMENDATION TO NATIONAL ACTION.' SHOWS
THE DEVELOPMENT OF THE COUNCIL OF EUROPE AND THE CONCEPTION,
DEVELOPMENT, STRUCTURE AND PROCEDURES OF THE WORKING PARTY,
AND ITS USE AS A PRESSURE GROUP ON THE NATIONAL LEVEL. CITES
ITS PROPAGANDISTIC FUNCTIONS AND CAPABILITIES.

1536 MUKERJI S.N. ED.
ADMINISTRATION OF EDUCATION IN INDIA.
BARODA: ACHARYA BOOK DEPOT, 1962, 679 PP.
DETAILED DISCUSSIONS OF EDUCATIONAL ADMINISTRATION STRES-
SING ADVANCES MADE IN FIELD DURING RECENT YEARS. DEAL
WITH GENERAL SUBJECT AREAS SUCH AS RELATIONS BETWEEN VARI-
OUS SUPERVISORY AGENCIES AND SCHOOLS, AND DIFFERENT AREAS
AND BRANCHES OF EDUCATION. SEPARATE SECTIONS ON EACH UNION
TERRITORY.

1537 MULLEY F.W.
THE POLITICS OF WESTERN DEFENSE.
NEW YORK: PRAEGER, 1962, 282 PP., $6.75.
DISCUSSES DEFENSE APPARATUS OF NATO. URGES DEVELOPMENT OF
SYSTEM OF JOINT POLITICAL CONTROL OVER USE AND DEPLOYMENT OF
TACTICAL AND STRATEGIC NUCLEAR WEAPONS IN ORDER TO STRENGTH-
EN ALLIANCE. ASSERTING THAT NATO IS PURELY A DEFENSIVE MIL-
ITARY ALLIANCE, PLEADS FOR POLITICAL CONSULTATIONS AMONG ITS
MEMBER STATES IN AN EFFORT TO COORDINATE INDIVIDUAL NATIONAL
POLICIES.

1538 MUNGER E.S.
AFRICAN FIELD REPORTS 1952-1961.
CAPETOWN: C STRUIK, 1961, 808 PP.
PERSONAL REPORTS COVERING WIDE RANGE OF POLITICAL DEVEL-
OPMENTS IN TROPICAL AFRICA AND SOUTH AFRICA, INCLUDING
LEADERS, EVENTS, AND CONDITIONS.

1539 MUNICIPAL MANPOWER COMMISSION
GOVERNMENTAL MANPOWER FOR TOMORROW'S CITIES: A REPORT.
NEW YORK: MCGRAW HILL, 1962, 201 PP., LC#62-20507.
ANALYZES PROBLEM URBAN GOVERNMENTS HAVE IN ATTRACTING AND
KEEPING QUALITY PERSONNEL, ESPECIALLY IN TECHNICAL AREAS.
STUDY PROPOSES PLAN TO GIVE LOCAL GOVERNMENTS GUIDELINES TO
FOLLOW IN SEEKING QUALIFIED AND TRAINED WORKERS.

1540 MUNRO L.
UNITED NATIONS, HOPE FOR A DIVIDED WORLD.
NEW YORK: HOLT, 1960, 185 PP.
OUTLINES UN SYSTEM AS TO ORGANIZATION AND FUNCTION. EX-
AMINING POSSIBILITY OF WORLD PEACE THROUGH INTERNATIONAL CO-
OPERATION, ASSESSES UN'S INFLUENCE ON WORLD SITUATIONS.

1541 MURACCIOLE L.
"LES CONSTITUTIONS DES ETATS AFRICAINS D'EXPRESSION FRAN-
CAISE: LA CONSTITUTION DU 16 AVRIL 1962 DE LA REPUBLIQUE DU"
TCHAD.
REV. JURID. POLIT. OUTREMER, 16 (APR.-JUNE 62), 265-78.
PRESENTS AND COMMENTS BRIEFLY ON NEW AND MORE COMPREHEN-
SIVE CONSTITUTION OF CHAD. COMMENTARY EMPHASIZES POWER OF
THE PRESIDENT. HIS POWERS MAY BE CENSURED AND MODIFIED BY
TWO-THIRDS MAJORITY VOTE OF THE ASSEMBLY.

1542 MURACCIOLE L.
"LES MODIFICATIONS DE LA CONSTITUTION MALGACHE."
REV. JURID. POLIT. OUTREMER, 16 (JULY-SEPT. 62), 424-8.
BRIEF HISTORICAL ANALYSIS OF THE CONSTITUTION OF MADAGAS-
CAR. FOCUSES ON REVISIONS OF JUNE 6, 1962. POINTS OUT ARTI-
CLES DEALING WITH FREEDOM OF SPEECH. ELABORATES LAWS AND
CONSTITUTIONAL POWERS OF REPUBLIC'S PRESIDENT. INCLUDES LIST
OF MODIFIED CONSTITUTIONAL ARTICLES.

1543 MURCHISON C.
PSYCHOLOGIES OF 1930.
WORCHESTER: CLARK U. PR., 1930, 497 PP.
SEVERAL ISSUES COVERING MAJOR PROBLEMS CONCERNED WITH
THEORY OF HUMAN BEHAVIOR. PURPOSE IS TO DEFINE A GENERAL
WORKING BASIS OF PRINCIPLE ABLE TO GUIDE US IN PROPERLY
PLANNING BEHAVIOR IN ADVANCE.

1544 MURDESHWAR A.K.
ADMINISTRATIVE PROBLEMS RELATING TO NATIONALISATION: WITH
SPECIAL REFERENCE TO INDIAN STATE ENTERPRISES.
BOMBAY: POPULAR BOOK DEPOT, 1957, 330 PP.
DEVELOPS THEORY REGARDING ORGANIZATION AND ADMINISTRATION
OF NATIONALIZED UNDERTAKINGS BASED ON EXPERIENCE OF NATION-
ALIZED CONCERNS AND STATE ENTERPRISES IN BRITAIN, FRANCE,
CZECHOSLOVAKIA AND US. DISCUSSES VARIOUS PROBLEMS OF ALL
NATIONALIZED ENTERPRISES AND INDIA'S IN PARTICULAR; THOSE OF
LABOR, COMPOSITION OF GOVERNING BOARD, PARLIAMENTARY CON-
TROL, VOICE OF CONSUMER, STAFF, FINANCE, PRICE, POLICY.

1545 MURDOCK J.C. ED., GRAVES J. ED.
RESEARCH AND REGIONS.
COLUMBIA: U OF MO, BUS & PUB ADM, 1966, 211 PP., LC#66-65231
A KWIC (KEYWORD-IN-CONTEXT) INDEXED BIBLIOGRAPHY OF MA-
TERIAL IN ECONOMIC AND ADMINISTRATIVE RESEARCH AND REGIONAL
DEVELOPMENT. APPLIES COMPUTER TECHNIQUES TO INFORMATION RE-
TRIEVAL. PART I LISTS ENTRIES BY SEVEN KEYWORDS; PART II IS
AUTHOR-ALPHABETIZED BIBLIOGRAPHY; PART III, AN AUTHOR CROSS
REFERENCE. INCLUDES LISTING OF RESEARCH FACILITIES.

1546 MURRAY D.
"CHINESE EDUCATION IN SOUTH-EAST ASIA."
CHINA QUART., 20 (1964), 67-95.
SURVEYS DEVELOPMENT OF CHINESE EDUCATION WITHIN SOUTH-

EAST ASIAN CHINESE SOCIETIES, BRIEFLY RELATING THIS TO INTE-
GRATION OF OVERSEAS CHINESE INTO THE INDIGENOUS SOCIETIES.

1547 MURRAY J.N.
THE UNITED NATIONS TRUSTEESHIP SYSTEM.
URBANA: ILL. U. PR., 1957, 283 PP.
DESCRIBES ORIGIN OF TRUSTEESHIP SYSTEM AND FUNCTIONING
OF TRUSTEESHIP COUNCIL. DETAILS COUNCIL STRUCTURE. DEMON-
STRATES ACTION IN CASE OF FORMER ITALIAN SOMALILAND.

1548 MURRAY R.
"SECOND THOUGHTS ON GHANA."
NEW LEFT REV., 42 (MAR.-APR. 67), 25-39.
DISCUSSES LIMITATIONS OF FITSCH AND OPPENHEIMER'S ANALY-
IS OF SOCIALISM UNDER NKRUMAH IN THE BOOK "GHANA: END OF AN
ILLUSION." SUGGESTS THAT GHANIAN SOCIALISM LACKED THE INTE-
GRATED SELF-ANALYSIS, ON AN IDEOLOGICAL LEVEL, NECESSARY TO
RELATE SUCCESSFULLY TO THE REVOLUTIONARY PROCESS, A FACTOR
NOT ANALYZED BY FITSCH AND OPPENHEIMER WITH SUFFICIENT
SUBTLETY AND DEPTH.

1549 MUSHKIN S.J.
STATE PROGRAMMING.
CHICAGO: COUNCIL OF STATE GOVTS, 1965, 45 PP.
EXAMINES CONCERN OF STATES OVER THEIR ROLE IN ECONOMIC
DEVELOPMENT AND PRESENTS SOME MAJOR OBJECTIVES AND TOOLS OF
A STATE'S ECONOMIC POLICY. FOCUSES ON ECONOMIC PROGRAMMING
AS BASIS FOR PREDICTING REVENUES AND EXPENDITURES AND ON
PROGRAM-PLANNING AND EXPENDITURE DECISIONS IN CONTEXT OF
STATE ECONOMIC OBJECTIVES. STUDIES DIFFERENCES OF ECONOMIC
OBJECTIVES OF STATE AND NATION. MANY PERSPECTIVES USED.

1550 MUSOLF L.D.
PROMOTING THE GENERAL WELFARE: GOVERNMENT AND THE ECONOMY.
GLENVIEW, ILL: SCOTT, FORESMAN, 1965, 204 PP.
EXPLORATION OF ECONOMIC ACTIVITIES OF FEDERAL GOVERNMENT
AS PROMOTER, REGULATOR, BUYER, AND MANAGER. DISCUSSES HOW
THESE OPERATIONS PROMOTE GENERAL WELFARE.

1551 MUSSO AMBROSI L.A. ED.
BIBLIOGRAFIA DE BIBLIOGRAFIAS URUGUAYAS.
MONTEVIDEO: AGRUPACION BIB, 1964, 102 PP.
URUGUAYAN BIBLIOGRAPHY OF BIBLIOGRAPHIES INCLUDING
BOOKS, PERIODICALS, PAMPHLETS, AND NEWSPAPER ARTICLES. OVER
200 ENTRIES ARE URUGUAYAN BIBLIOGRAPHIC PERIODICALS. ABOUT
650 MATERIALS LISTED.

1552 NADLER E.B.
"SOME ECONOMIC DISADVANTAGES OF THE ARMS RACE."
J. CONFL. RESOLUT., 7 (SEPT. 63), 503-09.
STUDIES WAYS IN WHICH GROWTH OF MILITARY-INDUSTRIAL COM-
PLEX PREVENTS EFFECTIVE CONTROL OF AMERICAN ECONOMY. PROBLEM
CONTRIBUTES TO BUSINESS STAGNATION AND UNEMPLOYMENT. OFFERS
SOLUTIONS.

1553 NARAIN J.P.
SWARAJ FOR THE PEOPLE.
RAJGHAT: AKHIL BHARAT SARVA SEVA, 1961, 32 PP.
ARGUMENTS AND PROPOSALS ON REFORMING INDIA'S POLITICAL
INSTITUTIONS AND PROCESSES TO MAKE THEM "MORE DEMOCRATIC,
EFFICIENT, ENDURING, AND MEANINGFUL." EMPHASIZES EDUCATION,
DISTRIBUTION OF POWER, DEVELOPMENT OF "SOCIAL CONSCIOUS-
NESS," ELIMINATION OF ELECTORAL CONTESTS IN VILLAGE COMMUNI-
TIES, ETC. CONCLUDES THAT PEOPLE MUST TAKE LARGER ROLE IN
SHAPING NATIONAL WILL.

1554 NARASIMHAN V.K.
THE PRESS, THE PUBLIC AND THE ADMINISTRATION (PAMPHLET)
NEW DELHI: INDIAN INST PUB ADMIN, 1961, 68 PP.
ANALYZES ROLE OF PRESS IN INDIA AS VITAL SOURCE OF COM-
MUNICATION BETWEEN PEOPLE AND GOVERNMENT. FEELS PRESS SHOULD
ACT AS "MEDIATOR" BETWEEN PUBLIC AND ADMINISTRATION, AND
SUGGESTS CHANGES NECESSARY FOR THIS FUNCTION. SEES THIS ROLE
AS BEST WAY PRESS CAN SERVE PEOPLE IN FUTURE.

1555 NARVER J.C.
CONGLOMERATE MERGERS AND MARKET COMPETITION.
BERKELEY: U OF CALIF PR, 1967, 155 PP., LC#67-11444.
AUTHOR DEFINES CONGLOMERATE FIRM AS "A MARKET DIVERSIFIED
FIRM" OPERATING IN "TWO OR MORE SEPARATE PRODUCT AND/OR GEO-
GRAPHIC MARKETS," AND HE DISCUSSES THE SEVERAL FACTORS IN
CONGLOMERATE MERGERS LEADING TO THEIR ABILITY TO AFFECT COM-
PETITION. ANALYZES UNDER WHAT CONDITIONS MERGERS INCREASE OR
LESSEN COMPETITION IN A MARKET, MARKET STRUCTURE, AND MANA-
GERIAL BEHAVIOR.

1556 NASA
CONFERENCE ON SPACE, SCIENCE, AND URBAN LIFE.
WASHINGTON: US GOVERNMENT, 1963, 254 PP.
EXAMINES POSSIBILITIES OF APPLYING SPACE EXPLORATION
PROGRAM TO PROBLEMS OF DAILY LIFE IN URBAN AREAS. SEEKS
WAYS TO USE NEW KNOWLEDGE DEVELOPING IN SCIENTIFIC AND
TECHNOLOGICAL REVOLUTION TO HELP FIND ANSWERS TO CRITICAL
ISSUES FACING URBAN POPULATIONS.

1557 NASH B.D.
STAFFING THE PRESIDENCY: PLANNING PAMPHLET NO. 80 (PAMPHLET)
WASHINGTON: NATL PLANNING ASSN, 1952, 78 PP.
CABINET HAS NOT REALLY HELPED PRESIDENT TO DEVELOP POLICY
OR ADMINISTER THE EXECUTIVE BRANCH. IT SHOULD BE EXPANDED TO
INCLUDE HEADS OF ALL AGENCIES AND DEPARTMENTS AND GIVEN
ADDITIONAL FUNCTIONS.

1558 NASH M.
"SOCIAL PREREQUISITES TO ECONOMIC GROWTH IN LATIN AMERICA
AND SOUTHEAST ASIA."
ECON. DEVELOP. CULT. CHANGE, 12(APR 64), 225-42.
COMPARATIVE STUDY OF MODERNIZING NATION IN LATIN
AMERICA AND A NEWLY INDEPENDENT NATION OF SOUTHEAST ASIA.
EMPLOYS MACRO-STRUCTURAL ANALYSIS AND MICRO-ANALYSIS TO FIT
ROLE PERCEPTIONS IN THEIR INSTUTIONAL CONTEXT.

1559 NATHAN M.
THE SOUTH AFRICAN COMMONWEALTH: CONSTITUTION, PROBLEMS,
SOCIAL CONDITIONS.
JOHANNESBURG: SPECIALTY PR S AFR, 1919, 483 PP.
DESCRIBES SYSTEM OF GOVERNMENT IN SOUTH AFRICA AS OF
1919; SHOWS RELATIONSHIP TO GREAT BRITAIN AND COMMONWEALTH.
AUTHOR FEELS ANCESTRY AND HISTORY OF PEOPLE ASSURES CON-
TINUATION OF IDEALS OF LIBERTY, CIVILIZATION, AND HONOR.

1560 NATIONAL BOOK CENTRE PAKISTAN
BOOKS ON PAKISTAN: A BIBLIOGRAPHY.
KARACHI: STERLING PRINTING & PUB, 1965, 71 PP.
EMPHASIZES CULTURAL ASPECTS; INCLUDES BOOKS ON PAKISTAN
PUBLISHED OUTSIDE THE COUNTRY. SECTIONS ON HISTORY, IDEOL-
OGY, AND POLITICS; CONSTITUTIONAL STUDIES; ADMINISTRATION
AND BASIC DEMOCRACY; SOCIOLOGY, CUSTOM AND FOLKLORE.
ALL PUBLICATIONS ARE IN ENGLISH. CONTAINS INDEXES OF PUB-
LISHERS AND TITLES.

1561 NATIONAL BOOK LEAGUE
THE COMMONWEALTH IN BOOKS: AN ANNOTATED LIST.
LONDON: NATL BOOK LEAGUE, 1964, 126 PP.
LISTS BOOKS ON GEOGRAPHY, HISTORY, SOCIOLOGY, POLITICS,
LAW, AND LOCAL GOVERNMENT; BOOKS IN FRENCH FROM CANADIAN
PUBLISHERS. ANNOTATED AND ARRANGED BY SUBJECT. CONTAINS
BOOKS PUBLISHED SINCE APPROXIMATELY 1950.

1562 NATIONAL BUREAU ECONOMIC RES
THE RATE AND DIRECTION OF INVENTIVE ACTIVITY: ECONOMIC AND
SOCIAL FACTORS.
PRINCETON: PRINCETON U PRESS, 1962, 626 PP., LC#62-7044.
SELECTION OF PAPERS FROM CONFERENCE OF UNIVERSITIES-NAT-
TIONAL BUREAU COMMITTEE FOR ECONOMIC RESEARCH AND COMMITTEE
ON ECONOMIC GROWTH OF SOCIAL SCIENCE RESEARCH COUNCIL. DEALS
WITH RECENT RESEARCH INTO PROCESS OF INVENTION IN ECONOMIC
GROWTH, INDUSTRIAL ORGANIZATION, DEFENSE ECONOMICS, AND
MANAGEMENT SCIENCE.

1563 NATIONAL COMN COMMUNITY HEALTH
ACTION - PLANNING FOR COMMUNITY HEALTH SERVICES (PAMPHLET)
WASHINGTON: PUBLIC AFFAIRS PRESS, 1967, 67 PP., LC#67-19824.
REPORTS ON COMMUNITY ACTION STUDIES PROJECT TO STUDY
COMMUNITY-SUPPORTED IMPROVEMENTS IN HEALTH SERVICES.
PRESENTS FINDINGS ON FUNCTIONING OF COMMUNITY ACTION
PROGRAMS, STEPS IN PROCESS, AND RESULTS IN INCREASED
SERVICES. DISCUSSES NEED FOR DEFINITION OF AREA INVOLVED,
COOPERATION OF HEALTH ASSOCIATIONS, DEFINITE BUDGET, CORRECT
TIMING, AND FAVORABLE PUBLIC OPINION.

1564 NEAL F.W.
TITOISM IN ACTION.
BERKELEY: U OF CALIF PR, 1958, 331 PP., LC#58-10291.
TRACES DEVELOPMENT OF NEW THEORIES OF COMMUNISM IN YUGO-
SLAVIA. EXAMINES EVOLUTION OF NEW POLITICAL STRUCTURE AND
ECONOMIC SYSTEM. ANALYZES THEORIES BEHIND NEW REFORMS,
AND EXPLAINS AND EVALUATES THEIR SIGNIFICANCE. WORK BASED
ON YUGOSLAV LAW, GOVERNMENT DOCUMENTS, AND JOURNALS.

1565 NEEDHAM T.
"SCIENCE AND SOCIETY IN EAST AND WEST."
SCI. SOC., 28 (64), 385-408.
DISCUSSES THE PROBLEM OF HUMANIZING BUREAUCRACY THROUGH-
OUT CHINESE HISTORY. 'CHINA WAS HOMEOSTATIC, CYBERNETIC IF
YOU LIKE, BUT NEVER STAGNANT.' CHINESE INVENTIONS THAT
SHOCKED EUROPEAN CULTURE TIME AFTER TIME WERE TAKEN IN
STRIDE BY CHINA. NOTES THOSE FEATURES OF CHINESE SOCIETY
WHICH ALLOW THE INTEGRATION AND ASSIMILATION OF IDEAS OF
SOCIAL CHANGE.

1566 NEEDLER M.C.
"THE POLITICAL DEVELOPMENT OF MEXICO."
AMER. POLIT. SCI. REV., 55 (JUNE 61), 308-12.
CONTENDS THAT MEXICO HAS BEEN MORE DEMOCRATIC AND
STABLE THAN OTHER LATIN AMERICAN COUNTRIES DUE TO SPECIAL
TYPE OF POLITICAL INSTITUTION.

1567 NEIBURG H.L.
"THE EISENHOWER AEC AND CONGRESS: A STUDY IN EXECUTIVE-LEG-
ISLATIVE RELATIONS."
MIDWEST J. OF POLI. SCI., 6 (MAY 62), 115-148.

SHOWS HOW POLICY-MAKING INITIATIVE DURING 1956-60 RESTED WITH CONGRESSIONAL JOINT COMMITTEE ON ATOMIC ENERGY RATHER THAN WITH EXECUTIVE BRANCH. USES MICROCOSM OF EISENHOWER ADMINISTRATION. COVERS AEC AND PRE-1953 RELATIONS WITH CONGRESS. ALSO, EFFECT OF DEMOCRATIC VICTORIES, AND ROLE OF LEWIS STRAUSS. CONCLUDES THAT STRONGER PRESIDENTIAL LEADERSHIP ISNECESSARY.

1568 NELSON D.H.
ADMINISTRATIVE AGENCIES OF THE USA: THEIR DECISIONS AND AUTHORITY.
DETROIT: WAYNE STATE U PR, 1964, 341 PP., LC#63-13433.
    BASICALLY FORMALISTIC TEXT REVIEWING THE ADJUDICATORY POWERS AND PROCEDURES OF ADMINISTRATIVE AGENCIES, INCLUDING A DESCRIPTION OF ADMINISTRATIVE LAW IN THE US.

1569 NELSON R.H.
"LEGISLATIVE PARTICIPATION IN THE TREATY AND AGREEMENT MAKING PROCESS."
WESTERN POLIT. STUD., 15 (MAR. 60), 154-172.
    STUDIES ROLE OF CONGRESS, THROUGH PARTICIPATION IN MAKING AND IMPLEMENTING TREATIES AND OTHER INTERNATIONAL AGREEMENTS, IN THE EXECUTION OF US FOREIGN POLICY.

1570 NEUBURGER O.
OFFICIAL PUBLICATIONS OF PRESENT-DAY GERMANY: GOVERNMENT, CORPORATE ORGANIZATIONS, AND NATIONAL SOCIALIST PARTY.
WASHINGTON: GOVT PR OFFICE, 1942, 130 PP., LC#41-50721.
    ANNOTATED BIBLIOGRAPHY OF PUBLICATIONS ISSUED BY THE GERMAN GOVERNMENT SINCE 1933. INCLUDES AN INTRODUCTORY GUIDE TO GOVERNMENTAL STRUCTURE, LISTS OF BIBLIOGRAPHIC AIDS AND GAZETTES OF OCCUPIED TERRITORIES, NAZI PARTY PUBLICATIONS, ETC. ALSO INDICATES METHOD OF PUBLICATION AND PROVIDES AN INDEX OF ORGANIZATIONS.

1571 NEUCHTERLEIN D.E.
"THAILAND* ANOTHER VIETNAM?"
MILITARY REV., 47 (JUNE 67), 59-63.
    NOTES INCREASE OF COMMUNIST INSURGENCY IN NORTHEASTERN AREA OF THAILAND AND GIVES BACKGROUND OF INFILTRATION. SURVEYS ADVANTAGES WHICH THAILAND HAS OVER VIETNAM: PROSPERITY, STABILITY, NATIONAL UNITY, EFFICIENT GOVERNMENT. DESCRIBES US FACILITIES AND POLICY. CONCLUDES THAT THE THAIS WITH THEIR LONG HISTORY OF NATIONHOOD CAN TAKE CARE OF THEMSELVES.

1572 NEUMANN F.L.
"APPROACHES TO THE STUDY OF POLITICAL POWER."
POLIT. SCI. QUART., 65 (JUNE 50), 161-180.
    REVIEWS THE DIFFERENT APPROACHES TO STUDY OF POLITICAL POWER: POLITICAL POWER AND PSYCHOLOGY, DIFFERENT PHILOSOPHERS' ATTITUDES TO POLITICAL POWER, SIGNIFICANCE OF POLITICAL POWER AND FIVE SOCIOLOGICAL GENERALIZATIONS, ROOTS OF POLITICAL POWER'-POLITICAL PARTY, PRIVATE PROPERTY, BUREAUCRACY; IDENTIFICATION OF POLITICAL POWER, AND POLITICAL POWER AND FREEDOM.

1573 NEUMANN R.G.
THE GOVERNMENT OF THE GERMAN FEDERAL REPUBLIC.
NEW YORK: HARPER & ROW, 1966, 192 PP., LC#66-22517.
    HISTORICAL INTRODUCTION TO GERMANY'S GOVERNMENTAL STRUCTURE, THE CONTROVERSIAL ISSUE OF REUNIFICATION AND ITS POLITICAL SIGNIFICANCE; GERMANY'S PLACE IN EUROPEAN AND ATLANTIC WORLDS. DISCUSSES REASONS FOR HER POLITICAL STABILITY AND INSTABILITY, AND POINTS OF COOPERATION AND FRICTION BETWEEN GERMANY AND HER NEIGHBORS. CONSIDERS WHICH ASPECTS OF ADENAUER REGIME WILL HAVE LASTING SIGNIFICANCE.

1574 NEUMANN S. ED.
"MODERN POLITICAL PARTIES: APPROACHES TO COMPARATIVE POLITIC
CHICAGO: U OF CHICAGO PRESS, 1956.
    ANTHOLOGY OF INDEPENDENT STUDIES WHICH ATTEMPTS TO PRESENT IN CONCRETE FORM CONSISTENT PATTERNS OF AND PROBLEMS OF MAJOR POLITICAL PARTIES. CONTAINS STUDY OF PARTY DEVELOPMENTS IN UK FROM STAGE OF GOVERNING ELITE TO ORGANIZED MASS PARTIES, ANALYSIS OF COMMONWEALTH POLITICS, FRENCH POLITICAL PARTIES, PARTY ORGANIZATION IN US, BELGIUM, SCANDINAVIA, USSR, JAPAN, GERMANY, AND EASTERN EUROPE. BIBLIOGRAPHY.

1575 NEUSTADT R.E.
PRESIDENTIAL POWER.
NEW YORK: SIGNET, 1964, 189 PP., $0.60.
    EXAMINES ASPECTS OF PRESIDENTIAL POWER: USES, SCOPE, LIMITATIONS, POTENTIALITIES. ILLUSTRATED THROUGH ANALYSES OF INCIDENTS IN TRUMAN AND EISENHOWER ADMINISTRATIONS. ON BASIS OF CONCLUSIONS DERIVED FROM STUDY, TRIES TO ASSESS STRENGTH OR WEAKNESS OF PRESIDENT.

1576 NEVINS A.
THE STATE UNIVERSITIES AND DEMOCRACY.
URBANA: U OF ILLINOIS PR, 1962, 171 PP., LC#62-13215.
    A SWIFT AND PERCEPTIVE SURVEY OF MAJOR MINDS AND MAJOR EVENTS IN THE HISTORY OF THE GREAT AMERICAN STATE INSTITUTIONS., INCLUDING THE PROMISE OF CORNELL, POPULAR CENSURE AND OPPOSITION TO LAND-GRANT COLLEGES FROM VARIOUS GROUPS, THE EFFECTS OF PUBLIC ENDOWMENT, THE RESULTANT

UPGRADING OF SECONDARY EDUCATION, EXTENSION TEACHING, THE ROLE OF STATE BOARDS, ADMINISTRATION, AND DEMOCRATIC IDEALS.

1577 NEW ZEALAND COMM OF ST SERVICE
THE STATE SERVICES IN NEW ZEALAND.
WELLINGTON, N.Z.: RE OWEN, 1962, 470 PP.
    REPORT OF ROYAL COMMISSION OF INQUIRY INTO ORGANIZATION, STAFFING, AND METHODS OF CONTROL AND OPERATION OF DEPARTMENTS OF STATE. RECOMMENDS SEVERAL CHANGES TOWARD INCREASED EFFICIENCY, ECONOMY, AND IMPROVED SERVICE IN DISCHARGE OF PUBLIC BUSINESS.

1578 NEWLYN W.T.
"MONETARY SYSTEMS AND INTEGRATION"
J. OF EAST AFRICAN ECONOMIC REV., 11 (JUNE 64), 41-58.
    DISCUSSION OF RELATIONSHIP BETWEEN POLITICAL INTEGRATION AND ECONOMIC INTEGRATION, WITH SPECIAL REFERENCE TO MONETARY SYSTEMS. ANALYSIS APPLIED TO EAST AFRICA.

1579 NEWMAN F.C., KEATON H.J.
"CONGRESS AND THE FAITHFUL EXECUTION OF LAWS - SHOULD LEGISLATORS SUPERVISE ADMINISTRATORS."
CALIF. LAW REV., 41 (1953), 565-578, 584-595.
    CONGRESS EXERCISES TOO MUCH PARTISAN POLITICAL CONTROL OVER ADMNISTRATIVE DECISION-MAKING. AS COMPETENT, NON-POLITICAL PUBLIC SERVANTS, AUMINISTRATORS CAN BEST MAKE DECISIONS WHICH ARE IN THE PUBLIC INTEREST.

1580 NICHOLAS H.G.
THE UNITED NATIONS AS A POLITICAL INSTITUTION.
LONDON: OXFORD U. PR., 1962, 232 PP., $1.75.
    EXPLORES ORIGIN AND TRACES HISTORICAL EVOLUTION OF UN. ANALYZES ITS CHARACTER IN TERMS OF INTERNATIONAL POLITICS.

1581 NIEBURG H.L.
IN THE NAME OF SCIENCE.
CHICAGO: QUADRANGLE BOOKS, INC, 1966, 431 PP., LC#66-11868.
    ANALYSIS OF US FEDERAL SCIENCE POLICIES AND GOVERNMENT CONTRACTS IN TECHNOLOGICAL AND SCIENTIFIC FIELDS. EXAMINES SOCIOLOGICAL IMPLICATIONS OF NATIONALIZATION OF SCIENCE AND NUMEROUS LARGE-SCALE TRANSACTIONS BETWEEN GOVERNMENT AND INDUSTRIAL PROFIT ORGANIZATIONS. ANALYZES FEDERAL CONTRACT AS POWERFUL SOCIAL MANAGEMENT TOOL IN STIMULATION OF ECONOMIC AND POLITICAL ACTIVITY AND IN DISTRIBUTION OF POWER.

1582 NIEDERHOFFER A.
BEHIND THE SHIELD; THE POLICE IN URBAN SOCIETY.
GARDEN CITY: DOUBLEDAY, 1967, 253 PP., LC#67-16896.
    FORMER NEW YORK CITY POLICEMAN DRAWS ON OWN EXPERIENCE AND INTERVIEWS TO EXPLAIN POLICE RESENTMENT OF CIVILIAN INTERFERENCE WITH THEIR DUTIES. CYNICAL ATTITUDES, VULNERABILITY TO CORRUPTION, AND CONDONEMENT OF ILLEGAL USE OF FORCE OF POLICE. DESCRIBES SOCIAL FORCES THAT SHAPE POLICE-PERSONALITY. PRESENTS POLICE "TYPES." EXAMINES CHANGES IN DEMANDS ON AND ROLE OF POLICE FORCE.

1583 NIELANDER W.A., MILLER R.W.
PUBLIC RELATIONS.
NEW YORK: RONALD PRESS, 1951, 398 PP.
    OUTLINES CONCEPTS AND AIMS OF PUBLIC RELATIONS. EXAMINES INTERNAL AND EXTERNAL PERSONAL RELATIONS FOUND IN BUSINESS FIRMS. DISCUSSES CORPORATE RELATIONS WITH GENERAL PUBLIC, PRIVATE ORGANIZATIONS, GOVERNMENT BODIES, AND FOREIGN ORGANIZATIONS. DESCRIBES ORGANIZATION AND FUNCTION OF A PUBLIC RELATIONS BODY AND DISCUSSES USE OF VARIOUS PUBLICITY TECHNIQUES AND OTHER PROFESSIONAL PRACTICES.

1584 NIVEN R.
NIGERIA.
NEW YORK: FREDERICK PRAEGER, 1967, 268 PP., LC#66-21789.
    CHAPTERS 19 TO 23 MOST RELEVANT TO RESEARCHER. COVERS POLITICAL STRUCTURE, PARTIES, CONSTITUTIONS, ADMINISTRATION, 1966 REVOLTS. ALSO HAS INFORMATION ABOUT EACH PROVINCE AND RELATION TO NATIONAL UNITY. TRACES DEVELOPMENT FROM TRIBAL FEDERATION TO NATIONAL STATE.

1585 NJ DEPARTMENT CIVIL SERV
THE CIVIL SERVICE RULES OF THE STATE OF NEW JERSEY.
TRENTON: N J DEPT CIVIL SERVICE, 1962, 56 PP.
    COLLECTS RULES RELATING TO NEW JERSEY CIVIL SERVICE CONCERNING STATE, COUNTY AND MUNICIPAL OPERATIONS AS DERIVED FROM CHAPTER 156,PL 1908, AND SUPPLEMENTARY ACTS.

1586 NJ DIVISION STATE-REGION PLAN
UTILIZATION OF NEW JERSEY'S DELAWARE RIVER WATERFRONT (PAMPHLET)
TRENTON: N J DEPT CONS & ECO DEV, 1965, 64 PP.
    INVENTORY OF EXISTING AND EMERGING PATTERNS OF LAND ALONG RIVER. AIMS TO KEEP ALL NEW NJ INDUSTRY "WATER-ORIENTED" BY ANALYZING CURRENT ACTIVITY OF RIVER AND GROWTH IN PAST. SUGGESTS CENTRALIZING CONTROL AND PLANNING OF ALL WATERFRONT LAND UNDER ONE AGENCY. RECOMMENDS USING MORE LAND FOR RECREATIONAL PURPOSES.

1587 NORDEN A.
WAR AND NAZI CRIMINALS IN WEST GERMANY: STATE, ECONOMY,

ADMINISTRATION, ARMY, JUSTICE, SCIENCE.
BERLIN: NATL FRONT DEM GERMANY, 1965, 402 PP.
CLAIMS THAT NAZI WAR CRIMINALS ARE TAKING OVER WEST GER-
MAN GOVERNMENT WHICH WILL PRECIPITATE WWIII. CASTI-
GATES BONN GOVERNMENT FOR CESSATION OF PROSECUTION OF WAR
CRIMINALS. DESCRIBES HITLER'S SECRET POLICE AND POLITICAL
MACHINE, AND HIS STAFF FOR EXTERMINATION OF JEWS. LISTS
SPECIFIC INDIVIDUALS, DESCRIBING FORMER NAZI ACTIVITIES AND
CURRENT POSITION IN GOVERNMENT.

1588 NORGREN P.H., HILL S.E.
"TOWARD FAIR EMPLOYMENT."
NEW YORK: COLUMBIA U PRESS, 1964.
CRITICAL STUDY AND APPRAISAL OF GOVERNMENTAL FAIR EMPLOY-
MENT AGENCIES AT FEDERAL, STATE, AND LOCAL LEVELS. CONTENDS
THAT ALTHOUGH GOVERNMENT FAIR EMPLOYMENT MEASURES CAN EXPE-
DITE THE PROCESS, THE ESSENTIAL KEY TO FULL EMPLOYMENT
EQUALITY FOR RACIAL MINORITIES IS TO BE FOUND IN CHANGING
LABOR MARKET BEHAVIOR AND EQUALIZATION OF EDUCATIONAL OPPOR-
TUNITIES. BIBLIOGRAPHY OF WORKS PUBLISHED FROM 1943-63.

1589 NORTH R.C.
"DIE DISKREPANZ ZWISCHEN REALITAT UND WUNSCHBILD ALS
INNENPOLITISCHER FAKTOR."
OSTEUROPA, 10 (NOV.-DEC. 60), 766-69.
CONSIDERS DIFFERENCES BETWEEN REAL AND IDEAL VALUES AS
INSTRUMENTAL IN CAUSING TENSION AND DISAPPOINTMENT. ARGUES
THAT PRODUCTIVE FUNCTIONS OF SOCIETY ARE AFFECTED IN DIRECT
RELATION TO MAGNITUDE OF DIFFERENCES. APPLIES CONCEPTUAL
MODEL TO ANALYSIS OF COMMUNIST CHINA.

1590 NORTH R.C.
"DECISION MAKING IN CRISIS: AN INTRODUCTION."
J. CONFL. RESOLUT., 6 (SEPT. 62), 197-200.
INTRODUCTION TO CONTEMPORARY STUDY OF INTERNATIONAL
CRISES. FOCUSES ON CLARIFYING THE RELATIONSHIP BETWEEN CON-
FLICT AND INTEGRATION AND TESTS A SERIES OF GENERAL HYPOTH-
ESES ABOUT THE BEHAVIOR OF STATES.

1591 NORTH R.C. ET AL.
CONTENT ANALYSIS: A HANDBOOK WITH APPLICATIONS FOR THE
STUDY OF INTERNATIONAL CRISIS.
EVANSTON: NORTHWESTERN U. PR., 1963, 182 PP., $2.95.
A VALUABLE INTRODUCTION TO A USEFUL RESEARCH TECHNIQUE.
INCLUDES CONCRETE ILLUSTRATIONS PLUS GUIDES 'FOR DECIDING
WHETHER, WHEN, AND WHAT FORM OF CONTENT ANALYSIS SHOULD BE
USED.' THE EXAMPLES COME FROM RESEARCH ON THE ORIGINS OF
WORLD WAR I AND ON CONTEMPORARY SINO-SOVIET RELATIONS.
SPECIAL FORMS DISCUSSED INCLUDE: THE CONVENTIONAL FREQUENCY
COUNT AND QUALITATIVE IDENTIFICATIONS, Q-SORTS, PAIR COM-
PARISONS, AND EVALUATIVE ASSERTION ANALYSIS.

1592 NORTHRUP H.R.
RESTRICTIVE LABOR PRACTICES IN THE SUPERMARKET INDUSTRY.
PHILA: U OF PENN PR, 1967, 202 PP., LC#67-26220.
STUDIES LABOR-MANAGEMENT RELATIONS AND PROBLEMS IN SUPER-
MARKET INDUSTRY. SEEKS TO DETERMINE WHETHER LABOR PRACTICES
WORK AGAINST CONSUMER INTERESTS AND EFFICIENT MARKETING
OPERATIONS. DISCUSSES POTENTIALS FOR CHANGE, PRESENTS DE-
TAILS OF TECHNOLOGICAL PROGRESS, AND SUGGESTS NEW APPROACH
TO LABOR RELATIONS. INCLUDES HISTORY OF DEVELOPMENT OF
SUPERMARKETS AND UNIONIZATION MOVEMENT.

1593 NOVE A.
"THE SOVIET MODEL AND UNDERDEVELOPED COUNTRIES."
INT. AFF., 37 (JAN. 61), 29-38.
ANALYZES FACTORS WEAKENING GROWTH OF ECONOMIC ACTIVITY
RELATING TO PARTICULAR COUNTRIES. COMPARES COMMUNIST AND
WESTERN PROPAGANDA METHODS, AND THEIR PURPOSE OF MOBILIZING
PEOPLE TO CARRY OUT DIFFICULT TASKS. WARNS THAT WEST'S
ALTERNATIVE SUGGESTIONS ARE NOT ALWAYS ATTUNED TO GOALS.

1594 NOVE A.
THE SOVIET ECONOMY.
NEW YORK: FREDERICK PRAEGER, 1961, 328 PP., LC#61-16579.
INTRODUCTION SURVEY OF SOVIET ECONOMY, INCLUDING ITS PRO-
DUCTIVE ENTERPRISES, ADMINISTRATION, CHANGING NATURE OF ITS
PROBLEMS, AND BASIC CONCEPTS OF SOVIET ECONOMICS.

1595 NUQUIST A.E.
TOWN GOVERNMENT IN VERMONT.
BURLINGTON: U OF VERMONT, 1964, 276 PP., LC#64-15447.
ANALYZES STRUCTURE OF TOWN GOVERNMENTS, MOST DEMOCRATIC
FORM OF GOVERNMENT IN US, IN VERMONT. COVERS TYPICAL TOWN
MEETING, OFFICIALS OF TOWN, THEIR FUNCTIONS, ANNUAL REPORTS,
AND SPECIFIC AREA PROBLEMS SUCH AS CONSERVATION, FORESTRY,
ETC; DEALS BRIEFLY WITH COUNTY ORGANIZATION.

1596 NYC TEMPORARY COMM CITY FINAN
MUNICIPAL COLLECTIVE BARGAINING (NO. 8)
NEW YORK: NY CITY TEMP COMM FIN, 1966, 65 PP.
STUDY OF FINANCIAL PROBLEMS OF NYC AND RECOMMENDED SOLU-
TIONS. DEALS WITH PROGRAMS AND REVENUES, INTERGOVERNMENTAL
FISCAL RELATIONS, CAPITAL DEVELOPMENT AND DEBT, FISCAL STA-
TUS OF EDUCATION, AND RELATED SUBJECTS.

1597 NYE J.S. JR.
"EAST AFRICAN ECONOMIC INTEGRATION."
J. MOD. AFRICAN STUD., 1 (DEC. 63), 475-502.
EVALUATES A LONG-TERM EXPERIMENT IN ECONOMIC AND ADMIN-
ISTRATIVE UNION AMONG KENYA, TANGANYIKA, UGANDA. ECONOMIC
INTEGRATION IS EXTENSIVE BUT THERE IS NO GOOD PROSPECT OF
CONTINUED STABILITY WITHOUT POLITICAL UNION--AND ECONOMIC
INTEGRATION HAS YET TO PRODUCE ANY FORCES LEADING AUTO-
MATICALLY IN THIS DIRECTION.

1598 NYE J.S.
"CORRUPTION AND POLITICAL DEVELOPMENT: A COST-BENEFIT
ANALYSIS."
AM. POL. SCI. REV., 61 (JUNE 67), 417-427.
STUDIES EFFECTS OF CORRUPTION, BENEFITS SUCH AS PROMOTING
ECONOMIC DEVELOPMENT, NATIONAL INTEGRATION, AND GOVERNMENTAL
CAPACITY TO DEAL WITH CHANGE AND COSTS SUCH AS WASTE OF RE-
SOURCES, INSTABILITY, AND REDUCTION OF GOVERNMENTAL CAPAC-
ITY. RESEARCH SHOWS THAT PROBABILITY IS GREATER THAT COSTS
WILL EXCEED BENEFITS OF CORRUPTION IN UNDERDEVELOPED
COUNTRIES.

1599 O'DELL J.H.
"THE JULY REBELLIONS AND THE 'MILITARY STATE'."
FREEDOMWAYS, 7 (FALL 67), 288-301.
ANTI-JOHNSON ADMINISTRATION ARTICLE DISCUSSES THE GROWING
POWER OF THE EXECUTIVE-MILITARY COALITION IN THE AREA OF
CIVIL RIGHTS AND IN VIETNAM. EMPHASIZES THE NEED FOR A
"RESISTANCE MOVEMENT" TO COMBAT TOTALITARIANISM AND
MILITARISM. CALLS FOR UNITY OF THE "OPPRESSED MASSES."

1600 O'HEARN P.J.T.
PEACE, ORDER AND GOOD GOVERNMENT; A NEW CONSTITUTION FOR
CANADA.
TORONTO: MACMILLAN CO OF CANADA, 1964, 325 PP.
PROPOSES CHANGES IN CANADIAN CONSTITUTION IN ALL AREAS;
SUPPLIES REASONS FOR CHANGES AND PRESENTS POSSIBILITIES OF
THESE TAKING PLACE.

1601 O'NEILL C.E.
CHURCH AND STATE IN FRENCH COLONIAL LOUISIANA: POLICY AND
POLITICS TO 1732.
NEW HAVEN: YALE U PR, 1966, 313 PP., LC#66-21529.
STUDIES ATTITUDES AND ACTIVITIES OF CIVIL AND RELIGIOUS
INSTITUTIONS IN FRENCH COLONY OF LOUISIANA FROM BEGINNING OF
COLONY TO RETROCESSION TO KING BY COMPANY OF INDIES; THEIR
COOPERATION AND CONFLICT, AND THEIR MOTIVES.

1602 OECD
MEDITERRANEAN REGIONAL PROJECT: TURKEY; EDUCATION AND
DEVELOPMENT.
PARIS: ORG FOR ECO COOP AND DEV, 1965, 189 PP.
REVIEWS PRESENT EDUCATIONAL STRUCTURE AND POLICY IN
TURKEY; TREATS ROLE OF EDUCATION IN SOCIAL AND ECONOMIC
DEVELOPMENT. DISCUSSES FACILITIES, TEACHER TRAINING AND
SUPPLY, AND ADMINISTRATION. EXAMINES COST OF EDUCATIONAL
DEVELOPMENT, PRESENT EXPENDITURES, AND FUTURE NEEDS. COVERS
ECONOMIC TARGETS AND MANPOWER, OCCUPATIONAL CLASSIFICATIONS,
DEMAND AND SUPPLY, AND PARTICIPATION.

1603 OECD SEMINAR REGIONAL DEV
REGIONAL DEVELOPMENT IN ISRAEL.
PARIS: ORG FOR ECO COOP AND DEV, 1964, 46 PP.
DISCUSSES INSTITUTIONS FOR REGIONAL PLANNING IN ISRAEL,
THEIR ADMINISTRATION AND IMPLEMENTATION OF PROGRAMS AT
NATIONAL AND REGIONAL LEVELS. STUDIES DEVELOPMENT IN LAKHISH
REGION IN PARTICULAR; OBJECTIVES AND ASPECTS OF PLAN AND
CHANGES ACCOMPLISHED BY DEVELOPMENT PROGRAM.

1604 OHLIN G.
AID AND INDEBTEDNESS.
PARIS: ORG FOR ECO COOP AND DEV, 1966, 55 PP.
ANALYSIS OF CURRENT INTERNATIONAL ECONOMIC AID SITUATION
FOCUSING ON RELATIONSHIPS BETWEEN AID REQUIREMENTS, TERMS OF
ASSISTANCE, AND PROBLEMS OF INDEBTEDNESS OF UNDERDEVELOPED
COUNTRIES.

1605 OLIVE B.A.
"THE ADMINISTRATION OF HIGHER EDUCATION: A BIBLIOGRAPHICAL
SURVEY."
ADMINISTRATIVE SCI. Q., 2 (MAR. 67), 671-677.
FOUR EXTENSIVE BIBLIOGRAPHICAL STUDIES WHICH EXAMINE THE
LITERATURE OF THE ADMINISTRATION OF HIGHER EDUCATION ARE
EVALUATED AND CURRENT INDEXING SOURCES ARE INDICATED. A SUR-
VEY OF THE RECENT EDUCATIONAL LITERATURE REVEALS THE EXIS-
TENCE OF FEW SIGNIFICANT RESEARCH PUBLICATIONS. REASONS FOR
THE PAUCITY OF RESEARCH IDENTIFIED AS THE NATURE OF THE UNI-
VERSITY ORGANIZATIONAL STRUCTURE AND FACULTY ATTITUDES.

1606 OLLE-LAPRUNE J.
LA STABILITE DES MINISTRES SOUS LA TROISIEME REPUBLIQUE,
1879-1940.
PARIS: PICHON ET DURAND-AUZIAS, 1962, 376 PP.
ANALYTICAL HISTORY OF MINISTERIAL TURNOVER DURING FRENCH
THIRD REPUBLIC, EMPHASIZING COMPARATIVE STABILITY DURING
PERIODS OF CRISIS AND NORMALITY, INCLUDING MECHANISMS AND

FORMS OF STABILITY.

1607 OLLERENSHAW K.
"SHARING RESPONSIBLITY."
PUBLIC ADMINISTRATION. 40 (SPRING 62), 43-54.
DISCUSSION OF RELATIONS BETWEEN EDUCATION ADMINISTRATORS
AND PUBLICLY ELECTED BOARD MEMBERS IN BRITISH PUBLIC
EDUCATION SYSTEMS. CALLS FOR INCREASED COOPERATION TO BEST
SERVE PUBLIC INTEREST.

1608 OLSON M. JR.
THE ECONOMICS OF WARTIME SHORTAGE.
DURHAM: DUKE U PR, 1963, 152 PP., LC#63-17328.
INVESTIGATES HISTORICALLY THE EFFECTS OF WAR UPON A NA-
TION AND TO WHAT EXTENT THAT NATION CAN ADJUST PHYSICALLY
AND ECONOMICALLY. SHOWS BRITAIN'S PROBLEMS IN REVOLUTIONARY
AND NAPOLEONIC WARS. THEN CONSIDERS POSITION OF UK
IN WWI AND COMPARES IT WITH GERMANY. FINALLY CONSIDERS
BRITAIN'S LOSSES IN FOOD IMPORTS DURING WWII AND DRAWS
THEORETICAL SPECULATIONS FROM RESULTS OF STUDY.

1609 OLSON M. JR.
DROIT PUBLIC.
PARIS: PR UNIV DE FRANCE, 1957, 438 PP.
PUBLIC RIGHT DEFINED AS RULES OF SOCIAL CONDUCT
ESTABLISHED AND SANCTIONED BY PUBLIC AUTHORITY. STUDY IS
DIVIDED INTO THREE BRANCHES: CONSTITUTIONAL RIGHTS,
ADMINISTRATIVE RIGHTS, AND FINANCIAL RIGHTS. DISCUSSES
EVOLUTION OF PUBLIC RIGHT FROM 1789.

1610 ONYEMELUKWE C.C.
PROBLEMS OF INDUSTRIAL PLANNING AND MANAGEMENT IN NIGERIA.
LONDON: LONGMANS, GREEN & CO, 1966, 330 PP.
STUDY OF BACKGROUND AND NATURE OF PROBLEMS OF INDUSTRI-
ALIZATION IN NIGERIA, A REPRESENTATIVE AFRICAN NATION. SHOWS
THAT SOCIAL CHANGES MUST TAKE PLACE ALONGSIDE TECHNOLOGICAL
OR PROGRESS WILL NOT TAKE PLACE. AUTHOR HOPES OTHER UNDER-
DEVELOPED NATIONS CAN LEARN FROM NIGERIA'S ATTEMPT TO SOLVE
MODERN PROBLEMS.

1611 OPERATIONS AND POLICY RESEARCH
PERU ELECTION MEMORANDA (PAMPHLET)
WASHINGTON: OPER & POL RES, INC, 1964, 38 PP.
STUDY OF GOVERNMENTAL STRUCTURE AND REPRESENTATION BY EX-
AMINATION OF 1963 PERUVIAN ELECTIONS. DISCUSSES LAWS GOV-
ERNING ELECTORAL QUALIFICATIONS AND PROCEDURES.

1612 OPERATIONS RESEARCH SOCIETY
A COMPREHENSIVE BIBLIOGRAPHY ON OPERATIONS RESEARCH; THROUGH
1956 WITH SUPPLEMENT FOR 1957.
CLEVELAND: CASE INST OF TECH, 1958, 188 PP., LC#58-9681.
CODED BIBLIOGRAPHY CONTAINING 3,000 TITLES OF BOOKS, AR-
TICLES, REPORTS, PROCEEDINGS, ETC. PUBLISHED THROUGH 1956.
INTENDED FOR AN OPERATIONS RESEARCH AUDIENCE. EACH AU-
THOR GIVEN A SERIAL WHICH REPRESENTS SHORTHAND VERSION OF
COMPLETE ENTRY; SERIALS USED FOR COMPUTERIZED CODING OF
CROSS REFERENCES. TEN-DIGIT CLASSIFICATION TO LEFT OF EACH
ENTRY INFORMS READER ON CONTENT OF WORK CITED.

1613 OPOTOWSKY S.
THE KENNEDY GOVERNMENT.
NEW YORK: EP DUTTON, 1961, 208 PP., LC#61-12465.
DISCUSSION OF FORMATION AND KEY POLICIES OF KENNEDY AD-
MINISTRATION WHICH CONSISTS LARGELY OF PROFILES OF PROFES-
SIONAL CAREERS OF CABINET HEADS AND OTHER ADMINISTRATION
OFFICIALS.

1614 ORG FOR ECO COOP AND DEVEL
THE MEDITERRANEAN REGIONAL PROJECT: AN EXPERIMENT IN
PLANNING BY SIX COUNTRIES.
PARIS: ORG FOR ECO COOP AND DEV, 1965, 39 PP.
RELATES EDUCATION TO ECONOMIC GROWTH AND SOCIAL ADVANCE-
MENT IN GREECE, YUGOSLAVIA, SPAIN, TURKEY, PORTUGAL, AND
ITALY. ESTIMATES FUTURE EDUCATIONAL NEEDS ACCORDING TO
ECONOMIC CRITERIA, SOCIAL AND CULTURAL OBJECTIVES, AND
DEMOGRAPHIC TRENDS. FORMULATES PROPOSALS FOR 1961-75.
ANALYZES COSTS, ADMINISTRATION, EDUCATIONAL STRUCTURE,
DEMAND AND SUPPLY, MANPOWER, AND ROLE OF TEACHERS.

1615 ORG FOR ECO COOP AND DEVEL
THE MEDITERRANEAN REGIONAL PROJECT: YUGOSLAVIA; EDUCATION
AND DEVELOPMENT.
PARIS: ORG FOR ECO COOP AND DEV, 1965, 143 PP.
REVIEWS ECONOMIC AND SOCIAL DEVELOPMENTS, PAST AND PRES-
ENT, AND SURVEYS YUGOSLAV EDUCATIONAL SYSTEM. DISCUSSES
ECONOMIC AND MANPOWER PROJECTIONS, 1961-75, AND SKILL
STRUCTURE; INCLUDES PROSPECTIVE VERSUS REQUIRED OUTPUTS OF
EDUCATIONAL SYSTEM FOR 1961-75 AND PRESENTS METHODOLOGICAL
APPROACH. CLOSING SECTION DEALS WITH TEACHING STAFF AND
FINANCIAL EXPENDITURE.

1616 ORTH C.D., BAILEY J.C., WOLEK F.W.
ADMINISTERING RESEARCH AND DEVELOPMENT.
HOMEWOOD: DORSEY, 1964, 585 PP., LC#64-24699.
DETAILED CASE STUDIES OF PROBLEMS IN MANAGEMENT OF RE-
SEARCH AND DEVELOPMENT GROUPS FOCUSING ON ADMINISTRATIVE AC-

TIVITIES OF SEVERAL LARGE CORPORATIONS. ALSO CONTAINS COL-
LECTIONS OF GENERAL DISCUSSIONS OF RESEARCH STUDIES PROBLEMS
AND CONCEPTUAL PROBLEMS.

1617 ORTIZ R.P.
ANNUARIO BIBLIOGRAFICO COLOMBIANO, 1951-1956.
BOGOTA: BOG INST CARA CUERNO, 1958, 334 PP.
LISTING OF BOOKS AND MONOGRAPHS PUBLISHED IN COLUMBIA OR
BY COLUMBIANS DURING PERIOD 1951-1956. MATERIAL ON
POLITICAL SCIENCE, SOCIOLOGY, STATISTICS, ECONOMICS, LAW,
PUBLIC ADMINISTRATION, SOCIAL WELFARE, EDUCATION, COMMERCE,
AND LINGUISTICS.

1618 OSTGAARD E.
"FACTORS INFLUENCING THE FLOW OF NEWS."
JOURNAL OF PEACE RESEARCH, (1965), 9-63.
FACTORS WHICH IMPAIR AND DISTORT NEWS AS IT IS FINALLY
PRESENTED BY NEWS MEDIA ARE PRESENTED TO SHOW HOW NEWS MEDIA
INFLUENCE WORKING OF INTERNATIONAL COMMUNITY. SUGGESTS
GENERAL HYPOTHESES CONCERNING EFFECTS OF NEWS MEDIA AND
POSSIBILITIES FOR FURTHER RESEARCH TO LEAD TO MINIMIZATION
OF SUCH EFFECTS.

1619 OVERSEAS DEVELOPMENT INST.
EFFECTIVE AID.
LONDON: MIN OF OVERSEAS DEVEL, 1967, 129 PP.
EXAMINES AID ADMINISTRATION, TERMS AND CONDITIONS OF
FOREIGN AID, AND TECHNICAL ASSISTANCE TO UNDERDEVELOPED NA-
TIONS. DISCUSSES PRACTICES IN GERMANY, FRANCE, UK, AND US.

1620 OWEN G.
INDUSTRY IN THE UNITED STATES.
BALTIMORE: PENGUIN BOOKS, 1966, 215 PP.
LOOK AT MANAGEMENT OF AMERICAN INDUSTRY STUDIES
DECISION-MAKING PROCESS AND TRAINING OF MANAGERS TO MAKE
DECISIONS. ATTRIBUTES SUCCESS OF AMERICAN BUSINESS TO HIGH
ESTEEM IN WHICH BUSINESS HAS BEEN HELD, HIGH CALIBER OF
BUSINESSMEN, AND GOVERNMENT'S CONTRIBUTION TO PROSPERITY.
COMPARES AMERICAN MEN AND METHODS TO BRITISH COUNTERPARTS
AND SUGGESTS MEANS FOR IMPROVEMENT IN BRITISH SYSTEM.

1621 PACKARD V.
THE PYRAMID CLIMBERS.
NEW YORK: MCGRAW HILL, 1962, 339 PP., LC#62-21117.
DISCUSSES INNER WORLD OF BUSINESS EXECUTIVES AND METHODS
AND CONDITIONS OF SUCCEEDING IN STRUGGLE FOR EXECUTIVE
POWER. EXAMINES TYPES OF EXECUTIVES, SEARCH FOR IDEAL TYPES,
AND EFFORTS TO DEVELOP LEADERS OF BREADTH AND IMAGINATION.

1622 PADELFORD N.J.
"REGIONAL COOPERATION IN THE SOUTH PACIFIC: THE SOUTH
PACIFIC COMMISSION."
INT. ORG., 13 (SUMMER 59), 380-393.
TRACES HISTORIC DEVELOPMENT, NATURE AND PURPOSE OF THE
COMMISSION. DESCRIBES ESTABLISHMENT OF THE RESEARCH COUNCIL
WHOSE OBJECTIVE IS AIDING AND BETTERING LIFE OF INHABITANTS
AND PREPARING THEM FOR EVENTUAL SELF-DETERMINATION.

1623 PADOVER S.K.
"PSYCHOLOGICAL WARFARE AND FOREIGN POLICY."
AMER. SCH., 20 (SPRING 61), 151-61.
STATES THAT TO BE EFFECTIVE, WORDS MUST BE COUPLED WITH
ACTION: HENCE PSYCHOLOGICAL WARFARE HAS TO BE CLOSELY TIED
TO POLITICAL OR MILITARY POLICY. CONCLUDES THAT AMERICAN
FOREIGN POLICY SUFFERS FROM INTELLECTUAL AND SPIRITUAL
EMPTINESS.

1624 PAGE T. ED.
THE PUBLIC PERSONNEL AGENCY AND THE CHIEF EXECUTIVE
(REPORT NO. 601)
CHICAGO: PUBLIC PERSONNEL ASSN, 1960, 40 PP.
CONSIDERS PROBLEM OF HOW BEST TO ORGANIZE THE PERSONNEL
FUNCTION OF INDUSTRY AND RELATIONSHIP BETWEEN PERSONNEL
AGENCY AND EXECUTIVES WITH DISCUSSING OF RELATIVE MERITS
OF AGENCIES HEADED BY SINGLE EXECUTIVE US COMMISSION.

1625 PAGE T.
STATE PERSONNEL REORGANIZATION IN ILLINOIS.
URBANA: U OF ILLINOIS PR, 1961, 154 PP.
EXAMINES SHIFT OF PERSONNEL FUNCTION IN STATE GOVERNMENT
FROM AN INDEPENDENT AGENCY TO THE GOVERNOR'S CABINET. SHOWS
CONDITIONS UNDER WHICH SHIFT TOOK PLACE, EXPECTATIONS OF AD-
MINISTRATIVE AND POLITICAL LEADERS INVOLVED, AND OPERATION
OF SYSTEM UNDER REVISED PATTERN OF ORGANIZATION.

1626 PALMER A.M.
ADMINISTRATION OF MEDICAL AND PHARMACEUTICAL PATENTS
(PAMPHLET)
WASHINGTON: NATL ACAD OF SCI, 1955, 69 PP., LC#55-60029.
INTERPRETIVE ANALYSES AND DESCRIPTIONS OF SITUATION AT
EACH OF 90 MEDICAL SCHOOLS AND 74 COLLEGES OF PHARMACY
REGARDING SPECIAL POLICIES AND PRACTICES FOR DEALING WITH
MEDICAL PATENTS. WHERE PERTINENT, INCLUDES VERBATIM EXCERPTS
FROM APPLICABLE GENERAL UNIVERSITY RESEARCH AND PATENT
POLICIES.

1627 PALMER J.M.
AMERICA IN ARMS: THE EXPERIENCE OF THE UNITED STATES WITH
MILITARY ORGANIZATION.
NEW HAVEN: YALE U PR, 1941, 207 PP.
DESCRIBES PERIODS OF HISTORY IN WHICH US HAS BEEN ARMED,
SHOWING EVOLUTION OF MILITARY ORGANIZATION WITHIN THE GOV-
ERNMENT. DISCUSSES GEORGE WASHINGTON'S MILITARY POLICY, ROLE
OF MILITIA IN REVOLUTION, WAR THEORIES OF KNOX AND STEUBEN.
ANALYZES US MILITARY ORGANIZATION DURING WAR OF 1812 AND
WWI. SPECULATES ON FUTURE OF MILITARY AFTER WWII.

1628 PALMER M.
"THE UNITED ARAB REPUBLIC* AN ASSESSMENT OF ITS FAILURE."
MIDDLE EAST J., 20 (WINTER 66), 50-67.
THE FORCES WHICH DROVE THE SYRIAN ELITES TO ACCEPTING
SUBMERGENCE WITHIN THE UAR LED TO EVEN GREATER FRACTIONING
AND COMPETITION AMONG THE ELITES, UNTIL EVEN GREAT POPULAR
SUPPORT FOR UNION COULD NOT MAKE UP FOR THE INADEQUACIES OF
THE ADMINISTRATIVE STRUCTURE. PALMER VIEWS THIS FAILURE AT
UNITY AS ILLUSTRATIVE OF GENERAL ARAB UNITY PROBLEMS.

1629 PALOTAI O.C.
PUBLICATIONS OF THE INSTITUTE OF GOVERNMENT, 1930-1962.
CHAPEL HILL: U OF N CAR INST GOV, 1963, 78 PP.
RECORD OF RESEARCH AND PUBLISHING ACTIVITIES OF THE
INSTITUTE OF GOVERNMENT. TOPICALLY CLASSIFIED LIST OF COM-
PARATIVE STUDIES IN THE STRUCTURE AND WORKINGS OF GOVERNMENT
AT ALL LEVELS, PRIMARILY STATE AND LOCAL ADMINISTRATION.
INCLUDES ANNOTATED SECTION ON SPECIAL STUDIES PUB-
LISHED BY THE INSTITUTE.

1630 PAN AMERICAN UNION
REPERTORIO DE PUBLICACIONES PERIODICAS ACTUALES LATINO-AMER-
ICANAS.
PARIS: UNESCO, 1958.
DIRECTORY OF LATIN AMERICAN PERIODICALS ARRANGED BY DEWEY
DECIMAL SYSTEM.

1631 PANJABI K.L. ED.
THE CIVIL SERVANT IN INDIA.
BOMBAY: BHARATIYI VIDYA BHAUAN, 1965, 356 PP.
COLLECTION OF STATEMENTS BY RETIRED MEMBERS OF CIVIL SER-
VICE, REVIEWING THEIR WORK IN THE SERVICE, TRAINING (FORMAL
AND PERSONAL), DISCIPLINE, WORKING CONDITIONS, AS WELL AS
TRIALS, COMPENSATIONS, AND CHERISHED IDEALS. MANY ARE HUMOR-
OUS AND PERSONAL REFLECTIONS, INTIMATELY PICTURING ADMINIS-
TRATION OF PRE-INDEPENDENCE INDIA.

1632 PARET P.
FRENCH REVOLUTIONARY WARFARE FROM INDOCHINA TO ALGERIA*
THE ANALYSIS OF A POLITICAL AND MILITARY DOCTRINE.
PRINCETON: CTR OF INTL STUDIES, 1964, 163 PP., LC#64-13381.
ANALYSIS OF FRENCH DOCTRINE FOR COMBATING UNCONVENTIONAL
SUBLIMITED WARFARE. PARET BELIEVES THAT IN ITS STRENGTHS
AND WEAKNESSES IT IS THE BEST GUIDE FOR OTHERS INVOLVED IN
THIS TYPE OF WAR. STRESSES INTERRELATION OF POLITICAL, PSY-
CHOLOGICAL, AND MILITARY MEASURES.

1633 PARK R.L. ED., TINKER I. ED.
LEADERSHIP AND POLITICAL INSTITUTIONS IN INDIA.
PRINCETON: U. PR., 1959, 486 PP.
TRADITIONS OF INDIAN LEADERSHIP ARE DISCUSSED ALONG WITH
AN EVALUATION OF PERSONAL QUALITIES OF THREE MAJOR POLITICAL
FIGURES. STUDY INCLUDES AN ANALYSIS OF PUBLIC ADMINISTRATION
AND RURAL DEVELOPMENT.

1634 PARKINSON C.N.
PARKINSON'S LAW.
BOSTON: HOUGHTON MIFFLIN, 1957, 110 PP., LC#57-09881.
DISCUSSES UNDERLYING PRINCIPLES OF ADMINISTRATION AND
WORK ORGANIZATION. ALSO COVERS TIME ALLOTMENT, FISCAL
FINANCIAL PLANNING, RETIREMENT PROGRAMS, AND EFFECT
OF GENERAL ATTITUDES UPON PUBLIC ADMINISTRATION.

1635 PARRISH W.E.
MISSOURI UNDER RADICAL RULE 1865-1870.
COLUMBIA: U OF MO PR, 1965, 385 PP., LC#65-21794.
STUDY OF FIVE-YEAR PERIOD DURING WHICH PROGRESSIVE RE-
FORMS WERE MADE IN FORWARDING NEGRO SUFFRAGE AND EDUCATION,
WHITE ACCEPTANCE OF NEGROES, AND ECONOMIC AND SOCIAL WELFARE
OF STATE. ATTEMPTS TO RESTORE BALANCE IN HISTORICAL OUTLOOK
UPON RADICALS' METHODS, POLITICS, AND CONTRIBUTIONS.

1636 PARSONS T.
THE STRUCTURE OF SOCIAL ACTION.
NEW YORK: MCGRAW HILL, 1937, 817 PP.
TRACES THE DEVELOPMENT OF THE POSITIVISTIC THEORY OF AC-
TION AND POINTS OUT THE EMERGENCE OF A REVOLUTIONARY THEORY
OF ACTION FROM THE POSITIVE TRADITION. ANALYZES THE PRINCI-
PLE CHARACTERISTICS OF CAPITALISM AND CONCLUDES WITH SYSTEM-
ATIC THEORY OF MAX WEBER'S DOCTRINE.

1637 PARSONS T.
"SUGGESTIONS FOR A SOCIOLOGICAL APPROACH TO THE THEORY OF
ORGANIZATIONS - I" (BMR)"
ADMINISTRATIVE SCI. Q., 1 (JUNE 56), 3-239.
ATTEMPTS TO OUTLINE AN APPROACH TO ANALYSIS OF FORMAL
ORGANIZATIONS IN TERMS OF A GENERAL THEORY OF SOCIAL SYS-
TEMS. ORGANIZATIONS AS DEFINED BY PARSONS ARE ANALYZED IN
TERMS OF AN INSTITUTIONALIZED VALUE SYSTEM, DEFINING AND
LEGITIMIZING ITS GOAL, AND OF MECHANISMS BY WHICH IT IS
ARTICULATED WITH SOCIETY IN WHICH IT OPERATES. AUTHOR
EXAMINES THE THREE PRIMARY CONTEXTS OF THIS ARTICULATION.

1638 PARSONS T.
"EVOLUTIONARY UNIVERSALS IN SOCIETY."
AMER. SOC. REV., 29 (JUNE 64), 339-57.
SIX CASES PRESENTED TO DEMONSTRATE A THEORY OF DEVEL-
OPMENTAL STAGES: STRATIFICATION, LEGITIMATION, BUREAUCRACY,
MONEY AND MARKETS, LAW, AND DEMOCRACY.

1639 PASLEY R.S.
"ORGANIZATIONAL CONFLICTS OF INTEREST IN GOVERNMENT CON-
TRACTS."
WISC. LAW REV., 67 (WINTER 67), 1-42.
THE GROWTH OF DEFENSE AND SPACE EFFORTS BY THE FEDERAL
GOVT. AND THE DEVELOPMENT OF AN IMMENSE MILITARY-INDUSTRIAL
OMPLEX HAVE BROUGHT WITH THEM THE ORGANIZATIONAL CONFLICT OF
INTEREST, WHICH ARISES WHEN AN INDUSTRY ENGAGES IN RESEARCH
AND DVLPMT. OF PRODUCTS AND THEN SUPPLIES THOSE PRODUCTS TO
THE GOVT. PASLEY DESCRIBES 2 MAJOR AREAS OF CONFLICT - PRO-
CUREMENT AND EMPLOYMENT.

1640 PASTUHOV V.D.
A GUIDE TO THE PRACTICE OF INTERNATIONAL CONFERENCES.
WASHINGTON: CARNEGIE ENDOWMENT, 1945, 275 PP.
DEALS WITH PLANNING, STAFFING, BUDGETING, ORGANIZING,
DIRECTING AND ACTUAL HOLDING OF INTERNATIONAL CONFERENCES
AND COMMITTEE MEETINGS, DEVOTING SPECIAL ATTENTION TO
FOLLOW-UP WORK. LINKS TECHNICAL PROCESSES WITH THEORY AND
REPRESENTATIVE LITERATURE IN THIS FIELD.

1641 PATRA A.C.
THE ADMINISTRATION OF JUSTICE UNDER THE EAST INDIA COMPANY
IN BENGAL, BIHAR AND ORISSA.
NEW YORK: ASIA PUBL HOUSE, 1963, 233 PP.
APPRAISAL OF DISPENSATION OF JUSTICE BY PRINCIPAL JUDI-
CIAL INSTITUTIONS OPERATING UNDER EAST INDIA COMPANY IN
BENGAL. FOCUSES ON AREA OF LEGAL ADMINISTRATION.

1642 PATTERSON C.P., MCALISTER S.B., HESTER G.C.
STATE AND LOCAL GOVERNMENT IN TEXAS (3RD ED.)
NEW YORK: MACMILLAN, 1940, 586 PP.
SURVEYS ALL ASPECTS OF TEXAS GOVERNMENT, INCLUDING ITS
CONSTITUTION, LEGISLATURE, ELECTIONS, TAXATION, EDUCA-
TION, WELFARE, POLICE, AND HIGHWAY SYSTEMS. EMPHASIS ON
STATE GOVERNMENT AS OPPOSED TO COUNTY AND MUNICIPAL GOVERN-
MENT.

1643 PATTERSON C.P.
PRESIDENTIAL GOVERNMENT IN THE UNITED STATES - THE UNWRITTEN
CONSTITUTION.
CHAPEL HILL: U OF N CAR PR, 1947, 301 PP.
ARGUES THAT PARTY POLITICS, AS INSTRUMENT OF ECONOMIC
FORCES, HAS TURNED AMERICAN POLITICAL SYSTEM INTO "UNLIMITED
DEMOCRACY" AND "UNWRITTEN CONSTITUTIONALISM," ENDING IN THE
ESTABLISHMENT OF THE POLITICAL HEGEMONY OF THE PRESIDENT. TO
REMEDY EVILS OF POSSIBLE ONE-MAN RULE UNDER STRONG
PRESIDENCY, SUGGESTS THAT THE PARTY BE MADE RESPONSIBLE BY
ESTABLISHING A MODIFIED FORM OF CABINET GOVERNMENT.

1644 PAULSEN F.R.
AMERICAN EDUCATION: CHALLENGES AND IMAGES.
TUCSON: U OF ARIZONA PR, 1967, 118 PP., LC#66-28787.
ANALYZES AND EVALUATES MODERN ISSUES OF EDUCATION, USING
FOUR BASIC CHALLENGES AS CRITERIA. EDUCATION SHOULD HELP
INDIVIDUAL UNDERSTAND HIMSELF AND COMMUNICATE WITH OTHERS.
IT SHOULD ALSO STRIVE FOR NATIONAL COHERENCE, AND DETERMINE
WAYS TO BRING ABOUT WORLD PEACE. BOTH TEACHERS AND ACTUAL
CLASSROOM SITUATIONS ARE STUDIED IN SERIOUS EFFORT TO HELP
EDUCATORS MEET CHALLENGES OF FUTURE.

1645 PAYNE J.L.
LABOR AND POLITICS IN PERU: THE SYSTEM OF POLITICAL
BARGAINING.
NEW HAVEN: YALE U PR, 1965, 292 PP., LC#65-22335.
DISCUSSES LABOR RELATIONS AND LABOR POLITICS AS ONE AREA.
COLLECTIVE BARGAINING IS MORE ACCURATELY POLITICAL
BARGAINING IN PERU WHERE POLITICS AND UNIONS ARE CLOSELY
TIED. EXAMINES RELATIONS BETWEEN LABOR AND EXTREMIST AND
MODERATE PARTIES, STRUCTURE AND LEADERSHIP OF LABOR
MOVEMENT, AND SYSTEM OF POLITICAL BARGAINING.

1646 PAYNE W.A.
"LOCAL GOVERNMENT STUDY COMMISSIONS: ORGANIZATION FOR
ACTION."
AMERICAN COUNTY GOVERNMENT, 32 (JULY 67), 15-19.
STUDIES CREATION, ORGANIZATION, AND OPERATION OF COUNTY
COMMISSIONS TO ANALYZE PROBLEMS OF LOCAL GOVERNMENT. COMMIS-
SIONS CAN BE ESTABLISHED BY STATE LEGISLATURE OR BY COUNTY
RESOLUTION. COMMITTEES ARE SET UP TO STUDY SEPARATE AREAS,
AND MASTER WORK PLAN IS CHOSEN. FINAL REPORT SUMMARIZES

FINDINGS AND GIVES SUGGESTIONS FOR CHANGES IN LOCAL GOVERN-
MENTAL SYSTEM.

1647 PEABODY R.L. ED., POLSBY N.W. ED.
NEW PERSPECTIVES ON THE HOUSE OF REPRESENTATIVES.
NEW YORK: RAND MCNALLY & CO, 1963, 381 PP., LC#63-17450.
    REAPPRAISAL OF POLITICS, PROCEDURES, AND TRADITIONS OF
HOUSE. INCLUDES ESSAYS ON ENLARGED RULES COMMITTEE, COM-
MITTEE ASSIGNMENTS, FEDERAL AID TO EDUCATION , AND MAKING
OF MILITARY POLICY.

1648 PEABODY R.L.
ORGANIZATIONAL AUTHORITY.
NEW YORK: ATHERTON PRESS, 1964, 163 PP., LC#64-19646.
    PRESENTS RESULTS OF EXPLORATORY STUDY OF AUTHORITY RELA-
TIONSHIPS IN THREE PUBLIC SERVICE ORGANIZATIONS: ELEMENTARY
SCHOOL, PUBLIC WELFARE AGENCY BRANCH OFFICE, AND MUNICIPAL
POLICE DEPARTMENT. DISTINGUISHES FUNCTIONAL AND FORMAL AU-
THORITY, BOTH NECESSARY FOR ACHIEVING GOALS AND SATISFYING
INDIVIDUAL NEEDS.

1649 PEARSON A.W.
"RESOURCE ALLOCATION."
J. MANAGEMENT STUDIES, 4 (OCT. 68), 332-353.
    CONSIDERS PROBLEM OF FACTOR UTILIZATION THAT GENERATES
ALTERNATE INVESTMENT POSSIBILITES, AND OF SELECTING ONE
THAT GIVES MAXIMUM POSSIBLE GROSS PROFIT. DISCUSSES VARIOUS
MODELS THAT CAN BE USED IN THIS DETERMINATION, ALONG WITH
THEIR EFFECTIVENESS AND PAST APPLICATIONS.

1650 PEASLEE A.J.
INTERNATIONAL GOVERNMENT ORGANIZATIONS, CONSTITUTIONAL
DOCUMENTS.
GENEVA: NIJHOFF, 1961, 2 VOLS.
    REFERENCE WORK ON SUBJECT DESCRIBES FUNCTIONS, PROTOCOL
ARRANGEMENTS, AND CONSTITUTIONAL OF SEVERAL HUNDRED ORGANI-
ZATIONS.

1651 PENICK J.L. JR. ED., PURSELL CW J.R. ED. ET AL.
THE POLITICS OF AMERICAN SCIENCE, 1939 TO THE PRESENT.
SKOKIE: RAND MCNALLY & CO, 1965, 287 PP., LC#65-14099.
    READINGS ON ISSUES OF PRESENT DAY (WELFARE STATE, COLD
WAR, INTERNATIONALISM, ETC.) THAT HAVE INFLUENCED AND
HELPED MOLD STRUCTURE OF US SCIENTIFIC COMMUNITY. ATTEMPTS
TO ILLUMINATE QUESTIONS OF POLICY AND ADMINISTRATION RATHER
THAN TECHNICAL PROBLEMS OF SCIENCE.

1652 PENNSYLVANIA ECONOMY LEAGUE
URBAN RENEWAL IMPACT STUDY: ADMINISTRATIVE-LEGAL-FISCAL.
PITTSBURGH: ACTION HOUSING, INC, 1960, 300 PP.
    ATTEMPTS TO PLACE MAJOR PHYSCIAL, SOCIAL, ECONOMIC, AND
ADMINISTRATIVE DIMENSIONS ON A COMPREHENSIVE RENEWAL PRO-
GRAM FOR ALLEGHENY COUNTY, PENNSYLVANIA. IDENTIFIES BASIC
PROBLEMS AND ISSUES AND POINTS WAY TOWARD MORE EFFECTIVELY
OVERCOMING BLIGHT AND DECAY. AMONG SUGGESTIONS ARE THOSE FOR
GREATER COOPERATION IN ADMINISTRATION, AND COMMUNITY PROGRAM
FINANCING SOCIAL AND ECONOMIC AS WELL AS PHYSICAL PLANNING.

1653 PENTONY D.E. ED.
UNITED STATES FOREIGN AID.
SAN FRANCISCO: CHANDLER, 1960, 147 PP., LC#60-07597.
    DISCUSSES OBJECTIVES OF US FOREIGN AID, MILITARY,
ECONOMIC, AND HUMANITARIAN. GIVES BACKGROUND OF FOREIGN
AID PROGRAM AND EXAMINES VARYING METHODS OF AID IN ITS
ADMINISTRATION. USES TWO CASE STUDIES OF AID TO ANALYZE
ITS EFFECTIVENESS.

1654 PERHAM M.
AFRICANS AND BRITISH RULE.
LONDON: OXFORD U PR, 1941, 98 PP.
    STUDIES GROWTH OF BRITAIN'S POLICIES TOWARD HER COLONIES
IN AFRICA. DESCRIBES CONTINENT AS IT WAS BEFORE EUROPEAN
OCCUPATION AND TRACES PROCESS BY WHICH BRITISH AFRICA WAS
GAINED AND HOW IT HAS BEEN GOVERNED. EXAMINES POLITICAL AND
ECONOMIC USES AND ABUSES OF IMPERIALISM. DESCRIBES HOW BRIT-
AIN RULES INDIRECTLY THROUGH AFRICAN SELF-GOVERNMENT. CALLS
FOR INCREASED EFFORTS TOWARD MUTUAL UNDERSTANDING.

1655 PERHAM M.
COLONIAL GOVERNMENT: ANNOTATED READING LIST ON BRITISH
COLONIAL GOVERNMENT.
LONDON: OXFORD U PR, 1950, 80 PP.
    SELECTED LIST OF PAMPHLETS, LEGISLATION, BIBLIOGRAPHIES,
CONFIDENTIAL MATERIAL, AND JOURNALS FOR STUDENTS OF BRITISH
COLONIALISM. NOT OVERLY SPECIALIZED; CONCENTRATES ON LARGER
COLONIES. MAINLY PRIMARY SOURCE MATERIAL FROM PUBLICATIONS
CIRCA 1950. INCLUDES A FEW PUBLICATIONS FROM OUTSIDE UNITED
KINGDOM.

1656 PERKINS J.A.
"CONGRESSIONAL INVESTIGATIONS OF MATTERS OF INTERNATIONAL
IMPORT."
AM. POL. SCI. REV., 34 (APR. 40), 284-294.
    MAINTAINS THAT INVESTIGATING COMMITTEES IN CONGRESS ARE
NOT USEFUL INSTRUMENTS FOR COLLECTING INFORMATION. INFORMA-
TION PROCURED SAID TO BE BIASED. CORRECTIVE LIES IN CON-

GRESS' ABILITY TO CURB MINORITY PARTY POWER.

1657 PERKINS J.A.
"ADMINISTRATION OF THE NATIONAL SECURITY PROGRAM."
PUBLIC ADMIN. REV., 13 (SPRING 53), 80-86.
    SECURITY POLICY DETERMINATION REQUIRES CHANGES IN FORM
AND FUNCTION: DISCUSSES ROLES OF DEFENSE DEPARTMENT, STATE
DEPARTMENT, NATIONAL SECURITY COUNCIL, AND CONGRESS IN
SECURITY PLANNING.

1658 PERKINS J.A.
THE UNIVERSITY IN TRANSITION.
PRINCETON: PRINCETON U PRESS, 1966, 89 PP., LC#66-15804.
    DISCUSSES FACTORS BEARING UPON UNIVERSITY GROWTH AND DE-
VELOPMENT AND PROBLEMS OF DIRECTING TRANSITION. NOTES STU-
DENT AND ADMINISTRATION PROBLEMS IN RELATING TO "OUTSIDE
WORLD." EXAMINES EDUCATIONAL AND ADMINISTRATIVE FACTORS IN
SEARCH FOR INTERNAL COHERENCE IN CHANGING TIMES. DISCUSSES
VARIOUS FORCES WHICH DETERMINE FORMAL UNIVERSITY ORGANIZA-
TION AND DEPARTMENTAL FUNCTIONS.

1659 PERLOFF H.S. ED., COHEN H. ED.
URBAN RESEARCH AND EDUCATION IN THE NEW YORK METROPOLITAN
REGION (VOL. II)
NEW YORK: REGIONAL PLANNING ASSN, 1965, 350 PP.
    PAPERS PREPARED FOR STUDY OF MEANS BY WHICH INTELLECTUAL
RESOURCES OF NEW YORK MIGHT BE MOBILIZED MORE EFFECTIVELY
TO COPE WITH DIFFICULT URBAN PROBLEMS. TOPICS COVERED ARE:
RELATION OF UNIVERSITIES TO THE COMMUNITY; PLANNING
DECISIONS AND PLANNING EDUCATION; SOCIAL, ECONOMIC, AND
POLITICAL FORCES; WAYS OF ORGANIZING INFORMATION; AND RE-
SEARCH AND TECHNICAL ASSISTANCE NEEDED.

1660 PERREN G.E., HOLLOWAY M.F.
LANGUAGE AND COMMUNICATION IN THE COMMONWEALTH (PAMPHLET)
LONDON: H M STATIONERY OFFICE, 1965, 54 PP.
    ANALYZES MAJOR LANGUAGE PROBLEMS IN COMMONWEALTH IN
GOVERNMENT, EDUCATION, AND INDUSTRIAL AREAS. FEELS THEY
HINDER DEVELOPMENT OF ORGANIZATION. URGES THAT WIDER METHODS
OF LANGUAGE TEACHING BE INTRODUCED FOR FUTURE PROGRESS.

1661 PERROW C., STREET D., VINTER R.D.
ORGANIZATION FOR TREATMENT: A COMPARATIVE STUDY OF INSTITU-
TIONS FOR DELINQUENTS.
NEW YORK: MACMILLAN, 1966, 330 PP., LC#66-17696.
    DETAILED EVALUATION OF CAPACITY OF JUVENILE CORRECTIONAL
INSTITUTIONS TO PREPARE INMATES FOR SUCCESSFUL PARTICIPATION
IN SOCIETY. INVESTIGATES PROBLEM ON EXECUTIVE, STAFF, AND
INMATE LEVELS AND EMPHASIZES NEED FOR OBJECTIVE GOALS AND
MEASURES OF EFFECTIVENESS RATHER THAN VAGUELY DEFINED "BE-
LIEF SYSTEMS" IN TREATMENT OF INMATES. POINTS OUT NEED FOR
COOPERATION BETWEEN INSTITUTIONS AND OUTSIDE AGENCIES.

1662 PETERSON F.
SURVEY OF LABOR ECONOMICS (REV. ED.)
NEW YORK: HARPER & ROW, 1951, 871 PP.
    ANALYZES BASIC DATA AND MAJOR THEORIES PERTAINING
TO ECONOMIC PHENOMENA RELATING TO LABOR. EMPHASIZES
HISTORICAL DEVELOPMENT OF CURRENT THEORIES, PRACTICES, AND
INSTITUTIONAL ARRANGEMENTS. COVERS EMPLOYMENT AND UNEMPLOY-
MENT, WAGES AND HOURS, LABOR UNIONS AND LABOR-MANAGEMENT
RELATIONS, AND SOCIAL SECURITY. REVISED EDITION IS UPDATED
AND CONTAINS MANY CHANGES AND ADDITIONS.

1663 PETRULLO L. ED., BASS B.M. ED.
LEADERSHIP AND INTERPERSONAL BEHAVIOR.
NEW YORK: HOLT RINEHART WINSTON, 1961, 385 PP., LC#61-6167.
    ANALYZES INTERACTION OF PERSON AND SITUATION IN LEADER-
HIP PROCESS. CONSIDERS ALSO ASPECTS OF LEADERSHIP AND INTER-
PERSONAL BEHAVIOR BASED ON CONCEPTS OF HOMEOSTASIS, REIN-
FORCEMENT, AUTOMATA THEORY, AND GROUP DYNAMICS. DISCUSSES
SMALL GROUP EXPERIMENTS IN LABORATORY AND FIELD AND LEADER-
SHIP PHENOMENA IN LARGE INDUSTRIAL AND MILITARY ORGANIZA-
TIONS.

1664 PETTEE G.S.
THE PROCESS OF REVOLUTION.
NEW YORK: HARPER, 1938, 167 PP.
    BELIEVES SOCIOLOGY OFFERS MOST ILLUMINATING AND COMPRE-
HENSIVE DEFINITION OF REVOLUTION. THEORY IS BASED UPON THREE
GREAT REVOLUTIONS: FRENCH, RUSSIAN, AND SPANISH. SURVEYS
FASCIST MOVEMENT AND NOTES POSSIBLE DEMOCRATIC ALTERNATIVE.

1665 PFIFFNER J.M.
RESEARCH METHODS IN PUBLIC ADMINISTRATION.
NEW YORK: RONALD PRESS, 1940, 447 PP.
    TEXTBOOK FOR TRAINING IN PRACTICAL OPERATING METHODS AND
TECHNIQUES OF FACT-FINDING IN PUBLIC ADMINISTRATION.
FOCUSES ON PROBLEMS OF MANAGEMENT. DESCRIBES CAREER
OPPORTUNITIES IN RESEARCH, AND STAFF RELATIONSHIPS WITHIN
ORGANIZATIONS. ANALYZES RESEARCH PLANNING, HANDLING OF DATA,
INTERVIEWS, QUESTIONNAIRES, AND METHODS OF PREPARING THE
RESEARCH REPORT.

1666 PFIFFNER J.M., PRESTHAUS R.V.
PUBLIC ADMINISTRATION.

NEW YORK: RONALD PRESS, 1960, 570 PP., LC#60-07771.
EXAMINES FIELD OF PUBLIC ADMINISTRATION AT ALL LEVELS OF
GOVERNMENT. RECOUNTS RISE OF BUREAUCRATIC STATE, ITS IMPACT
ON ADMINISTRATION THEORY AND PRACTICE, AND NATURE OF THE
NEW PUBLIC ADMINISTRATOR. DEALS WITH THREE TECHNICAL
ASPECTS OF ADMINISTRATION: ORGANIZATION, PERSONNEL, AND
FINANCE.

1667 PFIFFNER J.M.
"ADMINISTRATIVE RATIONALITY" (BMR)"
PUBLIC ADMIN. REV., 20 (SUMMER 60), 125-132.
DISCUSSES BASES OF ADMINISTRATIVE RATIONALITY IN
POLICY-MAKING. CLARIFIES PROCESS OVER WHICH ADMINISTRATOR
"PRESIDES." HOPES TO HELP ADMINISTRATOR ADJUST THE "MIX" OF
HIS RATIONALITY TO THE MOST SUCCESSFUL AND ETHICAL ENDS.
DISCUSSES CLASSICAL, NORMATIVE, AND BEHAVIORAL MODELS OF
RATIONALITY.

1668 PHELPS-FETHERS I.
SOVIET INTERNATIONAL FRONT ORGANIZATIONS* A CONCISE HANDBOOK
NEW YORK: FREDERICK PRAEGER, 1965, 178 PP., LC#65-20503.
PHELPS-FETHERSTON REVIEWS HISTORY OF FRONT MOVEMENT AND
ANALYZES SOVIET-CONTROLLED INTERNATIONAL FRONT ORGANIZATIONS
IN TERMS OF AIMS, MEMBERSHIP, PUBLICATIONS, SUCCESS, AND
STATUS IN THE SINO-SOVIET CONFLICT.

1669 PHILLIPS J.C.
MUNICIPAL GOVERNMENT AND ADMINISTRATION IN AMERICA.
NEW YORK: MACMILLAN, 1960, 648 PP., LC#60-5247.
STUDIES MUNICIPAL GOVERNMENT AND ADMINISTRATION WITH
REFERENCE TO INTERGOVERNMENTAL RELATIONS INVOLVING
MUNICIPALITIES. DISCUSSES CIVIL RIGHTS AT MUNICIPAL LEVEL,
PUBLIC RELATIONS, PLANNING URBAN RENEWAL, AND ZONING.

1670 PHILLIPS O.H.
CONSTITUTIONAL AND ADMINISTRATIVE LAW (3RD ED.)
LONDON: SWEET AND MAXWELL, LTD, 1962, 855 PP.
EXAMINES ENGLISH LAW, INCLUDING ANALYSIS OF CONSTITUTION
AND PARLIAMENT, CROWN AND CENTRAL GOVERNMENT, JUDICIAL SYS-
TEM, AND RIGHTS AND DUTIES OF CITIZENRY, AND ADMINISTRATIVE
LAW AND RELATION TO COMMONWELATH.

1671 PIERCE R.A.
RUSSIAN CENTRAL ASIA, 1867-1917: A SELECTED BIBLIOGRAPHY
(PAMPHLET)
BERKELEY: U OF CALIF PR, 1953, 28 PP.
SELECTED LIST OF MATERIAL DESIGNED TO AID SPECIALISTS IN
RESEARCH IN FIELD. MAIN STRESS IS ON DOMESTIC DEVELOPMENTS.
ITEMS ARE ARRANGED BY SUBJECT CONTENT: HISTORY, RUSSIAN CON-
QUEST, ADMINISTRATION, WWI IMPACT, ECONOMICS, ETHNOGRAPHY,
NATIVE LAW, CULTURAL DEVELOPMENT, EDUCATION, AND GEOG-
RAPHY. INCLUDES 483 ENTRIES.

1672 PIERCE R.A.
RUSSIAN CENTRAL ASIA, 1867-1917.
BERKELEY: U OF CALIF PR, 1960, 359 PP., LC#59-11314.
A SURVEY OF THE EXPANSION OF RUSSIA'S ASIAN FRONTIERS
AND COLONIZATION OF THE BORDERLANDS WHICH OCCURRED BETWEEN
1867-1917. TREATS TERRITORIAL CONQUEST AND ADMINISTRATION IN
TERMS OF STRUCTURE, ORGANIZATION, REFORM, AND DEVELOPMENT.
DISCUSSES COLONIZATION, URBAN DEVELOPMENT, ECONOMIC DEVELOP-
MENT, AND THE CLASH OF EASTERN AND WESTERN CULTURES. CON-
CLUDES WITH COLLAPSE OF TSAR AND COLONIAL INHERITANCE.

1673 PIERCE T.M.
FEDERAL, STATE, AND LOCAL GOVERNMENT IN EDUCATION.
WASHINGTON: CTR APPL RES EDUC, 1964, 120 PP.
DISCUSSES EXPANDING ROLE OF ALL LEVELS OF GOVERNMENT IN
SUPERVISION AND SUPPORT OF EDUCATION. EMPHASIZES GROWTH AND
IMPROVEMENT OF SCHOOL SYSTEMS UNDER GOVERNMENT AUSPICES. AD-
VOCATES INTEGRATION BETWEEN LEVELS AND BRANCHES OF GOVERN-
MENT IN EDUCATION PROGRAMS.

1674 PINNICK A.W.
COUNTRY PLANNERS IN ACTION.
SIDCUP, KENT, ENGL.: LAMBARDE PRESS, 1964, 128 PP.
DISCUSSES COUNTRY PLANNING PROGRAM IN DORSET TO ILLUS-
TRATE DECISION-MAKING PROCESS, CONTROL OF EXPERTS BY POLITI-
CIANS, AND DRASTIC NEED FOR CHANGE IN FINANCIAL BASIS OF
PROGRAM. INCLUDES PROPOSAL TO BUILD NEW TOWN. METHODS BY
WHICH INDUSTRY CREEPS INTO AREA TO AVOID BEING RESTRICTED,
AND PLANNING FOR CHILDREN, LEISURE, AND AMENITIES. ATTEMPTS
TO PROVIDE INFORMATION TO PUBLIC TO CHANGE ATTITUDES.

1675 PINTO F.B.M.
ENRIQUECIMENTO ILICITO NO EXERCICIO DE CARGOS PUBLICOS.
RIO DE JANEIRO: COM EDIT FORENSE, 1960, 411 PP.
ANALYZES CORRUPTION AND GRAFT OF PUBLIC OFFICIALS IN
AMERICAS, WITH EMPHASIS ON BRAZIL. COMPARES LATIN AMERICAN
COUNTRIES AND US. DISCUSSES CONSTITUTIONAL AND LEGAL CONTROL
AND RESTRICTION ON PUBLIC OFFICIALS AND HOW THESE ARE
VIOLATED. EXAMINES REASONS AND ETHICAL NORMS AS BASIS FOR
DEVELOPING SYSTEM TO COMBAT ABUSE OF PUBLIC POWER AND
POSITION.

1676 PIPER D.C.

"THE ROLE OF INTER-GOVERNMENTAL MACHINERY IN CANADIAN-
AMERICAN RELATIONS."
S. ATLANTIC QUART., 62 (FALL 63), 551-574.
DESCRIPTIVE ANALYSIS OF SCOPE AND NATURE OF TEN JOINT
BODIES WHICH CONDUCT EXTENSIVE INTERGOVERNMENTAL RELATIONS.
REVEALS STRESSES AND IRRITATIONS EXISTING BETWEEN THE TWO
COUNTRIES AS WELL AS CLOSE COOPERATION.

1677 PIPES R.
THE FORMATION OF THE SOVIET UNION.
CAMBRIDGE: HARVARD U. PR., 1964, 365 PP., $7.95.
HISTORICAL ACCOUNT OF THE DISINTEGRATION OF THE RUSSIAN
EMPIRE, AND ON ITS RUINS, THE ERECTION OF THE MULTINATIONAL
COMMUNIST STATE.

1678 PIQUEMAL M.
"LES PROBLEMES DES UNIONS D'ETATS EN AFRIQUE NOIRE."
REV. JURID. POLIT. OUTREMER, 16 (JAN.-MARCH 62), 21-58.
EXPLORES PROBLEMS FACING DEVELOPING AFRICAN COUNTRIES.
MAJOR DILEMMA IS WHETHER OR NOT TO ADOPT FEDERALIST SYSTEM.
SHOWS SOCIAL STRATIFICATION OF OLD COLONIAL SYSTEMS. PRE-
SENTS POLITICAL IDEOLOGIES OF AFRICAN LEADERS. DISCUSSES
POSSIBILITIES FOR ECONOMIC UNION, AND ANALYZES FRANCE'S ROLE
IN THIS PROJECT.

1679 PLANO J.C., RIGGS R.E.
FORGING WORLD ORDER: THE POLITICS OF INTERNATIONAL ORGANIZA-
TION.
NEW YORK: MACMILLAN, 1967, 600 PP., LC#67-18893.
INVESTIGATES CONTEMPORARY INTERNATIONAL ORGANIZATION
WITHOUT ATTACHMENT TO ANY SINGLE THEORY OF POLITICAL BEHAV-
IOR. DISCUSSION OF SETTING, PROBLEMS, AND PROCESSES OF IN-
TERNATIONAL ORGANIZATION. REVEALS INTERACTION OF POLITICAL
INSTITUTIONS AND INDIVIDUALS WHO SHAPE THEM --WHO GETS WHAT,
WHY, AND HOW.

1680 PLANTEY A.
TRAITE PRATIQUE DE LA FONCTION PUBLIQUE (2ND ED., 2 VOLS.)
PARIS: PICHON ET DURAND-AUZIAS, 1963, 637 PP.
SAYS STATE OF PUBLIC ADMINISTRATION IN FRANCE IN PAST 50
YEARS HAS BEEN DEPLORABLE. IT HAS NOT CHANGED WITH TIMES AND
NUMBER OF CIVIL SERVANTS IN PROPORTION TO POPULATION IS
HIGH. MOST STUDIES OF PROBLEMS HAVE BEEN JUDICIAL. THIS
STUDY PLACES EMPHASIS ON POLITICAL, ADMINISTRATIVE, AND
SOCIAL ROLES AND PROBLEMS OF THE PERSONNEL OF PUBLIC BODIES.

1681 PLATO
THE REPUBLIC.
NEW YORK: OXFORD U. PR., 1945, 366 PP.
STARTING FROM DISCUSSION OF CONCEPT OF JUSTICE, CON-
STRUCTS IDEAL STATE THAT ENABLES EACH MAN TO REALIZE POTEN-
TIAL. STATE ONLY POSSIBLE IF PHILOSOPHERS GIVEN POLITICAL
POWER.

1683 PLISCHKE E.
GOVERNMENT AND POLITICS OF CONTEMPORARY BERLIN.
THE HAGUE: MARTINUS NIJHOFF, 1963, 119 PP.
DESCRIBES POST-WWII POLITICAL DEVELOPMENT OF CITY, BUT
EMPHASIZES AND EVALUATES ADMINISTRATION SINCE 1945. ANALYZES
ALL GOVERNMENT FUNCTIONS, PROCEDURES, AND POLITICAL
IMPLICATIONS IN EACH CITY DEPARTMENT. ANALYZES POLITICS
OF BERLIN IN RELATION TO INFLUENCES OF ALLIES.
BIBLIOGRAPHY OF GOVERNMENT AND POLITICS OF BERLIN.

1684 PLISCHKE E.
SYSTEMS OF INTEGRATING THE INTERNATIONAL COMMUNITY.
PRINCETON: VAN NOSTRAND, 1964, 198 PP.
OVERVIEW OF MAIN CONTEMPORARY TYPES OF INTERSTATE INTE-
GRATION: CONFEDERATION, SUPRANATIONAL ASSOCIATION, FEDERA-
TION, AND POLITICAL ASSOCIATION FOUND WITHIN COMMUNIST BLOC.

1685 POLK W.R.
"PROBLEMS OF GOVERNMENT UTILIZATION OF SCHOLARLY RESEARCH
IN INTERNATIONAL AFFAIRS."
BACKGROUND, 9 (NOV. 65), 237-259.
THE GOVERNMENT ADMINISTRATOR AND RESEARCH SCHOLAR HAVE
DIFFERENT PERCEPTIONS REGARDING TIME AND PROBLEMS OF IMPORT,
WHICH MAKES FRUITFUL AND HONEST RELATIONS DIFFICULT. POLK
ANALYZES THE NEEDS AND ASSETS OF BOTH GROUPS, DANGERS THEY
PRESENT TO ONE ANOTHER, AND COMMUNICATIONS PROBLEMS.

1686 POLSBY N.W.
"BOOKS IN THE FIELD: POLITICAL SCIENCE."
WILSON LIBRARY BULLETIN, 40 (JAN. 66), 432-439.
AN ANNOTATED BIBLIOGRAPHY ON POLITICAL SCIENCE. ENGLISH-
LANGUAGE MATERIAL. RANGES FROM 1956 TO 1965. CONTAINS 25
ENTRIES. OUTLINED UNDER THREE HEADINGS: PEOPLE AND THE
AMERICAN POLITICAL PROCESS, ADMINISTRATIVE STRATEGY, AND
THE SUPREME COURT.

1687 POOL I., LERNER D.
SYMBOLS OF DEMOCRACY.
STANFORD: U. PR., 1952, 80 PP.
SURVEYING THE TERMINOLOGY OF DEMOCRACY, AUTHORS HAVE
NOTED AN INCREASING CONCERN WITH THE CONCEPT OF DEMOCRACY.
MAINTAIN THAT JUDGMENTS EXPRESSED CONCERNING DEMOCRACY ARE

STRONGLY FAVORABLE REGARDLESS OF THE PRACTICE IN ANY GIVEN
COUNTRY.

1688 POOL I. ET AL.
SATELLITE GENERALS: A STUDY OF MILITARY ELITES IN THE
SOVIET SPHERE.
STANFORD: U. PR., 1955, 165 PP.
STUDIES OF MILITARY LEADERS IN CZECHOSLOVAKIA, POLAND,
RUMANIA, HUNGARY, AND CHINA DETERMINE WHETHER KEY QUALIFICA-
TION IS MILITARY SKILL OR IDEOLOGICAL CONFORMITY. RELIES ON
BIOGRAPHICAL MATERIAL.

1689 POOLE D.C.
THE CONDUCT OF FOREIGN RELATIONS UNDER MODERN DEMOCRATIC
CONDITIONS.
NEW HAVEN: YALE U. PR., 1924, 197 PP.
CONSIDERS THE INSTRUMENTS AND PROCESSES OF FOREIGN POLICY
AND THE EFFECT OF NATIONAL AND INTERNATIONAL ORGANIZATION ON
IT. RELATES THE PROBLEMS OF OPEN DIPLOMACY AND THE METHODS
OF INFORMATION DISSEMINATION. CONCLUDES RESPONSIBILITY IN
WORLD AFFAIRS WILL GROW AS KNOWLEDGIBLE POPULAR JUDGEMENT IS
EXPRESSED.

1690 POOLE W.F., FLETCHER W.I.
INDEX TO PERIODICAL LITERATURE.
BOSTON: JAMES R OSGOOD & CO, 1882, 1442 PP.
UNANNOTATED CROSS-REFERENCED INDEX OF ARTICLES PUBLISHED
BEFORE 1881 IN ENGLISH LANGUAGE. ALL SUBJECTS INCLUDED WITH
INITIAL SUBJECT INDEX. INCLUSIVE DATES 1800 TO 1881;
INCLUDES BRITISH PERIODICALS.

1691 POOLEY B.J.
THE EVOLUTION OF BRITISH PLANNING LEGISLATION.
ANN ARBOR: U OF MICH LAW SCHOOL, 1960, 100 PP., LC#60-63300.
STUDIES HISTORY OF PLANNING IN GREAT BRITAIN; ANALYZES
STRUCTURE OF STATE AND LOCAL GOVERNMENT; AND DESCRIBES IN
DETAIL TOWN AND COUNTRY PLANNING ACTS OF 1947, 1953, AND
1954, SHOWING SOME OF BRITAIN'S STARTLING SOLUTIONS
TO METROPOLITAN PROBLEMS.

1692 POPPINO R.E.
INTERNATIONAL COMMUNISM IN LATIN AMERICA: A HISTORY OF THE
MOVEMENT 1917-1963.
NEW YORK: FREE PRESS OF GLENCOE, 1964, 247 PP., LC#64-21203.
DISCUSSES AND ANALYZES REASONS FOR COMMUNIST APPEAL
IN LATIN AMERICA; POLITICAL HERITAGE, PRESENT ROLE,
ORGANIZATION, AND TECHNIQUES OF COMMUNISTS; THEIR RELATION
TO THE USSR; AND THEIR POTENTIAL. ATTEMPTS TO SYNTHESIZE
EARLIER EXPLORATORY STUDIES AND PRESENT NEW MATERIAL WHILE
RELATING THE CURRENT HISTORY OF LATIN AMERICAN COMMUNISM AND
EFFORTS AT CONTAINING IT.

1693 POSNER M.V., WOOLF S.J.
ITALIAN PUBLIC ENTERPRISE.
CAMBRIDGE: HARVARD U PR, 1967, 170 PP.
STUDIES THE HISTORY, GROWTH, AND ROLE OF STATE ENTERPRISE
IN ITALY IN THE LAST 15 YEARS. TYPICAL EXAMPLES OF STATE
ENTERPRISES ANALYZED AS TO STRUCTURE, CONTROL, FINANCE, AND
PERFORMANCE.

1694 POSVAR W.W.
"NATIONAL SECURITY POLICY* THE REALM OF OBSCURITY."
ORBIS, 9 (FALL 65), 694-713.
ARTICLE'S CONCERN IS TO DEFINE EXTENT TO WHICH CRITICISM
OF LACK OF CLARITY IN NATIONAL POLICY MAY NOT BE JUSTIFIED.
DESCRIBES WORK BEING DONE BY EXPERTS IN PUBLIC ADMINISTRA-
TION, DECISION-MAKING THEORISTS, AND SYSTEMS ANALYSTS. THE
REALM OF OBSCURITY INVOLVES THE DIFFERENT DIMENSIONS THAT
POLICY-MAKERS OPERATE IN AND UNAVOIDABLE SUBJECTIVITY OF ALL
DECISION-MAKERS.

1695 POTTER D.C.
GOVERNMENT IN RURAL INDIA.
LONDON: LONDON SCHOOL ECONOMICS, 1964, 91 PP.
STUDY OF DISTRICT ADMINISTRATION IN RURAL INDIA. DEALS
WITH STRUCTURE OF LOCAL GOVERNMENT AND COMMUNITY DEVELOPMENT
AS ADMINISTRATIVE FUNCTION OF STATE GOVERNMENTS.

1696 POUND R.
JUSTICE ACCORDING TO LAW.
NEW HAVEN: YALE U PR, 1958, 98 PP.
GENERAL DISCUSSION OF PURPOSE, METHODS, AND PROBLEMS IN-
VOLVED IN LEGAL ADMINISTRATION OF JUSTICE. CONSISTS OF THREE
LECTURES DEFINING JUSITCE, LAW, AND LEGAL JUSTICE. APPROACH
IS THEORETICALLY AND HISTORICALLY ORIENTED.

1697 POWELL N.J.
PERSONNEL ADMINISTRATION IN GOVERNMENT.
ENGLEWOOD CLIFFS: PRENTICE HALL, 1956, 548 PP., LC#56-09003.
SETS FORTH BASIC IDEAS AND DATA FOR WORKING OUT EFFECTIVE
PERSONNEL PROGRAMS IN PUBLIC SERVICE. DISCUSSES RECRUITING,
PAY, TRAINING, PUBLIC RELATIONS, EFFECTS OF POLITICAL PAR-
TIES ON CIVIL SERVICE, RELATION TO JUDICIARY, AND HANDLING
OF RECRUITMENT.

1698 PRAKASH O.M.
THE THEORY AND WORKING OF STATE CORPORATIONS: WITH SPECIAL
REFERENCE TO INDIA.
LONDON: ALLEN & UNWIN, 1962, 272 PP.
ANALYZES GENERAL CHARACTERISTICS AND OPERATIONS OF STATE
CORPORATIONS, WHICH INCLUDE PUBLIC CORPORATIONS AND GOVERN-
MENT COMPANIES, IN INDIA, UK, AND US. CRITICALLY EXAMINES
SPECIFIC ISSUES RELATING TO FUNCTIONING OF THESE CORPORA-
TIONS, ONE US, AND ONE ENGLISH.

1699 PRATT R.C.
"THE ADMINISTRATION OF ECONOMIC PLANNING IN A NEWLY INDEPEND
ENT STATE* THE TANZANIAN EXPERIENCE 1963-1966."
J. COMMONWEALTH POL. ST., 5 (MAR. 67), 38-59.
PRAISES FIVE YEAR PLAN IN TANZANIA AS HIGHLY PROFESSIONAL
AND USEFUL OUTLINE FOR ALL ASPECTS OF DEVELOPMENT. RELATES
IT TO POLITICAL SITUATION, AND EXPLAINS FAILURE OF GOVERN-
MENT TO GIVE TOP PRIORITY TO PLAN IN ADMINISTRATIVE PROGRAM.
DISCUSSES REASONS AND POSSIBLE CORRECTIONS.

1700 PRESS C., WILLIAMS O.
STATE MANUALS, BLUE BOOKS AND ELECTION RESULTS.
BERKELEY: U CAL, INST GOVT STUD, 1962, 101 PP.
COMPREHENSIVE STATE-BY-STATE SURVEY OF ALL STATE LEGIS-
LATIVE MANUALS AND BLUEBOOKS. ANALYZES AND TABULATES THEIR
CONTENTS AND INDICATES FREQUENCY OF PUBLICATION AND PRICE.
COMPILATION OF STATE ELECTIONS RESULTS DESIGNED TO PROVIDE
FACTUAL MATERIALS USEFUL IN COMPARATIVE STUDIES OF DECISION-
MAKING.

1701 PRESS C.
A BIBLIOGRAPHIC INTRODUCTION TO AMERICAN STATE GOVERNMENT
AND POLITICS (PAMPHLET
E LANSING: MSU COMM DEV   SERV, 1964, 34 PP.
UNANNOTATED TOPICAL LISTING OF 500 BOOKS, SCHOLARLY
ARTICLES, TEXTBOOKS, CASE HISTORIES, AND BIBLIOGRAPHIES
PUBLISHED FROM 1935 TO 1964. EMPHASIS IS ON PARTY POLITICS
AND EXECUTIVE AND LEGISLATIVE BRANCHES OF GOVERNMENT.

1702 PREST A.R.
PUBLIC FINANCE IN UNDERDEVELOPED COUNTRIES.
NEW YORK: PRAEGER, 1963, 164 PP., $4.50.
TWO MAJOR PROBLEMS OF SUBJECT ARE LONG-TERM PRESSURE FOR
INCREASED GOVERNMENT SPENDING AND CONCURRENT INSTABILITY OF
GOVERNMENT FINANCES. RELATES PROBLEMS TO TAX SYSTEMS OF SUCH
COUNTRIES AND SUGGESTS DESIRABLE FEATURES.

1703 PRESTHUS R.
THE ORGANIZATIONAL SOCIETY.
NEW YORK: ALFRED KNOPF, 1962, 323 PP., LC#62-11232.
STUDIES LARGE ORGANIZATIONS AND THEIR INFLUENCE ON
INDIVIDUALS WHO WORK FOR THEM, DEFINING ORGANIZATIONS AS
MINIATURE SOCIETIES, DEVELOPING A THEORY OF ORGANIZATIONAL
BEHAVIOR, AND DESCRIBING PATTERNS OF ACCOMMODATION.

1704 PRESTHUS R.
BEHAVIORAL APPROACHES TO PUBLIC ADMINISTRATION.
UNIVERSITY: U ALABAMA PR, 1965, 158 PP., LC#64-66422.
ANALYZES BEHAVIORALISM AS MOOD AND METHOD. DESCRIBES BE-
HAVIORAL RESEARCH ON COMMUNITY POWER STRUCTURE, ON ORGANIZA-
TIONAL EFFECTIVENESS, AND ON BRITISH EXECUTIVES. INCLUDES
EXPOSITION ON THE USES OF BEHAVIORALISM. PROVIDES A SYSTEM-
ATIC COMPARISON OF THE RESULTS OF THE "REPUTATIONAL" AND
"DECISIONAL" METHODS FOR DETERMINING WHERE POWER LIES IN A
GIVEN COMMUNITY, AND COMPARES TWO COMMUNITIES.

1705 PRESTHUS R.V.
"BEHAVIOR AND BUREAUCRACY IN MANY CULTURES."
PUBLIC ADMIN. REV., 19 (WINTER 59), 25-35.
"COMPARATIVE ADMINISTRATION NEEDS AN EXPLICIT SYNTHESIS
BETWEEN CONCEPTUAL THEORY AND EMPIRICAL FIELD RESEARCH."

1706 PRICE D.K.
"THE PARLIAMENTARY AND PRESIDENTIAL SYSTEMS" (BMR)"
PUBLIC ADMIN. REV., 3 (FALL 43), 317-334.
EXAMINATION OF CLASSIC THEORY OF PARLIAMENTARY GOVERNMENT
WITH A VIEW TO ITS INAPPLICABILITY TO US LEGISLATIVE-
EXECUTIVE RELATIONS. CONTESTS ASSUMPTIONS THAT LEGISLATURE
ALONE REPRESENTS THE PEOPLE AND THAT ADMINISTRATIVE
OFFICIALS ARE RESPONSIBLE TO THE PEOPLE ONLY THROUGH THE
LEGISLATURE. THIS RELATIONSHIP HANDICAPS BOTH LEGISLATIVE
AND EXECUTIVE BRANCHES IN WORKING TOGETHER.

1707 PRINCE C.E.
NEW JERSEY'S JEFFERSONIAN REPUBLICANS; THE GENESIS OF AN
EARLY PARTY MACHINE (1789-1817)
CHAPEL HILL: U OF N CAR PR, 1967, 266 PP., LC#67-15103.
STUDIES CONTRIBUTIONS TO POLITICAL PARTY MACHINERY MADE
BY NEW JERSEY'S JEFFERSONIAN REPUBLICANS. STATES THAT PARTY
MANAGERS USED NEWSPAPER PROPAGANDA, PATRONAGE CONTROL, AND
OTHER TECHNIQUES TO GAIN ASCENDENCE. DISCUSSES FIRST STATE
NOMINATING COVENTION IN 1800 AND LOCAL ORGANIZATIONS AS
EVIDENCE OF POLITICAL SOPHISTICATION. TRACES ADVANCE OF
MACHINE TO ELECTION OF 1812 AND FOLLOWING DECLINE.

1708 PRINCETON U INDUSTRIAL REL SEC
SELECTED REFERENCES OF THE INDUSTRIAL RELATIONS SECTION OF

PRINCETON, NEW JERSEY.
PRINCETON: PRIN U INDUS REL CTR.
CONTAINS 100 BIBLIOGRAPHIES EACH CONTAINING APPROXIMATELY
30 ENTRIES ARRANGED TOPICALLY AND ALPHABETICALLY BY AUTHOR.
ENTRIES DATE 1940-60; INCLUDE BOOKS, JOURNAL ARTICLES, AND
GOVERNMENT DOCUMENTS DEALING WITH WIDE RANGE OF PROBLEMS IN
INDUSTRIAL RELATIONS. ALL ENTRIES ARE IN ENGLISH. PUBLISHED
BIMONTHLY 1944-61.

1709 PRINCETON U INDUSTRIAL REL SEC
OUTSTANDING BOOKS ON INDUSTRIAL RELATIONS, 1965
(PAMPHLET NO. 128)
PRINCETON: PRIN U INDUS REL CTR, 1966, 4 PP.
ANNOTATED BIBLIOGRAPHY OF BOOKS PUBLISHED IN ENGLISH IN
AND ARRANGED BY TOPIC.

1710 PRINCETON U INDUSTRIAL REL SEC
RECENT MATERIAL ON COLLECTIVE BARGAINING IN GOVERNMENT
(PAMPHLET NO. 130)
PRINCETON: PRIN U INDUS REL CTR, 1966, 4 PP.
ANNOTATED BIBLIOGRAPHY OF BOOKS, ARTICLES, AND DOCUMENTS
PUBLISHED IN ENGLISH, 1962-66; LISTED TOPICALLY.

1711 PRINCETON U INDUSTRIAL REL SEC
OUTSTANDING BOOKS ON INDUSTRIAL RELATIONS, 1966
(PAMPHLET NO. 134)
PRINCETON: PRIN U INDUS REL CTR, 1967, 4 PP.
ANNOTATED BIBLIOGRAPHY OF BOOKS PUBLISHED IN ENGLISH IN
1966; LISTED ALPHABETICALLY BY AUTHOR.

1712 PRINCETON UNIVERSITY
SELECTED REFERENCES: INDUSTRIAL RELATIONS SECTION.
PRINCETON: PRIN U INDUS REL CTR.
SELECTED ANNOTATED REFERENCES TO RECENT WORKS IN INDUS-
TRIAL RELATIONS: EMPLOYMENT AND INCOME; COLLECTIVE BARGAIN-
ING; WAGE POLICIES; ARBITRATION OF LABOR DISPUTES; ADMINIS-
TRATION OF UNION CONTRACTS; ETC.. FIRST PUBLISHED IN 1945
BY DEPARTMENT OF SOCIOLOGY AND ECONOMICS.

1713 PRUITT D.G.
"PROBLEM SOLVING IN THE DEPARTMENT OF STATE."
DENVER: U. PR., 1964-5, 55 PP.
TWENTY-EIGHT CASE-STUDIES SHOW VERTICAL AND HORIZONTAL
STRUCTURE AND FUNCTIONING OF STATE DEPARTMENT. FINDS THAT
EXPERTISE OF LOWER ECHELONS SUPPLY POLICY ALTERNATIVES
TO GENERALISTS AT TOP.

1714 PUBLIC ADMIN CLEARING HOUSE
PUBLIC ADMINISTRATIONS ORGANIZATIONS: A DIRECTORY, 1954.
CHICAGO: PUBLIC ADMIN CLEAR HSE, 1954, 150 PP.
SEVENTH EDITION OF DIRECTORY OF VOLUNTARY ORGANIZATIONS
WORKING IN PUBLIC ADMINISTRATION. EMPHASIZES NATIONAL
ORGANIZATIONS. PREVIOUS EDITIONS INCLUDE CANADA AS WELL
AS US. INCLUDES DESCRIPTIONS OF ACTIVITIES. DESCRIBES 513
NATIONAL ORGANIZATIONS; ARRANGEMENT IS ALPHABETICAL.

1715 PUBLIC ADMINISTRATION SERVICE
YOUR BUSINESS OF GOVERNMENT: A CATALOG OF PUBLICATIONS IN
THE FIELD OF PUBLIC ADMINISTRATION (PAMPHLET)
CHICAGO: PUBLIC ADMIN SERVICE, 1944, 30 PP.
UNANNOTATED BIBLIOGRAPHY OF PUBLICATIONS ISSUED BY 15
PRIVATE AND GOVERNMENTAL ASSOCIATIONS ON THE SUBJECT OF
GOVERNMENT ADMINISTRATION. INCLUDES PUBLICATIONS WHICH MAKE
AVAILABLE FOR GENERAL USE THE PRINCIPLES, FINDINGS, AND
RECOMMENDATIONS DEVELOPED AS A RESULT OF SURVEY, REORGANIZA-
TION, AND INSTALLATION PROJECTS. MOST WORKS POSTDATE 1934.
ARRANGED ALPHABETICALLY BY ISSUING ORGANIZATION.

1716 PUBLIC ADMINISTRATION SERVICE
CURRENT RESEARCH PROJECTS IN PUBLIC ADMINISTRATION
(PAMPHLET)
CHICAGO: PUBLIC ADMIN SERVICE, 1947, 39 PP.
RECORD OF PROJECTS INITIATED OR IN PROGRESS IN 1947 ON
RESEARCH PROJECTS IN SCHOOLS OF PUBLIC ADMINISTRATION AND
DEPARTMENTS OF POLITICAL SCIENCE, SOCIOLOGY, BUSINESS ADMIN-
ISTRATION, AND SOCIAL WORK. INCLUDES LISTINGS FROM INSTI-
TUTIONS OF EDUCATION IN HOUSING, PLANNING, ETC. INDICATES
DEGREE IN CONNECTION WITH WHICH PROJECT WAS UNDERTAKEN.
ANNUAL PUBLICATION FIRST APPEARED IN 1938.

1717 PUBLIC ADMINISTRATION SERVICE
SOURCE MATERIALS IN PUBLIC ADMINISTRATION: A SELECTED
BIBLIOGRAPHY (PAS PUBLICATION NO. 102)
CHICAGO: PUBLIC ADMIN SERVICE, 1948, 30 PP.
GUIDE TO CURRENT AND RECENT LITERATURE IN FIELD OF PUBLIC
ADMINISTRATION. SELECTIVE LISTS OF BASIC SOURCES AND REFER-
ENCE BOOKS, WITH BRIEF ANNOTATIONS AND COMPREHENSIVE LIST-
ING OF MORE RECENT TEXTS, TREATISES, AND SPECIAL STUDIES IN
FIELD; CLASSIFIED BY SUBJECT, AND SUBJECT BIBLIOGRAPHIES.
INCLUDES LIST OF PUBLISHERS AND PERIODICALS CITED.

1718 PUBLISHERS' CIRCULAR LIMITED
THE ENGLISH CATALOGUE OF BOOKS.
SURREY: PUBL CIRCULAR LTD.
YEARLY PUBLICATION SINCE 1836 LISTING ALL BOOKS PUBLISHED
IN UNITED KINGDOM DURING THAT CALENDAR YEAR. BOOKS ARE

LISTED BY AUTHOR AND TITLE AND INDEXED BY SUBJECT AT END
OF VOLUME. SEPARATE LISTING FOR PAPERBACKS. INCLUDES
MATERIALS ON ALL SUBJECTS.

1719 PUGET H. ED.
ESSAI DE BIBLIOGRAPHIE DES PRINCIPAUX OUVRAGES DE DROIT
PUBLIC... QUI ONT PARU HORS DE FRANCE DE 1945 A 1958.
PARIS: EDITIONS DE L'EPARGNE, 1961, 369 PP.
LISTING OF WORKS ON PUBLIC LAW AND ADMINISTRATION
PUBLISHED BETWEEN 1945 AND 1958 IN US AND WESTERN EUROPE.
CONTAINS 5,030 ENTRIES AND AUTHOR INDEX. SECTIONS ON
REFERENCE WORKS; CONSTITUTIONAL LAW AND POLITICAL SCIENCE;
ADMINISTRATIVE LAW AND MANAGEMENT.

1720 PULLEN W.R.
A CHECK LIST OF LEGISLATIVE JOURNALS ISSUED SINCE 1937 BY
THE STATES OF THE UNITED STATES OF AMERICA (PAMPHLET)
CHICAGO: AMER LIB ASSN, 1955, 60 PP., LC#55-8711.
AN UNANNOTATED BIBLIOGRAPHY ON LEGISLATIVE JOURNALS IS-
SUED SINCE 1937. MATERIAL IN ENGLISH LANGUAGE, RANGING FROM
1937-55. 1,160 ENTRIES. CONSISTS OF A CHECK LIST OF
JOURNALS OF VARIOUS STATE LEGISLATURES AND THE DATES OF IS-
SUANCE FROM 1937 TO 1955.

1721 PURCELL V.
THE MEMOIRS OF A MALAYAN OFFICIAL.
LONDON: CASSELL & CO LTD, 1965, 373 PP.
PERSONAL RECOLLECTIONS OF VICTOR PURCELL, MALAYAN ARMY
OFFICER, CIVIL SERVICE OFFICIAL, UN CONSULTANT, AND CAM-
BRIDGE DON. CENTERS ON DISCUSSION OF DUTIES AND EXPERIENCES
IN MALAYAN CIVIL SERVICE.

1722 PUSTAY J.S.
COUNTER-INSURGENCY WARFARE.
NEW YORK: FREE PR., 1965, 236 PP., $6.95.
REVIEWS EVOLUTION OF COMMUNIST THEORY ON INSURGENCY WAR-
FARE, AND POINTS TO CURRENT USE IN SPECIFIC UNDERDEVELOPED
AREAS. ANALYZES EXISTING METHODS AND TACTICS OF COUNTER-
INSURGENCY WARFARE AT EACH STAGE OF DEVELOPMENT.

1723 PYE L.W.
THE POLICY IMPLICATIONS OF SOCIAL CHANGE IN NON-WESTERN
SOCIETIES.
CAMBRIDGE: M I T PRESS, 1957, 80 PP.
EXAMINES PROCESS OF SOCIAL CHANGE UNIQUE TO ASIAN SOCI-
ETIES, AND SYSTEMATICALLY ARRANGES A SERIES OF HYPOTHESES
WHICH SHED LIGHT UPON FEATURES OF THEIR POLITICS. SETS FORTH
INSIGHTS OF VALUE IN MAKING OF AMERICAN POLICY TOWARD SUCH
SOCIETIES.

1724 PYE L.W.
SOUTHEAST ASIA'S POLITICAL SYSTEMS.
ENGLEWOOD CLIFFS: PRENTICE HALL, 1967, 97 PP., LC#67-20230.
DISCUSSES NATURE AND FUNCTION OF SOUTHEAST ASIAN
POLITICAL SYSTEMS, EMPHASIZING GEOGRAPHICAL, CULTURAL, AND
IDEOLOGICAL DIVERSITY. NOTES GOVERNMENTAL STRUCTURE, PARTY
SYSTEMS, AND LEADERSHIP. SEES FOUNDATIONS OF SYSTEMS IN
HISTORY, SOCIAL STRUCTURE, IDEOLOGIES, AND HUMAN ECOLOGIES.
COMMENTS ON PERFORMANCE OF GOVERNMENTS AND NOTES PROSPECTS
AND PROBLEMS FOR FUTURE. COMPARES GOVERNMENTS AND SYSTEMS.

1725 PYLEE M.V.
CONSTITUTIONAL GOVERNMENT IN INDIA (2ND REV. ED.)
BOMBAY: ASIA PUBL HOUSE, 1965, 824 PP.
DISCUSSES RISE AND NATURE OF CONSTITUTIONAL GOVERNMENT IN
INDIA. EXAMINES FUNDAMENTAL RIGHTS, OPERATION OF NATIONAL
AND STATE GOVERNMENTS, AND FEDERAL SYSTEM.

1726 QUADE Q.L.
"THE TRUMAN ADMINISTRATION AND THE SEPARATION OF POWERS:
THE CASE OF THE MARSHALL PLAN."
REV. POLIT., 27 (JAN. 65), 58-77.
GIVES INSIGHT INTO THE POLICY-MAKING PROCEDURES LEADING
TO THE FORMATION OF AMERICAN FOREIGN POLICY - USES MARSHALL
PLAN AS CASE STUDY BECAUSE OF ITS SIGNIFICANCE TO POST-WAR
ECONOMIC AND POLITICAL DEVELOPMENT AND THE CHANGE IN US FOR-
EIGN POLICY. GIVES INSIGHT INTO DESIGN AND STRUCTURE OF
MARSHALL PLAN AND ITS INCEPTION.

1727 QURESHI S.
INCENTIVES IN AMERICAN EMPLOYMENT (THESIS, UNIVERSITY
OF PENNSYLVANIA)
PHILA: UNIV OF PENNSYLVANIA, 1961, 188 PP.
DISCUSSES USE OF INCENTIVES IN FEDERAL CIVILIAN EMPLOY-
MENT. ANALYSIS OF HEALTH AND RETIREMENT PLANS, OVERTIME
PAY, AND IDEA AWARDS LEADS TO CONCLUSION THAT THE GENERAL
MONETARY LEVEL OF INCENTIVES SHOULD BE INCREASED AND THAT
SPECIAL SERVICES SHOULD BE PROVIDED TO UPPER LEVEL
ADMINISTRATORS.

1728 RAEFF M.
ORIGINS OF THE RUSSIAN INTELLIGENTSIA: THE
EIGHTEENTH-CENTURY NOBILITY.
NEW YORK: HARCOURT BRACE, 1966, 248 PP., LC#66-19152.
STUDIES ELEMENTS SHAPING LIFE OF THE 18TH-CENTURY RUSSIAN
NOBLEMAN. EXAMINES THE FAMILY, EDUCATION, RELATIONS TO

OTHER INDIVIDUALS, AND EXPERIENCES AS AN ACTIVE MEMBER
OF RUSSIAN SOCIETY. EMPHASIZES ROLE OF INTELLECTUAL EX-
PERIENCES ACQUIRED WITHIN FRAMEWORK. HISTORY BASED ON
OFFICIAL GOVERNMENT SOURCES; MEMOIRS, DIARIES AND
LETTERS; CONTEMPORARY LITERATURE; AND BIOGRAPHIES.

1729 RAI H.
"DISTRICT MAGISTRATE AND POLICE SUPERINTENDENT IN INDIA: THE
CONTROVERSY OF DUAL CONTROL"
J. OF ADMINISTRATION OVERSEAS, 6 (JULY 67), 192-199.
    PRESENTS BACKGROUND OF CONFLICT BETWEEN DISTRICT MAGIS-
TRATE AND POLICE SUPERINTENDENT OVER CONTROL OF POLICE
FORCE. BEGINS WITH POLICE ACT OF 1861 AND INCLUDES PRESENT
SITUATION OF MAGISTRATIVE DOMINANCE. GIVES ARGUMENTS ON BOTH
SIDES AND SUGGESTS NEW ARRANGEMENT.

1730 RALSTON D.B.
THE ARMY OF THE REPUBLIC; THE PLACE OF THE MILITARY IN THE
POLITICAL EVOLUTION OF FRANCE 1871-1914.
CAMBRIDGE: M I T PRESS, 1967, 395 PP., LC#67-16494.
    EXAMINES ROLE OF ARMY IN FRENCH THIRD REPUBLIC AFTER
FRANCO-PRUSSIAN WAR. DISCUSSES INCOMPATIBILITY OF HIGH COM-
MAND WITH CIVIL GOVERNMENT AND NECESSITY FOR LARGE STANDING
ARMY TO ENSURE NATIONAL SECURITY. ANALYZES MILITARY LEGISLA-
TION AND COMMENTS ON MILITARY INFLUENCE IN FORMATION OF
PUBLIC POLICY. NOTES DREYFUS AFFAIR, 1897-1900, AND VARIOUS
SPECIFIC PROBLEMS OF MILITARY ADMINISTRATION.

1731 RANSHOFFEN-WERTHEIMER EF
THE INTERNATIONAL SECRETARIAT: A GREAT EXPERIMENT IN
INTERNATIONAL ADMINISTRATION.
WASHINGTON: CARNEGIE ENDOWMENT, 1945, 500 PP.
    ANALYZES EXPERIENCE OF LEAGUE OF NATIONS' SECRETARIAT
IN INTERNATIONAL ADMINISTRATION. DISCUSSES HISTORY OF
SECRETARIAT: STRUCTURAL DEVELOPMENT, LEADERSHIP, AND PER-
SONNEL PROBLEMS.

1732 RANSONE C.B.
THE OFFICE OF GOVERNOR IN THE UNITED STATES.
UNIVERSITY: U ALABAMA PR, 1956, 417 PP., LC#56-7220.
    STUDY OF GOVERNOR'S ROLE IN THE DAY-TO-DAY CONDUCT
OF THE BUSINESS OF STATE GOVERNMENT. EXAMINES STATE PO-
LITICAL SETTING AS A CONTROLLING INFLUENCE UPON THE PERFOR-
MANCE OF GUBERNATORIAL FUNCTIONS. CONSIDERS THE GOVERNOR'S
ACCOUNTABILITY TO THE ELECTORATE, THE LEGISLATURE, AND THE
COURTS. BASED ON DATA COLLECTED IN INTERVIEWS WITH
GOVERNORS AND THEIR POLITICAL-ADMINISTRATIVE STAFF.

1733 RAO K.V.
PARLIAMENTARY DEMOCRACY OF INDIA.
CALCUTTA: WORLD PRESS LTD, 1961, 369 PP.
    CRITICAL STUDY OF INDIAN DEMOCRACY FOCUSES ON BOTH
LEGAL AND POLITICAL PROVISIONS OF INDIAN CONSTITUTION. AP-
PRAISES EXTENT TO WHICH CONSTITUTION HAS ENABLED ESTABLISH-
MENT OF DEMOCRATIC REPUBLIC IN INDIA. EXAMINES WORKING OF
EXECUTIVE STRUCTURE, PARLIAMENT, AND COURT SYSTEMS UNDER
PROVISIONS OF CONSTITUTION. ADVOCATES IMMEDIATE ATTENTION TO
THOSE PROVISIONS THAT REQUIRE AMENDMENT.

1734 RAO V.K.R.
INTERNATIONAL AID FOR ECONOMIC DEVELOPMENT - POSSIBILITIES
AND LIMITATIONS.
CAMBRIDGE: LEEDS U PRESS, 1960, 29 PP.
    DETAILED CRITICAL ANALYSIS OF INTERNATIONAL ECONOMIC AID
PROGRAMS EMPHASIZING OBLIGATIONS AND VITAL IMPORTANCE OF IN-
CREASED AID FROM DEVELOPED NATIONS. STRESSES LIMITATIONS IM-
POSED ON VOLUME AND EFFECTIVENESS OF ECONOMIC AID BY NUMER-
OUS POLITICAL AND SOCIAL AS WELL AS ECONOMIC FACTORS IN DE-
VELOPED AND UNDERDEVELOPED COUNTRIES. EXAMINES ACTIVITIES OF
UN AGENCIES AND OTHER INTERNATIONAL ECONOMIC BODIES.

1735 RAPAPORT R.N., RAPAPORT R.S.
"'DEMOCRATIZATION' AND AUTHORITY IN A THERAPEUTIC
COMMUNITY."
BEHAVIORAL SCIENCE, 2 (APR. 57), 128-133.
    DISCUSSES "DOCTOR'S ORDERS" AND AVOIDANCE OF COERCIVE
AUTHORITY AND RELATES THESE ISSUES TO EFFICIENCY. THE
ANSWER MAY BE THE "THERAPEUTIC COMMUNITY," WHICH "DIFFUSES
DECISION-MAKING RESPONSIBILITY AS WELL AS THERAPEUTIC ACT-
IVITY TO STAFF AND PATIENTS THROUGHOUT THE SOCIAL SYSTEM."
DESCRIBES SUCH UNIT ORGANIZED BY DR. MAXWELL JONES.

1736 RAPHAEL J.S.
GOVERNMENTAL REGULATION OF BUSINESS.
NEW YORK: FREE PRESS OF GLENCOE, 1966, 260 PP., LC#66-12081.
    SURVEYS LEGAL BACKGROUND OF GOVERNMENT CONTROL OF BUSI-
NESS. ANALYZES SOURCES OF POWER, SUCH AS CONSTITUTION.
EXAMINES ADMINISTRATIVE AGENCIES THAT ARE INSTRUMENTAL IN
ENFORCING LAWS. REVEALS DEVICES AVAILABLE TO COMPANIES
IF GOVERNMENT BECOMES TOO POWERFUL.

1737 RAPHAEL M.
PENSIONS AND PUBLIC SERVANTS.
HAGUE: MOUTON & CO, 1964, 171 PP.
    SURVEY OF ORIGINS OF OLD-AGE SCHEMES AND RETIREMENT PLANS
IN ENGLAND. EMPHASIS ON PUBLIC SUPERANNUATION METHOD COPIED

BY PRIVATE CONCERNS SINCE OLD AGE BECAME PROBLEM IN
ENGLAND. ONLY STUDY OF KIND; BASED ON MANUSCRIPTS, ETC.

1738 RAPHAELI N.
"SELECTED ARTICLES AND DOCUMENTS ON COMPARATIVE PUBLIC AD-
MINISTRATION."
AM. POL. SCI. REV., 60 (SEPT. 60), 755-756.
    AN UNANNOTATED BIBLIOGRAPHY ON COMPARATIVE PUBLIC ADMIN-
ISTRATION. ENGLISH-LANGUAGE AND SOME FRENCH SOURCES. RANGES
FROM 1965 TO 1966. 55 ENTRIES OUTLINED UNDER FIVE HEADINGS:
GENERAL WORKS, BUREAUCRATIC SYSTEMS, PERSONNEL AND FISCAL
ADMINISTRATION, DEVELOPMENT ADMINISTRATION, AND COMPARATIVE
LOCAL GOVERNMENT.

1739 RAPHAELI N.
"SELECTED ARTICLES AND DOCUMENTS ON COMPARATIVE PUBLIC
ADMINISTRATION."
AM. POL. SCI. REV., 59 (SEPT.66), 755-756.
    AN UNANNOTATED BIBLIOGRAPHY OF ARTICLES AND DOCUMENTS ON
PUBLIC ADMINISTRATION. INCLUDES ENGLISH-LANGUAGE AND SOME
FRENCH AND SPANISH MATERIAL. ITEMS GROUPED UNDER SIX HEAD-
INGS: GENERAL WORKS, BUREAUCRATIC SYSTEMS, PERSONNEL AND
FISCAL ADMINISTRATION, ADMINISTRATIVE RESPONSIBILITY AND
CONTROL, DEVELOPMENT ADMINISTRATION, COMPARATIVE LOCAL
GOVERNMENT. 58 ENTRIES. MATERIAL PUBLISHED 1963-65.

1740 RAPP W.F.
"MANAGEMENT ANALYSIS AT THE HEADQUARTERS OF FEDERAL
AGENCIES."
INT. REV. OF ADMIN. SCI., 26 (1960), 235-248.
    A SURVEY OF MANAGEMENT ANALYSIS STAFFS AND FUNCTIONS:
"COLLABORATIVE WORKING ARRANGEMENTS ARE TYPICAL, STAFFS ARE
SMALL, THERE ARE MANY CONCEPTS AND PRACTICES."

1741 RAPPARD W.E.
THE CRISIS OF DEMOCRACY.
CHICAGO: U. CHI. PR., 1938, 287 PP.
    FOCUSES ON CHANGES WHICH HAVE COME OVER MEN'S MINDS IN
ALL COUNTRIES SINCE THE WORLD WAR WITH RESPECT TO THE INSTI-
TUTIONS AND IDEALS OF POPULAR GOVERNMENTS.

1742 RAUDSEPP E.
MANAGING CREATIVE SCIENTISTS AND ENGINEERS.
NEW YORK: MACMILLAN, 1963, 249 PP., LC#63-07448.
    EXPLORES RELATIONSHIP BETWEEN RESEARCH AND MANAGEMENT IN
CONTEMPORARY US ECONOMY. DISCUSSES CREATIVE PROCESS AND
CHARACTERISTICS OF CREATIVE PROFESSIONAL; CREATIVITY IN CUL-
TURE AND INDUSTRY; AND MANAGING CREATIVE RESEARCH.

1743 RAUM O.
"THE MODERN LEADERSHIP GROUP AMONG THE SOUTH AFRICAN XHOSA."
SOCIOLOGUS, 17 (WINTER 67), 115-130.
    TRACES HISTORY OF LEADERSHIP OF S. AFRICAN XHOSA FROM
BEGINNINGS OF XHOSA CONTACT WITH WHITES. BEFORE 1870, THREE
IMAGINATIVE INDIVIDUALS WERE SUCCESSIVE LEADERS, AND THEIR
ROLES WERE NOT INSTITUTIONALIZED. AFTER 1870, AS CONTACT
BECAME MORE SIGNIFICANT, AGENTS AND INTERPRETERS ASSUMED
LEADERSHIP. FROM 1920, TEACHERS AND CLERGY BECAME ACCEPTED
LEADERS, AND ARE TODAY, ALONG WITH DOCTORS AND LAWYERS.

1744 RAVKIN A.
THE NEW STATES OF AFRICA (HEADLINE SERIES, NO. 183(
(PAMPHLET)
NEW YORK: FOREIGN POLICY ASSN, 1967, 63 PP., LC#67-25598.
    INTRODUCTION TO SITUATION AND PROBLEMS OF NEWLY-INDEPEN-
DENT AFRICAN STATES, INCLUDING POLITICAL, ECONOMIC, AND
SOCIAL ASPECTS. AFRICA EQUIPPED NEITHER TO ACCEPT MODERN
WORLD ORDER NOR TO CHANGE IT.

1745 RAWLINSON J.L.
CHINA'S STRUGGLE FOR NAVAL DEVELOPMENT 1839-1895.
CAMBRIDGE: HARVARD U PR, 1967, 318 PP., LC#66-10127.
    DESCRIBES CHINA'S EFFORT TO BUILD POWERFUL NAVAL FORCE
IN LATE 19TH CENTURY. DISCUSSES INABILITY TO CONTRAVENE
TRADITIONAL ORGANIZATION AS IT CONTRIBUTED TO FAILURE OF
EFFORT. DISCUSSES DAMAGING DEFEATS BY JAPAN IN 1894-5 THAT
ALTERED HISTORY OF PACIFIC AREA IN 20TH CENTURY.

1746 RAYMOND J.
POWER AT THE PENTAGON (1ST ED.)
NEW YORK: HARPER & ROW, 1964, 363 PP., LC#63-20297.
    DISCUSSION OF INCREASE IN PENTAGON'S POWER AS MILITARY
BUILDUP PLACED MORE AUTHORITY "IN THE HANDS OF OUR DEFEND-
ERS." TRACES THIS DEVELOPMENT FROM JUST BEFORE WWII TO
"MC NAMARA'S MONARCHY."

1747 READ W.H.
"UPWARD COMMUNICATION IN INDUSTRIAL HIERARCHIES."
HUMAN RELATIONS, 15 (1962), 3-15.
    CONCERNS COMMUNICATION IN LARGE ORGANIZATIONS. PARTICULAR
FOCUS IS UPON MOTIVATIONAL AND ATTITUDINAL FACTORS THAT
AFFECT THE ACCURACY WITH WHICH MEMBERS AT ONE ADMINISTRATIVE
LEVEL COMMUNICATE TO A HIGHER LEVEL. SIGNIFICANTLY NEGATIVE
RELATIONSHIP BETWEEN UPWARD-MOBILITY AND UPWARD-COMMUNICA-
TION WAS FOUND, A RELATIONSHIP MODIFIED BY THE TRUST THESE
EXECUTIVES HAD IN THEIR SUPERIORS.

1748 REAGAN M.O.
"THE POLITICAL STRUCTURE OF THE FEDERAL RESERVE SYSTEM."
AM. POL. SCI. REV., 55 (MAR. 61), 64-76.
HISTORY AND STRUCTURE OF THE FEDERAL RESERVE SYSTEM AND
WHERE ITS AUTHORITY LIES. FORMAL ROLES DO NOT REFLECT ACTUAL
DISTRIBUTION OF POWER IN THE SYSTEM.

1749 RECK D.
GOVERNMENT PURCHASING AND COMPETITION.
BERKELEY: U OF CALIF PR, 1954, 215 PP., LC#54-12093.
STUDY OF POLICIES ESTABLISHED BY CONGRESS TO GUIDE
PURCHASING OPERATIONS OF CIVILIAN AGENCIES OF FEDERAL
GOVERNMENT: LEGAL REQUIREMENT THAT SEALED BIDS BE USED IN
CONTRACTING, AND DELEGATION OF AUTHORITY TO CENTRALIZE
PURCHASES AND POLICIES TO GENERAL SERVICES ADMINISTRATION.
STUDY IS DESIGNED TO CONTRIBUTE TO UNDERSTANDING OF POLICIES
PURSUED BY OTHER LARGE-QUANTITY BUYERS.

1750 REDFIELD C.E.
COMMUNICATION IN MANAGEMENT.
CHICAGO: U OF CHICAGO PRESS, 1958, 314 PP., LC#58-11955.
ANALYSIS OF THEORY AND PRACTICE OF ADMINISTRATIVE COMMU-
NICATION. DISCUSSES GENERAL GUIDING PRINCIPLES AND VARIOUS
FORMS OF COMMUNICATION BETWEEN DIFFERENT ORGANIZATIONAL LEV-
ELS SUCH AS ORDER-GIVING, REPORTING, REVIEWING, AND CONFER-
RING. INTENDED AS GUIDEBOOK FOR ADMINISTRATORS.

1751 REDFORD D.R., ET A.L.
POLITICS AND GOVERNMENT IN THE UNITED STATES.
NEW YORK: HARCOURT BRACE, 1965, 1004 PP., LC#65-17518.
GENERAL DISCUSSION OF US POLITICAL INSTITUTIONS FROM
COLONIAL BEGINNINGS TO PRESENT. INCLUDES DISCUSSION OF STATE
AND LOCAL GOVERNMENTS.

1752 REDFORD E.S.
FIELD ADMINISTRATION OF WARTIME RATIONING.
WASHINGTON: US GOVERNMENT, 1947, 196 PP.
ANALYSIS AND EVALUATION OF ADMINISTRATIVE BEHAVIOR OF THE
CONSUMER RATIONING PROGRAM OPERATED BY OFFICE OF PRICE
ADMINISTRATION DURING WWII. STUDIES DEVELOPMENT OF AREAS OF
FIELD ADMINISTRATION, ORGANIZATIONAL PATTERN USED, RATIONING
DIVISION, ROLE OF LOCAL BOARD, BASIC COMMUNICATION AND
CONTROL, AND PROBLEM OF WORKLOAD. CONCLUDES THAT COOPERATION
MADE PROGRAM WORK.

1753 REDFORD E.S.
ADMINISTRATION OF NATIONAL ECONOMIC CONTROL.
NEW YORK: MACMILLAN, 1952, 403 PP.
FEATURES OF ADMINISTRATIVE SYSTEM IN USE IN ECONOMIC
CONTROL AND PROBLEMS OF ADMINISTERING ECONOMIC CONTROLS,
COURTS AND ADMINISTRATIVE PROCESS, INTEREST GROUPS AND
ADMINISTRATIVE DECISION-MAKING.

1754 REDFORD E.S. ED.
PUBLIC ADMINISTRATION AND POLICY FORMATION: STUDIES IN OIL,
GAS, BANKING, RIVER DEVELOPMENT AND CORPORATE INVESTIGATIONS
AUSTIN: U OF TEXAS PR, 1956, 319 PP., LC#56-7507.
FIVE CASE STUDIES OF ADMINISTRATIVE REGULATION EMPHASIZE
RELATIONSHIP BETWEEN CONTROL, EFFICIENCY, AND PUBLIC
INTEREST. DISCUSSES INTERRELATIONSHIPS BETWEEN AGENCIES,
CLIENTELE, AND SPECIFIC INDIVIDUALS.

1755 REDFORD E.S.
"THE NEVER-ENDING SEARCH FOR THE PUBLIC INTEREST" IN E. RED-
FORD, IDEALS AND PRACTICE IN PUBLIC ADMINISTRATION (BMR)"
UNIVERSITY: U ALABAMA PR, 1958.
FINDS THAT INDIVIDUALS AND GROUPS EXERT CONSTANT EFFORT
IN US TO BEND POLICY TOWARD SPECIAL INTERESTS. STATES THAT
AS A RESULT OF STRUCTURE OF SOCIETY AND GOVERNMENT, THERE IS
A GREAT DEAL OF PUBLIC INTEREST FOCUSED ON MAJOR PUBLIC
DECISIONS. ARGUES THAT MUCH RATIONALITY AND FRATERNITY ARE
EMBODIED IN TODAY'S POLITICAL ORDER: INSTITUTIONAL PROCESS
WILL YIELD PUBLIC GOOD IN THE FUTURE.

1756 REDFORD E.S.
IDEAL AND PRACTICE IN PUBLIC ADMINISTRATION.
UNIVERSITY: U ALABAMA PR, 1958, 155 PP.
ANALYSIS OF PUBLIC ADMINISTRATION, ITS GOALS, TASK, AND
METHODS. STUDIES RULE OF LAW VERSUS REAL MEN, RESPONSIBLE
ADMINISTRATION, DIRECTION OF DEMOCRACY, SEARCH FOR PUBLIC
INTEREST, AND THE REALITY OF THE IDEAL. CONCLUDES THAT
ADMINISTRATION IN A RESPONSIBLE GOVERNMENT WORKS FOR AND
ACHIEVES THE PUBLIC INTEREST.

1757 REDFORD E.S.
NATIONAL REGULATORY COMMISSIONS: NEED FOR A NEW LOOK
(PAMPHLET)
COLLEGE PARK: U MD, BUR PUB ADM, 1959, 23 PP., LC#59-63426.
REGULATORY AGENCIES SHOULD BE MORE DIRECTLY SUPERVISED BY
THE PRESIDENT TO INSURE THAT THE AGENCIES WILL ACT IN THE
PUBLIC INTEREST.

1758 REDFORD E.S.
"THE PROTECTION OF THE PUBLIC INTEREST WITH SPECIAL
REFERENCE TO ADMINISTRATIVE REGULATION."
AM. POL. SCI. REV., 48 (DEC.54), 1103-1113.

CRITICAL OF INTEREST GROUP THEORY IN PUBLIC ADMINISTRA-
TION. SUGGESTS CENTRALIZATION OF ADMINISTRATIVE MACHINERY
WOULD FACILITATE BROAD AND LONG VIEW OF SOCIAL INTERESTS.

1759 REDFORD E.S.
THE ROLE OF GOVERNMENT IN THE AMERICAN ECONOMY.
NEW YORK: MACMILLAN, 1966, 148 PP., LC#66-25280.
ANALYSIS OF INTERRELATIONSHIP BETWEEN US GOVERNMENT AND
AMERICAN ECONOMIC SYSTEM. EVOLUTION OF EFFECT THAT
GOVERNMENT HAS HAD IN DEVELOPMENT, REGULATION, AND
ADMINISTRATION OF ECONOMY. BASIC SYSTEM OF PRESENT DAY OF
THIS INTERACTION AND PERCEIVED FUTURE PROBLEMS.

1760 REDLICH F.
THE GERMAN MILITARY ENTERPRISER AND HIS WORK FORCE.
WIESBADEN: FRANK STEINER VERLAG, 1964, 532 PP.
A STUDY IN THE BORDER AREA BETWEEN MILITARY AND ECONOMIC
HISTORY, FOCUSING ON MILITARY OFFICER-ENTERPRISER, WHO
BOTH LED AND RAISED HIS ARMY. EXAMINES DEVELOPMENT OF THIS
SOCIAL AND OCCUPATIONAL TYPE AND VARIOUS SPECIFIC QUESTIONS:
ORGANIZATION OF BUSINESS, FINANCING OF IT, SOCIAL ASPECTS,
HUMAN RELATIONS AND MOTIVATION, SOLDIER-CIVILIAN RELATIONS.
A WORK IN COMPARATIVE HISTORIOGRAPHY.

1761 REES A.
"THE EFFECTS OF UNIONS ON RESOURCE ALLOCATION."
JOURNAL OF LAW AND ECONOMICS, 6 (OCT. 63), 69-78.
DISCUSSES EFFECTS OF LABOR UNIONS ON RESOURCE ALLOCATION
THROUGH CONTROL OVER WAGE INCREASES. EXAMINES RESULTS OF
COLLECTIVE BARGAINING ON INTER- AND INTRA-INDUSTRY WAGE
STRUCTURES. COMPARES WAGES AND EMPLOYMENT DISTRIBUTION UNDER
UNION AND OPEN COMPETIVE MARKET SYSTEMS. MAINTAINS THAT
BENEFICIAL ASPECTS OF BARGAINING ARE MORE IMPORTANT THAN ITS
EFFECT ON RESOURCE ALLOCATION.

1762 REICH C.A.
BUREAUCRACY AND THE FORESTS (PAMPHLET)
SANTA BARBARA: CTR DEMO INST, 1962, 13 PP.
ARGUES THAT MORE PUBLIC PARTICIPATION IS DESIRABLE IN
MANAGEMENT AND PLANNING FOR OUR FORESTS.

1763 REICH N.
LABOR RELATIONS IN REPUBLICAN GERMANY.
NEW YORK: OXFORD U PR, 1938, 292 PP.
TREATS EMPLOYER-EMPLOYEE RELATIONSHIPS, 1918-1933, IN
WEIMAR REPUBLIC. STUDIES COLLECTIVE ORGANIZATION OF INDUS-
TRIAL RELATIONS WITHIN FRAMEWORK OF TRADITIONAL POLITICAL
DEMOCRACY. ANALYZES ECONOMIC PROVISIONS OF WEIMAR CONSTITU-
TION, ROLE OF LABOR IN THE REPUBLIC, ARBITRATION METHODS,
ORGANIZATION WITHIN THE SHOPS, AND ULTIMATE FAILURE OF THE
REPUBLIC.

1764 REISCHAUER R.
"JAPAN'S GOVERNMENT--POLITICS."
LONDON: THOMAS NELSON & SONS, 1939.
EXAMINES FUNDAMENTALS OF JAPANESE POLITICAL THEORY AND
EVOLUTION OF STATE FROM PRIMITIVE TRIBAL FORM TO STRONGLY
CENTRALIZED GOVERNMENT OF 20TH CENTURY. ANALYZES POLITICAL
AND CULTURAL SIGNIFICANCE OF POLICY OF "THE IMPERIAL WAY."
LENGTHY DISCUSSION OF ORGANIZATION OF JAPANESE GOVERNMENT
IN 1939. SHORT SELECT BIBLIOGRAPHY IN ENGLISH.

1765 REISELBACH L.N.
"THE BASIS OF ISOLATIONIST BEHAVIOR."
PUB. OPIN. QUART., 24 (WINTER 60), 645-57.
SEEKS TO EXPLAIN THE CAUSES OF ISOLATIONISM IN TERMS OF
VARIABLES. ANALYZES ITS NATURAL DEVELOPMENT IN CONNECTION
WITH ECO/POLITICAL FACTORS. STUDY IS BASED ON POPULAR POLLS.

1766 REISS A.J. JR. ED.
SCHOOLS IN A CHANGING SOCIETY.
NEW YORK: FREE PRESS OF GLENCOE, 1965, 224 PP., LC#65-25255.
ESSAYS CONTRIBUTED TO A CONFERENCE ON RESEARCH IN THE
ADMINISTRATIVE ORGANIZATION OF SCHOOL SYSTEMS AND ON ITS
EFFECT ON THE SOCIALIZATION OF YOUTH IN THE SCHOOL AND THE
COMMUNITY. THEMES INCLUDE ORGANIZATIONAL DISPARITY, YOUTH
CULTURE, COMMUNITY LINKAGES OF PUBLIC SCHOOLS, SCHOOLS IN
A CHANGING SOCIETY, USES OF AUTHORITY, POLICE AND PROBATION,
INTEGRATION PLANS, CONTEMPORARY PROBLEMS, AND PUBLIC POLICY.

1767 REISSMAN L.
"A STUDY OF ROLE CONCEPTIONS IN BUREAUCRACY" (BMR)"
SOCIAL FORCES, 27 (MAR. 49), 305-310.
PRESENTS DATA ON AMERICAN BUREAUCRATS. EXAMINES
THEORETICAL FRAMEWORK WITHIN WHICH STUDY WAS CONDUCTED,
SUGGESTING A RESOLUTION OF METHODOLOGICALLY CREATED
DICHOTOMY OF INFORMAL-FORMAL STRUCTURES IN THE STUDY OF
BUREAUCRATIC ORGANIZATIONS. PROPOSES CONCEPT OF "ROLE" AS A
VALUABLE TOOL FOR STUDYING BUREAUCRACY.

1768 RHODE W.E.
"COMMITTEE CLEARANCE OF ADMINISTRATIVE DECISIONS."
E LANSING: MICH ST, BUR SOC& POL, 1959, 72 PP., LC#59-62974.
THE FIRST COMPREHENSIVE DISCUSSION OF THE HISTORY AND
OPERATION OF CONGRESSIONAL COMMITTEE CLEARANCE OF ADMINIS-
TRATIVE DECISIONS. SURVEYS AND ANALYZES ESTABLISHMENT AND

USE OF COMMITTEE CLEARANCE FROM INCEPTION IN LATE 1920'S
THROUGH 1957. EVALUATES OPERATION OF THIS DEVICE IN TERMS OF
ITS LEGITIMACY IN OUR SYSTEM OF GOVERNMENT. HEAVILY DOCU-
MENTED; MOST REFERENCES TO "CONGRESSIONAL RECORD."

1769 RHODES G.
PUBLIC SECTOR PENSIONS.
LONDON: ALLEN & UNWIN, 1965, 320 PP.
RESEARCH BY ROYAL INSTITUTE OF PUBLIC ADMINISTRATION
(GREAT BRITAIN) REVIEWING POLICIES IMPLICIT IN CURRENT
PUBLIC SECTOR PENSION SCHEMES. SCRUTINIZES COMPLEXITIES
OF ADMINISTRATION AND VARIETY OF METHODS OF FINANCING
SCHEMES. SETS PUBLIC SECTOR SCHEMES IN WIDER CONTEXT
OF NATIONAL PENSIONS POLICY.

1770 RHODESIA-NYASA NATL ARCHIVES
A SELECT BIBLIOGRAPHY OF RECENT PUBLICATIONS CONCERNING THE
FEDERATION OF RHODESIA AND NYASALAND (PAMPHLET)
SALISBURY: NAT ARCH RHODES NYAS, 1960, 13 PP.
UNANNOTATED CLASSIFIED BIBLIOGRAPHY OF POST-1950 PUB-
LICATIONS IN ENGLISH. COVERS OFFICIAL PERIODICAL PUBLICA-
TIONS, GOVERNMENT PUBLICATIONS ON SPECIAL TOPICS, NEWSPA-
PERS, PERIODICALS, AND BOOKS. SELECTIONS CONCERN SUBJECTS OF
HISTORICAL, POLITICAL, ECONOMIC, GEOLOGICAL, AND ANTHROPO-
LOGICAL INTEREST.

1772 RICH B.M.
"ADMINISTRATIVE REORGANIZATION IN NEW JERSEY" (BMR)
PUBLIC ADMIN.   REV., 7 (1947), P251-257.
DESCRIBES FEATURES OF REORGANIZATION AND REVISION OF
NEW JERSEY'S STATE GOVERNMENT, 1947-52. SHOWS HOW MUCH OF
THIS REORGANIZATION WAS RESULT OF CONSTITUTIONAL CHANGE.
ANALYZES OVER-ALL AND DETAILED STRUCTURAL PROBLEMS AND
METHODS THAT HAVE BEEN EMPLOYED TO SMOOTH OPERATIONS.

1773 RICHARD J.B.
GOVERNMENT AND POLITICS OF WYOMING.
DUBUQUE: WC BROWN, 1966, 105 PP.
OUTLINE OF GOVERNMENTAL AND POLITICAL SYSTEMS IN STATE OF
WYOMING. DESCRIBES POLITICAL PARTIES, ELECTIONS, AND INTER-
EST GROUPS; POLITICS AND LAW-MAKING IN STATE LEGISLATURE;
GOVERNOR'S POLITICS AND ADMINISTRATION; STATE JUDICIAL SYS-
TEM; AND SYSTEMS OF LOCAL GOVERNMENT.

1774 RICHARDS P.G.
PATRONAGE IN BRITISH GOVERNMENT.
TORONTO: U OF TORONTO PRESS, 1963, 284 PP.
DISCUSSION OF THE INFLUENCE OF PARTY POLITICS ON
GOVERNMENT APPOINTMENTS IN BRITAIN, TO THE ADMINISTRATIVE
BRANCHES, THE JUDICIARY, AND THE CHURCH. SAYS THAT ALTHOUGH
PATRONAGE STILL EXISTS, IT IS NOT DETRIMENTAL TO DEMOCRACY.

1775 RICHARDSON H.G., SAYLES G.O.
THE ADMINISTRATION OF IRELAND 1172-1377.
DUBLIN: IRISH MANUSCRIPTS COMN, 1963, 300 PP.
EXAMINATION OF IRISH ADMINISTRATION, 1172-1377, WITH
DESCRIPTION OF EACH IMPORTANT OFFICE AND BRANCH OF GOVERN-
MENT, INCLUDING LISTS OF MINISTER, IRISH TREASURER'S AC-
COUNTS, AND ILLUSTRATIVE DOCUMENTS.

1776 RICHARDSON I.L.
BIBLIOGRAFIA BRASILEIRA DE ADMINISTRACAO PUBLICA E
ASSUNTOS CORRELATOS.
RIO DE JAN: FUND GETULIO VARGAS, 1964, 840 PP.
BIBLIOGRAPHY OF 7,300 ITEMS ON BRAZILIAN DEVELOPMENT IN
FIELD OF PUBLIC ADMINISTRATION. COVERS PERIOD 1940-61.
CONTAINS REFERENCES TO CONSTITUTIONAL RIGHTS; POLITICAL
THEORY; CENTRAL GOVERNMENT ORGANIZATION; INTERNATIONAL
RELATIONS, LAWS, AND ORGANIZATIONS; STATE, LOCAL, AND TERRI-
TORIAL GOVERNMENTS; POLITICAL PARTIES AND ELECTIONS; ADMINIS-
TRATIVE LAW; PLANNING, ETC.

1777 RIDDICK F.M.
THE UNITED STATES CONGRESS ORGANIZATION AND PROCEDURE.
MANASSAS: NATL CAPITOL PUBL, 1949, 459 PP., LC#49-1982.
COMPREHENSIVE TREATMENT OF PROCEDURE IN CONGRESS INCLU-
DING FUNCTIONS AND POLITICAL ORGANIZATIONS OF CONGRESS,
PRESIDING OFFICERS, COMMITTEES, EMPLOYEES, INSTRUMENTS FOR
DETERMINATION OF LEGISLATION, ORDER OF PROCEDURE, STEPS OF
PASSAGE OF A BILL, AND THE PRESIDENT-CONGRESS RELATION.

1778 RIDDLE D.H.
THE TRUMAN COMMITTEE: A STUDY IN CONGRESSIONAL RESPONSIBILI-
TY.
NEW BRUNSWICK: RUTGERS U PR, 1964, 165 PP., LC#63-16306.
EXAMINATION OF TRUMAN COMMITTEE AND ITS WORK AS CASE
STUDY OF RESPONSIBLE INVESTIGATION. BASED ON INTERVIEWS,
PUBLISHED HEARINGS AND REPORTS, CONTEMPORARY BOOKS AND ARTI-
CLES. INCLUDES EXTENSIVE BIBLIOGRAPHY AND APPENDICES.

1779 RIDLEY C.E., SIMON H.A.
MEASURING MUNICIPAL ACTIVITIES (PAMPHLET)
CHICAGO: INT CITY MANAGER'S ASSN, 1943, 75 PP.
DEFINES CRITERIA BY WHICH MUNICIPAL SERVICES MAY BE
MEASURED AND PURPOSES OF SUCH MEASUREMENT. SERVICES
CONSIDERED ARE PUBLIC HEALTH, LIBRARIES, POLICE AND FIRE

PROTECTION, PLAYGROUNDS, WELFARE, AND SO ON. DIFFERENT
CRITERIA MUST BE EXAMINED FOR THEIR USEFULNESS IF A CITY
IS TO KNOW IT IS GETTING THE MOST BENEFIT FROM EACH TAX
DOLLAR.

1780 RIDLEY C.E., NOLTING O.F.
THE CITY-MANAGER PROFESSION.
CHICAGO: U OF CHICAGO PRESS, 1934, 143 PP.
DESCRIBES INCREASINGLY TECHNICAL NATURE OF CITY GOVERN-
MENT AND CONSEQUENT NEED TO HAVE TECHNICIANS ABLE TO
ADMINISTER A CITY. TRACES HISTORY OF IDEA OF A CITY-MANAGER
AND MAKES SUGGESTIONS HOW BEST A CITY MIGHT SELECT HIM.

1781 RIDLEY F., BLONDEL J.
PUBLIC ADMINISTRATION IN FRANCE.
LONDON: ROUTLEDGE & KEGAN PAUL, 1964, 336 PP.
DETAILED DESCRIPTION OF FRENCH ADMINISTRATIVE
ORGANIZATION, FUNCTIONS, POWERS. COMPARES EFFECT ON
REPRESENTATIVENESS OF ADMINISTRATION OF FRENCH TECHNOCRATIC
AND BRITISH LIBERAL IDEOLOGIES.

1782 RIES J.C.
THE MANAGEMENT OF DEFENSE: ORGANIZATION AND CONTROL OF THE
US ARMED SERVICES.
BALTIMORE: JOHNS HOPKINS PRESS, 1964, 212 PP., LC#64-18122.
REAPPRAISAL OF DEFENSE ORGANIZATION. FAVORS COMMITTEE
METHOD OF ORGANIZATION--CONCLUDING THAT AMERICAN POLITICAL
ENVIRONMENT DEMANDS PLURALISTIC DEFENSE STRUCTURE WHICH
ALLOCATES RESPONSIBILITY IN KEEPING WITH AUTHORITY. URGES
RATIONALIZATION OF DECISION-MAKING AND RESTORATION OF
ORGANIZATIONAL EQUILIBRIUM.

1783 RIESELBACH Z.N.
"QUANTITATIVE TECHNIQUES FOR STUDYING VOTING BEHAVIOR IN
THE UNITED NATIONS GENERAL ASSEMBLY."
INT. ORGAN., 14 (1960), 291-306.
DEALS WITH POSSIBLE MEANS OF SOLVING THE QUESTIONS
REGARDING BLOC-VOTING PATTERNS. DATA PRESENTED TO GIVE
OPPOSITION-VIEWER OPPORTUNITY TO REWORK THE FIGURES TO SUIT
HIS OWN STANDARDS.

1784 RIGBY T.H.
"TRADITIONAL, MARKET, AND ORGANIZATIONAL SOCIETIES AND
THE USSR."
WORLD POLIT., 16(JULY 64), 539-57.
DESCRIBES SOVIET SOCIETY AND PARTICULARLY THE SOVIET
POLITICAL SYSTEM IN TERMS OF A TYPOLOGY OF SOCIETY BASED
ON MODES OF COORDINATING SOCIAL ACTIVITY. INTENDED TO
COMPARE AND CONTRAST COMMUNIST AND NON-COMMUNIST INDUS-
TRIALIZED SOCIETIES. TREATS PARTICULARLY THE SOVIET SYSTEM
AS IT DEVELOPED UNDER STALIN.

1785 RIGGS F.W.
ADMINISTRATION IN DEVELOPING COUNTRIES.
BOSTON: HOUGHTON, 1964, 477 PP., $7.95.
OFFERS BOTH STRUCTURAL AND FUNCTIONAL APPROACH TO PROB-
LEMS OF ADMINISTRATION IN DEVELOPING COUNTRIES. PRESENTS
MODEL OF AGRARIAN SOCIETY IN PROCESS OF INDUSTRIALIZATION.

1786 RIGGS R.E.
THE MOVEMENT FOR ADMINISTRATIVE REORGANIZATION IN ARIZONA.
TUCSON: U OF ARIZONA PR, 1964, 86 PP., LC#64-64712.
SURVEYS NATURE OF PAST EFFORTS TO REORGANIZE
ADMINISTRATIVE SYSTEM TO AVOID DUPLICATION OF POSITIONS AND
TO ECONOMIZE. PRESENTED IN SEVERAL PARTY PLATFORMS OF BOTH
PARTIES AND IN BILLS TO LEGISLATURE. DISCUSSES REASONS FOR
FAILURE OF REFORMS, SUCH AS LEGISLATIVE JEALOUSY OF
EXECUTIVE POWER AND DEPARTMENT OPPOSITION. DRAWS
IMPLICATIONS FOR FUTURE REORGANIZATION PROGRAMS.

1787 RIKER W.H.
FEDERALISM.
BOSTON: LITTLE BROWN, 1964, 169 PP., LC#64-22483.
DISCUSSES ORIGIN, OPERATION, AND SIGNIFICANCE OF FEDERA-
LISM, INCLUDING THEORY OF FEDERALISM, ITS ORIGIN AND PUR-
POSES, ITS MAINTENANCE, ITS INSTITUTIONS IN US, FEDERALISM
OUTSIDE US, AND VALUE OF FEDERALISM.

1788 RILEY V., ALLEN R.L.
INTERINDUSTRY ECONOMIC STUDIES.
BALTIMORE: JOHNS HOPKINS PRESS, 1955, 280 PP.
ANNOTATED AND INDEXED BIBLIOGRAPHY ALSO PRESENTS AND
DISCUSSES ASPECTS OF INTERINDUSTRY ECONOMICS. DEALS WITH
THEORETICAL ECONOMY STRUCTURE, MATHEMATICAL AND COMPUTATION-
AL TECHNIQUES OF ANALYSIS, PROBLEMS AND MEANS OF CLASSIFICA-
TION, AS WELL AS SPECIFIC FACETS OF THE US ECONOMIC SYSTEM.
CONTAINS A SEPARATE SECTION OF GENERAL DISCUSSION AND IN-
CLUDES A LIST OF GENERAL REFERENCES.

1789 RIORDAN W.L. ED.
PLUNKITT OF TAMMANY HALL.
NEW YORK: MCCLURE, PHILLIPS & CO, 1905, 183 PP.
COLLECTED TALKS OF G.W. PLUNKITT, TAMMANY POLITICAL
LEADER, INCLUDING ATTITUDES TOWARD GRAFT, PATRONAGE,
REFORMERS, ORGANIZATION LEADERSHIP, THE ROLE OF BOSSES,
AND THE CURSE OF CIVIL SERVICE REFORM.

1790 RIPLEY R.B.
"INTERAGENCY COMMITTEES AND INCREMENTALISM: THE CASE OF AID
TO INDIA."
MIDWEST J. POLIT. SCI., 8 (MAY 64), 143-165.
STUDY OF THE AMERICAN AID PROGRAM TO INDIA FROM 1951-1962
AS A METHOD OF ANALYZING THE FUNCTIONING OF INTERAGENCY COM-
MITTEES. HYPOTHESES ARE EXAMINED THAT (1) THESE COMMITTEES
TEND TO REMAIN STABLE AND INERT, AND (2) THEY PRODUCE AN IN-
CREMENTAL SITUATION. AFFIRMATIVE CONCLUSIONS ARE DRAWN BUT
INCREMENTALISM IS DECLARED NOT INEVITABLE.

1791 ROBBINS L.
ECONOMIC PLANNING AND INTERNATIONAL ORDER.
NEW YORK: MACMILLAN, 1937, 330 PP.
VIEWS VARIOUS TYPES OF PLANNING: INDEPENDENT NATIONAL
PLANNING, PARTIAL INTERNATION AND COMPLETE INTERNATIONAL
PLANNING. POINTS OUT CHARACTERISTICS OF EACH TYPE. CONCLUDES
WITH ANALYSIS OF KEYNESIAN DOCTRINE.

1792 ROBERT J.
"LES ELECTIONS LEGISLATIVES DU 17 MAI 1963 ET L'EVOLUTION
POLITIQUE INTERNE DU MAROC."
REV. JURID. POLIT. OUTREMER, 17 (APR.-JUNE 63), 254-91.
VIEWS 1963 LEGISLATIVE ELECTIONS AND EVOLUTION OF POLI-
TICS IN MOROCCO. ANALYZES ELECTORAL PROCESS, FOCUSING ON
TECHNICALITIES OF BALLOTING. POINTS OUT POSITIONS OF POLITI-
CAL PARTIES AND OPINION GROUPS, TACTICS OF OPPOSITION AND
POLITICAL ATTITUDES OF THE KING. DISCUSSES ELECTION RETURNS.

1793 ROBERT J.
LA MONARCHIE MAROCAINE.
PARIS: PICHON ET DURAND-AUZIAS, 1963, 350 PP.
RECAPITULATES STUDIES ALREADY UNDERTAKEN ON MOROCCO.
AUTHOR POINTS OUT THAT THEY ARE ALMOST NONEXISTENT SINCE
MOROCCO'S INDEPENDENCE; HENCE IMPORTANCE OF THIS WORK.
COLLATES ALL OFFICIAL TEXTS ON ADMINISTRATIVE AND
CONSTITUTIONAL MATTERS TO GAIN AN EXACT DESCRIPTION OF THE
PRINCIPAL ORGANS OF THE STATE. ILLUMINATES PAPERS ON ALL
QUESTIONS FACING MOROCCO SINCE INDEPENDENCE.

1794 ROBERTS E.B.
"THE PROBLEM OF AGING ORGANIZATIONS."
BUSINESS HORIZONS, 10 (WINTER 67), 51-60.
DESCRIBES RISE AND FALL IN EFFICIENCY AND OUTPUT OF R&D
FIRMS. BASED ON INDUSTRIAL DYNAMICS, PROPOSES THAT PROBLEMS
ARE NATURAL OUTGROWTH OF FIRMS' DEVELOPMENT. DISCUSSES AP-
PLICATION OF FEEDBACK LOOPS AND EFFECT OF VARIOUS DIVI-
SIONS WITHIN THE ORGANIZATION UPON ONE ANOTHER, PROPOSING
SOLUTIONS AND CORRECTIVE MEASURES.

1795 ROBERTS J.C.
"CIVIL RESTRAINT, MENTAL ILLNESS, AND THE RIGHT TO
TREATMENT."
YALE LAW J., 77 (NOV. 67), 87-116.
EXAMINES INVOLUNTARY DETENTION IN MENTAL ILLNESS.
CLAIMS THAT THERE ARE DIFFICULTIES IN JUDICIAL
IMPLEMENTATION OF RIGHT TO TREATMENT, SUCH AS THE UNWILLING
PATIENT AND THE DETERMINATION OF BEST TREATMENT. SEES
CONSTITUTIONAL PROBLEMS IN CERTAIN APPROACHES NOW USED, FOR
EXAMPLE, DETAINING PERSONS FOR NON-TREATABLE ILLNESS ALONE.
ADVOCATES ADMINISTRATIVE SOLUTION, MUCH LIKE NEW YORK'S.

1796 ROBERTS S.H.
HISTORY OF FRENCH COLONIAL POLICY.
LONDON: KING, 1929, 741 PP.
HISTORICALLY REVIEWS THE FIFTY YEARS OF FRENCH COLONI-
ZATION AND DISCUSSES THE THEORIES BEHIND THE MOVEMENT.
ANALYZES ITS ECONOMIC,POLICAL AND ADMINISTRATIVE PROB-
LEMS. INCLUDES A STUDY OF FRENCH EMPIRE SINCE 1914.

1797 ROBINSON D.W.
PROMISING PRACTICES IN CIVIC EDUCATION.
NEW YORK: NATL COUN SOC STUDIES, 1967, 364 PP., LC#67-27006.
REPORT OF STUDY OF CIVIC EDUCATION, LEARNING, AND ACTION
IN US IN 1963. ANALYZES AND PRESENTS BEST SOCIO-CIVIC
QUALITIES AND COMPETENCIES AS ORGANIZED UNDER 11 CITIZENSHIP
GOALS ESSENTIAL FOR RESPONSIBLE CITIZENRY. AIMS TO PRESENT
DEFINITION OF CITIZENSHIP EDUCATION AS OBSERVED IN 83
SCHOOLS THROUGHOUT US.

1798 ROBINSON E.A.G.
THE STRUCTURE OF COMPETITIVE INDUSTRY.
NEW YORK: CAMBRIDGE U PRESS, 1953, 179 PP.
DISCUSSES MEANS AVAILABLE TO GREAT BRITAIN FOR INCREASING
ITS NATIONAL PRODUCT, THROUGH CONSIDERATION OF INDUSTRIAL
EFFICIENCY. DEFENDS FREE MARKET SYSTEM AS MOST EFFICIENT
BECAUSE IT ADJUSTS TO DEMANDS OF CONSUMER. ATTEMPTS TO
DEFINE AND DESCRIBE WORKINGS OF FREE MARKET SYSTEM.

1799 ROBINSON E.A.G.
ECONOMIC CONSEQUENCES OF THE SIZE OF NATIONS.
NEW YORK: ST MARTIN'S PRESS, 1960, 447 PP.
ANALYSIS OF RELATION OF SIZE OF NATIONS TO THEIR ECONOMIC
PROSPERITY. DISCUSSES SIZE IN RELATION TO ECONOMIC EFFICIEN-
CY, ADAPTABILITY, AND STABILITY AND TO PROBLEMS OF EXECUTIVE
ADMINISTRATION AND TO FOREIGN AID POLICIES.

1800 ROBINSON H.
DEVELOPMENT OF THE BRITISH EMPIRE.
BOSTON: HOUGHTON, 1936, 475 PP.
PRESENTS PROBLEMS OF COLONIAL GOVERNMENT, COLONIZATION OF
AMERICA AND REVOLUTION ON ATLANTIC SEABORD, CANADIAN INDE-
PENDENCE, ASIAN AND AFRICAN COLONIZATION, AND FINALLY MAN-
DATED TERRITORIES HELD UNDER CONTRACT WITH THE LEAGUE OF
NATIONS. THE ECONOMICS OF EMPIRE, WITH ITS CONFLICTING AND
DIVERSE INTERESTS AND GROWING NATIONALISM AMONG COLONIES IS
DISCUSSED.

1801 ROBINSON J.A.
"THE ROLE OF THE RULES COMMITTEE IN ARRANGING THE PROGRAM
OF THE UNITED STATES HOUSE OF REPRESENTATIVES."
WESTERN POLIT. QUART., 12 (SEPT. 59), 653-669.
ANALYZES THE ACTIVITIES OF THE HOUSE COMMITTEE ON RULES,
INSOFAR AS THEY RELATE TO SELECTING BILLS AND RESOLUTIONS
FOR CONSIDERATION BY THE HOUSE. ACTUALLY THE COMMITTEE WITH-
HOLDS ONLY A FEW BILLS EACH SESSION. THE COMMITTEE PERFORMS
A NECESSARY FUNCTION IN ARRANGING THE PROGRAM OF THE HOUSE.

1802 ROBINSON J.A.
"PROCESS SATISFACTION AND POLICY APPROVAL IN STATE DEPART-
MENT - CONGRESSIONAL RELATIONS."
AMER. J. PUBLIC HEALTH, 68 (NOV. 61), 278-283.
US CONGRESSMEN WHO ARE SATISFIED WITH INFORMATION
FURNISHED THEM BY DEPARTMENT OF STATE AND WEIGHT GIVEN TO
CONGRESSIONAL OPINION IN DEPARTMENTAL POLICY-MAKING, ARE
LIKELY TO APPROVE DEPARTMENTAL POLICY. PROPOSITION IS
MORE LIKELY, HOWEVER, WITH CONGRESSMEN OF POLITICAL PARTY
OPPOSITE THAT OF THE PRESIDENT.

1803 ROBINSON K. ED., MADDEN F. ED.
ESSAYS IN IMPERIAL GOVERNMENT.
NEW YORK: HUMANITIES PRESS, 1963, 293 PP.
STUDIES PROBLEMS OF COLONIALISM IN AFRICA. PRESENTS
HISTORICAL APPRAISAL, AND CONSIDERS POLITICAL
ADMINISTRATION, IMPERIAL PATERNALISM, ECONOMIC POLICY, AND
TRANSFER OF POWER. INCLUDES BIBLIOGRAPHY OF WORKS OF MARGERY
PURHAM, LEADING SCHOLAR ON AFRICAN GOVERNMENT.

1804 ROBINSON M.
THE COMING OF AGE OF THE LANGLEY PORTER CLINIC (PAMPHLET)
UNIVERSITY: U ALABAMA PR, 1962, 48 PP.
DEALS WITH ADMINISTRATIVE AND ORGANIZATIONAL ASPECTS OF
PLANNED CHANGES WITHIN A PUBLICLY ADMINISTERED AGENCY
(LANGLEY PORTER NEUROPSYCHIATRIC INSTITUTE). DESCRIBES
PROCESS OF REORGANIZATION FOLLOWING MANAGEMENT SURVEY, 1957.

1805 ROBINSON M.E.
EDUCATION FOR SOCIAL CHANGE: ESTABLISHING INSTITUTES OF PUB-
LIC AND BUSINESS ADMINISTRATION ABROAD (PAMPHLET)
WASHINGTON: BROOKINGS INST, 1961, 90 PP.
REPORT ON CONFERENCE OF REPRESENTATIVES OF AMERICAN UNI-
VERSITIES THAT HAVE HELPED TO ESTABLISH PUBLIC AND BUSINESS
ADMINISTRATION INSTITUTES ABROAD. AIMS OF CONFERENCE WERE TO
REVIEW PROGRESS AND STUDY PROCESS OF FOUNDING SUCH INSTITU-
TIONS AND THEIR EFFECT ON SOCIAL CHANGE.

1806 ROBSON W.A. ED.
"GREAT CITIES OF THE WORLD: THEIR GOVERNMENT, POLITICS, AND
PLANNING."
LONDON: ALLEN & UNWIN, 1954.
ATTEMPTS TO SHOW PROBLEMS OF GOVERNMENT, POLITICS, AND
PLANNING WHICH CONFRONT LARGE CITIES AND HOW THEY DEAL WITH
THEM. DESCRIPTIONS OF LOCAL GOVERNMENT OF REPRESENTATIVE
GROUP OF CITIES. SELECT BIBLIOGRAPHY AT CONCLUSION IS CLAS-
SIFIED BY CITY. PART ONE IS GENERAL ESSAY BY ROBSON ON
POLITICAL AND CIVIC CHARACTERISTICS OF LARGE METROPOLITAN
REGIONS.

1807 ROBSON W.A.
"TWO-LEVEL GOVERNMENT FOR METROPOLITAN AREAS."
WESTERN POLIT. QUART., 10 (JUNE 57), 442-444.
SUGGESTS METROPOLITAN GOVERNMENTAL STRUCTURE TO DEAL
WITH REGIONAL PROBLEMS AND LOCAL STRUCTURES FOR LOCAL
PROBLEMS. THE GOAL SHOULD BE TO "PROJECT LOCAL SELF-GOVERN-
MENT ONTO A REGIONAL PLANE."

1808 ROBSON W.A.
THE GOVERNORS AND THE GOVERNED.
BATON ROUGE: LOUISIANA ST U PR, 1964, 68 PP., LC#64-15876.
DEALS WITH RELATIONSHIP IN WESTERN DEMOCRACY, PARTICULAR-
LY IN US, OF EXECUTIVE TO PEOPLE, PROBLEMS OF BUREAUCRACY
AND ITS CONTROL, COMMUNICATION, CITIZENS' ATTITUDE TOWARD
POLITICS. CALLS FOR CITIZEN PARTICIPATION IN GOVERNMENT AS
WELL AS GREAT STATESMANSHIP FROM POLITICIANS.

1809 ROCHE J.P., LEVY L.W.
THE CONGRESS.
NEW YORK: HARCOURT BRACE, 1964, 212 PP., LC#64-12974.
A SELECTION OF SIXTEEN DOCUMENTS THAT ILLUSTRATE THE
ACTUAL OPERATION OF CONGRESS AND THE DISTRIBUTION OF POWER
WITHIN CONGRESS. EXAMINES THE LEGISLATIVE PROCESS, THE
IMPORTANCE OF SENIORITY AND OF THE REPUBLICAN-DIXIECRAT CO-
ALITION, CONGRESSIONAL INVESTIGATIONS, CONGRESS AND FOREIGN

POLICY. CONGRESS INSTITUTIONALIZES A BALANCE OF POLITICAL
FORCES DIFFERENT FROM THOSE OF THE NATION AS A WHOLE.

1810 ROCHE J.P., LEVY L.W.
THE PRESIDENCY.
NEW YORK: HARCOURT BRACE, 1964, 223 PP., LC#64-13913.
DISCUSSES CONSTITUTIONAL POWERS OF EXECUTIVE AND
THEIR RELATION TO THE CONDUCT OF FOREIGN POLICY, AS WELL
AS THE VETO POWER, REMOVAL POWER, AND GENERAL EMERGENCY
POWERS THAT HAVE DEVELOPED IN NATIONAL CRISES.

1811 ROEPKE W.
A HUMANE ECONOMY: THE SOCIAL FRAMEWORK OF THE FREE MARKET.
CHICAGO: REGNERY, 1960, 261 PP.
IMPASSIONED STATEMENT WITH REFERENCE TO TRIUMPH OF FREE-
MARKET ECONOMY AND CORRESPONDING FAILURE OF SOCIALIST
TECHNIQUES IN PAST 15 YEARS. ASSERTS THAT IT IS A PRECEPT
OF ETHICAL AND HUMANE BEHAVIOR AS WELL AS POLITICAL WISDOM
TO ADAPT ECONOMIC POLICY TO MAN INSTEAD OF CONVERSE. ADDS,
HOWEVER, THAT THE FREE-MARKET ECONOMY MUST ALSO FIND A
PLACE 'WITHIN THE HIGHER ORDER'.

1812 ROETTER C.
THE DIPLOMATIC ART.
PHILADELPHIA: MACRAE SMITH CO, 1963, 248 PP., LC#63-12444.
INFORMAL HISTORY OF WORLD DIPLOMACY WITH EMPHASIS ON DIP-
LOMATIC PROCEDURES AND MEANS OF TRAINING AND CHOOSING
DIPLOMATS IN NUCLEAR AGE.

1813 ROFF W.R.
THE ORIGINS OF MALAY NATIONALISM.
NEW HAVEN: YALE U PR, 1967, 297 PP., LC#67-13447.
STUDIES GROWTH OF NATIONALISM IN MALAY AND VOLUNTARY
ASSOCIATIONS THAT SERVE AS EXPRESSIONS OF THIS FEELING.
DISCUSSES GOVERNMENTAL STRUCTURE OF MALAY UNDER BRITISH.
FOCUSES ON THREE NEW ELITE GROUPS, MUSLIM BOURGEOISIE, MALAY
INTELLIGENTSIA, AND ENGLISH-SCHOOLED SCIONS OF MALAY RULING
HOUSES. TREATS THEIR RELATIONSHIP WITH TRADITIONAL ELITES
AND IMPACT ON SOCIAL CHANGE.

1814 ROGERS W.C.
INTERNATIONAL ADMINISTRATION: A BIBLIOGRAPHY (PUBLICATION
NO 92; A PAMPHLET)
CHICAGO: PUBLIC ADMIN SERVICE, 1945, 32 PP.
ENGLISH-LANGUAGE BIBLIOGRAPHY OF WORKS PUBLISHED BOTH
PRIOR TO 1939 AND IN PERIOD 1939-1945. INCLUDES BOOKS,
PAMPHLETS, AND PERIODICALS RELATED TO ADMINISTRATION OR
MANAGEMENT OF VARIED ACTIVITIES UNDERTAKEN BY PUBLIC AUTHOR-
ITIES ON CENTRAL, LOCAL, AND SPECIAL LEVELS INTERNA-
TIONALLY. EACH ITEM RECEIVES ANNOTATION OF SEVERAL LINES.

1815 ROGOW A.A., TEMPLE J.Y.
"CONGRESSIONAL GOVERNMENT: LEGISLATIVE POWER V. DOMESTIC
PROCESSES."
GEORGETOWN LAW J., 32 (JUNE 64), 947-953.
DEALS WITH THE DECLINE OF CONGRESS AS THE CHIEF INITIATOR
OF LEGISLATION AND POLICY AND THE PASSING OF THIS POWER TO
THE WHITE HOUSE AND THE EXECUTIVE DEPARTMENTS AND AGENCIES.
IN THE AREA OF FOREIGN POLICY THE CHIEF REASON FOR
THIS DECLINE IS THAT CONGRESS IS RESPONSIBLE TO CONSTITUENTS
IN DISTRICTS AND STATES WHILE THE PRESIDENT IS RESPONSIBLE
TO THE NATION AND THE WORLD. PRESIDENT NEEDS PARTY SUPPORT.

1816 ROMANO F.
CIVIL SERVICE AND PUBLIC EMPLOYEE LAW IN NEW JERSEY.
NEWARK: ASSOC LAWYERS PUBL CO, 1961, 464 PP.
TRIEATISE ON DIFFICULT PROBLEMS ARISING IN THE ADMIN-
ISTRATION AND INTERPRETATION OF CIVIL SERVICE AND PUBLIC
EMPLOYEE LAW. RECORDS ALL LEGISLATION RELEVANT TO MUNICIPAL
COUNTY, AND STATE EMPLOYEE LAW. ARRANGED IN SECTIONS
EACH DELAING WITH ONE TYPE OF WORKER: ELECTED OFFICIALS,
POLICE, FIREMEN, TEACHERS, ETC.; INCLUDES MORE GENERAL
SECTIONS ON TENURE, PENSIONS, CIVIL SERVICE, ETC.

1817 ROMASCO A.U.
THE POVERTY OF ABUNDANCE: HOOVER, THE NATION, THE DEPRESSION
NEW YORK: OXFORD U PR, 1965, 282 PP., LC#65-26565.
STUDIES CONSEQUENCES OF GREAT DEPRESSION, EXPLORING WAYS
IN WHICH AMERICAN LEADERS, FOLLOWING SUGGESTIONS OF PRESI-
DENT HOOVER, USED NATION'S EXISTING INSTITUTIONS TO MASTER
THE ECONOMIC COLLAPSE. RECREATES PROBLEMS FACING CONTEMPO-
RARY LEADERSHIP, SHOWS METHODS THEY USED, AND EVALUATES
PERFORMANCE.

1818 ROSE A.M.
"CONFIDENCE AND THE CORPORATION."
AMER. J. OF ECO. AND SOC., 26 (JULY 67), 231-236.
FOUNDATION OF THE CORPORATION IS CONFIDENCE. HOLDS THAT
IN PAST FEW YEARS DIRECTORS AND MANAGERS OF CORPORATIONS
HAVE PASSED BY-LAWS IN OWN FAVOR AND CHEATED STOCKHOLDERS.
RESULTING LOSS OF CONFIDENCE UNDERMINES CORPORATE SYSTEM.

1819 ROSE D.L., HOC V.V.
THE VIETNAMESE CIVIL SERVICE.
E LANSING: MICH ST VIET ADVISORY, 1961, 467 PP.
MANY DOCUMENTS AND INTERVIEWS, REVIEW NATURE AND SCOPE OF

SYSTEM, EMPLOYEE CLASSIFICATION AND COMPENSATION, PROCEDURE
OF RECRUITMENT, PROMOTIONS, AND OTHER ADMINISTRATIVE MAT-
TERS. INCLUDES CHARTS AND LISTS. AUTHOR EVALUATES SYSTEM
AS BASICALLY INEFFICIENT DUE TO ORIENTATION TOWARD
BENEFIT AND SECURITY OF WORKERS RATHER THAN UTILITY.

1820 ROSENBERG B., HOWTON F.W.
"ETHNIC LIBERALISM AND EMPLOYMENT DISCRIMINATION IN THE
NORTH."
AMER. J. OF ECO. AND SOC., 26 (OCT. 67), 387-398.
EXAMINES NATURE AND FUNCTION OF DE FACTO DISCRIMINATION.
SHOWS HOW PUTATIVELY LIBERAL NORTHERN EMPLOYER RATIONALIZES
HIS DISCRIMINATORY PRACTICES. DISCUSSES EXTENT TO WHICH HE
IS EMBARRASSED BY HIS INVOLVEMENT IN ACTIVITIES HIS
PROFESSED VALUES CONDEMN. FEELS EMPLOYERS MAY BE
SUFFICIENTLY AMBIVALENT TO MAKE THE SYSTEM SUSCEPTIBLE OF
CHANGE.

1821 ROSENFARB J.
FREEDOM AND THE ADMINISTRATIVE STATE.
NEW YORK: HARPER & ROW, 1948, 274 PP.
DEALS WITH EVOLUTION OF ADMINISTRATIVE STATE, STATUS OF
FREEDOM AND DEMOCRACY, POSITION OF LABOR, CONDITION OF LAW
AND GOVERNMENT IN ADMINISTRATIVE STATE. THE DRIVE TO MANAGED
ECONOMY IS EXAMINED AND RELATED TO CONDITION AND FREEDOM OF
DEMOCRATIC LIFE UNDER THIS SYSTEM. INDICATES THAT MANAGED
ECONOMY IS NECESSARY AND AT ODDS WITH CONCEPT OF DEMOCRATIC
REPRESENTATIVE GOVERNMENT.

1822 ROSENHAUPT H.W.
HOW TO WAGE PEACE.
NEW YORK: DAY, 1949, 249 PP.
ASSESSES THE NECESSITY OF CREATIVE COMMON ACTION IN ORDER
TO ACHIEVE POSITIVE RESULTS. ANALYZES INTRANATIONAL GROUPS
INTERESTED IN PROBLEM OF MAINTAINING PEACE. DISCUSSES RELE-
VANT POLITICAL MOVEMENTS WITHIN THE CONGRESS. EXPLORES CER-
TAIN RESEARCH INSTITUTES.

1823 ROSENZWEIG J.E.
"MANAGERS AND MANAGEMENT SCIENTISTS (TWO CULTURES)"
BUSINESS HORIZONS, 10 (FALL 67), 79-86.
EXAMINES DIFFERENCES IN METHODS, VOCABULARY, AND VALUES
OF MANAGERS AND MANAGEMENT SCIENTISTS, SEEKING REASONS FOR
LACK OF UTILIZATION OF LATTER BY FORMER. POINTS OUT DE-
FICIENCIES IN BOTH AND MEANS OF BRINGING THEM CLOSER TO-
GETHER TO IMPLEMENT PROGRESS IN MANAGERIAL EFFICIENCY.

1824 ROSHOLT R.L.
AN ADMINISTRATIVE HISTORY OF NASA, 1958-1963.
WASHINGTON: GOVT PR OFFICE, 1966, 381 PP., LC#66-60083.
HISTORICAL STUDY OF ADMINISTRATION OF NASA, ITS
ANTECEDENTS AND BEGINNING, AND CHANGES AS SPACE PROGRAM
ACCELERATED AND POLITICAL ADMINISTRATIONS CHANGED.

1825 ROSOLIO D.
TEN YEARS OF THE CIVIL SERVICE IN ISRAEL (1948-1958)
(PAMPHLET)
WASHINGTON: GOVT PR OFFICE, 1959, 23 PP.
RECORDS OF ESTABLISHMENT OF MINISTRIES AND PUBLIC SERV-
ICES IN 1948, NUMBERS AND CHARACTERISTICS OF CIVIL SERV-
ANTS, ADMINISTRATIVE PROCEDURE, WORKING CONDITIONS, AND
BENEFITS OF CIVIL SERVANTS. RECOMMENDS COMMISSION "KEEP
UP THE GOOD WORK" AND MAINTAIN ITS HIGH STANDARDS OF
SERVICE.

1826 ROSS P.
THE GOVERNMENT AS A SOURCE OF UNION POWER.
PROVIDENCE: BROWN U PRESS, 1965, 320 PP., LC#65-10155.
ANALYSIS OF GOVERNMENT INFLUENCE AND ACTIVITY IN LABOR-
MANAGEMENT COLLECTIVE BARGAINING. DISCUSSES LEGISLATION
REGARDING DUTY OF BOTH GROUPS TO BARGAIN IN GOOD FAITH.

1827 ROSS R.M., MILLSAP K.F.
STATE AND LOCAL GOVERNMENT AND ADMINISTRATION.
NEW YORK: RONALD PRESS, 1966, 705 PP., LC#66-20089.
EMPHASIZES ADMINISTRATIVE ASPECTS OF STATE AND LOCAL GOV-
ERNMENT, PRESENTING CONSIDERABLE MATERIAL ON GOVERNMENTAL
STRUCTURE. ALSO DISCUSSES ROLE COUNTIES PLAY, POSITION OF
MUNICIPALITIES AND SPECIAL DISTRICTS, AND PECULIAR PROBLEMS
OF URBAN AREAS. STRESSES IMPORTANCE OF INTERGOVERNMENTAL
COOPERATION AND GROWING RELATIONSHIP BETWEEN NATIONAL AND
LOCAL GOVERNMENTS.

1828 ROSSITER C.L.
CONSTITUTIONAL DICTATORSHIP; CRISIS GOVERNMENT IN THE MODERN
DEMOCRACIES.
PRINCETON: PRINCETON U PRESS, 1948, 322 PP.
STUDY OF NATURE OF CONSTITUTIONAL DICTATORSHIP IN HISTORY
AS EXAMINED IN PERIOD OF CRISIS IN GERMAN REPUBLIC, FRENCH
REPUBLIC, GREAT BRITAIN, AND US. COVERS CHANCES OF TIGHT
CONTROL FORMALLY OR INFORMALLY OBTAINED UNDER DEMOCRATIC
GOVERNMENT, AND DANGERS OF ITS APPLICATION TO WHOLE SYSTEM.

1829 ROSTOW W.W.
"ASIAN LEADERSHIP AND FREE-WORLD ALLIANCE."
CAMBRIDGE: M.I.T. PR., 1954, 22 PP.

MUST CONVINCE THE ASIAN INTELLECTUAL ELITE THAT USA INTERESTS AND OBJECTIVES CORRESPOND IN IMPORTANT RESPECTS TO THEIR OWN. THE FOUR KEY-ISSUES IN TERMS OF COMMON PROBLEMS ARE: COLONIALISM, ECONOMIC GROWTH, NATURE OF COMMUNISM AND THE 'DEMOCRATIC PROCESS.'

1830 ROSTOW W.W.
"RUSSIA AND CHINA UNDER COMMUNISM."
WORLD POLIT., 7 (JULY 55), 513-31.
SEEKS TO SET FORTH CERTAIN MAJOR SIMILARITIES AND DIF-FERENCES BETWEEN THESE COUNTRIES. EXAMINES (1) ROLE OF IN-TELLECTUALS (2) LEADERSHIP (3) PROBLEM OF EXTERNAL EXPANSION FOR INTERNATIONAL COMMUNISM. CONCLUDES WITH DIRECTION TOWARD A FOREIGN AMERICAN POLICY.

1831 ROTBERG R.
"THE FEDERATION MOVEMENT IN BRITISH EAST AND CENTRAL AFRICA."
J. COMMONWEALTH POLIT. STUD., 2 (MAY 64), 141-160.
COMPARES BRITISH CENTRAL AFRICA, WHERE WHITE DOMINATION INFLUENCED AND ASSERTED ITSELF IN THE DEVELOPMENT OF THE FEDERATION OF RHODESIA AND NYASALAND, AND BRITISH EAST AFRICA WHERE AFRICAN SENTIMENT PREVAILED AND BLOCKED THE FEDERATION OF KENYA, UGANDA AND TANGANYIKA.

1832 ROTBERG R.I.
A POLITICAL HISTORY OF TROPICAL AFRICA.
NEW YORK: HARCOURT BRACE, 1965, 429 PP., LC#65-21072.
COMPREHENSIVE DEVELOPMENT OF GOVERNMENT IN SOUTHERN AFRICA. EARLY EMPIRES, INTERNATIONAL SLAVE TRADE, COLONIAL-ISM, WESTERN INFLUENCES, AND INDEPENDENCE EXAMINED.

1833 ROTBERG R.I.
"COLONIALISM AND AFTER: THE POLITICAL LITERATURE OF CENTRAL AFRICA - A BIBLIOGRAPHIC ESSAY."
AFRICAN FORUM, 2 (WINTER 67), 66-73.
SELECTIVE SURVEY OF ABOUT 80 BOOKS AND ARTICLES IN ENG-LISH ON VARIOUS ASPECTS OF POLITICS IN ZAMBIA, MALAWI, AND RHODESIA. EXCLUDES GOVERNMENT DOCUMENTS.

1834 ROTHENBERG J.
ECONOMIC EVALUATION OF URBAN RENEWAL: CONCEPTUAL FOUNDATION OF BENEFIT-COST ANALYSIS.
WASHINGTON: BROOKINGS INST, 1967, 277 PP., LC#67-19190.
CONCENTRATES ON REDEVELOPMENT ASPECTS OF URBAN RENEWAL PROGRAM IN US. FORMULATES A PROCEDURE BY WHICH A BENEFIT-COST ANALYSIS OF URBAN RENEWAL CAN BE CARRIED OUT. ILLUSTRATES PROCEDURE BY ANALYSIS OF FIVE SELECTED RENEWAL PROJECTS.

1835 ROUGEMONT D.
"LES NOUVELLES CHANCES DE L'EUROPE."
TABLE RONDE, 18 (FEB. 63), 149-61.
EXAMINES THREE SIGNIFICANT FACTORS SHAPING SITUATION OF MODERN EUROPE: 1)EFFORTS FOR UNIFICATION OF EUROPEAN COMMUN-ITY 2)POLITICAL WITHDRAWAL OF EUROPE FROM FORMER COLONIES, COINCIDENT WITH ADOPTION BY THIRD WORLD OF EUROPEAN CIVILI-ZATION, AND 3)UNREGULARIZED SPREAD OF EUROPEAN ADMINISTRA-TIVE TECHNIQUES.

1836 ROURKE F.E.
"THE POLITICS OF ADMINISTRATIVE ORGANIZATION: A CASE HISTORY."
J. OF POLITICS, 19 (AUG. 57), 461-478.
CASE STUDY IN DEVELOPMENT OF NATIONAL EMPLOYMENT SECURITY POLICY DEMONSTRATING THAT, CONTRARY TO EXPECTATIONS, INFLU-ENCE OF GROUPS ALIGNING THEMSELVES IN OPPOSITION TO REORGAN-IZATION PLAN NO. 2 OF 1949 HAS INCREASED RATHER THAN DIMINISHED SINCE ITS APPROVAL.

1837 ROURKE F.E.
"ADMINISTRATIVE SECRECY: A CONGRESSIONAL DILEMMA."
AM. POL. SCI. REV., 54 (SEPT. 60), 684-694.
DEALS WITH THE LONG-STANDING CONGRESSIONAL RESENTMENT AGAINST ADMINISTRATIVE EFFORTS TO CONCEAL INFORMATION. GIVES SPECIFIC EXAMPLES OF LEGISLATIVE FUNCTIONS WHICH HAVE DE-MANDED ACCESS TO WHAT ONLY EXECUTIVE OFFICIALS COULD SUPPLY AND WHICH WERE HANDICAPPED BY EXECUTIVE SECRECY. YET, A WIDE RANGE OF CONGRESSIONAL STATUTES EXIST WHICH ALIGN CONGRESS ITSELF ON THE SIDE OF SECRECY.

1838 ROURKE F.E.
BUREAUCRATIC POWER IN NATIONAL POLITICS.
BOSTON: LITTLE BROWN, 1965, 199 PP., LC#65-21074.
A COLLECTION OF READINGS ON THE GROWTH, ORGANIZATION, AND LIMITATIONS OF BUREAUCRATIC POWER, AND WHAT SUSTAINS IT.

1839 ROWAT D.C. ED.
BASIC ISSUES IN PUBLIC ADMINISTRATION.
NEW YORK: MACMILLAN, 1961, 500 PP., LC#61-5280.
ESSAYS ON PRINCIPLES OF PUBLIC ADMINISTRATION DISCUSS VARIOUS ASPECTS OF BUREAUCRATIC ORGANIZATION AND DECISION-MAKING, THE DELEGATION OF LEGISLATIVE POWERS, AND THE THREAT BUREAUCRACY PRESENTS TO PRESERVATION OF DEMOCRACY.

1840 ROWAT D.C. ED.
THE OMBUDSMAN: CITIZEN'S DEFENDER.
TORONTO: U OF TORONTO PRESS, 1965, 348 PP.
STUDIES THAT OFFICER OF PARLIAMENT WHO INVESTIGATES COM-PLAINTS FROM CITIZENS AGAINST UNJUST ADMINISTRATIVE ACTION AND SEEKS A REMEDY. ANALYZES PRESENT OMBUDSMAN SYSTEMS, RELATED INSTITUTIONS, PROPOSED SCHEMES, AND DATA FROM OMBUDSMAN CASES IN SWEDEN, FINLAND, DENMARK, NORWAY, AND NEW ZEALAND. CONCLUDES THAT OMBUDSMAN SHOULD BE AN IMPORTANT ADDITION TO DEMOCRATIC GOVERNMENT.

1841 ROWAT D.C.
"RECENT DEVELOPMENTS IN OMBUDSMANSHIP* A REVIEW ARTICLE."
CAN. PUBLIC ADMIN., 10 (MAR. 67), 35-47.
REVIEWS LITERATURE ON "OMBUDSMANSHIP" AND EXAMINES MOST RECENT DEVELOPMENTS IN USA, CANADA, AND BRITAIN. THE IDEA OF CREATING A LIAISON OFFICE BETWEEN THE GOVERNMENT AND PUBLIC HAS BEEN READILY ACCEPTED, AND AUTHOR FINDS THAT ONE OF MOST INTERESTING DEVELOPMENTS HAS BEEN THE INSTITUTION OF OMBUDS-MEN IN THE USA AT A LOCAL LEVEL FIRST RATHER THAN AT A NA-TIONAL LEVEL THOUGH PROVISIONS EXIST NOW FOR ALL LEVELS.

1842 ROWE J.Z.
THE PUBLIC-PRIVATE CHARACTER OF UNITED STATES CENTRAL BANKING.
NEW BRUNSWICK: RUTGERS U PR, 1965, 210 PP., LC#68-28214.
DISCUSSION OF HISTORY OF CENTRAL BANKING SYSTEM IN US, INFLUENCE OF FOREIGN BANKS, ESTABLISHMENT OF FEDERAL RESERVE SYSTEM AND ITS MODIFICATIONS AND PROPOSALS TO ALTER PRESENT SYSTEM. MAIN EMPHASIS IS ON THE PUBLIC AND PRIVATE ASPECTS OF THE AMERICAN BANKING SYSTEM.

1843 ROY N.C.
THE CIVIL SERVICE IN INDIA.
CALCUTTA: FIRMA KL MUKHOPADHYAY, 1960, 355 PP.
DISCUSSES STRUCTURE OF INDIAN GOVERNMENT, RECRUITMENT OF CIVIL SERVANTS, SALARIES, PUBLIC SERVICE COMMISSIONS, AND POLITICAL CONTROL OVER ADMINISTRATIVE APPARATUS.

1844 ROYAL INST. INT. AFF.
THE COLONIAL PROBLEM.
LONDON: OXFORD U. PR., 1937, 448 PP.
SEVERAL PAPERS COVERING THE INTERNATIONAL ASPECT OF THE COLONIAL QUESTION, THE DIFFERENT FORMS OF COLONIAL ADMINIS-TRATION AND SUCH SPECIAL PROBLEMS AS COLONIAL INVESTMENT, TRADE, FINANCE AND SETTLEMENT.

1845 ROYAL INSTITUTE PUBLIC ADMIN
BRITISH PUBLIC ADMINISTRATION.
LONDON: LAWRENCE BROS, LTD, 1963, 27 PP.
SELECTED BIBLIOGRAPHY LISTS ABOUT 400 ITEMS DEALING WITH VARIOUS ASPECTS OF PUBLIC ADMINISTRATION IN THE UK. ARRANGED TOPICALLY, IT DEALS WITH SUCH AREAS AS PARLIAMENT, ELEC-TIONS, PRESSURE GROUPS, PARTIES, CIVIL SERVICE, NATIONALIZED INDUSTRY, PUBLIC FINANCE, LOCAL GOVERNMENT, ADMINISTRATIVE LAW, SOCIAL SERVICES, MANAGEMENT, ETC. INCLUDES REPORTS.

1846 RUBENSTEIN A.H. ED., HABERST C.T. ED.
SOME THEORIES OF ORGANIZATION.
HOMEWOOD: RICHARD IRWIN, 1960, 492 PP., LC#60-14052.
DEALS WITH THE NATURE OF ORGANIZATION THEORY, ORGANIZA-TIONAL STRUCTURE AND PROCESS, LEADERSHIP AND MORALE, COMMUNICATION, CONTROL AND EVALUATION, DECISION-MAKING AND RESEARCH TECHNIQUES.

1847 RUBENSTEIN R., LASSWELL H.D.
THE SHARING OF POWER IN A PSYCHIATRIC HOSPITAL.
NEW HAVEN: YALE U PR, 1966, 329 PP., LC#66-21534.
DISCUSSES SOCIAL AND PHYSICAL ENVIRONMENT AND PARTICI-PANTS IN YALE PSYCHIATRIC INSTITUTE COMMUNITY AND INNOVA-TIONS RESULTING FROM PATIENT-STAFF MEETINGS IN 1956. COVERS TRANSCRIPTS OF MEETINGS, VALUE-INSTITUTION ANALYSIS OF MEET-INGS, AND EFFECTS OF POWER SHARING ON PATIENTS AND STAFF.

1848 RUBIN A.P.
"UNITED STATES CONTEMPORARY PRACTICE RELATING TO INTERNATIONAL LAW."
AMER. J. INT. LAW, 59 (JAN. 65), 103-30.
LISTS AND BRIEFLY EXAMINES RECENT USA COURT DECISIONS IN LIGHT OF IMPACT ON INTERNATIONAL LAW - BOUNDARY CLAIMS, DIPLOMACY AND EXTRADITION. ALSO PUBLISHES EXECUTIVE DEPARTMENT VIEWS ON SUBJECTS RELATING TO INTERNATIONAL LAW.

1849 RUBIN H.
PENSIONS AND EMPLOYEE MOBILITY IN THE PUBLIC SERVICE.
NEW YORK: TWENTIETH CENT FUND, 1965, 105 PP.
STUDIES RETIREMENT PROGRAMS OF FIVE LARGEST CITIES, FIVE LARGEST STATES, AND VARIOUS UNITS OF FEDERAL GOVERNMENT IN RELATION TO EMPLOYEE MOBILITY. CONCLUDES THAT PENSION PLANS DO NOT SIGNIFICANTLY DETER MOBILITY WITHIN GOVERNMENT JOB MARKET. FINDS THAT EMPLOYEES OFTEN CHANGE JOBS WITHOUT CONCERN FOR THEIR PENSION RIGHTS.

1850 RUBIN R.I.
"THE LEGISLATIVE-EXECUTIVE RELATIONS OF THE UNITED STATES INFORMATION AGENCY."
PARLIMENTARY AFFAIRS, 2 (SPRING 67), 158-169.

STUDY OF ORGANIZATION OF USIA, CONGRESSIONAL RELATIONS
FUNCTION, COMMUNICATIONS NETWORK EXISTING BETWEEN THE AGENCY
AND CONGRESS, AND CONGRESSIONAL OPINION REGARDING RECORD OF
THE INFORMATION PROGRAM. AUTHOR DISCUSSES RESTRAINTS ON DO-
MESTIC ACTIVITIES OF USIA AND FINDS THAT CONGRESSIONAL LIAI-
SON FUNCTION IS CRUCIAL TO AGENCY'S SUCCESS AND RELATION BE-
TWEEN USIA AND CONGRESS SHOULD BE STRENGTHENED.

1851 RUBINSTEIN A.Z.
"YUGOSLAVIA'S OPENING SOCIETY."
CURR. HIST., 48 (MAR. 65), 149-153.
DURING PAST 15 YEARS YUGOSLAVIA HAS EXPERIENCED
TRANSFORMATION FROM STALINIST PROTOTYPE OF SOCIALISM TOWARD
ESTABLISHMENT OF INSTITUTIONS AND PROCEDURES COMMITTED TO
DEMOCRATIC PROCESS. INCREASINGLY NON-AUTHORITARIAN SOLUTION
TO ITS COMPLEX PROBLEMS. OPERATION OF NEW CONSTITUTION
WILL BE MEASURE OF SUCCESS.

1852 RUBINSTEIN A.Z. ED., THUMM G.W. ED.
THE CHALLENGE OF POLITICS: IDEAS AND ISSUES (2ND ED.)
ENGLEWOOD CLIFFS: PRENTICE HALL, 1965, 475 PP., LC#65-12155.
COLLECTION OF WRITINGS ON POLITICS DEALING WITH RELATION
OF MAN TO SOCIETY, POLITICAL EQUALITY, GOVERNMENTAL POWER,
FREEDOM VERSUS AUTHORITY, GOVERNMENTAL STRUCTURE, AND RELA-
TIONS AMONG STATES.

1853 RUDOLPH F.
THE AMERICAN COLLEGE AND UNIVERSITY.
NEW YORK: ALFRED KNOPF, 1962, 553 PP., LC#62-12991.
AFTER A HISTORICAL REVIEW, THE AUTHOR TAKES UP THE
SUBJECTS OF ACADEMIC BALANCE OF POWER, COLLEGE FINANCING,
COEDUCATION, THE IMPLICATIONS OF THE UNIVERSITY MOVEMENT,
THE IDEAL OF PUBLIC SERVICE AND PROGRESSIVISM, RESEARCH
AGENCIES AND THEIR PROLIFERATION AND CONTROL, FOUNDATIONS,
ORGANIZATION OF THE MODERN UNIVERSITY, GOVERNMENTAL IMPACT
AND THE INFLUENCE OF PUBLIC POLICIES AND ATTITUDES.

1854 RUDOLPH S.
"CONSENSUS AND CONFLICT IN INDIAN POLITICS."
WORLD POLIT., 13 (APR. 61), 385-99.
INDIAN DIFFIDENCE ABOUT AND CULTURAL EXPERIENCE WITH
POLITICAL CONFLICT DOES LITTLE TO LEGITIMIZE THE TYPES OF
LEADERS WHO FLOURISH IN CONTEXT OF DEMOCRATIC POLITICS.

1855 RUITENBEER H.M.
THE DILEMMA OF ORGANIZATIONAL SOCIETY.
NEW YORK: EP DUTTON, 1963, 220 PP., LC#63-24814.
EXPLORES EFFECTS OF MASS SOCIETY UPON INDIVIDUALS.
FRIEDRICH CONSIDERS LOYALTY AND AUTHORITY. REISMAN, WHYTE,
MERTON, AND MEAD COVER TECHNICAL ADVANCES, EDUCATION, AND
LEISURE, AND KARL JASPERS DISCUSSES BUREAUCRACY AS FORM OF
TOTALITARIANISM. ALSO CONSIDERS EFFECTS ON URBANISM AND
RELIGION.

1856 RUSK D.
"THE MAKING OF FOREIGN POLICY"
DEPT OF STATE BULLETIN, 50 (FEB. 64), 164-176.
TRANSCRIPT OF TELEVISION INTERVIEW BETWEEN DEAN RUSK AND
ERIC GOLDMAN. DISCUSSES DECISION-MAKING PROCESS, RELATION
OF DOMESTIC POLITICS TO FOREIGN POLICY, AND METHODS OF
IMPROVING ADMINISTRATION PROCEDURES. EXPLORES STAFFING
PROBLEMS, EXTENT OF AUTHORITY OF DEPARTMENT OF STATE, AND
RELATION OF FOREIGN POLICY TO PUBLIC OPINION.

1857 RUSSELL R.B.
UNITED NATIONS EXPERIENCE WITH MILITARY FORCES: POLITICAL
AND LEGAL ASPECTS.
WASHINGTON: BROOKINGS INST, 1964, 174 PP.
ANALYSIS OF UN'S INTERNATIONAL POLICE FORCE AND PEACE-
KEEPING MISSIONS. INCLUDES UNEF, UNOGIL, ONUC, AND UNSF,
WITH DISCUSSION OF AVAILABILITY OF FORCES, CHARTER
PROVISIONS CONCERNING ENFORCEMENT AND SANCTION, AND THE
NATURE OF AN INTERNATIONAL FORCE.

1858 RUSSETT B.M.
WORLD HANDBOOK OF POLITICAL AND SOCIAL INDICATORS.
NEW HAVEN: YALE U PR, 1964, 373 PP., LC#64-20933.
PRESENTS DATA SIGNIFICANT TO THE DEVELOPMENT OF THE SCI-
ENCE OF COMPARATIVE AND INTERNATIONAL POLITICS; ILLUSTRATES
A VARIETY OF MEANS FOR ANALYZING THIS DATA. COMPARES NATIONS
ON VARIOUS POLITICALLY RELEVANT INDEXES AND EXAMINES INTER-
RELATIONSHIPS OF DIFFERENT POLITICAL, ECONOMIC, SOCIAL, AND
CULTURAL DEVELOPMENTS. DATA SERIES SELECTED ACCORDING TO THE
CRITERIA OF ACCURACY AND AVAILABILITY.

1859 RUSTOW D.A.
THE POLITICS OF COMPROMISE.
PRINCETON: PRINCETON U PRESS, 1955, 257 PP., LC#55-6702.
STUDY OF PARTIES AND CABINET GOVERNMENT IN SWEDEN EMPHA-
SIZING NECESSITY AND EFFECTUALITY OF COMPROMISE POLICY IN
SWEDISH POLITICS. DISCUSSES SEVERAL SUCCESSFUL PROGRAMS IN
SOCIAL AND ECONOMIC PLANNING. PROVIDES CURSORY ACCOUNT OF
SOCIAL WELFARE, LABOR RELATIONS, AND FOREIGN POLICY. TRACES
DEVELOPMENT OF SWEDISH DEMOCRACY.

1860 RUSTOW D.A.

"THE MILITARY IN MIDDLE EASTERN SOCIETY AND POLITICS."
WASHINGTON: BROOKINGS INST., 1963, 20 PP.
TRACES PAST AND PRESENT HISTORY OF MILITARY INTERVENTION
IN COUNTRIES' INTERNAL AFFAIRS AND ASSESSES THEIR FUTURE
ROLES.

1861 SABLE M.H.
A GUIDE TO LATIN AMERICAN STUDIES (2 VOLS)
LOS ANGELES: U CAL LAT AM CTR, 1967, 783 PP., LC#67-63021.
AN ANNOTATED BIBLIOGRAPHY OF 5,000 BOOKS, MONOGRAPHS,
PERIODICALS, PAMPHLETS, AND GOVERNMENT DOCUMENTS ON LATIN
AMERICAN CIVILIZATION. PUBLICATIONS ENGLISH AND SPANISH PRI-
MARILY, BUT INCLUDES SOME FRENCH, GERMAN, AND PORTUGUESE
SOURCES. LARGE SECTION ON POLITICAL SCIENCE AND MANY ENTRIES
ON RELATED FIELDS. INDEXED BY SUBJECT AND COUNTRY.

1862 SALETAN E.N.
"ADMINISTRATIVE TRUSTIFICATION."
WESTERN POLIT. QUART., 11 (DEC. 58), 857-874.
GOVERNMENT HAS FAILED IN ATTEMPTS AT MEDIATING BETWEEN
INTEREST GROUPS: THE STRONGEST ALWAYS WINS. GOVERNMENT MUST
NOW DECIDE WHETHER IT WANTS TO REPRESENT PUBLIC INTEREST OR
PRIVATE GROUPS.

1863 SALISBURY R.H.
"URBAN POLITICS: THE NEW CONVERGENCE OF POWER."
J. OF POLITICS, 26 (NOV. 64), 775-797.
THIS STUDY TRACES THE DEVELOPMENT OF POWER HOLDERS IN
THE CITIES. THE "NEW CONVERGENCE OF POWER" INCLUDES THE
ELECTED OR APPOINTED CHIEF EXECUTIVE, THE LOCALLYORIENTED
ECONOMIC INTERESTS, AND THE PROFESSIONAL WORKERS IN
TECHNICAL CITY-RELATED PROGRAMS.

1864 SALMOND J.A.
THE CIVILIAN CONSERVATION CORPS, 1933-1942.
DURHAM: DUKE U PR, 1967, 240 PP., LC#66-30206.
STUDY OF CENTRAL ORGANIZATION OF CIVILIAN CONSERVATION
CORPS. FOCUSES ON ADMINISTRATIVE OPERATIONS AND FIELD WORK.
NOTES NEED FOR, AND CREATION OF, CCC; SHOWS HOW IT WAS MO-
BILIZED. DESCRIBES ADMINISTRATORS AND DETAILS POLICIES OF
EXPANSION AND PROBLEMS ENCOUNTERED.

1865 SALTER J.T. ED.
THE AMERICAN POLITICIAN.
CHAPEL HILL: U OF N CAR PR, 1938, 412 PP.
BIOGRAPHIC ESSAYS ON US 20TH-CENTURY POLITICAL LEADERS
SUCH AS NORMAN THOMAS, LA GUARDIA, AND JOHN L. LEWIS STUDY
POLITICAL POWER, ORGANIZATION, AND MOTIVATION. DISCUSS 19
PERSONALITIES, MANY OF WHOM ARE MAYORS AND GOVERNORS. SEEK
TO REPRESENT VARIETY OF POLITICAL VIEWS; INCLUDE TECHNIQUES
OF POLITICAL CAMPAIGNING AND ISSUES.

1866 SAMPSON A.
ANATOMY OF BRITAIN.
NEW YORK: HAWTHORNE BOOKS, 1962, 638 PP.
ANALYSIS OF POWER STRUCTURE OF BRITAIN. COVERED ARE
TRADITIONAL SEATS OF AUTHORITY, THRONE, ARISTOCRACY, PARLIA-
MENT, AND LESS WELL-KNOWN INFLUENCES, FINANCE, NATIONALIZED
INDUSTRIES, PRIVATE FIRMS, COMMUNICATIONS INDUSTRY. INFORMAL
AND READABLE ACCOUNT OF BRITISH POWER ELITES.

1867 SANDERSON E.
AFRICA IN THE NINETEENTH CENTURY.
NEW YORK: CHAS SCRIBNER'S SONS, 1900, 335 PP.
STORY OF THE NINETEENTH-CENTURY EXPLORATION AND PARTITION
OF AFRICA. CONCENTRATES ON THE ADVENTURES AND EXPLOITS OF
BRITISH AND FRENCH PIONEERS, SOLDIERS, AND ADMINISTRATORS.

1868 SAPIN B.M.
THE MAKING OF UNITED STATES FOREIGN POLICY.
WASHINGTON: BROOKINGS INST, 1966, 415 PP., LC#66-13626.
FOCUSES ON FORMULATION AND ADMINISTRATION OF US FOREIGN
POLICY, PARTICULARLY MAJOR POLICY DECISION-MAKING WITHIN
EXECUTIVE BRANCH AND IMPORTANT OVERSEAS PROGRAMS. CAREFULLY
EXAMINES NATIONAL SECURITY MACHINERY AT PRESIDENTIAL LEVEL,
PRESENT ORGANIZATIONAL ARRANGEMENTS, AND THEIR RECENT
ANTECEDENTS.

1869 SARROS P.P.
CONGRESS AND THE NEW DIPLOMACY: THE FORMULATION OF MUTUAL
SECURITY POLICY: 1953-60 (THESIS)
PRINCETON: PRIN U, DEPT OF POL, 1964, 425 PP.
EVALUATES ROLE OF CONGRESS IN FORMULATION OF MUTUAL SE-
CURITY POLICY 1953-60 AND ANALYZES EFFECTS OF PARTY AFFILIA-
TION, REGIONALISM, AND COMMITTEE WORK ON ACTIONS, USING TAB-
ULATIONS BASED ON VOTING RECORDS OF CONGRESSMEN.

1870 SATHYAMURTHY T.V.
"TWENTY YEARS OF UNESCO: AN INTERPRETATION."
INTL. ORGANIZATION, 21 (SUMMER 67), 614-633.
REVIEWS DEVELOPMENT OF UNESCO AGAINST IMPORTANT EVENTS OF
PAST 20 YEARS AND FOCUSES ON CHANGING AS WELL AS UNCHANGING
ASPECTS OF RATIONALE OF UNESCO. STATES THAT SOCIAL FORCES
MUST BE BALANCED AS WELL AS POLITICAL FORCES TO MAINTAIN
PEACE. DISCUSSES CONCEPT OF FUNCTION OF UNESCO HELD BY ITS
SEVERAL HEADS. STUDIES FUTURE OF ORGANIZATION.

1871 SAWYER R.A.
A LIST OF WORKS ON COUNTY GOVERNMENT.
PRINCETON: PRIN U INDUS REL CTR, 1915.
LISTS APPROXIMATELY 600 SOURCES INCLUDING BOOKS, JOURNAL
ARTICLES, AND OFFICIAL PUBLICATIONS DEALING WITH WIDE RANGE
OF POLITICAL AND LEGAL ASPECTS OF COUNTY GOVERNMENT IN US.
ARRANGED ACCORDING TO FOLLOWING TOPICS: GENERAL WORKS IN
COUNTY ADMINISTRATION, COUNTY ADMINISTRATION IN INDIVIDUAL
STATES, COUNTY OFFICES, AND COUNTY PUBLICATIONS. ALL ENTRIES
ARE IN ENGLISH AND WERE PUBLISHED FROM LATE 1800'S TO 1915.

1872 SAYER W.S., MOSHER F.C.
AN AGENDA FOR RESEARCH IN PUBLIC PERSONNEL ADMINISTRATION.
WASHINGTON: NATL PLANNING ASSN, 1959, 64 PP., LC#59-15954.
REPORT EXAMINES MAJOR TYPES OF NATIONWIDE RESEARCH NEED-
ED TO INCREASE BASIC KNOWLEDGE AND ACHIEVE FRESH PERSPEC-
TIVE ON US PUBLIC PERSONNEL ADMINISTRATION. SUGGESTS THAT
RESEARCH BE STIMULATED IN UNIVERSITIES, GOVERNMENT AGENCIES,
PRIVATE RESEARCH ORGANIZATIONS, BUSINESS PERSONNEL DEPART-
MENTS, AND LABOR UNIONS.

1873 SAYLES L.R., STRAUSS G.
THE LOCAL UNION.
NEW YORK: HARPER & ROW, 1953, 269 PP., LC#53-5477.
BOOK STUDIES LOCAL INDUSTRIAL UNIONS, GRIEVANCE PROCED-
URES AND GROUP PRESSURES, THE ROLES OF OFFICERS AND STEW-
ARDS, MEMBERSHIP AND UNION DEMOCRACY AND THUS PRESENTS A
VALUABLE SOURCE FOR STUDENTS OF REPRESENTATION. GRIEVANCE
PROCEDURES, THE DECLINE OF THE STEWARDS' COMMUNICATION
FUNCTION, CROSS-PRESSURES, UNION ELECTIONS, AND UPWARD
COMMUNICATIONS FROM MEMBERS AT UNION MEETINGS ARE DISCUSSED.

1874 SAYLES L.R.
MANAGERIAL BEHAVIOR: ADMINISTRATION IN COMPLEX ORGANIZATIONS
NEW YORK: MCGRAW HILL, 1964, 269 PP., LC#63-22424.
DEALS WITH ADMINISTRATIVE SKILL AND ACTION, SEEKING TO
EXPLAIN AND PREDICT THE RECURRING PATTERNS OR UNIFORMITIES
OF EXECUTIVE BEHAVIOR. EMPHASIS IS ON GENERAL THEORIES OF
ORGANIZATIONAL AND MANAGEMENT BEHAVIOR. IS CONCERNED WITH
LEADERSHIP, DECISION-MAKING, AND PERSONNEL RELATIONSHIPS.

1875 SAYRE W.S., KAUFMAN H.
GOVERNING NEW YORK CITY; POLITICS IN THE METROPOLIS.
NEW YORK: RUSSELL SAGE FDN, 1960, 815 PP., LC#60-8408.
EXAMINES PROCESS BY WHICH NEW YORK CITY IS GOVERNED.
DESCRIBES CITY, REWARDS FOR POLITICAL ACTION, AND KINDS OF
PEOPLE IN GOVERNMENT. STUDIES STRATEGIES USED BY POLITICIANS
TO BE ELECTED AND BY ALL CATEGORIES OF PARTICIPANTS TO
INFLUENCE DECISION-MAKERS. DESCRIBES SYSTEMS OF ELECTIONS
AND APPOINTMENTS AND TASKS OF BUREAUCRATIC AGENCIES,
POLITICAL PARTIES, COURTS, AND GOVERNOR.

1876 SCALAPINO R.A., MASUMI J.
PARTIES AND POLITICS IN CONTEMPORARY JAPAN.
BERKELEY: U OF CALIF PR, 1962, 190 PP., LC#61-14279.
ANALYSIS OF POSTWAR JAPANESE POLITICS REGARDING THEIR IN-
TERNATIONAL AND DOMESTIC ASPECTS. DESCRIBES COMPOSITION AND
ORGANIZATION OF JAPANESE POLITICAL PARTIES AND OPERATION OF
POLITICAL PROCESS.

1877 SCARROW H.A.
THE HIGHER PUBLIC SERVICE OF THE COMMONWEALTH OF AUSTRALIA.
DURHAM: DUKE U PR, 1957, 180 PP., LC#57-13024.
CASE STUDY OF PUBLIC SERVICE BUREAUCRACY IN AUSTRALIA,
FROM ITS BEGINNINGS AS MACHINERY WAS SET UP THROUGH ITS
GROWTH AND DEVELOPMENT TO PRESENT ORGANIZATION. DISCUSSES
COMPOSITION OF SERVICE AND ITS ROLE IN GOVERNMENTAL
STRUCTURE.

1878 SCHACHTER O.
"THE ENFORCEMENT OF INTERNATIONAL JUDICIAL AND ARBITRAL
DECISIONS."
AMER. J. INT. LAW, 54, (JAN. 60), 1-24.
DISCUSSING DIFFICULTIES FOUND IN ENFORCEMENT OF WORLD
COURT DECISIONS, ANALYZES PROBLEMS AND PROCEDURES CONNECTED
WITH SUCCESSFUL PARTIES CLAIMS. OUTLINES POSSIBLE REMEDIES
AVAILABLE THROUGH INTERNATIONAL ORGANIZATIONS.

1879 SCHAEFER W.V.
THE SUSPECT AND SOCIETY: CRIMINAL PROCEDURE AND CONVERGING
CONSTITUTIONAL DOCTRINES.
EVANSTON: NORTHWESTERN U PRESS, 1967, 99 PP.
DEALS WITH LEGAL PROBLEMS CENTERING ON POLICE
INTERROGATION OF PERSONS SUSPECTED OF HAVING COMMITTED
CRIMES. CONSIDERS CONSTITUTIONAL DOCTRINES THAT BEAR UPON
POLICE INTERROGATION AS IT HAS BEEN CONDUCTED IN THE PAST.
DISCUSSES MODEL CODE OF PROCEDURE ADVANCED BY AMERICAN LAW
INSTITUTE TO REGULATE POLICE CONDUCT IN TREATMENT OF
CRIMINAL.

1880 SCHAPIRO L.
THE GOVERNMENT AND POLITICS OF THE SOVIET UNION.
LONDON: HUTCHINSON & CO, 1965, 191 PP.
ACADEMIC ANALYSIS OF NATURE OF FUNCTIONS OF RUSSIA'S CEN-
TRAL AND LOCAL GOVERNMENT AND RELATIONS WITH PARTY POLICY.
TRIES TO DETERMINE REAL ESSENCE OF SOVIET POWER AND ITS DE-
VELOPMENT SINCE 1917. ANALYZES POLITICS BEHIND CHANGES IN
SOVIET LAW, POLICY, AND OFFICIALS SINCE REVOLUTION.

1881 SCHAPIRO L.
"THE COMMUNIST PARTY OF THE SOVIET UNION."
NEW YORK: RANDOM HOUSE, INC, 1960.
DISCUSSION OF EVOLUTION OF RUSSIAN COMMUNIST PARTY.
ANALYZES NATURE OF MOVEMENT FROM WHICH BOLSHEVIDS EMERGED,
METHOD OF GOVERNMENT LENIN EVOLVED AFTER 1917, THE PARTY
AFTER 1928 UNDER STALIN'S RULE. EPILOGUE TRACES PARTY
DEVELOPMENTS BETWEEN 1953 AND 1958. BIBLIOGRAPHY REFERS TO
NUMEROUS PRIMARY SOURCES AND PROVIDES SHORT GUIDE TO
LITERATURE IN THIS FIELD. SECONDARY SOURCES IN ENGLISH.

1882 SCHATTSCHNEIDER E.E., JONES V., BAILEY S.K.
A GUIDE TO THE STUDY OF PUBLIC AFFAIRS.
NY: WILLIAM SLOAN ASSOCIATES, 1952, 135 PP.
RESEARCH AID AND PROCEDURAL GUIDE TO FIELD OF PUB-
LIC AFFAIRS. COVERS RESEARCH METHOD AND TECHNIQUE IN THE
STUDY OF NEWSPAPERS, PRESSURE GROUPS, FEDERAL GOVERNMENT
AGENCIES, CONGRESSMEN, CITY GOVERNMENT, BUDGETS, STATUTES,
AND JUDICIAL DECISIONS.

1883 SCHATZ S.P.
"THE INFLENCE OF PLANNING ON DEVELOPMENT: THE NIGERIAN
EXPERIENCE."
SOC. RES., 27 (WINTER 60), 451-68.
REVEALS MANY DRAWBACKS OF DEVELOPMENT PLANS FORMULATED BY
UNDERDEVELOPED COUNTRIES AFTER WORLD WAR TWO. PINPOINTS THE
WEAKNESSES IN NIGERIAN PLANS WHICH ARE TRULY SERIES OF DE-
VELOPMENT SCHEMES. STATES LACK OF PERSONNEL AND EXPERIENCE
AS BEING MAIN FACTORS CONTRIBUTING TO INEFFICIENT PLANNING.

1884 SCHECHTER A.H.
INTERPRETATION OF AMBIGUOUS DOCUMENTS BY INTERNATIONAL
ADMINISTRATIVE TRIBUNALS.
NEW YORK: FREDERICK PRAEGER, 1964, 183 PP.
ANALYSIS OF INTERNATIONAL LEGAL DEVELOPMENTS SINCE WWII.
EXAMINES ACTIONS OF UN ADMINISTRATIVE TRIBUNAL, ILO ADMINIS-
TRATIVE TRIBUNAL, AND EUROPEAN COURT OF JUSTICE IN INTERPRE-
TATIONS OF INTERNATIONAL RULES AND REGULATIONS.

1885 SCHEINMAN L.
EURATOM* NUCLEAR INTEGRATION IN EUROPE.
NEW YORK: CARNEGIE ENDOWMENT, 1967, 66 PP.
AN ANALYSIS OF EURATOM REVOLVING AROUND FIVE FACTORS* THE
ENERGY CONTEXT, NATIONAL DISPARITIES, NUCLEAR NATIONALISM,
EXECUTIVE LEADERSHIP, AND THE NATURE OF THE BARGAIN IN CON-
TEXT. WHILE EURATOM IS UNLIKELY TO SURVIVE IN ITS PRESENT
FORM,AUTHOR SUGGESTS THAT EUROPEAN CONCERN ABOUT THE TECHNO-
LOGICAL GAP BETWEEN EUROPE AND THE US MIGHT PROVIDE THE IMPE
TUS FOR THE REBIRTH OF A RESTYLED SCIENTIFIC COMMUNITY.

1886 SCHER S.
"CONGRESSIONAL COMMITTEE MEMBERS AND INDEPENDENT AGENCY
OVERSEERS: A CASE STUDY."
AM. POL. SCI. REV., 54 (DEC. 60), 911-920.
TREATS BEHAVIOR OF MEMBERS OF A CONGRESSIONAL COMMITTEE
AS OVERSEERS OF AN INDEPENDENT REGULATORY COMMISSION. STUDY
EXAMINES THE HOUSE EDUCATION AND LABOR COMMITTEE AS IT RE-
VIEWED THE PERFORMANCE OF THE NATIONAL LABOR RELATIONS BOARD
IN 1953.

1887 SCHERMER G.
MEETING SOCIAL NEEDS IN THE PENJERDEL REGION.
PHILA: PENN-NJ-DEL METROPOL PROJ, 1964, 54 PP.
REPORT ON REGIONAL ASPECTS OF SOCIAL NEEDS AND PROGRAMS
IN 11-COUNTY AREA OF PENNSYLVANIA, NEW JERSEY, AND DELAWARE.
PRESENTS AN APPROACH TO SOCIAL PLANNING. STUDIES WELFARE
NEEDS OF A METROPOLITAN REGION, ORGANIZATION OF SERVICES,
FINANCING OF HEALTH AND WELFARE SERVICES. ASSUMES COMMUNITY
OF INTEREST THROUGHOUT THE REGION. STUDY WAS COMMISSIONED BY
PENJERDEL.

1888 SCHILLING W.R.
"THE H-BOMB: HOW TO DECIDE WITHOUT ACTUALLY CHOOSING."
POLIT. SCI. QUART., 76 (MAR. 61) 26-46.
CONTRASTS CONTENT AND FORM OF TRUMAN'S DECISION ON JAN.3,
1945 WITH POLICY DISCUSSION THAT HAD PRECEDED IT. ADVANCES
EXPLANATION FOR CHARACTER OF DECISION AND INDICATES POLIT-
ICAL CONSEQUENCES.

1889 SCHILLING W.R.
"SCIENTISTS, FOREIGN POLICY AND POLITICS."
AMER. POLIT. SCI. REV., 56 (JUNE 62), 287-300.
ASSERTS THE TECHNOLOGICAL ADVANCES OF THE TWENTIETH
CENTURY NECESSITATE A CLOSE RELATIONSHIP BETWEEN SCIENCE AND
GOVERNMENT. CONCLUDES STATESMEN WILL DETERMINE TO WHAT EX-
TENT SCIENCE WILL BE PUT TO FUTURE USE.

1890 SCHILLING W.R., HAMMOND P.Y., SNYDER O.H.
STRATEGY, POLITICS, AND DEFENSE BUDGETS.
NEW YORK: COLUMB. U. PR., 1962.
THREE STUDIES OF THE POLITICAL PROCESS AS IT OPERATED TO
DEFINE NATIONAL SECURITY IN THE CRITICAL PERIOD OF TRANSI-
TION FROM AMERICAN ATOMIC MONOPOLY TO THERMONUCLEAR WEAPONS

BEING ON BOTH SIDES. DEAL IN TURN WITH THE WARNING PHASE OF 1948-49, THE REACTION TO DRAMATIC EVENTS BEGINNING IN 1950, AND THE RESETTING OF MILITARY POLICY IN THE FIRST YEARS OF THE EISENHOWER ADMINISTRATION.

1891 SCHLESSINGER P.J.
ELEMENTS OF CALIFORNIA GOVERNMENT (2ND ED.)
NEW YORK: HOLT RINEHART WINSTON, 1966, 130 PP., LC#66-20524.
PRESENTS BROAD SWEEP OF GOVERNMENTAL INSTITUTIONS IN CALIFORNIA. TRACES LINE OF AUTHORITY FROM PEOPLE THROUGH STATE GOVERNMENT AND LOCAL JURISDICTIONS AND BACK TO PEOPLE. EXAMINES LEGISLATIVE, ADMINISTRATIVE, AND JUDICIAL PROCESSES, AND FUNCTIONS AND RELATIONS OF GOVERNMENTS.

1892 SCHLOCHAUER H.J.
OFFENTLICHES RECHT.
KARLSRUHE: VERL C F MULLER, 1957, 269 PP.
EXAMINES ORIGIN AND NATURE OF BASIC LAW OF FEDERAL REPUB-LIC OF WEST GERMANY. EXAMINES RELATION OF NATION AND STATES AND POSITION OF WEST GERMANY IN RELATION TO INTERNATIONAL COMMUNITY. STUDIES CONSTITUTIONAL ORGANS, CONSTITUTIONAL COURT, AND SYSTEM OF ADMINISTRATIVE ADJUDICATION.

1893 SCHLOSSBERG S.I.
ORGANIZING AND THE LAW.
WASHINGTON: BUREAU NATL AFFAIRS, 1967, 254 PP., LC#67-22857.
EXPLANATION OF PROVISIONS IN TAFT-HARTLEY ACT THAT AFFECT ORGANIZATION OF LABOR UNIONS. SHOWS HOW LAW CAN BE USED TO UNION AGENT'S ADVANTAGE. EXPLAINS RULES OF NATIONAL LABOR RELATIONS BOARD ON SOLICITATION; TELLS ORGANIZER HOW TO SPOT ILLEGAL CONDUCT BY EMPLOYER; EXPLAINS RULES ON BARGAINING UNITS.

1894 SCHMECKEBIER L., EASTIN R.
GOVERNMENT PUBLICATIONS AND THEIR USE.
WASHINGTON: BROOKINGS INST, 1961, 476 PP., LC#61-7718.
AIDS ACQUISITION AND USE OF GOVERNMENT PUBLICATIONS: DESCRIBES BASIC GUIDES TO THEM; INDICATES USES AND LIMITA-TIONS OF AVAILABLE INDEXES, CATALOGS, AND BIBLIOGRAPHIES; EXPLAINS SYSTEMS OF NUMBERING AND METHODS OF TITLING; CITES OUTSTANDING SERIES OR COMPILATIONS; TELLS HOW TO ACQUIRE THESE PUBLICATIONS, WHICH ORIGINATE IN ALL THREE BRANCHES OF THE US GOVERNMENT. LISTS DEPOSITORY LIBRARIES.

1895 SCHMIDT F. ED., WEINER H.N. ED.
PUBLIC RELATIONS IN HEALTH AND WELFARE.
NEW YORK: COLUMBIA U PRESS, 1966, 278 PP., LC#66-19480.
DEFINES ROLE OF THE PUBLIC RELATIONS PRACTITIONER IN PRIVATE AND PUBLIC HEALTH AND WELFARE ORGANIZATIONS. SELEC-TIONS ARE BASED UPON MATERIAL PRESENTED AT 1965 SUMMER WORK-SHOP AT THE COLUMBIA UNIVERSITY SCHOOL OF SOCIAL WORK.

1896 SCHMIDT K.M. ED.
AMERICAN STATE AND LOCAL GOVERNMENT IN ACTION.
BELMONT: DICKENSON PUBL CO, 1966, 365 PP., LC#66-23585.
SELECTION OF ARTICLES ON POLITICAL PROCESS AT STATE AND LOCAL LEVELS. INCLUDES ANALYSIS OF INTERGOVERNMENTAL RELA-TIONS, STATE AND LOCAL POLITICS, PRESSURE GROUPS, GOVERNMENT IN THE FIFTY STATES, AND THE COMMUNITY DECISION PROCESS. STUDIES ROLE OF GOVERNOR, STATE LEGISLATURE, STATE COURT, MAYOR, CITY COUNCIL, AND COUNTY BOARD. DISCUSSES URBAN RENEWAL AND CURES FOR CITY PROBLEMS.

1897 SCHMITT H.A.
"THE EUROPEAN COMMUNITIES."
CURR. HIST., 45 (NOV. 63), 257-263.
WITHIN COMMON MARKET MEMBERSHIP IS STAGNANT. TOO MANY OBSTACLES TO POLITICAL UNION. BRIEF SURVEY OF MARSHALL PLAN, SCHUMAN PLAN, EUROPEAN DEFENSE COMMUNITY, COMMON MARKET AND ECSC. PRESSURES AND FEARS HAVE RECEDED AND PROSPERITY IS ORDER OF DAY. IT APPEARS TO AUTHOR THAT EUROPE WILL PROGRESS TOWARD UNION ONLY UNDER LASH OF DISASTER.

1898 SCHNEIDER E.V.
INDUSTRIAL SOCIOLOGY: THE SOCIAL RELATIONS OF INDUSTRY AND COMMUNITY.
NEW YORK: MCGRAW HILL, 1957, 559 PP., LC#57-7242.
AN OVER-ALL VIEW OF INDUSTRIAL INSTITUTIONS, PAST AND PRESENT, AND THEIR INFLUENCE ON THE FAMILY, THE COMMUNITY, AND THE GOVERNMENT AS WELL AS INDUSTRY'S GENERAL ROLE IN SOCIAL CHANGE. DEALS WITH ROLE, STRATIFICATION, MINORITY GROUPS, AND GOVERNMENT REGULATION, AS WELL AS THE SOCIAL STRUCTURE AND FUNCTIONS OF TRADE UNIONISM.

1899 SCHOECK H. ED., WIGGINS J.W. ED.
THE NEW ARGUMENT IN ECONOMICS.
PRINCETON: VAN NOSTRAND, 1963, 264 PP.
ESSAYS PRESENTING VARIOUS VIEWS ON ECONOMIC ISSUES SUCH AS NEOMERCANTILISM, ECONOMIC ROLE OF STATE, PRIVATE AND PUBLIC EXPENDITURES, AND TRADE UNIONISM. ALSO DISCUSSES NATURAL RESOURCES, FOREIGN AID PROGRAM IN BOLIVIA, GROWTH OF BUREAUCRATIC POWER, AND PUBLIC VS. PRIVATE SECTOR IN BRITAIN.

1900 SCHRADER R.
SCIENCE AND POLICY.

NEW YORK: PERGAMON PRESS, 1963, 81 PP., LC#63-11117.
DISCUSSES INTERACTION OF SCIENTIFIC AND POLITICAL AFFAIRS. TREATS IMPACT OF SCIENCE AND TECHNOLOGY ON POLICY PROBLEMS, MILITARY AFFAIRS, ADMINISTRATION, INTERNATIONAL RELATIONS, AND UNDERDEVELOPED WORLD, PROPOSING NEW GOVERN-MENTAL POLICIES.

1901 SCHRAMM W., RILEY J.W. JR.
"COMMUNICATION IN THE SOVIETIZED STATE, AS DEMONSTRATED IN KOREA."
AMER. SOCIOL. REV., 16 (DEC. 51), 757-66.
BASED ON DATA FROM BOTH N. KOREA AND SOUTH KOREA DURING THE 90-DAY COMMUNIST OCCUPATION. THE EXTREMELY CENTRALISED CONTROL AND INTENSIVE USE FOR PROPAGANDA OF ALL COMMUNICATION CHANNELS FROM RADIO TO 'COMICS', IS ILLUS-TRATED. CONCLUDES THAT THE COMMUNISTS INTENDED TO KEEP THE KOREANS FROM ANY COUNTER-INFORMATION OR REBELLIOUS THOUGHTS.

1902 SCHRAMM W. ED.
"MASS COMMUNICATIONS: A BOOK OF READINGS (2ND ED.)"
URBANA: U OF ILLINOIS PR, 1960.
INTERPRETATION OF MASS COMMUNICATIONS AS BRANCH OF SOCIAL SCIENCES. EMPHASIS ON MASS MEDIA AS ORGANIZATIONS, ON STRUC-TURE AND FUNCTION OF MASS COMMUNICATIONS. NEW RE-EVALUATION OF CONCEPTION OF "THE TWO-STEP" FLOW OF COMMUNICATION. ADDITIONAL STUDIES OF RESPONSIBILITY AND ETHIC OF COMMUN-ICATIONS. ANTHOLOGY CONCLUDED WITH NOTE ON SUGGESTIONS FOR FURTHER READING.

1903 SCHUBERT G.
THE PUBLIC INTEREST.
NEW YORK: FREE PRESS OF GLENCOE, 1960, 244 PP., LC#60-10902.
ANALYZES AND TRACES DEVELOPMENT AND USE OF THE CONCEPT "PUBLIC INTEREST" IN CONTEMPORARY POLITICAL SCIENCE. IDENTIFYING THREE MAJOR SCHOOLS OF THOUGHT. SUGGESTS THAT FOCUS ON THE MOST "REPRESENTATIVE" INSTITUTION BE ELIMINATED, THAT THE CONCEPT OF PUBLIC INTEREST MAKES NO "OPERATIONAL SENSE."

1904 SCHUBERT G.A.
"'THE PUBLIC INTEREST' IN ADMINISTRATIVE DECISION-MAKING: THEOREM, THEOSOPHY OR THEORY"
AM. POL. SCI. REV., 51 (JUNE 57), 346-368.
THE PURPOSE OF THE PAPER IS TO ARRIVE AT A THEORY WHICH WOULD DESCRIBE "A RELATIONSHIP BETWEEN A CONCEPT OF THE PUB-LIC INTEREST AND OFFICIAL BEHAVIOR IN SUCH TERMS THAT IT MIGHT BE POSSIBLE TO COLLECT DATA FOR PURPOSE OF ATTEMPTING TO VALIDATE HYPOTHESIS CONCERNING THE RELATIONSHIP." DIS-CUSSES THE POLITICAL FUNCTION OF BUREAUCRACY AND EXECUTIVE POWER, AND THE NEED FOR A THEORY OF PUBLIC INTEREST.

1905 SCHULMAN S.
TOWARD JUDICIAL REFORM IN PENNSYLVANIA; A STUDY IN COURT REORGANIZATION.
PHILADELPHIA: U OF PENN LAW SCH, 1962, 281 PP., LC#62-18050.
EXPOSES DEFICIENCIES IN PENNSYLVANIA'S JUDICIAL SYSTEM AND DISCUSSES PREVIOUS RESEARCH, POSSIBLE IMPROVEMENTS, AND AREAS FOR FURTHER RESEARCH.

1906 SCHULTZ W.J., HARRIS C.L.
AMERICAN PUBLIC FINANCE.
ENGLEWOOD CLIFFS: PRENTICE HALL, 1949, 798 PP.
STUDY OF US PUBLIC FINANCE DEALING WITH GOVERNMENTAL EX-PENDITURE, TAXATION, GOVERNMENTAL BORROWING, FISCAL INTERRE-LATIONSHIPS ON ALL GOVERNMENTAL LEVELS, AND OVER-ALL FISCAL POLICY.

1907 SCHUMACHER B.G.
COMPUTER DYNAMICS IN PUBLIC ADMINISTRATION.
WASHINGTON: SPARTAN BOOKS, 1967, 195 PP., LC#67-17365.
TRACT URGING AUTOMATION OF PUBLIC AGENCIES ON ALL ADMINISTRATIVE LEVELS, DETAILING IMPLEMENTATION OF COMPUTER HARDWARE. EVALUATES COMPUTERS AND DISCUSSES EVOLUTIONARY STAGES OF USE IN PUBLIC SERVICE. ATTEMPTS TO PRESENT AS NEARLY COMPLETE TAXONOMIC STRUCTURE OF SYSTEMS AND THEORIES AS POSSIBLE. GLOSSARY.

1908 SCHURMANN F.
"ECONOMIC POLICY AND POLITICAL POWER IN COMMUNIST CHINA."
ANN. AMER. ACAD. POLIT. SOC. SCI., 349 (SEPT. 63), 49-69.
SCRUTINIZES WITHIN HISTORICAL CONTEXT THE TWO MAJOR STRATEGIES BEHIND CHINESE DEVELOPMENT AND DISCLOSES THEIR ULTIMATE SHORTCOMINGS. RELATES THE DECISIONS INVOLVED IN STRATEGY-DEVELOPMENT TO A COMPLEX OF IDEOLOGICAL, POLITICAL, AND SOCIAL VARIABLES. SUGGESTS THAT THE NON-ECONOMIC VARIABLES WILL BE AS IMPORTANT TO CHINA AS PURELY ECONOMIC.

1909 SCHURMANN F.
IDEOLOGY AND ORGANIZATION IN COMMUNIST CHINA.
BERKELEY: U OF CALIF PR, 1966, 540 PP., LC#66-15324.
THEORIZES THAT IDEOLOGY AND ORGANIZATION AROSE IN RED CHINA BECAUSE A TRADITIONAL SOCIAL SYSTEM NO LONGER EXISTED TO GIVE UNITY TO SOCIETY. TRACES STRUGGLE IN MAINLAND COUNTRYSIDE AND CITIES TO CREATE AND IMPOSE STRUCTURES OF ORGANIZATION ON THE NATION. STUDIES THE PARTY, GOVERNMENT BUREAUCRACY AND MANAGEMENT, CONCEPTS OF CONTROL, AND

ORGANIZATION OF CITIES AND VILLAGES.

1910 SCHURZ W.L.
AMERICAN FOREIGN AFFAIRS: A GUIDE TO INTERNATIONAL
AFFAIRS.
NEW YORK: DUTTON, 1959, 265 PP.
POINTS OUT BASIC ISSUES IN INTERNATIONAL AFFAIRS AS AN
INTRODUCTION TO THE FIELD OF POLICY MAKING. EMPHASIZING THE
IMPORTANCE OF PUBLIC OPINION, DISCUSSES THE INFLUENCE OF
VARIOUS ELEMENTS UPON US FOREIGN POLICY. E.G. INTERNATIONAL
OPINION, MASS MEDIA, CREATION OF NEW STATES AND POLITICS.

1911 SCHWARTZ B.
LAW AND THE EXECUTIVE IN BRITAIN: A COMPARATIVE STUDY.
NEW YORK: NEW YORK U PR, 1949, 388 PP.
STUDY OF EXECUTIVE POWER AND ADMINISTRATIVE LAW IN UK.
EXECUTIVE HAS INCREASED IN SIZE AND POWER AND TENDS TO MAKE
LAW AS WELL AS CARRY IT OUT; THERE IS NEED FOR ADDITIONAL
CONTROL OVER BUREAUCRACY.

1912 SCHWARTZ B.
FRENCH ADMINISTRATIVE LAW AND THE COMMON-LAW WORLD.
NEW YORK: NEW YORK U PR, 1954, 367 PP.
COMPARES FRENCH LAW WITH THE ANGLO-AMERICAN SYSTEM, WITH-
IN THE CONTEXT OF THEIR ECONOMIC, HISTORICAL, POLITICAL, AND
SOCIAL HERITAGES. PURPOSE IS TO FIND POSSIBLE AREAS OF IM-
PROVEMENT IN THE AMERICAN LEGAL SYSTEM. EMPHASIZES THE RELA-
TIONS OF THE THREE BRANCHES OF GOVERNMENT - LEGISLATIVE, EX-
ECUTIVE, AND JUDICIAL - TO EACH OTHER, AND THE INTERRELATION
OF LOCAL, STATE, AND FEDERAL GOVERNMENTS. CITES MANY CASES.

1913 SCHWARTZ B.
"LEGISLATIVE CONTROL OF ADMINISTRATIVE RULES AND REGULATIONS
THE AMERICAN EXPERIENCE."
NYU LAW REV., 30 (MAY 55), 1031-1045.
WITH GREAT INCREASE IN SIZE AND POWER OF BUREAUCRACY
EFFECTIVE MEANS OF CONTROL, ESPECIALY BY THE LEGISLATURE,
MUST BE DEVELOPED.

1914 SCHWARTZ B.
"THE INTELLIGENTSIA IN COMMUNIST CHINA: A TENTATIVE
COMPARISON."
DAEDALUS, 89 (SUMMER 60), 604-621.
COMPARES RUSSIAN INTELLIGENTSIA OF MID-NINETEENTH CENTURY
TO THEIR PRESENT CHINESE COUNTERPARTS WITH REFLECTIONS ON
POST-REVOLUTION SITUATION IN BOTH COUNTRIES. MOST FACTORS
SEEM TO INDICATE MORE COMPLIANT ATTITUDE TOWARD TOTALITAR-
IANISM ON THE PART OF THE CHINESE BUT AUTHOR CONCLUDES
THEY REMAIN AN INCALCULABLE QUANTITY.

1915 SCHWEBEL S.M.
"THE SECRETARY-GENERAL OF THE UN."
CAMBRIDGE: HARVARD U. PR., 1952, 299 PP.
CONSIDERS THE MOST SIGNIFICANT ASPECTS OF THE POSITION,
ITS POLITICAL POWERS AND PRACTICE. ANALYZES ITS
RELATION WITH THE GENERAL ASSEMBLY, WITH GOVERNMENT, WITH
NON-POLITICAL ORGANS AND OUTLINES FUTURE TRENDS.

1916 SCHWELB E.
"OPERATION OF THE EUROPEAN CONVENTION ON HUMAN RIGHTS."
INT. ORGAN., 18 (SUMMER 64), 558-85.
EFFECTIVENESS OF EUROPEAN COMMISSION OF HUMAN RIGHTS IS
ILLUSTRATED BY SELECTED CASES WHICH DEMONSTRATE HOW THE COM-
MISSION ENSURED OBSERVANCE OF OBLIGATIONS BETWEEN VARIOUS
PARTIES. CONCLUDES WORK OF COMMISSION IS SIGNIFICANT ADVANCE
IN INTERNATIONAL PROTECTION OF HUMAN RIGHTS.

1917 SCHWERIN K.
"LAW LIBRARIES AND FOREIGN LAW COLLECTION IN THE USA."
INT. AND COMP. LAW Q., 11 (APR. 62), 537-567.
STUDIES BOTH US LAW LIBRARIES IN GENERAL AND THEIR FOR-
EIGN LAW COLLECTIONS. REVIEWS SOME MAJOR LAW LIBRARIES AND
LIBRARY FACILITIES AND SYSTEMS. SURVEYS MAJOR COLLECTIONS
OF FOREIGN LAW, AND METHODS OF DEVELOPING THESE COLLECTIONS.

1918 SCOTT A.M.
THE REVOLUTION IN STATECRAFT: INFORMAL PENETRATION.
NEW YORK: RANDOM HOUSE, INC, 1965, 194 PP., LC#65-23340.
COMPREHENSIVE ANALYSIS OF A DEVELOPMENT THAT HAS
REVOLUTIONIZED MODERN STATECRAFT: ADVENT OF INFORMAL
RELATIONS BETWEEN NATIONS. DISCUSSES EVOLUTION OF INFORMAL
ACCESS TECHNIQUES, INCLUDING ECONOMIC AID, INFORMATION
PROGRAMS, POLITICAL WARFARE, MILITARY TRAINING OPERATIONS,
AND CULTURAL EXCHANGE PROGRAMS.

1919 SCOTT D.J.R.
RUSSIAN POLITICAL INSTITUTIONS.
NEW YORK: RINEHART, 1958, 265 PP., LC#58-4632.
STUDIES INTERNAL GOVERNMENT STRUCTURE AND ORGANIZATION,
POLITICAL PERIODS, THE UNION, COLLECTIVE ADMINISTRATION,
REPRESENTATIVE BODIES, AND METHODS USED TO SECURE COOPERA-
TION. BIBLIOGRAPHY OF 50 ENTRIES, 1902-65, IN ENGLISH,
LISTED TOPICALLY: TEXTBOOKS, STUDIES OF SOVIET POLITICS,
SPECIAL ASPECTS OF POLITICS, BACKGROUND, AND JOURNALS.

1920 SCOTT R.E.

"MEXICAN GOVERNMENT IN TRANSITION (REV ED)"
URBANA: U OF ILLINOIS PR, 1964.
STUDY OF MEXICO'S EVOLVING SYSTEM OF POLITICS THROUGH
GENERALIZING APPROACH. CONSIDERS SOCIAL, PSYCHOLOGICAL, AND
PHYSICAL CONDITIONS WHICH MAKE UP MEXICAN POLITICAL CULTURE
AND DISCUSSES THEM AS FACTORS IN GROUP APPROACH TO STUDY OF
POLITICAL PROCESS. CONTAINS ANALYSIS OF FORMAL CONSTITU-
TIONAL STRUCTURE AND GOVERNMENT AGENCIES. INCLUDES EXTENSIVE
BIBLIOGRAPHY IN SPANISH AND ENGLISH.

1921 SCOTT W.R., DORNBUSCH S.M., ET AL.
"ORGANIZATIONAL EVALUATION AND AUTHORITY."
ADMINISTRATIVE SCI. Q., 12 NO. 00003716 67).
TREATS EVALUATION OF SUBJECTS AS IT RELATES TO AUTHORITY
IN FORMAL ORGANIZATIONS. LISTS AUTHORITY RIGHTS: PERFORMANCE
EVALUATION, DIRECTION, AND DELEGATION OF POWER. DESCRIBES
"AUTHORITY SYSTEMS" COMPRISED OF AUTHORITY "LINKS" AND
RELATIONSHIPS. COMPARES CONCEPT WITH THEORIES OF WEBER,
RAVEN, EVAN, AND BARNARD. DESCRIBES INCOMPATIBILITY AND
HYPOTHESES FOR PREDICTION OF ORGANIZATIONAL INSTABILITIES.

1922 SEASHOLES B. ED.
VOTING, INTEREST GROUPS, AND PARTIES.
GLENVIEW, ILL: SCOTT, FORESMAN, 1966, 136 PP., LC#66-14833.
SELECTED READINGS TREAT THREE PRIME WAYS OF CITIZEN
PARTICIPATION IN US POLITICS: VOTING, WORKING AS MEMBERS OF
INTEREST GROUPS, AND JOINING PARTY ACTIVITIES. ALSO DISCUSS
POLITICAL APATHY AND NONPARTICIPATION. COVER ROLE OF
PARTIES, NATURE, FUNCTION, AND PARTY MACHINERY.

1923 SECKLER-HUDSON C.
BIBLIOGRAPHY ON PUBLIC ADMINISTRATION (4TH ED.)
WASHINGTON: AMERICAN U PR, 1953, 131 PP.
SELECTED, ANNOTATED, AND INDEXED BIBLIOGRAPHY OF OVER
1,100 REFERENCES TO PUBLIC ADMINISTRATION. INCLUDES GOVERN-
MENT PUBLICATIONS, PERIODICALS, REPORTS, BOOKS, AND OTHER
ITEMS ARRANGED ACCORDING TO CATEGORIES SUCH AS BUDGETARY
ADMINISTRATION, ORGANIZATION AND MANAGEMENT, PERSONNEL,
ADJUDICATION, ADMINISTRATIVE LAW, PUBLIC RELATIONS, INTER-
NATIONAL ADMINISTRATION, ETC.

1924 SEGUNDO-SANCHEZ M.
OBRAS (2 VOLS.)
CARACAS: BANCO CENTRAL VENEZ, 1964.
VOLUME I IS SUBTITLED (IN SPANISH) "CONTRIBUTION TO THE
KNOWLEDGE OF THE FOREIGN BOOKS CONCERNING VENEZUELA AND ITS
GREAT MEN, PUBLISHED OR REPRINTED, SINCE THE NINETEENTH CEN-
TURY." VOLUME II CONTAINS BIBLIOGRAPHIC AND HISTORICAL STUD-
IES. A SEPARATE ANALYTICAL AUTHOR-TITLE INDEX IS PROVIDED.

1925 SEIDMAN H.
"THE GOVERNMENT CORPORATION IN THE UNITED STATES."
PUBLIC ADMINISTRATION, 37 (SUMMER 59), 103-109.
GOVERNMENT CORPORATIONS IN THE US ARE SET UP TO HELP
PRIVATE ENTERPRISE. CONTROL OVER THESE CORPORATIONS IS LESS
SPECIFIC THAN IN BRITAIN, BUT CONGRESS AND THE PRESIDENT DO
HAVE SUFFICIENT CONTROL.

1926 SELF P., STORING H.J.
THE STATE AND THE FARMER.
BERKELEY: U OF CALIF PR, 1963, 251 PP.
DISCUSSES AGRICULTURAL POLICIES AND POLITICS IN GREAT
BRITAIN BETWEEN 1945-61. ANALYZES THE CLOSE AND PERVASIVE
COOPERATION BETWEEN GOVERNMENT AND PRINCIPAL AGRICULTURAL
ORGANIZATIONS. EXPLORES CHARACTER AND HISTORY OF PARTNERSHIP
AND REVIEWS PROBLEMS AND CONFLICTS OVER THE ADMINISTRATION
OF PUBLIC POLICY.

1927 SELZNICK
LEADERSHIP IN ADMINISTRATION: A SOCIOLOGICAL INTERPRETATION.
EVANSTON: ROW-PETERSON, 1957, 162 PP., LC#57-11350.
OUTLINES A PERSPECTIVE FOR STUDY OF LEADERSHIP IN ADMIN-
ISTRATIVE ORGANIZATIONS WITH REFERENCE TO ROUTINE AND CRIT-
ICAL DECISIONS, THE DEFINITION OF MISSION AND ROLE AND THE
EMBODIMENT OF PURPOSE. EXPLORES THE MEANING OF INSTITUTION-
AL LEADERSHIP IN ORDER TO ENCOURAGE REFLECTION AND SELF-
KNOWLEDGE.

1928 SELZNICK P.
"AN APPROACH TO A THEORY OF BUREAUCRACY."
AMER. SOCIOLOGICAL REV., 8 (FEB. 43), 47-59.
ANALYZES BUREAUCRACY AS SPECIAL CASE OF GENERAL THEORY
OF PURPOSIVE BEHAVIOR. DRAWS ON STUDIES BY ROETHLIS BERGER,
BARNARD, WEBER, FRIEDRICH, AND MICHELS, CONCENTRATING ON
EFFECT OF INFORMAL ORGANIZATION WITHIN A BUREAUCRACY AS IM-
PORTANT NEW FACTOR TO BE CONSIDERED.

1929 SELZNICK P.
THE ORGANIZATIONAL WEAPON: A STUDY OF BOLSHEVIK STRATEGY AND
TACTICS.
NEW YORK: MCGRAW HILL, 1952, 350 PP.
ANALYZES USE OF ORGANIZATIONS AND ORGANIZATIONAL
PRACTICES AS WEAPONS IN STRUGGLE FOR POWER AS USED BY
BOLSHEVIKS. CONCERNED WITH USE OF PARTY AS MEANS OF COMBAT,
NATURE OF CADRES, AND TOTAL CONTROL OF INDIVIDUALS. STUDIES
STRATEGIC PRINCIPLES, IMAGE OF THE MASS, AND UNITED FRONT

TACTICS. EXAMINES INSTITUTIONAL TARGETS, ROLE OF MASS POWER, DEFENSE AND COUNTEROFFENSE, AND QUALITY OF PARTICIPATION.

1930 SEYLER W.C.
"DOCTORAL DISSERTATIONS IN POLITICAL SCIENCE IN UNIVERSITIES OF THE UNITED STATES AND CANADA."
AM. POL. SCI. REV., 60 (SEPT. 66), 778-803.
AN UNANNOTATED BIBLIOGRAPHY OF DOCTORAL DISSERTATIONS IN POLITICAL SCIENCE. MATERIAL IS FROM LATE 1965 TO 1966. ENGLISH LANGUAGE. CONTAINS 1,150 ENTRIES.

1931 SHANKS M. ED.
THE LESSONS OF PUBLIC ENTERPRISE.
LONDON: JONATHAN CAPE, 1963, 313 PP.
EXAMINES STATE OF PUBLIC ENTERPRISE IN ENGLAND IN 1963, EVALUATING RELATIONSHIP WITH GOVERNMENT, THE PUBLIC, CUSTOMERS, WORKERS, AND PRIVATE INDUSTRIES. DISCUSSES PROBLEM OF WHO DECIDES PUBLIC INTEREST, PROBLEMS OF PARLIAMENTARY CONTROL; COMPARES WITH CASES ON CONTINENT.

1932 SHAPIRO D.
A SELECT BIBLIOGRAPHY OF WORKS IN ENGLISH ON RUSSIAN HISTORY, 1801-1917.
OXFORD: BLACKWELL, 1962, 106 PP.
BIBLIOGRAPHY OF 1,070 BOOKS AND ARTICLES IN ENGLISH. INCLUDES CROSS REFERENCES. ITEMS ARRANGED BY SUBJECT: GENERAL HISTORY, FOREIGN RELATIONS, EXPANSION, ADMINISTRATION AND LAW, ARMED FORCES AND CAMPAIGNS, SOCIETY AND INTELLIGENTSIA, ECONOMIC HISTORY, LAND AND PEASANTS, REVOLUTIONARY MOVEMENTS, NATIONALITIES AND BORDERLANDS, SOCIAL THOUGHT AND PHILOSOPHY.

1933 SHAPP W.R.
FIELD ADMINISTRATION IN THE UNITED NATIONS SYSTEM.
NEW YORK: FREDERICK PRAEGER, 1961, 570 PP.
SURVEYS UN FIELD ORGANIZATION, ITS RELATION TO CENTRAL CONTROL, AND WAY AID PROGRAMMES ARE MANAGED. FOCUSES ON METHODS OF IMPROVING EFFICIENCY IN OPERATIONS AND IN AID GATHERING. PRESENTS DATA FROM MANY INTERVIEWS WITH WORLD-WIDE PERSONNEL. CONSIDERS HAMPERING FACTORS TO BE INTERNAL INSTITUTIONAL RELATIONSHIPS AND NATIONAL AND BLOC POLITICS.

1934 SHARKANSKY I.
"FOUR AGENCIES AND AN APPROPRIATIONS SUBCOMMITTEE: A COMPARATIVE STUDY OF BUDGET STRATEGIES."
MIDWEST J. OF POLI. SCI., 9 (1965), 254-281.
CONCLUDES, "INTER ALIA," THAT THERE IS A CLEAR RANGE OF VARIATION AMONG AGENCIES IN THE ASSERTIVENESS WITH WHICH THEY APPROACH THEIR APPROPRIATIONS SUBCOMMITTEE AND THEIR RESPONSES TO THE SUPERVISORY AND CONTROL EFFORTS OF THE SUBCOMMITTEE.

1935 SHARMA M.P.
PUBLIC ADMINISTRATION IN THEORY AND PRACTICE.
ALLAHABAD, INDIA: KITAB MAHAL, 1958, 508 PP.
DISCUSSES THEORY OF PUBLIC ADMINISTRATION, ITS ORGANIZATION, VARIOUS REGULATORY AGENCIES AND COMMISSIONS, PERSONNEL ADMINISTRATION, AND ADMINISTRATIVE LAW AND RESPONSIBILITY IN CONTEXT OF INDIAN, BRITISH, AN US EXPERIENCE.

1936 SHARMA S.A.
PARLIAMENTARY GOVERNMENT IN INDIA.
ALLAHABAD: CENTRAL BOOK DEPT, 1965, 242 PP.
SURVEYS ALL ASPECTS OF INDIAN GOVERNMENT FROM MAKING OF CONSTITUTION TO DETAILS OF PUBLIC FINANCE AND LOCAL GOVERNMENTAL SYSTEMS. INCLUDES DISCUSSION OF JUDICIAL AND ADMINISTRATIVE TRIBUNALS AND WORK OF PLANNING COMMISSIONS.

1937 SHARMA S.R.
SOME ASPECTS OF THE INDIAN ADMINISTRATIVE SYSTEM.
NEW DELHI: INDIAN INST PUB ADMIN, 1957, 160 PP.
ANALYSIS OF INDIAN PUBLIC ADMINISTRATION REGARDING ITS ORGANIZATION, PARLIAMENTARY CONTROL, CIVIL SERVANTS, PLANNING, AND US APPRAISAL OF SYSTEM.

1938 SHARMA T.R.
THE WORKING OF STATE ENTERPRISES IN INDIA.
BOMBAY: VORA & CO, 1961, 232 PP.
STUDY OF GROWTH OF STATE INTEREST IN INDUSTRIES, LEADING TO EVENTUAL NATIONALIZATION. ANALYZES ADMINISTRATION OF SUCH INDUSTRIES, SHOWING EXTENT OF MINISTERIAL CONTROL, RELATIONSHIP AND RESPONSIBILITY OF STATE UNDERTAKINGS TO THE LEGISLATURE, LABOR PROBLEMS, AND PRICE POLICY. OBSERVES THAT PUBLIC UNDERSTANDING MUST SEE THAT INDIAN NATIONALIZATION IS INSPIRED BY FISCAL, SECURITY, AND SOCIAL MOTIVES.

1939 SHARP W.R.
FIELD ADMINISTRATION IN THE UNITED NATION SYSTEM: THE CONDUCT OF INTERNATIONAL ECONOMIC AND SOCIAL PROGRAMS.
NEW YORK: PRAEGER, 1961, 570 PP.
CLASSIFIES AND DESCRIBES THE VARIOUS FORMS OF FIELD ORGANIZATIONS WITHIN THE U.N., AND ANALYZES THEIR ADMINISTRATIVE AND PLANNING PROBLEMS. ALSO DISCUSSES THE FUTURE DEVELOPMENT OF THESE ORGANIZATIONS.

1940 SHAW S.J.

THE FINANCIAL AND ADMINISTRATIVE ORGANIZATION AND DEVELOPMENT OF OTTOMAN EGYPT 1517-1798.
PRINCETON: PRIN U ORIENTAL STUD, 1958.
EXAMINES TOTAL ADMINISTRATIVE SYSTEM OF EGYPT FROM OTTOMAN CONQUEST TO NAPOLEON'S EXPEDITION. CONCENTRATES ON OBJECTIVES OF REGIME AND DEGREE TO WHICH THEY WERE FULFILLED. COVERS REVENUES OF EMPIRE AND METHOD OF COLLECTING MORE FULLY THAN SPENDING. BIBLIOGRAPHY OF WORKS CITED AND REFERENCES USED.

1941 SHELTON W.L.
CHECKLIST OF NEW MEXICO PUBLICATIONS, 1850-1953.
ALBUQUERQUE: U OF N MEX PR, 1954, 240 PP., LC#54-12989.
INCLUDES ALL OFFICIAL DOCUMENTS PRINTED OR PUBLISHED BETWEEN 1850 AND 1953 BY OR FOR THE STATE OR DISTRIBUTED BY THE STATE. REPORTS LISTED UNDER NAME OF ISSUING BODY FOLLOWED BY OTHER PUBLICATIONS IN ALPHABETICAL ORDER. OMITS PUBLICATIONS OF STATE-SUPPORTED EDUCATIONAL INSTITUTIONS AND AGRICULTURAL EXPERIMENT STATIONS.

1942 SHERBENOU E.L.
"CLASS, PARTICIPATION, AND THE COUNCIL-MANAGER PLAN."
PUBLIC ADMIN. REV., 21 (SUMMER 61) 131-135.
THIS STUDY DISCLOSED THAT THE COUNCIL-MANAGER PLAN IS PREDOMINANT IN HIGHER INCOME COMMUNITIES. MANAGER CITIES ALSO HAD A LOWER AVERAGE NET MUNICIPAL DEBT PER CAPITA, A HIGHER AVERAGE TOTAL EXPENDITURE PER CAPITA, AND A HIGHER AVERAGE MUNICIPAL PROPERTY TAX PER CAPITA COMPARED TO NON-MANAGER CITIES. THE PLAN WAS COMMON IN CITIES HAVING GREATER CITIZEN PARTICIPATION IN LOCAL POLITICS.

1943 SHERIDAN R.G.
URBAN JUSTICE.
KNOXVILLE: U TENN, BUR PUB ADMIN, 1964, 101 PP., LC#64-64894
NOTES JURISDICTION, ORGANIZATIONAL STRUCTURE, ADMINTRATIVE PROCEDURES, TRIAL METHODS, AND SAFEGUARDS IN ADMINISTRATION OF JUSTICE IN TENNESSEE'S MUNICIPAL COURTS. MAKES RECOMMENDATIONS FOR PROCEDURAL AND SUBSTANTIVE CHANGES.

1944 SHERMAN H.
"IT ALL DEPENDS."
UNIVERSITY: U ALABAMA PR, 1966.
ANALYSIS BY PRACTITIONER OF SUCCESS AND FAILURE IN ORGANIZATION POLICY. DEFINES CONTENT TO ORGANIZATION, OFFERS STUDY OF ORGANIZATION OF PORT OF NEW YORK AUTHORITY AND AN EXTENSIVE BIBLIOGRAPHY ON PROBLEMS AND POLICIES OF ORGANIZATIONS.

1945 SHERWOOD F.P., BEST W.H.
SUPERVISORY METHODS IN MUNICIPAL ADMINISTRATION.
CHICAGO: INT CITY MANAGER'S ASSN, 1958, 302 PP., LC#58-11340
REFERENCE TEXT AND TRAINING MANUAL OUTLINING STRUCTURE OF SUPERVISOR'S ROLE IN MUNICIPAL ADMINISTRATION. PROVIDES INSTRUCTION IN TECHNICAL SKILLS NECESSARY AND USEFUL FOR MUNICIPAL SUPERVISOR; DEALS WITH "HUMAN RELATIONS" ASPECT OF DIRECT LEADERSHIP SITUATION.

1946 SHERWOOD R.E.
ROOSEVELT AND HOPKINS.
NEW YORK: HARPER, 1948, 979 PP.
THROUGH BIOGRAPHICAL TREATMENT OF HOPKINS, ONE OF ROOSEVELT'S CLOSEST AIDES, REVEALS RELATIONSHIP BETWEEN THE TWO MEN, AND CURRENT EVENTS OF THE TIME.

1947 SHILS E.A.
"THE LEGISLATOR AND HIS ENVIRONMENT."
UNIV. CHICAGO LAW REV., 58 (1951), 571-584.
EXPLORES FACTORS WHICH MAY ASSIST IN UNDERSTANDING OF PECULIARITIES AND EXCESSES OF CONGRESSIONAL INVESTIGATIONS. VIEWS THESE EXCESSES AS ARISING OUT OF THE CONDITIONS OF LIFE OF THE AMERICAN LEGISLATOR. ANALYZES WHAT CAUSED CERTAIN FEATURES OF THE INVESTIGATIVE PROCESS, WITH REFERENCE TO HOSTILITY TOWARD WITNESSES AND DISREGARD FOR STANDARDS OF PROPRIETY AND RESPECT NECESSARY TO A DEMOCRACY.

1948 SHIMKIN D.B.
"STRUCTURE OF SOVIET POWER."
QUART. REV. ECO. BUS., 3 (AUTUMN 63), 19-25.
DISCUSSES SOVIET OBJECTIVES IN INTERNATIONAL POWER POLITICS: INTERNAL SOURCES AND RESTRAINTS OF POWER, AND CURRENT SOVIET TECHNIQUES. WARNS USA TO BE PREPARED FOR A VARIETY OF RADICALLY DIFFERENT STRATEGIC SOVIET OBJECTIVES.

1949 SHISTER J.
ECONOMICS OF THE LABOR MARKET.
NEW YORK: J B LIPPINCOTT, 1949, 590 PP.
ANALYZES NATURE AND OPERATION OF THE LABOR MARKET. EXAMINES GROWTH OF TRADE UNIONS, THEIR LOCAL AND NATIONAL STRUCTURES AND BARGAINING POLICIES, MANAGEMENT'S RELATIONS WITH ORGANIZED AND UNORGANIZED LABOR, AND GOVERNMENT POLICY DISCUSSES OPERATION OF THE LABOR MARKET WITH RESPECT TO WAGES; SEASONAL, CYCLICAL, AND TECHNOLOGICAL ASPECTS OF VOLUME OF EMPLOYMENT; AND DISTRIBUTION OF INCOME.

1950 SHOEMAKER R.L.
"JAPANESE ARMY AND THE WEST."

MILITARY REV., 47 (MAY 67), 10-17.
SURVEYS ORIGIN AND DEVELOPMENT OF JAPANESE MILITARY FROM
THE RISE OF SHOGUNS AND SAMURAI TO ITS WESTERNIZATION AT
TURN OF CENTURY. POSES QUESTION OF WHY JAPAN DELAYED ITS
MILITARY DEVELOPMENT FOR TWO AND A HALF CENTURIES AFTER EX-
POSURE TO THE WEST, HOW IT DEVELOPED SO QUICKLY, AND WHY IT
CHOSE FRANCE AS MILITARY EXEMPLAR FOR REFORM. CONCLUDES,
AND SHOWS, THAT INTERNAL AND EXTERNAL FACTORS WERE IDEAL.

1951 SIDEY H.
JOHN F. KENNEDY, PRESIDENT.
NEW YORK: ATHENEUM PUBLISHERS, 1963, 400 PP., LC#63-7800.
A REPORTER'S CLOSE-HAND LOOK AT KENNEDY'S FIRST TWO YEARS
IN WHITE HOUSE AND HOW THE NEW PRESIDENT GREW TO BE AN
EXPERIENCED ONE. AUTHOR HAD TRAVELED WITH KENNEDY SINCE
1958, AND KNEW HIM AS WELL AS AN OUTSIDER COULD.

1952 SILBERMAN B.S. ED., HAROOTUNIAN H.D. ED.
MODERN JAPANESE LEADERSHIP; TRANSITION AND CHANGE.
TUCSON: U OF ARIZONA PR, 1966, 433 PP., LC#66-18532.
REVISED PAPERS DELIVERED AT CONFERENCE ON NINETEENTH-
CENTURY JAPANESE ELITES. EXAMINES THE TOKUGAWA VILLAGE HEAD-
MAN, THE TRANSFORMATION OF OUTCAST LEADERS, SOCIAL VALUES
AND LEADERSHIP IN LATE TOKUGAWA THOUGHT, CHRISTIAN SAMURAI,
ELITE TRANSFORMATION IN THE UPPER CIVIL SERVICE, TRANSFOR-
MATION OF MILITARY ELITE, AND GROWTH OF POLITICAL PARTIES
AND LEADERSHIP IN RURAL JAPAN.

1953 SILVERT K.H.
"AMERICAN ACADEMIC ETHICS AND SOCIAL RESEARCH ABROAD* THE
LESSON OF PROJECT CAMELOT."
BACKGROUND, 9 (NOV. 65), 215-236.
SCATHING CRITICISM OF THE MANAGEMENT OF PROJECT CAMELOT,
ESPECIALLY OF THE QUESTIONABLE ACADEMIC DIPLOMACY AND POOR
COMMUNICATIONS WITH CHILE. SILVERT ARTICULATES GENERAL RULES
AND FUNCTIONS FOR THE SCHOLAR DOING INTERNATIONAL RESEARCH
WHILE UNDER GOVERNMENT EMPLOY. LASTLY, HE COMMENTS ON THE
REASONS BEHIND THE GENERAL INEPTNESS OF THE LATIN AMERICAN
AREA PROGRAMS IN AMERICAN POLITICAL RESEARCH.

1954 SIMOES DOS REIS A.
BIBLIOGRAFIA DAS BIBLIOGRAFIAS BRASILEIRAS.
RIO DE JANEIRO: INST. NACIONAL DO LIVRO, 1942,186 PP.
BIBLIOGRAPHY OF BRAZILIAN BIBLIOGRAPHIES. INCLUDES
BOOKS AND PERIODICALS. ENTRIES ARE ARRANGED ALPHABETICALLY
BY AUTHOR.

1955 SIMON H.A.
"DECISION-MAKING AND ADMINISTRATIVE ORGANIZATION" (BMR)"
PUBLIC ADMIN. REV., 4 (WINTER 44), 17-30.
DISCUSSES ADMINISTRATIVE THEORY BY ANALYZING MANNER IN
WHICH DECISIONS AND BEHAVIOR OF OPERATIVE EMPLOYEES ARE
INFLUENCED BY THE ORGANIZATION. DESCRIBES ORGANIZATIONAL
INFLUENCES ON THE SUBORDINATE AND ADMINISTRATIVE PROCESSES
FOR INSURING CORRECT DECISIONS. SHOWS THAT WITHIN LIMITS
FIXED BY HIS SUPERIORS, EACH MEMBER OF AN ORGANIZATION
RETAINS A CERTAIN SPHERE OF DISCRETION.

1956 SIMON H.A.
ADMINISTRATIVE BEHAVIOR: A STUDY OF DECISION-MAKING PROCESS-
ES IN ADMINISTRATIVE ORGANIZATION.
LONDON: MACMILLAN, 1947, 259 PP., LC#47-30782.
ATTEMPTS TO CONSTRUCT ADEQUATE LINGUISTIC AND CONCEPTUAL
TOOLS FOR DESCRIBING ADMINISTRATIVE ORGANIZATION. DESCRIBES
IT IN A WAY THAT WILL PROVIDE THE BASIS OF SCIENTIFIC ANAL-
YSIS OF THE EFFECTIVENESS OF ITS STRUCTURE AND OPERATION
TION, TO PRACTICAL ADMINISTRATORS AND TO GRADUATE AND UNDER-
GRADUATE STUDENTS FOR A STUDY OF BEHAVIOR IN ADMINISTRATION.

1957 SIMON H.A., SMITHBURG D.W. ET AL.
"PUBLIC ADMINISTRATION."
NEW YORK: ALFRED KNOPF, 1950.
STUDY OF ORGANIZATION OF MAJOR GOVERNMENTAL STRUCTURES --
FEDERAL, STATE AND LOCAL; BEHAVIOR OF INDIVIDUAL WITHIN OR-
GANIZATIONAL STRUCTURE; RELATIONSHIP BETWEEN POLITICS AND
ADMINISTRATION. THE ROLE OF ADMINISTRATOR IN FORMATION OF
POLICY. EMPHASIZES PROBLEMS OF SMALL ORGANIZATIONS AS WELL
AS ISSUES OF EXECUTIVE ORGANIZATION. INCLUDES BIBLIOGRAPHIC
NOTES.

1959 SIMON H.A.
MODELS OF MAN, SOCIAL AND RATIONAL: MATHEMATICAL ESSAYS ON
RATIONAL HUMAN BEHAVIOR IN A SOCIAL SETTING.
NEW YORK: WILEY, 1957, 299 PP.
SIXTEEN ESSAYS DEALING WITH CAUSAL AND INFLUENTIAL RELA-
TIONSHIPS, SOCIAL PROCESSES, FACTORS AFFECTING MOTIVATION,
AND THE MAKING OF RATIONAL ADMINISTRATIVE DECISIONS. MATH-
EMATICS IS APPLIED TO A STUDY OF SOCIAL AND POLITICAL
PROCESSES.

1960 SIMON H.A.
"ADMINISTRATIVE DECISION-MAKING."
PUBLIC ADMIN. REV., 25 (MAR. 65), 31-37.
REVIEW OF THE DEVELOPMENT OF DECISION-MAKING AS A
METHODOLOGICAL TOOL FOR STUDYING PUBLIC ADMINISTRATION. NEW
TECHNIQUES HAVE INCREASED OUR UNDERSTANDING OF HOW PEOPLE

FUNCTION IN ORGANIZATIONS.

1961 SIMON R. ED.
PERSPECTIVES IN PUBLIC RELATIONS.
NORMAN: U OF OKLAHOMA PR, 1966, 353 PP., LC#65-24193.
COLLECTION OF ARTICLES, SPEECHES, DISCUSSIONS, AND CASE
STUDIES IN PUBLIC RELATIONS. OFFERS BROAD HISTORICAL VIEW
OF THE FIELD, ASSESSING RELATIONSHIP OF PUBLIC RELATIONS
PRACTITIONERS TO EACH OTHER AND TO THEIR ENVIRONMENT. ANA-
LYZES PROCESSES INVOLVED IN PLANNING, PROGRAMMING, AND
COMMUNICATING.

1962 SIMON Y.R.
A GENERAL THEORY OF AUTHORITY.
NOTRE DAME: U OF NOTRE DAME, 1962, 167 PP., LC#62-19020.
ESSAY ON PRINCIPLES OF AUTHORITY AND RELATION BETWEEN
AUTHORITY AND LIBERTY. DESCRIBE AUTHORITY AS MEANS OF
UNIFICATION FOR COMMON ACTION AND COMMON GOOD, REMOVING
PARADOX OF INDIVIDUAL FREEDOM AND AUTHORITY.

1963 SIMPSON R.L.
"VERTICAL AND HORIZONTAL COMMUNICATION IN FORMAL
ORGANIZATION"
ADMINISTRATIVE SCI. Q., 4 (SEPT. 59), 189-196.
TESTS ASSUMPTION THAT COMMUNICATION IN ORGANIZATIONS
MOVE VERTICALLY THROUGHOUT HIERARCHY RATHER THAN CUTTING
ACROSS LINES OF AUTHORITY. INTERVIEWS WITH SUPERVISORS IN
TEXTILE MILL SHOWED THAT COMMUNICATION AMONG FIRST-LINE
FOREMEN WAS HORIZONTAL. HYPOTHESIZES THAT MECHANIZATION
REDUCES NEED FOR CLOSE SUPERVISION AND VERTICAL
COMMUNICATION SINCE MACHINES, NOT FOREMEN, SET WORK PACE.

1964 SINGER J.D.
FINANCING INTERNATIONAL ORGANIZATION: THE UNITED NATIONS
BUDGET PROCESS.
GENEVA: NIJHOFF, 1961, 185 PP.
TRACES IN DETAIL SIX MAJOR EVOLUTIONARY PHASES OF FINAN-
CIAL SYSTEM. PUTS BUDGET PLANNING PROCESS IN SETTING OF
INTERNATIONAL RELATIONS. EMPHASIZES CYCLICAL DYNAMICS OF
UN BUDGET PROCESS.

1965 SINGER J.D. ED.
HUMAN BEHAVIOR AND INTERNATINAL POLITICS* CONTRIBUTIONS
FROM THE SOCIAL-PSYCHOLOGICAL SCIENCES.
NEW YORK: RAND MCNALLY & CO, 1965, 466 PP., LC#65-14105.
COLLECTION OF ESSAYS FROM THE BEHAVIORAL SCIENCES CONSID-
ERED RELEVANT TO INTERNATIONAL POLITICS THROUGH ANALOGY.
AUTHOR PROPOSES BERTALANFFY'S GENERAL SYSTEMS THEORY AS AN
INTEGRATING FRAMEWORK FOR THE VARIOUS DISCIPLINES: CONTRIBU-
TIONS ORGANIZED AROUND, THE INTERNATIONAL SYSTEM AS ENVIRON-
MENT, THE NATION-STATE AS PRIMARY ACTOR, POLITICS AS INTER-
ACTION, AND SYSTEM TRANSFORMATION. GOOD BIBLIOGRAPHY.

1966 SINGER K.
THE IDEA OF CONFLICT.
MELBOURNE: U. PR., 1949, 181 PP.
TRACES IDEA OF CONFLICT BY ANALYZING PAST STRIFE AND
SHOWING HOW EMBODIED IN PRESENT WORLD CONFLICTS. DENOTES
INTERPLAY OF FORCES AND VARIETY OF ORDINARY OCCASIONS
FROM WHICH CONFLICTS ARISE.

1967 SINGER M.R.
THE EMERGING ELITE: A STUDY OF POLITICAL LEADERSHIP IN
CEYLON.
CAMBRIDGE: M.I.T. PR., 1964, 203 PP.
IDENTIFIES SOCIOECONOMIC CHARACTERISTICS, ATTITUDES, AND
SELF-IMAGES OF CONTEMPORARY POLITICAL, CIVIL SERVICE, TRADE-
UNION, AND RURAL ELITES. EMERGING ELITES SYNTHESIZE TRADI-
TIONAL AND WESTERN VALUES, ARE ESSENTIALLY MIDDLE-CLASS,
REPRESENTING MIDDLE-CLASS INTERESTS.

1968 SINGH H.L.
PROBLEMS AND POLICIES OF THE BRITISH IN INDIA, 1885-1898.
NEW YORK: ASIA PUBL HOUSE, 1963, 284 PP.
EXAMINES INDO-BRITISH EMPIRE IN PERIOD OF ITS CLIMAX AND
INCREASED INDIAN DEMANDS FOR GREATER, MORE ACTIVE SHARE IN
GOVERNMENT AND ADMINISTRATION. DISCUSSES VASTNESS AND COM-
PLEXITY OF ADMINISTRATION PROBLEMS WHICH MADE SHARING OF
GOVERNMENT POWER WITH INDIANS IMPERATIVE. CRITICIZES ENGLISH
FAILURE TO ADJUST POLICIES TO CHANGING CIRCUMSTANCES. FOCUS-
ES ON CIVIL SERVICE, LEGISLATIVE, AND MILITARY ISSUES.

1969 SINGH M.M.
MUNICIPAL GOVERNMENT IN THE CALCUTTA METROPOLITAN DISTRICT
A PRELIMINARY SURVEY.
DUBLIN: INST PUBLIC ADMIN, 1963, 123 PP.
EXAMINES MUNICIPAL ORGANIZATION AND SERVICES OF 32 MUNIC-
IPALITIES IN INDIA GOVERNED UNDER BENGAL MUNICIPAL ACT OF
1932. DISCUSSES ROLE OF MUNICIPAL CORPORATIONS.

1970 SINGTON D., WEIDENFELD A.
THE GOEBBELS EXPERIMENT.
LONDON: JOHN MURRAY, 1942, 260 PP.
STUDY OF NAZI PROPAGANDA MACHINERY INCLUDES ORGANIZA-
TION, PARTY PRESS, PROPAGANDA MINISTRY, BROADCASTING, RELA-
TION TO ARMED FORCES, CONTROL, AND RELATION TO FINE ARTS.

1971 SINHA H.N.
      OUTLINES OF POLITICAL SCIENCE.
      BOMBAY: ASIA PUBL HOUSE, 1959, 247 PP.
         OUTLINES PRINCIPLES OF POLITICAL THEORY AND CENTRAL CON-
      CEPTS AS LIBERTY, SOVEREIGNTY, AND LAW. DISCUSSES POLITICAL
      INSTITUTIONS (EXECUTIVE, LEGISLATIVE, AND JUDICIAL) AND
      BRIEFLY EXAMINES ELECTORAL SYSTEM AND PRINCIPLE OF SEPARA-
      TION OF POWERS.

1972 SISSON C.H.
      THE SPIRIT OF BRITISH ADMINISTRATION AND SOME EUROPEAN
      COMPARISONS.
      LONDON: FABER AND FABER, 1959, 162 PP.
         ANALYSIS OF INDIVIDUAL IN, AND ORGANIZATION OF, BRITISH
      PUBLIC ADMINISTRATION AND ITS RELATION TO LAW AND POLITICS.
      COMPARES BRITISH SYSTEM WITH THAT OF FRANCE, GERMANY, AND
      SWEDEN.

1973 SKIDMORE T.E.
      POLITICS IN BRAZIL 1930-1964.
      NEW YORK: OXFORD U PR, 1967, 448 PP.
         COMPLETE STUDY OF BRAZILIAN POLITICS FOR THREE DECADES OF
      DEMOCRACY TO DETERMINE REASONS FOR CONSTITUTIONAL
      BREAKDOWN. ECONOMIC DIFFICULTIES AND POLITICAL ERRORS ARE
      CITED AS CAUSES FOR COUP D'ETAT. PROBLEMS ARISE FROM LAND
      DISTRIBUTION, UNFAVORABLE TRADE BALANCE, AND FLUCTUATING
      POLITICAL POWER.

1974 SKINNER G.W.
      LEADERSHIP AND POWER IN THE CHINESE COMMUNITY OF THAILAND.
      ITHACA: CORNELL U. PR., 1958.
         FIELD STUDY OF SOCIAL, POLITICAL, ECONOMIC, ORGANIZATION-
      AL, AND POWER ASPECTS OF CHINESE COMMUNITY. SUGGESTS THAT
      CHINESE COMMUNITY LEADERS ARE ENCOURAGING ASSIMILATION INTO
      THAI SOCIAL STRUCTURE.

1975 SKOLNICK J.H.
      "SOCIAL CONTROL IN THE ADVERSARY SYSTEM."
      J. OF CONFLICT RESOLUTION, 11 (MAR. 67), 52-70.
         DESCRIBES AND ANALYZES OUTSTANDING FEATURES OF THE
      ADVERSARY SYSTEM, AS OBSERVED IN OPERATION, THAT ARE
      RELEVANT TO SOCIAL CONTROL PROBLEM OF CONFLICT MAINTENANCE
      IN THE SYSTEM. EXAMINES PRESSURES ON PROSECUTOR TO REDUCE
      CONFLICT. ANALYZES CONFLICT MODEL FOR VARYING CATEGORIES OF
      DEFENSE ATTORNEY.

1976 SKOLNIKOFF E.B.
      "MAKING FOREIGN POLICY"
      CURRENT, (JAN. 67), 27-32.
         STRESSES IMPORTANCE OF SCIENCE AND TECHNOLOGY TO FOREIGN
      POLICY CONCERNS, ESPECIALLY IN NATIONAL DEFENSE. ADVOCATES
      REACTIVATION OF SCIENCE OFFICE AT STATE DEPT TO BE SOURCE OF
      CONSTANT RELEVANT INFORMATION. SCIENCE OFFICE FUNCTION IS TO
      CORRELATE ACTIVITIES OF VARIOUS AGENCIES AS WELL AS RESEARCH
      WORK AND DATA-GATHERING AROUND THE WORLD ABOUT TECHNOLOGICAL
      CHANGE.

1977 SLESSER H.
      THE ADMINISTRATION OF THE LAW.
      LONDON: HUTCHINSON U LIBRARY, 1948, 144 PP.
         A STUDY FOR LAYMEN OF THE ADMINISTRATION OF ENGLISH CIVIL
      AND CRIMINAL LAW. DESCRIBES THE CONSTITUTION OF COURTS, THE
      RECEPTION OF EVIDENCE, THE METHOD OF PROOF, AND THE MANNER
      IN WHICH JUDGES ARRIVE AT DECISIONS. INCLUDES A BRIEF
      OUTLINE OF BRITISH LEGAL HISTORY AND DEVELOPMENT AND OF
      HISTORICAL FORMS OF ACTION AND PROSECUTION.

1978 SLICHTER S.H.
      UNION POLICIES AND INDUSTRIAL MANAGEMENT.
      WASHINGTON: BROOKINGS INST, 1941, 597 PP.
         FOCUSES ON COLLECTIVE BARGAINING, ITS CONTENT AND PRO-
      CESS, TO PROVIDE WIDE-RANGE ANALYSIS OF RELATIONSHIPS BE-
      TWEEN TRADE UNIONISTS AND EMPLOYERS. CONSIDERS EFFECTS OF
      MODERN UNION UPON PRODUCTION IN HIRING, LAYOFFS, WORK RULES,
      AND WAGE PAYMENT. ALSO EXAMINES RELATION OF UNION AND NON-
      UNION PLANTS AND EMPLOYEES.

1979 SMIGEL E.O.
      "THE IMPACT OF RECRUITMENT ON THE ORGANIZATION OF THE LARGE
      LAW FIRM" (BMR)"
      AMER. SOCIOLOGICAL REV., 25 (FEB. 60), 56-66.
         CITES EVIDENCE INDICATING THAT RECRUITMENT COMPLEX WHICH
      MUST SATISFY DEMANDS OF BOTH FIRM AND RECRUIT IS BEING
      SEVERELY STRAINED BY INCREASED COMPETITION. TO MEET THIS,
      CHANGES HAVE BEEN MADE IN ORGANIZATION OF FIRMS. DISCUSSES
      FACT THAT PLANNED CHANGES OFTEN PRODUCED SIDE EFFECTS THAT
      HAVE INTERFERED WITH DESIRED GOAL.

1980 SMITH C. ED.
      THE OMBUDSMAN: A BIBLIOGRAPHY (PAMPHLET)
      RALEIGH: N CAR FRIEND COMM LEGIS, 1965, 7 PP.
         LISTS 100 ENTRIES PUBLISHED BETWEEN 1957 AND 1964 IN
      ENGLISH ALPHABETICALLY BY AUTHOR.

1981 SMITH H.E. ED.
      READINGS IN ECONOMIC DEVELOPMENT AND ADMINISTRATION IN

      TANZANIA.
      DAR SALAAM: U SALAAM PUB ADMIN, 1966, 598 PP.
         CREATES HEREWITH FIRST SOURCE BOOK FOR TANZANIAN ECONOMY,
      INCLUDING GOVERNMENT DOCUMENTS, RESEARCH REPORTS, AND
      JOURNALISTIC CONTRIBUTIONS. BRIEFLY DESCRIBES HISTORY AND
      SPECIFIC PROBLEMS, THEN DEALS WITH MONETARY SYSTEM, FINANCE,
      LABOR, INDUSTRIALIZATION, PLANNING, INTERNATIONAL TRADE, AND
      MUCH-DESIRED INTEGRATION OF EAST AFRICA.

1982 SMITH L.
      AMERICAN DEMOCRACY AND MILITARY POWER.
      CHICAGO: U. CHI. PR., 1951, 370 PP.
         DESCRIBES AMERICAN SYSTEM OF CIVIL CONTROL OF MILITARY
      POWER. ANALYZES THE PRESIDENCY AND ADMINISTRATION OF
      NATIONAL DEFENSE, CONGRESSIONAL COMMITTEES ON THE CONDUCT OF
      WAR, AND MILITARY INFLUENCE IN CONGRESS. CONCLUDES WITH
      ANALYSIS OF WAR-EMERGENCY AND CONSTITUTIONAL POWERS.

1983 SMITH M.G.
      GOVERNMENT IN ZAZZAU 1800-1950.
      LONDON: OXFORD U PR, 1960, 371 PP.
         STUDY OF GOVERNMENT IN ZARIA REGION OF NORTHERN NIGERIA,
      SHOWING ITS DEVELOPMENT IN 19TH CENTURY UNDER TRIBAL LEADER-
      SHIP, AND ITS PRESENT-DAY, POSTCOLONIAL COMPOSITION. THE-
      ORY OF STRUCTURAL CHANGE IS DEVELOPED THROUGH ANALYSIS OF
      CHANGES WHICH WERE PART OF PROCESS WHICH TRANSFORMED GOV-
      ERNMENT SYSTEMS.

1984 SMITH R.M.
      STATE GOVERNMENT IN TRANSITION.
      PHILA: U OF PENN PR, 1963, 309 PP., LC#63-07864.
         REJECTS ABSTRACT STUDY OF GOVERNMENT TO DISCUSS WHETHER
      ANY STATE GOVERNOR HAS MEANS AT HIS COMMAND TO PROPAGATE
      HIS PROGRAM. STUDY CENTERS AROUND PENNSYLVANIA AND REFORM
      OF STATE GOVERNMENT, ESPECIALLY UNDER LEADER'S
      GOVERNORSHIP.

1985 SMITH T.E.
      "ELECTIONS IN DEVELOPING COUNTRIES: A STUDY OF ELECTORAL
      PROCEDURES USED IN TOPICAL AFRICA, SOUTH-EAST ASIA..."
      NEW YORK: ST MARTIN'S PRESS, 1960.
         SUMMARY OF VARIOUS ELECTORAL METHODS WHICH HAVE BEEN
      TRIED IN INTRODUCING DEMOCRACY TO DEVELOPING COUNTRIES IN
      TROPICAL AFRICA, INDIA, SOUTH-EAST ASIA, AND BRITISH
      CARIBBEAN. CONTAINS INFORMATION ON ELECTORAL ADMINISTRATION
      AND GEOGRAPHY, REGISTRATION, FRANCHISE, MINORITIES AND ELEC-
      TORAL SYSTEM, ETC. BIBLIOGRAPHY ARRANGED BY COUNTRY.

1986 SMITH W.H.T.
      "THE IMPLICATIONS OF THE AMERICAN BAR ASSOCIATION ADVISORY
      COMMITTEE RECOMMENDATIONS FOR POLICE ADMINISTRATION."
      NOTRE DAME LAWYER, 42 (1967), 907-914.
         DISCUSSES EXTENT OF PRESS INFLUENCE ON FREE TRIALS,
      STATING THAT IN NEW YORK STATE LESS THAN 10 PER CENT OF
      CRIMINAL DEFENDANTS EVER COME TO TRIAL. INVESTIGATES EXTENT
      OF POLICE RESTRICTION OF INFORMATION ABOUT DEFENDANT.
      MAINTAINS THAT AMERICAN BAR ASSOCIATION RECOMMENDATIONS
      ARE NOT SOLUTION AND SUGGESTS VOLUNTARY CODE OF ETHICS.
         PRESS FORCES ADJUD ETHIC

1987 SMITHIES A.
      THE BUDGETARY PROCESS IN THE UNITED STATES.
      NEW YORK: MCGRAW HILL, 1955, 486 PP., LC#54-11767.
         HOW FEDERAL GOVERNMENT MAKES EXPENDITURE DECISIONS, IN-
      CLUDING PARTS PLAYED BY PRESIDENT, CONGRESS, AND DEPARTMENT-
      AL BUREAUS. MAKES RECOMMENDATIONS, STARTING WITH IDEA THAT
      DECISION-MAKING CAN BE IMPROVED BY CLEAR FORMULATION OF AL-
      TERNATIVES. COVERS DEFENSE AND NON-DEFENSE BUDGETS, ECONOMIC
      IMPACT OF BUDGET, HISTORY OF BUDGETARY PROCESS, RELATION TO
      NATIONAL POLICY, FORMULATION, EXECUTION, REVIEW OF BUDGET.

1988 SNIDER C.F.
      "AMERICAN COUNTY GOVERNMENT: A MID-CENTURY REVIEW" (BMR)"
      AM. POL. SCI. REV., 46 (MAR. 52), 66-80.
         REVIEWS THE US COUNTY, ATTEMPTING TO DETERMINE EXTENT
      OF MODERNIZATION AND DIRECTIONS OF FUTURE IMPROVEMENT.
      COMPARES COUNTY ADMINISTRATION OF 1950'S WITH THAT OF EARLY
      20TH CENTURY. PROPOSES CONSOLIDATION OF COUNTY AND CITY
      GOVERNMENTS IN HIGHLY URBANIZED AREAS, MORE GENERAL USE OF
      STATE SUPERVISION OVER COUNTIES, AND PROVISION FOR COUNTY
      EXECUTIVE WITH ADMINISTRATIVE AUTHORITY.

1989 SNIDER C.F.
      AMERICAN STATE AND LOCAL GOVERNMENT.
      NEW YORK: APPLETON, 1965, 735 PP., LC#65-25813.
         EXTENSIVE EXAMINATION OF ORGANIZATION, POWERS, POPULAR
      CONTROL, LAWS, FUNCTIONS, AND FINANCE OF STATE AND LOCAL
      GOVERNMENT IN US.

1990 SNOWISS L.M.
      "CONGRESSIONAL RECRUITMENT AND REPRESENTATION."
      AM. POL. SCI. REV., 60 (SEPT. 66), 627-639.
         CASE STUDY OF METROPOLITAN CHICAGO, SHOWING RELATIONSHIP
      BETWEEN LOCAL POLITICAL ORGANIZATION, CANDIDATE RECRUIT-
      MENT, AND REPRESENTATION IN HOUSE OF REPRESENTATIVES: DEMON-
      STRATES EFFECTS WHICH DIFFERENT SYSTEMS OF RECRUITMENT HAVE

UPON THE KINDS OF MEN ENTERING PUBLIC LIFE AND PUBLIC
POLICIES THEY ESPOUSE.

1991 SNYDER F.G.
ONE-PARTY GOVERNMENT IN MALI: TRANSITION TOWARD CONTROL.
NEW HAVEN: YALE U PR, 1965, 178 PP., LC#65-22341.
THESIS IS THAT FUTURE OF MALI - A COUNTRY WITH REMARKABLY
LITTLE ECONOMIC GROWTH OR POLITICAL STABILITY - WILL BE
DETERMINED BY THE HISTORY AND STRUCTURE OF THE UNION
SOUDANAISE PARTY. ARGUES PARTY STRUCTURE MUST LOOSEN.

1992 SNYDER R.C. ED., BRUCK H. ED., SAPIN B. ED.
FOREIGN POLICY DECISION-MAKING.
NEW YORK: FREE PRESS, 1962, 274 PP.
CONSTRUCT SCHEMA FOR ANALYSIS OF SUBJECT. EMPHASIZE
VARIABLES OF DECISION-MAKING. DEVELOP TESTABLE HYPOTHESIS
BY CONSIDERING CASE STUDIES AND ORGANIZATIONAL STUDIES.

1993 SOHN L.B.
BASIC DOCUMENTS OF THE UNITED NATIONS.
BROOKLYN: FOUND. PR., 1956, 307 PP.
COMPILATION OF DOCUMENTS INTENDED TO SERVE AS A REFERENCE
VOLUME. REPRODUCTION OF UN CHARTER ACCOMPANIED BY THIRTY-
EIGHT SUPPLEMENTARY RECORDS AND FIFTEEN EXPLANATORY NOTES.

1994 SOHN L.B. ED.
CASES ON UNITED NATIONS LAW.
BROOKLYN: FOUNDATION PRESS, 1956, 1048 PP.
CASEBOOK CENTERING ON LEGAL PROBLEMS WHICH HAVE ARISEN IN
WORK OF UN. EMPHASIZES MATERIAL WHICH PRESENTS CLEARLY THE
ARGUMENTS ON BOTH SIDES OF EACH CASE. CASES ARE GROUPED
IN A WAY THAT BRINGS TOGETHER DECISIONS WHICH ARE PARALLEL
N FACTS BUT OPPOSITE IN CONCLUSIONS OR POSITIONS. SELECTIONS
DEAL WITH PROBLEMS OF UN ORGANIZATION, FUNCTIONS AND POWERS
OF UN ORGANS, AND CURRENT PROBLEMS OF WORLD LAW.

1995 SOHN L.B.
"THE DEFINITION OF AGGRESSION."
VIRGINIA LAW REV., 45 (JUNE 59), 697-701.
DEMANDS THAT THE INTERNATIONAL COURTS BE STRENGTHENED, SO
THAT AGGRESSIVE NATIONS WILL BE PROSECUTED. FEELS THAT A
CLEARER UNDERSTANDING OF THE LAW IS NECESSARY IN ORDER TO
DO THIS.

1996 SOMERS H.M.
"THE PRESIDENT AS ADMINISTRATOR."
ANN. ACAD. POL. SOC. SCI., 283 (SEPT. 52), 104-114.
ARGUES THAT INCREASED PRESIDENTIAL CONTROL OVER
ADMINISTRATIVE AGENCIES TO INCREASE RESPONSIBILITY AND
AND EFFICIENCY: IN GENERAL AGREEMENT WITH HOOVER COMMISSION.

1997 SOROKIN P.
CONTEMPORARY SOCIOLOGICAL THEORIES.
NEW YORK: HARPER, 1928, 785 PP.
SURVEYS PRINCIPLE SOCIOLOGICAL THEORIES IN ORDER TO
ESTABLISH TO WHAT EXTENT THEY ARE SCIENTIFICALLY VALID.
DESCRIBES VARIOUS INTERPRETATIONS OF THE STRUGGLE FOR EXIST-
ENCE AND THE SOCIOLOGY OF WAR. CONCLUDES WITH ANALYSIS AND
DEFINITION OF SOCIOLOGY.

1998 SOUTH AFRICA COMMISSION ON FUT
INTERIM AND FINAL REPORTS ON FUTURE FORM OF GOVERNMENT IN
THE SOUTH-WEST AFRICAN PROTECTORATE (PAMPHLET)
CAPETOWN: UNION OF SOUTH AFRICA, 1921, 12 PP.
REPORT ON FUTURE FORM OF GOVERNMENT IN UNION OF SOUTH
AFRICA, METHOD OF REPRESENTATION OF PEOPLE, AND CHANGES IN
ADMINISTRATION OF WITHDRAWAL OF MARTIAL LAW.

1999 SOUTH AFRICAN CONGRESS OF DEM
FACE THE FUTURE.
JOHANNESBURG: S AFR CONG DEM, 1960, 19 PP.
CALL FROM ORGANIZATION OF BLACKS AND A FEW WHITES TO
STRIVE FOR ABOLITION OF APARTHEID AND FREEDOM FOR ALL RACES.
MUST BE ACHIEVED BY EDUCATION, UNDERSTANDING, AND COOPER-
ATION. INCLUDES FREEDOM CHARTER OF 1955, WHICH PUTS FORTH
STATEMENTS OF EQUAL RIGHTS, FRIENDSHIP, AND PEACE.

2000 SOUTH PACIFIC COMMISSION
INDEX OF SOCIAL SCIENCE RESEARCH THESES ON THE SOUTH PACIFIC
NOUMEA: SOUTH PACIFIC COMMISSION, 1957, 79 PP.
ANNOTATED LIST OF UNIVERSITY-HELD SOCIAL SCIENCE RESEARCH
THESES ON THE SOUTH PACIFIC WHICH HAVE SOME SOCIAL, POLITI-
CAL, OR ECONOMIC BEARING ON COMMISSION'S AREA OF CONCERN.
PROVIDES INFORMATION ON SIZE, SCOPE, AND INTENTION OF EACH
AUTHOR'S WORK; INCLUDES QUOTATIONS OF PASSAGES STATING
INTENTIONS WHEN AVAILABLE. NOT INDEXED.

2001 SOVIET-EAST EUROPEAN RES SERV
SOVIET SOCIETY.
NEW YORK: SOVIET RES TRANS SERV.
QUARTERLY ANNOTATED BIBLIOGRAPHY FIRST PUBLISHED IN
1961. REPRESENTS A SELECTIVE LIST OF ARTICLES PUBLISHED
IN CURRENT SOVIET PERIODICALS ON MATTERS CONCERNING EDUCA-
TION, SOCIOLOGY, PHILOSOPHY, PUBLIC ADMINISTRATION AND NON-
GOVERNMENTAL INSTITUTIONS WITH VIEW TO GIVING SURVEY OF
DAILY ISSUES AND PROBLEMS. OCCASIONAL ARTICLES FROM DAILY

PRESS INCLUDED.

2002 SPACKMAN A.
"THE SENATE OF TRINIDAD AND TOBAGO."
SOCIAL ECO. STUDIES, 16 (MAR. 67), 77-100.
AUTHOR DISCUSSES THE COMPOSITION AND THE FUNCTIONS OF THE
TRINIDAD SENATE IN TERMS OF INPUT AND OUTPUT EFFICIENCY, AND
CONCLUDES THAT A UNICAMERAL LEGISLATURE WOULD SERVE THE
COUNTRY BETTER.

2003 SPEAR P.
"NEHRU."
MODERN ASIAN STUDIES, 1 (JAN. 67), 15-29.
ASSESSES SUCCESSES AND FAILURES OF NEHRU'S "REIGN" AND
SPECULATES AS TO WHY HE IS HELD IN SUCH DISREGARD IN INDIA
TODAY. BLAMES NEHRU FOR LACK OF RELIANCE IN THE CIVIL SER-
VICE AND FOR DISTRUST OF TALENT NEAR HIM. CONCLUDES THAT
NEHRU'S GRAND DESIGN FOR WESTERNIZATION LACKED WIDE POPULAR
SUPPORT AND THAT HIS PERSONALITY WAS UNEQUAL TO FORMULATING
SUSTAINED POLICY OF REFORM.

2004 SPEECKAERT G.P.
SELECT BIBLIOGRAPHY ON INTERNATIONAL ORGANIZATION, 1885-1964
BRUSSELS: UNION OF INTL ASSN, 1965, 148 PP.
SOME 350 TITLES ARE LISTED ALPHABETICALLY BY AUTHOR FOR
WORKS DEALING WITH INTERNATIONAL ORGANIZATION IN GENERAL.
SOME 730 TITLES ARE LISTED RELATING TO 214 SPECIFIC ORGAN-
IZATIONS; HERE THE DIVISION IS FRENCH ALPHABETIZATION OF
ORGANIZATIONAL TITLES, THEN SUBDIVIDED CHRONOLOGICALLY TO
PROVIDE "HISTORY AT A GLANCE." NOT ANNOTATED.

2005 SPERO S.D.
GOVERNMENT AS EMPLOYER.
NEW YORK: REMSEN PR, 1948, 497 PP.
DISCUSSION OF ATTEMPTS AND RIGHTS OF CIVIL SERVANTS TO
ORGANIZE FOR COLLECTIVE BARGAINING AND THE US GOVERNMENT'S
CLAIM THAT RECOGNITION OF CIVIL SERVANTS' BARGAINING
ORGANIZATION WOULD BE A DEROGATION OF THE SOVEREIGNTY OF THE
GOVERNMENT.

2006 SPICER K.
A SAMARITAN STATE?
TORONTO: TORONTO UNIV PRESS, 1966, 272 PP.
DETAILED RECORDS OF CANADA'S AID PROGRAM IN PAST SIX
FORMATIVE YEARS. PREFACED BY FIRST CHAPTER WHICH POSES MAJOR
ISSUES OF POLICY FOR CANADIANS, THEN MOVES INTO HISTORY OF
CANADIAN AID.

2007 SPINELLI A.
THE EUROCRATS; CONFLICT AND CRISIS IN THE EUROPEAN
COMMUNITY (TRANS. BY C. GROVE HAINES)
BALTIMORE: JOHNS HOPKINS PRESS, 1966, 229 PP., LC#66-14379.
DESCRIBES CENTERS OF UNITED EUROPEAN ACTION; SHOWING WAY
THEY ARE INTERCONNECTED AND THEIR LIMITATIONS AND
POSSIBILITIES. PRESENTS ORIGINS OF EUROPEAN COMMUNITY IDEA;
GROUPS FORMED, SUCH AS EURATOM COMMISSION AND COMMON MARKET;
RELATIONSHIP OF NATIONAL BUREAUCRACIES; STRENGTH OF INTEREST
GROUPS; AND POLITICAL ORGANIZATION OF EUROPEAN COMMUNITY.

2008 SPIRO H.J.
GOVERNMENT BY CONSTITUTIONS: THE POLITICAL SYSTEMS OF
DEMOCRACY.
NEW YORK: RANDOM, 1959, 496 PP.
EXAMINES THE POLITICS, POLICIES, INSTITUTIONS, PRO-
CEDURES AND REPRESENTATION IN SYSTEMS OF CONSTITUTIONAL
GOVERNMENT. DEALS SPECIFICALLY WITH SWEDEN, ITALY,
SWITZERLAND, GERMANY, FRANCE, GREAT BRITAIN, CANADA AND THE
UNITED STATES. DISCUSSES CONDITIONS OF CONSTITUTIONAL
SUCCESS AND LOOKS AT FUTURE OF CONSTITUTIONAL SYSTEMS.

2009 SPITZ A.A., WEIDNER E.W.
"DEVELOPMENT ADMINISTRATION: AN ANNOTATED BIBLIOGRAPHY."
HONOLULU: EAST-WEST CENT. PR., 1963, 116 PP., $3.50.
A SELECTIVE BIBLIOGRAPHY ON PUBLIC ADMINISTRATION FOR
NEWLY EMERGING COUNTRIES. DESIGNED TO BE SUGGESTIVE
RATHER THAN DEFINITIVE. INCLUDES MATERIALS, PUBLISHED IN
ENGLISH, SINCE 1945.

2010 SPITZ D.
DEMOCRACY AND THE CHALLENGE OF POWER.
NEW YORK: COLUMB. U. PR., 1958, 228 PP.
ASSAYS THE ABUSES OF POWER IN A DEMOCRACY, CONTENDING
THEY ARISE FROM BOTH OPPRESSIVE ACTS OF GOVERNMENT AND ARBI-
TRARY PRACTICES OF INDIVIDUALS AND GROUPS. IN A DEMOCRACY,
NON-CONFORMISTS ARE OFTEN PERSECUTED AND PUBLIC OPINION CAN
OFTEN BE TYRANNICAL. STATES CONTROL IS DIFFICULT BECAUSE OF
THE WIDE DIFFUSION OF POWERS AND RESPONSIBILITIES.

2012 SPRING D.
THE ENGLISH LANDED ESTATE IN THE NINETEENTH CENTURY: ITS
ADMINISTRATION.
BALTIMORE: JOHNS HOPKINS PRESS, 1963, 216 PP., LC#63-10814.
ATTEMPTS TO DESCRIBE ENGLISH LANDOWNER OF 19TH CENTURY IN
HIS SOCIAL, ECONOMIC, AND POLITICAL FUNCTIONS, INCLUDING
ANATOMY OF ESTATE ADMINISTRATION, AND RELATION OF LANDOWNER
TO STATE.

2013 SPRINGER H.W.
"FEDERATION IN THE CARIBBEAN: AN ATTEMPT THAT FAILED."
INT. ORGAN., 16 (AUG. 62), 758-75.
TRACES EVOLUTION OF PLANS FOR CARIBBEAN FEDERATION AND
DISCUSSES THE FORCES WHICH WORKED FOR AND AGAINST ITS ESTAB-
LISHMENT.

2014 SRIVASTAVA G.L.
COLLECTIVE BARGAINING AND LABOR-MANAGEMENT RELATIONS IN
INDIA.
LONDON: BOOKLAND PRIVATE, LTD, 1962, 405 PP.
COMPARES COLLECTIVE BARGAINING METHODS AND THEORIES IN
INDIA, GREAT BRITAIN, AND US, USING CASE STUDIES FOR ILLUS-
TRATION. EVALUATES RELATIVE MERITS OF VOLUNTARY VS. COMPUL-
SORY ARBITRATION AND RESULTS OF BOTH AFFECTING LABOR AND
INDUSTRY.

2015 STAAR R.F.
"ELECTIONS IN COMMUNIST POLAND."
MIDWEST. J. POLIT. SCI., 2 (MAY 58), 57-75.
BRIEF HISTORY OF POSTWAR POLAND'S ELECTIONS AND REFEREN-
DUMS. EMPHASIZES EARLY COMMUNIST TECHNIQUES OF INTIMIDATION,
COERCION AND FRAUD TO WIN ELECTIONS. CONCLUDES WITH ANALYSIS
OF MORE RECENT DEMOCRATIC MACHINERY BEING USED NOW.

2016 STAHL O.G.
"DEMOCRACY AND PUBLIC EMPLOYEE MORALITY."
ANN. ACAD. POL. SOC. SCI., 297 (JAN. 55), 90-97.
PUBLIC INTEREST IS REPRESENTED MORE THAN PRIVATE
INTERESTS IN THE ACTIONS OF BUREAUCRATS, BUT THERE IS STILL
ROOM FOR IMPROVEMENT.

2017 STAHL O.G.
PUBLIC PERSONNEL ADMINISTRATION.
LONDON: HARPER & ROW, 1962, 531 PP., LC#62-19728.
TRACES TREND OF INCREASING PROFESSIONALISM IN GOVERNMENT
AND THE EXPANSION OF THE CIVIL SERVICE. EXAMINES CURRENT
METHODS OF RECRUITMENT AND TRAINING, AND DISCUSSES RECENT
INNOVATIONS IN MANAGEMENT. ALSO DESCRIBES SUCH OCCUPATIONAL
ASPECTS OF PUBLIC WORK AS WAGES, BENEFITS, AND TURNOVER.

2018 STANFORD RESEARCH INSTITUTE
AFRICAN DEVELOPMENT: A TEST FOR INTERNATIONAL COOPERATION.
MENLO PARK: STANFORD U RES INST, 1960, 170 PP.
COVERING ALL OF AFRICA BUT UAR AND UNION OF SOUTH AFRICA,
THIS STUDY EXAMINES CHARACTER OF AFRICAN DEVELOPMENT IN
LIGHT OF PAST ROLES OF ASSISTANCE, INVESTMENT, AND TRADE;
STEPS TAKEN TO MODIFY THESE EXTERNAL FACTORS, AND THOSE
SUGGESTED. EXAMINES EFFECTIVENESS OF MEASURES IN LIGHT OF
AFRICAN ATTITUDES AND ASPIRATIONS. INDICATES PROBLEMS
IMPEDING DEVELOPMENT OF AN EFFECTIVE WESTERN APPROACH.

2019 STANLEY D.T.
"EXCELLENCE IN PUBLIC SERVICE - HOW DO YOU REALLY KNOW?"
PUBLIC ADMIN. REV., 24 (SEPT. 64), 170-174.
AT PRESENT THERE IS NO EFFECTIVE EVALUATION PROCEDURE IN
USE: ARTICLE SUGGESTS SEVERAL.

2020 STANLEY D.T.
THE HIGHER CIVIL SERVICE: AN EVALUATION OF FEDERAL PERSONNEL
PRACTICES.
WASHINGTON: BROOKINGS INST, 1964, 145 PP., LC#64-66213.
STUDY OF HIGH-LEVEL CIVIL SERVICE EMPLOYEES, ANALYZING
THE OPERATION OF CIVIL SERVICE SYSTEM WITH REFERENCE TO
CRITERIA OF EFFECTIVE PERSONNEL SYSTEMS. WEIGHS VARIOUS AL-
TERNATIVE SYSTEMS. SUGGESTS THAT PROGRESS IN THE HIGHER
CIVIL SERVICE SYSTEM WILL REQUIRE MANY INNOVATIONS. SURVEYS
PRESENT AND PAST EMPLOYEES AND SOME OUTSIDERS.

2021 STANLEY D.T.
CHANGING ADMINISTRATIONS.
WASHINGTON: BROOKINGS INST, 1965, LC#65-28725.
STUDIES TRANSFER OF POWER AND CONTINUITY OF
ADMINISTRATION IN FEDERAL GOVERNMENT AFTER 1960 AND 1964
PRESIDENTIAL ELECTIONS. EVALUATES PRESIDENT AND ASSOCIATES
ON OVER-ALL PERFORMANCE. COVERS SIX DEPARTMENTS: STATE;
DEFENSE; INTERIOR; AGRICULTURE; HEALTH, EDUCATION, AND
WELFARE; AND FEDERAL AVIATION ADMINISTRATION.

2022 STANLEY T.W.
"DECENTRALIZING NUCLEAR CONTROL IN NATO."
ORBIS, 7 (SPRING 63), 41-48.
PROPOSES SEVERAL SEPARATE COMMAND AND CONTROL SYSTEMS FOR
NATO'S NUCLEAR FORCES. USA WOULD MAINTAIN CONTROL OVER MAJOR
NUCLEAR FORCES FOR COUNTERFORCE AND MEDIUM-RANGE MISSILES
AND TACTICAL AIRCRAFT IN EUROPE. OUTLINES HYPOTHETICAL CASES
PROVING VALUE AND FEASIBILITY OF PROPOSALS.

2023 STARR M.K. ED.
EXECUTIVE READINGS IN MANAGEMENT SCIENCE.
NEW YORK: MACMILLAN, 1965, 422 PP., LC#65-17820.
REPRINTS OF ARTICLES FROM JOURNAL "MANAGEMENT SCIENCE,"
WHICH EXPRESSES VIEWS OF ALL TYPES OF INDUSTRIAL AND
TECHNICAL MANAGERS. BELIEVES THAT SHARED MANAGEMENT
EXPERIENCES MAY IMPROVE WORKER ENVIRONMENT THROUGH
DEVELOPMENT OF COMMON DISCIPLINE.

2024 ILLINOIS, STATE OF
PUBLICATIONS OF THE STATE OF ILLINOIS.
SPRINGFIELD: ILLINOIS ST PUBL.
PAMPHLET ISSUED BIANNUALLY LISTING PUBLICATIONS OF
STATE OF ILLINOIS. INDICATES WHERE FEE IS CHARGED AND WHERE
DOCUMENT IS NOT AVAILABLE FOR DISTRIBUTION.

2025 STATIST REICHSAMTE
BIBLIOGRAPHIE DER STAATS- UND WIRSCHAFTSWISSENSCHAFTEN.
DRESDEN: BIBLIOG DES STAATS, 1941, 930 PP.
A COLLECTION OF MONTHLY PERIODICALS LISTING WORKS
PUBLISHED IN THE FIELDS OF ECONOMICS AND POLITICS. LISTING
LARGELY BOOKS AND PERIODICALS, IT IS CATEGORIZED INTO SUCH
FIELDS AS HISTORY OF SCIENCE, BUSINESS ADMINISTRATION,
ECONOMIC CONDITIONS, PUBLIC FINANCE, ETC. INCLUDES
FOREIGN MATERIAL AND COVERS WORKS PUBLISHED IN THE
PRECEDING ONE TO TWO YEARS; GERMAN PRIMARILY.

2026 STEIN E., HAY P.
"LEGAL REMEDIES OF ENTERPRISES IN THE EUROPEAN ECONOMIC
COMMUNITY."
AMER. J. COMP. LAW, 9 (SUMMER 60), 375-424.
SURVEYS GOALS OF EEC, CONSIDERING INTEGRATION OF NATIONAL
ECONOMIES OF FRANCE, GERMANY, ITALY AND BENELUX COUNTRIES
AS PRINCIPAL OBJECTIVE. ANALYZES LAW-MAKING POWERS VESTED BY
COMMON MARKET TREATY IN COMMUNITY'S MAIN INSTITUTIONS:
COUNCIL OF MINISTERS AND EUROPEAN COMMISSION. RAISES
QUESTIONS REGARDING JURISDICTION OF COMMUNITY JUSTICE COURT.

2027 STEIN H.
THE FOREIGN SERVICE ACT OF 1946.
INDIANAPOLIS: BOBBS-MERRILL, 1949, 201 PP.
HISTORY OF CREATION OF FOREIGN SERVICE ACT. TRACES
CONTROVERSY AND NEGOTIATIONS AMONG MEMBERS OF BUDGET
BUREAU AND FOREIGN SERVICE. CASE STUDY OFFERS MATERIAL FOR
EVALUATING BOTH THE GUILD NOTION OF ADMINISTRATIVE
ORGANIZATION AND THE COORDINATING ACTIVITIES OF BUDGET
BUREAU.

2028 STEIN H. ED.
AMERICAN CIVIL-MILITARY DECISION.
UNIVERSITY: U ALABAMA PR, 1963, 705 PP., LC#62-16825.
CASE STUDIES IN CIVILIAN-MILITARY RELATIONS IN US AS SEEN
IN ANALYSIS OF 20TH-CENTURY DECISIONS ON MILITARY POLICY AND
ORGANIZATION. DEALS WITH FOREIGN MILITARY AID, WAR STRAT-
EGY, AND MILITARY APPROPRIATIONS.

2029 STEINER G.A. ED.
THE CREATIVE ORGANIZATION.
CHICAGO: U OF CHICAGO PRESS, 1965, 267 PP., LC#65-17301.
COLLECTION OF ARTICLES ADDRESSES ITSELF TO PROBLEMS ARIS-
ING FROM THE INCREASING NEED FOR, AND EMPHASIS ON, CREATIV-
ITY IN BUSINESS OPERATIONS. DEALS WITH DEFINING, MEASURING,
AND FOSTERING CREATIVITY, AS WELL AS METHODS OF DISCOVERING
CREATIVE INDIVIDUALS IN MANAGEMENT SPHERES.

2030 STEINER K.
LOCAL GOVERNMENT IN JAPAN.
STANFORD: STANFORD U PRESS, 1965, 564 PP., LC#64-17005.
PROVIDES OVERVIEW OF ALL ASPECTS OF JAPANESE LOCAL
GOVERNMENT SYSTEM AND ATTEMPTS TO DETERMINE DEGREE OF LOCAL
AUTONOMY - IN LAW AND IN PRACTICE. APPRAISES POST-WAR
REFORMS. USES ELECTORAL STATISTICS EXTENSIVELY.

2031 STEINMETZ H.
"THE PROBLEMS OF THE LANDRAT: A STUDY OF COUNTY GOVERNMENT
IN THE US ZONE OF GERMANY."
J. OF POLITICS, 11 (MAY 49), 318-334.
DISCUSSES ROLE AND PROBLEMS OF COUNTY GOVERNMENT IN AMER-
ICAN OCCUPIED ZONES OF GERMANY AFTER WWII. MENTIONS HOUSING,
HEALTH, WELFARE, AND PRICE CONTROLS INITIATED AFTER WWII;
AND PROBLEM CREATED BY HITLER'S PLANNED, WARTIME ECONOMY.

2032 STENE E.O., FLORO G.K.
ABANDONMENTS OF THE MANAGER PLAN.
LAWRENCE: U KANSAS, GOV RES CTR, 1953, 107 PP.
STUDY OF FOUR SMALL, MIDWESTERN CITIES FINDS THAT THE
MAJOR REASON FOR THE DISSATISFACTION WITH THE PLAN COULD BE
TRACED TO THE BEHAVIOR OF THE MANAGER AND SUPPORTERS
OF THE MANAGER. GENERALLY, MINORITY GROUPS FELT UNREP-
RESENTED UNDER THE PLAN.

2033 STEPHENS O.
FACTS TO A CANDID WORLD.
STANFORD: STANFORD U PRESS, 1955, 164 PP., LC#55-11262.
INVESTIGATES AMERICAN PROPAGANDA OVERSEAS - ITS PUBLIC
OPINION, ORGANIZATION, AND OPERATION - THEN EVALUATES ITS
EFFECTIVENESS.

2034 STEVENSON A.E.
LOOKING OUTWARD: YEARS OF CRISIS AT THE UNITED NATIONS.
NEW YORK: HARPER, 1963, 295 PP.
SPEECHES AND WRITINGS RELATING TO THE UN SINCE
APPOINTMENT AS PERMANENT USA REPRESENTATIVE. 'IN A WORLD
MADE ONE BY SCIENCE AND THREATENED BY UNIVERSAL DESTRUCTION,
SOME PERSONAL RIGHTS - ABOVE ALL THE RIGHT TO LIFE AND

SECURITY - CAN NO LONGER BE SAFEGUARDED BY THE INDIVIDUAL
NATIONAL GOVERNMENT. WORLD SOCIETY HAS TO ACHIEVE THE
MINIMUM INSTITUTIONS OF ORDER.'

2035 STEWART D.D.
"THE PLACE OF VOLUNTEER PARTICIPATION IN BUREAUCRATIC
ORGANIZATION."
SOCIAL FORCES, 29 (MAR. 51), 311-317.
PROBES FUNCTION AND POWERS OF SELECTIVE SERVICE
SYSTEM LOCAL BOARDS COMPOSED OF VOLUNTEER ADMINISTRATORS.
DESCRIBES CHANGE OF ROLE OF BOARDS FROM COMMUNITY REPRESEN-
TATIVES TO BOARD REPRESENTATION OF THE SELECTIVE SERVICE
SYSTEM TO THE COMMUNITY DUE PARTLY TO THE LACK OF "AN
ORGANIZED, ARTICULATE GROUP WITH A VESTED INTEREST IN THE
MAINTENANCE OF THE AUTONOMY OF THE LOCAL BOARDS."

2036 STEWART F.M.
"A HALF CENTURY OF MUNICIPAL REFORM."
BERKELEY: U OF CALIF PR, 1950.
HISTORY OF NATIONAL MUNICIPAL LEAGUE. OUTLINES CONDITIONS
WHICH BROUGHT ORGANIZATION INTO EXISTENCE; DESCRIBES ITS
PROGRAM FOR IMPROVEMENT OF LOCAL GOVERNMENT; ANALYZES ITS
METHODS, TECHNIQUES AND PROBLEMS; AND ATTEMPTS TO EVALUATE
CONTRIBUTION OF LEAGUE TO FIFTY YEARS OF MUNICIPAL REFORM,
1894-1944. CONTAINS EXTENSIVE BIBLIOGRAPHY OF LITERATURE.

2037 STEWART I.
ORGANIZING SCIENTIFIC RESEARCH FOR WAR: ADMINISTRATIVE
HISTORY OF OFFICE OF SCIENTIFIC RESEARCH AND DEVELOPMENT.
BOSTON: LITTLE BROWN, 1948, 360 PP.
DESCRIBES ADMINISTRATIVE FRAMEWORK OF THE ORGANIZATION
THAT DEVELOPED, IMPROVED, AND BROUGHT INTO USE CERTAIN NEW
WEAPONS IN WWII. STUDIES BEGINNINGS AND NATURE OF OFFICE OF
SCIENTIFIC RESEARCH AND DEVELOPMENT. ANALYZES ITS FUNCTION
AS A LIAISON WITH ARMED SERVICES AND ALLIED GOVERNMENTS.
DISCUSSES FISCAL POLICY, SECURITY, LABOR, AND PUBLIC
RELATIONS OF OSRD.

2038 STEWART J.D.
BRITISH PRESSURE GROUPS: THEIR ROLE IN RELATION TO THE
HOUSE OF COMMONS.
NY & LONDON: ACADEMIC PRESS, 1958, 273 PP.
DISCUSSES PROPER, OFFICIAL, AND RECOGNIZED ACTIVITIES OF
PRESSURE GROUPS IN BRITAIN AND THEIR EFFECT UPON HOUSE OF
COMMONS' PROCEEDINGS. CONCENTRATES ON 1945-55 PERIOD.
ANALYZES PROCESS OF CONSULTATION, STRATEGIES,
PARLIAMENTARY ROUTINES, AND REPRESENTATION OF SEVERAL
IMPORTANT ORGANIZATIONS.

2039 STINCHCOMBE A.L.
"BUREAUCRATIC AND CRAFT ADMINISTRATION OF PRODUCTION: A
COMPARATIVE STUDY" (BMR).
ADMINISTRATIVE SCI. Q., 4 (SEPT. 59), 168-187.
COMPARES MASS PRODUCTION AND CONSTRUCTION INDUSTRIES WITH
RESPECT TO SOCIAL LOCATION OF WORK PLANNING, ADMINISTRATIVE
STATUS STRUCTURE, AND CONTENT OF ADMINISTRATIVE
COMMUNICATION. EXPLAINS LACK OF BUREAUCRACY IN CONSTRUCTION
BY ECONOMIC INSTABILITY. REVISES MAX WEBER'S IDEAL TYPE OF
BUREAUCRACY TO INCLUDE ONLY THOSE ELEMENTS PRESENT IN MASS
PRODUCTION AND ABSENT IN CONSTRUCTION.

2040 STOESSINGER J.G.
"THE INTERNATIONAL ATOMIC ENERGY AGENCY: THE FIRST PHASE."
INT. ORG., 13 (SUMMER 59), 394-411.
DESCRIBES AGENCY'S POLICY MAKING PROCESS, ADMINISTRATION,
RESEARCH PROBLEMS, COORDINATION WITH OTHER INTERNATIONAL
AGENCIES, AND ITS STRUGGLE TO MAINTAIN PEACE. EXAMINES
RELATIONSHIPS BETWEEN ATOMIC AND NON-ATOMIC NATIONS.
POINTS OUT WEAKNESS OF BILATERAL AGREEMENTS ON MATTERS OF
ATOMIC AID AND FAVORS AGREEMENTS ARRANGED THROUGH THE
AGENCY.

2041 STOICOIU V.
LEGAL SOURCES AND BIBLIOGRAPHY OF ROMANIA.
NEW YORK: FREDERICK PRAEGER, 1964, 237 PP., LC#64-15523.
COMPILES, ANNOTATES, AND THOROUGHLY INDEXES BY SUBJECT
AND AUTHOR MONOGRAPHS, SERIALS, BOOKS, ARTICLES, DOCUMENTS,
ETC. CONTAINS 1,589 ITEMS DEALING WITH THE PRINCIPLES AND
DEVELOPMENT OF ROMANIAN LAW SINCE ITS ACCEPTANCE OF THE
FRENCH LEGAL SYSTEM IN 1859 AND INCLUDING THE PERIOD
FOLLOWING SOVIET OCCUPATION. WRITINGS IN ROMANIAN AND MOST
OTHER EUROPEAN LANGUAGES.

2042 STOKE H.W.
"EXECUTIVE LEADERSHIP AND THE GROWTH OF PROPAGANDA."
AM. POL. SCI. REV., 35 (JUNE 41), 490-500.
SUGGESTS THAT TREMENDOUS GROWTH OF PUBLICITY ACTIVITIES
OF MODERN GOVERNMENT IS DIRECT CONSEQUENCE OF THE CONTINUED
ABSORPTION BY THE EXECUTIVE OF THE POWERS OF LEGISLATION.
CONTENDS THAT THIS IS GROWING TREND AND SEEKS REASONS FOR
THIS IN PROCESSES OF GOVERNMENT IN DEMOCRATIC SOCIETY.

2043 STOKES W.S.
BIBLIOGRAPHY OF STANDARD AND CLASSICAL WORKS IN THE FIELDS
OF AMERICAN POLITICAL SCIENCE.
WASHINGTON: PAN AMERICAN UNION, 1948, 30 PP.

CONTAINS 90 LISTINGS IN ENGLISH OF BOOKS AND US GOVERN-
MENT DOCUMENTS ON AMERICAN POLITICS. ARRANGED BY SUBJECT,
SELECTIVE. PUBLICATION DATES OF LISTINGS, 1900-47.

2044 STOKES W.S.
"HONDURAS: AN AREA STUDY IN GOVERNMENT."
MADISON: U OF WISCONSIN PR, 1950.
STUDY OF POLITICAL ROUTINE BASED ON LENGTHY FREE OBSER-
VATION AND SCHOLARLY RESEARCH. DISCUSSES GEOGRAPHICAL SET-
TING AND EVOLUTION OF GOVERNMENT AND POLITICS; EARLY CONSTI-
TUTIONS; LAW AND THE SYSTEM OF COLONIAL COURTS; ORGAN-
IZATION AND PROCEDURE OF MODERN COURTS; ADMINISTRATIVE UNITS
AND PROCEDURE; DEVELOPMENT OF POLITICAL PARTIES; ELECTORAL
SYSTEM AND REPRESENTATION. EXTENSIVE SPANISH BIBLIOGRAPHY.

2045 STOLPER W.
"SOCIAL FACTORS IN ECONOMIC PLANNING, WITH SPECIAL REFERENCE
TO NIGERIA."
S64 JOUE7 11 JUN- 1-17   00110
DISCUSSION OF NEED TO INCLUDE SOCIAL VARIABLES - LOCAL
CUSTOMS, HISTORIES, MANNERS - IN ECONOMIC PLANNING.

2046 STONE E.O.
"ADMINISTRATIVE INTEGRATION."
ANN. ACAD. POL. SOC. SCI., 292 (MAR. 54), 111-119.
INTEGRATION (CENTRALIZATION) OF THE BUREAUCRACY IS
BENEFICIAL TO PUBLIC INTEREST, AND PROGRESS HAS BEEN MADE,
BUT IT BECOMES HARDER AS SIZE OF BUREAUCRACY INCREASES.
ALSO PRIVATE INTEREST GROUPS OPPOSE INTEGRATION.

2047 STONE J.
QUEST FOR SURVIVAL.
CAMBRIDGE: HARVARD U. PR., 1961, 104 PP.
EVALUATES FEASIBILITY OF RULE OF LAW IN ARBITRATION OF
INTERNATIONAL DISPUTES, OUTLINING OBSTACLES TO THIRD-PARTY
SETTLEMENT. SURVEYS SCOPE AND ENFORCEMENT OF INTERNATIONAL
LAW. DEMONSTRATES FALLACIES OF CURRENT THOUGHT ON WORLD
PROBLEMS.

2048 STONE P.A.
"DECISION TECHNIQUES FOR TOWN DEVELOPMENT."
OPERATIONAL RESEARCH Q., 15 (SEPT. 64), 185-205.
QUANTITATIVE ANALYSIS OF CONSEQUENCES OF TOWN DEVELOPMENT
WITH PURPOSE OF REDUCING MASS OF PROBLEMS TO COMPREHENSIBLE
STATISTICS. DRAWS DISTINCTION BETWEEN COST-BENEFIT ANALYSIS,
COST-BENEFIT CRITERIA AND COSTS-IN-USE CRITERIA. CONTENDS
CONSEQUENCES CAN ONLY BE MEASURED BY TRACING THEIR INCIDENCE
BEYOND EFFECTS ON MARKET AND LOOKING AT THEIR TOTAL SOCIO-
ECONOMIC IMPACT BY EVALUATING THEIR COSTS AND BENEFITS.

2049 STOUT H.M.
BRITISH GOVERNMENT.
NEW YORK: OXFORD U PR, 1953, 433 PP., LC#52-14156.
DESCRIPTION OF THE PRESENT-DAY STRUCTURE AND PRACTICE
OF BRITISH GOVERNMENT, INTENDED FOR AMERICAN STUDENTS. EXAM-
INES THE GOVERNMENT IN LIGHT OF POSTWAR DEVELOPMENTS - NEW
ELECTIONS, EXPANSION OF GOVERNMENTAL FUNCTIONS UNDER THE
WELFARE STATE CONCEPT, NEW COMMONWEALTH RELATIONS, ETC. DIS-
CUSSES THE CONSTITUTION AND CONSTITUTIONAL RIGHTS, STRUCTURE
OF THE PRINCIPAL INSTITUTIONS, AND POLICY FORMATION.

2050 STOWELL E.C.
INTERVENTION IN INTERNATIONAL LAW.
WASHINGTON: BYRNE, 1921, 558 PP.
SETS FORTH THE OCCASIONS WHEN A STATE, THREATENED BY A-
NOTHER NATION, IS JUSTIFIED IN USING FORCE TO INFLUENCE THE
OTHER'S CONDUCT. ANALYZES INTERNATIONAL POLICE REGULATIONS,
SURVEYS POLITICAL REASONS FOR VIOLATION OF SOVEREIGNTY,
POINTS OUT PROBLEM OF BALANCE OF POWER.

2051 STRAUSS E.
THE RULING SERVANTS.
NEW YORK: PRAEGER, 1961, 307 PP.
DEALS WITH PROBLEM OF GROWTH OF POWERFUL BUREAUCRACIES IN
MODERN SOCIETY. ANALYZES GENERAL CAUSES OF THIS GROWTH AND
RESULTS OF THE TREND. SPECIFICALLY CONSIDERS FRENCH, RUSSIAN
AND BRITISH BUREAUCRACIES.

2052 STREET D., VINTER R.D., PERROW C.
ORGANIZATION FOR TREATMENT.
NEW YORK: FREE PRESS OF GLENCOE, 1966, 330 PP., LC#66-17696.
COMPARATIVE STUDY OF SIX INSTITUTIONS FOR MALE
DELINQUENTS, DEALING WITH ADMINISTRATIVE STRATEGY, GOALS
AND THEIR EFFECTS ON INMATE SOCIAL SYSTEMS AND REHABILITA-
TION POLICIES. POWER DISTRIBUTION, ORGANIZATION STRUCTURE,
ROLES, CONFLICT, AND PERSPECTIVES AS WELL AS SOCIAL CONTROLS
ARE EXAMINED FROM BOTH INMATE AND STAFF POINT OF VIEW.
CONTAINS VALUABLE BIBLIOGRAPHY AND REFERENCES.

2053 SUBRAMANIAM V.
"REPRESENTATIVE BUREAUCRACY: A REASSESSMENT."
AM. POL. SCI. REV., (FALL 67), 1010-1019.
DISCUSSES TERM "REPRESENTATIVE BUREAUCRACY" AND NATURE
AND DESIRABILITY OF SYSTEM IT IMPLIES. SAYS TERM REFERS TO
CIVIL SERVICE IN WHICH RATIO OF UPPER, MIDDLE, LOWER CLASS
EMPLOYEES IS SAME AS CLASS RATIO OF POPULATION; IN FACT,

MOST CIVIL SERVICES ARE RUN BY MIDDLE CLASS, AND ARE REP-
RESENTATIVE ONLY IN MIDDLE-CLASS NATIONS LIKE US. DOUBTS AD-
VANTAGES OF REPRESENTATIVE BUREAUCRACY, WERE IT FEASIBLE.

2054 SULLIVAN G.
THE STORY OF THE PEACE CORPS.
NEW YORK: FLEET, 1964, 156 PP.
DISCUSSES HISTORY AND ORGANIZATION OF PEACE CORPS, WITH
EMPHASIS ON PROJECTS AND PROGRAMS.

2055 SURRENCY E.C., FELD B., CREA J.
A GUIDE TO LEGAL RESEARCH.
NEW YORK: OCEANA PUBLISHING, 1959, 124 PP.
DISCUSSES METHODS OF LEGAL RESEARCH UNDER SEPARATE CHAP-
TERS ACCORDING TO TYPE OF LAW BOOKS: RESEARCH IN STATE
STATUTORY LAW, STATE DECISIONAL LAW, FEDERAL LAW, FEDERAL
ADMINISTRATIVE LAW. MENTIONS MAJOR SOURCES WHICH MIGHT BE
CONSULTED AND INCLUDES SAMPLE PAGES FROM MANY VOLUMES DIS-
CUSSED.

2056 SUTHERLAND G.
CONSTITUTIONAL POWER AND WORLD AFFAIRS.
NEW YORK: COLUMBIA U. PR., 1919, 202 PP.
DEALS WITH WORLD WAR ONE AND ITS EFFECTS ON AMERICAN FO-
REIGN RELATIONS. DEPICTS NATURE OF INTERNAL AND EXTERNAL
POWERS OF THE NATIONAL GOVERNMENT. SURVEYS THE POLITICAL
DIVISION BETWEEN PRESIDENT AND CONGRESS. CALLS FOR A LIBERAL
CONSTITUTIONAL CONSTRUCTION IN EXTERNAL AFFAIRS.

2057 SUTTON F.X.
"REPRESENTATION AND THE NATURE OF POLITICAL SYSTEMS."
COMP. STUD. SOC. HIST., 2 (OCT. 59), 1-10.
TRACES DEVELOPMENT OF POLITICAL REPRESENTATION FROM
PRIMITIVE SOCIETY TO MODERN INDUSTRIAL SOCIETY. ALSO
DIFFERENTIATES BETWEEN THAT WHICH IS REPRESENTATIVE ACTION
AND THAT WHICH IS AUTONOMOUS ACTIVITY OF INDIVIDUALS IN
COLLECTIVITY.

2058 SWEARER H.R.
"AFTER KHRUSHCHEV: WHAT NEXT."
CURR. HIST., 47 (NOV. 64), 257-265.
THE PARTY WILL DETERMINE OUTCOME OF ANY LEADERSHIP
STRUGGLE. SECRETARIAT WAS LAUNCHING PAD FOR STALIN AND
KHRUSHCHEV. POSSIBLE HEIRS TO KHRUSHCHEV'S POST LISTED.

2059 SWEENEY S.B. ED., DAVY T.J.
EDUCATION FOR ADMINISTRATIVE CAREERS IN GOVERNMENT SERVICE.
PHILA: U OF PENN PR, 1958, 366 PP., LC#58-12719.
RESULTS OF RESEARCH-CONFERENCE PROGRAM CONDUCTED 1956-57
TO DETERMINE BEST TRAINING FOR ADMINISTRATIVE CAREERS IN
LOCAL AND STATE GOVERNMENT. DEFINES ADMINISTRATIVE POLICY-
MAKING OFFICER AND EXAMINES TRENDS IN OFFICER EDUCATION.
PRESENTS DESIRABLE EDUCATION PROGRAM FOR UNDERGRADUATE AND
GRADUATE LEVELS.

2060 SWEENEY S.B. ED., CHARLESWORTH J.C. ED.
ACHIEVING EXCELLENCE IN PUBLIC SERVICE.
PHILA: AMER ACAD POL & SOC SCI, 1963, 209 PP.
ATTEMPTS TO CALL ATTENTION TO LAG BETWEEN NEEDS OF
PUBLIC ADMINISTION AND QUALITY OF ITS PERSONNEL. URGES
NEW ACTION PROGRAMS AND ARTICLES ON GOVERNMENT SYSTEM.
DISCUSSES KINDS OF PEOPLE NEEDED, PRESENT INADEQUACIES, AND
FUTURE PROGRAMS.

2061 SWENSON R.J.
FEDERAL ADMINISTRATIVE LAW: A STUDY OF THE GROWTH, NATURE,
AND CONTROL OF ADMINISTRATIVE ACTION.
NEW YORK: RONALD PRESS, 1952, 376 PP., LC#52-9466.
DISCUSSES RISE OF ADMINISTRATIVE LAW, JUDICIAL AND LEGIS-
LATIVE CONTROL OF ADMINISTRATIVE PROCESS, AND TRANSFORMATION
OF PUBLIC IDEOLOGY FROM "RUGGED INDIVIDUALISM" TO MODERN
"SERVICE STATE."

2062 SWERDLOW I. ED.
DEVELOPMENT ADMINISTRATION: CONCEPTS AND PROBLEMS.
SYRACUSE: U. PR., 1963, $3.95.
ESSAYS ON MAJOR PROBLEMS OF PUBLIC ADMINISTRATION IN
NEW AND DEVELOPING COUNTRIES. DEMONSTRATES THAT POOR
COUNTRIES HAVE SPECIAL CHARACTERISTICS THAT TEND TO CREATE
A DIFFERENT ROLE FOR GOVERNMENT.

2063 SWISHER C.B.
THE THEORY AND PRACTICE OF AMERICAN NATIONAL GOVERNMENT.
BOSTON: HOUGHTON MIFFLIN, 1951, 949 PP.
EXAMINES AMERICAN POLITICS, LAW, AND ADMINISTRATION IN
ACTION, AS WELL AS THE MACHINERY AND THE THEORY OF GOVERN-
MENT. SURVEYS FEDERAL AND STATE PROCESSES, AND FOREIGN
RELATIONS IN WAR AND IN PEACE. CONCLUDES WITH QUESTIONS
OF LIBERTY AND WORLD PEACE IN A WORLD WITH CONFLICTING
CULTURES; UPHOLDS THE BASIC PRINCIPLES OF AMERICAN
DEMOCRACY.

2064 SYMONDS R.
"REFLECTIONS IN LOCALISATION."
J. COMMONWEALTH POLIT. STUD., 2 (NOV. 64), 219-234.
STUDIES THE TRANSFER OF ADMINISTRATIVE POWER IN FORMER
BRITISH COLONIES BY WHICH NATIONALS REPLACED EXPATRIATES.
BRITISH POLICY IS COMPARED IN EACH COLONY AS TO DEGREE OF
EDUCATION, POLITICAL AWARENESS AND ADMINISTRATIVE TRAINING
ACHIEVED.

2065 SZLADITS C.
BIBLIOGRAPHY ON FOREIGN AND COMPARATIVE LAW: BOOKS AND
ARTICLES IN ENGLISH (SUPPLEMENT 1962)
NEW YORK: OCEANA PUBLISHING, 1964, 134 PP., LC#55-11076.
ANNOTATES AND LISTS 3,431 ITEMS ARRANGED TOPICALLY;
BOOKS, ARTICLES, PAMPHLETS, SERIALS, DOCUMENTS, ETC.,
PERTINENT TO COMPARATIVE LAW, PUBLIC LAW, INTERNATIONAL LAW,
COMMERCIAL LAW, CRIMINAL LAW, AND PRIVATE LAW. INCLUDES
BIBLIOGRAPHIES, REFERENCES, LISTS OF INSTITUTIONS OF
COMPARATIVE LAW, ETC.

2066 SZLADITS C.
A BIBLIOGRAPHY ON FOREIGN AND COMPARATIVE LAW (SUPPLEMENT
1964)
NEW YORK: OCEANA PUBLISHING, 1966, 119 PP., LC#55-11076.
ANNOTATED BIBLIOGRAPHY ON BOOKS AND ARTICLES IN ENGLISH
FROM 1960-66. SOURCES ON COMPARATIVE LAW, GENERAL WORKS,
PRIVATE LAW, COMMERCIAL LAW, LABOR LAW, LAW OF PROCEDURE,
CRIMINAL LAW, CRIMINAL PROCEDURE, PUBLIC LAW, AND PRIVATE
INTERNATIONAL LAW. PUBLISHED FOR PARKER SCHOOL OF FOREIGN
AND COMPARATIVE LAW, COLUMBIA UNIVERSITY.

2067 TABORSKY E.
"CHANGE IN CZECHOSLOVAKIA."
CURR. HIST., 48 (MAR. 65), 168-174.
LIBERAL TRENDS PERMEATING INTELLECTUAL SCENE HAVE NOT YET
FOUND WAY INTO ACTUAL POLITICAL PRACTICE WHICH REMAINS AS
RIGID AND TOTALITARIAN AS EVER. GOVERNMENT FOUND DEFERRING
FAITHFULLY TO SOVIET LINE IN ALL SIGNIFICANT MATTERS OF
COMMUNIST POLICY AND STRATEGY.

2068 TACHERON D.G., UDALL M.K.
"THE JOB OF THE CONGRESSMAN: AN INTRODUCTION TO SERVICES IN
THE US HOUSE OF REPRESENTATIVES."
INDIANAPOLIS: BOBBS-MERRILL, 1966.
PROVIDES BASIC INFORMATION ABOUT OPERATING PROBLEMS OF
PARTICULAR CONCERN TO NEWLY ELECTED CONGRESSMAN. INCLUDES
PROCEDURAL INSTRUCTIONS ON SETTING UP AND MANAGING A CON-
GRESSIONAL OFFICE, CONDUCTING LEGISLATIVE BUSINESS, AND
SERVING A CONSTITUENCY. BIBLIOGRAPHY CONTAINS A COMPREHEN-
SIVE LISTING OF MAJOR WORKS ON CONGRESSIONAL FUNCTIONS AND
OPERATIONS IN THE 1960'S; MODERN CRITICAL WORKS INCLUDED.

2069 TACKABERRY R.B.
"ORGANIZING AND TRAINING PEACE-KEEPING FORCES: THE CANADIAN
VIEW."
INTERNATIONAL JOURNAL, 22 (SPRING 67), 195-209.
OUTLINES MILITARY TRAINING PROCEDURE OF CANADIAN ARMED
FORCES WHICH HAVE CONTRIBUTED TO THEIR SUCCESS IN PEACE-
KEEPING OPERATIONS. ADVOCATES SIMILAR ORGANIZING AND TRAIN-
ING OF UN FORCES. CALLS FOR UN COMMITTEE TO PLAN AND ES-
TABLISH PERMANENT PEACE-KEEPING FORCES.

2070 TAMBIAH S.J.
"THE POLITICS OF LANGUAGE IN INDIA AND CEYLON."
MODERN ASIAN STUDIES, 1 (JULY 67), 215-240.
ARGUES THAT LANGUAGE PLAYS TREMENDOUS ROLE IN POLITICS
IN INDIA AND CEYLON, BOTH IN PARTY AND ADMINISTRATIVE ROLES
STATES THAT MAJOR PROBLEM IS THE FIGHTING OF MODERN BATTLES
WITH TRADITIONALISTIC SLOGANS AND REVIVALISTIC DOGMA.

2071 TANG P.S.H.
"COMMUNIST CHINA TODAY: DOMESTIC AND FOREIGN POLICIES."
NEW YORK: FREDERICK PRAEGER, 1957.
ANALYSIS OF INTERNATIONAL COMMUNISM AND ITS MANIFESTA-
TIONS AND OPERATIONS ON THE CHINESE MAINLAND. INTERPRETATION
OF COMMUNISM IN ACTION IN CHINA AND PEKING'S ROLE IN THE
MOSCOW-PEKING AXIS AND ITS IMPACT ON FREE WORLD. CHARTS AND
TABLES INCLUDED TO CLARIFY ORGANIZATIONAL COMPLEXITIES OF
PARTY AND STATE STRUCTURE. VOLUME II IS A DOCUMENTARY AND
CHRONOLOGICAL INDEX. SELECT BIBLIOGRAPHY OF BOOKS.

2072 TANNENBAUM A.S.
"CONTROL AND EFFECTIVENESS IN A VOLUNTARY ORGANIZATION."
AMER. J. OF SOCIOLOGY, 67 (JULY 61), 33-46.
FROM THE RELATIVELY AUTONOMOUS LOCAL LEAGUES WITHIN US
LEAGUE OF WOMEN VOTERS, A PROBABILITY SAMPLE WAS TAKEN
TO TEST TWO HYPOTHESES CONCERNING THE CAUSES AND EFFECTS OF
VARYING PATTERNS OF CONTROL IN ORGANIZATIONS. THE HYPOTHESES
STATE THAT THE EFFECTIVENESS OF THE LOCAL LEAGUE WILL VARY
DIRECTLY WITH THE AVERAGE POSITIVE SLOPE AND THE HEIGHT OF
THE LOCAL LEAGUE'S CONTROL CURVES. DATA SUPPORTS HYPOTHESES.

2073 TANNENBAUM A.S.
"CONTROL IN ORGANIZATIONS: INDIVIDUAL ADJUSTMENT AND
ORGANIZATIONAL PERFORMANCE."
ADMINISTRATIVE SCI. Q., 7 (SEPT. 62), 236-257.
A SYNTHESIS OF RECENT RESEARCH. SOME EVIDENCE SUGGESTS
THAT INCREASED CONTROL EXERCISED BY ALL LEVELS OF THE
ORGANIZATION HIERARCHY IS ASSOCIATED WITH INCREASED
ORGANIZATIONAL EFFECTIVENESS. HOWEVER, A RELATIVELY HIGH

LEVEL OF TOTAL CONTROL "MAY REFLECT INCREASED PARTICIPATION
AND MUTUAL INFLUENCE THROUGHOUT THE ORGANIZATION AND A
GREATER DEGREE OF INTEGRATION OF ALL MEMBERS."

2074 TANNENBAUM R., MASSARIK F.
"PARTICIPATION BY SUBORDINATES IN THE MANAGERIAL DECISION-
MAKING PROCESS" (BMR)"
CAN. J. OF ECO. AND POL. SCI., 16 (AUG. 50), 408-418.
DISCUSSES ROLE OF "PARTICIPATION" BY INDIVIDUALS OR
GROUPS IN INDUSTRIAL ORGANIZATIONS. ATTEMPTS TO DEVELOP AN
OPERATIONAL DEFINITION OF THE CONCEPT AND A PRECISE SET OF
HYPOTHESES REGARDING ITS DYNAMICS. ANALYZES POSSIBLE
ADVANTAGES OF PARTICIPATION AS A MANAGERIAL DEVICE. TREATS
THE PSYCHOLOGICAL AND EXTRA-PARTICIPATIONAL CONDITIONS FOR
EFFECTIVE PARTICIPATION.

2075 TANNENBAUM R., ET A.L.
LEADERSHIP AND ORGANIZATION.
NEW YORK: MCGRAW HILL, 1961, 480 PP., LC#60-14804.
PRODUCED BY UCLA HUMAN RELATIONS RESEARCH GROUP.
PRESENTS MATERIALS ON THEORIES OF LEADERSHIP, "SENSITIVITY
TRAINING," WITH METHODOLOGICAL AND CONCEPTUAL EMPHASIS. A
HEAVY SUMMARY OF A HEAVILY RESEARCHED FIELD THAT WILL NEVER
BOW TO SUCCINCT EFFECTIVE STATEMENT. DOES CONTAIN RELEVANT
STATEMENTS ON EMPATHY, PARTICIPATION OF SUBORDINATES,
MANAGERIAL DECISION-MAKING, AND BUREAUCRACY.

2076 TANSKY L.
US AND USSR AID TO DEVELOPING COUNTRIES.
NEW YORK: FREDERICK PRAEGER, 1966, 192 PP., LC#66-26574.
COMPARES ALL AREAS OF RUSSIAN AND US FOREIGN AID: MAGNI-
TUDE AND GEOGRAPHIC DISTRIBUTION, OBJECTIVES, FINANCIAL DIS-
TRIBUTION METHODS, CREDIT SYSTEMS. CASE STUDIES OF TURKEY,
INDIA, AND UAR SHOW DIFFERENCES IN METHODS, IMPACT, AND EF-
FECT. DISCUSSES TRENDS OF AID PROGRAMS IN BOTH COUNTRIES.

2077 TANZER L. ED.
THE KENNEDY CIRCLE.
NEW YORK: VAN REES PRESS, 1961, 315 PP., LC#61-14134.
PROFILES OF KENNEDY AND HIS ADMINISTRATION. FOURTEEN RE-
PORTERS DISCUSS JFK, HIS CABINET, AND ADVISERS. SOME OF
THOSE DISCUSSED ARE SORENSEN, BUNDY, SALINGER, RUSK, DILLON,
MCNAMARA, RFK, FREEMAN, GOLDBERG, RIBICOFF, AND UDALL.
EMPHASIZES THE PROCESSES AND IN-GROUP BEHAVIOR OF THE
EXECUTIVE ESTABLISHMENT.

2078 TAPPAN P.W.
DELINQUENT GIRLS IN COURT.
NEW YORK: COLUMBIA U PRESS, 1947, 249 PP.
STUDIES FUNCTIONS AND PROCESSES OF WAYWARD MINORS COURT
IN NYC. ATTEMPTING TO TAKE PREVENTATIVE AS WELL AS PUNITIVE
ACTION, THIS COURT STRIVES TO TREAT CASES INDIVIDUALLY IN
ORDER TO PREVENT OFFENDERS FROM JOINING, OR BEING FORCED
INTO, DELINQUENT SUBCULTURE. DESCRIBES LEGAL AND SOCIAL OB-
JECTIVES, FACILITIES, PERSONNEL, AND ADMINISTRATIVE PRAC-
TICES OF THE COURTS.

2079 TARKOWSKI Z.M., TURNBULL A.V.
"SCIENTISTS VERSUS ADMINISTRATORS: AN APPROACH TOWARD
ACHIEVING GREATER UNDERSTANDING."
PUBLIC ADMINISTRATION, 37 (SUMMER 59), 213-259.
IN BRITISH GOVERNMENT, SCIENTISTS TEND TO PURSUE OWN
GOALS WHILE ADMINISTRATORS ARE MORE LOYAL TO THEIR
ORGANIZATION AND MORE RESPONSIVE TO PARLIAMENT: THERE IS
MUCH FRICTION BETWEEN THE TWO GROUPS. ARTICLE SUGGESTS
WAYS OF IMPROVING COMMUNICATIONS BETWEEN THE TWO GROUPS.

2080 TARLING N.
"A CONCISE HISTORY OF SOUTHEAST ASIA."
NEW YORK: FREDERICK PRAEGER, 1966.
A HISTORY OF SOUTHEAST ASIA FROM VIEWPOINT OF AUSTRAL-
ASIAN HISTORIAN. ATTEMPTS TO PROVIDE FRAMEWORK FOR APPRAIS-
ING INTERACTION OF EXTERNAL INFLUENCES AND GIVEN CONDITIONS
OF SOUTHEAST ASIAN FRONTIER AREA. TRACES HISTORY OF AREA
FROM 13TH CENTURY TO 1965; EMPHASIS ON INDIVIDUAL COUN-
TRIES SINCE 1942. BIBLIOGRAPHICAL APPENDIX OF WORKS IN ENG-
LISH PUBLISHED SINCE 1922; CONCENTRATION ON RECENT WORKS.

2081 TATOMIR N.
"ORGANIZATIA INTERNATIONALA A MUNCII: ASPECTE NOI ALE PRO-
BLEMEI IMBUNATATIRII MECANISMULUI EI."
ANNU. STIINT. UNIV. IASI, STIINT. SOC., 8 (62), 133-43.
OUTLINES HISTORY OF OIT AND EXAMINES ITS STRUCTURE. IN-
DICATES AREAS NEEDING REFORMS. STATES THAT COMPOSITION OF
ITS ORGANS BEARS NO RELATION TO REALITIES OF CONTEMPORARY
WORLD.

2082 TATU M.
"URSS: LES FLOTTEMENTS DE LA DIRECTION COLLEGIALE."
REALITES, (NOV. 67), 62-65.
ANALYZES SOVIET POLICY ERRORS. BELIEVES THAT SOVIET IN-
VOLVEMENT IN ARAB-ISRAELI CRISIS WAS A MISTAKE, THAT ITS
POLICY WAS IMPROVISED, IRRESPONSIBLE, AND FACILE. KHRUSH-
CHEV MADE ERRORS IN HIS CALCULATIONS, BUT SOVIET LEADERS
TODAY ARE CHARACTERIZED BY A COLLECTIVE PARALYSIS IN
DECISION-MAKING. BREZHNEV HAS CONSIDERED YOUNGER LEADERS

WITH IDEAS OF REFORM A THREAT TO HIM.

2083 TAUBENFELD H.J.
"OUTER SPACE--PAST POLITICS AND FUTURE POLICY."
PROC. AMER. SOC. INT. LAW., 55 (APR. 61), 176-89.
OUTLINES THE INHERENT DANGER OF NUCLEAR POWERS USING
SPACE AS A HIGHWAY FOR DESTRUCTIVE MECHANISMS. SPECULATES
THAT LIMITED CONFLICTS ARISING IN THE FUTURE IN OUTER
SPACE MAY BE EXTENDED. ADVOCATES ATTAINMENT OF SPECIFIC REG-
ULATIONS WITHIN LEGISLATIVE AND ENFORCEMENT FRAMEWORK OF
AN INTERNATIONAL COSMIC SURVEILLANCE AUTHORITY.

2084 TAYLOR D.
THE BRITISH IN AFRICA.
CHESTER SPRINGS: DUFOUR, 1962, 185 PP., LC#64-22679.
TRACES BRITISH COLONIALISM IN AFRICA FROM INCEPTION. SLA-
VERY, DOMINATION, "WHITE MAN'S BURDEN," ADMINISTRATION, ECO-
NOMIC POLICIES, AND PREPARATION FOR SOVEREIGNTY EXAMINED.
VIEWS LASTING EFFECT OF BRITAIN UPON POLITICAL, ECONOMIC,
AND CULTURAL PRACTICES.

2085 TAYLOR D.W., FAUST W.L.
"TWENTY QUESTIONS: EFFICIENCY IN PROBLEM SOLVING AS A
FUNCTION OF SIZE OF GROUP"
J. OF EXPER. PSYCH., 44 (NOV. 52), 360-368.
REPORTS EXPERIMENT USING "TWENTY QUESTIONS," STUDYING
RAPIDITY WITH WHICH SKILL INVOLVED IN GAME IS LEARNED,
VARIATION OF EFFICIENCY IN PROBLEM-SOLVING WITH GROUP SIZE,
AND RELATIVE RATES OF IMPROVEMENT IN INDIVIDUAL PERFORMANCE
WHEN PRACTICE WAS ALONE OR AS PART OF GROUP. PRIMARILY
GROUPS OF DIFFERENT SIZE PERFORMED EQUALLY WELL, AND BETTER
THAN INDIVIDUALS.

2086 TAYLOR H.
THE STATESMAN.
NEW YORK: MENTOR, 1958, 159 PP., $0.50.
FORERUNNER OF MODERN SUCCESS LITERATURE (WRITTEN IN 1836)
YET RELEVANT TO CONTEMPORARY POLITICS. 'BOLD VENTURE INTO
THE ART OF STRATEGY', BOOK COVERS SUCH TACTICS AS HOW TO:
MAKE A DECISION, NEGOTIATE A QUARREL, ADVANCE A REPUTATION,
AND CRITICIZE OFFICIALLY. CONCERNS THE CONSCIENCE OF A
STATESMAN, ETHICS OF POLITICS, AND 'EVLIS WHICH ENSUE FROM
MEN'S AUTHORITY BEING IN INVERSE RATIO OF THEIR ABILITIES.'

2087 TAYLOR J.K.L. ED.
ATTITUDES AND METHODS OF COMMUNICATION AND CONSULTATION BE-
TWEEN EMPLOYERS AND WORKERS AT INDIVIDUAL FIRM LEVEL.
PARIS: ORG FOR ECO COOP AND DEV, 1962, 121 PP.
PAPERS GIVEN AT INTERNATIONAL JOINT SEMINAR OF THE ORGAN-
IZATION FOR ECONOMIC COOPERATION AND DEVELOPMENT IN LONDON,
FEB. 26 TO MAR. 2, 1962, STUDYING COMMUNICATION SYSTEMS WITH
PURPOSES OF FURTHERING GENERAL WELFARE, USING WORKERS EFFI-
CIENTLY, AND REDUCING COSTS.

2088 TAYLOR M.G.
"THE ROLE OF THE MEDICAL PROFESSION IN THE FORMULATION AND
EXECUTION OF PUBLIC POLICY" (BMR)"
CAN. J. OF ECO. AND POL. SCI., 26 (FEB. 60), 108-127.
EXAMINES RELATION OF MEDICAL PROFESSION TO CANADIAN
GOVERNMENT. DISCUSSES ROLE OF PROFESSION AS SELF-GOVERNING
GROUP AND ITS RESISTANCE TO OUTSIDE CONTROL. TREATS CANADIAN
MEDICAL ASSOCIATION'S FUNCTION AS INTEREST OR PRESSURE
GROUP IN AREAS OF MEDICAL PRACTICES AND STANDARDS AND
ORGANIZING AND FINANCING OF MEDICAL SERVICES. REVEALS GROUP
INVOLVEMENT IN PUBLIC ADMINISTRATION IN SEVERAL AREAS.

2089 TAYLOR P.S.
"THE RELATION OF RESEARCH TO LEGISLATIVE AND ADMINISTRATIVE
DECISIONS."
J. SOCIAL ISSUES, 3 (FALL 57).
SOCIAL SCIENTISTS CONTRIBUTE TO INTELLIGENT POLITICAL
DECISIONS, BUT MUCH MUST STILL BE DONE TO UNDERSTAND DECI-
SION PROCESS, TO CLARIFY ISSUES, AND TO DEVELOP POLICY
ALTERNATIVES.

2090 TAYLOR R.W.
"ARTHUR F. BENTLEY'S POLITICAL SCIENCE" (BMR)"
WESTERN POLIT. QUART., 5 (JUNE 52), 214-230.
SUGGESTS HOW BENTLEY'S THEORY MAY PROVE USEFUL TO
POLITICAL SCIENCE. DISCUSSES BENTLEY'S APPROACH AS IT
APPEARED IN "THE PROCESS OF GOVERNMENT." ANALYZES CRITICISMS
OF THIS BOOK AND INDICATES IMPORTANT ISSUES RAISED BY HIS
THEORY. SHOWS HOW THEORY APPLIES TO VARIOUS CLASSIFICATIONS
USED IN DESCRIPTIONS OF THE POLICY-MAKING PROCESS.

2091 TERRIEN F.W., MILLS D.L.
"THE EFFECT OF CHANGING SIZE UPON THE INTERNAL STRUCTURE OF
ORGANIZATIONS" (BMR)"
AMER. SOCIOLOGICAL REV., 20 (FEB. 55), 11-13.
EXAMINES EFFECT OF SIZE OF ADMINISTRATIVE COMPONENTS UPON
NATURE OF INTRA-ORGANIZATIONAL STRUCTURE. MAINTAINS THAT THE
RELATIONSHIP IS SUCH THAT THE LARGER THE SIZE OF CONTAINING
ORGANIZATION THE GREATER WILL BE THE PROPORTION GIVEN OVER
TO ITS ADMINISTRATIVE COMPONENT.

2092 THARAMATHAJ C.

A STUDY OF THE COMPOSITION OF THE THAI CIVIL SERVICE (PAPER)
BANGKOK: THAMMASAT U. PUB. ADMIN., 1959, 85 PP.
DESCRIBES COMPOSITION OF THAI CIVIL SERVICE AND DRAWS
CONCLUSIONS AS TO SIZE, ROLE OF FEMALE EMPLOYEES,
RELATIONSHIP OF AREAS OF CIVIL SERVICE, AND SALARY.

2093 THAYER L.O.
ADMINISTRATIVE COMMUNICATION.
HOMEWOOD: RICHARD IRWIN, 1961, 344 PP., LC#61-6986.
DETAILED ANALYSIS OF FUNCTIONS, METHODS, AND ADMINISTRA-
TIVE PROBLEMS OF COMMUNICATIONS IN LARGE ORGANIZATIONS.
DESCRIBES COMMUNICATION AS PRIMARY ADMINISTRATIVE TOOL.
DISCUSSES BASIC CONCEPTS INTENDED AS PRACTICAL GUIDE FOR
ADMINISTRATORS AND STUDENTS.

2094 THE BRITISH COUNCIL
PUBLIC ADMINISTRATION: A SELECT LIST OF BOOKS AND PERIOD-
ICALS.
LONDON: LONGMANS, GREEN & CO, 1964, 120 PP.
UNANNOTATED LISTING OF 1,500 BOOKS AND PERIODICALS PRI-
MARILY AUTHORED BY COMMONWEALTH WRITERS ON ALL PHASES OF
PUBLIC ADMINISTRATION. TOPICAL LISTING OF ITEMS PUBLISHED
FROM 1870-1964, WITH EMPHASIS ON 1950'S AND 1960'S.
BIBLIOGRAPHIES AND YEARBOOKS ARE ALSO INCLUDED. WORKS CON-
CERNED WITH INDIGENOUS PUBLIC ADMINISTRATION.

2095 THE TAX FOUNDATION
STUDIES IN ECONOMY AND EFFICIENCY IN GOVERNMENT.
NEW YORK: TAX FOUNDATION, 1941, 89 PP.
UNANNOTATED BIBLIOGRAPHIC SURVEY OF RECENTLY COMPLETED
AND CURRENT STUDIES ON GOVERNMENT FINANCE AND PUBLIC ADMIN-
ISTRATION. STUDIES DIRECTLY RELATED TO TOPIC CLASSIFIED BY
STATE AND INSTITUTION AND THEN BY SUBJECT; INDIRECTLY RE-
LATED STUDIES CLASSIFIED ONLY BY STATE AND INSTITUTION.
NATION-WIDE IN SCOPE.

2096 THIERRY S.S.
LE VATICAN SECRET.
PARIS: CALMAN-LEVY, 1962, 233 PP.
DESCRIBES AND ANALYZES ADMINISTRATION AND DECISION-MAKING
PROCESS OF VATICAN CITY. TREATS DELIBERATIVE PROCESS AND
EXECUTIVE MANAGEMENT FROM HISTORICAL AND EVOLUTIONARY
PERSPECTIVE.

2097 THOENES P.
THE ELITE IN THE WELFARE STATE ,TRANS. BY J BINGHAM; ED. BY.
NEW YORK: FREE PRESS OF GLENCOE, 1966, 236 PP.
A DUTCH SOCIOLOGIST PROBES THE CONFLICT BETWEEN
UNDERLYING ASSUMPTIONS OF EQUALITY AND THE COMMON GOOD IN A
WELFARE STATE AND THE USE OF THIS STATE BY AN ELITE OF
TRAINED PERSONNEL TO EXECUTE POLICY AS AN ADMINISTRATIVE
TECHNOCRACY.

2098 THOMAS F.
THE ENVIRONMENTAL BASIS OF SOCIETY.
NEW YORK: CENTURY, 1925, 336 PP.
STUDY PRESENTS, IN APPROPRIATE HISTORICAL AND CULTURAL
SETTINGS, THEORIES THAT ATTEMPT TO EXPLAIN PHENOMENA OF IN-
DIVIDUAL AND SOCIAL LIFE IN TERMS OF GEOGRAPHIC ENVIRONMENT.

2099 THOMAS F.C. JR.
"THE PEACE CORPS IN MOROCCO."
MIDDLE EAST J., 19 (SUMMER 65), 273-283.
CRITIQUE OF FIRST PEACE CORPS MISSION TO MOROCCO BY ITS
DIRECTOR. NOTES PROBLEMS OF FITTING IDEALISTIC SELF-HELP-
ORIENTED PERSONNEL INTO PRE-EXISTING FORMALIZED FRENCH FOR-
EIGN AID TECHNICAL PROGRAMS. MORE GENERAL PROBLEMS OF DEVIS-
ING SUCCESSFUL PEACE CORPS PROGRAM ALSO DISCUSSED.

2100 THOMAS S.B.
GOVERNMENT AND ADMINISTRATION IN COMMUNIST CHINA (MONOGRAPH)
NEW YORK: INST OF PACIFIC RELNS, 1953, 150 PP.
RELATIVELY FORMALIST IN HISTORY AND ANALYSIS OF COMMUNIST
CHINESE GOVERNMENT, ITS RISE TO POWER, CLAIMS TO
FUNCTIONALLY REPRESENT ALL THE PEOPLE, BY SUBORDINATION TO
PARTY CONTROL.

2101 THOMETZ C.E.
THE DECISION-MAKERS: THE POWER STRUCTURE OF DALLAS.
DALLAS: SOUTHERN METHODIST U PR, 1963, 141 PP., LC#63-21184.
AN ATTEMPT TO FORM A THEORY OF COMMUNITY POWER USING THE
CITY OF DALLAS AS A TEST COMMUNITY. SEEKS TO DETERMINE WHO
THE DECISION-MAKERS ARE, HOW THEY OPERATE, WHO DIAGNOSES
PROBLEMS, AND WHO DECIDES WHEN AND IF THEY WILL BE FACED.

2102 THOMPSON H.C.
RHODESIA AND ITS GOVERNMENT.
LONDON: SMITH, ELDER & CO, 1898, 352 PP.
CALLS FOR MATURE, STERN, AND IMPECCABLY JUST IMPERIAL
POLICY IN AFRICA. BRITAIN MUST EXTEND HER SPHERE OF INFLU-
ENCE IN ORDER THAT NATIVES MAY PROSPER UNDER FAIR RULE.
CONCENTRATES ON POLICIES IN MASHONALAND.

2103 THOMPSON J.D.
"ORGANIZATIONAL MANAGEMENT OF CONFLICT" (BMR)"
ADMINISTRATIVE SCI. Q., 4 (MAR. 60), 389-409.

FOCUSES ON ORGANIZATION-WIDE MANAGEMENT OF CONFLICT.
SUGGESTS THAT CONFLICT GENERATED BY ADMINISTRATIVE
ALLOCATIONS IS ROOTED IN TECHNOLOGY AND CONTROLLED BY
STRUCTURE OF ORGANIZATION. DISCUSSES LATENT ROLE CONFLICT
AND CONFLICT OCCASIONED BY COMPETING PRESSURES ON MEMBERS.
ADVANCES PROPOSITIONS TO ILLUSTRATE THAT VARIOUS TYPES OF
ORGANIZATIONS HAVE DIFFERENT VULNERABILITIES AND DEFENSES.

2104 THOMPSON K.W.
"MORAL PURPOSE IN FOREIGN POLICY: REALITIES AND ILLUSIONS."
SOC. RES., 27 (AUTUMN 60), 261-276.
RAISES QUESTION OF POLITICS AND ETHICS. ANALYZES GOALS
AND PURPOSES OF BROADER INTERNATIONAL COMMUNITY IN THE FACE
OF HARSH REALITIES OF INTERNATIONAL POLITICS. CONSIDERS
LEGAL AND MORAL IMPLICATIONS REGARDING DELICATE SITUATIONS
LIKE U2. DISUSSES FUNDAMENTAL PROBLEMS OF POLICY COORDINA-
TION AND DECISION-MAKING IN FOREIGN AFFAIRS. QUESTIONS ROLE
OF PRIVATE CITIZEN IN VAST AND SPRAWLING POLITICAL SYSTEM.

2105 THOMPSON V.A.
MODERN ORGANIZATION.
NEW YORK: ALFRED KNOPF, 1961, 197 PP.
GENERAL WORK ON THE NATURE AND FORMS OF MODERN
BUREAUCRACY.

2106 THOMPSON V.A.
"HIERARACHY, SPECIALIZATION, AND ORGANIZATIONAL CONFLICT"
(BMR)"
ADMINISTRATIVE SCI. Q., 5 (MAR. 61), 485-521.
STATES THAT COMBINATION IN MODERN BUREAUCRACY OF
TECHNOLOGICAL SPECIALIZATION AND HIERARCHY HAS PRODUCED AN
ORGANIZATIONALLY DETERMINED PATTERN OF CONFLICT, WHICH
ULTIMATELY REFLECTS GROWING GAP BETWEEN AUTHORITY AND
PERCEPTIONS OF TECHNICAL NEEDS. DISCUSSES SPECIFIC CAUSES OF
INTRAORGANIZATIONAL CONFLICT.

2107 THOMPSON V.A.
"ADMINISTRATIVE OBJECTIVES FOR DEVELOPMENT ADMINISTRA-
TION."
ADMIN. SCI. QUART., 9 (JUNE 64), 91-108.
ADMINISTRATIVE PRACTICES AND PRINCIPLES OF THE WEST
HAVE DERIVED FROM PREOCCUPATION WITH CONTROL AND THEREFORE
HAVE LITTLE VALUE FOR DEVELOPMENT ADMINISTRATION IN UNDER-
DEVELOPED COUNTRIES WHERE THE NEED IS FOR AN ADOPTIVE
ADMINISTRATION, ONE THAT CAN INCORPORATE CONSTANT CHANGE.

2108 THORELLI H.B., GRAVES R.L., HOWELLS L.T.
INTOP: INTERNATIONAL OPERATIONS SIMULATION: PLAYER'S MANUAL.
NEW YORK: FREE PRESS OF GLENCOE, 1963, 58 PP., LC#63-13249.
PLAYER'S MANUAL FOR ONE OF THE FIRST MAJOR BUSINESS
SIMULATION EXERCISES ORIENTED TOWARD SPECIFIC PROBLEM OF
INTERNATIONAL AND OVERSEAS OPERATIONS; DESIGNED TO INCREASE
UNDERSTANDING OF PROBLEMS OF MULTINATIONAL CORPORATIONS AND
TO YIELD SUBSTANTIAL PAYOFF IN GENERAL MANAGEMENT TRAINING.

2109 THORNTON M.L.
OFFICIAL PUBLICATIONS OF THE COLONY AND STATE OF NORTH CARO-
LINA, 1749-1939.
PRINCETON* UNIV. REF. SYSTEM, 1954, 347 PP.
A BIBLIOGRAPHY AND CHECKLIST OF 4,143 PUBLICATIONS ISSUED
BY STATE-SUPPORTED DEPARTMENTS AND INSTITUTIONS OF NORTH
CAROLINA. NO DOCUMENTS PUBLISHED AFTER DECEMBER 1939 ARE
INCLUDED. ALPHABETICALLY ARRANGED.

2110 TILMAN R.O.
BUREAUCRATIC TRANSITION IN MALAYA.
DURHAM: DUKE U PR, 1964, 175 PP., LC#64-20418.
TRACES TRANSITIONAL PROCESS OF BUREAUCRACY IN MALAYA FROM
BEGINNING OF BRITISH COLONIALISM UNTIL CREATION OF
FEDERATION OF MALAYSIA IN 1963. DEMONSTRATES PROCESS OF
SYNTHESIS OF BRITISH SYSTEM AND SOUTHEAST ASIAN SOCIETY TO
CREATE VERY EFFICIENT, LARGELY INDIGENOUS, BUREAUCRACY.

2111 TINBERGEN J.
CENTRAL PLANNING.
NEW HAVEN: YALE U PR, 1964, 150 PP., LC#64-20938.
CENTRAL PLANNING IS A FEATURE OF EVERY INDUSTRIALIZED
STATE. PLANNING PROCESS CONFRONTS PROBLEMS OF CENTRALIZA-
TION OF DECISION-MAKING, OF DETERMINING THE ROLES OF INTER-
EST GROUPS IN DRAWING UP PLAN, OF UTILITY OF FORECASTS.
PRESENTS DATA ON PLANNING PROGRAMS COLLECTED BY QUESTION-
NAIRES TO WESTERN,, DEVELOPING, AND COMMUNIST NATIONS. POL-
ICY SHOULD BE CARRIED OUT PARTLY BY SUPERNATIONAL ORGANS.

2112 TIVEY L.
"THE POLITICAL CONSEQUENCES OF ECONOMIC PLANNING."
PARLIAMENTARY AFFAIRS, 20 (FALL 67), 297-314.
BELIEVES THAT POLITICAL VALUES IN ECONOMIC PLANNING HAVE
BEEN NEGLECTED. MAIN PROBLEM LIES WITH FACT THAT GOVERNMENT
HAS NEITHER CONTROL NOR PREROGATIVE OVER THE PRIME AGENTS OF
PRODUCTION. INTEREST GROUPS PLAY TOO GREAT A ROLE IN PLAN-
NING. BELIEVES THAT PRIMACY OF TRADITIONAL POLITICAL PROCESS
MUST BE MAINTAINED, AND THAT FINAL AUTHORITY ON ECONOMIC
PLANNING MATTERS MUST REST WITH GOVERNMENT.

2113 TOMA P.A.

THE POLITICS OF FOOD FOR PEACE; EXECUTIVE-LEGISLATIVE
INTERACTION.
TUCSON: U OF ARIZONA PR, 1967, 195 PP., LC#67-20091.
   DISCUSSES 1964 SWING IN CONGRESSIONAL ATTITUDES AWAY FROM
EXPANSION OF FOOD FOR PEACE PROGRAM. PRESENTS POSSIBLE
TRENDS IN US FOREIGN AID POLICY ON QUESTION OF FOOD AID.
INVESTIGATES LARGE GOVERNMENT SURPLUSES AND RISING WORLDWIDE
FOOD DEFICIT. ANALYZES CONGRESSIONAL DEBATE AND VOTING
PATTERNS TO DETERMINE FACTORS AFFECTING CONGRESSIONAL
DECISIONS AND RESULTS OF EXECUTIVE SUGGESTIONS ON POLICY.

2114 TOMASIC D.
"POLITICAL LEADERSHIP IN CONTEMPORARY POLAND."
J. HUM. RELAT., 9 (NO.2, 61), 191-206.
   ATTEMPTS TO SHOW WHICH CONDITIONS, CIRCUMSTANCES AND SOC-
IAL FORCES HAVE RESISTED SOVIETIZATION AND WHICH HAVE PRO-
MOTED IT IN CONTEMPORARY POLAND. ANALYZES BACKGROUNDS OF
POLISH LEADERS WITH RESPECT TO THEIR LIFE-LONG AFFILIATIONS
WITH COMMUNISM. APPRAISES INFLUENCE OF CHURCH, PARTY POWER
AND ORGANIZATION, GEOGRAPHIC HISTORY, AND CULTURE.

2115 TOMPKINS D.C.
CIVIL DEFENSE IN THE STATES: A BIBLIOGRAPHY (DEFENSE
BIBLIOGRAPHIES NO. 3; PAMPHLET)
BERKELEY: U CALIF. BUR PUB ADMIN, 1953, 56 PP., LC#53-62488.
   LISTING OF CURRENT LITERATURE AND BACKGROUND OF DOMESTIC
ASPECTS OF NATIONAL DEFENSE AND WAR ADMINISTRATION. CONTAINS
MATERIAL ON FEDERAL CIVIL DEFENSE ADMINISTRATION; STATE
CIVIL DEFENSE PROGRAMS AND LEGISLATION; MUTUAL AID; WORK-
MAN'S COMPENSATION FOR VOLUNTEERS. INCLUDES SELECTED
BIBLIOGRAPHY ON STATE CIVIL DEFENSE.

2116 TOMPKINS D.C.
STATE GOVERNMENT AND ADMINISTRATION: A BIBLIOGRAPHY.
BERKELEY: U CALIF. BUR PUB ADMIN, 1954, 269 PP.
   GUIDE TO PRIMARY SOURCES OF IMFORMATION WHICH ARE BASIC
TO A STUDY OF STATE GOVERNMENT AND ADMINISTRATION. DRAWS
ON MATERIALS ISSUED SINCE 1930. ANNOTATIONS CLARIFY
OBSCURE TITLES OR INDICATE CONTENT. CONTAINS AUTHOR AND
SUBJECT INDEX. SECOND PART OF VOLUME IS DEVOTED TO LEGIS-
LATIVE PROCESS, WITH PARTICULAR REFERENCE TO ORGANIZATION
AND PROCEDURE OF LEGISLATIVE AND JUDICIAL ADMINISTRATION.

2117 TOMPKINS D.C.
CONFLICT OF INTEREST IN THE FEDERAL GOVERNMENT: A BIBLIOG-
RAPHY.
BERKELEY: U CALIF. BUR PUB ADMIN, 1961, 66 PP.
   BIBLIOGRAPHY OF CONFLICT OF INTEREST LAWS STRESSES THE
PERIOD SINCE 1950 AND INCLUDES EXPLANATORY AND SUPPLEMEN-
TARY TEXT WITH REFERENCES DRAWN FROM THE UNIVERSITY OF
CALIFORNIA LIBRARIES. DEALS WITH LAWS, PERSONS AFFECTED
AND EXEMPT, REGULATIONS OF EXECUTIVE EMPLOYEES' CONDUCT,
ROLE OF CONGRESS, THE SHERMAN ADAMS CASE, AND THE PRESI-
DENT'S 1961 PROGRAM.

2118 TOMPKINS D.C. ED.
PROBATION SINCE WORLD WAR II.
BERKELEY: U CAL, INST GOVT STUD, 1964, 311 PP.
   BIBLIOGRAPHY DEALING WITH PROBATION AND PAROLE, LISTED
TOPICALLY: PROBATION, ADMINISTRATION OF PROBATION SYMPTOMS,
FACTORS IN CORRECTIVE PROCESS, PROBATION OFFICERS, AND
PROBATIONERS. BOOKS, ARTICLES, JOURNALS, 1945-64, IN
ENGLISH.

2119 TORRE M.
"PSYCHIATRIC OBSERVATIONS OF INTERNATIONAL CONFERENCES."
INT. J. SOC. PSYCHIAT., 1(NO.3, 55), 48-53.
   BELIEVES A COMBINATION OF ALL SKILLS IS ESSENTIAL FOR
THE UNDERSTANDING AND OPERATION OF INTERNATIONAL CONFERENCES
AND THIS COMBINED SOCIAL SCIENCE APPROACH OFFERS GREATEST
PROMISE FOR DEVELOPMENT OF THE CONFERENCE IN FURTHERING
INTERNATIONAL COLLABORATION.

2120 TOTMAN C.
POLITICS IN THE TOKUGAWA BAKUFU, 1600-1843.
CAMBRIDGE: HARVARD U PR, 1967, 320 PP.
   DESCRIBES POLITICAL ORGANIZATION AND LEADERSHIP OF ADMIN-
ISTRATIVE STRUCTURE OF LEADING RULING FAMILY OF EARLY MODERN
JAPAN. COMPARISIONS O CONTEMPORARY INSTITUTIONS IN EUROPE
AND TO OTHER ASIAN POLITICAL SYSTEMS. TREATS EVOLUTION OF
SYSTEM.

2121 TOTOK W., WEITZEL R.
HANDBUCH DER BIBLIOGRAPHISCHEN NACHSCHLAGEWERKE.
FRANKFURT: V KLOSTERMANN, 1954, 258 PP.
   BIBLIOGRAPHY OF GERMAN BIBLIOGRAPHIES IN GENERAL
AND SPECIFIC SUBJECTS.

2122 TOTTEN G.O.
THE SOCIAL DEMOCRATIC MOVEMENT IN PREWAR JAPAN.
NEW HAVEN: YALE U PR, 1966, 455 PP., LC#66-12515.
   DISCUSSES THE RISE OF NON-COMMUNIST PROLETARIAN PARTIES
DURING THE 1920'S. CONSIDERS THE PROBLEM OF ORGANIZATION,
SINCE SOCIAL DEMOCRACY IMPLIED A LIMITING OF THE EMPEROR'S
POWER. FINDS THAT IT WAS TO GAIN THE EMPEROR'S SUPPORT THAT
THE SOCIAL DEMOCRATS SUPPORTED THE WAR IN MANCHURIA AT A
TIME WHEN THEY HAD THE MOST STRENGTH IN THE DIET AND THE
COUNTRY.

2123 TOURNELLE G.
"DIPLOMATIE D' HIER ET D'AUJOURD' HUI."
TABLE RONDE, 229 (FEB. 67), 7-23.
   A STUDY OF PAST AND PRESENT DIPLOMATIC AGENTS--THEIR ROLE
IN INFORMATION GATHERING AND NEGOTIATION, THE QUALITIES THEY
POSSESS AND THE ROLES THEY MUST FOLLOW. CONCLUDES THAT
WHILE CONDITIONS HAVE CHANGED WITH THE ADVENT OF MORE RAPID
COMMUNICATION, THE EVOLUTION OF INTERNATIONAL DIPLOMACY
ETC., THE GOAL, PEACE, REMAINS THE SAME.

2124 TOWSTER J.
POLITICAL POWER IN THE USSR: 1917-1947.
NEW YORK: OXFORD U PR, 1948, 443 PP.
   A STUDY OF THE DEVELOPMENT OF THEORY AND STRUCTURE OF THE
SOVIET GOVERNMENT. TRACES THE EVOLUTION OF BASIC CONCEPTS
OF STATE AND LAW, CONSTITUTION, CLASS, AND NATIONALITY.
DESCRIBES THE STRUCTURAL ARRANGEMENTS OF POWER AND THE
ROLE OF DIVERSE SOCIAL, POLITICAL, AND IDEOLOGICAL FORCES.
ANALYZES PAST AND PROSPECTIVE TRENDS IN TERMS OF AUTHORITY
AND LIBERTY, POLITICAL CONTROL, AND CAPACITY FOR CHANGE.

2125 TRAVERS H. JR.
"AN EXAMINATION OF THE CAB'S MERGER POLICY."
U. KANSAS LAW J., 15 (MAR. 67), 227-263.
   EXAMINES 3 RECENT CASES TO DETERMINE CAB'S POLICY AND
STANDARDS FOR DECISION REGARDING AIRLINE MERGERS. DISCUSSES
POLICY PRIOR TO 1938, CIVIL AERONAUTICS ACT, ECONOMIC DETER-
MINANTS OF POLICY, STRUCTURE OF AIRLINES INDUSTRY, COMPETI-
TION, IMPACT OF MERGERS, AND ANTI-MONOPOLY PROVISO. AUTHOR
PRESENTS IDEAS FOR REFORM.

2126 TRECKER H.B.
NEW UNDERSTANDING OF ADMINISTRATION.
NEW YORK: ASSOCIATION PRESS, 1961, 245 PP., LC#61-7111.
   WRITTEN FOR LEADERSHIP IN VOLUNTARY ASSOCIATIONS AND
COMMUNITY SERVICES, THIS BOOK DEALS WITH DECISION-MAKING IN
A DEMOCRATIC CONTEXT, THE ROLES AND RESPONSIBILITIES OF
ORGANIZATION PARTICIPANTS AND GROUP BEHAVIOR. CHAPTERS ON
IN-GROUP COMMUNICATION AND ON WORK WITH BOARDS, COMMITTEES,
AND MEMBERS ARE ESPECIALLY RELEVANT.

2127 TREITSCHKE H.
POLITICS.
NEW YORK: MACMILLAN, 1916, 1049 PP.
   TREATS THE NATURE AND SOCIAL FOUNDATIONS OF THE STATE.
ANALYZES SOME VARIETIES OF POLITICAL CONSTITUTIONS. CONSI-
DERS STATE'S INFLUENCE UPON RULERS AND RULED. POINTS OUT
GOVERNMENT FUNCTIONS IN RELATION TO INTERNATIONAL INTER-
COURSE.

2128 TREVELYAN G.M.
THE TWO-PARTY SYSTEM IN ENGLISH POLITICAL HISTORY
(PAMPHLET)
LONDON: OXFORD U PR, 1926, 27 PP.
   LECTURE ON HISTORY OF TWO-PARTY SYSTEM IN ENGLISH POLI-
TICS EXPLORES BOTH CONTINUITY OF PARTIES IN BRITISH HISTORY
BEFORE PRESENT CENTURY, AND BASIS FOR WHIG AND TORY POWER
THROUGH TWO CENTURIES.

2129 TRUMAN D.
"THE DOMESTIC POLITICS OF FOREIGN AID."
PROC. ACAD. POLIT. SCI., 27 (JAN. 62), 86-91.
   EXAMINES EFFECT OF FOREIGN AID POLICY ON DOMESTIC POLI-
TICS. STUDIES VOTING PATTERNS IN HOUSE OF REPRESENTATVES ON
FOREIGN AID. AID PROGRAM TARGET OF MOST CRITICISM, BUT
GENERALLY CONCEDED TO BE NESCESSARY AND BILLS ARE
PASSED BY CONGRESS.

2130 TRUMAN D.B.
"PUBLIC OPINION RESEARCH AS A TOOL OF PUBLIC ADMINISTRATION"
PUBLIC ADMIN. REV., 5 (WINTER 45).
   USES OF OPINION RESEARCH IN ADMINISTRATION FOR TESTING
HYPOTHESES, PRE-TESTING PROJECTED PROGRAMS, EVALUATING
ONGOING PROGRAMS, AND FACILITATING INFORMATIONAL ASPECTS OF
OPERATING POLICY. ACADEMIC ANALYSTS CAN USE OPINION RESEARCH
TO NARROW THE AREA OF UNSUPPORTED ASSUMPTIONS.

2131 TRUMAN D.B.
"THE GOVERNMENTAL PROCESS: POLITICAL INTERESTS AND PUBLIC
OPINION."
NEW YORK: ALFRED KNOPF, 1962.
   EXAMINES ROLE OF INTEREST GROUPS IN OPERATION OF COMPLEX
SOCIETY AND CIRCUMSTANCES OF THEIR INVOLVEMENT IN GOVERNING
PROCESS. INTRODUCES AND DEVELOPS IMPLICATIONS OF OVERLAP-
PING GROUP MEMBERSHIP. ANALYZES TACTICS OF INTEREST GROUPS
IN GOVERNMENTAL AREA AND THEIR DEPENDENCE UPON PUBLIC
OPINION AND PROPAGANDA TECHNIQUES. CONTAINS SHORT SELECT
BIBLIOGRAPHY.

2132 TSOU T.
AMERICA'S FAILURE IN CHINA, 1941-1950.
CHICAGO: U. CHI. PR., 1963, 696 PP., $12.50.
   ANALYZES AMERICA'S FOREIGN POLICY AND POINTS OUT WEAK-

NESSES AND INACTION WHICH LEAD TO THE CREATION OF ANIMOSITY
BETWEEN THE TWO NATIONS. CRITIQUE OF AMERICA'S LACK OF A
FAR-REACHING INTELLIGENT ASIAN POLICY DURING CHINA'S CRITI-
CAL YEARS.

2133 TSUJI K.
"THE CABINET, ADMINISTRATIVE ORGANIZATION, AND THE
BUREAUCRACY."
ANN. ACAD. POL. SOC. SCI., 308 (NOV. 56), 10-17.
DEVELOPMENT OF BUREAUCRATIC ORGANIZATION AND CONTROL OF
IT FROM MEIJI RESTORATION TO 1954. PRIME MINISTER AND DIET
TRADITIONALLY WEAK, BUT THERE IS CHANGE TOWARD GIVING BOTH
DIRECT CONTROL OVER BUREAUCRACY.

2134 TUCKER R.C.
THE SOVIET POLITICAL MIND.
NEW YORK: PRAEGER, 1963, 238 PP.
STUDY OF STALINISM AND OF POST-STALINIST CHANGES IN THE
USSR INCLUDING: THE POLITICS OF DE-STALINIZATION, STALIN AND
THE USES OF PSYCHOLOGY, AND STALINISM AND THE COLD WAR.

2135 TUCKER R.C.
THE SOVIET POLITICAL MIND.
NEW YORK: PRAEGER, 1963, 238 PP.
EXPLORES PATTERNS OF THOUGHT, WAYS OF PERCEIVING THE
WORLD, PSYCHOLOGICAL ATTITUDES, IDEOLOGICAL PREMISES AND
WORKING THEORIES. DISTINGUISHES RELATIONSHIP BETWEEN IDEOLO-
GY AND POLICY UNDER SOVIET-COMMUNIST SYSTEM. POINTS OUT
DISCREPANCY BETWEEN POLITICAL OUTLOOKS OF STATE AND
CITIZEN 'OFFICIAL RUSSIA AND POPULAR RUSSIA).

2136 TULLY A., BRITTEN M.
WHERE DID YOUR MONEY GO.
NEW YORK: SIMON AND SCHUSTER, 1964, 223 PP., LC#64-15351.
EXAMINES WASTE IN FOREIGN AID PROGRAM, FAILURES IN ADMIN-
ISTRATION, PLANNING, AND CONTROL. ANALYZES US FOREIGN AID
BY COUNTRY, REGION, CATEGORY AND EFFECTIVENESS. COMPARES US
AND SOVIET FOREIGN AID PROGRAMS AND THEIR RELATIVE
EFFECTIVENESS.

2137 TURNER F.C. JR.
"EXPERIMENT IN INTER-AMERICAN PEACE-KEEPING."
ARMY, 17 (JUNE 67), 34-39.
A BRIEF REPORT ON THE INTER-AMERICAN PEACE FORCE STA-
TIONED IN THE DOMINICAN REPUBLIC, 1965-66, WHICH VIEWS THIS
OPERATION AS SETTING A PRECEDENT FOR HEMISPHERIC COOPERATION
IN PEACEFUL SETTLEMENT OF DOMESTIC DISPUTES. SURVEYS THE
COMMAND STRUCTURE, GENERAL ORGANIZATION, AND LOGISTICS OF
THE IAPF, AND BRIEFLY NOTES SOME OF THE PROBLEMS ENCOUNTERED
IN THE OPERATION.

2138 TURNER H.A., VIEG J.A.
THE GOVERNMENT AND POLITICS OF CALIFORNIA (2ND ED.)
NEW YORK: MCGRAW HILL, 1964, 286 PP., LC#60-12784.
DELINEATES STATE AND LOCAL GOVERNMENTAL STRUCTURE AND
POLITICAL SYSTEM IN CALIFORNIA, EMPHASIZING ACTUAL FUNCTION-
ING OF GOVERNMENT; CRITICALLY MEASURES ITS EFFECTIVENESS
AGAINST HIGH STANDARDS.

2139 TURNER M.C. ED.
LIBROS EN VENTA EN HISPANOAMERICA Y ESPANA.
NEW YORK: RR BOWKER, 1964, 1891 PP.
EXTENSIVE LIST OF SPANISH-LANGUAGE BOOKS IN PRINT. DIVID-
ED INTO AUTHOR AND SUBJECT INDEXES.

2140 TURNER R.H.
"THE NAVY DISBURSING OFFICER AS A BUREAUCRAT" (BMR)"
AMER. SOCIOLOGICAL REV., 12 (JUNE 47), 342-348.
DESCRIBES SOCIOLOGICALLY RELEVANT INFLUENCES THAT BEAR
ON ONE BUREAUCRATIC OFFICER: THE NAVY DISBURSING OFFICER.
STATES THAT DURING WWII, CERTAIN INFLUENCES DIVERTED HIM
FROM FUNCTIONING AS AN IDEAL, TYPICAL BUREAUCRAT. HE
BEGAN TO FUNCTION IN A PERSONAL WAY, RELEGATING SYSTEMATIC,
BUREAUCRATIC RULES TO A SECONDARY ROLE.

2141 TYBOUT R.A.
ECONOMICS OF RESEARCH AND DEVELOPMENT.
COLUMBUS: OHIO STATE U PR, 1965, 458 PP., LC#65-18734.
TOPICS INCLUDE6 HISTORY OF SCIENCE, INDUSTRIAL R&D,
INTERNATIONAL ORGANIZATION, PUBLIC POLICY, MILITARY R&D,
INTERNATIONAL COLLABORATION, AND THE EMERGENT NATIONS.
RESULTS OF A CONFERENCE. INCLUDES COMMENTS ON PAPERS.

2142 U OF MICHIGAN LAW SCHOOL
ATOMS AND THE LAW.
ANN ARBOR: U OF MICH LAW SCHOOL, 1959, 1512 PP.
CONCERNS LEGAL PROBLEMS INVOLVED IN PEACEFUL USES OF
ATOMIC ENERGY. CONCENTRATES ON TORT LIABILITY FOR RADIATION
INJURIES, WORKMEN'S COMPENSATION, FEDERAL STATUTORY AND
ADMINISTRATIVE PROVISIONS REGULATING ATOMIC ACTIVITIES, AND
STATE REGULATION OF ATOMIC ENERGY. INCLUDES ESSAYS ON
INTERNATIONAL ASPECTS OF THE SUBJECT.

2143 UDY S.H. JR.
THE ORGANIZATION OF PRODUCTION IN NONINDUSTRIAL CULTURE.
PRINCETON: PRIN U, DEPT OF ECO, 1957, 300 PP.

COMPARATIVE ANALYSIS OF 320 NONINDUSTRIAL PRODUCTION
ORGANIZATIONS. TESTS HYPOTHESIS THAT NATURE OF THESE
ORGANIZATIONS IS DEFINED BY THE TECHNOLOGICAL PROCESS
EACH DIRECTS, BY ITS INSTITUTIONAL SETTING, AND BY THE
EFFECT UPON THE REWARD SYSTEM OF ALL THESE DETERMINING
FACTORS. THE EVIDENCE SUPPORTS THE HYPOTHESIS.

2144 UDY S.H. JR.
"'BUREAUCRACY' AND 'RATIONALITY' IN WEBER'S ORGANIZATION
THEORY: AN EMPIRICAL STUDY" (BMR)"
AMER. SOCIOLOGICAL REV., 24 (DEC. 59), 791-795.
REFORMULATES SEVEN OF MAX WEBER'S IDEAL-TYPICAL
SPECIFICATIONS FOR "RATIONAL BUREAUCRACY" INTO A SYSTEM OF
THREE "BUREAUCRATIC" AND FOUR "RATIONAL" VARIABLES. PROPOSES
THAT BUREAUCRATIC VARIABLES ARE POSITIVELY ASSOCIATED, AND
RATIONAL VARIABLES ARE POSITIVELY ASSOCIATED, BUT RATIONAL
VARIABLES ARE NEGATIVELY ASSOCIATED WITH BUREAUCRATIC
VARIABLES. DEVELOPS GENERAL ORGANIZATIONAL MODEL.

2145 ULAM A.B.
TITOISM AND THE COMINFORM.
CAMBRIDGE: HARVARD U. PR., 1952, 243 PP.
ANALYZES YUGOSLAV COMMUNIST PARTY IN COMPARISON WITH
OTHER COMMUNIST GOVERNMENTS. EVALUATES SOVIET-
YUGOSLAV DISPUTE. DISCUSSES COMINFORM AND 'PEOPLE'S
DEMOCRACIES'.

2146 UN DEPARTMENT PUBLIC INF
SELECTED BIBLIOGRAPHY OF THE SPECIALIZED AGENCIES RELATED
TO THE UNITED NATIONS (PAMPHLET)
NEW YORK: UNITED NATIONS, 1949, 28 PP.
INCLUDES OFFICIAL DOCUMENTS OF UN, SPECIALIZED AGENCIES,
PUBLICATIONS OF MEMBER GOVERNMENTS, AS WELL AS BOOKS,
PAMPHLETS, AND MAGAZINE ARTICLES. BASIC DOCUMENTS COVER
STRUCTURE, HISTORY OF ACTIVITIES, FUNCTIONS, AND PROGRAMS OF
SPECIALIZED AGENCIES TOGETHER WITH OFFICIAL RECORDS, PERIOD-
ICALS, AND SERIAL PUBLICATIONS ISSUED BY THEM. PERIOD REPRE-
SENTED IS 1945-JANUARY, 1949.

2147 UN ECAFE
ADMINISTRATIVE ASPECTS OF FAMILY PLANNING PROGRAMMES
(PAMPHLET)
NEW YORK: UNITED NATIONS, 1966, 64 PP.
REPORT OF MEETING OF ECAFE IN 1966 AIMED AT DISCUSSING
EXPERIENCES AND PROBLEMS IN ADMINISTERING POPULATION CONTROL
PROGRAMS. REPRESENTATIVES FROM 23 NATIONS TRIED TO
COLLABORATE ON REGIONAL PROGRAMS, GOVERNMENT ACTION, AND
NEED FOR INTERNATIONAL AID.

2148 UN ECONOMIC AND SOCIAL COUNCIL
BIBLIOGRAPHY OF PUBLICATIONS OF THE UN AND SPECIALIZED AGEN-
CIES IN THE SOCIAL WELFARE FIELD: 1946-1952.
NEW YORK: UNITED NATIONS, 1955, 270 PP.
SPECIAL ISSUE OF THE "SOCIAL WELFARE INFORMATION SERIES,"
DESIGNED FOR THOSE CONCERNED WITH SPECIFIC BRANCHES OF SO-
CIAL WELFARE. CLASSIFIES 704 ANNOTATED ENTRIES CONCERNING
INTERNATIONAL PROGRAMS, BIBLIOGRAPHIES, AND DIRECTORIES OF
ORGANIZATIONS DEALING WITH THE HANDICAPPED; FAMILY, YOUTH,
AND CHILD WELFARE; TRAINING FOR SOCIAL WORK; ETC. CONTAINS A
SUBJECT CLASSIFICATION OUTLINE AND A CUMULATIVE INDEX.

2149 UN HEADQUARTERS LIBRARY
BIBLIOGRAPHIE DE LA CHARTE DES NATIONS UNIES.
NEW YORK: UNITED NATIONS, 1955, 128 PP.
COMPILES, ANNOTATES, AND INDEXES 2,059 ITEMS (BOOKS, DOC-
UMENTS, ARTICLES, PAMPHLETS, ETC.) DEALING WITH, OR DEVOTED
TO, THE HISTORY, PRINCIPLES, PURPOSES, ORGANS, MEMBERSHIP,
AND ORGANIZATION OF THE UN, AS DEFINED BY ITS CHARTER AND
THE PROPOSALS, CONFERENCES, AND COMMITTEES PRECEDING ITS
DRAFTING. ARRANGED ACCORDING TO CHARTER PROVISIONS. IN
FRENCH.

2150 UN PUB. INFORM. ORGAN.
EVERY MAN'S UNITED NATIONS.
NEW YORK: UN, 1964, 593 PP.
COMPREHENSIVE ANALYSIS OF FUNCTIONS AND ACTIVITIES OF UN.
DESCRIBES THEIR PRINCIPAL ORGANS SUCH AS GENERAL ASSEMBLY,
SECURITY COUNCIL, AND INTERNATIONAL COURT OF JUSTICE.
FOCUSES ON QUESTIONS RELATED TO PROBLEMS OF INTERNATIONAL
SECURITY. INCLUDES LIST OF INTER-GOVERNMENTAL AGENCIES CON-
NECTED WITH UN ORGANIZATION.

2151 UN SECRETARY GENERAL
PLANNING FOR ECONOMIC DEVELOPMENT.
NEW YORK: UNITED NATIONS, 1963, 156 PP.
REPORTS ON ECONOMIC PLANNING AND TECHNIQUES USED IN
SEVERAL COUNTRIES. EXAMINES ORGANIZATION AND MANAGEMENT OF
PLANS, AS WELL AS NATIONAL AND INTERNATIONAL POLICIES.

2152 UNECA LIBRARY
NEW ACQUISITIONS IN THE UNECA LIBRARY.
NEW YORK: UNITED NATIONS, 1962.
PERIODICAL LISTING OF RECENT BOOKS, MONOGRAPHS, SERIAL
PUBLICATIONS AND PERIODICALS COVERING CURRENT SOCIAL, ECO-
NOMIC, CULTURAL, AND TECHNICAL PROBLEMS OF WORLD WITH SPE-
CIAL ATTENTION TO AFRICA AND DEVELOPING NATIONS. FIRST PUB-

LISHED 1962. ITEMS, IN ALL LANGUAGES, ARRANGED BY SUBJECT.

2153 UNESCO
INTERNATIONAL BIBLIOGRAPHY OF POLITICAL SCIENCE
(VOLUMES 1-8)
PARIS: UNESCO.
AN ANNUAL PUBLICATION IN THE SERIES OF THE GENERAL PRO-
GRAM FOR SOCIAL SCIENCE DOCUMENTATION. AN INTERNATIONAL CUR-
RENT BIBLIOGRAPHY CONTAINING BOOKS AND PERIODICAL ARTICLES
ARRANGED IN A CLASSIFIED SCHEME WITH INDEXES BY AUTHOR AND
SUBJECT. ALSO INCLUDES RELEVANT GOVERNMENT DOCUMENTS. UNAN-
NOTATED. BEGINNING WITH VOLUME 9, 1960, PUBLISHED IN LONDON
BY STEVENS & SONS AND IN CHICAGO BY ALDINE PUBLISHING CO.

2154 UNESCO
REPERTOIRE DES BIBLIOTHEQUES DE FRANCE: CENTRES ET SERVICES
DE DOCUMENTATION DE FRANCE.
PARIS: UNESCO, 1951, 288 PP.
REPORTS ON BIBLIOGRAPHIC SERVICES IN FRANCE. FOR EACH
SUBJECT HEADING, DESCRIBES THE NAME OF THE DOCUMENTATION
SERVICE, ITS FUNCTIONS, PUBLICATIONS, METHODS, ADMINISTRA-
TION, AND DOCUMENTS AT ITS DISPOSAL. LISTS 309 SUBJECT
HEADINGS: 127 IN THE PUBLIC SECTOR, 40 IN COMMERCE AND
INDUSTRY, 132 IN LEARNED SOCIETIES. ALSO INCLUDES A SUP-
PLEMENTARY LIST.

2155 UNESCO
THESES DE SCIENCES SOCIALES: CATALOGUE ANALYTIQUE INTERNA-
TIONAL DE THESES INEDITES DE DOCTORAT, 1940-1950.
PARIS: UNESCO, 1952, 236 PP.
3,215 ITEMS DESCRIBING DOCTORAL THESES IN THE SOCIAL
SCIENCES FROM 23 MEMBERS PARTICIPATING IN PROGRAM ORGAN-
IZED BY UNESCO. BILINGUAL CATALOGUE, WITH TITLES EITHER IN
FRENCH OR ENGLISH. CLASSIFICATION ACCORDING TO MAJOR DIS-
CIPLINE AS PRESCRIBED BY UNIVERSAL DECIMAL SYSTEM. CONTAINS
SUBJECT, AUTHOR, AND GEOGRAPHICAL INDEXES AND TABLE OF
LANGUAGES.

2156 UNESCO
UNESCO PUBLICATIONS: CHECK LIST (2ND REV. ED.)
PARIS: UNESCO, 1958, 32 PP.
CONTAINS LISTS OF PUBLICATIONS, SERIES, AND COLLECTIONS.
DIVIDED INTO LANGUAGE OF PUBLICATION: ENGLISH, FRENCH, AND
SPANISH. ITEMS ARRANGED BY SUBJECT.

2157 UNESCO
INTERNATIONAL ORGANIZATIONS IN THE SOCIAL SCIENCES(REV. ED.)
PARIS: UNESCO, 1965, 147 PP.
SUMMARY DESCRIPTION OF THE STRUCTURE AND ACTIVITIES OF
NONGOVERNMENTAL ORGANIZATIONS SPECIALIZING IN SOCIAL
SCIENCES AND IN CONSULTATIVE RELATIONSHIP WITH UNESCO. THIS
BILINGUAL EDITION COMPRISES 14 INTERNATIONAL SOCIAL SCIENCE
ORGANIZATIONS HAVING CONSULTATIVE AND ASSOCIATE OR INFORMA-
TION AND CONSULTATIVE RELATIONS WITH UNESCO. LISTS THEIR
GEOGRAPHICAL EXTENSION, AFFILIATED BODIES, STRUCTURE, ETC.

2158 UNION OF SOUTH AFRICA
REPORT CONCERNING ADMINISTRATION OF SOUTH WEST AFRICA
(6 VOLS.)
PRETORIA: U OF SOUTH AFRICA, 1937, 3000 PP.
YEARLY REPORTS, 1922-37, BY GOVERNMENT OF UNION OF SOUTH
AFRICA TO COUNCIL OF LEAGUE OF NATIONS CONCERNING
ADMINISTRATION OF SOUTH WEST AFRICA. COVERS TOPICS OF
LEGISLATION, INTERNATIONAL RELATIONS, CONSTITUTION, COURT
SYSTEM, PRISONS, ARMS AND POLICE, DEMOGRAPHY, FINANCE AND
TAXES, INDUSTRY, AGRICULTURE, NATIVE AFFAIRS, HEALTH, TRADE,
MISSIONS, AND ECONOMY.

2159 UNITED NATIONS
OFFICIAL RECORDS OF THE UNITED NATIONS' GENERAL ASSEMBLY.
NEW YORK: UNITED NATIONS.
OFFICIAL RECORDS OF GENERAL ASSEMBLY CONSIST OF SUMMARY
OR VERBATIM REPORTS OF PLENARY MEETINGS OF THE GENERAL
COMMITTEE, THE SIX MAIN COMMITTEES, AND SESSIONAL COMMIT-
TEES; ANNEXES OF MOST SIGNIFICANT AND PERTINENT DOCUMENTS;
SUPPLEMENTS INCLUDING RESOLUTIONS ADOPTED BY THE SESSION;
ANNUAL REPORT AND BUDGET BY THE SECRETARY-GENERAL, COUNCIL
REPORTS, COMMITTEE REPORTS, ETC. ANNUAL PUBLICATIONS.

2160 UNITED NATIONS
UNITED NATIONS PUBLICATIONS.
NEW YORK: UNITED NATIONS.
ANNUAL PUBLICATION, FIRST PUBLISHED 1945, LISTING ALL
MATERIALS PUBLISHED DURING YEAR BY ALL UN DEPARTMENTS AND
AGENCIES.

2161 UNITED NATIONS
BIBLIOGRAPHY ON INDUSTRIALIZATION IN UNDER-DEVELOPED
COUNTRIES.
NEW YORK: UNITED NATIONS, 1956, 216 PP.
A BIBLIOGRAPHY IN ENGLISH, FRENCH, AND SPANISH COVERING
PUBLICATIONS OF THE UNITED NATIONS, OTHER PUBLICATIONS, AND
UNPUBLISHED RESEARCH. BESIDES GENERAL WORKS, IT INCLUDES
MATERIAL ON AFRICA, THE MIDDLE EAST, ASIA AND THE FAR EAST,
EUROPE, AND LATIN AMERICA AND THE CARIBBEAN. HAS INDEXES
OF PERSONAL AND GENERAL NAMES.

2162 UNITED NATIONS
UNITED NATIONS PUBLICATIONS: 1945-1966.
NEW YORK: UNITED NATIONS, 1967, 175 PP.
INCLUDES UN AND INTERNATIONAL COURT OF JUSTICE SALES PUB-
LICATIONS ISSUED FROM 1945-66 AND EXCLUDES MIMEOGRAPHED DOC-
UMENTS OF THE ECONOMIC COMMISSION FOR EUROPE. ARRANGEMENT
IS TOPICAL: ECONOMIC DEVELOPMENT, WORLD ECONOMY, TRADE,
FINANCE, PUBLIC ADMINISTRATION, SOCIAL QUESTIONS, CARTOG-
RAPHY, DEMOGRAPHY, HEALTH SERVICES, UN ORGANS AND ORGANIZA-
TION, STATISTICS, LEAGUE OF NATIONS, ETC. INCLUDES APPENDIX.

2163 UNIVERSAL REFERENCE SYSTEM
INTERNATIONAL AFFAIRS: VOLUME I IN THE POLITICAL SCIENCE,
GOVERNMENT, AND PUBLIC POLICY SERIES.
PRINCETON: UNIVERSAL REF SYSTEM, 1965, 1205 PP., LC#65-19793
COMPUTERIZED INFORMATION RETRIEVAL SYSTEM FOR THE SOCIAL
AND BEHAVIORAL SCIENCES; ANNOTATED AND INTENSIVELY INDEXED
UTILYZING THE "TOPICAL-METHODOLOGICAL INDEX" DEVELOPED
BY PROFESSOR ALFRED DE GRAZIA. VOLUME CARRIES 3,000 REFEREN-
CES IN INTERNATIONAL AFFAIRS. QUARTERLY GAZETTES BEGAN IN
AUGUST, 1967.

2164 UNIVERSAL REFERENCE SYSTEM
ADMINISTRATIVE MANAGEMENT: PUBLIC AND PRIVATE BUREAUCRACY
(VOLUME IV)
PRINCETON* UNIV. REF. SYSTEM, 1967, 1200 PP.
COMPUTERIZED INFORMATION RETRIEVAL SYSTEM. ANNOTATED AND
EXTENSIVELY INDEXED, UTILIZING "TOPICAL-METHODOLOGICAL IN-
DEX" DEVELOPED BY PROFESSOR ALFRED DE GRAZIA. APPROXIMATELY
3,000 CITATIONS FROM BOOKS, GOVERNMENT PUBLICATIONS, AND
JOURNALS. ENGLISH AND EUROPEAN LANGUAGES. MATERIALS SELECT-
ED FROM CLASSICAL SOURCES THROUGH 1967. TO BE PUBLISHED
EARLY 1968, WITH SUBSEQUENT QUARTERLY GAZETTES.

2165 UNIVERSAL REFERENCE SYSTEM
PUBLIC POLICY AND THE MANAGEMENT OF SCIENCE (VOLUME IX)
PRINCETON* UNIV. REF. SYSTEM, 1967, 1200 PP.
ABOUT 3000 SELECTED BOOKS, ARTICLES, AND DOCUMENTS CON-
CERNED WITH INSTITUTIONAL AND BEHAVIORAL PROCESS OF SCIEN-
TIFIC DECISION-MAKING. MAJORITY OF ITEMS FROM 1960'S; IN-
CLUDES ENGLISH-LANGUAGE AND EUROPEAN SOURCES. USES PROFESSOR
ALFRED DE GRAZIA'S "TOPICAL-METHODOLOGICAL INDEX." TO BE
PUBLISHED EARLY 1968. QUARTERLY GAZETTES BEGAN AUG., 1967.

2166 UNIVERSITY MICROFILMS INC
DISSERTATION ABSTRACTS: ABSTRACTS OF DISSERTATIONS AND MONO-
GRAPHS IN MICROFILM.
ANN ARBOR: U MICROFILMS, INC.
MONTHLY COMPILATION OF ABSTRACTS OF DOCTORAL DISSERTA-
TIONS SUBMITTED TO UNIVERSITY MICROFILMS, INC. ARRANGEMENT
IS ALPHABETICAL UNDER SUBJECT HEADING. ALPHABETICAL AUTHOR
INDEX INCLUDED FOLLOWING ABSTRACTS. FIRST PUBLISHED 1938.
CONFINED TO AMERICAN AND CANADIAN INSTITUTIONS.

2167 UNIVERSITY OF FLORIDA
CARIBBEAN ACQUISITIONS: MATERIALS ACQUIRED BY THE UNI-
VERSITY OF FLORIDA 1957-1960.
GAINESVILLE: U OF FLORIDA LIB.
LIST OF MATERIALS ACQUIRED BY THE UNIVERSITY OF
FLORIDA UNDER THE FARMINGTON PLAN AND THE UNIVERSITY'S
EMPHASIS ON LATIN AMERICAN STUDIES. ANNUAL SUPPLEMENTS
UPDATE LIST.

2168 UNIVERSITY OF LONDON
THE FAR EAST AND SOUTH-EAST ASIA: A CUMULATED LIST OF
PERIODICAL ARTICLES, MAY 1956-APRIL 1957.
LONDON: U LON, ORIENT + AFR STUD, 1958, 123 PP.
THIRD ANNUAL CUMULATION OF PERIODICAL ARTICLES IN WESTERN
LANGUAGES. CONTAINS 2,000 ITEMS ON ANTHROPOLOGY, SOCIOLOGY
AND FOLKLORE; GEOGRAPHY AND HISTORY; AND SOCIAL SCIENCES.
MATERIAL IS CLASSIFIED BY GEOGRAPHIC REGION. INCLUDES
AUTHOR INDEX.

2169 UNIVERSITY PITT INST LOC GOVT
THE COUNCIL-MANAGER FORM OF GOVERNMENT IN PENNSYLVANIA
(PAMPHLET)
PITTSBURGH: U PITT, INST LOC GOV, 1962, 50 PP.
DESCRIBES AND ANALYZES THIS UNIQUE FORM OF LOCAL GOVERN-
MENT. EXPLAINS PLAN OF GOVERNMENT AND SETS UP "MODEL"
ORDINANCE OUTLINING POWERS OF MUNICIPAL MANAGER AND HIS RE-
SPONSIBILITIES TO LOCAL GOVERNMENT BODY AND CONSTITUENTS.

2170 US ADMINISTRATIVE CONFERENCE
FINAL REPORT OF THE ADMINISTRATIVE CONFERENCE OF THE US;
SUGGESTIONS FOR IMPROVING PROCESSES - ADMIN. AGENCIES.
WASHINGTON: US GOVERNMENT, 1962, 120 PP.
PART I SUMMARIZES ACTIVITIES OF ADMINISTRATIVE
CONFERENCE OF THE US, WHICH SOUGHT WAYS TO DEVELOP SENSE
OF UNITY IN ADMINISTRATIVE AGENCIES AND DEGREE OF UNIFORM-
ITY IN PROCEDURES. INCLUDES RECOMMENDATIONS AND SUMMARY
OF PROCEDURES. PART II CONTAINS CONFERENCE'S SUGGESTIONS
FOR FUTURE IMPROVEMENT OF PROCESSES OF THESE AGENCIES.

2171 US ADVISORY COMN INTERGOV REL
ALTERNATIVE APPROACHES TO GOVERNMENTAL REORGANIZATION IN
METROPOLITAN AREAS (PAMPHLET)

WASHINGTON: US GOVERNMENT, 1962, 88 PP.
THE STRENGTHS AND WEAKNESSES OF 10 DIFFERENT APPROACHES
TO GOVERNMENTAL REORGANIZATION ARE COVERED. A MODEL FOR
STATE LEGISLATION ON EXTRATERRITORIAL PLANNING, ZONING, AND
SUBDIVISION REGULATIONS IS INCLUDED.

2172 US ADVISORY COMN INTERGOV REL
STATE CONSTITUTIONAL AND STATUTORY RESTRICTIONS UPON THE
STRUCTURAL, FUNCTIONAL, AND PERSONAL POWERS OF LOCAL GOV'T.
WASHINGTON: US GOVERNMENT, 1962, 80 PP.
REVIEWS STATE CONSTITUTIONAL AND STATUTORY LIMITATIONS
UPON LOCAL GOVERNMENT IN HISTORICAL, THEORETICAL, POLITICAL,
LEGAL CONTEXT. EXPLORES NATURE AND FUNCTIONS OF LOCAL GOV-
ERNMENT; NATURE OF RESTRICTIONS, WHICH IMPAIR INITIATIVE;
DETERMINES BEST COURSES FOR IMPLEMENTING REVISIONS IN THESE
LIMITATIONS; DEVELOPS POSSIBLE COURSES OF ACTION FOR ELIMIN-
ATING UNJUSTIFIED RESTRICTIONS.

2173 US BOARD GOVERNORS FEDL RESRV
SELECTED BIBLIOGRAPHY ON MONETARY POLICY AND MANAGEMENT OF
THE PUBLIC DEBT 1947-1960 AND 1961-1963 SUPPLEMENT (PAMPH.)
WASHINGTON: US GOVERNMENT, 1964, 20 PP.
BIBLIOGRAPHY OF APPROXIMATELY 200 BOOKS, ARTICLES, AND
GOVERNMENT PUBLICATIONS IN ENGLISH; ARRANGED ALPHABETICALLY
BY AUTHOR ON TOPICS OF MONETARY POLICY AND MANAGEMENT OF
PUBLIC DEBT FROM 1947-63.

2174 US BUREAU OF THE BUDGET
THE ADMINISTRATION OF GOVERNMENT SUPPORTED RESEARCH AT
UNIVERSITIES (PAMPHLET)
WASHINGTON: GOVT PR OFFICE, 1966, 141 PP.
REPORT UNDERTAKEN IN RESPONSE TO EXECUTIVE BRANCH'S CON-
TINUING CONCERN THAT ITS RESEARCH BE WELL MANAGED.
IDENTIFIES ADMINISTRATIVE PROCEDURES WHICH FOSTER GOOD RE-
SEARCH, HELP INSTITUTION, AND GUARANTEE PRUDENT STEWARDSHIP
OF PUBLIC FUNDS. PARTICULARLY CONCERNED WITH MANAGEMENT
OF FEDERALLY-FUNDED RESEARCH PROGRAMS IN PHYSICAL, LIFE,
AND BEHAVIORAL SCIENCES.

2175 US CIVIL SERVICE COMMISSION
A BIBLIOGRAPHY OF PUBLIC PERSONNEL ADMINISTRATION LITERATURE
WASHINGTON: US GOVERNMENT.
BIBLIOGRAPHY OF BOOKS, ARTICLES, AND REPORTS. FIRST
VOLUME PUBLISHED 1949 WITH EIGHT SUPPLEMENTS THROUGH 1958.

2176 US CIVIL SERVICE COMMISSION
DISSERTATIONS AND THESES RELATING TO PERSONNEL ADMIN-
ISTRATION (PAMPHLET)
WASHINGTON: US GOVERNMENT, 1957.
UNANNOTATED ANNUAL BIBLIOGRAPHY FIRST ISSUED IN 1957.
MATERIAL SELECTED FROM THESES LISTED IN A VARIETY OF BUSI-
ESS, ECONOMIC, SOCIOLOGICAL, AND POLITICAL SCIENCE JOURNALS.
SELECTION AND CLASSIFICATION MADE ON BASIS OF TITLE ONLY.

2177 US CIVIL SERVICE COMMISSION
CONGRESSIONAL DOCUMENTS RELATING TO CIVIL SERVICE.
WASHINGTON: US GOVERNMENT, 1959, 254 PP.
ANNOTATED BIBLIOGRAPHY OF APPROXIMATELY 3,000 DOCUMENTS,
REPORTS, AND HEARINGS DEALING WITH US CIVIL SERVICE.
ARTICLES IN ENGLISH AND DATE FROM 1826 TO 1959.

2178 US CONGRESS JT COMM ECO GOVT
BACKGROUND MATERIAL ON ECONOMY IN GOVERNMENT 1967 (PAMPHLET)
WASHINGTON: US GOVERNMENT, 1967, 229 PP.
ANALYSIS OF FEDERAL PROPERTY HOLDINGS AND PROPERTY MAN-
AGEMENT ACTIVITIES IN ORDER TO IMPROVE OPERATIONS AND LOWER
COSTS. LISTS AMOUNT AND COST OF REAL PROPERTY HOLDINGS AND
EXTENT OF DEFENSE DEPARTMENT PROPERTY ACTIVITIES AND YEARLY
EXPENDITURES.

2179 US CONGRESS: SENATE
HEARINGS OF THE COMMITTEE ON THE JUDICIARY.
WASHINGTON: GOVT PR OFFICE, 1963, 1185 PP.
APPENDIX VOLUME II OF HEARINGS BEFORE SUBCOMMITTEE TO
INVESTIGATE ADMINISTRATION OF INTERNAL SECURITY ACT DEALING
WITH DEPARTMENTAL AND AGENCY RULES AND REGULATIONS. COLLEC-
TION OF DOCUMENTS ON US PERSONNEL SECURITY PRACTICES. SUB-
COMMITTEE HEADED BY JAMES O. EASTMAN AND THOMAS J. DODD.

2180 US DEPARTMENT HEALTH EDUC WELF
NEW PROGRAMS IN HEALTH, EDUCATION, WELFARE, HOUSING AND UR-
BAN DEVELOPMENT FOR PERSONS AND FAMILIES -LOW, MOD' INCOME.
WASHINGTON: US GOVERNMENT, 1967, 50 PP.
DESCRIBES NEW AND EXPANDED PROGRAMS WITHIN DEPARTMENT OF
HEALTH, EDUCATION, AND WELFARE AND DEPARTMENT OF HOUSING
AND URBAN DEVELOPMENT. TELLS WHERE TO OBTAIN INFORMATION,
LISTS REGIONAL OFFICES OF EACH DEPARTMENT, PROVIDES DETAILED
INFORMATION ABOUT REGIONAL HOUSING ASSISTANCE OFFICES, LISTS
STATE NURSING ORGANIZATIONS IN US AND TERRITORIES.

2181 US DEPARTMENT OF JUSTICE
ANNUAL REPORT OF THE OFFICE OF ADMINISTRATIVE PROCEDURE.
WASHINGTON: US GOVERNMENT, 1967.
FIRST ISSUED IN 1957, REPORTS ACTIVITIES OF THE OFFICE OF
ADMINISTRATIVE PROCEDURE: ORGANIZATION OF THE OFFICE, REC-
OGNITION AND DISCIPLINE OF ATTORNEYS, UNIFORM RULES

STUDIES, STATISTICAL INFORMATION.

2182 US DEPARTMENT OF STATE
RESEARCH ON EASTERN EUROPE (EXCLUDING USSR)
WASHINGTON: DEPT OF STATE, 1952.
LISTING OF COMPLETED AND IN PROGRESS RESEARCH PROJECTS
REPORTED BY SCHOLARS TO EXTERNAL RESEARCH STAFF. PUBLISHED
ERRATICALLY FROM 1952-58. PUBLISHED LARGELY TO INDICATE
COMPLETION AND AVAILABILITY OF NEW RESEARCH. RESEARCH IS
LISTED BY COUNTRY WITH WHICH IT IS CONCERNED. INCLUDES SOME
PROJECTS BEGUN AS EARLY AS 1941 BUT BELIEVED NOT TO HAVE
BEEN PUBLISHED. PUBLISHED IN 10 PARTS.

2183 US DEPARTMENT OF THE ARMY
SELECT BIBLIOGRAPHY ON ADMINISTRATIVE ORGANIZATION(PAMPHLET)
WASHINGTON: DEPT OF THE ARMY, 1960, 38 PP.
ANNOTATED BIBLIOGRAPHY OF SELECTED BOOKS, PAMPHLETS,
PERIODICALS, AND ARTICLES CONCERNED WITH MILITARY ADMINIS-
TRATIVE ORGANIZATION. MUCH LITERATURE ON BUSINESS AND IN-
DUSTRY IS PRESENTED FOR ORGANIZATIONAL CONCEPTS, CRITERIA,
AND DOCTRINE. INCLUDES INDEXES AND GUIDES AND LISTS APPROX-
IMATELY 235 SOURCES.

2184 US DEPARTMENT OF THE ARMY
COMMUNIST CHINA: A STRATEGIC SURVEY: A BIBLIOGRAPHY
(PAMPHLET NO. 20-67)
WASHINGTON: DEPT OF THE ARMY, 1966, 143 PP.
BIBLIOGRAPHIC PROBE INTO THE ECONOMIC, SOCIOLOGICAL, MIL-
ITARY, AND POLITICAL MAKE-UP OF COMMUNIST CHINA. FOCUSES ON
EMERGENCE AS STRATEGIC THREAT. ABSTRACTS FROM OVER 650 PER-
IODICAL ARTICLES, BOOKS, AND STUDIES IN ENGLISH. INCLUDES
CHINA'S POLICY TO SOUTH ASIA AS A WHOLE AND TO INDIVIDUAL
COUNTRIES. MAPS, CHARTS, AND DATA APPENDED.

2185 US DEPARTMENT OF THE ARMY
CIVILIAN IN PEACE, SOLDIER IN WAR: A BIBLIOGRAPHIC SURVEY OF
THE ARMY AND AIR NATIONAL GUARD (PAMPHLET, NOS. 130-2)
WASHINGTON: DEPT OF THE ARMY, 1967, 192 PP.
ANNOTATED BIBLIOGRAPHY OF PERIODICAL ARTICLES, BOOKS, UN-
PUBLISHED MATERIALS, AND GOVERNMENT PUBLICATIONS PERTAINING
TO THE ROLE AND FUNCTIONS OF THE MILITARY IN THE US. SOURCES
CITED PUBLISHED 1938 THROUGH 1966. OVER 800 ITEMS ARRANGED
BY SUBJECT. INCLUDES SECTION ON MILITIAS OF FOREIGN COUN-
TRIES AND ONE ON STATE MILITIAS. MAJORITY OF ENTRIES ARE
GOVERNMENT PUBLICATIONS.

2186 US GENERAL ACCOUNTING OFFICE
EXAMINATION OF ECONOMIC AND TECHNICAL ASSISTANCE PROGRAM FOR
IRAN.
WASHINGTON: US GOVERNMENT, 1961, 80 PP.
REPORTS ON ADMINISTRATION OF FOREIGN AID TO IRAN, BREAK-
ING DOWN NATURE AND AMOUNT OF AID, SPENDING PRACTICES, WAS-
TAGE, AND PROBLEMS OF CONTROL. CASE STUDIES GIVE SPECIFIC
ILLUSTRATIONS OF USAGE AND EFFECT OF US AID.

2187 US HOUSE COM ON ED AND LABOR
ADMINISTRATION OF AGING.
WASHINGTON: US GOVERNMENT, 1963, 260 PP.
REPORTS ON HEARINGS DISCUSSING DEVELOPMENT OF NEW OR IM-
PROVED PROGRAMS TO HELP AGED THROUGH GRANTS TO STATES FOR
PLANNING, RESEARCH, AND TRAINING PROGRAMS.

2188 US HOUSE COMM EDUC AND LABOR
ADMINISTRATION OF THE NATIONAL LABOR RELATIONS ACT.
WASHINGTON: US GOVERNMENT, 1965, 326 PP.
REPORTS INVESTIGATION OF NATIONAL LABOR RELATIONS BOARD
IN ADMINISTERING NATIONAL LABOR RELATIONS ACT. INCLUDES
BY VARIOUS LEADERS, AND SPECIFIC CASES ILLUSTRATING
OF CERTAIN INCIDENTS.

2189 US HOUSE COMM GOVT OPERATIONS
HEARINGS BEFORE A SUBCOMMITTEE OF THE COMMITTEE ON GOVERN-
MENT OPERATIONS.
WASHINGTON: GOVT PR OFFICE, 1958, 1301 PP.
STATEMENTS AND TESTIMONIES BY PUBLIC AND PRIVATE OFFI-
CIALS ON FOREIGN AID CONSTRUCTION PROJECTS IN CAMBODIA AND
PHILIPPINES. EXAMINES DEFENSE SUPPORT, ECONOMIC AID, AND
TECHNICAL ASSISTANCE IN BROAD PERSPECTIVE. INVESTIGATES
OPERATIONAL EFFICIENCY IN ROAD PROJECTS.

2190 US HOUSE COMM GOVT OPERATIONS
UNITED STATES AID OPERATIONS IN LAOS.
WASHINGTON: US GOVERNMENT, 1959, 983 PP.
HEARINGS ON US AID TO LAOS. INVESTIGATES EFFECT OF MILI-
TARY AID ON ECONOMIC AND POLITICAL STABILITY AND METHODS
OF IMPROVING ADMINISTRATION OF PROGRAM TO FURTHER POLITICAL
OBJECTIVES.

2191 US HOUSE COMM GOVT OPERATIONS
AN INVESTIGATION OF THE US ECONOMIC AND MILITARY ASSISTANCE
PROGRAMS IN VIETNAM.
WASHINGTON: US GOVERNMENT, 1966, 130 PP.
REPORTS ON US AID PROGRAM IN VIETNAM. MAINTAINS THAT IN-
CREASED ECONOMIC AID IS NECESSARY IF POLITICAL AND MILITARY
VICTORIES ARE TO BE ACHIEVED. EXAMINES IMPORT PROGRAM, CON-
TROL OF MONEY, AUDITS AND INSPECTIONS, AID MANAGEMENT, PORT

SITUATION, CIVILIAN MEDICAL PROGRAM, PACIFICATION, MILITARY
CONSTRUCTION, AND ILLICIT PRACTICES AFFECTING US AID.

2192 US HOUSE COMM ON COMMERCE
ADMINISTRATIVE PROCESS AND ETHICAL QUESTIONS.
WASHINGTON: US GOVERNMENT, 1958, 256 PP.
HEARINGS BEFORE SUBCOMMITTEE OF COMMITTEE ON INTERSTATE
AND FOREIGN COMMERCE HEADED BY OREN HARRIS, INCLUDING PANEL
DISCUSSION BY REPRESENTATIVES OF LAW SCHOOLS, GOVERNMENT AND
BAR ON CONTROL OF JUDICIAL FUNCTIONS OF ADMINISTRATIVE
AGENCIES, RESTRICTION OF THEIR LEGISLATIVE FUNCTIONS, AND
CONTROL OF IMPROPER PROCEDURES.

2193 US HOUSE COMM ON POST OFFICE
MANPOWER UTILIZATION IN THE FEDERAL GOVERNMENT.
WASHINGTON: US GOVERNMENT, 1957, 318 PP.
HEARINGS BEFORE SUBCOMMITTEE ON MANPOWER UTILIZATION OF
COMMITTEE ON POST OFFICE AND CIVIL SERVICE HEADED BY JAMES
C. DAVIS ON DEFENSE DEPARTMENT'S USE OF ENGINEERING AND SCI-
ENTIFIC MANPOWER UNDER CONDITION OF UNLIMITED DEFENSE FUNDS.
MUST ECONOMIZE AND INCREASE EFFICIENCY TO DEVELOP DOMESTIC
PROGRAMS AND STILL ADVANCE DEFENSE PROGRAM.

2194 US HOUSE COMM ON POST OFFICE
TO PROVIDE AN EFFECTIVE SYSTEM OF PERSONNEL ADMINISTRATION.
WASHINGTON: US GOVERNMENT, 1958, 195 PP.
HEARINGS BEFORE SUBCOMMITTEE OF COMMITTEE ON POST OFFICE
AND CIVIL SERVICE OF US SENATE HEADED BY JOSEPH S. CLARK ON
BILL S. 3888 PROVIDING FOR EFFECTIVE SYSTEM OF PERSONNEL
ADMINISTRATION IN ALL EXECUTIVE AGENCIES. ESTABLISHES
POLICY DECLARATION THAT ALL AGENCIES ARE UNDER CONTROL OF
PRESIDENT, AND FORMS CAREER SERVICE POSITIONS FROM CIVIL
SERVICE AND OFFICE OF PERSONNEL MANAGEMENT.

2195 US HOUSE COMM ON POST OFFICE
MANPOWER UTILIZATION IN THE FEDERAL GOVERNMENT.
WASHINGTON: GOVT PR OFFICE, 1958, 401 PP.
HEARINGS BEFORE SUBCOMMITTEE ON MANPOWER UTILIZATION, OF
THE HOUSE COMMITTEE ON POST OFFICE AND CIVIL SERVICE OF THE
85TH CONGRESS. HEARINGS HELD DECEMBER, 1958, WEIGHED ACTIONS
TAKEN ON VARIOUS EXECUTIVE ORDERS; HEARD REPORTS OF SPECIAL
STUDIES OF WASTE AND INEFFICIENCY IN FEDERAL EMPLOYMENT.
RECOMMENDATIONS MADE FOR MORE EFFICIENCY IN CIVIL SERVICE
PROGRAMS.

2196 US HOUSE COMM ON POST OFFICE
MANPOWER UTILIZATION IN THE FEDERAL GOVERNMENT.
WASHINGTON: GOVT PR OFFICE, 1958, 200 PP.
HEARINGS BEFORE SUBCOMMITTEE ON MANPOWER UTILIZATION, OF
THE HOUSE COMMITTEE ON POST OFFICE AND CIVIL SERVICE OF THE
85TH CONGRESS. HEARINGS HELD APRIL AND MAY, 1958,
CONSIDERED PROPOSAL THAT A CAREER EXECUTIVE PROGRAM BE SET
UP TO TRAIN CAREER CIVIL SERVANTS FOR SERVICE IN
ADMINISTRATIVE AND MANAGERIAL POSITIONS.

2197 US HOUSE COMM ON POST OFFICE
TRAINING OF FEDERAL EMPLOYEES.
WASHINGTON: GOVT PR OFFICE, 1958, 126 PP.
HEARINGS BEFORE HOUSE COMMITTEE ON POST OFFICE AND CIVIL
SERVICE, MAY AND JUNE, 1958, DEBATING PROPOSED BILL
TO INCREASE EFFICIENCY AND ECONOMY IN GOVERNMENT
BY PROVIDING FOR PROGRAMS TO TRAIN CIVILIAN OFFICERS AND
EMPLOYEES TO PERFORM OFFICIAL DUTIES.

2198 US HOUSE COMM SCI ASTRONAUT
GOVERNMENT, SCIENCE, AND INTERNATIONAL POLICY.
WASHINGTON: US GOVERNMENT, 1967, 220 PP.
PROCEEDINGS BEFORE CONGRESSIONAL COMMITTEE ON SCIENCE AND
ASTRONAUTICS. PURPOSE WAS TO IDENTIFY SPHERES OF RESEARCH
WHICH OFFER EXCEPTIONAL PROMISE; DISCUSS CURRENT METHODS OF
RESEARCH; PROVIDE INFORMATION ON AVAILABILITY OF SCIENTIFIC
MANPOWER AND EDUCATIONAL NEEDS; PROVIDE INFORMATION ON MAT-
TERS OF INTERNATIONAL COOPERATION AND ORGANIZATION.

2199 US HOUSE RULES COMM
HEARINGS BEFORE A SPECIAL SUBCOMMITTEE: ESTABLISHMENT OF A
STANDING COMMITTEE ON ADMINISTRATIVE PROCEDURE, PRACTICE.
WASHINGTON: US GOVERNMENT, 1956, 88 PP.
TRANSCRIPTS OF TESTIMONY ON HOUSE RESOLUTION 462, TO
ESTABLISH STANDING COMMITTEE TO STUDY ABUSES OF ADMINIS-
TRATIVE AUTHORITY, AND NEED FOR LEGISLATIVE STANDARDS TO
LIMIT EXERCISE OF ADMINISTRATIVE DISCRETION IN AREAS OF DEL-
EGATED POWER, STUDY PROCEDURES AND PRACTICES OF ADMINISTRA-
TIVE AGENCIES, AND EVALUATE EFFECTS OF LAWS REGULATING
PROCEDURES.

2200 US LIBRARY OF CONGRESS
CATALOG OF THE PUBLIC DOCUMENTS OF THE UNITED STATES, 1893-
1940.
WASHINGTON: LIBRARY OF CONGRESS.
CATALOG OF US GOVERNMENT PUBLICATIONS DURING YEARS 1893-
1940 AND CUMULATED EVERY TWO YEARS. ITEMS ENTERED BY SUB-
JECT, TITLE, AUTHOR, AND GOVERNMENTAL AGENCY. LARGELY A
DUPLICATE OF THE "MONTHLY CATALOG."

2201 US LIBRARY OF CONGRESS
LIST OF REFERENCES ON A LEAGUE OF NATIONS.
WASHINGTON: LIBRARY OF CONGRESS, 1918, 59 PP.
COMPILATION OF BOOKS, ARTICLES, DOCUMENTS, AND SPEECHES.
ARRANGED ALPHABETICALLY BY AUTHOR. PUBLICATION DATES RANGE
FROM 1915 THROUH 1930; 800 ENTRIES.

2202 US LIBRARY OF CONGRESS
CLASSIFIED GUIDE TO MATERIAL IN THE LIBRARY OF CONGRESS
COVERING URBAN COMMUNITY DEVELOPMENT.
WASHINGTON: US NATL RESOURC COMM, 1936, 102 PP.
LISTS NO BOOKS, BUT CONSISTS OF 850 SUBJECT HEADINGS AND
SUBHEADINGS RELATED TO URBAN MATTERS, CHOSEN FROM LIST OF
SUBJECT HEADINGS USED IN DICTIONARY CATALOGUES OF LIBRARY OF
CONGRESS. ARRANGED BY ANALOGICAL LIST OF CLASSES OF RELATED
SUBJECTS; BY CALL NUMBERS CORRESPONDING TO SUBJECT HEADINGS,
ARRANGED ACCORDING TO ALPHABETICAL AND NUMERICAL SEQUENCE OF
LIBRARY-CONGRESS CLASSIFICATIONS; ALPHABETICAL BY SUBJECT.

2203 US LIBRARY OF CONGRESS
BRAZIL: A GUIDE TO THE OFFICIAL PUBLICATIONS OF BRAZIL.
WASHINGTON: LIBRARY OF CONGRESS, 1948, 224 PP.
BIBLIOGRAPHY OF MATERIALS IN LIBRARY OF CONGRESS PUB-
LISHED BY BRAZILIAN GOVERNMENT IN 19TH AND 20TH CENTURIES;
ALL IN SPANISH AND PORTUGUESE, ARRANGED ACCORDING TO BRANCH
OF GOVERNMENT: EXECUTIVE, LEGISLATIVE, JUDICIAL; APPROXI-
MATELY 2,000 ITEMS.

2204 US LIBRARY OF CONGRESS
EAST EUROPEAN ACCESSIONS LIST (VOL. I)
WASHINGTON: LIBRARY OF CONGRESS, 1951, 1500 PP., LC#51-60032
RECORD OF EASTERN EUROPEAN MONOGRAPHS AND PERIODICALS
SINCE 1939 IN ENGLISH AND LANGUAGE OF ORIGINAL COUNTRY; AR-
RANGED BY COUNTRY AND DIVIDED INTO PERIODICALS AND MONO-
GRAPHS WHICH ARE FURTHER DIVIDED INTO SUBJECTS.

2205 US LIBRARY OF CONGRESS
INDEX TO LATIN AMERICAN LEGISLATION: 1950-1960 (2 VOLS.)
WASHINGTON: LIBRARY OF CONGRESS, 1960, 1474 PP.
COMPREHENSIVE AND TOPICALLY ARRANGED INDEX TO IMPORTANT
AND RELEVANT LEGISLATION ENACTED BY LATIN AMERICAN GOVERN-
MENTS; INDEXES 30,000 ITEMS. INCLUDES "MATTERS
OF GENERAL INTEREST, BASIC CODES, AND ORGANIC LAWS WITH
THEIR AMENDMENTS"; EXCLUDES PRIVATE LEGISLATION, CONFERRING
OF HONORS, APPOINTMENTS, DISMISSALS, ETC.

2206 US LIBRARY OF CONGRESS
A LIST OF AMERICAN DOCTORAL DISSERTATIONS ON AFRICA.
WASHINGTON: LIBRARY OF CONGRESS, 1962, 69 PP., LC#62-60088.
700 THESES, ON SUBJECTS RELATING TO AFRICA, WHICH HAVE
BEEN ACCEPTED BY US AND CANADIAN UNIVERSITIES FROM LATE
19TH CENTURY TO 1961. ARRANGED ALPHABETICALLY BY AUTHOR.

2207 US LIBRARY OF CONGRESS
NIGERIA: A GUIDE TO OFFICIAL PUBLICATIONS.
WASHINGTON: LIBRARY OF CONGRESS, 1966, 166 PP., LC#66-61703.
REVISION OF A SIMILAR GUIDE PUBLISHED IN 1959 WHICH
COVERS PUBLICATIONS ISSUED BY NIGERIAN GOVERNMENTS FROM
THE ESTABLISHMENT OF BRITISH ADMINISTRATION IN NIGERIA IN
1861 TO 1865. ALSO LISTS SELECTION OF DOCUMENTS RELEVANT TO
NIGERIA AND THE BRITISH CAMEROONS ISSUED BY VARIOUS BRITISH
GOVERNMENT OFFICES AND BY THE LEAGUE OF NATIONS AND UN.

2208 US PRES COMM STUDY MIL ASSIST
COMPOSITE REPORT.
WASHINGTON: U.S. PRES. COMM. STUDY MILITARY ASSISTANCE,1959, 600PP.
REPORTS ON ORGANIZATION OF US MILITARY ASSISTANCE PROGRAM
AND ORGANIZATIONAL ASPECTS OF ECONOMIC AID PROGRAM. EMPHA-
SIZES NEED FOR EFFECTIVE ADMINISTRATION AND LONG-RANGE PLAN-
NING. TABLES, CHARTS, FIGURES.

2209 US PRES CONF ADMIN PROCEDURE
REPORT (PAMPHLET)
WASHINGTON, D.C.: CONF. ADMIN. PROCEDURE, 1953,94 PP.
RECOMMENDATIONS TO PRESIDENT ON WAYS TO REDUCE DELAY, EX-
PENSE, AND VOLUME OF RECORDS IN ADJUDICATORY PROCEEDINGS OF
GOVERNMENT AGENCIES, INCLUDING JUDICIAL CONFERENCE, CIVIL
SERVICE COMMISSION, GENERAL SERVICES ADMINISTRATION, AND ALL
GOVERNMENTAL AGENCIES.

2210 US SENATE COMM AERO SPACE SCI
AERONAUTICAL RESEARCH AND DEVELOPMENT POLICY; HEARINGS,
COMM ON AERONAUTICAL AND SPACE SCIENCES...1967 (PAMPHLET)
WASHINGTON: GOVT PR OFFICE, 1967, 189 PP.
HEARINGS DEALT WITH ADEQUACY OF POLICY PLANNING IN AERO-
NAUTICAL RESEARCH AND DEVELOPMENT, AND WITH PROPER ROLES OF
CONGRESS, EXECUTIVE BRANCH, AND PRIVATE INDUSTRY. BOTH
SPACE AND NONSPACE ACTIVITIES TREATED.

2211 US SENATE COMM APPROPRIATIONS
PERSONNEL ADMINISTRATION AND OPERATIONS OF AGENCY FOR INTER-
NATIONAL DEVELOPMENT: SPECIAL HEARING.
WASHINGTON: GOVT PR OFFICE, 1963, 404 PP.
ANALYSIS OF PEOPLE WHO ARE APPOINTED TO AID AGENCY TO
ADMINISTER FOREIGN AID FUNDS AND PROGRAMS. FEELS PEOPLE ARE
INEFFICIENT AND UNDESERVING, AND WASTE US MONEY. SUGGESTS
AGENCY PEOPLE HAVE CIVIL SERVICE STATUS AND BE OF TOP

QUALITY. INVESTIGATES CERTAIN NATIONS, THEIR PROGRAMS, AND
LEADERS.

2212 US SENATE COMM GOVT OPERATIONS
ADMINISTRATION OF NATIONAL SECURITY.
WASHINGTON: GOVT PR OFFICE, 1962, 201 PP.
DESCRIBES ADMINISTRATION OF SECURITY PROGRAMS UNDER
KENNEDY AND EFFECT OF THIS ON FOREIGN POLICY DEVELOPMENT
IN THAT PERIOD. INCLUDES TEXTS OF RELEVANT OFFICIAL
STATEMENTS BY JFK, RUSK, MCNAMARA, AND BUNDY. ALSO GIVES
RECENT COMMENTS BY ACHESON, NEUSTADT, AND HERTER.

2213 US SENATE COMM GOVT OPERATIONS
ADMINISTRATION OF NATIONAL SECURITY (9 PARTS)
WASHINGTON: US GOVERNMENT, 1963, 600 PP.
COLLECTION OF US GOVERNMENT DOCUMENTS OF THE HEARINGS
BEFORE SUBCOMMITTEE ON NATIONAL SECURITY STAFFING AND
OPERATIONS DURING THE 88TH CONGRESS, FIRST AND SECOND SES-
SIONS. CONTAINS OPENING STATEMENTS, TESTIMONY, MEMORANDA,
EXHIBITS, AND COMMENTARY OF PARTICIPANTS IN THE INVESTIGA-
TION. COMMITTEE CHAIRED BY JOHN L. MCCLELLAN OF ARKANSAS.

2214 US SENATE COMM GOVT OPERATIONS
METROPOLITAN AMERICA: A SELECTED BIBLIOGRAPHY (PAMPHLET)
WASHINGTON: US GOVERNMENT, 1964, 37 PP.
TOPICALLY ARRANGED AND ANNOTATED BIBLIOGRAPHY OF
BOOKS, REPORTS, AND MONOGRAPHS ON GOVERNMENT OF METRO-
POLITAN AMERICA. TOPICS INCLUDE ORIGIN AND GROWTH OF
CITIES; METROPOLITAN ORGANIZATIONS; INTERGOVERNMENTAL
RELATIONS; DECISION-MAKING; FINANCES; AIR POLLUTION; EDUCA-
TION AND HOUSING; TRANSPORTATION; URBAN RENEWAL; ETC.

2215 US SENATE COMM GOVT OPERATIONS
THE SECRETARY OF STATE AND THE AMBASSADOR.
NEW YORK: FREDERICK PRAEGER, 1964, 203 PP., LC#64-8342.
ANTHOLOGY OF SUBCOMMITTEE'S PAPERS ON THE CONDUCT OF US
FOREIGN POLICY. DISCUSSES ROLES OF STATE DEPARTMENT, THE
PRESIDENT, AND THE AMERICAN AMBASSADOR IN FOREIGN POLICY OP-
ERATIONS. INCLUDES OBSERVATIONS BY DEAN RUSK ON THE NATIONAL
SECURITY POLICY PROCESS.

2216 US SENATE COMM GOVT OPERATIONS
ADMINISTRATION OF NATIONAL SECURITY.
WASHINGTON: US GOVERNMENT, 1964, 190 PP.
REPRODUCES OFFICIAL DOCUMENTS AND STATEMENTS ON STAFFING
AND MANAGEMENT OF FOREIGN AFFAIRS AND DEFENSE, AND RECENT
COMMENTS BY FORMER OFFICIALS AND STUDENTS OF THE POLICY-
MAKING PROCESS. DOCUMENTS COVER PERIOD FROM 1960-64, WITH
STATEMENTS BY JFK, MCNAMARA, KENNAN, AND ACHESON.

2217 US SENATE COMM GOVT OPERATIONS
ORGANIZATION OF FEDERAL EXECUTIVE DEPARTMENTS AND AGENCIES:
REPORT OF MARCH 23, 1965.
WASHINGTON: GOVT PR OFFICE, 1965, 67 PP.
REVIEWS ORGANIZATIONAL CHANGES IN EXECUTIVE BRANCH DURING
1964. IS 25TH OF SERIES. DETAILED ORGANIZATION CHART. COVERS
BUREAUS OF DEPARTMENTS OF AGRICULTURE, COMMERCE, DEFENSE,
THREE MILITARY DEPARTMENTS, HEALTH, EDUCATION, AND WELFARE,
INTERIOR, LABOR, POST OFFICE, STATE, TREASURY, ALSO
INDEPENDENT AGENCIES; ALSO EMPLOYEE STATISTICS AND SUMMARY
CHARTS.

2218 US SENATE COMM GOVT OPERATIONS
ADMINISTRATION OF NATIONAL SECURITY.
WASHINGTON: GOVT PR OFFICE, 1965, 600 PP.
STAFF REPORTS AND HEARINGS SUBMITTED TO COMMITTEE ON
GOVERNMENT OPERATIONS BY ITS SUBCOMMITTEE ON NATIONAL
SECURITY STAFFING AND OPERATIONS. INVESTIGATES ROLE OF
SECRETARY OF STATE AND HIS DEPARTMENT IN POLICY OF NATIONAL
SECURITY, AND ROLE OF US AMBASSADORS IN CONDUCT OF US
FOREIGN RELATIONS.

2219 US SENATE COMM GOVT OPERATIONS
INTERGOVERNMENTAL PERSONNEL ACT OF 1966.
WASHINGTON: GOVT PR OFFICE, 1966, 277 PP.
HEARINGS BEFORE SENATE SUBCOMMITTEE ON INTERGOVERNMENTAL
RELATIONS, OF COMMITTEE ON GOVERNMENT OPERATIONS, APRIL,
1966.CONCERNS BILL TO STRENGTHEN COOPERATION AND ADMINIS-
TRATION OF GRANT-IN-AID PROGRAMS, TO EXTEND STATE MERIT
SYSTEMS (FINANCED FEDERALLY), AND TO PROVIDE FUNDS FOR
IMPROVEMENT OF PERSONNEL ADMINISTRATION.

2220 US SENATE COMM ON FOREIGN REL
REVIEW OF THE UNITED NATIONS CHARTER: A COLLECTION OF
DOCUMENTS.
WASHINGTON: US GOVERNMENT, 1954, 895 PP.
DOCUMENTS USED BY SENATE SUBCOMMITTEE ON THE UNITED
NATIONS CHARTER IN CONSIDERATION OF CONDITIONS OF ITS
RENEWAL. INCLUDES TEXT OF BASIC INTERNATIONAL INSTRUMENTS
RELATED TO ADOPTION OF CHARTER; DOCUMENTARY HISTORY OF LEG-
ISLATION SINCE 1943 WHICH RELATES TO CHARTER; ILLUSTRATIVE
SELECTION OF OFFICIAL STUDIES, ACTS, ETC., RELATED TO RE-
NEWAL AND UN MEMBERS' VIEWS ON CHARTER REVIEW.

2221 US SENATE COMM ON FOREIGN REL
HEARINGS ON S 2859 AND S 2861.
WASHINGTON: GOVT PR OFFICE, 1966, 752 PP.
STATEMENTS BY PUBLIC AND PRIVATE OFFICIALS ON MILITARY
AND ECONOMIC AID, NATURE AND EXTENT OF SOVIET AID, DEVELOP-
MENT LOANS, ROLE OF PRIVATE ENTERPRISE, VALUE OF MILITARY
ASSISTANCE, AND GENERAL ASPECTS OF INTERNATIONAL SECURITY.

2222 US SENATE COMM ON FOREIGN REL
ARMS SALES AND FOREIGN POLICY (PAMPHLET)
WASHINGTON: US GOVERNMENT, 1967, 13 PP.
STAFF STUDY OF COMMITTEE ON FOREIGN POLICY. CONCLUDES
THAT SALE OF ARMS HAS REPLACED GIVING ARMS AS PREDOMINANT
FORM OF US MILITARY ASSISTANCE. BELIEVES THAT US
MUST REAPPRAISE ADEQUACY OF PRESENT MACHINERY OF POLICY
CONTROL AND LEGISLATIVE OVERSIGHT GOVERNING SALE OF
ARMS. MAKES SPECIFIC RECOMMENDATIONS FOR IMPROVEMENT.

2223 US SENATE COMM ON FOREIGN REL
THE UNITED NATIONS AT TWENTY-ONE (PAMPHLET)
WASHINGTON: US GOVERNMENT, 1967, 46 PP.
REPORT ON UN BY SENATOR FRANK CHURCH TO SENATE COMMITTEE
ON FOREIGN RELATIONS. DISCUSSES FOUNDING OF UN, CHANGES
IN WORLD SITUATION SINCE THEN, AND FUNCTIONING OF UN AS
PEACEKEEPING FORCE. MAINTAINS NEED FOR GREATER UNDERSTANDING
IN CONGRESS OF POTENTIAL AND LIMITS OF UN AS PEACEKEEPER.

2224 US SENATE COMM ON FOREIGN REL
THE UNITED NATIONS PEACEKEEPING DILEMMA (PAMPHLET)
WASHINGTON: US GOVERNMENT, 1967, 32 PP.
REPORT BY SENATOR CLIFFORD P. CASE TO SENATE COMMITTEE
ON FOREIGN RELATIONS ON UN. DISCUSSES UN'S RESPONSIBILITIES
IN PEACEKEEPING AND UN ACTIONS IN MIDDLE EAST IN 1956 AND IN
CONGO. GIVES US OBJECTIVES IN SOLVING UN'S PEACEKEEPING
PROBLEMS OF COOPERATION AND FINANCING ACTIONS.

2225 US SENATE COMM ON FOREIGN REL
HUMAN RIGHTS CONVENTIONS.
WASHINGTON: US GOVERNMENT, 1967, 227 PP.
SUBCOMMITTEE HEARINGS OF COMMITTEE ON FOREIGN RELATIONS
HELD FEBRUARY AND MARCH, 1967, J.W. FULLBRIGHT PRESIDING.
TESTIMONY DEALS WITH CONVENTION ON THE POLITICAL RIGHTS OF
WOMEN, CONVENTION CONCERNING THE ABOLITION OF FORCED LABOR,
AND A SUPPLEMENTARY SLAVERY CONVENTION. RECOMMENDING SENATE
RATIFICATION ARE AJ. GOLDBERG, BAR ASSOCIATION REPRESENTA-
TIVES, AND AFL-CIO MEMBERS.

2226 US SENATE COMM ON JUDICIARY
FEDERAL ADMINISTRATIVE PROCEDURE.
WASHINGTON: GOVT PR OFFICE, 1960, 343 PP.
RECORD OF HEARINGS BEFORE SUBCOMMITTEE ON ADMINISTRATIVE
PRACTICE AND PROCEDURE ON PROCEDURAL PROBLEMS IN ADMINIS-
TRATIVE AGENCIES. INCLUDES TESTIMONY OF WITNESSES AND
EXHIBITS.

2227 US SENATE COMM ON JUDICIARY
ADMINISTRATIVE PROCEDURE LEGISLATION.
WASHINGTON: GOVT PR OFFICE, 1960, 429 PP.
RECORD OF HEARINGS BEFORE SUBCOMMITTEE ON ADMINISTRATIVE
PRACTICE AND PROCEDURE, ON LEGISLATION TO ESTABLISH OFFICE
OF FEDERAL ADMINISTRATIVE PRACTICE AND STANDARDS OF CONDUCT
FOR AGENCY HEARING PROCEEDINGS. INCLUDES TESTIMONY OF WIT-
NESSES AND EXHIBITS.

2228 US SENATE COMM ON JUDICIARY
STATE DEPARTMENT SECURITY.
WASHINGTON: GOVT. PR. OFFICE, 1962, 676 PP.
REPORTS ORIGINAL HEARINGS ON ADMINISTRATION OF INTERNAL
SECURITY ACT AND OTHER LAWS. ALSO REVIEWS ATTEMPTS BY
KENNEDY TO SUSPEND ITS OPERATIONS AND RESULTANT OUTCRY FROM
PRESS AND SENATE.

2229 US SENATE COMM ON JUDICIARY
ADMINISTERED PRICES.
WASHINGTON: GOVT PR OFFICE, 1963, 276 PP.
LEGAL AND ECONOMIC AUTHORITIES DISCUSS APPROPRIATE
PUBLIC POLICY WITH REGARD TO ADMINISTERED PRICES. CASE
STUDIES, CELLER-KEFAUVER ACT, AND ANTI-TRUST LAWS ARE
INCLUDED.

2230 US SENATE COMM ON JUDICIARY
ADMINISTRATIVE CONFERENCE OF THE UNITED STATES.
WASHINGTON: GOVT PR OFFICE, 1963, 151 PP.
RECORD OF HEARINGS BEFORE SUBCOMMITTEE ON ADMINISTRATIVE
PRACTICE AND PROCEDURE ON LEGISLATION TO IMPROVE ADMINIS-
TRATION OF FEDERAL AGENCIES THROUGH CREATION OF ADMINISTRA-
TIVE CONFERENCE OF US. INCLUDES TESTIMONY OF WITNESSES.

2231 US SENATE COMM ON JUDICIARY
ADMINISTRATIVE PROCEDURE ACT.
WASHINGTON: GOVT PR OFFICE, 1964, 693 PP.
RECORD OF HEARINGS BEFORE SUBCOMMITTEE ON ADMINISTRATIVE
PRACTICE AND PROCEDURE ON AMENDMENT TO ADMINISTRATIVE PRO-
CEDURE ACT. INCLUDES TESTIMONY OF WITNESSES, TEXTS OF BILLS
UNDER DISCUSSION, AND EXHIBITS.

2232 US SENATE COMM ON JUDICIARY
HEARINGS BEFORE SUBCOMMITTEE ON ADMINISTRATIVE PRACTICE AND

PROCEDURE ABOUT ADMINISTRATIVE PROCEDURE ACT 1965.
WASHINGTON: GOVT PR OFFICE, 1965, 572 PP.
TRANSCRIPT OF HEARINGS IN MAY, 1965, ON FOUR BILLS TO
AMEND THE ADMINISTRATIVE PROCEDURE ACT OF 1946. INCLUDES
TEXTS OF BILLS, STATEMENTS OF WITNESSES, AND COMMENTS
OF FEDERAL AGENCIES, BAR ASSOCIATIONS, AND VARIOUS COM-
PANIES. BILLS CONCERN IMPROVING RULES GOVERNING PROCEDURES
BEFORE FEDERAL ADMINISTRATIVE AGENCIES, FREEDOM OF INFORMA-
TION ABOUT GOVERNMENT ACTIVITIES, ATTORNEYS' PRACTICE.

2233 US SENATE COMM ON POST OFFICE
TO PROVIDE FOR AN EFFECTIVE SYSTEM OF PERSONNEL
ADMINISTRATION.
WASHINGTON: US GOVERNMENT, 1959, 140 PP.
HEARINGS BEFORE SUBCOMMITTEE ON CIVIL SERVICE OF
COMMITTEE ON POST OFFICE AND CIVIL SERVICE OF US SENATE
HEADED BY RALPH YARBOROUGH, ON BILL S. 1638 PROVIDING FOR
EFFECTIVE SYSTEM OF PERSONNEL ADMINISTRATION FOR EXECUTIVE
BRANCH BY ESTABLISHING AGENCIES TO CONTROL MANAGEMENT OF
DEPARTMENTS.

2234 US SENATE COMM POST OFFICE
TO PROVIDE AN EFFECTIVE SYSTEM OF PERSONNEL ADMINISTRATION.
WASHINGTON: US GOVERNMENT, 1958, 195 PP.
RECORD OF HEARINGS BEFORE SENATE POST OFFICE AND CIVIL
SERVICE COMMITTEE ON BILL TO PROVIDE EFFECTIVE SYSTEM OF
PERSONNEL FOR EXECUTIVE BRANCH. INCLUDES REPORTS AND
TESTIMONY.

2235 US SENATE COMM. GOVT. OPER.
"REVISION OF THE UN CHARTER."
WASHINGTON: G.P.O., 1950, 64 PP.
DEALS WITH EAST-WEST TENSION AND PRESSURE FOR ACTION, AND
THE UN IN RELATION TO US FOREIGN POLICY. GIVES INSIGHT INTO
SENATE CONCURRENT RESOLUTIONS. CONCLUDES WITH STUDY OF
RESPONSIBILITIES OF THE EXECUTIVE AND CONGRESS.

2236 US SENATE COMM. GOVT. OPER.
ORGANIZING FOR NATIONAL SECURITY.
WASHINGTON: G.P.O., 1960, 180 PP.
DISCUSSES ORGANIZATION, FUNCTION AND DEFICIENCIES OF NA-
TIONAL SECURITY COUNCIL. EMPHASIZING HEAVY AGENDA AND COM-
PLEX PROCEDURES, SUGGESTS IMPROVEMENTS.

2237 US STATE DEPT.
PEACE AND WAR: UNITED STATES FOREIGN POLICY, 1931-41.
WASHINGTON: G.P.O., 1942, 144 PP.
DESCRIBES IMPORTANT FACTORS INFLUENCING THE CONDUCT OF
OUR FOREIGN RELATIONS. SHOWS HOW OUR FOREIGN POLICY HAD TO
MOVE WITHIN THE FRAMEWORK OF A GRADUAL EVOLUTION OF PUBLIC
OPINION. ANALYZES COLLECTION OF DOCUMENTS RELATED TO THE
DECADE UNDER CONSIDERATION.

2238 US SUPERINTENDENT OF DOCUMENTS
EDUCATION (PRICE LIST 31)
WASHINGTON: GOVT PR OFFICE.
A SERIES PUBLICATION OF US GOVERNMENT PUBLICATIONS CUR-
RENTLY AVAILABLE FOR SALE. INCLUDES MATERIALS ON TOPICS SUCH
AS CIVIL DEFENSE, CIVIL RIGHTS AND EDUCATION, SECONDARY AND
HIGHER EDUCATION, FEDERAL AID, FOREIGN EDUCATION, DEBATES,
SCHOOL FINANCE, AND NATIONAL SCIENCE FOUNDATION PUBLICA-
TIONS. ENTRIES LISTED BY SUBJECT. 53 EDITIONS TO DATE. CUR-
RENT EDITION COVERS MATERIALS FROM 1958 THROUGH 1966.

2239 US SUPERINTENDENT OF DOCUMENTS
INTERSTATE COMMERCE (PRICE LIST 59)
WASHINGTON: GOVT PR OFFICE.
SERIES PUBLICATION OF US GOVERNMENT LISTING GOVERNMENT
PUBLICATIONS CURRENTLY AVAILABLE FOR SALE. 48 EDITIONS TO
DATE. LATEST ISSUE CONTAINS PUBLICATIONS FROM 1949 THROUGH
1966. MAJORITY OF ENTRIES ANNOTATED; GROUPED BY SUBJECTS
SUCH AS ACCIDENTS AND SAFETY, INTERSTATE COMMERCE COMMIS-
SION, LOCOMOTIVES AND RAILROADS, LEGISLATION, STATE TAXA-
TION, AND TARIFF CIRCULARS.

2240 US SUPERINTENDENT OF DOCUMENTS
LABOR (PRICE LIST 33)
WASHINGTON: GOVT PR OFFICE.
SERIES PUBLICATION OF US GOVERNMENT LISTING GOVERNMENT
PUBLICATIONS CURRENTLY AVAILABLE FOR SALE. ENTRIES GROUPED
BY SUBJECT: INCLUDE TOPICS SUCH AS COLLECTIVE BARGAINING,
LABOR DEPARTMENT, NATIONAL LABOR RELATIONS ACT AND BOARD,
PUBLIC WORKS, UNIONS, WAGES, EMPLOYMENT AND UNEMPLOYMENT,
PRODUCTIVITY, AND PUBLIC WORKS. 45 EDITIONS TO DATE. MATE-
RIALS IN LATEST ISSUE PUBLISHED 1958 THROUGH 1966.

2241 US SUPERINTENDENT OF DOCUMENTS
POLITICAL SCIENCE: GOVERNMENT, CRIME, DISTRICT OF COLUMBIA
(PRICE LIST 54)
WASHINGTON: GOVT PR OFFICE.
SERIES PUBLICATION LISTING US GOVERNMENT DOCUMENTS CUR-
RENTLY AVAILABLE FOR SALE. ITEMS ARRANGED BY SUBJECT COVER
TOPICS SUCH AS STATE DEPARTMENT, JUSTICE DEPARTMENT, CIVIL
PROCEDURE, CONSTITUTIONAL RIGHTS, GOVERNMENT ORGANIZATION,
SUPREME COURT, VOTING, GOVERNMENT EMPLOYEES, AND CRIME AND
CRIMINAL PROCEDURE. ITEMS ARE ARRANGED BY SUBJECT. 44 EDI-

TIONS TO DATE. CURRENT ISSUE CONTAINS 1959-66 SOURCES.

2242 US SUPERINTENDENT OF DOCUMENTS
TARIFF AND TAXATION (PRICE LIST 37)
WASHINGTON: GOVT PR OFFICE.
SERIES PUBLICATION OF US GOVERNMENT PUBLICATIONS CURRENT-
LY AVAILABLE FOR SALE LISTING ITEMS BY SUBJECT. TOPICS IN-
CLUDE US CUSTOMS COURT REPORTS, REPORT OF CASES ADJUDGED BE-
FORE CUSTOMS AND PATENT APPEALS COURT, INTERNAL REVENUE BU-
REAU, TARIFF AND TRADE, TAX COURT, TARIFF COMMISSION, PROP-
ERTY TAX, ETC. 46 EDITIONS TO DATE. LATEST ISSUE COVERS MA-
TERIALS PUBLISHED FROM 1951 THROUGH 1966.

2243 US SUPERINTENDENT OF DOCUMENTS
TRANSPORTATION: HIGHWAYS, ROADS, AND POSTAL SERVICE (PRICE
LIST 25)
WASHINGTON: GOVT PR OFFICE.
SERIES PUBLICATION OF US GOVERNMENT LISTING MATERIALS
CURRENTLY AVAILABLE FOR SALE. ENTRIES GROUPED BY SUBJECT:
INCLUDE TOPICS SUCH AS FEDERAL MARITIME COMMISSION, MARITIME
ADMINISTRATION, PORTS, POSTAL SERVICE, NAVIGATION, MERCHANT
MARINE, PUBLIC ROADS BUREAU, RAILROADS, FIRST AID AT SEA,
AND INTRACOASTAL WATERWAY. 50 EDITIONS TO DATE. MATERIALS
PUBLISHED 1952 THROUGH 1967.

2244 US SUPERINTENDENT OF DOCUMENTS
SPACE: MISSILES, THE MOON, NASA, AND SATELLITES (PRICE
LIST 79A)
WASHINGTON: GOVT PR OFFICE, 1967, 21 PP.
FIRST EDITION OF US GOVERNMENT SERIES LISTING GOVERNMENT
MATERIALS CURRENTLY AVAILABLE FOR SALE. MAJORITY OF SOURCES
ANNOTATED; ENTRIES PUBLISHED 1959 THROUGH 1966. TOPICS IN-
CLUDE SPACE EDUCATION, EXPLORATION, RESEARCH TECHNOLOGY,
NASA CONGRESSIONAL REPORTS, PROJECT APOLLO AND GEMINI, COM-
MUNICATIONS SATELLITES, INSPECTION, INTERNATIONAL COOPERA-
TION, ETC.

2245 US TARIFF COMMISSION
LIST OF PUBLICATIONS OF THE TARIFF COMMISSION (PAMPHLET)
WASHINGTON: US GOVERNMENT, 1951, 29 PP.
A TABULATED, UNANNOTATED LIST OF PUBLICATIONS RELEASED BY
THE TARIFF COMMISSION BETWEEN 1940-51. LISTED ALPHABETICALLY
BY SUBJECT AND REPORT DESIGNATION.

2246 US TARIFF COMMISSION
THE TARIFF; A BIBLIOGRAPHY: A SELECT LIST OF REFERENCES.
WASHINGTON: US GOVERNMENT, 1934, 980 PP.
ALPHABETICAL LISTING OF 6,500 ITEMS, BOOKS, PAMPHLETS,
AND PERIODICALS AVAILABLE IN US. INCLUDES REFERENCE TO
HISTORY, STATE, FEDERAL, AND INTERNATIONAL; THEORY AND
POLICY; PRACTICE; TREATIES, ADMINISTRATION; AND ECONOMIC
IMPLICATIONS OF TARIFF LAWS. CONTAINS AUTHOR AND SUBJECT
INDEXES. INCLUDES ANNOTATIONS WHERE WORK IS NOTABLE OR
TITLE OBSCURE.

2247 USEEM J., USEEM R., DONOGHUE J.
"MEN IN THE MIDDLE OF THE THIRD CULTURE: THE ROLES OF
AMERICAN AND NON-WESTERN PEOPLE IN CROSS-CULTURAL ADMINIS-."
TRATION.
HUM. ORGAN., 22 (FALL 63), 169-79.
DEFINES A BINATIONAL THIRD CULTURE, DESCRIBES ITS
MEMBERS, PARTICULARLY THE AMERICAN COMMUNITY ABROAD, ANA-
LYSES THEMES RELATING TO COORDINATION AND THE IMPLEMENTING
OF PROGRAMS, AND OUTLINES THEORETICAL IMPLICATIONS FOR
CROSS-CULTURAL ADMINISTRATION.

2248 VAID K.N.
STATE AND LABOR IN INDIA.
NEW YORK: ASIA PUBL HOUSE, 1965, 279 PP.
TREATS ROLE OF STATE IN GUIDING EMPLOYER-EMPLOYEE
RELATIONSHIP AND IN SETTING STANDARDS FOR WORKING CONDITIONS
AND WAGES. EXAMINES LEGISLATION RELATING TO HOURS, WELFARE,
SOCIAL SECURITY, WAGES, DISPUTES, AND UNIONS.

2249 VALEN H., KATZ D.
POLITICAL PARTIES IN NORWAY.
OSLO: J CHR GUNDERSON, 1964, 383 PP.
EXAMINES POLITICAL PARTIES ON THE LOCAL LEVEL. ANALYZES
THEIR STRUCTURE AND METHODS, AND DISCUSSES THE CHARACTER
OF LOCAL LEADERS. THEN VIEWS NORWEGIAN POLITICS AT A
GRASS ROOTS LEVEL. STATISTICS ARE BASED ON A 1957-58
ELECTION.

2250 VAN DER SPRENKEL S.
"LEGAL INSTITUTIONS IN MANCHU CHINA."
LONDON: ATHLONE PRESS, 1962.
PRELIMINARY SURVEY OF COMPLEX OF LEGAL AND QUASI-LEGAL
INSTITUTIONS OF MANCHU PERIOD. DESCRIPTION OF THEORY AND
FUNCTIONS OF GOVERNMENT IN CHINA. STRUCTURE OF ADMINISTRA-
TION. DISCUSSES CODIFIED LAW, JUDICIAL PROCEDURE, JURISDIC-
TIONAL ASPECTS OF THE "TSU" AND GUILD SYSTEM, LOCAL AND
CUSTOMARY JURISDICTION. CONCLUDING CHAPTER ON LAW AS ETHI-
CAL FOUNDATION OF SOCIETY. BIBLIOGRAPHY INCLUDED.

2251 VAN RIPER P.P.
HISTORY OF THE UNITED STATES CIVIL SERVICE.

EVANSTON: ROW-PETERSON, 1958, 588 PP., LC#58-5927.
STORY OF US ADMINISTRATIVE SYSTEM AS IT DEVELOPED, AS IT RESPONDED TO VARIOUS POLITICAL AND SOCIAL PRESSURES, AND AS IT FUNCTIONED FROM DAY TO DAY. STRESSES NATURE OF CIVIL SERVICE AS A POLITICAL INSTITUTION, REFLECTING POLICIES OF THE DEMOCRATIC SYSTEM. DISCUSSES SOME BUREAUCRATIC PROBLEMS AND OFFERS SUGGESTIONS FOR SOLVING THEM.

2252 VAN RIPER P.P., GUNTER E. ET AL.
THE MERIT SYSTEM: FOUNDATION FOR RESPONSIBLE PUBLIC MANAGEMENT (PAMPHLET)
CHICAGO: PUBLIC PERSONNEL ASSN, 1963, 25 PP.
FIVE SHORTRTICLES ON HOW A MERIT SYSTEM OF APPOINTMENT AND PROMOTION PROVIDES MORE EFFICNT PUBLIC ADMINISTRATION AND FURTHERS THE PUBLIC INTEREST.

2253 VAN SLYCK P.
PEACE: THE CONTROL OF NATIONAL POWER.
BOSTON: BEACON PRESS, 1963, 186 PP., LC#63-21565.
SUBTITLED "A GUIDE FOR THE CONCERNED CITIZEN ON PROBLEMS OF DISARMAMENT AND STRENGTHENING OF THE UNITED NATIONS." ANALYZES MAJOR ISSUES IN WORLD AFFAIRS AND PROPOSALS FOR RESTRUCTURING PRESENT WORLD. ISSUES INCLUDE CUBAN MISSILE CRISIS, INTERNATIONAL LAW AND CONTROL OF FORCE, FINANCING PEACE, PROBLEMS OF WORLD AUTHORITY, ROLE OF UN, AND PROBLEMS OF FACTS AND PROSPECTS FOR ARMS CONTROL.

2254 VANDENBOSCH A., HOGAN W.N.
THE UN: BACKGROUND, ORGANIZATION, FUNCTIONS, ACTIVITIES.
NEW YORK: MCGRAW HILL, 1952, 456 PP.
OUTLINES COMPLEX OF FACTORS INVOLVED IN UN PROCEDURES AND PRACTISES. EMPHASIZES THAT FIRST PURPOSE OF UN SYSTEM IS COLLECTIVE SECURITY. TRACES DEVELOPMENT OF INTERNATIONAL CO-OPERATION TO PRESERVE HUMAN RIGHTS AND FUNDAMENTAL FREEDOMS.

2255 VASEY W.
GOVERNMENT AND SOCIAL WELFARE: ROLES OF FEDERAL , STATE AND LOCAL GOVERNMENTS IN ADMINISTERING WELFARE SERVICES.
NEW YORK: HOLT RINEHART WINSTON, 1958, 506 PP., LC#58-6336.
DISCUSSION OF BASIC GORAGIZATIONAL PROBLEM OF SOCIAL WELFARE AGENCIES OF TRYING TO REPRESENT BOTH THE PUBLIC AND THE AGENCY'S SPECIFIC CLIENTELE.

2256 VECCHIO G.D.
L'ETAT ET LE DROIT.
PARIS: DALLOZ, 1964, 184 PP.
DISCUSSES BASIC ELEMENTS OF STATE (TERRITORY, PEOPLE, SOVEREIGNTY), HISTORICAL EVOLUTION, EXECUTIVE, LEGISLATIVE, AND JUDICIAL FUNCTIONS, INTERNATIONAL LEGAL COMMUNITY WITH PARTICULAR REFERENCE TO UN, AND CONCLUDES WITH DISCUSSION OF AIM OF STATE. INCLUDES BRIEF ANALYSIS OF FUNCTION OF ITALIAN LEGISLATURE UNDER CONSTITUTION.

2257 VEINOTT A.F. JR. ED.
MATHEMATICAL STUDIES IN MANAGEMENT SCIENCE.
NEW YORK: MACMILLAN, 1965, 481 PP., LC#55-17819.
SURVEY OF CURRENT TOPICS OF DISCUSSION IN MANAGEMENT SCIENCES. PAPERS DEAL WITH DETERMINISTIC DECISION MODELS AND STOCHASTIC DECISION MODELS; TREAT TRANSPORTATION AND NETWORK PROBLEMS, TOPICS IN LINEAR AND QUADRATIC PROGRAMMING, AND PRODUCTION AND INVENTORY CONTROL; ANALYZE PROGRAMMING UNDER UNCERTAINTY, AND INVENTORY MODELS.

2258 VENKATESAN S.L. ED., PARANTAPE H.K. ED.
BIBLIOGRAPHY ON PUBLIC ENTERPRISES IN INDIA.
NEW DELHI: INDIAN INST PUB ADMIN, 1961, 106 PP.
ABOUT 800 ITEMS IN ENGLISH COVERING HALF A CENTURY BUT CHIEFLY SINCE INDEPENDENCE. INDEXED BY AUTHOR AND SUBJECT. INCLUDES BOOKS, ARTICLES, PAMPHLETS, REPORTS, AND A LIST OF JOURNALS.

2259 VERBA S.
"SMALL GROUPS AND POLITICAL BEHAVIOR: A STUDY OF LEADERSHIP"
PRINCETON: PRINCETON U PRESS, 1961.
EXPLORES RELEVANCE FOR POLITICAL SCIENCE OF THEORY OF BEHAVIOR OF SMALL FACE-TO-FACE GROUPS. METHOD BASED ON CONTROLLED EXPERIMENTAL STUDY OF INTERACTION IN SMALL GROUPS. ARGUES FOR IMPORTANCE OF PRIMARY GROUP IN POLITICS AND DISCUSSES FUNCTIONS OF FACE-TO-FACE GROUP AND PLACE WITHIN POLITICAL SYSTEM. SPECIAL DISCUSSIONS OF METHOD AND ITS APPLICATIONS. CONTAINS EXTENSIVE BIBLIOGRAPHY.

2260 VERGIN R.C.
"COMPUTER INDUCED ORGANIZATION CHANGES."
BUSINESS TOPICS, 15 (SUMMER 67), 60-68.
EXAMINES EFFECT OF COMPUTER ON DECISION-MAKING, CONCOMITANT CHANGES IN STRUCTURE OF ORGANIZATION, AND POSITION OF DATA PROCESSING. DISCUSSES MIDDLE MANAGEMENT, DECENTRALIZATION, AND RESISTANCE TO ORGANIZATIONAL CHANGE. COMMENTS ON IMPACT OF COMPUTER IN FUTURE.

2261 VERNON R.
THE MYTH AND REALITY OF OUR URBAN PROBLEMS (PAMPHLET)
CAMBRIDGE, MASS.: JOINT CTR. URBAN STUD., 1962, 84 PP.
STAFFORD LITTLE LECTURES PRESENTED AT PRINCETON UNIVERSITY, 1961. OFFER PRESCRIPTION FOR, RATHER THAN PROG-

NOSIS OF, METROPOLITAN ILLS. PROPOSE SEVERAL PROGRAMS, INCLUDING LAND-USE PLANNING, REBUILDING CITIES, GOVERNMENT INTERVENTION, AND THE LIKE.

2262 VINER J.
"ECONOMIC FOREIGN POLICY ON THE NEW FRONTIER."
FOR. AFF., 39 (JULY 61), 560-77.
SCORES KENNEDY ON PROTECTIONIST COMMERCIAL POLICY TO PROMOTE TARIFF REDUCTION AND FOR CONTINUING ILLOGICAL FARM PROGRAM. COMMENDS KENNEDY ON PROPOSALS REORGANIZING FOREIGN AID PROGRAM. ANALYZES REMEDIES TO BALANCE-OF-PAYMENT DEFICIT.

2263 VIORST M.
HOSTILE ALLIES: FDR AND DE GAULLE.
NEW YORK: MACMILLAN, 1965, 280 PP., $6.95.
PRESENTS PERSONALITIES, MOTIVATIONS, POLICY CONFLICTS OF TOP EXECUTIVES FROM MAY 1940 TO SEPT. 1945. POWER CONFLICT SET OFF BY DETAILED ACCOUNTS OF WW 2 STRATEGIES AND POLITICAL EVENTS.

2264 VIRALLY M.
"VERS UNE REFORME DU SECRETARIAT DES NATIONS UNIES."
INT. ORGAN., 15 (SPRING 61), 236-55.
EXAMINES ROLE OF UN SECRETARY GENERAL. ASSUMES THAT AUTHORITY HE HAS ACQUIRED HAS BECOME KEYSTONE OF UN DIPLOMACY. STATES THAT SOVIET PROPOSAL WOULD DESTROY INTERNATIONAL CHARACTER OF THE SECRETARIAT.

2265 VIRGINIA STATE LIBRARY
CHECK-LIST OF VIRGINIA STATE PUBLICATIONS.
RICHMOND: VIRGINIA STATE LIB.
A CURRENT BIBLIOGRAPHY OF VIRGINIA OFFICIAL PUBLICATIONS, ISSUED ANNUALLY SINCE 1926, AND COVERING ALL DOCUMENTS SINCE 1776. APPROXIMATELY 600 PUBLICATIONS ARE ANNOTATED AND CLASSIFIED ALPHABETICALLY BY DEPARTMENT EACH YEAR.

2266 VON HOFFMAN N.
THE MULTIVERSITY; A PERSONAL REPORT ON WHAT HAPPENS TO TODAY'S STUDENTS AT AMERICAN UNIVERSITIES.
NEW YORK: HOLT RINEHART WINSTON, 1966, 201 PP., LC#66-14222.
RELATES EXPERIENCES OF YOUNG PEOPLE IN LARGE UNIVERSITY. REPORTS ON REACTION OF STUDENTS TO EMPHASIS ON EDUCATION AS STEPPING STONE TO JOB, FEELING OF ANONYMITY, HOSTILITY TO ADMINISTRATION, AND CONCERN FOR POLITICAL AND SOCIAL CAUSES. PROFESSORS SPEAK ABOUT ACADEMIC FREEDOM, TEACHING VERSUS RESEARCH, CAMPUS MORALITY, AND STUDENT INERTIA. ROLE OF UNIVERSITY IN SOCIETY IS DISCUSSED.

2267 VONGLAHN G.
LAW AMONG NATIONS: AN INTRODUCTION TO PUBLIC INTERNATIONAL LAW.
NEW YORK: MACMILLAN, 1965, 768 PP., $9.95.
PRESENTS ISSUES OF FOLLOWING TOPICS: LAW OF NATIONS, INTERNATIONAL LAW, LAW AND THE INDIVIDUAL, TERRITORIAL QUESTIONS, INTERNATIONAL TRANSACTIONS, AND WAR. GIVES FACTS, DECISIONS, AND REASONING OF SIGNIFICANT CASES.

2268 VOOS H.
ORGANIZATIONAL COMMUNICATION: A BIBLIOGRAPHY.
NEW BRUNSWICK: RUTGERS U PR, 1967, 265 PP., LC#67-63681.
REVIEWS LITERATURE OF RESEARCH RELATING TO COMMUNICATION WITHIN AND AMONG GROUPS. INCLUDES EXPERIMENTAL, SCIENTIFIC, AND INDUSTRIAL GROUPS.

2269 WADE E.C.S., PHILLIPS G.G.
CONSTITUTIONAL LAW; AN OUTLINE OF THE LAW AND PRACTICE OF THE CONSTITUTION.
LONDON: LONGMANS, GREEN & CO, 1950, 535 PP.
EXAMINES THE ENGLISH SYSTEM OF GOVERNMENT. BROAD STUDY INCLUDES NATURE OF CONSTITUTION AND GENERAL PRINCIPLES FOR AUTHORITY, PARLIAMENT, EXECUTIVE, AND JUDICIARY; DESCRIBES GOVERNMENT ON LOCAL LEVEL. CONSIDERS ADMINISTRATIVE LAW, CITIZEN AND STATE, MILITARY FORCES, AND RELATIONS WITH THE COMMONWEALTH.

2270 WADE H.W.R.
TOWARDS ADMINISTRATIVE JUSTICE.
ANN ARBOR: U OF MICH PR, 1963, 138 PP., LC#63-9896.
FIVE LECTURES (THE THOMAS M. COOLEY LECTURES), DELIVERED AT THE UNIVERSITY OF MICHIGAN IN OCTOBER, 1961, BY PROFESSOR WADE OF OXFORD UNIVERSITY, ATTEMPT TO EXPLAIN SOME OF PRESENT PROBLEMS OF ADMINISTRATIVE LAW IN BRITAIN AND BRITISH ATTEMPTS TO SOLVE THEM. MAKES COMPARISONS BETWEEN AMERICAN AND BRITISH INSTITUTIONS. INCLUDES TABLES OF STATUTES AND CASES, AND AN INDEX.

2271 WADIA M.
THE NATURE AND SCOPE OF MANAGEMENT.
GLENVIEW, ILL: SCOTT, FORESMAN, 1966, 356 PP.
PRESENTS INTRODUCTORY THEORIES OF MANAGEMENT AND ITS OBJECTIVES. DISCUSSES FUNCTIONAL APPROACH AND PRACTICAL MATTERS AS WELL AS PRESENTING RECENT DEVELOPMENTS IN MANAGEMENT EDUCATION AND PRACTICE.

2272 WAGER P.W. ED.

"COUNTY GOVERNMENT ACROSS THE NATION."
PRINCETON* UNIV. REF. SYSTEM, 1950.
    DESCRIPTION OF ORGANIZATION AND OPERATIONS OF PARTICULAR
COUNTY GOVERNMENTS IN 48 STATES WITH THE EXCLUSION OF METRO-
POLITAN COUNTIES. INTRODUCTION SURVEYS GENERAL FEATURES OF
COUNTY GOVERNMENT: SCHOOL DISTRICTS, TOWNSHIP GOVERNMENTS,
TOWN GOVERNMENT, STATE ADMINISTRATIVE SUPERVISION, REVENUES
AND EXPENDITURES, COURTS AND COURT OFFICIALS, ETC. SHORT
GENERAL BIBLIOGRAPHY INCLUDED.

2273 WAGLEY C.
AMAZON TOWN: A STUDY OF MAN IN THE TROPICS.
NEW YORK: MACMILLAN, 1953, 305 PP.
    STUDY BY AUTHOR OF LIFE IN RURAL UNDEVELOPED BRAZILIAN
COMMUNITY ON AMAZON RIVER. ANALYSIS OF CULTURE AND STRUCTURE
OF SOCIETY BY RESIDENCE IN COMMUNITY AND INFORMATION GAINED
FROM OTHERS IN THE AREA.

2274 WAGRET M.
"L'ASCENSION POLITIQUE DE L'U.D.D.I.A. (CONGO) ET SA PRISE
DU POUVOIR (1956-1959)."
REV. JURID. POLIT. OUTREMER, 17 (APR.-JUNE 63), 334-44.
    REVEALS SOCIAL AND ECONOMIC BACKGROUND OF THE UNION FOR
DEFENSE OF AFRICAN INTERESTS. RELATES ITS POLICIES TO FRENCH
POLITICAL CRISIS WHICH GAVE RISE TO FIFTH REPUBLIC. DIS-
CUSSES FOUNDATION OF CONGOLESE REPUBLIC AND POWER STRUGGLES
WITHIN POLITICAL ORGANIZATION.

2275 WAINHOUSE D.W.
REMNANTS OF EMPIRE: THE UNITED NATIONS AND THE END OF
COLONIALISM.
NEW YORK: HARPER ROW, 1964, 153 PP.
    CONSIDERS BALANCE SHEET OF WESTERN COLONIALISM AND
RELATIONSHIPS BEING DEVELOPED IN PROCESS OF LIQUIDATING LAST
VESTIGES OF EMPIRE. DISCUSSES TERRITORIES RANGING FROM
LARGE DEPENDENCIES TO TINY ISLANDS, IN FRAMEWORK OF
PRESSING ISSUES AND METROPOLES INVOLVED.

2276 WALDO D. ED.
THE RESEARCH FUNCTION OF UNIVERSITY BUREAUS AND INSTITUTES
FOR GOVERNMENTAL-RELATED RESEARCH.
BERKELEY: U CALIF, BUR PUB ADMIN, 1960.
    ISSUED BY BUREAU OF PUBLIC ADMINISTRATION, BOOK IS
RESULT OF A 1959 CONFERENCE AT UNIVERSITY OF CALIFORNIA.
DEALS WITH RESEARCH IN PUBLIC ADMINISTRATION, POLITICS,
COMPARATIVE GOVERNMENTS, METROPOLISES, AND PUBLIC POLICY.
ALSO DEALS WITH METHODS OF RESEARCH. THE RELATION BETWEEN
THEIR OUTPUT AND THE HOW AND WHY OF THEIR ORGANIZATION IS
NOT ADEQUATELY EXPLAINED.

2277 WALINE M.
LE CONTROLE JURIDICTIONNEL DE L'ADMINISTRATION.
CAIRO: UNIVERSITE FOUAD 1ER, 1949, 208 PP.
    EXAMINES ORGANIZATION OF ADMINISTRATIVE JURISDICTION,
ESPECIALLY "COUNSEIL D'ETATS." IN FRANCE, BELGIUM, AND
EGYPT. CONSIDERS HOW ADMINISTRATIVE ACTS, WHEN BEYOND THEIR
JURISDICTION, CAN BE ANNULLED THROUGH JUDICIAL PROCESSES.

2278 WALKER A.A. ED.
OFFICIAL PUBLICATIONS OF SIERRA LEONE AND GAMBIA.
WASHINGTON: LIBRARY OF CONGRESS, 1963, 92 PP., LC#63-60090.
    BIBLIOGRAPHY OF DOCUMENTS PUBLISHED SINCE ESTABLISHMENT
OF CENTRAL GOVERNMENT AND PERTINENT PUBLICATIONS OF BRITISH
GOVERNMENT RELATED TO ITS COLONIAL ADMINISTRATION. ARRANGED
BY COUNTRY AND SUBDIVIDED ALPHABETICALLY BY AUTHOR AND TITLE
UNDER PUBLISHER. CENSUS AND DEVELOPMENT PLANNING UNDER
SEPARATE TOPIC. AUTHOR AND SUBJECT INDEX INCLUDED. CONTAINS
730 ITEMS IN ENGLISH.

2279 WALKER H.
"THE LEGISLATIVE PROCESS: LAWMAKING IN THE UNITED STATES."
NEW YORK: RONALD PRESS, 1948.
    A DESCRIPTION OF THE MACHINERY SET UP IN THE US FOR DE-
TERMINING AND DECLARING THE WILL OF THE PEOPLE. EVALUATES
DEFECTS WITHIN THE LEGISLATIVE PROCESS AND SUGGESTS A DIREC-
TION FOR FUTURE REFORMS. UNANNOTATED BIBLIOGRAPHY OF AP-
PROXIMATELY 200 BOOKS IN ENGLISH, ARRANGED ALPHABETICALLY BY
AUTHOR WITHIN EACH CHAPTER DIVISION; LISTS WORKS PUBLISHED
FROM 1876 THROUGH 1946.

2280 WALKER N.
MORALE IN THE CIVIL SERVICE.
EDINBURGH: EDINBURGH U PR, 1961, 302 PP.
    ANALYSIS OF PSYCHOLOGICAL MORALE OF DESK WORKER IN CIVIL
SERVICE OF GREAT BRITAIN. EXAMINES CAUSES OF FAVORABLE AND
UNFAVORABLE ATTITUDES ON PART OF ORGANIZATIONAL WORKER. DIS-
CUSSES OUTSIDE INFLUENCE AND BENEFITS OF WORKER ON HIS MO-
RALE AND JOB SATISFACTION.

2281 WALL E.H.
THE COURT OF JUSTICE IN THE EUROPEAN COMMUNITIES:
JURISDICTION AND PROCEDURE.
LONDON, WASH, DC: BUTTERWORTHS, 1966, 321 PP.
    INTERPRETS RESULTS OF ATTEMPTS BY THE COURT OF JUSTICE
TO RECONCILE LEGAL CONCEPTS THAT DIFFER AMONG MEMBER
COUNTRIES. LOOKS INTO OPERATION OF CONTINENTAL

ADMINISTRATIVE LAW AND ITS CREATION BY EUROPEAN JUDGES.
DESCRIBES ORGANIZATION OF THE COURT, PROCEDURE BEFORE THE
COURT, AND THE GENERAL TASK OF THE COURT.

2282 WALL N.L.
MUNICIPAL REPORTING TO THE PUBLIC (PAMPHLET)
CHICAGO: INT CITY MANAGER'S ASSN, 1963, 71 PP.
    GUIDE FOR MUNICIPAL OFFICERS BY WHICH TO PLAN ANNUAL
REPORTS. FEELS TRADITIONAL REPORT OF DEPARTMENT STATISTICS
AND FINANCIAL DATA IS OBSOLETE AND DOES NOT INFORM CITIZENS.
SUGGESTS REPORTING ON PROGRAMS OF CITIZENS' CONCERN RATHER
THAN ON DEPARTMENTAL FUNCTIONS. PROVIDES METHODS FOR
PLANNING AND ILLUSTRATING REPORTS.

2283 WALLER D.J.
"CHINA: RED OR EXPERT."
POLIT. QUART., 38 (APR.-JUNE 67), 122-131.
    CONCLUDES THAT IN CHINA IN LAST DECADE, STRESS IN BOTH
ARMY AND BUREAUCRACY INTELLIGENTSIA HAS BEEN IN FAVOR OF
POLITICALLY RED AS OPPOSED TO PROFESSIONALS. FROM THIS
VIEWPOINT CULTURAL REVOLUTION CAN BE VIEWED AS CONTINUATION
OF POLICY OF ELIMINATING PROFESSIONALS FROM POSITIONS OF
POWER. HOWEVER, THE ANALOGY MUST NOT BE CARRIED TOO FAR.

2284 WALTER B.
COMMUNICATIONS AND INFLUENCE: DECISION MAKING IN A
MUNICIPAL ADMINISTRATIVE HIERARCHY (PH.D. DISS., UNPUBL.)
EVANSTON, ILL: NORTHWESTERN U, 1960.
    TRACES THE FLOW OF INFLUENCE WITHIN AN ADMINSTRATIVE
ORGANIZATION BY OBSERVING AND MAPPING CHANNELS TRAVELED BY
VARIOUS TYPES OF FACTUAL - AND VALUE-DECISION PREMISES. THE
OBJECT IS TO SEE WHICH WERE ACCEPTED, REJECTED, OR
MODIFIED.

2285 WALTON R.E., MCKERSIE R.B.
A BEHAVIORAL THEORY OF LABOR NEGOTIATIONS: AN ANALYSIS OF A
SOCIAL INTERACTION SYSTEM.
NEW YORK: MCGRAW HILL, 1965, 437 PP., LC#64-66050.
    BEHAVIORAL THEORY OF LABOR-MANAGEMENT BARGAINING APPLIED
TO FOUR SYSTEMS OF ACTIVITIES: DISTRIBUTIVE BARGAINING, IN-
TEGRATIVE BARGAINING, ATTITUDINAL STRUCTURING, AND INTRAOR-
GANIZATIONAL BARGAINING; HOW NEGOTIATOR MUST BALANCE HIS
SEPARATE CONCERNS AND ACHIEVE GREATEST GOOD FOR GREATEST
NUMBER.

2286 WANGSNESS P.H.
THE POWER OF THE CITY MANAGER.
BERKELEY: U CALIF, BUR PUB ADMIN, 1962, 101 PP.
    ANALYZES NATURE AND SOURCES OF POWER FOR CITY MANAGER IN
VARIOUS ROLES HE ASSUMES TO PERFORM HIS DUTIES. FINDS THAT
TRADITIONAL CONCEPTS OF WAY MANAGER FUNCTIONS ARE FALSE.
FEELS NO NEED FOR STRONG MANAGER, TO HAVE EFFECTIVE GOVERN-
MENT. DOES NOT FEEL COUNCIL-MANAGER TYPE OF GOVERNMENT IS
BENEFICIAL TO CITY.

2287 WARBURG J.P.
THE UNITED STATES IN THE POSTWAR WORLD.
NEW YORK: ATHENEUM PUBLISHERS, 1966, 327 PP., LC#66-23577.
    REVIEWS ORIGINS OF US POSTWAR FOREIGN POLICY AND EXAMINES
ITS EFFECTS; DESCRIBES WHAT HAS BEEN DONE AND WHAT IS LEFT
TO DO. ANALYZES HOW AND BY WHOM FOREIGN POLICY HAS BEEN
SHAPED, AND EXAMINES CRITICISM OF US POLICY FROM OTHER
COUNTRIES.

2288 WARD R.
BACKGROUND MATERIAL ON ECONOMIC IMPACT OF FEDERAL PROCURE-
MENT - 1965: FOR JOINT ECONOMIC COMMITTEE US CONGRESS.
WASHINGTON: US GOVERNMENT, 1965, 251 PP.
    DESCRIPTION OF AND STATISTICS ON US PROCUREMENT AND PROP-
ERTY MANAGEMENT IN AREAS OF MOST WASTE IN PAST FIVE YEARS.
PREPARED FOR HEARINGS TO REDUCE WASTE AND INCREASE EFFICIEN-
CY IN AREAS WHERE GOVERNMENT HAS GREATEST MONETARY OBLIGA-
TIONS, PRIMARILY MILITARY. EMPHASIZES ECONOMIC ASPECTS OF
PROCUREMENT AND RELATED SUPPLY MANAGEMENT MATTERS.

2289 WARD R.E. ED.
A GUIDE TO JAPANESE REFERENCE AND RESEARCH MATERIALS IN THE
FIELD OF POLITICAL SCIENCE.
ANN ARBOR: U OF MICH PR, 1950, 104 PP.
    SELECTED ANNOTATED BIBLIOGRAPHY. REFERS ONLY TO POLITICAL
DEVELOPMENTS SINCE 1868 AND INCLUDES FEW WORKS PUBLISHED
AFTER 1940. ITEMS IN FIELDS OF HISTORY, ECONOMY, METHOD-
OLOGY, AND GENERAL BACKGROUND. GREAT MAJORITY OF WORKS IN
JAPANESE WITH EXCEPTIONS IN FIELD OF METHODOLOGY. NO WORKS
ON FOREIGN RELATIONS INCLUDED. ARRANGED TOPICALLY. CONTAINS
LIST OF PUBLISHERS.

2290 WARD R.E., WATANABE H.
JAPANESE POLITICAL SCIENCE: A GUIDE TO JAPANESE REFERENCE
AND RESEARCH MATERIALS (2ND ED.)
ANN ARBOR: U OF MICH PR, 1961, 210 PP.
    A BRIEFLY ANNOTATED BIBLIOGRAPHY OF 1,759 ITEMS, LARGELY
LIMITED TO JAPANESE TITLES WHICH TREAT POLITICAL SCIENCE
SUBJECTS AND DEVELOPMENTS IN JAPAN SINCE THE MEIJI RESTORA-
TION (1868). FOCUSES UPON RESULTS OF POST-1945 SCHOLARSHIP
WHICH APPEAR IN BOOK RATHER THAN ARTICLE FORM. ARRANGED INTO

27 TOPICAL HEADINGS, AND INDEXED BY AUTHOR AND EDITOR. ANNO-
TATIONS EVALUATE UTILITY OF ITEM FOR REFERENCE PURPOSES.

2291 WARD W.E.
GOVERNMENT IN WEST AFRICA.
LONDON: ALLEN & UNWIN, 1965, 269 PP.
   DISCUSSES COMPARATIVE SYSTEMS OF GOVERNMENT AND POLITICAL
INTERACTION IN EACH. RELATES GENERAL CONCEPTS TO AFRICA IN
ORDER TO JUDGE CONSTITUTIONAL AND POLITICAL SITUATION IN
CHANGE FROM COLONIAL TO INDEPENDENT RULE.

2292 WARNER A.W., FUCHS V.R.
CONCEPTS AND CASES IN ECONOMIC ANALYSIS.
NEW YORK: HARCOURT BRACE, 1958, 288 PP., LC#58-9446.
   ATTEMPTS TO DEFINE BASIC ECONOMIC THEORY THROUGH USE OF
CONCEPTS AND METHODS OF ECONOMIC ANALYSIS. FOCUSES ON ACTUAL
ECONOMIC SITUATIONS RATHER THAN BROAD PROBLEM AREAS. SOME
CONCEPTS DISCUSSED INCLUDE DEMAND, ELASTICITY, EQUILIBRIUM,
AND MARGINAL ANALYSIS. EACH SECTION INCLUDES SEVERAL REAL
CASE PROBLEMS TAKEN FROM PUBLISHED SOURCES WHICH REQUIRE
APPLICATION OF ONE OF THE CONCEPTUAL TOOLS DISCUSSED.

2293 WARNER W.L., LOW J.O.
THE SOCIAL SYSTEM OF THE MODERN FACTORY; THE STRIKE: AN
ANALYSIS.
NEW HAVEN: YALE U PR, 1947, 245 PP.
   STUDIES SOCIAL ORGANIZATION OF FACTORY. SHOWS LABOR'S
RELATIONS WITH MANAGEMENT AND POSITION OF FACTORY AND
WORKERS IN COMMUNITY BY EXAMPLE OF STRIKE IN SHOE FACTORY.
EXAMINES CAUSES OF STRIKE AND REASONS FOR ITS SUCCESS.
DESCRIBES FOUNDATION OF STRONG UNION AGAINST ALL EFFORTS OF
MANAGEMENT, AND CHANGE OF YANKEE CITY FROM NONUNION TO
UNION TOWN.

2294 WARNER W.L. ED., MARTIN N.H., ED.
INDUSTRIAL MAN.
NEW YORK: HARPER & ROW, 1959, 580 PP., LC#58-07023.
   PSYCHO-SOCIAL INVESTIGATION OF WHAT LEADS TO SUCCESS IN
AMERICAN BUSINESSMAN FROM PERSONALITY TO SOCIAL ORIGINS.
INCLUDES PATTERNS OF MOBILITY, BUREAUCRATIC STRUCTURE
AND PERSONALITY, GOALS OF MANAGEMENT, RELATION OF MANAGER TO
WORKER, AND ROLD OF UNIONS IN AFFECTING MODERN EXECUTIVES.

2295 WARNER W.L., VAN RIPER P.P. ET AL.
THE AMERICAN FEDERAL EXECUTIVE.
NEW HAVEN: YALE U PR, 1963, 405 PP., LC#63-7952.
   ANALYZES ROLE AND IMAGE OF THE GOVERNMENTAL BUREAUCRAT,
INCLUDING RESEARCH ON SOCIAL ORIGIN OF THE FEDERAL EXECU-
TIVE. EXPLAINING THEORY AND METHOD OF TECHNIQUE USED IN
ASSESSMENT, DISCUSSES CAREER AND LIFE OF THE EXECUTIVE
IN SETTING OF FAMILY OCCUPATION, REGION OF ORIGIN, INFLU-
ENCE OF MARRIAGE, AND LEVEL AND TYPE OF EDUCATION.

2296 WARREN R.O.
GOVERNMENT IN METROPOLITAN REGIONS: A REAPPRAISAL OF FRAC-
TIONATED POLITICAL ORGANIZATION.
DAVIS: U OF CAL, INST GOVT AFF, 1966, 327 PP., LC#66-64381.
   REVIEWS WORK THAT HAS BEEN DONE IN FIELD OF GOVERNMENTAL
ORGANIZATION IN URBAN AREAS. IDENTIFIES GENERALLY ACCEPTED
ASSUMPTIONS ABOUT METROPOLITAN ORGANIZATION AND RELATES
THESE TO GOVERNMENTAL EXPERIENCE OF A SPECIFIC URBAN REGION.
SHOWS CAPACITIES AND CHARACTERISTICS OF FRACTIONATED SYSTEM
OF GOVERNMENT.

2297 WARREN S.
THE AMERICAN PRESIDENT.
ENGLEWOOD CLIFFS: PRENTICE HALL, 1967, 176 PP., LC#67-25927.
   EXAMINES EVOLUTION OF US PRESIDENCY TO PRESENT STATE OF
IMPORTANCE. DEALS WITH PLACE OF PRESIDENCY IN CONSTITUTION,
GIVING EXAMPLES OF HOW SOME MEN WHO OCCUPIED IT VIEWED ITS
NATURE. INCLUDES OUTSIDERS' COMMENTS ON THE OFFICE, WHICH
IS FURTHER EVALUATED BY MEANS OF OFFICIAL STATEMENTS AND
OF POLICIES FELT TO REFLECT THE RANGE OF ROLES REQUIRED BY
CIRCUMSTANCES AND PRECEDENT.

2298 WASHINGTON S.H. ED.
BIBLIOGRAPHY: LABOR-MANAGEMENT RELATIONS ACT, 1947 AS AMEND-
ED BY LABOR-MANAGEMENT REPORTING AND DISCLOSURE ACT, 1959.
WASHINGTON: NATL LAB REL BOARD, 1966, 117 PP.
   BIBLIOGRAPHICAL LISTING OF MATERIALS PUBLISHED ON LABOR
LAW AND RELATED AREAS FROM 1959-1966. ENTRIES DIVIDED INTO
FIVE MAJOR CLASSIFICATIONS: GOVERNMENT PUBLICATIONS, BOOKS
AND PAMPHLETS, GENERAL AND TRADE PERIODICALS, LEGAL PERIOD-
ICAL ARTICLES, AND CASE COMMENTS-LEGAL PERIODICALS. SUBJECT
INDEX PROVIDED. SUPPLEMENTS PLANNED. CONTAINS 1,075 ENTRIES.

2299 WASSERMAN P.
INFORMATION FOR ADMINISTRATORS: A GUIDE TO PUBLICATIONS AND
SERVICES FOR MANAGEMENT IN BUSINESS AND GOVERNMENT.
ITHACA, NY: CORNELL SCH BUS ADM, 1956, 375 PP.
   OUTLINES SOURCES OF INFORMATION USEFUL IN BUSINESS AND
GOVERNMENTAL MANAGEMENT. DISCUSSES PARTICULAR UTILITY OF
EACH KIND OF PUBLICATION LISTED. INCLUDES LIBRARIES, GOVERN-
MENT PUBLICATIONS, PERIODICALS AND NEWSPAPERS, SOURCES OF
STATISTICAL DATA, AND PUBLICATIONS ASSOCIATED WITH CHAMBERS
OF COMMERCE, PROFESSIONAL ORGANIZATIONS, VARIOUS RESEARCH

INSTITUTIONS, AND BUSINESS AND PUBLIC ADMINISTRATION GROUPS.

2300 WASSERMAN P. ED.
MEASUREMENT AND ANALYSIS OF ORGANIZATIONAL PERFORMANCE.
ITHACA, NY: CORNELL SCH BUS ADM, 1959, 109 PP.
   COVERS TOTAL, UNIT, AND INDIVIDUAL EFFICIENCY IN ORGAN-
IZATIONS OF ALL TYPES. GENERAL AND THEORETICAL MATERIAL ON
IMPROVEMENT OF EFFICIENCY.

2301 WATERS M.
THE UNITED NATIONS* INTERNATIONAL ORGANIZATION AND ADMINIS-
TRATION.
NEW YORK: MACMILLAN, 1967, 512 PP.
   A COLLECTION OF READINGS, SPEECHES, AND DOCUMENTS ON
EVERY PHASE OF UN ORGANIZATION AND OPERATION. TRACES HIS-
TORICAL DEVELOPMENT OF INTERNATIONAL ORGANIZATION, UN AS A
CONSTITUTIONAL AND POLITICAL SYSTEM, INTERNAL AND EXTERNAL
ASPECTS OF ORGANIZATION. UN AND ROLE OF LAW, ETC. EVERY
AGENCY OF THE UN IS COVERED AS IS GENERAL ASSEMBLY AND
SECRETARIAT.

2302 WATERSTON A.
"PLANNING IN MOROCCO, ORGANIZATION AND IMPLEMENTATION.
BALTIMORE: HOPKINS ECON. DEVELOP. INT. BANK FOR."
RECON. AND DEV., 1962, 72 PP., $2.50.
   DISCUSSES THE ORGANIZATIONAL AND ADMINISTRATIVE
ASPECTS OF PLANNING AND THE DESIGN OF POLICIES, PROCEDURES
AND INSTITUTIONAL ARRANGEMENTS FOR IMPLEMENTING DEVELOP-
MENT PLANS IN MOROCCO.

2303 WATERSTON A.
DEVELOPMENT PLANNING* LESSONS OF EXPERIENCE.
BALTIMORE: JOHNS HOPKINS PRESS, 1965, 706 PP., LC#65-26180.
   A COMPARISON OF A NUMBER OF TYPES OF NATIONAL ECONOMIC
PLANS, THEIR MACHINERY AND IMPLEMENTATION. PLANNING AS ECO-
NOMIC FUNCTION DISCUSSED AND ITS HISTORY TRACED. MANY CASES
EXAMINED, WEALTH OF INTERACTING DETAILS PRESENTED IN ORGAN-
IZED FASHION, WITH GOOD INDEX AND BIBLIOGRAPHY.

2304 WAUGH E.W.
SECOND CONSUL.
INDIANAPOLIS: BOBBS-MERRILL, 1956, 244 PP., LC#56-13043.
   STIMULATED BY EISENHOWER'S HEART ATTACK, DISCUSSES PROB-
LEM OF THE VICE-PRESIDENCY, INCLUDING PAST HISTORY, DECLINE,
PROBLEMS OF ELECTION, DIFFICULTIES OF SUCCESSION, AND
RELATIVE POWER, WITH SUGGESTED ALTERNATIVES.

2305 WEBER M.
STAATSSOZIOLOGIE.
BERLIN: DUNCKER & HUMBLOT, 1956, 129 PP.
   DISCUSSES CENTRAL CONCEPTS OF STATE ORGANIZATION FROM
SOCIOLOGICAL POINT OF VIEW. EXAMINES QUESTION OF LEGITIMACY
AND BUREAUCRATIC ADMINISTRATION. INCLUDES DISCUSSION OF
PARTY ORGANIZATION AND PARLIAMENTARY RULE. DISTINGUISHES
LEGAL, TRADITIONAL, AND CHARISMATIC RULE.

2306 WEBER W., NEESSE G. ET AL.
DER DEUTSCHE BEAMTE HEUTE.
BADEN-BADEN: VERLAG A LUTZEYER, 1959, 75 PP.
   DISCUSSES ROLE OF CIVIL SERVICE OFFICIALS IN WEST GERMANY
AND MAKES RECOMMENDATIONS FOR HIERARCHY OF CIVIL INSTITU-
TIONS DEVOTED TO EFFICIENT ADMINISTRATION OF PUBLIC GOOD,
INDEPENDENT OF PARTY PRESSURE.

2307 WEBSTER J.A.
A GENERAL STUDY OF THE DEPARTMENT OF DEFENSE INTERNAL
SECURITY PROGRAM.
LOS ANGELES: U OF S CALIF PR, 1960, 78 PP.
   EXAMINES ADMINISTRATIVE SUCCESS, PROBLEMS, AND FAILINGS
OF INDUSTRIAL SECURITY PROGRAM. CONSIDERS COST OF ADMIN-
ISTRATION, NEED FOR SECURITY, LEGAL ASPECTS OF SECURITY,
AND RELATION OF JUDICIAL TO EXECUTIVE BRANCHES IN THESE
PROBLEMS.

2308 WEDDING N., LESSLER R.S.
ADVERTISING MANAGEMENT.
NEW YORK: RONALD PRESS, 1962, 629 PP., LC#62-19340.
   MANAGEMENT-ORIENTED TEXT DEVELOPS DECISION-MAKING
TECHNIQUES FOR PROFITABLE USES OF ADVERTISING. INCLUDES
EVALUATION OF ITS EFFECTIVENESS. COVERS BUDGETING, PLANNING,
AND PROMOTION.

2309 WEIDENBAUM M.L., SALOMA JS
CONGRESS AND THE FEDERAL BUDGET: FEDERAL BUDGETING AND THE
RESPONSIBLE USE OF POWER.
WASHINGTON: AMER ENTERPRISE INST, 1964, 99 PP.
   DISCUSSES THE PRESSURES FOR GOVERNMENT SPENDING, FEDERAL
SPENDING AND THE LOCALITY, THE MECHANICS OF GOVERNMENT
SPENDING, BUILT-IN RIGIDITIES IN THE FEDERAL BUDGET, THE
CONGRESSIONAL BUDGET PROCESS, AND ATTEMPTS AT ITS REFORM.

2310 WEIDLUND J. ED., ET A.L.
COMPARATIVE PUBLIC ADMINISTRATION.
ANN ARBOR: U OF MICH PR, 1957, 76 PP.
   SELECTIVE COMPILING OF RECENT AUTHORITATIVE WORKS
GROUPED TOPICALLY UNDER HEADINGS MOST OFTEN USED IN STUDYING

PUBLIC ADMINISTRATION. CONTAINS 600 ENTRIES WHICH COMPARE
PATTERNS OF ADMINISTRATION IN DIFFERENT COUNTRIES. INCLUDES
SECTION OF PERIODICALS AND LIST OF BIBLIOGRAPHIES FOR
FURTHER STUDY.

2311 WEIDNER E.W.
INTERGOVERNMENTAL RELATIONS AS SEEN BY PUBLIC OFFICIALS.
MINNEAPOLIS: U OF MINN PR, 1960, 162 PP., LC#60-11688.
QUESTIONNAIRE SURVEY OF ATTITUDES OF, INFLUENCES ON,
STATE GOVERNMENT PERSONNEL IN MINNESSOTA, AND THEIR VIEWS
OF RELATIONS BETWEEN GOVERNMENT AGENCIES.

2312 WEIGLEY R.F.
HISTORY OF THE UNITED STATES ARMY.
NEW YORK: MACMILLAN, 1967, 688 PP.
EMPHASIZES INTERNAL, INSTITUTIONAL DEVELOPMENT OF THE AR-
MY RATHER THAN STRESSING BATTLES AND CAMPAIGNS. CONSIDERS
PLACE OF ARMY WITHIN AMERICAN GOVERNMENT AND SOCIETY AT
LARGE AND INCLUDES METHODS OF WARMAKING.

2313 WEIL G.L.
"THE MERGER OF THE INSTITUTIONS OF THE EUROPEAN COMMUNITIES"
AMER. J. OF INT. LAW, 61 (JAN. 67), 57-65.
REPORTS ON NATURE AND SIGNIFICANCE OF MERGER TREATY OF
1965 WHICH REPLACED EEC, EURATOM, AND ECSC WITH A SINGLE
COUNCIL AND COMMISSION. THIS SINGLE COMMISSION DEALING WITH
EUROPEAN NATURAL POWER CONTROL IS CONSIDERED AS A MAJOR
CONSTITUTIONAL DEVELOPMENT IN PROGRESS TOWARD EUROPEAN UNI-
TY.

2314 WEINBERG M. ED.
SCHOOL INTEGRATION: A COMPREHENSIVE CLASSIFIED BIBLIOGRAPHY
OF 3,100 REFERENCES.
CHICAGO: INTEGRATED EDUC ASSOC, 1967, 137 PP., LC#67-29000.
LISTS BOOKS, ARTICLES, AND GOVERNMENT PUBLICATIONS
IN ENGLISH FROM 1954-67 ON SCHOOL INTEGRATION.
REFERENCES ARRANGED ALPHABETICALLY UNDER TOPICS, INCLUDING
PRACTICES, NEW APPROACHES, DEPRIVATION, AND SPANISH-
AMERICANS.

2315 WEINER M.
POLITICAL CHANGE IN SOUTH ASIA.
CALCUTTA: FIRMA KL MUKHOPADHYAY, 1963, 285 PP.
ESSAYS CONCERNING POLITICAL CHANGE PRIMARILY IN INDIA.
DESCRIBES CULTURAL BACKGROUND AND GOVERNMENTAL STRUCTURES.
COMPARES POLITICAL CHANGE IN PAKISTAN AND CEYLON WITH INDIA.
COVERS ECONOMIC DEVELOPMENT AND POLITICAL STABILITY.

2316 WEISS R.S., JACOBSON E.
"A METHOD FOR THE ANALYSIS OF THE STRUCTURE OF COMPLEX
ORGANIZATIONS."
AMER. SOCIOL. REV., 20 (DEC. 55), 661-668.
PROPOSES USE OF SOCIOMETRIC TECHNIQUES IN THE ANALYSIS OF
ROLE RELATIONSHIPS OF MEMBERS OF THE ORGANIZATIONS TO BETTER
UNDERSTAND GROUP STRUCTURE, GOALS AND METHODS OF OPERATION.

2317 WELCH S.R.
PORTUGUESE RULE AND SPANISH CROWN IN SOUTH AFRICA 1581-1640.
CAPETOWN: JUTA & CO. LTD., 1950, 634 PP.
DISCUSSES HISTORY OF PORTUGUESE AND SPANISH TRADE, MIS-
SIONARY ACTIVITIES, WARS, AND SERVICES IN SOUTH AFRICA BE-
TWEEN 1581 AND 1640. EXAMINES IN DETAIL PORTUGUESE ADMINIS-
TRATION OF COLONIAL LANDS.

2318 WELLEQUET J.
LE CONGO BELGE ET LA WELTPOLITIK (1894-1914.
BRUSSELS: PR UNIV DE BRUXELLES, 1962, 499 PP.
WORK ON WHAT GERMANY THOUGHT OF CONGO BETWEEN 1894-1914
WHEN GERMANY WAS FOLLOWING ITS "WELTPOLITIK." EXTENSIVELY
DOCUMENTS ANTI-CONGOLESE CAMPAIGN AND GERMAN CONQUERING
AMBITIONS.

2319 WELLISZ S.
THE ECONOMICS OF THE SOVIET BLOC.
NEW YORK: MCGRAW HILL, 1964, 245 PP., LC#63-1762.
STUDY OF SOVIET ECONOMICS AIMING TO SHOW HOW SYSTEM WORKS
AND ANALYZING HOW ECONOMIC DECISIONS ARE REACHED AND PUT
INTO PRACTICE. SHOWS HOW SOVIET-TYPE ECONOMY ALLOCATES RE-
SOURCES AND DECIDES UPON PRODUCT MIX, METHOD OF PRODUCTION,
AND DISTRIBUTION.

2320 WELLS A.J. ED.
THE BRITISH NATIONAL BIBLIOGRAPHY CUMULATED SUBJECT
CATALOGUE, 1951-1954.
LONDON: COUN BRIT NATL BIBLIOG, 1958, 190 PP.
DETAILED BIBLIOGRAPHY OF BRITISH PUBLICATIONS. ITEMS
ARRANGED BY SUBJECT.

2321 WELTON H.
THE THIRD WORLD WAR; TRADE AND INDUSTRY, THE NEW
BATTLEGROUND.
NEW YORK: PHILOSOPHICAL LIB, 1959, 330 PP.
CLAIMS NO MILITARY CONFLICT WILL DEVELOP BETWEEN COM-
MUNIST AND WESTERN NATIONS, SINCE WAR, ALREADY IN PROGRESS
IN TRADE AND INDUSTRY, WILL ITSELF DETERMINE FUTURE OF
WORLD. DEFEAT IS BASED ON ECONOMIC DESTRUCTION BY DISPLACE-

MENT OF EXPORTS IN WORLD MARKETS.

2322 WENDT P.F.
HOUSING POLICY - THE SEARCH FOR SOLUTIONS.
BERKELEY: U CAL BUR BUS ECON RES, 1962, 283 PP., LC#62-11497
EVALUATES NATIONAL HOUSING PROGRAMS AND POLICIES IN UK,
SWEDEN, WEST GERMANY, AND US SINCE WWII. COMPARES POSTWAR
POLICIES, PRODUCTION, AND RELATIVE IMPROVEMENT IN HOUSING
STANDARDS AMONG ALTERNATIVE POLICIES. EXAMINES RELATION
BETWEEN HOUSING AND GENERAL ECONOMIC POLICIES.

2323 WERNETTE J.P.
GOVERNMENT AND BUSINESS.
NEW YORK: MACMILLAN, 1964, 534 PP., LC#64-12864.
STUDY OF RELATIONSHIPS BETWEEN GOVERNMENT AND BUSINESS,
ENABLING THE "THOUGHTFUL CITIZEN" TO BETTER UNDERSTAND PUB-
LIC PROBLEMS AND GOVERNMENT ACTION. COVERS SUCH TOPICS AS
COMPETITION AND MONOPOLY, ECONOMIC GROWTH, PROTECTIVE LABOR
LEGISLATION, CONSERVATION, INTERNATIONAL TRADE POLICIES, AND
REGULATION OF PRIVATE FINANCIAL ACTIVITIES.

2324 WESSON R.G.
THE IMPERIAL ORDER.
BERKELEY: U OF CALIF PR, 1967, 547 PP., LC#67-11938.
DISCUSSES THEORY OF POLITICAL POWER. ARGUES THAT THE
DEGREE TO WHICH POWER OR POLITICAL MOTIVATION DOMINATES
SOCIETY DEPENDS LARGELY UPON THE DEGREE TO WHICH IT IS
CHECKED BY CONTRARY POWER, THAT IS, THE DEGREE TO WHICH
POWER IS DIVIDED. DESCRIBES IMPERIAL SYSTEMS THROUGHOUT
HISTORY, WHERE A SINGLE WILL MOBILIZES THE POTENCY OF THE
MASSES WHO ARE OTHERWISE UNABLE TO GOVERN THEMSEVLES.

2325 WEST F.J.
POLITICAL ADVANCEMENT IN THE SOUTH PACIFIC.
MELBOURNE, OXFORD U. PR., 1961, 186 PP.
DESCRIBES COLONIAL ADMINISTRATION OF FIJI, TAHITI AND
SAMOA AND ANALYZES THE DEGREE AND EFFECTIVENESS OF LOCAL
SELF-GOVERNMENT. CONCLUDES THAT A PARTIAL SUCCESS HAS BEEN
ACHIEVED IN THIS AREA, WITH RESPONSIBILITY FOR FUTURE DEVEL-
OPMENT RESTING WITH NATIVE LEADERS AS WELL AS WITH THE AD-
MINISTRATIVE POWERS.

2326 WESTIN A.F.
THE ANATOMY OF A CONSTITUTIONAL LAW CASE.
NEW YORK: MACMILLAN, 1958, 183 PP., LC#58-9839.
DOCUMENTARY PRESENTATION OF "YOUNGSTOWN SHEET & TUBE CO
V. SAWYER" SUPREME COURT CASE. INTENDED TO PORTRAY THE WORK-
INGS OF THE AMERICAN CONSTITUTIONAL PROCESS. TRACES DEVELOP-
MENT OF CASE FROM ITS BEGINNING AS STEEL INDUSTRY DISPUTE IN
1952 TO AFTERMATH OF SUPREME COURT DECISION. DISCUSSES MEANS
BY WHICH POLITICAL AND SOCIAL PRESSURES ARE BROUGHT TO BEAR
ON LEGAL CASES AT SUPREME COURT LEVEL.

2327 WESTON J.F.
THE SCOPE AND METHODOLOGY OF FINANCE.
ENGLEWOOD CLIFFS: PRENTICE HALL, 1966, 143 PP., LC#66-19883.
STUDIES CHANGE IN FIELD OF FINANCE FROM CONCERN WITH
PROCUREMENT OF FUNDS TO ANALYSIS OF MOST VALUABLE USE OF
THESE FUNDS FOR FIRM. EXPLAINS CHANGES IN WHOLE ECONOMY
SINCE WWII, ALONG WITH NEW METHODS AND TOOLS OF ANALYSIS
THAT HAVE CAUSED CHANGES. EMPHASIZES NEED FOR FINANCIAL
MANAGERS TO SELECT RIGHT TYPE OF METHODS OF ANALYSIS BE-
CAUSE OF VARIETY OF RESULTS POSSIBLE.

2328 WESTON P.B., WELLS K.M.
THE ADMINISTRATION OF JUSTICE.
ENGLEWOOD CLIFFS: PRENTICE HALL, 1967, 257 PP., LC#67-19788.
DETAILS US SYSTEM FOR ADMINISTRATION OF CRIMINAL JUSTICE.
DESCRIBES BASIC FUNCTIONAL AREAS: POLICE, PROSECUTOR,
COURTS, PROBATION, PAROLE, AND CORRECTION (INSTITUTIONS).
DETAILS VARIOUS COURT AND JUDICIAL SYSTEMS AND PROCEDURES
FROM ARREST TO FINAL DISPOSITION. INVESTIGATES PRINCIPLES OF
FEDERAL, CONSTITUTIONAL, AND STATE LAWS. DESCRIBES PRE AND
POST-TRIAL WRITS, MOTIONS, AND APPEALS.

2329 WHEARE K.C.
GOVERNMENT BY COMMITTEE; AN ESSAY ON THE BRITISH
CONSTITUTION.
LONDON: OXFORD U PR, 1955, 264 PP.
EXAMINES CONDUCT OF GOVERNMENT THROUGH GROUPS OF PEOPLE
ACTING COLLECTIVELY IN COMMITTEES. STUDIES SIX TYPES OF
COMMITTEES ACCORDING TO THEIR FUNCTIONS - COMMITTEES TO
ADVISE, INQUIRE, NEGOTIATE, LEGISLATE, ADMINISTER, AND
CONTROL. COMPARES COMMITTEES ON THEIR EFFECTIVENESS AND
SHORTCOMINGS. ALSO COMPARES OFFICERS OF COMMITTEES. STATES
THAT WELL-LED COMMITTEES ENSURE DEMOCRACY.

2330 WHEARE K.C.
THE CONSTITUTIONAL STRUCTURE OF THE COMMONWEALTH.
LONDON: OXFORD U PR, 1960, 201 PP.
DESCRIBES CONSTITUTIONAL STRUCTURE OF COMMONWEALTH AS OF
MARCH, 1960; PRESENTS CONCEPTS AND CASES OF AUTONOMY,
AUTOCHTHONY, EQUALITY, AND COOPERATION AMONG MEMBER
STATES. DETAILS PSYCHOLOGY AND PRACTICE OF LOYALTY TO QUEEN,
AND OTHER SYMBOLIC EXPRESSIONS OF UNITY.

2331 WHEARE K.C.
FEDERAL GOVERNMENT (4TH ED.)
NEW YORK: OXFORD U PR, 1964, 266 PP.
COMPARES AND CONTRASTS ORGANIZATION, INSTITUTIONS, DIVI-
SION OF POWERS, BASIC PRINCIPLES, CONSTITUTIONS, ROLE OF
GOVERNMENT IN ECONOMY, AND DEVELOPMENT OF COUNTRIES IN
WORLD WITH FEDERAL SYSTEM OF GOVERNMENT. ESTABLISHES RE-
QUIREMENTS FOR A FEDERAL SYSTEM.

2332 WHEELER-BENNETT J.W.
THE NEMESIS OF POWER (2ND ED.)
NEW YORK: ST MARTIN'S PRESS, 1964, 831 PP.
HISTORY OF GERMAN ARMY, FROM DEFEAT IN WWI TO ITS
REESTABLISHMENT IN WEST GERMANY. EMPHASIZES ROLE OF OFFICER
CORPS AS RESPONSIBLE FOR NATURE AND CONTINUITY OF ARMY'S
EMBROILMENT IN POLITICS. PRIMARILY COVERS WWII PERIOD. THE
PECULIAR RELATIONSHIP BETWEEN HITLER AND THE GENERAL STAFF.

2334 WHITE J.
GERMAN AID.
LONDON: MIN OF OVERSEAS DEVEL, 1965, 217 PP.
SURVEYS SOURCES, POLICY, AND STRUCTURE OF GERMAN AID AND
ATTITUDE OF GERMAN PEOPLE TOWARD IT. DISCUSSES THEORETICAL
RESULTS OF FOREIGN AID, ROLE OF TECHNICAL DEVELOPMENT, AND
ITS IMPORTANCE TO TRADE FOR DONOR AND RECEIVER.

2335 WHITE L.D.
"CONGRESSIONAL CONTROL OF THE PUBLIC SERVICE."
AM. POL. SCI. REV., 39 (FEB. 45), 1-11.
SEES CONGRESS DECLINING IN PUBLIC ESTEEM AND IN ITS CON-
TROL OF THE ADMINISTRATION. SUGGESTS REFORMS FOR CONGRESS SO
IT MAY REGAIN THE CONTROL WHICH IS DEMOCRATICALLY ESSENTIAL
TO ENSURE THAT ITS MANDATES ON PUBLIC POLICY PREVAIL AND TO
ENSURE THAT THE EXECUTION OF PUBLIC POLICY AVOIDS WASTE, IN-
COMPETENCE, AND UNNECESSARY PUBLIC INCONVENIENCE.

2336 WHITE L.D.
INTRODUCTION TO THE STUDY OF PUBLIC ADMINISTRATION.
LONDON: MACMILLAN, 1948, 612 PP.
ANALYZES PUBLIC ADMINISTRATION: FORM AND TRENDS, STRUC-
TURE AND ORGANIZATION. TREATS THE DYNAMICS OF MANAGEMENT,
FISCAL MANAGEMENT, PERSONNEL MANAGEMENT, ADMINISTRATIVE
POWERS, AND THE SYSTEM OF RESPONSIBILITY. DWELLS ON THE
ADMINISTRATIVE INADEQUACY IN THE UNITED STATES.

2337 WHITE L.D.
THE FEDERALISTS: A STUDY IN ADMINISTRATIVE HISTORY.
NEW YORK: MACMILLAN, 1948, 538 PP.
STUDIES PREVAILING VALUES AND EVENTS, PERSONALITIES, AND
INSTITUTIONS OF US GOVERNMENT, 1789-1801. FOCUSES ON
PRACTICAL PROBLEMS OF GOVERNMENT AND FORMULATION OF IDEAS AS
PROBLEMS WERE SURMOUNTED. DISCUSSES WASHINGTON AND HIS
ASSISTANTS, GROWTH OF CONGRESS, DEVELOPMENT OF DEPARTMENTS
AND AGENCIES, AND HAMILTON'S CONFLICTS WITH JEFFERSON AND
ADAMS.

2338 WHITE L.D.
THE JEFFERSONIANS: A STUDY IN ADMINISTRATIVE HISTORY 1801-
1829.
NEW YORK: MACMILLAN, 1951, 572 PP.
BELIEVES THAT JEFFERSONIAN ERA IN FIELD OF
ADMINISTRATION WAS LARGELY A PROJECTION OF FEDERALIST IDEAS
AND PRACTICE. DESCRIBES ERA'S MAJOR PERSONALITIES, EVENTS,
AND "TEMPER." TREATS GENERAL ADMINISTRATIVE RELATIONSHIPS
BETWEEN EXECUTIVE AND LEGISLATIVE BRANCHES, OPERATIONS OF
DEPARTMENTS, AND FISCAL SYSTEM. STUDIES PERSONNEL SYSTEM,
AND DESCRIBES SOME ADMINISTRATIVE PROBLEMS.

2339 WHITE L.D.
THE JACKSONIANS: A STUDY IN ADMINISTRATIVE HISTORY 1829-1861
NEW YORK: MACMILLAN, 1954, 593 PP.
STUDIES ADMINISTRATIVE HISTORY OF PERIOD WHEN INDUSTRY,
TRANSPORTATION, AND POLITICAL LIFE OF US WERE UNDERGOING
GREAT CHANGES. SHOWS THAT YEARS WERE FULL OF CONSTITUTIONAL
DEBATE, PARTY CONFLICT, AND SECTIONAL STRIFE, COMPRISING AN
ERA OF TENSION OVERSHADOWING NORMAL GOVERNMENT OPERATIONS.
STUDIES PRESIDENCY, MANAGEMENT PROBLEMS IN GOVERNMENT
AGENCIES, ECONOMIC PROBLEMS, AND PUBLIC SERVICE ETHICS.

2340 WHITE L.D.
THE REPUBLICAN ERA: 1869-1901, A STUDY IN ADMINISTRATIVE
HISTORY.
NEW YORK: MACMILLAN, 1958, 406 PP., LC#58-6209.
EXAMINES PROBLEMS FACING EXECUTIVE AND LEGISLATIVE
BRANCHES OF AMERICAN GOVERNMENT. EMPHASIZES CIVIL SERVICE
AND ETHICS OF PUBLIC-OFFICE HOLDERS.

2341 WHITEHEAD T.N.
LEADERSHIP IN A FREE SOCIETY; A STUDY IN HUMAN RELATIONS
BASED ON AN ANALYSIS OF PRESENT-DAY INDUSTRIAL CIVILIZATION.
CAMBRIDGE: HARVARD U PR, 1947, 266 PP.
CONCERNED WITH IMPACT OF BUSINESS AND INDUSTRIAL
INSTITUTIONS ON SOCIETY AND WITH TYPE OF SOCIAL STRUCTURE
WHICH CAN MAINTAIN ITSELF BEST IN TECHNOLOGICALLY DEVELOPING
WORLD. STUDIES FUNCTIONING OF WORKING GROUPS AND ROLE OF
LEADERSHIP IN COLLECTIVE ACTION; INVESTIGATES INTERACTION
BETWEEN HUMAN MOTIVES AND SHAPE AND DEVELOPMENT OF ORGANIZED
INSTITUTIONS. REVIEWS TYPES OF SOCIAL SYSTEMS.

2342 WHITNAH D.R.
SAFER SKYWAYS.
AMES: IOWA STATE U PR, 1966, 417 PP., LC#66-24402.
EXAMINES FEDERAL CONTROL OF AVIATION IN US 1926-66.
TRACING TECHNOLOGICAL ADVANCES SINCE THEN, UNDERSCORES
PRIMARY PURPOSE OF GOVERNMENTAL REGULATION - MAKING
AIRWAYS SAFER. ALSO CONSIDERS PROBLEMS OF PERSONNEL AND
ADMINISTRATION IN RAPIDLY GROWING CONCERNS. NOTES
INTERACTION OF FAA-CAB AND MILITARY.

2343 WHYTE W.H. JR.
THE ORGANIZATION MAN.
NEW YORK: SIMON AND SCHUSTER, 1956, 429 PP., LC#56-9926.
A CRITIQUE OF "EMPLOYEESHIP" APPLICABLE TO THOSE IN
ANY LARGE COLLECTIVE ORGANIZATION. IT DESCRIBES THE NEW
ETHIC OF BELIEVING IN GROUP BELONGINGNESS AND MAKING IT
THE SOURCE OF CREATIVITY, AND MAKES A PLEA FOR THE PRESER-
VATION OF THE INDIVIDUAL. DESCRIBES FASHIONABLE TONING-
DOWN OF LEADERSHIP FUNCTIONS. AMBITION, OVERWORK, AND GENIUS
WITH RESULTING BUREAUCRATIZATION, AND COMMONALITY.

2344 WIGGINS J.R.
FREEDOM OR SECRECY.
NEW YORK: OXFORD U PR, 1956, 242 PP., LC#56-11115.
STUDY OF CENSORSHIP AND POPULAR INFORMATION THAT DIMIN-
ISHES WITH GROWING NATIONAL SECRECY. DEALS WITH PRIVATE
TRANSACTIONS, USE OF CAMERAS IN COURT, REPRISAL FOR
PUBLICATION, AND RIGHT OF DISTRIBUTION.

2345 WILCOX J.K.
GUIDE TO THE OFFICIAL PUBLICATIONS OF THE NEW DEAL
ADMINISTRATION (2 VOLS.)
CHICAGO: AMER LIB ASSN, 1934.
FAIRLY COMPLETE CHECKLIST OF MIMEOGRAPHED AND PRINTED
OFFICIAL PUBLICATIONS OF ALL EMERGENCY ADMINISTRATIONS FROM
MARCH 1933 TO APRIL 1934. A SUPPLEMENT COVERS PERIOD
THROUGH 1935. MATERIAL IS ARRANGED ALPHABETICALLY WITHOUT
INDEXES. INCLUDES EXTENSIVE BIBLIOGRAPHIC INFORMATION.
DESIGNED TO SERVE AS REFERENCE GUIDE FOR STUDENT OF NEW
DEAL AND IS STILL VALUABLE AS SUCH TODAY.

2346 WILCOX J.K. ED.
MANUAL ON THE USE OF STATE PUBLICATIONS.
CHICAGO: AMER LIB ASSN, 1940, 342 PP., LC#40-16350.
COMPREHENSIVE ANNOTATED MANUAL ON THE USE OF STATE PUBLI-
CATIONS AS SOURCES OF RESEARCH. PART II, BIBLIOGRAPHICAL
AIDS, IS A COMPILATION OF STATE GOVERNMENT ORGANIZATIONS AND
BIBLIOGRAPHIES OF INDIVIDUAL STATE LISTS OF ALL PUBLICATIONS
AND IMPORTANT ARTICLES. PART III, BASIC STATE PUBLICATIONS,
IS ATTEMPT TO BRING TOGETHER ALL RECENT INFORMATION ON STATE
FUNCTIONS IN DIRECTORIES, DIGESTS, AND BIBLIOGRAPHIES.

2347 WILCOX J.K.
OFFICIAL DEFENSE PUBLICATIONS, 1941-1945 (NINE VOLS.)
BERKELEY: U OF CALIF PR, 1946.
AN ANNOTATED GUIDE TO OFFICIAL DEFENSE AND WAR PUBLICA-
TIONS OF FEDERAL, STATE, AND CANADIAN AGENCIES, COVERING THE
PERIOD FROM JUNE 1940 TO JANUARY 1945. THE NINE-VOLUME SET
LISTS 19,000 ITEMS, OF WHICH 655 ARE CANADIAN, 4,887 STATE,
AND 13,392 FEDERAL. MATERIAL LISTED ALPHABETICALLY BY NAME
OF ISSUING AGENCY; BOTH AUTHOR AND SUBJECT INDEX APPENDED TO
GUIDE.

2348 WILDAVSKY A.
LEADERSHIP IN A SMALL TOWN.
TOTOWA: BEDMINSTER PR, 1964, 388 PP., LC#64-19860.
ANALYZES MUNICIPAL STRUCTURE OF OBERLIN, OHIO, IN DETAIL.
EXAMINES WATER AND POWER OPERATIONS, NEGROES AND HOUSING,
ZONING, AND LOCAL ELECTIONS. DISCUSSES AND EXPLAINS LEADER-
SHIP STRUCTURE, INCLUDING INDIVIDUAL LEADERS. GENERALIZES
ON PLURALISM IN AMERICAN CITIES AS WELL AS POLITICAL
PARTICIPATIONS.

2349 WILDER B.E.
BIBLIOGRAPHY OF THE OFFICIAL PUBLICATIONS OF KANSAS,
1854-1958.
LAWRENCE: U KANSAS, GOV RES CTR, 1965, 318 PP., LC#65-63730.
TWO-VOLUME BIBLIOGRAPHY OF STATE AND TERRITORIAL PUBLICA-
TIONS AND OFFICIAL LITERATURE OF STATE INSTITUTIONS AND
SOCIETIES. COMPRISES OVER 20,000 PRINTED ITEMS, MIMEOGRAPHED
AND TYPEWRITTEN PUBLICATIONS. DOES NOT LIST LEGISLATIVE
BILLS. LIST ARRANGED ALPHABETICALLY.

2350 WILDING N., LAUNDY P.
"AN ENCYCLOPEDIA OF PARLIAMENT."
LONDON: CASSELL & CO LTD, 1958.
COLLECTION OF INFORMATION RELATING TO PARLIAMENT AND ITS
ASSOCIATED SUBJECTS. HEADINGS ARE ARRANGED IN ONE ALPHABET-
ICAL SEQUENCE. ENTRIES CHOSEN FOR THEIR RELEVANCE TO THE
CREATION AND GROWTH OF POWERS, PRIVILEGES, AND PRECEDENTS OF
PARLIAMENT, OR FOR THEIR INFLUENCE ON ITS CUSTOMS AND PRO-
CEDURES. UNANNOTATED BIBLIOGRAPHY OF POLITICAL BIOGRAPHIES
AND WORKS CONCERNING THE PARLIAMENTS OF UK.

2351 WILENSKY H.L.
SYLLABUS OF INDUSTRIAL RELATIONS: A GUIDE TO READING
AND RESEARCH.
CHICAGO: U OF CHICAGO PRESS, 1954, 305 PP.
   GUIDE TO READING AND RESEARCH IN INDUSTRIAL RELATIONS.
REFERENCES TO MATERIAL ON STUDY OF INDUSTRIAL RELATIONS;
URBAN INDUSTRIAL SETTING; ORGANIZATION OF WORK; TRADE
UNION HISTORY, ORGANIZATION, ADMINISTRATION AND IMPACT;
COLLECTIVE BARGAINING SYSTEMS, PROCESSES AND ISSUES;
PUBLIC POLICY AND INDUSTRIAL RELATIONS.

2352 WILENSKY H.L., LEBEAUX C.N.
INDUSTRIAL SOCIETY AND SOCIAL WELFARE: IMPACT OF INDUSTRIAL-
IZATION ON SUPPLY AND ORGANIZATION OF SOC WELF SERVICES.
NEW YORK: RUSSELL SAGE FDN, 1958, 401 PP., LC#58-8637.
   AN ACCOUNT OF THE EFFECTS OF INDUSTRIALIZATION ON SOCIAL
INSTITUTIONS IN US: FAVORABLE AND ADVERSE EFFECTS; DEVELOP-
MENT OF SOCIAL WELFARE; SOCIAL WORK AS A PROFESSION.

2353 WILLIAMS S.
"NEGOTIATING INVESTMENT IN EMERGING COUNTRIES."
HARVARD BUS. REV., 43 (JAN. - FEB. 65), 89 PP.
   NOTES PRESSURES AND TENSIONS IN THE DECISION TO INVEST
IN UNDERDEVELOPED AREAS. ASSERTS THAT 'THE ART OF POLITICS
AND THE CONCEPTS OF SOCIAL SCIENCE CAN BECOME AS IMPORTANT
AS HARDHEADED TECHNICAL AND FINANCIAL CALCULATIONS....'

2354 WILLIAMSON O.E.
THE ECONOMICS OF DISCRETIONARY BEHAVIOR: MANAGERIAL OBJEC-
TIVES IN A THEORY OF THE FIRM.
ENGLEWOOD CLIFFS: PRENTICE HALL, 1964, 182 PP., LC#64-18412.
   FORD FOUNDATION DOCTORAL DISSERTATION. CENTERS ATTENTION
ON DISCRETIONARY BEHAVIOR OF MANAGERS IN THEIR OPERATION OF
BUSINESS FIRMS. OBJECTIVES: TO INDICATE IN WHAT WAY MANAGERS
ARE MOTIVATED TO ATTEND TO OTHER THAN PROFIT GOALS, TO
TRANSLATE MOTIVATION OF MANAGERS TO ANALYSIS OF OPERATIONS
CONTEXT, TO IDENTIFY CONDITIONS FOR DISCRETIONARY BEHAVIOR
TO BE OF QUANTITATIVE IMPORTANCE, AND TO DEVELOP A THEORY.

2355 WILLNER A.R.
THE NEOTRADITIONAL ACCOMMODATION TO POLITICAL INDEPENDENCE*
THE CASE OF INDONESIA * RESEARCH MONOGRAPH NO. 26.
PRINCETON: CTR OF INTL STUDIES, 1966, 71 PP.
   THESIS6 THAT MANY NEW STATES WHEN INDEPENDENT SUPERIMPOSE
INDIGENOUS VALUES AND TRADITIONAL BEHAVIOR PATTERNS ON THE
MODERN ORGANIZATIONAL STRUCTURES BEQUEATHED THEM BY CO-
ONIALISM. MOREOVER, THIS OCCURS MOST FREQUENTLY IN THE BU-
REAUCRACIES WHICH MUST IMPLEMENT POLICY. INDONESIA'S DEVEL-
OPMENT AS A GUIDED DEMOCRACY IS OFFERED AS A CASE STUDY.

2356 WILLOUGHBY W.F.
PRINCIPLES OF PUBLIC ADMINISTRATION WITH SPECIAL REFERENCE
TO THE NATIONAL AND STATE GOVERNMENTS OF THE UNITED STATES.
WASHINGTON: BROOKINGS INST, 1927, 720 PP.
   A STUDY OF THE ORGANIZATION AND CONDUCT OF FEDERAL AND
STATE ADMINISTRATIONS, WITH EMPHASIS ON ROLES AND PRACTICES
OF THE EXECUTIVE AND LEGISLATIVE BRANCHES AND THEIR RELATED
AGENCIES. EXAMINES INTERNAL ORGANIZATION AND OPERATING
SERVICES, PERSONNEL, MATERIEL, AND FINANCE PROCEDURES AND
CONTROL.

2357 WILLOUGHBY W.R.
THE ST LAWRENCE WATERWAY: A STUDY IN POLITICS AND DIPLOM-
ACY.
MADISON: U. WISCONSIN PR., 1961, 381 PP.
   EMPHASIZES THE BEHIND-THE-SCENES POLITICAL DEVELOPMENTS
(POLITICAL ECONOMICS, PRESSURE GROUPS, LEGISLATION) WHICH
LED UP TO THE CREATION OF THE MODERN WATERWAY SYSTEM.

2358 WILLSON F.M.G.
ADMINISTRATORS IN ACTION.
TORONTO: TORONTO UNIV PRESS, 1961, 349 PP.
   CASE STUDIES OF BRITISH ADMINISTRATION SYSTEM DESIGNED TO
TEACH MANAGEMENT TECHNIQUES.

2359 WILSON G.
CASES AND MATERIALS ON CONSTITUTIONAL AND ADMINISTRATIVE LAW
NEW YORK: CAMBRIDGE U PRESS, 1966, 609 PP., LC#66-10244.
   DISCUSSES PROBLEMS OF LAW IN RELATION TO ADMINISTRATION
AND CONSTITUTIONAL AUTHORITY. BASED ON ENGLISH LAW, INCLU-
DING CENTRAL GOVERNMENT, CIVIL SERVICE, PARLIAMENT, COURTS,
LIBERTIES AND ORDER, FOREIGN AFFAIRS, AND CROWN PROCEEDINGS.

2360 WILSON L.
THE ACADEMIC MAN.
NEW YORK: OCTAGON PUBL CO, 1964, 248 PP., LC#64-24851.
   CONCERNED PRIMARILY WITH INTERNAL VARIABLES IN UNIVERSITY
ORGANIZATION. DESCRIBES THE RISE TO FULL PROFESSIONAL
STATUS AND THE "PROFESSOR ADMINISTRANT" AND DISCUSSES HIER-
ARCHIES OF ADMINISTRATION, THE ROLE OF FACULTY GROUPS,
AUTHORITARIANISM AND IMPLICATIONS OF PROFESSIONAL STATUS.
CONTAINS AAUP PROFESSIONAL CODE OF ETHICS.

2361 WILSON P. ED.
GOVERNMENT AND POLITICS OF INDIA AND PAKISTAN: 1885-1955;
A BIBLIOGRAPHY OF WORKS IN WESTERN LANGUAGES.

BERKELEY: U CAL INST ASIA STUD, 1956, 357 PP., LC#56-63303.
   BIBLIOGRAPHY INCLUDES BOOKS, PAMPHLETS, AND NONSERIAL
GOVERNMENT PUBLICATIONS. WORKS ARRANGED UNDER BROAD SUBJECT
DIVISIONS AND CHRONOLOGICALLY BY DATE OF PUBLICATION. WORKS
INDEXED BY AUTHOR, TITLE, BY SERIES, AND PUBLISHER. INCLUDES
5,294 ITEMS ON GENERAL HISTORY, POLITICS, CONSTITUTIONAL
HISTORY, GOVERNMENT AND ADMINISTRATION, AND INTERNATIONAL
RELATIONS.

2362 WILSON W.
CONSTITUTIONAL GOVERNMENT IN THE UNITED STATES.
NY: LEMCKE, LEMCKE & BEUCHNER, 1908, 236 PP.
   WOODROW WILSON'S STUDY OF US GOVERNMENT INCLUDES
DISCUSSION OF CONSTITUTIONAL GOVERNMENT IN GENERAL, PLACE OF
US IN CONSTITUTIONAL DEVELOPMENT, BRANCHES OF GOVERNMENT,
FEDERAL-STATE RELATIONS, AND POLITICAL PARTIES.

2363 WILSON W.
THE STATE: ELEMENTS OF HISTORICAL AND PRACTICAL POLITICS.
BOSTON: D C HEATH, 1918, 554 PP.
   DISCUSSES OBJECTS AND FUNCTIONS OF GOVERNMENT, NATURE OF
LAW; EXAMINES STRUCTURE OF GOVERNMENT OF MAJOR BELLIGERENT
POWERS OF WWI, INCLUDING US.

2364 WILSON W.
CONGRESSIONAL GOVERNMENT.
NEW YORK: NOONDAY PRESS, 1956, 222 PP., LC#56-6567.
   A STUDY OF AMERICAN POLITICS FROM THE CIVIL WAR TO THE
1880'S. IT IS A STUDY OF PRESIDENTIAL WEAKNESS IN THE FACE
OF AN ALL- POWERFUL CONGRESS AND ITS STANDING COMMITTEES.

2365 WINGFIELD C.J.
"POWER STRUCTURE AND DECISION-MAKING IN CITY PLANNING."
PUBLIC ADMIN. REV., 23 (JUNE 63), 74-81.
   TO BE EFFECTIVE IN THE COMMUNITY POWER STRUCTURE, THE
PLANNER TRANSLATES HIS EXPERTISE INTO POWER. THIS CAN BE
DONE IF THE PLANNER EDUCATES THE PUBLIC IN AN ACTIVE WAY,
RESULTING IN AN "UPGRADING OF CONSTITUENTS' VALUES SUCH THAT
DECISIONS MADE IN THE PRIVATE SECTOR ARE MORE LIKELY TO BE
IN ACCORD WITH PUBLIC PLANS."

2366 WINTHROP H.
"THE MEANING OF DECENTRALIZATION FOR TWENTIETH-CENTURY MAN."
AMER. J. OF ECO. AND SOC., 26 (OCT. 67), 351-366.
   EXAMINES ASPECTS OF MODERN DECENTRALIST THOUGHT.
CONSIDERS NEW DECENTRALISM AS ONE OF MANY PHILOSOPHIES
PRESENTLY COMPETING FOR THE RIGHT TO STRUCTURE
THE COMING SOCIAL ORDER. STATES THAT DECENTRALIZATION, WITH
THE HELP OF SCIENCE AND TECHNOLOGY, CAN FURNISH SOLUTIONS TO
MANY MODERN PROBLEMS, ADMINISTRATIVE, EDUCATIONAL, AND
POLITICAL.

2367 WITHERELL J.W.
OFFICIAL PUBLICATIONS OF FRENCH EQUATORIAL AFRICA, FRENCH
CAMEROONS, AND TOGO, 1946-1958 (PAMPHLET)
WASHINGTON: LIBRARY OF CONGRESS, 1964, 78 PP., LC#64-60029.
   AN ANNOTATED BIBLIOGRAPHY OF 405 PUBLICATIONS CONCERNED
WITH AFRIQUE EQUATORIALE FRANCAISE AND THE TRUST TERRITORIES
WHICH WERE ISSUED DURING THE TERM OF THE FOURTH REPUBLIC.
COVERS PUBLICATIONS OF GOVERNMENT GENERAL OF FRENCH EQUATO-
RIAL AFRICA, GOVERNMENTS OF FOUR TERRITORIES WHICH COM-
PRISED AEF, AND THE ADMINISTRATIONS IN THE CAMEROONS AND
TOGO FROM 1946-58. SOURCES IN FRENCH AND ENGLISH.

2368 WITHERELL J.W. ED.
MADAGASCAR AND ADJACENT ISLANDS; A GUIDE TO OFFICIAL
PUBLICATIONS (PAMPHLET)
WASHINGTON: LIBRARY OF CONGRESS, 1965, 58 PP., LC#65-61703.
   BIBLIOGRAPHY OF 927 ITEMS DATING FROM ESTABLISHMENTS OF
FRENCH ADMINISTRATIONS IN MADAGASCAR, COMORO ISLANDS, AND
REUNION, AND BRITISH ADMINISTRATIONS IN MAURITIUS AND
SEYCHELLES. TERMINAL DATE FOR MADAGASCAR IS 1958. OTHERS
CONTINUE TO PRESENT. INCLUDES PUBLICATIONS OF COLONIAL AND
LOCAL GOVERNMENT. ARRANGED ALPHABETICALLY BY AUTHOR AND
TITLE UNDER LOCALE. AUTHOR AND SUBJECT INDEXES INCLUDED.

2369 WITTFOGEL K.A.
"RUSSIA AND ASIA: PROBLEMS OF CONTEMPORARY AREA STUDIES
AND INTERNATIONAL RELATIONS."
WORLD POLIT., 2 (JULY 50), 445-462.
   MUST UNDERSTAND THE INFLUENCE OF ASIAN DESPOTISM ON
RUSSIAN SOCIETY. SOVIET GOVERNMENTAL MANAGEMENT OF AGRI-
CULTURE AND THE CONTINUED BUREAUCRATIC CONTROL OF THE
ECONOMY DESPITE INDUSTRIALIZATION REFLECT THE ORIENTAL
INFLUENCE. BROAD KNOWLEDGE OF FOREIGN COUNTRIES CALLED FOR
IN ORDER TO MAKE USA FOREIGN-AID AN EFFECTIVE WEAPON.

2370 WOLFERS A.
"COLLECTIVE SECURITY AND THE WAR IN KOREA."
YALE REV., 43 (JUNE 54), 487-496.
   DEFINES COLLECTIVE SECURITY TO DETERMINE WHETHER THE UN
ACTION IN KOREA JUSTIFIES BEING HERALDED AS FIRST EXPERIMENT
IN COLLECTIVE SECURITY. CONCLUDES THAT ACTION IN KOREA IS
EXAMPLE OF COLLECTIVE MILITARY DEFENSE BASED ON TRADITIONAL
POWER POLITICS.

2371 WOLFINGER R.E., FIELD J.O.
"POLITICAL ETHOS AND THE STRUCTURE OF CITY GOVERNMENT."
AM. POL. SCI. REV., 60 (JUNE 66), 306-326.
THIS STUDY USES DEMOGRAPHIC DATA TO TEST THE THEORY THAT
AMERICAN CITIES ARE GOVERNED IN ACCORDANCE WITH A
POLITICAL ETHOS THAT IS EITHER "PUBLIC-REGARDING" OR
"PRIVATE-REGARDING " DEPENDING TO A LARGE EXTENT ON THE
ETHNIC COMPOSITION OF THE POPULATION. THE THEORY IS FOUND
IN NEED OF A GOOD DEAL OF MODIFICATION.

2372 WOLL P.
AMERICAN BUREAUCRACY.
NEW YORK: W W NORTON, 1963, 184 PP., LC#63-8039.
EXAMINES THE GROWTH OF THE NATIONAL BUREAUCRACY TO A
POSITION OF DOMINANCE IN AREAS RESERVED TO THE CONGRESS, THE
PRESIDENT, AND THE JUDICIARY.

2373 WOLL P.
ADMINISTRATIVE LAW: THE INFORMAL PROCESS.
BERKELEY: U OF CALIF PR, 1963, 203 PP., LC#63-10409.
DISCUSSION OF THE ADJUDICATIVE FUNCTION OF
ADMINISTRATIVE AGENCIES. SAYS THAT REQUIREMENTS OF PUBLIC
POLICY, SPEED, AND TECHNICAL SKILLS HAVE MADE
ADMINISTRATIVE ADJUDICATION LARGELY INFORMAL IN PRACTICE.

2374 WORLD PEACE FOUNDATION
DOCUMENTS OF INTERNATIONAL ORGANIZATIONS: A SELECTED BIBLIO-
GRAPHY.
BOSTON: WORLD PEACE FOUNDATION.
QUARTERLY BIBLIOGRAPHY, FIRST PUBLISHED IN 1947, IS LIM-
ITED TO OFFICIAL DOCUMENTATION OF UN, ITS SPECIALIZED AGEN-
CIES, LEAGUE OF NATIONS, REGIONAL ORGANIZATIONS, WAR AND
TRANSITIONAL ORGANIZATIONS AND OTHER FUNCTIONAL ORGANIZA-
TIONS. MATERIALS GROUPED BY ORGANIZATION AND TOPIC. ANNOTA-
TIONS USED SPARINGLY. PUBLICATION CONTINUED FOR 3 YEARS.
LIMITED TO MATERIALS IN LIBRARY OF WORLD PIECE FOUNDATION.

2375 WORLD PEACE FOUNDATION
"INTERNATIONAL ORGANIZATIONS: SUMMARY OF ACTIVITIES."
INT. ORGAN., 18 (SPRING 64), 302-485.
GIVES COMPLETE BREAK-DOWN OF UN'S ORGANIZATION AND FUNC-
TIONS THROUGH A STUDY OF MEMBERS, GENERAL ASSEMBLY, SECUR-
ITY COUNCIL AND SPECIFIC EXAMPLES OF PAST POLICIES AND PRO-
CEDURES, E.G. INDIA-PAKISTAN DISPUTE, CYPRUS-TURKISH QUES-
TION.

2376 WORLEY P.
ASIA TODAY (REV. ED.) (PAMPHLET)
TRENTON: TRENTON STATE COL, 1960, 35 PP.
BIBLIOGRAPHICAL GUIDE TO THE MOST GENERALLY USEFUL MATE-
RIALS IN THE TRENTON STATE COLLEGE LIBRARY FOR STUDENTS OF
ASIAN AFFAIRS. BOOKS RANGE FROM TRAVEL GUIDES TO TECHNICAL
ECONOMIC AND SOCIOLOGICAL AREA STUDIES, VIRTUALLY ALL OF
WHICH BEAR POST-1950 PUBLICATION DATES. ENTRIES BOTH CRITI-
CALLY AND DESCRIPTIVELY ANNOTATED, AND ARRANGED BY GEOGRAPH-
ICAL AREA.

2377 WRAITH R., SIMPKINS E.
CORRUPTION IN DEVELOPING COUNTRIES.
NEW YORK: W W NORTON, 1964, 211 PP.
EXAMINES PATTERN OF CORRUPTION IN BRITISH INSTITUTIONAL
SYSTEM DURING 18TH AND 19TH CENTURIES AND INFLUENCE ON
AFRICAN SYSTEMS, ESPECIALLY IN NIGERIA, DURING 20TH
CENTURY.

2378 WRIGHT D.M.
THE CREATION OF PURCHASING POWER.
CAMBRIDGE: HARVARD U PR, 1942, 251 PP.
EXAMINES CREATION OF PURCHASING POWER AS STIMULUS TO STOP
DEPRESSIONS. CONSIDERS PURCHASING POWER AS PROBLEM OF
PRODUCTION, AS MONEY, IN TERMS OF PRICES AND INCOME, AND AS
ABILITY AND WILLINGNESS TO BUY. DEFINES INFLATION AND
EVALUATES THEORIES OF BANK CREDIT AND POLICY, VELOCITY
STIMULATORS, AND PURCHASING POWER INJECTORS. INCLUDES
DEFICIT FINANCING, DISTRIBUTION, AND ADMINISTRATION.

2379 WRIGHT D.S., MCANAW R.L.
AMERICAN STATE ADMINISTRATORS (PAMPHLET)
NEW YORK: PUBLISHED BY AUTHOR, 1965, 40 PP.
STUDIES CODE AND MARGINAL TABULATIONS FOR STATE
ADMINISTRATIVE OFFICIALS QUESTIONNAIRE ON PERSONAL,
PROFESSIONAL, AND ATTITUDINAL DIMENSIONS OF STATE
ADMINISTRATORS. PRESENTS QUESTIONNAIRE AND IBM CARD CODES.

2380 WRIGHT F.K.
"INVESTMENT CRITERIA AND THE COST OF CAPITAL."
J. MANAGEMENT STUDIES, 4 (OCT. 67), 251-269.
ANALYZES RELATIONSHIP BETWEEN INVESTMENT RETURNS AND
CAPITAL COST TO DETERMINE BY WHAT CRITERIA MANAGERS SHOULD
DECIDE. EXAMINES EFFECT OF COMPANY OBJECTIVES AND LIMITA-
TIONS UPON THEM, STRESSING NEED FOR DEFINING THEM CLEARLY
BEFORE MAKING SECONDARY POLICY DECISIONS.

2381 WRIGHT H.R.
SOCIAL SERVICE IN WARTIME.
CHICAGO: U OF CHICAGO PRESS, 1944, 201 PP.

AN ACCOUNT OF WHAT SOCIAL WORKERS WERE DOING TO
ALLEVIATE FREEDOM FROM WANT. THE RED CROSS, TRAVELERS AID
SERVICE, PUBLIC ASSISTANCE PROGRAMS, AND FEDERATED FINANCING
OF SOCIAL WORK ARE A FEW PHASES OF WARTIME SOCIAL WORK
DISCUSSED.

2382 WRIGHT J.H., CHRISTIAN B.H.
PUBLIC RELATIONS IN MANAGEMENT.
NEW YORK: MCGRAW HILL, 1949, 229 PP.
EXPLAINS PUBLIC RELATIONS AS NECESSARY FUNCTION OF
BUSINESS, WHICH MAINTAINS GOOD COMMUNICATION WITH PUBLIC IN
ORDER TO BUILD CONFIDENCE AND UNDERSTANDING AS NECESSARY
PART OF COMPANY PLANS. REQUIRES BUSINESS TO KEEP EMPLOYEES
AND PUBLIC INFORMED OF ITS ACTIVITIES TO IMPROVE ITSELF AND
CONTRIBUTE TO COMMUNITY DEVELOPMENT.

2383 WRIGHT Q. ED.
GOLD AND MONETARY STABILIZATION.
CHICAGO: U. CHI. PR., 1932, 174 PP.
SERIES OF LECTURES COVERS INTERNATIONAL ASPECTS
OF THE GOLD STANDARD, MONEY AND BUSINESS CYCLE, FEDERAL
RESERVE POLICY IN DEPRESSION, THE FUTURE OF GOLD STANDARD,
AND MONETARY STABILITY AND THE GOLD STANDARD.

2384 WRIGHT Q.
"CONGRESS AND THE TREATY-MAKING POWER."
PROC. AMER. SOC. INT. LAW, 1952, 43-69.
DEALS WITH STATEMENT CONCERNING CONSTITUTIONAL POWERS OF
THE PRESIDENT AND THE CONGRESS, INDICATING POSSIBLIITY OR
PROBABILITY OF FREQUENT CONFLICTS. PRESENTS DIRECTIONS FOR
CONSTITUTIONAL AMENDMENTS TO IMPROVE CONDUCT OF FOREIGN
RELATIONS.

2385 WRIGHT Q.
"THE PEACEFUL ADJUSTMENT OF INTERNATIONAL RELATIONS:
PROBLEMS AND RESEARCH APPROACHES."
J. SOC. ISSUES, 11 (1955), 3-12.
SEES PROBLEM SOLUTION FOR PEACEFUL WORLD AS VARIED, AND
THEREFORE TYPES OF RESEARCH RELEVANT TO EACH CLASS OF PROB-
LEMS AS VARIED ALSO. DEVISES SCHEME OF CLASSIFICATION OF
PROBLEMS IN INTERNATIONAL RELATIONS INTO 4 TYPES, AS WELL AS
CLASSIFICATION OF 4 TYPES OF RESEARCH.

2386 WU E.
LEADERS OF TWENTIETH-CENTURY CHINA; AN ANNOTATED BIBLIOGRA-
PHY OF SELECTED CHINESE BIOGRAPHICAL WORKS IN HOOVER LIBRARY
STANFORD: HOOVER INSTITUTE, 1956, 106 PP.
ANNOTATED BIBLIOGRAPHICAL GUIDE IN CHINESE, ENGLISH, AND
TRANSLITERATED CHINESE TO THE CHIEF CHINESE BIOGRAPHICAL
COMPENDIA RESOURCES IN THE HOOVER LIBRARY. LISTS 500 ITEMS
PUBLISHED SINCE 1900, ARRANGED ALPHABETICALLY BY AUTHOR, IN
BOTH ROMANIZATION AND CHARACTERS. DESCRIPTIVE ANNOTATIONS
IN ENGLISH.

2387 WYLIE C.M. ED.
RESEARCH IN PUBLIC HEALTH ADMINISTRATION; SELECTED RECENT
ABSTRACTS IV (PAMPHLET)
BALTIMORE: J HOPKINS SCHOOL HYG, 1966, 60 PP.
125 ABSTRACTS OF BOOKS, GOVERNMENT PUBLICATIONS, AND PER-
IODICAL ARTICLES DATED 1963-65. ENTRIES GROUPED BY SUBJECT.
INCLUDES: GENERAL RESEARCH, ADMINISTRATION OF RESEARCH, STA-
TISTICS, ADMINISTRATIVE AND OPERATIONS RESEARCH, AND ROLE OF
COMMUNITY HEALTH AGENCIES.

2388 YALE UNIV BUR OF HIGHWAY TRAF
URBAN TRANSPORTATION ADMINISTRATION.
NEW HAVEN: YALE U PR, 1959, 134 PP.
STUDIES WAYS IN WHICH GOVERNMENTAL ORGANIZATION CAN BET-
TER SERVE NEEDS OF URBAN TRANSPORTATION. LIMITED PRIMARILY
TO ORGANIZATIONAL PATTERNS AND ADMINISTRATIVE PRACTICES IN
INDIVIDUAL COMMUNITIES. SUGGESTIONS ARE MADE FOR STREAMLIN-
ING ADMINISTRATION OF URBAN TRANSPORTATION THROUGH COORDINA-
TING EXISTING BODIES.

2389 YANG C.K.
A CHINESE VILLAGE IN EARLY COMMUNIST TRANSITION.
CAMBRIDGE: TECHNOLOGY PR., 1959, 284 PP.
SURVEYS CHANGES IN PEASANT VILLAGE, NEAR CANTON, CHINA,
AS RESULT OF COMMUNIST RISE TO POWER. ANALYZES ECONOMIC,
SOCIAL, AND POLITICAL STRUCTURES IN RELATION TO NATIONAL
CHANGES. EMPHASIZES AGRICULTURAL TECHNOLOGY, FAMILY
STRUCTURE, AND POWER GROUPINGS.

2390 YATES M., GILCHRIST M.
ADMINISTRATIVE REORGANIZATION OF STATE GOVERNMENTS: A
BIBLIOGRAPHY (PAMPHLET)
CHICAGO: COUNCIL OF STATE GOVTS, 1948, 12 PP.
COMPREHENSIVE COVERAGE OF ALL REPORTS ON COMPLETE SURVEYS
OF STATE ADMINISTRATION. CITATIONS INCLUDE REPORTS, BOOKS,
AND ARTICLES WHERE NO COMPLETE SURVEY HAD BEEN MADE.
MATERIAL ARRANGED BY STATE.

2391 YOUNG C.
POLITICS IN THE CONGO* DECOLONIZATION AND INDEPENDENCE.
PRINCETON: PRINCETON U PRESS, 1965, 659 PP., LC#65-10843.
IN THIS MASSIVE STUDY THIS AUTHOR PRESENTS THE MANY

FACTORS AT WORK IN THE CONGO TOWARD THE DEVELOPMENT OF A
POLITICAL SYSTEM OUT OF THE DISARRAY LEFT BY HURRIED DE-
COLONIZATION. FACTIOUS ELITES AND POLITICAL PARTIES, ARBI-
TRARY BOUNDARIES, AND MANY OTHER PROBLEMS MAKE THIS A STUDY
OF DYNAMIC FLUX AND CHANGE RATHER THAN STABLE INSTITUTIONS.

2392 YOUNG G.
FEDERALISM AND FREEDOM.
LONDON: OXFORD U. PR., 1941, 204 PP.
BRIEF HISTORY OF POLITICAL TRENDS OF EUROPEAN COUNTRIES.
EVALUATES GROWTH OF GERMAN INDUSTRIAL STRENGTH, THE WORKING
OF AMERICAN FEDERATION AND THE RUSSIAN PROBLEM. SURVEYS
RELATIONSHIP BETWEEN ETHICS AND ECONOMICS. CONCLUDES WITH
DIAGNOSIS OF ECONOMIC DISORDERS.

2393 YOUNG R.
THIS IS CONGRESS.
NEW YORK: ALFRED KNOPF, 1943, 267 PP.
EXAMINES THE PLACE OF CONGRESS IN THE GOVERNMENTAL SYS-
TEM. TRIES TO EXPLAIN TO THE LAYMAN HOW CONGRESS OPERATES
AND SUGGESTS REFORMS WHICH MIGHT BETTER GEAR CONGRESS TO THE
DEMANDS OF BIG GOVERNMENT. RATHER THAN A LEGISLATIVE BODY,
CONGRESS IS NOW, TO A GREAT EXTENT, A REVISIONARY BODY
WHICH INFLUENCES BUT DOES NOT ITSELF MAKE PUBLIC POLICY.
IT HAS AN ITEM VETO OVER PRESIDENTIAL PROPOSALS.

2394 YOUNG S.
MANAGEMENT: A SYSTEMS ANALYSIS.
GLENVIEW, ILL: SCOTT, FORESMAN, 1966, 445 PP.
DESIGN, IMPLEMENTATION, OPERATION, AND CONTROL OF A MAN-
AGEMENT SYSTEM IS DISCUSSED, WITH EMPHASIS ON ORGANIZATIONAL
PROBLEM-SOLVING. SYSTEMS APPROACH UTILIZED TO CONSIDER MANA-
GERIAL DECISION-MAKING AS A TOTAL OPERATING SYSTEM; THE
RELATIONSHIP OF PARTS TO WHOLE IS ALSO ANALYZED. INCLUDES
CASES.

2395 YOUNG W. ED.
EXISTING MECHANISMS OF ARMS CONTROL.
NEW YORK: PERGAMON PRESS, 1966, 150 PP., LC#65-25010.
FOR NEW ARMS CONTROL MEASURES TO WORK THEY NEED TO BE
BASED ON EXPERIENCE AS WELL AS ANALOGY AND IMAGINATION. EDI-
TOR YOUNG HAS COLLECTED ESSAYS ON EXPERIENCES OF 5 INSTITU-
TIONS IN CONTROLLING THE WARLIKE USES OF FISSIONABLE MATTER.
CONTRIBUTORS: MEN SUCH AS SEABORG EXPERIENCED IN THE OPERA-
TIONS OF THE ATOMIC ENERGY COMMISSION, EURATON, ETC.

2396 ZABEL O.H.
GOD AND CAESAR IN NEBRASKA: A STUDY OF LEGAL RELATIONSHIP
OF CHURCH AND STATE, 1854-1954.
LINCOLN: U OF NEB PR, 1955, 198 PP.
STUDIES LEGAL RELATIONSHIP OF CHURCH AND STATE FROM 1854-
1954 IN NEBRASKA. EXAMINES BOTH STATE'S RECOGNITION OF
RELIGIOUS FREEDOM AND RELIGION'S ROLE IN ADMINISTRATIVE
DECISIONS. DISCUSSES SUNDAY LAWS AND PROVIDES DETAILED
STUDY OF EDUCATION AS IT RELATES TO CHURCH AND STATE.
COMPARES NEBRASKA'S SITUATION TO THOSE OF OTHER STATES.

2397 ZALEZNIK A.
HUMAN DILEMMAS OF LEADERSHIP.
NEW YORK: HARPER & ROW, 1966, 237 PP., LC#66-11480.
PSYCHOLOGICAL STUDY OF LEADERSHIP AND SPECIAL PROBLEMS OF
INDIVIDUALS CALLED UPON TO EXERCISE AUTHORITY. COVERS CON-
FLICTS OF AUTHORITY AND SELF-ESTEEM, SELF-ESTEEM AND STATUS,
USE OF POWER IN INTERPERSONAL RELATIONS, AND BASIC GROUP
STRUCTURES IN INDUSTRY.

2398 ZASLOW M.
"RECENT CONSTITUTIONAL DEVELOPMENTS IN CANADA'S NORTHERN
TERRITORIES."
CAN. PUBLIC ADMIN., 10 (JUNE 67), 167-180.
EXAMINES ADMINISTRATION OF YUKON AND NORTHWEST CANADIAN
TERRITORIES. SHOWS RECENT CONSTITUTIONAL CHANGES, ROLE OF
TERRITORIAL COUNCILS, AND FUNCTIONS OF LOCAL EXECUTIVE
OFFICERS. POINTS OUT STEADY ADVANCEMENT TOWARD FULLER
SELF-GOVERNMENT, AND CONSIDERS POSSIBILITIES OF FRACTION-
ALISM.

2399 ZAUBERMAN A.
"SOVIET BLOC ECONOMIC INTEGRATION."
PROBL. COMMUNISM, 8 (JULY-AUG. 59) 23-29.
ASSERTS THAT BLOCK ECONOMIC INTEGRATION
HAS FAR-REACHING POLITICAL IMPLICATIONS. INDICATES THAT IT
MAY COMMEND ITSELF TO SOVIET POLICY-MAKERS AS MEANS OF
STRENGTHENING INTRA-BLOC TIES AND THEREBY CONSOLIDATING
SOVIET POLITICAL HEGEMONY OVER EASTERN EUROPE.

2400 ZELERMYER W. ED.
BUSINESS LAW: NEW PERSPECTIVES IN BUSINESS ECONOMICS.
BOSTON: D C HEATH, 1967, 120 PP., LC#67-16812.
RECENT WORKS BY NINE AUTHORS REPRESENTING CURRENT THOUGHT
ON CHANGING ASPECTS OF BUSINESS LAW. INCLUDES READINGS ON
PROPERTY, UNIFORM COMMERCIAL CODE, ANTITRUST LAWS, AND LABOR
POLICY AND ARBITRATION.

2401 ZELLER B. ED.
"AMERICAN STATE LEGISLATURES: REPORT ON THE COMMITTEE ON

AMERICAN LEGISLATURES."
NEW YORK: THOMAS Y CROWELL, 1954.
PRESENTS RESULTS OF FOUR-YEAR STUDY OF STATE LEGISLA-
TURES. CONCLUDES THAT STATE LEGISLATURES ARE POORLY EQUIPPED
TO SERVE AS POLICY-MAKING AGENCIES. EXTENSIVE BIBLIOGRAPHY
COVERS FIELDS OF REPRESENTATION, ORGANIZATION, PROCEDURE,
LEGISLATIVE AIDS, EXECUTIVE-LEGISLATIVE RELATIONS. APPEN-
DIXES DEVOTED TO RESULTS OF CASE STUDIES IN NEBRASKA,
MAINE, CONNECTICUT, AND MASSACHUSETTS.

2402 ZIMMERN A. ED.
MODERN POLITICAL DOCTRINE.
LONDON: OXFORD U. PR., 1939, 306 PP.
ELABORATES ON GOVERNMENTS' ECONOMIC PROBLEMS OF PROCESSES
AND METHODS AND POINTS OUT POLITICAL DIFFICULTIES ENCOUN-
TERED IN THEIR ATTEMPT TO MAINTAIN WORLD ECONOMIC INTER-
DEPENDENCE.

2403 ZINK H.
CITY BOSSES IN THE UNITED STATES: A STUDY OF TWENTY
MUNICIPAL BOSSES.
DURHAM: DUKE U PR, 1930, 368 PP., LC#30-31996.
ANALYZES SPECIFIC GROUP OF CITY BOSSES OF MAJOR AMERICAN
CITIES. SHOWS THEIR PERSONAL BACKGROUNDS AND
CHARACTERISTICS, DOMESTIC AND SOCIAL RELATIONS, AND THEIR
RELATIONS WITH BUSINESS. DISCUSSES GENERAL PATTERN OF RISE
TO POWER, POLITICAL LEADERSHIP, AND QUESTION OF THEIR
TYPICALITY.

2404 ZINKIN T.
CHALLENGES IN INDIA.
NEW YORK: WALKER, 1966, 248 PP.
DISCUSSES INDIAN DOMESTIC ISSUES AND EVENTS SINCE THE
DEATH OF NEHRU. ANALYZES EFFECTS OF HIS ADMINISTRATION
AND CHANGES SHASTRI INTRODUCED. CONSIDERS PROBLEMS OF
AGRICULTURAL SELF-SUFFICIENCY AND INDUSTRIALIZATION FROM
PRE-INDEPENDENCE TO SHASTRI. RELATED PROBLEMS OF CIVIL
SERVICE CORRUPTION AND INDIAN-PAKISTANI RELATIONS ARE ALSO
INCLUDED.

2405 ZOETEWEIJ B.
"INCOME POLICIES ABROAD: AN INTERIM REPORT."
INDUST. LABOR REL. REV., 20 (JULY 67), 650-664
COMPARES PURPOSES AND METHODS OF SEVERAL WESTERN EUROPEAN
COUNTRIES IN SETTING NORMS FOR WAGE AND PRICE ADJUSTMENTS.
EVALUATES EFFECTIVENESS OF VARIOUS TECHNIQUES. CONSIDERS IN-
COME POLICY AS INSTRUMENT FOR AVOIDING INFLATION AS DIS-
TINCT FROM CHANGING OVER-ALL INCOME OR INCREASING INVEST-
MENTS. FINDS LONG-TERM CENTRAL COORDINATION OF WAGE CLAIMS
IMPOSSIBLE. SUGGESTS COMPROMISE ALTERNATIVES.

2406 ZONDAG C.H.
THE BOLIVIAN ECONOMY 1952-65.
NEW YORK: FREDERICK PRAEGER, 1967, 262 PP., LC#66-14090.
DISCUSSES ECONOMIC EFFECTS OF SOCIAL REVOLUTION. INCLUDES
DESCRIPTION OF SITUATION CAUSING REVOLUTION. INFLATION,
PUBLIC ADMINISTRATION, INDUSTRY, FOREIGN TRADE ARE EXTEN-
SIVELY ANALYZED. EXPOSITION OF FUTURE PROSPECTS AND POLICIES
OF BOLIVIAN GOVERNMENT.

2407 ZUCKERT E.M.
"THE SERVICE SECRETARY* HAS HE A USEFUL ROLE?"
FOREIGN AFFAIRS, 44 (APR. 66), 458-479.
FORMER SECRETARY OF THE AIR FORCE UNDER KENNEDY- JOHNSON
ADMINISTRATION EXPLAINS CHANGES IN DEFENSE ORGANIZATION
AND OPERATIONS PUT IN FORCE BY MC NAMARA. IN B-70 AND TFX
CASES HE ANALYZES PROBLEMS OF THE NEW "SECRETARY" AS MIDDLE-
MAN BETWEEN CIVILIAN CONTROL TECHNIQUES OF SECRETARY OF DE-
FENSE AND TRADITIONAL OPERATION DEMANDS OF AIR FORCE.

INDEX OF DOCUMENTS

AARON T.J. B0049

ABA....AMERICAN BAR ASSOCIATION

S67
SMITH W.H.T.,"THE IMPLICATIONS OF THE AMERICAN BAR   EDU/PROP
ASSOCIATION ADVISORY COMMITTEE RECOMMENDATIONS FOR   CONTROL
POLICE ADMINISTRATION." ADMIN...JURID 20 ABA.   GP/REL
PAGE 98 B1986   ORD/FREE

ABBOT F.C. B0050

ABEL T. B0051

ABELS J. B0052

ABERLE D.F. B0053

ABERNATHY B.R. B0054

ABILITY TESTS....SEE KNO/TEST

ABLARD C.D. B0055

ABM/DEFSYS....ANTI-BALLISTIC MISSILE DEFENSE SYSTEMS

ABORIGINES....ABORIGINES (AUSTRALIA)

B65
BERNDT R.M.,ABORIGINAL MAN IN AUSTRALIA. LAW DOMIN   SOC
ADMIN COLONIAL MARRIAGE HABITAT ORD/FREE...LING   CULTURE
CHARTS ANTHOL BIBLIOG WORSHIP 20 AUSTRAL ABORIGINES   SOCIETY
MUSIC ELKIN/AP. PAGE 11 B0225   STRUCT

ABORTION....ABORTION

ABRIKOSSOV, DIMITRI....SEE ABRIKSSV/D

ABRIKSSV/D....DIMITRI ABRIKOSSOV

ACAD/ASST....ACADEMIC ASSISTANCE COUNCIL (U.K.)

ACADEM....UNIVERSITY, COLLEGE, GRADUATE SCHOOL, HIGHER
     EDUCATION

N
DEUTSCHE BUCHEREI,JAHRESVERZEICHNIS DER DEUTSCHEN   BIBLIOG
HOCHSCHULSCHRIFTEN. EUR+WWI GERMANY LAW ADMIN   WRITING
PERSON...MGT SOC 19/20. PAGE 28 B0579   ACADEM
                                                      INTELL
N
KENTUCKY STATE ARCHIVES,CHECKLIST OF KENTUCKY STATE   BIBLIOG/A
PUBLICATIONS AND STATE DIRECTORY. USA+45 LAW ACADEM   PROVS
EX/STRUC LEGIS EDU/PROP LEAD...JURID 20. PAGE 59   PUB/INST
B1196   ADMIN
N
MINISTERE DE L'EDUC NATIONALE,CATALOGUE DES THESES   BIBLIOG
DE DOCTORAT SOUTENUES DEVANT LES UNIVERSITAIRES   ACADEM
FRANCAISES. FRANCE LAW DIPLOM ADMIN...HUM SOC 20.   KNOWL
PAGE 74 B1490   NAT/G
N
UNIVERSITY MICROFILMS INC,DISSERTATION ABSTRACTS: BIBLIOG/A
ABSTRACTS OF DISSERTATIONS AND MONOGRAPHS IN   ACADEM
MICROFILM. CANADA DIPLOM ADMIN...INDEX 20. PAGE 107   PRESS
B2166   WRITING
N
US SUPERINTENDENT OF DOCUMENTS,EDUCATION (PRICE   BIBLIOG/A
LIST 31). USA+45 LAW FINAN LOC/G NAT/G DEBATE ADMIN   EDU/PROP
LEAD RACE/REL FEDERAL HEALTH POLICY. PAGE 111 B2238   ACADEM
                                                      SCHOOL
N19
BOHLKE R.H.,BUREAUCRATS AND INTELLECTUALS: A   PERSON
CRITIQUE OF C. WRIGHT MILLS (PAMPHLET). ADMIN   SOC
SOCISM. PAGE 13 B0266   ELITES
                                                      ACADEM
B46
BIBLIOGRAFIIA DISSERTATSII: DOKTORSKIE DISSERTATSII   BIBLIOG
ZA 19411944 (2 VOLS.). COM USSR LAW POL/PAR DIPLOM   ACADEM
ADMIN LEAD...PHIL/SCI SOC 20. PAGE 2 B0035   KNOWL
                                                      MARXIST
B49
MCLEAN J.M.,THE PUBLIC SERVICE AND UNIVERSITY   ACADEM
EDUCATION. UK USA-45 DELIB/GP EX/STRUC TOP/EX ADMIN   NAT/G
...GOV/COMP METH/COMP NAT/COMP ANTHOL 20. PAGE 72   EXEC
B1455   EDU/PROP
C50
MORLAN R.L.,"INTERGOVERNMENTAL RELATIONS IN   SCHOOL
EDUCATION." USA+45 FINAN LOC/G MUNIC NAT/G FORCES   GOV/REL
PROB/SOLV RECEIVE ADMIN RACE/REL COST...BIBLIOG   ACADEM
INDIAN/AM. PAGE 76 B1526   POLICY
B51
UNESCO,REPERTOIRE DES BIBLIOTHEQUES DE FRANCE: BIBLIOG
CENTRES ET SERVICES DE DOCUMENTATION DE FRANCE.   ADMIN
FRANCE INDUS ACADEM NAT/G INT/TRADE 20 UNESCO.

B52
SCHATTSCHNEIDER E.E.,A GUIDE TO THE STUDY OF PUBLIC   ACT/RES
AFFAIRS. LAW LOC/G NAT/G LEGIS BUDGET PRESS ADMIN   INTELL
LOBBY...JURID CHARTS 20. PAGE 93 B1882   ACADEM
                                                      METH/COMP
B52
UNESCO,THESES DE SCIENCES SOCIALES: CATALOGUE   BIBLIOG
ANALYTIQUE INTERNATIONAL DE THESES INEDITES DE   ACADEM
DOCTORAT, 1940-1950. INT/ORG DIPLOM EDU/PROP...GEOG   WRITING
INT/LAW MGT PSY SOC 20. PAGE 107 B2155
B54
THORNTON M.L.,OFFICIAL PUBLICATIONS OF THE COLONY   BIBLIOG
AND STATE OF NORTH CAROLINA, 1749-1939. USA+45   ADMIN
USA-45 LEGIS LEAD GOV/REL ATTIT 18/20. PAGE 104   PROVS
B2109   ACADEM
B55
PALMER A.M.,ADMINISTRATION OF MEDICAL AND   HEAL
PHARMACEUTICAL PATENTS (PAMPHLET). USA+45 PROF/ORG   ACADEM
ADMIN PHIL/SCI. PAGE 80 B1626   LAW
                                                      LICENSE
B56
ECOLE NAT'L D'ADMINISTRATION,RECRUITMENT AND   ADMIN
TRAINING FOR THE HIGHER CIVIL SERVICE IN FRANCE.   MGT
FRANCE EX/STRUC PLAN EDU/PROP CONTROL ROUTINE TASK   EXEC
COST...METH 20 CIVIL/SERV. PAGE 32 B0650   ACADEM
B57
CENTRAL ASIAN RESEARCH CENTRE,BIBLIOGRAPHY OF   BIBLIOG/A
RECENT SOVIET SOURCE MATERIAL ON SOVIET CENTRAL   COM
ASIA AND THE BORDERLANDS. AFGHANISTN INDIA PAKISTAN   CULTURE
UAR USSR ECO/UNDEV AGRI EXTR/IND INDUS ACADEM ADMIN   NAT/G
...HEAL HUM LING CON/ANAL 20. PAGE 19 B0399
B57
SOUTH PACIFIC COMMISSION,INDEX OF SOCIAL SCIENCE   BIBLIOG/A
RESEARCH THESES ON THE SOUTH PACIFIC. S/ASIA ACADEM   ACT/RES
ADMIN COLONIAL...SOC 20. PAGE 99 B2000   SECT
                                                      CULTURE
B58
AMERICAN SOCIETY PUBLIC ADMIN,STRENGTHENING   ADMIN
MANAGEMENT FOR DEMOCRATIC GOVERNMENT. USA+45 ACADEM   NAT/G
EX/STRUC WORKER PLAN BUDGET CONFER CT/SYS   EXEC
EFFICIENCY ANTHOL. PAGE 4 B0088   MGT
B58
SWEENEY S.B.,EDUCATION FOR ADMINISTRATIVE CAREERS   EDU/PROP
IN GOVERNMENT SERVICE. USA+45 ACADEM CONSULT CREATE   ADMIN
PLAN CONFER SKILL...TREND IDEA/COMP METH 20   NAT/G
CIVIL/SERV. PAGE 102 B2059   LOC/G
B59
CONOVER H.F.,NIGERIAN OFFICIAL PUBLICATIONS,   BIBLIOG
1869-1959: A GUIDE. NIGER CONSTN FINAN ACADEM   NAT/G
SCHOOL FORCES PRESS ADMIN COLONIAL...HIST/WRIT   CON/ANAL
19/20. PAGE 23 B0466
B59
MOOS M.,THE CAMPUS AND THE STATE. LAW FINAN   EDU/PROP
DELIB/GP LEGIS EXEC LOBBY GP/REL PWR...POLICY   ACADEM
BIBLIOG. PAGE 75 B1517   PROVS
                                                      CONTROL
B59
SAYER W.S.,AN AGENDA FOR RESEARCH IN PUBLIC   WORKER
PERSONNEL ADMINISTRATION. FUT USA+45 ACADEM LABOR   ADMIN
LOC/G NAT/G POL/PAR DELIB/GP MGT. PAGE 93 B1872   ACT/RES
                                                      CONSULT
B59
SURRENCY E.C.,A GUIDE TO LEGAL RESEARCH. USA+45   NAT/G
ACADEM LEGIS ACT/RES ADMIN...DECISION METH/COMP   PROVS
BIBLIOG METH. PAGE 102 B2055   ADJUD
                                                      JURID
B60
CORSON J.J.,GOVERNANCE OF COLLEGES AND   ADMIN
UNIVERSITIES. STRUCT FINAN DELIB/GP DOMIN EDU/PROP   EXEC
LEAD CHOOSE GP/REL CENTRAL COST PRIVIL SUPEGO   ACADEM
ORD/FREE PWR...DECISION BIBLIOG. PAGE 24 B0481   HABITAT
B60
FLORES R.H.,CATALOGO DE TESIS DOCTORALES DE LAS   BIBLIOG
FACULTADES DE LA UNIVERSIDAD DE EL SALVADOR.   ACADEM
EL/SALVADR LAW DIPLOM ADMIN LEAD GOV/REL...SOC   L/A+17C
19/20. PAGE 36 B0730   NAT/G
B60
LEYDER J.,BIBLIOGRAPHIE DE L'ENSEIGNEMENT SUPERIEUR   BIBLIOG/A
ET DE LA RECHERCHE SCIENTIFIQUE EN AFRIQUE   ACT/RES
INTERTROPICALE (2 VOLS.). AFR CULTURE ECO/UNDEV   ACADEM
AGRI PLAN EDU/PROP ADMIN COLONIAL...GEOG SOC/INTEG   R+D
20 NEGRO. PAGE 65 B1309
B60
WALDO D.,THE RESEARCH FUNCTION OF UNIVERSITY   ADMIN
BUREAUS AND INSTITUTES FOR GOVERNMENTAL-RELATED   R+D
RESEARCH. FINAN ACADEM NAT/G INGP/REL ROLE...POLICY   MUNIC
CLASSIF GOV/COMP. PAGE 113 B2276
B61
ROBINSON M.E.,EDUCATION FOR SOCIAL CHANGE: FOR/AID
ESTABLISHING INSTITUTES OF PUBLIC AND BUSINESS   EDU/PROP
ADMINISTRATION ABROAD (PAMPHLET). WOR+45 SOCIETY   MGT
ACADEM CONFER INGP/REL ROLE...SOC CHARTS BIBLIOG 20   ADJUST
ICA. PAGE 89 B1805
B62
BOWEN W.G.,THE FEDERAL GOVERNMENT AND PRINCETON   NAT/G

UNIVERSITY. USA+45 FINAN ACT/RES PROB/SOLV ADMIN
CONTROL COST...POLICY 20 PRINCETN/U. PAGE 14 B0285
ACADEM
GP/REL
OP/RES

B62
DODDS H.W.,THE ACADEMIC PRESIDENT "EDUCATOR OR
CARETAKER? FINAN DELIB/GP EDU/PROP PARTIC ATTIT
ROLE PWR...POLICY RECORD INT. PAGE 30 B0601
ACADEM
ADMIN
LEAD
CONTROL

B62
FRIEDLANDER W.A.,INDIVIDUALISM AND SOCIAL WELFARE.
FRANCE ACADEM OP/RES ADMIN AGE/Y AGE/A ORD/FREE 20.
PAGE 37 B0756
GIVE
SOC/WK
SOC/EXP
FINAN

B62
INTERNAT CONGRESS OF JURISTS,EXECUTIVE ACTION AND
THE RULE OF RULE: REPORTION PROCEEDINGS OF INT'T
CONGRESS OF JURISTS.--RIO DE JANEIRO, BRAZIL. WOR+45
ACADEM CONSULT JUDGE EDU/PROP ADJUD CT/SYS INGP/REL
PERSON DEPT/DEFEN. PAGE 54 B1094
JURID
EXEC
ORD/FREE
CONTROL

B62
MUKERJI S.N.,ADMINISTRATION OF EDUCATION IN INDIA.
ACADEM LOC/G PROVS ROUTINE...POLICY STAT CHARTS 20.
PAGE 76 B1536
SCHOOL
ADMIN
NAT/G
EDU/PROP

B62
NEVINS A.,THE STATE UNIVERSITIES AND DEMOCRACY.
AGRI FINAN SCHOOL ADMIN EXEC EFFICIENCY ATTIT.
PAGE 78 B1576
ACADEM
PROVS
EDU/PROP
POLICY

B62
RUDOLPH F.,THE AMERICAN COLLEGE AND UNIVERSITY.
CLIENT FINAN PUB/INST DELIB/GP EDU/PROP CONTROL
EXEC CONSEN ATTIT POLICY. PAGE 92 B1853
ACADEM
INGP/REL
PWR
ADMIN

B62
US LIBRARY OF CONGRESS,A LIST OF AMERICAN DOCTORAL
DISSERTATIONS ON AFRICA. SOCIETY SECT DIPLOM
EDU/PROP ADMIN...GEOG 19/20. PAGE 109 B2206
BIBLIOG
AFR
ACADEM
CULTURE

L62
SCHWERIN K.,"LAW LIBRARIES AND FOREIGN LAW
COLLECTION IN THE USA." USA+45 USA-45...INT/LAW
STAT 20. PAGE 95 B1917
BIBLIOG
LAW
ACADEM
ADMIN

B63
CHOJNACKI S.,REGISTER ON CURRENT RESEARCH ON
ETHIOPIA AND THE HORN OF AFRICA. ETHIOPIA LAW
CULTURE AGRI SECT EDU/PROP ADMIN...GEOG HEAL LING
20. PAGE 21 B0426
BIBLIOG
ACT/RES
INTELL
ACADEM

B63
INTL INST ADMIN SCIENCES,EDUCATION IN PUBLIC
ADMINISTRATION: A SYMPOSIUM ON TEACHING METHODS AND
MATERIALS. WOR+45 SCHOOL CONSULT CREATE CONFER
SKILL...OBS TREND IDEA/COMP METH/COMP 20. PAGE 54
B1100
EDU/PROP
METH
ADMIN
ACADEM

B63
NASA,CONFERENCE ON SPACE, SCIENCE, AND URBAN LIFE.
USA+45 SOCIETY INDUS ACADEM ACT/RES ECO/TAC ADMIN
20. PAGE 77 B1556
MUNIC
SPACE
TEC/DEV
PROB/SOLV

B64
RECENT PUBLICATIONS ON GOVERNMENTAL PROBLEMS. FINAN
INDUS ACADEM PLAN PROB/SOLV EDU/PROP ADJUD ADMIN
BIO/SOC...MGT SOC. PAGE 2 B0040
BIBLIOG
AUTOMAT
LEGIS
JURID

B64
AVASTHI A.,ASPECTS OF ADMINISTRATION. INDIA UK
USA+45 FINAN ACADEM DELIB/GP LEGIS RECEIVE
PARL/PROC PRIVIL...NAT/COMP 20. PAGE 7 B0150
MGT
ADMIN
SOC/WK
ORD/FREE

B64
VALEN H.,POLITICAL PARTIES IN NORWAY. NORWAY ACADEM
PARTIC ROUTINE INGP/REL KNOWL...QU 20. PAGE 111
B2249
LOC/G
POL/PAR
PERSON

B64
WILSON L.,THE ACADEMIC MAN. STRUCT FINAN PROF/ORG
OP/RES ADMIN AUTHORIT ROLE RESPECT...SOC STAT.
PAGE 117 B2360
ACADEM
INGP/REL
STRATA
DELIB/GP

B65
BARNETT V.M. JR.,THE REPRESENTATION OF THE UNITED
STATES ABROAD* REVISED EDITION. ECO/UNDEV ACADEM
INT/ORG FORCES ACT/RES CREATE OP/RES FOR/AID REGION
CENTRAL...CLASSIF ANTHOL. PAGE 9 B0189
USA+45
DIPLOM
ADMIN

B65
CRAMER J.F.,CONTEMPORARY EDUCATION: A COMPARATIVE
STUDY OF NATIONAL SYSTEMS (2ND ED.). CHINA/COM
EUR+WWI INDIA USA+45 FINAN PROB/SOLV ADMIN CONTROL
ATTIT...IDEA/COMP METH/COMP 20 CHINJAP. PAGE 25
B0502
EDU/PROP
NAT/COMP
SCHOOL
ACADEM

B65
JONES A.G.,THE EVOLUTION OF PERSONNEL SYSTEMS FOR
US FOREIGN AFFAIRS* A HISTORY OF REFORM EFFORTS.
USA+45 USA-45 ACADEM OP/RES GOV/REL...MGT CONGRESS.
PAGE 57 B1149
DIPLOM
ADMIN
ACT/RES
EFFICIENCY

B65
LIPSET S.M.,THE BERKELEY STUDENT REVOLT: FACTS AND
INTERPRETATIONS. USA+45 INTELL VOL/ASSN CONSULT
EDU/PROP PRESS DEBATE ADMIN REV HAPPINESS
RIGID/FLEX MAJORIT. PAGE 65 B1322
CROWD
ACADEM
ATTIT
GP/REL

B65
LYONS G.M.,SCHOOLS FOR STRATEGY* EDUCATION AND
RESEARCH IN NATIONAL SECURITY AFFAIRS. USA+45 FINAN
NAT/G VOL/ASSN FORCES TEC/DEV ADMIN WAR...GP/COMP
IDEA/COMP PERS/COMP COLD/WAR. PAGE 67 B1351
ACADEM
ACT/RES
INTELL

B65
NORDEN A.,WAR AND NAZI CRIMINALS IN WEST GERMANY:
STATE, ECONOMY, ADMINISTRATION, ARMY, JUSTICE,
SCIENCE. GERMANY GERMANY/W MOD/EUR ECO/DEV ACADEM
EX/STRUC FORCES DOMIN ADMIN CT/SYS...POLICY MAJORIT
PACIFIST 20. PAGE 78 B1587
FASCIST
WAR
NAT/G
TOP/EX

B65
OECD,MEDITERRANEAN REGIONAL PROJECT: TURKEY;
EDUCATION AND DEVELOPMENT. FUT TURKEY SOCIETY
STRATA FINAN NAT/G PROF/ORG PLAN PROB/SOLV ADMIN
COST...STAT CHARTS 20 OECD. PAGE 79 B1602
EDU/PROP
ACADEM
SCHOOL
ECO/UNDEV

B65
ORG FOR ECO COOP AND DEVEL,THE MEDITERRANEAN
REGIONAL PROJECT: AN EXPERIMENT IN PLANNING BY SIX
COUNTRIES. FUT GREECE SPAIN TURKEY YUGOSLAVIA
SOCIETY FINAN NAT/G PROF/ORG EDU/PROP ADMIN REGION
COST...POLICY STAT CHARTS 20 OECD. PAGE 80 B1614
PLAN
ECO/UNDEV
ACADEM
SCHOOL

B65
ORG FOR ECO COOP AND DEVEL,THE MEDITERRANEAN
REGIONAL PROJECT: YUGOSLAVIA; EDUCATION AND
DEVELOPMENT. YUGOSLAVIA SOCIETY FINAN PROF/ORG PLAN
ADMIN COST DEMAND MARXISM...STAT TREND CHARTS METH
20 OECD. PAGE 80 B1615
EDU/PROP
ACADEM
SCHOOL
ECO/UNDEV

B65
PERLOFF H.S.,URBAN RESEARCH AND EDUCATION IN THE
NEW YORK METROPOLITAN REGION (VOL. II). FUT USA+45
NEIGH PROF/ORG ACT/RES PROB/SOLV EDU/PROP ADMIN
...STAT BIBLIOG 20 NEWYORK/C. PAGE 82 B1659
MUNIC
PLAN
ACADEM
GP/REL

L65
HOOK S.,"SECOND THOUGHTS ON BERKELEY" USA+45 ELITES
INTELL LEGIT ADMIN COERCE REPRESENT GP/REL INGP/REL
TOTALISM AGE/Y MARXISM 20 BERKELEY FREE/SPEE
STUDNT/PWR. PAGE 51 B1040
ACADEM
ORD/FREE
POLICY
CREATE

S65
"FURTHER READING." INDIA NAT/G ADMIN 20. PAGE 2
B0043
BIBLIOG
EDU/PROP
SCHOOL
ACADEM

S65
POLK W.R.,"PROBLEMS OF GOVERNMENT UTILIZATION OF
SCHOLARLY RESEARCH IN INTERNATIONAL AFFAIRS." FINAN
NAT/G EDU/PROP CONTROL TASK GP/REL ATTIT PERCEPT
KNOWL...POLICY TIME. PAGE 83 B1685
ACT/RES
ACADEM
PLAN
ADMIN

S65
SILVERT K.H.,"AMERICAN ACADEMIC ETHICS AND SOCIAL
RESEARCH ABROAD* THE LESSON OF PROJECT CAMELOT."
CHILE L/A+17C USA+45 FINAN ADMIN...PHIL/SCI SOC
GEN/LAWS CAMELOT. PAGE 97 B1953
ACADEM
NAT/G
ACT/RES
POLICY

B66
ANDREWS K.R.,THE EFFECTIVENESS OF UNIVERSITY
MANAGEMENT DEVELOPMENT PROGRAMS. FUT USA+45 ECO/TAC
ADMIN...MGT QU METH/COMP 20. PAGE 5 B0103
ECO/DEV
ACADEM
TOP/EX
ATTIT

B66
BRAIBANTI R.,RESEARCH ON THE BUREAUCRACY OF
PAKISTAN. PAKISTAN LAW CULTURE INTELL ACADEM LOC/G
SECT PRESS CT/SYS...LING CHARTS 20 BUREAUCRCY.
PAGE 15 B0279
HABITAT
NAT/G
ADMIN
CONSTN

B66
GLAZER M.,THE FEDERAL GOVERNMENT AND THE
UNIVERSITY. CHILE PROB/SOLV DIPLOM GIVE ADMIN WAR
...POLICY SOC 20. PAGE 40 B0810
BIBLIOG/A
NAT/G
PLAN
ACADEM

B66
PERKINS J.A.,THE UNIVERSITY IN TRANSITION. USA+45
SOCIETY FINAN INDUS NAT/G EX/STRUC ADMIN INGP/REL
COST EFFICIENCY ATTIT 20. PAGE 82 B1658
ACADEM
ORD/FREE
CREATE
ROLE

B66
SCHMIDT F.,PUBLIC RELATIONS IN HEALTH AND WELFARE.
USA+45 ACADEM RECEIVE PRESS FEEDBACK GOV/REL
PERS/REL DEMAND EFFICIENCY ATTIT PERCEPT WEALTH 20
PUBLIC/REL. PAGE 94 B1895
PROF/ORG
EDU/PROP
ADMIN
HEALTH

B66
US BUREAU OF THE BUDGET,THE ADMINISTRATION OF
GOVERNMENT SUPPORTED RESEARCH AT UNIVERSITIES
(PAMPHLET). USA+45 CONSULT TOP/EX ADMIN INCOME
WEALTH...MGT PHIL/SCI INT. PAGE 108 B2174
ACT/RES
NAT/G
ACADEM
GP/REL

B66
VON HOFFMAN N.,THE MULTIVERSITY; A PERSONAL REPORT
ON WHAT HAPPENS TO TODAY'S STUDENTS AT AMERICAN
UNIVERSITIES. USA+45 SOCIETY ROUTINE ANOMIE ROLE
MORAL ORD/FREE SKILL...INT 20. PAGE 112 B2266
EDU/PROP
ACADEM
ATTIT
STRANGE

L66
AMERICAN ECONOMIC REVIEW,"SIXTY-THIRD LIST OF
DOCTORAL DISSERTATIONS IN POLITICAL ECONOMY IN
BIBLIOG/A
CONCPT

AMERICAN UNIVERSITIES AND COLLEGES." ECO/DEV AGRI ACADEM
FINAN LABOR WORKER PLAN BUDGET INT/TRADE ADMIN
DEMAND...MGT STAT 20. PAGE 4 B0084
                                                                B67
HOROWITZ I.L.,"THE RISE AND FALL OF PROJECT CAMELOT: NAT/G
STUDIES IN THE RELATIONSHIP BETWEEN SOCIAL SCIENCE   ACADEM
AND PRACTICAL POLITICS. USA+45 WOR+45 CULTURE   ACT/RES
FORCES LEGIS EXEC CIVMIL/REL KNOWL...POLICY SOC   GP/REL
METH/CNCPT 20. PAGE 51 B1043
                                                                S67
ATKIN J.M.,"THE FEDERAL GOVERNMENT, BIG BUSINESS,   SCHOOL
AND COLLEGES OF EDUCATION." PROF/ORG CONSULT CREATE ACADEM
PLAN PROB/SOLV ADMIN EFFICIENCY. PAGE 7 B0144   NAT/G
                                                     INDUS
                                                                S67
BASTID M.,"ORIGINES ET DEVELOPMENT DE LA REVOLUTION REV
CULTURELLE." CHINA/COM DOMIN ADMIN CONTROL LEAD   CULTURE
COERCE CROWD ATTIT DRIVE MARXISM...POLICY 20.   ACADEM
PAGE 10 B0195   WORKER
                                                                S67
DOERN G.B.,"THE ROYAL COMMISSIONS IN THE GENERAL   R+D
POLICY PROCESS AND IN FEDERAL-PROVINCIAL   EX/STRUC
RELATIONS." CANADA CONSTN ACADEM PROVS CONSULT   GOV/REL
DELIB/GP LEGIS ACT/RES PROB/SOLV CONFER CONTROL   NAT/G
EFFICIENCY...METH/COMP 20 SENATE ROYAL/COMM.
PAGE 30 B0603
                                                                S67
LA PORTE T.,"DIFFUSION AND DISCONTINUITY IN   INTELL
SCIENCE, TECHNOLOGY AND PUBLIC AFFAIRS: RESULTS OF   ADMIN
A SEARCH IN THE FIELD." USA+45 ACT/RES TEC/DEV   ACADEM
PERS/REL ATTIT PHIL/SCI. PAGE 62 B1249   GP/REL
                                                                S67
MONEYPENNY P.,"UNIVERSITY PURPOSE, DISCIPLINE, AND   ACADEM
DUE PROCESS." USA+45 EDU/PROP ADJUD LEISURE   AGE/Y
ORD/FREE. PAGE 74 B1500   CONTROL
                                                     ADMIN
                                                                S67
OLIVE B.A.,"THE ADMINISTRATION OF HIGHER EDUCATION: ACADEM
A BIBLIOGRAPHICAL SURVEY." USA+45 ATTIT. PAGE 79   ADMIN
B1605   OP/RES

ACADEM/SCI....ACADEMY OF SCIENCES (U.S.S.R.)

ACADEMIC ASSISTANCE COUNCIL (U.K.)....SEE ACAD/ASST

ACADEMY OF SCIENCES (U.S.S.R.)....SEE ACADEM/SCI

ACBC....ACTION COUNCIL FOR BETTER CITIES

ACCOUNTING....SEE ACCT

ACCT....ACCOUNTING, BOOKKEEPING

ACCULTURATION....SEE CULTURE

ACD....UNITED STATES ARMS CONTROL AND DISARMAMENT AGENCY

ACHESON/D....DEAN ACHESON

ACKOFF R.L. B0056

ACLU....AMERICAN CIVIL LIBERTIES UNION
                                                                B38
BALDWIN R.N.,CIVIL LIBERTIES AND INDUSTRIAL   LABOR
CONFLICT. USA+45 STRATA WORKER INGP/REL...MGT 20   LG/CO
ACLU CIVIL/LIB. PAGE 9 B0175   INDUS
                                                     GP/REL
                                                                B52
MILLER M.,THE JUDGES AND THE JUDGED. USA+45 LG/CO   COM/IND
ACT/RES TV ROUTINE SANCTION NAT/LISM ATTIT ORD/FREE DISCRIM
...POLICY ACLU. PAGE 73 B1481   EDU/PROP
                                                     MARXISM

ACQUAINTANCE GROUP....SEE FACE/GP

ACT/RES....RESEARCH FACILITATING SOCIAL ACTION

ACTION COUNCIL FOR BETTER CITIES....SEE ACBC

ACTION....ALLEGHENY COUNCIL TO IMPROVE OUR NEIGHBORHOODS

ACTON/LORD....LORD ACTON
                                                                B52
HIMMELFARB G.,LORD ACTON: A STUDY IN CONSCIENCE AND PWR
POLITICS. MOD/EUR NAT/G POL/PAR SECT LEGIS TOP/EX   BIOG
EDU/PROP ADMIN NAT/LISM ATTIT PERSON SUPEGO MORAL
ORD/FREE...CONCPT PARLIAMENT 19 ACTON/LORD. PAGE 50
B1014

ADA....AMERICANS FOR DEMOCRATIC ACTION

ADAMOVITCH A. B0807

ADAMS J.C. B0057

ADAMS V. B0058

ADAMS/J....PRESIDENT JOHN ADAMS

ADAMS/JQ....PRESIDENT JOHN QUINCY ADAMS

ADAMS/SAM....SAMUEL ADAMS

ADDICTION....ADDICTION

ADENAUER/K....KONRAD ADENAUER
                                                                L63
FREUND G.,"ADENAUER AND THE FUTURE OF GERMANY."   NAT/G
EUR+WWI FUT GERMANY/W FORCES LEGIT ADMIN ROUTINE   BIOG
ATTIT DRIVE PERSON PWR...POLICY TIME/SEQ TREND   DIPLOM
VAL/FREE 20 ADENAUER/K. PAGE 37 B0753   GERMANY
                                                                S63
ANTHON C.G.,"THE END OF THE ADENAUER ERA." EUR+WWI   NAT/G
GERMANY/W CONSTN EX/STRUC CREATE DIPLOM LEGIT ATTIT TOP/EX
PERSON ALL/VALS...RECORD 20 ADENAUER/K. PAGE 6   BAL/PWR
B0113   GERMANY
                                                                B66
NEUMANN R.G.,THE GOVERNMENT OF THE GERMAN FEDERAL   NAT/G
REPUBLIC. EUR+WWI GERMANY/W LOC/G EX/STRUC LEGIS   POL/PAR
CT/SYS INGP/REL PWR...BIBLIOG 20 ADENAUER/K.   DIPLOM
PAGE 78 B1573   CONSTN

ADJUD....JUDICIAL AND ADJUDICATIVE PROCESSES
                                                                N
US SUPERINTENDENT OF DOCUMENTS,POLITICAL SCIENCE: BIBLIOG/A
GOVERNMENT, CRIME, DISTRICT OF COLUMBIA (PRICE LIST NAT/G
54). USA+45 LAW CONSTN EX/STRUC WORKER ADJUD ADMIN   CRIME
CT/SYS CHOOSE INGP/REL RACE/REL CONGRESS PRESIDENT.
PAGE 111 B2241
                                                                N
US SUPERINTENDENT OF DOCUMENTS,TARIFF AND TAXATION   BIBLIOG/A
(PRICE LIST 37). USA+45 LAW INT/TRADE ADJUD ADMIN   TAX
CT/SYS INCOME OWN...DECISION GATT. PAGE 111 B2242   TARIFFS
                                                     NAT/G
                                                                N
VIRGINIA STATE LIBRARY,CHECK-LIST OF VIRGINIA STATE BIBLIOG/A
PUBLICATIONS. USA+45 USA-45 ECO/DEV POL/PAR LEGIS   PROVS
ADJUD LEAD 18/20. PAGE 112 B2265   ADMIN
                                                     GOV/REL
                                                                B08
THE GOVERNMENT OF SOUTH AFRICA (VOL. II). SOUTH/AFR CONSTN
STRATA EXTR/IND EX/STRUC TOP/EX BUDGET ADJUD ADMIN   FINAN
CT/SYS PRODUC...CORREL CENSUS 19 RAILROAD   LEGIS
CIVIL/SERV POSTAL/SYS. PAGE 2 B0033   NAT/G
                                                                B08
WILSON W.,CONSTITUTIONAL GOVERNMENT IN THE UNITED   NAT/G
STATES. USA-45 LAW POL/PAR PROVS CHIEF LEGIS   GOV/REL
BAL/PWR ADJUD EXEC FEDERAL PWR 18/20 SUPREME/CT   CONSTN
HOUSE/REP SENATE. PAGE 117 B2362   PARL/PROC
                                                                B09
HARVARD UNIVERSITY LAW LIBRARY,CATALOGUE OF THE   BIBLIOG/A
LIBRARY OF THE LAW SCHOOL OF HARVARD UNIVERSITY (3   LAW
VOLS.). UK USA-45 LEGIS JUDGE ADJUD CT/SYS...JURID   ADMIN
CHARTS 14/20. PAGE 48 B0963
                                                                N19
PERREN G.E.,LANGUAGE AND COMMUNICATION IN THE   EDU/PROP
COMMONWEALTH (PAMPHLET). FUT UK LAW ECO/DEV PRESS   LING
TV WRITING ADJUD ADMIN COLONIAL CONTROL 20   GOV/REL
CMN/WLTH. PAGE 82 B1660   COM/IND
                                                                B24
HOLDSWORTH W.S.,A HISTORY OF ENGLISH LAW; THE   LAW
COMMON LAW AND ITS RIVALS (VOL. V). UK SEA EX/STRUC LEGIS
WRITING ADMIN...INT/LAW JURID CONCPT IDEA/COMP   ADJUD
WORSHIP 16/17 PARLIAMENT ENGLSH/LAW COMMON/LAW.   CT/SYS
PAGE 51 B1033
                                                                B24
HOLDSWORTH W.S.,A HISTORY OF ENGLISH LAW; THE   LAW
COMMON LAW AND ITS RIVALS (VOL. VI). UK STRATA   CONSTN
EX/STRUC ADJUD ADMIN CONTROL CT/SYS...JURID CONCPT   LEGIS
GEN/LAWS 17 COMMONWLTH PARLIAMENT ENGLSH/LAW   CHIEF
COMMON/LAW. PAGE 51 B1034
                                                                B25
MATHEWS J.M.,AMERICAN STATE GOVERNMENT. USA-45   PROVS
LOC/G CHIEF EX/STRUC LEGIS ADJUD CONTROL CT/SYS   ADMIN
ROUTINE GOV/REL PWR 20 GOVERNOR. PAGE 71 B1426   FEDERAL
                                                     CONSTN
                                                                B27
DICKINSON J.,ADMINISTRATIVE JUSTICE AND THE   CT/SYS
SUPREMACY OF LAW IN THE UNITED STATES. USA-45 LAW   ADJUD
INDUS DOMIN EDU/PROP CONTROL EXEC GP/REL ORD/FREE   ADMIN
...POLICY JURID 19/20. PAGE 29 B0586   NAT/G
                                                                B28
HARDMAN J.B.,AMERICAN LABOR DYNAMICS. WORKER   LABOR
ECO/TAC DOMIN ADJUD LEAD LOBBY PWR...POLICY MGT.   INGP/REL
PAGE 47 B0944   ATTIT
                                                     GP/REL
                                                                B29
MOLEY R.,POLITICS AND CRIMINAL PROSECUTION. USA-45   PWR
POL/PAR EX/STRUC LEGIT CONTROL LEAD ROUTINE CHOOSE   CT/SYS

INGP/REL...JURID CHARTS 20. PAGE 74 B1497
CRIME
ADJUD
B32

MCKISACK M.,THE PARLIAMENTARY REPRESENTATION OF THE
ENGLISH BOROUGHS DURING THE MIDDLE AGES. UK CONSTN
CULTURE ELITES EX/STRUC TAX PAY ADJUD PARL/PROC
APPORT FEDERAL...POLICY 13/15 PARLIAMENT. PAGE 72
B1454
NAT/G
MUNIC
LEGIS
CHOOSE
B33

ENSOR R.C.K.,COURTS AND JUDGES IN FRANCE, GERMANY,
AND ENGLAND. FRANCE GERMANY UK LAW PROB/SOLV ADMIN
ROUTINE CRIME ROLE...METH/COMP 20 CIVIL/LAW.
PAGE 33 B0676
CT/SYS
EX/STRUC
ADJUD
NAT/COMP
B37

BUREAU OF NATIONAL AFFAIRS,LABOR RELATIONS
REFERENCE MANUAL VOL 1, 1935-1937. BARGAIN DEBATE
ROUTINE INGP/REL 20 NLRB. PAGE 17 B0351
LABOR
ADMIN
ADJUD
NAT/G
B37

UNION OF SOUTH AFRICA,REPORT CONCERNING
ADMINISTRATION OF SOUTH WEST AFRICA (6 VOLS.).
SOUTH/AFR INDUS PUB/INST FORCES LEGIS BUDGET DIPLOM
EDU/PROP ADJUD CT/SYS...GEOG CHARTS 20 AFRICA/SW
LEAGUE/NAT. PAGE 107 B2158
NAT/G
ADMIN
COLONIAL
CONSTN
B38

FIELD G.L.,THE SYNDICAL AND CORPORATIVE
INSTITUTIONS OF ITALIAN FASCISM. ITALY CONSTN
STRATA LABOR EX/STRUC TOP/EX ADJUD ADMIN LEAD
TOTALISM AUTHORIT...MGT 20 MUSSOLIN/B. PAGE 35
B0716
FASCISM
INDUS
NAT/G
WORKER
B40

HART J.,AN INTRODUCTION TO ADMINISTRATIVE LAW, WITH
SELECTED CASES. USA-45 CONSTN SOCIETY NAT/C
EX/STRUC ADJUD CT/SYS LEAD CRIME ORD/FREE
...DECISION JURID 20 CASEBOOK. PAGE 47 B0958
LAW
ADMIN
LEGIS
PWR
B41

GELLHORN W.,FEDERAL ADMINISTRATIVE PROCEEDINGS.
USA+45 CLIENT FACE/GP NAT/G LOBBY REPRESENT PWR 20.
PAGE 39 B0788
EX/STRUC
LAW
ADJUD
POLICY
B44

DAVIS H.E.,PIONEERS IN WORLD ORDER. WOR-45 CONSTN
ECO/TAC DOMIN EDU/PROP LEGIT ADJUD ADMIN ARMS/CONT
CHOOSE KNOWL ORD/FREE...POLICY JURID SOC STAT OBS
CENSUS TIME/SE● ANTHOL LEAGUE/NAT 20. PAGE 26 B0537
INT/ORG
ROUTINE
B45

MILLIS H.A.,ORGANIZED LABOR (FIRST ED.). LAW STRUCT
DELIB/GP WORKER ECO/TAC ADJUD CONTROL REPRESENT
INGP/REL INCOME MGT. PAGE 74 B1485
LABOR
POLICY
ROUTINE
GP/REL
B47

PATTERSON C.P.,PRESIDENTIAL GOVERNMENT IN THE
UNITED STATES - THE UNWRITTEN CONSTITUTION. USA+45
DELIB/GP EX/STRUC ADJUD ADMIN EXEC...DECISION
PRESIDENT. PAGE 81 B1643
CHIEF
NAT/G
CONSTN
POL/PAR
B47

TAPPAN P.W.,DELINQUENT GIRLS IN COURT. USA-45 MUNIC
EX/STRUC FORCES ADMIN EXEC ADJUST SEX RESPECT
...JURID SOC/WK 20 NEWYORK/C FEMALE/SEX. PAGE 103
B2078
CT/SYS
AGE/Y
CRIME
ADJUD
B48

BISHOP H.M.,BASIC ISSUES OF AMERICAN DEMOCRACY.
USA+45 USA-45 POL/PAR EX/STRUC LEGIS ADJUD FEDERAL
...BIBLIOG 18/20. PAGE 12 B0244
NAT/G
PARL/PROC
CONSTN
B48

HART J.,THE AMERICAN PRESIDENCY IN ACTION 1789: A
STUDY IN CONSTITUTIONAL HISTORY. USA-45 POL/PAR
DELIB/GP FORCES LEGIS ADJUD ADMIN LEAD GP/REL
PERS/REL 18 PRESIDENT CONGRESS. PAGE 47 B0959
NAT/G
CONSTN
CHIEF
EX/STRUC
B48

SLESSER H.,THE ADMINISTRATION OF THE LAW. UK CONSTN
EX/STRUC OP/RES PROB/SOLV CRIME ROLE...DECISION
METH/COMP 20 CIVIL/LAW ENGLSH/LAW CIVIL/LAW.
PAGE 98 B1977
LAW
CT/SYS
ADJUD
B49

DENNING A.,FREEDOM UNDER THE LAW. MOD/EUR UK LAW
SOCIETY CHIEF EX/STRUC LEGIS ADJUD CT/SYS PERS/REL
PERSON 17/20 ENGLSH/LAW. PAGE 28 B0573
ORD/FREE
JURID
NAT/G
B49

WALINE M.,LE CONTROLE JURIDICTIONNEL DE
L'ADMINISTRATION. BELGIUM FRANCE UAR JUDGE BAL/PWR
ADJUD CONTROL CT/SYS...GP/COMP 20. PAGE 113 B2277
JURID
ADMIN
PWR
ORD/FREE
B50

GRAVES W.B.,PUBLIC ADMINISTRATION: A COMPREHENSIVE
BIBLIOGRAPHY ON PUBLIC ADMINISTRATION IN THE UNITED
STATES (PAMPHLET). USA+45 USA-45 LOC/G NAT/G LEGIS
ADJUD INGP/REL...MGT 20. PAGE 42 B0858
BIBLIOG
FINAN
CONTROL
ADMIN
B50

MCCAMY J.,THE ADMINISTRATION OF AMERICAN FOREIGN
AFFAIRS. USA+45 SOCIETY INT/ORG NAT/G ACT/RES PLAN
INT/TRADE EDU/PROP ADJUD ALL/VALS...METH/CNCPT
TIME/SEQ CONGRESS 20. PAGE 71 B1441
EXEC
STRUCT
DIPLOM
B51

ANDERSON W.,STATE AND LOCAL GOVERNMENT IN THE
UNITED STATES. USA+45 CONSTN POL/PAR EX/STRUC LEGIS
LOC/G
MUNIC

BUDGET TAX ADJUD CT/SYS CHOOSE...CHARTS T 20.
PAGE 5 B0100
PROVS
GOV/REL
B51

ANDERSON W.,GOVERNMENT IN THE FIFTY STATES. LAW
CONSTN FINAN POL/PAR LEGIS EDU/PROP ADJUD ADMIN
CT/SYS CHOOSE...CHARTS 20. PAGE 5 B0101
LOC/G
PROVS
GOV/REL
B51

DAVIS K.C.,ADMINISTRATIVE LAW. USA+45 USA-45 NAT/G
PROB/SOLV BAL/PWR CONTROL ORD/FREE...POLICY 20
SUPREME/CT. PAGE 26 B0539
ADMIN
JURID
EX/STRUC
ADJUD
B51

SWISHER C.B.,THE THEORY AND PRACTICE OF AMERICAN
NATIONAL GOVERNMENT. CULTURE LEGIS DIPLOM ADJUD
ADMIN WAR PEACE ORD/FREE...MAJORIT 17/20. PAGE 102
B2063
CONSTN
NAT/G
GOV/REL
GEN/LAWS
S51

COHEN M.B.,"PERSONALITY AS A FACTOR IN
ADMINISTRATIVE DECISIONS." ADJUD PERS/REL ANOMIE
SUPEGO...OBS SELF/OBS INT. PAGE 22 B0446
PERSON
ADMIN
PROB/SOLV
PSY
B52

DE GRAZIA A.,POLITICAL ORGANIZATION. CONSTN LOC/G
MUNIC NAT/G CHIEF LEGIS TOP/EX ADJUD CT/SYS
PERS/REL...INT/LAW MYTH UN. PAGE 27 B0553
FEDERAL
LAW
ADMIN
B52

DONHAM W.B.,ADMINISTRATION AND BLIND SPOTS. LG/CO
EX/STRUC BARGAIN ADJUD ROUTINE ROLE SUPEGO 20.
PAGE 30 B0605
ADMIN
TOP/EX
DECISION
POLICY
B52

REDFORD E.S.,ADMINISTRATION OF NATIONAL ECONOMIC
CONTROL. ECO/DEV DELIB/GP ADJUD CONTROL EQUILIB 20.
PAGE 87 B1753
ADMIN
ROUTINE
GOV/REL
LOBBY
B52

SWENSON R.J.,FEDERAL ADMINISTRATIVE LAW: A STUDY OF
THE GROWTH, NATURE, AND CONTROL OF ADMINISTRATIVE
ACTION. USA-45 JUDGE ADMIN GOV/REL EFFICIENCY
PRIVIL ATTIT NEW/LIB SUPREME/CT. PAGE 102 B2061
JURID
CONSTN
LEGIS
ADJUD
S52

EDELMAN M.,"GOVERNMENTAL ORGANIZATION AND PUBLIC
POLICY." DELIB/GP ADJUD DECISION. PAGE 32 B0652
ADMIN
PLURIST
LOBBY
EX/STRUC
B53

MAJUMDAR B.B.,PROBLEMS OF PUBLIC ADMINISTRATION IN
INDIA. INDIA INDUS PLAN BUDGET ADJUD CENTRAL DEMAND
WEALTH...WELF/ST ANTHOL 20 CIVIL/SERV. PAGE 68
B1384
ECO/UNDEV
GOV/REL
ADMIN
MUNIC
B53

SAYLES L.R.,THE LOCAL UNION. CONSTN CULTURE
DELIB/GP PARTIC CHOOSE GP/REL INGP/REL ATTIT ROLE
...MAJORIT DECISION MGT. PAGE 93 B1873
LABOR
LEAD
ADJUD
ROUTINE
B53

SECKLER-HUDSON C.,BIBLIOGRAPHY ON PUBLIC
ADMINISTRATION (4TH ED.). USA+45 LAW POL/PAR
DELIB/GP BUDGET ADJUD LOBBY GOV/REL GP/REL ATTIT
...JURID 20. PAGE 95 B1923
BIBLIOG/A
ADMIN
NAT/G
MGT
N53

US PRES CONF ADMIN PROCEDURE,REPORT (PAMPHLET).
USA+45 CONFER ADJUD...METH/COMP 20 PRESIDENT.
PAGE 109 B2209
NAT/G
DELIB/GP
ADJUST
ADMIN
B54

BENTLEY A.F.,INQUIRY INTO INQUIRIES: ESSAYS IN
SOCIAL THEORY. UNIV LEGIS ADJUD ADMIN LOBBY
...PHIL/SCI PSY NEW/IDEA LING METH 20. PAGE 11
B0220
EPIST
SOC
CONCPT
B54

JENNINGS I.,THE QUEEN'S GOVERNMENT. UK POL/PAR
DELIB/GP ADJUD ADMIN CT/SYS PARL/PROC REPRESENT
CONSERVE 13/20 PARLIAMENT. PAGE 56 B1132
NAT/G
CONSTN
LEGIS
CHIEF
B54

MILLARD E.L.,FREEDOM IN A FEDERAL WORLD. FUT WOR+45
VOL/ASSN TOP/EX LEGIT ROUTINE FEDERAL PEACE ATTIT
DISPL ORD/FREE PWR...MAJORIT INT/LAW JURID TREND
COLD/WAR 20. PAGE 73 B1479
INT/ORG
CREATE
ADJUD
BAL/PWR
B54

SCHWARTZ B.,FRENCH ADMINISTRATIVE LAW AND THE
COMMON-LAW WORLD. FRANCE CULTURE LOC/G NAT/G PROVS
DELIB/GP EX/STRUC LEGIS PROB/SOLV CT/SYS EXEC
GOV/REL...IDEA/COMP ENGLSH/LAW. PAGE 95 B1912
JURID
LAW
METH/COMP
ADJUD
S54

COOPER L.,"ADMINISTRATIVE JUSTICE." UK ADMIN
REPRESENT PWR...POLICY 20. PAGE 23 B0475
LAW
ADJUD
CONTROL
EX/STRUC
B55

BRAUN K.,LABOR DISPUTES AND THEIR SETTLEMENT.
ECO/TAC ROUTINE TASK GP/REL...DECISION GEN/LAWS.
PAGE 15 B0301
INDUS
LABOR
BARGAIN
ADJUD

CHOWDHURI R.N.,INTERNATIONAL MANDATES AND
TRUSTEESHIP SYSTEMS. WOR+45 STRUCT ECO/UNDEV
INT/ORG LEGIS DOMIN EDU/PROP LEGIT ADJUD EXEC PWR
...CONCPT TIME/SEQ UN 20. PAGE 21 B0427
B55
DELIB/GP
PLAN
SOVEREIGN

CRAIG J.,BIBLIOGRAPHY OF PUBLIC ADMINISTRATION IN
AUSTRALIA. CONSTN FINAN EX/STRUC LEGIS PLAN DIPLOM
RECEIVE ADJUD ROUTINE...HEAL 19/20 AUSTRAL
PARLIAMENT. PAGE 24 B0500
B55
BIBLIOG
GOV/REL
ADMIN
NAT/G

DE ARAGAO J.G.,LA JURIDICTION ADMINISTRATIVE AU
BRESIL. BRAZIL ADJUD COLONIAL CT/SYS REV FEDERAL
ORD/FREE...BIBLIOG 19/20. PAGE 27 B0549
B55
EX/STRUC
ADMIN
NAT/G

PULLEN W.R.,A CHECK LIST OF LEGISLATIVE JOURNALS
ISSUED SINCE 1937 BY THE STATES OF THE UNITED
STATES OF AMERICA (PAMPHLET). USA+45 USA-45 LAW
WRITING ADJUD ADMIN...JURID 20. PAGE 85 B1720
B55
BIBLIOG
PROVS
EDU/PROP
LEGIS

WHEARE K.C.,GOVERNMENT BY COMMITTEE; AN ESSAY ON
THE BRITISH CONSTITUTION. UK NAT/G LEGIS INSPECT
CONFER ADJUD ADMIN CONTROL TASK EFFICIENCY ROLE
POPULISM 20. PAGE 115 B2329
B55
DELIB/GP
CONSTN
LEAD
GP/COMP

WRIGHT Q.,"THE PEACEFUL ADJUSTMENT OF INTERNATIONAL
RELATIONS: PROBLEMS AND RESEARCH APPROACHES." UNIV
INTELL EDU/PROP ADJUD ROUTINE KNOWL SKILL...INT/LAW
JURID PHIL/SCI CLASSIF 20. PAGE 118 B2385
S55
R+D
METH/CNCPT
PEACE

SOHN L.B.,CASES ON UNITED NATIONS LAW. STRUCT
DELIB/GP WAR PEACE ORD/FREE...DECISION ANTHOL 20
UN. PAGE 99 B1994
B56
INT/ORG
INT/LAW
ADMIN
ADJUD

US HOUSE RULES COMM,HEARINGS BEFORE A SPECIAL
SUBCOMMITTEE: ESTABLISHMENT OF A STANDING COMMITTEE
ON ADMINISTRATIVE PROCEDURE. PRACTICE. USA+45 LAW
EX/STRUC ADJUD CONTROL EXEC GOV/REL EFFICIENCY PWR
...POLICY INT 20 CONGRESS. PAGE 109 B2199
B56
ADMIN
DOMIN
DELIB/GP
NAT/G

WIGGINS J.R.,FREEDOM OR SECRECY. USA+45 USA-45
DELIB/GP EX/STRUC FORCES ADJUD SANCTION KNOWL PWR
...AUD/VIS CONGRESS 20. PAGE 116 B2344
B56
ORD/FREE
PRESS
NAT/G
CONTROL

EISENTADT S.N.,"POLITICAL STRUGGLE IN BUREAUCRATIC
SOCIETIES" ASIA CULTURE ADJUD SANCTION PWR
BUREAUCRCY OTTOMAN BYZANTINE. PAGE 33 B0661
L56
ADMIN
CHIEF
CONTROL
ROUTINE

AUMANN F.R.,"THE ISTRUMENTALITIES OF JUSTICE: THEIR
FORMS, FUNCTIONS, AND LIMITATIONS." WOR+45 WOR-45
JUDGE PROB/SOLV ROUTINE ATTIT...BIBLIOG 20. PAGE 7
B0147
C56
JURID
ADMIN
CT/SYS
ADJUD

CHICAGO U LAW SCHOOL,CONFERENCE ON JUDICIAL
ADMINISTRATION. LOC/G MUNIC NAT/G PROVS...ANTHOL
20. PAGE 21 B0421
B57
CT/SYS
ADJUD
ADMIN
GOV/REL

COOPER F.E.,THE LAWYER AND ADMINISTRATIVE AGENCIES.
USA+45 CLIENT LAW PROB/SOLV CT/SYS PERSON ROLE.
PAGE 23 B0473
B57
CONSULT
ADMIN
ADJUD
DELIB/GP

HINDERLING A.,DIE REFORMATORISCHE
VERWALTUNGSGERICHTSBARKEIT. GERMANY/W PROB/SOLV
ADJUD SUPEGO PWR...CONCPT 20. PAGE 50 B1015
B57
ADMIN
CT/SYS
JURID
CONTROL

MEYER P.,ADMINISTRATIVE ORGANIZATION: A COMPARATIVE
STUDY OF THE ORGANIZATION OF PUBLIC ADMINISTRATION.
DENMARK FRANCE NORWAY SWEDEN UK USA+45 ELITES LOC/G
CONSULT LEGIS ADJUD CONTROL LEAD PWR SKILL
DECISION. PAGE 73 B1475
B57
ADMIN
METH/COMP
NAT/G
CENTRAL

HAILEY,"TOMORROW IN AFRICA." CONSTN SOCIETY LOC/G
NAT/G DOMIN ADJUD ADMIN GP/REL DISCRIM NAT/LISM
ATTIT MORAL ORD/FREE...PSY SOC CONCPT OBS RECORD
TREND GEN/LAWS CMN/WLTH 20. PAGE 45 B0917
S57
AFR
PERSON
ELITES
RACE/REL

CHARLES R.,LA JUSTICE EN FRANCE. FRANCE LAW CONSTN
DELIB/GP CRIME 20. PAGE 20 B0413
B58
JURID
ADMIN
CT/SYS
ADJUD

DAVIS K.C.,ADMINISTRATIVE LAW TREATISE (VOLS. I AND
IV). NAT/G JUDGE PROB/SOLV ADJUD GP/REL 20
SUPREME/CT. PAGE 26 B0540
B58
ADMIN
JURID
CT/SYS
EX/STRUC

DAVIS K.C.,ADMINISTRATIVE LAW; CASES, TEXT,
PROBLEMS. LAW LOC/G NAT/G TOP/EX PAY CONTROL
GOV/REL INGP/REL FEDERAL 20 SUPREME/CT. PAGE 27
B0541
B58
ADJUD
JURID
CT/SYS
ADMIN

KAPLAN H.E.,THE LAW OF CIVIL SERVICE. USA+45 LAW
POL/PAR CT/SYS CRIME GOV/REL...POLICY JURID 20.
PAGE 58 B1167
B58
ADJUD
NAT/G
ADMIN
CONSTN

LAW COMMISSION OF INDIA,REFORM OF JUDICIAL
ADMINISTRATION. INDIA TOP/EX ADMIN DISCRIM
EFFICIENCY...METH/COMP 20. PAGE 63 B1276
B58
CT/SYS
ADJUD
GOV/REL
CONTROL

POUND R.,JUSTICE ACCORDING TO LAW. LAW SOCIETY
CT/SYS 20. PAGE 84 B1696
B58
CONCPT
JURID
ADJUD
ADMIN

SHARMA M.P.,PUBLIC ADMINISTRATION IN THEORY AND
PRACTICE. INDIA UK USA+45 USA-45 EX/STRUC ADJUD
...POLICY CONCPT NAT/COMP 20. PAGE 96 B1935
B58
MGT
ADMIN
DELIB/GP
JURID

SPITZ D.,DEMOCRACY AND THE CHALLANGE OF POWER. FUT
USA+45 USA-45 LAW SOCIETY STRUCT LOC/G POL/PAR
PROVS DELIB/GP EX/STRUC LEGIS TOP/EX ACT/RES CREATE
DOMIN EDU/PROP LEGIT ADJUD ADMIN ATTIT DRIVE MORAL
ORD/FREE TOT/POP. PAGE 99 B2010
B58
NAT/G
PWR

US HOUSE COMM ON COMMERCE,ADMINISTRATIVE PROCESS
AND ETHICAL QUESTIONS. USA+45 LAW LEGIS INT/TRADE
CONTROL 20 CONGRESS. PAGE 109 B2192
B58
POLICY
ADMIN
DELIB/GP
ADJUD

WESTIN A.F.,THE ANATOMY OF A CONSTITUTIONAL LAW
CASE. USA+45 LAW LEGIS ADMIN EXEC...DECISION MGT
SOC RECORD 20 SUPREME/CT. PAGE 115 B2326
B58
CT/SYS
INDUS
ADJUD
CONSTN

JONAS F.H.,"BIBLIOGRAPHY ON WESTERN POLITICS."
USA+45 USA-45 ELITES MUNIC POL/PAR LEGIS ADJUD
ADMIN 20. PAGE 57 B1148
L58
BIBLIOG/A
LOC/G
NAT/G
LAW

DIAMANT A.,"A CASE STUDY OF ADMINISTRATIVE
AUTONOMY: CONTROLS AND TENSIONS IN FRENCH
ADMINISTRATION." FRANCE ADJUD LOBBY DEMAND
EFFICIENCY 20. PAGE 29 B0585
S58
ADMIN
CONTROL
LEGIS
EXEC

STAAR R.F.,"ELECTIONS IN COMMUNIST POLAND." EUR+WWI
SOCIETY INT/ORG NAT/G POL/PAR LEGIS ACT/RES ECO/TAC
EDU/PROP ADJUD ADMIN ROUTINE COERCE TOTALISM ATTIT
ORD/FREE PWR 20. PAGE 100 B2015
S58
COM
CHOOSE
POLAND

COUNCIL OF STATE GOVERNORS,AMERICAN LEGISLATURES:
STRUCTURE AND PROCEDURES. SUMMARY AND TABULATIONS
OF A 1959 SURVEY. PUERT/RICO USA+45 PAY ADJUD ADMIN
APPORT...IDEA/COMP 20 GUAM VIRGIN/ISL. PAGE 24
B0495
B59
LEGIS
CHARTS
PROVS
REPRESENT

DAVIS K.C.,ADMINISTRATIVE LAW TEXT. USA+45 NAT/G
DELIB/GP EX/STRUC CONTROL ORD/FREE...T 20
SUPREME/CT. PAGE 27 B0542
B59
ADJUD
ADMIN
JURID
CT/SYS

DESMITH S.A.,JUDICIAL REVIEW OF ADMINISTRATIVE
ACTION. UK LOC/G CONSULT DELIB/GP ADMIN PWR
...DECISION JURID 20 ENGLSH/LAW. PAGE 28 B0576
B59
ADJUD
NAT/G
PROB/SOLV
CT/SYS

ELLIOTT S.D.,IMPROVING OUR COURTS. LAW EX/STRUC
PLAN PROB/SOLV ADJUD ADMIN TASK CRIME EFFICIENCY
ORD/FREE 20. PAGE 33 B0669
B59
CT/SYS
JURID
GOV/REL
NAT/G

GORDENKER L.,THE UNITED NATIONS AND THE PEACEFUL
UNIFICATION OF KOREA. ASIA LAW LOC/G CONSULT
ACT/RES DIPLOM DOMIN LEGIT ADJUD ADMIN ORD/FREE
SOVEREIGN...INT GEN/METH UN COLD/WAR 20. PAGE 41
B0829
B59
DELIB/GP
KOREA
INT/ORG

MACIVER R.M.,THE NATIONS AND THE UN. WOR+45 NAT/G
CONSULT ADJUD ADMIN ALL/VALS...CONCPT DEEP/QU UN
TOT/POP UNESCO 20. PAGE 67 B1362
B59
INT/ORG
ATTIT
DIPLOM

REDFORD E.S.,NATIONAL REGULATORY COMMISSIONS: NEED
FOR A NEW LOOK (PAMPHLET). USA+45 CLIENT PROB/SOLV
ADJUD LOBBY EFFICIENCY...POLICY 20. PAGE 87 B1757
B59
REPRESENT
CONTROL
EXEC
NAT/G

SURRENCY E.C.,A GUIDE TO LEGAL RESEARCH. USA+45
ACADEM LEGIS ACT/RES ADMIN...DECISION METH/COMP
BIBLIOG METH. PAGE 102 B2055
B59
NAT/G
PROVS
ADJUD
JURID

HECTOR L.J.,"GOVERNMENT BY ANONYMITY: WHO WRITES
OUR REGULATORY OPINIONS?" USA+45 NAT/G TOP/EX
CONTROL EXEC. PAGE 49 B0987
L59
ADJUD
REPRESENT
EX/STRUC

ADMIN
S59

LASSWELL H.D.,"UNIVERSALITY IN PERSPECTIVE." FUT
UNIV SOCIETY CONSULT TOP/EX PLAN EDU/PROP ADJUD
ROUTINE ARMS/CONT COERCE PEACE ATTIT PERSON
ALL/VALS. PAGE 63 B1271
INT/ORG
JURID
TOTALISM

S59

SOHN L.B.,"THE DEFINITION OF AGGRESSION." FUT LAW
FORCES LEGIT ADJUD ROUTINE COERCE ORD/FREE PWR
...MAJORIT JURID QUANT COLD/WAR 20. PAGE 99 B1995
INT/ORG
CT/SYS
DETER
SOVEREIGN

B60

ADRIAN C.R.,STATE AND LOCAL GOVERNMENTS: A STUDY IN
THE POLITICAL PROCESS. USA+45 LAW FINAN MUNIC
POL/PAR LEGIS ADJUD EXEC CHOOSE REPRESENT. PAGE 3
B0060
LOC/G
PROVS
GOV/REL
ATTIT

B60

DAVIS K.C.,ADMINISTRATIVE LAW AND GOVERNMENT.
USA+45 EX/STRUC PROB/SOLV ADJUD GP/REL PWR...POLICY
20 SUPREME/CT. PAGE 27 B0543
ADMIN
JURID
CT/SYS
NAT/G

B60

ELKOURI F.,HOW ARBITRATION WORKS (REV. ED.). LAW
INDUS BARGAIN 20. PAGE 33 B0667
MGT
LABOR
ADJUD
GP/REL

B60

HODGETTS J.E.,CANADIAN PUBLIC ADMINISTRATION.
CANADA CONTROL LOBBY EFFICIENCY 20. PAGE 50 B1024
REPRESENT
ADMIN
EX/STRUC
ADJUD

B60

PENNSYLVANIA ECONOMY LEAGUE.URBAN RENEWAL IMPACT
STUDY: ADMINISTRATIVE-LEGAL-FISCAL. USA+45 FINAN
LOC/G NEIGH ADMIN EFFICIENCY...CENSUS CHARTS 20
PENNSYLVAN. PAGE 82 B1652
PLAN
BUDGET
MUNIC
ADJUD

B60

PFIFFNER J.M.,PUBLIC ADMINISTRATION. USA+45 FINAN
WORKER PLAN PROB/SOLV ADJUD CONTROL EXEC...T 20.
PAGE 82 B1666
ADMIN
NAT/G
LOC/G
MGT

B60

SCHUBERT G.,THE PUBLIC INTEREST. USA+45 CONSULT
PLAN PROB/SOLV ADJUD ADMIN GP/REL PWR ALL/IDEOS 20.
PAGE 94 B1903
POLICY
DELIB/GP
REPRESENT
POL/PAR

B60

WEBSTER J.A.,A GENERAL STUDY OF THE DEPARTMENT OF
DEFENSE INTERNAL SECURITY PROGRAM. USA+45 WORKER
TEC/DEV ADJUD CONTROL CT/SYS EXEC GOV/REL COST
...POLICY DECISION MGT 20 DEPT/DEFEN SUPREME/CT.
PAGE 114 B2307
ORD/FREE
PLAN
ADMIN
NAT/G

L60

DEAN A.W.,"SECOND GENEVA CONFERENCE OF THE LAW OF
THE SEA: THE FIGHT FOR FREEDOM OF THE SEAS." FUT
USA+45 USSR WOR-45 SEA CONSTN STRUCT PLAN
INT/TRADE ADJUD ADMIN ORD/FREE...DECISION RECORD
TREND GEN/LAWS 20 TREATY. PAGE 28 B0564
INT/ORG
JURID
INT/LAW

L60

FUCHS R.F.,"FAIRNESS AND EFFECTIVENESS IN
ADMINISTRATIVE AGENCY ORGANIZATION AND PROCEDURES."
USA+45 ADJUD ADMIN REPRESENT. PAGE 38 B0764
EFFICIENCY
EX/STRUC
EXEC
POLICY

L60

STEIN E.,"LEGAL REMEDIES OF ENTERPRISES IN THE
EUROPEAN ECONOMIC COMMUNITY." EUR+WWI FUT ECO/DEV
INDUS PLAN ECO/TAC ADMIN PWR...MGT MATH STAT TREND
CON/ANAL EEC 20. PAGE 115 B2026
MARKET
ADJUD

S60

BOGARDUS E.S.,"THE SOCIOLOGY OF A STRUCTURED
PEACE." FUT SOCIETY CREATE DIPLOM EDU/PROP ADJUD
ROUTINE ATTIT RIGID/FLEX KNOWL ORD/FREE RESPECT
...POLICY INT/LAW JURID NEW/IDEA SELF/OBS TOT/POP
20 UN. PAGE 13 B0264
INT/ORG
SOC
NAT/LISM
PEACE

S60

MARSHALL G.,"POLICE RESPONSIBILITY." UK LOC/G ADJUD
ADMIN EXEC 20. PAGE 70 B1409
CONTROL
REPRESENT
LAW
FORCES

S60

SCHACHTER O.,"THE ENFORCEMENT OF INTERNATIONAL
JUDICIAL AND ARBITRAL DECISIONS." WOR+45 NAT/G
ECO/TAC DOMIN LEGIT ROUTINE COERCE ATTIT DRIVE
ALL/VALS PWR...METH/CNCPT TREND TOT/POP 20 UN.
PAGE 93 B1878
INT/ORG
ADJUD
INT/LAW

S60

SCHER S.,"CONGRESSIONAL COMMITTEE MEMBERS AND
INDEPENDENT AGENCY OVERSEERS: A·CASE STUDY."
DELIB/GP EX/STRUC JUDGE TOP/EX DOMIN ADMIN CONTROL
PWR...SOC/EXP HOUSE/REP CONGRESS. PAGE 93 B1886
LEGIS
GOV/REL
LABOR
ADJUD

S60

THOMPSON K.W.,"MORAL PURPOSE IN FOREIGN POLICY:
REALITIES AND ILLUSIONS." WOR+45 WOR-45 LAW CULTURE
SOCIETY INT/ORG PLAN ADJUD ADMIN COERCE RIGID/FLEX
SUPEGO KNOWL ORD/FREE PWR...SOC TREND SOC/EXP
TOT/POP 20. PAGE 104 B2104
MORAL
JURID
DIPLOM

B61

AUERBACH C.A.,THE LEGAL PROCESS. USA+45 DELIB/GP
JUDGE CONFER ADJUD CONTROL...DECISION 20
SUPREME/CT. PAGE 7 B0146
JURID
ADMIN
LEGIS
CT/SYS

B61

BAINS J.S.,STUDIES IN POLITICAL SCIENCE. INDIA
WOR+45 WOR-45 CONSTN BAL/PWR ADJUD ADMIN PARL/PROC
SOVEREIGN...SOC METH/COMP ANTHOL 17/20 UN. PAGE 8
B0165
DIPLOM
INT/LAW
NAT/G

B61

BEASLEY K.E.,STATE SUPERVISION OF MUNICIPAL DEBT IN
KANSAS - A CASE STUDY. USA+45 USA-45 FINAN PROVS
BUDGET TAX ADJUD ADMIN CONTROL SUPEGO. PAGE 10
B0201
MUNIC
LOC/G
LEGIS
JURID

B61

CARROTHERS A.W.R.,LABOR ARBITRATION IN CANADA.
CANADA LAW NAT/G CONSULT LEGIS WORKER ADJUD ADMIN
CT/SYS 20. PAGE 19 B0386
LABOR
MGT
GP/REL
BARGAIN

B61

DARRAH E.L.,FIFTY STATE GOVERNMENTS: A COMPILATION
OF EXECUTIVE ORGANIZATION CHARTS. USA+45 LOC/G
DELIB/GP LEGIS ADJUD LEAD PWR 20 GOVERNOR. PAGE 26
B0530
EX/STRUC
ADMIN
ORG/CHARTS
PROVS

B61

RAO K.V.,PARLIAMENTARY DEMOCRACY OF INDIA. INDIA
EX/STRUC TOP/EX COLONIAL CT/SYS PARL/PROC ORD/FREE
...POLICY CONCPT TREND 20 PARLIAMENT. PAGE 86 B1733
CONSTN
ADJUD
NAT/G
FEDERAL

B61

ROMANO F.,CIVIL SERVICE AND PUBLIC EMPLOYEE LAW IN
NEW JERSEY. CONSTN MUNIC WORKER GIVE PAY CHOOSE
UTIL 20. PAGE 90 B1816
ADMIN
PROVS
ADJUD
LOC/G

B61

ROWAT D.C.,BASIC ISSUES IN PUBLIC ADMINISTRATION.
STRUCT EX/STRUC PWR CONSERVE...MAJORIT DECISION MGT
T 20 BUREAUCRCY. PAGE 91 B1839
NAT/G
ADJUD
ADMIN

B61

STONE J.,QUEST FOR SURVIVAL. WOR+45 NAT/G VOL/ASSN
LEGIT ADMIN ARMS/CONT COERCE DISPL ORD/FREE PWR
...POLICY INT/LAW JURID COLD/WAR 20. PAGE 101 B2047
INT/ORG
ADJUD
SOVEREIGN

B61

TOMPKINS D.C.,CONFLICT OF INTEREST IN THE FEDERAL
GOVERNMENT: A BIBLIOGRAPHY. USA+45 EX/STRUC LEGIS
ADJUD ADMIN CRIME CONGRESS PRESIDENT. PAGE 105
B2117
BIBLIOG
ROLE
NAT/G
LAW

S61

ABLARD C.D.,"EX PARTE CONTACTS WITH FEDERAL
ADMINISTRATIVE AGENCIES." USA+45 CLIENT NAT/G
DELIB/GP ADMIN PWR 20. PAGE 3 B0055
EXEC
ADJUD
LOBBY
REPRESENT

B62

CARTER G.M.,THE GOVERNMENT OF THE SOVIET UNION.
USSR CULTURE LOC/G DIPLOM ECO/TAC ADJUD CT/SYS LEAD
WEALTH...CHARTS T 20 COM/PARTY. PAGE 19 B0390
NAT/G
MARXISM
POL/PAR
EX/STRUC

B62

DELANY V.T.H.,THE ADMINISTRATION OF JUSTICE IN
IRELAND. IRELAND CONSTN FINAN JUDGE COLONIAL CRIME
...CRIMLGY 19/20. PAGE 28 B0571
ADMIN
JURID
CT/SYS
ADJUD

B62

GROGAN V.,ADMINISTRATIVE TRIBUNALS IN THE PUBLIC
SERVICE. IRELAND UK NAT/G CONTROL CT/SYS...JURID
GOV/COMP 20. PAGE 44 B0884
ADMIN
LAW
ADJUD
DELIB/GP

B62

INTERNAT CONGRESS OF JURISTS.EXECUTIVE ACTION AND
THE RULE OF RULE: REPORTION PROCEEDINGS OF INT'T
CONGRESS OF JURISTS,-RIO DE JANEIRO, BRAZIL. WOR+45
ACADEM CONSULT JUDGE EDU/PROP ADJUD CT/SYS INGP/REL
PERSON DEPT/DEFEN. PAGE 54 B1094
JURID
EXEC
ORD/FREE
CONTROL

B62

LYNCH J.,ADMINISTRATION COLONIAL ESPANOLA
1782-1810. SPAIN PROVS TOP/EX PARTIC 18/19 ARGEN.
PAGE 67 B1349
COLONIAL
CONTROL
ADJUD
ADMIN

B62

MARS D.,SUGGESTED LIBRARY IN PUBLIC ADMINISTRATION.
FINAN DELIB/GP EX/STRUC WORKER COMPUTER ADJUD
...DECISION PSY SOC METH/COMP 20. PAGE 69 B1403
BIBLIOG
ADMIN
METH
MGT

B62

PHILLIPS O.H.,CONSTITUTIONAL AND ADMINISTRATIVE LAW
(3RD ED.). UK INT/ORG LOC/G CHIEF EX/STRUC LEGIS
BAL/PWR ADJUD COLONIAL CT/SYS PWR...CHARTS 20.
PAGE 83 B1670
JURID
ADMIN
CONSTN
NAT/G

B62

SRIVASTAVA G.L.,COLLECTIVE BARGAINING AND LABOR-
MANAGEMENT RELATIONS IN INDIA. INDIA UK USA+45
INDUS LEGIS WORKER ADJUD EFFICIENCY PRODUC
...METH/COMP 20. PAGE 100 B2014
LABOR
MGT
BARGAIN
GP/REL

L62

ERDMANN H.H.,"ADMINISTRATIVE LAW AND FARM
AGRI

ECONOMICS." USA+45 LOC/G NAT/G PLAN PROB/SOLV LOBBY ADMIN
...DECISION ANTHOL 20. PAGE 33 B0680
ADJUD
POLICY
S62

FESLER J.W.,"FRENCH FIELD ADMINISTRATION: THE EX/STRUC
BEGINNINGS." CHRIST-17C CULTURE SOCIETY STRATA FRANCE
NAT/G ECO/TAC DOMIN EDU/PROP LEGIT ADJUD COERCE
ATTIT ALL/VALS...TIME/SEQ CON/ANAL GEN/METH
VAL/FREE 13/15. PAGE 35 B0714
C62

TRUMAN D.B.,"THE GOVERNMENTAL PROCESS: POLITICAL LOBBY
INTERESTS AND PUBLIC OPINION." POL/PAR ADJUD ADMIN EDU/PROP
EXEC LEAD ROUTINE CHOOSE REPRESENT GOV/REL GP/REL
RIGID/FLEX...POLICY BIBLIOG/A 20. PAGE 105 B2131 LEGIS
C62

VAN DER SPRENKEL S.,"LEGAL INSTITUTIONS IN MANCHU LAW
CHINA." ASIA STRUCT CT/SYS ROUTINE GOV/REL GP/REL JURID
...CONCPT BIBLIOG 17/20. PAGE 111 B2250 ADMIN
ADJUD
B63

BOWETT D.W.,THE LAW OF INTERNATIONAL INSTITUTIONS. INT/ORG
WOR+45 WOR-45 CONSTN DELIB/GP EX/STRUC JUDGE ADJUD
EDU/PROP LEGIT CT/SYS EXEC ROUTINE RIGID/FLEX DIPLOM
ORD/FREE PWR...JURID CONCPT ORG/CHARTS GEN/METH
LEAGUE/NAT OAS OEEC 20 UN. PAGE 14 B0286
B63

BURRUS B.R.,ADMINSTRATIVE LAW AND LOCAL GOVERNMENT. EX/STRUC
USA+45 PROVS LEGIS LICENSE ADJUD ORD/FREE 20. LOC/G
PAGE 17 B0356 JURID
CONSTN
B63

COUNCIL STATE GOVERNMENTS,HANDBOOK FOR LEGISLATIVE LEGIS
COMMITTEES. USA+45 LAW DELIB/GP EX/STRUC TOP/EX PARL/PROC
CHOOSE PWR...METH/COMP 20. PAGE 24 B0496 PROVS
ADJUD
B63

ECOLE NATIONALE D'ADMIN,BIBLIOGRAPHIE SELECTIVE BIBLIOG
D'OUVRAGES DE LANGUE FRANCAISE TRAITANT DES AFR
PROBLEMES GOUVERNEMENTAUX ET ADMINISTRATIFS. NAT/G ADMIN
FORCES ACT/RES OP/RES PLAN PROB/SOLV BUDGET ADJUD EX/STRUC
COLONIAL LEAD 20. PAGE 32 B0651
B63

ELIAS T.O.,THE NIGERIAN LEGAL SYSTEM. NIGERIA LAW CT/SYS
FAM KIN SECT ADMIN NAT/LISM...JURID 18/20. ADJUD
ENGLSH/LAW COMMON/LAW. PAGE 33 B0665 COLONIAL
PROF/ORG
B63

GARNER U.F.,ADMINISTRATIVE LAW. UK LAW LOC/G NAT/G ADMIN
EX/STRUC LEGIS JUDGE BAL/PWR BUDGET ADJUD CONTROL JURID
CT/SYS...BIBLIOG 20. PAGE 39 B0783 PWR
GOV/REL
B63

GRIFFITH J.A.G.,PRINCIPLES OF ADMINISTRATIVE LAW JURID
(3RD ED.). UK CONSTN EX/STRUC LEGIS ADJUD CONTROL ADMIN
CT/SYS PWR...CHARTS 20. PAGE 43 B0879 NAT/G
BAL/PWR
B63

HOUGHTELING J.L. JR.,THE LEGAL ENVIRONMENT OF LAW
BUSINESS. LG/CO NAT/G CONSULT AGREE CONTROL MGT
...DICTIONARY T 20. PAGE 52 B1047 ADJUD
JURID
B63

KLEIN F.J.,JUDICIAL ADMINISTRATION AND THE LEGAL BIBLIOG/A
PROFESSION. USA+45 ADMIN CONTROL EFFICIENCY CT/SYS
...POLICY 20. PAGE 60 B1217 ADJUD
JUDGE
B63

KLESMENT J.,LEGAL SOURCES AND BIBLIOGRAPHY OF THE BIBLIOG/A
BALTIC STATES (ESTONIA, LATVIA, LITHUANIA). COM JURID
ESTONIA LATVIA LITHUANIA LAW FINAN ADJUD CT/SYS CONSTN
REGION CENTRAL MARXISM 19/20. PAGE 60 B1218 ADMIN
B63

KULZ H.R.,STAATSBURGER UND STAATSGEWALT (2 VOLS.). ADMIN
GERMANY SWITZERLND UK USSR CONSTN DELIB/GP TARIFFS ADJUD
TAX...JURID 20. PAGE 61 B1242 CT/SYS
NAT/COMP
B63

PATRA A.C.,THE ADMINISTRATION OF JUSTICE UNDER THE ADMIN
EAST INDIA COMPANY IN BENGAL, BIHAR AND ORISSA. JURID
INDIA UK LG/CO CAP/ISM INT/TRADE ADJUD COLONIAL CONCPT
CONTROL CT/SYS...POLICY 20. PAGE 81 B1641
B63

US SENATE COMM ON JUDICIARY,ADMINISTERED PRICES. LG/CO
USA+45 RATION ADJUD CONTROL LOBBY...POLICY 20 PRICE
SENATE MONOPOLY. PAGE 110 B2229 ADMIN
DECISION
B63

WADE H.W.R.,TOWARDS ADMINISTRATIVE JUSTICE. UK ADJUD
USA+45 CONSTN CONSULT PROB/SOLV CT/SYS PARL/PROC IDEA/COMP
...POLICY JURID METH/COMP 20 ENGLSH/LAW. PAGE 112 ADMIN
B2270
B63

WOLL P.,AMERICAN BUREAUCRACY. USA+45 USA-45 CONSTN LEGIS
NAT/G ADJUD PWR OBJECTIVE...MGT GP/COMP. PAGE 118 EX/STRUC
B2372 ADMIN
GP/REL

B63
WOLL P.,ADMINISTRATIVE LAW: THE INFORMAL PROCESS. ADMIN
USA+45 NAT/G CONTROL EFFICIENCY 20. PAGE 118 B2373 ADJUD
REPRESENT
EX/STRUC
L63

BOLGAR V.,"THE PUBLIC INTEREST: A JURISPRUDENTIAL CONCPT
AND COMPARATIVE OVERVIEW OF SYMPOSIUM ON ORD/FREE
FUNDAMENTAL CONCEPTS OF PUBLIC LAW" COM FRANCE CONTROL
GERMANY SWITZERLND LAW ADJUD ADMIN AGREE LAISSEZ NAT/COMP
...JURID GEN/LAWS 20 EUROPE/E. PAGE 13 B0268
L63

LIVERNASH E.R.,"THE RELATION OF POWER TO THE LABOR
STRUCTURE AND PROCESS OF COLLECTIVE BARGAINING." GP/REL
ADJUD ORD/FREE...POLICY MGT CLASSIF GP/COMP. PWR
PAGE 66 B1330 ECO/TAC
B64

RECENT PUBLICATIONS ON GOVERNMENTAL PROBLEMS. FINAN BIBLIOG
INDUS ACADEM PLAN PROB/SOLV EDU/PROP ADJUD ADMIN AUTOMAT
BIO/SOC...MGT SOC. PAGE 2 B0040 LEGIS
JURID
B64

BENNETT H.A.,THE COMMISSION AND THE COMMON LAW: A ADJUD
STUDY IN ADMINISTRATIVE ADJUDICATION. LAW ADMIN DELIB/GP
CT/SYS LOBBY SANCTION GOV/REL 20 COMMON/LAW. DIST/IND
PAGE 10 B0212 POLICY
B64

BLAKE R.R.,MANAGING INTERGROUP CONFLICT IN CREATE
INDUSTRY. INDUS DELIB/GP EX/STRUC GP/REL PERS/REL PROB/SOLV
GAME. PAGE 12 B0250 OP/RES
ADJUD
B64

ENDACOTT G.B.,GOVERNMENT AND PEOPLE IN HONG KONG CONSTN
1841-1962: A CONSTITUTIONAL HISTORY. UK LEGIS ADJUD COLONIAL
REPRESENT ATTIT 19/20 HONG/KONG. PAGE 33 B0674 CONTROL
ADMIN
B64

GJUPANOVIC H.,LEGAL SOURCES AND BIBLIOGRAPHY OF BIBLIOG/A
YUGOSLAVIA. COM YUGOSLAVIA LAW LEGIS DIPLOM ADMIN JURID
PARL/PROC REGION CRIME CENTRAL 20. PAGE 40 B0807 CONSTN
ADJUD
B64

GRZYBOWSKI K.,THE SOCIALIST COMMONWEALTH OF INT/LAW
NATIONS: ORGANIZATIONS AND INSTITUTIONS. FORCES COM
DIPLOM INT/TRADE ADJUD ADMIN LEAD WAR MARXISM REGION
SOCISM...BIBLIOG 20 COMECON WARSAW/P. PAGE 44 B0898 INT/ORG
B64

HALLER W.,DER SCHWEDISCHE JUSTITIEOMBUDSMAN. JURID
DENMARK FINLAND NORWAY SWEDEN LEGIS ADJUD CONTROL PARL/PROC
PERSON ORD/FREE...NAT/COMP 20 OMBUDSMAN. PAGE 46 ADMIN
B0926 CHIEF
B64

JACKSON R.M.,THE MACHINERY OF JUSTICE IN ENGLAND. CT/SYS
UK EDU/PROP CONTROL COST ORD/FREE...MGT 20 ADJUD
ENGLSH/LAW. PAGE 55 B1109 JUDGE
JURID
B64

KAHNG T.J.,LAW, POLITICS, AND THE SECURITY COUNCIL* DELIB/GP
AN INQUIRY INTO THE HANDLING OF LEGAL QUESTIONS. ADJUD
LAW CONSTN NAT/G ACT/RES OP/RES CT/SYS TASK PWR ROUTINE
...INT/LAW BIBLIOG UN. PAGE 57 B1160
B64

KARLEN D.,THE CITIZEN IN COURT. USA+45 LAW ADMIN CT/SYS
ROUTINE CRIME GP/REL...JURID 20. PAGE 58 B1175 ADJUD
GOV/REL
JUDGE
B64

NELSON D.H.,ADMINISTRATIVE AGENCIES OF THE USA: ADMIN
THEIR DECISIONS AND AUTHORITY. USA+45 NAT/G CONTROL EX/STRUC
CT/SYS REPRESENT...DECISION 20. PAGE 78 B1568 ADJUD
LAW
B64

PRESS C.,A BIBLIOGRAPHIC INTRODUCTION TO AMERICAN BIBLIOG
STATE GOVERNMENT AND POLITICS (PAMPHLET). USA+45 LEGIS
USA-45 EX/STRUC ADJUD INGP/REL FEDERAL ORD/FREE 20. LOC/G
PAGE 84 B1701 POL/PAR
B64

ROCHE J.P.,THE CONGRESS. EX/STRUC BAL/PWR DIPLOM INGP/REL
DEBATE ADJUD LEAD PWR. PAGE 89 B1809 LEGIS
DELIB/GP
SENIOR
B64

SCHECHTER A.H.,INTERPRETATION OF AMBIGUOUS INT/LAW
DOCUMENTS BY INTERNATIONAL ADMINISTRATIVE DIPLOM
TRIBUNALS. WOR+45 EX/STRUC INT/TRADE CT/SYS INT/ORG
SOVEREIGN 20 UN ILO EURCT/JUST. PAGE 93 B1884 ADJUD
B64

SHERIDAN R.G.,URBAN JUSTICE. USA+45 PROVS CREATE LOC/G
ADMIN CT/SYS ORD/FREE 20 TENNESSEE. PAGE 96 B1943 JURID
ADJUD
MUNIC
B64

STOICOIU V.,LEGAL SOURCES AND BIBLIOGRAPHY OF BIBLIOG/A
ROMANIA. COM ROMANIA LAW FINAN POL/PAR LEGIS JUDGE JURID
ADJUD CT/SYS PARL/PROC MARXISM 20. PAGE 101 B2041 CONSTN
ADMIN

B64
SZLADITS C.,BIBLIOGRAPHY ON FOREIGN AND COMPARATIVE BIBLIOG/A
LAW: BOOKS AND ARTICLES IN ENGLISH (SUPPLEMENT JURID
1962). FINAN INDUS JUDGE LICENSE ADMIN CT/SYS ADJUD
PARL/PROC OWN...INT/LAW CLASSIF METH/COMP NAT/COMP LAW
20. PAGE 102 B2065

S64
LIPSET S.M.,"SOCIOLOGY AND POLITICAL SCIENCE: A BIBLIOG/A
BIBLIOGRAPHICAL NOTE." WOR+45 ELITES LEGIS ADJUD SOC
ADMIN ATTIT IDEA/COMP. PAGE 65 B1321 METH/COMP

S64
PARSONS T.,"EVOLUTIONARY UNIVERSALS IN SOCIETY." SOC
UNIV SOCIETY STRATA MARKET EDU/PROP LEGIT ADJUD CONCPT
ADMIN ALL/VALS...JURID OBS GEN/LAWS VAL/FREE 20.
PAGE 81 B1638

S64
SCHWELB E.,"OPERATION OF THE EUROPEAN CONVENTION ON INT/ORG
HUMAN RIGHTS." EUR+WWI LAW SOCIETY CREATE EDU/PROP MORAL
ADJUD ADMIN PEACE ATTIT ORD/FREE PWR...POLICY
INT/LAW CONCPT OBS GEN/LAWS UN VAL/FREE ILO 20
ECHR. PAGE 95 B1916

B65
CAVERS D.F.,THE CHOICE-OF-LAW PROCESS. PROB/SOLV JURID
ADJUD CT/SYS CHOOSE RATIONAL...IDEA/COMP 16/20 DECISION
TREATY. PAGE 19 B0396 METH/COMP
ADMIN

B65
COOPER F.E.,STATE ADMINISTRATIVE LAW (2 VOLS.). LAW JURID
LEGIS PLAN TAX ADJUD CT/SYS FEDERAL PWR...CONCPT CONSTN
20. PAGE 23 B0474 ADMIN
PROVS

B65
EVERETT R.O.,URBAN PROBLEMS AND PROSPECTS. USA+45 MUNIC
CREATE TEC/DEV EDU/PROP ADJUD ADMIN GOV/REL ATTIT PLAN
...ANTHOL 20 URBAN/RNWL. PAGE 34 B0691 PROB/SOLV
NEIGH

B65
FRIEDMAN L.,SOUTHERN JUSTICE. USA+45 PUB/INST LEGIT ADJUD
ADMIN CT/SYS DISCRIM...DECISION ANTHOL 20 NEGRO LAW
SOUTH/US CIV/RIGHTS. PAGE 37 B0758 CONSTN
RACE/REL

B65
FRYE R.J.,HOUSING AND URBAN RENEWAL IN ALABAMA. MUNIC
USA+45 NEIGH LEGIS BUDGET ADJUD ADMIN PARTIC...MGT PROB/SOLV
20 ALABAMA URBAN/RNWL. PAGE 38 B0762 PLAN
GOV/REL

B65
INST INTL DES CIVILISATION DIF.THE CONSTITUTIONS CONSTN
AND ADMINISTRATIVE INSTITUTIONS OF THE NEW STATES. ADMIN
AFR ISLAM S/ASIA NAT/G POL/PAR DELIB/GP EX/STRUC ADJUD
CONFER EFFICIENCY NAT/LISM...JURID SOC 20. PAGE 54 ECO/UNDEV
B1088

B65
KAAS L.,DIE GEISTLICHE GERICHTSBARKEIT DER JURID
KATHOLISCHEN KIRCHE IN PREUSSEN (2 VOLS.). PRUSSIA CATHISM
CONSTN NAT/G PROVS SECT ADJUD ADMIN ATTIT 16/20. GP/REL
PAGE 57 B1158 CT/SYS

B65
LATHAM E.,THE GROUP BASIS OF POLITICS: A STUDY IN LEGIS
BASING-POINT LEGISLATION. INDUS MARKET POL/PAR GP/COMP
DELIB/GP EX/STRUC DEBATE ADJUD...CHARTS PRESIDENT. GP/REL
PAGE 63 B1274

B65
SMITH C.,THE OMBUDSMAN: A BIBLIOGRAPHY (PAMPHLET). BIBLIOG
DENMARK SWEDEN USA+45 LAW LEGIS JUDGE GOV/REL ADMIN
GP/REL...JURID 20. PAGE 98 B1980 CT/SYS
ADJUD

B65
US SENATE COMM ON JUDICIARY,HEARINGS BEFORE ROUTINE
SUBCOMMITTEE ON ADMINISTRATIVE PRACTICE AND DELIB/GP
PROCEDURE ABOUT ADMINISTRATIVE PROCEDURE ACT 1965. ADMIN
USA+45 LEGIS EDU/PROP ADJUD GOV/REL INGP/REL NAT/G
EFFICIENCY...POLICY INT 20 CONGRESS. PAGE 110 B2232

B65
VAID K.N.,STATE AND LABOR IN INDIA. INDIA INDUS LAW
WORKER PAY PRICE ADJUD CONTROL PARL/PROC GP/REL LABOR
ORD/FREE 20. PAGE 111 B2248 MGT
NEW/LIB

B65
WILDER B.E.,BIBLIOGRAPHY OF THE OFFICIAL BIBLIOG
PUBLICATIONS OF KANSAS, 1854-1958. USA+45 USA-45 PROVS
ECO/DEV POL/PAR EX/STRUC LEGIS ADJUD ATTIT 19/20. GOV/REL
PAGE 116 B2349 ADMIN

S65
LONG T.G.,"THE ADMINISTRATIVE PROCESS: AGONIZING ADJUD
REAPPRAISAL IN THE FTC." NAT/G REPRESENT 20 FTC. LOBBY
PAGE 66 B1339 ADMIN
EX/STRUC

B66
O'NEILL C.E.,CHURCH AND STATE IN FRENCH COLONIAL COLONIAL
LOUISIANA: POLICY AND POLITICS TO 1732. PROVS NAT/G
VOL/ASSN DELIB/GP ADJUD ADMIN GP/REL ATTIT DRIVE SECT
...POLICY BIBLIOG 17/18 LOUISIANA CHURCH/STA. PWR
PAGE 79 B1601

B66
RAPHAEL J.S.,GOVERNMENTAL REGULATION OF BUSINESS. LG/CO

USA+45 LAW CONSTN TAX ADJUD ADMIN EFFICIENCY PWR GOV/REL
20. PAGE 86 B1736 CONTROL
ECO/DEV

B66
SCHLESSINGER P.J.,ELEMENTS OF CALIFORNIA GOVERNMENT LOC/G
(2ND ED.). USA+45 LAW ADJUD ADMIN CONTROL CT/SYS PROVS
EFFICIENCY...BIBLIOG T CALIFORNIA. PAGE 94 B1891 GOV/REL
LEGIS

B66
SCHMIDT K.M.,AMERICAN STATE AND LOCAL GOVERNMENT IN PROVS
ACTION. USA+45 CONSTN LOC/G POL/PAR CHIEF LEGIS ADMIN
PROB/SOLV ADJUD LOBBY GOV/REL...DECISION ANTHOL 20 MUNIC
GOVERNOR MAYOR URBAN/RNWL. PAGE 94 B1896 PLAN

B66
WALL E.H.,THE COURT OF JUSTICE IN THE EUROPEAN CT/SYS
COMMUNITIES: JURISDICTION AND PROCEDURE. EUR+WWI INT/ORG
DIPLOM ADJUD ADMIN ROUTINE TASK...CONCPT LING 20. LAW
PAGE 113 B2281 OP/RES

B66
WASHINGTON S.H.,BIBLIOGRAPHY: LABOR-MANAGEMENT BIBLIOG
RELATIONS ACT, 1947 AS AMENDED BY LABOR-MANAGEMENT LAW
REPORTING AND DISCLOSURE ACT, 1959. USA+45 CONSTN LABOR
INDUS DELIB/GP LEGIS WORKER BARGAIN ECO/TAC ADJUD MGT
GP/REL NEW/LIB...JURID CONGRESS. PAGE 114 B2298

B66
WILSON G.,CASES AND MATERIALS ON CONSTITUTIONAL AND JURID
ADMINISTRATIVE LAW. UK LAW NAT/G EX/STRUC LEGIS ADMIN
BAL/PWR BUDGET DIPLOM ADJUD CONTROL CT/SYS GOV/REL CONSTN
ORD/FREE 20 PARLIAMENT ENGLSH/LAW. PAGE 117 B2359 PWR

S66
POLSBY N.W.,"BOOKS IN THE FIELD: POLITICAL BIBLIOG/A
SCIENCE." LAW CONSTN LOC/G NAT/G LEGIS ADJUD PWR 20 ATTIT
SUPREME/CT. PAGE 83 B1686 ADMIN
JURID

B67
GELLHORN W.,OMBUDSMEN AND OTHERS: CITIZENS' NAT/COMP
PROTECTORS IN NINE COUNTRIES. WOR+45 LAW CONSTN REPRESENT
LEGIS INSPECT ADJUD ADMIN CONTROL CT/SYS CHOOSE INGP/REL
PERS/REL...STAT CHARTS 20. PAGE 39 B0789 PROB/SOLV

B67
HEWITT W.H.,ADMINISTRATION OF CRIMINAL JUSTICE IN CRIME
NEW YORK. LAW PROB/SOLV ADJUD ADMIN...CRIMLGY ROLE
CHARTS T 20 NEW/YORK. PAGE 49 B1001 CT/SYS
FORCES

B67
KATZ J.,PSYCHOANALYSIS, PSYCHIATRY, AND LAW. USA+45 LAW
LOC/G NAT/G PUB/INST PROB/SOLV ADMIN HEALTH PSY
...CRIMLGY CONCPT SAMP/SIZ IDEA/COMP. PAGE 58 B1180 CT/SYS
ADJUD

B67
LEACH R.H.,GOVERNING THE AMERICAN NATION. FUT NAT/G
USA+45 USA-45 CONSTN POL/PAR PLAN ADJUD EXEC CONSEN LEGIS
CONGRESS PRESIDENT. PAGE 63 B1278 PWR

B67
LENG S.C.,JUSTICE IN COMMUNIST CHINA: A SURVEY OF CT/SYS
THE JUDICIAL SYSTEM OF THE CHINESE PEOPLE'S ADJUD
REPUBLIC. CHINA/COM LAW CONSTN LOC/G NAT/G PROF/ORG JURID
CONSULT FORCES ADMIN CRIME ORD/FREE...BIBLIOG 20 MARXISM
MAO. PAGE 64 B1290

B67
NIEDERHOFFER A.,BEHIND THE SHIELD; THE POLICE IN FORCES
URBAN SOCIETY. USA+45 LEGIT ADJUD ROUTINE COERCE PERSON
CRIME ADJUST...INT CHARTS 20 NEWYORK/C. PAGE 78 SOCIETY
B1582 ATTIT

B67
US SENATE COMM ON FOREIGN REL,HUMAN RIGHTS LEGIS
CONVENTIONS. USA+45 LABOR VOL/ASSN DELIB/GP DOMIN ORD/FREE
ADJUD REPRESENT...INT/LAW MGT CONGRESS. PAGE 110 WORKER
B2225 LOBBY

B67
WATERS M.,THE UNITED NATIONS* INTERNATIONAL CONSTN
ORGANIZATION AND ADMINISTRATION. WOR+45 EX/STRUC INT/ORG
FORCES DIPLOM LEAD REGION ARMS/CONT REPRESENT ADMIN
INGP/REL ROLE...METH/COMP ANTHOL 20 UN LEAGUE/NAT. ADJUD
PAGE 114 B2301

B67
WESTON P.B.,THE ADMINISTRATION OF JUSTICE. USA+45 CRIME
CONSTN MUNIC NAT/G PROVS EX/STRUC JUDGE ADMIN CT/SYS
CONTROL SANCTION ORD/FREE...CHARTS 20. PAGE 115 JURID
B2328 ADJUD

L67
"A PROPOS DES INCITATIONS FINANCIERES AUX LOC/G
GROUPEMENTS DES COMMUNES: ESSAI D'INTERPRETATION." ECO/TAC
FRANCE NAT/G LEGIS ADMIN GOV/REL CENTRAL 20. PAGE 2 APPORT
B0046 ADJUD

L67
"RESTRICTIVE SOVEREIGN IMMUNITY, THE STATE SOVEREIGN
DEPARTMENT, AND THE COURTS." USA+45 USA-45 EX/STRUC ORD/FREE
DIPLOM ADJUD CONTROL GOV/REL 19/20 DEPT/STATE PRIVIL
SUPREME/CT. PAGE 2 B0047 CT/SYS

L67
BERGER R.,"ADMINISTRATIVE ARBITRARINESS* A SEQUEL." LAW
USA+45 CONSTN ADJUD CT/SYS SANCTION INGP/REL LABOR
...POLICY JURID. PAGE 11 B0222 BARGAIN
ADMIN

BLUMBERG A.S.,"THE PRACTICE OF LAW AS CONFIDENCE GAME: ORGANIZATIONAL COOPTATION OF A PROFESSION." USA+45 CLIENT SOCIETY CONSULT ROLE JURID. PAGE 13 B0260
L67
CT/SYS
ADJUD
GP/REL
ADMIN

CAHIERS P.,"LE RECOURS EN CONSTATATION DE MANQUEMENTS DES ETATS MEMBRES DEVANT LA COUR DES COMMUNAUTES EUROPEENNES." LAW PROB/SOLV DIPLOM ADMIN CT/SYS SANCTION ATTIT...POLICY DECISION JURID ECSC EEC. PAGE 18 B0362
L67
INT/ORG
CONSTN
ROUTINE
ADJUD

CARMICHAEL D.M.,"FORTY YEARS OF WATER POLLUTION CONTROL IN WISCONSIN: A CASE STUDY." LAW EXTR/IND INDUS MUNIC DELIB/GP PLAN PROB/SOLV SANCTION ...CENSUS CHARTS 20 WISCONSIN. PAGE 19 B0382
L67
HEALTH
CONTROL
ADMIN
ADJUD

GAINES J.E.,"THE YOUTH COURT CONCEPT AND ITS IMPLEMENTATION IN TOMPKINS COUNTY, NEW YORK." USA+45 LAW CONSTN JUDGE WORKER ADJUD ADMIN CHOOSE PERSON...JURID NEW/YORK. PAGE 38 B0772
L67
CT/SYS
AGE/Y
INGP/REL
CRIME

GOULD W.B.,"THE STATUS OF UNAUTHORIZED AND 'WILDCAT' STRIKES UNDER THE NATIONAL LABOR RELATIONS ACT." USA+45 ACT/RES BARGAIN ECO/TAC LEGIT ADJUD ADMIN GP/REL MGT. PAGE 42 B0842
L67
ECO/DEV
INDUS
LABOR
POLICY

JACOBY S.B.,"THE 89TH CONGRESS AND GOVERNMENT LITIGATION." USA+45 ADMIN COST...JURID 20 CONGRESS. PAGE 55 B1117
L67
LAW
NAT/G
ADJUD
SANCTION

TRAVERS H. JR.,"AN EXAMINATION OF THE CAB'S MERGER POLICY." USA+45 USA-45 LAW NAT/G LEGIS PLAN ADMIN ...DECISION 20 CONGRESS. PAGE 105 B2125
L67
ADJUD
LG/CO
POLICY
DIST/IND

KRARUP O.,"JUDICIAL REVIEW OF ADMINISTRATIVE ACTION IN DENMARK." DENMARK LAW CT/SYS...JURID CONCPT 19/20. PAGE 61 B1234
S67
ADJUD
CONTROL
EXEC
DECISION

MELTZER B.D.,"RUMINATIONS ABOUT IDEOLOGY, LAW, AND LABOR ARBITRATION." USA+45 ECO/DEV PROB/SOLV CONFER MGT. PAGE 73 B1466
S67
JURID
ADJUD
LABOR
CONSULT

MONEYPENNY P.,"UNIVERSITY PURPOSE, DISCIPLINE, AND DUE PROCESS." USA+45 EDU/PROP ADJUD LEISURE ORD/FREE. PAGE 74 B1500
S67
ACADEM
AGE/Y
CONTROL
ADMIN

SKOLNICK J.H.,"SOCIAL CONTROL IN THE ADVERSARY SYSTEM." USA+45 CONSULT OP/RES ADMIN CONTROL. PAGE 98 B1975
S67
PROB/SOLV
PERS/REL
ADJUD
CT/SYS

SPEAR P.,"NEHRU." INDIA NAT/G POL/PAR ECO/TAC ADJUD GOV/REL CENTRAL RIGID/FLEX 20 NEHRU/J. PAGE 99 B2003
S67
CHIEF
ATTIT
ADMIN
CREATE

TACKABERRY R.B.,"ORGANIZING AND TRAINING PEACE-KEEPING FORCES* THE CANADIAN VIEW." CANADA PLAN DIPLOM CONFER ADJUD ADMIN CIVMIL/REL 20 UN. PAGE 102 B2069
S67
PEACE
FORCES
INT/ORG
CONSULT

TURNER F.C. JR.,"EXPERIMENT IN INTER-AMERICAN PEACE-KEEPING." DOMIN/REP ADMIN ROUTINE REV ORD/FREE OAS 20. PAGE 106 B2137
S67
FORCES
ADJUD
PEACE

GOODNOW F.J.,"AN EXECUTIVE AND THE COURTS: JUDICIAL REMEDIES AGAINST ADMINISTRATIVE ACTION" FRANCE UK USA-45 WOR-45 LAW CONSTN SANCTION ORD/FREE 19. PAGE 41 B0823
L86
CT/SYS
GOV/REL
ADMIN
ADJUD

ADJUST....SOCIAL ADJUSTMENT, SOCIALIZATION. SEE ALSO INGP/REL

STOLPER W.,"SOCIAL FACTORS IN ECONOMIC PLANNING, WITH SPECIAL REFERENCE TO NIGERIA" AFR NIGER CULTURE FAM SECT RECEIVE ETIQUET ADMIN DEMAND 20. PAGE 101 B2045
NCO
ECO/UNDEV
PLAN
ADJUST
RISK

MARX F.M.,"POLICY FORMULATION AND THE ADMINISTRATIVE PROCESS" ROUTINE ADJUST EFFICIENCY OPTIMAL PRIVIL DRIVE PERSON OBJECTIVE...DECISION OBS GEN/METH. PAGE 70 B1418
S39
ADMIN
LEAD
INGP/REL
MGT

BAKER H.,PROBLEMS OF REEMPLOYMENT AND RETRAINING OF MANPOWER DURING THE TRANSITION FROM WAR TO PEACE. USA+45 INDUS LABOR LG/CO NAT/G PLAN ADMIN PEACE ...POLICY MGT 20. PAGE 8 B0167
B45
BIBLIOG/A
ADJUST
WAR
PROB/SOLV

REDFORD E.S.,FIELD ADMINISTRATION OF WARTIME RATIONING. USA-45 CONSTN ELITES DIST/IND WORKER
B47
ADMIN
NAT/G

CONTROL WAR GOV/REL ADJUST RIGID/FLEX 20 OPA. PAGE 87 B1752
PROB/SOLV
RATION
B47

TAPPAN P.W.,DELINQUENT GIRLS IN COURT. USA-45 MUNIC EX/STRUC FORCES ADMIN EXEC ADJUST SEX RESPECT ...JURID SOC/WK 20 NEWYORK/C FEMALE/SEX. PAGE 103 B2078
CT/SYS
AGE/Y
CRIME
ADJUD

ARGYRIS C.,EXECUTIVE LEADERSHIP: AN APPRAISAL OF A MANAGER IN ACTION. TOP/EX ADMIN LEAD ADJUST ATTIT ...METH 20. PAGE 6 B0127
B53
MGT
EX/STRUC
WORKER
PERS/REL

MILLIKAN M.F.,INCOME STABILIZATION FOR A DEVELOPING DEMOCRACY. USA+45 ECO/DEV LABOR BUDGET ECO/TAC TAX ADMIN ADJUST PRODUC WEALTH...POLICY TREND 20. PAGE 73 B1484
B53
ANTHOL
MARKET
EQUILIB
EFFICIENCY
N53

US PRES CONF ADMIN PROCEDURE,REPORT (PAMPHLET). USA+45 CONFER ADJUD...METH/COMP 20 PRESIDENT. PAGE 109 B2209
NAT/G
DELIB/GP
ADJUST
ADMIN
B55

BERNAYS E.L.,THE ENGINEERING OF CONSENT. VOL/ASSN OP/RES ROUTINE INGP/REL ATTIT RESPECT...POLICY METH/CNCPT METH/COMP 20. PAGE 11 B0224
GP/REL
PLAN
ACT/RES
ADJUST
B56

HOWARD L.V.,TULANE STUDIES IN POLITICAL SCIENCE: CIVIL SERVICE DEVELOPMENT IN LOUISIANA VOLUME 3. LAW POL/PAR LEGIS CT/SYS ADJUST ORD/FREE...STAT CHARTS 19/20 LOUISIANA CIVIL/SERV. PAGE 52 B1050
ADMIN
GOV/REL
PROVS
POLICY
S58

ARGYRIS C.,"SOME PROBLEMS IN CONCEPTUALIZING ORGANIZATIONAL CLIMATE: A CASE STUDY OF A BANK" (BMR)" USA+45 EX/STRUC ADMIN PERS/REL ADJUST PERSON ...POLICY HYPO/EXP SIMUL 20. PAGE 6 B0129
FINAN
CONCPT
LG/CO
INGP/REL
B59

COUNCIL OF STATE GOVERNMENTS,STATE GOVERNMENT: AN ANNOTATED BIBLIOGRAPHY (PAMPHLET). USA+45 LAW AGRI INDUS WORKER PLAN TAX ADJUST AGE/Y ORD/FREE...HEAL MGT 20. PAGE 24 B0494
BIBLIOG/A
PROVS
LOC/G
ADMIN
B60

FRANKE W.,THE REFORM AND ABOLITION OF THE TRADITIONAL CHINESE EXAMINATION SYSTEM. ASIA STRUCT 19/20 CIVIL/SERV. PAGE 37 B0750
ADJUST
ADMIN
TESTS
STRATA
B61

BIRNBACH B.,NEO-FREUDIAN SOCIAL PHILOSOPHY. TEC/DEV INGP/REL ADJUST HAPPINESS SUPEGO HEALTH...CONCPT GEN/LAWS BIBLIOG 20. PAGE 12 B0242
SOCIETY
PSY
PERSON
ADMIN
B61

JACOBS J.,THE DEATH AND LIFE OF GREAT AMERICAN CITIES. USA+45 SOCIETY DIST/IND CREATE PROB/SOLV ADMIN...GEOG SOC CENSUS 20 URBAN/RNWL. PAGE 55 B1113
MUNIC
PLAN
ADJUST
HABITAT
B61

PAGE T.,STATE PERSONNEL REORGANIZATION IN ILLINOIS. USA+45 POL/PAR CHIEF TEC/DEV LEAD ADJUST 20. PAGE 80 B1625
ADMIN
PROVS
WORKER
DELIB/GP
B61

ROBINSON M.E.,EDUCATION FOR SOCIAL CHANGE: ESTABLISHING INSTITUTES OF PUBLIC AND BUSINESS ADMINISTRATION ABROAD (PAMPHLET). WOR+45 SOCIETY ACADEM CONFER INGP/REL ROLE...SOC CHARTS BIBLIOG 20 ICA. PAGE 89 B1805
FOR/AID
EDU/PROP
MGT
ADJUST
B63

COSTELLO T.W.,PSYCHOLOGY IN ADMINISTRATION: A RESEARCH ORIENTATION. CREATE PROB/SOLV PERS/REL ADJUST ANOMIE ATTIT DRIVE PERCEPT ROLE...DECISION BIBLIOG T 20. PAGE 24 B0488
PSY
MGT
EXEC
ADMIN
B63

HEYEL C.,THE ENCYCLOPEDIA OF MANAGEMENT. WOR+45 MARKET TOP/EX TEC/DEV AUTOMAT LEAD ADJUST...STAT CHARTS GAME ANTHOL BIBLIOG. PAGE 49 B1002
MGT
INDUS
ADMIN
FINAN
B63

KORNHAUSER W.,SCIENTISTS IN INDUSTRY: CONFLICT AND ACCOMMODATION. USA+45 R+D LG/CO NAT/G TEC/DEV CONTROL ADJUST ATTIT...MGT STAT INT BIBLIOG 20. PAGE 61 B1229
CREATE
INDUS
PROF/ORG
GP/REL
B63

LITTERER J.A.,ORGANIZATIONS: STRUCTURE AND BEHAVIOR. PLAN DOMIN CONTROL LEAD ROUTINE SANCTION INGP/REL EFFICIENCY PRODUC DRIVE RIGID/FLEX PWR. PAGE 66 B1325
ADMIN
CREATE
MGT
ADJUST
B63

OLSON M. JR.,THE ECONOMICS OF WARTIME SHORTAGE. FRANCE GERMANY MOD/EUR UK AGRI PROB/SOLV ADMIN DEMAND WEALTH...POLICY OLD/LIB 17/20. PAGE 80 B1608
WAR
ADJUST
ECO/TAC
NAT/COMP
B63

SINGH H.L.,PROBLEMS AND POLICIES OF THE BRITISH IN INDIA, 1885-1898. INDIA UK NAT/G FORCES LEGIS
COLONIAL
PWR

PROB/SOLV CONTROL RACE/REL ADJUST DISCRIM NAT/LISM POLICY
RIGID/FLEX...MGT 19 CIVIL/SERV. PAGE 97 B1968 ADMIN
B64

ARGYRIS C.,INTEGRATING THE INDIVIDUAL AND THE ADMIN
ORGANIZATION. WORKER PROB/SOLV LEAD SANCTION PERS/REL
REPRESENT ADJUST EFFICIENCY DRIVE PERSON...PSY VOL/ASSN
METH/CNCPT ORG/CHARTS. PAGE 6 B0132 PARTIC
B64

BANTON M.,THE POLICEMAN IN THE COMMUNITY. UK USA+45 FORCES
STRUCT PROF/ORG WORKER LOBBY ROUTINE COERCE CROWD ADMIN
GP/REL ADJUST DISCRIM PERCEPT 20. PAGE 9 B0181 ROLE
RACE/REL
B64

CULLINGWORTH J.B.,TOWN AND COUNTRY PLANNING IN MUNIC
ENGLAND AND WALES. UK LAW SOCIETY CONSULT ACT/RES PLAN
ADMIN ROUTINE LEISURE INGP/REL ADJUST PWR...GEOG 20 NAT/G
OPEN/SPACE URBAN/RNWL. PAGE 25 B0512 PROB/SOLV
B64

INST D'ETUDE POL L'U GRENOBLE,ADMINISTRATION ADMIN
TRADITIONELLE ET PLANIFICATION REGIONALE. FRANCE MUNIC
LAW POL/PAR PROB/SOLV ADJUST RIGID/FLEX...CHARTS PLAN
ANTHOL BIBLIOG T 20 REFORMERS. PAGE 54 B1087 CREATE
B65

ELDER R.E.,OVERSEAS REPRESENTATION AND SERVICES FOR OP/RES
FEDERAL DOMESTIC AGENCIES. USA+45 NAT/G ACT/RES DIPLOM
FOR/AID EDU/PROP SENIOR ROUTINE TASK ADJUST...MGT GOV/REL
ORG/CHARTS. PAGE 33 B0663 ADMIN
B65

KASER M.,COMECON* INTEGRATION PROBLEMS OF THE PLAN
PLANNED ECONOMIES. INT/ORG TEC/DEV INT/TRADE PRICE ECO/DEV
ADMIN ADJUST CENTRAL...STAT TIME/SEQ ORG/CHARTS COM
COMECON. PAGE 58 B1177 REGION
B65

KOUSOULAS D.G.,REVOLUTION AND DEFEAT; THE STORY OF REV
THE GREEK COMMUNIST PARTY. GREECE INT/ORG EX/STRUC MARXISM
DIPLOM FOR/AID EDU/PROP PARL/PROC ADJUST ATTIT 20 POL/PAR
COM/PARTY. PAGE 61 B1230 ORD/FREE
B65

REISS A.J. JR.,SCHOOLS IN A CHANGING SOCIETY. SCHOOL
CULTURE PROB/SOLV INSPECT DOMIN CONFER INGP/REL EX/STRUC
RACE/REL AGE/C AGE/Y ALL/VALS...ANTHOL SOC/INTEG 20 ADJUST
NEWYORK/C. PAGE 87 B1766 ADMIN
S65

THOMAS F.C. JR.,"THE PEACE CORPS IN MOROCCO." MOROCCO
CULTURE MUNIC PROVS CREATE ROUTINE TASK ADJUST FRANCE
STRANGE...OBS PEACE/CORP. PAGE 104 B2099 FOR/AID
EDU/PROP
B66

DAVIS J.A.,SOUTHERN AFRICA IN TRANSITION. SOUTH/AFR AFR
USA+45 FINAN NAT/G DELIB/GP EDU/PROP ADMIN COLONIAL ADJUST
REGION RACE/REL ATTIT SOVEREIGN...ANTHOL 20 CONSTN
RESOURCE/N. PAGE 26 B0538
B66

FISK E.K.,NEW GUINEA ON THE THRESHOLD; ASPECTS OF ECO/UNDEV
SOCIAL, POLITICAL, AND ECONOMIC DEVELOPMENT. AGRI SOCIETY
NAT/G INT/TRADE ADMIN ADJUST LITERACY ROLE...CHARTS
ANTHOL 20 NEW/GUINEA. PAGE 36 B0726
B66

MACFARQUHAR R.,CHINA UNDER MAO: POLITICS TAKES ECO/UNDEV
COMMAND. CHINA/COM COM AGRI INDUS CHIEF FORCES TEC/DEV
DIPLOM INT/TRADE EDU/PROP TASK REV ADJUST...ANTHOL ECO/TAC
20 MAO. PAGE 67 B1359 ADMIN
B66

ONYEMELUKWE C.C.,PROBLEMS OF INDUSTRIAL PLANNING ECO/UNDEV
AND MANAGEMENT IN NIGERIA. AFR FINAN LABOR DELIB/GP ECO/TAC
TEC/DEV ADJUST...MGT TREND BIBLIOG. PAGE 80 B1610 INDUS
PLAN
B66

ROSHOLT R.L.,AN ADMINISTRATIVE HISTORY OF NASA, ADMIN
1958-1963. SPACE USA+45 FINAN LEAD...MGT CHARTS EX/STRUC
BIBLIOG 20 NASA. PAGE 90 B1824 ADJUST
DELIB/GP
B66

SILBERMAN B.S.,MODERN JAPANESE LEADERSHIP; LEAD
TRANSITION AND CHANGE. NAT/G POL/PAR CHIEF ADMIN CULTURE
REPRESENT GP/REL ADJUST RIGID/FLEX...SOC METH/COMP ELITES
ANTHOL 19/20 CHINJAP CHRISTIAN. PAGE 97 B1952 MUNIC
B67

BENNETT J.W.,HUTTERIAN BRETHREN; THE AGRICULTURAL SECT
ECONOMY AND SOCIAL ORGANIZATION OF A COMMUNAL AGRI
PEOPLE. USA+45 SOCIETY FAM KIN TEC/DEV ADJUST...MGT STRUCT
AUD/VIS GP/COMP 20. PAGE 10 B0213 GP/REL
B67

CECIL L.,ALBERT BALLIN; BUSINESS AND POLITICS IN DIPLOM
IMPERIAL GERMANY 1888-1918. GERMANY UK INT/TRADE CONSTN
LEAD WAR PERS/REL ADJUST PWR WEALTH...MGT BIBLIOG ECO/DEV
19/20. PAGE 19 B0397 TOP/EX
B67

EDUCATION, INTERACTION, AND SOCIAL CHANGE. STRATA EDU/PROP
MUNIC SCHOOL ADMIN RIGID/FLEX ROLE 20. PAGE 49 ADJUST
B0991 SOC
ACT/RES
B67

NIEDERHOFFER A.,BEHIND THE SHIELD; THE POLICE IN FORCES
URBAN SOCIETY. USA+45 LEGIT ADJUD ROUTINE COERCE PERSON
CRIME ADJUST...INT CHARTS 20 NEWYORK/C. PAGE 78 SOCIETY

B1582 ATTIT
B67

ROBINSON D.W.,PROMISING PRACTICES IN CIVIC EDU/PROP
EDUCATION. FUT USA+45 CONTROL PARTIC GOV/REL...OBS NAT/G
AUD/VIS 20. PAGE 89 B1797 ADJUST
ADMIN
S67

HUGON P.,"BLOCAGES ET DESEQUILIBRES DE LA ECO/UNDEV
CROISSANCE ECONOMIQUE EN AFRIQUE NOIRE." AFR KIN COLONIAL
MUNIC CREATE PLAN INT/TRADE REGION ADJUST CENTRAL STRUCT
EQUILIB NAT/LISM ORD/FREE 20. PAGE 52 B1060 ADMIN
S67

LIU K.C.,"DISINTEGRATION OF THE OLD ORDER." ASIA ADJUST
SOCIETY PROB/SOLV ADMIN REGION TOTALISM ORD/FREE NAT/LISM
MARXISM 19/20. PAGE 66 B1329
S67

LLOYD K.,"URBAN RACE RIOTS V EFFECTIVE ANTI- GP/REL
DISCRIMINATION AGENCIES* AN END OR A BEGINNING?" DISCRIM
USA+45 STRATA ACT/RES ADMIN ADJUST ORD/FREE RESPECT LOC/G
...PLURIST DECISION SOC SOC/WK. PAGE 66 B1332 CROWD
S67

VERGIN R.C.,"COMPUTER INDUCED ORGANIZATION COMPUTER
CHANGES." FUT USA+45 R+D CREATE OP/RES TEC/DEV DECISION
ADJUST CENTRAL...MGT INT CON/ANAL COMPUT/IR. AUTOMAT
PAGE 112 B2260 EX/STRUC
N67

NATIONAL COMN COMMUNITY HEALTH,ACTION - PLANNING PLAN
FOR COMMUNITY HEALTH SERVICES (PAMPHLET). USA+45 MUNIC
PROF/ORG DELIB/GP BUDGET ROUTINE GP/REL ATTIT HEALTH
...HEAL SOC SOC/WK CHARTS TIME 20. PAGE 77 B1563 ADJUST

ADJUSTMENT, SOCIAL....SEE ADJUST

ADLER/A....ALFRED ADLER

ADMIN....ORGANIZATIONAL BEHAVIOR, NONEXECUTIVE

ADMINISTRATIVE STAFF COLLEGE B0059

ADMINISTRATIVE MANAGEMENT....SEE MGT

ADOLESCENCE....SEE AGE/Y

ADRIAN C.R. B0060,B0061,B0275

ADU A.L. B0062

ADVERT/ADV....ADVERTISING ADVISORY COMMISSION

ADVERTISING....SEE SERV/IND+EDU/PROP; SEE ALSO TV, PRESS

ADVISORY COMMISSION ON INTERGOVERNMENTAL RELATIONS....SEE
     INTGOV/REL

AEA....ATOMIC ENERGY AUTHORITY OF UN; SEE ALSO NUC/PWR

AEC....ATOMIC ENERGY COMMISSION; SEE ALSO NUC/PWR

L62

CAVERS D.F.,"ADMINISTRATIVE DECISION-MAKING IN REPRESENT
NUCLEAR FACILITIES LICENSING." USA+45 CLIENT ADMIN LOBBY
EXEC 20 AEC. PAGE 19 B0395 PWR
CONTROL
L62

NEIBURG H.L.,"THE EISENHOWER AEC AND CONGRESS: A CHIEF
STUDY IN EXECUTIVE-LEGISLATIVE RELATIONS." USA+45 LEGIS
NAT/G POL/PAR DELIB/GP EX/STRUC TOP/EX ADMIN EXEC GOV/REL
LEAD ROUTINE PWR...POLICY COLD/WAR CONGRESS NUC/PWR
PRESIDENT AEC. PAGE 77 B1567

AFGHANISTN....SEE ALSO ISLAM, ASIA

B57

CENTRAL ASIAN RESEARCH CENTRE,BIBLIOGRAPHY OF BIBLIOG/A
RECENT SOVIET SOURCE MATERIAL ON SOVIET CENTRAL COM
ASIA AND THE BORDERLANDS. AFGHANISTN INDIA PAKISTAN CULTURE
UAR USSR ECO/UNDEV AGRI EXTR/IND INDUS ACADEM ADMIN NAT/G
...HEAL HUM LING CON/ANAL 20. PAGE 19 B0399

AFL/CIO....AMERICAN FEDERATION OF LABOR, CONGRESS OF
     INDUSTRIAL ORGANIZATIONS

B51

PETERSON F.,SURVEY OF LABOR ECONOMICS (REV. ED.). WORKER
STRATA ECO/DEV LABOR INSPECT BARGAIN PAY PRICE EXEC DEMAND
ROUTINE GP/REL ALL/VALS ORD/FREE 20 AFL/CIO IDEA/COMP
DEPT/LABOR. PAGE 82 B1662 T
S66

JACOBSON J.,"COALITIONISM: FROM PROTEST TO RACE/REL
POLITICKING" USA+45 ELITES NAT/G POL/PAR PROB/SOLV LABOR
ADMIN LEAD DISCRIM ORD/FREE PWR CONSERVE 20 NEGRO SOCIALIST
AFL/CIO CIV/RIGHTS BLACK/PWR. PAGE 55 B1116 VOL/ASSN

AFLAK/M....MICHEL AFLAK

AFR....AFRICA

NCO
STOLPER W.,"SOCIAL FACTORS IN ECONOMIC PLANNING, ECO/UNDEV
WITH SPECIAL REFERENCE TO NIGERIA" AFR NIGER PLAN
CULTURE FAM SECT RECEIVE ETIQUET ADMIN DEMAND 20. ADJUST
PAGE 101 B2045 RISK

B00
SANDERSON E.,AFRICA IN THE NINETEENTH CENTURY. COLONIAL
FRANCE UK EXTR/IND FORCES LEGIS ADMIN WAR DISCRIM AFR
ORD/FREE...GEOG GP/COMP SOC/INTEG 19. PAGE 92 B1867 DIPLOM

B02
MOREL E.D.,AFFAIRS OF WEST AFRICA. UK FINAN INDUS COLONIAL
FAM KIN SECT CHIEF WORKER DIPLOM RACE/REL LITERACY ADMIN
HEALTH...CHARTS 18/20 AFRICA/W NEGRO. PAGE 75 B1521 AFR

B26
MOON P.T.,IMPERIALISM AND WORLD POLITICS. AFR ASIA WEALTH
ISLAM MOD/EUR S/ASIA USA-45 SOCIETY NAT/G EX/STRUC TIME/SEQ
BAL/PWR DOMIN COLONIAL NAT/LISM ATTIT DRIVE PWR CAP/ISM
...GEOG SOC 20. PAGE 75 B1510 DIPLOM

B28
BUELL R.,THE NATIVE PROBLEM IN AFRICA. KIN LABOR AFR
LOC/G ECO/TAC ROUTINE ORD/FREE...REC/INT KNO/TEST CULTURE
CENSUS TREND CHARTS SOC/EXP STERTYP 20. PAGE 17
B0339

B29
ROBERTS S.H.,HISTORY OF FRENCH COLONIAL POLICY. AFR INT/ORG
ASIA L/A+17C S/ASIA CULTURE ECO/DEV ECO/UNDEV FINAN ACT/RES
NAT/G PLAN ECO/TAC DOMIN ROUTINE SOVEREIGN...OBS FRANCE
HIST/WRIT TREND CHARTS VAL/FREE 19/20. PAGE 89 COLONIAL
B1796

B32
CARDINALL AW.A BIBLIOGRAPHY OF THE GOLD COAST. AFR BIBLIOG
UK NAT/G EX/STRUC ATTIT...POLICY 19/20. PAGE 18 ADMIN
B0376 COLONIAL
DIPLOM

B35
GORER G.,AFRICA DANCES: A BOOK ABOUT WEST AFRICAN AFR
NEGROES. STRUCT LOC/G SECT FORCES TAX ADMIN ATTIT
COLONIAL...ART/METH MYTH WORSHIP 20 NEGRO AFRICA/W CULTURE
CHRISTIAN RITUAL. PAGE 41 B0835 SOCIETY

B41
PERHAM M.,AFRICANS AND BRITISH RULE. AFR UK ECO/TAC DIPLOM
CONTROL GP/REL ATTIT 20. PAGE 82 B1654 COLONIAL
ADMIN
ECO/UNDEV

B43
LEWIN E.,ROYAL EMPIRE SOCIETY BIBLIOGRAPHIES NO. 9: BIBLIOG
SUB-SAHARA AFRICA. ECO/UNDEV TEC/DEV DIPLOM ADMIN AFR
COLONIAL LEAD 20. PAGE 64 B1303 NAT/G
SOCIETY

B47
CROCKER W.R.,ON GOVERNING COLONIES: BEING AN COLONIAL
OUTLINE OF THE REAL ISSUES AND A COMPARISON OF THE POLICY
BRITISH, FRENCH, AND BELGIAN... AFR BELGIUM FRANCE GOV/COMP
UK CULTURE SOVEREIGN...OBS 20. PAGE 25 B0505 ADMIN

B48
MEEK C.K.,COLONIAL LAW: A BIBLIOGRAPHY WITH SPECIAL COLONIAL
REFERENCE TO NATIVE AFRICAN SYSTEMS OF LAW AND LAND ADMIN
TENURE. AFR ECO/UNDEV AGRI CT/SYS...JURID SOC 20. LAW
PAGE 72 B1462 CONSTN

B55
APTER D.E.,THE GOLD COAST IN TRANSITION. FUT CONSTN AFR
CULTURE SOCIETY ECO/UNDEV FAM KIN LOC/G NAT/G SOVEREIGN
POL/PAR LEGIS TOP/EX EDU/PROP LEGIT ADMIN ATTIT
PERSON PWR...CONCPT STAT INT CENSUS TOT/POP
VAL/FREE. PAGE 6 B0120

B56
CENTRAL AFRICAN ARCHIVES,A GUIDE TO THE PUBLIC BIBLIOG/A
RECORDS OF SOUTHERN RHODESIA UNDER THE REGIME OF COLONIAL
THE BRITISH SOUTH AFRICA COMPANY, 1890-1923. UK ADMIN
STRUCT NAT/G WRITING GP/REL 19/20. PAGE 19 B0398 AFR

B56
INTERNATIONAL AFRICAN INST.SELECT ANNOTATED BIBLIOG/A
BIBLIOGRAPHY OF TROPICAL AFRICA. NAT/G EDU/PROP AFR
ADMIN HEALTH. PAGE 54 B1095 SOC
HABITAT

B56
MANNONI D.O.,PROSPERO AND CALIBAN: THE PSYCHOLOGY CULTURE
OF COLONIZATION. AFR EUR+WWI FAM KIN MUNIC SECT COLONIAL
DOMIN ADMIN ATTIT DRIVE LOVE PWR RESPECT...PSY SOC
CONCPT MYTH OBS DEEP/INT BIOG GEN/METH MALAGASY 20.
PAGE 69 B1394

S56
KHAMA T.,"POLITICAL CHANGE IN AFRICAN SOCIETY." AFR
CONSTN SOCIETY LOC/G NAT/G POL/PAR EX/STRUC LEGIS ELITES
LEGIT ADMIN CHOOSE REPRESENT NAT/LISM MORAL
ORD/FREE PWR...CONCPT OBS TREND GEN/METH CMN/WLTH
17/20. PAGE 59 B1201

B57
MURRAY J.N.,THE UNITED NATIONS TRUSTEESHIP SYSTEM. INT/ORG
AFR WOR+45 CONSTN CONSULT LEGIS EDU/PROP LEGIT EXEC DELIB/GP
ROUTINE...INT TIME/SEQ SOMALI UN 20. PAGE 77 B1547

S57
HAILEY,"TOMORROW IN AFRICA." CONSTN SOCIETY LOC/G AFR
NAT/G DOMIN ADJUD ADMIN GP/REL DISCRIM NAT/LISM PERSON
ATTIT MORAL ORD/FREE...PSY SOC CONCPT OBS RECORD ELITES
TREND GEN/LAWS CMN/WLTH 20. PAGE 45 B0917 RACE/REL

B58
CARTER G.M.,TRANSITION IN AFRICA: STUDIES IN NAT/COMP
POLITICAL ADAPTATION. AFR CENTRL/AFR GHANA NIGERIA PWR
CONSTN LOC/G POL/PAR ADMIN GP/REL FEDERAL...MAJORIT CONTROL
BIBLIOG 20. PAGE 19 B0389 NAT/G

B58
COLEMAN J.S.,NIGERIA: BACKGROUND TO NATIONALISM. NAT/G
AFR SOCIETY ECO/DEV KIN LOC/G POL/PAR TEC/DEV DOMIN NAT/LISM
ADMIN DRIVE PWR RESPECT...TRADIT SOC INT SAMP NIGERIA
TIME/SEQ 20. PAGE 22 B0452

B58
COWAN L.G.,LOCAL GOVERNMENT IN WEST AFRICA. AFR LOC/G
FRANCE UK CULTURE KIN POL/PAR CHIEF LEGIS CREATE COLONIAL
ADMIN PARTIC GOV/REL GP/REL...METH/COMP 20. PAGE 24 SOVEREIGN
B0498 REPRESENT

S58
MAIR L.P.,"REPRESENTATIVE LOCAL GOVERNMENT AS A AFR
PROBLEM IN SOCIAL CHANGE." ECO/UNDEV KIN LOC/G PWR
NAT/G SCHOOL JUDGE ADMIN ROUTINE REPRESENT ELITES
RIGID/FLEX RESPECT...CONCPT STERTYP CMN/WLTH 20.
PAGE 68 B1383

B60
ASPREMONT-LYNDEN H.,RAPPORT SUR L'ADMINISTRATION AFR
BELGE DU RUANDA-URUNDI PENDANT L'ANNEE 1959. COLONIAL
BELGIUM RWANDA AGRI INDUS DIPLOM ECO/TAC INT/TRADE ECO/UNDEV
DOMIN ADMIN RACE/REL...GEOG CENSUS 20 UN. PAGE 7 INT/ORG
B0143

B60
EASTON S.C.,THE TWILIGHT OF EUROPEAN COLONIALISM. FINAN
AFR S/ASIA CONSTN SOCIETY STRUCT ECO/UNDEV INDUS ADMIN
NAT/G FORCES ECO/TAC COLONIAL CT/SYS ATTIT KNOWL
ORD/FREE PWR...SOCIALIST TIME/SEQ TREND CON/ANAL
20. PAGE 32 B0645

B60
LEYDER J.,BIBLIOGRAPHIE DE L'ENSEIGNEMENT SUPERIEUR BIBLIOG/A
ET DE LA RECHERCHE SCIENTIFIQUE EN AFRIQUE ACT/RES
INTERTROPICALE (2 VOLS.). AFR CULTURE ECO/UNDEV ACADEM
AGRI PLAN EDU/PROP ADMIN COLONIAL...GEOG SOC/INTEG R+D
20 NEGRO. PAGE 65 B1309

B60
LIPSET S.M.,POLITICAL MAN. AFR COM EUR+WWI L/A+17C PWR
MOD/EUR S/ASIA USA+45 STRUCT ECO/DEV SOC
ECO/UNDEV POL/PAR SECT ADMIN WEALTH...CONCPT WORK
TOT/POP 20. PAGE 65 B1320

B60
STANFORD RESEARCH INSTITUTE,AFRICAN DEVELOPMENT: A FOR/AID
TEST FOR INTERNATIONAL COOPERATION. AFR USA+45 ECO/UNDEV
WOR+45 FINAN INT/ORG PLAN PROB/SOLV ECO/TAC ATTIT
INT/TRADE ADMIN...CHARTS 20. PAGE 100 B2018 DIPLOM

S60
APTER D.E.,"THE ROLE OF TRADITIONALISM IN THE CONSERVE
POLITICAL MODERNIZATION OF GHANA AND UGANDA" (BMR)" ADMIN
AFR GHANA UGANDA CULTURE NAT/G POL/PAR NAT/LISM GOV/COMP
...CON/ANAL 20. PAGE 6 B0121 PROB/SOLV

S60
EMERSON R.,"THE EROSION OF DEMOCRACY." AFR FUT LAW S/ASIA
CULTURE INTELL SOCIETY ECO/UNDEV FAM LOC/G NAT/G POL/PAR
FORCES PLAN TEC/DEV ECO/TAC ADMIN CT/SYS ATTIT
ORD/FREE PWR...SOCIALIST SOC CONCPT STAND/INT
TIME/SEQ WORK 20. PAGE 33 B0671

S60
FRANKEL S.H.,"ECONOMIC ASPECTS OF POLITICAL NAT/G
INDEPENDENCE IN AFRICA." AFR FUT SOCIETY ECO/UNDEV FOR/AID
COM/IND FINAN LEGIS PLAN TEC/DEV CAP/ISM ECO/TAC
INT/TRADE ADMIN ATTIT DRIVE RIGID/FLEX PWR WEALTH
...MGT NEW/IDEA MATH TIME/SEQ VAL/FREE 20. PAGE 37
B0751

S60
GARNICK D.H.,"ON THE ECONOMIC FEASIBILITY OF A MARKET
MIDDLE EASTERN COMMON MARKET." AFR ISLAM CULTURE INT/TRADE
INDUS NAT/G PLAN TEC/DEV ECO/TAC ADMIN ATTIT DRIVE
RIGID/FLEX...PLURIST STAT TREND GEN/LAWS 20.
PAGE 39 B0784

S60
SCHATZ S.P.,"THE INFLENCE OF PLANNING ON ECO/UNDEV
DEVELOPMENT: THE NIGERIAN EXPERIENCE." AFR FUT PLAN
FINAN INDUS NAT/G EX/STRUC ECO/TAC ADMIN ATTIT NIGERIA
PERCEPT ORD/FREE PWR...MATH TREND CON/ANAL SIMUL
VAL/FREE 20. PAGE 93 B1883

C60
SMITH T.E.,"ELECTIONS IN DEVELOPING COUNTRIES: A ECO/UNDEV
STUDY OF ELECTORAL PROCEDURES USED IN TOPICAL CHOOSE
AFRICA, SOUTH-EAST ASIA..." AFR S/ASIA UK ROUTINE REPRESENT
GOV/REL RACE/REL...GOV/COMP BIBLIOG 20. PAGE 98 ADMIN
B1985

B61
MUNGER E.S.,AFRICAN FIELD REPORTS 1952-1961. AFR
SOUTH/AFR SOCIETY ECO/UNDEV NAT/G POL/PAR COLONIAL DISCRIM
EXEC PARL/PROC GUERRILLA RACE/REL ALL/IDEOS...SOC RECORD
AUD/VIS 20. PAGE 76 B1538

S61
LIEBENOW J.G.,"LEGITIMACY OF ALIEN RELATIONSHIP: COLONIAL
THE NYATURU OF TANGANYIKA" (BMR)" AFR UK ADMIN LEAD DOMIN
CHOOSE 20 NYATURU TANGANYIKA. PAGE 65 B1312 LEGIT
PWR

S61
MILLER E.,"LEGAL ASPECTS OF UN ACTION IN THE   INT/ORG
CONGO." AFR CULTURE ADMIN PEACE DRIVE RIGID/FLEX   LEGIT
ORD/FREE...WELF/ST JURID OBS UN CONGO 20. PAGE 73
B1480

B62
CARSON P.,MATERIALS FOR WEST AFRICAN HISTORY IN THE   BIBLIOG/A
ARCHIVES OF BELGIUM AND HOLLAND. CLIENT INDUS   COLONIAL
INT/TRADE ADMIN 17/19. PAGE 19 B0387   AFR
                                                       ECO/UNDEV

B62
INGHAM K.,A HISTORY OF EAST AFRICA. NAT/G DIPLOM   AFR
ADMIN WAR NAT/LISM...SOC BIOG BIBLIOG. PAGE 54   CONSTN
B1085   COLONIAL

B62
MORE S.S.,REMODELLING OF DEMOCRACY FOR AFRO-ASIAN   ORD/FREE
NATIONS. AFR INDIA S/ASIA SOUTH/AFR CONSTN EX/STRUC   ECO/UNDEV
COLONIAL CHOOSE TOTALISM SOVEREIGN NEW/LIB SOCISM   ADMIN
...SOC/WK 20. PAGE 75 B1520   LEGIS

B62
TAYLOR D.,THE BRITISH IN AFRICA. UK CULTURE   AFR
ECO/UNDEV INDUS DIPLOM INT/TRADE ADMIN WAR RACE/REL   COLONIAL
ORD/FREE SOVEREIGN...POLICY BIBLIOG 15/20 CMN/WLTH.   DOMIN
PAGE 103 B2084

B62
UNECA LIBRARY,NEW ACQUISITIONS IN THE UNECA   BIBLIOG
LIBRARY. LAW NAT/G PLAN PROB/SOLV TEC/DEV ADMIN   AFR
REGION...GEOG SOC 20 UN. PAGE 106 B2152   ECO/UNDEV
                                                       INT/ORG

B62
US LIBRARY OF CONGRESS,A LIST OF AMERICAN DOCTORAL   BIBLIOG
DISSERTATIONS ON AFRICA. SOCIETY SECT DIPLOM   AFR
EDU/PROP ADMIN...GEOG 19/20. PAGE 109 B2206   ACADEM
                                                       CULTURE

L62
HOFFHERR R.,"LE PROBLEME DE L'ENCADREMENT DANS LES   AFR
JEUNES ETATS DE LANGUE FRANCAISE EN AFRIQUE   STRUCT
CENTRALE ET A MADAGASCAR." FUT ECO/UNDEV CONSULT   FRANCE
PLAN ECO/TAC COLONIAL ATTIT...MGT TIME/SEQ VAL/FREE
20. PAGE 51 B1028

L62
MANGIN G.,"L'ORGANIZATION JUDICIAIRE DES ETATS   AFR
D'AFRIQUE ET DE MADAGASCAR." ISLAM WOR+45 STRATA   LEGIS
STRUCT ECO/UNDEV NAT/G LEGIT EXEC...JURID TIME/SEQ   COLONIAL
TOT/POP 20 SUPREME/CT. PAGE 69 B1387   MADAGASCAR

S62
JACOBSON H.K.,"THE UNITED NATIONS AND COLONIALISM: INT/ORG
A TENTATIVE APPRAISAL." AFR FUT S/ASIA USSR   CONCPT
WOR+45 NAT/G DELIB/GP PLAN DIPLOM ECO/TAC DOMIN   COLONIAL
ADMIN ROUTINE COERCE ATTIT RIGID/FLEX ORD/FREE PWR
...OBS STERTYP UN 20. PAGE 55 B1115

S62
MANGIN G.,"LES ACCORDS DE COOPERATION EN MATIERE DE   INT/ORG
JUSTICE ENTRE LA FRANCE ET LES ETATS AFRICAINS ET   LAW
MALGACHE." AFR ISLAM WOR+45 STRUCT ECO/UNDEV NAT/G   FRANCE
DELIB/GP PERCEPT ALL/VALS...JURID MGT TIME/SEQ 20.
PAGE 69 B1386

S62
MURACCIOLE L.,"LES CONSTITUTIONS DES ETATS   NAT/G
AFRICAINS D'EXPRESSION FRANCAISE: LA CONSTITUTION   CONSTN
DU 16 AVRIL 1962 DE LA REPUBLIQUE DU" AFR CHAD
CHIEF LEGIS LEGIT COLONIAL EXEC ROUTINE ORD/FREE
SOVEREIGN...SOC CONCPT 20. PAGE 76 B1541

S62
MURACCIOLE L.,"LES MODIFICATIONS DE LA CONSTITUTION   NAT/G
MALGACHE." AFR WOR+45 ECO/UNDEV LEGIT EXEC ALL/VALS   STRUCT
...JURID 20. PAGE 76 B1542   SOVEREIGN
                                                       MADAGASCAR

S62
PIQUEMAL M.,"LES PROBLEMES DES UNIONS D'ETATS EN   AFR
AFRIQUE NOIRE." FRANCE SOCIETY INT/ORG NAT/G   ECO/UNDEV
DELIB/GP PLAN LEGIT ADMIN COLONIAL ROUTINE ATTIT   REGION
ORD/FREE PWR...GEOG METH/CNCPT 20. PAGE 83 B1678

B63
ECOLE NATIONALE D'ADMIN,BIBLIOGRAPHIE SELECTIVE   BIBLIOG
D'OUVRAGES DE LANGUE FRANCAISE TRAITANT DES   AFR
PROBLEMES GOUVERNEMENTAUX ET ADMINISTRATIFS. NAT/G   ADMIN
FORCES ACT/RES OP/RES PLAN PROB/SOLV BUDGET ADJUD   EX/STRUC
COLONIAL LEAD 20. PAGE 32 B0651

B63
GALBRAITH J.S.,RELUCTANT EMPIRE: BRITISH POLICY OF   COLONIAL
THE SOUTH AFRICAN FRONTIER, 1834-1854. AFR   ADMIN
SOUTH/AFR UK GP/REL RACE/REL DISCRIM...CHARTS   POLICY
BIBLIOG 19 MISSION. PAGE 38 B0774   SECT

B63
HAUSMAN W.H.,MANAGING ECONOMIC DEVELOPMENT IN   ECO/UNDEV
AFRICA. AFR USA+45 LAW FINAN WORKER TEC/DEV WEALTH   PLAN
...ANTHOL 20. PAGE 48 B0970   FOR/AID
                                                       MGT

B63
HEUSSLER R.,YESTERDAY'S RULERS: THE MAKING OF THE   EX/STRUC
BRITISH COLONIAL SERVICE. AFR EUR+WWI UK STRATA   MORAL
SECT DELIB/GP PLAN DOMIN EDU/PROP ATTIT PERCEPT   ELITES
PERSON SUPEGO KNOWL ORD/FREE PWR...MGT SOC OBS INT
TIME/SEQ 20 CMN/WLTH. PAGE 49 B1000

B63
ROBINSON K.,ESSAYS IN IMPERIAL GOVERNMENT. CAMEROON   COLONIAL
NIGERIA UK CONSTN LOC/G LEGIS ADMIN GOV/REL PWR   AFR
...POLICY ANTHOL BIBLIOG 17/20 PURHAM/M. PAGE 89   DOMIN
B1803

S63
BANFIELD J.,"FEDERATION IN EAST-AFRICA." AFR UGANDA   EX/STRUC
ELITES INT/ORG NAT/G VOL/ASSN LEGIS ECO/TAC FEDERAL   PWR
ATTIT SOVEREIGN TOT/POP 20 TANGANYIKA. PAGE 9 B0180   REGION

S63
NYE J.S. JR.,"EAST AFRICAN ECONOMIC INTEGRATION."   ECO/UNDEV
AFR UGANDA PROVS DELIB/GP PLAN ECO/TAC INT/TRADE   INT/ORG
ADMIN ROUTINE ORD/FREE PWR WEALTH...OBS TIME/SEQ
VAL/FREE 20. PAGE 79 B1597

S63
WAGRET M.,"L'ASCENSION POLITIQUE DE L'U.D.D.I.A.   EX/STRUC
(CONGO) ET SA PRISE DU POUVOIR (1956-1959)." AFR   CHOOSE
WOR+45 NAT/G POL/PAR CONSULT DELIB/GP LEGIS PERCEPT   FRANCE
ALL/VALS SOVEREIGN...TIME/SEQ CONGO. PAGE 113 B2274

B64
THE SPECIAL COMMONWEALTH AFRICAN ASSISTANCE PLAN.   ECO/UNDEV
AFR CANADA INDIA NIGERIA UK FINAN SCHOOL...CHARTS   TREND
20 COMMONWLTH. PAGE 2 B0041   FOR/AID
                                                       ADMIN

B64
BROWN C.V.,GOVERNMENT AND BANKING IN WESTERN   ADMIN
NIGERIA. AFR NIGERIA GOV/REL GP/REL...POLICY 20.   ECO/UNDEV
PAGE 16 B0321   FINAN
                                                       NAT/G

B64
HANNA W.J.,INDEPENDENT BLACK AFRICA: THE POLITICS   AFR
OF FREEDOM. ELITES INDUS KIN CHIEF COLONIAL CHOOSE   ECO/UNDEV
GOV/REL RACE/REL NAT/LISM ATTIT PERSON 20 NEGRO.   ADMIN
PAGE 46 B0938   PROB/SOLV

B64
HERSKOVITS M.J.,ECONOMIC TRANSITION IN AFRICA. FUT   AFR
INT/ORG NAT/G WORKER PROB/SOLV TEC/DEV INT/TRADE   ECO/UNDEV
EQUILIB INCOME...ANTHOL 20. PAGE 49 B0996   PLAN
                                                       ADMIN

B64
KIESER P.J.,THE COST OF ADMINISTRATION, SUPERVISION   AFR
AND SERVICES IN URBAN BANTU TOWNSHIPS. SOUTH/AFR   MGT
SERV/IND MUNIC PROVS ADMIN COST...OBS QU CHARTS 20   FINAN
BANTU. PAGE 60 B1203

B64
LITTLE I.M.D.,AID TO AFRICA. AFR UK TEC/DEV DIPLOM   FOR/AID
ECO/TAC INCOME WEALTH 20. PAGE 66 B1326   ECO/UNDEV
                                                       ADMIN
                                                       POLICY

B64
RUSSELL R.B.,UNITED NATIONS EXPERIENCE WITH   FORCES
MILITARY FORCES: POLITICAL AND LEGAL ASPECTS. AFR   DIPLOM
KOREA WOR+45 LEGIS PROB/SOLV ADMIN CONTROL   SANCTION
EFFICIENCY PEACE...POLICY INT/LAW BIBLIOG UN.   ORD/FREE
PAGE 92 B1857

B64
WITHERELL J.W.,OFFICIAL PUBLICATIONS OF FRENCH   BIBLIOG/A
EQUATORIAL AFRICA, FRENCH CAMEROONS, AND TOGO,   AFR
1946-1958 (PAMPHLET). CAMEROON CHAD FRANCE GABON   NAT/G
TOGO LAW ECO/UNDEV EXTR/IND INT/TRADE...GEOG HEAL   ADMIN
20. PAGE 117 B2367

L64
MACKINTOSH J.P.,"NIGERIA'S EXTERNAL AFFAIRS." UK   AFR
CULTURE ECO/UNDEV NAT/G VOL/ASSN EDU/PROP LEGIT   DIPLOM
ADMIN ATTIT ORD/FREE PWR 20. PAGE 68 B1365   NIGERIA

L64
ROTBERG R.,"THE FEDERATION MOVEMENT IN BRITISH EAST   VOL/ASSN
AND CENTRAL AFRICA." AFR RHODESIA UGANDA ECO/UNDEV   PWR
NAT/G POL/PAR FORCES DOMIN LEGIT ADMIN COERCE ATTIT   REGION
...CONCPT TREND 20 TANGANYIKA. PAGE 91 B1831

L64
SYMONDS R.,"REFLECTIONS IN LOCALISATION." AFR   ADMIN
S/ASIA UK STRATA INT/ORG NAT/G SCHOOL EDU/PROP   MGT
LEGIT KNOWL ORD/FREE PWR RESPECT CMN/WLTH 20.   COLONIAL
PAGE 102 B2064

S64
CLIGNET R.,"POTENTIAL ELITES IN GHANA AND THE IVORY   PWR
COAST: A PRELIMINARY SURVEY." AFR CULTURE ELITES   LEGIT
STRATA KIN NAT/G SECT DOMIN EXEC ORD/FREE RESPECT   IVORY/CST
SKILL...POLICY RELATIV GP/COMP NAT/COMP 20. PAGE 21   GHANA
B0438

S64
LOW D.A.,"LION RAMPANT." EUR+WWI MOD/EUR S/ASIA   AFR
ECO/UNDEV NAT/G FORCES TEC/DEV ECO/TAC LEGIT ADMIN   DOMIN
COLONIAL COERCE ORD/FREE RESPECT 19/20. PAGE 67   DIPLOM
B1344   UK

S64
NEWLYN W.T.,"MONETARY SYSTEMS AND INTEGRATION" AFR   ECO/UNDEV
BUDGET ADMIN FEDERAL PRODUC PROFIT UTIL...CHARTS 20   REGION
AFRICA/E. PAGE 78 B1578   METH/COMP
                                                       FINAN

B65
ADU A.L.,THE CIVIL SERVICE IN NEW AFRICAN STATES.   ECO/UNDEV
AFR GHANA FINAN SOVEREIGN...POLICY 20 CIVIL/SERV   ADMIN
AFRICA/E AFRICA/W. PAGE 3 B0062   COLONIAL
                                                       NAT/G

B65
BARISH N.N.,MANAGEMENT SCIENCES IN THE EMERGING
COUNTRIES. AFR CHINA/COM WOR+45 FINAN INDUS PLAN
PRODUC HABITAT...ANTHOL 20. PAGE 9 B0184

ECO/UNDEV
OP/RES
MGT
TEC/DEV

B65
FOLTZ W.J.,FROM FRENCH WEST AFRICA TO THE MALI
FEDERATION. AFR FRANCE MALI ADMIN CONTROL FEDERAL
...DECISION 20. PAGE 36 B0734

EXEC
TOP/EX
ELITES
LEAD

B65
INST INTL DES CIVILISATION DIF,THE CONSTITUTIONS
AND ADMINISTRATIVE INSTITUTIONS OF THE NEW STATES.
AFR ISLAM S/ASIA NAT/G POL/PAR DELIB/GP EX/STRUC
CONFER EFFICIENCY NAT/LISM...JURID SOC 20. PAGE 54
B1088

CONSTN
ADMIN
ADJUD
ECO/UNDEV

B65
ROTBERG R.I.,A POLITICAL HISTORY OF TROPICAL
AFRICA. EX/STRUC DIPLOM INT/TRADE DOMIN ADMIN
RACE/REL NAT/LISM PWR SOVEREIGN...GEOG TIME/SEQ
BIBLIOG 1/20. PAGE 91 B1832

AFR
CULTURE
COLONIAL

B66
DAVIS J.A.,SOUTHERN AFRICA IN TRANSITION. SOUTH/AFR
USA+45 FINAN NAT/G DELIB/GP EDU/PROP ADMIN COLONIAL
REGION RACE/REL ATTIT SOVEREIGN...ANTHOL 20
RESOURCE/N. PAGE 26 B0538

AFR
ADJUST
CONSTN

B66
DILLEY M.R.,BRITISH POLICY IN KENYA COLONY (2ND
ED.). AFR INDIA UK LABOR BUDGET TAX ADMIN PARL/PROC
GP/REL...BIBLIOG 20 PARLIAMENT. PAGE 29 B0594

COLONIAL
REPRESENT
SOVEREIGN

B66
HAYER T.,FRENCH AID. AFR FRANCE AGRI FINAN BUDGET
ADMIN WAR PRODUC...CHARTS 18/20 THIRD/WRLD
OVRSEA/DEV. PAGE 48 B0975

TEC/DEV
COLONIAL
FOR/AID
ECO/UNDEV

B66
KAUNDA K.,ZAMBIA: INDEPENDENCE AND BEYOND: THE
SPEECHES OF KENNETH KAUNDA. AFR FUT ZAMBIA SOCIETY
ECO/UNDEV NAT/G PROB/SOLV ECO/TAC ADMIN RACE/REL
SOVEREIGN 20. PAGE 59 B1183

ORD/FREE
COLONIAL
CONSTN
LEAD

B66
ONYEMELUKWE C.C.,PROBLEMS OF INDUSTRIAL PLANNING
AND MANAGEMENT IN NIGERIA. AFR FINAN LABOR DELIB/GP
TEC/DEV ADJUST...MGT TREND BIBLIOG. PAGE 80 B1610

ECO/UNDEV
ECO/TAC
INDUS
PLAN

B66
SPICER K.,A SAMARITAN STATE? AFR CANADA INDIA
PAKISTAN UK USA+45 FINAN INDUS PRODUC...CHARTS 20
NATO. PAGE 99 B2006

DIPLOM
FOR/AID
ECO/DEV
ADMIN

L66
LEMARCHAND R.,"SOCIAL CHANGE AND POLITICAL
MODERNISATION IN BURUNDI." AFR BURUNDI STRATA CHIEF
EX/STRUC RIGID/FLEX PWR...SOC 20. PAGE 64 B1285

NAT/G
STRUCT
ELITES
CONSERVE

L66
MCAUSLAN J.P.W.,"CONSTITUTIONAL INNOVATION AND
POLITICAL STABILITY IN TANZANIA: A PRELIMINARY
ASSESSMENT." AFR TANZANIA ELITES CHIEF EX/STRUC
RIGID/FLEX PWR 20 PRESIDENT BUREAUCRCY. PAGE 71
B1440

CONSTN
NAT/G
EXEC
POL/PAR

S66
AFRICAN BIBLIOGRAPHIC CENTER,"A CURRENT VIEW OF
AFRICANA: A SELECT AND ANNOTATED BIBLIOGRAPHICAL
PUBLISHING GUIDE, 1965-1966." AFR CULTURE INDUS
LABOR SECT FOR/AID ADMIN COLONIAL REV RACE/REL
SOCISM...LING 20. PAGE 3 B0063

BIBLIOG/A
NAT/G
TEC/DEV
POL/PAR

S66
MATTHEWS D.G.,"PRELUDE-COUP D'ETAT-MILITARY
GOVERNMENT: A BIBLIOGRAPHICAL AND RESEARCH GUIDE TO
NIGERIAN POL AND GOVT, JAN, 1965-66." AFR NIGER LAW
CONSTN POL/PAR LEGIS CIVMIL/REL GOV/REL...STAT 20.
PAGE 71 B1430

BIBLIOG
NAT/G
ADMIN
CHOOSE

B67
GIFFORD P.,BRITAIN AND GERMANY IN AFRICA. AFR
GERMANY UK ECO/UNDEV LEAD WAR NAT/LISM ATTIT
...POLICY HIST/WRIT METH/COMP ANTHOL BIBLIOG 19/20
WWI. PAGE 39 B0797

COLONIAL
ADMIN
DIPLOM
NAT/COMP

B67
RAVKIN A.,THE NEW STATES OF AFRICA (HEADLINE
SERIES, NO. 183((PAMPHLET). CULTURE STRUCT INDUS
COLONIAL NAT/LISM...SOC 20. PAGE 86 B1744

AFR
ECO/UNDEV
SOCIETY
ADMIN

S67
GRUNDY K.W.,"THE POLITICAL USES OF IMAGINATION."
GHANA ELITES SOCIETY NAT/G DOMIN EDU/PROP COLONIAL
REGION REPRESENT GP/REL CENTRAL PWR MARXISM 20.
PAGE 44 B0897

NAT/LISM
EX/STRUC
AFR
LEAD

S67
HUGON P.,"BLOCAGES ET DESEQUILIBRES DE LA
CROISSANCE ECONOMIQUE EN AFRIQUE NOIRE." AFR KIN
MUNIC CREATE PLAN INT/TRADE REGION ADJUST CENTRAL
EQUILIB NAT/LISM ORD/FREE 20. PAGE 52 B1060

ECO/UNDEV
COLONIAL
STRUCT
ADMIN

S67
IDENBURG P.J.,"POLITICAL STRUCTURAL DEVELOPMENT IN
TROPICAL AFRICA." UK ECO/UNDEV KIN POL/PAR CHIEF

AFR
CONSTN

EX/STRUC CREATE COLONIAL CONTROL REPRESENT RACE/REL
...MAJORIT TREND 20. PAGE 53 B1074

NAT/G
GOV/COMP

S67
MURRAY R.,"SECOND THOUGHTS ON GHANA." AFR GHANA
NAT/G POL/PAR ADMIN REV GP/REL CENTRAL...SOCIALIST
CONCPT METH 20. PAGE 77 B1548

COLONIAL
CONTROL
REGION
SOCISM

S67
PRATT R.C.,"THE ADMINISTRATION OF ECONOMIC PLANNING
IN A NEWLY INDEPEND ENT STATE* THE TANZANIAN
EXPERIENCE 1963-1966." AFR TANZANIA ECO/UNDEV PLAN
CONTROL ROUTINE TASK EFFICIENCY 20. PAGE 84 B1699

NAT/G
DELIB/GP
ADMIN
TEC/DEV

S67
ROTBERG R.I.,"COLONIALISM AND AFTER: THE POLITICAL
LITERATURE OF CENTRAL AFRICA - A BIBLIOGRAPHIC
ESSAY." AFR CHIEF EX/STRUC REV INGP/REL RACE/REL
SOVEREIGN 20. PAGE 91 B1833

BIBLIOG/A
COLONIAL
DIPLOM
NAT/G

B82
MACDONALD D.,AFRICANA; OR, THE HEART OF HEATHEN
AFRICA, VOL. II: MISSION LIFE. SOCIETY STRATA KIN
CREATE EDU/PROP ADMIN COERCE LITERACY HEALTH...MYTH
WORSHIP 19 LIVNGSTN/D MISSION NEGRO. PAGE 67 B1355

SECT
AFR
CULTURE
ORD/FREE

B95
LATIMER E.W.,EUROPE IN AFRICA IN THE NINETEENTH
CENTURY. ECO/UNDEV KIN SECT DIPLOM DOMIN ADMIN
DISCRIM 17/18. PAGE 63 B1275

AFR
COLONIAL
WAR
FINAN

B98
THOMPSON H.C.,RHODESIA AND ITS GOVERNMENT. AFR
RHODESIA ECO/UNDEV INDUS KIN WORKER INT/TRADE
DISCRIM LITERACY ORD/FREE 19. PAGE 104 B2102

COLONIAL
ADMIN
POLICY
ELITES

AFR/STATES....ORGANIZATION OF AFRICAN STATES

AFRICA/CEN....CENTRAL AFRICA

AFRICA/E....EAST AFRICA

S64
NEWLYN W.T.,"MONETARY SYSTEMS AND INTEGRATION" AFR
BUDGET ADMIN FEDERAL PRODUC PROFIT UTIL...CHARTS 20
AFRICA/E. PAGE 78 B1578

ECO/UNDEV
REGION
METH/COMP
FINAN

B65
ADU A.L.,THE CIVIL SERVICE IN NEW AFRICAN STATES.
AFR GHANA FINAN SOVEREIGN...POLICY 20 CIVIL/SERV
AFRICA/E AFRICA/W. PAGE 3 B0062

ECO/UNDEV
ADMIN
COLONIAL
NAT/G

B65
LEYS C.T.,FEDERATION IN EAST AFRICA. LAW AGRI
DIST/IND FINAN INT/ORG LABOR INT/TRADE CONFER ADMIN
CONTROL GP/REL...ANTHOL 20 AFRICA/E. PAGE 65 B1310

FEDERAL
REGION
ECO/UNDEV
PLAN

B66
SMITH H.E.,READINGS IN ECONOMIC DEVELOPMENT AND
ADMINISTRATION IN TANZANIA. TANZANIA FINAN INDUS
LABOR NAT/G PLAN PROB/SOLV INT/TRADE COLONIAL
REGION...ANTHOL BIBLIOG 20 AFRICA/E. PAGE 98 B1981

TEC/DEV
ADMIN
GOV/REL

AFRICA/N....NORTH AFRICA

B63
DIESNER H.J.,KIRCHE UND STAAT IM SPATROMISCHEN
REICH. ROMAN/EMP EX/STRUC COLONIAL COERCE ATTIT
CATHISM 4/5 AFRICA/N CHURCH/STA. PAGE 29 B0592

SECT
GP/REL
DOMIN
JURID

AFRICA/SW....SOUTH WEST AFRICA

N19
SOUTH AFRICA COMMISSION ON FUT,INTERIM AND FINAL
REPORTS ON FUTURE FORM OF GOVERNMENT IN THE SOUTH-
WEST AFRICAN PROTECTORATE (PAMPHLET). SOUTH/AFR
NAT/G FORCES CONFER COLONIAL CONTROL 20 AFRICA/SW.
PAGE 99 B1998

CONSTN
REPRESENT
ADMIN
PROB/SOLV

B37
UNION OF SOUTH AFRICA,REPORT CONCERNING
ADMINISTRATION OF SOUTH WEST AFRICA (6 VOLS.).
SOUTH/AFR INDUS PUB/INST FORCES LEGIS BUDGET DIPLOM
EDU/PROP ADJUD CT/SYS...GEOG CHARTS 20 AFRICA/SW
LEAGUE/NAT. PAGE 107 B2158

NAT/G
ADMIN
COLONIAL
CONSTN

AFRICA/W....WEST AFRICA

B02
MOREL E.D.,AFFAIRS OF WEST AFRICA. UK FINAN INDUS
FAM KIN SECT CHIEF WORKER DIPLOM RACE/REL LITERACY
HEALTH...CHARTS 18/20 AFRICA/W NEGRO. PAGE 75 B1521

COLONIAL
ADMIN
AFR

B35
GORER G.,AFRICA DANCES: A BOOK ABOUT WEST AFRICAN
NEGROES. STRUCT LOC/G SECT FORCES TAX ADMIN
COLONIAL...ART/METH MYTH WORSHIP 20 NEGRO AFRICA/W
CHRISTIAN RITUAL. PAGE 41 B0835

AFR
ATTIT
CULTURE
SOCIETY

B65
ADU A.L.,THE CIVIL SERVICE IN NEW AFRICAN STATES.   ECO/UNDEV

WORKER

AFR GHANA FINAN SOVEREIGN...POLICY 20 CIVIL/SERV ADMIN
AFRICA/E AFRICA/W. PAGE 3 B0062 COLONIAL
NAT/G
B65

WARD W.E.,GOVERNMENT IN WEST AFRICA. WOR+45 POL/PAR GOV/COMP
EX/STRUC PLAN PARTIC GP/REL SOVEREIGN 20 AFRICA/W. CONSTN
PAGE 114 B2291 COLONIAL
ECO/UNDEV

AFRICAN BIBLIOGRAPHIC CENTER B0063

AFTA....ATLANTIC FREE TRADE AREA

AGARWAL R.C. B0064

AGE....AGE FACTORS

B57
DE GRAZIA A.,GRASS ROOTS PRIVATE WELFARE. LOC/G NEW/LIB
SCHOOL ACT/RES EDU/PROP ROUTINE CROWD GP/REL HEALTH
DISCRIM HAPPINESS ILLEGIT AGE HABITAT. PAGE 27 MUNIC
B0554 VOL/ASSN
B64
TOMPKINS D.C.,PROBATION SINCE WORLD WAR II. USA+45 BIBLIOG
FORCES ADMIN ROUTINE PERS/REL AGE...CRIMLGY HEAL PUB/INST
20. PAGE 105 B2118 ORD/FREE
CRIME
S64
EAKIN T.C.,"LEGISLATIVE POLITICS -- I AND II THE PROVS
WESTERN STATES, 19581964" (SUPPLEMENT)" USA+45 LEGIS
POL/PAR SCHOOL CONTROL LOBBY CHOOSE AGE. PAGE 32 ROUTINE
B0641 STRUCT

AGE/A....ADULTS

B62
FRIEDLANDER W.A.,INDIVIDUALISM AND SOCIAL WELFARE. GIVE
FRANCE ACADEM OP/RES ADMIN AGE/Y AGE/A ORD/FREE 20. SOC/WK
PAGE 37 B0756 SOC/EXP
FINAN

AGE/C....INFANTS AND CHILDREN

B55
UN ECONOMIC AND SOCIAL COUNCIL,BIBLIOGRAPHY OF BIBLIOG/A
PUBLICATIONS OF THE UN AND SPECIALIZED AGENCIES IN SOC/WK
THE SOCIAL WELFARE FIELD, 1946-1952. WOR+45 FAM ADMIN
INT/ORG MUNIC ACT/RES PLAN PROB/SOLV EDU/PROP AGE/C WEALTH
AGE/Y HABITAT...HEAL UN. PAGE 106 B2148
B61
CONFREY E.A.,ADMINISTRATION OF COMMUNITY HEALTH HEAL
SERVICES. USA+45 R+D PUB/INST DELIB/GP PLAN BUDGET ADMIN
ROUTINE AGE/C HEALTH...MGT SOC/WK METH/COMP 20. MUNIC
PAGE 23 B0461 BIO/SOC
B64
PINNICK A.W.,COUNTRY PLANNERS IN ACTION. UK FINAN MUNIC
SERV/IND NAT/G CONSULT DELIB/GP PRICE CONTROL PLAN
ROUTINE LEISURE AGE/C...GEOG 20 URBAN/RNWL. PAGE 83 INDUS
B1674 ATTIT
B65
HUGHES J.M.,EDUCATION IN AMERICA (2ND ED.). USA+45 EDU/PROP
USA-45 GP/REL INGP/REL AGE/C AGE/Y ROLE...IDEA/COMP SCHOOL
BIBLIOG T 20. PAGE 52 B1059 ADMIN
METH/COMP
B65
REISS A.J. JR.,SCHOOLS IN A CHANGING SOCIETY. SCHOOL
CULTURE PROB/SOLV INSPECT DOMIN CONFER INGP/REL EX/STRUC
RACE/REL AGE/C AGE/Y ALL/VALS...ANTHOL SOC/INTEG 20 ADJUST
NEWYORK/C. PAGE 87 B1766 ADMIN
B67
PAULSEN F.R.,AMERICAN EDUCATION: CHALLENGES AND EDU/PROP
IMAGES. FUT USA+45 ADMIN AGE/C AGE/Y SUPEGO HEALTH SCHOOL
...ANTHOL 20. PAGE 81 B1644 ORD/FREE
GOV/REL
B67
WEINBERG M.,SCHOOL INTEGRATION: A COMPREHENSIVE BIBLIOG
CLASSIFIED BIBLIOGRAPHY OF 3,100 REFERENCES. USA+45 SCHOOL
LAW NAT/G NEIGH SECT PLAN ROUTINE AGE/C WEALTH DISCRIM
SOC/INTEG INDIAN/AM. PAGE 115 B2314 RACE/REL

AGE/O....OLD PEOPLE

B63
US HOUSE COM ON ED AND LABOR,ADMINISTRATION OF AGE/O
AGING. USA+45 R+D EX/STRUC PLAN BUDGET PAY EDU/PROP ADMIN
ROUTINE COST CONGRESS. PAGE 108 B2187 DELIB/GP
GIVE
B64
RAPHAEL M.,PENSIONS AND PUBLIC SERVANTS. UK PLAN ADMIN
EDU/PROP PARTIC GOV/REL HEALTH...POLICY CHARTS SENIOR
17/20 CIVIL/SERV. PAGE 86 B1737 PAY
AGE/O
B65
RHODES G.,PUBLIC SECTOR PENSIONS. UK FINAN LEGIS ADMIN
BUDGET TAX PAY INCOME...CHARTS 20 CIVIL/SERV. RECEIVE
PAGE 88 B1769 AGE/O

AGE/Y....YOUTH AND ADOLESCENCE

S40
GERTH H.,"THE NAZI PARTY: ITS LEADERSHIP AND POL/PAR
COMPOSITION" (BMR)" GERMANY ELITES STRATA STRUCT DOMIN
EX/STRUC FORCES ECO/TAC CT/SYS CHOOSE TOTALISM LEAD
AGE/Y AUTHORIT PWR 20. PAGE 39 B0792 ADMIN
B47
TAPPAN P.W.,DELINQUENT GIRLS IN COURT. USA+45 MUNIC CT/SYS
EX/STRUC FORCES ADMIN EXEC ADJUST SEX RESPECT AGE/Y
...JURID SOC/WK 20 NEWYORK/C FEMALE/SEX. PAGE 103 CRIME
B2078 ADJUD
B55
UN ECONOMIC AND SOCIAL COUNCIL,BIBLIOGRAPHY OF BIBLIOG/A
PUBLICATIONS OF THE UN AND SPECIALIZED AGENCIES IN SOC/WK
THE SOCIAL WELFARE FIELD, 1946-1952. WOR+45 FAM ADMIN
INT/ORG MUNIC ACT/RES PLAN PROB/SOLV EDU/PROP AGE/C WEALTH
AGE/Y HABITAT...HEAL UN. PAGE 106 B2148
B59
COUNCIL OF STATE GOVERNMENTS,STATE GOVERNMENT: AN BIBLIOG/A
ANNOTATED BIBLIOGRAPHY (PAMPHLET). USA+45 LAW AGRI PROVS
INDUS WORKER PLAN TAX ADJUST AGE/Y ORD/FREE...HEAL LOC/G
MGT 20. PAGE 24 B0494 ADMIN
B59
EPSTEIN F.T.,EAST GERMANY: A SELECTED BIBLIOGRAPHY BIBLIOG/A
(PAMPHLET). COM GERMANY/E LAW AGRI FINAN INDUS INTELL
LABOR POL/PAR EDU/PROP ADMIN AGE/Y 20. PAGE 33 MARXISM
B0677 NAT/G
B60
FRYE R.J.,GOVERNMENT AND LABOR: THE ALABAMA ADMIN
PROGRAM. USA+45 INDUS R+D LABOR WORKER BUDGET LEGIS
EFFICIENCY AGE/Y HEALTH...CHARTS 20 ALABAMA. LOC/G
PAGE 38 B0761 PROVS
B62
FRIEDLANDER W.A.,INDIVIDUALISM AND SOCIAL WELFARE. GIVE
FRANCE ACADEM OP/RES ADMIN AGE/Y AGE/A ORD/FREE 20. SOC/WK
PAGE 37 B0756 SOC/EXP
FINAN
B65
HUGHES J.M.,EDUCATION IN AMERICA (2ND ED.). USA+45 EDU/PROP
USA-45 GP/REL INGP/REL AGE/C AGE/Y ROLE...IDEA/COMP SCHOOL
BIBLIOG T 20. PAGE 52 B1059 ADMIN
METH/COMP
B65
REISS A.J. JR.,SCHOOLS IN A CHANGING SOCIETY. SCHOOL
CULTURE PROB/SOLV INSPECT DOMIN CONFER INGP/REL EX/STRUC
RACE/REL AGE/C AGE/Y ALL/VALS...ANTHOL SOC/INTEG 20 ADJUST
NEWYORK/C. PAGE 87 B1766 ADMIN
L65
HOOK S.,"SECOND THOUGHTS ON BERKELEY" USA+45 ELITES ACADEM
INTELL LEGIT ADMIN COERCE REPRESENT GP/REL INGP/REL ORD/FREE
TOTALISM AGE/Y MARXISM 20 BERKELEY FREE/SPEE POLICY
STUDNT/PWR. PAGE 51 B1040 CREATE
B66
PERROW C.,ORGANIZATION FOR TREATMENT: A COMPARATIVE AGE/Y
STUDY OF INSTITUTIONS FOR DELINQUENTS. LAW PSY
PROB/SOLV ADMIN CRIME PERSON MORAL...SOC/WK OBS PUB/INST
DEEP/QU CHARTS SOC/EXP SOC/INTEG 20. PAGE 82 B1661
B66
STREET D.,ORGANIZATION FOR TREATMENT. CLIENT PROVS GP/COMP
PUB/INST PLAN CONTROL PARTIC REPRESENT ATTIT PWR AGE/Y
...POLICY BIBLIOG. PAGE 101 B2052 ADMIN
VOL/ASSN
B67
PAULSEN F.R.,AMERICAN EDUCATION: CHALLENGES AND EDU/PROP
IMAGES. FUT USA+45 ADMIN AGE/C AGE/Y SUPEGO HEALTH SCHOOL
...ANTHOL 20. PAGE 81 B1644 ORD/FREE
GOV/REL
L67
GAINES J.E.,"THE YOUTH COURT CONCEPT AND ITS CT/SYS
IMPLEMENTATION IN TOMPKINS COUNTY, NEW YORK." AGE/Y
USA+45 LAW CONSTN JUDGE WORKER ADJUD ADMIN CHOOSE INGP/REL
PERSON...JURID NEW/YORK. PAGE 38 B0772 CRIME
S67
MONEYPENNY P.,"UNIVERSITY PURPOSE, DISCIPLINE, AND ACADEM
DUE PROCESS." USA+45 EDU/PROP ADJUD LEISURE AGE/Y
ORD/FREE. PAGE 74 B1500 CONTROL
ADMIN

AGGRESSION....SEE WAR, COERCE+INT/REL

AGGRESSION, PHYSICAL....SEE COERCE, DRIVE

AGREE....AGREEMENTS, CONTRACTS, TREATIES, CONCORDATS,
INTERSTATE COMPACTS

B61
LAHAYE R.,LES ENTREPRISES PUBLIQUES AU MAROC. NAT/G
FRANCE MOROCCO LAW DIST/IND EXTR/IND FINAN CONSULT INDUS
PLAN TEC/DEV ADMIN AGREE CONTROL OWN...POLICY 20. ECO/UNDEV
PAGE 62 B1250 ECO/TAC
B63
HOUGHTELING J.L. JR.,THE LEGAL ENVIRONMENT OF LAW
BUSINESS. LG/CO NAT/G CONSULT AGREE CONTROL MGT

...DICTIONARY T 20. PAGE 52 B1047
ADJUD
JURID
L63

BOLGAR V.,"THE PUBLIC INTEREST: A JURISPRUDENTIAL
AND COMPARATIVE OVERVIEW OF SYMPOSIUM ON
FUNDAMENTAL CONCEPTS OF PUBLIC LAW" COM FRANCE
GERMANY SWITZERLND LAW ADJUD ADMIN AGREE LAISSEZ
...JURID GEN/LAWS 20 EUROPE/E. PAGE 13 B0268
CONCPT
ORD/FREE
CONTROL
NAT/COMP
B65

MACDONALD R.W.,THE LEAGUE OF ARAB STATES: A STUDY
IN THE DYNAMICS OF REGIONAL ORGANIZATION. ISRAEL
UAR USSR FINAN INT/ORG DELIB/GP ECO/TAC AGREE
NEUTRAL ORD/FREE PWR...DECISION BIBLIOG 20 TREATY
UN. PAGE 67 B1358
ISLAM
REGION
DIPLOM
ADMIN
B66

LEE L.T.,VIENNA CONVENTION ON CONSULAR RELATIONS.
WOR+45 LAW INT/ORG CONFER GP/REL PRIVIL...INT/LAW
20 TREATY VIENNA/CNV. PAGE 63 B1279
AGREE
DIPLOM
ADMIN
B67

GABRIEL P.P.,THE INTERNATIONAL TRANSFER OF
CORPORATE SKILLS: MANAGEMENT CONTRACTS IN LESS
DEVELOPED COUNTRIES. CLIENT INDUS LG/CO PLAN
PROB/SOLV CAP/ISM ECO/TAC FOR/AID INT/TRADE RENT
ADMIN SKILL 20. PAGE 38 B0771
ECO/UNDEV
AGREE
MGT
CONSULT

L67

COHEN M.,"THE DEMISE OF UNEF." CONSTN DIPLOM ADMIN
AGREE LEAD COERCE 20 UNEF U/THANT HAMMARSK/D.
PAGE 22 B0445
INT/ORG
FORCES
PEACE
POLICY

AGRI....AGRICULTURE (INCLUDING HUNTING AND GATHERING)

THE JAPAN SCIENCE REVIEW: LAW AND POLITICS: LIST OF
BOOKS AND ARTICLES ON LAW AND POLITICS. CONSTN AGRI
INDUS LABOR DIPLOM TAX ADMIN CRIME...INT/LAW SOC 20
CHINJAP. PAGE 1 B0025
BIBLIOG
LAW
S/ASIA
PHIL/SCI

ECONOMIC LIBRARY SELECTIONS. AGRI INDUS MARKET
ADMIN...STAT NAT/COMP 20. PAGE 2 B0026
BIBLIOG/A
WRITING
FINAN
N

KYRIAK T.E.,EAST EUROPE: BIBLIOGRAPHY--INDEX TO US
JPRS RESEARCH TRANSLATIONS. ALBANIA BULGARIA COM
CZECHOSLVK HUNGARY POLAND ROMANIA AGRI EXTR/IND
FINAN SERV/IND INT/TRADE WEAPON...GEOG MGT SOC 20.
PAGE 62 B1247
BIBLIOG/A
PRESS
MARXISM
INDUS

N

UNITED NATIONS,UNITED NATIONS PUBLICATIONS. WOR+45
ECO/UNDEV AGRI FINAN FORCES ADMIN LEAD WAR PEACE
...POLICY INT/LAW 20 UN. PAGE 107 B2160
BIBLIOG
INT/ORG
DIPLOM

N

US LIBRARY OF CONGRESS,CATALOG OF THE PUBLIC
DOCUMENTS OF THE UNITED STATES, 18931940. USA-45
LAW ECO/DEV AGRI PLAN PROB/SOLV ADMIN LEAD GOV/REL
ATTIT 19/20. PAGE 109 B2200
BIBLIOG
NAT/G
POLICY
LOC/G

N

US SUPERINTENDENT OF DOCUMENTS,LABOR (PRICE LIST
33). USA+45 LAW AGRI CONSTRUC INDUS NAT/G BARGAIN
PRICE ADMIN AUTOMAT PRODUC MGT. PAGE 111 B2240
BIBLIOG/A
WORKER
LABOR
LEGIS

N

WORLD PEACE FOUNDATION,DOCUMENTS OF INTERNATIONAL
ORGANIZATIONS: A SELECTED BIBLIOGRAPHY. WOR+45
WOR-45 AGRI FINAN ACT/RES OP/RES INT/TRADE ADMIN
...CON/ANAL 20 UN UNESCO LEAGUE/NAT. PAGE 118 B2374
BIBLIOG
DIPLOM
INT/ORG
REGION

N19

EAST KENTUCKY REGIONAL PLAN,PROGRAM 60: A DECADE OF
ACTION FOR PROGRESS IN EASTERN KENTUCKY (PAMPHLET).
USA+45 AGRI CONSTRUC INDUS CONSULT ACT/RES
PROB/SOLV EDU/PROP GOV/REL HEALTH KENTUCKY. PAGE 32
B0643
REGION
ADMIN
PLAN
ECO/UNDEV

B39

BAKER G.,THE COUNTY AGENT. USA-45 LOC/G NAT/G
PROB/SOLV ADMIN...POLICY 20 ROOSEVLT/F NEW/DEAL
COUNTY/AGT. PAGE 8 B0166
AGRI
CONSULT
GOV/REL
EDU/PROP

B40

GAUS J.M.,PUBLIC ADMINISTRATION AND THE UNITED
STATES DEPARTMENT OF AGRICULTURE. USA-45 STRUCT
DIST/IND FINAN MARKET EX/STRUC PROB/SOLV GIVE
PRODUC...POLICY GEOG CHARTS 20 DEPT/AGRI. PAGE 39
B0786
ADMIN
AGRI
DELIB/GP
OP/RES

B44

BIENSTOCK G.,MANAGEMENT IN RUSSIAN INDUSTRY AND
AGRICULTURE. USSR CONSULT WORKER LEAD COST PROFIT
ATTIT DRIVE PWR...MGT METH/COMP DICTIONARY 20.
PAGE 12 B0236
ADMIN
MARXISM
SML/CO
AGRI

L44

HAILEY,"THE FUTURE OF COLONIAL PEOPLES." WOR-45
CONSTN CULTURE ECO/UNDEV AGRI MARKET INT/ORG NAT/G
SECT CONSULT ECO/TAC LEGIT ADMIN NAT/LISM ALL/VALS
...SOC OBS TREND STERTYP CMN/WLTH LEAGUE/NAT
PARLIAMENT 20. PAGE 45 B0916
PLAN
CONCPT
DIPLOM
UK

B46

WILCOX J.K.,OFFICIAL DEFENSE PUBLICATIONS.
BIBLIOG/A

1941-1945 (NINE VOLS.). USA-45 AGRI INDUS R+D LABOR
FORCES TEC/DEV EFFICIENCY PRODUC SKILL WEALTH 20.
PAGE 116 B2347
WAR
CIVMIL/REL
ADMIN
B48

MEEK C.K.,COLONIAL LAW: A BIBLIOGRAPHY WITH SPECIAL
REFERENCE TO NATIVE AFRICAN SYSTEMS OF LAW AND LAND
TENURE. AFR ECO/UNDEV AGRI CT/SYS...JURID SOC 20.
PAGE 72 B1462
COLONIAL
ADMIN
LAW
CONSTN
B50

COMMONS J.R.,THE ECONOMICS OF COLLECTIVE ACTION.
USA-45 AGRI INDUS LABOR NAT/G LEGIS ADMIN
EFFICIENCY...MGT METH/COMP BIBLIOG 20. PAGE 22
B0458
ECO/DEV
CAP/ISM
ACT/RES
CONCPT
B51

US TARIFF COMMISSION,LIST OF PUBLICATIONS OF THE
TARIFF COMMISSION (PAMPHLET). USA+45 USA-45 AGRI
EXTR/IND INDUS INT/TRADE...STAT 20. PAGE 111 B2245
BIBLIOG
TARIFFS
NAT/G
ADMIN

C52

LANCASTER L.W.,"GOVERNMENT IN RURAL AMERICA."
USA+45 ECO/DEV AGRI SCHOOL FORCES LEGIS JUDGE
BUDGET TAX CT/SYS...CHARTS BIBLIOG. PAGE 62 B1253
GOV/REL
LOC/G
MUNIC
ADMIN

B53

WAGLEY C.,AMAZON TOWN: A STUDY OF MAN IN THE
TROPICS. BRAZIL L/A+17C STRATA STRUCT ECO/UNDEV
AGRI EX/STRUC RACE/REL DISCRIM HABITAT WEALTH...OBS
SOC/EXP 20. PAGE 113 B2273
SOC
NEIGH
CULTURE
INGP/REL

B54

CHICAGO JOINT REFERENCE LIB,FEDERAL-STATE-LOCAL
RELATIONS: A SELECTED BIBLIOGRAPHY. USA+45 AGRI
LABOR LOC/G MUNIC EX/STRUC ADMIN REGION HEALTH
CON/ANAL. PAGE 21 B0419
BIBLIOG
FEDERAL
GOV/REL

B55

SMITHIES A.,THE BUDGETARY PROCESS IN THE UNITED
STATES. ECO/DEV AGRI EX/STRUC FORCES LEGIS
PROB/SOLV TAX ROUTINE EFFICIENCY...MGT CONGRESS
PRESIDENT. PAGE 98 B1987
NAT/G
ADMIN
BUDGET
GOV/REL

S55

BUNZEL J.H.,"THE GENERAL IDEOLOGY OF AMERICAN SMALL
BUSINESS"(BMR)" USA+45 USA-45 AGRI GP/REL INGP/REL
PERSON...MGT IDEA/COMP 18/20. PAGE 17 B0345
ALL/IDEOS
ATTIT
SML/CO
INDUS

B57

CENTRAL ASIAN RESEARCH CENTRE,BIBLIOGRAPHY OF
RECENT SOVIET SOURCE MATERIAL ON SOVIET CENTRAL
ASIA AND THE BORDERLANDS. AFGHANISTN INDIA PAKISTAN
UAR USSR ECO/UNDEV AGRI EXTR/IND INDUS ACADEM ADMIN
...HEAL HUM LING CON/ANAL 20. PAGE 19 B0399
BIBLIOG/A
COM
CULTURE
NAT/G

B57

IKE N.,JAPANESE POLITICS. INTELL STRUCT AGRI INDUS
FAM KIN LABOR PRESS CHOOSE ATTIT...DECISION BIBLIOG
19/20 CHINJAP. PAGE 53 B1075
NAT/G
ADMIN
POL/PAR
CULTURE

B58

NEAL F.W.,TITOISM IN ACTION. COM YUGOSLAVIA AGRI
LOC/G DIPLOM TOTALISM...BIBLIOG 20 TITO/MARSH.
PAGE 77 B1564
MARXISM
POL/PAR
CHIEF
ADMIN

B58

SCOTT D.J.R.,RUSSIAN POLITICAL INSTITUTIONS. RUSSIA
USSR CONSTN AGRI DELIB/GP PLAN EDU/PROP CONTROL
CHOOSE EFFICIENCY ATTIT MARXISM...BIBLIOG/A 13/20.
PAGE 95 B1919
NAT/G
POL/PAR
ADMIN
DECISION

B59

CHRISTENSON R.M.,THE BRANNAN PLAN: FARM POLITICS
AND POLICY. USA+45 ECO/DEV CONSULT PLAN PAY GOV/REL
...POLICY 20. PAGE 21 B0429
AGRI
NAT/G
ADMIN
ECO/TAC

B59

COUNCIL OF STATE GOVERNMENTS,STATE GOVERNMENT: AN
ANNOTATED BIBLIOGRAPHY (PAMPHLET). USA+45 LAW AGRI
INDUS WORKER PLAN TAX ADJUST AGE/Y ORD/FREE...HEAL
MGT 20. PAGE 24 B0494
BIBLIOG/A
PROVS
LOC/G
ADMIN

B59

EPSTEIN F.T.,EAST GERMANY: A SELECTED BIBLIOGRAPHY
(PAMPHLET). COM GERMANY/E LAW AGRI FINAN INDUS
LABOR POL/PAR EDU/PROP ADMIN AGE/Y 20. PAGE 33
B0677
BIBLIOG/A
INTELL
MARXISM
NAT/G

B59

LEMBERG E.,DIE VERTRIEBENEN IN WESTDEUTSCHLAND (3
VOLS.). GERMANY/W CULTURE STRUCT AGRI PROVS ADMIN
...JURID 20 MIGRATION. PAGE 64 B1287
GP/REL
INGP/REL
SOCIETY

B59

YANG C.K.,A CHINESE VILLAGE IN EARLY COMMUNIST
TRANSITION. ECO/UNDEV AGRI FAM KIN MUNIC FORCES
PLAN ECO/TAC DOMIN EDU/PROP ATTIT DRIVE PWR RESPECT
...SOC CONCPT METH/CNCPT OBS RECORD CON/ANAL CHARTS
WORK 20. PAGE 118 B2389
ASIA
ROUTINE
SOCISM

B60

ASPREMONT-LYNDEN H.,RAPPORT SUR L'ADMINISTRATION
BELGE DU RUANDA-URUNDI PENDANT L'ANNEE 1959.
BELGIUM RWANDA AGRI INDUS DIPLOM ECO/TAC INT/TRADE
DOMIN ADMIN RACE/REL...GEOG CENSUS 20 UN. PAGE 7
B0143
AFR
COLONIAL
ECO/UNDEV
INT/ORG

B60

DRAPER T.,AMERICAN COMMUNISM AND SOVIET RUSSIA.   COM
EUR+WWI USA+45 USSR INTELL AGRI COM/IND FINAN INDUS   POL/PAR
LABOR PROF/ORG VOL/ASSN PLAN TEC/DEV DOMIN EDU/PROP
ADMIN COERCE REV PERSON PWR...POLICY CONCPT MYTH
19/20. PAGE 30 B0617

B60

LEYDER J.,BIBLIOGRAPHIE DE L'ENSEIGNEMENT SUPERIEUR   BIBLIOG/A
ET DE LA RECHERCHE SCIENTIFIQUE EN AFRIQUE   ACT/RES
INTERTROPICALE (2 VOLS.). AFR CULTURE ECO/UNDEV   ACADEM
AGRI PLAN EDU/PROP ADMIN COLONIAL...GEOG SOC/INTEG   R+D
20 NEGRO. PAGE 65 B1309

B60

PIERCE R.A.,RUSSIAN CENTRAL ASIA, 1867-1917. ASIA   COLONIAL
RUSSIA CULTURE AGRI INDUS EDU/PROP REV NAT/LISM   DOMIN
...CHARTS BIBLIOG 19/20 BOLSHEVISM INTERVENT.   ADMIN
PAGE 83 B1672   ECO/UNDEV

B60

ROBINSON E.A.G.,ECONOMIC CONSEQUENCES OF THE SIZE   CONCPT
OF NATIONS. AGRI INDUS DELIB/GP FOR/AID ADMIN   INT/ORG
EFFICIENCY...METH/COMP 20. PAGE 89 B1799   NAT/COMP

B60

WORLEY P.,ASIA TODAY (REV. ED.) (PAMPHLET). COM   BIBLIOG/A
ECO/UNDEV AGRI FINAN INDUS POL/PAR FOR/AID ADMIN   ASIA
MARXISM 20. PAGE 118 B2376   DIPLOM
                                                              NAT/G

S60

HERZ J.H.,"EAST GERMANY: PROGRESS AND PROSPECTS."   POL/PAR
COM AGRI FINAN INDUS LOC/G NAT/G FORCES PLAN   STRUCT
TEC/DEV DOMIN ADMIN COERCE DRIVE PERCEPT RIGID/FLEX   GERMANY
MORAL ORD/FREE PWR...MARXIST PSY SOC RECORD STERTYP
WORK. PAGE 49 B0997

B61

BRADY R.A.,ORGANIZATION, AUTOMATION, AND SOCIETY.   TEC/DEV
USA+45 AGRI COM/IND DIST/IND MARKET CREATE   INDUS
...DECISION MGT 20. PAGE 14 B0296   AUTOMAT
                                                              ADMIN

B61

BULLIS H.A.,MANIFESTO FOR AMERICANS. USA+45 AGRI   ECO/TAC
LABOR NAT/G NEIGH FOR/AID INT/TRADE TAX EDU/PROP   SOCIETY
CHOOSE...POLICY MGT 20 UN UNESCO. PAGE 17 B0342   INDUS
                                                             CAP/ISM

B61

DRURY J.W.,THE GOVERNMENT OF KANSAS. USA+45 AGRI   PROVS
INDUS CHIEF LEGIS WORKER PLAN BUDGET GIVE CT/SYS   CONSTN
GOV/REL...T 20 KANSAS GOVERNOR CITY/MGT. PAGE 31   ADMIN
B0621   LOC/G

B61

HARRISON S.,INDIA AND THE UNITED STATES. FUT S/ASIA   DELIB/GP
USA+45 WOR+45 INTELL ECO/DEV ECO/UNDEV AGRI INDUS   ACT/RES
INT/ORG NAT/G CONSULT EX/STRUC TOP/EX PLAN ECO/TAC   FOR/AID
NEUTRAL ALL/VALS...MGT TOT/POP 20. PAGE 47 B0956   INDIA

B61

HART H.C.,ADMINISTRATIVE ASPECTS OF RIVER VALLEY   ADMIN
DEVELOPMENT. INDIA USA+45 INDUS CONTROL EFFICIENCY   PLAN
OPTIMAL PRODUC 20 TVA. PAGE 47 B0957   METH/COMP
                                                         AGRI

B61

HORVATH B.,THE CHARACTERISTICS OF YUGOSLAV ECONOMIC   ACT/RES
DEVELOPMENT. COM ECO/UNDEV AGRI INDUS PLAN CAP/ISM   YUGOSLAVIA
ECO/TAC ROUTINE WEALTH...SOCIALIST STAT CHARTS
STERTYP WORK 20. PAGE 52 B1045

B61

KOESTLER A.,THE LOTUS AND THE ROBOT. ASIA INDIA   SECT
S/ASIA SOCIETY STRATA ECO/DEV AGRI INDUS FAM CREATE   ECO/UNDEV
DOMIN EDU/PROP ADMIN COERCE ATTIT DRIVE SUPEGO
ORD/FREE PWR RESPECT WEALTH...MYTH OBS 20 CHINJAP.
PAGE 61 B1226

B61

MARX K.,THE COMMUNIST MANIFESTO. IN (MENDEL A.   COM
ESSENTIAL WORKS OF MARXISM, NEW YORK: BANTAM. FUT   NEW/IDEA
MOD/EUR CULTURE ECO/DEV ECO/UNDEV AGRI FINAN INDUS   CAP/ISM
MARKET PROC/MFG LABOR MUNIC POL/PAR CONSULT FORCES   REV
CREATE PLAN ADMIN ATTIT DRIVE RIGID/FLEX ORD/FREE
PWR RESPECT MARX/KARL WORK. PAGE 70 B1421

B61

US GENERAL ACCOUNTING OFFICE,EXAMINATION OF   FOR/AID
ECONOMIC AND TECHNICAL ASSISTANCE PROGRAM FOR IRAN.   ADMIN
IRAN USA+45 AGRI INDUS DIPLOM CONTROL COST 20.   TEC/DEV
PAGE 108 B2186   ECO/UNDEV

S61

VINER J.,"ECONOMIC FOREIGN POLICY ON THE NEW   TOP/EX
FRONTIER." USA+45 ECO/UNDEV AGRI FINAN INDUS MARKET   ECO/TAC
INT/ORG NAT/G FOR/AID INT/TRADE ADMIN ATTIT PWR 20   BAL/PAY
KENNEDY/JF. PAGE 112 B2262   TARIFFS

B62

BRIMMER B.,A GUIDE TO THE USE OF UNITED NATIONS   BIBLIOG/A
DOCUMENTS. WOR+45 ECO/UNDEV AGRI EX/STRUC FORCES   INT/ORG
PROB/SOLV ADMIN WAR PEACE WEALTH...POLICY UN.   DIPLOM
PAGE 15 B0310

B62

GALENSON W.,LABOR IN DEVELOPING COUNTRIES. BRAZIL   LABOR
INDONESIA ISRAEL PAKISTAN TURKEY AGRI INDUS WORKER   ECO/UNDEV
PAY PRICE GP/REL WEALTH...MGT CHARTS METH/COMP   BARGAIN
NAT/COMP 20. PAGE 38 B0775   POL/PAR

B62

KENNEDY J.F.,TO TURN THE TIDE. SPACE AGRI INT/ORG   DIPLOM
FORCES TEC/DEV ADMIN NUC/PWR PEACE WEALTH...ANTHOL   CHIEF
20 KENNEDY/JF CIV/RIGHTS. PAGE 59 B1193   POLICY
                                                     NAT/G

B62

NEVINS A.,THE STATE UNIVERSITIES AND DEMOCRACY.   ACADEM
AGRI FINAN SCHOOL ADMIN EXEC EFFICIENCY ATTIT.   PROVS
PAGE 78 B1576   EDU/PROP
                                                     POLICY

L62

BELSHAW D.G.R.,"PUBLIC INVESTMENT IN AGRICULTURE   ECO/UNDEV
AND ECONOMIC DEVELOPMENT OF UGANDA" UGANDA AGRI   PLAN
INDUS R+D ECO/TAC RATION TAX PAY COLONIAL 20   ADMIN
WORLD/BANK. PAGE 10 B0209   CENTRAL

L62

ERDMANN H.H.,"ADMINISTRATIVE LAW AND FARM   AGRI
ECONOMICS." USA+45 LOC/G NAT/G PLAN PROB/SOLV LOBBY ADMIN
...DECISION ANTHOL 20. PAGE 33 B0680   ADJUD
                                                     POLICY

L62

WATERSTON A.,"PLANNING IN MOROCCO, ORGANIZATION AND NAT/G
IMPLEMENTATION. BALTIMORE: HOPKINS ECON. DEVELOP.   PLAN
INT. BANK FOR." ISLAM ECO/DEV AGRI DIST/IND INDUS   MOROCCO
PROC/MFG SERV/IND LOC/G EX/STRUC ECO/TAC PWR WEALTH
TOT/POP VAL/FREE 20. PAGE 114 B2302

B63

CHOJNACKI S.,REGISTER ON CURRENT RESEARCH ON   BIBLIOG
ETHIOPIA AND THE HORN OF AFRICA. ETHIOPIA LAW   ACT/RES
CULTURE AGRI SECT EDU/PROP ADMIN...GEOG HEAL LING   INTELL
20. PAGE 21 B0426   ACADEM

B63

CONF ON FUTURE OF COMMONWEALTH,THE FUTURE OF THE   DIPLOM
COMMONWEALTH. UK ECO/UNDEV AGRI EDU/PROP ADMIN   RACE/REL
SOC/INTEG 20 COMMONWLTH. PAGE 23 B0460   ORD/FREE
                                                     TEC/DEV

B63

GOURNAY B.,PUBLIC ADMINISTRATION. FRANCE LAW CONSTN BIBLIOG/A
AGRI FINAN LABOR SCHOOL EX/STRUC CHOOSE...MGT   ADMIN
METH/COMP 20. PAGE 42 B0846   NAT/G
                                                     LOC/G

B63

HATHAWAY D.A.,GOVERNMENT AND AGRICULTURE: PUBLIC   AGRI
POLICY IN A DEMOCRATIC SOCIETY. USA+45 LEGIS ADMIN   GOV/REL
EXEC LOBBY REPRESENT PWR 20. PAGE 48 B0967   PROB/SOLV
                                                     EX/STRUC

B63

INDIAN INSTITUTE PUBLIC ADMIN,CASES IN INDIAN   DECISION
ADMINISTRATION. INDIA AGRI NAT/G PROB/SOLV TEC/DEV   PLAN
ECO/TAC ADMIN...ANTHOL METH 20. PAGE 53 B1083   MGT
                                                     ECO/UNDEV

B63

OLSON M. JR.,THE ECONOMICS OF WARTIME SHORTAGE.   WAR
FRANCE GERMANY MOD/EUR UK AGRI PROB/SOLV ADMIN   ADJUST
DEMAND WEALTH...POLICY OLD/LIB 17/20. PAGE 80 B1608 ECO/TAC
                                                     NAT/COMP

B63

PEABODY R.L.,NEW PERSPECTIVES ON THE HOUSE OF   NEW/IDEA
REPRESENTATIVES. AGRI FINAN SCHOOL FORCES CONFER   LEGIS
LEAD CHOOSE REPRESENT FEDERAL...POLICY DECISION   PWR
HOUSE/REP. PAGE 82 B1647   ADMIN

B63

SELF P.,THE STATE AND THE FARMER. UK ECO/DEV MARKET AGRI
WORKER PRICE CONTROL GP/REL...WELF/ST 20 DEPT/AGRI. NAT/G
PAGE 95 B1926   ADMIN
                                                     VOL/ASSN

B63

SPRING D.,THE ENGLISH LANDED ESTATE IN THE   STRATA
NINETEENTH CENTURY: ITS ADMINISTRATION. UK ELITES   PERS/REL
STRUCT AGRI NAT/G GP/REL OWN PWR WEALTH...BIBLIOG   MGT
19 HOUSE/LORD. PAGE 99 B2012

S63

DELLIN L.A.D.,"BULGARIA UNDER SOVIET LEADERSHIP."   AGRI
BULGARIA COM USA+45 USSR ECO/DEV INDUS POL/PAR   NAT/G
EX/STRUC TOP/EX COERCE RIGID/FLEX...POLICY   TOTALISM
TIME/SEQ 20. PAGE 28 B0572

S63

SCHURMANN F.,"ECONOMIC POLICY AND POLITICAL POWER   PLAN
IN COMMUNIST CHINA." ASIA CHINA/COM USSR SOCIETY   ECO/TAC
ECO/UNDEV AGRI INDUS CREATE ADMIN ROUTINE ATTIT
DRIVE RIGID/FLEX PWR WEALTH...HIST/WRIT TREND
CHARTS WORK 20. PAGE 94 B1908

N63

GREAT BRITAIN DEPT TECH COOP,PUBLIC ADMINISTRATION: BIBLIOG/A
A SELECT BIBLIOGRAPHY (PAMPHLET). WOR+45 AGRI FINAN ADMIN
INDUS EX/STRUC OP/RES ECO/TAC...MGT METH/COMP   NAT/G
NAT/COMP. PAGE 43 B0861   LOC/G

B64

ALDERFER H.O.,LOCAL GOVERNMENT IN DEVELOPING   ADMIN
COUNTRIES. ASIA COM L/A+17C S/ASIA AGRI LOC/G MUNIC ROUTINE
PROVS DOMIN CHOOSE PWR...POLICY MGT CONCPT 20.
PAGE 3 B0070

B64

FAINSOD M.,HOW RUSSIA IS RULED (REV. ED.). RUSSIA   NAT/G
USSR AGRI PROC/MFG LABOR POL/PAR EX/STRUC CONTROL   REV
PWR...POLICY BIBLIOG 19/20 KHRUSH/N COM/PARTY.   MARXISM

PAGE 34 B0700

B64

GRAVIER J.F.,AMENAGEMENT DU TERRITOIRE ET L'AVENIR PLAN
DES REGIONS FRANCAISES. FRANCE ECO/DEV AGRI INDUS MUNIC
CREATE...GEOG CHARTS 20. PAGE 42 B0859 NEIGH
ADMIN

B64

HAMBRIDGE G.,DYNAMICS OF DEVELOPMENT. AGRI FINAN ECO/UNDEV
INDUS LABOR INT/TRADE EDU/PROP ADMIN LEAD OWN ECO/TAC
HEALTH...ANTHOL BIBLIOG 20. PAGE 46 B0930 OP/RES
ACT/RES

B64

HICKEY G.C.,VILLAGE IN VIETNAM. USA+45 VIETNAM LAW CULTURE
AGRI FAM SECT ADMIN ATTIT...SOC CHARTS WORSHIP 20. SOCIETY
PAGE 49 B1003 STRUCT
S/ASIA

B64

LI C.M.,INDUSTRIAL DEVELOPMENT IN COMMUNIST CHINA. ASIA
CHINA/COM ECO/DEV ECO/UNDEV AGRI FINAN INDUS MARKET TEC/DEV
LABOR NAT/G ECO/TAC INT/TRADE EXEC ALL/VALS
...POLICY RELATIV TREND WORK TOT/POP VAL/FREE 20.
PAGE 65 B1311

B64

RIGGS F.W.,ADMINISTRATION IN DEVELOPING COUNTRIES. ECO/UNDEV
FUT WOR+45 STRUCT AGRI INDUS NAT/G PLAN TEC/DEV ADMIN
ECO/TAC EDU/PROP RIGID/FLEX KNOWL WEALTH...POLICY
MGT CONCPT METH/CNCPT TREND 20. PAGE 88 B1785

B64

SINGER M.R.,THE EMERGING ELITE: A STUDY OF TOP/EX
POLITICAL LEADERSHIP IN CEYLON. S/ASIA ECO/UNDEV STRATA
AGRI KIN NAT/G SECT EX/STRUC LEGIT ATTIT PWR NAT/LISM
RESPECT...SOC STAT CHARTS 20. PAGE 97 B1967 CEYLON

S64

FLORINSKY M.T.,"TRENDS IN THE SOVIET ECONOMY." COM ECO/DEV
USA+45 USSR INDUS LABOR NAT/G PLAN TEC/DEV ECO/TAC AGRI
ALL/VALS SOCISM...MGT METH/CNCPT STYLE CON/ANAL
GEN/METH WORK 20. PAGE 36 B0731

S64

HUELIN D.,"ECONOMIC INTEGRATION IN LATIN AMERICAN: MARKET
PROGRESS AND PROBLEMS." L/A+17C ECO/DEV AGRI ECO/UNDEV
DIST/IND FINAN INDUS NAT/G VOL/ASSN CONSULT INT/TRADE
DELIB/GP EX/STRUC ACT/RES PLAN TEC/DEV ECO/TAC
ROUTINE BAL/PAY WEALTH WORK 20. PAGE 52 B1058

S64

KASSOF A.,"THE ADMINISTERED SOCIETY: SOCIETY
TOTALITARIANISM WITHOUT TERROR." COM USSR STRATA DOMIN
AGRI INDUS NAT/G PERF/ART SCHOOL TOP/EX EDU/PROP TOTALISM
ADMIN ORD/FREE PWR...POLICY SOC TIME/SEQ GEN/LAWS
VAL/FREE 20. PAGE 58 B1178

S64

NASH M.,"SOCIAL PREREQUISITES TO ECONOMIC GROWTH IN ECO/DEV
LATIN AMERICA AND SOUTHEAST ASIA." L/A+17C S/ASIA PERCEPT
CULTURE SOCIETY ECO/UNDEV AGRI INDUS NAT/G PLAN
TEC/DEV EDU/PROP ROUTINE ALL/VALS...POLICY RELATIV
SOC NAT/COMP WORK TOT/POP 20. PAGE 77 B1558

B65

AMERICAN ECONOMIC ASSOCIATION,INDEX OF ECONOMIC BIBLIOG
JOURNALS 1886-1965 (7 VOLS.). UK USA+45 AGRI WRITING
FINAN PLAN ECO/TAC INT/TRADE ADMIN...STAT CENSUS INDUS
19/20. PAGE 4 B0083

B65

HADWIGER D.F.,PRESSURES AND PROTEST. NAT/G LEGIS AGRI
PLAN LEAD PARTIC ROUTINE ATTIT POLICY. PAGE 45 GP/REL
B0913 LOBBY
CHOOSE

B65

INT. BANK RECONSTR. DEVELOP.,ECONOMIC DEVELOPMENT INDUS
OF KUWAIT. ISLAM KUWAIT AGRI FINAN MARKET EX/STRUC NAT/G
TEC/DEV ECO/TAC ADMIN WEALTH...OBS CON/ANAL CHARTS
20. PAGE 54 B1092

B65

LEYS C.T.,FEDERATION IN EAST AFRICA. LAW AGRI FEDERAL
DIST/IND FINAN INT/ORG LABOR INT/TRADE CONFER ADMIN REGION
CONTROL GP/REL...ANTHOL 20 AFRICA/E. PAGE 65 B1310 ECO/UNDEV
PLAN

B65

ROMASCO A.U.,THE POVERTY OF ABUNDANCE: HOOVER, THE ECO/TAC
NATION, THE DEPRESSION. USA-45 AGRI LEGIS WORKER ADMIN
GIVE PRESS LEAD 20 HOOVER/H. PAGE 90 B1817 NAT/G
FINAN

L65

HAMMOND A.,"COMPREHENSIVE VERSUS INCREMENTAL TOP/EX
BUDGETING IN THE DEPARTMENT OF AGRICULTURE" USA+45 EX/STRUC
GP/REL ATTIT...PSY INT 20 DEPT/AGRI. PAGE 46 B0934 AGRI
BUDGET

S65

TABORSKY E.,"CHANGE IN CZECHOSLOVAKIA." COM USSR ECO/DEV
ELITES INTELL AGRI INDUS NAT/G DELIB/GP EX/STRUC PLAN
ECO/TAC TOTALISM ATTIT RIGID/FLEX SOCISM...MGT CZECHOSLVK
CONCPT TREND 20. PAGE 102 B2067

B66

BIRKHEAD G.S.,ADMINISTRATIVE PROBLEMS IN PAKISTAN. ADMIN
PAKISTAN AGRI FINAN INDUS LG/CO ECO/TAC CONTROL PWR NAT/G
...CHARTS ANTHOL 20. PAGE 12 B0241 ORD/FREE
ECO/UNDEV

B66

FISK E.K.,NEW GUINEA ON THE THRESHOLD; ASPECTS OF ECO/UNDEV
SOCIAL, POLITICAL, AND ECONOMIC DEVELOPMENT. AGRI SOCIETY
NAT/G INT/TRADE ADMIN ADJUST LITERACY ROLE...CHARTS
ANTHOL 20 NEW/GUINEA. PAGE 36 B0726

B66

FOX K.A.,THE THEORY OF QUANTITATIVE ECONOMIC POLICY ECO/TAC
WITH APPLICATIONS TO ECONOMIC GROWTH AND ECOMETRIC
STABILIZATION. ECO/DEV AGRI NAT/G PLAN ADMIN RISK EQUILIB
...DECISION IDEA/COMP SIMUL T. PAGE 37 B0746 GEN/LAWS

B66

HAYER T.,FRENCH AID. AFR FRANCE AGRI FINAN BUDGET TEC/DEV
ADMIN WAR PRODUC...CHARTS 18/20 THIRD/WRLD COLONIAL
OVRSEA/DEV. PAGE 48 B0975 FOR/AID
ECO/UNDEV

B66

KIRDAR U.,THE STRUCTURE OF UNITED NATIONS ECONOMIC INT/ORG
AID TO UNDERDEVELOPED COUNTRIES. AGRI FINAN INDUS FOR/AID
NAT/G EX/STRUC PLAN GIVE TASK...POLICY 20 UN. ECO/UNDEV
PAGE 60 B1213 ADMIN

B66

MACFARQUHAR R.,CHINA UNDER MAO: POLITICS TAKES ECO/UNDEV
COMMAND. CHINA/COM COM AGRI INDUS CHIEF FORCES TEC/DEV
DIPLOM INT/TRADE EDU/PROP TASK REV ADJUST...ANTHOL ECO/TAC
20 MAO. PAGE 67 B1359 ADMIN

B66

MONTGOMERY J.D.,APPROACHES TO DEVELOPMENT: ECO/UNDEV
POLITICS, ADMINISTRATION AND CHANGE. USA+45 AGRI ADMIN
FOR/AID ORD/FREE...CONCPT IDEA/COMP METH/COMP POLICY
ANTHOL. PAGE 75 B1507 ECO/TAC

B66

MURDOCK J.C.,RESEARCH AND REGIONS. AGRI FINAN INDUS BIBLIOG
LOC/G MUNIC NAT/G PROB/SOLV TEC/DEV ADMIN REGION ECO/DEV
20. PAGE 76 B1545 COMPUT/IR
R+D

B66

ZINKIN T.,CHALLENGES IN INDIA. INDIA PAKISTAN LAW NAT/G
AGRI FINAN INDUS TOP/EX TEC/DEV CONTROL ROUTINE ECO/TAC
ORD/FREE PWR 20 NEHRU/J SHASTRI/LB CIVIL/SERV. POLICY
PAGE 119 B2404 ADMIN

L66

AMERICAN ECONOMIC REVIEW,"SIXTY-THIRD LIST OF BIBLIOG/A
DOCTORAL DISSERTATIONS IN POLITICAL ECONOMY IN CONCPT
AMERICAN UNIVERSITIES AND COLLEGES." ECO/DEV AGRI ACADEM
FINAN LABOR WORKER PLAN BUDGET INT/TRADE ADMIN
DEMAND...MGT STAT 20. PAGE 4 B0084

S66

MATTHEWS D.G.,"ETHIOPIAN OUTLINE: A BIBLIOGRAPHIC BIBLIOG
RESEARCH GUIDE." ETHIOPIA LAW STRUCT ECO/UNDEV AGRI NAT/G
LABOR SECT CHIEF DELIB/GP EX/STRUC ADMIN...LING DIPLOM
ORG/CHARTS 20. PAGE 71 B1429 POL/PAR

B67

BALDWIN G.B.,PLANNING AND DEVELOPMENT IN IRAN. IRAN PLAN
AGRI INDUS CONSULT WORKER EDU/PROP BAL/PAY...CHARTS ECO/UNDEV
20. PAGE 8 B0173 ADMIN
PROB/SOLV

B67

BENNETT J.W.,HUTTERIAN BRETHREN; THE AGRICULTURAL SECT
ECONOMY AND SOCIAL ORGANIZATION OF A COMMUNAL AGRI
PEOPLE. USA+45 SOCIETY FAM KIN TEC/DEV ADJUST...MGT STRUCT
AUD/VIS GP/COMP 20. PAGE 10 B0213 GP/REL

B67

GREENE L.S.,AMERICAN GOVERNMENT POLICIES AND POLICY
FUNCTIONS. USA+45 LAW AGRI DIST/IND LABOR MUNIC NAT/G
BUDGET DIPLOM EDU/PROP ORD/FREE...BIBLIOG T 20. ADMIN
PAGE 43 B0867 DECISION

B67

JAKUBAUSKAS E.B.,HUMAN RESOURCES DEVELOPMENT. PROB/SOLV
USA+45 AGRI INDUS SERV/IND ACT/RES PLAN ADMIN ECO/TAC
RACE/REL DISCRIM...TREND GEN/LAWS. PAGE 55 B1119 EDU/PROP
WORKER

B67

SALMOND J.A.,THE CIVILIAN CONSERVATION CORPS, ADMIN
1933-1942. USA-45 NAT/G CREATE EXEC EFFICIENCY ECO/TAC
WEALTH...BIBLIOG 20 ROOSEVLT/F. PAGE 92 B1864 TASK
AGRI

B67

TOMA P.A.,THE POLITICS OF FOOD FOR PEACE; FOR/AID
EXECUTIVE-LEGISLATIVE INTERACTION. USA+45 ECO/UNDEV POLICY
POL/PAR DEBATE EXEC LOBBY CHOOSE PEACE...DECISION LEGIS
CHARTS. PAGE 104 B2113 AGRI

S67

FOX R.G.,"FAMILY, CASTE, AND COMMERCE IN A NORTH CULTURE
INDIAN MARKET TOWN." INDIA STRATA AGRI FACE/GP FAM GP/REL
NEIGH OP/RES BARGAIN ADMIN ROUTINE WEALTH...SOC ECO/UNDEV
CHARTS 20. PAGE 37 B0747 DIST/IND

S67

FRYKENBURG R.E.,"STUDIES OF LAND CONTROL IN INDIAN ECO/UNDEV
HISTORY: REVIEW ARTICLE." INDIA UK STRATA AGRI CONTROL
MUNIC OP/RES COLONIAL REGION EFFICIENCY OWN HABITAT ADMIN
...CONCPT 16/20. PAGE 38 B0763

AGRICULTURE....SEE AGRI

AHMAD M. B0065

AHRCO....ALLEGHENY HOUSING REHABILITATION CORPORATION

AID

B63
US SENATE COMM APPROPRIATIONS,PERSONNEL   ADMIN
ADMINISTRATION AND OPERATIONS OF AGENCY FOR   FOR/AID
INTERNATIONAL DEVELOPMENT: SPECIAL HEARING. FINAN   EFFICIENCY
LEAD COST UTIL SKILL...CHARTS 20 CONGRESS AID   DIPLOM
CIVIL/SERV. PAGE 109 B2211

B66
US HOUSE COMM GOVT OPERATIONS,AN INVESTIGATION OF   FOR/AID
THE US ECONOMIC AND MILITARY ASSISTANCE PROGRAMS IN   ECO/UNDEV
VIETNAM. USA+45 VIETNAM/S SOCIETY CONSTRUC FINAN   WAR
FORCES BUDGET INT/TRADE PEACE HEALTH...MGT   INSPECT
HOUSE/REP AID. PAGE 108 B2191

AIKEN C. B0066

AIR POLLUTION....SEE POLLUTION

AIR....LOCALE OF SUBJECT ACTIVITY IS AERIAL

B54
LOCKLIN D.P.,ECONOMICS OF TRANSPORTATION (4TH ED.).   ECO/DEV
USA+45 USA-45 SEA AIR LAW FINAN LG/CO EX/STRUC   DIST/IND
ADMIN CONTROL...STAT CHARTS 19/20 RAILROAD   ECO/TAC
PUB/TRANS. PAGE 66 B1335   TEC/DEV

B60
KINGSTON-MCCLOUG E.,DEFENSE; POLICY AND STRATEGY.   FORCES
UK SEA AIR TEC/DEV DIPLOM ADMIN LEAD WAR ORD/FREE   PLAN
...CHARTS 20. PAGE 60 B1209   POLICY
                                                       DECISION

S61
TAUBENFELD H.J.,"OUTER SPACE--PAST POLITICS AND   PLAN
FUTURE POLICY." FUT USA+45 USA-45 WOR+45 AIR INTELL   SPACE
STRUCT ECO/DEV NAT/G TOP/EX ACT/RES ADMIN ROUTINE   INT/ORG
NUC/PWR ATTIT DRIVE...CONCPT TIME/SEQ TREND TOT/POP
20. PAGE 103 B2083

B64
FISK W.M.,ADMINISTRATIVE PROCEDURE IN A REGULATORY   SERV/IND
AGENCY: THE CAB AND THE NEW YORK-CHICAGO CASE   ECO/DEV
(PAMPHLET). USA+45 DIST/IND ADMIN CONTROL LOBBY   AIR
GP/REL ROLE ORD/FREE NEWYORK/C CHICAGO CAB. PAGE 36   JURID
B0727

B66
WHITNAH D.R.,SAFER SKYWAYS. DIST/IND DELIB/GP   ADMIN
FORCES TOP/EX WORKER TEC/DEV ROUTINE WAR CIVMIL/REL   NAT/G
COST...TIME/SEQ 20 FAA CAB. PAGE 116 B2342   AIR
                                                       GOV/REL

S67
GOLIGHTLY H.O.,"THE AIRLINES: A CASE STUDY IN   DIST/IND
MANAGEMENT INNOVATION." USA+45 AIR FINAN INDUS   MARKET
TOP/EX CREATE PLAN PROB/SOLV ADMIN EXEC PROFIT   MGT
...DECISION 20. PAGE 40 B0820   TEC/DEV

AIYAR S.P. B0067

AJAO/A....ADEROGBA AJAO

ALABAMA....ALABAMA

B60
FRYE R.J.,GOVERNMENT AND LABOR: THE ALABAMA   ADMIN
PROGRAM. USA+45 INDUS R+D LABOR WORKER BUDGET   LEGIS
EFFICIENCY AGE/Y HEALTH...CHARTS 20 ALABAMA.   LOC/G
PAGE 38 B0761   PROVS

B65
FRYE R.J.,HOUSING AND URBAN RENEWAL IN ALABAMA.   MUNIC
USA+45 NEIGH LEGIS BUDGET ADJUD ADMIN PARTIC...MGT   PROB/SOLV
20 ALABAMA URBAN/RNWL. PAGE 38 B0762   PLAN
                                                       GOV/REL

ALASKA....ALASKA

ALBANIA....SEE ALSO COM

N
KYRIAK T.E.,EAST EUROPE: BIBLIOGRAPHY--INDEX TO US   BIBLIOG/A
JPRS RESEARCH TRANSLATIONS. ALBANIA BULGARIA COM   PRESS
CZECHOSLVK HUNGARY POLAND ROMANIA AGRI EXTR/IND   MARXISM
FINAN SERV/IND INT/TRADE WEAPON...GEOG MGT SOC 20.   INDUS
PAGE 62 B1247

ALBERTA....ALBERTA

ALBI F. B0068

ALBONETTI A. B0069

ALCOHOLISM....SEE BIO/SOC

ALDERFER H.F. B0070

ALDERSON W. B0071,B0499

ALEMBERT/J....JEAN LE ROND D'ALEMBERT

ALEXANDER R.S. B0072

ALEXANDER T. B0073

ALEXANDER Y. B0074

ALGER C.F. B0075,B0076

ALGERIA....SEE ALSO ISLAM

B62
ANDREWS W.G.,FRENCH POLITICS AND ALGERIA: THE   GOV/COMP
PROCESS OF POLICY FORMATION 1954-1962. ALGERIA   EXEC
FRANCE CONSTN ELITES POL/PAR CHIEF DELIB/GP LEGIS   COLONIAL
DIPLOM PRESS CHOOSE 20. PAGE 5 B0105

B64
PARET P.,FRENCH REVOLUTIONARY WARFARE FROM   FRANCE
INDOCHINA TO ALGERIA* THE ANALYSIS OF A POLITICAL   GUERRILLA
AND MILITARY DOCTRINE. ALGERIA VIETNAM FORCES   GEN/LAWS
OP/RES TEC/DEV ROUTINE REV ATTIT...PSY BIBLIOG.
PAGE 81 B1632

ALGIER/CHR....CHARTER OF ALGIERS

ALI S. B0077

ALIANZA POPULAR REVOLUCIONARIA AMERICANA (PERU)....SEE APRA

ALIENATION....SEE STRANGE

ALL/IDEOS....CONCERNS THREE OR MORE OF THE TERMS LISTED IN
     THE IDEOLOGICAL TOPIC INDEX, P. XIII

N
REVIEW OF POLITICS. WOR+45 WOR-45 CONSTN LEGIS   BIBLIOG/A
PROB/SOLV ADMIN LEAD ALL/IDEOS...PHIL/SCI 20.   DIPLOM
PAGE 1 B0006   INT/ORG
                                                      NAT/G

N
CUMULATIVE BOOK INDEX. WOR+45 WOR-45 ADMIN PERSON   INDEX
ALL/VALS ALL/IDEOS...HUM PHIL/SCI SOC LING 19/20.   NAT/G
PAGE 1 B0012   DIPLOM

N
PUBLISHERS' TRADE LIST ANNUAL. LAW POL/PAR ADMIN   BIBLIOG
PERSON ALL/IDEOS...HUM SOC 19/20. PAGE 1 B0020   NAT/G
                                                      DIPLOM
                                                      POLICY

N
PUBLISHERS' CIRCULAR LIMITED,THE ENGLISH CATALOGUE   BIBLIOG
OF BOOKS. UK WOR+45 WOR-45 LAW CULTURE LOC/G NAT/G   ALL/VALS
ADMIN LEAD...MGT 19/20. PAGE 85 B1718   ALL/IDEOS
                                                      SOCIETY

S55
BUNZEL J.H.,"THE GENERAL IDEOLOGY OF AMERICAN SMALL   ALL/IDEOS
BUSINESS"(BMR)" USA+45 USA-45 AGRI GP/REL INGP/REL   ATTIT
PERSON...MGT IDEA/COMP 18/20. PAGE 17 B0345   SML/CO
                                                      INDUS

B60
SCHUBERT G.,THE PUBLIC INTEREST. USA+45 CONSULT   POLICY
PLAN PROB/SOLV ADJUD ADMIN GP/REL PWR ALL/IDEOS 20.   DELIB/GP
PAGE 94 B1903   REPRESENT
                                                      POL/PAR

B61
MUNGER E.S.,AFRICAN FIELD REPORTS 1952-1961.   AFR
SOUTH/AFR SOCIETY ECO/UNDEV NAT/G POL/PAR COLONIAL   DISCRIM
EXEC PARL/PROC GUERRILLA RACE/REL ALL/IDEOS...SOC   RECORD
AUD/VIS 20. PAGE 76 B1538

B63
FRIED R.C.,THE ITALIAN PREFECTS. ITALY STRATA   ADMIN
ECO/DEV NAT/LISM ALL/IDEOS...TREND CHARTS METH/COMP   NAT/G
BIBLIOG 17/20 PREFECT. PAGE 37 B0755   EFFICIENCY

B63
SCHOECK H.,THE NEW ARGUMENT IN ECONOMICS. UK USA+45   WELF/ST
INDUS MARKET LABOR NAT/G ECO/TAC ADMIN ROUTINE   FOR/AID
BAL/PAY PWR...POLICY BOLIV. PAGE 94 B1899   ECO/DEV
                                                     ALL/IDEOS

B64
HARMON R.B.,BIBLIOGRAPHY OF BIBLIOGRAPHIES IN   BIBLIOG
POLITICAL SCIENCE (MIMEOGRAPHED PAPER: LIMITED   NAT/G
EDITION). WOR+45 WOR-45 INT/ORG POL/PAR GOV/REL   DIPLOM
ALL/IDEOS...INT/LAW JURID MGT 19/20. PAGE 47 B0949   LOC/G

B66
HARMON R.B.,SOURCES AND PROBLEMS OF BIBLIOGRAPHY IN   BIBLIOG
POLITICAL SCIENCE (PAMPHLET). INT/ORG LOC/G MUNIC   DIPLOM
POL/PAR ADMIN GOV/REL ALL/IDEOS...JURID MGT CONCPT   INT/LAW
19/20. PAGE 47 B0951   NAT/G

B67
PYE L.W.,SOUTHEAST ASIA'S POLITICAL SYSTEMS. ASIA   NAT/G
S/ASIA STRUCT ECO/UNDEV EX/STRUC CAP/ISM DIPLOM   POL/PAR
ALL/IDEOS...TREND CHARTS. PAGE 85 B1724   GOV/COMP

S67
JAVITS J.K.,"THE USE OF AMERICAN PLURALISM." USA+45   CENTRAL
ECO/DEV BUDGET ADMIN ALL/IDEOS...DECISION TREND.   ATTIT
PAGE 56 B1127   POLICY

NAT/G

ALL/PROG....ALLIANCE FOR PROGRESS

ALL/VALS....CONCERNS SIX OR MORE OF THE TERMS LISTED IN
THE VALUES INDEX, P. XIII

N

CUMULATIVE BOOK INDEX. WOR-45 ADMIN PERSON ALL/VALS INDEX
ALL/IDEOS...HUM PHIL/SCI SOC LING 19/20. PAGE 1   DIPLOM
B0012

N

PUBLISHERS' CIRCULAR LIMITED.THE ENGLISH CATALOGUE   BIBLIOG
OF BOOKS. UK WOR-45 LAW CULTURE LOC/G ADMIN LEAD   ALL/VALS
...MGT 19/20. PAGE 85 B1718   ALL/IDEOS
                                                     SOCIETY
B0C

MORRIS H.C.,THE HISTORY OF COLONIZATION. WOR+45   DOMIN
WOR-45 ECO/DEV ECO/UNDEV INT/ORG ACT/RES PLAN   SOVEREIGN
ECO/TAC LEGIT ROUTINE COERCE ATTIT DRIVE ALL/VALS   COLONIAL
...GEOG TREND 19. PAGE 76 B1528
B05

RIORDAN W.L.,PLUNKITT OF TAMMANY HALL. USA-45   POL/PAR
SOCIETY PROB/SOLV EXEC LEAD TASK CHOOSE ALL/VALS   MUNIC
...RECORD ANTHOL 20 REFORMERS TAMMANY NEWYORK/C   CHIEF
PLUNKITT/G. PAGE 88 B1789   ATTIT
B19

SUTHERLAND G.,CONSTITUTIONAL POWER AND WORLD   USA-45
AFFAIRS. CONSTN STRUCT INT/ORG NAT/G CHIEF LEGIS   EXEC
ACT/RES PLAN GOV/REL ALL/VALS...OBS TIME/SEQ   DIPLOM
CONGRESS VAL/FREE 20 PRESIDENT. PAGE 102 B2056
B23

FRANK T.,A HISTORY OF ROME. MEDIT-7 INTELL SOCIETY   EXEC
LOC/G NAT/G POL/PAR FORCES LEGIS DOMIN LEGIT   STRUCT
ALL/VALS...POLICY CONCPT TIME/SEQ GEN/LAWS ROM/EMP   ELITES
ROM/EMP. PAGE 37 B0749
B24

MERRIAM C.E.,A HISTORY OF POLITICAL THEORIES -   UNIV
RECENT TIMES. USA-45 WOR-45 CULTURE SOCIETY ECO/DEV INTELL
R+D EDU/PROP ROUTINE CHOOSE ATTIT PERSON ALL/VALS
...POLICY SOC CONCPT METH/CNCPT OBS HIST/WRIT
TIME/SEQ TREND. PAGE 73 B1471
B25

THOMAS F.,THE ENVIRONMENTAL BASIS OF SOCIETY.   SOCIETY
USA-45 WOR-45 STRATA ECO/DEV EXTR/IND CONSULT   GEOG
ECO/TAC ROUTINE ATTIT ALL/VALS...SOC TIME/SEQ.
PAGE 104 B2098
B28

HALL W.P.,EMPIRE TO COMMONWEALTH. FUT WOR-45 CONSTN VOL/ASSN
ECO/DEV ECO/UNDEV INT/ORG PROVS PLAN DIPLOM   NAT/G
EDU/PROP ADMIN COLONIAL PEACE PERSON ALL/VALS   UK
...POLICY GEOG SOC OBS RECORD TREND CMN/WLTH
PARLIAMENT 19/20. PAGE 46 B0925
B31

HILL N.,INTERNATIONAL ADMINISTRATION. WOR-45   INT/ORG
DELIB/GP DIPLOM EDU/PROP ALL/VALS...MGT TIME/SEQ   ADMIN
LEAGUE/NAT TOT/POP VAL/FREE 20. PAGE 50 B1011
B37

PARSONS T.,THE STRUCTURE OF SOCIAL ACTION. UNIV   CULTURE
INTELL SOCIETY INDUS MARKET ECO/TAC ROUTINE CHOOSE   ATTIT
ALL/VALS...CONCPT OBS BIOG TREND GEN/LAWS 20.   CAP/ISM
PAGE 81 B1636
B37

ROYAL INST. INT. AFF.,THE COLONIAL PROBLEM. WOR-45   INT/ORG
LAW ECO/DEV ECO/UNDEV NAT/G PLAN ECO/TAC EDU/PROP   ACT/RES
ADMIN ATTIT ALL/VALS...CONCPT 20. PAGE 91 B1844   SOVEREIGN
                                                     COLONIAL
B38

LANGE O.,ON THE ECONOMIC THEORY OF SOCIALISM. UNIV   MARKET
ECO/DEV FINAN INDUS INT/ORG PUB/INST ROUTINE ATTIT   ECO/TAC
ALL/VALS...SOC CONCPT STAT TREND 20. PAGE 62 B1258   INT/TRADE
                                                     SOCISM
B38

RAPPARD W.E.,THE CRISIS OF DEMOCRACY. EUR+WWI UNIV   NAT/G
WOR-45 CULTURE SOCIETY ECO/DEV INT/ORG POL/PAR   CONCPT
ACT/RES EDU/PROP EXEC CHOOSE ATTIT ALL/VALS...SOC
OBS HIST/WRIT TIME/SEQ LEAGUE/NAT NAZI TOT/POP 20.
PAGE 86 B1741
B41

YOUNG G.,FEDERALISM AND FREEDOM. EUR+WWI MOD/EUR   NAT/G
RUSSIA USA-45 WOR-45 SOCIETY STRUCT ECO/DEV INT/ORG WAR
EXEC FEDERAL ATTIT PERSON ALL/VALS...OLD/LIB CONCPT
OBS TREND LEAGUE/NAT TOT/POP. PAGE 119 B2392
B42

JONES V.,METROPOLITAN GOVERNMENT. HABITAT ALL/VALS   LOC/G
...MGT SOC CHARTS. PAGE 57 B1151   MUNIC
                                                     ADMIN
                                                     TECHRACY
L44

HAILEY,"THE FUTURE OF COLONIAL PEOPLES." WOR-45   PLAN
CONSTN CULTURE ECO/UNDEV AGRI MARKET INT/ORG NAT/G   CONCPT
SECT CONSULT ECO/TAC LEGIT ADMIN NAT/LISM ALL/VALS   DIPLOM
...SOC OBS TREND STERTYP CMN/WLTH LEAGUE/NAT   UK
PARLIAMENT 20. PAGE 45 B0916
B46

GRIFFIN G.G.,A GUIDE TO MANUSCRIPTS RELATING TO   BIBLIOG/A

AMERICAN HISTORY IN BRITISH DEPOSITORIES. CANADA   ALL/VALS
IRELAND MOD/EUR UK USA-45 LAW DIPLOM ADMIN COLONIAL
WAR NAT/LISM SOVEREIGN...GEOG INT/LAW 15/19
CMN/WLTH. PAGE 43 B0876
B48

BONAPARTE M.,MYTHS OF WAR. GERMANY WOR-45 CULTURE   ROUTINE
SOCIETY FORCES LEGIT ATTIT ALL/VALS...CONCPT   MYTH
HIST/WRIT TIME/SEQ 20 JEWS. PAGE 13 B0271   WAR
B49

ROSENHAUPT H.W.,HOW TO WAGE PEACE. USA+45 SOCIETY   INTELL
STRATA STRUCT R+D INT/ORG POL/PAR LEGIS ACT/RES   CONCPT
CREATE PLAN EDU/PROP ADMIN EXEC ATTIT ALL/VALS   DIPLOM
...TIME/SEQ TREND COLD/WAR 20. PAGE 90 B1822
B49

SINGER K.,THE IDEA OF CONFLICT. INTELL INT/ORG PLAN ACT/RES
ROUTINE ATTIT DRIVE ALL/VALS...POLICY CONCPT   SOC
TIME/SEQ. PAGE 97 B1966
B50

LITTLE HOOVER COMM.HOW TO ACHIEVE GREATER   TOP/EX
EFFICIENCY AND ECONOMY IN MINNESOTA'S GOVERNMENT   LOC/G
(PAMPHLET). PLAN BUDGET ADMIN CHOOSE EFFICIENCY   GOV/REL
ALL/VALS 20 MINNESOTA. PAGE 66 B1327   PROVS
B50

MCCAMY J.,THE ADMINISTRATION OF AMERICAN FOREIGN   EXEC
AFFAIRS. USA+45 SOCIETY INT/ORG NAT/G ACT/RES PLAN   STRUCT
INT/TRADE EDU/PROP ADJUD ALL/VALS...METH/CNCPT   DIPLOM
TIME/SEQ CONGRESS 20. PAGE 71 B1441
L50

US SENATE COMM. GOVT. OPER.,"REVISION OF THE UN   INT/ORG
CHARTER." FUT USA+45 WOR+45 CONSTN ECO/DEV   LEGIS
ECO/UNDEV NAT/G DELIB/GP ACT/RES CREATE PLAN EXEC   PEACE
ROUTINE CHOOSE ALL/VALS...POLICY CONCPT CONGRESS UN
TOT/POP 20 COLD/WAR. PAGE 111 B2235
C50

SIMON H.A.,"PUBLIC ADMINISTRATION." LG/CO SML/CO   MGT
PLAN DOMIN LEAD GP/REL DRIVE PERCEPT ALL/VALS   ADMIN
...POLICY BIBLIOG/A 20. PAGE 97 B1957   DECISION
                                                     EX/STRUC
B51

LASSWELL H.D.,THE POLITICAL WRITINGS OF HAROLD D   PERSON
LASSWELL. UNIV DOMIN EXEC LEAD RATIONAL ATTIT DRIVE PSY
ROLE ALL/VALS...OBS BIOG 20. PAGE 63 B1269   INGP/REL
                                                     CONCPT
B51

LEITES N.,THE OPERATIONAL CODE OF THE POLITBURO.   DELIB/GP
COM USSR CREATE PLAN DOMIN LEGIT COERCE ALL/VALS   ADMIN
...SOC CONCPT MYTH TREND CON/ANAL GEN/LAWS 20   SOCISM
LENIN/VI STALIN/J. PAGE 64 B1284
B51

PETERSON F.,SURVEY OF LABOR ECONOMICS (REV. ED.).   WORKER
STRATA ECO/DEV LABOR INSPECT BARGAIN PAY PRICE EXEC DEMAND
ROUTINE GP/REL ALL/VALS ORD/FREE 20 AFL/CIO   IDEA/COMP
DEPT/LABOR. PAGE 82 B1662   T
B51

SMITH L.,AMERICAN DEMOCRACY AND MILITARY POWER.   FORCES
USA+45 USA-45 CONSTN STRATA NAT/G LEGIS ACT/RES   STRUCT
LEGIT ADMIN EXEC GOV/REL ALL/VALS...CONCPT   WAR
HIST/WRIT CONGRESS 20. PAGE 98 B1982
B52

ULAM A.B.,TITOISM AND THE COMINFORM. USSR WOR+45   COM
STRUCT INT/ORG NAT/G ACT/RES PLAN EXEC ATTIT DRIVE   POL/PAR
ALL/VALS...CONCPT OBS VAL/FREE 20 COMINTERN   TOTALISM
TITO/MARSH. PAGE 106 B2145   YUGOSLAVIA
B52

VANDENBOSCH A.,THE UN: BACKGROUND, ORGANIZATION,   DELIB/GP
FUNCTIONS, ACTIVITIES. WOR+45 WOR-45 CONSTN STRUCT   TIME/SEQ
INT/ORG CONSULT BAL/PWR EDU/PROP EXEC ALL/VALS   PEACE
...POLICY CONCPT UN 20. PAGE 112 B2254
B53

GROSS B.M.,THE LEGISLATIVE STRUGGLE: A STUDY IN   LEGIS
SOCIAL COMBAT. STRUCT LOC/G POL/PAR JUDGE EDU/PROP   DECISION
DEBATE ETIQUET ADMIN LOBBY CHOOSE GOV/REL INGP/REL   PERSON
HEREDITY ALL/VALS...SOC PRESIDENT. PAGE 44 B0885   LEAD
S53

MORRIS B.S.,"THE COMINFORM: A FIVE YEAR   VOL/ASSN
PERSPECTIVE." COM UNIV USSR WOR+45 ECO/DEV POL/PAR   EDU/PROP
TOP/EX PLAN DOMIN ADMIN TOTALISM ATTIT ALL/VALS   DIPLOM
...CONCPT TIME/SEQ TREND CON/ANAL WORK VAL/FREE 20.
PAGE 76 B1527
B54

MATTHEWS D.R.,THE SOCIAL BACKGROUND OF POLITICAL   DECISION
DECISION-MAKERS. CULTURE SOCIETY STRATA FAM   BIOG
EX/STRUC LEAD ATTIT BIO/SOC DRIVE PERSON ALL/VALS   SOC
HIST/WRIT. PAGE 71 B1431
L54

ARCIENEGAS G.,"POST-WAR SOVIET FOREIGN POLICY: A   INTELL
WORLD PERSPECTIVE." COM USA+45 STRUCT NAT/G POL/PAR ACT/RES
TOP/EX PLAN ADMIN ALL/VALS...TREND COLD/WAR TOT/POP USSR
20. PAGE 6 B0124
B55

MAZZINI J.,THE DUTIES OF MAN. MOD/EUR LAW SOCIETY   SUPEGO
FAM NAT/G POL/PAR SECT VOL/ASSN EX/STRUC ACT/RES   CONCPT
CREATE REV PEACE ATTIT ALL/VALS...GEN/LAWS WORK 19. NAT/LISM
PAGE 71 B1439
L55

KISER M.,"ORGANIZATION OF AMERICAN STATES." L/A+17C VOL/ASSN

USA+45 ECO/UNDEV INT/ORG NAT/G PLAN TEC/DEV DIPLOM ECO/DEV
ECO/TAC INT/TRADE EDU/PROP ADMIN ALL/VALS...POLICY REGION
MGT RECORD ORG/CHARTS OAS 20. PAGE 60 B1215

L55
ROSTOW W.W.,"RUSSIA AND CHINA UNDER COMMUNISM." COM
CHINA/COM USSR INTELL STRUCT INT/ORG NAT/G POL/PAR ASIA
TOP/EX ACT/RES PLAN ADMIN ATTIT ALL/VALS MARXISM
...CONCPT OBS TIME/SEQ TREND GOV/COMP VAL/FREE 20.
PAGE 91 B1830

B56
JENNINGS W.I.,THE APPROACH TO SELF-GOVERNMENT. NAT/G
CEYLON INDIA PAKISTAN S/ASIA UK SOCIETY POL/PAR CONSTN
DELIB/GP LEGIS ECO/TAC EDU/PROP ADMIN EXEC CHOOSE COLONIAL
ATTIT ALL/VALS...JURID CONCPT GEN/METH TOT/POP 20.
PAGE 56 B1136

L56
PARSONS T.,"SUGGESTIONS FOR A SOCIOLOGICAL APPROACH SOC
TO THE THEORY OF ORGANIZATIONS - I" (BMR)" FINAN CONCPT
EX/STRUC LEGIT ALL/VALS...POLICY DECISION 20. ADMIN
PAGE 81 B1637 STRUCT

B59
ELLIOTT O.,MEN AT THE TOP. USA+45 CULTURE EX/STRUC TOP/EX
PRESS GOV/REL ATTIT ALL/VALS...OBS INT QU 20. PERSON
PAGE 33 B0668 LEAD
POLICY

B59
JOYCE J.A.,RED CROSS INTERNATIONAL AND THE STRATEGY VOL/ASSN
OF PEACE. WOR+45 WOR-45 EX/STRUC SUPEGO ALL/VALS HEALTH
...CONCPT GEN/LAWS TOT/POP 19/20 RED/CROSS. PAGE 57
B1155

B59
MACIVER R.M.,THE NATIONS AND THE UN. WOR+45 NAT/G INT/ORG
CONSULT ADJUD ADMIN ALL/VALS...CONCPT DEEP/QU UN ATTIT
TOT/POP UNESCO 20. PAGE 67 B1362 DIPLOM

S59
LASSWELL H.D.,"UNIVERSALITY IN PERSPECTIVE." FUT INT/ORG
UNIV SOCIETY CONSULT TOP/EX PLAN EDU/PROP ADJUD JURID
ROUTINE ARMS/CONT COERCE PEACE ATTIT PERSON TOTALISM
ALL/VALS. PAGE 63 B1271

B60
HYDE L.K.G.,THE US AND THE UN. WOR+45 STRUCT USA+45
ECO/DEV ECO/UNDEV NAT/G ACT/RES PLAN DIPLOM INT/ORG
EDU/PROP ADMIN ALL/VALS...CONCPT TIME/SEQ GEN/LAWS FOR/AID
UN VAL/FREE 20. PAGE 53 B1070

B60
LENCZOWSKI G.,OIL AND STATE IN THE MIDDLE EAST. FUT ISLAM
IRAN LAW ECO/UNDEV EXTR/IND NAT/G TOP/EX PLAN INDUS
TEC/DEV ECO/TAC LEGIT ADMIN COERCE ATTIT ALL/VALS NAT/LISM
PWR...CHARTS 20. PAGE 64 B1288

S60
HALPERIN M.H.,"IS THE SENATE'S FOREIGN RELATIONS PLAN
RESEARCH WORTHWHILE." COM FUT USA+45 USSR ACT/RES DIPLOM
BAL/PWR EDU/PROP ADMIN ALL/VALS CONGRESS VAL/FREE
20 COLD/WAR. PAGE 46 B0927

S60
SCHACHTER O.,"THE ENFORCEMENT OF INTERNATIONAL INT/ORG
JUDICIAL AND ARBITRAL DECISIONS." WOR+45 NAT/G ADJUD
ECO/TAC DOMIN LEGIT ROUTINE COERCE ATTIT DRIVE INT/LAW
ALL/VALS PWR...METH/CNCPT TREND TOT/POP 20 UN.
PAGE 93 B1878

B61
HARRISON S.,INDIA AND THE UNITED STATES. FUT S/ASIA DELIB/GP
USA+45 WOR+45 INTELL ECO/DEV ECO/UNDEV AGRI INDUS ACT/RES
INT/ORG NAT/G CONSULT EX/STRUC TOP/EX PLAN ECO/TAC FOR/AID
NEUTRAL ALL/VALS...MGT TOT/POP 20. PAGE 47 B0956 INDIA

S61
ALGER C.F.,"NON-RESOLUTION CONSEQUENCES OF THE INT/ORG
UNITED NATIONS AND THEIR EFFECT ON INTERNATIONAL DRIVE
CONFLICT." WOR+45 CONSTN ECO/DEV NAT/G CONSULT BAL/PWR
DELIB/GP TOP/EX ACT/RES PLAN DIPLOM EDU/PROP
ROUTINE ATTIT ALL/VALS...INT/LAW TOT/POP UN 20.
PAGE 4 B0075

S61
JACKSON E.,"CONSTITUTIONAL DEVELOPMENTS OF THE INT/ORG
UNITED NATIONS: THE GROWTH OF ITS EXECUTIVE EXEC
CAPACITY." FUT WOR+45 CONSTN STRUCT ACT/RES PLAN
ALL/VALS...NEW/IDEA OBS COLD/WAR UN 20. PAGE 55
B1106

S61
LEWY G.,"SUPERIOR ORDERS, NUCLEAR WARFARE AND THE DETER
DICTATES OF CONSCIENCE: THE DILEMMA OF MILITARY INT/ORG
OBEDIENCE IN THE ATOMIC." FUT UNIV WOR+45 INTELL LAW
SOCIETY FORCES TOP/EX ACT/RES ADMIN ROUTINE NUC/PWR INT/LAW
PERCEPT RIGID/FLEX ALL/VALS...POLICY CONCPT 20.
PAGE 65 B1308

S61
RUDOLPH S.,"CONSENSUS AND CONFLICT IN INDIAN POL/PAR
POLITICS." S/ASIA WOR+45 NAT/G DELIB/GP DIPLOM PERCEPT
EDU/PROP ADMIN CONSEN PERSON ALL/VALS...OBS TREND INDIA
TOT/POP VAL/FREE 20. PAGE 92 B1854

S61
VIRALLY M.,"VERS UNE REFORME DU SECRETARIAT DES INT/ORG
NATIONS UNIES." FUT WOR+45 CONSTN ECO/DEV TOP/EX INTELL
BAL/PWR ADMIN ALL/VALS...CONCPT BIOG UN VAL/FREE DIPLOM
20. PAGE 112 B2264

C61
VERBA S.,"SMALL GROUPS AND POLITICAL BEHAVIOR: A LEAD
STUDY OF LEADERSHIP" DOMIN PARTIC ROUTINE GP/REL ELITES
ATTIT DRIVE ALL/VALS...CONCPT IDEA/COMP LAB/EXP FACE/GP
BIBLIOG METH. PAGE 112 B2259

B62
PRESTHUS R.,THE ORGANIZATIONAL SOCIETY. USA+45 LG/CO
STRUCT ECO/DEV ADMIN ATTIT ALL/VALS...PSY SOC 20. WORKER
PAGE 84 B1703 PERS/REL
DRIVE

S62
FESLER J.W.,"FRENCH FIELD ADMINISTRATION: THE EX/STRUC
BEGINNINGS." CHRIST-17C CULTURE SOCIETY STRATA FRANCE
NAT/G ECO/TAC DOMIN EDU/PROP LEGIT ADJUD COERCE
ATTIT ALL/VALS...TIME/SEQ CON/ANAL GEN/METH
VAL/FREE 13/15. PAGE 35 B0714

S62
IKLE F.C.,"POLITICAL NEGOTIATION AS A PROCESS OF ROUTINE
MODIFYING UTILITIES." WOR+45 FACE/GP LABOR NAT/G DECISION
FORCES ACT/RES EDU/PROP DETER PERCEPT ALL/VALS DIPLOM
...PSY NEW/IDEA HYPO/EXP GEN/METH 20. PAGE 53 B1076

S62
MANGIN G.,"LES ACCORDS DE COOPERATION EN MATIERE DE INT/ORG
JUSTICE ENTRE LA FRANCE ET LES ETATS AFRICAINS ET LAW
MALGACHE." AFR ISLAM WOR+45 STRUCT ECO/UNDEV NAT/G FRANCE
DELIB/GP PERCEPT ALL/VALS...JURID MGT TIME/SEQ 20.
PAGE 69 B1386

S62
MURACCIOLE L.,"LES MODIFICATIONS DE LA CONSTITUTION NAT/G
MALGACHE." AFR WOR+45 ECO/UNDEV LEGIT EXEC ALL/VALS STRUCT
...JURID 20. PAGE 76 B1542 SOVEREIGN
MADAGASCAR

B63
CHARLES S.,MINISTER OF RELIEF: HARRY HOPKINS AND ADMIN
THE DEPRESSION. EX/STRUC PROB/SOLV RATION PARL/PROC ECO/TAC
PERS/REL ALL/VALS 20 HOPKINS/H NRA. PAGE 20 B0414 PLAN
BIOG

B63
DEBRAY P.,LE PORTUGAL ENTRE DEUX REVOLUTIONS. NAT/G
EUR+WWI PORTUGAL CONSTN LEGIT ADMIN ATTIT ALL/VALS DELIB/GP
...DECISION CONCPT 20 SALAZAR/A. PAGE 28 B0567 TOP/EX

B63
KAPP W.K.,HINDU CULTURE: ECONOMIC DEVELOPMENT AND SECT
ECONOMIC PLANNING IN INDIA. INDIA S/ASIA CULTURE ECO/UNDEV
ECO/TAC EDU/PROP ADMIN ALL/VALS...POLICY MGT
TIME/SEQ VAL/FREE 20. PAGE 58 B1171

B63
LANGROD G.,THE INTERNATIONAL CIVIL SERVICE: ITS INT/ORG
ORIGINS, ITS NATURE, ITS EVALUATION. FUT WOR+45 ADMIN
WOR-45 DELIB/GP ACT/RES DOMIN LEGIT ATTIT
RIGID/FLEX SUPEGO ALL/VALS...MGT CONCPT STAT
TIME/SEQ ILO LEAGUE/NAT VAL/FREE 20 UN. PAGE 62
B1259

B63
MCKIE R.,MALAYSIA IN FOCUS. INDONESIA WOR+45 S/ASIA
ECO/UNDEV FINAN NAT/G POL/PAR SECT FORCES PLAN NAT/LISM
ADMIN COLONIAL COERCE DRIVE ALL/VALS...POLICY MALAYSIA
RECORD CENSUS TIME/SEQ CMN/WLTH 20. PAGE 72 B1453

B63
NORTH R.C.,CONTENT ANALYSIS: A HANDBOOK WITH METH/CNCPT
APPLICATIONS FOR THE STUDY OF INTERNATIONAL CRISIS. COMPUT/IR
ASIA COM EUR+WWI MOD/EUR INT/ORG TEC/DEV DOMIN USSR
EDU/PROP ROUTINE COERCE PERCEPT RIGID/FLEX ALL/VALS
...QUANT TESTS CON/ANAL SIMUL GEN/LAWS VAL/FREE.
PAGE 79 B1591

B63
STEVENSON A.E.,LOOKING OUTWARD: YEARS OF CRISIS AT INT/ORG
THE UNITED NATIONS. COM CUBA USA+45 WOR+45 SOCIETY CONCPT
NAT/G EX/STRUC ACT/RES LEGIT COLONIAL ATTIT PERSON ARMS/CONT
SUPEGO ALL/VALS...POLICY HUM UN COLD/WAR CONGO 20.
PAGE 100 B2034

B63
WARNER W.L.,THE AMERICAN FEDERAL EXECUTIVE. USA+45 ELITES
USA-45 CONSULT EX/STRUC GP/REL DRIVE ALL/VALS...PSY NAT/G
DEEP/QU CHARTS 19/20 PRESIDENT. PAGE 114 B2295 TOP/EX
ADMIN

L63
EMERSON R.,"POLITICAL MODERNIZATION." WOR+45 POL/PAR
CULTURE ECO/UNDEV NAT/G FORCES ECO/TAC DOMIN ADMIN
EDU/PROP LEGIT COERCE ALL/VALS...CONCPT TIME/SEQ
VAL/FREE 20. PAGE 33 B0672

L63
ROBERT J.,"LES ELECTIONS LEGISLATIVES DU 17 MAI CHOOSE
1963 ET L'EVOLUTION POLITIQUE INTERNE DU MAROC." MOROCCO
ISLAM WOR+45 NAT/G POL/PAR EXEC ALL/VALS 20.
PAGE 89 B1792

L63
SPITZ A.A.,"DEVELOPMENT ADMINISTRATION: AN ADMIN
ANNOTATED BIBLIOGRAPHY." WOR+45 CULTURE SOCIETY ECO/UNDEV
STRATA DELIB/GP EX/STRUC TOP/EX ACT/RES ECO/TAC
DOMIN EDU/PROP LEGIT COERCE ATTIT ALL/VALS...MGT
VAL/FREE. PAGE 99 B2009

S63
ANTHON C.G.,"THE END OF THE ADENAUER ERA." EUR+WWI NAT/G
GERMANY/W CONSTN EX/STRUC CREATE DIPLOM LEGIT ATTIT TOP/EX
PERSON ALL/VALS...RECORD 20 ADENAUER/K. PAGE 6 BAL/PWR

B0113 GERMANY
  S63

ARASTEH R.,"THE ROLE OF INTELLECTUALS IN INTELL
ADMINISTRATIVE DEVELOPMENT AND SOCIAL CHANGE IN ADMIN
MODERN IRAN." ISLAM CULTURE NAT/G CONSULT ACT/RES IRAN
EDU/PROP EXEC ATTIT BIO/SOC PERCEPT SUPEGO ALL/VALS
...POLICY MGT PSY SOC CONCPT 20. PAGE 6 B0123
  S63

HARRIS R.L.,"A COMPARATIVE ANALYSIS OF THE DELIB/GP
ADMINISTRATIVE SYSTEMS OF CANADA AND CEYLON." EX/STRUC
S/ASIA CULTURE SOCIETY STRATA TOP/EX ACT/RES DOMIN CANADA
EDU/PROP LEGIT COERCE ATTIT SUPEGO ALL/VALS...MGT CEYLON
CHARTS GEN/LAWS VAL/FREE 20. PAGE 47 B0955
  S63

MODELSKI G.,"STUDY OF ALLIANCES." WOR+45 WOR-45 VOL/ASSN
INT/ORG NAT/G FORCES LEGIT ADMIN CHOOSE ALL/VALS CON/ANAL
PWR SKILL...INT/LAW CONCPT GEN/LAWS 20 TREATY. DIPLOM
PAGE 74 B1495
  S63

SCHMITT H.A.,"THE EUROPEAN COMMUNITIES." EUR+WWI VOL/ASSN
FRANCE DELIB/GP EX/STRUC TOP/EX CREATE TEC/DEV ECO/DEV
ECO/TAC LEGIT REGION COERCE DRIVE ALL/VALS
...METH/CNCPT EEC 20. PAGE 94 B1897
  S63

USEEM J.,"MEN IN THE MIDDLE OF THE THIRD CULTURE: ADMIN
THE ROLES OF AMERICAN AND NON-WESTERN PEOPLE IN SOCIETY
CROSS-CULTURAL ADMINIS-." FUT WOR+45 DELIB/GP PERSON
EX/STRUC LEGIS ATTIT ALL/VALS...MGT INT TIME/SEQ
GEN/LAWS VAL/FREE. PAGE 111 B2247
  S63

WAGRET M.,"L'ASCENSION POLITIQUE DE L'U.D.D.I.A. EX/STRUC
(CONGO) ET SA PRISE DU POUVOIR (1956-1959)." AFR CHOOSE
WOR+45 NAT/G POL/PAR CONSULT DELIB/GP LEGIS PERCEPT FRANCE
ALL/VALS SOVEREIGN...TIME/SEQ CONGO. PAGE 113 B2274
  B64

APTER D.E.,IDEOLOGY AND DISCONTENT. FUT WOR+45 ACT/RES
CONSTN CULTURE INTELL SOCIETY STRUCT INT/ORG NAT/G ATTIT
DELIB/GP LEGIS CREATE PLAN TEC/DEV EDU/PROP EXEC
PERCEPT PERSON RIGID/FLEX ALL/VALS...POLICY
TOT/POP. PAGE 6 B0122
  B64

EATON H.,PRESIDENTIAL TIMBER: A HISTORY OF DELIB/GP
NOMINATING CONVENTIONS, 1868-1960. USA+45 USA-45 CHOOSE
POL/PAR EX/STRUC DEBATE LOBBY ATTIT PERSON ALL/VALS CHIEF
...MYTH 19/20 PRESIDENT. PAGE 32 B0646 NAT/G
  B64

GUTTSMAN W.L.,THE BRITISH POLITICAL ELITE. EUR+WWI NAT/G
MOD/EUR STRATA FAM LABOR POL/PAR SCHOOL VOL/ASSN SOC
DELIB/GP LEGIS LEGIT EXEC CHOOSE ATTIT ALL/VALS UK
...STAT BIOG TIME/SEQ CHARTS VAL/FREE. PAGE 45 ELITES
B0905
  B64

LI C.M.,INDUSTRIAL DEVELOPMENT IN COMMUNIST CHINA. ASIA
CHINA/COM ECO/DEV ECO/UNDEV AGRI FINAN INDUS MARKET TEC/DEV
LABOR NAT/G ECO/TAC INT/TRADE EXEC ALL/VALS
...POLICY RELATIV TREND WORK TOT/POP VAL/FREE 20.
PAGE 65 B1311
  B64

MERILLAT H.C.L.,LEGAL ADVISERS AND FOREIGN AFFAIRS. CONSULT
WOR+45 WOR-45 ELITES INTELL NAT/G LEGIT ADMIN EX/STRUC
PERCEPT ALL/VALS...MGT NEW/IDEA RECORD 20. PAGE 73 DIPLOM
B1469
  B64

PIPES R.,THE FORMATION OF THE SOVIET UNION. EUR+WWI COM
MOD/EUR STRUCT ECO/UNDEV NAT/G LEGIS DOMIN LEGIT USSR
CT/SYS EXEC COERCE ALL/VALS...POLICY RELATIV RUSSIA
HIST/WRIT TIME/SEQ TOT/POP 19/20. PAGE 83 B1677
  B64

SULLIVAN G.,THE STORY OF THE PEACE CORPS. USA+45 INT/ORG
WOR+45 INTELL FACE/GP NAT/G SCHOOL VOL/ASSN CONSULT ECO/UNDEV
EX/STRUC PLAN EDU/PROP ADMIN ATTIT DRIVE ALL/VALS FOR/AID
...POLICY HEAL SOC CONCPT INT QU BIOG TREND SOC/EXP PEACE
WORK. PAGE 102 B2054
  B64

UN PUB. INFORM. ORGAN.,EVERY MAN'S UNITED NATIONS. INT/ORG
UNIV WOR+45 CONSTN CULTURE SOCIETY ECO/DEV ROUTINE
ECO/UNDEV NAT/G ACT/RES PLAN ECO/TAC INT/TRADE
EDU/PROP LEGIT PEACE ATTIT ALL/VALS...POLICY HUM
INT/LAW CONCPT CHARTS UN TOT/POP 20. PAGE 106 B2150
  S64

FLORINSKY M.T.,"TRENDS IN THE SOVIET ECONOMY." COM ECO/DEV
USA+45 USSR INDUS LABOR NAT/G PLAN TEC/DEV ECO/TAC AGRI
ALL/VALS SOCISM...MGT METH/CNCPT STYLE CON/ANAL
GEN/METH WORK 20. PAGE 36 B0731
  S64

NASH M.,"SOCIAL PREREQUISITES TO ECONOMIC GROWTH IN ECO/DEV
LATIN AMERICA AND SOUTHEAST ASIA." L/A+17C S/ASIA PERCEPT
CULTURE SOCIETY ECO/UNDEV AGRI NAT/G PLAN
TEC/DEV EDU/PROP ROUTINE ALL/VALS...POLICY RELATIV
SOC NAT/COMP WORK TOT/POP 20. PAGE 77 B1558
  S64

NEEDHAM T.,"SCIENCE AND SOCIETY IN EAST AND WEST." ASIA
INTELL STRATA R+D LOC/G NAT/G PROVS CONSULT ACT/RES STRUCT
CREATE PLAN TEC/DEV EDU/PROP ADMIN ATTIT ALL/VALS
...POLICY RELATIV MGT CONCPT NEW/IDEA TIME/SEQ WORK
WORK. PAGE 77 B1565

  S64

PARSONS T.,"EVOLUTIONARY UNIVERSALS IN SOCIETY." SOC
UNIV SOCIETY STRATA MARKET EDU/PROP LEGIT ADJUD CONCPT
ADMIN ALL/VALS...JURID OBS GEN/LAWS VAL/FREE 20.
PAGE 81 B1638
  B65

REISS A.J. JR.,SCHOOLS IN A CHANGING SOCIETY. SCHOOL
CULTURE PROB/SOLV INSPECT DOMIN CONFER INGP/REL EX/STRUC
RACE/REL AGE/C AGE/Y ALL/VALS...ANTHOL SOC/INTEG 20 ADJUST
NEWYORK/C. PAGE 87 B1766 ADMIN
  S65

RUBINSTEIN A.Z.,"YUGOSLAVIA'S OPENING SOCIETY." COM CONSTN
USSR INTELL NAT/G LEGIS TOP/EX LEGIT CT/SYS EX/STRUC
RIGID/FLEX ALL/VALS SOCISM...HUM TIME/SEQ TREND 20. YUGOSLAVIA
PAGE 92 B1851
  B66

WILLNER A.R.,THE NEOTRADITIONAL ACCOMMODATION TO INDONESIA
POLITICAL INDEPENDENCE* THE CASE OF INDONESIA * CONSERVE
RESEARCH MONOGRAPH NO. 26. CULTURE ECO/UNDEV CREATE ELITES
PROB/SOLV FOR/AID LEGIT COLONIAL EFFICIENCY ADMIN
NAT/LISM ALL/VALS SOC. PAGE 117 B2355
  S67

LASLETT J.H.M.,"SOCIALISM AND THE AMERICAN LABOR LABOR
MOVEMENT* SOME NEW REFLECTIONS." USA-45 VOL/ASSN ROUTINE
LOBBY PARTIC CENTRAL ALL/VALS SOCISM...GP/COMP 20. ATTIT
PAGE 63 B1265 GP/REL
  B82

POOLE W.F.,INDEX TO PERIODICAL LITERATURE. LOC/G BIBLIOG
NAT/G DIPLOM ADMIN...HUM PHIL/SCI SOC 19. PAGE 84 USA-45
B1690 ALL/VALS
  SOCIETY

ALLEGHENY COUNCIL TO IMPROVE OUR NEIGHBORHOODS....SEE
 ACTION

ALLEGHENY HOUSING REHABILITATION CORPORATION....SEE AHRCO

ALLEN R.L. B1788

ALLIANCE FOR PROGRESS....SEE ALL/PROG

ALLIANCES, MILITARY....SEE FORCES+INT/REL

ALLPORT G.W. B0078

ALMOND G.A. B0079

ALPANDER G.G. B0080

ALTO/ADIGE....ALTO-ADIGE REGION OF ITALY

AM/LEGION....AMERICAN LEGION

AMA....AMERICAN MEDICAL ASSOCIATION

AMBITION....SEE DRIVE

AMEND/I....CONCERNED WITH FREEDOMS GRANTED IN THE
 FIRST AMENDMENT

AMEND/IV....CONCERNED WITH FREEDOMS GRANTED IN THE
 FOURTH AMENDMENT

AMEND/V....CONCERNED WITH FREEDOMS GRANTED IN THE
 FIFTH AMENDMENT

AMEND/VI....CONCERNED WITH FREEDOMS GRANTED IN THE
 SIXTH AMENDMENT

AMEND/XIV....CONCERNED WITH FREEDOMS GRANTED IN THE
 FOURTEENTH AMENDMENT

AMER ENTERPRISE INST PUB POL B0081

AMERICAN BAR ASSOCIATION....SEE ABA

AMERICAN CIVIL LIBERTIES UNION....SEE ACLU

AMERICAN FARM BUREAU FEDERATION....SEE FARM/BUR

AMERICAN FEDERATION OF LABOR, CONGRESS OF INDUSTRIAL
 ORGANIZATIONS....SEE AFL/CIO, LABOR

AMERICAN INDIANS....SEE INDIAN/AM

AMERICAN LEGION....SEE AM/LEGION

AMERICAN POLITICAL SCIENCE ASSOCIATION....SEE APSA

AMERICAN TELEPHONE AND TELEGRAPH....SEE AT+T

AMERICAN ASSEMBLY COLUMBIA U B0082

AMERICAN ECONOMIC ASSOCIATION B0083

AMERICAN ECONOMIC REVIEW B0084

AMERICAN FRIENDS SERVICE COMM B0085

AMERICAN MANAGEMENT ASSN B0086

AMERICAN POLITICAL SCI ASSN B0087

AMERICAN SOCIETY PUBLIC ADMIN B0088,B0089

AMERICAS, PRE/EUROPEAN....SEE PRE/AMER

AMLUND C.A. B0090

AMMAN/MAX....MAX AMMAN

ANARCH....ANARCHISM; SEE ALSO ATTIT, VALUES INDEX

ANARCHISM....SEE ANARCH

ANCIENT EGYPT....SEE EGYPT/ANC

ANCIENT GREECE....SEE GREECE/ANC

ANDALUSIA....SEE ALSO SPAIN

ANDERSON C.W. B0091

ANDERSON D.L. B0092

ANDERSON J. B0093

ANDERSON L.G. B0094

ANDERSON M. B0095

ANDERSON S.V. B0096

ANDERSON T.J. B0097

ANDERSON W. B0098,B0099,B0100,B0101

ANDORRA....SEE ALSO APPROPRIATE TIME/SPACE/CULTURE INDEX

ANDREN N. B0102

ANDREWS K.R. B0103

ANDREWS W.G. B0104,B0105

ANDRIOT J.L. B0106,B0107

ANGEL D.D. B0108

ANGELL N. B0109

ANGELL R. B0110

ANGERS F.A. B0111

ANGLIN D. B0112

ANGLO/SAX....ANGLO-SAXON

ANGOLA....ANGOLA

ANNEXATION....ANNEXATION

ANOMIE....GENERALIZED PERSONAL ANXIETY; SEE DISPL

S51
COHEN M.B.,"PERSONALITY AS A FACTOR IN   PERSON
ADMINISTRATIVE DECISIONS." ADJUD PERS/REL ANOMIE   ADMIN
SUPEGO...OBS SELF/OBS INT. PAGE 22 B0446   PROB/SOLV
                                                    PSY
B54
LAPIERRE R.T.,A THEORY OF SOCIAL CONTROL. STRUCT   CONTROL
ADMIN ROUTINE SANCTION ANOMIE AUTHORIT DRIVE PERSON VOL/ASSN
PWR...MAJORIT CONCPT CLASSIF. PAGE 62 B1260   CULTURE
B58
WILENSKY H.L.,INDUSTRIAL SOCIETY AND SOCIAL   INDUS
WELFARE: IMPACT OF INDUSTRIALIZATION ON SUPPLY AND ECO/DEV
ORGANIZATION OF SOC WELF SERVICES. ELITES SOCIETY RECEIVE
STRATA SERV/IND FAM MUNIC PUB/INST CONSULT WORKER PROF/ORG
ADMIN AUTOMAT ANOMIE 20. PAGE 117 B2352
S58
MITCHELL W.C.,"OCCUPATIONAL ROLE STRAINS: THE   ANOMIE
AMERICAN ELECTIVE PUBLIC OFFICIAL." CONTROL   DRIVE
RIGID/FLEX SUPEGO HEALTH ORD/FREE...SOC INT QU.   ROUTINE
PAGE 74 B1492   PERSON
B63
COSTELLO T.W.,PSYCHOLOGY IN ADMINISTRATION: A   PSY
RESEARCH ORIENTATION. CREATE PROB/SOLV PERS/REL   MGT
ADJUST ANOMIE ATTIT DRIVE PERCEPT ROLE...DECISION EXEC
BIBLIOG T 20. PAGE 24 B0488   ADMIN
B66
DICKSON W.J.,COUNSELING IN AN ORGANIZATION: A   INDUS
SEQUEL TO THE HAWTHORNE RESEARCHES. CLIENT VOL/ASSN WORKER

B66
ACT/RES PROB/SOLV AUTOMAT ROUTINE PERS/REL   PSY
HAPPINESS ANOMIE ROLE...OBS CHARTS 20 AT+T. PAGE 29 MGT
B0588
B66
MCKENZIE J.L.,AUTHORITY IN THE CHURCH. STRUCT LEAD SECT
INGP/REL PERS/REL CENTRAL ANOMIE ATTIT ORD/FREE   AUTHORIT
RESPECT CATH. PAGE 72 B1452   PWR
                                                    ADMIN
B66
VON HOFFMAN N.,THE MULTIVERSITY; A PERSONAL REPORT EDU/PROP
ON WHAT HAPPENS TO TODAY'S STUDENTS AT AMERICAN   ACADEM
UNIVERSITIES. USA+45 SOCIETY ROUTINE ANOMIE ROLE   ATTIT
MORAL ORD/FREE SKILL...INT 20. PAGE 112 B2266   STRANGE

ANTARCTICA

ANTHOL....ANTHOLOGY, SYMPOSIUM, PANEL OF WRITERS

B05
RIORDAN W.L.,PLUNKITT OF TAMMANY HALL. USA-45   POL/PAR
SOCIETY PROB/SOLV EXEC LEAD TASK CHOOSE ALL/VALS   MUNIC
...RECORD ANTHOL 20 REFORMERS TAMMANY NEWYORK/C   CHIEF
PLUNKITT/G. PAGE 88 B1789   ATTIT
N19
FOLSOM M.B.,BETTER MANAGEMENT OF THE PUBLIC'S   ADMIN
BUSINESS (PAMPHLET). USA+45 NAT/G DELIB/GP PAY CONFER NAT/G
CONTROL REGION GP/REL...METH/COMP ANTHOL 20.   MGT
PAGE 36 B0733   PROB/SOLV
B38
SALTER J.T.,THE AMERICAN POLITICIAN. USA-45 LABOR BIOG
POL/PAR EDU/PROP ADMIN CHOOSE ATTIT DRIVE PERSON   LEAD
PWR...POLICY ANTHOL 20 THOMAS/N LEWIS/JL LAGUARD/F PROVS
GOVERNOR MAYOR. PAGE 92 B1865   LOC/G
B44
DAVIS H.E.,PIONEERS IN WORLD ORDER. WOR-45 CONSTN INT/ORG
ECO/TAC DOMIN EDU/PROP LEGIT ADJUD ADMIN ARMS/CONT ROUTINE
CHOOSE KNOWL ORD/FREE...POLICY JURID SOC STAT OBS
CENSUS TIME/SEQ ANTHOL LEAGUE/NAT 20. PAGE 26 B0537
B49
MCLEAN J.M.,THE PUBLIC SERVICE AND UNIVERSITY   ACADEM
EDUCATION. UK USA-45 DELIB/GP EX/STRUC TOP/EX ADMIN NAT/G
...GOV/COMP METH/COMP NAT/COMP ANTHOL 20. PAGE 72 EXEC
B1455   EDU/PROP
B53
MAJUMDAR B.B.,PROBLEMS OF PUBLIC ADMINISTRATION IN ECO/UNDEV
INDIA. INDIA INDUS PLAN BUDGET ADJUD CENTRAL DEMAND GOV/REL
WEALTH...WELF/ST ANTHOL 20 CIVIL/SERV. PAGE 68   ADMIN
B1384   MUNIC
B53
MILLIKAN M.F.,INCOME STABILIZATION FOR A DEVELOPING ANTHOL
DEMOCRACY. USA+45 ECO/DEV LABOR BUDGET ECO/TAC TAX MARKET
ADMIN ADJUST PRODUC WEALTH...POLICY TREND 20.   EQUILIB
PAGE 73 B1484   EFFICIENCY
B54
MCCLOSKEY J.F.,OPERATIONS RESEARCH FOR MANAGEMENT. OP/RES
STRUCT COMPUTER ADMIN ROUTINE...PHIL/SCI CONCPT   MGT
METH/CNCPT TREND ANTHOL BIBLIOG 20. PAGE 72 B1445 METH/COMP
                                                   TEC/DEV
C54
ROBSON W.A.,"GREAT CITIES OF THE WORLD: THEIR   LOC/G
GOVERNMENT, POLITICS, AND PLANNING." CONSTN FINAN MUNIC
EX/STRUC ADMIN EXEC CHOOSE GOV/REL...STAT TREND   PLAN
ANTHOL BIBLIOG 20. PAGE 89 B1806   PROB/SOLV
B55
BAILEY S.K.,RESEARCH FRONTIERS IN POLITICS AND   R+D
GOVERNMENT. CONSTN LEGIS ADMIN REV CHOOSE...CONCPT METH
IDEA/COMP GAME ANTHOL 20. PAGE 8 B0164   NAT/G
B56
CONAWAY O.B.,DEMOCRACY IN FEDERAL ADMINISTRATION   ADMIN
(PAMPHLET). USA+45 LEGIS PARTIC ATTIT...TREND   SERV/IND
ANTHOL 20. PAGE 23 B0459   NAT/G
                                                   GP/REL
B56
DEGRAS J.,THE COMMUNIST INTERNATIONAL, 1919-1943: COM
DOCUMENTS (3 VOLS.). EX/STRUC...ANTHOL BIBLIOG 20. DIPLOM
PAGE 28 B0569   POLICY
                                                   POL/PAR
B56
SOHN L.B.,BASIC DOCUMENTS OF THE UNITED NATIONS.   DELIB/GP
WOR+45 LAW INT/ORG LEGIT EXEC ROUTINE CHOOSE PWR   CONSTN
...JURID CONCPT GEN/LAWS ANTHOL UN TOT/POP OAS FAO
ILO 20. PAGE 99 B1993
B56
SOHN L.B.,CASES ON UNITED NATIONS LAW. STRUCT   INT/ORG
DELIB/GP WAR PEACE ORD/FREE...DECISION ANTHOL 20   INT/LAW
UN. PAGE 99 B1994   ADMIN
                                                   ADJUD
C56
NEUMANN S.,"MODERN POLITICAL PARTIES: APPROACHES TO POL/PAR
COMPARATIVE POLITIC. FRANCE UK EX/STRUC DOMIN ADMIN GOV/COMP
LEAD REPRESENT TOTALISM ATTIT...POLICY TREND   ELITES
METH/COMP ANTHOL BIBLIOG/A 20 CMN/WLTH. PAGE 78   MAJORIT
B1574
B57
CHICAGO U LAW SCHOOL,CONFERENCE ON JUDICIAL   CT/SYS
ADMINISTRATION. LOC/G MUNIC NAT/G PROVS...ANTHOL   ADJUD

20. PAGE 21 B0421   ADMIN
                                                     GOV/REL
                                                          B58
AMERICAN SOCIETY PUBLIC ADMIN,STRENGTHENING   ADMIN
MANAGEMENT FOR DEMOCRATIC GOVERNMENT. USA+45 ACADEM NAT/G
EX/STRUC WORKER PLAN BUDGET CONFER CT/SYS   EXEC
EFFICIENCY ANTHOL. PAGE 4 B0088   MGT
                                                          B58
ATOMIC INDUSTRIAL FORUM,MANAGEMENT AND ATOMIC   NUC/PWR
ENERGY. WOR+45 SEA LAW MARKET NAT/G TEC/DEV INSPECT INDUS
INT/TRADE CONFER PEACE HEALTH...ANTHOL 20. PAGE 7   MGT
B0145   ECO/TAC
                                                          B59
GINSBURG M.,LAW AND OPINION IN ENGLAND. UK CULTURE   JURID
KIN LABOR LEGIS EDU/PROP ADMIN CT/SYS CRIME OWN   POLICY
HEALTH...ANTHOL 20 ENGLSH/LAW. PAGE 40 B0802   ECO/TAC
                                                          B59
U OF MICHIGAN LAW SCHOOL,ATOMS AND THE LAW. USA+45   NUC/PWR
PROVS WORKER PROB/SOLV DIPLOM ADMIN GOV/REL ANTHOL. NAT/G
PAGE 106 B2142   CONTROL
                                                     LAW
                                                          B59
WARNER W.L.,INDUSTRIAL MAN. USA+45 USA-45 ELITES   EXEC
INDUS LABOR TOP/EX WORKER ADMIN INGP/REL PERS/REL   LEAD
...CHARTS ANTHOL 20. PAGE 114 B2294   PERSON
                                                     MGT
                                                          B60
JUNZ A.J., PRESENT TRENDS IN AMERICAN NATIONAL   POL/PAR
GOVERNMENT. LEGIS DIPLOM ADMIN CT/SYS ORD/FREE   CHOOSE
...CONCPT ANTHOL 20 CONGRESS PRESIDENT SUPREME/CT.   CONSTN
PAGE 2 B0048   NAT/G
                                                          B60
ARROW K.J.,MATHEMATICAL METHODS IN THE SOCIAL   MATH
SCIENCES, 1959. TEC/DEV CHOOSE UTIL PERCEPT   PSY
...KNO/TEST GAME SIMUL ANTHOL. PAGE 7 B0137   MGT
                                                          B60
BRISTOL L.H. JR.,DEVELOPING THE CORPORATE IMAGE.   LG/CO
USA+45 SOCIETY ECO/DEV COM/IND SCHOOL EDU/PROP   ATTIT
PRESS TV...AUD/VIS ANTHOL. PAGE 15 B0312   MGT
                                                     ECO/TAC
                                                          B60
PAGE T.,THE PUBLIC PERSONNEL AGENCY AND THE CHIEF   WORKER
EXECUTIVE (REPORT NO. 601). USA+45 LOC/G NAT/G   EXEC
GP/REL PERS/REL...ANTHOL 20. PAGE 80 B1624   ADMIN
                                                     MGT
                                                          B60
PENTONY D.E.,UNITED STATES FOREIGN AID. INDIA LAOS   FOR/AID
USA+45 ECO/UNDEV INT/TRADE ADMIN PEACE ATTIT   DIPLOM
...POLICY METH/COMP ANTHOL 20. PAGE 82 B1653   ECO/TAC
                                                          C60
SCHRAMM W.,"MASS COMMUNICATIONS: A BOOK OF READINGS COM/IND
(2ND ED.)" LG/CO PRESS ADMIN CONTROL ROUTINE ATTIT   EDU/PROP
ROLE SUPEGO...CHARTS ANTHOL BIBLIOG 20. PAGE 94   CROWD
B1902   MAJORIT
                                                          B61
BAINS J.S.,STUDIES IN POLITICAL SCIENCE. INDIA   DIPLOM
WOR+45 WOR-45 CONSTN BAL/PWR ADJUD ADMIN PARL/PROC   INT/LAW
SOVEREIGN...SOC METH/COMP ANTHOL 17/20 UN. PAGE 8   NAT/G
B0165
                                                          B61
PROCEEDINGS OF THE CONFERENCE ON BUSINESS GAMES AS   GAME
TEACHING DEVICES. PROB/SOLV ECO/TAC CONFER ADMIN   DECISION
TASK...MGT ANTHOL 20. PAGE 29 B0593   EDU/PROP
                                                     EFFICIENCY
                                                          B61
DUBIN R.,HUMAN RELATIONS IN ADMINISTRATION. USA+45   PERS/REL
INDUS LABOR LG/CO EX/STRUC GP/REL DRIVE PWR   MGT
...DECISION SOC CHARTS ANTHOL 20. PAGE 31 B0623   ADMIN
                                                     EXEC
                                                          B61
HAMILTON A.,THE FEDERALIST. USA-45 NAT/G VOL/ASSN   EX/STRUC
LEGIS TOP/EX EDU/PROP LEGIT CHOOSE ATTIT RIGID/FLEX CONSTN
ORD/FREE PWR...MAJORIT JURID CONCPT ANTHOL. PAGE 46
B0931
                                                          B61
INTL UNION LOCAL AUTHORITIES,LOCAL GOVERNMENT IN   LOC/G
THE USA. USA+45 PUB/INST DELIB/GP CONFER AUTOMAT   MUNIC
GP/REL POPULISM...ANTHOL 20 CITY/MGT. PAGE 54 B1101 ADMIN
                                                     GOV/REL
                                                          B61
KERTESZ S.D.,AMERICAN DIPLOMACY IN A NEW ERA. COM   ANTHOL
S/ASIA UK USA+45 FORCES PROB/SOLV BAL/PWR ECO/TAC   DIPLOM
ADMIN COLONIAL WAR PEACE ORD/FREE 20 NATO CONGRESS   TREND
UN COLD/WAR. PAGE 59 B1199
                                                          B61
NARASIMHAN V.K.,THE PRESS, THE PUBLIC AND THE   NAT/G
ADMINISTRATION (PAMPHLET). INDIA COM/IND CONTROL   ADMIN
REPRESENT GOV/REL EFFICIENCY...ANTHOL 20. PAGE 77   PRESS
B1554   NEW/LIB
                                                          B61
TANZER L.,THE KENNEDY CIRCLE. INTELL CONSULT   EX/STRUC
DELIB/GP TOP/EX CONTROL EXEC INGP/REL PERS/REL PWR   NAT/G
...BIOG IDEA/COMP ANTHOL 20 KENNEDY/JF PRESIDENT   CHIEF
DEMOCRAT MCNAMARA/R RUSK/D. PAGE 103 B2077
                                                          B62
HATTERY L.H.,INFORMATION RETRIEVAL MANAGEMENT.   R+D

CLIENT INDUS TOP/EX COMPUTER OP/RES TEC/DEV ROUTINE COMPUT/IR
COST EFFICIENCY RIGID/FLEX...METH/COMP ANTHOL 20.   MGT
PAGE 48 B0968   CREATE
                                                          B62
INAYATULLAH,BUREAUCRACY AND DEVELOPMENT IN   EX/STRUC
PAKISTAN. PAKISTAN ECO/UNDEV EDU/PROP CONFER   ADMIN
...ANTHOL DICTIONARY 20 BUREAUCRCY. PAGE 53 B1078   NAT/G
                                                     LOC/G
                                                          B62
KENNEDY J.F.,TO TURN THE TIDE. SPACE AGRI INT/ORG   DIPLOM
FORCES TEC/DEV ADMIN NUC/PWR PEACE WEALTH...ANTHOL   CHIEF
20 KENNEDY/JF CIV/RIGHTS. PAGE 59 B1193   POLICY
                                                     NAT/G
                                                          B62
KUHN T.E.,PUBLIC ENTERPRISES. PROJECT PLANNING AND   ECO/DEV
ECONOMIC DEVELOPMENT (PAMPHLET). ECO/UNDEV FINAN   ECO/TAC
PLAN ADMIN EFFICIENCY OWN...MGT STAT CHARTS ANTHOL   LG/CO
20. PAGE 61 B1240   NAT/G
                                                          B62
NJ DEPARTMENT CIVIL SERV,THE CIVIL SERVICE RULES OF ADMIN
THE STATE OF NEW JERSEY. USA+45 USA-45 PAY...JURID   PROVS
ANTHOL 20 CIVIL/SERV NEW/JERSEY. PAGE 78 B1585   ROUTINE
                                                     WORKER
                                                          L62
ERDMANN H.H.,"ADMINISTRATIVE LAW AND FARM   AGRI
ECONOMICS." USA+45 LOC/G NAT/G PLAN PROB/SOLV LOBBY ADMIN
...DECISION ANTHOL 20. PAGE 33 B0680   ADJUD
                                                     POLICY
                                                          B63
DALAND R.T.,PERSPECTIVES OF BRAZILIAN PUBLIC   ADMIN
ADMINISTRATION (VOL. I). BRAZIL LAW ECO/UNDEV   NAT/G
SCHOOL CHIEF TEC/DEV CONFER CONTROL GP/REL ATTIT   PLAN
ROLE...ANTHOL 20. PAGE 26 B0525   GOV/REL
                                                          B63
DE GUZMAN R.P.,PATTERNS IN DECISION-MAKING: CASE   ADMIN
STUDIES IN PHILIPPINE PUBLIC ADMINISTRATION.   DECISION
PHILIPPINE LAW CHIEF PROB/SOLV INGP/REL DRIVE   POLICY
PERCEPT ROLE...ANTHOL T 20. PAGE 27 B0557   GOV/REL
                                                          B63
DE VRIES E.,SOCIAL ASPECTS OF ECONOMIC DEVELOPMENT   L/A+17C
IN LATIN AMERICA. CULTURE SOCIETY STRATA FINAN   ECO/UNDEV
INDUS INT/ORG DELIB/GP ACT/RES ECO/TAC EDU/PROP
ADMIN ATTIT SUPEGO HEALTH KNOWL ORD/FREE...SOC STAT
TREND ANTHOL TOT/POP VAL/FREE. PAGE 28 B0562
                                                          B63
HANSON A.H.,NATIONALIZATION: A BOOK OF READINGS.   NAT/G
WOR+45 FINAN DELIB/GP LEGIS WORKER BUDGET ADMIN   OWN
GP/REL EFFICIENCY SOCISM...MGT ANTHOL. PAGE 46   INDUS
B0941   CONTROL
                                                          B63
HAUSMAN W.H.,MANAGING ECONOMIC DEVELOPMENT IN   ECO/UNDEV
AFRICA. AFR USA+45 LAW FINAN WORKER TEC/DEV WEALTH   PLAN
...ANTHOL 20. PAGE 48 B0970   FOR/AID
                                                     MGT
                                                          B63
HEYEL C.,THE ENCYCLOPEDIA OF MANAGEMENT. WOR+45   MGT
MARKET TOP/EX TEC/DEV AUTOMAT LEAD ADJUST...STAT   INDUS
CHARTS GAME ANTHOL BIBLIOG. PAGE 49 B1002   ADMIN
                                                     FINAN
                                                          B63
INDIAN INSTITUTE PUBLIC ADMIN,CASES IN INDIAN   DECISION
ADMINISTRATION. INDIA AGRI NAT/G PROB/SOLV TEC/DEV   PLAN
ECO/TAC ADMIN...ANTHOL METH 20. PAGE 53 B1083   MGT
                                                     ECO/UNDEV
                                                          B63
KAST F.E.,SCIENCE, TECHNOLOGY, AND MANAGEMENT.   MGT
SPACE USA+45 FORCES CONFER DETER NUC/PWR...PHIL/SCI PLAN
CHARTS ANTHOL BIBLIOG 20 NASA. PAGE 58 B1179   TEC/DEV
                                                     PROB/SOLV
                                                          B63
MENZEL J.M.,THE CHINESE CIVIL SERVICE: CAREER OPEN   ADMIN
TO TALENT? ASIA ROUTINE INGP/REL DISCRIM ATTIT ROLE NAT/G
KNOWL ANTHOL. PAGE 73 B1468   DECISION
                                                     ELITES
                                                          B63
ROBINSON K.,ESSAYS IN IMPERIAL GOVERNMENT. CAMEROON COLONIAL
NIGERIA UK CONSTN LOC/G LEGIS ADMIN GOV/REL PWR   AFR
...POLICY ANTHOL BIBLIOG 17/20 PURHAM/M. PAGE 89   DOMIN
B1803
                                                          B63
SHANKS M.,THE LESSONS OF PUBLIC ENTERPRISE. UK   SOCISM
LEGIS WORKER ECO/TAC ADMIN PARL/PROC GOV/REL ATTIT   OWN
...POLICY MGT METH/COMP NAT/COMP ANTHOL 20   NAT/G
PARLIAMENT. PAGE 96 B1931   INDUS
                                                          B63
SWEENEY S.B.,ACHIEVING EXCELLENCE IN PUBLIC   ADMIN
SERVICE. FUT USA+45 NAT/G ACT/RES GOV/REL...POLICY   WORKER
ANTHOL 20 CIVIL/SERV. PAGE 102 B2060   TASK
                                                     PLAN
                                                          B63
SWERDLOW I.,DEVELOPMENT ADMINISTRATION: CONCEPTS   ECO/UNDEV
AND PROBLEMS. WOR+45 CULTURE SOCIETY STRATA   ADMIN
DELIB/GP EX/STRUC ACT/RES PLAN ECO/TAC DOMIN LEGIT
ATTIT RIGID/FLEX SUPEGO HEALTH PWR...MGT CONCPT
ANTHOL VAL/FREE. PAGE 102 B2062

B63

WEINER M.,POLITICAL CHANGE IN SOUTH ASIA. CEYLON   NAT/G
INDIA PAKISTAN S/ASIA CULTURE ELITES ECO/UNDEV   CONSTN
EX/STRUC ADMIN CONTROL CHOOSE CONSERVE...GOV/COMP   TEC/DEV
ANTHOL 20. PAGE 115 B2315

B64

CHANDLER A.D. JR.,GIANT ENTERPRISE: FORD, GENERAL   LG/CO
MOTORS, AND THE AUTOMOBILE INDUSTRY; SOURCES AND   DIST/IND
READINGS. USA+45 USA-45 FINAN MARKET CREATE ADMIN   LABOR
...TIME/SEQ ANTHOL 20 AUTOMOBILE. PAGE 20 B0404   MGT

B64

COX R.,THEORY IN MARKETING. FUT USA+45 SOCIETY   MARKET
ECO/DEV PROB/SOLV PRICE RISK PRODUC ATTIT...ANTHOL ECO/TAC
20. PAGE 24 B0499   PHIL/SCI
                                                    MGT

B64

GOLDWIN R.A.,POLITICAL PARTIES, USA. USA+45 USA-45 POL/PAR
LOC/G ADMIN LEAD EFFICIENCY ATTIT PWR...POLICY STAT PARTIC
ANTHOL 18/20 CONGRESS. PAGE 40 B0818   NAT/G
                                                    CONSTN

B64

HAMBRIDGE G.,DYNAMICS OF DEVELOPMENT. AGRI FINAN   ECO/UNDEV
INDUS LABOR INT/TRADE EDU/PROP ADMIN LEAD OWN   ECO/TAC
HEALTH...ANTHOL BIBLIOG 20. PAGE 46 B0930   OP/RES
                                                    ACT/RES

B64

HERSKOVITS M.J.,ECONOMIC TRANSITION IN AFRICA. FUT AFR
INT/ORG NAT/G WORKER PROB/SOLV TEC/DEV INT/TRADE   ECO/UNDEV
EQUILIB INCOME...ANTHOL 20. PAGE 49 B0996   PLAN
                                                    ADMIN

B64

INST D'ETUDE POL L'U GRENOBLE,ADMINISTRATION   ADMIN
TRADITIONELLE ET PLANIFICATION REGIONALE. FRANCE   MUNIC
LAW POL/PAR PROB/SOLV ADJUST RIGID/FLEX...CHARTS   PLAN
ANTHOL BIBLIOG T 20 REFORMERS. PAGE 54 B1087   CREATE

B64

JACKSON H.M.,THE SECRETARY OF STATE AND THE   GOV/REL
AMBASSADOR* JACKSON SUBCOMMITTEE PAPERS ON THE   DIPLOM
CONDUCT OF AMERICAN FOREIGN POLICY. USA+45 NAT/G   ADMIN
FORCES ACT/RES OP/RES EDU/PROP CENTRAL EFFICIENCY   EX/STRUC
ORD/FREE...OBS RECORD ANTHOL CONGRESS PRESIDENT.
PAGE 55 B1107

B64

PLISCHKE E.,SYSTEMS OF INTEGRATING THE   INT/ORG
INTERNATIONAL COMMUNITY. WOR+45 NAT/G VOL/ASSN   EX/STRUC
ECO/TAC LEGIT PWR WEALTH...TIME/SEQ ANTHOL UN   REGION
TOT/POP 20. PAGE 83 B1684

B64

US SENATE COMM GOVT OPERATIONS,THE SECRETARY OF   DIPLOM
STATE AND THE AMBASSADOR. USA+45 CHIEF CONSULT   DELIB/GP
EX/STRUC FORCES PLAN ADMIN EXEC INGP/REL ROLE   NAT/G
...ANTHOL 20 PRESIDENT DEPT/STATE. PAGE 110 B2215

B65

AIYAR S.P.,STUDIES IN INDIAN DEMOCRACY. INDIA   ORD/FREE
STRATA ECO/UNDEV LABOR POL/PAR LEGIS DIPLOM LOBBY   REPRESENT
REGION CHOOSE ATTIT SOCISM...ANTHOL 20. PAGE 3   ADMIN
B0067   NAT/G

B65

BARISH N.N.,MANAGEMENT SCIENCES IN THE EMERGING   ECO/UNDEV
COUNTRIES. AFR CHINA/COM WOR+45 FINAN INDUS PLAN   OP/RES
PRODUC HABITAT...ANTHOL 20. PAGE 9 B0184   MGT
                                                    TEC/DEV

B65

BARNETT V.M. JR.,THE REPRESENTATION OF THE UNITED   USA+45
STATES ABROAD* REVISED EDITION. ECO/UNDEV ACADEM   DIPLOM
INT/ORG FORCES ACT/RES CREATE OP/RES FOR/AID REGION ADMIN
CENTRAL...CLASSIF ANTHOL. PAGE 9 B0189

B65

BERNDT R.M.,ABORIGINAL MAN IN AUSTRALIA. LAW DOMIN SOC
ADMIN COLONIAL MARRIAGE HABITAT ORD/FREE...LING   CULTURE
CHARTS ANTHOL BIBLIOG WORSHIP 20 AUSTRAL ABORIGINES SOCIETY
MUSIC ELKIN/AP. PAGE 11 B0225   STRUCT

B65

BOCK E.,GOVERNMENT REGULATION OF BUSINESS. USA+45   MGT
LAW EX/STRUC LEGIS EXEC ORD/FREE PWR...ANTHOL   ADMIN
CONGRESS. PAGE 13 B0261   NAT/G
                                                    CONTROL

B65

EVERETT R.O.,URBAN PROBLEMS AND PROSPECTS. USA+45   MUNIC
CREATE TEC/DEV EDU/PROP ADJUD ADMIN GOV/REL ATTIT   PLAN
...ANTHOL 20 URBAN/RNWL. PAGE 34 B0691   PROB/SOLV
                                                    NEIGH

B65

FRIEDMAN L.,SOUTHERN JUSTICE. USA+45 PUB/INST LEGIT ADJUD
ADMIN CT/SYS DISCRIM...DECISION ANTHOL 20 NEGRO   LAW
SOUTH/US CIV/RIGHTS. PAGE 37 B0758   CONSTN
                                                    RACE/REL

B65

LEYS C.T.,FEDERATION IN EAST AFRICA. LAW AGRI   FEDERAL
DIST/IND FINAN INT/ORG LABOR INT/TRADE CONFER ADMIN REGION
CONTROL GP/REL...ANTHOL 20 AFRICA/E. PAGE 65 B1310 ECO/UNDEV
                                                    PLAN

B65

MEISEL J.H.,PARETO & MOSCA. ITALY STRUCT ADMIN   PWR
...SOC CON/ANAL ANTHOL BIBLIOG 19/20. PAGE 72 B1463 ELITES
                                                    CONTROL

LAISSEZ
B65

PENNICK JL J.R.,THE POLITICS OF AMERICAN SCIENCE,   POLICY
1939 TO THE PRESENT. USA+45 USA-45 INTELL TEC/DEV   ADMIN
DIPLOM NEW/LIB...ANTHOL 20 COLD/WAR. PAGE 82 B1651 PHIL/SCI
                                                    NAT/G

B65

REISS A.J. JR.,SCHOOLS IN A CHANGING SOCIETY.   SCHOOL
CULTURE PROB/SOLV INSPECT DOMIN CONFER INGP/REL   EX/STRUC
RACE/REL AGE/C AGE/Y ALL/VALS...ANTHOL SOC/INTEG 20 ADJUST
NEWYORK/C. PAGE 87 B1766   ADMIN

B65

ROWAT D.C.,THE OMBUDSMAN: CITIZEN'S DEFENDER.   INSPECT
DENMARK FINLAND NEW/ZEALND NORWAY SWEDEN CONSULT   CONSTN
PROB/SOLV FEEDBACK PARTIC GP/REL...SOC CONCPT   NAT/G
NEW/IDEA METH/COMP ANTHOL BIBLIOG 20. PAGE 91 B1840 ADMIN

B65

RUBINSTEIN A.Z.,THE CHALLENGE OF POLITICS: IDEAS   NAT/G
AND ISSUES (2ND ED.). UNIV ELITES SOCIETY EX/STRUC DIPLOM
BAL/PWR PARL/PROC AUTHORIT...DECISION ANTHOL 20.   GP/REL
PAGE 92 B1852   ORD/FREE

B65

SINGER J.D.,HUMAN BEHAVIOR AND INTERNATINAL   DIPLOM
POLITICS* CONTRIBUTIONS FROM THE SOCIAL-   PHIL/SCI
PSYCHOLOGICAL SCIENCES. ACT/RES PLAN EDU/PROP ADMIN QUANT
KNOWL...DECISION PSY SOC NET/THEORY HYPO/EXP   SIMUL
LAB/EXP SOC/EXP GEN/METH ANTHOL BIBLIOG. PAGE 97
B1965

B65

STARR M.K.,EXECUTIVE READINGS IN MANAGEMENT   MGT
SCIENCE. TOP/EX WORKER EDU/PROP ADMIN...DECISION   EX/STRUC
GEN/LAWS ANTHOL METH T 20. PAGE 100 B2023   PLAN
                                                    LG/CO

B66

BALDWIN D.A.,FOREIGN AID AND AMERICAN FOREIGN   FOR/AID
POLICY; A DOCUMENTARY ANALYSIS. USA+45 ECO/UNDEV   DIPLOM
ADMIN...ECOMETRIC STAT STYLE CHARTS PROG/TEAC   IDEA/COMP
GEN/LAWS ANTHOL. PAGE 8 B0172

B66

BIRKHEAD G.S.,ADMINISTRATIVE PROBLEMS IN PAKISTAN. ADMIN
PAKISTAN AGRI FINAN INDUS LG/CO ECO/TAC CONTROL PWR NAT/G
...CHARTS ANTHOL 20. PAGE 12 B0241   ORD/FREE
                                                    ECO/UNDEV

B66

BOYD H.W.,MARKETING MANAGEMENT: CASES FROM EMERGING MGT
COUNTRIES. BRAZIL GHANA ISRAEL WOR+45 ADMIN   ECO/UNDEV
PERS/REL ATTIT HABITAT WEALTH...ANTHOL 20 ARGEN   PROB/SOLV
CASEBOOK. PAGE 14 B0292   MARKET

B66

BURNS A.C.,PARLIAMENT AS AN EXPORT. WOR+45 CONSTN   PARL/PROC
BARGAIN DEBATE ROUTINE GOV/REL EFFICIENCY...ANTHOL POL/PAR
COMMONWLTH PARLIAMENT. PAGE 17 B0353   CT/SYS
                                                    CHIEF

B66

COOK P.W. JR.,PROBLEMS OF CORPORATE POWER. WOR+45   ADMIN
FINAN INDUS BARGAIN GP/REL...MGT ANTHOL. PAGE 23   LG/CO
B0471   PWR
                                                    ECO/TAC

B66

DAVIS J.A.,SOUTHERN AFRICA IN TRANSITION. SOUTH/AFR AFR
USA+45 NAT/G DELIB/GP EDU/PROP ADMIN COLONIAL   ADJUST
REGION RACE/REL ATTIT SOVEREIGN...ANTHOL 20   CONSTN
RESOURCE/N. PAGE 26 B0538

B66

FISK E.K.,NEW GUINEA ON THE THRESHOLD; ASPECTS OF   ECO/UNDEV
SOCIAL, POLITICAL, AND ECONOMIC DEVELOPMENT. AGRI   SOCIETY
NAT/G INT/TRADE ADMIN ADJUST LITERACY ROLE...CHARTS
ANTHOL 20 NEW/GUINEA. PAGE 36 B0726

B66

HAWLEY C.E.,ADMINISTRATIVE QUESTIONS AND POLITICAL ADMIN
ANSWERS. USA+45 STRUCT WORKER EDU/PROP...GP/COMP   GEN/LAWS
ANTHOL 20. PAGE 48 B0973   GP/REL

B66

MACFARQUHAR R.,CHINA UNDER MAO: POLITICS TAKES   ECO/UNDEV
COMMAND. CHINA/COM COM AGRI INDUS CHIEF FORCES   TEC/DEV
DIPLOM INT/TRADE EDU/PROP TASK REV ADJUST...ANTHOL ECO/TAC
20 MAO. PAGE 67 B1359   ADMIN

B66

MONTGOMERY J.D.,APPROACHES TO DEVELOPMENT: ECO/UNDEV
POLITICS, ADMINISTRATION AND CHANGE. USA+45 AGRI   ADMIN
FOR/AID ORD/FREE...CONCPT IDEA/COMP METH/COMP   POLICY
ANTHOL. PAGE 75 B1507   ECO/TAC

B66

SCHMIDT K.M.,AMERICAN STATE AND LOCAL GOVERNMENT IN PROVS
ACTION. USA+45 CONSTN LOC/G POL/PAR CHIEF LEGIS   ADMIN
PROB/SOLV ADJUD LOBBY GOV/REL...DECISION ANTHOL 20 MUNIC
GOVERNOR MAYOR URBAN/RNWL. PAGE 94 B1896   PLAN

B66

SEASHOLES B.,VOTING, INTEREST GROUPS, AND PARTIES. CHOOSE
USA+45 FINAN LOC/G NAT/G ADMIN LEAD GP/REL INGP/REL POL/PAR
ROLE...CHARTS ANTHOL 20. PAGE 95 B1922   LOBBY
                                                    PARTIC

B66

SILBERMAN B.S.,MODERN JAPANESE LEADERSHIP;   LEAD
TRANSITION AND CHANGE. NAT/G POL/PAR CHIEF ADMIN   CULTURE
REPRESENT GP/REL ADJUST RIGID/FLEX...SOC METH/COMP ELITES

ANTHOL 19/20 CHINJAP CHRISTIAN. PAGE 97 B1952   MUNIC

B66
SMITH H.E.,READINGS IN ECONOMIC DEVELOPMENT AND   TEC/DEV
ADMINISTRATION IN TANZANIA. TANZANIA FINAN INDUS   ADMIN
LABOR NAT/G PLAN PROB/SOLV INT/TRADE COLONIAL   GOV/REL
REGION...ANTHOL BIBLIOG 20 AFRICA/E. PAGE 98 B1981

B66
WADIA M.,THE NATURE AND SCOPE OF MANAGEMENT.   MGT
DELIB/GP EX/STRUC CREATE AUTOMAT CONTROL EFFICIENCY   PROB/SOLV
...ANTHOL 20. PAGE 112 B2271   IDEA/COMP
ECO/TAC

B67
CROTTY W.J.,APPROACHES TO THE STUDY OF PARTY   POL/PAR
ORGANIZATION. USA+45 SOCIETY GP/REL...ANTHOL 20.   STRUCT
PAGE 25 B0509   GEN/LAWS
ADMIN

B67
DUN J.L.,THE ESSENCE OF CHINESE CIVILIZATION. ASIA   CULTURE
FAM NAT/G TEC/DEV ADMIN SANCTION WAR HABITAT   SOCIETY
...ANTHOL WORSHIP. PAGE 31 B0630

B67
FARRIS M.T.,MODERN TRANSPORTATION: SELECTED   DIST/IND
READINGS. UNIV CONTROL...POLICY ANTHOL T 20.   MGT
PAGE 35 B0706   COST

B67
GIFFORD P.,BRITAIN AND GERMANY IN AFRICA. AFR   COLONIAL
GERMANY UK ECO/UNDEV LEAD WAR NAT/LISM ATTIT   ADMIN
...POLICY HIST/WRIT METH/COMP ANTHOL BIBLIOG 19/20   DIPLOM
WWI. PAGE 39 B0797   NAT/COMP

B67
PAULSEN F.R.,AMERICAN EDUCATION: CHALLENGES AND   EDU/PROP
IMAGES. FUT USA+45 ADMIN AGE/C AGE/Y SUPEGO HEALTH   SCHOOL
...ANTHOL 20. PAGE 81 B1644   ORD/FREE
GOV/REL

B67
WARREN S.,THE AMERICAN PRESIDENT. POL/PAR FORCES   CHIEF
LEGIS DIPLOM ECO/TAC ADMIN EXEC PWR...ANTHOL 18/20   LEAD
ROOSEVLT/F KENNEDY/JF JOHNSON/LB TRUMAN/HS   NAT/G
WILSON/W. PAGE 114 B2297   CONSTN

B67
WATERS M.,THE UNITED NATIONS* INTERNATIONAL   CONSTN
ORGANIZATION AND ADMINISTRATION. WOR+45 EX/STRUC   INT/ORG
FORCES DIPLOM LEAD REGION ARMS/CONT REPRESENT   ADMIN
INGP/REL ROLE...METH/COMP ANTHOL 20 UN LEAGUE/NAT.   ADJUD
PAGE 114 B2301

B67
ZELERMYER W.,BUSINESS LAW: NEW PERSPECTIVES IN   LABOR
BUSINESS ECONOMICS. USA+45 LAW INDUS DELIB/GP   CAP/ISM
...JURID MGT ANTHOL BIBLIOG 20 NLRB. PAGE 119 B2400 LG/CO

ANTHON C.G. B0113

ANTHONY R.N. B0114

ANTHROPOLOGY, CULTURAL....SEE SOC

ANTHROPOLOGY, PSYCHOLOGICAL....SEE PSY

ANTI/SEMIT....ANTI-SEMITISM; SEE ALSO JEWS, GP/REL

ANTIBALLISTIC MISSILE DEFENSE SYSTEMS....SEE ABM/DEFSYS

ANTI-SEMITISM....SEE JEWS, GP/REL, ANTI/SEMIT

ANTI-TRUST ACTIONS....SEE MONOPOLY, INDUS, CONTROL

ANXIETY....SEE ANOMIE

APACHE....APACHE INDIANS

APARTHEID....APARTHEID

APPALACHIA

APPELLATE COURT SYSTEM....SEE CT/APPEALS, CT/SYS

APPLEBY P.H. B0115,B0116,B0117,B0118,B0119

APPORT....DELINEATION OF LEGISLATIVE DISTRICTS

N19
OPERATIONS AND POLICY RESEARCH,PERU ELECTION   CHOOSE
MEMORANDA (PAMPHLET). L/A+17C PERU POL/PAR LEGIS   CONSTN
EXEC APPORT REPRESENT 20. PAGE 80 B1611   SUFF
NAT/G

B32
MCKISACK M.,THE PARLIAMENTARY REPRESENTATION OF THE NAT/G
ENGLISH BOROUGHS DURING THE MIDDLE AGES. UK CONSTN   MUNIC
CULTURE ELITES EX/STRUC TAX PAY ADJUD PARL/PROC   LEGIS
APPORT FEDERAL...POLICY 13/15 PARLIAMENT. PAGE 72   CHOOSE
B1454

B48
STOKES W.S.,BIBLIOGRAPHY OF STANDARD AND CLASSICAL BIBLIOG
WORKS IN THE FIELDS OF AMERICAN POLITICAL SCIENCE. NAT/G
USA+45 USA-45 POL/PAR PROVS FORCES DIPLOM ADMIN   LOC/G
CT/SYS APPORT 20 CONGRESS PRESIDENT. PAGE 101 B2043 CONSTN

B52
LEGISLATIVE REFERENCE SERVICE,PROBLEMS OF   BIBLIOG
LEGISLATIVE APPORTIONMENT ON BOTH FEDERAL AND STATE REPRESENT
LEVELS: SELECTED REFERENCES (PAMPHLET). USA+45   CHOOSE
USA-45 LOC/G NAT/G LEGIS WRITING ADMIN APPORT 20   PROVS
CONGRESS. PAGE 63 B1282

C54
ZELLER B.,"AMERICAN STATE LEGISLATURES: REPORT ON REPRESENT
THE COMMITTEE ON AMERICAN LEGISLATURES." CONSTN   LEGIS
POL/PAR EX/STRUC CONFER ADMIN CONTROL EXEC LOBBY   PROVS
ROUTINE GOV/REL...POLICY BIBLIOG 20. PAGE 119 B2401 APPORT

B57
KNEIER C.M.,CITY GOVERNMENT IN THE UNITED STATES   MUNIC
(3RD ED.). USA-45 FINAN NAT/G POL/PAR LEGIS   LOC/G
EDU/PROP LEAD APPORT REPRESENT ATTIT...MGT 20   ADMIN
CITY/MGT. PAGE 60 B1219   GOV/REL

B59
COUNCIL OF STATE GOVERNORS,AMERICAN LEGISLATURES: LEGIS
STRUCTURE AND PROCEDURES. SUMMARY AND TABULATIONS CHARTS
OF A 1959 SURVEY. PUERT/RICO USA+45 PAY ADJUD ADMIN PROVS
APPORT...IDEA/COMP 20 GUAM VIRGIN/ISL. PAGE 24   REPRESENT
B0495

B66
FINK M.,A SELECTIVE BIBLIOGRAPHY ON STATE   BIBLIOG
CONSTITUTIONAL REVISION (PAMPHLET). USA+45 FINAN   PROVS
EX/STRUC LEGIS EDU/PROP ADMIN CT/SYS APPORT CHOOSE LOC/G
GOV/REL 20. PAGE 35 B0720   CONSTN

B66
RICHARD J.B.,GOVERNMENT AND POLITICS OF WYOMING.   PROVS
USA+45 POL/PAR EX/STRUC LEGIS CT/SYS LOBBY APPORT   LOC/G
CHOOSE REPRESENT 20 WYOMING GOVERNOR. PAGE 88 B1773 ADMIN

B67
BUREAU GOVERNMENT RES AND SERV,COUNTY GOVERNMENT   BIBLIOG/A
REORGANIZATION - A SELECTED ANNOTATED BIBLIOGRAPHY APPORT
(PAPER). USA+45 USA-45 LAW CONSTN MUNIC PROVS   LOC/G
EX/STRUC CREATE PLAN PROB/SOLV REPRESENT GOV/REL   ADMIN
20. PAGE 17 B0349

L67
"A PROPOS DES INCITATIONS FINANCIERES AUX   LOC/G
GROUPEMENTS DES COMMUNES: ESSAI D'INTERPRETATION." ECO/TAC
FRANCE NAT/G LEGIS ADMIN GOV/REL CENTRAL 20. PAGE 2 APPORT
B0046   ADJUD

APRA....ALIANZA POPULAR REVOLUCIONARIA AMERICANA, A PERUVIAN
POLITICAL PARTY

APSA....AMERICAN POLITICAL SCIENCE ASSOCIATION

APT/TEST....APTITUDE TESTS

B45
BENJAMIN H.C.,EMPLOYMENT TESTS IN INDUSTRY AND   BIBLIOG/A
BUSINESS. LG/CO WORKER ROUTINE...MGT PSY SOC   METH
CLASSIF PROBABIL STAT APT/TEST KNO/TEST PERS/TEST   TESTS
20. PAGE 10 B0211   INDUS

B62
CHICAGO U CTR PROG GOVT ADMIN,EDUCATION FOR   EDU/PROP
INNOVATIVE BEHAVIOR IN EXECUTIVES. UNIV ELITES   CREATE
ADMIN EFFICIENCY DRIVE PERSON...MGT APT/TEST   EXEC
PERS/TEST CHARTS LAB/EXP BIBLIOG 20. PAGE 21 B0420 STAT

APTER D.E. B0120,B0121,B0122

APTITUDE TESTS....SEE APT/TEST

AQUINAS/T....SAINT THOMAS AQUINAS

ARA....AREA REDEVELOPMENT ACT

ARABIA/SOU....SOUTH ARABIA

ARABS....ARAB WORLD, INCLUDING ITS CULTURE

B63
BADI J.,THE GOVERNMENT OF THE STATE OF ISRAEL: A   NAT/G
CRITICAL ACCOUNT OF ITS PARLIAMENT, EXECUTIVE, AND CONSTN
JUDICIARY. ISRAEL ECO/DEV CHIEF DELIB/GP LEGIS   EX/STRUC
DIPLOM CT/SYS INGP/REL PEACE ORD/FREE...BIBLIOG 20 POL/PAR
PARLIAMENT ARABS MIGRATION. PAGE 8 B0157

ARASTEH R. B0123

ARBITRATION....SEE DELIB/GP, CONSULT, AND FUNCTIONAL GROUP
CONCERNED (E.G., LABOR)

ARCIENEGAS G. B0124

ARCO EDITORIAL BOARD B0125

AREA STUDIES....SEE NAT/COMP

ARGAL R. B0126

ARGENTINA....SEE ALSO L/A&17C

B41

CHILDS J.B.,A GUIDE TO THE OFFICIAL PUBLICATIONS OF NAT/G
THE OTHER AMERICAN REPUBLICS: ARGENTINA. CHIEF   EX/STRUC
DIPLOM GOV/REL...BIBLIOG 18/19 ARGEN. PAGE 21 B0422 METH/CNCPT
                                                    LEGIS

B62

FORD A.G.,THE GOLD STANDARD 1880-1914: BRITAIN AND FINAN
ARGENTINA. UK ECO/UNDEV INT/TRADE ADMIN GOV/REL   ECO/TAC
DEMAND EFFICIENCY...STAT CHARTS 19/20 ARGEN   BUDGET
GOLD/STAND. PAGE 36 B0737   BAL/PAY

B62

LYNCH J.,ADMINISTRATION COLONIAL ESPANOLA   COLONIAL
1782-1810. SPAIN PROVS TOP/EX PARTIC 18/19 ARGEN.   CONTROL
PAGE 67 B1349   ADJUD
                                                    ADMIN

B66

BOYD H.W.,MARKETING MANAGEMENT: CASES FROM EMERGING MGT
COUNTRIES. BRAZIL GHANA ISRAEL WOR+45 ADMIN   ECO/UNDEV
PERS/REL ATTIT HABITAT WEALTH...ANTHOL 20 ARGEN   PROB/SOLV
CASEBOOK. PAGE 14 B0292   MARKET

ARGYRIS C. B0127,B0128,B0129,B0130,B0131,B0132

ARISTOCRATIC....SEE TRADIT, STRATA, ELITES

ARISTOTLE....ARISTOTLE

B60

GRUNDLICH T.,DIE TECHNIK DER DIKTATUR. ADMIN   COERCE
TOTALISM ATTIT PWR...MGT CONCPT ARISTOTLE. PAGE 44 DOMIN
B0896   ORD/FREE
                                                    WAR

ARIZONA....ARIZONA

B64

RIGGS R.E.,THE MOVEMENT FOR ADMINISTRATIVE   ADMIN
REORGANIZATION IN ARIZONA. USA+45 LAW POL/PAR   PROVS
DELIB/GP LEGIS PROB/SOLV CONTROL RIGID/FLEX PWR   CREATE
...ORG/CHARTS 20 ARIZONA DEMOCRAT REPUBLICAN.   PLAN
PAGE 88 B1786

ARKANSAS....ARKANSAS

ARMED FORCES....SEE FORCES

ARMS CONTROL....SEE ARMS/CONT, ACD

ARMS CONTROL AND DISARMAMENT AGENCY (U.S.)....SEE ACD

ARMS/CONT....ARMS CONTROL, DISARMAMENT

B44

DAVIS H.E.,PIONEERS IN WORLD ORDER. WOR-45 CONSTN   INT/ORG
ECO/TAC DOMIN EDU/PROP LEGIT ADJUD ADMIN ARMS/CONT ROUTINE
CHOOSE KNOWL ORD/FREE...POLICY JURID SOC STAT OBS
CENSUS TIME/SEQ ANTHOL LEAGUE/NAT 20. PAGE 26 B0537

B54

US SENATE COMM ON FOREIGN REL,REVIEW OF THE UNITED BIBLIOG
NATIONS CHARTER: A COLLECTION OF DOCUMENTS. LEGIS   CONSTN
DIPLOM ADMIN ARMS/CONT WAR REPRESENT SOVEREIGN   INT/ORG
...INT/LAW 20 UN. PAGE 110 B2220   DEBATE

B58

CONSERVATIVE POLITICAL CENTRE,A WORLD SECURITY   ORD/FREE
AUTHORITY? WOR+45 CONSTN ELITES FINAN DELIB/GP PLAN CONSERVE
PROB/SOLV ADMIN CONTROL NUC/PWR GP/REL...IDEA/COMP FORCES
20. PAGE 23 B0468   ARMS/CONT

B58

HENKIN L.,ARMS CONTROL AND INSPECTION IN AMERICAN   USA+45
LAW. LAW CONSTN INT/ORG LOC/G MUNIC NAT/G PROVS   JURID
EDU/PROP LEGIT EXEC NUC/PWR KNOWL ORD/FREE...OBS   ARMS/CONT
TOT/POP CONGRESS 20. PAGE 49 B0990

S59

LASSWELL H.D.,"UNIVERSALITY IN PERSPECTIVE." FUT   INT/ORG
UNIV SOCIETY CONSULT TOP/EX PLAN EDU/PROP ADJUD   JURID
ROUTINE ARMS/CONT COERCE PEACE ATTIT PERSON   TOTALISM
ALL/VALS. PAGE 63 B1271

B60

MORISON E.E.,TURMOIL AND TRADITION: A STUDY OF THE BIOG
LIFE AND TIMES OF HENRY L. STIMSON. USA+45 USA-45   NAT/G
POL/PAR CHIEF DELIB/GP FORCES BAL/PWR DIPLOM   EX/STRUC
ARMS/CONT WAR PEACE 19/20 STIMSON/HL ROOSEVLT/F
TAFT/WH HOOVER/H REPUBLICAN. PAGE 75 B1525

L60

BRENNAN D.G.,"SETTING AND GOALS OF ARMS CONTROL."   FORCES
FUT USA+45 USSR WOR+45 INTELL INT/ORG NAT/G   COERCE
VOL/ASSN CONSULT PLAN DIPLOM ECO/TAC ADMIN KNOWL   ARMS/CONT
PWR...POLICY CONCPT TREND COLD/WAR 20. PAGE 15   DETER
B0305

B61

STONE J.,QUEST FOR SURVIVAL. WOR+45 NAT/G VOL/ASSN INT/ORG
LEGIT ADMIN ARMS/CONT COERCE DISPL ORD/FREE PWR   ADJUD
...POLICY INT/LAW JURID COLD/WAR 20. PAGE 101 B2047 SOVEREIGN

S61

CARLETON W.G.,"AMERICAN FOREIGN POLICY: MYTHS AND   PLAN
REALITIES." FUT USA+45 WOR+45 ECO/UNDEV INT/ORG   MYTH
EX/STRUC ARMS/CONT NUC/PWR WAR ATTIT...POLICY   DIPLOM
CONCPT CONT/OBS GEN/METH COLD/WAR TOT/POP 20.
PAGE 19 B0378

S62

MARTIN L.W.,"POLITICAL SETTLEMENTS AND ARMS   CONCPT
CONTROL." COM EUR+WWI GERMANY USA+45 PROVS FORCES   ARMS/CONT
TOP/EX ACT/RES CREATE DOMIN LEGIT ROUTINE COERCE
ATTIT RIGID/FLEX ORD/FREE PWR...METH/CNCPT RECORD
GEN/LAWS 20. PAGE 70 B1410

B63

BOISSIER P.,HISTORIE DU COMITE INTERNATIONAL DE LA INT/ORG
CROIX ROUGE. MOD/EUR WOR-45 CONSULT FORCES PLAN   HEALTH
DIPLOM EDU/PROP ADMIN MORAL ORD/FREE...SOC CONCPT   ARMS/CONT
RECORD TIME/SEQ GEN/LAWS TOT/POP VAL/FREE 19/20.   WAR
PAGE 13 B0267

B63

STEVENSON A.E.,LOOKING OUTWARD: YEARS OF CRISIS AT INT/ORG
THE UNITED NATIONS. COM CUBA USA+45 WOR+45 SOCIETY CONCPT
NAT/G EX/STRUC ACT/RES LEGIT COLONIAL ATTIT PERSON ARMS/CONT
SUPEGO ALL/VALS...POLICY HUM UN COLD/WAR CONGO 20.
PAGE 100 B2034

B63

VAN SLYCK P.,PEACE: THE CONTROL OF NATIONAL POWER. ARMS/CONT
CUBA WOR+45 FINAN NAT/G FORCES PROB/SOLV TEC/DEV   PEACE
BAL/PWR ADMIN CONTROL ORD/FREE...POLICY INT/LAW UN INT/ORG
COLD/WAR TREATY. PAGE 112 B2253   DIPLOM

S63

BECHHOEFER B.G.,"UNITED NATIONS PROCEDURES IN CASE INT/ORG
OF VIOLATIONS OF DISARMAMENT AGREEMENTS." COM   DELIB/GP
USA+45 USSR LAW CONSTN NAT/G EX/STRUC FORCES LEGIS
BAL/PWR EDU/PROP CT/SYS ARMS/CONT ORD/FREE PWR
...POLICY STERTYP UN VAL/FREE 20. PAGE 10 B0204

S63

MORGENTHAU H.J.,"THE POLITICAL CONDITIONS FOR AN   INT/ORG
INTERNATIONAL POLICE FORCE." FUT WOR+45 CREATE   FORCES
LEGIT ADMIN PEACE ORD/FREE 20. PAGE 75 B1524   ARMS/CONT
                                                    DETER

B64

RAYMOND J.,POWER AT THE PENTAGON (1ST ED.). ELITES PWR
NAT/G PLAN EDU/PROP ARMS/CONT DETER WAR WEAPON   CIVMIL/REL
...TIME/SEQ 20 PENTAGON MCNAMARA/R. PAGE 86 B1746   EX/STRUC
                                                    FORCES

S64

GALTUNE J.,"BALANCE OF POWER AND THE PROBLEM OF   PWR
PERCEPTION. A LOGICAL ANALYSIS." WOR+45 CONSTN   PSY
SOCIETY NAT/G DELIB/GP EX/STRUC LEGIS DOMIN ADMIN   ARMS/CONT
COERCE DRIVE ORD/FREE...POLICY CONCPT OBS TREND   WAR
GEN/LAWS. PAGE 38 B0778

B65

GOTLIEB A.,DISARMAMENT AND INTERNATIONAL LAW* A   INT/LAW
STUDY OF THE ROLE OF LAW IN THE DISARMAMENT   INT/ORG
PROCESS. USA+45 USSR PROB/SOLV CONFER ADMIN ROUTINE ARMS/CONT
NUC/PWR ORD/FREE SOVEREIGN UN TREATY. PAGE 42 B0841 IDEA/COMP

B66

EPSTEIN F.T.,THE AMERICAN BIBLIOGRAPHY OF RUSSIAN   BIBLIOG
AND EAST EUROPEAN STUDIES FOR 1964. USSR LOC/G   COM
NAT/G POL/PAR FORCES ADMIN ARMS/CONT...JURID CONCPT MARXISM
20 UN. PAGE 33 B0678   DIPLOM

B66

YOUNG W.,EXISTING MECHANISMS OF ARMS CONTROL.   ARMS/CONT
PROC/MFG OP/RES DIPLOM TASK CENTRAL...MGT TREATY.   ADMIN
PAGE 119 B2395   NUC/PWR
                                                    ROUTINE

B67

WATERS M.,THE UNITED NATIONS* INTERNATIONAL   CONSTN
ORGANIZATION AND ADMINISTRATION. WOR+45 EX/STRUC   INT/ORG
FORCES DIPLOM LEAD REGION ARMS/CONT REPRESENT   ADMIN
INGP/REL ROLE...METH/COMP ANTHOL 20 UN LEAGUE/NAT. ADJUD
PAGE 114 B2301

S67

LALL B.G.,"GAPS IN THE ABM DEBATE." NAT/G DIPLOM   NUC/PWR
DETER CIVMIL/REL 20. PAGE 62 B1251   ARMS/CONT
                                                    EX/STRUC
                                                    FORCES

N67

US SENATE COMM ON FOREIGN REL,ARMS SALES AND   ARMS/CONT
FOREIGN POLICY (PAMPHLET). FINAN FOR/AID CONTROL   ADMIN
20. PAGE 110 B2222   OP/RES
                                                    DIPLOM

ARMSTRONG J.A. B0134

ARMY....ARMY (ALL NATIONS)

ARNOLD/M....MATTHEW ARNOLD

ARNOW K. B0135

ARON R. B0136

ARROW K.J. B0137

ART/METH....FINE AND PERFORMING ARTS

N

UNIVERSITY OF FLORIDA,CARIBBEAN ACQUISITIONS: BIBLIOG
MATERIALS ACQUIRED BY THE UNIVERSITY OF FLORIDA   ECO/UNDEV
1957-1960. L/A+17C...ART/METH GEOG MGT 20. PAGE 107   EDU/PROP
B2167   JURID

B35

GORER G.,AFRICA DANCES: A BOOK ABOUT WEST AFRICAN   AFR
NEGROES. STRUCT LOC/G SECT FORCES TAX ADMIN   ATTIT
COLONIAL...ART/METH MYTH WORSHIP 20 NEGRO AFRICA/W   CULTURE
CHRISTIAN RITUAL. PAGE 41 B0835   SOCIETY

B42

SINGTON D.,THE GOEBBELS EXPERIMENT. GERMANY MOD/EUR   FASCISM
NAT/G EX/STRUC FORCES CONTROL ROUTINE WAR TOTALISM   EDU/PROP
PWR...ART/METH HUM 20 NAZI GOEBBELS/J. PAGE 97   ATTIT
B1970   COM/IND

B61

FREYRE G.,THE PORTUGUESE AND THE TROPICS. L/A+17C   COLONIAL
PORTUGAL SOCIETY PERF/ART ADMIN TASK GP/REL   METH
...ART/METH CONCPT SOC/INTEG 20. PAGE 37 B0754   PLAN
                                                       CULTURE

ARTHUR D LITTLE INC B0138

ARTHUR/CA....PRESIDENT CHESTER ALAN ARTHUR

ARTIFACTS....SEE THING/STOR

ARTISTIC ACHIEVEMENT....SEE CREATE

ASHER R.E. B0139

ASHFORD D.E. B0140

ASHRAF A. B0141

ASIA....SEE ALSO APPROPRIATE TIME/SPACE/CULTURE INDEX

N

SUMMARIES OF SELECTED JAPANESE MAGAZINES. LAW   BIBLIOG/A
CULTURE ADMIN LEAD 20 CHINJAP. PAGE 1 B0024   ATTIT
                                                       NAT/G
                                                       ASIA

B26

MOON P.T.,IMPERIALISM AND WORLD POLITICS. AFR ASIA   WEALTH
ISLAM MOD/EUR S/ASIA USA-45 SOCIETY NAT/G EX/STRUC   TIME/SEQ
BAL/PWR DOMIN COLONIAL NAT/LISM ATTIT DRIVE PWR   CAP/ISM
...GEOG SOC 20. PAGE 75 B1510   DIPLOM

B29

ROBERTS S.H.,HISTORY OF FRENCH COLONIAL POLICY. AFR   INT/ORG
ASIA L/A+17C S/ASIA CULTURE ECO/DEV ECO/UNDEV FINAN   ACT/RES
NAT/G PLAN ECO/TAC DOMIN ROUTINE SOVEREIGN...OBS   FRANCE
HIST/WRIT TREND CHARTS VAL/FREE 19/20. PAGE 89   COLONIAL
B1796

C40

FAHS C.B.,"GOVERNMENT IN JAPAN." FINAN FORCES LEGIS   ASIA
TOP/EX BUDGET INT/TRADE EDU/PROP SOVEREIGN   DIPLOM
...CON/ANAL BIBLIOG/A 20 CHINJAP. PAGE 34 B0698   NAT/G
                                                       ADMIN

B50

WARD R.E.,A GUIDE TO JAPANESE REFERENCE AND   BIBLIOG/A
RESEARCH MATERIALS IN THE FIELD OF POLITICAL   ASIA
SCIENCE. LAW CONSTN LOC/G PRESS ADMIN...SOC   NAT/G
CON/ANAL METH 19/20 CHINJAP. PAGE 113 B2289

S50

WITTFOGEL K.A.,"RUSSIA AND ASIA: PROBLEMS OF   ECO/DEV
CONTEMPORARY AREA STUDIES AND INTERNATIONAL   ADMIN
RELATIONS." ASIA COM USA+45 SOCIETY NAT/G DIPLOM   RUSSIA
ECO/TAC FOR/AID EDU/PROP KNOWL...HIST/WRIT TOT/POP   USSR
20. PAGE 117 B2369

B51

BERTON P.A.,MANCHURIA: AN ANNOTATED BIBLIOGRAPHY.   BIBLIOG/A
ASIA DIST/IND ADMIN...SOC 20. PAGE 11 B0231   MARXISM
                                                       ECO/UNDEV
                                                       COLONIAL

S51

SCHRAMM W.,"COMMUNICATION IN THE SOVIETIZED STATE,   ATTIT
AS DEMONSTRATED IN KOREA." ASIA COM KOREA COM/IND   EDU/PROP
FACE/GP POL/PAR SCHOOL FORCES ADMIN PWR MARXISM   TOTALISM
...SOC CONCPT MYTH INT BIOG TOT/POP 20. PAGE 94
B1901

C53

KRACKE E.A. JR.,"CIVIL SERVICE IN EARLY SUNG CHINA,   ADMIN
960-1067." ASIA GP/REL...BIBLIOG/A 10/11. PAGE 61   NAT/G
B1231   WORKER
                                                       CONTROL

L54

ROSTOW W.W.,"ASIAN LEADERSHIP AND FREE-WORLD   ATTIT
ALLIANCE." ASIA COM USA+45 CULTURE ELITES INTELL   LEGIT
NAT/G TEC/DEV ECO/TAC EDU/PROP COLONIAL PARL/PROC   DIPLOM
ROUTINE COERCE DRIVE ORD/FREE MARXISM...PSY CONCPT.
PAGE 90 B1829

S54

WOLFERS A.,"COLLECTIVE SECURITY AND THE WAR IN   ACT/RES
KOREA." ASIA KOREA USA+45 INT/ORG DIPLOM ROUTINE   LEGIT
...GEN/LAWS UN COLD/WAR 20. PAGE 117 B2370

B55

POOL I.,SATELLITE GENERALS: A STUDY OF MILITARY   FORCES
ELITES IN THE SOVIET SPHERE. ASIA CHINA/COM COM   CHOOSE
CZECHOSLVK FUT HUNGARY POLAND ROMANIA USSR ELITES
STRATA ADMIN ATTIT PWR SKILL...METH/CNCPT BIOG 20.
PAGE 84 B1688

L55

ROSTOW W.W.,"RUSSIA AND CHINA UNDER COMMUNISM."   COM
CHINA/COM USSR INTELL STRUCT INT/ORG NAT/G POL/PAR   ASIA
TOP/EX ACT/RES PLAN ADMIN ATTIT ALL/VALS MARXISM
...CONCPT OBS TIME/SEQ TREND GOV/COMP VAL/FREE 20.
PAGE 91 B1830

S55

KAUTSKY J.H.,"THE NEW STRATEGY OF INTERNATIONAL   COM
COMMUNISM." ASIA CHINA/COM FUT WOR+45 WOR-45 ADMIN   POL/PAR
ROUTINE PERSON MARXISM SOCISM...TREND IDEA/COMP 20   TOTALISM
LENIN/VI MAO. PAGE 59 B1184   USSR

B56

KIRK G.,THE CHANGING ENVIRONMENT OF INTERNATIONAL   FUT
RELATIONS. ASIA S/ASIA USA+45 WOR+45 ECO/UNDEV   EXEC
INT/ORG NAT/G FOR/AID EDU/PROP PEACE KNOWL   DIPLOM
...PLURIST COLD/WAR TOT/POP 20. PAGE 60 B1214

B56

WU E.,LEADERS OF TWENTIETH-CENTURY CHINA; AN   BIBLIOG/A
ANNOTATED BIBLIOGRAPHY OF SELECTED CHINESE   BIOG
BIOGRAPHICAL WORKS IN HOOVER LIBRARY. ASIA INDUS   INTELL
POL/PAR DIPLOM ADMIN REV WAR...HUM MGT 20. PAGE 118   CHIEF
B2386

L56

EISENTADT S.N.,"POLITICAL STRUGGLE IN BUREAUCRATIC   ADMIN
SOCIETIES" ASIA CULTURE ADJUD SANCTION PWR   CHIEF
BUREAUCRCY OTTOMAN BYZANTINE. PAGE 33 B0661   CONTROL
                                                       ROUTINE

B57

PYE L.W.,THE POLICY IMPLICATIONS OF SOCIAL CHANGE   SOCIETY
IN NON-WESTERN SOCIETIES. ASIA USA+45 CULTURE   ORD/FREE
STRUCT NAT/G ECO/TAC ADMIN ROLE...POLICY SOC.   ECO/UNDEV
PAGE 85 B1723   DIPLOM

S57

BAUER R.A.,"BRAINWASHING: PSYCHOLOGY OR   EDU/PROP
DEMONOLOGY." ASIA CHINA/COM COM POL/PAR ECO/TAC   PSY
ADMIN COERCE ATTIT DRIVE ORD/FREE...CONCPT MYTH 20.   TOTALISM
PAGE 10 B0196

B58

SKINNER G.W.,LEADERSHIP AND POWER IN THE CHINESE   SOC
COMMUNITY OF THAILAND. ASIA S/ASIA STRATA FACE/GP   ELITES
KIN PROF/ORG VOL/ASSN EX/STRUC DOMIN PERSON RESPECT   THAILAND
...METH/CNCPT STAT INT QU BIOG CHARTS 20. PAGE 98
B1974

B58

UNIVERSITY OF LONDON,THE FAR EAST AND SOUTH-EAST   BIBLIOG
ASIA: A CUMULATED LIST OF PERIODICAL ARTICLES, MAY   SOC
1956-APRIL 1957. ASIA S/ASIA LAW ADMIN...LING 20.
PAGE 107 B2168

S58

JORDAN A.,"MILITARY ASSISTANCE AND NATIONAL   FORCES
POLICY." ASIA FUT USA+45 WOR+45 ECO/DEV ECO/UNDEV   POLICY
INT/ORG NAT/G PLAN ECO/TAC ROUTINE WEAPON ATTIT   FOR/AID
RIGID/FLEX PWR...CONCPT TREND 20. PAGE 57 B1153   DIPLOM

B59

CHINA INSTITUTE OF AMERICA,,CHINA AND THE UNITED   ASIA
NATIONS. CHINA/COM FUT STRUCT EDU/PROP LEGIT ADMIN   INT/ORG
ATTIT KNOWL ORD/FREE PWR...OBS RECORD STAND/INT
TIME/SEQ UN LEAGUE/NAT UNESCO 20. PAGE 21 B0425

B59

GORDENKER L.,THE UNITED NATIONS AND THE PEACEFUL   DELIB/GP
UNIFICATION OF KOREA. ASIA LAW LOC/G CONSULT   KOREA
ACT/RES DIPLOM DOMIN LEGIT ADJUD ADMIN ORD/FREE   INT/ORG
SOVEREIGN...INT GEN/METH UN COLD/WAR 20. PAGE 41
B0829

B59

YANG C.K.,A CHINESE VILLAGE IN EARLY COMMUNIST   ASIA
TRANSITION. ECO/UNDEV AGRI FAM KIN MUNIC FORCES   ROUTINE
PLAN ECO/TAC DOMIN EDU/PROP ATTIT DRIVE PWR RESPECT   SOCISM
...SOC CONCPT METH/CNCPT OBS RECORD CON/ANAL CHARTS
WORK 20. PAGE 118 B2389

B60

FRANKE W.,THE REFORM AND ABOLITION OF THE   ADJUST
TRADITIONAL CHINESE EXAMINATION SYSTEM. ASIA STRUCT   ADMIN
19/20 CIVIL/SERV. PAGE 37 B0750   TESTS
                                                       STRATA

B60

PIERCE R.A.,RUSSIAN CENTRAL ASIA, 1867-1917. ASIA   COLONIAL
RUSSIA CULTURE AGRI INDUS EDU/PROP REV NAT/LISM   DOMIN
...CHARTS BIBLIOG 19/20 BOLSHEVISM INTERVENT.   ADMIN
PAGE 83 B1672   ECO/UNDEV

B60

WORLEY P.,ASIA TODAY (REV. ED.) (PAMPHLET). COM   BIBLIOG/A
ECO/UNDEV AGRI FINAN INDUS POL/PAR FOR/AID ADMIN   ASIA
MARXISM 20. PAGE 118 B2376   DIPLOM
                                                       NAT/G

S60

NORTH R.C.,"DIE DISKREPANZ ZWISCHEN REALITAT UND   SOCIETY
WUNSCHBILD ALS INNENPOLITISCHER FAKTOR." ASIA   ECO/TAC
CHINA/COM COM FUT ECO/UNDEV NAT/G PLAN DOMIN ADMIN
COERCE PERCEPT...SOC MYTH GEN/METH WORK TOT/POP 20.

PAGE 79 B1589

S60
SCHWARTZ B.,"THE INTELLIGENTSIA IN COMMUNIST CHINA: INTELL
A TENTATIVE COMPARISON." ASIA CHINA/COM COM RUSSIA RIGID/FLEX
ELITES SOCIETY STRATA POL/PAR VOL/ASSN CREATE ADMIN REV
COERCE NAT/LISM TOTALISM...POLICY TREND 20. PAGE 95
B1914

B61
FRIEDMANN W.G.,JOINT INTERNATIONAL BUSINESS ECO/UNDEV
VENTURES. ASIA ISLAM L/A+17C ECO/DEV DIST/IND FINAN INT/TRADE
PROC/MFG FACE/GP LG/CO NAT/G VOL/ASSN CONSULT
EX/STRUC PLAN ADMIN ROUTINE WEALTH...OLD/LIB WORK
20. PAGE 37 B0760

B61
KOESTLER A.,THE LOTUS AND THE ROBOT. ASIA INDIA SECT
S/ASIA SOCIETY STRATA ECO/DEV AGRI INDUS FAM CREATE ECO/UNDEV
DOMIN EDU/PROP ADMIN COERCE ATTIT DRIVE SUPEGO
ORD/FREE PWR RESPECT WEALTH...MYTH OBS 20 CHINJAP.
PAGE 61 B1226

B61
MARSH R.M.,THE MANDARINS: THE CIRCULATION OF ELITES ELITES
IN CHINA, 1600-1900. ASIA STRUCT PROF/ORG...SOC ADMIN
CHARTS BIBLIOG DICTIONARY 17/20. PAGE 70 B1406 FAM
STRATA

S61
MARSH R.M.,"FORMAL ORGANIZATION AND PROMOTION IN A ADMIN
PRE-INDUSTRIAL SOCIETY" (BMR)" ASIA FAM EX/STRUC STRUCT
LEAD...SOC CHARTS 19 WEBER/MAX. PAGE 70 B1407 ECO/UNDEV
STRATA

L62
ABERLE D.F.,"CHAHAR AND DAGOR MONGOL BUREAUCRATIC EX/STRUC
ADMINISTRATION: 19621945." ASIA MUNIC TOP/EX PWR STRATA
...MGT OBS INT MONGOL 20. PAGE 3 B0053

C62
VAN DER SPRENKEL S.,"LEGAL INSTITUTIONS IN MANCHU LAW
CHINA." ASIA STRUCT CT/SYS ROUTINE GOV/REL GP/REL JURID
...CONCPT BIBLIOG 17/20. PAGE 111 B2250 ADMIN
ADJUD

B63
LEWIS J.W.,LEADERSHIP IN COMMUNIST CHINA. ASIA POL/PAR
INTELL ECO/UNDEV LOC/G MUNIC NAT/G PROVS ECO/TAC DOMIN
EDU/PROP LEGIT ADMIN COERCE ATTIT ORD/FREE PWR ELITES
...INT TIME/SEQ CHARTS TOT/POP VAL/FREE. PAGE 65
B1304

B63
MENZEL J.M.,THE CHINESE CIVIL SERVICE: CAREER OPEN ADMIN
TO TALENT? ASIA ROUTINE INGP/REL DISCRIM ATTIT ROLE NAT/G
KNOWL ANTHOL. PAGE 73 B1468 DECISION
ELITES

B63
NORTH R.C.,CONTENT ANALYSIS: A HANDBOOK WITH METH/CNCPT
APPLICATIONS FOR THE STUDY OF INTERNATIONAL CRISIS. COMPUT/IR
ASIA COM EUR+WWI MOD/EUR INT/ORG TEC/DEV DOMIN USSR
EDU/PROP ROUTINE COERCE PERCEPT RIGID/FLEX ALL/VALS
...QUANT TESTS CON/ANAL SIMUL GEN/LAWS VAL/FREE.
PAGE 79 B1591

B63
TSOU T.,AMERICA'S FAILURE IN CHINA, 1941-1950. ASIA
USA+45 USA-45 NAT/G ACT/RES PLAN DOMIN EDU/PROP PERCEPT
ADMIN ROUTINE ATTIT PERSON ORD/FREE...DECISION DIPLOM
CONCPT MYTH TIME/SEQ TREND STERTYP 20. PAGE 105
B2132

S63
ETIENNE G.,"'LOIS OBJECTIVES' ET PROBLEMES DE TOTALISM
DEVELOPPEMENT DANS LE CONTEXTE CHINE-URSS." ASIA USSR
CHINA/COM COM FUT STRUCT INT/ORG VOL/ASSN TOP/EX
TEC/DEV ECO/TAC ATTIT RIGID/FLEX...GEOG MGT
TIME/SEQ TOT/POP 20. PAGE 34 B0682

S63
SCHURMANN F.,"ECONOMIC POLICY AND POLITICAL POWER PLAN
IN COMMUNIST CHINA." ASIA CHINA/COM USSR SOCIETY ECO/TAC
ECO/UNDEV AGRI INDUS CREATE ADMIN ROUTINE ATTIT
DRIVE RIGID/FLEX PWR WEALTH...HIST/WRIT TREND
CHARTS WORK 20. PAGE 94 B1908

B64
ALDERFER H.O.,LOCAL GOVERNMENT IN DEVELOPING ADMIN
COUNTRIES. ASIA COM L/A+17C S/ASIA AGRI LOC/G MUNIC ROUTINE
PROVS DOMIN CHOOSE PWR...POLICY MGT CONCPT 20.
PAGE 3 B0070

B64
LI C.M.,INDUSTRIAL DEVELOPMENT IN COMMUNIST CHINA. ASIA
CHINA/COM ECO/DEV ECO/UNDEV AGRI FINAN INDUS MARKET TEC/DEV
LABOR NAT/G ECO/TAC INT/TRADE EXEC ALL/VALS
...POLICY RELATIV TREND WORK TOT/POP VAL/FREE 20.
PAGE 65 B1311

S64
KENNAN G.F.,"POLYCENTRISM AND WESTERN POLICY." ASIA RIGID/FLEX
CHINA/COM COM FUT USA+45 USSR NAT/G ACT/RES DOMIN ATTIT
EDU/PROP EXEC COERCE DISPL PERCEPT...POLICY DIPLOM
COLD/WAR 20. PAGE 59 B1192

S64
MURRAY D.,"CHINESE EDUCATION IN SOUTH-EAST ASIA." S/ASIA
SOCIETY NEIGH EDU/PROP ROUTINE PERSON KNOWL SCHOOL
...OBS/ENVIR STERTYP. PAGE 76 B1546 REGION
ASIA

S64
NEEDHAM T.,"SCIENCE AND SOCIETY IN EAST AND WEST." ASIA
INTELL STRATA R+D LOC/G NAT/G PROVS CONSULT ACT/RES STRUCT
CREATE PLAN TEC/DEV EDU/PROP ADMIN ATTIT ALL/VALS
...POLICY RELATIV MGT CONCPT NEW/IDEA TIME/SEQ WORK
WORK. PAGE 77 B1565

B65
MORGENTHAU H.,MORGENTHAU DIARY (CHINA) (2 VOLS.). DIPLOM
ASIA USA+45 USA-45 LAW DELIB/GP EX/STRUC PLAN ADMIN
FOR/AID INT/TRADE CONFER WAR MARXISM 20 CHINJAP.
PAGE 75 B1523

B65
PHELPS-FETHERS I.,SOVIET INTERNATIONAL FRONT USSR
ORGANIZATIONS* A CONCISE HANDBOOK. DIPLOM DOMIN EDU/PROP
LEGIT ADMIN EXEC GP/REL PEACE MARXISM...TIME/SEQ ASIA
GP/COMP. PAGE 83 B1668 COM

B66
TOTTEN G.O.,THE SOCIAL DEMOCRATIC MOVEMENT IN POL/PAR
PREWAR JAPAN. ASIA CHIEF EX/STRUC LEGIS DOMIN LEAD SOCISM
ROUTINE WAR 20 CHINJAP. PAGE 105 B2122 PARTIC
STRATA

B66
UN ECAFE,ADMINISTRATIVE ASPECTS OF FAMILY PLANNING PLAN
PROGRAMMES (PAMPHLET). ASIA THAILAND WOR+45 CENSUS
VOL/ASSN PROB/SOLV BUDGET FOR/AID EDU/PROP CONFER FAM
CONTROL GOV/REL TIME 20 UN BIRTH/CON. PAGE 106 ADMIN
B2147

B67
DUN J.L.,THE ESSENCE OF CHINESE CIVILIZATION. ASIA CULTURE
FAM NAT/G TEC/DEV ADMIN SANCTION WAR HABITAT SOCIETY
...ANTHOL WORSHIP. PAGE 31 B0630

B67
PYE L.W.,SOUTHEAST ASIA'S POLITICAL SYSTEMS. ASIA NAT/G
S/ASIA STRUCT ECO/UNDEV EX/STRUC CAP/ISM DIPLOM POL/PAR
ALL/IDEOS...TREND CHARTS. PAGE 85 B1724 GOV/COMP

B67
RAWLINSON J.L.,CHINA'S STRUGGLE FOR NAVAL SEA
DEVELOPMENT 1839-1895. ASIA DIPLOM ADMIN WAR FORCES
...BIBLIOG DICTIONARY 19 CHINJAP. PAGE 86 B1745 PWR

S67
LIU K.C.,"DISINTEGRATION OF THE OLD ORDER." ASIA ADJUST
SOCIETY PROB/SOLV ADMIN REGION TOTALISM ORD/FREE NAT/LISM
MARXISM 19/20. PAGE 66 B1329

S67
SHOEMAKER R.L.,"JAPANESE ARMY AND THE WEST." ASIA FORCES
ELITES EX/STRUC DIPLOM DOMIN EDU/PROP COERCE ATTIT TEC/DEV
AUTHORIT PWR 1/20 CHINJAP. PAGE 96 B1950 WAR
TOTALISM

ASIANS....ASIANS, ASIAN MINORITIES

ASPINALL A. B0142

ASPREMONT-LYNDEN H. B0143

ASQUITH/HH....HERBERT HENRY ASQUITH

ASSASSINATION....SEE MURDER

ASSIMILATION....SEE GP/REL+INGP/REL

ASSOCIATIONS....SEE VOL/ASSN

AT+T....AMERICAN TELEPHONE AND TELEGRAPH

B66
DICKSON W.J.,COUNSELING IN AN ORGANIZATION: A INDUS
SEQUEL TO THE HAWTHORNE RESEARCHES. CLIENT VOL/ASSN WORKER
ACT/RES PROB/SOLV AUTOMAT ROUTINE PERS/REL PSY
HAPPINESS ANOMIE ROLE...OBS CHARTS 20 AT+T. PAGE 29 MGT
B0588

ATATURK/MK....MUSTAFA KEMAL ATATURK

ATHENS....ATHENS, GREECE

ATKIN J.M. B0144

ATLAN/ALL....ATLANTIC ALLIANCE

ATLANTA....ATLANTA, GEORGIA

ATLANTIC ALLIANCE....SEE ATLAN/ALL

ATLANTIC FREE TRADE AREA....SEE AFTA

ATLASES....SEE MAPS

ATOM BOMB....SEE NUC/PWR

ATOMIC ENERGY AUTHORITY OF UN....SEE AEA

ATOMIC ENERGY COMMISSION....SEE AEC + COUNTRY'S NAME

ATOMIC INDUSTRIAL FORUM B0145

ATTENTION....SEE PERCEPT

ATTIT....ATTITUDES, OPINIONS, IDEOLOGY

N
MONPIED E.,BIBLIOGRAPHIE FEDERALISTE: ARTICLES ET   BIBLIOG/A
DOCUMENTS PUBLIES DANS LES PERIODIQUES PARUS EN   FEDERAL
FRANCE NOV. 1945-OCT. 1950. EUR+WWI WOR+45 ADMIN   CENTRAL
REGION ATTIT MARXISM PACIFISM 20 EEC. PAGE 74 B1501   INT/ORG

N
READERS GUIDE TO PERIODICAL LITERATURE. WOR+45   BIBLIOG
WOR-45 LAW ADMIN ATTIT PERSON...HUM PSY SOC 20.   WRITING
PAGE 1 B0021   DIPLOM
  NAT/G

N
SUMMARIES OF SELECTED JAPANESE MAGAZINES. LAW   BIBLIOG/A
CULTURE ADMIN LEAD 20 CHINJAP. PAGE 1 B0024   ATTIT
  NAT/G
  ASIA

N
PERSONNEL. USA+45 LAW LABOR LG/CO WORKER CREATE   BIBLIOG/A
GOV/REL PERS/REL ATTIT WEALTH. PAGE 2 B0030   ADMIN
  MGT
  GP/REL

DEUTSCHE BUCHEREI,DEUTSCHES BUCHERVERZEICHNIS.   BIBLIOG
GERMANY LAW CULTURE POL/PAR ADMIN LEAD ATTIT PERSON   NAT/G
...SOC 20. PAGE 29 B0581   DIPLOM
  ECO/DEV

N
FAUNT J.R.,A CHECKLIST OF SOUTH CAROLINA STATE   BIBLIOG
PUBLICATIONS. USA+45 CONSTN LEGIS ADMIN ATTIT 20.   PROVS
PAGE 35 B0708   LOC/G
  GOV/REL

N
US LIBRARY OF CONGRESS,CATALOG OF THE PUBLIC   BIBLIOG
DOCUMENTS OF THE UNITED STATES, 18931940. USA-45   NAT/G
LAW ECO/DEV AGRI PLAN PROB/SOLV ADMIN LEAD GOV/REL   POLICY
ATTIT 19/20. PAGE 109 B2200   LOC/G

B00
MORRIS H.C.,THE HISTORY OF COLONIZATION. WOR+45   DOMIN
WOR-45 ECO/DEV ECO/UNDEV INT/ORG ACT/RES PLAN   SOVEREIGN
ECO/TAC LEGIT ROUTINE COERCE ATTIT DRIVE ALL/VALS   COLONIAL
...GEOG TREND 19. PAGE 76 B1528

B05
RIORDAN W.L.,PLUNKITT OF TAMMANY HALL. USA-45   POL/PAR
SOCIETY PROB/SOLV EXEC LEAD TASK CHOOSE ALL/VALS   MUNIC
...RECORD ANTHOL 20 REFORMERS TAMMANY NEWYORK/C   CHIEF
PLUNKITT/G. PAGE 88 B1789   ATTIT

B16
TREITSCHKE H.,POLITICS. UNIV SOCIETY STRATA NAT/G   EXEC
EX/STRUC LEGIS DOMIN EDU/PROP ATTIT PWR RESPECT   ELITES
...CONCPT TIME/SEQ GEN/LAWS TOT/POP 20. PAGE 105   GERMANY
B2127

N19
WRIGHT D.S.,AMERICAN STATE ADMINISTRATORS   QU
(PAMPHLET). USA+45 ATTIT PERSON...SAMP/SIZ CHARTS   TOP/EX
SOC/EXP METH 20. PAGE 118 B2379   ADMIN
  PROVS

B20
HALDANE R.B.,BEFORE THE WAR. MOD/EUR SOCIETY   POLICY
INT/ORG NAT/G DELIB/GP PLAN DOMIN EDU/PROP LEGIT   DIPLOM
ADMIN COERCE DRIVE MORAL ORD/FREE PWR...SOC   UK
CONCPT SELF/OBS RECORD BIOG TIME/SEQ. PAGE 45 B0921

B24
MERRIAM C.E.,A HISTORY OF POLITICAL THEORIES -   UNIV
RECENT TIMES. USA-45 WOR-45 CULTURE SOCIETY ECO/DEV   INTELL
R+D EDU/PROP ROUTINE CHOOSE ATTIT PERSON ALL/VALS
...POLICY SOC CONCPT METH/CNCPT OBS HIST/WRIT
TIME/SEQ TREND. PAGE 73 B1471

B25
THOMAS F.,THE ENVIRONMENTAL BASIS OF SOCIETY.   SOCIETY
USA-45 WOR-45 STRATA ECO/DEV EXTR/IND CONSULT   GEOG
ECO/TAC ROUTINE ATTIT ALL/VALS...SOC TIME/SEQ.
PAGE 104 B2098

B26
INTERNATIONAL BIBLIOGRAPHY OF POLITICAL SCIENCE.   BIBLIOG
WOR+45 NAT/G POL/PAR EX/STRUC LEGIS CT/SYS LEAD   DIPLOM
CHOOSE GOV/REL ATTIT...PHIL/SCI 20. PAGE 2 B0034   CONCPT
  ADMIN

B26
MOON P.T.,IMPERIALISM AND WORLD POLITICS. AFR ASIA   WEALTH
ISLAM MOD/EUR S/ASIA USA+45 SOCIETY NAT/G EX/STRUC   TIME/SEQ
BAL/PWR DOMIN COLONIAL NAT/LISM ATTIT DRIVE PWR   CAP/ISM
...GEOG SOC 20. PAGE 75 B1510   DIPLOM

B27
ANGELL N.,THE PUBLIC MIND. USA-45 SOCIETY EDU/PROP   PERCEPT
ROUTINE SUPEGO KNOWL...POLICY CONCPT MYTH OBS/ENVIR   ATTIT
EUR+WW1 TOT/POP 20. PAGE 5 B0109   DIPLOM
  NAT/LISM

B28
HARDMAN J.B.,AMERICAN LABOR DYNAMICS. WORKER   LABOR
ECO/TAC DOMIN ADJUD LEAD LOBBY PWR...POLICY MGT.   INGP/REL
PAGE 47 B0944   ATTIT
  GP/REL

B28
SOROKIN P.,CONTEMPORARY SOCIOLOGICAL THEORIES.   CULTURE
MOD/EUR UNIV SOCIETY R+D SCHOOL LEWIS/C ECO/TAC EDU/PROP   SOC
ROUTINE ATTIT DRIVE...PSY CONCPT TIME/SEQ TREND   WAR
GEN/LAWS 20. PAGE 99 B1997

B29
BUELL R.,INTERNATIONAL RELATIONS. WOR+45 WOR-45   INT/ORG
CONSTN STRATA FORCES TOP/EX ADMIN ATTIT DRIVE   BAL/PWR
SUPEGO MORAL ORD/FREE PWR SOVEREIGN...JURID SOC   DIPLOM
CONCPT 20. PAGE 17 B0340

B32
CARDINALL AW,A BIBLIOGRAPHY OF THE GOLD COAST. AFR   BIBLIOG
UK NAT/G EX/STRUC ATTIT...POLICY 19/20. PAGE 18   ADMIN
B0376   COLONIAL
  DIPLOM

B32
WRIGHT Q.,GOLD AND MONETARY STABILIZATION. FUT   FINAN
USA+45 WOR-45 INTELL ECO/DEV INT/ORG NAT/G CONSULT   POLICY
PLAN ECO/TAC ADMIN ATTIT WEALTH...CONCPT TREND 20.
PAGE 118 B2383

B33
DANGERFIELD R.,IN DEFENSE OF THE SENATE. USA-45   LEGIS
CONSTN NAT/G EX/STRUC TOP/EX ATTIT KNOWL   DELIB/GP
...METH/CNCPT STAT TIME/SEQ TREND CON/ANAL CHARTS   DIPLOM
CONGRESS 20 TREATY. PAGE 26 B0528

B34
DE CENIVAL P.,BIBLIOGRAPHIE MAROCAINE: 1923-1933.   BIBLIOG/A
FRANCE MOROCCO SECT ADMIN LEAD GP/REL ATTIT...LING   ISLAM
20. PAGE 27 B0551   NAT/G
  COLONIAL

B35
GORER G.,AFRICA DANCES: A BOOK ABOUT WEST AFRICAN   AFR
NEGROES. STRUCT LOC/G SECT FORCES TAX ADMIN   ATTIT
COLONIAL...ART/METH MYTH WORSHIP 20 NEGRO AFRICA/W   CULTURE
CHRISTIAN RITUAL. PAGE 41 B0835   SOCIETY

B37
PARSONS T.,THE STRUCTURE OF SOCIAL ACTION. UNIV   CULTURE
INTELL SOCIETY INDUS MARKET ECO/TAC ROUTINE CHOOSE   ATTIT
ALL/VALS...CONCPT OBS BIOG TREND GEN/LAWS 20.   CAP/ISM
PAGE 81 B1636

B37
ROYAL INST. INT. AFF.,THE COLONIAL PROBLEM. WOR-45   INT/ORG
LAW ECO/DEV ECO/UNDEV NAT/G PLAN ECO/TAC EDU/PROP   ACT/RES
ADMIN ATTIT ALL/VALS...CONCPT 20. PAGE 91 B1844   SOVEREIGN
  COLONIAL

B38
LANGE O.,ON THE ECONOMIC THEORY OF SOCIALISM. UNIV   MARKET
ECO/DEV FINAN INDUS INT/ORG PUB/INST ROUTINE ATTIT   ECO/TAC
ALL/VALS...SOC CONCPT STAT TREND 20. PAGE 62 B1258   INT/TRADE
  SOCISM

B38
MACDONALD G.E.,CHECK LIST OF LEGISLATIVE JOURNALS   BIBLIOG
OF THE STATES OF THE UNITED STATES OF AMERICA.   PROVS
USA+45 ADMIN GOV/REL ATTIT...POLICY 18/20. PAGE 67   LEGIS
B1356   LOC/G

B38
RAPPARD W.E.,THE CRISIS OF DEMOCRACY. EUR+WWI UNIV   NAT/G
WOR-45 CULTURE SOCIETY ECO/DEV INT/ORG POL/PAR   CONCPT
ACT/RES EDU/PROP EXEC CHOOSE ATTIT ALL/VALS...SOC
OBS HIST/WRIT TIME/SEQ LEAGUE/NAT NAZI TOT/POP 20.
PAGE 86 B1741

B38
SALTER J.T.,THE AMERICAN POLITICIAN. USA-45 LABOR   BIOG
POL/PAR EDU/PROP ADMIN CHOOSE ATTIT DRIVE PERSON   LEAD
PWR...POLICY ANTHOL 20 THOMAS/N LEWIS/JL LAGUARD/F   PROVS
GOVERNOR MAYOR. PAGE 92 B1865   LOC/G

B39
HITLER A.,MEIN KAMPF. EUR+WWI FUT MOD/EUR STRUCT   PWR
INT/ORG LABOR NAT/G POL/PAR FORCES CREATE PLAN   NEW/IDEA
BAL/PWR DIPLOM ECO/TAC DOMIN EDU/PROP ADMIN COERCE   WAR
ATTIT...SOCIALIST BIOG TREND NAZI. PAGE 50 B1020

B39
MCCAMY J.L.,GOVERNMENT PUBLICITY: ITS PRACTICE IN   EDU/PROP
FEDERAL ADMINISTRATION. USA+45 COM/IND ADMIN   NAT/G
CONTROL EXEC PARTIC INGP/REL...SOC 20. PAGE 71   PLAN
B1442   ATTIT

B39
ZIMMERN A.,MODERN POLITICAL DOCTRINE. WOR-45   NAT/G
CULTURE SOCIETY ECO/UNDEV DELIB/GP EX/STRUC CREATE   ECO/TAC
DOMIN COERCE NAT/LISM ATTIT RIGID/FLEX ORD/FREE PWR   BAL/PWR
WEALTH...POLICY CONCPT OBS TIME/SEQ TREND TOT/POP   INT/TRADE
LEAGUE/NAT 20. PAGE 119 B2402

B41
BURTON M.E.,THE ASSEMBLY OF THE LEAGUE OF NATIONS.   DELIB/GP
WOR-45 CONSTN SOCIETY STRUCT INT/ORG NAT/G CREATE   EX/STRUC
ATTIT RIGID/FLEX PWR...POLICY TIME/SEQ LEAGUE/NAT   DIPLOM
20. PAGE 18 B0359

B41
PERHAM M.,AFRICANS AND BRITISH RULE. AFR UK ECO/TAC   DIPLOM
CONTROL GP/REL ATTIT 20. PAGE 82 B1654   COLONIAL
  ADMIN
  ECO/UNDEV

B41
YOUNG G.,FEDERALISM AND FREEDOM. EUR+WWI MOD/EUR   NAT/G
RUSSIA USA-45 WOR-45 SOCIETY STRUCT ECO/DEV INT/ORG   WAR
EXEC FEDERAL ATTIT PERSON ALL/VALS...OLD/LIB CONCPT

OBS TREND LEAGUE/NAT TOT/POP. PAGE 119 B2392

B42
HARLOW R.F.,PUBLIC RELATIONS IN WAR AND PEACE. FUT WAR
USA-45 ECO/DEV ECO/TAC ROUTINE 20. PAGE 47 B0947   ATTIT
SOCIETY
INGP/REL

B42
SINGTON D.,THE GOEBBELS EXPERIMENT. GERMANY MOD/EUR FASCISM
NAT/G EX/STRUC FORCES CONTROL ROUTINE WAR TOTALISM NAT/G
PWR...ART/METH HUM 20 NAZI GOEBBELS/J. PAGE 97   EDU/PROP
B1970   ATTIT
COM/IND

B42
US STATE DEPT.,PEACE AND WAR: UNITED STATES FOREIGN DIPLOM
POLICY, 1931-41. CULTURE FORCES ROUTINE CHOOSE   USA-45
ATTIT DRIVE PERSON 20. PAGE 111 B2237   PLAN

S42
HUZAR E.,"LEGISLATIVE CONTROL OVER ADMINISTRATION: ADMIN
CONGRESS AND WPA" USA-45 FINAN DELIB/GP LOBBY   EX/STRUC
GOV/REL EFFICIENCY ATTIT...POLICY CONGRESS. PAGE 53 CONTROL
B1069   LEGIS

B43
LEVY H.P.,A STUDY IN PUBLIC RELATIONS: CASE HISTORY ATTIT
OF THE RELATIONS MAINTAINED BETWEEN A DEPT OF   RECEIVE
PUBLIC ASSISTANCE AND PEOPLE. USA-45 NAT/G PRESS   WEALTH
ADMIN LOBBY GP/REL DISCRIM...SOC/WK LING AUD/VIS 20 SERV/IND
PENNSYLVAN. PAGE 64 B1302

B44
BIENSTOCK G.,MANAGEMENT IN RUSSIAN INDUSTRY AND   ADMIN
AGRICULTURE. USSR CONSULT WORKER LEAD COST PROFIT   MARXISM
ATTIT DRIVE PWR...MGT METH/COMP DICTIONARY 20.   SML/CO
PAGE 12 B0236   AGRI

S44
SIMON H.A.,"DECISION-MAKING AND ADMINISTRATIVE   DECISION
ORGANIZATION" (BMR)" WOR-45 CHOOSE INGP/REL   ADMIN
EFFICIENCY ATTIT RESPECT...MGT 20. PAGE 97 B1955   CONTROL
WORKER

B45
BUSH V.,SCIENCE, THE ENDLESS FRONTIER. FUT USA-45   R+D
INTELL STRATA ACT/RES CREATE PLAN EDU/PROP ADMIN   NAT/G
NUC/PWR PEACE ATTIT HEALTH KNOWL...MAJORIT HEAL MGT
PHIL/SCI CONCPT OBS TREND 20. PAGE 18 B0360

B45
PLATO,THE REPUBLIC. MEDIT-7 UNIV SOCIETY STRUCT   PERSON
EX/STRUC FORCES UTOPIA ATTIT PERCEPT HEALTH KNOWL   PHIL/SCI
ORD/FREE PWR...HUM CONCPT STERTYP TOT/POP. PAGE 83
B1681

S45
KRIESBERG M.,"WHAT CONGRESSMEN AND ADMINISTRATORS   LEGIS
THINK OF THE POLLS." USA-45 CONTROL PWR...INT QU.   ATTIT
PAGE 61 B1236   EDU/PROP
ADMIN

S45
TRUMAN D.B.,"PUBLIC OPINION RESEARCH AS A TOOL OF   REPRESENT
PUBLIC ADMINISTRATION" ADMIN PARTIC ROLE...DECISION METH/CNCPT
20. PAGE 105 B2130   ATTIT
EX/STRUC

B46
CLOUGH S.B.,ECONOMIC HISTORY OF EUROPE. CHRIST-17C   ECO/TAC
EUR+WWI MOD/EUR WOR+45 SOCIETY EXEC ATTIT WEALTH   CAP/ISM
...CONCPT GEN/LAWS WORK TOT/POP VAL/FREE 7/20.
PAGE 22 B0440

B46
DAVIES E.,NATIONAL ENTERPRISE: THE DEVELOPMENT OF   ADMIN
THE PUBLIC CORPORATION. UK LG/CO EX/STRUC WORKER   NAT/G
PROB/SOLV COST ATTIT SOCISM 20. PAGE 26 B0536   CONTROL
INDUS

B47
BARNARD C.,THE FUNCTIONS OF THE EXECUTIVE. USA+45   EXEC
ELITES INTELL LEGIT ATTIT DRIVE PERSON SKILL...PSY   EX/STRUC
SOC METH/CNCPT SOC/EXP GEN/METH VAL/FREE 20. PAGE 9 ROUTINE
B0187

B47
BORGESE G.,COMMON CAUSE. LAW CONSTN SOCIETY STRATA   WOR+45
ECO/DEV INT/ORG POL/PAR FORCES LEGIS TOP/EX CAP/ISM NAT/G
DIPLOM ADMIN EXEC ATTIT PWR 20. PAGE 14 B0279   SOVEREIGN
REGION

B47
GAUS J.M.,REFLECTIONS ON PUBLIC ADMINISTRATION.   MGT
USA+45 CONTROL GOV/REL CENTRAL FEDERAL ATTIT WEALTH POLICY
...DECISION 20. PAGE 39 B0787   EX/STRUC
ADMIN

B47
LASSWELL H.D.,THE ANALYSIS OF POLITICAL BEHAVIOUR: R+D
AN EMPIRICAL APPROACH. WOR+45 CULTURE NAT/G FORCES   ACT/RES
EDU/PROP ADMIN ATTIT PERCEPT KNOWL...PHIL/SCI PSY   ELITES
SOC NEW/IDEA OBS INT GEN/METH NAZI 20. PAGE 63
B1267

B48
BONAPARTE M.,MYTHS OF WAR. GERMANY WOR+45 WOR-45   ROUTINE
CULTURE SOCIETY NAT/G FORCES LEGIT ATTIT ALL/VALS   MYTH
...CONCPT HIST/WRIT TIME/SEQ 20 JEWS. PAGE 13 B0271 WAR

B48
HULL C.,THE MEMOIRS OF CORDELL HULL (VOLUME ONE).   BIOG
USA-45 WOR-45 CONSTN FAM LOC/G NAT/G PROVS DELIB/GP DIPLOM
FORCES LEGIS TOP/EX BAL/PWR LEGIT ADMIN EXEC WAR
ATTIT ORD/FREE PWR...MAJORIT SELF/OBS TIME/SEQ

TREND NAZI 20. PAGE 52 B1062

B48
TOWSTER J.,POLITICAL POWER IN THE USSR: 1917-1947.   EX/STRUC
USSR CONSTN CULTURE ELITES CREATE PLAN COERCE   NAT/G
CENTRAL ATTIT RIGID/FLEX ORD/FREE...BIBLIOG   MARXISM
SOC/INTEG 20 LENIN/VI STALIN/J. PAGE 105 B2124   PWR

B49
ASPINALL A.,POLITICS AND THE PRESS 1780-1850. UK   PRESS
LAW ELITES FINAN PROF/ORG LEGIS ADMIN ATTIT   CONTROL
...POLICY 18/19. PAGE 7 B0142   POL/PAR
ORD/FREE

B49
BUSH V.,MODERN ARMS AND FREE MEN. WOR-45 SOCIETY   TEC/DEV
NAT/G ECO/TAC DOMIN LEGIT EXEC COERCE DETER ATTIT   FORCES
DRIVE ORD/FREE PWR...CONCPT MYTH COLD/WAR 20   NUC/PWR
COLD/WAR. PAGE 18 B0361   WAR

B49
GLOVER J.D.,THE ADMINISTRATOR. ELITES LG/CO   ADMIN
EX/STRUC ACT/RES CONTROL GP/REL INGP/REL PERS/REL   MGT
AUTHORIT...POLICY CONCPT HIST/WRIT. PAGE 40 B0811   ATTIT
PROF/ORG

B49
KENT S.,STRATEGIC INTELLIGENCE FOR AMERICAN WORLD   ACT/RES
POLICY. FUT USA+45 NAT/G ATTIT PERCEPT ORD/FREE   EX/STRUC
...OBS 20. PAGE 59 B1195   DIPLOM

B49
ROSENHAUPT H.W.,HOW TO WAGE PEACE. USA+45 SOCIETY   INTELL
STRATA STRUCT R+D INT/ORG POL/PAR LEGIS ACT/RES   CONCPT
CREATE PLAN EDU/PROP ADMIN EXEC ATTIT ALL/VALS   DIPLOM
...TIME/SEQ TREND COLD/WAR 20. PAGE 90 B1822

B49
SINGER K.,THE IDEA OF CONFLICT. UNIV INTELL INT/ORG ACT/RES
NAT/G PLAN ROUTINE ATTIT DRIVE ALL/VALS...POLICY   SOC
CONCPT TIME/SEQ. PAGE 97 B1966

B49
WRIGHT J.H.,PUBLIC RELATIONS IN MANAGEMENT. USA+45   MGT
USA-45 ECO/DEV LG/CO SML/CO CONSULT EXEC TASK   PLAN
PROFIT ATTIT ROLE 20. PAGE 118 B2382   EDU/PROP
PARTIC

B50
HYNEMAN C.S.,BUREAUCRACY IN A DEMOCRACY. CHIEF   NAT/G
LEGIS ADMIN CONTROL LEAD ROUTINE PERS/REL COST   CENTRAL
EFFICIENCY UTIL ATTIT AUTHORIT PERSON MORAL.   EX/STRUC
PAGE 53 B1071   MYTH

B50
KOENIG L.W.,THE SALE OF THE TANKERS. USA+45 SEA   NAT/G
DIST/IND POL/PAR DIPLOM ADMIN CIVMIL/REL ATTIT   POLICY
...DECISION 20 PRESIDENT DEPT/STATE. PAGE 60 B1223   PLAN
GOV/REL

B50
MANNHEIM K.,FREEDOM, POWER, AND DEMOCRATIC   TEC/DEV
PLANNING. FUT USSR WOR+45 ELITES INTELL SOCIETY   PLAN
NAT/G EDU/PROP ROUTINE ATTIT DRIVE SUPEGO SKILL   CAP/ISM
...POLICY PSY CONCPT TREND GEN/LAWS 20. PAGE 69   UK
B1393

B50
MONPIED E.,BIBLIOGRAPHIE FEDERALISTE: OUVRAGES   BIBLIOG/A
CHOISIS (VOL. I, MIMEOGRAPHED PAPER). EUR+WWI   FEDERAL
DIPLOM ADMIN REGION ATTIT PACIFISM SOCISM...INT/LAW CENTRAL
19/20. PAGE 74 B1502   INT/ORG

S50
DALTON M.,"CONFLICTS BETWEEN STAFF AND LINE   MGT
MANAGERIAL OFFICERS" (BMR). USA+45 USA-45 ELITES   ATTIT
LG/CO WORKER PROB/SOLV ADMIN EXEC EFFICIENCY PRODUC GP/REL
...GP/COMP 20. PAGE 26 B0526   INDUS

S50
HUMPHREY H.H.,"THE SENATE ON TRIAL." USA+45 POL/PAR PARL/PROC
DEBATE REPRESENT EFFICIENCY ATTIT RIGID/FLEX   ROUTINE
...TRADIT SENATE. PAGE 52 B1064   PWR
LEGIS

S50
NEUMANN F.L.,"APPROACHES TO THE STUDY OF POLITICAL   PWR
POWER." POL/PAR TOP/EX ADMIN LEAD ATTIT ORD/FREE   IDEA/COMP
CONSERVE LAISSEZ MARXISM...PSY SOC. PAGE 78 B1572   CONCPT

B51
GUETZKOW H.,GROUPS, LEADERSHIP, AND MEN. FACE/GP   ATTIT
SECT EDU/PROP EXEC PERSON RESPECT...PERS/TEST   SOC
GEN/METH 20. PAGE 44 B0901   ELITES

B51
LASSWELL H.D.,THE POLITICAL WRITINGS OF HAROLD D   PERSON
LASSWELL. UNIV DOMIN EXEC LEAD RATIONAL ATTIT DRIVE PSY
ROLE ALL/VALS...OBS BIOG 20. PAGE 63 B1269   INGP/REL
CONCPT

L51
MANGONE G.,"THE IDEA AND PRACTICE OF WORLD   INT/ORG
GOVERNMENT." FUT WOR+45 WOR-45 ECO/DEV LEGIS CREATE SOCIETY
LEGIT ROUTINE ATTIT MORAL PWR WEALTH...CONCPT   INT/LAW
GEN/LAWS 20. PAGE 69 B1388

S51
INKELES A.,"UNDERSTANDING A FOREIGN SOCIETY: A   SOC
SOCIOLOGIST'S VIEW." SOCIETY ROUTINE KNOWL...PSY   METH/CNCPT
CONCPT GEN/METH 20. PAGE 54 B1086   PERCEPT
ATTIT

S51
SCHRAMM W.,"COMMUNICATION IN THE SOVIETIZED STATE,   ATTIT
AS DEMONSTRATED IN KOREA." ASIA COM KOREA COM/IND   EDU/PROP

FACE/GP POL/PAR SCHOOL FORCES ADMIN PWR MARXISM   TOTALISM
...SOC CONCPT MYTH INT BIOG TOT/POP 20. PAGE 94
B1901
                                                                    S51
STEWART D.D.,"THE PLACE OF VOLUNTEER PARTICIPATION   ADMIN
IN BUREAUCRATIC ORGANIZATION." NAT/G DELIB/GP   PARTIC
OP/RES DOMIN LOBBY WAR ATTIT ROLE PWR. PAGE 101   VOL/ASSN
B2035   FORCES
                                                                    C51
MOORE B.,"SOVIET POLITICS - THE DILEMMA OF POWER: ATTIT
THE ROLE OF IDEAS IN SOCIAL CHANGE." USSR PROB/SOLV   PWR
DIPLOM EDU/PROP ADMIN LEAD ROUTINE REV...POLICY   CONCPT
DECISION BIBLIOG 20. PAGE 75 B1512   MARXISM
                                                                    B52
DAY E.E.,EDUCATION FOR FREEDOM AND RESPONSIBILITY.   SCHOOL
FUT USA+45 CULTURE CONSULT EDU/PROP ATTIT SKILL   KNOWL
...MGT CONCPT OBS GEN/LAWS COLD/WAR 20. PAGE 27
B0547
                                                                    B52
HIMMELFARB G.,LORD ACTON: A STUDY IN CONSCIENCE AND   PWR
POLITICS. MOD/EUR NAT/G POL/PAR SECT LEGIS TOP/EX   BIOG
EDU/PROP ADMIN NAT/LISM ATTIT PERSON SUPEGO MORAL
ORD/FREE...CONCPT PARLIAMENT 19 ACTON/LORD. PAGE 50
B1014
                                                                    B52
MAIER N.R.F.,PRINCIPLES OF HUMAN RELATIONS. WOR+45   INDUS
WOR+45 CULTURE SOCIETY ROUTINE ATTIT DRIVE PERCEPT
PERSON RIGID/FLEX SUPEGO PWR...PSY CONT/OBS RECORD
TOT/POP VAL/FREE 20. PAGE 68 B1379
                                                                    B52
MILLER M.,THE JUDGES AND THE JUDGED. USA+45 LG/CO   COM/IND
ACT/RES TV ROUTINE SANCTION NAT/LISM ATTIT ORD/FREE   DISCRIM
...POLICY ACLU. PAGE 73 B1481   EDU/PROP
                                                        MARXISM
                                                                    B52
SELZNICK P.,THE ORGANIZATIONAL WEAPON: A STUDY OF   MARXISM
BOLSHEVIK STRATEGY AND TACTICS. USSR SOCIETY STRATA   POL/PAR
LABOR DOMIN EDU/PROP PARTIC REV ATTIT PWR...POLICY   LEAD
MGT CONCPT 20 BOLSHEVISM. PAGE 95 B1929   TOTALISM
                                                                    B52
SWENSON R.J.,FEDERAL ADMINISTRATIVE LAW: A STUDY OF   JURID
THE GROWTH, NATURE, AND CONTROL OF ADMINISTRATIVE   CONSTN
ACTION. USA-45 JUDGE ADMIN GOV/REL EFFICIENCY   LEGIS
PRIVIL ATTIT NEW/LIB SUPREME/CT. PAGE 102 B2061   ADJUD
                                                                    B52
ULAM A.B.,TITOISM AND THE COMINFORM. USSR WOR+45   COM
STRUCT INT/ORG NAT/G ACT/RES PLAN EXEC ATTIT DRIVE   POL/PAR
ALL/VALS...CONCPT OBS VAL/FREE 20 COMINTERN   TOTALISM
TITO/MARSH. PAGE 106 B2145   YUGOSLAVIA
                                                                    S52
BRUEGEL J.W.,"DIE INTERNAZIONALE   VOL/ASSN
GEWERKSCHAFTSBEWEGUNG." COM EUR+WWI USA+45 WOR+45   LABOR
DELIB/GP EX/STRUC ECO/TAC EDU/PROP ATTIT PWR   TOTALISM
RESPECT SKILL WEALTH WORK 20. PAGE 16 B0330
                                                                    S52
SCHWEBEL S.M.,"THE SECRETARY-GENERAL OF THE UN."   INT/ORG
FUT INTELL CONSULT DELIB/GP ADMIN PEACE ATTIT   TOP/EX
...JURID MGT CONCPT TREND UN CONGRESS 20. PAGE 95
B1915
                                                                    C52
LASSWELL H.D.,"THE COMPARATIVE STUDY OF ELITES: AN   ELITES
INTRODUCTION AND BIBLIOGRAPHY." STRATA POL/PAR   LEAD
EDU/PROP ADMIN LOBBY COERCE ATTIT PERSON PWR   CONCPT
...BIBLIOG 20. PAGE 63 B1270   DOMIN
                                                                    B53
A BIBLIOGRAPHY AND SUBJECT INDEX OF PUBLICATIONS OF   BIBLIOG
FLORIDA STATE AGENCIES. USA+45 LOC/G LEAD ATTIT 20   PROVS
FLORIDA. PAGE 2 B0036   GOV/REL
                                                        ADMIN
                                                                    B53
APPLEBY P.H.,PUBLIC ADMINISTRATION IN INDIA: REPORT   ADMIN
OF A SURVEY. INDIA LOC/G OP/RES ATTIT ORD/FREE 20.   NAT/G
PAGE 6 B0118   EX/STRUC
                                                        GOV/REL
                                                                    B53
ARGYRIS C.,EXECUTIVE LEADERSHIP: AN APPRAISAL OF A   MGT
MANAGER IN ACTION. TOP/EX ADMIN LEAD ADJUST ATTIT   EX/STRUC
...METH 20. PAGE 6 B0127   WORKER
                                                        PERS/REL
                                                                    B53
MEYER P.,THE JEWS IN THE SOVIET SATELLITES.   COM
CZECHOSLVK POLAND SOCIETY STRATA NAT/G BAL/PWR   SECT
ECO/TAC EDU/PROP LEGIT ADMIN COERCE ATTIT DISPL   TOTALISM
PERCEPT HEALTH PWR RESPECT WEALTH...METH/CNCPT JEWS   USSR
VAL/FREE NAZI 20. PAGE 73 B1474
                                                                    B53
SAYLES L.R.,THE LOCAL UNION. CONSTN CULTURE   LABOR
DELIB/GP PARTIC CHOOSE GP/REL INGP/REL ATTIT ROLE   LEAD
...MAJORIT DECISION MGT. PAGE 93 B1873   ADJUD
                                                        ROUTINE
                                                                    B53
SECKLER-HUDSON C.,BIBLIOGRAPHY ON PUBLIC   BIBLIOG/A
ADMINISTRATION (4TH ED.). USA+45 LAW POL/PAR   ADMIN
DELIB/GP BUDGET ADJUD LOBBY GOV/REL GP/REL ATTIT   NAT/G
...JURID 20. PAGE 95 B1923   MGT

                                                                    S53
CORY R.H. JR.,"FORGING A PUBLIC INFORMATION POLICY   INT/ORG
FOR THE UNITED NATIONS." FUT WOR+45 SOCIETY ADMIN   EDU/PROP
PEACE ATTIT PERSON SKILL...CONCPT 20 UN. PAGE 24   BAL/PWR
B0486
                                                                    S53
MORRIS B.S.,"THE COMINFORM: A FIVE YEAR   VOL/ASSN
PERSPECTIVE." COM UNIV USSR WOR+45 ECO/DEV POL/PAR   EDU/PROP
TOP/EX PLAN DOMIN ADMIN TOTALISM ATTIT ALL/VALS   DIPLOM
...CONCPT TIME/SEQ TREND CON/ANAL WORK VAL/FREE 20.
PAGE 76 B1527
                                                                    C53
BULNER-THOMAS I.,"THE PARTY SYSTEM IN GREAT   NAT/G
BRITAIN." UK CONSTN SECT PRESS CONFER GP/REL ATTIT   POL/PAR
...POLICY TREND BIBLIOG 19/20 PARLIAMENT. PAGE 17   ADMIN
B0343   ROUTINE
                                                                    B54
ALLPORT G.W.,THE NATURE OF PREJUDICE. USA+45 WOR+45   CULTURE
STRATA FACE/GP KIN NEIGH SECT ADMIN GP/REL DISCRIM   PERSON
ATTIT DRIVE LOVE RESPECT...PSY SOC MYTH QU/SEMANT   RACE/REL
20. PAGE 4 B0078
                                                                    B54
CONWAY O.B. JR.,LEGISLATIVE-EXECUTIVE RELATIONS IN   BAL/PWR
THE GOVERNMENT OF THE UNITED STATES (PAMPHLET).   FEDERAL
BUDGET ATTIT PERCEPT...DECISION 20. PAGE 23 B0470   GOV/REL
                                                        EX/STRUC
                                                                    B54
DUVERGER M.,POLITICAL PARTIES: THEIR ORGANIZATION   POL/PAR
AND ACTIVITY IN THE MODERN STATE. EUR+WWI MOD/EUR   EX/STRUC
USA+45 USA-45 EDU/PROP ADMIN ROUTINE ATTIT DRIVE   ELITES
ORD/FREE PWR...SOC CONCPT MATH STAT TIME/SEQ
TOT/POP 19/20. PAGE 31 B0635
                                                                    B54
GOULDNER A.W.,WILDCAT STRIKE. LABOR TEC/DEV PAY   INDUS
ADMIN LEAD PERS/REL ATTIT RIGID/FLEX PWR...MGT   WORKER
CONCPT. PAGE 40 B0816   GP/REL
                                                        SOC
                                                                    B54
GOULDNER A.W.,PATTERNS OF INDUSTRIAL BUREAUCRACY.   ADMIN
DOMIN ATTIT DRIVE...BIBLIOG 20 BUREAUCRCY. PAGE 42   INDUS
B0844   OP/RES
                                                        WORKER
                                                                    B54
MATTHEWS D.R.,THE SOCIAL BACKGROUND OF POLITICAL   DECISION
DECISION-MAKERS. CULTURE SOCIETY STRATA FAM   BIOG
EX/STRUC LEAD ATTIT BIO/SOC DRIVE PERSON ALL/VALS   SOC
HIST/WRIT. PAGE 71 B1431
                                                                    B54
MILLARD E.L.,FREEDOM IN A FEDERAL WORLD. FUT WOR+45   INT/ORG
VOL/ASSN TOP/EX LEGIT ROUTINE FEDERAL PEACE ATTIT   CREATE
DISPL ORD/FREE PWR...MAJORIT INT/LAW JURID TREND   ADJUD
COLD/WAR 20. PAGE 73 B1479   BAL/PWR
                                                                    B54
MOSK S.A.,INDUSTRIAL REVOLUTION IN MEXICO. MARKET   INDUS
LABOR CREATE CAP/ISM ADMIN ATTIT SOCISM...POLICY 20   TEC/DEV
MEXIC/AMER. PAGE 76 B1533   ECO/UNDEV
                                                        NAT/G
                                                                    B54
THORNTON M.L.,OFFICIAL PUBLICATIONS OF THE COLONY   BIBLIOG
AND STATE OF NORTH CAROLINA, 1749-1939. USA+45   ADMIN
USA-45 LEGIS LEAD GOV/REL ATTIT 18/20. PAGE 104   PROVS
B2109   ACADEM
                                                                    L54
FURNISS E.S.,"WEAKNESSES IN FRENCH FOREIGN POLICY-   NAT/G
MAKING." EUR+WWI LEGIS LEGIT EXEC ATTIT RIGID/FLEX   STRUCT
ORD/FREE...SOC CONCPT METH/CNCPT OBS 20. PAGE 38   DIPLOM
B0766   FRANCE
                                                                    L54
ROSTOW W.W.,"ASIAN LEADERSHIP AND FREE-WORLD   ATTIT
ALLIANCE." ASIA COM USA+45 CULTURE ELITES INTELL   LEGIT
NAT/G TEC/DEV ECO/TAC EDU/PROP COLONIAL PARL/PROC   DIPLOM
ROUTINE COERCE DRIVE ORD/FREE MARXISM...PSY CONCPT.
PAGE 90 B1829
                                                                    C54
GOULDNER A.W.,"PATTERNS OF INDUSTRIAL BUREAUCRACY."   ADMIN
GP/REL CONSEN ATTIT DRIVE...BIBLIOG 20. PAGE 42   INDUS
B0843   OP/RES
                                                        WORKER
                                                                    B55
APTER D.E.,THE GOLD COAST IN TRANSITION. FUT CONSTN   AFR
CULTURE SOCIETY ECO/UNDEV FAM KIN LOC/G NAT/G   SOVEREIGN
POL/PAR LEGIS TOP/EX EDU/PROP LEGIT ADMIN ATTIT
PERSON PWR...CONCPT STAT INT CENSUS TOT/POP
VAL/FREE. PAGE 6 B0120
                                                                    B55
BERNAYS E.L.,THE ENGINEERING OF CONSENT. VOL/ASSN   GP/REL
OP/RES ROUTINE INGP/REL ATTIT RESPECT...POLICY   PLAN
METH/CNCPT METH/COMP 20. PAGE 11 B0224   ACT/RES
                                                        ADJUST
                                                                    B55
MAZZINI J.,THE DUTIES OF MAN. MOD/EUR LAW SOCIETY   SUPEGO
FAM NAT/G POL/PAR SECT VOL/ASSN EX/STRUC ACT/RES   CONCPT
CREATE REV PEACE ATTIT ALL/VALS...GEN/LAWS WORK 19.   NAT/LISM
PAGE 71 B1439
                                                                    B55
POOL I.,SATELLITE GENERALS: A STUDY OF MILITARY   FORCES

ELITES IN THE SOVIET SPHERE. ASIA CHINA/COM COM
CZECHOSLVK FUT HUNGARY POLAND ROMANIA USSR ELITES
STRATA ADMIN ATTIT PWR SKILL...METH/CNCPT BIOG 20.
PAGE 84 B1688
    CHOOSE

    B55
STEPHENS O.,FACTS TO A CANDID WORLD. USA+45 WOR+45
COM/IND EX/STRUC PRESS ROUTINE EFFICIENCY ATTIT
...PSY 20. PAGE 100 B2033
    EDU/PROP
    PHIL/SCI
    NAT/G
    DIPLOM

    B55
UN HEADQUARTERS LIBRARY,BIBLIOGRAPHIE DE LA CHARTE
DES NATIONS UNIES. CHINA/COM KOREA WOR+45 VOL/ASSN
CONFER ADMIN COERCE PEACE ATTIT ORD/FREE SOVEREIGN
...INT/LAW 20 UNESCO UN. PAGE 106 B2149
    BIBLIOG/A
    INT/ORG
    DIPLOM

    L55
ROSTOW W.W.,"RUSSIA AND CHINA UNDER COMMUNISM."
CHINA/COM USSR INTELL STRUCT INT/ORG NAT/G POL/PAR
TOP/EX ACT/RES PLAN ADMIN ATTIT ALL/VALS MARXISM
...CONCPT OBS TIME/SEQ TREND GOV/COMP VAL/FREE 20.
PAGE 91 B1830
    COM
    ASIA

    S55
ANGELL R.,"GOVERNMENTS AND PEOPLES AS A FOCI FOR
PEACE-ORIENTED RESEARCH." WOR+45 CULTURE SOCIETY
FACE/GP ACT/RES CREATE PLAN DIPLOM EDU/PROP ROUTINE
ATTIT PERCEPT SKILL...POLICY CONCPT OBS TREND
GEN/METH 20. PAGE 5 B0110
    FUT
    SOC
    PEACE

    S55
BUNZEL J.H.,"THE GENERAL IDEOLOGY OF AMERICAN SMALL
BUSINESS"(BMR)" USA+45 USA-45 AGRI GP/REL INGP/REL
PERSON...MGT IDEA/COMP 18/20. PAGE 17 B0345
    ALL/IDEOS
    ATTIT
    SML/CO
    INDUS

    S55
CROCKETT W.H.,"EMERGENT LEADERSHIP IN SMALL
DECISION MAKING GROUPS." ACT/RES ROUTINE PERS/REL
ATTIT...STAT CONT/OBS SOC/EXP SIMUL. PAGE 25 B0507
    DELIB/GP
    ADMIN
    PSY
    DECISION

    S55
TORRE M.,"PSYCHIATRIC OBSERVATIONS OF INTERNATIONAL
CONFERENCES." WOR+45 INT/ORG PROF/ORG VOL/ASSN
CONSULT EDU/PROP ROUTINE ATTIT DRIVE KNOWL...PSY
METH/CNCPT OBS/ENVIR STERTYP 20. PAGE 105 B2119
    DELIB/GP
    OBS
    DIPLOM

    B56
CONAWAY O.B.,DEMOCRACY IN FEDERAL ADMINISTRATION
(PAMPHLET). USA+45 LEGIS PARTIC ATTIT...TREND
ANTHOL 20. PAGE 23 B0459
    ADMIN
    SERV/IND
    NAT/G
    GP/REL

    B56
JENNINGS W.I.,THE APPROACH TO SELF-GOVERNMENT.
CEYLON INDIA PAKISTAN S/ASIA UK SOCIETY POL/PAR
DELIB/GP LEGIS ECO/TAC EDU/PROP ADMIN EXEC CHOOSE
ATTIT ALL/VALS...JURID CONCPT GEN/METH TOT/POP 20.
PAGE 56 B1136
    NAT/G
    CONSTN
    COLONIAL

    B56
KAUFMANN W.W.,MILITARY POLICY AND NATIONAL
SECURITY. USA+45 ELITES INTELL NAT/G TOP/EX PLAN
BAL/PWR DIPLOM ROUTINE COERCE NUC/PWR ATTIT
ORD/FREE PWR 20 COLD/WAR. PAGE 58 B1182
    FORCES
    CREATE

    B56
MANNONI D.O.,PROSPERO AND CALIBAN: THE PSYCHOLOGY
OF COLONIZATION. AFR EUR+WWI FAM KIN MUNIC SECT
DOMIN ADMIN ATTIT DRIVE LOVE PWR RESPECT...PSY SOC
CONCPT MYTH OBS DEEP/INT BIOG GEN/METH MALAGASY 20.
PAGE 69 B1394
    CULTURE
    COLONIAL

    B56
WAUGH E.W.,SECOND CONSUL. USA+45 USA-45 CONSTN
POL/PAR PROB/SOLV PARL/PROC CHOOSE PERS/REL ATTIT
...BIBLIOG 18/20 VICE/PRES. PAGE 114 B2304
    NAT/G
    EX/STRUC
    PWR
    CHIEF

    B56
WILSON W.,CONGRESSIONAL GOVERNMENT. USA-45 NAT/G
ADMIN EXEC PARL/PROC GP/REL MAJORITY ATTIT 19
SENATE HOUSE/REP. PAGE 117 B2364
    LEGIS
    CHIEF
    CONSTN
    PWR

    S56
HEADY F.,"THE MICHIGAN DEPARTMENT OF
ADMINISTRATION; A CASE STUDY IN THE POLITICS OF
ADMINISTRATION" (BMR)" USA+45 POL/PAR PROVS CHIEF
LEGIS GP/REL ATTIT 20 MICHIGAN. PAGE 48 B0980
    ADMIN
    DELIB/GP
    LOC/G

    S56
KAUFMAN H.,"EMERGING CONFLICTS IN THE DOCTRINES OF
PUBLIC ADMINISTRATION" (BMR)" USA+45 USA-45 NAT/G
EX/STRUC LEGIS CONTROL NEUTRAL ATTIT PWR...TREND
20. PAGE 58 B1181
    ADMIN
    ORD/FREE
    REPRESENT
    LEAD

    C56
AUMANN F.R.,"THE ISTRUMENTALITIES OF JUSTICE: THEIR
FORMS, FUNCTIONS, AND LIMITATIONS." WOR+45 WOR-45
JUDGE PROB/SOLV ROUTINE ATTIT...BIBLIOG 20. PAGE 7
B0147
    JURID
    ADMIN
    CT/SYS
    ADJUD

    C56
FALL B.B.,"THE VIET-MINH REGIME." VIETNAM LAW
ECO/UNDEV POL/PAR FORCES DOMIN WAR ATTIT MARXISM
...BIOG PREDICT BIBLIOG/A 20. PAGE 35 B0703
    NAT/G
    ADMIN
    EX/STRUC
    LEAD

    C56
NEUMANN S.,"MODERN POLITICAL PARTIES: APPROACHES TO
COMPARATIVE POLITIC. FRANCE UK EX/STRUC DOMIN ADMIN
    POL/PAR
    GOV/COMP

LEAD REPRESENT TOTALISM ATTIT...POLICY TREND
METH/COMP ANTHOL BIBLIOG/A 20 CMN/WLTH. PAGE 78
B1574
    ELITES
    MAJORIT

    B57
BERGER M.,BUREAUCRACY AND SOCIETY IN MODERN EGYPT;
A STUDY OF THE HIGHER CIVIL SERVICE. UAR REPRESENT
...QU 20. PAGE 11 B0221
    ATTIT
    EXEC
    ADMIN
    ROUTINE

    B57
DJILAS M.,THE NEW CLASS: AN ANALYSIS OF THE
COMMUNIST SYSTEM. STRATA CAP/ISM ECO/TAC DOMIN
EDU/PROP LEGIT EXEC COERCE ATTIT PWR MARXISM
...MARXIST MGT CONCPT TIME/SEQ GEN/LAWS 20. PAGE 29
B0600
    COM
    POL/PAR
    USSR
    YUGOSLAVIA

    B57
HOLCOMBE A.N.,STRENGTHENING THE UNITED NATIONS.
USA+45 ACT/RES CREATE PLAN EDU/PROP ATTIT PERCEPT
PWR...METH/CNCPT CONT/OBS RECORD UN COLD/WAR 20.
PAGE 51 B1032
    INT/ORG
    ROUTINE

    B57
HUNTINGTON S.P.,THE SOLDIER AND THE STATE: THE
THEORY AND POLITICS OF CIVIL-MILITARY RELATIONS.
USA+45 USA-45 NAT/G PROF/ORG CONSULT DOMIN LEGIT
ROUTINE ATTIT PWR...CONCPT TIME/SEQ COLD/WAR 20.
PAGE 53 B1065
    ACT/RES
    FORCES

    B57
IKE N.,JAPANESE POLITICS. INTELL STRUCT AGRI INDUS
FAM KIN LABOR PRESS CHOOSE ATTIT...DECISION BIBLIOG
19/20 CHINJAP. PAGE 53 B1075
    NAT/G
    ADMIN
    POL/PAR
    CULTURE

    B57
KAPLAN M.A.,SYSTEM AND PROCESS OF INTERNATIONAL
POLITICS. FUT WOR+45 WOR-45 SOCIETY PLAN BAL/PWR
ADMIN ATTIT PERSON RIGID/FLEX PWR SOVEREIGN
...DECISION TREND VAL/FREE. PAGE 58 B1168
    INT/ORG
    DIPLOM

    B57
KNEIER C.M.,CITY GOVERNMENT IN THE UNITED STATES
(3RD ED.). USA-45 FINAN NAT/G POL/PAR LEGIS
EDU/PROP LEAD APPORT REPRESENT ATTIT...MGT 20
CITY/MGT. PAGE 60 B1219
    MUNIC
    LOC/G
    ADMIN
    GOV/REL

    B57
LOEWENSTEIN K.,POLITICAL POWER AND THE GOVERNMENTAL
PROCESS. WOR+45 CONSTN NAT/G POL/PAR
EX/STRUC LEGIS TOP/EX DOMIN EDU/PROP LEGIT ADMIN
REGION CHOOSE ATTIT...JURID STERTYP GEN/LAWS 20.
PAGE 66 B1336
    PWR
    CONCPT

    B57
PARKINSON C.N.,PARKINSON'S LAW. UNIV EX/STRUC PLAN
ATTIT PERSON TIME. PAGE 81 B1634
    ADMIN
    EXEC
    FINAN
    ECOMETRIC

    B57
SHARMA S.R.,SOME ASPECTS OF THE INDIAN
ADMINISTRATIVE SYSTEM. INDIA WOR+45 TEC/DEV BUDGET
LEGIT ROUTINE ATTIT. PAGE 96 B1937
    EXEC
    DECISION
    ADMIN
    INGP/REL

    B57
SIMON H.A.,MODELS OF MAN, SOCIAL AND RATIONAL:
MATHEMATICAL ESSAYS ON RATIONAL HUMAN BEHAVIOR IN A
SOCIAL SETTING. UNIV LAW SOCIETY FACE/GP VOL/ASSN
CONSULT EX/STRUC LEGIS CREATE ADMIN ROUTINE ATTIT
DRIVE PWR...SOC CONCPT METH/CNCPT QUANT STAT
TOT/POP VAL/FREE 20. PAGE 97 B1959
    MATH
    SIMUL

    L57
HAAS E.B.,"REGIONAL INTEGRATION AND NATIONAL
POLICY." WOR+45 VOL/ASSN DELIB/GP EX/STRUC ECO/TAC
DOMIN EDU/PROP LEGIT COERCE ATTIT PERCEPT KNOWL
...TIME/SEQ COLD/WAR 20 UN. PAGE 45 B0908
    INT/ORG
    ORD/FREE
    REGION

    S57
BAUER R.A.,"BRAINWASHING: PSYCHOLOGY OR
DEMONOLOGY." ASIA CHINA/COM COM POL/PAR ECO/TAC
ADMIN COERCE ATTIT DRIVE ORD/FREE...CONCPT MYTH 20.
PAGE 10 B0196
    EDU/PROP
    PSY
    TOTALISM

    S57
COTTER C.P.,"ADMINISTRATIVE ACCOUNTABILITY;
REPORTING TO CONGRESS." USA+45 CONSULT DELIB/GP
PARL/PROC PARTIC GOV/REL ATTIT PWR DECISION.
PAGE 24 B0490
    LEGIS
    EX/STRUC
    REPRESENT
    CONTROL

    S57
HAILEY,"TOMORROW IN AFRICA." CONSTN SOCIETY LOC/G
NAT/G DOMIN ADJUD ADMIN GP/REL DISCRIM NAT/LISM
ATTIT MORAL ORD/FREE...PSY SOC CONCPT OBS RECORD
TREND GEN/LAWS CMN/WLTH 20. PAGE 45 B0917
    AFR
    PERSON
    ELITES
    RACE/REL

    S57
JANOWITZ M.,"THE BUREAUCRAT AND THE PUBLIC: A STUDY
OF INFORMATIONAL PERSPECTIVES." USA+45 PROB/SOLV
ATTIT 20. PAGE 55 B1120
    REPRESENT
    ADMIN
    EX/STRUC
    CLIENT

    S57
RAPAPORT R.N.,"'DEMOCRATIZATION' AND AUTHORITY IN A
THERAPEUTIC COMMUNITY." OP/RES ADMIN PARTIC CENTRAL
ATTIT...POLICY DECISION. PAGE 86 B1735
    PUB/INST
    HEALTH
    DOMIN
    CLIENT

    S57
ROURKE F.E.,"THE POLITICS OF ADMINISTRATIVE
ORGANIZATION: A CASE HISTORY." USA+45 LABOR WORKER
    POLICY
    ATTIT

PLAN ADMIN TASK EFFICIENCY 20 DEPT/LABOR CONGRESS. MGT
PAGE 91 B1836   GP/COMP
                                                        B58
LAQUER W.Z.,THE MIDDLE EAST IN TRANSITION. COM USSR ISLAM
ECO/UNDEV NAT/G VOL/ASSN EDU/PROP EXEC ATTIT DRIVE   TREND
PWR MARXISM COLD/WAR TOT/POP 20. PAGE 62 B1261   NAT/LISM
                                                        B58
LOVEJOY D.S.,RHODE ISLAND POLITICS AND THE AMERICAN REV
REVOLUTION 1760-1776. UK USA+45 ELITES EX/STRUC TAX COLONIAL
LEAD REPRESENT GOV/REL GP/REL ATTIT 18 RHODE/ISL.   ECO/TAC
PAGE 67 B1343   SOVEREIGN
                                                        B58
MARCH J.G.,ORGANIZATIONS. USA+45 CREATE OP/RES PLAN MGT
PROB/SOLV PARTIC ROUTINE RATIONAL ATTIT PERCEPT   PERSON
...DECISION BIBLIOG. PAGE 69 B1397   DRIVE
                                                     CONCPT
                                                        B58
MILLS C.W.,THE CAUSES OF WORLD WAR THREE. FUT   CONSULT
USA+45 INTELL NAT/G DOMIN EDU/PROP ADMIN WAR ATTIT   PWR
SOC. PAGE 74 B1487   ELITES
                                                     PEACE
                                                        B58
REDFORD E.S.,IDEAL AND PRACTICE IN PUBLIC   POLICY
ADMINISTRATION. CONSTN ELITES NAT/G CONSULT   EX/STRUC
DELIB/GP LEAD UTOPIA ATTIT POPULISM...DECISION   PLAN
METH/COMP 20. PAGE 87 B1756   ADMIN
                                                        B58
SCOTT D.J.R.,RUSSIAN POLITICAL INSTITUTIONS. RUSSIA NAT/G
USSR CONSTN AGRI DELIB/GP PLAN EDU/PROP CONTROL   POL/PAR
CHOOSE EFFICIENCY ATTIT MARXISM...BIBLIOG/A 13/20.   ADMIN
PAGE 95 B1919   DECISION
                                                        B58
SPITZ D.,DEMOCRACY AND THE CHALLANGE OF POWER. FUT   NAT/G
USA+45 LAW SOCIETY STRUCT LOC/G POL/PAR   PWR
PROVS DELIB/GP EX/STRUC LEGIS TOP/EX ACT/RES CREATE
DOMIN EDU/PROP LEGIT ADJUD ADMIN ATTIT DRIVE MORAL
ORD/FREE TOT/POP. PAGE 99 B2010
                                                        B58
STEWART J.D.,BRITISH PRESSURE GROUPS: THEIR ROLE IN LOBBY
RELATION TO THE HOUSE OF COMMONS. UK CONSULT   LEGIS
DELIB/GP ADMIN ROUTINE CHOOSE REPRESENT ATTIT ROLE   PLAN
20 HOUSE/CMNS PARLIAMENT. PAGE 101 B2038   PARL/PROC
                                                        B58
TAYLOR H.,THE STATESMAN. MOD/EUR FACE/GP FAM NAT/G   EXEC
POL/PAR DELIB/GP LEGIS ATTIT PERSON PWR...POLICY   STRUCT
CONCPT OBS GEN/LAWS. PAGE 103 B2086
                                                        L58
HAVILAND H.F.,"FOREIGN AID AND THE POLICY PROCESS: LEGIS
1957." USA+45 FACE/GP POL/PAR VOL/ASSN CHIEF   PLAN
DELIB/GP ACT/RES LEGIT EXEC GOV/REL ATTIT DRIVE PWR FOR/AID
...POLICY TESTS CONGRESS 20. PAGE 48 B0971
                                                        S58
JORDAN A.,"MILITARY ASSISTANCE AND NATIONAL   FORCES
POLICY." ASIA FUT USA+45 WOR+45 ECO/DEV ECO/UNDEV   POLICY
INT/ORG NAT/G PLAN ECO/TAC ROUTINE WEAPON ATTIT   FOR/AID
RIGID/FLEX PWR...CONCPT TREND 20. PAGE 57 B1153   DIPLOM
                                                        S58
STAAR R.F.,"ELECTIONS IN COMMUNIST POLAND." EUR+WWI COM
SOCIETY INT/ORG NAT/G POL/PAR LEGIS ACT/RES ECO/TAC CHOOSE
EDU/PROP ADJUD ADMIN ROUTINE COERCE TOTALISM ATTIT   POLAND
ORD/FREE PWR 20. PAGE 100 B2015
                                                        C58
REDFORD E.S.,"THE NEVER-ENDING SEARCH FOR THE   LOBBY
PUBLIC INTEREST" IN E. REDFORD, IDEALS AND PRACTICE POLICY
IN PUBLIC ADMINISTRATION (BMR)" USA+45 USA-45   ADMIN
SOCIETY PARTIC GP/REL ATTIT PLURISM...DECISION SOC   MAJORIT
20. PAGE 87 B1755
                                                        B59
BOWLES C.,THE COMING POLITICAL BREAKTHROUGH. USA+45 DIPLOM
ECO/DEV EX/STRUC ATTIT...CONCPT OBS 20. PAGE 14   CHOOSE
B0288   PREDICT
                                                     POL/PAR
                                                        B59
CHINA INSTITUTE OF AMERICA.,CHINA AND THE UNITED   ASIA
NATIONS. CHINA/COM FUT STRUCT EDU/PROP LEGIT ADMIN   INT/ORG
ATTIT KNOWL ORD/FREE PWR...OBS RECORD STAND/INT
TIME/SEQ UN LEAGUE/NAT UNESCO 20. PAGE 21 B0425
                                                        B59
ELLIOTT O.,MEN AT THE TOP. USA+45 CULTURE EX/STRUC   TOP/EX
PRESS GOV/REL ATTIT ALL/VALS...OBS INT QU 20.   PERSON
PAGE 33 B0668   LEAD
                                                     POLICY
                                                        B59
FAYERWEATHER J.,THE EXECUTIVE OVERSEAS: INT/TRADE
ADMINISTRATIVE ATTITUDES AND RELATIONSHIPS IN A   TOP/EX
FOREIGN CULTURE. USA+45 WOR+45 CULTURE LG/CO SML/CO NAT/COMP
ATTIT...MGT PERS/COMP 20 MEXIC/AMER. PAGE 35 B0709   PERS/REL
                                                        B59
GRABER D.,CRISIS DIPLOMACY. L/A+17C USA+45 USA-45   ROUTINE
NAT/G TOP/EX ECO/TAC COERCE ATTIT ORD/FREE...CONCPT MORAL
MYTH TIME/SEQ COLD/WAR 20. PAGE 42 B0848   DIPLOM
                                                        B59
MACIVER R.M.,THE NATIONS AND THE UN. WOR+45 NAT/G   INT/ORG
CONSULT ADJUD ADMIN ALL/VALS...CONCPT DEEP/QU UN   ATTIT
TOT/POP UNESCO 20. PAGE 67 B1362   DIPLOM

                                                        B59
MAYNTZ R.,PARTEIGRUPPEN IN DER GROSSSTADT. GERMANY   MUNIC
STRATA STRUCT DOMIN CHOOSE 20. PAGE 71 B1437   MGT
                                                     POL/PAR
                                                     ATTIT
                                                        B59
SCHURZ W.L.,AMERICAN FOREIGN AFFAIRS: A GUIDE TO   INT/ORG
INTERNATIONAL AFFAIRS. USA+45 WOR+45 WOR-45 NAT/G   SOCIETY
FORCES LEGIS TOP/EX PLAN EDU/PROP LEGIT ADMIN   DIPLOM
ROUTINE ATTIT ORD/FREE PWR...SOC CONCPT STAT
SAMP/SIZ CHARTS STERTYP 20. PAGE 95 B1910
                                                        B59
SISSON C.H.,THE SPIRIT OF BRITISH ADMINISTRATION   GOV/COMP
AND SOME EUROPEAN COMPARISONS. FRANCE GERMANY/W   ADMIN
SWEDEN UK LAW EX/STRUC INGP/REL EFFICIENCY ORD/FREE ELITES
...DECISION 20. PAGE 98 B1972   ATTIT
                                                        B59
WEBER W.,DER DEUTSCHE BEAMTE HEUTE. GERMANY/W NAT/G MGT
DELIB/GP LEGIS CONFER ATTIT SUPEGO...JURID 20.   EFFICIENCY
CIVIL/SERV. PAGE 114 B2306   ELITES
                                                     GP/REL
                                                        B59
YANG C.K.,A CHINESE VILLAGE IN EARLY COMMUNIST   ASIA
TRANSITION. ECO/UNDEV AGRI FAM KIN MUNIC FORCES   ROUTINE
PLAN ECO/TAC DOMIN EDU/PROP ATTIT DRIVE PWR RESPECT SOCISM
...SOC CONCPT METH/CNCPT OBS RECORD CON/ANAL CHARTS
WORK 20. PAGE 118 B2389
                                                        S59
BAILEY S.D.,"THE FUTURE COMPOSITION OF THE   INT/ORG
TRUSTEESHIP COUNCIL." FUT WOR+45 CONSTN VOL/ASSN   NAT/LISM
ADMIN ATTIT PWR...OBS TREND CON/ANAL VAL/FREE UN   SOVEREIGN
20. PAGE 8 B0101
                                                        S59
BENDIX R.,"INDUSTRIALIZATION, IDEOLOGIES, AND   INDUS
SOCIAL STRUCTURE" (BMR)" UK USA+45 USSR STRUCT   ATTIT
WORKER GP/REL EFFICIENCY...IDEA/COMP 20. PAGE 10   MGT
B0210   ADMIN
                                                        S59
DWYER R.J.,"THE ADMINISTRATIVE ROLE IN   ADMIN
DESEGREGATION." USA+45 LAW PROB/SOLV LEAD RACE/REL   SCHOOL
ISOLAT STRANGE ROLE...POLICY SOC/INTEG MISSOURI   DISCRIM
NEGRO CIV/RIGHTS. PAGE 31 B0638   ATTIT
                                                        S59
KISSINGER H.A.,"THE POLICYMAKER AND THE   INTELL
INTELLECTUAL." USA+45 CONSULT DELIB/GP ACT/RES   CREATE
ADMIN ATTIT DRIVE RIGID/FLEX KNOWL PWR...POLICY
PLURIST MGT METH/CNCPT GEN/LAWS GEN/METH 20.
PAGE 60 B1216
                                                        S59
LASSWELL H.D.,"UNIVERSALITY IN PERSPECTIVE." FUT   INT/ORG
UNIV SOCIETY CONSULT TOP/EX PLAN EDU/PROP ADJUD   JURID
ROUTINE ARMS/CONT COERCE PEACE ATTIT PERSON   TOTALISM
ALL/VALS. PAGE 63 B1271
                                                        S59
LENGYEL P.,"SOME TRENDS IN THE INTERNATIONAL CIVIL   ADMIN
SERVICE." FUT WOR+45 INT/ORG CONSULT ATTIT...MGT   EXEC
OBS TREND CON/ANAL LEAGUE/NAT UNESCO 20. PAGE 64
B1291
                                                        S59
SUTTON F.X.,"REPRESENTATION AND THE NATURE OF   NAT/G
POLITICAL SYSTEMS." UNIV WOR-45 CULTURE SOCIETY   CONCPT
STRATA INT/ORG FORCES JUDGE DOMIN LEGIT EXEC REGION
REPRESENT ATTIT ORD/FREE RESPECT...SOC HIST/WRIT
TIME/SEQ. PAGE 102 B2057
                                                        S59
ZAUBERMAN A.,"SOVIET BLOC ECONOMIC INTEGRATION."   MARKET
COM CULTURE INTELL ECO/DEV INDUS TOP/EX ACT/RES   INT/ORG
PLAN ECO/TAC INT/TRADE ROUTINE CHOOSE ATTIT   USSR
...TIME/SEQ 20. PAGE 119 B2399   TOTALISM
                                                        B60
ADRIAN C.R.,STATE AND LOCAL GOVERNMENTS: A STUDY IN LOC/G
THE POLITICAL PROCESS. USA+45 LAW FINAN MUNIC   PROVS
POL/PAR LEGIS ADJUD EXEC CHOOSE REPRESENT. PAGE 3   GOV/REL
B0060   ATTIT
                                                        B60
BAERWALD F.,ECONOMIC SYSTEM ANALYSIS: CONCEPTS AND   ACT/RES
PERSPECTIVES. USA+45 ECO/DEV NAT/G COMPUTER EQUILIB ECO/TAC
INCOME ATTIT...DECISION CONCPT IDEA/COMP. PAGE 8   ROUTINE
B0159   FINAN
                                                        B60
BERNSTEIN I.,THE LEAN YEARS. SOCIETY STRATA PARTIC   WORKER
GP/REL ATTIT...SOC 20 DEPRESSION. PAGE 11 B0227   LABOR
                                                     WEALTH
                                                     MGT
                                                        B60
BRISTOL L.H. JR.,DEVELOPING THE CORPORATE IMAGE.   LG/CO
USA+45 SOCIETY ECO/DEV COM/IND SCHOOL EDU/PROP   ATTIT
PRESS TV...AUD/VIS ANTHOL. PAGE 15 B0312   MGT
                                                     ECO/TAC
                                                        B60
EASTON S.C.,THE TWILIGHT OF EUROPEAN COLONIALISM.   FINAN
AFR S/ASIA CONSTN SOCIETY STRUCT ECO/UNDEV INDUS   ADMIN
NAT/G FORCES ECO/TAC COLONIAL CT/SYS ATTIT KNOWL
ORD/FREE PWR...SOCIALIST TIME/SEQ TREND CON/ANAL
20. PAGE 32 B0645

B60
ECKHOFF T.,RATIONALITY AND RESPONSIBILITY IN   ADMIN
ADMINISTRATIVE AND JUDICIAL DECISION-MAKING. ELITES   PROB/SOLV
LEAD INGP/REL ATTIT PWR...MGT METH/COMP GAME 20.   DECISION
PAGE 32 B0649   METH/CNCPT
                                                      B60
FURNISS E.S.,FRANCE, TROUBLED ALLY. EUR+WWI FUT   NAT/G
CULTURE SOCIETY BAL/PWR ADMIN ATTIT DRIVE PWR   FRANCE
...TREND TOT/POP 20 DEGAULLE/C. PAGE 38 B0767
                                                      B60
GLOVER J.D.,A CASE STUDY OF HIGH LEVEL   ADMIN
ADMINISTRATION IN A LARGE ORGANIZATION. EX/STRUC   TOP/EX
EXEC LEAD ROUTINE INGP/REL OPTIMAL ATTIT PERSON   FORCES
...POLICY DECISION INT QU. PAGE 40 B0812   NAT/G
                                                      B60
GRANICK D.,THE RED EXECUTIVE. COM USA+45 SOCIETY   PWR
ECO/DEV INDUS NAT/G POL/PAR EX/STRUC PLAN ECO/TAC   STRATA
EDU/PROP ADMIN EXEC ATTIT DRIVE...GP/COMP 20.   USSR
PAGE 42 B0851   ELITES
                                                      B60
GRUNDLICH T.,DIE TECHNIK DER DIKTATUR. ADMIN   COERCE
TOTALISM ATTIT PWR...MGT CONCPT ARISTOTLE. PAGE 44   DOMIN
B0896   ORD/FREE
                                                      WAR
                                                      B60
HAUSER O.,PREUSSISCHE STAATSRASON UND NATIONALER   NAT/LISM
GEDANKE. PRUSSIA SOCIETY PRESS ADMIN...CONCPT   NAT/G
19/20. PAGE 48 B0969   ATTIT
                                                      PROVS
                                                      B60
LENCZOWSKI G.,OIL AND STATE IN THE MIDDLE EAST. FUT   ISLAM
IRAN LAW ECO/UNDEV EXTR/IND NAT/G TOP/EX PLAN   INDUS
TEC/DEV ECO/TAC LEGIT ADMIN COERCE ATTIT ALL/VALS   NAT/LISM
PWR...CHARTS 20. PAGE 64 B1288
                                                      B60
LERNER A.P.,THE ECONOMICS OF CONTROL. USA+45   ECO/DEV
ECO/UNDEV INT/ORG ACT/RES PLAN CAP/ISM INT/TRADE   ROUTINE
ATTIT WEALTH...SOC MATH STAT GEN/LAWS INDEX 20.   ECO/TAC
PAGE 64 B1295   SOCISM
                                                      B60
LINDSAY K.,EUROPEAN ASSEMBLIES: THE EXPERIMENTAL   VOL/ASSN
PERIOD 1949-1959. EUR+WWI ECO/DEV NAT/G POL/PAR   INT/ORG
LEGIS TOP/EX ACT/RES PLAN ECO/TAC DOMIN LEGIT   REGION
ROUTINE ATTIT DRIVE ORD/FREE PWR SKILL...SOC CONCPT
TREND CHARTS GEN/LAWS VAL/FREE. PAGE 65 B1315
                                                      B60
LISKA G.,THE NEW STATECRAFT. WOR+45 WOR-45 LEGIS   ECO/TAC
DIPLOM ADMIN ATTIT WEALTH...HIST/WRIT TREND   CONCPT
COLD/WAR 20. PAGE 66 B1323   FOR/AID
                                                      B60
MCGREGOR D.,THE HUMAN SIDE OF ENTERPRISE. USA+45   MGT
LEAD ROUTINE GP/REL INGP/REL...CONCPT GEN/LAWS 20.   ATTIT
PAGE 72 B1449   SKILL
                                                      EDU/PROP
                                                      B60
MEEHAN E.J.,THE BRITISH LEFT WING AND FOREIGN   ACT/RES
POLICY: A STUDY OF THE INFLUENCE OF IDEOLOGY. FUT   ATTIT
UK UNIV WOR+45 INTELL TOP/EX PLAN ADMIN ROUTINE   DIPLOM
DRIVE...OBS TIME/SEQ GEN/LAWS PARLIAMENT 20.
PAGE 72 B1461
                                                      B60
MEYRIAT J.,LA SCIENCE POLITIQUE EN FRANCE,   BIBLIOG/A
1945-1958; BIBLIOGRAPHIES FRANCAISES DE SCIENCES   NAT/G
SOCIALES (VOL. I). EUR+WWI FRANCE POL/PAR DIPLOM   CONCPT
ADMIN CHOOSE ATTIT...IDEA/COMP METH/COMP NAT/COMP   PHIL/SCI
20. PAGE 73 B1478
                                                      B60
MOORE W.E.,LABOR COMMITMENT AND SOCIAL CHANGE IN   LABOR
DEVELOPING AREAS. SOCIETY STRATA ECO/UNDEV MARKET   ORD/FREE
VOL/ASSN WORKER AUTHORIT SKILL...MGT NAT/COMP   ATTIT
SOC/INTEG 20. PAGE 75 B1514   INDUS
                                                      B60
MUNRO L.,UNITED NATIONS, HOPE FOR A DIVIDED WORLD.   INT/ORG
FUT WOR+45 CONSTN DELIB/GP CREATE TEC/DEV DIPLOM   ROUTINE
EDU/PROP LEGIT PEACE ATTIT HEALTH ORD/FREE PWR
...CONCPT TREND UN VAL/FREE 20. PAGE 76 B1540
                                                      B60
PENTONY D.E.,UNITED STATES FOREIGN AID. INDIA LAOS   FOR/AID
USA+45 ECO/UNDEV INT/TRADE ADMIN PEACE ATTIT   DIPLOM
...POLICY METH/COMP ANTHOL 20. PAGE 82 B1653   ECO/TAC
                                                      B60
ROEPKE W.,A HUMANE ECONOMY: THE SOCIAL FRAMEWORK OF   DRIVE
THE FREE MARKET. FUT USSR WOR+45 CULTURE SOCIETY   EDU/PROP
ECO/DEV PLAN ECO/TAC ADMIN ATTIT PERSON RIGID/FLEX   CAP/ISM
SUPEGO MORAL WEALTH SOCISM...POLICY OLD/LIB CONCPT
TREND GEN/LAWS 20. PAGE 90 B1811
                                                      B60
RUBENSTEIN A.H.,SOME THEORIES OF ORGANIZATION.   SOCIETY
ROUTINE ATTIT...DECISION ECOMETRIC. PAGE 91 B1846   ECO/DEV
                                                      INDUS
                                                      TOP/EX
                                                      B60
SOUTH AFRICAN CONGRESS OF DEM,FACE THE FUTURE.   RACE/REL
SOUTH/AFR ELITES LEGIS ADMIN REGION COERCE PEACE   DISCRIM
ATTIT 20. PAGE 99 B1999   CONSTN
                                                      NAT/G

                                                      B60
STANFORD RESEARCH INSTITUTE,AFRICAN DEVELOPMENT: A   FOR/AID
TEST FOR INTERNATIONAL COOPERATION. AFR USA+45   ECO/UNDEV
WOR+45 FINAN INT/ORG PLAN PROB/SOLV ECO/TAC   ATTIT
INT/TRADE ADMIN...CHARTS 20. PAGE 100 B2018   DIPLOM
                                                      B60
US SENATE COMM. GOVT. OPER.,ORGANIZING FOR NATIONAL   CONSULT
SECURITY. USA+45 USA-45 INTELL STRUCT SML/CO   EXEC
ACT/RES ADMIN ATTIT PERSON PWR SKILL...DECISION 20.
PAGE 111 B2236
                                                      B60
WEIDNER E.W.,INTERGOVERNMENTAL RELATIONS AS SEEN BY   ATTIT
PUBLIC OFFICIALS. USA+45 PROVS EX/STRUC EXEC   GP/REL
FEDERAL...QU 20. PAGE 115 B2311   GOV/REL
                                                      ADMIN
                                                      S60
BOGARDUS E.S.,"THE SOCIOLOGY OF A STRUCTURED   INT/ORG
PEACE." FUT SOCIETY CREATE DIPLOM EDU/PROP ADJUD   SOC
ROUTINE ATTIT RIGID/FLEX KNOWL ORD/FREE RESPECT   NAT/LISM
...POLICY INT/LAW JURID NEW/IDEA SELF/OBS TOT/POP   PEACE
20 UN. PAGE 13 B0264
                                                      S60
BOYER W.W.,"POLICY MAKING BY GOVERNMENT AGENCIES."   NAT/G
USA+45 WOR+45 R+D DELIB/GP TOP/EX EDU/PROP ROUTINE   DIPLOM
ATTIT BIO/SOC DRIVE...CONCPT TREND TOT/POP 20.
PAGE 14 B0293
                                                      S60
EMERSON R.,"THE EROSION OF DEMOCRACY." AFR FUT LAW   S/ASIA
CULTURE INTELL SOCIETY ECO/UNDEV FAM LOC/G NAT/G   POL/PAR
FORCES PLAN TEC/DEV ECO/TAC ADMIN CT/SYS ATTIT
ORD/FREE PWR...SOCIALIST SOC CONCPT STAND/INT
TIME/SEQ WORK 20. PAGE 33 B0671
                                                      S60
FRANKEL S.H.,"ECONOMIC ASPECTS OF POLITICAL   NAT/G
INDEPENDENCE IN AFRICA." AFR FUT SOCIETY ECO/UNDEV   FOR/AID
COM/IND FINAN LEGIS PLAN TEC/DEV CAP/ISM ECO/TAC
INT/TRADE ADMIN ATTIT DRIVE RIGID/FLEX PWR WEALTH
...MGT NEW/IDEA MATH TIME/SEQ VAL/FREE 20. PAGE 37
B0751
                                                      S60
GARNICK D.H.,"ON THE ECONOMIC FEASIBILITY OF A   MARKET
MIDDLE EASTERN COMMON MARKET." AFR ISLAM CULTURE   INT/TRADE
INDUS NAT/G PLAN TEC/DEV ECO/TAC ADMIN ATTIT DRIVE
RIGID/FLEX...PLURIST STAT TREND GEN/LAWS 20.
PAGE 39 B0784
                                                      S60
HUTCHINSON C.E.,"AN INSTITUTE FOR NATIONAL SECURITY   POLICY
AFFAIRS." USA+45 R+D NAT/G CONSULT TOP/EX ACT/RES   METH/CNCPT
CREATE PLAN TEC/DEV EDU/PROP ROUTINE NUC/PWR ATTIT   ELITES
ORD/FREE PWR...DECISION MGT PHIL/SCI CONCPT RECORD   DIPLOM
GEN/LAWS GEN/METH 20. PAGE 53 B1068
                                                      S60
MODELSKI G.,"AUSTRALIA AND SEATO." S/ASIA USA+45   INT/ORG
CULTURE INTELL ECO/DEV NAT/G PLAN DIPLOM ADMIN   ACT/RES
ROUTINE ATTIT SKILL...MGT TIME/SEQ AUSTRAL 20
SEATO. PAGE 74 B1493
                                                      S60
REISELBACH L.N.,"THE BASIS OF ISOLATIONIST   ATTIT
BEHAVIOR." USA+45 USA-45 CULTURE ECO/DEV LOC/G   DIPLOM
NAT/G ADMIN CHOOSE BIO/SOC DRIVE RIGID/FLEX   ECO/TAC
...CENSUS SAMP TREND CHARTS TOT/POP 20. PAGE 87
B1765
                                                      S60
ROURKE F.E.,"ADMINISTRATIVE SECRECY: A   LEGIS
CONGRESSIONAL DILEMMA." DELIB/GP CT/SYS ATTIT   EXEC
...MAJORIT DECISION JURID. PAGE 91 B1837   ORD/FREE
                                                      POLICY
                                                      S60
SCHACHTER O.,"THE ENFORCEMENT OF INTERNATIONAL   INT/ORG
JUDICIAL AND ARBITRAL DECISIONS." WOR+45 NAT/G   ADJUD
ECO/TAC DOMIN LEGIT ROUTINE COERCE ATTIT DRIVE   INT/LAW
ALL/VALS PWR...METH/CNCPT TREND TOT/POP 20 UN.
PAGE 93 B1878
                                                      S60
SCHATZ S.P.,"THE INFLENCE OF PLANNING ON   ECO/UNDEV
DEVELOPMENT: THE NIGERIAN EXPERIENCE." AFR FUT   PLAN
FINAN INDUS NAT/G EX/STRUC ECO/TAC ADMIN ATTIT   NIGERIA
PERCEPT ORD/FREE PWR...MATH TREND CON/ANAL SIMUL
VAL/FREE 20. PAGE 93 B1883
                                                      S60
THOMPSON J.D.,"ORGANIZATIONAL MANAGEMENT OF   PROB/SOLV
CONFLICT" (BMR)" WOR+45 STRUCT LABOR LG/CO WORKER   PERS/REL
TEC/DEV INGP/REL ATTIT GP/COMP. PAGE 104 B2103   ADMIN
                                                      MGT
                                                      C60
FITZSIMMONS T.,"USSR: ITS PEOPLE, ITS SOCIETY, ITS   CULTURE
CULTURE." USSR FAM SECT DIPLOM EDU/PROP ADMIN   STRUCT
RACE/REL ATTIT...POLICY CHARTS BIBLIOG 20. PAGE 36   SOCIETY
B0728   COM
                                                      C60
SCHAPIRO L.B.,"THE COMMUNIST PARTY OF THE SOVIET   POL/PAR
UNION." USSR INTELL CHIEF EX/STRUC FORCES DOMIN   COM
ADMIN LEAD WAR ATTIT SOVEREIGN...POLICY BIBLIOG 20.   REV
PAGE 93 B1881
                                                      C60
SCHRAMM W.,"MASS COMMUNICATIONS: A BOOK OF READINGS   COM/IND

(2ND ED.)" LG/CO PRESS ADMIN CONTROL ROUTINE ATTIT EDU/PROP
ROLE SUPEGO...CHARTS ANTHOL BIBLIOG 20. PAGE 94 CROWD
B1902 MAJORIT
B61

AMERICAN MANAGEMENT ASSN.SUPERIOR-SUBORDINATE MGT
COMMUNICATION IN MANAGEMENT. STRATA FINAN INDUS ACT/RES
SML/CO WORKER CONTROL EXEC ATTIT 20. PAGE 4 B0086 PERS/REL
LG/CO
B61

BARNES W.,THE FOREIGN SERVICE OF THE UNITED STATES. NAT/G
USA+45 USA-45 CONSTN INT/ORG POL/PAR CONSULT MGT
DELIB/GP LEGIS DOMIN EDU/PROP EXEC ATTIT RIGID/FLEX DIPLOM
ORD/FREE PWR...POLICY CONCPT STAT OBS RECORD BIOG
TIME/SEQ TREND. PAGE 9 B0188
B61

BARRASH J.,LABOR'S GRASS ROOTS: A STUDY OF THE LABOR
LOCAL UNION. STRATA BARGAIN LEAD REPRESENT DEMAND USA+45
ATTIT PWR. PAGE 9 B0190 INGP/REL
EXEC
B61

BURDETTE F.L.,POLITICAL SCIENCE: A SELECTED BIBLIOG/A
BIBLIOGRAPHY OF BOOKS IN PRINT, WITH ANNOTATIONS GOV/COMP
(PAMPHLET). LAW LOC/G NAT/G POL/PAR PROVS DIPLOM CONCPT
EDU/PROP ADMIN CHOOSE ATTIT 20. PAGE 17 B0347 ROUTINE
B61

CATHERINE R.,LE FONCTIONNAIRE FRANCAIS. FRANCE ADMIN
NAT/G INGP/REL ATTIT MORAL ORD/FREE...T CIVIL/SERV. GP/REL
PAGE 19 B0394 LEAD
SUPEGO
B61

DRAGNICH A.N.,MAJOR EUROPEAN GOVERNMENTS. FRANCE NAT/G
GERMANY/W UK USSR LOC/G EX/STRUC CT/SYS PARL/PROC LEGIS
ATTIT MARXISM...JURID MGT NAT/COMP 19/20. PAGE 30 CONSTN
B0615 POL/PAR
B61

HAMILTON A.,THE FEDERALIST. USA-45 NAT/G VOL/ASSN EX/STRUC
LEGIS TOP/EX EDU/PROP LEGIT CHOOSE ATTIT RIGID/FLEX CONSTN
ORD/FREE PWR...MAJORIT JURID CONCPT ANTHOL. PAGE 46
B0931
B61

HASAN H.S.,PAKISTAN AND THE UN. ISLAM WOR+45 INT/ORG
ECO/DEV ECO/UNDEV NAT/G TOP/EX ECO/TAC FOR/AID ATTIT
EDU/PROP ADMIN DRIVE PERCEPT...OBS TIME/SEQ UN 20. PAKISTAN
PAGE 48 B0965
B61

HOUN F.W.,TO CHANGE A NATION: PROPAGANDA AND DOMIN
INDOCTRINATION IN COMMUNIST CHINA. CHINA/COM COM EDU/PROP
ACT/RES PLAN PRESS ADMIN FEEDBACK CENTRAL TOTALISM
EFFICIENCY ATTIT...PSY SOC 20. PAGE 52 B1048 MARXISM
B61

KOESTLER A.,THE LOTUS AND THE ROBOT. ASIA INDIA SECT
S/ASIA SOCIETY STRATA ECO/DEV AGRI INDUS FAM CREATE ECO/UNDEV
DOMIN EDU/PROP ADMIN COERCE ATTIT DRIVE SUPEGO
ORD/FREE PWR RESPECT WEALTH...MYTH OBS 20 CHINJAP.
PAGE 61 B1226
B61

KRUPP S.,PATTERN IN ORGANIZATIONAL ANALYSIS: A MGT
CRITICAL EXAMINATION. INGP/REL PERS/REL RATIONAL CONTROL
ATTIT AUTHORIT DRIVE PWR...DECISION PHIL/SCI SOC CONCPT
IDEA/COMP. PAGE 61 B1239 METH/CNCPT
B61

LASSWELL H.D.,PSYCOPATHOLOGY AND POLITICS. WOR-45 ATTIT
CULTURE SOCIETY FACE/GP NAT/G CONSULT CREATE GEN/METH
EDU/PROP EXEC ROUTINE DISPL DRIVE PERSON PWR
RESPECT...PSY CONCPT METH/CNCPT METH. PAGE 63 B1272
B61

LOSCHELDER W.,AUSBILDUNG UND AUSLESE DER BEAMTEN. PROF/ORG
GERMANY/W ELITES NAT/G ADMIN GP/REL ATTIT...JURID EDU/PROP
20 CIVIL/SERV. PAGE 67 B1341 EX/STRUC
CHOOSE
B61

MACRIDIS R.C.,COMPARATIVE POLITICS: NOTES AND POL/PAR
READINGS. WOR+45 LOC/G MUNIC NAT/G PROVS VOL/ASSN CHOOSE
EDU/PROP ADMIN ATTIT PERSON ORD/FREE...SOC CONCPT
OBS RECORD TREND 20. PAGE 68 B1376
B61

MARVICK D.,POLITICAL DECISION-MAKERS. INTELL STRATA TOP/EX
NAT/G POL/PAR EX/STRUC LEGIS DOMIN EDU/PROP ATTIT BIOG
PERSON PWR...PSY STAT OBS CONT/OBS STAND/INT ELITES
UNPLAN/INT TIME/SEQ CHARTS STERTYP VAL/FREE.
PAGE 70 B1416
B61

MARX K.,THE COMMUNIST MANIFESTO. IN (MENDEL A. COM
ESSENTIAL WORKS OF MARXISM, NEW YORK: BANTAM. FUT NEW/IDEA
MOD/EUR CULTURE ECO/DEV ECO/UNDEV AGRI FINAN CAP/ISM
MARKET PROC/MFG LABOR MUNIC POL/PAR CONSULT FORCES REV
CREATE PLAN ADMIN ATTIT DRIVE RIGID/FLEX ORD/FREE
PWR RESPECT MARX/KARL WORK. PAGE 70 B1421
B61

MOLLAU G.,INTERNATIONAL COMMUNISM AND WORLD COM
REVOLUTION: HISTORY AND METHODS. RUSSIA USSR REV
INT/ORG NAT/G POL/PAR VOL/ASSN FORCES BAL/PWR
DIPLOM EXEC REGION WAR ATTIT PWR MARXISM...CONCPT
TIME/SEQ COLD/WAR 19/20. PAGE 74 B1498
B61

NARAIN J.P.,SWARAJ FOR THE PEOPLE. INDIA CONSTN NAT/G

LOC/G MUNIC POL/PAR CHOOSE REPRESENT EFFICIENCY ORD/FREE
ATTIT PWR SOVEREIGN 20. PAGE 77 B1553 EDU/PROP
EX/STRUC
B61

PETRULLO L.,LEADERSHIP AND INTERPERSONAL BEHAVIOR. PERSON
FACE/GP FAM PROF/ORG EX/STRUC FORCES DOMIN WAR ATTIT
GP/REL PERS/REL EFFICIENCY PRODUC PWR...MGT PSY. LEAD
PAGE 82 B1663 HABITAT
B61

SHARMA T.R.,THE WORKING OF STATE ENTERPRISES IN NAT/G
INDIA. INDIA DELIB/GP LEGIS WORKER BUDGET PRICE INDUS
CONTROL GP/REL OWN ATTIT...MGT CHARTS 20. PAGE 96 ADMIN
B1938 SOCISM
B61

SINGER J.D.,FINANCING INTERNATIONAL ORGANIZATION: INT/ORG
THE UNITED NATIONS BUDGET PROCESS. WOR+45 FINAN MGT
ACT/RES CREATE PLAN BUDGET ECO/TAC ADMIN ROUTINE
ATTIT KNOWL...DECISION METH/CNCPT TIME/SEQ UN 20.
PAGE 97 B1964
B61

TANNENBAUM R.,LEADERSHIP AND ORGANIZATION. STRUCT LEAD
ADMIN INGP/REL ATTIT PERCEPT...DECISION METH/CNCPT MGT
OBS CHARTS BIBLIOG. PAGE 103 B2075 RESPECT
ROLE
B61

WALKER N.,MORALE IN THE CIVIL SERVICE. UK EXEC LEAD ATTIT
INGP/REL EFFICIENCY HAPPINESS 20. PAGE 113 B2280 WORKER
ADMIN
PSY
L61

THOMPSON V.A.,"HIERARACHY, SPECIALIZATION, AND PERS/REL
ORGANIZATIONAL CONFLICT" (BMR)" WOR+45 STRATA PROB/SOLV
STRUCT WORKER TEC/DEV GP/REL INGP/REL ATTIT ADMIN
AUTHORIT 20 BUREAUCRCY. PAGE 104 B2106 EX/STRUC
S61

ALGER C.F.,"NON-RESOLUTION CONSEQUENCES OF THE INT/ORG
UNITED NATIONS AND THEIR EFFECT ON INTERNATIONAL DRIVE
CONFLICT." WOR+45 CONSTN ECO/DEV NAT/G CONSULT BAL/PWR
DELIB/GP TOP/EX ACT/RES PLAN DIPLOM EDU/PROP
ROUTINE ATTIT ALL/VALS...INT/LAW TOT/POP UN 20.
PAGE 4 B0075
S61

ANGLIN D.,"UNITED STATES OPPOSITION TO CANADIAN INT/ORG
MEMBERSHIP IN THE PAN AMERICAN UNION: A CANADIAN CANADA
VIEW." L/A+17C UK USA+45 VOL/ASSN DELIB/GP EX/STRUC
PLAN DIPLOM DOMIN REGION ATTIT RIGID/FLEX PWR
...RELATIV CONCPT STERTYP CMN/WLTH OAS 20. PAGE 5
B0112
S61

CARLETON W.G.,"AMERICAN FOREIGN POLICY: MYTHS AND PLAN
REALITIES." FUT USA+45 WOR+45 ECO/UNDEV INT/ORG MYTH
EX/STRUC ARMS/CONT NUC/PWR WAR ATTIT...POLICY DIPLOM
CONCPT CONT/OBS GEN/METH COLD/WAR TOT/POP 20.
PAGE 19 B0378
S61

DEXTER L.A.,"HAS THE PUBLIC OFFICIAL ON OBLIGATION ADMIN
TO RESTRICT HIS FRIENDSHIPS?" NAT/G EX/STRUC TOP/EX ATTIT
20. PAGE 29 B0584 REPRESENT
POLICY
S61

EVAN W.M.,"A LABORATORY EXPERIMENT ON BUREAUCRATIC ADMIN
AUTHORITY" WORKER CONTROL EXEC PRODUC ATTIT PERSON LEGIT
...PSY SOC CHARTS SIMUL 20 WEBER/MAX. PAGE 34 B0687 LAB/EXP
EFFICIENCY
S61

GORDON L.,"ECONOMIC REGIONALISM RECONSIDERED." FUT ECO/DEV
USA+45 WOR+45 INDUS NAT/G TEC/DEV DIPLOM ROUTINE ATTIT
PERCEPT WEALTH...WELF/ST METH/CNCPT WORK 20. CAP/ISM
PAGE 41 B0830 REGION
S61

HAAS E.B.,"INTERNATIONAL INTEGRATION: THE EUROPEAN INT/ORG
AND THE UNIVERSAL PROCESS." EUR+WWI FUT WOR+45 TREND
NAT/G EX/STRUC ATTIT DRIVE ORD/FREE PWR...CONCPT REGION
GEN/LAWS OEEC 20 NATO COUNCL/EUR. PAGE 45 B0909
S61

JUVILER P.H.,"INTERPARLIAMENTARY CONTACTS IN SOVIET INT/ORG
FOREIGN POLICY." COM FUT WOR+45 WOR-45 SOCIETY DELIB/GP
CONSULT ACT/RES DIPLOM ADMIN PEACE ATTIT RIGID/FLEX USSR
WEALTH...WELF/ST SOC TOT/POP CONGRESS 19/20.
PAGE 57 B1156
S61

SHERBENOU E.L.,"CLASS, PARTICIPATION, AND THE REPRESENT
COUNCIL-MANAGER PLAN." ELITES STRUCT LEAD GP/REL MUNIC
ATTIT PWR DECISION. PAGE 96 B1942 EXEC
S61

TAUBENFELD H.J.,"OUTER SPACE--PAST POLITICS AND PLAN
FUTURE POLICY." FUT USA-45 WOR+45 AIR INTELL SPACE
STRUCT ECO/DEV NAT/G TOP/EX ACT/RES ADMIN ROUTINE INT/ORG
NUC/PWR ATTIT DRIVE...CONCPT TIME/SEQ TREND TOT/POP
20. PAGE 103 B2083
S61

VINER J.,"ECONOMIC FOREIGN POLICY ON THE NEW TOP/EX
FRONTIER." USA+45 ECO/UNDEV AGRI FINAN INDUS MARKET ECO/TAC
INT/ORG NAT/G FOR/AID INT/TRADE ADMIN ATTIT PWR 20 BAL/PAY
KENNEDY/JF. PAGE 112 B2262 TARIFFS

ETZIONI A.,"A COMPARATIVE ANALYSIS OF COMPLEX
ORGANIZATIONS: ON POWER, INVOLVEMENT AND THEIR
CORRELATES." ELITES CREATE OP/RES ROUTINE INGP/REL
PERS/REL CONSEN ATTIT DRIVE PWR...CONCPT BIBLIOG.
PAGE 34 B0684
C61 CON/ANAL SOC LEAD CONTROL

VERBA S.,"SMALL GROUPS AND POLITICAL BEHAVIOR: A
STUDY OF LEADERSHIP" DOMIN PARTIC ROUTINE GP/REL
ATTIT DRIVE ALL/VALS...CONCPT IDEA/COMP LAB/EXP
BIBLIOG METH. PAGE 112 B2259
C61 LEAD ELITES FACE/GP

BAILEY S.D.,THE SECRETARIAT OF THE UNITED NATIONS.
FUT WOR+45 DELIB/GP PLAN BAL/PWR DOMIN EDU/PROP
ADMIN PEACE ATTIT PWR...DECISION CONCPT TREND
CON/ANAL CHARTS UN VAL/FREE COLD/WAR 20. PAGE 8
B0162
B62 INT/ORG EXEC DIPLOM

BECKMAN T.N.,MARKETING (7TH ED.). USA+45 SOCIETY
ECO/DEV NAT/G PRICE EFFICIENCY INCOME ATTIT WEALTH
...MGT BIBLIOG 20. PAGE 10 B0205
B62 MARKET ECO/TAC DIST/IND POLICY

BENSON E.T.,CROSS FIRE: THE EIGHT YEARS WITH
EISENHOWER. USA+45 DIPLOM LEAD ATTIT PERSON
CONSERVE...TRADIT BIOG 20 EISNHWR/DD PRESIDENT
TAFT/RA DULLES/JF NIXON/RM. PAGE 11 B0218
B62 ADMIN POLICY DELIB/GP TOP/EX

BROWN L.C.,LATIN AMERICA, A BIBLIOGRAPHY. EX/STRUC
ADMIN LEAD ATTIT...POLICY 20. PAGE 16 B0323
B62 BIBLIOG L/A+17C DIPLOM NAT/G

CAIRNCROSS A.K.,FACTORS IN ECONOMIC DEVELOPMENT.
WOR+45 ECO/UNDEV INDUS R+D LG/CO NAT/G EX/STRUC
PLAN TEC/DEV ECO/TAC ATTIT HEALTH KNOWL PWR WEALTH
...TIME/SEQ GEN/LAWS TOT/POP VAL/FREE 20. PAGE 18
B0363
B62 MARKET ECO/DEV

CARPER E.T.,ILLINOIS GOES TO CONGRESS FOR ARMY
LAND. USA+45 LAW EXTR/IND PROVS REGION CIVMIL/REL
GOV/REL FEDERAL ATTIT 20 ILLINOIS SENATE CONGRESS
DIRKSEN/E DOUGLAS/P. PAGE 19 B0385
B62 ADMIN LOBBY GEOG LEGIS

DODDS H.W.,THE ACADEMIC PRESIDENT "EDUCATOR OR
CARETAKER? FINAN DELIB/GP EDU/PROP PARTIC ATTIT
ROLE PWR...POLICY RECORD INT. PAGE 30 B0601
B62 ACADEM ADMIN LEAD CONTROL

ESCUELA SUPERIOR DE ADMIN PUBL,INFORME DEL
SEMINARIO SOBRE SERVICIO CIVIL O CARRERA
ADMINISTRATIVA. L/A+17C ELITES STRATA CONFER
CONTROL GOV/REL INGP/REL SUPEGO 20 CENTRAL/AM
CIVIL/SERV. PAGE 33 B0681
B62 ADMIN NAT/G PROB/SOLV ATTIT

FRIEDMANN W.,METHODS AND POLICIES OF PRINCIPAL
DONOR COUNTRIES IN PUBLIC INTERNATIONAL DEVELOPMENT
FINANCING: PRELIMINARY APPRAISAL. FRANCE GERMANY/W
UK USA+45 USSR WOR+45 FINAN CAP/ISM DIPLOM ADMIN
ECO/TAC ATTIT 20 EEC. PAGE 37 B0759
B62 INT/ORG FOR/AID NAT/COMP ADMIN

JEWELL M.E.,SENATORIAL POLITICS AND FOREIGN POLICY.
NAT/G POL/PAR CHIEF DELIB/GP TOP/EX FOR/AID
EDU/PROP ROUTINE ATTIT PWR SKILL...MAJORIT
METH/CNCPT TIME/SEQ CONGRESS 20 PRESIDENT. PAGE 56
B1138
B62 USA+45 LEGIS DIPLOM

KARNJAHAPRAKORN C.,MUNICIPAL GOVERNMENT IN THAILAND
AS AN INSTITUTION AND PROCESS OF SELF-GOVERNMENT.
THAILAND CULTURE FINAN EX/STRUC LEGIS PLAN CONTROL
GOV/REL EFFICIENCY ATTIT...POLICY 20. PAGE 58 B1176
B62 LOC/G MUNIC ORD/FREE ADMIN

LIPPMANN W.,PREFACE TO POLITICS. LABOR CHIEF
CONTROL LEAD...MYTH IDEA/COMP 19/20 ROOSEVLT/T
TAMMANY WILSON/H SANTAYAN/G BERGSON/H. PAGE 65
B1318
B62 PARTIC ATTIT ADMIN

MULLEY F.W.,THE POLITICS OF WESTERN DEFENSE.
EUR+WWI USA-45 WOR+45 VOL/ASSN EX/STRUC FORCES
COERCE DETER PEACE ATTIT ORD/FREE PWR...RECORD
TIME/SEQ CHARTS COLD/WAR 20 NATO. PAGE 76 B1537
B62 INT/ORG DELIB/GP NUC/PWR

NEVINS A.,THE STATE UNIVERSITIES AND DEMOCRACY.
AGRI FINAN SCHOOL ADMIN EXEC EFFICIENCY ATTIT.
PAGE 78 B1576
B62 ACADEM PROVS EDU/PROP POLICY

PACKARD V.,THE PYRAMID CLIMBERS: USA+45 ELITES
SOCIETY CREATE PROB/SOLV EFFICIENCY ATTIT...MGT 20.
PAGE 80 B1621
B62 INDUS TOP/EX PERS/REL DRIVE

PRESTHUS R.,THE ORGANIZATIONAL SOCIETY. USA+45
STRUCT ECO/DEV ADMIN ATTIT ALL/VALS...PSY SOC 20.
PAGE 84 B1703
B62 LG/CO WORKER PERS/REL DRIVE

RUDOLPH F.,THE AMERICAN COLLEGE AND UNIVERSITY.
CLIENT FINAN PUB/INST DELIB/GP EDU/PROP CONTROL
EXEC CONSEN ATTIT POLICY. PAGE 92 B1853
B62 ACADEM INGP/REL PWR ADMIN

SCALAPINO R.A.,PARTIES AND POLITICS IN CONTEMPORARY
JAPAN. EX/STRUC DIPLOM CHOOSE NAT/LISM ATTIT
...POLICY 20 CHINJAP. PAGE 93 B1876
B62 POL/PAR PARL/PROC ELITES DECISION

SHAPIRO D.,A SELECT BIBLIOGRAPHY OF WORKS IN
ENGLISH ON RUSSIAN HISTORY, 1801-1917. COM USSR
STRATA FORCES EDU/PROP ADMIN REV RACE/REL ATTIT
19/20. PAGE 96 B1932
B62 BIBLIOG DIPLOM COLONIAL

TAYLOR J.K.L.,ATTITUDES AND METHODS OF
COMMUNICATION AND CONSULTATION BETWEEN EMPLOYERS
AND WORKERS AT INDIVIDUAL FIRM LEVEL. WOR+45 STRUCT
INDUS LABOR CONFER TASK GP/REL EFFICIENCY...MGT
BIBLIOG METH 20 OECD. PAGE 103 B2087
B62 WORKER ADMIN ATTIT EDU/PROP

US SENATE COMM GOVT OPERATIONS.ADMINISTRATION OF
NATIONAL SECURITY. USA+45 CHIEF PLAN PROB/SOLV
TEC/DEV DIPLOM ATTIT...POLICY DECISION 20
KENNEDY/JF RUSK/D MCNAMARA/R BUNDY/M HERTER/C.
PAGE 110 B2212
B62 ORD/FREE ADMIN NAT/G CONTROL

US SENATE COMM ON JUDICIARY.STATE DEPARTMENT
SECURITY. USA+45 CHIEF TEC/DEV DOMIN ADMIN EXEC
ATTIT ORD/FREE...POLICY CONGRESS DEPT/STATE
PRESIDENT KENNEDY/JF KENNEDY/JF SENATE 20. PAGE 110
B2228
B62 CONTROL WORKER NAT/G GOV/REL

WEDDING N.,ADVERTISING MANAGEMENT. USA+45 ECO/DEV
BUDGET CAP/ISM PRODUC PROFIT ATTIT...DECISION MGT
PSY 20. PAGE 114 B2308
B62 ECO/TAC COM/IND PLAN EDU/PROP

WELLEQUET J.,LE CONGO BELGE ET LA WELTPOLITIK
(1894-1914. GERMANY DOMIN EDU/PROP WAR ATTIT
...BIBLIOG T CONGO/LEOP. PAGE 115 B2318
B62 ADMIN DIPLOM GP/REL COLONIAL

GALBRAITH J.K.,"ECONOMIC DEVELOPMENT IN
PERSPECTIVE." CAP/ISM ECO/TAC ROUTINE ATTIT WEALTH
...TREND CHARTS SOC/EXP WORK 20. PAGE 38 B0773
L62 ECO/UNDEV PLAN

HOFFHERR R.,"LE PROBLEME DE L'ENCADREMENT DANS LES
JEUNES ETATS DE LANGUE FRANCAISE EN AFRIQUE
CENTRALE ET A MADAGASCAR." FUT ECO/UNDEV CONSULT
PLAN ECO/TAC COLONIAL ATTIT...MGT TIME/SEQ VAL/FREE
20. PAGE 51 B1028
L62 AFR STRUCT FRANCE

ALBONETTI A.,"IL SECONDO PROGRAMMA QUINQUENNALE
1963-67 ED IL BILANCIO RICERCHE ED INVESTIMENTI PER
IL 1963 DELL'ERATOM." EUR+WWI FUT ITALY WOR+45
ECO/DEV SERV/IND INT/ORG TEC/DEV ECO/TAC ATTIT
SKILL WEALTH...MGT TIME/SEQ OEEC 20. PAGE 3 B0069
S62 R+D PLAN NUC/PWR

ALGER C.F.,"THE EXTERNAL BUREAUCRACY IN UNITED
STATES FOREIGN AFFAIRS." USA+45 WOR+45 SOCIETY
COM/IND INT/ORG NAT/G CONSULT EX/STRUC ACT/RES
...MGT SOC CONCPT TREND 20. PAGE 4 B0076
S62 ADMIN ATTIT DIPLOM

BRZEZINSKI Z.K.,"DEVIATION CONTROL: A STUDY IN THE
DYNAMICS OF DOCTRINAL CONFLICT." WOR+45 WOR-45
VOL/ASSN CREATE BAL/PWR DOMIN EXEC DRIVE PERCEPT
PWR...METH/CNCPT TIME/SEQ TREND 20. PAGE 16 B0333
S62 RIGID/FLEX ATTIT

FESLER J.W.,"FRENCH FIELD ADMINISTRATION: THE
BEGINNINGS." CHRIST-17C CULTURE SOCIETY STRATA
NAT/G ECO/TAC DOMIN EDU/PROP LEGIT ADJUD COERCE
ATTIT ALL/VALS...TIME/SEQ CON/ANAL GEN/METH
VAL/FREE 13/15. PAGE 35 B0714
S62 EX/STRUC FRANCE

GUYOT J.F.,"GOVERNMENT BUREAUCRATS ARE DIFFERENT."
USA+45 REPRESENT PWR 20. PAGE 45 B0906
S62 ATTIT DRIVE TOP/EX ADMIN

HUDSON G.F.,"SOVIET FEARS OF THE WEST." COM USA+45
SOCIETY DELIB/GP EX/STRUC TOP/EX ACT/RES CREATE
DOMIN EDU/PROP LEGIT ADMIN ROUTINE DRIVE PERSON
RIGID/FLEX PWR...RECORD TIME/SEQ TOT/POP 20
STALIN/J. PAGE 52 B1057
S62 ATTIT MYTH GERMANY USSR

IOVTCHOUK M.T.,"ON SOME THEORETICAL PRINCIPLES AND
METHODS OF SOCIOLOGICAL INVESTIGATIONS (IN
RUSSIAN)." FUT USA+45 STRATA R+D NAT/G POL/PAR
TOP/EX ACT/RES PLAN ECO/TAC EDU/PROP ROUTINE ATTIT
RIGID/FLEX MARXISM SOCISM...MARXIST METH/CNCPT OBS
TREND NAT/COMP GEN/LAWS 20. PAGE 54 B1102
S62 COM ECO/DEV CAP/ISM USSR

JACOBSON H.K.,"THE UNITED NATIONS AND COLONIALISM:
A TENTATIVE APPRAISAL." AFR FUT S/ASIA USA+45 USSR
S62 INT/ORG CONCPT

WOR+45 NAT/G DELIB/GP PLAN DIPLOM ECO/TAC DOMIN   COLONIAL
ADMIN ROUTINE COERCE ATTIT RIGID/FLEX ORD/FREE PWR
...OBS STERTYP UN 20. PAGE 55 B1115

                                                        S62
JOHNSON H.."CANADA IN A CHANGING WORLD." EUR+WWI   ECO/DEV
USA+45 NAT/G CAP/ISM ECO/TAC ADMIN ATTIT WEALTH   PLAN
...TREND TOT/POP 20 EEC. PAGE 57 B1143   CANADA

                                                        S62
MARTIN L.W.,"POLITICAL SETTLEMENTS AND ARMS   CONCPT
CONTROL." COM EUR+WWI GERMANY USA+45 PROVS FORCES   ARMS/CONT
TOP/EX ACT/RES CREATE DOMIN LEGIT ROUTINE COERCE
ATTIT RIGID/FLEX ORD/FREE PWR...METH/CNCPT RECORD
GEN/LAWS 20. PAGE 70 B1410

                                                        S62
PIQUEMAL M.,"LES PROBLEMES DES UNIONS D'ETATS EN   AFR
AFRIQUE NOIRE." FRANCE SOCIETY INT/ORG NAT/G   ECO/UNDEV
DELIB/GP PLAN LEGIT ADMIN COLONIAL ROUTINE ATTIT   REGION
ORD/FREE PWR...GEOG METH/CNCPT 20. PAGE 83 B1678

                                                        S62
READ W.H.,"UPWARD COMMUNICATION IN INDUSTRIAL   ADMIN
HIERARCHIES." LG/CO TOP/EX PROB/SOLV DOMIN EXEC   INGP/REL
PERS/REL ATTIT DRIVE PERCEPT...CORREL STAT CHARTS   PSY
20. PAGE 86 B1747   MGT

                                                        S62
SPRINGER H.W.,"FEDERATION IN THE CARIBBEAN: AN   VOL/ASSN
ATTEMPT THAT FAILED." L/A+17C ECO/UNDEV INT/ORG   NAT/G
POL/PAR PROVS LEGIS CREATE PLAN LEGIT ADMIN FEDERAL   REGION
ATTIT DRIVE PERSON ORD/FREE PWR...POLICY GEOG PSY
CONCPT OBS CARIBBEAN CMN/WLTH 20. PAGE 100 B2013

                                                        S62
TANNENBAUM A.S.,"CONTROL IN ORGANIZATIONS: ADMIN
INDIVIDUAL ADJUSTMENT AND ORGANIZATIONAL   MGT
PERFORMANCE." DOMIN PARTIC REPRESENT INGP/REL   STRUCT
PRODUC ATTIT DRIVE PWR...PSY CORREL. PAGE 102 B2073   CONTROL

                                                        S62
TRUMAN D.,"THE DOMESTIC POLITICS OF FOREIGN AID."   ROUTINE
USA+45 WOR+45 NAT/G POL/PAR LEGIS DIPLOM ECO/TAC   FOR/AID
EDU/PROP ADMIN CHOOSE ATTIT PWR CONGRESS 20
CONGRESS. PAGE 105 B2129

                                                        C62
BLAU P.M.,"FORMAL ORGANIZATIONS." WOR+45 SOCIETY   ADMIN
STRUCT ECO/DEV GP/REL ATTIT...METH/CNCPT BIBLIOG   SOC
20. PAGE 12 B0253   GEN/METH
                                                        INGP/REL
                                                        C62
DE GRAZIA A.,"POLITICAL BEHAVIOR (REV. ED.)" STRATA   PHIL/SCI
POL/PAR LEAD LOBBY ROUTINE WAR CHOOSE REPRESENT   OP/RES
CONSEN ATTIT ORD/FREE BIBLIOG. PAGE 27 B0555   CONCPT

                                                        B63
BANFIELD E.C.,CITY POLITICS. CULTURE LABOR LOC/G   MUNIC
POL/PAR LEGIS EXEC LEAD CHOOSE...DECISION NEGRO.   RIGID/FLEX
PAGE 9 B0178   ATTIT
                                                        B63
BOCK E.A., STATE AND LOCAL GOVERNMENT; A CASE BOOK.   LOC/G
USA+45 MUNIC PROVS CONSULT GP/REL ATTIT...MGT 20   ADMIN
CASEBOOK GOVERNOR MAYOR. PAGE 12 B0254   PROB/SOLV
                                                        CHIEF
                                                        B63
BOCK E.A.,STATE AND LOCAL GOVERNMENT: A CASE BOOK.   PROVS
USA+45 FINAN CHIEF PROB/SOLV TAX ATTIT...POLICY 20   LOC/G
CASEBOOK. PAGE 13 B0263   ADMIN
                                                        GOV/REL
                                                        B63
BONINI C.P.,SIMULATION OF INFORMATION AND DECISION   INDUS
SYSTEMS IN THE FIRM. MARKET BUDGET DOMIN EDU/PROP   SIMUL
ADMIN COST ATTIT HABITAT PERCEPT PWR...CONCPT   DECISION
PROBABIL QUANT PREDICT HYPO/EXP BIBLIOG. PAGE 13   MGT
B0273
                                                        B63
CORLEY R.N.,THE LEGAL ENVIRONMENT OF BUSINESS.   NAT/G
CONSTN LEGIS TAX ADMIN CT/SYS DISCRIM ATTIT PWR   INDUS
...TREND 18/20. PAGE 23 B0477   JURID
                                                        DECISION
                                                        B63
COSTELLO T.W.,PSYCHOLOGY IN ADMINISTRATION: A   PSY
RESEARCH ORIENTATION. CREATE PROB/SOLV PERS/REL   MGT
ADJUST ANOMIE ATTIT DRIVE PERCEPT ROLE...DECISION   EXEC
BIBLIOG T 20. PAGE 24 B0488   ADMIN
                                                        B63
DALAND R.T.,PERSPECTIVES OF BRAZILIAN PUBLIC   ADMIN
ADMINISTRATION (VOL. I). BRAZIL LAW ECO/UNDEV   NAT/G
SCHOOL CHIEF TEC/DEV CONFER CONTROL GP/REL ATTIT   PLAN
ROLE PWR...ANTHOL 20. PAGE 26 B0525   GOV/REL
                                                        B63
DE VRIES E.,SOCIAL ASPECTS OF ECONOMIC DEVELOPMENT   L/A+17C
IN LATIN AMERICA. CULTURE SOCIETY STRATA FINAN   ECO/UNDEV
INDUS INT/ORG DELIB/GP ACT/RES ECO/TAC EDU/PROP
ADMIN ATTIT SUPEGO HEALTH KNOWL ORD/FREE...SOC STAT
TREND ANTHOL TOT/POP VAL/FREE. PAGE 28 B0562
                                                        B63
DEBRAY P.,LE PORTUGAL ENTRE DEUX REVOLUTIONS.   NAT/G
EUR+WWI PORTUGAL CONSTN ADMIN ATTIT ALL/VALS   DELIB/GP
...DECISION CONCPT 20 SALAZAR/A. PAGE 28 B0567   TOP/EX
                                                        B63
DIESNER H.J.,KIRCHE UND STAAT IM SPATROMISCHEN   SECT
REICH. ROMAN/EMP EX/STRUC COLONIAL COERCE ATTIT   GP/REL

CATHISM 4/5 AFRICA/N CHURCH/STA. PAGE 29 B0592   DOMIN
                                                        JURID
                                                        B63
GRANT D.R.,STATE AND LOCAL GOVERNMENT IN AMERICA.   PROVS
USA+45 FINAN LOC/G MUNIC EX/STRUC FORCES EDU/PROP   POL/PAR
ADMIN CHOOSE FEDERAL ATTIT...JURID 20. PAGE 42   LEGIS
B0853   CONSTN
                                                        B63
HEUSSLER R.,YESTERDAY'S RULERS: THE MAKING OF THE   EX/STRUC
BRITISH COLONIAL SERVICE. AFR EUR+WWI UK STRATA   MORAL
SECT DELIB/GP PLAN DOMIN EDU/PROP ATTIT PERCEPT   ELITES
PERSON SUPEGO KNOWL ORD/FREE PWR...MGT SOC OBS INT
TIME/SEQ 20 CMN/WLTH. PAGE 49 B1000
                                                        B63
HOWER R.M.,MANAGERS AND SCIENTISTS. EX/STRUC CREATE   R+D
ADMIN REPRESENT ATTIT DRIVE ROLE PWR SKILL...SOC   MGT
INT. PAGE 52 B1052   PERS/REL
                                                        INGP/REL
                                                        B63
KORNHAUSER W.,SCIENTISTS IN INDUSTRY: CONFLICT AND   CREATE
ACCOMMODATION. USA+45 R+D LG/CO NAT/G TEC/DEV   INDUS
CONTROL ADJUST ATTIT...MGT STAT INT BIBLIOG 20.   PROF/ORG
PAGE 61 B1229   GP/REL
                                                        B63
LANGROD G.,THE INTERNATIONAL CIVIL SERVICE: ITS   INT/ORG
ORIGINS, ITS NATURE, ITS EVALUATION. FUT WOR+45   ADMIN
WOR-45 DELIB/GP ACT/RES DOMIN LEGIT ATTIT
RIGID/FLEX SUPEGO ALL/VALS...MGT CONCPT STAT
TIME/SEQ ILO LEAGUE/NAT VAL/FREE 20 UN. PAGE 62
B1259
                                                        B63
LEWIS J.W.,LEADERSHIP IN COMMUNIST CHINA. ASIA   POL/PAR
INTELL ECO/UNDEV LOC/G MUNIC NAT/G PROVS ECO/TAC   DOMIN
EDU/PROP LEGIT ADMIN COERCE ATTIT ORD/FREE PWR   ELITES
...INT TIME/SEQ CHARTS TOT/POP VAL/FREE. PAGE 65
B1304
                                                        B63
MENZEL J.M.,THE CHINESE CIVIL SERVICE: CAREER OPEN   ADMIN
TO TALENT? ASIA ROUTINE INGP/REL DISCRIM ATTIT ROLE   NAT/G
KNOWL ANTHOL. PAGE 73 B1468   DECISION
                                                        ELITES
                                                        B63
PLANTEY A.,TRAITE PRATIQUE DE LA FONCTION PUBLIQUE   ADMIN
(2ND ED., 2 VOLS.). FRANCE FINAN EX/STRUC PROB/SOLV   SUPEGO
GP/REL ATTIT...SOC 20 CIVIL/SERV. PAGE 83 B1680   JURID
                                                        B63
SHANKS M.,THE LESSONS OF PUBLIC ENTERPRISE. UK   SOCISM
LEGIS WORKER ECO/TAC ADMIN PARL/PROC GOV/REL ATTIT   OWN
...POLICY MGT METH/COMP NAT/COMP ANTHOL 20   NAT/G
PARLIAMENT. PAGE 96 B1931   INDUS
                                                        B63
STEIN H.,AMERICAN CIVIL-MILITARY DECISION. USA+45   CIVMIL/REL
USA-45 EX/STRUC FORCES LEGIS TOP/EX PLAN DIPLOM   DECISION
FOR/AID ATTIT 20 CONGRESS. PAGE 100 B2028   WAR
                                                        BUDGET
                                                        B63
STEVENSON A.E.,LOOKING OUTWARD: YEARS OF CRISIS AT   INT/ORG
THE UNITED NATIONS. COM CUBA USA+45 WOR+45 SOCIETY   CONCPT
NAT/G EX/STRUC ACT/RES LEGIT COLONIAL ATTIT PERSON   ARMS/CONT
SUPEGO ALL/VALS...POLICY HUM UN COLD/WAR CONGO 20.
PAGE 100 B2034
                                                        B63
SWERDLOW I.,DEVELOPMENT ADMINISTRATION: CONCEPTS   ECO/UNDEV
AND PROBLEMS. WOR+45 CULTURE SOCIETY STRATA   ADMIN
DELIB/GP EX/STRUC ACT/RES PLAN ECO/TAC DOMIN LEGIT
ATTIT RIGID/FLEX SUPEGO HEALTH PWR...MGT CONCPT
ANTHOL VAL/FREE. PAGE 102 B2062
                                                        B63
THOMETZ C.E.,THE DECISION-MAKERS: THE POWER   ELITES
STRUCTURE OF DALLAS. USA+45 CULTURE EX/STRUC DOMIN   MUNIC
LEGIT GP/REL ATTIT OBJECTIVE...INT CHARTS GP/COMP.   PWR
PAGE 104 B2101   DECISION
                                                        B63
TSOU T.,AMERICA'S FAILURE IN CHINA, 1941-1950.   ASIA
USA+45 USA-45 NAT/G ACT/RES PLAN DOMIN EDU/PROP   PERCEPT
ADMIN ROUTINE ATTIT PERSON ORD/FREE...DECISION   DIPLOM
CONCPT MYTH TIME/SEQ TREND STERTYP 20. PAGE 105
B2132
                                                        B63
TUCKER R.C.,THE SOVIET POLITICAL MIND. COM INTELL   STRUCT
NAT/G TOP/EX EDU/PROP ADMIN COERCE TOTALISM ATTIT   RIGID/FLEX
PWR MARXISM...PSY MYTH HYPO/EXP 20. PAGE 106 B2135   ELITES
                                                        USSR
                                                        L63
BEGUIN H.,"ASPECTS GEOGRAPHIQUE DE LA   ECO/UNDEV
POLARISATION." FUT WOR+45 SOCIETY STRUCT ECO/DEV   GEOG
R+D BAL/PWR ADMIN ATTIT RIGID/FLEX HEALTH WEALTH   DIPLOM
...CHARTS 20. PAGE 10 B0206
                                                        L63
FREUND G.,"ADENAUER AND THE FUTURE OF GERMANY."   NAT/G
EUR+WWI FUT GERMANY/W FORCES LEGIT ADMIN ROUTINE   BIOG
ATTIT DRIVE PERSON PWR...POLICY TIME/SEQ TREND   DIPLOM
VAL/FREE 20 ADENAUER/K. PAGE 37 B0753   GERMANY
                                                        L63
SPITZ A.A.,"DEVELOPMENT ADMINISTRATION: AN   ADMIN
ANNOTATED BIBLIOGRAPHY." WOR+45 CULTURE SOCIETY   ECO/UNDEV

STRATA DELIB/GP EX/STRUC TOP/EX ACT/RES ECO/TAC
DOMIN EDU/PROP LEGIT COERCE ATTIT ALL/VALS...MGT
VAL/FREE. PAGE 99 B2009

S63
ANTHON C.G.,"THE END OF THE ADENAUER ERA." EUR+WWI   NAT/G
GERMANY/W CONSTN EX/STRUC CREATE DIPLOM LEGIT ATTIT   TOP/EX
PERSON ALL/VALS...RECORD 20 ADENAUER/K. PAGE 6   BAL/PWR
B0113   GERMANY

S63
ARASTEH R.,"THE ROLE OF INTELLECTUALS IN   INTELL
ADMINISTRATIVE DEVELOPMENT AND SOCIAL CHANGE IN   ADMIN
MODERN IRAN." ISLAM CULTURE NAT/G CONSULT ACT/RES   IRAN
EDU/PROP EXEC ATTIT BIO/SOC PERCEPT SUPEGO ALL/VALS
...POLICY MGT PSY SOC CONCPT 20. PAGE 6 B0123

S63
BANFIELD J.,"FEDERATION IN EAST-AFRICA." AFR UGANDA   EX/STRUC
ELITES INT/ORG NAT/G VOL/ASSN LEGIS ECO/TAC FEDERAL   PWR
ATTIT SOVEREIGN TOT/POP 20 TANGANYIKA. PAGE 9 B0180   REGION

S63
BOWIE R.,"STRATEGY AND THE ATLANTIC ALLIANCE."   FORCES
EUR+WWI VOL/ASSN BAL/PWR COERCE NUC/PWR ATTIT   ROUTINE
ORD/FREE PWR...DECISION GEN/LAWS NATO COLD/WAR 20.
PAGE 14 B0287

S63
DELLIN L.A.D.,"BULGARIA UNDER SOVIET LEADERSHIP."   AGRI
BULGARIA COM USA+45 USSR ECO/DEV ECO/DEV INDUS POL/PAR NAT/G
EX/STRUC TOP/EX COERCE ATTIT RIGID/FLEX...POLICY   TOTALISM
TIME/SEQ 20. PAGE 28 B0572

S63
ETIENNE G.,"'LOIS OBJECTIVES' ET PROBLEMES DE   TOTALISM
DEVELOPPEMENT DANS LE CONTEXTE CHINE-URSS." ASIA   USSR
CHINA/COM COM FUT STRUCT INT/ORG VOL/ASSN TOP/EX
TEC/DEV ECO/TAC ATTIT RIGID/FLEX...GEOG MGT
TIME/SEQ TOT/POP 20. PAGE 34 B0682

S63
GITTELL M.,"METROPOLITAN MAYOR: DEAD END." LOC/G   MUNIC
PARTIC REGION ATTIT PWR GP/COMP. PAGE 40 B0804   LEAD
                                                      EXEC

S63
HARRIS R.L.,"A COMPARATIVE ANALYSIS OF THE   DELIB/GP
ADMINISTRATIVE SYSTEMS OF CANADA AND CEYLON."   EX/STRUC
S/ASIA CULTURE SOCIETY STRATA TOP/EX ACT/RES DOMIN   CANADA
EDU/PROP LEGIT COERCE ATTIT SUPEGO ALL/VALS...MGT   CEYLON
CHARTS GEN/LAWS VAL/FREE 20. PAGE 47 B0955

S63
HAVILAND H.F.,"BUILDING A POLITICAL COMMUNITY."   VOL/ASSN
EUR+WWI FUT UK USA+45 ECO/DEV ECO/UNDEV INT/ORG   DIPLOM
NAT/G DELIB/GP BAL/PWR ECO/TAC NEUTRAL ROUTINE
ATTIT PWR WEALTH...CONCPT COLD/WAR TOT/POP 20.
PAGE 48 B0972

S63
MANGONE G.,"THE UNITED NATIONS AND UNITED STATES   INT/ORG
FOREIGN POLICY." USA+45 WOR+45 ECO/UNDEV NAT/G   ECO/TAC
DIPLOM LEGIT ROUTINE ATTIT DRIVE...TIME/SEQ UN   FOR/AID
COLD/WAR 20. PAGE 69 B1390

S63
ROUGEMONT D.,"LES NOUVELLES CHANCES DE L'EUROPE."   ECO/UNDEV
EUR+WWI FUT ECO/DEV INT/ORG NAT/G ACT/RES PLAN   PERCEPT
TEC/DEV EDU/PROP ADMIN COLONIAL FEDERAL ATTIT PWR
SKILL...TREND 20. PAGE 91 B1835

S63
RUSTOW D.A.,"THE MILITARY IN MIDDLE EASTERN SOCIETY   FORCES
AND POLITICS." FUT ISLAM CONSTN SOCIETY FACE/GP   ELITES
NAT/G POL/PAR PROF/ORG CONSULT DOMIN ADMIN EXEC
REGION COERCE NAT/LISM ATTIT DRIVE PERSON ORD/FREE
PWR...POLICY CONCPT OBS STERTYP 20. PAGE 92 B1860

S63
SCHURMANN F.,"ECONOMIC POLICY AND POLITICAL POWER   PLAN
IN COMMUNIST CHINA." ASIA CHINA/COM USSR SOCIETY   ECO/TAC
ECO/UNDEV AGRI INDUS CREATE ADMIN ROUTINE ATTIT
DRIVE RIGID/FLEX PWR WEALTH...HIST/WRIT TREND
CHARTS WORK 20. PAGE 94 B1908

S63
SHIMKIN D.B.,"STRUCTURE OF SOVIET POWER." COM FUT   PWR
USA+45 USSR WOR+45 NAT/G FORCES ECO/TAC DOMIN EXEC
COERCE CHOOSE ATTIT WEALTH...TIME/SEQ COLD/WAR
TOT/POP VAL/FREE 20. PAGE 96 B1948

S63
STANLEY T.W.,"DECENTRALIZING NUCLEAR CONTROL IN   INT/ORG
NATO." EUR+WWI USA+45 ELITES FORCES ACT/RES ATTIT   EX/STRUC
ORD/FREE PWR...NEW/IDEA HYPO/EXP TOT/POP 20 NATO.   NUC/PWR
PAGE 100 B2022

S63
USEEM J.,"MEN IN THE MIDDLE OF THE THIRD CULTURE: ADMIN
THE ROLES OF AMERICAN AND NON-WESTERN PEOPLE IN   SOCIETY
CROSS-CULTURAL ADMINIS-." FUT WOR+45 DELIB/GP   PERSON
EX/STRUC LEGIS ATTIT ALL/VALS...MGT INT TIME/SEQ
GEN/LAWS VAL/FREE. PAGE 111 B2247

S63
WINGFIELD C.J.,"POWER STRUCTURE AND DECISION-MAKING   MUNIC
IN CITY PLANNING." EDU/PROP ADMIN LEAD PARTIC   PLAN
GP/REL ATTIT. PAGE 117 B2365   DECISION
                                                      PWR

C63
CARLISLE D.,"PARTY LOYALTY; THE ELECTION PROCESS IN   CHOOSE
SOUTH CAROLINA." USA+45 LOC/G ADMIN ATTIT...TREND   POL/PAR

CHARTS BIBLIOG 17/20. PAGE 19 B0380   PROVS
                                                      SUFF

B64
AHMAD M.,THE CIVIL SERVANT IN PAKISTAN. PAKISTAN   WELF/ST
ECO/UNDEV COLONIAL INGP/REL...SOC CHARTS BIBLIOG 20   ADMIN
CIVIL/SERV. PAGE 3 B0065   ATTIT
                                                      STRATA

B64
ANDREN N.,GOVERNMENT AND POLITICS IN THE NORDIC   CONSTN
COUNTRIES: DENMARK, FINLAND, ICELAND, NORWAY,   NAT/G
SWEDEN. DENMARK FINLAND ICELAND NORWAY SWEDEN   CULTURE
POL/PAR CHIEF LEGIS ADMIN REGION REPRESENT ATTIT   GOV/COMP
CONSERVE...CHARTS BIBLIOG/A 20. PAGE 5 B0102

B64
APTER D.E.,IDEOLOGY AND DISCONTENT. FUT WOR+45   ACT/RES
CONSTN CULTURE INTELL SOCIETY STRUCT INT/ORG NAT/G   ATTIT
DELIB/GP LEGIS CREATE PLAN TEC/DEV EDU/PROP EXEC
PERCEPT PERSON RIGID/FLEX ALL/VALS...POLICY
TOT/POP. PAGE 6 B0122

B64
CLARK J.S.,CONGRESS: THE SAPLESS BRANCH. DELIB/GP   LEGIS
SENIOR ATTIT CONGRESS. PAGE 21 B0432   ROUTINE
                                                      ADMIN
                                                      POL/PAR

B64
COTTER C.P.,POLITICS WITHOUT POWER: THE NATIONAL   CHOOSE
PARTY COMMITTEES. USA+45 FINAN NAT/G LOBBY ROUTINE   POL/PAR
GP/REL ATTIT ROLE SUPEGO PWR 20. PAGE 24 B0491   REPRESENT
                                                      DELIB/GP

B64
COTTRELL A.J.,THE POLITICS OF THE ATLANTIC   VOL/ASSN
ALLIANCE. EUR+WWI USA+45 INT/ORG NAT/G DELIB/GP   FORCES
EX/STRUC BAL/PWR DIPLOM REGION DETER ATTIT ORD/FREE
...CONCPT RECORD GEN/LAWS GEN/METH NATO 20. PAGE 24
B0493

B64
COX R.,THEORY IN MARKETING. FUT USA+45 SOCIETY   MARKET
ECO/DEV PROB/SOLV PRICE RISK PRODUC ATTIT...ANTHOL   ECO/TAC
20. PAGE 24 B0499   PHIL/SCI
                                                      MGT

B64
EATON H.,PRESIDENTIAL TIMBER: A HISTORY OF   DELIB/GP
NOMINATING CONVENTIONS, 1868-1960. USA+45 USA-45   CHOOSE
POL/PAR EX/STRUC DEBATE LOBBY ATTIT PERSON ALL/VALS   CHIEF
...MYTH 19/20 PRESIDENT. PAGE 32 B0646   NAT/G

B64
ENDACOTT G.B.,GOVERNMENT AND PEOPLE IN HONG KONG   CONSTN
1841-1962: A CONSTITUTIONAL HISTORY. UK LEGIS ADJUD   COLONIAL
REPRESENT ATTIT 19/20 HONG/KONG. PAGE 33 B0674   CONTROL
                                                      ADMIN

B64
EWING D.W.,THE MANAGERIAL MIND. SOCIETY STRUCT   MGT
INDUS PERSON KNOWL 20. PAGE 34 B0692   ATTIT
                                                      CREATE
                                                      EFFICIENCY

B64
GOLDWIN R.A.,POLITICAL PARTIES, USA. USA+45 USA-45   POL/PAR
LOC/G ADMIN LEAD EFFICIENCY ATTIT PWR...POLICY STAT   PARTIC
ANTHOL 18/20 CONGRESS. PAGE 40 B0818   NAT/G
                                                      CONSTN

B64
GREBLER L.,URBAN RENEWAL IN EUROPEAN COUNTRIES: ITS   MUNIC
EMERGENCE AND POTENTIALS. EUR+WWI UK ECO/DEV LOC/G   PLAN
NEIGH CREATE ADMIN ATTIT...TREND NAT/COMP 20   CONSTRUC
URBAN/RNWL. PAGE 43 B0863   NAT/G

B64
GUTTSMAN W.L.,THE BRITISH POLITICAL ELITE. EUR+WWI   NAT/G
MOD/EUR STRATA FAM LABOR POL/PAR SCHOOL VOL/ASSN   SOC
DELIB/GP LEGIS LEGIT EXEC CHOOSE ATTIT ALL/VALS   UK
...STAT BIOG TIME/SEQ CHARTS VAL/FREE. PAGE 45   ELITES
B0905

B64
HANNA W.J.,INDEPENDENT BLACK AFRICA: THE POLITICS   AFR
OF FREEDOM. ELITES INDUS KIN CHIEF COLONIAL CHOOSE   ECO/UNDEV
GOV/REL RACE/REL NAT/LISM ATTIT PERSON 20 NEGRO.   ADMIN
PAGE 46 B0938   PROB/SOLV

B64
HICKEY G.C.,VILLAGE IN VIETNAM. USA+45 VIETNAM LAW   CULTURE
AGRI FAM SECT ADMIN ATTIT...SOC CHARTS WORSHIP 20.   SOCIETY
PAGE 49 B1003   STRUCT
                                                      S/ASIA

B64
INDIAN COMM PREVENTION CORRUPT,REPORT, 1964. INDIA   CRIME
NAT/G GOV/REL ATTIT ORD/FREE...CRIMLGY METH 20.   ADMIN
PAGE 53 B1079   LEGIS
                                                      LOC/G

B64
KILPATRICKFP,SOURCE BOOK OF OCCUPATIONAL VALUES AND   NAT/G
THE IMAGE OF THE FEDERAL SERVICE. USA+45 EX/STRUC   ATTIT
...POLICY MGT INT METH/COMP 20. PAGE 60 B1205   ADMIN
                                                      WORKER

B64
KILPATRICKFP,THE IMAGE OF THE FEDERAL SERVICE.   NAT/G
USA+45 EX/STRUC...POLICY MGT INT METH/COMP 20.   ATTIT
PAGE 60 B1206   ADMIN
                                                      WORKER

KIMBROUGH R.B.,POLITICAL POWER AND EDUCATIONAL DECISION-MAKING. USA+45 FINAN ADMIN LEAD GP/REL ATTIT PWR PROG/TEAC. PAGE 60 B1207
B64
EDU/PROP
PROB/SOLV
DECISION
SCHOOL

MAHAR J.M.,INDIA: A CRITICAL BIBLIOGRAPHY. INDIA PAKISTAN CULTURE ECO/UNDEV LOC/G POL/PAR SECT PROB/SOLV DIPLOM ADMIN COLONIAL PARL/PROC ATTIT 20. PAGE 68 B1377
B64
BIBLIOG/A
S/ASIA
NAT/G
LEAD

MUSSO AMBROSI L.A.,BIBLIOGRAFIA DE BIBLIOGRAFIAS URUGUAYAS. URUGUAY DIPLOM ADMIN ATTIT...SOC 20. PAGE 77 B1551
B64
BIBLIOG
NAT/G
L/A+17C
PRESS

NEUSTADT R.,PRESIDENTIAL POWER. USA+45 CONSTN NAT/G CHIEF LEGIS CREATE EDU/PROP LEGIT ADMIN EXEC COERCE ATTIT PERSON RIGID/FLEX PWR CONGRESS 20 PRESIDENT TRUMAN/HS EISNHWR/DD. PAGE 78 B1575
B64
TOP/EX
SKILL

PARET P.,FRENCH REVOLUTIONARY WARFARE FROM INDOCHINA TO ALGERIA* THE ANALYSIS OF A POLITICAL AND MILITARY DOCTRINE. ALGERIA VIETNAM FORCES OP/RES TEC/DEV ROUTINE REV ATTIT...PSY BIBLIOG. PAGE 81 B1632
B64
FRANCE
GUERRILLA
GEN/LAWS

PINNICK A.W.,COUNTRY PLANNERS IN ACTION. UK FINAN SERV/IND NAT/G CONSULT DELIB/GP PRICE CONTROL ROUTINE LEISURE AGE/C...GEOG 20 URBAN/RNWL. PAGE 83 B1674
B64
MUNIC
PLAN
INDUS
ATTIT

POPPINO R.E.,INTERNATIONAL COMMUNISM IN LATIN AMERICA: A HISTORY OF THE MOVEMENT 1917-1963. CHINA/COM USSR INTELL STRATA LABOR WORKER ADMIN REV ATTIT...POLICY 20 COLD/WAR. PAGE 84 B1692
B64
MARXISM
POL/PAR
L/A+17C

POTTER D.C.,GOVERNMENT IN RURAL INDIA. INDIA LEGIT INGP/REL EFFICIENCY ATTIT 20. PAGE 84 B1695
B64
LOC/G
ADMIN
TAX
PROB/SOLV

RICHARDSON I.L.,BIBLIOGRAFIA BRASILEIRA DE ADMINISTRACAO PUBLICA E ASSUNTOS CORRELATOS. BRAZIL CONSTN FINAN LOC/G NAT/G POL/PAR DIPLOM RECEIVE ATTIT...METH 20. PAGE 88 B1776
B64
BIBLIOG
MGT
ADMIN
LAW

ROBSON W.A.,THE GOVERNORS AND THE GOVERNED. USA+45 PROB/SOLV DOMIN ADMIN CONTROL CHOOSE...POLICY PRESIDENT. PAGE 89 B1808
B64
EX/STRUC
ATTIT
PARTIC
LEAD

SINGER M.R.,THE EMERGING ELITE: A STUDY OF POLITICAL LEADERSHIP IN CEYLON. S/ASIA ECO/UNDEV AGRI KIN NAT/G SECT EX/STRUC LEGIT ATTIT PWR RESPECT...SOC STAT CHARTS 20. PAGE 97 B1967
B64
TOP/EX
STRATA
NAT/LISM
CEYLON

SULLIVAN G.,THE STORY OF THE PEACE CORPS. USA+45 WOR+45 INTELL FACE/GP NAT/G SCHOOL VOL/ASSN CONSULT EX/STRUC PLAN EDU/PROP ADMIN ATTIT DRIVE ALL/VALS ...POLICY HEAL SOC CONCPT INT QU BIOG TREND SOC/EXP WORK. PAGE 102 B2054
B64
INT/ORG
ECO/UNDEV
FOR/AID
PEACE

UN PUB. INFORM. ORGAN.,EVERY MAN'S UNITED NATIONS. UNIV WOR+45 CONSTN CULTURE SOCIETY ECO/DEV ECO/UNDEV NAT/G ACT/RES PLAN ECO/TAC INT/TRADE EDU/PROP LEGIT PEACE ATTIT ALL/VALS...POLICY HUM INT/LAW CONCPT CHARTS UN TOT/POP 20. PAGE 106 B2150
B64
INT/ORG
ROUTINE

WAINHOUSE D.W.,REMNANTS OF EMPIRE: THE UNITED NATIONS AND THE END OF COLONIALISM. FUT PORTUGAL WOR+45 NAT/G CONSULT DOMIN LEGIT ADMIN ROUTINE ATTIT ORD/FREE...POLICY JURID RECORD INT TIME/SEQ UN CMN/WLTH 20. PAGE 113 B2275
B64
INT/ORG
TREND
COLONIAL

WRAITH R.,CORRUPTION IN DEVELOPING COUNTRIES. NIGERIA UK LAW ELITES STRATA INDUS LOC/G NAT/G SECT FORCES EDU/PROP ADMIN PWR WEALTH 18/20. PAGE 118 B2377
B64
ECO/UNDEV
CRIME
SANCTION
ATTIT

HAAS E.B.,"ECONOMICS AND DIFFERENTIAL PATTERNS OF POLITICAL INTEGRATION: PROJECTIONS ABOUT UNITY IN LATIN AMERICA." SOCIETY NAT/G DELIB/GP ACT/RES CREATE PLAN ECO/TAC REGION ROUTINE ATTIT DRIVE PWR WEALTH...CONCPT TREND CHARTS LAFTA 20. PAGE 45 B0910
L64
L/A+17C
INT/ORG
MARKET

MACKINTOSH J.P.,"NIGERIA'S EXTERNAL AFFAIRS." UK CULTURE ECO/UNDEV NAT/G VOL/ASSN EDU/PROP LEGIT ADMIN ATTIT ORD/FREE PWR 20. PAGE 68 B1365
L64
AFR
DIPLOM
NIGERIA

MILLIS W.,"THE DEMILITARIZED WORLD." COM USA+45 USSR WOR+45 CONSTN NAT/G EX/STRUC PLAN LEGIT ATTIT DRIVE...CONCPT TIME/SEQ STERTYP TOT/POP COLD/WAR 20. PAGE 74 B1486
L64
FUT
INT/ORG
BAL/PWR
PEACE

RIPLEY R.B.,"INTERAGENCY COMMITTEES AND INCREMENTALISM: THE CASE OF AID TO INDIA." INDIA USA+45 INTELL NAT/G DELIB/GP ACT/RES DIPLOM ROUTINE NAT/LISM ATTIT PWR...SOC CONCPT NEW/IDEA TIME/SEQ CON/ANAL VAL/FREE 20. PAGE 89 B1790
L64
EXEC
MGT
FOR/AID

ROTBERG R.,"THE FEDERATION MOVEMENT IN BRITISH EAST AND CENTRAL AFRICA." AFR RHODESIA UGANDA ECO/UNDEV NAT/G POL/PAR FORCES DOMIN LEGIT ADMIN COERCE ATTIT ...CONCPT TREND 20 TANGANYIKA. PAGE 91 B1831
L64
VOL/ASSN
PWR
REGION

GROSS J.A.,"WHITEHALL AND THE COMMONWEALTH." EUR+WWI MOD/EUR INT/ORG NAT/G CONSULT DELIB/GP LEGIS DOMIN ADMIN COLONIAL ROUTINE PWR CMN/WLTH 19/20. PAGE 44 B0890
S64
EX/STRUC
ATTIT
TREND

HADY T.F.,"CONGRESSIONAL TOWNSHIPS AS INCORPORATED MUNICIPALITIES." NEIGH ADMIN REPRESENT ATTIT GEOG. PAGE 45 B0914
S64
MUNIC
REGION
LOC/G
GOV/COMP

JOHNSON K.F.,"CAUSAL FACTORS IN LATIN AMERICAN POLITICAL INSTABILITY." CULTURE NAT/G VOL/ASSN EX/STRUC FORCES EDU/PROP LEGIT ADMIN COERCE REV ATTIT KNOWL PWR...STYLE RECORD CHARTS WORK 20. PAGE 57 B1144
S64
L/A+17C
PERCEPT
ELITES

KAMMERER G.M.,"ROLE DIVERSITY OF CITY MANAGERS." LOC/G ADMIN LEAD PERCEPT PWR GP/COMP. PAGE 57 B1163
S64
MUNIC
EXEC
ATTIT
ROLE

KENNAN G.F.,"POLYCENTRISM AND WESTERN POLICY." ASIA CHINA/COM COM FUT USA+45 USSR NAT/G ACT/RES DOMIN EDU/PROP EXEC COERCE DISPL PERCEPT...POLICY COLD/WAR 20. PAGE 59 B1192
S64
RIGID/FLEX
ATTIT
DIPLOM

LIPSET S.M.,"SOCIOLOGY AND POLITICAL SCIENCE: A BIBLIOGRAPHICAL NOTE." WOR+45 ELITES LEGIS ADJUD ADMIN ATTIT IDEA/COMP. PAGE 65 B1321
S64
BIBLIOG/A
SOC
METH/COMP

MOWER A.G.,"THE OFFICIAL PRESSURE GROUP OF THE COUNCIL OF EUROPE'S CONSULATIVE ASSEMBLY." EUR+WWI SOCIETY STRUCT FINAN CONSULT ECO/TAC ADMIN ROUTINE ATTIT PWR WEALTH...STAT CHARTS 20 COUNCL/EUR. PAGE 76 B1535
S64
INT/ORG
EDU/PROP

NEEDHAM T.,"SCIENCE AND SOCIETY IN EAST AND WEST." ASIA INTELL STRATA R+D LOC/G NAT/G PROVS CONSULT ACT/RES CREATE PLAN TEC/DEV EDU/PROP ADMIN ATTIT ALL/VALS ...POLICY RELATIV MGT CONCPT NEW/IDEA TIME/SEQ WORK WORK. PAGE 77 B1565
S64
ASIA
STRUCT

RUSK D.,"THE MAKING OF FOREIGN POLICY" USA+45 CHIEF DELIB/GP WORKER PROB/SOLV ADMIN ATTIT PWR ...DECISION 20 DEPT/STATE RUSK/D GOLDMAN/E. PAGE 92 B1856
S64
DIPLOM
INT
POLICY

SCHWELB E.,"OPERATION OF THE EUROPEAN CONVENTION ON HUMAN RIGHTS." EUR+WWI LAW SOCIETY CREATE EDU/PROP ADJUD ADMIN PEACE ATTIT ORD/FREE PWR...POLICY INT/LAW CONCPT OBS GEN/LAWS UN VAL/FREE ILO 20 ECHR. PAGE 95 B1916
S64
INT/ORG
MORAL

THOMPSON V.A.,"ADMINISTRATIVE OBJECTIVES FOR DEVELOPMENT ADMINISTRATION." WOR+45 CREATE PLAN DOMIN EDU/PROP EXEC ROUTINE ATTIT ORD/FREE PWR ...POLICY GEN/LAWS VAL/FREE. PAGE 104 B2107
S64
ECO/UNDEV
MGT

NORGREN P.H.,"TOWARD FAIR EMPLOYMENT." USA+45 LAW STRATA LABOR NAT/G FORCES ACT/RES ADMIN ATTIT ...POLICY BIBLIOG 20 NEGRO. PAGE 79 B1588
C64
RACE/REL
DISCRIM
WORKER
MGT

AIYAR S.P.,STUDIES IN INDIAN DEMOCRACY. INDIA STRATA ECO/UNDEV LABOR POL/PAR LEGIS DIPLOM LOBBY REGION CHOOSE ATTIT SOCISM...ANTHOL 20. PAGE 3 B0067
B65
ORD/FREE
REPRESENT
ADMIN
NAT/G

ALDERSON W.,DYNAMIC MARKETING BEHAVIOR. USA+45 FINAN CREATE TEC/DEV EDU/PROP PRICE COST 20. PAGE 3 B0071
B65
MGT
MARKET
ATTIT
CAP/ISM

CONRAD J.P.,CRIME AND ITS CORRECTION: AN INTERNATIONAL SURVEY OF ATTITUDES AND PRACTICES. EUR+WWI NETHERLAND USA+45 USSR ATTIT MORAL 20 SCANDINAV. PAGE 23 B0467
B65
CRIME
PUB/INST
POLICY
ADMIN

CRAMER J.F.,CONTEMPORARY EDUCATION: A COMPARATIVE STUDY OF NATIONAL SYSTEMS (2ND ED.). CHINA/COM EUR+WWI INDIA USA+45 FINAN PROB/SOLV ADMIN CONTROL ATTIT...IDEA/COMP METH/COMP 20 CHINJAP. PAGE 25 B0502
B65
EDU/PROP
NAT/COMP
SCHOOL
ACADEM

EVERETT R.O.,URBAN PROBLEMS AND PROSPECTS. USA+45 MUNIC
CREATE TEC/DEV EDU/PROP ADJUD ADMIN GOV/REL ATTIT PLAN
...ANTHOL 20 URBAN/RNWL. PAGE 34 B0691 PROB/SOLV
NEIGH
B65

GOPAL S.,BRITISH POLICY IN INDIA 1858-1905. INDIA COLONIAL
UK ELITES CHIEF DELIB/GP ECO/TAC GP/REL DISCRIM ADMIN
ATTIT...IDEA/COMP NAT/COMP PERS/COMP BIBLIOG/A POL/PAR
19/20. PAGE 41 B0828 ECO/UNDEV
B65

HADWIGER D.F.,PRESSURES AND PROTEST. NAT/G LEGIS AGRI
PLAN LEAD PARTIC ROUTINE ATTIT POLICY. PAGE 45 GP/REL
B0913 LOBBY
CHOOSE
B65

HARR J.E.,THE DEVELOPMENT OF CAREERS IN THE FOREIGN OP/RES
SERVICE. CREATE SENIOR EXEC FEEDBACK GOV/REL MGT
EFFICIENCY ATTIT RESPECT ORG/CHARTS. PAGE 47 B0953 ADMIN
DIPLOM
B65

KAAS L.,DIE GEISTLICHE GERICHTSBARKEIT DER JURID
KATHOLISCHEN KIRCHE IN PREUSSEN (2 VOLS.). PRUSSIA CATHISM
CONSTN NAT/G PROVS SECT ADJUD ADMIN ATTIT 16/20. GP/REL
PAGE 57 B1158 CT/SYS
B65

KOUSOULAS D.G.,REVOLUTION AND DEFEAT; THE STORY OF REV
THE GREEK COMMUNIST PARTY. GREECE INT/ORG EX/STRUC MARXISM
DIPLOM FOR/AID EDU/PROP PARL/PROC ADJUST ATTIT 20 POL/PAR
COM/PARTY. PAGE 61 B1230 ORD/FREE
B65

KWEDER J.B.,THE ROLES OF THE MANAGER, MAYOR, AND MUNIC
COUNCILMEN IN POLICYMAKING. LEGIS PERS/REL ATTIT EXEC
ROLE PWR GP/COMP. PAGE 62 B1246 LEAD
DECISION
B65

LIPSET S.M.,THE BERKELEY STUDENT REVOLT: FACTS AND CROWD
INTERPRETATIONS. USA+45 INTELL VOL/ASSN CONSULT ACADEM
EDU/PROP PRESS DEBATE ADMIN REV HAPPINESS ATTIT
RIGID/FLEX MAJORIT. PAGE 65 B1322 GP/REL
B65

MASTERS N.A.,COMMITTEE ASSIGNMENTS IN THE HOUSE OF LEAD
REPRESENTATIVES (BMR). USA+45 ELITES POL/PAR LEGIS
EX/STRUC PARTIC REPRESENT GP/REL PERS/REL ATTIT PWR CHOOSE
...STAT CHARTS 20 HOUSE/REP. PAGE 71 B1425 DELIB/GP
B65

MEYERHOFF A.E.,THE STRATEGY OF PERSUASION. USA+45 EDU/PROP
COM/IND CONSULT FOR/AID CONTROL COERCE COST ATTIT EFFICIENCY
PERCEPT MARXISM 20 COLD/WAR. PAGE 73 B1476 OP/RES
ADMIN
B65

NATIONAL BOOK CENTRE PAKISTAN,BOOKS ON PAKISTAN: A BIBLIOG
BIBLIOGRAPHY. PAKISTAN CULTURE DIPLOM ADMIN ATTIT CONSTN
...MAJORIT SOC CONCPT 20. PAGE 77 B1560 S/ASIA
NAT/G
B65

PARRISH W.E.,MISSOURI UNDER RADICAL RULE 1865-1870. PROVS
USA-45 SOCIETY INDUS LOC/G POL/PAR WORKER EDU/PROP ADMIN
SUFF REV/REL ATTIT...BIBLIOG 19 NEGRO MISSOURI. RACE/REL
PAGE 81 B1635 ORD/FREE
B65

PUSTAY J.S.,COUNTER-INSURGENCY WARFARE. COM USA+45 FORCES
LOC/G NAT/G ACT/RES EDU/PROP ADMIN COERCE ATTIT PWR
...CONCPT MARX/KARL 20. PAGE 85 B1722 GUERRILLA
B65

UNESCO,INTERNATIONAL ORGANIZATIONS IN THE SOCIAL INT/ORG
SCIENCES(REV. ED.). LAW ADMIN ATTIT...CRIMLGY GEOG R+D
INT/LAW PSY SOC STAT 20 UNESCO. PAGE 107 B2157 PROF/ORG
ACT/RES
B65

WHITE J.,GERMAN AID. GERMANY/W FINAN PLAN TEC/DEV FOR/AID
INT/TRADE ADMIN ATTIT...POLICY 20. PAGE 116 B2334 ECO/UNDEV
DIPLOM
ECO/TAC
B65

WILDER B.E.,BIBLIOGRAPHY OF THE OFFICIAL BIBLIOG
PUBLICATIONS OF KANSAS, 1854-1958. USA+45 USA-45 PROVS
ECO/DEV POL/PAR EX/STRUC LEGIS ADJUD ATTIT 19/20. GOV/REL
PAGE 116 B2349 ADMIN
L65

HAMMOND A.,"COMPREHENSIVE VERSUS INCREMENTAL TOP/EX
BUDGETING IN THE DEPARTMENT OF AGRICULTURE" USA+45 EX/STRUC
GP/REL ATTIT...PSY INT 20 DEPT/AGRI. PAGE 46 B0934 AGRI
BUDGET
L65

LASSWELL H.D.,"THE POLICY SCIENCES OF DEVELOPMENT." PWR
CULTURE SOCIETY EX/STRUC CREATE ADMIN ATTIT KNOWL METH/CNCPT
...SOC CONCPT SIMUL GEN/METH. PAGE 63 B1273 DIPLOM
S65

"FURTHER READING." INDIA ADMIN COLONIAL WAR GOV/REL BIBLIOG
ATTIT 20. PAGE 2 B0044 DIPLOM
NAT/G
POLICY
S65

OSTGAARD E.,"FACTORS INFLUENCING THE FLOW OF NEWS." EDU/PROP
COM/IND BUDGET DIPLOM EXEC GP/REL COST ATTIT SAMP. PERCEPT

PAGE 80 B1618 RECORD
S65

POLK W.R.,"PROBLEMS OF GOVERNMENT UTILIZATION OF ACT/RES
SCHOLARLY RESEARCH IN INTERNATIONAL AFFAIRS." FINAN ACADEM
NAT/G EDU/PROP CONTROL TASK GP/REL ATTIT PERCEPT PLAN
KNOWL...POLICY TIME. PAGE 83 B1685 ADMIN
S65

TABORSKY E.,"CHANGE IN CZECHOSLOVAKIA." COM USSR ECO/DEV
ELITES INTELL AGRI INDUS NAT/G DELIB/GP EX/STRUC PLAN
ECO/TAC TOTALISM ATTIT RIGID/FLEX SOCISM...MGT CZECHOSLVK
CONCPT TREND 20. PAGE 102 B2067
B66

ANDERSON D.L.,MUNICIPAL PUBLIC RELATIONS (1ST ED.). MUNIC
USA+45 SOCIETY CONSULT FORCES PRESS ADMIN...CHARTS INGP/REL
BIBLIOG/A 20. PAGE 4 B0092 EDU/PROP
ATTIT
B66

ANDREWS K.R.,THE EFFECTIVENESS OF UNIVERSITY ECO/DEV
MANAGEMENT DEVELOPMENT PROGRAMS. FUT USA+45 ECO/TAC ACADEM
ADMIN...MGT QU METH/COMP 20. PAGE 5 B0103 TOP/EX
ATTIT
B66

BAKKE E.W.,MUTUAL SURVIVAL; THE GOAL OF UNION AND MGT
MANAGEMENT (2ND ED.). USA+45 ELITES ECO/DEV ECO/TAC LABOR
CONFER ADMIN REPRESENT GP/REL INGP/REL ATTIT BARGAIN
...GP/COMP 20. PAGE 8 B0170 INDUS
B66

BARBER W.F.,INTERNAL SECURITY AND MILITARY POWER* L/A+17C
COUNTERINSURGENCY AND CIVIC ACTION IN LATIN FORCES
AMERICA. ECO/UNDEV CREATE ADMIN REV ATTIT ORD/FREE
RIGID/FLEX MARXISM...INT BIBLIOG OAS. PAGE 9 B0183 TASK
B66

BEAUFRE A.,NATO AND EUROPE. WOR+45 PLAN CONFER EXEC INT/ORG
NUC/PWR ATTIT...POLICY 20 NATO EUROPE. PAGE 10 DETER
B0203 DIPLOM
ADMIN
B66

BOYD H.W.,MARKETING MANAGEMENT: CASES FROM EMERGING MGT
COUNTRIES. BRAZIL GHANA ISRAEL WOR+45 ADMIN ECO/UNDEV
PERS/REL ATTIT HABITAT WEALTH...ANTHOL 20 ARGEN PROB/SOLV
CASEBOOK. PAGE 14 B0292 MARKET
B66

CARALEY D.,PARTY POLITICS AND NATIONAL ELECTIONS. POL/PAR
USA+45 STRATA LOC/G PROVS EX/STRUC BARGAIN ADMIN CHOOSE
SANCTION GP/REL ATTIT 20 DEMOCRAT REPUBLICAN. REPRESENT
PAGE 18 B0375 NAT/G
B66

DAVIDSON R.H.,CONGRESS IN CRISIS: POLITICS AND LEGIS
CONGRESSIONAL REFORM. USA+45 SOCIETY POL/PAR PARL/PROC
CONTROL LEAD ROUTINE GOV/REL ATTIT PWR...POLICY 20 PROB/SOLV
CONGRESS. PAGE 26 B0535 NAT/G
B66

DAVIS J.A.,SOUTHERN AFRICA IN TRANSITION. SOUTH/AFR AFR
USA+45 FINAN NAT/G DELIB/GP EDU/PROP ADMIN COLONIAL ADJUST
REGION RACE/REL ATTIT SOVEREIGN...ANTHOL 20 CONSTN
RESOURCE/N. PAGE 26 B0538
B66

FABAR R.,THE VISION AND THE NEED: LATE VICTORIAN COLONIAL
IMPERIALIST AIMS. MOD/EUR UK WOR-45 CULTURE NAT/G CONCPT
DIPLOM...TIME/SEQ METH/COMP 19 KIPLING/R ADMIN
COMMONWLTH. PAGE 34 B0693 ATTIT
B66

FINNISH POLITICAL SCIENCE ASSN,SCANDINAVIAN ATTIT
POLITICAL STUDIES (VOL. I). FINLAND DIPLOM ADMIN POL/PAR
LOBBY PARL/PROC...CHARTS BIBLIOG 20 SCANDINAV. ACT/RES
PAGE 36 B0721 CHOOSE
B66

HIDAYATULLAH M.,DEMOCRACY IN INDIA AND THE JUDICIAL NAT/G
PROCESS. INDIA EX/STRUC LEGIS LEAD GOV/REL ATTIT CT/SYS
ORD/FREE...MAJORIT CONCPT 20 NEHRU/J. PAGE 50 B1007 CONSTN
JURID
B66

MCKENZIE J.L.,AUTHORITY IN THE CHURCH. STRUCT LEAD SECT
INGP/REL PERS/REL CENTRAL ANOMIE ATTIT ORD/FREE AUTHORIT
RESPECT CATH. PAGE 72 B1452 PWR
ADMIN
B66

O'NEILL C.E.,CHURCH AND STATE IN FRENCH COLONIAL COLONIAL
LOUISIANA: POLICY AND POLITICS TO 1732. PROVS NAT/G
VOL/ASSN DELIB/GP ADJUD ADMIN GP/REL ATTIT DRIVE SECT
...POLICY BIBLIOG 17/18 LOUISIANA CHURCH/STA. PWR
PAGE 79 B1601
B66

PERKINS J.A.,THE UNIVERSITY IN TRANSITION. USA+45 ACADEM
SOCIETY FINAN INDUS NAT/G EX/STRUC ADMIN INGP/REL ORD/FREE
COST EFFICIENCY ATTIT 20. PAGE 82 B1658 CREATE
ROLE
B66

RAEFF M.,ORIGINS OF THE RUSSIAN INTELLIGENTSIA: THE INTELL
EIGHTEENTH-CENTURY NOBILITY. RUSSIA FAM NAT/G ELITES
EDU/PROP ADMIN PERS/REL ATTIT...HUM BIOG 18. STRATA
PAGE 85 B1728 CONSERVE
B66

RUBENSTEIN R.,THE SHARING OF POWER IN A PSYCHIATRIC ADMIN
HOSPITAL. CLIENT PROF/ORG PUB/INST INGP/REL ATTIT PARTIC
PWR...DECISION OBS RECORD. PAGE 91 B1847 HEALTH

CONCPT
B66
SCHMIDT F.,PUBLIC RELATIONS IN HEALTH AND WELFARE. PROF/ORG
USA+45 ACADEM RECEIVE PRESS FEEDBACK GOV/REL EDU/PROP
PERS/REL DEMAND EFFICIENCY ATTIT PERCEPT WEALTH 20 ADMIN
PUBLIC/REL. PAGE 94 B1895 HEALTH
B66
SCHURMANN F.,IDEOLOGY AND ORGANIZATION IN COMMUNIST MARXISM
CHINA. CHINA/COM LOC/G MUNIC POL/PAR ECO/TAC STRUCT
CONTROL ATTIT...MGT STERTYP 20 COM/PARTY. PAGE 94 ADMIN
B1909 NAT/G
B66
SIMON R.,PERSPECTIVES IN PUBLIC RELATIONS. USA+45 GP/REL
INDUS ACT/RES PLAN ADMIN ATTIT MGT. PAGE 97 B1961 PERS/REL
COM/IND
SOCIETY
B66
STREET D.,ORGANIZATION FOR TREATMENT. CLIENT PROVS GP/COMP
PUB/INST PLAN CONTROL PARTIC REPRESENT ATTIT PWR AGE/Y
...POLICY BIBLIOG. PAGE 101 B2052 ADMIN
VOL/ASSN
B66
US DEPARTMENT OF THE ARMY,COMMUNIST CHINA: A BIBLIOG/A
STRATEGIC SURVEY: A BIBLIOGRAPHY (PAMPHLET NO. MARXISM
20-67). CHINA/COM COM INDIA USSR NAT/G POL/PAR S/ASIA
EX/STRUC FORCES NUC/PWR REV ATTIT...POLICY GEOG DIPLOM
CHARTS. PAGE 108 B2184
B66
VON HOFFMAN N.,THE MULTIVERSITY; A PERSONAL REPORT EDU/PROP
ON WHAT HAPPENS TO TODAY'S STUDENTS AT AMERICAN ACADEM
UNIVERSITIES. USA+45 SOCIETY ROUTINE ANOMIE ROLE ATTIT
MORAL ORD/FREE SKILL...INT 20. PAGE 112 B2266 STRANGE
B66
ZALEZNIK A.,HUMAN DILEMMAS OF LEADERSHIP. ELITES LEAD
INDUS EX/STRUC INGP/REL ATTIT...PSY 20. PAGE 119 PERSON
B2397 EXEC
MGT
L66
CRAIN R.L.,"STRUCTURE AND VALUES IN LOCAL POLITICAL MUNIC
SYSTEMS: THE CASE OF FLUORIDATION DECISIONS." EDU/PROP
EX/STRUC LEGIS LEAD PARTIC REPRESENT PWR...DECISION LOC/G
GOV/COMP. PAGE 25 B0501 ATTIT
S66
PALMER M.,"THE UNITED ARAB REPUBLIC* AN ASSESSMENT UAR
OF ITS FAILURE." ELITES ECO/UNDEV POL/PAR FORCES SYRIA
ECO/TAC RUMOR ADMIN EXEC EFFICIENCY ATTIT SOCISM REGION
...INT NASSER/G. PAGE 81 B1628 FEDERAL
S66
POLSBY N.W.,"BOOKS IN THE FIELD: POLITICAL BIBLIOG/A
SCIENCE." LAW CONSTN LOC/G NAT/G LEGIS ADJUD PWR 20 ATTIT
SUPREME/CT. PAGE 83 B1686 ADMIN
JURID
S66
WOLFINGER R.E.,"POLITICAL ETHOS AND THE STRUCTURE MUNIC
OF CITY GOVERNMENT." POL/PAR EX/STRUC REPRESENT ATTIT
GP/REL PERS/REL RIGID/FLEX PWR. PAGE 118 B2371 STRATA
GOV/COMP
B67
BRAYMAN H.,CORPORATE MANAGEMENT IN A WORLD OF MGT
POLITICS. USA+45 ELITES MARKET CREATE BARGAIN ECO/DEV
DIPLOM INT/TRADE ATTIT SKILL 20. PAGE 15 B0302 CAP/ISM
INDUS
B67
BUDER S.,PULLMAN: AN EXPERIMENT IN INDUSTRIAL ORDER DIST/IND
AND COMMUNITY PLANNING, 1880-1930. USA+45 SOCIETY INDUS
LABOR LG/CO CREATE PROB/SOLV CONTROL GP/REL MUNIC
EFFICIENCY ATTIT...MGT BIBLIOG 19/20 PULLMAN. PLAN
PAGE 17 B0337
B67
GIFFORD P.,BRITAIN AND GERMANY IN AFRICA. AFR COLONIAL
GERMANY UK ECO/UNDEV LEAD WAR NAT/LISM ATTIT ADMIN
...POLICY HIST/WRIT METH/COMP ANTHOL BIBLIOG 19/20 DIPLOM
WWI. PAGE 39 B0797 NAT/COMP
B67
GITTELL M.,PARTICIPANTS AND PARTICIPATION: A STUDY SCHOOL
OF SCHOOL POLICY IN NEW YORK. USA+45 MUNIC EX/STRUC DECISION
BUDGET PAY ATTIT...POLICY 20 NEWYORK/C. PAGE 40 PARTIC
B0806 ADMIN
B67
JHANGIANI M.A.,JANA SANGH AND SWATANTRA: A PROFILE POL/PAR
OF THE RIGHTIST PARTIES IN INDIA. INDIA ADMIN LAISSEZ
CHOOSE MARXISM SOCISM...INT CHARTS BIBLIOG 20. NAT/LISM
PAGE 56 B1140 ATTIT
B67
NIEDERHOFFER A.,BEHIND THE SHIELD; THE POLICE IN FORCES
URBAN SOCIETY. USA+45 LEGIT ADJUD ROUTINE COERCE PERSON
CRIME ADJUST...INT CHARTS 20 NEWYORK/C. PAGE 78 SOCIETY
B1582 ATTIT
B67
SKIDMORE T.E.,POLITICS IN BRAZIL 1930-1964. BRAZIL CONSTN
L/A+17C INDUS NAT/G PROB/SOLV ATTIT 20. PAGE 98 ECO/TAC
B1973 ADMIN
B67
US DEPARTMENT OF THE ARMY,CIVILIAN IN PEACE, BIBLIOG/A
SOLDIER IN WAR: A BIBLIOGRAPHIC SURVEY OF THE ARMY FORCES
AND AIR NATIONAL GUARD (PAMPHLET, NOS. 130-2). ROLE

USA+45 USA-45 LOC/G NAT/G PROVS LEGIS PLAN ADMIN DIPLOM
ATTIT ORD/FREE...POLICY 19/20. PAGE 108 B2185
L67
CAHIERS P.,"LE RECOURS EN CONSTATATION DE INT/ORG
MANQUEMENTS DES ETATS MEMBRES DEVANT LA COUR DES CONSTN
COMMUNAUTES EUROPEENNES." LAW PROB/SOLV DIPLOM ROUTINE
ADMIN CT/SYS SANCTION ATTIT...POLICY DECISION JURID ADJUD
ECSC EEC. PAGE 18 B0362
S67
ALPANDER G.G.,"ENTREPRENEURS AND PRIVATE ENTERPRISE ECO/UNDEV
IN TURKEY." TURKEY INDUS PROC/MFG EDU/PROP ATTIT LG/CO
DRIVE WEALTH...GEOG MGT SOC STAT TREND CHARTS 20. NAT/G
PAGE 4 B0080 POLICY
S67
ANDERSON M.,"THE FRENCH PARLIAMENT." EUR+WWI FRANCE PARL/PROC
MOD/EUR CONSTN POL/PAR CHIEF LEGIS LOBBY ATTIT ROLE LEAD
PWR 19/20. PAGE 5 B0095 GOV/COMP
EX/STRUC
S67
BASTID M.,"ORIGINES ET DEVELOPMENT DE LA REVOLUTION REV
CULTURELLE." CHINA/COM DOMIN ADMIN CONTROL LEAD CULTURE
COERCE CROWD ATTIT DRIVE MARXISM...POLICY 20. ACADEM
PAGE 10 B0195 WORKER
S67
BEASLEY W.G.,"POLITICS AND THE SAMURAI CLASS ELITES
STRUCTURE IN SATSUMA, 18581868." STRATA FORCES STRUCT
DOMIN LEGIT ADMIN LEAD 19 CHINJAP. PAGE 10 B0202 ATTIT
PRIVIL
S67
BREGMAN A.,"WHITHER RUSSIA?" COM RUSSIA INTELL MARXISM
POL/PAR DIPLOM PARTIC NAT/LISM TOTALISM ATTIT ELITES
ORD/FREE 20. PAGE 15 B0304 ADMIN
CREATE
S67
CHAMBERLAIN N.W.,"STRIKES IN CONTEMPORARY CONTEXT." LABOR
LAW INDUS NAT/G CHIEF CONFER COST ATTIT ORD/FREE BARGAIN
...POLICY MGT 20. PAGE 20 B0400 EFFICIENCY
PROB/SOLV
S67
DRAPER A.P.,"UNIONS AND THE WAR IN VIETNAM." USA+45 LABOR
CONFER ADMIN LEAD WAR ORD/FREE PACIFIST 20. PAGE 30 PACIFISM
B0616 ATTIT
ELITES
S67
GITTELL M.,"PROFESSIONALISM AND PUBLIC DECISION
PARTICIPATION IN EDUCATIONAL POLICY MAKING." STRUCT PLAN
ADMIN GP/REL ATTIT PWR 20. PAGE 40 B0805 EDU/PROP
MUNIC
S67
GOBER J.L.,"FEDERALISM AT WORK." USA+45 NAT/G MUNIC
CONSULT ACT/RES PLAN CONFER ADMIN LEAD PARTIC TEC/DEV
FEDERAL ATTIT. PAGE 40 B0813 R+D
GOV/REL
S67
HSUEH C.T.,"THE CULTURAL REVOLUTION AND LEADERSHIP LEAD
CRISIS IN COMMUNIST CHINA." CHINA/COM POL/PAR REV
EX/STRUC FORCES EDU/PROP ATTIT PWR...POLICY 20. CULTURE
PAGE 52 B1054 MARXISM
S67
JAVITS J.K.,"THE USE OF AMERICAN PLURALISM." USA+45 CENTRAL
ECO/DEV BUDGET ADMIN ALL/IDEOS...DECISION TREND. ATTIT
PAGE 56 B1127 POLICY
NAT/G
S67
JENCKS C.E.,"SOCIAL STATUS OF COAL MINERS IN EXTR/IND
BRITAIN SINCE NATIONALIZATION." UK STRATA STRUCT WORKER
LABOR RECEIVE GP/REL INCOME OWN ATTIT HABITAT...MGT CONTROL
T 20. PAGE 56 B1128 NAT/G
S67
LA PORTE T.,"DIFFUSION AND DISCONTINUITY IN INTELL
SCIENCE, TECHNOLOGY AND PUBLIC AFFAIRS: RESULTS OF ADMIN
A SEARCH IN THE FIELD." USA+45 ACT/RES TEC/DEV ACADEM
PERS/REL ATTIT PHIL/SCI. PAGE 62 B1249 GP/REL
S67
LASLETT J.H.M.,"SOCIALISM AND THE AMERICAN LABOR LABOR
MOVEMENT* SOME NEW REFLECTIONS." USA-45 VOL/ASSN ROUTINE
LOBBY PARTIC CENTRAL ALL/VALS SOCISM...GP/COMP 20. ATTIT
PAGE 63 B1265 GP/REL
S67
LEWIS P.H.,"LEADERSHIP AND CONFLICT WITHIN POL/PAR
FEBRERISTA PARTY OF PARAGUAY." L/A+17C PARAGUAY ELITES
EX/STRUC DOMIN SENIOR CONTROL INGP/REL CENTRAL LEAD
FEDERAL 20. PAGE 65 B1305
S67
OLIVE B.A.,"THE ADMINISTRATION OF HIGHER EDUCATION: ACADEM
A BIBLIOGRAPHICAL SURVEY." USA+45 ATTIT. PAGE 79 ADMIN
B1605 OP/RES
S67
ROSENBERG B.,"ETHNIC LIBERALISM AND EMPLOYMENT RACE/REL
DISCRIMINATION IN THE NORTH." USA+45 TOP/EX ATTIT
PROB/SOLV ADMIN REGION PERS/REL DISCRIM...INT WORKER
IDEA/COMP. PAGE 90 B1820 EXEC
S67
RUBIN R.I.,"THE LEGISLATIVE-EXECUTIVE RELATIONS OF LEGIS
THE UNITED STATES INFORMATION AGENCY." USA+45 EX/STRUC
EDU/PROP TASK INGP/REL EFFICIENCY ISOLAT ATTIT ROLE GP/REL

USIA CONGRESS. PAGE 91 B1850   PROF/ORG

SCOTT W.R.,"ORGANIZATIONAL EVALUATION AND   S67
AUTHORITY." CONTROL SANCTION PERS/REL ATTIT DRIVE   EXEC
...SOC CONCPT OBS CHARTS IDEA/COMP 20. PAGE 95   WORKER
B1921   INSPECT
                                                      EX/STRUC
                                                      S67
SHOEMAKER R.L.,"JAPANESE ARMY AND THE WEST." ASIA   FORCES
ELITES EX/STRUC DIPLOM DOMIN EDU/PROP COERCE ATTIT   TEC/DEV
AUTHORIT PWR 1/20 CHINJAP. PAGE 96 B1950   WAR
                                                      TOTALISM
                                                      S67
SPEAR P.,"NEHRU." INDIA NAT/G POL/PAR ECO/TAC ADJUD   CHIEF
GOV/REL CENTRAL RIGID/FLEX 20 NEHRU/J. PAGE 99   ATTIT
B2003   ADMIN
                                                      CREATE
                                                      S67
WALLER D.J.,"CHINA: RED OR EXPERT." CHINA/COM   CONTROL
INTELL DOMIN REV ATTIT MARXISM 20. PAGE 113 B2283   FORCES
                                                      ADMIN
                                                      POL/PAR
                                                      N67
NATIONAL COMN COMMUNITY HEALTH,ACTION - PLANNING   PLAN
FOR COMMUNITY HEALTH SERVICES (PAMPHLET). USA+45   MUNIC
PROF/ORG DELIB/GP BUDGET ROUTINE GP/REL ATTIT   HEALTH
...HEAL SOC SOC/WK CHARTS TIME 20. PAGE 77 B1563   ADJUST

ATTLEE/C....CLEMENT ATLEE

ATTORNEY GENERAL....SEE ATTRNY/GEN

ATTRNY/GEN....ATTORNEY GENERAL

AUD/VIS....FILM AND SOUND (INCLUDING PHOTOGRAPHY)

                                                      N19
WALL N.L.,MUNICIPAL REPORTING TO THE PUBLIC   METH
(PAMPHLET). LOC/G PLAN WRITING ADMIN REPRESENT   MUNIC
EFFICIENCY...AUD/VIS CHARTS 20. PAGE 113 B2282   GP/REL
                                                      COM/IND
                                                      B43
LEVY H.P.,A STUDY IN PUBLIC RELATIONS: CASE HISTORY   ATTIT
OF THE RELATIONS MAINTAINED BETWEEN A DEPT OF   RECEIVE
PUBLIC ASSISTANCE AND PEOPLE. USA+45 NAT/G PRESS   WEALTH
ADMIN LOBBY GP/REL DISCRIM...SOC/WK LING AUD/VIS 20   SERV/IND
PENNSYLVAN. PAGE 64 B1302
                                                      B50
DEES J.W. JR.,URBAN SOCIOLOGY AND THE EMERGING   PLAN
ATOMIC MEGALOPOLIS, PART I. USA+45 TEC/DEV ADMIN   NEIGH
NUC/PWR HABITAT...SOC AUD/VIS CHARTS GEN/LAWS 20   MUNIC
WATER. PAGE 28 B0568   PROB/SOLV
                                                      B50
JENKINS W.S.,A GUIDE TO THE MICROFILM COLLECTION OF   BIBLIOG
EARLY STATE RECORDS. USA+45 CONSTN MUNIC LEGIS   PROVS
PRESS ADMIN CT/SYS 18/20. PAGE 56 B1130   AUD/VIS
                                                      B56
WIGGINS J.R.,FREEDOM OR SECRECY. USA+45 USA-45   ORD/FREE
DELIB/GP EX/STRUC FORCES ADJUD SANCTION KNOWL PWR   PRESS
...AUD/VIS CONGRESS 20. PAGE 116 B2344   NAT/G
                                                      CONTROL
                                                      B59
BONNETT C.E.,LABOR-MANAGEMENT RELATIONS. USA+45   MGT
OP/RES PROB/SOLV EDU/PROP...AUD/VIS CHARTS 20.   LABOR
PAGE 13 B0274   INDUS
                                                      GP/REL
                                                      B60
BRISTOL L.H. JR.,DEVELOPING THE CORPORATE IMAGE.   LG/CO
USA+45 SOCIETY ECO/DEV COM/IND SCHOOL EDU/PROP   ATTIT
PRESS TV...AUD/VIS ANTHOL. PAGE 15 B0312   MGT
                                                      ECO/TAC
                                                      B61
MUNGER E.S.,AFRICAN FIELD REPORTS 1952-1961.   AFR
SOUTH/AFR SOCIETY ECO/UNDEV NAT/G POL/PAR COLONIAL   DISCRIM
EXEC PARL/PROC GUERRILLA RACE/REL ALL/IDEOS...SOC   RECORD
AUD/VIS 20. PAGE 76 B1538
                                                      B62
MORTON L.,STRATEGY AND COMMAND: THE FIRST TWO   WAR
YEARS. USA-45 NAT/G CONTROL EXEC LEAD WEAPON   FORCES
CIVMIL/REL PWR...POLICY AUD/VIS CHARTS 20 CHINJAP.   PLAN
PAGE 76 B1532   DIPLOM
                                                      N63
INTERNATIONAL CITY MGRS ASSN,POST-ENTRY TRAINING IN   LOC/G
THE LOCAL PUBLIC SERVICE (PAMPHLET). SCHOOL PLAN   WORKER
PROB/SOLV TEC/DEV ADMIN EFFICIENCY SKILL...POLICY   EDU/PROP
AUD/VIS CHARTS BIBLIOG 20 CITY/MGT. PAGE 54 B1096   METH/COMP
                                                      B65
CAMPBELL G.A.,THE CIVIL SERVICE IN BRITAIN (2ND   ADMIN
ED.). UK DELIB/GP FORCES WORKER' CREATE PLAN   LEGIS
...POLICY AUD/VIS 19/20 CIVIL/SERV. PAGE 18 B0370   NAT/G
                                                      FINAN
                                                      B67
BENNETT J.W.,HUTTERIAN BRETHREN; THE AGRICULTURAL   SECT
ECONOMY AND SOCIAL ORGANIZATION OF A COMMUNAL   AGRI
PEOPLE. USA+45 SOCIETY FAM KIN TEC/DEV ADJUST...MGT   STRUCT
AUD/VIS GP/COMP 20. PAGE 10 B0213   GP/REL

                                                      B67
ROBINSON D.W.,PROMISING PRACTICES IN CIVIC   EDU/PROP
EDUCATION. FUT USA+45 CONTROL PARTIC GOV/REL...OBS   NAT/G
AUD/VIS 20. PAGE 89 B1797   ADJUST
                                                      ADMIN

AUERBACH C.A. B0146

AUGUSTINE....SAINT AUGUSTINE

AUMANN F.R. B0147

AUSLAND J.C. B0148

AUST/HUNG....AUSTRIA-HUNGARY

AUSTRALIA....SEE ALSO S/ASIA, COMMONWLTH

                                                      N
AUSTRALIAN NATIONAL RES COUN,AUSTRALIAN SOCIAL   BIBLIOG/A
SCIENCE ABSTRACTS. NEW/ZEALND CULTURE SOCIETY LOC/G   POLICY
CT/SYS PARL/PROC...HEAL JURID PSY SOC 20 AUSTRAL.   NAT/G
PAGE 7 B0149   ADMIN
                                                      B21
BRYCE J.,MODERN DEMOCRACIES. FUT NEW/ZEALND USA-45   NAT/G
LAW CONSTN POL/PAR PROVS VOL/ASSN EX/STRUC LEGIS   TREND
LEGIT CT/SYS EXEC KNOWL CONGRESS AUSTRAL 20.
PAGE 16 B0332
                                                      B55
CRAIG J.,BIBLIOGRAPHY OF PUBLIC ADMINISTRATION IN   BIBLIOG
AUSTRALIA. CONSTN FINAN EX/STRUC LEGIS PLAN DIPLOM   GOV/REL
RECEIVE ADJUD ROUTINE...HEAL 19/20 AUSTRAL   ADMIN
PARLIAMENT. PAGE 24 B0500   NAT/G
                                                      B57
SCARROW H.A.,THE HIGHER PUBLIC SERVICE OF THE   ADMIN
COMMONWEALTH OF AUSTRALIA. LAW SENIOR LOBBY ROLE 20   NAT/G
AUSTRAL CIVIL/SERV COMMONWLTH. PAGE 93 B1877   EX/STRUC
                                                      GOV/COMP
                                                      B58
BLAIR L.,THE COMMONWEALTH PUBLIC SERVICE. LAW   ADMIN
WORKER...MGT CHARTS GOV/COMP 20 COMMONWLTH AUSTRAL   NAT/G
CIVIL/SERV. PAGE 12 B0248   EX/STRUC
                                                      INGP/REL
                                                      S59
PADELFORD N.J.,"REGIONAL COOPERATION IN THE SOUTH   INT/ORG
PACIFIC: THE SOUTH PACIFIC COMMISSION." FUT   ADMIN
NEW/ZEALND UK WOR+45 CULTURE ECO/UNDEV LOC/G
VOL/ASSN...OBS CON/ANAL UNESCO VAL/FREE AUSTRAL 20.
PAGE 80 B1622
                                                      S60
MODELSKI G.,"AUSTRALIA AND SEATO." S/ASIA USA+45   INT/ORG
CULTURE INTELL ECO/DEV NAT/G PLAN DIPLOM ADMIN   ACT/RES
ROUTINE ATTIT SKILL...MGT TIME/SEQ AUSTRAL 20
SEATO. PAGE 74 B1493
                                                      B65
BERNDT R.M.,ABORIGINAL MAN IN AUSTRALIA. LAW DOMIN   SOC
ADMIN COLONIAL MARRIAGE HABITAT ORD/FREE...LING   CULTURE
CHARTS ANTHOL BIBLIOG WORSHIP 20 AUSTRAL ABORIGINES   SOCIETY
MUSIC ELKIN/AP. PAGE 11 B0225   STRUCT

AUSTRALIAN NATIONAL RES COUN B0149

AUSTRIA....SEE ALSO APPROPRIATE TIME/SPACE/CULTURE INDEX

                                                      N
DEUTSCHE BUCHEREI,JAHRESVERZEICHNIS DES DEUTSCHEN   BIBLIOG
SCHRIFTUMS. AUSTRIA EUR+WWI GERMANY SWITZERLND LAW   WRITING
LOC/G DIPLOM ADMIN...MGT SOC 19/20. PAGE 29 B0580   NAT/G
                                                      B61
KEE R.,REFUGEE WORLD. AUSTRIA EUR+WWI GERMANY NEIGH   NAT/G
EX/STRUC WORKER PROB/SOLV ECO/TAC RENT EDU/PROP   GIVE
INGP/REL COST LITERACY HABITAT 20 MIGRATION.   WEALTH
PAGE 59 B1186   STRANGE
                                                      B62
BROWN B.E.,NEW DIRECTIONS IN COMPARATIVE POLITICS.   NAT/COMP
AUSTRIA FRANCE GERMANY UK WOR+45 EX/STRUC LEGIS   METH
ORD/FREE 20. PAGE 16 B0320   POL/PAR
                                                      FORCES
                                                      B66
OHLIN G.,AID AND INDEBTEDNESS. AUSTRIA FINAN   FOR/AID
INT/ORG PLAN DIPLOM GIVE...POLICY MATH CHARTS 20.   ECO/UNDEV
PAGE 79 B1604   ADMIN
                                                      WEALTH

AUSTRIA-HUNGARY....SEE AUST/HUNG

AUTHORIT....AUTHORITARIANISM, PERSONAL; SEE ALSO DOMIN

                                                      B38
FIELD G.L.,THE SYNDICAL AND CORPORATIVE   FASCISM
INSTITUTIONS OF ITALIAN FASCISM. ITALY CONSTN   INDUS
STRATA LABOR EX/STRUC TOP/EX ADJUD ADMIN LEAD   NAT/G
TOTALISM AUTHORIT...MGT 20 MUSSOLIN/B. PAGE 35   WORKER
B0716

S40
GERTH H.,"THE NAZI PARTY: ITS LEADERSHIP AND   POL/PAR
COMPOSITION" (BMR)" GERMANY ELITES STRATA STRUCT   DOMIN
EX/STRUC FORCES ECO/TAC CT/SYS CHOOSE TOTALISM   LEAD
AGE/Y AUTHORIT PWR 20. PAGE 39 B0792   ADMIN

B48
ROSSITER C.L.,CONSTITUTIONAL DICTATORSHIP; CRISIS   NAT/G
GOVERNMENT IN THE MODERN DEMOCRACIES. FRANCE   AUTHORIT
GERMANY UK USA-45 WOR-45 EX/STRUC BAL/PWR CONTROL   CONSTN
COERCE WAR CENTRAL ORD/FREE...DECISION 19/20.   TOTALISM
PAGE 90 B1828

B49
GLOVER J.D.,THE ADMINISTRATOR. ELITES LG/CO   ADMIN
EX/STRUC ACT/RES CONTROL GP/REL INGP/REL PERS/REL   MGT
AUTHORIT...POLICY CONCPT HIST/WRIT. PAGE 40 B0811   ATTIT
    PROF/ORG
B50
HYNEMAN C.S.,BUREAUCRACY IN A DEMOCRACY. CHIEF   NAT/G
LEGIS ADMIN CONTROL LEAD ROUTINE PERS/REL COST   CENTRAL
EFFICIENCY UTIL ATTIT AUTHORIT PERSON MORAL.   EX/STRUC
PAGE 53 B1071   MYTH

S52
JOSEPHSON E.,"IRRATIONAL LEADERSHIP IN FORMAL   ADMIN
ORGANIZATIONS." EX/STRUC PLAN LEAD GP/REL INGP/REL   RATIONAL
EFFICIENCY AUTHORIT DRIVE PSY. PAGE 57 B1154   CONCPT
    PERSON
B54
LAPIERRE R.T.,A THEORY OF SOCIAL CONTROL. STRUCT   CONTROL
ADMIN ROUTINE SANCTION ANOMIE AUTHORIT DRIVE PERSON   VOL/ASSN
PWR...MAJORIT CONCPT CLASSIF. PAGE 62 B1260   CULTURE

S59
JANOWITZ M.,"CHANGING PATTERNS OF ORGANIZATIONAL   FORCES
AUTHORITY: THE MILITARY ESTABLISHMENT" (BMR)"   AUTHORIT
USA-45 ELITES STRUCT EX/STRUC PLAN DOMIN AUTOMAT   ADMIN
NUC/PWR WEAPON 20. PAGE 55 B1122   TEC/DEV

S59
ROBINSON J.A.,"THE ROLE OF THE RULES COMMITTEE IN   PARL/PROC
ARRANGING THE PROGRAM OF THE UNITED STATES HOUSE OF   DELIB/GP
REPRESENTATIVES." USA+45 DEBATE CONTROL AUTHORIT   ROUTINE
HOUSE/REP. PAGE 89 B1801   LEGIS

B60
MOORE W.E.,LABOR COMMITMENT AND SOCIAL CHANGE IN   LABOR
DEVELOPING AREAS. SOCIETY STRATA ECO/UNDEV MARKET   ORD/FREE
VOL/ASSN WORKER AUTHORIT SKILL...MGT NAT/COMP   ATTIT
SOC/INTEG 20. PAGE 75 B1514   INDUS

C60
MCCLEERY R.,"COMMUNICATION PATTERNS AS BASES OF   PERS/REL
SYSTEMS OF AUTHORITY AND POWER" IN THEORETICAL   PUB/INST
STUDIES IN SOCIAL ORGAN. OF PRISON-BMR. USA+45   PWR
SOCIETY STRUCT EDU/PROP ADMIN CONTROL COERCE CRIME   DOMIN
GP/REL AUTHORIT...SOC 20. PAGE 71 B1443

B61
KRUPP S.,PATTERN IN ORGANIZATIONAL ANALYSIS: A   MGT
CRITICAL EXAMINATION. INGP/REL PERS/REL RATIONAL   CONTROL
ATTIT AUTHORIT DRIVE PWR...DECISION PHIL/SCI SOC   CONCPT
IDEA/COMP. PAGE 61 B1239   METH/CNCPT

L61
THOMPSON V.A.,"HIERARACHY, SPECIALIZATION, AND   PERS/REL
ORGANIZATIONAL CONFLICT" (BMR) USA+45 STRATA   PROB/SOLV
STRUCT WORKER TEC/DEV GP/REL INGP/REL ATTIT   ADMIN
AUTHORIT 20 BUREAUCRCY. PAGE 104 B2106   EX/STRUC

S62
GIDWANI K.A.,"LEADER BEHAVIOUR IN ELECTED AND NON-   LEAD
ELECTED GROUPS." DELIB/GP ROUTINE TASK HAPPINESS   INGP/REL
AUTHORIT...SOC STAT CHARTS SOC/EXP. PAGE 39 B0796   GP/COMP
    CHOOSE
B63
BERNE E.,THE STRUCTURE AND DYNAMICS OF   INGP/REL
ORGANIZATIONS AND GROUPS. CLIENT PARTIC DRIVE   AUTHORIT
HEALTH...MGT PSY ORG/CHARTS. PAGE 11 B0226   ROUTINE
    CLASSIF
B63
DOUGLASS H.R.,MODERN ADMINISTRATION OF SECONDARY   EDU/PROP
SCHOOLS. CLIENT DELIB/GP WORKER REPRESENT INGP/REL   ADMIN
AUTHORIT...TREND BIBLIOG. PAGE 30 B0613   SCHOOL
    MGT
B64
ETZIONI A.,MODERN ORGANIZATIONS. CLIENT STRUCT   MGT
DOMIN CONTROL LEAD PERS/REL AUTHORIT...CLASSIF   ADMIN
BUREAUCRCY. PAGE 34 B0685   PLAN
    CULTURE
B64
WILSON L.,THE ACADEMIC MAN. STRUCT FINAN PROF/ORG   ACADEM
OP/RES ADMIN AUTHORIT ROLE RESPECT...SOC STAT.   INGP/REL
PAGE 117 B2360   STRATA
    DELIB/GP
B65
GOULDNER A.W.,STUDIES IN LEADERSHIP. LABOR EDU/PROP   LEAD
CONTROL PARTIC...CONCPT CLASSIF. PAGE 42 B0845   ADMIN
    AUTHORIT
B65
RUBINSTEIN A.Z.,THE CHALLENGE OF POLITICS: IDEAS   NAT/G
AND ISSUES (2ND ED.). UNIV ELITES SOCIETY EX/STRUC   DIPLOM
BAL/PWR PARL/PROC AUTHORIT...DECISION ANTHOL 20.   GP/REL
PAGE 92 B1852   ORD/FREE

B66
MCKENZIE J.L.,AUTHORITY IN THE CHURCH. STRUCT LEAD   SECT
INGP/REL PERS/REL CENTRAL ANOMIE ATTIT ORD/FREE   AUTHORIT
RESPECT CATH. PAGE 72 B1452   PWR
    ADMIN
S67
SHOEMAKER R.L.,"JAPANESE ARMY AND THE WEST." ASIA   FORCES
ELITES EX/STRUC DIPLOM DOMIN EDU/PROP COERCE ATTIT   TEC/DEV
AUTHORIT PWR 1/20 CHINJAP. PAGE 96 B1950   WAR
    TOTALISM

AUTHORITY....SEE DOMIN

AUTOMAT....AUTOMATION; SEE ALSO COMPUTER, PLAN

N
US SUPERINTENDENT OF DOCUMENTS,LABOR (PRICE LIST   BIBLIOG/A
33). USA+45 LAW AGRI CONSTRUC INDUS NAT/G BARGAIN   WORKER
PRICE ADMIN AUTOMAT PRODUC MGT. PAGE 111 B2240   LABOR
    LEGIS
B56
GLADDEN E.N.,CIVIL SERVICE OR BUREAUCRACY? UK LAW   ADMIN
STRATA LABOR TOP/EX PLAN SENIOR AUTOMAT CONTROL   GOV/REL
PARTIC CHOOSE HAPPINESS...CHARTS 19/20 CIVIL/SERV   EFFICIENCY
BUREAUCRCY. PAGE 40 B0808   PROVS

B58
BRIGHT J.R.,AUTOMATION AND MANAGEMENT. INDUS LABOR   AUTOMAT
WORKER OP/RES TEC/DEV INSPECT 20. PAGE 15 B0307   COMPUTER
    PLAN
    MGT
B58
CHEEK G.,ECONOMIC AND SOCIAL IMPLICATIONS OF   BIBLIOG/A
AUTOMATION: A BIBLIOGRAPHIC REVIEW (PAMPHLET).   SOCIETY
USA+45 LG/CO WORKER CREATE PLAN CONTROL ROUTINE   INDUS
PERS/REL EFFICIENCY PRODUC...METH/COMP 20. PAGE 20   AUTOMAT
B0416

B58
WILENSKY H.L.,INDUSTRIAL SOCIETY AND SOCIAL   INDUS
WELFARE: IMPACT OF INDUSTRIALIZATION ON SUPPLY AND   ECO/DEV
ORGANIZATION OF SOC WELF SERVICES. ELITES SOCIETY   RECEIVE
STRATA SERV/IND FAM MUNIC PUB/INST CONSULT WORKER   PROF/ORG
ADMIN AUTOMAT ANOMIE 20. PAGE 117 B2352

S58
MANSFIELD E.,"A STUDY OF DECISION-MAKING WITHIN THE   OP/RES
FIRM." LG/CO WORKER INGP/REL COST EFFICIENCY PRODUC   PROB/SOLV
...CHARTS 20. PAGE 69 B1395   AUTOMAT
    ROUTINE
S59
JANOWITZ M.,"CHANGING PATTERNS OF ORGANIZATIONAL   FORCES
AUTHORITY: THE MILITARY ESTABLISHMENT" (BMR)"   AUTHORIT
USA+45 ELITES STRUCT EX/STRUC PLAN DOMIN AUTOMAT   ADMIN
NUC/PWR WEAPON 20. PAGE 55 B1122   TEC/DEV

S59
SIMPSON R.L.,"VERTICAL AND HORIZONTAL COMMUNICATION   PERS/REL
IN FORMAL ORGANIZATION" USA+45 LG/CO EX/STRUC DOMIN   AUTOMAT
CONTROL TASK INGP/REL TIME 20. PAGE 97 B1963   INDUS
    WORKER
B60
MORRIS W.T.,ENGINEERING ECONOMY. AUTOMAT RISK   OP/RES
RATIONAL...PROBABIL STAT CHARTS GAME SIMUL BIBLIOG   DECISION
T 20. PAGE 76 B1529   MGT
    PROB/SOLV
B61
BRADY R.A.,ORGANIZATION, AUTOMATION, AND SOCIETY.   TEC/DEV
USA+45 AGRI COM/IND DIST/IND MARKET CREATE   INDUS
...DECISION MGT 20. PAGE 14 B0296   AUTOMAT
    ADMIN
B61
INTL UNION LOCAL AUTHORITIES,LOCAL GOVERNMENT IN   LOC/G
THE USA. USA+45 PUB/INST DELIB/GP CONFER AUTOMAT   MUNIC
GP/REL POPULISM...ANTHOL 20 CITY/MGT. PAGE 54 B1101   ADMIN
    GOV/REL
B63
HEARLE E.F.R.,A DATA PROCESSING SYSTEM FOR STATE   LOC/G
AND LOCAL GOVERNMENTS. PLAN TEC/DEV AUTOMAT ROUTINE   PROVS
...MGT METH/CNCPT CLASSIF 20. PAGE 49 B0984   COMPUTER
    COMPUT/IR
B63
HEYEL C.,THE ENCYCLOPEDIA OF MANAGEMENT. WOR+45   MGT
MARKET TOP/EX TEC/DEV AUTOMAT LEAD ADJUST...STAT   INDUS
CHARTS GAME ANTHOL BIBLIOG. PAGE 49 B1002   ADMIN
    FINAN
B63
MCDONOUGH A.M.,INFORMATION ECONOMICS AND MANAGEMENT   COMPUT/IR
SYSTEMS. ECO/DEV OP/RES AUTOMAT EFFICIENCY 20.   MGT
PAGE 72 B1448   CONCPT
    COMPUTER
B64
RECENT PUBLICATIONS ON GOVERNMENTAL PROBLEMS. FINAN   BIBLIOG
INDUS ACADEM PLAN PROB/SOLV EDU/PROP ADJUD ADMIN   AUTOMAT
BIO/SOC...MGT SOC. PAGE 2 B0040   LEGIS
    JURID
B64
BRIGHT J.R.,RESEARCH, DEVELOPMENT AND TECHNOLOGICAL   TEC/DEV
INNOVATION. CULTURE R+D CREATE PLAN PROB/SOLV   NEW/IDEA
AUTOMAT RISK PERSON...DECISION CONCPT PREDICT   INDUS

BIBLIOG. PAGE 15 B0308 — MGT

B64
DIEBOLD J.,BEYOND AUTOMATION: MANAGERIAL PROBLEMS OF AN EXPLODING TECHNOLOGY. SOCIETY ECO/DEV CREATE ECO/TAC AUTOMAT SKILL...TECHNIC MGT WORK. PAGE 29 B0589 — FUT INDUS PROVS NAT/G

B64
WERNETTE J.P.,GOVERNMENT AND BUSINESS. LABOR CAP/ISM ECO/TAC INT/TRADE TAX ADMIN AUTOMAT NUC/PWR CIVMIL/REL DEMAND...MGT 20 MONOPOLY. PAGE 115 B2323 — NAT/G FINAN ECO/DEV CONTROL

B65
BOGUSLAW R.,THE NEW UTOPIANS. OP/RES ADMIN CONTROL PWR...IDEA/COMP SIMUL 20. PAGE 13 B0265 — UTOPIA AUTOMAT COMPUTER PLAN

B66
DICKSON W.J.,COUNSELING IN AN ORGANIZATION: A SEQUEL TO THE HAWTHORNE RESEARCHES. CLIENT VOL/ASSN ACT/RES PROB/SOLV AUTOMAT ROUTINE PERS/REL HAPPINESS ANOMIE ROLE...OBS CHARTS 20 AT+T. PAGE 29 B0588 — INDUS WORKER PSY MGT

B66
NIEBURG H.L.,IN THE NAME OF SCIENCE. USA+45 EX/STRUC LEGIS TEC/DEV BUDGET PAY AUTOMAT LOBBY PWR ...OBS 20. PAGE 78 B1581 — NAT/G INDUS TECHRACY

B66
US SENATE COMM GOVT OPERATIONS,INTERGOVERNMENTAL PERSONNEL ACT OF 1966. USA+45 NAT/G CONSULT DELIB/GP WORKER TEC/DEV PAY AUTOMAT UTIL 20 CONGRESS. PAGE 110 B2219 — ADMIN LEGIS EFFICIENCY EDU/PROP

B66
WADIA M.,THE NATURE AND SCOPE OF MANAGEMENT. DELIB/GP EX/STRUC CREATE AUTOMAT CONTROL EFFICIENCY ...ANTHOL 20. PAGE 112 B2271 — MGT PROB/SOLV IDEA/COMP ECO/TAC

B67
SCHUMACHER B.G.,COMPUTER DYNAMICS IN PUBLIC ADMINISTRATION. USA+45 CREATE PLAN TEC/DEV...MGT LING CON/ANAL BIBLIOG/A 20. PAGE 94 B1907 — COMPUTER COMPUT/IR ADMIN AUTOMAT

S67
MOOR E.J.,"THE INTERNATIONAL IMPACT OF AUTOMATION." WOR+45 ACT/RES COMPUTER CREATE PLAN CAP/ISM ROUTINE EFFICIENCY PREDICT. PAGE 75 B1511 — TEC/DEV OP/RES AUTOMAT INDUS

S67
MORTON J.A.,"A SYSTEMS APPROACH TO THE INNOVATION PROCESS: ITS USE IN THE BELL SYSTEM." USA+45 INTELL INDUS LG/CO CONSULT WORKER COMPUTER AUTOMAT DEMAND ...MGT CHARTS 20. PAGE 76 B1531 — TEC/DEV GEN/METH R+D COM/IND

S67
VERGIN R.C.,"COMPUTER INDUCED ORGANIZATION CHANGES." FUT USA+45 R+D CREATE OP/RES TEC/DEV ADJUST CENTRAL...MGT INT CON/ANAL COMPUT/IR. PAGE 112 B2260 — COMPUTER DECISION AUTOMAT EX/STRUC

AUTOMOBILE....AUTOMOBILE

B64
CHANDLER A.D. JR.,GIANT ENTERPRISE: FORD, GENERAL MOTORS, AND THE AUTOMOBILE INDUSTRY; SOURCES AND READINGS. USA+45 USA-45 FINAN MARKET CREATE ADMIN ...TIME/SEQ ANTHOL 20 AUTOMOBILE. PAGE 20 B0404 — LG/CO DIST/IND LABOR MGT

AVASTHI A. B0150

AVERAGE....MEAN, AVERAGE BEHAVIORS

AVERY M.W. B0151

AVERY R.S. B0866

AYEARST M. B0152

AYLMER G. B0153

AZERBAIJAN....AZERBAIJAN, IRAN

———— B ————

BA/MBUTI....BA MBUTI - THE FOREST PEOPLE (CONGO)

BABCOCK R.S. B0154

BABIES....SEE AGE/C

BACHELDER G.L. B0155

BACHRACH P. B0156

BACKUS/I....ISAAC BACKUS

BACON/F....FRANCIS BACON

BADEN....BADEN

BADI J. B0157

BAERWALD F. B0158,B0159

BAGEHOT W. B0160

BAGHDAD....BAGHDAD, IRAQ

BAHAWALPUR....BAHAWALPUR, PAKISTAN

BAHIA....BAHIA

B65
BOXER C.R.,PORTUGUESE SOCIETY IN THE TROPICS - THE MUNICIPAL COUNCILS OF GAO, MACAO, BAHIA, AND LUANDA, 1510-1800. EUR+WWI MOD/EUR PORTUGAL CONSTN EX/STRUC DOMIN CONTROL ROUTINE REPRESENT PRIVIL ...BIBLIOG/A 16/19 GENACCOUNT MACAO BAHIA LUANDA. PAGE 14 B0290 — MUNIC ADMIN COLONIAL DELIB/GP

BAIL....BAIL

BAILEY J.C. B1616

BAILEY S.D. B0161,B0162,B0163

BAILEY S.K. B0164,B1882

BAILEY/JM....JOHN MORAN BAILEY

BAILEY/S....S. BAILEY

BAILEY/T....THOMAS BAILEY

BAINS J.S. B0165

BAKER G. B0166

BAKER H. B0167

BAKER J.K. B0538

BAKER R.J. B0168

BAKKE E.W. B0169,B0170

BAKUBA....BAKUBA TRIBE

BAL/PAY....BALANCE OF PAYMENTS

B50
HARTLAND P.C.,BALANCE OF INTERREGIONAL PAYMENTS OF NEW ENGLAND. USA+45 TEC/DEV ECO/TAC LEGIT ROUTINE BAL/PAY PROFIT 20 NEW/ENGLND FED/RESERV. PAGE 47 B0962 — ECO/DEV FINAN REGION PLAN

S53
BLOUGH R.,"THE ROLE OF THE ECONOMIST IN FEDERAL POLICY MAKING." USA+45 ELITES INTELL ECO/DEV NAT/G CONSULT EX/STRUC ACT/RES PLAN INT/TRADE BAL/PAY WEALTH...POLICY CONGRESS 20. PAGE 13 B0256 — DELIB/GP ECO/TAC

B58
CHANG C.,THE INFLATIONARY SPIRAL: THE EXPERIENCE IN CHINA 1939-50. CHINA/COM BUDGET INT/TRADE PRICE ADMIN CONTROL WAR DEMAND...POLICY CHARTS 20. PAGE 20 B0406 — FINAN ECO/TAC BAL/PAY GOV/REL

S61
HALPERIN M.H.,"THE GAITHER COMMITTEE AND THE POLICY PROCESS." USA+45 NAT/G TOP/EX ACT/RES LEGIT ADMIN BAL/PAY PERCEPT...CONCPT TOT/POP 20. PAGE 46 B0928 — PLAN POLICY NUC/PWR DELIB/GP

S61
VINER J.,"ECONOMIC FOREIGN POLICY ON THE NEW FRONTIER." USA+45 ECO/UNDEV AGRI FINAN INDUS MARKET INT/ORG NAT/G FOR/AID INT/TRADE ADMIN ATTIT PWR 20 KENNEDY/JF. PAGE 112 B2262 — TOP/EX ECO/TAC BAL/PAY TARIFFS

B62
FORD A.G.,THE GOLD STANDARD 1880-1914: BRITAIN AND ARGENTINA. UK ECO/UNDEV INT/TRADE ADMIN GOV/REL DEMAND EFFICIENCY...STAT CHARTS 19/20 ARGEN GOLD/STAND. PAGE 36 B0737 — FINAN ECO/TAC BUDGET BAL/PAY

B62
INST TRAINING MUNICIPAL ADMIN,MUNICIPAL FINANCE ADMINISTRATION (6TH ED.). USA+45 ELITES ECO/DEV LEGIS PLAN BUDGET TAX GP/REL BAL/PAY COST...POLICY 20 CITY/MGT. PAGE 54 B1089 — MUNIC ADMIN FINAN LOC/G

B63
SCHOECK H.,THE NEW ARGUMENT IN ECONOMICS. UK USA+45 INDUS MARKET LABOR NAT/G ECO/TAC ADMIN ROUTINE BAL/PAY PWR...POLICY BOLIV. PAGE 94 B1899 — WELF/ST FOR/AID ECO/DEV ALL/IDEOS

S63
NADLER E.B.,"SOME ECONOMIC DISADVANTAGES OF THE ARMS RACE." USA+45 INDUS R+D FORCES PLAN TEC/DEV ECO/TAC FOR/AID EDU/PROP PWR WEALTH...TREND COLD/WAR 20. PAGE 77 B1552 — ECO/DEV MGT BAL/PAY

S64
HUELIN D.,"ECONOMIC INTEGRATION IN LATIN AMERICAN: PROGRESS AND PROBLEMS." L/A+17C ECO/DEV AGRI — MARKET ECO/UNDEV

DIST/IND FINAN INDUS NAT/G VOL/ASSN CONSULT   INT/TRADE
DELIB/GP EX/STRUC ACT/RES PLAN TEC/DEV ECO/TAC
ROUTINE BAL/PAY WEALTH WORK 20. PAGE 52 B1058
                                                           B65

EDELMAN M.,THE POLITICS OF WAGE-PRICE DECISIONS.   GOV/COMP
GERMANY ITALY NETHERLAND UK INDUS LABOR POL/PAR   CONTROL
PROB/SOLV BARGAIN PRICE ROUTINE BAL/PAY COST DEMAND ECO/TAC
20. PAGE 32 B0654   PLAN
                                                           B67

BALDWIN G.B.,PLANNING AND DEVELOPMENT IN IRAN. IRAN PLAN
AGRI INDUS CONSULT WORKER EDU/PROP BAL/PAY...CHARTS ECO/UNDEV
20. PAGE 8 B0173   ADMIN
                                                   PROB/SOLV
                                                           B67

ENKE S.,DEFENSE MANAGEMENT. USA+45 R+D FORCES   DECISION
WORKER PLAN ECO/TAC ADMIN NUC/PWR BAL/PAY UTIL   DELIB/GP
WEALTH...MGT DEPT/DEFEN. PAGE 33 B0675   EFFICIENCY
                                                   BUDGET
                                                           B67

KARDOUCHE G.K.,THE UAR IN DEVELOPMENT. UAR ECO/TAC FINAN
INT/TRADE BAL/PAY...STAT CHARTS BIBLIOG 20. PAGE 58 MGT
B1172   CAP/ISM
                                                   ECO/UNDEV
                                                           S67

DUGGAR J.W.,"THE DEVELOPMENT OF MONEY SUPPLY IN   ECO/UNDEV
ETHIOPIA." ETHIOPIA ISLAM CONSULT OP/RES BUDGET   FINAN
CONTROL ROUTINE EFFICIENCY EQUILIB WEALTH...MGT 20. BAL/PAY
PAGE 31 B0629   ECOMETRIC

BAL/PWR....BALANCE OF POWER

GOODNOW F.J.,THE PRINCIPLES OF THE ADMINISTRATIVE ADMIN
LAW OF THE UNITED STATES. USA-45 LAW STRUCT   NAT/G
EX/STRUC LEGIS BAL/PWR CONTROL GOV/REL PWR...JURID PROVS
19/20 CIVIL/SERV. PAGE 41 B0822   LOC/G
                                                           B08

WILSON W.,CONSTITUTIONAL GOVERNMENT IN THE UNITED NAT/G
STATES. USA-45 LAW POL/PAR PROVS CHIEF LEGIS   GOV/REL
BAL/PWR ADJUD EXEC FEDERAL PWR 18/20 SUPREME/CT   CONSTN
HOUSE/REP SENATE. PAGE 117 B2362   PARL/PROC
                                                           B21

STOWELL E.C.,INTERVENTION IN INTERNATIONAL LAW.   BAL/PWR
UNIV LAW SOCIETY INT/ORG ACT/RES PLAN LEGIT ROUTINE SOVEREIGN
WAR...JURID OBS GEN/LAWS 20. PAGE 101 B2050
                                                           B24

BAGEHOT W.,THE ENGLISH CONSTITUTION AND OTHER   NAT/G
POLITICAL ESSAYS. UK DELIB/GP BAL/PWR ADMIN CONTROL STRUCT
EXEC ROUTINE CONSERVE...METH PARLIAMENT 19/20.   CONCPT
PAGE 8 B0160
                                                           B26

MOON P.T.,IMPERIALISM AND WORLD POLITICS. AFR ASIA WEALTH
ISLAM MOD/EUR S/ASIA USA-45 SOCIETY NAT/G EX/STRUC TIME/SEQ
BAL/PWR DOMIN COLONIAL NAT/LISM ATTIT DRIVE PWR   CAP/ISM
...GEOG SOC 20. PAGE 75 B1510   DIPLOM
                                                           B29

BUELL R.,INTERNATIONAL RELATIONS. WOR+45 WOR-45   INT/ORG
CONSTN STRATA FORCES TOP/EX ADMIN ATTIT DRIVE   BAL/PWR
SUPEGO MORAL ORD/FREE PWR SOVEREIGN...JURID SOC   DIPLOM
CONCPT 20. PAGE 17 B0340
                                                           B39

HITLER A.,MEIN KAMPF. EUR+WWI FUT MOD/EUR STRUCT   PWR
INT/ORG LABOR NAT/G POL/PAR FORCES CREATE PLAN   NEW/IDEA
BAL/PWR DIPLOM ECO/TAC DOMIN EDU/PROP ADMIN COERCE WAR
ATTIT...SOCIALIST BIOG TREND NAZI. PAGE 50 B1020
                                                           B39

ZIMMERN A.,MODERN POLITICAL DOCTRINE. WOR-45   NAT/G
CULTURE SOCIETY ECO/UNDEV DELIB/GP EX/STRUC CREATE ECO/TAC
DOMIN COERCE NAT/LISM RIGID/FLEX ORD/FREE PWR   BAL/PWR
WEALTH...POLICY CONCPT OBS TIME/SEQ TREND TOT/POP INT/TRADE
LEAGUE/NAT 20. PAGE 119 B2402
                                                           B48

HULL C.,THE MEMOIRS OF CORDELL HULL (VOLUME ONE). BIOG
USA-45 WOR+45 CONSTN FAM LOC/G NAT/G PROVS DELIB/GP DIPLOM
FORCES LEGIS TOP/EX BAL/PWR LEGIT ADMIN EXEC WAR
ATTIT ORD/FREE PWR...MAJORIT SELF/OBS TIME/SEQ
TREND NAZI 20. PAGE 52 B1062
                                                           B48

ROSSITER C.L.,CONSTITUTIONAL DICTATORSHIP; CRISIS NAT/G
GOVERNMENT IN THE MODERN DEMOCRACIES. FRANCE   AUTHORIT
GERMANY UK USA-45 WOR+45 EX/STRUC BAL/PWR CONTROL CONSTN
COERCE WAR CENTRAL ORD/FREE...DECISION 19/20.   TOTALISM
PAGE 90 B1828
                                                           B49

WALINE M.,LE CONTROLE JURIDICTIONNEL DE   JURID
L'ADMINISTRATION. BELGIUM FRANCE UAR JUDGE BAL/PWR ADMIN
ADJUD CONTROL CT/SYS...GP/COMP 20. PAGE 113 B2277 PWR
                                                   ORD/FREE
                                                           B50

LASSWELL H.D.,NATIONAL SECURITY AND INDIVIDUAL   FACE/GP
FREEDOM. USA+45 R+D NAT/G VOL/ASSN CONSULT DELIB/GP ROUTINE
LEGIT ADMIN KNOWL ORD/FREE PWR...PLURIST TOT/POP   BAL/PWR
COLD/WAR 20. PAGE 63 B1268
                                                           B51

DAVIS K.C.,ADMINISTRATIVE LAW. USA+45 USA-45 NAT/G ADMIN
PROB/SOLV BAL/PWR CONTROL ORD/FREE...POLICY 20   JURID

SUPREME/CT. PAGE 26 B0539   EX/STRUC
                                                   ADJUD
                                                           B52

VANDENBOSCH A.,THE UN: BACKGROUND, ORGANIZATION,   DELIB/GP
FUNCTIONS, ACTIVITIES. WOR+45 LAW CONSTN STRUCT   TIME/SEQ
INT/ORG CONSULT BAL/PWR LEGIT ADMIN EXEC ALL/VALS PEACE
...POLICY CONCPT UN 20. PAGE 112 B2254
                                                           B53

MEYER P.,THE JEWS IN THE SOVIET SATELLITES.   COM
CZECHOSLVK POLAND SOCIETY STRATA NAT/G BAL/PWR   SECT
ECO/TAC EDU/PROP LEGIT ADMIN COERCE ATTIT DISPL   TOTALISM
PERCEPT HEALTH PWR RESPECT WEALTH...METH/CNCPT JEWS USSR
VAL/FREE NAZI 20. PAGE 73 B1474
                                                           S53

CORY R.H. JR.,"FORGING A PUBLIC INFORMATION POLICY INT/ORG
FOR THE UNITED NATIONS." FUT WOR+45 SOCIETY ADMIN EDU/PROP
PEACE ATTIT PERSON SKILL...CONCPT 20 UN. PAGE 24   BAL/PWR
B0486
                                                           S53

DRUCKER P.F.,"THE EMPLOYEE SOCIETY." STRUCT BAL/PWR LABOR
PARTIC REPRESENT PWR...DECISION CONCPT. PAGE 30   MGT
B0619   WORKER
                                                   CULTURE
                                                           B54

CONWAY O.B. JR.,LEGISLATIVE-EXECUTIVE RELATIONS IN BAL/PWR
THE GOVERNMENT OF THE UNITED STATES (PAMPHLET).   FEDERAL
BUDGET ATTIT PERCEPT...DECISION 20. PAGE 23 B0470 GOV/REL
                                                   EX/STRUC
                                                           B54

MILLARD E.L.,FREEDOM IN A FEDERAL WORLD. FUT WOR+45 INT/ORG
VOL/ASSN TOP/EX LEGIT ROUTINE FEDERAL PEACE ATTIT CREATE
DISPL ORD/FREE PWR...MAJORIT INT/LAW JURID TREND   ADJUD
COLD/WAR 20. PAGE 73 B1479   BAL/PWR
                                                           B55

GUAITA A.,BIBLIOGRAFIA ESPANOLA DE DERECHO   BIBLIOG
ADMINISTRATIVO (PAMPHLET). SPAIN LOC/G MUNIC NAT/G ADMIN
PROVS JUDGE BAL/PWR GOV/REL OWN...JURID 18/19.   CONSTN
PAGE 44 B0900   PWR
                                                           B56

KAUFMANN W.W.,MILITARY POLICY AND NATIONAL   FORCES
SECURITY. USA+45 ELITES INTELL NAT/G TOP/EX PLAN   CREATE
BAL/PWR DIPLOM ROUTINE COERCE NUC/PWR ATTIT
ORD/FREE PWR 20 COLD/WAR. PAGE 58 B1182
                                                           B57

KAPLAN M.A.,SYSTEM AND PROCESS OF INTERNATIONAL   INT/ORG
POLITICS. FUT WOR+45 WOR-45 SOCIETY PLAN BAL/PWR   DIPLOM
ADMIN ATTIT PERSON RIGID/FLEX PWR SOVEREIGN
...DECISION TREND VAL/FREE. PAGE 58 B1168
                                                           B59

MAASS A.,AREA AND POWER: A THEORY OF LOCAL   LOC/G
GOVERNMENT. MUNIC PROVS EX/STRUC LEGIS CT/SYS   FEDERAL
CHOOSE PWR 20. PAGE 67 B1354   BAL/PWR
                                                   GOV/REL
                                                           S59

STOESSINGER J.G.,"THE INTERNATIONAL ATOMIC ENERGY INT/ORG
AGENCY: THE FIRST PHASE." FUT WOR+45 NAT/G VOL/ASSN ECO/DEV
DELIB/GP BAL/PWR LEGIT ADMIN ROUTINE PWR...OBS   FOR/AID
CON/ANAL GEN/LAWS VAL/FREE 20 IAEA. PAGE 101 B2040 NUC/PWR
                                                           B60

BROOKINGS INSTITUTION.UNITED STATES FOREIGN POLICY: DIPLOM
STUDY NO 9: THE FORMULATION AND ADMINISTRATION OF INT/ORG
UNITED STATES FOREIGN POLICY. USA+45 WOR+45   CREATE
EX/STRUC LEGIS BAL/PWR FOR/AID EDU/PROP CIVMIL/REL
GOV/REL...INT COLD/WAR. PAGE 16 B0317
                                                           B60

FURNISS E.S.,FRANCE, TROUBLED ALLY. EUR+WWI FUT   NAT/G
CULTURE SOCIETY BAL/PWR ADMIN ATTIT DRIVE PWR   FRANCE
...TREND TOT/POP 20 DEGAULLE/C. PAGE 38 B0767
                                                           B60

MORISON E.E.,TURMOIL AND TRADITION: A STUDY OF THE BIOG
LIFE AND TIMES OF HENRY L. STIMSON. USA+45 USA-45 NAT/G
POL/PAR CHIEF DELIB/GP FORCES BAL/PWR DIPLOM   EX/STRUC
ARMS/CONT WAR PEACE 19/20 STIMSON/HL ROOSEVLT/F
TAFT/WH HOOVER/H REPUBLICAN. PAGE 75 B1525
                                                           L60

GRODZINS M.,"AMERICAN POLITICAL PARTIES AND THE   POL/PAR
AMERICAN SYSTEM" (BMR)" USA+45 LOC/G NAT/G LEGIS   FEDERAL
BAL/PWR ADMIN ROLE PWR...DECISION 20. PAGE 44 B0883 CENTRAL
                                                   GOV/REL
                                                           S60

HALPERIN M.H.,"IS THE SENATE'S FOREIGN RELATIONS   PLAN
RESEARCH WORTHWHILE." COM FUT USA+45 USSR ACT/RES DIPLOM
BAL/PWR EDU/PROP ADMIN ALL/VALS CONGRESS VAL/FREE
20 COLD/WAR. PAGE 46 B0927
                                                           S60

MORA J.A.,"THE ORGANIZATION OF AMERICAN STATES."   L/A+17C
USA+45 LAW ECO/UNDEV VOL/ASSN DELIB/GP PLAN BAL/PWR INT/ORG
EDU/PROP ADMIN DRIVE RIGID/FLEX ORD/FREE WEALTH   REGION
...TIME/SEQ GEN/LAWS OAS 20. PAGE 75 B1518
                                                           S60

RIESELBACH Z.N.,"QUANTITATIVE TECHNIQUES FOR   QUANT
STUDYING VOTING BEHAVIOR IN THE UNITED NATIONS   CHOOSE
GENERAL ASSEMBLY." FUT S/ASIA USA+45 INT/ORG
BAL/PWR DIPLOM ECO/TAC FOR/AID ADMIN PWR...POLICY
METH/CNCPT METH UN 20. PAGE 88 B1783

B61
BAINS J.S.,,STUDIES IN POLITICAL SCIENCE. INDIA   DIPLOM
WOR+45 WOR-45 CONSTN BAL/PWR ADJUD ADMIN PARL/PROC   INT/LAW
SOVEREIGN...SOC METH/COMP ANTHOL 17/20 UN. PAGE 8   NAT/G
B0165

B61
KERTESZ S.D.,,AMERICAN DIPLOMACY IN A NEW ERA. COM   ANTHOL
S/ASIA UK USA+45 FORCES PROB/SOLV BAL/PWR ECO/TAC   DIPLOM
ADMIN COLONIAL WAR PEACE ORD/FREE 20 NATO CONGRESS   TREND
UN COLD/WAR. PAGE 59 B1199

B61
MOLLAU G.,,INTERNATIONAL COMMUNISM AND WORLD   COM
REVOLUTION: HISTORY AND METHODS. RUSSIA USSR   REV
INT/ORG NAT/G POL/PAR VOL/ASSN FORCES BAL/PWR
DIPLOM EXEC REGION WAR ATTIT PWR MARXISM...CONCPT
TIME/SEQ COLD/WAR 19/20. PAGE 74 B1498

S61
ALGER C.F.,,"NON-RESOLUTION CONSEQUENCES OF THE   INT/ORG
UNITED NATIONS AND THEIR EFFECT ON INTERNATIONAL   DRIVE
CONFLICT." WOR+45 CONSTN ECO/DEV NAT/G CONSULT   BAL/PWR
DELIB/GP TOP/EX ACT/RES PLAN DIPLOM EDU/PROP
ROUTINE ATTIT ALL/VALS...INT/LAW TOT/POP UN 20.
PAGE 4 B0075

S61
DEVINS J.H.,,"THE INITIATIVE." COM USA+45 USA-45   FORCES
USSR SOCIETY NAT/G ACT/RES CREATE BAL/PWR ROUTINE   CONCPT
COERCE DETER RIGID/FLEX SKILL...STERTYP COLD/WAR   WAR
20. PAGE 29 B0582

S61
VIRALLY M.,,"VERS UNE REFORME DU SECRETARIAT DES   INT/ORG
NATIONS UNIES." FUT WOR+45 CONSTN ECO/DEV TOP/EX   INTELL
BAL/PWR ADMIN ALL/VALS...CONCPT BIOG UN VAL/FREE   DIPLOM
20. PAGE 112 B2264

B62
BAILEY S.D.,,THE SECRETARIAT OF THE UNITED NATIONS. INT/ORG
FUT WOR+45 DELIB/GP PLAN BAL/PWR DOMIN EDU/PROP   EXEC
ADMIN PEACE ATTIT PWR...DECISION CONCPT TREND   DIPLOM
CON/ANAL CHARTS UN VAL/FREE COLD/WAR 20. PAGE 8
B0162

B62
PHILLIPS O.H.,,CONSTITUTIONAL AND ADMINISTRATIVE LAW JURID
(3RD ED.). UK INT/ORG LOC/G CHIEF EX/STRUC LEGIS   ADMIN
BAL/PWR ADJUD COLONIAL CT/SYS PWR...CHARTS 20.   CONSTN
PAGE 83 B1670   NAT/G

B62
SCHILLING W.R.,,STRATEGY, POLITICS, AND DEFENSE   ROUTINE
BUDGETS. USA+45 R+D NAT/G CONSULT DELIB/GP FORCES   POLICY
LEGIS ACT/RES PLAN BAL/PWR LEGIT EXEC NUC/PWR
RIGID/FLEX PWR...TREND COLD/WAR CONGRESS 20
EISNHWR/DD. PAGE 93 B1890

B62
WANGSNESS P.H.,,THE POWER OF THE CITY MANAGER.   PWR
USA+45 EX/STRUC BAL/PWR BUDGET TAX ADMIN REPRESENT   TOP/EX
CENTRAL EFFICIENCY DRIVE ROLE...POLICY 20 CITY/MGT. MUNIC
PAGE 113 B2286   LOC/G

S62
BRZEZINSKI Z.K.,,"DEVIATION CONTROL: A STUDY IN THE RIGID/FLEX
DYNAMICS OF DOCTRINAL CONFLICT." WOR+45 WOR-45   ATTIT
VOL/ASSN CREATE BAL/PWR DOMIN EXEC DRIVE PERCEPT
PWR...METH/CNCPT TIME/SEQ TREND 20. PAGE 16 B0333

B63
CROZIER B.,,THE MORNING AFTER; A STUDY OF   SOVEREIGN
INDEPENDENCE. WOR+45 EX/STRUC PLAN BAL/PWR COLONIAL NAT/LISM
GP/REL 20 COLD/WAR. PAGE 25 B0511   NAT/G
                                                     DIPLOM

B63
GARNER U.F.,,ADMINISTRATIVE LAW. UK LAW LOC/G NAT/G ADMIN
EX/STRUC LEGIS JUDGE BAL/PWR BUDGET ADJUD CONTROL   JURID
CT/SYS...BIBLIOG 20. PAGE 39 B0783   PWR
                                                     GOV/REL

B63
GRIFFITH J.A.G.,,PRINCIPLES OF ADMINISTRATIVE LAW   JURID
(3RD ED.). UK CONSTN EX/STRUC LEGIS ADJUD CONTROL   ADMIN
CT/SYS PWR...CHARTS 20. PAGE 43 B0879   NAT/G
                                                     BAL/PWR

B63
VAN SLYCK P.,,PEACE: THE CONTROL OF NATIONAL POWER. ARMS/CONT
CUBA WOR+45 FINAN NAT/G FORCES PROB/SOLV TEC/DEV   PEACE
BAL/PWR ADMIN CONTROL ORD/FREE...POLICY INT/LAW UN   INT/ORG
COLD/WAR TREATY. PAGE 112 B2253   DIPLOM

L63
BEGUIN H.,,"ASPECTS GEOGRAPHIQUE DE LA   ECO/UNDEV
POLARISATION." FUT WOR+45 SOCIETY STRUCT ECO/DEV   GEOG
R+D BAL/PWR ADMIN ATTIT RIGID/FLEX HEALTH WEALTH   DIPLOM
...CHARTS 20. PAGE 10 B0206

S63
ANTHON C.G.,,"THE END OF THE ADENAUER ERA." EUR+WWI NAT/G
GERMANY/W CONSTN EX/STRUC CREATE DIPLOM LEGIT ATTIT TOP/EX
PERSON ALL/VALS...RECORD 20 ADENAUER/K. PAGE 6   BAL/PWR
B0113   GERMANY

S63
BECHHOEFER B.G.,,"UNITED NATIONS PROCEDURES IN CASE INT/ORG
OF VIOLATIONS OF DISARMAMENT AGREEMENTS." COM   DELIB/GP
USA+45 USSR LAW CONSTN NAT/G EX/STRUC FORCES LEGIS
BAL/PWR EDU/PROP CT/SYS ARMS/CONT ORD/FREE PWR
...POLICY STERTYP UN VAL/FREE 20. PAGE 10 B0204

S63
BOWIE R.,,"STRATEGY AND THE ATLANTIC ALLIANCE."   FORCES
EUR+WWI VOL/ASSN BAL/PWR COERCE NUC/PWR ATTIT   ROUTINE
ORD/FREE PWR...DECISION GEN/LAWS NATO COLD/WAR 20.
PAGE 14 B0287

S63
HAVILAND H.F.,,"BUILDING A POLITICAL COMMUNITY."   VOL/ASSN
EUR+WWI FUT UK USA+45 ECO/DEV ECO/UNDEV INT/ORG   DIPLOM
NAT/G DELIB/GP BAL/PWR ECO/TAC NEUTRAL ROUTINE
ATTIT PWR WEALTH...CONCPT COLD/WAR TOT/POP 20.
PAGE 48 B0972

B64
COTTRELL A.J.,,THE POLITICS OF THE ATLANTIC   VOL/ASSN
ALLIANCE. EUR+WWI USA+45 INT/ORG NAT/G DELIB/GP   FORCES
EX/STRUC BAL/PWR DIPLOM REGION DETER ATTIT ORD/FREE
...CONCPT RECORD GEN/LAWS GEN/METH NATO 20. PAGE 24
B0493

B64
LOWI T.J.,,AT THE PLEASURE OF THE MAYOR. EX/STRUC   LOBBY
PROB/SOLV BAL/PWR ADMIN PARTIC CHOOSE GP/REL   LOC/G
...CONT/OBS NET/THEORY CHARTS 20 NEWYORK/C MAYOR.   PWR
PAGE 67 B1346   MUNIC

B64
ROCHE J.P.,,THE CONGRESS. EX/STRUC BAL/PWR DIPLOM   INGP/REL
DEBATE ADJUD LEAD PWR. PAGE 89 B1809   LEGIS
                                                     DELIB/GP
                                                     SENIOR

B64
ROCHE J.P.,,THE PRESIDENCY. USA+45 USA-45 CONSTN   EX/STRUC
NAT/G CHIEF BAL/PWR DIPLOM GP/REL 18/20 PRESIDENT.   PWR
PAGE 90 B1810

B64
WHEARE K.C.,,FEDERAL GOVERNMENT (4TH ED.). WOR+45   FEDERAL
WOR-45 POL/PAR LEGIS BAL/PWR CT/SYS...POLICY JURID   CONSTN
CONCPT GOV/COMP 17/20. PAGE 116 B2331   EX/STRUC
                                                     NAT/COMP

L64
MILLIS W.,,"THE DEMILITARIZED WORLD." COM USA+45   FUT
USSR WOR+45 CONSTN NAT/G EX/STRUC PLAN LEGIT ATTIT   INT/ORG
DRIVE...CONCPT TIME/SEQ STERTYP TOT/POP COLD/WAR   BAL/PWR
20. PAGE 74 B1486   PEACE

B65
RUBINSTEIN A.Z.,,THE CHALLENGE OF POLITICS: IDEAS   NAT/G
AND ISSUES (2ND ED.). UNIV ELITES SOCIETY EX/STRUC   DIPLOM
BAL/PWR PARL/PROC AUTHORIT...DECISION ANTHOL 20.   GP/REL
PAGE 92 B1852   ORD/FREE

S65
BROWN S.,,"AN ALTERNATIVE TO THE GRAND DESIGN."   VOL/ASSN
EUR+WWI FUT USA+45 INT/ORG NAT/G EX/STRUC FORCES   CONCPT
CREATE BAL/PWR DOMIN RIGID/FLEX ORD/FREE PWR   DIPLOM
...NEW/IDEA RECORD EEC NATO 20. PAGE 16 B0327

B66
LIVINGSTON J.C.,,THE CONSENT OF THE GOVERNED. USA+45 NAT/G
EX/STRUC BAL/PWR DOMIN CENTRAL PERSON PWR...POLICY   LOBBY
CONCPT OBS IDEA/COMP 20 CONGRESS. PAGE 66 B1331   MAJORIT
                                                     PARTIC

B66
WILSON G.,,CASES AND MATERIALS ON CONSTITUTIONAL AND JURID
ADMINISTRATIVE LAW. UK LAW NAT/G EX/STRUC LEGIS   ADMIN
BAL/PWR BUDGET DIPLOM ADJUD CONTROL CT/SYS GOV/REL   CONSTN
ORD/FREE 20 PARLIAMENT ENGLSH/LAW. PAGE 117 B2359   PWR

S66
BURDETTE F.L.,,"SELECTED ARTICLES AND DOCUMENTS ON   BIBLIOG
AMERICAN GOVERNMENT AND POLITICS." LAW LOC/G MUNIC   USA+45
NAT/G POL/PAR PROVS LEGIS BAL/PWR ADMIN EXEC   JURID
REPRESENT MGT. PAGE 17 B0348   CONSTN

B67
IANNACCONE L.,,POLITICS IN EDUCATION. USA+45 LOC/G   EDU/PROP
PROF/ORG BAL/PWR ADMIN...CHARTS SIMUL. PAGE 53   GEN/LAWS
B1072   PROVS

S67
GORMAN W.,,"ELLUL - A PROPHETIC VOICE." WOR+45   CREATE
ELITES SOCIETY ACT/RES PLAN BAL/PWR DOMIN CONTROL   ORD/FREE
PARTIC TOTALISM PWR 20. PAGE 41 B0837   EX/STRUC
                                                     UTOPIA

BALANCE OF PAYMENTS....SEE BAL/PAY

BALANCE OF POWER....SEE BAL/PWR

BALDWIN D.A. B0171,B0172

BALDWIN G.B. B0173

BALDWIN H. B0174

BALDWIN R.N. B0175

BALDWIN/J....JAMES BALDWIN

BALKANS....BALKANS

BALTIMORE....BALTIMORE, MD.

BANDA/HK....H.K. BANDA, PRIME MINISTER OF MALAWI

BANFIELD E.C. B0176,B0177,B0178,B0179

BANFIELD J. B0180

BANK/ENGL....THE BANK OF ENGLAND

BANKING....SEE FINAN

BANKRUPTCY....BANKRUPTCY

BANTON M. B0181

BANTU....BANTU NATION AND CULTURE

KIESER P.J.,THE COST OF ADMINISTRATION, SUPERVISION AFR
AND SERVICES IN URBAN BANTU TOWNSHIPS. SOUTH/AFR   MGT
SERV/IND MUNIC PROVS ADMIN COST...OBS QU CHARTS 20 FINAN
BANTU. PAGE 60 B1203

B64 (placed at right above KIESER entry)

BANTUSTANS....BANTUSTANS, REPUBLIC OF SOUTH AFRICA

BAO/DAI....BAO DAI

BARATZ M.S. B0156

BARBARIAN....BARBARIAN

BARBASH J. B0182

BARBER W.F. B0183

BARGAIN....BARGAINING; SEE ALSO ECO/TAC, MARKET, DIPLOM

US SUPERINTENDENT OF DOCUMENTS,LABOR (PRICE LIST BIBLIOG/A
33). USA+45 LAW AGRI CONSTRUC INDUS NAT/G BARGAIN WORKER
PRICE ADMIN AUTOMAT PRODUC MGT. PAGE 111 B2240   LABOR
                                                  LEGIS
                                                     B37
BUREAU OF NATIONAL AFFAIRS,LABOR RELATIONS   LABOR
REFERENCE MANUAL VOL 1, 1935-1937. BARGAIN DEBATE ADMIN
ROUTINE INGP/REL 20 NLRB. PAGE 17 B0351   ADJUD
                                                  NAT/G
                                                     B38
REICH N.,LABOR RELATIONS IN REPUBLICAN GERMANY.   WORKER
GERMANY CONSTN ECO/DEV INDUS NAT/G ADMIN CONTROL MGT
GP/REL FASCISM POPULISM 20 WEIMAR/REP. PAGE 87   LABOR
B1763   BARGAIN
                                                     B40
BURT F.A.,AMERICAN ADVERTISING AGENCIES. BARGAIN LG/CO
BUDGET LICENSE WRITING PRICE PERS/REL COST DEMAND COM/IND
...ORG/CHARTS BIBLIOG 20. PAGE 18 B0358   ADMIN
                                                  EFFICIENCY
                                                     B41
LESTER R.A.,ECONOMICS OF LABOR. UK USA-45 TEC/DEV LABOR
BARGAIN PAY INGP/REL INCOME...MGT 19/20. PAGE 64 ECO/DEV
B1298   INDUS
                                                  WORKER
                                                     B41
SLICHTER S.H.,UNION POLICIES AND INDUSTRIAL   BARGAIN
MANAGEMENT. USA-45 INDUS TEC/DEV PAY GP/REL   LABOR
INGP/REL COST EFFICIENCY PRODUC...POLICY 20.   MGT
PAGE 98 B1978   WORKER
                                                     B42
LEISERSON A.,ADMINISTRATIVE REGULATION: A STUDY IN LOBBY
REPRESENTATION OF INTERESTS. NAT/G EX/STRUC   ADMIN
PROB/SOLV BARGAIN CONFER ROUTINE REPRESENT PERS/REL GP/REL
UTIL PWR POLICY. PAGE 63 B1283   GOV/REL
                                                     B49
SHISTER J.,ECONOMICS OF THE LABOR MARKET. LOC/G   MARKET
NAT/G WORKER TEC/DEV BARGAIN PAY PRICE EXEC GP/REL LABOR
INCOME...MGT T 20. PAGE 96 B1949   INDUS
                                                     B51
DIMOCK M.E.,FREE ENTERPRISE AND THE ADMINISTRATIVE CAP/ISM
STATE. FINAN LG/CO BARGAIN BUDGET DOMIN CONTROL   ADMIN
INGP/REL EFFICIENCY 20. PAGE 29 B0595   MGT
                                                  MARKET
                                                     B51
PETERSON F.,SURVEY OF LABOR ECONOMICS (REV. ED.). WORKER
STRATA ECO/DEV LABOR INSPECT BARGAIN PAY PRICE EXEC DEMAND
ROUTINE GP/REL ALL/VALS ORD/FREE 20 AFL/CIO   IDEA/COMP
DEPT/LABOR. PAGE 82 B1662   T
                                                     B52
DONHAM W.B.,ADMINISTRATION AND BLIND SPOTS. LG/CO ADMIN
EX/STRUC BARGAIN ADJUD ROUTINE ROLE SUPEGO 20.   TOP/EX
PAGE 30 B0605   DECISION
                                                  POLICY
                                                     B55
BRAUN K.,LABOR DISPUTES AND THEIR SETTLEMENT.   INDUS
ECO/TAC ROUTINE TASK GP/REL...DECISION GEN/LAWS. LABOR
PAGE 15 B0301   BARGAIN
                                                  ADJUD
                                                     B58
LESTER R.A.,AS UNIONS MATURE. POL/PAR BARGAIN LEAD LABOR
PARTIC GP/REL CENTRAL...MAJORIT TIME/SEQ METH/COMP. INDUS

PAGE 64 B1299   POLICY
                                                  MGT
                                                     B58
WARNER A.W.,CONCEPTS AND CASES IN ECONOMIC   ECO/TAC
ANALYSIS. PROB/SOLV BARGAIN CONTROL INCOME PRODUC DEMAND
...ECOMETRIC MGT CONCPT CLASSIF CHARTS 20   EQUILIB
KEYNES/JM. PAGE 114 B2292   COST
                                                     B60
ELKOURI F.,HOW ARBITRATION WORKS (REV. ED.). LAW MGT
INDUS BARGAIN 20. PAGE 33 B0667   LABOR
                                                  ADJUD
                                                  GP/REL
                                                     B61
BARRASH J.,LABOR'S GRASS ROOTS; A STUDY OF THE   LABOR
LOCAL UNION. STRATA BARGAIN LEAD REPRESENT DEMAND USA+45
ATTIT PWR. PAGE 9 B0190   INGP/REL
                                                  EXEC
                                                     B61
CARROTHERS A.W.R.,LABOR ARBITRATION IN CANADA.   LABOR
CANADA LAW NAT/G CONSULT LEGIS WORKER ADJUD ADMIN MGT
CT/SYS 20. PAGE 19 B0386   GP/REL
                                                  BARGAIN
                                                     B61
MACMAHON A.W.,DELEGATION AND AUTONOMY. INDIA STRUCT ADMIN
LEGIS BARGAIN BUDGET ECO/TAC LEGIT EXEC REPRESENT PLAN
GOV/REL CENTRAL DEMAND EFFICIENCY PRODUC. PAGE 68 FEDERAL
B1373
                                                     B62
GALENSON W.,LABOR IN DEVELOPING COUNTRIES. BRAZIL LABOR
INDONESIA ISRAEL PAKISTAN TURKEY AGRI INDUS WORKER ECO/UNDEV
PAY PRICE GP/REL WEALTH...MGT CHARTS METH/COMP   BARGAIN
NAT/COMP 20. PAGE 38 B0775   POL/PAR
                                                     B62
SRIVASTAVA G.L.,COLLECTIVE BARGAINING AND LABOR- LABOR
MANAGEMENT RELATIONS IN INDIA. INDIA UK USA+45   MGT
INDUS LEGIS WORKER ADJUD EFFICIENCY PRODUC   BARGAIN
...METH/COMP 20. PAGE 100 B2014   GP/REL
                                                     563
REES A.,"THE EFFECTS OF UNIONS ON RESOURCE   LABOR
ALLOCATION." USA+45 WORKER PRICE CONTROL GP/REL   BARGAIN
...MGT METH/COMP 20. PAGE 87 B1761   RATION
                                                  INCOME
                                                     B65
EDELMAN M.,THE POLITICS OF WAGE-PRICE DECISIONS. GOV/COMP
GERMANY ITALY NETHERLAND UK INDUS LABOR POL/PAR   CONTROL
PROB/SOLV BARGAIN PRICE ROUTINE BAL/PAY COST DEMAND ECO/TAC
20. PAGE 32 B0654   PLAN
                                                     B65
PAYNE J.L.,LABOR AND POLITICS IN PERU; THE SYSTEM LABOR
OF POLITICAL BARGAINING. PERU CONSTN VOL/ASSN   POL/PAR
EX/STRUC LEAD PWR...CHARTS 20. PAGE 81 B1645   BARGAIN
                                                  GP/REL
                                                     B65
ROSS P.,THE GOVERNMENT AS A SOURCE OF UNION POWER. LABOR
USA+45 LAW ECO/DEV PROB/SOLV ECO/TAC LEAD GP/REL BARGAIN
...MGT 20. PAGE 90 B1826   POLICY
                                                  NAT/G
                                                     B65
US HOUSE COMM EDUC AND LABOR,ADMINISTRATION OF THE ADMIN
NATIONAL LABOR RELATIONS ACT. USA+45 DELIB/GP   LABOR
WORKER PROB/SOLV BARGAIN PAY CONTROL 20 NLRB   GP/REL
CONGRESS. PAGE 108 B2188   INDUS
                                                     B65
WALTON R.E.,A BEHAVIORAL THEORY OF LABOR   SOC
NEGOTIATIONS: AN ANALYSIS OF A SOCIAL INTERACTION LABOR
SYSTEM. USA+45 FINAN PROB/SOLV ECO/TAC GP/REL   BARGAIN
INGP/REL...DECISION BIBLIOG. PAGE 113 B2285   ADMIN
                                                     B66
BAKKE E.W.,MUTUAL SURVIVAL; THE GOAL OF UNION AND MGT
MANAGEMENT (2ND ED.). USA+45 ELITES ECO/DEV ECO/TAC LABOR
CONFER ADMIN REPRESENT GP/REL INGP/REL ATTIT   BARGAIN
...GP/COMP 20. PAGE 8 B0170   INDUS
                                                     B66
BURNS A.C.,PARLIAMENT AS AN EXPORT. WOR+45 CONSTN PARL/PROC
BARGAIN DEBATE ROUTINE GOV/REL EFFICIENCY...ANTHOL POL/PAR
COMMONWLTH PARLIAMENT. PAGE 17 B0353   CT/SYS
                                                  CHIEF
                                                     B66
CARALEY D.,PARTY POLITICS AND NATIONAL ELECTIONS. POL/PAR
USA+45 STRATA LOC/G PROVS EX/STRUC BARGAIN ADMIN CHOOSE
SANCTION GP/REL ATTIT 20 DEMOCRAT REPUBLICAN.   REPRESENT
PAGE 18 B0375   NAT/G
                                                     B66
COOK P.W. JR.,PROBLEMS OF CORPORATE POWER. WOR+45 ADMIN
FINAN INDUS BARGAIN GP/REL...MGT ANTHOL. PAGE 23 LG/CO
B0471   PWR
                                                  ECO/TAC
                                                     B66
NYC TEMPORARY COMM CITY FINAN,MUNICIPAL COLLECTIVE MUNIC
BARGAINING (NO. 8). USA+45 PLAN PROB/SOLV BARGAIN FINAN
BUDGET TAX EDU/PROP GOV/REL COST...MGT 20   ADMIN
NEWYORK/C. PAGE 79 B1596   LOC/G
                                                     B66
WASHINGTON S.H.,BIBLIOGRAPHY: LABOR-MANAGEMENT   BIBLIOG
RELATIONS ACT, 1947 AS AMENDED BY LABOR-MANAGEMENT LAW
REPORTING AND DISCLOSURE ACT, 1959. USA+45 CONSTN LABOR

INDUS DELIB/GP LEGIS WORKER BARGAIN ECO/TAC ADJUD GP/REL NEW/LIB...JURID CONGRESS. PAGE 114 B2298 — MGT

S66
BALDWIN D.A.,"CONGRESSIONAL INITIATIVE IN FOREIGN POLICY." NAT/G BARGAIN DIPLOM FOR/AID RENT GIVE ...DECISION CONGRESS. PAGE 8 B0171 — EXEC TOP/EX GOV/REL

N66
PRINCETON U INDUSTRIAL REL SEC,OUTSTANDING BOOKS ON INDUSTRIAL RELATIONS, 1965 (PAMPHLET NO. 128). WOR+45 LABOR BARGAIN GOV/REL RACE/REL HEALTH PWR ...MGT 20. PAGE 85 B1709 — BIBLIOG/A INDUS GP/REL POLICY

N66
PRINCETON U INDUSTRIAL REL SEC,RECENT MATERIAL ON COLLECTIVE BARGAINING IN GOVERNMENT (PAMPHLET NO. 130). USA+45 ECO/DEV LABOR WORKER ECO/TAC GOV/REL ...MGT 20. PAGE 85 B1710 — BIBLIOG/A BARGAIN NAT/G GP/REL

B67
BRAYMAN H.,CORPORATE MANAGEMENT IN A WORLD OF POLITICS. USA+45 ELITES MARKET CREATE BARGAIN DIPLOM INT/TRADE ATTIT SKILL 20. PAGE 15 B0302 — MGT ECO/DEV CAP/ISM INDUS

B67
NORTHRUP H.R.,RESTRICTIVE LABOR PRACTICES IN THE SUPERMARKET INDUSTRY. USA+45 INDUS WORKER TEC/DEV BARGAIN PAY CONTROL GP/REL COST...STAT CHARTS NLRB. PAGE 79 B1592 — DIST/IND MARKET LABOR MGT

B67
SCHLOSSBERG S.I.,ORGANIZING AND THE LAW. USA+45 WORKER PLAN LEGIT REPRESENT GP/REL...JURID MGT 20 NLRB. PAGE 94 B1893 — LABOR CONSULT BARGAIN PRIVIL

L67
BERGER R.,"ADMINISTRATIVE ARBITRARINESS* A SEQUEL." USA+45 CONSTN ADJUD CT/SYS SANCTION INGP/REL ...POLICY JURID. PAGE 11 B0222 — LAW LABOR BARGAIN ADMIN

L67
GOULD W.B.,"THE STATUS OF UNAUTHORIZED AND 'WILDCAT' STRIKES UNDER THE NATIONAL LABOR RELATIONS ACT." USA+45 ACT/RES BARGAIN ECO/TAC LEGIT ADJUD ADMIN GP/REL MGT. PAGE 42 B0842 — ECO/DEV INDUS LABOR POLICY

S67
BERRODIN E.F.,"AT THE BARGAINING TABLE." LABOR DIPLOM ECO/TAC ADMIN...MGT 20 MICHIGAN. PAGE 11 B0230 — PROVS WORKER LAW BARGAIN

S67
CHAMBERLAIN N.W.,"STRIKES IN CONTEMPORARY CONTEXT." LABOR LAW INDUS NAT/G CHIEF CONFER COST ATTIT ORD/FREE ...POLICY MGT 20. PAGE 20 B0400 — BARGAIN EFFICIENCY PROB/SOLV

S67
FERGUSON H.,"3-CITY CONSOLIDATION." USA+45 CONSTN INDUS BARGAIN BUDGET CONFER ADMIN INGP/REL COST UTIL. PAGE 35 B0712 — MUNIC CHOOSE CREATE PROB/SOLV

S67
FOX R.G.,"FAMILY, CASTE, AND COMMERCE IN A NORTH INDIAN MARKET TOWN." INDIA STRATA AGRI FACE/GP FAM NEIGH OP/RES BARGAIN ADMIN ROUTINE WEALTH...SOC CHARTS 20. PAGE 37 B0747 — CULTURE GP/REL ECO/UNDEV DIST/IND

S67
HALL B.,"THE COALITION AGAINST DISHWASHERS." USA+45 POL/PAR PROB/SOLV BARGAIN LEAD CHOOSE REPRESENT GP/REL ORD/FREE PWR...POLICY 20. PAGE 46 B0923 — LABOR ADMIN DOMIN WORKER

S67
ZOETEWEIJ B.,"INCOME POLICIES ABROAD: AN INTERIM REPORT." NAT/G PROB/SOLV BARGAIN BUDGET PRICE RISK CENTRAL EFFICIENCY EQUILIB...MGT NAT/COMP 20. PAGE 119 B2405 — METH/COMP INCOME POLICY LABOR

N67
US CONGRESS JT COMM ECO GOVT,BACKGROUND MATERIAL ON ECONOMY IN GOVERNMENT 1967 (PAMPHLET). WOR+45 ECO/DEV BARGAIN PRICE DEMAND OPTIMAL...STAT DEPT/DEFEN. PAGE 108 B2178 — BUDGET COST MGT NAT/G

BARILE P. B0057

BARISH N.N. B0184

BARKER E. B0185

BARNARD C.I. B0187

BARNARD/C....CHESTER I. BARNARD

S43
SELZNICK P.,"AN APPROACH TO A THEORY OF BUREAUCRACY." INDUS WORKER CONTROL LEAD EFFICIENCY OPTIMAL...SOC METH 20 BARNARD/C BUREAUCRCY WEBER/MAX FRIEDRCH/C MICHELS/R. PAGE 95 B1928 — ROUTINE ADMIN MGT EX/STRUC

BARNES H.E. B1471

BARNES W. B0188

BARNETT V.M. B0189

BARNETT/R....ROSS BARNETT

BAROTSE....BAROTSE TRIBE OF RHODESIA

BARRASH J. B0190

BARTLEY H.J. B0191

BARZANSKI S. B0192

BASHILELE....BASHILELE TRIBE

BASS B.M. B0193,B1663

BASS M.E. B0194

BASTID M. B0195

BATAK....BATAK TRIBE, PHILIPPINES

BATISTA/J....JUAN BATISTA

BAUER R.A. B0196

BAUM R.D. B0197

BAUMEL C.P. B1119

BAUMGARTEL H. B0198

BAVARIA....BAVARIA

BAVELAS A. B0199

BAWONGO....BAWONGO TRIBE

BAYESIAN INFLUENCE....SEE SIMUL

BEAL J.R. B0200

BEARD/CA....CHARLES A. BEARD

BEASLEY K.E. B0201

BEASLEY W.G. B0202

BEAUFRE A. B0203

BECCARIA/C....CAESARE BONESARA BECCARIA

BECHHOEFER B.G. B0204

BECKER/E....ERNEST BECKER

BECKMAN T.N. B0205

BEGUIN H. B0206

BEHAV/SCI....BEHAVIORAL SCIENCES

BEHAVIOR TESTS....SEE PERS/TEST

BEHAVIORAL SCIENCES....SEE BEHAV/SCI

BEHAVIORSM....BEHAVIORISM

BEISEL A.R. B0207

BELGIUM....BELGIUM

B47
CONOVER H.F.,NON-SELF-GOVERNING AREAS. BELGIUM FRANCE ITALY UK WOR+45 CULTURE ECO/UNDEV INT/ORG LOC/G NAT/G ECO/TAC INT/TRADE ADMIN HEALTH...SOC UN. PAGE 23 B0465 — BIBLIOG/A COLONIAL DIPLOM

B47
CROCKER W.R.,ON GOVERNING COLONIES: BEING AN OUTLINE OF THE REAL ISSUES AND A COMPARISON OF THE BRITISH, FRENCH, AND BELGIAN... AFR BELGIUM FRANCE UK CULTURE SOVEREIGN...OBS 20. PAGE 25 B0505 — COLONIAL POLICY GOV/COMP ADMIN

B49
WALINE M.,LE CONTROLE JURIDICTIONNEL DE L'ADMINISTRATION. BELGIUM FRANCE UAR JUDGE BAL/PWR ADJUD CONTROL CT/SYS...GP/COMP 20. PAGE 113 B2277 — JURID ADMIN PWR ORD/FREE

B60
ASPREMONT-LYNDEN H.,RAPPORT SUR L'ADMINISTRATION BELGE DU RUANDA-URUNDI PENDANT L'ANNEE 1959. BELGIUM RWANDA AGRI INDUS DIPLOM ECO/TAC INT/TRADE DOMIN ADMIN RACE/REL...GEOG CENSUS 20 UN. PAGE 7 B0143 — AFR COLONIAL ECO/UNDEV INT/ORG

B62
GRANICK D.,THE EUROPEAN EXECUTIVE. BELGIUM FRANCE GERMANY/W UK INDUS LABOR LG/CO SML/CO EX/STRUC PLAN — MGT ECO/DEV

TEC/DEV CAP/ISM COST DEMAND...POLICY CHARTS 20.   ECO/TAC
PAGE 42 B0852   EXEC
                                                         B65
YOUNG C.,POLITICS IN THE CONGO* DECOLONIZATION AND   BELGIUM
INDEPENDENCE. ELITES STRATA FORCES ADMIN REV   COLONIAL
RACE/REL FEDERAL SOVEREIGN...OBS INT CHARTS   NAT/LISM
CONGO/LEOP. PAGE 118 B2391

BELIEF....SEE SECT, ATTIT

BELL J. B0208

BELLAS/HES....NATIONAL BELLAS HESS

BELSHAW D.G.R. B0209

BEN/BELLA....AHMED BEN BELLA

BENDIX R. B0210

BENESE....BENES

BENGAL....BENGAL + BENGALIS

BENIN....BENIN - DISTRICT IN NIGERIA

BENJAMIN H.C. B0211

BENNETT H.A. B0212

BENNETT J.W. B0213

BENNIS W.G. B0214,B0215,B0216

BENOIT E. B0217

BENSON E.T. B0218

BENTHAM/J....JEREMY BENTHAM

BENTLEY A.F. B0220

BENTLEY/AF....ARTHUR F. BENTLEY
                                                         S52
TAYLOR R.W.,"ARTHUR F. BENTLEY'S POLITICAL SCIENCE"   GEN/LAWS
(BMR)" USA+45 INTELL NAT/G...DECISION CLASSIF   POLICY
IDEA/COMP 20 BENTLEY/AF. PAGE 103 B2090   ADMIN

BERGER M. B0221

BERGER R. B0222

BERGSON/H....HENRI BERGSON
                                                         B62
LIPPMANN W.,PREFACE TO POLITICS. LABOR CHIEF   PARTIC
CONTROL LEAD...MYTH IDEA/COMP 19/20 ROOSEVLT/T   ATTIT
TAMMANY WILSON/H SANTAYAN/G BERGSON/H. PAGE 65   ADMIN
B1318

BERGSON/WJ....W. JAMES BERGSON

BERKELEY....BERKELEY, CALIFORNIA
                                                         L65
HOOK S.,"SECOND THOUGHTS ON BERKELEY" USA+45 ELITES   ACADEM
INTELL LEGIT ADMIN COERCE REPRESENT GP/REL INGP/REL   ORD/FREE
TOTALISM AGE/Y MARXISM 20 BERKELEY FREE/SPEE   POLICY
STUDNT/PWR. PAGE 51 B1040   CREATE

BERLIN....BERLIN
                                                         B63
PLISCHKE E.,GOVERNMENT AND POLITICS OF CONTEMPORARY   MUNIC
BERLIN. GERMANY LAW CONSTN POL/PAR LEGIS WAR CHOOSE   LOC/G
REPRESENT GOV/REL...CHARTS BIBLIOG 20 BERLIN.   POLICY
PAGE 83 B1683   ADMIN
                                                         S66
AUSLAND J.C.,"CRISIS MANAGEMENT* BERLIN, CYPRUS,   OP/RES
LAOS." CYPRUS LAOS FORCES CREATE PLAN EDU/PROP TASK   DIPLOM
CENTRAL PERSON RIGID/FLEX...DECISION MGT 20 BERLIN   RISK
KENNEDY/JF MCNAMARA/R RUSK. PAGE 7 B0148   ADMIN

BERLIN/BLO....BERLIN BLOCKADE

BERLINER J.S. B0223

BERNAYS E.L. B0224

BERNAYS/EL....EDWARD L. BERNAYS

BERNDT C.H. B0225

BERNDT R.M. B0225

BERNE E. B0226

BERNSTEIN I. B0227

BERNSTEIN M.H. B0228

BERNTHAL W.F. B0229

BERRIEN W. B0276

BERRODIN E.F. B0230

BERTON P.A. B0231

BESCOBY I. B0232

BESSARABIA....BESSARABIA; SEE ALSO USSR

BEST W.H. B1945

BHALERAO C.N. B0233

BHAMBHRI C.P. B0234,B0235

BHUMIBOL/A....BHUMIBOL ADULYADEJ

BHUTAN....SEE ALSO ASIA

BIAFRA....BIAFRA

BIBLE....BIBLE: OLD AND NEW TESTAMENTS

BIBLIOG....BIBLIOGRAPHY OVER 50 ITEMS
                                                         N
WELLS A.J.,THE BRITISH NATIONAL BIBLIOGRAPHY   BIBLIOG
CUMULATED SUBJECT CATALOGUE, 1951-1954. UK WOR+45   NAT/G
LAW ADMIN LEAD...HUM SOC 20. PAGE 115 B2320
                                                         B
DEUTSCHE BIBLIOTH FRANKF A M,DEUTSCHE   BIBLIOG
BIBLIOGRAPHIE. EUR+WWI GERMANY ECO/DEV FORCES   LAW
DIPLOM LEAD...POLICY PHIL/SCI SOC 20. PAGE 28 B0578   ADMIN
                                                     NAT/G
                                                         N
CONGRESSIONAL MONITOR. CONSULT DELIB/GP PROB/SOLV   BIBLIOG
PRESS DEBATE ROUTINE...POLICY CONGRESS. PAGE 1   LEGIS
B0002   REPRESENT
                                                     USA+45
                                                         N
INTERNATIONAL BIBLIOGRAPHY OF ECONOMICS. WOR+45   BIBLIOG
FINAN MARKET ADMIN DEMAND INCOME PRODUC...POLICY   ECO/DEV
IDEA/COMP METH. PAGE 1 B0003   ECO/UNDEV
                                                     INT/TRADE
                                                         N
BIBLIO. CATALOGUE DES OUVRAGES PARUS EN LANGUE   BIBLIOG
FRANCAISE DANS LE MONDE ENTIER. FRANCE WOR+45 ADMIN   NAT/G
LEAD PERSON...SOC 20. PAGE 1 B0008   DIPLOM
                                                     ECO/DEV
                                                         N
BULLETIN OF THE PUBLIC AFFAIRS INFORMATION SERVICE.   BIBLIOG
WOR+45 WOR-45 ECO/UNDEV FINAN LABOR LOC/G PROVS   NAT/G
TEC/DEV DIPLOM EDU/PROP SOC. PAGE 1 B0010   ECO/DEV
                                                     ADMIN
                                                         N
DEUTSCHE BIBLIOGRAPHIE, HALBJAHRESVERZEICHNIS.   BIBLIOG
WOR+45 LAW ADMIN PERSON. PAGE 1 B0013   NAT/G
                                                     DIPLOM
                                                         N
PUBLISHERS' TRADE LIST ANNUAL. LAW POL/PAR ADMIN   BIBLIOG
PERSON ALL/IDEOS...HUM SOC 19/20. PAGE 1 B0020   NAT/G
                                                     DIPLOM
                                                     POLICY
                                                         N
READERS GUIDE TO PERIODICAL LITERATURE. WOR+45   BIBLIOG
WOR-45 LAW ADMIN ATTIT PERSON...HUM PSY SOC 20.   WRITING
PAGE 1 B0021   DIPLOM
                                                     NAT/G
                                                         N
SUBJECT GUIDE TO BOOKS IN PRINT: AN INDEX TO THE   BIBLIOG
PUBLISHERS' TRADE LIST ANNUAL. UNIV LAW LOC/G   ECO/DEV
DIPLOM WRITING ADMIN LEAD PERSON...MGT SOC. PAGE 1   POL/PAR
B0023   NAT/G
                                                         N
THE JAPAN SCIENCE REVIEW: LAW AND POLITICS: LIST OF   BIBLIOG
BOOKS AND ARTICLES ON LAW AND POLITICS. CONSTN AGRI   LAW
INDUS LABOR DIPLOM TAX ADMIN CRIME...INT/LAW SOC 20   S/ASIA
CHINJAP. PAGE 1 B0025   PHIL/SCI
                                                         N
SUBJECT GUIDE TO BOOKS IN PRINT: AN INDEX TO THE   BIBLIOG
PUBLISHERS' TRADE LIST ANNUAL. WOR+45 WOR-45 LAW   NAT/G
CULTURE ADMIN LEAD PERSON...HUM MGT SOC. PAGE 2   DIPLOM
B0029
                                                         N
FINANCIAL INDEX. CANADA UK USA+45 ECO/DEV LG/CO   BIBLIOG
ADMIN 20. PAGE 2 B0032   INDUS
                                                     FINAN

PRESS
N

CARLETON UNIVERSITY LIBRARY,SELECTED LIST OF
CURRENT MATERIALS ON CANADIAN PUBLIC
ADMINISTRATION. CANADA LEGIS WORKER PLAN BUDGET 20.
PAGE 19 B0379
BIBLIOG
ADMIN
LOC/G
MUNIC
N

DEUTSCHE BUCHEREI,JAHRESVERZEICHNIS DER DEUTSCHEN
HOCHSCHULSCHRIFTEN. EUR+WWI GERMANY LAW ADMIN
PERSON...MGT SOC 19/20. PAGE 28 B0579
BIBLIOG
WRITING
ACADEM
INTELL
N

DEUTSCHE BUCHEREI,JAHRESVERZEICHNIS DES DEUTSCHEN
SCHRIFTUMS. AUSTRIA EUR+WWI GERMANY SWITZERLND LAW
LOC/G DIPLOM ADMIN...MGT SOC 19/20. PAGE 29 B0580
BIBLIOG
WRITING
NAT/G
N

DEUTSCHE BUCHEREI,DEUTSCHES BUCHERVERZEICHNIS.
GERMANY LAW CULTURE POL/PAR ADMIN LEAD ATTIT PERSON
...SOC 20. PAGE 29 B0581
BIBLIOG
NAT/G
DIPLOM
ECO/DEV
N

DOHERTY D.K.,PRELIMINARY BIBLIOGRAPHY OF
COLONIZATION AND SETTLEMENT IN LATIN AMERICA AND
ANGLO-AMERICA. L/A+17C PRE/AMER USA-45 ECO/UNDEV
NAT/G 15/20. PAGE 30 B0604
BIBLIOG
COLONIAL
ADMIN
DIPLOM
N

FAUNT J.R.,A CHECKLIST OF SOUTH CAROLINA STATE
PUBLICATIONS. USA+45 CONSTN LEGIS ADMIN ATTIT 20.
PAGE 35 B0708
BIBLIOG
PROVS
LOC/G
GOV/REL
N

MARTIN W.O. JR.,STATE OF LOUISIANA OFFICIAL
PUBLICATIONS. USA+45 USA-45 LEGIS ADMIN LEAD 19/20.
PAGE 70 B1415
BIBLIOG
PROVS
GOV/REL
N

MINISTERE DE L'EDUC NATIONALE,CATALOGUE DES THESES
DE DOCTORAT SOUTENNES DEVANT LES UNIVERSITAIRES
FRANCAISES. FRANCE LAW DIPLOM ADMIN...HUM SOC 20.
PAGE 74 B1490
BIBLIOG
ACADEM
KNOWL
NAT/G
N

PUBLISHERS' CIRCULAR LIMITED,THE ENGLISH CATALOGUE
OF BOOKS. UK WOR+45 WOR-45 LAW CULTURE LOC/G NAT/G
ADMIN LEAD...MGT 19/20. PAGE 85 B1718
BIBLIOG
ALL/VALS
ALL/IDEOS
SOCIETY
N

STATE OF ILLINOIS,PUBLICATIONS OF THE STATE OF
ILLINOIS. USA+45 FINAN POL/PAR ADMIN LEAD 20
ILLINOIS. PAGE 100 B2024
BIBLIOG
PROVS
LOC/G
GOV/REL
N

UNESCO,INTERNATIONAL BIBLIOGRAPHY OF POLITICAL
SCIENCE (VOLUMES 1-8). WOR+45 LAW NAT/G EX/STRUC
LEGIS PROB/SOLV DIPLOM ADMIN GOV/REL 20 UNESCO.
PAGE 107 B2153
BIBLIOG
CONCPT
IDEA/COMP
N

UNITED NATIONS,UNITED NATIONS PUBLICATIONS. WOR+45
ECO/UNDEV AGRI FINAN FORCES ADMIN LEAD WAR PEACE
...POLICY INT/LAW 20 UN. PAGE 107 B2160
BIBLIOG
INT/ORG
DIPLOM
N

UNIVERSITY OF FLORIDA,CARIBBEAN ACQUISITIONS:
MATERIALS ACQUIRED BY THE UNIVERSITY OF FLORIDA
1957-1960. L/A+17C...ART/METH GEOG MGT 20. PAGE 107
B2167
BIBLIOG
ECO/UNDEV
EDU/PROP
JURID
N

US CIVIL SERVICE COMMISSION,A BIBLIOGRAPHY OF
PUBLIC PERSONNEL ADMINISTRATION LITERATURE. WOR+45
EFFICIENCY...POLICY MGT. PAGE 108 B2175
BIBLIOG
ADMIN
WORKER
PLAN
N

US LIBRARY OF CONGRESS,CATALOG OF THE PUBLIC
DOCUMENTS OF THE UNITED STATES, 1893-1940. USA-45
LAW ECO/DEV AGRI PLAN PROB/SOLV ADMIN LEAD GOV/REL
ATTIT 19/20. PAGE 109 B2200
BIBLIOG
NAT/G
POLICY
LOC/G
N

WORLD PEACE FOUNDATION,DOCUMENTS OF INTERNATIONAL
ORGANIZATIONS: A SELECTED BIBLIOGRAPHY. WOR+45
WOR-45 AGRI FINAN ACT/RES OP/RES INT/TRADE ADMIN
...CON/ANAL 20 UN UNESCO LEAGUE/NAT. PAGE 118 B2374
BIBLIOG
DIPLOM
INT/ORG
REGION
B07

HAASE A.R.,INDEX OF ECONOMIC MATERIAL IN DOCUMENTS
OF STATES OF THE UNITED STATES (13 VOLS.). USA-45
NAT/G GOV/REL...POLICY 18/20. PAGE 45 B0911
BIBLIOG
ECO/DEV
PROVS
ADMIN
B13

MEYER H.H.B.,SELECT LIST OF REFERENCES ON
COMMISSION GOVERNMENT FOR CITIES (PAMPHLET). USA-45
EX/STRUC ADMIN 20. PAGE 73 B1473
BIBLIOG
LOC/G
MUNIC
DELIB/GP
B18

US LIBRARY OF CONGRESS,LIST OF REFERENCES ON A
LEAGUE OF NATIONS. DIPLOM WAR PEACE 20 LEAGUE/NAT.
PAGE 109 B2201
BIBLIOG
INT/ORG
ADMIN
EX/STRUC
N19

FAHRNKOPF N.,STATE AND LOCAL GOVERNMENT IN ILLINOIS
(PAMPHLET). CONSTN ADMIN PARTIC CHOOSE REPRESENT
BIBLIOG
LOC/G

GOV/REL...JURID MGT 20 ILLINOIS. PAGE 34 B0696
LEGIS
CT/SYS
B26

INTERNATIONAL BIBLIOGRAPHY OF POLITICAL SCIENCE.
WOR+45 NAT/G POL/PAR EX/STRUC LEGIS CT/SYS LEAD
CHOOSE GOV/REL ATTIT...PHIL/SCI 20. PAGE 2 B0034
BIBLIOG
DIPLOM
CONCPT
ADMIN
C27

HSIAO K.C.,"POLITICAL PLURALISM." LAW CONSTN
POL/PAR LEGIS PLAN ADMIN CENTRAL SOVEREIGN
...INT/LAW BIBLIOG 19/20. PAGE 52 B1053
STRUCT
GEN/LAWS
PLURISM
B29

BOUDET P.,BIBLIOGRAPHIE DE L'INDOCHINE FRANCAISE.
S/ASIA VIETNAM SECT...GEOG LING 20. PAGE 14 B0282
BIBLIOG
ADMIN
COLONIAL
DIPLOM
B30

FAIRLIE J.A.,COUNTY GOVERNMENT AND ADMINISTRATION.
UK USA-45 NAT/G SCHOOL FORCES BUDGET TAX CT/SYS
CHOOSE...JURID BIBLIOG 11/20. PAGE 35 B0701
ADMIN
GOV/REL
LOC/G
MUNIC
B32

CARDINALL A,,A BIBLIOGRAPHY OF THE GOLD COAST. AFR
UK NAT/G EX/STRUC ATTIT...POLICY 19/20. PAGE 18
B0376
BIBLIOG
ADMIN
COLONIAL
DIPLOM
B33

BROMAGE A.W.,AMERICAN COUNTY GOVERNMENT. USA-45
NAT/G LEAD GOV/REL CENTRAL PWR...MGT BIBLIOG 18/20.
PAGE 15 B0314
LOC/G
CREATE
ADMIN
MUNIC
B34

RIDLEY C.E.,THE CITY-MANAGER PROFESSION. CHIEF PLAN
ADMIN CONTROL ROUTINE CHOOSE...TECHNIC CHARTS
GOV/COMP BIBLIOG 20. PAGE 88 B1780
MUNIC
EX/STRUC
LOC/G
EXEC
B34

WILCOX J.K.,GUIDE TO THE OFFICIAL PUBLICATIONS OF
THE NEW DEAL ADMINISTRATION (2 VOLS.). USA-45 CHIEF
LEGIS ADMIN...POLICY 20 CONGRESS ROOSEVLT/F.
PAGE 116 B2345
BIBLIOG
NAT/G
NEW/LIB
RECEIVE
B36

US LIBRARY OF CONGRESS,CLASSIFIED GUIDE TO MATERIAL
IN THE LIBRARY OF CONGRESS COVERING URBAN COMMUNITY
DEVELOPMENT. USA+45 CREATE PROB/SOLV ADMIN 20.
PAGE 109 B2202
BIBLIOG
CLASSIF
MUNIC
PLAN
B37

HODGSON J.G.,THE OFFICIAL PUBLICATIONS OF AMERICAN
COUNTIES: A UNION LIST. SCHOOL BUDGET...HEAL MGT
SOC/WK 19/20. PAGE 51 B1026
BIBLIOG
LOC/G
PUB/INST
B38

MACDONALD G.E.,CHECK LIST OF LEGISLATIVE JOURNALS
OF THE STATES OF THE UNITED STATES OF AMERICA.
USA-45 ADMIN GOV/REL ATTIT...POLICY 18/20. PAGE 67
B1356
BIBLIOG
PROVS
LEGIS
LOC/G
C39

REISCHAUER R.,"JAPAN'S GOVERNMENT--POLITICS."
CONSTN STRATA POL/PAR FORCES LEGIS DIPLOM ADMIN
EXEC CENTRAL...POLICY BIBLIOG 20 CHINJAP. PAGE 87
B1764
NAT/G
S/ASIA
CONCPT
ROUTINE
B40

BURT F.A.,AMERICAN ADVERTISING AGENCIES. BARGAIN
BUDGET LICENSE WRITING PRICE PERS/REL COST DEMAND
...ORG/CHARTS BIBLIOG 20. PAGE 18 B0358
LG/CO
COM/IND
ADMIN
EFFICIENCY
B41

CHILDS J.B.,A GUIDE TO THE OFFICIAL PUBLICATIONS OF
THE OTHER AMERICAN REPUBLICS: ARGENTINA. CHIEF
DIPLOM GOV/REL...BIBLIOG 18/19 ARGEN. PAGE 21 B0422
NAT/G
EX/STRUC
METH/CNCPT
LEGIS
B41

COHEN E.W.,THE GROWTH OF THE BRITISH CIVIL SERVICE
1780-1939. UK NAT/G SENIOR ROUTINE GOV/REL...MGT
METH/COMP BIBLIOG 18/20. PAGE 22 B0442
OP/RES
TIME/SEQ
CENTRAL
ADMIN
B41

STATIST REICHSAMTE,BIBLIOGRAPHIE DER STAATS- UND
WIRSCHAFTSWISSENSCHAFTEN. EUR+WWI GERMANY FINAN
ADMIN. PAGE 100 B2025
BIBLIOG
ECO/DEV
NAT/G
POLICY
B41

THE TAX FOUNDATION,STUDIES IN ECONOMY AND
EFFICIENCY IN GOVERNMENT. FINAN R+D OP/RES BUDGET
TAX 20. PAGE 104 B2095
BIBLIOG
ADMIN
EFFICIENCY
NAT/G
B42

BROWN A.D.,LIST OF REFERENCES ON THE CIVIL SERVICE
AND PERSONNEL ADMINISTRATION IN THE UNITED STATES
(2ND MIMEOGRAPHED SUPPLEMENT). USA-45 LOC/G POL/PAR
PROVS FEDERAL...TESTS 20. PAGE 16 B0319
BIBLIOG
ADMIN
MGT
NAT/G
B42

SIMOES DOS REIS A.,BIBLIOGRAFIA DAS BIBLIOGRAFIAS
BRASILEIRAS. BRAZIL ADMIN COLONIAL 20. PAGE 97
B1954
BIBLIOG
NAT/G
DIPLOM
L/A+17C

B42

WRIGHT D.M.,THE CREATION OF PURCHASING POWER. FINAN
USA-45 NAT/G PRICE ADMIN WAR INCOME PRODUC...POLICY ECO/TAC
CONCPT IDEA/COMP BIBLIOG 20 MONEY. PAGE 118 B2378 ECO/DEV
CREATE

B43

CARLO A.M.,ENSAYO DE UNA BIBLIOGRAFIA DE BIBLIOG
BIBLIOGRAFIAS MEXICANAS. ECO/UNDEV LOC/G ADMIN LEAD L/A+17C
20 MEXIC/AMER. PAGE 19 B0381 NAT/G
DIPLOM

B43

LEWIN E.,ROYAL EMPIRE SOCIETY BIBLIOGRAPHIES NO. 9: BIBLIOG
SUB-SAHARA AFRICA. ECO/UNDEV TEC/DEV DIPLOM ADMIN AFR
COLONIAL LEAD 20. PAGE 64 B1303 NAT/G
SOCIETY

B44

PUBLIC ADMINISTRATION SERVICE,YOUR BUSINESS OF BIBLIOG
GOVERNMENT: A CATALOG OF PUBLICATIONS IN THE FIELD ADMIN
OF PUBLIC ADMINISTRATION (PAMPHLET). FINAN R+D NAT/G
LOC/G ACT/RES OP/RES PLAN 20. PAGE 85 B1715 MUNIC

B45

CONOVER H.F.,THE GOVERNMENTS OF THE MAJOR FOREIGN BIBLIOG
POWERS: A BIBLIOGRAPHY. FRANCE GERMANY ITALY UK NAT/G
USSR CONSTN LOC/G POL/PAR EX/STRUC FORCES ADMIN DIPLOM
CT/SYS CIVMIL/REL TOTALISM...POLICY 19/20. PAGE 23
B0464

C45

FISHER M.J.,"PARTIES AND POLITICS IN THE LOCAL CHOOSE
COMMUNITY." USA-45 NAT/G SCHOOL ADMIN PARTIC LOC/G
REPRESENT KNOWL...BIBLIOG 20. PAGE 36 B0724 POL/PAR
ROUTINE

B46

BIBLIOGRAFIIA DISSERTATSII: DOKTORSKIE DISSERTATSII BIBLIOG
ZA 19411944 (2 VOLS). COM USSR LAW POL/PAR DIPLOM ACADEM
ADMIN LEAD...PHIL/SCI SOC 20. PAGE 2 B0035 KNOWL
MARXIST

C46

GOODRICH L.M.,"CHARTER OF THE UNITED NATIONS: CONSTN
COMMENTARY AND DOCUMENTS." EX/STRUC ADMIN...INT/LAW INT/ORG
CON/ANAL BIBLIOG 20 UN. PAGE 41 B0826 DIPLOM

B47

BAERWALD F.,FUNDAMENTALS OF LABOR ECONOMICS. LAW ECO/DEV
INDUS LABOR LG/CO CONTROL GP/REL INCOME TOTALISM WORKER
...MGT CHARTS GEN/LAWS BIBLIOG 20. PAGE 8 B0158 MARKET

B47

HIRSHBERG H.S.,SUBJECT GUIDE TO UNITED STATES BIBLIOG
GOVERNMENT PUBLICATIONS. USA+45 USA-45 LAW ADMIN NAT/G
...SOC 20. PAGE 50 B1017 DIPLOM
LOC/G

B47

JENKINS W.S.,COLLECTED PUBLIC DOCUMENTS OF THE BIBLIOG
STATES: A CHECK LIST. USA-45 ECO/DEV NAT/G ADMIN PROVS
GOV/REL 20. PAGE 56 B1129 LEGIS
TOP/EX

B47

PUBLIC ADMINISTRATION SERVICE,CURRENT RESEARCH BIBLIOG
PROJECTS IN PUBLIC ADMINISTRATION (PAMPHLET). LAW R+D
CONSTN COM/IND LABOR LOC/G MUNIC PROVS ACT/RES MGT
DIPLOM RECEIVE EDU/PROP WAR 20. PAGE 85 B1716 ADMIN

B48

BISHOP H.M.,BASIC ISSUES OF AMERICAN DEMOCRACY. NAT/G
USA+45 USA-45 POL/PAR EX/STRUC LEGIS ADJUD FEDERAL PARL/PROC
...BIBLIOG 18/20. PAGE 12 B0244 CONSTN

B48

STOKES W.S.,BIBLIOGRAPHY OF STANDARD AND CLASSICAL BIBLIOG
WORKS IN THE FIELDS OF AMERICAN POLITICAL SCIENCE. NAT/G
USA+45 USA-45 POL/PAR PROVS FORCES DIPLOM ADMIN LOC/G
CT/SYS APPORT 20 CONGRESS PRESIDENT. PAGE 101 B2043 CONSTN

B48

TOWSTER J.,POLITICAL POWER IN THE USSR: 1917-1947. EX/STRUC
USSR CONSTN CULTURE ELITES CREATE PLAN COERCE NAT/G
CENTRAL ATTIT RIGID/FLEX ORD/FREE...BIBLIOG MARXISM
SOC/INTEG 20 LENIN/VI STALIN/J. PAGE 105 B2124 PWR

C48

BOLLENS J.C.,"THE PROBLEM OF GOVERNMENT IN THE SAN USA+45
FRANCISCO BAY REGION." INDUS PROVS ADMIN GOV/REL MUNIC
...SOC CHARTS BIBLIOG 20. PAGE 13 B0270 LOC/G
PROB/SOLV

C48

WALKER H.,"THE LEGISLATIVE PROCESS; LAWMAKING IN PARL/PROC
THE UNITED STATES." NAT/G POL/PAR PROVS EX/STRUC LEGIS
OP/RES PROB/SOLV CT/SYS LOBBY GOV/REL...CHARTS LAW
BIBLIOG T 18/20 CONGRESS. PAGE 113 B2279 CONSTN

N48

YATES M.,ADMINISTRATIVE REORGANIZATION OF STATE BIBLIOG
GOVERNMENTS: A BIBLIOGRAPHY (PAMPHLET). USA+45 LOC/G
USA-45 CONSTN OP/RES PLAN CONFER...POLICY 20. ADMIN
PAGE 118 B2390 PROVS

B49

BORBA DE MORAES R.,MANUAL BIBLIOGRAFICO DE ESTUDOS BIBLIOG
BRASILEIROS. BRAZIL DIPLOM ADMIN LEAD...SOC 20. L/A+17C
PAGE 14 B0276 NAT/G
ECO/UNDEV

B49

HEADLAM-MORLEY,BIBLIOGRAPHY IN POLITICS FOR THE BIBLIOG
HONOUR SCHOOL OF PHILOSOPHY, POLITICS AND ECONOMICS NAT/G

(PAMPHLET). UK CONSTN LABOR MUNIC DIPLOM ADMIN PHIL/SCI
19/20. PAGE 48 B0979 GOV/REL

N49

UN DEPARTMENT PUBLIC INF,SELECTED BIBLIOGRAPHY OF BIBLIOG
THE SPECIALIZED AGENCIES RELATED TO THE UNITED INT/ORG
NATIONS (PAMPHLET). USA+45 ROLE 20 UN. PAGE 106 EX/STRUC
B2146 ADMIN

B50

COMMONS J.R.,THE ECONOMICS OF COLLECTIVE ACTION. ECO/DEV
USA-45 AGRI INDUS LABOR NAT/G LEGIS ADMIN CAP/ISM
EFFICIENCY...MGT METH/COMP BIBLIOG 20. PAGE 22 ACT/RES
B0458 CONCPT

B50

FIGANIERE J.C.,BIBLIOTHECA HISTORICA PORTUGUEZA. BIBLIOG
BRAZIL PORTUGAL SECT ADMIN. PAGE 35 B0717 NAT/G
DIPLOM
COLONIAL

B50

GRAVES W.B.,PUBLIC ADMINISTRATION: A COMPREHENSIVE BIBLIOG
BIBLIOGRAPHY ON PUBLIC ADMINISTRATION IN THE UNITED FINAN
STATES (PAMPHLET). USA+45 USA-45 LOC/G NAT/G LEGIS CONTROL
ADJUD INGP/REL...MGT 20. PAGE 42 B0858 ADMIN

B50

GREAT BRITAIN TREASURY,PUBLIC ADMINISTRATION: A BIBLIOG
BIBLIOGRAPHY FOR ORGANISATION AND METHODS PLAN
(PAMPHLET). LOC/G NAT/G CONSULT EX/STRUC CONFER CONTROL
ROUTINE TASK EFFICIENCY...MGT 20. PAGE 43 B0862 ADMIN

B50

JENKINS W.S.,A GUIDE TO THE MICROFILM COLLECTION OF BIBLIOG
EARLY STATE RECORDS. USA+45 CONSTN MUNIC LEGIS PROVS
PRESS ADMIN CT/SYS 18/20. PAGE 56 B1130 AUD/VIS

C50

HOLCOMBE A.,"OUR MORE PERFECT UNION." USA+45 USA-45 CONSTN
POL/PAR JUDGE CT/SYS EQUILIB FEDERAL PWR...MAJORIT NAT/G
TREND BIBLIOG 18/20 CONGRESS PRESIDENT. PAGE 51 ADMIN
B1031 PLAN

C50

MORLAN R.L.,"INTERGOVERNMENTAL RELATIONS IN SCHOOL
EDUCATION." USA+45 FINAN LOC/G MUNIC NAT/G FORCES GOV/REL
PROB/SOLV RECEIVE ADMIN RACE/REL COST...BIBLIOG ACADEM
INDIAN/AM. PAGE 76 B1526 POLICY

C50

STEWART F.M.,"A HALF CENTURY OF MUNICIPAL REFORM." LOC/G
USA+45 CONSTN FINAN SCHOOL EX/STRUC PLAN PROB/SOLV VOL/ASSN
EDU/PROP ADMIN CHOOSE GOV/REL BIBLIOG. PAGE 101 MUNIC
B2036 POLICY

C50

STOKES W.S.,"HONDURAS: AN AREA STUDY IN CONSTN
GOVERNMENT." HONDURAS NAT/G POL/PAR COLONIAL CT/SYS LAW
ROUTINE CHOOSE REPRESENT...GEOG RECORD BIBLIOG L/A+17C
19/20. PAGE 101 B2044 ADMIN

C50

WAGER P.W.,"COUNTY GOVERNMENT ACROSS THE NATION." LOC/G
USA+45 CONSTN COM/IND FINAN SCHOOL DOMIN CT/SYS PROVS
LEAD GOV/REL...STAT BIBLIOG 20. PAGE 112 B2272 ADMIN
ROUTINE

B51

UNESCO,REPERTOIRE DES BIBLIOTHEQUES DE FRANCE: BIBLIOG
CENTRES ET SERVICES DE DOCUMENTATION DE FRANCE. ADMIN
FRANCE INDUS ACADEM NAT/G INT/TRADE 20 UNESCO.
PAGE 107 B2154

B51

US TARIFF COMMISSION,LIST OF PUBLICATIONS OF THE BIBLIOG
TARIFF COMMISSION (PAMPHLET). USA+45 USA-45 AGRI TARIFFS
EXTR/IND INDUS INT/TRADE...STAT 20. PAGE 111 B2245 NAT/G
ADMIN

C51

MOORE B.,"SOVIET POLITICS - THE DILEMMA OF POWER: ATTIT
THE ROLE OF IDEAS IN SOCIAL CHANGE." USSR PROB/SOLV PWR
DIPLOM EDU/PROP ADMIN LEAD ROUTINE REV...POLICY CONCPT
DECISION BIBLIOG 20. PAGE 75 B1512 MARXISM

B52

GOLDSTEIN J.,THE GOVERNMENT OF BRITISH TRADE LABOR
UNIONS. UK ECO/DEV EX/STRUC INGP/REL...BIBLIOG 20. PARTIC
PAGE 40 B0817

B52

LEGISLATIVE REFERENCE SERVICE,PROBLEMS OF BIBLIOG
LEGISLATIVE APPORTIONMENT ON BOTH FEDERAL AND STATE REPRESENT
LEVELS: SELECTED REFERENCES (PAMPHLET). USA+45 CHOOSE
USA-45 LOC/G NAT/G LEGIS WRITING ADMIN APPORT 20 PROVS
CONGRESS. PAGE 63 B1282

B52

UNESCO,THESES DE SCIENCES SOCIALES: CATALOGUE BIBLIOG
ANALYTIQUE INTERNATIONAL DE THESES INEDITES DE ACADEM
DOCTORAT, 1940-1950. INT/ORG DIPLOM EDU/PROP...GEOG WRITING
INT/LAW MGT PSY SOC 20. PAGE 107 B2155

B52

US DEPARTMENT OF STATE,RESEARCH ON EASTERN EUROPE BIBLIOG
(EXCLUDING USSR). EUR+WWI LAW ECO/DEV NAT/G R+D
PROB/SOLV DIPLOM ADMIN LEAD MARXISM...TREND 19/20. ACT/RES
PAGE 108 B2182 COM

C52

LANCASTER L.W.,"GOVERNMENT IN RURAL AMERICA." GOV/REL
USA+45 ECO/DEV AGRI SCHOOL FORCES LEGIS JUDGE LOC/G
BUDGET TAX CT/SYS...CHARTS BIBLIOG. PAGE 62 B1253 MUNIC
ADMIN

LASSWELL H.D.,"THE COMPARATIVE STUDY OF ELITES: AN
INTRODUCTION AND BIBLIOGRAPHY." STRATA POL/PAR
EDU/PROP ADMIN LOBBY COERCE ATTIT PERSON PWR
...BIBLIOG 20. PAGE 63 B1270
C52 ELITES LEAD CONCPT DOMIN

A BIBLIOGRAPHY AND SUBJECT INDEX OF PUBLICATIONS OF
FLORIDA STATE AGENCIES. USA+45 LOC/G LEAD ATTIT 20
FLORIDA. PAGE 2 B0036
B53 BIBLIOG PROVS GOV/REL ADMIN

GREENE K.R.C.,INSTITUTIONS AND INDIVIDUALS: AN
ANNOTATED LIST OF DIRECTORIES USEFUL IN
INTERNATIONAL ADMINISTRATION. USA+45 NAT/G VOL/ASSN
...INDEX 20. PAGE 43 B0865
B53 BIBLIOG INT/ORG ADMIN DIPLOM

PIERCE R.A.,RUSSIAN CENTRAL ASIA, 1867-1917: A
SELECTED BIBLIOGRAPHY (PAMPHLET). USSR LAW CULTURE
NAT/G EDU/PROP WAR...GEOG SOC 19/20. PAGE 83 B1671
B53 BIBLIOG COLONIAL ADMIN COM

STOUT H.M.,BRITISH GOVERNMENT. UK FINAN LOC/G
POL/PAR DELIB/GP DIPLOM ADMIN COLONIAL CHOOSE
ORD/FREE...JURID BIBLIOG 20 COMMONWLTH. PAGE 101
B2049
B53 NAT/G PARL/PROC CONSTN NEW/LIB

TOMPKINS D.C.,CIVIL DEFENSE IN THE STATES: A
BIBLIOGRAPHY (DEFENSE BIBLIOGRAPHIES NO. 3;
PAMPHLET). USA+45 LABOR LOC/G NAT/G PROVS LEGIS.
PAGE 105 B2115
B53 BIBLIOG WAR ORD/FREE ADMIN

BULNER-THOMAS I.,"THE PARTY SYSTEM IN GREAT
BRITAIN." UK CONSTN SECT PRESS CONFER GP/REL ATTIT
...POLICY TREND BIBLIOG 19/20 PARLIAMENT. PAGE 17
B0343
C53 NAT/G POL/PAR ADMIN ROUTINE

DORWART R.A.,"THE ADMINISTRATIVE REFORMS OF
FREDRICK WILLIAM I OF PRUSSIA. GERMANY MOD/EUR
CHIEF CONTROL PWR...BIBLIOG 16/18. PAGE 30 B0608
C53 ADMIN NAT/G CENTRAL GOV/REL

CHICAGO JOINT REFERENCE LIB,FEDERAL-STATE-LOCAL
RELATIONS; A SELECTED BIBLIOGRAPHY. USA+45 AGRI
LABOR LOC/G MUNIC EX/STRUC ADMIN REGION HEALTH
CON/ANAL. PAGE 21 B0419
B54 BIBLIOG FEDERAL GOV/REL

GOULDNER A.W.,PATTERNS OF INDUSTRIAL BUREAUCRACY.
DOMIN ATTIT DRIVE...BIBLIOG 20 BUREAUCRCY. PAGE 42
B0844
B54 ADMIN INDUS OP/RES WORKER

MCCLOSKEY J.F.,OPERATIONS RESEARCH FOR MANAGEMENT.
STRUCT COMPUTER ADMIN ROUTINE...PHIL/SCI CONCPT
METH/CNCPT TREND ANTHOL BIBLIOG 20. PAGE 72 B1445
B54 OP/RES MGT METH/COMP TEC/DEV

SHELTON W.L.,CHECKLIST OF NEW MEXICO PUBLICATIONS,
1850-1953. USA+45 USA-45 LEGIS ADMIN LEAD 19/20.
PAGE 96 B1941
B54 BIBLIOG PROVS GOV/REL

THORNTON M.L.,OFFICIAL PUBLICATIONS OF THE COLONY
AND STATE OF NORTH CAROLINA, 1749-1939. USA+45
USA-45 LEGIS LEAD GOV/REL ATTIT 18/20. PAGE 104
B2109
B54 BIBLIOG ADMIN PROVS ACADEM

US SENATE COMM ON FOREIGN REL,REVIEW OF THE UNITED
NATIONS CHARTER: A COLLECTION OF DOCUMENTS. LEGIS
DIPLOM ADMIN ARMS/CONT WAR REPRESENT SOVEREIGN
...INT/LAW 20 UN. PAGE 110 B2220
B54 BIBLIOG CONSTN INT/ORG DEBATE

WILENSKY H.L.,SYLLABUS OF INDUSTRIAL RELATIONS: A
GUIDE TO READING AND RESEARCH. USA+45 MUNIC ADMIN
INGP/REL...POLICY MGT PHIL/SCI 20. PAGE 117 B2351
B54 BIBLIOG INDUS LABOR WORKER

CALDWELL L.K.,"THE GOVERNMENT AND ADMINISTRATION OF
NEW YORK." LOC/G MUNIC POL/PAR SCHOOL CHIEF LEGIS
PLAN TAX CT/SYS...MGT SOC/WK BIBLIOG 20 NEWYORK/C.
PAGE 18 B0366
C54 PROVS ADMIN CONSTN EX/STRUC

GOULDNER A.W.,"PATTERNS OF INDUSTRIAL BUREAUCRACY."
GP/REL CONSEN ATTIT DRIVE...BIBLIOG 20. PAGE 42
B0843
C54 ADMIN INDUS OP/RES WORKER

LANDAU J.M.,"PARLIAMENTS AND PARTIES IN EGYPT." UAR
NAT/G SECT CONSULT LEGIS TOP/EX PROB/SOLV ADMIN
COLONIAL...GEN/LAWS BIBLIOG 19/20. PAGE 62 B1254
C54 ISLAM NAT/LISM PARL/PROC POL/PAR

ROBSON W.A.,"GREAT CITIES OF THE WORLD: THEIR
GOVERNMENT, POLITICS, AND PLANNING." CONSTN FINAN
EX/STRUC ADMIN EXEC CHOOSE GOV/REL...STAT TREND
ANTHOL BIBLIOG 20. PAGE 89 B1806
C54 LOC/G MUNIC PLAN PROB/SOLV

ZELLER B.,"AMERICAN STATE LEGISLATURES: REPORT ON
C54 REPRESENT

THE COMMITTEE ON AMERICAN LEGISLATURES." CONSTN
POL/PAR EX/STRUC CONFER ADMIN CONTROL EXEC LOBBY
ROUTINE GOV/REL...POLICY BIBLIOG 20. PAGE 119 B2401
LEGIS PROVS APPORT

CRAIG J.,BIBLIOGRAPHY OF PUBLIC ADMINISTRATION IN
AUSTRALIA. CONSTN FINAN EX/STRUC LEGIS PLAN DIPLOM
RECEIVE ADJUD ROUTINE...HEAL 19/20 AUSTRAL
PARLIAMENT. PAGE 24 B0500
B55 BIBLIOG GOV/REL ADMIN NAT/G

DE ARAGAO J.G.,LA JURIDICTION ADMINISTRATIVE AU
BRESIL. BRAZIL ADJUD COLONIAL CT/SYS REV FEDERAL
ORD/FREE...BIBLIOG 19/20. PAGE 27 B0549
B55 EX/STRUC ADMIN NAT/G

GUAITA A.,BIBLIOGRAFIA ESPANOLA DE DERECHO
ADMINISTRATIVO (PAMPHLET). SPAIN LOC/G MUNIC NAT/G
PROVS JUDGE BAL/PWR GOV/REL OWN...JURID 18/19.
PAGE 44 B0900
B55 BIBLIOG ADMIN CONSTN PWR

GULICK C.A.,HISTORY AND THEORIES OF WORKING-CLASS
MOVEMENTS: A SELECT BIBLIOGRAPHY. EUR+WWI MOD/EUR
UK USA-45 INT/ORG. PAGE 44 B0902
B55 BIBLIOG WORKER LABOR ADMIN

JAPAN MOMBUSHO DAIGAKU GAKIYUT,BIBLIOGRAPHY OF THE
STUDIES ON LAW AND POLITICS (PAMPHLET). CONSTN
INDUS LABOR DIPLOM TAX ADMIN...CRIMLGY INT/LAW 20
CHINJAP. PAGE 56 B1126
B55 BIBLIOG LAW PHIL/SCI

PULLEN W.R.,A CHECK LIST OF LEGISLATIVE JOURNALS
ISSUED SINCE 1937 BY THE STATES OF THE UNITED
STATES OF AMERICA (PAMPHLET). USA+45 USA-45 LAW
WRITING ADJUD ADMIN...JURID 20. PAGE 85 B1720
B55 BIBLIOG PROVS EDU/PROP LEGIS

RILEY V.,INTERINDUSTRY ECONOMIC STUDIES. USA+45
COMPUTER ADMIN OPTIMAL PRODUC...MGT CLASSIF STAT.
PAGE 88 B1788
B55 BIBLIOG ECO/DEV PLAN STRUCT

BONER H.A.,"HUNGRY GENERATIONS." UK WOR+45 WOR-45
STRATA INDUS FAM LABOR CAP/ISM...MGT BIBLIOG 19/20.
PAGE 13 B0272
C55 ECO/DEV PHIL/SCI CONCPT WEALTH

BARBASH J.,THE PRACTICE OF UNIONISM. ECO/TAC LEAD
LOBBY GP/REL INGP/REL DRIVE MARXISM BIBLIOG. PAGE 9
B0182
B56 LABOR REPRESENT CONTROL ADMIN

DEGRAS J.,THE COMMUNIST INTERNATIONAL, 1919-1943:
DOCUMENTS (3 VOLS.). EX/STRUC...ANTHOL BIBLIOG 20.
PAGE 28 B0569
B56 COM DIPLOM POLICY POL/PAR

UNITED NATIONS,BIBLIOGRAPHY ON INDUSTRIALIZATION IN
UNDER-DEVELOPED COUNTRIES. WOR+45 R+D INT/ORG NAT/G
FOR/AID ADMIN LEAD 20 UN. PAGE 107 B2161
B56 BIBLIOG ECO/UNDEV INDUS TEC/DEV

WASSERMAN P.,INFORMATION FOR ADMINISTRATORS: A
GUIDE TO PUBLICATIONS AND SERVICES FOR MANAGEMENT
IN BUSINESS AND GOVERNMENT. R+D LOC/G NAT/G
PROF/ORG VOL/ASSN PRESS...PSY SOC STAT 20. PAGE 114
B2299
B56 BIBLIOG MGT KNOWL EDU/PROP

WAUGH E.W.,SECOND CONSUL. USA+45 USA-45 CONSTN
POL/PAR PROB/SOLV PARL/PROC CHOOSE PERS/REL ATTIT
...BIBLIOG 18/20 VICE/PRES. PAGE 114 B2304
B56 NAT/G EX/STRUC PWR CHIEF

WILSON P.,GOVERNMENT AND POLITICS OF INDIA AND
PAKISTAN: 1885-1955; A BIBLIOGRAPHY OF WORKS IN
WESTERN LANGUAGES. INDIA PAKISTAN CONSTN LOC/G
POL/PAR FORCES DIPLOM ADMIN WAR CHOOSE...BIOG
CON/ANAL 19/20. PAGE 117 B2361
B56 BIBLIOG COLONIAL NAT/G S/ASIA

AUMANN F.R.,"THE ISTRUMENTALITIES OF JUSTICE: THEIR
FORMS, FUNCTIONS, AND LIMITATIONS." WOR+45 WOR-45
JUDGE PROB/SOLV ROUTINE ATTIT...BIBLIOG 20. PAGE 7
B0147
C56 JURID ADMIN CT/SYS ADJUD

BABCOCK R.S.,STATE & LOCAL GOVERNMENT AND POLITICS.
USA+45 CONSTN POL/PAR EX/STRUC LEGIS BUDGET LOBBY
CHOOSE SUFF...CHARTS BIBLIOG T 20. PAGE 8 B0154
B57 PROVS LOC/G GOV/REL

BISHOP O.B.,PUBLICATIONS OF THE GOVERNMENTS OF NOVA
SCOTIA, PRINCE EDWARD ISLAND, NEW BRUNSWICK
1758-1952. CANADA UK ADMIN COLONIAL LEAD...POLICY
18/20. PAGE 12 B0245
B57 BIBLIOG NAT/G DIPLOM

IKE N.,JAPANESE POLITICS. INTELL STRUCT AGRI INDUS
FAM KIN LABOR PRESS CHOOSE ATTIT...DECISION BIBLIOG
19/20 CHINJAP. PAGE 53 B1075
B57 NAT/G ADMIN POL/PAR CULTURE

KIETH-LUCAS A.,DECISIONS ABOUT PEOPLE IN NEED, A
STUDY OF ADMINISTRATIVE RESPONSIVENESS IN PUBLIC
B57 ADMIN RIGID/FLEX

ASSISTANCE. USA+45 GIVE RECEIVE INGP/REL PERS/REL   SOC/WK
MORAL RESPECT WEALTH...SOC OBS BIBLIOG 20. PAGE 60   DECISION
B1204

B57

SCHNEIDER E.V.,INDUSTRIAL SOCIOLOGY: THE SOCIAL   LABOR
RELATIONS OF INDUSTRY AND COMMUNITY. STRATA INDUS   MGT
NAT/G NEIGH CREATE ADMIN PARTIC GP/REL RACE/REL   INGP/REL
ROLE PWR...POLICY BIBLIOG. PAGE 94 B1898   STRUCT

B57

UDY S.H. JR.,THE ORGANIZATION OF PRODUCTION IN   METH/COMP
NONINDUSTRIAL CULTURE. VOL/ASSN DELIB/GP TEC/DEV   ECO/UNDEV
...CHARTS BIBLIOG. PAGE 106 B2143   PRODUC
                                                          ADMIN
B57

US CIVIL SERVICE COMMISSION,DISSERTATIONS AND   BIBLIOG
THESES RELATING TO PERSONNEL ADMINISTRATION   ADMIN
(PAMPHLET). USA+45 COM/IND LABOR EX/STRUC GP/REL   MGT
INGP/REL DECISION. PAGE 108 B2176   WORKER

C57

TANG P.S.H.,"COMMUNIST CHINA TODAY: DOMESTIC AND   POL/PAR
FOREIGN POLICIES." CHINA/COM COM S/ASIA USSR STRATA   LEAD
FORCES DIPLOM EDU/PROP COERCE GOV/REL...POLICY   ADMIN
MAJORIT BIBLIOG 20. PAGE 102 B2071   CONSTN

B58

LIST OF PUBLICATIONS (PERIODICAL OR AD HOC) ISSUED   BIBLIOG
BY VARIOUS MINISTRIES OF THE GOVERNMENT OF INDIA   NAT/G
(3RD ED.). INDIA ECO/UNDEV PLAN...POLICY MGT 20.   ADMIN
PAGE 2 B0037

B58

CARTER G.M.,TRANSITION IN AFRICA; STUDIES IN   NAT/COMP
POLITICAL ADAPTATION. AFR CENTRL/AFR GHANA NIGERIA   PWR
CONSTN LOC/G POL/PAR ADMIN GP/REL FEDERAL...MAJORIT   CONTROL
BIBLIOG 20. PAGE 19 B0389   NAT/G

B58

DWARKADAS R.,ROLE OF HIGHER CIVIL SERVICE IN INDIA.   ADMIN
INDIA ECO/UNDEV LEGIS PROB/SOLV GP/REL PERS/REL   NAT/G
...POLICY WELF/ST DECISION ORG/CHARTS BIBLIOG 20   ROLE
CIVIL/SERV INTRVN/ECO. PAGE 31 B0637   PLAN

B58

GROSSMAN J.,BIBLIOGRAPHY ON PUBLIC ADMINISTRATION   BIBLIOG
IN LATIN AMERICA. ECO/UNDEV FINAN PLAN BUDGET   L/A+17C
ECO/TAC TARIFFS TAX...STAT 20. PAGE 44 B0893   NAT/G
                                                          ADMIN
B58

MARCH J.G.,ORGANIZATIONS. USA+45 CREATE OP/RES PLAN   MGT
PROB/SOLV PARTIC ROUTINE RATIONAL ATTIT PERCEPT   PERSON
...DECISION BIBLIOG. PAGE 69 B1397   DRIVE
                                                          CONCPT
B58

NEAL F.W.,TITOISM IN ACTION. COM YUGOSLAVIA AGRI   MARXISM
LOC/G DIPLOM TOTALISM...BIBLIOG 20 TITO/MARSH.   POL/PAR
PAGE 77 B1564   CHIEF
                                                          ADMIN
B58

ORTIZ R.P.,ANNUARIO BIBLIOGRAFICO COLOMBIANO,   BIBLIOG
1951-1956. LAW RECEIVE EDU/PROP ADMIN...LING STAT   SOC
20 COLOMB. PAGE 80 B1617

B58

PAN AMERICAN UNION,REPERTORIO DE PUBLICACIONES   BIBLIOG
PERIODICAS ACTUALES LATINO-AMERICANAS. CULTURE   L/A+17C
ECO/UNDEV ADMIN LEAD GOV/REL 20 OAS. PAGE 81 B1630   NAT/G
                                                          DIPLOM
B58

SHAW S.J.,THE FINANCIAL AND ADMINISTRATIVE   FINAN
ORGANIZATION AND DEVELOPMENT OF OTTOMAN EGYPT   ADMIN
1517-1798. UAR LOC/G FORCES BUDGET INT/TRADE TAX   GOV/REL
EATING INCOME WEALTH...CHARTS BIBLIOG 16/18 OTTOMAN   CULTURE
NAPOLEON/B. PAGE 96 B1940

B58

UNESCO,UNESCO PUBLICATIONS: CHECK LIST (2ND REV.   BIBLIOG
ED.). WOR+45 DIPLOM FOR/AID WEALTH...POLICY SOC   INT/ORG
UNESCO. PAGE 107 B2156   ECO/UNDEV
                                                          ADMIN
B58

UNIVERSITY OF LONDON,THE FAR EAST AND SOUTH-EAST   BIBLIOG
ASIA: A CUMULATED LIST OF PERIODICAL ARTICLES, MAY   SOC
1956-APRIL 1957. ASIA S/ASIA LAW ADMIN...LING 20.
PAGE 107 B2168

C58

GOLAY J.F.,"THE FOUNDING OF THE FEDERAL REPUBLIC OF   FEDERAL
GERMANY." GERMANY/W CONSTN EX/STRUC DIPLOM ADMIN   NAT/G
CHOOSE...DECISION BIBLIOG 20. PAGE 40 B0814   PARL/PROC
                                                          POL/PAR
C58

WILDING N.,"AN ENCYCLOPEDIA OF PARLIAMENT." UK LAW   PARL/PROC
CONSTN CHIEF PROB/SOLV DIPLOM DEBATE WAR INGP/REL   POL/PAR
PRIVIL...BIBLIOG DICTIONARY 13/20 CMN/WLTH   NAT/G
PARLIAMENT. PAGE 116 B2350   ADMIN

B59

CONOVER H.F.,NIGERIAN OFFICIAL PUBLICATIONS,   BIBLIOG
1869-1959: A GUIDE. NIGER CONSTN FINAN ACADEM   NAT/G
SCHOOL FORCES PRESS ADMIN COLONIAL...HIST/WRIT   CON/ANAL
19/20. PAGE 23 B0466

B59

MOOS M.,THE CAMPUS AND THE STATE. LAW FINAN   EDU/PROP
DELIB/GP LEGIS EXEC LOBBY GP/REL PWR...POLICY   ACADEM

BIBLIOG. PAGE 75 B1517   PROVS
                                                          CONTROL
B59

SURRENCY E.C.,A GUIDE TO LEGAL RESEARCH. USA+45   NAT/G
ACADEM LEGIS ACT/RES ADMIN...DECISION METH/COMP   PROVS
BIBLIOG METH. PAGE 102 B2055   ADJUD
                                                          JURID
B60

ANGERS F.A.,ESSAI SUR LA CENTRALISATION: ANALYSE   CENTRAL
DES PRINCIPES ET PERSPECTIVES CANADIENNES. CANADA   ADMIN
ECO/TAC CONTROL...SOC IDEA/COMP BIBLIOG 20. PAGE 5
B0111

B60

AYEARST M.,THE BRITISH WEST INDIES: THE SEARCH FOR   CONSTN
SELF-GOVERNMENT. FUT WEST/IND LOC/G POL/PAR   COLONIAL
EX/STRUC LEGIS CHOOSE FEDERAL...NAT/COMP BIBLIOG   REPRESENT
17/20. PAGE 7 B0152   NAT/G

B60

CORSON J.J.,GOVERNANCE OF COLLEGES AND   ADMIN
UNIVERSITIES. STRUCT FINAN DELIB/GP DOMIN EDU/PROP   EXEC
LEAD CHOOSE GP/REL CENTRAL COST PRIVIL SUPEGO   ACADEM
ORD/FREE PWR...DECISION BIBLIOG. PAGE 24 B0481   HABITAT

B60

FLORES R.H.,CATALOGO DE TESIS DOCTORALES DE LAS   BIBLIOG
FACULTADES DE LA UNIVERSIDAD DE EL SALVADOR.   ACADEM
EL/SALVADR LAW DIPLOM ADMIN LEAD GOV/REL...SOC   L/A+17C
19/20. PAGE 36 B0730   NAT/G

B60

JONES V.,METROPOLITAN COMMUNITIES: A BIBLIOGRAPHY   BIBLIOG
WITH SPECIAL EMPHASIS UPON GOVERNMENT AND POLITICS,   LOC/G
1955-1957. STRUCT ECO/DEV FINAN FORCES PLAN   MUNIC
PROB/SOLV RECEIVE EDU/PROP CT/SYS...GEOG HEAL 20.   ADMIN
PAGE 57 B1152

B60

KERSELL J.E.,PARLIAMENTARY SUPERVISION OF DELEGATED   LEGIS
LEGISLATION. UK EFFICIENCY PWR...POLICY CHARTS   CONTROL
BIBLIOG METH 20 PARLIAMENT. PAGE 59 B1198   NAT/G
                                                       EX/STRUC
B60

LINDVEIT E.N.,SCIENTISTS IN GOVERNMENT. USA+45 PAY   TEC/DEV
EDU/PROP ADMIN DRIVE HABITAT ROLE...TECHNIC BIBLIOG   ECO/TAC
20. PAGE 65 B1316   PHIL/SCI
                                                       GOV/REL
B60

MORRIS W.T.,ENGINEERING ECONOMY. AUTOMAT RISK   OP/RES
RATIONAL...PROBABIL STAT CHARTS GAME SIMUL BIBLIOG   DECISION
T 20. PAGE 76 B1529   MGT
                                                       PROB/SOLV
B60

PIERCE R.A.,RUSSIAN CENTRAL ASIA, 1867-1917. ASIA   COLONIAL
RUSSIA CULTURE AGRI INDUS EDU/PROP REV NAT/LISM   DOMIN
...CHARTS BIBLIOG 19/20 BOLSHEVISM INTERVENT.   ADMIN
PAGE 83 B1672   ECO/UNDEV
                                                       B60

SAYRE W.S.,GOVERNING NEW YORK CITY; POLITICS IN THE   MUNIC
METROPOLIS. POL/PAR CHIEF DELIB/GP LEGIS PLAN   ADMIN
CT/SYS LEAD PARTIC CHOOSE...DECISION CHARTS BIBLIOG   PROB/SOLV
20 NEWYORK/C BUREAUCRCY. PAGE 93 B1875

S60

HEADY F.,"RECENT LITERATURE ON COMPARATIVE PUBLIC   GOV/COMP
ADMINISTRATION." EXEC 20. PAGE 48 B0981   ADMIN
                                                       EX/STRUC
                                                       BIBLIOG
S60

RAPHAELI N.,"SELECTED ARTICLES AND DOCUMENTS ON   BIBLIOG
COMPARATIVE PUBLIC ADMINISTRATION." USA+45 FINAN   MGT
LOC/G TOP/EX TEC/DEV EXEC GP/REL INGP/REL...GP/COMP   ADMIN
GOV/COMP METH/COMP. PAGE 86 B1738   EX/STRUC
                                                       C60

FITZSIMMONS T.,"USSR: ITS PEOPLE, ITS SOCIETY, ITS   CULTURE
CULTURE." USSR FAM SECT DIPLOM EDU/PROP ADMIN   STRUCT
RACE/REL ATTIT...POLICY CHARTS BIBLIOG 20. PAGE 36   SOCIETY
B0728   COM

C60

SCHAPIRO L.B.,"THE COMMUNIST PARTY OF THE SOVIET   POL/PAR
UNION." USSR INTELL CHIEF EX/STRUC FORCES DOMIN   COM
ADMIN LEAD WAR ATTIT SOVEREIGN...POLICY BIBLIOG 20.   REV
PAGE 93 B1881

C60

SCHRAMM W.,"MASS COMMUNICATIONS: A BOOK OF READINGS   COM/IND
(2ND ED.)" LG/CO PRESS ADMIN CONTROL ROUTINE ATTIT   EDU/PROP
ROLE SUPEGO...CHARTS ANTHOL BIBLIOG 20. PAGE 94   CROWD
B1902   MAJORIT

C60

SMITH T.E.,"ELECTIONS IN DEVELOPING COUNTRIES: A   ECO/UNDEV
STUDY OF ELECTORAL PROCEDURES USED IN TOPICAL   CHOOSE
AFRICA, SOUTH-EAST ASIA..." AFR S/ASIA UK ROUTINE   REPRESENT
GOV/REL RACE/REL...GOV/COMP BIBLIOG 20. PAGE 98   ADMIN
B1985

N60

RHODESIA-NYASA NATL ARCHIVES,A SELECT BIBLIOGRAPHY   BIBLIOG
OF RECENT PUBLICATIONS CONCERNING THE FEDERATION OF   ADMIN
RHODESIA AND NYASALAND (PAMPHLET). MALAWI RHODESIA   ORD/FREE
LAW CULTURE STRUCT ECO/UNDEV LEGIS...GEOG 20.   NAT/G
PAGE 88 B1770

B61
AGARWAL R.C.,STATE ENTERPRISE IN INDIA. FUT INDIA   ECO/UNDEV
UK FINAN INDUS ADMIN CONTROL OWN...POLICY CHARTS   SOCISM
BIBLIOG 20 RAILROAD. PAGE 3 B0064   GOV/REL
                                                          LG/CO
B61
BIRNBACH B.,NEO-FREUDIAN SOCIAL PHILOSOPHY. TEC/DEV   SOCIETY
INGP/REL ADJUST HAPPINESS SUPEGO HEALTH...CONCPT   PSY
GEN/LAWS BIBLIOG 20. PAGE 12 B0242   PERSON
                                                          ADMIN
B61
CARNEY D.E.,GOVERNMENT AND ECONOMY IN BRITISH WEST   METH/COMP
AFRICA. GAMBIA GHANA NIGERIA SIER/LEONE DOMIN ADMIN   COLONIAL
GOV/REL SOVEREIGN WEALTH LAISSEZ...BIBLIOG 20   ECO/TAC
CMN/WLTH. PAGE 19 B0384   ECO/UNDEV
B61
MARSH R.M.,THE MANDARINS: THE CIRCULATION OF ELITES   ELITES
IN CHINA, 1600-1900. ASIA STRUCT PROF/ORG...SOC   ADMIN
CHARTS BIBLIOG DICTIONARY 17/20. PAGE 70 B1406   FAM
                                                          STRATA
B61
NOVE A.,THE SOVIET ECONOMY. USSR ECO/DEV FINAN   PLAN
NAT/G ECO/TAC PRICE ADMIN EFFICIENCY MARXISM   PRODUC
...TREND BIBLIOG 20. PAGE 79 B1594   POLICY
B61
PUGET H.,ESSAI DE BIBLIOGRAPHIE DES PRINCIPAUX   BIBLIOG
OUVRAGES DE DROIT PUBLIC... QUI ONT PARU HORS DE   MGT
FRANCE DE 1945 A 1958. EUR+WWI USA+45 CONSTN LOC/G   ADMIN
...METH 20. PAGE 85 B1719   LAW
B61
ROBINSON M.E.,EDUCATION FOR SOCIAL CHANGE: FOR/AID
ESTABLISHING INSTITUTES OF PUBLIC AND BUSINESS   EDU/PROP
ADMINISTRATION ABROAD (PAMPHLET). WOR+45 SOCIETY   MGT
ACADEM CONFER INGP/REL ROLE...SOC CHARTS BIBLIOG 20   ADJUST
ICA. PAGE 89 B1805
B61
TANNENBAUM R.,LEADERSHIP AND ORGANIZATION. STRUCT   LEAD
ADMIN INGP/REL ATTIT PERCEPT...DECISION METH/CNCPT   MGT
OBS CHARTS BIBLIOG. PAGE 103 B2075   RESPECT
                                                          ROLE
B61
TOMPKINS D.C.,CONFLICT OF INTEREST IN THE FEDERAL   BIBLIOG
GOVERNMENT: A BIBLIOGRAPHY. USA+45 EX/STRUC LEGIS   ROLE
ADJUD ADMIN CRIME CONGRESS PRESIDENT. PAGE 105   NAT/G
B2117   LAW
B61
TRECKER H.B.,NEW UNDERSTANDING OF ADMINISTRATION.   VOL/ASSN
NEIGH DELIB/GP CONTROL LEAD GP/REL INGP/REL   PROF/ORG
...POLICY DECISION BIBLIOG. PAGE 105 B2126   ADMIN
                                                          PARTIC
C61
ETZIONI A.,"A COMPARATIVE ANALYSIS OF COMPLEX   CON/ANAL
ORGANIZATIONS: ON POWER, INVOLVEMENT AND THEIR   SOC
CORRELATES." ELITES CREATE OP/RES ROUTINE INGP/REL   LEAD
PERS/REL CONSEN ATTIT DRIVE PWR...CONCPT BIBLIOG.   CONTROL
PAGE 34 B0684
C61
MOODIE G.C.,"THE GOVERNMENT OF GREAT BRITAIN." UK   NAT/G
LAW STRUCT LOC/G POL/PAR DIPLOM RECEIVE ADMIN   SOCIETY
COLONIAL CHOOSE...BIBLIOG 20 PARLIAMENT. PAGE 75   PARL/PROC
B1508   GOV/COMP
C61
VERBA S.,"SMALL GROUPS AND POLITICAL BEHAVIOR: A   LEAD
STUDY OF LEADERSHIP" DOMIN PARTIC ROUTINE GP/REL   ELITES
ATTIT DRIVE ALL/VALS...CONCPT IDEA/COMP LAB/EXP   FACE/GP
BIBLIOG METH. PAGE 112 B2259
B62
BECKMAN T.N.,MARKETING (7TH ED.). USA+45 SOCIETY   MARKET
ECO/DEV NAT/G PRICE EFFICIENCY INCOME ATTIT WEALTH   ECO/TAC
...MGT BIBLIOG 20. PAGE 10 B0205   DIST/IND
                                                          POLICY
B62
BROWN L.C.,LATIN AMERICA, A BIBLIOGRAPHY. EX/STRUC   BIBLIOG
ADMIN LEAD ATTIT...POLICY 20. PAGE 16 B0323   L/A+17C
                                                          DIPLOM
                                                          NAT/G
B62
CHICAGO U CTR PROG GOVT ADMIN,EDUCATION FOR   EDU/PROP
INNOVATIVE BEHAVIOR IN EXECUTIVES. UNIV ELITES   CREATE
ADMIN EFFICIENCY DRIVE PERSON...MGT APT/TEST   EXEC
PERS/TEST CHARTS LAB/EXP BIBLIOG 20. PAGE 21 B0420   STAT
B62
GROVE J.W.,GOVERNMENT AND INDUSTRY IN BRITAIN. UK   ECO/TAC
FINAN LOC/G CONSULT DELIB/GP INT/TRADE ADMIN   INDUS
CONTROL...BIBLIOG 20. PAGE 44 B0894   NAT/G
                                                          GP/REL
B62
INGHAM K.,A HISTORY OF EAST AFRICA. NAT/G DIPLOM   AFR
ADMIN WAR NAT/LISM...SOC BIOG BIBLIOG. PAGE 54   CONSTN
B1085   COLONIAL
B62
INTERNATIONAL LABOR OFFICE,WORKERS' MANAGEMENT IN   WORKER
YUGOSLAVIA. COM YUGOSLAVIA LABOR DELIB/GP EX/STRUC   CONTROL
PROB/SOLV ADMIN PWR MARXISM...CHARTS ORG/CHARTS   MGT
BIBLIOG 20. PAGE 54 B1098   INDUS

B62
MARS D.,SUGGESTED LIBRARY IN PUBLIC ADMINISTRATION.   BIBLIOG
FINAN DELIB/GP EX/STRUC WORKER COMPUTER ADJUD   ADMIN
...DECISION PSY SOC METH/COMP 20. PAGE 69 B1403   METH
                                                          MGT
B62
NEW ZEALAND COMM OF ST SERVICE,THE STATE SERVICES   ADMIN
IN NEW ZEALAND. NEW/ZEALND CONSULT EX/STRUC ACT/RES   WORKER
...BIBLIOG 20. PAGE 78 B1577   TEC/DEV
                                                          NAT/G
B62
PRESS C.,STATE MANUALS, BLUE BOOKS AND ELECTION   BIBLIOG
RESULTS. LAW LOC/G MUNIC LEGIS WRITING FEDERAL   PROVS
SOVEREIGN...DECISION STAT CHARTS 20. PAGE 84 B1700   ADMIN
                                                          CHOOSE
B62
SHAPIRO D.,A SELECT BIBLIOGRAPHY OF WORKS IN   BIBLIOG
ENGLISH ON RUSSIAN HISTORY, 1801-1917. COM USSR   DIPLOM
STRATA FORCES EDU/PROP ADMIN REV RACE/REL ATTIT   COLONIAL
19/20. PAGE 96 B1932
B62
TAYLOR D.,THE BRITISH IN AFRICA. UK CULTURE   AFR
ECO/UNDEV INDUS DIPLOM INT/TRADE ADMIN WAR RACE/REL   COLONIAL
ORD/FREE SOVEREIGN...POLICY BIBLIOG 15/20 CMN/WLTH. DOMIN
PAGE 103 B2084
B62
TAYLOR J.K.L.,ATTITUDES AND METHODS OF   WORKER
COMMUNICATION AND CONSULTATION BETWEEN EMPLOYERS   ADMIN
AND WORKERS AT INDIVIDUAL FIRM LEVEL. WOR+45 STRUCT   ATTIT
INDUS LABOR CONFER TASK GP/REL EFFICIENCY...MGT   EDU/PROP
BIBLIOG METH 20 OECD. PAGE 103 B2087
B62
UNECA LIBRARY,NEW ACQUISITIONS IN THE UNECA   BIBLIOG
LIBRARY. LAW NAT/G PLAN PROB/SOLV TEC/DEV ADMIN   AFR
REGION...GEOG SOC 20 UN. PAGE 106 B2152   ECO/UNDEV
                                                          INT/ORG
B62
US LIBRARY OF CONGRESS,A LIST OF AMERICAN DOCTORAL   BIBLIOG
DISSERTATIONS ON AFRICA. SOCIETY SECT DIPLOM   AFR
EDU/PROP ADMIN...GEOG 19/20. PAGE 109 B2206   ACADEM
                                                          CULTURE
B62
WELLEQUET J.,LE CONGO BELGE ET LA WELTPOLITIK   ADMIN
(1894-1914. GERMANY DOMIN EDU/PROP WAR ATTIT   DIPLOM
...BIBLIOG T CONGO/LEOP. PAGE 115 B2318   GP/REL
                                                          COLONIAL
L62
SCHWERIN K.,"LAW LIBRARIES AND FOREIGN LAW   BIBLIOG
COLLECTION IN THE USA." USA+45 USA-45...INT/LAW   LAW
STAT 20. PAGE 95 B1917   ACADEM
                                                          ADMIN
C62
BLAU P.M.,"FORMAL ORGANIZATIONS." WOR+45 SOCIETY   ADMIN
STRUCT ECO/DEV GP/REL ATTIT...METH/CNCPT BIBLIOG   SOC
20. PAGE 12 B0253   GEN/METH
                                                          INGP/REL
C62
DE GRAZIA A.,"POLITICAL BEHAVIOR (REV. ED.)" STRATA   PHIL/SCI
POL/PAR LEAD LOBBY ROUTINE WAR CHOOSE REPRESENT   OP/RES
CONSEN ATTIT ORD/FREE BIBLIOG. PAGE 27 B0555   CONCPT
C62
MORGAN G.G.,"SOVIET ADMINISTRATIVE LEGALITY: THE   LAW
ROLE OF THE ATTORNEY GENERAL'S OFFICE." COM USSR   CONSTN
CONTROL ROUTINE...CONCPT BIBLIOG 18/20. PAGE 75   LEGIS
B1522   ADMIN
C62
VAN DER SPRENKEL S.,"LEGAL INSTITUTIONS IN MANCHU   LAW
CHINA." ASIA STRUCT CT/SYS ROUTINE GOV/REL GP/REL   JURID
...CONCPT BIBLIOG 17/20. PAGE 111 B2250   ADMIN
                                                          ADJUD
B63
BADI J.,THE GOVERNMENT OF THE STATE OF ISRAEL: A   NAT/G
CRITICAL ACCOUNT OF ITS PARLIAMENT, EXECUTIVE, AND   CONSTN
JUDICIARY. ISRAEL ECO/DEV CHIEF DELIB/GP LEGIS   EX/STRUC
DIPLOM CT/SYS INGP/REL PEACE ORD/FREE...BIBLIOG 20   POL/PAR
PARLIAMENT ARABS MIGRATION. PAGE 8 B0157
B63
BASS M.E.,SELECTIVE BIBLIOGRAPHY ON MUNICIPAL   BIBLIOG
GOVERNMENT FROM THE FILES OF THE MUNICIPAL   LOC/G
TECHNICAL ADVISORY SERVICE. USA+45 FINAN SERV/IND   ADMIN
PLAN 20. PAGE 9 B0194   MUNIC
B63
BLONDEL J.,VOTERS, PARTIES, AND LEADERS. UK ELITES   POL/PAR
LOC/G NAT/G PROVS ACT/RES DOMIN REPRESENT GP/REL   STRATA
INGP/REL...SOC BIBLIOG 20. PAGE 12 B0255   LEGIS
                                                          ADMIN
B63
BONINI C.P.,SIMULATION OF INFORMATION AND DECISION   INDUS
SYSTEMS IN THE FIRM. MARKET BUDGET DOMIN EDU/PROP   SIMUL
ADMIN COST ATTIT HABITAT PERCEPT PWR...CONCPT   DECISION
PROBABIL QUANT PREDICT HYPO/EXP BIBLIOG. PAGE 13   MGT
B0273
B63
CHOJNACKI S.,REGISTER ON CURRENT RESEARCH ON   BIBLIOG
ETHIOPIA AND THE HORN OF AFRICA. ETHIOPIA LAW   ACT/RES
CULTURE AGRI SECT EDU/PROP ADMIN...GEOG HEAL LING   INTELL

20. PAGE 21 B0426   ACADEM

B63

COMISION DE HISTORIO,GUIA DE LOS DOCUMENTOS BIBLIOG
MICROFOTOGRAFIADOS POR LA UNIDAD MOVIL DE LA NAT/G
UNESCO. SOCIETY ECO/UNDEV INT/ORG ADMIN...SOC 20 L/A+17C
UNESCO. PAGE 22 B0456 DIPLOM

B63

COSTELLO T.W.,PSYCHOLOGY IN ADMINISTRATION: A PSY
RESEARCH ORIENTATION. CREATE PROB/SOLV PERS/REL MGT
ADJUST ANOMIE ATTIT DRIVE PERCEPT ROLE...DECISION EXEC
BIBLIOG T 20. PAGE 24 B0488 ADMIN

B63

CROUCH W.W.,SOUTHERN CALIFORNIA METROPOLIS: A STUDY LOC/G
IN DEVELOPMENT OF GOVERNMENT FOR A METROPOLITAN MUNIC
AREA. USA+45 USA-45 PROB/SOLV ADMIN LOBBY PARTIC LEGIS
CENTRAL ORD/FREE PWR...BIBLIOG 20 PROGRSV/M. DECISION
PAGE 25 B0510

B63

DEAN A.L.,FEDERAL AGENCY APPROACHES TO FIELD ADMIN
MANAGEMENT (PAMPHLET). R+D DELIB/GP EX/STRUC MGT
PROB/SOLV GOV/REL...CLASSIF BIBLIOG 20 FAA NASA NAT/G
DEPT/HEW POSTAL/SYS IRS. PAGE 28 B0563 OP/RES

B63

DOUGLASS H.R.,MODERN ADMINISTRATION OF SECONDARY EDU/PROP
SCHOOLS. CLIENT DELIB/GP WORKER REPRESENT INGP/REL ADMIN
AUTHORIT...TREND BIBLIOG. PAGE 30 B0613 SCHOOL
    MGT

B63

ECOLE NATIONALE D'ADMIN,BIBLIOGRAPHIE SELECTIVE BIBLIOG
D'OUVRAGES DE LANGUE FRANCAISE TRAITANT DES AFR
PROBLEMES GOUVERNEMENTAUX ET ADMINISTRATIFS. NAT/G ADMIN
FORCES ACT/RES OP/RES PLAN PROB/SOLV BUDGET ADJUD EX/STRUC
COLONIAL LEAD 20. PAGE 32 B0651

B63

FRIED R.C.,THE ITALIAN PREFECTS. ITALY STRATA ADMIN
ECO/DEV NAT/LISM ALL/IDEOS...TREND CHARTS METH/COMP NAT/G
BIBLIOG 17/20 PREFECT. PAGE 37 B0755 EFFICIENCY

B63

GALBRAITH J.S.,RELUCTANT EMPIRE: BRITISH POLICY OF COLONIAL
THE SOUTH AFRICAN FRONTIER, 1834-1854. AFR ADMIN
SOUTH/AFR UK GP/REL RACE/REL DISCRIM...CHARTS POLICY
BIBLIOG 19 MISSION. PAGE 38 B0774 SECT

B63

GANGULY D.S.,PUBLIC CORPORATIONS IN A NATIONAL ECO/UNDEV
ECONOMY. INDIA WOR+45 FINAN INDUS TOP/EX PRICE LG/CO
EFFICIENCY...MGT STAT CHARTS BIBLIOG 20. PAGE 38 SOCISM
B0779 GOV/REL

B63

GARNER U.F.,ADMINISTRATIVE LAW. UK LAW LOC/G NAT/G ADMIN
EX/STRUC LEGIS JUDGE BAL/PWR BUDGET ADJUD CONTROL JURID
CT/SYS...BIBLIOG 20. PAGE 39 B0783 PWR
    GOV/REL

B63

HERNDON J.,A SELECTED BIBLIOGRAPHY OF MATERIALS IN BIBLIOG
STATE GOVERNMENT AND POLITICS (PAMPHLET). USA+45 GOV/COMP
POL/PAR LEGIS ADMIN CHOOSE MGT. PAGE 49 B0993 PROVS
    DECISION

B63

HEYEL C.,THE ENCYCLOPEDIA OF MANAGEMENT. WOR+45 MGT
MARKET TOP/EX TEC/DEV AUTOMAT LEAD ADJUST...STAT INDUS
CHARTS GAME ANTHOL BIBLIOG. PAGE 49 B1002 ADMIN
    FINAN

B63

HONORD S.,PUBLIC RELATIONS IN ADMINISTRATION. PRESS
WOR+45 NAT/G...SOC/WK BIBLIOG 20. PAGE 51 B1039 DIPLOM
    MGT
    METH/COMP

B63

JOHNS R.,CONFRONTING ORGANIZATIONAL CHANGE. NEIGH SOC/WK
DELIB/GP CREATE OP/RES ADMIN GP/REL DRIVE...WELF/ST WEALTH
SOC RECORD BIBLIOG. PAGE 56 B1142 LEAD
    VOL/ASSN

B63

KAST F.E.,SCIENCE, TECHNOLOGY, AND MANAGEMENT. MGT
SPACE USA+45 FORCES CONFER DETER NUC/PWR...PHIL/SCI PLAN
CHARTS ANTHOL BIBLIOG 20 NASA. PAGE 58 B1179 TEC/DEV
    PROB/SOLV

B63

KORNHAUSER W.,SCIENTISTS IN INDUSTRY: CONFLICT AND CREATE
ACCOMMODATION. USA+45 R+D LG/CO NAT/G TEC/DEV INDUS
CONTROL ADJUST ATTIT...MGT STAT INT BIBLIOG 20. PROF/ORG
PAGE 61 B1229 GP/REL

B63

LOCKARD D.,THE POLITICS OF STATE AND LOCAL LOC/G
GOVERNMENT. USA+45 CONSTN EX/STRUC LEGIS CT/SYS PROVS
FEDERAL...CHARTS BIBLIOG 20. PAGE 66 B1334 OP/RES
    ADMIN

B63

PLISCHKE E.,GOVERNMENT AND POLITICS OF CONTEMPORARY MUNIC
BERLIN. GERMANY LAW CONSTN POL/PAR LEGIS WAR CHOOSE LOC/G
REPRESENT GOV/REL...CHARTS BIBLIOG 20 BERLIN. POLICY
PAGE 83 B1683 ADMIN

B63

RICHARDSON H.G.,THE ADMINISTRATION OF IRELAND ADMIN
1172-1377. IRELAND CONSTN EX/STRUC LEGIS JUDGE NAT/G
CT/SYS PARL/PROC...CHARTS BIBLIOG 12/14. PAGE 88 PWR

B1775

B63

ROBINSON K.,ESSAYS IN IMPERIAL GOVERNMENT. CAMEROON COLONIAL
NIGERIA UK CONSTN LOC/G LEGIS ADMIN GOV/REL PWR AFR
...POLICY ANTHOL BIBLIOG 17/20 PURHAM/M. PAGE 89 DOMIN
B1803

B63

ROYAL INSTITUTE PUBLIC ADMIN,BRITISH PUBLIC BIBLIOG
ADMINISTRATION. UK LAW FINAN INDUS LOC/G POL/PAR ADMIN
LEGIS LOBBY PARL/PROC CHOOSE JURID. PAGE 91 B1845 MGT
    NAT/G

B63

SCHRADER R.,SCIENCE AND POLICY. WOR+45 ECO/DEV TEC/DEV
ECO/UNDEV R+D FORCES PLAN DIPLOM GOV/REL TECHRACY NAT/G
BIBLIOG. PAGE 94 B1900 POLICY
    ADMIN

B63

SPRING D.,THE ENGLISH LANDED ESTATE IN THE STRATA
NINETEENTH CENTURY: ITS ADMINISTRATION. UK ELITES PERS/REL
STRUCT AGRI NAT/G GP/REL OWN PWR WEALTH...BIBLIOG MGT
19 HOUSE/LORD. PAGE 99 B2012

B63

WALKER A.A.,OFFICIAL PUBLICATIONS OF SIERRA LEONE BIBLIOG
AND GAMBIA. GAMBIA SIER/LEONE UK LAW CONSTN LEGIS NAT/G
PLAN BUDGET DIPLOM...SOC SAMP CON/ANAL 20. PAGE 113 COLONIAL
B2278 ADMIN

C63

BLUM J.M.,"THE NATIONAL EXPERIENCE." USA+45 USA-45 ADMIN
ECO/DEV DIPLOM WAR NAT/LISM...POLICY CHARTS BIBLIOG NAT/G
T 16/20 CONGRESS PRESIDENT COLD/WAR. PAGE 13 B0258 LEGIS
    CHIEF

C63

CARLISLE D.,"PARTY LOYALTY; THE ELECTION PROCESS IN CHOOSE
SOUTH CAROLINA." USA+45 LOC/G ADMIN ATTIT...TREND POL/PAR
CHARTS BIBLIOG 17/20. PAGE 19 B0380 PROVS
    SUFF

N63

INTERNATIONAL CITY MGRS ASSN,POST-ENTRY TRAINING IN LOC/G
THE LOCAL PUBLIC SERVICE (PAMPHLET). SCHOOL PLAN WORKER
PROB/SOLV TEC/DEV ADMIN EFFICIENCY SKILL...POLICY EDU/PROP
AUD/VIS CHARTS BIBLIOG 20 CITY/MGT. PAGE 54 B1096 METH/COMP

B64

RECENT PUBLICATIONS ON GOVERNMENTAL PROBLEMS. FINAN BIBLIOG
INDUS ACADEM PLAN PROB/SOLV EDU/PROP ADJUD ADMIN AUTOMAT
BIO/SOC...MGT SOC. PAGE 2 B0040 LEGIS
    JURID

B64

AHMAD M.,THE CIVIL SERVANT IN PAKISTAN. PAKISTAN WELF/ST
ECO/UNDEV COLONIAL INGP/REL...SOC CHARTS BIBLIOG 20 ADMIN
CIVIL/SERV. PAGE 3 B0065 ATTIT
    STRATA

B64

BOTTOMORE T.B.,ELITES AND SOCIETY. INTELL STRATA ELITES
ECO/DEV ECO/UNDEV ADMIN GP/REL ORD/FREE...CONCPT IDEA/COMP
BIBLIOG 20. PAGE 14 B0281 SOCIETY
    SOC

B64

BOUVIER-AJAM M.,MANUEL TECHNIQUE ET PRATIQUE DU MUNIC
MAIRE ET DES ELUS ET AGENTS COMMUNAUX. FRANCE LOC/G ADMIN
BUDGET CHOOSE GP/REL SUPEGO...JURID BIBLIOG 20 CHIEF
MAYOR COMMUNES. PAGE 14 B0284 NEIGH

B64

BRIGHT J.R.,RESEARCH, DEVELOPMENT AND TECHNOLOGICAL TEC/DEV
INNOVATION. CULTURE R+D CREATE PLAN PROB/SOLV NEW/IDEA
AUTOMAT RISK PERSON...DECISION CONCPT PREDICT INDUS
BIBLIOG. PAGE 15 B0308 MGT

B64

FAINSOD M.,HOW RUSSIA IS RULED (REV. ED.). RUSSIA NAT/G
USSR AGRI PROC/MFG LABOR POL/PAR EX/STRUC CONTROL REV
PWR...POLICY BIBLIOG 19/20 KHRUSH/N COM/PARTY. MARXISM
PAGE 34 B0700

B64

FLORENCE P.S.,ECONOMICS AND SOCIOLOGY OF INDUSTRY; INDUS
A REALISTIC ANALYSIS OF DEVELOPMENT. ECO/UNDEV SOC
LG/CO NAT/G PLAN...GEOG MGT BIBLIOG 20. PAGE 36 ADMIN
B0729

B64

FORBES A.H.,CURRENT RESEARCH IN BRITISH STUDIES. UK BIBLIOG
CONSTN CULTURE POL/PAR SECT DIPLOM ADMIN...JURID PERSON
BIOG WORSHIP 20. PAGE 36 B0736 NAT/G
    PARL/PROC

B64

GOODNOW H.F.,THE CIVIL SERVICE OF PAKISTAN: ADMIN
BUREAUCRACY IN A NEW NATION. INDIA PAKISTAN S/ASIA GOV/REL
ECO/UNDEV PROVS CHIEF PARTIC CHOOSE EFFICIENCY PWR LAW
...BIBLIOG 20. PAGE 41 B0824 NAT/G

B64

GRZYBOWSKI K.,THE SOCIALIST COMMONWEALTH OF INT/LAW
NATIONS: ORGANIZATIONS AND INSTITUTIONS. FORCES COM
DIPLOM INT/TRADE ADJUD INT/LAW WAR MARXISM REGION
SOCISM...BIBLIOG 20 COMECON WARSAW/P. PAGE 44 B0898 INT/ORG

B64

HAMBRIDGE G.,DYNAMICS OF DEVELOPMENT. AGRI FINAN ECO/UNDEV
INDUS LABOR INT/TRADE EDU/PROP ADMIN LEAD OWN ECO/TAC
HEALTH...ANTHOL BIBLIOG 20. PAGE 46 B0930 OP/RES
    ACT/RES

HAMILTON B.L.S.,PROBLEMS OF ADMINISTRATION IN AN ADMIN B64
EMERGENT NATION: CASE STUDY OF JAMAICA. JAMAICA UK ECO/UNDEV
WOR+45 MUNIC COLONIAL HABITAT...CHARTS BIBLIOG 20 GOV/REL
CIVIL/SERV. PAGE 46 B0932 NAT/G

HARMON R.B.,BIBLIOGRAPHY OF BIBLIOGRAPHIES IN BIBLIOG B64
POLITICAL SCIENCE (MIMEOGRAPHED PAPER: LIMITED NAT/G
EDITION). WOR+45 WOR-45 INT/ORG POL/PAR GOV/REL DIPLOM
ALL/IDEOS...INT/LAW JURID MGT 19/20. PAGE 47 B0949 LOC/G

IBERO-AMERICAN INSTITUTES,IBEROAMERICANA. STRUCT BIBLIOG B64
ADMIN SOC. PAGE 53 B1073 L/A+17C
NAT/G
DIPLOM

INST D'ETUDE POL L'U GRENOBLE,ADMINISTRATION ADMIN B64
TRADITIONELLE ET PLANIFICATION REGIONALE. FRANCE MUNIC
LAW POL/PAR PROB/SOLV ADJUST RIGID/FLEX...CHARTS PLAN
ANTHOL BIBLIOG T 20 REFORMERS. PAGE 54 B1087 CREATE

JACKSON W.V.,LIBRARY GUIDE FOR BRAZILIAN STUDIES. BIBLIOG B64
BRAZIL USA+45 STRUCT DIPLOM ADMIN...SOC 20. PAGE 55 L/A+17C
B1110 NAT/G
LOC/G

KAHNG T.J.,LAW, POLITICS, AND THE SECURITY COUNCIL* DELIB/GP B64
AN INQUIRY INTO THE HANDLING OF LEGAL QUESTIONS. ADJUD
LAW CONSTN NAT/G ACT/RES OP/RES CT/SYS TASK PWR ROUTINE
...INT/LAW BIBLIOG UN. PAGE 57 B1160

MARRIS R.,THE ECONOMIC THEORY OF "MANAGERIAL" CAP/ISM B64
CAPITALISM. USA+45 ECO/DEV LG/CO ECO/TAC DEMAND MGT
...CHARTS BIBLIOG 20. PAGE 69 B1402 CONTROL
OP/RES

MCNULTY J.E.,SOME ECONOMIC ASPECTS OF BUSINESS ADMIN B64
ORGANIZATION. ECO/DEV UTIL...MGT CHARTS BIBLIOG LG/CO
METH 20. PAGE 72 B1458 GEN/LAWS

MUSSO AMBROSI L.A.,BIBLIOGRAFIA DE BIBLIOGRAFIAS BIBLIOG B64
URUGUAYAS. URUGUAY DIPLOM ADMIN ATTIT...SOC 20. NAT/G
PAGE 77 B1551 L/A+17C
PRESS

O'HEARN P.J.T.,PEACE, ORDER AND GOOD GOVERNMENT; A NAT/G B64
NEW CONSTITUTION FOR CANADA. CANADA EX/STRUC LEGIS CONSTN
CT/SYS PARL/PROC...BIBLIOG 20. PAGE 79 B1600 LAW
CREATE

PARET P.,FRENCH REVOLUTIONARY WARFARE FROM FRANCE B64
INDOCHINA TO ALGERIA* THE ANALYSIS OF A POLITICAL GUERRILLA
AND MILITARY DOCTRINE. ALGERIA VIETNAM FORCES GEN/LAWS
OP/RES TEC/DEV ROUTINE REV ATTIT...PSY BIBLIOG.
PAGE 81 B1632

PEABODY R.L.,ORGANIZATIONAL AUTHORITY. SCHOOL ADMIN B64
WORKER PLAN SENIOR GOV/REL UTIL DRIVE PWR...PSY EFFICIENCY
CHARTS BIBLIOG 20. PAGE 82 B1648 TASK
GP/REL

PRESS C.,A BIBLIOGRAPHIC INTRODUCTION TO AMERICAN BIBLIOG B64
STATE GOVERNMENT AND POLITICS (PAMPHLET). USA+45 LEGIS
USA-45 EX/STRUC ADJUD INGP/REL FEDERAL ORD/FREE 20. LOC/G
PAGE 84 B1701 POL/PAR

RICHARDSON I.L.,BIBLIOGRAFIA BRASILEIRA DE BIBLIOG B64
ADMINISTRACAO PUBLICA E ASSUNTOS CORRELATOS. BRAZIL MGT
CONSTN FINAN LOC/G NAT/G POL/PAR PLAN DIPLOM ADMIN
RECEIVE ATTIT...METH 20. PAGE 88 B1776 LAW

RIDDLE D.H.,THE TRUMAN COMMITTEE: A STUDY IN LEGIS B64
CONGRESSIONAL RESPONSIBILITY. INDUS FORCES OP/RES DELIB/GP
DOMIN ADMIN LEAD PARL/PROC WAR PRODUC SUPEGO CONFER
...BIBLIOG CONGRESS. PAGE 88 B1778

RIES J.C.,THE MANAGEMENT OF DEFENSE: ORGANIZATION FORCES B64
AND CONTROL OF THE US ARMED SERVICES. PROF/ORG ACT/RES
DELIB/GP EX/STRUC LEGIS GOV/REL PERS/REL CENTRAL DECISION
RATIONAL PWR...POLICY TREND GOV/COMP BIBLIOG. CONTROL
PAGE 88 B1782

RUSSELL R.B.,UNITED NATIONS EXPERIENCE WITH FORCES B64
MILITARY FORCES: POLITICAL AND LEGAL ASPECTS. AFR DIPLOM
KOREA WOR+45 LEGIS PROB/SOLV ADMIN CONTROL SANCTION
EFFICIENCY PEACE...POLICY INT/LAW BIBLIOG UN. ORD/FREE
PAGE 92 B1857

SEGUNDO-SANCHEZ M.,OBRAS (2 VOLS.). VENEZUELA BIBLIOG B64
EX/STRUC DIPLOM ADMIN 19/20. PAGE 95 B1924 LEAD
NAT/G
L/A+17C

THE BRITISH COUNCIL,PUBLIC ADMINISTRATION: A SELECT BIBLIOG B64
LIST OF BOOKS AND PERIODICALS. LAW CONSTN FINAN ADMIN
POL/PAR SCHOOL CHOOSE...HEAL MGT METH/COMP 19/20 LOC/G

CMN/WLTH. PAGE 104 B2094 INDUS

TILMAN R.O.,BUREAUCRATIC TRANSITION IN MALAYA. ADMIN B64
MALAYSIA S/ASIA UK NAT/G EX/STRUC DIPLOM...CHARTS COLONIAL
BIBLIOG 20. PAGE 104 B2110 SOVEREIGN
EFFICIENCY

TOMPKINS D.C.,PROBATION SINCE WORLD WAR II. USA+45 BIBLIOG B64
FORCES ADMIN ROUTINE PERS/REL AGE...CRIMLGY HEAL PUB/INST
20. PAGE 105 B2118 ORD/FREE
CRIME

TURNER M.C.,LIBROS EN VENTA EN HISPANOAMERICA Y BIBLIOG B64
ESPANA. SPAIN LAW CONSTN CULTURE ADMIN LEAD...HUM L/A+17C
SOC 20. PAGE 106 B2139 NAT/G
DIPLOM

WILLIAMSON O.E.,THE ECONOMICS OF DISCRETIONARY EFFICIENCY B64
BEHAVIOR: MANAGERIAL OBJECTIVES IN A THEORY OF THE MGT
FIRM. MARKET BUDGET CAP/ISM PRODUC DRIVE PERSON ECO/TAC
...STAT CHARTS BIBLIOG METH 20. PAGE 117 B2354 CHOOSE

STONE P.A.,"DECISION TECHNIQUES FOR TOWN OP/RES S64
DEVELOPMENT." PLAN COST PROFIT...DECISION MGT MUNIC
CON/ANAL CHARTS METH/COMP BIBLIOG 20. PAGE 101 ADMIN
B2048 PROB/SOLV

NORGREN P.H.,"TOWARD FAIR EMPLOYMENT." USA+45 LAW RACE/REL C64
STRATA LABOR NAT/G FORCES ACT/RES ADMIN ATTIT DISCRIM
...POLICY BIBLIOG 20 NEGRO. PAGE 79 B1588 WORKER
MGT

SCOTT R.E.,"MEXICAN GOVERNMENT IN TRANSITION (REV NAT/G C64
ED)." CULTURE STRUCT POL/PAR CHIEF ADMIN LOBBY REV L/A+17C
CHOOSE GP/REL DRIVE...BIBLIOG METH 20 MEXIC/AMER. ROUTINE
PAGE 95 B1920 CONSTN

US BOARD GOVERNORS FEDL RESRV,SELECTED BIBLIOGRAPHY BIBLIOG N64
ON MONETARY POLICY AND MANAGEMENT OF THE PUBLIC FINAN
DEBT 1947-1960 AND 1961-1963 SUPPLEMENT (PAMPH.). NAT/G
USA+45 PLAN...POLICY MGT 20. PAGE 108 B2173

AMERICAN ECONOMIC ASSOCIATION,INDEX OF ECONOMIC BIBLIOG B65
JOURNALS 1886-1965 (7 VOLS.). UK USA+45 USA-45 AGRI WRITING
FINAN PLAN ECO/TAC INT/TRADE ADMIN...STAT CENSUS INDUS
19/20. PAGE 4 B0083

BERNDT R.M.,ABORIGINAL MAN IN AUSTRALIA. LAW DOMIN SOC B65
ADMIN COLONIAL MARRIAGE HABITAT ORD/FREE...LING CULTURE
CHARTS ANTHOL BIBLIOG WORSHIP 20 AUSTRAL ABORIGINES SOCIETY
MUSIC ELKIN/AP. PAGE 11 B0225 STRUCT

DE GRAZIA A.,REPUBLIC IN CRISIS: CONGRESS AGAINST LEGIS B65
THE EXECUTIVE FORCE. USA+45 USA-45 SOCIETY POL/PAR EXEC
CHIEF DOMIN ROLE ORD/FREE PWR...CONCPT MYTH BIBLIOG GOV/REL
20 CONGRESS. PAGE 27 B0556 CONTROL

EAST J.P.,COUNCIL-MANAGER GOVERNMENT: THE POLITICAL SIMUL B65
THOUGHT OF ITS FOUNDER, RICHARD S. CHILDS. USA+45 LOC/G
CREATE ADMIN CHOOSE...BIOG GEN/LAWS BIBLIOG MUNIC
CHILDS/RS CITY/MGT. PAGE 32 B0642 EX/STRUC

FEERICK J.D.,FROM FAILING HANDS: THE STUDY OF EX/STRUC B65
PRESIDENTIAL SUCCESSION. CONSTN NAT/G PROB/SOLV CHIEF
LEAD PARL/PROC MURDER CHOOSE...NEW/IDEA BIBLIOG 20 LAW
KENNEDY/JF JOHNSON/LB PRESIDENT PRE/US/AM LEGIS
VICE/PRES. PAGE 35 B0710

HARMON R.B.,POLITICAL SCIENCE: A BIBLIOGRAPHICAL BIBLIOG B65
GUIDE TO THE LITERATURE. WOR+45 WOR-45 R+D INT/ORG POL/PAR
LOC/G NAT/G DIPLOM ADMIN...CONCPT METH. PAGE 47 LAW
B0950 GOV/COMP

HISPANIC SOCIETY OF AMERICA,CATALOGUE (10 VOLS.). BIBLIOG B65
PORTUGAL PRE/AMER SPAIN NAT/G ADMIN...POLICY SOC L/A+17C
15/20. PAGE 50 B1018 COLONIAL
DIPLOM

HUGHES J.M.,EDUCATION IN AMERICA (2ND ED.). USA+45 EDU/PROP B65
USA-45 GP/REL INGP/REL AGE/C AGE/Y ROLE...IDEA/COMP SCHOOL
BIBLIOG T 20. PAGE 52 B1059 ADMIN
METH/COMP

KELLEY E.J.,MARKETING: STRATEGY AND FUNCTIONS. MARKET B65
ECO/DEV INDUS PLAN PRICE CONTROL ROUTINE...MGT DIST/IND
BIBLIOG 20. PAGE 59 B1191 POLICY
ECO/TAC

MACDONALD R.W.,THE LEAGUE OF ARAB STATES: A STUDY ISLAM B65
IN THE DYNAMICS OF REGIONAL ORGANIZATION. ISRAEL REGION
UAR USSR FINAN INT/ORG DELIB/GP ECO/TAC AGREE DIPLOM
NEUTRAL ORD/FREE PWR...DECISION BIBLIOG 20 TREATY ADMIN
UN. PAGE 67 B1358

MEISEL J.H.,PARETO & MOSCA. ITALY STRUCT ADMIN PWR B65
...SOC CON/ANAL ANTHOL BIBLIOG 19/20. PAGE 72 B1463 ELITES

MUSHKIN S.J.,STATE PROGRAMMING. USA+45 PLAN BUDGET TAX ADMIN REGION GOV/REL...BIBLIOG 20. PAGE 77 B1549
CONTROL LAISSEZ B65
PROVS POLICY CREATE ECO/DEV

NATIONAL BOOK CENTRE PAKISTAN,BOOKS ON PAKISTAN: A BIBLIOGRAPHY. PAKISTAN CULTURE DIPLOM ADMIN ATTIT ...MAJORIT SOC CONCPT 20. PAGE 77 B1560
B65
BIBLIOG CONSTN S/ASIA NAT/G

PARRISH W.E.,MISSOURI UNDER RADICAL RULE 1865-1870. USA-45 SOCIETY INDUS LOC/G POL/PAR WORKER EDU/PROP SUFF INGP/REL ATTIT...BIBLIOG 19 NEGRO MISSOURI. PAGE 81 B1635
B65
PROVS ADMIN RACE/REL ORD/FREE

PERLOFF H.S.,URBAN RESEARCH AND EDUCATION IN THE NEW YORK METROPOLITAN REGION (VOL. II). FUT USA+45 NEIGH PROF/ORG ACT/RES PROB/SOLV EDU/PROP ADMIN ...STAT BIBLIOG 20 NEWYORK/C. PAGE 82 B1659
B65
MUNIC PLAN ACADEM GP/REL

ROTBERG R.I.,A POLITICAL HISTORY OF TROPICAL AFRICA. EX/STRUC DIPLOM INT/TRADE DOMIN ADMIN RACE/REL NAT/LISM PWR SOVEREIGN...GEOG TIME/SEQ BIBLIOG 1/20. PAGE 91 B1832
B65
AFR CULTURE COLONIAL

ROWAT D.C.,THE OMBUDSMAN: CITIZEN'S DEFENDER. DENMARK FINLAND NEW/ZEALND NORWAY SWEDEN CONSULT PROB/SOLV FEEDBACK PARTIC GP/REL...SOC CONCPT NEW/IDEA METH/COMP ANTHOL BIBLIOG 20. PAGE 91 B1840
B65
INSPECT CONSTN NAT/G ADMIN

ROWE J.Z.,THE PUBLIC-PRIVATE CHARACTER OF UNITED STATES CENTRAL BANKING. USA+45 NAT/G EX/STRUC ...BIBLIOG 20 FED/RESERV. PAGE 91 B1842
B65
FINAN PLAN FEDERAL LAW

SCOTT A.M.,THE REVOLUTION IN STATECRAFT: INFORMAL PENETRATION. WOR+45 WOR-45 CULTURE INT/ORG FORCES ECO/TAC ROUTINE...BIBLIOG 20. PAGE 95 B1918
B65
DIPLOM EDU/PROP FOR/AID

SINGER J.D.,HUMAN BEHAVIOR AND INTERNATIONAL POLITICS* CONTRIBUTIONS FROM THE SOCIAL-PSYCHOLOGICAL SCIENCES. ACT/RES PLAN EDU/PROP ADMIN KNOWL...DECISION PSY SOC NET/THEORY HYPO/EXP LAB/EXP SOC/EXP GEN/METH ANTHOL BIBLIOG. PAGE 97 B1965
B65
DIPLOM PHIL/SCI QUANT SIMUL

SMITH C.,THE OMBUDSMAN: A BIBLIOGRAPHY (PAMPHLET). DENMARK SWEDEN USA+45 LAW LEGIS JUDGE GOV/REL GP/REL...JURID 20. PAGE 98 B1980
B65
BIBLIOG ADMIN CT/SYS ADJUD

SPEECKAERT G.P.,SELECT BIBLIOGRAPHY ON INTERNATIONAL ORGANIZATION, 1885-1964. WOR+45 WOR-45 EX/STRUC DIPLOM ADMIN REGION 19/20 UN. PAGE 99 B2004
B65
BIBLIOG INT/ORG GEN/LAWS STRATA

WALTON R.E.,A BEHAVIORAL THEORY OF LABOR NEGOTIATIONS: AN ANALYSIS OF A SOCIAL INTERACTION SYSTEM. USA+45 FINAN PROB/SOLV ECO/TAC GP/REL INGP/REL...DECISION BIBLIOG. PAGE 113 B2285
B65
SOC LABOR BARGAIN ADMIN

WATERSTON A.,DEVELOPMENT PLANNING* LESSONS OF EXPERIENCE. ECO/TAC CENTRAL...MGT QUANT BIBLIOG. PAGE 114 B2303
B65
ECO/UNDEV CREATE PLAN ADMIN

WILDER B.E.,BIBLIOGRAPHY OF THE OFFICIAL PUBLICATIONS OF KANSAS, 1854-1958. USA+45 USA-45 ECO/DEV POL/PAR EX/STRUC LEGIS ADJUD ATTIT 19/20. PAGE 116 B2349
B65
BIBLIOG PROVS GOV/REL ADMIN

WITHERELL J.W.,MADAGASCAR AND ADJACENT ISLANDS; A GUIDE TO OFFICIAL PUBLICATIONS (PAMPHLET). FRANCE MADAGASCAR S/ASIA UK LAW OP/RES PLAN DIPLOM ...POLICY CON/ANAL 19/20. PAGE 117 B2368
B65
BIBLIOG COLONIAL LOC/G ADMIN

"FURTHER READING." INDIA STRUCT FINAN WORKER ADMIN COST 20. PAGE 2 B0042
S65
BIBLIOG MGT ECO/UNDEV EFFICIENCY

"FURTHER READING." INDIA NAT/G ADMIN 20. PAGE 2 B0043
S65
BIBLIOG EDU/PROP SCHOOL ACADEM

"FURTHER READING." INDIA ADMIN COLONIAL WAR GOV/REL ATTIT 20. PAGE 2 B0044
S65
BIBLIOG DIPLOM NAT/G POLICY

RAPHAELI N.,"SELECTED ARTICLES AND DOCUMENTS ON COMPARATIVE PUBLIC ADMINISTRATION." USA+45 FINAN
S65
BIBLIOG ADMIN

LOC/G WORKER TEC/DEV CONTROL LEAD...SOC/WK GOV/COMP METH/COMP. PAGE 86 B1739
NAT/G MGT B66

ADAMS J.C.,THE GOVERNMENT OF REPUBLICAN ITALY (2ND ED.). ITALY LOC/G POL/PAR DELIB/GP LEGIS WORKER ADMIN CT/SYS FASCISM...CHARTS BIBLIOG 20 PARLIAMENT. PAGE 3 B0057
NAT/G CHOOSE EX/STRUC CONSTN B66

ASHRAF A.,THE CITY GOVERNMENT OF CALCUTTA: A STUDY OF INERTIA. INDIA ELITES INDUS NAT/G EX/STRUC ACT/RES PLAN PROB/SOLV LEAD HABITAT...BIBLIOG 20 CALCUTTA. PAGE 7 B0141
LOC/G MUNIC ADMIN ECO/UNDEV B66

BARBER W.F.,INTERNAL SECURITY AND MILITARY POWER* COUNTERINSURGENCY AND CIVIC ACTION IN LATIN AMERICA. ECO/UNDEV CREATE ADMIN REV ATTIT RIGID/FLEX MARXISM...INT BIBLIOG OAS. PAGE 9 B0183
L/A+17C FORCES ORD/FREE TASK B66

CHAPMAN B.,THE PROFESSION OF GOVERNMENT: THE PUBLIC SERVICE IN EUROPE. CONSTN NAT/G POL/PAR EX/STRUC LEGIS TOP/EX PROB/SOLV DEBATE EXEC PARL/PROC PARTIC 20. PAGE 20 B0411
BIBLIOG ADMIN EUR+WWI GOV/COMP B66

DAHLBERG J.S.,THE NEW YORK BUREAU OF MUNICIPAL RESEARCH: PIONEER IN GOVERNMENT ADMINISTRATION. CONSTN R+D BUDGET EDU/PROP PARTIC REPRESENT EFFICIENCY ORD/FREE...BIBLIOG METH 20 NEW/YORK NIPA. PAGE 26 B0522
PROVS MUNIC DELIB/GP ADMIN B66

DEBENKO E.,RESEARCH SOURCES FOR SOUTH ASIAN STUDIES IN ECONOMIC DEVELOPMENT: A SELECT BIBLIOGRAPHY OF SERIAL PUBLICATIONS. CEYLON INDIA NEPAL PAKISTAN PROB/SOLV ADMIN...POLICY 20. PAGE 28 B0566
BIBLIOG ECO/UNDEV S/ASIA PLAN B66

DILLEY M.R.,BRITISH POLICY IN KENYA COLONY (2ND ED.). AFR INDIA UK LABOR BUDGET TAX ADMIN PARL/PROC GP/REL...BIBLIOG 20 PARLIAMENT. PAGE 29 B0594
COLONIAL REPRESENT SOVEREIGN B66

EPSTEIN F.T.,THE AMERICAN BIBLIOGRAPHY OF RUSSIAN AND EAST EUROPEAN STUDIES FOR 1964. USSR LOC/G NAT/G POL/PAR FORCES ADMIN ARMS/CONT...JURID CONCPT 20 UN. PAGE 33 B0678
BIBLIOG COM MARXISM DIPLOM B66

FINK M.,A SELECTIVE BIBLIOGRAPHY ON STATE CONSTITUTIONAL REVISION (PAMPHLET). USA+45 FINAN EX/STRUC LEGIS EDU/PROP ADMIN CT/SYS APPORT CHOOSE GOV/REL 20. PAGE 35 B0720
BIBLIOG PROVS LOC/G CONSTN B66

FINNISH POLITICAL SCIENCE ASSN,SCANDINAVIAN POLITICAL STUDIES (VOL. I). FINLAND DIPLOM ADMIN LOBBY PARL/PROC...CHARTS BIBLIOG 20 SCANDINAV. PAGE 36 B0721
ATTIT POL/PAR ACT/RES CHOOSE B66

HARMON R.B.,SOURCES AND PROBLEMS OF BIBLIOGRAPHY IN POLITICAL SCIENCE (PAMPHLET). INT/ORG LOC/G MUNIC POL/PAR ADMIN GOV/REL ALL/IDEOS...JURID MGT CONCPT 19/20. PAGE 47 B0951
BIBLIOG DIPLOM INT/LAW NAT/G B66

HASTINGS P.G.,THE MANAGEMENT OF BUSINESS FINANCE. ECO/DEV PLAN BUDGET CONTROL COST...DECISION CHARTS BIBLIOG T 20. PAGE 48 B0966
FINAN MGT INDUS ECO/TAC B66

KAESTNER K.,GESAMTWIRTSCHAFTLICHE PLANUNG IN EINER GEMISCHTEN WIRTSCHAFTSORDNUNG (WIRTSCHAFTSPOLITISCHE STUDIEN 5). GERMANY/W WOR+45 WOR-45 INDUS MARKET NAT/G ACT/RES GP/REL INGP/REL PRODUC...ECOMETRIC MGT BIBLIOG 20. PAGE 57 B1159
ECO/TAC PLAN POLICY PREDICT B66

MURDOCK J.C.,RESEARCH AND REGIONS. AGRI FINAN INDUS LOC/G MUNIC NAT/G PROB/SOLV TEC/DEV ADMIN REGION 20. PAGE 76 B1545
BIBLIOG ECO/DEV COMPUT/IR R+D B66

NEUMANN R.G.,THE GOVERNMENT OF THE GERMAN FEDERAL REPUBLIC. EUR+WWI GERMANY/W LOC/G EX/STRUC LEGIS CT/SYS INGP/REL PWR...BIBLIOG 20 ADENAUER/K. PAGE 78 B1573
NAT/G POL/PAR DIPLOM CONSTN B66

O'NEILL C.E.,CHURCH AND STATE IN FRENCH COLONIAL LOUISIANA: POLICY AND POLITICS TO 1732. PROVS VOL/ASSN DELIB/GP ADJUD ADMIN GP/REL ATTIT DRIVE ...POLICY BIBLIOG 17/18 LOUISIANA CHURCH/STA. PAGE 79 B1601
COLONIAL NAT/G SECT PWR B66

ONYEMELUKWE C.C.,PROBLEMS OF INDUSTRIAL PLANNING AND MANAGEMENT IN NIGERIA. AFR FINAN LABOR DELIB/GP TEC/DEV ADJUST...MGT TREND BIBLIOG. PAGE 80 B1610
ECO/UNDEV ECO/TAC INDUS PLAN B66

ROSHOLT R.L.,AN ADMINISTRATIVE HISTORY OF NASA, 1958-1963. SPACE USA+45 FINAN LEAD...MGT CHARTS BIBLIOG 20 NASA. PAGE 90 B1824
ADMIN EX/STRUC ADJUST DELIB/GP B66

SCHLESSINGER P.J.,ELEMENTS OF CALIFORNIA GOVERNMENT LOC/G

(2ND ED.). USA+45 LAW ADJUD ADMIN CONTROL CT/SYS
EFFICIENCY...BIBLIOG T CALIFORNIA. PAGE 94 B1891
PROVS GOV/REL LEGIS

B66

SMITH H.E.,READINGS IN ECONOMIC DEVELOPMENT AND
ADMINISTRATION IN TANZANIA. TANZANIA FINAN INDUS
LABOR NAT/G PLAN PROB/SOLV INT/TRADE COLONIAL
REGION...ANTHOL BIBLIOG 20 AFRICA/E. PAGE 98 B1981
TEC/DEV ADMIN GOV/REL

B66

STREET D.,ORGANIZATION FOR TREATMENT. CLIENT PROVS
PUB/INST PLAN CONTROL PARTIC REPRESENT ATTIT PWR
...POLICY BIBLIOG. PAGE 101 B2052
GP/COMP AGE/Y ADMIN VOL/ASSN

B66

US LIBRARY OF CONGRESS,NIGERIA: A GUIDE TO OFFICIAL
PUBLICATIONS. CAMEROON NIGERIA UK DIPLOM...POLICY
19/20 UN LEAGUE/NAT. PAGE 109 B2207
BIBLIOG ADMIN NAT/G COLONIAL

B66

WARREN R.O.,GOVERNMENT IN METROPOLITAN REGIONS: A
REAPPRAISAL OF FRACTIONATED POLITICAL ORGANIZATION.
USA+45 ACT/RES PROB/SOLV REGION...CHARTS METH/COMP
BIBLIOG CITY/MGT. PAGE 114 B2296
LOC/G MUNIC EX/STRUC PLAN

B66

WASHINGTON S.H.,BIBLIOGRAPHY: LABOR-MANAGEMENT
RELATIONS ACT, 1947 AS AMENDED BY LABOR-MANAGEMENT
REPORTING AND DISCLOSURE ACT, 1959. USA+45 CONSTN
INDUS DELIB/GP LEGIS WORKER BARGAIN ECO/TAC ADJUD
GP/REL NEW/LIB...JURID CONGRESS. PAGE 114 B2298
BIBLIOG LAW LABOR MGT

L66

SEYLER W.C.,"DOCTORAL DISSERTATIONS IN POLITICAL
SCIENCE IN UNIVERSITIES OF THE UNITED STATES AND
CANADA." INT/ORG LOC/G ADMIN...INT/LAW MGT
GOV/COMP. PAGE 96 B1930
BIBLIOG LAW NAT/G

S66

"FURTHER READING." INDIA LOC/G NAT/G PLAN ADMIN
WEALTH...GEOG SOC CONCPT CENSUS 20. PAGE 2 B0045
BIBLIOG ECO/UNDEV TEC/DEV PROVS

S66

BURDETTE F.L.,"SELECTED ARTICLES AND DOCUMENTS ON
AMERICAN GOVERNMENT AND POLITICS." LAW LOC/G MUNIC
NAT/G POL/PAR PROVS LEGIS BAL/PWR ADMIN EXEC
REPRESENT MGT. PAGE 17 B0348
BIBLIOG USA+45 JURID CONSTN

S66

MATTHEWS D.G.,"ETHIOPIAN OUTLINE: A BIBLIOGRAPHIC
RESEARCH GUIDE." ETHIOPIA LAW STRUCT ECO/UNDEV AGRI
LABOR SECT CHIEF DELIB/GP EX/STRUC ADMIN...LING
ORG/CHARTS 20. PAGE 71 B1429
BIBLIOG NAT/G DIPLOM POL/PAR

S66

MATTHEWS D.G.,"PRELUDE-COUP D'ETAT-MILITARY
GOVERNMENT: A BIBLIOGRAPHICAL AND RESEARCH GUIDE TO
NIGERIAN POL AND GOVT, JAN. 1965-66." AFR NIGER LAW
CONSTN POL/PAR LEGIS CIVMIL/REL GOV/REL...STAT 20.
PAGE 71 B1430
BIBLIOG NAT/G ADMIN CHOOSE

C66

SHERMAN H.,"IT ALL DEPENDS." USA+45 FINAN MARKET
PLAN PROB/SOLV EXEC PARTIC INGP/REL SUPEGO
...DECISION BIBLIOG 20. PAGE 96 B1944
LG/CO MGT ADMIN POLICY

C66

TACHERON D.G.,"THE JOB OF THE CONGRESSMAN: AN
INTRODUCTION TO SERVICES IN THE US HOUSE OF
REPRESENTATIVES." DELIB/GP EX/STRUC PRESS SENIOR
CT/SYS LOBBY CHOOSE GOV/REL...BIBLIOG 20 CONGRESS
HOUSE/REP SENATE. PAGE 102 B2068
LEGIS PARL/PROC ADMIN POL/PAR

N66

BACHELDER G.L.,THE LITERATURE OF FEDERALISM: A
SELECTED BIBLIOGRAPHY (REV ED) (A PAMPHLET). USA+45
USA-45 WOR+45 WOR-45 LAW CONSTN PROVS ADMIN CT/SYS
GOV/REL ROLE...CONCPT 19/20. PAGE 8 B0155
BIBLIOG FEDERAL NAT/G LOC/G

B67

ANDRIOT J.L.,GUIDE TO US GOVERNMENT SERIALS AND
PERIODICALS (VOL. IV). USA+45 COM/IND PRESS ADMIN.
PAGE 5 B0107
BIBLIOG NAT/G

B67

BUDER S.,PULLMAN: AN EXPERIMENT IN INDUSTRIAL ORDER
AND COMMUNITY PLANNING, 1880-1930. USA-45 SOCIETY
LABOR LG/CO CREATE PROB/SOLV CONTROL GP/REL
EFFICIENCY ATTIT...MGT BIBLIOG 19/20 PULLMAN.
PAGE 17 B0337
DIST/IND INDUS MUNIC PLAN

B67

CECIL L.,ALBERT BALLIN: BUSINESS AND POLITICS IN
IMPERIAL GERMANY 1888-1918. GERMANY UK INT/TRADE
LEAD WAR PERS/REL ADJUST PWR WEALTH...MGT BIBLIOG
19/20. PAGE 19 B0397
DIPLOM CONSTN ECO/DEV TOP/EX

B67

COHEN R.,COMPARATIVE POLITICAL SYSTEMS: STUDIES IN
THE POLITICS OF PRE-INDUSTRIAL SOCIETIES. WOR+45
WOR-45 CULTURE FAM KIN LOC/G NEIGH ADMIN LEAD
MARRIAGE...BIBLIOG 20. PAGE 22 B0447
ECO/UNDEV STRUCT SOCIETY GP/COMP

B67

DICKSON P.G.M.,THE FINANCIAL REVOLUTION IN ENGLAND.
UK NAT/G TEC/DEV ADMIN GOV/REL...SOC METH/CNCPT
CHARTS GP/COMP BIBLIOG 17/18. PAGE 29 B0587
ECO/DEV FINAN CAP/ISM MGT

B67

DOSSICK J.J.,DOCTORAL RESEARCH ON PUERTO RICO AND
PUERTO RICANS. PUERT/RICO USA+45 USA-45 ADMIN 20.
PAGE 30 B0609
BIBLIOG CONSTN POL/PAR DIPLOM

B67

EVANS R.H.,COEXISTENCE: COMMUNISM AND ITS PRACTICE
IN BOLOGNA, 1945-1965. ITALY CAP/ISM ADMIN CHOOSE
PEACE ORD/FREE...SOC STAT DEEP/INT SAMP CHARTS
BIBLIOG 20. PAGE 34 B0690
MARXISM CULTURE MUNIC POL/PAR

B67

FINCHER F.,THE GOVERNMENT OF THE UNITED STATES.
USA+45 USA-45 POL/PAR CHIEF CT/SYS LOBBY GP/REL
INGP/REL...CONCPT CHARTS BIBLIOG T 18/20 PRESIDENT
CONGRESS SUPREME/CT. PAGE 35 B0719
NAT/G EX/STRUC LEGIS OP/RES

B67

GIFFORD P.,BRITAIN AND GERMANY IN AFRICA. AFR
GERMANY UK ECO/UNDEV LEAD WAR NAT/LISM ATTIT
...POLICY HIST/WRIT METH/COMP ANTHOL BIBLIOG 19/20
WWI. PAGE 39 B0797
COLONIAL ADMIN DIPLOM NAT/COMP

B67

GREENE L.S.,AMERICAN GOVERNMENT POLICIES AND
FUNCTIONS. USA+45 LAW AGRI DIST/IND LABOR MUNIC
BUDGET DIPLOM EDU/PROP ORD/FREE...BIBLIOG T 20.
PAGE 43 B0867
POLICY NAT/G ADMIN DECISION

B67

JHANGIANI M.A.,JANA SANGH AND SWATANTRA: A PROFILE
OF THE RIGHTIST PARTIES IN INDIA. INDIA ADMIN
CHOOSE MARXISM SOCISM...INT CHARTS BIBLIOG 20.
PAGE 56 B1140
POL/PAR LAISSEZ NAT/LISM ATTIT

B67

KARDOUCHE G.K.,THE UAR IN DEVELOPMENT. UAR ECO/TAC
INT/TRADE BAL/PAY...STAT CHARTS BIBLIOG 20. PAGE 58
B1172
FINAN MGT CAP/ISM ECO/UNDEV

B67

KONCZACKI Z.A.,PUBLIC FINANCE AND ECONOMIC
DEVELOPMENT OF NATAL 1893-1910. TAX ADMIN COLONIAL
...STAT CHARTS BIBLIOG 19/20 NATAL. PAGE 61 B1228
ECO/TAC FINAN NAT/G ECO/UNDEV

B67

LENG S.C.,JUSTICE IN COMMUNIST CHINA: A SURVEY OF
THE JUDICIAL SYSTEM OF THE CHINESE PEOPLE'S
REPUBLIC. CHINA/COM LAW CONSTN LOC/G NAT/G PROF/ORG
CONSULT FORCES ADMIN CRIME ORD/FREE...BIBLIOG 20
MAO. PAGE 64 B1290
CT/SYS ADJUD JURID MARXISM

B67

NARVER J.C.,CONGLOMERATE MERGERS AND MARKET
COMPETITION. USA+45 LAW STRUCT ADMIN LEAD RISK COST
PROFIT WEALTH...POLICY CHARTS BIBLIOG. PAGE 77
B1555
DEMAND LG/CO MARKET MGT

B67

PLANO J.C.,FORGING WORLD ORDER: THE POLITICS OF
INTERNATIONAL ORGANIZATION. PROB/SOLV DIPLOM
CONTROL CENTRAL RATIONAL ORD/FREE...INT/LAW CHARTS
BIBLIOG 20 UN LEAGUE/NAT. PAGE 83 B1679
INT/ORG ADMIN JURID

B67

RALSTON D.B.,THE ARMY OF THE REPUBLIC; THE PLACE OF
THE MILITARY IN THE POLITICAL EVOLUTION OF FRANCE
1871-1914. FRANCE MOD/EUR EX/STRUC LEGIS TOP/EX
DIPLOM ADMIN WAR GP/REL ROLE...BIBLIOG 19/20.
PAGE 86 B1730
FORCES NAT/G CIVMIL/REL POLICY

B67

RAWLINSON J.L.,CHINA'S STRUGGLE FOR NAVAL
DEVELOPMENT 1839-1895. ASIA DIPLOM ADMIN WAR
...BIBLIOG DICTIONARY 19 CHINJAP. PAGE 86 B1745
SEA FORCES PWR

B67

ROFF W.R.,THE ORIGINS OF MALAY NATIONALISM.
MALAYSIA INTELL NAT/G ADMIN COLONIAL...BIBLIOG
DICTIONARY 20 CMN/WLTH. PAGE 90 B1813
NAT/LISM ELITES VOL/ASSN SOCIETY

B67

SALMOND J.A.,THE CIVILIAN CONSERVATION CORPS,
1933-1942. USA-45 NAT/G CREATE EXEC EFFICIENCY
WEALTH...BIBLIOG 20 ROOSEVLT/F. PAGE 92 B1864
ADMIN ECO/TAC TASK AGRI

B67

WEINBERG M.,SCHOOL INTEGRATION: A COMPREHENSIVE
CLASSIFIED BIBLIOGRAPHY OF 3,100 REFERENCES. USA+45
LAW NAT/G NEIGH SECT PLAN ROUTINE AGE/C WEALTH
SOC/INTEG INDIAN/AM. PAGE 115 B2314
BIBLIOG SCHOOL DISCRIM RACE/REL

B67

WESSON R.G.,THE IMPERIAL ORDER. WOR-45 STRUCT SECT
DOMIN ADMIN COLONIAL LEAD CONSERVE...CONCPT BIBLIOG
20. PAGE 115 B2324
PWR CHIEF CONTROL SOCIETY

B67

ZELERMYER W.,BUSINESS LAW: NEW PERSPECTIVES IN
BUSINESS ECONOMICS. USA+45 LAW INDUS DELIB/GP
...JURID MGT ANTHOL BIBLIOG 20 NLRB. PAGE 119 B2400
LABOR CAP/ISM LG/CO

B67

ZONDAG C.H.,THE BOLIVIAN ECONOMY 1952-65. L/A+17C
TEC/DEV FOR/AID ADMIN...OBS TREND CHARTS BIBLIOG 20
BOLIV. PAGE 119 B2406
ECO/UNDEV INDUS PRODUC

S67

DANELSKI D.J.,"CONFLICT AND ITS RESOLUTION IN THE
ROLE

SUPREME COURT." PROB/SOLV LEAD ROUTINE PERSON...PSY JURID
PERS/COMP BIBLIOG 20. PAGE 26 B0527   JUDGE
                                      INGP/REL
                                             B82

POOLE W.F.,INDEX TO PERIODICAL LITERATURE. LOC/G   BIBLIOG
NAT/G DIPLOM ADMIN...HUM PHIL/SCI SOC 19. PAGE 84   USA-45
B1690   ALL/VALS
                                                   SOCIETY

BIBLIOG/A....BIBLIOGRAPHY OVER 50 ITEMS ANNOTATED

                                                        N
AUSTRALIAN NATIONAL RES COUN,AUSTRALIAN SOCIAL   BIBLIOG/A
SCIENCE ABSTRACTS. NEW/ZEALND CULTURE SOCIETY LOC/G POLICY
CT/SYS PARL/PROC...HEAL JURID PSY SOC 20 AUSTRAL. NAT/G
PAGE 7 B0149   ADMIN

                                                        N
CONOVER H.F.,MADAGASCAR: A SELECTED LIST OF   BIBLIOG/A
REFERENCES. MADAGASCAR STRUCT ECO/UNDEV NAT/G ADMIN SOCIETY
...SOC 19/20. PAGE 23 B0463   CULTURE
                                                   COLONIAL

                                                        N
MONPIED E.,BIBLIOGRAPHIE FEDERALISTE: ARTICLES ET BIBLIOG/A
DOCUMENTS PUBLIES DANS LES PERIODIQUES PARUS EN   FEDERAL
FRANCE NOV. 1945-OCT. 1950. EUR+WWI WOR+45 ADMIN   CENTRAL
REGION ATTIT MARXISM PACIFISM 20 EEC. PAGE 74 B1501 INT/ORG
                                                        N
PRINCETON U INDUSTRIAL REL SEC,SELECTED REFERENCES BIBLIOG/A
OF THE INDUSTRIAL RELATIONS SECTION OF PRINCETON, INDUS
NEW JERSEY. LG/CO NAT/G LEGIS WORKER PLAN PROB/SOLV LABOR
PAY ADMIN ROUTINE TASK GP/REL...PSY 20. PAGE 84   MGT
B1708

SOVIET-EAST EUROPEAN RES SERV,SOVIET SOCIETY. USSR BIBLIOG/A
LABOR POL/PAR PRESS MARXISM...MARXIST 20. PAGE 99 EDU/PROP
B2001   ADMIN
                                                   SOC
                                                        N
VENKATESAN S.L.,BIBLIOGRAPHY ON PUBLIC ENTERPRISES BIBLIOG/A
IN INDIA. INDIA S/ASIA FINAN LG/CO LOC/G PLAN   ADMIN
BUDGET SOCISM...MGT 20. PAGE 112 B2258   ECO/UNDEV
                                                   INDUS
                                                        N
AMERICAN POLITICAL SCIENCE REVIEW. USA+45 USA-45   BIBLIOG/A
WOR+45 WOR-45 INT/ORG ADMIN...INT/LAW PHIL/SCI   DIPLOM
CONCPT METH 20 UN. PAGE 1 B0001   NAT/G
                                                   GOV/COMP
                                                        N
INTERNATIONAL REVIEW OF ADMINISTRATIVE SCIENCES.   BIBLIOG/A
WOR+45 WOR-45 STRATA ECO/DEV ECO/UNDEV CREATE PLAN ADMIN
PROB/SOLV DIPLOM CONTROL REPRESENT...MGT 20. PAGE 1 INT/ORG
B0004   NAT/G
                                                        N
JOURNAL OF POLITICS. USA+45 USA-45 CONSTN POL/PAR BIBLIOG/A
EX/STRUC LEGIS PROB/SOLV DIPLOM CT/SYS CHOOSE   NAT/G
RACE/REL 20. PAGE 1 B0005   LAW
                                                   LOC/G
                                                        N
REVIEW OF POLITICS. WOR+45 WOR-45 CONSTN LEGIS   BIBLIOG/A
PROB/SOLV ADMIN LEAD ALL/IDEOS...PHIL/SCI 20.   DIPLOM
PAGE 1 B0006   INT/ORG
                                                   NAT/G
                                                        N
THE AMERICAN CITY. INDUS PROF/ORG PLAN GOV/REL   BIBLIOG/A
...MGT 20. PAGE 1 B0007   ADMIN
                                                   TEC/DEV
                                                   MUNIC
                                                        N
WHITAKER'S CUMULATIVE BOOKLIST. UK ADMIN...HUM SOC BIBLIOG/A
20. PAGE 1 B0009   WRITING
                                                   CON/ANAL
                                                        N
CIVIL SERVICE JOURNAL. PARTIC INGP/REL PERS/REL   ADMIN
...MGT BIBLIOG/A 20. PAGE 1 B0011   NAT/G
                                                   SERV/IND
                                                   WORKER
                                                        N
HANDBOOK OF LATIN AMERICAN STUDIES. LAW CULTURE   BIBLIOG/A
ECO/UNDEV POL/PAR ADMIN LEAD...SOC 20. PAGE 1 B0014 L/A+17C
                                                   NAT/G
                                                   DIPLOM
                                                        N
JOURNAL OF PUBLIC ADMINISTRATION: JOURNAL OF THE   BIBLIOG/A
ROYAL INSTITUTE OF PUBLIC ADMINISTRATION. UK PLAN ADMIN
GP/REL INGP/REL 20. PAGE 1 B0015   NAT/G
                                                   MGT

LOCAL GOVERNMENT SERVICE....SOC'BIBLIOG/A 20.   LOC/G
PAGE 1 B0016   ADMIN
                                                   MUNIC
                                                   GOV/REL
                                                        N
THE MANAGEMENT REVIEW. FINAN EX/STRUC PROFIT   LABOR
BIBLIOG/A. PAGE 1 B0017   MGT
                                                   ADMIN
                                                   MARKET

                                                        N
MARKETING INFORMATION GUIDE. USA+45 ECO/DEV FINAN BIBLIOG/A
ADMIN GP/REL. PAGE 1 B0018   DIST/IND
                                                   MARKET
                                                   ECO/TAC
                                                        N
PUBLIC ADMINISTRATION ABSTRACTS AND INDEX OF   BIBLIOG/A
ARTICLES. WOR+45 PLAN PROB/SOLV...POLICY 20. PAGE 1 ADMIN
B0019   ECO/UNDEV
                                                   NAT/G
                                                        N
REVUE FRANCAISE DE SCIENCE POLITIQUE. FRANCE UK   NAT/G
...BIBLIOG/A 20. PAGE 1 B0022   DIPLOM
                                                   CONCPT
                                                   ROUTINE
                                                        N
SUMMARIES OF SELECTED JAPANESE MAGAZINES. LAW   BIBLIOG/A
CULTURE ADMIN LEAD 20 CHINJAP. PAGE 1 B0024   ATTIT
                                                   NAT/G
                                                   ASIA
                                                        N
ECONOMIC LIBRARY SELECTIONS. AGRI INDUS MARKET   BIBLIOG/A
ADMIN...STAT NAT/COMP 20. PAGE 2 B0026   WRITING
                                                   FINAN
                                                        N
NEUE POLITISCHE LITERATUR; BERICHTE UBER DAS   BIBLIOG/A
INTERNATIONALE SCHRIFTTUM ZUR POLITIK. WOR+45 LAW DIPLOM
CONSTN POL/PAR ADMIN LEAD GOV/REL...POLICY   NAT/G
IDEA/COMP. PAGE 2 B0027   NAT/COMP
                                                        N
PERSONNEL ADMINISTRATION: THE JOURNAL OF THE   WORKER
SOCIETY FOR PERSONNEL ADMINISTRATION. USA+45 INDUS MGT
LG/CO SML/CO...BIBLIOG/A 20. PAGE 2 B0028   ADMIN
                                                   EX/STRUC
                                                        N
PERSONNEL. USA+45 LAW LABOR LG/CO WORKER CREATE   BIBLIOG/A
GOV/REL PERS/REL ATTIT WEALTH. PAGE 2 B0030   ADMIN
                                                   MGT
                                                   GP/REL
                                                        N
BUSINESS LITERATURE. WOR+45 MARKET ADMIN MGT.   BIBLIOG/A
PAGE 2 B0031   INDUS
                                                   FINAN
                                                   POLICY
                                                        N
CATHERINE R.,LA REVUE ADMINISTRATIVE. FRANCE LAW   ADMIN
NAT/G LEGIS...JURID BIBLIOG/A 20. PAGE 19 B0393   MGT
                                                   FINAN
                                                   METH/COMP
                                                        N
KENTUCKY STATE ARCHIVES,CHECKLIST OF KENTUCKY STATE BIBLIOG/A
PUBLICATIONS AND STATE DIRECTORY. USA+45 LAW ACADEM PROVS
EX/STRUC LEGIS EDU/PROP LEAD...JURID 20. PAGE 59   PUB/INST
B1196   ADMIN
                                                        N
KYRIAK T.E.,EAST EUROPE: BIBLIOGRAPHY--INDEX TO US BIBLIOG/A
JPRS RESEARCH TRANSLATIONS. ALBANIA BULGARIA COM   PRESS
CZECHOSLVK HUNGARY POLAND ROMANIA AGRI EXTR/IND   MARXISM
FINAN SERV/IND INT/TRADE WEAPON...GEOG MGT SOC 20. INDUS
PAGE 62 B1247
                                                        N
PRINCETON UNIVERSITY,SELECTED REFERENCES: BIBLIOG/A
INDUSTRIAL RELATIONS SECTION. USA+45 EX/STRUC   LABOR
WORKER TEC/DEV...MGT 20. PAGE 85 B1712   INDUS
                                                   GP/REL
                                                        N
UNIVERSITY MICROFILMS INC,DISSERTATION ABSTRACTS: BIBLIOG/A
ABSTRACTS OF DISSERTATIONS AND MONOGRAPHS IN   ACADEM
MICROFILM. CANADA DIPLOM ADMIN...INDEX 20. PAGE 107 PRESS
B2166   WRITING
                                                        N
US SUPERINTENDENT OF DOCUMENTS,EDUCATION (PRICE   BIBLIOG/A
LIST 31). USA+45 LAW FINAN LOC/G NAT/G DEBATE ADMIN EDU/PROP
LEAD RACE/REL FEDERAL HEALTH POLICY. PAGE 111 B2238 ACADEM
                                                   SCHOOL
                                                        N
US SUPERINTENDENT OF DOCUMENTS,INTERSTATE COMMERCE BIBLIOG/A
(PRICE LIST 59). USA+45 LAW LOC/G NAT/G LEGIS   DIST/IND
TARIFFS TAX ADMIN CONTROL HEALTH DECISION. PAGE 111 GOV/REL
B2239   PROVS
                                                        N
US SUPERINTENDENT OF DOCUMENTS,LABOR (PRICE LIST   BIBLIOG/A
33). USA+45 LAW AGRI CONSTRUC INDUS NAT/G BARGAIN WORKER
PRICE ADMIN AUTOMAT PRODUC MGT. PAGE 111 B2240   LABOR
                                                   LEGIS
                                                        N
US SUPERINTENDENT OF DOCUMENTS,POLITICAL SCIENCE: BIBLIOG/A
GOVERNMENT, CRIME, DISTRICT OF COLUMBIA (PRICE LIST NAT/G
54). USA+45 LAW CONSTN EX/STRUC WORKER ADJUD ADMIN CRIME
CT/SYS CHOOSE INGP/REL RACE/REL CONGRESS PRESIDENT.
PAGE 111 B2241
                                                        N
US SUPERINTENDENT OF DOCUMENTS,TARIFF AND TAXATION BIBLIOG/A
(PRICE LIST 37). USA+45 LAW INT/TRADE ADJUD ADMIN TAX
CT/SYS INCOME OWN...DECISION GATT. PAGE 111 B2242 TARIFFS
                                                   NAT/G

US SUPERINTENDENT OF DOCUMENTS,TRANSPORTATION: BIBLIOG/A N
HIGHWAYS, ROADS, AND POSTAL SERVICE (PRICE LIST DIST/IND
25). PANAMA USA+45 LAW FORCES DIPLOM ADMIN GOV/REL SERV/IND
HEALTH MGT. PAGE 111 B2243 NAT/G

VIRGINIA STATE LIBRARY,CHECK-LIST OF VIRGINIA STATE BIBLIOG/A N
PUBLICATIONS. USA+45 USA-45 ECO/DEV POL/PAR LEGIS PROVS
ADJUD LEAD 18/20. PAGE 112 B2265 ADMIN
GOV/REL
B03

GRIFFIN A.P.C.,LIST OF BOOKS ON THE CABINETS OF BIBLIOG/A
ENGLAND AND AMERICA (PAMPHLET). MOD/EUR UK USA-45 GOV/COMP
CONSTN NAT/G CONSULT EX/STRUC 19/20. PAGE 43 B0875 ADMIN
DELIB/GP
B09

HARVARD UNIVERSITY LAW LIBRARY,CATALOGUE OF THE BIBLIOG/A
LIBRARY OF THE LAW SCHOOL OF HARVARD UNIVERSITY (3 LAW
VOLS.). UK USA-45 LEGIS JUDGE ADJUD CT/SYS...JURID ADMIN
CHARTS 14/20. PAGE 48 B0963
B15

SAWYER R.A.,A LIST OF WORKS ON COUNTY GOVERNMENT. BIBLIOG/A
LAW FINAN MUNIC TOP/EX ROUTINE CRIME...CLASSIF LOC/G
RECORD 19/20. PAGE 93 B1871 GOV/REL
ADMIN
C20

BLACHLY F.F.,"THE GOVERNMENT AND ADMINISTRATION OF NAT/G
GERMANY." GERMANY CONSTN LOC/G PROVS DELIB/GP GOV/REL
EX/STRUC FORCES LEGIS TOP/EX CT/SYS...BIBLIOG/A ADMIN
19/20. PAGE 12 B0246 PHIL/SCI
B31

BORCHARD E.H.,GUIDE TO THE LAW AND LEGAL LITERATURE BIBLIOG/A
OF FRANCE. FRANCE FINAN INDUS LABOR SECT LEGIS LAW
ADMIN COLONIAL CRIME OWN...INT/LAW 20. PAGE 14 CONSTN
B0277 METH
B33

GREER S.,A BIBLIOGRAPHY OF PUBLIC ADMINISTRATION. BIBLIOG/A
WOR-45 CONSTN LOC/G MUNIC EX/STRUC LEGIS...CONCPT ADMIN
20. PAGE 43 B0869 MGT
NAT/G
B34

DE CENIVAL P.,BIBLIOGRAPHIE MAROCAINE: 1923-1933. BIBLIOG/A
FRANCE MOROCCO SECT ADMIN LEAD GP/REL ATTIT...LING ISLAM
20. PAGE 27 B0551 NAT/G
COLONIAL
B34

US TARIFF COMMISSION,THE TARIFF; A BIBLIOGRAPHY: A BIBLIOG/A
SELECT LIST OF REFERENCES. USA-45 LAW DIPLOM TAX TARIFFS
ADMIN...POLICY TREATY 20. PAGE 111 B2246 ECO/TAC
B35

GREER S.,BIBLIOGRAPHY ON CIVIL SERVICE AND BIBLIOG/A
PERSONNEL ADMINISTRATION. USA-45 LOC/G PROVS WORKER ADMIN
PRICE SENIOR DRIVE...MGT 20. PAGE 43 B0870 NAT/G
ROUTINE
B36

GRAVES W.B.,AMERICAN STATE GOVERNMENT. CONSTN FINAN NAT/G
EX/STRUC FORCES LEGIS BUDGET TAX CT/SYS REPRESENT PROVS
GOV/REL...BIBLIOG/A 19/20. PAGE 42 B0855 ADMIN
FEDERAL
B37

GALLOWAY G.B.,AMERICAN PAMPHLET LITERATURE OF BIBLIOG/A
PUBLIC AFFAIRS (PAMPHLET). USA-45 ECO/DEV LABOR PLAN
ADMIN...MGT 20. PAGE 38 B0776 DIPLOM
NAT/G
B40

WILCOX J.K.,MANUAL ON THE USE OF STATE BIBLIOG/A
PUBLICATIONS. USA-45 FINAN LEGIS TAX GOV/REL PROVS
...CHARTS 20. PAGE 116 B2346 ADMIN
LAW
C40

FAHS C.B.,"GOVERNMENT IN JAPAN." FINAN FORCES LEGIS ASIA
TOP/EX BUDGET INT/TRADE EDU/PROP SOVEREIGN DIPLOM
...CON/ANAL BIBLIOG/A 20 CHINJAP. PAGE 34 B0698 NAT/G
ADMIN
N40

COUNTY GOVERNMENT IN THE UNITED STATES: A LIST OF BIBLIOG/A
RECENT REFERENCES (PAMPHLET). USA-45 LAW PUB/INST LOC/G
PLAN BUDGET CT/SYS CENTRAL 20. PAGE 49 B0988 ADMIN
MUNIC
B42

CHAMBERLIN W.,INDUSTRIAL RELATIONS IN GERMANY BIBLIOG/A
1914-1939. GERMANY 20. PAGE 20 B0401 LABOR
MGT
GP/REL
B42

NEUBURGER O.,OFFICIAL PUBLICATIONS OF PRESENT-DAY BIBLIOG/A
GERMANY: GOVERNMENT, CORPORATE ORGANIZATIONS, AND FASCISM
NATIONAL SOCIALIST PARTY. GERMANY CONSTN COM/IND NAT/G
POL/PAR EDU/PROP PRESS 20 NAZI. PAGE 78 B1570 ADMIN
B43

CLARKE M.P.,PARLIAMENTARY PRIVILEGE IN THE AMERICAN LEGIS
COLONIES. PROVS DOMIN ADMIN REPRESENT GOV/REL PWR
ORD/FREE...BIBLIOG/A 17/18. PAGE 21 B0433 COLONIAL
PARL/PROC
B44

DAHL D.,SICKNESS BENEFITS AND GROUP PURCHASE OF BIBLIOG/A

MEDICAL CARE FOR INDUSTRIAL EMPLOYEES. FAM LABOR INDUS
NAT/G PLAN...POLICY MGT SOC STAT 20. PAGE 25 B0519 WORKER
HEAL
B45

BAKER H.,PROBLEMS OF REEMPLOYMENT AND RETRAINING OF BIBLIOG/A
MANPOWER DURING THE TRANSITION FROM WAR TO PEACE. ADJUST
USA+45 INDUS LABOR LG/CO NAT/G PLAN ADMIN PEACE WAR
...POLICY MGT 20. PAGE 8 B0167 PROB/SOLV
B45

BENJAMIN H.C.,EMPLOYMENT TESTS IN INDUSTRY AND BIBLIOG/A
BUSINESS. LG/CO WORKER ROUTINE...MGT PSY SOC METH
CLASSIF PROBABIL STAT APT/TEST KNO/TEST PERS/TEST TESTS
20. PAGE 10 B0211 INDUS
B45

ROGERS W.C.,INTERNATIONAL ADMINISTRATION: A BIBLIOG/A
BIBLIOGRAPHY (PUBLICATION NO 92; A PAMPHLET). ADMIN
WOR-45 INT/ORG LOC/G NAT/G CENTRAL 20. PAGE 90 MGT
B1814 DIPLOM
B46

GRIFFIN G.G.,A GUIDE TO MANUSCRIPTS RELATING TO BIBLIOG/A
AMERICAN HISTORY IN BRITISH DEPOSITORIES. CANADA ALL/VALS
IRELAND MOD/EUR UK USA-45 LAW DIPLOM ADMIN COLONIAL NAT/G
WAR NAT/LISM SOVEREIGN...GEOG INT/LAW 15/19
CMN/WLTH. PAGE 43 B0876
B46

WILCOX J.K.,OFFICIAL DEFENSE PUBLICATIONS. BIBLIOG/A
1941-1945 (NINE VOLS.). USA-45 AGRI INDUS R+D LABOR WAR
FORCES TEC/DEV EFFICIENCY PRODUC SKILL WEALTH 20. CIVMIL/REL
PAGE 116 B2347 ADMIN
B47

CONOVER H.F.,NON-SELF-GOVERNING AREAS. BELGIUM BIBLIOG/A
FRANCE ITALY UK WOR+45 CULTURE ECO/UNDEV INT/ORG COLONIAL
LOC/G NAT/G ECO/TAC INT/TRADE ADMIN HEALTH...SOC DIPLOM
UN. PAGE 23 B0465
B47

DE NOIA J.,GUIDE TO OFFICIAL PUBLICATIONS OF THE BIBLIOG/A
OTHER AMERICAN REPUBLICS: EL SALVADOR. EL/SALVADR CONSTN
LAW LEGIS EDU/PROP CT/SYS 20. PAGE 27 B0558 NAT/G
ADMIN
B47

DE NOIA J.,GUIDE TO OFFICIAL PUBLICATIONS OF THE BIBLIOG/A
OTHER AMERICAN REPUBLICS: NICARAGUA (VOL. XIV). EDU/PROP
NICARAGUA LAW LEGIS ADMIN CT/SYS...JURID 19/20. NAT/G
PAGE 27 B0559 CONSTN
B47

DE NOIA J.,GUIDE TO OFFICIAL PUBLICATIONS OF THE BIBLIOG/A
OTHER AMERICAN REPUBLICS: PANAMA (VOL. XV). PANAMA CONSTN
LAW LEGIS EDU/PROP CT/SYS 20. PAGE 27 B0560 ADMIN
NAT/G
B48

DE NOIA J.,GUIDE TO OFFICIAL PUBLICATIONS OF OTHER BIBLIOG/A
AMERICAN REPUBLICS: PERU (VOL. XVII). PERU LAW CONSTN
LEGIS ADMIN CT/SYS...JURID 19/20. PAGE 28 B0561 NAT/G
EDU/PROP
B48

PUBLIC ADMINISTRATION SERVICE,SOURCE MATERIALS IN BIBLIOG/A
PUBLIC ADMINISTRATION: A SELECTED BIBLIOGRAPHY (PAS GOV/REL
PUBLICATION NO. 102). USA+45 LAW FINAN LOC/G MUNIC MGT
NAT/G PLAN RECEIVE EDU/PROP CT/SYS CHOOSE HEALTH ADMIN
20. PAGE 85 B1717
B48

US LIBRARY OF CONGRESS,BRAZIL: A GUIDE TO THE BIBLIOG/A
OFFICIAL PUBLICATIONS OF BRAZIL. BRAZIL L/A+17C NAT/G
CONSULT DELIB/GP LEGIS CT/SYS 19/20. PAGE 109 B2203 ADMIN
TOP/EX
B49

BOYD A.M.,UNITED STATES GOVERNMENT PUBLICATIONS BIBLIOG/A
(3RD ED.). USA+45 EX/STRUC LEGIS ADMIN...JURID PRESS
CHARTS 20. PAGE 14 B0291 NAT/G
EDU/PROP
B49

DE GRAZIA A.,HUMAN RELATIONS IN PUBLIC BIBLIOG/A
ADMINISTRATION. INDUS ACT/RES CREATE PLAN PROB/SOLV ADMIN
TEC/DEV INGP/REL PERS/REL DRIVE...POLICY SOC 20. PHIL/SCI
PAGE 27 B0552 OP/RES
B49

GRAVES W.B.,BASIC INFORMATION ON THE REORGANIZATION BIBLIOG/A
OF THE EXECUTIVE BRANCH: 1912-1948. USA-45 BUDGET EX/STRUC
ADMIN CONTROL GP/REL EFFICIENCY...MGT CHARTS NAT/G
ORG/CHARTS 20 PRESIDENT. PAGE 42 B0857 CHIEF
B50

BROWN E.S.,MANUAL OF GOVERNMENT PUBLICATIONS. BIBLIOG/A
WOR+45 WOR-45 CONSTN INT/ORG MUNIC PROVS DIPLOM NAT/G
ADMIN 20. PAGE 16 B0322 LAW
B50

MONPIED E.,BIBLIOGRAPHIE FEDERALISTE: OUVRAGES BIBLIOG/A
CHOISIS (VOL. I, MIMEOGRAPHED PAPER). EUR+WWI FEDERAL
DIPLOM ADMIN REGION ATTIT PACIFISM SOCISM...INT/LAW CENTRAL
19/20. PAGE 74 B1502 INT/ORG
B50

PERHAM M.,COLONIAL GOVERNMENT: ANNOTATED READING BIBLIOG/A
LIST ON BRITISH COLONIAL GOVERNMENT. UK WOR+45 COLONIAL
WOR-45 ECO/UNDEV INT/ORG LEGIS FOR/AID INT/TRADE GOV/REL
DOMIN ADMIN REV 20. PAGE 82 B1655 NAT/G
B50

WARD R.E.,A GUIDE TO JAPANESE REFERENCE AND BIBLIOG/A

RESEARCH MATERIALS IN THE FIELD OF POLITICAL
SCIENCE. LAW CONSTN LOC/G PRESS ADMIN...SOC
CON/ANAL METH 19/20 CHINJAP. PAGE 113 B2289
ASIA
NAT/G

C50

SIMON H.A.,"PUBLIC ADMINISTRATION." LG/CO SML/CO
PLAN DOMIN LEAD GP/REL DRIVE PERCEPT ALL/VALS
...POLICY BIBLIOG/A 20. PAGE 97 B1957
MGT
ADMIN
DECISION
EX/STRUC

B51

BERTON P.A.,MANCHURIA: AN ANNOTATED BIBLIOGRAPHY.
ASIA DIST/IND ADMIN...SOC 20. PAGE 11 B0231
BIBLIOG/A
MARXISM
ECO/UNDEV
COLONIAL

B51

US LIBRARY OF CONGRESS,EAST EUROPEAN ACCESSIONS
LIST (VOL. I). POL/PAR DIPLOM ADMIN LEAD 20.
PAGE 109 B2204
BIBLIOG/A
COM
SOCIETY
NAT/G

B52

JANSE R.S.,SOVIET TRANSPORTATION AND
COMMUNICATIONS: A BIBLIOGRAPHY. COM USSR PLAN
...DICTIONARY 20. PAGE 56 B1124
BIBLIOG/A
COM/IND
LEGIS
ADMIN

B53

CALDWELL L.K.,RESEARCH METHODS IN PUBLIC
ADMINISTRATION: AN OUTLINE OF TOPICS AND READINGS
(PAMPHLET). LAW ACT/RES COMPUTER KNOWL...SOC STAT
GEN/METH 20. PAGE 18 B0365
BIBLIOG/A
METH/COMP
ADMIN
OP/RES

B53

LARSEN K.,NATIONAL BIBLIOGRAPHIC SERVICES: THEIR
CREATION AND OPERATION. WOR+45 COM/IND CREATE PLAN
DIPLOM PRESS ADMIN ROUTINE...MGT UNESCO. PAGE 62
B1262
BIBLIOG/A
INT/ORG
WRITING

B53

SECKLER-HUDSON C.,BIBLIOGRAPHY ON PUBLIC
ADMINISTRATION (4TH ED.). USA+45 LAW POL/PAR
DELIB/GP BUDGET ADJUD LOBBY GOV/REL GP/REL ATTIT
...JURID 20. PAGE 95 B1923
BIBLIOG/A
ADMIN
NAT/G
MGT

C53

KRACKE E.A. JR.,"CIVIL SERVICE IN EARLY SUNG CHINA,
960-1067." ASIA GP/REL...BIBLIOG/A 10/11. PAGE 61
B1231
ADMIN
NAT/G
WORKER
CONTROL

B54

TOMPKINS D.C.,STATE GOVERNMENT AND ADMINISTRATION:
A BIBLIOGRAPHY. USA+45 USA-45 CONSTN LEGIS JUDGE
BUDGET CT/SYS LOBBY...CHARTS 20. PAGE 105 B2116
BIBLIOG/A
LOC/G
PROVS
ADMIN

B54

TOTOK W.,HANDBUCH DER BIBLIOGRAPHISCHEN
NACHSCHLAGEWERKE. GERMANY LAW CULTURE ADMIN...SOC
20. PAGE 105 B2121
BIBLIOG/A
NAT/G
DIPLOM
POLICY

B55

HOROWITZ M.,INCENTIVE WAGE SYSTEMS. INDUS LG/CO
WORKER CONTROL GP/REL...MGT PSY 20. PAGE 51 B1044
BIBLIOG/A
PAY
PLAN
TASK

B55

UN ECONOMIC AND SOCIAL COUNCIL,BIBLIOGRAPHY OF
PUBLICATIONS OF THE UN AND SPECIALIZED AGENCIES IN
THE SOCIAL WELFARE FIELD, 1946-1952. WOR+45 FAM
INT/ORG MUNIC ACT/RES PLAN PROB/SOLV EDU/PROP AGE/C
AGE/Y HABITAT...HEAL UN. PAGE 106 B2148
BIBLIOG/A
SOC/WK
ADMIN
WEALTH

B55

UN HEADQUARTERS LIBRARY,BIBLIOGRAPHIE DE LA CHARTE
DES NATIONS UNIES. CHINA/COM KOREA WOR+45 VOL/ASSN
CONFER ADMIN COERCE PEACE ATTIT ORD/FREE SOVEREIGN
...INT/LAW 20 UNESCO UN. PAGE 106 B2149
BIBLIOG/A
INT/ORG
DIPLOM

C55

GRASSMUCK G.L.,"A MANUAL OF LEBANESE
ADMINISTRATION." LEBANON PLAN...CHARTS BIBLIOG/A
20. PAGE 42 B0854
ADMIN
NAT/G
ISLAM
EX/STRUC

B56

CENTRAL AFRICAN ARCHIVES,A GUIDE TO THE PUBLIC
RECORDS OF SOUTHERN RHODESIA UNDER THE REGIME OF
THE BRITISH SOUTH AFRICA COMPANY, 1890-1923. UK
STRUCT NAT/G WRITING GP/REL 19/20. PAGE 19 B0398
BIBLIOG/A
COLONIAL
ADMIN
AFR

B56

INTERNATIONAL AFRICAN INST,SELECT ANNOTATED
BIBLIOGRAPHY OF TROPICAL AFRICA. NAT/G EDU/PROP
ADMIN HEALTH. PAGE 54 B1095
BIBLIOG/A
AFR
SOC
HABITAT

B56

IRIKURA J.K.,SOUTHEAST ASIA: SELECTED ANNOTATED
BIBLIOGRAPHY OF JAPANESE PUBLICATIONS. CULTURE
ADMIN RACE/REL 20 CHINJAP. PAGE 55 B1104
BIBLIOG/A
S/ASIA
DIPLOM

B56

WU E.,LEADERS OF TWENTIETH-CENTURY CHINA; AN
ANNOTATED BIBLIOGRAPHY OF SELECTED CHINESE
BIOGRAPHICAL WORKS IN HOOVER LIBRARY. ASIA INDUS
POL/PAR DIPLOM ADMIN REV WAR...HUM MGT 20. PAGE 118
B2386
BIBLIOG/A
BIOG
INTELL
CHIEF

C56

FALL B.B.,"THE VIET-MINH REGIME." VIETNAM LAW
NAT/G

ECO/UNDEV POL/PAR FORCES DOMIN WAR ATTIT MARXISM
...BIOG PREDICT BIBLIOG/A 20. PAGE 35 B0703
ADMIN
EX/STRUC
LEAD

C56

NEUMANN S.,"MODERN POLITICAL PARTIES: APPROACHES TO
COMPARATIVE POLITIC. FRANCE UK EX/STRUC DOMIN ADMIN
LEAD REPRESENT TOTALISM ATTIT...POLICY TREND
METH/COMP ANTHOL BIBLIOG/A 20 CMN/WLTH. PAGE 78
B1574
POL/PAR
GOV/COMP
ELITES
MAJORIT

B57

CENTRAL ASIAN RESEARCH CENTRE,BIBLIOGRAPHY OF
RECENT SOVIET SOURCE MATERIAL ON SOVIET CENTRAL
ASIA AND THE BORDERLANDS. AFGHANISTN INDIA PAKISTAN
UAR USSR ECO/UNDEV AGRI EXTR/IND INDUS ACADEM ADMIN
...HEAL HUM LING CON/ANAL 20. PAGE 19 B0399
BIBLIOG/A
COM
CULTURE
NAT/G

B57

CHANDRA S.,PARTIES AND POLITICS AT THE MUGHAL
COURT: 1707-1740. INDIA CULTURE EX/STRUC CREATE
PLAN PWR...BIBLIOG/A 18. PAGE 20 B0405
POL/PAR
ELITES
NAT/G

B57

SOUTH PACIFIC COMMISSION,INDEX OF SOCIAL SCIENCE
RESEARCH THESES ON THE SOUTH PACIFIC. S/ASIA ACADEM
ADMIN COLONIAL...SOC 20. PAGE 99 B2000
BIBLIOG/A
ACT/RES
SECT
CULTURE

B57

WEIDLUND J.,COMPARATIVE PUBLIC ADMINISTRATION.
EX/STRUC METH/COMP. PAGE 114 B2310
ADMIN
NAT/G
GOV/COMP
BIBLIOG/A

B58

CHEEK G.,ECONOMIC AND SOCIAL IMPLICATIONS OF
AUTOMATION: A BIBLIOGRAPHIC REVIEW (PAMPHLET).
USA+45 LG/CO WORKER CREATE PLAN CONTROL ROUTINE
PERS/REL EFFICIENCY PRODUC...METH/COMP 20. PAGE 20
B0416
BIBLIOG/A
SOCIETY
INDUS
AUTOMAT

B58

MASON J.B.,THAILAND BIBLIOGRAPHY. S/ASIA THAILAND
CULTURE EDU/PROP ADMIN...GEOG SOC LING 20. PAGE 70
B1423
BIBLIOG/A
ECO/UNDEV
DIPLOM
NAT/G

B58

OPERATIONS RESEARCH SOCIETY,A COMPREHENSIVE
BIBLIOGRAPHY ON OPERATIONS RESEARCH: THROUGH 1956
WITH SUPPLEMENT FOR 1957. COM/IND DIST/IND INDUS
ADMIN...DECISION MATH STAT METH 20. PAGE 80 B1612
BIBLIOG/A
COMPUT/IR
OP/RES
MGT

B58

SCOTT D.J.R.,RUSSIAN POLITICAL INSTITUTIONS. RUSSIA
USSR CONSTN AGRI DELIB/GP PLAN EDU/PROP CONTROL
CHOOSE EFFICIENCY ATTIT MARXISM...BIBLIOG/A 13/20.
PAGE 95 B1919
NAT/G
POL/PAR
ADMIN
DECISION

L58

EISENSTADT S.N.,"BUREAUCRACY AND
BUREAUCRATIZATION." WOR+45 ECO/DEV INDUS R+D PLAN
GOV/REL...WELF/ST TREND BIBLIOG/A 20. PAGE 32 B0659
ADMIN
OP/RES
MGT
PHIL/SCI

L58

JONAS F.H.,"BIBLIOGRAPHY ON WESTERN POLITICS."
USA+45 USA-45 ELITES MUNIC POL/PAR LEGIS ADJUD
ADMIN 20. PAGE 57 B1148
BIBLIOG/A
LOC/G
NAT/G
LAW

B59

COUNCIL OF STATE GOVERNMENTS,STATE GOVERNMENT: AN
ANNOTATED BIBLIOGRAPHY (PAMPHLET). USA+45 LAW AGRI
INDUS WORKER PLAN TAX ADJUST AGE/Y ORD/FREE...HEAL
MGT 20. PAGE 24 B0494
BIBLIOG/A
PROVS
LOC/G
ADMIN

B59

EPSTEIN F.T.,EAST GERMANY: A SELECTED BIBLIOGRAPHY
(PAMPHLET). COM GERMANY/E LAW AGRI FINAN INDUS
LABOR POL/PAR EDU/PROP ADMIN AGE/Y 20. PAGE 33
B0677
BIBLIOG/A
INTELL
MARXISM
NAT/G

B59

INTERAMERICAN CULTURAL COUN,LISTA DE LIBROS
REPRESENTAVOS DE AMERICA. CULTURE DIPLOM ADMIN 20.
PAGE 54 B1093
BIBLIOG/A
NAT/G
L/A+17C
SOC

B59

US CIVIL SERVICE COMMISSION,CONGRESSIONAL DOCUMENTS
RELATING TO CIVIL SERVICE. USA+45 USA-45 CONFER
19/20 CONGRESS. PAGE 108 B2177
BIBLIOG/A
ADMIN
NAT/G
LEGIS

B59

WASSERMAN P.,MEASUREMENT AND ANALYSIS OF
ORGANIZATIONAL PERFORMANCE. FINAN MARKET EX/STRUC
TEC/DEV EDU/PROP CONTROL ROUTINE TASK...MGT 20.
PAGE 114 B2300
BIBLIOG/A
ECO/TAC
OP/RES
EFFICIENCY

L59

"A BIBLIOGRAPHICAL ESSAY ON DECISION MAKING."
WOR+45 WOR-45 STRUCT OP/RES GP/REL...CONCPT
IDEA/COMP METH 20. PAGE 2 B0038
BIBLIOG/A
DECISION
ADMIN
LEAD

C59

DAHL R.A.,"SOCIAL SCIENCE RESEARCH ON BUSINESS:
PRODUCT AND POTENTIAL" INDUS MARKET OP/RES CAP/ISM
ADMIN LOBBY DRIVE...PSY CONCPT BIBLIOG/A 20.
PAGE 26 B0521
MGT
EFFICIENCY
PROB/SOLV
EX/STRUC

ANDRIOT J.L.,GUIDE TO POPULAR GOVERNMENT
PUBLICATIONS. USA+45 CONSTN ADMIN 20. PAGE 5 B0106
B60
BIBLIOG/A
PRESS
NAT/G

CRAUMER L.V.,BUSINESS PERIODICALS INDEX (8VOLS.).
USA+45 LABOR TAX 20. PAGE 25 B0503
B60
BIBLIOG/A
FINAN
ECO/DEV
MGT

LEWIS P.R.,LITERATURE OF THE SOCIAL SCIENCES: AN
INTRODUCTORY SURVEY AND GUIDE. UK LAW INDUS DIPLOM
INT/TRADE ADMIN...MGT 19/20. PAGE 65 B1306
B60
BIBLIOG/A
SOC

LEYDER J.,BIBLIOGRAPHIE DE L'ENSEIGNEMENT SUPERIEUR
ET DE LA RECHERCHE SCIENTIFIQUE EN AFRIQUE
INTERTROPICALE (2 VOLS.). AFR CULTURE ECO/UNDEV
AGRI PLAN EDU/PROP ADMIN COLONIAL...GEOG SOC/INTEG
20 NEGRO. PAGE 65 B1309
B60
BIBLIOG/A
ACT/RES
ACADEM
R+D

MEYRIAT J.,LA SCIENCE POLITIQUE EN FRANCE,
1945-1958; BIBLIOGRAPHIES FRANCAISES DE SCIENCES
SOCIALES (VOL. I). EUR+WWI FRANCE POL/PAR DIPLOM
ADMIN CHOOSE ATTIT...IDEA/COMP METH/COMP NAT/COMP
20. PAGE 73 B1478
B60
BIBLIOG/A
NAT/G
CONCPT
PHIL/SCI

US DEPARTMENT OF THE ARMY,SELECT BIBLIOGRAPHY ON
ADMINISTRATIVE ORGANIZATION(PAMPHLET). USA+45 INDUS
NAT/G EX/STRUC OP/RES CIVMIL/REL EFFICIENCY
ORD/FREE. PAGE 108 B2183
B60
BIBLIOG/A
ADMIN
CONCPT
FORCES

US LIBRARY OF CONGRESS,INDEX TO LATIN AMERICAN
LEGISLATION: 1950-1960 (2 VOLS.). NAT/G DELIB/GP
ADMIN PARL/PROC 20. PAGE 109 B2205
B60
BIBLIOG/A
LEGIS
L/A+17C
JURID

WORLEY P.,ASIA TODAY (REV. ED.) (PAMPHLET). COM
ECO/UNDEV AGRI FINAN INDUS POL/PAR FOR/AID ADMIN
MARXISM 20. PAGE 118 B2376
B60
BIBLIOG/A
ASIA
DIPLOM
NAT/G

ARMSTRONG J.A.,AN ESSAY ON SOURCES FOR THE STUDY OF
THE COMMUNIST PARTY OF THE SOVIET UNION, 1934-1960
(EXTERNAL RESEARCH PAPER 137). USSR EX/STRUC ADMIN
LEAD REV 20. PAGE 7 B0134
B61
BIBLIOG/A
COM
POL/PAR
MARXISM

BURDETTE F.L.,POLITICAL SCIENCE: A SELECTED
BIBLIOGRAPHY OF BOOKS IN PRINT, WITH ANNOTATIONS
(PAMPHLET). LAW LOC/G NAT/G POL/PAR PROVS DIPLOM
EDU/PROP ADMIN CHOOSE ATTIT 20. PAGE 17 B0347
B61
BIBLIOG/A
GOV/COMP
CONCPT
ROUTINE

COHN B.S.,DEVELOPMENT AND IMPACT OF BRITISH
ADMINISTRATION IN INDIA: A BIBLIOGRAPHIC ESSAY.
INDIA UK ECO/UNDEV NAT/G DOMIN...POLICY MGT SOC
19/20. PAGE 22 B0448
B61
BIBLIOG/A
COLONIAL
S/ASIA
ADMIN

LEE R.R.,ENGINEERING-ECONOMIC PLANNING
MISCELLANEOUS SUBJECTS: A SELECTED BIBLIOGRAPHY
(MIMEOGRAPHED). FINAN LOC/G MUNIC NEIGH ADMIN
CONTROL INGP/REL HABITAT...GEOG MGT SOC/WK 20
RESOURCE/N. PAGE 63 B1280
B61
BIBLIOG/A
PLAN
REGION

SCHMECKEBIER L.,GOVERNMENT PUBLICATIONS AND THEIR
USE. USA+45 LEGIS ACT/RES CT/SYS EXEC INGP/REL 20.
PAGE 94 B1894
B61
BIBLIOG/A
EDU/PROP
NAT/G
ADMIN

WARD R.E.,JAPANESE POLITICAL SCIENCE: A GUIDE TO
JAPANESE REFERENCE AND RESEARCH MATERIALS (2ND
ED.). LAW CONSTN STRATA NAT/G POL/PAR DELIB/GP
LEGIS ADMIN CHOOSE GP/REL...INT/LAW 19/20 CHINJAP.
PAGE 113 B2290
B61
BIBLIOG/A
PHIL/SCI

BRIMMER B.,A GUIDE TO THE USE OF UNITED NATIONS
DOCUMENTS. WOR+45 ECO/UNDEV AGRI EX/STRUC FORCES
PROB/SOLV ADMIN WAR PEACE WEALTH...POLICY UN.
PAGE 15 B0310
B62
BIBLIOG/A
INT/ORG
DIPLOM

CARSON P.,MATERIALS FOR WEST AFRICAN HISTORY IN THE
ARCHIVES OF BELGIUM AND HOLLAND. CLIENT INDUS
INT/TRADE ADMIN 17/19. PAGE 19 B0387
B62
BIBLIOG/A
COLONIAL
AFR
ECO/UNDEV

COSTA RICA UNIVERSIDAD BIBL,LISTA DE TESIS DE GRADO
DE LA UNIVERSIDAD DE COSTA RICA. COSTA/RICA LAW
LOC/G ADMIN LEAD...SOC 20. PAGE 24 B0487
B62
BIBLIOG/A
NAT/G
DIPLOM
ECO/UNDEV

TRUMAN D.B.,"THE GOVERNMENTAL PROCESS: POLITICAL
INTERESTS AND PUBLIC OPINION." POL/PAR ADJUD ADMIN
EXEC LEAD ROUTINE CHOOSE REPRESENT GOV/REL
RIGID/FLEX...POLICY BIBLIOG 20. PAGE 105 B2131
C62
LOBBY
EDU/PROP
GP/REL
LEGIS

COM INTERNAT DES MOUVEMENTS,REPERTOIRE
INTERNATIONAL DES SOURCES POUR L'ETUDE DES
MOUVEMENTS SOCIAUX AUX XIXE ET XXE SIECLES (VOL.
B63
BIBLIOG/A
MARXISM
POL/PAR

III). MOD/EUR ADMIN...SOC 19. PAGE 22 B0454
LABOR

GOURNAY B.,PUBLIC ADMINISTRATION. FRANCE LAW CONSTN
AGRI FINAN LABOR SCHOOL EX/STRUC CHOOSE...MGT
METH/COMP 20. PAGE 42 B0846
B63
BIBLIOG/A
ADMIN
NAT/G
LOC/G

KLEIN F.J.,JUDICIAL ADMINISTRATION AND THE LEGAL
PROFESSION. USA+45 ADMIN CONTROL EFFICIENCY
...POLICY 20. PAGE 60 B1217
B63
BIBLIOG/A
CT/SYS
ADJUD
JUDGE

KLESMENT J.,LEGAL SOURCES AND BIBLIOGRAPHY OF THE
BALTIC STATES (ESTONIA, LATVIA, LITHUANIA). COM
ESTONIA LATVIA LITHUANIA LAW FINAN ADJUD CT/SYS
REGION CENTRAL MARXISM 19/20. PAGE 60 B1218
B63
BIBLIOG/A
JURID
CONSTN
ADMIN

PALOTAI O.C.,PUBLICATIONS OF THE INSTITUTE OF
GOVERNMENT, 1930-1962. LAW PROVS SCHOOL WORKER
ACT/RES OP/RES CT/SYS GOV/REL...CRIMLGY SOC/WK.
PAGE 81 B1629
B63
BIBLIOG/A
ADMIN
LOC/G
FINAN

GREAT BRITAIN DEPT TECH COOP,PUBLIC ADMINISTRATION:
A SELECT BIBLIOGRAPHY (PAMPHLET). WOR+45 AGRI FINAN
INDUS EX/STRUC OP/RES ECO/TAC...MGT METH/COMP
NAT/COMP. PAGE 43 B0861
N63
BIBLIOG/A
ADMIN
NAT/G
LOC/G

ANDREN N.,GOVERNMENT AND POLITICS IN THE NORDIC
COUNTRIES: DENMARK, FINLAND, ICELAND, NORWAY,
SWEDEN. DENMARK FINLAND ICELAND NORWAY SWEDEN
POL/PAR CHIEF LEGIS ADMIN REGION REPRESENT ATTIT
CONSERVE...CHARTS BIBLIOG/A 20. PAGE 5 B0102
B64
CONSTN
NAT/G
CULTURE
GOV/COMP

FALK L.A.,ADMINISTRATIVE ASPECTS OF GROUP PRACTICE.
USA+45 FINAN PROF/ORG PLAN MGT. PAGE 35 B0702
B64
BIBLIOG/A
HEAL
ADMIN
SERV/IND

GESELLSCHAFT RECHTSVERGLEICH,BIBLIOGRAPHIE DES
DEUTSCHEN RECHTS (BIBLIOGRAPHY OF GERMAN LAW,
TRANS. BY COURTLAND PETERSON). GERMANY FINAN INDUS
LABOR SECT FORCES CT/SYS PARL/PROC CRIME...INT/LAW
SOC NAT/COMP 20. PAGE 39 B0794
B64
BIBLIOG/A
JURID
CONSTN
ADMIN

GJUPANOVIC H.,LEGAL SOURCES AND BIBLIOGRAPHY OF
YUGOSLAVIA. COM YUGOSLAVIA LAW LEGIS DIPLOM ADMIN
PARL/PROC REGION CRIME CENTRAL 20. PAGE 40 B0807
B64
BIBLIOG/A
JURID
CONSTN
ADJUD

GROSS B.M.,THE MANAGING OF ORGANIZATIONS (VOL. II).
FUT USA+45 ECO/DEV EDU/PROP EFFICIENCY...MGT
BIBLIOG/A 20. PAGE 44 B0887
B64
ECO/TAC
ADMIN
INDUS
POLICY

KNOX V.H.,PUBLIC FINANCE: INFORMATION SOURCES.
USA+45 DIPLOM ADMIN GOV/REL COST...POLICY 20.
PAGE 60 B1221
B64
BIBLIOG/A
FINAN
TAX
BUDGET

MAHAR J.M.,INDIA: A CRITICAL BIBLIOGRAPHY. INDIA
PAKISTAN CULTURE ECO/UNDEV LOC/G POL/PAR SECT
PROB/SOLV DIPLOM ADMIN COLONIAL PARL/PROC ATTIT 20.
PAGE 68 B1377
B64
BIBLIOG/A
S/ASIA
NAT/G
LEAD

NATIONAL BOOK LEAGUE,THE COMMONWEALTH IN BOOKS: AN
ANNOTATED LIST. CANADA UK LOC/G SECT ADMIN...SOC
BIOG 20 CMN/WLTH. PAGE 77 B1561
B64
BIBLIOG/A
JURID
NAT/G

RIKER W.H.,FEDERALISM. WOR+45 WOR-45 CONSTN CHIEF
LEGIS ADMIN COLONIAL CONTROL CT/SYS PWR...BIBLIOG/A
18/20. PAGE 88 B1787
B64
FEDERAL
NAT/G
ORD/FREE
CENTRAL

STOICOIU V.,LEGAL SOURCES AND BIBLIOGRAPHY OF
ROMANIA. COM ROMANIA LAW FINAN POL/PAR LEGIS JUDGE
ADJUD CT/SYS PARL/PROC MARXISM 20. PAGE 101 B2041
B64
BIBLIOG/A
JURID
CONSTN
ADMIN

SZLADITS C.,BIBLIOGRAPHY ON FOREIGN AND COMPARATIVE
LAW: BOOKS AND ARTICLES IN ENGLISH (SUPPLEMENT
1962). FINAN INDUS JUDGE LICENSE ADMIN CT/SYS
PARL/PROC OWN...INT/LAW CLASSIF METH/COMP NAT/COMP
20. PAGE 102 B2065
B64
BIBLIOG/A
JURID
ADJUD
LAW

WITHERELL J.W.,OFFICIAL PUBLICATIONS OF FRENCH
EQUATORIAL AFRICA, FRENCH CAMEROONS, AND TOGO,
1946-1958 (PAMPHLET). CAMEROON CHAD FRANCE GABON
TOGO LAW ECO/UNDEV EXTR/IND INT/TRADE...GEOG HEAL
20. PAGE 117 B2367
B64
BIBLIOG/A
AFR
NAT/G
ADMIN

HORECKY P.L.,"LIBRARY OF CONGRESS PUBLICATIONS IN
AID OF USSR AND EAST EUROPEAN RESEARCH." BULGARIA
CZECHOSLVK POLAND USSR YUGOSLAVIA NAT/G POL/PAR
DIPLOM ADMIN GOV/REL...CLASSIF 20. PAGE 51 B1042
S64
BIBLIOG/A
COM
MARXISM

LIPSET S.M.,"SOCIOLOGY AND POLITICAL SCIENCE: A
S64
BIBLIOG/A

BIBLIOGRAPHICAL NOTE." WOR+45 ELITES LEGIS ADJUD   SOC
ADMIN ATTIT IDEA/COMP. PAGE 65 B1321   METH/COMP
                                                              N64
US SENATE COMM GOVT OPERATIONS,METROPOLITAN   BIBLIOG/A
AMERICA: A SELECTED BIBLIOGRAPHY (PAMPHLET). USA+45   MUNIC
DIST/IND FINAN LOC/G EDU/PROP ADMIN HEALTH 20.   GOV/REL
PAGE 110 B2214   DECISION
                                                              B65
BOXER C.R.,PORTUGUESE SOCIETY IN THE TROPICS - THE   MUNIC
MUNICIPAL COUNCILS OF GAO, MACAO, BAHIA, AND   ADMIN
LUANDA, 1510-1800. EUR+WWI MOD/EUR PORTUGAL CONSTN   COLONIAL
EX/STRUC DOMIN CONTROL ROUTINE REPRESENT PRIVIL   DELIB/GP
...BIBLIOG/A 16/19 GENACCOUNT MACAO BAHIA LUANDA.
PAGE 14 B0290
                                                              B65
CUTLIP S.M.,A PUBLIC RELATIONS BIBLIOGRAPHY. INDUS   BIBLIOG/A
LABOR NAT/G PROF/ORG SCHOOL DIPLOM PRESS TV GOV/REL   MGT
GP/REL...PSY SOC/WK 20. PAGE 25 B0515   COM/IND
                                                         ADMIN
                                                              B65
GOPAL S.,BRITISH POLICY IN INDIA 1858-1905. INDIA   COLONIAL
UK ELITES CHIEF DELIB/GP ECO/TAC GP/REL DISCRIM   ADMIN
ATTIT...IDEA/COMP NAT/COMP PERS/COMP BIBLIOG/A   POL/PAR
19/20. PAGE 41 B0828   ECO/UNDEV
                                                              B65
INTERNATIONAL CITY MGRS ASSN,COUNCIL-MANAGER   BIBLIOG/A
GOVERNMENT, 1940-64: AN ANNOTATED BIBLIOGRAPHY.   MUNIC
USA+45 ADMIN GOV/REL ROLE...MGT 20. PAGE 54 B1097   CONSULT
                                                         PLAN
                                                              B65
UNIVERSAL REFERENCE SYSTEM,INTERNATIONAL AFFAIRS: BIBLIOG/A
VOLUME I IN THE POLITICAL SCIENCE, GOVERNMENT, AND   GEN/METH
PUBLIC POLICY SERIES...DECISION ECOMETRIC GEOG   COMPUT/IR
INT/LAW JURID MGT PHIL/SCI PSY SOC. PAGE 107 B2163   DIPLOM
                                                              L65
MATTHEWS D.G.,"A CURRENT BIBLIOGRAPHY ON ETHIOPIAN   BIBLIOG/A
AFFAIRS: A SELECT BIBLIOGRAPHY FROM 1950-1964."   ADMIN
ETHIOPIA LAW CULTURE ECO/UNDEV INDUS LABOR SECT   POL/PAR
FORCES DIPLOM CIVMIL/REL RACE/REL...LING STAT 20.   NAT/G
PAGE 71 B1428
                                                              B66
ALI S.,PLANNING, DEVELOPMENT AND CHANGE: AN   BIBLIOG/A
ANNOTATED BIBLIOGRAPHY ON DEVELOPMENTAL   ADMIN
ADMINISTRATION. PAKISTAN SOCIETY ORD/FREE 20.   ECO/UNDEV
PAGE 4 B0077   PLAN
                                                              B66
ANDERSON D.L.,MUNICIPAL PUBLIC RELATIONS (1ST ED.).   MUNIC
USA+45 SOCIETY CONSULT FORCES PRESS ADMIN...CHARTS   INGP/REL
BIBLIOG/A 20. PAGE 4 B0092   EDU/PROP
                                                         ATTIT
                                                              B66
GLAZER M.,THE FEDERAL GOVERNMENT AND THE   BIBLIOG/A
UNIVERSITY. CHILE PROB/SOLV DIPLOM GIVE ADMIN WAR   NAT/G
...POLICY SOC 20. PAGE 40 B0810   PLAN
                                                         ACADEM
                                                              B66
GROSS C.,A BIBLIOGRAPHY OF BRITISH MUNICIPAL   BIBLIOG/A
HISTORY (2ND ED.). UK LOC/G ADMIN 11/19. PAGE 44   MUNIC
B0888   CONSTN
                                                              B66
HANKE L.,HANDBOOK OF LATIN AMERICAN STUDIES.   BIBLIOG/A
ECO/UNDEV ADMIN LEAD...HUM SOC 20. PAGE 46 B0937   L/A+17C
                                                         INDEX
                                                         NAT/G
                                                              B66
LINDFORS G.V.,INTERCOLLEGIATE BIBLIOGRAPHY; CASES   BIBLIOG/A
IN BUSINESS ADMINISTRATION (VOL. X). FINAN MARKET   ADMIN
LABOR CONSULT PLAN GP/REL PRODUC 20. PAGE 65 B1314   MGT
                                                         OP/RES
                                                              B66
SZLADITS C.,A BIBLIOGRAPHY ON FOREIGN AND   BIBLIOG/A
COMPARATIVE LAW (SUPPLEMENT 1964). FINAN FAM LABOR   CT/SYS
LG/CO LEGIS JUDGE ADMIN CRIME...CRIMLGY 20.   INT/LAW
PAGE 102 B2066
                                                              B66
US DEPARTMENT OF THE ARMY,COMMUNIST CHINA: A   BIBLIOG/A
STRATEGIC SURVEY: A BIBLIOGRAPHY (PAMPHLET NO.   MARXISM
20-67). CHINA/COM COM INDIA USSR NAT/G POL/PAR   S/ASIA
EX/STRUC FORCES NUC/PWR REV ATTIT...POLICY GEOG   DIPLOM
CHARTS. PAGE 108 B2184
                                                              B66
WYLIE C.M.,RESEARCH IN PUBLIC HEALTH   BIBLIOG/A
ADMINISTRATION; SELECTED RECENT ABSTRACTS IV   R+D
(PAMPHLET). USA+45 MUNIC PUB/INST ACT/RES CREATE   HEAL
OP/RES TEC/DEV GP/REL ROLE...MGT PHIL/SCI STAT.   ADMIN
PAGE 118 B2387
                                                              L66
AMERICAN ECONOMIC REVIEW,"SIXTY-THIRD LIST OF   BIBLIOG/A
DOCTORAL DISSERTATIONS IN POLITICAL ECONOMY IN   CONCPT
AMERICAN UNIVERSITIES AND COLLEGES." ECO/DEV AGRI   ACADEM
FINAN LABOR WORKER PLAN BUDGET INT/TRADE ADMIN
DEMAND...MGT STAT 20. PAGE 4 B0084
                                                              S66
AFRICAN BIBLIOGRAPHIC CENTER,"A CURRENT VIEW OF   BIBLIOG/A
AFRICANA: A SELECT AND ANNOTATED BIBLIOGRAPHICAL   NAT/G
PUBLISHING GUIDE, 1965-1966." AFR CULTURE INDUS   TEC/DEV

LABOR SECT FOR/AID ADMIN COLONIAL REV RACE/REL   POL/PAR
SOCISM...LING 20. PAGE 3 B0063
                                                              S66
POLSBY N.W.,"BOOKS IN THE FIELD: POLITICAL   BIBLIOG/A
SCIENCE." LAW CONSTN LOC/G NAT/G LEGIS ADJUD PWR 20   ATTIT
SUPREME/CT. PAGE 83 B1686   ADMIN
                                                       JURID
                                                              N66
PRINCETON U INDUSTRIAL REL SEC,OUTSTANDING BOOKS ON   BIBLIOG/A
INDUSTRIAL RELATIONS, 1965 (PAMPHLET NO. 128).   INDUS
WOR+45 LABOR BARGAIN GOV/REL RACE/REL HEALTH PWR   GP/REL
...MGT 20. PAGE 85 B1709   POLICY
                                                              N66
PRINCETON U INDUSTRIAL REL SEC,RECENT MATERIAL ON   BIBLIOG/A
COLLECTIVE BARGAINING IN GOVERNMENT (PAMPHLET NO.   BARGAIN
130). USA+45 ECO/DEV LABOR WORKER ECO/TAC GOV/REL   NAT/G
...MGT 20. PAGE 85 B1710   GP/REL
                                                              B67
BUREAU GOVERNMENT RES AND SERV,COUNTY GOVERNMENT   BIBLIOG/A
REORGANIZATION - A SELECTED ANNOTATED BIBLIOGRAPHY   APPORT
(PAPER). USA+45 USA-45 LAW CONSTN MUNIC PROVS   LOC/G
EX/STRUC CREATE PLAN PROB/SOLV REPRESENT GOV/REL   ADMIN
20. PAGE 17 B0349
                                                              B67
SABLE M.H.,A GUIDE TO LATIN AMERICAN STUDIES (2   BIBLIOG/A
VOLS). CONSTN FINAN INT/ORG LABOR MUNIC POL/PAR   L/A+17C
FORCES CAP/ISM FOR/AID ADMIN MARXISM SOCISM OAS.   DIPLOM
PAGE 92 B1861   NAT/LISM
                                                              B67
SCHUMACHER B.G.,COMPUTER DYNAMICS IN PUBLIC   COMPUTER
ADMINISTRATION. USA+45 CREATE PLAN TEC/DEV...MGT   COMPUT/IR
LING CON/ANAL BIBLIOG/A 20. PAGE 94 B1907   ADMIN
                                                       AUTOMAT
                                                              B67
UNITED NATIONS,UNITED NATIONS PUBLICATIONS: BIBLIOG/A
1945-1966. WOR+45 COM/IND DIST/IND FINAN TEC/DEV   INT/ORG
ADMIN...POLICY INT/LAW MGT CHARTS 20. UN UNESCO.   DIPLOM
PAGE 107 B2162   WRITING
                                                              B67
UNIVERSAL REFERENCE SYSTEM,ADMINISTRATIVE   BIBLIOG/A
MANAGEMENT: PUBLIC AND PRIVATE BUREAUCRACY (VOLUME   MGT
IV). WOR+45 WOR-45 ECO/DEV LG/CO LOC/G PUB/INST   ADMIN
VOL/ASSN GOV/REL...COMPUT/IR GEN/METH. PAGE 107   NAT/G
B2164
                                                              B67
UNIVERSAL REFERENCE SYSTEM,PUBLIC POLICY AND THE   BIBLIOG/A
MANAGEMENT OF SCIENCE (VOLUME IX). FUT SPACE WOR+45   POLICY
LAW NAT/G TEC/DEV CONTROL NUC/PWR GOV/REL   MGT
...COMPUT/IR GEN/METH. PAGE 107 B2165   PHIL/SCI
                                                              B67
US DEPARTMENT OF THE ARMY,CIVILIAN IN PEACE,   BIBLIOG/A
SOLDIER IN WAR: A BIBLIOGRAPHIC SURVEY OF THE ARMY   FORCES
AND AIR NATIONAL GUARD (PAMPHLET NOS. 130-2).   ROLE
USA+45 USA-45 LOC/G NAT/G PROVS LEGIS PLAN ADMIN   DIPLOM
ATTIT ORD/FREE...POLICY 19/20. PAGE 108 B2185
                                                              B67
VOOS H.,ORGANIZATIONAL COMMUNICATION: A   BIBLIOG/A
BIBLIOGRAPHY. WOR+45 STRATA R+D PROB/SOLV FEEDBACK   INDUS
COERCE...MGT PSY NET/THEORY HYPO/EXP. PAGE 112   COM/IND
B2268   VOL/ASSN
                                                              S67
ROTBERG R.I.,"COLONIALISM AND AFTER: THE POLITICAL   BIBLIOG/A
LITERATURE OF CENTRAL AFRICA - A BIBLIOGRAPHIC   COLONIAL
ESSAY." AFR CHIEF EX/STRUC REV INGP/REL RACE/REL   DIPLOM
SOVEREIGN 20. PAGE 91 B1833   NAT/G
                                                              N67
US SUPERINTENDENT OF DOCUMENTS,SPACE: MISSILES, THE   BIBLIOG/A
MOON, NASA, AND SATELLITES (PRICE LIST 79A). USA+45   SPACE
COM/IND R+D NAT/G DIPLOM EDU/PROP ADMIN CONTROL   TEC/DEV
HEALTH...POLICY SIMUL NASA CONGRESS. PAGE 111 B2244   PEACE
                                                              N67
PRINCETON U INDUSTRIAL REL SEC,OUTSTANDING BOOKS ON   BIBLIOG/A
INDUSTRIAL RELATIONS, 1966 (PAMPHLET NO. 134).   INDUS
WOR+45 LABOR WORKER PLAN PRICE CONTROL INCOME...MGT   GP/REL
20. PAGE 85 B1711   POLICY

BICAMERALISM....SEE LEGIS, CONGRESS, HOUSE/REP, SENATE

BIENSTOCK G. B0236

BIESANZ J. B0237

BIGLER/W....WILLIAM BIGLER

BILL/RIGHT....BILL OF RIGHTS
                                                              B59
LOEWENSTEIN K.,VERFASSUNGSRECHT UND   CONSTN
VERFASSUNGSPRAXIS DER VEREINIGTEN STAATEN. USA+45   POL/PAR
USA-45 COLONIAL CT/SYS GP/REL RACE/REL ORD/FREE   EX/STRUC
...JURID 18/20 SUPREME/CT CONGRESS PRESIDENT   NAT/G
BILL/RIGHT CIVIL/LIB. PAGE 66 B1337

BINANI G.D. B0238

BINDER L. B0239

BINGHAM A.M. B0240

BINNS/JJ....JOSEPH J. BINNS

BIO/SOC....BIO-SOCIAL PROCESSES, DRUGS, SEXUALITY

B30
MURCHISON C.,PSYCHOLOGIES OF 1930. UNIV USA-45 CREATE
CULTURE INTELL SOCIETY STRATA FAM ROUTINE BIO/SOC PERSON
DRIVE RIGID/FLEX SUPEGO...NEW/IDEA OBS SELF/OBS
CONT/OBS 20. PAGE 76 B1543

B54
MATTHEWS D.R.,THE SOCIAL BACKGROUND OF POLITICAL DECISION
DECISION-MAKERS. CULTURE SOCIETY STRATA FAM BIOG
EX/STRUC LEAD ATTIT BIO/SOC DRIVE PERSON ALL/VALS SOC
HIST/WRIT. PAGE 71 B1431

S60
BOYER W.W.,"POLICY MAKING BY GOVERNMENT AGENCIES." NAT/G
USA+45 WOR+45 R+D DELIB/GP TOP/EX EDU/PROP ROUTINE DIPLOM
ATTIT BIO/SOC DRIVE...CONCPT TREND TOT/POP 20.
PAGE 14 B0293

S60
REISELBACH L.N.,"THE BASIS OF ISOLATIONIST ATTIT
BEHAVIOR." USA+45 USA-45 CULTURE ECO/DEV LOC/G DIPLOM
NAT/G ADMIN ROUTINE CHOOSE BIO/SOC DRIVE RIGID/FLEX ECO/TAC
...CENSUS SAMP TREND CHARTS TOT/POP 20. PAGE 87
B1765

B61
CONFREY E.A.,ADMINISTRATION OF COMMUNITY HEALTH HEAL
SERVICES. USA+45 R+D PUB/INST DELIB/GP PLAN BUDGET ADMIN
ROUTINE AGE/C HEALTH...MGT SOC/WK METH/COMP 20. MUNIC
PAGE 23 B0461 BIO/SOC

S63
ARASTEH R.,"THE ROLE OF INTELLECTUALS IN INTELL
ADMINISTRATIVE DEVELOPMENT AND SOCIAL CHANGE IN ADMIN
MODERN IRAN." ISLAM CULTURE NAT/G CONSULT ACT/RES IRAN
EDU/PROP EXEC ATTIT BIO/SOC PERCEPT SUPEGO ALL/VALS
...POLICY MGT PSY SOC CONCPT 20. PAGE 6 B0123

B64
RECENT PUBLICATIONS ON GOVERNMENTAL PROBLEMS. FINAN BIBLIOG
INDUS ACADEM PLAN PROB/SOLV EDU/PROP ADJUD ADMIN AUTOMAT
BIO/SOC...MGT SOC. PAGE 2 B0040 LEGIS
JURID

B67
MINTZ M.,BY PRESCRIPTION ONLY. USA+45 NAT/G BIO/SOC
EX/STRUC PLAN TEC/DEV EXEC EFFICIENCY HEALTH...MGT PROC/MFG
SOC/WK 20. PAGE 74 B1491 CONTROL
POLICY

BIOG....BIOGRAPHY (INCLUDES PSYCHOANALYSIS)

B20
HALDANE R.B.,BEFORE THE WAR. MOD/EUR SOCIETY POLICY
INT/ORG NAT/G DELIB/GP PLAN DOMIN EDU/PROP LEGIT DIPLOM
ADMIN COERCE ATTIT DRIVE MORAL ORD/FREE PWR...SOC UK
CONCPT SELF/OBS RECORD BIOG TIME/SEQ. PAGE 45 B0921

B30
ZINK H.,CITY BOSSES IN THE UNITED STATES: A STUDY LOC/G
OF TWENTY MUNICIPAL BOSSES. USA-45 INDUS MUNIC DOMIN
NEIGH POL/PAR ADMIN CRIME INGP/REL PERS/REL PWR BIOG
...PERS/COMP 20 BOSSISM. PAGE 119 B2403 LEAD

B37
PARSONS T.,THE STRUCTURE OF SOCIAL ACTION. UNIV CULTURE
INTELL SOCIETY INDUS MARKET ECO/TAC ROUTINE CHOOSE ATTIT
ALL/VALS...CONCPT OBS BIOG TREND GEN/LAWS 20. CAP/ISM
PAGE 81 B1636

S37
LASSWELL H.D.,"GOVERNMENTAL AND PARTY LEADERS IN ELITES
FASCIST ITALY." ITALY CRIME SKILL...BIOG CHARTS FASCISM
GP/COMP 20. PAGE 63 B1266 ADMIN

B38
SALTER J.T.,THE AMERICAN POLITICIAN. USA-45 LABOR BIOG
POL/PAR EDU/PROP ADMIN CHOOSE ATTIT DRIVE PERSON LEAD
PWR...POLICY ANTHOL 20 THOMAS/N LEWIS/JL LAGUARD/F PROVS
GOVERNOR MAYOR. PAGE 92 B1865 LOC/G

B39
HITLER A.,MEIN KAMPF. EUR+WWI FUT MOD/EUR STRUCT PWR
INT/ORG LABOR NAT/G POL/PAR FORCES CREATE PLAN NEW/IDEA
BAL/PWR DIPLOM ECO/TAC DOMIN EDU/PROP ADMIN COERCE WAR
ATTIT...SOCIALIST BIOG TREND NAZI. PAGE 50 B1020

B39
MACMAHON A.W.,FEDERAL ADMINISTRATORS: A BIOG
BIOGRAPHICAL APPROACH TO THE PROBLEM OF ADMIN
DEPARTMENTAL MANAGEMENT. USA-45 DELIB/GP EX/STRUC NAT/G
WORKER LEAD...TIME/SEQ 19/20. PAGE 68 B1366 MGT

B47
FLYNN E.J.,YOU'RE THE BOSS. USA-45 ELITES TOP/EX LOC/G
DOMIN CONTROL EXEC LEAD REPRESENT 19/20 NEWYORK/C MUNIC
ROOSEVLT/F FLYNN/BOSS BOSSISM. PAGE 36 B0732 BIOG
POL/PAR

B48
HULL C.,THE MEMOIRS OF CORDELL HULL (VOLUME ONE). BIOG
USA-45 WOR-45 CONSTN FAM LOC/G NAT/G PROVS DELIB/GP DIPLOM
FORCES LEGIS TOP/EX BAL/PWR LEGIT ADMIN EXEC WAR
ATTIT ORD/FREE PWR...MAJORIT SELF/OBS TIME/SEQ
TREND NAZI 20. PAGE 52 B1062

B48
SHERWOOD R.E.,ROOSEVELT AND HOPKINS. UK USA+45 USSR TOP/EX
NAT/G EX/STRUC FORCES ADMIN ROUTINE PERSON PWR BIOG
...TIME/SEQ 20 ROOSEVLT/F HOPKINS/H. PAGE 96 B1946 DIPLOM
WAR

B48
WHITE L.D.,THE FEDERALISTS: A STUDY IN ADMIN
ADMINISTRATIVE HISTORY. STRUCT DELIB/GP LEGIS NAT/G
BUDGET ROUTINE GOV/REL GP/REL PERS/REL PWR...BIOG POLICY
18/19 PRESIDENT CONGRESS WASHINGT/G JEFFERSN/T PROB/SOLV
HAMILTON/A. PAGE 116 B2337

B50
MONTGOMERY H.,CRACKER PARTIES. CULTURE EX/STRUC POL/PAR
LEAD PWR POPULISM...TIME/SEQ 19 GEORGIA CALHOUN/JC PROVS
COBB/HOWLL JACKSON/A. PAGE 74 B1505 ELITES
BIOG

B51
LASSWELL H.D.,THE POLITICAL WRITINGS OF HAROLD D PERSON
LASSWELL. UNIV DOMIN EXEC LEAD RATIONAL ATTIT DRIVE PSY
ROLE ALL/VALS...OBS BIOG 20. PAGE 63 B1269 INGP/REL
CONCPT

B51
WHITE L.D.,THE JEFFERSONIANS: A STUDY IN ADMIN
ADMINISTRATIVE HISTORY 18011829. USA-45 DELIB/GP NAT/G
LEGIS TOP/EX PROB/SOLV BUDGET ECO/TAC GP/REL POLICY
FEDERAL...BIOG IDEA/COMP 19 PRESIDENT CONGRESS POL/PAR
JEFFERSN/T. PAGE 116 B2338

S51
SCHRAMM W.,"COMMUNICATION IN THE SOVIETIZED STATE, ATTIT
AS DEMONSTRATED IN KOREA." ASIA COM KOREA COM/IND EDU/PROP
FACE/GP POL/PAR SCHOOL FORCES ADMIN PWR MARXISM TOTALISM
...SOC CONCPT MYTH INT BIOG TOT/POP 20. PAGE 94
B1901

B52
HIMMELFARB G.,LORD ACTON: A STUDY IN CONSCIENCE AND PWR
POLITICS. MOD/EUR NAT/G POL/PAR SECT LEGIS TOP/EX BIOG
EDU/PROP ADMIN NAT/LISM ATTIT PERSON SUPEGO MORAL
ORD/FREE...CONCPT PARLIAMENT 19 ACTON/LORD. PAGE 50
B1014

B54
COMBS C.H.,DECISION PROCESSES. INTELL SOCIETY MATH
DELIB/GP CREATE TEC/DEV DOMIN LEGIT EXEC CHOOSE DECISION
DRIVE RIGID/FLEX KNOWL PWR...PHIL/SCI SOC
METH/CNCPT CONT/OBS REC/INT PERS/TEST SAMP/SIZ BIOG
SOC/EXP WORK. PAGE 22 B0455

B54
MATTHEWS D.R.,THE SOCIAL BACKGROUND OF POLITICAL DECISION
DECISION-MAKERS. CULTURE SOCIETY STRATA FAM BIOG
EX/STRUC LEAD ATTIT BIO/SOC DRIVE PERSON ALL/VALS SOC
HIST/WRIT. PAGE 71 B1431

B55
POOL I.,SATELLITE GENERALS: A STUDY OF MILITARY FORCES
ELITES IN THE SOVIET SPHERE. ASIA CHINA/COM COM CHOOSE
CZECHOSLVK FUT HUNGARY POLAND ROMANIA USSR ELITES
STRATA ADMIN ATTIT PWR SKILL...METH/CNCPT BIOG 20.
PAGE 84 B1688

B56
MANNONI D.O.,PROSPERO AND CALIBAN: THE PSYCHOLOGY CULTURE
OF COLONIZATION. AFR EUR+WWI FAM KIN MUNIC SECT COLONIAL
DOMIN ADMIN ATTIT DRIVE LOVE PWR RESPECT...PSY SOC
CONCPT MYTH OBS DEEP/INT BIOG GEN/METH MALAGASY 20.
PAGE 69 B1394

B56
WILSON P.,GOVERNMENT AND POLITICS OF INDIA AND BIBLIOG
PAKISTAN: 1885-1955; A BIBLIOGRAPHY OF WORKS IN COLONIAL
WESTERN LANGUAGES. INDIA PAKISTAN CONSTN LOC/G NAT/G
POL/PAR FORCES DIPLOM ADMIN WAR CHOOSE...BIOG S/ASIA
CON/ANAL 19/20. PAGE 117 B2361

B56
WU E.,LEADERS OF TWENTIETH-CENTURY CHINA; AN BIBLIOG/A
ANNOTATED BIBLIOGRAPHY OF SELECTED CHINESE BIOG
BIOGRAPHICAL WORKS IN HOOVER LIBRARY. ASIA INDUS INTELL
POL/PAR DIPLOM ADMIN REV WAR...HUM MGT 20. PAGE 118 CHIEF
B2386

L56
MACMAHON A.W.,"WOODROW WILSON AS LEGISLATIVE LEADER LEGIS
AND ADMINISTRATOR." CONSTN POL/PAR ADMIN...POLICY CHIEF
HIST/WRIT WILSON/W PRESIDENT. PAGE 68 B1371 LEAD
BIOG

C56
FALL B.B.,"THE VIET-MINH REGIME." VIETNAM LAW NAT/G
ECO/UNDEV POL/PAR FORCES DOMIN WAR ATTIT MARXISM ADMIN
...BIOG PREDICT BIBLIOG/A 20. PAGE 35 B0703 EX/STRUC
LEAD

B57
BEAL J.R.,JOHN FOSTER DULLES, A BIOGRAPHY. USA+45 BIOG
USSR WOR+45 CONSTN INT/ORG NAT/G EX/STRUC LEGIT DIPLOM
ADMIN NUC/PWR DISPL PERSON ORD/FREE PWR SKILL
...POLICY PSY OBS RECORD COLD/WAR UN 20 DULLES/JF.
PAGE 10 B0200

B58
SKINNER G.W.,LEADERSHIP AND POWER IN THE CHINESE SOC
COMMUNITY OF THAILAND. ASIA S/ASIA STRATA FACE/GP ELITES
KIN PROF/ORG VOL/ASSN EX/STRUC DOMIN PERSON RESPECT THAILAND
...METH/CNCPT STAT INT QU BIOG CHARTS 20. PAGE 98
B1974

B59

PARK R.L.,LEADERSHIP AND POLITICAL INSTITUTIONS IN   NAT/G
INDIA. S/ASIA CULTURE ECO/UNDEV LOC/G MUNIC PROVS   EXEC
LEGIS PLAN ADMIN LEAD ORD/FREE WEALTH...GEOG SOC   INDIA
BIOG TOT/POP VAL/FREE 20. PAGE 81 B1633

B60

MORISON E.E.,TURMOIL AND TRADITION: A STUDY OF THE   BIOG
LIFE AND TIMES OF HENRY L. STIMSON. USA+45 USA-45   NAT/G
POL/PAR CHIEF DELIB/GP FORCES BAL/PWR DIPLOM   EX/STRUC
ARMS/CONT WAR PEACE 19/20 STIMSON/HL ROOSEVLT/F
TAFT/WH HOOVER/H REPUBLICAN. PAGE 75 B1525

B61

BARNES W.,THE FOREIGN SERVICE OF THE UNITED STATES.   NAT/G
USA+45 USA-45 CONSTN INT/ORG POL/PAR CONSULT   MGT
DELIB/GP LEGIS DOMIN EDU/PROP EXEC ATTIT RIGID/FLEX   DIPLOM
ORD/FREE PWR...POLICY CONCPT STAT OBS RECORD BIOG
TIME/SEQ TREND. PAGE 9 B0188

B61

MARKMANN C.L.,JOHN F. KENNEDY: A SENSE OF PURPOSE.   CHIEF
USA+45 INTELL FAM CONSULT DELIB/GP LEGIS PERSON   TOP/EX
SKILL 20 KENNEDY/JF EISNHWR/DD ROOSEVLT/F   ADMIN
NEW/FRONTR PRESIDENT. PAGE 69 B1399   BIOG

B61

MARVICK D.,POLITICAL DECISION-MAKERS. INTELL STRATA   TOP/EX
NAT/G POL/PAR EX/STRUC LEGIS DOMIN EDU/PROP ATTIT   BIOG
PERSON PWR...PSY STAT OBS CONT/OBS STAND/INT   ELITES
UNPLAN/INT TIME/SEQ CHARTS STERTYP VAL/FREE.
PAGE 70 B1416

B61

OPOTOWSKY S.,THE KENNEDY GOVERNMENT. NAT/G CONSULT   ADMIN
EX/STRUC LEAD PERSON...POLICY 20 KENNEDY/JF   BIOG
CONGRESS CABINET. PAGE 80 B1613   ELITES
                                                       TOP/EX

B61

TANZER L.,THE KENNEDY CIRCLE. INTELL CONSULT   EX/STRUC
DELIB/GP TOP/EX CONTROL EXEC INGP/REL PERS/REL PWR   NAT/G
...BIOG IDEA/COMP ANTHOL 20 KENNEDY/JF PRESIDENT   CHIEF
DEMOCRAT MCNAMARA/R RUSK/D. PAGE 103 B2077

S61

VIRALLY M.,"VERS UNE REFORME DU SECRETARIAT DES   INT/ORG
NATIONS UNIES." FUT WOR+45 CONSTN ECO/DEV TOP/EX   INTELL
BAL/PWR ADMIN ALL/VALS...CONCPT BIOG UN VAL/FREE   DIPLOM
20. PAGE 112 B2264

B62

BENSON E.T.,CROSS FIRE: THE EIGHT YEARS WITH   ADMIN
EISENHOWER. USA+45 DIPLOM LEAD ATTIT PERSON   POLICY
CONSERVE...TRADIT BIOG 20 EISNHWR/DD PRESIDENT   DELIB/GP
TAFT/RA DULLES/JF NIXON/RM. PAGE 11 B0218   TOP/EX

B62

INGHAM K.,A HISTORY OF EAST AFRICA. NAT/G DIPLOM   AFR
ADMIN WAR NAT/LISM...SOC BIOG BIBLIOG. PAGE 54   CONSTN
B1085   COLONIAL

B63

CHARLES S.,MINISTER OF RELIEF: HARRY HOPKINS AND   ADMIN
THE DEPRESSION. EX/STRUC PROB/SOLV RATION PARL/PROC   ECO/TAC
PERS/REL ALL/VALS 20 HOPKINS/H NRA. PAGE 20 B0414   PLAN
                                                       BIOG

B63

KARL B.D.,EXECUTIVE REORGANIZATION AND REFORM IN   BIOG
THE NEW DEAL. ECO/DEV INDUS DELIB/GP EX/STRUC PLAN   EXEC
BUDGET ADMIN EFFICIENCY PWR POPULISM...POLICY 20   CREATE
PRESIDENT ROOSEVLT/F WILSON/W NEW/DEAL. PAGE 58   CONTROL
B1174

B63

SIDEY H.,JOHN F. KENNEDY, PRESIDENT. USA+45 INTELL   BIOG
FAM CONSULT DELIB/GP LEGIS ADMIN LEAD 20 KENNEDY/JF   TOP/EX
PRESIDENT. PAGE 97 B1951   SKILL
                                                       PERSON

B63

TUCKER R.C.,THE SOVIET POLITICAL MIND. WOR+45   COM
ELITES INT/ORG NAT/G POL/PAR DIPLOM ECO/TAC   TOP/EX
DOMIN ADMIN NUC/PWR REV DRIVE PERSON SUPEGO PWR   USSR
WEALTH...POLICY MGT PSY CONCPT OBS BIOG TREND
COLD/WAR MARX/KARL 20. PAGE 106 B2134

L63

FREUND G.,"ADENAUER AND THE FUTURE OF GERMANY."   NAT/G
EUR+WWI FUT GERMANY/W FORCES LEGIT ADMIN ROUTINE   BIOG
ATTIT DRIVE PERSON PWR...POLICY TIME/SEQ TREND   DIPLOM
VAL/FREE 20 ADENAUER/K. PAGE 37 B0753   GERMANY

B64

FORBES A.H.,CURRENT RESEARCH IN BRITISH STUDIES. UK   BIBLIOG
CONSTN CULTURE POL/PAR SECT DIPLOM ADMIN...JURID   PERSON
BIOG WORSHIP 20. PAGE 36 B0736   NAT/G
                                                       PARL/PROC

B64

GUTTSMAN W.L.,THE BRITISH POLITICAL ELITE. EUR+WWI   NAT/G
MOD/EUR STRATA FAM LABOR POL/PAR SCHOOL VOL/ASSN   SOC
DELIB/GP LEGIS LEGIT EXEC CHOOSE ATTIT ALL/VALS   UK
...STAT BIOG TIME/SEQ CHARTS VAL/FREE. PAGE 45   ELITES
B0905

B64

NATIONAL BOOK LEAGUE,THE COMMONWEALTH IN BOOKS: AN   BIBLIOG/A
ANNOTATED LIST. CANADA UK LOC/G SECT ADMIN...SOC   JURID
BIOG 20 CMN/WLTH. PAGE 77 B1561   NAT/G

B64

SULLIVAN G.,THE STORY OF THE PEACE CORPS. USA+45   INT/ORG

WOR+45 INTELL FACE/GP NAT/G SCHOOL VOL/ASSN CONSULT   ECO/UNDEV
EX/STRUC PLAN EDU/PROP ADMIN ATTIT DRIVE ALL/VALS   FOR/AID
...POLICY HEAL SOC CONCPT INT QU BIOG TREND SOC/EXP   PEACE
WORK. PAGE 102 B2054

S64

CASE H.L.,"GORDON R. CLAPP: THE ROLE OF FAITH,   ADMIN
PURPOSES AND PEOPLE IN ADMINISTRATION." INDUS MUNIC   BIOG
PROVS...POLICY 20. PAGE 19 B0391   EX/STRUC
                                                       DECISION

S64

KHAN M.Z.,"THE PRESIDENT OF THE GENERAL ASSEMBLY."   INT/ORG
WOR+45 CONSTN DELIB/GP EDU/PROP LEGIT ROUTINE PWR   TOP/EX
RESPECT SKILL...DECISION SOC BIOG TREND UN 20.
PAGE 59 B1202

B65

EAST J.P.,COUNCIL-MANAGER GOVERNMENT: THE POLITICAL   SIMUL
THOUGHT OF ITS FOUNDER, RICHARD S. CHILDS. USA+45   LOC/G
CREATE ADMIN CHOOSE...BIOG GEN/LAWS BIBLIOG 20   MUNIC
CHILDS/RS CITY/MGT. PAGE 32 B0642   EX/STRUC

B65

PANJABI K.L.,THE CIVIL SERVANT IN INDIA. INDIA UK   ADMIN
NAT/G CONSULT EX/STRUC REGION GP/REL RACE/REL 20.   WORKER
PAGE 81 B1631   BIOG
                                                       COLONIAL

B65

PURCELL V.,THE MEMOIRS OF A MALAYAN OFFICIAL.   BIOG
MALAYSIA UK ECO/UNDEV INDUS LABOR EDU/PROP COLONIAL   ADMIN
CT/SYS WAR NAT/LISM TOTALSM ORD/FREE SOVEREIGN 20   JURID
UN CIVIL/SERV. PAGE 85 B1721   FORCES

B65

VIORST M.,HOSTILE ALLIES: FDR AND DE GAULLE.   TOP/EX
EUR+WWI USA-45 ELITES NAT/G VOL/ASSN FORCES LEGIS   PWR
PLAN LEGIT ADMIN COERCE PERSON...BIOG TIME/SEQ 20   WAR
ROOSEVLT/F DEGAULLE/C. PAGE 112 B2263   FRANCE

B66

RAEFF M.,ORIGINS OF THE RUSSIAN INTELLIGENTSIA: THE   INTELL
EIGHTEENTH-CENTURY NOBILITY. RUSSIA FAM NAT/G   ELITES
EDU/PROP ADMIN PERS/REL ATTIT...HUM BIOG 18.   STRATA
PAGE 85 B1728   CONSERVE

B67

ANGEL D.D.,ROMNEY. LABOR LG/CO NAT/G EXEC WAR   BIOG
RACE/REL PERSON ORD/FREE...MGT WORSHIP 20   CHIEF
ROMNEY/GEO CIV/RIGHTS MORMON GOVERNOR. PAGE 5 B0108   PROVS
                                                       POLICY

B67

FARNSWORTH B.,WILLIAM C. BULLITT AND THE SOVIET   DIPLOM
UNION. COM USA-45 USSR NAT/G CHIEF CONSULT DELIB/GP   BIOG
EX/STRUC WAR REPRESENT MARXISM 20 WILSON/W   POLICY
ROOSEVLT/F STALIN/J BULLITT/WC. PAGE 35 B0705

BIRCH/SOC....JOHN BIRCH SOCIETY

BIRKHEAD G.S. B0241

BIRNBACH B. B0242

BIRTH/CON....BIRTH CONTROL POLICIES AND TECHNIQUES

B66

UN ECAFE,ADMINISTRATIVE ASPECTS OF FAMILY PLANNING   PLAN
PROGRAMMES (PAMPHLET). ASIA THAILAND WOR+45   CENSUS
VOL/ASSN PROB/SOLV BUDGET FOR/AID EDU/PROP CONFER   FAM
CONTROL GOV/REL TIME 20 UN BIRTH/CON. PAGE 106   ADMIN
B2147

BISHOP D.G. B0243

BISHOP H.M. B0244

BISHOP O.B. B0245

BISMARCK/O....OTTO VON BISMARCK

B63

JACOB H.,GERMAN ADMINISTRATION SINCE BISMARCK: ADMIN
CENTRAL AUTHORITY VERSUS LOCAL AUTONOMY. GERMANY   NAT/G
GERMANY/W LAW POL/PAR CONTROL CENTRAL TOTALSM   LOC/G
FASCISM...MAJORIT DECISION STAT CHARTS GOV/COMP   POLICY
19/20 BISMARCK/O HITLER/A WEIMAR/REP. PAGE 55 B1111

BLACHLY F.F. B0246

BLACK R.L. B0477

BLACK/EUG....EUGENE BLACK

BLACK/HL....HUGO L. BLACK

BLACK/MUS....BLACK MUSLIMS

BLACK/PWR....BLACK POWER; SEE ALSO NEGRO

S66

JACOBSON J.,"COALITIONISM: FROM PROTEST TO   RACE/REL
POLITICKING" USA+45 ELITES NAT/G POL/PAR PROB/SOLV   LABOR
ADMIN LEAD DISCRIM ORD/FREE PWR CONSERVE 20 NEGRO   SOCIALIST

AFL/CIO CIV/RIGHTS BLACK/PWR. PAGE 55 B1116   VOL/ASSN

BLACK/ZION....BLACK ZIONISM

BLACKSTN/W....SIR WILLIAM BLACKSTONE

BLACKSTOCK P.W. B0247

BLACKSTONE, SIR WILLIAM....SEE BLACKSTN/W

BLAIR L. B0248

BLAISDELL D.C. B0249

BLAKE R.R. B0250

BLAU P.M. B0251,B0252,B0253

BLOCH/E....ERNEST BLOCH

BLOCK E.A. B0254

BLONDEL J. B0255,B1781

BLOUGH R. B0256

BLUEPRINTS....SEE ORG/CHARTS

BLUM H.L. B0257

BLUM J.M. B0258

BLUMBERG A.S. B0259,B0260

BMA....BRITISH MEDICAL ASSOCIATION

BOARD....SEE DELIB/GP

BOARD/MDCN....BOARD ON MEDICINE

BOAS/FRANZ....FRANZ BOAS

BOCK E. B0261

BOCK E.A. B0262,B0263

BODIN/JEAN....JEAN BODIN

BOER/WAR....BOER WAR

BOGARDUS E.S. B0264

BOGARDUS....BOGARDUS SCALE

BOGUSLAW R. B0265

BOHLKE R.H. B0266

BOHME/H....HELMUT BOHME

BOISSIER P. B0267

BOLGAR V. B0268

BOLINGBROKE H ST J. B0269

BOLIVIA....SEE ALSO L/A&17C

                                                        B63
    SCHOECK H..THE NEW ARGUMENT IN ECONOMICS. UK USA+45 WELF/ST
    INDUS MARKET LABOR NAT/G ECO/TAC ADMIN ROUTINE   FOR/AID
    BAL/PAY PWR...POLICY BOLIV. PAGE 94 B1899   ECO/DEV
                                                         ALL/IDEOS
                                                        B67
    ZONDAG C.H..THE BOLIVIAN ECONOMY 1952-65. L/A+17C   ECO/UNDEV
    TEC/DEV FOR/AID ADMIN...OBS TREND CHARTS BIBLIOG 20 INDUS
    BOLIV. PAGE 119 B2406   PRODUC

BOLLENS J.C. B0270

BOLSHEVISM....BOLSHEVISM AND BOLSHEVISTS

                                                        B52
    SELZNICK P..THE ORGANIZATIONAL WEAPON: A STUDY OF   MARXISM
    BOLSHEVIK STRATEGY AND TACTICS. USSR SOCIETY STRATA POL/PAR
    LABOR DOMIN EDU/PROP PARTIC REV ATTIT PWR...POLICY   LEAD
    MGT CONCPT 20 BOLSHEVISM. PAGE 95 B1929   TOTALISM
                                                        B60
    PIERCE R.A..RUSSIAN CENTRAL ASIA, 1867-1917. ASIA   COLONIAL
    RUSSIA CULTURE AGRI INDUS EDU/PROP REV NAT/LISM   DOMIN
    ...CHARTS BIBLIOG 19/20 BOLSHEVISM INTERVENT.   ADMIN
    PAGE 83 B1672   ECO/UNDEV

BONAPART/L....LOUIS BONAPARTE (KING OF HOLLAND)

BONAPARTE M. B0271

BONER H.A. B0272

BONINI C.P. B0273

BONNETT C.E. B0274

BONTOC....BONTOC, A MOUNTAIN TRIBE OF LUZON, PHILIPPINES

BOOKS....SEE OLD/STOR

BOONE/DANL....DANIEL BOONE

BOOTH D.A. B0275

BORBA DE MORAES R. B0276

BORCHARD E.H. B0277

BORCHARDT K. B0278

BORDEN/R....SIR ROBERT BORDEN

BORGESE G. B0279

BORNEO....SEE ALSO S/ASIA

BOSCH/JUAN....JUAN BOSCH

BOSSISM....BOSSISM; MONOPOLY OF POLITICAL POWER (U.S.)

                                                        B30
    ZINK H..CITY BOSSES IN THE UNITED STATES: A STUDY   LOC/G
    OF TWENTY MUNICIPAL BOSSES. USA-45 INDUS MUNIC   DOMIN
    NEIGH POL/PAR ADMIN CRIME INGP/REL PERS/REL PWR   BIOG
    ...PERS/COMP 20 BOSSISM. PAGE 119 B2403   LEAD
                                                        B47
    FLYNN E.J..YOU'RE THE BOSS. USA-45 ELITES TOP/EX   LOC/G
    DOMIN CONTROL EXEC LEAD REPRESENT 19/20 NEWYORK/C   MUNIC
    ROOSEVLT/F FLYNN/BOSS BOSSISM. PAGE 36 B0732   BIOG
                                                        POL/PAR

BOSTON....BOSTON, MASSACHUSETTS

                                                        B65
    GREER S..URBAN RENEWAL AND AMERICAN CITIES: THE   MUNIC
    DILEMMA OF DEMOCRATIC INTERVENTION. USA+45 R+D   PROB/SOLV
    LOC/G VOL/ASSN ACT/RES BUDGET ADMIN GOV/REL...SOC   PLAN
    INT SAMP 20 BOSTON CHICAGO MIAMI URBAN/RNWL.   NAT/G
    PAGE 43 B0871

BOSWORTH K.A. B0280

BOTSWANA....BOTSWANA

BOTTOMORE T.B. B0281

BOUDET P. B0282

BOULDER....BOULDER, COLORADO

BOULDING K.E. B0283

BOURASSA/H....HENRI BOURASSA

BOURGEOIS R. B0282

BOUSSER M. B0551

BOUVIER-AJAM M. B0284

BOWEN W.G. B0285

BOWETT D.W. B0286

BOWIE R. B0287

BOWLES C. B0288

BOXER C.R. B0290

BOXER/REBL....BOXER REBELLION

BOYD A.M. B0291

BOYD H.W. B0292

BOYER W.W. B0293,B0294

BRADLEY A.W. B0295

BRADLEY/FH....FRANCIS HERBERT BRADLEY

BRADY R.A. B0296

BRADY R.H. B0297

BRAHMIN....BRAHMIN CASTE

BRAIBANTI R.J.D. B0298,B0299,B0300

BRAINWASHING....SEE EDU/PROP

BRANDEIS/L....LOUIS BRANDEIS

BRANNAN/C....CHARLES BRANNAN (SECRETARY OF AGRICULTURE)

BRAUN K. B0301

BRAYMAN H. B0302

BRAZIL....SEE ALSO L/A+17C

                                           B42
SIMOES DOS REIS A.,BIBLIOGRAFIA DAS BIBLIOGRAFIAS   BIBLIOG
BRASILEIRAS. BRAZIL ADMIN COLONIAL 20. PAGE 97   NAT/G
B1954   DIPLOM
                                         L/A+17C
                                         B48
US LIBRARY OF CONGRESS,BRAZIL: A GUIDE TO THE   BIBLIOG/A
OFFICIAL PUBLICATIONS OF BRAZIL. BRAZIL L/A+17C   NAT/G
CONSULT DELIB/GP LEGIS CT/SYS 19/20. PAGE 109 B2203 ADMIN
                                         TOP/EX
                                         B49
BORBA DE MORAES R.,MANUAL BIBLIOGRAFICO DE ESTUDOS BIBLIOG
BRASILEIROS. BRAZIL DIPLOM ADMIN LEAD...SOC 20.   L/A+17C
PAGE 14 B0276   NAT/G
                                       ECO/UNDEV
                                       B50
FIGANIERE J.C.,BIBLIOTHECA HISTORICA PORTUGUEZA.   BIBLIOG
BRAZIL PORTUGAL SECT ADMIN. PAGE 35 B0717   NAT/G
                                         DIPLOM
                                       COLONIAL
                                       B53
WAGLEY C.,AMAZON TOWN: A STUDY OF MAN IN THE   SOC
TROPICS. BRAZIL L/A+17C STRATA STRUCT ECO/UNDEV   NEIGH
AGRI EX/STRUC RACE/REL DISCRIM HABITAT WEALTH...OBS CULTURE
SOC/EXP 20. PAGE 113 B2273   INGP/REL
                                       B55
DE ARAGAO J.G.,LA JURIDICTION ADMINISTRATIVE AU   EX/STRUC
BRESIL. BRAZIL ADJUD COLONIAL CT/SYS REV FEDERAL   ADMIN
ORD/FREE...BIBLIOG 19/20. PAGE 27 B0549   NAT/G
                                       B60
PINTO F.B.M.,ENRIQUECIMENTO ILICITO NO EXERCICIO DE ADMIN
CARGOS PUBLICOS. BRAZIL L/A+17C USA+45 ELITES   NAT/G
TRIBUTE CONTROL INGP/REL ORD/FREE PWR...NAT/COMP   CRIME
20. PAGE 83 B1675   LAW
                                       B62
GALENSON W.,LABOR IN DEVELOPING COUNTRIES. BRAZIL   LABOR
INDONESIA ISRAEL PAKISTAN TURKEY AGRI INDUS WORKER ECO/UNDEV
PAY PRICE GP/REL WEALTH...MGT CHARTS METH/COMP   BARGAIN
NAT/COMP 20. PAGE 38 B0775   POL/PAR
                                       B63
DALAND R.T.,PERSPECTIVES OF BRAZILIAN PUBLIC   ADMIN
ADMINISTRATION (VOL. I). BRAZIL LAW ECO/UNDEV   NAT/G
SCHOOL CHIEF TEC/DEV CONFER CONTROL GP/REL ATTIT   PLAN
ROLE PWR...ANTHOL 20. PAGE 26 B0525   GOV/REL
                                       B63
FORTES A.B.,HISTORIA ADMINISTRATIVA, JUDICIARIA E   PROVS
ECLESIASTICA DO RIO GRANDE DO SUL. BRAZIL L/A+17C ADMIN
LOC/G SECT COLONIAL CT/SYS ORD/FREE CATHISM 16/20. JURID
PAGE 37 B0742
                                       B63
THORELLI H.B.,INTOP: INTERNATIONAL OPERATIONS   GAME
SIMULATION: PLAYER'S MANUAL. BRAZIL FINAN OP/RES   INT/TRADE
ADMIN GP/REL INGP/REL PRODUC PERCEPT...DECISION MGT EDU/PROP
EEC. PAGE 104 B2108   LG/CO
                                       B64
JACKSON W.V.,LIBRARY GUIDE FOR BRAZILIAN STUDIES.   BIBLIOG
BRAZIL USA+45 STRUCT DIPLOM ADMIN...SOC 20. PAGE 55 L/A+17C
B1110   NAT/G
                                       LOC/G
                                       B64
RICHARDSON I.L.,BIBLIOGRAFIA BRASILEIRA DE   BIBLIOG
ADMINISTRACAO PUBLICA E ASSUNTOS CORRELATOS. BRAZIL MGT
CONSTN FINAN LOC/G NAT/G POL/PAR PLAN DIPLOM   ADMIN
RECEIVE ATTIT...METH 20. PAGE 88 B1776   LAW
                                       B66
BOYD H.W.,MARKETING MANAGEMENT: CASES FROM EMERGING MGT
COUNTRIES. BRAZIL GHANA ISRAEL WOR+45 ADMIN   ECO/UNDEV
PERS/REL ATTIT HABITAT WEALTH...ANTHOL 20 ARGEN   PROB/SOLV
CASEBOOK. PAGE 14 B0292   MARKET
                                       B67
SKIDMORE T.E.,POLITICS IN BRAZIL 1930-1964. BRAZIL   CONSTN
L/A+17C INDUS NAT/G PROB/SOLV ATTIT 20. PAGE 98   ECO/TAC
B1973   ADMIN

BRECHT A. B0303

BREGMAN A. B0304

BREHON....BREHON LAW (ANCIENT CELTIC)

BRENNAN D.G. B0305

BRIAND/A....ARISTIDE BRIAND

BRIDGEPORT....BRIDGEPORT, CONNECTICUT

BRIEFS H.W. B0306

BRIGHT J.R. B0307,B0308

BRIMMER A.F. B0309

BRIMMER B. B0310

BRINTON C. B0311

BRISTOL L.H. B0312

BRIT/COLUM....BRITISH COLUMBIA, CANADA

BRITISH COLUMBIA, CANADA....SEE BRIT/COLUM

BRITISH COMMONWEALTH OF NATIONS....SEE COMMONWLTH

BRITISH GUIANA....SEE GUIANA/BR + GUY NA

BRITISH MEDICAL ASSOCIATION....SEE BMA

BRITTEN M. B2136

BROGAN D.W. B0313

BROMAGE A.W. B0314,B0315

BROOK/EDGR....EDGAR H. BROOKES

BROOKINGS INSTITUTION B0316,B0317

BROOKINGS....BROOKINGS INSTITUTION, THE

BROOKS R.R. B0318

BROWN A.D. B0319

BROWN B.E. B0320,B1376

BROWN C.V. B0321

BROWN E.S. B0322

BROWN L.C. B0323

BROWN L.N. B0324

BROWN M. B0325

BROWN R.E. B0326

BROWN S. B0327

BROWN W.O. B0389

BROWN/JOHN....JOHN BROWN

BROWNE C.G. B0328

BROWNE D.G. B0329

BROWNE G.S. B0502

BROWNELL/H....HERBERT BROWNELL

BRUCK H. B1992

BRUEGEL J.W. B0330

BRUNTON R.L. B0331

BRYAN/WJ....WILLIAM JENNINGS BRYAN

BRYCE J. B0332

BRYCE/J....JAMES BRYCE

BRZEZINSKI Z.K. B0333,B0334,B0335,B0336

BRZEZNSK/Z....ZBIGNIEW K. BRZEZINSKI

BUCHANAN/J....PRESIDENT JAMES BUCHANAN

BUCKLEY/WF....WILLIAM F. BUCKLEY

BUDDHISM....BUDDHISM

BUDER S. B0337

BUDGET....BUDGETING, BUDGETS, FISCAL PLANNING

VENKATESAN S.L.,BIBLIOGRAPHY ON PUBLIC ENTERPRISES IN INDIA. INDIA S/ASIA FINAN LG/CO LOC/G PLAN BUDGET SOCISM...MGT 20. PAGE 112 B2258
N
BIBLIOG/A
ADMIN
ECO/UNDEV
INDUS

CARLETON UNIVERSITY LIBRARY,SELECTED LIST OF CURRENT MATERIALS ON CANADIAN PUBLIC ADMINISTRATION. CANADA LEGIS WORKER PLAN BUDGET 20. PAGE 19 B0379
N
BIBLIOG
ADMIN
LOC/G
MUNIC

UNITED NATIONS,OFFICIAL RECORDS OF THE UNITED NATIONS' GENERAL ASSEMBLY. WOR+45 BUDGET DIPLOM ADMIN 20 UN. PAGE 107 B2159
N
INT/ORG
DELIB/GP
INT/LAW
WRITING

THE GOVERNMENT OF SOUTH AFRICA (VOL. II). SOUTH/AFR STRATA EXTR/IND EX/STRUC TOP/EX BUDGET ADJUD ADMIN CT/SYS PRODUC...CORREL CENSUS 19 RAILROAD CIVIL/SERV POSTAL/SYS. PAGE 2 B0033
B08
CONSTN
FINAN
LEGIS
NAT/G

NATHAN M.,THE SOUTH AFRICAN COMMONWEALTH: CONSTITUTION, PROBLEMS, SOCIAL CONDITIONS. SOUTH/AFR UK CULTURE INDUS EX/STRUC LEGIS BUDGET EDU/PROP ADMIN CT/SYS GP/REL RACE/REL...LING 19/20 CMN/WLTH. PAGE 77 B1559
B19
CONSTN
NAT/G
POL/PAR
SOCIETY

FIKS M.,PUBLIC ADMINISTRATION IN ISRAEL (PAMPHLET). ISRAEL SCHOOL EX/STRUC BUDGET PAY INGP/REL ...DECISION 20 CIVIL/SERV. PAGE 35 B0718
N19
EDU/PROP
NAT/G
ADMIN
WORKER

MARSH J.F. JR.,THE FBI RETIREMENT BILL (PAMPHLET). USA+45 EX/STRUC WORKER PLAN PROB/SOLV BUDGET LEAD LOBBY PARL/PROC PERS/REL RIGID/FLEX...POLICY 20 FBI PRESIDENT BUR/BUDGET. PAGE 70 B1405
N19
ADMIN
NAT/G
SENIOR
GOV/REL

KENT F.R.,THE GREAT GAME OF POLITICS. USA-45 LOC/G NAT/G POL/PAR EX/STRUC PROB/SOLV BUDGET CHOOSE GOV/REL 20. PAGE 59 B1194
B24
ADMIN
OP/RES
STRUCT

WILLOUGHBY W.F.,PRINCIPLES OF PUBLIC ADMINISTRATION WITH SPECIAL REFERENCE TO THE NATIONAL AND STATE GOVERNMENTS OF THE UNITED STATES. FINAN PROVS CHIEF CONSULT LEGIS CREATE BUDGET EXEC ROUTINE GOV/REL CENTRAL...MGT 20 BUR/BUDGET CONGRESS PRESIDENT. PAGE 117 B2356
B27
NAT/G
EX/STRUC
OP/RES
ADMIN

FAIRLIE J.A.,COUNTY GOVERNMENT AND ADMINISTRATION. UK USA-45 NAT/G SCHOOL FORCES BUDGET TAX CT/SYS CHOOSE...JURID BIBLIOG 11/20. PAGE 35 B0701
B30
ADMIN
GOV/REL
LOC/G
MUNIC

CRAWFORD F.G.,"THE EXECUTIVE BUDGET DECISION IN NEW YORK." LEGIS EXEC PWR NEW/YORK. PAGE 25 B0504
S30
LEAD
BUDGET
PROVS
PROB/SOLV

GRAVES W.B.,AMERICAN STATE GOVERNMENT. CONSTN FINAN EX/STRUC FORCES LEGIS BUDGET TAX CT/SYS REPRESENT GOV/REL...BIBLIOG/A 19/20. PAGE 42 B0855
B36
NAT/G
PROVS
ADMIN
FEDERAL

HODGSON J.G.,THE OFFICIAL PUBLICATIONS OF AMERICAN COUNTIES: A UNION LIST. SCHOOL BUDGET...HEAL MGT SOC/WK 19/20. PAGE 51 B1026
B37
BIBLIOG
LOC/G
PUB/INST

UNION OF SOUTH AFRICA,REPORT CONCERNING ADMINISTRATION OF SOUTH WEST AFRICA (6 VOLS.). SOUTH/AFR INDUS PUB/INST FORCES LEGIS BUDGET DIPLOM EDU/PROP ADJUD CT/SYS...GEOG CHARTS 20 AFRICA/SW LEAGUE/NAT. PAGE 107 B2158
B37
NAT/G
ADMIN
COLONIAL
CONSTN

JENNINGS W.I.,PARLIAMENT. UK POL/PAR OP/RES BUDGET LEAD CHOOSE GP/REL...MGT 20 PARLIAMENT HOUSE/LORD HOUSE/CMNS. PAGE 56 B1135
B39
PARL/PROC
LEGIS
CONSTN
NAT/G

BURT F.A.,AMERICAN ADVERTISING AGENCIES. BARGAIN BUDGET LICENSE WRITING PRICE PERS/REL COST DEMAND ...ORG/CHARTS BIBLIOG 20. PAGE 18 B0358
B40
LG/CO
COM/IND
ADMIN
EFFICIENCY

FAHS C.B.,"GOVERNMENT IN JAPAN." FINAN FORCES LEGIS TOP/EX BUDGET INT/TRADE EDU/PROP SOVEREIGN ...CON/ANAL BIBLIOG/A 20 CHINJAP. PAGE 34 B0698
C40
ASIA
DIPLOM
NAT/G
ADMIN

COUNTY GOVERNMENT IN THE UNITED STATES: A LIST OF RECENT REFERENCES (PAMPHLET). USA-45 LAW PUB/INST PLAN BUDGET CT/SYS CENTRAL 20. PAGE 49 B0988
N40
BIBLIOG/A
LOC/G
ADMIN
MUNIC

MACMAHON A.W.,THE ADMINISTRATION OF FEDERAL WORK RELIEF. USA-45 EX/STRUC WORKER BUDGET EFFICIENCY ...CONT/OBS CHARTS 20 WPA. PAGE 68 B1367
B41
ADMIN
NAT/G
MGT
GIVE

THE TAX FOUNDATION,STUDIES IN ECONOMY AND EFFICIENCY IN GOVERNMENT. FINAN R+D OP/RES BUDGET TAX 20. PAGE 104 B2095
B41
BIBLIOG
ADMIN
EFFICIENCY
NAT/G

MACMAHON A.W.,"CONGRESSIONAL OVERSIGHT OF ADMINISTRATION: THE POWER OF THE PURSE." USA-45 BUDGET ROUTINE GOV/REL PWR...POLICY CONGRESS. PAGE 68 B1368
L43
LEGIS
DELIB/GP
ADMIN
CONTROL

CALDWELL L.K.,"STRENGTHENING STATE LEGISLATURES" FUT DELIB/GP WEALTH REFORMERS. PAGE 18 B0364
S47
PROVS
LEGIS
ROUTINE
BUDGET

STEWART I.,ORGANIZING SCIENTIFIC RESEARCH FOR WAR: ADMINISTRATIVE HISTORY OF OFFICE OF SCIENTIFIC RESEARCH AND DEVELOPMENT. USA-45 INTELL R+D LABOR WORKER CREATE BUDGET WEAPON CIVMIL/REL GP/REL EFFICIENCY...POLICY 20. PAGE 101 B2037
B48
DELIB/GP
ADMIN
WAR
TEC/DEV

WHITE L.D.,THE FEDERALISTS: A STUDY IN ADMINISTRATIVE HISTORY. STRUCT DELIB/GP LEGIS BUDGET ROUTINE GOV/REL GP/REL PERS/REL PWR...BIOG 18/19 PRESIDENT CONGRESS WASHINGT/G JEFFERSN/T HAMILTON/A. PAGE 116 B2337
B48
ADMIN
NAT/G
POLICY
PROB/SOLV

GRAVES W.B.,BASIC INFORMATION ON THE REORGANIZATION OF THE EXECUTIVE BRANCH: 1912-1948. USA-45 BUDGET ADMIN CONTROL GP/REL EFFICIENCY...MGT CHARTS ORG/CHARTS 20 PRESIDENT. PAGE 42 B0857
B49
BIBLIOG/A
EX/STRUC
NAT/G
CHIEF

LITTLE HOOVER COMM,HOW TO ACHIEVE GREATER EFFICIENCY AND ECONOMY IN MINNESOTA'S GOVERNMENT (PAMPHLET). PLAN BUDGET ADMIN CHOOSE EFFICIENCY ALL/VALS 20 MINNESOTA. PAGE 66 B1327
B50
TOP/EX
LOC/G
GOV/REL
PROVS

ANDERSON W.,STATE AND LOCAL GOVERNMENT IN THE UNITED STATES. USA+45 CONSTN POL/PAR EX/STRUC LEGIS BUDGET TAX ADJUD CT/SYS CHOOSE...CHARTS T 20. PAGE 5 B0100
B51
LOC/G
MUNIC
PROVS
GOV/REL

DIMOCK M.E.,FREE ENTERPRISE AND THE ADMINISTRATIVE STATE. FINAN LG/CO BARGAIN BUDGET DOMIN CONTROL INGP/REL EFFICIENCY 20. PAGE 29 B0595
B51
CAP/ISM
ADMIN
MGT
MARKET

WHITE L.D.,THE JEFFERSONIANS: A STUDY IN ADMINISTRATIVE HISTORY 18011829. USA-45 DELIB/GP LEGIS TOP/EX PROB/SOLV BUDGET ECO/TAC GP/REL FEDERAL...BIOG IDEA/COMP 19 PRESIDENT CONGRESS JEFFERSN/T. PAGE 116 B2338
B51
ADMIN
NAT/G
POLICY
POL/PAR

SCHATTSCHNEIDER E.E.,A GUIDE TO THE STUDY OF PUBLIC AFFAIRS. LAW LOC/G NAT/G LEGIS BUDGET PRESS ADMIN LOBBY...JURID CHARTS 20. PAGE 93 B1882
B52
ACT/RES
INTELL
ACADEM
METH/COMP

RICH B.M.,"ADMINISTRATION REORGANIZATION IN NEW JERSEY" (BMR) USA+45 DELIB/GP EX/STRUC WORKER OP/RES BUDGET 20 NEW/JERSEY. PAGE 88 B1772
S52
ADMIN
CONSTN
PROB/SOLV
PROVS

SNIDER C.F.,"AMERICAN COUNTY GOVERNMENT: A MID-CENTURY REVIEW" (BMR)" USA+45 USA-45 PROVS DELIB/GP EX/STRUC BUDGET TAX PWR 20. PAGE 98 B1988
S52
LOC/G
ADMIN
GOV/REL
REGION

LANCASTER L.W.,"GOVERNMENT IN RURAL AMERICA." USA+45 ECO/DEV AGRI SCHOOL FORCES LEGIS JUDGE BUDGET TAX CT/SYS...CHARTS BIBLIOG. PAGE 62 B1253
C52
GOV/REL
LOC/G
MUNIC
ADMIN

DIMOCK M.E.,PUBLIC ADMINISTRATION. USA+45 FINAN WORKER BUDGET CONTROL CHOOSE...T 20. PAGE 29 B0596
B53
ADMIN
STRUCT
OP/RES
POLICY

MAJUMDAR B.B.,PROBLEMS OF PUBLIC ADMINISTRATION IN INDIA. INDIA INDUS PLAN BUDGET ADJUD CENTRAL DEMAND WEALTH...WELF/ST ANTHOL 20 CIVIL/SERV. PAGE 68 B1384
B53
ECO/UNDEV
GOV/REL
ADMIN
MUNIC

MILLIKAN M.F.,INCOME STABILIZATION FOR A DEVELOPING DEMOCRACY. USA+45 ECO/DEV LABOR BUDGET ECO/TAC TAX
B53
ANTHOL
MARKET

ADMIN ADJUST PRODUC WEALTH...POLICY TREND 20.
PAGE 73 B1484

EQUILIB
EFFICIENCY
B53

SECKLER-HUDSON C.,BIBLIOGRAPHY ON PUBLIC
ADMINISTRATION (4TH ED.). USA+45 LAW POL/PAR
DELIB/GP BUDGET ADJUD LOBBY GOV/REL GP/REL ATTIT
...JURID 20. PAGE 95 B1923

BIBLIOG/A
ADMIN
NAT/G
MGT
B54

CONWAY O.B. JR.,LEGISLATIVE-EXECUTIVE RELATIONS IN
THE GOVERNMENT OF THE UNITED STATES (PAMPHLET).
BUDGET ATTIT PERCEPT...DECISION 20. PAGE 23 B0470

BAL/PWR
FEDERAL
GOV/REL
EX/STRUC
B54

HOBBS E.H.,BEHIND THE PRESIDENT - A STUDY OF
EXECUTIVE OFFICE AGENCIES. USA+45 NAT/G PLAN BUDGET
ECO/TAC EXEC ORD/FREE 20 BUR/BUDGET. PAGE 50 B1022

EX/STRUC
DELIB/GP
CONFER
CONSULT
B54

TOMPKINS D.C.,STATE GOVERNMENT AND ADMINISTRATION:
A BIBLIOGRAPHY. USA+45 USA-45 CONSTN LEGIS JUDGE
BUDGET CT/SYS LOBBY...CHARTS 20. PAGE 105 B2116

BIBLIOG/A
LOC/G
PROVS
ADMIN
B55

SMITHIES A.,THE BUDGETARY PROCESS IN THE UNITED
STATES. ECO/DEV AGRI EX/STRUC FORCES LEGIS
PROB/SOLV TAX ROUTINE EFFICIENCY...MGT CONGRESS
PRESIDENT. PAGE 98 B1987

NAT/G
ADMIN
BUDGET
GOV/REL
S56

MARGOLIS J.,"ON MUNICIPAL LAND POLICY FOR FISCAL
GAINS." USA+45 MUNIC PLAN TAX COST EFFICIENCY
HABITAT KNOWL...MGT 20. PAGE 69 B1398

BUDGET
POLICY
GEOG
LOC/G
S56

MILNE R.S.,"CONTROL OF GOVERNMENT CORPORATIONS IN
THE UNITED STATES." USA+45 NAT/G CHIEF LEGIS BUDGET
20 GENACCOUNT. PAGE 74 B1488

CONTROL
EX/STRUC
GOV/REL
PWR
B57

BABCOCK R.S.,STATE & LOCAL GOVERNMENT AND POLITICS.
USA+45 CONSTN POL/PAR EX/STRUC LEGIS BUDGET LOBBY
CHOOSE SUFF...CHARTS BIBLIOG T 20. PAGE 8 B0154

PROVS
LOC/G
GOV/REL
B57

MURDESHWAR A.K.,ADMINISTRATIVE PROBLEMS RELATING TO
NATIONALISATION: WITH SPECIAL REFERENCE TO INDIAN
STATE ENTERPRISES. CZECHOSLVK FRANCE INDIA UK
USA+45 LEGIS WORKER PROB/SOLV BUDGET PRICE CONTROL
...MGT GEN/LAWS 20 PARLIAMENT. PAGE 76 B1544

NAT/G
OWN
INDUS
ADMIN

B57

SHARMA S.R.,SOME ASPECTS OF THE INDIAN
ADMINISTRATIVE SYSTEM. INDIA WOR+45 TEC/DEV BUDGET
LEGIT ROUTINE ATTIT. PAGE 96 B1937

EXEC
DECISION
ADMIN
INGP/REL
B58

AMERICAN SOCIETY PUBLIC ADMIN,STRENGTHENING
MANAGEMENT FOR DEMOCRATIC GOVERNMENT. USA+45 ACADEM
EX/STRUC WORKER PLAN BUDGET CONFER CT/SYS
EFFICIENCY ANTHOL. PAGE 4 B0088

ADMIN
NAT/G
EXEC
MGT
B58

CHANG C.,THE INFLATIONARY SPIRAL: THE EXPERIENCE IN
CHINA 1939-50. CHINA/COM BUDGET INT/TRADE PRICE
ADMIN CONTROL WAR DEMAND...POLICY CHARTS 20.
PAGE 20 B0406

FINAN
ECO/TAC
BAL/PAY
GOV/REL
B58

GROSSMAN J.,BIBLIOGRAPHY ON PUBLIC ADMINISTRATION
IN LATIN AMERICA. ECO/UNDEV FINAN PLAN BUDGET
ECO/TAC TARIFFS TAX...STAT 20. PAGE 44 B0893

BIBLIOG
L/A+17C
NAT/G
ADMIN
B58

INDIAN INST OF PUBLIC ADMIN,IMPROVING CITY
GOVERNMENT. INDIA ECO/UNDEV PLAN BUDGET PARTIC
GP/REL 20. PAGE 53 B1080

LOC/G
MUNIC
PROB/SOLV
ADMIN
B58

SHAW S.J.,THE FINANCIAL AND ADMINISTRATIVE
ORGANIZATION AND DEVELOPMENT OF OTTOMAN EGYPT
1517-1798. UAR LOC/G FORCES BUDGET INT/TRADE TAX
EATING INCOME WEALTH...CHARTS BIBLIOG 16/18 OTTOMAN
NAPOLEON/B. PAGE 96 B1940

FINAN
ADMIN
GOV/REL
CULTURE

B59

BRUNTON R.L.,MANAGEMENT PRACTICES FOR SMALLER
CITIES. USA+45 MUNIC CONSULT PLAN BUDGET PERS/REL
20 CITY/MGT. PAGE 16 B0331

ADMIN
LOC/G
MGT
TOP/EX
B59

IPSEN H.P.,HAMBURGISCHES STAATS- UND
VERWALTUNGSRECHT. CONSTN LOC/G FORCES BUDGET CT/SYS
...JURID 20 HAMBURG. PAGE 54 B1103

ADMIN
PROVS
LEGIS
FINAN
B59

JENNINGS W.I.,CABINET GOVERNMENT (3RD ED.). UK
POL/PAR CHIEF BUDGET ADMIN CHOOSE GP/REL 20.
PAGE 56 B1137

DELIB/GP
NAT/G
CONSTN
OP/RES
B59

US PRES COMM STUDY MIL ASSIST,COMPOSITE REPORT.
USA+45 ECO/UNDEV PLAN BUDGET DIPLOM EFFICIENCY

FOR/AID
FORCES

...POLICY MGT 20. PAGE 109 B2208

WEAPON
ORD/FREE
B59

YALE UNIV BUR OF HIGHWAY TRAF,URBAN TRANSPORTATION
ADMINISTRATION. FUT USA+45 CONSTRUC ACT/RES BUDGET
...CENSUS 20 PUB/TRANS. PAGE 118 B2388

ADMIN
DIST/IND
LOC/G
PLAN
L59

RHODE W.E.,"COMMITTEE CLEARANCE OF ADMINISTRATIVE
DECISIONS." DELIB/GP LEGIS BUDGET DOMIN CIVMIL/REL
20 CONGRESS. PAGE 87 B1768

DECISION
ADMIN
OP/RES
NAT/G
B60

ALBI F.,TRATADO DE LOS MODOS DE GESTION DE LAS
CORPORACIONES LOCALES. SPAIN FINAN NAT/G BUDGET
CONTROL EXEC ROUTINE GOV/REL ORD/FREE SOVEREIGN
...MGT 20. PAGE 3 B0068

LOC/G
LAW
ADMIN
MUNIC
B60

ARGAL R.,MUNICIPAL GOVERNMENT IN INDIA. INDIA
BUDGET TAX ADMIN EXEC 19/20. PAGE 6 B0126

LOC/G
MUNIC
DELIB/GP
CONTROL
B60

FRYE R.J.,GOVERNMENT AND LABOR: THE ALABAMA
PROGRAM. USA+45 INDUS R+D LABOR WORKER BUDGET
EFFICIENCY AGE/Y HEALTH...CHARTS 20 ALABAMA.
PAGE 38 B0761

ADMIN
LEGIS
LOC/G
PROVS
B60

MARSHALL A.H.,FINANCIAL ADMINISTRATION IN LOCAL
GOVERNMENT. UK DELIB/GP CONFER COST INCOME PERSON
...JURID 20. PAGE 70 B1408

FINAN
LOC/G
BUDGET
ADMIN
B60

MATTOD P.K.,A STUDY OF LOCAL SELF GOVERNMENT IN
URBAN INDIA. INDIA FINAN DELIB/GP LEGIS BUDGET TAX
SOVERFIGN...MGT GP/COMP 20. PAGE 71 B1432

MUNIC
CONSTN
LOC/G
ADMIN
B60

PENNSYLVANIA ECONOMY LEAGUE,URBAN RENEWAL IMPACT
STUDY: ADMINISTRATIVE-LEGAL-FISCAL. USA+45 FINAN
LOC/G NEIGH ADMIN EFFICIENCY...CENSUS CHARTS 20
PENNSYLVAN. PAGE 82 B1652

PLAN
BUDGET
MUNIC
ADJUD
B61

BEASLEY K.E.,STATE SUPERVISION OF MUNICIPAL DEBT IN
KANSAS - A CASE STUDY. USA+45 USA-45 FINAN PROVS
BUDGET TAX ADJUD ADMIN CONTROL SUPEGO. PAGE 10
B0201

MUNIC
LOC/G
LEGIS
JURID
B61

CONFREY E.A.,ADMINISTRATION OF COMMUNITY HEALTH
SERVICES. USA+45 R+D PUB/INST DELIB/GP PLAN BUDGET
ROUTINE AGE/C HEALTH...MGT SOC/WK METH/COMP 20.
PAGE 23 B0461

HEAL
ADMIN
MUNIC
BIO/SOC
B61

DRURY J.W.,THE GOVERNMENT OF KANSAS. USA+45 AGRI
INDUS CHIEF LEGIS WORKER PLAN BUDGET GIVE CT/SYS
GOV/REL...T 20 KANSAS GOVERNOR CITY/MGT. PAGE 31
B0621

PROVS
CONSTN
ADMIN
LOC/G
B61

GRIFFITH E.S.,CONGRESS: ITS CONTEMPORARY ROLE.
CONSTN POL/PAR CHIEF PLAN BUDGET DIPLOM CONFER
ADMIN LOBBY...DECISION CONGRESS. PAGE 43 B0878

PARL/PROC
EX/STRUC
TOP/EX
LEGIS
B61

MACMAHON A.W.,DELEGATION AND AUTONOMY. INDIA STRUCT
LEGIS BARGAIN BUDGET ECO/TAC LEGIT EXEC REPRESENT
GOV/REL CENTRAL DEMAND EFFICIENCY PRODUC. PAGE 68
B1373

ADMIN
PLAN
FEDERAL

B61

QURESHI S.,INCENTIVES IN AMERICAN EMPLOYMENT
(THESIS, UNIVERSITY OF PENNSYLVANIA). DELIB/GP
TOP/EX BUDGET ROUTINE SANCTION COST TECHRACY MGT.
PAGE 85 B1727

SERV/IND
ADMIN
PAY
EX/STRUC
B61

SHARMA T.R.,THE WORKING OF STATE ENTERPRISES IN
INDIA. INDIA DELIB/GP LEGIS WORKER BUDGET PRICE
CONTROL GP/REL OWN ATTIT...MGT CHARTS 20. PAGE 96
B1938

NAT/G
INDUS
ADMIN
SOCISM
B61

SINGER J.D.,FINANCING INTERNATIONAL ORGANIZATION:
THE UNITED NATIONS BUDGET PROCESS. WOR+45 FINAN
ACT/RES CREATE PLAN BUDGET ECO/TAC ADMIN ROUTINE
ATTIT KNOWL...DECISION METH/CNCPT TIME/SEQ UN 20.
PAGE 97 B1964

INT/ORG
MGT

B62

ARCO EDITORIAL BOARD,PUBLIC MANAGEMENT AND
ADMINISTRATION. PLAN BUDGET WRITING CONTROL ROUTINE
...TESTS CHARTS METH T 20. PAGE 6 B0125

MGT
ADMIN
NAT/G
LOC/G
B62

FORD A.G.,THE GOLD STANDARD 1880-1914: BRITAIN AND
ARGENTINA. UK ECO/UNDEV INT/TRADE ADMIN GOV/REL
DEMAND EFFICIENCY...STAT CHARTS 19/20 ARGEN
GOLD/STAND. PAGE 36 B0737

FINAN
ECO/TAC
BUDGET
BAL/PAY
B62

INST TRAINING MUNICIPAL ADMIN,MUNICIPAL FINANCE
ADMINISTRATION (6TH ED.). USA+45 ELITES ECO/DEV

MUNIC
ADMIN

LEGIS PLAN BUDGET TAX GP/REL BAL/PAY COST...POLICY
20 CITY/MGT. PAGE 54 B1089

FINAN
LOC/G

B62

WANGSNESS P.H.,THE POWER OF THE CITY MANAGER.
USA+45 EX/STRUC BAL/PWR BUDGET TAX ADMIN REPRESENT
CENTRAL EFFICIENCY DRIVE ROLE...POLICY 20 CITY/MGT.
PAGE 113 B2286

PWR
TOP/EX
MUNIC
LOC/G

B62

WEDDING N.,ADVERTISING MANAGEMENT. USA+45 ECO/DEV
BUDGET CAP/ISM PRODUC PROFIT ATTIT...DECISION MGT
PSY 20. PAGE 114 B2308

ECO/TAC
COM/IND
PLAN
EDU/PROP

B63

BONINI C.P.,SIMULATION OF INFORMATION AND DECISION
SYSTEMS IN THE FIRM. MARKET BUDGET DOMIN EDU/PROP
ADMIN COST ATTII HABITAT PERCEPT PWR...CONCPT
PROBABIL QUANT PREDICT HYPO/EXP BIBLIOG. PAGE 13
B0273

INDUS
SIMUL
DECISION
MGT

B63

DUE J.F.,STATE SALES TAX ADMINISTRATION. OP/RES
BUDGET PAY ADMIN EXEC ROUTINE COST EFFICIENCY
PROFIT...CHARTS METH/COMP 20. PAGE 31 B0626

PROVS
TAX
STAT
GOV/COMP

B63

ECOLE NATIONALE D'ADMIN.BIBLIOGRAPHIE SELECTIVE
D'OUVRAGES DE LANGUE FRANCAISE TRAITANT DES
PROBLEMES GOUVERNEMENTAUX ET ADMINISTRATIFS. NAT/G
FORCES ACT/RES OP/RES PLAN PROB/SOLV BUDGET ADJUD
COLONIAL LEAD 20. PAGE 32 B0651

BIBLIOG
AFR
ADMIN
EX/STRUC

B63

GARNER U.F.,ADMINISTRATIVE LAW. UK LAW LOC/G NAT/G
EX/STRUC LEGIS JUDGE BAL/PWR BUDGET ADJUD CONTROL
CT/SYS...BIBLIOG 20. PAGE 39 B0783

ADMIN
JURID
PWR
GOV/REL

B63

HANSON A.H.,NATIONALIZATION: A BOOK OF READINGS.
WOR+45 FINAN DELIB/GP LEGIS WORKER BUDGET
GP/REL EFFICIENCY SOCISM...MGT ANTHOL. PAGE 46
B0941

NAT/G
OWN
INDUS
CONTROL

B63

KARL B.D.,EXECUTIVE REORGANIZATION AND REFORM IN
THE NEW DEAL. ECO/DEV INDUS DELIB/GP EX/STRUC PLAN
BUDGET ADMIN EFFICIENCY PWR POPULISM...POLICY 20
PRESIDENT ROOSEVLT/F WILSON/W NEW/DEAL. PAGE 58
B1174

BIOG
EXEC
CREATE
CONTROL

B63

MAHESHWARI B.,STUDIES IN PANCHAYATI RAJ. INDIA
POL/PAR EX/STRUC BUDGET EXEC REPRESENT CENTRAL
EFFICIENCY...DECISION 20. PAGE 68 B1378

FEDERAL
LOC/G
GOV/REL
LEAD

B63

SINGH M.M.,MUNICIPAL GOVERNMENT IN THE CALCUTTA
METROPOLITAN DISTRICT A PRELIMINARY SURVEY. FINAN
LG/CO DELIB/GP BUDGET TAX ADMIN GP/REL 20 CALCUTTA.
PAGE 97 B1969

LOC/G
HEALTH
MUNIC
JURID

B63

STEIN H.,AMERICAN CIVIL-MILITARY DECISION. USA+45
USA-45 EX/STRUC FORCES LEGIS TOP/EX PLAN DIPLOM
FOR/AID ATTIT 20 CONGRESS. PAGE 100 B2028

CIVMIL/REL
DECISION
WAR
BUDGET

B63

UN SECRETARY GENERAL,PLANNING FOR ECONOMIC
DEVELOPMENT. ECO/UNDEV FINAN BUDGET INT/TRADE
TARIFFS TAX ADMIN 20 UN. PAGE 106 B2151

PLAN
ECO/TAC
MGT
NAT/COMP

B63

US HOUSE COM ON ED AND LABOR,ADMINISTRATION OF
AGING. USA+45 R+D EX/STRUC PLAN BUDGET PAY EDU/PROP
ROUTINE COST CONGRESS. PAGE 108 B2187

AGE/O
ADMIN
DELIB/GP
GIVE

B63

WALKER A.A.,OFFICIAL PUBLICATIONS OF SIERRA LEONE
AND GAMBIA. GAMBIA SIER/LEONE UK LAW CONSTN LEGIS
PLAN BUDGET DIPLOM...SOC SAMP CON/ANAL 20. PAGE 113
B2278

BIBLIOG
NAT/G
COLONIAL
ADMIN

B64

BOUVIER-AJAM M.,MANUEL TECHNIQUE ET PRATIQUE DU
MAIRE ET DES ELUS ET AGENTS COMMUNAUX. FRANCE LOC/G
BUDGET CHOOSE GP/REL SUPEGO...JURID BIBLIOG 20
MAYOR COMMUNES. PAGE 14 B0284

MUNIC
ADMIN
CHIEF
NEIGH

B64

FATOUROS A.A.,CANADA'S OVERSEAS AID. CANADA WOR+45
ECO/DEV FINAN NAT/G BUDGET ECO/TAC CONFER ADMIN 20.
PAGE 35 B0707

FOR/AID
DIPLOM
ECO/UNDEV
POLICY

B64

FONTENEAU J.,LE CONSEIL MUNICIPAL: LE MAIRE-LES
ADJOINTS. FRANCE FINAN DELIB/GP EX/STRUC BUDGET TAX
TASK COST INCOME ROLE SUPEGO 20 MAYOR. PAGE 36
B0735

MUNIC
NEIGH
ADMIN
TOP/EX

B64

KNOX V.H.,PUBLIC FINANCE: INFORMATION SOURCES.
USA+45 DIPLOM ADMIN GOV/REL COST...POLICY 20.
PAGE 60 B1221

BIBLIOG/A
FINAN
TAX
BUDGET

B64

NUQUIST A.E.,TOWN GOVERNMENT IN VERMONT. USA+45
FINAN TOP/EX PROB/SOLV BUDGET TAX REPRESENT SUFF
EFFICIENCY...OBS INT 20 VERMONT. PAGE 79 B1595

LOC/G
MUNIC
POPULISM
ADMIN

B64

WEIDENBAUM M.L.,CONGRESS AND THE FEDERAL BUDGET:
FEDERAL BUDGETING AND THE RESPONSIBLE USE OF POWER.
LOC/G PLAN TAX CONGRESS. PAGE 114 B2309

LEGIS
EX/STRUC
BUDGET
ADMIN

B64

WELLISZ S.,THE ECONOMICS OF THE SOVIET BLOC. COM
USSR INDUS WORKER PLAN BUDGET INT/TRADE TAX PRICE
PRODUC WEALTH MARXISM...METH/COMP 20. PAGE 115
B2319

EFFICIENCY
ADMIN
MARKET

B64

WILLIAMSON O.E.,THE ECONOMICS OF DISCRETIONARY
BEHAVIOR: MANAGERIAL OBJECTIVES IN A THEORY OF THE
FIRM. MARKET BUDGET CAP/ISM PRODUC DRIVE PERSON
...STAT CHARTS BIBLIOG METH 20. PAGE 117 B2354

EFFICIENCY
MGT
ECO/TAC
CHOOSE

S64

CARNEGIE ENDOWMENT INT. PEACE,"ADMINISTRATION AND
BUDGET (ISSUES BEFORE THE NINETEENTH GENERAL
ASSEMBLY)." WOR+45 FINAN BUDGET ECO/TAC ROUTINE
COST...STAT RECORD UN. PAGE 19 B0383

INT/ORG
ADMIN

S64

NEWLYN W.T.,"MONETARY SYSTEMS AND INTEGRATION" AFR
BUDGET ADMIN FEDERAL PRODUC PROFIT UTIL...CHARTS 20
AFRICA/E. PAGE 78 B1578

ECO/UNDEV
REGION
METH/COMP
FINAN

B65

DUGGAR G.S.,RENEWAL OF TOWN AND VILLAGE I: A WORLD-
WIDE SURVEY OF LOCAL GOVERNMENT EXPERIENCE. WOR+45
CONSTRUC INDUS CREATE BUDGET REGION GOV/REL...QU
NAT/COMP 20 URBAN/RNWL. PAGE 31 B0628

MUNIC
NEIGH
PLAN
ADMIN

B65

FISCHER F.C.,THE GOVERNMENT OF MICHIGAN. USA+45
NAT/G PUB/INST EX/STRUC LEGIS BUDGET GIVE EDU/PROP
CT/SYS CHOOSE GOV/REL...T MICHIGAN. PAGE 36 B0723

PROVS
LOC/G
ADMIN
CONSTN

B65

FRYE R.J.,HOUSING AND URBAN RENEWAL IN ALABAMA.
USA+45 NEIGH LEGIS BUDGET ADJUD ADMIN PARTIC...MGT
20 ALABAMA URBAN/RNWL. PAGE 38 B0762

MUNIC
PROB/SOLV
PLAN
GOV/REL

B65

GOODSELL C.T.,ADMINISTRATION OF A REVOLUTION.
PUERT/RICO ECO/UNDEV FINAN MUNIC POL/PAR PROVS
LEGIS PLAN BUDGET RECEIVE ADMIN COLONIAL LEAD 20
ROOSEVLT/F. PAGE 41 B0827

EXEC
SOC

B65

GREER S.,URBAN RENEWAL AND AMERICAN CITIES: THE
DILEMMA OF DEMOCRATIC INTERVENTION. USA+45 R+D
LOC/G VOL/ASSN ACT/RES BUDGET ADMIN GOV/REL...SOC
INT SAMP 20 BOSTON CHICAGO MIAMI URBAN/RNWL.
PAGE 43 B0871

MUNIC
PROB/SOLV
PLAN
NAT/G

B65

GT BRIT ADMIN STAFF COLLEGE,THE ACCOUNTABILITY OF
PUBLIC CORPORATIONS (REV. ED.). UK ECO/DEV FINAN
DELIB/GP EX/STRUC BUDGET CAP/ISM CONFER PRICE
PARL/PROC 20. PAGE 44 B0899

LG/CO
NAT/G
ADMIN
CONTROL

B65

MELMANS S.,OUR DEPLETED SOCIETY. SPACE USA+45
ECO/DEV FORCES BUDGET ECO/TAC ADMIN WEAPON
EFFICIENCY 20 COLD/WAR. PAGE 73 B1465

CIVMIL/REL
INDUS
EDU/PROP
CONTROL

B65

MUSHKIN S.J.,STATE PROGRAMMING. USA+45 PLAN BUDGET
TAX ADMIN REGION GOV/REL...BIBLIOG 20. PAGE 77
B1549

PROVS
POLICY
CREATE
ECO/DEV

B65

RHODES G.,PUBLIC SECTOR PENSIONS. UK FINAN LEGIS
BUDGET TAX PAY INCOME...CHARTS 20 CIVIL/SERV.
PAGE 88 B1769

ADMIN
RECEIVE
AGE/O
WORKER

B65

STANLEY D.T.,CHANGING ADMINISTRATIONS. USA+45
POL/PAR DELIB/GP TOP/EX BUDGET GOV/REL GP/REL
PERS/REL PWR...MAJORIT DECISION MGT 20 PRESIDENT
SUCCESSION DEPT/STATE DEPT/DEFEN DEPT/HEW. PAGE 100
B2021

NAT/G
CHIEF
ADMIN
EX/STRUC

L65

HAMMOND A.,"COMPREHENSIVE VERSUS INCREMENTAL
BUDGETING IN THE DEPARTMENT OF AGRICULTURE" USA+45
GP/REL ATTIT...PSY INT 20 DEPT/AGRI. PAGE 46 B0934

TOP/EX
EX/STRUC
AGRI
BUDGET

S65

OSTGAARD E.,"FACTORS INFLUENCING THE FLOW OF NEWS."
COM/IND BUDGET DIPLOM EXEC GP/REL COST ATTIT SAMP.
PAGE 80 B1618

EDU/PROP
PERCEPT
RECORD

B66

CLEGG R.K.,THE ADMINISTRATOR IN PUBLIC WELFARE.
USA+45 STRUCT NAT/G PROVS PROB/SOLV BUDGET ECO/TAC
GP/REL ROLE...SOC/WK 20 PUBLIC/REL. PAGE 21 B0434

ADMIN
GIVE
GOV/REL
OP/RES

B66
DAHLBERG J.S.,THE NEW YORK BUREAU OF MUNICIPAL PROVS
RESEARCH: PIONEER IN GOVERNMENT ADMINISTRATION. MUNIC
CONSTN R+D BUDGET EDU/PROP PARTIC REPRESENT DELIB/GP
EFFICIENCY ORD/FREE...BIBLIOG METH 20 NEW/YORK ADMIN
NIPA. PAGE 26 B0522

B66
DILLEY M.R.,BRITISH POLICY IN KENYA COLONY (2ND COLONIAL
ED.). AFR INDIA UK LABOR BUDGET TAX ADMIN PARL/PROC REPRESENT
GP/REL...BIBLIOG 20 PARLIAMENT. PAGE 29 B0594 SOVEREIGN

B66
GHOSH P.K.,THE CONSTITUTION OF INDIA: HOW IT HAS CONSTN
BEEN FRAMED. INDIA LOC/G DELIB/GP EX/STRUC NAT/G
PROB/SOLV BUDGET INT/TRADE CT/SYS CHOOSE...LING 20. LEGIS
PAGE 39 B0795 FEDERAL

B66
GREENE L.E.,GOVERNMENT IN TENNESSEE (2ND ED.). PROVS
USA+45 DIST/IND INDUS POL/PAR EX/STRUC LEGIS PLAN LOC/G
BUDGET GIVE CT/SYS...MGT T 20 TENNESSEE. PAGE 43 CONSTN
B0866 ADMIN

B66
HASTINGS P.G.,THE MANAGEMENT OF BUSINESS FINANCE. FINAN
ECO/DEV PLAN BUDGET CONTROL COST...DECISION CHARTS MGT
BIBLIOG T 20. PAGE 48 B0966 INDUS
ECO/TAC

B66
HAYER T.,FRENCH AID. AFR FRANCE AGRI FINAN BUDGET TEC/DEV
ADMIN WAR PRODUC...CHARTS 18/20 THIRD/WRLD COLONIAL
OVRSEA/DEV. PAGE 48 B0975 FOR/AID
ECO/UNDEV

B66
INTERPARLIAMENTARY UNION.PARLIAMENTS: COMPARATIVE PARL/PROC
STUDY ON STRUCTURE AND FUNCTIONING OF LEGIS
REPRESENTATIVE INSTITUTIONS IN FIFTY-FIVE GOV/COMP
COUNTRIES. WOR+45 POL/PAR DELIB/GP BUDGET ADMIN EX/STRUC
CONTROL CHOOSE. PAGE 54 B1099

B66
JOHNSON N.,PARLIAMENT AND ADMINISTRATION: THE LEGIS
ESTIMATES COMMITTEE 1945-65. FUT UK NAT/G EX/STRUC ADMIN
PLAN BUDGET ORD/FREE...T 20 PARLIAMENT HOUSE/CMNS. FINAN
PAGE 57 B1147 DELIB/GP

B66
MANGONE G.J.,UN ADMINISTRATION OF ECONOMIC AND ADMIN
SOCIAL PROGRAMS. CONSULT BUDGET INT/TRADE REGION 20 MGT
UN. PAGE 69 B1391 ECO/TAC
DELIB/GP

B66
NIEBURG H.L.,IN THE NAME OF SCIENCE. USA+45 NAT/G
EX/STRUC LEGIS TEC/DEV BUDGET PAY AUTOMAT LOBBY PWR INDUS
...OBS 20. PAGE 78 B1581 TECHRACY

B66
NYC TEMPORARY COMM CITY FINAN.MUNICIPAL COLLECTIVE MUNIC
BARGAINING (NO. 8). USA+45 PLAN PROB/SOLV BARGAIN FINAN
BUDGET TAX EDU/PROP GOV/REL COST...MGT 20 ADMIN
NEWYORK/C. PAGE 79 B1596 LOC/G

B66
ROSS R.M.,STATE AND LOCAL GOVERNMENT AND LOC/G
ADMINISTRATION. USA+45 CONSTN POL/PAR EX/STRUC PROVS
LEGIS BUDGET EDU/PROP CONTROL CT/SYS CHOOSE GOV/REL MUNIC
T. PAGE 90 B1827 ADMIN

B66
UN ECAFE.ADMINISTRATIVE ASPECTS OF FAMILY PLANNING PLAN
PROGRAMMES (PAMPHLET). ASIA THAILAND WOR+45 CENSUS
VOL/ASSN PROB/SOLV BUDGET FOR/AID EDU/PROP CONFER FAM
CONTROL GOV/REL TIME 20 UN BIRTH/CON. PAGE 106 ADMIN
B2147

B66
US HOUSE COMM GOVT OPERATIONS.AN INVESTIGATION OF FOR/AID
THE US ECONOMIC AND MILITARY ASSISTANCE PROGRAMS IN ECO/UNDEV
VIETNAM. USA+45 VIETNAM/S SOCIETY CONSTRUC FINAN WAR
FORCES BUDGET INT/TRADE PEACE HEALTH...MGT INSPECT
HOUSE/REP AID. PAGE 108 B2191

B66
US SENATE COMM ON FOREIGN REL.HEARINGS ON S 2859 FOR/AID
AND S 2861. USA+45 WOR+45 FORCES BUDGET CAP/ISM DIPLOM
ADMIN DETER WEAPON TOTALISM...NAT/COMP 20 UN ORD/FREE
CONGRESS. PAGE 110 B2221 ECO/UNDEV

B66
WILSON G.,CASES AND MATERIALS ON CONSTITUTIONAL AND JURID
ADMINISTRATIVE LAW. UK LAW NAT/G EX/STRUC LEGIS ADMIN
BAL/PWR BUDGET DIPLOM ADJUD CONTROL CT/SYS GOV/REL CONSTN
ORD/FREE 20 PARLIAMENT ENGLSH/LAW. PAGE 117 B2359 PWR

L66
AMERICAN ECONOMIC REVIEW.,"SIXTY-THIRD LIST OF BIBLIOG/A
DOCTORAL DISSERTATIONS IN POLITICAL ECONOMY IN CONCPT
AMERICAN UNIVERSITIES AND COLLEGES." ECO/DEV AGRI ACADEM
FINAN LABOR WORKER PLAN BUDGET INT/TRADE ADMIN
DEMAND...MGT STAT 20. PAGE 4 B0084

C66
JACOB H.,"DIMENSIONS OF STATE POLITICS HEARD A. ED. PROVS
STATE LEGIWLATURES IN AMERICAN POLITICS." CULTURE LEGIS
STRATA POL/PAR BUDGET TAX LOBBY ROUTINE GOV/REL ROLE
...TRADIT DECISION GEOG. PAGE 55 B1112 REPRESENT

B67
ENKE S.,DEFENSE MANAGEMENT. USA+45 R+D FORCES DECISION
WORKER PLAN ECO/TAC ADMIN NUC/PWR BAL/PAY UTIL DELIB/GP

WEALTH...MGT DEPT/DEFEN. PAGE 33 B0675 EFFICIENCY
BUDGET

B67
GITTELL M.,PARTICIPANTS AND PARTICIPATION: A STUDY SCHOOL
OF SCHOOL POLICY IN NEW YORK. USA+45 MUNIC EX/STRUC DECISION
BUDGET PAY ATTIT...POLICY 20 NEWYORK/C. PAGE 40 PARTIC
B0806 ADMIN

B67
GREENE L.S.,AMERICAN GOVERNMENT POLICIES AND POLICY
FUNCTIONS. USA+45 LAW AGRI DIST/IND LABOR MUNIC NAT/G
BUDGET DIPLOM EDU/PROP ORD/FREE...BIBLIOG T 20. ADMIN
PAGE 43 B0867 DECISION

B67
JAIN R.K.,MANAGEMENT OF STATE ENTERPRISES. INDIA NAT/G
SOCIETY FINAN WORKER BUDGET ADMIN CONTROL OWN 20. SOCISM
PAGE 55 B1118 INDUS
MGT

S67
DUGGAR J.W.,"THE DEVELOPMENT OF MONEY SUPPLY IN ECO/UNDEV
ETHIOPIA." ETHIOPIA ISLAM CONSULT OP/RES BUDGET FINAN
CONTROL ROUTINE EFFICIENCY EQUILIB WEALTH...MGT 20. BAL/PAY
PAGE 31 B0629 ECOMETRIC

S67
FERGUSON H.,"3-CITY CONSOLIDATION." USA+45 CONSTN MUNIC
INDUS BARGAIN BUDGET CONFER ADMIN INGP/REL COST CHOOSE
UTIL. PAGE 35 B0712 CREATE
PROB/SOLV

S67
GORHAM W.,"NOTES OF A PRACTITIONER." USA+45 BUDGET DECISION
ADMIN COST...CON/ANAL METH/COMP 20 JOHNSON/LB. NAT/G
PAGE 41 B0836 DELIB/GP
EFFICIENCY

S67
HUMPHREY H.,"A MORE PERFECT UNION." USA+45 LOC/G GOV/REL
NAT/G ACT/RES BUDGET RECEIVE CENTRAL CONGRESS. FEDERAL
PAGE 52 B1063 ADMIN
PROB/SOLV

S67
JAVITS J.K.,"THE USE OF AMERICAN PLURALISM." USA+45 CENTRAL
ECO/DEV BUDGET ADMIN ALL/IDEOS...DECISION TREND. ATTIT
PAGE 56 B1127 POLICY
NAT/G

S67
KAYSEN C.,"DATA BANKS AND DOSSIERS." FUT USA+45 CENTRAL
COM/IND NAT/G PLAN PROB/SOLV TEC/DEV BUDGET ADMIN EFFICIENCY
ROUTINE. PAGE 59 B1185 CENSUS
ACT/RES

S67
KURON J.,"AN OPEN LETTER TO THE PARTY." CONSTN ELITES
WORKER BUDGET EDU/PROP ADMIN REPRESENT SUFF OWN STRUCT
...SOCIALIST 20. PAGE 62 B1244 POL/PAR
ECO/TAC

S67
LEES J.P.,"LEGISLATIVE REVIEW AND BUREAUCRATIC SUPEGO
RESPONSIBILITY." USA+45 FINAN NAT/G DELIB/GP PLAN BUDGET
PROB/SOLV CONFER CONTROL GP/REL DEMAND...DECISION LEGIS
20 CONGRESS PRESIDENT HOUSE/REP BUREAUCRCY. PAGE 63 EXEC
B1281

S67
LERNER A.P.,"EMPLOYMENT THEORY AND EMPLOYMENT CAP/ISM
POLICY." ECO/DEV INDUS LABOR LG/CO BUDGET ADMIN WORKER
DEMAND PROFIT WEALTH LAISSEZ METH/COMP. PAGE 64 CONCPT
B1296

S67
LINEBERRY R.L.,"REFORMISM AND PUBLIC POLICIES IN DECISION
AMERICAN CITIES." USA+45 POL/PAR EX/STRUC LEGIS POLICY
BUDGET TAX GP/REL...STAT CHARTS. PAGE 65 B1317 MUNIC
LOC/G

S67
MACDONALD G.J.F.,"SCIENCE AND SPACE POLICY. HOW SPACE
DOES IT GET PLANNED?" R+D CREATE TEC/DEV BUDGET PLAN
ADMIN ROUTINE...DECISION NASA. PAGE 67 B1357 MGT
EX/STRUC

S67
MERON T.,"THE UN'S 'COMMON SYSTEM' OF SALARY, ADMIN
ALLOWANCE, AND BENEFITS: CRITICAL APPR'SAL OF COORD EX/STRUC
IN PERSONNEL MATTERS." VOL/ASSN PAY EFFICIENCY INT/ORG
...CHARTS 20 UN. PAGE 73 B1470 BUDGET

S67
WRIGHT F.K.,"INVESTMENT CRITERIA AND THE COST OF COST
CAPITAL." FINAN PLAN BUDGET OPTIMAL PRODUC...POLICY PROFIT
DECISION 20. PAGE 118 B2380 INDUS
MGT

S67
ZOETEWEIJ B.,"INCOME POLICIES ABROAD: AN INTERIM METH/COMP
REPORT." NAT/G PROB/SOLV BARGAIN BUDGET PRICE RISK INCOME
CENTRAL EFFICIENCY EQUILIB...MGT NAT/COMP 20. POLICY
PAGE 119 B2405 LABOR

N67
NATIONAL COMN COMMUNITY HEALTH.ACTION - PLANNING PLAN
FOR COMMUNITY HEALTH SERVICES (PAMPHLET). USA+45 MUNIC
PROF/ORG DELIB/GP BUDGET ROUTINE GP/REL ATTIT HEALTH
...HEAL SOC SOC/WK CHARTS TIME 20. PAGE 77 B1563 ADJUST

N67
US CONGRESS JT COMM ECO GOVT.BACKGROUND MATERIAL ON BUDGET
ECONOMY IN GOVERNMENT 1967 (PAMPHLET). WOR+45 COST

ECO/DEV BARGAIN PRICE DEMAND OPTIMAL...STAT   MGT
DEPT/DEFEN. PAGE 108 B2178   NAT/G

                                                    N67
US SENATE COMM ON FOREIGN REL,THE UNITED NATIONS AT INT/ORG
TWENTY-ONE (PAMPHLET). WOR+45 BUDGET ADMIN SENATE   DIPLOM
UN. PAGE 110 B2223   PEACE

                                                    N67
US SENATE COMM ON FOREIGN REL,THE UNITED NATIONS   INT/ORG
PEACEKEEPING DILEMMA (PAMPHLET). ISLAM WOR+45   DIPLOM
PROB/SOLV BUDGET ADMIN SENATE UN. PAGE 110 B2224   PEACE

                                                    S68
PEARSON A.W.,"RESOURCE ALLOCATION." PLAN PROB/SOLV PROFIT
BUDGET ADMIN CONTROL CHOOSE EFFICIENCY...DECISION   OPTIMAL
MGT 20. PAGE 82 B1649   COST
                                                    INDUS

BUECHNER J.C. B0338

BUELL R. B0339,B0340

BUENO M. B0341

BUENOS/AIR....BUENOS AIRES, ARGENTINA

BUGANDA....BUGANDA, UGANDA

BUKHARIN/N....NIKOLAI BUKHARIN

BULGARIA....BULGARIA; SEE ALSO COM

                                                    N
KYRIAK T.L.,EAST EUROPE: BIBLIOGRAPHY--INDEX TO US BIBLIOG/A
JPRS RESEARCH TRANSLATIONS. ALBANIA BULGARIA COM   PRESS
CZECHOSLVK HUNGARY POLAND ROMANIA AGRI EXTR/IND   MARXISM
FINAN SERV/IND INT/TRADE WEAPON...GEOG MGT SOC 20. INDUS
PAGE 62 B1247

                                                    S63
DELLIN L.A.D.,"BULGARIA UNDER SOVIET LEADERSHIP."   AGRI
BULGARIA COM USA+45 USSR ECO/DEV INDUS POL/PAR   NAT/G
EX/STRUC TOP/EX COERCE ATTIT RIGID/FLEX...POLICY   TOTALISM
TIME/SEQ 20. PAGE 28 B0572

                                                    S64
HORECKY P.L.,"LIBRARY OF CONGRESS PUBLICATIONS IN   BIBLIOG/A
AID OF USSR AND EAST EUROPEAN RESEARCH." BULGARIA   COM
CZECHOSLVK POLAND USSR YUGOSLAVIA NAT/G POL/PAR   MARXISM
DIPLOM ADMIN GOV/REL...CLASSIF 20. PAGE 51 B1042

BULLIS H.A. B0342

BULLITT/WC....WILLIAM C. BULLITT

                                                    B67
FARNSWORTH B.,WILLIAM C. BULLITT AND THE SOVIET   DIPLOM
UNION. COM USA-45 USSR NAT/G CHIEF CONSULT DELIB/GP BIOG
EX/STRUC WAR REPRESENT MARXISM 20 WILSON/W   POLICY
ROOSEVLT/F STALIN/J BULLITT/WC. PAGE 35 B0705

BULMER-THOMAS I. B0343

BULPITT J.G. B0344

BUNCHE/R....RALPH BUNCHE

BUNDY/M....MCGEORGE BUNDY

                                                    B62
US SENATE COMM GOVT OPERATIONS,ADMINISTRATION OF   ORD/FREE
NATIONAL SECURITY. USA+45 CHIEF PLAN PROB/SOLV   ADMIN
TEC/DEV DIPLOM ATTIT...POLICY DECISION 20   NAT/G
KENNEDY/JF RUSK/D MCNAMARA/R BUNDY/M HERTER/C.   CONTROL
PAGE 110 B2212

BUNZEL J.H. B0345

BUR/BUDGET....BUREAU OF THE BUDGET

                                                    N19
DOTSON A.,PRODUCTION PLANNING IN THE PATENT OFFICE EFFICIENCY
(PAMPHLET). USA+45 DIST/IND PROB/SOLV PRODUC...MGT PLAN
PHIL/SCI 20 BUR/BUDGET PATENT/OFF. PAGE 30 B0610   NAT/G
                                                    ADMIN

                                                    N19
MARSH J.F. JR.,THE FBI RETIREMENT BILL (PAMPHLET). ADMIN
USA+45 EX/STRUC WORKER PLAN PROB/SOLV BUDGET LEAD   NAT/G
LOBBY PARL/PROC PERS/REL RIGID/FLEX...POLICY 20 FBI SENIOR
PRESIDENT BUR/BUDGET. PAGE 70 B1405   GOV/REL

                                                    B27
WILLOUGHBY W.F.,PRINCIPLES OF PUBLIC ADMINISTRATION NAT/G
WITH SPECIAL REFERENCE TO THE NATIONAL AND STATE   EX/STRUC
GOVERNMENTS OF THE UNITED STATES. FINAN PROVS CHIEF OP/RES
CONSULT LEGIS CREATE BUDGET EXEC ROUTINE GOV/REL   ADMIN
CENTRAL...MGT 20 BUR/BUDGET CONGRESS PRESIDENT.
PAGE 117 B2356

                                                    B49
STEIN H.,THE FOREIGN SERVICE ACT OF 1946. USA+45   DIPLOM
ELITES EX/STRUC PLAN PROB/SOLV LOBBY GOV/REL   LAW
PERS/REL RIGID/FLEX...POLICY IDEA/COMP 20 CONGRESS NAT/G
BUR/BUDGET. PAGE 100 B2027   ADMIN

                                                    B54
HOBBS E.H.,BEHIND THE PRESIDENT - A STUDY OF   EX/STRUC
EXECUTIVE OFFICE AGENCIES. USA+45 NAT/G PLAN BUDGET DELIB/GP
ECO/TAC EXEC ORD/FREE 20 BUR/BUDGET. PAGE 50 B1022 CONFER
                                                    CONSULT

BUR/STNDRD....BUREAU OF STANDARDS

BURACK E.H. B0346

BURAGR/ECO....BUREAU OF AGRICULTURAL ECONOMICS

BURDETTE F.L. B0347,B0348

BUREAU OF AGRICULTURAL ECONOMICS....SEE BURAGR/ECO

BUREAU OF STANDARDS....SEE BUR/STNDRD

BUREAU OF THE BUDGET....SEE BUR/BUDGET

BUREAU GOVERNMENT RES AND SERV B0349

BUREAU OF NATIONAL AFFAIRS B0350,B0351

BUREAUCRCY....BUREAUCRACY; SEE ALSO ADMIN

                                                    S43
SELZNICK P.,"AN APPROACH TO A THEORY OF   ROUTINE
BUREAUCRACY." INDUS WORKER CONTROL LEAD EFFICIENCY ADMIN
OPTIMAL...SCC METH 20 BARNARD/C BUREAUCRCY   MGT
WEBER/MAX FRIEDRCH/C MICHELS/R. PAGE 95 B1928   EX/STRUC

                                                    S47
TURNER R.H.,"THE NAVY DISBURSING OFFICER AS A   FORCES
BUREAUCRAT" (BMR)" USA-45 LAW STRATA DIST/IND WAR   ADMIN
PWR...SOC 20 BUREAUCRCY. PAGE 106 B2140   PERSON
                                                    ROLE

                                                    B48
ROSENFARB J.,FREEDOM AND THE ADMINISTRATIVE STATE. ECO/DEV
NAT/G ROUTINE EFFICIENCY PRODUC RATIONAL UTIL   INDUS
...TECHNIC WELF/ST MGT 20 BUREAUCRCY. PAGE 90 B1821 PLAN
                                                    WEALTH

                                                    S49
REISSMAN L.,"A STUDY OF ROLE CONCEPTIONS IN   ADMIN
BUREAUCRACY" (BMR)" PERS/REL ROLE...SOC CONCPT   METH/CNCPT
NEW/IDEA IDEA/COMP SOC/EXP 20 BUREAUCRCY. PAGE 87   GEN/LAWS
B1767   PROB/SOLV

                                                    B54
GOULDNER A.W.,PATTERNS OF INDUSTRIAL BUREAUCRACY.   ADMIN
DOMIN ATTIT DRIVE...BIBLIOG 20 BUREAUCRCY. PAGE 42 INDUS
B0844   OP/RES
                                                    WORKER

                                                    B56
BLAU P.M.,BUREAUCRACY IN MODERN SOCIETY. STRUCT   SOC
INDUS LABOR LG/CO LOC/G NAT/G FORCES EDU/PROP   EX/STRUC
ROUTINE ORD/FREE 20 BUREAUCRCY. PAGE 12 B0252   ADMIN
                                                    EFFICIENCY

                                                    B56
GLADDEN E.N.,CIVIL SERVICE OR BUREAUCRACY? UK LAW   ADMIN
STRATA LABOR TOP/EX PLAN SENIOR AUTOMAT CONTROL   GOV/REL
PARTIC CHOOSE HAPPINESS...CHARTS 19/20 CIVIL/SERV   EFFICIENCY
BUREAUCRCY. PAGE 40 B0808   PROVS

                                                    L56
EISENTADT S.N.,"POLITICAL STRUGGLE IN BUREAUCRATIC ADMIN
SOCIETIES" ASIA CULTURE ADJUD SANCTION PWR   CHIEF
BUREAUCRCY OTTOMAN BYZANTINE. PAGE 33 B0661   CONTROL
                                                    ROUTINE

                                                    S59
UDY S.H. JR.,"'BUREAUCRACY' AND 'RATIONALITY' IN   GEN/LAWS
WEBER'S ORGANIZATION THEORY: AN EMPIRICAL STUDY"   METH/CNCPT
(BMR)" UNIV STRUCT INDUS LG/CO SML/CO VOL/ASSN   ADMIN
...SOC SIMUL 20 WEBER/MAX BUREAUCRCY. PAGE 106   RATIONAL
B2144

                                                    B60
SAYRE W.S.,GOVERNING NEW YORK CITY; POLITICS IN THE MUNIC
METROPOLIS. POL/PAR CHIEF DELIB/GP LEGIS PLAN   ADMIN
CT/SYS LEAD PARTIC CHOOSE...DECISION CHARTS BIBLIOG PROB/SOLV
20 NEWYORK/C BUREAUCRCY. PAGE 93 B1875

                                                    B61
ETZIONI A.,COMPLEX ORGANIZATIONS: A SOCIOLOGICAL   VOL/ASSN
READER. CLIENT CULTURE STRATA CREATE OP/RES ADMIN   STRUCT
...POLICY METH/CNCPT BUREAUCRCY. PAGE 34 B0683   CLASSIF
                                                    PROF/ORG

                                                    B61
ROWAT D.C.,BASIC ISSUES IN PUBLIC ADMINISTRATION.   NAT/G
STRUCT EX/STRUC PWR CONSERVE...MAJORIT DECISION MGT ADJUD
T 20 BUREAUCRCY. PAGE 91 B1839   ADMIN

                                                    L61
THOMPSON V.A.,"HIERARCHY, SPECIALIZATION, AND   PERS/REL
ORGANIZATIONAL CONFLICT" (BMR)" WOR+45 STRATA   PROB/SOLV

STRUCT WORKER TEC/DEV GP/REL INGP/REL ATTIT
AUTHORIT 20 BUREAUCRCY. PAGE 104 B2106 — ADMIN EX/STRUC

S61

EHRMANN H.W.,"FRENCH BUREAUCRACY AND ORGANIZED
INTERESTS" (BMR)" FRANCE NAT/G DELIB/GP ROUTINE
...INT 20 BUREAUCRCY CIVIL/SERV. PAGE 32 B0657 — ADMIN DECISION PLURISM LOBBY

B62

INAYATULLAH,BUREAUCRACY AND DEVELOPMENT IN
PAKISTAN. PAKISIAN ECO/UNDEV EDU/PROP CONFER
...ANTHOL DICTIONARY 20 BUREAUCRCY. PAGE 53 B1078 — EX/STRUC ADMIN NAT/G LOC/G

S62

MAINZER L.C.,"INJUSTICE AND BUREAUCRACY." ELITES
STRATA STRUCT EX/STRUC SENIOR CONTROL EXEC LEAD
ROUTINE INGP/REL ORD/FREE...CONCPT 20 BUREAUCRCY.
PAGE 68 B1381 — MORAL MGT ADMIN

B64

ETZIONI A.,MODERN ORGANIZATIONS. CLIENT STRUCT
DOMIN CONTROL LEAD PERS/REL AUTHORIT...CLASSIF
BUREAUCRCY. PAGE 34 B0685 — MGT ADMIN PLAN CULTURE

B65

GOLEMBIEWSKI R.T.,MEN, MANAGEMENT, AND MORALITY;
TOWARD A NEW ORGANIZATIONAL ETHIC. CONSTN EX/STRUC
CREATE ADMIN CONTROL INGP/REL PERSON SUPEGO MORAL
PWR...GOV/COMP METH/COMP 20 BUREAUCRCY. PAGE 40
B0819 — LG/CO MGT PROB/SOLV

B66

BRAIBANTI R.,RESEARCH ON THE BUREAUCRACY OF
PAKISTAN. PAKISIAN LAW CULTURE INTELL ACADEM LOC/G
SECT PRESS CT/SYS...LING CHARTS 20 BUREAUCRCY.
PAGE 15 B0299 — HABITAT NAT/G ADMIN CONSTN

B66

HEADY F.,PUBLIC ADMINISTRATION: A COMPARATIVE
PERSPECTIVE. ECO/DEV ECO/UNDEV...GOV/COMP 20
BUREAUCRCY. PAGE 48 B0982 — ADMIN NAT/COMP NAT/G CIVMIL/REL

L66

MCAUSLAN J.P.W.,"CONSTITUTIONAL INNOVATION AND
POLITICAL STABILITY IN TANZANIA: A PRELIMINARY
ASSESSMENT." AFR TANZANIA ELITES CHIEF EX/STRUC
RIGID/FLEX PWR 20 PRESIDENT BUREAUCRCY. PAGE 71
B1440 — CONSTN NAT/G EXEC POL/PAR

S67

LEES J.P.,"LEGISLATIVE REVIEW AND BUREAUCRATIC
RESPONSIBILITY." USA+45 FINAN NAT/G DELIB/GP PLAN
PROB/SOLV CONFER CONTROL GP/REL DEMAND...DECISION
20 CONGRESS PRESIDENT HOUSE/REP BUREAUCRCY. PAGE 63
B1281 — SUPEGO BUDGET LEGIS EXEC

S67

SUBRAMANIAM V.,"REPRESENTATIVE BUREAUCRACY: A
REASSESSMENT." USA+45 ELITES LOC/G NAT/G ADMIN
GOV/REL PRIVIL DRIVE ROLE...POLICY CENSUS 20
CIVIL/SERV BUREAUCRCY. PAGE 101 B2053 — STRATA GP/REL MGT GOV/COMP

BURKE E.M. B0352

BURKE/EDM....EDMUND BURKE

BURMA....BURMA

C66

TARLING N.,"A CONCISE HISTORY OF SOUTHEAST ASIA."
BURMA CAMBODIA LAOS S/ASIA THAILAND VIETNAM
ECO/UNDEV POL/PAR FORCES ADMIN REV WAR CIVMIL/REL
ORD/FREE MARXISM SOCISM 13/20. PAGE 103 B2080 — COLONIAL DOMIN INT/TRADE NAT/LISM

BURNS A.C. B0353

BURNS J.M. B0354

BURR/AARON....AARON BURR

BURRUS B.R. B0355,B0356

BURSK E.C. B0357

BURT F.A. B0358

BURTON M.E. B0359

BURUNDI....SEE ALSO AFR

L66

LEMARCHAND R.,"SOCIAL CHANGE AND POLITICAL
MODERNISATION IN BURUNDI." AFR BURUNDI STRATA CHIEF
EX/STRUC RIGID/FLEX PWR...SOC 20. PAGE 64 B1285 — NAT/G STRUCT ELITES CONSERVE

BUSH V. B0360,B0361

BUSINESS CYCLE....SEE ECO, FINAN

BUSINESS MANAGEMENT....SEE MGT

BYZANTINE....BYZANTINE EMPIRE

L56

EISENTADT S.N.,"POLITICAL STRUGGLE IN BUREAUCRATIC
SOCIETIES" ASIA CULTURE ADJUD SANCTION PWR
BUREAUCRCY OTTOMAN BYZANTINE. PAGE 33 B0661 — ADMIN CHIEF CONTROL ROUTINE

C

CAB....CIVIL AERONAUTICS BOARD

B64

FISK W.M.,ADMINISTRATIVE PROCEDURE IN A REGULATORY
AGENCY: THE CAB AND THE NEW YORK-CHICAGO CASE
(PAMPHLET). USA+45 DIST/IND ADMIN CONTROL LOBBY
GP/REL ROLE ORD/FREE NEWYORK/C CHICAGO CAB. PAGE 36
B0727 — SERV/IND ECO/DEV AIR JURID

B66

WHITNAH D.R.,SAFER SKYWAYS. DIST/IND DELIB/GP
FORCES TOP/EX WORKER TEC/DEV ROUTINE WAR CIVMIL/REL
COST...TIME/SEQ 20 FAA CAB. PAGE 116 B2342 — ADMIN NAT/G AIR GOV/REL

CABINET....SEE ALSO EX/STRUC, DELIB/GP, CONSULT

B61

OPOTOWSKY S.,THE KENNEDY GOVERNMENT. NAT/G CONSULT
EX/STRUC LEAD PERSON...POLICY 20 KENNEDY/JF
CONGRESS CABINET. PAGE 80 B1613 — ADMIN BIOG ELITES TOP/EX

B62

GRAY R.K.,EIGHTEEN ACRES UNDER GLASS. ELITES
CONSULT EX/STRUC DIPLOM PRESS CONFER WAR PERS/REL
PERSON 20 EISNHWR/DD TRUMAN/HS CABINET. PAGE 43
B0860 — CHIEF ADMIN TOP/EX NAT/G

CAESAR/JUL....JULIUS CAESAR

CAHIER P. B0362

CAIRNCROSS A.K. B0363

CAIRO....CAIRO, EGYPT

CALCUTTA....CALCUTTA, INDIA

B63

SINGH M.M.,MUNICIPAL GOVERNMENT IN THE CALCUTTA
METROPOLITAN DISTRICT A PRELIMINARY SURVEY. FINAN
LG/CO DELIB/GP BUDGET TAX ADMIN GP/REL 20 CALCUTTA.
PAGE 97 B1969 — LOC/G HEALTH MUNIC JURID

B66

ASHRAF A.,THE CITY GOVERNMENT OF CALCUTTA: A STUDY
OF INERTIA. INDIA ELITES INDUS NAT/G EX/STRUC
ACT/RES PLAN PROB/SOLV LEAD HABITAT...BIBLIOG 20
CALCUTTA. PAGE 7 B0141 — LOC/G MUNIC ADMIN ECO/UNDEV

CALDWELL L.K. B0364,B0365,B0366

CALHOUN/JC....JOHN C. CALHOUN

B50

MONTGOMERY H.,CRACKER PARTIES. CULTURE EX/STRUC
LEAD PWR POPULISM...TIME/SEQ 19 GEORGIA CALHOUN/JC
COBB/HOWLL JACKSON/A. PAGE 74 B1505 — POL/PAR PROVS ELITES BIOG

CALIFORNIA....CALIFORNIA

B62

FOSS P.O.,REORGANIZATION AND REASSIGNMENT IN THE
CALIFORNIA HIGHWAY PATROL (PAMPHLET). USA+45 STRUCT
WORKER EDU/PROP CONTROL COERCE INGP/REL ORD/FREE
PWR...DECISION 20 CALIFORNIA. PAGE 37 B0744 — FORCES ADMIN PROVS PLAN

B62

ROBINSON M.,THE COMING OF AGE OF THE LANGLEY PORTER
CLINIC (PAMPHLET). USA+45 PROF/ORG PROVS PLAN...MGT
PSY 20 CALIFORNIA LANGLEY. PAGE 89 B1804 — PUB/INST ADMIN EFFICIENCY HEAL

B64

TURNER H.A.,THE GOVERNMENT AND POLITICS OF
CALIFORNIA (2ND ED.). LAW FINAN MUNIC POL/PAR
SCHOOL EX/STRUC LEGIS LOBBY CHOOSE...CHARTS T 20
CALIFORNIA. PAGE 106 B2138 — PROVS ADMIN LOC/G CONSTN

B65

ARTHUR D LITTLE INC,SAN FRANCISCO COMMUNITY RENEWAL
PROGRAM. USA+45 FINAN PROVS ADMIN INCOME...CHARTS
20 CALIFORNIA SAN/FRAN URBAN/RNWL. PAGE 7 B0138 — HABITAT MUNIC PLAN PROB/SOLV

B66

SCHLESSINGER P.J.,ELEMENTS OF CALIFORNIA GOVERNMENT
(2ND ED.). USA+45 LAW ADJUD ADMIN CONTROL CT/SYS
EFFICIENCY...BIBLIOG T CALIFORNIA. PAGE 94 B1891 — LOC/G PROVS GOV/REL LEGIS

CALKINS E.E. B0367

CALKINS R.D. B0368

CALVIN/J....JOHN CALVIN

B63
MONTER W.,THE GOVERNMENT OF GENEVA, 1536-1605   SECT
(DOCTORAL THESIS). SWITZERLND DIPLOM LEAD ORD/FREE   FINAN
SOVEREIGN 16/17 CALVIN/J ROME. PAGE 74 B1504   LOC/G
   ADMIN

CAMB/SOMER....CAMBRIDGE-SOMERVILLE YOUTH STUDY

CAMBODIA....SEE ALSO S/ASIA

B58
US HOUSE COMM GOVT OPERATIONS,HEARINGS BEFORE A   FOR/AID
SUBCOMMITTEE OF THE COMMITTEE ON GOVERNMENT   DIPLOM
OPERATIONS. CAMBODIA PHILIPPINE USA+45 CONSTRUC   ORD/FREE
TEC/DEV ADMIN CONTROL WEAPON EFFICIENCY HOUSE/REP.   ECO/UNDEV
PAGE 108 B2189

C66
TARLING N.,"A CONCISE HISTORY OF SOUTHEAST ASIA."   COLONIAL
BURMA CAMBODIA LAOS S/ASIA THAILAND VIETNAM   DOMIN
ECO/UNDEV POL/PAR FORCES ADMIN REV WAR CIVMIL/REL   INT/TRADE
ORD/FREE MARXISM SOCISM 13/20. PAGE 103 B2080   NAT/LISM

CAMBRIDGE-SOMERVILLE YOUTH STUDY....SEE CAMB/SOMER

CAMELOT....PROJECT CAMELOT (CHILE)

S65
SILVERT K.H.,"AMERICAN ACADEMIC ETHICS AND SOCIAL   ACADEM
RESEARCH ABROAD* THE LESSON OF PROJECT CAMELOT."   NAT/G
CHILE L/A+17C USA+45 FINAN ADMIN...PHIL/SCI SOC   ACT/RES
GEN/LAWS CAMELOT. PAGE 97 B1953   POLICY

CAMEROON....SEE ALSO AFR

B63
ROBINSON K.,ESSAYS IN IMPERIAL GOVERNMENT. CAMEROON COLONIAL
NIGERIA UK CONSIN LOC/G LEGIS ADMIN GOV/REL PWR   AFR
...POLICY ANTHOL BIBLIOG 17/20 PURHAM/M. PAGE 89   DOMIN
B1803

B64
WITHERELL J.W.,OFFICIAL PUBLICATIONS OF FRENCH   BIBLIOG/A
EQUATORIAL AFRICA, FRENCH CAMEROONS, AND TOGO,   AFR
1946-1958 (PAMPHLET). CAMEROON CHAD FRANCE GABON   NAT/G
TOGO EURO ECO/UNDEV EXTR/IND INT/TRADE...GEOG HEAL   ADMIN
20. PAGE 117 B2367

B66
US LIBRARY OF CONGRESS,NIGERIA: A GUIDE TO OFFICIAL BIBLIOG
PUBLICATIONS. CAMEROON NIGERIA UK DIPLOM...POLICY   ADMIN
19/20 UN LEAGUE/NAT. PAGE 109 B2207   NAT/G
   COLONIAL

CAMPBELL A. B0369

CAMPBELL A.K. B0262

CAMPBELL G.A. B0370

CAMPBELL R.W. B0371

CANAD/CRWN....CANADIAN CROWN CORPORATIONS

CANADA....SEE ALSO COMMONWLTH

N
FINANCIAL INDEX. CANADA UK USA+45 ECO/DEV LG/CO   BIBLIOG
ADMIN 20. PAGE 2 B0032   INDUS
   FINAN
   PRESS

N
CARLETON UNIVERSITY LIBRARY,SELECTED LIST OF   BIBLIOG
CURRENT MATERIALS ON CANADIAN PUBLIC   ADMIN
ADMINISTRATION. CANADA LEGIS WORKER PLAN BUDGET 20. LOC/G
PAGE 19 B0379   MUNIC

N
UNIVERSITY MICROFILMS INC,DISSERTATION ABSTRACTS: BIBLIOG/A
ABSTRACTS OF DISSERTATIONS AND MONOGRAPHS IN   ACADEM
MICROFILM. CANADA DIPLOM ADMIN...INDEX 20. PAGE 107 PRESS
B2166   WRITING

N19
CANADA CIVIL SERV COMM,THE ANALYSIS OF ORGANIZATION NAT/G
IN THE GOVERNMENT OF CANADA (PAMPHLET). CANADA   MGT
CONSTN EX/STRUC LEGIS TOP/EX CREATE PLAN CONTROL   ADMIN
GP/REL 20. PAGE 18 B0372   DELIB/GP

B46
GRIFFIN G.G.,A GUIDE TO MANUSCRIPTS RELATING TO   BIBLIOG/A
AMERICAN HISTORY IN BRITISH DEPOSITORIES. CANADA   ALL/VALS
IRELAND MOD/EUR UK USA-45 LAW DIPLOM ADMIN COLONIAL NAT/G
WAR NAT/LISM SOVEREIGN...GEOG INT/LAW 15/19
CMN/WLTH. PAGE 43 B0876

B50
MCHENRY D.E.,THE THIRD FORCE IN CANADA: THE   POL/PAR
COOPERATIVE COMMONWEALTH FEDERATION, 1932-1948.   ADMIN

CANADA EX/STRUC LEGIS REPRESENT 20 LABOR/PAR.   CHOOSE
PAGE 72 B1451   POLICY
   B57

BISHOP O.B.,PUBLICATIONS OF THE GOVERNMENTS OF NOVA BIBLIOG
SCOTIA, PRINCE EDWARD ISLAND, NEW BRUNSWICK   NAT/G
1758-1952. CANADA UK ADMIN COLONIAL LEAD...POLICY   DIPLOM
18/20. PAGE 12 B0245
   S57

HODGETTS J.E.,"THE CIVIL SERVICE AND POLICY   ADMIN
FORMATION." CANADA NAT/G EX/STRUC ROUTINE GOV/REL   DECISION
20. PAGE 50 B1023   EFFICIENCY
   POLICY
   B59

SPIRO H.J.,GOVERNMENT BY CONSTITUTIONS: THE   NAT/G
POLITICAL SYSTEMS OF DEMOCRACY. CANADA EUR+WWI FUT   CONSTN
USA+45 WOR+45 WOR-45 LEGIS TOP/EX LEGIT ADMIN
CT/SYS ORD/FREE PWR...TREND TOT/POP VAL/FREE 20.
PAGE 99 B2008
   B60

ANGERS F.A.,ESSAI SUR LA CENTRALISATION: ANALYSE   CENTRAL
DES PRINCIPES ET PERSPECTIVES CANADIENNES. CANADA   ADMIN
ECO/TAC CONTROL...SOC IDEA/COMP BIBLIOG 20. PAGE 5
B0111
   B60

HODGETTS J.E.,CANADIAN PUBLIC ADMINISTRATION.   REPRESENT
CANADA CONTROL LOBBY EFFICIENCY 20. PAGE 50 B1024   ADMIN
   EX/STRUC
   ADJUD
   S60

TAYLOR M.G.,"THE ROLE OF THE MEDICAL PROFESSION IN   PROF/ORG
THE FORMULATION AND EXECUTION OF PUBLIC POLICY"   HEALTH
(BMR)" CANADA NAT/G CONSULT ADMIN REPRESENT GP/REL   LOBBY
ROLE SOVEREIGN...DECISION 20 CMA. PAGE 103 B2088   POLICY
   B61

CARROTHERS A.W.R.,LABOR ARBITRATION IN CANADA.   LABOR
CANADA LAW NAT/G CONSULT LEGIS WORKER ADJUD ADMIN   MGT
CT/SYS 20. PAGE 19 B0386   GP/REL
   BARGAIN
   B61

HALL M.,DISTRIBUTION IN GREAT BRITAIN AND NORTH   DIST/IND
AMERICA. CANADA UK USA+45 ECO/DEV INDUS MARKET   PRODUC
EFFICIENCY PROFIT...MGT CHARTS 20. PAGE 46 B0924   ECO/TAC
   CAP/ISM
   B61

WILLOUGHBY W.R.,THE ST LAWRENCE WATERWAY: A STUDY   LEGIS
IN POLITICS AND DIPLOMACY. USA+45 ECO/DEV COM/IND   INT/TRADE
INT/ORG CONSULT DELIB/GP ACT/RES TEC/DEV DIPLOM   CANADA
ECO/TAC ROUTINE...TIME/SEQ 20. PAGE 117 B2357   DIST/IND
   S61

ANGLIN D.,"UNITED STATES OPPOSITION TO CANADIAN   INT/ORG
MEMBERSHIP IN THE PAN AMERICAN UNION: A CANADIAN   CANADA
VIEW." L/A+17C UK USA+45 VOL/ASSN DELIB/GP EX/STRUC
PLAN DIPLOM DOMIN REGION ATTIT RIGID/FLEX PWR
...RELATIV CONCPT STERTYP CMN/WLTH OAS 20. PAGE 5
B0112
   S62

JOHNSON H.,"CANADA IN A CHANGING WORLD." EUR+WWI   ECO/DEV
USA+45 NAT/G CAP/ISM ECO/TAC ADMIN ATTIT WEALTH   PLAN
...TREND TOT/POP 20 EEC. PAGE 57 B1143   CANADA
   S63

HARRIS R.L.,"A COMPARATIVE ANALYSIS OF THE   DELIB/GP
ADMINISTRATIVE SYSTEMS OF CANADA AND CEYLON."   EX/STRUC
S/ASIA CULTURE SOCIETY STRATA TOP/EX ACT/RES DOMIN   CANADA
EDU/PROP LEGIT COERCE ATTIT SUPEGO ALL/VALS...MGT   CEYLON
CHARTS GEN/LAWS VAL/FREE 20. PAGE 47 B0955
   S63

PIPER D.C.,"THE ROLE OF INTER-GOVERNMENTAL   GOV/REL
MACHINERY IN CANADIANAMERICAN RELATIONS." CANADA   ADMIN
USA+45 PROB/SOLV REPRESENT 20. PAGE 83 B1676   EX/STRUC
   CONFER
   B64

THE SPECIAL COMMONWEALTH AFRICAN ASSISTANCE PLAN.   ECO/UNDEV
AFR CANADA INDIA NIGERIA UK FINAN SCHOOL...CHARTS   TREND
20 COMMONWLTH. PAGE 2 B0041   FOR/AID
   ADMIN
   B64

FATOUROS A.A.,CANADA'S OVERSEAS AID. CANADA WOR+45   FOR/AID
ECO/DEV FINAN NAT/G BUDGET ECO/TAC CONFER ADMIN 20. DIPLOM
PAGE 35 B0707   ECO/UNDEV
   POLICY
   B64

NATIONAL BOOK LEAGUE,THE COMMONWEALTH IN BOOKS: AN   BIBLIOG/A
ANNOTATED LIST. CANADA UK LOC/G SECT ADMIN...SOC   JURID
BIOG 20 CMN/WLTH. PAGE 77 B1561   NAT/G
   B64

O'HEARN P.J.T.,PEACE, ORDER AND GOOD GOVERNMENT; A   NAT/G
NEW CONSTITUTION FOR CANADA. CANADA EX/STRUC LEGIS   CONSTN
CT/SYS PARL/PROC...BIBLIOG 20. PAGE 79 B1600   LAW
   CREATE
   N64

CANADA NATL JT COUN PUB SERV,THE CANADA NATIONAL   GP/REL
JOINT COUNCIL OF THE PUBLIC SERVICE 1944-1964   NAT/G
(PAMPHLET). CANADA EX/STRUC PERS/REL DRIVE...MGT 20 LABOR
PEARSON/L. PAGE 18 B0373   EFFICIENCY
   B66

ANDERSON S.V.,CANADIAN OMBUDSMAN PROPOSALS. CANADA   NAT/G

LEGIS DEBATE PARL/PROC...MAJORIT JURID TIME/SEQ
IDEA/COMP 20 OMBUDSMAN PARLIAMENT. PAGE 5 B0096
CREATE
ADMIN
POL/PAR
B66

SPICER K.,A SAMARITAN STATE? AFR CANADA INDIA
PAKISTAN UK USA+45 FINAN INDUS PRODUC...CHARTS 20
NATO. PAGE 99 B2006
DIPLOM
FOR/AID
ECO/DEV
ADMIN
B67

KAPLAN H.,URBAN POLITICAL SYSTEMS: A FUNCTIONAL
ANALYSIS OF METRO TORONTO. CANADA STRUCT NEIGH PLAN
ADMIN...POLICY METH 20 TORONTO. PAGE 58 B1166
GEN/LAWS
MUNIC
LOC/G
FEDERAL
L67

BESCOBY I.,"A COLONIAL ADMINISTRATION* AN ANALYSIS
OF ADMINISTRATION IN BRITISH COLUMBIA 1869-1871."
UK STRATA EX/STRUC LEGIS TASK GOV/REL EFFICIENCY
ROLE...MGT CHARTS 19. PAGE 11 B0232
ADMIN
CANADA
COLONIAL
LEAD
S67

DOERN G.B.,"THE ROYAL COMMISSIONS IN THE GENERAL
POLICY PROCESS AND IN FEDERAL-PROVINCIAL
RELATIONS." CANADA CONSTN ACADEM PROVS CONSULT
DELIB/GP LEGIS ACT/RES PROB/SOLV CONFER CONTROL
EFFICIENCY...METH/COMP 20 SENATE ROYAL/COMM.
PAGE 30 B0603
R+D
EX/STRUC
GOV/REL
NAT/G
S67

ROWAT D.C.,"RECENT DEVELOPMENTS IN OMBUDSMANSHIP* A
REVIEW ARTICLE." UK USA+45 STRUCT CONSULT INSPECT
TASK EFFICIENCY...NEW/IDEA 20. PAGE 91 B1841
CANADA
ADMIN
LOC/G
NAT/G
S67

TACKABERRY R.B.,"ORGANIZING AND TRAINING PEACE-
KEEPING FORCES* THE CANADIAN VIEW." CANADA PLAN
DIPLOM CONFER ADJUD ADMIN CIVMIL/REL 20 UN.
PAGE 102 B2069
PEACE
FORCES
INT/ORG
CONSULT
S67

ZASLOW M.,"RECENT CONSTITUTIONAL DEVELOPMENTS IN
CANADA'S NORTHERN TERRITORIES." CANADA LOC/G
DELIB/GP EX/STRUC LEGIS ADMIN ORD/FREE...TREND 20.
PAGE 119 B2398
GOV/REL
REGION
CONSTN
FEDERAL

CANADA CIVIL SERV COMM B0372

CANADA NATL JT COUN PUB SERV B0373

CANADIAN CROWN CORPORATIONS....SEE CANAD/CRWN

CANADIAN MEDICAL ASSOCIATION....SEE CMA

CANAL/ZONE....CANAL ZONE

CANNON/JG....JOSEPH G. CANNON

CANON/LAW....CANON LAW

CANTRIL/H....HADLEY CANTRIL

CAP/ISM....CAPITALISM

MOON P.T.,IMPERIALISM AND WORLD POLITICS. AFR ASIA
ISLAM MOD/EUR S/ASIA USA-45 SOCIETY NAT/G EX/STRUC
BAL/PWR DOMIN COLONIAL NAT/LISM ATTIT DRIVE PWR
...GEOG SOC 20. PAGE 75 B1510
WEALTH
TIME/SEQ
CAP/ISM
DIPLOM
B26

HETTINGER H.S.,A DECADE OF RADIO ADVERTISING.
USA-45 ECO/DEV CAP/ISM PRICE...CHARTS 20. PAGE 49
B0999
EDU/PROP
COM/IND
ECO/TAC
ROUTINE
B33

PARSONS T.,THE STRUCTURE OF SOCIAL ACTION. UNIV
INTELL SOCIETY INDUS MARKET ECO/TAC ROUTINE CHOOSE
ALL/VALS...CONCPT OBS BIOG TREND GEN/LAWS 20.
PAGE 81 B1636
CULTURE
ATTIT
CAP/ISM
B37

CLOUGH S.B.,ECONOMIC HISTORY OF EUROPE. CHRIST-17C
EUR+WWI MOD/EUR WOR-45 SOCIETY EXEC ATTIT WEALTH
...CONCPT GEN/LAWS WORK TOT/POP VAL/FREE 7/20.
PAGE 22 B0440
ECO/TAC
CAP/ISM
B46

BORGESE G.,COMMON CAUSE. LAW CONSTN SOCIETY STRATA
ECO/DEV INT/ORG POL/PAR FORCES LEGIS TOP/EX CAP/ISM
DIPLOM ADMIN EXEC ATTIT PWR 20. PAGE 14 B0279
WOR+45
NAT/G
SOVEREIGN
REGION
B47

FORD FOUNDATION,REPORT OF THE STUDY FOR THE FORD
FOUNDATION ON POLICY AND PROGRAM. SOCIETY R+D
ACT/RES CAP/ISM FOR/AID EDU/PROP ADMIN KNOWL
...POLICY PSY SOC 20. PAGE 36 B0739
WEALTH
GEN/LAWS
B49

COMMONS J.R.,THE ECONOMICS OF COLLECTIVE ACTION.
USA-45 AGRI INDUS LABOR NAT/G LEGIS ADMIN
EFFICIENCY...MGT METH/COMP BIBLIOG 20. PAGE 22
B0458
ECO/DEV
CAP/ISM
ACT/RES
CONCPT
B50

MANNHEIM K.,FREEDOM, POWER, AND DEMOCRATIC
TEC/DEV

PLANNING. FUT USSR WOR+45 ELITES INTELL SOCIETY
NAT/G EDU/PROP ROUTINE ATTIT DRIVE SUPEGO SKILL
...POLICY PSY CONCPT TREND GEN/LAWS 20. PAGE 69
B1393
PLAN
CAP/ISM
UK
B51

DIMOCK M.E.,FREE ENTERPRISE AND THE ADMINISTRATIVE
STATE. FINAN LG/CO BARGAIN BUDGET DOMIN CONTROL
INGP/REL EFFICIENCY 20. PAGE 29 B0595
CAP/ISM
ADMIN
MGT
MARKET
B52

EGLE W.P.,ECONOMIC STABILIZATION. USA+45 SOCIETY
FINAN MARKET PLAN ECO/TAC DOMIN EDU/PROP LEGIT EXEC
WEALTH...CONCPT METH/CNCPT TREND HYPO/EXP GEN/METH
TOT/POP VAL/FREE 20. PAGE 32 B0656
NAT/G
ECO/DEV
CAP/ISM
B54

MOSK S.A.,INDUSTRIAL REVOLUTION IN MEXICO. MARKET
LABOR CREATE CAP/ISM ADMIN ATTIT SOCISM...POLICY 20
MEXIC/AMER. PAGE 76 B1533
INDUS
TEC/DEV
ECO/UNDEV
NAT/G
B54

RECK D.,GOVERNMENT PURCHASING AND COMPETITION.
USA+45 LEGIS CAP/ISM ECO/TAC GOV/REL CENTRAL
...POLICY 20 CONGRESS. PAGE 87 B1749
NAT/G
FINAN
MGT
COST
C55

BONER H.A.,"HUNGRY GENERATIONS." UK WOR+45 WOR-45
STRATA INDUS FAM LABOR CAP/ISM...MGT BIBLIOG 19/20.
PAGE 13 B0272
ECO/DEV
PHIL/SCI
CONCPT
WEALTH
B56

ALEXANDER R.S.,INDUSTRIAL MARKETING. USA+45 ECO/DEV
DIST/IND FINAN NAT/G ACT/RES CAP/ISM PRICE CONTROL
...POLICY MGT 20. PAGE 4 B0072
INDUS
MARKET
ECO/TAC
PLAN
B57

DJILAS M.,THE NEW CLASS: AN ANALYSIS OF THE
COMMUNIST SYSTEM. STRATA CAP/ISM ECO/TAC DOMIN
EDU/PROP LEGIT EXEC COERCE ATTIT PWR MARXISM
...MARXIST MGT CONCPT TIME/SEQ GEN/LAWS 20. PAGE 29
B0600
COM
POL/PAR
USSR
YUGOSLAVIA
B57

MORSTEIN-MARX F.,THE ADMINISTRATIVE STATE: AN
INTRODUCTION TO BUREAUCRACY. EUR+WWI FUT MOD/EUR
USA+45 USA-45 NAT/G CONSULT ADMIN ROUTINE TOTALISM
DRIVE SKILL...TREND 19/20. PAGE 76 B1530
EXEC
MGT
CAP/ISM
ELITES
C59

DAHL R.A.,"SOCIAL SCIENCE RESEARCH ON BUSINESS:
PRODUCT AND POTENTIAL" INDUS MARKET OP/RES CAP/ISM
ADMIN LOBBY DRIVE...PSY CONCPT BIBLIOG/A 20.
PAGE 26 B0521
MGT
EFFICIENCY
PROB/SOLV
EX/STRUC
B60

CAMPBELL R.W.,SOVIET ECONOMIC POWER. COM USA+45
DIST/IND MARKET TOP/EX ACT/RES CAP/ISM ECO/TAC
DOMIN EDU/PROP ADMIN ROUTINE DRIVE...MATH TIME/SEQ
CHARTS WORK 20. PAGE 18 B0371
ECO/DEV
PLAN
SOCISM
USSR
B60

LERNER A.P.,THE ECONOMICS OF CONTROL. USA+45
ECO/UNDEV INT/ORG ACT/RES PLAN CAP/ISM INT/TRADE
ATTIT WEALTH...SOC MATH STAT GEN/LAWS INDEX 20.
PAGE 64 B1295
ECO/DEV
ROUTINE
ECO/TAC
SOCISM
B60

ROEPKE W.,A HUMANE ECONOMY: THE SOCIAL FRAMEWORK OF
THE FREE MARKET. FUT USSR WOR+45 CULTURE SOCIETY
ECO/DEV PLAN ECO/TAC ADMIN ATTIT PERSON RIGID/FLEX
SUPEGO MORAL WEALTH SOCISM...POLICY OLD/LIB CONCPT
TREND GEN/LAWS 20. PAGE 90 B1811
DRIVE
EDU/PROP
CAP/ISM
L60

MACPHERSON C.,"TECHNICAL CHANGE AND POLITICAL
DECISION." WOR+45 NAT/G CREATE CAP/ISM DIPLOM
ROUTINE RIGID/FLEX...CONCPT OBS GEN/METH 20.
PAGE 68 B1375
TEC/DEV
ADMIN
S60

FRANKEL S.H.,"ECONOMIC ASPECTS OF POLITICAL
INDEPENDENCE IN AFRICA." AFR FUT SOCIETY ECO/UNDEV
COM/IND FINAN LEGIS PLAN TEC/DEV CAP/ISM ECO/TAC
INT/TRADE ADMIN ATTIT DRIVE RIGID/FLEX PWR WEALTH
...MGT NEW/IDEA MATH TIME/SEQ VAL/FREE 20. PAGE 37
B0751
NAT/G
FOR/AID
B61

BULLIS H.A.,MANIFESTO FOR AMERICANS. USA+45 AGRI
LABOR NAT/G NEIGH FOR/AID INT/TRADE TAX EDU/PROP
CHOOSE...POLICY MGT 20 UN UNESCO. PAGE 17 B0342
ECO/TAC
SOCIETY
INDUS
CAP/ISM
B61

HALL M.,DISTRIBUTION IN GREAT BRITAIN AND NORTH
AMERICA. CANADA UK USA+45 ECO/DEV INDUS MARKET
EFFICIENCY PROFIT...MGT CHARTS 20. PAGE 46 B0924
DIST/IND
PRODUC
ECO/TAC
CAP/ISM
B61

HORVATH B.,THE CHARACTERISTICS OF YUGOSLAV ECONOMIC
DEVELOPMENT. COM ECO/UNDEV AGRI INDUS PLAN CAP/ISM
ECO/TAC ROUTINE WEALTH...SOCIALIST STAT CHARTS
STERTYP WORK 20. PAGE 52 B1045
ACT/RES
YUGOSLAVIA
B61

LENIN V.I.,WHAT IS TO BE DONE? (1902). RUSSIA LABOR
NAT/G POL/PAR WORKER CAP/ISM ECO/TAC ADMIN PARTIC
EDU/PROP
PRESS

...MARXIST IDEA/COMP GEN/LAWS 19/20. PAGE 64 B1292 MARXISM METH/COMP

B61

MARX K.,THE COMMUNIST MANIFESTO. IN (MENDEL A. COM
ESSENTIAL WORKS OF MARXISM, NEW YORK: BANTAM. FUT NEW/IDEA
MOD/EUR CULTURE ECO/DEV ECO/UNDEV AGRI FINAN INDUS CAP/ISM
MARKET PROC/MFG LABOR MUNIC POL/PAR CONSULT FORCES REV
CREATE PLAN ADMIN ATTIT DRIVE RIGID/FLEX ORD/FREE
PWR RESPECT MARX/KARL WORK. PAGE 70 B1421

S61

GORDON L.,"ECONOMIC REGIONALISM RECONSIDERED." FUT ECO/DEV
USA+45 WOR+45 INDUS NAT/G TEC/DEV DIPLOM ROUTINE ATTIT
PERCEPT WEALTH...WELF/ST METH/CNCPT WORK 20. CAP/ISM
PAGE 41 B0830 REGION

B62

FRIEDMANN W.,METHODS AND POLICIES OF PRINCIPAL INT/ORG
DONOR COUNTRIES IN PUBLIC INTERNATIONAL DEVELOPMENT FOR/AID
FINANCING: PRELIMINARY APPRAISAL. FRANCE GERMANY/W NAT/COMP
UK USA+45 USSR WOR+45 FINAN TEC/DEV CAP/ISM DIPLOM ADMIN
ECO/TAC ATTIT 20 EEC. PAGE 37 B0759

B62

GRANICK D.,THE EUROPEAN EXECUTIVE. BELGIUM FRANCE MGT
GERMANY/W UK INDUS LABOR LG/CO SML/CO EX/STRUC PLAN ECO/DEV
TEC/DEV CAP/ISM COST DEMAND...POLICY CHARTS 20. ECO/TAC
PAGE 42 B0852 EXEC

B62

MEANS G.C.,THE CORPORATE REVOLUTION IN AMERICA: LG/CO
ECONOMIC REALITY VS. ECONOMIC THEORY. USA+45 USA-45 MARKET
INDUS WORKER PLAN CAP/ISM ADMIN...IDEA/COMP 20. CONTROL
PAGE 72 B1459 PRICE

B62

WEDDING N.,ADVERTISING MANAGEMENT. USA+45 ECO/DEV ECO/TAC
BUDGET CAP/ISM PRODUC PROFIT ATTIT...DECISION MGT COM/IND
PSY 20. PAGE 114 B2308 PLAN
EDU/PROP

L62

GALBRAITH J.K.,"ECONOMIC DEVELOPMENT IN ECO/UNDEV
PERSPECTIVE." CAP/ISM ECO/TAC ROUTINE ATTIT WEALTH PLAN
...TREND CHARTS SOC/EXP WORK 20. PAGE 38 B0773

S62

IOVTCHOUK M.T.,"ON SOME THEORETICAL PRINCIPLES AND COM
METHODS OF SOCIOLOGICAL INVESTIGATIONS (IN ECO/DEV
RUSSIAN)." FUT USA+45 STRATA R+D NAT/G POL/PAR CAP/ISM
TOP/EX ACT/RES PLAN ECO/TAC EDU/PROP ROUTINE ATTIT USSR
RIGID/FLEX MARXISM SOCISM...MARXIST METH/CNCPT OBS
TREND NAT/COMP GEN/LAWS 20. PAGE 54 B1102

S62

JOHNSON H.,"CANADA IN A CHANGING WORLD." EUR+WWI ECO/DEV
USA+45 NAT/G CAP/ISM ECO/TAC ADMIN ATTIT WEALTH PLAN
...TREND TOT/POP 20 EEC. PAGE 57 B1143 CANADA

B63

PATRA A.C.,THE ADMINISTRATION OF JUSTICE UNDER THE ADMIN
EAST INDIA COMPANY IN BENGAL, BIHAR AND ORISSA. JURID
INDIA UK LG/CO CAP/ISM INT/TRADE ADJUD COLONIAL CONCPT
CONTROL CT/SYS...POLICY 20. PAGE 81 B1641

B64

GROSS B.M.,THE MANAGING OF ORGANIZATIONS (VOL. I). ECO/TAC
USA+45 ECO/DEV LG/CO CAP/ISM EFFICIENCY ROLE...MGT ADMIN
20. PAGE 44 B0886 INDUS
POLICY

B64

MARRIS R.,THE ECONOMIC THEORY OF "MANAGERIAL" CAP/ISM
CAPITALISM. USA+45 ECO/DEV LG/CO ECO/TAC DEMAND MGT
...CHARTS BIBLIOG 20. PAGE 69 B1402 CONTROL
OP/RES

B64

WERNETTE J.P.,GOVERNMENT AND BUSINESS. LABOR NAT/G
CAP/ISM ECO/TAC INT/TRADE TAX ADMIN AUTOMAT NUC/PWR FINAN
CIVMIL/REL DEMAND...MGT 20 MONOPOLY. PAGE 115 B2323 ECO/DEV
CONTROL

B64

WILLIAMSON O.E.,THE ECONOMICS OF DISCRETIONARY EFFICIENCY
BEHAVIOR: MANAGERIAL OBJECTIVES IN A THEORY OF THE MGT
FIRM. MARKET BUDGET CAP/ISM PRODUC DRIVE PERSON ECO/TAC
...STAT CHARTS BIBLIOG METH 20. PAGE 117 B2354 CHOOSE

B65

ALDERSON W.,DYNAMIC MARKETING BEHAVIOR. USA+45 MGT
FINAN CREATE TEC/DEV EDU/PROP PRICE COST 20. PAGE 3 MARKET
B0071 ATTIT
CAP/ISM

B65

COPELAND M.A.,OUR FREE ENTERPRISE ECONOMY. USA+45 CAP/ISM
INDUS LABOR ADMIN CONTROL GP/REL MGT. PAGE 23 B0476 PLAN
FINAN
ECO/DEV

B65

GT BRIT ADMIN STAFF COLLEGE,THE ACCOUNTABILITY OF LG/CO
PUBLIC CORPORATIONS (REV. ED.). UK ECO/DEV FINAN NAT/G
DELIB/GP EX/STRUC BUDGET CAP/ISM CONFER PRICE ADMIN
PARL/PROC 20. PAGE 44 B0899 CONTROL

B65

MUSOLF L.D.,PROMOTING THE GENERAL WELFARE: ECO/TAC
GOVERNMENT AND THE ECONOMY. USA+45 ECO/DEV CAP/ISM NAT/G
DEMAND OPTIMAL 20. PAGE 77 B1550 EX/STRUC
NEW/LIB

B65

STEINER G.A.,THE CREATIVE ORGANIZATION. ELITES CREATE
LG/CO PLAN PROB/SOLV TEC/DEV INSPECT CAP/ISM MGT
CONTROL EXEC PERSON...METH/COMP HYPO/EXP 20. ADMIN
PAGE 100 B2029 SOC

L65

WILLIAMS S.,"NEGOTIATING INVESTMENT IN EMERGING FINAN
COUNTRIES." USA+45 WOR+45 INDUS MARKET NAT/G TOP/EX ECO/UNDEV
TEC/DEV CAP/ISM ECO/TAC ADMIN SKILL WEALTH...POLICY
RELATIV MGT WORK 20. PAGE 117 B2353

B66

GRETHER E.T.,MARKETING AND PUBLIC POLICY. USA+45 MARKET
ECO/DEV DIST/IND NAT/G PLAN CAP/ISM PRICE CONTROL PROB/SOLV
...GEOG MGT 20. PAGE 43 B0874 ECO/TAC
POLICY

B66

REDFORD E.S.,THE ROLE OF GOVERNMENT IN THE AMERICAN NAT/G
ECONOMY. USA+45 USA-45 FINAN INDUS LG/CO PROB/SOLV ECO/DEV
ADMIN INGP/REL INCOME PRODUC 18/20. PAGE 87 B1759 CAP/ISM
ECO/TAC

B66

US SENATE COMM ON FOREIGN REL,HEARINGS ON S 2859 FOR/AID
AND S 2861. USA+45 WOR+45 FORCES BUDGET CAP/ISM DIPLOM
ADMIN DETER WEAPON TOTALISM...NAT/COMP 20 UN ORD/FREE
CONGRESS. PAGE 110 B2221 ECO/UNDEV

S66

JACOBS P.,"RE-RADICALIZING THE DE-RADICALIZED." NAT/G
USA+45 SOCIETY STRUCT FINAN PLAN PROB/SOLV CAP/ISM POLICY
WEALTH CONSERVE NEW/LIB 20. PAGE 55 B1114 MARXIST
ADMIN

B67

BRAYMAN H.,CORPORATE MANAGEMENT IN A WORLD OF MGT
POLITICS. USA+45 ELITES MARKET CREATE BARGAIN ECO/DEV
DIPLOM INT/TRADE ATTIT SKILL 20. PAGE 15 B0302 CAP/ISM
INDUS

B67

DICKSON P.G.M.,THE FINANCIAL REVOLUTION IN ENGLAND. ECO/DEV
UK NAT/G TEC/DEV ADMIN GOV/REL...SOC METH/CNCPT FINAN
CHARTS GP/COMP BIBLIOG 17/18. PAGE 29 B0587 CAP/ISM
MGT

B67

EVANS R.H.,COEXISTENCE: COMMUNISM AND ITS PRACTICE MARXISM
IN BOLOGNA, 1945-1965. ITALY CAP/ISM ADMIN CHOOSE CULTURE
PEACE ORD/FREE...SOC STAT DEEP/INT SAMP CHARTS MUNIC
BIBLIOG 20. PAGE 34 B0690 POL/PAR

B67

GABRIEL P.P.,THE INTERNATIONAL TRANSFER OF ECO/UNDEV
CORPORATE SKILLS: MANAGEMENT CONTRACTS IN LESS AGREE
DEVELOPED COUNTRIES. CLIENT INDUS LG/CO PLAN MGT
PROB/SOLV CAP/ISM ECO/TAC FOR/AID INT/TRADE RENT CONSULT
ADMIN SKILL 20. PAGE 38 B0771

B67

GROSSMAN G.,ECONOMIC SYSTEMS. USA+45 USA-45 USSR ECO/DEV
YUGOSLAVIA WORKER CAP/ISM PRICE GP/REL EQUILIB PLAN
WEALTH MARXISM SOCISM...MGT METH/COMP 19/20. TEC/DEV
PAGE 44 B0892 DEMAND

B67

KARDOUCHE G.K.,THE UAR IN DEVELOPMENT. UAR ECO/TAC FINAN
INT/TRADE BAL/PAY...STAT CHARTS BIBLIOG 20. PAGE 58 MGT
B1172 CAP/ISM
ECO/UNDEV

B67

POSNER M.V.,ITALIAN PUBLIC ENTERPRISE. ITALY NAT/G
ECO/DEV FINAN INDUS CREATE ECO/TAC ADMIN CONTROL PLAN
EFFICIENCY PRODUC...TREND CHARTS 20. PAGE 84 B1693 CAP/ISM
SOCISM

B67

PYE L.W.,SOUTHEAST ASIA'S POLITICAL SYSTEMS. ASIA NAT/G
S/ASIA STRUCT ECO/UNDEV EX/STRUC CAP/ISM DIPLOM POL/PAR
ALL/IDEOS...TREND CHARTS. PAGE 85 B1724 GOV/COMP

B67

SABLE M.H.,A GUIDE TO LATIN AMERICAN STUDIES (2 BIBLIOG/A
VOLS). CONSTN FINAN INT/ORG LABOR MUNIC POL/PAR L/A+17C
FORCES CAP/ISM FOR/AID ADMIN MARXISM SOCISM OAS. DIPLOM
PAGE 92 B1861 NAT/LISM

B67

TANSKY L.,US AND USSR AID TO DEVELOPING COUNTRIES. FOR/AID
INDIA TURKEY UAR USA+45 USSR FINAN PLAN TEC/DEV ECO/UNDEV
ADMIN WEALTH...TREND METH/COMP 20. PAGE 103 B2076 MARXISM
CAP/ISM

B67

ZELERMYER W.,BUSINESS LAW: NEW PERSPECTIVES IN LABOR
BUSINESS ECONOMICS. USA+45 LAW INDUS DELIB/GP CAP/ISM
...JURID MGT ANTHOL BIBLIOG 20 NLRB. PAGE 119 B2400 LG/CO

L67

MANNE H.G.,"OUR TWO CORPORATION SYSTEMS* LAW AND INDUS
ECONOMICS." LAW CONTROL SANCTION GP/REL...JURID 20. ELITES
PAGE 69 B1392 CAP/ISM
ADMIN

S67

LERNER A.P.,"EMPLOYMENT THEORY AND EMPLOYMENT CAP/ISM
POLICY." ECO/DEV INDUS LABOR LG/CO BUDGET ADMIN WORKER
DEMAND PROFIT WEALTH LAISSEZ METH/COMP. PAGE 64 CONCPT
B1296

S67

MOOR E.J.,"THE INTERNATIONAL IMPACT OF AUTOMATION." TEC/DEV

WOR+45 ACT/RES COMPUTER CREATE PLAN CAP/ISM ROUTINE OP/RES
EFFICIENCY PREDICT. PAGE 75 B1511   AUTOMAT
                                                       INDUS

CAPE W.H. B0704

CAPE/HOPE....CAPE OF GOOD HOPE

CAPITAL....SEE FINAN, ECO

CAPITALISM....SEE CAP/ISM

CAPLOW T. B0374

CAPODIST/J....JOHN CAPODISTRIAS

CAPONE/AL....AL CAPONE

CARALEY D. B0375

CARDINALL AW B0376

CARDOZA/JN....JACOB N. CARDOZA

CARIAS B. B0377

CARIBBEAN....CARIBBEAN

                                                         S62
   SPRINGER H.W.,"FEDERATION IN THE CARIBBEAN: AN   VOL/ASSN
   ATTEMPT THAT FAILED." L/A+17C ECO/UNDEV INT/ORG   NAT/G
   POL/PAR PROVS LEGIS CREATE PLAN LEGIT ADMIN FEDERAL REGION
   ATTIT DRIVE PERSON ORD/FREE PWR...POLICY GEOG PSY
   CONCPT OBS CARIBBEAN CMN/WLTH 20. PAGE 100 B2013

CARLETON W.G. B0378

CARLETON UNIVERSITY LIBRARY B0379

CARLISLE D. B0380

CARLO A.M. B0381

CARMICHAEL D.M. B0382

CARNEG/COM....CARNEGIE COMMISSION

CARNEGIE COMMISSION....SEE CARNEG/COM

CARNEGIE ENDOWMENT INT. PEACE B0383

CARNEY D.E. B0384

CARPER E.T. B0385

CARRANZA/V....VENUSTIANZO CARRANZA

CARRELL J.J. B0331

CARROTHERS A.W.R. B0386

CARSON P. B0387

CARTER B.E. B0388

CARTER G.M. B0389,B0390

CASE H.L. B0391

CASE STUDIES....CARRIED UNDER THE SPECIAL TECHNIQUES USED,
   OR TOPICS COVERED

CASEBOOK....CASEBOOK, SUCH AS LEGAL OR SOCIOLOGICAL CASEBOOK

                                                         B40
   HART J.,AN INTRODUCTION TO ADMINISTRATIVE LAW, WITH LAW
   SELECTED CASES. USA-45 CONSTN SOCIETY NAT/G   ADMIN
   EX/STRUC ADJUD CT/SYS LEGIS LEAD CRIME ORD/FREE   LEGIS
   ...DECISION JURID 20 CASEBOOK. PAGE 47 B0958   PWR
                                                         B55
   CUSHMAN R.E.,LEADING CONSTITUTIONAL DECISIONS.   CONSTN
   USA+45 USA-45 NAT/G EX/STRUC LEGIS JUDGE TAX   PROB/SOLV
   FEDERAL...DECISION 20 SUPREME/CT CASEBOOK. PAGE 25 JURID
   B0513   CT/SYS
                                                         B62
   BOCK E.A.,CASE STUDIES IN AMERICAN GOVERNMENT.   POLICY
   USA+45 ECO/DEV CHIEF EDU/PROP CT/SYS RACE/REL   LEGIS
   ORD/FREE...JURID MGT PHIL/SCI PRESIDENT CASEBOOK.   IDEA/COMP
   PAGE 13 B0262   NAT/G
                                                         B63
   BOCK E.A., STATE AND LOCAL GOVERNMENT: A CASE BOOK. LOC/G
   USA+45 MUNIC PROVS CONSULT GP/REL ATTIT...MGT 20   ADMIN
   CASEBOOK GOVERNOR MAYOR. PAGE 12 B0254   PROB/SOLV
                                                       CHIEF
                                                         B63
   BOCK E.A.,STATE AND LOCAL GOVERNMENT: A CASE BOOK. PROVS

   USA+45 FINAN CHIEF PROB/SOLV TAX ATTIT...POLICY 20 LOC/G
   CASEBOOK. PAGE 13 B0263   ADMIN
                                                       GOV/REL
                                                         B66
   BOYD H.W.,MARKETING MANAGEMENT: CASES FROM EMERGING MGT
   COUNTRIES. BRAZIL GHANA ISRAEL WOR+45 ADMIN   ECO/UNDEV
   PERS/REL ATTIT HABITAT WEALTH...ANTHOL 20 ARGEN   PROB/SOLV
   CASEBOOK. PAGE 14 B0292   MARKET
                                                         B66
   FENN DH J.R.,BUSINESS DECISION MAKING AND   DECISION
   GOVERNMENT POLICY. SERV/IND LEGIS LICENSE ADMIN   PLAN
   CONTROL GP/REL INGP/REL 20 CASEBOOK. PAGE 35 B0711 NAT/G
                                                       LG/CO

CASTE....SEE INDIA + STRATA, HINDU

CASTRO/F....FIDEL CASTRO

CATEGORY (AS CONCEPT)....SEE METH/CNCPT

CATER D. B0392

CATH....ROMAN CATHOLIC

                                                         B66
   MCKENZIE J.L.,AUTHORITY IN THE CHURCH. STRUCT LEAD SECT
   INGP/REL PERS/REL CENTRAL ANOMIE ATTIT ORD/FREE   AUTHORIT
   RESPECT CATH. PAGE 72 B1452   PWR
                                                       ADMIN

CATHERINE R. B0393,B0394

CATHISM....ROMAN CATHOLICISM

                                                         B62
   THIERRY S.S.,LE VATICAN SECRET. CHRIST-17C EUR+WWI ADMIN
   MOD/EUR VATICAN NAT/G SECT DELIB/GP DOMIN LEGIT   EX/STRUC
   SOVEREIGN. PAGE 104 B2096   CATHISM
                                                       DECISION
                                                         B63
   DIESNER H.J.,KIRCHE UND STAAT IM SPATROMISCHEN   SECT
   REICH. ROMAN/EMP EX/STRUC COLONIAL COERCE ATTIT   GP/REL
   CATHISM 4/5 AFRICA/N CHURCH/STA. PAGE 29 B0592   DOMIN
                                                       JURID
                                                         B63
   FORTES A.B.,HISTORIA ADMINISTRATIVA, JUDICIARIA E   PROVS
   ECLESIASTICA DO RIO GRANDE DO SUL. BRAZIL L/A+17C   ADMIN
   LOC/G SECT COLONIAL CT/SYS ORD/FREE CATHISM 16/20. JURID
   PAGE 37 B0742
                                                         B65
   COHN H.J.,THE GOVERNMENT OF THE RHINE PALATINATE IN PROVS
   THE FIFTEENTH CENTURY. GERMANY FINAN LOC/G DELIB/GP JURID
   LEGIS CT/SYS CHOOSE CATHISM 14/15 PALATINATE.   GP/REL
   PAGE 22 B0449   ADMIN
                                                         B65
   HAINES R.M.,THE ADMINISTRATION OF THE DIOCESE OF   ADMIN
   WORCESTER IN THE FIRST HALF OF THE FOURTEENTH   EX/STRUC
   CENTURY. UK CATHISM...METH/COMP 13/15. PAGE 45   SECT
   B0918   DELIB/GP
                                                         B65
   KAAS L.,DIE GEISTLICHE GERICHTSBARKEIT DER   JURID
   KATHOLISCHEN KIRCHE IN PREUSSEN (2 VOLS.). PRUSSIA CATHISM
   CONSTN NAT/G PROVS SECT ADJUD ADMIN ATTIT 16/20.   GP/REL
   PAGE 57 B1158   CT/SYS

CATHOLICISM....SEE CATH, CATHISM

CATTON B. B0258

CAUCUS....SEE PARL/PROC

CAVERS D.F. B0395,B0396

CECIL L. B0397

CED....COMMITTEE FOR ECONOMIC DEVELOPMENT

CENSORSHIP....SEE EDU/PROP

CENSUS....POPULATION ENUMERATION

                                                         B08
   THE GOVERNMENT OF SOUTH AFRICA (VOL. II). SOUTH/AFR CONSTN
   STRATA EXTR/IND EX/STRUC TOP/EX BUDGET ADJUD ADMIN FINAN
   CT/SYS PRODUC...CORREL CENSUS 19 RAILROAD   LEGIS
   CIVIL/SERV POSTAL/SYS. PAGE 2 B0033   NAT/G
                                                         N19
   ANDERSON W.,THE UNITS OF GOVERNMENT IN THE UNITED   LOC/G
   STATES (PAMPHLET). USA-45 NAT/G PROVS EFFICIENCY   CENSUS
   ...CHARTS 20. PAGE 5 B0098   ADMIN
                                                       GOV/REL
                                                         B28
   BUELL R.,THE NATIVE PROBLEM IN AFRICA. KIN LABOR   AFR
   LOC/G ECO/TAC ROUTINE ORD/FREE...REC/INT KNO/TEST   CULTURE
   CENSUS TREND CHARTS SOC/EXP STERTYP 20. PAGE 17
   B0339

B44
DAVIS H.E.,PIONEERS IN WORLD ORDER. WOR-45 CONSTN   INT/ORG
ECO/TAC DOMIN EDU/PROP LEGIT ADJUD ADMIN ARMS/CONT   ROUTINE
CHOOSE KNOWL ORD/FREE...POLICY JURID SOC STAT OBS
CENSUS TIME/SEQ ANTHOL LEAGUE/NAT 20. PAGE 26 B0537

B55
APTER D.E.,THE GOLD COAST IN TRANSITION. FUT CONSTN AFR
CULTURE SOCIETY ECO/UNDEV FAM KIN LOC/G NAT/G   SOVEREIGN
POL/PAR LEGIS TOP/EX EDU/PROP LEGIT ADMIN ATTIT
PERSON PWR...CONCPT STAT INT CENSUS TOT/POP
VAL/FREE. PAGE 6 B0120

B59
YALE UNIV BUR OF HIGHWAY TRAF,URBAN TRANSPORTATION   ADMIN
ADMINISTRATION. FUT USA+45 CONSTRUC ACT/RES BUDGET   DIST/IND
...CENSUS 20 PUB/TRANS. PAGE 118 B2388   LOC/G
                                                          PLAN
B60
ASPREMONT-LYNDEN H.,RAPPORT SUR L'ADMINISTRATION   AFR
BELGE DU RUANDA-URUNDI PENDANT L'ANNEE 1959.   COLONIAL
BELGIUM RWANDA AGRI INDUS DIPLOM ECO/TAC INT/TRADE   ECO/UNDEV
DOMIN ADMIN RACE/REL...GEOG CENSUS 20 UN. PAGE 7   INT/ORG
B0143

B60
PENNSYLVANIA ECONOMY LEAGUE,URBAN RENEWAL IMPACT   PLAN
STUDY: ADMINISTRATIVE-LEGAL-FISCAL. USA+45 FINAN   BUDGET
LOC/G NEIGH ADMIN EFFICIENCY...CENSUS CHARTS 20   MUNIC
PENNSYLVAN. PAGE 82 B1652   ADJUD

S60
BANFIELD E.C.,"THE POLITICAL IMPLICATIONS OF   TASK
METROPOLITAN GROWTH" (BMR)" UK USA+45 LOC/G   MUNIC
PROB/SOLV ADMIN GP/REL...METH/COMP NAT/COMP 20.   GOV/COMP
PAGE 9 B0176   CENSUS

S60
REISELBACH L.N.,"THE BASIS OF ISOLATIONIST   ATTIT
BEHAVIOR." USA+45 USA-45 CULTURE ECO/DEV LOC/G   DIPLOM
NAT/G ADMIN ROUTINE CHOOSE BIO/SOC DRIVE RIGID/FLEX   ECO/TAC
...CENSUS SAMP TREND CHARTS TOT/POP 20. PAGE 87
B1765

B61
JACOBS J.,THE DEATH AND LIFE OF GREAT AMERICAN   MUNIC
CITIES. USA+45 SOCIETY DIST/IND CREATE PROB/SOLV   PLAN
ADMIN...GEOG SOC CENSUS 20 URBAN/RNWL. PAGE 55   ADJUST
B1113   HABITAT

B62
CHERNICK J.,THE SELECTION OF TRAINEES UNDER MDTA.   EDU/PROP
USA+45 NAT/G LEGIS PERSON...CENSUS 20 CIVIL/SERV   WORKER
MDTA. PAGE 20 B0418   ADMIN
                                                        DELIB/GP
B63
MCKIE R.,MALAYSIA IN FOCUS. INDONESIA WOR+45   S/ASIA
ECO/UNDEV FINAN NAT/G POL/PAR SECT FORCES PLAN   NAT/LISM
ADMIN COLONIAL COERCE DRIVE ALL/VALS...POLICY   MALAYSIA
RECORD CENSUS TIME/SEQ CMN/WLTH 20. PAGE 72 B1453

B64
BROMAGE A.W.,MANAGER PLAN ABANDONMENTS: WHY A FEW   MUNIC
HAVE DROPPED COUNCILMANAGER GOVERNMENT. USA+45   PLAN
CREATE PARTIC CHOOSE...MGT CENSUS CHARTS 20.   CONSULT
PAGE 15 B0315   LOC/G

B65
AMERICAN ECONOMIC ASSOCIATION,INDEX OF ECONOMIC   BIBLIOG
JOURNALS 1886-1965 (7 VOLS.). UK USA+45 USA-45 AGRI   WRITING
FINAN PLAN ECO/TAC INT/TRADE ADMIN...STAT CENSUS   INDUS
19/20. PAGE 4 B0083

B65
MATRAS J.,SOCIAL CHANGE IN ISRAEL. ISRAEL STRATA   SECT
FAM ACT/RES EDU/PROP ADMIN CHOOSE...STAT CENSUS   NAT/LISM
19/20 JEWS. PAGE 71 B1427   GEOG
                                                       STRUCT
B66
UN ECAFE,ADMINISTRATIVE ASPECTS OF FAMILY PLANNING   PLAN
PROGRAMMES (PAMPHLET). ASIA THAILAND WOR+45   CENSUS
VOL/ASSN PROB/SOLV BUDGET FOR/AID EDU/PROP CONFER   FAM
CONTROL GOV/REL TIME 20 UN BIRTH/CON. PAGE 106   ADMIN
B2147

S66
"FURTHER READING." INDIA LOC/G NAT/G PLAN ADMIN   BIBLIOG
WEALTH...GEOG SOC CONCPT CENSUS 20. PAGE 2 B0045   ECO/UNDEV
                                                      TEC/DEV
                                                      PROVS
L67
CARMICHAEL D.M.,"FORTY YEARS OF WATER POLLUTION   HEALTH
CONTROL IN WISCONSIN: A CASE STUDY." LAW EXTR/IND   CONTROL
INDUS MUNIC DELIB/GP PLAN PROB/SOLV SANCTION   ADMIN
...CENSUS CHARTS 20 WISCONSIN. PAGE 19 B0382   ADJUD

S67
KAYSEN C.,"DATA BANKS AND DOSSIERS." FUT USA+45   CENTRAL
COM/IND NAT/G PLAN PROB/SOLV TEC/DEV BUDGET ADMIN   EFFICIENCY
ROUTINE. PAGE 59 B1185   CENSUS
                                                      ACT/RES
S67
SUBRAMANIAM V.,"REPRESENTATIVE BUREAUCRACY: A   STRATA
REASSESSMENT." USA+45 ELITES LOC/G NAT/G ADMIN   GP/REL
GOV/REL PRIVIL DRIVE ROLE...POLICY CENSUS 20   MGT
CIVIL/SERV BUREAUCRCY. PAGE 101 B2053   GOV/COMP

CENTER/PAR....CENTER PARTY (ALL NATIONS)

CENTO....CENTRAL TREATY ORGANIZATION

CENTRAL AFRICA....SEE AFRICA/CEN

CENTRAL AFRICAN REPUBLIC....SEE CENTRL/AFR

CENTRAL INTELLIGENCE AGENCY....SEE CIA

CENTRAL TREATY ORGANIZATION....SEE CENTO

CENTRAL....CENTRALIZATION

N
MONPIED E.,BIBLIOGRAPHIE FEDERALISTE: ARTICLES ET   BIBLIOG/A
DOCUMENTS PUBLIES DANS LES PERIODIQUES PARUS EN   FEDERAL
FRANCE NOV. 1945-OCT. 1950. EUR+WWI WOR+45 ADMIN   CENTRAL
REGION ATTIT MARXISM PACIFISM 20 EEC. PAGE 74 B1501   INT/ORG

N19
ANDERSON J.,THE ORGANIZATION OF ECONOMIC STUDIES IN   ECO/TAC
RELATION TO THE PROBLEMS OF GOVERNMENT (PAMPHLET).   ACT/RES
UK FINAN INDUS DELIB/GP PLAN PROB/SOLV ADMIN 20.   NAT/G
PAGE 5 B0093   CENTRAL

B27
WILLOUGHBY W.F.,PRINCIPLES OF PUBLIC ADMINISTRATION   NAT/G
WITH SPECIAL REFERENCE TO THE NATIONAL AND STATE   EX/STRUC
GOVERNMENTS OF THE UNITED STATES. FINAN PROVS CHIEF   OP/RES
CONSULT LEGIS CREATE BUDGET EXEC ROUTINE GOV/REL   ADMIN
CENTRAL...MGT 20 BUR/BUDGET CONGRESS PRESIDENT.
PAGE 117 B2356

C27
HSIAO K.C.,"POLITICAL PLURALISM." LAW CONSTN   STRUCT
POL/PAR LEGIS PLAN ADMIN CENTRAL SOVEREIGN   GEN/LAWS
...INT/LAW BIBLIOG 19/20. PAGE 52 B1053   PLURISM

B33
BROMAGE A.W.,AMERICAN COUNTY GOVERNMENT. USA-45   LOC/G
NAT/G LEAD GOV/REL CENTRAL PWR...MGT BIBLIOG 18/20.   CREATE
PAGE 15 B0314   ADMIN
                                                       MUNIC
B39
ANDERSON W.,LOCAL GOVERNMENT IN EUROPE. FRANCE   GOV/COMP
GERMANY ITALY UK USSR MUNIC PROVS ADMIN GOV/REL   NAT/COMP
CENTRAL SOVEREIGN 20. PAGE 5 B0099   LOC/G
                                                       CONSTN
C39
REISCHAUER R.,"JAPAN'S GOVERNMENT--POLITICS."   NAT/G
CONSTN STRATA POL/PAR FORCES LEGIS DIPLOM ADMIN   S/ASIA
EXEC CENTRAL...POLICY BIBLIOG 20 CHINJAP. PAGE 87   CONCPT
B1764   ROUTINE

N40
COUNTY GOVERNMENT IN THE UNITED STATES: A LIST OF   BIBLIOG/A
RECENT REFERENCES (PAMPHLET). USA-45 LAW PUB/INST   LOC/G
PLAN BUDGET CT/SYS CENTRAL 20. PAGE 49 B0988   ADMIN
                                                       MUNIC
B41
COHEN E.W.,THE GROWTH OF THE BRITISH CIVIL SERVICE   OP/RES
1780-1939. UK NAT/G SENIOR ROUTINE GOV/REL...MGT   TIME/SEQ
METH/COMP BIBLIOG 18/20. PAGE 22 B0442   CENTRAL
                                                       ADMIN
B45
ROGERS W.C.,INTERNATIONAL ADMINISTRATION: A   BIBLIOG/A
BIBLIOGRAPHY (PUBLICATION NO 92: A PAMPHLET).   ADMIN
WOR-45 INT/ORG LOC/G NAT/G CENTRAL 20. PAGE 90   MGT
B1814   DIPLOM

C45
MCDIARMID J.,"THE MOBILIZATION OF SOCIAL   INTELL
SCIENTISTS," IN L. WHITE'S CIVIL CIVIL SERVICE IN   WAR
WARTIME." USA-45 TEC/DEV CENTRAL...SOC 20   DELIB/GP
CIVIL/SERV. PAGE 72 B1447   ADMIN

B47
GAUS J.M.,REFLECTIONS ON PUBLIC ADMINISTRATION.   MGT
USA+45 CONTROL GOV/REL CENTRAL FEDERAL ATTIT WEALTH   POLICY
...DECISION 20. PAGE 39 B0787   EX/STRUC
                                                      ADMIN
B48
ROSSITER C.L.,CONSTITUTIONAL DICTATORSHIP: CRISIS   NAT/G
GOVERNMENT IN THE MODERN DEMOCRACIES. FRANCE   AUTHORIT
GERMANY UK USA-45 WOR+45 EX/STRUC BAL/PWR CONTROL   CONSTN
COERCE WAR CENTRAL ORD/FREE...DECISION 19/20.   TOTALISM
PAGE 90 B1828

B48
TOWSTER J.,POLITICAL POWER IN THE USSR: 1917-1947.   EX/STRUC
USSR CONSTN CULTURE ELITES CREATE PLAN COERCE   NAT/G
CENTRAL ATTIT RIGID/FLEX ORD/FREE...BIBLIOG   MARXISM
SOC/INTEG 20 LENIN/VI STALIN/J. PAGE 105 B2124   PWR

L49
FAINSED M.,"RECENT DEVELOPMENTS IN SOVIET PUBLIC   DOMIN
ADMINISTRATION." USSR EXEC 20. PAGE 34 B0699   CONTROL
                                                      CENTRAL
                                                      EX/STRUC
B50
HYNEMAN C.S.,BUREAUCRACY IN A DEMOCRACY. CHIEF   NAT/G
LEGIS ADMIN CONTROL LEAD ROUTINE PERS/REL COST   CENTRAL
EFFICIENCY UTIL ATTIT AUTHORIT PERSON MORAL.   EX/STRUC
PAGE 53 B1071   MYTH

B50
MONPIED E.,BIBLIOGRAPHIE FEDERALISTE: OUVRAGES   BIBLIOG/A

CHOISIS (VOL. I, MIMEOGRAPHED PAPER). EUR+WWI
DIPLOM ADMIN REGION ATTIT PACIFISM SOCISM...INT/LAW
19/20. PAGE 74 B1502

FEDERAL
CENTRAL
INT/ORG
B53

MAJUMDAR B.B.,PROBLEMS OF PUBLIC ADMINISTRATION IN
INDIA. INDIA INDUS PLAN BUDGET ADJUD CENTRAL DEMAND
WEALTH...WELF/ST ANTHOL 20 CIVIL/SERV. PAGE 68
B1384

ECO/UNDEV
GOV/REL
ADMIN
MUNIC
C53

DORWART R.A.,"THE ADMINISTRATIVE REFORMS OF
FREDRICK WILLIAM I OF PRUSSIA. GERMANY MOD/EUR
CHIEF CONTROL PWR...BIBLIOG 16/18. PAGE 30 B0608

ADMIN
NAT/G
CENTRAL
GOV/REL
B54

RECK D.,GOVERNMENT PURCHASING AND COMPETITION.
USA+45 LEGIS CAP/ISM ECO/TAC GOV/REL CENTRAL
...POLICY 20 CONGRESS. PAGE 87 B1749

NAT/G
FINAN
MGT
COST
S54

STONE E.O.,"ADMINISTRATIVE INTEGRATION." USA+45
NAT/G ADMIN CONTROL CENTRAL 20. PAGE 101 B2046

REPRESENT
EFFICIENCY
LOBBY
EX/STRUC
B57

MEYER P.,ADMINISTRATIVE ORGANIZATION: A COMPARATIVE
STUDY OF THE ORGANIZATION OF PUBLIC ADMINISTRATION.
DENMARK FRANCE NORWAY SWEDEN UK USA+45 ELITES LOC/G
CONSULT LEGIS ADJUD CONTROL LEAD PWR SKILL
DECISION. PAGE 73 B1475

ADMIN
METH/COMP
NAT/G
CENTRAL
S57

RAPAPORT R.N.,"'DEMOCRATIZATION' AND AUTHORITY IN A
THERAPEUTIC COMMUNITY." OP/RES ADMIN PARTIC CENTRAL
ATTIT...POLICY DECISION. PAGE 86 B1735

PUB/INST
HEALTH
DOMIN
CLIENT
B58

LESTER F.A.,AS UNIONS MATURE. POL/PAR BARGAIN LEAD
PARTIC GP/REL CENTRAL...MAJORIT TIME/SEQ METH/COMP.
PAGE 64 B1299

LABOR
INDUS
POLICY
MGT
S58

EISENSTADT S.N.,"INTERNAL CONTRADICTIONS IN
BUREAUCRATIC POLITICS." ADMIN EXEC CENTRAL. PAGE 32
B0658

ELITES
LEAD
PWR
EX/STRUC
B60

ANGERS F.A.,ESSAI SUR LA CENTRALISATION: ANALYSE
DES PRINCIPES ET PERSPECTIVES CANADIENNES. CANADA
ECO/TAC CONTROL...SOC IDEA/COMP BIBLIOG 20. PAGE 5
B0111

CENTRAL
ADMIN
B60

CORSON J.J.,GOVERNANCE OF COLLEGES AND
UNIVERSITIES. STRUCT FINAN DELIB/GP DOMIN EDU/PROP
LEAD CHOOSE GP/REL CENTRAL COST PRIVIL SUPEGO
ORD/FREE PWR...DECISION BIBLIOG. PAGE 24 B0481

ADMIN
EXEC
ACADEM
HABITAT
L60

GRODZINS M.,"AMERICAN POLITICAL PARTIES AND THE
AMERICAN SYSTEM" (BMR)" USA+45 LOC/G NAT/G LEGIS
BAL/PWR ADMIN ROLE PWR...DECISION 20. PAGE 44 B0883

POL/PAR
FEDERAL
CENTRAL
GOV/REL
B61

HOUN F.W.,TO CHANGE A NATION; PROPAGANDA AND
INDOCTRINATION IN COMMUNIST CHINA. CHINA/COM COM
ACT/RES PLAN PRESS ADMIN FEEDBACK CENTRAL
EFFICIENCY ATTIT...PSY SOC 20. PAGE 52 B1048

DOMIN
EDU/PROP
TOTALISM
MARXISM
B61

MACMAHON A.W.,DELEGATION AND AUTONOMY. INDIA STRUCT
LEGIS BARGAIN BUDGET ECO/TAC LEGIT EXEC REPRESENT
GOV/REL CENTRAL DEMAND EFFICIENCY PRODUC. PAGE 68
B1373

ADMIN
PLAN
FEDERAL
B62

BINDER L.,IRAN: POLITICAL DEVELOPMENT IN A CHANGING
SOCIETY. IRAN OP/RES REV GP/REL CENTRAL RATIONAL
PWR...PHIL/SCI NAT/COMP GEN/LAWS 20. PAGE 12 B0239

LEGIT
NAT/G
ADMIN
STRUCT
B62

DIMOCK M.E.,THE NEW AMERICAN POLITICAL ECONOMY: A
SYNTHESIS OF POLITICS AND ECONOMICS. USA+45 FINAN
LG/CO PLAN ADMIN REGION GP/REL CENTRAL MORAL 20.
PAGE 29 B0598

FEDERAL
ECO/TAC
NAT/G
PARTIC
B62

EVANS M.S.,THE FRINGE ON TOP. USSR EX/STRUC FORCES
DIPLOM ECO/TAC PEACE CONSERVE SOCISM...TREND 20
KENNEDY/JF. PAGE 34 B0689

NAT/G
PWR
CENTRAL
POLICY
B62

WANGSNESS P.H.,THE POWER OF THE CITY MANAGER.
USA+45 EX/STRUC BAL/PWR BUDGET TAX ADMIN REPRESENT
CENTRAL EFFICIENCY DRIVE ROLE...POLICY 20 CITY/MGT.
PAGE 113 B2286

PWR
TOP/EX
MUNIC
LOC/G
L62

BELSHAW D.G.R.,"PUBLIC INVESTMENT IN AGRICULTURE
AND ECONOMIC DEVELOPMENT OF UGANDA" UGANDA AGRI
INDUS R+D ECO/TAC RATION TAX PAY COLONIAL 20
WORLD/BANK. PAGE 10 B0209

ECO/UNDEV
PLAN
ADMIN
CENTRAL
B63

CORSON J.J.,PUBLIC ADMINISTRATION IN MODERN

MGT

SOCIETY. INDUS FORCES CONTROL CENTRAL EFFICIENCY
20. PAGE 24 B0482

NAT/G
PROB/SOLV
INGP/REL
B63

CROUCH W.W.,SOUTHERN CALIFORNIA METROPOLIS: A STUDY
IN DEVELOPMENT OF GOVERNMENT FOR A METROPOLITAN
AREA. USA+45 USA-45 PROB/SOLV ADMIN LOBBY PARTIC
CENTRAL ORD/FREE PWR...BIBLIOG 20 PROGRSV/M.
PAGE 25 B0510

LOC/G
MUNIC
LEGIS
DECISION
B63

JACOB H.,GERMAN ADMINISTRATION SINCE BISMARCK:
CENTRAL AUTHORITY VERSUS LOCAL AUTONOMY. GERMANY
GERMANY/W LAW POL/PAR CONTROL CENTRAL TOTALISM
FASCISM...MAJORIT DECISION STAT CHARTS GOV/COMP
19/20 BISMARCK/O HITLER/A WEIMAR/REP. PAGE 55 B1111

ADMIN
NAT/G
LOC/G
POLICY
B63

KLESMENT J.,LEGAL SOURCES AND BIBLIOGRAPHY OF THE
BALTIC STATES (ESTONIA, LATVIA, LITHUANIA). COM
ESTONIA LATVIA LITHUANIA LAW FINAN ADJUD CT/SYS
REGION CENTRAL MARXISM 19/20. PAGE 60 B1218

BIBLIOG/A
JURID
CONSTN
ADMIN
B63

MAHESHWARI B.,STUDIES IN PANCHAYATI RAJ. INDIA
POL/PAR EX/STRUC BUDGET EXEC REPRESENT CENTRAL
EFFICIENCY...DECISION 20. PAGE 68 B1378

FEDERAL
LOC/G
GOV/REL
LEAD
B64

GJUPANOVIC H.,LEGAL SOURCES AND BIBLIOGRAPHY OF
YUGOSLAVIA. COM YUGOSLAVIA LAW LEGIS DIPLOM ADMIN
PARL/PROC REGION CRIME CENTRAL 20. PAGE 40 B0807

BIBLIOG/A
JURID
CONSTN
ADJUD
B64

JACKSON H.M.,THE SECRETARY OF STATE AND THE
AMBASSADOR* JACKSON SUBCOMMITTEE PAPERS ON THE
CONDUCT OF AMERICAN FOREIGN POLICY. USA+45 NAT/G
FORCES ACT/RES OP/RES EDU/PROP CENTRAL EFFICIENCY
ORD/FREE...OBS RECORD ANTHOL CONGRESS PRESIDENT.
PAGE 55 B1107

GOV/REL
DIPLOM
ADMIN
EX/STRUC
B64

KAPP E.,THE MERGER OF THE EXECUTIVES OF THE
EUROPEAN COMMUNITIES. LAW CONSTN STRUCT ACT/RES
PLAN PROB/SOLV ADMIN REGION TASK...INT/LAW MGT ECSC
EEC. PAGE 58 B1170

CENTRAL
EX/STRUC
B64

PIERCE T.M.,FEDERAL, STATE, AND LOCAL GOVERNMENT IN
EDUCATION. FINAN LOC/G PROVS LEGIS PLAN EDU/PROP
ADMIN CONTROL CENTRAL COST KNOWL 20. PAGE 83 B1673

NAT/G
POLICY
SCHOOL
GOV/REL
B64

RIES J.C.,THE MANAGEMENT OF DEFENSE: ORGANIZATION
AND CONTROL OF THE US ARMED SERVICES. PROF/ORG
DELIB/GP EX/STRUC LEGIS GOV/REL PERS/REL CENTRAL
RATIONAL PWR...POLICY TREND GOV/COMP BIBLIOG.
PAGE 88 B1782

FORCES
ACT/RES
DECISION
CONTROL
B64

RIKER W.H.,FEDERALISM. WOR+45 WOR-45 CONSTN CHIEF
LEGIS ADMIN COLONIAL CONTROL CT/SYS PWR...BIBLIOG/A
18/20. PAGE 88 B1787

FEDERAL
NAT/G
ORD/FREE
B64

STANLEY D.T.,THE HIGHER CIVIL SERVICE: AN
EVALUATION OF FEDERAL PERSONNEL PRACTICES. USA+45
CREATE EXEC ROUTINE CENTRAL...MGT SAMP IDEA/COMP
METH/COMP 20 CIVIL/SERV. PAGE 100 B2020

NAT/G
ADMIN
CONTROL
EFFICIENCY
B64

TINBERGEN J.,CENTRAL PLANNING. COM INTELL ECO/DEV
ECO/UNDEV FINAN INT/ORG PROB/SOLV ECO/TAC CONTROL
EXEC ROUTINE DECISION. PAGE 104 B2111

PLAN
INDUS
MGT
CENTRAL
B65

BARNETT V.M. JR.,THE REPRESENTATION OF THE UNITED
STATES ABROAD* REVISED EDITION. ECO/UNDEV ACADEM
INT/ORG FORCES ACT/RES CREATE OP/RES FOR/AID REGION
CENTRAL...CLASSIF ANTHOL. PAGE 9 B0189

USA+45
DIPLOM
ADMIN
B65

CHANDA A.,FEDERALISM IN INDIA. INDIA UK ELITES
FINAN NAT/G POL/PAR EX/STRUC LEGIS DIPLOM TAX
GOV/REL POPULISM...POLICY 20. PAGE 20 B0402

CONSTN
CENTRAL
FEDERAL
B65

KASER M.,COMECON* INTEGRATION PROBLEMS OF THE
PLANNED ECONOMIES. INT/ORG TEC/DEV INT/TRADE PRICE
ADMIN ADJUST CENTRAL...STAT TIME/SEQ ORG/CHARTS
COMECON. PAGE 58 B1177

PLAN
ECO/DEV
COM
REGION
B65

WATERSTON A.,DEVELOPMENT PLANNING* LESSONS OF
EXPERIENCE. ECO/TAC CENTRAL...MGT QUANT BIBLIOG.
PAGE 114 B2303

ECO/UNDEV
CREATE
PLAN
ADMIN
S65

BALDWIN H.,"SLOW-DOWN IN THE PENTAGON." USA+45
CREATE PLAN GOV/REL CENTRAL COST EFFICIENCY PWR
...MGT MCNAMARA/R. PAGE 9 B0174

RECORD
R+D
WEAPON
ADMIN
B66

LIVINGSTON J.C.,THE CONSENT OF THE GOVERNED. USA+45
EX/STRUC BAL/PWR DOMIN CENTRAL PERSON PWR...POLICY
CONCPT OBS IDEA/COMP 20 CONGRESS. PAGE 66 B1331

NAT/G
LOBBY
MAJORIT

PARTIC
B66

MCKENZIE J.L.,AUTHORITY IN THE CHURCH. STRUCT LEAD | SECT
INGP/REL PERS/REL CENTRAL ANOMIE ATTIT ORD/FREE | AUTHORIT
RESPECT CATH. PAGE 72 B1452 | PWR
ADMIN
B66

YOUNG W.,EXISTING MECHANISMS OF ARMS CONTROL. | ARMS/CONT
PROC/MFG OP/RES DIPLOM TASK CENTRAL...MGT TREATY. | ADMIN
PAGE 119 B2395 | NUC/PWR
ROUTINE
S66

AUSLAND J.C.,"CRISIS MANAGEMENT* BERLIN, CYPRUS, | OP/RES
LAOS." CYPRUS LAOS FORCES CREATE PLAN EDU/PROP TASK | DIPLOM
CENTRAL PERSON RIGID/FLEX...DECISION MGT 20 BERLIN | RISK
KENNEDY/JF MCNAMARA/R RUSK. PAGE 7 B0148 | ADMIN
B67

PLANO J.C.,FORGING WORLD ORDER: THE POLITICS OF | INT/ORG
INTERNATIONAL ORGANIZATION. PROB/SOLV DIPLOM | ADMIN
CONTROL CENTRAL RATIONAL ORD/FREE...INT/LAW CHARTS | JURID
BIBLIOG 20 UN LEAGUE/NAT. PAGE 83 B1679
L67

"A PROPOS DES INCITATIONS FINANCIERES AUX | LOC/G
GROUPEMENTS DES COMMUNES: ESSAI D'INTERPRETATION." | ECO/TAC
FRANCE NAT/G LEGIS ADMIN GOV/REL CENTRAL 20. PAGE 2 | APPORT
B0046 | ADJUD
S67

GRUNDY K.W.,"THE POLITICAL USES OF IMAGINATION." | NAT/LISM
GHANA ELITES SOCIETY NAT/G DOMIN EDU/PROP COLONIAL | EX/STRUC
REGION REPRESENT GP/REL CENTRAL PWR MARXISM 20. | AFR
PAGE 44 B0897 | LEAD
S67

HOFMANN W.,"THE PUBLIC INTEREST PRESSURE GROUP: THE | LOC/G
CASE OF THE DEUTSCHE STADTETAG." GERMANY GERMANY/W | VOL/ASSN
CONSTN STRUCT NAT/G CENTRAL FEDERAL PWR...TIME/SEQ | LOBBY
20. PAGE 51 B1030 | ADMIN
S67

HUDDLESTON J.,"TRADE UNIONS IN THE GERMAN FEDERAL | LABOR
REPUBLIC." EUR+WWI GERMANY/W UK LAW INDUS WORKER | GP/REL
CREATE CENTRAL...MGT GP/COMP 20. PAGE 52 B1056 | SCHOOL
ROLE
S67

HUGON P.,"BLOCAGES ET DESEQUILIBRES DE LA | ECO/UNDEV
CROISSANCE ECONOMIQUE EN AFRIQUE NOIRE." AFR KIN | COLONIAL
MUNIC CREATE PLAN INT/TRADE REGION ADJUST CENTRAL | STRUCT
EQUILIB NAT/LISM ORD/FREE 20. PAGE 52 B1060 | ADMIN
S67

HUMPHREY H.,"A MORE PERFECT UNION." USA+45 LOC/G | GOV/REL
NAT/G ACT/RES BUDGET RECEIVE CENTRAL CONGRESS. | FEDERAL
PAGE 52 B1063 | ADMIN
PROB/SOLV
S67

JAVITS J.K.,"THE USE OF AMERICAN PLURALISM." USA+45 | CENTRAL
ECO/DEV BUDGET ADMIN ALL/IDEOS...DECISION TREND. | ATTIT
PAGE 56 B1127 | POLICY
NAT/G
S67

KAYSEN C.,"DATA BANKS AND DOSSIERS." FUT USA+45 | CENTRAL
COM/IND NAT/G PLAN PROB/SOLV TEC/DEV BUDGET ADMIN | EFFICIENCY
ROUTINE. PAGE 59 B1185 | CENSUS
ACT/RES
S67

LASLETT J.H.M.,"SOCIALISM AND THE AMERICAN LABOR | LABOR
MOVEMENT* SOME NEW REFLECTIONS." USA-45 VOL/ASSN | ROUTINE
LOBBY PARTIC CENTRAL ALL/VALS SOCISM...GP/COMP 20. | ATTIT
PAGE 63 B1265 | GP/REL
S67

LENDVAI P.,"HUNGARY* CHANGE VS. IMMOBILISM." | ECO/DEV
HUNGARY LABOR NAT/G PLAN DEBATE ADMIN ROUTINE | MGT
CENTRAL EFFICIENCY MARXISM PLURISM...PREDICT 20. | CHOOSE
PAGE 64 B1289
S67

LEVCIK B.,"WAGES AND EMPLOYMENT PROBLEMS IN THE NEW | MARXISM
SYSTEM OF PLANNED MANAGEMENT IN CZECHOSLOVAKIA." | WORKER
CZECHOSLVK EUR+WWI NAT/G OP/RES PLAN ADMIN ROUTINE | MGT
INGP/REL CENTRAL EFFICIENCY PRODUC DECISION. | PAY
PAGE 64 B1300
S67

LEWIS P.H.,"LEADERSHIP AND CONFLICT WITHIN | POL/PAR
FEBRERISTA PARTY OF PARAGUAY." L/A+17C PARAGUAY | ELITES
EX/STRUC DOMIN SENIOR CONTROL INGP/REL CENTRAL | LEAD
FEDERAL ATTIT 20. PAGE 65 B1305
S67

MURRAY R.,"SECOND THOUGHTS ON GHANA." AFR GHANA | COLONIAL
NAT/G POL/PAR ADMIN REV GP/REL CENTRAL...SOCIALIST | CONTROL
CONCPT METH 20. PAGE 77 B1548 | REGION
SOCISM
S67

NEUCHTERLEIN D.E.,"THAILAND* ANOTHER VIETNAM?" | WAR
THAILAND ECO/UNDEV DIPLOM ADMIN REGION CENTRAL | GUERRILLA
NAT/LISM...POLICY 20. PAGE 78 B1571 | S/ASIA
NAT/G
S67

SPEAR P.,"NEHRU." INDIA NAT/G POL/PAR ECO/TAC ADJUD | CHIEF
GOV/REL CENTRAL RIGID/FLEX 20 NEHRU/J. PAGE 99 | ATTIT
B2003 | ADMIN

CREATE
S67

VERGIN R.C.,"COMPUTER INDUCED ORGANIZATION | COMPUTER
CHANGES." FUT USA+45 R+D CREATE OP/RES TEC/DEV | DECISION
ADJUST CENTRAL...MGT INT CON/ANAL COMPUT/IR. | AUTOMAT
PAGE 112 B2260 | EX/STRUC
S67

WEIL G.L.,"THE MERGER OF THE INSTITUTIONS OF THE | ECO/TAC
EUROPEAN COMMUNITIES" EUR+WWI ECO/DEV INT/TRADE | INT/ORG
CONSEN PLURISM...DECISION MGT 20 EEC EURATOM ECSC | CENTRAL
TREATY. PAGE 115 B2313 | INT/LAW
S67

WINTHROP H.,"THE MEANING OF DECENTRALIZATION FOR | ADMIN
TWENTIETH-CENTURY MAN." FUT WOR+45 SOCIETY TEC/DEV. | STRUCT
PAGE 117 B2366 | CENTRAL
PROB/SOLV
S67

ZOETEWEIJ B.,"INCOME POLICIES ABROAD: AN INTERIM | METH/COMP
REPORT." NAT/G PROB/SOLV BARGAIN BUDGET PRICE RISK | INCOME
CENTRAL EFFICIENCY EQUILIB...MGT NAT/COMP 20. | POLICY
PAGE 119 B2405 | LABOR

CENTRAL AFRICAN ARCHIVES B0398

CENTRAL ASIAN RESEARCH CENTRE B0399

CENTRAL/AM....CENTRAL AMERICA

B62

ESCUELA SUPERIOR DE ADMIN PUBL,INFORME DEL | ADMIN
SEMINARIO SOBRE SERVICIO CIVIL O CARRERA | NAT/G
ADMINISTRATIVA. L/A+17C ELITES STRATA CONFER | PROB/SOLV
CONTROL GOV/REL INGP/REL SUPEGO 20 CENTRAL/AM | ATTIT
CIVIL/SERV. PAGE 33 B0681

CENTRL/AFR....CENTRAL AFRICAN REPUBLIC

B58

CARTER G.M.,TRANSITION IN AFRICA; STUDIES IN | NAT/COMP
POLITICAL ADAPTATION. AFR CENTRL/AFR GHANA NIGERIA | PWR
CONSTN LOC/G POL/PAR ADMIN GP/REL FEDERAL...MAJORIT | CONTROL
BIBLIOG 20. PAGE 19 B0389 | NAT/G

CERMAK/AJ....ANTON J. CERMAK

CEWA....CEWA (AFRICAN TRIBE)

CEYLON....CEYLON

B56

JENNINGS W.I.,THE APPROACH TO SELF-GOVERNMENT. | NAT/G
CEYLON INDIA PAKISTAN S/ASIA UK SOCIETY POL/PAR | CONSTN
DELIB/GP LEGIS ECO/TAC EDU/PROP ADMIN EXEC CHOOSE | COLONIAL
ATTIT ALL/VALS...JURID CONCPT GEN/METH TOT/POP 20.
PAGE 56 B1136
B63

WEINER M.,POLITICAL CHANGE IN SOUTH ASIA. CEYLON | NAT/G
INDIA PAKISTAN S/ASIA CULTURE ELITES ECO/UNDEV | CONSTN
EX/STRUC ADMIN CONTROL CHOOSE CONSERVE...GOV/COMP | TEC/DEV
ANTHOL 20. PAGE 115 B2315
S63

HARRIS R.L.,"A COMPARATIVE ANALYSIS OF THE | DELIB/GP
ADMINISTRATIVE SYSTEMS OF CANADA AND CEYLON." | EX/STRUC
S/ASIA CULTURE SOCIETY STRATA TOP/EX ACT/RES DOMIN | CANADA
EDU/PROP LEGIT COERCE ATTIT SUPEGO ALL/VALS...MGT | CEYLON
CHARTS GEN/LAWS VAL/FREE 20. PAGE 47 B0955
B64

SINGER M.R.,THE EMERGING ELITE: A STUDY OF | TOP/EX
POLITICAL LEADERSHIP IN CEYLON. S/ASIA ECO/UNDEV | STRATA
AGRI KIN NAT/G SECT EX/STRUC LEGIT ATTIT PWR | NAT/LISM
RESPECT...SOC STAT CHARTS 20. PAGE 97 B1967 | CEYLON
B66

DEBENKO E.,RESEARCH SOURCES FOR SOUTH ASIAN STUDIES | BIBLIOG
IN ECONOMIC DEVELOPMENT: A SELECT BIBLIOGRAPHY OF | ECO/UNDEV
SERIAL PUBLICATIONS. CEYLON INDIA NEPAL PAKISTAN | S/ASIA
PROB/SOLV ADMIN...POLICY 20. PAGE 28 B0566 | PLAN
L67

TAMBIAH S.J.,"THE POLITICS OF LANGUAGE IN INDIA AND | POL/PAR
CEYLON." CEYLON INDIA NAT/G DOMIN ADMIN...SOC 20. | LING
PAGE 102 B2070 | NAT/LISM
REGION

CHACO/WAR....CHACO WAR

CHAD....SEE ALSO AFR

S62

MURACCIOLE L.,"LES CONSTITUTIONS DES ETATS | NAT/G
AFRICAINS D'EXPRESSION FRANCAISE: LA CONSTITUTION | CONSTN
DU 16 AVRIL 1962 DE LA REPUBLIQUE DU" AFR CHAD
CHIEF LEGIS LEGIT COLONIAL EXEC ROUTINE ORD/FREE
SOVEREIGN...SOC CONCPT 20. PAGE 76 B1541
B64

WITHERELL J.W.,OFFICIAL PUBLICATIONS OF FRENCH | BIBLIOG/A
EQUATORIAL AFRICA, FRENCH CAMEROONS, AND TOGO, | AFR
1946-1958 (PAMPHLET). CAMEROON CHAD FRANCE GABON | NAT/G

TOGO LAW ECO/UNDEV EXTR/IND INT/TRADE...GEOG HEAL   ADMIN
20. PAGE 117 B2367

CHAMBERLAIN N.W. B0400

CHAMBERLIN W. B0401

CHAMBERS/J....JORDAN CHAMBERS

CHAMBR/DEP....CHAMBER OF DEPUTIES (FRANCE)

CHAMBRLN/J....JOSEPH CHAMBERLAIN

CHAMBRLN/N....NEVILLE CHAMBERLAIN

CHANDA A. B0402

CHANDLER A.D. B0403,B0404

CHANDRA S. B0405

CHANG C. B0406

CHANGE (AS GOAL)....SEE ORD/FREE

CHANGE (AS INNOVATION)....SEE CREATE

CHANGE (SOCIAL MOBILITY)....SEE GEOG, STRATA

CHAPIN F.S. B0407

CHAPMAN B. B0408,B0409,B0410,B0411

CHAPMAN J.F. B0357

CHAPPLE E.D. B0412

CHARACTER....SEE PERSON

CHARISMA....CHARISMA

CHARLES R. B0413

CHARLES S. B0414

CHARLES/I....CHARLES I OF ENGLAND

                                                    B61
AYLMER G.,THE KING'S SERVANTS. UK ELITES CHIEF PAY   ADMIN
CT/SYS WEALTH 17 CROMWELL/O CHARLES/I. PAGE 7 B0153   ROUTINE
                                                     EX/STRUC
                                                     NAT/G

CHARLESWORTH J.C. B0415,B2060

CHARTISM....CHARTISM

CHARTS....GRAPHS, CHARTS, DIAGRAMS, MAPS

CHASE/S....STUART CHASE

CHATEAUB/F....VICOMTE FRANCOIS RENE DE CHATEAUBRIAND

CHATTANOOG....CHATTANOOGA, TENNESSEE

CHECKS AND BALANCES SYSTEM....SEE BAL/PWR

CHEEK G. B0416

CHEN T.H. B0417

CHEN/YUN....CH'EN YUN

CHERNICK J. B0418

CHIANG....CHIANG KAI-SHEK

CHICAGO....CHICAGO, ILLINOIS

                                                    B29
MERRIAM C.E.,CHICAGO: A MORE INTIMATE VIEW OF URBAN   STRUCT
POLITICS. USA-45 CONSTN POL/PAR LEGIS ADMIN CRIME   GP/REL
INGP/REL 18/20 CHICAGO. PAGE 73 B1472   MUNIC
                                                    B64
FISK W.M.,ADMINISTRATIVE PROCEDURE IN A REGULATORY   SERV/IND
AGENCY: THE CAB AND THE NEW YORK-CHICAGO CASE   ECO/DEV
(PAMPHLET). USA+45 DIST/IND ADMIN CONTROL LOBBY   AIR
GP/REL ROLE ORD/FREE NEWYORK/C CHICAGO CAB. PAGE 36 JURID
B0727
                                                    B65
GREER S.,URBAN RENEWAL AND AMERICAN CITIES: THE   MUNIC
DILEMMA OF DEMOCRATIC INTERVENTION. USA+45 R+D   PROB/SOLV
LOC/G VOL/ASSN ACT/RES BUDGET ADMIN GOV/REL...SOC   PLAN
INT SAMP 20 BOSTON CHICAGO MIAMI URBAN/RNWL.   NAT/G
PAGE 43 B0871

                                                    S66
SNOWISS L.M.,"CONGRESSIONAL RECRUITMENT AND   LEGIS
REPRESENTATION." USA+45 LG/CO MUNIC POL/PAR ADMIN   REPRESENT
REGION CONGRESS CHICAGO. PAGE 98 B1990   CHOOSE
                                                     LOC/G

CHICAGO JOINT REFERENCE LIB B0419

CHICAGO U CTR PROG GOVT ADMIN B0420

CHICAGO U LAW SCHOOL B0421

CHIEF....PRESIDENT, MONARCH, PRESIDENCY, PREMIER, CHIEF
    OFFICER OF ANY GOVERNMENT

                                                    B02
MOREL E.D.,AFFAIRS OF WEST AFRICA. UK FINAN INDUS   COLONIAL
FAM KIN SECT CHIEF WORKER DIPLOM RACE/REL LITERACY   ADMIN
HEALTH...CHARTS 18/20 AFRICA/W NEGRO. PAGE 75 B1521 AFR
                                                    B05
RIORDAN W.L.,PLUNKITT OF TAMMANY HALL. USA-45   POL/PAR
SOCIETY PROB/SOLV EXEC LEAD TASK CHOOSE ALL/VALS   MUNIC
...RECORD ANTHOL 20 REFORMERS TAMMANY NEWYORK/C   CHIEF
PLUNKITT/G. PAGE 88 B1789   ATTIT
                                                    B08
WILSON W.,CONSTITUTIONAL GOVERNMENT IN THE UNITED   NAT/G
STATES. USA-45 LAW POL/PAR PROVS CHIEF LEGIS   GOV/REL
BAL/PWR ADJUD EXEC FEDERAL PWR 18/20 SUPREME/CT   CONSTN
HOUSE/REP SENATE. PAGE 117 B2362   PARL/PROC
                                                    B17
CORWIN E.S.,THE PRESIDENT'S CONTROL OF FOREIGN   TOP/EX
RELATIONS. FUT USA-45 CONSTN STRATA NAT/G CHIEF   PWR
EX/STRUC LEGIS KNOWL RESPECT...JURID CONCPT TREND   DIPLOM
CONGRESS VAL/FREE 20 PRESIDENT. PAGE 24 B0483
                                                    B19
SUTHERLAND G.,CONSTITUTIONAL POWER AND WORLD   USA-45
AFFAIRS. CONSTN STRUCT INT/ORG NAT/G CHIEF LEGIS   EXEC
ACT/RES PLAN GOV/REL ALL/VALS...OBS TIME/SEQ   DIPLOM
CONGRESS VAL/FREE 20 PRESIDENT. PAGE 102 B2056
                                                    N19
TREVELYAN G.M.,THE TWO-PARTY SYSTEM IN ENGLISH   PARL/PROC
POLITICAL HISTORY (PAMPHLET). UK CHIEF LEGIS   POL/PAR
COLONIAL EXEC REV CHOOSE 17/19. PAGE 105 B2128   NAT/G
                                                     PWR
                                                    B24
HOLDSWORTH W.S.,A HISTORY OF ENGLISH LAW; THE   LAW
COMMON LAW AND ITS RIVALS (VOL. VI). UK STRATA   CONSTN
EX/STRUC ADJUD ADMIN CONTROL CT/SYS...JURID CONCPT   LEGIS
GEN/LAWS 17 COMMONWLTH PARLIAMENT ENGLSH/LAW   CHIEF
COMMON/LAW. PAGE 51 B1034
                                                    B25
MATHEWS J.M.,AMERICAN STATE GOVERNMENT. USA-45   PROVS
LOC/G CHIEF EX/STRUC LEGIS ADJUD CONTROL CT/SYS   ADMIN
ROUTINE GOV/REL PWR 20 GOVERNOR. PAGE 71 B1426   FEDERAL
                                                     CONSTN
                                                    B27
WILLOUGHBY W.F.,PRINCIPLES OF PUBLIC ADMINISTRATION   NAT/G
WITH SPECIAL REFERENCE TO THE NATIONAL AND STATE   EX/STRUC
GOVERNMENTS OF THE UNITED STATES. FINAN PROVS CHIEF OP/RES
CONSULT LEGIS CREATE BUDGET EXEC ROUTINE GOV/REL   ADMIN
CENTRAL...MGT 20 BUR/BUDGET CONGRESS PRESIDENT.
PAGE 117 B2356
                                                    B34
RIDLEY C.E.,THE CITY-MANAGER PROFESSION. CHIEF PLAN   MUNIC
ADMIN CONTROL ROUTINE CHOOSE...TECHNIC CHARTS   EX/STRUC
GOV/COMP BIBLIOG 20. PAGE 88 B1780   LOC/G
                                                     EXEC
                                                    B34
WILCOX J.K.,GUIDE TO THE OFFICIAL PUBLICATIONS OF   BIBLIOG
THE NEW DEAL ADMINISTRATION (2 VOLS.). USA-45 CHIEF NAT/G
LEGIS ADMIN...POLICY 20 CONGRESS ROOSEVLT/F.   NEW/LIB
PAGE 116 B2345   RECEIVE
                                                    B41
CHILDS J.B.,A GUIDE TO THE OFFICIAL PUBLICATIONS OF   NAT/G
THE OTHER AMERICAN REPUBLICS: ARGENTINA. CHIEF   EX/STRUC
DIPLOM GOV/REL...BIBLIOG 18/19 ARGEN. PAGE 21 B0422 METH/CNCPT
                                                     LEGIS
                                                    B43
YOUNG R.,THIS IS CONGRESS. FUT SENIOR ADMIN GP/REL   LEGIS
PWR...DECISION REFORMERS CONGRESS. PAGE 119 B2393   DELIB/GP
                                                     CHIEF
                                                     ROUTINE
                                                    S44
GRIFFITH E.S.,"THE CHANGING PATTERN OF PUBLIC   LAW
POLICY FORMATION." MOD/EUR WOR+45 FINAN CHIEF   POLICY
CONFER ADMIN LEAD CONSERVE SOCISM TECHRACY...SOC   TEC/DEV
CHARTS CONGRESS. PAGE 43 B0877
                                                    B47
MARX F.M.,THE PRESIDENT AND HIS STAFF SERVICES   CONSTN
PUBLIC ADMINISTRATION SERVICES NUMBER 98   CHIEF
(PAMPHLET). FINAN ADMIN CT/SYS REPRESENT PWR 20   NAT/G
PRESIDENT. PAGE 70 B1419   EX/STRUC
                                                    B47
PATTERSON C.P.,PRESIDENTIAL GOVERNMENT IN THE   CHIEF
UNITED STATES - THE UNWRITTEN CONSTITUTION. USA+45   NAT/G
DELIB/GP EX/STRUC ADJUD ADMIN EXEC...DECISION   CONSTN

PRESIDENT. PAGE 81 B1643   POL/PAR

B1224

B48
HART J.,THE AMERICAN PRESIDENCY IN ACTION 1789: A   NAT/G
STUDY IN CONSTITUTIONAL HISTORY. USA-45 POL/PAR   CONSTN
DELIB/GP FORCES LEGIS ADJUD ADMIN LEAD GP/REL   CHIEF
PERS/REL 18 PRESIDENT CONGRESS. PAGE 47 B0959   EX/STRUC

B49
DENNING A.,FREEDOM UNDER THE LAW. MOD/EUR UK LAW   ORD/FREE
SOCIETY CHIEF EX/STRUC LEGIS ADJUD CT/SYS PERS/REL   JURID
PERSON 17/20 ENGLSH/LAW. PAGE 28 B0573   NAT/G

B49
GRAVES W.B.,BASIC INFORMATION ON THE REORGANIZATION   BIBLIOG/A
OF THE EXECUTIVE BRANCH: 1912-1948. USA-45 BUDGET   EX/STRUC
ADMIN CONTROL GP/REL EFFICIENCY...MGT CHARTS   NAT/G
ORG/CHARTS 20 PRESIDENT. PAGE 42 B0857   CHIEF

B49
RIDDICK F.M.,THE UNITED STATES CONGRESS   LEGIS
ORGANIZATION AND PROCEDURE. POL/PAR DELIB/GP   PARL/PROC
PROB/SOLV DEBATE CONTROL EXEC LEAD INGP/REL PWR   CHIEF
...MAJORIT DECISION CONGRESS PRESIDENT. PAGE 88   EX/STRUC
B1777

S49
CORWIN E.S.,"THE PRESIDENCY IN PERSPECTIVE." USA+45   CHIEF
USA-45 NAT/G LEAD 20 PRESIDENT. PAGE 24 B0485   PWR
                                                          REPRESENT
                                                          EXEC

B50
HYNEMAN C.S.,BUREAUCRACY IN A DEMOCRACY. CHIEF   NAT/G
LEGIS ADMIN CONTROL LEAD ROUTINE PERS/REL COST   CENTRAL
EFFICIENCY UTIL ATTIT AUTHORIT PERSON MORAL.   EX/STRUC
PAGE 53 B1071   MYTH

S51
MARX F.M.,"SIGNIFICANCE FOR THE ADMINISTRATIVE   LEGIS
PROCESS." POL/PAR LEAD PARL/PROC GOV/REL EFFICIENCY   ADMIN
SUPEGO...POLICY CONGRESS. PAGE 70 B1420   CHIEF

B52
CORSON J.J.,EXECUTIVES FOR THE FEDERAL SERVICE.   LOBBY
USA+45 CHIEF...MGT 20. PAGE 24 B0480   ADMIN
                                                          EX/STRUC
                                                          PERS/REL

B52
DE GRAZIA A.,POLITICAL ORGANIZATION. CONSTN LOC/G   FEDERAL
MUNIC NAT/G CHIEF LEGIS TOP/EX ADJUD CT/SYS   LAW
PERS/REL...INT/LAW MYTH UN. PAGE 27 B0553   ADMIN

B52
NASH B.D.,STAFFING THE PRESIDENCY: PLANNING   EX/STRUC
PAMPHLET NO. 80 (PAMPHLET). NAT/G CHIEF CONSULT   EXEC
DELIB/GP CONFER ADMIN 20 PRESIDENT. PAGE 77 B1557   TOP/EX
                                                          ROLE

L52
WRIGHT Q.,"CONGRESS AND THE TREATY-MAKING POWER."   ROUTINE
USA+45 WOR+45 CONSTN INTELL NAT/G CHIEF CONSULT   DIPLOM
EX/STRUC LEGIS TOP/EX CREATE GOV/REL DISPL DRIVE   INT/LAW
RIGID/FLEX...TREND TOT/POP CONGRESS CONGRESS 20   DELIB/GP
TREATY. PAGE 118 B2384

C53
DORWART R.A.,"THE ADMINISTRATIVE REFORMS OF   ADMIN
FREDRICK WILLIAM I OF PRUSSIA. GERMANY MOD/EUR   NAT/G
CHIEF CONTROL PWR...BIBLIOG 16/18. PAGE 30 B0608   CENTRAL
                                                          GOV/REL

B54
JENNINGS I.,THE QUEEN'S GOVERNMENT. UK POL/PAR   NAT/G
DELIB/GP ADJUD ADMIN CT/SYS PARL/PROC REPRESENT   CONSTN
CONSERVE 13/20 PARLIAMENT. PAGE 56 B1132   LEGIS
                                                          CHIEF

B54
WHITE L.D.,THE JACKSONIANS: A STUDY IN   NAT/G
ADMINISTRATIVE HISTORY 1829-1861. USA-45 CONSTN   ADMIN
POL/PAR CHIEF DELIB/GP LEGIS CREATE PROB/SOLV   POLICY
ECO/TAC LEAD REGION GP/REL 19 PRESIDENT CONGRESS
JACKSON/A. PAGE 116 B2339

C54
CALDWELL L.K.,"THE GOVERNMENT AND ADMINISTRATION OF   PROVS
NEW YORK." LOC/G MUNIC POL/PAR SCHOOL CHIEF LEGIS   ADMIN
PLAN TAX CT/SYS...MGT SOC/WK BIBLIOG 20 NEWYORK/C.   CONSTN
PAGE 18 B0366   EX/STRUC

B56
ABELS J.,THE TRUMAN SCANDALS. USA+45 USA-45 POL/PAR   CRIME
TAX LEGIT CT/SYS CHOOSE PRIVIL MORAL WEALTH 20   ADMIN
TRUMAN/HS PRESIDENT CONGRESS. PAGE 3 B0052   CHIEF
                                                          TRIBUTE

B56
BROWNE D.G.,THE RISE OF SCOTLAND YARD: A HISTORY OF   CRIMLGY
THE METROPOLITAN POLICE. UK MUNIC CHIEF ADMIN CRIME   LEGIS
GP/REL 19/20. PAGE 16 B0329   CONTROL
                                                          FORCES

B56
CARTER B.E.,THE OFFICE OF THE PRIME MINISTER. UK   GOV/REL
ADMIN REPRESENT PARLIAMENT 20. PAGE 19 B0388   CHIEF
                                                          EX/STRUC
                                                          LEAD

B56
KOENIG L.W.,THE TRUMAN ADMINISTRATION: ITS   ADMIN
PRINCIPLES AND PRACTICE. USA+45 POL/PAR CHIEF LEGIS   POLICY
DIPLOM DEATH NUC/PWR WAR CIVMIL/REL PEACE   EX/STRUC
...DECISION 20 TRUMAN/HS PRESIDENT TREATY. PAGE 61   GOV/REL

B56
WAUGH E.W.,SECOND CONSUL. USA+45 USA-45 CONSTN   NAT/G
POL/PAR PROB/SOLV PARL/PROC CHOOSE PERS/REL ATTIT   EX/STRUC
...BIBLIOG 18/20 VICE/PRES. PAGE 114 B2304   PWR
                                                          CHIEF

B56
WILSON W.,CONGRESSIONAL GOVERNMENT. USA-45 NAT/G   LEGIS
ADMIN EXEC PARL/PROC GP/REL MAJORITY ATTIT 19   CHIEF
SENATE HOUSE/REP. PAGE 117 B2364   CONSTN
                                                          PWR

B56
WU E.,LEADERS OF TWENTIETH-CENTURY CHINA; AN   BIBLIOG/A
ANNOTATED BIBLIOGRAPHY OF SELECTED CHINESE   BIOG
BIOGRAPHICAL WORKS IN HOOVER LIBRARY. ASIA INDUS   INTELL
POL/PAR DIPLOM ADMIN REV WAR...HUM MGT 20. PAGE 118   CHIEF
B2386

L56
EISENTADT S.N.,"POLITICAL STRUGGLE IN BUREAUCRATIC   ADMIN
SOCIETIES" ASIA CULTURE ADJUD SANCTION PWR   CHIEF
BUREAUCRCY OTTOMAN BYZANTINE. PAGE 33 B0661   CONTROL
                                                          ROUTINE

L56
MACMAHON A.W.,"WOODROW WILSON AS LEGISLATIVE LEADER   LEGIS
AND ADMINISTRATOR." CONSTN POL/PAR ADMIN...POLICY   CHIEF
HIST/WRIT WILSON/W PRESIDENT. PAGE 68 B1371   LEAD
                                                          BIOG

S56
CLEVELAND H.,"THE EXECUTIVE AND THE PUBLIC   LOBBY
INTEREST." USA+45 DOMIN ADMIN PWR...POLICY 20.   REPRESENT
PAGE 21 B0437   CHIEF
                                                          EXEC

S56
HEADY F.,"THE MICHIGAN DEPARTMENT OF   ADMIN
ADMINISTRATION; A CASE STUDY IN THE POLITICS OF   DELIB/GP
ADMINISTRATION" (BMR)" USA+45 POL/PAR PROVS CHIEF   LOC/G
LEGIS GP/REL ATTIT 20 MICHIGAN. PAGE 48 B0980

S56
MILNE R.S.,"CONTROL OF GOVERNMENT CORPORATIONS IN   CONTROL
THE UNITED STATES." USA+45 NAT/G CHIEF LEGIS BUDGET   EX/STRUC
20 GENACCOUNT. PAGE 74 B1488   GOV/REL
                                                          PWR

N57
MACMAHON A.W.,ADMINISTRATION AND FOREIGN POLICY   DIPLOM
(PAMPHLET). USA+45 CHIEF OP/RES ADMIN 20. PAGE 68   EX/STRUC
B1372   DECISION
                                                          CONFER

B58
BERNSTEIN M.H.,THE JOB OF THE FEDERAL EXECUTIVE.   NAT/G
POL/PAR CHIEF LEGIS ADMIN EXEC LOBBY CHOOSE GOV/REL   TOP/EX
ORD/FREE PWR...MGT TREND. PAGE 11 B0228   PERS/COMP

B58
COWAN L.G.,LOCAL GOVERNMENT IN WEST AFRICA. AFR   LOC/G
FRANCE UK CULTURE KIN POL/PAR CHIEF LEGIS CREATE   COLONIAL
ADMIN PARTIC GOV/REL GP/REL...METH/COMP 20. PAGE 24   SOVEREIGN
B0498   REPRESENT

B58
MOEN N.W.,THE GOVERNMENT OF SCOTLAND 1603 - 1625.   CHIEF
UK JUDGE ADMIN GP/REL PWR 17 SCOTLAND COMMON/LAW.   JURID
PAGE 74 B1496   CONTROL
                                                          PARL/PROC

B58
NEAL F.W.,TITOISM IN ACTION. COM YUGOSLAVIA AGRI   MARXISM
LOC/G DIPLOM TOTALISM...BIBLIOG 20 TITO/MARSH.   POL/PAR
PAGE 77 B1564   CHIEF
                                                          ADMIN

L58
HAVILAND H.F.,"FOREIGN AID AND THE POLICY PROCESS: LEGIS
1957." USA+45 FACE/GP POL/PAR VOL/ASSN CHIEF   PLAN
DELIB/GP ACT/RES LEGIT EXEC GOV/REL ATTIT DRIVE PWR   FOR/AID
...POLICY TESTS CONGRESS 20. PAGE 48 B0971

S58
FREEMAN J.L.,"THE BUREAUCRACY IN PRESSURE   CONTROL
POLITICS." USA+45 NAT/G CHIEF ADMIN EXEC 20.   EX/STRUC
PAGE 37 B0752   REPRESENT
                                                          LOBBY

C58
WILDING N.,"AN ENCYCLOPEDIA OF PARLIAMENT." UK LAW   PARL/PROC
CONSTN CHIEF PROB/SOLV DIPLOM DEBATE WAR INGP/REL   POL/PAR
PRIVIL...BIBLIOG DICTIONARY 13/20 CMN/WLTH   NAT/G
PARLIAMENT. PAGE 116 B2350   ADMIN

B59
DUVERGER M.,LA CINQUIEME REPUBLIQUE. FRANCE WOR+45   NAT/G
POL/PAR CHIEF EX/STRUC LOBBY. PAGE 31 B0636   CONSTN
                                                          GOV/REL
                                                          PARL/PROC

B59
JENNINGS W.I.,CABINET GOVERNMENT (3RD ED.). UK   DELIB/GP
POL/PAR CHIEF BUDGET ADMIN CHOOSE GP/REL 20.   NAT/G
PAGE 56 B1137   CONSTN
                                                          OP/RES

B60
MORISON E.E.,TURMOIL AND TRADITION: A STUDY OF THE   BIOG
LIFE AND TIMES OF HENRY L. STIMSON. USA+45 USA-45   NAT/G
POL/PAR CHIEF DELIB/GP FORCES BAL/PWR DIPLOM   EX/STRUC
ARMS/CONT WAR PEACE 19/20 STIMSON/HL ROOSEVLT/F

TAFT/WH HOOVER/H REPUBLICAN. PAGE 75 B1525

B60

SAYRE W.S.,GOVERNING NEW YORK CITY; POLITICS IN THE MUNIC
METROPOLIS. POL/PAR CHIEF DELIB/GP LEGIS PLAN ADMIN
CT/SYS LEAD PARTIC CHOOSE...DECISION CHARTS BIBLIOG PROB/SOLV
20 NEWYORK/C BUREAUCRCY. PAGE 93 B1875

C60

SCHAPIRO L.B.,"THE COMMUNIST PARTY OF THE SOVIET POL/PAR
UNION." USSR INTELL CHIEF EX/STRUC FORCES DOMIN COM
ADMIN LEAD WAR ATTIT SOVEREIGN...POLICY BIBLIOG 20. REV
PAGE 93 B1881

B61

AYLMER G.,THE KING'S SERVANTS. UK ELITES CHIEF PAY ADMIN
CT/SYS WEALTH 17 CROMWELL/O CHARLES/I. PAGE 7 B0153 ROUTINE
EX/STRUC
NAT/G

B61

DRURY J.W.,THE GOVERNMENT OF KANSAS. USA+45 AGRI PROVS
INDUS CHIEF LEGIS WORKER PLAN BUDGET GIVE CT/SYS CONSTN
GOV/REL...T 20 KANSAS GOVERNOR CITY/MGT. PAGE 31 ADMIN
B0621 LOC/G

B61

GRIFFITH E.S.,CONGRESS: ITS CONTEMPORARY ROLE. PARL/PROC
CONSTN POL/PAR CHIEF PLAN BUDGET DIPLOM CONFER EX/STRUC
ADMIN LOBBY...DECISION CONGRESS. PAGE 43 B0878 TOP/EX
LEGIS

B61

MARKMANN C.L.,JOHN F. KENNEDY: A SENSE OF PURPOSE. CHIEF
USA+45 INTELL FAM CONSULT DELIB/GP LEGIS PERSON TOP/EX
SKILL 20 KENNEDY/JF EISNHWR/DD ROOSEVLT/F ADMIN
NEW/FRONTR PRESIDENT. PAGE 69 B1399 BIOG

B61

PAGE T.,STATE PERSONNEL REORGANIZATION IN ILLINOIS. ADMIN
USA+45 POL/PAR CHIEF TEC/DEV LEAD ADJUST 20. PROVS
PAGE 80 B1625 WORKER
DELIB/GP

B61

TANZER L.,THE KENNEDY CIRCLE. INTELL CONSULT EX/STRUC
DELIB/GP TOP/EX CONTROL EXEC INGP/REL PERS/REL PWR NAT/G
...BIOG IDEA/COMP ANTHOL 20 KENNEDY/JF PRESIDENT CHIEF
DEMOCRAT MCNAMARA/R RUSK/D. PAGE 103 B2077

L61

KRAMER R.,"EXECUTIVE PRIVILEGE - A STUDY OF THE REPRESENT
PERIOD 1953-1960." NAT/G CHIEF EX/STRUC LEGIS PWR. LEAD
PAGE 61 B1233 EXEC
GOV/REL

S61

KUIC V.,"THEORY AND PRACTICE OF THE AMERICAN EXEC
PRESIDENCY." USA+45 USA-45 NAT/G ADMIN REPRESENT EX/STRUC
...PLURIST 20 PRESIDENT. PAGE 61 B1241 PWR
CHIEF

S61

ROBINSON J.A.,"PROCESS SATISFACTION AND POLICY GOV/REL
APPROVAL IN STATE DEPARTMENT - CONGRESSIONAL EX/STRUC
RELATIONS." ELITES CHIEF LEGIS CONFER DEBATE ADMIN POL/PAR
FEEDBACK ROLE...CHARTS 20 CONGRESS PRESIDENT DECISION
DEPT/STATE. PAGE 89 B1802

B62

ANDREWS W.G.,FRENCH POLITICS AND ALGERIA: THE GOV/COMP
PROCESS OF POLICY FORMATION 1954-1962. ALGERIA EXEC
FRANCE CONSTN ELITES POL/PAR CHIEF DELIB/GP LEGIS COLONIAL
DIPLOM PRESS CHOOSE 20. PAGE 5 B0105

B62

BOCK E.A.,CASE STUDIES IN AMERICAN GOVERNMENT. POLICY
USA+45 ECO/DEV CHIEF EDU/PROP CT/SYS RACE/REL LEGIS
ORD/FREE...JURID MGT PHIL/SCI PRESIDENT CASEBOOK. IDEA/COMP
PAGE 13 B0262 NAT/G

B62

FARBER W.O.,GOVERNMENT OF SOUTH DAKOTA. USA+45 PROVS
DIST/IND POL/PAR CHIEF EX/STRUC LEGIS ECO/TAC GIVE LOC/G
EDU/PROP CT/SYS PARTIC...T 20 SOUTH/DAK GOVERNOR. ADMIN
PAGE 35 B0704 CONSTN

B62

GRAY R.K.,EIGHTEEN ACRES UNDER GLASS. ELITES CHIEF
CONSULT EX/STRUC DIPLOM PRESS CONFER WAR PERS/REL ADMIN
PERSON 20 EISNHWR/DD TRUMAN/HS CABINET. PAGE 43 TOP/EX
B0860 NAT/G

B62

HARARI M.,GOVERNMENT AND POLITICS OF THE MIDDLE DIPLOM
EAST. ISLAM USA+45 NAT/G SECT CHIEF ADMIN ORD/FREE ECO/UNDEV
20. PAGE 47 B0943 TEC/DEV
POLICY

B62

HSUEH S.-.S.,GOVERNMENT AND ADMINISTRATION OF HONG ADMIN
KONG. CHIEF DELIB/GP LEGIS CT/SYS REPRESENT GOV/REL LOC/G
20 HONG/KONG CITY/MGT CIVIL/SERV GOVERNOR. PAGE 52 COLONIAL
B1055 EX/STRUC

B62

JEWELL M.E.,SENATORIAL POLITICS AND FOREIGN POLICY. USA+45
NAT/G POL/PAR CHIEF DELIB/GP TOP/EX FOR/AID LEGIS
EDU/PROP ROUTINE ATTIT PWR SKILL...MAJORIT DIPLOM
METH/CNCPT TIME/SEQ CONGRESS 20 PRESIDENT. PAGE 56
B1138

B62

KENNEDY J.F.,TO TURN THE TIDE. SPACE AGRI INT/ORG DIPLOM
FORCES TEC/DEV ADMIN NUC/PWR PEACE WEALTH...ANTHOL CHIEF

20 KENNEDY/JF CIV/RIGHTS. PAGE 59 B1193 POLICY
NAT/G

B62

LIPPMANN W.,PREFACE TO POLITICS. LABOR CHIEF PARTIC
CONTROL LEAD...MYTH IDEA/COMP 19/20 ROOSEVLT/T ATTIT
TAMMANY WILSON/H SANTAYAN/G BERGSON/H. PAGE 65 ADMIN
B1318

B62

PHILLIPS O.H.,CONSTITUTIONAL AND ADMINISTRATIVE LAW JURID
(3RD ED.). UK INT/ORG LOC/G CHIEF EX/STRUC LEGIS ADMIN
BAL/PWR ADJUD COLONIAL CT/SYS PWR...CHARTS 20. CONSTN
PAGE 83 B1670 NAT/G

B62

US SENATE COMM GOVT OPERATIONS,ADMINISTRATION OF ORD/FREE
NATIONAL SECURITY. USA+45 CHIEF PLAN PROB/SOLV ADMIN
TEC/DEV DIPLOM ATTIT...POLICY DECISION 20 NAT/G
KENNEDY/JF RUSK/D MCNAMARA/R BUNDY/M HERTER/C. CONTROL
PAGE 110 B2212

B62

US SENATE COMM ON JUDICIARY,STATE DEPARTMENT CONTROL
SECURITY. USA+45 CHIEF TEC/DEV DOMIN ADMIN EXEC WORKER
ATTIT ORD/FREE...POLICY CONGRESS DEPT/STATE NAT/G
PRESIDENT KENNEDY/JF KENNEDY/JF SENATE 20. PAGE 110 GOV/REL
B2228

L62

NEIBURG H.L.,"THE EISENHOWER AEC AND CONGRESS: A CHIEF
STUDY IN EXECUTIVE-LEGISLATIVE RELATIONS." USA+45 LEGIS
NAT/G POL/PAR DELIB/GP EX/STRUC TOP/EX ADMIN EXEC GOV/REL
LEAD ROUTINE PWR...POLICY COLD/WAR CONGRESS NUC/PWR
PRESIDENT AEC. PAGE 77 B1567

S62

MURACCIOLE L.,"LES CONSTITUTIONS DES ETATS NAT/G
AFRICAINS D'EXPRESSION FRANCAISE: LA CONSTITUTION CONSTN
DU 16 AVRIL 1962 DE LA REPUBLIQUE DU" AFR CHAD
CHIEF LEGIS LEGIT COLONIAL EXEC ROUTINE ORD/FREE
SOVEREIGN...SOC CONCPT 20. PAGE 76 B1541

B63

BADI J.,THE GOVERNMENT OF THE STATE OF ISRAEL: A NAT/G
CRITICAL ACCOUNT OF ITS PARLIAMENT, EXECUTIVE, AND CONSTN
JUDICIARY. ISRAEL ECO/DEV CHIEF DELIB/GP LEGIS EX/STRUC
DIPLOM CT/SYS INGP/REL PEACE ORD/FREE...BIBLIOG 20 POL/PAR
PARLIAMENT ARABS MIGRATION. PAGE 8 B0157

B63

BOCK E.A., STATE AND LOCAL GOVERNMENT: A CASE BOOK. LOC/G
USA+45 MUNIC PROVS CONSULT GP/REL ATTIT...MGT 20 ADMIN
CASEBOOK GOVERNOR MAYOR. PAGE 12 B0254 PROB/SOLV
CHIEF

B63

BOCK E.A.,STATE AND LOCAL GOVERNMENT: A CASE BOOK. PROVS
USA+45 FINAN CHIEF PROB/SOLV TAX ATTIT...POLICY 20 LOC/G
CASEBOOK. PAGE 13 B0263 ADMIN
GOV/REL

B63

DALAND R.T.,PERSPECTIVES OF BRAZILIAN PUBLIC ADMIN
ADMINISTRATION (VOL. I). BRAZIL LAW ECO/UNDEV NAT/G
SCHOOL CHIEF TEC/DEV CONFER CONTROL GP/REL ATTIT PLAN
ROLE PWR...ANTHOL 20. PAGE 26 B0525 GOV/REL

B63

DE GUZMAN R.P.,PATTERNS IN DECISION-MAKING: CASE ADMIN
STUDIES IN PHILIPPINE PUBLIC ADMINISTRATION. DECISION
PHILIPPINE LAW CHIEF PROB/SOLV INGP/REL DRIVE POLICY
PERCEPT ROLE...ANTHOL T 20. PAGE 27 B0557 GOV/REL

B63

ROBERT J.,LA MONARCHIE MAROCAINE. MOROCCO LABOR CHIEF
MUNIC POL/PAR EX/STRUC ORD/FREE PWR...JURID TREND T CONSERVE
20. PAGE 89 B1793 ADMIN
CONSTN

C63

BLUM J.M.,"THE NATIONAL EXPERIENCE." USA+45 USA-45 ADMIN
ECO/DEV DIPLOM WAR NAT/LISM...POLICY CHARTS BIBLIOG NAT/G
T 16/20 CONGRESS PRESIDENT COLD/WAR. PAGE 13 B0258 LEGIS
CHIEF

B64

ANDREN N.,GOVERNMENT AND POLITICS IN THE NORDIC CONSTN
COUNTRIES: DENMARK, FINLAND, ICELAND, NORWAY, NAT/G
SWEDEN. DENMARK FINLAND ICELAND NORWAY SWEDEN CULTURE
POL/PAR CHIEF LEGIS ADMIN REGION REPRESENT ATTIT GOV/COMP
CONSERVE...CHARTS BIBLIOG/A 20. PAGE 5 B0102

B64

BOUVIER-AJAM M.,MANUEL TECHNIQUE ET PRATIQUE DU MUNIC
MAIRE ET DES ELUS ET AGENTS COMMUNAUX. FRANCE LOC/G ADMIN
BUDGET CHOOSE GP/REL SUPEGO...JURID BIBLIOG 20 CHIEF
MAYOR COMMUNES. PAGE 14 B0284 NEIGH

B64

COMMITTEE ECONOMIC DEVELOPMENT,IMPROVING EXECUTIVE EXEC
MANAGEMENT IN THE FEDERAL GOVERNMENT. USA+45 CHIEF MGT
DELIB/GP WORKER PLAN PAY SENIOR ADMIN EFFICIENCY 20 TOP/EX
PRESIDENT. PAGE 22 B0457 NAT/G

B64

EATON H.,PRESIDENTIAL TIMBER: A HISTORY OF DELIB/GP
NOMINATING CONVENTIONS, 1868-1960. USA+45 USA-45 CHOOSE
POL/PAR EX/STRUC DEBATE LOBBY ATTIT PERSON ALL/VALS CHIEF
...MYTH 19/20 PRESIDENT. PAGE 32 B0646 NAT/G

B64

GOODMAN W.,THE TWO-PARTY SYSTEM IN THE UNITED POL/PAR
STATES. USA+45 USA-45 STRATA LOC/G CHIEF EDU/PROP REPRESENT

ADMIN COST PWR POPULISM...PLURIST 18/20 PRESIDENT. — CHOOSE NAT/G
PAGE 41 B0821
B64

GOODNOW H.F.,THE CIVIL SERVICE OF PAKISTAN: — ADMIN GOV/REL LAW NAT/G
BUREAUCRACY IN A NEW NATION. INDIA PAKISTAN S/ASIA
ECO/UNDEV PROVS CHIEF PARTIC CHOOSE EFFICIENCY PWR
...BIBLIOG 20. PAGE 41 B0824
B64

HALLER W.,DER SCHWEDISCHE JUSTITIEOMBUDSMAN. — JURID PARL/PROC ADMIN CHIEF
DENMARK FINLAND NORWAY SWEDEN LEGIS ADJUD CONTROL
PERSON ORD/FREE...NAT/COMP 20 OMBUDSMAN. PAGE 46
B0926
B64

HANNA W.J.,INDEPENDENT BLACK AFRICA: THE POLITICS — AFR ECO/UNDEV ADMIN PROB/SOLV
OF FREEDOM. ELITES INDUS KIN CHIEF COLONIAL CHOOSE
GOV/REL RACE/REL NAT/LISM ATTIT PERSON 20 NEGRO.
PAGE 46 B0938
B64

NEUSTADT R.,PRESIDENTIAL POWER. USA+45 CONSTN NAT/G — TOP/EX SKILL
CHIEF LEGIS CREATE EDU/PROP LEGIT ADMIN EXEC COERCE
ATTIT PERSON RIGID/FLEX PWR CONGRESS 20 PRESIDENT
TRUMAN/HS EISNHWR/DD. PAGE 78 B1575
B64

RIKER W.H.,FEDERALISM. WOR+45 WOR-45 CONSTN CHIEF — FEDERAL NAT/G ORD/FREE CENTRAL
LEGIS ADMIN COLONIAL CONTROL CT/SYS PWR...BIBLIOG/A
18/20. PAGE 88 B1787
B64

ROCHE J.P.,THE PRESIDENCY. USA+45 USA-45 CONSTN — EX/STRUC PWR
NAT/G CHIEF BAL/PWR DIPLOM GP/REL 18/20 PRESIDENT.
PAGE 90 B1810
B64

SARROS P.P.,CONGRESS AND THE NEW DIPLOMACY: THE — DIPLOM POL/PAR NAT/G
FORMULATION OF MUTUAL SECURITY POLICY: 1953-60
(THESIS). USA+45 CHIEF EX/STRUC REGION ROUTINE
CHOOSE GOV/REL PEACE ROLE...POLICY 20 PRESIDENT
CONGRESS. PAGE 92 B1869
B64

US SENATE COMM GOVT OPERATIONS,THE SECRETARY OF — DIPLOM DELIB/GP NAT/G
STATE AND THE AMBASSADOR. USA+45 CHIEF CONSULT
EX/STRUC FORCES PLAN ADMIN EXEC INGP/REL ROLE
...ANTHOL 20 PRESIDENT DEPT/STATE. PAGE 110 B2215
B64

US SENATE COMM GOVT OPERATIONS,ADMINISTRATION OF — ADMIN FORCES ORD/FREE NAT/G
NATIONAL SECURITY. USA+45 CHIEF TOP/EX PLAN DIPLOM
CONTROL PEACE...POLICY DECISION 20 PRESIDENT
CONGRESS. PAGE 110 B2216
S64

ROGOW A.A.,"CONGRESSIONAL GOVERNMENT: LEGISLATIVE — PWR DIPLOM LEGIS POLICY
POWER V. DOMESTIC PROCESSES." USA+45 CHIEF DELIB/GP
ADMIN GOV/REL CONGRESS. PAGE 90 B1815
S64

RUSK D.,"THE MAKING OF FOREIGN POLICY" USA+45 CHIEF — DIPLOM INT POLICY
DELIB/GP WORKER PROB/SOLV ADMIN ATTIT PWR
...DECISION 20 DEPT/STATE RUSK/D GOLDMAN/E. PAGE 92
B1856
S64

SWEARER H.R.,"AFTER KHRUSHCHEV: WHAT NEXT." COM FUT — EX/STRUC PWR
USSR CONSTN ELITES NAT/G POL/PAR CHIEF DELIB/GP
LEGIS DOMIN LEAD...RECORD TREND STERTYP GEN/METH
20. PAGE 102 B2058
C64

SCOTT R.E.,"MEXICAN GOVERNMENT IN TRANSITION (REV — NAT/G L/A+17C ROUTINE CONSTN
ED)" CULTURE STRUCT POL/PAR CHIEF ADMIN LOBBY REV
CHOOSE GP/REL DRIVE...BIBLIOG METH 20 MEXIC/AMER.
PAGE 95 B1920
B65

DE GRAZIA A.,REPUBLIC IN CRISIS: CONGRESS AGAINST — LEGIS EXEC GOV/REL CONTROL
THE EXECUTIVE FORCE. USA+45 USA-45 SOCIETY POL/PAR
CHIEF DOMIN ROLE ORD/FREE PWR...CONCPT MYTH BIBLIOG
20 CONGRESS. PAGE 27 B0556
B65

FEERICK J.D.,FROM FAILING HANDS: THE STUDY OF — EX/STRUC CHIEF LAW LEGIS
PRESIDENTIAL SUCCESSION. CONSTN NAT/G PROB/SOLV
LEAD PARL/PROC MURDER CHOOSE...NEW/IDEA BIBLIOG 20
KENNEDY/JF JOHNSON/LB PRESIDENT PRE/US/AM
VICE/PRES. PAGE 35 B0710
B65

GOPAL S.,BRITISH POLICY IN INDIA 1858-1905. INDIA — COLONIAL ADMIN POL/PAR ECO/UNDEV
UK ELITES CHIEF DELIB/GP ECO/TAC GP/REL DISCRIM
ATTIT...IDEA/COMP NAT/COMP PERS/COMP BIBLIOG/A
19/20. PAGE 41 B0828
B65

GREGG J.L.,POLITICAL PARTIES AND PARTY SYSTEMS IN — LEAD POL/PAR NAT/G CHIEF
GUATEMALA. 1944-1963. GUATEMALA L/A+17C EX/STRUC
FORCES CREATE CONTROL REV CHOOSE PWR...TREND
IDEA/COMP 20. PAGE 43 B0872
B65

HAIGHT D.E.,THE PRESIDENT; ROLES AND POWERS. USA+45 — CHIEF LEGIS TOP/EX EX/STRUC
USA-45 POL/PAR PLAN DIPLOM CHOOSE PERS/REL PWR
18/20 PRESIDENT CONGRESS. PAGE 45 B0915
B65

KOENIG C.W.,OFFICIAL MAKERS OF PUBLIC POLICY: — CHIEF LEGIS
CONGRESS AND THE PRESIDENT. USA+45 USA-45 NAT/G

EX/STRUC PROB/SOLV PWR. PAGE 60 B1222 — GOV/REL PLURISM
B65

KOENIG L.W.,OFFICIAL MAKERS OF PUBLIC POLICY: — POLICY LEGIS CHIEF NAT/G
CONGRESS AND THE PRESIDENT. USA+45 USA-45 EX/STRUC
ADMIN CONTROL GOV/REL PWR 18/20 CONGRESS PRESIDENT.
PAGE 61 B1225
B65

SNIDER C.F.,AMERICAN STATE AND LOCAL GOVERNMENT. — GOV/REL MUNIC PROVS LOC/G
USA+45 FINAN CHIEF EX/STRUC TAX ADMIN CONTROL SUFF
INGP/REL PWR 20. PAGE 98 B1989
B65

STANLEY D.T.,CHANGING ADMINISTRATIONS. USA+45 — NAT/G CHIEF ADMIN EX/STRUC
POL/PAR DELIB/GP TOP/EX BUDGET GOV/REL GP/REL
PERS/REL PWR...MAJORIT DECISION MGT 20 PRESIDENT
SUCCESSION DEPT/STATE DEPT/DEFEN DEPT/HEW. PAGE 100
B2021
B66

BURNS A.C.,PARLIAMENT AS AN EXPORT. WOR+45 CONSTN — PARL/PROC POL/PAR CT/SYS CHIEF
BARGAIN DEBATE ROUTINE GOV/REL EFFICIENCY...ANTHOL
COMMONWLTH PARLIAMENT. PAGE 17 B0353
B66

CORNWELL E.E. JR.,THE AMERICAN PRESIDENCY: VITAL — CHIEF EX/STRUC NAT/G ADMIN
CENTER. USA+45 USA-45 POL/PAR LEGIS PROB/SOLV
CONTROL PARTIC GOV/REL 18/20 PRESIDENT. PAGE 23
B0478
B66

GERBERDING W.P.,UNITED STATES FOREIGN POLICY: — PROB/SOLV CHIEF EX/STRUC CONTROL
PERSPECTIVES AND ANALYSIS. USA+45 LEGIS EXEC LEAD
REPRESENT PWR 20. PAGE 39 B0791
B66

MACFARQUHAR R.,CHINA UNDER MAO: POLITICS TAKES — ECO/UNDEV TEC/DEV ECO/TAC ADMIN
COMMAND. CHINA/COM COM AGRI INDUS CHIEF FORCES
DIPLOM INT/TRADE EDU/PROP TASK REV ADJUST...ANTHOL
20 MAO. PAGE 67 B1359
B66

SCHMIDT K.M.,AMERICAN STATE AND LOCAL GOVERNMENT IN — PROVS ADMIN MUNIC PLAN
ACTION. USA+45 CONSTN LOC/G POL/PAR CHIEF LEGIS
PROB/SOLV ADJUD LOBBY GOV/REL...DECISION ANTHOL 20
GOVERNOR MAYOR URBAN/RNWL. PAGE 94 B1896
B66

SILBERMAN B.S.,MODERN JAPANESE LEADERSHIP: — LEAD CULTURE ELITES MUNIC
TRANSITION AND CHANGE. NAT/G POL/PAR CHIEF ADMIN
REPRESENT GP/REL ADJUST RIGID/FLEX...SOC METH/COMP
ANTHOL 19/20 CHINJAP CHRISTIAN. PAGE 97 B1952
B66

TOTTEN G.O.,THE SOCIAL DEMOCRATIC MOVEMENT IN — POL/PAR SOCISM PARTIC STRATA
PREWAR JAPAN. ASIA CHIEF EX/STRUC LEGIS DOMIN LEAD
ROUTINE WAR 20 CHINJAP. PAGE 105 B2122
L66

LEMARCHAND R.,"SOCIAL CHANGE AND POLITICAL — NAT/G STRUCT ELITES CONSERVE
MODERNISATION IN BURUNDI." AFR BURUNDI STRATA CHIEF
EX/STRUC RIGID/FLEX PWR...SOC 20. PAGE 64 B1285
L66

MCAUSLAN J.P.W.,"CONSTITUTIONAL INNOVATION AND — CONSTN NAT/G EXEC POL/PAR
POLITICAL STABILITY IN TANZANIA: A PRELIMINARY
ASSESSMENT." AFR TANZANIA ELITES CHIEF EX/STRUC
RIGID/FLEX PWR 20 PRESIDENT BUREAUCRCY. PAGE 71
B1440
S66

MATTHEWS D.G.,"ETHIOPIAN OUTLINE: A BIBLIOGRAPHIC — BIBLIOG NAT/G DIPLOM POL/PAR
RESEARCH GUIDE." ETHIOPIA LAW STRUCT ECO/UNDEV AGRI
LABOR SECT CHIEF DELIB/GP EX/STRUC ADMIN...LING
ORG/CHARTS 20. PAGE 71 B1429
B67

ANGEL D.D.,ROMNEY. LABOR LG/CO NAT/G EXEC WAR — BIOG CHIEF PROVS POLICY
RACE/REL PERSON ORD/FREE...MGT WORSHIP 20
ROMNEY/GEO CIV/RIGHTS MORMON GOVERNOR. PAGE 5 B0108
B67

BRZEZINSKI Z.K.,THE SOVIET BLOC: UNITY AND CONFLICT — NAT/G DIPLOM
(2ND ED., REV., ENLARGED). COM POLAND USSR INTELL
CHIEF EX/STRUC CONTROL EXEC GOV/REL PWR MARXISM
...TREND IDEA/COMP 20 LENIN/VI MARX/KARL STALIN/J.
PAGE 16 B0336
B67

FARNSWORTH B.,WILLIAM C. BULLITT AND THE SOVIET — DIPLOM BIOG POLICY
UNION. COM USA-45 USSR NAT/G CHIEF CONSULT DELIB/GP
EX/STRUC WAR REPRESENT MARXISM 20 WILSON/W
ROOSEVLT/F STALIN/J BULLITT/WC. PAGE 35 B0705
B67

FINCHER F.,THE GOVERNMENT OF THE UNITED STATES. — NAT/G EX/STRUC LEGIS OP/RES
USA+45 USA-45 POL/PAR CHIEF CT/SYS LOBBY GP/REL
INGP/REL...CONCPT CHARTS BIBLIOG T 18/20 PRESIDENT
CONGRESS SUPREME/CT. PAGE 35 B0719
B67

MCCONNELL G.,THE MODERN PRESIDENCY. USA+45 CONSTN — NAT/G CHIEF EX/STRUC
TOP/EX DOMIN EXEC CHOOSE PWR...MGT 20. PAGE 72
B1446
B67

WARREN S.,THE AMERICAN PRESIDENT. POL/PAR FORCES — CHIEF

LEGIS DIPLOM ECO/TAC ADMIN EXEC PWR...ANTHOL 18/20
ROOSEVLT/F KENNEDY/JF JOHNSON/LB TRUMAN/HS
WILSON/W. PAGE 114 B2297
LEAD
NAT/G
CONSTN

B67
WESSON R.G.,THE IMPERIAL ORDER. WOR-45 STRUCT SECT
DOMIN ADMIN COLONIAL LEAD CONSERVE...CONCPT BIBLIOG
20. PAGE 115 B2324
PWR
CHIEF
CONTROL
SOCIETY

S67
ANDERSON M.,"THE FRENCH PARLIAMENT." EUR+WWI FRANCE
MOD/EUR CONSTN POL/PAR CHIEF LEGIS LOBBY ATTIT ROLE
PWR 19/20. PAGE 5 B0095
PARL/PROC
LEAD
GOV/COMP
EX/STRUC

S67
BRADLEY A.W.,"CONSTITUTION-MAKING IN UGANDA."
UGANDA LAW CHIEF DELIB/GP LEGIS ADMIN EXEC
PARL/PROC RACE/REL ORD/FREE...GOV/COMP 20. PAGE 14
B0295
NAT/G
CREATE
CONSTN
FEDERAL

S67
CHAMBERLAIN N.W.,"STRIKES IN CONTEMPORARY CONTEXT."
LAW INDUS NAT/G CHIEF CONFER COST ATTIT ORD/FREE
...POLICY MGT 20. PAGE 20 B0400
LABOR
BARGAIN
EFFICIENCY
PROB/SOLV

S67
HALL B.,"THE PAINTER'S UNION: A PARTIAL VICTORY."
USA+45 PROB/SOLV LEGIT ADMIN REPRESENT 20. PAGE 45
B0922
LABOR
CHIEF
CHOOSE
CRIME

S67
IDENBURG P.J.,"POLITICAL STRUCTURAL DEVELOPMENT IN
TROPICAL AFRICA." UK ECO/UNDEV KIN POL/PAR CHIEF
EX/STRUC CREATE COLONIAL CONTROL REPRESENT RACE/REL
...MAJORIT TREND 20. PAGE 53 B1074
AFR
CONSTN
NAT/G
GOV/COMP

S67
O'DELL J.H.,"THE JULY REBELLIONS AND THE 'MILITARY
STATE'." USA+45 VIETNAM STRATA CHIEF WORKER
COLONIAL EXEC CROWD CIVMIL/REL RACE/REL TOTALISM
...WELF/ST PACIFIST 20 NEGRO JOHNSON/LB PRESIDENT
CIV/RIGHTS. PAGE 79 B1599
PWR
NAT/G
COERCE
FORCES

S67
ROTBERG R.I.,"COLONIALISM AND AFTER: THE POLITICAL
LITERATURE OF CENTRAL AFRICA - A BIBLIOGRAPHIC
ESSAY." AFR CHIEF EX/STRUC REV INGP/REL RACE/REL
SOVEREIGN 20. PAGE 91 B1833
BIBLIOG/A
COLONIAL
DIPLOM
NAT/G

S67
SPEAR P.,"NEHRU." INDIA NAT/G POL/PAR ECO/TAC ADJUD
GOV/REL CENTRAL RIGID/FLEX 20 NEHRU/J. PAGE 99
B2003
CHIEF
ATTIT
ADMIN
CREATE

S67
TATU M.,"URSS: LES FLOTTEMENTS DE LA DIRECTION
COLLEGIALE." UAR USSR CHIEF LEAD INGP/REL
EFFICIENCY...DECISION TREND 20 MID/EAST. PAGE 103
B2082
POLICY
NAT/G
EX/STRUC
DIPLOM

B86
BOLINSBROKE H ST J.,A DISSERTATION UPON PARTIES
(1729). UK LEGIS CHOOSE GOV/REL SOVEREIGN...TRADIT
18 PARLIAMENT. PAGE 13 B0269
CONSERVE
POL/PAR
CHIEF
EX/STRUC

CHILDPEN....SEE AGE/C

CHILDS J.B. B0422,B0558

CHILDS J.R. B0423

CHILDS R.S. B0424

CHILDS/RS....RICHARD SPENCER CHILDS

B65
EAST J.P.,COUNCIL-MANAGER GOVERNMENT: THE POLITICAL
THOUGHT OF ITS FOUNDER, RICHARD S. CHILDS. USA+45
CREATE ADMIN CHOOSE...BIOG GEN/LAWS BIBLIOG 20
CHILDS/RS CITY/MGT. PAGE 32 B0642
SIMUL
LOC/G
MUNIC
EX/STRUC

CHILE....SEE ALSO L/A+17C

S65
SILVERT K.H.,"AMERICAN ACADEMIC ETHICS AND SOCIAL
RESEARCH ABROAD* THE LESSON OF PROJECT CAMELOT."
CHILE L/A+17C USA+45 FINAN ADMIN...PHIL/SCI SOC
GEN/LAWS CAMELOT. PAGE 97 B1953
ACADEM
NAT/G
ACT/RES
POLICY

B66
GLAZER M.,THE FEDERAL GOVERNMENT AND THE
UNIVERSITY. CHILE PROB/SOLV DIPLOM GIVE ADMIN WAR
...POLICY SOC 20. PAGE 40 B0810
BIBLIOG/A
NAT/G
PLAN
ACADEM

CHINA....CHINA IN GENERAL; SEE ALSO ASIA,CHINA/COM,TAIWAN

CHINA INSTITUTE OF AMERICA. B0425

CHINA/COM....COMMUNIST CHINA

B53
THOMAS S.B.,GOVERNMENT AND ADMINISTRATION IN
COMMUNIST CHINA (MONOGRAPH). CHINA/COM PROB/SOLV
EDU/PROP 20. PAGE 104 B2100
PWR
EX/STRUC
REPRESENT
ELITES

B55
POOL I.,SATELLITE GENERALS: A STUDY OF MILITARY
ELITES IN THE SOVIET SPHERE. ASIA CHINA/COM COM
CZECHOSLVK FUT HUNGARY POLAND ROMANIA USSR ELITES
STRATA ADMIN ATTIT PWR SKILL...METH/CNCPT BIOG 20.
PAGE 84 B1688
FORCES
CHOOSE

B55
UN HEADQUARTERS LIBRARY,BIBLIOGRAPHIE DE LA CHARTE
DES NATIONS UNIES. CHINA/COM KOREA WOR+45 VOL/ASSN
CONFER ADMIN COERCE PEACE ATTIT ORD/FREE SOVEREIGN
...INT/LAW 20 UNESCO UN. PAGE 106 B2149
BIBLIOG/A
INT/ORG
DIPLOM

L55
ROSTOW W.W.,"RUSSIA AND CHINA UNDER COMMUNISM."
CHINA/COM USSR INTELL STRUCT INT/ORG NAT/G POL/PAR
TOP/EX ACT/RES PLAN ADMIN ATTIT ALL/VALS MARXISM
...CONCPT OBS TIME/SEQ TREND GOV/COMP VAL/FREE 20.
PAGE 91 B1830
COM
ASIA

S55
KAUTSKY J.H.,"THE NEW STRATEGY OF INTERNATIONAL
COMMUNISM." ASIA CHINA/COM FUT WOR+45 WOR-45 ADMIN
ROUTINE PERSON MARXISM SOCISM...TREND IDEA/COMP 20
LENIN/VI MAO. PAGE 59 B1184
COM
POL/PAR
TOTALISM
USSR

S57
BAUER R.A.,"BRAINWASHING: PSYCHOLOGY OR
DEMONOLOGY." ASIA CHINA/COM COM POL/PAR ECO/TAC
ADMIN COERCE ATTIT DRIVE ORD/FREE...CONCPT MYTH 20.
PAGE 10 B0196
EDU/PROP
PSY
TOTALISM

C57
TANG P.S.H.,"COMMUNIST CHINA TODAY: DOMESTIC AND
FOREIGN POLICIES." CHINA/COM COM S/ASIA USSR STRATA
FORCES DIPLOM EDU/PROP COERCE GOV/REL...POLICY
MAJORIT BIBLIOG 20. PAGE 102 B2071
POL/PAR
LEAD
ADMIN
CONSTN

B58
CHANG C.,THE INFLATIONARY SPIRAL: THE EXPERIENCE IN
CHINA 1939-50. CHINA/COM BUDGET INT/TRADE PRICE
ADMIN CONTROL WAR DEMAND...POLICY CHARTS 20.
PAGE 20 B0406
FINAN
ECO/TAC
BAL/PAY
GOV/REL

B59
CHINA INSTITUTE OF AMERICA.,CHINA AND THE UNITED
NATIONS. CHINA/COM FUT STRUCT EDU/PROP LEGIT ADMIN
ATTIT KNOWL ORD/FREE PWR...OBS RECORD STAND/INT
TIME/SEQ UN LEAGUE/NAT UNESCO 20. PAGE 21 B0425
ASIA
INT/ORG

S60
NORTH R.C.,"DIE DISKREPANZ ZWISCHEN REALITAT UND
WUNSCHBILD ALS INNENPOLITISCHER FAKTOR." ASIA
CHINA/COM COM FUT ECO/UNDEV NAT/G PLAN DOMIN ADMIN
COERCE PERCEPT...SOC MYTH GEN/METH WORK TOT/POP 20.
PAGE 79 B1589
SOCIETY
ECO/TAC

S60
SCHWARTZ B.,"THE INTELLIGENTSIA IN COMMUNIST CHINA:
A TENTATIVE COMPARISON." ASIA CHINA/COM COM RUSSIA
ELITES SOCIETY STRATA POL/PAR VOL/ASSN CREATE ADMIN
COERCE NAT/LISM TOTALISM...POLICY TREND 20. PAGE 95
B1914
INTELL
RIGID/FLEX
REV

B61
HOUN F.W.,TO CHANGE A NATION; PROPAGANDA AND
INDOCTRINATION IN COMMUNIST CHINA. CHINA/COM COM
ACT/RES PLAN PRESS ADMIN FEEDBACK CENTRAL
EFFICIENCY ATTIT...PSY SOC 20. PAGE 52 B1048
DOMIN
EDU/PROP
TOTALISM
MARXISM

S63
ETIENNE G.,"'LOIS OBJECTIVES' ET PROBLEMES DE
DEVELOPPEMENT DANS LE CONTEXTE CHINE-URSS." ASIA
CHINA/COM COM FUT STRUCT INT/ORG VOL/ASSN TOP/EX
TEC/DEV ECO/TAC ATTIT RIGID/FLEX...GEOG MGT
TIME/SEQ TOT/POP 20. PAGE 34 B0682
TOTALISM
USSR

S63
SCHURMANN F.,"ECONOMIC POLICY AND POLITICAL POWER
IN COMMUNIST CHINA." ASIA CHINA/COM USSR SOCIETY
ECO/UNDEV AGRI INDUS CREATE ADMIN ROUTINE ATTIT
DRIVE RIGID/FLEX PWR WEALTH...HIST/WRIT TREND
CHARTS WORK 20. PAGE 94 B1908
PLAN
ECO/TAC

B64
LI C.M.,INDUSTRIAL DEVELOPMENT IN COMMUNIST CHINA.
CHINA/COM ECO/DEV ECO/UNDEV AGRI FINAN INDUS MARKET
LABOR NAT/G ECO/TAC INT/TRADE EXEC ALL/VALS
...POLICY RELATIV TREND WORK TOT/POP VAL/FREE 20.
PAGE 65 B1311
ASIA
TEC/DEV

B64
POPPINO R.E.,INTERNATIONAL COMMUNISM IN LATIN
AMERICA: A HISTORY OF THE MOVEMENT 1917-1963.
CHINA/COM USSR INTELL STRATA LABOR WORKER ADMIN REV
ATTIT...POLICY 20 COLD/WAR. PAGE 84 B1692
MARXISM
POL/PAR
L/A+17C

S64
KENNAN G.F.,"POLYCENTRISM AND WESTERN POLICY." ASIA
CHINA/COM COM FUT USA+45 USSR NAT/G ACT/RES DOMIN
EDU/PROP EXEC COERCE DISPL PERCEPT...POLICY
COLD/WAR 20. PAGE 59 B1192
RIGID/FLEX
ATTIT
DIPLOM

B65
BARISH N.N.,MANAGEMENT SCIENCES IN THE EMERGING
COUNTRIES. AFR CHINA/COM WOR+45 FINAN INDUS PLAN
PRODUC HABITAT...ANTHOL 20. PAGE 9 B0184
ECO/UNDEV
OP/RES
MGT

CHEN T.H.,THE CHINESE COMMUNIST REGIME: A
DOCUMENTARY STUDY (2 VOLS.). CHINA/COM LAW CONSTN
ELITES ECO/UNDEV LEGIS ECO/TAC ADMIN CONTROL PWR
...SOC 20. PAGE 20 B0417

TEC/DEV
B65
MARXISM
POL/PAR
NAT/G

CRAMER J.F.,CONTEMPORARY EDUCATION: A COMPARATIVE
STUDY OF NATIONAL SYSTEMS (2ND ED.). CHINA/COM
EUR+WWI INDIA USA+45 FINAN PROB/SOLV ADMIN CONTROL
ATTIT...IDEA/COMP METH/COMP 20 CHINJAP. PAGE 25
B0502

B65
EDU/PROP
NAT/COMP
SCHOOL
ACADEM

MACFARQUHAR R.,CHINA UNDER MAO: POLITICS TAKES
COMMAND. CHINA/COM COM AGRI INDUS CHIEF FORCES
DIPLOM INT/TRADE EDU/PROP TASK REV ADJUST...ANTHOL
20 MAO. PAGE 67 B1359

B66
ECO/UNDEV
TEC/DEV
ECO/TAC
ADMIN

SCHURMANN F.,IDEOLOGY AND ORGANIZATION IN COMMUNIST
CHINA. CHINA/COM LOC/G MUNIC POL/PAR ECO/TAC
CONTROL ATTIT...MGT STERTYP 20 COM/PARTY. PAGE 94
B1909

B66
MARXISM
STRUCT
ADMIN
NAT/G

US DEPARTMENT OF THE ARMY,COMMUNIST CHINA: A
STRATEGIC SURVEY: A BIBLIOGRAPHY (PAMPHLET NO.
20-67). CHINA/COM COM INDIA USSR NAT/G POL/PAR
EX/STRUC FORCES NUC/PWR REV ATTIT...POLICY GEOG
CHARTS. PAGE 108 B2184

B66
BIBLIOG/A
MARXISM
S/ASIA
DIPLOM

LENG S.C.,JUSTICE IN COMMUNIST CHINA: A SURVEY OF
THE JUDICIAL SYSTEM OF THE CHINESE PEOPLE'S
REPUBLIC. CHINA/COM LAW CONSTN LOC/G NAT/G PROF/ORG
CONSULT FORCES ADMIN CRIME ORD/FREE...BIBLIOG 20
MAO. PAGE 64 B1290

B67
CT/SYS
ADJUD
JURID
MARXISM

BASTID M.,"ORIGINES ET DEVELOPMENT DE LA REVOLUTION
CULTURELLE." CHINA/COM DOMIN ADMIN CONTROL LEAD
COERCE CROWD ATTIT DRIVE MARXISM...POLICY 20.
PAGE 10 B0195

S67
REV
CULTURE
ACADEM
WORKER

BAUM R.D.,"IDEOLOGY REDIVIVUS." CHINA/COM NAT/G
EDU/PROP ADMIN 20. PAGE 10 B0197

S67
REV
MARXISM
CREATE
TEC/DEV

HSUEH C.T.,"THE CULTURAL REVOLUTION AND LEADERSHIP
CRISIS IN COMMUNIST CHINA." CHINA/COM POL/PAR
EX/STRUC FORCES EDU/PROP ATTIT PWR...POLICY 20.
PAGE 52 B1054

S67
LEAD
REV
CULTURE
MARXISM

WALLER D.J.,"CHINA: RED OR EXPERT." CHINA/COM
INTELL DOMIN REV ATTIT MARXISM 20. PAGE 113 B2283

S67
CONTROL
FORCES
ADMIN
POL/PAR

CHINESE/AM....CHINESE IMMIGRANTS TO US AND THEIR DESCENDANTS

CHITTAGONG....CHITTAGONG HILL TRIBES

CHOICE (IN DECISION-MAKING)....SEE PROB/SOLV

CHOJNACKI S. B0426

CHOOSE....CHOICE, ELECTION

JOURNAL OF POLITICS. USA-45 USA-45 CONSTN POL/PAR
EX/STRUC LEGIS PROB/SOLV DIPLOM CT/SYS CHOOSE
RACE/REL 20. PAGE 1 B0005

N
BIBLIOG/A
NAT/G
LAW
LOC/G

US SUPERINTENDENT OF DOCUMENTS,POLITICAL SCIENCE:
GOVERNMENT, CRIME, DISTRICT OF COLUMBIA (PRICE LIST
54). USA+45 LAW CONSTN EX/STRUC WORKER ADJUD ADMIN
CT/SYS CHOOSE INGP/REL RACE/REL CONGRESS PRESIDENT.
PAGE 111 B2241

N
BIBLIOG/A
NAT/G
CRIME

RIORDAN W.L.,PLUNKITT OF TAMMANY HALL. USA-45
SOCIETY PROB/SOLV EXEC LEAD TASK CHOOSE ALL/VALS
...RECORD ANTHOL 20 REFORMERS TAMMANY NEWYORK/C
PLUNKITT/G. PAGE 88 B1789

B05
POL/PAR
MUNIC
CHIEF
ATTIT

FAHRNKOPF N.,STATE AND LOCAL GOVERNMENT IN ILLINOIS
(PAMPHLET). CONSTN ADMIN PARTIC CHOOSE REPRESENT
GOV/REL...JURID MGT 20 ILLINOIS. PAGE 34 B0696

N19
BIBLIOG
LOC/G
LEGIS
CT/SYS

GRIFFITH W.,THE PUBLIC SERVICE (PAMPHLET). UK LAW
LOC/G NAT/G PARTIC CHOOSE DRIVE ROLE SKILL...CHARTS
20 CIVIL/SERV. PAGE 44 B0880

N19
ADMIN
EFFICIENCY
EDU/PROP
GOV/REL

OPERATIONS AND POLICY RESEARCH,PERU ELECTION
MEMORANDA (PAMPHLET). L/A+17C PERU POL/PAR LEGIS
EXEC APPORT REPRESENT 20. PAGE 80 B1611

N19
CHOOSE
CONSTN
SUFF
NAT/G

TREVELYAN G.M.,THE TWO-PARTY SYSTEM IN ENGLISH
POLITICAL HISTORY (PAMPHLET). UK CHIEF LEGIS
COLONIAL EXEC REV CHOOSE 17/19. PAGE 105 B2128

N19
PARL/PROC
POL/PAR
NAT/G
PWR

KENT F.R.,THE GREAT GAME OF POLITICS. USA-45 LOC/G
NAT/G POL/PAR EX/STRUC PROB/SOLV BUDGET CHOOSE
GOV/REL 20. PAGE 59 B1194

B24
ADMIN
OP/RES
STRUCT

MERRIAM C.E.,A HISTORY OF POLITICAL THEORIES -
RECENT TIMES. USA-45 WOR-45 CULTURE SOCIETY ECO/DEV
R+D EDU/PROP ROUTINE CHOOSE ATTIT PERSON ALL/VALS
...POLICY SOC CONCPT METH/CNCPT OBS HIST/WRIT
TIME/SEQ TREND. PAGE 73 B1471

B24
UNIV
INTELL

INTERNATIONAL BIBLIOGRAPHY OF POLITICAL SCIENCE.
WOR+45 NAT/G POL/PAR EX/STRUC LEGIS CT/SYS LEAD
CHOOSE GOV/REL ATTIT...PHIL/SCI 20. PAGE 2 B0034

B26
BIBLIOG
DIPLOM
CONCPT
ADMIN

FYFE H.,THE BRITISH LIBERAL PARTY. UK SECT ADMIN
LEAD CHOOSE GP/REL PWR SOCISM...MAJORIT TIME/SEQ
19/20 LIB/PARTY CONSRV/PAR. PAGE 38 B0768

B28
POL/PAR
NAT/G
REPRESENT
POPULISM

MOLEY R.,POLITICS AND CRIMINAL PROSECUTION. USA-45
POL/PAR EX/STRUC LEGIT CONTROL LEAD ROUTINE CHOOSE
INGP/REL...JURID CHARTS 20. PAGE 74 B1497

B29
PWR
CT/SYS
CRIME
ADJUD

FAIRLIE J.A.,COUNTY GOVERNMENT AND ADMINISTRATION.
UK USA-45 NAT/G SCHOOL FORCES BUDGET TAX CT/SYS
CHOOSE...JURID BIBLIOG 11/20. PAGE 35 B0701

B30
ADMIN
GOV/REL
LOC/G
MUNIC

MCKISACK M.,THE PARLIAMENTARY REPRESENTATION OF THE
ENGLISH BOROUGHS DURING THE MIDDLE AGES. UK CONSTN
CULTURE ELITES EX/STRUC TAX PAY ADJUD PARL/PROC
APPORT FEDERAL...POLICY 13/15 PARLIAMENT. PAGE 72
B1454

B32
NAT/G
MUNIC
LEGIS
CHOOSE

RIDLEY C.E.,THE CITY-MANAGER PROFESSION. CHIEF PLAN
ADMIN CONTROL ROUTINE CHOOSE...TECHNIC CHARTS
GOV/COMP BIBLIOG 20. PAGE 88 B1780

B34
MUNIC
EX/STRUC
LOC/G
EXEC

GOSNELL H.F.,MACHINE POLITICS: CHICAGO MODEL.
COM/IND FACE/GP LOC/G EX/STRUC LEAD ROUTINE
SANCTION REPRESENT GOV/REL PWR...POLICY MATH OBS
INT CHARTS. PAGE 41 B0840

B37
POL/PAR
MUNIC
ADMIN
CHOOSE

PARSONS T.,THE STRUCTURE OF SOCIAL ACTION. UNIV
INTELL SOCIETY INDUS MARKET ECO/TAC ROUTINE CHOOSE
ALL/VALS...CONCPT OBS BIOG TREND GEN/LAWS 20.
PAGE 81 B1636

B37
CULTURE
ATTIT
CAP/ISM

RAPPARD W.E.,THE CRISIS OF DEMOCRACY. EUR+WWI UNIV
WOR-45 CULTURE SOCIETY ECO/DEV INT/ORG POL/PAR
ACT/RES EDU/PROP EXEC CHOOSE ATTIT ALL/VALS...SOC
OBS HIST/WRIT TIME/SEQ LEAGUE/NAT NAZI TOT/POP 20.
PAGE 86 B1741

B38
NAT/G
CONCPT

SALTER J.T.,THE AMERICAN POLITICIAN. USA-45 LABOR
POL/PAR EDU/PROP ADMIN CHOOSE ATTIT DRIVE PERSON
PWR...POLICY ANTHOL 20 THOMAS/N LEWIS/JL LAGUARD/F
GOVERNOR MAYOR. PAGE 92 B1865

B38
BIOG
LEAD
PROVS
LOC/G

JENNINGS W.I.,PARLIAMENT. UK POL/PAR OP/RES BUDGET
LEAD CHOOSE GP/REL...MGT 20 PARLIAMENT HOUSE/LORD
HOUSE/CMNS. PAGE 56 B1135

B39
PARL/PROC
LEGIS
CONSTN
NAT/G

MCHENRY D.E.,HIS MAJESTY'S OPPOSITION: STRUCTURE
AND PROBLEMS OF THE BRITISH LABOUR PARTY 1931-1938.
UK FINAN LABOR LOC/G DELIB/GP LEGIS EDU/PROP LEAD
PARTIC CHOOSE GP/REL SOCISM...TREND 20 LABOR/PAR.
PAGE 72 B1450

B40
POL/PAR
MGT
NAT/G
POLICY

PATTERSON C.P.,STATE AND LOCAL GOVERNMENT IN TEXAS
(3RD ED.). USA-45 EX/STRUC LEGIS CT/SYS CHOOSE 20
TEXAS. PAGE 81 B1642

B40
CONSTN
PROVS
GOV/REL
LOC/G

GERTH H.,"THE NAZI PARTY: ITS LEADERSHIP AND
COMPOSITION" (BMR)" GERMANY ELITES STRATA STRUCT
EX/STRUC FORCES ECO/TAC CT/SYS CHOOSE TOTALISM
AGE/Y AUTHORIT PWR 20. PAGE 39 B0792

S40
POL/PAR
DOMIN
LEAD
ADMIN

BINGHAM A.M.,THE TECHNIQUES OF DEMOCRACY. USA-45
CONSTN STRUCT POL/PAR LEGIS PLAN PARTIC CHOOSE
REPRESENT NAT/LISM TOTALISM...MGT 20. PAGE 12 B0240

B42
POPULISM
ORD/FREE
ADMIN
NAT/G

DENNISON E.,THE SENATE FOREIGN RELATIONS COMMITTEE.
USA-45 NAT/G DELIB/GP ROUTINE CHOOSE PWR CONGRESS

B42
LEGIS
ACT/RES

20. PAGE 28 B0574

DIPLOM

ROUTINE
B53

B42

US STATE DEPT.,PEACE AND WAR: UNITED STATES FOREIGN DIPLOM
POLICY, 1931-41. CULTURE FORCES ROUTINE CHOOSE USA-45
ATTIT DRIVE PERSON 20. PAGE 111 B2237 PLAN

B44

DAVIS H.E.,PIONEERS IN WORLD ORDER. WOR-45 CONSTN INT/ORG
ECO/TAC DOMIN EDU/PROP LEGIT ADJUD ADMIN ARMS/CONT ROUTINE
CHOOSE KNOWL ORD/FREE...POLICY JURID SOC STAT OBS
CENSUS TIME/SEQ ANTHOL LEAGUE/NAT 20. PAGE 26 B0537

S44

SIMON H.A.,"DECISION-MAKING AND ADMINISTRATIVE DECISION
ORGANIZATION" (BMR) WOR-45 CHOOSE INGP/REL ADMIN
EFFICIENCY ATTIT RESPECT...MGT 20. PAGE 97 B1955 CONTROL
WORKER

C45

FISHER M.J.,"PARTIES AND POLITICS IN THE LOCAL CHOOSE
COMMUNITY." USA-45 NAT/G SCHOOL ADMIN PARTIC LOC/G
REPRESENT KNOWL...BIBLIOG 20. PAGE 36 B0724 POL/PAR
ROUTINE

B47

KEFAUVER E.,A TWENTIETH-CENTURY CONGRESS. POL/PAR LEGIS
EX/STRUC SENIOR ADMIN CONTROL EXEC LOBBY CHOOSE DELIB/GP
EFFICIENCY PWR. PAGE 59 B1189 ROUTINE
TOP/EX

B48

PUBLIC ADMINISTRATION SERVICE,SOURCE MATERIALS IN BIBLIOG/A
PUBLIC ADMINISTRATION: A SELECTED BIBLIOGRAPHY (PAS GOV/REL
PUBLICATION NO. 102). USA+45 LAW FINAN LOC/G MUNIC MGT
NAT/G PLAN RECEIVE EDU/PROP CT/SYS CHOOSE HEALTH ADMIN
20. PAGE 85 B1717

B50

AMERICAN POLITICAL SCI ASSN,TOWARD A MORE POL/PAR
RESPONSIBLE TWO-PARTY SYSTEM. USA+45 CONSTN TASK
VOL/ASSN LEGIS LEAD CHOOSE...POLICY MGT 20. PAGE 4 PARTIC
B0087 ACT/RES

B50

LITTLE HOOVER COMM,HOW TO ACHIEVE GREATER TOP/EX
EFFICIENCY AND ECONOMY IN MINNESOTA'S GOVERNMENT LOC/G
(PAMPHLET). PLAN BUDGET ADMIN CHOOSE EFFICIENCY GOV/REL
ALL/VALS 20 MINNESOTA. PAGE 66 B1327 PROVS

B50

MCHENRY D.E.,THE THIRD FORCE IN CANADA: THE POL/PAR
COOPERATIVE COMMONWEALTH FEDERATION, 1932-1948. ADMIN
CANADA EX/STRUC LEGIS REPRESENT 20 LABOR/PAR. CHOOSE
PAGE 72 B1451 POLICY

L50

US SENATE COMM. GOVT. OPER.,"REVISION OF THE UN INT/ORG
CHARTER." FUT USA+45 WOR+45 CONSTN ECO/DEV LEGIS
ECO/UNDEV NAT/G DELIB/GP ACT/RES CREATE PLAN EXEC PEACE
ROUTINE CHOOSE ALL/VALS...POLICY CONCPT CONGRESS UN
TOT/POP 20 COLD/WAR. PAGE 111 B2235

S50

EPSTEIN L.D.,"POLITICAL STERILIZATION OF CIVIL ADMIN
SERVANTS: THE UNITED STATES AND GREAT BRITAIN." UK LEGIS
USA+45 USA-45 STRUCT TOP/EX OP/RES PARTIC CHOOSE DECISION
NAT/LISM 20 CONGRESS CIVIL/SERV. PAGE 33 B0679 POL/PAR

C50

STEWART F.M.,"A HALF CENTURY OF MUNICIPAL REFORM." LOC/G
USA+45 CONSTN FINAN SCHOOL EX/STRUC PLAN PROB/SOLV VOL/ASSN
EDU/PROP ADMIN CHOOSE GOV/REL BIBLIOG. PAGE 101 MUNIC
B2036 POLICY

C50

STOKES W.S.,"HONDURAS: AN AREA STUDY IN CONSTN
GOVERNMENT." HONDURAS NAT/G POL/PAR COLONIAL CT/SYS LAW
ROUTINE CHOOSE REPRESENT...GEOG RECORD BIBLIOG L/A+17C
19/20. PAGE 101 B2044 ADMIN

B51

ANDERSON W.,STATE AND LOCAL GOVERNMENT IN THE LOC/G
UNITED STATES. USA+45 CONSTN POL/PAR EX/STRUC LEGIS MUNIC
BUDGET TAX ADJUD CT/SYS CHOOSE...CHARTS T 20. PROVS
PAGE 5 B0100 GOV/REL

B51

ANDERSON W.,GOVERNMENT IN THE FIFTY STATES. LAW LOC/G
CONSTN FINAN POL/PAR LEGIS EDU/PROP ADJUD ADMIN PROVS
CT/SYS CHOOSE...CHARTS 20. PAGE 5 B0101 GOV/REL

B52

LEGISLATIVE REFERENCE SERVICE,PROBLEMS OF BIBLIOG
LEGISLATIVE APPORTIONMENT ON BOTH FEDERAL AND STATE REPRESENT
LEVELS: SELECTED REFERENCES (PAMPHLET). USA+45 CHOOSE
USA-45 LOC/G NAT/G LEGIS WRITING ADMIN APPORT 20 PROVS
CONGRESS. PAGE 63 B1282

B53

DIMOCK M.E.,PUBLIC ADMINISTRATION. USA+45 FINAN ADMIN
WORKER BUDGET CONTROL CHOOSE...T 20. PAGE 29 B0596 STRUCT
OP/RES
POLICY

B53

GROSS B.M.,THE LEGISLATIVE STRUGGLE: A STUDY IN LEGIS
SOCIAL COMBAT. STRUCT LOC/G POL/PAR JUDGE EDU/PROP DECISION
DEBATE ETIQUET ADMIN LOBBY CHOOSE GOV/REL INGP/REL PERSON
HEREDITY ALL/VALS...SOC PRESIDENT. PAGE 44 B0885 LEAD

B53

SAYLES L.R.,THE LOCAL UNION. CONSTN CULTURE LABOR
DELIB/GP PARTIC CHOOSE GP/REL INGP/REL ATTIT ROLE LEAD
...MAJORIT DECISION MGT. PAGE 93 B1873 ADJUD

STOUT H.M.,BRITISH GOVERNMENT. UK FINAN LOC/G NAT/G
POL/PAR DELIB/GP DIPLOM ADMIN COLONIAL CHOOSE PARL/PROC
ORD/FREE...JURID BIBLIOG 20 COMMONWLTH. PAGE 101 CONSTN
B2049 NEW/LIB

B54

COMBS C.H.,DECISION PROCESSES. INTELL SOCIETY MATH
DELIB/GP CREATE TEC/DEV DOMIN LEGIT EXEC CHOOSE DECISION
DRIVE RIGID/FLEX KNOWL PWR...PHIL/SCI SOC
METH/CNCPT CONT/OBS REC/INT PERS/TEST SAMP/SIZ BIOG
SOC/EXP WORK. PAGE 22 B0455

S54

CHILDS R.S.,"CITIZEN ORGANIZATION FOR CONTROL OF CHOOSE
GOVERNMENT." USA+45 POL/PAR CONTROL LOBBY...MAJORIT REPRESENT
20. PAGE 21 B0424 ADMIN
EX/STRUC

C54

ROBSON W.A.,"GREAT CITIES OF THE WORLD: THEIR LOC/G
GOVERNMENT, POLITICS, AND PLANNING." CONSTN FINAN MUNIC
EX/STRUC ADMIN EXEC CHOOSE GOV/REL...STAT TREND PLAN
ANTHOL BIBLIOG 20. PAGE 89 B1806 PROB/SOLV

B55

BAILEY S.K.,RESEARCH FRONTIERS IN POLITICS AND R+D
GOVERNMENT. CONSTN LEGIS ADMIN REV CHOOSE...CONCPT METH
IDEA/COMP GAME ANTHOL 20. PAGE 8 B0164 NAT/G

B55

POOL I.,SATELLITE GENERALS: A STUDY OF MILITARY FORCES
ELITES IN THE SOVIET SPHERE. ASIA CHINA/COM COM CHOOSE
CZECHOSLVK FUT HUNGARY POLAND ROMANIA USSR ELITES
STRATA ADMIN ATTIT PWR SKILL...METH/CNCPT BIOG 20.
PAGE 84 B1688

B56

ABELS J.,THE TRUMAN SCANDALS. USA+45 USA-45 POL/PAR CRIME
TAX LEGIT CT/SYS CHOOSE PRIVIL MORAL WEALTH 20 ADMIN
TRUMAN/HS PRESIDENT CONGRESS. PAGE 3 B0052 CHIEF
TRIBUTE

B56

GLADDEN E.N.,CIVIL SERVICE OR BUREAUCRACY? UK LAW ADMIN
STRATA LABOR TOP/EX PLAN SENIOR AUTOMAT CONTROL GOV/REL
PARTIC CHOOSE HAPPINESS...CHARTS 19/20 CIVIL/SERV EFFICIENCY
BUREAUCRCY. PAGE 40 B0808 PROVS

B56

JENNINGS W.I.,THE APPROACH TO SELF-GOVERNMENT. NAT/G
CEYLON INDIA PAKISTAN S/ASIA UK SOCIETY POL/PAR CONSTN
DELIB/GP LEGIS ECO/TAC EDU/PROP ADMIN EXEC CHOOSE COLONIAL
ATTIT ALL/VALS...JURID CONCPT GEN/METH TOT/POP 20.
PAGE 56 B1136

B56

SOHN L.B.,BASIC DOCUMENTS OF THE UNITED NATIONS. DELIB/GP
WOR+45 LAW INT/ORG LEGIT EXEC ROUTINE CHOOSE PWR CONSTN
...JURID CONCPT GEN/LAWS ANTHOL UN TOT/POP OAS FAO
ILO 20. PAGE 99 B1993

B56

WAUGH E.W.,SECOND CONSUL. USA+45 USA-45 CONSTN NAT/G
POL/PAR PROB/SOLV PARL/PROC CHOOSE PERS/REL ATTIT EX/STRUC
...BIBLIOG 18/20 VICE/PRES. PAGE 114 B2304 PWR
CHIEF

B56

WILSON P.,GOVERNMENT AND POLITICS OF INDIA AND BIBLIOG
PAKISTAN: 1885-1955; A BIBLIOGRAPHY OF WORKS IN COLONIAL
WESTERN LANGUAGES. INDIA PAKISTAN CONSTN LOC/G NAT/G
POL/PAR DIPLOM ADMIN WAR CHOOSE...BIOG S/ASIA
CON/ANAL 19/20. PAGE 117 B2361

S56

KHAMA T.,"POLITICAL CHANGE IN AFRICAN SOCIETY." AFR
CONSTN SOCIETY LOC/G NAT/G POL/PAR EX/STRUC LEGIS ELITES
LEGIT ADMIN CHOOSE REPRESENT NAT/LISM MORAL
ORD/FREE PWR...CONCPT OBS TREND GEN/METH CMN/WLTH
17/20. PAGE 59 B1201

B57

BABCOCK R.S.,STATE & LOCAL GOVERNMENT AND POLITICS. PROVS
USA+45 CONSTN POL/PAR EX/STRUC LEGIS BUDGET LOBBY LOC/G
CHOOSE SUFF...CHARTS BIBLIOG T 20. PAGE 8 B0154 GOV/REL

B57

CRONBACK L.J.,PSYCHOLOGICAL TESTS AND PERSONNEL MATH
DECISIONS. OP/RES PROB/SOLV CHOOSE PERSON...PSY DECISION
STAT TESTS 20. PAGE 25 B0508 WORKER
MGT

B57

IKE N.,JAPANESE POLITICS. INTELL STRUCT AGRI INDUS NAT/G
FAM KIN LABOR PRESS CHOOSE ATTIT...DECISION BIBLIOG ADMIN
19/20 CHINJAP. PAGE 53 B1075 POL/PAR
CULTURE

B57

LOEWENSTEIN K.,POLITICAL POWER AND THE GOVERNMENTAL PWR
PROCESS. WOR+45 WOR-45 CONSTN NAT/G POL/PAR CONCPT
EX/STRUC LEGIS TOP/EX DOMIN EDU/PROP LEGIT ADMIN
REGION CHOOSE ATTIT...JURID STERTYP GEN/LAWS 20.
PAGE 66 B1336

S57

GULICK L.,"METROPOLITAN ORGANIZATION." LEGIS EXEC REGION
PARTIC CHOOSE REPRESENT GOV/REL...MAJORIT DECISION. LOC/G
PAGE 45 B0904 MUNIC

S57

TAYLOR P.S.,"THE RELATION OF RESEARCH TO DECISION

LEGISLATIVE AND ADMINISTRATIVE DECISIONS." ELITES
ACT/RES PLAN PROB/SOLV CONFER CHOOSE POLICY.
PAGE 103 B2089
LEGIS
MGT
PWR
B58

BERNSTEIN M.H.,THE JOB OF THE FEDERAL EXECUTIVE.
POL/PAR CHIEF LEGIS ADMIN EXEC LOBBY CHOOSE GOV/REL
ORD/FREE PWR...MGT TREND. PAGE 11 B0228
NAT/G
TOP/EX
PERS/COMP
B58

SCOTT D.J.R.,RUSSIAN POLITICAL INSTITUTIONS. RUSSIA
USSR CONSTN AGRI DELIB/GP PLAN EDU/PROP CONTROL
CHOOSE EFFICIENCY ATTIT MARXISM...BIBLIOG/A 13/20.
PAGE 95 B1919
NAT/G
POL/PAR
ADMIN
DECISION
B58

STEWART J.D.,BRITISH PRESSURE GROUPS: THEIR ROLE IN
RELATION TO THE HOUSE OF COMMONS. UK CONSULT
DELIB/GP ADMIN ROUTINE CHOOSE REPRESENT ATTIT ROLE
20 HOUSE/CMNS PARLIAMENT. PAGE 101 B2038
LOBBY
LEGIS
PLAN
PARL/PROC
S58

BLAISDELL D.C.,"PRESSURE GROUPS, FOREIGN POLICIES,
AND INTERNATIONAL POLITICS." USA+45 WOR+45 INT/ORG
PLAN DOMIN EDU/PROP LEGIT ADMIN ROUTINE CHOOSE
...DECISION MGT METH/CNCPT CON/ANAL 20. PAGE 12
B0249
PROF/ORG
PWR
S58

STAAR R.F.,"ELECTIONS IN COMMUNIST POLAND." EUR+WWI
SOCIETY INT/ORG NAT/G POL/PAR LEGIS ACT/RES ECO/TAC
EDU/PROP ADJUD ADMIN ROUTINE COERCE TOTALISM ATTIT
ORD/FREE PWR 20. PAGE 100 B2015
COM
CHOOSE
POLAND
C58

GOLAY J.F.,"THE FOUNDING OF THE FEDERAL REPUBLIC OF
GERMANY." GERMANY/W CONSTN EX/STRUC DIPLOM ADMIN
CHOOSE...DECISION BIBLIOG 20. PAGE 40 B0814
FEDERAL
NAT/G
PARL/PROC
POL/PAR
B59

BOWLES C.,THE COMING POLITICAL BREAKTHROUGH. USA+45
ECO/DEV EX/STRUC ATTIT...CONCPT OBS 20. PAGE 14
B0288
DIPLOM
CHOOSE
PREDICT
POL/PAR
B59

JENNINGS W.I.,CABINET GOVERNMENT (3RD ED.). UK
POL/PAR CHIEF BUDGET ADMIN CHOOSE GP/REL 20.
PAGE 56 B1137
DELIB/GP
NAT/G
CONSTN
OP/RES
B59

MAASS A.,AREA AND POWER: A THEORY OF LOCAL
GOVERNMENT. MUNIC PROVS EX/STRUC LEGIS CT/SYS
CHOOSE PWR 20. PAGE 67 B1354
LOC/G
FEDERAL
BAL/PWR
GOV/REL
B59

MAYNTZ R.,PARTEIGRUPPEN IN DER GROSSSTADT. GERMANY
STRATA STRUCT DOMIN CHOOSE 20. PAGE 71 B1437
MUNIC
MGT
POL/PAR
ATTIT
B59

SINHA H.N.,OUTLINES OF POLITICAL SCIENCE. NAT/G
POL/PAR EX/STRUC LEGIS CT/SYS CHOOSE REPRESENT 20.
PAGE 98 B1971
JURID
CONCPT
ORD/FREE
SOVEREIGN
S59

ZAUBERMAN A.,"SOVIET BLOC ECONOMIC INTEGRATION."
COM CULTURE INTELL ECO/DEV INDUS TOP/EX ACT/RES
PLAN ECO/TAC INT/TRADE ROUTINE CHOOSE ATTIT
...TIME/SEQ 20. PAGE 119 B2399
MARKET
INT/ORG
USSR
TOTALISM
B60

JUNZ A.J., PRESENT TRENDS IN AMERICAN NATIONAL
GOVERNMENT. LEGIS DIPLOM ADMIN CT/SYS ORD/FREE
...CONCPT ANTHOL 20 CONGRESS PRESIDENT SUPREME/CT.
PAGE 2 B0048
POL/PAR
CHOOSE
CONSTN
NAT/G
B60

ADRIAN C.R.,STATE AND LOCAL GOVERNMENTS: A STUDY IN
THE POLITICAL PROCESS. USA+45 LAW FINAN MUNIC
POL/PAR LEGIS ADJUD EXEC CHOOSE REPRESENT. PAGE 3
B0060
LOC/G
PROVS
GOV/REL
ATTIT
B60

ARROW K.J.,MATHEMATICAL METHODS IN THE SOCIAL
SCIENCES, 1959. TEC/DEV CHOOSE UTIL PERCEPT
...KNO/TEST GAME SIMUL ANTHOL. PAGE 7 B0137
MATH
PSY
MGT
B60

AYEARST M.,THE BRITISH WEST INDIES: THE SEARCH FOR
SELF-GOVERNMENT. FUT WEST/IND LOC/G POL/PAR
EX/STRUC LEGIS CHOOSE FEDERAL...NAT/COMP BIBLIOG
17/20. PAGE 7 B0152
CONSTN
COLONIAL
REPRESENT
NAT/G
B60

BASS B.M.,LEADERSHIP, PSYCHOLOGY, AND
ORGANIZATIONAL BEHAVIOR. DOMIN CHOOSE DRIVE PERSON
PWR RESPECT SKILL...SOC METH/CNCPT OBS. PAGE 9
B0193
UNIV
FACE/GP
DELIB/GP
ROUTINE
B60

CORSON J.J.,GOVERNANCE OF COLLEGES AND
UNIVERSITIES. STRUCT FINAN DELIB/GP DOMIN EDU/PROP
LEAD CHOOSE GP/REL CENTRAL COST PRIVIL SUPEGO
ORD/FREE PWR...DECISION BIBLIOG. PAGE 24 B0481
ADMIN
EXEC
ACADEM
HABITAT
B60

GRAHAM G.A.,AMERICA'S CAPACITY TO GOVERN: SOME
PRELIMINARY THOUGHTS FOR PROSPECTIVE
ADMINISTRATORS. USA+45 SOCIETY DELIB/GP TOP/EX
MGT
LEAD
CHOOSE

CREATE PROB/SOLV RATIONAL 20. PAGE 42 B0849
ADMIN
B60

HAYEK F.A.,THE CONSTITUTION OF LIBERTY. UNIV LAW
CONSTN WORKER TAX EDU/PROP ADMIN CT/SYS COERCE
DISCRIM...IDEA/COMP 20. PAGE 48 B0974
ORD/FREE
CHOOSE
NAT/G
CONCPT
B60

HAYNES G.H.,THE SENATE OF THE UNITED STATES: ITS
HISTORY AND PRACTICE. CONSTN EX/STRUC TOP/EX CONFER
DEBATE LEAD LOBBY PARL/PROC CHOOSE PWR SENATE
CONGRESS. PAGE 48 B0977
LEGIS
DELIB/GP
B60

MEYRIAT J.,LA SCIENCE POLITIQUE EN FRANCE.
1945-1958; BIBLIOGRAPHIES FRANCAISES DE SCIENCES
SOCIALES (VOL. I). EUR+WWI FRANCE POL/PAR DIPLOM
ADMIN CHOOSE ATTIT...IDEA/COMP METH/COMP NAT/COMP
20. PAGE 73 B1478
BIBLIOG/A
NAT/G
CONCPT
PHIL/SCI
B60

SAYRE W.S.,GOVERNING NEW YORK CITY; POLITICS IN THE
METROPOLIS. POL/PAR CHIEF DELIB/GP LEGIS PLAN
CT/SYS LEAD PARTIC CHOOSE...DECISION CHARTS BIBLIOG
20 NEWYORK/C BUREAUCRCY. PAGE 93 B1875
MUNIC
ADMIN
PROB/SOLV
B60

WALTER B.,COMMUNICATIONS AND INFLUENCE: DEXISION
MAKING IN A MUNICIPAL ADMINISTRATIVE HIERARCHY
(PH.D. DISS., UNPUBL.). LEAD CHOOSE PWR METH/CNCPT.
PAGE 113 B2284
MUNIC
DECISION
ADMIN
STRUCT
S60

HUNTINGTON S.P.,"STRATEGIC PLANNING AND THE
POLITICAL PROCESS." USA+45 NAT/G DELIB/GP LEGIS
ACT/RES ECO/TAC LEGIT ROUTINE CHOOSE RIGID/FLEX PWR
...POLICY MAJORIT MGT 20. PAGE 53 B1066
EXEC
FORCES
NUC/PWR
WAR
S60

REISELBACH L.N.,"THE BASIS OF ISOLATIONIST
BEHAVIOR." USA+45 USA-45 CULTURE ECO/DEV LOC/G
NAT/G ADMIN ROUTINE CHOOSE BIO/SOC DRIVE RIGID/FLEX
...CENSUS SAMP TREND CHARTS TOT/POP 20. PAGE 87
B1765
ATTIT
DIPLOM
ECO/TAC
S60

RIESELBACH Z.N.,"QUANTITATIVE TECHNIQUES FOR
STUDYING VOTING BEHAVIOR IN THE UNITED NATIONS
GENERAL ASSEMBLY." FUT S/ASIA USA+45 INT/ORG
BAL/PWR DIPLOM ECO/TAC FOR/AID ADMIN PWR...POLICY
METH/CNCPT METH UN 20. PAGE 88 B1783
QUANT
CHOOSE
C60

SMITH T.E.,"ELECTIONS IN DEVELOPING COUNTRIES: A
STUDY OF ELECTORAL PROCEDURES USED IN TOPICAL
AFRICA, SOUTH-EAST ASIA..." AFR S/ASIA UK ROUTINE
GOV/REL RACE/REL...GOV/COMP BIBLIOG 20. PAGE 98
B1985
ECO/UNDEV
CHOOSE
REPRESENT
ADMIN
B61

BANFIELD E.C.,URBAN GOVERNMENT; A READER IN
POLITICS AND ADMINISTRATION. ELITES LABOR POL/PAR
EXEC CHOOSE REPRESENT GP/REL PWR PLURISM...PSY SOC.
PAGE 9 B0177
MUNIC
GEN/METH
DECISION
B61

BENOIT E.,EUROPE AT SIXES AND SEVENS: THE COMMON
MARKET, THE FREE TRADE ASSOCIATION AND THE UNITED
STATES. EUR+WWI FUT USA+45 INDUS CONSULT DELIB/GP
EX/STRUC TOP/EX ACT/RES ECO/TAC EDU/PROP ROUTINE
CHOOSE PERCEPT WEALTH...MGT TREND EEC TOT/POP 20
EFTA. PAGE 11 B0217
FINAN
ECO/DEV
VOL/ASSN
B61

BULLIS H.A.,MANIFESTO FOR AMERICANS. USA+45 AGRI
LABOR NAT/G NEIGH FOR/AID INT/TRADE TAX EDU/PROP
CHOOSE...POLICY MGT 20 UN UNESCO. PAGE 17 B0342
ECO/TAC
SOCIETY
INDUS
CAP/ISM
B61

BURDETTE F.L.,POLITICAL SCIENCE: A SELECTED
BIBLIOGRAPHY OF BOOKS IN PRINT, WITH ANNOTATIONS
(PAMPHLET). LAW LOC/G NAT/G POL/PAR PROVS DIPLOM
EDU/PROP ADMIN CHOOSE ATTIT 20. PAGE 17 B0347
BIBLIOG/A
GOV/COMP
CONCPT
ROUTINE
B61

HAMILTON A.,THE FEDERALIST. USA-45 NAT/G VOL/ASSN
LEGIS TOP/EX EDU/PROP LEGIT CHOOSE ATTIT RIGID/FLEX
ORD/FREE PWR...MAJORIT JURID CONCPT ANTHOL. PAGE 46
B0931
EX/STRUC
CONSTN
B61

JANOWITZ M.,COMMUNITY POLITICAL SYSTEMS. USA+45
SOCIETY INDUS VOL/ASSN TEC/DEV ADMIN LEAD CHOOSE
...SOC SOC/WK 20. PAGE 56 B1123
MUNIC
STRUCT
POL/PAR
B61

LOSCHELDER W.,AUSBILDUNG UND AUSLESE DER BEAMTEN.
GERMANY/W ELITES NAT/G ADMIN GP/REL ATTIT...JURID
20 CIVIL/SERV. PAGE 67 B1341
PROF/ORG
EDU/PROP
EX/STRUC
CHOOSE
B61

MACRIDIS R.C.,COMPARATIVE POLITICS: NOTES AND
READINGS. WOR+45 LOC/G MUNIC NAT/G PROVS VOL/ASSN
EDU/PROP ADMIN ATTIT PERSON ORD/FREE...SOC CONCPT
OBS RECORD TREND 20. PAGE 68 B1376
POL/PAR
CHOOSE
B61

NARAIN J.P.,SWARAJ FOR THE PEOPLE. INDIA CONSTN
LOC/G MUNIC POL/PAR CHOOSE REPRESENT EFFICIENCY
ATTIT PWR SOVEREIGN 20. PAGE 77 B1553
NAT/G
ORD/FREE
EDU/PROP
EX/STRUC

ROMANO F.,CIVIL SERVICE AND PUBLIC EMPLOYEE LAW IN
NEW JERSEY. CONSTN MUNIC WORKER GIVE PAY CHOOSE
UTIL 20. PAGE 90 B1816
ADMIN PROVS ADJUD LOC/G
B61

WARD R.E.,JAPANESE POLITICAL SCIENCE: A GUIDE TO
JAPANESE REFERENCE AND RESEARCH MATERIALS (2ND
ED.). LAW CONSTN STRATA NAT/G POL/PAR DELIB/GP
LEGIS ADMIN CHOOSE GP/REL...INT/LAW 19/20 CHINJAP.
PAGE 113 B2290
BIBLIOG/A PHIL/SCI
B61

WEST F.J.,POLITICAL ADVANCEMENT IN THE SOUTH
PACIFIC. CONSTN CULTURE POL/PAR LEGIS DOMIN ADMIN
CHOOSE SOVEREIGN VAL/FREE 20 FIJI TAHITI SAMOA.
PAGE 115 B2325
S/ASIA LOC/G COLONIAL
B61

LIEBENOW J.G.,"LEGITIMACY OF ALIEN RELATIONSHIP:
THE NYATURU OF TANGANYIKA" (BMR)" AFR UK ADMIN LEAD
CHOOSE 20 NYATURU TANGANYIKA. PAGE 65 B1312
S61 COLONIAL DOMIN LEGIT PWR

MOODIE G.C.,"THE GOVERNMENT OF GREAT BRITAIN." UK
LAW STRUCT LOC/G POL/PAR DIPLOM RECEIVE ADMIN
COLONIAL CHOOSE...BIBLIOG 20 PARLIAMENT. PAGE 75
B1508
C61 NAT/G SOCIETY PARL/PROC GOV/COMP

ANDREWS W.G.,EUROPEAN POLITICAL INSTITUTIONS.
FRANCE GERMANY UK USSR TOP/EX LEAD PARL/PROC CHOOSE
20. PAGE 5 B0104
B62 NAT/COMP POL/PAR EX/STRUC LEGIS

ANDREWS W.G.,FRENCH POLITICS AND ALGERIA: THE
PROCESS OF POLICY FORMATION 1954-1962. ALGERIA
FRANCE CONSTN ELITES POL/PAR CHIEF DELIB/GP LEGIS
DIPLOM PRESS CHOOSE 20. PAGE 5 B0105
B62 GOV/COMP EXEC COLONIAL

HITCHNER D.G.,MODERN GOVERNMENT: A SURVEY OF
POLITICAL SCIENCE. WOR+45 INT/ORG LEGIS ADMIN
CT/SYS EXEC CHOOSE TOTALISM POPULISM...INT/LAW
PHIL/SCI METH 20. PAGE 50 B1019
B62 CONCPT NAT/G STRUCT

KAMMERER G.M.,CITY MANAGERS IN POLITICS: AN
ANALYSIS OF MANAGER TENURE AND TERMINATION. POL/PAR
LEGIS PARTIC CHOOSE PWR...DECISION GEOG METH/CNCPT.
PAGE 57 B1161
B62 MUNIC LEAD EXEC

LOWI T.J.,LEGISLATIVE POLITICS U.S.A. LAW LEGIS
DIPLOM EXEC LOBBY CHOOSE SUFF FEDERAL PWR 19/20
CONGRESS. PAGE 67 B1345
B62 PARL/PROC REPRESENT POLICY ROUTINE

MORE S.S.,REMODELLING OF DEMOCRACY FOR AFRO-ASIAN
NATIONS. AFR INDIA S/ASIA SOUTH/AFR CONSTN EX/STRUC
COLONIAL CHOOSE TOTALISM SOVEREIGN NEW/LIB SOCISM
...SOC/WK 20. PAGE 75 B1520
B62 ORD/FREE ECO/UNDEV ADMIN LEGIS

PRESS C.,STATE MANUALS, BLUE BOOKS AND ELECTION
RESULTS. LAW LOC/G MUNIC LEGIS WRITING FEDERAL
SOVEREIGN...DECISION STAT CHARTS 20. PAGE 84 B1700
B62 BIBLIOG PROVS ADMIN CHOOSE

SCALAPINO R.A.,PARTIES AND POLITICS IN CONTEMPORARY
JAPAN. EX/STRUC DIPLOM CHOOSE NAT/LISM ATTIT
...POLICY 20 CHINJAP. PAGE 93 B1876
B62 POL/PAR PARL/PROC ELITES DECISION

BAILEY S.D.,"THE TROIKA AND THE FUTURE OF THE UN."
CONSTN CREATE LEGIT EXEC CHOOSE ORD/FREE PWR
...CONCPT NEW/IDEA UN COLD/WAR 20. PAGE 8 B0163
L62 FUT INT/ORG USSR

GIDWANI K.A.,"LEADER BEHAVIOUR IN ELECTED AND NON-
ELECTED GROUPS." DELIB/GP ROUTINE TASK HAPPINESS
AUTHORIT...SOC STAT CHARTS SOC/EXP. PAGE 39 B0796
S62 LEAD INGP/REL GP/COMP CHOOSE

TRUMAN D.,"THE DOMESTIC POLITICS OF FOREIGN AID."
USA+45 WOR+45 NAT/G POL/PAR LEGIS DIPLOM ECO/TAC
EDU/PROP ADMIN CHOOSE ATTIT PWR CONGRESS 20
CONGRESS. PAGE 105 B2129
S62 ROUTINE FOR/AID

= GRAZIA A.,"POLITICAL BEHAVIOR (REV. ED.)" STRATA
..L/PAR LEAD LOBBY ROUTINE WAR CHOOSE REPRESENT
CO..SEN ATTIT ORD/FREE BIBLIOG. PAGE 27 B0555
C62 PHIL/SCI OP/RES CONCPT

TRUMAN D.B.,"THE GOVERNMENTAL PROCESS: POLITICAL
INTERESTS AND PUBLIC OPINION." POL/PAR ADJUD ADMIN
EXEC LEAD ROUTINE CHOOSE REPRESENT GOV/REL
RIGID/FLEX...POLICY BIBLIOG/A 20. PAGE 105 B2131
C62 LOBBY EDU/PROP GP/REL LEGIS

BANFIELD E.C.,CITY POLITICS. CULTURE LABOR LOC/G
POL/PAR LEGIS EXEC LEAD CHOOSE...DECISION NEGRO.
PAGE 9 B0178
B63 MUNIC RIGID/FLEX ATTIT

CLARK J.S.,THE SENATE ESTABLISHMENT. USA+45 NAT/G
POL/PAR ADMIN CHOOSE PERSON SENATE. PAGE 21 B0431
B63 LEGIS ROUTINE

LEAD SENIOR
B63

COUNCIL STATE GOVERNMENTS,HANDBOOK FOR LEGISLATIVE
COMMITTEES. USA+45 LAW DELIB/GP EX/STRUC TOP/EX
CHOOSE PWR...METH/COMP 20. PAGE 24 B0496
LEGIS PARL/PROC PROVS ADJUD

GOURNAY B.,PUBLIC ADMINISTRATION. FRANCE LAW CONSTN
AGRI FINAN LABOR SCHOOL EX/STRUC CHOOSE...MGT
METH/COMP 20. PAGE 42 B0846
B63 BIBLIOG/A ADMIN NAT/G LOC/G

GRANT D.R.,STATE AND LOCAL GOVERNMENT IN AMERICA.
USA+45 FINAN LOC/G MUNIC EX/STRUC FORCES EDU/PROP
ADMIN CHOOSE FEDERAL ATTIT...JURID 20. PAGE 42
B0853
B63 PROVS POL/PAR LEGIS CONSTN

HERNDON J.,A SELECTED BIBLIOGRAPHY OF MATERIALS IN
STATE GOVERNMENT AND POLITICS (PAMPHLET). USA+45
POL/PAR LEGIS ADMIN CHOOSE MGT. PAGE 49 B0993
B63 BIBLIOG GOV/COMP PROVS DECISION

HIGA M.,POLITICS AND PARTIES IN POSTWAR OKINAWA.
USA+45 VOL/ASSN LEGIS CONTROL LOBBY CHOOSE NAT/LISM
PWR SOVEREIGN MARXISM SOCISM 20 OKINAWA CHINJAP.
PAGE 50 B1008
B63 GOV/REL POL/PAR ADMIN FORCES

MACNEIL N.,FORGE OF DEMOCRACY: THE HOUSE OF
REPRESENTATIVES. POL/PAR EX/STRUC TOP/EX DEBATE
LEAD PARL/PROC CHOOSE GOV/REL PWR...OBS HOUSE/REP.
PAGE 68 B1374
B63 LEGIS DELIB/GP

PEABODY R.L.,NEW PERSPECTIVES ON THE HOUSE OF
REPRESENTATIVES. AGRI FINAN SCHOOL FORCES CONFER
LEAD CHOOSE REPRESENT FEDERAL...POLICY DECISION
HOUSE/REP. PAGE 82 B1647
B63 NEW/IDEA LEGIS PWR ADMIN

PLISCHKE E.,GOVERNMENT AND POLITICS OF CONTEMPORARY
BERLIN. GERMANY LAW CONSTN POL/PAR LEGIS WAR CHOOSE
REPRESENT GOV/REL...CHARTS BIBLIOG 20 BERLIN.
PAGE 83 B1683
B63 MUNIC LOC/G POLICY ADMIN

ROYAL INSTITUTE PUBLIC ADMIN,BRITISH PUBLIC
ADMINISTRATION. UK LAW FINAN INDUS LOC/G POL/PAR
LEGIS LOBBY PARL/PROC CHOOSE JURID. PAGE 91 B1845
B63 BIBLIOG ADMIN MGT NAT/G

WEINER M.,POLITICAL CHANGE IN SOUTH ASIA. CEYLON
INDIA PAKISTAN S/ASIA CULTURE ELITES ECO/UNDEV
EX/STRUC ADMIN CONTROL CHOOSE CONSERVE...GOV/COMP
ANTHOL 20. PAGE 115 B2315
B63 NAT/G CONSTN TEC/DEV

ROBERT J.,"LES ELECTIONS LEGISLATIVES DU 17 MAI
1963 ET L'EVOLUTION POLITIQUE INTERNE DU MAROC."
ISLAM WOR+45 NAT/G POL/PAR EXEC ALL/VALS 20.
PAGE 89 B1792
L63 CHOOSE MOROCCO

BRZEZINSKI Z.K.,"CINCINNATUS AND THE APPARATCHIK."
COM USA+45 USA-45 ELITES LOC/G NAT/G PROVS CONSULT
LEGIS DOMIN LEGIT EXEC ROUTINE CHOOSE DRIVE PWR
SKILL...CONCPT CHARTS VAL/FREE COLD/WAR 20. PAGE 16
B0334
S63 POL/PAR USSR

MODELSKI G.,"STUDY OF ALLIANCES." WOR+45 WOR-45
INT/ORG NAT/G FORCES LEGIT ADMIN CHOOSE ALL/VALS
PWR SKILL...INT/LAW CONCPT GEN/LAWS 20 TREATY.
PAGE 74 B1495
S63 VOL/ASSN CON/ANAL DIPLOM

SHIMKIN D.B.,"STRUCTURE OF SOVIET POWER." COM FUT
USA+45 USSR WOR+45 NAT/G FORCES ECO/TAC DOMIN EXEC
COERCE CHOOSE ATTIT WEALTH...TIME/SEQ COLD/WAR
TOT/POP VAL/FREE 20. PAGE 96 B1948
S63 PWR

WAGRET M.,"L'ASCENSION POLITIQUE DE L'U.D.D.I.A.
(CONGO) ET SA PRISE DU POUVOIR (1956-1959)." AFR
WOR+45 NAT/G POL/PAR CONSULT DELIB/GP LEGIS PERCEPT
ALL/VALS SOVEREIGN...TIME/SEQ CONGO. PAGE 113 B2274
S63 EX/STRUC CHOOSE FRANCE

CARLISLE D.,"PARTY LOYALTY: THE ELECTION PROCESS IN
SOUTH CAROLINA." USA+45 LOC/G ADMIN ATTIT...TREND
CHARTS BIBLIOG 17/20. PAGE 19 B0380
C63 CHOOSE POL/PAR PROVS SUFF

ALDERFER H.O.,LOCAL GOVERNMENT IN DEVELOPING
COUNTRIES. ASIA COM L/A+17C S/ASIA AGRI LOC/G MUNIC
PROVS DOMIN CHOOSE PWR...POLICY MGT CONCPT 20.
PAGE 3 B0070
B64 ADMIN ROUTINE

BOUVIER-AJAM M.,MANUEL TECHNIQUE ET PRATIQUE DU
MAIRE ET DES ELUS ET AGENTS COMMUNAUX. FRANCE LOC/G
BUDGET CHOOSE GP/REL SUPEGO...JURID BIBLIOG 20
MAYOR COMMUNES. PAGE 14 B0284
B64 MUNIC ADMIN CHIEF NEIGH

BROMAGE A.W.,MANAGER PLAN ABANDONMENTS: WHY A FEW
HAVE DROPPED COUNCILMANAGER GOVERNMENT. USA+45
B64 MUNIC PLAN

CREATE PARTIC CHOOSE...MGT CENSUS CHARTS 20.
PAGE 15 B0315
CONSULT
LOC/G

B64
CONNECTICUT U INST PUBLIC SERV,SUMMARY OF CHARTER
PROVISIONS IN CONNECTICUT LOCAL GOVERNMENT
(PAMPHLET). USA+45 DELIB/GP LEGIS TOP/EX CHOOSE
REPRESENT 20 CONNECTICT CITY/MGT MAYOR. PAGE 23
B0462
CONSTN
MUNIC
LOC/G
EX/STRUC

B64
COTTER C.P.,POLITICS WITHOUT POWER: THE NATIONAL
PARTY COMMITTEES. USA+45 FINAN NAT/G LOBBY ROUTINE
GP/REL ATTIT ROLE SUPEGO PWR 20. PAGE 24 B0491
CHOOSE
POL/PAR
REPRESENT
DELIB/GP

B64
EATON H.,PRESIDENTIAL TIMBER: A HISTORY OF
NOMINATING CONVENTIONS, 1868-1960. USA+45 USA-45
POL/PAR EX/STRUC DEBATE LOBBY ATTIT PERSON ALL/VALS
...MYTH 19/20 PRESIDENT. PAGE 32 B0646
DELIB/GP
CHOOSE
CHIEF
NAT/G

B64
GOODMAN W.,THE TWO-PARTY SYSTEM IN THE UNITED
STATES. USA+45 USA-45 STRATA LOC/G CHIEF EDU/PROP
ADMIN COST PWR POPULISM...PLURIST 18/20 PRESIDENT.
PAGE 41 B0821
POL/PAR
REPRESENT
CHOOSE
NAT/G

B64
GOODNOW H.F.,THE CIVIL SERVICE OF PAKISTAN:
BUREAUCRACY IN A NEW NATION. INDIA PAKISTAN S/ASIA
ECO/UNDEV PROVS CHIEF PARTIC CHOOSE EFFICIENCY PWR
...BIBLIOG 20. PAGE 41 B0824
ADMIN
GOV/REL
LAW
NAT/G

B64
GUTTSMAN W.L.,THE BRITISH POLITICAL ELITE. EUR+WWI
MOD/EUR STRATA FAM LABOR POL/PAR SCHOOL VOL/ASSN
DELIB/GP LEGIS LEGIT EXEC CHOOSE ATTIT ALL/VALS
...STAT BIOG TIME/SEQ CHARTS VAL/FREE. PAGE 45
B0905
NAT/G
SOC
UK
ELITES

B64
HANNA W.J.,INDEPENDENT BLACK AFRICA: THE POLITICS
OF FREEDOM. ELITES INDUS KIN CHIEF COLONIAL CHOOSE
GOV/REL RACE/REL NAT/LISM ATTIT PERSON 20 NEGRO.
PAGE 46 B0938
AFR
ECO/UNDEV
ADMIN
PROB/SOLV

B64
KAACK H.,DIE PARTEIEN IN DER
VERFASSUNGSWIRKLICHKEIT DER BUNDESREPUBLIK.
GERMANY/W ADMIN PARL/PROC CHOOSE...JURID 20.
PAGE 57 B1157
POL/PAR
PROVS
NAT/G

B64
LOWI T.J.,AT THE PLEASURE OF THE MAYOR. EX/STRUC
PROB/SOLV BAL/PWR ADMIN PARTIC CHOOSE GP/REL
...CONT/OBS NET/THEORY CHARTS 20 NEWYORK/C MAYOR.
PAGE 67 B1346
LOBBY
LOC/G
PWR
MUNIC

B64
ROBSON W.A.,THE GOVERNORS AND THE GOVERNED. USA+45
PROB/SOLV DOMIN ADMIN CONTROL CHOOSE...POLICY
PRESIDENT. PAGE 89 B1808
EX/STRUC
ATTIT
PARTIC
LEAD

B64
SARROS P.P.,CONGRESS AND THE NEW DIPLOMACY: THE
FORMULATION OF MUTUAL SECURITY POLICY: 1953-60
(THESIS). USA+45 CHIEF EX/STRUC REGION ROUTINE
CHOOSE GOV/REL PEACE ROLE...POLICY 20 PRESIDENT
CONGRESS. PAGE 92 B1869
DIPLOM
POL/PAR
NAT/G

B64
THE BRITISH COUNCIL,PUBLIC ADMINISTRATION: A SELECT
LIST OF BOOKS AND PERIODICALS. LAW CONSTN FINAN
POL/PAR SCHOOL CHOOSE...HEAL MGT METH/COMP 19/20
CMN/WLTH. PAGE 104 B2094
BIBLIOG
ADMIN
LOC/G
INDUS

B64
TURNER H.A.,THE GOVERNMENT AND POLITICS OF
CALIFORNIA (2ND ED.). LAW FINAN MUNIC POL/PAR
SCHOOL EX/STRUC LEGIS LOBBY CHOOSE...CHARTS T 20
CALIFORNIA. PAGE 106 B2138
PROVS
ADMIN
LOC/G
CONSTN

B64
WILLIAMSON O.E.,THE ECONOMICS OF DISCRETIONARY
BEHAVIOR: MANAGERIAL OBJECTIVES IN A THEORY OF THE
FIRM. MARKET BUDGET CAP/ISM PRODUC DRIVE PERSON
...STAT CHARTS BIBLIOG METH 20. PAGE 117 B2354
EFFICIENCY
MGT
ECO/TAC
CHOOSE

L64
GILBERT C.E.,"NATIONAL POLITICAL ALIGNMENTS AND THE
POLITICS OF LARGE CITIES." ELITES LOC/G NAT/G LEGIS
EXEC LEAD PLURISM GOV/COMP. PAGE 39 B0800
MUNIC
CHOOSE
POL/PAR
PWR

S64
EAKIN T.C.,"LEGISLATIVE POLITICS -- I AND II THE
WESTERN STATES, 1958-1964" (SUPPLEMENT)" USA+45
POL/PAR SCHOOL CONTROL LOBBY CHOOSE AGE. PAGE 32
B0641
PROVS
LEGIS
ROUTINE
STRUCT

C64
SCOTT R.E.,"MEXICAN GOVERNMENT IN TRANSITION (REV
ED)" CULTURE STRUCT POL/PAR CHIEF ADMIN LOBBY REV
CHOOSE GP/REL DRIVE...BIBLIOG METH 20 MEXIC/AMER.
PAGE 95 B1920
NAT/G
L/A+17C
ROUTINE
CONSTN

B65
AIYAR S.P.,STUDIES IN INDIAN DEMOCRACY. INDIA
STRATA ECO/UNDEV LABOR POL/PAR LEGIS DIPLOM LOBBY
REGION CHOOSE ATTIT SOCISM...ANTHOL 20. PAGE 3
B0067
ORD/FREE
REPRESENT
ADMIN
NAT/G

B65
BANFIELD E.C.,BIG CITY POLITICS. USA+45 CONSTN
POL/PAR ADMIN LOBBY CHOOSE SUFF INGP/REL PWR...GEOG
20. PAGE 9 B0179
METH/COMP
MUNIC
STRUCT

B65
CAVERS D.F.,THE CHOICE-OF-LAW PROCESS. PROB/SOLV
ADJUD CT/SYS CHOOSE RATIONAL...IDEA/COMP 16/20
TREATY. PAGE 19 B0396
JURID
DECISION
METH/COMP
ADMIN

B65
COHN H.J.,THE GOVERNMENT OF THE RHINE PALATINATE IN
THE FIFTEENTH CENTURY. GERMANY FINAN LOC/G DELIB/GP
LEGIS CT/SYS CHOOSE CATHISM 14/15 PALATINATE.
PAGE 22 B0449
PROVS
JURID
GP/REL
ADMIN

B65
EAST J.P.,COUNCIL-MANAGER GOVERNMENT: THE POLITICAL
THOUGHT OF ITS FOUNDER, RICHARD S. CHILDS. USA+45
CREATE ADMIN CHOOSE...BIOG GEN/LAWS BIBLIOG 20
CHILDS/RS CITY/MGT. PAGE 32 B0642
SIMUL
LOC/G
MUNIC
EX/STRUC

B65
FEERICK J.D.,FROM FAILING HANDS: THE STUDY OF
PRESIDENTIAL SUCCESSION. CONSTN NAT/G PROB/SOLV
LEAD PARL/PROC MURDER CHOOSE...NEW/IDEA BIBLIOG 20
KENNEDY/JF JOHNSON/LB PRESIDENT PRE/US/AM
VICE/PRES. PAGE 35 B0710
EX/STRUC
CHIEF
LAW
LEGIS

B65
FISCHER F.C.,THE GOVERNMENT OF MICHIGAN. USA+45
NAT/G PUB/INST EX/STRUC LEGIS BUDGET GIVE EDU/PROP
CT/SYS CHOOSE GOV/REL...T MICHIGAN. PAGE 36 B0723
PROVS
LOC/G
ADMIN
CONSTN

B65
GREGG J.L.,POLITICAL PARTIES AND PARTY SYSTEMS IN
GUATEMALA, 1944-1963. GUATEMALA L/A+17C EX/STRUC
FORCES CREATE CONTROL REV CHOOSE PWR...TREND
IDEA/COMP 20. PAGE 43 B0872
LEAD
POL/PAR
NAT/G
CHIEF

B65
HADWIGER D.F.,PRESSURES AND PROTEST. NAT/G LEGIS
PLAN LEAD PARTIC ROUTINE ATTIT POLICY. PAGE 45
B0913
AGRI
GP/REL
LOBBY
CHOOSE

B65
HAIGHT D.E.,THE PRESIDENT; ROLES AND POWERS. USA+45
USA-45 POL/PAR PLAN DIPLOM CHOOSE PERS/REL PWR
18/20 PRESIDENT CONGRESS. PAGE 45 B0915
CHIEF
LEGIS
TOP/EX
EX/STRUC

B65
MASTERS N.A.,COMMITTEE ASSIGNMENTS IN THE HOUSE OF
REPRESENTATIVES (BMR). USA+45 ELITES POL/PAR
EX/STRUC PARTIC REPRESENT GP/REL PERS/REL ATTIT PWR
...STAT CHARTS 20 HOUSE/REP. PAGE 71 B1425
LEAD
LEGIS
CHOOSE
DELIB/GP

B65
MATRAS J.,SOCIAL CHANGE IN ISRAEL. ISRAEL STRATA
FAM ACT/RES EDU/PROP ADMIN CHOOSE...STAT CENSUS
19/20 JEWS. PAGE 71 B1427
SECT
NAT/LISM
GEOG
STRUCT

B65
SCHAPIRO L.,THE GOVERNMENT AND POLITICS OF THE
SOVIET UNION. USSR WOR+45 WOR-45 ADMIN PARTIC REV
CHOOSE REPRESENT PWR...POLICY IDEA/COMP 20. PAGE 93
B1880
MARXISM
GOV/REL
NAT/G
LOC/G

B65
STEINER K.,LOCAL GOVERNMENT IN JAPAN. CONSTN
CULTURE NAT/G ADMIN CHOOSE...SOC STAT 20 CHINJAP.
PAGE 100 B2030
LOC/G
SOCIETY
JURID
ORD/FREE

N65
MOTE M.E.,SOVIET LOCAL AND REPUBLIC ELECTIONS. COM
USSR NAT/G PLAN PARTIC GOV/REL TOTALISM PWR
...CHARTS 20. PAGE 76 B1534
CHOOSE
ADMIN
CONTROL
LOC/G

B66
ADAMS J.C.,THE GOVERNMENT OF REPUBLICAN ITALY (2ND
ED.). ITALY LOC/G POL/PAR DELIB/GP LEGIS WORKER
ADMIN CT/SYS FASCISM...CHARTS BIBLIOG 20
PARLIAMENT. PAGE 3 B0057
NAT/G
CHOOSE
EX/STRUC
CONSTN

B66
BHALERAO C.N.,PUBLIC SERVICE COMMISSIONS OF INDIA:
A STUDY. INDIA SERV/IND EX/STRUC ROUTINE CHOOSE
GOV/REL INGP/REL...KNO/TEST EXHIBIT 20. PAGE 11
B0233
NAT/G
OP/RES
LOC/G
ADMIN

B66
CARALEY D.,PARTY POLITICS AND NATIONAL ELECTIONS.
USA+45 STRATA LOC/G PROVS EX/STRUC BARGAIN ADMIN
SANCTION GP/REL ATTIT 20 DEMOCRAT REPUBLICAN.
PAGE 18 B0375
POL/PAR
CHOOSE
REPRESENT
NAT/G

B66
FINK M.,A SELECTIVE BIBLIOGRAPHY ON STATE
CONSTITUTIONAL REVISION (PAMPHLET). USA+45 FINAN
EX/STRUC LEGIS EDU/PROP ADMIN CT/SYS APPORT CHOOSE
GOV/REL 20. PAGE 35 B0720
BIBLIOG
PROVS
LOC/G
CONSTN

B66
FINNISH POLITICAL SCIENCE ASSN,SCANDINAVIAN
POLITICAL STUDIES (VOL. I). FINLAND DIPLOM ADMIN
LOBBY PARL/PROC...CHARTS BIBLIOG 20 SCANDINAV.
PAGE 36 B0721
ATTIT
POL/PAR
ACT/RES
CHOOSE

B66
GHOSH P.K.,THE CONSTITUTION OF INDIA: HOW IT HAS BEEN FRAMED. INDIA LOC/G DELIB/GP EX/STRUC PROB/SOLV BUDGET INT/TRADE CT/SYS CHOOSE...LING 20. PAGE 39 B0795 — CONSTN NAT/G LEGIS FEDERAL

B66
HESSLER I.O.,29 WAYS TO GOVERN A CITY. EX/STRUC TOP/EX PROB/SOLV PARTIC CHOOSE REPRESENT EFFICIENCY ...CHARTS 20 CITY/MGT MAYOR. PAGE 49 B0998 — MUNIC GOV/COMP LOC/G ADMIN

B66
INTERPARLIAMENTARY UNION,PARLIAMENTS: COMPARATIVE STUDY ON STRUCTURE AND FUNCTIONING OF REPRESENTATIVE INSTITUTIONS IN FIFTY-FIVE COUNTRIES. WOR+45 POL/PAR DELIB/GP BUDGET ADMIN CONTROL CHOOSE. PAGE 54 B1099 — PARL/PROC LEGIS GOV/COMP EX/STRUC

B66
RICHARD J.B.,GOVERNMENT AND POLITICS OF WYOMING. USA+45 POL/PAR EX/STRUC LEGIS CT/SYS LOBBY APPORT CHOOSE REPRESENT 20 WYOMING GOVERNOR. PAGE 88 B1773 — PROVS LOC/G ADMIN

B66
ROSS R.M.,STATE AND LOCAL GOVERNMENT AND ADMINISTRATION. USA+45 CONSTN POL/PAR EX/STRUC LEGIS BUDGET EDU/PROP CONTROL CT/SYS CHOOSE GOV/REL T. PAGE 90 B1827 — LOC/G PROVS MUNIC ADMIN

B66
SEASHOLES B.,VOTING, INTEREST GROUPS, AND PARTIES. USA+45 FINAN LOC/G NAT/G ADMIN LEAD GP/REL INGP/REL ROLE...CHARTS ANTHOL 20. PAGE 95 B1922 — CHOOSE POL/PAR LOBBY PARTIC

S66
MATTHEWS D.G.,"PRELUDE-COUP D'ETAT-MILITARY GOVERNMENT: A BIBLIOGRAPHICAL AND RESEARCH GUIDE TO NIGERIAN POL AND GOVT, JAN. 1965-66." AFR NIGER LAW CONSTN POL/PAR LEGIS CIVMIL/REL GOV/REL...STAT 20. PAGE 71 B1430 — BIBLIOG NAT/G ADMIN CHOOSE

S66
SNOWISS L.M.,"CONGRESSIONAL RECRUITMENT AND REPRESENTATION." USA+45 LG/CO MUNIC POL/PAR ADMIN REGION CONGRESS CHICAGO. PAGE 98 B1990 — LEGIS REPRESENT CHOOSE LOC/G

C66
TACHERON D.G.,"THE JOB OF THE CONGRESSMAN: AN INTRODUCTION TO SERVICES IN THE US HOUSE OF REPRESENTATIVES." DELIB/GP EX/STRUC PRESS SENIOR CT/SYS LOBBY CHOOSE GOV/REL...BIBLIOG 20 CONGRESS HOUSE/REP SENATE. PAGE 102 B2068 — LEGIS PARL/PROC ADMIN POL/PAR

B67
BULPITT J.G.,PARTY POLITICS IN ENGLISH LOCAL GOVERNMENT. UK CONSTN ACT/RES TAX CONTROL CHOOSE REPRESENT GOV/REL KNOWL 20. PAGE 17 B0344 — POL/PAR LOC/G ELITES EX/STRUC

B67
EVANS R.H.,COEXISTENCE: COMMUNISM AND ITS PRACTICE IN BOLOGNA, 1945-1965. ITALY CAP/ISM ADMIN CHOOSE PEACE ORD/FREE...SOC STAT DEEP/INT SAMP CHARTS BIBLIOG 20. PAGE 34 B0690 — MARXISM CULTURE MUNIC POL/PAR

B67
FESLER J.W.,THE FIFTY STATES AND THEIR LOCAL GOVERNMENTS. FUT USA+45 POL/PAR LEGIS PROB/SOLV ADMIN CT/SYS CHOOSE GOV/REL FEDERAL...POLICY CHARTS 20 SUPREME/CT. PAGE 35 B0715 — PROVS LOC/G

B67
GELLHORN W.,OMBUDSMEN AND OTHERS: CITIZENS' PROTECTORS IN NINE COUNTRIES. WOR+45 LAW CONSTN LEGIS INSPECT ADJUD ADMIN CONTROL CT/SYS CHOOSE PERS/REL...STAT CHARTS 20. PAGE 39 B0789 — NAT/COMP REPRESENT INGP/REL PROB/SOLV

B67
ILLINOIS COMMISSION,IMPROVING THE STATE LEGISLATURE. USA+45 LAW CONSTN NAT/G PROB/SOLV EDU/PROP ADMIN TASK CHOOSE INGP/REL EFFICIENCY ILLINOIS. PAGE 53 B1077 — PROVS LEGIS REPRESENT PLAN

B67
JHANGIANI M.A.,JANA SANGH AND SWATANTRA: A PROFILE OF THE RIGHTIST PARTIES IN INDIA. INDIA ADMIN CHOOSE MARXISM SOCISM...INT CHARTS BIBLIOG 20. PAGE 56 B1140 — POL/PAR LAISSEZ NAT/LISM ATTIT

B67
MCCONNELL G.,THE MODERN PRESIDENCY. USA+45 CONSTN TOP/EX DOMIN EXEC CHOOSE PWR...MGT 20. PAGE 72 B1446 — NAT/G CHIEF EX/STRUC

B67
NIVEN R.,NIGERIA. NIGERIA CONSTN INDUS EX/STRUC COLONIAL REV NAT/LISM...CHARTS 19/20. PAGE 78 B1584 — NAT/G REGION CHOOSE GP/REL

B67
PRINCE C.E.,NEW JERSEY'S JEFFERSONIAN REPUBLICANS; THE GENESIS OF AN EARLY PARTY MACHINE (1789-1817). USA-45 LOC/G EDU/PROP PRESS CONTROL CHOOSE...CHARTS 18/19 NEW/JERSEY REPUBLICAN. PAGE 84 B1707 — POL/PAR CONSTN ADMIN PROVS

B67
TOMA P.A.,THE POLITICS OF FOOD FOR PEACE: EXECUTIVE-LEGISLATIVE INTERACTION. USA+45 ECO/UNDEV POL/PAR DEBATE EXEC LOBBY CHOOSE PEACE...DECISION CHARTS. PAGE 104 B2113 — FOR/AID POLICY LEGIS AGRI

L67
GAINES J.E.,"THE YOUTH COURT CONCEPT AND ITS IMPLEMENTATION IN TOMPKINS COUNTY, NEW YORK." USA+45 LAW CONSTN JUDGE WORKER ADJUD ADMIN CHOOSE PERSON...JURID NEW/YORK. PAGE 38 B0772 — CT/SYS AGE/Y INGP/REL CRIME

S67
FERGUSON H.,"3-CITY CONSOLIDATION." USA+45 CONSTN INDUS BARGAIN BUDGET CONFER ADMIN INGP/REL COST UTIL. PAGE 35 B0712 — MUNIC CHOOSE CREATE PROB/SOLV

S67
HALL B.,"THE PAINTER'S UNION: A PARTIAL VICTORY." USA+45 PROB/SOLV LEGIT ADMIN REPRESENT 20. PAGE 45 B0922 — LABOR CHIEF CHOOSE CRIME

S67
HALL B.,"THE COALITION AGAINST DISHWASHERS." USA+45 POL/PAR PROB/SOLV BARGAIN LEAD CHOOSE REPRESENT GP/REL ORD/FREE PWR...POLICY 20. PAGE 46 B0923 — LABOR ADMIN DOMIN WORKER

S67
LENDVAI P.,"HUNGARY* CHANGE VS. IMMOBILISM." HUNGARY LABOR NAT/G PLAN DEBATE ADMIN ROUTINE CENTRAL EFFICIENCY MARXISM PLURISM...PREDICT 20. PAGE 64 B1289 — ECO/DEV MGT CHOOSE

S68
PEARSON A.W.,"RESOURCE ALLOCATION." PLAN PROB/SOLV BUDGET ADMIN CONTROL CHOOSE EFFICIENCY...DECISION MGT 20. PAGE 82 B1649 — PROFIT OPTIMAL COST INDUS

B86
BOLINSBROKE H ST J.,A DISSERTATION UPON PARTIES (1729). UK LEGIS CHOOSE GOV/REL SOVEREIGN...TRADIT 18 PARLIAMENT. PAGE 13 B0269 — CONSERVE POL/PAR CHIEF EX/STRUC

CHOU/ENLAI....CHOU EN-LAI

CHOWDHURI R.N. B0427

CHOWDRY K. B0796

CHRIS/DEM....CHRISTIAN DEMOCRATIC PARTY (ALL NATIONS)

CHRISTENSEN A.N. B0428

CHRISTENSON R.M. B0429

CHRISTIAN B.H. B2382

CHRISTIAN DEMOCRATIC PARTY....SEE CHRIS/DEM

CHRISTIAN....CHRISTIAN BELIEFS OR CHURCHES

B35
GORER G.,AFRICA DANCES: A BOOK ABOUT WEST AFRICAN NEGROES. STRUCT LOC/G SECT FORCES TAX ADMIN COLONIAL...ART/METH MYTH WORSHIP 20 NEGRO AFRICA/W CHRISTIAN RITUAL. PAGE 41 B0835 — AFR ATTIT CULTURE SOCIETY

B66
SILBERMAN B.S.,MODERN JAPANESE LEADERSHIP; TRANSITION AND CHANGE. NAT/G POL/PAR CHIEF ADMIN REPRESENT GP/REL ADJUST RIGID/FLEX...SOC METH/COMP ANTHOL 19/20 CHINJAP CHRISTIAN. PAGE 97 B1952 — LEAD CULTURE ELITES MUNIC

CHRIST-17C.... CHRISTENDOM TO 1700

B05
MACHIAVELLI N.,THE ART OF WAR. CHRIST-17C TOP/EX DRIVE ORD/FREE PWR SKILL...MGT CHARTS. PAGE 67 B1360 — NAT/G FORCES WAR ITALY

B38
DAY C.,A HISTORY OF COMMERCE. CHRIST-17C EUR+WWI ISLAM MEDIT-7 MOD/EUR USA-45 ECO/DEV FINAN NAT/G ECO/TAC EXEC ROUTINE PWR WEALTH HIST/WRIT. PAGE 27 B0546 — MARKET INT/TRADE

B46
CLOUGH S.B.,ECONOMIC HISTORY OF EUROPE. CHRIST-17C EUR+WWI MOD/EUR WOR-45 SOCIETY EXEC ATTIT WEALTH ...CONCPT GEN/LAWS WORK TOT/POP VAL/FREE 7/20. PAGE 22 B0440 — ECO/TAC CAP/ISM

B62
THIERRY S.S.,LE VATICAN SECRET. CHRIST-17C EUR+WWI MOD/EUR VATICAN NAT/G SECT DELIB/GP DOMIN LEGIT SOVEREIGN. PAGE 104 B2096 — ADMIN EX/STRUC CATHISM DECISION

S62
FESLER J.W.,"FRENCH FIELD ADMINISTRATION: THE BEGINNINGS." CHRIST-17C CULTURE SOCIETY STRATA NAT/G ECO/TAC DOMIN EDU/PROP LEGIT ADJUD COERCE ATTIT ALL/VALS...TIME/SEQ CON/ANAL GEN/METH VAL/FREE 13/15. PAGE 35 B0714 — EX/STRUC FRANCE

B64
REDLICH F.,THE GERMAN MILITARY ENTERPRISER AND HIS WORK FORCE. CHRIST-17C GERMANY ELITES SOCIETY FINAN — EX/STRUC FORCES

ECO/TAC CIVMIL/REL GP/REL INGP/REL...HIST/WRIT METH/COMP 14/17. PAGE 87 B1760 — PROFIT WORKER

CHRONOLOGY....SEE TIME/SEQ

CHURCH....SEE SECT

CHURCH/STA....CHURCH-STATE RELATIONS (ALL NATIONS)

B63
DIESNER H.J.,KIRCHE UND STAAT IM SPATROMISCHEN REICH. ROMAN/EMP EX/STRUC COLONIAL COERCE ATTIT CATHISM 4/5 AFRICA/N CHURCH/STA. PAGE 29 B0592 — SECT GP/REL DOMIN JURID

B66
O'NEILL C.E.,CHURCH AND STATE IN FRENCH COLONIAL LOUISIANA: POLICY AND POLITICS TO 1732. PROVS VOL/ASSN DELIB/GP ADJUD ADMIN GP/REL ATTIT DRIVE ...POLICY BIBLIOG 17/18 LOUISIANA CHURCH/STA. PAGE 79 B1601 — COLONIAL NAT/G SECT PWR

CHURCHLL/W....SIR WINSTON CHURCHILL

CIA....CENTRAL INTELLIGENCE AGENCY

B64
BLACKSTOCK P.W.,THE STRATEGY OF SUBVERSION. USA+45 FORCES EDU/PROP ADMIN COERCE GOV/REL...DECISION MGT 20 DEPT/DEFEN CIA DEPT/STATE. PAGE 12 B0247 — ORD/FREE DIPLOM CONTROL

CICERO....CICERO

CINCINNATI....CINCINNATI, OHIO

CINEMA....SEE FILM

CITIES....SEE MUNIC

CITIZENSHIP....SEE CITIZENSHP

CITIZENSHP....CITIZENSHIP

CITY/MGT....CITY MANAGEMENT, CITY MANAGERS; SEE ALSO MUNIC, ADMIN, MGT, LOC/G

N19
ABBOT F.C.,THE CAMBRIDGE CITY MANAGER (PAMPHLET). PROB/SOLV ADMIN PERS/REL RIGID/FLEX PWR...MGT 20 MASSACHU CITY/MGT. PAGE 2 B0050 — MUNIC EX/STRUC TOP/EX GP/REL

B57
KNEIER C.M.,CITY GOVERNMENT IN THE UNITED STATES (3RD ED.). USA+45 FINAN NAT/G POL/PAR LEGIS EDU/PROP LEAD APPORT REPRESENT ATTIT...MGT 20 CITY/MGT. PAGE 60 B1219 — MUNIC LOC/G ADMIN GOV/REL

B58
SHERWOOD F.P.,SUPERVISORY METHODS IN MUNICIPAL ADMINISTRATION. USA+45 MUNIC WORKER EDU/PROP PARTIC INGP/REL PERS/REL 20 CITY/MGT. PAGE 96 B1945 — EX/STRUC LEAD ADMIN LOC/G

B59
BRUNTON R.L.,MANAGEMENT PRACTICES FOR SMALLER CITIES. USA+45 MUNIC CONSULT PLAN BUDGET PERS/REL 20 CITY/MGT. PAGE 16 B0331 — ADMIN LOC/G MGT TOP/EX

B61
DRURY J.W.,THE GOVERNMENT OF KANSAS. USA+45 AGRI INDUS CHIEF LEGIS WORKER PLAN BUDGET GIVE CT/SYS GOV/REL...T 20 KANSAS GOVERNOR CITY/MGT. PAGE 31 B0621 — PROVS CONSTN ADMIN LOC/G

B61
INTL UNION LOCAL AUTHORITIES,LOCAL GOVERNMENT IN THE USA. USA+45 PUB/INST DELIB/GP CONFER AUTOMAT GP/REL POPULISM...ANTHOL 20 CITY/MGT. PAGE 54 B1101 — LOC/G MUNIC ADMIN GOV/REL

B62
HSUEH S.-S.,GOVERNMENT AND ADMINISTRATION OF HONG KONG. CHIEF DELIB/GP LEGIS CT/SYS REPRESENT GOV/REL 20 HONG/KONG CITY/MGT CIVIL/SERV GOVERNOR. PAGE 52 B1055 — ADMIN LOC/G COLONIAL EX/STRUC

B62
INST TRAINING MUNICIPAL ADMIN,MUNICIPAL FINANCE ADMINISTRATION (6TH ED.). USA+45 ELITES ECO/DEV LEGIS PLAN BUDGET TAX GP/REL BAL/PAY COST...POLICY 20 CITY/MGT. PAGE 54 B1089 — MUNIC ADMIN FINAN LOC/G

B62
WANGSNESS P.H.,THE POWER OF THE CITY MANAGER. USA+45 EX/STRUC BAL/PWR BUDGET TAX ADMIN REPRESENT CENTRAL EFFICIENCY DRIVE ROLE...POLICY 20 CITY/MGT. PAGE 113 B2286 — PWR TOP/EX MUNIC LOC/G

N62
UNIVERSITY PITT INST LOC GOVT,THE COUNCIL-MANAGER FORM OF GOVERNMENT IN PENNSYLVANIA (PAMPHLET). PROVS EX/STRUC REPRESENT GOV/REL EFFICIENCY ...CHARTS SIMUL 20 PENNSYLVAN CITY/MGT. PAGE 107 B2169 — LOC/G TOP/EX MUNIC PWR

N63
INTERNATIONAL CITY MGRS ASSN,POST-ENTRY TRAINING IN THE LOCAL PUBLIC SERVICE (PAMPHLET). SCHOOL PLAN PROB/SOLV TEC/DEV ADMIN EFFICIENCY SKILL...POLICY AUD/VIS CHARTS BIBLIOG 20 CITY/MGT. PAGE 54 B1096 — LOC/G WORKER EDU/PROP METH/COMP

B64
CONNECTICUT U INST PUBLIC SERV,SUMMARY OF CHARTER PROVISIONS IN CONNECTICUT LOCAL GOVERNMENT (PAMPHLET). USA+45 DELIB/GP LEGIS TOP/EX CHOOSE REPRESENT 20 CONNECTICT CITY/MGT MAYOR. PAGE 23 B0462 — CONSTN MUNIC LOC/G EX/STRUC

B64
WILDAVSKY A.,LEADERSHIP IN A SMALL TOWN. USA+45 STRUCT PROB/SOLV EXEC PARTIC RACE/REL PWR PLURISM ...SOC 20 NEGRO WATER CIV/RIGHTS OBERLIN CITY/MGT. PAGE 116 B2348 — LEAD MUNIC ELITES

B65
BUECHNER J.C.,DIFFERENCES IN ROLE PERCEPTIONS IN COLORADO COUNCIL-MANAGER CITIES. USA+45 ADMIN ROUTINE GP/REL CONSEN PERCEPT PERSON ROLE ...DECISION MGT STAT INT QU CHARTS 20 COLORADO CITY/MGT. PAGE 17 B0338 — MUNIC CONSULT LOC/G IDEA/COMP

B65
EAST J.P.,COUNCIL-MANAGER GOVERNMENT: THE POLITICAL THOUGHT OF ITS FOUNDER, RICHARD S. CHILDS. USA+45 CREATE ADMIN CHOOSE....BIOG GEN/LAWS BIBLIOG 20 CHILDS/RS CITY/MGT. PAGE 32 B0642 — SIMUL LOC/G MUNIC EX/STRUC

B66
HESSLER I.O.,29 WAYS TO GOVERN A CITY. EX/STRUC TOP/EX PROB/SOLV PARTIC CHOOSE REPRESENT EFFICIENCY ...CHARTS 20 CITY/MGT MAYOR. PAGE 49 B0998 — MUNIC GOV/COMP LOC/G ADMIN

B66
WARREN R.O.,GOVERNMENT IN METROPOLITAN REGIONS: A REAPPRAISAL OF FRACTIONATED POLITICAL ORGANIZATION. USA+45 ACT/RES PROB/SOLV REGION...CHARTS METH/COMP BIBLIOG CITY/MGT. PAGE 114 B2296 — LOC/G MUNIC EX/STRUC PLAN

CIV/DEFENS....CIVIL DEFENSE (SYSTEMS, PLANNING, AND

CIV/DISOBD....CIVIL DISOBEDIENCE

CIV/RIGHTS....CIVIL RIGHTS: CONTEMPORARY CIVIL RIGHTS MOVEMENTS; SEE ALSO RACE/REL, CONSTN + LAW

N19
BUREAU OF NAT'L AFFAIRS INC.,A CURRENT LOOK AT: (1) THE NEGRO AND TITLE VII, (2) SEX AND TITLE VII (PAMPHLET). LAW LG/CO SML/CO RACE/REL...POLICY SOC STAT DEEP/QU TREND CON/ANAL CHARTS 20 NEGRO CIV/RIGHTS. PAGE 17 B0350 — DISCRIM SEX WORKER MGT

S59
DWYER R.J.,"THE ADMINISTRATIVE ROLE IN DESEGREGATION." USA+45 LAW PROB/SOLV LEAD RACE/REL ISOLAT STRANGE ROLE...POLICY SOC/INTEG MISSOURI NEGRO CIV/RIGHTS. PAGE 31 B0638 — ADMIN SCHOOL DISCRIM ATTIT

B62
KENNEDY J.F.,TO TURN THE TIDE. SPACE AGRI INT/ORG FORCES TEC/DEV ADMIN NUC/PWR PEACE WEALTH...ANTHOL 20 KENNEDY/JF CIV/RIGHTS. PAGE 59 B1193 — DIPLOM CHIEF POLICY NAT/G

B64
WILDAVSKY A.,LEADERSHIP IN A SMALL TOWN. USA+45 STRUCT PROB/SOLV EXEC PARTIC RACE/REL PWR PLURISM ...SOC 20 NEGRO WATER CIV/RIGHTS OBERLIN CITY/MGT. PAGE 116 B2348 — LEAD MUNIC ELITES

B65
FRIEDMAN L.,SOUTHERN JUSTICE. USA+45 PUB/INST LEGIT ADMIN CT/SYS DISCRIM...DECISION ANTHOL 20 NEGRO SOUTH/US CIV/RIGHTS. PAGE 37 B0758 — ADJUD LAW CONSTN RACE/REL

S66
JACOBSON J.,"COALITIONISM: FROM PROTEST TO POLITICKING" USA+45 ELITES NAT/G POL/PAR PROB/SOLV ADMIN LEAD DISCRIM ORD/FREE PWR CONSERVE 20 NEGRO AFL/CIO CIV/RIGHTS BLACK/PWR. PAGE 55 B1116 — RACE/REL LABOR SOCIALIST VOL/ASSN

B67
ANGEL D.D.,ROMNEY. LABOR LG/CO NAT/G EXEC WAR RACE/REL PERSON ORD/FREE...MGT WORSHIP 20 ROMNEY/GEO CIV/RIGHTS MORMON GOVERNOR. PAGE 5 B0108 — BIOG CHIEF PROVS POLICY

S67
O'DELL J.H.,"THE JULY REBELLIONS AND THE 'MILITARY STATE'." USA+45 VIETNAM STRATA CHIEF WORKER COLONIAL EXEC CROWD CIVMIL/REL RACE/REL TOTALISM ...WELF/ST PACIFIST 20 NEGRO JOHNSON/LB PRESIDENT CIV/RIGHTS. PAGE 79 B1599 — PWR NAT/G COERCE FORCES

CIVIL AERONAUTICS BOARD....SEE CAB

CIVIL DEFENSE....SEE CIV/DEFENS

CIVIL DISOBEDIENCE....SEE CIV/DISOBD

CIVIL RIGHTS....SEE CIV/RIGHTS

CIVIL SERVICE....SEE ADMIN

CIVIL/CODE....CIVIL CODE (FRANCE)

CIVIL/LAW....CIVIL LAW

B33
ENSOR R.C.K..COURTS AND JUDGES IN FRANCE, GERMANY, CT/SYS
AND ENGLAND. FRANCE GERMANY UK LAW PROB/SOLV ADMIN EX/STRUC
ROUTINE CRIME ROLE...METH/COMP 20 CIVIL/LAW. ADJUD
PAGE 33 B0676 NAT/COMP

B48
SLESSER H..THE ADMINISTRATION OF THE LAW. UK CONSTN LAW
EX/STRUC OP/RES PROB/SOLV CRIME ROLE...DECISION CT/SYS
METH/COMP 20 CIVIL/LAW ENGLSH/LAW CIVIL/LAW. ADJUD
PAGE 98 B1977

B48
SLESSER H..THE ADMINISTRATION OF THE LAW. UK CONSTN LAW
EX/STRUC OP/RES PROB/SOLV CRIME ROLE...DECISION CT/SYS
METH/COMP 20 CIVIL/LAW ENGLSH/LAW CIVIL/LAW. ADJUD
PAGE 98 B1977

CIVIL/LIB....CIVIL LIBERTIES; SEE ALSO CONSTN + LAW

B38
BALDWIN R.N..CIVIL LIBERTIES AND INDUSTRIAL LABOR
CONFLICT. USA+45 STRATA WORKER INGP/REL...MGT 20 LG/CO
ACLU CIVIL/LIB. PAGE 9 B0175 INDUS
GP/REL

B59
LOEWENSTEIN K..VERFASSUNGSRECHT UND CONSTN
VERFASSUNGSPRAXIS DER VEREINIGTEN STAATEN. USA+45 POL/PAR
USA-45 COLONIAL CT/SYS GP/REL RACE/REL ORD/FREE EX/STRUC
...JURID 18/20 SUPREME/CT CONGRESS PRESIDENT NAT/G
BILL/RIGHT CIVIL/LIB. PAGE 66 B1337

B60
PHILLIPS J.C..MUNICIPAL GOVERNMENT AND MUNIC
ADMINISTRATION IN AMERICA. USA+45 LAW CONSTN FINAN GOV/REL
FORCES PLAN RECEIVE OWN ORD/FREE 20 CIVIL/LIB. LOC/G
PAGE 83 B1669 ADMIN

CIVIL/SERV....CIVIL SERVICE; SEE ALSO ADMIN

B05
GOODNOW F.J..THE PRINCIPLES OF THE ADMINISTRATIVE ADMIN
LAW OF THE UNITED STATES. USA-45 LAW STRUCT NAT/G
EX/STRUC LEGIS BAL/PWR CONTROL GOV/REL PWR...JURID PROVS
19/20 CIVIL/SERV. PAGE 41 B0822 LOC/G

B08
THE GOVERNMENT OF SOUTH AFRICA (VOL. II). SOUTH/AFR CONSTN
STRATA EXTR/IND EX/STRUC TOP/EX BUDGET ADJUD ADMIN FINAN
CT/SYS PRODUC...CORREL CENSUS 19 RAILROAD LEGIS
CIVIL/SERV POSTAL/SYS. PAGE 2 B0033 NAT/G

N19
FIKS M..PUBLIC ADMINISTRATION IN ISRAEL (PAMPHLET). EDU/PROP
ISRAEL SCHOOL EX/STRUC BUDGET PAY INGP/REL NAT/G
...DECISION 20 CIVIL/SERV. PAGE 35 B0718 ADMIN
WORKER

N19
GINZBERG E..MANPOWER FOR GOVERNMENT (PAMPHLET). WORKER
USA+45 FORCES PLAN PROB/SOLV PAY EDU/PROP ADMIN CONSULT
GP/REL COST...MGT PREDICT TREND 20 CIVIL/SERV. NAT/G
PAGE 40 B0803 LOC/G

N19
GRIFFITH W..THE PUBLIC SERVICE (PAMPHLET). UK LAW ADMIN
LOC/G NAT/G PARTIC CHOOSE DRIVE ROLE SKILL...CHARTS EFFICIENCY
20 CIVIL/SERV. PAGE 44 B0880 EDU/PROP
GOV/REL

C45
MCDIARMID J.."THE MOBILIZATION OF SOCIAL INTELL
SCIENTISTS," IN L. WHITE'S CIVIL CIVIL SERVICE IN WAR
WARTIME." USA-45 TEC/DEV CENTRAL...SOC 20 DELIB/GP
CIVIL/SERV. PAGE 72 B1447 ADMIN

B48
CHILDS J.R..AMERICAN FOREIGN SERVICE. USA+45 DIPLOM
SOCIETY NAT/G ROUTINE GOV/REL 20 DEPT/STATE ADMIN
CIVIL/SERV. PAGE 21 B0423 GP/REL

S50
EPSTEIN L.D.."POLITICAL STERILIZATION OF CIVIL ADMIN
SERVANTS: THE UNITED STATES AND GREAT BRITAIN." UK LEGIS
USA+45 USA-45 STRUCT TOP/EX OP/RES PARTIC CHOOSE DECISION
NAT/LISM 20 CONGRESS CIVIL/SERV. PAGE 33 B0679 POL/PAR

B53
MAJUMDAR B.B..PROBLEMS OF PUBLIC ADMINISTRATION IN ECO/UNDEV
INDIA. INDIA INDUS PLAN BUDGET ADJUD CENTRAL DEMAND GOV/REL
WEALTH...WELF/ST ANTHOL 20 CIVIL/SERV. PAGE 68 ADMIN
B1384 MUNIC

B56
DUNNILL F..THE CIVIL SERVICE. UK LAW PLAN ADMIN PERSON
EFFICIENCY DRIVE NEW/LIB...STAT CHARTS 20 WORKER
PARLIAMENT CIVIL/SERV. PAGE 31 B0633 STRATA
SOC/WK

B56
ECOLE NAT'L D'ADMINISTRATION.RECRUITMENT AND ADMIN
TRAINING FOR THE HIGHER CIVIL SERVICE IN FRANCE. MGT
FRANCE EX/STRUC PLAN EDU/PROP CONTROL ROUTINE TASK EXEC

COST...METH 20 CIVIL/SERV. PAGE 32 B0650 ACADEM
B56
GLADDEN E.N..CIVIL SERVICE OR BUREAUCRACY? UK LAW ADMIN
STRATA LABOR TOP/EX PLAN SENIOR AUTOMAT CONTROL GOV/REL
PARTIC CHOOSE HAPPINESS...CHARTS 19/20 CIVIL/SERV EFFICIENCY
BUREAUCRCY. PAGE 40 B0808 PROVS

B56
HOWARD L.V..TULANE STUDIES IN POLITICAL SCIENCE: ADMIN
CIVIL SERVICE DEVELOPMENT IN LOUISIANA VOLUME 3. GOV/REL
LAW POL/PAR LEGIS CT/SYS ADJUST ORD/FREE...STAT PROVS
CHARTS 19/20 LOUISIANA CIVIL/SERV. PAGE 52 B1050 POLICY

B56
POWELL N.J..PERSONNEL ADMINISTRATION IN GOVERNMENT. ADMIN
COM/IND POL/PAR LEGIS PAY CT/SYS ROUTINE GP/REL WORKER
PERS/REL...POLICY METH 20 CIVIL/SERV. PAGE 84 B1697 LOC/G
NAT/G

B57
SCARROW H.A..THE HIGHER PUBLIC SERVICE OF THE ADMIN
COMMONWEALTH OF AUSTRALIA. LAW SENIOR LOBBY ROLE 20 NAT/G
AUSTRAL CIVIL/SERV COMMONWLTH. PAGE 93 B1877 EX/STRUC
GOV/COMP

B57
US HOUSE COMM ON POST OFFICE.MANPOWER UTILIZATION NAT/G
IN THE FEDERAL GOVERNMENT. USA+45 FORCES WORKER ADMIN
CREATE PLAN EFFICIENCY UTIL 20 CONGRESS CIVIL/SERV LABOR
POSTAL/SYS DEPT/DEFEN. PAGE 109 B2193 EX/STRUC

B58
BLAIR L..THE COMMONWEALTH PUBLIC SERVICE. LAW ADMIN
WORKER...MGT CHARTS GOV/COMP 20 COMMONWLTH AUSTRAL NAT/G
CIVIL/SERV. PAGE 12 B0248 EX/STRUC
INGP/REL

B58
DWARKADAS R..ROLE OF HIGHER CIVIL SERVICE IN INDIA. ADMIN
INDIA ECO/UNDEV LEGIS PROB/SOLV GP/REL PERS/REL NAT/G
...POLICY WELF/ST DECISION ORG/CHARTS BIBLIOG 20 ROLE
CIVIL/SERV INTRVN/ECO. PAGE 31 B0637 PLAN

B58
SWEENEY S.B..EDUCATION FOR ADMINISTRATIVE CAREERS EDU/PROP
IN GOVERNMENT SERVICE. USA+45 ACADEM CONSULT CREATE ADMIN
PLAN CONFER SKILL...TREND IDEA/COMP METH 20 NAT/G
CIVIL/SERV. PAGE 102 B2059 LOC/G

B58
US HOUSE COMM ON POST OFFICE.TO PROVIDE AN ADMIN
EFFECTIVE SYSTEM OF PERSONNEL ADMINISTRATION. NAT/G
USA+45 DELIB/GP CONTROL EFFICIENCY 20 CONGRESS EX/STRUC
PRESIDENT CIVIL/SERV POSTAL/SYS. PAGE 109 B2194 LAW

B58
US HOUSE COMM POST OFFICE.MANPOWER UTILIZATION IN ADMIN
THE FEDERAL GOVERNMENT. USA+45 DIST/IND EX/STRUC WORKER
LEGIS CONFER EFFICIENCY 20 CONGRESS CIVIL/SERV. DELIB/GP
PAGE 109 B2195 NAT/G

B58
US HOUSE COMM POST OFFICE.MANPOWER UTILIZATION IN ADMIN
THE FEDERAL GOVERNMENT. USA+45 DIST/IND EX/STRUC WORKER
LEGIS CONFER EFFICIENCY 20 CONGRESS CIVIL/SERV. DELIB/GP
PAGE 109 B2196 NAT/G

B58
US HOUSE COMM POST OFFICE.TRAINING OF FEDERAL LEGIS
EMPLOYEES. USA+45 DIST/IND NAT/G EX/STRUC EDU/PROP DELIB/GP
CONFER GOV/REL EFFICIENCY SKILL 20 CONGRESS WORKER
CIVIL/SERV. PAGE 109 B2197 ADMIN

B58
US SENATE COMM POST OFFICE.TO PROVIDE AN EFFECTIVE INT
SYSTEM OF PERSONNEL ADMINISTRATION. USA+45 NAT/G LEGIS
EX/STRUC PARL/PROC GOV/REL...JURID 20 SENATE CONFER
CIVIL/SERV. PAGE 111 B2234 ADMIN

B58
VAN RIPER P.P..HISTORY OF THE UNITED STATES CIVIL ADMIN
SERVICE. USA+45 USA-45 LABOR LOC/G DELIB/GP LEGIS WORKER
PROB/SOLV LOBBY GOV/REL GP/REL INCOME...POLICY NAT/G
18/20 PRESIDENT CIVIL/SERV. PAGE 111 B2251

B58
WHITE L.D..THE REPUBLICAN ERA: 1869-1901, A STUDY MGT
IN ADMINISTRATIVE HISTORY. USA-45 FINAN PLAN PWR
NEUTRAL CRIME GP/REL MORAL LAISSEZ PRESIDENT DELIB/GP
REFORMERS 19 CONGRESS CIVIL/SERV. PAGE 116 B2340 ADMIN

B59
CHAPMAN B..THE PROFESSION OF GOVERNMENT: THE PUBLIC ADMIN
SERVICE IN EUROPE. MOD/EUR LABOR CT/SYS...T 20 CONTROL
CIVIL/SERV. PAGE 20 B0409 ROUTINE
EX/STRUC

B59
INDIAN INSTITUTE PUBLIC ADMIN.MORALE IN THE PUBLIC HAPPINESS
SERVICES: REPORT OF A CONFERENCE JAN., 3-4, 1959. ADMIN
INDIA S/ASIA ECO/UNDEV PROVS PLAN EDU/PROP CONFER WORKER
GOV/REL EFFICIENCY DRIVE ROLE 20 CIVIL/SERV. INGP/REL
PAGE 53 B1082

B59
THARAMATHAJ C..A STUDY OF THE COMPOSITION OF THE ADMIN
THAI CIVIL SERVICE (PAPER). THAILAND PAY ROLE EX/STRUC
...CHARTS 20 CIVIL/SERV FEMALE/SEX. PAGE 103 B2092 STRATA
INGP/REL

B59
US SENATE COMM ON POST OFFICE.TO PROVIDE FOR AN ADMIN
EFFECTIVE SYSTEM OF PERSONNEL ADMINISTRATION. NAT/G
EFFICIENCY...MGT 20 CONGRESS CIVIL/SERV POSTAL/SYS EX/STRUC

YARBROGH/R. PAGE 111 B2233   LAW
                                                              B59
WEBER W..DER DEUTSCHE BEAMTE HEUTE. GERMANY/W NAT/G MGT
DELIB/GP LEGIS CONFER ATTIT SUPEGO...JURID 20   EFFICIENCY
CIVIL/SERV. PAGE 114 B2306   ELITES
                                                   GP/REL
                                                              B60
FRANKE W..THE REFORM AND ABOLITION OF THE   ADJUST
TRADITIONAL CHINESE EXAMINATION SYSTEM. ASIA STRUCT ADMIN
19/20 CIVIL/SERV. PAGE 37 B0750   TESTS
                                                   STRATA
                                                              B60
ROY N.C..THE CIVIL SERVICE IN INDIA. INDIA POL/PAR ADMIN
ECO/TAC INCOME...JURID MGT 20 CIVIL/SERV. PAGE 91   NAT/G
B1843   DELIB/GP
                                                   CONFER
                                                              B61
CATHERINE R..LE FONCTIONNAIRE FRANCAIS. FRANCE   ADMIN
NAT/G INGP/REL ATTIT MORAL ORD/FREE...T CIVIL/SERV. GP/REL
PAGE 19 B0394   LEAD
                                                   SUPEGO
                                                              B61
LOSCHELDER W..AUSBILDUNG UND AUSLESE DER BEAMTEN.   PROF/ORG
GERMANY/W ELITES NAT/G ADMIN GP/REL ATTIT...JURID   EDU/PROP
20 CIVIL/SERV. PAGE 67 B1341   EX/STRUC
                                                   CHOOSE
                                                              S61
EHRMANN H.W.."FRENCH BUREAUCRACY AND ORGANIZED   ADMIN
INTERESTS" (BMR)" FRANCE NAT/G DELIB/GP ROUTINE   DECISION
...INT 20 BUREAUCRCY CIVIL/SERV. PAGE 32 B0657   PLURISM
                                                   LOBBY
                                                              B62
CHERNICK J..THE SELECTION OF TRAINEES UNDER MDTA.   EDU/PROP
USA+45 NAT/G LEGIS PERSON...CENSUS 20 CIVIL/SERV   WORKER
MDTA. PAGE 20 B0418   ADMIN
                                                   DELIB/GP
                                                              B62
ESCUELA SUPERIOR DE ADMIN PUBL.INFORME DEL   ADMIN
SEMINARIO SOBRE SERVICIO CIVIL O CARRERA   NAT/G
ADMINISTRATIVA. L/A+17C ELITES STRATA CONFER   PROB/SOLV
CONTROL GOV/REL INGP/REL SUPEGO 20 CENTRAL/AM   ATTIT
CIVIL/SERV. PAGE 33 B0681
                                                              B62
HSUEH S.--S.,GOVERNMENT AND ADMINISTRATION OF HONG ADMIN
KONG. CHIEF DELIB/GP LEGIS CT/SYS REPRESENT GOV/REL LOC/G
20 HONG/KONG CITY/MGT CIVIL/SERV GOVERNOR. PAGE 52 COLONIAL
B1055   EX/STRUC
                                                              B62
INSTITUTE OF PUBLIC ADMIN.A SHORT HISTORY OF THE   ADMIN
PUBLIC SERVICE IN IRELAND. IRELAND UK DIST/IND   WORKER
INGP/REL FEDERAL 13/20 CIVIL/SERV. PAGE 54 B1091   GOV/REL
                                                   NAT/G
                                                              B62
NJ DEPARTMENT CIVIL SERV.THE CIVIL SERVICE RULES OF ADMIN
THE STATE OF NEW JERSEY. USA+45 USA-45 PAY...JURID PROVS
ANTHOL 20 CIVIL/SERV NEW/JERSEY. PAGE 78 B1585   ROUTINE
                                                   WORKER
                                                              B63
PLANTEY A..TRAITE PRATIQUE DE LA FONCTION PUBLIQUE ADMIN
(2ND ED., 2 VOLS.). FRANCE FINAN EX/STRUC PROB/SOLV SUPEGO
GP/REL ATTIT...SOC 20 CIVIL/SERV. PAGE 83 B1680   JURID
                                                              B63
SINGH H.L..PROBLEMS AND POLICIES OF THE BRITISH IN COLONIAL
INDIA, 1885-1898. INDIA UK NAT/G FORCES LEGIS   PWR
PROB/SOLV CONTROL RACE/REL ADJUST DISCRIM NAT/LISM POLICY
RIGID/FLEX...MGT 19 CIVIL/SERV. PAGE 97 B1968   ADMIN
                                                              B63
SWEENEY S.B..ACHIEVING EXCELLENCE IN PUBLIC   ADMIN
SERVICE. FUT USA+45 NAT/G ACT/RES GOV/REL...POLICY WORKER
ANTHOL 20 CIVIL/SERV. PAGE 102 B2060   TASK
                                                   PLAN
                                                              B63
US SENATE COMM APPROPRIATIONS.PERSONNEL   ADMIN
ADMINISTRATION AND OPERATIONS OF AGENCY FOR   FOR/AID
INTERNATIONAL DEVELOPMENT: SPECIAL HEARING. FINAN   EFFICIENCY
LEAD COST UTIL SKILL...CHARTS 20 CONGRESS AID   DIPLOM
CIVIL/SERV. PAGE 109 B2211
                                                              S63
MEDALIA N.Z.."POSITION AND PROSPECTS OF   NAT/G
SOCIOLOGISTS IN FEDERAL EMPLOYMENT." USA+45 CONSULT WORKER
PAY SENIOR ADMIN GOV/REL...TREND CHARTS 20   SOC
CIVIL/SERV. PAGE 72 B1460   SKILL
                                                              B64
AHMAD M..THE CIVIL SERVANT IN PAKISTAN. PAKISTAN   WELF/ST
ECO/UNDEV COLONIAL INGP/REL...SOC CHARTS BIBLIOG 20 ADMIN
CIVIL/SERV. PAGE 3 B0065   ATTIT
                                                   STRATA
                                                              B64
HAMILTON B.L.S..PROBLEMS OF ADMINISTRATION IN AN   ADMIN
EMERGENT NATION: CASE STUDY OF JAMAICA. JAMAICA UK ECO/UNDEV
WOR+45 MUNIC COLONIAL HABITAT...CHARTS BIBLIOG 20   GOV/REL
CIVIL/SERV. PAGE 46 B0932   NAT/G
                                                              B64
RAPHAEL M..PENSIONS AND PUBLIC SERVANTS. UK PLAN   ADMIN
EDU/PROP PARTIC GOV/REL HEALTH...POLICY CHARTS   SENIOR
17/20 CIVIL/SERV. PAGE 86 B1737   PAY

                                                   AGE/O
                                                              B64
STANLEY D.T..THE HIGHER CIVIL SERVICE: AN   NAT/G
EVALUATION OF FEDERAL PERSONNEL PRACTICES. USA+45   ADMIN
CREATE EXEC ROUTINE CENTRAL...MGT SAMP IDEA/COMP   CONTROL
METH/COMP 20 CIVIL/SERV. PAGE 100 B2020   EFFICIENCY
                                                              B65
ADU A.L..THE CIVIL SERVICE IN NEW AFRICAN STATES.   ECO/UNDEV
AFR GHANA FINAN SOVEREIGN...POLICY 20 CIVIL/SERV   ADMIN
AFRICA/E AFRICA/W. PAGE 3 B0062   COLONIAL
                                                   NAT/G
                                                              B65
CAMPBELL G.A..THE CIVIL SERVICE IN BRITAIN (2ND   ADMIN
ED.). UK DELIB/GP FORCES WORKER CREATE PLAN   LEGIS
...POLICY AUD/VIS 19/20 CIVIL/SERV. PAGE 18 B0370   NAT/G
                                                   FINAN
                                                              B65
KRIESBERG M..PUBLIC ADMINISTRATION IN DEVELOPING   NAT/G
COUNTRIES: PROCEEDINGS OF AN INTERNATIONAL   ECO/UNDEV
CONFERENCE HELD IN BOGOTA, COLUMBIA,1963. FUT   SOCIETY
EDU/PROP ORD/FREE...MGT 20 CIVIL/SERV. PAGE 61   ADMIN
B1237
                                                              B65
PURCELL V..THE MEMOIRS OF A MALAYAN OFFICIAL.   BIOG
MALAYSIA UK ECO/UNDEV INDUS LABOR EDU/PROP COLONIAL ADMIN
CT/SYS WAR NAT/LISM TOTALISM ORD/FREE SOVEREIGN 20 JURID
UN CIVIL/SERV. PAGE 85 B1721   FORCES
                                                              B65
RHODES G..PUBLIC SECTOR PENSIONS. UK FINAN LEGIS   ADMIN
BUDGET TAX PAY INCOME...CHARTS 20 CIVIL/SERV.   RECEIVE
PAGE 88 B1769   AGE/O
                                                   WORKER
                                                              B66
ZINKIN T..CHALLENGES IN INDIA. INDIA PAKISTAN LAW   NAT/G
AGRI FINAN INDUS TOP/EX TEC/DEV CONTROL ROUTINE   ECO/TAC
ORD/FREE PWR 20 NEHRU/J SHASTRI/LB CIVIL/SERV.   POLICY
PAGE 119 B2404   ADMIN
                                                              B67
KRISLOV S..THE NEGRO IN FEDERAL EMPLOYMENT. LAW   WORKER
STRATA LOC/G CREATE PROB/SOLV INSPECT GOV/REL   NAT/G
DISCRIM ROLE...DECISION INT TREND 20 NEGRO WWI   ADMIN
CIVIL/SERV. PAGE 61 B1238   RACE/REL
                                                              S67
SUBRAMANIAM V.."REPRESENTATIVE BUREAUCRACY: A   STRATA
REASSESSMENT." USA+45 ELITES LOC/G NAT/G ADMIN   GP/REL
GOV/REL PRIVIL DRIVE ROLE...POLICY CENSUS 20   MGT
CIVIL/SERV BUREAUCRCY. PAGE 101 B2053   GOV/COMP

                                                              N
WEIGLEY R.F..HISTORY OF THE UNITED STATES ARMY.   FORCES
USA+45 USA-45 SOCIETY NAT/G LEAD WAR GP/REL PWR   ADMIN
...SOC METH/COMP COLD/WAR. PAGE 115 B2312   ROLE
                                                   CIVMIL/REL
                                                              B45
CONOVER H.F..THE GOVERNMENTS OF THE MAJOR FOREIGN   BIBLIOG
POWERS: A BIBLIOGRAPHY. FRANCE GERMANY ITALY UK   NAT/G
USSR CONSTN LOC/G POL/PAR EX/STRUC FORCES ADMIN   DIPLOM
CT/SYS CIVMIL/REL TOTALISM...POLICY 19/20. PAGE 23
B0464
                                                              B46
WILCOX J.K..OFFICIAL DEFENSE PUBLICATIONS,   BIBLIOG/A
1941-1945 (NINE VOLS.). USA-45 AGRI INDUS R+D LABOR WAR
FORCES TEC/DEV EFFICIENCY PRODUC SKILL WEALTH 20.   CIVMIL/REL
PAGE 116 B2347   ADMIN
                                                              B48
STEWART I..ORGANIZING SCIENTIFIC RESEARCH FOR WAR: DELIB/GP
ADMINISTRATIVE HISTORY OF OFFICE OF SCIENTIFIC   ADMIN
RESEARCH AND DEVELOPMENT. USA-45 INTELL R+D LABOR   WAR
WORKER CREATE BUDGET WEAPON CIVMIL/REL GP/REL   TEC/DEV
EFFICIENCY...POLICY 20. PAGE 101 B2037
                                                              B50
KOENIG L.W..THE SALE OF THE TANKERS. USA+45 SEA   NAT/G
DIST/IND POL/PAR DIPLOM ADMIN CIVMIL/REL ATTIT   POLICY
...DECISION 20 PRESIDENT DEPT/STATE. PAGE 60 B1223 PLAN
                                                   GOV/REL
                                                              S52
MASLAND J.W.."THE NATIONAL WAR COLLEGE AND THE   CIVMIL/REL
ADMINISTRATION OF FOREIGN AFFAIRS." USA+45 NAT/G   EX/STRUC
FORCES EXEC 20. PAGE 70 B1422   REPRESENT
                                                   PROB/SOLV
                                                              S53
PERKINS J.A.."ADMINISTRATION OF THE NATIONAL   CONTROL
SECURITY PROGRAM." USA+45 EX/STRUC FORCES ADMIN   GP/REL
CIVMIL/REL ORD/FREE 20. PAGE 82 B1657   REPRESENT
                                                   PROB/SOLV
                                                              B56
KOENIG L.W..THE TRUMAN ADMINISTRATION: ITS   ADMIN
PRINCIPLES AND PRACTICE. USA+45 POL/PAR CHIEF LEGIS POLICY
DIPLOM DEATH NUC/PWR WAR CIVMIL/REL PEACE   EX/STRUC
...DECISION 20 TRUMAN/HS PRESIDENT TREATY. PAGE 61 GOV/REL

B1224

KAMPELMAN M.M.,"CONGRESSIONAL CONTROL VS EXECUTIVE
FLEXIBILITY." USA+45 NAT/G 20. PAGE 58 B1165

S58
CIVMIL/REL
ADMIN
EX/STRUC
CONTROL

RHODE W.E.,"COMMITTEE CLEARANCE OF ADMINISTRATIVE
DECISIONS." DELIB/GP LEGIS BUDGET DOMIN CIVMIL/REL
20 CONGRESS. PAGE 87 B1768

L59
DECISION
ADMIN
OP/RES
NAT/G

BROOKINGS INSTITUTION.UNITED STATES FOREIGN POLICY:
STUDY NO 9: THE FORMULATION AND ADMINISTRATION OF
UNITED STATES FOREIGN POLICY. USA+45 WOR+45
EX/STRUC LEGIS BAL/PWR FOR/AID EDU/PROP CIVMIL/REL
GOV/REL...INT COLD/WAR. PAGE 16 B0317

B60
DIPLOM
INT/ORG
CREATE

US DEPARTMENT OF THE ARMY.SELECT BIBLIOGRAPHY ON
ADMINISTRATIVE ORGANIZATION(PAMPHLET). USA+45 INDUS
NAT/G EX/STRUC OP/RES CIVMIL/REL EFFICIENCY
ORD/FREE. PAGE 108 B2183

B60
BIBLIOG/A
ADMIN
CONCPT
FORCES

LYONS G.M.,"THE NEW CIVIL-MILITARY RELATIONS."
USA+45 NAT/G EX/STRUC TOP/EX PROB/SOLV ADMIN EXEC
PARTIC 20. PAGE 67 B1350

S61
CIVMIL/REL
PWR
REPRESENT

CARPER E.T.,ILLINOIS GOES TO CONGRESS FOR ARMY
LAND. USA+45 LAW EXTR/IND PROVS REGION CIVMIL/REL
GOV/REL FEDERAL ATTIT 20 ILLINOIS SENATE CONGRESS
DIRKSEN/E DOUGLAS/P. PAGE 19 B0385

B62
ADMIN
LOBBY
GEOG
LEGIS

MORTON L.,STRATEGY AND COMMAND: THE FIRST TWO
YEARS. USA+45 NAT/G CONTROL EXEC LEAD WEAPON
CIVMIL/REL PWR...POLICY AUD/VIS CHARTS 20 CHINJAP.
PAGE 76 B1532

B62
WAR
FORCES
PLAN
DIPLOM

STEIN H.,AMERICAN CIVIL-MILITARY DECISION. USA+45
USA-45 EX/STRUC FORCES LEGIS TOP/EX PLAN DIPLOM
FOR/AID ATTIT 20 CONGRESS. PAGE 100 B2028

B63
CIVMIL/REL
DECISION
WAR
BUDGET

RAYMOND J.,POWER AT THE PENTAGON (1ST ED.). ELITES
NAT/G PLAN EDU/PROP ARMS/CONT DETER WAR WEAPON
...TIME/SEQ 20 PENTAGON MCNAMARA/R. PAGE 86 B1746

B64
PWR
CIVMIL/REL
EX/STRUC
FORCES

REDLICH F.,THE GERMAN MILITARY ENTERPRISER AND HIS
WORK FORCE. CHRIST-17C GERMANY ELITES SOCIETY FINAN
ECO/TAC CIVMIL/REL GP/REL INGP/REL...HIST/WRIT
METH/COMP 14/17. PAGE 87 B1760

B64
EX/STRUC
FORCES
PROFIT
WORKER

WERNETTE J.P.,GOVERNMENT AND BUSINESS. LABOR
CAP/ISM ECO/TAC INT/TRADE TAX ADMIN AUTOMAT NUC/PWR
CIVMIL/REL DEMAND...MGT 20 MONOPOLY. PAGE 115 B2323

B64
NAT/G
FINAN
ECO/DEV
CONTROL

ECCLES H.E.,MILITARY CONCEPTS AND PHILOSOPHY.
USA+45 STRUCT EXEC ROUTINE COERCE WAR CIVMIL/REL
COST...OBS GEN/LAWS COLD/WAR. PAGE 32 B0648

B65
PLAN
DRIVE
LEAD
FORCES

MELMANS S.,OUR DEPLETED SOCIETY. SPACE USA+45
ECO/DEV FORCES BUDGET ECO/TAC ADMIN WEAPON
EFFICIENCY 20 COLD/WAR. PAGE 73 B1465

B65
CIVMIL/REL
INDUS
EDU/PROP
CONTROL

US SENATE COMM GOVT OPERATIONS.ORGANIZATION OF
FEDERAL EXECUTIVE DEPARTMENTS AND AGENCIES: REPORT
OF MARCH 23, 1965. USA+45 FORCES LEGIS DIPLOM
ROUTINE CIVMIL/REL EFFICIENCY FEDERAL...MGT STAT.
PAGE 110 B2217

B65
ADMIN
EX/STRUC
GOV/REL
ORG/CHARTS

WARD R.,BACKGROUND MATERIAL ON ECONOMIC IMPACT OF
FEDERAL PROCUREMENT - 1965: FOR JOINT ECONOMIC
COMMITTEE US CONGRESS. FINAN ROUTINE WEAPON
CIVMIL/REL EFFICIENCY...STAT CHARTS 20 CONGRESS.
PAGE 113 B2288

B65
ECO/DEV
NAT/G
OWN
GOV/REL

MATTHEWS D.G.,"A CURRENT BIBLIOGRAPHY ON ETHIOPIAN
AFFAIRS: A SELECT BIBLIOGRAPHY FROM 1950-1964."
ETHIOPIA LAW CULTURE ECO/UNDEV INDUS LABOR SECT
FORCES DIPLOM CIVMIL/REL RACE/REL...LING STAT 20.
PAGE 71 B1428

L65
BIBLIOG/A
ADMIN
POL/PAR
NAT/G

HEADY F.,PUBLIC ADMINISTRATION: A COMPARATIVE
PERSPECTIVE. ECO/DEV ECO/UNDEV...GOV/COMP 20
BUREAUCRCY. PAGE 48 B0982

B66
ADMIN
NAT/COMP
NAT/G
CIVMIL/REL

SAPIN B.M.,THE MAKING OF UNITED STATES FOREIGN
POLICY. USA+45 INT/ORG DELIB/GP FORCES PLAN ECO/TAC
CIVMIL/REL PRESIDENT. PAGE 92 B1868

B66
DIPLOM
EX/STRUC
DECISION
NAT/G

WHITNAH D.R.,SAFER SKYWAYS. DIST/IND DELIB/GP

B66
ADMIN

FORCES TOP/EX WORKER TEC/DEV ROUTINE WAR CIVMIL/REL
COST...TIME/SEQ 20 FAA CAB. PAGE 116 B2342

NAT/G
AIR
GOV/REL

MATTHEWS D.G.,"PRELUDE-COUP D'ETAT-MILITARY
GOVERNMENT: A BIBLIOGRAPHICAL AND RESEARCH GUIDE TO
NIGERIAN POL AND GOVT, JAN. 1965-66." AFR NIGER LAW
CONSTN POL/PAR LEGIS CIVMIL/REL GOV/REL...STAT 20.
PAGE 71 B1430

S66
BIBLIOG
NAT/G
ADMIN
CHOOSE

TARLING N.,"A CONCISE HISTORY OF SOUTHEAST ASIA."
BURMA CAMBODIA LAOS S/ASIA THAILAND VIETNAM
ECO/UNDEV POL/PAR FORCES ADMIN REV WAR CIVMIL/REL
ORD/FREE MARXISM SOCISM 13/20. PAGE 103 B2080

C66
COLONIAL
DOMIN
INT/TRADE
NAT/LISM

HOROWITZ I.L.,THE RISE AND FALL OF PROJECT CAMELOT:
STUDIES IN THE RELATIONSHIP BETWEEN SOCIAL SCIENCE
AND PRACTICAL POLITICS. USA+45 WOR+45 CULTURE
FORCES LEGIS EXEC CIVMIL/REL KNOWL...POLICY SOC
METH/CNCPT 20. PAGE 51 B1043

B67
NAT/G
ACADEM
ACT/RES
GP/REL

MACKINTOSH J.M.,JUGGERNAUT. USSR NAT/G POL/PAR
ADMIN LEAD CIVMIL/REL COST TOTALISM PWR MARXISM
...GOV/COMP 20. PAGE 68 B1364

B67
WAR
FORCES
COM
PROF/ORG

RALSTON D.B.,THE ARMY OF THE REPUBLIC; THE PLACE OF
THE MILITARY IN THE POLITICAL EVOLUTION OF FRANCE
1871-1914. FRANCE MOD/EUR EX/STRUC LEGIS TOP/EX
DIPLOM ADMIN WAR GP/REL ROLE...BIBLIOG 19/20.
PAGE 86 B1730

B67
FORCES
NAT/G
CIVMIL/REL
POLICY

LALL B.G.,"GAPS IN THE ABM DEBATE." NAT/G DIPLOM
DETER CIVMIL/REL 20. PAGE 62 B1251

S67
NUC/PWR
ARMS/CONT
EX/STRUC
FORCES

O'DELL J.H.,"THE JULY REBELLIONS AND THE 'MILITARY
STATE'." USA+45 VIETNAM STRATA CHIEF WORKER
COLONIAL EXEC CROWD CIVMIL/REL RACE/REL TOTALISM
...WELF/ST PACIFIST 20 NEGRO JOHNSON/LB PRESIDENT
CIV/RIGHTS. PAGE 79 B1599

S67
PWR
NAT/G
COERCE
FORCES

TACKABERRY R.B.,"ORGANIZING AND TRAINING PEACE-
KEEPING FORCES* THE CANADIAN VIEW." CANADA PLAN
DIPLOM CONFER ADJUD ADMIN CIVMIL/REL 20 UN.
PAGE 102 B2069

S67
PEACE
FORCES
INT/ORG
CONSULT

CLAN....SEE KIN

CLAPP G.R. B0430

CLARK J.S. B0431,B0432

CLARK/JB....JOHN BATES CLARK

CLARKE M.P. B0433

CLASS DIVISION....SEE STRATA

CLASS, SOCIAL....SEE STRATA

CLASSIF....CLASSIFICATION, TYPOLOGY, SET THEORY

SAWYER R.A.,A LIST OF WORKS ON COUNTY GOVERNMENT.
LAW FINAN MUNIC TOP/EX ROUTINE CRIME...CLASSIF
RECORD 19/20. PAGE 93 B1871

B15
BIBLIOG/A
LOC/G
GOV/REL
ADMIN

DOUGLAS P.H.,"OCCUPATIONAL V PROPORTIONAL
REPRESENTATION." INDUS NAT/G PLAN ROUTINE SUFF
CONSEN DRIVE...CONCPT CLASSIF. PAGE 30 B0612

L23
REPRESENT
PROF/ORG
DOMIN
INGP/REL

US LIBRARY OF CONGRESS.CLASSIFIED GUIDE TO MATERIAL
IN THE LIBRARY OF CONGRESS COVERING URBAN COMMUNITY
DEVELOPMENT. USA+45 CREATE PROB/SOLV ADMIN 20.
PAGE 109 B2202

B36
BIBLIOG
CLASSIF
MUNIC
PLAN

BENJAMIN H.C.,EMPLOYMENT TESTS IN INDUSTRY AND
BUSINESS. LG/CO WORKER ROUTINE...MGT PSY SOC
CLASSIF PROBABIL STAT APT/TEST KNO/TEST PERS/TEST
20. PAGE 10 B0211

B45
BIBLIOG/A
METH
TESTS
INDUS

GRAVES W.B.,"LEGISLATIVE REFERENCE SYSTEM FOR THE
CONGRESS OF THE UNITED STATES." ROUTINE...CLASSIF
TREND EXHIBIT CONGRESS. PAGE 42 B0856

S47
LEGIS
STRUCT

KNICKERBOCKER I.,"LEADERSHIP: A CONCEPTION AND SOME
IMPLICATIONS." INDUS OP/RES REPRESENT INGP/REL
DRIVE...MGT CLASSIF. PAGE 60 B1220

S48
LEAD
CONCPT
PERSON
ROLE

TAYLOR R.W.,"ARTHUR F. BENTLEY'S POLITICAL SCIENCE"
(BMR)" USA+45 INTELL NAT/G...DECISION CLASSIF

S52
GEN/LAWS
POLICY

IDEA/COMP 20 BENTLEY/AF. PAGE 103 B2090   ADMIN

                                                                    B54
LAPIERRE R.T.,,A THEORY OF SOCIAL CONTROL. STRUCT   CONTROL
ADMIN ROUTINE SANCTION ANOMIE AUTHORIT DRIVE PERSON   VOL/ASSN
PWR...MAJORIT CONCPT CLASSIF. PAGE 62 B1260   CULTURE

                                                                    B55
RILEY V.,INTERINDUSTRY ECONOMIC STUDIES. USA+45   BIBLIOG
COMPUTER ADMIN OPTIMAL PRODUC...MGT CLASSIF STAT.   ECO/DEV
PAGE 88 B1788   PLAN
                                                          STRUCT

                                                                    S55
CHAPIN F.S.,,"FORMALIZATION OBSERVED IN TEN   VOL/ASSN
VOLUNTARY ORGANIZATIONS: CONCEPTS, MORPHOLOGY,   ROUTINE
PROCESS." STRUCT INGP/REL PERS/REL...METH/CNCPT   CONTROL
CLASSIF OBS RECORD. PAGE 20 B0407   OP/RES

                                                                    S55
WRIGHT Q.,,"THE PEACEFUL ADJUSTMENT OF INTERNATIONAL   R+D
RELATIONS: PROBLEMS AND RESEARCH APPROACHES." UNIV   METH/CNCPT
INTELL EDU/PROP ADJUD ROUTINE KNOWL SKILL...INT/LAW   PEACE
JURID PHIL/SCI CLASSIF 20. PAGE 118 B2385

                                                                    B58
WARNER A.W.,,CONCEPTS AND CASES IN ECONOMIC   ECO/TAC
ANALYSIS. PROB/SOLV BARGAIN CONTROL INCOME PRODUC   DEMAND
...ECOMETRIC MGT CONCPT CLASSIF CHARTS 20   EQUILIB
KEYNES/JM. PAGE 114 B2292   COST

                                                                    B59
DAHRENDORF R.,CLASS AND CLASS CONFLICT IN   VOL/ASSN
INDUSTRIAL SOCIETY. LABOR NAT/G COERCE ROLE PLURISM   STRUCT
...POLICY MGT CONCPT CLASSIF. PAGE 26 B0523   SOC
                                                         GP/REL

                                                                    S59
STINCHCOMBE A.L.,,"BUREAUCRATIC AND CRAFT   CONSTRUC
ADMINISTRATION OF PRODUCTION: A COMPARATIVE STUDY"   PROC/MFG
(BMR)" USA+45 STRUCT EX/STRUC ECO/TAC GP/REL   ADMIN
...CLASSIF GP/COMP IDEA/COMP GEN/LAWS 20 WEBER/MAX.   PLAN
PAGE 101 B2039

                                                                    B60
WALDO D.,THE RESEARCH FUNCTION OF UNIVERSITY   ADMIN
BUREAUS AND INSTITUTES FOR GOVERNMENTAL-RELATED   R+D
RESEARCH. FINAN ACADEM NAT/G INGP/REL ROLE...POLICY   MUNIC
CLASSIF GOV/COMP. PAGE 113 B2276

                                                                    B61
ETZIONI A.,COMPLEX ORGANIZATIONS: A SOCIOLOGICAL   VOL/ASSN
READER. CLIENT CULTURE STRATA CREATE OP/RES ADMIN   STRUCT
...POLICY METH/CNCPT BUREAUCRCY. PAGE 34 B0683   CLASSIF
                                                         PROF/ORG

                                                                    B63
BERNE E.,THE STRUCTURE AND DYNAMICS OF   INGP/REL
ORGANIZATIONS AND GROUPS. CLIENT PARTIC DRIVE   AUTHORIT
HEALTH...MGT PSY ORG/CHARTS. PAGE 11 B0226   ROUTINE
                                                         CLASSIF

                                                                    B63
DEAN A.L.,FEDERAL AGENCY APPROACHES TO FIELD   ADMIN
MANAGEMENT (PAMPHLET). R+D DELIB/GP EX/STRUC   MGT
PROB/SOLV GOV/REL...CLASSIF BIBLIOG 20 FAA NASA   NAT/G
DEPT/HEW POSTAL/SYS IRS. PAGE 28 B0563   OP/RES

                                                                    B63
HEARLE E.F.R.,A DATA PROCESSING SYSTEM FOR STATE   LOC/G
AND LOCAL GOVERNMENTS. PLAN TEC/DEV AUTOMAT ROUTINE   PROVS
...MGT METH/CNCPT CLASSIF 20. PAGE 49 B0984   COMPUTER
                                                         COMPUT/IR

                                                                    L63
LIVERNASH E.R.,,"THE RELATION OF POWER TO THE   LABOR
STRUCTURE AND PROCESS OF COLLECTIVE BARGAINING."   GP/REL
ADJUD ORD/FREE...POLICY MGT CLASSIF GP/COMP.   PWR
PAGE 66 B1330   ECO/TAC

                                                                    B64
COOMBS C.H.,A THEORY OF DATA....MGT PHIL/SCI SOC   CON/ANAL
CLASSIF MATH PROBABIL STAT QU. PAGE 23 B0472   GEN/METH
                                                         TESTS
                                                         PSY

                                                                    B64
ETZIONI A.,MODERN ORGANIZATIONS. CLIENT STRUCT   MGT
DOMIN CONTROL LEAD PERS/REL AUTHORIT...CLASSIF   ADMIN
BUREAUCRCY. PAGE 34 B0685   PLAN
                                                         CULTURE

                                                                    B64
SZLADITS C.,BIBLIOGRAPHY ON FOREIGN AND COMPARATIVE   BIBLIOG/A
LAW: BOOKS AND ARTICLES IN ENGLISH (SUPPLEMENT   JURID
1962). FINAN INDUS JUDGE LICENSE ADMIN CT/SYS   ADJUD
PARL/PROC OWN...INT/LAW CLASSIF METH/COMP NAT/COMP   LAW
20. PAGE 102 B2065

                                                                    S64
HORECKY P.L.,,"LIBRARY OF CONGRESS PUBLICATIONS IN   BIBLIOG/A
AID OF USSR AND EAST EUROPEAN RESEARCH." BULGARIA   COM
CZECHOSLVK POLAND USSR YUGOSLAVIA NAT/G POL/PAR   MARXISM
DIPLOM ADMIN GOV/REL...CLASSIF 20. PAGE 51 B1042

                                                                    B65
BARNETT V.M. JR.,THE REPRESENTATION OF THE UNITED   USA+45
STATES ABROAD* REVISED EDITION. ECO/UNDEV ACADEM   DIPLOM
INT/ORG FORCES ACT/RES CREATE OP/RES FOR/AID REGION   ADMIN
CENTRAL....CLASSIF ANTHOL. PAGE 9 B0189

                                                                    B65
GOULDNER A.W.,STUDIES IN LEADERSHIP. LABOR EDU/PROP   LEAD
CONTROL PARTIC...CONCPT CLASSIF. PAGE 42 B0845   ADMIN
                                                         AUTHORIT

                                                                    S67
SKOLNIKOFF E.B.,,"MAKING FOREIGN POLICY" PROB/SOLV   TEC/DEV
EFFICIENCY PERCEPT PWR...MGT METH/CNCPT CLASSIF 20.   CONTROL
PAGE 98 B1976   USA+45
                                                         NAT/G

CLAUSWTZ/K....KARL VON CLAUSEWITZ

CLEGG R.K. B0434

CLEMENCE/G....GEORGES CLEMENCEAU

CLEMENCEAU, GEORGES....SEE CLEMENCE/G

CLEMENTS R.V. B0435

CLEMHOUT S. B0436

CLEMSON....CLEMSON UNIVERSITY

CLEVELAND H. B0437

CLEVELAND....CLEVELAND, OHIO

CLEVELND/G....PRESIDENT GROVER CLEVELAND

CLIENT....CLIENTS, CLIENTELE (BUT NOT CUSTOMERS)

                                                                    B19
DUNN A.,SCIENTIFIC SELLING AND ADVERTISING. CLIENT   LG/CO
ADMIN DEMAND EFFICIENCY 20. PAGE 31 B0632   PERCEPT
                                                        PERS/REL
                                                        TASK

                                                                    B41
GELLHORN W.,FEDERAL ADMINISTRATIVE PROCEEDINGS.   EX/STRUC
USA+45 CLIENT FACE/GP NAT/G LOBBY REPRESENT PWR 20.   LAW
PAGE 39 B0788   ADJUD
                                                        POLICY

                                                                    B49
APPLEBY P.H.,,POLICY AND ADMINISTRATION. USA+45   REPRESENT
NAT/G LOBBY PWR 20. PAGE 6 B0116   EXEC
                                                        ADMIN
                                                        CLIENT

                                                                    B52
APPLEBY P.H.,,MORALITY AND ADMINISTRATION IN   REPRESENT
DEMOCRATIC GOVERNMENT. USA+45 CLIENT NAT/G EXEC   LOBBY
EFFICIENCY 20. PAGE 6 B0117   ADMIN
                                                        EX/STRUC

                                                                    B55
BLAU P.M.,THE DYNAMICS OF BUREAUCRACY: A STUDY OF   CLIENT
INTERPERSONAL RELATIONS IN TWO GOVERNMENT AGENCIES.   ADMIN
USA+45 EX/STRUC REPRESENT INGP/REL PERS/REL.   EXEC
PAGE 12 B0251   ROUTINE

                                                                    B56
FRANCIS R.G.,SERVICE AND PROCEDURE IN BUREAUCRACY.   CLIENT
EXEC LEAD ROUTINE...QU 20. PAGE 37 B0748   ADMIN
                                                        INGP/REL
                                                        REPRESENT

                                                                    B56
REDFORD E.S.,PUBLIC ADMINISTRATION AND POLICY   EX/STRUC
FORMATION: STUDIES IN OIL, GAS, BANKING, RIVER   PROB/SOLV
DEVELOPMENT AND CORPORATE INVESTIGATIONS. USA+45   CONTROL
CLIENT NAT/G ADMIN LOBBY REPRESENT GOV/REL INGP/REL   EXEC
20. PAGE 87 B1754

                                                                    B57
COOPER F.E.,THE LAWYER AND ADMINISTRATIVE AGENCIES.   CONSULT
USA+45 CLIENT LAW PROB/SOLV CT/SYS PERSON ROLE.   ADMIN
PAGE 23 B0473   ADJUD
                                                        DELIB/GP

                                                                    S57
JANOWITZ M.,,"THE BUREAUCRAT AND THE PUBLIC: A STUDY   REPRESENT
OF INFORMATIONAL PERSPECTIVES." USA+45 PROB/SOLV   ADMIN
ATTIT 20. PAGE 55 B1120   EX/STRUC
                                                        CLIENT

                                                                    S57
RAPAPORT R.N.,,"'DEMOCRATIZATION' AND AUTHORITY IN A   PUB/INST
THERAPEUTIC COMMUNITY." OP/RES ADMIN PARTIC CENTRAL   HEALTH
ATTIT...POLICY DECISION. PAGE 86 B1735   DOMIN
                                                        CLIENT

                                                                    B59
REDFORD E.S.,NATIONAL REGULATORY COMMISSIONS: NEED   REPRESENT
FOR A NEW LOOK (PAMPHLET). USA+45 CLIENT PROB/SOLV   CONTROL
ADJUD LOBBY EFFICIENCY...POLICY 20. PAGE 87 B1757   EXEC
                                                        NAT/G

                                                                    B61
ETZIONI A.,COMPLEX ORGANIZATIONS: A SOCIOLOGICAL   VOL/ASSN
READER. CLIENT CULTURE STRATA CREATE OP/RES ADMIN   STRUCT
...POLICY METH/CNCPT BUREAUCRCY. PAGE 34 B0683   CLASSIF
                                                        PROF/ORG

                                                                    S61
ABLARD C.D.,,"EX PARTE CONTACTS WITH FEDERAL   EXEC
ADMINISTRATIVE AGENCIES." USA+45 CLIENT NAT/G   ADJUD
DELIB/GP ADMIN PWR 20. PAGE 3 B0055   LOBBY
                                                        REPRESENT

                                                                    B62
CARSON P.,MATERIALS FOR WEST AFRICAN HISTORY IN THE   BIBLIOG/A

ARCHIVES OF BELGIUM AND HOLLAND. CLIENT INDUS
INT/TRADE ADMIN 17/19. PAGE 19 B0387
COLONIAL
AFR
ECO/UNDEV

B62
HATTERY L.H.,INFORMATION RETRIEVAL MANAGEMENT.
CLIENT INDUS TOP/EX COMPUTER OP/RES TEC/DEV ROUTINE
COST EFFICIENCY RIGID/FLEX...METH/COMP ANTHOL 20.
PAGE 48 B0968
R+D
COMPUT/IR
MGT
CREATE

B62
RUDOLPH F.,THE AMERICAN COLLEGE AND UNIVERSITY.
CLIENT FINAN PUB/INST DELIB/GP EDU/PROP CONTROL
EXEC CONSEN ATTIT POLICY. PAGE 92 B1853
ACADEM
INGP/REL
PWR
ADMIN

L62
CAVERS D.F.,"ADMINISTRATIVE DECISION-MAKING IN
NUCLEAR FACILITIES LICENSING." USA+45 CLIENT ADMIN
EXEC 20 AEC. PAGE 19 B0395
REPRESENT
LOBBY
PWR
CONTROL

B63
BERNE E.,THE STRUCTURE AND DYNAMICS OF
ORGANIZATIONS AND GROUPS. CLIENT PARTIC DRIVE
HEALTH...MGT PSY ORG/CHARTS. PAGE 11 B0226
INGP/REL
AUTHORIT
ROUTINE
CLASSIF

B63
DOUGLASS H.R.,MODERN ADMINISTRATION OF SECONDARY
SCHOOLS. CLIENT DELIB/GP WORKER REPRESENT INGP/REL
AUTHORIT...TREND BIBLIOG. PAGE 30 B0613
EDU/PROP
ADMIN
SCHOOL
MGT

S63
HILLS R.J.,"THE REPRESENTATIVE FUNCTION: NEGLECTED
DIMENSION OF LEADERSHIP BEHAVIOR" USA+45 CLIENT
STRUC SCHOOL PERS/REL...STAT QU SAMP LAB/EXP 20.
PAGE 50 B1012
LEAD
ADMIN
EXEC
ACT/RES

B64
EDELMAN M.,THE SYMBOLIC USES OF POWER. USA+45
EX/STRUC CONTROL GP/REL INGP/REL...MGT T. PAGE 32
B0653
CLIENT
PWR
EXEC
ELITES

B64
ETZIONI A.,MODERN ORGANIZATIONS. CLIENT STRUCT
DOMIN CONTROL LEAD PERS/REL AUTHORIT...CLASSIF
BUREAUCRCY. PAGE 34 B0685
MGT
ADMIN
PLAN
CULTURE

B65
COHEN H.,THE DEMONICS OF BUREAUCRACY: PROBLEMS OF
CHANGE IN A GOVERNMENT AGENCY. USA+45 CLIENT
ROUTINE REPRESENT 20. PAGE 22 B0443
EXEC
EX/STRUC
INGP/REL
ADMIN

B66
DICKSON W.J.,COUNSELING IN AN ORGANIZATION: A
SEQUEL TO THE HAWTHORNE RESEARCHES. CLIENT VOL/ASSN
ACT/RES PROB/SOLV AUTOMAT ROUTINE PERS/REL
HAPPINESS ANOMIE ROLE...OBS CHARTS 20 AT+T. PAGE 29
B0588
INDUS
WORKER
PSY
MGT

B66
RUBENSTEIN R.,THE SHARING OF POWER IN A PSYCHIATRIC
HOSPITAL. CLIENT PROF/ORG PUB/INST INGP/REL ATTIT
PWR...DECISION OBS RECORD. PAGE 91 B1847
ADMIN
PARTIC
HEALTH
CONCPT

B66
STREET D.,ORGANIZATION FOR TREATMENT. CLIENT PROVS
PUB/INST PLAN CONTROL PARTIC REPRESENT ATTIT PWR
...POLICY BIBLIOG. PAGE 101 B2052
GP/COMP
AGE/Y
ADMIN
VOL/ASSN

B67
BLUMBERG A.S.,CRIMINAL JUSTICE. USA+45 CLIENT LAW
LOC/G FORCES JUDGE ACT/RES LEGIT ADMIN RATIONAL
MYTH. PAGE 13 B0259
JURID
CT/SYS
PROF/ORG
CRIME

B67
GABRIEL P.P.,THE INTERNATIONAL TRANSFER OF
CORPORATE SKILLS: MANAGEMENT CONTRACTS IN LESS
DEVELOPED COUNTRIES. CLIENT INDUS LG/CO PLAN
PROB/SOLV CAP/ISM ECO/TAC FOR/AID INT/TRADE RENT
ADMIN SKILL 20. PAGE 38 B0771
ECO/UNDEV
AGREE
MGT
CONSULT

L67
BLUMBERG A.S.,"THE PRACTICE OF LAW AS CONFIDENCE
GAME: ORGANIZATIONAL COOPTATION OF A PROFESSION."
USA+45 CLIENT SOCIETY CONSULT ROLE JURID. PAGE 13
B0260
CT/SYS
ADJUD
GP/REL
ADMIN

CLIFFORD/C.,...CLARK CLIFFORD

CLIGNET R. B0438

CLIQUES....SEE FACE/GP

CLOKIE H.M. B0439

CLOUGH S.B. B0440

CLUBS....SEE VOL/ASSN, FACE/GP

CMA....CANADIAN MEDICAL ASSOCIATION

S60
TAYLOR M.G.,"THE ROLE OF THE MEDICAL PROFESSION IN
THE FORMULATION AND EXECUTION OF PUBLIC POLICY
(BMR)" CANADA NAT/G CONSULT ADMIN REPRESENT GP/REL
ROLE SOVEREIGN...DECISION 20 CMA. PAGE 103 B2088
PROF/ORG
HEALTH
LOBBY
POLICY

CMN/WLTH....BRITISH COMMONWEALTH OF NATIONS; SEE
ALSO VOL/ASSN, APPROPRIATE NATIONS, COMMONWLTH

B19
NATHAN M.,THE SOUTH AFRICAN COMMONWEALTH:
CONSTITUTION, PROBLEMS, SOCIAL CONDITIONS.
SOUTH/AFR UK CULTURE INDUS EX/STRUC LEGIS BUDGET
EDU/PROP ADMIN CT/SYS GP/REL RACE/REL...LING 19/20
CMN/WLTH. PAGE 77 B1559
CONSTN
NAT/G
POL/PAR
SOCIETY

N19
PERREN G.E.,LANGUAGE AND COMMUNICATION IN THE
COMMONWEALTH (PAMPHLET). FUT UK LAW ECO/DEV PRESS
TV WRITING ADJUD ADMIN COLONIAL CONTROL 20
CMN/WLTH. PAGE 82 B1660
EDU/PROP
LING
GOV/REL
COM/IND

B28
HALL W.P.,EMPIRE TO COMMONWEALTH. FUT WOR-45 CONSTN
ECO/DEV ECO/UNDEV INT/ORG PROVS PLAN DIPLOM
EDU/PROP ADMIN COLONIAL PEACE PERSON ALL/VALS
...POLICY GEOG SOC OBS RECORD TREND CMN/WLTH
PARLIAMENT 19/20. PAGE 46 B0925
VOL/ASSN
NAT/G
UK

B36
ROBINSON H.,DEVELOPMENT OF THE BRITISH EMPIRE.
WOR-45 CULTURE SOCIETY STRUCT ECO/DEV ECO/UNDEV
INT/ORG VOL/ASSN FORCES CREATE PLAN DOMIN EDU/PROP
ADMIN COLONIAL PWR WEALTH...POLICY GEOG CHARTS
CMN/WLTH 16/20. PAGE 89 B1800
NAT/G
HIST/WRIT
UK

L44
HAILEY,"THE FUTURE OF COLONIAL PEOPLES." WOR-45
CONSTN CULTURE ECO/UNDEV AGRI MARKET INT/ORG NAT/G
SECT CONSULT ECO/TAC LEGIT ADMIN NAT/LISM ALL/VALS
...SOC OBS TREND STERTYP CMN/WLTH LEAGUE/NAT
PARLIAMENT 20. PAGE 45 B0916
PLAN
CONCPT
DIPLOM
UK

B46
GRIFFIN G.G.,A GUIDE TO MANUSCRIPTS RELATING TO
AMERICAN HISTORY IN BRITISH DEPOSITORIES. CANADA
IRELAND MOD/EUR UK USA-45 LAW DIPLOM ADMIN COLONIAL
WAR NAT/LISM SOVEREIGN...GEOG INT/LAW 15/19
CMN/WLTH. PAGE 43 B0876
BIBLIOG/A
ALL/VALS
NAT/G

B50
WADE E.C.S.,CONSTITUTIONAL LAW: AN OUTLINE OF THE
LAW AND PRACTICE OF THE CONSTITUTION. UK LEGIS
DOMIN ADMIN GP/REL 16/20 CMN/WLTH PARLIAMENT
ENGLSH/LAW. PAGE 112 B2269
CONSTN
NAT/G
PARL/PROC
LAW

S56
KHAMA T.,"POLITICAL CHANGE IN AFRICAN SOCIETY."
CONSTN SOCIETY LOC/G NAT/G POL/PAR EX/STRUC LEGIS
LEGIT ADMIN CHOOSE REPRESENT NAT/LISM MORAL
ORD/FREE PWR...CONCPT OBS TREND GEN/METH CMN/WLTH
17/20. PAGE 59 B1201
AFR
ELITES

C56
NEUMANN S.,"MODERN POLITICAL PARTIES: APPROACHES TO
COMPARATIVE POLITIC. FRANCE UK EX/STRUC DOMIN ADMIN
LEAD REPRESENT TOTALISM ATTIT...POLICY TREND
METH/COMP ANTHOL BIBLIOG/A 20 CMN/WLTH. PAGE 78
B1574
POL/PAR
GOV/COMP
ELITES
MAJORIT

S57
HAILEY,"TOMORROW IN AFRICA." CONSTN SOCIETY LOC/G
NAT/G DOMIN ADJUD ADMIN GP/REL DISCRIM NAT/LISM
ATTIT MORAL ORD/FREE...PSY SOC CONCPT OBS RECORD
TREND GEN/LAWS CMN/WLTH 20. PAGE 45 B0917
AFR
PERSON
ELITES
RACE/REL

S58
MAIR L.P.,"REPRESENTATIVE LOCAL GOVERNMENT AS A
PROBLEM IN SOCIAL CHANGE." ECO/UNDEV KIN LOC/G
NAT/G SCHOOL JUDGE ADMIN ROUTINE REPRESENT
RIGID/FLEX RESPECT...CONCPT STERTYP CMN/WLTH 20.
PAGE 68 B1383
AFR
PWR
ELITES

C58
WILDING N.,"AN ENCYCLOPEDIA OF PARLIAMENT." UK LAW
CONSTN CHIEF PROB/SOLV DIPLOM DEBATE WAR INGP/REL
PRIVIL...BIBLIOG DICTIONARY 13/20 CMN/WLTH
PARLIAMENT. PAGE 116 B2350
PARL/PROC
POL/PAR
NAT/G
ADMIN

B60
WHEARE K.C.,THE CONSTITUTIONAL STRUCTURE OF THE
COMMONWEALTH. UK EX/STRUC DIPLOM DOMIN ADMIN
COLONIAL CONTROL LEAD INGP/REL SUPEGO 20 CMN/WLTH.
PAGE 115 B2330
CONSTN
INT/ORG
VOL/ASSN
SOVEREIGN

B61
CARNEY D.E.,GOVERNMENT AND ECONOMY IN BRITISH WEST
AFRICA. GAMBIA GHANA NIGERIA SIER/LEONE DOMIN ADMIN
GOV/REL SOVEREIGN WEALTH LAISSEZ...BIBLIOG 20
CMN/WLTH. PAGE 19 B0384
METH/COMP
COLONIAL
ECO/TAC
ECO/UNDEV

B61
HICKS U.K.,DEVELOPMENT FROM BELOW. UK INDUS ADMIN
COLONIAL ROUTINE GOV/REL...POLICY METH/CNCPT CHARTS
19/20 CMN/WLTH. PAGE 50 B1006
ECO/UNDEV
LOC/G
GOV/COMP
METH/COMP

S61
ANGLIN D.,"UNITED STATES OPPOSITION TO CANADIAN
MEMBERSHIP IN THE PAN AMERICAN UNION: A CANADIAN
VIEW." L/A+17C UK USA+45 VOL/ASSN DELIB/GP EX/STRUC
PLAN DIPLOM DOMIN REGION ATTIT RIGID/FLEX PWR
INT/ORG
CANADA

...RELATIV CONCPT STERTYP CMN/WLTH OAS 20. PAGE 5
B0112

B62
TAYLOR D.,THE BRITISH IN AFRICA. UK CULTURE   AFR
ECO/UNDEV INDUS DIPLOM INT/TRADE ADMIN WAR RACE/REL   COLONIAL
ORD/FREE SOVEREIGN...POLICY BIBLIOG 15/20 CMN/WLTH.   DOMIN
PAGE 103 B2084

S62
SPRINGER H.W.,"FEDERATION IN THE CARIBBEAN: AN   VOL/ASSN
ATTEMPT THAT FAILED." L/A+17C ECO/UNDEV INT/ORG   NAT/G
POL/PAR PROVS LEGIS CREATE PLAN LEGIT ADMIN FEDERAL   REGION
ATTIT DRIVE PERSON ORD/FREE PWR...POLICY GEOG PSY
CONCPT OBS CARIBBEAN CMN/WLTH 20. PAGE 100 B2013

B63
HEUSSLER R.,YESTERDAY'S RULERS: THE MAKING OF THE   EX/STRUC
BRITISH COLONIAL SERVICE. AFR EUR+WWI UK STRATA   MORAL
SECT DELIB/GP PWR DOMIN EDU/PROP ATTIT PERCEPT   ELITES
PERSON SUPEGO KNOWL ORD/FREE PWR...MGT SOC OBS INT
TIME/SEQ 20 CMN/WLTH. PAGE 49 B1000

B63
MCKIE R.,MALAYSIA IN FOCUS. INDONESIA WOR+45   S/ASIA
ECO/UNDEV FINAN NAT/G POL/PAR SECT FORCES PLAN   NAT/LISM
ADMIN COLONIAL COERCE DRIVE ALL/VALS...POLICY   MALAYSIA
RECORD CENSUS TIME/SEQ CMN/WLTH 20. PAGE 72 B1453

B64
NATIONAL BOOK LEAGUE,THE COMMONWEALTH IN BOOKS: AN   BIBLIOG/A
ANNOTATED LIST. CANADA UK LOC/G SECT ADMIN...SOC   JURID
BIOG 20 CMN/WLTH. PAGE 77 B1561   NAT/G

B64
THE BRITISH COUNCIL,PUBLIC ADMINISTRATION: A SELECT   BIBLIOG
LIST OF BOOKS AND PERIODICALS. LAW CONSTN FINAN   ADMIN
POL/PAR SCHOOL CHOOSE...HEAL MGT METH/COMP 19/20   LOC/G
CMN/WLTH. PAGE 104 B2094   INDUS

B64
WAINHOUSE D.W.,REMNANTS OF EMPIRE: THE UNITED   INT/ORG
NATIONS AND THE END OF COLONIALISM. FUT PORTUGAL   TREND
WOR+45 CONSULT DOMIN LEGIT ADMIN ROUTINE   COLONIAL
ATTIT ORD/FREE...POLICY JURID RECORD INT TIME/SEQ
UN CMN/WLTH 20. PAGE 113 B2275

L64
SYMONDS R.,"REFLECTIONS IN LOCALISATION." AFR   ADMIN
S/ASIA UK STRATA INT/ORG NAT/G SCHOOL EDU/PROP   MGT
LEGIT KNOWL ORD/FREE PWR RESPECT CMN/WLTH 20.   COLONIAL
PAGE 102 B2064

S64
GROSS J.A.,"WHITEHALL AND THE COMMONWEALTH."   EX/STRUC
EUR+WWI MOD/EUR INT/ORG NAT/G CONSULT DELIB/GP   ATTIT
LEGIS DOMIN ADMIN COLONIAL ROUTINE PWR CMN/WLTH   TREND
19/20. PAGE 44 B0890

B67
ROFF W.R.,THE ORIGINS OF MALAY NATIONALISM.   NAT/LISM
MALAYSIA INTELL NAT/G ADMIN COLONIAL...BIBLIOG   ELITES
DICTIONARY 20 CMN/WLTH. PAGE 90 B1813   VOL/ASSN
                                                       SOCIETY

COALITIONS....SEE VOL/ASSN+POL

COASTGUARD....COAST GUARD

COBB/HOWLL....HOWELL COBB

B50
MONTGOMERY H.,CRACKER PARTIES. CULTURE EX/STRUC   POL/PAR
LEAD PWR POPULISM...TIME/SEQ 19 GEORGIA CALHOUN/JC   PROVS
COBB/HOWLL JACKSON/A. PAGE 74 B1505   ELITES
                                                       BIOG

COCH L. B0441

COERCE....COERCION, VIOLENCE; SEE ALSO FORCES,
    PROCESSES AND PRACTICES INDEX, PART G, P. XIII

B00
MORRIS H.C.,THE HISTORY OF COLONIZATION. WOR+45   DOMIN
WOR-45 ECO/DEV ECO/UNDEV INT/ORG ACT/RES PLAN   SOVEREIGN
ECO/TAC LEGIT ROUTINE COERCE ATTIT DRIVE ALL/VALS   COLONIAL
...GEOG TREND 19. PAGE 76 B1528

B20
HALDANE R.B.,BEFORE THE WAR. MOD/EUR SOCIETY   POLICY
INT/ORG NAT/G DELIB/GP PLAN DOMIN EDU/PROP LEGIT   DIPLOM
ADMIN COERCE ATTIT DRIVE MORAL ORD/FREE PWR...SOC   UK
CONCPT SELF/OBS RECORD BIOG TIME/SEQ. PAGE 45 B0921

B38
PETTEE G.S.,THE PROCESS OF REVOLUTION. COM FRANCE   COERCE
ITALY MOD/EUR RUSSIA SPAIN WOR-45 ELITES INTELL   CONCPT
SOCIETY STRATA STRUCT INT/ORG NAT/G POL/PAR ACT/RES   REV
PLAN EDU/PROP LEGIT EXEC...SOC MYTH TIME/SEQ
TOT/POP 18/20. PAGE 82 B1664

B39
HITLER A.,MEIN KAMPF. EUR+WWI FUT MOD/EUR STRUCT   PWR
INT/ORG LABOR NAT/G POL/PAR FORCES CREATE PLAN   NEW/IDEA
BAL/PWR DIPLOM ECO/TAC DOMIN EDU/PROP ADMIN COERCE   WAR
ATTIT...SOCIALIST BIOG TREND NAZI. PAGE 50 B1020

B39
ZIMMERN A.,MODERN POLITICAL DOCTRINE. WOR-45   NAT/G
CULTURE SOCIETY ECO/UNDEV DELIB/GP EX/STRUC CREATE   ECO/TAC
DOMIN COERCE NAT/LISM ATTIT RIGID/FLEX ORD/FREE PWR   BAL/PWR
WEALTH...POLICY CONCPT OBS TIME/SEQ TREND TOT/POP   INT/TRADE
LEAGUE/NAT 20. PAGE 119 B2402

S41
ABEL T.,"THE ELEMENT OF DECISION IN THE PATTERN OF   TEC/DEV
WAR." EUR+WWI FUT NAT/G TOP/EX DIPLOM ROUTINE   FORCES
COERCE DISPL PERCEPT PWR...SOC METH/CNCPT HIST/WRIT   WAR
TREND GEN/LAWS 20. PAGE 2 B0051

B48
ROSSITER C.L.,CONSTITUTIONAL DICTATORSHIP; CRISIS   NAT/G
GOVERNMENT IN THE MODERN DEMOCRACIES. FRANCE   AUTHORIT
GERMANY UK USA-45 WOR-45 EX/STRUC BAL/PWR CONTROL   CONSTN
COERCE WAR CENTRAL ORD/FREE...DECISION 19/20.   TOTALISM
PAGE 90 B1828

B48
TOWSTER J.,POLITICAL POWER IN THE USSR: 1917-1947.   EX/STRUC
USSR CONSTN CULTURE ELITES CREATE PLAN COERCE   NAT/G
CENTRAL ATTIT RIGID/FLEX ORD/FREE...BIBLIOG   MARXISM
SOC/INTEG 20 LENIN/VI STALIN/J. PAGE 105 B2124   PWR

B49
BUSH V.,MODERN ARMS AND FREE MEN. WOR-45 SOCIETY   TEC/DEV
NAT/G ECO/TAC DOMIN LEGIT EXEC COERCE DETER ATTIT   FORCES
DRIVE ORD/FREE PWR...CONCPT MYTH COLD/WAR 20   NUC/PWR
COLD/WAR. PAGE 18 B0361   WAR

B51
LEITES N.,THE OPERATIONAL CODE OF THE POLITBURO.   DELIB/GP
COM USSR CREATE PLAN DOMIN LEGIT COERCE ALL/VALS   ADMIN
...SOC CONCPT MYTH TREND CON/ANAL GEN/LAWS 20   SOCISM
LENIN/VI STALIN/J. PAGE 64 B1284

B52
BRINTON C.,THE ANATOMY OF REVOLUTION. FRANCE UK   SOCIETY
USA-45 USSR WOR-45 ELITES INTELL ECO/DEV NAT/G   CONCPT
EX/STRUC FORCES COERCE DRIVE ORD/FREE PWR SOVEREIGN   REV
...MYTH HIST/WRIT GEN/LAWS. PAGE 15 B0311

C52
LASSWELL H.D.,"THE COMPARATIVE STUDY OF ELITES: AN   ELITES
INTRODUCTION AND BIBLIOGRAPHY." STRATA POL/PAR   LEAD
EDU/PROP ADMIN LOBBY COERCE ATTIT PERSON PWR   CONCPT
...BIBLIOG 20. PAGE 63 B1270   DOMIN

B53
MEYER P.,THE JEWS IN THE SOVIET SATELLITES.   COM
CZECHOSLVK POLAND SOCIETY STRATA NAT/G BAL/PWR   SECT
ECO/TAC EDU/PROP LEGIT ADMIN COERCE ATTIT DISPL   TOTALISM
PERCEPT HEALTH PWR RESPECT WEALTH...METH/CNCPT JEWS   USSR
VAL/FREE NAZI 20. PAGE 73 B1474

L54
ROSTOW W.W.,"ASIAN LEADERSHIP AND FREE-WORLD   ATTIT
ALLIANCE." ASIA COM USA+45 CULTURE ELITES INTELL   LEGIT
NAT/G TEC/DEV ECO/TAC EDU/PROP COLONIAL PARL/PROC   DIPLOM
ROUTINE COERCE DRIVE ORD/FREE MARXISM...PSY CONCPT.
PAGE 90 B1829

B55
UN HEADQUARTERS LIBRARY,BIBLIOGRAPHIE DE LA CHARTE   BIBLIOG/A
DES NATIONS UNIES. CHINA/COM KOREA WOR+45 VOL/ASSN   INT/ORG
CONFER ADMIN COERCE PEACE ATTIT ORD/FREE SOVEREIGN   DIPLOM
...INT/LAW 20 UNESCO UN. PAGE 106 B2149

B56
KAUFMANN W.W.,MILITARY POLICY AND NATIONAL   FORCES
SECURITY. USA+45 ELITES INTELL NAT/G TOP/EX PLAN   CREATE
BAL/PWR DIPLOM ROUTINE COERCE NUC/PWR ATTIT
ORD/FREE PWR 20 COLD/WAR. PAGE 58 B1182

B57
DJILAS M.,THE NEW CLASS: AN ANALYSIS OF THE   COM
COMMUNIST SYSTEM. STRATA CAP/ISM ECO/TAC DOMIN   POL/PAR
EDU/PROP LEGIT EXEC COERCE ATTIT PWR MARXISM   USSR
...MARXIST MGT CONCPT TIME/SEQ GEN/LAWS 20. PAGE 29   YUGOSLAVIA
B0600

L57
HAAS E.B.,"REGIONAL INTEGRATION AND NATIONAL   INT/ORG
POLICY." WOR+45 VOL/ASSN DELIB/GP EX/STRUC ECO/TAC   ORD/FREE
DOMIN EDU/PROP LEGIT COERCE ATTIT PERCEPT KNOWL   REGION
...TIME/SEQ COLD/WAR 20 UN. PAGE 45 B0908

S57
BAUER R.A.,"BRAINWASHING: PSYCHOLOGY OR   EDU/PROP
DEMONOLOGY." ASIA CHINA/COM COM POL/PAR ECO/TAC   PSY
ADMIN COERCE ATTIT DRIVE ORD/FREE...CONCPT MYTH 20.   TOTALISM
PAGE 10 B0196

C57
TANG P.S.H.,"COMMUNIST CHINA TODAY: DOMESTIC AND   POL/PAR
FOREIGN POLICIES." CHINA/COM COM S/ASIA USSR STRATA   LEAD
FORCES DIPLOM EDU/PROP COERCE GOV/REL...POLICY   ADMIN
MAJORIT BIBLIOG 20. PAGE 102 B2071   CONSTN

S58
STAAR R.F.,"ELECTIONS IN COMMUNIST POLAND." EUR+WWI   COM
SOCIETY NAT/G POL/PAR LEGIS ACT/RES ECO/TAC CHOOSE   CHOOSE
EDU/PROP ADJUD ADMIN ROUTINE COERCE TOTALISM ATTIT   POLAND
ORD/FREE PWR 20. PAGE 100 B2015

B59
BHAMBHRI C.P.,SUBSTANCE OF HINDU POLITY. INDIA   GOV/REL
S/ASIA LAW EX/STRUC JUDGE TAX COERCE GP/REL   WRITING
POPULISM 20 HINDU. PAGE 11 B0234   SECT
                                                       PROVS

B59

DAHRENDORF R.,CLASS AND CLASS CONFLICT IN INDUSTRIAL SOCIETY. LABOR NAT/G COERCE ROLE PLURISM ...POLICY MGT CONCPT CLASSIF. PAGE 26 B0523
VOL/ASSN STRUCT SOC GP/REL

B59

GOODRICH L.,THE UNITED NATIONS. WOR+45 CONSTN STRUCT ACT/RES LEGIT COERCE KNOWL ORD/FREE PWR ...GEN/LAWS UN 20. PAGE 41 B0825
INT/ORG ROUTINE

B59

GRABER D.,CRISIS DIPLOMACY. L/A+17C USA+45 USA-45 NAT/G TOP/EX ECO/TAC COERCE ATTIT ORD/FREE...CONCPT MYTH TIME/SEQ COLD/WAR 20. PAGE 42 B0848
ROUTINE MORAL DIPLOM

B59

JANOWITZ M.,SOCIOLOGY AND THE MILITARY ESTABLISHMENT. USA+45 WOR+45 CULTURE SOCIETY PROF/ORG CONSULT EX/STRUC PLAN TEC/DEV DIPLOM DOMIN COERCE DRIVE RIGID/FLEX ORD/FREE PWR SKILL COLD/WAR 20. PAGE 55 B1121
FORCES SOC

S59

LASSWELL H.D.,"UNIVERSALITY IN PERSPECTIVE." FUT UNIV SOCIETY CONSULT TOP/EX PLAN EDU/PROP ADJUD ROUTINE ARMS/CONT COERCE PEACE ATTIT PERSON ALL/VALS. PAGE 63 B1271
INT/ORG JURID TOTALISM

S59

SOHN L.B.,"THE DEFINITION OF AGGRESSION." FUT LAW FORCES LEGIT ADJUD ROUTINE COERCE ORD/FREE PWR ...MAJORIT JURID QUANT COLD/WAR 20. PAGE 99 B1995
INT/ORG CT/SYS DETER SOVEREIGN

B60

DRAPER T.,AMERICAN COMMUNISM AND SOVIET RUSSIA. EUR+WWI USA+45 USSR COM/IND COM/IND INDUS LABOR PROF/ORG VOL/ASSN PLAN TEC/DEV DOMIN EDU/PROP ADMIN COERCE REV PERSON PWR...POLICY CONCPT MYTH 19/20. PAGE 30 B0617
COM POL/PAR

B60

GRUNDLICH T.,DIE TECHNIK DER DIKTATUR. ADMIN TOTALISM ATTIT PWR...MGT CONCPT ARISTOTLE. PAGE 44 B0896
COERCE DOMIN ORD/FREE WAR

B60

HAYEK F.A.,THE CONSTITUTION OF LIBERTY. UNIV LAW CONSTN WORKER TAX EDU/PROP ADMIN CT/SYS COERCE DISCRIM...IDEA/COMP 20. PAGE 48 B0974
ORD/FREE CHOOSE NAT/G CONCPT

B60

LENCZOWSKI G.,OIL AND STATE IN THE MIDDLE EAST. FUT IRAN LAW ECO/UNDEV EXTR/IND NAT/G TOP/EX PLAN TEC/DEV ECO/TAC LEGIT ADMIN COERCE ATTIT ALL/VALS PWR...CHARTS 20. PAGE 64 B1288
ISLAM INDUS NAT/LISM

B60

SOUTH AFRICAN CONGRESS OF DEM,FACE THE FUTURE. SOUTH/AFR ELITES LEGIS ADMIN REGION COERCE PEACE ATTIT 20. PAGE 99 B1999
RACE/REL DISCRIM CONSTN NAT/G

L60

BRENNAN D.G.,"SETTING AND GOALS OF ARMS CONTROL." FUT USA+45 USSR WOR+45 INTELL INT/ORG NAT/G VOL/ASSN CONSULT PLAN DIPLOM ECO/TAC ADMIN KNOWL PWR...POLICY CONCPT TREND COLD/WAR 20. PAGE 15 B0305
FORCES COERCE ARMS/CONT DETER

S60

HERZ J.H.,"EAST GERMANY: PROGRESS AND PROSPECTS." COM AGRI FINAN INDUS LOC/G NAT/G FORCES PLAN TEC/DEV DOMIN ADMIN COERCE DRIVE PERCEPT RIGID/FLEX MORAL ORD/FREE PWR...MARXIST PSY SOC RECORD STERTYP WORK. PAGE 49 B0997
POL/PAR STRUCT GERMANY

S60

NORTH R.C.,"DIE DISKREPANZ ZWISCHEN REALITAT UND WUNSCHBILD ALS INNENPOLITISCHER FAKTOR." ASIA CHINA/COM COM FUT ECO/UNDEV NAT/G PLAN DOMIN ADMIN COERCE PERCEPT...SOC MYTH GEN/METH WORK TOT/POP 20. PAGE 79 B1589
SOCIETY ECO/TAC

S60

SCHACHTER O.,"THE ENFORCEMENT OF INTERNATIONAL JUDICIAL AND ARBITRAL DECISIONS." WOR+45 NAT/G ECO/TAC DOMIN LEGIT ROUTINE COERCE ATTIT DRIVE ALL/VALS PWR...METH/CNCPT TREND TOT/POP 20 UN. PAGE 93 B1878
INT/ORG ADJUD INT/LAW

S60

SCHWARTZ B.,"THE INTELLIGENTSIA IN COMMUNIST CHINA: A TENTATIVE COMPARISON." ASIA CHINA/COM COM RUSSIA ELITES SOCIETY STRATA POL/PAR VOL/ASSN CREATE ADMIN COERCE NAT/LISM TOTALISM...POLICY TREND 20. PAGE 95 B1914
INTELL RIGID/FLEX REV

S60

THOMPSON K.W.,"MORAL PURPOSE IN FOREIGN POLICY: REALITIES AND ILLUSIONS." WOR+45 WOR-45 LAW CULTURE SOCIETY INT/ORG PLAN ADJUD ADMIN COERCE RIGID/FLEX SUPEGO KNOWL ORD/FREE PWR...SOC TREND SOC/EXP TOT/POP 20. PAGE 104 B2104
MORAL JURID DIPLOM

C60

MCCLEERY R.,"COMMUNICATION PATTERNS AS BASES OF SYSTEMS OF AUTHORITY AND POWER" IN THEORETICAL STUDIES IN SOCIAL ORGAN. OF PRISON-BMR. USA+45 SOCIETY STRUCT EDU/PROP ADMIN CONTROL COERCE CRIME
PERS/REL PUB/INST PWR DOMIN

GP/REL AUTHORIT...SOC 20. PAGE 71 B1443

B61

BISHOP D.G.,THE ADMINISTRATION OF BRITISH FOREIGN RELATIONS. EUR+WWI MOD/EUR INT/ORG NAT/G POL/PAR DELIB/GP LEGIS TOP/EX ECO/TAC DOMIN EDU/PROP ADMIN COERCE 20. PAGE 12 B0243
ROUTINE PWR DIPLOM UK

B61

KOESTLER A.,THE LOTUS AND THE ROBOT. ASIA INDIA S/ASIA SOCIETY STRATA ECO/DEV AGRI INDUS FAM CREATE DOMIN EDU/PROP ADMIN COERCE ATTIT DRIVE SUPEGO ORD/FREE PWR RESPECT WEALTH...MYTH OBS 20 CHINJAP. PAGE 61 B1226
SECT ECO/UNDEV

B61

MONAS S.,THE THIRD SECTION: POLICE AND SOCIETY IN RUSSIA UNDER NICHOLAS I. MOD/EUR RUSSIA ELITES STRUCT NAT/G EX/STRUC ADMIN CONTROL PWR CONSERVE ...DECISION 19 NICHOLAS/I. PAGE 74 B1499
ORD/FREE COM FORCES COERCE

B61

STONE J.,QUEST FOR SURVIVAL. WOR+45 NAT/G VOL/ASSN LEGIT ADMIN ARMS/CONT COERCE DISPL ORD/FREE PWR ...POLICY INT/LAW JURID COLD/WAR 20. PAGE 101 B2047
INT/ORG ADJUD SOVEREIGN

S61

DEVINS J.H.,"THE INITIATIVE." COM USA+45 USA-45 USSR SOCIETY NAT/G ACT/RES CREATE BAL/PWR ROUTINE COERCE DETER RIGID/FLEX SKILL...STERTYP COLD/WAR 20. PAGE 29 B0582
FORCES CONCPT WAR

B62

FOSS P.O.,REORGANIZATION AND REASSIGNMENT IN THE CALIFORNIA HIGHWAY PATROL (PAMPHLET). USA+45 STRUCT WORKER EDU/PROP CONTROL COERCE INGP/REL ORD/FREE PWR...DECISION 20 CALIFORNIA. PAGE 37 B0744
FORCES ADMIN PROVS PLAN

B62

MULLEY F.W.,THE POLITICS OF WESTERN DEFENSE. EUR+WWI USA-45 WOR+45 VOL/ASSN EX/STRUC FORCES COERCE DETER PEACE ATTIT ORD/FREE PWR...RECORD TIME/SEQ CHARTS COLD/WAR 20 NATO. PAGE 76 B1537
INT/ORG DELIB/GP NUC/PWR

S62

FESLER J.W.,"FRENCH FIELD ADMINISTRATION: THE BEGINNINGS." CHRIST-17C CULTURE SOCIETY STRATA NAT/G ECO/TAC DOMIN EDU/PROP LEGIT ADJUD COERCE ATTIT ALL/VALS...TIME/SEQ CON/ANAL GEN/METH VAL/FREE 13/15. PAGE 35 B0714
EX/STRUC FRANCE

S62

JACOBSON H.K.,"THE UNITED NATIONS AND COLONIALISM: A TENTATIVE APPRAISAL." AFR FUT S/ASIA USA+45 USSR WOR+45 NAT/G DELIB/GP PLAN DIPLOM ECO/TAC DOMIN ADMIN ROUTINE COERCE ATTIT RIGID/FLEX ORD/FREE PWR ...OBS STERTYP UN 20. PAGE 55 B1115
INT/ORG CONCPT COLONIAL

S62

MARTIN L.W.,"POLITICAL SETTLEMENTS AND ARMS CONTROL." COM EUR+WWI GERMANY USA+45 PROVS FORCES TOP/EX ACT/RES CREATE DOMIN LEGIT ROUTINE COERCE ATTIT RIGID/FLEX ORD/FREE PWR...METH/CNCPT RECORD GEN/LAWS 20. PAGE 70 B1410
CONCPT ARMS/CONT

B63

DIESNER H.J.,KIRCHE UND STAAT IM SPATROMISCHEN REICH. ROMAN/EMP EX/STRUC COLONIAL COERCE ATTIT CATHISM 4/5 AFRICA/N CHURCH/STA. PAGE 29 B0592
SECT GP/REL DOMIN JURID

B63

FISHER S.N.,THE MILITARY IN THE MIDDLE EAST: PROBLEMS IN SOCIETY AND GOVERNMENT. ISLAM USA+45 NAT/G DOMIN LEGIT COERCE ORD/FREE PWP...TIME/SEQ VAL/FREE 20. PAGE 36 B0725
EX/STRUC FORCES

B63

LEWIS J.W.,LEADERSHIP IN COMMUNIST CHINA. ASIA INTELL ECO/UNDEV LOC/G MUNIC NAT/G PROVS ECO/TAC EDU/PROP LEGIT ADMIN COERCE ATTIT ORD/FREE PWR ...INT TIME/SEQ CHARTS TOT/POP VAL/FREE. PAGE 65 B1304
POL/PAR DOMIN ELITES

B63

MCKIE R.,MALAYSIA IN FOCUS. INDONESIA WOR+45 ECO/UNDEV FINAN NAT/G POL/PAR SECT FORCES PLAN ADMIN COLONIAL COERCE DRIVE ALL/VALS...POLICY RECORD CENSUS TIME/SEQ CMN/WLTH 20. PAGE 72 B1453
S/ASIA NAT/LISM MALAYSIA

B63

NORTH R.C.,CONTENT ANALYSIS: A HANDBOOK WITH APPLICATIONS FOR THE STUDY OF INTERNATIONAL CRISIS. ASIA COM EUR+WWI MOD/EUR INT/ORG TEC/DEV DOMIN EDU/PROP ROUTINE COERCE PERCEPT RIGID/FLEX ALL/VALS ...QUANT TESTS CON/ANAL SIMUL GEN/LAWS VAL/FREE. PAGE 79 B1591
METH/CNCPT COMPUT/IR USSR

B63

TUCKER R.C.,THE SOVIET POLITICAL MIND. COM INTELL NAT/G TOP/EX EDU/PROP ADMIN COERCE TOTALISM ATTIT PWR MARXISM...PSY MYTH HYPO/EXP 20. PAGE 106 B2135
STRUCT RIGID/FLEX ELITES USSR

L63

EMERSON R.,"POLITICAL MODERNIZATION." WOR+45 CULTURE ECO/UNDEV NAT/G FORCES ECO/TAC DOMIN EDU/PROP LEGIT ADMIN COERCE ALL/VALS...CONCPT TIME/SEQ VAL/FREE 20. PAGE 33 B0672
POL/PAR ADMIN

L63

SPITZ A.A.,"DEVELOPMENT ADMINISTRATION: AN ANNOTATED BIBLIOGRAPHY." WOR+45 CULTURE SOCIETY STRATA DELIB/GP EX/STRUC TOP/EX ACT/RES ECO/TAC
ADMIN ECO/UNDEV

DOMIN EDU/PROP LEGIT COERCE ATTIT ALL/VALS...MGT
VAL/FREE. PAGE 99 B2009

S63
BACHRACH P.,"DECISIONS AND NONDECISIONS: AN   PWR
ANALYTICAL FRAMEWORK." UNIV SOCIETY CREATE LEGIT   HYPO/EXP
ADMIN EXEC COERCE...DECISION PSY CONCPT CHARTS.
PAGE 8 B0156

S63
BOWIE R.,"STRATEGY AND THE ATLANTIC ALLIANCE."   FORCES
EUR+WWI VOL/ASSN BAL/PWR COERCE NUC/PWR ATTIT   ROUTINE
ORD/FREE PWR...DECISION GEN/LAWS NATO COLD/WAR 20.
PAGE 14 B0287

S63
DELLIN L.A.D.,"BULGARIA UNDER SOVIET LEADERSHIP."   AGRI
BULGARIA COM USA+45 USSR ECO/DEV INDUS POL/PAR   NAT/G
EX/STRUC TOP/EX COERCE ATTIT RIGID/FLEX...POLICY   TOTALISM
TIME/SEQ 20. PAGE 28 B0572

S63
HARRIS R.L.,"A COMPARATIVE ANALYSIS OF THE   DELIB/GP
ADMINISTRATIVE SYSTEMS OF CANADA AND CEYLON."   EX/STRUC
S/ASIA CULTURE SOCIETY STRATA TOP/EX ACT/RES DOMIN   CANADA
EDU/PROP LEGIT COERCE ATTIT SUPEGO ALL/VALS...MGT   CEYLON
CHARTS GEN/LAWS VAL/FREE 20. PAGE 47 B0955

S63
RUSTOW D.A.,"THE MILITARY IN MIDDLE EASTERN SOCIETY   FORCES
AND POLITICS." FUT ISLAM CONSTN SOCIETY FACE/GP   ELITES
NAT/G POL/PAR PROF/ORG CONSULT DOMIN ADMIN EXEC
REGION COERCE NAT/LISM ATTIT DRIVE PERSON ORD/FREE
PWR...POLICY CONCPT OBS STERTYP 20. PAGE 92 B1860

S63
SCHMITT H.A.,"THE EUROPEAN COMMUNITIES." EUR+WWI   VOL/ASSN
FRANCE DELIB/GP EX/STRUC TOP/EX CREATE TEC/DEV   ECO/DEV
ECO/TAC LEGIT REGION COERCE DRIVE ALL/VALS
...METH/CNCPT EEC 20. PAGE 94 B1897

S63
SHIMKIN D.B.,"STRUCTURE OF SOVIET POWER." COM FUT   PWR
USA+45 USSR WOR+45 NAT/G FORCES ECO/DEV DOMIN EXEC
COERCE CHOOSE ATTIT WEALTH...TIME/SEQ COLD/WAR
TOT/POP VAL/FREE 20. PAGE 96 B1948

B64
BANTON M.,THE POLICEMAN IN THE COMMUNITY. UK USA+45   FORCES
STRUCT PROF/ORG WORKER LOBBY ROUTINE COERCE CROWD   ADMIN
GP/REL ADJUST DISCRIM PERCEPT 20. PAGE 9 B0181   ROLE
                                                      RACE/REL
B64
BLACKSTOCK P.W.,THE STRATEGY OF SUBVERSION. USA+45   ORD/FREE
FORCES EDU/PROP ADMIN COERCE GOV/REL...DECISION MGT   DIPLOM
20 DEPT/DEFEN CIA DEPT/STATE. PAGE 12 B0247   CONTROL

B64
NEUSTADT R.,PRESIDENTIAL POWER. USA+45 CONSTN NAT/G   TOP/EX
CHIEF LEGIS CREATE EDU/PROP LEGIT ADMIN EXEC COERCE   SKILL
ATTIT PERSON RIGID/FLEX PWR CONGRESS 20 PRESIDENT
TRUMAN/HS EISNHWR/DD. PAGE 78 B1575

B64
PIPES R.,THE FORMATION OF THE SOVIET UNION. EUR+WWI   COM
MOD/EUR STRUCT ECO/UNDEV NAT/G LEGIS DOMIN LEGIT   USSR
CT/SYS EXEC COERCE ALL/VALS...POLICY RELATIV   RUSSIA
HIST/WRIT TIME/SEQ TOT/POP 19/20. PAGE 83 B1677

L64
ROTBERG R.,"THE FEDERATION MOVEMENT IN BRITISH EAST   VOL/ASSN
AND CENTRAL AFRICA." AFR RHODESIA UGANDA ECO/UNDEV   PWR
NAT/G POL/PAR FORCES DOMIN LEGIT ADMIN COERCE ATTIT   REGION
...CONCPT TREND 20 TANGANYIKA. PAGE 91 B1831

S64
GALTUNE J.,"BALANCE OF POWER AND THE PROBLEM OF   PWR
PERCEPTION. A LOGICAL ANALYSIS." WOR+45 CONSTN   PSY
SOCIETY NAT/G DELIB/GP EX/STRUC LEGIS DOMIN ADMIN   ARMS/CONT
COERCE DRIVE ORD/FREE...POLICY CONCPT OBS TREND   WAR
GEN/LAWS. PAGE 38 B0778

S64
JOHNSON K.F.,"CAUSAL FACTORS IN LATIN AMERICAN   L/A+17C
POLITICAL INSTABILITY." CULTURE NAT/G VOL/ASSN   PERCEPT
EX/STRUC FORCES EDU/PROP LEGIT ADMIN COERCE REV   ELITES
ATTIT KNOWL PWR...STYLE RECORD CHARTS WORK 20.
PAGE 57 B1144

S64
KENNAN G.F.,"POLYCENTRISM AND WESTERN POLICY." ASIA   RIGID/FLEX
CHINA/COM COM FUT USA+45 USSR NAT/G ACT/RES DOMIN   ATTIT
EDU/PROP EXEC COERCE DISPL PERCEPT...POLICY   DIPLOM
COLD/WAR 20. PAGE 59 B1192

S64
LOW D.A.,"LION RAMPANT." EUR+WWI MOD/EUR S/ASIA   AFR
ECO/UNDEV NAT/G FORCES TEC/DEV ECO/TAC LEGIT ADMIN   DOMIN
COLONIAL COERCE ORD/FREE RESPECT 19/20. PAGE 67   DIPLOM
B1344   UK

B65
ECCLES H.E.,MILITARY CONCEPTS AND PHILOSOPHY.   PLAN
USA+45 STRUCT EXEC ROUTINE COERCE WAR CIVMIL/REL   DRIVE
COST...OBS GEN/LAWS COLD/WAR. PAGE 32 B0648   LEAD
                                                      FORCES
B65
MEYERHOFF A.E.,THE STRATEGY OF PERSUASION. USA+45   EDU/PROP
COM/IND CONSULT FOR/AID CONTROL COERCE COST ATTIT   EFFICIENCY
PERCEPT MARXISM 20 COLD/WAR. PAGE 73 B1476   OP/RES
                                                      ADMIN

B65
PUSTAY J.S.,COUNTER-INSURGENCY WARFARE. COM USA+45   FORCES
LOC/G NAT/G ACT/RES EDU/PROP ADMIN COERCE ATTIT   PWR
...CONCPT MARX/KARL 20. PAGE 85 B1722   GUERRILLA

B65
VIORST M.,HOSTILE ALLIES: FDR AND DE GAULLE.   TOP/EX
EUR+WWI USA-45 ELITES NAT/G VOL/ASSN FORCES LEGIS   PWR
PLAN LEGIT ADMIN COERCE PERSON...BIOG TIME/SEQ 20   WAR
ROOSEVLT/F DEGAULLE/C. PAGE 112 B2263   FRANCE

L65
HOOK S.,"SECOND THOUGHTS ON BERKELEY" USA+45 ELITES   ACADEM
INTELL LEGIT ADMIN COERCE REPRESENT GP/REL INGP/REL   ORD/FREE
TOTALISM AGE/Y MARXISM 20 BERKELEY FREE/SPEE   POLICY
STUDNT/PWR. PAGE 51 B1040   CREATE

B67
NIEDERHOFFER A.,BEHIND THE SHIELD; THE POLICE IN   FORCES
URBAN SOCIETY. USA+45 LEGIT ADJUD ROUTINE COERCE   PERSON
CRIME ADJUST...INT CHARTS 20 NEWYORK/C. PAGE 78   SOCIETY
B1582   ATTIT

B67
VOOS H.,ORGANIZATIONAL COMMUNICATION: A   BIBLIOG/A
BIBLIOGRAPHY. WOR+45 STRATA R+D PROB/SOLV FEEDBACK   INDUS
COERCE...MGT PSY NET/THEORY HYPO/EXP. PAGE 112   COM/IND
B2268   VOL/ASSN

L67
COHEN M.,"THE DEMISE OF UNEF." CONSTN DIPLOM ADMIN   INT/ORG
AGREE LEAD COERCE 20 UNEF U/THANT HAMMARSK/D.   FORCES
PAGE 22 B0445   PEACE
                                                      POLICY

L67
ROBERTS J.C.,"CIVIL RESTRAINT, MENTAL ILLNESS, AND   HEALTH
THE RIGHT TO TREATMENT." PROB/SOLV ADMIN PERSON   ORD/FREE
HEAL. PAGE 89 B1795   COERCE
                                                      LAW

S67
BASTID M.,"ORIGINES ET DEVELOPMENT DE LA REVOLUTION   REV
CULTURELLE." CHINA/COM DOMIN ADMIN CONTROL LEAD   CULTURE
COERCE CROWD ATTIT DRIVE MARXISM...POLICY 20.   ACADEM
PAGE 10 B0195   WORKER

S67
O'DELL J.H.,"THE JULY REBELLIONS AND THE 'MILITARY   PWR
STATE'." USA+45 VIETNAM STRATA CHIEF WORKER   NAT/G
COLONIAL EXEC CROWD CIVMIL/REL RACE/REL TOTALISM   COERCE
...WELF/ST PACIFIST 20 NEGRO JOHNSON/LB PRESIDENT   FORCES
CIV/RIGHTS. PAGE 79 B1599

S67
SHOEMAKER R.L.,"JAPANESE ARMY AND THE WEST." ASIA   FORCES
ELITES EX/STRUC DIPLOM DOMIN EDU/PROP COERCE ATTIT   TEC/DEV
AUTHORIT PWR 1/20 CHINJAP. PAGE 96 B1950   WAR
                                                      TOTALISM

B82
MACDONALD D.,AFRICANA; OR, THE HEART OF HEATHEN   SECT
AFRICA. VOL. II: MISSION LIFE. SOCIETY STRATA KIN   AFR
CREATE EDU/PROP ADMIN COERCE LITERACY HEALTH...MYTH   CULTURE
WORSHIP 19 LIVNGSTN/D MISSION NEGRO. PAGE 67 B1355   ORD/FREE

COERCION....SEE COERCE

COEXIST....COEXISTENCE; SEE ALSO COLD/WAR, PEACE

COEXISTENCE....SEE COLD/WAR, PEACE, COEXIST

COFFIN/WS....WILLIAM SLOANE COFFIN, JR.

COGNITION....SEE PERCEPT

COGNITIVE DISSONANCE....SEE PERCEPT, ROLE

COHEN E.W. B0442

COHEN H. B0443,B1659

COHEN K.J. B0444

COHEN M. B0445

COHEN M.B. B0446

COHEN R. B0447

COHEN R.A. B0446

COHESION....SEE CONSEN

COHN B.S. B0448

COHN H.J. B0449

COHN T.S. B0328

COLD/WAR....COLD WAR

N
WEIGLEY R.F.,HISTORY OF THE UNITED STATES ARMY.   FORCES
USA+45 USA-45 SOCIETY NAT/G LEAD WAR GP/REL PWR   ADMIN
...SOC METH/COMP COLD/WAR. PAGE 115 B2312   ROLE

CIVMIL/REL
B49
BUSH V.,MODERN ARMS AND FREE MEN. WOR-45 SOCIETY | TEC/DEV
NAT/G ECO/TAC DOMIN LEGIT EXEC COERCE DETER ATTIT | FORCES
DRIVE ORD/FREE PWR...CONCPT MYTH COLD/WAR 20 | NUC/PWR
COLD/WAR. PAGE 18 B0361 | WAR

B49
BUSH V.,MODERN ARMS AND FREE MEN. WOR-45 SOCIETY | TEC/DEV
NAT/G ECO/TAC DOMIN LEGIT EXEC COERCE DETER ATTIT | FORCES
DRIVE ORD/FREE PWR...CONCPT MYTH COLD/WAR 20 | NUC/PWR
COLD/WAR. PAGE 18 B0361 | WAR

B49
ROSENHAUPT H.W.,HOW TO WAGE PEACE. USA+45 SOCIETY | INTELL
STRATA STRUCT R+D INT/ORG POL/PAR LEGIS ACT/RES | CONCPT
CREATE PLAN EDU/PROP ADMIN EXEC ATTIT ALL/VALS | DIPLOM
...TIME/SEQ TREND COLD/WAR 20. PAGE 90 B1822

B50
LASSWELL H.D.,NATIONAL SECURITY AND INDIVIDUAL | FACE/GP
FREEDOM. USA+45 R+D NAT/G VOL/ASSN CONSULT DELIB/GP | ROUTINE
LEGIT ADMIN KNOWL ORD/FREE PWR...PLURIST TOT/POP | BAL/PWR
COLD/WAR 20. PAGE 63 B1268

L50
US SENATE COMM. GOVT. OPER.,"REVISION OF THE UN | INT/ORG
CHARTER." FUT USA+45 WOR+45 CONSTN ECO/DEV | LEGIS
ECO/UNDEV NAT/G DELIB/GP ACT/RES CREATE PLAN EXEC | PEACE
ROUTINE CHOOSE ALL/VALS...POLICY CONCPT CONGRESS UN
TOT/POP 20 COLD/WAR. PAGE 111 B2235

B52
DAY E.E.,EDUCATION FOR FREEDOM AND RESPONSIBILITY. | SCHOOL
FUT USA+45 CULTURE CONSULT EDU/PROP ATTIT SKILL | KNOWL
...MGT CONCPT OBS GEN/LAWS COLD/WAR 20. PAGE 27
B0547

B54
MILLARD E.L.,FREEDOM IN A FEDERAL WORLD. FUT WOR+45 | INT/ORG
VOL/ASSN TOP/EX LEGIT ROUTINE FEDERAL PEACE ATTIT | CREATE
DISPL ORD/FREE PWR...MAJORIT INT/LAW JURID TREND | ADJUD
COLD/WAR 20. PAGE 73 B1479 | BAL/PWR

L54
ARCIENEGAS G.,"POST-WAR SOVIET FOREIGN POLICY: A | INTELL
WORLD PERSPECTIVE." COM USA+45 STRUCT NAT/G POL/PAR | ACT/RES
TOP/EX PLAN ADMIN ALL/VALS...TREND COLD/WAR TOT/POP | USSR
20. PAGE 6 B0124

S54
WOLFERS A.,"COLLECTIVE SECURITY AND THE WAR IN | ACT/RES
KOREA." ASIA KOREA USA+45 INT/ORG DIPLOM ROUTINE | LEGIT
...GEN/LAWS UN COLD/WAR 20. PAGE 117 B2370

B56
KAUFMANN W.W.,MILITARY POLICY AND NATIONAL | FORCES
SECURITY. USA+45 ELITES INTELL NAT/G TOP/EX PLAN | CREATE
BAL/PWR DIPLOM ROUTINE COERCE NUC/PWR ATTIT
ORD/FREE PWR 20 COLD/WAR. PAGE 58 B1182

B56
KIRK G.,THE CHANGING ENVIRONMENT OF INTERNATIONAL | FUT
RELATIONS. ASIA S/ASIA WOR+45 ECO/UNDEV | EXEC
INT/ORG NAT/G FOR/AID EDU/PROP PEACE KNOWL | DIPLOM
...PLURIST COLD/WAR TOT/POP 20. PAGE 60 B1214

B57
BEAL J.R.,JOHN FOSTER DULLES, A BIOGRAPHY. USA+45 | BIOG
USSR WOR+45 CONSTN INT/ORG NAT/G EX/STRUC LEGIT | DIPLOM
ADMIN NUC/PWR DISPL PERSON ORD/FREE PWR SKILL
...POLICY PSY OBS RECORD COLD/WAR UN 20 DULLES/JF.
PAGE 10 B0200

B57
HOLCOMBE A.N.,STRENGTHENING THE UNITED NATIONS. | INT/ORG
USA+45 ACT/RES CREATE PLAN EDU/PROP ATTIT PERCEPT | ROUTINE
PWR...METH/CNCPT CONT/OBS RECORD UN COLD/WAR 20.
PAGE 51 B1032

B57
HUNTINGTON S.P.,THE SOLDIER AND THE STATE: THE | ACT/RES
THEORY AND POLITICS OF CIVIL-MILITARY RELATIONS. | FORCES
USA+45 USA-45 NAT/G PROF/ORG CONSULT DOMIN LEGIT
ROUTINE ATTIT PWR...CONCPT TIME/SEQ COLD/WAR 20.
PAGE 53 B1065

L57
HAAS E.B.,"REGIONAL INTEGRATION AND NATIONAL | INT/ORG
POLICY." WOR+45 VOL/ASSN DELIB/GP EX/STRUC ECO/TAC | ORD/FREE
DOMIN EDU/PROP LEGIT COERCE ATTIT PERCEPT KNOWL | REGION
...TIME/SEQ COLD/WAR 20 UN. PAGE 45 B0908

B58
KINTNER W.R.,ORGANIZING FOR CONFLICT: A PROPOSAL. | USA+45
USSR STRUCT NAT/G LEGIS ADMIN EXEC PEACE ORD/FREE | PLAN
PWR...CONCPT OBS TREND NAT/COMP VAL/FREE COLD/WAR | DIPLOM
20. PAGE 60 B1211

B58
LAQUER W.Z.,THE MIDDLE EAST IN TRANSITION. COM USSR | ISLAM
ECO/UNDEV NAT/G VOL/ASSN EDU/PROP EXEC ATTIT DRIVE | TREND
PWR MARXISM COLD/WAR TOT/POP 20. PAGE 62 B1261 | NAT/LISM

S58
DAVENPORT J.,"ARMS AND THE WELFARE STATE." INTELL | USA+45
STRUCT FORCES CREATE ECO/TAC FOR/AID DOMIN LEGIT | NAT/G
ADMIN WAR ORD/FREE PWR...POLICY SOC CONCPT MYTH OBS | USSR
TREND COLD/WAR TOT/POP 20. PAGE 26 B0533

B59
GORDENKER L.,THE UNITED NATIONS AND THE PEACEFUL | DELIB/GP
UNIFICATION OF KOREA. ASIA LAW LOC/G CONSULT | KOREA
ACT/RES DIPLOM DOMIN LEGIT ADJUD ADMIN ORD/FREE | INT/ORG

SOVEREIGN...INT GEN/METH UN COLD/WAR 20. PAGE 41
B0829

B59
GRABER D.,CRISIS DIPLOMACY. L/A+17C USA+45 USA-45 | ROUTINE
NAT/G TOP/EX ECO/TAC COERCE ATTIT ORD/FREE...CONCPT | MORAL
MYTH TIME/SEQ COLD/WAR 20. PAGE 42 B0848 | DIPLOM

B59
JANOWITZ M.,SOCIOLOGY AND THE MILITARY | FORCES
ESTABLISHMENT. USA+45 WOR+45 CULTURE SOCIETY | SOC
PROF/ORG CONSULT EX/STRUC PLAN TEC/DEV DIPLOM DOMIN
COERCE DRIVE RIGID/FLEX ORD/FREE PWR SKILL COLD/WAR
20. PAGE 55 B1121

B59
WELTON H.,THE THIRD WORLD WAR: TRADE AND INDUSTRY, | INT/TRADE
THE NEW BATTLEGROUND. WOR+45 ECO/DEV INDUS MARKET | PLAN
TASK...MGT IDEA/COMP COLD/WAR. PAGE 115 B2321 | DIPLOM

S59
HILSMAN R.,"THE FOREIGN-POLICY CONSENSUS: AN | PROB/SOLV
INTERIM RESEARCH REPORT." USA+45 INT/ORG LEGIS | NAT/G
TEC/DEV WAR CONSEN KNOWL...DECISION COLD/WAR. | DELIB/GP
PAGE 50 B1013 | DIPLOM

S59
HOFFMANN S.,"IMPLEMENTATION OF INTERNATIONAL | INT/ORG
INSTRUMENTS ON HUMAN RIGHTS." WOR+45 VOL/ASSN | MORAL
DELIB/GP JUDGE EDU/PROP LEGIT ROUTINE PEACE
COLD/WAR 20. PAGE 51 B1029

S59
SOHN L.B.,"THE DEFINITION OF AGGRESSION." FUT LAW | INT/ORG
FORCES LEGIT ADJUD ROUTINE COERCE ORD/FREE PWR | CT/SYS
...MAJORIT JURID QUANT COLD/WAR 20. PAGE 99 B1995 | DETER
| SOVEREIGN

B60
BROOKINGS INSTITUTION.UNITED STATES FOREIGN POLICY: | DIPLOM
STUDY NO 9: THE FORMULATION AND ADMINISTRATION OF | INT/ORG
UNITED STATES FOREIGN POLICY. USA+45 WOR+45 | CREATE
EX/STRUC LEGIS BAL/PWR FOR/AID EDU/PROP CIVMIL/REL
GOV/REL...INT COLD/WAR. PAGE 16 B0317

B60
LISKA G.,THE NEW STATECRAFT. WOR+45 WOR-45 LEGIS | ECO/TAC
DIPLOM ADMIN ATTIT PWR WEALTH...HIST/WRIT TREND | CONCPT
COLD/WAR 20. PAGE 66 B1323 | FOR/AID

L60
BRENNAN D.G.,"SETTING AND GOALS OF ARMS CONTROL." | FORCES
FUT USA+45 USSR WOR+45 INTELL INT/ORG NAT/G | COERCE
VOL/ASSN CONSULT PLAN DIPLOM ECO/TAC ADMIN KNOWL | ARMS/CONT
PWR...POLICY CONCPT TREND COLD/WAR 20. PAGE 15 | DETER
B0305

S60
GROSSMAN G.,"SOVIET GROWTH: ROUTINE, INERTIA, AND | POL/PAR
PRESSURE." COM STRATA NAT/G DELIB/GP PLAN TEC/DEV | ECO/DEV
ECO/TAC EDU/PROP ADMIN ROUTINE DRIVE WEALTH | USSR
COLD/WAR 20. PAGE 44 B0891

S60
HALPERIN M.H.,"IS THE SENATE'S FOREIGN RELATIONS | PLAN
RESEARCH WORTHWHILE." COM FUT USA+45 USSR ACT/RES | DIPLOM
BAL/PWR EDU/PROP ADMIN ALL/VALS CONGRESS VAL/FREE
20 COLD/WAR. PAGE 46 B0927

B61
KERTESZ S.D.,AMERICAN DIPLOMACY IN A NEW ERA. COM | ANTHOL
S/ASIA UK USA+45 FORCES PROB/SOLV BAL/PWR ECO/TAC | DIPLOM
ADMIN COLONIAL WAR PEACE ORD/FREE 20 NATO CONGRESS | TREND
UN COLD/WAR. PAGE 59 B1199

B61
MOLLAU G.,INTERNATIONAL COMMUNISM AND WORLD | COM
REVOLUTION: HISTORY AND METHODS. RUSSIA USSR | REV
INT/ORG NAT/G POL/PAR VOL/ASSN FORCES BAL/PWR
DIPLOM EXEC REGION WAR ATTIT PWR MARXISM...CONCPT
TIME/SEQ COLD/WAR 19/20. PAGE 74 B1498

B61
STONE J.,QUEST FOR SURVIVAL. WOR+45 NAT/G VOL/ASSN | INT/ORG
LEGIT ADMIN ARMS/CONT COERCE DISPL ORD/FREE PWR | ADJUD
...POLICY INT/LAW JURID COLD/WAR 20. PAGE 101 B2047 | SOVEREIGN

S61
CARLETON W.G.,"AMERICAN FOREIGN POLICY: MYTHS AND | PLAN
REALITIES." FUT USA+45 WOR+45 ECO/UNDEV INT/ORG | MYTH
EX/STRUC ARMS/CONT NUC/PWR WAR ATTIT...POLICY | DIPLOM
CONCPT CONT/OBS GEN/METH COLD/WAR TOT/POP 20.
PAGE 19 B0378

S61
DEVINS J.H.,"THE INITIATIVE." COM USA+45 USA-45 | FORCES
USSR SOCIETY NAT/G ACT/RES CREATE BAL/PWR ROUTINE | CONCPT
COERCE DETER RIGID/FLEX SKILL...STERTYP COLD/WAR | WAR
20. PAGE 29 B0582

S61
JACKSON E.,"CONSTITUTIONAL DEVELOPMENTS OF THE | INT/ORG
UNITED NATIONS: THE GROWTH OF ITS EXECUTIVE | EXEC
CAPACITY." FUT WOR+45 CONSTN STRUCT ACT/RES PLAN
ALL/VALS...NEW/IDEA OBS COLD/WAR UN 20. PAGE 55
B1106

B62
BAILEY S.D.,THE SECRETARIAT OF THE UNITED NATIONS. | INT/ORG
FUT WOR+45 DELIB/GP PLAN BAL/PWR DOMIN EDU/PROP | EXEC
ADMIN PEACE ATTIT PWR...DECISION CONCPT TREND | DIPLOM
CON/ANAL CHARTS UN VAL/FREE COLD/WAR 20. PAGE 8
B0162

B62
LAWSON R.,INTERNATIONAL REGIONAL ORGANIZATIONS.   INT/ORG
WOR+45 NAT/G VOL/ASSN CONSULT LEGIS EDU/PROP LEGIT   DELIB/GP
ADMIN EXEC ROUTINE HEALTH PWR WEALTH...JURID EEC   REGION
COLD/WAR 20 UN. PAGE 63 B1277

B62
MODELSKI G.,A THEORY OF FOREIGN POLICY. WOR+45   PLAN
WOR-45 NAT/G DELIB/GP EX/STRUC TOP/EX EDU/PROP   PWR
LEGIT ROUTINE...POLICY CONCPT TOT/POP COLD/WAR 20.   DIPLOM
PAGE 74 B1494

B62
MULLEY F.W.,THE POLITICS OF WESTERN DEFENSE.   INT/ORG
EUR+WWI USA-45 WOR+45 VOL/ASSN EX/STRUC FORCES   DELIB/GP
COERCE DETER PEACE ATTIT ORD/FREE PWR...RECORD   NUC/PWR
TIME/SEQ CHARTS COLD/WAR 20 NATO. PAGE 76 B1537

B62
SCHILLING W.R.,STRATEGY, POLITICS, AND DEFENSE   ROUTINE
BUDGETS. USA+45 R+D NAT/G CONSULT DELIB/GP FORCES   POLICY
LEGIS ACT/RES PLAN BAL/PWR LEGIT EXEC NUC/PWR
RIGID/FLEX PWR...TREND COLD/WAR CONGRESS 20
EISNHWR/DD. PAGE 93 B1890

L62
BAILEY S.D.,"THE TROIKA AND THE FUTURE OF THE UN."   FUT
CONSTN CREATE LEGIT EXEC CHOOSE ORD/FREE PWR   INT/ORG
...CONCPT NEW/IDEA UN COLD/WAR 20. PAGE 8 B0163   USSR

L62
NEIBURG H.L.,"THE EISENHOWER AEC AND CONGRESS: A   CHIEF
STUDY IN EXECUTIVE-LEGISLATIVE RELATIONS." USA+45   LEGIS
NAT/G POL/PAR DELIB/GP EX/STRUC TOP/EX ADMIN EXEC   GOV/REL
LEAD ROUTINE PWR...POLICY COLD/WAR CONGRESS   NUC/PWR
PRESIDENT AEC. PAGE 77 B1567

B63
CROZIER B.,THE MORNING AFTER; A STUDY OF   SOVEREIGN
INDEPENDENCE. WOR+45 EX/STRUC PLAN BAL/PWR COLONIAL   NAT/LISM
GP/REL 20 COLD/WAR. PAGE 25 B0511   NAT/G
DIPLOM

B63
STEVENSON A.E.,LOOKING OUTWARD: YEARS OF CRISIS AT   INT/ORG
THE UNITED NATIONS. COM CUBA USA+45 WOR+45 SOCIETY   CONCPT
NAT/G EX/STRUC ACT/RES LEGIT COLONIAL ATTIT PERSON   ARMS/CONT
SUPEGO ALL/VALS...POLICY HUM UN COLD/WAR CONGO 20.
PAGE 100 B2034

B63
TUCKER R.C.,THE SOVIET POLITICAL MIND. WOR+45   COM
ELITES INT/ORG NAT/G POL/PAR PLAN DIPLOM ECO/TAC   TOP/EX
DOMIN ADMIN NUC/PWR REV DRIVE PERSON SUPEGO PWR   USSR
WEALTH...POLICY MGT PSY CONCPT OBS BIOG TREND
COLD/WAR MARX/KARL 20. PAGE 106 B2134

B63
VAN SLYCK P.,PEACE: THE CONTROL OF NATIONAL POWER.   ARMS/CONT
CUBA WOR+45 FINAN NAT/G FORCES PROB/SOLV TEC/DEV   PEACE
BAL/PWR ADMIN CONTROL ORD/FREE...POLICY INT/LAW UN   INT/ORG
COLD/WAR TREATY. PAGE 112 B2253   DIPLOM

S63
BOWIE R.,"STRATEGY AND THE ATLANTIC ALLIANCE."   FORCES
EUR+WWI VOL/ASSN BAL/PWR COERCE NUC/PWR ATTIT   ROUTINE
ORD/FREE PWR...DECISION GEN/LAWS NATO COLD/WAR 20.
PAGE 14 B0287

S63
BRZEZINSKI Z.K.,"CINCINNATUS AND THE APPARATCHIK."   POL/PAR
COM USA+45 USA-45 ELITES LOC/G NAT/G PROVS CONSULT   USSR
LEGIS DOMIN LEGIT EXEC ROUTINE CHOOSE DRIVE PWR
SKILL...CONCPT CHARTS VAL/FREE COLD/WAR 20. PAGE 16
B0334

S63
HAVILAND H.F.,"BUILDING A POLITICAL COMMUNITY."   VOL/ASSN
EUR+WWI FUT UK USA+45 ECO/DEV ECO/UNDEV INT/ORG   DIPLOM
NAT/G DELIB/GP BAL/PWR ECO/TAC NEUTRAL ROUTINE
ATTIT PWR WEALTH...CONCPT COLD/WAR TOT/POP 20.
PAGE 48 B0972

S63
MANGONE G.,"THE UNITED NATIONS AND UNITED STATES   INT/ORG
FOREIGN POLICY." USA+45 WOR+45 ECO/UNDEV NAT/G   ECO/TAC
DIPLOM LEGIT ROUTINE ATTIT DRIVE...TIME/SEQ UN   FOR/AID
COLD/WAR 20. PAGE 69 B1390

S63
NADLER E.B.,"SOME ECONOMIC DISADVANTAGES OF THE   ECO/DEV
ARMS RACE." USA+45 INDUS R+D FORCES PLAN TEC/DEV   MGT
ECO/TAC FOR/AID EDU/PROP PWR WEALTH...TREND   BAL/PAY
COLD/WAR 20. PAGE 77 B1552

S63
SHIMKIN D.B.,"STRUCTURE OF SOVIET POWER." COM FUT   PWR
USA+45 USSR WOR+45 NAT/G FORCES ECO/TAC DOMIN EXEC
COERCE CHOOSE ATTIT WEALTH...TIME/SEQ COLD/WAR
TOT/POP VAL/FREE 20. PAGE 96 B1948

C63
BLUM J.M.,"THE NATIONAL EXPERIENCE." USA+45 USA-45   ADMIN
ECO/DEV DIPLOM WAR NAT/LISM...POLICY CHARTS BIBLIOG   NAT/G
T 16/20 CONGRESS PRESIDENT COLD/WAR. PAGE 13 B0258   LEGIS
CHIEF

B64
POPPINO R.E.,INTERNATIONAL COMMUNISM IN LATIN   MARXISM
AMERICA: A HISTORY OF THE MOVEMENT 1917-1963.   POL/PAR
CHINA/COM USSR INTELL STRATA LABOR WORKER ADMIN REV   L/A+17C
ATTIT...POLICY 20 COLD/WAR. PAGE 84 B1692

L64
MILLIS W.,"THE DEMILITARIZED WORLD." COM USA+45   FUT
USSR WOR+45 CONSTN NAT/G EX/STRUC PLAN LEGIT ATTIT   INT/ORG
DRIVE...CONCPT TIME/SEQ STERTYP TOT/POP COLD/WAR   BAL/PWR
20. PAGE 74 B1486   PEACE

S64
KENNAN G.F.,"POLYCENTRISM AND WESTERN POLICY."   RIGID/FLEX
ASIA CHINA/COM COM FUT USA+45 USSR NAT/G ACT/RES DOMIN   ATTIT
EDU/PROP EXEC COERCE DISPL PERCEPT...POLICY   DIPLOM
COLD/WAR 20. PAGE 59 B1192

B65
ECCLES H.E.,MILITARY CONCEPTS AND PHILOSOPHY.   PLAN
USA+45 STRUCT EXEC ROUTINE COERCE WAR CIVMIL/REL   DRIVE
COST...OBS GEN/LAWS COLD/WAR. PAGE 32 B0648   LEAD
FORCES

B65
LYONS G.M.,SCHOOLS FOR STRATEGY* EDUCATION AND   ACADEM
RESEARCH IN NATIONAL SECURITY AFFAIRS. USA+45 FINAN   ACT/RES
NAT/G VOL/ASSN FORCES TEC/DEV ADMIN WAR...GP/COMP   INTELL
IDEA/COMP PERS/COMP COLD/WAR. PAGE 67 B1351

B65
MELMANS S.,OUR DEPLETED SOCIETY. SPACE USA+45   CIVMIL/REL
ECO/DEV FORCES BUDGET ECO/TAC ADMIN WEAPON   INDUS
EFFICIENCY 20 COLD/WAR. PAGE 73 B1465   EDU/PROP
CONTROL

B65
MEYERHOFF A.E.,THE STRATEGY OF PERSUASION. USA+45   EDU/PROP
COM/IND CONSULT FOR/AID CONTROL COERCE COST ATTIT   EFFICIENCY
PERCEPT MARXISM 20 COLD/WAR. PAGE 73 B1476   OP/RES
ADMIN

B65
PENNICK JL J.R.,THE POLITICS OF AMERICAN SCIENCE,   POLICY
1939 TO THE PRESENT. USA+45 USA-45 INTELL TEC/DEV   ADMIN
DIPLOM NEW/LIB...ANTHOL 20 COLD/WAR. PAGE 82 B1651   PHIL/SCI
NAT/G

L65
RUBIN A.P.,"UNITED STATES CONTEMPORARY PRACTICE   LAW
RELATING TO INTERNATIONAL LAW." USA+45 WOR+45   LEGIT
CONSTN INT/ORG NAT/G DELIB/GP EX/STRUC DIPLOM DOMIN   INT/LAW
CT/SYS ROUTINE ORD/FREE...CONCPT COLD/WAR 20.
PAGE 91 B1848

B66
MARTIN L.W.,DIPLOMACY IN MODERN EUROPEAN HISTORY.   DIPLOM
EUR+WWI MOD/EUR INT/ORG NAT/G EX/STRUC ROUTINE WAR   POLICY
PEACE TOTALISM PWR 15/20 COLD/WAR EUROPE/W. PAGE 70
B1411

B66
WARBURG J.P.,THE UNITED STATES IN THE POSTWAR   FOR/AID
WORLD. USA+45 ECO/TAC...POLICY 20 COLD/WAR.   DIPLOM
PAGE 113 B2287   PLAN
ADMIN

COLE C.W. B0440

COLE T. B0450

COLE/GEO....GEORGE COLE

COLEGROVE K.W. B0451

COLEMAN J.S. B0452

COLLECTIVE BARGAINING....SEE BARGAIN+LABOR+GP/REL

COLLECTIVE SECURITY....SEE INT/ORG+FORCES

COLLEGES....SEE ACADEM

COLLINS B.E. B0453

COLOMBIA....SEE ALSO L/A&17C

B58
ORTIZ R.P.,ANNUARIO BIBLIOGRAFICO COLOMBIANO,   BIBLIOG
1951-1956. LAW RECEIVE EDU/PROP ADMIN...LING STAT   SOC
20 COLOMB. PAGE 80 B1617

S67
FABREGA J.,"ANTECEDENTES EXTRANJEROS EN LA   CONSTN
CONSTITUCION PANAMENA." CUBA L/A+17C PANAMA URUGUAY   JURID
EX/STRUC LEGIS DIPLOM ORD/FREE 19/20 COLOMB   NAT/G
MEXIC/AMER. PAGE 34 B0694   PARL/PROC

S67
MCNAMARA R.L.,"THE NEED FOR INNOVATIVENESS IN   PROB/SOLV
DEVELOPING SOCIETIES." L/A+17C EDU/PROP ADMIN LEAD   PLAN
WEALTH...POLICY PSY SOC METH 20 COLOMB. PAGE 72   ECO/UNDEV
B1456   NEW/IDEA

COLONIAL AMERICA....SEE PRE/US/AM, PRE/AMER

COLONIAL....COLONIALISM; SEE ALSO DOMIN

N
CONOVER H.F.,MADAGASCAR: A SELECTED LIST OF   BIBLIOG/A
REFERENCES. MADAGASCAR STRUCT ECO/UNDEV NAT/G ADMIN   SOCIETY

...SOC 19/20. PAGE 23 B0463 | CULTURE COLONIAL N

DOHERTY D.K.,PRELIMINARY BIBLIOGRAPHY OF COLONIZATION AND SETTLEMENT IN LATIN AMERICA AND ANGLO-AMERICA. L/A+17C PRE/AMER USA-45 ECO/UNDEV NAT/G 15/20. PAGE 30 B0604 | BIBLIOG COLONIAL ADMIN DIPLOM B00

MORRIS H.C.,THE HISTORY OF COLONIZATION. WOR+45 WOR-45 ECO/DEV ECO/UNDEV INT/ORG ACT/RES PLAN ECO/TAC LEGIT ROUTINE COERCE ATTIT DRIVE ALL/VALS ...GEOG TREND 19. PAGE 76 B1528 | DOMIN SOVEREIGN COLONIAL B00

SANDERSON E.,AFRICA IN THE NINETEENTH CENTURY. FRANCE UK EXTR/IND FORCES LEGIS ADMIN WAR DISCRIM ORD/FREE...GEOG GP/COMP SOC/INTEG 19. PAGE 92 B1867 | COLONIAL AFR DIPLOM B02

MOREL E.D.,AFFAIRS OF WEST AFRICA. UK FINAN INDUS FAM KIN SECT CHIEF WORKER DIPLOM RACE/REL LITERACY HEALTH...CHARTS 18/20 AFRICA/W NEGRO. PAGE 75 B1521 | COLONIAL ADMIN AFR B17

HARLOW R.V.,THE HISTORY OF LEGISLATIVE METHODS IN THE PERIOD BEFORE 1825. USA-45 EX/STRUC ADMIN COLONIAL LEAD PARL/PROC ROUTINE...GP/COMP GOV/COMP HOUSE/REP. PAGE 47 B0948 | LEGIS DELIB/GP PROVS POL/PAR N19

PERREN G.E.,LANGUAGE AND COMMUNICATION IN THE COMMONWEALTH (PAMPHLET). FUT UK LAW ECO/DEV PRESS TV WRITING ADJUD ADMIN COLONIAL CONTROL 20 CMN/WLTH. PAGE 82 B1660 | EDU/PROP LING GOV/REL COM/IND N19

SOUTH AFRICA COMMISSION ON FUT,INTERIM AND FINAL REPORTS ON FUTURE FORM OF GOVERNMENT IN THE SOUTH-WEST AFRICAN PROTECTORATE (PAMPHLET). SOUTH/AFR NAT/G FORCES CONFER COLONIAL CONTROL 20 AFRICA/SW. PAGE 99 B1998 | CONSTN REPRESENT ADMIN PROB/SOLV N19

TREVELYAN G.M.,THE TWO-PARTY SYSTEM IN ENGLISH POLITICAL HISTORY (PAMPHLET). UK CHIEF LEGIS COLONIAL EXEC REV CHOOSE 17/19. PAGE 105 B2128 | PARL/PROC POL/PAR NAT/G PWR B26

MOON P.T.,IMPERIALISM AND WORLD POLITICS. AFR ASIA ISLAM MOD/EUR S/ASIA USA-45 SOCIETY NAT/G EX/STRUC BAL/PWR DOMIN COLONIAL NAT/LISM ATTIT DRIVE PWR ...GEOG SOC 20. PAGE 75 B1510 | WEALTH TIME/SEQ CAP/ISM DIPLOM B28

HALL W.P.,EMPIRE TO COMMONWEALTH. FUT WOR+45 CONSTN ECO/DEV ECO/UNDEV INT/ORG PROVS PLAN DIPLOM EDU/PROP ADMIN COLONIAL PEACE PERSON ALL/VALS ...POLICY GEOG SOC OBS RECORD TREND CMN/WLTH PARLIAMENT 19/20. PAGE 46 B0925 | VOL/ASSN NAT/G UK B29

BOUDET P.,BIBLIOGRAPHIE DE L'INDOCHINE FRANCAISE. S/ASIA VIETNAM SECT...GEOG LING 20. PAGE 14 B0282 | BIBLIOG ADMIN COLONIAL DIPLOM B29

ROBERTS S.H.,HISTORY OF FRENCH COLONIAL POLICY. AFR ASIA L/A+17C S/ASIA CULTURE ECO/DEV ECO/UNDEV FINAN NAT/G PLAN ECO/TAC DOMIN ROUTINE SOVEREIGN...OBS HIST/WRIT TREND CHARTS VAL/FREE 19/20. PAGE 89 B1796 | INT/ORG ACT/RES FRANCE COLONIAL B31

BORCHARD E.H.,GUIDE TO THE LAW AND LEGAL LITERATURE OF FRANCE. FRANCE FINAN INDUS LABOR SECT LEGIS ADMIN COLONIAL CRIME OWN...INT/LAW 20. PAGE 14 B0277 | BIBLIOG/A LAW CONSTN METH B31

DEKAT A.D.A.,COLONIAL POLICY. S/ASIA CULTURE EX/STRUC ECO/TAC DOMIN ADMIN COLONIAL ROUTINE SOVEREIGN WEALTH...POLICY MGT RECORD KNO/TEST SAMP. PAGE 28 B0570 | DRIVE PWR INDONESIA NETHERLAND B32

CARDINALL AW.,A BIBLIOGRAPHY OF THE GOLD COAST. AFR UK NAT/G EX/STRUC ATTIT...POLICY 19/20. PAGE 18 B0376 | BIBLIOG ADMIN COLONIAL DIPLOM B34

DE CENIVAL P.,BIBLIOGRAPHIE MAROCAINE: 1923-1933. FRANCE MOROCCO SECT ADMIN LEAD GP/REL ATTIT...LING 20. PAGE 27 B0551 | BIBLIOG/A ISLAM NAT/G COLONIAL B35

GORER G.,AFRICA DANCES: A BOOK ABOUT WEST AFRICAN NEGROES. STRUCT LOC/G SECT FORCES TAX ADMIN COLONIAL...ART/METH MYTH WORSHIP 20 NEGRO AFRICA/W CHRISTIAN RITUAL. PAGE 41 B0835 | AFR ATTIT CULTURE SOCIETY B36

ROBINSON H.,DEVELOPMENT OF THE BRITISH EMPIRE. WOR-45 CULTURE SOCIETY STRUCT ECO/DEV ECO/UNDEV INT/ORG VOL/ASSN FORCES CREATE PLAN DOMIN EDU/PROP ADMIN COLONIAL PWR WEALTH...POLICY GEOG CHARTS CMN/WLTH 16/20. PAGE 89 B1800 | NAT/G HIST/WRIT UK B37

ROYAL INST. INT. AFF.,THE COLONIAL PROBLEM. WOR-45 | INT/ORG

LAW ECO/DEV ECO/UNDEV NAT/G PLAN ECO/TAC EDU/PROP ADMIN ATTIT ALL/VALS...CONCPT 20. PAGE 91 B1844 | ACT/RES SOVEREIGN COLONIAL B37

UNION OF SOUTH AFRICA,REPORT CONCERNING ADMINISTRATION OF SOUTH WEST AFRICA (6 VOLS.). SOUTH/AFR INDUS PUB/INST FORCES LEGIS BUDGET DIPLOM EDU/PROP ADJUD CT/SYS...GEOG CHARTS 20 AFRICA/SW LEAGUE/NAT. PAGE 107 B2158 | NAT/G ADMIN COLONIAL CONSTN B41

PERHAM M.,AFRICANS AND BRITISH RULE. AFR UK ECO/TAC CONTROL GP/REL ATTIT 20. PAGE 82 B1654 | DIPLOM COLONIAL ADMIN ECO/UNDEV B42

SIMOES DOS REIS A.,BIBLIOGRAFIA DAS BIBLIOGRAFIAS BRASILEIRAS. BRAZIL ADMIN COLONIAL 20. PAGE 97 B1954 | BIBLIOG NAT/G DIPLOM L/A+17C B43

CLARKE M.P.,PARLIAMENTARY PRIVILEGE IN THE AMERICAN COLONIES. PROVS DOMIN ADMIN REPRESENT GOV/REL ORD/FREE...BIBLIOG/A 17/18. PAGE 21 B0433 | LEGIS PWR COLONIAL PARL/PROC B43

LEWIN E.,ROYAL EMPIRE SOCIETY BIBLIOGRAPHIES NO. 9: SUB-SAHARA AFRICA. ECO/UNDEV TEC/DEV DIPLOM ADMIN COLONIAL LEAD 20. PAGE 64 B1303 | BIBLIOG AFR NAT/G SOCIETY B46

GRIFFIN G.G.,A GUIDE TO MANUSCRIPTS RELATING TO AMERICAN HISTORY IN BRITISH DEPOSITORIES. CANADA IRELAND MOD/EUR UK USA-45 LAW DIPLOM ADMIN COLONIAL WAR NAT/LISM SOVEREIGN...GEOG INT/LAW 15/19 CMN/WLTH. PAGE 43 B0876 | BIBLIOG/A ALL/VALS NAT/G B47

CONOVER H.F.,NON-SELF-GOVERNING AREAS. BELGIUM FRANCE ITALY UK WOR+45 CULTURE ECO/UNDEV INT/ORG LOC/G NAT/G ECO/TAC INT/TRADE ADMIN HEALTH...SOC UN. PAGE 23 B0465 | BIBLIOG/A COLONIAL DIPLOM B47

CROCKER W.R.,ON GOVERNING COLONIES: BEING AN OUTLINE OF THE REAL ISSUES AND A COMPARISON OF THE BRITISH, FRENCH, AND BELGIAN... AFR BELGIUM FRANCE UK CULTURE SOVEREIGN...OBS 20. PAGE 25 B0505 | COLONIAL POLICY GOV/COMP ADMIN B48

DAY P.,CRISIS IN SOUTH AFRICA. SOUTH/AFR UK KIN MUNIC ECO/TAC RECEIVE 20 SMUTS/JAN MIGRATION. PAGE 27 B0548 | RACE/REL COLONIAL ADMIN EXTR/IND B48

MEEK C.K.,COLONIAL LAW: A BIBLIOGRAPHY WITH SPECIAL REFERENCE TO NATIVE AFRICAN SYSTEMS OF LAW AND LAND TENURE. AFR ECO/UNDEV AGRI CT/SYS...JURID SOC 20. PAGE 72 B1462 | COLONIAL ADMIN LAW CONSTN S49

STEINMETZ H.,"THE PROBLEMS OF THE LANDRAT: A STUDY OF COUNTY GOVERNMENT IN THE US ZONE OF GERMANY." GERMANY/W USA+45 INDUS PLAN DIPLOM EDU/PROP CONTROL WAR GOV/REL FEDERAL WEALTH PLURISM...GOV/COMP 20 LANDRAT. PAGE 100 B2031 | LOC/G COLONIAL MGT TOP/EX B50

FIGANIERE J.C.,BIBLIOTHECA HISTORICA PORTUGUEZA. BRAZIL PORTUGAL SECT ADMIN. PAGE 35 B0717 | BIBLIOG NAT/G DIPLOM COLONIAL B50

PERHAM M.,COLONIAL GOVERNMENT: ANNOTATED READING LIST ON BRITISH COLONIAL GOVERNMENT. UK WOR+45 WOR-45 ECO/UNDEV INT/ORG LEGIS FOR/AID INT/TRADE DOMIN ADMIN REV 20. PAGE 82 B1655 | BIBLIOG/A COLONIAL GOV/REL NAT/G B50

WELCH S.R.,PORTUGUESE RULE AND SPANISH CROWN IN SOUTH AFRICA 1581-1640. PORTUGAL SOUTH/AFR SPAIN SOCIETY KIN NEIGH SECT INT/TRADE ADMIN 16/17 MISSION. PAGE 115 B2317 | DIPLOM COLONIAL WAR PEACE C50

STOKES W.S.,"HONDURAS: AN AREA STUDY IN GOVERNMENT." HONDURAS NAT/G POL/PAR COLONIAL CT/SYS ROUTINE CHOOSE REPRESENT...GEOG RECORD BIBLIOG 19/20. PAGE 101 B2044 | CONSTN LAW L/A+17C ADMIN B51

BERTON P.A.,MANCHURIA: AN ANNOTATED BIBLIOGRAPHY. ASIA DIST/IND ADMIN...SOC 20. PAGE 11 B0231 | BIBLIOG/A MARXISM ECO/UNDEV COLONIAL B53

PIERCE R.A.,RUSSIAN CENTRAL ASIA, 1867-1917: A SELECTED BIBLIOGRAPHY (PAMPHLET). USSR LAW CULTURE NAT/G EDU/PROP WAR...GEOG SOC 19/20. PAGE 83 B1671 | BIBLIOG COLONIAL ADMIN COM B53

STOUT H.M.,BRITISH GOVERNMENT. UK FINAN LOC/G POL/PAR DELIB/GP DIPLOM ADMIN COLONIAL CHOOSE ORD/FREE...JURID BIBLIOG 20 COMMONWLTH. PAGE 101 B2049 | NAT/G PARL/PROC CONSTN NEW/LIB

ROSTOW W.W.,"ASIAN LEADERSHIP AND FREE-WORLD
ALLIANCE." ASIA COM USA+45 CULTURE ELITES INTELL
NAT/G TEC/DEV ECO/TAC EDU/PROP COLONIAL PARL/PROC
ROUTINE COERCE DRIVE ORD/FREE MARXISM...PSY CONCPT.
PAGE 90 B1829
L54
ATTIT
LEGIT
DIPLOM

LANDAU J.M.,"PARLIAMENTS AND PARTIES IN EGYPT." UAR
NAT/G SECT CONSULT LEGIS TOP/EX PROB/SOLV ADMIN
COLONIAL...GEN/LAWS BIBLIOG 19/20. PAGE 62 B1254
C54
ISLAM
NAT/LISM
PARL/PROC
POL/PAR

DE ARAGAO J.G.,LA JURIDICTION ADMINISTRATIVE AU
BRESIL. BRAZIL ADJUD COLONIAL CT/SYS REV FEDERAL
ORD/FREE...BIBLIOG 19/20. PAGE 27 B0549
B55
EX/STRUC
ADMIN
NAT/G

CENTRAL AFRICAN ARCHIVES,A GUIDE TO THE PUBLIC
RECORDS OF SOUTHERN RHODESIA UNDER THE REGIME OF
THE BRITISH SOUTH AFRICA COMPANY, 1890-1923. UK
STRUCT NAT/G WRITING GP/REL 19/20. PAGE 19 B0398
B56
BIBLIOG/A
COLONIAL
ADMIN
AFR

JENNINGS W.I.,THE APPROACH TO SELF-GOVERNMENT.
CEYLON INDIA PAKISTAN S/ASIA UK SOCIETY POL/PAR
DELIB/GP LEGIS ECO/TAC EDU/PROP ADMIN EXEC CHOOSE
ATTIT ALL/VALS...JURID CONCPT GEN/METH TOT/POP 20.
PAGE 56 B1136
B56
NAT/G
CONSTN
COLONIAL

MANNONI D.O.,PROSPERO AND CALIBAN: THE PSYCHOLOGY
OF COLONIZATION. AFR EUR+WWI FAM KIN MUNIC SECT
DOMIN ADMIN ATTIT DRIVE LOVE PWR RESPECT...PSY SOC
CONCPT MYTH OBS DEEP/INT BIOG GEN/METH MALAGASY 20.
PAGE 69 B1394
B56
CULTURE
COLONIAL

WILSON P.,GOVERNMENT AND POLITICS OF INDIA AND
PAKISTAN: 1885-1955; A BIBLIOGRAPHY OF WORKS IN
WESTERN LANGUAGES. INDIA PAKISTAN CONSTN LOC/G
POL/PAR FORCES DIPLOM ADMIN WAR CHOOSE...BIOG
CON/ANAL 19/20. PAGE 117 B2361
B56
BIBLIOG
COLONIAL
NAT/G
S/ASIA

BISHOP O.B.,PUBLICATIONS OF THE GOVERNMENTS OF NOVA
SCOTIA, PRINCE EDWARD ISLAND, NEW BRUNSWICK
1758-1952. CANADA UK ADMIN COLONIAL LEAD...POLICY
18/20. PAGE 12 B0245
B57
BIBLIOG
NAT/G
DIPLOM

SOUTH PACIFIC COMMISSION,INDEX OF SOCIAL SCIENCE
RESEARCH THESES ON THE SOUTH PACIFIC. S/ASIA ACADEM
ADMIN COLONIAL...SOC 20. PAGE 99 B2000
B57
BIBLIOG/A
ACT/RES
SECT
CULTURE

COWAN L.G.,LOCAL GOVERNMENT IN WEST AFRICA. AFR
FRANCE UK CULTURE KIN POL/PAR CHIEF LEGIS CREATE
ADMIN PARTIC GOV/REL GP/REL...METH/COMP 20. PAGE 24
B0498
B58
LOC/G
COLONIAL
SOVEREIGN
REPRESENT

LOVEJOY D.S.,RHODE ISLAND POLITICS AND THE AMERICAN
REVOLUTION 1760-1776. UK USA-45 ELITES EX/STRUC TAX
LEAD REPRESENT GOV/REL GP/REL ATTIT 18 RHODE/ISL.
PAGE 67 B1343
B58
REV
COLONIAL
ECO/TAC
SOVEREIGN

CONOVER H.F.,NIGERIAN OFFICIAL PUBLICATIONS,
1869-1959: A GUIDE. NIGER CONSTN FINAN ACADEM
SCHOOL FORCES PRESS ADMIN COLONIAL...HIST/WRIT
19/20. PAGE 23 B0466
B59
BIBLIOG
NAT/G
CON/ANAL

LOEWENSTEIN K.,VERFASSUNGSRECHT UND
VERFASSUNGSPRAXIS DER VEREINIGTEN STAATEN. USA+45
USA-45 COLONIAL CT/SYS GP/REL RACE/REL ORD/FREE
...JURID 18/20 SUPREME/CT CONGRESS PRESIDENT
BILL/RIGHT CIVIL/LIB. PAGE 66 B1337
B59
CONSTN
POL/PAR
EX/STRUC
NAT/G

ASPREMONT-LYNDEN H.,RAPPORT SUR L'ADMINISTRATION
BELGE DU RUANDA-URUNDI PENDANT L'ANNEE 1959.
BELGIUM RWANDA AGRI INDUS DIPLOM ECO/TAC INT/TRADE
DOMIN ADMIN RACE/REL...GEOG CENSUS 20 UN. PAGE 7
B0143
B60
AFR
COLONIAL
ECO/UNDEV
INT/ORG

AYEARST M.,THE BRITISH WEST INDIES: THE SEARCH FOR
SELF-GOVERNMENT. FUT WEST/IND LOC/G POL/PAR
EX/STRUC LEGIS CHOOSE FEDERAL...NAT/COMP BIBLIOG
17/20. PAGE 7 B0152
B60
CONSTN
COLONIAL
REPRESENT
NAT/G

EASTON S.C.,THE TWILIGHT OF EUROPEAN COLONIALISM.
AFR S/ASIA CONSIN SOCIETY STRUCT ECO/UNDEV INDUS
NAT/G FORCES ECO/TAC COLONIAL CT/SYS ATTIT KNOWL
ORD/FREE PWR...SOCIALIST TIME/SEQ TREND CON/ANAL
20. PAGE 32 B0645
B60
FINAN
ADMIN

LEYDER J.,BIBLIOGRAPHIE DE L'ENSEIGNEMENT SUPERIEUR
ET DE LA RECHERCHE SCIENTIFIQUE EN AFRIQUE
INTERTROPICALE (2 VOLS.). AFR CULTURE ECO/UNDEV
AGRI PLAN EDU/PROP ADMIN COLONIAL...GEOG SOC/INTEG
20 NEGRO. PAGE 65 B1309
B60
BIBLIOG/A
ACT/RES
ACADEM
R+D

PIERCE R.A.,RUSSIAN CENTRAL ASIA, 1867-1917. ASIA
RUSSIA CULTURE AGRI INDUS EDU/PROP REV NAT/LISM
...CHARTS BIBLIOG 19/20 BOLSHEVISM INTERVENT.
B60
COLONIAL
DOMIN
ADMIN

PAGE 83 B1672
ECO/UNDEV

SMITH M.G.,GOVERNMENT IN ZAZZAU 1800-1950. NIGERIA
UK CULTURE SOCIETY LOC/G ADMIN COLONIAL
...METH/CNCPT NEW/IDEA METH 19/20. PAGE 98 B1983
B60
REGION
CONSTN
KIN
ECO/UNDEV

WHEARE K.C.,THE CONSTITUTIONAL STRUCTURE OF THE
COMMONWEALTH. UK EX/STRUC DIPLOM DOMIN ADMIN
COLONIAL CONTROL LEAD INGP/REL SUPEGO 20 CMN/WLTH.
PAGE 115 B2330
B60
CONSTN
INT/ORG
VOL/ASSN
SOVEREIGN

CARNEY D.E.,GOVERNMENT AND ECONOMY IN BRITISH WEST
AFRICA. GAMBIA GHANA NIGERIA SIER/LEONE DOMIN ADMIN
GOV/REL SOVEREIGN WEALTH LAISSEZ...BIBLIOG 20
CMN/WLTH. PAGE 19 B0384
B61
METH/COMP
COLONIAL
ECO/TAC
ECO/UNDEV

COHN B.S.,DEVELOPMENT AND IMPACT OF BRITISH
ADMINISTRATION IN INDIA: A BIBLIOGRAPHIC ESSAY.
INDIA UK ECO/UNDEV NAT/G DOMIN...POLICY MGT SOC
19/20. PAGE 22 B0448
B61
BIBLIOG/A
COLONIAL
S/ASIA
ADMIN

FREYRE G.,THE PORTUGUESE AND THE TROPICS. L/A+17C
PORTUGAL SOCIETY PERF/ART ADMIN TASK GP/REL
...ART/METH CONCPT SOC/INTEG 20. PAGE 37 B0754
B61
COLONIAL
METH
PLAN
CULTURE

HICKS U.K.,DEVELOPMENT FROM BELOW. UK INDUS ADMIN
COLONIAL ROUTINE GOV/REL...POLICY METH/CNCPT CHARTS
19/20 CMN/WLTH. PAGE 50 B1006
B61
ECO/UNDEV
LOC/G
GOV/COMP
METH/COMP

KERTESZ S.D.,AMERICAN DIPLOMACY IN A NEW ERA. COM
S/ASIA USA+45 FORCES PROB/SOLV BAL/PWR ECO/TAC
ADMIN COLONIAL WAR PEACE ORD/FREE 20 NATO CONGRESS
UN COLD/WAR. PAGE 59 B1199
B61
ANTHOL
DIPLOM
TREND

MUNGER E.S.,AFRICAN FIELD REPORTS 1952-1961.
SOUTH/AFR SOCIETY ECO/UNDEV NAT/G POL/PAR COLONIAL
EXEC PARL/PROC GUERRILLA RACE/REL ALL/IDEOS...SOC
AUD/VIS 20. PAGE 76 B1538
B61
AFR
DISCRIM
RECORD

RAO K.V.,PARLIAMENTARY DEMOCRACY OF INDIA. INDIA
EX/STRUC TOP/EX COLONIAL CT/SYS PARL/PROC ORD/FREE
...POLICY CONCPT TREND 20 PARLIAMENT. PAGE 86 B1733
B61
CONSTN
ADJUD
NAT/G
FEDERAL

ROSE D.L.,THE VIETNAMESE CIVIL SERVICE. VIETNAM
CONSULT DELIB/GP GIVE PAY EDU/PROP COLONIAL GOV/REL
UTIL...CHARTS 20. PAGE 90 B1819
B61
ADMIN
EFFICIENCY
STAT
NAT/G

WEST F.J.,POLITICAL ADVANCEMENT IN THE SOUTH
PACIFIC. CONSTN CULTURE POL/PAR LEGIS DOMIN ADMIN
CHOOSE SOVEREIGN VAL/FREE 20 FIJI TAHITI SAMOA.
PAGE 115 B2325
B61
S/ASIA
LOC/G
COLONIAL

LIEBENOW J.G.,"LEGITIMACY OF ALIEN RELATIONSHIP:
THE NYATURU OF TANGANYIKA" (BMR)" AFR UK ADMIN LEAD
CHOOSE 20 NYATURU TANGANYIKA. PAGE 65 B1312
S61
COLONIAL
DOMIN
LEGIT
PWR

MOODIE G.C.,"THE GOVERNMENT OF GREAT BRITAIN." UK
LAW STRUCT LOC/G POL/PAR DIPLOM RECEIVE ADMIN
COLONIAL CHOOSE...BIBLIOG 20 PARLIAMENT. PAGE 75
B1508
C61
NAT/G
SOCIETY
PARL/PROC
GOV/COMP

ANDREWS W.G.,FRENCH POLITICS AND ALGERIA: THE
PROCESS OF POLICY FORMATION 1954-1962. ALGERIA
FRANCE CONSTN ELITES POL/PAR CHIEF DELIB/GP LEGIS
DIPLOM PRESS CHOOSE 20. PAGE 5 B0105
B62
GOV/COMP
EXEC
COLONIAL

CARSON P.,MATERIALS FOR WEST AFRICAN HISTORY IN THE
ARCHIVES OF BELGIUM AND HOLLAND. CLIENT INDUS
INT/TRADE ADMIN 17/19. PAGE 19 B0387
B62
BIBLIOG/A
COLONIAL
AFR
ECO/UNDEV

DELANY V.T.H.,THE ADMINISTRATION OF JUSTICE IN
IRELAND. IRELAND CONSTN FINAN JUDGE COLONIAL CRIME
...CRIMLGY 19/20. PAGE 28 B0571
B62
ADMIN
JURID
CT/SYS
ADJUD

HSUEH S.-S.,GOVERNMENT AND ADMINISTRATION OF HONG
KONG. CHIEF DELIB/GP LEGIS CT/SYS REPRESENT GOV/REL
20 HONG/KONG CITY/MGT CIVIL/SERV GOVERNOR. PAGE 52
B1055
B62
ADMIN
LOC/G
COLONIAL
EX/STRUC

INGHAM K.,A HISTORY OF EAST AFRICA. NAT/G DIPLOM
ADMIN WAR NAT/LISM...SOC BIOG BIBLIOG. PAGE 54
B1085
B62
AFR
CONSTN
COLONIAL

LYNCH J.,ADMINISTRATION COLONIAL ESPANOLA
1782-1810. SPAIN PROVS TOP/EX PARTIC 18/19 ARGEN.
PAGE 67 B1349
B62
COLONIAL
CONTROL
ADJUD
ADMIN

MORE S.S.,REMODELLING OF DEMOCRACY FOR AFRO-ASIAN   ORD/FREE
NATIONS. AFR INDIA S/ASIA SOUTH/AFR CONSTN EX/STRUC   ECO/UNDEV
COLONIAL CHOOSE TOTALISM SOVEREIGN NEW/LIB SOCISM   ADMIN
...SOC/WK 20. PAGE 75 B1520   LEGIS
                                                     B62
PHILLIPS O.H.,CONSTITUTIONAL AND ADMINISTRATIVE LAW JURID
(3RD ED.). UK INT/ORG LOC/G CHIEF EX/STRUC LEGIS   ADMIN
BAL/PWR ADJUD COLONIAL CT/SYS PWR...CHARTS 20.   CONSTN
PAGE 83 B1670   NAT/G
                                                     B62
SHAPIRO D.,A SELECT BIBLIOGRAPHY OF WORKS IN   BIBLIOG
ENGLISH ON RUSSIAN HISTORY, 1801-1917. COM USSR   DIPLOM
STRATA FORCES EDU/PROP ADMIN REV RACE/REL ATTIT   COLONIAL
19/20. PAGE 96 B1932
                                                     B62
TAYLOR D.,THE BRITISH IN AFRICA. UK CULTURE   AFR
ECO/UNDEV INDUS DIPLOM INT/TRADE ADMIN WAR RACE/REL COLONIAL
ORD/FREE SOVEREIGN...POLICY BIBLIOG 15/20 CMN/WLTH. DOMIN
PAGE 103 B2084
                                                     B62
WELLEQUET J.,LE CONGO BELGE ET LA WELTPOLITIK   ADMIN
(1894-1914). GERMANY DOMIN EDU/PROP WAR ATTIT   DIPLOM
...BIBLIOG T CONGO/LEOP. PAGE 115 B2318   GP/REL
                                                     COLONIAL
                                                     L62
BELSHAW D.G.R.,"PUBLIC INVESTMENT IN AGRICULTURE   ECO/UNDEV
AND ECONOMIC DEVELOPMENT OF UGANDA" UGANDA AGRI   PLAN
INDUS R+D ECO/TAC RATION TAX PAY COLONIAL 20   ADMIN
WORLD/BANK. PAGE 10 B0209   CENTRAL
                                                     L62
HOFFHERR R.,"LE PROBLEME DE L'ENCADREMENT DANS LES   AFR
JEUNES ETATS DE LANGUE FRANCAISE EN AFRIQUE   STRUCT
CENTRALE ET A MADAGASCAR." FUT ECO/UNDEV CONSULT   FRANCE
PLAN ECO/TAC COLONIAL ATTIT...MGT TIME/SEQ VAL/FREE
20. PAGE 51 B1028
                                                     L62
MANGIN G.,"L'ORGANIZATION JUDICIAIRE DES ETATS   AFR
D'AFRIQUE ET DE MADAGASCAR." ISLAM WOR+45 STRATA   LEGIS
STRUCT ECO/UNDEV NAT/G LEGIT EXEC...JURID TIME/SEQ   COLONIAL
TOT/POP 20 SUPREME/CT. PAGE 69 B1387   MADAGASCAR
                                                     S62
JACOBSON H.K.,"THE UNITED NATIONS AND COLONIALISM: INT/ORG
A TENTATIVE APPRAISAL." AFR FUT S/ASIA USA+45 USSR   CONCPT
WOR+45 NAT/G DELIB/GP PLAN DIPLOM ECO/TAC DOMIN   COLONIAL
ADMIN ROUTINE COERCE ATTIT RIGID/FLEX ORD/FREE PWR
...OBS STERTYP UN 20. PAGE 55 B1115
                                                     S62
MURACCIOLE L.,"LES CONSTITUTIONS DES ETATS   NAT/G
AFRICAINS D'EXPRESSION FRANCAISE: LA CONSTITUTION   CONSTN
DU 16 AVRIL 1962 DE LA REPUBLIQUE DU" AFR CHAD
CHIEF LEGIS LEGIT COLONIAL EXEC ROUTINE ORD/FREE
SOVEREIGN...SOC CONCPT 20. PAGE 76 B1541
                                                     S62
PIQUEMAL M.,"LES PROBLEMES DES UNIONS D'ETATS EN   AFR
AFRIQUE NOIRE." FRANCE SOCIETY INT/ORG NAT/G   ECO/UNDEV
DELIB/GP PLAN LEGIT ADMIN COLONIAL ROUTINE ATTIT   REGION
ORD/FREE PWR...GEOG METH/CNCPT 20. PAGE 83 B1678
                                                     B63
CROZIER B.,THE MORNING AFTER: A STUDY OF   SOVEREIGN
INDEPENDENCE. WOR+45 EX/STRUC PLAN BAL/PWR COLONIAL NAT/LISM
GP/REL 20 COLD/WAR. PAGE 25 B0511   NAT/G
                                                     DIPLOM
                                                     B63
DIESNER H.J.,KIRCHE UND STAAT IM SPATROMISCHEN   SECT
REICH. ROMAN/EMP EX/STRUC COLONIAL COERCE ATTIT   GP/REL
CATHISM 4/5 AFRICA/N CHURCH/STA. PAGE 29 B0592   DOMIN
                                                     JURID
                                                     B63
ECOLE NATIONALE D'ADMIN,BIBLIOGRAPHIE SELECTIVE   BIBLIOG
D'OUVRAGES DE LANGUE FRANCAISE TRAITANT DES   AFR
PROBLEMES GOUVERNEMENTAUX ET ADMINISTRATIFS. NAT/G   ADMIN
FORCES ACT/RES UP/RES PLAN PROB/SOLV BUDGET ADJUD   EX/STRUC
COLONIAL LEAD 20. PAGE 32 B0651
                                                     B63
ELIAS T.O.,THE NIGERIAN LEGAL SYSTEM. NIGERIA LAW   CT/SYS
FAM KIN SECT ADMIN NAT/LISM...JURID 18/20   ADJUD
ENGLSH/LAW COMMUN/LAW. PAGE 33 B0665   COLONIAL
                                                     PROF/ORG
                                                     B63
FORTES A.B.,HISTORIA ADMINISTRATIVA, JUDICIARIA E   PROVS
ECLESIASTICA DO RIO GRANDE DO SUL. BRAZIL L/A+17C   ADMIN
LOC/G SECT COLONIAL CT/SYS ORD/FREE CATHISM 16/20.   JURID
PAGE 37 B0742
                                                     B63
GALBRAITH J.S.,RELUCTANT EMPIRE: BRITISH POLICY OF   COLONIAL
THE SOUTH AFRICAN FRONTIER, 1834-1854. AFR   ADMIN
SOUTH/AFR UK GP/REL RACE/REL DISCRIM...CHARTS   POLICY
BIBLIOG 19 MISSION. PAGE 38 B0774   SECT
                                                     B63
MCKIE R.,MALAYSIA IN FOCUS. INDONESIA WOR+45   S/ASIA
ECO/UNDEV FINAN NAT/G POL/PAR SECT FORCES PLAN   NAT/LISM
ADMIN COLONIAL COERCE DRIVE ALL/VALS...POLICY   MALAYSIA
RECORD CENSUS TIME/SEQ CMN/WLTH 20. PAGE 72 B1453
                                                     B63
PATRA A.C.,THE ADMINISTRATION OF JUSTICE UNDER THE   ADMIN

EAST INDIA COMPANY IN BENGAL, BIHAR AND ORISSA.   JURID
INDIA UK LG/CO CAP/ISM INT/TRADE ADJUD COLONIAL   CONCPT
CONTROL CT/SYS...POLICY 20. PAGE 81 B1641
                                                     B63
ROBINSON K.,ESSAYS IN IMPERIAL GOVERNMENT. CAMEROON COLONIAL
NIGERIA UK CONSTN LOC/G LEGIS ADMIN GOV/REL PWR   AFR
...POLICY ANTHOL BIBLIOG 17/20 PURHAM/M. PAGE 89   DOMIN
B1803
                                                     B63
SINGH H.L.,PROBLEMS AND POLICIES OF THE BRITISH IN   COLONIAL
INDIA, 1885-1898. INDIA UK NAT/G FORCES LEGIS   PWR
PROB/SOLV CONTROL RACE/REL ADJUST DISCRIM NAT/LISM   POLICY
RIGID/FLEX...MGT 19 CIVIL/SERV. PAGE 97 B1968   ADMIN
                                                     B63
STEVENSON A.E.,LOOKING OUTWARD: YEARS OF CRISIS AT   INT/ORG
THE UNITED NATIONS. COM CUBA USA+45 WOR+45 SOCIETY   CONCPT
NAT/G EX/STRUC ACT/RES LEGIT COLONIAL ATTIT PERSON   ARMS/CONT
SUPEGO ALL/VALS...POLICY HUM UN COLD/WAR CONGO 20.
PAGE 100 B2034
                                                     B63
WALKER A.A.,OFFICIAL PUBLICATIONS OF SIERRA LEONE   BIBLIOG
AND GAMBIA. GAMBIA SIER/LEONE UK LAW CONSTN LEGIS   NAT/G
PLAN BUDGET DIPLOM...SOC SAMP CON/ANAL 20. PAGE 113 COLONIAL
B2278   ADMIN
                                                     S63
ROUGEMONT D.,"LES NOUVELLES CHANCES DE L'EUROPE."   ECO/UNDEV
EUR+WWI FUT ECO/DEV INT/ORG NAT/G ACT/RES PLAN   PERCEPT
TEC/DEV EDU/PROP ADMIN COLONIAL FEDERAL ATTIT PWR
SKILL...TREND 20. PAGE 91 B1835
                                                     B64
AHMAD M.,THE CIVIL SERVANT IN PAKISTAN. PAKISTAN   WELF/ST
ECO/UNDEV COLONIAL INGP/REL...SOC CHARTS BIBLIOG 20 ADMIN
CIVIL/SERV. PAGE 3 B0065   ATTIT
                                                     STRATA
                                                     B64
DAS M.N.,INDIA UNDER MORLEY AND MINTO. INDIA UK   GOV/REL
ECO/UNDEV MUNIC PROVS EX/STRUC LEGIS DIPLOM CONTROL COLONIAL
REV 20 MORLEY/J. PAGE 26 B0531   POLICY
                                                     ADMIN
                                                     B64
DUROSELLE J.B.,POLITIQUES NATIONALES ENVERS LES   DIPLOM
JEUNES ETATS. FRANCE ISRAEL ITALY UK USA+45 USSR   ECO/UNDEV
YUGOSLAVIA ECO/DEV FINAN ECO/TAC INT/TRADE ADMIN   COLONIAL
PWR 20. PAGE 31 B0634   DOMIN
                                                     B64
ENDACOTT G.B.,GOVERNMENT AND PEOPLE IN HONG KONG   CONSTN
1841-1962: A CONSTITUTIONAL HISTORY. UK LEGIS ADJUD COLONIAL
REPRESENT ATTIT 19/20 HONG/KONG. PAGE 33 B0674   CONTROL
                                                     ADMIN
                                                     B64
HAMILTON B.L.S.,PROBLEMS OF ADMINISTRATION IN AN   ADMIN
EMERGENT NATION: CASE STUDY OF JAMAICA. JAMAICA UK   ECO/UNDEV
WOR+45 MUNIC COLONIAL HABITAT...CHARTS BIBLIOG 20   GOV/REL
CIVIL/SERV. PAGE 46 B0932   NAT/G
                                                     B64
HANNA W.J.,INDEPENDENT BLACK AFRICA: THE POLITICS   AFR
OF FREEDOM. ELITES INDUS KIN CHIEF COLONIAL CHOOSE   ECO/UNDEV
GOV/REL RACE/REL NAT/LISM ATTIT PERSON 20 NEGRO.   ADMIN
PAGE 46 B0938   PROB/SOLV
                                                     B64
MAHAR J.M.,INDIA: A CRITICAL BIBLIOGRAPHY. INDIA   BIBLIOG/A
PAKISTAN CULTURE ECO/UNDEV LOC/G POL/PAR SECT   S/ASIA
PROB/SOLV DIPLOM ADMIN COLONIAL PARL/PROC ATTIT 20. NAT/G
PAGE 68 B1377   LEAD
                                                     B64
RIKER W.H.,FEDERALISM. WOR+45 WOR-45 CONSTN CHIEF   FEDERAL
LEGIS ADMIN COLONIAL CONTROL CT/SYS PWR...BIBLIOG/A NAT/G
18/20. PAGE 88 B1787   ORD/FREE
                                                     CENTRAL
                                                     B64
TILMAN R.O.,BUREAUCRATIC TRANSITION IN MALAYA.   ADMIN
MALAYSIA S/ASIA UK NAT/G EX/STRUC DIPLOM...CHARTS   COLONIAL
BIBLIOG 20. PAGE 104 B2110   SOVEREIGN
                                                     EFFICIENCY
                                                     B64
WAINHOUSE D.W.,REMNANTS OF EMPIRE: THE UNITED   INT/ORG
NATIONS AND THE END OF COLONIALISM. FUT PORTUGAL   TREND
WOR+45 NAT/G CONSULT DOMIN LEGIT ADMIN ROUTINE   COLONIAL
ATTIT ORD/FREE...POLICY JURID RECORD INT TIME/SEQ
UN CMN/WLTH 20. PAGE 113 B2275
                                                     L64
SYMONDS R.,"REFLECTIONS IN LOCALISATION." AFR   ADMIN
S/ASIA UK STRATA INT/ORG NAT/G SCHOOL EDU/PROP   MGT
LEGIT KNOWL ORD/FREE PWR RESPECT CMN/WLTH 20.   COLONIAL
PAGE 102 B2064
                                                     S64
GROSS J.A.,"WHITEHALL AND THE COMMONWEALTH."   EX/STRUC
EUR+WWI MOD/EUR INT/ORG NAT/G CONSULT DELIB/GP   ATTIT
LEGIS DOMIN ADMIN COLONIAL ROUTINE PWR CMN/WLTH   TREND
19/20. PAGE 44 B0890
                                                     S64
LOW D.A.,"LION RAMPANT." EUR+WWI MOD/EUR S/ASIA   AFR
ECO/UNDEV NAT/G FORCES TEC/DEV ECO/TAC LEGIT ADMIN   DOMIN
COLONIAL COERCE ORD/FREE RESPECT 19/20. PAGE 67   DIPLOM
B1344   UK

ADU A.L.,THE CIVIL SERVICE IN NEW AFRICAN STATES. | ECO/UNDEV
AFR GHANA FINAN SOVEREIGN...POLICY 20 CIVIL/SERV | ADMIN
AFRICA/E AFRICA/W. PAGE 3 B0062 | COLONIAL
B65 | NAT/G

BERNDT R.M.,ABORIGINAL MAN IN AUSTRALIA. LAW DOMIN | SOC
ADMIN COLONIAL MARRIAGE HABITAT ORD/FREE...LING | CULTURE
CHARTS ANTHOL BIBLIOG WORSHIP 20 AUSTRAL ABORIGINES | SOCIETY
MUSIC ELKIN/AP. PAGE 11 B0225 | STRUCT
B65

BOXER C.R.,PORTUGUESE SOCIETY IN THE TROPICS - THE | MUNIC
MUNICIPAL COUNCILS OF GAO, MACAO, BAHIA, AND | ADMIN
LUANDA, 1510-1800. EUR+WWI MOD/EUR PORTUGAL CONSTN | COLONIAL
EX/STRUC DOMIN CONTROL ROUTINE REPRESENT PRIVIL | DELIB/GP
...BIBLIOG/A 16/19 GENACCOUNT MACAO BAHIA LUANDA.
PAGE 14 B0290
B65

GOODSELL C.T.,ADMINISTRATION OF A REVOLUTION. | EXEC
PUERT/RICO ECO/UNDEV FINAN MUNIC POL/PAR PROVS | SOC
LEGIS PLAN BUDGET RECEIVE ADMIN COLONIAL LEAD 20
ROOSEVLT/F. PAGE 41 B0827
B65

GOPAL S.,BRITISH POLICY IN INDIA 1858-1905. INDIA | COLONIAL
UK ELITES CHIEF DELIB/GP ECO/TAC GP/REL DISCRIM | ADMIN
ATTIT...IDEA/COMP NAT/COMP PERS/COMP BIBLIOG/A | POL/PAR
19/20. PAGE 41 B0828 | ECO/UNDEV
B65

HISPANIC SOCIETY OF AMERICA,CATALOGUE (10 VOLS.). | BIBLIOG
PORTUGAL PRE/AMER SPAIN NAT/G ADMIN...POLICY SOC | L/A+17C
15/20. PAGE 50 B1018 | COLONIAL
B65 | DIPLOM

LEMAY G.H.,BRITISH SUPREMACY IN SOUTH AFRICA | WAR
1899-1907. SOUTH/AFR UK ADMIN CONTROL LEAD GP/REL | COLONIAL
ORD/FREE 19/20. PAGE 64 B1286 | DOMIN
B65 | POLICY

MOORE C.H.,TUNISIA SINCE INDEPENDENCE. ELITES LOC/G | NAT/G
POL/PAR ADMIN COLONIAL CONTROL.EXEC GOV/REL | EX/STRUC
TOTALISM MARXISM...INT 20 TUNIS. PAGE 75 B1513 | SOCISM
B65

PANJABI K.L.,THE CIVIL SERVANT IN INDIA. INDIA UK | ADMIN
NAT/G CONSULT EX/STRUC REGION GP/REL RACE/REL 20. | WORKER
PAGE 81 B1631 | BIOG
B65 | COLONIAL

PURCELL V.,THE MEMOIRS OF A MALAYAN OFFICIAL. | BIOG
MALAYSIA UK ECO/UNDEV INDUS LABOR EDU/PROP COLONIAL | ADMIN
CT/SYS WAR NAT/LISM TOTALISM ORD/FREE SOVEREIGN 20 | JURID
UN CIVIL/SERV. PAGE 85 B1721 | FORCES
B65

PYLEE M.V.,CONSTITUTIONAL GOVERNMENT IN INDIA (2ND | CONSTN
REV. ED.). INDIA POL/PAR EX/STRUC DIPLOM COLONIAL | NAT/G
CT/SYS PARL/PROC PRIVIL...JURID 16/20. PAGE 85 | PROVS
B1725 | FEDERAL
B65

ROTBERG R.I.,A POLITICAL HISTORY OF TROPICAL | AFR
AFRICA. EX/STRUC DIPLOM INT/TRADE DOMIN ADMIN | CULTURE
RACE/REL NAT/LISM PWR SOVEREIGN...GEOG TIME/SEQ | COLONIAL
BIBLIOG 1/20. PAGE 91 B1832
B65

WARD W.E.,GOVERNMENT IN WEST AFRICA. WOR+45 POL/PAR | GOV/COMP
EX/STRUC PLAN PARTIC GP/REL SOVEREIGN 20 AFRICA/W. | CONSTN
PAGE 114 B2291 | COLONIAL
B65 | ECO/UNDEV

WITHERELL J.W.,MADAGASCAR AND ADJACENT ISLANDS; A | BIBLIOG
GUIDE TO OFFICIAL PUBLICATIONS (PAMPHLET). FRANCE | COLONIAL
MADAGASCAR S/ASIA UK LAW OP/RES PLAN DIPLOM | LOC/G
...POLICY CON/ANAL 19/20. PAGE 117 B2368 | ADMIN
B65

YOUNG C.,POLITICS IN THE CONGO* DECOLONIZATION AND | BELGIUM
INDEPENDENCE. ELITES STRATA FORCES ADMIN REV | COLONIAL
RACE/REL FEDERAL SOVEREIGN...OBS INT CHARTS | NAT/LISM
CONGO/LEOP. PAGE 118 B2391
S65

"FURTHER READING." INDIA ADMIN COLONIAL WAR GOV/REL | BIBLIOG
ATTIT 20. PAGE 2 B0044 | DIPLOM
| NAT/G
| POLICY
B66

DAVIS J.A.,SOUTHERN AFRICA IN TRANSITION. SOUTH/AFR | AFR
USA+45 FINAN NAT/G DELIB/GP EDU/PROP ADMIN COLONIAL | ADJUST
REGION RACE/REL ATTIT SOVEREIGN...ANTHOL 20 | CONSTN
RESOURCE/N. PAGE 26 B0538
B66

DILLEY M.R.,BRITISH POLICY IN KENYA COLONY (2ND | COLONIAL
ED.). AFR INDIA UK LABOR BUDGET TAX ADMIN PARL/PROC | REPRESENT
GP/REL...BIBLIOG 20 PARLIAMENT. PAGE 29 B0594 | SOVEREIGN
B66

FABAR R.,THE VISION AND THE NEED: LATE VICTORIAN | COLONIAL
IMPERIALIST AIMS. MOD/EUR UK WOR-45 CULTURE NAT/G | CONCPT
DIPLOM...TIME/SEQ METH/COMP 19 KIPLING/R | ADMIN
COMMONWLTH. PAGE 34 B0693 | ATTIT

HAYER T.,FRENCH AID. AFR FRANCE AGRI FINAN BUDGET | TEC/DEV
ADMIN WAR PRODUC...CHARTS 18/20 THIRD/WRLD | COLONIAL
OVRSEA/DEV. PAGE 48 B0975 | FOR/AID
B66 | ECO/UNDEV

KAUNDA K.,ZAMBIA: INDEPENDENCE AND BEYOND: THE | ORD/FREE
SPEECHES OF KENNETH KAUNDA. AFR FUT ZAMBIA SOCIETY | COLONIAL
ECO/UNDEV NAT/G PROB/SOLV ECO/TAC ADMIN RACE/REL | CONSTN
SOVEREIGN 20. PAGE 59 B1183 | LEAD
B66

O'NEILL C.E.,CHURCH AND STATE IN FRENCH COLONIAL | COLONIAL
LOUISIANA: POLICY AND POLITICS TO 1732. PROVS | NAT/G
VOL/ASSN DELIB/GP ADJUD ADMIN GP/REL ATTIT DRIVE | SECT
...POLICY BIBLIOG 17/18 LOUISIANA CHURCH/STA. | PWR
PAGE 79 B1601
B66

SMITH H.E.,READINGS IN ECONOMIC DEVELOPMENT AND | TEC/DEV
ADMINISTRATION IN TANZANIA. TANZANIA FINAN INDUS | ADMIN
LABOR ADMIN PLAN PROB/SOLV INT/TRADE COLONIAL | GOV/REL
REGION...ANTHOL BIBLIOG 20 AFRICA/E. PAGE 98 B1981
B66

US LIBRARY OF CONGRESS,NIGERIA: A GUIDE TO OFFICIAL | BIBLIOG
PUBLICATIONS. CAMERCON NIGERIA UK DIPLOM...POLICY | ADMIN
19/20 UN LEAGUE/NAT. PAGE 109 B2207 | NAT/G
| COLONIAL
B66

WILLNER A.R.,THE NEOTRADITIONAL ACCOMMODATION TO | INDONESIA
POLITICAL INDEPENDENCE* THE CASE OF INDONESIA * | CONSERVE
RESEARCH MONOGRAPH NO. 26. CULTURE ECO/UNDEV CREATE | ELITES
PROB/SOLV FOR/AID LEGIT COLONIAL EFFICIENCY | ADMIN
NAT/LISM ALL/VALS SOC. PAGE 117 B2355
S66

AFRICAN BIBLIOGRAPHIC CENTER,"A CURRENT VIEW OF | BIBLIOG/A
AFRICANA: A SELECT AND ANNOTATED BIBLIOGRAPHICAL | NAT/G
PUBLISHING GUIDE, 1965-1966." AFR CULTURE INDUS | TEC/DEV
LABOR SECT FOR/AID ADMIN COLONIAL REV RACE/REL | POL/PAR
SOCISM...LING 20. PAGE 3 B0063
C66

TARLING N.,"A CONCISE HISTORY OF SOUTHEAST ASIA." | COLONIAL
BURMA CAMBODIA LAOS S/ASIA THAILAND VIETNAM | DOMIN
ECO/UNDEV POL/PAR FORCES ADMIN REV WAR CIVMIL/REL | INT/TRADE
ORD/FREE MARXISM SOCISM 13/20. PAGE 82 B2080 | NAT/LISM
B67

DE BLIJ H.J.,SYSTEMATIC POLITICAL GEOGRAPHY. WOR+45 | GEOG
STRUCT INT/ORG NAT/G EDU/PROP ADMIN COLONIAL | CONCPT
ROUTINE ORD/FREE PWR...IDEA/COMP T 20. PAGE 27 | METH
B0550

GIFFORD P.,BRITAIN AND GERMANY IN AFRICA. AFR | COLONIAL
GERMANY UK ECO/UNDEV LEAD WAR NAT/LISM ATTIT | ADMIN
...POLICY HIST/WRIT METH/COMP ANTHOL BIBLIOG 19/20 | DIPLOM
WWI. PAGE 39 B0797 | NAT/COMP
B67

KONCZACKI Z.A.,PUBLIC FINANCE AND ECONOMIC | ECO/TAC
DEVELOPMENT OF NATAL 1893-1910. TAX ADMIN COLONIAL | FINAN
...STAT CHARTS BIBLIOG 19/20 NATAL. PAGE 61 B1228 | NAT/G
| ECO/UNDEV
B67

NIVEN R.,NIGERIA. NIGERIA CONSTN INDUS EX/STRUC | NAT/G
COLONIAL REV NAT/LISM...CHARTS 19/20. PAGE 78 B1584 | REGION
| CHOOSE
| GP/REL
B67

RAVKIN A.,THE NEW STATES OF AFRICA (HEADLINE | AFR
SERIES. NO. 183((PAMPHLET). CULTURE STRUCT INDUS | ECO/UNDEV
COLONIAL NAT/LISM...SOC 20. PAGE 86 B1744 | SOCIETY
| ADMIN
B67

ROFF W.R.,THE ORIGINS OF MALAY NATIONALISM. | NAT/LISM
MALAYSIA INTELL NAT/G ADMIN COLONIAL...BIBLIOG | ELITES
DICTIONARY 20 CMN/WLTH. PAGE 90 B1813 | VOL/ASSN
| SOCIETY
B67

WESSON R.G.,THE IMPERIAL ORDER. WOR-45 STRUCT SECT | PWR
DOMIN ADMIN COLONIAL LEAD CONSERVE...CONCPT BIBLIOG | CHIEF
20. PAGE 115 B2324 | CONTROL
| SOCIETY
L67

BESCOBY I.,"A COLONIAL ADMINISTRATION* AN ANALYSIS | ADMIN
OF ADMINISTRATION IN BRITISH COLUMBIA 1869-1871." | CANADA
UK STRATA EX/STRUC LEGIS TASK GOV/REL EFFICIENCY | COLONIAL
ROLE...MGT CHARTS 19. PAGE 11 B0232 | LEAD
S67

FRYKENBURG R.E.,"STUDIES OF LAND CONTROL IN INDIAN | ECO/UNDEV
HISTORY: REVIEW ARTICLE." INDIA UK STRATA AGRI | CONTROL
MUNIC OP/RES COLONIAL REGION EFFICIENCY OWN HABITAT | ADMIN
...CONCPT 16/20. PAGE 38 B0763
S67

GRUNDY K.W.,"THE POLITICAL USES OF IMAGINATION." | NAT/LISM
GHANA ELITES SOCIETY NAT/G DOMIN EDU/PROP COLONIAL | EX/STRUC
REGION REPRESENT GP/REL CENTRAL PWR MARXISM 20. | AFR
PAGE 44 B0897 | LEAD
S67

HUGON P.,"BLOCAGES ET DESEQUILIBRES DE LA | ECO/UNDEV
CROISSANCE ECONOMIQUE EN AFRIQUE NOIRE." AFR KIN | COLONIAL

MUNIC CREATE PLAN INT/TRADE REGION ADJUST CENTRAL STRUCT
EQUILIB NAT/LISM ORD/FREE 20. PAGE 52 B1060 ADMIN
S67

IDENBURG P.J.,"POLITICAL STRUCTURAL DEVELOPMENT IN AFR
TROPICAL AFRICA." UK ECO/UNDEV KIN POL/PAR CHIEF CONSTN
EX/STRUC CREATE COLONIAL CONTROL REPRESENT RACE/REL NAT/G
...MAJORIT TREND 20. PAGE 53 B1074 GOV/COMP
S67

MURRAY R.,"SECOND THOUGHTS ON GHANA." AFR GHANA COLONIAL
NAT/G POL/PAR ADMIN REV GP/REL CENTRAL...SOCIALIST CONTROL
CONCPT METH 20. PAGE 77 B1548 REGION
SOCISM
S67

O'DELL J.H.,"THE JULY REBELLIONS AND THE 'MILITARY PWR
STATE'." USA+45 VIETNAM STRATA CHIEF WORKER NAT/G
COLONIAL EXEC CROWD CIVMIL/REL RACE/REL TOTALISM COERCE
...WELF/ST PACIFIST 20 NEGRO JOHNSON/LB PRESIDENT FORCES
CIV/RIGHTS. PAGE 79 B1599
S67

ROTBERG R.I.,"COLONIALISM AND AFTER: THE POLITICAL BIBLIOG/A
LITERATURE OF CENTRAL AFRICA - A BIBLIOGRAPHIC COLONIAL
ESSAY." AFR CHIEF EX/STRUC REV INGP/REL RACE/REL DIPLOM
SOVEREIGN 20. PAGE 91 B1833 NAT/G
B95

LATIMER E.W.,EUROPE IN AFRICA IN THE NINETEENTH AFR
CENTURY. ECO/UNDEV KIN SECT DIPLOM DOMIN ADMIN COLONIAL
DISCRIM 17/18. PAGE 63 B1275 WAR
FINAN
B98

THOMPSON H.C.,RHODESIA AND ITS GOVERNMENT. AFR COLONIAL
RHODESIA ECO/UNDEV INDUS KIN WORKER INT/TRADE ADMIN
DISCRIM LITERACY ORD/FREE 19. PAGE 104 B2102 POLICY
ELITES

COLORADO....COLORADO

B65

BUECHNER J.C.,DIFFERENCES IN ROLE PERCEPTIONS IN MUNIC
COLORADO COUNCIL-MANAGER CITIES. USA+45 ADMIN CONSULT
ROUTINE GP/REL CONSEN PERCEPT PERSON ROLE LOC/G
...DECISION MGT STAT INT QU CHARTS 20 COLORADO IDEA/COMP
CITY/MGT. PAGE 17 B0338

COLUMBIA/U....COLUMBIA UNIVERSITY

COM....COMMUNIST COUNTRIES, EXCEPT CHINA; SEE ALSO
        APPROPRIATE NATIONS, MARXISM

N

KYRIAK T.E.,EAST EUROPE: BIBLIOGRAPHY--INDEX TO US BIBLIOG/A
JPRS RESEARCH TRANSLATIONS. ALBANIA BULGARIA COM PRESS
CZECHOSLVK HUNGARY POLAND ROMANIA AGRI EXTR/IND MARXISM
FINAN SERV/IND INT/TRADE WEAPON...GEOG MGT SOC 20. INDUS
PAGE 62 B1247
B38

HARPER S.N.,THE GOVERNMENT OF THE SOVIET UNION. COM MARXISM
USSR LAW CONSTN ECO/DEV PLAN TEC/DEV DIPLOM NAT/G
INT/TRADE ADMIN REV NAT/LISM...POLICY 20. PAGE 47 LEAD
B0952 POL/PAR
B38

PETTEE G.S.,THE PROCESS OF REVOLUTION. COM FRANCE COERCE
ITALY MOD/EUR RUSSIA SPAIN WOR-45 ELITES INTELL CONCPT
SOCIETY STRATA STRUC INT/ORG NAT/G POL/PAR ACT/RES REV
PLAN EDU/PROP LEGIT EXEC...SOC MYTH TIME/SEQ
TOT/POP 18/20. PAGE 82 B1664
B46

BIBLIOGRAFIIA DISSERTATSII: DOKTORSKIE DISSERTATSII BIBLIOG
ZA 19411944 (2 VOLS.). COM USSR LAW POL/PAR DIPLOM ACADEM
ADMIN LEAD...PHIL/SCI SOC 20. PAGE 2 B0035 KNOWL
MARXIST
S50

WITTFOGEL K.A.,"RUSSIA AND ASIA: PROBLEMS OF ECO/DEV
CONTEMPORARY AREA STUDIES AND INTERNATIONAL ADMIN
RELATIONS." ASIA COM USA+45 SOCIETY NAT/G DIPLOM RUSSIA
ECO/TAC FOR/AID EDU/PROP KNOWL...HIST/WRIT TOT/POP USSR
20. PAGE 117 B2369
B51

LEITES N.,THE OPERATIONAL CODE OF THE POLITBURO. DELIB/GP
COM USSR CREATE PLAN DOMIN LEGIT COERCE ALL/VALS ADMIN
...SOC CONCPT MYTH TREND CON/ANAL GEN/LAWS 20 SOCISM
LENIN/VI STALIN/J. PAGE 64 B1284
B51

US LIBRARY OF CONGRESS,EAST EUROPEAN ACCESSIONS BIBLIOG/A
LIST (VOL. I). POL/PAR DIPLOM ADMIN LEAD 20. COM
PAGE 109 B2204 SOCIETY
NAT/G
S51

SCHRAMM W.,"COMMUNICATION IN THE SOVIETIZED STATE, ATTIT
AS DEMONSTRATED IN KOREA." ASIA COM KOREA COM/IND EDU/PROP
FACE/GP POL/PAR SCHOOL FORCES ADMIN PWR MARXISM TOTALISM
...SOC CONCPT MYTH INT BIOG TOT/POP 20. PAGE 94
B1901
B52

JANSE R.S.,SOVIET TRANSPORTATION AND BIBLIOG/A
COMMUNICATIONS: A BIBLIOGRAPHY. COM USSR PLAN COM/IND
...DICTIONARY 20. PAGE 56 B1124 LEGIS

ADMIN
B52

ULAM A.B.,TITOISM AND THE COMINFORM. USSR WOR+45 COM
STRUCT INT/ORG NAT/G ACT/RES PLAN EXEC ATTIT DRIVE POL/PAR
ALL/VALS...CONCPT OBS VAL/FREE 20 COMINTERN TOTALISM
TITO/MARSH. PAGE 106 B2145 YUGOSLAVIA
B52

US DEPARTMENT OF STATE,RESEARCH ON EASTERN EUROPE BIBLIOG
(EXCLUDING USSR). EUR+WWI LAW ECO/DEV NAT/G R+D
PROB/SOLV DIPLOM ADMIN LEAD MARXISM...TREND 19/20. ACT/RES
PAGE 108 B2182 COM
S52

BRUEGEL J.W.,"DIE INTERNAZIONALE VOL/ASSN
GEWERKSCHAFTSBEWEGUNG." COM EUR+WWI USA+45 WOR+45 LABOR
DELIB/GP EX/STRUC ECO/TAC EDU/PROP ATTIT PWR TOTALISM
RESPECT SKILL WEALTH WORK 20. PAGE 16 B0330
B53

MEYER P.,THE JEWS IN THE SOVIET SATELLITES. COM
CZECHOSLVK POLAND SOCIETY STRATA NAT/G BAL/PWR SECT
ECO/TAC EDU/PROP LEGIT ADMIN COERCE ATTIT DISPL TOTALISM
PERCEPT HEALTH PWR RESPECT WEALTH...METH/CNCPT JEWS USSR
VAL/FREE NAZI 20. PAGE 73 B1474
B53

PIERCE R.A.,RUSSIAN CENTRAL ASIA, 1867-1917: A BIBLIOG
SELECTED BIBLIOGRAPHY (PAMPHLET). USSR LAW CULTURE COLONIAL
NAT/G EDU/PROP WAR...GEOG SOC 19/20. PAGE 83 B1671 ADMIN
COM
S53

MORRIS B.S.,"THE COMINFORM: A FIVE YEAR VOL/ASSN
PERSPECTIVE." COM UNIV USSR WOR+45 ECO/DEV POL/PAR EDU/PROP
TOP/EX PLAN DOMIN ADMIN TOTALISM ATTIT ALL/VALS DIPLOM
...CONCPT TIME/SEQ TREND CON/ANAL WORK VAL/FREE 20.
PAGE 76 B1527
B54

BIESANZ J.,MODERN SOCIETY: AN INTRODUCTION TO SOCIETY
SOCIAL SCIENCE. COM CONSTN STRUCT FAM MUNIC NAT/G PROB/SOLV
SECT EX/STRUC LEGIS GP/REL PERSON...SOC 20. PAGE 12 CULTURE
B0237
L54

ARCIENEGAS G.,"POST-WAR SOVIET FOREIGN POLICY: A INTELL
WORLD PERSPECTIVE." COM USA+45 STRUCT NAT/G POL/PAR ACT/RES
TOP/EX PLAN ADMIN ALL/VALS...TREND COLD/WAR TOT/POP USSR
20. PAGE 6 B0124
L54

ROSTOW W.W.,"ASIAN LEADERSHIP AND FREE-WORLD ATTIT
ALLIANCE." ASIA COM USA+45 CULTURE ELITES INTELL LEGIT
NAT/G TEC/DEV ECO/TAC EDU/PROP COLONIAL PARL/PROC DIPLOM
ROUTINE COERCE DRIVE ORD/FREE MARXISM...PSY CONCPT.
PAGE 90 B1829
B55

POOL I.,SATELLITE GENERALS: A STUDY OF MILITARY FORCES
ELITES IN THE SOVIET SPHERE. ASIA CHINA/COM COM CHOOSE
CZECHOSLVK FUT HUNGARY POLAND ROMANIA USSR ELITES
STRATA ADMIN ATTIT PWR SKILL...METH/CNCPT BIOG 20.
PAGE 84 B1688
L55

ROSTOW W.W.,"RUSSIA AND CHINA UNDER COMMUNISM." COM
CHINA/COM USSR INTELL STRUCT INT/ORG NAT/G POL/PAR ASIA
TOP/EX ACT/RES PLAN ADMIN ATTIT ALL/VALS MARXISM
...CONCPT OBS TIME/SEQ TREND GOV/COMP VAL/FREE 20.
PAGE 91 B1830
S55

KAUTSKY J.H.,"THE NEW STRATEGY OF INTERNATIONAL COM
COMMUNISM." ASIA CHINA/COM FUT WOR+45 WOR-45 ADMIN POL/PAR
ROUTINE PERSON MARXISM SOCISM...TREND IDEA/COMP 20 TOTALISM
LENIN/VI MAC. PAGE 59 B1184 USSR
B56

DEGRAS J.,THE COMMUNIST INTERNATIONAL, 1919-1943: COM
DOCUMENTS (3 VOLS.). EX/STRUC...ANTHOL BIBLIOG 20. DIPLOM
PAGE 28 B0569 POLICY
POL/PAR
B57

CENTRAL ASIAN RESEARCH CENTRE,BIBLIOGRAPHY OF BIBLIOG/A
RECENT SOVIET SOURCE MATERIAL ON SOVIET CENTRAL COM
ASIA AND THE BORDERLANDS. AFGHANISTN INDIA PAKISTAN CULTURE
UAR USSR ECO/UNDEV AGRI EXTR/IND INDUS ACADEM ADMIN NAT/G
...HEAL HUM LING CON/ANAL 20. PAGE 19 B0399
B57

DJILAS M.,THE NEW CLASS: AN ANALYSIS OF THE COM
COMMUNIST SYSTEM. STRATA CAP/ISM ECO/TAC DOMIN POL/PAR
EDU/PROP LEGIT EXEC COERCE ATTIT PWR MARXISM USSR
...MARXIST MGT CONCPT TIME/SEQ GEN/LAWS 20. PAGE 29 YUGOSLAVIA
B0600
S57

BAUER R.A.,"BRAINWASHING: PSYCHOLOGY OR EDU/PROP
DEMONOLOGY." ASIA CHINA/COM COM POL/PAR ECO/TAC PSY
ADMIN COERCE ATTIT DRIVE ORD/FREE...CONCPT MYTH 20. TOTALISM
PAGE 10 B0196
C57

TANG P.S.H.,"COMMUNIST CHINA TODAY: DOMESTIC AND POL/PAR
FOREIGN POLICIES." CHINA/COM COM S/ASIA USSR STRATA LEAD
FORCES DIPLOM EDU/PROP COERCE GOV/REL...POLICY ADMIN
MAJORIT BIBLIOG 20. PAGE 102 B2071 CONSTN
B58

LAQUER W.Z.,THE MIDDLE EAST IN TRANSITION. COM USSR ISLAM
ECO/UNDEV NAT/G VOL/ASSN EDU/PROP EXEC ATTIT DRIVE TREND

PWR MARXISM COLD/WAR TOT/POP 20. PAGE 62 B1261 — NAT/LISM

B58
NEAL F.W.,"TITOISM IN ACTION. COM YUGOSLAVIA AGRI LOC/G DIPLOM TOTALISM...BIBLIOG 20 TITO/MARSH. PAGE 77 B1564 — MARXISM POL/PAR CHIEF ADMIN

S58
STAAR R.F.,"ELECTIONS IN COMMUNIST POLAND." EUR+WWI SOCIETY INT/ORG NAT/G POL/PAR LEGIS ACT/RES ECO/TAC EDU/PROP ADJUD ADMIN ROUTINE COERCE TOTALISM ATTIT ORD/FREE PWR 20. PAGE 100 B2015 — COM CHOOSE POLAND

B59
EPSTEIN F.T.,EAST GERMANY: A SELECTED BIBLIOGRAPHY (PAMPHLET). COM GERMANY/E LAW AGRI FINAN INDUS LABOR POL/PAR EDU/PROP ADMIN AGE/Y 20. PAGE 33 B0677 — BIBLIOG/A INTELL MARXISM NAT/G

S59
ZAUBERMAN A.,"SOVIET BLOC ECONOMIC INTEGRATION." COM CULTURE INTELL ECO/DEV INDUS TOP/EX ACT/RES PLAN ECO/TAC INT/TRADE ROUTINE CHOOSE ATTIT ...TIME/SEQ 20. PAGE 119 B2399 — MARKET INT/ORG USSR TOTALISM

B60
CAMPBELL R.W.,SOVIET ECONOMIC POWER. COM USA+45 DIST/IND MARKET TOP/EX ACT/RES CAP/ISM ECO/TAC DOMIN EDU/PROP ADMIN ROUTINE DRIVE...MATH TIME/SEQ CHARTS WORK 20. PAGE 18 B0371 — ECO/DEV PLAN SOCISM USSR

B60
DRAPER T.,AMERICAN COMMUNISM AND SOVIET RUSSIA. EUR+WWI USA+45 USSR INTELL AGRI COM/IND FINAN INDUS LABOR PROF/ORG VOL/ASSN PLAN TEC/DEV DOMIN EDU/PROP ADMIN COERCE REV PERSON PWR...POLICY CONCPT MYTH 19/20. PAGE 30 B0617 — COM POL/PAR

B60
GRANICK D.,THE RED EXECUTIVE. COM USA+45 SOCIETY ECO/DEV INDUS NAT/G POL/PAR EX/STRUC PLAN ECO/TAC EDU/PROP ADMIN EXEC ATTIT DRIVE...GP/COMP 20. PAGE 42 B0851 — PWR STRATA USSR ELITES

B60
LIPSET S.M.,POLITICAL MAN. AFR COM EUR+WWI L/A+17C MOD/EUR S/ASIA USA+45 USA-45 STRUCT ECO/DEV ECO/UNDEV POL/PAR SECT ADMIN WEALTH...CONCPT WORK TOT/POP 20. PAGE 65 B1320 — PWR SOC

B60
WORLEY P.,ASIA TODAY (REV. ED.) (PAMPHLET). COM ECO/UNDEV AGRI FINAN INDUS POL/PAR FOR/AID ADMIN MARXISM 20. PAGE 118 B2376 — BIBLIOG/A ASIA DIPLOM NAT/G

S60
GROSSMAN G.,"SOVIET GROWTH: ROUTINE, INERTIA, AND PRESSURE." COM STRATA NAT/G DELIB/GP PLAN TEC/DEV ECO/TAC EDU/PROP ADMIN ROUTINE DRIVE WEALTH COLD/WAR 20. PAGE 44 B0891 — POL/PAR ECO/DEV USSR

S60
HALPERIN M.H.,"IS THE SENATE'S FOREIGN RELATIONS RESEARCH WORTHWHILE." COM FUT USA+45 USSR ACT/RES BAL/PWR EDU/PROP ADMIN ALL/VALS CONGRESS VAL/FREE 20 COLD/WAR. PAGE 46 B0927 — PLAN DIPLOM

S60
HERZ J.H.,"EAST GERMANY: PROGRESS AND PROSPECTS." COM AGRI FINAN INDUS LOC/G NAT/G FORCES PLAN TEC/DEV DOMIN ADMIN COERCE DRIVE PERCEPT RIGID/FLEX MORAL ORD/FREE PWR...MARXIST PSY SOC RECORD STERTYP WORK. PAGE 49 B0997 — POL/PAR STRUCT GERMANY

S60
NORTH R.C.,"DIE DISKREPANZ ZWISCHEN REALITAT UND WUNSCHBILD ALS INNENPOLITISCHER FAKTOR." ASIA CHINA/COM COM FUT ECO/UNDEV NAT/G PLAN DOMIN ADMIN COERCE PERCEPT...SOC MYTH GEN/METH WORK TOT/POP 20. PAGE 79 B1589 — SOCIETY ECO/TAC

S60
SCHWARTZ B.,"THE INTELLIGENTSIA IN COMMUNIST CHINA: A TENTATIVE COMPARISON." ASIA CHINA/COM COM RUSSIA ELITES SOCIETY STRATA POL/PAR VOL/ASSN CREATE ADMIN COERCE NAT/LISM TOTALISM...POLICY TREND 20. PAGE 95 B1914 — INTELL RIGID/FLEX REV

C60
FITZSIMMONS T.,"USSR: ITS PEOPLE, ITS SOCIETY, ITS CULTURE." USSR FAM SECT DIPLOM EDU/PROP ADMIN RACE/REL ATTIT...POLICY CHARTS BIBLIOG 20. PAGE 36 B0728 — CULTURE STRUCT SOCIETY COM

C60
SCHAPIRO L.B.,"THE COMMUNIST PARTY OF THE SOVIET UNION." USSR INTELL CHIEF EX/STRUC FORCES DOMIN ADMIN LEAD WAR ATTIT SOVEREIGN...POLICY BIBLIOG 20. PAGE 93 B1881 — POL/PAR COM REV

B61
ARMSTRONG J.A.,AN ESSAY ON SOURCES FOR THE STUDY OF THE COMMUNIST PARTY OF THE SOVIET UNION, 1934-1960 (EXTERNAL RESEARCH PAPER 137). USSR EX/STRUC ADMIN LEAD REV 20. PAGE 7 B0134 — BIBLIOG/A COM POL/PAR MARXISM

B61
HORVATH B.,THE CHARACTERISTICS OF YUGOSLAV ECONOMIC DEVELOPMENT. COM ECO/UNDEV AGRI INDUS PLAN CAP/ISM ECO/TAC ROUTINE WEALTH...SOCIALIST STAT CHARTS STERTYP WORK 20. PAGE 52 B1045 — ACT/RES YUGOSLAVIA

B61
HOUN F.W.,TO CHANGE A NATION: PROPAGANDA AND INDOCTRINATION IN COMMUNIST CHINA. CHINA/COM COM ACT/RES PLAN PRESS ADMIN FEEDBACK CENTRAL EFFICIENCY ATTIT...PSY SOC 20. PAGE 52 B1048 — DOMIN EDU/PROP TOTALISM MARXISM

B61
KERTESZ S.D.,AMERICAN DIPLOMACY IN A NEW ERA. COM S/ASIA UK USA+45 FORCES PROB/SOLV BAL/PWR ECO/TAC ADMIN COLONIAL WAR PEACE ORD/FREE 20 NATO CONGRESS UN COLD/WAR. PAGE 59 B1199 — ANTHOL DIPLOM TREND

B61
MARX K.,THE COMMUNIST MANIFESTO. IN (MENDEL A. ESSENTIAL WORKS OF MARXISM. NEW YORK: BANTAM. FUT MOD/EUR CULTURE ECO/DEV ECO/UNDEV AGRI FINAN INDUS MARKET PROC/MFG LABOR MUNIC POL/PAR CONSULT FORCES CREATE PLAN ADMIN ATTIT DRIVE RIGID/FLEX ORD/FREE PWR RESPECT MARX/KARL WORK. PAGE 70 B1421 — COM NEW/IDEA CAP/ISM REV

B61
MOLLAU G.,INTERNATIONAL COMMUNISM AND WORLD REVOLUTION: HISTORY AND METHODS. RUSSIA USSR INT/ORG NAT/G POL/PAR VOL/ASSN FORCES BAL/PWR DIPLOM EXEC REGION WAR ATTIT PWR MARXISM...CONCPT TIME/SEQ COLD/WAR 19/20. PAGE 74 B1498 — COM REV

B61
MONAS S.,THE THIRD SECTION: POLICE AND SOCIETY IN RUSSIA UNDER NICHOLAS I. MOD/EUR RUSSIA STRUCT NAT/G EX/STRUC ADMIN CONTROL PWR CONSERVE ...DECISION 19 NICHOLAS/I. PAGE 74 B1499 — ORD/FREE COM FORCES COERCE

S61
DEVINS J.H.,"THE INITIATIVE." COM USA+45 USA-45 USSR SOCIETY NAT/G ACT/RES CREATE BAL/PWR ROUTINE COERCE DETER RIGID/FLEX SKILL...STERTYP COLD/WAR 20. PAGE 29 B0582 — FORCES CONCPT WAR

S61
JUVILER P.H.,"INTERPARLIAMENTARY CONTACTS IN SOVIET FOREIGN POLICY." COM FUT WOR+45 WOR-45 SOCIETY CONSULT ACT/RES DIPLOM ADMIN PEACE ATTIT RIGID/FLEX WEALTH...WELF/ST SOC TOT/POP CONGRESS 19/20. PAGE 57 B1156 — INT/ORG DELIB/GP USSR

S61
NOVE A.,"THE SOVIET MODEL AND UNDERDEVELOPED COUNTRIES." COM FUT USSR WOR+45 CULTURE ECO/DEV POL/PAR FOR/AID EDU/PROP ADMIN MORAL WEALTH ...POLICY RECORD HIST/WRIT 20. PAGE 79 B1593 — ECO/UNDEV PLAN

S61
TOMASIC D.,"POLITICAL LEADERSHIP IN CONTEMPORARY POLAND." COM EUR+WWI GERMANY NAT/G POL/PAR SECT DELIB/GP PLAN ECO/TAC DOMIN EDU/PROP PWR MARXISM ...MARXIST GEOG MGT CONCPT TIME/SEQ STERTYP 20. PAGE 105 B2114 — SOCIETY ROUTINE USSR POLAND

B62
INTERNATIONAL LABOR OFFICE,WORKERS' MANAGEMENT IN YUGOSLAVIA. COM YUGOSLAVIA LABOR DELIB/GP EX/STRUC PROB/SOLV ADMIN PWR MARXISM...CHARTS ORG/CHARTS BIBLIOG 20. PAGE 54 B1098 — WORKER CONTROL MGT INDUS

B62
SHAPIRO D.,A SELECT BIBLIOGRAPHY OF WORKS IN ENGLISH ON RUSSIAN HISTORY, 1801-1917. COM USSR STRATA FORCES EDU/PROP ADMIN REV RACE/REL ATTIT 19/20. PAGE 96 B1932 — BIBLIOG DIPLOM COLONIAL

S62
HUDSON G.F.,"SOVIET FEARS OF THE WEST." COM USA+45 SOCIETY DELIB/GP EX/STRUC TOP/EX ACT/RES CREATE DOMIN EDU/PROP LEGIT ADMIN ROUTINE DRIVE PERSON RIGID/FLEX PWR...RECORD TIME/SEQ TOT/POP 20 STALIN/J. PAGE 52 B1057 — ATTIT MYTH GERMANY USSR

S62
IOVTCHOUK M.T.,"ON SOME THEORETICAL PRINCIPLES AND METHODS OF SOCIOLOGICAL INVESTIGATIONS (IN RUSSIAN)." FUT USA+45 STRATA R+D NAT/G POL/PAR TOP/EX ACT/RES PLAN ECO/TAC EDU/PROP ROUTINE ATTIT RIGID/FLEX MARXISM SOCISM...MARXIST METH/CNCPT OBS TREND NAT/COMP GEN/LAWS 20. PAGE 54 B1102 — COM ECO/DEV CAP/ISM USSR

S62
MARTIN L.W.,"POLITICAL SETTLEMENTS AND ARMS CONTROL." COM EUR+WWI GERMANY USA+45 PROVS FORCES TOP/EX ACT/RES CREATE DOMIN LEGIT ROUTINE COERCE ATTIT RIGID/FLEX ORD/FREE PWR...METH/CNCPT RECORD GEN/LAWS 20. PAGE 70 B1410 — CONCPT ARMS/CONT

C62
MORGAN G.G.,"SOVIET ADMINISTRATIVE LEGALITY: THE ROLE OF THE ATTORNEY GENERAL'S OFFICE." COM USSR CONTROL ROUTINE...CONCPT BIBLIOG 18/20. PAGE 75 B1522 — LAW CONSTN LEGIS ADMIN

C63
BROGAN D.W.,POLITICAL PATTERNS IN TODAY'S WORLD. FRANCE USA+45 USSR WOR+45 CONSTN STRUCT PLAN DIPLOM ADMIN LEAD ROLE SUPEGO...PHIL/SCI 20. PAGE 15 B0313 — NAT/COMP NEW/LIB COM TOTALISM

B63
KLESMENT J.,LEGAL SOURCES AND BIBLIOGRAPHY OF THE BALTIC STATES (ESTONIA, LATVIA, LITHUANIA). COM ESTONIA LATVIA LITHUANIA LAW FINAN ADJUD CT/SYS REGION CENTRAL MARXISM 19/20. PAGE 60 B1218 — BIBLIOG/A JURID CONSTN ADMIN

B63
NORTH R.C.,CONTENT ANALYSIS: A HANDBOOK WITH — METH/CNCPT

APPLICATIONS FOR THE STUDY OF INTERNATIONAL CRISIS. COMPUT/IR
ASIA COM EUR+WWI MOD/EUR INT/ORG TEC/DEV DOMIN   USSR
EDU/PROP ROUTINE COERCE PERCEPT RIGID/FLEX ALL/VALS
...QUANT TESTS CON/ANAL SIMUL GEN/LAWS VAL/FREE.
PAGE 79 B1591

B63
STEVENSON A.E.,LOOKING OUTWARD: YEARS OF CRISIS AT   INT/ORG
THE UNITED NATIONS. COM CUBA USA+45 WOR+45 SOCIETY   CONCPT
NAT/G EX/STRUC ACT/RES LEGIT COLONIAL ATTIT PERSON   ARMS/CONT
SUPEGO ALL/VALS...POLICY HUM UN COLD/WAR CONGO 20.
PAGE 100 B2034

B63
TUCKER R.C.,THE SOVIET POLITICAL MIND. WOR+45   COM
ELITES INT/ORG NAT/G POL/PAR PLAN DIPLOM ECO/TAC   TOP/EX
DOMIN ADMIN NUC/PWR REV DRIVE PERSON SUPEGO PWR   USSR
WEALTH...POLICY MGT PSY CONCPT OBS BIOG TREND
COLD/WAR MARX/KARL 20. PAGE 106 B2134

B63
TUCKER R.C.,THE SOVIET POLITICAL MIND. COM INTELL   STRUCT
NAT/G TOP/EX EDU/PROP ADMIN COERCE TOTALSM ATTIT   RIGID/FLEX
PWR MARXISM...PSY MYTH HYPO/EXP 20. PAGE 106 B2135   ELITES
                                                      USSR

L63
BOLGAR V.,"THE PUBLIC INTEREST: A JURISPRUDENTIAL   CONCPT
AND COMPARATIVE OVERVIEW OF SYMPOSIUM ON   ORD/FREE
FUNDAMENTAL CONCEPTS OF PUBLIC LAW" COM FRANCE   CONTROL
GERMANY SWITZERLND LAW ADJUD ADMIN AGREE LAISSEZ   NAT/COMP
...JURID GEN/LAWS 20 EUROPE/E. PAGE 13 B0268

S63
BECHHOEFER B.G.,"UNITED NATIONS PROCEDURES IN CASE   INT/ORG
OF VIOLATIONS OF DISARMAMENT AGREEMENTS." COM   DELIB/GP
USA+45 USSR CONSTN NAT/G EX/STRUC FORCES LEGIS
BAL/PWR EDU/PROP CT/SYS ARMS/CONT ORD/FREE PWR
...POLICY STERTYP UN VAL/FREE 20. PAGE 10 B0204

S63
BRZEZINSKI Z.K.,"CINCINNATUS AND THE APPARATCHIK."   POL/PAR
COM USA+45 ELITES LOC/G NAT/G PROVS CONSULT   USSR
LEGIS DOMIN LEGIT EXEC ROUTINE CHOOSE DRIVE PWR
SKILL...CONCPT CHARTS VAL/FREE COLD/WAR 20. PAGE 16
B0334

S63
DELLIN L.A.D.,"BULGARIA UNDER SOVIET LEADERSHIP."   AGRI
BULGARIA COM USA+45 USSR ECO/DEV INDUS POL/PAR   NAT/G
EX/STRUC TOP/EX COERCE ATTIT RIGID/FLEX...POLICY   TOTALISM
TIME/SEQ 20. PAGE 28 B0572

S63
ETIENNE G.,"'LOIS OBJECTIVES' ET PROBLEMES DE   TOTALISM
DEVELOPPEMENT DANS LE CONTEXTE CHINE-URSS." ASIA   USSR
CHINA/COM COM FUT STRUCT INT/ORG VOL/ASSN TOP/EX
TEC/DEV ECO/TAC ATTIT RIGID/FLEX...GEOG MGT
TIME/SEQ TOT/POP 20. PAGE 34 B0682

S63
SHIMKIN D.B.,"STRUCTURE OF SOVIET POWER." COM FUT   PWR
USA+45 USSR WOR+45 NAT/G FORCES ECO/TAC DOMIN EXEC
COERCE CHOOSE ATTIT WEALTH...TIME/SEQ COLD/WAR
TOT/POP VAL/FREE 20. PAGE 96 B1948

B64
ALDERFER H.O.,LOCAL GOVERNMENT IN DEVELOPING   ADMIN
COUNTRIES. ASIA COM L/A+17C S/ASIA AGRI LOC/G MUNIC   ROUTINE
PROVS DOMIN CHOOSE PWR...POLICY MGT CONCPT 20.
PAGE 3 B0070

B64
GJUPANOVIC H.,LEGAL SOURCES AND BIBLIOGRAPHY OF   BIBLIOG/A
YUGOSLAVIA. COM YUGOSLAVIA LAW LEGIS DIPLOM ADMIN   JURID
PARL/PROC REGION CRIME CENTRAL 20. PAGE 40 B0807   CONSTN
                                                      ADJUD

B64
GRZYBOWSKI K.,THE SOCIALIST COMMONWEALTH OF   INT/LAW
NATIONS: ORGANIZATIONS AND INSTITUTIONS. FORCES   COM
DIPLOM INT/TRADE ADJUD ADMIN LEAD WAR MARXISM   REGION
SOCISM...BIBLIOG 20 COMECON WARSAW/P. PAGE 44 B0898   INT/ORG

B64
PIPES R.,THE FORMATION OF THE SOVIET UNION. EUR+WWI   COM
MOD/EUR STRUCT ECO/UNDEV NAT/G LEGIS DOMIN LEGIT   USSR
CT/SYS EXEC COERCE ALL/VALS...POLICY RELATIV   RUSSIA
HIST/WRIT TIME/SEQ TOT/POP 19/20. PAGE 83 B1677

B64
STOICOIU V.,LEGAL SOURCES AND BIBLIOGRAPHY OF   BIBLIOG/A
ROMANIA. COM ROMANIA LAW FINAN POL/PAR LEGIS JUDGE   JURID
ADJUD CT/SYS PARL/PROC MARXISM 20. PAGE 101 B2041   CONSTN
                                                      ADMIN

B64
TINBERGEN J.,CENTRAL PLANNING. COM INTELL ECO/DEV   PLAN
ECO/UNDEV FINAN INT/ORG PROB/SOLV ECO/TAC CONTROL   INDUS
EXEC ROUTINE DECISION. PAGE 104 B2111   MGT
                                                      CENTRAL

B64
WELLISZ S.,THE ECONOMICS OF THE SOVIET BLOC. COM   EFFICIENCY
USSR INDUS WORKER PLAN BUDGET INT/TRADE TAX PRICE   ADMIN
PRODUC WEALTH MARXISM...METH/COMP 20. PAGE 115   MARKET
B2319

L64
MILLIS W.,"THE DEMILITARIZED WORLD." COM USA+45   FUT
USSR WOR+45 CONSTN NAT/G EX/STRUC PLAN LEGIT ATTIT   INT/ORG
DRIVE...CONCPT TIME/SEQ STERTYP TOT/POP COLD/WAR   BAL/PWR
20. PAGE 74 B1486   PEACE

S64
FLORINSKY M.T.,"TRENDS IN THE SOVIET ECONOMY." COM   ECO/DEV
USA+45 USSR INDUS LABOR NAT/G PLAN TEC/DEV ECO/TAC   AGRI
ALL/VALS SOCISM...MGT METH/CNCPT STYLE CON/ANAL
GEN/METH WORK 20. PAGE 36 B0731

S64
HORECKY P.L.,"LIBRARY OF CONGRESS PUBLICATIONS IN   BIBLIOG/A
AID OF USSR AND EAST EUROPEAN RESEARCH." BULGARIA   COM
CZECHOSLVK POLAND USSR YUGOSLAVIA NAT/G POL/PAR   MARXISM
DIPLOM ADMIN GOV/REL...CLASSIF 20. PAGE 51 B1042

S64
KAPLAN N.,"RESEARCH ADMINISTRATION AND THE   R+D
ADMINISTRATOR: USSR AND US." COM USA+45 INTELL   ADMIN
EX/STRUC KNOWL...MGT 20. PAGE 58 B1169   USSR

S64
KASSOF A.,"THE ADMINISTERED SOCIETY: SOCIETY
TOTALITARIANISM WITHOUT TERROR." COM USSR STRATA   DOMIN
AGRI INDUS NAT/G PERF/ART SCHOOL TOP/EX EDU/PROP   TOTALISM
ADMIN ORD/FREE PWR...POLICY SOC TIME/SEQ GEN/LAWS
VAL/FREE 20. PAGE 58 B1178

S64
KENNAN G.F.,"POLYCENTRISM AND WESTERN POLICY." ASIA   RIGID/FLEX
CHINA/COM COM FUT USA+45 USSR NAT/G ACT/RES DOMIN   ATTIT
EDU/PROP EXEC COERCE DISPL PERCEPT...POLICY   DIPLOM
COLD/WAR 20. PAGE 59 B1192

S64
RIGBY T.H.,"TRADITIONAL, MARKET, AND ORGANIZATIONAL   MARKET
SOCIETIES AND THE USSR." COM ECO/DEV NAT/G POL/PAR   ADMIN
ECO/TAC DOMIN ORD/FREE PWR WEALTH...TIME/SEQ   USSR
GEN/LAWS VAL/FREE 20 STALIN/J. PAGE 88 B1784

S64
SWEARER H.R.,"AFTER KHRUSHCHEV: WHAT NEXT." COM FUT   EX/STRUC
USSR CONSTN ELITES NAT/G POL/PAR CHIEF DELIB/GP   PWR
LEGIS DOMIN LEAD...RECORD TREND STERTYP GEN/METH
20. PAGE 102 B2058

B65
DAVISON W.P.,INTERNATIONAL POLITICAL COMMUNICATION.   EDU/PROP
COM USA+45 WOR+45 CULTURE ECO/UNDEV NAT/G PROB/SOLV   DIPLOM
PRESS TV ADMIN 20 FILM. PAGE 27 B0545   PERS/REL
                                                      COM/IND

B65
KASER M.,COMECON* INTEGRATION PROBLEMS OF THE   PLAN
PLANNED ECONOMIES. INT/ORG TEC/DEV INT/TRADE PRICE   ECO/DEV
ADMIN ADJUST CENTRAL...STAT TIME/SEQ ORG/CHARTS   COM
COMECON. PAGE 58 B1177   REGION

B65
PHELPS-FETHERS I.,SOVIET INTERNATIONAL FRONT   USSR
ORGANIZATIONS* A CONCISE HANDBOOK. DIPLOM DOMIN   EDU/PROP
LEGIT ADMIN EXEC GP/REL PEACE MARXISM...TIME/SEQ   ASIA
GP/COMP. PAGE 83 B1668   COM

B65
PUSTAY J.S.,COUNTER-INSURGENCY WARFARE. COM USA+45   FORCES
LOC/G NAT/G ACT/RES EDU/PROP ADMIN COERCE ATTIT   PWR
...CONCPT MARX/KARL 20. PAGE 85 B1722   GUERRILLA

S65
RUBINSTEIN A.Z.,"YUGOSLAVIA'S OPENING SOCIETY." COM   CONSTN
USSR INTELL NAT/G LEGIS TOP/EX LEGIT CT/SYS   EX/STRUC
RIGID/FLEX ALL/VALS SOCISM...HUM TIME/SEQ TREND 20.   YUGOSLAVIA
PAGE 92 B1851

S65
TABORSKY E.,"CHANGE IN CZECHOSLOVAKIA." COM USSR   ECO/DEV
ELITES INTELL AGRI.INDUS NAT/G DELIB/GP EX/STRUC   PLAN
ECO/TAC TOTALISM ATTIT RIGID/FLEX SOCISM...MGT   CZECHOSLVK
CONCPT TREND 20. PAGE 102 B2067

N65
MOTE M.E.,SOVIET LOCAL AND REPUBLIC ELECTIONS. COM   CHOOSE
USSR NAT/G PLAN PARTIC GOV/REL TOTALISM PWR   ADMIN
...CHARTS 20. PAGE 76 B1534   CONTROL
                                                      LOC/G

B66
EPSTEIN F.T.,THE AMERICAN BIBLIOGRAPHY OF RUSSIAN   BIBLIOG
AND EAST EUROPEAN STUDIES FOR 1964. USSR LOC/G   COM
NAT/G POL/PAR FORCES ADMIN ARMS/CONT...JURID CONCPT   MARXISM
20 UN. PAGE 33 B0678   DIPLOM

B66
MACFARQUHAR R.,CHINA UNDER MAO: POLITICS TAKES   ECO/UNDEV
COMMAND. CHINA/COM COM AGRI INDUS CHIEF FORCES   TEC/DEV
DIPLOM INT/TRADE EDU/PROP TASK REV ADJUST...ANTHOL   ECO/TAC
20 MAO. PAGE 67 B1359   ADMIN

B66
US DEPARTMENT OF THE ARMY,COMMUNIST CHINA: A   BIBLIOG/A
STRATEGIC SURVEY: A BIBLIOGRAPHY (PAMPHLET NO.   MARXISM
20-67). CHINA/COM COM INDIA USSR NAT/G POL/PAR   S/ASIA
EX/STRUC FORCES NUC/PWR REV ATTIT...POLICY GEOG   DIPLOM
CHARTS. PAGE 108 B2184

S66
MARKSHAK J.,"ECONOMIC PLANNING AND THE COST OF   ECO/UNDEV
THINKING." COM MARKET EX/STRUC...DECISION GEN/LAWS.   ECO/TAC
PAGE 69 B1400   PLAN
                                                      ECO/DEV

B67
BRZEZINSKI Z.K.,THE SOVIET BLOC: UNITY AND CONFLICT   NAT/G
(2ND ED., REV., ENLARGED). COM POLAND USSR INTELL   DIPLOM
CHIEF EX/STRUC CONTROL EXEC GOV/REL PWR MARXISM
...TREND IDEA/COMP 20 LENIN/VI MARX/KARL STALIN/J.
PAGE 16 B0336

FARNSWORTH B.,WILLIAM C. BULLITT AND THE SOVIET UNION. COM USA-45 USSR NAT/G CHIEF CONSULT DELIB/GP EX/STRUC WAR REPRESENT MARXISM 20 WILSON/W ROOSEVLT/F STALIN/J BULLITT/WC. PAGE 35 B0705
B67 DIPLOM BIOG POLICY

GRUBER H.,INTERNATIONAL COMMUNISM IN THE ERA OF LENIN. COM ADMIN REV GP/REL 20. PAGE 44 B0895
B67 MARXISM HIST/WRIT POL/PAR

MACKINTOSH J.M.,JUGGERNAUT. USSR NAT/G POL/PAR ADMIN LEAD CIVMIL/REL COST TOTALISM PWR MARXISM ...GOV/COMP 20. PAGE 68 B1364
B67 WAR FORCES COM PROF/ORG

BREGMAN A.,"WHITHER RUSSIA?" COM RUSSIA INTELL POL/PAR DIPLOM PARTIC NAT/LISM TOTALISM ATTIT ORD/FREE 20. PAGE 15 B0304
S67 MARXISM ELITES ADMIN CREATE

COM INTERNAT DES MOUVEMENTS B0454

COM/IND....COMMUNICATIONS INDUSTRY

PERREN G.E.,LANGUAGE AND COMMUNICATION IN THE COMMONWEALTH (PAMPHLET). FUT UK LAW ECO/DEV PRESS TV WRITING ADJUD ADMIN COLONIAL CONTROL 20 CMN/WLTH. PAGE 82 B1660
N19 EDU/PROP LING GOV/REL COM/IND

WALL N.L.,MUNICIPAL REPORTING TO THE PUBLIC (PAMPHLET). LOC/G PLAN WRITING ADMIN REPRESENT EFFICIENCY...AUD/VIS CHARTS 20. PAGE 113 B2282
N19 METH MUNIC GP/REL COM/IND

HETTINGER H.S.,A DECADE OF RADIO ADVERTISING. USA-45 ECO/DEV CAP/ISM PRICE...CHARTS 20. PAGE 49 B0999
B33 EDU/PROP COM/IND ECO/TAC ROUTINE

GOSNELL H.F.,MACHINE POLITICS: CHICAGO MODEL. COM/IND FACE/GP LOC/G EX/STRUC LEAD ROUTINE SANCTION REPRESENT GOV/REL PWR...POLICY MATH OBS INT CHARTS. PAGE 41 B0840
B37 POL/PAR MUNIC ADMIN CHOOSE

MCCAMY J.L.,GOVERNMENT PUBLICITY: ITS PRACTICE IN FEDERAL ADMINISTRATION. USA-45 COM/IND ADMIN CONTROL EXEC PARTIC INGP/REL...SOC 20. PAGE 71 B1442
B39 EDU/PROP NAT/G PLAN ATTIT

BURT F.A.,AMERICAN ADVERTISING AGENCIES. BARGAIN BUDGET LICENSE WRITING PRICE PERS/REL COST DEMAND ...ORG/CHARTS BIBLIOG 20. PAGE 18 B0358
B40 LG/CO COM/IND ADMIN EFFICIENCY

NEUBURGER O.,OFFICIAL PUBLICATIONS OF PRESENT-DAY GERMANY: GOVERNMENT, CORPORATE ORGANIZATIONS, AND NATIONAL SOCIALIST PARTY. GERMANY CONSTN COM/IND POL/PAR EDU/PROP PRESS 20 NAZI. PAGE 78 B1570
B42 BIBLIOG/A FASCISM NAT/G ADMIN

SINGTON D.,THE GOEBBELS EXPERIMENT. GERMANY MOD/EUR NAT/G EX/STRUC FORCES CONTROL ROUTINE WAR TOTALISM PWR...ART/METH HUM 20 NAZI GOEBBELS/J. PAGE 97 B1970
B42 FASCISM EDU/PROP ATTIT COM/IND

PUBLIC ADMINISTRATION SERVICE,CURRENT RESEARCH PROJECTS IN PUBLIC ADMINISTRATION (PAMPHLET). LAW CONSTN COM/IND LABOR LOC/G MUNIC PROVS ACT/RES DIPLOM RECEIVE EDU/PROP WAR 20. PAGE 85 B1716
B47 BIBLIOG R+D MGT ADMIN

SIMON H.A.,ADMINISTRATIVE BEHAVIOR: A STUDY OF DECISION-MAKING PROCESSES IN ADMINISTRATIVE ORGANIZATION. STRUCT COM/IND OP/RES PROB/SOLV EFFICIENCY EQUILIB UTIL...PHIL/SCI PSY STYLE. PAGE 97 B1956
B47 DECISION NEW/IDEA ADMIN RATIONAL

BAKKE E.W.,BONDS OF ORGANIZATION (2ND ED.). USA+45 COM/IND FINAN ADMIN LEAD PERS/REL...INT SOC/INTEG 20. PAGE 8 B0169
B50 ECO/DEV MGT LABOR GP/REL

WAGER P.W.,"COUNTY GOVERNMENT ACROSS THE NATION." USA+45 CONSTN COM/IND FINAN SCHOOL DOMIN CT/SYS LEAD GOV/REL...STAT BIBLIOG 20. PAGE 112 B2272
C50 LOC/G PROVS ADMIN ROUTINE

NIELANDER W.A.,PUBLIC RELATIONS. USA+45 COM/IND LOC/G NAT/G VOL/ASSN EX/STRUC DIPLOM EDU/PROP PRESS TV...METH/CNCPT T 20. PAGE 78 B1583
B51 PERS/REL GP/REL LG/CO ROUTINE

SCHRAMM W.,"COMMUNICATION IN THE SOVIETIZED STATE, AS DEMONSTRATED IN KOREA." ASIA COM KOREA COM/IND FACE/GP POL/PAR SCHOOL FORCES ADMIN PWR MARXISM ...SOC CONCPT MYTH INT BIOG TOT/POP 20. PAGE 94 B1901
S51 ATTIT EDU/PROP TOTALISM

JANSE R.S.,SOVIET TRANSPORTATION AND COMMUNICATIONS: A BIBLIOGRAPHY. COM USSR PLAN ...DICTIONARY 20. PAGE 56 B1124
B52 BIBLIOG/A COM/IND LEGIS ADMIN

MILLER M.,THE JUDGES AND THE JUDGED. USA+45 LG/CO ACT/RES TV ROUTINE SANCTION NAT/LISM ATTIT ORD/FREE ...POLICY ACLU. PAGE 73 B1481
B52 COM/IND DISCRIM EDU/PROP MARXISM

LARSEN K.,NATIONAL BIBLIOGRAPHIC SERVICES: THEIR CREATION AND OPERATION. WOR+45 COM/IND CREATE PLAN DIPLOM PRESS ADMIN ROUTINE...MGT UNESCO. PAGE 62 B1262
B53 BIBLIOG/A INT/ORG WRITING

BINANI G.D.,INDIA AT A GLANCE (REV. ED.). INDIA COM/IND FINAN INDUS LABOR PROVS SCHOOL PLAN DIPLOM INT/TRADE ADMIN...JURID 20. PAGE 12 B0238
B54 INDEX CON/ANAL NAT/G ECO/UNDEV

STEPHENS O.,FACTS TO A CANDID WORLD. USA+45 WOR+45 COM/IND EX/STRUC PRESS ROUTINE EFFICIENCY ATTIT ...PSY 20. PAGE 100 B2033
B55 EDU/PROP PHIL/SCI NAT/G DIPLOM

POWELL N.J.,PERSONNEL ADMINISTRATION IN GOVERNMENT. COM/IND POL/PAR LEGIS PAY CT/SYS ROUTINE GP/REL PERS/REL...POLICY METH 20 CIVIL/SERV. PAGE 84 B1697
B56 ADMIN WORKER LOC/G NAT/G

US CIVIL SERVICE COMMISSION,DISSERTATIONS AND THESES RELATING TO PERSONNEL ADMINISTRATION (PAMPHLET). USA+45 COM/IND LABOR EX/STRUC GP/REL INGP/REL DECISION. PAGE 108 B2176
B57 BIBLIOG ADMIN MGT WORKER

OPERATIONS RESEARCH SOCIETY,A COMPREHENSIVE BIBLIOGRAPHY ON OPERATIONS RESEARCH; THROUGH 1956 WITH SUPPLEMENT FOR 1957. COM/IND DIST/IND INDUS ADMIN...DECISION MATH STAT METH 20. PAGE 80 B1612
B58 BIBLIOG/A COMPUT/IR OP/RES MGT

REDFIELD C.E.,COMMUNICATION IN MANAGEMENT. DELIB/GP EX/STRUC WRITING LEAD PERS/REL...PSY INT METH 20. PAGE 87 B1750
B58 COM/IND MGT LG/CO ADMIN

BRISTOL L.H. JR.,DEVELOPING THE CORPORATE IMAGE. USA+45 SOCIETY ECO/DEV COM/IND SCHOOL EDU/PROP PRESS TV...AUD/VIS ANTHOL. PAGE 15 B0312
B60 LG/CO ATTIT MGT ECO/TAC

DRAPER T.,AMERICAN COMMUNISM AND SOVIET RUSSIA. EUR+WWI USA+45 USSR INTELL AGRI COM/IND FINAN INDUS LABOR PROF/ORG VOL/ASSN PLAN TEC/DEV DOMIN EDU/PROP ADMIN COERCE REV PERSON PWR...POLICY CONCPT MYTH 19/20. PAGE 30 B0617
B60 COM POL/PAR

FRANKEL S.H.,"ECONOMIC ASPECTS OF POLITICAL INDEPENDENCE IN AFRICA." AFR FUT SOCIETY ECO/UNDEV COM/IND FINAN LEGIS PLAN TEC/DEV CAP/ISM ECO/TAC INT/TRADE ADMIN ATTIT DRIVE RIGID/FLEX PWR WEALTH ...MGT NEW/IDEA MATH TIME/SEQ VAL/FREE 20. PAGE 37 B0751
S60 NAT/G FOR/AID

SCHRAMM W.,"MASS COMMUNICATIONS: A BOOK OF READINGS (2ND ED.)" LG/CO PRESS ADMIN CONTROL ROUTINE ATTIT ROLE SUPEGO...CHARTS ANTHOL BIBLIOG 20. PAGE 94 B1902
C60 COM/IND EDU/PROP CROWD MAJORIT

BRADY R.A.,ORGANIZATION, AUTOMATION, AND SOCIETY. USA+45 AGRI COM/IND DIST/IND MARKET CREATE ...DECISION MGT 20. PAGE 14 B0296
B61 TEC/DEV INDUS AUTOMAT ADMIN

NARASIMHAN V.K.,THE PRESS, THE PUBLIC AND THE ADMINISTRATION (PAMPHLET). INDIA COM/IND CONTROL REPRESENT GOV/REL EFFICIENCY...ANTHOL 20. PAGE 77 B1554
B61 NAT/G ADMIN PRESS NEW/LIB

WILLOUGHBY W.R.,THE ST LAWRENCE WATERWAY: A STUDY IN POLITICS AND DIPLOMACY. USA+45 ECO/DEV COM/IND INT/ORG CONSULT DELIB/GP ACT/RES TEC/DEV DIPLOM ECO/TAC ROUTINE...TIME/SEQ 20. PAGE 117 B2357
B61 LEGIS INT/TRADE CANADA DIST/IND

SAMPSON A.,ANATOMY OF BRITAIN. UK LAW COM/IND FINAN INDUS MARKET MUNIC POL/PAR EX/STRUC TOP/EX DIPLOM LEAD REPRESENT PERSON PARLIAMENT WORSHIP. PAGE 92 B1866
B62 ELITES PWR STRUCT FORCES

WEDDING N.,ADVERTISING MANAGEMENT. USA+45 ECO/DEV BUDGET CAP/ISM PRODUC PROFIT ATTIT...DECISION MGT PSY 20. PAGE 114 B2308
B62 ECO/TAC COM/IND PLAN EDU/PROP

ALGER C.F.,"THE EXTERNAL BUREAUCRACY IN UNITED STATES FOREIGN AFFAIRS." USA+45 WOR+45 SOCIETY
S62 ADMIN ATTIT

COM/IND INT/ORG NAT/G CONSULT EX/STRUC ACT/RES ...MGT SOC CONCPT TREND 20. PAGE 4 B0076
DIPLOM
S63

COUTY P.,"L'ASSISTANCE POUR LE DEVELOPPEMENT: POINT DE VUE SCANDINAVES." EUR+WWI FINLAND FUT SWEDEN WOR+45 ECO/DEV ECO/UNDEV COM/IND LABOR NAT/G PROF/ORG ACT/RES SKILL WEALTH TOT/POP 20. PAGE 24 B0497
FINAN
ROUTINE
FOR/AID

DUCROS B.,"MOBILISATION DES RESSOURCES PRODUCTIVES ET DEVELOPPEMENT." FUT INTELL SOCIETY COM/IND DIST/IND FINAN INDUS ROUTINE WEALTH ...METH/CNCPT OBS 20. PAGE 31 B0625
S63
ECO/UNDEV
TEC/DEV

RUSSET B.M.,WORLD HANDBOOK OF POLITICAL AND SOCIAL INDICATORS. WOR+45 COM/IND ADMIN WEALTH...GEOG 20. PAGE 92 B1858
B64
DIPLOM
STAT
NAT/G
NAT/COMP

CUTLIP S.M.,A PUBLIC RELATIONS BIBLIOGRAPHY. INDUS LABOR NAT/G PROF/ORG SCHOOL DIPLOM PRESS TV GOV/REL GP/REL...PSY SOC/WK 20. PAGE 25 B0515
B65
BIBLIOG/A
MGT
COM/IND
ADMIN

DAVISON W.P.,INTERNATIONAL POLITICAL COMMUNICATION. COM USA+45 WOR+45 CULTURE ECO/UNDEV NAT/G PROB/SOLV PRESS TV ADMIN 20 FILM. PAGE 27 B0545
B65
EDU/PROP
DIPLOM
PERS/REL
COM/IND

MEYERHOFF A.E.,THE STRATEGY OF PERSUASION. USA+45 COM/IND CONSULT FOR/AID CONTROL COERCE COST ATTIT PERCEPT MARXISM 20 COLD/WAR. PAGE 73 B1476
B65
EDU/PROP
EFFICIENCY
OP/RES
ADMIN

OSTGAARD E.,"FACTORS INFLUENCING THE FLOW OF NEWS." COM/IND BUDGET DIPLOM EXEC GP/REL COST ATTIT SAMP. PAGE 80 B1618
S65
EDU/PROP
PERCEPT
RECORD

SIMON R.,PERSPECTIVES IN PUBLIC RELATIONS. USA+45 INDUS ACT/RES PLAN ADMIN ATTIT MGT. PAGE 97 B1961
B66
GP/REL
PERS/REL
COM/IND
SOCIETY

ANDRIOT J.L.,GUIDE TO US GOVERNMENT SERIALS AND PERIODICALS (VOL. IV). USA+45 COM/IND PRESS ADMIN. PAGE 5 B0107
B67
BIBLIOG
NAT/G

UNITED NATIONS,UNITED NATIONS PUBLICATIONS: 1945-1966. WOR+45 COM/IND DIST/IND FINAN TEC/DEV ADMIN...POLICY INT/LAW MGT CHARTS 20 UN UNESCO. PAGE 107 B2162
B67
BIBLIOG/A
INT/ORG
DIPLOM
WRITING

VOOS H.,ORGANIZATIONAL COMMUNICATION: A BIBLIOGRAPHY. WOR+45 STRATA R+D PROB/SOLV FEEDBACK COERCE...MGT PSY NET/THEORY HYPO/EXP. PAGE 112 B2268
B67
BIBLIOG/A
INDUS
COM/IND
VOL/ASSN

KAYSEN C.,"DATA BANKS AND DOSSIERS." FUT USA+45 COM/IND NAT/G PLAN PROB/SOLV TEC/DEV BUDGET ADMIN ROUTINE. PAGE 59 B1185
S67
CENTRAL
EFFICIENCY
CENSUS
ACT/RES

MORTON J.A.,"A SYSTEMS APPROACH TO THE INNOVATION PROCESS: ITS USE IN THE BELL SYSTEM." USA+45 INTELL INDUS LG/CO CONSULT WORKER COMPUTER AUTOMAT DEMAND ...MGT CHARTS 20. PAGE 76 B1531
S67
TEC/DEV
GEN/METH
R+D
COM/IND

US SUPERINTENDENT OF DOCUMENTS,SPACE: MISSILES, THE MOON, NASA, AND SATELLITES (PRICE LIST 79A). USA+45 COM/IND R+D NAT/G DIPLOM EDU/PROP ADMIN CONTROL HEALTH...POLICY SIMUL NASA CONGRESS. PAGE 111 B2244
N67
BIBLIOG/A
SPACE
TEC/DEV
PEACE

COM/PARTY....COMMUNIST PARTY (ALL NATIONS)

CARTER G.M.,THE GOVERNMENT OF THE SOVIET UNION. USSR CULTURE LOC/G DIPLOM ECO/TAC ADJUD CT/SYS LEAD WEALTH...CHARTS T 20 COM/PARTY. PAGE 19 B0390
B62
NAT/G
MARXISM
POL/PAR
EX/STRUC

FAINSOD M.,HOW RUSSIA IS RULED (REV. ED.). RUSSIA USSR AGRI PROC/MFG LABOR POL/PAR EX/STRUC CONTROL PWR...POLICY BIBLIOG 19/20 KHRUSH/N COM/PARTY. PAGE 34 B0700
B64
NAT/G
REV
MARXISM

KOUSOULAS D.G.,REVOLUTION AND DEFEAT; THE STORY OF THE GREEK COMMUNIST PARTY. GREECE INT/ORG EX/STRUC DIPLOM FOR/AID EDU/PROP PARL/PROC ADJUST ATTIT 20 COM/PARTY. PAGE 61 B1230
B65
REV
MARXISM
POL/PAR
ORD/FREE

SCHURMANN F.,IDEOLOGY AND ORGANIZATION IN COMMUNIST CHINA. CHINA/COM LOC/G MUNIC POL/PAR ECO/TAC CONTROL ATTIT...MGT STERTYP 20 COM/PARTY. PAGE 94 B1909
B66
MARXISM
STRUCT
ADMIN
NAT/G

COM/SCITEC....COMMITTEE ON SCIENCE AND TECHNOLOGY (OF

COMBS C.H. B0455

COMECON....COMMUNIST ECONOMIC ORGANIZATION EAST EUROPE

GRZYBOWSKI K.,THE SOCIALIST COMMONWEALTH OF NATIONS: ORGANIZATIONS AND INSTITUTIONS. FORCES DIPLOM INT/TRADE ADJUD ADMIN LEAD WAR MARXISM SOCISM...BIBLIOG 20 COMECON WARSAW/P. PAGE 44 B0898
B64
INT/LAW
COM
REGION
INT/ORG

KASER M.,COMECON* INTEGRATION PROBLEMS OF THE PLANNED ECONOMIES. INT/ORG TEC/DEV INT/TRADE PRICE ADMIN ADJUST CENTRAL...STAT TIME/SEQ ORG/CHARTS COMECON. PAGE 58 B1177
B65
PLAN
ECO/DEV
COM
REGION

COMINFORM....COMMUNIST INFORMATION BUREAU

COMINTERN....COMMUNIST THIRD INTERNATIONAL

ULAM A.B.,TITOISM AND THE COMINFORM. USSR WOR+45 STRUCT INT/ORG NAT/G ACT/RES PLAN EXEC ATTIT DRIVE ALL/VALS...CONCPT OBS VAL/FREE 20 COMINTERN TITO/MARSH. PAGE 106 B2145
B52
COM
POL/PAR
TOTALISM
YUGOSLAVIA

COMISION DE HISTORIO B0456

COMM/SPACE....COMMITTEE ON SPACE RESEARCH

COMMANDS....SEE LEAD, DOMIN

COMMISSIONS....SEE CONFER, DELIB/GP

COMMITTEE ECONOMIC DEVELOPMENT B0457

COMMITTEE FOR ECONOMIC DEVELOPMENT....SEE CED

COMMITTEE ON SCIENCE AND TECHNOLOGY (OF THE BRITISH PARLIAMENT)....SEE COM/SCITEC

COMMITTEES....SEE CONFER, DELIB/GP

COMMON/LAW....COMMON LAW

HOLDSWORTH W.S.,A HISTORY OF ENGLISH LAW; THE COMMON LAW AND ITS RIVALS (VOL. V). UK SEA EX/STRUC WRITING ADMIN...INT/LAW JURID CONCPT IDEA/COMP WORSHIP 16/17 PARLIAMENT ENGLSH/LAW COMMON/LAW. PAGE 51 B1033
B24
LAW
LEGIS
ADJUD
CT/SYS

HOLDSWORTH W.S.,A HISTORY OF ENGLISH LAW; THE COMMON LAW AND ITS RIVALS (VOL. VI). UK STRATA EX/STRUC ADJUD ADMIN CONTROL CT/SYS...JURID CONCPT GEN/LAWS 17 COMMONWLTH PARLIAMENT ENGLSH/LAW COMMON/LAW. PAGE 51 B1034
B24
LAW
CONSTN
LEGIS
CHIEF

MOEN N.W.,THE GOVERNMENT OF SCOTLAND 1603 - 1625. UK JUDGE ADMIN GP/REL PWR 17 SCOTLAND COMMON/LAW. PAGE 74 B1496
B58
CHIEF
JURID
CONTROL
PARL/PROC

HANBURY H.G.,ENGLISH COURTS OF LAW. UK EX/STRUC LEGIS CRIME ROLE 12/20 COMMON/LAW ENGLSH/LAW. PAGE 46 B0936
B60
JURID
CT/SYS
CONSTN
GOV/REL

ELIAS T.O.,THE NIGERIAN LEGAL SYSTEM. NIGERIA LAW FAM KIN SECT ADMIN NAT/LISM...JURID 18/20 ENGLSH/LAW COMMON/LAW. PAGE 33 B0665
B63
CT/SYS
ADJUD
COLONIAL
PROF/ORG

BENNETT H.A.,THE COMMISSION AND THE COMMON LAW: A STUDY IN ADMINISTRATIVE ADJUDICATION. LAW ADMIN CT/SYS LOBBY SANCTION GOV/REL 20 COMMON/LAW. PAGE 10 B0212
B64
ADJUD
DELIB/GP
DIST/IND
POLICY

COMMONS J.R. B0458

COMMONWEALTH....SEE COMMONWLTH

COMMONWLTH....BRITISH COMMONWEALTH OF NATIONS; SEE ALSO VOL/ASSN, APPROPRIATE NATIONS, CMN/WLTH

HOLDSWORTH W.S.,A HISTORY OF ENGLISH LAW; THE COMMON LAW AND ITS RIVALS (VOL. VI). UK STRATA EX/STRUC ADJUD ADMIN CONTROL CT/SYS...JURID CONCPT GEN/LAWS 17 COMMONWLTH PARLIAMENT ENGLSH/LAW COMMON/LAW. PAGE 51 B1034
B24
LAW
CONSTN
LEGIS
CHIEF

STOUT H.M.,BRITISH GOVERNMENT. UK FINAN LOC/G POL/PAR DELIB/GP DIPLOM ADMIN COLONIAL CHOOSE ORD/FREE...JURID BIBLIOG 20 COMMONWLTH. PAGE 101 B2049
B53
NAT/G
PARL/PROC
CONSTN
NEW/LIB

SCARROW H.A.,THE HIGHER PUBLIC SERVICE OF THE
COMMONWEALTH OF AUSTRALIA. LAW SENIOR LOBBY ROLE 20
AUSTRAL CIVIL/SERV COMMONWLTH. PAGE 93 B1877
B57
ADMIN
NAT/G
EX/STRUC
GOV/COMP

BLAIR L.,THE COMMONWEALTH PUBLIC SERVICE. LAW
WORKER...MGT CHARTS GOV/COMP 20 COMMONWLTH AUSTRAL
CIVIL/SERV. PAGE 12 B0248
B58
ADMIN
NAT/G
EX/STRUC
INGP/REL

CONF ON FUTURE OF COMMONWEALTH,THE FUTURE OF THE
COMMONWEALTH. UK ECO/UNDEV AGRI EDU/PROP ADMIN
SOC/INTEG 20 COMMONWLTH. PAGE 23 B0460
B63
DIPLOM
RACE/REL
ORD/FREE
TEC/DEV

THE SPECIAL COMMONWEALTH AFRICAN ASSISTANCE PLAN.
AFR CANADA INDIA NIGERIA UK FINAN SCHOOL...CHARTS
20 COMMONWLTH. PAGE 2 B0041
B64
ECO/UNDEV
TREND
FOR/AID
ADMIN

BURNS A.C.,PARLIAMENT AS AN EXPORT. WOR+45 CONSTN
BARGAIN DEBATE ROUTINE GOV/REL EFFICIENCY...ANTHOL
COMMONWLTH PARLIAMENT. PAGE 17 B0353
B66
PARL/PROC
POL/PAR
CT/SYS
CHIEF

FABAR R.,THE VISION AND THE NEED: LATE VICTORIAN
IMPERIALIST AIMS. MOD/EUR WOR-45 CULTURE NAT/G
DIPLOM...TIME/SEQ METH/COMP 19 KIPLING/R
COMMONWLTH. PAGE 34 B0693
B66
COLONIAL
CONCPT
ADMIN
ATTIT

COMMUN/DEV....COMMUNITY DEVELOPMENT MOVEMENT IN INDIA

COMMUNES....COMMUNES

BOUVIER-AJAM M.,MANUEL TECHNIQUE ET PRATIQUE DU
MAIRE ET DES ELUS ET AGENTS COMMUNAUX. FRANCE LOC/G
BUDGET CHOOSE GP/REL SUPEGO...JURID BIBLIOG 20
MAYOR COMMUNES. PAGE 14 B0284
B64
MUNIC
ADMIN
CHIEF
NEIGH

COMMUNICATION, MASS....SEE EDU/PROP

COMMUNICATION, PERSONAL....SEE PERS/REL

COMMUNICATION, POLITICAL....SEE EDU/PROP

COMMUNICATIONS INDUSTRY....SEE COM/IND

COMMUNISM....SEE MARXISM

COMMUNIST CHINA....SEE CHINA/COM

COMMUNIST COUNTRIES (EXCEPT CHINA)....SEE COM

COMMUNIST ECONOMIC ORGANIZATION....SEE COMECON

COMMUNIST INFORMATION BUREAU....SEE COMINFORM

COMMUNIST THIRD INTERNATIONAL....SEE COMINTERN

COMMUNITY....SEE NEIGH

COMPANY, LARGE....SEE LG/CO

COMPANY, SMALL....SEE SML/CO

COMPARATIVE....SEE APPROPRIATE COMPARATIVE ANALYSIS INDEX

COMPETITION....SEE APPROPRIATE RELATIONS AND VALUES INDEXES

COMPNY/ACT....COMPANIES ACT (U.K., 1882)

COMPULSORY NATIONAL SERVICE....SEE NAT/SERV

COMPUT/IR....INFORMATION RETRIEVAL

OPERATIONS RESEARCH SOCIETY,A COMPREHENSIVE
BIBLIOGRAPHY ON OPERATIONS RESEARCH; THROUGH 1956
WITH SUPPLEMENT FOR 1957. COM/IND DIST/IND INDUS
ADMIN...DECISION MATH STAT METH 20. PAGE 80 B1612
B58
BIBLIOG/A
COMPUT/IR
OP/RES
MGT

HATTERY L.H.,INFORMATION RETRIEVAL MANAGEMENT.
CLIENT INDUS TOP/EX COMPUTER OP/RES TEC/DEV ROUTINE
COST EFFICIENCY RIGID/FLEX...METH/COMP ANTHOL 20.
PAGE 48 B0968
B62
R+D
COMPUT/IR
MGT
CREATE

HEARLE E.F.R.,A DATA PROCESSING SYSTEM FOR STATE
AND LOCAL GOVERNMENTS. PLAN TEC/DEV AUTOMAT ROUTINE
...MGT METH/CNCPT CLASSIF 20. PAGE 49 B0984
B63
LOC/G
PROVS
COMPUTER
COMPUT/IR

MCDONOUGH A.M.,INFORMATION ECONOMICS AND MANAGEMENT
SYSTEMS. ECO/DEV OP/RES AUTOMAT EFFICIENCY 20.
PAGE 72 B1448
B63
COMPUT/IR
MGT
CONCPT

NORTH R.C.,CONTENT ANALYSIS: A HANDBOOK WITH
APPLICATIONS FOR THE STUDY OF INTERNATIONAL CRISIS.
ASIA COM EUR+WWI MOD/EUR INT/ORG TEC/DEV DOMIN
EDU/PROP ROUTINE COERCE PERCEPT RIGID/FLEX ALL/VALS
...QUANT TESTS CON/ANAL SIMUL GEN/LAWS VAL/FREE.
PAGE 79 B1591
COMPUTER
B63
METH/CNCPT
COMPUT/IR
USSR

UNIVERSAL REFERENCE SYSTEM,INTERNATIONAL AFFAIRS:
VOLUME I IN THE POLITICAL SCIENCE, GOVERNMENT, AND
PUBLIC POLICY SERIES...DECISION ECOMETRIC GEOG
INT/LAW JURID MGT PHIL/SCI PSY SOC. PAGE 107 B2163
B65
BIBLIOG/A
GEN/METH
COMPUT/IR
DIPLOM

HOLSTI O.R.,"THE 1914 CASE." MOD/EUR COMPUTER
DIPLOM EDU/PROP EXEC...DECISION PSY PROBABIL STAT
COMPUT/IR SOC/EXP TIME. PAGE 51 B1036
S65
CON/ANAL
PERCEPT
WAR

MURDOCK J.C.,RESEARCH AND REGIONS. AGRI FINAN INDUS
LOC/G MUNIC NAT/G PROB/SOLV TEC/DEV ADMIN REGION
20. PAGE 76 B1545
B66
BIBLIOG
ECO/DEV
COMPUT/IR
R+D

SCHUMACHER B.G.,COMPUTER DYNAMICS IN PUBLIC
ADMINISTRATION. USA+45 CREATE PLAN TEC/DEV...MGT
LING CON/ANAL BIBLIOG/A 20. PAGE 94 B1907
B67
COMPUTER
COMPUT/IR
ADMIN
AUTOMAT

UNIVERSAL REFERENCE SYSTEM,ADMINISTRATIVE
MANAGEMENT: PUBLIC AND PRIVATE BUREAUCRACY (VOLUME
IV). WOR+45 WOR-45 ECO/DEV LG/CO LOC/G PUB/INST
VOL/ASSN GOV/REL...COMPUT/IR GEN/METH. PAGE 107
B2164
B67
BIBLIOG/A
MGT
ADMIN
NAT/G

UNIVERSAL REFERENCE SYSTEM,PUBLIC POLICY AND THE
MANAGEMENT OF SCIENCE (VOLUME IX). FUT SPACE WOR+45
LAW NAT/G TEC/DEV CONTROL NUC/PWR GOV/REL
...COMPUT/IR GEN/METH. PAGE 107 B2165
B67
BIBLIOG/A
POLICY
MGT
PHIL/SCI

VERGIN R.C.,"COMPUTER INDUCED ORGANIZATION
CHANGES." FUT USA+45 R+D CREATE OP/RES TEC/DEV
ADJUST CENTRAL...MGT INT CON/ANAL COMPUT/IR.
PAGE 112 B2260
S67
COMPUTER
DECISION
AUTOMAT
EX/STRUC

COMPUTER....COMPUTER TECHNIQUES AND TECHNOLOGY

CALDWELL L.K.,RESEARCH METHODS IN PUBLIC
ADMINISTRATION; AN OUTLINE OF TOPICS AND READINGS
(PAMPHLET). LAW ACT/RES COMPUTER KNOWL...SOC STAT
GEN/METH 20. PAGE 18 B0365
B53
BIBLIOG/A
METH/COMP
ADMIN
OP/RES

MCCLOSKEY J.F.,OPERATIONS RESEARCH FOR MANAGEMENT.
STRUCT COMPUTER ADMIN ROUTINE...PHIL/SCI CONCPT
METH/CNCPT TREND ANTHOL BIBLIOG 20. PAGE 72 B1445
B54
OP/RES
MGT
METH/COMP
TEC/DEV

RILEY V.,INTERINDUSTRY ECONOMIC STUDIES. USA+45
COMPUTER ADMIN OPTIMAL PRODUC...MGT CLASSIF STAT.
PAGE 88 B1788
B55
BIBLIOG
ECO/DEV
PLAN
STRUCT

BRIGHT J.R.,AUTOMATION AND MANAGEMENT. INDUS LABOR
WORKER OP/RES TEC/DEV INSPECT 20. PAGE 15 B0307
B58
AUTOMAT
COMPUTER
PLAN
MGT

BAERWALD F.,ECONOMIC SYSTEM ANALYSIS: CONCEPTS AND
PERSPECTIVES. USA+45 ECO/DEV NAT/G COMPUTER EQUILIB
INCOME ATTIT...DECISION CONCPT IDEA/COMP. PAGE 8
B0159
B60
ACT/RES
ECO/TAC
ROUTINE
FINAN

BOULDING K.E.,LINEAR PROGRAMMING AND THE THEORY OF
THE FIRM. ACT/RES PLAN...MGT MATH. PAGE 14 B0283
B60
LG/CO
NEW/IDEA
COMPUTER

HATTERY L.H.,INFORMATION RETRIEVAL MANAGEMENT.
CLIENT INDUS TOP/EX COMPUTER OP/RES TEC/DEV ROUTINE
COST EFFICIENCY RIGID/FLEX...METH/COMP ANTHOL 20.
PAGE 48 B0968
B62
R+D
COMPUT/IR
MGT
CREATE

MARS D.,SUGGESTED LIBRARY IN PUBLIC ADMINISTRATION.
FINAN DELIB/GP EX/STRUC WORKER COMPUTER ADJUD
...DECISION PSY SOC METH/COMP 20. PAGE 69 B1403
B62
BIBLIOG
ADMIN
METH
MGT

BURSK E.C.,NEW DECISION-MAKING TOOLS FOR MANAGERS.
COMPUTER PLAN PROB/SOLV ROUTINE COST. PAGE 18 B0357
B63
DECISION
MGT
MATH
RIGID/FLEX

HEARLE E.F.R.,A DATA PROCESSING SYSTEM FOR STATE
AND LOCAL GOVERNMENTS. PLAN TEC/DEV AUTOMAT ROUTINE
...MGT METH/CNCPT CLASSIF 20. PAGE 49 B0984
B63
LOC/G
PROVS
COMPUTER
COMPUT/IR

MCDONOUGH A.M.,INFORMATION ECONOMICS AND MANAGEMENT
SYSTEMS. ECO/DEV OP/RES AUTOMAT EFFICIENCY 20.
PAGE 72 B1448

B63
COMPUT/IR
MGT
CONCPT
COMPUTER

BOGUSLAW R.,THE NEW UTOPIANS. OP/RES ADMIN CONTROL
PWR...IDEA/COMP SIMUL 20. PAGE 13 B0265

B65
UTOPIA
AUTOMAT
COMPUTER
PLAN

VEINOTT A.F. JR.,MATHEMATICAL STUDIES IN MANAGEMENT
SCIENCE. UNIV INDUS COMPUTER ADMIN...DECISION
NET/THEORY SIMUL 20. PAGE 112 B2257

B65
MATH
MGT
PLAN
PRODUC

HOLSTI O.R.,"THE 1914 CASE." MOD/EUR COMPUTER
DIPLOM EDU/PROP EXEC...DECISION PSY PROBABIL STAT
COMPUT/IR SOC/EXP TIME. PAGE 51 B1036

S65
CON/ANAL
PERCEPT
WAR

MANSFIELD E.,MANAGERIAL ECONOMICS AND OPERATIONS
RESEARCH; A NONMATHEMATICAL INTRODUCTION. USA+45
ELITES ECO/DEV CONSULT EX/STRUC PROB/SOLV ROUTINE
EFFICIENCY OPTIMAL...GAME T 20. PAGE 69 B1396

B66
ECO/TAC
OP/RES
MGT
COMPUTER

DIEBOLD J.,"COMPUTERS, PROGRAM MANAGEMENT AND
FOREIGN AFFAIRS." USA+45 INDUS OP/RES TEC/DEV...MGT
GP/COMP GEN/LAWS. PAGE 29 B0590

S66
COMPUTER
DIPLOM
ROUTINE
ACT/RES

SCHUMACHER B.G.,COMPUTER DYNAMICS IN PUBLIC
ADMINISTRATION. USA+45 CREATE PLAN TEC/DEV...MGT
LING CON/ANAL BIBLIOG/A 20. PAGE 94 B1907

B67
COMPUTER
COMPUT/IR
ADMIN
AUTOMAT

BRADY R.H.,"COMPUTERS IN TOP-LEVEL DECISION MAKING"
FUT WOR+45 CONTROL...PREDICT CHARTS. PAGE 15 B0297

S67
COMPUTER
MGT
DECISION
TEC/DEV

DROR Y.,"POLICY ANALYSTS." USA+45 COMPUTER OP/RES
ECO/TAC ADMIN ROUTINE...ECOMETRIC METH/COMP SIMUL
20. PAGE 30 B0618

S67
NAT/G
POLICY
PLAN
DECISION

MOOR E.J.,"THE INTERNATIONAL IMPACT OF AUTOMATION."
WOR+45 ACT/RES COMPUTER CREATE PLAN CAP/ISM ROUTINE
EFFICIENCY PREDICT. PAGE 75 B1511

S67
TEC/DEV
OP/RES
AUTOMAT
INDUS

MORTON J.A.,"A SYSTEMS APPROACH TO THE INNOVATION
PROCESS: ITS USE IN THE BELL SYSTEM." USA+45 INTELL
INDUS LG/CO CONSULT WORKER COMPUTER AUTOMAT DEMAND
...MGT CHARTS 20. PAGE 76 B1531

S67
TEC/DEV
GEN/METH
R+D
COM/IND

VERGIN R.C.,"COMPUTER INDUCED ORGANIZATION
CHANGES." FUT USA+45 R+D CREATE OP/RES TEC/DEV
ADJUST CENTRAL...MGT INT CON/ANAL COMPUT/IR.
PAGE 112 B2260

S67
COMPUTER
DECISION
AUTOMAT
EX/STRUC

COMTE/A....AUGUST COMTE

CON/ANAL....QUANTITATIVE CONTENT ANALYSIS

WHITAKER'S CUMULATIVE BOOKLIST. UK ADMIN...HUM SOC
20. PAGE 1 B0009

N
BIBLIOG/A
WRITING
CON/ANAL

WORLD PEACE FOUNDATION,DOCUMENTS OF INTERNATIONAL
ORGANIZATIONS: A SELECTED BIBLIOGRAPHY. WOR+45
WOR-45 AGRI FINAN ACT/RES OP/RES INT/TRADE ADMIN
...CON/ANAL 20 UN UNESCO LEAGUE/NAT. PAGE 118 B2374

N
BIBLIOG
DIPLOM
INT/ORG
REGION

BUREAU OF NAT'L AFFAIRS INC.,A CURRENT LOOK AT:
(1) THE NEGRO AND TITLE VII, (2) SEX AND TITLE VII
(PAMPHLET). LAW LG/CO SML/CO RACE/REL...POLICY SOC
STAT DEEP/QU TREND CON/ANAL CHARTS 20 NEGRO
CIV/RIGHTS. PAGE 17 B0350

N19
DISCRIM
SEX
WORKER
MGT

DANGERFIELD R.,IN DEFENSE OF THE SENATE. USA-45
CONSTN NAT/G EX/STRUC TOP/EX ATTIT KNOWL
...METH/CNCPT STAT TIME/SEQ TREND CON/ANAL CHARTS
CONGRESS 20 TREATY. PAGE 26 B0528

B33
LEGIS
DELIB/GP
DIPLOM

FAHS C.B.,"GOVERNMENT IN JAPAN." FINAN FORCES LEGIS
TOP/EX BUDGET INT/TRADE EDU/PROP SOVEREIGN
...CON/ANAL BIBLIOG/A 20 CHINJAP. PAGE 34 B0698

C40
ASIA
DIPLOM
NAT/G
ADMIN

CORWIN E.S.,"THE CONSTITUTION AND WORLD
ORGANIZATION." FUT USA+45 USA-45 NAT/G EX/STRUC
LEGIS PEACE KNOWL...CON/ANAL UN 20. PAGE 24 B0484

L44
INT/ORG
CONSTN
SOVEREIGN

GOODRICH L.M.,"CHARTER OF THE UNITED NATIONS:
COMMENTARY AND DOCUMENTS." EX/STRUC ADMIN...INT/LAW

C46
CONSTN
INT/ORG

CON/ANAL BIBLIOG 20 UN. PAGE 41 B0826

DIPLOM

WARD R.E.,A GUIDE TO JAPANESE REFERENCE AND
RESEARCH MATERIALS IN THE FIELD OF POLITICAL
SCIENCE. LAW CONSTN LOC/G PRESS ADMIN...SOC
CON/ANAL METH 19/20 CHINJAP. PAGE 113 B2289

B50
BIBLIOG/A
ASIA
NAT/G

LEITES N.,THE OPERATIONAL CODE OF THE POLITBURO.
COM USSR CREATE PLAN DOMIN LEGIT COERCE ALL/VALS
...SOC CONCPT MYTH TREND CON/ANAL GEN/LAWS 20
LENIN/VI STALIN/J. PAGE 64 B1284

B51
DELIB/GP
ADMIN
SOCISM

MORRIS B.S.,"THE COMINFORM: A FIVE YEAR
PERSPECTIVE." COM UNIV USSR WOR+45 ECO/DEV POL/PAR
TOP/EX PLAN DOMIN ADMIN TOTALISM ATTIT ALL/VALS
...CONCPT TIME/SEQ TREND CON/ANAL WORK VAL/FREE 20.
PAGE 76 B1527

S53
VOL/ASSN
EDU/PROP
DIPLOM

BINANI G.D.,INDIA AT A GLANCE (REV. ED.). INDIA
COM/IND FINAN INDUS LABOR PROVS SCHOOL PLAN DIPLOM
INT/TRADE ADMIN...JURID 20. PAGE 12 B0238

B54
INDEX
CON/ANAL
NAT/G
ECO/UNDEV

CHICAGO JOINT REFERENCE LIB,FEDERAL-STATE-LOCAL
RELATIONS; A SELECTED BIBLIOGRAPHY. USA+45 AGRI
LABOR LOC/G MUNIC EX/STRUC ADMIN REGION HEALTH
CON/ANAL. PAGE 21 B0419

B54
BIBLIOG
FEDERAL
GOV/REL

LOVEDAY A.,REFLECTIONS ON INTERNATIONAL
ADMINISTRATION. WOR+45 WOR-45 DELIB/GP ACT/RES
ADMIN EXEC ROUTINE DRIVE...METH/CNCPT TIME/SEQ
CON/ANAL SIMUL TOT/POP 20. PAGE 67 B1342

B56
INT/ORG
MGT

WILSON P.,GOVERNMENT AND POLITICS OF INDIA AND
PAKISTAN: 1885-1955; A BIBLIOGRAPHY OF WORKS IN
WESTERN LANGUAGES. INDIA PAKISTAN CONSTN LOC/G
POL/PAR FORCES DIPLOM ADMIN WAR CHOOSE...BIOG
CON/ANAL 19/20. PAGE 117 B2361

B56
BIBLIOG
COLONIAL
NAT/G
S/ASIA

CENTRAL ASIAN RESEARCH CENTRE,BIBLIOGRAPHY OF
RECENT SOVIET SOURCE MATERIAL ON SOVIET CENTRAL
ASIA AND THE BORDERLANDS. AFGHANISTN INDIA PAKISTAN
UAR USSR ECO/UNDEV AGRI EXTR/IND INDUS ACADEM ADMIN
...HEAL HUM LING CON/ANAL 20. PAGE 19 B0399

B57
BIBLIOG/A
COM
CULTURE
NAT/G

BLAISDELL D.C.,"PRESSURE GROUPS, FOREIGN POLICIES,
AND INTERNATIONAL POLITICS." USA+45 WOR+45 INT/ORG
PLAN DOMIN EDU/PROP LEGIT ADMIN ROUTINE CHOOSE
...DECISION MGT METH/CNCPT CON/ANAL 20. PAGE 12
B0249

S58
PROF/ORG
PWR

CONOVER H.F.,NIGERIAN OFFICIAL PUBLICATIONS,
1869-1959: A GUIDE. NIGER CONSTN FINAN ACADEM
SCHOOL FORCES PRESS ADMIN COLONIAL...HIST/WRIT
19/20. PAGE 23 B0466

B59
BIBLIOG
NAT/G
CON/ANAL

YANG C.K.,A CHINESE VILLAGE IN EARLY COMMUNIST
TRANSITION. ECO/UNDEV AGRI FAM KIN MUNIC FORCES
PLAN ECO/TAC DOMIN EDU/PROP ATTIT DRIVE PWR RESPECT
...SOC CONCPT METH/CNCPT OBS RECORD CON/ANAL CHARTS
WORK 20. PAGE 118 B2389

B59
ASIA
ROUTINE
SOCISM

BAILEY S.D.,"THE FUTURE COMPOSITION OF THE
TRUSTEESHIP COUNCIL." FUT WOR+45 CONSTN VOL/ASSN
ADMIN ATTIT PWR...OBS TREND CON/ANAL VAL/FREE UN
20. PAGE 8 B0161

S59
INT/ORG
NAT/LISM
SOVEREIGN

CALKINS R.D.,"THE DECISION PROCESS IN
ADMINISTRATION." EX/STRUC PROB/SOLV ROUTINE MGT.
PAGE 18 B0368

S59
ADMIN
OP/RES
DECISION
CON/ANAL

LENGYEL P.,"SOME TRENDS IN THE INTERNATIONAL CIVIL
SERVICE." FUT WOR+45 INT/ORG CONSULT ATTIT...MGT
OBS TREND CON/ANAL LEAGUE/NAT UNESCO 20. PAGE 64
B1291

S59
ADMIN
EXEC

PADELFORD N.J.,"REGIONAL COOPERATION IN THE SOUTH
PACIFIC: THE SOUTH PACIFIC COMMISSION." FUT
NEW/ZEALND UK WOR+45 CULTURE ECO/UNDEV LOC/G
VOL/ASSN...OBS CON/ANAL UNESCO VAL/FREE AUSTRAL 20.
PAGE 80 B1622

S59
INT/ORG
ADMIN

STOESSINGER J.G.,"THE INTERNATIONAL ATOMIC ENERGY
AGENCY: THE FIRST PHASE." FUT WOR+45 NAT/G VOL/ASSN
DELIB/GP BAL/PWR LEGIT ADMIN ROUTINE PWR...OBS
CON/ANAL GEN/LAWS VAL/FREE 20 IAEA. PAGE 101 B2048

S59
INT/ORG
ECO/DEV
FOR/AID
NUC/PWR

EASTON S.C.,THE TWILIGHT OF EUROPEAN COLONIALISM.
AFR S/ASIA CONSTN SOCIETY STRUCT ECO/UNDEV INDUS
NAT/G FORCES ECO/TAC COLONIAL CT/SYS ATTIT KNOWL
ORD/FREE PWR...SOCIALIST TIME/SEQ TREND CON/ANAL
20. PAGE 32 B0645

B60
FINAN
ADMIN

STEIN E.,"LEGAL REMEDIES OF ENTERPRISES IN THE
EUROPEAN ECONOMIC COMMUNITY." EUR+WWI FUT ECO/DEV

L60
MARKET
ADJUD

INDUS PLAN ECO/TAC ADMIN PWR...MGT MATH STAT TREND
CON/ANAL EEC 20. PAGE 100 B2026

S60
APTER D.E.,"THE ROLE OF TRADITIONALISM IN THE   CONSERVE
POLITICAL MODERNIZATION OF GHANA AND UGANDA" (BMR)"   ADMIN
AFR GHANA UGANDA CULTURE NAT/G POL/PAR NAT/LISM   GOV/COMP
...CON/ANAL 20. PAGE 6 B0121   PROB/SOLV

S60
SCHATZ S.P.,"THE INFLENCE OF PLANNING ON   ECO/UNDEV
DEVELOPMENT: THE NIGERIAN EXPERIENCE." AFR FUT   PLAN
FINAN INDUS NAT/G EX/STRUC ECO/TAC ADMIN ATTIT   NIGERIA
PERCEPT ORD/FREE PWR...MATH TREND CON/ANAL SIMUL
VAL/FREE 20. PAGE 93 B1883

C61
ETZIONI A.,"A COMPARATIVE ANALYSIS OF COMPLEX   CON/ANAL
ORGANIZATIONS: ON POWER, INVOLVEMENT AND THEIR   SOC
CORRELATES." ELITES CREATE OP/RES ROUTINE INGP/REL   LEAD
PERS/REL CONSEN ATTIT DRIVE PWR...CONCPT BIBLIOG.   CONTROL
PAGE 34 B0684

B62
BAILEY S.D.,THE SECRETARIAT OF THE UNITED NATIONS.   INT/ORG
FUT WOR+45 DELIB/GP PLAN BAL/PWR DOMIN EDU/PROP   EXEC
ADMIN PEACE ATTIT PWR...DECISION CONCPT TREND   DIPLOM
CON/ANAL CHARTS UN VAL/FREE COLD/WAR 20. PAGE 8
B0162

B62
NICHOLAS H.G.,THE UNITED NATIONS AS A POLITICAL   INT/ORG
INSTITUTION. WOR+45 CONSTN EX/STRUC ACT/RES LEGIT   ROUTINE
PERCEPT KNOWL PWR...CONCPT TIME/SEQ CON/ANAL
ORG/CHARTS UN 20. PAGE 78 B1580

B62
SNYDER R.C.,FOREIGN POLICY DECISION-MAKING. FUT   TEC/DEV
KOREA WOR+45 R+D CREATE ADMIN ROUTINE PWR   HYPO/EXP
...DECISION PSY SOC CONCPT METH/CNCPT CON/ANAL   DIPLOM
CHARTS GEN/METH METH 20. PAGE 99 B1992

S62
FESLER J.W.,"FRENCH FIELD ADMINISTRATION: THE   EX/STRUC
BEGINNINGS." CHRIST-17C CULTURE SOCIETY STRATA   FRANCE
NAT/G ECO/TAC DOMIN EDU/PROP LEGIT ADJUD COERCE
ATTIT ALL/VALS...TIME/SEQ CON/ANAL GEN/METH
VAL/FREE 13/15. PAGE 35 B0714

B63
NORTH R.C.,CONTENT ANALYSIS: A HANDBOOK WITH   METH/CNCPT
APPLICATIONS FOR THE STUDY OF INTERNATIONAL CRISIS.   COMPUT/IR
ASIA COM EUR+WWI MOD/EUR INT/ORG TEC/DEV DOMIN   USSR
EDU/PROP ROUTINE COERCE PERCEPT RIGID/FLEX ALL/VALS
...QUANT TESTS CON/ANAL SIMUL GEN/LAWS VAL/FREE.
PAGE 79 B1591

B63
WALKER A.A.,OFFICIAL PUBLICATIONS OF SIERRA LEONE   BIBLIOG
AND GAMBIA. GAMBIA SIER/LEONE UK LAW CONSTN LEGIS   NAT/G
PLAN BUDGET DIPLOM...SOC SAMP CON/ANAL 20. PAGE 113   COLONIAL
B2278   ADMIN

S63
CLEMHOUT S.,"PRODUCTION FUNCTION ANALYSIS APPLIED   ECO/DEV
TO THE LEONTIEF SCARCE-FACTOR PARADOX OF   ECO/TAC
INTERNATIONAL TRADE." EUR+WWI USA+45 DIST/IND NAT/G
PLAN TEC/DEV DIPLOM PWR WEALTH...MGT METH/CNCPT
CONT/OBS CON/ANAL CHARTS SIMUL GEN/LAWS 20. PAGE 21
B0436

S63
MODELSKI G.,"STUDY OF ALLIANCES." WOR+45 WOR-45   VOL/ASSN
INT/ORG NAT/G FORCES LEGIT ADMIN CHOOSE ALL/VALS   CON/ANAL
PWR SKILL...INT/LAW CONCPT GEN/LAWS 20 TREATY.   DIPLOM
PAGE 74 B1495

B64
COOMBS C.H.,A THEORY OF DATA....MGT PHIL/SCI SOC   CON/ANAL
CLASSIF MATH PROBABIL STAT QU. PAGE 23 B0472   GEN/METH
                                                        TESTS
                                                        PSY

L64
RIPLEY R.B.,"INTERAGENCY COMMITTEES AND   EXEC
INCREMENTALISM: THE CASE OF AID TO INDIA." INDIA   MGT
USA+45 INTELL NAT/G DELIB/GP ACT/RES DIPLOM ROUTINE   FOR/AID
NAT/LISM ATTIT PWR...SOC CONCPT NEW/IDEA TIME/SEQ
CON/ANAL VAL/FREE 20. PAGE 89 B1790

S64
FLORINSKY M.T.,"TRENDS IN THE SOVIET ECONOMY." COM   ECO/DEV
USA+45 USSR INDUS LABOR NAT/G PLAN TEC/DEV ECO/TAC   AGRI
ALL/VALS SOCISM...MGT METH/CNCPT STYLE CON/ANAL
GEN/METH WORK 20. PAGE 36 B0731

S64
STONE P.A.,"DECISION TECHNIQUES FOR TOWN   OP/RES
DEVELOPMENT." PLAN COST PROFIT...DECISION MGT   MUNIC
CON/ANAL CHARTS METH/COMP BIBLIOG 20. PAGE 101   ADMIN
B2048   PROB/SOLV

B65
INT. BANK. RECONSTR. DEVELOP.,ECONOMIC DEVELOPMENT   INDUS
OF KUWAIT. ISLAM KUWAIT AGRI FINAN MARKET EX/STRUC   NAT/G
TEC/DEV ECO/TAC ADMIN WEALTH...OBS CON/ANAL CHARTS
20. PAGE 54 B1092

B65
MEISEL J.H.,PARETO & MOSCA. ITALY STRUCT ADMIN   PWR
...SOC CON/ANAL ANTHOL BIBLIOG 19/20. PAGE 72 B1463   ELITES
                                                      CONTROL
                                                      LAISSEZ

B65
WITHERELL J.W.,MADAGASCAR AND ADJACENT ISLANDS; A   BIBLIOG
GUIDE TO OFFICIAL PUBLICATIONS (PAMPHLET). FRANCE   COLONIAL
MADAGASCAR S/ASIA UK LAW OP/RES PLAN DIPLOM   LOC/G
...POLICY CON/ANAL 19/20. PAGE 117 B2368   ADMIN

S65
HOLSTI O.R.,"THE 1914 CASE." MOD/EUR COMPUTER   CON/ANAL
DIPLOM EDU/PROP EXEC...DECISION PSY PROBABIL STAT   PERCEPT
COMPUT/IR SOC/EXP TIME. PAGE 51 B1036   WAR

B67
SCHUMACHER B.G.,COMPUTER DYNAMICS IN PUBLIC   COMPUTER
ADMINISTRATION. USA+45 CREATE PLAN TEC/DEV...MGT   COMPUT/IR
LING CON/ANAL BIBLIOG/A 20. PAGE 94 B1907   ADMIN
                                                     AUTOMAT

S67
GORHAM W.,"NOTES OF A PRACTITIONER." USA+45 BUDGET   DECISION
ADMIN COST...CON/ANAL METH/COMP 20 JOHNSON/LB.   NAT/G
PAGE 41 B0836   DELIB/GP
                                                     EFFICIENCY

S67
VERGIN R.C.,"COMPUTER INDUCED ORGANIZATION   COMPUTER
CHANGES." FUT USA+45 R+D CREATE OP/RES TEC/DEV   DECISION
ADJUST CENTRAL...MGT INT CON/ANAL COMPUT/IR.   AUTOMAT
PAGE 112 B2260   EX/STRUC

CON/INTERP....CONSTITUTIONAL INTERPRETATION

CONAWAY O.B. B0459

CONCEN/CMP....CONCENTRATION CAMPS

CONCEPT....SEE CONCPT

CONCPT....SUBJECT-MATTER CONCEPTS

CONDEMNATION OF LAND OR PROPERTY....SEE CONDEMNATN

CONDEMNATN....CONDEMNATION OF LAND OR PROPERTY

CONDOTTIER....CONDOTTIERI - HIRED MILITIA

CONF ON FUTURE OF COMMONWEALTH B0460

CONFER....CONFERENCES; SEE ALSO DELIB/GP

N19
FOLSOM M.B.,BETTER MANAGEMENT OF THE PUBLIC'S   ADMIN
BUSINESS (PAMPHLET). USA+45 DELIB/GP PAY CONFER   NAT/G
CONTROL REGION GP/REL...METH/COMP ANTHOL 20.   MGT
PAGE 36 B0733   PROB/SOLV

N19
SOUTH AFRICA COMMISSION ON FUT,INTERIM AND FINAL   CONSTN
REPORTS ON FUTURE FORM OF GOVERNMENT IN THE SOUTH-   REPRESENT
WEST AFRICAN PROTECTORATE (PAMPHLET). SOUTH/AFR   ADMIN
NAT/G FORCES CONFER COLONIAL CONTROL 20 AFRICA/SW.   PROB/SOLV
PAGE 99 B1998

B37
CLOKIE H.M.,ROYAL COMMISSIONS OF INQUIRY; THE   NAT/G
SIGNIFICANCE OF INVESTIGATIONS IN BRITISH POLITICS.   DELIB/GP
UK POL/PAR CONFER ROUTINE...POLICY DECISION   INSPECT
TIME/SEQ 16/20. PAGE 22 B0439

B42
LEISERSON A.,ADMINISTRATIVE REGULATION: A STUDY IN   LOBBY
REPRESENTATION OF INTERESTS. NAT/G EX/STRUC   ADMIN
PROB/SOLV BARGAIN CONFER ROUTINE REPRESENT PERS/REL   GP/REL
UTIL PWR POLICY. PAGE 63 B1283   GOV/REL

S44
GRIFFITH E.S.,"THE CHANGING PATTERN OF PUBLIC   LAW
POLICY FORMATION." MOD/EUR WOR+45 FINAN CHIEF   POLICY
CONFER ADMIN LEAD CONSERVE SOCISM TECHRACY...SOC   TEC/DEV
CHARTS CONGRESS. PAGE 43 B0877

S44
KEFAUVER E.,"THE NEED FOR BETTER EXECUTIVE-   LEGIS
LEGISLATIVE TEAMWORK IN THE NATIONAL GOVERNMENT."   EXEC
USA-45 CONSTN NAT/G ROUTINE...TRADIT CONGRESS   CONFER
REFORMERS. PAGE 59 B1188   LEAD

B48
SPERO S.D.,GOVERNMENT AS EMPLOYER. USA+45 NAT/G   SOVEREIGN
EX/STRUC ADMIN CONTROL EXEC 20. PAGE 99 B2005   INGP/REL
                                                     REPRESENT
                                                     CONFER

N48
YATES M.,ADMINISTRATIVE REORGANIZATION OF STATE   BIBLIOG
GOVERNMENTS: A BIBLIOGRAPHY (PAMPHLET). USA+45   LOC/G
USA-45 CONSTN OP/RES PLAN CONFER...POLICY 20.   ADMIN
PAGE 118 B2390   PROVS

B50
GREAT BRITAIN TREASURY,PUBLIC ADMINISTRATION: A   BIBLIOG
BIBLIOGRAPHY FOR ORGANISATION AND METHODS   PLAN
(PAMPHLET). LOC/G NAT/G CONSULT EX/STRUC CONFER   CONTROL
ROUTINE TASK EFFICIENCY...MGT 20. PAGE 43 B0862   ADMIN

B51
SHILS E.A.,"THE LEGISLATOR AND HIS ENVIRONMENT."   LEGIS
EX/STRUC DOMIN CONFER EFFICIENCY PWR MAJORIT.   TOP/EX
PAGE 96 B1947   ADMIN
                                                     DELIB/GP

NASH B.D.,STAFFING THE PRESIDENCY: PLANNING
PAMPHLET NO. 80 (PAMPHLET). NAT/G CHIEF CONSULT
DELIB/GP CONFER ADMIN 20 PRESIDENT. PAGE 77 B1557
B52 EX/STRUC EXEC TOP/EX ROLE

TAYLOR D.W.,"TWENTY QUESTIONS: EFFICIENCY IN
PROBLEM SOLVING AS A FUNCTION OF SIZE OF GROUP"
WOR+45 CONFER ROUTINE INGP/REL...PSY GP/COMP 20.
PAGE 103 B2085
S52 PROB/SOLV EFFICIENCY SKILL PERCEPT

BULNER-THOMAS I.,"THE PARTY SYSTEM IN GREAT
BRITAIN." UK CONSTN SECT PRESS CONFER GP/REL ATTIT
...POLICY TREND BIBLIOG 19/20 PARLIAMENT. PAGE 17
B0343
C53 NAT/G POL/PAR ADMIN ROUTINE

US PRES CONF ADMIN PROCEDURE,REPORT (PAMPHLET).
USA+45 CONFER ADJUD...METH/COMP 20 PRESIDENT.
PAGE 109 B2209
N53 NAT/G DELIB/GP ADJUST ADMIN

HOBBS E.H.,BEHIND THE PRESIDENT - A STUDY OF
EXECUTIVE OFFICE AGENCIES. USA+45 NAT/G PLAN BUDGET
ECO/TAC EXEC ORD/FREE 20 BUR/BUDGET. PAGE 50 B1022
B54 EX/STRUC DELIB/GP CONFER CONSULT

ZELLER B.,"AMERICAN STATE LEGISLATURES: REPORT ON
THE COMMITTEE ON AMERICAN LEGISLATURES." CONSTN
POL/PAR EX/STRUC CONFER ADMIN CONTROL EXEC LOBBY
ROUTINE GOV/REL...POLICY BIBLIOG 20. PAGE 119 B2401
C54 REPRESENT LEGIS PROVS APPORT

UN HEADQUARTERS LIBRARY,BIBLIOGRAPHIE DE LA CHARTE
DES NATIONS UNIES. CHINA/COM KOREA WOR+45 VOL/ASSN
CONFER ADMIN COERCE PEACE ATTIT ORD/FREE SOVEREIGN
...INT/LAW 20 UNESCO UN. PAGE 106 B2149
B55 BIBLIOG/A INT/ORG DIPLOM

WHEARE K.C.,GOVERNMENT BY COMMITTEE; AN ESSAY ON
THE BRITISH CONSTITUTION. UK NAT/G LEGIS INSPECT
CONFER ADJUD ADMIN CONTROL TASK EFFICIENCY ROLE
POPULISM 20. PAGE 115 B2329
B55 DELIB/GP CONSTN LEAD GP/COMP

TAYLOR P.S.,"THE RELATION OF RESEARCH TO
LEGISLATIVE AND ADMINISTRATIVE DECISIONS." ELITES
ACT/RES PLAN PROB/SOLV CONFER CHOOSE POLICY.
PAGE 103 B2089
S57 DECISION LEGIS MGT PWR

MACMAHON A.W.,ADMINISTRATION AND FOREIGN POLICY
(PAMPHLET). USA+45 CHIEF OP/RES ADMIN 20. PAGE 68
B1372
N57 DIPLOM EX/STRUC DECISION CONFER

AMERICAN SOCIETY PUBLIC ADMIN,STRENGTHENING
MANAGEMENT FOR DEMOCRATIC GOVERNMENT. USA+45 ACADEM
EX/STRUC WORKER PLAN BUDGET CONFER CT/SYS
EFFICIENCY ANTHOL. PAGE 4 B0088
B58 ADMIN NAT/G EXEC MGT

ATOMIC INDUSTRIAL FORUM,MANAGEMENT AND ATOMIC
ENERGY. WOR+45 SEA LAW MARKET NAT/G TEC/DEV INSPECT
INT/TRADE CONFER PEACE HEALTH...ANTHOL 20. PAGE 7
B0145
B58 NUC/PWR INDUS MGT ECO/TAC

KRAINES O.,CONGRESS AND THE CHALLENGE OF BIG
GOVERNMENT. USA-45 EX/STRUC CONFER DEBATE
EFFICIENCY. PAGE 61 B1232
B58 LEGIS DELIB/GP ADMIN

SWEENEY S.B.,EDUCATION FOR ADMINISTRATIVE CAREERS
IN GOVERNMENT SERVICE. USA+45 ACADEM CONSULT CREATE
PLAN CONFER SKILL...TREND IDEA/COMP METH 20
CIVIL/SERV. PAGE 102 B2059
B58 EDU/PROP ADMIN NAT/G LOC/G

US HOUSE COMM POST OFFICE,MANPOWER UTILIZATION IN
THE FEDERAL GOVERNMENT. USA+45 DIST/IND EX/STRUC
LEGIS CONFER EFFICIENCY 20 CONGRESS CIVIL/SERV.
PAGE 109 B2195
B58 ADMIN WORKER DELIB/GP NAT/G

US HOUSE COMM POST OFFICE,MANPOWER UTILIZATION IN
THE FEDERAL GOVERNMENT. USA+45 DIST/IND EX/STRUC
LEGIS CONFER EFFICIENCY 20 CONGRESS CIVIL/SERV.
PAGE 109 B2196
B58 ADMIN WORKER DELIB/GP NAT/G

US HOUSE COMM POST OFFICE,TRAINING OF FEDERAL
EMPLOYEES. USA+45 DIST/IND NAT/G EX/STRUC EDU/PROP
CONFER GOV/REL EFFICIENCY SKILL 20 CONGRESS
CIVIL/SERV. PAGE 109 B2197
B58 LEGIS DELIB/GP WORKER ADMIN

US SENATE COMM POST OFFICE,TO PROVIDE AN EFFECTIVE
SYSTEM OF PERSONNEL ADMINISTRATION. USA+45 NAT/G
EX/STRUC PARL/PROC GOV/REL...JURID 20 SENATE.
PAGE 111 B2234
B58 INT LEGIS CONFER ADMIN

INDIAN INSTITUTE PUBLIC ADMIN,MORALE IN THE PUBLIC
SERVICES: REPORT OF A CONFERENCE JAN., 3-4, 1959.
INDIA S/ASIA ECO/UNDEV PROVS PLAN EDU/PROP CONFER
GOV/REL EFFICIENCY DRIVE ROLE 20 CIVIL/SERV.
PAGE 53 B1082
B59 HAPPINESS ADMIN WORKER INGP/REL

US CIVIL SERVICE COMMISSION,CONGRESSIONAL DOCUMENTS
RELATING TO CIVIL SERVICE. USA+45 USA-45 CONFER
19/20 CONGRESS. PAGE 108 B2177
B59 BIBLIOG/A ADMIN NAT/G LEGIS

WEBER W.,DER DEUTSCHE BEAMTE HEUTE. GERMANY/W NAT/G
DELIB/GP LEGIS CONFER ATTIT SUPEGO...JURID 20
CIVIL/SERV. PAGE 114 B2306
B59 MGT EFFICIENCY ELITES GP/REL

HAYNES G.H.,THE SENATE OF THE UNITED STATES: ITS
HISTORY AND PRACTICE. CONSTN EX/STRUC TOP/EX CONFER
DEBATE LEAD LOBBY PARL/PROC CHOOSE PWR SENATE
CONGRESS. PAGE 48 B0977
B60 LEGIS DELIB/GP

INDIAN INST OF PUBLIC ADMIN,STATE UNDERTAKINGS:
REPORT OF A CONFERENCE, DECEMBER 19-20, 1959
(PAMPHLET). INDIA LG/CO DELIB/GP CONFER PARL/PROC
EFFICIENCY OWN...MGT 20. PAGE 53 B1081
B60 GOV/REL ADMIN NAT/G LEGIS

MARSHALL A.H.,FINANCIAL ADMINISTRATION IN LOCAL
GOVERNMENT. UK DELIB/GP CONFER COST INCOME PERSON
...JURID 20. PAGE 70 B1408
B60 FINAN LOC/G BUDGET ADMIN

ROY N.C.,THE CIVIL SERVICE IN INDIA. INDIA POL/PAR
ECO/TAC INCOME...JURID MGT 20 CIVIL/SERV. PAGE 91
B1843
B60 ADMIN NAT/G DELIB/GP CONFER

US SENATE COMM ON JUDICIARY,FEDERAL ADMINISTRATIVE
PROCEDURE. USA+45 CONSTN NAT/G PROB/SOLV CONFER
GOV/REL...JURID INT 20 SENATE. PAGE 110 B2226
B60 PARL/PROC LEGIS ADMIN LAW

US SENATE COMM ON JUDICIARY,ADMINISTRATIVE
PROCEDURE LEGISLATION. USA+45 CONSTN NAT/G
PROB/SOLV CONFER ROUTINE GOV/REL...INT 20 SENATE.
PAGE 110 B2227
B60 PARL/PROC LEGIS ADMIN JURID

AUERBACH C.A.,THE LEGAL PROCESS. USA+45 DELIB/GP
JUDGE CONFER ADJUD CONTROL...DECISION 20
SUPREME/CT. PAGE 7 B0146
B61 JURID ADMIN LEGIS CT/SYS

PROCEEDINGS OF THE CONFERENCE ON BUSINESS GAMES AS
TEACHING DEVICES. PROB/SOLV ECO/TAC CONFER ADMIN
TASK...MGT ANTHOL 20. PAGE 29 B0593
B61 GAME DECISION EDU/PROP EFFICIENCY

GRIFFITH E.S.,CONGRESS: ITS CONTEMPORARY ROLE.
CONSTN POL/PAR CHIEF PLAN BUDGET DIPLOM CONFER
ADMIN LOBBY...DECISION CONGRESS. PAGE 43 B0878
B61 PARL/PROC EX/STRUC TOP/EX LEGIS

INTL UNION LOCAL AUTHORITIES,LOCAL GOVERNMENT IN
THE USA. USA+45 PUB/INST DELIB/GP CONFER AUTOMAT
GP/REL POPULISM...ANTHOL 20 CITY/MGT. PAGE 54 B1101
B61 LOC/G MUNIC ADMIN GOV/REL

ROBINSON M.E.,EDUCATION FOR SOCIAL CHANGE:
ESTABLISHING INSTITUTES OF PUBLIC AND BUSINESS
ADMINISTRATION ABROAD (PAMPHLET). WOR+45 SOCIETY
ACADEM CONFER INGP/REL ROLE...SOC CHARTS BIBLIOG 20
ICA. PAGE 89 B1805
B61 FOR/AID EDU/PROP MGT ADJUST

ROBINSON J.A.,"PROCESS SATISFACTION AND POLICY
APPROVAL IN STATE DEPARTMENT - CONGRESSIONAL
RELATIONS." ELITES CHIEF LEGIS CONFER DEBATE ADMIN
FEEDBACK ROLE...CHARTS 20 CONGRESS PRESIDENT
DEPT/STATE. PAGE 89 B1802
S61 GOV/REL EX/STRUC POL/PAR DECISION

ESCUELA SUPERIOR DE ADMIN PUBL,INFORME DEL
SEMINARIO SOBRE SERVICIO CIVIL O CARRERA
ADMINISTRATIVA. L/A+17C ELITES STRATA CONFER
CONTROL GOV/REL INGP/REL SUPEGO 20 CENTRAL/AM
CIVIL/SERV. PAGE 33 B0681
B62 ADMIN NAT/G PROB/SOLV ATTIT

GRAY R.K.,EIGHTEEN ACRES UNDER GLASS. ELITES
CONSULT EX/STRUC DIPLOM PRESS CONFER WAR PERS/REL
PERSON 20 EISNHWR/DD TRUMAN/HS CABINET. PAGE 43
B0860
B62 CHIEF ADMIN TOP/EX NAT/G

INAYATULLAH,BUREAUCRACY AND DEVELOPMENT IN
PAKISTAN. PAKISTAN ECO/UNDEV EDU/PROP CONFER
...ANTHOL DICTIONARY 20 BUREAUCRCY. PAGE 53 B1078
B62 EX/STRUC ADMIN NAT/G LOC/G

TAYLOR J.K.L.,ATTITUDES AND METHODS OF
COMMUNICATION AND CONSULTATION BETWEEN EMPLOYERS
AND WORKERS AT INDIVIDUAL FIRM LEVEL. WOR+45 STRUCT
INDUS LABOR CONFER TASK GP/REL EFFICIENCY...MGT
BIBLIOG METH 20 OECD. PAGE 103 B2087
B62 WORKER ADMIN ATTIT EDU/PROP

DALAND R.T.,PERSPECTIVES OF BRAZILIAN PUBLIC
B63 ADMIN

ADMINISTRATION (VOL. I). BRAZIL LAW ECO/UNDEV SCHOOL CHIEF TEC/DEV CONFER CONTROL GP/REL ATTIT ROLE PWR...ANTHOL 20. PAGE 26 B0525
NAT/G
PLAN
GOV/REL

B63

HARGROVE M.M.,BUSINESS POLICY CASES-WITH BEHAVIORAL SCIENCE IMPLICATIONS. LG/CO SML/CO EX/STRUC TOP/EX PLAN PROB/SOLV CONFER ADMIN CONTROL ROUTINE EFFICIENCY. PAGE 47 B0946
SOC/EXP
INDUS
DECISION
MGT

B63

INTL INST ADMIN SCIENCES,EDUCATION IN PUBLIC ADMINISTRATION: A SYMPOSIUM ON TEACHING METHODS AND MATERIALS. WOR+45 SCHOOL CONSULT CREATE CONFER SKILL...OBS TREND IDEA/COMP METH/COMP 20. PAGE 54 B1100
EDU/PROP
METH
ADMIN
ACADEM

B63

KAST F.E.,SCIENCE, TECHNOLOGY, AND MANAGEMENT. SPACE USA+45 FORCES CONFER DETER NUC/PWR...PHIL/SCI CHARTS ANTHOL BIBLIOG 20 NASA. PAGE 58 B1179
MGT
PLAN
TEC/DEV
PROB/SOLV

B63

PEABODY R.L.,NEW PERSPECTIVES ON THE HOUSE OF REPRESENTATIVES. AGRI FINAN SCHOOL FORCES CONFER LEAD CHOOSE REPRESENT FEDERAL...POLICY DECISION HOUSE/REP. PAGE 82 B1647
NEW/IDEA
LEGIS
PWR
ADMIN

B63

US SENATE COMM ON JUDICIARY,ADMINISTRATIVE CONFERENCE OF THE UNITED STATES. USA+45 CONSTN NAT/G PROB/SOLV CONFER GOV/REL...INT 20 SENATE. PAGE 110 B2230
PARL/PROC
JURID
ADMIN
LEGIS

S63

PIPER D.C.,"THE ROLE OF INTER-GOVERNMENTAL MACHINERY IN CANADIANAMERICAN RELATIONS." CANADA USA+45 PROB/SOLV REPRESENT 20. PAGE 83 B1676
GOV/REL
ADMIN
EX/STRUC
CONFER

B64

FATOUROS A.A.,CANADA'S OVERSEAS AID. CANADA WOR+45 ECO/DEV FINAN NAT/G BUDGET ECO/TAC CONFER ADMIN 20. PAGE 35 B0707
FOR/AID
DIPLOM
ECO/UNDEV
POLICY

B64

RIDDLE D.H.,THE TRUMAN COMMITTEE: A STUDY IN CONGRESSIONAL RESPONSIBILITY. INDUS FORCES OP/RES DOMIN ADMIN LEAD WAR PRODUC SUPEGO ...BIBLIOG CONGRESS. PAGE 88 B1778
LEGIS
DELIB/GP
CONFER

B64

US SENATE COMM ON JUDICIARY,ADMINISTRATIVE PROCEDURE ACT. USA+45 CONSTN NAT/G PROB/SOLV CONFER GOV/REL PWR...INT 20 SENATE. PAGE 110 B2231
PARL/PROC
LEGIS
JURID
ADMIN

B65

GOTLIEB A.,DISARMAMENT AND INTERNATIONAL LAW* A STUDY OF THE ROLE OF LAW IN THE DISARMAMENT PROCESS. USA+45 USSR PROB/SOLV CONFER ADMIN ROUTINE NUC/PWR ORD/FREE SOVEREIGN UN TREATY. PAGE 42 B0841
INT/LAW
INT/ORG
ARMS/CONT
IDEA/COMP

B65

GT BRIT ADMIN STAFF COLLEGE,THE ACCOUNTABILITY OF PUBLIC CORPORATIONS (REV. ED.). UK ECO/DEV FINAN DELIB/GP EX/STRUC BUDGET CAP/ISM CONFER PRICE PARL/PROC 20. PAGE 44 B0899
LG/CO
NAT/G
ADMIN
CONTROL

B65

INST INTL DES CIVILISATION DIF,THE CONSTITUTIONS AND ADMINISTRATIVE INSTITUTIONS OF THE NEW STATES. AFR ISLAM S/ASIA NAT/G POL/PAR DELIB/GP EX/STRUC CONFER EFFICIENCY NAT/LISM...JURID SOC 20. PAGE 54 B1088
CONSTN
ADMIN
ADJUD
ECO/UNDEV

B65

LEYS C.T.,FEDERATION IN EAST AFRICA. LAW AGRI DIST/IND FINAN INT/ORG LABOR INT/TRADE CONFER ADMIN CONTROL GP/REL...ANTHOL 20 AFRICA/E. PAGE 65 B1310
FEDERAL
REGION
ECO/UNDEV
PLAN

B65

MORGENTHAU H.,MORGENTHAU DIARY (CHINA) (2 VOLS.). ASIA USA+45 USA-45 LAW DELIB/GP EX/STRUC PLAN FOR/AID INT/TRADE CONFER WAR MARXISM 20 CHINJAP. PAGE 75 B1523
DIPLOM
ADMIN

B65

REISS A.J. JR.,SCHOOLS IN A CHANGING SOCIETY. CULTURE PROB/SOLV INSPECT DOMIN CONFER INGP/REL RACE/REL AGE/C AGE/Y ALL/VALS...ANTHOL SOC/INTEG 20 NEWYORK/C. PAGE 87 B1766
SCHOOL
EX/STRUC
ADJUST
ADMIN

B66

BAKKE E.W.,MUTUAL SURVIVAL; THE GOAL OF UNION AND MANAGEMENT (2ND ED.). USA+45 ELITES ECO/DEV ECO/TAC CONFER ADMIN REPRESENT GP/REL INGP/REL ATTIT ...GP/COMP 20. PAGE 8 B0170
MGT
LABOR
BARGAIN
INDUS

B66

BEAUFRE A.,NATO AND EUROPE. WOR+45 PLAN CONFER EXEC NUC/PWR ATTIT...POLICY 20 NATO EUROPE. PAGE 10 B0203
INT/ORG
DETER
DIPLOM
ADMIN

B66

LEE L.T.,VIENNA CONVENTION ON CONSULAR RELATIONS. WOR+45 LAW INT/ORG CONFER GP/REL PRIVIL...INT/LAW 20 TREATY VIENNA/CNV. PAGE 63 B1279
AGREE
DIPLOM
ADMIN

B66

UN ECAFE,ADMINISTRATIVE ASPECTS OF FAMILY PLANNING
PLAN

PROGRAMMES (PAMPHLET). ASIA THAILAND WOR+45 VOL/ASSN PROB/SOLV BUDGET FOR/AID EDU/PROP CONFER CONTROL GOV/REL TIME 20 UN BIRTH/CON. PAGE 106 B2147
CENSUS
FAM
ADMIN

N66

AMERICAN SOCIETY PUBLIC ADMIN,PUBLIC ADMINISTRATION AND THE WAR ON POVERTY (PAMPHLET). USA+45 SOCIETY ECO/DEV FINAN LOC/G LEGIS CREATE EDU/PROP CONFER GOV/REL GP/REL ROLE 20 POVRTY/WAR. PAGE 4 B0089
WEALTH
NAT/G
PLAN
ADMIN

S67

CHAMBERLAIN N.W.,"STRIKES IN CONTEMPORARY CONTEXT." LAW INDUS NAT/G CHIEF CONFER COST ATTIT ORD/FREE ...POLICY MGT 20. PAGE 20 B0400
LABOR
BARGAIN
EFFICIENCY
PROB/SOLV

S67

CONWAY J.E.,"MAKING RESEARCH EFFECTIVE IN LEGISLATION." LAW R+D CONSULT EX/STRUC PLAN CONFER ADMIN LEAD ROUTINE TASK INGP/REL DECISION. PAGE 23 B0469
ACT/RES
POLICY
LEGIS
PROB/SOLV

S67

DOERN G.B.,"THE ROYAL COMMISSIONS IN THE GENERAL POLICY PROCESS AND IN FEDERAL-PROVINCIAL RELATIONS." CANADA CONSTN ACADEM PROVS CONSULT DELIB/GP LEGIS ACT/RES PROB/SOLV CONFER CONTROL EFFICIENCY...METH/COMP 20 SENATE ROYAL/COMM. PAGE 30 B0603
R+D
EX/STRUC
GOV/REL
NAT/G

S67

DRAPER A.P.,"UNIONS AND THE WAR IN VIETNAM." USA+45 CONFER ADMIN LEAD WAR ORD/FREE PACIFIST 20. PAGE 30 B0616
LABOR
PACIFISM
ATTIT
ELITES

S67

FERGUSON H.,"3-CITY CONSOLIDATION." USA+45 CONSTN INDUS BARGAIN BUDGET CONFER ADMIN INGP/REL COST UTIL. PAGE 35 B0712
MUNIC
CHOOSE
CREATE
PROB/SOLV

S67

GOBER J.L.,"FEDERALISM AT WORK." USA+45 NAT/G CONSULT ACT/RES PLAN CONFER ADMIN LEAD PARTIC FEDERAL ATTIT. PAGE 40 B0813
MUNIC
TEC/DEV
R+D
GOV/REL

S67

LEES J.P.,"LEGISLATIVE REVIEW AND BUREAUCRATIC RESPONSIBILITY." USA+45 FINAN NAT/G DELIB/GP PLAN PROB/SOLV CONFER CONTROL GP/REL DEMAND...DECISION 20 CONGRESS PRESIDENT HOUSE/REP BUREAUCRCY. PAGE 63 B1281
SUPEGO
BUDGET
LEGIS
EXEC

S67

MELTZER B.D.,"RUMINATIONS ABOUT IDEOLOGY, LAW, AND LABOR ARBITRATION." USA+45 ECO/DEV PROB/SOLV CONFER MGT. PAGE 73 B1466
JURID
ADJUD
LABOR
CONSULT

S67

TACKABERRY R.B.,"ORGANIZING AND TRAINING PEACE-KEEPING FORCES* THE CANADIAN VIEW." CANADA PLAN DIPLOM CONFER ADJUD ADMIN CIVMIL/REL 20 UN. PAGE 102 B2069
PEACE
FORCES
INT/ORG
CONSULT

S67

TOURNELLE G.,"DIPLOMATIE D' HIER ET D'AUJOURD' HUI." CONFER ADMIN ROUTINE PEACE. PAGE 105 B2123
DIPLOM
ROLE
INT/ORG

CONFERENCES....SEE CONFER, DELIB/GP

CONFIDENCE, PERSONAL....SEE SUPEGO

CONFLICT, MILITARY....SEE WAR, FORCES+COERCE

CONFLICT, PERSONAL....SEE PERS/REL, ROLE

CONFLICT....CONFLICT THEORY

CONFORMITY....SEE CONSEN, DOMIN

CONFREY E.A. B0461

CONFRONTATION....SEE CONFRONTN

CONFRONTN....CONFRONTATION

CONFUCIUS....CONFUCIUS

CONGO....CONGO, PRE-INDEPENDENCE OR GENERAL

S61

MILLER E.,"LEGAL ASPECTS OF UN ACTION IN THE CONGO." AFR CULTURE ADMIN PEACE DRIVE RIGID/FLEX ORD/FREE...WELF/ST JURID OBS UN CONGO 20. PAGE 73 B1480
INT/ORG
LEGIT

B63

STEVENSON A.E.,LOOKING OUTWARD: YEARS OF CRISIS AT THE UNITED NATIONS. COM CUBA USA+45 WOR+45 SOCIETY NAT/G EX/STRUC ACT/RES LEGIT COLONIAL ATTIT PERSON SUPEGO ALL/VALS...POLICY HUM UN COLD/WAR CONGO 20. PAGE 100 B2034
INT/ORG
CONCPT
ARMS/CONT

S63
WAGRET M.,"L'ASCENSION POLITIQUE DE L'U.D.D.I.A. (CONGO) ET SA PRISE DU POUVOIR (1956-1959)." AFR WOR+45 NAT/G POL/PAR CONSULT DELIB/GP LEGIS PERCEPT ALL/VALS SOVEREIGN...TIME/SEQ CONGO. PAGE 113 B2274
EX/STRUC
CHOOSE
FRANCE

CONGO/BRAZ....CONGO, BRAZZAVILLE; SEE ALSO AFR

CONGO/KINS....CONGO, KINSHASA; SEE ALSO AFR

B62
WELLEQUET J.,LE CONGO BELGE ET LA WELTPOLITIK (1894-1914. GERMANY DOMIN EDU/PROP WAR ATTIT ...BIBLIOG T CONGO/KINS. PAGE 115 B2318
ADMIN
DIPLOM
GP/REL
COLONIAL

B65
YOUNG C.,POLITICS IN THE CONGO* DECOLONIZATION AND INDEPENDENCE. ELITES STRATA FORCES ADMIN REV RACE/REL FEDERAL SOVEREIGN...OBS INT CHARTS CONGO/KINS. PAGE 118 B2391
BELGIUM
COLONIAL
NAT/LISM

CONGRESS OF RACIAL EQUALITY....SEE CORE

CONGRESS....CONGRESS (ALL NATIONS); SEE ALSO LEGIS, HOUSE/REP, SENATE, DELIB/GP

N
CONGRESSIONAL MONITOR. CONSULT DELIB/GP PROB/SOLV PRESS DEBATE ROUTINE...POLICY CONGRESS. PAGE 1 B0002
BIBLIOG
LEGIS
REPRESENT
USA+45

N
US SUPERINTENDENT OF DOCUMENTS,POLITICAL SCIENCE: GOVERNMENT, CRIME, DISTRICT OF COLUMBIA (PRICE LIST 54). USA+45 LAW CONSTN EX/STRUC WORKER ADJUD ADMIN CT/SYS CHOOSE INGP/REL RACE/REL CONGRESS PRESIDENT. PAGE 111 B2241
BIBLIOG/A
NAT/G
CRIME

B17
CORWIN E.S.,THE PRESIDENT'S CONTROL OF FOREIGN RELATIONS. FUT USA-45 CONSTN STRATA NAT/G CHIEF EX/STRUC LEGIS KNOWL RESPECT...JURID CONCPT TREND CONGRESS VAL/FREE 20 PRESIDENT. PAGE 24 B0483
TOP/EX
PWR
DIPLOM

B19
SUTHERLAND G.,CONSTITUTIONAL POWER AND WORLD AFFAIRS. CONSTN STRUCT INT/ORG NAT/G CHIEF LEGIS ACT/RES PLAN GOV/REL ALL/VALS...OBS TIME/SEQ CONGRESS VAL/FREE 20 PRESIDENT. PAGE 102 B2056
USA-45
EXEC
DIPLOM

B21
BRYCE J.,MODERN DEMOCRACIES. FUT NEW/ZEALND USA-45 LAW CONSTN POL/PAR PROVS VOL/ASSN EX/STRUC LEGIS LEGIT CT/SYS EXEC KNOWL CONGRESS AUSTRAL 20. PAGE 16 B0332
NAT/G
TREND

B27
WILLOUGHBY W.F.,PRINCIPLES OF PUBLIC ADMINISTRATION WITH SPECIAL REFERENCE TO THE NATIONAL AND STATE GOVERNMENTS OF THE UNITED STATES. FINAN PROVS CHIEF CONSULT LEGIS CREATE BUDGET EXEC ROUTINE GOV/REL CENTRAL...MGT 20 BUR/BUDGET CONGRESS PRESIDENT. PAGE 117 B2341
NAT/G
EX/STRUC
OP/RES
ADMIN

B33
DANGERFIELD R.,IN DEFENSE OF THE SENATE. USA-45 CONSTN NAT/G EX/STRUC TOP/EX ATTIT KNOWL ...METH/CNCPT STAT TIME/SEQ TREND CON/ANAL CHARTS CONGRESS 20 TREATY. PAGE 26 B0528
LEGIS
DELIB/GP
DIPLOM

B34
WILCOX J.K.,GUIDE TO THE OFFICIAL PUBLICATIONS OF THE NEW DEAL ADMINISTRATION (2 VOLS.). USA-45 CHIEF LEGIS ADMIN...POLICY 20 CONGRESS ROOSEVLT/F. PAGE 116 B2345
BIBLIOG
NAT/G
NEW/LIB
RECEIVE

S40
PERKINS J.A.,"CONGRESSIONAL INVESTIGATIONS OF MATTERS OF INTERNATIONAL IMPORT." DELIB/GP DIPLOM ADMIN CONTROL 20 CONGRESS. PAGE 82 B1656
POL/PAR
DECISION
PARL/PROC
GOV/REL

B42
DENNISON E.,THE SENATE FOREIGN RELATIONS COMMITTEE. USA-45 NAT/G DELIB/GP ROUTINE CHOOSE PWR CONGRESS 20. PAGE 28 B0574
LEGIS
ACT/RES
DIPLOM

S42
HUZAR E.,"LEGISLATIVE CONTROL OVER ADMINISTRATION: CONGRESS AND WPA" USA-45 FINAN DELIB/GP LOBBY GOV/REL EFFICIENCY ATTIT...POLICY CONGRESS. PAGE 53 B1069
ADMIN
EX/STRUC
CONTROL
LEGIS

B43
YOUNG R.,THIS IS CONGRESS. FUT SENIOR ADMIN GP/REL PWR...DECISION REFORMERS CONGRESS. PAGE 119 B2393
LEGIS
DELIB/GP
CHIEF
ROUTINE

L43
MACMAHON A.W.,"CONGRESSIONAL OVERSIGHT OF ADMINISTRATION: THE POWER OF THE PURSE." USA-45 BUDGET ROUTINE GOV/REL PWR...POLICY CONGRESS. PAGE 68 B1368
LEGIS
DELIB/GP
ADMIN
CONTROL

S43
PRICE D.K.,"THE PARLIAMENTARY AND PRESIDENTIAL SYSTEMS" (BMR)" USA-45 NAT/G EX/STRUC PARL/PROC GOV/REL PWR 20 PRESIDENT CONGRESS PARLIAMENT. PAGE 84 B1706
LEGIS
REPRESENT
ADMIN
GOV/COMP

S44
COLEGROVE K.W.,"THE ROLE OF CONGRESS AND PUBLIC OPINION IN FORMULATING FOREIGN POLICY." USA+45 WAR ...DECISION UN CONGRESS. PAGE 22 B0451
EX/STRUC
DIPLOM
LEGIS
PWR

S44
GRIFFITH E.S.,"THE CHANGING PATTERN OF PUBLIC POLICY FORMATION." MOD/EUR WOR+45 FINAN CHIEF CONFER ADMIN LEAD CONSERVE SOCISM TECHRACY...SOC CHARTS CONGRESS. PAGE 43 B0877
LAW
POLICY
TEC/DEV

S44
KEFAUVER E.,"THE NEED FOR BETTER EXECUTIVE-LEGISLATIVE TEAMWORK IN THE NATIONAL GOVERNMENT." USA-45 CONSTN NAT/G ROUTINE...TRADIT CONGRESS REFORMERS. PAGE 59 B1188
LEGIS
EXEC
CONFER
LEAD

S45
WHITE L.D.,"CONGRESSIONAL CONTROL OF THE PUBLIC SERVICE." USA-45 NAT/G CONSULT DELIB/GP PLAN SENIOR CONGRESS. PAGE 116 B2335
LEGIS
EXEC
POLICY
CONTROL

S47
GRAVES W.B.,"LEGISLATIVE REFERENCE SYSTEM FOR THE CONGRESS OF THE UNITED STATES." ROUTINE...CLASSIF TREND EXHIBIT CONGRESS. PAGE 42 B0856
LEGIS
STRUCT

B48
HART J.,THE AMERICAN PRESIDENCY IN ACTION 1789: A STUDY IN CONSTITUTIONAL HISTORY. USA-45 POL/PAR DELIB/GP FORCES LEGIS ADJUD ADMIN LEAD GP/REL PERS/REL 18 PRESIDENT CONGRESS. PAGE 47 B0959
NAT/G
CONSTN
CHIEF
EX/STRUC

B48
STOKES W.S.,BIBLIOGRAPHY OF STANDARD AND CLASSICAL WORKS IN THE FIELDS OF AMERICAN POLITICAL SCIENCE. USA+45 USA-45 POL/PAR PROVS FORCES DIPLOM CT/SYS APPORT 20 CONGRESS PRESIDENT. PAGE 101 B2043
BIBLIOG
NAT/G
LOC/G
CONSTN

B48
WHITE L.D.,THE FEDERALISTS: A STUDY IN ADMINISTRATIVE HISTORY. STRUCT DELIB/GP LEGIS BUDGET ROUTINE GOV/REL GP/REL PERS/REL PWR...BIOG 18/19 PRESIDENT CONGRESS WASHINGT/G JEFFERSN/T HAMILTON/A. PAGE 116 B2337
ADMIN
NAT/G
POLICY
PROB/SOLV

C48
WALKER H.,"THE LEGISLATIVE PROCESS; LAWMAKING IN THE UNITED STATES." NAT/G POL/PAR PROVS EX/STRUC OP/RES PROB/SOLV CT/SYS LOBBY GOV/REL...CHARTS BIBLIOG T 18/20 CONGRESS. PAGE 113 B2279
PARL/PROC
LEGIS
LAW
CONSTN

B49
RIDDICK F.M.,THE UNITED STATES CONGRESS ORGANIZATION AND PROCEDURE. POL/PAR DELIB/GP PROB/SOLV DEBATE CONTROL EXEC LEAD INGP/REL PWR ...MAJORIT DECISION CONGRESS PRESIDENT. PAGE 88 B1777
LEGIS
PARL/PROC
CHIEF
EX/STRUC

B49
STEIN H.,THE FOREIGN SERVICE ACT OF 1946. USA+45 ELITES EX/STRUC PLAN PROB/SOLV LOBBY GOV/REL PERS/REL RIGID/FLEX...POLICY IDEA/COMP 20 CONGRESS BUR/BUDGET. PAGE 100 B2027
DIPLOM
LAW
NAT/G
ADMIN

L49
BROOKINGS INST.,"GOVERNMENT MECHANISM FOR CONDUCT OF US FOREIGN RELATIONS." USA+45 CONSTN NAT/G LEGIS CT/SYS...MGT TIME/SEQ CONGRESS TOT/POP 20. PAGE 15 B0316
EXEC
STRUCT
DIPLOM

B50
MCCAMY J.,THE ADMINISTRATION OF AMERICAN FOREIGN AFFAIRS. USA+45 SOCIETY INT/ORG NAT/G ACT/RES PLAN INT/TRADE EDU/PROP ADJUD ALL/VALS...METH/CNCPT TIME/SEQ CONGRESS 20. PAGE 71 B1441
EXEC
STRUCT
DIPLOM

L50
US SENATE COMM. GOVT. OPER.,"REVISION OF THE UN CHARTER." FUT USA+45 WOR+45 CONSTN ECO/DEV ECO/UNDEV NAT/G DELIB/GP ACT/RES CREATE PLAN EXEC ROUTINE CHOOSE ALL/VALS...POLICY CONCPT CONGRESS UN TOT/POP 20 COLD/WAR. PAGE 111 B2235
INT/ORG
LEGIS
PEACE

S50
EPSTEIN L.D.,"POLITICAL STERILIZATION OF CIVIL SERVANTS: THE UNITED STATES AND GREAT BRITAIN." UK USA+45 USA-45 STRUCT TOP/EX OP/RES PARTIC CHOOSE NAT/LISM 20 CONGRESS CIVIL/SERV. PAGE 33 B0679
ADMIN
LEGIS
DECISION
POL/PAR

C50
HOLCOMBE A.,"OUR MORE PERFECT UNION." USA+45 USA-45 POL/PAR JUDGE CT/SYS EQUILIB FEDERAL PWR...MAJORIT TREND BIBLIOG 18/20 CONGRESS PRESIDENT. PAGE 51 B1031
CONSTN
NAT/G
ADMIN
PLAN

B51
SMITH L.,AMERICAN DEMOCRACY AND MILITARY POWER. USA+45 USA-45 CONSTN STRATA NAT/G LEGIS ACT/RES LEGIT ADMIN EXEC GOV/REL ALL/VALS...CONCPT HIST/WRIT CONGRESS 20. PAGE 98 B1982
FORCES
STRUCT
WAR

B51
WHITE L.D.,THE JEFFERSONIANS: A STUDY IN ADMINISTRATIVE HISTORY 18011829. USA-45 DELIB/GP LEGIS TOP/EX PROB/SOLV BUDGET ECO/TAC GP/REL
ADMIN
NAT/G
POLICY

FEDERAL...BIOG IDEA/COMP 19 PRESIDENT CONGRESS   POL/PAR
JEFFERSN/T. PAGE 116 B2338

                                                       S51
MARX F.M.,"SIGNIFICANCE FOR THE ADMINISTRATIVE   LEGIS
PROCESS." POL/PAR LEAD PARL/PROC GOV/REL EFFICIENCY   ADMIN
SUPEGO...POLICY CONGRESS. PAGE 70 B1420   CHIEF

                                                       B52
ELLIOTT W.,UNITED STATES FOREIGN POLICY, ITS   LEGIS
ORGANIZATION AND CONTROL. USA+45 USA-45 CONSTN   EX/STRUC
NAT/G FORCES TOP/EX PEACE...TIME/SEQ CONGRESS   DIPLOM
LEAGUE/NAT 20. PAGE 33 B0670

                                                       B52
LEGISLATIVE REFERENCE SERVICE,PROBLEMS OF   BIBLIOG
LEGISLATIVE APPORTIONMENT ON BOTH FEDERAL AND STATE   REPRESENT
LEVELS: SELECTED REFERENCES (PAMPHLET). USA+45   CHOOSE
USA-45 LOC/G NAT/G LEGIS WRITING ADMIN APPORT 20   PROVS
CONGRESS. PAGE 63 B1282

                                                       L52
WRIGHT Q.,"CONGRESS AND THE TREATY-MAKING POWER."   ROUTINE
USA+45 WOR+45 CONSTN INTELL NAT/G CHIEF CONSULT   DIPLOM
EX/STRUC LEGIS TOP/EX CREATE GOV/REL DISPL DRIVE   INT/LAW
RIGID/FLEX...TREND TOT/POP CONGRESS CONGRESS 20   DELIB/GP
TREATY. PAGE 118 B2384

                                                       L52
WRIGHT Q.,"CONGRESS AND THE TREATY-MAKING POWER."   ROUTINE
USA+45 WOR+45 CONSTN INTELL NAT/G CHIEF CONSULT   DIPLOM
EX/STRUC LEGIS TOP/EX CREATE GOV/REL DISPL DRIVE   INT/LAW
RIGID/FLEX...TREND TOT/POP CONGRESS CONGRESS 20   DELIB/GP
TREATY. PAGE 118 B2384

                                                       S52
SCHWEBEL S.M.,"THE SECRETARY-GENERAL OF THE UN."   INT/ORG
FUT INTELL CONSULT DELIB/GP ADMIN PEACE ATTIT   TOP/EX
...JURID MGT CONCPT TREND UN CONGRESS 20. PAGE 95
B1915

                                                       S53
BLOUGH R.,"THE ROLE OF THE ECONOMIST IN FEDERAL   DELIB/GP
POLICY MAKING." USA+45 ELITES INTELL ECO/DEV NAT/G   ECO/TAC
CONSULT EX/STRUC ACT/RES PLAN INT/TRADE BAL/PAY
WEALTH...POLICY CONGRESS 20. PAGE 13 B0256

                                                       S53
GABLE R.W.,"NAM: INFLUENTIAL LOBBY OR KISS OF   LOBBY
DEATH?" (BMR)" USA+45 LAW INSPECT EDU/PROP ADMIN   LEGIS
CONTROL INGP/REL EFFICIENCY PWR 20 CONGRESS NAM   INDUS
TAFT/HART. PAGE 38 B0769   LG/CO

                                                       B54
RECK D.,GOVERNMENT PURCHASING AND COMPETITION.   NAT/G
USA+45 LEGIS CAP/ISM ECO/TAC GOV/REL CENTRAL   FINAN
...POLICY 20 CONGRESS. PAGE 87 B1749   MGT
                                                       COST
                                                       B54
WHITE L.D.,THE JACKSONIANS: A STUDY IN   NAT/G
ADMINISTRATIVE HISTORY 1829-1861. USA+45 CONSTN   ADMIN
POL/PAR CHIEF DELIB/GP LEGIS CREATE PROB/SOLV   POLICY
ECO/TAC LEAD REGION GP/REL 19 PRESIDENT CONGRESS
JACKSON/A. PAGE 116 B2339

                                                       B55
GALLOWAY G.B.,CONGRESS AND PARLIAMENT: THEIR   DELIB/GP
ORGANIZATION AND OPERATION IN THE US AND THE UK: LEGIS
PLANNING PAMPHLET NO. 93. POL/PAR EX/STRUC DEBATE   PARL/PROC
CONTROL LEAD ROUTINE EFFICIENCY PWR...POLICY   GOV/COMP
CONGRESS PARLIAMENT. PAGE 38 B0777

                                                       B55
SMITHIES A.,THE BUDGETARY PROCESS IN THE UNITED   NAT/G
STATES. ECO/DEV AGRI EX/STRUC FORCES LEGIS   ADMIN
PROB/SOLV TAX ROUTINE EFFICIENCY...MGT CONGRESS   BUDGET
PRESIDENT. PAGE 98 B1987   GOV/REL

                                                       B56
ABELS J.,THE TRUMAN SCANDALS. USA+45 USA-45 POL/PAR   CRIME
TAX LEGIT CT/SYS CHOOSE PRIVIL MORAL WEALTH 20   ADMIN
TRUMAN/HS PRESIDENT CONGRESS. PAGE 3 B0052   CHIEF
                                                       TRIBUTE
                                                       B56
US HOUSE RULES COMM,HEARINGS BEFORE A SPECIAL   ADMIN
SUBCOMMITTEE: ESTABLISHMENT OF A STANDING COMMITTEE   DOMIN
ON ADMINISTRATIVE PROCEDURE, PRACTICE. USA+45 LAW   DELIB/GP
EX/STRUC ADJUD CONTROL EXEC GOV/REL EFFICIENCY PWR   NAT/G
...POLICY INT 20 CONGRESS. PAGE 109 B2199

                                                       B56
WIGGINS J.R.,FREEDOM OR SECRECY. USA+45 USA-45   ORD/FREE
DELIB/GP EX/STRUC FORCES ADJUD SANCTION KNOWL PWR   PRESS
...AUD/VIS CONGRESS 20. PAGE 116 B2344   NAT/G
                                                       CONTROL
                                                       B57
US HOUSE COMM ON POST OFFICE,MANPOWER UTILIZATION   NAT/G
IN THE FEDERAL GOVERNMENT. USA+45 FORCES WORKER   ADMIN
CREATE PLAN EFFICIENCY UTIL 20 CONGRESS CIVIL/SERV   LABOR
POSTAL/SYS DEPT/DEFEN. PAGE 109 B2193   EX/STRUC

                                                       S57
ROURKE F.E.,"THE POLITICS OF ADMINISTRATIVE   POLICY
ORGANIZATION: A CASE HISTORY." USA+45 LABOR WORKER   ATTIT
PLAN ADMIN TASK EFFICIENCY 20 DEPT/LABOR CONGRESS.   MGT
PAGE 91 B1836   GP/COMP

                                                       B58
HENKIN L.,ARMS CONTROL AND INSPECTION IN AMERICAN   USA+45
LAW. LAW CONSTN INT/ORG LOC/G MUNIC NAT/G PROVS   JURID
EDU/PROP LEGIT EXEC NUC/PWR KNOWL ORD/FREE...OBS   ARMS/CONT

TOT/POP CONGRESS 20. PAGE 49 B0990

                                                       B58
US HOUSE COMM ON COMMERCE,ADMINISTRATIVE PROCESS   POLICY
AND ETHICAL QUESTIONS. USA+45 LAW LEGIS INT/TRADE   ADMIN
CONTROL 20 CONGRESS. PAGE 109 B2192   DELIB/GP
                                                       ADJUD
                                                       B58
US HOUSE COMM ON POST OFFICE,TO PROVIDE AN   ADMIN
EFFECTIVE SYSTEM OF PERSONNEL ADMINISTRATION.   NAT/G
USA+45 DELIB/GP CONTROL EFFICIENCY 20 CONGRESS   EX/STRUC
PRESIDENT CIVIL/SERV POSTAL/SYS. PAGE 109 B2194   LAW

                                                       B58
US HOUSE COMM POST OFFICE,MANPOWER UTILIZATION IN   ADMIN
THE FEDERAL GOVERNMENT. USA+45 DIST/IND EX/STRUC   WORKER
LEGIS CONFER EFFICIENCY 20 CONGRESS CIVIL/SERV.   DELIB/GP
PAGE 109 B2195   NAT/G
                                                       B58
US HOUSE COMM POST OFFICE,MANPOWER UTILIZATION IN   ADMIN
THE FEDERAL GOVERNMENT. USA+45 DIST/IND EX/STRUC   WORKER
LEGIS CONFER EFFICIENCY 20 CONGRESS CIVIL/SERV.   DELIB/GP
PAGE 109 B2196   NAT/G
                                                       B58
US HOUSE COMM POST OFFICE,TRAINING OF FEDERAL   LEGIS
EMPLOYEES. USA+45 DIST/IND NAT/G EX/STRUC EDU/PROP   DELIB/GP
CONFER GOV/REL EFFICIENCY SKILL 20 CONGRESS   WORKER
CIVIL/SERV. PAGE 109 B2197   ADMIN
                                                       B58
WHITE L.D.,THE REPUBLICAN ERA: 1869-1901, A STUDY   MGT
IN ADMINISTRATIVE HISTORY. USA+45 FINAN PLAN   PWR
NEUTRAL CRIME GP/REL MORAL LAISSEZ PRESIDENT   DELIB/GP
REFORMERS 19 CONGRESS CIVIL/SERV. PAGE 116 B2340   ADMIN
                                                       L58
HAVILAND H.F.,"FOREIGN AID AND THE POLICY PROCESS: LEGIS
1957." USA+45 FACE/GP POL/PAR VOL/ASSN CHIEF   PLAN
DELIB/GP ACT/RES LEGIT EXEC GOV/REL ATTIT DRIVE PWR   FOR/AID
...POLICY TESTS CONGRESS 20. PAGE 48 B0971

                                                       B59
LOEWENSTEIN K.,VERFASSUNGSRECHT UND   CONSTN
VERFASSUNGSPRAXIS DER VEREINIGTEN STAATEN. USA+45   POL/PAR
USA-45 COLONIAL CT/SYS GP/REL RACE/REL ORD/FREE   EX/STRUC
...JURID 18/20 SUPREME/CT CONGRESS PRESIDENT   NAT/G
BILL/RIGHT CIVIL/LIB. PAGE 66 B1337
                                                       B59
US CIVIL SERVICE COMMISSION,CONGRESSIONAL DOCUMENTS   BIBLIOG/A
RELATING TO CIVIL SERVICE. USA+45 USA-45 CONFER   ADMIN
19/20 CONGRESS. PAGE 108 B2177   NAT/G
                                                       LEGIS
                                                       B59
US SENATE COMM ON POST OFFICE,TO PROVIDE FOR AN   ADMIN
EFFECTIVE SYSTEM OF PERSONNEL ADMINISTRATION.   NAT/G
EFFICIENCY...MGT 20 CONGRESS CIVIL/SERV POSTAL/SYS   EX/STRUC
YARBROGH/R. PAGE 111 B2233   LAW
                                                       L59
RHODE W.E.,"COMMITTEE CLEARANCE OF ADMINISTRATIVE   DECISION
DECISIONS." DELIB/GP LEGIS BUDGET DOMIN CIVMIL/REL   ADMIN
20 CONGRESS. PAGE 87 B1768   OP/RES
                                                       NAT/G
                                                       B60
JUNZ A.J., PRESENT TRENDS IN AMERICAN NATIONAL   POL/PAR
GOVERNMENT. LEGIS DIPLOM ADMIN CT/SYS ORD/FREE   CHOOSE
...CONCPT ANTHOL 20 CONGRESS PRESIDENT SUPREME/CT.   CONSTN
PAGE 2 B0048   NAT/G
                                                       B60
HAYNES G.H.,THE SENATE OF THE UNITED STATES: ITS   LEGIS
HISTORY AND PRACTICE. CONSTN EX/STRUC TOP/EX CONFER   DELIB/GP
DEBATE LEAD LOBBY PARL/PROC CHOOSE PWR SENATE
CONGRESS. PAGE 48 B0977

                                                       S60
HALPERIN M.H.,"IS THE SENATE'S FOREIGN RELATIONS   PLAN
RESEARCH WORTHWHILE." COM FUT USA+45 USSR ACT/RES   DIPLOM
BAL/PWR EDU/PROP ADMIN ALL/VALS CONGRESS VAL/FREE
20 COLD/WAR. PAGE 46 B0927

                                                       S60
NELSON R.H.,"LEGISLATIVE PARTICIPATION IN THE   LEGIS
TREATY AND AGREEMENT MAKING PROCESS." CONSTN   PEACE
POL/PAR PLAN EXEC PWR FAO UN CONGRESS. PAGE 78   DECISION
B1569   DIPLOM
                                                       S60
SCHER S.,"CONGRESSIONAL COMMITTEE MEMBERS AND   LEGIS
INDEPENDENT AGENCY OVERSEERS: A CASE STUDY."   GOV/REL
DELIB/GP EX/STRUC JUDGE TOP/EX DOMIN ADMIN CONTROL   LABOR
PWR...SOC/EXP HOUSE/REP CONGRESS. PAGE 93 B1886   ADJUD
                                                       B61
GRIFFITH E.S.,CONGRESS: ITS CONTEMPORARY ROLE.   PARL/PROC
CONSTN POL/PAR CHIEF PLAN BUDGET DIPLOM CONFER   EX/STRUC
ADMIN LOBBY...DECISION CONGRESS. PAGE 43 B0878   TOP/EX
                                                       LEGIS
                                                       B61
KERTESZ S.D.,AMERICAN DIPLOMACY IN A NEW ERA. COM   ANTHOL
S/ASIA UK USA+45 FORCES PROB/SOLV BAL/PWR ECO/TAC   DIPLOM
ADMIN COLONIAL WAR PEACE ORD/FREE 20 NATO CONGRESS   TREND
UN COLD/WAR. PAGE 59 B1199
                                                       B61
OPOTOWSKY S.,THE KENNEDY GOVERNMENT. NAT/G CONSULT   ADMIN
EX/STRUC LEAD PERSON...POLICY 20 KENNEDY/JF   BIOG
CONGRESS CABINET. PAGE 80 B1613   ELITES

TOP/EX
B61
TOMPKINS D.C.,CONFLICT OF INTEREST IN THE FEDERAL
GOVERNMENT: A BIBLIOGRAPHY. USA+45 EX/STRUC LEGIS
ADJUD ADMIN CRIME CONGRESS PRESIDENT. PAGE 105
B2117
BIBLIOG
ROLE
NAT/G
LAW

S61
JUVILER P.H.,"INTERPARLIAMENTARY CONTACTS IN SOVIET
FOREIGN POLICY." COM FUT WOR+45 WOR-45 SOCIETY
CONSULT ACT/RES DIPLOM ADMIN PEACE ATTIT RIGID/FLEX
WEALTH...WELF/ST SOC TOT/POP CONGRESS 19/20.
PAGE 57 B1156
INT/ORG
DELIB/GP
USSR

S61
ROBINSON J.A.,"PROCESS SATISFACTION AND POLICY
APPROVAL IN STATE DEPARTMENT - CONGRESSIONAL
RELATIONS." ELITES CHIEF LEGIS CONFER DEBATE ADMIN
FEEDBACK ROLE...CHARTS 20 CONGRESS PRESIDENT
DEPT/STATE. PAGE 89 B1802
GOV/REL
EX/STRUC
POL/PAR
DECISION

B62
CARPER E.T.,ILLINOIS GOES TO CONGRESS FOR ARMY
LAND. USA+45 LAW EXTR/IND PROVS REGION CIVMIL/REL
GOV/REL FEDERAL ATTIT 20 ILLINOIS SENATE CONGRESS
DIRKSEN/E DOUGLAS/P. PAGE 19 B0385
ADMIN
LOBBY
GEOG
LEGIS

B62
JEWELL M.E.,SENATORIAL POLITICS AND FOREIGN POLICY. USA+45
NAT/G POL/PAR CHIEF DELIB/GP TOP/EX FOR/AID
EDU/PROP ROUTINE ATTIT PWR SKILL...MAJORIT
METH/CNCPT TIME/SEQ CONGRESS 20 PRESIDENT. PAGE 56
B1138
LEGIS
DIPLOM

B62
LOWI T.J.,LEGISLATIVE POLITICS U.S.A. LAW LEGIS
DIPLOM EXEC LOBBY CHOOSE SUFF FEDERAL PWR 19/20
CONGRESS. PAGE 67 B1345
PARL/PROC
REPRESENT
POLICY
ROUTINE

B62
SCHILLING W.R.,STRATEGY, POLITICS, AND DEFENSE
BUDGETS. USA+45 R+D NAT/G CONSULT DELIB/GP FORCES
LEGIS ACT/RES PLAN BAL/PWR LEGIT EXEC NUC/PWR
RIGID/FLEX PWR...TREND COLD/WAR CONGRESS 20
EISNHWR/DD. PAGE 93 B1890
ROUTINE
POLICY

B62
US SENATE COMM ON JUDICIARY,STATE DEPARTMENT
SECURITY. USA+45 CHIEF TEC/DEV DOMIN ADMIN EXEC
ATTIT ORD/FREE...POLICY CONGRESS DEPT/STATE
PRESIDENT KENNEDY/JF KENNEDY/JF SENATE 20. PAGE 110
B2228
CONTROL
WORKER
NAT/G
GOV/REL

L62
NEIBURG H.L.,"THE EISENHOWER AEC AND CONGRESS: A
STUDY IN EXECUTIVE-LEGISLATIVE RELATIONS." USA+45
NAT/G POL/PAR DELIB/GP EX/STRUC TOP/EX ADMIN EXEC
LEAD ROUTINE PWR...POLICY COLD/WAR CONGRESS
PRESIDENT AEC. PAGE 77 B1567
CHIEF
LEGIS
GOV/REL
NUC/PWR

S62
TRUMAN D.,"THE DOMESTIC POLITICS OF FOREIGN AID."
USA+45 WOR+45 NAT/G POL/PAR LEGIS DIPLOM ECO/TAC
EDU/PROP ADMIN CHOOSE ATTIT PWR CONGRESS 20
CONGRESS. PAGE 105 B2129
ROUTINE
FOR/AID

S62
TRUMAN D.,"THE DOMESTIC POLITICS OF FOREIGN AID."
USA+45 WOR+45 NAT/G POL/PAR LEGIS DIPLOM ECO/TAC
EDU/PROP ADMIN CHOOSE ATTIT PWR CONGRESS 20
CONGRESS. PAGE 105 B2129
ROUTINE
FOR/AID

B63
GREEN H.P.,GOVERNMENT OF THE ATOM. USA+45 LEGIS
PROB/SOLV ADMIN CONTROL PWR...POLICY DECISION 20
PRESIDENT CONGRESS. PAGE 43 B0864
GOV/REL
EX/STRUC
NUC/PWR
DELIB/GP

B63
STEIN H.,AMERICAN CIVIL-MILITARY DECISION. USA+45
USA-45 EX/STRUC FORCES LEGIS TOP/EX PLAN DIPLOM
FOR/AID ATTIT 20 CONGRESS. PAGE 100 B2028
CIVMIL/REL
DECISION
WAR
BUDGET

B63
US CONGRESS: SENATE,HEARINGS OF THE COMMITTEE ON
THE JUDICIARY. USA+45 CONSTN NAT/G ADMIN GOV/REL 20
CONGRESS. PAGE 108 B2179
LEGIS
LAW
ORD/FREE
DELIB/GP

B63
US HOUSE COM ON ED AND LABOR,ADMINISTRATION OF
AGING. USA+45 R+D EX/STRUC PLAN BUDGET PAY EDU/PROP
ROUTINE COST CONGRESS. PAGE 108 B2187
AGE/O
ADMIN
DELIB/GP
GIVE

B63
US SENATE COMM APPROPRIATIONS,PERSONNEL
ADMINISTRATION AND OPERATIONS OF AGENCY FOR
INTERNATIONAL DEVELOPMENT: SPECIAL HEARING. FINAN
LEAD COST UTIL SKILL...CHARTS 20 CONGRESS AID
CIVIL/SERV. PAGE 109 B2211
ADMIN
FOR/AID
EFFICIENCY
DIPLOM

B63
US SENATE COMM GOVT OPERATIONS,ADMINISTRATION OF
NATIONAL SECURITY (9 PARTS). ADMIN...INT REC/INT
CHARTS 20 SENATE CONGRESS. PAGE 110 B2213
DELIB/GP
NAT/G
OP/RES
ORD/FREE

C63
BLUM J.M.,"THE NATIONAL EXPERIENCE." USA+45 USA-45
ECO/DEV DIPLOM WAR NAT/LISM...POLICY CHARTS BIBLIOG
ADMIN
NAT/G

T 16/20 CONGRESS PRESIDENT COLD/WAR. PAGE 13 B0258
LEGIS
CHIEF

B64
CLARK J.S.,CONGRESS: THE SAPLESS BRANCH. DELIB/GP
SENIOR ATTIT CONGRESS. PAGE 21 B0432
LEGIS
ROUTINE
ADMIN
POL/PAR

B64
GOLDWIN R.A.,POLITICAL PARTIES, USA. USA+45 USA-45
LOC/G ADMIN LEAD EFFICIENCY ATTIT PWR...POLICY STAT
ANTHOL 18/20 CONGRESS. PAGE 40 B0818
POL/PAR
PARTIC
NAT/G
CONSTN

B64
JACKSON H.M.,THE SECRETARY OF STATE AND THE
AMBASSADOR* JACKSON SUBCOMMITTEE PAPERS ON THE
CONDUCT OF AMERICAN FOREIGN POLICY. USA+45 NAT/G
FORCES ACT/RES OP/RES EDU/PROP CENTRAL EFFICIENCY
ORD/FREE...OBS RECORD ANTHOL CONGRESS PRESIDENT.
PAGE 55 B1107
GOV/REL
DIPLOM
ADMIN
EX/STRUC

B64
KEEFE W.J.,THE AMERICAN LEGISLATIVE PROCESS:
CONGRESS AND THE STATES. USA+45 LAW POL/PAR
DELIB/GP DEBATE ADMIN LOBBY REPRESENT CONGRESS
PRESIDENT. PAGE 59 B1187
LEGIS
DECISION
PWR
PROVS

B64
NEUSTADT R.,PRESIDENTIAL POWER. USA+45 CONSTN NAT/G
CHIEF LEGIS CREATE EDU/PROP LEGIT ADMIN EXEC COERCE
ATTIT PERSON RIGID/FLEX PWR CONGRESS 20 PRESIDENT
TRUMAN/HS EISNHWR/DD. PAGE 78 B1575
TOP/EX
SKILL

B64
RIDDLE D.H.,THE TRUMAN COMMITTEE: A STUDY IN
CONGRESSIONAL RESPONSIBILITY. INDUS FORCES OP/RES
DOMIN ADMIN LEAD PARL/PROC WAR PRODUC SUPEGO
...BIBLIOG CONGRESS. PAGE 88 B1778
LEGIS
DELIB/GP
CONFER

B64
SARROS P.P.,CONGRESS AND THE NEW DIPLOMACY: THE
FORMULATION OF MUTUAL SECURITY POLICY: 1953-60
(THESIS). USA+45 CHIEF EX/STRUC REGION ROUTINE
CHOOSE GOV/REL PEACE ROLE...POLICY 20 PRESIDENT
CONGRESS. PAGE 92 B1869
DIPLOM
POL/PAR
NAT/G

B64
US SENATE COMM GOVT OPERATIONS,ADMINISTRATION OF
NATIONAL SECURITY. USA+45 CHIEF TOP/EX PLAN DIPLOM
CONTROL PEACE...POLICY DECISION 20 PRESIDENT
CONGRESS. PAGE 110 B2216
ADMIN
FORCES
ORD/FREE
NAT/G

B64
WEIDENBAUM M.L.,CONGRESS AND THE FEDERAL BUDGET:
FEDERAL BUDGETING AND THE RESPONSIBLE USE OF POWER.
LOC/G PLAN TAX CONGRESS. PAGE 114 B2309
LEGIS
EX/STRUC
BUDGET
ADMIN

S64
ROGOW A.A.,"CONGRESSIONAL GOVERNMENT: LEGISLATIVE
POWER V. DOMESTIC PROCESSES." USA+45 CHIEF DELIB/GP
ADMIN GOV/REL CONGRESS. PAGE 90 B1815
PWR
DIPLOM
LEGIS
POLICY

B65
BOCK E.,GOVERNMENT REGULATION OF BUSINESS. USA+45
LAW EX/STRUC LEGIS EXEC ORD/FREE PWR...ANTHOL
CONGRESS. PAGE 13 B0261
MGT
ADMIN
NAT/G
CONTROL

B65
DE GRAZIA A.,REPUBLIC IN CRISIS: CONGRESS AGAINST
THE EXECUTIVE FORCE. USA+45 USA-45 SOCIETY POL/PAR
CHIEF DOMIN ROLE ORD/FREE PWR...CONCPT MYTH BIBLIOG
20 CONGRESS. PAGE 27 B0556
LEGIS
EXEC
GOV/REL
CONTROL

B65
HAIGHT D.E.,THE PRESIDENT: ROLES AND POWERS. USA+45
USA-45 POL/PAR PLAN DIPLOM CHOOSE PERS/REL PWR
18/20 PRESIDENT CONGRESS. PAGE 45 B0915
CHIEF
LEGIS
TOP/EX
EX/STRUC

B65
JONES A.G.,THE EVOLUTION OF PERSONNEL SYSTEMS FOR
US FOREIGN AFFAIRS* A HISTORY OF REFORM EFFORTS.
USA+45 USA-45 ACADEM OP/RES GOV/REL...MGT CONGRESS.
PAGE 57 B1149
DIPLOM
ADMIN
ACT/RES
EFFICIENCY

B65
KOENIG L.W.,OFFICIAL MAKERS OF PUBLIC POLICY:
CONGRESS AND THE PRESIDENT. USA+45 USA-45 EX/STRUC
ADMIN CONTROL GOV/REL PWR 18/20 CONGRESS PRESIDENT.
PAGE 61 B1225
POLICY
LEGIS
CHIEF
NAT/G

B65
US HOUSE COMM EDUC AND LABOR,ADMINISTRATION OF THE
NATIONAL LABOR RELATIONS ACT. USA+45 DELIB/GP
WORKER PROB/SOLV BARGAIN PAY CONTROL 20 NLRB
CONGRESS. PAGE 108 B2188
ADMIN
LABOR
GP/REL
INDUS

B65
US SENATE COMM ON JUDICIARY,HEARINGS BEFORE
SUBCOMMITTEE ON ADMINISTRATIVE PRACTICE AND
PROCEDURE ABOUT ADMINISTRATIVE PROCEDURE ACT 1965.
USA+45 LEGIS EDU/PROP ADJUD GOV/REL INGP/REL
EFFICIENCY...POLICY INT 20 CONGRESS. PAGE 110 B2232
ROUTINE
DELIB/GP
ADMIN
NAT/G

B65
WARD R.,BACKGROUND MATERIAL ON ECONOMIC IMPACT OF
FEDERAL PROCUREMENT - 1965: FOR JOINT ECONOMIC
COMMITTEE US CONGRESS. FINAN ROUTINE WEAPON
CIVMIL/REL EFFICIENCY...STAT CHARTS 20 CONGRESS.
ECO/DEV
NAT/G
OWN
GOV/REL

PAGE 113 B2288

USIA CONGRESS. PAGE 91 B1850   PROF/ORG
                                                                    N67
US SUPERINTENDENT OF DOCUMENTS,SPACE: MISSILES, THE   BIBLIOG/A
MOON, NASA, AND SATELLITES (PRICE LIST 79A). USA+45   SPACE
COM/IND R+D NAT/G DIPLOM EDU/PROP ADMIN CONTROL   TEC/DEV
HEALTH...POLICY SIMUL NASA CONGRESS. PAGE 111 B2244   PEACE
                                                                    N67
US SENATE COMM AERO SPACE SCI,AERONAUTICAL RESEARCH   DIST/IND
AND DEVELOPMENT POLICY: HEARINGS, COMM ON   SPACE
AERONAUTICAL AND SPACE SCIENCES...1967 (PAMPHLET).   NAT/G
R+D PROB/SOLV EXEC GOV/REL 20 DEPT/DEFEN FAA NASA   PLAN
CONGRESS. PAGE 109 B2210

CONGRESS/P....CONGRESS PARTY (ALL NATIONS)

CONNECTICT....CONNECTICUT

                                                                    B64
CONNECTICUT U INST PUBLIC SERV,SUMMARY OF CHARTER   CONSTN
PROVISIONS IN CONNECTICUT LOCAL GOVERNMENT   MUNIC
(PAMPHLET). USA+45 DELIB/GP LEGIS TOP/EX CHOOSE   LOC/G
REPRESENT 20 CONNECTICT CITY/MGT MAYOR. PAGE 23   EX/STRUC
B0462

CONNECTICUT U INST PUBLIC SERV B0462

CONOVER H.F. B0463,B0464,B0465,B0466

CONRAD J.P. B0467

CONRAD/JOS....JOSEPH CONRAD

CONSCIENCE....SEE SUPEGO

CONSCN/OBJ....CONSCIENTIOUS OBJECTION TO WAR AND KILLING

CONSCRIPTN....CONSCRIPTION

CONSEN....CONSENSUS

                                                                    N19
ADMINISTRATIVE STAFF COLLEGE,THE ACCOUNTABILITY OF   PARL/PROC
GOVERNMENT DEPARTMENTS (PAMPHLET) (REV. ED.). UK   ELITES
CONSTN FINAN NAT/G CONSULT ADMIN INGP/REL CONSEN   SANCTION
PRIVIL 20 PARLIAMENT. PAGE 3 B0059   PROB/SOLV
                                                                    L23
DOUGLAS P.H.,"OCCUPATIONAL V PROPORTIONAL   REPRESENT
REPRESENTATION." INDUS NAT/G PLAN ROUTINE SUFF   PROF/ORG
CONSEN DRIVE...CONCPT CLASSIF. PAGE 30 B0612   DOMIN
                                                       INGP/REL
                                                                    C54
GCULDNER A.W.,"PATTERNS OF INDUSTRIAL BUREAUCRACY."   ADMIN
GP/REL CONSEN ATTIT DRIVE...BIBLIOG 20. PAGE 42   INDUS
B0843   OP/RES
                                                       WORKER
                                                                    B56
WHYTE W.H. JR.,THE ORGANIZATION MAN. CULTURE FINAN   ADMIN
VOL/ASSN DOMIN EDU/PROP EXEC DISPL HABITAT ROLE   LG/CO
...PERS/TEST STERTYP. PAGE 116 B2343   PERSON
                                                       CONSEN
                                                                    S59
HILSMAN R.,"THE FOREIGN-POLICY CONSENSUS: AN   PROB/SOLV
INTERIM RESEARCH REPORT." USA+45 INT/ORG LEGIS   NAT/G
TEC/DEV EXEC WAR CONSEN KNOWL...DECISION COLD/WAR.   DELIB/GP
PAGE 50 B1013   DIPLOM
                                                                    S61
RUDOLPH S.,"CONSENSUS AND CONFLICT IN INDIAN   POL/PAR
POLITICS." S/ASIA WOR+45 NAT/G DELIB/GP DIPLOM   PERCEPT
EDU/PROP ADMIN CONSEN PERSON ALL/VALS...OBS TREND   INDIA
TOT/POP VAL/FREE 20. PAGE 92 B1854
                                                                    C61
ETZIONI A.,"A COMPARATIVE ANALYSIS OF COMPLEX   CON/ANAL
ORGANIZATIONS: ON POWER, INVOLVEMENT AND THEIR   SOC
CORRELATES." ELITES CREATE OP/RES ROUTINE INGP/REL   LEAD
PERS/REL CONSEN ATTIT DRIVE PWR...CONCPT BIBLIOG.   CONTROL
PAGE 34 B0684
                                                                    B62
RUDOLPH F.,THE AMERICAN COLLEGE AND UNIVERSITY.   ACADEM
CLIENT FINAN PUB/INST DELIB/GP EDU/PROP CONTROL   INGP/REL
EXEC CONSEN ATTIT POLICY. PAGE 92 B1853   PWR
                                                       ADMIN
                                                                    C62
DE GRAZIA A.,"POLITICAL BEHAVIOR (REV. ED.)" STRATA   PHIL/SCI
POL/PAR LEAD LOBBY ROUTINE WAR CHOOSE REPRESENT   OP/RES
CONSEN ATTIT ORD/FREE BIBLIOG. PAGE 27 B0555   CONCPT
                                                                    B65
BUECHNER J.C.,DIFFERENCES IN ROLE PERCEPTIONS IN   MUNIC
COLORADO COUNCIL-MANAGER CITIES. USA+45 ADMIN   CONSULT
ROUTINE GP/REL CONSEN PERCEPT PERSON ROLE   LOC/G
...DECISION MGT STAT INT QU CHARTS 20 COLORADO   IDEA/COMP
CITY/MGT. PAGE 17 B0338
                                                                    B65
LAMBIRI I.,SOCIAL CHANGE IN A GREEK COUNTRY TOWN.   INDUS
GREECE FAM PROB/SOLV ROUTINE TASK LEISURE INGP/REL   WORKER
CONSEN ORD/FREE...SOC INT QU CHARTS 20. PAGE 62   CULTURE
B1252   NEIGH

                                                                    L65
SHARKANSKY I.,"FOUR AGENCIES AND AN APPROPRIATIONS   ADMIN
SUBCOMMITTEE: A COMPARATIVE STUDY OF BDUGET   EDU/PROP
STRATEGIES." USA+45 EX/STRUC TOP/EX PROB/SOLV   NAT/G
CONTROL ROUTINE CONGRESS. PAGE 96 B1934   LEGIS
                                                                    S65
HAMMOND P.Y.,"FOREIGN POLICY-MAKING AND   DIPLOM
ADMINISTRATIVE POLITICS." CREATE ADMIN COST   STRUCT
...DECISION CONCPT GAME CONGRESS PRESIDENT. PAGE 46   IDEA/COMP
B0935   OP/RES
                                                                    C65
HUNTINGTON S.P.,"CONGRESSIONAL RESPONSES TO THE   FUT
TWENTIETH CENTURY IN D. TRUMAN. ED. THE CONGRESS   LEAD
AND AMERICA'S FUTURE." USA+45 USA-45 DIPLOM SENIOR   NAT/G
ADMIN EXEC PWR...SOC 20 CONGRESS. PAGE 53 B1067   LEGIS
                                                                    B66
DAVIDSON R.H.,CONGRESS IN CRISIS: POLITICS AND   LEGIS
CONGRESSIONAL REFORM. USA+45 SOCIETY POL/PAR   PARL/PROC
CONTROL LEAD ROUTINE GOV/REL ATTIT PWR...POLICY 20   PROB/SOLV
CONGRESS. PAGE 26 B0535   NAT/G
                                                                    B66
LIVINGSTON J.C.,THE CONSENT OF THE GOVERNED. USA+45   NAT/G
EX/STRUC BAL/PWR DOMIN CENTRAL PERSON PWR...POLICY   LOBBY
CONCPT OBS IDEA/COMP 20 CONGRESS. PAGE 66 B1331   MAJORIT
                                                       PARTIC
                                                                    B66
US SENATE COMM GOVT OPERATIONS,INTERGOVERNMENTAL   ADMIN
PERSONNEL ACT OF 1966. USA+45 NAT/G CONSULT   LEGIS
DELIB/GP WORKER TEC/DEV PAY AUTOMAT UTIL 20   EFFICIENCY
CONGRESS. PAGE 110 B2219   EDU/PROP
                                                                    B66
US SENATE COMM ON FOREIGN REL,HEARINGS ON S 2859   FOR/AID
AND S 2861. USA+45 WOR+45 FORCES BUDGET CAP/ISM   DIPLOM
ADMIN DETER WEAPON TOTALISM...NAT/COMP 20 UN   ORD/FREE
CONGRESS. PAGE 110 B2221   ECO/UNDEV
                                                                    B66
WASHINGTON S.H.,BIBLIOGRAPHY: LABOR-MANAGEMENT   BIBLIOG
RELATIONS ACT, 1947 AS AMENDED BY LABOR-MANAGEMENT   LAW
REPORTING AND DISCLOSURE ACT, 1959. USA+45 CONSTN   LABOR
INDUS DELIB/GP LEGIS WORKER BARGAIN ECO/TAC ADJUD   MGT
GP/REL NEW/LIB...JURID CONGRESS. PAGE 114 B2298
                                                                    S66
BALDWIN D.A.,"CONGRESSIONAL INITIATIVE IN FOREIGN   EXEC
POLICY." NAT/G BARGAIN DIPLOM FOR/AID RENT GIVE   TOP/EX
...DECISION CONGRESS. PAGE 8 B0171   GOV/REL
                                                                    S66
SNOWISS L.M.,"CONGRESSIONAL RECRUITMENT AND   LEGIS
REPRESENTATION." USA+45 LG/CO MUNIC POL/PAR ADMIN   REPRESENT
REGION CONGRESS CHICAGO. PAGE 98 B1990   CHOOSE
                                                       LOC/G
                                                                    C66
TACHERON D.G.,"THE JOB OF THE CONGRESSMAN: AN   LEGIS
INTRODUCTION TO SERVICES IN THE US HOUSE OF   PARL/PROC
REPRESENTATIVES." DELIB/GP EX/STRUC PRESS SENIOR   ADMIN
CT/SYS LOBBY CHOOSE GOV/REL...BIBLIOG 20 CONGRESS   POL/PAR
HOUSE/REP SENATE. PAGE 102 B2068
                                                                    B67
FINCHER F.,THE GOVERNMENT OF THE UNITED STATES.   NAT/G
USA+45 USA-45 POL/PAR CHIEF CT/SYS LOBBY GP/REL   EX/STRUC
INGP/REL...CONCPT CHARTS BIBLIOG T 18/20 PRESIDENT   LEGIS
CONGRESS SUPREME/CT. PAGE 35 B0719   OP/RES
                                                                    B67
LEACH R.H.,GOVERNING THE AMERICAN NATION. FUT   NAT/G
USA+45 USA-45 CONSTN POL/PAR PLAN ADJUD EXEC CONSEN   LEGIS
CONGRESS PRESIDENT. PAGE 63 B1278   PWR
                                                                    B67
US SENATE COMM ON FOREIGN REL,HUMAN RIGHTS   LEGIS
CONVENTIONS. USA+45 LABOR VOL/ASSN DELIB/GP DOMIN   ORD/FREE
ADJUD REPRESENT...INT/LAW MGT CONGRESS. PAGE 110   WORKER
B2225   LOBBY
                                                                    L67
JACOBY S.B.,"THE 89TH CONGRESS AND GOVERNMENT   LAW
LITIGATION." USA+45 ADMIN COST...JURID 20 CONGRESS.   NAT/G
PAGE 55 B1117   ADJUD
                                                       SANCTION
                                                                    L67
TRAVERS H. JR.,"AN EXAMINATION OF THE CAB'S MERGER   ADJUD
POLICY." USA+45 USA-45 LAW NAT/G LEGIS PLAN ADMIN   LG/CO
...DECISION 20 CONGRESS. PAGE 105 B2125   POLICY
                                                       DIST/IND
                                                                    S67
HUMPHREY H.,"A MORE PERFECT UNION." USA+45 LOC/G   GOV/REL
NAT/G ACT/RES BUDGET RECEIVE CENTRAL CONGRESS.   FEDERAL
PAGE 52 B1063   ADMIN
                                                       PROB/SOLV
                                                                    S67
LEES J.P.,"LEGISLATIVE REVIEW AND BUREAUCRATIC   SUPEGO
RESPONSIBILITY." USA+45 FINAN NAT/G DELIB/GP PLAN   BUDGET
PROB/SOLV CONFER CONTROL GP/REL DEMAND...DECISION   LEGIS
20 CONGRESS PRESIDENT HOUSE/REP BUREAUCRCY. PAGE 63   EXEC
B1281
                                                                    S67
RUBIN R.I.,"THE LEGISLATIVE-EXECUTIVE RELATIONS OF   LEGIS
THE UNITED STATES INFORMATION AGENCY." USA+45   EX/STRUC
EDU/PROP TASK INGP/REL EFFICIENCY ISOLAT ATTIT ROLE   GP/REL

S66

HANSON A.H.,"PLANNING AND THE POLITICIANS* SOME
REFLECTIONS ON ECONOMIC PLANNING IN WESTERN
EUROPE." MARKET NAT/G TEC/DEV CONSEN ROLE
...METH/COMP NAT/COMP. PAGE 46 B0942

PLAN
ECO/DEV
EUR+WWI
ADMIN

B67

LEACH R.H.,GOVERNING THE AMERICAN NATION. FUT
USA+45 USA-45 CONSTN POL/PAR PLAN ADJUD EXEC CONSEN
CONGRESS PRESIDENT. PAGE 63 B1278

NAT/G
LEGIS
PWR

S67

WEIL G.L.,"THE MERGER OF THE INSTITUTIONS OF THE
EUROPEAN COMMUNITIES" EUR+WWI ECO/DEV INT/TRADE
CONSEN PLURISM...DECISION MGT 20 EEC EURATOM ECSC
TREATY. PAGE 115 B2313

ECO/TAC
INT/ORG
CENTRAL
INT/LAW

CONSENSUS....SEE CONSEN

CONSERVATIVE POLITICAL CENTRE B0468

CONSERVATISM....SEE CONSERVE

CONSERVE....TRADITIONALISM

B24

BAGEHOT W.,THE ENGLISH CONSTITUTION AND OTHER
POLITICAL ESSAYS. UK DELIB/GP BAL/PWR ADMIN CONTROL
EXEC ROUTINE CONSERVE...METH PARLIAMENT 19/20.
PAGE 8 B0160

NAT/G
STRUCT
CONCPT

S44

GRIFFITH E.S.,"THE CHANGING PATTERN OF PUBLIC
POLICY FORMATION." MOD/EUR WOR+45 FINAN CHIEF
CONFER ADMIN LEAD CONSERVE SOCISM TECHRACY...SOC
CHARTS CONGRESS. PAGE 43 B0877

LAW
POLICY
TEC/DEV

S50

NEUMANN F.L.,"APPROACHES TO THE STUDY OF POLITICAL
POWER." POL/PAR TOP/EX ADMIN LEAD ATTIT ORD/FREE
CONSERVE LAISSEZ MARXISM...PSY SOC. PAGE 78 B1572

PWR
IDEA/COMP
CONCPT

B54

JENNINGS I.,THE QUEEN'S GOVERNMENT. UK POL/PAR
DELIB/GP ADJUD ADMIN CT/SYS PARL/PROC REPRESENT
CONSERVE 13/20 PARLIAMENT. PAGE 56 B1132

NAT/G
CONSTN
LEGIS
CHIEF

B56

WEBER M.,STAATSSOZIOLOGIE. STRUCT LEGIT ADMIN
PARL/PROC SUPEGO CONSERVE JURID. PAGE 114 B2305

SOC
NAT/G
POL/PAR
LEAD

B58

CONSERVATIVE POLITICAL CENTRE,A WORLD SECURITY
AUTHORITY? WOR+45 CONSTN ELITES FINAN DELIB/GP PLAN
PROB/SOLV ADMIN CONTROL NUC/PWR GP/REL...IDEA/COMP
20. PAGE 23 B0468

ORD/FREE
CONSERVE
FORCES
ARMS/CONT

S60

APTER D.E.,"THE ROLE OF TRADITIONALISM IN THE
POLITICAL MODERNIZATION OF GHANA AND UGANDA" (BMR)"
AFR GHANA UGANDA CULTURE NAT/G POL/PAR NAT/LISM
...CON/ANAL 20. PAGE 6 B0121

CONSERVE
ADMIN
GOV/COMP
PROB/SOLV

B61

MONAS S.,THE THIRD SECTION: POLICE AND SOCIETY IN
RUSSIA UNDER NICHOLAS I. MOD/EUR RUSSIA ELITES
STRUCT NAT/G EX/STRUC ADMIN CONTROL PWR CONSERVE
...DECISION 19 NICHOLAS/I. PAGE 74 B1499

ORD/FREE
COM
FORCES
COERCE

B61

ROWAT D.C.,BASIC ISSUES IN PUBLIC ADMINISTRATION.
STRUCT EX/STRUC PWR CONSERVE...MAJORIT DECISION MGT
T 20 BUREAUCRCY. PAGE 91 B1839

NAT/G
ADJUD
ADMIN

B62

BENSON E.T.,CROSS FIRE: THE EIGHT YEARS WITH
EISENHOWER. USA+45 DIPLOM LEAD ATTIT PERSON
CONSERVE...TRADIT BIOG 20 EISNHWR/DD PRESIDENT
TAFT/RA DULLES/JF NIXON/RM. PAGE 11 B0218

ADMIN
POLICY
DELIB/GP
TOP/EX

B62

EVANS M.S.,THE FRINGE ON TOP. USSR EX/STRUC FORCES
DIPLOM ECO/TAC PEACE CONSERVE SOCISM...TREND 20
KENNEDY/JF. PAGE 34 B0689

NAT/G
PWR
CENTRAL
POLICY

B63

ROBERT J.,LA MONARCHIE MAROCAINE. MOROCCO LABOR
MUNIC POL/PAR EX/STRUC ORD/FREE PWR...JURID TREND T
20. PAGE 89 B1793

CHIEF
CONSERVE
ADMIN
CONSTN

B63

WEINER M.,POLITICAL CHANGE IN SOUTH ASIA. CEYLON
INDIA PAKISTAN S/ASIA CULTURE ELITES ECO/UNDEV
EX/STRUC ADMIN CONTROL CHOOSE CONSERVE...GOV/COMP
ANTHOL 20. PAGE 115 B2315

NAT/G
CONSTN
TEC/DEV

B64

ANDREN N.,GOVERNMENT AND POLITICS IN THE NORDIC
COUNTRIES: DENMARK, FINLAND, ICELAND, NORWAY,
SWEDEN. DENMARK FINLAND ICELAND NORWAY SWEDEN
POL/PAR CHIEF LEGIS ADMIN REGION REPRESENT ATTIT
CONSERVE...CHARTS BIBLIOG/A 20. PAGE 5 B0102

CONSTN
NAT/G
CULTURE
GOV/COMP

S65

HAMILTON R.F.,"SKILL LEVEL AND POLITICS." USA+45
CULTURE STRATA STRUCT LABOR CONSERVE NEW/LIB.
PAGE 46 B0933

SKILL
ADMIN

S65

POSVAR W.W.,"NATIONAL SECURITY POLICY* THE REALM OF
OBSCURITY." CREATE PLAN PROB/SOLV ADMIN LEAD GP/REL
CONSERVE...DECISION GEOG. PAGE 84 B1694

DIPLOM
USA+45
RECORD

B66

RAEFF M.,ORIGINS OF THE RUSSIAN INTELLIGENTSIA: THE
EIGHTEENTH-CENTURY NOBILITY. RUSSIA FAM NAT/G
EDU/PROP ADMIN PERS/REL ATTIT...HUM BIOG 18.
PAGE 85 B1728

INTELL
ELITES
STRATA
CONSERVE

B66

WILLNER A.R.,THE NEOTRADITIONAL ACCOMMODATION TO
POLITICAL INDEPENDENCE* THE CASE OF INDONESIA *
RESEARCH MONOGRAPH NO. 26. CULTURE ECO/UNDEV CREATE
PROB/SOLV FOR/AID LEGIT COLONIAL EFFICIENCY
NAT/LISM ALL/VALS SOC. PAGE 117 B2355

INDONESIA
CONSERVE
ELITES
ADMIN

L66

LEMARCHAND R.,"SOCIAL CHANGE AND POLITICAL
MODERNISATION IN BURUNDI." AFR BURUNDI STRATA CHIEF
EX/STRUC RIGID/FLEX PWR...SOC 20. PAGE 64 B1285

NAT/G
STRUCT
ELITES
CONSERVE

S66

JACOBS P.,"RE-RADICALIZING THE DE-RADICALIZED."
USA+45 SOCIETY STRUCT FINAN PLAN PROB/SOLV CAP/ISM
WEALTH CONSERVE NEW/LIB 20. PAGE 55 B1114

NAT/G
POLICY
MARXIST
ADMIN

S66

JACOBSON J.,"COALITIONISM: FROM PROTEST TO
POLITICKING" USA+45 ELITES NAT/G POL/PAR PROB/SOLV
ADMIN LEAD DISCRIM ORD/FREE PWR CONSERVE 20 NEGRO
AFL/CIO CIV/RIGHTS BLACK/PWR. PAGE 55 B1116

RACE/REL
LABOR
SOCIALIST
VOL/ASSN

B67

WESSON R.G.,THE IMPERIAL ORDER. WOR-45 STRUCT SECT
DOMIN ADMIN COLONIAL LEAD CONSERVE...CONCPT BIBLIOG
20. PAGE 115 B2324

PWR
CHIEF
CONTROL
SOCIETY

B86

BOLINSBROKE H ST J.,A DISSERTATION UPON PARTIES
(1729). UK LEGIS CHOOSE GOV/REL SOVEREIGN...TRADIT
18 PARLIAMENT. PAGE 13 B0269

CONSERVE
POL/PAR
CHIEF
EX/STRUC

CONSRV/PAR....CONSERVATIVE PARTY (ALL NATIONS)

B28

FYFE H.,THE BRITISH LIBERAL PARTY. UK SECT ADMIN
LEAD CHOOSE GP/REL PWR SOCISM...MAJORIT TIME/SEQ
19/20 LIB/PARTY CONSRV/PAR. PAGE 38 B0768

POL/PAR
NAT/G
REPRESENT
POPULISM

CONSTITUTION....SEE CONSTN

CONSTN....CONSTITUTIONS

N

JOURNAL OF POLITICS. USA+45 USA-45 CONSTN POL/PAR
EX/STRUC LEGIS PROB/SOLV DIPLOM CT/SYS CHOOSE
RACE/REL 20. PAGE 1 B0005

BIBLIOG/A
NAT/G
LAW
LOC/G

N

REVIEW OF POLITICS. WOR+45 WOR-45 CONSTN LEGIS
PROB/SOLV ADMIN LEAD ALL/IDEOS...PHIL/SCI 20.
PAGE 1 B0006

BIBLIOG/A
DIPLOM
INT/ORG
NAT/G

N

THE JAPAN SCIENCE REVIEW: LAW AND POLITICS: LIST OF
BOOKS AND ARTICLES ON LAW AND POLITICS. CONSTN AGRI
INDUS LABOR DIPLOM TAX ADMIN CRIME...INT/LAW SOC 20
CHINJAP. PAGE 1 B0025

BIBLIOG
LAW
S/ASIA
PHIL/SCI

N

NEUE POLITISCHE LITERATUR; BERICHTE UBER DAS
INTERNATIONALE SCHRIFTTUM ZUR POLITIK. WOR+45 LAW
CONSTN POL/PAR ADMIN LEAD GOV/REL...POLICY
IDEA/COMP. PAGE 2 B0027

BIBLIOG/A
DIPLOM
NAT/G
NAT/COMP

N

FAUNT J.R.,A CHECKLIST OF SOUTH CAROLINA STATE
PUBLICATIONS. USA+45 CONSTN LEGIS ADMIN ATTIT 20.
PAGE 35 B0708

BIBLIOG
PROVS
LOC/G
GOV/REL

N

US SUPERINTENDENT OF DOCUMENTS,POLITICAL SCIENCE:
GOVERNMENT, CRIME. DISTRICT OF COLUMBIA (PRICE LIST
54). USA+45 LAW CONSTN EX/STRUC WORKER ADJUD ADMIN
CT/SYS CHOOSE INGP/REL RACE/REL CONGRESS PRESIDENT.
PAGE 111 B2241

BIBLIOG/A
NAT/G
CRIME

B03

GRIFFIN A.P.C.,LIST OF BOOKS ON THE CABINETS OF
ENGLAND AND AMERICA (PAMPHLET). MOD/EUR UK USA-45
CONSTN NAT/G CONSULT EX/STRUC 19/20. PAGE 43 B0875

BIBLIOG/A
GOV/COMP
ADMIN
DELIB/GP

B08

THE GOVERNMENT OF SOUTH AFRICA (VOL. II). SOUTH/AFR
STRATA EXTR/IND EX/STRUC TOP/EX BUDGET ADJUD ADMIN
CT/SYS PRODUC...CORREL CENSUS 19 RAILROAD
CIVIL/SERV POSTAL/SYS. PAGE 2 B0033

CONSTN
FINAN
LEGIS
NAT/G

B08

WILSON W.,CONSTITUTIONAL GOVERNMENT IN THE UNITED

NAT/G

STATES. USA-45 LAW POL/PAR PROVS CHIEF LEGIS   GOV/REL
BAL/PWR ADJUD EXEC FEDERAL PWR 18/20 SUPREME/CT   CONSTN
HOUSE/REP SENATE. PAGE 117 B2362   PARL/PROC

B17
CORWIN E.S.,THE PRESIDENT'S CONTROL OF FOREIGN   TOP/EX
RELATIONS. FUT USA-45 CONSTN STRATA NAT/G CHIEF   PWR
EX/STRUC LEGIS KNOWL RESPECT...JURID CONCPT TREND   DIPLOM
CONGRESS VAL/FREE 20 PRESIDENT. PAGE 24 B0483

B18
WILSON W.,THE STATE: ELEMENTS OF HISTORICAL AND   NAT/G
PRACTICAL POLITICS. FRANCE GERMANY ITALY UK USSR   JURID
CONSTN EX/STRUC LEGIS CT/SYS WAR PWR...POLICY   CONCPT
GOV/COMP 20. PAGE 117 B2363   NAT/COMP

B19
NATHAN M.,THE SOUTH AFRICAN COMMONWEALTH: CONSTN
CONSTITUTION, PROBLEMS, SOCIAL CONDITIONS.   NAT/G
SOUTH/AFR UK CULTURE INDUS EX/STRUC LEGIS BUDGET   POL/PAR
EDU/PROP ADMIN CT/SYS GP/REL RACE/REL...LING 19/20   SOCIETY
CMN/WLTH. PAGE 77 B1559

B19
SUTHERLAND G.,CONSTITUTIONAL POWER AND WORLD   USA-45
AFFAIRS. CONSTN STRUCT INT/ORG NAT/G CHIEF LEGIS   EXEC
ACT/RES PLAN GOV/REL ALL/VALS...OBS TIME/SEQ   DIPLOM
CONGRESS VAL/FREE 20 PRESIDENT. PAGE 102 B2056

N19
ABERNATHY B.R.,SOME PERSISTING QUESTIONS CONCERNING   PROVS
THE CONSTITUTIONAL STATE EXECUTIVE (PAMPHLET).   EX/STRUC
CONSTN TOP/EX TEC/DEV GOV/REL EFFICIENCY TIME 20   PROB/SOLV
GOVERNOR. PAGE 3 B0054   PWR

N19
ADMINISTRATIVE STAFF COLLEGE,THE ACCOUNTABILITY OF   PARL/PROC
GOVERNMENT DEPARTMENTS (PAMPHLET) (REV. ED.). UK   ELITES
CONSTN FINAN NAT/G CONSULT ADMIN INGP/REL CONSEN   SANCTION
PRIVIL 20 PARLIAMENT. PAGE 3 B0059   PROB/SOLV

N19
CANADA CIVIL SERV COMM,THE ANALYSIS OF ORGANIZATION   NAT/G
IN THE GOVERNMENT OF CANADA (PAMPHLET). CANADA   MGT
CONSTN EX/STRUC LEGIS TOP/EX CREATE PLAN CONTROL   ADMIN
GP/REL 20. PAGE 18 B0372   DELIB/GP

N19
FAHRNKOPF N.,STATE AND LOCAL GOVERNMENT IN ILLINOIS   BIBLIOG
(PAMPHLET). CONSTN ADMIN PARTIC CHOOSE REPRESENT   LOC/G
GOV/REL...JURID MGT 20 ILLINOIS. PAGE 34 B0696   LEGIS
  CT/SYS

N19
OPERATIONS AND POLICY RESEARCH,PERU ELECTION   CHOOSE
MEMORANDA (PAMPHLET). L/A+17C PERU POL/PAR LEGIS   CONSTN
EXEC APPORT REPRESENT 20. PAGE 80 B1611   SUFF
  NAT/G

N19
SOUTH AFRICA COMMISSION ON FUT,INTERIM AND FINAL   CONSTN
REPORTS ON FUTURE FORM OF GOVERNMENT IN THE SOUTH-   REPRESENT
WEST AFRICAN PROTECTORATE (PAMPHLET). SOUTH/AFR   ADMIN
NAT/G FORCES CONFER COLONIAL CONTROL 20 AFRICA/SW.   PROB/SOLV
PAGE 99 B1998

C20
BLACHLY F.F.,"THE GOVERNMENT AND ADMINISTRATION OF   NAT/G
GERMANY." GERMANY CONSTN LOC/G PROVS DELIB/GP   GOV/REL
EX/STRUC FORCES LEGIS TOP/EX CT/SYS...BIBLIOG/A   ADMIN
19/20. PAGE 12 B0246   PHIL/SCI

B21
BRYCE J.,MODERN DEMOCRACIES. FUT NEW/ZEALND USA-45   NAT/G
LAW CONSTN POL/PAR PROVS VOL/ASSN EX/STRUC LEGIS   TREND
LEGIT CT/SYS EXEC KNOWL CONGRESS AUSTRAL 20.
PAGE 16 B0332

B24
HOLDSWORTH W.S.,A HISTORY OF ENGLISH LAW; THE   LAW
COMMON LAW AND ITS RIVALS (VOL. VI). UK STRATA   CONSTN
EX/STRUC ADJUD ADMIN CONTROL CT/SYS...JURID CONCPT   LEGIS
GEN/LAWS 17 COMMONWLTH PARLIAMENT ENGLSH/LAW   CHIEF
COMMON/LAW. PAGE 51 B1034

B25
MATHEWS J.M.,AMERICAN STATE GOVERNMENT. USA-45   PROVS
LOC/G CHIEF EX/STRUC LEGIS ADJUD CONTROL CT/SYS   ADMIN
ROUTINE GOV/REL PWR 20 GOVERNOR. PAGE 71 B1426   FEDERAL
  CONSTN

B26
LUCE R.,CONGRESS: AN EXPLANATION. USA-45 CONSTN   DECISION
FINAN ADMIN LEAD. PAGE 67 B1347   LEGIS
  CREATE
  REPRESENT

C27
HSIAO K.C.,"POLITICAL PLURALISM." LAW CONSTN   STRUCT
POL/PAR LEGIS PLAN ADMIN CENTRAL SOVEREIGN   GEN/LAWS
...INT/LAW BIBLIOG 19/20. PAGE 52 B1053   PLURISM

B28
HALL W.P.,EMPIRE TO COMMONWEALTH. FUT WOR-45 CONSTN   VOL/ASSN
ECO/DEV ECO/UNDEV INT/ORG PROVS PLAN DIPLOM   NAT/G
EDU/PROP ADMIN COLONIAL PEACE PERSON ALL/VALS   UK
...POLICY GEOG SOC OBS RECORD TREND CMN/WLTH
PARLIAMENT 19/20. PAGE 46 B0925

B29
BUELL R.,INTERNATIONAL RELATIONS. WOR+45 WOR-45   INT/ORG
CONSTN STRATA FORCES TOP/EX ADMIN ATTIT DRIVE   BAL/PWR
SUPEGO MORAL ORD/FREE PWR SOVEREIGN...JURID SOC   DIPLOM
CONCPT 20. PAGE 17 B0340

B29
MERRIAM C.E.,CHICAGO: A MORE INTIMATE VIEW OF URBAN   STRUCT
POLITICS. USA-45 CONSTN POL/PAR LEGIS ADMIN CRIME   GP/REL
INGP/REL 18/20 CHICAGO. PAGE 73 B1472   MUNIC

B31
BORCHARD E.H.,GUIDE TO THE LAW AND LEGAL LITERATURE   BIBLIOG/A
OF FRANCE. FRANCE FINAN INDUS LABOR SECT LEGIS   LAW
ADMIN COLONIAL CRIME OWN...INT/LAW 20. PAGE 14   CONSTN
B0277   METH

B32
MCKISACK M.,THE PARLIAMENTARY REPRESENTATION OF THE   NAT/G
ENGLISH BOROUGHS DURING THE MIDDLE AGES. UK CONSTN   MUNIC
CULTURE ELITES EX/STRUC TAX PAY ADJUD PARL/PROC   LEGIS
APPORT FEDERAL...POLICY 13/15 PARLIAMENT. PAGE 72   CHOOSE
B1454

B33
DANGERFIELD R.,IN DEFENSE OF THE SENATE. USA-45   LEGIS
CONSTN NAT/G EX/STRUC TOP/EX ATTIT KNOWL   DELIB/GP
...METH/CNCPT STAT TIME/SEQ TREND CON/ANAL CHARTS   DIPLOM
CONGRESS 20 TREATY. PAGE 26 B0528

B33
GREER S.,A BIBLIOGRAPHY OF PUBLIC ADMINISTRATION.   BIBLIOG/A
WOR-45 CONSTN LOC/G MUNIC EX/STRUC LEGIS...CONCPT   ADMIN
20. PAGE 43 B0869   MGT
  NAT/G

L34
GOSNELL H.F.,"BRITISH ROYAL COMMISSIONS OF INQUIRY"   DELIB/GP
UK CONSTN LEGIS PRESS ADMIN PARL/PROC...DECISION 20   INSPECT
PARLIAMENT. PAGE 41 B0839   POLICY
  NAT/G

B36
GRAVES W.B.,AMERICAN STATE GOVERNMENT. CONSTN FINAN   NAT/G
EX/STRUC FORCES LEGIS BUDGET TAX CT/SYS REPRESENT   PROVS
GOV/REL...BIBLIOG/A 19/20. PAGE 42 B0855   ADMIN
  FEDERAL

B37
UNION OF SOUTH AFRICA,REPORT CONCERNING   NAT/G
ADMINISTRATION OF SOUTH WEST AFRICA (6 VOLS.).   ADMIN
SOUTH/AFR INDUS PUB/INST FORCES LEGIS BUDGET DIPLOM   COLONIAL
EDU/PROP ADJUD CT/SYS...GEOG CHARTS 20 AFRICA/SW   CONSTN
LEAGUE/NAT. PAGE 107 B2158

B38
FIELD G.L.,THE SYNDICAL AND CORPORATIVE   FASCISM
INSTITUTIONS OF ITALIAN FASCISM. ITALY CONSTN   INDUS
STRATA LABOR EX/STRUC TOP/EX ADJUD ADMIN LEAD   NAT/G
TOTALISM AUTHORIT...MGT 20 MUSSOLIN/B. PAGE 35   WORKER
B0716

B38
HARPER S.N.,THE GOVERNMENT OF THE SOVIET UNION. COM   MARXISM
USSR LAW CONSTN ECO/DEV PLAN TEC/DEV DIPLOM   NAT/G
INT/TRADE ADMIN REV NAT/LISM...POLICY 20. PAGE 47   LEAD
B0952   POL/PAR

B38
REICH N.,LABOR RELATIONS IN REPUBLICAN GERMANY.   WORKER
GERMANY CONSTN ECO/DEV INDUS NAT/G ADMIN CONTROL   MGT
GP/REL FASCISM POPULISM 20 WEIMAR/REP. PAGE 87   LABOR
B1763   BARGAIN

B39
ANDERSON W.,LOCAL GOVERNMENT IN EUROPE. FRANCE   GOV/COMP
GERMANY ITALY UK USSR MUNIC PROVS ADMIN GOV/REL   NAT/COMP
CENTRAL SOVEREIGN 20. PAGE 5 B0099   LOC/G
  CONSTN

B39
JENNINGS W.I.,PARLIAMENT. UK POL/PAR OP/RES BUDGET   PARL/PROC
LEAD CHOOSE GP/REL...MGT 20 PARLIAMENT HOUSE/LORD   LEGIS
HOUSE/CMNS. PAGE 56 B1135   CONSTN
  NAT/G

C39
REISCHAUER R.,"JAPAN'S GOVERNMENT--POLITICS."   NAT/G
CONSTN STRATA POL/PAR FORCES LEGIS DIPLOM ADMIN   S/ASIA
EXEC CENTRAL...POLICY BIBLIOG 20 CHINJAP. PAGE 87   CONCPT
B1764   ROUTINE

B40
HART J.,AN INTRODUCTION TO ADMINISTRATIVE LAW, WITH   LAW
SELECTED CASES. USA-45 CONSTN SOCIETY NAT/G   ADMIN
EX/STRUC ADJUD CT/SYS LEAD CRIME ORD/FREE   LEGIS
...DECISION JURID 20 CASEBOOK. PAGE 47 B0958   PWR

B40
PATTERSON C.P.,STATE AND LOCAL GOVERNMENT IN TEXAS   CONSTN
(3RD ED.). USA-45 EX/STRUC LEGIS CT/SYS CHOOSE 20   PROVS
TEXAS. PAGE 81 B1642   GOV/REL
  LOC/G

B41
BURTON M.E.,THE ASSEMBLY OF THE LEAGUE OF NATIONS.   DELIB/GP
WOR-45 CONSTN SOCIETY STRUCT INT/ORG NAT/G CREATE   EX/STRUC
ATTIT RIGID/FLEX PWR...POLICY TIME/SEQ LEAGUE/NAT   DIPLOM
20. PAGE 18 B0359

B42
BINGHAM A.M.,THE TECHNIQUES OF DEMOCRACY. USA-45   POPULISM
CONSTN STRUCT POL/PAR LEGIS PLAN PARTIC CHOOSE   ORD/FREE
REPRESENT NAT/LISM TOTALISM...MGT 20. PAGE 12 B0240   ADMIN
  NAT/G

B42
NEUBURGER O.,OFFICIAL PUBLICATIONS OF PRESENT-DAY   BIBLIOG/A
GERMANY: GOVERNMENT, CORPORATE ORGANIZATIONS, AND   FASCISM
NATIONAL SOCIALIST PARTY. GERMANY CONSTN COM/IND   NAT/G

POL/PAR EDU/PROP PRESS 20 NAZI. PAGE 78 B1570　　ADMIN

B44

DAVIS H.E.,PIONEERS IN WORLD ORDER. WOR-45 CONSTN　INT/ORG
ECO/TAC DOMIN EDU/PROP LEGIT ADJUD ADMIN ARMS/CONT　ROUTINE
CHOOSE KNOWL ORD/FREE...POLICY JURID SOC STAT OBS
CENSUS TIME/SEQ ANTHOL LEAGUE/NAT 20. PAGE 26 B0537

L44

CORWIN E.S.,"THE CONSTITUTION AND WORLD　　　　　　INT/ORG
ORGANIZATION." FUT USA+45 USA-45 NAT/G EX/STRUC　　CONSTN
LEGIS PEACE KNOWL...CON/ANAL UN 20. PAGE 24 B0484　SOVEREIGN

L44

HAILEY,"THE FUTURE OF COLONIAL PEOPLES." WOR-45　　PLAN
CONSTN CULTURE ECO/UNDEV AGRI MARKET INT/ORG NAT/G　CONCPT
SECT CONSULT ECO/TAC LEGIT ADMIN NAT/LISM ALL/VALS　DIPLOM
...SOC OBS TREND STERTYP CMN/WLTH LEAGUE/NAT　　　　　UK
PARLIAMENT 20. PAGE 45 B0916

S44

KEFAUVER E.,"THE NEED FOR BETTER EXECUTIVE-　　　　LEGIS
LEGISLATIVE TEAMWORK IN THE NATIONAL GOVERNMENT."　EXEC
USA-45 CONSTN NAT/G ROUTINE...TRADIT CONGRESS　　　CONFER
REFORMERS. PAGE 59 B1188　　　　　　　　　　　　　　LEAD

B45

BRECHT A.,FEDERALISM AND REGIONALISM IN GERMANY;　FEDERAL
THE DIVISION OF PRUSSIA. GERMANY PRUSSIA WOR-45　　REGION
CREATE ADMIN WAR TOTALISM PWR...CHARTS 20 HITLER/A.　PROB/SOLV
PAGE 15 B0303　　　　　　　　　　　　　　　　　　　CONSTN

B45

CONOVER H.F.,THE GOVERNMENTS OF THE MAJOR FOREIGN　BIBLIOG
POWERS: A BIBLIOGRAPHY. FRANCE GERMANY ITALY UK　　NAT/G
USSR CONSTN LOC/G POL/PAR EX/STRUC FORCES ADMIN　　DIPLOM
CT/SYS CIVMIL/REL TOTALISM...POLICY 19/20. PAGE 23
B0464

B45

RANSHOFFEN-WERTHEIMER EF,THE INTERNATIONAL　　　　INT/ORG
SECRETARIAT: A GREAT EXPERIMENT IN INTERNATIONAL　EXEC
ADMINISTRATION. EUR+WWI FUT CONSTN FACE/GP CONSULT
DELIB/GP ACT/RES ADMIN ROUTINE PEACE ORD/FREE...MGT
RECORD ORG/CHARTS LEAGUE/NAT WORK 20. PAGE 86 B1731

B46

CORRY J.A.,DEMOCRATIC GOVERNMENT AND POLITICS.　　NAT/G
WOR-45 EX/STRUC LOBBY TOTALISM...MAJORIT CONCPT　　CONSTN
METH/COMP NAT/COMP 20. PAGE 24 B0479　　　　　　　POL/PAR
　　　　　　　　　　　　　　　　　　　　　　　　　JURID

C46

GOODRICH L.M.,"CHARTER OF THE UNITED NATIONS:　　EX/STRUC
COMMENTARY AND DOCUMENTS." EX/STRUC ADMIN...INT/LAW　INT/ORG
CON/ANAL BIBLIOG 20 UN. PAGE 41 B0826　　　　　　　DIPLOM

B47

BORGESE G.,COMMON CAUSE. LAW CONSTN SOCIETY STRATA　WOR+45
ECO/DEV INT/ORG POL/PAR FORCES LEGIS TOP/EX CAP/ISM　NAT/G
DIPLOM ADMIN EXEC ATTIT PWR 20. PAGE 14 B0279　　　SOVEREIGN
　　　　　　　　　　　　　　　　　　　　　　　　　REGION

B47

DE NOIA J.,GUIDE TO OFFICIAL PUBLICATIONS OF THE　BIBLIOG/A
OTHER AMERICAN REPUBLICS: EL SALVADOR. EL/SALVADR　CONSTN
LAW LEGIS EDU/PROP CT/SYS 20. PAGE 27 B0558　　　　NAT/G
　　　　　　　　　　　　　　　　　　　　　　　　　ADMIN

B47

DE NOIA J.,GUIDE TO OFFICIAL PUBLICATIONS OF THE　BIBLIOG/A
OTHER AMERICAN REPUBLICS: NICARAGUA (VOL. XIV).　　EDU/PROP
NICARAGUA LAW LEGIS ADMIN CT/SYS...JURID 19/20.　　NAT/G
PAGE 27 B0559　　　　　　　　　　　　　　　　　　CONSTN

B47

DE NOIA J.,GUIDE TO OFFICIAL PUBLICATIONS OF THE　BIBLIOG/A
OTHER AMERICAN REPUBLICS: PANAMA (VOL. XV). PANAMA　CONSTN
LAW LEGIS EDU/PROP CT/SYS 20. PAGE 27 B0560　　　　ADMIN
　　　　　　　　　　　　　　　　　　　　　　　　　NAT/G

B47

MARX F.M.,THE PRESIDENT AND HIS STAFF SERVICES　　CONSTN
PUBLIC ADMINISTRATION SERVICES NUMBER 98　　　　　CHIEF
(PAMPHLET). FINAN ADMIN CT/SYS REPRESENT PWR 20　　NAT/G
PRESIDENT. PAGE 70 B1419　　　　　　　　　　　　　EX/STRUC

B47

PATTERSON C.P.,PRESIDENTIAL GOVERNMENT IN THE　　CHIEF
UNITED STATES - THE UNWRITTEN CONSTITUTION. USA+45　NAT/G
DELIB/GP EX/STRUC ADJUD ADMIN EXEC...DECISION　　　CONSTN
PRESIDENT. PAGE 81 B1643　　　　　　　　　　　　　POL/PAR

B47

PUBLIC ADMINISTRATION SERVICE,CURRENT RESEARCH　　BIBLIOG
PROJECTS IN PUBLIC ADMINISTRATION (PAMPHLET). LAW　R+D
CONSTN COM/IND LABOR LOC/G MUNIC PROVS ACT/RES　　MGT
DIPLOM RECEIVE EDU/PROP WAR 20. PAGE 85 B1716　　　ADMIN

B47

REDFORD E.S.,FIELD ADMINISTRATION OF WARTIME　　　ADMIN
RATIONING. USA-45 CONSTN ELITES DIST/IND WORKER　　NAT/G
CONTROL WAR GOV/REL ADJUST RIGID/FLEX 20 OPA.　　　PROB/SOLV
PAGE 87 B1752　　　　　　　　　　　　　　　　　　RATION

B48

BISHOP H.M.,BASIC ISSUES OF AMERICAN DEMOCRACY.　　NAT/G
USA+45 USA-45 POL/PAR EX/STRUC LEGIS ADJUD FEDERAL　PARL/PROC
...BIBLIOG 18/20. PAGE 12 B0244　　　　　　　　　CONSTN

B48

DE NOIA J.,GUIDE TO OFFICIAL PUBLICATIONS OF OTHER　BIBLIOG/A
AMERICAN REPUBLICS: PERU (VOL. XVII). PERU LAW　　CONSTN
LEGIS ADMIN CT/SYS...JURID 19/20. PAGE 28 B0561　　NAT/G
　　　　　　　　　　　　　　　　　　　　　　　　　EDU/PROP

B48

HART J.,THE AMERICAN PRESIDENCY IN ACTION 1789: A　NAT/G
STUDY IN CONSTITUTIONAL HISTORY. USA-45 POL/PAR　　CONSTN
DELIB/GP FORCES LEGIS ADJUD ADMIN LEAD GP/REL　　　CHIEF
PERS/REL 18 PRESIDENT CONGRESS. PAGE 47 B0959　　　EX/STRUC

B48

HULL C.,THE MEMOIRS OF CORDELL HULL (VOLUME ONE).　BIOG
USA-45 WOR-45 CONSTN FAM LOC/G NAT/G PROVS DELIB/GP　DIPLOM
FORCES LEGIS TOP/EX BAL/PWR LEGIT ADMIN EXEC WAR
ATTIT ORD/FREE PWR...MAJORIT SELF/OBS TIME/SEQ
TREND NAZI 20. PAGE 52 B1062

B48

MEEK C.K.,COLONIAL LAW: A BIBLIOGRAPHY WITH SPECIAL　COLONIAL
REFERENCE TO NATIVE AFRICAN SYSTEMS OF LAW AND LAND　ADMIN
TENURE. AFR ECO/UNDEV AGRI CT/SYS...JURID SOC 20.　LAW
PAGE 72 B1462　　　　　　　　　　　　　　　　　　CONSTN

B48

ROSSITER C.L.,CONSTITUTIONAL DICTATORSHIP; CRISIS　NAT/G
GOVERNMENT IN THE MODERN DEMOCRACIES. FRANCE　　　AUTHORIT
GERMANY UK USA-45 WOR-45 EX/STRUC BAL/PWR CONTROL　CONSTN
COERCE WAR CENTRAL ORD/FREE...DECISION 19/20.　　　TOTALISM
PAGE 90 B1828

B48

SLESSER H.,THE ADMINISTRATION OF THE LAW. UK CONSTN　LAW
EX/STRUC OP/RES PROB/SOLV CRIME ROLE...DECISION　　CT/SYS
METH/COMP 20 CIVIL/LAW ENGLSH/LAW CIVIL/LAW.　　　ADJUD
PAGE 98 B1977

B48

STOKES W.S.,BIBLIOGRAPHY OF STANDARD AND CLASSICAL　BIBLIOG
WORKS IN THE FIELDS OF AMERICAN POLITICAL SCIENCE.　NAT/G
USA+45 USA-45 POL/PAR PROVS FORCES DIPLOM ADMIN　　LOC/G
CT/SYS APPORT 20 CONGRESS PRESIDENT. PAGE 101 B2043　CONSTN

B48

TOWSTER J.,POLITICAL POWER IN THE USSR: 1917-1947.　EX/STRUC
USSR CONSTN CULTURE ELITES CREATE PLAN COERCE　　　NAT/G
CENTRAL ATTIT RIGID/FLEX ORD/FREE...BIBLIOG　　　　MARXISM
SOC/INTEG 20 LENIN/VI STALIN/J. PAGE 105 B2124　　PWR

C48

WALKER H.,"THE LEGISLATIVE PROCESS; LAWMAKING IN　PARL/PROC
THE UNITED STATES." NAT/G POL/PAR PROVS EX/STRUC　LEGIS
OP/RES PROB/SOLV CT/SYS LOBBY GOV/REL...CHARTS　　LAW
BIBLIOG T 18/20 CONGRESS. PAGE 113 B2279　　　　　CONSTN

N48

YATES M.,ADMINISTRATIVE REORGANIZATION OF STATE　　BIBLIOG
GOVERNMENTS: A BIBLIOGRAPHY (PAMPHLET). USA+45　　LOC/G
USA-45 CONSTN OP/RES PLAN CONFER...POLICY 20.　　ADMIN
PAGE 118 B2390　　　　　　　　　　　　　　　　　PROVS

B49

HEADLAM-MORLEY,BIBLIOGRAPHY IN POLITICS FOR THE　　BIBLIOG
HONOUR SCHOOL OF PHILOSOPHY, POLITICS AND ECONOMICS　NAT/G
(PAMPHLET). UK CONSTN LABOR MUNIC DIPLOM ADMIN　　PHIL/SCI
19/20. PAGE 48 B0979　　　　　　　　　　　　　　GOV/REL

L49

BROOKINGS INST.,"GOVERNMENT MECHANISM FOR CONDUCT　EXEC
OF US FOREIGN RELATIONS." USA+45 CONSTN NAT/G LEGIS　STRUCT
CT/SYS...MGT TIME/SEQ CONGRESS TOT/POP 20. PAGE 15　DIPLOM
B0316

B50

AMERICAN POLITICAL SCI ASSN,TOWARD A MORE　　　　POL/PAR
RESPONSIBLE TWO-PARTY SYSTEM. USA+45 CONSTN　　　TASK
VOL/ASSN LEGIS LEAD CHOOSE...POLICY MGT 20. PAGE 4　PARTIC
B0087　　　　　　　　　　　　　　　　　　　　　ACT/RES

B50

BROWN E.S.,MANUAL OF GOVERNMENT PUBLICATIONS.　　BIBLIOG/A
WOR+45 WOR-45 CONSTN INT/ORG MUNIC PROVS DIPLOM　　NAT/G
ADMIN 20. PAGE 16 B0322　　　　　　　　　　　　　LAW

B50

JENKINS W.S.,A GUIDE TO THE MICROFILM COLLECTION OF　BIBLIOG
EARLY STATE RECORDS. USA+45 CONSTN MUNIC LEGIS　　PROVS
PRESS ADMIN CT/SYS 18/20. PAGE 56 B1130　　　　　AUD/VIS

B50

WADE E.C.S.,CONSTITUTIONAL LAW; AN OUTLINE OF THE　CONSTN
LAW AND PRACTICE OF THE CONSTITUTION. UK LEGIS　　NAT/G
DOMIN ADMIN GP/REL 16/20 CMN/WLTH PARLIAMENT　　　PARL/PROC
ENGLSH/LAW. PAGE 112 B2269　　　　　　　　　　　LAW

B50

WARD R.E.,A GUIDE TO JAPANESE REFERENCE AND　　　BIBLIOG/A
RESEARCH MATERIALS IN THE FIELD OF POLITICAL　　　ASIA
SCIENCE. LAW CONSTN LOC/G PRESS ADMIN...SOC　　　NAT/G
CON/ANAL METH 19/20 CHINJAP. PAGE 113 B2289

L50

US SENATE COMM. GOVT. OPER.,"REVISION OF THE UN　INT/ORG
CHARTER." FUT USA+45 WOR+45 CONSTN ECO/DEV　　　　LEGIS
ECO/UNDEV NAT/G DELIB/GP ACT/RES CREATE PLAN EXEC　PEACE
ROUTINE CHOOSE ALL/VALS...POLICY CONCPT CONGRESS UN
TOT/POP 20 COLD/WAR. PAGE 111 B2235

C50

HOLCOMBE A.,"OUR MORE PERFECT UNION." USA+45 USA-45　CONSTN
POL/PAR JUDGE CT/SYS EQUILIB FEDERAL PWR...MAJORIT　NAT/G
TREND BIBLIOG 18/20 CONGRESS PRESIDENT. PAGE 51　　ADMIN
B1031　　　　　　　　　　　　　　　　　　　　　PLAN

C50

STEWART F.M.,"A HALF CENTURY OF MUNICIPAL REFORM."　LOC/G
USA+45 CONSTN FINAN SCHOOL EX/STRUC PLAN PROB/SOLV　VOL/ASSN
EDU/PROP ADMIN CHOOSE GOV/REL BIBLIOG. PAGE 101　　MUNIC
B2036　　　　　　　　　　　　　　　　　　　　　POLICY

C50
STOKES W.S.,"HONDURAS: AN AREA STUDY IN   CONSTN
GOVERNMENT." HONDURAS NAT/G POL/PAR COLONIAL CT/SYS   LAW
ROUTINE CHOOSE REPRESENT...GEOG RECORD BIBLIOG   L/A+17C
19/20. PAGE 101 B2044   ADMIN

C50
WAGER P.W.,"COUNTY GOVERNMENT ACROSS THE NATION."   LOC/G
USA+45 CONSTN COM/IND FINAN SCHOOL DOMIN CT/SYS   PROVS
LEAD GOV/REL...STAT BIBLIOG 20. PAGE 112 B2272   ADMIN
                                                          ROUTINE

B51
ANDERSON W.,STATE AND LOCAL GOVERNMENT IN THE   LOC/G
UNITED STATES. USA+45 CONSTN POL/PAR EX/STRUC LEGIS   MUNIC
BUDGET TAX ADJUD CT/SYS CHOOSE...CHARTS T 20.   PROVS
PAGE 5 B0100   GOV/REL

B51
ANDERSON W.,GOVERNMENT IN THE FIFTY STATES. LAW   LOC/G
CONSTN FINAN POL/PAR LEGIS EDU/PROP ADJUD ADMIN   PROVS
CT/SYS CHOOSE...CHARTS 20. PAGE 5 B0101   GOV/REL

B51
CHRISTENSEN A.N.,THE EVOLUTION OF LATIN AMERICAN   NAT/G
GOVERNMENT: A BOOK OF READINGS. ECO/UNDEV INDUS   CONSTN
LOC/G POL/PAR EX/STRUC LEGIS FOR/AID CT/SYS   DIPLOM
...SOC/WK 20 SOUTH/AMER. PAGE 21 B0428   L/A+17C

B51
SMITH L.,AMERICAN DEMOCRACY AND MILITARY POWER.   FORCES
USA+45 USA-45 CONSTN STRATA NAT/G LEGIS ACT/RES   STRUCT
LEGIT ADMIN EXEC GOV/REL ALL/VALS...CONCPT   WAR
HIST/WRIT CONGRESS 20. PAGE 98 B1982

B51
SWISHER C.B.,THE THEORY AND PRACTICE OF AMERICAN   CONSTN
NATIONAL GOVERNMENT. CULTURE LEGIS DIPLOM ADJUD   NAT/G
ADMIN WAR PEACE ORD/FREE...MAJORIT 17/20. PAGE 102   GOV/REL
B2063   GEN/LAWS

B52
DE GRAZIA A.,POLITICAL ORGANIZATION. CONSTN LOC/G   FEDERAL
MUNIC NAT/G CHIEF LEGIS TOP/EX ADJUD CT/SYS   LAW
PERS/REL...INT/LAW MYTH UN. PAGE 27 B0553   ADMIN

B52
ELLIOTT W.,UNITED STATES FOREIGN POLICY. ITS   LEGIS
ORGANIZATION AND CONTROL. USA+45 USA-45 CONSTN   EX/STRUC
NAT/G FORCES TOP/EX PEACE...TIME/SEQ CONGRESS   DIPLOM
LEAGUE/NAT 20. PAGE 33 B0670

B52
SWENSON R.J.,FEDERAL ADMINISTRATIVE LAW: A STUDY OF   JURID
THE GROWTH, NATURE, AND CONTROL OF ADMINISTRATIVE   CONSTN
ACTION. USA-45 JUDGE ADMIN GOV/REL EFFICIENCY   LEGIS
PRIVIL ATTIT NEW/LIB SUPREME/CT. PAGE 102 B2061   ADJUD

B52
VANDENBOSCH A.,THE UN: BACKGROUND, ORGANIZATION,   DELIB/GP
FUNCTIONS, ACTIVITIES. WOR+45 LAW CONSTN STRUCT   TIME/SEQ
INT/ORG CONSULT BAL/PWR EDU/PROP EXEC ALL/VALS   PEACE
...POLICY CONCPT UN 20. PAGE 112 B2254

L52
WRIGHT Q.,"CONGRESS AND THE TREATY-MAKING POWER."   ROUTINE
USA+45 WOR+45 CONSTN INTELL NAT/G CHIEF CONSULT   DIPLOM
EX/STRUC LEGIS TOP/EX CREATE GOV/REL DISPL DRIVE   INT/LAW
RIGID/FLEX...TREND TOT/POP CONGRESS CONGRESS 20   DELIB/GP
TREATY. PAGE 118 B2384

S52
RICH B.M.,"ADMINISTRATION REORGANIZATION IN NEW   ADMIN
JERSEY" (BMR)" USA+45 DELIB/GP EX/STRUC WORKER   CONSTN
OP/RES BUDGET 20 NEW/JERSEY. PAGE 88 B1772   PROB/SOLV
                                                         PROVS

B53
SAYLES L.R.,THE LOCAL UNION. CONSTN CULTURE   LABOR
DELIB/GP PARTIC CHOOSE GP/REL INGP/REL ATTIT ROLE   LEAD
...MAJORIT DECISION MGT. PAGE 93 B1873   ADJUD
                                                         ROUTINE

B53
STOUT H.M.,BRITISH GOVERNMENT. UK FINAN LOC/G   NAT/G
POL/PAR DELIB/GP DIPLOM ADMIN COLONIAL CHOOSE   PARL/PROC
ORD/FREE...JURID BIBLIOG 20 COMMONWLTH. PAGE 101   CONSTN
B2049   NEW/LIB

C53
BULNER-THOMAS I.,"THE PARTY SYSTEM IN GREAT   NAT/G
BRITAIN." UK CONSTN SECT PRESS CONFER GP/REL ATTIT   POL/PAR
...POLICY TREND BIBLIOG 19/20 PARLIAMENT. PAGE 17   ADMIN
B0343   ROUTINE

B54
BIESANZ J.,MODERN SOCIETY: AN INTRODUCTION TO   SOCIETY
SOCIAL SCIENCE. COM CONSTN STRUCT FAM MUNIC NAT/G   PROB/SOLV
SECT EX/STRUC LEGIS GP/REL PERSON...SOC 20. PAGE 12   CULTURE
B0237

B54
JENNINGS I.,THE QUEEN'S GOVERNMENT. UK POL/PAR   NAT/G
DELIB/GP ADJUD ADMIN CT/SYS PARL/PROC REPRESENT   CONSTN
CONSERVE 13/20 PARLIAMENT. PAGE 56 B1132   LEGIS
                                                         CHIEF

B54
TOMPKINS D.C.,STATE GOVERNMENT AND ADMINISTRATION: BIBLIOG/A
A BIBLIOGRAPHY. USA+45 USA-45 CONSTN LEGIS JUDGE   LOC/G
BUDGET CT/SYS LOBBY...CHARTS 20. PAGE 105 B2116   PROVS
                                                         ADMIN

B54
US SENATE COMM ON FOREIGN REL,REVIEW OF THE UNITED   BIBLIOG

NATIONS CHARTER: A COLLECTION OF DOCUMENTS. LEGIS   CONSTN
DIPLOM ADMIN ARMS/CONT WAR REPRESENT SOVEREIGN   INT/ORG
...INT/LAW 20 UN. PAGE 110 B2220   DEBATE

B54
WHITE L.D.,THE JACKSONIANS: A STUDY IN   NAT/G
ADMINISTRATIVE HISTORY 1829-1861. USA-45 CONSTN   ADMIN
POL/PAR CHIEF DELIB/GP LEGIS CREATE PROB/SOLV   POLICY
ECO/TAC LEAD REGION GP/REL 19 PRESIDENT CONGRESS
JACKSON/A. PAGE 116 B2339

C54
CALDWELL L.K.,"THE GOVERNMENT AND ADMINISTRATION OF   PROVS
NEW YORK." LOC/G MUNIC POL/PAR SCHOOL CHIEF LEGIS   ADMIN
PLAN TAX CT/SYS...MGT SOC/WK BIBLIOG 20 NEWYORK/C.   CONSTN
PAGE 18 B0366   EX/STRUC

C54
ROBSON W.A.,"GREAT CITIES OF THE WORLD: THEIR   LOC/G
GOVERNMENT, POLITICS, AND PLANNING." CONSTN FINAN   MUNIC
EX/STRUC ADMIN EXEC CHOOSE GOV/REL...STAT TREND   PLAN
ANTHOL BIBLIOG 20. PAGE 89 B1806   PROB/SOLV

C54
ZELLER B.,"AMERICAN STATE LEGISLATURES: REPORT ON   REPRESENT
THE COMMITTEE ON AMERICAN LEGISLATURES." CONSTN   LEGIS
POL/PAR EX/STRUC CONFER ADMIN CONTROL EXEC LOBBY   PROVS
ROUTINE GOV/REL...POLICY BIBLIOG 20. PAGE 119 B2401   APPORT

B55
APTER D.E.,THE GOLD COAST IN TRANSITION. FUT CONSTN   AFR
CULTURE SOCIETY ECO/UNDEV FAM KIN LOC/G NAT/G   SOVEREIGN
POL/PAR LEGIS TOP/EX EDU/PROP LEGIT ADMIN ATTIT
PERSON PWR...CONCPT STAT INT CENSUS TOT/POP
VAL/FREE. PAGE 6 B0120

B55
BAILEY S.K.,RESEARCH FRONTIERS IN POLITICS AND   R+D
GOVERNMENT. CONSTN LEGIS ADMIN REV CHOOSE...CONCPT   METH
IDEA/COMP GAME ANTHOL 20. PAGE 8 B0164   NAT/G

B55
BEISEL A.R.,CONTROL OVER ILLEGAL ENFORCEMENT OF THE   ORD/FREE
CRIMINAL LAW: ROLE OF THE SUPREME COURT. CONSTN   LAW
ROUTINE MORAL PWR...SOC 20 SUPREME/CT. PAGE 10   CRIME
B0207

B55
CRAIG J.,BIBLIOGRAPHY OF PUBLIC ADMINISTRATION IN   BIBLIOG
AUSTRALIA. CONSTN FINAN EX/STRUC LEGIS PLAN DIPLOM   GOV/REL
RECEIVE ADJUD ROUTINE...HEAL 19/20 AUSTRAL   ADMIN
PARLIAMENT. PAGE 24 B0500   NAT/G

B55
CUSHMAN R.E.,LEADING CONSTITUTIONAL DECISIONS.   CONSTN
USA+45 USA-45 NAT/G EX/STRUC LEGIS JUDGE TAX   PROB/SOLV
FEDERAL...DECISION 20 SUPREME/CT CASEBOOK. PAGE 25   JURID
B0513   CT/SYS

B55
GUAITA A.,BIBLIOGRAFIA ESPANOLA DE DERECHO   BIBLIOG
ADMINISTRATIVO (PAMPHLET). SPAIN LOC/G MUNIC NAT/G   ADMIN
PROVS JUDGE BAL/PWR GOV/REL OWN...JURID 18/19.   CONSTN
PAGE 44 B0900   PWR

B55
JAPAN MOMBUSHO DAIGAKU GAKIYUT,BIBLIOGRAPHY OF THE   BIBLIOG
STUDIES ON LAW AND POLITICS (PAMPHLET). CONSTN   LAW
INDUS LABOR DIPLOM TAX ADMIN...CRIMLGY INT/LAW 20   PHIL/SCI
CHINJAP. PAGE 56 B1126

B55
WHEARE K.C.,GOVERNMENT BY COMMITTEE; AN ESSAY ON   DELIB/GP
THE BRITISH CONSTITUTION. UK NAT/G LEGIS INSPECT   CONSTN
CONFER ADJUD ADMIN CONTROL TASK EFFICIENCY ROLE   LEAD
POPULISM 20. PAGE 115 B2329   GP/COMP

B56
JENNINGS W.I.,THE APPROACH TO SELF-GOVERNMENT.   NAT/G
CEYLON INDIA PAKISTAN S/ASIA UK SOCIETY POL/PAR   CONSTN
DELIB/GP LEGIS ECO/TAC EDU/PROP ADMIN EXEC CHOOSE   COLONIAL
ATTIT ALL/VALS...JURID CONCPT GEN/METH TOT/POP 20.
PAGE 56 B1136

B56
SOHN L.B.,BASIC DOCUMENTS OF THE UNITED NATIONS.   DELIB/GP
WOR+45 LAW INT/ORG LEGIT EXEC ROUTINE CHOOSE PWR   CONSTN
...JURID CONCPT GEN/LAWS ANTHOL UN TOT/POP OAS FAO
ILO 20. PAGE 99 B1993

B56
WAUGH E.W.,SECOND CONSUL. USA+45 USA-45 CONSTN   NAT/G
POL/PAR PROB/SOLV PARL/PROC CHOOSE PERS/REL ATTIT   EX/STRUC
...BIBLIOG 18/20 VICE/PRES. PAGE 114 B2304   PWR
                                                         CHIEF

B56
WILSON P.,GOVERNMENT AND POLITICS OF INDIA AND   BIBLIOG
PAKISTAN: 1885-1955; A BIBLIOGRAPHY OF WORKS IN   COLONIAL
WESTERN LANGUAGES. INDIA PAKISTAN CONSTN LOC/G   NAT/G
POL/PAR FORCES DIPLOM ADMIN WAR CHOOSE...BIOG   S/ASIA
CON/ANAL 19/20. PAGE 117 B2361

B56
WILSON W.,CONGRESSIONAL GOVERNMENT. USA-45 NAT/G   LEGIS
ADMIN EXEC PARL/PROC GP/REL MAJORITY ATTIT 19   CHIEF
SENATE HOUSE/REP. PAGE 117 B2364   CONSTN
                                                         PWR

L56
MACMAHON A.W.,"WOODROW WILSON AS LEGISLATIVE LEADER   LEGIS
AND ADMINISTRATOR." CONSTN POL/PAR ADMIN...POLICY   CHIEF
HIST/WRIT WILSON/W PRESIDENT. PAGE 68 B1371   LEAD
                                                         BIOG

S56

KHAMA T.,"POLITICAL CHANGE IN AFRICAN SOCIETY." AFR
CONSTN SOCIETY LOC/G NAT/G POL/PAR EX/STRUC LEGIS ELITES
LEGIT ADMIN CHOOSE REPRESENT NAT/LISM MORAL
ORD/FREE PWR...CONCPT OBS TREND GEN/METH CMN/WLTH
17/20. PAGE 59 B1201

B57

BABCOCK R.S.,STATE & LOCAL GOVERNMENT AND POLITICS. PROVS
USA+45 CONSTN POL/PAR EX/STRUC LEGIS BUDGET LOBBY LOC/G
CHOOSE SUFF...CHARTS BIBLIOG T 20. PAGE 8 B0154 GOV/REL

B57

BEAL J.R.,JOHN FOSTER DULLES, A BIOGRAPHY. USA+45 BIOG
USSR WOR+45 CONSTN INT/ORG NAT/G EX/STRUC LEGIT DIPLOM
ADMIN NUC/PWR DISPL PERSON ORD/FREE PWR SKILL
...POLICY PSY OBS RECORD COLD/WAR UN 20 DULLES/JF.
PAGE 10 B0200

B57

LOEWENSTEIN K.,POLITICAL POWER AND THE GOVERNMENTAL PWR
PROCESS. WOR+45 WOR-45 CONSTN NAT/G POL/PAR CONCPT
EX/STRUC LEGIS TOP/EX DOMIN EDU/PROP LEGIT ADMIN
REGION CHOOSE ATTIT...JURID STERTYP GEN/LAWS 20.
PAGE 66 B1336

B57

MURRAY J.N.,THE UNITED NATIONS TRUSTEESHIP SYSTEM. INT/ORG
AFR WOR+45 CONSTN CONSULT LEGIS EDU/PROP LEGIT EXEC DELIB/GP
ROUTINE...INT TIME/SEQ SOMALI UN 20. PAGE 77 B1547

B57

SCHLOCHAUER H.J.,OFFENTLICHES RECHT. GERMANY/W CONSTN
FINAN EX/STRUC LEGIS DIPLOM FEDERAL ORD/FREE JURID
...INT/LAW 20. PAGE 94 B1892 ADMIN
CT/SYS

S57

HAILEY,"TOMORROW IN AFRICA." CONSTN SOCIETY LOC/G AFR
NAT/G DOMIN ADJUD ADMIN GP/REL DISCRIM NAT/LISM PERSON
ATTIT MORAL ORD/FREE...PSY SOC CONCPT OBS RECORD ELITES
TREND GEN/LAWS CMN/WLTH 20. PAGE 45 B0917 RACE/REL

C57

TANG P.S.H.,"COMMUNIST CHINA TODAY: DOMESTIC AND POL/PAR
FOREIGN POLICIES." CHINA/COM COM S/ASIA USSR STRATA LEAD
FORCES DIPLOM EDU/PROP COERCE GOV/REL...POLICY ADMIN
MAJORIT BIBLIOG 20. PAGE 102 B2071 CONSTN

B58

CARTER G.M.,TRANSITION IN AFRICA; STUDIES IN NAT/COMP
POLITICAL ADAPTATION. AFR CENTRL/AFR GHANA NIGERIA PWR
CONSTN LOC/G POL/PAR ADMIN GP/REL FEDERAL...MAJORIT CONTROL
BIBLIOG 20. PAGE 19 B0389 NAT/G

B58

CHARLES R.,LA JUSTICE EN FRANCE. FRANCE LAW CONSTN JURID
DELIB/GP CRIME 20. PAGE 20 B0413 ADMIN
CT/SYS
ADJUD

B58

CONSERVATIVE POLITICAL CENTRE,A WORLD SECURITY ORD/FREE
AUTHORITY? WOR+45 CONSTN ELITES FINAN DELIB/GP PLAN CONSERVE
PROB/SOLV ADMIN CONTROL NUC/PWR GP/REL...IDEA/COMP FORCES
20. PAGE 23 B0468 ARMS/CONT

B58

HENKIN L.,ARMS CONTROL AND INSPECTION IN AMERICAN USA+45
LAW. LAW CONSTN INT/ORG LOC/G MUNIC NAT/G PROVS JURID
EDU/PROP LEGIT EXEC NUC/PWR KNOWL ORD/FREE...OBS ARMS/CONT
TOT/POP CONGRESS 20. PAGE 49 B0990

B58

JAPAN MINISTRY OF JUSTICE,CRIMINAL JUSTICE IN CONSTN
JAPAN. LAW PROF/ORG PUB/INST FORCES CONTROL CT/SYS CRIME
PARL/PROC 20 CHINJAP. PAGE 56 B1125 JURID
ADMIN

B58

KAPLAN H.E.,THE LAW OF CIVIL SERVICE. USA+45 LAW ADJUD
POL/PAR CT/SYS CRIME GOV/REL...POLICY JURID 20. NAT/G
PAGE 58 B1167 ADMIN
CONSTN

B58

REDFORD E.S.,IDEAL AND PRACTICE IN PUBLIC POLICY
ADMINISTRATION. CONSTN ELITES NAT/G CONSULT EX/STRUC
DELIB/GP LEAD UTOPIA ATTIT POPULISM...DECISION PLAN
METH/COMP 20. PAGE 87 B1756 ADMIN

B58

SCOTT D.J.R.,RUSSIAN POLITICAL INSTITUTIONS. RUSSIA NAT/G
USSR CONSTN AGRI DELIB/GP PLAN EDU/PROP CONTROL POL/PAR
CHOOSE EFFICIENCY ATTIT MARXISM...BIBLIOG/A 13/20. ADMIN
PAGE 95 B1919 DECISION

B58

WESTIN A.F.,THE ANATOMY OF A CONSTITUTIONAL LAW CT/SYS
CASE. USA+45 LAW LEGIS ADMIN EXEC...DECISION MGT INDUS
SOC RECORD 20 SUPREME/CT. PAGE 115 B2326 ADJUD
CONSTN

S58

ELKIN A.B.,"OEEC-ITS STRUCTURE AND POWERS." EUR+WWI ECO/DEV
CONSTN INDUS INT/ORG NAT/G VOL/ASSN DELIB/GP EX/STRUC
ACT/RES PLAN ORD/FREE WEALTH...CHARTS ORG/CHARTS
OEEC 20. PAGE 33 B0666

C58

GOLAY J.F.,"THE FOUNDING OF THE FEDERAL REPUBLIC OF FEDERAL
GERMANY." GERMANY/W CONSTN EX/STRUC DIPLOM ADMIN NAT/G
CHOOSE...DECISION BIBLIOG 20. PAGE 40 B0814 PARL/PROC
POL/PAR

C58

WILDING N.,"AN ENCYCLOPEDIA OF PARLIAMENT." UK LAW PARL/PROC
CONSTN CHIEF PROB/SOLV DIPLOM DEBATE WAR INGP/REL POL/PAR
PRIVIL...BIBLIOG DICTIONARY 13/20 CMN/WLTH NAT/G
PARLIAMENT. PAGE 116 B2350 ADMIN

B59

CONOVER H.F.,NIGERIAN OFFICIAL PUBLICATIONS, BIBLIOG
1869-1959: A GUIDE. NIGER CONSTN FINAN ACADEM NAT/G
SCHOOL FORCES PRESS ADMIN COLONIAL...HIST/WRIT CON/ANAL
19/20. PAGE 23 B0466

B59

DUVERGER M.,LA CINQUIEME REPUBLIQUE. FRANCE WOR+45 NAT/G
POL/PAR CHIEF EX/STRUC LOBBY. PAGE 31 B0636 CONSTN
GOV/REL
PARL/PROC

B59

GOODRICH L.,THE UNITED NATIONS. WOR+45 CONSTN INT/ORG
STRUCT ACT/RES LEGIT COERCE KNOWL ORD/FREE PWR ROUTINE
...GEN/LAWS UN 20. PAGE 41 B0825

B59

IPSEN H.P.,HAMBURGISCHES STAATS- UND ADMIN
VERWALTUNGSRECHT. CONSTN LOC/G FORCES BUDGET CT/SYS PROVS
...JURID 20 HAMBURG. PAGE 54 B1103 LEGIS
FINAN

B59

JENNINGS W.I.,CABINET GOVERNMENT (3RD ED.). UK DELIB/GP
POL/PAR CHIEF BUDGET ADMIN CHOOSE GP/REL 20. NAT/G
PAGE 56 B1137 CONSTN
OP/RES

B59

LOEWENSTEIN K.,VERFASSUNGSRECHT UND CONSTN
VERFASSUNGSPRAXIS DER VEREINIGTEN STAATEN. USA+45 POL/PAR
USA-45 COLONIAL CT/SYS GP/REL RACE/REL ORD/FREE EX/STRUC
...JURID 18/20 SUPREME/CT CONGRESS PRESIDENT NAT/G
BILL/RIGHT CIVIL/LIB. PAGE 66 B1337

B59

MILLETT J.D.,GOVERNMENT AND PUBLIC ADMINISTRATION; ADMIN
THE QUEST FOR RESPONSIBLE PERFORMANCE. USA+45 NAT/G PWR
DELIB/GP LEGIS CT/SYS EXEC...DECISION MGT. PAGE 73 CONSTN
B1483 ROLE

B59

SPIRO H.J.,GOVERNMENT BY CONSTITUTIONS: THE NAT/G
POLITICAL SYSTEMS OF DEMOCRACY. CANADA EUR+WWI FUT CONSTN
USA+45 WOR+45 WOR-45 LEGIS TOP/EX LEGIT ADMIN
CT/SYS ORD/FREE PWR...TREND TOT/POP VAL/FREE 20.
PAGE 99 B2008

S59

BAILEY S.D.,"THE FUTURE COMPOSITION OF THE INT/ORG
TRUSTEESHIP COUNCIL." FUT WOR+45 CONSTN VOL/ASSN NAT/LISM
ADMIN ATTIT PWR...OBS TREND CON/ANAL VAL/FREE UN SOVEREIGN
20. PAGE 8 B0161

B60

JUNZ A.J., PRESENT TRENDS IN AMERICAN NATIONAL POL/PAR
GOVERNMENT. LEGIS DIPLOM ADMIN CT/SYS ORD/FREE CHOOSE
...CONCPT ANTHOL 20 CONGRESS PRESIDENT SUPREME/CT. CONSTN
PAGE 2 B0048 NAT/G

B60

ANDRIOT J.L.,GUIDE TO POPULAR GOVERNMENT BIBLIOG/A
PUBLICATIONS. USA+45 CONSTN ADMIN 20. PAGE 5 B0106 PRESS
NAT/G

B60

AYEARST M.,THE BRITISH WEST INDIES: THE SEARCH FOR CONSTN
SELF-GOVERNMENT. FUT WEST/IND LOC/G POL/PAR COLONIAL
EX/STRUC LEGIS CHOOSE FEDERAL...NAT/COMP BIBLIOG REPRESENT
17/20. PAGE 7 B0152 NAT/G

B60

EASTON S.C.,THE TWILIGHT OF EUROPEAN COLONIALISM. FINAN
AFR S/ASIA CONSTN SOCIETY STRUCT ECO/UNDEV INDUS ADMIN
NAT/G FORCES ECO/TAC COLONIAL CT/SYS ATTIT KNOWL
ORD/FREE PWR...SOCIALIST TIME/SEQ TREND CON/ANAL
20. PAGE 32 B0645

B60

HANBURY H.G.,ENGLISH COURTS OF LAW. UK EX/STRUC JURID
LEGIS CRIME ROLE 12/20 COMMON/LAW ENGLSH/LAW. CT/SYS
PAGE 46 B0936 CONSTN
GOV/REL

B60

HAYEK F.A.,THE CONSTITUTION OF LIBERTY. UNIV LAW ORD/FREE
CONSTN WORKER TAX EDU/PROP ADMIN CT/SYS COERCE CHOOSE
DISCRIM...IDEA/COMP 20. PAGE 48 B0974 NAT/G
CONCPT

B60

HAYNES G.H.,THE SENATE OF THE UNITED STATES: ITS LEGIS
HISTORY AND PRACTICE. CONSTN EX/STRUC TOP/EX CONFER DELIB/GP
DEBATE LEAD LOBBY PARL/PROC CHOOSE PWR SENATE
CONGRESS. PAGE 48 B0977

B60

MATTOD P.K.,A STUDY OF LOCAL SELF GOVERNMENT IN MUNIC
URBAN INDIA. INDIA FINAN DELIB/GP LEGIS BUDGET TAX CONSTN
SOVEREIGN...MGT GP/COMP 20. PAGE 71 B1432 LOC/G
ADMIN

B60

MUNRO L.,UNITED NATIONS, HOPE FOR A DIVIDED WORLD. INT/ORG
FUT WOR+45 CONSTN DELIB/GP CREATE TEC/DEV DIPLOM ROUTINE
EDU/PROP LEGIT PEACE ATTIT HEALTH ORD/FREE PWR
...CONCPT TREND UN VAL/FREE 20. PAGE 76 B1540

                                                                                                    LOC/G
                                                            B60   B61
PHILLIPS J.C.,MUNICIPAL GOVERNMENT AND   MUNIC   SHARP W.R.,FIELD ADMINISTRATION IN THE UNITED   INT/ORG
ADMINISTRATION IN AMERICA. USA+45 LAW CONSTN FINAN GOV/REL NATION SYSTEM: THE CONDUCT OF INTERNATIONAL   CONSULT
FORCES PLAN RECEIVE OWN ORD/FREE 20 CIVIL/LIB.   LOC/G   ECONOMIC AND SOCIAL PROGRAMS. FUT WOR+45 CONSTN
PAGE 83 B1669   ADMIN   SOCIETY ECO/UNDEV R+D DELIB/GP ACT/RES PLAN TEC/DEV
                                                            EDU/PROP EXEC ROUTINE HEALTH WEALTH...HUM CONCPT
                                                            B60   CHARTS METH ILO UNESCO VAL/FREE UN 20. PAGE 96
SMITH M.G.,GOVERNMENT IN ZAZZAU 1800-1950. NIGERIA REGION   B1939
UK CULTURE SOCIETY LOC/G ADMIN COLONIAL   CONSTN   B61
...METH/CNCPT NEW/IDEA METH 19/20. PAGE 98 B1983 KIN   WARD R.E.,JAPANESE POLITICAL SCIENCE: A GUIDE TO   BIBLIOG/A
                                                 ECO/UNDEV JAPANESE REFERENCE AND RESEARCH MATERIALS (2ND   PHIL/SCI
                                                            B60   ED.). LAW CONSTN STRATA NAT/G POL/PAR DELIB/GP
SOUTH AFRICAN CONGRESS OF DEM,FACE THE FUTURE.   RACE/REL   LEGIS ADMIN CHOOSE GP/REL...INT/LAW 19/20 CHINJAP.
SOUTH/AFR ELITES LEGIS ADMIN REGION COERCE PEACE DISCRIM   PAGE 113 B2290
ATTIT 20. PAGE 99 B1999   CONSTN   B61
                                                 NAT/G   WEST F.J.,POLITICAL ADVANCEMENT IN THE SOUTH   S/ASIA
                                                            B60   PACIFIC. CONSTN CULTURE POL/PAR LEGIS DOMIN ADMIN LOC/G
US SENATE COMM ON JUDICIARY,FEDERAL ADMINISTRATIVE PARL/PROC CHOOSE SOVEREIGN VAL/FREE 20 FIJI TAHITI SAMOA.   COLONIAL
PROCEDURE. USA+45 CONSTN NAT/G PROB/SOLV CONFER   LEGIS   PAGE 115 B2325
GOV/REL...JURID INT 20 SENATE. PAGE 110 B2226   ADMIN   B61
                                                 LAW   WILLSON F.M.G.,ADMINISTRATORS IN ACTION. UK MARKET ADMIN
                                                            B60   TEC/DEV PARL/PROC 20. PAGE 117 B2358   NAT/G
US SENATE COMM ON JUDICIARY,ADMINISTRATIVE   PARL/PROC   CONSTN
PROCEDURE LEGISLATION. USA+45 CONSTN NAT/G   LEGIS   L61
PROB/SOLV CONFER ROUTINE GOV/REL...INT 20 SENATE. ADMIN   GERWIG R.,"PUBLIC AUTHORITIES IN THE UNITED   LOC/G
PAGE 110 B2227   JURID   STATES." LAW CONSTN PROVS TAX ADMIN FEDERAL.   MUNIC
                                                            B60   PAGE 39 B0793   GOV/REL
WHEARE K.C.,THE CONSTITUTIONAL STRUCTURE OF THE CONSTN   PWR
COMMONWEALTH. UK EX/STRUC DIPLOM DOMIN ADMIN   INT/ORG   S61
COLONIAL CONTROL LEAD INGP/REL SUPEGO 20 CMN/WLTH. VOL/ASSN ALGER C.F.,"NON-RESOLUTION CONSEQUENCES OF THE   INT/ORG
PAGE 115 B2330   SOVEREIGN UNITED NATIONS AND THEIR EFFECT ON INTERNATIONAL DRIVE
                                                            L60   CONFLICT." WOR+45 CONSTN ECO/DEV NAT/G CONSULT   BAL/PWR
DEAN A.W.,"SECOND GENEVA CONFERENCE OF THE LAW OF INT/ORG   DELIB/GP TOP/EX ACT/RES PLAN DIPLOM EDU/PROP
THE SEA: THE FIGHT FOR FREEDOM OF THE SEAS." FUT JURID   ROUTINE ATTIT ALL/VALS...INT/LAW TOT/POP UN 20.
USA+45 USSR WOR+45 WOR-45 SEA CONSTN STRUCT PLAN INT/LAW   PAGE 4 B0075
INT/TRADE ADJUD ADMIN ORD/FREE...DECISION RECORD   S61
TREND GEN/LAWS 20 TREATY. PAGE 28 B0564   JACKSON E.,"CONSTITUTIONAL DEVELOPMENTS OF THE   INT/ORG
                                                            S60   UNITED NATIONS: THE GROWTH OF ITS EXECUTIVE   EXEC
NELSON R.H.,"LEGISLATIVE PARTICIPATION IN THE   LEGIS   CAPACITY." FUT WOR+45 CONSTN STRUCT ACT/RES PLAN
TREATY AND AGREEMENT MAKING PROCESS." CONSTN   PEACE   ALL/VALS...NEW/IDEA OBS COLD/WAR UN 20. PAGE 55
POL/PAR PLAN EXEC PWR FAO UN CONGRESS. PAGE 78   DECISION   B1106
B1569   DIPLOM   S61
                                                            B61   VIRALLY M.,"VERS UNE REFORME DU SECRETARIAT DES INT/ORG
BAINS J.S.,STUDIES IN POLITICAL SCIENCE. INDIA   DIPLOM   NATIONS UNIES." FUT WOR+45 CONSTN ECO/DEV TOP/EX   INTELL
WOR+45 WOR-45 CONSTN BAL/PWR ADJUD ADMIN PARL/PROC INT/LAW BAL/PWR ADMIN ALL/VALS...CONCPT BIOG UN VAL/FREE   DIPLOM
SOVEREIGN...SOC METH/COMP ANTHOL 17/20 UN. PAGE 8 NAT/G   20. PAGE 112 B2264
B0165   B62
                                                            B61   ANDREWS W.G.,FRENCH POLITICS AND ALGERIA: THE   GOV/COMP
BARNES W.,THE FOREIGN SERVICE OF THE UNITED STATES. NAT/G   PROCESS OF POLICY FORMATION 1954-1962. ALGERIA   EXEC
USA+45 USA-45 CONSTN INT/ORG POL/PAR CONSULT   MGT   FRANCE CONSTN ELITES POL/PAR CHIEF DELIB/GP LEGIS COLONIAL
DELIB/GP LEGIS DOMIN EDU/PROP EXEC ATTIT RIGID/FLEX DIPLOM DIPLOM PRESS CHOOSE 20. PAGE 5 B0105
ORD/FREE PWR...POLICY CONCPT STAT OBS RECORD BIOG   B62
TIME/SEQ TREND. PAGE 9 B0188   DELANY V.T.H.,THE ADMINISTRATION OF JUSTICE IN   ADMIN
                                                            B61   IRELAND. IRELAND CONSTN FINAN JUDGE COLONIAL CRIME JURID
DRAGNICH A.N.,MAJOR EUROPEAN GOVERNMENTS. FRANCE NAT/G   ...CRIMLGY 19/20. PAGE 28 B0571   CT/SYS
GERMANY/W UK USSR LOC/G EX/STRUC CT/SYS PARL/PROC LEGIS   ADJUD
ATTIT MARXISM...JURID MGT NAT/COMP 19/20. PAGE 30 CONSTN   B62
B0615   POL/PAR   FARBER W.O.,GOVERNMENT OF SOUTH DAKOTA. USA+45   PROVS
                                                            B61   DIST/IND IND/PAR CHIEF EX/STRUC LEGIS ECO/TAC GIVE LOC/G
DRURY J.W.,THE GOVERNMENT OF KANSAS. USA+45 AGRI PROVS   EDU/PROP CT/SYS PARTIC...T 20 SOUTH/DAK GOVERNOR. ADMIN
INDUS CHIEF LEGIS WORKER PLAN BUDGET GIVE CT/SYS CONSTN   PAGE 35 B0704   CONSTN
GOV/REL...T 20 KANSAS GOVERNOR CITY/MGT. PAGE 31 ADMIN   B62
B0621   LOC/G   INGHAM K.,A HISTORY OF EAST AFRICA. NAT/G DIPLOM   AFR
                                                            B61   ADMIN WAR NAT/LISM...SOC BIOG BIBLIOG. PAGE 54   CONSTN
GRIFFITH E.S.,CONGRESS: ITS CONTEMPORARY ROLE.   PARL/PROC B1085   COLONIAL
CONSTN POL/PAR CHIEF PLAN BUDGET DIPLOM CONFER   EX/STRUC   B62
ADMIN LOBBY...DECISION CONGRESS. PAGE 43 B0878   TOP/EX   INSTITUTE JUDICIAL ADMIN,JUDGES: THEIR TEMPORARY   NAT/G
                                                 LEGIS   APPOINTMENT, ASSIGNMENT AND TRANSFER: SURVEY OF FED LOC/G
                                                            B61   AND STATE CONSTN'S STATUTES. ROLES OF CT. USA+45 JUDGE
HAMILTON A.,THE FEDERALIST. USA-45 NAT/G VOL/ASSN EX/STRUC CONSTN PROVS CT/SYS GOV/REL PWR JURID. PAGE 54   ADMIN
LEGIS TOP/EX EDU/PROP LEGIT CHOOSE ATTIT RIGID/FLEX CONSTN B1090
ORD/FREE PWR...MAJORIT JURID CONCPT ANTHOL. PAGE 46   B62
B0931   MORE S.S.,REMODELLING OF DEMOCRACY FOR AFRO-ASIAN ORD/FREE
                                                            B61   NATIONS. AFR INDIA S/ASIA SOUTH/AFR CONSTN EX/STRUC ECO/UNDEV
NARAIN J.P.,SWARAJ FOR THE PEOPLE. INDIA CONSTN NAT/G   COLONIAL CHOOSE TOTALISM SOVEREIGN NEW/LIB SOCISM ADMIN
LOC/G MUNIC POL/PAR CHOOSE REPRESENT EFFICIENCY ORD/FREE   ...SOC/WK 20. PAGE 75 B1520   LEGIS
ATTIT PWR SOVEREIGN 20. PAGE 77 B1553   EDU/PROP   B62
                                                 EX/STRUC   NICHOLAS H.G.,THE UNITED NATIONS AS A POLITICAL   INT/ORG
                                                            B61   INSTITUTION. WOR+45 CONSTN EX/STRUC ACT/RES LEGIT ROUTINE
PEASLEE A.J.,INTERNATIONAL GOVERNMENT   INT/ORG   PERCEPT KNOWL PWR...CONCPT TIME/SEQ CON/ANAL
ORGANIZATIONS, CONSTITUTIONAL DOCUMENTS. WOR+45 STRUCT   ORG/CHARTS UN 20. PAGE 78 B1580
WOR-45 CONSTN VOL/ASSN DELIB/GP EX/STRUC ROUTINE   B62
KNOWL TOT/POP 20. PAGE 82 B1650   OLLE-LAPRUNE J.,LA STABILITE DES MINISTRES SOUS LA LEGIS
                                                            B61   TROISIEME REPUBLIQUE, 1879-1940. FRANCE CONSTN   NAT/G
PUGET H.,ESSAI DE BIBLIOGRAPHIE DES PRINCIPAUX   BIBLIOG   POL/PAR LEAD WAR INGP/REL RIGID/FLEX PWR...POLICY ADMIN
OUVRAGES DE DROIT PUBLIC... QUI ONT PARU HORS DE MGT   CHARTS 19/20. PAGE 79 B1606   PERSON
FRANCE DE 1945 A 1958. EUR+WWI USA+45 CONSTN LOC/G ADMIN   B62
...METH 20. PAGE 85 B1719   LAW   PHILLIPS O.H.,CONSTITUTIONAL AND ADMINISTRATIVE LAW JURID
                                                            B61   (3RD ED.). UK INT/ORG LOC/G CHIEF EX/STRUC LEGIS ADMIN
RAO K.V.,PARLIAMENTARY DEMOCRACY OF INDIA. INDIA CONSTN   BAL/PWR ADJUD COLONIAL CT/SYS PWR...CHARTS 20.   CONSTN
EX/STRUC TOP/EX COLONIAL CT/SYS PARL/PROC ORD/FREE ADJUD   PAGE 83 B1670   NAT/G
...POLICY CONCPT TREND 20 PARLIAMENT. PAGE 86 B1733 NAT/G   B62
                                                 FEDERAL   SCHULMAN S.,TOWARD JUDICIAL REFORM IN PENNSYLVANIA: CT/SYS
                                                            B61   A STUDY IN COURT REORGANIZATION. USA+45 CONSTN   ACT/RES
ROMANO F.,CIVIL SERVICE AND PUBLIC EMPLOYEE LAW IN ADMIN   JUDGE PLAN ADMIN LOBBY SANCTION PRIVIL PWR...JURID PROB/SOLV
NEW JERSEY. CONSTN MUNIC WORKER GIVE PAY CHOOSE PROVS
UTIL 20. PAGE 90 B1816   ADJUD

20 PENNSYLVAN. PAGE 94 B1905

B62

US ADVISORY COMN INTERGOV REL,STATE CONSTITUTIONAL AND STATUTORY RESTRICTIONS UPON THE STRUCTURAL, FUNCTIONAL, AND PERSONAL POWERS OF LOCAL GOV'T. EX/STRUC ACT/RES DOMIN GOV/REL PWR...POLICY DECISION 17/20. PAGE 108 B2172
LOC/G CONSTN PROVS LAW

L62

BAILEY S.D.,"THE TROIKA AND THE FUTURE OF THE UN." CONSTN CREATE LEGIT EXEC CHOOSE ORD/FREE PWR ...CONCPT NEW/IDEA UN COLD/WAR 20. PAGE 8 B0163
FUT INT/ORG USSR

L62

MALINOWSKI W.R.,"CENTRALIZATION AND DE-CENTRALIZATION IN THE UNITED NATIONS' ECONOMIC AND SOCIAL ACTIVITIES." WOR+45 CONSTN ECO/UNDEV INT/ORG VOL/ASSN DELIB/GP ECO/TAC EDU/PROP ADMIN RIGID/FLEX ...OBS CHARTS UNESCO UN EEC OAS OEEC 20. PAGE 69 B1385
CREATE GEN/LAWS

S62

MURACCIOLE L.,"LES CONSTITUTIONS DES ETATS AFRICAINS D'EXPRESSION FRANCAISE: LA CONSTITUTION DU 16 AVRIL 1962 DE LA REPUBLIQUE DU" AFR CHAD CHIEF LEGIS LEGIT COLONIAL EXEC ROUTINE ORD/FREE SOVEREIGN...SOC CONCPT 20. PAGE 76 B1541
NAT/G CONSTN

C62

MORGAN G.G.,"SOVIET ADMINISTRATIVE LEGALITY: THE ROLE OF THE ATTORNEY GENERAL'S OFFICE." COM USSR CONTROL ROUTINE...CONCPT BIBLIOG 18/20. PAGE 75 B1522
LAW CONSTN LEGIS ADMIN

B63

ADRIAN C.R.,GOVERNING OVER FIFTY STATES AND THEIR COMMUNITIES. USA+45 CONSTN FINAN MUNIC NAT/G POL/PAR EX/STRUC LEGIS ADMIN CONTROL CT/SYS ...CHARTS 20. PAGE 3 B0061
PROVS LOC/G GOV/REL GOV/COMP

B63

BADI J.,THE GOVERNMENT OF THE STATE OF ISRAEL: A CRITICAL ACCOUNT OF ITS PARLIAMENT, EXECUTIVE, AND JUDICIARY. ISRAEL ECO/DEV CHIEF DELIB/GP LEGIS DIPLOM CT/SYS INGP/REL PEACE ORD/FREE...BIBLIOG 20 PARLIAMENT ARABS MIGRATION. PAGE 8 B0157
NAT/G CONSTN EX/STRUC POL/PAR

B63

BOWETT D.W.,THE LAW OF INTERNATIONAL INSTITUTIONS. WOR+45 WOR-45 CONSTN DELIB/GP EX/STRUC JUDGE EDU/PROP LEGIT CT/SYS EXEC ROUTINE RIGID/FLEX ORD/FREE PWR...JURID CONCPT ORG/CHARTS GEN/METH LEAGUE/NAT OAS OEEC 20 UN. PAGE 14 B0286
INT/ORG ADJUD DIPLOM

B63

BROGAN D.W.,POLITICAL PATTERNS IN TODAY'S WORLD. FRANCE USA+45 USSR WOR+45 CONSTN STRUCT PLAN DIPLOM ADMIN LEAD ROLE SUPEGO...PHIL/SCI 20. PAGE 15 B0313
NAT/COMP NEW/LIB COM TOTALISM

B63

BURRUS B.R.,ADMINSTRATIVE LAW AND LOCAL GOVERNMENT. USA+45 PROVS LEGIS LICENSE ADJUD ORD/FREE 20. PAGE 17 B0356
EX/STRUC LOC/G JURID CONSTN

B63

CORLEY R.N.,THE LEGAL ENVIRONMENT OF BUSINESS. CONSTN LEGIS TAX ADMIN CT/SYS DISCRIM ATTIT PWR ...TREND 18/20. PAGE 23 B0477
NAT/G INDUS JURID DECISION

B63

DEBRAY P.,LE PORTUGAL ENTRE DEUX REVOLUTIONS. EUR+WWI PORTUGAL CONSTN LEGIT ADMIN ATTIT ALL/VALS ...DECISION CONCPT 20 SALAZAR/A. PAGE 28 B0567
NAT/G DELIB/GP TOP/EX

B63

GOURNAY B.,PUBLIC ADMINISTRATION. FRANCE LAW CONSTN AGRI FINAN LABOR SCHOOL EX/STRUC CHOOSE...MGT METH/COMP 20. PAGE 42 B0846
BIBLIOG/A ADMIN NAT/G LOC/G

B63

GRANT D.R.,STATE AND LOCAL GOVERNMENT IN AMERICA. USA+45 FINAN LOC/G MUNIC EX/STRUC FORCES EDU/PROP ADMIN CHOOSE FEDERAL ATTIT...JURID 20. PAGE 42 B0853
PROVS POL/PAR LEGIS CONSTN

B63

GRIFFITH J.A.G.,PRINCIPLES OF ADMINISTRATIVE LAW (3RD ED.). UK CONSTN EX/STRUC LEGIS ADJUD CONTROL CT/SYS PWR...CHARTS 20. PAGE 43 B0879
JURID ADMIN NAT/G BAL/PWR

B63

KLESMENT J.,LEGAL SOURCES AND BIBLIOGRAPHY OF THE BALTIC STATES (ESTONIA, LATVIA, LITHUANIA). COM ESTONIA LATVIA LITHUANIA LAW FINAN ADJUD CT/SYS REGION CENTRAL MARXISM 19/20. PAGE 60 B1218
BIBLIOG/A JURID CONSTN ADMIN

B63

KULZ H.R.,STAATSBURGER UND STAATSGEWALT (2 VOLS.). GERMANY SWITZERLND UK USSR CONSTN DELIB/GP TARIFFS TAX...JURID 20. PAGE 61 B1242
ADMIN ADJUD CT/SYS NAT/COMP

B63

LOCKARD D.,THE POLITICS OF STATE AND LOCAL GOVERNMENT. USA+45 CONSTN EX/STRUC LEGIS CT/SYS FEDERAL...CHARTS BIBLIOG 20. PAGE 66 B1334
LOC/G PROVS OP/RES ADMIN

B63

MAYNE R.,THE COMMUNITY OF EUROPE. UK CONSTN NAT/G CONSULT DELIB/GP CREATE PLAN ECO/TAC LEGIT ADMIN ROUTINE ORD/FREE PWR WEALTH...CONCPT TIME/SEQ EEC EURATOM 20. PAGE 71 B1436
EUR+WWI INT/ORG REGION

B63

PLISCHKE E.,GOVERNMENT AND POLITICS OF CONTEMPORARY BERLIN. GERMANY LAW CONSTN POL/PAR LEGIS WAR CHOOSE REPRESENT GOV/REL...CHARTS BIBLIOG 20 BERLIN. PAGE 83 B1683
MUNIC LOC/G POLICY ADMIN

B63

RICHARDSON H.G.,THE ADMINISTRATION OF IRELAND 1172-1377. IRELAND CONSTN EX/STRUC LEGIS JUDGE CT/SYS PARL/PROC...CHARTS BIBLIOG 12/14. PAGE 88 B1775
ADMIN NAT/G PWR

B63

ROBERT J.,LA MONARCHIE MAROCAINE. MOROCCO LABOR MUNIC POL/PAR EX/STRUC ORD/FREE PWR...JURID TREND T 20. PAGE 89 B1793
CHIEF CONSERVE ADMIN CONSTN

B63

ROBINSON K.,ESSAYS IN IMPERIAL GOVERNMENT. CAMEROON NIGERIA UK CONSTN LOC/G LEGIS ADMIN GOV/REL PWR ...POLICY ANTHOL BIBLIOG 17/20 PURHAM/M. PAGE 89 B1803
COLONIAL AFR DOMIN

B63

US CONGRESS: SENATE,HEARINGS OF THE COMMITTEE ON THE JUDICIARY. USA+45 CONSTN NAT/G ADMIN GOV/REL 20 CONGRESS. PAGE 108 B2179
LEGIS LAW ORD/FREE DELIB/GP

B63

US SENATE COMM ON JUDICIARY,ADMINISTRATIVE CONFERENCE OF THE UNITED STATES. USA+45 CONSTN NAT/G PROB/SOLV CONFER GOV/REL...INT 20 SENATE. PAGE 110 B2230
PARL/PROC JURID ADMIN LEGIS

B63

WADE H.W.R.,TOWARDS ADMINISTRATIVE JUSTICE. UK USA+45 CONSTN CONSULT PROB/SOLV CT/SYS PARL/PROC ...POLICY JURID METH/COMP 20 ENGLSH/LAW. PAGE 112 B2270
ADJUD IDEA/COMP ADMIN

B63

WALKER A.A.,OFFICIAL PUBLICATIONS OF SIERRA LEONE AND GAMBIA. GAMBIA SIER/LEONE UK LAW CONSTN LEGIS PLAN BUDGET DIPLOM...SOC SAMP CON/ANAL 20. PAGE 113 B2278
BIBLIOG NAT/G COLONIAL ADMIN

B63

WEINER M.,POLITICAL CHANGE IN SOUTH ASIA. CEYLON INDIA PAKISTAN S/ASIA CULTURE ELITES ECO/UNDEV EX/STRUC ADMIN CONTROL CHOOSE CONSERVE...GOV/COMP ANTHOL 20. PAGE 115 B2315
NAT/G CONSTN TEC/DEV

B63

WOLL P.,AMERICAN BUREAUCRACY. USA+45 USA-45 CONSTN NAT/G ADJUD PWR OBJECTIVE...MGT GP/COMP. PAGE 118 B2372
LEGIS EX/STRUC ADMIN GP/REL

S63

ANTHON C.G.,"THE END OF THE ADENAUER ERA." EUR+WWI GERMANY/W CONSTN EX/STRUC CREATE DIPLOM LEGIT ATTIT PERSON ALL/VALS...RECORD 20 ADENAUER/K. PAGE 6 B0113
NAT/G TOP/EX BAL/PWR GERMANY

S63

BECHHOEFER B.G.,"UNITED NATIONS PROCEDURES IN CASE OF VIOLATIONS OF DISARMAMENT AGREEMENTS." COM USA+45 USSR LAW CONSTN NAT/G EX/STRUC FORCES LEGIS BAL/PWR EDU/PROP CT/SYS ARMS/CONT ORD/FREE PWR ...POLICY STERTYP UN VAL/FREE 20. PAGE 10 B0204
INT/ORG DELIB/GP

S63

RUSTOW D.A.,"THE MILITARY IN MIDDLE EASTERN SOCIETY AND POLITICS." FUT ISLAM CONSTN SOCIETY FACE/GP NAT/G POL/PAR PROF/ORG CONSULT DOMIN ADMIN EXEC REGION COERCE NAT/LISM ATTIT DRIVE PERSON ORD/FREE PWR...POLICY CONCPT OBS STERTYP 20. PAGE 92 B1860
FORCES ELITES

B64

ANDREN N.,GOVERNMENT AND POLITICS IN THE NORDIC COUNTRIES: DENMARK, FINLAND, ICELAND, NORWAY, SWEDEN. DENMARK FINLAND ICELAND NORWAY SWEDEN POL/PAR CHIEF LEGIS ADMIN REGION REPRESENT ATTIT CONSERVE...CHARTS BIBLIOG/A 20. PAGE 5 B0102
CONSTN NAT/G CULTURE GOV/COMP

B64

APTER D.E.,IDEOLOGY AND DISCONTENT. FUT WOR+45 CONSTN CULTURE INTELL SOCIETY STRUCT INT/ORG NAT/G DELIB/GP LEGIS CREATE PLAN TEC/DEV EDU/PROP EXEC PERCEPT PERSON RIGID/FLEX ALL/VALS...POLICY TOT/POP. PAGE 6 B0122
ACT/RES ATTIT

B64

CONNECTICUT U INST PUBLIC SERV,SUMMARY OF CHARTER PROVISIONS IN CONNECTICUT LOCAL GOVERNMENT (PAMPHLET). USA+45 DELIB/GP LEGIS TOP/EX CHOOSE REPRESENT 20 CONNECTICT CITY/MGT MAYOR. PAGE 23 B0462
CONSTN MUNIC LOC/G EX/STRUC

B64

ENDACOTT G.B.,GOVERNMENT AND PEOPLE IN HONG KONG 1841-1962: A CONSTITUTIONAL HISTORY. UK LEGIS ADJUD REPRESENT ATTIT 19/20 HONG/KONG. PAGE 33 B0674
CONSTN COLONIAL CONTROL ADMIN

B64
FORBES A.H.,CURRENT RESEARCH IN BRITISH STUDIES. UK BIBLIOG
CONSTN CULTURE POL/PAR SECT DIPLOM ADMIN...JURID PERSON
BIOG WORSHIP 20. PAGE 36 B0736 NAT/G
PARL/PROC

B64
GESELLSCHAFT RECHTSVERGLEICH,BIBLIOGRAPHIE DES BIBLIOG/A
DEUTSCHEN RECHTS (BIBLIOGRAPHY OF GERMAN LAW, JURID
TRANS. BY COURTLAND PETERSON). GERMANY FINAN INDUS CONSTN
LABOR SECT FORCES CT/SYS PARL/PROC CRIME...INT/LAW ADMIN
SOC NAT/COMP 20. PAGE 39 B0794

B64
GJUPANOVIC H.,LEGAL SOURCES AND BIBLIOGRAPHY OF BIBLIOG/A
YUGOSLAVIA. COM YUGOSLAVIA LAW LEGIS DIPLOM ADMIN JURID
PARL/PROC REGION CRIME CENTRAL 20. PAGE 40 B0807 CONSTN
ADJUD

B64
GOLDWIN R.A.,POLITICAL PARTIES. USA. USA+45 USA-45 POL/PAR
LOC/G ADMIN LEAD EFFICIENCY ATTIT PWR...POLICY STAT PARTIC
ANTHOL 18/20 CONGRESS. PAGE 40 B0818 NAT/G
CONSTN

B64
KAHNG T.J.,LAW, POLITICS, AND THE SECURITY COUNCIL* DELIB/GP
AN INQUIRY INTO THE HANDLING OF LEGAL QUESTIONS. ADJUD
LAW CONSTN NAT/G ACT/RES OP/RES CT/SYS TASK PWR ROUTINE
...INT/LAW BIBLIOG UN. PAGE 57 B1160

B64
KAPP E.,THE MERGER OF THE EXECUTIVES OF THE CENTRAL
EUROPEAN COMMUNITIES. LAW CONSTN STRUCT ACT/RES EX/STRUC
PLAN PROB/SOLV ADMIN REGION TASK...INT/LAW MGT ECSC
EEC. PAGE 58 B1170

B64
KARIEL H.S.,IN SEARCH OF AUTHORITY: TWENTIETH- CONSTN
CENTURY POLITICAL THOUGHT. WOR+45 WOR-45 NAT/G CONCPT
EX/STRUC TOTALISM DRIVE PWR...MGT PHIL/SCI GEN/LAWS ORD/FREE
19/20 NIETZSCH/F FREUD/S WEBER/MAX NIEBUHR/R IDEA/COMP
MARITAIN/J. PAGE 58 B1173

B64
MARSH D.C.,THE FUTURE OF THE WELFARE STATE. UK NEW/LIB
CONSTN NAT/G POL/PAR...POLICY WELF/ST 20. PAGE 69 ADMIN
B1404 CONCPT
INSPECT

B64
NEUSTADT R.,PRESIDENTIAL POWER. USA+45 CONSTN NAT/G TOP/EX
CHIEF LEGIS CREATE EDU/PROP LEGIT ADMIN EXEC COERCE SKILL
ATTIT PERSON RIGID/FLEX PWR CONGRESS 20 PRESIDENT
TRUMAN/HS EISNHWR/DD. PAGE 78 B1575

B64
O'HEARN P.J.T.,PEACE, ORDER AND GOOD GOVERNMENT; A NAT/G
NEW CONSTITUTION FOR CANADA. CANADA EX/STRUC LEGIS CONSTN
CT/SYS PARL/PROC...BIBLIOG 20. PAGE 79 B1600 LAW
CREATE

B64
RICHARDSON I.L.,BIBLIOGRAFIA BRASILEIRA DE BIBLIOG
ADMINISTRACAO PUBLICA E ASSUNTOS CORRELATOS. BRAZIL MGT
CONSTN FINAN LOC/G NAT/G POL/PAR PLAN DIPLOM ADMIN
RECEIVE ATTIT...METH 20. PAGE 88 B1776 LAW

B64
RIKER W.H.,FEDERALISM. WOR+45 WOR-45 CONSTN CHIEF FEDERAL
LEGIS ADMIN COLONIAL CONTROL CT/SYS PWR...BIBLIOG/A NAT/G
18/20. PAGE 88 B1787 ORD/FREE
CENTRAL

B64
ROCHE J.P.,THE PRESIDENCY. USA+45 USA-45 CONSTN EX/STRUC
NAT/G CHIEF BAL/PWR DIPLOM GP/REL 18/20 PRESIDENT. PWR
PAGE 90 B1810

B64
STOICOIU V.,LEGAL SOURCES AND BIBLIOGRAPHY OF BIBLIOG/A
ROMANIA. COM ROMANIA LAW FINAN POL/PAR LEGIS JUDGE JURID
ADJUD CT/SYS PARL/PROC MARXISM 20. PAGE 101 B2041 CONSTN
ADMIN

B64
THE BRITISH COUNCIL,PUBLIC ADMINISTRATION: A SELECT BIBLIOG
LIST OF BOOKS AND PERIODICALS. LAW CONSTN FINAN ADMIN
POL/PAR SCHOOL CHOOSE...HEAL MGT METH/COMP 19/20 LOC/G
CMN/WLTH. PAGE 104 B2094 INDUS

B64
TURNER H.A.,THE GOVERNMENT AND POLITICS OF PROVS
CALIFORNIA (2ND ED.). LAW FINAN MUNIC POL/PAR ADMIN
SCHOOL EX/STRUC LEGIS LOBBY CHOOSE...CHARTS T 20 LOC/G
CALIFORNIA. PAGE 106 B2138 CONSTN

B64
TURNER M.C.,LIBROS EN VENTA EN HISPANOAMERICA Y BIBLIOG
ESPANA. SPAIN LAW CONSTN CULTURE ADMIN LEAD...HUM L/A+17C
SOC 20. PAGE 106 B2139 NAT/G
DIPLOM

B64
UN PUB. INFORM. ORGAN.,EVERY MAN'S UNITED NATIONS. INT/ORG
UNIV WOR+45 CONSTN CULTURE SOCIETY ECO/DEV ROUTINE
ECO/UNDEV NAT/G ACT/RES PLAN ECO/TAC INT/TRADE
EDU/PROP LEGIT PEACE ATTIT ALL/VALS...POLICY HUM
INT/LAW CONCPT CHARTS UN TOT/POP 20. PAGE 106 B2150

B64
US SENATE COMM ON JUDICIARY,ADMINISTRATIVE PARL/PROC
PROCEDURE ACT. USA+45 CONSTN NAT/G PROB/SOLV CONFER LEGIS
GOV/REL PWR...INT 20 SENATE. PAGE 110 B2231 JURID

ADMIN
B64
VECCHIO G.D.,L'ETAT ET LE DROIT. ITALY CONSTN NAT/G
EX/STRUC LEGIS DIPLOM CT/SYS...JURID 20 UN. SOVEREIGN
PAGE 112 B2256 CONCPT
INT/LAW

B64
WHEARE K.C.,FEDERAL GOVERNMENT (4TH ED.). WOR+45 FEDERAL
WOR-45 POL/PAR LEGIS BAL/PWR CT/SYS...POLICY JURID CONSTN
CONCPT GOV/COMP 17/20. PAGE 116 B2331 EX/STRUC
NAT/COMP

L64
MILLIS W.,"THE DEMILITARIZED WORLD." COM USA+45 FUT
USSR WOR+45 CONSTN NAT/G EX/STRUC PLAN LEGIT ATTIT INT/ORG
DRIVE...CONCPT TIME/SEQ STERTYP TOT/POP COLD/WAR BAL/PWR
20. PAGE 74 B1486 PEACE

L64
WORLD PEACE FOUNDATION,"INTERNATIONAL INT/ORG
ORGANIZATIONS: SUMMARY OF ACTIVITIES." INDIA ROUTINE
PAKISTAN TURKEY WOR+45 CONSTN CONSULT EX/STRUC
ECO/TAC EDU/PROP LEGIT ORD/FREE...JURID SOC UN 20
CYPRESS. PAGE 118 B2375

S64
GALTUNG J.,"BALANCE OF POWER AND THE PROBLEM OF PWR
PERCEPTION. A LOGICAL ANALYSIS." WOR+45 CONSTN PSY
SOCIETY NAT/G DELIB/GP EX/STRUC LEGIS DOMIN ADMIN ARMS/CONT
COERCE DRIVE ORD/FREE...POLICY CONCPT OBS TREND WAR
GEN/LAWS. PAGE 38 B0778

S64
KHAN M.Z.,"THE PRESIDENT OF THE GENERAL ASSEMBLY." INT/ORG
WOR+45 CONSTN DELIB/GP EDU/PROP LEGIT ROUTINE PWR TOP/EX
RESPECT SKILL...DECISION SOC BIOG TREND UN 20.
PAGE 59 B1202

S64
SWEARER H.R.,"AFTER KHRUSHCHEV: WHAT NEXT." COM FUT EX/STRUC
USSR CONSTN ELITES NAT/G POL/PAR CHIEF DELIB/GP PWR
LEGIS DOMIN LEAD...RECORD TREND STERTYP GEN/METH
20. PAGE 102 B2058

C64
SCOTT R.E.,"MEXICAN GOVERNMENT IN TRANSITION (REV NAT/G
ED)" CULTURE STRUCT POL/PAR CHIEF ADMIN LOBBY REV L/A+17C
CHOOSE GP/REL DRIVE...BIBLIOG METH 20 MEXIC/AMER. ROUTINE
PAGE 95 B1920 CONSTN

B65
BANFIELD E.C.,BIG CITY POLITICS. USA+45 CONSTN METH/COMP
POL/PAR ADMIN LOBBY CHOOSE SUFF INGP/REL PWR...GEOG MUNIC
20. PAGE 9 B0179 STRUCT

B65
BOXER C.R.,PORTUGUESE SOCIETY IN THE TROPICS - THE MUNIC
MUNICIPAL COUNCILS OF GAO, MACAO, BAHIA, AND ADMIN
LUANDA, 1510-1800. EUR+WWI MOD/EUR PORTUGAL CONSTN COLONIAL
EX/STRUC DOMIN CONTROL ROUTINE REPRESENT PRIVIL DELIB/GP
...BIBLIOG/A 16/19 GENACCOUNT MACAO BAHIA LUANDA.
PAGE 14 B0290

B65
CHANDA A.,FEDERALISM IN INDIA. INDIA UK ELITES CONSTN
FINAN NAT/G POL/PAR EX/STRUC LEGIS DIPLOM TAX CENTRAL
GOV/REL POPULISM...POLICY 20. PAGE 20 B0402 FEDERAL

B65
CHEN T.H.,THE CHINESE COMMUNIST REGIME: A MARXISM
DOCUMENTARY STUDY (2 VOLS.). CHINA/COM LAW CONSTN POL/PAR
ELITES ECO/UNDEV LEGIS ECO/TAC ADMIN CONTROL PWR NAT/G
...SOC 20. PAGE 20 B0417

B65
COOPER F.E.,STATE ADMINISTRATIVE LAW (2 VOLS.). LAW JURID
LEGIS PLAN TAX ADJUD CT/SYS FEDERAL PWR...CONCPT CONSTN
20. PAGE 23 B0474 ADMIN
PROVS

B65
FEERICK J.D.,FROM FAILING HANDS: THE STUDY OF EX/STRUC
PRESIDENTIAL SUCCESSION. CONSTN NAT/G PROB/SOLV CHIEF
LEAD PARL/PROC MURDER CHOOSE...NEW/IDEA BIBLIOG 20 LAW
KENNEDY/JF JOHNSON/LB PRESIDENT PRE/US/AM LEGIS
VICE/PRES. PAGE 35 B0710

B65
FISCHER F.C.,THE GOVERNMENT OF MICHIGAN. USA+45 PROVS
NAT/G PUB/INST EX/STRUC LEGIS BUDGET GIVE EDU/PROP LOC/G
CT/SYS CHOOSE GOV/REL...T MICHIGAN. PAGE 36 B0723 ADMIN
CONSTN

B65
FRIEDMAN L.,SOUTHERN JUSTICE. USA+45 PUB/INST LEGIT ADJUD
ADMIN CT/SYS DISCRIM...DECISION ANTHOL 20 NEGRO LAW
SOUTH/US CIV/RIGHTS. PAGE 37 B0758 CONSTN
RACE/REL

B65
GOLEMBIEWSKI R.T.,MEN, MANAGEMENT, AND MORALITY; LG/CO
TOWARD A NEW ORGANIZATIONAL ETHIC. CONSTN EX/STRUC MGT
CREATE ADMIN CONTROL INGP/REL PERSON SUPEGO MORAL PROB/SOLV
PWR...GOV/COMP METH/COMP 20 BUREAUCRCY. PAGE 40
B0819

B65
INST INTL DES CIVILISATION DIF,THE CONSTITUTIONS CONSTN
AND ADMINISTRATIVE INSTITUTIONS OF THE NEW STATES. ADMIN
AFR ISLAM S/ASIA NAT/G POL/PAR DELIB/GP EX/STRUC ADJUD
CONFER EFFICIENCY NAT/LISM...JURID SOC 20. PAGE 54 ECO/UNDEV
B1088

KAAS L.,DIE GEISTLICHE GERICHTSBARKEIT DER
KATHOLISCHEN KIRCHE IN PREUSSEN (2 VOLS.). PRUSSIA
CONSTN NAT/G PROVS SECT ADJUD ADMIN ATTIT 16/20.
PAGE 57 B1158
JURID
CATHISM
GP/REL
CT/SYS

B65

NATIONAL BOOK CENTRE PAKISTAN,BOOKS ON PAKISTAN: A
BIBLIOGRAPHY. PAKISTAN CULTURE DIPLOM ADMIN ATTIT
...MAJORIT SOC CONCPT 20. PAGE 77 B1560
BIBLIOG
CONSTN
S/ASIA
NAT/G

B65

OLSON M. JR.,DROIT PUBLIC. FRANCE NAT/G LEGIS SUFF
GP/REL PRIVIL...TREND 18/20. PAGE 80 B1609
CONSTN
FINAN
ADMIN
ORD/FREE

B65

PAYNE J.L.,LABOR AND POLITICS IN PERU; THE SYSTEM
OF POLITICAL BARGAINING. PERU CONSTN VOL/ASSN
EX/STRUC LEAD PWR...CHARTS 20. PAGE 81 B1645
LABOR
POL/PAR
BARGAIN
GP/REL

B65

PYLEE M.V.,CONSTITUTIONAL GOVERNMENT IN INDIA (2ND
REV. ED.). INDIA POL/PAR EX/STRUC DIPLOM COLONIAL
CT/SYS PARL/PROC PRIVIL...JURID 16/20. PAGE 85
B1725
CONSTN
NAT/G
PROVS
FEDERAL

B65

ROWAT D.C.,THE OMBUDSMAN: CITIZEN'S DEFENDER.
DENMARK FINLAND NEW/ZEALND NORWAY SWEDEN CONSULT
PROB/SOLV FEEDBACK PARTIC GP/REL...SOC CONCPT
NEW/IDEA METH/COMP ANTHOL BIBLIOG 20. PAGE 91 B1840
INSPECT
CONSTN
NAT/G
ADMIN

B65

SHARMA S.A.,PARLIAMENTARY GOVERNMENT IN INDIA.
INDIA FINAN LOC/G PROVS DELIB/GP PLAN ADMIN CT/SYS
FEDERAL...JURID 20. PAGE 96 B1936
NAT/G
CONSTN
PARL/PROC
LEGIS

B65

STEINER K.,LOCAL GOVERNMENT IN JAPAN. CONSTN
CULTURE NAT/G ADMIN CHOOSE...SOC STAT 20 CHINJAP.
PAGE 100 B2030
LOC/G
SOCIETY
JURID
ORD/FREE

B65

VONGLAHN G.,LAW AMONG NATIONS: AN INTRODUCTION TO
PUBLIC INTERNATIONAL LAW. UNIV WOR+45 LAW INT/ORG
NAT/G LEGIT EXEC RIGID/FLEX...CONCPT TIME/SEQ
GEN/LAWS UN TOT/POP 20. PAGE 112 B2267
CONSTN
JURID
INT/LAW

B65

WARD W.E.,GOVERNMENT IN WEST AFRICA. WOR+45 POL/PAR
EX/STRUC PLAN PARTIC GP/REL SOVEREIGN 20 AFRICA/W.
PAGE 114 B2291
GOV/COMP
CONSTN
COLONIAL
ECO/UNDEV

L65

RUBIN A.P.,"UNITED STATES CONTEMPORARY PRACTICE
RELATING TO INTERNATIONAL LAW." USA+45 WOR+45
CONSTN INT/ORG NAT/G DELIB/GP EX/STRUC DIPLOM DOMIN
CT/SYS ROUTINE ORD/FREE...CONCPT COLD/WAR 20.
PAGE 91 B1848
LAW
LEGIT
INT/LAW

S65

RUBINSTEIN A.Z.,"YUGOSLAVIA'S OPENING SOCIETY." COM
USSR INTELL CONSTN NAT/G LEGIS TOP/EX LEGIT CT/SYS
RIGID/FLEX ALL/VALS SOCISM...HUM TIME/SEQ TREND 20.
PAGE 92 B1851
CONSTN
EX/STRUC
YUGOSLAVIA

B66

ADAMS J.C.,THE GOVERNMENT OF REPUBLICAN ITALY (2ND
ED.). ITALY LOC/G POL/PAR DELIB/GP LEGIS WORKER
ADMIN CT/SYS FASCISM...CHARTS BIBLIOG 20.
PARLIAMENT. PAGE 3 B0057
NAT/G
CHOOSE
EX/STRUC
CONSTN

B66

BRAIBANTI R.,RESEARCH ON THE BUREAUCRACY OF
PAKISTAN. PAKISTAN LAW CULTURE INTELL ACADEM LOC/G
SECT PRESS CT/SYS...LING CHARTS 20 BUREAUCRCY.
PAGE 15 B0299
HABITAT
NAT/G
ADMIN
CONSTN

B66

BURNS A.C.,PARLIAMENT AS AN EXPORT. WOR+45 CONSTN
BARGAIN DEBATE ROUTINE GOV/REL EFFICIENCY...ANTHOL
COMMONWLTH PARLIAMENT. PAGE 17 B0353
PARL/PROC
POL/PAR
CT/SYS
CHIEF

B66

CHAPMAN B.,THE PROFESSION OF GOVERNMENT: THE PUBLIC
SERVICE IN EUROPE. CONSTN NAT/G POL/PAR EX/STRUC
LEGIS TOP/EX PROB/SOLV DEBATE EXEC PARL/PROC PARTIC
20. PAGE 20 B0411
BIBLIOG
ADMIN
EUR+WWI
GOV/COMP

B66

DAHLBERG J.S.,THE NEW YORK BUREAU OF MUNICIPAL
RESEARCH: PIONEER IN GOVERNMENT ADMINISTRATION.
CONSTN R+D BUDGET EDU/PROP PARTIC REPRESENT
EFFICIENCY ORD/FREE...BIBLIOG METH 20 NEW/YORK
NIPA. PAGE 26 B0522
PROVS
MUNIC
DELIB/GP
ADMIN

B66

DAVIS J.A.,SOUTHERN AFRICA IN TRANSITION. SOUTH/AFR
USA+45 FINAN NAT/G DELIB/GP EDU/PROP ADMIN COLONIAL
REGION RACE/REL ATTIT SOVEREIGN...ANTHOL 20
RESOURCE/N. PAGE 26 B0538
AFR
ADJUST
CONSTN

B66

FINK M.,A SELECTIVE BIBLIOGRAPHY ON STATE
CONSTITUTIONAL REVISION (PAMPHLET). USA+45 FINAN
EX/STRUC LEGIS EDU/PROP ADMIN CT/SYS APPORT CHOOSE
BIBLIOG
PROVS
LOC/G

GOV/REL 20. PAGE 35 B0720
CONSTN

B66

GHOSH P.K.,THE CONSTITUTION OF INDIA: HOW IT HAS
BEEN FRAMED. INDIA LOC/G DELIB/GP EX/STRUC
PROB/SOLV BUDGET INT/TRADE CT/SYS CHOOSE...LING 20.
PAGE 39 B0795
CONSTN
NAT/G
LEGIS
FEDERAL

B66

GREENE L.E.,GOVERNMENT IN TENNESSEE (2ND ED.).
USA+45 DIST/IND INDUS POL/PAR EX/STRUC LEGIS PLAN
BUDGET GIVE CT/SYS...MGT T 20 TENNESSEE. PAGE 43
B0866
PROVS
LOC/G
CONSTN
ADMIN

B66

GROSS C.,A BIBLIOGRAPHY OF BRITISH MUNICIPAL
HISTORY (2ND ED.). UK LOC/G ADMIN 11/19. PAGE 44
B0888
BIBLIOG/A
MUNIC
CONSTN

B66

HIDAYATULLAH M.,DEMOCRACY IN INDIA AND THE JUDICIAL
PROCESS. INDIA EX/STRUC LEGIS LEAD GOV/REL ATTIT
ORD/FREE...MAJORIT CONCPT 20 NEHRU/J. PAGE 50 B1007
NAT/G
CT/SYS
CONSTN
JURID

B66

KAUNDA K.,ZAMBIA: INDEPENDENCE AND BEYOND: THE
SPEECHES OF KENNETH KAUNDA. AFR FUT ZAMBIA SOCIETY
ECO/UNDEV NAT/G PROB/SOLV ECO/TAC ADMIN RACE/REL
SOVEREIGN 20. PAGE 59 B1183
ORD/FREE
COLONIAL
CONSTN
LEAD

B66

NEUMANN R.G.,THE GOVERNMENT OF THE GERMAN FEDERAL
REPUBLIC. EUR+WWI GERMANY/W LOC/G EX/STRUC LEGIS
CT/SYS INGP/REL PWR...BIBLIOG 20 ADENAUER/K.
PAGE 78 B1573
NAT/G
POL/PAR
DIPLOM
CONSTN

B66

RAPHAEL J.S.,GOVERNMENTAL REGULATION OF BUSINESS.
USA+45 LAW CONSTN TAX ADJUD ADMIN EFFICIENCY PWR
20. PAGE 86 B1736
LG/CO
GOV/REL
CONTROL
ECO/DEV

B66

ROSS R.M.,STATE AND LOCAL GOVERNMENT AND
ADMINISTRATION. USA+45 CONSTN POL/PAR EX/STRUC
LEGIS BUDGET EDU/PROP CONTROL CT/SYS CHOOSE GOV/REL
T. PAGE 90 B1827
LOC/G
PROVS
MUNIC
ADMIN

B66

SCHMIDT K.M.,AMERICAN STATE AND LOCAL GOVERNMENT IN
ACTION. USA+45 CONSTN LOC/G POL/PAR CHIEF LEGIS
PROB/SOLV ADJUD LOBBY GOV/REL...DECISION ANTHOL 20
GOVERNOR MAYOR URBAN/RNWL. PAGE 94 B1896
PROVS
ADMIN
MUNIC
PLAN

B66

SPINELLI A.,THE EUROCRATS: CONFLICT AND CRISIS IN
THE EUROPEAN COMMUNITY (TRANS. BY C. GROVE HAINES).
EUR+WWI MARKET POL/PAR ECO/TAC PARL/PROC EEC OEEC
ECSC EURATOM. PAGE 99 B2007
INT/ORG
INGP/REL
CONSTN
ADMIN

B66

WASHINGTON S.H.,BIBLIOGRAPHY: LABOR-MANAGEMENT
RELATIONS ACT, 1947 AS AMENDED BY LABOR-MANAGEMENT
REPORTING AND DISCLOSURE ACT, 1959. USA+45 CONSTN
INDUS DELIB/GP LEGIS WORKER BARGAIN ECO/TAC ADJUD
GP/REL NEW/LIB...JURID CONGRESS. PAGE 114 B2298
BIBLIOG
LAW
LABOR
MGT

B66

WILSON G.,CASES AND MATERIALS ON CONSTITUTIONAL AND
ADMINISTRATIVE LAW. UK LAW NAT/G EX/STRUC LEGIS
BAL/PWR BUDGET DIPLOM ADJUD CONTROL CT/SYS GOV/REL
ORD/FREE 20 PARLIAMENT ENGLSH/LAW. PAGE 117 B2359
JURID
ADMIN
CONSTN
PWR

L66

MCAUSLAN J.P.W.,"CONSTITUTIONAL INNOVATION AND
POLITICAL STABILITY IN TANZANIA: A PRELIMINARY
ASSESSMENT." AFR TANZANIA ELITES CHIEF EX/STRUC
RIGID/FLEX PWR 20 PRESIDENT BUREAUCRCY. PAGE 71
B1440
CONSTN
NAT/G
EXEC
POL/PAR

S66

BURDETTE F.L.,"SELECTED ARTICLES AND DOCUMENTS ON
AMERICAN GOVERNMENT AND POLITICS." LAW LOC/G MUNIC
NAT/G POL/PAR PROVS LEGIS BAL/PWR ADMIN EXEC
REPRESENT MGT. PAGE 17 B0348
BIBLIOG
USA+45
JURID
CONSTN

S66

MATTHEWS D.G.,"PRELUDE-COUP D'ETAT-MILITARY
GOVERNMENT: A BIBLIOGRAPHICAL AND RESEARCH GUIDE TO
NIGERIAN POL AND GOVT, JAN, 1965-66." AFR NIGER LAW
CONSTN POL/PAR LEGIS CIVMIL/REL GOV/REL...STAT 20.
PAGE 71 B1430
BIBLIOG
NAT/G
ADMIN
CHOOSE

S66

POLSBY N.W.,"BOOKS IN THE FIELD: POLITICAL
SCIENCE." LAW CONSTN LOC/G NAT/G LEGIS ADJUD PWR 20
SUPREME/CT. PAGE 83 B1686
BIBLIOG/A
ATTIT
ADMIN
JURID

N66

BACHELDER G.L.,THE LITERATURE OF FEDERALISM: A
SELECTED BIBLIOGRAPHY (REV ED) (A PAMPHLET). USA+45
USA-45 WOR-45 LAW CONSTN PROVS ADMIN CT/SYS
GOV/REL ROLE...CONCPT 19/20. PAGE 8 B0155
BIBLIOG
FEDERAL
NAT/G
LOC/G

B67

BROWN L.N.,FRENCH ADMINISTRATIVE LAW. FRANCE UK
CONSTN NAT/G LEGIS DOMIN CONTROL EXEC PARL/PROC PWR
...JURID METH/COMP GEN/METH. PAGE 16 B0324
EX/STRUC
LAW
IDEA/COMP
CT/SYS

B67

BULPITT J.G.,PARTY POLITICS IN ENGLISH LOCAL
GOVERNMENT. UK CONSTN ACT/RES TAX CONTROL CHOOSE
POL/PAR
LOC/G

REPRESENT GOV/REL KNOWL 20. PAGE 17 B0344 ELITES EX/STRUC

B67
BUREAU GOVERNMENT RES AND SERV,COUNTY GOVERNMENT REORGANIZATION - A SELECTED ANNOTATED BIBLIOGRAPHY (PAPER). USA+45 USA-45 LAW CONSTN MUNIC PROVS EX/STRUC CREATE PLAN PROB/SOLV REPRESENT GOV/REL 20. PAGE 17 B0349 BIBLIOG/A APPORT LOC/G ADMIN

B67
CECIL L.,ALBERT BALLIN; BUSINESS AND POLITICS IN IMPERIAL GERMANY 1888-1918. GERMANY UK INT/TRADE LEAD WAR PERS/REL ADJUST PWR WEALTH...MGT BIBLIOG 19/20. PAGE 19 B0397 DIPLOM CONSTN ECO/DEV TOP/EX

B67
DOSSICK J.J.,DOCTORAL RESEARCH ON PUERTO RICO AND PUERTO RICANS. PUERT/RICO USA+45 USA-45 ADMIN 20. PAGE 30 B0609 BIBLIOG CONSTN POL/PAR DIPLOM

B67
GELLHORN W.,OMBUDSMEN AND OTHERS: CITIZENS' PROTECTORS IN NINE COUNTRIES. WOR+45 LAW CONSTN LEGIS INSPECT ADJUD ADMIN CONTROL CT/SYS CHOOSE PERS/REL...STAT CHARTS 20. PAGE 39 B0789 NAT/COMP REPRESENT INGP/REL PROB/SOLV

B67
ILLINOIS COMMISSION,IMPROVING THE STATE LEGISLATURE. USA+45 LAW CONSTN NAT/G PROB/SOLV EDU/PROP ADMIN TASK CHOOSE INGP/REL EFFICIENCY ILLINOIS. PAGE 53 B1077 PROVS LEGIS REPRESENT PLAN

B67
LEACH R.H.,GOVERNING THE AMERICAN NATION. FUT USA+45 USA-45 CONSTN POL/PAR PLAN ADJUD EXEC CONSEN CONGRESS PRESIDENT. PAGE 63 B1278 NAT/G LEGIS PWR

B67
LENG S.C.,JUSTICE IN COMMUNIST CHINA: A SURVEY OF THE JUDICIAL SYSTEM OF THE CHINESE PEOPLE'S REPUBLIC. CHINA/COM LAW CONSTN LOC/G NAT/G PROF/ORG CONSULT FORCES ADMIN CRIME ORD/FREE...BIBLIOG 20 MAO. PAGE 64 B1290 CT/SYS ADJUD JURID MARXISM

B67
MCCONNELL G.,THE MODERN PRESIDENCY. USA+45 CONSTN TOP/EX DOMIN EXEC CHOOSE PWR...MGT 20. PAGE 72 B1446 NAT/G CHIEF EX/STRUC

B67
NIVEN R.,NIGERIA. NIGERIA CONSTN INDUS EX/STRUC COLONIAL REV NAT/LISM...CHARTS 19/20. PAGE 78 B1584 NAT/G REGION CHOOSE GP/REL

B67
PRINCE C.E.,NEW JERSEY'S JEFFERSONIAN REPUBLICANS; THE GENESIS OF AN EARLY PARTY MACHINE (1789-1817). USA-45 LOC/G EDU/PROP PRESS CONTROL CHOOSE...CHARTS 18/19 NEW/JERSEY REPUBLICAN. PAGE 84 B1707 POL/PAR CONSTN ADMIN PROVS

B67
SABLE M.H.,A GUIDE TO LATIN AMERICAN STUDIES (2 VOLS). CONSTN FINAN INT/ORG LABOR MUNIC POL/PAR FORCES CAP/ISM FOR/AID ADMIN MARXISM SOCISM OAS. PAGE 92 B1861 BIBLIOG/A L/A+17C DIPLOM NAT/LISM

B67
SCHAEFER W.V.,THE SUSPECT AND SOCIETY: CRIMINAL PROCEDURE AND CONVERGING CONSTITUTIONAL DOCTRINES. USA+45 TEC/DEV LOBBY ROUTINE SANCTION...INT 20. PAGE 93 B1879 CRIME FORCES CONSTN JURID

B67
SKIDMORE T.E.,POLITICS IN BRAZIL 1930-1964. BRAZIL L/A+17C INDUS NAT/G PROB/SOLV ATTIT 20. PAGE 98 B1973 CONSTN ECO/TAC ADMIN

B67
WARREN S.,THE AMERICAN PRESIDENT. POL/PAR FORCES LEGIS DIPLOM ECO/TAC ADMIN EXEC PWR...ANTHOL 18/20 ROOSEVLT/F KENNEDY/JF JOHNSON/LB TRUMAN/HS WILSON/W. PAGE 114 B2297 CHIEF LEAD NAT/G CONSTN

B67
WATERS M.,THE UNITED NATIONS* INTERNATIONAL ORGANIZATION AND ADMINISTRATION. WOR+45 EX/STRUC FORCES DIPLOM LEAD REGION ARMS/CONT REPRESENT INGP/REL ROLE...METH/COMP ANTHOL 20 UN LEAGUE/NAT. PAGE 114 B2301 CONSTN INT/ORG ADMIN ADJUD

B67
WESTON P.B.,THE ADMINISTRATION OF JUSTICE. USA+45 CONSTN MUNIC NAT/G PROVS EX/STRUC JUDGE ADMIN CONTROL SANCTION ORD/FREE...CHARTS 20. PAGE 115 B2328 CRIME CT/SYS JURID ADJUD

L67
BERGER R.,"ADMINISTRATIVE ARBITRARINESS* A SEQUEL." USA+45 CONSTN ADJUD CT/SYS SANCTION INGP/REL ...POLICY JURID. PAGE 11 B0222 LAW LABOR BARGAIN ADMIN

L67
CAHIERS P.,"LE RECOURS EN CONSTATATION DE MANQUEMENTS DES ETATS MEMBRES DEVANT LA COUR DES COMMUNAUTES EUROPEENNES." LAW PROB/SOLV DIPLOM ADMIN CT/SYS SANCTION ATTIT...POLICY DECISION JURID ECSC EEC. PAGE 18 B0362 INT/ORG CONSTN ROUTINE ADJUD

L67
COHEN M.,"THE DEMISE OF UNEF." CONSTN DIPLOM ADMIN AGREE LEAD COERCE 20 UNEF U/THANT HAMMARSK/D. PAGE 22 B0445 INT/ORG FORCES PEACE POLICY

L67
GAINES J.E.,"THE YOUTH COURT CONCEPT AND ITS IMPLEMENTATION IN TOMPKINS COUNTY, NEW YORK." USA+45 LAW CONSTN JUDGE WORKER ADJUD ADMIN CHOOSE PERSON...JURID NEW/YORK. PAGE 38 B0772 CT/SYS AGE/Y INGP/REL CRIME

S67
ANDERSON M.,"THE FRENCH PARLIAMENT." EUR+WWI FRANCE MOD/EUR CONSTN POL/PAR CHIEF LEGIS LOBBY ATTIT ROLE PWR 19/20. PAGE 5 B0095 PARL/PROC LEAD GOV/COMP EX/STRUC

S67
BRADLEY A.W.,"CONSTITUTION-MAKING IN UGANDA." UGANDA LAW CHIEF DELIB/GP LEGIS ADMIN EXEC PARL/PROC RACE/REL ORD/FREE...GOV/COMP 20. PAGE 14 B0295 NAT/G CREATE CONSTN FEDERAL

S67
DOERN G.B.,"THE ROYAL COMMISSIONS IN THE GENERAL POLICY PROCESS AND IN FEDERAL-PROVINCIAL RELATIONS." CANADA CONSTN ACADEM PROVS CONSULT DELIB/GP LEGIS ACT/RES PROB/SOLV CONFER CONTROL EFFICIENCY...METH/COMP 20 SENATE ROYAL/COMM. PAGE 30 B0603 R+D EX/STRUC GOV/REL NAT/G

S67
FABREGA J.,"ANTECEDENTES EXTRANJEROS EN LA CONSTITUCION PANAMENA." CUBA L/A+17C PANAMA URUGUAY EX/STRUC LEGIS DIPLOM ORD/FREE 19/20 COLOMB MEXIC/AMER. PAGE 34 B0694 CONSTN JURID NAT/G PARL/PROC

S67
FERGUSON H.,"3-CITY CONSOLIDATION." USA+45 CONSTN INDUS BARGAIN BUDGET CONFER ADMIN INGP/REL COST UTIL. PAGE 35 B0712 MUNIC CHOOSE CREATE PROB/SOLV

S67
HOFMANN W.,"THE PUBLIC INTEREST PRESSURE GROUP: THE CASE OF THE DEUTSCHE STADTETAG." GERMANY GERMANY/W CONSTN STRUCT NAT/G CENTRAL FEDERAL PWR...TIME/SEQ 20. PAGE 51 B1030 LOC/G VOL/ASSN LOBBY ADMIN

S67
IDENBURG P.J.,"POLITICAL STRUCTURAL DEVELOPMENT IN TROPICAL AFRICA." UK ECO/UNDEV KIN POL/PAR CHIEF EX/STRUC CREATE COLONIAL CONTROL REPRESENT RACE/REL ...MAJORIT TREND 20. PAGE 53 B1074 AFR CONSTN NAT/G GOV/COMP

S67
KURON J.,"AN OPEN LETTER TO THE PARTY." CONSTN WORKER BUDGET EDU/PROP ADMIN REPRESENT SUFF OWN ...SOCIALIST 20. PAGE 62 B1244 ELITES STRUCT POL/PAR ECO/TAC

S67
SATHYAMURTHY T.V.,"TWENTY YEARS OF UNESCO: AN INTERPRETATION." SOCIETY PROB/SOLV LEAD PEACE UNESCO. PAGE 92 B1870 ADMIN CONSTN INT/ORG TIME/SEQ

S67
TIVEY L.,"THE POLITICAL CONSEQUENCES OF ECONOMIC PLANNING." UK CONSTN INDUS ACT/RES ADMIN CONTROL LOBBY REPRESENT EFFICIENCY SUPEGO SOVEREIGN ...DECISION 20. PAGE 104 B2112 PLAN POLICY NAT/G

S67
ZASLOW M.,"RECENT CONSTITUTIONAL DEVELOPMENTS IN CANADA'S NORTHERN TERRITORIES." CANADA LOC/G DELIB/GP EX/STRUC LEGIS ADMIN ORD/FREE...TREND 20. PAGE 119 B2398 GOV/REL REGION CONSTN FEDERAL

L86
GOODNOW F.J.,"AN EXECUTIVE AND THE COURTS: JUDICIAL REMEDIES AGAINST ADMINISTRATIVE ACTION" FRANCE UK USA-45 WOR-45 LAW CONSTN SANCTION ORD/FREE 19. PAGE 41 B0823 CT/SYS GOV/REL ADMIN ADJUD

B87
KINNEAR J.B.,PRINCIPLES OF CIVIL GOVERNMENT. MOD/EUR USA-45 CONSTN LOC/G EX/STRUC ADMIN PARL/PROC RACE/REL...CONCPT 18/19. PAGE 60 B1210 POL/PAR NAT/G GOV/COMP REPRESENT

CONSTN/CNV....CONSTITUTIONAL CONVENTION

CONSTRUC....CONSTRUCTION INDUSTRY

N
US SUPERINTENDENT OF DOCUMENTS,LABOR (PRICE LIST 33). USA+45 LAW AGRI CONSTRUC INDUS NAT/G BARGAIN PRICE ADMIN AUTOMAT PRODUC MGT. PAGE 111 B2240 BIBLIOG/A WORKER LABOR LEGIS

N19
EAST KENTUCKY REGIONAL PLAN,PROGRAM 60: A DECADE OF ACTION FOR PROGRESS IN EASTERN KENTUCKY (PAMPHLET). USA+45 AGRI CONSTRUC INDUS CONSULT ACT/RES PROB/SOLV EDU/PROP GOV/REL HEALTH KENTUCKY. PAGE 32 B0643 REGION ADMIN PLAN ECO/UNDEV

N19
EAST KENTUCKY REGIONAL PLAN,PROGRAM 60 REPORT: ACTION FOR PORGRESS IN EASTERN KENTUCKY (PAMPHLET). USA+45 CONSTRUC INDUS ACT/RES PROB/SOLV EDU/PROP ADMIN GOV/REL KENTUCKY. PAGE 32 B0644 REGION PLAN ECO/UNDEV CONSULT

B51

MAASS A.,MUDDY WATERS: THE ARMY ENGINEERS AND THE
NATIONS RIVERS. USA-45 PROF/ORG CONSULT LEGIS ADMIN
EXEC ROLE PWR...SOC PRESIDENT 20. PAGE 67 B1353

FORCES
GP/REL
LOBBY
CONSTRUC

B58

US HOUSE COMM GOVT OPERATIONS,HEARINGS BEFORE A
SUBCOMMITTEE OF THE COMMITTEE ON GOVERNMENT
OPERATIONS. CAMBODIA PHILIPPINE USA+45 CONSTRUC
TEC/DEV ADMIN CONTROL WEAPON EFFICIENCY HOUSE/REP.
PAGE 108 B2189

FOR/AID
DIPLOM
ORD/FREE
ECO/UNDEV

B59

YALE UNIV BUR OF HIGHWAY TRAF,URBAN TRANSPORTATION
ADMINISTRATION. FUT USA+45 CONSTRUC ACT/RES BUDGET
...CENSUS 20 PUB/TRANS. PAGE 118 B2388

ADMIN
DIST/IND
LOC/G
PLAN

S59

STINCHCOMBE A.L.,"BUREAUCRATIC AND CRAFT
ADMINISTRATION OF PRODUCTION: A COMPARATIVE STUDY"
(BMR)" USA+45 STRUCT EX/STRUC ECO/TAC GP/REL
...CLASSIF GP/COMP IDEA/COMP GEN/LAWS 20 WEBER/MAX.
PAGE 101 B2039

CONSTRUC
PROC/MFG
ADMIN
PLAN

B64

GREBLER L.,URBAN RENEWAL IN EUROPEAN COUNTRIES: ITS
EMERGENCE AND POTENTIALS. EUR+WWI UK ECO/DEV LOC/G
NEIGH CREATE ADMIN ATTIT...TREND NAT/COMP 20
URBAN/RNWL. PAGE 43 B0863

MUNIC
PLAN
CONSTRUC
NAT/G

B65

DUGGAR G.S.,RENEWAL OF TOWN AND VILLAGE I: A WORLD-
WIDE SURVEY OF LOCAL GOVERNMENT EXPERIENCE. WOR+45
CONSTRUC INDUS CREATE BUDGET REGION GOV/REL...QU
NAT/COMP 20 URBAN/RNWL. PAGE 31 B0628

MUNIC
NEIGH
PLAN
ADMIN

B66

US HOUSE COMM GOVT OPERATIONS,AN INVESTIGATION OF
THE US ECONOMIC AND MILITARY ASSISTANCE PROGRAMS IN
VIETNAM. USA+45 VIETNAM/S SOCIETY CONSTRUC FINAN
FORCES BUDGET INT/TRADE PEACE HEALTH...MGT
HOUSE/REP AID. PAGE 108 B2191

FOR/AID
ECO/UNDEV
WAR
INSPECT

CONSTRUCTION INDUSTRY....SEE CONSTRUC

CONSULT....CONSULTANTS

N

CONGRESSIONAL MONITOR. CONSULT DELIB/GP PROB/SOLV
PRESS DEBATE ROUTINE...POLICY CONGRESS. PAGE 1
B0002

BIBLIOG
LEGIS
REPRESENT
USA+45

B03

GRIFFIN A.P.C.,LIST OF BOOKS ON THE CABINETS OF
ENGLAND AND AMERICA (PAMPHLET). MOD/EUR UK USA-45
CONSTN NAT/G CONSULT EX/STRUC 19/20. PAGE 43 B0875

BIBLIOG/A
GOV/COMP
ADMIN
DELIB/GP

N19

ADMINISTRATIVE STAFF COLLEGE,THE ACCOUNTABILITY OF
GOVERNMENT DEPARTMENTS (PAMPHLET) (REV. ED.). UK
CONSTN FINAN NAT/G CONSULT ADMIN INGP/REL CONSEN
PRIVIL 20 PARLIAMENT. PAGE 3 B0059

PARL/PROC
ELITES
SANCTION
PROB/SOLV

N19

EAST KENTUCKY REGIONAL PLAN,PROGRAM 60: A DECADE OF
ACTION FOR PROGRESS IN EASTERN KENTUCKY (PAMPHLET).
USA+45 AGRI CONSTRUC INDUS CONSULT ACT/RES
PROB/SOLV EDU/PROP GOV/REL HEALTH KENTUCKY. PAGE 32
B0643

REGION
ADMIN
PLAN
ECO/UNDEV

N19

EAST KENTUCKY REGIONAL PLAN,PROGRAM 60 REPORT:
ACTION FOR PORGRESS IN EASTERN KENTUCKY (PAMPHLET).
USA+45 CONSTRUC INDUS ACT/RES PROB/SOLV EDU/PROP
ADMIN GOV/REL KENTUCKY. PAGE 32 B0644

REGION
PLAN
ECO/UNDEV
CONSULT

N19

GINZBERG E.,MANPOWER FOR GOVERNMENT (PAMPHLET).
USA+45 FORCES PLAN PROB/SOLV PAY EDU/PROP ADMIN
GP/REL COST...MGT PREDICT TREND 20 CIVIL/SERV.
PAGE 40 B0803

WORKER
CONSULT
NAT/G
LOC/G

B25

THOMAS F.,THE ENVIRONMENTAL BASIS OF SOCIETY.
USA-45 WOR-45 STRATA ECO/DEV EXTR/IND CONSULT
ECO/TAC ROUTINE ATTIT ALL/VALS...SOC TIME/SEQ.
PAGE 104 B2098

SOCIETY
GEOG

B27

WILLOUGHBY W.F.,PRINCIPLES OF PUBLIC ADMINISTRATION
WITH SPECIAL REFERENCE TO THE NATIONAL AND STATE
GOVERNMENTS OF THE UNITED STATES. FINAN PROVS CHIEF
CONSULT LEGIS CREATE BUDGET EXEC ROUTINE GOV/REL
CENTRAL...MGT 20 BUR/BUDGET CONGRESS PRESIDENT.
PAGE 117 B2356

NAT/G
EX/STRUC
OP/RES
ADMIN

B32

WRIGHT Q.,GOLD AND MONETARY STABILIZATION. FUT
USA-45 WOR-45 INTELL ECO/DEV INT/ORG NAT/G CONSULT
PLAN ECO/TAC ADMIN ATTIT WEALTH...CONCPT TREND 20.
PAGE 118 B2383

FINAN
POLICY

B39

BAKER G.,THE COUNTY AGENT. USA-45 LOC/G NAT/G
PROB/SOLV ADMIN...POLICY 20 ROOSEVLT/F NEW/DEAL
COUNTY/AGT. PAGE 8 B0166

AGRI
CONSULT
GOV/REL
EDU/PROP

B44

BIENSTOCK G.,MANAGEMENT IN RUSSIAN INDUSTRY AND
AGRICULTURE. USSR CONSULT WORKER LEAD COST PROFIT
ATTIT DRIVE PWR...MGT METH/COMP DICTIONARY 20.
PAGE 12 B0236

ADMIN
MARXISM
SML/CO
AGRI

L44

HAILEY,"THE FUTURE OF COLONIAL PEOPLES." WOR-45
CONSTN CULTURE ECO/UNDEV AGRI MARKET INT/ORG NAT/G
SECT CONSULT ECO/TAC LEGIT ADMIN NAT/LISM ALL/VALS
...SOC OBS TREND STERTYP CMN/WLTH LEAGUE/NAT
PARLIAMENT 20. PAGE 45 B0916

PLAN
CONCPT
DIPLOM
UK

B45

RANSHOFFEN-WERTHEIMER EF,THE INTERNATIONAL
SECRETARIAT: A GREAT EXPERIMENT IN INTERNATIONAL
ADMINISTRATION. EUR+WWI FUT CONSTN FACE/GP CONSULT
DELIB/GP ACT/RES ADMIN ROUTINE PEACE ORD/FREE...MGT
RECORD ORG/CHARTS LEAGUE/NAT WORK 20. PAGE 86 B1731

INT/ORG
EXEC

S45

WHITE L.D.,"CONGRESSIONAL CONTROL OF THE PUBLIC
SERVICE." USA-45 NAT/G CONSULT DELIB/GP PLAN SENIOR
CONGRESS. PAGE 116 B2335

LEGIS
EXEC
POLICY
CONTROL

B47

MILLETT J.D.,THE PROCESS AND ORGANIZATION OF
GOVERNMENT PLANNING. USA+45 DELIB/GP ACT/RES LEAD
LOBBY TASK...POLICY GEOG TIME 20 RESOURCE/N.
PAGE 73 B1482

ADMIN
NAT/G
PLAN
CONSULT

B48

US LIBRARY OF CONGRESS,BRAZIL: A GUIDE TO THE
OFFICIAL PUBLICATIONS OF BRAZIL. BRAZIL L/A+17C
CONSULT DELIB/GP LEGIS CT/SYS 19/20. PAGE 109 B2203

BIBLIOG/A
NAT/G
ADMIN
TOP/EX

S48

COCH L.,"OVERCOMING RESISTANCE TO CHANGE" (BMR)"
USA+45 CONSULT ADMIN ROUTINE GP/REL EFFICIENCY
PRODUC PERCEPT SKILL...CHARTS SOC/EXP 20. PAGE 22
B0441

WORKER
OP/RES
PROC/MFG
RIGID/FLEX

B49

WRIGHT J.H.,PUBLIC RELATIONS IN MANAGEMENT. USA+45
USA-45 ECO/DEV LG/CO SML/CO CONSULT EXEC TASK
PROFIT ATTIT ROLE 20. PAGE 118 B2382

MGT
PLAN
EDU/PROP
PARTIC

B50

GREAT BRITAIN TREASURY,PUBLIC ADMINISTRATION: A
BIBLIOGRAPHY FOR ORGANISATION AND METHODS
(PAMPHLET). LOC/G NAT/G CONSULT EX/STRUC CONFER
ROUTINE TASK EFFICIENCY...MGT 20. PAGE 43 B0862

BIBLIOG
PLAN
CONTROL
ADMIN

B50

LASSWELL H.D.,NATIONAL SECURITY AND INDIVIDUAL
FREEDOM. USA+45 R+D NAT/G VOL/ASSN CONSULT DELIB/GP
LEGIT ADMIN KNOWL ORD/FREE PWR...PLURIST TOT/POP
COLD/WAR 20. PAGE 63 B1268

FACE/GP
ROUTINE
BAL/PWR

B51

MAASS A.,MUDDY WATERS: THE ARMY ENGINEERS AND THE
NATIONS RIVERS. USA-45 PROF/ORG CONSULT LEGIS ADMIN
EXEC ROLE PWR...SOC PRESIDENT 20. PAGE 67 B1353

FORCES
GP/REL
LOBBY
CONSTRUC

S51

LERNER D.,"THE POLICY SCIENCES: RECENT DEVELOPMENTS
IN SCOPE AND METHODS." R+D SERV/IND CREATE DIPLOM
ROUTINE PWR...METH/CNCPT TREND GEN/LAWS METH 20.
PAGE 64 B1297

CONSULT
SOC

B52

DAY E.E.,EDUCATION FOR FREEDOM AND RESPONSIBILITY.
FUT USA+45 CULTURE CONSULT EDU/PROP ATTIT SKILL
...MGT CONCPT OBS GEN/LAWS COLD/WAR 20. PAGE 27
B0547

SCHOOL
KNOWL

B52

NASH B.D.,STAFFING THE PRESIDENCY: PLANNING
PAMPHLET NO. 80 (PAMPHLET). NAT/G CHIEF CONSULT
DELIB/GP CONFER ADMIN 20 PRESIDENT. PAGE 77 B1557

EX/STRUC
EXEC
TOP/EX
ROLE

B52

VANDENBOSCH A.,THE UN: BACKGROUND, ORGANIZATION,
FUNCTIONS, ACTIVITIES. WOR+45 LAW CONSTN STRUCT
INT/ORG CONSULT BAL/PWR EDU/PROP EXEC ALL/VALS
...POLICY CONCPT UN 20. PAGE 112 B2254

DELIB/GP
TIME/SEQ
PEACE

L52

WRIGHT Q.,"CONGRESS AND THE TREATY-MAKING POWER."
USA+45 WOR+45 CONSTN INTELL NAT/G CHIEF CONSULT
EX/STRUC LEGIS TOP/EX CREATE GOV/REL DISPL DRIVE
RIGID/FLEX...TREND TOT/POP CONGRESS CONGRESS 20
TREATY. PAGE 118 B2384

ROUTINE
DIPLOM
INT/LAW
DELIB/GP

S52

SCHWEBEL S.M.,"THE SECRETARY-GENERAL OF THE UN."
FUT INTELL CONSULT DELIB/GP ADMIN PEACE ATTIT
...JURID MGT CONCPT TREND UN CONGRESS 20. PAGE 95
B1915

INT/ORG
TOP/EX

B53

MACMAHON A.W.,ADMINISTRATION IN FOREIGN AFFAIRS.
NAT/G CONSULT DELIB/GP LEGIS ACT/RES CREATE ADMIN
EXEC RIGID/FLEX PWR...METH/CNCPT TIME/SEQ TOT/POP
VAL/FREE 20. PAGE 68 B1369

USA+45
ROUTINE
FOR/AID
DIPLOM

S53

BLOUGH R.,"THE ROLE OF THE ECONOMIST IN FEDERAL
POLICY MAKING." USA+45 ELITES INTELL ECO/DEV NAT/G

DELIB/GP
ECO/TAC

CONSULT EX/STRUC ACT/RES PLAN INT/TRADE BAL/PAY
WEALTH...POLICY CONGRESS 20. PAGE 13 B0256

B54
HOBBS E.H.,BEHIND THE PRESIDENT - A STUDY OF   EX/STRUC
EXECUTIVE OFFICE AGENCIES. USA+45 NAT/G PLAN BUDGET   DELIB/GP
ECO/TAC EXEC ORD/FREE 20 BUR/BUDGET. PAGE 50 B1022   CONFER
                                                      CONSULT

C54
LANDAU J.M.,"PARLIAMENTS AND PARTIES IN EGYPT." UAR   ISLAM
NAT/G SECT CONSULT LEGIS TOP/EX PROB/SOLV ADMIN   NAT/LISM
COLONIAL...GEN/LAWS BIBLIOG 19/20. PAGE 62 B1254   PARL/PROC
                                                      POL/PAR

S55
TORRE M.,"PSYCHIATRIC OBSERVATIONS OF INTERNATIONAL   DELIB/GP
CONFERENCES." WOR+45 INT/ORG PROF/ORG VOL/ASSN   OBS
CONSULT EDU/PROP ROUTINE ATTIT DRIVE KNOWL...PSY   DIPLOM
METH/CNCPT OBS/ENVIR STERTYP 20. PAGE 105 B2119

S56
CUTLER R.,"THE DEVELOPMENT OF THE NATIONAL SECURITY   ORD/FREE
COUNCIL." USA+45 INTELL CONSULT EX/STRUC DIPLOM   DELIB/GP
LEAD 20 TRUMAN/HS EISNHWR/DD NSC. PAGE 25 B0514   PROB/SOLV
                                                      NAT/G

B57
ASHER R.E.,THE UNITED NATIONS AND THE PROMOTION OF   INT/ORG
THE GENERAL WELFARE. WOR+45 WOR-45 ECO/UNDEV   CONSULT
EX/STRUC ACT/RES PLAN EDU/PROP ROUTINE HEALTH...HUM
CONCPT CHARTS UNESCO UN ILO 20. PAGE 7 B0139

B57
COOPER F.E.,THE LAWYER AND ADMINISTRATIVE AGENCIES.   CONSULT
USA+45 CLIENT LAW PROB/SOLV CT/SYS PERSON ROLE.   ADMIN
PAGE 23 B0473   ADJUD
                                                      DELIB/GP

B57
HUNTINGTON S.P.,THE SOLDIER AND THE STATE: THE   ACT/RES
THEORY AND POLITICS OF CIVIL-MILITARY RELATIONS.   FORCES
USA+45 USA-45 NAT/G PROF/ORG CONSULT DOMIN LEGIT
ROUTINE ATTIT PWR...CONCPT TIME/SEQ COLD/WAR 20.
PAGE 53 B1065

B57
MEYER P.,ADMINISTRATIVE ORGANIZATION: A COMPARATIVE   ADMIN
STUDY OF THE ORGANIZATION OF PUBLIC ADMINISTRATION.   METH/COMP
DENMARK FRANCE NORWAY SWEDEN UK USA+45 ELITES LOC/G   NAT/G
CONSULT LEGIS ADJUD CONTROL LEAD PWR SKILL   CENTRAL
DECISION. PAGE 73 B1475

B57
MORSTEIN-MARX F.,THE ADMINISTRATIVE STATE: AN   EXEC
INTRODUCTION TO BUREAUCRACY. EUR+WWI FUT MOD/EUR   MGT
USA+45 USA-45 NAT/G CONSULT ADMIN ROUTINE TOTALISM   CAP/ISM
DRIVE SKILL...TREND 19/20. PAGE 76 B1530   ELITES

B57
MURRAY J.N.,THE UNITED NATIONS TRUSTEESHIP SYSTEM.   INT/ORG
AFR WOR+45 CONSIN CONSULT LEGIS EDU/PROP LEGIT EXEC   DELIB/GP
ROUTINE...INT TIME/SEQ SOMALI UN 20. PAGE 77 B1547

B57
SIMON H.A.,MODELS OF MAN, SOCIAL AND RATIONAL: MATH
MATHEMATICAL ESSAYS ON RATIONAL HUMAN BEHAVIOR IN A   SIMUL
SOCIAL SETTING. UNIV LAW SOCIETY FACE/GP VOL/ASSN
CONSULT EX/STRUC LEGIS CREATE ADMIN ROUTINE ATTIT
DRIVE PWR...SOC CONCPT METH/CNCPT QUANT STAT
TOT/POP VAL/FREE 20. PAGE 97 B1959

S57
COTTER C.P.,"ADMINISTRATIVE ACCOUNTABILITY: LEGIS
REPORTING TO CONGRESS." USA+45 CONSULT DELIB/GP   EX/STRUC
PARL/PROC PARTIC GOV/REL ATTIT PWR DECISION.   REPRESENT
PAGE 24 B0490   CONTROL

B58
MILLS C.W.,THE CAUSES OF WORLD WAR THREE. FUT   CONSULT
USA+45 INTELL NAT/G DOMIN EDU/PROP ADMIN WAR ATTIT   PWR
SOC. PAGE 74 B1487   ELITES
                                                     PEACE

B58
REDFORD E.S.,IDEAL AND PRACTICE IN PUBLIC   POLICY
ADMINISTRATION. CONSTN ELITES NAT/G CONSULT   EX/STRUC
DELIB/GP LEAD UTOPIA ATTIT POPULISM...DECISION   PLAN
METH/COMP 20. PAGE 87 B1756   ADMIN

B58
STEWART J.D.,BRITISH PRESSURE GROUPS: THEIR ROLE IN LOBBY
RELATION TO THE HOUSE OF COMMONS. UK CONSULT   LEGIS
DELIB/GP ADMIN ROUTINE CHOOSE REPRESENT ATTIT ROLE   PLAN
20 HOUSE/CMNS PARLIAMENT. PAGE 101 B2038   PARL/PROC

B58
SWEENEY S.B.,EDUCATION FOR ADMINISTRATIVE CAREERS   EDU/PROP
IN GOVERNMENT SERVICE. USA+45 ACADEM CONSULT CREATE   ADMIN
PLAN CONFER SKILL...TREND IDEA/COMP METH 20   NAT/G
CIVIL/SERV. PAGE 102 B2059   LOC/G

B58
WILENSKY H.L.,INDUSTRIAL SOCIETY AND SOCIAL   INDUS
WELFARE: IMPACT OF INDUSTRIALIZATION ON SUPPLY AND   ECO/DEV
ORGANIZATION OF SOC WELF SERVICES. ELITES SOCIETY   RECEIVE
STRATA SERV/IND FAM MUNIC PUB/INST CONSULT WORKER   PROF/ORG
ADMIN AUTOMAT ANOMIE 20. PAGE 117 B2352

B59
BRUNTON R.L.,MANAGEMENT PRACTICES FOR SMALLER   ADMIN
CITIES. USA+45 MUNIC CONSULT PLAN BUDGET PERS/REL   LOC/G
20 CITY/MGT. PAGE 16 B0331   MGT
                                                     TOP/EX

B59
CHRISTENSON R.M.,THE BRANNAN PLAN: FARM POLITICS   AGRI
AND POLICY. USA+45 ECO/DEV CONSULT PLAN PAY GOV/REL   NAT/G
...POLICY 20. PAGE 21 B0429   ADMIN
                                                     ECO/TAC

B59
DESMITH S.A.,JUDICIAL REVIEW OF ADMINISTRATIVE   ADJUD
ACTION. UK LOC/G CONSULT DELIB/GP ADMIN PWR   NAT/G
...DECISION JURID 20 ENGLSH/LAW. PAGE 28 B0576   PROB/SOLV
                                                     CT/SYS

B59
DIEBOLD W. JR.,THE SCHUMAN PLAN: A STUDY IN   INT/ORG
ECONOMIC COOPERATION, 1950-1959. EUR+WWI FRANCE   REGION
GERMANY USA+45 EXTR/IND CONSULT DELIB/GP PLAN
DIPLOM ECO/TAC INT/TRADE ROUTINE ORD/FREE WEALTH
...METH/CNCPT STAT CONT/OBS INT TIME/SEQ ECSC 20.
PAGE 29 B0591

B59
GORDENKER L.,THE UNITED NATIONS AND THE PEACEFUL   DELIB/GP
UNIFICATION OF KOREA. ASIA LAW LOC/G CONSULT   KOREA
ACT/RES DIPLOM DOMIN LEGIT ADJUD ADMIN ORD/FREE   INT/ORG
SOVERFIGN...INT GEN/METH UN COLD/WAR 20. PAGE 41
B0829

B59
JANOWITZ M.,SOCIOLOGY AND THE MILITARY   FORCES
ESTABLISHMENT. USA+45 WOR+45 CULTURE SOCIETY   SOC
PROF/ORG CONSULT EX/STRUC PLAN TEC/DEV DIPLOM DOMIN
COERCE DRIVE RIGID/FLEX ORD/FREE PWR SKILL COLD/WAR
20. PAGE 55 B1121

B59
MACIVER R.M.,THE NATIONS AND THE UN. WOR+45 NAT/G   INT/ORG
CONSULT ADJUD ADMIN ALL/VALS...CONCPT DEEP/QU UN   ATTIT
TOT/POP UNESCO 20. PAGE 67 B1362   DIPLOM

B59
SAYER W.S.,AN AGENDA FOR RESEARCH IN PUBLIC   WORKER
PERSONNEL ADMINISTRATION. FUT USA+45 ACADEM LABOR   ADMIN
LOC/G NAT/G POL/PAR DELIB/GP MGT. PAGE 93 B1872   ACT/RES
                                                     CONSULT

S59
CHAPMAN B.,"THE FRENCH CONSEIL D'ETAT." FRANCE   ADMIN
NAT/G CONSULT OP/RES PROB/SOLV PWR...OBS 20.   LAW
PAGE 20 B0410   CT/SYS
                                                     LEGIS

S59
KISSINGER H.A.,"THE POLICYMAKER AND THE   INTELL
INTELLECTUAL." USA+45 CONSULT DELIB/GP ACT/RES   CREATE
ADMIN ATTIT DRIVE RIGID/FLEX KNOWL PWR...POLICY
PLURIST MGT METH/CNCPT GEN/LAWS GEN/METH 20.
PAGE 60 B1216

S59
LASSWELL H.D.,"UNIVERSALITY IN PERSPECTIVE." FUT   INT/ORG
UNIV SOCIETY CONSULT TOP/EX PLAN EDU/PROP ADJUD   JURID
ROUTINE ARMS/CONT COERCE PEACE ATTIT PERSON   TOTALISM
ALL/VALS. PAGE 63 B1271

S59
LENGYEL P.,"SOME TRENDS IN THE INTERNATIONAL CIVIL ADMIN
SERVICE." FUT WOR+45 INT/ORG CONSULT ATTIT...MGT   EXEC
OBS TREND CON/ANAL LEAGUE/NAT UNESCO 20. PAGE 64
B1291

B60
POOLEY B.J.,THE EVOLUTION OF BRITISH PLANNING   PLAN
LEGISLATION. UK ECO/DEV LOC/G CONSULT DELIB/GP   MUNIC
ADMIN 20 URBAN/RNWL. PAGE 84 B1691   LEGIS
                                                     PROB/SOLV

B60
SCHUBERT G.,THE PUBLIC INTEREST. USA+45 CONSULT   POLICY
PLAN PROB/SOLV ADJUD ADMIN GP/REL PWR ALL/IDEOS 20.   DELIB/GP
PAGE 94 B1903   REPRESENT
                                                     POL/PAR

B60
US SENATE COMM. GOVT. OPER.,ORGANIZING FOR NATIONAL CONSULT
SECURITY. USA+45 USA-45 INTELL STRUCT SML/CO   EXEC
ACT/RES ADMIN ATTIT PERSON PWR SKILL...DECISION 20.
PAGE 111 B2236

L60
BRENNAN D.G.,"SETTING AND GOALS OF ARMS CONTROL."   FORCES
FUT USA+45 USSR WOR+45 INTELL INT/ORG NAT/G   COERCE
VOL/ASSN CONSULT PLAN DIPLOM ECO/TAC ADMIN KNOWL   ARMS/CONT
PWR...POLICY CONCPT TREND COLD/WAR 20. PAGE 15   DETER
B0305

S60
HERRERA F.,"THE INTER-AMERICAN DEVELOPMENT BANK."   L/A+17C
USA+45 ECO/UNDEV INT/ORG CONSULT DELIB/GP PLAN   FINAN
ECO/TAC INT/TRADE ROUTINE WEALTH...STAT 20. PAGE 49   FOR/AID
B0994   REGION

S60
HUTCHINSON C.E.,"AN INSTITUTE FOR NATIONAL SECURITY POLICY
AFFAIRS." USA+45 R+D NAT/G CONSULT TOP/EX ACT/RES   METH/CNCPT
CREATE PLAN TEC/DEV EDU/PROP ROUTINE NUC/PWR ATTIT   ELITES
ORD/FREE PWR...DECISION MGT PHIL/SCI CONCPT RECORD   DIPLOM
GEN/LAWS GEN/METH 20. PAGE 53 B1068

S60
SMIGEL E.O.,"THE IMPACT OF RECRUITMENT ON THE   LG/CO
ORGANIZATION OF THE LARGE LAW FIRM" (BMR)" USA+45   ADMIN
STRUCT CONSULT PLAN GP/REL EFFICIENCY JURID.   LAW
PAGE 98 B1979   WORKER

S60

TAYLOR M.G.,"THE ROLE OF THE MEDICAL PROFESSION IN THE FORMULATION AND EXECUTION OF PUBLIC POLICY" (BMR)" CANADA NAT/G CONSULT ADMIN REPRESENT GP/REL ROLE SOVEREIGN...DECISION 20 CMA. PAGE 103 B2088
PROF/ORG
HEALTH
LOBBY
POLICY

B61

BARNES W.,THE FOREIGN SERVICE OF THE UNITED STATES. USA+45 USA-45 CONSTN INT/ORG POL/PAR CONSULT DELIB/GP LEGIS DOMIN EDU/PROP EXEC ATTIT RIGID/FLEX ORD/FREE PWR...POLICY CONCPT STAT OBS RECORD BIOG TIME/SEQ TREND. PAGE 9 B0188
NAT/G
MGT
DIPLOM

B61

BENOIT E.,EUROPE AT SIXES AND SEVENS: THE COMMON MARKET, THE FREE TRADE ASSOCIATION AND THE UNITED STATES. EUR+WWI FUT USA+45 INDUS CONSULT DELIB/GP EX/STRUC TOP/EX ACT/RES ECO/TAC EDU/PROP ROUTINE CHOOSE PERCEPT WEALTH...MGT TREND EEC TOT/POP 20 EFTA. PAGE 11 B0217
FINAN
ECO/DEV
VOL/ASSN

B61

CARROTHERS A.W.R.,LABOR ARBITRATION IN CANADA. CANADA LAW NAT/G CONSULT LEGIS WORKER ADJUD ADMIN CT/SYS 20. PAGE 19 B0386
LABOR
MGT
GP/REL
BARGAIN

B61

FRIEDMANN W.G.,JOINT INTERNATIONAL BUSINESS VENTURES. ASIA ISLAM L/A+17C ECO/DEV DIST/IND FINAN PROC/MFG FACE/GP LG/CO NAT/G VOL/ASSN CONSULT EX/STRUC PLAN ADMIN ROUTINE WEALTH...OLD/LIB WORK 20. PAGE 37 B0760
ECO/UNDEV
INT/TRADE

B61

HARRISON S.,INDIA AND THE UNITED STATES. FUT S/ASIA USA+45 WOR+45 INTELL ECO/DEV ECO/UNDEV AGRI INDUS INT/ORG NAT/G CONSULT EX/STRUC TOP/EX PLAN ECO/TAC NEUTRAL ALL/VALS...MGT TOT/POP 20. PAGE 47 B0956
DELIB/GP
ACT/RES
FOR/AID
INDIA

B61

LAHAYE R.,LES ENTREPRISES PUBLIQUES AU MAROC. FRANCE MOROCCO LAW DIST/IND EXTR/IND FINAN CONSULT PLAN TEC/DEV ADMIN AGREE CONTROL OWN...POLICY 20. PAGE 62 B1250
NAT/G
INDUS
ECO/UNDEV
ECO/TAC

B61

LASSWELL H.D.,PSYCOPATHOLOGY AND POLITICS. WOR-45 CULTURE SOCIETY FACE/GP NAT/G CONSULT CREATE EDU/PROP EXEC ROUTINE DISPL DRIVE PERSON PWR RESPECT...PSY CUNCPT METH/CNCPT METH. PAGE 63 B1272
ATTIT
GEN/METH

B61

MARKMANN C.L.,JOHN F. KENNEDY: A SENSE OF PURPOSE. USA+45 INTELL FAM CONSULT DELIB/GP LEGIS PERSON SKILL 20 KENNEDY/JF EISNHWR/DD ROOSEVLT/F NEW/FRONTR PRESIDENT. PAGE 69 B1399
CHIEF
TOP/EX
ADMIN
BIOG

B61

MARX K.,THE COMMUNIST MANIFESTO. IN (MENDEL A. ESSENTIAL WORKS OF MARXISM, NEW YORK: BANTAM. FUT MOD/EUR CULTURE ECO/DEV ECO/UNDEV AGRI FINAN INDUS MARKET PROC/MFG LABOR MUNIC POL/PAR CONSULT FORCES CREATE PLAN ADMIN ATTIT DRIVE RIGID/FLEX ORD/FREE PWR RESPECT MARX/KARL WORK. PAGE 70 B1421
COM
NEW/IDEA
CAP/ISM
REV

B61

OPOTOWSKY S.,THE KENNEDY GOVERNMENT. NAT/G CONSULT EX/STRUC LEAD PERSON...POLICY 20 KENNEDY/JF CONGRESS CABINET. PAGE 80 B1613
ADMIN
BIOG
ELITES
TOP/EX

B61

ROSE D.L.,THE VIETNAMESE CIVIL SERVICE. VIETNAM CONSULT DELIB/GP GIVE PAY EDU/PROP COLONIAL GOV/REL UTIL...CHARTS 20. PAGE 90 B1819
ADMIN
EFFICIENCY
STAT
NAT/G

B61

SHARP W.R.,FIELD ADMINISTRATION IN THE UNITED NATION SYSTEM: THE CONDUCT OF INTERNATIONAL ECONOMIC AND SOCIAL PROGRAMS. FUT WOR+45 CONSTN SOCIETY ECO/UNDEV R+D DELIB/GP ACT/RES PLAN TEC/DEV EDU/PROP EXEC ROUTINE HEALTH WEALTH...HUM CONCPT CHARTS METH ILO UNESCO VAL/FREE UN 20. PAGE 96 B1939
INT/ORG
CONSULT

B61

STRAUSS E.,THE RULING SERVANTS. FRANCE UK USSR WOR+45 WOR-45 NAT/G CONSULT DELIB/GP EX/STRUC TOP/EX DOMIN EDU/PROP LEGIT ROUTINE...MGT TIME/SEQ STERTYP 20. PAGE 101 B2051
ADMIN
PWR
ELITES

B61

TANZER L.,THE KENNEDY CIRCLE. INTELL CONSULT DELIB/GP TOP/EX CONTROL EXEC INGP/REL PERS/REL PWR ...BIOG IDEA/COMP ANTHOL 20 KENNEDY/JF PRESIDENT DEMOCRAT MCNAMARA/R RUSK/D. PAGE 103 B2077
EX/STRUC
NAT/G
CHIEF

B61

WILLOUGHBY W.R.,THE ST LAWRENCE WATERWAY: A STUDY IN POLITICS AND DIPLOMACY. USA+45 ECO/DEV COM/IND INT/ORG CONSULT DELIB/GP ACT/RES TEC/DEV DIPLOM ECO/TAC ROUTINE...TIME/SEQ 20. PAGE 117 B2357
LEGIS
INT/TRADE
CANADA
DIST/IND

S61

ALGER C.F.,"NON-RESOLUTION CONSEQUENCES OF THE UNITED NATIONS AND THEIR EFFECT ON INTERNATIONAL CONFLICT." WOR+45 WOR-45 CONSTN ECO/DEV NAT/G CONSULT DELIB/GP TOP/EX ACT/RES PLAN DIPLOM EDU/PROP ROUTINE ATTIT ALL/VALS...INT/LAW TOT/POP UN 20. PAGE 4 B0075
INT/ORG
DRIVE
BAL/PWR

S61

DYKMAN J.W.,"REVIEW ARTICLE* PLANNING AND DECISION THEORY." ELITES LOC/G MUNIC CONSULT ADMIN...POLICY MGT. PAGE 31 B0640
DECISION
PLAN
RATIONAL

S61

JUVILER P.H.,"INTERPARLIAMENTARY CONTACTS IN SOVIET FOREIGN POLICY." COM FUT WOR+45 WOR-45 SOCIETY CONSULT ACT/RES DIPLOM ADMIN PEACE ATTIT RIGID/FLEX WEALTH...WELF/ST SOC TOT/POP CONGRESS 19/20. PAGE 57 B1156
INT/ORG
DELIB/GP
USSR

S61

SCHILLING W.R.,"THE H-BOMB: HOW TO DECIDE WITHOUT ACTUALLY CHOOSING." FUT USA+45 INTELL CONSULT ADMIN CT/SYS MORAL...JURID OBS 20 TRUMAN/HS. PAGE 93 B1888
PERSON
LEGIT
NUC/PWR

B62

ARGYRIS C.,INTERPERSONAL COMPETENCE AND ORGANIZATIONAL EFFECTIVENESS. CREATE PLAN PROB/SOLV EDU/PROP INGP/REL PERS/REL PRODUC...OBS INT SIMUL 20. PAGE 6 B0131
EX/STRUC
ADMIN
CONSULT
EFFICIENCY

B62

GRAY R.K.,EIGHTEEN ACRES UNDER GLASS. ELITES CONSULT EX/STRUC DIPLOM PRESS CONFER WAR PERS/REL PERSON 20 EISNHWR/DD TRUMAN/HS CABINET. PAGE 43 B0860
CHIEF
ADMIN
TOP/EX
NAT/G

B62

GROVE J.W.,GOVERNMENT AND INDUSTRY IN BRITAIN. UK FINAN LOC/G CONSULT DELIB/GP INT/TRADE ADMIN CONTROL...BIBLIOG 20. PAGE 44 B0894
ECO/TAC
INDUS
NAT/G
GP/REL

B62

INTERNAT CONGRESS OF JURISTS,EXECUTIVE ACTION AND THE RULE OF RULE: REPORTION PROCEEDINGS OF INT'T CONGRESS OF JURISTS.-RIO DE JANEIRO, BRAZIL. WOR+45 ACADEM CONSULT JUDGE EDU/PROP ADJUD CT/SYS INGP/REL PERSON DEPT/DEFEN. PAGE 54 B1094
JURID
EXEC
ORD/FREE
CONTROL

B62

LAWSON R.,INTERNATIONAL REGIONAL ORGANIZATIONS. WOR+45 NAT/G VOL/ASSN CONSULT LEGIS EDU/PROP LEGIT ADMIN EXEC ROUTINE HEALTH PWR WEALTH...JURID EEC COLD/WAR 20 UN. PAGE 63 B1277
INT/ORG
DELIB/GP
REGION

B62

NEW ZEALAND COMM OF ST SERVICE,THE STATE SERVICES IN NEW ZEALAND. NEW/ZEALND CONSULT EX/STRUC ACT/RES ...BIBLIOG 20. PAGE 78 B1577
ADMIN
WORKER
TEC/DEV
NAT/G

B62

SCHILLING W.R.,STRATEGY, POLITICS, AND DEFENSE BUDGETS. USA+45 R+D NAT/G CONSULT DELIB/GP FORCES LEGIS ACT/RES PLAN BAL/PWR LEGIT EXEC NUC/PWR RIGID/FLEX PWR...TREND COLD/WAR CONGRESS 20 EISNHWR/DD. PAGE 93 B1890
ROUTINE
POLICY

L62

HOFFHERR R.,"LE PROBLEME DE L'ENCADREMENT DANS LES JEUNES ETATS DE LANGUE FRANCAISE EN AFRIQUE CENTRALE ET A MADAGASCAR." FUT ECO/UNDEV CONSULT PLAN ECO/TAC COLONIAL ATTIT...MGT TIME/SEQ VAL/FREE 20. PAGE 51 B1028
AFR
STRUCT
FRANCE

S62

ALGER C.F.,"THE EXTERNAL BUREAUCRACY IN UNITED STATES FOREIGN AFFAIRS." USA+45 WOR+45 SOCIETY COM/IND INT/ORG NAT/G CONSULT EX/STRUC ACT/RES ...MGT SOC CONCPT TREND 20. PAGE 4 B0076
ADMIN
ATTIT
DIPLOM

S62

BUENO M.,"ASPECTOS SOCIOLOGICOS DE LA EDUCACION." FUT UNIV INTELL R+D SERV/IND SCHOOL CONSULT EX/STRUC ACT/RES PLAN...METH/CNCPT OBS 20. PAGE 17 B0341
SOCIETY
EDU/PROP
PERSON

S62

NORTH R.C.,"DECISION MAKING IN CRISIS: AN INTRODUCTION." WOR+45 WOR-45 NAT/G CONSULT DELIB/GP TEC/DEV PERCEPT KNOWL...POLICY DECISION PSY METH/CNCPT CONT/OBS TREND VAL/FREE 20. PAGE 79 B1590
INT/ORG
ROUTINE
DIPLOM

S62

SCHILLING W.R.,"SCIENTISTS, FOREIGN POLICY AND POLITICS." WOR+45 WOR-45 INTELL INT/ORG CONSULT TOP/EX ACT/RES PLAN ADMIN KNOWL...CONCPT OBS TREND LEAGUE/NAT 20. PAGE 93 B1889
NAT/G
TEC/DEV
DIPLOM
NUC/PWR

B63

BOCK E.A., STATE AND LOCAL GOVERNMENT: A CASE BOOK. USA+45 MUNIC PROVS CONSULT GP/REL ATTIT...MGT 20 CASEBOOK GOVERNOR MAYOR. PAGE 12 B0254
LOC/G
ADMIN
PROB/SOLV
CHIEF

B63

BOISSIER P.,HISTORIE DU COMITE INTERNATIONAL DE LA CROIX ROUGE. MOD/EUR WOR-45 CONSULT FORCES PLAN DIPLOM EDU/PROP ADMIN MORAL ORD/FREE...SOC CONCPT RECORD TIME/SEQ GEN/LAWS TOT/POP VAL/FREE 19/20. PAGE 13 B0267
INT/ORG
HEALTH
ARMS/CONT
WAR

B63

HOUGHTELING J.L. JR.,THE LEGAL ENVIRONMENT OF BUSINESS. LG/CO NAT/G CONSULT AGREE CONTROL ...DICTIONARY T 20. PAGE 52 B1047
LAW
MGT
ADJUD
JURID

B63

INTL INST ADMIN SCIENCES,EDUCATION IN PUBLIC ADMINISTRATION: A SYMPOSIUM ON TEACHING METHODS AND MATERIALS. WOR+45 SCHOOL CONSULT CREATE CONFER SKILL...OBS TREND IDEA/COMP METH/COMP 20. PAGE 54 B1100
EDU/PROP METH ADMIN ACADEM

B63

MAYNE R.,THE COMMUNITY OF EUROPE. UK CONSTN NAT/G CONSULT DELIB/GP CREATE PLAN ECO/TAC LEGIT ADMIN ROUTINE ORD/FREE PWR WEALTH...CONCPT TIME/SEQ EEC EURATOM 20. PAGE 71 B1436
EUR+WWI INT/ORG REGION

B63

SIDEY H.,JOHN F. KENNEDY, PRESIDENT. USA+45 INTELL FAM CONSULT DELIB/GP LEGIS ADMIN LEAD 20 KENNEDY/JF PRESIDENT. PAGE 97 B1951
BIOG TOP/EX SKILL PERSON

B63

WADE H.W.R.,TOWARDS ADMINISTRATIVE JUSTICE. UK USA+45 CONSTN CONSULT PROB/SOLV CT/SYS PARL/PROC ...POLICY JURID METH/COMP 20 ENGLSH/LAW. PAGE 112 B2270
ADJUD IDEA/COMP ADMIN

B63

WARNER W.L.,THE AMERICAN FEDERAL EXECUTIVE. USA+45 USA-45 CONSULT EX/STRUC GP/REL DRIVE ALL/VALS...PSY DEEP/QU CHARTS 19/20 PRESIDENT. PAGE 114 B2295
ELITES NAT/G TOP/EX ADMIN

S63

ARASTEH R.,"THE ROLE OF INTELLECTUALS IN ADMINISTRATIVE DEVELOPMENT AND SOCIAL CHANGE IN MODERN IRAN." ISLAM CULTURE NAT/G CONSULT ACT/RES EDU/PROP EXEC ATTIT BIO/SOC PERCEPT SUPEGO ALL/VALS ...POLICY MGT PSY SOC CONCPT 20. PAGE 6 B0123
INTELL ADMIN IRAN

S63

BARZANSKI S.,"REGIONAL UNDERDEVELOPMENT IN THE EUROPEAN ECONOMIC COMMUNITY." EUR+WWI ELITES DIST/IND MARKET VOL/ASSN CONSULT EX/STRUC ECO/TAC RIGID/FLEX WEALTH EEC OEEC 20. PAGE 9 B0192
ECO/UNDEV PLAN

S63

BRZEZINSKI Z.K.,"CINCINNATUS AND THE APPARATCHIK." COM USA+45 USA-45 ELITES LOC/G NAT/G PROVS CONSULT LEGIS DOMIN LEGIT EXEC ROUTINE CHOOSE DRIVE PWR SKILL...CONCPT CHARTS VAL/FREE COLD/WAR 20. PAGE 16 B0334
POL/PAR USSR

S63

MEDALIA N.Z.,"POSITION AND PROSPECTS OF SOCIOLOGISTS IN FEDERAL EMPLOYMENT." USA+45 CONSULT PAY SENIOR ADMIN GOV/REL...TREND CHARTS 20 CIVIL/SERV. PAGE 72 B1460
NAT/G WORKER SOC SKILL

S63

RUSTOW D.A.,"THE MILITARY IN MIDDLE EASTERN SOCIETY AND POLITICS." FUT ISLAM CONSTN SOCIETY FACE/GP NAT/G POL/PAR PROF/ORG CONSULT DOMIN ADMIN EXEC REGION COERCE NAT/LISM ATTIT DRIVE PERSON ORD/FREE PWR...POLICY CONCPT OBS STERTYP 20. PAGE 92 B1860
FORCES ELITES

S63

WAGRET M.,"L'ASCENSION POLITIQUE DE L'U.D.D.I.A. (CONGO) ET SA PRISE DU POUVOIR (1956-1959)." AFR WOR+45 NAT/G POL/PAR CONSULT DELIB/GP LEGIS PERCEPT ALL/VALS SOVEREIGN...TIME/SEQ CONGO. PAGE 113 B2274
EX/STRUC CHOOSE FRANCE

B64

BROMAGE A.W.,MANAGER PLAN ABANDONMENTS: WHY A FEW HAVE DROPPED COUNCILMANAGER GOVERNMENT. USA+45 CREATE PARTIC CHOOSE...MGT CENSUS CHARTS 20. PAGE 15 B0315
MUNIC PLAN CONSULT LOC/G

B64

CULLINGWORTH J.B.,TOWN AND COUNTRY PLANNING IN ENGLAND AND WALES. UK LAW SOCIETY CONSULT ACT/RES ADMIN ROUTINE LEISURE INGP/REL ADJUST PWR...GEOG 20 OPEN/SPACE URBAN/RNWL. PAGE 25 B0512
MUNIC PLAN NAT/G PROB/SOLV

B64

MERILLAT H.C.L.,LEGAL ADVISERS AND FOREIGN AFFAIRS. WOR+45 WOR-45 ELITES INTELL NAT/G LEGIT ADMIN PERCEPT ALL/VALS...MGT NEW/IDEA RECORD 20. PAGE 73 B1469
CONSULT EX/STRUC DIPLOM

B64

PINNICK A.W.,COUNTRY PLANNERS IN ACTION. UK FINAN SERV/IND NAT/G CONSULT DELIB/GP PRICE CONTROL ROUTINE LEISURE AGE/C...GEOG 20 URBAN/RNWL. PAGE 83 B1674
MUNIC PLAN INDUS ATTIT

B64

SULLIVAN G.,THE STORY OF THE PEACE CORPS. USA+45 WOR+45 INTELL FACE/GP NAT/G SCHOOL VOL/ASSN CONSULT EX/STRUC PLAN EDU/PROP ADMIN ATTIT DRIVE ALL/VALS ...POLICY HEAL SOC CONCPT INT QU BIOG TREND SOC/EXP WORK. PAGE 102 B2054
INT/ORG ECO/UNDEV FOR/AID PEACE

B64

US SENATE COMM GOVT OPERATIONS,THE SECRETARY OF STATE AND THE AMBASSADOR. USA+45 CHIEF CONSULT EX/STRUC FORCES PLAN ADMIN EXEC INGP/REL ROLE ...ANTHOL 20 PRESIDENT DEPT/STATE. PAGE 110 B2215
DIPLOM DELIB/GP NAT/G

B64

WAINHOUSE D.W.,REMNANTS OF EMPIRE: THE UNITED NATIONS AND THE END OF COLONIALISM. FUT PORTUGAL WOR+45 NAT/G CONSULT DOMIN LEGIT ADMIN ROUTINE ATTIT ORD/FREE...POLICY JURID RECORD INT TIME/SEQ UN CMN/WLTH 20. PAGE 113 B2275
INT/ORG TREND COLONIAL

L64

PRUITT D.G.,"PROBLEM SOLVING IN THE DEPARTMENT OF STATE." USA+45 NAT/G CONSULT PROB/SOLV EXEC PWR ...DECISION INT ORG/CHARTS 20. PAGE 85 B1713
ROUTINE MGT DIPLOM

L64

WORLD PEACE FOUNDATION,"INTERNATIONAL ORGANIZATIONS: SUMMARY OF ACTIVITIES." INDIA PAKISTAN TURKEY WOR+45 CONSTN CONSULT EX/STRUC ECO/TAC EDU/PROP LEGIT ORD/FREE...JURID SOC UN 20 CYPRESS. PAGE 118 B2375
INT/ORG ROUTINE

S64

GROSS J.A.,"WHITEHALL AND THE COMMONWEALTH." EUR+WWI MOD/EUR INT/ORG NAT/G CONSULT DELIB/GP LEGIS DOMIN ADMIN COLONIAL ROUTINE PWR CMN/WLTH 19/20. PAGE 44 B0890
EX/STRUC ATTIT TREND

S64

HUELIN D.,"ECONOMIC INTEGRATION IN LATIN AMERICAN: PROGRESS AND PROBLEMS." L/A+17C ECO/DEV AGRI DIST/IND FINAN INDUS NAT/G VOL/ASSN CONSULT DELIB/GP EX/STRUC ACT/RES PLAN TEC/DEV ECO/TAC ROUTINE BAL/PAY WEALTH WORK 20. PAGE 52 B1058
MARKET ECO/UNDEV INT/TRADE

S64

MOWER A.G.,"THE OFFICIAL PRESSURE GROUP OF THE COUNCIL OF EUROPE'S CONSULATIVE ASSEMBLY." EUR+WWI SOCIETY STRUCT FINAN CONSULT ECO/TAC ADMIN ROUTINE ATTIT PWR WEALTH...STAT CHARTS 20 COUNCL/EUR. PAGE 76 B1535
INT/ORG EDU/PROP

S64

NEEDHAM T.,"SCIENCE AND SOCIETY IN EAST AND WEST." ASIA INTELL STRATA R+D LOC/G NAT/G PROVS CONSULT ACT/RES STRUCT CREATE PLAN TEC/DEV EDU/PROP ADMIN ATTIT ALL/VALS ...POLICY RELATIV MGT CONCPT NEW/IDEA TIME/SEQ WORK WORK. PAGE 77 B1565

B65

BUECHNER J.C.,DIFFERENCES IN ROLE PERCEPTIONS IN COLORADO COUNCIL-MANAGER CITIES. USA+45 ADMIN ROUTINE GP/REL PERCEPT PERSON ROLE ...DECISION MGT STAT INT QU CHARTS 20 COLORADO CITY/MGT. PAGE 17 B0338
MUNIC CONSULT LOC/G IDEA/COMP

B65

INTERNATIONAL CITY MGRS ASSN,COUNCIL-MANAGER GOVERNMENT, 1940-64: AN ANNOTATED BIBLIOGRAPHY. USA+45 ADMIN GOV/REL ROLE...MGT 20. PAGE 54 B1097
BIBLIOG/A MUNIC CONSULT PLAN

B65

LIPSET S.M.,THE BERKELEY STUDENT REVOLT: FACTS AND INTERPRETATIONS. USA+45 INTELL VOL/ASSN CONSULT EDU/PROP PRESS DEBATE ATTIT REV HAPPINESS RIGID/FLEX MAJORIT. PAGE 65 B1322
CROWD ACADEM ATTIT GP/REL

B65

MEYERHOFF A.E.,THE STRATEGY OF PERSUASION. USA+45 COM/IND CONSULT FOR/AID CONTROL COERCE COST ATTIT PERCEPT MARXISM 20 COLD/WAR. PAGE 73 B1476
EDU/PROP EFFICIENCY OP/RES ADMIN

B65

PANJABI K.L.,THE CIVIL SERVANT IN INDIA. INDIA UK NAT/G CONSULT EX/STRUC REGION GP/REL RACE/REL 20. PAGE 81 B1631
ADMIN WORKER BIOG COLONIAL

B65

ROWAT D.C.,THE OMBUDSMAN: CITIZEN'S DEFENDER. DENMARK FINLAND NEW/ZEALND NORWAY SWEDEN CONSULT PROB/SOLV FEEDBACK PARTIC GP/REL...SOC CONCPT NEW/IDEA METH/COMP ANTHOL BIBLIOG 20. PAGE 91 B1840
INSPECT CONSTN NAT/G ADMIN

S65

ALEXANDER T.,"SYNECTICS: INVENTING BY THE MADNESS METHOD." DELIB/GP TOP/EX ACT/RES TEC/DEV EXEC TASK KNOWL...MGT METH/COMP 20. PAGE 4 B0073
PROB/SOLV OP/RES CREATE CONSULT

S65

QUADE Q.L.,"THE TRUMAN ADMINISTRATION AND THE SEPARATION OF POWERS: THE CASE OF THE MARSHALL PLAN." SOCIETY INT/ORG NAT/G CONSULT DELIB/GP LEGIS PLAN ECO/TAC ROUTINE DRIVE PERCEPT RIGID/FLEX ORD/FREE PWR WEALTH...DECISION GEOG NEW/IDEA TREND 20 TRUMAN/HS. PAGE 85 B1726
USA+45 ECO/UNDEV DIPLOM

B66

ALEXANDER Y.,INTERNATIONAL TECHNICAL ASSISTANCE EXPERTS* A CASE STUDY OF THE U.N. EXPERIENCE. ECO/UNDEV CONSULT EX/STRUC CREATE PLAN DIPLOM FOR/AID TASK EFFICIENCY...ORG/CHARTS UN. PAGE 4 B0074
ECO/TAC INT/ORG ADMIN MGT

B66

ANDERSON D.L.,MUNICIPAL PUBLIC RELATIONS (1ST ED.). USA+45 SOCIETY CONSULT FORCES PRESS ADMIN...CHARTS BIBLIOG/A 20. PAGE 4 B0092
MUNIC INGP/REL EDU/PROP ATTIT

B66

LINDFORS G.V.,INTERCOLLEGIATE BIBLIOGRAPHY; CASES IN BUSINESS ADMINISTRATION (VOL. X). FINAN MARKET LABOR CONSULT PLAN GP/REL PRODUC 20. PAGE 65 B1314
BIBLIOG/A ADMIN MGT OP/RES

B66

MANGONE G.J.,UN ADMINISTRATION OF ECONOMIC AND AOCIAL PROGRAMS. CONSULT BUDGET INT/TRADE REGION 20 UN. PAGE 69 B1391
ADMIN MGT ECO/TAC

DELIB/GP
B66

MANSFIELD E.,MANAGERIAL ECONOMICS AND OPERATIONS RESEARCH; A NONMATHEMATICAL INTRODUCTION. USA+45 ELITES ECO/DEV CONSULT EX/STRUC PROB/SOLV ROUTINE EFFICIENCY OPTIMAL...GAME T 20. PAGE 69 B1396
ECO/TAC
OP/RES
MGT
COMPUTER
B66

US BUREAU OF THE BUDGET,THE ADMINISTRATION OF GOVERNMENT SUPPORTED RESEARCH AT UNIVERSITIES (PAMPHLET). USA+45 CONSULT TOP/EX ADMIN INCOME WEALTH...MGT PHIL/SCI INT. PAGE 108 B2174
ACT/RES
NAT/G
ACADEM
GP/REL
B66

US SENATE COMM GOVT OPERATIONS,INTERGOVERNMENTAL PERSONNEL ACT OF 1966. USA+45 NAT/G CONSULT DELIB/GP WORKER TEC/DEV PAY AUTOMAT UTIL 20 CONGRESS. PAGE 110 B2219
ADMIN
LEGIS
EFFICIENCY
EDU/PROP
B67

BALDWIN G.B.,PLANNING AND DEVELOPMENT IN IRAN. IRAN AGRI INDUS CONSULT WORKER EDU/PROP BAL/PAY...CHARTS 20. PAGE 8 B0173
PLAN
ECO/UNDEV
ADMIN
PROB/SOLV
B67

FARNSWORTH B.,WILLIAM C. BULLITT AND THE SOVIET UNION. COM USA-45 USSR NAT/G CHIEF CONSULT DELIB/GP EX/STRUC WAR REPRESENT MARXISM 20 WILSON/W ROOSEVLT/F STALIN/J BULLITT/WC. PAGE 35 B0705
DIPLOM
BIOG
POLICY
B67

GABRIEL P.P.,THE INTERNATIONAL TRANSFER OF CORPORATE SKILLS: MANAGEMENT CONTRACTS IN LESS DEVELOPED COUNTRIES. CLIENT INDUS LG/CO PLAN PROB/SOLV CAP/ISM ECO/TAC FOR/AID INT/TRADE RENT ADMIN SKILL 20. PAGE 38 B0771
ECO/UNDEV
AGREE
MGT
CONSULT
B67

HIRSCHMAN A.O.,DEVELOPMENT PROJECTS OBSERVED. INDUS INT/ORG CONSULT EX/STRUC CREATE OP/RES ECO/TAC DEMAND...POLICY MGT METH/COMP 20 WORLD/BANK. PAGE 50 B1016
ECO/UNDEV
R+D
FINAN
PLAN
B67

LENG S.C.,JUSTICE IN COMMUNIST CHINA: A SURVEY OF THE JUDICIAL SYSTEM OF THE CHINESE PEOPLE'S REPUBLIC. CHINA/COM LAW CONSTN LOC/G NAT/G PROF/ORG CONSULT FORCES ADMIN CRIME ORD/FREE...BIBLIOG 20 MAO. PAGE 64 B1290
CT/SYS
ADJUD
JURID
MARXISM
B67

SCHLOSSBERG S.I.,ORGANIZING AND THE LAW. USA+45 WORKER PLAN LEGIT REPRESENT GP/REL...JURID MGT 20 NLRB. PAGE 94 B1893
LABOR
CONSULT
BARGAIN
PRIVIL
L67

BLUMBERG A.S.,"THE PRACTICE OF LAW AS CONFIDENCE GAME; ORGANIZATIONAL COOPTATION OF A PROFESSION." USA+45 CLIENT SUCIETY CONSULT ROLE JURID. PAGE 13 B0260
CT/SYS
ADJUD
GP/REL
ADMIN
S67

ATKIN J.M.,"THE FEDERAL GOVERNMENT, BIG BUSINESS, AND COLLEGES OF EDUCATION." PROF/ORG CONSULT CREATE PLAN PROB/SOLV ADMIN EFFICIENCY. PAGE 7 B0144
SCHOOL
ACADEM
NAT/G
INDUS
S67

CONWAY J.E.,"MAKING RESEARCH EFFECTIVE IN LEGISLATION." LAW R+D CONSULT EX/STRUC PLAN CONFER ADMIN LEAD ROUTINE TASK INGP/REL DECISION. PAGE 23 B0469
ACT/RES
POLICY
LEGIS
PROB/SOLV
S67

DOERN G.B.,"THE ROYAL COMMISSIONS IN THE GENERAL POLICY PROCESS AND IN FEDERAL-PROVINCIAL RELATIONS." CANADA CONSTN ACADEM PROVS CONSULT DELIB/GP LEGIS ACT/RES PROB/SOLV CONFER CONTROL EFFICIENCY...METH/COMP 20 SENATE ROYAL/COMM. PAGE 30 B0603
R+D
EX/STRUC
GOV/REL
NAT/G
S67

DUGGAR J.W.,"THE DEVELOPMENT OF MONEY SUPPLY IN ETHIOPIA." ETHIOPIA ISLAM CONSULT OP/RES BUDGET CONTROL ROUTINE EFFICIENCY EQUILIB WEALTH...MGT 20. PAGE 31 B0629
ECO/UNDEV
FINAN
BAL/PAY
ECOMETRIC
S67

GOBER J.L.,"FEDERALISM AT WORK." USA+45 NAT/G CONSULT ACT/RES PLAN CONFER ADMIN LEAD PARTIC FEDERAL ATTIT. PAGE 40 B0813
MUNIC
TEC/DEV
R+D
GOV/REL
S67

MELTZER B.D.,"RUMINATIONS ABOUT IDEOLOGY, LAW, AND LABOR ARBITRATION." USA+45 ECO/DEV PROB/SOLV CONFER MGT. PAGE 73 B1466
JURID
ADJUD
LABOR
CONSULT
S67

MORTON J.A.,"A SYSTEMS APPROACH TO THE INNOVATION PROCESS: ITS USE IN THE BELL SYSTEM." USA+45 INTELL INDUS LG/CO CONSULT WORKER COMPUTER AUTOMAT DEMAND ...MGT CHARTS 20. PAGE 76 B1531
TEC/DEV
GEN/METH
R+D
COM/IND
S67

ROWAT D.C.,"RECENT DEVELOPMENTS IN OMBUDSMANSHIP* A REVIEW ARTICLE." UK USA+45 STRUCT CONSULT INSPECT TASK EFFICIENCY...NEW/IDEA 20. PAGE 91 B1841
CANADA
ADMIN
LOC/G
NAT/G

S67

SKOLNICK J.H.,"SOCIAL CONTROL IN THE ADVERSARY SYSTEM." USA+45 CONSULT OP/RES ADMIN CONTROL. PAGE 98 B1975
PROB/SOLV
PERS/REL
ADJUD
CT/SYS
S67

TACKABERRY R.B.,"ORGANIZING AND TRAINING PEACE-KEEPING FORCES* THE CANADIAN VIEW." CANADA PLAN DIPLOM CONFER ADJUD ADMIN CIVMIL/REL 20 UN. PAGE 102 B2069
PEACE
FORCES
INT/ORG
CONSULT

CONSULTANTS....SEE CONSULT

CONSUMER....SEE MARKET, ECO

CONT/OBS....CONTROLLED DIRECT OBSERVATION

B30

MURCHISON C.,PSYCHOLOGIES OF 1930. UNIV USA-45 CULTURE INTELL SOCIETY STRATA FAM ROUTINE BIO/SOC DRIVE RIGID/FLEX SUPEGO...NEW/IDEA OBS SELF/OBS CONT/OBS 20. PAGE 76 B1543
CREATE
PERSON
B41

MACMAHON A.W.,THE ADMINISTRATION OF FEDERAL WORK RELIEF. USA-45 EX/STRUC WORKER BUDGET EFFICIENCY ...CONT/OBS CHARTS 20 WPA. PAGE 68 B1367
ADMIN
NAT/G
MGT
GIVE
B52

MAIER N.R.F.,PRINCIPLES OF HUMAN RELATIONS. WOR+45 WOR-45 CULTURE SOCIETY ROUTINE ATTIT DRIVE PERCEPT PERSON RIGID/FLEX SUPEGO PWR...PSY CONT/OBS RECORD TOT/POP VAL/FREE 20. PAGE 68 B1379
INDUS
B53

MACK R.T.,RAISING THE WORLDS STANDARD OF LIVING. IRAN INT/ORG VOL/ASSN EX/STRUC ECO/TAC WEALTH...MGT METH/CNCPT STAT CONT/OBS INT TOT/POP VAL/FREE 20 UN. PAGE 67 B1363
WOR+45
FOR/AID
INT/TRADE
B54

COMBS C.H.,DECISION PROCESSES. INTELL SOCIETY DELIB/GP CREATE TEC/DEV DOMIN LEGIT EXEC CHOOSE DRIVE RIGID/FLEX KNOWL PWR...PHIL/SCI SOC METH/CNCPT CONT/OBS REC/INT PERS/TEST SAMP/SIZ BIOG SOC/EXP WORK. PAGE 22 B0455
MATH
DECISION
S55

CROCKETT W.H.,"EMERGENT LEADERSHIP IN SMALL DECISION MAKING GROUPS." ACT/RES ROUTINE PERS/REL ATTIT...STAT CONT/OBS SOC/EXP SIMUL. PAGE 25 B0507
DELIB/GP
ADMIN
PSY
DECISION
S56

GORE W.J.,"ADMINISTRATIVE DECISION-MAKING IN FEDERAL FIELD OFFICES." USA+45 PROVS PWR CONT/OBS. PAGE 41 B0833
DECISION
PROB/SOLV
FEDERAL
ADMIN
B57

HOLCOMBE A.N.,STRENGTHENING THE UNITED NATIONS. USA+45 ACT/RES CREATE PLAN EDU/PROP ATTIT PERCEPT PWR...METH/CNCPT CONT/OBS RECORD UN COLD/WAR 20. PAGE 51 B1032
INT/ORG
ROUTINE
B58

BROWNE C.G.,THE CONCEPT OF LEADERSHIP. UNIV FACE/GP DOMIN EDU/PROP LEGIT LEAD DRIVE PERSON PWR...MGT SOC OBS SELF/OBS CONT/OBS INT PERS/TEST STERTYP GEN/LAWS. PAGE 16 B0328
EXEC
CONCPT
B59

DIEBOLD W. JR.,THE SCHUMAN PLAN: A STUDY IN ECONOMIC COOPERATION, 1950-1959. EUR+WWI FRANCE GERMANY USA+45 EXTR/IND CONSULT DELIB/GP PLAN DIPLOM ECO/TAC INT/TRADE ROUTINE ORD/FREE WEALTH ...METH/CNCPT STAT CONT/OBS INT TIME/SEQ ECSC 20. PAGE 29 B0591
INT/ORG
REGION
S60

MORALES C.J.,"TRADE AND ECONOMIC INTEGRATION IN LATIN AMERICA." FUT L/A+17C LAW STRATA ECO/UNDEV DIST/IND INDUS LABOR NAT/G LEGIS ECO/TAC ADMIN RIGID/FLEX WEALTH...CONCPT NEW/IDEA CONT/OBS TIME/SEQ WORK 20. PAGE 75 B1519
FINAN
INT/TRADE
REGION
B61

HAIRE M.,MODERN ORGANIZATION THEORY. LABOR ROUTINE MAJORITY...CONCPT MODAL OBS CONT/OBS. PAGE 45 B0919
PERS/REL
GP/REL
MGT
DECISION
B61

MARVICK D.,POLITICAL DECISION-MAKERS. INTELL STRATA NAT/G POL/PAR EX/STRUC LEGIS DOMIN EDU/PROP ATTIT PERSON PWR...PSY STAT OBS CONT/OBS STAND/INT UNPLAN/INT TIME/SEQ CHARTS STERTYP VAL/FREE. PAGE 70 B1416
TOP/EX
BIOG
ELITES
S61

CARLETON W.G.,"AMERICAN FOREIGN POLICY: MYTHS AND REALITIES." FUT USA+45 WOR+45 ECO/UNDEV INT/ORG EX/STRUC ARMS/CONT NUC/PWR WAR ATTIT...POLICY CONCPT CONT/OBS GEN/METH COLD/WAR TOT/POP 20. PAGE 19 B0378
PLAN
MYTH
DIPLOM
S62

NORTH R.C.,"DECISION MAKING IN CRISIS: AN INTRODUCTION." WOR+45 WOR-45 NAT/G CONSULT DELIB/GP
INT/ORG
ROUTINE

TEC/DEV PERCEPT KNOWL...POLICY DECISION PSY   DIPLOM
METH/CNCPT CONT/OBS TREND VAL/FREE 20. PAGE 79
B1590
                                                                        S63
CLEMHOUT S.,"PRODUCTION FUNCTION ANALYSIS APPLIED   ECO/DEV
TO THE LEONTIEF SCARCE-FACTOR PARADOX OF   ECO/TAC
INTERNATIONAL TRADE." EUR+WWI USA+45 DIST/IND NAT/G
PLAN TEC/DEV DIPLOM PWR WEALTH...MGT METH/CNCPT
CONT/OBS CON/ANAL CHARTS SIMUL GEN/LAWS 20. PAGE 21
B0436
                                                                        B64
LOWI T.J.,AT THE PLEASURE OF THE MAYOR. EX/STRUC   LOBBY
PROB/SOLV BAL/PWR ADMIN PARTIC CHOOSE GP/REL   LOC/G
...CONT/OBS NET/THEORY CHARTS 20 NEWYORK/C MAYOR.   PWR
PAGE 67 B1346   MUNIC

CONTEMPT....SEE RESPECT

CONTENT ANALYSIS....SEE CON/ANAL

CONTROL....CONTROL OF HUMAN GROUP OPERATIONS

                                                                        N
INTERNATIONAL REVIEW OF ADMINISTRATIVE SCIENCES.   BIBLIOG/A
WOR+45 WOR-45 STRATA ECO/DEV ECO/UNDEV CREATE PLAN   ADMIN
PROB/SOLV DIPLOM CONTROL REPRESENT...MGT 20. PAGE 1 INT/ORG
B0004   NAT/G
                                                                        N
US SUPERINTENDENT OF DOCUMENTS,INTERSTATE COMMERCE   BIBLIOG/A
(PRICE LIST 59). USA+45 LAW LOC/G NAT/G LEGIS   DIST/IND
TARIFFS TAX ADMIN CONTROL HEALTH DECISION. PAGE 111 GOV/REL
B2239   PROVS
                                                                        B05
GOODNOW F.J.,THE PRINCIPLES OF THE ADMINISTRATIVE   ADMIN
LAW OF THE UNITED STATES. USA+45 LAW STRUCT   NAT/G
EX/STRUC LEGIS BAL/PWR CONTROL GOV/REL PWR...JURID   PROVS
19/20 CIVIL/SERV. PAGE 41 B0822   LOC/G
                                                                        N19
BURRUS B.R.,INVESTIGATION AND DISCOVERY IN STATE   NAT/G
ANTITRUST (PAMPHLET). USA+45 USA-45 LEGIS ECO/TAC   PROVS
ADMIN CONTROL CT/SYS CRIME GOV/REL PWR...JURID   LAW
CHARTS 19/20 FTC MONOPOLY. PAGE 17 B0355   INSPECT
                                                                        N19
CANADA CIVIL SERV COMM,THE ANALYSIS OF ORGANIZATION NAT/G
IN THE GOVERNMENT OF CANADA (PAMPHLET). CANADA   MGT
CONSTN EX/STRUC LEGIS TOP/EX CREATE PLAN CONTROL   ADMIN
GP/REL 20. PAGE 18 B0372   DELIB/GP
                                                                        N19
FOLSOM M.B.,BETTER MANAGEMENT OF THE PUBLIC'S   ADMIN
BUSINESS (PAMPHLET). USA+45 DELIB/GP PAY CONFER   NAT/G
CONTROL REGION GP/REL...METH/COMP ANTHOL 20.   MGT
PAGE 36 B0733   PROB/SOLV
                                                                        N19
GORWALA A.D.,THE ADMINISTRATIVE JUNGLE (PAMPHLET).   ADMIN
INDIA NAT/G LEGIS ECO/TAC CONTROL GOV/REL   POLICY
...METH/COMP 20. PAGE 41 B0838   PLAN
                                                     ECO/UNDEV
                                                                        N19
JACKSON R.G.A.,THE CASE FOR AN INTERNATIONAL   FOR/AID
DEVELOPMENT AUTHORITY (PAMPHLET). WOR+45 ECO/DEV   INT/ORG
DIPLOM GIVE CONTROL GP/REL EFFICIENCY NAT/LISM   ECO/UNDEV
SOVEREIGN 20. PAGE 55 B1108   ADMIN
                                                                        N19
PERREN G.E.,LANGUAGE AND COMMUNICATION IN THE   EDU/PROP
COMMONWEALTH (PAMPHLET). FUT UK LAW ECO/DEV PRESS   LING
TV WRITING ADJUD ADMIN COLONIAL CONTROL 20   GOV/REL
CMN/WLTH. PAGE 82 B1660   COM/IND
                                                                        N19
SOUTH AFRICA COMMISSION ON FUT,INTERIM AND FINAL   CONSTN
REPORTS ON FUTURE FORM OF GOVERNMENT IN THE SOUTH-   REPRESENT
WEST AFRICAN PROTECTORATE (PAMPHLET). SOUTH/AFR   ADMIN
NAT/G FORCES CONFER COLONIAL CONTROL 20 AFRICA/SW.   PROB/SOLV
PAGE 99 B1998
                                                                        B24
BAGEHOT W.,THE ENGLISH CONSTITUTION AND OTHER   NAT/G
POLITICAL ESSAYS. UK DELIB/GP BAL/PWR ADMIN CONTROL STRUCT
EXEC ROUTINE CONSERVE...METH PARLIAMENT 19/20.   CONCPT
PAGE 8 B0160
                                                                        B24
HOLDSWORTH W.S.,A HISTORY OF ENGLISH LAW; THE   LAW
COMMON LAW AND ITS RIVALS (VOL. VI). UK STRATA   CONSTN
EX/STRUC ADJUD ADMIN CONTROL CT/SYS...JURID CONCPT   LEGIS
GEN/LAWS 17 COMMONWLTH PARLIAMENT ENGLSH/LAW   CHIEF
COMMON/LAW. PAGE 51 B1034
                                                                        B25
MATHEWS J.M.,AMERICAN STATE GOVERNMENT. USA+45   PROVS
LOC/G CHIEF EX/STRUC LEGIS ADJUD CONTROL CT/SYS   ADMIN
ROUTINE GOV/REL PWR 20 GOVERNOR. PAGE 71 B1426   FEDERAL
                                                     CONSTN
                                                                        B27
DICKINSON J.,ADMINISTRATIVE JUSTICE AND THE   CT/SYS
SUPREMACY OF LAW IN THE UNITED STATES. USA+45 LAW   ADJUD
INDUS DOMIN EDU/PROP CONTROL EXEC GP/REL ORD/FREE   ADMIN
...POLICY JURID 19/20. PAGE 29 B0586   NAT/G
                                                                        B29
MOLEY R.,POLITICS AND CRIMINAL PROSECUTION. USA+45   PWR

POL/PAR EX/STRUC LEGIT CONTROL LEAD ROUTINE CHOOSE   CT/SYS
INGP/REL...JURID CHARTS 20. PAGE 74 B1497   CRIME
                                                     ADJUD
                                                                        B34
RIDLEY C.E.,THE CITY-MANAGER PROFESSION. CHIEF PLAN MUNIC
ADMIN CONTROL ROUTINE CHOOSE...TECHNIC CHARTS   EX/STRUC
GOV/COMP BIBLIOG 20. PAGE 88 B1780   LOC/G
                                                     EXEC
                                                                        B37
GULICK L.,PAPERS ON THE SCIENCE OF ADMINISTRATION.   OP/RES
INDUS PROB/SOLV TEC/DEV COST EFFICIENCY PRODUC   CONTROL
HABITAT...PHIL/SCI METH/COMP 20. PAGE 45 B0903   ADMIN
                                                     MGT
                                                                        B38
REICH N.,LABOR RELATIONS IN REPUBLICAN GERMANY.   WORKER
GERMANY CONSTN ECO/DEV INDUS NAT/G ADMIN CONTROL   MGT
GP/REL FASCISM POPULISM 20 WEIMAR/REP. PAGE 87   LABOR
B1763   BARGAIN
                                                                        B39
MCCAMY J.L.,GOVERNMENT PUBLICITY: ITS PRACTICE IN   EDU/PROP
FEDERAL ADMINISTRATION. USA+45 COM/IND ADMIN   NAT/G
CONTROL EXEC PARTIC INGP/REL...SOC 20. PAGE 71   PLAN
B1442   ATTIT
                                                                        S40
PERKINS J.A.,"CONGRESSIONAL INVESTIGATIONS OF   POL/PAR
MATTERS OF INTERNATIONAL IMPORT." DELIB/GP DIPLOM   DECISION
ADMIN CONTROL 20 CONGRESS. PAGE 82 B1656   PARL/PROC
                                                     GOV/REL
                                                                        B41
PERHAM M.,AFRICANS AND BRITISH RULE. AFR UK ECO/TAC DIPLOM
CONTROL GP/REL ATTIT 20. PAGE 82 B1654   COLONIAL
                                                     ADMIN
                                                     ECO/UNDEV
                                                                        B42
SINGTON D.,THE GOEBBELS EXPERIMENT. GERMANY MOD/EUR FASCISM
NAT/G EX/STRUC FORCES CONTROL ROUTINE WAR TOTALISM   EDU/PROP
PWR...ART/METH HUM 20 NAZI GOEBBELS/J. PAGE 97   ATTIT
B1970   COM/IND
                                                                        S42
HUZAR E.,"LEGISLATIVE CONTROL OVER ADMINISTRATION: ADMIN
CONGRESS AND WPA" USA+45 FINAN DELIB/GP LOBBY   EX/STRUC
GOV/REL EFFICIENCY ATTIT...POLICY CONGRESS. PAGE 53 CONTROL
B1069   LEGIS
                                                                        L43
MACMAHON A.W.,"CONGRESSIONAL OVERSIGHT OF   LEGIS
ADMINISTRATION: THE POWER OF THE PURSE." USA+45   DELIB/GP
BUDGET ROUTINE GOV/REL PWR...POLICY CONGRESS.   ADMIN
PAGE 68 B1368   CONTROL
                                                                        S43
SELZNICK P.,"AN APPROACH TO A THEORY OF   ROUTINE
BUREAUCRACY." INDUS WORKER CONTROL LEAD EFFICIENCY   ADMIN
OPTIMAL...SOC METH 20 BARNARD/C BUREAUCRCY   MGT
WEBER/MAX FRIEDRCH/C MICHELS/R. PAGE 95 B1928   EX/STRUC
                                                                        B44
BARKER E.,THE DEVELOPMENT OF PUBLIC SERVICES IN   GOV/COMP
WESTERN EUROPE: 1660-1930. FRANCE GERMANY UK SCHOOL ADMIN
CONTROL REPRESENT ROLE...WELF/ST 17/20. PAGE 9   EX/STRUC
B0185
                                                                        S44
SIMON H.A.,"DECISION-MAKING AND ADMINISTRATIVE   DECISION
ORGANIZATION" (BMR)" WOR-45 CHOOSE INGP/REL   ADMIN
EFFICIENCY ATTIT RESPECT...MGT 20. PAGE 97 B1955   CONTROL
                                                     WORKER
                                                                        B45
MILLIS H.A.,ORGANIZED LABOR (FIRST ED.). LAW STRUCT LABOR
DELIB/GP WORKER ECO/TAC ADJUD CONTROL REPRESENT   POLICY
INGP/REL INCOME MGT. PAGE 74 B1485   ROUTINE
                                                     GP/REL
                                                                        S45
KRIESBERG M.,"WHAT CONGRESSMEN AND ADMINISTRATORS   LEGIS
THINK OF THE POLLS." USA+45 CONTROL PWR...INT QU.   ATTIT
PAGE 61 B1236   EDU/PROP
                                                     ADMIN
                                                                        S45
WHITE L.D.,"CONGRESSIONAL CONTROL OF THE PUBLIC   LEGIS
SERVICE." USA+45 NAT/G CONSULT DELIB/GP PLAN SENIOR EXEC
CONGRESS. PAGE 116 B2335   POLICY
                                                     CONTROL
                                                                        B46
DAVIES E.,NATIONAL ENTERPRISE: THE DEVELOPMENT OF   ADMIN
THE PUBLIC CORPORATION. UK LG/CO EX/STRUC WORKER   NAT/G
PROB/SOLV COST ATTIT SOCISM 20. PAGE 26 B0536   CONTROL
                                                     INDUS
                                                                        B47
BAERWALD F.,FUNDAMENTALS OF LABOR ECONOMICS. LAW   ECO/DEV
INDUS LABOR LG/CO CONTROL GP/REL INCOME TOTALISM   WORKER
...MGT CHARTS GEN/LAWS BIBLIOG 20. PAGE 8 B0158   MARKET
                                                                        B47
FLYNN E.J.,YOU'RE THE BOSS. USA+45 ELITES TOP/EX   LOC/G
DOMIN CONTROL EXEC LEAD REPRESENT 19/20 NEWYORK/C   MUNIC
ROOSEVLT/F FLYNN/BOSS BOSSISM. PAGE 36 B0732   BIOG
                                                     POL/PAR
                                                                        B47
GAUS J.M.,REFLECTIONS ON PUBLIC ADMINISTRATION.   MGT
USA+45 CONTROL GOV/REL CENTRAL FEDERAL ATTIT WEALTH POLICY
...DECISION 20. PAGE 39 B0787   EX/STRUC

KEFAUVER E.,A TWENTIETH-CENTURY CONGRESS. POL/PAR EX/STRUC SENIOR ADMIN CONTROL EXEC LOBBY CHOOSE EFFICIENCY PWR. PAGE 59 B1189
ADMIN
B47
LEGIS
DELIB/GP
ROUTINE
TOP/EX

REDFORD E.S.,FIELD ADMINISTRATION OF WARTIME RATIONING. USA-45 CONSTN ELITES DIST/IND WORKER CONTROL WAR GOV/REL ADJUST RIGID/FLEX 20 OPA. PAGE 87 B1752
B47
ADMIN
NAT/G
PROB/SOLV
RATION

ROSSITER C.L.,CONSTITUTIONAL DICTATORSHIP: CRISIS GOVERNMENT IN THE MODERN DEMOCRACIES. FRANCE GERMANY UK USA-45 WOR-45 EX/STRUC BAL/PWR CONTROL COERCE WAR CENTRAL ORD/FREE...DECISION 19/20. PAGE 90 B1828
B48
NAT/G
AUTHORIT
CONSTN
TOTALISM

SPERO S.D.,GOVERNMENT AS EMPLOYER. USA+45 NAT/G EX/STRUC ADMIN CONTROL EXEC 20. PAGE 99 B2005
B48
SOVEREIGN
INGP/REL
REPRESENT
CONFER

ASPINALL A.,POLITICS AND THE PRESS 1780-1850. UK LAW ELITES FINAN PROF/ORG LEGIS ADMIN ATTIT ...POLICY 18/19. PAGE 7 B0142
B49
PRESS
CONTROL
POL/PAR
ORD/FREE

GLOVER J.D.,THE ADMINISTRATOR. ELITES LG/CO EX/STRUC ACT/RES CONTROL GP/REL INGP/REL PERS/REL AUTHORIT...POLICY CONCPT HIST/WRIT. PAGE 40 B0811
B49
ADMIN
MGT
ATTIT
PROF/ORG

GRAVES W.B.,BASIC INFORMATION ON THE REORGANIZATION OF THE EXECUTIVE BRANCH: 1912-1948. USA-45 BUDGET ADMIN CONTROL GP/REL EFFICIENCY...MGT CHARTS ORG/CHARTS 20 PRESIDENT. PAGE 42 B0857
B49
BIBLIOG/A
EX/STRUC
NAT/G
CHIEF

RIDDICK F.M.,THE UNITED STATES CONGRESS ORGANIZATION AND PROCEDURE. POL/PAR DELIB/GP PROB/SOLV DEBATE CONTROL EXEC LEAD INGP/REL PWR ...MAJORIT DECISION CONGRESS PRESIDENT. PAGE 88 B1777
B49
LEGIS
PARL/PROC
CHIEF
EX/STRUC

SCHWARTZ B.,LAW AND THE EXECUTIVE IN BRITAIN: A COMPARATIVE STUDY. UK USA+45 LAW EX/STRUC PWR ...GOV/COMP 20. PAGE 95 B1911
B49
ADMIN
EXEC
CONTROL
REPRESENT

WALINE M.,LE CONTROLE JURIDICTIONNEL DE L'ADMINISTRATION. BELGIUM FRANCE UAR JUDGE BAL/PWR ADJUD CONTROL CT/SYS...GP/COMP 20. PAGE 113 B2277
B49
JURID
ADMIN
PWR
ORD/FREE

FAINSED M.,"RECENT DEVELOPMENTS IN SOVIET PUBLIC ADMINISTRATION." USSR EXEC 20. PAGE 34 B0699
L49
DOMIN
CONTROL
CENTRAL
EX/STRUC

STEINMETZ H.,"THE PROBLEMS OF THE LANDRAT: A STUDY OF COUNTY GOVERNMENT IN THE US ZONE OF GERMANY." GERMANY/W USA+45 INDUS PLAN DIPLOM EDU/PROP CONTROL WAR GOV/REL FEDERAL WEALTH PLURISM...GOV/COMP 20 LANDRAT. PAGE 100 B2031
S49
LOC/G
COLONIAL
MGT
TOP/EX

GRAVES W.B.,PUBLIC ADMINISTRATION: A COMPREHENSIVE BIBLIOGRAPHY ON PUBLIC ADMINISTRATION IN THE UNITED STATES (PAMPHLET). USA+45 USA-45 LOC/G NAT/G LEGIS ADJUD INGP/REL...MGT 20. PAGE 42 B0858
B50
BIBLIOG
FINAN
CONTROL
ADMIN

GREAT BRITAIN TREASURY.PUBLIC ADMINISTRATION: A BIBLIOGRAPHY FOR ORGANISATION AND METHODS (PAMPHLET). LOC/G NAT/G CONSULT EX/STRUC CONFER ROUTINE TASK EFFICIENCY...MGT 20. PAGE 43 B0862
B50
BIBLIOG
PLAN
CONTROL
ADMIN

HYNEMAN C.S.,BUREAUCRACY IN A DEMOCRACY. CHIEF LEGIS ADMIN CONTROL LEAD ROUTINE PERS/REL COST EFFICIENCY UTIL ATTIT AUTHORIT PERSON MORAL. PAGE 53 B1071
B50
NAT/G
CENTRAL
EX/STRUC
MYTH

DAVIS K.C.,ADMINISTRATIVE LAW. USA+45 USA-45 NAT/G PROB/SOLV BAL/PWR CONTROL ORD/FREE...POLICY 20 SUPREME/CT. PAGE 26 B0539
B51
ADMIN
JURID
EX/STRUC
ADJUD

DIMOCK M.E.,FREE ENTERPRISE AND THE ADMINISTRATIVE STATE. FINAN LG/CO BARGAIN BUDGET DOMIN CONTROL INGP/REL EFFICIENCY 20. PAGE 29 B0595
B51
CAP/ISM
ADMIN
MGT
MARKET

REDFORD E.S.,ADMINISTRATION OF NATIONAL ECONOMIC CONTROL. ECO/DEV DELIB/GP ADJUD CONTROL EQUILIB 20. PAGE 87 B1753
B52
ADMIN
ROUTINE
GOV/REL
LOBBY

LIPSET S.M.,"DEMOCRACY IN PRIVATE GOVERNMENT; (A
S52
LABOR

CASE STUDY OF THE INTERNATIONAL TYPOGRAPHICAL UNION)" (BMR)" POL/PAR CONTROL LEAD INGP/REL PWR ...MAJORIT DECISION PREDICT 20. PAGE 65 B1319
ADMIN
ELITES
REPRESENT

SOMERS H.M.,"THE PRESIDENT AS ADMINISTRATOR." USA+45 NAT/G ADMIN REPRESENT GOV/REL 20 PRESIDENT. PAGE 99 B1996
S52
CONTROL
EFFICIENCY
EX/STRUC
EXEC

DIMOCK M.E.,PUBLIC ADMINISTRATION. USA+45 FINAN WORKER BUDGET CONTROL CHOOSE...T 20. PAGE 29 B0596
B53
ADMIN
STRUCT
OP/RES
POLICY

NEWMAN F.C.,"CONGRESS AND THE FAITHFUL EXECUTION OF LAWS - SHOULD LEGISLATORS SUPERVISE ADMINISTRATORS." USA+45 NAT/G EX/STRUC EXEC PWR POLICY. PAGE 78 B1579
L53
REPRESENT
CONTROL
ADMIN
LEGIS

GABLE R.W.,"NAM: INFLUENTIAL LOBBY OR KISS OF DEATH?" (BMR)" USA+45 LAW INSPECT EDU/PROP ADMIN CONTROL INGP/REL EFFICIENCY PWR 20 CONGRESS NAM TAFT/HART. PAGE 38 B0769
S53
LOBBY
LEGIS
INDUS
LG/CO

PERKINS J.A.,"ADMINISTRATION OF THE NATIONAL SECURITY PROGRAM." USA+45 EX/STRUC FORCES ADMIN CIVMIL/REL ORD/FREE 20. PAGE 82 B1657
S53
CONTROL
GP/REL
REPRESENT
PROB/SOLV

DORWART R.A.,"THE ADMINISTRATIVE REFORMS OF FREDRICK WILLIAM I OF PRUSSIA. GERMANY MOD/EUR CHIEF CONTROL PWR...BIBLIOG 16/18. PAGE 30 B0608
C53
ADMIN
NAT/G
CENTRAL
GOV/REL

KRACKE E.A. JR.,"CIVIL SERVICE IN EARLY SUNG CHINA, 960-1067." ASIA GP/REL...BIBLIOG/A 10/11. PAGE 61 B1231
C53
ADMIN
NAT/G
WORKER
CONTROL

LAPIERRE R.T.,A THEORY OF SOCIAL CONTROL. STRUCT ADMIN ROUTINE SANCTION ANOMIE AUTHORIT DRIVE PERSON PWR...MAJORIT CONCPT CLASSIF. PAGE 62 B1260
B54
CONTROL
VOL/ASSN
CULTURE

LOCKLIN D.P.,ECONOMICS OF TRANSPORTATION (4TH ED.). USA+45 USA-45 SEA AIR LAW FINAN LG/CO EX/STRUC ADMIN CONTROL...STAT CHARTS 19/20 RAILROAD PUB/TRANS. PAGE 66 B1335
B54
ECO/DEV
DIST/IND
ECO/TAC
TEC/DEV

APPLEBY P.H.,"BUREAUCRACY AND THE FUTURE." USA+45 NAT/G CONTROL EXEC...MAJORIT 20. PAGE 6 B0119
S54
EX/STRUC
LOBBY
REPRESENT
ADMIN

CHILDS R.S.,"CITIZEN ORGANIZATION FOR CONTROL OF GOVERNMENT." USA+45 POL/PAR CONTROL LOBBY...MAJORIT 20. PAGE 21 B0424
S54
CHOOSE
REPRESENT
ADMIN
EX/STRUC

COOPER L.,"ADMINISTRATIVE JUSTICE." UK ADMIN REPRESENT PWR...POLICY 20. PAGE 23 B0475
S54
LAW
ADJUD
CONTROL
EX/STRUC

GILBERT C.E.,"LEGISLATIVE CONTROL OF THE BUREAUCRACY." USA+45 NAT/G ADMIN EXEC 20. PAGE 39 B0798
S54
CONTROL
EX/STRUC
REPRESENT
GOV/REL

STONE E.O.,"ADMINISTRATIVE INTEGRATION." USA+45 NAT/G ADMIN CONTROL CENTRAL 20. PAGE 101 B2046
S54
REPRESENT
EFFICIENCY
LOBBY
EX/STRUC

ZELLER B.,"AMERICAN STATE LEGISLATURES: REPORT ON THE COMMITTEE ON AMERICAN LEGISLATURES." CONSTN POL/PAR EX/STRUC CONFER ADMIN CONTROL EXEC LOBBY ROUTINE GOV/REL...POLICY BIBLIOG 20. PAGE 119 B2401
C54
REPRESENT
LEGIS
PROVS
APPORT

GALLOWAY G.B.,CONGRESS AND PARLIAMENT: THEIR ORGANIZATION AND OPERATION IN THE US AND THE UK: PLANNING PAMPHLET NO. 93. POL/PAR EX/STRUC DEBATE CONTROL LEAD ROUTINE EFFICIENCY PWR...POLICY CONGRESS PARLIAMENT. PAGE 38 B0777
B55
DELIB/GP
LEGIS
PARL/PROC
GOV/COMP

HOROWITZ M.,INCENTIVE WAGE SYSTEMS. INDUS LG/CO WORKER CONTROL GP/REL...MGT PSY 20. PAGE 51 B1044
B55
BIBLIOG/A
PAY
PLAN
TASK

WHEARE K.C.,GOVERNMENT BY COMMITTEE; AN ESSAY ON THE BRITISH CONSTITUTION. UK NAT/G LEGIS INSPECT CONFER ADJUD ADMIN CONTROL TASK EFFICIENCY ROLE POPULISM 20. PAGE 115 B2329
B55
DELIB/GP
CONSTN
LEAD
GP/COMP

ZABEL O.H.,GOD AND CAESAR IN NEBRASKA: A STUDY OF LEGAL RELATIONSHIP OF CHURCH AND STATE, 1854-1954.
B55
SECT
PROVS

TAX GIVE ADMIN CONTROL GP/REL ROLE...GP/COMP 19/20   LAW
NEBRASKA. PAGE 119 B2396   EDU/PROP

                                                    S55
CHAPIN F.S.,"FORMALIZATION OBSERVED IN TEN   VOL/ASSN
VOLUNTARY ORGANIZATIONS: CONCEPTS, MORPHOLOGY,   ROUTINE
PROCESS." STRUCT INGP/REL PERS/REL...METH/CNCPT   CONTROL
CLASSIF OBS RECORD. PAGE 20 B0407   OP/RES

                                                    S55
SCHWARTZ B.,"LEGISLATIVE CONTROL OF ADMINISTRATIVE CONTROL
RULES AND REGULATIONS THE AMERICAN EXPERIENCE."   ADMIN
USA+45 GOV/REL...GOV/COMP 20. PAGE 95 B1913   EX/STRUC
                                                    LEGIS

                                                    B56
ALEXANDER R.S.,INDUSTRIAL MARKETING. USA+45 ECO/DEV INDUS
DIST/IND FINAN NAT/G ACT/RES CAP/ISM PRICE CONTROL MARKET
...POLICY MGT 20. PAGE 4 B0072   ECO/TAC
                                                    PLAN

                                                    B56
BARBASH J.,THE PRACTICE OF UNIONISM. ECO/TAC LEAD   LABOR
LOBBY GP/REL INGP/REL DRIVE MARXISM BIBLIOG. PAGE 9 REPRESENT
B0182   CONTROL
                                                    ADMIN

                                                    B56
BROWNE D.G.,THE RISE OF SCOTLAND YARD: A HISTORY OF CRIMLGY
THE METROPOLITAN POLICE. UK MUNIC CHIEF ADMIN CRIME LEGIS
GP/REL 19/20. PAGE 16 B0329   CONTROL
                                                    FORCES

                                                    B56
ECOLE NAT'L D'ADMINISTRATION,RECRUITMENT AND   ADMIN
TRAINING FOR THE HIGHER CIVIL SERVICE IN FRANCE.   MGT
FRANCE EX/STRUC PLAN EDU/PROP CONTROL ROUTINE TASK EXEC
COST...METH 20 CIVIL/SERV. PAGE 32 B0650   ACADEM

                                                    B56
GLADDEN E.N.,CIVIL SERVICE OR BUREAUCRACY? UK LAW   ADMIN
STRATA LABOR TOP/EX PLAN SENIOR AUTOMAT CONTROL   GOV/REL
PARTIC CHOOSE HAPPINESS...CHARTS 19/20 CIVIL/SERV   EFFICIENCY
BUREAUCRCY. PAGE 40 B0808   PROVS

                                                    B56
HICKMAN C.A.,INDIVIDUALS, GROUPS, AND ECONOMIC   MGT
BEHAVIOR. WORKER PAY CONTROL EXEC GP/REL INGP/REL   ADMIN
PERSON ROLE...PSY SOC PERS/COMP METH 20. PAGE 50   ECO/TAC
B1005   PLAN

                                                    B56
REDFORD E.S.,PUBLIC ADMINISTRATION AND POLICY   EX/STRUC
FORMATION: STUDIES IN OIL, GAS, BANKING, RIVER   PROB/SOLV
DEVELOPMENT AND CORPORATE INVESTIGATIONS. USA+45   CONTROL
CLIENT NAT/G ADMIN LOBBY REPRESENT GOV/REL INGP/REL EXEC
20. PAGE 87 B1754

                                                    B56
US HOUSE RULES COMM,HEARINGS BEFORE A SPECIAL   ADMIN
SUBCOMMITTEE: ESTABLISHMENT OF A STANDING COMMITTEE DOMIN
ON ADMINISTRATIVE PROCEDURE, PRACTICE. USA+45 LAW   DELIB/GP
EX/STRUC ADMIN CONTROL EXEC GOV/REL EFFICIENCY PWR NAT/G
...POLICY INT 20 CONGRESS. PAGE 109 B2199

                                                    B56
WIGGINS J.R.,FREEDOM OR SECRECY. USA+45 USA-45   ORD/FREE
DELIB/GP EX/STRUC FORCES ADJUD SANCTION KNOWL PWR   PRESS
...AUD/VIS CONGRESS 20. PAGE 116 B2344   NAT/G
                                                    CONTROL

                                                    L56
EISENTADT S.N.,"POLITICAL STRUGGLE IN BUREAUCRATIC ADMIN
SOCIETIES" ASIA CULTURE ADJUD SANCTION PWR   CHIEF
BUREAUCRCY OTTOMAN BYZANTINE. PAGE 33 B0661   CONTROL
                                                    ROUTINE

                                                    S56
COTTER C.P.,"ADMINISTRATIVE ACCOUNTABILITY TO   CONTROL
CONGRESS: THE CONCURRENT RESOLUTION." USA+45 NAT/G GOV/REL
EXEC REPRESENT PWR 20. PAGE 24 B0489   LEGIS
                                                    EX/STRUC

                                                    S56
KAUFMAN H.,"EMERGING CONFLICTS IN THE DOCTRINES OF ADMIN
PUBLIC ADMINISTRATION" (BMR)" USA+45 USA-45 NAT/G   ORD/FREE
EX/STRUC LEGIS CONTROL NEUTRAL ATTIT PWR...TREND   REPRESENT
20. PAGE 58 B1181   LEAD

                                                    S56
MILNE R.S.,"CONTROL OF GOVERNMENT CORPORATIONS IN   CONTROL
THE UNITED STATES." USA+45 NAT/G CHIEF LEGIS BUDGET EX/STRUC
20 GENACCOUNT. PAGE 74 B1488   GOV/REL
                                                    PWR

                                                    B57
HINDERLING A.,DIE REFORMATORISCHE   ADMIN
VERWALTUNGSGERICHTSBARKEIT. GERMANY/W PROB/SOLV   CT/SYS
ADJUD SUPEGO PWR...CONCPT 20. PAGE 50 B1015   JURID
                                                    CONTROL

                                                    B57
JENNINGS I.,PARLIAMENT. UK FINAN INDUS POL/PAR   PARL/PROC
DELIB/GP EX/STRUC PLAN CONTROL...MAJORIT JURID   TOP/EX
PARLIAMENT. PAGE 56 B1133   MGT
                                                    LEGIS

                                                    B57
MEYER P.,ADMINISTRATIVE ORGANIZATION: A COMPARATIVE ADMIN
STUDY OF THE ORGANIZATION OF PUBLIC ADMINISTRATION. METH/COMP
DENMARK FRANCE NORWAY SWEDEN UK USA+45 ELITES LOC/G NAT/G
CONSULT LEGIS ADJUD CONTROL LEAD PWR SKILL   CENTRAL
DECISION. PAGE 73 B1475

                                                    B57
MURDESHWAR A.K.,ADMINISTRATIVE PROBLEMS RELATING TO NAT/G
NATIONALISATION: WITH SPECIAL REFERENCE TO INDIAN   OWN
STATE ENTERPRISES. CZECHOSLVK FRANCE INDIA UK   INDUS
USA+45 LEGIS WORKER PROB/SOLV BUDGET PRICE CONTROL ADMIN
...MGT GEN/LAWS 20 PARLIAMENT. PAGE 76 B1544

                                                    L57
DOTSON A.,"FUNDAMENTAL APPROACHES TO   ADMIN
RESPONSIBILITY." USA+45 NAT/G PWR 20. PAGE 30 B0611 REPRESENT
                                                    EXEC
                                                    CONTROL

                                                    S57
ARGYRIS C.,"THE INDIVIDUAL AND ORGANIZATION: SOME   PERSON
PROBLEMS OF MUTUAL ADJUSTMENT" (BMR)" USA+45   METH
PROB/SOLV ADMIN CONTROL 20. PAGE 6 B0128   INGP/REL
                                                    TASK

                                                    S57
COTTER C.P.,"ADMINISTRATIVE ACCOUNTABILITY: LEGIS
REPORTING TO CONGRESS." USA+45 CONSULT DELIB/GP   EX/STRUC
PARL/PROC PARTIC GOV/REL ATTIT PWR DECISION.   REPRESENT
PAGE 24 B0490   CONTROL

                                                    S57
DANIELSON L.E.,"SUPERVISORY PROBLEMS IN DECISION   PROB/SOLV
MAKING." WORKER ADMIN ROUTINE TASK MGT. PAGE 26   DECISION
B0529   CONTROL
                                                    GP/REL

                                                    S57
HARRIS J.P.,"LEGISLATIVE CONTROL OF ADMINISTRATION: LEGIS
SOME COMPARISONS OF AMERICAN AND EUROPEAN   CONTROL
PRACTICES." DEBATE PARL/PROC ROUTINE GOV/REL   EX/STRUC
EFFICIENCY SUPEGO DECISION. PAGE 47 B0954   REPRESENT

                                                    B58
CARTER G.M.,TRANSITION IN AFRICA; STUDIES IN   NAT/COMP
POLITICAL ADAPTATION. AFR CENTRL/AFR GHANA NIGERIA PWR
CONSTN LOC/G POL/PAR ADMIN GP/REL FEDERAL...MAJORIT CONTROL
BIBLIOG 20. PAGE 19 B0389   NAT/G

                                                    B58
CHANG C.,THE INFLATIONARY SPIRAL: THE EXPERIENCE IN FINAN
CHINA 1939-50. CHINA/COM BUDGET INT/TRADE PRICE   ECO/TAC
ADMIN CONTROL WAR DEMAND...POLICY CHARTS 20.   BAL/PAY
PAGE 20 B0406   GOV/REL

                                                    B58
CHEEK G.,ECONOMIC AND SOCIAL IMPLICATIONS OF   BIBLIOG/A
AUTOMATION: A BIBLIOGRAPHIC REVIEW (PAMPHLET).   SOCIETY
USA+45 LG/CO WORKER CREATE PLAN CONTROL ROUTINE   INDUS
PERS/REL EFFICIENCY PRODUC...METH/COMP 20. PAGE 20 AUTOMAT
B0416

                                                    B58
CONSERVATIVE POLITICAL CENTRE,A WORLD SECURITY   ORD/FREE
AUTHORITY? WOR+45 CONSTN ELITES FINAN DELIB/GP PLAN CONSERVE
PROB/SOLV ADMIN CONTROL NUC/PWR GP/REL...IDEA/COMP FORCES
20. PAGE 23 B0468   ARMS/CONT

                                                    B58
DAVIS K.C.,ADMINISTRATIVE LAW: CASES, TEXT,   ADJUD
PROBLEMS. LAW LOC/G NAT/G TOP/EX PAY CONTROL   JURID
GOV/REL INGP/REL FEDERAL 20 SUPREME/CT. PAGE 27   CT/SYS
B0541   ADMIN

                                                    B58
JAPAN MINISTRY OF JUSTICE,CRIMINAL JUSTICE IN   CONSTN
JAPAN. LAW PROF/ORG PUB/INST FORCES CONTROL CT/SYS CRIME
PARL/PROC 20 CHINJAP. PAGE 56 B1125   JURID
                                                    ADMIN

                                                    B58
LAW COMMISSION OF INDIA,REFORM OF JUDICIAL   CT/SYS
ADMINISTRATION. INDIA TOP/EX ADMIN DISCRIM   ADJUD
EFFICIENCY...METH/COMP 20. PAGE 63 B1276   GOV/REL
                                                    CONTROL

                                                    B58
MOEN N.W.,THE GOVERNMENT OF SCOTLAND 1603 - 1625.   CHIEF
UK JUDGE ADMIN GP/REL PWR 17 SCOTLAND COMMON/LAW.   JURID
PAGE 74 B1496   CONTROL
                                                    PARL/PROC

                                                    B58
SCOTT D.J.R.,RUSSIAN POLITICAL INSTITUTIONS. RUSSIA NAT/G
USSR CONSTN AGRI DELIB/GP PLAN EDU/PROP CONTROL   POL/PAR
CHOOSE EFFICIENCY ATTIT MARXISM...BIBLIOG/A 13/20. ADMIN
PAGE 95 B1919   DECISION

                                                    B58
US HOUSE COMM GOVT OPERATIONS,HEARINGS BEFORE A   FOR/AID
SUBCOMMITTEE OF THE COMMITTEE ON GOVERNMENT   DIPLOM
OPERATIONS. CAMBODIA PHILIPPINE USA+45 CONSTRUC   ORD/FREE
TEC/DEV ADMIN CONTROL WEAPON EFFICIENCY HOUSE/REP. ECO/UNDEV
PAGE 108 B2189

                                                    B58
US HOUSE COMM ON COMMERCE,ADMINISTRATIVE PROCESS   POLICY
AND ETHICAL QUESTIONS. USA+45 LAW LEGIS INT/TRADE   ADMIN
CONTROL 20 CONGRESS. PAGE 109 B2192   DELIB/GP
                                                    ADJUD

                                                    B58
US HOUSE COMM ON POST OFFICE,TO PROVIDE AN   ADMIN
EFFECTIVE SYSTEM OF PERSONNEL ADMINISTRATION.   NAT/G
USA+45 DELIB/GP CONTROL EFFICIENCY 20 CONGRESS   EX/STRUC
PRESIDENT CIVIL/SERV POSTAL/SYS. PAGE 109 B2194   LAW
                                                    B58
WARNER A.W.,CONCEPTS AND CASES IN ECONOMIC   ECO/TAC
ANALYSIS. PROB/SOLV BARGAIN CONTROL INCOME PRODUC   DEMAND

...ECOMETRIC MGT CONCPT CLASSIF CHARTS 20
KEYNES/JM. PAGE 114 B2292

EQUILIB
COST
S58

DIAMANT A.."A CASE STUDY OF ADMINISTRATIVE
AUTONOMY: CONTROLS AND TENSIONS IN FRENCH
ADMINISTRATION." FRANCE ADJUD LOBBY DEMAND
EFFICIENCY 20. PAGE 29 B0585

ADMIN
CONTROL
LEGIS
EXEC
S58

FREEMAN J.L.."THE BUREAUCRACY IN PRESSURE
POLITICS." USA+45 NAT/G CHIEF ADMIN EXEC 20.
PAGE 37 B0752

CONTROL
EX/STRUC
REPRESENT
LOBBY
S58

KAMPELMAN M.M.."CONGRESSIONAL CONTROL VS EXECUTIVE
FLEXIBILITY." USA+45 NAT/G 20. PAGE 58 B1165

CIVMIL/REL
ADMIN
EX/STRUC
CONTROL
S58

KEISER N.F.."PUBLIC RESPONSIBILITY AND FEDERAL
ADVISORY GROUPS: A CASE STUDY." NAT/G ADMIN CONTROL
LOBBY...POLICY 20. PAGE 59 B1190

REPRESENT
ELITES
GP/REL
EX/STRUC
S58

MITCHELL W.C.."OCCUPATIONAL ROLE STRAINS: THE
AMERICAN ELECTIVE PUBLIC OFFICIAL." CONTROL
RIGID/FLEX SUPEGO HEALTH ORD/FREE...SOC INT QU.
PAGE 74 B1492

ANOMIE
DRIVE
ROUTINE
PERSON
S58

SALETAN E.N.."ADMINISTRATIVE TRUSTIFICATION." NAT/G
EX/STRUC ADMIN 20. PAGE 92 B1862

LOBBY
PWR
CONTROL
REPRESENT
B59

CHAPMAN B..THE PROFESSION OF GOVERNMENT: THE PUBLIC
SERVICE IN EUROPE. MOD/EUR LABOR CT/SYS...T 20
CIVIL/SERV. PAGE 20 B0409

ADMIN
CONTROL
ROUTINE
EX/STRUC
B59

DAVIS K.C.,ADMINISTRATIVE LAW TEXT. USA+45 NAT/G
DELIB/GP EX/STRUC CONTROL ORD/FREE...T 20
SUPREME/CT. PAGE 27 B0542

ADJUD
ADMIN
JURID
CT/SYS
B59

HANSON A.H.,THE STRUCTURE AND CONTROL OF STATE
ENTERPRISES IN TURKEY. TURKEY LAW ADMIN GOV/REL
EFFICIENCY...CHARTS 20. PAGE 46 B0939

NAT/G
LG/CO
OWN
CONTROL
B59

MOOS M.,THE CAMPUS AND THE STATE. LAW FINAN
DELIB/GP LEGIS EXEC LOBBY GP/REL PWR...POLICY
BIBLIOG. PAGE 75 B1517

EDU/PROP
ACADEM
PROVS
CONTROL
B59

REDFORD E.S.,NATIONAL REGULATORY COMMISSIONS: NEED
FOR A NEW LOOK (PAMPHLET). USA+45 CLIENT PROB/SOLV
ADJUD LOBBY EFFICIENCY...POLICY 20. PAGE 87 B1757

REPRESENT
CONTROL
EXEC
NAT/G
B59

U OF MICHIGAN LAW SCHOOL,ATOMS AND THE LAW. USA+45
PROVS WORKER PROB/SOLV DIPLOM ADMIN GOV/REL ANTHOL.
PAGE 106 B2142

NUC/PWR
NAT/G
CONTROL
LAW
B59

WASSERMAN P.,MEASUREMENT AND ANALYSIS OF
ORGANIZATIONAL PERFORMANCE. FINAN MARKET EX/STRUC
TEC/DEV EDU/PROP CONTROL ROUTINE TASK...MGT 20.
PAGE 114 B2300

BIBLIOG/A
ECO/TAC
OP/RES
EFFICIENCY
L59

GILBERT C.E.,"THE FRAMEWORK OF ADMINISTRATIVE
RESPONSIBILITY." USA+45 20. PAGE 39 B0799

REPRESENT
EXEC
EX/STRUC
CONTROL
L59

HECTOR L.J.,"GOVERNMENT BY ANONYMITY: WHO WRITES
OUR REGULATORY OPINIONS?" USA+45 NAT/G TOP/EX
CONTROL EXEC. PAGE 49 B0987

ADJUD
REPRESENT
EX/STRUC
ADMIN
S59

JEWELL M.R.,"THE SENATE REPUBLICAN POLICY COMMITTEE
AND FOREIGN POLICY." PLAN ADMIN CONTROL LEAD LOBBY
EFFICIENCY PRESIDENT 20 REPUBLICAN. PAGE 56 B1139

POL/PAR
NAT/G
DELIB/GP
POLICY
S59

ROBINSON J.A.,"THE ROLE OF THE RULES COMMITTEE IN
ARRANGING THE PROGRAM OF THE UNITED STATES HOUSE OF
REPRESENTATIVES." USA+45 DEBATE CONTROL AUTHORIT
HOUSE/REP. PAGE 89 B1801

PARL/PROC
DELIB/GP
ROUTINE
LEGIS
S59

SEIDMAN H.,"THE GOVERNMENT CORPORATION IN THE
UNITED STATES." USA+45 LEGIS ADMIN PLURISM 20.
PAGE 95 B1925

CONTROL
GOV/REL
EX/STRUC
EXEC
S59

SIMPSON R.L.,"VERTICAL AND HORIZONTAL COMMUNICATION
IN FORMAL ORGANIZATION" USA+45 LG/CO EX/STRUC DOMIN
CONTROL TASK INGP/REL TIME 20. PAGE 97 B1963

PERS/REL
AUTOMAT
INDUS

WORKER
B60

ALBI F.,TRATADO DE LOS MODOS DE GESTION DE LAS
CORPORACIONES LOCALES. SPAIN FINAN NAT/G BUDGET
CONTROL EXEC ROUTINE GOV/REL ORD/FREE SOVEREIGN
...MGT 20. PAGE 3 B0068

LOC/G
LAW
ADMIN
MUNIC
B60

ANGERS F.A.,ESSAI SUR LA CENTRALISATION: ANALYSE
DES PRINCIPES ET PERSPECTIVES CANADIENNES. CANADA
ECO/TAC CONTROL...SOC IDEA/COMP BIBLIOG 20. PAGE 5
B0111

CENTRAL
ADMIN
B60

ARGAL P.,MUNICIPAL GOVERNMENT IN INDIA. INDIA
BUDGET TAX ADMIN EXEC 19/20. PAGE 6 B0126

LOC/G
MUNIC
DELIB/GP
CONTROL
B60

BHAMBHRI C.P.,PARLIAMENTARY CONTROL OVER STATE
ENTERPRISE IN INDIA. INDIA DELIB/GP ADMIN CONTROL
INGP/REL EFFICIENCY 20 PARLIAMENT. PAGE 11 B0235

NAT/G
OWN
INDUS
PARL/PROC
B60

HEAP D.,AN OUTLINE OF PLANNING LAW (3RD ED.). UK
LAW PROB/SOLV ADMIN CONTROL 20. PAGE 49 B0983

MUNIC
PLAN
JURID
LOC/G
B60

HODGETTS J.E.,CANADIAN PUBLIC ADMINISTRATION.
CANADA CONTROL LOBBY EFFICIENCY 20. PAGE 50 B1024

REPRESENT
ADMIN
EX/STRUC
ADJUD
B60

KERSELL J.E.,PARLIAMENTARY SUPERVISION OF DELEGATED
LEGISLATION. UK EFFICIENCY PWR...POLICY CHARTS
BIBLIOG METH 20 PARLIAMENT. PAGE 59 B1198

LEGIS
CONTROL
NAT/G
EX/STRUC
B60

PFIFFNER J.M.,PUBLIC ADMINISTRATION. USA+45 FINAN
WORKER PLAN PROB/SOLV ADJUD CONTROL EXEC...T 20.
PAGE 82 B1666

ADMIN
NAT/G
LOC/G
MGT
B60

PINTO F.B.M.,ENRIQUECIMENTO ILICITO NO EXERCICIO DE
CARGOS PUBLICOS. BRAZIL L/A+17C USA+45 ELITES
TRIBUTE CONTROL INGP/REL ORD/FREE PWR...NAT/COMP
20. PAGE 83 B1675

ADMIN
NAT/G
CRIME
LAW
B60

WEBSTER J.A.,A GENERAL STUDY OF THE DEPARTMENT OF
DEFENSE INTERNAL SECURITY PROGRAM. USA+45 WORKER
TEC/DEV ADJUD CONTROL CT/SYS EXEC GOV/REL COST
...POLICY DECISION MGT 20 DEPT/DEFEN SUPREME/CT.
PAGE 114 B2307

ORD/FREE
PLAN
ADMIN
NAT/G
B60

WHEARE K.C.,THE CONSTITUTIONAL STRUCTURE OF THE
COMMONWEALTH. UK EX/STRUC DIPLOM DOMIN ADMIN
COLONIAL CONTROL LEAD INGP/REL SUPEGO 20 CMN/WLTH.
PAGE 115 B2330

CONSTN
INT/ORG
VOL/ASSN
SOVEREIGN
S60

BAVELAS A.,"LEADERSHIP: MAN AND FUNCTION." WORKER
CREATE PLAN CONTROL PERS/REL PERSON PWR...MGT 20.
PAGE 10 B0199

LEAD
ADMIN
ROUTINE
ROLE
S60

MARSHALL G.,"POLICE RESPONSIBILITY." UK LOC/G ADJUD
ADMIN EXEC 20. PAGE 70 B1409

CONTROL
REPRESENT
LAW
FORCES
S60

PFIFFNER J.M.,"ADMINISTRATIVE RATIONALITY" (BMR)"
UNIV CONTROL...POLICY IDEA/COMP SIMUL. PAGE 83
B1667

ADMIN
DECISION
RATIONAL
S60

SCHER S.,"CONGRESSIONAL COMMITTEE MEMBERS AND
INDEPENDENT AGENCY OVERSEERS: A CASE STUDY."
DELIB/GP EX/STRUC JUDGE TOP/EX DOMIN ADMIN CONTROL
PWR...SOC/EXP HOUSE/REP CONGRESS. PAGE 93 B1886

LEGIS
GOV/REL
LABOR
ADJUD
C60

MCCLEERY R.,"COMMUNICATION PATTERNS AS BASES OF
SYSTEMS OF AUTHORITY AND POWER" IN THEORETICAL
STUDIES IN SOCIAL ORGAN. OF PRISON-BMR. USA+45
SOCIETY STRUCT EDU/PROP ADMIN CONTROL COERCE CRIME
GP/REL AUTHORIT...SOC 20. PAGE 71 B1443

PERS/REL
PUB/INST
PWR
DOMIN
C60

SCHRAMM W.,"MASS COMMUNICATIONS: A BOOK OF READINGS
(2ND ED.)" LG/CO PRESS ADMIN CONTROL ROUTINE ATTIT
ROLE SUPEGO...CHARTS ANTHOL BIBLIOG 20. PAGE 94
B1902

COM/IND
EDU/PROP
CROWD
MAJORIT
B61

AGARWAL R.C.,STATE ENTERPRISE IN INDIA. FUT INDIA
UK FINAN INDUS ADMIN CONTROL OWN...POLICY CHARTS
BIBLIOG 20 RAILROAD. PAGE 3 B0064

ECO/UNDEV
SOCISM
GOV/REL
LG/CO
B61

AMERICAN MANAGEMENT ASSN,SUPERIOR-SUBORDINATE
COMMUNICATION IN MANAGEMENT. STRATA FINAN INDUS
SML/CO WORKER CONTROL EXEC ATTIT 20. PAGE 4 B0086

MGT
ACT/RES
PERS/REL

LG/CO
B61
AUERBACH C.A.,THE LEGAL PROCESS. USA+45 DELIB/GP JUDGE CONFER ADJUD CONTROL...DECISION 20 SUPREME/CT. PAGE 7 B0146
JURID ADMIN LEGIS CT/SYS

B61
BEASLEY K.E.,STATE SUPERVISION OF MUNICIPAL DEBT IN KANSAS - A CASE STUDY. USA+45 USA-45 FINAN PROVS BUDGET TAX ADJUD ADMIN CONTROL SUPEGO. PAGE 10 B0201
MUNIC LOC/G LEGIS JURID

B61
GORDON R.A.,BUSINESS LEADERSHIP IN THE LARGE CORPORATION. USA+45 SOCIETY EX/STRUC ADMIN CONTROL ROUTINE GP/REL PWR...MGT 20. PAGE 41 B0831
LG/CO LEAD DECISION LOBBY

B61
HART H.C.,ADMINISTRATIVE ASPECTS OF RIVER VALLEY DEVELOPMENT. INDIA USA+45 INDUS CONTROL EFFICIENCY OPTIMAL PRODUC 20 TVA. PAGE 47 B0957
ADMIN PLAN METH/COMP AGRI

B61
KRUPP S.,PATTERN IN ORGANIZATIONAL ANALYSIS: A CRITICAL EXAMINATION. INGP/REL PERS/REL RATIONAL ATTIT AUTHORIT DRIVE PWR...DECISION PHIL/SCI SOC IDEA/COMP. PAGE 61 B1239
MGT CONTROL CONCPT METH/CNCPT

B61
LAHAYE R.,LES ENTREPRISES PUBLIQUES AU MAROC. FRANCE MOROCCO LAW DIST/IND EXTR/IND FINAN CONSULT PLAN TEC/DEV ADMIN AGREE CONTROL OWN...POLICY 20. PAGE 62 B1250
NAT/G INDUS ECO/UNDEV ECO/TAC

B61
LEE R.R.,ENGINEERING-ECONOMIC PLANNING MISCELLANEOUS SUBJECTS: A SELECTED BIBLIOGRAPHY (MIMEOGRAPHED). FINAN LOC/G MUNIC NEIGH ADMIN CONTROL INGP/REL HABITAT...GEOG MGT SOC/WK 20 RESOURCE/N. PAGE 63 B1280
BIBLIOG/A PLAN REGION

B61
MONAS S.,THE THIRD SECTION: POLICE AND SOCIETY IN RUSSIA UNDER NICHOLAS I. MOD/EUR RUSSIA ELITES STRUC NAT/G EX/STRUC ADMIN CONTROL PWR CONSERVE ...DECISION 19 NICHOLAS/I. PAGE 74 B1499
ORD/FREE COM FORCES COERCE

B61
NARASIMHAN V.K.,THE PRESS, THE PUBLIC AND THE ADMINISTRATION (PAMPHLET). INDIA COM/IND CONTROL REPRESENT GOV/REL EFFICIENCY...ANTHOL 20. PAGE 77 B1554
NAT/G ADMIN PRESS NEW/LIB

B61
SHARMA T.R.,THE WORKING OF STATE ENTERPRISES IN INDIA. INDIA DELIB/GP LEGIS WORKER BUDGET PRICE CONTROL GP/REL OWN ATTIT...MGT CHARTS 20. PAGE 96 B1938
NAT/G INDUS ADMIN SOCISM

B61
TANZER L.,THE KENNEDY CIRCLE. INTELL CONSULT DELIB/GP TOP/EX CONTROL EXEC INGP/REL PERS/REL PWR ...BIOG IDEA/COMP ANTHOL 20 KENNEDY/JF PRESIDENT DEMOCRAT MCNAMARA/R RUSK/D. PAGE 103 B2077
EX/STRUC NAT/G CHIEF

B61
TRECKER H.B.,NEW UNDERSTANDING OF ADMINISTRATION. NEIGH DELIB/GP CONTROL LEAD GP/REL INGP/REL ...POLICY DECISION BIBLIOG. PAGE 105 B2126
VOL/ASSN PROF/ORG ADMIN PARTIC

B61
US GENERAL ACCOUNTING OFFICE,EXAMINATION OF ECONOMIC AND TECHNICAL ASSISTANCE PROGRAM FOR IRAN. IRAN USA+45 AGRI INDUS DIPLOM CONTROL COST 20. PAGE 108 B2186
FOR/AID ADMIN TEC/DEV ECO/UNDEV

L61
MCNAMEE B.J.,"CONFLICT OF INTEREST: STATE GOVERNMENT EMPLOYEES." USA+45 PROVS 20. PAGE 72 B1457
LAW REPRESENT ADMIN CONTROL

S61
EVAN W.M.,"A LABORATORY EXPERIMENT ON BUREAUCRATIC AUTHORITY" WORKER CONTROL EXEC PRODUC ATTIT PERSON ...PSY SOC CHARTS SIMUL 20 WEBER/MAX. PAGE 34 B0687
ADMIN LEGIT LAB/EXP EFFICIENCY

S61
JOHNSON N.,"PARLIAMENTARY QUESTIONS AND THE CONDUCT OF ADMINISTRATION." UK REPRESENT PARLIAMENT 20. PAGE 57 B1146
CONTROL EXEC EX/STRUC

S61
TANNENBAUM A.S.,"CONTROL AND EFFECTIVENESS IN A VOLUNTARY ORGANIZATION." USA+45 ADMIN...CORREL MATH REGRESS STAT TESTS SAMP/SIZ CHARTS SOC/EXP INDEX 20 LEAGUE/WV. PAGE 102 B2072
EFFICIENCY VOL/ASSN CONTROL INGP/REL

C61
ETZIONI A.,"A COMPARATIVE ANALYSIS OF COMPLEX ORGANIZATIONS: ON POWER, INVOLVEMENT AND THEIR CORRELATES." ELITES CREATE OP/RES ROUTINE INGP/REL PERS/REL CONSEN ATTIT DRIVE PWR...CONCPT BIBLIOG. PAGE 34 B0684
CON/ANAL SOC LEAD CONTROL

B62
ARCO EDITORIAL BOARD,PUBLIC MANAGEMENT AND ADMINISTRATION. PLAN BUDGET WRITING CONTROL ROUTINE ...TESTS CHARTS METH T 20. PAGE 6 B0125
MGT ADMIN NAT/G

LOC/G
B62
BOWEN W.G.,THE FEDERAL GOVERNMENT AND PRINCETON UNIVERSITY. USA+45 FINAN ACT/RES PROB/SOLV ADMIN CONTROL COST...POLICY 20 PRINCETN/U. PAGE 14 B0285
NAT/G ACADEM GP/REL OP/RES

B62
BRIEFS H.W.,PRICING POWER AND "ADMINISTRATIVE" INFLATION (PAMPHLET). USA+45 PROC/MFG CONTROL EFFICIENCY MONEY GOLD/STAND. PAGE 15 B0306
ECO/DEV PRICE POLICY EXEC

B62
DODDS H.W.,THE ACADEMIC PRESIDENT "EDUCATOR OR CARETAKER? FINAN DELIB/GP EDU/PROP PARTIC ATTIT ROLE PWR...POLICY RECORD INT. PAGE 30 B0601
ACADEM ADMIN LEAD CONTROL

B62
ESCUELA SUPERIOR DE ADMIN PUBL,INFORME DEL SEMINARIO SOBRE SERVICIO CIVIL O CARRERA ADMINISTRATIVA. L/A+17C ELITES STRATA CONFER CONTROL GOV/REL INGP/REL SUPEGO 20 CENTRAL/AM CIVIL/SERV. PAGE 33 B0681
ADMIN NAT/G PROB/SOLV ATTIT

B62
FOSS P.O.,REORGANIZATION AND REASSIGNMENT IN THE CALIFORNIA HIGHWAY PATROL (PAMPHLET). USA+45 STRUC WORKER EDU/PROP CONTROL COERCE INGP/REL ORD/FREE PWR...DECISION 20 CALIFORNIA. PAGE 37 B0744
FORCES ADMIN PROVS PLAN

B62
GROGAN V.,ADMINISTRATIVE TRIBUNALS IN THE PUBLIC SERVICE. IRELAND UK NAT/G CONTROL CT/SYS...JURID GOV/COMP 20. PAGE 44 B0884
ADMIN LAW ADJUD DELIB/GP

B62
GROVE J.W.,GOVERNMENT AND INDUSTRY IN BRITAIN. UK FINAN LOC/G CONSULT DELIB/GP INT/TRADE ADMIN CONTROL...BIBLIOG 20. PAGE 44 B0894
ECO/TAC INDUS NAT/G GP/REL

B62
INTERNAT CONGRESS OF JURISTS,EXECUTIVE ACTION AND THE RULE OF RULE: REPORTION PROCEEDINGS OF INT'T CONGRESS OF JURISTS,-RIO DE JANEIRO, BRAZIL. WOR+45 ACADEM CONSULT JUDGE EDU/PROP ADJUD CT/SYS INGP/REL PERSON DEPT/DEFEN. PAGE 54 B1094
JURID EXEC ORD/FREE CONTROL

B62
INTERNATIONAL LABOR OFFICE,WORKERS' MANAGEMENT IN YUGOSLAVIA. COM YUGOSLAVIA LABOR DELIB/GP EX/STRUC PROB/SOLV ADMIN PWR MARXISM...CHARTS ORG/CHARTS BIBLIOG 20. PAGE 54 B1098
WORKER CONTROL MGT INDUS

B62
JENNINGS E.E.,THE EXECUTIVE: AUTOCRAT, BUREAUCRAT, DEMOCRAT. LEAD EFFICIENCY DRIVE 20. PAGE 56 B1131
EX/STRUC INGP/REL TOP/EX CONTROL

B62
KARNJAHAPRAKORN C.,MUNICIPAL GOVERNMENT IN THAILAND AS AN INSTITUTION AND PROCESS OF SELF-GOVERNMENT. THAILAND CULTURE FINAN EX/STRUC LEGIS PLAN CONTROL GOV/REL EFFICIENCY ATTIT...POLICY 20. PAGE 58 B1176
LOC/G MUNIC ORD/FREE ADMIN

B62
LIPPMANN W.,PREFACE TO POLITICS. LABOR CHIEF CONTROL LEAD...MYTH IDEA/COMP 19/20 ROOSEVLT/T TAMMANY WILSON/H SANTAYAN/G BERGSON/H. PAGE 65 B1318
PARTIC ATTIT ADMIN

B62
LITTLEFIELD N.,METROPOLITAN AREA PROBLEMS AND MUNICIPAL HOME RULE. USA+45 PROVS ADMIN CONTROL GP/REL PWR. PAGE 66 B1328
LOC/G SOVEREIGN JURID LEGIS

B62
LYNCH J.,ADMINISTRATION COLONIAL ESPANOLA 1782-1810. SPAIN PROVS TOP/EX PARTIC 18/19 ARGEN. PAGE 67 B1349
COLONIAL CONTROL ADJUD ADMIN

B62
MEANS G.C.,THE CORPORATE REVOLUTION IN AMERICA: ECONOMIC REALITY VS. ECONOMIC THEORY. USA+45 USA-45 INDUS WORKER PLAN CAP/ISM ADMIN...IDEA/COMP 20. PAGE 72 B1459
LG/CO MARKET CONTROL PRICE

B62
MORTON L.,STRATEGY AND COMMAND: THE FIRST TWO YEARS. USA-45 NAT/G CONTROL EXEC LEAD WEAPON CIVMIL/REL PWR...POLICY AUD/VIS CHARTS 20 CHINJAP. PAGE 76 B1532
WAR FORCES PLAN DIPLOM

B62
REICH C.A.,BUREAUCRACY AND THE FORESTS (PAMPHLET). USA+45 LOBBY...POLICY MGT 20. PAGE 87 B1762
ADMIN CONTROL EX/STRUC REPRESENT

B62
RUDOLPH F.,THE AMERICAN COLLEGE AND UNIVERSITY. CLIENT FINAN PUB/INST DELIB/GP EDU/PROP CONTROL EXEC CONSEN ATTIT POLICY. PAGE 92 B1853
ACADEM INGP/REL PWR ADMIN

B62
US SENATE COMM GOVT OPERATIONS,ADMINISTRATION OF NATIONAL SECURITY. USA+45 CHIEF PLAN PROB/SOLV
ORD/FREE ADMIN

TEC/DEV DIPLOM ATTIT...POLICY DECISION 20 KENNEDY/JF RUSK/D MCNAMARA/R BUNDY/M HERTER/C. PAGE 110 B2212
NAT/G CONTROL

B62

US SENATE COMM ON JUDICIARY,STATE DEPARTMENT SECURITY. USA+45 CHIEF TEC/DEV DOMIN ADMIN EXEC ATTIT ORD/FREE...POLICY CONGRESS DEPT/STATE PRESIDENT KENNEDY/JF KENNEDY/JF SENATE 20. PAGE 110 B2228
CONTROL WORKER NAT/G GOV/REL

L62

BORCHARDT K.,"CONGRESSIONAL USE OF ADMINISTRATIVE ORGANIZATION AND PROCEDURE FOR POLICY-MAKING PURPOSES." USA+45 NAT/G EXEC LOBBY. PAGE 14 B0278
ADMIN LEGIS REPRESENT CONTROL

L62

CAVERS D.F.,"ADMINISTRATIVE DECISION-MAKING IN NUCLEAR FACILITIES LICENSING." USA+45 CLIENT ADMIN EXEC 20 AEC. PAGE 19 B0395
REPRESENT LOBBY PWR CONTROL

S62

BRAIBANTI R.,"REFLECTIONS ON BUREAUCRATIC CORRPUTION." LAW REPRESENT 20. PAGE 15 B0298
CONTROL MORAL ADMIN GOV/COMP

S62

MAINZER L.C.,"INJUSTICE AND BUREAUCRACY." ELITES STRATA STRUCT EX/STRUC SENIOR CONTROL EXEC LEAD ROUTINE INGP/REL ORD/FREE...CONCPT 20 BUREAUCRCY. PAGE 68 B1381
MORAL MGT ADMIN

S62

TANNENBAUM A.S.,"CONTROL IN ORGANIZATIONS: INDIVIDUAL ADJUSTMENT AND ORGANIZATIONAL PERFORMANCE." DOMIN PARTIC REPRESENT INGP/REL PRODUC ATTIT DRIVE PWR...PSY CORREL. PAGE 102 B2073
ADMIN MGT STRUCT CONTROL

C62

MORGAN G.G.,"SOVIET ADMINISTRATIVE LEGALITY: THE ROLE OF THE ATTORNEY GENERAL'S OFFICE." COM USSR CONTROL ROUTINE...CONCPT BIBLIOG 18/20. PAGE 75 B1522
LAW CONSTN LEGIS ADMIN

B63

ADRIAN C.R.,GOVERNING OVER FIFTY STATES AND THEIR COMMUNITIES. USA+45 CONSTN FINAN MUNIC NAT/G POL/PAR EX/STRUC LEGIS ADMIN CONTROL CT/SYS ...CHARTS 20. PAGE 3 B0061
PROVS LOC/G GOV/REL GOV/COMP

B63

CORSON J.J.,PUBLIC ADMINISTRATION IN MODERN SOCIETY. INDUS FORCES CONTROL CENTRAL EFFICIENCY 20. PAGE 24 B0482
MGT NAT/G PROB/SOLV INGP/REL

B63

DALAND R.T.,PERSPECTIVES OF BRAZILIAN PUBLIC ADMINISTRATION (VOL. I). BRAZIL LAW ECO/UNDEV SCHOOL CHIEF TEC/DEV CONFER CONTROL GP/REL ATTIT ROLE PWR...ANTHOL 20. PAGE 26 B0525
ADMIN NAT/G PLAN GOV/REL

B63

GARNER U.F.,ADMINISTRATIVE LAW. UK LAW LOC/G NAT/G EX/STRUC LEGIS JUDGE BAL/PWR BUDGET ADJUD CONTROL CT/SYS...BIBLIOG 20. PAGE 39 B0783
ADMIN JURID PWR GOV/REL

B63

GREEN H.P.,GOVERNMENT OF THE ATOM. USA+45 LEGIS PROB/SOLV ADMIN CONTROL PWR...POLICY DECISION 20 PRESIDENT CONGRESS. PAGE 43 B0864
GOV/REL EX/STRUC NUC/PWR DELIB/GP

B63

GRIFFITH J.A.G.,PRINCIPLES OF ADMINISTRATIVE LAW (3RD ED.). UK CONSTN EX/STRUC LEGIS ADJUD CONTROL CT/SYS PWR...CHARTS 20. PAGE 43 B0879
JURID ADMIN NAT/G BAL/PWR

B63

HANSON A.H.,NATIONALIZATION: A BOOK OF READINGS. WOR+45 FINAN DELIB/GP LEGIS WORKER BUDGET ADMIN GP/REL EFFICIENCY SOCISM...MGT ANTHOL. PAGE 46 B0941
NAT/G OWN INDUS CONTROL

B63

HARGROVE M.M.,BUSINESS POLICY CASES-WITH BEHAVIORAL SCIENCE IMPLICATIONS. LG/CO SML/CO EX/STRUC TOP/EX PLAN PROB/SOLV CONFER ADMIN CONTROL ROUTINE EFFICIENCY. PAGE 47 B0946
SOC/EXP INDUS DECISION MGT

B63

HAYMAN D.,POLITICAL ACTIVITY RESTRICTION; AN ANALYSIS WITH RECOMMENDATIONS (PAMPHLET). USA+45 EXEC PARTIC ROLE PWR 20. PAGE 48 B0976
CONTROL ADMIN INGP/REL REPRESENT

B63

HIGA M.,POLITICS AND PARTIES IN POSTWAR OKINAWA. USA+45 VOL/ASSN LEGIS CONTROL LOBBY CHOOSE NAT/LISM PWR SOVEREIGN MARXISM SOCISM 20 OKINAWA CHINJAP. PAGE 50 B1008
GOV/REL POL/PAR ADMIN FORCES

B63

HOUGHTELING J.L. JR.,THE LEGAL ENVIRONMENT OF BUSINESS. LG/CO NAT/G CONSULT AGREE CONTROL ...DICTIONARY T 20. PAGE 52 B1047
LAW MGT ADJUD JURID

B63

JACOB H.,GERMAN ADMINISTRATION SINCE BISMARCK: CENTRAL AUTHORITY VERSUS LOCAL AUTONOMY. GERMANY GERMANY/W LAW POL/PAR CONTROL CENTRAL TOTALISM FASCISM...MAJORIT DECISION STAT CHARTS GOV/COMP 19/20 BISMARCK/O HITLER/A WEIMAR/REP. PAGE 55 B1111
ADMIN NAT/G LOC/G POLICY

B63

KARL B.D.,EXECUTIVE REORGANIZATION AND REFORM IN THE NEW DEAL. ECO/DEV INDUS DELIB/GP EX/STRUC PLAN BUDGET ADMIN EFFICIENCY PWR POPULISM...POLICY 20 PRESIDENT ROOSEVLT/F WILSON/W NEW/DEAL. PAGE 58 B1174
BIOG EXEC CREATE CONTROL

B63

KLEIN F.J.,JUDICIAL ADMINISTRATION AND THE LEGAL PROFESSION. USA+45 ADMIN CONTROL EFFICIENCY ...POLICY 20. PAGE 60 B1217
BIBLIOG/A CT/SYS ADJUD JUDGE

B63

KORNHAUSER W.,SCIENTISTS IN INDUSTRY: CONFLICT AND ACCOMMODATION. USA+45 R+D LG/CO NAT/G TEC/DEV CONTROL ADJUST ATTIT...MGT STAT INT BIBLIOG 20. PAGE 61 B1229
CREATE INDUS PROF/ORG GP/REL

B63

LITTERER J.A.,ORGANIZATIONS: STRUCTURE AND BEHAVIOR. PLAN DOMIN CONTROL LEAD ROUTINE SANCTION INGP/REL EFFICIENCY PRODUC DRIVE RIGID/FLEX PWR. PAGE 66 B1325
ADMIN CREATE MGT ADJUST

B63

MOORE W.E.,MAN, TIME, AND SOCIETY. UNIV STRUCT FAM MUNIC VOL/ASSN ADMIN...SOC NEW/IDEA TIME/SEQ TREND TIME 20. PAGE 75 B1515
CONCPT SOCIETY CONTROL

B63

PATRA A.C.,THE ADMINISTRATION OF JUSTICE UNDER THE EAST INDIA COMPANY IN BENGAL, BIHAR AND ORISSA. INDIA UK LG/CO CAP/ISM INT/TRADE ADJUD COLONIAL CONTROL CT/SYS...POLICY 20. PAGE 81 B1641
ADMIN JURID CONCPT

B63

RICHARDS P.G.,PATRONAGE IN BRITISH GOVERNMENT. ELITES DELIB/GP TOP/EX PROB/SOLV CONTROL CT/SYS EXEC PWR. PAGE 88 B1774
EX/STRUC REPRESENT POL/PAR ADMIN

B63

SELF P.,THE STATE AND THE FARMER. UK ECO/DEV MARKET WORKER PRICE CONTROL GP/REL...WELF/ST 20 DEPT/AGRI. PAGE 95 B1926
AGRI NAT/G ADMIN VOL/ASSN

B63

SINGH H.L.,PROBLEMS AND POLICIES OF THE BRITISH IN INDIA, 1885-1898. INDIA UK NAT/G FORCES LEGIS PROB/SOLV CONTROL RACE/REL ADJUST DISCRIM NAT/LISM RIGID/FLEX...MGT 19 CIVIL/SERV. PAGE 97 B1968
COLONIAL PWR POLICY ADMIN

B63

US SENATE COMM ON JUDICIARY,ADMINISTERED PRICES. USA+45 RATION ADJUD CONTROL LOBBY...POLICY 20 SENATE MONOPOLY. PAGE 110 B2229
LG/CO PRICE ADMIN DECISION

B63

VAN SLYCK P.,PEACE: THE CONTROL OF NATIONAL POWER. CUBA WOR+45 FINAN NAT/G FORCES PROB/SOLV TEC/DEV BAL/PWR ADMIN CONTROL ORD/FREE...POLICY INT/LAW UN COLD/WAR TREATY. PAGE 112 B2253
ARMS/CONT PEACE INT/ORG DIPLOM

B63

WEINER M.,POLITICAL CHANGE IN SOUTH ASIA. CEYLON INDIA PAKISTAN S/ASIA CULTURE ELITES ECO/UNDEV EX/STRUC ADMIN CONTROL CHOOSE CONSERVE...GOV/COMP ANTHOL 20. PAGE 115 B2315
NAT/G CONSTN TEC/DEV

B63

WOLL P.,ADMINISTRATIVE LAW: THE INFORMAL PROCESS. USA+45 NAT/G CONTROL EFFICIENCY 20. PAGE 118 B2373
ADMIN ADJUD REPRESENT EX/STRUC

L63

BOLGAR V.,"THE PUBLIC INTEREST: A JURISPRUDENTIAL AND COMPARATIVE OVERVIEW OF SYMPOSIUM ON FUNDAMENTAL CONCEPTS OF PUBLIC LAW" COM FRANCE GERMANY SWITZERLND LAW ADJUD ADMIN AGREE LAISSEZ ...JURID GEN/LAWS 20 EUROPE/E. PAGE 13 B0268
CONCPT ORD/FREE CONTROL NAT/COMP

S63

BAKER R.J.,"DISCUSSION AND DECISION-MAKING IN THE CIVIL SERVICE." UK CONTROL REPRESENT INGP/REL PERS/REL EFFICIENCY 20. PAGE 8 B0168
EXEC EX/STRUC PROB/SOLV ADMIN

S63

REES A.,"THE EFFECTS OF UNIONS ON RESOURCE ALLOCATION." USA+45 WORKER PRICE CONTROL GP/REL ...MGT METH/COMP 20. PAGE 87 B1761
LABOR BARGAIN RATION INCOME

B64

BLACKSTOCK P.W.,THE STRATEGY OF SUBVERSION. USA+45 FORCES EDU/PROP ADMIN COERCE GOV/REL...DECISION MGT 20 DEPT/DEFEN CIA DEPT/STATE. PAGE 12 B0247
ORD/FREE DIPLOM CONTROL

B64

DAS M.N.,INDIA UNDER MORLEY AND MINTO. INDIA UK ECO/UNDEV MUNIC PROVS EX/STRUC LEGIS DIPLOM CONTROL REV 20 MORLEY/J. PAGE 26 B0531
GOV/REL COLONIAL POLICY ADMIN

B64

EDELMAN M.,THE SYMBOLIC USES OF POWER. USA+45
CLIENT

EX/STRUC CONTROL GP/REL INGP/REL...MGT T. PAGE 32 — PWR EXEC ELITES B64
B0653

ENDACOTT G.B.,GOVERNMENT AND PEOPLE IN HONG KONG — CONSTN COLONIAL CONTROL ADMIN B64
1841-1962: A CONSTITUTIONAL HISTORY. UK LEGIS ADJUD
REPRESENT ATTIT 19/20 HONG/KONG. PAGE 33 B0674

ETZIONI A.,MODERN ORGANIZATIONS. CLIENT STRUCT — MGT ADMIN PLAN CULTURE B64
DOMIN CONTROL LEAD PERS/REL AUTHORIT...CLASSIF
BUREAUCRCY. PAGE 34 B0685

FAINSOD M.,HOW RUSSIA IS RULED (REV. ED.). RUSSIA — NAT/G REV MARXISM B64
USSR AGRI PROC/MFG LABOR POL/PAR EX/STRUC CONTROL
PWR...POLICY BIBLIOG 19/20 KHRUSH/N COM/PARTY.
PAGE 34 B0700

FISK W.M.,ADMINISTRATIVE PROCEDURE IN A REGULATORY — SERV/IND ECO/DEV AIR JURID B64
AGENCY: THE CAB AND THE NEW YORK-CHICAGO CASE
(PAMPHLET). USA+45 DIST/IND ADMIN CONTROL LOBBY
GP/REL ROLE ORD/FREE NEWYORK/C CHICAGO CAB. PAGE 36
B0727

HALLER W.,DER SCHWEDISCHE JUSTITIEOMBUDSMAN. — JURID PARL/PROC ADMIN CHIEF B64
DENMARK FINLAND NORWAY SWEDEN LEGIS ADJUD CONTROL
PERSON ORD/FREE...NAT/COMP 20 OMBUDSMAN. PAGE 46
B0926

JACKSON R.M.,THE MACHINERY OF JUSTICE IN ENGLAND. — CT/SYS ADJUD JUDGE JURID B64
UK EDU/PROP CONTROL COST ORD/FREE...MGT 20
ENGLSH/LAW. PAGE 55 B1109

MARRIS R.,THE ECONOMIC THEORY OF "MANAGERIAL" — CAP/ISM MGT CONTROL OP/RES B64
CAPITALISM. USA+45 ECO/DEV LG/CO ECO/TAC DEMAND
...CHARTS BIBLIOG 20. PAGE 69 B1402

NELSON D.H.,ADMINISTRATIVE AGENCIES OF THE USA: — ADMIN EX/STRUC ADJUD LAW B64
THEIR DECISIONS AND AUTHORITY. USA+45 NAT/G CONTROL
CT/SYS REPRESENT...DECISION 20. PAGE 78 B1568

PIERCE T.M.,FEDERAL, STATE, AND LOCAL GOVERNMENT IN — NAT/G POLICY SCHOOL GOV/REL B64
EDUCATION. FINAN LOC/G PROVS LEGIS PLAN EDU/PROP
ADMIN CONTROL CENTRAL COST KNOWL 20. PAGE 83 B1673

PINNICK A.W.,COUNTRY PLANNERS IN ACTION. UK FINAN — MUNIC PLAN INDUS ATTIT B64
SERV/IND NAT/G CONSULT DELIB/GP PRICE CONTROL
ROUTINE LEISURE AGE/C...GEOG 20 URBAN/RNWL. PAGE 83
B1674

RIDLEY F.,PUBLIC ADMINISTRATION IN FRANCE. FRANCE — ADMIN REPRESENT GOV/COMP PWR B64
UK EX/STRUC CONTROL PARTIC EFFICIENCY 20. PAGE 88
B1781

RIES J.C.,THE MANAGEMENT OF DEFENSE: ORGANIZATION — FORCES ACT/RES DECISION CONTROL B64
AND CONTROL OF THE US ARMED SERVICES. PROF/ORG
DELIB/GP EX/STRUC LEGIS GOV/REL PERS/REL CENTRAL
RATIONAL PWR...POLICY TREND GOV/COMP BIBLIOG.
PAGE 88 B1782

RIGGS R.E.,THE MOVEMENT FOR ADMINISTRATIVE — ADMIN PROVS CREATE PLAN B64
REORGANIZATION IN ARIZONA. USA+45 LAW POL/PAR
DELIB/GP LEGIS PROB/SOLV CONTROL RIGID/FLEX PWR
...ORG/CHARTS 20 ARIZONA DEMOCRAT REPUBLICAN.
PAGE 88 B1786

RIKER W.H.,FEDERALISM. WOR+45 WOR-45 CONSTN CHIEF — FEDERAL NAT/G ORD/FREE CENTRAL B64
LEGIS ADMIN COLONIAL CONTROL CT/SYS PWR...BIBLIOG/A
18/20. PAGE 88 B1787

ROBSON W.A.,THE GOVERNORS AND THE GOVERNED. USA+45 — EX/STRUC ATTIT PARTIC LEAD B64
PROB/SOLV DOMIN ADMIN CONTROL CHOOSE...POLICY
PRESIDENT. PAGE 89 B1808

RUSSELL R.B.,UNITED NATIONS EXPERIENCE WITH — FORCES DIPLOM SANCTION ORD/FREE B64
MILITARY FORCES: POLITICAL AND LEGAL ASPECTS. AFR
KOREA WOR+45 LEGIS PROB/SOLV ADMIN CONTROL
EFFICIENCY PEACE...POLICY INT/LAW BIBLIOG UN.
PAGE 92 B1857

SAYLES L.R.,MANAGERIAL BEHAVIOR: ADMINISTRATION IN — CONCPT ADMIN TOP/EX EX/STRUC B64
COMPLEX ORGANIZATIONS. INDUS LG/CO PROB/SOLV
CONTROL EXEC INGP/REL PERS/REL SKILL...MGT OBS
PREDICT GEN/LAWS 20. PAGE 93 B1874

STANLEY D.T.,THE HIGHER CIVIL SERVICE: AN — NAT/G ADMIN CONTROL B64
EVALUATION OF FEDERAL PERSONNEL PRACTICES. USA+45
CREATE EXEC ROUTINE CENTRAL...MGT SAMP IDEA/COMP

METH/COMP 20 CIVIL/SERV. PAGE 100 B2020 — EFFICIENCY B64

TINBERGEN J.,CENTRAL PLANNING. COM INTELL ECO/DEV — PLAN INDUS MGT CENTRAL B64
ECO/UNDEV FINAN INT/ORG PROB/SOLV ECO/TAC CONTROL
EXEC ROUTINE DECISION. PAGE 104 B2111

TULLY A.,WHERE DID YOUR MONEY GO. USA+45 USSR — FOR/AID DIPLOM CONTROL B64
ECO/UNDEV ADMIN EFFICIENCY WEALTH...METH/COMP 20.
PAGE 106 B2136

US SENATE COMM GOVT OPERATIONS,ADMINISTRATION OF — ADMIN FORCES ORD/FREE NAT/G B64
NATIONAL SECURITY. USA+45 CHIEF TOP/EX PLAN DIPLOM
CONTROL PEACE...POLICY DECISION 20 PRESIDENT
CONGRESS. PAGE 110 B2216

WERNETTE J.P.,GOVERNMENT AND BUSINESS. LABOR — NAT/G FINAN ECO/DEV CONTROL L64
CAP/ISM ECO/TAC INT/TRADE TAX ADMIN AUTOMAT NUC/PWR
CIVMIL/REL DEMAND...MGT 20 MONOPOLY. PAGE 115 B2323

FOX G.H.,"PERCEPTIONS OF THE VIETNAMESE PUBLIC — ADMIN EX/STRUC INGP/REL ROLE S64
ADMINISTRATION SYSTEM" VIETNAM ELITES CONTROL EXEC
LEAD PWR...INT 20. PAGE 37 B0745

EAKIN T.C.,"LEGISLATIVE POLITICS -- I AND II THE — PROVS LEGIS ROUTINE STRUCT S64
WESTERN STATES, 19581964" (SUPPLEMENT)" USA+45
POL/PAR SCHOOL CONTROL LOBBY CHOOSE AGE. PAGE 32
B0641

STANLEY D.T.,"EXCELLENCE IN PUBLIC SERVICE - HOW DO — EFFICIENCY EX/STRUC ADMIN CONTROL B65
YOU REALLY KNOW?" EXEC 20. PAGE 100 B2019

ANTHONY R.N.,PLANNING AND CONTROL SYSTEMS. UNIV — CONTROL PLAN METH HYPO/EXP B65
OP/RES...DECISION MGT LING. PAGE 6 B0114

BOCK E.,GOVERNMENT REGULATION OF BUSINESS. USA+45 — MGT ADMIN NAT/G CONTROL B65
LAW EX/STRUC LEGIS EXEC ORD/FREE PWR...ANTHOL
CONGRESS. PAGE 13 B0261

BOGUSLAW R.,THE NEW UTOPIANS. OP/RES ADMIN CONTROL — UTOPIA AUTOMAT COMPUTER PLAN B65
PWR...IDEA/COMP SIMUL 20. PAGE 13 B0265

BOXER C.R.,PORTUGUESE SOCIETY IN THE TROPICS - THE — MUNIC ADMIN COLONIAL DELIB/GP B65
MUNICIPAL COUNCILS OF GAO, MACAO, BAHIA, AND
LUANDA, 1510-1800. EUR+WWI MOD/EUR PORTUGAL CONSTN
EX/STRUC DOMIN CONTROL ROUTINE REPRESENT PRIVIL
...BIBLIOG/A 16/19 GENACCOUNT MACAO BAHIA LUANDA.
PAGE 14 B0290

CHEN T.H.,THE CHINESE COMMUNIST REGIME: A — MARXISM POL/PAR NAT/G B65
DOCUMENTARY STUDY (2 VOLS.). CHINA/COM LAW CONSTN
ELITES ECO/UNDEV LEGIS ECO/TAC ADMIN CONTROL PWR
...SOC 20. PAGE 20 B0417

COPELAND M.A.,OUR FREE ENTERPRISE ECONOMY. USA+45 — CAP/ISM PLAN FINAN ECO/DEV B65
INDUS LABOR ADMIN CONTROL GP/REL MGT. PAGE 23 B0476

CRAMER J.F.,CONTEMPORARY EDUCATION: A COMPARATIVE — EDU/PROP NAT/COMP SCHOOL ACADEM B65
STUDY OF NATIONAL SYSTEMS (2ND ED.). CHINA/COM
EUR+WWI INDIA USA+45 FINAN PROB/SOLV ADMIN CONTROL
ATTIT...IDEA/COMP METH/COMP 20 CHINJAP. PAGE 25
B0502

DE GRAZIA A.,REPUBLIC IN CRISIS: CONGRESS AGAINST — LEGIS EXEC GOV/REL CONTROL B65
THE EXECUTIVE FORCE. USA+45 USA-45 SOCIETY POL/PAR
CHIEF DOMIN ROLE ORD/FREE PWR...CONCPT MYTH BIBLIOG
20 CONGRESS. PAGE 27 B0556

DYER F.C.,BUREAUCRACY VS CREATIVITY. UNIV CONTROL — ADMIN DECISION METH/COMP CREATE B65
LEAD INGP/REL EFFICIENCY MGT. PAGE 31 B0639

EDELMAN M.,THE POLITICS OF WAGE-PRICE DECISIONS. — GOV/COMP CONTROL ECO/TAC PLAN B65
GERMANY ITALY NETHERLAND UK INDUS LABOR POL/PAR
PROB/SOLV BARGAIN PRICE ROUTINE BAL/PAY COST DEMAND
20. PAGE 32 B0654

FOLTZ W.J.,FROM FRENCH WEST AFRICA TO THE MALI — EXEC TOP/EX ELITES LEAD B65
FEDERATION. AFR FRANCE MALI ADMIN CONTROL FEDERAL
...DECISION 20. PAGE 36 B0734

GOLEMBIEWSKI R.T.,MEN, MANAGEMENT, AND MORALITY: — LG/CO MGT B65
TOWARD A NEW ORGANIZATIONAL ETHIC. CONSTN EX/STRUC

CREATE ADMIN CONTROL INGP/REL PERSON SUPEGO MORAL PWR...GOV/COMP METH/COMP 20 BUREAUCRCY. PAGE 40 B0819 — PROB/SOLV

GOULDNER A.W.,STUDIES IN LEADERSHIP. LABOR EDU/PROP CONTROL PARTIC...CONCPT CLASSIF. PAGE 42 B0845 — LEAD ADMIN AUTHORIT
B65

GREGG J.L.,POLITICAL PARTIES AND PARTY SYSTEMS IN GUATEMALA, 1944-1963. GUATEMALA L/A+17C EX/STRUC FORCES CREATE CONTROL REV CHOOSE PWR...TREND IDEA/COMP 20. PAGE 43 B0872 — LEAD POL/PAR NAT/G CHIEF
B65

GT BRIT ADMIN STAFF COLLEGE,THE ACCOUNTABILITY OF PUBLIC CORPORATIONS (REV. ED.). UK ECO/DEV FINAN DELIB/GP EX/STRUC BUDGET CAP/ISM CONFER PRICE PARL/PROC 20. PAGE 44 B0899 — LG/CO NAT/G ADMIN CONTROL
B65

KELLEY E.J.,MARKETING: STRATEGY AND FUNCTIONS. ECO/DEV INDUS PLAN PRICE CONTROL ROUTINE...MGT BIBLIOG 20. PAGE 59 B1191 — MARKET DIST/IND POLICY ECO/TAC
B65

KOENIG L.W.,OFFICIAL MAKERS OF PUBLIC POLICY: CONGRESS AND THE PRESIDENT. USA+45 USA-45 EX/STRUC ADMIN CONTROL GOV/REL PWR 18/20 CONGRESS PRESIDENT. PAGE 61 B1225 — POLICY LEGIS CHIEF NAT/G
B65

LEMAY G.H.,BRITISH SUPREMACY IN SOUTH AFRICA 1899-1907. SOUTH/AFR UK ADMIN CONTROL LEAD GP/REL ORD/FREE 19/20. PAGE 64 B1286 — WAR COLONIAL DOMIN POLICY
B65

LEYS C.T.,FEDERATION IN EAST AFRICA. LAW AGRI DIST/IND FINAN INT/ORG LABOR INT/TRADE CONFER ADMIN CONTROL GP/REL...ANTHOL 20 AFRICA/E. PAGE 65 B1310 — FEDERAL REGION ECO/UNDEV PLAN
B65

MEISEL J.H.,PARETO & MOSCA. ITALY STRUCT ADMIN ...SOC CON/ANAL ANTHOL BIBLIOG 19/20. PAGE 72 B1463 — PWR ELITES CONTROL LAISSEZ
B65

MELMANS S.,OUR DEPLETED SOCIETY. SPACE USA+45 ECO/DEV FORCES BUDGET ECO/TAC ADMIN WEAPON EFFICIENCY 20 COLD/WAR. PAGE 73 B1465 — CIVMIL/REL INDUS EDU/PROP CONTROL
B65

MEYERHOFF A.E.,THE STRATEGY OF PERSUASION. USA+45 COM/IND CONSULT FOR/AID CONTROL COERCE COST ATTIT PERCEPT MARXISM 20 COLD/WAR. PAGE 73 B1476 — EDU/PROP EFFICIENCY OP/RES ADMIN
B65

MOORE C.H.,TUNISIA SINCE INDEPENDENCE. ELITES LOC/G POL/PAR ADMIN COLONIAL CONTROL EXEC GOV/REL TOTALISM MARXISM...INT 20 TUNIS. PAGE 75 B1513 — NAT/G EX/STRUC SOCISM
B65

ROURKE F.E.,BUREAUCRATIC POWER IN NATIONAL POLITICS. ADMIN CONTROL EXEC GOV/REL INGP/REL 20. PAGE 91 B1838 — EX/STRUC EFFICIENCY REPRESENT PWR
B65

SNIDER C.F.,AMERICAN STATE AND LOCAL GOVERNMENT. USA+45 FINAN CHIEF EX/STRUC TAX ADMIN CONTROL SUFF INGP/REL PWR 20. PAGE 98 B1989 — GOV/REL MUNIC PROVS LOC/G
B65

STEINER G.A.,THE CREATIVE ORGANIZATION. ELITES LG/CO PLAN PROB/SOLV TEC/DEV INSPECT CAP/ISM CONTROL EXEC PERSON...METH/COMP HYPO/EXP 20. PAGE 100 B2029 — CREATE MGT ADMIN SOC
B65

US HOUSE COMM EDUC AND LABOR,ADMINISTRATION OF THE NATIONAL LABOR RELATIONS ACT. USA+45 DELIB/GP WORKER PROB/SOLV BARGAIN PAY CONTROL 20 NLRB CONGRESS. PAGE 108 B2188 — ADMIN LABOR GP/REL INDUS
B65

VAID K.N.,STATE AND LABOR IN INDIA. INDIA INDUS WORKER PAY PRICE ADJUD CONTROL PARL/PROC GP/REL ORD/FREE 20. PAGE 111 B2248 — LAW LABOR MGT NEW/LIB
L65

SHARKANSKY I.,"FOUR AGENCIES AND AN APPROPRIATIONS SUBCOMMITTEE: A COMPARATIVE STUDY OF BUDGET STRATEGIES." USA+45 EX/STRUC TOP/EX PROB/SOLV CONTROL ROUTINE CONGRESS. PAGE 96 B1934 — ADMIN EDU/PROP NAT/G LEGIS
S65

POLK W.R.,"PROBLEMS OF GOVERNMENT UTILIZATION OF SCHOLARLY RESEARCH IN INTERNATIONAL AFFAIRS." FINAN NAT/G EDU/PROP CONTROL TASK GP/REL ATTIT PERCEPT KNOWL...POLICY TIME. PAGE 83 B1685 — ACT/RES ACADEM PLAN ADMIN
S65

RAPHAELI N.,"SELECTED ARTICLES AND DOCUMENTS ON COMPARATIVE PUBLIC ADMINISTRATION." USA+45 FINAN LOC/G WORKER TEC/DEV CONTROL LEAD...SOC/WK GOV/COMP METH/COMP. PAGE 86 B1739 — BIBLIOG ADMIN NAT/G MGT

MOTE M.E.,SOVIET LOCAL AND REPUBLIC ELECTIONS. COM USSR NAT/G PLAN PARTIC GOV/REL TOTALISM PWR ...CHARTS 20. PAGE 76 B1534 — N65 CHOOSE ADMIN CONTROL LOC/G
B66

AARON T.J.,THE CONTROL OF POLICE DISCRETION: THE DANISH EXPERIENCE. DENMARK LAW CREATE ADMIN INGP/REL SUPEGO PWR 20 OMBUDSMAN. PAGE 2 B0049 — CONTROL FORCES REPRESENT PROB/SOLV
B66

AMER ENTERPRISE INST PUB POL,CONGRESS: THE FIRST BRANCH OF GOVERNMENT. EX/STRUC FEEDBACK REPRESENT INGP/REL PWR...DECISION METH/CNCPT PREDICT. PAGE 4 B0081 — EFFICIENCY LEGIS DELIB/GP CONTROL
B66

BIRKHEAD G.S.,ADMINISTRATIVE PROBLEMS IN PAKISTAN. PAKISTAN AGRI FINAN INDUS LG/CO ECO/TAC CONTROL PWR ...CHARTS ANTHOL 20. PAGE 12 B0241 — ADMIN NAT/G ORD/FREE ECO/UNDEV
B66

CORNWELL E.E. JR.,THE AMERICAN PRESIDENCY: VITAL CENTER. USA+45 USA-45 POL/PAR LEGIS PROB/SOLV CONTROL PARTIC GOV/REL 18/20 PRESIDENT. PAGE 23 B0478 — CHIEF EX/STRUC NAT/G ADMIN
B66

DAVIDSON R.H.,CONGRESS IN CRISIS: POLITICS AND CONGRESSIONAL REFORM. USA+45 SOCIETY POL/PAR CONTROL LEAD ROUTINE GOV/REL ATTIT PWR...POLICY 20 CONGRESS. PAGE 26 B0535 — LEGIS PARL/PROC PROB/SOLV NAT/G
B66

DAVIS R.G.,PLANNING HUMAN RESOURCE DEVELOPMENT, EDUCATIONAL MODELS AND SCHEMATA. WORKER OP/RES ECO/TAC EDU/PROP CONTROL COST PRODUC...GEOG STAT CHARTS 20. PAGE 27 B0544 — PLAN EFFICIENCY SIMUL ROUTINE
B66

FENN DH J.R.,BUSINESS DECISION MAKING AND GOVERNMENT POLICY. SERV/IND LEGIS LICENSE ADMIN CONTROL GP/REL INGP/REL 20 CASEBOOK. PAGE 35 B0711 — DECISION PLAN NAT/G LG/CO
B66

GERBERDING W.P.,UNITED STATES FOREIGN POLICY: PERSPECTIVES AND ANALYSIS. USA+45 LEGIS EXEC LEAD REPRESENT PWR 20. PAGE 39 B0791 — PROB/SOLV CHIEF EX/STRUC CONTROL
B66

GRETHER E.T.,MARKETING AND PUBLIC POLICY. USA+45 ECO/DEV DIST/IND NAT/G PLAN CAP/ISM PRICE CONTROL ...GEOG MGT 20. PAGE 43 B0874 — MARKET PROB/SOLV ECO/TAC POLICY
B66

HASTINGS P.G.,THE MANAGEMENT OF BUSINESS FINANCE. ECO/DEV PLAN BUDGET CONTROL COST...DECISION CHARTS BIBLIOG T 20. PAGE 48 B0966 — FINAN MGT INDUS ECO/TAC
B66

INTERPARLIAMENTARY UNION,PARLIAMENTS: COMPARATIVE STUDY ON STRUCTURE AND FUNCTIONING OF REPRESENTATIVE INSTITUTIONS IN FIFTY-FIVE COUNTRIES. WOR+45 POL/PAR DELIB/GP BUDGET ADMIN CONTROL CHOOSE. PAGE 54 B1099 — PARL/PROC LEGIS GOV/COMP EX/STRUC
B66

MONTEIRO J.B.,CORRUPTION: CONTROL OF MALADMINISTRATION. EUR+WWI INDIA USA+45 USSR NAT/G DELIB/GP ADMIN...GP/COMP 20 OMBUDSMAN. PAGE 74 B1503 — CONTROL CRIME PROB/SOLV
B66

RAPHAEL J.S.,GOVERNMENTAL REGULATION OF BUSINESS. USA+45 LAW CONSTN TAX ADJUD ADMIN EFFICIENCY PWR 20. PAGE 86 B1736 — LG/CO GOV/REL CONTROL ECO/DEV
B66

ROSS R.M.,STATE AND LOCAL GOVERNMENT AND ADMINISTRATION. USA+45 CONSTN POL/PAR EX/STRUC LEGIS BUDGET EDU/PROP CONTROL CT/SYS CHOOSE GOV/REL T. PAGE 90 B1827 — LOC/G PROVS MUNIC ADMIN
B66

SCHLESSINGER P.J.,ELEMENTS OF CALIFORNIA GOVERNMENT (2ND ED.). USA+45 LAW ADJUD ADMIN CONTROL CT/SYS EFFICIENCY...BIBLIOG T CALIFORNIA. PAGE 94 B1891 — LOC/G PROVS GOV/REL LEGIS
B66

SCHURMANN F.,IDEOLOGY AND ORGANIZATION IN COMMUNIST CHINA. CHINA/COM LOC/G MUNIC POL/PAR ECO/TAC CONTROL ATTIT...MGT STERTYP 20 COM/PARTY. PAGE 94 B1909 — MARXISM STRUCT ADMIN NAT/G
B66

STREET D.,ORGANIZATION FOR TREATMENT. CLIENT PROVS PUB/INST PLAN CONTROL PARTIC REPRESENT ATTIT PWR ...POLICY BIBLIOG. PAGE 101 B2052 — GP/COMP AGE/Y ADMIN VOL/ASSN
B66

UN ECAFE,ADMINISTRATIVE ASPECTS OF FAMILY PLANNING PROGRAMMES (PAMPHLET). ASIA THAILAND WOR+45 VOL/ASSN PROB/SOLV BUDGET FOR/AID EDU/PROP CONFER CONTROL GOV/REL TIME 20 UN BIRTH/CON. PAGE 106 — PLAN CENSUS FAM ADMIN

B2147

WADIA M.,THE NATURE AND SCOPE OF MANAGEMENT.
DELIB/GP EX/STRUC CREATE AUTOMAT CONTROL EFFICIENCY
...ANTHOL 20. PAGE 112 B2271
   B66
MGT
PROB/SOLV
IDEA/COMP
ECO/TAC

WESTON J.F.,THE SCOPE AND METHODOLOGY OF FINANCE.
PLAN TEC/DEV CONTROL EFFICIENCY INCOME UTIL...MGT
CONCPT MATH STAT TREND METH 20. PAGE 115 B2327
   B66
FINAN
ECO/DEV
POLICY
PRICE

WILSON G.,CASES AND MATERIALS ON CONSTITUTIONAL AND
ADMINISTRATIVE LAW. UK LAW NAT/G EX/STRUC LEGIS
BAL/PWR BUDGET DIPLOM ADJUD CONTROL CT/SYS GOV/REL
ORD/FREE 20 PARLIAMENT ENGLSH/LAW. PAGE 117 B2359
   B66
JURID
ADMIN
CONSTN
PWR

YOUNG S.,MANAGEMENT: A SYSTEMS ANALYSIS. DELIB/GP
EX/STRUC ECO/TAC CONTROL EFFICIENCY...NET/THEORY
20. PAGE 119 B2394
   B66
PROB/SOLV
MGT
DECISION
SIMUL

ZINKIN T.,CHALLENGES IN INDIA. INDIA PAKISTAN LAW
AGRI FINAN INDUS TOP/EX TEC/DEV CONTROL ROUTINE
ORD/FREE PWR 20 NEHRU/J SHASTRI/LB CIVIL/SERV.
PAGE 119 B2404
   B66
NAT/G
ECO/TAC
POLICY
ADMIN

BROWN L.N.,FRENCH ADMINISTRATIVE LAW. FRANCE UK
CONSTN NAT/G LEGIS DOMIN CONTROL EXEC PARL/PROC PWR
...JURID METH/COMP GEN/METH. PAGE 16 B0324
   B67
EX/STRUC
LAW
IDEA/COMP
CT/SYS

BRZEZINSKI Z.K.,THE SOVIET BLOC: UNITY AND CONFLICT
(2ND ED., REV., ENLARGED). COM POLAND USSR INTELL
CHIEF EX/STRUC CONTROL EXEC GOV/REL PWR MARXISM
...TREND IDEA/COMP 20 LENIN/VI MARX/KARL STALIN/J.
PAGE 16 B0336
   B67
NAT/G
DIPLOM

BUDER S.,PULLMAN: AN EXPERIMENT IN INDUSTRIAL ORDER
AND COMMUNITY PLANNING, 1880-1930. USA-45 SOCIETY
LABOR LG/CO CREATE PROB/SOLV CONTROL GP/REL
EFFICIENCY ATTIT...MGT BIBLIOG 19/20 PULLMAN.
PAGE 17 B0337
   B67
DIST/IND
INDUS
MUNIC
PLAN

BULPITT J.G.,PARTY POLITICS IN ENGLISH LOCAL
GOVERNMENT. UK CONSTN ACT/RES TAX CONTROL CHOOSE
REPRESENT GOV/REL KNOWL 20. PAGE 17 B0344
   B67
POL/PAR
LOC/G
ELITES
EX/STRUC

FARRIS M.T.,MODERN TRANSPORTATION: SELECTED
READINGS. UNIV CONTROL...POLICY ANTHOL T 20.
PAGE 35 B0706
   B67
DIST/IND
MGT
COST

GELLHORN W.,OMBUDSMEN AND OTHERS: CITIZENS'
PROTECTORS IN NINE COUNTRIES. WOR+45 LAW CONSTN
LEGIS INSPECT ADJUD ADMIN CONTROL CT/SYS CHOOSE
PERS/REL...STAT CHARTS 20. PAGE 39 B0789
   B67
NAT/COMP
REPRESENT
INGP/REL
PROB/SOLV

JAIN R.K.,MANAGEMENT OF STATE ENTERPRISES. INDIA
SOCIETY FINAN WORKER BUDGET ADMIN CONTROL OWN 20.
PAGE 55 B1118
   B67
NAT/G
SOCISM
INDUS
MGT

MINTZ M.,BY PRESCRIPTION ONLY. USA+45 NAT/G
EX/STRUC PLAN TEC/DEV EXEC EFFICIENCY HEALTH...MGT
SOC/WK 20. PAGE 74 B1491
   B67
BIO/SOC
PROC/MFG
CONTROL
POLICY

NORTHRUP H.R.,RESTRICTIVE LABOR PRACTICES IN THE
SUPERMARKET INDUSTRY. USA+45 INDUS WORKER TEC/DEV
BARGAIN PAY CONTROL GP/REL COST...STAT CHARTS NLRB.
PAGE 79 B1592
   B67
DIST/IND
MARKET
LABOR
MGT

PLANO J.C.,FORGING WORLD ORDER: THE POLITICS OF
INTERNATIONAL ORGANIZATION. PROB/SOLV DIPLOM
CONTROL CENTRAL RATIONAL ORD/FREE...INT/LAW CHARTS
BIBLIOG 20 UN LEAGUE/NAT. PAGE 83 B1679
   B67
INT/ORG
ADMIN
JURID

POSNER M.V.,ITALIAN PUBLIC ENTERPRISE. ITALY
ECO/DEV FINAN INDUS CREATE ECO/TAC ADMIN CONTROL
EFFICIENCY PRODUC...TREND CHARTS 20. PAGE 84 B1693
   B67
NAT/G
PLAN
CAP/ISM
SOCISM

PRINCE C.E.,NEW JERSEY'S JEFFERSONIAN REPUBLICANS:
THE GENESIS OF AN EARLY PARTY MACHINE (1789-1817).
USA-45 LOC/G EDU/PROP PRESS CONTROL CHOOSE...CHARTS
18/19 NEW/JERSEY REPUBLICAN. PAGE 84 B1707
   B67
POL/PAR
CONSTN
ADMIN
PROVS

ROBINSON D.W.,PROMISING PRACTICES IN CIVIC
EDUCATION. FUT USA+45 CONTROL PARTIC GOV/REL...OBS
AUD/VIS 20. PAGE 89 B1797
   B67
EDU/PROP
NAT/G
ADJUST
ADMIN

UNIVERSAL REFERENCE SYSTEM,PUBLIC POLICY AND THE
MANAGEMENT OF SCIENCE (VOLUME IX). FUT SPACE WOR+45
LAW NAT/G TEC/DEV CONTROL NUC/PWR GOV/REL
   B67
BIBLIOG/A
POLICY
MGT

...COMPUT/IR GEN/METH. PAGE 107 B2165
   PHIL/SCI

WESSON R.G.,THE IMPERIAL ORDER. WOR-45 STRUCT SECT
DOMIN ADMIN COLONIAL LEAD CONSERVE...CONCPT BIBLIOG
20. PAGE 115 B2324
   B67
PWR
CHIEF
CONTROL
SOCIETY

WESTON P.B.,THE ADMINISTRATION OF JUSTICE. USA+45
CONSTN MUNIC NAT/G PROVS EX/STRUC JUDGE ADMIN
CONTROL SANCTION ORD/FREE...CHARTS 20. PAGE 115
B2328
   B67
CRIME
CT/SYS
JURID
ADJUD

"RESTRICTIVE SOVEREIGN IMMUNITY, THE STATE
DEPARTMENT, AND THE COURTS." USA+45 USA-45 EX/STRUC
DIPLOM ADJUD CONTROL GOV/REL 19/20 DEPT/STATE
SUPREME/CT. PAGE 2 B0047
   L67
SOVEREIGN
ORD/FREE
PRIVIL
CT/SYS

CARMICHAEL D.M.,"FORTY YEARS OF WATER POLLUTION
CONTROL IN WISCONSIN: A CASE STUDY." LAW EXTR/IND
INDUS MUNIC DELIB/GP PLAN PROB/SOLV SANCTION
...CENSUS CHARTS 20 WISCONSIN. PAGE 19 B0382
   L67
HEALTH
CONTROL
ADMIN
ADJUD

MANNE H.G.,"OUR TWO CORPORATION SYSTEMS* LAW AND
ECONOMICS." LAW CONTROL SANCTION GP/REL...JURID 20.
PAGE 69 B1392
   L67
INDUS
ELITES
CAP/ISM
ADMIN

PASLEY R.S.,"ORGANIZATIONAL CONFLICTS OF INTEREST
IN GOVERNMENT CONTRACTS." ELITES R+D ROUTINE
NUC/PWR DEMAND EFFICIENCY 20. PAGE 81 B1639
   L67
NAT/G
ECO/TAC
RATION
CONTROL

BASTID M.,"ORIGINES ET DEVELOPMENT DE LA REVOLUTION
CULTURELLE." CHINA/COM DOMIN ADMIN CONTROL LEAD
COERCE CROWD ATTIT DRIVE MARXISM...POLICY 20.
PAGE 10 B0195
   S67
REV
CULTURE
ACADEM
WORKER

BERLINER J.S.,"RUSSIA'S BUREAUCRATS - WHY THEY'RE
REACTIONARY." USSR NAT/G OP/RES PROB/SOLV TEC/DEV
CONTROL SANCTION EFFICIENCY DRIVE PERSON...TECHNIC
SOC 20. PAGE 11 B0223
   S67
CREATE
ADMIN
INDUS
PRODUC

BRADY R.H.,"COMPUTERS IN TOP-LEVEL DECISION MAKING"
FUT WOR+45 CONTROL...PREDICT CHARTS. PAGE 15 B0297
   S67
COMPUTER
MGT
DECISION
TEC/DEV

BRIMMER A.F.,"INITIATIVE AND INNOVATION IN CENTRAL
BANKING." USA+45 ECO/DEV MARKET ECO/TAC TAX CONTROL
DEMAND...MGT CHARTS FED/RESERV. PAGE 15 B0309
   S67
FINAN
CREATE
NAT/G
POLICY

BURKE E.M.,"THE SEARCH FOR AUTHORITY IN PLANNING."
MUNIC NEIGH CREATE PROB/SOLV LEGIT ADMIN CONTROL
EFFICIENCY PWR...METH/COMP SIMUL 20. PAGE 17 B0352
   S67
DECISION
PLAN
LOC/G
METH

CARIAS B.,"EL CONTROL DE LAS EMPRESAS PUBLICAS POR
GRUPOS DE INTERESES DE LA COMUNIDAD." FRANCE UK
VENEZUELA INDUS NAT/G CONTROL OWN PWR...DECISION
NAT/COMP 20. PAGE 18 B0377
   S67
WORKER
REPRESENT
MGT
SOCISM

DIXON O.F.,"A SOCIAL SYSTEMS APPROACH TO
MARKETING." ECO/DEV ECO/TAC CONTROL EFFICIENCY
...DECISION 20. PAGE 29 B0599
   S67
MARKET
SOCIETY
GP/REL
MGT

DOERN G.B.,"THE ROYAL COMMISSIONS IN THE GENERAL
POLICY PROCESS AND IN FEDERAL-PROVINCIAL
RELATIONS." CANADA CONSTN ACADEM PROVS CONSULT
DELIB/GP LEGIS ACT/RES PROB/SOLV CONFER CONTROL
EFFICIENCY...METH/COMP 20 SENATE ROYAL/COMM.
PAGE 30 B0603
   S67
R+D
EX/STRUC
GOV/REL
NAT/G

DRYDEN S.,"LOCAL GOVERNMENT IN TANZANIA PART II"
TANZANIA LAW NAT/G POL/PAR CONTROL PARTIC REPRESENT
...DECISION 20. PAGE 31 B0622
   S67
LOC/G
GOV/REL
ADMIN
STRUCT

DUGGAR J.W.,"THE DEVELOPMENT OF MONEY SUPPLY IN
ETHIOPIA." ETHIOPIA ISLAM CONSULT OP/RES BUDGET
CONTROL ROUTINE EFFICIENCY EQUILIB WEALTH...MGT 20.
PAGE 31 B0629
   S67
ECO/UNDEV
FINAN
BAL/PAY
ECOMETRIC

FRYKENBURG R.E.,"STUDIES OF LAND CONTROL IN INDIAN
HISTORY: REVIEW ARTICLE." INDIA UK STRATA AGRI
MUNIC OP/RES COLONIAL REGION EFFICIENCY OWN HABITAT
...CONCPT 16/20. PAGE 38 B0763
   S67
ECO/UNDEV
CONTROL
ADMIN

GORMAN W.,"ELLUL - A PROPHETIC VOICE." WOR+45
ELITES SOCIETY ACT/RES PLAN BAL/PWR DOMIN CONTROL
PARTIC TOTALISM PWR 20. PAGE 41 B0837
   S67
CREATE
ORD/FREE
EX/STRUC
UTOPIA

HILL F.G.,"VEBLEN, BERLE AND THE MODERN
CORPORATION." FINAN ECO/TAC CONTROL OWN...MGT 20.
   S67
LG/CO
ROLE

PAGE 50 B1010 | INDUS
ECO/DEV

S67

IDENBURG P.J.,"POLITICAL STRUCTURAL DEVELOPMENT IN AFR
TROPICAL AFRICA." UK ECO/UNDEV KIN POL/PAR CHIEF CONSTN
EX/STRUC CREATE COLONIAL CONTROL REPRESENT RACE/REL NAT/G
...MAJORIT TREND 20. PAGE 53 B1074 GOV/COMP

S67

JENCKS C.E.,"SOCIAL STATUS OF COAL MINERS IN EXTR/IND
BRITAIN SINCE NATIONALIZATION." UK STRATA STRUCT WORKER
LABOR RECEIVE GP/REL INCOME OWN ATTIT HABITAT...MGT CONTROL
T 20. PAGE 56 B1128 NAT/G

S67

KRARUP O.,"JUDICIAL REVIEW OF ADMINISTRATIVE ACTION ADJUD
IN DENMARK." DENMARK LAW CT/SYS...JURID CONCPT CONTROL
19/20. PAGE 61 B1234 EXEC
DECISION

S67

LEES J.P.,"LEGISLATIVE REVIEW AND BUREAUCRATIC SUPEGO
RESPONSIBILITY." USA+45 FINAN NAT/G DELIB/GP PLAN BUDGET
PROB/SOLV CONFER CONTROL GP/REL DEMAND...DECISION LEGIS
20 CONGRESS PRESIDENT HOUSE/REP BUREAUCRCY. PAGE 63 EXEC
B1281

S67

LEWIS P.H.,"LEADERSHIP AND CONFLICT WITHIN POL/PAR
FEBRERISTA PARTY OF PARAGUAY." L/A+17C PARAGUAY ELITES
EX/STRUC DOMIN SENIOR CONTROL INGP/REL CENTRAL LEAD
FEDERAL ATTIT 20. PAGE 65 B1305

S67

MONEYPENNY P.,"UNIVERSITY PURPOSE, DISCIPLINE, AND ACADEM
DUE PROCESS." USA+45 EDU/PROP ADJUD LEISURE AGE/Y
ORD/FREE. PAGE 74 B1500 CONTROL
ADMIN

S67

MURRAY R.,"SECOND THOUGHTS ON GHANA." AFR GHANA COLONIAL
NAT/G POL/PAR ADMIN REV GP/REL CENTRAL...SOCIALIST CONTROL
CONCPT METH 20. PAGE 77 B1548 REGION
SOCISM

S67

NYE J.S.,"CORRUPTION AND POLITICAL DEVELOPMENT: A ECO/UNDEV
COST-BENEFIT ANALYSIS." WOR+45 SOCIETY TRIBUTE NAT/G
ADMIN CONTROL COST...CHARTS 20. PAGE 79 B1598 CRIME
ACT/RES

S67

PRATT R.C.,"THE ADMINISTRATION OF ECONOMIC PLANNING NAT/G
IN A NEWLY INDEPEND ENT STATE* THE TANZANIAN DELIB/GP
EXPERIENCE 1963-1966." AFR TANZANIA ECO/UNDEV PLAN ADMIN
CONTROL ROUTINE TASK EFFICIENCY 20. PAGE 84 B1699 TEC/DEV

S67

RAI H.,"DISTRICT MAGISTRATE AND POLICE STRUCT
SUPERINTENDENT IN INDIA: THE CONTROVERSY OF DUAL CONTROL
CONTROL" INDIA LAW PROVS ADMIN PWR 19/20. PAGE 86 ROLE
B1729 FORCES

S67

ROSE A.M.,"CONFIDENCE AND THE CORPORATION." LG/CO INDUS
CONTROL CRIME INCOME PROFIT 20. PAGE 90 B1818 EX/STRUC
VOL/ASSN
RESPECT

S67

SCOTT W.R.,"ORGANIZATIONAL EVALUATION AND EXEC
AUTHORITY." CONTROL SANCTION PERS/REL ATTIT DRIVE WORKER
...SOC CONCPT OBS CHARTS IDEA/COMP 20. PAGE 95 INSPECT
B1921 EX/STRUC

S67

SKOLNICK J.H.,"SOCIAL CONTROL IN THE ADVERSARY PROB/SOLV
SYSTEM." USA+45 CONSULT OP/RES ADMIN CONTROL. PERS/REL
PAGE 98 B1975 ADJUD
CT/SYS

S67

SKOLNIKOFF E.B.,"MAKING FOREIGN POLICY" PROB/SOLV TEC/DEV
EFFICIENCY PERCEPT PWR...MGT METH/CNCPT CLASSIF 20. CONTROL
PAGE 98 B1976 USA+45
NAT/G

S67

SMITH W.H.T.,"THE IMPLICATIONS OF THE AMERICAN BAR EDU/PROP
ASSOCIATION ADVISORY COMMITTEE RECOMMENDATIONS FOR CONTROL
POLICE ADMINISTRATION." ADMIN...JURID 20 ABA. GP/REL
PAGE 98 B1986 ORD/FREE

S67

TIVEY L.,"THE POLITICAL CONSEQUENCES OF ECONOMIC PLAN
PLANNING." UK CONSTN INDUS ACT/RES ADMIN CONTROL POLICY
LOBBY REPRESENT EFFICIENCY SUPEGO SOVEREIGN NAT/G
...DECISION 20. PAGE 104 B2112

S67

WALLER D.J.,"CHINA: RED OR EXPERT." CHINA/COM CONTROL
INTELL DOMIN REV ATTIT MARXISM 20. PAGE 113 B2283 FORCES
ADMIN
POL/PAR

N67

US SUPERINTENDENT OF DOCUMENTS,SPACE: MISSILES, THE BIBLIOG/A
MOON, AND SATELLITES (PRICE LIST 79A). USA+45 SPACE
COM/IND R+D NAT/G DIPLOM EDU/PROP ADMIN CONTROL TEC/DEV
HEALTH...POLICY SIMUL NASA CONGRESS. PAGE 111 B2244 PEACE

N67

PRINCETON U INDUSTRIAL REL SEC,OUTSTANDING BOOKS ON BIBLIOG/A
INDUSTRIAL RELATIONS, 1966 (PAMPHLET NO. 134). INDUS

WOR+45 LABOR WORKER PLAN PRICE CONTROL INCOME...MGT GP/REL
20. PAGE 85 B1711 POLICY

N67

US SENATE COMM ON FOREIGN REL,ARMS SALES AND ARMS/CONT
FOREIGN POLICY (PAMPHLET). FINAN FOR/AID CONTROL ADMIN
20. PAGE 110 B2222 OP/RES
DIPLOM

S68

GRAM H.A.,"BUSINESS ETHICS AND THE CORPORATION." POLICY
LG/CO SECT PROB/SOLV CONTROL EXEC GP/REL INGP/REL ADMIN
PERS/REL ROLE MORAL PWR...DECISION 20. PAGE 42 MGT
B0850

S68

PEARSON A.W.,"RESOURCE ALLOCATION." PLAN PROB/SOLV PROFIT
BUDGET ADMIN CONTROL CHOOSE EFFICIENCY...DECISION OPTIMAL
MGT 20. PAGE 82 B1649 COST
INDUS

CONTROLLED DIRECT OBSERVATION....SEE CONT/OBS

CONV/LEASE....CONVICT LEASE SYSTEM IN SOUTH

CONVENTIONAL....SEE CONVNTL

CONVNTL....CONVENTIONAL

CONWAY J.E. B0469

CONWAY O.B. B0470

COOK P.W. B0471

COOLIDGE/C....CALVIN COOLIDGE

COOMBS C.H. B0472

COOPER F.E. B0473,B0474

COOPER L. B0475

COOPERATION....SEE AGREE

COOPERATIVE....SEE VOL/ASSN

COORDINATION....SEE CENTRAL

COPELAND M.A. B0476

COPYRIGHT....COPYRIGHT

CORBETT D.C. B1024

CORE....CONGRESS OF RACIAL EQUALITY

CORLEY R.N. B0477

CORN/LAWS....CORN LAWS (U.K.)

CORNELL/U....CORNELL UNIVERSITY

CORNWELL E.E. B0478

CORONATIONS....SEE INAUGURATE

CORPORATION....SEE CORPORATN

CORPORATN....CORPORATION

CORRECTIONAL INSTITUTION....SEE PUB/INST

CORREL....STATISTICAL CORRELATIONS

B08

THE GOVERNMENT OF SOUTH AFRICA (VOL. II). SOUTH/AFR CONSTN
STRATA EXTR/IND EX/STRUC TOP/EX BUDGET ADJUD ADMIN FINAN
CT/SYS PRODUC...CORREL CENSUS 19 RAILROAD LEGIS
CIVIL/SERV POSTAL/SYS. PAGE 2 B0033 NAT/G

S61

TANNENBAUM A.S.,"CONTROL AND EFFECTIVENESS IN A EFFICIENCY
VOLUNTARY ORGANIZATION." USA+45 ADMIN...CORREL MATH VOL/ASSN
REGRESS STAT TESTS SAMP/SIZ CHARTS SOC/EXP INDEX 20 CONTROL
LEAGUE/WV. PAGE 102 B2072 INGP/REL

S62

READ W.H.,"UPWARD COMMUNICATION IN INDUSTRIAL ADMIN
HIERARCHIES." LG/CO TOP/EX PROB/SOLV DOMIN EXEC INGP/REL
PERS/REL ATTIT DRIVE PERCEPT...CORREL STAT CHARTS PSY
20. PAGE 86 B1747 MGT

S62

TANNENBAUM A.S.,"CONTROL IN ORGANIZATIONS: ADMIN
INDIVIDUAL ADJUSTMENT AND ORGANIZATIONAL MGT
PERFORMANCE." DOMIN PARTIC REPRESENT INGP/REL STRUCT
PRODUC ATTIT DRIVE PWR...PSY CORREL. PAGE 102 B2073 CONTROL

CORRY J.A. B0479

CORSON J.J. B0480,B0481,B0482

CORWIN E.S. B0483,B0484,B0485

CORY R.H. B0486

COST....ECONOMIC VALUE; SEE ALSO PROFIT, ECO

GINZBERG E.,MANPOWER FOR GOVERNMENT (PAMPHLET).   N19
USA+45 FORCES PLAN PROB/SOLV PAY EDU/PROP ADMIN   WORKER
GP/REL COST...MGT PREDICT TREND 20 CIVIL/SERV.   CONSULT
PAGE 40 B0803   NAT/G
                                                       LOC/G
                                                            N19
VERNON R.,THE MYTH AND REALITY OF OUR URBAN   PLAN
PROBLEMS (PAMPHLET). USA+45 SOCIETY LOC/G ADMIN   MUNIC
COST 20 PRINCETN/U INTERVENT URBAN/RNWL. PAGE 112   HABITAT
B2261   PROB/SOLV
                                                            B28
CALKINS E.E.,BUSINESS THE CIVILIZER. INDUS MARKET   LAISSEZ
WORKER TAX PAY ROUTINE COST DEMAND MORAL 19/20.   POLICY
PAGE 18 B0367   WEALTH
                                                       PROFIT
                                                            B37
GULICK L.,PAPERS ON THE SCIENCE OF ADMINISTRATION.   OP/RES
INDUS PROB/SOLV TEC/DEV COST EFFICIENCY PRODUC   CONTROL
HABITAT...PHIL/SCI METH/COMP 20. PAGE 45 B0903   ADMIN
                                                       MGT
                                                            B40
BURT F.A.,AMERICAN ADVERTISING AGENCIES. BARGAIN   LG/CO
BUDGET LICENSE WRITING PRICE PERS/REL COST DEMAND   COM/IND
...ORG/CHARTS BIBLIOG 20. PAGE 18 B0358   ADMIN
                                                       EFFICIENCY
                                                            B41
SLICHTER S.H.,UNION POLICIES AND INDUSTRIAL   BARGAIN
MANAGEMENT. USA-45 INDUS TEC/DEV PAY GP/REL   LABOR
INGP/REL COST EFFICIENCY PRODUC...POLICY 20.   MGT
PAGE 98 B1978   WORKER
                                                            B44
BIENSTOCK G.,MANAGEMENT IN RUSSIAN INDUSTRY AND   ADMIN
AGRICULTURE. USSR CONSULT WORKER LEAD COST PROFIT   MARXISM
ATTIT DRIVE PWR...MGT METH/COMP DICTIONARY 20.   SML/CO
PAGE 12 B0236   AGRI
                                                            B46
DAVIES E.,NATIONAL ENTERPRISE: THE DEVELOPMENT OF   ADMIN
THE PUBLIC CORPURATION. UK LG/CO EX/STRUC WORKER   NAT/G
PROB/SOLV COST ATTIT SOCISM 20. PAGE 26 B0536   CONTROL
                                                       INDUS
                                                            B48
HOOVER E.M.,THE LOCATION OF ECONOMIC ACTIVITY.   HABITAT
WOR+45 MARKET MUNIC WORKER PROB/SOLV INT/TRADE   INDUS
ADMIN COST...POLICY CHARTS T 20. PAGE 51 B1041   ECO/TAC
                                                       GEOG
                                                            B49
LEPAWSKY A.,ADMINISTRATION. FINAN INDUS LG/CO   ADMIN
SML/CO INGP/REL PERS/REL COST EFFICIENCY OPTIMAL   MGT
SKILL 20. PAGE 64 B1294   WORKER
                                                       EX/STRUC
                                                            B50
HYNEMAN C.S.,BUREAUCRACY IN A DEMOCRACY. CHIEF   NAT/G
LEGIS ADMIN CONTROL LEAD ROUTINE PERS/REL COST   CENTRAL
EFFICIENCY UTIL ATTIT AUTHORIT PERSON MORAL.   EX/STRUC
PAGE 53 B1071   MYTH
                                                            C50
MORLAN R.L.,"INTERGOVERNMENTAL RELATIONS IN   SCHOOL
EDUCATION." USA+45 FINAN LOC/G MUNIC NAT/G FORCES   GOV/REL
PROB/SOLV RECEIVE ADMIN RACE/REL COST...BIBLIOG   ACADEM
INDIAN/AM. PAGE 76 B1526   POLICY
                                                            B54
RECK D.,GOVERNMENT PURCHASING AND COMPETITION.   NAT/G
USA+45 LEGIS CAP/ISM ECO/TAC GOV/REL CENTRAL   FINAN
...POLICY 20 CONGRESS. PAGE 87 B1749   MGT
                                                       COST
                                                            B56
ECOLE NAT'L D'ADMINISTRATION,RECRUITMENT AND   ADMIN
TRAINING FOR THE HIGHER CIVIL SERVICE IN FRANCE.   MGT
FRANCE EX/STRUC PLAN EDU/PROP CONTROL ROUTINE TASK   EXEC
COST...METH 20 CIVIL/SERV. PAGE 32 B0650   ACADEM
                                                            S56
MARGOLIS J.,"ON MUNICIPAL LAND POLICY FOR FISCAL   BUDGET
GAINS." USA+45 MUNIC PLAN TAX COST EFFICIENCY   POLICY
HABITAT KNOWL...MGT 20. PAGE 69 B1398   GEOG
                                                       LOC/G
                                                            B58
WARNER A.W.,CONCEPTS AND CASES IN ECONOMIC   ECO/TAC
ANALYSIS. PROB/SOLV BARGAIN CONTROL INCOME PRODUC   DEMAND
...ECOMETRIC MGT CONCPT CLASSIF CHARTS 20   EQUILIB
KEYNES/JM. PAGE 114 B2292   COST
                                                            S58
MANSFIELD E.,"A STUDY OF DECISION-MAKING WITHIN THE   OP/RES
FIRM." LG/CO WORKER INGP/REL COST EFFICIENCY PRODUC   PROB/SOLV
...CHARTS 20. PAGE 69 B1395   AUTOMAT
                                                       ROUTINE
                                                            B60
CORSON J.J.,GOVERNANCE OF COLLEGES AND   ADMIN
UNIVERSITIES. STRUCT FINAN DELIB/GP DOMIN EDU/PROP   EXEC
LEAD CHOOSE GP/REL CENTRAL COST PRIVIL SUPEGO   ACADEM
ORD/FREE PWR...DECISION BIBLIOG. PAGE 24 B0481   HABITAT

                                                            B60
MARSHALL A.H.,FINANCIAL ADMINISTRATION IN LOCAL   FINAN
GOVERNMENT. UK DELIB/GP CONFER COST INCOME PERSON   LOC/G
...JURID 20. PAGE 70 B1408   BUDGET
                                                       ADMIN
                                                            B60
WEBSTER J.A.,A GENERAL STUDY OF THE DEPARTMENT OF   ORD/FREE
DEFENSE INTERNAL SECURITY PROGRAM. USA+45 WORKER   PLAN
TEC/DEV ADJUD CONTROL CT/SYS EXEC GOV/REL COST   ADMIN
...POLICY DECISION MGT 20 DEPT/DEFEN SUPREME/CT.   NAT/G
PAGE 114 B2307
                                                            B61
KEE R.,REFUGEE WORLD. AUSTRIA EUR+WWI GERMANY NEIGH   NAT/G
EX/STRUC WORKER PROB/SOLV ECO/TAC RENT EDU/PROP   GIVE
INGP/REL COST LITERACY HABITAT 20 MIGRATION.   WEALTH
PAGE 59 B1186   STRANGE
                                                            B61
QURESHI S.,INCENTIVES IN AMERICAN EMPLOYMENT   SERV/IND
(THESIS, UNIVERSITY OF PENNSYLVANIA). DELIB/GP   ADMIN
TOP/EX BUDGET ROUTINE SANCTION COST TECHRACY MGT.   PAY
PAGE 85 B1727   EX/STRUC
                                                            B61
US GENERAL ACCOUNTING OFFICE,EXAMINATION OF   FOR/AID
ECONOMIC AND TECHNICAL ASSISTANCE PROGRAM FOR IRAN.   ADMIN
IRAN USA+45 AGRI INDUS DIPLOM CONTROL COST 20.   TEC/DEV
PAGE 108 B2186   ECO/UNDEV
                                                            B62
BOWEN W.G.,THE FEDERAL GOVERNMENT AND PRINCETON   NAT/G
UNIVERSITY. USA+45 FINAN ACT/RES PROB/SOLV ADMIN   ACADEM
CONTROL COST...POLICY 20 PRINCETN/U. PAGE 14 B0285   GP/REL
                                                       OP/RES
                                                            B62
GRANICK D.,THE EUROPEAN EXECUTIVE. BELGIUM FRANCE   MGT
GERMANY/W UK INDUS LABOR LG/CO SML/CO EX/STRUC PLAN   ECO/DEV
TEC/DEV CAP/ISM COST DEMAND...POLICY CHARTS 20.   ECO/TAC
PAGE 42 B0852   EXEC
                                                            B62
HATTERY L.H.,INFORMATION RETRIEVAL MANAGEMENT.   R+D
CLIENT INDUS TOP/EX COMPUTER OP/RES TEC/DEV ROUTINE   COMPUT/IR
COST EFFICIENCY RIGID/FLEX...METH/COMP ANTHOL 20.   MGT
PAGE 48 B0968   CREATE
                                                            B62
INST TRAINING MUNICIPAL ADMIN,MUNICIPAL FINANCE   MUNIC
ADMINISTRATION (6TH ED.). USA+45 ELITES ECO/DEV   ADMIN
LEGIS PLAN BUDGET TAX GP/REL BAL/PAY COST...POLICY   FINAN
20 CITY/MGT. PAGE 54 B1089   LOC/G
                                                            B63
BONINI C.P.,SIMULATION OF INFORMATION AND DECISION   INDUS
SYSTEMS IN THE FIRM. MARKET BUDGET DOMIN EDU/PROP   SIMUL
ADMIN COST ATTIT HABITAT PERCEPT PWR...CONCPT   DECISION
PROBABIL QUANT PREDICT HYPO/EXP BIBLIOG. PAGE 13   MGT
B0273
                                                            B63
BURSK E.C.,NEW DECISION-MAKING TOOLS FOR MANAGERS.   DECISION
COMPUTER PLAN PROB/SOLV ROUTINE COST. PAGE 18 B0357   MGT
                                                       MATH
                                                       RIGID/FLEX
                                                            B63
DUE J.F.,STATE SALES TAX ADMINISTRATION. OP/RES   PROVS
BUDGET PAY ADMIN EXEC ROUTINE COST EFFICIENCY   TAX
PROFIT...CHARTS METH/COMP 20. PAGE 31 B0626   STAT
                                                       GOV/COMP
                                                            B63
US HOUSE COM ON ED AND LABOR,ADMINISTRATION OF   AGE/O
AGING. USA+45 R+D EX/STRUC PLAN BUDGET PAY EDU/PROP   ADMIN
ROUTINE COST CONGRESS. PAGE 108 B2187   DELIB/GP
                                                       GIVE
                                                            B63
US SENATE COMM APPROPRIATIONS,PERSONNEL   ADMIN
ADMINISTRATION AND OPERATIONS OF AGENCY FOR   FOR/AID
INTERNATIONAL DEVELOPMENT: SPECIAL HEARING. FINAN   EFFICIENCY
LEAD COST UTIL SKILL...CHARTS 20 CONGRESS AID   DIPLOM
CIVIL/SERV. PAGE 109 B2211
                                                            B64
FONTENEAU J.,LE CONSEIL MUNICIPAL: LE MAIRE-LES   MUNIC
ADJOINTS. FRANCE FINAN DELIB/GP EX/STRUC BUDGET TAX   NEIGH
TASK COST INCOME ROLE SUPEGO 20 MAYOR. PAGE 36   ADMIN
B0735   TOP/EX
                                                            B64
GARFIELD PJ   LOVEJOY WF,PUBLIC UTILITY   T
ECONOMICS. DIST/IND FINAN MARKET MUNIC ADMIN COST   ECO/TAC
DEMAND...TECHNIC JURID 20 MONOPOLY. PAGE 39 B0782   OWN
                                                     SERV/IND
                                                            B64
GOODMAN W.,THE TWO-PARTY SYSTEM IN THE UNITED   POL/PAR
STATES. USA+45 USA-45 STRATA LOC/G CHIEF EDU/PROP   REPRESENT
ADMIN COST PWR POPULISM...PLURIST 18/20 PRESIDENT.   CHOOSE
PAGE 41 B0821   NAT/G
                                                            B64
JACKSON R.M.,THE MACHINERY OF JUSTICE IN ENGLAND.   CT/SYS
UK EDU/PROP CONTROL COST ORD/FREE...MGT 20   ADJUD
ENGLSH/LAW. PAGE 55 B1109   JUDGE
                                                     JURID
                                                            B64
KIESER P.J.,THE COST OF ADMINISTRATION, SUPERVISION AFR
AND SERVICES IN URBAN BANTU TOWNSHIPS. SOUTH/AFR   MGT

SERV/IND MUNIC PROVS ADMIN COST...OBS QU CHARTS 20 FINAN
BANTU. PAGE 60 B1203
           B64

KNOX V.H.,PUBLIC FINANCE: INFORMATION SOURCES.   BIBLIOG/A
USA+45 DIPLOM ADMIN GOV/REL COST...POLICY 20.   FINAN
PAGE 60 B1221   TAX
                                            BUDGET
           B64

MAYER C.S.,INTERVIEWING COSTS IN SURVEY RESEARCH. SIMUL
USA+45 PLAN COST...MGT REC/INT SAMP METH/COMP   INT
HYPO/EXP METH 20. PAGE 71 B1434   R+D
                                           EFFICIENCY
           B64

PIERCE T.M.,FEDERAL, STATE, AND LOCAL GOVERNMENT IN NAT/G
EDUCATION. FINAN LOC/G PROVS LEGIS PLAN EDU/PROP POLICY
ADMIN CONTROL CENTRAL COST KNOWL 20. PAGE 83 B1673 SCHOOL
                                           GOV/REL
           S64

CARNEGIE ENDOWMENT INT. PEACE,"ADMINISTRATION AND INT/ORG
BUDGET (ISSUES BEFORE THE NINETEENTH GENERAL   ADMIN
ASSEMBLY)." WOR+45 FINAN BUDGET ECO/TAC ROUTINE
COST...STAT RECORD UN. PAGE 19 B0383
           S64

STONE P.A.,"DECISION TECHNIQUES FOR TOWN   OP/RES
DEVELOPMENT." PLAN COST PROFIT...DECISION MGT   MUNIC
CON/ANAL CHARTS METH/COMP BIBLIOG 20. PAGE 101 ADMIN
B2048   PROB/SOLV
           B65

ALDERSON W.,DYNAMIC MARKETING BEHAVIOR. USA+45   MGT
FINAN CREATE TEC/DEV EDU/PROP PRICE COST 20. PAGE 3 MARKET
B0071   ATTIT
                                           CAP/ISM
           B65

ECCLES H.E.,MILITARY CONCEPTS AND PHILOSOPHY.   PLAN
USA+45 STRUCT EXEC ROUTINE COERCE WAR CIVMIL/REL DRIVE
COST...OBS GEN/LAWS COLD/WAR. PAGE 32 B0648   LEAD
                                           FORCES
           B65

EDELMAN M.,THE POLITICS OF WAGE-PRICE DECISIONS. GOV/COMP
GERMANY ITALY NETHERLAND UK INDUS LABOR POL/PAR   CONTROL
PROB/SOLV BARGAIN PRICE ROUTINE BAL/PAY COST DEMAND ECO/TAC
20. PAGE 32 B0654   PLAN
           B65

MEYERHOFF A.E.,THE STRATEGY OF PERSUASION. USA+45 EDU/PROP
COM/IND CONSULT FOR/AID CONTROL COERCE COST ATTIT EFFICIENCY
PERCEPT MARXISM 20 COLD/WAR. PAGE 73 B1476   OP/RES
                                           ADMIN
           B65

OECD,MEDITERRANEAN REGIONAL PROJECT: TURKEY;   EDU/PROP
EDUCATION AND DEVELOPMENT. FUT TURKEY SOCIETY   ACADEM
STRATA FINAN NAT/G PROF/ORG PLAN PROB/SOLV ADMIN SCHOOL
COST...STAT CHARTS 20 OECD. PAGE 79 B1602   ECO/UNDEV
           B65

ORG FOR ECO COOP AND DEVEL,THE MEDITERRANEAN   PLAN
REGIONAL PROJECT: AN EXPERIMENT IN PLANNING BY SIX ECO/UNDEV
COUNTRIES. FUT GREECE SPAIN TURKEY YUGOSLAVIA   ACADEM
SOCIETY FINAN NAT/G PROF/ORG EDU/PROP ADMIN REGION SCHOOL
COST...POLICY STAT CHARTS 20 OECD. PAGE 80 B1614
           B65

ORG FOR ECO COOP AND DEVEL,THE MEDITERRANEAN   EDU/PROP
REGIONAL PROJECT: YUGOSLAVIA; EDUCATION AND   ACADEM
DEVELOPMENT. YUGOSLAVIA SOCIETY FINAN PROF/ORG PLAN SCHOOL
ADMIN COST DEMAND MARXISM...STAT TREND CHARTS METH ECO/UNDEV
20 OECD. PAGE 80 B1615
           S65

"FURTHER READING." INDIA STRUCT FINAN WORKER ADMIN BIBLIOG
COST 20. PAGE 2 B0042   MGT
                                           ECO/UNDEV
                                           EFFICIENCY
           S65

BALDWIN H.,"SLOW-DOWN IN THE PENTAGON." USA+45   RECORD
CREATE PLAN GOV/REL CENTRAL COST EFFICIENCY PWR   R+D
...MGT MCNAMARA/R. PAGE 9 B0174   WEAPON
                                           ADMIN
           S65

HAMMOND P.Y.,"FOREIGN POLICY-MAKING AND   DIPLOM
ADMINISTRATIVE POLITICS." CREATE ADMIN COST   STRUCT
...DECISION CONCPT GAME CONGRESS PRESIDENT. PAGE 46 IDEA/COMP
B0935   OP/RES
           S65

OSTGAARD E.,"FACTORS INFLUENCING THE FLOW OF NEWS." EDU/PROP
COM/IND BUDGET DIPLOM EXEC GP/REL COST ATTIT SAMP. PERCEPT
PAGE 80 B1618   RECORD
           B66

DAVIS R.G.,PLANNING HUMAN RESOURCE DEVELOPMENT,   PLAN
EDUCATIONAL MODELS AND SCHEMATA. WORKER OP/RES   EFFICIENCY
ECO/TAC EDU/PROP CONTROL COST PRODUC...GEOG STAT SIMUL
CHARTS 20. PAGE 27 B0544   ROUTINE
           B66

GROSS H.,MAKE OR BUY. USA+45 FINAN INDUS CREATE   ECO/TAC
PRICE PRODUC 20. PAGE 44 B0889   PLAN
                                           MGT
                                         COST
           B66

HASTINGS P.G.,THE MANAGEMENT OF BUSINESS FINANCE. FINAN
ECO/DEV PLAN BUDGET CONTROL COST...DECISION CHARTS MGT

BIBLIOG T 20. PAGE 48 B0966   INDUS
                                           ECO/TAC
           B66

KURAKOV I.G.,SCIENCE, TECHNOLOGY AND COMMUNISM;   CREATE
SOME QUESTIONS OF DEVELOPMENT (TRANS. BY CARIN   TEC/DEV
DEDIJER). USSR INDUS PLAN PROB/SOLV COST PRODUC   MARXISM
...MGT MATH CHARTS METH 20. PAGE 61 B1243   ECO/TAC
           B66

NYC TEMPORARY COMM CITY FINAN,MUNICIPAL COLLECTIVE MUNIC
BARGAINING (NO. 8). USA+45 PLAN PROB/SOLV BARGAIN FINAN
BUDGET TAX EDU/PROP GOV/REL COST...MGT 20   ADMIN
NEWYORK/C. PAGE 79 B1596   LOC/G
           B66

PERKINS J.A.,THE UNIVERSITY IN TRANSITION. USA+45 ACADEM
SOCIETY FINAN INDUS NAT/G EX/STRUC ADMIN INGP/REL ORD/FREE
COST EFFICIENCY ATTIT 20. PAGE 82 B1658   CREATE
                                           ROLE
           B66

WHITNAH D.R.,SAFER SKYWAYS. DIST/IND DELIB/GP   ADMIN
FORCES TOP/EX WORKER TEC/DEV ROUTINE WAR CIVMIL/REL NAT/G
COST...TIME/SEQ 20 FAA CAB. PAGE 116 B2342   AIR
                                           GOV/REL
           B67

FARRIS M.T.,MODERN TRANSPORTATION: SELECTED   DIST/IND
READINGS. UNIV CONTROL...POLICY ANTHOL T 20.   MGT
PAGE 35 B0706   COST
           B67

MACKINTOSH J.M.,JUGGERNAUT. USSR NAT/G POL/PAR   WAR
ADMIN LEAD CIVMIL/REL COST TOTALISM PWR MARXISM   FORCES
...GOV/COMP 20. PAGE 68 B1364   COM
                                           PROF/ORG
           B67

MARRIS P.,DILEMMAS OF SOCIAL REFORM: POVERTY AND STRUCT
COMMUNITY ACTION IN THE UNITED STATES. USA+45 NAT/G MUNIC
OP/RES ADMIN PARTIC EFFICIENCY WEALTH...SOC   PROB/SOLV
METH/COMP T 20 REFORMERS. PAGE 69 B1401   COST
           B67

NARVER J.C.,CONGLOMERATE MERGERS AND MARKET   DEMAND
COMPETITION. USA+45 LAW STRUCT ADMIN LEAD RISK COST LG/CO
PROFIT WEALTH...POLICY CHARTS BIBLIOG. PAGE 77   MARKET
B1555   MGT
           B67

NORTHRUP H.R.,RESTRICTIVE LABOR PRACTICES IN THE DIST/IND
SUPERMARKET INDUSTRY. USA+45 INDUS WORKER TEC/DEV MARKET
BARGAIN PAY CONTROL GP/REL COST...STAT CHARTS NLRB. LABOR
PAGE 79 B1592   MGT
           B67

ROTHENBERG J.,ECONOMIC EVALUATION OF URBAN RENEWAL: PLAN
CONCEPTUAL FOUNDATION OF BENEFIT-COST ANALYSIS.   MUNIC
USA+45 ECO/DEV NEIGH TEC/DEV ADMIN GEN/LAWS.   PROB/SOLV
PAGE 91 B1834   COST
           L67

JACOBY S.B.,"THE 89TH CONGRESS AND GOVERNMENT   LAW
LITIGATION." USA+45 ADMIN COST...JURID 20 CONGRESS. NAT/G
PAGE 55 B1117   ADJUD
                                           SANCTION
           S67

CHAMBERLAIN N.W.,"STRIKES IN CONTEMPORARY CONTEXT." LABOR
LAW INDUS NAT/G CHIEF CONFER COST ATTIT ORD/FREE   BARGAIN
...POLICY MGT 20. PAGE 20 B0400   EFFICIENCY
                                           PROB/SOLV
           S67

FERGUSON H.,"3-CITY CONSOLIDATION." USA+45 CONSTN MUNIC
INDUS BARGAIN BUDGET CONFER ADMIN INGP/REL COST   CHOOSE
UTIL. PAGE 35 B0712   CREATE
                                         PROB/SOLV
           S67

GORHAM W.,"NOTES OF A PRACTITIONER." USA+45 BUDGET DECISION
ADMIN COST...CON/ANAL METH/COMP 20 JOHNSON/LB.   NAT/G
PAGE 41 B0836   DELIB/GP
                                           EFFICIENCY
           S67

GRINYER P.H.,"THE SYSTEMATIC EVALUATION OF METHODS OP/RES
OF WAGE PAYMENT." UK INDUS WORKER ADMIN EFFICIENCY COST
...MGT METH/COMP 20. PAGE 44 B0882   PAY
                                           PRODUC
           S67

HAIRE M.,"MANAGING MANAGEMENT MANPOWER." EX/STRUC MGT
OP/RES PAY EDU/PROP COST EFFICIENCY...PREDICT SIMUL EXEC
20. PAGE 45 B0920   LEAD
                                         INDUS
           S67

NYE J.S.,"CORRUPTION AND POLITICAL DEVELOPMENT: A ECO/UNDEV
COST-BENEFIT ANALYSIS." WOR+45 SOCIETY TRIBUTE   NAT/G
ADMIN CONTROL COST...CHARTS 20. PAGE 79 B1598   CRIME
                                           ACT/RES
           S67

WRIGHT F.K.,"INVESTMENT CRITERIA AND THE COST OF COST
CAPITAL." FINAN PLAN BUDGET OPTIMAL PRODUC...POLICY PROFIT
DECISION 20. PAGE 118 B2380   INDUS
                                           MGT
           N67

US CONGRESS JT COMM ECO GOVT,BACKGROUND MATERIAL ON BUDGET
ECONOMY IN GOVERNMENT 1967 (PAMPHLET). WOR+45 STAT COST
ECO/DEV BARGAIN PRICE DEMAND OPTIMAL...STAT   MGT
DEPT/DEFEN. PAGE 108 B2178   NAT/G

S68
PEARSON A.W.,"RESOURCE ALLOCATION." PLAN PROB/SOLV   PROFIT
BUDGET ADMIN CONTROL CHOOSE EFFICIENCY...DECISION   OPTIMAL
MGT 20. PAGE 82 B1649   COST
                                                     INDUS

COSTA RICA UNIVERSIDAD BIBL B0487

COSTA/RICA....SEE ALSO L/A+17C

                                                     B62
COSTA RICA UNIVERSIDAD BIBL,LISTA DE TESIS DE GRADO   BIBLIOG/A
DE LA UNIVERSIDAD DE COSTA RICA. COSTA/RICA LAW   NAT/G
LOC/G ADMIN LEAD...SOC 20. PAGE 24 B0487   DIPLOM
                                                     ECO/UNDEV
                                                     S67
EDWARDS H.T.,"POWER STRUCTURE AND ITS COMMUNICATION   ELITES
IN SAN JOSE, COSTA RICA." COSTA/RICA L/A+17C STRATA   INGP/REL
FACE/GP POL/PAR EX/STRUC PROB/SOLV ADMIN LEAD   MUNIC
GP/REL PWR...STAT INT 20. PAGE 32 B0655   DOMIN

COSTELLO T.W. B0488

COTTER C.P. B0489,B0490,B0491, B0492

COTTRELL A.J. B0493

COUGHLIN/C....CHARLES EDWARD COUGHLIN

COUNCIL OF STATE GOVERNMENTS B0494

COUNCIL OF STATE GOVERNORS B0495

COUNCIL STATE GOVERNMENTS B0496

COUNCIL-MANAGER SYSTEM OF LOCAL GOVERNMENT....SEE
     COUNCL/MGR

COUNCL/EUR....COUNCIL OF EUROPE

                                                     S61
HAAS E.B.,"INTERNATIONAL INTEGRATION: THE EUROPEAN   INT/ORG
AND THE UNIVERSAL PROCESS." EUR+WWI FUT WOR+45   TREND
NAT/G EX/STRUC ATTIT DRIVE ORD/FREE PWR...CONCPT   REGION
GEN/LAWS OEEC 20 NATO COUNCL/EUR. PAGE 45 B0909

                                                     S64
MOWER A.G.,"THE OFFICIAL PRESSURE GROUP OF THE   INT/ORG
COUNCIL OF EUROPE'S CONSULATIVE ASSEMBLY." EUR+WWI   EDU/PROP
SOCIETY STRUCT FINAN CONSULT ECO/TAC ADMIN ROUTINE
ATTIT PWR WEALTH...STAT CHARTS 20 COUNCL/EUR.
PAGE 76 B1535

COUNCL/MGR....COUNCIL-MANAGER SYSTEM OF LOCAL GOVERNMENT

COUNTIES....SEE LOC/G

COUNTY AGRICULTURAL AGENT....SEE COUNTY/AGT

COUNTY/AGT....COUNTY AGRICULTURAL AGENT

                                                     B39
BAKER G.,THE COUNTY AGENT. USA-45 LOC/G NAT/G   AGRI
PROB/SOLV ADMIN...POLICY 20 ROOSEVLT/F NEW/DEAL   CONSULT
COUNTY/AGT. PAGE 8 B0166   GOV/REL
                                                     EDU/PROP

COURAGE....SEE DRIVE

COURT OF APPEALS....SEE CT/APPEALS

COURT SYSTEMS....SEE CT/SYS

COURT/DIST....DISTRICT COURTS

COURTS OF WESTMINSTER HALL....SEE CTS/WESTM

COUTY P. B0497

COWAN L.G. B0498

COWPER/W....WILLIAM COWPER

COX R. B0499

CRAIG J. B0500

CRAIG R. B0418

CRAIN R.L. B0501

CRAMER J.F. B0502

CRAUMER L.V. B0503

CRAWFORD F.G. B0504

CREA J. B2055

CREATE....CREATIVE PROCESSES

                                                     N
INTERNATIONAL REVIEW OF ADMINISTRATIVE SCIENCES.   BIBLIOG/A
WOR+45 WOR-45 STRATA ECO/DEV ECO/UNDEV CREATE PLAN   ADMIN
PROB/SOLV DIPLOM CONTROL REPRESENT...MGT 20. PAGE 1   INT/ORG
B0004   NAT/G

                                                     N
PERSONNEL. USA+45 LAW LABOR LG/CO WORKER CREATE   BIBLIOG/A
GOV/REL PERS/REL ATTIT WEALTH. PAGE 2 B0030   ADMIN
                                                     MGT
                                                     GP/REL

                                                     N19
CANADA CIVIL SERV COMM,THE ANALYSIS OF ORGANIZATION   NAT/G
IN THE GOVERNMENT OF CANADA (PAMPHLET). CANADA   MGT
CONSTN EX/STRUC LEGIS TOP/EX CREATE PLAN CONTROL   ADMIN
GP/REL 20. PAGE 18 B0372   DELIB/GP

                                                     N19
FIRMALINO T.,THE DISTRICT SCHOOL SUPERVISOR VS.   RIGID/FLEX
TEACHERS AND PARENTS: A PHILIPPINE CASE STUDY   SCHOOL
(PAMPHLET) (BMR). PHILIPPINE LOC/G PLAN EDU/PROP   ADMIN
LOBBY REGION PERS/REL 20. PAGE 36 B0722   CREATE

                                                     B26
LUCE R.,CONGRESS: AN EXPLANATION. USA-45 CONSTN   DECISION
FINAN ADMIN LEAD. PAGE 67 B1347   LEGIS
                                                     CREATE
                                                     REPRESENT
                                                     B27
WILLOUGHBY W.F.,PRINCIPLES OF PUBLIC ADMINISTRATION   NAT/G
WITH SPECIAL REFERENCE TO THE NATIONAL AND STATE   EX/STRUC
GOVERNMENTS OF THE UNITED STATES. FINAN PROVS CHIEF   OP/RES
CONSULT LEGIS CREATE BUDGET EXEC ROUTINE GOV/REL   ADMIN
CENTRAL...MGT 20 BUR/BUDGET CONGRESS PRESIDENT.
PAGE 117 B2356

                                                     B30
MURCHISON C.,PSYCHOLOGIES OF 1930. UNIV USA-45   CREATE
CULTURE INTELL SOCIETY STRATA FAM ROUTINE BIO/SOC   PERSON
DRIVE RIGID/FLEX SUPEGO...NEW/IDEA OBS SELF/OBS
CONT/OBS 20. PAGE 76 B1543

                                                     B33
BROMAGE A.W.,AMERICAN COUNTY GOVERNMENT. USA-45   LOC/G
NAT/G LEAD GOV/REL CENTRAL PWR...MGT BIBLIOG 18/20.   CREATE
PAGE 15 B0314   ADMIN
                                                     MUNIC
                                                     B36
ROBINSON H.,DEVELOPMENT OF THE BRITISH EMPIRE.   NAT/G
WOR-45 CULTURE SOCIETY STRUCT ECO/DEV ECO/UNDEV   HIST/WRIT
INT/ORG VOL/ASSN FORCES CREATE PLAN DOMIN EDU/PROP   UK
ADMIN COLONIAL PWR WEALTH...POLICY GEOG CHARTS
CMN/WLTH 16/20. PAGE 89 B1800

                                                     B36
US LIBRARY OF CONGRESS,CLASSIFIED GUIDE TO MATERIAL   BIBLIOG
IN THE LIBRARY OF CONGRESS COVERING URBAN COMMUNITY   CLASSIF
DEVELOPMENT. USA+45 CREATE PROB/SOLV ADMIN 20.   MUNIC
PAGE 109 B2202   PLAN

                                                     B39
HITLER A.,MEIN KAMPF. EUR+WWI FUT MOD/EUR STRUCT   PWR
INT/ORG LABOR NAT/G POL/PAR FORCES CREATE PLAN   NEW/IDEA
BAL/PWR DIPLOM ECO/TAC DOMIN EDU/PROP ADMIN COERCE   WAR
ATTIT...SOCIALIST BIOG TREND NAZI. PAGE 50 B1020

                                                     B39
ZIMMERN A.,MODERN POLITICAL DOCTRINE. WOR-45   NAT/G
CULTURE SOCIETY ECO/UNDEV DELIB/GP EX/STRUC CREATE   ECO/TAC
DOMIN COERCE NAT/LISM ATTIT RIGID/FLEX ORD/FREE PWR   BAL/PWR
WEALTH...POLICY CONCPT OBS TIME/SEQ TREND TOT/POP   INT/TRADE
LEAGUE/NAT 20. PAGE 119 B2402

                                                     B41
BURTON M.E.,THE ASSEMBLY OF THE LEAGUE OF NATIONS.   DELIB/GP
WOR-45 CONSTN SOCIETY STRUCT INT/ORG NAT/G CREATE   EX/STRUC
ATTIT RIGID/FLEX PWR...POLICY TIME/SEQ LEAGUE/NAT   DIPLOM
20. PAGE 18 B0359

                                                     B42
WRIGHT D.M.,THE CREATION OF PURCHASING POWER.   FINAN
USA-45 NAT/G PRICE ADMIN WAR INCOME PRODUC...POLICY   ECO/TAC
CONCPT IDEA/COMP BIBLIOG 20 MONEY. PAGE 118 B2378   ECO/DEV
                                                     CREATE
                                                     B45
BRECHT A.,FEDERALISM AND REGIONALISM IN GERMANY: FEDERAL
THE DIVISION OF PRUSSIA. GERMANY PRUSSIA WOR-45   REGION
CREATE ADMIN WAR TOTALISM PWR...CHARTS 20 HITLER/A.   PROB/SOLV
PAGE 15 B0303   CONSTN
                                                     B45
BUSH V.,SCIENCE, THE ENDLESS FRONTIER. FUT USA-45   R+D
INTELL STRATA ACT/RES CREATE PLAN NUC/PWR PEACE   NAT/G
ATTIT HEALTH KNOWL...MAJORIT HEAL MGT
PHIL/SCI CONCPT OBS TREND 20. PAGE 18 B0360

                                                     B48
STEWART I.,ORGANIZING SCIENTIFIC RESEARCH FOR WAR: DELIB/GP
ADMINISTRATIVE HISTORY OF OFFICE OF SCIENTIFIC   ADMIN
RESEARCH AND DEVELOPMENT. USA-45 INTELL R+D LABOR   WAR
WORKER CREATE BUDGET WEAPON CIVMIL/REL GP/REL   TEC/DEV
EFFICIENCY...POLICY 20. PAGE 101 B2037

B48
TOWSTER J.,POLITICAL POWER IN THE USSR: 1917-1947.   EX/STRUC
USSR CONSTN CULTURE ELITES CREATE PLAN COERCE   NAT/G
CENTRAL ATTIT RIGID/FLEX ORD/FREE...BIBLIOG   MARXISM
SOC/INTEG 20 LENIN/VI STALIN/J. PAGE 105 B2124   PWR

B49
DE GRAZIA A.,HUMAN RELATIONS IN PUBLIC   BIBLIOG/A
ADMINISTRATION. INDUS ACT/RES CREATE PLAN PROB/SOLV ADMIN
TEC/DEV INGP/REL PERS/REL DRIVE...POLICY SOC 20.   PHIL/SCI
PAGE 27 B0552   OP/RES

B49
ROSENHAUPT H.W.,HOW TO WAGE PEACE. USA+45 SOCIETY   INTELL
STRATA STRUCT R+D INT/ORG POL/PAR LEGIS ACT/RES   CONCPT
CREATE PLAN EDU/PROP ADMIN EXEC ATTIT ALL/VALS   DIPLOM
...TIME/SEQ TREND COLD/WAR 20. PAGE 90 B1822

L50
US SENATE COMM. GOVT. OPER.,"REVISION OF THE UN   INT/ORG
CHARTER." FUT USA+45 WOR+45 CONSTN ECO/DEV   LEGIS
ECO/UNDEV NAT/G DELIB/GP ACT/RES CREATE PLAN EXEC PEACE
ROUTINE CHOOSE ALL/VALS...POLICY CONCPT CONGRESS UN
TOT/POP 20 COLD/WAR. PAGE 111 B2235

B51
LEITES N.,THE OPERATIONAL CODE OF THE POLITBURO.   DELIB/GP
COM USSR CREATE PLAN DOMIN LEGIT COERCE ALL/VALS   ADMIN
...SOC CONCPT MYTH TREND CON/ANAL GEN/LAWS 20   SOCISM
LENIN/VI STALIN/J. PAGE 64 B1284

L51
MANGONE G.,"THE IDEA AND PRACTICE OF WORLD   INT/ORG
GOVERNMENT." FUT WOR+45 WOR-45 ECO/DEV LEGIS CREATE SOCIETY
LEGIT ROUTINE ATTIT MORAL PWR WEALTH...CONCPT   INT/LAW
GEN/LAWS 20. PAGE 69 B1388

S51
LERNER D.,"THE POLICY SCIENCES: RECENT DEVELOPMENTS CONSULT
IN SCOPE AND METHODS." R+D SERV/IND CREATE DIPLOM SOC
ROUTINE PWR...METH/CNCPT TREND GEN/LAWS METH 20.
PAGE 64 B1297

L52
WRIGHT Q.,"CONGRESS AND THE TREATY-MAKING POWER." ROUTINE
USA+45 WOR+45 CONSTN INTELL NAT/G CHIEF CONSULT   DIPLOM
EX/STRUC LEGIS TOP/EX CREATE GOV/REL DISPL DRIVE   INT/LAW
RIGID/FLEX...TREND TOT/POP CONGRESS CONGRESS 20   DELIB/GP
TREATY. PAGE 118 B2384

B53
LARSEN K.,NATIONAL BIBLIOGRAPHIC SERVICES: THEIR   BIBLIOG/A
CREATION AND OPERATION. WOR+45 COM/IND CREATE PLAN INT/ORG
DIPLOM PRESS ADMIN ROUTINE...MGT UNESCO. PAGE 62   WRITING
B1262

B53
MACMAHON A.W.,ADMINISTRATION IN FOREIGN AFFAIRS.   USA+45
NAT/G CONSULT DELIB/GP LEGIS ACT/RES CREATE ADMIN ROUTINE
EXEC RIGID/FLEX LEGIS PWR...METH/CNCPT TIME/SEQ TOT/POP FOR/AID
VAL/FREE 20. PAGE 68 B1369   DIPLOM

B54
COMBS C.H.,DECISION PROCESSES. INTELL SOCIETY   MATH
DELIB/GP CREATE TEC/DEV DOMIN LEGIT EXEC CHOOSE   DECISION
DRIVE RIGID/FLEX KNOWL PWR...PHIL/SCI SOC
METH/CNCPT CONT/OBS REC/INT PERS/TEST SAMP/SIZ BIOG
SOC/EXP WORK. PAGE 22 B0455

B54
MANGONE G.,A SHORT HISTORY OF INTERNATIONAL   INT/ORG
ORGANIZATION. MOD/EUR USA+45 USA-45 WOR+45 WOR-45 INT/LAW
LAW LEGIS CREATE LEGIT ROUTINE RIGID/FLEX PWR
...JURID CONCPT OBS TIME/SEQ STERTYP GEN/LAWS UN
TOT/POP VAL/FREE 18/20. PAGE 69 B1389

B54
MILLARD E.L.,FREEDOM IN A FEDERAL WORLD. FUT WOR+45 INT/ORG
VOL/ASSN TOP/EX LEGIT ROUTINE FEDERAL PEACE ATTIT CREATE
DISPL ORD/FREE PWR...MAJORIT INT/LAW JURID TREND   ADJUD
COLD/WAR 20. PAGE 73 B1479   BAL/PWR

B54
MOSK S.A.,INDUSTRIAL REVOLUTION IN MEXICO. MARKET INDUS
LABOR CREATE CAP/ISM ADMIN ATTIT SOCISM...POLICY 20 TEC/DEV
MEXIC/AMER. PAGE 76 B1533   ECO/UNDEV
                                                   NAT/G

B54
WHITE L.D.,THE JACKSONIANS: A STUDY IN   NAT/G
ADMINISTRATIVE HISTORY 1829-1861. USA-45 CONSTN   ADMIN
POL/PAR CHIEF DELIB/GP LEGIS CREATE PROB/SOLV   POLICY
ECO/TAC LEAD REGION GP/REL 19 PRESIDENT CONGRESS
JACKSON/A. PAGE 116 B2339

B55
MAZZINI J.,THE DUTIES OF MAN. MOD/EUR LAW SOCIETY SUPEGO
FAM NAT/G POL/PAR SECT VOL/ASSN EX/STRUC ACT/RES   CONCPT
CREATE REV PEACE ATTIT ALL/VALS...GEN/LAWS WORK 19. NAT/LISM
PAGE 71 B1439

S55
ANGELL R.,"GOVERNMENTS AND PEOPLES AS A FOCI FOR   FUT
PEACE-ORIENTED RESEARCH." WOR+45 CULTURE SOCIETY   SOC
FACE/GP ACT/RES CREATE PLAN DIPLOM EDU/PROP ROUTINE PEACE
ATTIT PERCEPT SKILL...POLICY CONCPT OBS TREND
GEN/METH 20. PAGE 5 B0110

B56
KAUFMANN W.W.,MILITARY POLICY AND NATIONAL   FORCES
SECURITY. USA+45 ELITES INTELL NAT/G TOP/EX PLAN   CREATE
BAL/PWR DIPLOM ROUTINE COERCE NUC/PWR ATTIT
ORD/FREE PWR 20 COLD/WAR. PAGE 58 B1182

B57
CHANDRA S.,PARTIES AND POLITICS AT THE MUGHAL   POL/PAR
COURT: 1707-1740. INDIA CULTURE EX/STRUC CREATE   ELITES
PLAN PWR...BIBLIOG/A 18. PAGE 20 B0405   NAT/G

B57
HEATH S.,CITADEL, MARKET, AND ALTAR; EMERGING   NEW/IDEA
SOCIETY. SOCIETY ADMIN OPTIMAL OWN RATIONAL   STRUCT
ORD/FREE...SOC LOG PREDICT GEN/LAWS DICTIONARY 20. UTOPIA
PAGE 49 B0985   CREATE

B57
HOLCOMBE A.N.,STRENGTHENING THE UNITED NATIONS.   INT/ORG
USA+45 ACT/RES CREATE PLAN EDU/PROP ATTIT PERCEPT ROUTINE
PWR...METH/CNCPT CONT/OBS RECORD UN COLD/WAR 20.
PAGE 51 B1032

B57
SCHNEIDER E.V.,INDUSTRIAL SOCIOLOGY: THE SOCIAL   LABOR
RELATIONS OF INDUSTRY AND COMMUNITY. STRATA INDUS MGT
NAT/G NEIGH CREATE ADMIN PARTIC GP/REL RACE/REL   INGP/REL
ROLE PWR...POLICY BIBLIOG. PAGE 94 B1898   STRUCT

B57
SELZNICK,LEADERSHIP IN ADMINISTRATION: A   LEAD
SOCIOLOGICAL INTERPRETATION. CREATE PROB/SOLV EXEC ADMIN
ROUTINE EFFICIENCY RATIONAL KNOWL...POLICY PSY.   DECISION
PAGE 95 B1927   NAT/G

B57
SIMON H.A.,MODELS OF MAN, SOCIAL AND RATIONAL: MATH
MATHEMATICAL ESSAYS ON RATIONAL HUMAN BEHAVIOR IN A SIMUL
SOCIAL SETTING. UNIV LAW SOCIETY FACE/GP VOL/ASSN
CONSULT EX/STRUC LEGIS CREATE ADMIN ROUTINE ATTIT
DRIVE PWR...SOC CONCPT METH/CNCPT QUANT STAT
TOT/POP VAL/FREE 20. PAGE 97 B1959

B57
US HOUSE COMM ON POST OFFICE,MANPOWER UTILIZATION NAT/G
IN THE FEDERAL GOVERNMENT. USA+45 FORCES WORKER   ADMIN
CREATE PLAN EFFICIENCY UTIL 20 CONGRESS CIVIL/SERV LABOR
POSTAL/SYS DEPT/DEFEN. PAGE 109 B2193   EX/STRUC

B58
CHEEK G.,ECONOMIC AND SOCIAL IMPLICATIONS OF   BIBLIOG/A
AUTOMATION: A BIBLIOGRAPHIC REVIEW (PAMPHLET).   SOCIETY
USA+45 LG/CO WORKER CREATE PLAN CONTROL ROUTINE   INDUS
PERS/REL EFFICIENCY PRODUC...METH/COMP 20. PAGE 20 AUTOMAT
B0416

B58
COWAN L.G.,LOCAL GOVERNMENT IN WEST AFRICA. AFR   LOC/G
FRANCE UK CULTURE KIN POL/PAR CHIEF LEGIS CREATE   COLONIAL
ADMIN PARTIC GOV/REL GP/REL...METH/COMP 20. PAGE 24 SOVEREIGN
B0498   REPRESENT

B58
MARCH J.G.,ORGANIZATIONS. USA+45 CREATE OP/RES PLAN MGT
PROB/SOLV PARTIC ROUTINE RATIONAL ATTIT PERCEPT   PERSON
...DECISION BIBLIOG. PAGE 69 B1397   DRIVE
                                                   CONCPT

B58
SPITZ D.,DEMOCRACY AND THE CHALLANGE OF POWER. FUT NAT/G
USA+45 USA-45 LAW SOCIETY STRUCT LOC/G POL/PAR   PWR
PROVS DELIB/GP EX/STRUC LEGIS TOP/EX ACT/RES CREATE
DOMIN EDU/PROP LEGIT ADJUD ADMIN ATTIT DRIVE MORAL
ORD/FREE TOT/POP. PAGE 99 B2010

B58
SWEENEY S.B.,EDUCATION FOR ADMINISTRATIVE CAREERS EDU/PROP
IN GOVERNMENT SERVICE. USA+45 ACADEM CONSULT CREATE ADMIN
PLAN CONFER SKILL...TREND IDEA/COMP METH 20   NAT/G
CIVIL/SERV. PAGE 102 B2059   LOC/G

S58
DAVENPORT J.,"ARMS AND THE WELFARE STATE." INTELL USA+45
STRUCT FORCES CREATE ECO/TAC FOR/AID DOMIN LEGIT   NAT/G
ADMIN WAR ORD/FREE PWR...POLICY SOC CONCPT MYTH OBS USSR
TREND COLD/WAR TOT/POP 20. PAGE 26 B0533

S59
KISSINGER H.A.,"THE POLICYMAKER AND THE   INTELL
INTELLECTUAL." USA+45 CONSULT DELIB/GP ACT/RES   CREATE
ADMIN ATTIT DRIVE RIGID/FLEX KNOWL PWR...POLICY
PLURIST MGT METH/CNCPT GEN/LAWS GEN/METH 20.
PAGE 60 B1216

B60
BROOKINGS INSTITUTION,UNITED STATES FOREIGN POLICY: DIPLOM
STUDY NO 9: THE FORMULATION AND ADMINISTRATION OF INT/ORG
UNITED STATES FOREIGN POLICY. USA+45 WOR+45   CREATE
EX/STRUC LEGIS BAL/PWR FOR/AID EDU/PROP CIVMIL/REL
GOV/REL...INT COLD/WAR. PAGE 16 B0317

B60
GILMORE D.R.,DEVELOPING THE "LITTLE" ECONOMIES.   ECO/TAC
USA+45 FINAN LG/CO PROF/ORG VOL/ASSN CREATE ADMIN. LOC/G
PAGE 40 B0801   PROVS
                                                   PLAN

B60
GRAHAM G.A.,AMERICA'S CAPACITY TO GOVERN: SOME   MGT
PRELIMINARY THOUGHTS FOR PROSPECTIVE   LEAD
ADMINISTRATORS. USA+45 SOCIETY DELIB/GP TOP/EX   CHOOSE
CREATE PROB/SOLV RATIONAL 20. PAGE 42 B0849   ADMIN

B60
MUNRO L.,UNITED NATIONS, HOPE FOR A DIVIDED WORLD. INT/ORG
FUT WOR+45 CONSTN DELIB/GP CREATE TEC/DEV DIPLOM   ROUTINE
EDU/PROP LEGIT PEACE ATTIT HEALTH ORD/FREE PWR
...CONCPT TREND UN VAL/FREE 20. PAGE 76 B1540

L60
MACPHERSON C.,"TECHNICAL CHANGE AND POLITICAL   TEC/DEV
DECISION." WOR+45 NAT/G CREATE CAP/ISM DIPLOM   ADMIN
ROUTINE RIGID/FLEX...CONCPT OBS GEN/METH 20.
PAGE 68 B1375

S60
BAVELAS A.,"LEADERSHIP: MAN AND FUNCTION." WORKER   LEAD
CREATE PLAN CONTROL PERS/REL PERSON PWR...MGT 20.   ADMIN
PAGE 10 B0199   ROUTINE
                                                       ROLE

S60
BOGARDUS E.S.,"THE SOCIOLOGY OF A STRUCTURED   INT/ORG
PEACE." FUT SOCIETY CREATE DIPLOM EDU/PROP ADJUD   SOC
ROUTINE ATTIT RIGID/FLEX KNOWL ORD/FREE RESPECT   NAT/LISM
...POLICY INT/LAW JURID NEW/IDEA SELF/OBS TOT/POP   PEACE
20 UN. PAGE 13 B0264

S60
HUTCHINSON C.E.,"AN INSTITUTE FOR NATIONAL SECURITY   POLICY
AFFAIRS." USA+45 R+D NAT/G CONSULT TOP/EX ACT/RES   METH/CNCPT
CREATE PLAN TEC/DEV EDU/PROP ROUTINE NUC/PWR ATTIT   ELITES
ORD/FREE PWR...DECISION MGT PHIL/SCI CONCPT RECORD   DIPLOM
GEN/LAWS GEN/METH 20. PAGE 53 B1068

S60
SCHWARTZ B.,"THE INTELLIGENTSIA IN COMMUNIST CHINA: INTELL
A TENTATIVE COMPARISON." ASIA CHINA/COM COM RUSSIA   RIGID/FLEX
ELITES SOCIETY STRATA POL/PAR VOL/ASSN CREATE ADMIN   REV
COERCE NAT/LISM TOTALISM...POLICY TREND 20. PAGE 95
B1914

B61
BRADY R.A.,ORGANIZATION, AUTOMATION, AND SOCIETY.   TEC/DEV
USA+45 AGRI COM/IND DIST/IND MARKET CREATE   INDUS
...DECISION MGT 20. PAGE 14 B0296   AUTOMAT
                                                       ADMIN

B61
ETZIONI A.,COMPLEX ORGANIZATIONS: A SOCIOLOGICAL   VOL/ASSN
READER. CLIENT CULTURE STRATA CREATE OP/RES ADMIN   STRUCT
...POLICY METH/CNCPT BUREAUCRCY. PAGE 34 B0683   CLASSIF
                                                       PROF/ORG

B61
GORDON W.J.J.,SYNECTICS; THE DEVELOPMENT OF   CREATE
CREATIVE CAPACITY. USA+45 PLAN TEC/DEV KNOWL WEALTH   PROB/SOLV
...DECISION MGT 20. PAGE 41 B0832   ACT/RES
                                                       TOP/EX

B61
JACOBS J.,THE DEATH AND LIFE OF GREAT AMERICAN   MUNIC
CITIES. USA+45 SOCIETY DIST/IND CREATE PROB/SOLV   PLAN
ADMIN...GEOG SOC CENSUS 20 URBAN/RNWL. PAGE 55   ADJUST
B1113   HABITAT

B61
KOESTLER A.,THE LOTUS AND THE ROBOT. ASIA INDIA   SECT
S/ASIA SOCIETY STRATA ECO/DEV AGRI INDUS FAM CREATE   ECO/UNDEV
DOMIN EDU/PROP ADMIN COERCE ATTIT DRIVE SUPEGO
ORD/FREE PWR RESPECT WEALTH...MYTH OBS 20 CHINJAP.
PAGE 61 B1226

B61
LASSWELL H.D.,PSYCOPATHOLOGY AND POLITICS. WOR-45   ATTIT
CULTURE SOCIETY FACE/GP NAT/G CONSULT CREATE   GEN/METH
EDU/PROP EXEC ROUTINE DISPL DRIVE PERSON PWR
RESPECT...PSY CONCPT METH/CNCPT METH. PAGE 63 B1272

B61
MARX K.,THE COMMUNIST MANIFESTO. IN (MENDEL A.   COM
ESSENTIAL WORKS OF MARXISM, NEW YORK: BANTAM. FUT   NEW/IDEA
MOD/EUR CULTURE ECO/DEV ECO/UNDEV AGRI FINAN INDUS   CAP/ISM
MARKET PROC/MFG LABOR MUNIC POL/PAR CONSULT FORCES   REV
CREATE PLAN ADMIN ATTIT DRIVE RIGID/FLEX ORD/FREE
PWR RESPECT MARX/KARL WORK. PAGE 70 B1421

B61
MAYNE A.,DESIGNING AND ADMINISTERING A REGIONAL   ECO/UNDEV
ECONOMIC DEVELOPMENT PLAN WITH SPECIFIC REFERENCE   PLAN
TO PUERTO RICO (PAMPHLET). PUERT/RICO SOCIETY NAT/G   CREATE
DELIB/GP REGION...DECISION 20. PAGE 71 B1435   ADMIN

B61
SINGER J.D.,FINANCING INTERNATIONAL ORGANIZATION: INT/ORG
THE UNITED NATIONS BUDGET PROCESS. WOR+45 FINAN   MGT
ACT/RES CREATE PLAN BUDGET ECO/TAC ADMIN ROUTINE
ATTIT KNOWL...DECISION METH/CNCPT TIME/SEQ UN 20.
PAGE 97 B1964

S61
DEVINS J.H.,"THE INITIATIVE." COM USA+45 USA-45   FORCES
USSR SOCIETY NAT/G ACT/RES CREATE BAL/PWR ROUTINE   CONCPT
COERCE DETER RIGID/FLEX SKILL...STERTYP COLD/WAR   WAR
20. PAGE 29 B0582

S61
PADOVER S.K.,"PSYCHOLOGICAL WARFARE AND FOREIGN   ROUTINE
POLICY." FUT UNIV USA+45 INTELL SOCIETY CREATE   DIPLOM
EDU/PROP ADMIN WAR PEACE PERCEPT...POLICY
METH/CNCPT TESTS TIME/SEQ 20. PAGE 80 B1623

C61
ETZIONI A.,"A COMPARATIVE ANALYSIS OF COMPLEX   CON/ANAL
ORGANIZATIONS: ON POWER, INVOLVEMENT AND THEIR   SOC
CORRELATES." ELITES CREATE OP/RES ROUTINE INGP/REL   LEAD
PERS/REL CONSEN ATTIT DRIVE PWR...CONCPT BIBLIOG.   CONTROL
PAGE 34 B0684

B62
ARGYRIS C.,INTERPERSONAL COMPETENCE AND   EX/STRUC
ORGANIZATIONAL EFFECTIVENESS. CREATE PLAN PROB/SOLV   ADMIN

EDU/PROP INGP/REL PERS/REL PRODUC...OBS INT SIMUL   CONSULT
20. PAGE 6 B0131   EFFICIENCY

B62
CHICAGO U CTR PROG GOVT ADMIN.EDUCATION FOR   EDU/PROP
INNOVATIVE BEHAVIOR IN EXECUTIVES. UNIV ELITES   CREATE
ADMIN EFFICIENCY DRIVE PERSON...MGT APT/TEST   EXEC
PERS/TEST CHARTS LAB/EXP BIBLIOG 20. PAGE 21 B0420   STAT

B62
HATTERY L.H.,INFORMATION RETRIEVAL MANAGEMENT.   R+D
CLIENT INDUS TOP/EX COMPUTER OP/RES TEC/DEV ROUTINE   COMPUT/IR
COST EFFICIENCY RIGID/FLEX...METH/COMP ANTHOL 20.   MGT
PAGE 48 B0968   CREATE

B62
NATIONAL BUREAU ECONOMIC RES.THE RATE AND DIRECTION   DECISION
OF INVENTIVE ACTIVITY: ECONOMIC AND SOCIAL FACTORS.   PROB/SOLV
STRUCT INDUS MARKET R+D CREATE OP/RES TEC/DEV   MGT
EFFICIENCY PRODUC RATIONAL UTIL...WELF/ST PHIL/SCI
METH/CNCPT TIME. PAGE 77 B1562

B62
PACKARD V.,THE PYRAMID CLIMBERS. USA+45 ELITES   INDUS
SOCIETY CREATE PROB/SOLV EFFICIENCY ATTIT...MGT 20.   TOP/EX
PAGE 80 B1621   PERS/REL
                                                       DRIVE

B62
SNYDER R.C.,FOREIGN POLICY DECISION-MAKING. FUT   TEC/DEV
KOREA WOR+45 R+D CREATE ADMIN ROUTINE PWR   HYPO/EXP
...DECISION PSY SOC CONCPT METH/CNCPT CON/ANAL   DIPLOM
CHARTS GEN/METH METH 20. PAGE 99 B1992

B62
STAHL O.G.,PUBLIC PERSONNEL ADMINISTRATION. LOC/G   ADMIN
TOP/EX CREATE PLAN ROUTINE...TECHNIC MGT T.   WORKER
PAGE 100 B2017   EX/STRUC
                                                       NAT/G

L62
BAILEY S.D.,"THE TROIKA AND THE FUTURE OF THE UN."   FUT
CONSTN CREATE LEGIT EXEC CHOOSE ORD/FREE PWR   INT/ORG
...CONCPT NEW/IDEA UN COLD/WAR 20. PAGE 8 B0163   USSR

L62
MALINOWSKI W.R.,"CENTRALIZATION AND DE-   CREATE
CENTRALIZATION IN THE UNITED NATIONS' ECONOMIC AND   GEN/LAWS
SOCIAL ACTIVITIES." WOR+45 CONSTN ECO/UNDEV INT/ORG
VOL/ASSN DELIB/GP ECO/TAC EDU/PROP ADMIN RIGID/FLEX
...OBS CHARTS UNESCO UN EEC OAS OEEC 20. PAGE 69
B1385

S62
BRZEZINSKI Z.K.,"DEVIATION CONTROL: A STUDY IN THE   RIGID/FLEX
DYNAMICS OF DOCTRINAL CONFLICT." WOR+45 WOR-45   ATTIT
VOL/ASSN CREATE BAL/PWR DOMIN EXEC DRIVE PERCEPT
PWR...METH/CNCPT TIME/SEQ TREND 20. PAGE 16 B0333

S62
DUFTY N.F.,"THE IMPLEMENTATION OF A DECISION."   DECISION
STRATA ACT/RES...MGT CHARTS SOC/EXP ORG/CHARTS.   CREATE
PAGE 31 B0627   METH/CNCPT
                                                       SOC

S62
HUDSON G.F.,"SOVIET FEARS OF THE WEST." COM USA+45   ATTIT
SOCIETY DELIB/GP EX/STRUC TOP/EX ACT/RES CREATE   MYTH
DOMIN EDU/PROP LEGIT ADMIN ROUTINE DRIVE PERSON   GERMANY
RIGID/FLEX PWR...RECORD TIME/SEQ TOT/POP 20   USSR
STALIN/J. PAGE 52 B1057

S62
MARTIN L.W.,"POLITICAL SETTLEMENTS AND ARMS   CONCPT
CONTROL." COM EUR+WWI GERMANY USA+45 PROVS FORCES   ARMS/CONT
TOP/EX ACT/RES CREATE DOMIN LEGIT ROUTINE COERCE
ATTIT RIGID/FLEX ORD/FREE PWR...METH/CNCPT RECORD
GEN/LAWS 20. PAGE 70 B1410

S62
SPRINGER H.W.,"FEDERATION IN THE CARIBBEAN: AN   VOL/ASSN
ATTEMPT THAT FAILED." L/A+17C ECO/UNDEV INT/ORG   NAT/G
POL/PAR PROVS LEGIS CREATE PLAN LEGIT ADMIN FEDERAL   REGION
ATTIT DRIVE PERSON ORD/FREE PWR...POLICY GEOG PSY
CONCPT OBS CARIBBEAN CMN/WLTH 20. PAGE 100 B2013

B63
COSTELLO T.W.,PSYCHOLOGY IN ADMINISTRATION: A   PSY
RESEARCH ORIENTATION. CREATE PROB/SOLV PERS/REL   MGT
ADJUST ANOMIE ATTIT DRIVE PERCEPT ROLE...DECISION   EXEC
BIBLIOG T 20. PAGE 24 B0488   ADMIN

B63
HOWER R.M.,MANAGERS AND SCIENTISTS. EX/STRUC CREATE   R+D
ADMIN REPRESENT ATTIT DRIVE ROLE PWR SKILL...SOC   MGT
INT. PAGE 52 B1052   PERS/REL
                                                       INGP/REL

B63
INTL INST ADMIN SCIENCES.EDUCATION IN PUBLIC   EDU/PROP
ADMINISTRATION: A SYMPOSIUM ON TEACHING METHODS AND   METH
MATERIALS. WOR+45 SCHOOL CONSULT CREATE CONFER   ADMIN
SKILL...OBS TREND IDEA/COMP METH/COMP 20. PAGE 54   ACADEM
B1100

B63
JOHNS R.,CONFRONTING ORGANIZATIONAL CHANGE. NEIGH   SOC/WK
DELIB/GP CREATE OP/RES ADMIN GP/REL DRIVE...WELF/ST   WEALTH
SOC RECORD BIBLIOG. PAGE 56 B1142   LEAD
                                                       VOL/ASSN

B63
KARL B.D.,EXECUTIVE REORGANIZATION AND REFORM IN   BIOG
THE NEW DEAL. ECO/DEV INDUS DELIB/GP EX/STRUC PLAN   EXEC

BUDGET ADMIN EFFICIENCY PWR POPULISM...POLICY 20 CREATE
PRESIDENT ROOSEVLT/F WILSON/W NEW/DEAL. PAGE 58 CONTROL
B1174

B63
KORNHAUSER W.,SCIENTISTS IN INDUSTRY: CONFLICT AND CREATE
ACCOMMODATION. USA+45 R+D LG/CO NAT/G TEC/DEV INDUS
CONTROL ADJUST ATTIT...MGT STAT INT BIBLIOG 20. PROF/ORG
PAGE 61 B1229 GP/REL

B63
LITTERER J.A.,ORGANIZATIONS: STRUCTURE AND ADMIN
BEHAVIOR. PLAN DOMIN CONTROL LEAD ROUTINE SANCTION CREATE
INGP/REL EFFICIENCY PRODUC DRIVE RIGID/FLEX PWR. MGT
PAGE 66 B1325 ADJUST

B63
MAYNE R.,THE COMMUNITY OF EUROPE. UK CONSTN NAT/G EUR+WWI
CONSULT DELIB/GP CREATE PLAN ECO/TAC LEGIT ADMIN INT/ORG
ROUTINE ORD/FREE PWR WEALTH...CONCPT TIME/SEQ EEC REGION
EURATOM 20. PAGE 71 B1436

B63
RAUDSEPP E.,MANAGING CREATIVE SCIENTISTS AND MGT
ENGINEERS. USA+45 ECO/DEV LG/CO GP/REL PERS/REL CREATE
PRODUC. PAGE 86 B1742 R+D
ECO/TAC

L63
BENNIS W.G.,"A NEW ROLE FOR THE BEHAVIORAL METH/CNCPT
SCIENCES: EFFECTING ORGANIZATIONAL CHANGE." ACT/RES CREATE
...MGT GP/COMP PERS/COMP SOC/EXP ORG/CHARTS. STRUCT
PAGE 11 B0216 SOC

S63
ANTHON C.G.,"THE END OF THE ADENAUER ERA." EUR+WWI NAT/G
GERMANY/W CONSTN EX/STRUC CREATE DIPLOM LEGIT ATTIT TOP/EX
PERSON ALL/VALS...RECORD 20 ADENAUER/K. PAGE 6 BAL/PWR
B0113 GERMANY

S63
BACHRACH P.,"DECISIONS AND NONDECISIONS: AN PWR
ANALYTICAL FRAMEWORK." UNIV SOCIETY CREATE LEGIT HYPO/EXP
ADMIN EXEC COERCE...DECISION PSY CONCPT CHARTS.
PAGE 8 B0156

S63
MASSART L.,"L'ORGANISATION DE LA RECHERCHE R+D
SCIENTIFIQUE EN EUROPE." EUR+WWI WOR+45 ACT/RES CREATE
PLAN TEC/DEV EDU/PROP EXEC KNOWL...METH/CNCPT EEC
20. PAGE 70 B1424

S63
MORGENTHAU H.J.,"THE POLITICAL CONDITIONS FOR AN INT/ORG
INTERNATIONAL POLICE FORCE." FUT WOR+45 CREATE FORCES
LEGIT ADMIN PEACE ORD/FREE 20. PAGE 75 B1524 ARMS/CONT
DETER

S63
SCHMITT H.A.,"THE EUROPEAN COMMUNITIES." EUR+WWI VOL/ASSN
FRANCE DELIB/GP EX/STRUC TOP/EX CREATE TEC/DEV ECO/DEV
ECO/TAC LEGIT REGION COERCE DRIVE ALL/VALS
...METH/CNCPT EEC 20. PAGE 94 B1897

S63
SCHURMANN F.,"ECONOMIC POLICY AND POLITICAL POWER PLAN
IN COMMUNIST CHINA." ASIA CHINA/COM USSR SOCIETY ECO/TAC
ECO/UNDEV AGRI INDUS CREATE ADMIN ROUTINE ATTIT
DRIVE RIGID/FLEX PWR WEALTH...HIST/WRIT TREND
CHARTS WORK 20. PAGE 94 B1908

B64
APTER D.E.,IDEOLOGY AND DISCONTENT. FUT WOR+45 ACT/RES
CONSTN CULTURE INTELL SOCIETY STRUCT INT/ORG NAT/G ATTIT
DELIB/GP LEGIS CREATE PLAN TEC/DEV EDU/PROP EXEC
PERCEPT PERSON RIGID/FLEX ALL/VALS...POLICY
TOT/POP. PAGE 6 B0122

B64
BLAKE R.R.,MANAGING INTERGROUP CONFLICT IN CREATE
INDUSTRY. INDUS DELIB/GP EX/STRUC GP/REL PERS/REL PROB/SOLV
GAME. PAGE 12 B0250 OP/RES
ADJUD

B64
BRIGHT J.R.,RESEARCH, DEVELOPMENT AND TECHNOLOGICAL TEC/DEV
INNOVATION. CULTURE R+D CREATE PLAN PROB/SOLV NEW/IDEA
AUTOMAT RISK PERSON...DECISION CONCPT PREDICT INDUS
BIBLIOG. PAGE 15 B0308 MGT

B64
BROMAGE A.W.,MANAGER PLAN ABANDONMENTS: WHY A FEW MUNIC
HAVE DROPPED COUNCILMANAGER GOVERNMENT. USA+45 PLAN
CREATE PARTIC CHOOSE...MGT CENSUS CHARTS 20. CONSULT
PAGE 15 B0315 LOC/G

B64
CAPLOW T.,PRINCIPLES OF ORGANIZATION. UNIV CULTURE VOL/ASSN
STRUCT CREATE INGP/REL UTOPIA...GEN/LAWS TIME. CONCPT
PAGE 18 B0374 SIMUL
EX/STRUC

B64
CHANDLER A.D. JR.,GIANT ENTERPRISE: FORD, GENERAL LG/CO
MOTORS, AND THE AUTOMOBILE INDUSTRY; SOURCES AND DIST/IND
READINGS. USA+45 USA-45 FINAN MARKET CREATE ADMIN LABOR
...TIME/SEQ ANTHOL 20 AUTOMOBILE. PAGE 20 B0404 MGT

B64
DIEBOLD J.,BEYOND AUTOMATION: MANAGERIAL PROBLEMS FUT
OF AN EXPLODING TECHNOLOGY. SOCIETY ECO/DEV CREATE INDUS
ECO/TAC AUTOMAT SKILL...TECHNIC MGT WORK. PAGE 29 PROVS
B0589 NAT/G

B64
EWING D.W.,THE MANAGERIAL MIND. SOCIETY STRUCT MGT
INDUS PERSON KNOWL 20. PAGE 34 B0692 ATTIT
CREATE
EFFICIENCY

B64
GRAVIER J.F.,AMENAGEMENT DU TERRITOIRE ET L'AVENIR PLAN
DES REGIONS FRANCAISES. FRANCE ECO/DEV AGRI INDUS MUNIC
CREATE...GEOG CHARTS 20. PAGE 42 B0859 NEIGH
ADMIN

B64
GREBLER L.,URBAN RENEWAL IN EUROPEAN COUNTRIES: ITS MUNIC
EMERGENCE AND POTENTIALS. EUR+WWI UK ECO/DEV LOC/G PLAN
NEIGH CREATE ADMIN ATTIT...TREND NAT/COMP 20 CONSTRUC
URBAN/RNWL. PAGE 43 B0863 NAT/G

B64
INST D'ETUDE POL L'U GRENOBLE,ADMINISTRATION ADMIN
TRADITIONELLE ET PLANIFICATION REGIONALE. FRANCE MUNIC
LAW POL/PAR PROB/SOLV ADJUST RIGID/FLEX...CHARTS PLAN
ANTHOL BIBLIOG T 20 REFORMERS. PAGE 54 B1087 CREATE

B64
NEUSTADT R.,PRESIDENTIAL POWER. USA+45 CONSTN NAT/G TOP/EX
CHIEF LEGIS CREATE EDU/PROP LEGIT ADMIN EXEC COERCE SKILL
ATTIT PERSON RIGID/FLEX PWR CONGRESS 20 PRESIDENT
TRUMAN/HS EISNHWR/DD. PAGE 78 B1575

B64
O'HEARN P.J.T.,PEACE, ORDER AND GOOD GOVERNMENT; A NAT/G
NEW CONSTITUTION FOR CANADA. CANADA EX/STRUC LEGIS CONSTN
CT/SYS PARL/PROC...BIBLIOG 20. PAGE 79 B1600 LAW
CREATE

B64
RIGGS R.E.,THE MOVEMENT FOR ADMINISTRATIVE ADMIN
REORGANIZATION IN ARIZONA. USA+45 LAW POL/PAR PROVS
DELIB/GP LEGIS PROB/SOLV CONTROL RIGID/FLEX PWR CREATE
...ORG/CHARTS 20 ARIZONA DEMOCRAT REPUBLICAN. PLAN
PAGE 88 B1786

B64
SHERIDAN R.G.,URBAN JUSTICE. USA+45 PROVS CREATE LOC/G
ADMIN CT/SYS ORD/FREE 20 TENNESSEE. PAGE 96 B1943 JURID
ADJUD
MUNIC

B64
STANLEY D.T.,THE HIGHER CIVIL SERVICE: AN NAT/G
EVALUATION OF FEDERAL PERSONNEL PRACTICES. USA+45 ADMIN
CREATE EXEC ROUTINE CENTRAL...MGT SAMP IDEA/COMP CONTROL
METH/COMP 20 CIVIL/SERV. PAGE 100 B2020 EFFICIENCY

L64
HAAS E.B.,"ECONOMICS AND DIFFERENTIAL PATTERNS OF L/A+17C
POLITICAL INTEGRATION: PROJECTIONS ABOUT UNITY IN INT/ORG
LATIN AMERICA." SOCIETY NAT/G DELIB/GP ACT/RES MARKET
CREATE PLAN ECO/TAC REGION ROUTINE ATTIT DRIVE PWR
WEALTH...CONCPT TREND CHARTS LAFTA 20. PAGE 45
B0910

S64
NEEDHAM T.,"SCIENCE AND SOCIETY IN EAST AND WEST." ASIA
INTELL STRATA R+D LOC/G NAT/G PROVS CONSULT ACT/RES STRUCT
CREATE PLAN TEC/DEV EDU/PROP ADMIN ATTIT ALL/VALS
...POLICY RELATIV MGT CONCPT NEW/IDEA TIME/SEQ WORK
WORK. PAGE 77 B1565

S64
SCHWELB E.,"OPERATION OF THE EUROPEAN CONVENTION ON INT/ORG
HUMAN RIGHTS." EUR+WWI LAW SOCIETY CREATE EDU/PROP MORAL
ADJUD ADMIN PEACE ATTIT ORD/FREE PWR...POLICY
INT/LAW CONCPT OBS GEN/LAWS UN VAL/FREE ILO 20
ECHR. PAGE 95 B1916

S64
THOMPSON V.A.,"ADMINISTRATIVE OBJECTIVES FOR ECO/UNDEV
DEVELOPMENT ADMINISTRATION." WOR+45 CREATE PLAN MGT
DOMIN EDU/PROP EXEC ROUTINE ATTIT ORD/FREE PWR
...POLICY GEN/LAWS VAL/FREE. PAGE 104 B2107

B65
ALDERSON W.,DYNAMIC MARKETING BEHAVIOR. USA+45 MGT
FINAN CREATE TEC/DEV EDU/PROP PRICE COST 20. PAGE 3 MARKET
B0071 ATTIT
CAP/ISM

B65
BARNETT V.M. JR.,THE REPRESENTATION OF THE UNITED USA+45
STATES ABROAD* REVISED EDITION. ECO/UNDEV ACADEM DIPLOM
INT/ORG FORCES ACT/RES CREATE OP/RES FOR/AID REGION ADMIN
CENTRAL...CLASSIF ANTHOL. PAGE 9 B0189

B65
CAMPBELL G.A.,THE CIVIL SERVICE IN BRITAIN (2ND ADMIN
ED.). UK DELIB/GP FORCES WORKER CREATE PLAN LEGIS
...POLICY AUD/VIS 19/20 CIVIL/SERV. PAGE 18 B0370 NAT/G
FINAN

B65
DUGGAR G.S.,RENEWAL OF TOWN AND VILLAGE I: A WORLD- MUNIC
WIDE SURVEY OF LOCAL GOVERNMENT EXPERIENCE. WOR+45 NEIGH
CONSTRUC INDUS CREATE BUDGET REGION GOV/REL...QU PLAN
NAT/COMP 20 URBAN/RNWL. PAGE 31 B0628 ADMIN

B65
DYER F.C.,BUREAUCRACY VS CREATIVITY. UNIV CONTROL ADMIN
LEAD INGP/REL EFFICIENCY MGT. PAGE 31 B0639 DECISION
METH/COMP
CREATE

EAST J.P.,COUNCIL-MANAGER GOVERNMENT: THE POLITICAL SIMUL
THOUGHT OF ITS FOUNDER, RICHARD S. CHILDS. USA+45   LOC/G
CREATE ADMIN CHOOSE...BIOG GEN/LAWS BIBLIOG 20   MUNIC
CHILDS/RS CITY/MGT. PAGE 32 B0642   EX/STRUC
                                                       B65

EVERETT R.O.,URBAN PROBLEMS AND PROSPECTS. USA+45   MUNIC
CREATE TEC/DEV EDU/PROP ADJUD ADMIN GOV/REL ATTIT   PLAN
...ANTHOL 20 URBAN/RNWL. PAGE 34 B0691   PROB/SOLV
                                                       NEIGH
                                                       B65

GOLEMBIEWSKI R.I.,MEN, MANAGEMENT, AND MORALITY;   LG/CO
TOWARD A NEW ORGANIZATIONAL ETHIC. CONSTN EX/STRUC   MGT
CREATE ADMIN CONTROL INGP/REL PERSON SUPEGO MORAL   PROB/SOLV
PWR...GOV/COMP METH/COMP 20 BUREAUCRCY. PAGE 40
B0819
                                                       B65

GREGG J.L.,POLITICAL PARTIES AND PARTY SYSTEMS IN   LEAD
GUATEMALA, 1944-1963. GUATEMALA L/A+17C EX/STRUC   POL/PAR
FORCES CREATE CONTROL REV CHOOSE PWR...TREND   NAT/G
IDEA/COMP 20. PAGE 43 B0872   CHIEF
                                                       B65

HARR J.E.,THE DEVELOPMENT OF CAREERS IN THE FOREIGN   OP/RES
SERVICE. CREATE SENIOR EXEC FEEDBACK GOV/REL   MGT
EFFICIENCY ATTIT RESPECT ORG/CHARTS. PAGE 47 B0953   ADMIN
                                                       DIPLOM
                                                       B65

MUSHKIN S.J.,STATE PROGRAMMING. USA+45 PLAN BUDGET   PROVS
TAX ADMIN REGION GOV/REL...BIBLIOG 20. PAGE 77   POLICY
B1549   CREATE
                                                       ECO/DEV
                                                       B65

STEINER G.A.,THE CREATIVE ORGANIZATION. ELITES   CREATE
LG/CO PLAN PROB/SOLV TEC/DEV INSPECT CAP/ISM   MGT
CONTROL EXEC PERSON...METH/COMP HYPO/EXP 20.   ADMIN
PAGE 100 B2029   SOC
                                                       B65

WATERSTON A.,DEVELOPMENT PLANNING* LESSONS OF   ECO/UNDEV
EXPERIENCE. ECO/TAC CENTRAL...MGT QUANT BIBLIOG.   CREATE
PAGE 114 B2303   PLAN
                                                       ADMIN

HOOK S.,"SECOND THOUGHTS ON BERKELEY" USA+45 ELITES   ACADEM
INTELL LEGIT ADMIN COERCE REPRESENT GP/REL INGP/REL   ORD/FREE
TOTALISM AGE/Y MARXISM 20 BERKELEY FREE/SPEE   POLICY
STUDNT/PWR. PAGE 51 B1040   CREATE
                                                       L65

LASSWELL H.D.,"THE POLICY SCIENCES OF DEVELOPMENT."   PWR
CULTURE SOCIETY EX/STRUC CREATE ADMIN ATTIT KNOWL   METH/CNCPT
...SOC CONCPT SIMUL GEN/METH. PAGE 63 B1273   DIPLOM
                                                       S65

ALEXANDER T.,"SYNECTICS: INVENTING BY THE MADNESS   PROB/SOLV
METHOD." DELIB/GP TOP/EX ACT/RES TEC/DEV EXEC TASK   OP/RES
KNOWL...MGT METH/COMP 20. PAGE 4 B0073   CREATE
                                                       CONSULT
                                                       S65

BALDWIN H.,"SLOW-DOWN IN THE PENTAGON." USA+45   RECORD
CREATE PLAN GOV/REL CENTRAL COST EFFICIENCY PWR   R+D
...MGT MCNAMARA/R. PAGE 9 B0174   WEAPON
                                                       ADMIN
                                                       S65

BROWN S.,"AN ALTERNATIVE TO THE GRAND DESIGN."   VOL/ASSN
EUR+WWI FUT USA+45 INT/ORG NAT/G EX/STRUC FORCES   CONCPT
CREATE BAL/PWR DOMIN RIGID/FLEX ORD/FREE PWR   DIPLOM
...NEW/IDEA RECORD EEC NATO 20. PAGE 16 B0327
                                                       S65

HAMMOND P.Y.,"FOREIGN POLICY-MAKING AND   DIPLOM
ADMINISTRATIVE POLITICS." CREATE ADMIN COST   STRUCT
...DECISION CONCPT GAME CONGRESS PRESIDENT. PAGE 46   IDEA/COMP
B0935   OP/RES
                                                       S65

POSVAR W.W.,"NATIONAL SECURITY POLICY* THE REALM OF   DIPLOM
OBSCURITY." CREATE PLAN PROB/SOLV ADMIN LEAD GP/REL   USA+45
CONSERVE...DECISION GEOG. PAGE 84 B1694   RECORD
                                                       S65

THOMAS F.C. JR.,"THE PEACE CORPS IN MOROCCO."   MOROCCO
CULTURE MUNIC PROVS CREATE ROUTINE TASK ADJUST   FRANCE
STRANGE...OBS PEACE/CORP. PAGE 104 B2099   FOR/AID
                                                       EDU/PROP
                                                       B66

AARON T.J.,THE CONTROL OF POLICE DISCRETION: THE   CONTROL
DANISH EXPERIENCE. DENMARK LAW CREATE ADMIN   FORCES
INGP/REL SUPEGO PWR 20 OMBUDSMAN. PAGE 2 B0049   REPRESENT
                                                       PROB/SOLV
                                                       B66

ALEXANDER Y.,INTERNATIONAL TECHNICAL ASSISTANCE   ECO/TAC
EXPERTS* A CASE STUDY OF THE U.N. EXPERIENCE.   INT/ORG
ECO/UNDEV CONSULT EX/STRUC CREATE PLAN DIPLOM   ADMIN
FOR/AID TASK EFFICIENCY...ORG/CHARTS UN. PAGE 4   MGT
B0074
                                                       B66

ANDERSON S.V.,CANADIAN OMBUDSMAN PROPOSALS. CANADA   NAT/G
LEGIS DEBATE PARL/PROC...MAJORIT JURID TIME/SEQ   CREATE
IDEA/COMP 20 OMBUDSMAN PARLIAMENT. PAGE 5 B0096   ADMIN
                                                       POL/PAR

BARBER W.F.,INTERNAL SECURITY AND MILITARY POWER*   L/A+17C
COUNTERINSURGENCY AND CIVIC ACTION IN LATIN   FORCES
AMERICA. ECO/UNDEV CREATE ADMIN REV ATTIT   ORD/FREE
RIGID/FLEX MARXISM...INT BIBLIOG OAS. PAGE 9 B0183   TASK
                                                       B66

GROSS H.,MAKE OR BUY. USA+45 FINAN INDUS CREATE   ECO/TAC
PRICE PRODUC 20. PAGE 44 B0889   PLAN
                                                       MGT
                                                       COST
                                                       B66

KURAKOV I.G.,SCIENCE, TECHNOLOGY AND COMMUNISM;   CREATE
SOME QUESTIONS OF DEVELOPMENT (TRANS. BY CARIN   TEC/DEV
DEDIJER). USSR INDUS PLAN PROB/SOLV COST PRODUC   MARXISM
...MGT MATH CHARTS METH 20. PAGE 61 B1243   ECO/TAC
                                                       B66

LEWIS W.A.,DEVELOPMENT PLANNING; THE ESSENTIALS OF   PLAN
ECONOMIC POLICY. USA+45 FINAN INDUS NAT/G WORKER   ECO/DEV
FOR/AID INT/TRADE ADMIN ROUTINE WEALTH...CONCPT   POLICY
STAT. PAGE 65 B1307   CREATE
                                                       B66

PERKINS J.A.,THE UNIVERSITY IN TRANSITION. USA+45   ACADEM
SOCIETY FINAN INDUS NAT/G EX/STRUC ADMIN INGP/REL   ORD/FREE
COST EFFICIENCY ATTIT 20. PAGE 82 B1658   CREATE
                                                       ROLE
                                                       B66

WADIA M.,THE NATURE AND SCOPE OF MANAGEMENT.   MGT
DELIB/GP EX/STRUC CREATE AUTOMAT CONTROL EFFICIENCY   PROB/SOLV
...ANTHOL 20. PAGE 112 B2271   IDEA/COMP
                                                       ECO/TAC
                                                       B66

WILLNER A.R.,THE NEOTRADITIONAL ACCOMMODATION TO   INDONESIA
POLITICAL INDEPENDENCE* THE CASE OF INDONESIA *   CONSERVE
RESEARCH MONOGRAPH NO. 26. CULTURE ECO/UNDEV CREATE   ELITES
PROB/SOLV FOR/AID LEGIT COLONIAL EFFICIENCY   ADMIN
NAT/LISM ALL/VALS SOC. PAGE 117 B2355
                                                       B66

WYLIE C.M.,RESEARCH IN PUBLIC HEALTH   BIBLIOG/A
ADMINISTRATION; SELECTED RECENT ABSTRACTS IV   R+D
(PAMPHLET). USA+45 MUNIC PUB/INST ACT/RES CREATE   HEAL
OP/RES TEC/DEV GP/REL ROLE...MGT PHIL/SCI STAT.   ADMIN
PAGE 118 B2387
                                                       S66

AUSLAND J.C.,"CRISIS MANAGEMENT* BERLIN, CYPRUS,   OP/RES
LAOS." CYPRUS LAOS FORCES CREATE PLAN EDU/PROP TASK   DIPLOM
CENTRAL PERSON RIGID/FLEX...DECISION MGT 20 BERLIN   RISK
KENNEDY/JF MCNAMARA/R RUSK. PAGE 7 B0148   ADMIN

AMERICAN SOCIETY PUBLIC ADMIN,PUBLIC ADMINISTRATION   WEALTH
AND THE WAR ON POVERTY (PAMPHLET). USA+45 SOCIETY   NAT/G
ECO/DEV FINAN LOC/G LEGIS CREATE EDU/PROP CONFER   PLAN
GOV/REL GP/REL ROLE 20 POVRTY/WAR. PAGE 4 B0089   ADMIN
                                                       B67

BRAYMAN H.,CORPORATE MANAGEMENT IN A WORLD OF   MGT
POLITICS. USA+45 ELITES MARKET CREATE BARGAIN   ECO/DEV
DIPLOM INT/TRADE ATTIT SKILL 20. PAGE 15 B0302   CAP/ISM
                                                       INDUS
                                                       B67

BUDER S.,PULLMAN: AN EXPERIMENT IN INDUSTRIAL ORDER   DIST/IND
AND COMMUNITY PLANNING, 1880-1930. USA+45 SOCIETY   INDUS
LABOR LG/CO CREATE PROB/SOLV CONTROL GP/REL   MUNIC
EFFICIENCY ATTIT...MGT BIBLIOG 19/20 PULLMAN.   PLAN
PAGE 17 B0337
                                                       B67

BUREAU GOVERNMENT RES AND SERV,COUNTY GOVERNMENT   BIBLIOG/A
REORGANIZATION - A SELECTED ANNOTATED BIBLIOGRAPHY   APPORT
(PAPER). USA+45 USA-45 LAW CONSTN MUNIC PROVS   LOC/G
EX/STRUC CREATE PLAN PROB/SOLV REPRESENT GOV/REL   ADMIN
20. PAGE 17 B0349
                                                       B67

HIRSCHMAN A.O.,DEVELOPMENT PROJECTS OBSERVED. INDUS   ECO/UNDEV
INT/ORG CONSULT EX/STRUC CREATE OP/RES ECO/TAC   R+D
DEMAND...POLICY MGT METH/COMP 20 WORLD/BANK.   FINAN
PAGE 50 B1016   PLAN
                                                       B67

KRISLOV S.,THE NEGRO IN FEDERAL EMPLOYMENT. LAW   WORKER
STRATA LOC/G CREATE PROB/SOLV INSPECT GOV/REL   NAT/G
DISCRIM ROLE...DECISION INT TREND 20 NEGRO WWI   ADMIN
CIVIL/SERV. PAGE 61 B1238   RACE/REL
                                                       B67

POSNER M.V.,ITALIAN PUBLIC ENTERPRISE. ITALY   NAT/G
ECO/DEV FINAN INDUS CREATE ECO/TAC ADMIN CONTROL   PLAN
EFFICIENCY PRODUC...TREND CHARTS 20. PAGE 84 B1693   CAP/ISM
                                                       SOCISM
                                                       B67

SALMOND J.A.,THE CIVILIAN CONSERVATION CORPS,   ADMIN
1933-1942. USA-45 NAT/G CREATE EXEC EFFICIENCY   ECO/TAC
WEALTH...BIBLIOG 20 ROOSEVLT/F. PAGE 92 B1864   TASK
                                                       AGRI
                                                       B67

SCHUMACHER B.G.,COMPUTER DYNAMICS IN PUBLIC   COMPUTER
ADMINISTRATION. USA+45 CREATE PLAN TEC/DEV...MGT   COMPUT/IR
LING CON/ANAL BIBLIOG/A 20. PAGE 94 B1907   ADMIN
                                                       AUTOMAT
                                                       S67

ATKIN J.M.,"THE FEDERAL GOVERNMENT, BIG BUSINESS,   SCHOOL

AND COLLEGES OF EDUCATION." PROF/ORG CONSULT CREATE ACADEM PLAN PROB/SOLV ADMIN EFFICIENCY. PAGE 7 B0144 NAT/G INDUS
S67

BAUM R.D.,"IDEOLOGY REDIVIVUS." CHINA/COM NAT/G REV EDU/PROP ADMIN 20. PAGE 10 B0197 MARXISM CREATE TEC/DEV
S67

BERLINER J.S.,"RUSSIA'S BUREAUCRATS - WHY THEY'RE CREATE REACTIONARY." USSR NAT/G OP/RES PROB/SOLV TEC/DEV ADMIN CONTROL SANCTION EFFICIENCY DRIVE PERSON...TECHNIC INDUS. SOC 20. PAGE 11 B0223 PRODUC
S67

BRADLEY A.W.,"CONSTITUTION-MAKING IN UGANDA." NAT/G UGANDA LAW CHIEF DELIB/GP LEGIS ADMIN EXEC CREATE PARL/PROC RACE/REL ORD/FREE...GOV/COMP 20. PAGE 14 CONSTN B0295 FEDERAL
S67

BREGMAN A.,"WHITHER RUSSIA?" COM RUSSIA INTELL MARXISM POL/PAR DIPLOM PARTIC NAT/LISM TOTALS ATTIT ELITES ORD/FREE 20. PAGE 15 B0304 ADMIN CREATE
S67

BRIMMER A.F.,"INITIATIVE AND INNOVATION IN CENTRAL FINAN BANKING." USA+45 ECO/DEV MARKET ECO/TAC TAX CONTROL CREATE DEMAND...MGT CHARTS FED/RESERV. PAGE 15 B0309 NAT/G POLICY
S67

BURACK E.H.,"INDUSTRIAL MANAGEMENT IN ADVANCED ADMIN PRODUCTION SYSTEMS: SOME THEORETICAL CONCEPTS AND MGT PRELIMINARY FINDINGS." INDUS CREATE PLAN PRODUC TEC/DEV ROLE...OBS STAND/INT DEEP/QU HYPO/EXP ORG/CHARTS EX/STRUC 20. PAGE 17 B0346
S67

BURKE E.M.,"THE SEARCH FOR AUTHORITY IN PLANNING." DECISION MUNIC NEIGH CREATE PROB/SOLV LEGIT ADMIN CONTROL PLAN EFFICIENCY PWR...METH/COMP SIMUL 20. PAGE 17 B0352 LOC/G METH
S67

FERGUSON H.,"3-CITY CONSOLIDATION." USA+45 CONSTN MUNIC INDUS BARGAIN BUDGET CONFER ADMIN INGP/REL COST CHOOSE UTIL. PAGE 35 B0712 CREATE PROB/SOLV
S67

GOLIGHTLY H.O.,"THE AIRLINES: A CASE STUDY IN DIST/IND MANAGEMENT INNOVATION." USA+45 AIR FINAN INDUS MARKET TOP/EX CREATE PLAN PROB/SOLV ADMIN EXEC PROFIT MGT ...DECISION 20. PAGE 40 B0820 TEC/DEV
S67

GORMAN W.,"ELLUL - A PROPHETIC VOICE." WOR+45 CREATE ELITES SOCIETY ACT/RES PLAN BAL/PWR DOMIN CONTROL ORD/FREE PARTIC TOTALISM PWR 20. PAGE 41 B0837 EX/STRUC UTOPIA
S67

HUDDLESTON J.,"TRADE UNIONS IN THE GERMAN FEDERAL LABOR REPUBLIC." EUR+WWI GERMANY/W UK LAW INDUS WORKER GP/REL CREATE CENTRAL...MGT GP/COMP 20. PAGE 52 B1056 SCHOOL ROLE
S67

HUGON P.,"BLOCAGES ET DESEQUILIBRES DE LA ECO/UNDEV CROISSANCE ECONOMIQUE EN AFRIQUE NOIRE." AFR KIN COLONIAL MUNIC CREATE PLAN INT/TRADE REGION ADJUST CENTRAL STRUCT EQUILIB NAT/LISM ORD/FREE 20. PAGE 52 B1060 ADMIN
S67

IDENBURG P.J.,"POLITICAL STRUCTURAL DEVELOPMENT IN AFR TROPICAL AFRICA." UK ECO/UNDEV KIN POL/PAR CHIEF CONSTN EX/STRUC CREATE COLONIAL CONTROL REPRESENT RACE/REL NAT/G ...MAJORIT TREND 20. PAGE 53 B1074 GOV/COMP
S67

MACDONALD G.J.F.,"SCIENCE AND SPACE POLICY* HOW SPACE DOES IT GET PLANNED?" R+D CREATE TEC/DEV BUDGET PLAN ADMIN ROUTINE...DECISION NASA. PAGE 67 B1357 MGT EX/STRUC
S67

MOOR E.J.,"THE INTERNATIONAL IMPACT OF AUTOMATION." TEC/DEV WOR+45 ACT/RES COMPUTER CREATE PLAN CAP/ISM ROUTINE OP/RES EFFICIENCY PREDICT. PAGE 75 B1511 AUTOMAT INDUS
S67

ROSENZWEIG J.E.,"MANAGERS AND MANAGEMENT SCIENTISTS EFFICIENCY (TWO CULTURES)" INDUS CREATE TEC/DEV OPTIMAL MGT ...NEW/IDEA 20. PAGE 90 B1823 INTELL METH/COMP
S67

SPEAR P.,"NEHRU." INDIA NAT/G POL/PAR ECO/TAC ADJUD CHIEF GOV/REL CENTRAL RIGID/FLEX 20 NEHRU/J. PAGE 99 ATTIT B2003 ADMIN CREATE
S67

VERGIN R.C.,"COMPUTER INDUCED ORGANIZATION COMPUTER CHANGES." FUT USA+45 R+D CREATE OP/RES TEC/DEV DECISION ADJUST CENTRAL...MGT INT CON/ANAL COMPUT/IR. AUTOMAT PAGE 112 B2260 EX/STRUC
S68

GUZZARDI W. JR.,"THE SECOND BATTLE OF BRITAIN." UK FINAN

STRATA LABOR WORKER CREATE PROB/SOLV EDU/PROP ADMIN ECO/TAC LEAD LOBBY...MGT SOC 20 GOLD/STAND. PAGE 45 B0907 ECO/DEV STRUCT
B82

MACDONALD D.,AFRICANA; OR, THE HEART OF HEATHEN SECT AFRICA, VOL. II: MISSION LIFE. SOCIETY STRATA KIN AFR CREATE EDU/PROP ADMIN COERCE LITERACY HEALTH...MYTH CULTURE WORSHIP 19 LIVNGSTN/D MISSION NEGRO. PAGE 67 B1355 ORD/FREE

CREDIT....CREDIT

CRIME....SEE ALSO ANOMIE

N
THE JAPAN SCIENCE REVIEW: LAW AND POLITICS: LIST OF BIBLIOG BOOKS AND ARTICLES ON LAW AND POLITICS. CONSTN AGRI LAW INDUS LABOR DIPLOM TAX ADMIN CRIME...INT/LAW SOC 20 S/ASIA CHINJAP. PAGE 1 B0025 PHIL/SCI
N

US SUPERINTENDENT OF DOCUMENTS,POLITICAL SCIENCE: BIBLIOG/A GOVERNMENT, CRIME, DISTRICT OF COLUMBIA (PRICE LIST NAT/G 54). USA+45 LAW CONSTN EX/STRUC WORKER ADJUD ADMIN CRIME CT/SYS CHOOSE INGP/REL RACE/REL CONGRESS PRESIDENT. PAGE 111 B2241
B15

SAWYER R.A.,A LIST OF WORKS ON COUNTY GOVERNMENT. BIBLIOG/A LAW FINAN MUNIC TOP/EX ROUTINE CRIME...CLASSIF LOC/G RECORD 19/20. PAGE 93 B1871 GOV/REL ADMIN
N19

BURRUS B.R.,INVESTIGATION AND DISCOVERY IN STATE NAT/G ANTITRUST (PAMPHLET). USA+45 USA-45 LEGIS ECO/TAC PROVS ADMIN CONTROL CT/SYS CRIME GOV/REL PWR...JURID LAW CHARTS 19/20 FTC MONOPOLY. PAGE 17 B0355 INSPECT
B29

MERRIAM C.E.,CHICAGO: A MORE INTIMATE VIEW OF URBAN STRUCT POLITICS. USA-45 CONSTN POL/PAR LEGIS ADMIN CRIME GP/REL INGP/REL 18/20 CHICAGO. PAGE 73 B1472 MUNIC
B29

MOLEY R.,POLITICS AND CRIMINAL PROSECUTION. USA-45 PWR POL/PAR EX/STRUC LEGIT CONTROL LEAD ROUTINE CHOOSE CT/SYS INGP/REL...JURID CHARTS 20. PAGE 74 B1497 CRIME ADJUD
B30

ZINK H.,CITY BOSSES IN THE UNITED STATES: A STUDY LOC/G OF TWENTY MUNICIPAL BOSSES. USA-45 INDUS MUNIC DOMIN NEIGH POL/PAR ADMIN CRIME INGP/REL PERS/REL PWR BIOG ...PERS/COMP 20 BOSSISM. PAGE 119 B2403 LEAD
B31

BORCHARD E.H.,GUIDE TO THE LAW AND LEGAL LITERATURE BIBLIOG/A OF FRANCE. FRANCE FINAN INDUS LABOR SECT LEGIS LAW ADMIN COLONIAL CRIME OWN...INT/LAW 20. PAGE 14 CONSTN B0277 METH
B33

ENSOR R.C.K.,COURTS AND JUDGES IN FRANCE, GERMANY, CT/SYS AND ENGLAND. FRANCE GERMANY UK LAW PROB/SOLV ADMIN EX/STRUC ROUTIN CRIME ROLE...METH/COMP 20 CIVIL/LAW. ADJUD PAGE 33 B0676 NAT/COMP
S37

LASSWELL H.D.,"GOVERNMENTAL AND PARTY LEADERS IN ELITES FASCIST ITALY." ITALY CRIME SKILL...BIOG CHARTS FASCISM GP/COMP 20. PAGE 63 B1266 ADMIN
B40

HART J.,AN INTRODUCTION TO ADMINISTRATIVE LAW, WITH LAW SELECTED CASES. USA-45 CONSTN SOCIETY NAT/G ADMIN EX/STRUC ADJUD CT/SYS LEAD CRIME ORD/FREE LEGIS ...DECISION JURID 20 CASEBOOK. PAGE 47 B0958 PWR
B47

TAPPAN P.W.,DELINQUENT GIRLS IN COURT. USA-45 MUNIC CT/SYS EX/STRUC FORCES ADMIN EXEC ADJUST SEX RESPECT AGE/Y ...JURID SOC/WK 20 NEWYORK/C FEMALE/SEX. PAGE 103 CRIME B2078 ADJUD
B48

SLESSER H.,THE ADMINISTRATION OF THE LAW. UK CONSTN LAW EX/STRUC OP/RES PROB/SOLV CRIME ROLE...DECISION CT/SYS METH/COMP 20 CIVIL/LAW ENGLSH/LAW CIVIL/LAW. ADJUD PAGE 98 B1977
B55

BEISEL A.R.,CONTROL OVER ILLEGAL ENFORCEMENT OF THE ORD/FREE CRIMINAL LAW: ROLE OF THE SUPREME COURT. CONSTN LAW ROUTINE MORAL PWR...SOC 20 SUPREME/CT. PAGE 10 CRIME B0207
B56

ABELS J.,THE TRUMAN SCANDALS. USA+45 USA-45 POL/PAR CRIME TAX LEGIT CT/SYS CHOOSE PRIVIL MORAL WEALTH 20 ADMIN TRUMAN/HS PRESIDENT CONGRESS. PAGE 3 B0052 CHIEF TRIBUTE
B56

BROWNE D.G.,THE RISE OF SCOTLAND YARD: A HISTORY OF CRIMLGY THE METROPOLITAN POLICE. UK MUNIC CHIEF ADMIN CRIME LEGIS GP/REL 19/20. PAGE 16 B0329 CONTROL FORCES
B58

CHARLES R.,LA JUSTICE EN FRANCE. FRANCE LAW CONSTN JURID DELIB/GP CRIME 20. PAGE 20 B0413 ADMIN CT/SYS

DEVLIN P.,THE CRIMINAL PROSECUTION IN ENGLAND. UK
NAT/G ADMIN ROUTINE EFFICIENCY...JURID SOC 20.
PAGE 29 B0583
`ADJUD B58 CRIME LAW METH CT/SYS`

JAPAN MINISTRY OF JUSTICE,CRIMINAL JUSTICE IN
JAPAN. LAW PROF/ORG PUB/INST FORCES CONTROL CT/SYS
PARL/PROC 20 CHINJAP. PAGE 56 B1125
`B58 CONSTN CRIME JURID ADMIN`

KAPLAN H.E.,THE LAW OF CIVIL SERVICE. USA+45 LAW
POL/PAR CT/SYS CRIME GOV/REL...POLICY JURID 20.
PAGE 58 B1167
`B58 ADJUD NAT/G ADMIN CONSTN`

WHITE L.D.,THE REPUBLICAN ERA: 1869-1901. A STUDY
IN ADMINISTRATIVE HISTORY. USA+45 FINAN PLAN
NEUTRAL CRIME GP/REL MORAL LAISSEZ PRESIDENT
REFORMERS 19 CONGRESS CIVIL/SERV. PAGE 116 B2340
`B58 MGT PWR DELIB/GP ADMIN`

ELLIOTT S.D.,IMPROVING OUR COURTS. LAW EX/STRUC
PLAN PROB/SOLV ADJUD ADMIN TASK CRIME EFFICIENCY
ORD/FREE 20. PAGE 33 B0669
`B59 CT/SYS JURID GOV/REL NAT/G`

GINSBURG M.,LAW AND OPINION IN ENGLAND. UK CULTURE
KIN LABOR LEGIS EDU/PROP ADMIN CT/SYS CRIME OWN
HEALTH...ANTHOL 20 ENGLSH/LAW. PAGE 40 B0802
`B59 JURID POLICY ECO/TAC`

HANBURY H.G.,ENGLISH COURTS OF LAW. UK EX/STRUC
LEGIS CRIME ROLE 12/20 COMMON/LAW ENGLSH/LAW.
PAGE 46 B0936
`B60 JURID CT/SYS CONSTN GOV/REL`

PINTO F.B.M.,ENRIQUECIMENTO ILICITO NO EXERCICIO DE
CARGOS PUBLICOS. BRAZIL L/A+17C USA+45 ELITES
TRIBUTE CONTROL INGP/REL ORD/FREE PWR...NAT/COMP
20. PAGE 83 B1675
`B60 ADMIN NAT/G CRIME LAW`

MCCLEERY R.,"COMMUNICATION PATTERNS AS BASES OF
SYSTEMS OF AUTHORITY AND POWER" IN THEORETICAL
STUDIES IN SOCIAL ORGAN. OF PRISON-BMR. USA+45
SOCIETY STRUCT EDU/PROP ADMIN CONTROL COERCE CRIME
GP/REL AUTHORIT...SOC 20. PAGE 71 B1443
`C60 PERS/REL PUB/INST PWR DOMIN`

TOMPKINS D.C.,CONFLICT OF INTEREST IN THE FEDERAL
GOVERNMENT: A BIBLIOGRAPHY. USA+45 EX/STRUC LEGIS
ADJUD ADMIN CRIME CONGRESS PRESIDENT. PAGE 105
B2117
`B61 BIBLIOG ROLE NAT/G LAW`

DELANY V.T.H.,THE ADMINISTRATION OF JUSTICE IN
IRELAND. IRELAND CONSTN FINAN JUDGE COLONIAL CRIME
...CRIMLGY 19/20. PAGE 28 B0571
`B62 ADMIN JURID CT/SYS ADJUD`

GESELLSCHAFT RECHTSVERGLEICH,BIBLIOGRAPHIE DES
DEUTSCHEN RECHTS (BIBLIOGRAPHY OF GERMAN LAW,
TRANS. BY COURTLAND PETERSON). GERMANY FINAN INDUS
LABOR SECT FORCES CT/SYS PARL/PROC CRIME...INT/LAW
SOC NAT/COMP 20. PAGE 39 B0794
`B64 BIBLIOG/A JURID CONSTN ADMIN`

GJUPANOVIC H.,LEGAL SOURCES AND BIBLIOGRAPHY OF
YUGOSLAVIA. COM YUGOSLAVIA LAW LEGIS DIPLOM ADMIN
PARL/PROC REGION CRIME CENTRAL 20. PAGE 40 B0807
`B64 BIBLIOG/A JURID CONSTN ADJUD`

INDIAN COMM PREVENTION CORRUPT,REPORT, 1964. INDIA
NAT/G GOV/REL ATTIT ORD/FREE...CRIMLGY METH 20.
PAGE 53 B1079
`B64 CRIME ADMIN LEGIS LOC/G`

KARLEN D.,THE CITIZEN IN COURT. USA+45 LAW ADMIN
ROUTINE CRIME GP/REL...JURID 20. PAGE 58 B1175
`B64 CT/SYS ADJUD GOV/REL JUDGE`

TOMPKINS D.C.,PROBATION SINCE WORLD WAR II. USA+45
FORCES ADMIN ROUTINE PERS/REL AGE...CRIMLGY HEAL
20. PAGE 105 B2118
`B64 BIBLIOG PUB/INST ORD/FREE CRIME`

WRAITH R.,CORRUPTION IN DEVELOPING COUNTRIES.
NIGERIA UK LAW ELITES STRATA INDUS LOC/G NAT/G SECT
FORCES EDU/PROP ADMIN PWR WEALTH 18/20. PAGE 118
B2377
`B64 ECO/UNDEV CRIME SANCTION ATTIT`

CONRAD J.P.,CRIME AND ITS CORRECTION: AN
INTERNATIONAL SURVEY OF ATTITUDES AND PRACTICES.
EUR+WWI NETHERLAND USA+45 USSR ATTIT MORAL 20
SCANDINAV. PAGE 23 B0467
`B65 CRIME PUB/INST POLICY ADMIN`

HOWE R.,THE STORY OF SCOTLAND YARD: A HISTORY OF
THE CID FROM THE EARLIEST TIMES TO THE PRESENT DAY.
UK MUNIC EDU/PROP 6/20 SCOT/YARD. PAGE 52 B1051
`B65 CRIMLGY CRIME FORCES`

MONTEIRO J.B.,CORRUPTION: CONTROL OF
MALADMINISTRATION. EUR+WWI INDIA USA+45 USSR NAT/G
DELIB/GP ADMIN...GP/COMP 20 OMBUDSMAN. PAGE 74
B1503
`ADMIN B66 CONTROL CRIME PROB/SOLV`

PERROW C.,ORGANIZATION FOR TREATMENT: A COMPARATIVE
STUDY OF INSTITUTIONS FOR DELINQUENTS. LAW
PROB/SOLV ADMIN CRIME PERSON MORAL...SOC/WK OBS
DEEP/QU CHARTS SOC/EXP SOC/INTEG 20. PAGE 82 B1661
`B66 AGE/Y PSY PUB/INST`

SZLADITS C.,A BIBLIOGRAPHY ON FOREIGN AND
COMPARATIVE LAW (SUPPLEMENT 1964). FINAN FAM LABOR
LG/CO LEGIS JUDGE ADMIN CRIME...CRIMLGY 20.
PAGE 102 B2066
`B66 BIBLIOG/A CT/SYS INT/LAW`

BLUMBERG A.S.,CRIMINAL JUSTICE. USA+45 CLIENT LAW
LOC/G FORCES JUDGE ACT/RES LEGIT ADMIN RATIONAL
MYTH. PAGE 13 B0259
`B67 JURID CT/SYS PROF/ORG CRIME`

HEWITT W.H.,ADMINISTRATION OF CRIMINAL JUSTICE IN
NEW YORK. LAW PROB/SOLV ADJUD ADMIN...CRIMLGY
CHARTS T 20 NEW/YORK. PAGE 49 B1001
`B67 CRIME ROLE CT/SYS FORCES`

LENG S.C.,JUSTICE IN COMMUNIST CHINA: A SURVEY OF
THE JUDICIAL SYSTEM OF THE CHINESE PEOPLE'S
REPUBLIC. CHINA/COM LAW CONSTN LOC/G NAT/G PROF/ORG
CONSULT FORCES ADMIN CRIME ORD/FREE...BIBLIOG 20
MAO. PAGE 64 B1290
`B67 CT/SYS ADJUD JURID MARXISM`

NIEDERHOFFER A.,BEHIND THE SHIELD; THE POLICE IN
URBAN SOCIETY. USA+45 LEGIT ADJUD ROUTINE COERCE
CRIME ADJUST...INT CHARTS 20 NEWYORK/C. PAGE 78
B1582
`B67 FORCES PERSON SOCIETY ATTIT`

SCHAEFER W.V.,THE SUSPECT AND SOCIETY: CRIMINAL
PROCEDURE AND CONVERGING CONSTITUTIONAL DOCTRINES.
USA+45 TEC/DEV LOBBY ROUTINE SANCTION...INT 20.
PAGE 93 B1879
`B67 CRIME FORCES CONSTN JURID`

WESTON P.B.,THE ADMINISTRATION OF JUSTICE. USA+45
CONSTN MUNIC NAT/G PROVS EX/STRUC JUDGE ADMIN
CONTROL SANCTION ORD/FREE...CHARTS 20. PAGE 115
B2328
`B67 CRIME CT/SYS JURID ADJUD`

GAINES J.E.,"THE YOUTH COURT CONCEPT AND ITS
IMPLEMENTATION IN TOMPKINS COUNTY, NEW YORK."
USA+45 LAW CONSTN JUDGE WORKER ADJUD ADMIN CHOOSE
PERSON...JURID NEW/YORK. PAGE 38 B0772
`L67 CT/SYS AGE/Y INGP/REL CRIME`

HALL B.,"THE PAINTER'S UNION: A PARTIAL VICTORY."
USA+45 PROB/SOLV LEGIT ADMIN REPRESENT 20. PAGE 45
B0922
`S67 LABOR CHIEF CHOOSE CRIME`

NYE J.S.,"CORRUPTION AND POLITICAL DEVELOPMENT: A
COST-BENEFIT ANALYSIS." WOR+45 SOCIETY TRIBUTE
ADMIN CONTROL COST...CHARTS 20. PAGE 79 B1598
`S67 ECO/UNDEV NAT/G CRIME ACT/RES`

ROSE A.M.,"CONFIDENCE AND THE CORPORATION." LG/CO
CONTROL CRIME INCOME PROFIT 20. PAGE 90 B1818
`S67 INDUS EX/STRUC VOL/ASSN RESPECT`

CRIMINOLOGY....SEE CRIMLGY

CRIMLGY....CRIMINOLOGY

JAPAN MOMBUSHO DAIGAKU GAKIYUT,BIBLIOGRAPHY OF THE
STUDIES ON LAW AND POLITICS (PAMPHLET). CONSTN
INDUS LABOR DIPLOM TAX ADMIN...CRIMLGY INT/LAW 20
CHINJAP. PAGE 56 B1126
`B55 BIBLIOG LAW PHIL/SCI`

BROWNE D.G.,THE RISE OF SCOTLAND YARD: A HISTORY OF
THE METROPOLITAN POLICE. UK MUNIC CHIEF ADMIN CRIME
GP/REL 19/20. PAGE 16 B0329
`B56 CRIMLGY LEGIS CONTROL FORCES`

DELANY V.T.H.,THE ADMINISTRATION OF JUSTICE IN
IRELAND. IRELAND CONSTN FINAN JUDGE COLONIAL CRIME
...CRIMLGY 19/20. PAGE 28 B0571
`B62 ADMIN JURID CT/SYS ADJUD`

EATON J.W.,STONE WALLS NOT A PRISON MAKE: THE
ANATOMY OF PLANNED ADMINISTRATIVE CHANGE. USA+45
PROVS EDU/PROP 20. PAGE 32 B0647
`B62 CRIMLGY ADMIN EXEC POLICY`

PALOTAI O.C.,PUBLICATIONS OF THE INSTITUTE OF
GOVERNMENT, 1930-1962. LAW PROVS SCHOOL WORKER
ACT/RES OP/RES CT/SYS GOV/REL...CRIMLGY SOC/WK.
`B63 BIBLIOG/A ADMIN LOC/G`

PAGE 81 B1629   FINAN
                                                           B64
INDIAN COMM PREVENTION CORRUPT,REPORT, 1964. INDIA   CRIME
NAT/G GOV/REL ATTIT ORD/FREE...CRIMLGY METH 20.   ADMIN
PAGE 53 B1079   LEGIS
                                                       LOC/G
                                                           B64
TOMPKINS D.C.,PROBATION SINCE WORLD WAR II. USA+45   BIBLIOG
FORCES ADMIN ROUTINE PERS/REL AGE...CRIMLGY HEAL   PUB/INST
20. PAGE 105 B2118   ORD/FREE
                                                       CRIME
                                                           B65
HOWE R.,THE STORY OF SCOTLAND YARD: A HISTORY OF   CRIMLGY
THE CID FROM THE EARLIEST TIMES TO THE PRESENT DAY.   CRIME
UK MUNIC EDU/PROP 6/20 SCOT/YARD. PAGE 52 B1051   FORCES
                                                       ADMIN
                                                           B65
UNESCO,INTERNATIONAL ORGANIZATIONS IN THE SOCIAL   INT/ORG
SCIENCES(REV. ED.). LAW ADMIN ATTIT...CRIMLGY GEOG   R+D
INT/LAW PSY SOC STAT 20 UNESCO. PAGE 107 B2157   PROF/ORG
                                                       ACT/RES
                                                           B66
SZLADITS C.,A BIBLIOGRAPHY ON FOREIGN AND   BIBLIOG/A
COMPARATIVE LAW (SUPPLEMENT 1964). FINAN FAM LABOR   CT/SYS
LG/CO LEGIS JUDGE ADMIN CRIME...CRIMLGY 20.   INT/LAW
PAGE 102 B2066
                                                           B67
HEWITT W.H.,ADMINISTRATION OF CRIMINAL JUSTICE IN   CRIME
NEW YORK. LAW PROB/SOLV ADJUD ADMIN...CRIMLGY   ROLE
CHARTS T 20 NEW/YORK. PAGE 49 B1001   CT/SYS
                                                       FORCES
                                                           B67
KATZ J.,PSYCHOANALYSIS, PSYCHIATRY, AND LAW. USA+45   LAW
LOC/G NAT/G PUB/INST PROB/SOLV ADMIN HEALTH   PSY
...CRIMLGY CONCPT SAMP/SIZ IDEA/COMP. PAGE 58 B1180   CT/SYS
                                                       ADJUD

CRIMNL/LAW....CRIMINAL LAW

CROCKER W.R. B0505

CROCKETT D.G. B0506

CROCKETT W.H. B0507

CROMWELL/O....OLIVER CROMWELL

                                                           B61
AYLMER G.,THE KING'S SERVANTS. UK ELITES CHIEF PAY   ADMIN
CT/SYS WEALTH 17 CROMWELL/O CHARLES/I. PAGE 7 B0153   ROUTINE
                                                       EX/STRUC
                                                       NAT/G

CRONBACK L.J. B0508

CROSS J.S. B0072

CROSS-PRESSURES .... SEE ROLE

CROTTY W.J. B0509

CROUCH W.W. B0510

CROWD....MOB BEHAVIOR, MASS BEHAVIOR

                                                           B45
MAYO E.,THE SOCIAL PROBLEMS OF AN INDUSTRIAL   INDUS
CIVILIZATION. USA+45 SOCIETY LABOR CROWD PERS/REL   GP/REL
LAISSEZ. PAGE 71 B1438   MGT
                                                       WORKER
                                                           B57
DE GRAZIA A.,GRASS ROOTS PRIVATE WELFARE. LOC/G   NEW/LIB
SCHOOL ACT/RES EDU/PROP ROUTINE CROWD GP/REL   HEALTH
DISCRIM HAPPINESS ILLEGIT AGE HABITAT. PAGE 27   MUNIC
B0554   VOL/ASSN
                                                           C60
SCHRAMM W.,"MASS COMMUNICATIONS: A BOOK OF READINGS   COM/IND
(2ND ED.)" LG/CO PRESS ADMIN CONTROL ROUTINE ATTIT   EDU/PROP
ROLE SUPEGO...CHARTS ANTHOL BIBLIOG 20. PAGE 94   CROWD
B1902   MAJORIT
                                                           B64
BANTON M.,THE POLICEMAN IN THE COMMUNITY. UK USA+45   FORCES
STRUCT PROF/ORG WORKER LOBBY ROUTINE COERCE CROWD   ADMIN
GP/REL ADJUST DISCRIM PERCEPT 20. PAGE 9 B0181   ROLE
                                                       RACE/REL
                                                           B65
LIPSET S.M.,THE BERKELEY STUDENT REVOLT: FACTS AND   CROWD
INTERPRETATIONS. USA+45 INTELL VOL/ASSN CONSULT   ACADEM
EDU/PROP PRESS DEBATE ADMIN REV HAPPINESS   ATTIT
RIGID/FLEX MAJORIT. PAGE 65 B1322   GP/REL
                                                           S67
BASTID M.,"ORIGINES ET DEVELOPMENT DE LA REVOLUTION   REV
CULTURELLE." CHINA/COM DOMIN ADMIN CONTROL LEAD   CULTURE
COERCE CROWD ATTIT DRIVE MARXISM...POLICY 20.   ACADEM
PAGE 10 B0195   WORKER

                                                           S67
LLOYD K.,"URBAN RACE RIOTS V EFFECTIVE ANTI-   GP/REL
DISCRIMINATION AGENCIES* AN END OR A BEGINNING?"   DISCRIM
USA+45 STRATA ACT/RES ADMIN ADJUST ORD/FREE RESPECT   LOC/G
...PLURIST DECISION SOC SOC/WK. PAGE 66 B1332   CROWD
                                                           S67
O'DELL J.H.,"THE JULY REBELLIONS AND THE 'MILITARY   PWR
STATE'." USA+45 VIETNAM STRATA CHIEF WORKER   NAT/G
COLONIAL EXEC CROWD CIVMIL/REL RACE/REL TOTALISM   COERCE
...WELF/ST PACIFIST 20 NEGRO JOHNSON/LB PRESIDENT   FORCES
CIV/RIGHTS. PAGE 79 B1599

CROZIER B. B0511

CRUMP/ED....EDWARD H. CRUMP

CRUSADES....CRUSADES, CRUSADERS OF HOLY WARS; ALSO KNIGHTS

CT/APPEALS....COURT CF APPEALS AND APPELLATE COURT SYSTEM

CT/SYS....COURT SYSTEMS

                                                           N
AUSTRALIAN NATIONAL RES COUN,AUSTRALIAN SOCIAL   BIBLIOG/A
SCIENCE ABSTRACTS. NEW/ZEALND CULTURE SOCIETY LOC/G   POLICY
CT/SYS PARL/PROC...HEAL JURID PSY SOC 20 AUSTRAL.   NAT/G
PAGE 7 B0149   ADMIN
                                                           N
JOURNAL OF POLITICS. USA+45 USA-45 CONSTN POL/PAR   BIBLIOG/A
EX/STRUC LEGIS PROB/SOLV DIPLOM CT/SYS CHOOSE   NAT/G
RACE/REL 20. PAGE 1 B0005   LAW
                                                       LOC/G
                                                           N
US SUPERINTENDENT OF DOCUMENTS,POLITICAL SCIENCE: BIBLIOG/A
GOVERNMENT, CRIME, DISTRICT OF COLUMBIA (PRICE LIST   NAT/G
54). USA+45 LAW CONSTN EX/STRUC WORKER ADJUD ADMIN   CRIME
CT/SYS CHOOSE INGP/REL RACE/REL CONGRESS PRESIDENT.
PAGE 111 B2241
                                                           N
US SUPERINTENDENT CF DOCUMENTS,TARIFF AND TAXATION   BIBLIOG/A
(PRICE LIST 37). USA+45 LAW INT/TRADE ADJUD ADMIN   TAX
CT/SYS INCOME OWN...DECISION GATT. PAGE 111 B2242   TARIFFS
                                                       NAT/G
                                                           B08
THE GOVERNMENT OF SOUTH AFRICA (VOL. II). SOUTH/AFR   CONSTN
STRATA EXTR/IND EX/STRUC TOP/EX BUDGET ADJUD ADMIN   FINAN
CT/SYS PRODUC...CORREL CENSUS 19 RAILROAD   LEGIS
CIVIL/SERV POSTAL/SYS. PAGE 2 B0033   NAT/G
                                                           B09
HARVARD UNIVERSITY LAW LIBRARY,CATALOGUE OF THE   BIBLIOG/A
LIBRARY OF THE LAW SCHOOL OF HARVARD UNIVERSITY (3   LAW
VOLS.). UK USA-45 LEGIS JUDGE ADJUD CT/SYS...JURID   ADMIN
CHARTS 14/20. PAGE 48 B0963
                                                           B18
WILSON W.,THE STATE: ELEMENTS OF HISTORICAL AND   NAT/G
PRACTICAL POLITICS. FRANCE GERMANY ITALY UK USSR   JURID
CONSTN EX/STRUC LEGIS CT/SYS WAR PWR...POLICY   CONCPT
GOV/COMP 20. PAGE 117 B2363   NAT/COMP
                                                           B19
NATHAN M.,THE SOUTH AFRICAN COMMONWEALTH: CONSTN
CONSTITUTION, PROBLEMS, SOCIAL CONDITIONS.   NAT/G
SOUTH/AFR UK CULTURE INDUS EX/STRUC LEGIS BUDGET   POL/PAR
EDU/PROP ADMIN CT/SYS GP/REL RACE/REL...LING 19/20   SOCIETY
CMN/WLTH. PAGE 77 B1559
                                                           N19
BURRUS B.R.,INVESTIGATION AND DISCOVERY IN STATE   NAT/G
ANTITRUST (PAMPHLET). USA+45 USA-45 LEGIS ECO/TAC   PROVS
ADMIN CONTROL CT/SYS CRIME GOV/REL PWR...JURID   LAW
CHARTS 19/20 FTC MONOPOLY. PAGE 17 B0355   INSPECT
                                                           N19
FAHRNKOPF N.,STATE AND LOCAL GOVERNMENT IN ILLINOIS BIBLIOG
(PAMPHLET). CONSTN ADMIN PARTIC CHOOSE REPRESENT   LOC/G
GOV/REL...JURID MGT 20 ILLINOIS. PAGE 34 B0696   LEGIS
                                                       CT/SYS
                                                           C20
BLACHLY F.F.,"THE GOVERNMENT AND ADMINISTRATION OF   NAT/G
GERMANY." GERMANY CONSTN LOC/G PROVS DELIB/GP   GOV/REL
EX/STRUC FORCES LEGIS TOP/EX CT/SYS...BIBLIOG/A   ADMIN
19/20. PAGE 12 B0246   PHIL/SCI
                                                           B21
BRYCE J.,MODERN DEMOCRACIES. FUT NEW/ZEALND USA-45   NAT/G
LAW CONSTN POL/PAR PROVS VOL/ASSN EX/STRUC LEGIS   TREND
LEGIT CT/SYS EXEC KNOWL CONGRESS AUSTRAL 20.
PAGE 16 B0332
                                                           B24
HOLDSWORTH W.S.,A HISTORY OF ENGLISH LAW; THE   LAW
COMMON LAW AND ITS RIVALS (VOL. V). UK SEA EX/STRUC   LEGIS
WRITING ADMIN...INT/LAW JURID CONCPT IDEA/COMP   ADJUD
WORSHIP 16/17 PARLIAMENT ENGLSH/LAW COMMON/LAW.   CT/SYS
PAGE 51 B1033
                                                           B24
HOLDSWORTH W.S.,A HISTORY OF ENGLISH LAW; THE   LAW
COMMON LAW AND ITS RIVALS (VOL. VI). UK STRATA   CONSTN
EX/STRUC ADJUD ADMIN CONTROL CT/SYS...JURID CONCPT   LEGIS
GEN/LAWS 17 COMMONWLTH PARLIAMENT ENGLSH/LAW   CHIEF
COMMON/LAW. PAGE 51 B1034

B25

MATHEWS J.M.,AMERICAN STATE GOVERNMENT. USA-45   PROVS
LOC/G CHIEF EX/STRUC LEGIS ADJUD CONTROL CT/SYS   ADMIN
ROUTINE GOV/REL PWR 20 GOVERNOR. PAGE 71 B1426   FEDERAL
                                                          CONSTN
                                                             B26

INTERNATIONAL BIBLIOGRAPHY OF POLITICAL SCIENCE.   BIBLIOG
WOR+45 NAT/G POL/PAR EX/STRUC LEGIS CT/SYS LEAD   DIPLOM
CHOOSE GOV/REL ATTIT...PHIL/SCI 20. PAGE 2 B0034   CONCPT
                                                          ADMIN
                                                             B27

DICKINSON J.,ADMINISTRATIVE JUSTICE AND THE   CT/SYS
SUPREMACY OF LAW IN THE UNITED STATES. USA-45 LAW   ADJUD
INDUS DOMIN EDU/PROP CONTROL EXEC GP/REL ORD/FREE   ADMIN
...POLICY JURID 19/20. PAGE 29 B0586   NAT/G
                                                             B29

MOLEY R.,POLITICS AND CRIMINAL PROSECUTION. USA-45   PWR
POL/PAR EX/STRUC LEGIT CONTROL LEAD ROUTINE CHOOSE   CT/SYS
INGP/REL...JURID CHARTS 20. PAGE 74 B1497   CRIME
                                                          ADJUD
                                                             B30

FAIRLIE J.A.,COUNTY GOVERNMENT AND ADMINISTRATION.   ADMIN
UK USA-45 NAT/G SCHOOL FORCES BUDGET TAX CT/SYS   GOV/REL
CHOOSE...JURID BIBLIOG 11/20. PAGE 35 B0701   LOC/G
                                                          MUNIC
                                                             B33

ENSOR R.C.K.,COURTS AND JUDGES IN FRANCE, GERMANY,   CT/SYS
AND ENGLAND. FRANCE GERMANY UK LAW PROB/SOLV ADMIN   EX/STRUC
ROUTINE CRIME ROLE...METH/COMP 20 CIVIL/LAW.   ADJUD
PAGE 33 B0676   NAT/COMP
                                                             B36

GRAVES W.B.,AMERICAN STATE GOVERNMENT. CONSTN FINAN   NAT/G
EX/STRUC FORCES LEGIS BUDGET TAX CT/SYS REPRESENT   PROVS
GOV/REL...BIBLIOG/A 19/20. PAGE 42 B0855   ADMIN
                                                          FEDERAL
                                                             B37

UNION OF SOUTH AFRICA,REPORT CONCERNING   NAT/G
ADMINISTRATION OF SOUTH WEST AFRICA (6 VOLS.).   ADMIN
SOUTH/AFR INDUS PUB/INST FORCES LEGIS BUDGET DIPLOM   COLONIAL
EDU/PROP ADJUD CT/SYS...GEOG CHARTS 20 AFRICA/SW   CONSTN
LEAGUE/NAT. PAGE 107 B2158
                                                             B40

HART J.,AN INTRODUCTION TO ADMINISTRATIVE LAW, WITH   LAW
SELECTED CASES. USA-45 CONSTN SOCIETY NAT/G   ADMIN
EX/STRUC ADJUD CT/SYS LEAD CRIME ORD/FREE   LEGIS
...DECISION JURID 20 CASEBOOK. PAGE 47 B0958   PWR
                                                             B40

PATTERSON C.P.,STATE AND LOCAL GOVERNMENT IN TEXAS   CONSTN
(3RD ED.). USA-45 EX/STRUC LEGIS CT/SYS CHOOSE 20   PROVS
TEXAS. PAGE 81 B1642   GOV/REL
                                                          LOC/G
                                                             S40

GERTH H.,"THE NAZI PARTY: ITS LEADERSHIP AND   POL/PAR
COMPOSITION" (BMR)" GERMANY ELITES STRATA STRUCT   DOMIN
EX/STRUC FORCES ECO/TAC CT/SYS CHOOSE TOTALISM   LEAD
AGE/Y AUTHORIT PWR 20. PAGE 39 B0792   ADMIN
                                                             N40

COUNTY GOVERNMENT IN THE UNITED STATES: A LIST OF   BIBLIOG/A
RECENT REFERENCES (PAMPHLET). USA-45 LAW PUB/INST   LOC/G
PLAN BUDGET CT/SYS CENTRAL 20. PAGE 49 B0988   ADMIN
                                                          MUNIC
                                                             B45

CONOVER H.F.,THE GOVERNMENTS OF THE MAJOR FOREIGN   BIBLIOG
POWERS: A BIBLIOGRAPHY. FRANCE GERMANY ITALY UK   NAT/G
USSR CONSTN LOC/G POL/PAR EX/STRUC FORCES ADMIN   DIPLOM
CT/SYS CIVMIL/REL TOTALISM...POLICY 19/20. PAGE 23
B0464
                                                             B47

DE NOIA J.,GUIDE TO OFFICIAL PUBLICATIONS OF THE   BIBLIOG/A
OTHER AMERICAN REPUBLICS: EL SALVADOR. EL/SALVADR   CONSTN
LAW LEGIS EDU/PROP CT/SYS 20. PAGE 27 B0558   NAT/G
                                                          ADMIN
                                                             B47

DE NOIA J.,GUIDE TO OFFICIAL PUBLICATIONS OF THE   BIBLIOG/A
OTHER AMERICAN REPUBLICS: NICARAGUA (VOL. XIV).   EDU/PROP
NICARAGUA LAW LEGIS ADMIN CT/SYS...JURID 19/20.   NAT/G
PAGE 27 B0559   CONSTN
                                                             B47

DE NOIA J.,GUIDE TO OFFICIAL PUBLICATIONS OF THE   BIBLIOG/A
OTHER AMERICAN REPUBLICS: PANAMA (VOL. XV). PANAMA   CONSTN
LAW LEGIS EDU/PROP CT/SYS 20. PAGE 27 B0560   ADMIN
                                                          NAT/G
                                                             B47

MARX F.M.,THE PRESIDENT AND HIS STAFF SERVICES   CONSTN
PUBLIC ADMINISTRATION SERVICES NUMBER 98   CHIEF
(PAMPHLET). FINAN ADMIN CT/SYS REPRESENT PWR 20   NAT/G
PRESIDENT. PAGE 70 B1419   EX/STRUC
                                                             B47

TAPPAN P.W.,DELINQUENT GIRLS IN COURT. USA-45 MUNIC   CT/SYS
EX/STRUC FORCES ADMIN EXEC ADJUST SEX RESPECT   AGE/Y
...JURID SOC/WK 20 NEWYORK/C FEMALE/SEX. PAGE 103   CRIME
B2078   ADJUD
                                                             B48

DE NOIA J.,GUIDE TO OFFICIAL PUBLICATIONS OF OTHER   BIBLIOG/A
AMERICAN REPUBLICS: PERU (VOL. XVII). PERU LAW   CONSTN
LEGIS ADMIN CT/SYS...JURID 19/20. PAGE 28 B0561   NAT/G

EDU/PROP
                                                             B48

MEEK C.K.,COLONIAL LAW; A BIBLIOGRAPHY WITH SPECIAL   COLONIAL
REFERENCE TO NATIVE AFRICAN SYSTEMS OF LAW AND LAND   ADMIN
TENURE. AFR ECO/UNDEV AGRI CT/SYS...JURID SOC 20.   LAW
PAGE 72 B1462   CONSTN
                                                             B48

PUBLIC ADMINISTRATION SERVICE,SOURCE MATERIALS IN   BIBLIOG/A
PUBLIC ADMINISTRATION: A SELECTED BIBLIOGRAPHY (PAS   GOV/REL
PUBLICATION NO. 102). USA+45 LAW FINAN LOC/G MUNIC   MGT
NAT/G PLAN RECEIVE EDU/PROP CT/SYS CHOOSE HEALTH   ADMIN
20. PAGE 85 B1717
                                                             B48

SLESSER H.,THE ADMINISTRATION OF THE LAW. UK CONSTN   LAW
EX/STRUC OP/RES PROB/SOLV CRIME ROLE...DECISION   CT/SYS
METH/COMP 20 CIVIL/LAW ENGLSH/LAW CIVIL/LAW.   ADJUD
PAGE 98 B1977
                                                             B48

STOKES W.S.,BIBLIOGRAPHY OF STANDARD AND CLASSICAL   BIBLIOG
WORKS IN THE FIELDS OF AMERICAN POLITICAL SCIENCE.   NAT/G
USA+45 USA-45 POL/PAR PROVS FORCES DIPLOM ADMIN   LOC/G
CT/SYS APPORT 20 CONGRESS PRESIDENT. PAGE 101 B2043   CONSTN
                                                             B48

US LIBRARY OF CONGRESS,BRAZIL: A GUIDE TO THE   BIBLIOG/A
OFFICIAL PUBLICATIONS OF BRAZIL. BRAZIL L/A+17C   NAT/G
CONSULT DELIB/GP LEGIS CT/SYS 19/20. PAGE 109 B2203   ADMIN
                                                          TOP/EX
                                                             C48

WALKER H.,"THE LEGISLATIVE PROCESS; LAWMAKING IN   PARL/PROC
THE UNITED STATES." NAT/G POL/PAR PROVS EX/STRUC   LEGIS
OP/RES PROB/SOLV CT/SYS LOBBY GOV/REL...CHARTS   LAW
BIBLIOG T 18/20 CONGRESS. PAGE 113 B2279   CONSTN
                                                             B49

DENNING A.,FREEDOM UNDER THE LAW. MOD/EUR UK LAW   ORD/FREE
SOCIETY CHIEF EX/STRUC LEGIS ADJUD CT/SYS PERS/REL   JURID
PERSON 17/20 ENGLSH/LAW. PAGE 28 B0573   NAT/G
                                                             B49

WALINE M.,LE CONTROLE JURIDICTIONNEL DE   JURID
L'ADMINISTRATION. BELGIUM FRANCE UAR JUDGE BAL/PWR   ADMIN
ADJUD CONTROL CT/SYS...GP/COMP 20. PAGE 113 B2277   PWR
                                                          ORD/FREE
                                                             L49

BROOKINGS INST.,"GOVERNMENT MECHANISM FOR CONDUCT   EXEC
OF US FOREIGN RELATIONS." USA+45 CONSTN NAT/G LEGIS   STRUCT
CT/SYS...MGT TIME/SEQ CONGRESS TOT/POP 20. PAGE 15   DIPLOM
B0316
                                                             B50

JENKINS W.S.,A GUIDE TO THE MICROFILM COLLECTION OF   BIBLIOG
EARLY STATE RECORDS. USA+45 CONSTN MUNIC LEGIS   PROVS
PRESS ADMIN CT/SYS 18/20. PAGE 56 B1130   AUD/VIS
                                                             C50

HOLCOMBE A.,"OUR MORE PERFECT UNION." USA+45 USA-45   CONSTN
POL/PAR JUDGE CT/SYS EQUILIB FEDERAL PWR...MAJORIT   NAT/G
TREND BIBLIOG 18/20 CONGRESS PRESIDENT. PAGE 51   ADMIN
B1031   PLAN
                                                             C50

STOKES W.S.,"HONDURAS: AN AREA STUDY IN   CONSTN
GOVERNMENT." HONDURAS NAT/G POL/PAR COLONIAL CT/SYS   LAW
ROUTINE CHOOSE REPRESENT...GEOG RECORD BIBLIOG   L/A+17C
19/20. PAGE 101 B2044   ADMIN
                                                             C50

WAGER P.W.,"COUNTY GOVERNMENT ACROSS THE NATION."   LOC/G
USA+45 CONSTN COM/IND FINAN SCHOOL DOMIN CT/SYS   PROVS
LEAD GOV/REL...STAT BIBLIOG 20. PAGE 112 B2272   ADMIN
                                                          ROUTINE
                                                             B51

ANDERSON W.,STATE AND LOCAL GOVERNMENT IN THE   LOC/G
UNITED STATES. USA+45 CONSTN POL/PAR EX/STRUC LEGIS   MUNIC
BUDGET TAX ADJUD CT/SYS CHOOSE...CHARTS T 20.   PROVS
PAGE 5 B0100   GOV/REL
                                                             B51

ANDERSON W.,GOVERNMENT IN THE FIFTY STATES. LAW   LOC/G
CONSTN FINAN POL/PAR LEGIS EDU/PROP ADJUD ADMIN   PROVS
CT/SYS CHOOSE...CHARTS 20. PAGE 5 B0101   GOV/REL
                                                             B51

CHRISTENSEN A.N.,THE EVOLUTION OF LATIN AMERICAN   NAT/G
GOVERNMENT: A BOOK OF READINGS. ECO/UNDEV INDUS   CONSTN
LOC/G POL/PAR EX/STRUC LEGIS FOR/AID CT/SYS   DIPLOM
...SOC/WK 20 SOUTH/AMER. PAGE 21 B0428   L/A+17C
                                                             B52

DE GRAZIA A.,POLITICAL ORGANIZATION. CONSTN LOC/G   FEDERAL
MUNIC NAT/G CHIEF LEGIS TOP/EX ADJUD CT/SYS   LAW
PERS/REL...INT/LAW MYTH UN. PAGE 27 B0553   ADMIN
                                                             C52

LANCASTER L.W.,"GOVERNMENT IN RURAL AMERICA."   GOV/REL
USA+45 ECO/DEV AGRI SCHOOL FORCES LEGIS JUDGE   LOC/G
BUDGET TAX CT/SYS...CHARTS BIBLIOG. PAGE 62 B1253   MUNIC
                                                          ADMIN
                                                             B54

JENNINGS I.,THE QUEEN'S GOVERNMENT. UK POL/PAR   NAT/G
DELIB/GP ADJUD ADMIN CT/SYS PARL/PROC REPRESENT   CONSTN
CONSERVE 13/20 PARLIAMENT. PAGE 56 B1132   LEGIS
                                                          CHIEF
                                                             B54

SCHWARTZ B.,FRENCH ADMINISTRATIVE LAW AND THE   JURID
COMMON-LAW WORLD. FRANCE CULTURE LOC/G NAT/G PROVS   LAW

DELIB/GP EX/STRUC LEGIS PROB/SOLV CT/SYS EXEC GOV/REL...IDEA/COMP ENGLSH/LAW. PAGE 95 B1912
METH/COMP
ADJUD

B54
TOMPKINS D.C.,STATE GOVERNMENT AND ADMINISTRATION: A BIBLIOGRAPHY. USA+45 USA-45 CONSTN LEGIS JUDGE BUDGET CT/SYS LOBBY...CHARTS 20. PAGE 105 B2116
BIBLIOG/A
LOC/G
PROVS
ADMIN

S54
HART J.,"ADMINISTRATION AND THE COURTS." USA+45 NAT/G REPRESENT 20. PAGE 47 B0960
ADMIN
GOV/REL
CT/SYS
FEDERAL

C54
CALDWELL L.K.,"THE GOVERNMENT AND ADMINISTRATION OF NEW YORK." LOC/G MUNIC POL/PAR SCHOOL CHIEF LEGIS PLAN TAX CT/SYS...MGT SOC/WK BIBLIOG 20 NEWYORK/C. PAGE 18 B0366
PROVS
ADMIN
CONSTN
EX/STRUC

B55
CUSHMAN R.E.,LEADING CONSTITUTIONAL DECISIONS. USA+45 USA-45 NAT/G EX/STRUC LEGIS JUDGE TAX FEDERAL...DECISION 20 SUPREME/CT CASEBOOK. PAGE 25 B0513
CONSTN
PROB/SOLV
JURID
CT/SYS

B55
DE ARAGAO J.G.,LA JURIDICTION ADMINISTRATIVE AU BRESIL. BRAZIL ADJUD COLONIAL CT/SYS REV FEDERAL ORD/FREE...BIBLIO 19/20. PAGE 27 B0549
EX/STRUC
ADMIN
NAT/G

B56
ABELS J.,THE TRUMAN SCANDALS. USA+45 USA-45 POL/PAR TAX LEGIT CT/SYS CHOOSE PRIVIL MORAL WEALTH 20 TRUMAN/HS PRESIDENT CONGRESS. PAGE 3 B0052
CRIME
ADMIN
CHIEF
TRIBUTE

B56
HOWARD L.V.,TULANE STUDIES IN POLITICAL SCIENCE: CIVIL SERVICE DEVELOPMENT IN LOUISIANA VOLUME 3. LAW POL/PAR LEGIS CT/SYS ADJUST ORD/FREE...STAT CHARTS 19/20 LOUISIANA CIVIL/SERV. PAGE 52 B1050
ADMIN
GOV/REL
PROVS
POLICY

B56
POWELL N.J.,PERSONNEL ADMINISTRATION IN GOVERNMENT. COM/IND POL/PAR LEGIS PAY CT/SYS ROUTINE GP/REL PERS/REL...POLICY METH 20 CIVIL/SERV. PAGE 84 B1697
ADMIN
WORKER
LOC/G
NAT/G

C56
AUMANN F.R.,"THE ISTRUMENTALITIES OF JUSTICE: THEIR FORMS, FUNCTIONS, AND LIMITATIONS." WOR+45 WOR-45 JUDGE PROB/SOLV ROUTINE ATTIT...BIBLIOG 20. PAGE 7 B0147
JURID
ADMIN
CT/SYS
ADJUD

B57
CHICAGO U LAW SCHOOL,CONFERENCE ON JUDICIAL ADMINISTRATION. LOC/G MUNIC NAT/G PROVS...ANTHOL 20. PAGE 21 B0421
CT/SYS
ADJUD
ADMIN
GOV/REL

B57
COOPER F.E.,THE LAWYER AND ADMINISTRATIVE AGENCIES. USA+45 CLIENT LAW PROB/SOLV CT/SYS PERSON ROLE. PAGE 23 B0473
CONSULT
ADMIN
ADJUD
DELIB/GP

B57
HINDERLING A.,DIE REFORMATORISCHE VERWALTUNGSGERICHTSBARKEIT. GERMANY/W PROB/SOLV ADJUD SUPEGO PWR...CONCPT 20. PAGE 50 B1015
ADMIN
CT/SYS
JURID
CONTROL

B57
SCHLOCHAUER H.J.,OFFENTLICHES RECHT. GERMANY/W FINAN EX/STRUC LEGIS DIPLOM FEDERAL ORD/FREE ...INT/LAW 20. PAGE 94 B1892
CONSTN
JURID
ADMIN
CT/SYS

B58
AMERICAN SOCIETY PUBLIC ADMIN,STRENGTHENING MANAGEMENT FOR DEMOCRATIC GOVERNMENT. USA+45 ACADEM EX/STRUC WORKER PLAN BUDGET CONFER CT/SYS EFFICIENCY ANTHOL. PAGE 4 B0088
ADMIN
NAT/G
EXEC
MGT

B58
CHARLES R.,LA JUSTICE EN FRANCE. FRANCE LAW CONSTN DELIB/GP CRIME 20. PAGE 20 B0413
JURID
ADMIN
CT/SYS
ADJUD

B58
DAVIS K.C.,ADMINISTRATIVE LAW TREATISE (VOLS. I AND IV). NAT/G JUDGE PROB/SOLV ADJUD GP/REL 20 SUPREME/CT. PAGE 26 B0540
ADMIN
JURID
CT/SYS
EX/STRUC

B58
DAVIS K.C.,ADMINISTRATIVE LAW; CASES, TEXT, PROBLEMS. LAW LOC/G NAT/G TOP/EX PAY CONTROL GOV/REL INGP/REL FEDERAL 20 SUPREME/CT. PAGE 27 B0541
ADJUD
JURID
CT/SYS
ADMIN

B58
DEVLIN P.,THE CRIMINAL PROSECUTION IN ENGLAND. UK NAT/G ADMIN ROUTINE EFFICIENCY...JURID SOC 20. PAGE 29 B0583
CRIME
LAW
METH
CT/SYS

B58
JAPAN MINISTRY OF JUSTICE,CRIMINAL JUSTICE IN JAPAN. LAW PROF/ORG PUB/INST FORCES CONTROL CT/SYS PARL/PROC 20 CHINJAP. PAGE 56 B1125
CONSTN
CRIME
JURID
ADMIN

B58
KAPLAN H.E.,THE LAW OF CIVIL SERVICE. USA+45 LAW POL/PAR CT/SYS CRIME GOV/REL...POLICY JURID 20. PAGE 58 B1167
ADJUD
NAT/G
ADMIN
CONSTN

B58
LAW COMMISSION OF INDIA,REFORM OF JUDICIAL ADMINISTRATION. INDIA TOP/EX ADMIN DISCRIM EFFICIENCY...METH/COMP 20. PAGE 63 B1276
CT/SYS
ADJUD
GOV/REL
CONTROL

B58
POUND R.,JUSTICE ACCORDING TO LAW. LAW SOCIETY CT/SYS 20. PAGE 84 B1696
CONCPT
JURID
ADJUD
ADMIN

B58
WESTIN A.F.,THE ANATOMY OF A CONSTITUTIONAL LAW CASE. USA+45 LAW LEGIS ADMIN EXEC...DECISION MGT SOC RECORD 20 SUPREME/CT. PAGE 115 B2326
CT/SYS
INDUS
ADJUD
CONSTN

B59
CHAPMAN B.,THE PROFESSION OF GOVERNMENT: THE PUBLIC SERVICE IN EUROPE. MOD/EUR LABOR CT/SYS...T 20 CIVIL/SERV. PAGE 20 B0409
ADMIN
CONTROL
ROUTINE
EX/STRUC

B59
DAVIS K.C.,ADMINISTRATIVE LAW TEXT. USA+45 NAT/G DELIB/GP EX/STRUC CONTROL ORD/FREE...T 20 SUPREME/CT. PAGE 27 B0542
ADJUD
ADMIN
JURID
CT/SYS

B59
DESMITH S.A.,JUDICIAL REVIEW OF ADMINISTRATIVE ACTION. UK LOC/G CONSULT DELIB/GP ADMIN PWR ...DECISION JURID 20 ENGLSH/LAW. PAGE 28 B0576
ADJUD
NAT/G
PROB/SOLV
CT/SYS

B59
ELLIOTT S.D.,IMPROVING OUR COURTS. LAW EX/STRUC PLAN PROB/SOLV ADJUD ADMIN TASK CRIME EFFICIENCY ORD/FREE 20. PAGE 33 B0669
CT/SYS
JURID
GOV/REL
NAT/G

B59
GINSBURG M.,LAW AND OPINION IN ENGLAND. UK CULTURE KIN LABOR LEGIS EDU/PROP ADMIN CT/SYS CRIME OWN HEALTH...ANTHOL 20 ENGLSH/LAW. PAGE 40 B0802
JURID
POLICY
ECO/TAC

B59
IPSEN H.P.,HAMBURGISCHES STAATS- UND VERWALTUNGSRECHT. CONSTN LOC/G FORCES BUDGET CT/SYS ...JURID 20 HAMBURG. PAGE 54 B1103
ADMIN
PROVS
LEGIS
FINAN

B59
LOEWENSTEIN K.,VERFASSUNGSRECHT UND VERFASSUNGSPRAXIS DER VEREINIGTEN STAATEN. USA+45 USA-45 COLONIAL CT/SYS GP/REL RACE/REL ORD/FREE ...JURID 18/20 SUPREME/CT CONGRESS PRESIDENT BILL/RIGHT CIVIL/LIB. PAGE 66 B1337
CONSTN
POL/PAR
EX/STRUC
NAT/G

B59
MAASS A.,AREA AND POWER: A THEORY OF LOCAL GOVERNMENT. MUNIC PROVS EX/STRUC LEGIS CT/SYS CHOOSE PWR 20. PAGE 67 B1354
LOC/G
FEDERAL
BAL/PWR
GOV/REL

B59
MILLETT J.D.,GOVERNMENT AND PUBLIC ADMINISTRATION: THE QUEST FOR RESPONSIBLE PERFORMANCE. USA+45 NAT/G DELIB/GP LEGIS CT/SYS EXEC...DECISION MGT. PAGE 73 B1483
ADMIN
PWR
CONSTN
ROLE

B59
SINHA H.N.,OUTLINES OF POLITICAL SCIENCE. NAT/G POL/PAR EX/STRUC LEGIS CT/SYS CHOOSE REPRESENT 20. PAGE 98 B1971
JURID
CONCPT
ORD/FREE
SOVEREIGN

B59
SPIRO H.J.,GOVERNMENT BY CONSTITUTIONS: THE POLITICAL SYSTEMS OF DEMOCRACY. CANADA EUR+WWI FUT USA+45 WOR+45 WOR-45 LEGIS TOP/EX LEGIT ADMIN CT/SYS ORD/FREE PWR...TREND TOT/POP VAL/FREE 20. PAGE 99 B2008
NAT/G
CONSTN

S59
CHAPMAN B.,"THE FRENCH CONSEIL D'ETAT." FRANCE NAT/G CONSULT OP/RES PROB/SOLV PWR...OBS 20. PAGE 20 B0410
ADMIN
LAW
CT/SYS
LEGIS

S59
SOHN L.B.,"THE DEFINITION OF AGGRESSION." FUT LAW FORCES LEGIT ADJUD ROUTINE COERCE ORD/FREE PWR ...MAJORIT JURID QUANT COLD/WAR 20. PAGE 99 B1995
INT/ORG
CT/SYS
DETER
SOVEREIGN

B60
JUNZ A.J., PRESENT TRENDS IN AMERICAN NATIONAL GOVERNMENT. LEGIS DIPLOM ADMIN CT/SYS ORD/FREE ...CONCPT ANTHOL 20 CONGRESS PRESIDENT SUPREME/CT. PAGE 2 B0048
POL/PAR
CHOOSE
CONSTN
NAT/G

B60
DAVIS K.C.,ADMINISTRATIVE LAW AND GOVERNMENT. USA+45 EX/STRUC PROB/SOLV ADJUD GP/REL PWR...POLICY 20 SUPREME/CT. PAGE 27 B0543
ADMIN
JURID
CT/SYS
NAT/G

EASTON S.C.,THE TWILIGHT OF EUROPEAN COLONIALISM.   FINAN
AFR S/ASIA CONSIN SOCIETY STRUCT ECO/UNDEV INDUS   ADMIN
NAT/G FORCES ECO/TAC COLONIAL CT/SYS ATTIT KNOWL
ORD/FREE PWR...SOCIALIST TIME/SEQ TREND CON/ANAL
20. PAGE 32 B0645

                                    B60

HANBURY H.G.,ENGLISH COURTS OF LAW. UK EX/STRUC   JURID
LEGIS CRIME ROLE 12/20 COMMON/LAW ENGLSH/LAW.   CT/SYS
PAGE 46 B0936   CONSTN
                 GOV/REL
                                    B60

HAYEK F.A.,THE CONSTITUTION OF LIBERTY. UNIV LAW   ORD/FREE
CONSTN WORKER TAX EDU/PROP ADMIN CT/SYS COERCE   CHOOSE
DISCRIM...IDEA/COMP 20. PAGE 48 B0974   NAT/G
                                   CONCPT
                                     B60

JONES V.,METROPOLITAN COMMUNITIES: A BIBLIOGRAPHY   BIBLIOG
WITH SPECIAL EMPHASIS UPON GOVERNMENT AND POLITICS,   LOC/G
1955-1957. STRUCT ECO/DEV FINAN FORCES PLAN   MUNIC
PROB/SOLV RECEIVE EDU/PROP CT/SYS...GEOG HEAL 20.   ADMIN
PAGE 57 B1152

                                     B60

SAYRE W.S.,GOVERNING NEW YORK CITY: POLITICS IN THE   MUNIC
METROPOLIS. POL/PAR CHIEF DELIB/GP LEGIS PLAN   ADMIN
CT/SYS LEAD PARTIC CHOOSE...DECISION CHARTS BIBLIOG   PROB/SOLV
20 NEWYORK/C BUREAUCRCY. PAGE 93 B1875

                                     B60

WEBSTER J.A.,A GENERAL STUDY OF THE DEPARTMENT OF   ORD/FREE
DEFENSE INTERNAL SECURITY PROGRAM. USA+45 WORKER   PLAN
TEC/DEV ADJUD CONTROL CT/SYS EXEC GOV/REL COST   ADMIN
...POLICY DECISION MGT 20 DEPT/DEFEN SUPREME/CT.   NAT/G
PAGE 114 B2307

                                     S60

EMERSON R.,"THE EROSION OF DEMOCRACY." AFR FUT LAW   S/ASIA
CULTURE INTELL SOCIETY ECO/UNDEV FAM LOC/G NAT/G   POL/PAR
FORCES PLAN TEC/DEV ECO/TAC ADMIN CT/SYS ATTIT
ORD/FREE PWR...SOCIALIST SOC CONCPT STAND/INT
TIME/SEQ WORK 20. PAGE 33 B0671

                                     S60

ROURKE F.E.,"ADMINISTRATIVE SECRECY: A   LEGIS
CONGRESSIONAL DILEMMA." DELIB/GP CT/SYS ATTIT   EXEC
...MAJORIT DECISION JURID. PAGE 91 B1837   ORD/FREE
                                   POLICY
                                   B61

AUERBACH C.A.,THE LEGAL PROCESS. USA+45 DELIB/GP   JURID
JUDGE CONFER ADJUD CONTROL...DECISION 20   ADMIN
SUPREME/CT. PAGE 7 B0146   LEGIS
                                   CT/SYS
                                   B61

AVERY M.W.,GOVERNMENT OF WASHINGTON STATE. USA+45   PROVS
MUNIC DELIB/GP EX/STRUC LEGIS GIVE CT/SYS PARTIC   LOC/G
REGION EFFICIENCY 20 WASHINGT/G GOVERNOR. PAGE 7   ADMIN
B0151   GOV/REL
                                   B61

AYLMER G.,THE KING'S SERVANTS. UK ELITES CHIEF PAY   ADMIN
CT/SYS WEALTH 1/ CROMWELL/O CHARLES/I. PAGE 7 B0153   ROUTINE
                                   EX/STRUC
                                   NAT/G
                                   B61

CARROTHERS A.W.R.,LABOR ARBITRATION IN CANADA.   LABOR
CANADA LAW NAT/G CONSULT LEGIS WORKER ADJUD ADMIN   MGT
CT/SYS 20. PAGE 19 B0386   GP/REL
                                   BARGAIN
                                   B61

DRAGNICH A.N.,MAJOR EUROPEAN GOVERNMENTS. FRANCE   NAT/G
GERMANY/W UK USSR LOC/G EX/STRUC CT/SYS PARL/PROC   LEGIS
ATTIT MARXISM...JURID MGT NAT/COMP 19/20. PAGE 30   CONSTN
B0615   POL/PAR
                                   B61

DRURY J.W.,THE GOVERNMENT OF KANSAS. USA+45 AGRI   PROVS
INDUS CHIEF LEGIS WORKER PLAN BUDGET GIVE CT/SYS   CONSTN
GOV/REL...T 20 KANSAS GOVERNOR CITY/MGT. PAGE 31   ADMIN
B0621   LOC/G
                                   B61

RAO K.V.,PARLIAMENTARY DEMOCRACY OF INDIA. INDIA   CONSTN
EX/STRUC TOP/EX COLONIAL CT/SYS PARL/PROC ORD/FREE   ADJUD
...POLICY CONCPT TREND 20 PARLIAMENT. PAGE 86 B1733   NAT/G
                                   FEDERAL
                                   B61

SCHMECKEBIER L.,GOVERNMENT PUBLICATIONS AND THEIR   BIBLIOG/A
USE. USA+45 LEGIS ACT/RES CT/SYS EXEC INGP/REL 20.   EDU/PROP
PAGE 94 B1894   NAT/G
                                   ADMIN
                                   S61

SCHILLING W.R.,"THE H-BOMB: HOW TO DECIDE WITHOUT   PERSON
ACTUALLY CHOOSING." FUT USA+45 INTELL CONSULT ADMIN   LEGIT
CT/SYS MORAL...JURID OBS 20 TRUMAN/HS. PAGE 93   NUC/PWR
B1888
                                   B62

BOCK E.A.,CASE STUDIES IN AMERICAN GOVERNMENT.   POLICY
USA+45 ECO/DEV CHIEF EDU/PROP CT/SYS RACE/REL   LEGIS
ORD/FREE...JURID MGT PHIL/SCI PRESIDENT CASEBOOK.   IDEA/COMP
PAGE 13 B0262   NAT/G
                                   B62

CARTER G.M.,THE GOVERNMENT OF THE SOVIET UNION.   NAT/G

USSR CULTURE LOC/G DIPLOM ECO/TAC ADJUD CT/SYS LEAD   MARXISM
WEALTH...CHARTS T 20 COM/PARTY. PAGE 19 B0390   POL/PAR
                                   EX/STRUC
                                   B62

DELANY V.T.H.,THE ADMINISTRATION OF JUSTICE IN   ADMIN
IRELAND. IRELAND CONSTN FINAN JUDGE COLONIAL CRIME   JURID
...CRIMLGY 19/20. PAGE 28 B0571   CT/SYS
                                   ADJUD
                                   B62

FARBER W.O.,GOVERNMENT OF SOUTH DAKOTA. USA+45   PROVS
DIST/IND POL/PAR CHIEF EX/STRUC LEGIS ECO/TAC GIVE   LOC/G
EDU/PROP CT/SYS PARTIC...T 20 SOUTH/DAK GOVERNOR.   ADMIN
PAGE 35 B0704   CONSTN
                                   B62

GROGAN V.,ADMINISTRATIVE TRIBUNALS IN THE PUBLIC   ADMIN
SERVICE. IRELAND UK NAT/G CONTROL CT/SYS...JURID   LAW
GOV/COMP 20. PAGE 44 B0884   ADJUD
                                   DELIB/GP
                                   B62

HITCHNER D.G.,MODERN GOVERNMENT: A SURVEY OF   CONCPT
POLITICAL SCIENCE. WOR+45 INT/ORG LEGIS ADMIN   NAT/G
CT/SYS EXEC CHOOSE TOTALISM POPULISM...INT/LAW   STRUCT
PHIL/SCI METH 20. PAGE 50 B1019
                                   B62

HSUEH S.-.S.,GOVERNMENT AND ADMINISTRATION OF HONG   ADMIN
KONG. CHIEF DELIB/GP LEGIS CT/SYS REPRESENT GOV/REL   LOC/G
20 HONG/KONG CITY/MGT CIVIL/SERV GOVERNOR. PAGE 52   COLONIAL
B1055   EX/STRUC
                                   B62

INSTITUTE JUDICIAL ADMIN,JUDGES: THEIR TEMPORARY   NAT/G
APPOINTMENT, ASSIGNMENT AND TRANSFER: SURVEY OF FED   LOC/G
AND STATE CONSTN'S STATUTES, ROLES OF CT. USA+45   JUDGE
CONSTN PROVS CT/SYS GOV/REL PWR JURID. PAGE 54   ADMIN
B1090
                                   B62

INTERNAT CONGRESS OF JURISTS,EXECUTIVE ACTION AND   JURID
THE RULE OF LAW: REPORTION PROCEEDINGS OF INT'T   EXEC
CONGRESS OF JURISTS--RIO DE JANEIRO, BRAZIL. WOR+45   ORD/FREE
ACADEM CONSULT JUDGE EDU/PROP ADJUD CT/SYS INGP/REL   CONTROL
PERSON DEPT/DEFEN. PAGE 54 B1094
                                   B62

PHILLIPS O.H.,CONSTITUTIONAL AND ADMINISTRATIVE LAW   JURID
(3RD ED.). UK INT/ORG LOC/G CHIEF EX/STRUC LEGIS   ADMIN
BAL/PWR ADJUD COLONIAL CT/SYS PWR...CHARTS 20.   CONSTN
PAGE 83 B1670   NAT/G
                                   B62

SCHULMAN S.,TOWARD JUDICIAL REFORM IN PENNSYLVANIA: CT/SYS
A STUDY IN COURT REORGANIZATION. USA+45 CONSTN   ACT/RES
JUDGE PLAN ADMIN LOBBY SANCTION PRIVIL PWR...JURID   PROB/SOLV
20 PENNSYLVAN. PAGE 94 B1905
                                   C62

VAN DER SPRENKEL S.,"LEGAL INSTITUTIONS IN MANCHU   LAW
CHINA." ASIA STRUCT CT/SYS ROUTINE GOV/REL GP/REL   JURID
...CONCPT BIBLIOG 17/20. PAGE 111 B2250   ADMIN
                                   ADJUD
                                   B63

ADRIAN C.R.,GOVERNING OVER FIFTY STATES AND THEIR   PROVS
COMMUNITIES. USA+45 CONSTN FINAN MUNIC NAT/G   LOC/G
POL/PAR EX/STRUC LEGIS ADMIN CONTROL CT/SYS   GOV/REL
...CHARTS 20. PAGE 3 B0061   GOV/COMP
                                   B63

BADI J.,THE GOVERNMENT OF THE STATE OF ISRAEL: A   NAT/G
CRITICAL ACCOUNT OF ITS PARLIAMENT, EXECUTIVE, AND   CONSTN
JUDICIARY. ISRAEL ECO/DEV CHIEF DELIB/GP LEGIS   EX/STRUC
DIPLOM CT/SYS INGP/REL PEACE ORD/FREE...BIBLIOG 20   POL/PAR
PARLIAMENT ARABS MIGRATION. PAGE 8 B0157
                                   B63

BOWETT D.W.,THE LAW OF INTERNATIONAL INSTITUTIONS.   INT/ORG
WOR+45 WOR-45 CONSTN DELIB/GP EX/STRUC JUDGE   ADJUD
EDU/PROP LEGIT CT/SYS EXEC ROUTINE RIGID/FLEX   DIPLOM
ORD/FREE PWR...JURID CONCPT ORG/CHARTS GEN/METH
LEAGUE/NAT OAS OEEC 20 UN. PAGE 14 B0286
                                   B63

CORLEY R.N.,THE LEGAL ENVIRONMENT OF BUSINESS.   NAT/G
CONSTN LEGIS TAX ADMIN CT/SYS DISCRIM ATTIT PWR   INDUS
...TREND 18/20. PAGE 23 B0477   JURID
                                   DECISION
                                   B63

ELIAS T.O.,THE NIGERIAN LEGAL SYSTEM. NIGERIA LAW   CT/SYS
FAM KIN SECT ADMIN NAT/LISM...JURID 18/20   ADJUD
ENGLSH/LAW COMMON/LAW. PAGE 33 B0665   COLONIAL
                                   PROF/ORG
                                   B63

FORTES A.B.,HISTORIA ADMINISTRATIVA, JUDICIARIA E   PROVS
ECLESIASTICA DO RIO GRANDE DO SUL. BRAZIL L/A+17C   ADMIN
LOC/G SECT COLONIAL CT/SYS ORD/FREE CATHISM 16/20.   JURID
PAGE 37 B0742
                                   B63

GARNER U.F.,ADMINISTRATIVE LAW. UK LAW LOC/G NAT/G   ADMIN
EX/STRUC LEGIS JUDGE BAL/PWR BUDGET ADJUD CONTROL   JURID
CT/SYS...BIBLIOG 20. PAGE 39 B0783   PWR
                                   GOV/REL
                                   B63

GRIFFITH J.A.G.,PRINCIPLES OF ADMINISTRATIVE LAW   JURID
(3RD ED.). UK CONSTN EX/STRUC LEGIS ADJUD CONTROL   ADMIN
CT/SYS PWR...CHARTS 20. PAGE 43 B0879   NAT/G

KLEIN F.J.,JUDICIAL ADMINISTRATION AND THE LEGAL
PROFESSION. USA+45 ADMIN CONTROL EFFICIENCY
...POLICY 20. PAGE 60 B1217
BAL/PWR
B63
BIBLIOG/A
CT/SYS
ADJUD
JUDGE

KLESMENT J.,LEGAL SOURCES AND BIBLIOGRAPHY OF THE
BALTIC STATES (ESTONIA, LATVIA, LITHUANIA). COM
ESTONIA LATVIA LITHUANIA LAW FINAN ADJUD CT/SYS
REGION CENTRAL MARXISM 19/20. PAGE 60 B1218
B63
BIBLIOG/A
JURID
CONSTN
ADMIN

KULZ H.R.,STAATSBURGER UND STAATSGEWALT (2 VOLS.).
GERMANY SWITZERLND UK USSR CONSTN DELIB/GP TARIFFS
TAX...JURID 20. PAGE 61 B1242
ADMIN
ADJUD
CT/SYS
NAT/COMP

LOCKARD D.,THE POLITICS OF STATE AND LOCAL
GOVERNMENT. USA+45 CONSTN EX/STRUC LEGIS CT/SYS
FEDERAL...CHARTS BIBLIOG 20. PAGE 66 B1334
B63
LOC/G
PROVS
OP/RES
ADMIN

PALOTAI O.C.,PUBLICATIONS OF THE INSTITUTE OF
GOVERNMENT, 1930-1962. LAW PROVS SCHOOL WORKER
ACT/RES OP/RES CT/SYS GOV/REL...CRIMLGY SOC/WK.
PAGE 81 B1629
B63
BIBLIOG/A
ADMIN
LOC/G
FINAN

PATRA A.C.,THE ADMINISTRATION OF JUSTICE UNDER THE
EAST INDIA COMPANY IN BENGAL, BIHAR AND ORISSA.
INDIA UK LG/CO CAP/ISM INT/TRADE ADJUD COLONIAL
CONTROL CT/SYS...POLICY 20. PAGE 81 B1641
ADMIN
JURID
CONCPT

RICHARDS P.G.,PATRONAGE IN BRITISH GOVERNMENT.
ELITES DELIB/GP TOP/EX PROB/SOLV CONTROL CT/SYS
EXEC PWR. PAGE 88 B1774
B63
EX/STRUC
REPRESENT
POL/PAR
ADMIN

RICHARDSON H.G.,THE ADMINISTRATION OF IRELAND
1172-1377. IRELAND CONSTN EX/STRUC LEGIS JUDGE
CT/SYS PARL/PROC...CHARTS BIBLIOG 12/14. PAGE 88
B1775
B63
ADMIN
NAT/G
PWR

WADE H.W.R.,TOWARDS ADMINISTRATIVE JUSTICE. UK
USA+45 CONSTN CONSULT PROB/SOLV CT/SYS PARL/PROC
...POLICY JURID METH/COMP 20 ENGLSH/LAW. PAGE 112
B2270
B63
ADJUD
IDEA/COMP
ADMIN

BECHHOEFER B.G.,"UNITED NATIONS PROCEDURES IN CASE
OF VIOLATIONS OF DISARMAMENT AGREEMENTS." COM
USA+45 USSR LAW CONSTN NAT/G EX/STRUC FORCES LEGIS
BAL/PWR EDU/PROP CT/SYS ARMS/CONT ORD/FREE PWR
...POLICY STERTYP UN VAL/FREE 20. PAGE 10 B0204
S63
INT/ORG
DELIB/GP

BENNETT H.A.,THE COMMISSION AND THE COMMON LAW: A
STUDY IN ADMINISTRATIVE ADJUDICATION. LAW ADMIN
CT/SYS LOBBY SANCTION GOV/REL 20 COMMON/LAW.
PAGE 10 B0212
B64
ADJUD
DELIB/GP
DIST/IND
POLICY

GESELLSCHAFT RECHTSVERGLEICH,BIBLIOGRAPHIE DES
DEUTSCHEN RECHTS (BIBLIOGRAPHY OF GERMAN LAW,
TRANS. BY COURTLAND PETERSON). GERMANY FINAN INDUS
LABOR SECT FORCES CT/SYS PARL/PROC CRIME...INT/LAW
SOC NAT/COMP 20. PAGE 39 B0794
B64
BIBLIOG/A
JURID
CONSTN
ADMIN

JACKSON R.M.,THE MACHINERY OF JUSTICE IN ENGLAND.
UK EDU/PROP CONTROL COST ORD/FREE...MGT 20
ENGLSH/LAW. PAGE 55 B1109
B64
CT/SYS
ADJUD
JUDGE
JURID

KAHNG T.J.,LAW, POLITICS, AND THE SECURITY COUNCIL*
AN INQUIRY INTO THE HANDLING OF LEGAL QUESTIONS.
LAW CONSTN NAT/G ACT/RES OP/RES CT/SYS TASK PWR
...INT/LAW BIBLIOG UN. PAGE 57 B1160
B64
DELIB/GP
ADJUD
ROUTINE

KARLEN D.,THE CITIZEN IN COURT. USA+45 LAW ADMIN
ROUTINE CRIME GP/REL...JURID 20. PAGE 58 B1175
B64
CT/SYS
ADJUD
GOV/REL
JUDGE

NELSON D.H.,ADMINISTRATIVE AGENCIES OF THE USA:
THEIR DECISIONS AND AUTHORITY. USA+45 NAT/G CONTROL
CT/SYS REPRESENT...DECISION 20. PAGE 78 B1568
B64
ADMIN
EX/STRUC
ADJUD
LAW

O'HEARN P.J.T.,PEACE, ORDER AND GOOD GOVERNMENT; A
NEW CONSTITUTION FOR CANADA. CANADA EX/STRUC LEGIS
CT/SYS PARL/PROC...BIBLIOG 20. PAGE 79 B1600
B64
NAT/G
CONSTN
LAW
CREATE

PIPES R.,THE FORMATION OF THE SOVIET UNION. EUR+WWI
MOD/EUR STRUCT ECO/UNDEV NAT/G LEGIS DOMIN LEGIT
CT/SYS EXEC COERCE ALL/VALS...POLICY RELATIV
HIST/WRIT TIME/SEQ TOT/POP 19/20. PAGE 83 B1677
B64
COM
USSR
RUSSIA

RIKER W.H.,FEDERALISM. WOR+45 WOR-45 CONSTN CHIEF
LEGIS ADMIN COLONIAL CONTROL CT/SYS PWR...BIBLIOG/A
B64
FEDERAL
NAT/G

18/20. PAGE 88 B1787
ORD/FREE
CENTRAL

SCHECHTER A.H.,INTERPRETATION OF AMBIGUOUS
DOCUMENTS BY INTERNATIONAL ADMINISTRATIVE
TRIBUNALS. WOR+45 EX/STRUC INT/TRADE CT/SYS
SOVEREIGN 20 UN ILO EURCT/JUST. PAGE 93 B1884
B64
INT/LAW
DIPLOM
INT/ORG
ADJUD

SHERIDAN R.G.,URBAN JUSTICE. USA+45 PROVS CREATE
ADMIN CT/SYS ORD/FREE 20 TENNESSEE. PAGE 96 B1943
B64
LOC/G
JURID
ADJUD
MUNIC

STOICOIU V.,LEGAL SOURCES AND BIBLIOGRAPHY OF
ROMANIA. COM ROMANIA LAW FINAN POL/PAR LEGIS JUDGE
ADJUD CT/SYS PARL/PROC MARXISM 20. PAGE 101 B2041
B64
BIBLIOG/A
JURID
CONSTN
ADMIN

SZLADITS C.,BIBLIOGRAPHY ON FOREIGN AND COMPARATIVE
LAW: BOOKS AND ARTICLES IN ENGLISH (SUPPLEMENT
1962). FINAN INDUS JUDGE LICENSE ADMIN CT/SYS
PARL/PROC OWN...INT/LAW CLASSIF METH/COMP NAT/COMP
20. PAGE 102 B2065
B64
BIBLIOG/A
JURID
ADJUD
LAW

VECCHIO G.D.,L'ETAT ET LE DROIT. ITALY CONSTN
EX/STRUC LEGIS DIPLOM CT/SYS...JURID 20 UN.
PAGE 112 B2256
B64
NAT/G
SOVEREIGN
CONCPT
INT/LAW

WHEARE K.C.,FEDERAL GOVERNMENT (4TH ED.). WOR+45
WOR-45 POL/PAR LEGIS BAL/PWR CT/SYS...POLICY JURID
CONCPT GOV/COMP 17/20. PAGE 116 B2331
B64
FEDERAL
CONSTN
EX/STRUC
NAT/COMP

CAVERS D.F.,THE CHOICE-OF-LAW PROCESS. PROB/SOLV
ADJUD CT/SYS CHOOSE RATIONAL...IDEA/COMP 16/20
TREATY. PAGE 19 B0396
B65
JURID
DECISION
METH/COMP
ADMIN

COHN H.J.,THE GOVERNMENT OF THE RHINE PALATINATE IN
THE FIFTEENTH CENTURY. GERMANY FINAN LOC/G DELIB/GP
LEGIS CT/SYS CHOOSE CATHISM 14/15 PALATINATE.
PAGE 22 B0449
B65
PROVS
JURID
GP/REL
ADMIN

COOPER F.E.,STATE ADMINISTRATIVE LAW (2 VOLS.). LAW
LEGIS PLAN TAX ADJUD CT/SYS FEDERAL PWR...CONCPT
20. PAGE 23 B0474
B65
JURID
CONSTN
ADMIN
PROVS

FISCHER F.C.,THE GOVERNMENT OF MICHIGAN. USA+45
NAT/G PUB/INST EX/STRUC LEGIS BUDGET GIVE EDU/PROP
CT/SYS CHOOSE GOV/REL...T MICHIGAN. PAGE 36 B0723
B65
PROVS
LOC/G
ADMIN
CONSTN

FRIEDMAN L.,SOUTHERN JUSTICE. USA+45 PUB/INST LEGIT
ADMIN CT/SYS DISCRIM...DECISION ANTHOL 20 NEGRO
SOUTH/US CIV/RIGHTS. PAGE 37 B0758
B65
ADJUD
LAW
CONSTN
RACE/REL

KAAS L.,DIE GEISTLICHE GERICHTSBARKEIT DER
KATHOLISCHEN KIRCHE IN PREUSSEN (2 VOLS.). PRUSSIA
CONSTN NAT/G PROVS SECT ADJUD ADMIN ATTIT 16/20.
PAGE 57 B1158
B65
JURID
CATHISM
GP/REL
CT/SYS

NORDEN A.,WAR AND NAZI CRIMINALS IN WEST GERMANY:
STATE, ECONOMY, ADMINISTRATION, ARMY, JUSTICE,
SCIENCE. GERMANY GERMANY/W MOD/EUR ECO/DEV ACADEM
EX/STRUC FORCES DOMIN CT/SYS...POLICY MAJORIT
PACIFIST 20. PAGE 78 B1587
B65
FASCIST
WAR
NAT/G
TOP/EX

PURCELL V.,THE MEMOIRS OF A MALAYAN OFFICIAL.
MALAYSIA UK ECO/UNDEV INDUS LABOR EDU/PROP COLONIAL
CT/SYS WAR NAT/LISM TOTALISM ORD/FREE SOVEREIGN 20
UN CIVIL/SERV. PAGE 85 B1721
B65
BIOG
ADMIN
JURID
FORCES

PYLEE M.V.,CONSTITUTIONAL GOVERNMENT IN INDIA (2ND
REV. ED.). INDIA POL/PAR EX/STRUC DIPLOM COLONIAL
CT/SYS PARL/PROC PRIVIL...JURID 16/20. PAGE 85
B1725
B65
CONSTN
NAT/G
PROVS
FEDERAL

REDFORD D.R.,POLITICS AND GOVERNMENT IN THE UNITED
STATES. USA+45 USA-45 LOC/G PROVS FORCES DIPLOM
CT/SYS LOBBY...JURID SUPREME/CT PRESIDENT. PAGE 87
B1751
B65
NAT/G
POL/PAR
EX/STRUC
LEGIS

SHARMA S.A.,PARLIAMENTARY GOVERNMENT IN INDIA.
INDIA FINAN LOC/G PROVS DELIB/GP PLAN ADMIN CT/SYS
FEDERAL...JURID 20. PAGE 96 B1936
B65
NAT/G
CONSTN
PARL/PROC
LEGIS

SMITH C.,THE OMBUDSMAN: A BIBLIOGRAPHY (PAMPHLET).
DENMARK SWEDEN USA+45 LAW LEGIS JUDGE GOV/REL
GP/REL...JURID 20. PAGE 98 B1980
B65
BIBLIOG
ADMIN
CT/SYS
ADJUD

RUBIN A.P.,"UNITED STATES CONTEMPORARY PRACTICE
L65
LAW

RELATING TO INTERNATIONAL LAW." USA+45 WOR+45   LEGIT
CONSTN INT/ORG NAT/G DELIB/GP EX/STRUC DIPLOM DOMIN INT/LAW
CT/SYS ROUTINE ORD/FREE...CONCPT COLD/WAR 20.
PAGE 91 B1848

                                                 S65

RUBINSTEIN A.Z.,"YUGOSLAVIA'S OPENING SOCIETY." COM CONSTN
USSR INTELL NAT/G LEGIS TOP/EX LEGIT CT/SYS   EX/STRUC
RIGID/FLEX ALL/VALS SOCISM...HUM TIME/SEQ TREND 20. YUGOSLAVIA
PAGE 92 B1851

                                                 B66

ADAMS J.C.,THE GOVERNMENT OF REPUBLICAN ITALY (2ND NAT/G
ED.). ITALY LOC/G POL/PAR DELIB/GP LEGIS WORKER   CHOOSE
ADMIN CT/SYS FASCISM...CHARTS BIBLIOG 20   EX/STRUC
PARLIAMENT. PAGE 3 B0057   CONSTN

                                                 B66

BRAIBANTI R.,RESEARCH ON THE BUREAUCRACY OF   HABITAT
PAKISTAN. PAKISTAN LAW CULTURE INTELL ACADEM LOC/G NAT/G
SECT PRESS CT/SYS...LING CHARTS 20 BUREAUCRCY.   ADMIN
PAGE 15 B0299   CONSTN

                                                 B66

BURNS A.C.,PARLIAMENT AS AN EXPORT. WOR+45 CONSTN   PARL/PROC
BARGAIN DEBATE ROUTINE GOV/REL EFFICIENCY...ANTHOL POL/PAR
COMMONWLTH PARLIAMENT. PAGE 17 B0353   CT/SYS
                                             CHIEF

                                                 B66

DUNCOMBE H.S.,COUNTY GOVERNMENT IN AMERICA. USA+45 LOC/G
FINAN MUNIC ADMIN ROUTINE GOV/REL...GOV/COMP 20.   PROVS
PAGE 31 B0631   CT/SYS
                                             TOP/EX

                                                 B66

FINK M.,A SELECTIVE BIBLIOGRAPHY ON STATE   BIBLIOG
CONSTITUTIONAL REVISION (PAMPHLET). USA+45 FINAN   PROVS
EX/STRUC LEGIS EDU/PROP ADMIN CT/SYS APPORT CHOOSE LOC/G
GOV/REL 20. PAGE 35 B0720   CONSTN

                                                 B66

GHOSH P.K.,THE CONSTITUTION OF INDIA: HOW IT HAS   CONSTN
BEEN FRAMED. INDIA LOC/G DELIB/GP EX/STRUC   NAT/G
PROB/SOLV BUDGET INT/TRADE CT/SYS CHOOSE...LING 20. LEGIS
PAGE 39 B0795   FEDERAL

                                                 B66

GREENE L.E.,GOVERNMENT IN TENNESSEE (2ND ED.).   PROVS
USA+45 DIST/IND INDUS POL/PAR EX/STRUC LEGIS PLAN   LOC/G
BUDGET GIVE CT/SYS...MGT T 20 TENNESSEE. PAGE 43   CONSTN
B0866   ADMIN

                                                 B66

HIDAYATULLAH M.,DEMOCRACY IN INDIA AND THE JUDICIAL NAT/G
PROCESS. INDIA EX/STRUC LEGIS LEAD GOV/REL ATTIT   CT/SYS
ORD/FREE...MAJORIT CONCPT 20 NEHRU/J. PAGE 50 B1007 CONSTN
                                             JURID

                                                 B66

NEUMANN R.G.,THE GOVERNMENT OF THE GERMAN FEDERAL   NAT/G
REPUBLIC. EUR+WWI GERMANY/W LOC/G EX/STRUC LEGIS   POL/PAR
CT/SYS INGP/REL PWR...BIBLIOG 20 ADENAUER/K.   DIPLOM
PAGE 78 B1573   CONSTN

                                                 B66

RICHARD J.B.,GOVERNMENT AND POLITICS OF WYOMING.   PROVS
USA+45 POL/PAR EX/STRUC LEGIS CT/SYS LOBBY APPORT   LOC/G
CHOOSE REPRESENT 20 WYOMING GOVERNOR. PAGE 88 B1773 ADMIN

                                                 B66

ROSS R.M.,STATE AND LOCAL GOVERNMENT AND   LOC/G
ADMINISTRATION. USA+45 CONSTN POL/PAR EX/STRUC   PROVS
LEGIS BUDGET EDU/PROP CONTROL CT/SYS CHOOSE GOV/REL MUNIC
T. PAGE 90 B1827   ADMIN

                                                 B66

SCHLESSINGER P.J.,ELEMENTS OF CALIFORNIA GOVERNMENT LOC/G
(2ND ED.). USA+45 LAW ADJUD ADMIN CONTROL CT/SYS   PROVS
EFFICIENCY...BIBLIOG T CALIFORNIA. PAGE 94 B1891   GOV/REL
                                             LEGIS

                                                 B66

SZLADITS C.,A BIBLIOGRAPHY ON FOREIGN AND   BIBLIOG/A
COMPARATIVE LAW (SUPPLEMENT 1964). FINAN FAM LABOR CT/SYS
LG/CO LEGIS JUDGE ADMIN CRIME...CRIMLGY 20.   INT/LAW
PAGE 102 B2066

                                                 B66

WALL E.H.,THE COURT OF JUSTICE IN THE EUROPEAN   CT/SYS
COMMUNITIES: JURISDICTION AND PROCEDURE. EUR+WWI   INT/ORG
DIPLOM ADJUD ADMIN ROUTINE TASK...CONCPT LING 20.   LAW
PAGE 113 B2281   OP/RES

                                                 B66

WILSON G.,CASES AND MATERIALS ON CONSTITUTIONAL AND JURID
ADMINISTRATIVE LAW. UK LAW NAT/G EX/STRUC LEGIS   ADMIN
BAL/PWR BUDGET DIPLOM ADJUD CONTROL CT/SYS GOV/REL CONSTN
ORD/FREE 20 PARLIAMENT ENGLSH/LAW. PAGE 117 B2359 PWR

                                                 C66

TACHERON D.G.,"THE JOB OF THE CONGRESSMAN: AN   LEGIS
INTRODUCTION TO SERVICES IN THE US HOUSE OF   PARL/PROC
REPRESENTATIVES." DELIB/GP EX/STRUC PRESS SENIOR   ADMIN
CT/SYS LOBBY CHOOSE GOV/REL...BIBLIOG 20 CONGRESS   POL/PAR
HOUSE/REP SENATE. PAGE 102 B2068

                                                 N66

BACHELDER G.L.,THE LITERATURE OF FEDERALISM: A   BIBLIOG
SELECTED BIBLIOGRAPHY (REV ED) (A PAMPHLET). USA+45 FEDERAL
USA-45 WOR+45 WOR-45 LAW CONSTN PROVS ADMIN CT/SYS NAT/G
GOV/REL ROLE...CONCPT 19/20. PAGE 8 B0155   LOC/G

                                                 B67

BLUMBERG A.S.,CRIMINAL JUSTICE. USA+45 CLIENT LAW   JURID

LOC/G FORCES JUDGE ACT/RES LEGIT ADMIN RATIONAL   CT/SYS
MYTH. PAGE 13 B0259   PROF/ORG
                                                CRIME

                                                 B67

BROWN L.N.,FRENCH ADMINISTRATIVE LAW. FRANCE UK   EX/STRUC
CONSTN NAT/G LEGIS DOMIN CONTROL EXEC PARL/PROC PWR LAW
...JURID METH/COMP GEN/METH. PAGE 16 B0324   IDEA/COMP
                                               CT/SYS

                                                 B67

FESLER J.W.,THE FIFTY STATES AND THEIR LOCAL   PROVS
GOVERNMENTS. FUT USA+45 POL/PAR LEGIS PROB/SOLV   LOC/G
ADMIN CT/SYS CHOOSE GOV/REL FEDERAL...POLICY CHARTS
20 SUPREME/CT. PAGE 35 B0715

                                                 B67

FINCHER F.,THE GOVERNMENT OF THE UNITED STATES.   NAT/G
USA+45 USA-45 POL/PAR CHIEF CT/SYS LOBBY GP/REL   EX/STRUC
INGP/REL...CONCPT CHARTS BIBLIOG T 18/20 PRESIDENT LEGIS
CONGRESS SUPREME/CT. PAGE 35 B0719   OP/RES

                                                 B67

GELLHORN W.,OMBUDSMEN AND OTHERS: CITIZENS'   NAT/COMP
PROTECTORS IN NINE COUNTRIES. WOR+45 LAW CONSTN   REPRESENT
LEGIS INSPECT ADJUD ADMIN CONTROL CT/SYS CHOOSE   INGP/REL
PERS/REL...STAT CHARTS 20. PAGE 39 B0789   PROB/SOLV

                                                 B67

HEWITT W.H.,ADMINISTRATION OF CRIMINAL JUSTICE IN   CRIME
NEW YORK. LAW PROB/SOLV ADJUD ADMIN...CRIMLGY   ROLE
CHARTS T 20 NEW/YORK. PAGE 49 B1001   CT/SYS
                                              FORCES

                                                 B67

KATZ J.,PSYCHOANALYSIS, PSYCHIATRY, AND LAW. USA+45 LAW
LOC/G NAT/G PUB/INST PROB/SOLV ADMIN HEALTH   PSY
...CRIMLGY CONCPT SAMP/SIZ IDEA/COMP. PAGE 58 B1180 CT/SYS
                                                ADJUD

                                                 B67

LENG S.C.,JUSTICE IN COMMUNIST CHINA: A SURVEY OF   CT/SYS
THE JUDICIAL SYSTEM OF THE CHINESE PEOPLE'S   ADJUD
REPUBLIC. CHINA/COM LAW CONSTN LOC/G NAT/G PROF/ORG JURID
CONSULT FORCES ADMIN CRIME ORD/FREE...BIBLIOG 20   MARXISM
MAO. PAGE 64 B1290

                                                 B67

WESTON P.B.,THE ADMINISTRATION OF JUSTICE. USA+45   CRIME
CONSTN MUNIC NAT/G PROVS EX/STRUC JUDGE ADMIN   CT/SYS
CONTROL SANCTION ORD/FREE...CHARTS 20. PAGE 115   JURID
B2328   ADJUD

                                                 L67

"RESTRICTIVE SOVEREIGN IMMUNITY, THE STATE   SOVEREIGN
DEPARTMENT, AND THE COURTS." USA+45 USA-45 EX/STRUC ORD/FREE
DIPLOM ADJUD CONTROL GOV/REL 19/20 DEPT/STATE   PRIVIL
SUPREME/CT. PAGE 2 B0047   CT/SYS

                                                 L67

BERGER R.,"ADMINISTRATIVE ARBITRARINESS* A SEQUEL." LAW
USA+45 CONSTN ADJUD CT/SYS SANCTION INGP/REL   LABOR
...POLICY JURID. PAGE 11 B0222   BARGAIN
                                             ADMIN

                                                 L67

BLUMBERG A.S.,"THE PRACTICE OF LAW AS CONFIDENCE   CT/SYS
GAME: ORGANIZATIONAL COOPTATION OF A PROFESSION." ADJUD
USA+45 CLIENT SOCIETY CONSULT ROLE JURID. PAGE 13 GP/REL
B0260   ADMIN

                                                 L67

CAHIERS P.,"LE RECOURS EN CONSTATATION DE   INT/ORG
MANQUEMENTS DES ETATS MEMBRES DEVANT LA COUR DES   CONSTN
COMMUNAUTES EUROPEENNES." LAW PROB/SOLV DIPLOM   ROUTINE
ADMIN CT/SYS SANCTION ATTIT...POLICY DECISION JURID ADJUD
ECSC EEC. PAGE 18 B0362

                                                 L67

GAINES J.E.,"THE YOUTH COURT CONCEPT AND ITS   CT/SYS
IMPLEMENTATION IN TOMPKINS COUNTY, NEW YORK."   AGE/Y
USA+45 LAW CONSTN JUDGE WORKER ADJUD ADMIN CHOOSE   INGP/REL
PERSON...JURID NEW/YORK. PAGE 38 B0772   CRIME

                                                 S67

KRARUP O.,"JUDICIAL REVIEW OF ADMINISTRATIVE ACTION ADJUD
IN DENMARK." DENMARK LAW CT/SYS...JURID CONCPT   CONTROL
19/20. PAGE 61 B1234   EXEC
                                              DECISION

                                                 S67

SKOLNICK J.H.,"SOCIAL CONTROL IN THE ADVERSARY   PROB/SOLV
SYSTEM." USA+45 CONSULT OP/RES ADMIN CONTROL.   PERS/REL
PAGE 98 B1975   ADJUD
                                                CT/SYS

                                                 L86

GOODNOW F.J.,"AN EXECUTIVE AND THE COURTS: JUDICIAL CT/SYS
REMEDIES AGAINST ADMINISTRATIVE ACTION" FRANCE UK GOV/REL
USA-45 WOR-45 LAW CONSTN SANCTION ORD/FREE 19.   ADMIN
PAGE 41 B0823   ADJUD

CTS/WESTM....COURTS OF WESTMINSTER HALL

CUBA....SEE ALSO L/A+17C

                                                 B63

STEVENSON A.E.,LOOKING OUTWARD: YEARS OF CRISIS AT INT/ORG
THE UNITED NATIONS. COM CUBA USA+45 WOR+45 SOCIETY CONCPT
NAT/G EX/STRUC ACT/RES LEGIT COLONIAL ATTIT PERSON ARMS/CONT
SUPEGO ALL/VALS...POLICY HUM UN COLD/WAR CONGO 20.
PAGE 100 B2034

B63
VAN SLYCK P.,PEACE: THE CONTROL OF NATIONAL POWER.   ARMS/CONT
CUBA WOR+45 FINAN NAT/G FORCES PROB/SOLV TEC/DEV   PEACE
BAL/PWR ADMIN CONTROL ORD/FREE...POLICY INT/LAW UN   INT/ORG
COLD/WAR TREATY. PAGE 112 B2253   DIPLOM

567
FABREGA J.,"ANTECEDENTES EXTRANJEROS EN LA   CONSTN
CONSTITUCION PANAMENA." CUBA L/A+17C PANAMA URUGUAY   JURID
EX/STRUC LEGIS DIPLOM ORD/FREE 19/20 COLOMB   NAT/G
MEXIC/AMER. PAGE 34 B0694   PARL/PROC

CUBAN CRISIS....SEE INT/REL+APPROPRIATE NATIONS+COLD WAR

CULLINGWORTH J.B. B0512

CULTS....SEE SECT

CULTUR/REV....CULTURAL REVOLUTION IN CHINA

CULTURAL REVOLUTION IN CHINA....SEE CULTUR/REV

CULTURE....CULTURAL PATTERNS

N
AUSTRALIAN NATIONAL RES COUN,AUSTRALIAN SOCIAL   BIBLIOG/A
SCIENCE ABSTRACTS. NEW/ZEALD CULTURE SOCIETY LOC/G   POLICY
CT/SYS PARL/PROC...HEAL JURID PSY SOC 20 AUSTRAL.   NAT/G
PAGE 7 B0149   ADMIN

N
CONOVER H.F.,MADAGASCAR: A SELECTED LIST OF   BIBLIOG/A
REFERENCES. MADAGASCAR STRUCT ECO/UNDEV NAT/G ADMIN   SOCIETY
...SOC 19/20. PAGE 23 B0463   CULTURE
                                                      COLONIAL
N
HANDBOOK OF LATIN AMERICAN STUDIES. LAW CULTURE   BIBLIOG/A
ECO/UNDEV POL/PAR ADMIN LEAD...SOC 20. PAGE 1 B0014   L/A+17C
                                                      NAT/G
                                                      DIPLOM
N
SUMMARIES OF SELECTED JAPANESE MAGAZINES. LAW   BIBLIOG/A
CULTURE ADMIN LEAD 20 CHINJAP. PAGE 1 B0024   ATTIT
                                                      NAT/G
                                                      ASIA
N
SUBJECT GUIDE TO BOOKS IN PRINT: AN INDEX TO THE   BIBLIOG
PUBLISHERS' TRADE LIST ANNUAL. WOR+45 WOR-45 LAW   NAT/G
CULTURE ADMIN LEAD PERSON...HUM MGT SOC. PAGE 2   DIPLOM
B0029
N
DEUTSCHE BUCHEREI,DEUTSCHES BUCHERVERZEICHNIS.   BIBLIOG
GERMANY LAW CULTURE POL/PAR ADMIN LEAD ATTIT PERSON NAT/G
...SOC 20. PAGE 29 B0581   DIPLOM
                                                      ECO/DEV
N
PUBLISHERS' CIRCULAR LIMITED,THE ENGLISH CATALOGUE   BIBLIOG
OF BOOKS. UK WOR+45 WOR-45 LAW CULTURE LOC/G NAT/G   ALL/VALS
ADMIN LEAD...MGT 19/20. PAGE 85 B1718   ALL/IDEOS
                                                      SOCIETY
NCO
STOLPER W.,"SOCIAL FACTORS IN ECONOMIC PLANNING,   ECO/UNDEV
WITH SPECIAL REFERENCE TO NIGERIA" AFR NIGER   PLAN
CULTURE FAM SECT RECEIVE ETIQUET ADMIN DEMAND 20.   ADJUST
PAGE 101 B2045   RISK
                                                      B19
NATHAN M.,THE SOUTH AFRICAN COMMONWEALTH: CONSTN
CONSTITUTION, PROBLEMS, SOCIAL CONDITIONS.   NAT/G
SOUTH/AFR UK CULTURE INDUS EX/STRUC LEGIS BUDGET   POL/PAR
EDU/PROP ADMIN CT/SYS GP/REL RACE/REL...LING 19/20   SOCIETY
CMN/WLTH. PAGE 77 B1559
                                                      B24
MERRIAM C.E.,A HISTORY OF POLITICAL THEORIES -   UNIV
RECENT TIMES. USA-45 WOR-45 CULTURE SOCIETY ECO/DEV INTELL
R+D EDU/PROP ROUTINE CHOOSE ATTIT PERSON ALL/VALS
...POLICY SOC CONCPT METH/CNCPT OBS HIST/WRIT
TIME/SEQ TREND. PAGE 73 B1471
                                                      B28
BUELL R.,THE NATIVE PROBLEM IN AFRICA. KIN LABOR   AFR
LOC/G ECO/TAC ROUTINE ORD/FREE...REC/INT KNO/TEST   CULTURE
CENSUS TREND CHARTS SOC/EXP STERTYP 20. PAGE 17
B0339
                                                      B28
SOROKIN P.,CONTEMPORARY SOCIOLOGICAL THEORIES.   CULTURE
MOD/EUR UNIV SOCIETY R+D SCHOOL ECO/TAC EDU/PROP   SOC
ROUTINE ATTIT DRIVE...PSY CONCPT TIME/SEQ TREND   WAR
GEN/LAWS 20. PAGE 99 B1997
                                                      B29
ROBERTS S.H.,HISTORY OF FRENCH COLONIAL POLICY. AFR INT/ORG
ASIA L/A+17C S/ASIA CULTURE ECO/DEV ECO/UNDEV FINAN ACT/RES
NAT/G PLAN ECO/TAC DOMIN ROUTINE SOVEREIGN...OBS   FRANCE
HIST/WRIT TREND CHARTS VAL/FREE 19/20. PAGE 89   COLONIAL
B1796
                                                      B30
MURCHISON C.,PSYCHOLOGIES OF 1930. UNIV USA-45   CREATE
CULTURE INTELL SOCIETY STRATA FAM ROUTINE BIO/SOC   PERSON
DRIVE RIGID/FLEX SUPEGO...NEW/IDEA OBS SELF/OBS
CONT/OBS 20. PAGE 76 B1543

B31
DEKAT A.D.A.,COLONIAL POLICY. S/ASIA CULTURE   DRIVE
EX/STRUC ECO/TAC DOMIN ADMIN COLONIAL ROUTINE   PWR
SOVEREIGN WEALTH...POLICY MGT RECORD KNO/TEST SAMP. INDONESIA
PAGE 28 B0570   NETHERLAND
                                                      B32
MCKISACK M.,THE PARLIAMENTARY REPRESENTATION OF THE NAT/G
ENGLISH BOROUGHS DURING THE MIDDLE AGES. UK CONSTN MUNIC
CULTURE ELITES EX/STRUC TAX PAY ADJUD PARL/PROC   LEGIS
APPORT FEDERAL...POLICY 13/15 PARLIAMENT. PAGE 72   CHOOSE
B1454
                                                      B35
GORER G.,AFRICA DANCES: A BOOK ABOUT WEST AFRICAN   AFR
NEGROES. STRUCT LOC/G SECT FORCES TAX ADMIN   ATTIT
COLONIAL...ART/METH MYTH WORSHIP 20 NEGRO AFRICA/W CULTURE
CHRISTIAN RITUAL. PAGE 41 B0835   SOCIETY
                                                      B36
ROBINSON H.,DEVELOPMENT OF THE BRITISH EMPIRE.   NAT/G
WOR-45 CULTURE SOCIETY STRUCT ECO/DEV ECO/UNDEV   HIST/WRIT
INT/ORG VOL/ASSN FORCES CREATE PLAN DOMIN EDU/PROP UK
ADMIN COLONIAL PWR WEALTH...POLICY GEOG CHARTS
CMN/WLTH 16/20. PAGE 89 B1800
                                                      B37
PARSONS T.,THE STRUCTURE OF SOCIAL ACTION. UNIV   CULTURE
INTELL SOCIETY INDUS MARKET ECO/TAC ROUTINE CHOOSE ATTIT
ALL/VALS...CONCPT OBS BIOG TREND GEN/LAWS 20.   CAP/ISM
PAGE 81 B1636
                                                      B38
RAPPARD W.E.,THE CRISIS OF DEMOCRACY. EUR+WWI UNIV NAT/G
WOR-45 CULTURE SOCIETY ECO/DEV INT/ORG POL/PAR   CONCPT
ACT/RES EDU/PROP EXEC CHOOSE ATTIT ALL/VALS...SOC
OBS HIST/WRIT TIME/SEQ LEAGUE/NAT NAZI TOT/POP 20.
PAGE 86 B1741
                                                      B39
ZIMMERN A.,MODERN POLITICAL DOCTRINE. WOR-45   NAT/G
CULTURE SOCIETY ECO/UNDEV DELIB/GP EX/STRUC CREATE ECO/TAC
DOMIN COERCE NAT/LISM ATTIT RIGID/FLEX ORD/FREE PWR BAL/PWR
WEALTH...POLICY CONCPT OBS TIME/SEQ TREND TOT/POP   INT/TRADE
LEAGUE/NAT 20. PAGE 119 B2402
                                                      B42
US STATE DEPT.,PEACE AND WAR: UNITED STATES FOREIGN DIPLOM
POLICY, 1931-41. CULTURE FORCES ROUTINE CHOOSE   USA-45
ATTIT DRIVE PERSON 20. PAGE 111 B2237   PLAN
                                                      L44
HAILEY,"THE FUTURE OF COLONIAL PEOPLES." WOR-45   PLAN
CONSTN CULTURE ECO/UNDEV AGRI MARKET INT/ORG NAT/G CONCPT
SECT CONSULT ECO/TAC LEGIT ADMIN NAT/LISM ALL/VALS DIPLOM
...SOC OBS TREND STERTYP CMN/WLTH LEAGUE/NAT   UK
PARLIAMENT 20. PAGE 45 B0916
                                                      B47
CONOVER H.F.,NON-SELF-GOVERNING AREAS. BELGIUM   BIBLIOG/A
FRANCE ITALY UK WOR-45 CULTURE ECO/UNDEV INT/ORG   COLONIAL
LOC/G NAT/G ECO/TAC INT/TRADE ADMIN HEALTH...SOC   DIPLOM
UN. PAGE 23 B0465
                                                      B47
CROCKER W.R.,ON GOVERNING COLONIES: BEING AN   COLONIAL
OUTLINE OF THE REAL ISSUES AND A COMPARISON OF THE POLICY
BRITISH, FRENCH, AND BELGIAN... AFR BELGIUM FRANCE GOV/COMP
UK CULTURE SOVEREIGN...OBS 20. PAGE 25 B0505   ADMIN
                                                      B47
LASSWELL H.D.,THE ANALYSIS OF POLITICAL BEHAVIOUR: R+D
AN EMPIRICAL APPROACH. WOR+45 CULTURE NAT/G FORCES ACT/RES
EDU/PROP ADMIN ATTIT PERCEPT KNOWL...PHIL/SCI PSY   ELITES
SOC NEW/IDEA OBS INT GEN/METH NAZI 20. PAGE 63
B1267
                                                      B48
BONAPARTE M.,MYTHS OF WAR. GERMANY WOR+45 WOR-45   ROUTINE
CULTURE SOCIETY NAT/G FORCES LEGIT ATTIT ALL/VALS   MYTH
...CONCPT HIST/WRIT TIME/SEQ 20 JEWS. PAGE 13 B0271 WAR
                                                      B48
TOWSTER J.,POLITICAL POWER IN THE USSR: 1917-1947. EX/STRUC
USSR CONSTN CULTURE ELITES CREATE PLAN COERCE   NAT/G
CENTRAL ATTIT RIGID/FLEX ORD/FREE...BIBLIOG   MARXISM
SOC/INTEG 20 LENIN/VI STALIN/J. PAGE 105 B2124   PWR
                                                      B50
MONTGOMERY H.,CRACKER PARTIES. CULTURE EX/STRUC   POL/PAR
LEAD PWR POPULISM...TIME/SEQ 19 GEORGIA CALHOUN/JC PROVS
COBB/HOWLL JACKSON/A. PAGE 74 B1505   ELITES
                                                      BIOG
                                                      B51
SWISHER C.B.,THE THEORY AND PRACTICE OF AMERICAN   CONSTN
NATIONAL GOVERNMENT. CULTURE LEGIS DIPLOM ADJUD   NAT/G
ADMIN WAR PEACE ORD/FREE...MAJORIT 17/20. PAGE 102 GOV/REL
B2063   GEN/LAWS
                                                      B52
DAY E.E.,EDUCATION FOR FREEDOM AND RESPONSIBILITY. SCHOOL
FUT USA+45 CULTURE CONSULT EDU/PROP ATTIT SKILL   KNOWL
...MGT CONCPT OBS GEN/LAWS COLD/WAR 20. PAGE 27
B0547
                                                      B52
MAIER N.R.F.,PRINCIPLES OF HUMAN RELATIONS. WOR+45 INDUS
WOR-45 CULTURE SOCIETY ROUTINE ATTIT DRIVE PERCEPT
PERSON RIGID/FLEX SUPEGO PWR...PSY CONT/OBS RECORD
TOT/POP VAL/FREE 20. PAGE 68 B1379
                                                      B53
PIERCE R.A.,RUSSIAN CENTRAL ASIA, 1867-1917: A   BIBLIOG

SELECTED BIBLIOGRAPHY (PAMPHLET). USSR LAW CULTURE COLONIAL
NAT/G EDU/PROP WAR...GEOG SOC 19/20. PAGE 83 B1671 ADMIN
                                                    COM
                                                    B53
SAYLES L.R..THE LOCAL UNION. CONSTN CULTURE   LABOR
DELIB/GP PARTIC CHOOSE GP/REL INGP/REL ATTIT ROLE   LEAD
...MAJORIT DECISION MGT. PAGE 93 B1873   ADJUD
                                                    ROUTINE
                                                    B53
WAGLEY C..AMAZON TOWN: A STUDY OF MAN IN THE   SOC
TROPICS. BRAZIL L/A+17C STRATA STRUCT ECO/UNDEV   NEIGH
AGRI EX/STRUC RACE/REL DISCRIM HABITAT WEALTH...OBS CULTURE
SOC/EXP 20. PAGE 113 B2273   INGP/REL
                                                    S53
DRUCKER P.F.."THE EMPLOYEE SOCIETY." STRUCT BAL/PWR LABOR
PARTIC REPRESENT PWR...DECISION CONCPT. PAGE 30   MGT
B0619   WORKER
                                                    CULTURE
                                                    B54
ALLPORT G.W..THE NATURE OF PREJUDICE. USA+45 WOR+45 CULTURE
STRATA FACE/GP KIN NEIGH SECT ADMIN GP/REL DISCRIM PERSON
ATTIT DRIVE LOVE RESPECT...PSY SOC MYTH QU/SEMANT   RACE/REL
20. PAGE 4 B0078   B54
BIESANZ J..MODERN SOCIETY: AN INTRODUCTION TO   SOCIETY
SOCIAL SCIENCE. COM CONSTN STRUCT FAM MUNIC NAT/G   PROB/SOLV
SECT EX/STRUC LEGIS GP/REL PERSON...SOC 20. PAGE 12 CULTURE
B0237   B54
LAPIERRE R.T..A THEORY OF SOCIAL CONTROL. STRUCT   CONTROL
ADMIN ROUTINE SANCTION ANOMIE AUTHORIT DRIVE PERSON VOL/ASSN
PWR...MAJORIT CONCPT CLASSIF. PAGE 62 B1260   CULTURE
                                                    B54
MATTHEWS D.R..THE SOCIAL BACKGROUND OF POLITICAL   DECISION
DECISION-MAKERS. CULTURE SOCIETY STRATA FAM   BIOG
EX/STRUC LEAD ATTIT BIO/SOC DRIVE PERSON ALL/VALS   SOC
HIST/WRIT. PAGE 71 B1431   B54
SCHWARTZ B..FRENCH ADMINISTRATIVE LAW AND THE   JURID
COMMON-LAW WORLD. FRANCE CULTURE LOC/G NAT/G PROVS LAW
DELIB/GP EX/STRUC LEGIS PROB/SOLV CT/SYS EXEC   METH/COMP
GOV/REL...IDEA/COMP ENGLSH/LAW. PAGE 95 B1912   ADJUD
                                                    B54
TOTOK W..HANDBUCH DER BIBLIOGRAPHISCHEN   BIBLIOG/A
NACHSCHLAGEWERKE. GERMANY LAW CULTURE ADMIN...SOC   NAT/G
20. PAGE 105 B2121   DIPLOM
                                                    POLICY
                                                    L54
ROSTOW W.W.."ASIAN LEADERSHIP AND FREE-WORLD   ATTIT
ALLIANCE." ASIA COM USA+45 CULTURE ELITES INTELL   LEGIT
NAT/G TEC/DEV ECO/TAC COLONIAL PARL/PROC   DIPLOM
ROUTINE COERCE DRIVE ORD/FREE MARXISM...PSY CONCPT.
PAGE 90 B1829
                                                    B55
APTER D.E..THE GOLD COAST IN TRANSITION. FUT CONSTN AFR
CULTURE SOCIETY ECO/UNDEV FAM KIN LOC/G NAT/G   SOVEREIGN
POL/PAR LEGIS TOP/EX EDU/PROP LEGIT ADMIN ATTIT
PERSON PWR...CONCPT STAT INT CENSUS TOT/POP
VAL/FREE. PAGE 6 B0120
                                                    S55
ANGELL R.."GOVERNMENTS AND PEOPLES AS A FOCI FOR   FUT
PEACE-ORIENTED RESEARCH." WOR+45 CULTURE SOCIETY   SOC
FACE/GP ACT/RES CREATE PLAN DIPLOM EDU/PROP ROUTINE PEACE
ATTIT PERCEPT SKILL...POLICY CONCPT OBS TREND
GEN/METH 20. PAGE 5 B0110
                                                    B56
IRIKURA J.K..SOUTHEAST ASIA: SELECTED ANNOTATED   BIBLIOG/A
BIBLIOGRAPHY OF JAPANESE PUBLICATIONS. CULTURE   S/ASIA
ADMIN RACE/REL 20 CHINJAP. PAGE 55 B1104   DIPLOM
                                                    B56
MANNONI D.O..PROSPERO AND CALIBAN: THE PSYCHOLOGY   CULTURE
OF COLONIZATION. AFR EUR+WWI FAM KIN MUNIC SECT   COLONIAL
DOMIN ADMIN ATTIT DRIVE LOVE PWR RESPECT...PSY SOC
CONCPT MYTH OBS DEEP/INT BIOG GEN/METH MALAGASY 20.
PAGE 69 B1394
                                                    B56
WHYTE W.H. JR..THE ORGANIZATION MAN. CULTURE FINAN ADMIN
VOL/ASSN DOMIN EDU/PROP EXEC DISPL HABITAT ROLE   LG/CO
...PERS/TEST STERTYP. PAGE 116 B2343   PERSON
                                                    CONSEN
                                                    L56
EISENTADT S.N.."POLITICAL STRUGGLE IN BUREAUCRATIC ADMIN
SOCIETIES" ASIA CULTURE ADJUD SANCTION PWR   CHIEF
BUREAUCRCY OTTOMAN BYZANTINE. PAGE 33 B0661   CONTROL
                                                    ROUTINE
                                                    B57
CENTRAL ASIAN RESEARCH CENTRE.BIBLIOGRAPHY OF   BIBLIOG/A
RECENT SOVIET SOURCE MATERIAL ON SOVIET CENTRAL   COM
ASIA AND THE BORDERLANDS. AFGHANISTN INDIA PAKISTAN CULTURE
UAR USSR ECO/UNDEV AGRI EXTR/IND INDUS ACADEM ADMIN NAT/G
...HEAL HUM LING CON/ANAL 20. PAGE 19 B0399
                                                    B57
CHANDRA S..PARTIES AND POLITICS AT THE MUGHAL   POL/PAR
COURT: 1707-1740. INDIA CULTURE EX/STRUC CREATE   ELITES
PLAN PWR...BIBLIOG/A 18. PAGE 20 B0405   NAT/G

                                                    B57
IKE N..JAPANESE POLITICS. INTELL STRUCT AGRI INDUS NAT/G
FAM KIN LABOR PRESS CHOOSE ATTIT...DECISION BIBLIOG ADMIN
19/20 CHINJAP. PAGE 53 B1075   POL/PAR
                                                    CULTURE
                                                    B57
PYE L.W..THE POLICY IMPLICATIONS OF SOCIAL CHANGE   SOCIETY
IN NON-WESTERN SOCIETIES. ASIA USA+45 CULTURE   ORD/FREE
STRUCT NAT/G ECO/TAC ADMIN ROLE...POLICY SOC.   ECO/UNDEV
PAGE 85 B1723   DIPLOM
                                                    B57
SOUTH PACIFIC COMMISSION.INDEX OF SOCIAL SCIENCE   BIBLIOG/A
RESEARCH THESES ON THE SOUTH PACIFIC. S/ASIA ACADEM ACT/RES
ADMIN COLONIAL...SOC 20. PAGE 99 B2000   SECT
                                                    CULTURE
                                                    B58
COWAN L.G..LOCAL GOVERNMENT IN WEST AFRICA. AFR   LOC/G
FRANCE UK CULTURE KIN POL/PAR CHIEF LEGIS CREATE   COLONIAL
ADMIN PARTIC GOV/REL GP/REL...METH/COMP 20. PAGE 24 SOVEREIGN
B0498   REPRESENT
                                                    B58
MASON J.B..THAILAND BIBLIOGRAPHY. S/ASIA THAILAND   BIBLIOG/A
CULTURE EDU/PROP ADMIN...GEOG SOC LING 20. PAGE 70 ECO/UNDEV
B1423   DIPLOM
                                                    NAT/G
                                                    B58
PAN AMERICAN UNION.REPERTORIO DE PUBLICACIONES   BIBLIOG
PERIODICAS ACTUALES LATINO-AMERICANAS. CULTURE   L/A+17C
ECO/UNDEV ADMIN LEAD GOV/REL 20 OAS. PAGE 81 B1630 NAT/G
                                                    DIPLOM
                                                    B58
SHAW S.J..THE FINANCIAL AND ADMINISTRATIVE   FINAN
ORGANIZATION AND DEVELOPMENT OF OTTOMAN EGYPT   ADMIN
1517-1798. UAR LOC/G FORCES BUDGET INT/TRADE TAX   GOV/REL
EATING INCOME WEALTH...CHARTS BIBLIOG 16/18 OTTOMAN CULTURE
NAPOLEON/B. PAGE 96 B1940
                                                    B59
ELLIOTT O..MEN AT THE TOP. USA+45 CULTURE EX/STRUC TOP/EX
PRESS GOV/REL ATTIT ALL/VALS...OBS INT QU 20.   PERSON
PAGE 33 B0668   LEAD
                                                    POLICY
                                                    B59
FAYERWEATHER J..THE EXECUTIVE OVERSEAS: INT/TRADE
ADMINISTRATIVE ATTITUDES AND RELATIONSHIPS IN A   TOP/EX
FOREIGN CULTURE. USA+45 WOR+45 CULTURE LG/CO SML/CO NAT/COMP
ATTIT...MGT PERS/COMP 20 MEXIC/AMER. PAGE 35 B0709 PERS/REL
                                                    B59
GINSBURG M..LAW AND OPINION IN ENGLAND. UK CULTURE JURID
KIN LABOR LEGIS EDU/PROP ADMIN CT/SYS CRIME OWN   POLICY
HEALTH...ANTHOL 20 ENGLSH/LAW. PAGE 40 B0802   ECO/TAC
                                                    B59
INTERAMERICAN CULTURAL COUN.LISTA DE LIBROS   BIBLIOG/A
REPRESENTAVOS DE AMERICA. CULTURE DIPLOM ADMIN 20. NAT/G
PAGE 54 B1093   L/A+17C
                                                    SOC
                                                    B59
JANOWITZ M..SOCIOLOGY AND THE MILITARY   FORCES
ESTABLISHMENT. USA+45 WOR+45 CULTURE SOCIETY   SOC
PROF/ORG CONSULT EX/STRUC PLAN TEC/DEV DIPLOM DOMIN
COERCE DRIVE RIGID/FLEX ORD/FREE PWR SKILL COLD/WAR
20. PAGE 55 B1121
                                                    B59
LEMBERG E..DIE VERTRIEBENEN IN WESTDEUTSCHLAND (3   GP/REL
VOLS.). GERMANY/W CULTURE STRUCT AGRI PROVS ADMIN   INGP/REL
...JURID 20 MIGRATION. PAGE 64 B1287   SOCIETY
                                                    B59
PARK R.L..LEADERSHIP AND POLITICAL INSTITUTIONS IN NAT/G
INDIA. S/ASIA CULTURE ECO/UNDEV LOC/G MUNIC PROVS   EXEC
LEGIS PLAN ADMIN LEAD ORD/FREE WEALTH...GEOG SOC   INDIA
BIOG TOT/POP VAL/FREE 20. PAGE 81 B1633
                                                    S59
GABLE R.W.."CULTURE AND ADMINISTRATION IN IRAN."   ADMIN
IRAN EXEC PARTIC REPRESENT PWR. PAGE 38 B0770   CULTURE
                                                    EX/STRUC
                                                    INGP/REL
                                                    S59
PADELFORD N.J.."REGIONAL COOPERATION IN THE SOUTH   INT/ORG
PACIFIC: THE SOUTH PACIFIC COMMISSION." FUT   ADMIN
NEW/ZEALND UK WOR+45 CULTURE ECO/UNDEV LOC/G
VOL/ASSN CON/ANAL UNESCO VAL/FREE AUSTRAL 20.
PAGE 80 B1622
                                                    S59
SUTTON F.X.."REPRESENTATION AND THE NATURE OF   NAT/G
POLITICAL SYSTEMS." UNIV WOR-45 CULTURE SOCIETY   CONCPT
STRATA INT/ORG FORCES JUDGE DOMIN LEGIT EXEC REGION
REPRESENT ATTIT ORD/FREE RESPECT...SOC HIST/WRIT
TIME/SEQ. PAGE 102 B2057
                                                    S59
ZAUBERMAN A.."SOVIET BLOC ECONOMIC INTEGRATION."   MARKET
COM CULTURE INTELL ECO/DEV INDUS TOP/EX ACT/RES   INT/ORG
PLAN ECO/TAC INT/TRADE ROUTINE CHOOSE ATTIT   USSR
...TIME/SEQ 20. PAGE 119 B2399   TOTALISM
                                                    B60
FURNISS E.S..FRANCE, TROUBLED ALLY. EUR+WWI FUT   NAT/G
CULTURE SOCIETY BAL/PWR ADMIN ATTIT DRIVE PWR   FRANCE
...TREND TOT/POP 20 DEGAULLE/C. PAGE 38 B0767

KERR C.,INDUSTRIALISM AND INDUSTRIAL MAN. CULTURE
SOCIETY ECO/UNDEV NAT/G ADMIN PRODUC WEALTH
...PREDICT TREND NAT/COMP 19/20. PAGE 59 B1197
B60
WORKER
MGT
ECO/DEV
INDUS

LEYDER J.,BIBLIOGRAPHIE DE L'ENSEIGNEMENT SUPERIEUR
ET DE LA RECHERCHE SCIENTIFIQUE EN AFRIQUE
INTERTROPICALE (2 VOLS.). AFR CULTURE ECO/UNDEV
AGRI PLAN EDU/PROP ADMIN COLONIAL...GEOG SOC/INTEG
20 NEGRO. PAGE 65 B1309
B60
BIBLIOG/A
ACT/RES
ACADEM
R+D

PIERCE R.A.,RUSSIAN CENTRAL ASIA, 1867-1917. ASIA
RUSSIA CULTURE AGRI INDUS EDU/PROP REV NAT/LISM
...CHARTS BIBLIOG 19/20 BOLSHEVISM INTERVENT.
PAGE 83 B1672
B60
COLONIAL
DOMIN
ADMIN
ECO/UNDEV

ROEPKE W.,A HUMANE ECONOMY: THE SOCIAL FRAMEWORK OF
THE FREE MARKET. FUT USSR WOR+45 CULTURE SOCIETY
ECO/DEV PLAN ECO/TAC ADMIN ATTIT PERSON RIGID/FLEX
SUPEGO MORAL WEALTH SOCISM...POLICY OLD/LIB CONCPT
TREND GEN/LAWS 20. PAGE 90 B1811
B60
DRIVE
EDU/PROP
CAP/ISM

SMITH M.G.,GOVERNMENT IN ZAZZAU 1800-1950. NIGERIA
UK CULTURE SOCIETY LOC/G ADMIN COLONIAL
...METH/CNCPT NEW/IDEA METH 19/20. PAGE 98 B1983
B60
REGION
CONSTN
KIN
ECO/UNDEV

APTER D.E.,"THE ROLE OF TRADITIONALISM IN THE
POLITICAL MODERNIZATION OF GHANA AND UGANDA" (BMR)"
AFR GHANA UGANDA CULTURE NAT/G POL/PAR NAT/LISM
...CON/ANAL 20. PAGE 6 B0121
S60
CONSERVE
ADMIN
GOV/COMP
PROB/SOLV

EMERSON R.,"THE EROSION OF DEMOCRACY." AFR FUT LAW
CULTURE INTELL SOCIETY ECO/UNDEV FAM LOC/G NAT/G
FORCES PLAN TEC/DEV ECO/TAC ADMIN CT/SYS ATTIT
ORD/FREE PWR...SOCIALIST SOC CONCPT STAND/INT
TIME/SEQ WORK 20. PAGE 33 B0671
S60
S/ASIA
POL/PAR

GARNICK D.H.,"ON THE ECONOMIC FEASIBILITY OF A
MIDDLE EASTERN COMMON MARKET." AFR ISLAM CULTURE
INDUS NAT/G PLAN TEC/DEV ECO/TAC ADMIN ATTIT DRIVE
RIGID/FLEX...PLURIST STAT TREND GEN/LAWS 20.
PAGE 39 B0784
S60
MARKET
INT/TRADE

MODELSKI G.,"AUSTRALIA AND SEATO." S/ASIA USA+45
CULTURE INTELL ECO/DEV NAT/G PLAN DIPLOM ADMIN
ROUTINE ATTIT SKILL...MGT TIME/SEQ AUSTRAL 20
SEATO. PAGE 74 B1493
S60
INT/ORG
ACT/RES

REISELBACH L.N.,"THE BASIS OF ISOLATIONIST
BEHAVIOR." USA+45 USA-45 CULTURE ECO/DEV LOC/G
NAT/G ADMIN ROUTINE CHOOSE BIO/SOC DRIVE RIGID/FLEX
...CENSUS SAMP TREND CHARTS TOT/POP 20. PAGE 87
B1765
S60
ATTIT
DIPLOM
ECO/TAC

THOMPSON K.W.,"MORAL PURPOSE IN FOREIGN POLICY:
REALITIES AND ILLUSIONS." WOR+45 WOR-45 LAW CULTURE
SOCIETY INT/ORG PLAN ADJUD ADMIN COERCE RIGID/FLEX
SUPEGO KNOWL ORD/FREE PWR...SOC TREND SOC/EXP
TOT/POP 20. PAGE 104 B2104
S60
MORAL
JURID
DIPLOM

FITZSIMMONS T.,"USSR: ITS PEOPLE, ITS SOCIETY, ITS
CULTURE." USSR FAM SECT DIPLOM EDU/PROP ADMIN
RACE/REL ATTIT...POLICY CHARTS BIBLIOG 20. PAGE 36
B0728
C60
CULTURE
STRUCT
SOCIETY
COM

RHODESIA-NYASA NATL ARCHIVES,A SELECT BIBLIOGRAPHY
OF RECENT PUBLICATIONS CONCERNING THE FEDERATION OF
RHODESIA AND NYASALAND (PAMPHLET). MALAWI RHODESIA
LAW CULTURE STRUCT ECO/UNDEV LEGIS...GEOG 20.
PAGE 88 B1770
N60
BIBLIOG
ADMIN
ORD/FREE
NAT/G

ETZIONI A.,COMPLEX ORGANIZATIONS: A SOCIOLOGICAL
READER. CLIENT CULTURE STRATA CREATE OP/RES ADMIN
...POLICY METH/CNCPT BUREAUCRCY. PAGE 34 B0683
B61
VOL/ASSN
STRUCT
CLASSIF
PROF/ORG

FREYRE G.,THE PORTUGUESE AND THE TROPICS. L/A+17C
PORTUGAL SOCIETY PERF/ART ADMIN TASK GP/REL
...ART/METH CONCPT SOC/INTEG 20. PAGE 37 B0754
B61
COLONIAL
METH
PLAN
CULTURE

LASSWELL H.D.,PSYCOPATHOLOGY AND POLITICS. WOR-45
CULTURE SOCIETY FACE/GP NAT/G CONSULT CREATE
EDU/PROP EXEC ROUTINE DISPL DRIVE PERSON PWR
RESPECT...PSY CONCPT METH/CNCPT METH. PAGE 63 B1272
B61
ATTIT
GEN/METH

MARX K.,THE COMMUNIST MANIFESTO. IN (MENDEL A.
ESSENTIAL WORKS OF MARXISM, NEW YORK: BANTAM. FUT
MOD/EUR CULTURE ECO/DEV ECO/UNDEV AGRI FINAN INDUS
MARKET PROC/MFG LABOR MUNIC POL/PAR CONSULT FORCES
CREATE PLAN ADMIN ATTIT DRIVE RIGID/FLEX ORD/FREE
PWR RESPECT MARX/KARL WORK. PAGE 70 B1421
B61
COM
NEW/IDEA
CAP/ISM
REV

WEST F.J.,POLITICAL ADVANCEMENT IN THE SOUTH
B61
S/ASIA

PACIFIC. CONSTN CULTURE POL/PAR LEGIS DOMIN ADMIN
CHOOSE SOVEREIGN VAL/FREE 20 FIJI TAHITI SAMOA.
PAGE 115 B2325
LOC/G
COLONIAL

MILLER E.,"LEGAL ASPECTS OF UN ACTION IN THE
CONGO." AFR CULTURE ADMIN PEACE DRIVE RIGID/FLEX
ORD/FREE...WELF/ST JURID OBS UN CONGO 20. PAGE 73
B1480
S61
INT/ORG
LEGIT

NOVE A.,"THE SOVIET MODEL AND UNDERDEVELOPED
COUNTRIES." COM FUT USSR WOR+45 CULTURE ECO/DEV
POL/PAR FOR/AID EDU/PROP ADMIN MORAL WEALTH
...POLICY RECORD HIST/WRIT 20. PAGE 79 B1593
S61
ECO/UNDEV
PLAN

CARTER G.M.,THE GOVERNMENT OF THE SOVIET UNION.
USSR CULTURE LOC/G DIPLOM ECO/TAC ADJUD CT/SYS LEAD
WEALTH...CHARTS T 20 COM/PARTY. PAGE 19 B0390
B62
NAT/G
MARXISM
POL/PAR
EX/STRUC

KARNJAHAPRAKORN C.,MUNICIPAL GOVERNMENT IN THAILAND
AS AN INSTITUTION AND PROCESS OF SELF-GOVERNMENT.
THAILAND CULTURE FINAN EX/STRUC LEGIS PLAN CONTROL
GOV/REL EFFICIENCY ATTIT...POLICY 20. PAGE 58 B1176
B62
LOC/G
MUNIC
ORD/FREE
ADMIN

TAYLOR D.,THE BRITISH IN AFRICA. UK CULTURE
ECO/UNDEV INDUS DIPLOM INT/TRADE ADMIN WAR RACE/REL
ORD/FREE SOVEREIGN...POLICY BIBLIOG 15/20 CMN/WLTH.
PAGE 103 B2084
B62
AFR
COLONIAL
DOMIN

US LIBRARY OF CONGRESS,A LIST OF AMERICAN DOCTORAL
DISSERTATIONS ON AFRICA. SOCIETY SECT DIPLOM
EDU/PROP ADMIN...GEOG 19/20. PAGE 109 B2206
B62
BIBLIOG
AFR
ACADEM
CULTURE

FESLER J.W.,"FRENCH FIELD ADMINISTRATION: THE
BEGINNINGS." CHRIST-17C CULTURE SOCIETY STRATA
NAT/G ECO/TAC DOMIN EDU/PROP LEGIT ADJUD COERCE
ATTIT ALL/VALS...TIME/SEQ CON/ANAL GEN/METH
VAL/FREE 13/15. PAGE 35 B0714
S62
EX/STRUC
FRANCE

BANFIELD E.C.,CITY POLITICS. CULTURE LABOR LOC/G
POL/PAR LEGIS EXEC LEAD CHOOSE...DECISION NEGRO.
PAGE 9 B0178
B63
MUNIC
RIGID/FLEX
ATTIT

CHOJNACKI S.,REGISTER ON CURRENT RESEARCH ON
ETHIOPIA AND THE HORN OF AFRICA. ETHIOPIA LAW
CULTURE AGRI SECT EDU/PROP ADMIN...GEOG HEAL LING
20. PAGE 21 B0426
B63
BIBLIOG
ACT/RES
INTELL
ACADEM

DE VRIES E.,SOCIAL ASPECTS OF ECONOMIC DEVELOPMENT
IN LATIN AMERICA. CULTURE SOCIETY STRATA FINAN
INDUS INT/ORG DELIB/GP ACT/RES ECO/TAC EDU/PROP
ADMIN ATTIT SUPEGO HEALTH KNOWL ORD/FREE...SOC STAT
TREND ANTHOL TOT/POP VAL/FREE. PAGE 28 B0562
B63
L/A+17C
ECO/UNDEV

KAPP W.K.,HINDU CULTURE: ECONOMIC DEVELOPMENT AND
ECONOMIC PLANNING IN INDIA. INDIA S/ASIA CULTURE
ECO/TAC EDU/PROP ADMIN ALL/VALS...POLICY MGT
TIME/SEQ VAL/FREE 20. PAGE 58 B1171
B63
SECT
ECO/UNDEV

RUITENBEER H.M.,THE DILEMMA OF ORGANIZATIONAL
SOCIETY. CULTURE ECO/DEV MUNIC SECT TEC/DEV
EDU/PROP NAT/LISM ORD/FREE...NAT/COMP 20 RIESMAN/D
WHYTE/WF MERTON/R MEAD/MARG JASPERS/K. PAGE 92
B1855
B63
PERSON
ROLE
ADMIN
WORKER

SWERDLOW I.,DEVELOPMENT ADMINISTRATION: CONCEPTS
AND PROBLEMS. WOR+45 CULTURE SOCIETY STRATA
DELIB/GP EX/STRUC ACT/RES PLAN ECO/TAC DOMIN LEGIT
ATTIT RIGID/FLEX SUPEGO HEALTH PWR...MGT CONCPT
ANTHOL VAL/FREE. PAGE 102 B2062
B63
ECO/UNDEV
ADMIN

THOMETZ C.E.,THE DECISION-MAKERS: THE POWER
STRUCTURE OF DALLAS. USA+45 CULTURE EX/STRUC DOMIN
LEGIT GP/REL ATTIT OBJECTIVE...INT CHARTS GP/COMP.
PAGE 104 B2101
B63
ELITES
MUNIC
PWR
DECISION

WEINER M.,POLITICAL CHANGE IN SOUTH ASIA. CEYLON
INDIA PAKISTAN S/ASIA CULTURE ELITES ECO/UNDEV
EX/STRUC ADMIN CONTROL CHOOSE CONSERVE...GOV/COMP
ANTHOL 20. PAGE 115 B2315
B63
NAT/G
CONSTN
TEC/DEV

EMERSON R.,"POLITICAL MODERNIZATION." WOR+45
CULTURE ECO/UNDEV NAT/G FORCES ECO/TAC DOMIN
EDU/PROP LEGIT COERCE ALL/VALS...CONCPT TIME/SEQ
VAL/FREE 20. PAGE 33 B0672
L63
POL/PAR
ADMIN

SPITZ A.A.,"DEVELOPMENT ADMINISTRATION: AN
ANNOTATED BIBLIOGRAPHY." WOR+45 CULTURE SOCIETY
STRATA DELIB/GP EX/STRUC TOP/EX ACT/RES ECO/TAC
DOMIN EDU/PROP LEGIT COERCE ATTIT ALL/VALS...MGT
VAL/FREE. PAGE 99 B2009
L63
ADMIN
ECO/UNDEV

ARASTEH R.,"THE ROLE OF INTELLECTUALS IN
ADMINISTRATIVE DEVELOPMENT AND SOCIAL CHANGE IN
MODERN IRAN." ISLAM CULTURE NAT/G CONSULT ACT/RES
S63
INTELL
ADMIN
IRAN

EDU/PROP EXEC ATTIT BIO/SOC PERCEPT SUPEGO ALL/VALS
...POLICY MGT PSY SOC CONCPT 20. PAGE 6 B0123

S63
HARRIS R.L.,."A COMPARATIVE ANALYSIS OF THE   DELIB/GP
ADMINISTRATIVE SYSTEMS OF CANADA AND CEYLON."   EX/STRUC
S/ASIA CULTURE SOCIETY STRATA TOP/EX ACT/RES DOMIN   CANADA
EDU/PROP LEGIT COERCE ATTIT SUPEGO ALL/VALS...MGT   CEYLON
CHARTS GEN/LAWS VAL/FREE 20. PAGE 47 B0955

B64
ANDREN N.,.GOVERNMENT AND POLITICS IN THE NORDIC   CONSTN
COUNTRIES: DENMARK, FINLAND, ICELAND, NORWAY,   NAT/G
SWEDEN. DENMARK FINLAND ICELAND NORWAY SWEDEN   CULTURE
POL/PAR CHIEF LEGIS ADMIN REGION REPRESENT ATTIT   GOV/COMP
CONSERVE...CHARTS BIBLIOG/A 20. PAGE 5 B0102

B64
APTER D.E.,.IDEOLOGY AND DISCONTENT. FUT WOR+45   ACT/RES
CONSTN CULTURE INTELL SOCIETY STRUCT INT/ORG NAT/G   ATTIT
DELIB/GP LEGIS CREATE PLAN TEC/DEV EDU/PROP EXEC
PERCEPT PERSON RIGID/FLEX ALL/VALS...POLICY
TOT/POP. PAGE 6 B0122

B64
BRIGHT J.R.,.RESEARCH, DEVELOPMENT AND TECHNOLOGICAL   TEC/DEV
INNOVATION. CULTURE R+D CREATE PLAN PROB/SOLV   NEW/IDEA
AUTOMAT RISK PERSON...DECISION CONCPT PREDICT   INDUS
BIBLIOG. PAGE 15 B0308   MGT

B64
CAPLOW T.,.PRINCIPLES OF ORGANIZATION. UNIV CULTURE   VOL/ASSN
STRUCT CREATE INGP/REL UTOPIA...GEN/LAWS TIME.   CONCPT
PAGE 18 B0374   SIMUL
                                                               EX/STRUC
B64
ETZIONI A.,.MODERN ORGANIZATIONS. CLIENT STRUCT   MGT
DOMIN CONTROL LEAD PERS/REL AUTHORIT...CLASSIF   ADMIN
BUREAUCRCY. PAGE 34 B0685   PLAN
                                                               CULTURE
B64
FORBES A.H.,.CURRENT RESEARCH IN BRITISH STUDIES. UK   BIBLIOG
CONSTN CULTURE POL/PAR SECT DIPLOM ADMIN...JURID   PERSON
BIOG WORSHIP 20. PAGE 36 B0736   NAT/G
                                                               PARL/PROC
B64
HICKEY G.C.,.VILLAGE IN VIETNAM. USA+45 VIETNAM LAW   CULTURE
AGRI FAM SECT ADMIN ATTIT...SOC CHARTS WORSHIP 20.   SOCIETY
PAGE 49 B1003   STRUCT
                                                               S/ASIA
B64
MAHAR J.M.,.INDIA: A CRITICAL BIBLIOGRAPHY. INDIA   BIBLIOG/A
PAKISTAN CULTURE ECO/UNDEV LOC/G POL/PAR SECT   S/ASIA
PROB/SOLV DIPLOM ADMIN COLONIAL PARL/PROC ATTIT 20.   NAT/G
PAGE 68 B1377   LEAD

B64
TURNER M.C.,.LIBROS EN VENTA EN HISPANOAMERICA Y   BIBLIOG
ESPANA. SPAIN LAW CONSTN CULTURE ADMIN LEAD...HUM   L/A+17C
SOC 20. PAGE 106 B2139   NAT/G
                                                               DIPLOM
B64
UN PUB. INFORM. ORGAN.,.EVERY MAN'S UNITED NATIONS.   INT/ORG
UNIV WOR+45 CONSTN CULTURE SOCIETY ECO/DEV   ROUTINE
ECO/UNDEV NAT/G ACT/RES PLAN ECO/TAC INT/TRADE
EDU/PROP LEGIT PEACE ATTIT ALL/VALS...POLICY HUM
INT/LAW CONCPT CHARTS UN TOT/POP 20. PAGE 106 B2150

L64
MACKINTOSH J.P.,."NIGERIA'S EXTERNAL AFFAIRS." UK   AFR
CULTURE ECO/UNDEV NAT/G VOL/ASSN EDU/PROP LEGIT   DIPLOM
ADMIN ATTIT ORD/FREE PWR 20. PAGE 68 B1365   NIGERIA

S64
CLIGNET R.,."POTENTIAL ELITES IN GHANA AND THE IVORY   PWR
COAST: A PRELIMINARY SURVEY." AFR CULTURE ELITES   LEGIT
STRATA KIN NAT/G SECT DOMIN EXEC ORD/FREE RESPECT   IVORY/CST
SKILL...POLICY RELATIV GP/COMP NAT/COMP 20. PAGE 21   GHANA
B0438

S64
JOHNSON K.F.,."CAUSAL FACTORS IN LATIN AMERICAN   L/A+17C
POLITICAL INSTABILITY." CULTURE NAT/G VOL/ASSN   PERCEPT
EX/STRUC FORCES EDU/PROP LEGIT ADMIN COERCE REV   ELITES
ATTIT KNOWL PWR...STYLE RECORD CHARTS WORK 20.
PAGE 57 B1144

S64
NASH M.,."SOCIAL PREREQUISITES TO ECONOMIC GROWTH IN ECO/DEV
LATIN AMERICA AND SOUTHEAST ASIA." L/A+17C S/ASIA   PERCEPT
CULTURE SOCIETY ECO/UNDEV AGRI INDUS NAT/G PLAN
TEC/DEV EDU/PROP ROUTINE ALL/VALS...POLICY RELATIV
SOC NAT/COMP WORK TOT/POP 20. PAGE 77 B1558

C64
SCOTT R.E.,."MEXICAN GOVERNMENT IN TRANSITION (REV   NAT/G
ED)" CULTURE STRUCT POL/PAR CHIEF ADMIN LOBBY REV   L/A+17C
CHOOSE GP/REL DRIVE...BIBLIOG METH 20 MEXIC/AMER.   ROUTINE
PAGE 95 B1920   CONSTN

B65
BERNDT R.M.,.ABORIGINAL MAN IN AUSTRALIA. LAW DOMIN   SOC
ADMIN COLONIAL MARRIAGE HABITAT ORD/FREE...LING   CULTURE
CHARTS ANTHOL BIBLIOG WORSHIP 20 AUSTRAL ABORIGINES   SOCIETY
MUSIC ELKIN/AP. PAGE 11 B0225   STRUCT

B65
DAVISON W.P.,.INTERNATIONAL POLITICAL COMMUNICATION.   EDU/PROP
COM USA+45 WOR+45 CULTURE ECO/UNDEV NAT/G PROB/SOLV   DIPLOM

PRESS TV ADMIN 20 FILM. PAGE 27 B0545   PERS/REL
                                                               COM/IND
B65
LAMBIRI I.,.SOCIAL CHANGE IN A GREEK COUNTRY TOWN.   INDUS
GREECE FAM PROB/SOLV ROUTINE TASK LEISURE INGP/REL   WORKER
CONSEN ORD/FREE...SOC INT QU CHARTS 20. PAGE 62   CULTURE
B1252   NEIGH

B65
MOORE W.E.,.THE IMPACT OF INDUSTRY. CULTURE STRUCT   INDUS
ORD/FREE...TREND 20. PAGE 75 B1516   MGT
                                                               TEC/DEV
                                                               ECO/UNDEV
B65
NATIONAL BOOK CENTRE PAKISTAN,.BOOKS ON PAKISTAN: A   BIBLIOG
BIBLIOGRAPHY. PAKISTAN CULTURE DIPLOM ADMIN ATTIT   CONSTN
...MAJORIT SOC CONCPT 20. PAGE 77 B1560   S/ASIA
                                                               NAT/G
B65
REISS A.J. JR.,.SCHOOLS IN A CHANGING SOCIETY.   SCHOOL
CULTURE PROB/SOLV INSPECT DOMIN CONFER INGP/REL   EX/STRUC
RACE/REL AGE/C AGE/Y ALL/VALS...ANTHOL SOC/INTEG 20   ADJUST
NEWYORK/C. PAGE 87 B1766   ADMIN

B65
ROTBERG R.I.,.A POLITICAL HISTORY OF TROPICAL   AFR
AFRICA. EX/STRUC DIPLOM INT/TRADE DOMIN ADMIN   CULTURE
RACE/REL NAT/LISM PWR SOVEREIGN...GEOG TIME/SEQ   COLONIAL
BIBLIOG 1/20. PAGE 91 B1832

B65
SCOTT A.M.,.THE REVOLUTION IN STATECRAFT: INFORMAL   DIPLOM
PENETRATION. WOR+45 WOR-45 CULTURE INT/ORG FORCES   EDU/PROP
ECO/TAC ROUTINE...BIBLIOG 20. PAGE 95 B1918   FOR/AID

B65
STEINER K.,.LOCAL GOVERNMENT IN JAPAN. CONSTN   LOC/G
CULTURE NAT/G ADMIN CHOOSE...SOC STAT 20 CHINJAP.   SOCIETY
PAGE 100 B2030   JURID
                                                               ORD/FREE
L65
LASSWELL H.D.,."THE POLICY SCIENCES OF DEVELOPMENT."   PWR
CULTURE SOCIETY EX/STRUC CREATE ADMIN ATTIT KNOWL   METH/CNCPT
...SOC CONCPT SIMUL GEN/METH. PAGE 63 B1273   DIPLOM

L65
MATTHEWS D.G.,."A CURRENT BIBLIOGRAPHY ON ETHIOPIAN   BIBLIOG/A
AFFAIRS: A SELECT BIBLIOGRAPHY FROM 1950-1964."   ADMIN
ETHIOPIA LAW CULTURE ECO/UNDEV INDUS LABOR SECT   POL/PAR
FORCES DIPLOM CIVMIL/REL RACE/REL...LING STAT 20.   NAT/G
PAGE 71 B1428

S65
HAMILTON R.F.,."SKILL LEVEL AND POLITICS." USA+45   SKILL
CULTURE STRATA STRUCT LABOR CONSERVE NEW/LIB.   ADMIN
PAGE 46 B0933

S65
THOMAS F.C. JR.,."THE PEACE CORPS IN MOROCCO."   MOROCCO
CULTURE MUNIC PROVS CREATE ROUTINE TASK ADJUST   FRANCE
STRANGE...OBS PEACE/CORP. PAGE 104 B2099   FOR/AID
                                                               EDU/PROP
B66
BRAIBANTI R.,.RESEARCH ON THE BUREAUCRACY OF   HABITAT
PAKISTAN. PAKISTAN LAW CULTURE INTELL ACADEM LOC/G   NAT/G
SECT PRESS CT/SYS...LING CHARTS 20 BUREAUCRCY.   ADMIN
PAGE 15 B0294   CONSTN

B66
FABAR R.,.THE VISION AND THE NEED: LATE VICTORIAN   COLONIAL
IMPERIALIST AIMS. MOD/EUR UK WOR+45 CULTURE NAT/G   CONCPT
DIPLOM...TIME/SEQ METH/COMP 19 KIPLING/R   ADMIN
COMMONWLTH. PAGE 34 B0693   ATTIT

B66
SILBERMAN B.S.,.MODERN JAPANESE LEADERSHIP: LEAD
TRANSITION AND CHANGE. NAT/G POL/PAR CHIEF ADMIN   CULTURE
REPRESENT GP/REL ADJUST RIGID/FLEX...SOC METH/COMP   ELITES
ANTHOL 19/20 CHINJAP CHRISTIAN. PAGE 97 B1952   MUNIC

B66
WILLNER A.R.,.THE NEOTRADITIONAL ACCOMMODATION TO   INDONESIA
POLITICAL INDEPENDENCE* THE CASE OF INDONESIA *   CONSERVE
RESEARCH MONOGRAPH NO. 26. CULTURE ECO/UNDEV CREATE   ELITES
PROB/SOLV FOR/AID LEGIT COLONIAL EFFICIENCY   ADMIN
NAT/LISM ALL/VALS SOC. PAGE 117 B2355

S66
AFRICAN BIBLIOGRAPHIC CENTER,."A CURRENT VIEW OF   BIBLIOG/A
AFRICANA: A SELECT AND ANNOTATED BIBLIOGRAPHICAL   NAT/G
PUBLISHING GUIDE, 1965-1966." AFR CULTURE INDUS   TEC/DEV
LABOR SECT FOR/AID ADMIN COLONIAL REV RACE/REL   POL/PAR
SOCISM...LING 20. PAGE 3 B0063

C66
JACOB H.,."DIMENSIONS OF STATE POLITICS HEARD A. ED.   PROVS
STATE LEGIWLATURES IN AMERICAN POLIITCS." CULTURE   LEGIS
STRATA POL/PAR BUDGET TAX LOBBY ROUTINE GOV/REL   ROLE
...TRADIT DECISION GEOG. PAGE 55 B1112   REPRESENT

B67
COHEN R.,.COMPARATIVE POLITICAL SYSTEMS: STUDIES IN   ECO/UNDEV
THE POLITICS OF PRE-INDUSTRIAL SOCIETIES. WOR+45   STRUCT
WOR-45 CULTURE FAM KIN LOC/G ADMIN LEAD   SOCIETY
MARRIAGE...BIBLIOG 20. PAGE 22 B0447   GP/COMP

B67
DUN J.L.,.THE ESSENCE OF CHINESE CIVILIZATION. ASIA   CULTURE
FAM NAT/G TEC/DEV ADMIN SANCTION WAR HABITAT   SOCIETY
...ANTHOL WORSHIP. PAGE 31 B0630

EVANS R.H.,COEXISTENCE: COMMUNISM AND ITS PRACTICE IN BOLOGNA, 1945-1965. ITALY CAP/ISM ADMIN CHOOSE PEACE ORD/FREE...SOC STAT DEEP/INT SAMP CHARTS BIBLIOG 20. PAGE 34 B0690
B67 MARXISM CULTURE MUNIC POL/PAR

HOROWITZ I.L.,THE RISE AND FALL OF PROJECT CAMELOT: STUDIES IN THE RELATIONSHIP BETWEEN SOCIAL SCIENCE AND PRACTICAL POLITICS. USA+45 WOR+45 CULTURE FORCES LEGIS EXEC CIVMIL/REL KNOWL...POLICY SOC METH/CNCPT 20. PAGE 51 B1043
B67 NAT/G ACADEM ACT/RES GP/REL

RAVKIN A.,THE NEW STATES OF AFRICA (HEADLINE SERIES, NO. 183((PAMPHLET). CULTURE STRUCT INDUS COLONIAL NAT/LISM...SOC 20. PAGE 86 B1744
B67 AFR ECO/UNDEV SOCIETY ADMIN

BASTID M.,"ORIGINES ET DEVELOPMENT DE LA REVOLUTION CULTURELLE." CHINA/COM DOMIN ADMIN CONTROL LEAD COERCE CROWD ATTIT DRIVE MARXISM...POLICY 20. PAGE 10 B0195
S67 REV CULTURE ACADEM WORKER

FOX R.G.,"FAMILY, CASTE, AND COMMERCE IN A NORTH INDIAN MARKET TOWN." INDIA STRATA AGRI FACE/GP FAM NEIGH OP/RES BARGAIN ADMIN ROUTINE WEALTH...SOC CHARTS 20. PAGE 37 B0747
S67 CULTURE GP/REL ECO/UNDEV DIST/IND

HSUEH C.T.,"THE CULTURAL REVOLUTION AND LEADERSHIP CRISIS IN COMMUNIST CHINA." CHINA/COM POL/PAR EX/STRUC FORCES EDU/PROP ATTIT PWR...POLICY 20. PAGE 52 B1054
S67 LEAD REV CULTURE MARXISM

RAUM O.,"THE MODERN LEADERSHIP GROUP AMONG THE SOUTH AFRICAN XHOSA." SOUTH/AFR SOCIETY SECT EX/STRUC REPRESENT GP/REL INGP/REL PERSON ...METH/COMP 17/20 XHOSA NEGRO. PAGE 86 B1743
S67 RACE/REL KIN LEAD CULTURE

MACDONALD D.,AFRICANA; OR, THE HEART OF HEATHEN AFRICA. VOL. II: MISSION LIFE. SOCIETY STRATA KIN CREATE EDU/PROP ADMIN COERCE LITERACY HEALTH...MYTH WORSHIP 19 LIVNGSTN/D MISSION NEGRO. PAGE 67 B1355
B82 SECT AFR CULTURE ORD/FREE

CUMMINGS M.C. B1205,B1206

CUNNINGHAM R.M. B0072

CURLEY/JM....JAMES M. CURLEY

CURRENT EVENTS....SEE HIST

CURZON/GN....GEORGE NATHANIEL CURZON

CUSHMAN R.E. B0513

CUTLER R. B0514

CUTLIP S.M. B0515

CYBERNETICS....SEE FEEDBACK, SIMUL, CONTROL

CYCLES....SEE TIME/SEQ

CYERT R.M. B0516,B0517,B0518

CYPRUS....SEE ALSO APPROPRIATE TIME/SPACE/CULTURE INDEX

WORLD PEACE FOUNDATION,"INTERNATIONAL ORGANIZATIONS: SUMMARY OF ACTIVITIES." INDIA PAKISTAN TURKEY WOR+45 CONSTN CONSULT EX/STRUC ECO/TAC EDU/PROP LEGIT ORD/FREE...JURID SOC UN 20 CYPRESS. PAGE 118 B2375
L64 INT/ORG ROUTINE

AUSLAND J.C.,"CRISIS MANAGEMENT* BERLIN, CYPRUS, LAOS." CYPRUS LAOS FORCES CREATE PLAN EDU/PROP TASK CENTRAL PERSON RIGID/FLEX...DECISION MGT 20 BERLIN KENNEDY/JF MCNAMARA/R RUSK. PAGE 7 B0148
S66 OP/RES DIPLOM RISK ADMIN

CZECHOSLVK....CZECHOSLOVAKIA; SEE ALSO COM

KYRIAK T.E.,EAST EUROPE: BIBLIOGRAPHY--INDEX TO US JPRS RESEARCH TRANSLATIONS. ALBANIA BULGARIA COM CZECHOSLVK HUNGARY POLAND ROMANIA AGRI EXTR/IND FINAN SERV/IND INT/TRADE WEAPON...GEOG MGT SOC 20. PAGE 62 B1247
N BIBLIOG/A PRESS MARXISM INDUS

MEYER P.,THE JEWS IN THE SOVIET SATELLITES. CZECHOSLVK POLAND SOCIETY STRATA NAT/G BAL/PWR ECO/TAC EDU/PROP LEGIT ADMIN COERCE ATTIT DISPL PERCEPT HEALTH PWR RESPECT WEALTH...METH/CNCPT JEWS VAL/FREE NAZI 20. PAGE 73 B1474
B53 COM SECT TOTALISM USSR

POOL I.,SATELLITE GENERALS: A STUDY OF MILITARY ELITES IN THE SOVIET SPHERE. ASIA CHINA/COM COM CZECHOSLVK FUT HUNGARY POLAND ROMANIA USSR ELITES STRATA ADMIN ATTIT PWR SKILL...METH/CNCPT BIOG 20. PAGE 84 B1688
B55 FORCES CHOOSE

MURDESHWAR A.K.,ADMINISTRATIVE PROBLEMS RELATING TO NATIONALISATION: WITH SPECIAL REFERENCE TO INDIAN STATE ENTERPRISES. CZECHOSLVK FRANCE INDIA UK USA+45 LEGIS WORKER PROB/SOLV BUDGET PRICE CONTROL ...MGT GEN/LAWS 20 PARLIAMENT. PAGE 76 B1544
B57 NAT/G OWN INDUS ADMIN

HORECKY P.L.,"LIBRARY OF CONGRESS PUBLICATIONS IN AID OF USSR AND EAST EUROPEAN RESEARCH." BULGARIA CZECHOSLVK POLAND USSR YUGOSLAVIA NAT/G POL/PAR DIPLOM ADMIN GOV/REL...CLASSIF 20. PAGE 51 B1042
S64 BIBLIOG/A COM MARXISM

TABORSKY E.,"CHANGE IN CZECHOSLOVAKIA." COM USSR ELITES INTELL AGRI INDUS NAT/G DELIB/GP EX/STRUC ECO/TAC TOTALISM ATTIT RIGID/FLEX SOCISM...MGT CONCPT TREND 20. PAGE 102 B2067
S65 ECO/DEV PLAN CZECHOSLVK

LEVCIK B.,"WAGES AND EMPLOYMENT PROBLEMS IN THE NEW SYSTEM OF PLANNED MANAGEMENT IN CZECHOSLOVAKIA." CZECHOSLVK EUR+WWI NAT/G OP/RES PLAN ADMIN ROUTINE INGP/REL CENTRAL EFFICIENCY PRODUC DECISION. PAGE 64 B1300
S67 MARXISM WORKER MGT PAY

─────D─────────

DAC....DEVELOPMENT ASSISTANCE COMMITTEE (PART OF OECD)

DAHL D. B0519

DAHL R.A. B0520,B0521

DAHLBERG J.S. B0522

DAHOMEY....SEE ALSO AFR

DAHRENDORF R. B0523

DAKAR....DAKAR, SENEGAL

DAKIN R.E. B0524

DALAND R.T. B0525

DALTON M. B0526

DANELSKI D.J. B0527

DANGERFIELD R. B0528

DANIEL/Y....YULI DANIEL

DANIELSON L.E. B0529

DANTE....DANTE ALIGHIERI

DARRAH E.L. B0530

DARWIN/C....CHARLES DARWIN

DAS M.N. B0531

DATA ANALYSIS....SEE CON/ANAL, STAT, MATH, COMPUTER

DAVEE R. B0532

DAVENPORT J. B0533

DAVID P.T. B0534

DAVIDSON R.H. B0535

DAVIDSON W.R. B0205

DAVIES E. B0536

DAVIS H.E. B0537

DAVIS J.A. B0538

DAVIS K.C. B0539,B0540,B0541,B0542,B0543

DAVIS R.G. B0544

DAVIS R.L. B0455

DAVIS/JEFF....JEFFERSON DAVIS

DAVIS/W....WARREN DAVIS

DAVISON W.P. B0545

DAVY T.J. B2059

DAY C. B0546

DAY E.E. B0547

DAY P. B0548

DE ARAGAO J.G. B0549

DE BLIJ H.J. B0550

DE CENIVAL P. B0551

DE GRAZIA A. B0552,B0553,B0554,B0555,B0556

DE GUZMAN R.P. B0557

DE NOIA J. B0558,B0559,B0560,B0561

DE VRIES E. B0562

DEAN A.L. B0563

DEAN A.W. B0564

DEAN B.V. B0565

DEATH....DEATH

B56
KOENIG L.W.,THE TRUMAN ADMINISTRATION: ITS   ADMIN
PRINCIPLES AND PRACTICE. USA+45 POL/PAR CHIEF LEGIS   POLICY
DIPLOM DEATH NUC/PWR WAR CIVMIL/REL PEACE   EX/STRUC
...DECISION 20 TRUMAN/HS PRESIDENT TREATY. PAGE 61   GOV/REL
B1224

DEBATE....ORGANIZED COLLECTIVE ARGUMENT

N
CONGRESSIONAL MONITOR. CONSULT DELIB/GP PROB/SOLV   BIBLIOG
PRESS DEBATE ROUTINE...POLICY CONGRESS. PAGE 1   LEGIS
B0002   REPRESENT
   USA+45
N
US SUPERINTENDENT OF DOCUMENTS,EDUCATION (PRICE   BIBLIOG/A
LIST 31). USA+45 LAW FINAN LOC/G NAT/G DEBATE ADMIN EDU/PROP
LEAD RACE/REL FEDERAL HEALTH POLICY. PAGE 111 B2238 ACADEM
   SCHOOL
B37
BUREAU OF NATIONAL AFFAIRS,LABOR RELATIONS   LABOR
REFERENCE MANUAL VOL 1, 1935-1937. BARGAIN DEBATE ADMIN
ROUTINE INGP/REL 20 NLRB. PAGE 17 B0351   ADJUD
   NAT/G
B49
RIDDICK F.M.,THE UNITED STATES CONGRESS   LEGIS
ORGANIZATION AND PROCEDURE. POL/PAR DELIB/GP   PARL/PROC
PROB/SOLV DEBATE CONTROL EXEC LEAD INGP/REL PWR   CHIEF
...MAJORIT DECISION CONGRESS PRESIDENT. PAGE 88   EX/STRUC
B1777
S50
HUMPHREY H.H.,"THE SENATE ON TRIAL." USA+45 POL/PAR PARL/PROC
DEBATE REPRESENT EFFICIENCY ATTIT RIGID/FLEX   ROUTINE
...TRADIT SENATE. PAGE 52 B1064   PWR
   LEGIS
B53
GROSS B.M.,THE LEGISLATIVE STRUGGLE: A STUDY IN   LEGIS
SOCIAL COMBAT. STRUCT LOC/G POL/PAR JUDGE EDU/PROP DECISION
DEBATE ETIQUET ADMIN LOBBY CHOOSE GOV/REL INGP/REL PERSON
HEREDITY ALL/VALS...SOC PRESIDENT. PAGE 44 B0885   LEAD
B54
US SENATE COMM ON FOREIGN REL,REVIEW OF THE UNITED BIBLIOG
NATIONS CHARTER: A COLLECTION OF DOCUMENTS. LEGIS CONSTN
DIPLOM ADMIN ARMS/CONT WAR REPRESENT SOVEREIGN   INT/ORG
...INT/LAW 20 UN. PAGE 110 B2220   DEBATE
B55
GALLOWAY G.B.,CONGRESS AND PARLIAMENT: THEIR   DELIB/GP
ORGANIZATION AND OPERATION IN THE US AND THE UK: LEGIS
PLANNING PAMPHLET NO. 93. POL/PAR EX/STRUC DEBATE   PARL/PROC
CONTROL LEAD ROUTINE EFFICIENCY PWR...POLICY   GOV/COMP
CONGRESS PARLIAMENT. PAGE 38 B0777
S57
HARRIS J.P.,"LEGISLATIVE CONTROL OF ADMINISTRATION: LEGIS
SOME COMPARISONS OF AMERICAN AND EUROPEAN   CONTROL
PRACTICES." DEBATE PARL/PROC ROUTINE GOV/REL   EX/STRUC
EFFICIENCY SUPEGO DECISION. PAGE 47 B0954   REPRESENT
B58
KRAINES O.,CONGRESS AND THE CHALLENGE OF BIG   LEGIS
GOVERNMENT. USA-45 EX/STRUC CONFER DEBATE   DELIB/GP
EFFICIENCY. PAGE 61 B1232   ADMIN
C58
WILDING N.,"AN ENCYCLOPEDIA OF PARLIAMENT." UK LAW PARL/PROC
CONSTN CHIEF PROB/SOLV DIPLOM DEBATE WAR INGP/REL POL/PAR
PRIVIL...BIBLIOG DICTIONARY 13/20 CMN/WLTH   NAT/G
PARLIAMENT. PAGE 116 B2350   ADMIN
S59
ROBINSON J.A.,"THE ROLE OF THE RULES COMMITTEE IN   PARL/PROC
ARRANGING THE PROGRAM OF THE UNITED STATES HOUSE OF DELIB/GP

REPRESENTATIVES." USA+45 DEBATE CONTROL AUTHORIT   ROUTINE
HOUSE/REP. PAGE 89 B1801   LEGIS
B60
HAYNES G.H.,THE SENATE OF THE UNITED STATES: ITS   LEGIS
HISTORY AND PRACTICE. CONSTN EX/STRUC TOP/EX CONFER DELIB/GP
DEBATE LEAD LOBBY PARL/PROC CHOOSE PWR SENATE
CONGRESS. PAGE 48 B0977
S61
ROBINSON J.A.,"PROCESS SATISFACTION AND POLICY   GOV/REL
APPROVAL IN STATE DEPARTMENT - CONGRESSIONAL   EX/STRUC
RELATIONS." ELITES CHIEF LEGIS CONFER DEBATE ADMIN POL/PAR
FEEDBACK ROLE...CHARTS 20 CONGRESS PRESIDENT   DECISION
DEPT/STATE. PAGE 89 B1802
B63
MACNEIL N.,FORGE OF DEMOCRACY: THE HOUSE OF   LEGIS
REPRESENTATIVES. POL/PAR EX/STRUC TOP/EX DEBATE   DELIB/GP
LEAD PARL/PROC CHOOSE GOV/REL PWR...OBS HOUSE/REP.
PAGE 68 B1374
B64
EATON H.,PRESIDENTIAL TIMBER: A HISTORY OF   DELIB/GP
NOMINATING CONVENTIONS, 1868-1960. USA+45 USA-45 CHOOSE
POL/PAR EX/STRUC DEBATE LOBBY ATTIT PERSON ALL/VALS CHIEF
...MYTH 19/20 PRESIDENT. PAGE 32 B0646   NAT/G
B64
KEEFE W.J.,THE AMERICAN LEGISLATIVE PROCESS: LEGIS
CONGRESS AND THE STATES. USA+45 LAW POL/PAR   DECISION
DELIB/GP DEBATE ADMIN LOBBY REPRESENT CONGRESS   PWR
PRESIDENT. PAGE 59 B1187   PROVS
B64
ROCHE J.P.,THE CONGRESS. EX/STRUC BAL/PWR DIPLOM   INGP/REL
DEBATE ADJUD LEAD PWR. PAGE 89 B1809   LEGIS
   DELIB/GP
   SENIOR
B65
LATHAM E.,THE GROUP BASIS OF POLITICS: A STUDY IN   LEGIS
BASING-POINT LEGISLATION. INDUS MARKET POL/PAR   GP/COMP
DELIB/GP EX/STRUC DEBATE ADJUD...CHARTS PRESIDENT. GP/REL
PAGE 63 B1274
B65
LIPSET S.M.,THE BERKELEY STUDENT REVOLT: FACTS AND CROWD
INTERPRETATIONS. USA+45 INTELL VOL/ASSN CONSULT   ACADEM
EDU/PROP PRESS DEBATE ADMIN REV HAPPINESS   ATTIT
RIGID/FLEX MAJORIT. PAGE 65 B1322   GP/REL
B66
ANDERSON S.V.,CANADIAN OMBUDSMAN PROPOSALS. CANADA NAT/G
LEGIS DEBATE PARL/PROC...MAJORIT JURID TIME/SEQ   CREATE
IDEA/COMP 20 OMBUDSMAN PARLIAMENT. PAGE 5 B0096   ADMIN
   POL/PAR
B66
BURNS A.C.,PARLIAMENT AS AN EXPORT. WOR+45 CONSTN   PARL/PROC
BARGAIN DEBATE ROUTINE GOV/REL EFFICIENCY...ANTHOL POL/PAR
COMMONWLTH PARLIAMENT. PAGE 17 B0353   CT/SYS
   CHIEF
B66
CHAPMAN B.,THE PROFESSION OF GOVERNMENT: THE PUBLIC BIBLIOG
SERVICE IN EUROPE. CONSTN NAT/G POL/PAR EX/STRUC   ADMIN
LEGIS TOP/EX PROB/SOLV DEBATE EXEC PARL/PROC PARTIC EUR+WWI
20. PAGE 20 B0411   GOV/COMP
B67
TOMA P.A.,THE POLITICS OF FOOD FOR PEACE: FOR/AID
EXECUTIVE-LEGISLATIVE INTERACTION. USA+45 ECO/UNDEV POLICY
POL/PAR DEBATE EXEC LOBBY CHOOSE PEACE...DECISION LEGIS
CHARTS. PAGE 104 B2113   AGRI
S67
LENDVAI P.,"HUNGARY* CHANGE VS. IMMOBILISM."   ECO/DEV
HUNGARY LABOR NAT/G PLAN DEBATE ADMIN ROUTINE   MGT
CENTRAL EFFICIENCY MARXISM PLURISM...PREDICT 20.   CHOOSE
PAGE 64 B1289

DEBENKO E. B0566

DEBRAY P. B0567

DEBS/E....EUGENE DEBS

DEBT....PUBLIC DEBT, INCLUDING NATIONAL DEBT; SEE ALSO
  ECO + NAT/G

DECISION....DECISION-MAKING AND GAME THEORY; SEE ALSO GAME

N
US SUPERINTENDENT OF DOCUMENTS,INTERSTATE COMMERCE BIBLIOG/A
(PRICE LIST 59). USA+45 LAW LOC/G NAT/G LEGIS   DIST/IND
TARIFFS TAX ADMIN CONTROL HEALTH DECISION. PAGE 111 GOV/REL
B2239   PROVS
N
US SUPERINTENDENT OF DOCUMENTS,TARIFF AND TAXATION BIBLIOG/A
(PRICE LIST 37). USA+45 LAW INT/TRADE ADJUD ADMIN   TAX
CT/SYS INCOME OWN...DECISION GATT. PAGE 111 B2242   TARIFFS
   NAT/G
N19
FIKS M.,PUBLIC ADMINISTRATION IN ISRAEL (PAMPHLET). EDU/PROP
ISRAEL SCHOOL EX/STRUC BUDGET PAY INGP/REL   NAT/G
...DECISION 20 CIVIL/SERV. PAGE 35 B0718   ADMIN
   WORKER

KRIESBERG M.,CANCELLATION OF THE RATION STAMPS (PAMPHLET). USA+45 USA-45 MARKET PROB/SOLV PRICE GOV/REL RIGID/FLEX 20 OPA. PAGE 61 B1235
N19 RATION DECISION ADMIN NAT/G

LUCE R.,CONGRESS: AN EXPLANATION. USA-45 CONSTN FINAN ADMIN LEAD. PAGE 67 B1347
B26 DECISION LEGIS CREATE REPRESENT

GOSNELL H.F.,"BRITISH ROYAL COMMISSIONS OF INQUIRY" UK CONSTN LEGIS PRESS ADMIN PARL/PROC...DECISION 20 PARLIAMENT. PAGE 41 B0839
L34 DELIB/GP INSPECT POLICY NAT/G

HERRING E.P.,PUBLIC ADMINISTRATION AND THE PUBLIC INTEREST. LABOR NAT/G PARTIC EFFICIENCY 20. PAGE 49 B0995
B36 GP/REL DECISION PROB/SOLV ADMIN

CLOKIE H.M.,ROYAL COMMISSIONS OF INQUIRY; THE SIGNIFICANCE OF INVESTIGATIONS IN BRITISH POLITICS. UK POL/PAR CONFER ROUTINE...POLICY DECISION TIME/SEQ 16/20. PAGE 22 B0439
B37 NAT/G DELIB/GP INSPECT

MARX F.M.,"POLICY FORMULATION AND THE ADMINISTRATIVE PROCESS" ROUTINE ADJUST EFFICIENCY OPTIMAL PRIVIL DRIVE PERSON OBJECTIVE...DECISION OBS GEN/METH. PAGE 70 B1418
S39 ADMIN LEAD INGP/REL MGT

HART J.,AN INTRODUCTION TO ADMINISTRATIVE LAW, WITH SELECTED CASES. USA-45 CONSTN SOCIETY NAT/G EX/STRUC ADJUD CT/SYS LEAD CRIME ORD/FREE ...DECISION JURID 20 CASEBOOK. PAGE 47 B0958
B40 LAW ADMIN LEGIS PWR

PERKINS J.A.,"CONGRESSIONAL INVESTIGATIONS OF MATTERS OF INTERNATIONAL IMPORT." DELIB/GP DIPLOM ADMIN CONTROL 20 CONGRESS. PAGE 82 B1656
S40 POL/PAR DECISION PARL/PROC GOV/REL

YOUNG R.,THIS IS CONGRESS. FUT SENIOR ADMIN GP/REL PWR...DECISION REFORMERS CONGRESS. PAGE 119 B2393
B43 LEGIS DELIB/GP CHIEF ROUTINE

COLEGROVE K.W.,"THE ROLE OF CONGRESS AND PUBLIC OPINION IN FORMULATING FOREIGN POLICY." USA+45 WAR ...DECISION UN CONGRESS. PAGE 22 B0451
S44 EX/STRUC DIPLOM LEGIS PWR

SIMON H.A.,"DECISION-MAKING AND ADMINISTRATIVE ORGANIZATION" (BMR)" WOR-45 CHOOSE INGP/REL EFFICIENCY ATTIT RESPECT...MGT 20. PAGE 97 B1955
S44 DECISION ADMIN CONTROL WORKER

TRUMAN D.B.,"PUBLIC OPINION RESEARCH AS A TOOL OF PUBLIC ADMINISTRATION" ADMIN PARTIC ROLE...DECISION 20. PAGE 105 B2130
S45 REPRESENT METH/CNCPT ATTIT EX/STRUC

CAMPBELL A.,"THE USES OF INTERVIEW SURVEYS IN FEDERAL ADMNISTRATION" PROB/SOLV EXEC PARTIC DECISION. PAGE 18 B0369
S46 INT ADMIN EX/STRUC REPRESENT

GAUS J.M.,REFLECTIONS ON PUBLIC ADMINISTRATION. USA+45 CONTROL GOV/REL CENTRAL FEDERAL ATTIT WEALTH ...DECISION 20. PAGE 39 B0787
B47 MGT POLICY EX/STRUC ADMIN

PATTERSON C.P.,PRESIDENTIAL GOVERNMENT IN THE UNITED STATES - THE UNWRITTEN CONSTITUTION. USA+45 DELIB/GP EX/STRUC ADJUD ADMIN EXEC...DECISION PRESIDENT. PAGE 81 B1643
B47 CHIEF NAT/G CONSTN POL/PAR

SIMON H.A.,ADMINISTRATIVE BEHAVIOR: A STUDY OF DECISION-MAKING PROCESSES IN ADMINISTRATIVE ORGANIZATION. STRUCT COM/IND OP/RES PROB/SOLV EFFICIENCY EQUILIB UTIL...PHIL/SCI PSY STYLE. PAGE 97 B1956
B47 DECISION NEW/IDEA ADMIN RATIONAL

ROSSITER C.L.,CONSTITUTIONAL DICTATORSHIP; CRISIS GOVERNMENT IN THE MODERN DEMOCRACIES. FRANCE GERMANY UK USA-45 WOR-45 EX/STRUC BAL/PWR CONTROL COERCE WAR CENTRAL ORD/FREE...DECISION 19/20. PAGE 90 B1828
B48 NAT/G AUTHORIT CONSTN TOTALISM

SLESSER H.,THE ADMINISTRATION OF THE LAW. UK CONSTN EX/STRUC OP/RES PROB/SOLV CRIME ROLE...DECISION METH/COMP 20 CIVIL/LAW ENGLSH/LAW CIVIL/LAW. PAGE 98 B1977
B48 LAW CT/SYS ADJUD

RIDDICK F.M.,THE UNITED STATES CONGRESS ORGANIZATION AND PROCEDURE. POL/PAR DELIB/GP PROB/SOLV DEBATE CONTROL EXEC LEAD INGP/REL PWR
B49 LEGIS PARL/PROC CHIEF

...MAJORIT DECISION CONGRESS PRESIDENT. PAGE 88 B1777
EX/STRUC

KOENIG L.W.,THE SALE OF THE TANKERS. USA+45 SEA DIST/IND POL/PAR DIPLOM ADMIN CIVMIL/REL ATTIT ...DECISION 20 PRESIDENT DEPT/STATE. PAGE 60 B1223
B50 NAT/G POLICY PLAN GOV/REL

EPSTEIN L.D.,"POLITICAL STERILIZATION OF CIVIL SERVANTS: THE UNITED STATES AND GREAT BRITAIN." UK USA+45 USA-45 STRUCT TOP/EX OP/RES PARTIC CHOOSE NAT/LISM 20 CONGRESS CIVIL/SERV. PAGE 33 B0679
S50 ADMIN LEGIS DECISION POL/PAR

TANNENBAUM R.,"PARTICIPATION BY SUBORDINATES IN THE MANAGERIAL DECISIONMAKING PROCESS" (BMR)" WOR+45 INDUS SML/CO WORKER INGP/REL...CONCPT GEN/LAWS 20. PAGE 103 B2074
S50 PARTIC DECISION MGT LG/CO

SIMON H.A.,"PUBLIC ADMINISTRATION." LG/CO SML/CO PLAN DOMIN LEAD GP/REL DRIVE PERCEPT ALL/VALS ...POLICY BIBLIOG/A 20. PAGE 97 B1957
C50 MGT ADMIN DECISION EX/STRUC

MOORE B.,"SOVIET POLITICS - THE DILEMMA OF POWER: THE ROLE OF IDEAS IN SOCIAL CHANGE." USSR PROB/SOLV DIPLOM EDU/PROP ADMIN LEAD ROUTINE REV...POLICY DECISION BIBLIOG 20. PAGE 75 B1512
C51 ATTIT PWR CONCPT MARXISM

DONHAM W.B.,ADMINISTRATION AND BLIND SPOTS. LG/CO EX/STRUC BARGAIN ADJUD ROUTINE ROLE SUPEGO 20. PAGE 30 B0605
B52 ADMIN TOP/EX DECISION POLICY

EDELMAN M.,"GOVERNMENTAL ORGANIZATION AND PUBLIC POLICY." DELIB/GP ADJUD DECISION. PAGE 32 B0652
S52 ADMIN PLURIST LOBBY EX/STRUC

LIPSET S.M.,"DEMOCRACY IN PRIVATE GOVERNMENT; (A CASE STUDY OF THE INTERNATIONAL TYPOGRAPHICAL UNION)" (BMR)" POL/PAR CONTROL LEAD INGP/REL PWR ...MAJORIT DECISION PREDICT 20. PAGE 65 B1319
S52 LABOR ADMIN ELITES REPRESENT

TAYLOR R.W.,"ARTHUR F. BENTLEY'S POLITICAL SCIENCE" (BMR)" USA+45 INTELL NAT/G...DECISION CLASSIF IDEA/COMP 20 BENTLEY/AF. PAGE 103 B2090
S52 GEN/LAWS POLICY ADMIN

GROSS B.M.,THE LEGISLATIVE STRUGGLE: A STUDY IN SOCIAL COMBAT. STRUCT LOC/G POL/PAR JUDGE EDU/PROP DEBATE ETIQUET ADMIN LOBBY CHOOSE GOV/REL INGP/REL HEREDITY ALL/VALS...SOC PRESIDENT. PAGE 44 B0885
B53 LEGIS DECISION PERSON LEAD

SAYLES L.R.,THE LOCAL UNION. CONSTN CULTURE DELIB/GP PARTIC CHOOSE GP/REL INGP/REL ATTIT ROLE ...MAJORIT DECISION MGT. PAGE 93 B1873
B53 LABOR LEAD ADJUD ROUTINE

STENE E.O.,ABANDONMENTS OF THE MANAGER PLAN. LEGIS LEAD GP/REL PWR DECISION. PAGE 100 B2032
B53 MUNIC EX/STRUC REPRESENT ADMIN

DRUCKER P.F.,"THE EMPLOYEE SOCIETY." STRUCT BAL/PWR PARTIC REPRESENT PWR...DECISION CONCPT. PAGE 30 B0619
S53 LABOR MGT WORKER CULTURE

COMBS C.H.,DECISION PROCESSES. INTELL SOCIETY DELIB/GP CREATE TEC/DEV DOMIN LEGIT EXEC CHOOSE DRIVE RIGID/FLEX KNOWL PWR...PHIL/SCI SOC METH/CNCPT CONT/OBS REC/INT PERS/TEST SAMP/SIZ BIOG SOC/EXP WORK. PAGE 22 B0455
B54 MATH DECISION

CONWAY O.B. JR.,LEGISLATIVE-EXECUTIVE RELATIONS IN THE GOVERNMENT OF THE UNITED STATES (PAMPHLET). BUDGET ATTIT PERCEPT...DECISION 20. PAGE 23 B0470
B54 BAL/PWR FEDERAL GOV/REL EX/STRUC

MATTHEWS D.R.,THE SOCIAL BACKGROUND OF POLITICAL DECISION-MAKERS. CULTURE SOCIETY STRATA FAM EX/STRUC LEAD ATTIT BIO/SOC DRIVE PERSON ALL/VALS HIST/WRIT. PAGE 71 B1431
B54 DECISION BIOG SOC

BRAUN K.,LABOR DISPUTES AND THEIR SETTLEMENT. ECO/TAC ROUTINE TASK GP/REL...DECISION GEN/LAWS. PAGE 15 B0301
B55 INDUS LABOR BARGAIN ADJUD

CUSHMAN R.E.,LEADING CONSTITUTIONAL DECISIONS. USA+45 USA-45 NAT/G EX/STRUC LEGIS JUDGE TAX FEDERAL...DECISION 20 SUPREME/CT CASEBOOK. PAGE 25 B0513
B55 CONSTN PROB/SOLV JURID CT/SYS

CROCKETT W.H.,"EMERGENT LEADERSHIP IN SMALL DECISION MAKING GROUPS." ACT/RES ROUTINE PERS/REL ATTIT...STAT CONT/OBS SOC/EXP SIMUL. PAGE 25 B0507
S55 DELIB/GP ADMIN PSY

DECISION
S55

DRUCKER P.F.,"'MANAGEMENT SCIENCE' AND THE MGT
MANAGER." PLAN ROUTINE RIGID/FLEX...METH/CNCPT LOG STRUCT
HYPO/EXP. PAGE 30 B0620 DECISION
RATIONAL
B56

KOENIG L.W.,THE TRUMAN ADMINISTRATION: ITS ADMIN
PRINCIPLES AND PRACTICE. USA+45 POL/PAR CHIEF LEGIS POLICY
DIPLOM DEATH NUC/PWR WAR CIVMIL/REL PEACE EX/STRUC
...DECISION 20 TRUMAN/HS PRESIDENT TREATY. PAGE 61 GOV/REL
B1224
B56

SOHN L.B.,CASES ON UNITED NATIONS LAW. STRUCT INT/ORG
DELIB/GP WAR PEACE ORD/FREE...DECISION ANTHOL 20 INT/LAW
UN. PAGE 99 B1994 ADMIN
ADJUD
L56

PARSONS T.,"SUGGESTIONS FOR A SOCIOLOGICAL APPROACH SOC
TO THE THEORY OF ORGANIZATIONS - I" (BMR)" FINAN CONCPT
EX/STRUC LEGIT ALL/VALS...POLICY DECISION 20. ADMIN
PAGE 81 B1637 STRUCT
S56

GORE W.J.,"ADMINISTRATIVE DECISION-MAKING IN DECISION
FEDERAL FIELD OFFICES." USA+45 PROVS PWR CONT/OBS. PROB/SOLV
PAGE 41 B0833 FEDERAL
ADMIN
B57

CRONBACK L.J.,PSYCHOLOGICAL TESTS AND PERSONNEL MATH
DECISIONS. OP/RES PROB/SOLV CHOOSE PERSON...PSY DECISION
STAT TESTS 20. PAGE 25 B0508 WORKER
MGT
B57

IKE N.,JAPANESE POLITICS. INTELL STRUCT AGRI INDUS NAT/G
FAM KIN LABOR PRESS CHOOSE ATTIT...DECISION BIBLIOG ADMIN
19/20 CHINJAP. PAGE 53 B1075 POL/PAR
CULTURE
B57

KAPLAN M.A.,SYSTEM AND PROCESS OF INTERNATIONAL INT/ORG
POLITICS. FUT WOR+45 WOR-45 SOCIETY PLAN BAL/PWR DIPLOM
ADMIN ATTIT PERSON RIGID/FLEX PWR SOVEREIGN
...DECISION TREND VAL/FREE. PAGE 58 B1168
B57

KIETH-LUCAS A.,DECISIONS ABOUT PEOPLE IN NEED, A ADMIN
STUDY OF ADMINISTRATIVE RESPONSIVENESS IN PUBLIC RIGID/FLEX
ASSISTANCE. USA+45 GIVE RECEIVE INGP/REL PERS/REL SOC/WK
MORAL RESPECT WEALTH...SOC OBS BIBLIOG 20. PAGE 60 DECISION
B1204
B57

MEYER P.,ADMINISTRATIVE ORGANIZATION: A COMPARATIVE ADMIN
STUDY OF THE ORGANIZATION OF PUBLIC ADMINISTRATION. METH/COMP
DENMARK FRANCE NORWAY SWEDEN UK USA+45 ELITES LOC/G NAT/G
CONSULT LEGIS ADJUD CONTROL LEAD PWR SKILL CENTRAL
DECISION. PAGE 73 B1475
B57

SELZNICK,LEADERSHIP IN ADMINISTRATION: A LEAD
SOCIOLOGICAL INTERPRETATION. CREATE PROB/SOLV EXEC ADMIN
ROUTINE EFFICIENCY RATIONAL KNOWL...POLICY PSY. DECISION
PAGE 95 B1927 NAT/G
B57

SHARMA S.R.,SOME ASPECTS OF THE INDIAN EXEC
ADMINISTRATIVE SYSTEM. INDIA WOR+45 TEC/DEV BUDGET DECISION
LEGIT ROUTINE ATTIT. PAGE 96 B1937 ADMIN
INGP/REL
B57

US CIVIL SERVICE COMMISSION,DISSERTATIONS AND BIBLIOG
THESES RELATING TO PERSONNEL ADMINISTRATION ADMIN
(PAMPHLET). USA+45 COM/IND LABOR EX/STRUC GP/REL MGT
INGP/REL DECISION. PAGE 108 B2176 WORKER
S57

COTTER C.P.,"ADMINISTRATIVE ACCOUNTABILITY; LEGIS
REPORTING TO CONGRESS." USA+45 CONSULT DELIB/GP EX/STRUC
PARL/PROC PARTIC GOV/REL ATTIT PWR DECISION. REPRESENT
PAGE 24 B0490 CONTROL
S57

DANIELSON L.E.,"SUPERVISORY PROBLEMS IN DECISION PROB/SOLV
MAKING." WORKER ADMIN ROUTINE TASK MGT. PAGE 26 DECISION
B0529 CONTROL
GP/REL
S57

FESLER J.W.,"ADMINISTRATIVE LITERATURE AND THE ADMIN
SECOND HOOVER COMMISSION REPORTS" (BMR)" USA+45 NAT/G
EX/STRUC LEGIS WRITING...DECISION METH 20. PAGE 35 OP/RES
B0713 DELIB/GP
S57

GULICK L.,"METROPOLITAN ORGANIZATION." LEGIS EXEC REGION
PARTIC CHOOSE REPRESENT GOV/REL...MAJORIT DECISION. LOC/G
PAGE 45 B0904 MUNIC
S57

HARRIS J.P.,"LEGISLATIVE CONTROL OF ADMINISTRATION: LEGIS
SOME COMPARISONS OF AMERICAN AND EUROPEAN CONTROL
PRACTICES." DEBATE PARL/PROC ROUTINE GOV/REL EX/STRUC
EFFICIENCY SUPEGO DECISION. PAGE 47 B0954 REPRESENT
S57

HODGETTS J.E.,"THE CIVIL SERVICE AND POLICY ADMIN
FORMATION." CANADA NAT/G EX/STRUC ROUTINE GOV/REL DECISION

---

20. PAGE 50 B1023 EFFICIENCY
POLICY
S57

RAPAPORT R.N.,"'DEMOCRATIZATION' AND AUTHORITY IN A PUB/INST
THERAPEUTIC COMMUNITY." OP/RES ADMIN PARTIC CENTRAL HEALTH
ATTIT...POLICY DECISION. PAGE 86 B1735 DOMIN
CLIENT
S57

SCHUBERT G.A.,"'THE PUBLIC INTEREST' IN ADMIN
ADMINISTRATIVE DECISION-MAKING: THEOREM, THEOSOPHY DECISION
OR THEORY" USA+45 EX/STRUC PROB/SOLV...METH/CNCPT POLICY
STAT. PAGE 94 B1904 EXEC
S57

TAYLOR P.S.,"THE RELATION OF RESEARCH TO DECISION
LEGISLATIVE AND ADMINISTRATIVE DECISIONS." ELITES LEGIS
ACT/RES PLAN PROB/SOLV CONFER CHOOSE POLICY. MGT
PAGE 103 B2089 PWR
N57

MACMAHON A.W.,ADMINISTRATION AND FOREIGN POLICY DIPLOM
(PAMPHLET). USA+45 CHIEF OP/RES ADMIN 20. PAGE 68 EX/STRUC
B1372 DECISION
CONFER
B58

DWARKADAS R.,ROLE OF HIGHER CIVIL SERVICE IN INDIA. ADMIN
INDIA ECO/UNDEV LEGIS PROB/SOLV GP/REL PERS/REL NAT/G
...POLICY WELF/ST DECISION ORG/CHARTS BIBLIOG 20 ROLE
CIVIL/SERV INTRVN/ECO. PAGE 31 B0637 PLAN
B58

MARCH J.G.,ORGANIZATIONS. USA+45 CREATE OP/RES PLAN MGT
PROB/SOLV PARTIC ROUTINE RATIONAL ATTIT PERCEPT PERSON
...DECISION BIBLIOG. PAGE 69 B1397 DRIVE
CONCPT
B58

MELMAN S.,DECISION-MAKING AND PRODUCTIVITY. INDUS LABOR
EX/STRUC WORKER OP/RES PROB/SOLV TEC/DEV ADMIN PRODUC
ROUTINE RIGID/FLEX GP/COMP. PAGE 73 B1464 DECISION
MGT
B58

OPERATIONS RESEARCH SOCIETY,A COMPREHENSIVE BIBLIOG/A
BIBLIOGRAPHY ON OPERATIONS RESEARCH; THROUGH 1956 COMPUT/IR
WITH SUPPLEMENT FOR 1957. COM/IND DIST/IND INDUS OP/RES
ADMIN...DECISION MATH STAT METH 20. PAGE 80 B1612 MGT
B58

REDFORD E.S.,IDEAL AND PRACTICE IN PUBLIC POLICY
ADMINISTRATION. CONSTN ELITES NAT/G CONSULT EX/STRUC
DELIB/GP LEAD UTOPIA ATTIT POPULISM...DECISION PLAN
METH/COMP 20. PAGE 87 B1756 ADMIN
B58

SCOTT D.J.R.,RUSSIAN POLITICAL INSTITUTIONS. RUSSIA NAT/G
USSR CONSTN AGRI DELIB/GP PLAN EDU/PROP CONTROL POL/PAR
CHOOSE EFFICIENCY ATTIT MARXISM...BIBLIOG/A 13/20. ADMIN
PAGE 95 B1919 DECISION
B58

WESTIN A.F.,THE ANATOMY OF A CONSTITUTIONAL LAW CT/SYS
CASE. USA+45 LAW LEGIS ADMIN EXEC...DECISION MGT INDUS
SOC RECORD 20 SUPREME/CT. PAGE 115 B2326 ADJUD
CONSTN
L58

CYERT R.M.,"THE ROLE OF EXPECTATIONS IN BUSINESS LG/CO
DECISION-MAKING." PROB/SOLV PRICE RIGID/FLEX. DECISION
PAGE 25 B0516 ROUTINE
EXEC
S58

BLAISDELL D.C.,"PRESSURE GROUPS, FOREIGN POLICIES, PROF/ORG
AND INTERNATIONAL POLITICS." USA+45 WOR+45 INT/ORG PWR
PLAN DOMIN EDU/PROP LEGIT ADMIN ROUTINE CHOOSE
...DECISION MGT METH/CNCPT CON/ANAL 20. PAGE 12
B0249
S58

DEAN B.V.,"APPLICATION OF OPERATIONS RESEARCH TO DECISION
MANAGERIAL DECISION MAKING" STRATA ACT/RES OP/RES
PROB/SOLV ROLE...SOC PREDICT SIMUL 20. PAGE 28 MGT
B0565 METH/CNCPT
C58

GOLAY J.F.,"THE FOUNDING OF THE FEDERAL REPUBLIC OF FEDERAL
GERMANY." GERMANY/W CONSTN EX/STRUC DIPLOM ADMIN NAT/G
CHOOSE...DECISION BIBLIOG 20. PAGE 40 B0814 PARL/PROC
POL/PAR
C58

REDFORD E.S.,"THE NEVER-ENDING SEARCH FOR THE LOBBY
PUBLIC INTEREST" IN E. REDFORD, IDEALS AND PRACTICE POLICY
IN PUBLIC ADMINISTRATION (BMR)" USA+45 USA-45 ADMIN
SOCIETY PARTIC GP/REL ATTIT PLURISM...DECISION SOC MAJORIT
20. PAGE 87 B1755
B59

DESMITH S.A.,JUDICIAL REVIEW OF ADMINISTRATIVE ADJUD
ACTION. UK LOC/G CONSULT DELIB/GP ADMIN PWR NAT/G
...DECISION JURID 20 ENGLSH/LAW. PAGE 28 B0576 PROB/SOLV
CT/SYS
B59

MILLETT J.D.,GOVERNMENT AND PUBLIC ADMINISTRATION; ADMIN
THE QUEST FOR RESPONSIBLE PERFORMANCE. USA+45 NAT/G PWR
DELIB/GP LEGIS CT/SYS EXEC...DECISION MGT. PAGE 73 CONSTN
B1483 ROLE
B59

MONTGOMERY J.D.,CASES IN VIETNAMESE ADMINISTRATION. ADMIN

VIETNAM/S EX/STRUC 20. PAGE 75 B1506
DECISION
PROB/SOLV
LEAD
B59

SISSON C.H.,THE SPIRIT OF BRITISH ADMINISTRATION
AND SOME EUROPEAN COMPARISONS. FRANCE GERMANY/W
SWEDEN UK LAW EX/STRUC INGP/REL EFFICIENCY ORD/FREE
...DECISION 20. PAGE 98 B1972
GOV/COMP
ADMIN
ELITES
ATTIT
B59

SURRENCY E.C.,A GUIDE TO LEGAL RESEARCH. USA+45
ACADEM LEGIS ACT/RES ADMIN...DECISION METH/COMP
BIBLIOG METH. PAGE 102 B2055
NAT/G
PROVS
ADJUD
JURID
L59

"A BIBLIOGRAPHICAL ESSAY ON DECISION MAKING."
WOR+45 WOR-45 STRUCT OP/RES GP/REL...CONCPT
IDEA/COMP METH 20. PAGE 2 B0038
BIBLIOG/A
DECISION
ADMIN
LEAD
L59

RHODE W.E.,"COMMITTEE CLEARANCE OF ADMINISTRATIVE
DECISIONS." DELIB/GP LEGIS BUDGET DOMIN CIVMIL/REL
20 CONGRESS. PAGE 87 B1768
DECISION
ADMIN
OP/RES
NAT/G
S59

CALKINS R.D.,"THE DECISION PROCESS IN
ADMINISTRATION." EX/STRUC PROB/SOLV ROUTINE MGT.
PAGE 18 B0368
ADMIN
OP/RES
DECISION
CON/ANAL
S59

CYERT R.M.,"MODELS IN A BEHAVIORAL THEORY OF THE
FIRM." ROUTINE...DECISION MGT METH/CNCPT MATH.
PAGE 25 B0517
SIMUL
GAME
PREDICT
INDUS
S59

HILSMAN R.,"THE FOREIGN-POLICY CONSENSUS: AN
INTERIM RESEARCH REPORT." USA+45 INT/ORG LEGIS
TEC/DEV EXEC WAR CONSEN KNOWL...DECISION COLD/WAR.
PAGE 50 B1013
PROB/SOLV
NAT/G
DELIB/GP
DIPLOM
B60

BAERWALD F.,ECONOMIC SYSTEM ANALYSIS: CONCEPTS AND
PERSPECTIVES. USA+45 ECO/DEV NAT/G COMPUTER EQUILIB
INCOME ATTIT...DECISION CONCPT IDEA/COMP. PAGE 8
B0159
ACT/RES
ECO/TAC
ROUTINE
FINAN
B60

CORSON J.J.,GOVERNANCE OF COLLEGES AND
UNIVERSITIES. STRUCT FINAN DELIB/GP DOMIN EDU/PROP
LEAD CHOOSE GP/REL CENTRAL COST PRIVIL SUPEGO
ORD/FREE PWR...DECISION BIBLIOG. PAGE 24 B0481
ADMIN
EXEC
ACADEM
HABITAT
B60

ECKHOFF T.,RATIONALITY AND RESPONSIBILITY IN
ADMINISTRATIVE AND JUDICIAL DECISION-MAKING. ELITES
LEAD INGP/REL ATTIT PWR...MGT METH/COMP GAME 20.
PAGE 32 B0649
ADMIN
PROB/SOLV
DECISION
METH/CNCPT
B60

FOSS P.,POLITICS AND GRASS: THE ADMINISTRATION OF
GRAZING ON THE PUBLIC DOMAIN. USA+45 LEGIS TOP/EX
EXEC...DECISION 20. PAGE 37 B0743
REPRESENT
ADMIN
LOBBY
EX/STRUC
B60

GLOVER J.D.,A CASE STUDY OF HIGH LEVEL
ADMINISTRATION IN A LARGE ORGANIZATION. EX/STRUC
EXEC LEAD ROUTINE INGP/REL OPTIMAL ATTIT PERSON
...POLICY DECISION INT QU. PAGE 40 B0812
ADMIN
TOP/EX
FORCES
NAT/G
B60

KINGSTON-MCCLOUG E.,DEFENSE; POLICY AND STRATEGY.
UK SEA AIR TEC/DEV DIPLOM ADMIN LEAD WAR ORD/FREE
...CHARTS 20. PAGE 60 B1209
FORCES
PLAN
POLICY
DECISION
B60

MORRIS W.T.,ENGINEERING ECONOMY. AUTOMAT RISK
RATIONAL...PROBABIL STAT CHARTS GAME SIMUL BIBLIOG
T 20. PAGE 76 B1529
OP/RES
DECISION
MGT
PROB/SOLV
B60

RUBENSTEIN A.H.,SOME THEORIES OF ORGANIZATION.
ROUTINE ATTIT...DECISION ECOMETRIC. PAGE 91 B1846
SOCIETY
ECO/DEV
INDUS
TOP/EX
B60

SAYRE W.S.,GOVERNING NEW YORK CITY; POLITICS IN THE
METROPOLIS. POL/PAR CHIEF DELIB/GP LEGIS DRAM
CT/SYS LEAD PARTIC CHOOSE...DECISION CHARTS BIBLIOG
20 NEWYORK/C BUREAUCRCY. PAGE 93 B1875
MUNIC
ADMIN
PROB/SOLV
B60

US SENATE COMM. GOVT. OPER.,ORGANIZING FOR NATIONAL
SECURITY. USA+45 USA-45 INTELL STRUCT SML/CO
ACT/RES ADMIN ATTIT PERSON PWR SKILL...DECISION 20.
PAGE 111 B2236
CONSULT
EXEC
B60

WALTER B.,COMMUNICATIONS AND INFLUENCE: DEXISION
MAKING IN A MUNICIPAL ADMINISTRATIVE HIERARCHY
(PH.D. DISS., UNPUBL.). LEAD CHOOSE PWR METH/CNCPT.
PAGE 113 B2284
MUNIC
DECISION
ADMIN
STRUCT
B60

WEBSTER J.A.,A GENERAL STUDY OF THE DEPARTMENT OF
DEFENSE INTERNAL SECURITY PROGRAM. USA+45 WORKER
ORD/FREE
PLAN

TEC/DEV ADJUD CONTROL CT/SYS EXEC GOV/REL COST
...POLICY DECISION MGT 20 DEPT/DEFEN SUPREME/CT.
PAGE 114 B2307
ADMIN
NAT/G
L60

DEAN A.W.,"SECOND GENEVA CONFERENCE OF THE LAW OF
THE SEA: THE FIGHT FOR FREEDOM OF THE SEAS." FUT
USA+45 USSR WOR+45 WOR-45 SEA CONSTN STRUCT PLAN
INT/TRADE ADJUD ADMIN ORD/FREE...DECISION RECORD
TREND GEN/LAWS 20 TREATY. PAGE 28 B0564
INT/ORG
JURID
INT/LAW
L60

GRODZINS M.,"AMERICAN POLITICAL PARTIES AND THE
AMERICAN SYSTEM" (BMR)" USA+45 LOC/G NAT/G LEGIS
BAL/PWR ADMIN ROLE PWR...DECISION 20. PAGE 44 B0883
POL/PAR
FEDERAL
CENTRAL
GOV/REL
S60

FRIEDMAN L.,"DECISION MAKING IN COMPETITIVE
SITUATIONS" OP/RES...MGT PROBABIL METH/COMP SIMUL
20. PAGE 37 B0757
DECISION
UTIL
OPTIMAL
GAME
S60

HUTCHINSON C.E.,"AN INSTITUTE FOR NATIONAL SECURITY
AFFAIRS." USA+45 R+D NAT/G CONSULT TOP/EX ACT/RES
CREATE PLAN TEC/DEV EDU/PROP ROUTINE NUC/PWR ATTIT
ORD/FREE PWR...DECISION MGT PHIL/SCI CONCPT RECORD
GEN/LAWS GEN/METH 20. PAGE 53 B1068
POLICY
METH/CNCPT
ELITES
DIPLOM
S60

NELSON R.H.,"LEGISLATIVE PARTICIPATION IN THE
TREATY AND AGREEMENT MAKING PROCESS." CONSTN
POL/PAR PLAN EXEC PWR FAO UN CONGRESS. PAGE 78
B1569
LEGIS
PEACE
DECISION
DIPLOM
S60

PFIFFNER J.M.,"ADMINISTRATIVE RATIONALITY" (BMR)"
UNIV CONTROL...POLICY IDEA/COMP SIMUL. PAGE 83
B1667
ADMIN
DECISION
RATIONAL
S60

ROURKE F.E.,"ADMINISTRATIVE SECRECY: A
CONGRESSIONAL DILEMMA." DELIB/GP CT/SYS ATTIT
...MAJORIT DECISION JURID. PAGE 91 B1837
LEGIS
EXEC
ORD/FREE
POLICY
S60

TAYLOR M.G.,"THE ROLE OF THE MEDICAL PROFESSION IN
THE FORMULATION AND EXECUTION OF PUBLIC POLICY"
(BMR)" CANADA NAT/G CONSULT ADMIN REPRESENT GP/REL
ROLE SOVEREIGN...DECISION 20 CMA. PAGE 103 B2088
PROF/ORG
HEALTH
LOBBY
POLICY
B61

AUERBACH C.A.,THE LEGAL PROCESS. USA+45 DELIB/GP
JUDGE CONFER ADJUD CONTROL...DECISION 20
SUPREME/CT. PAGE 7 B0146
JURID
ADMIN
LEGIS
CT/SYS
B61

BANFIELD E.C.,URBAN GOVERNMENT; A READER IN
POLITICS AND ADMINISTRATION. ELITES LABOR POL/PAR
EXEC CHOOSE REPRESENT GP/REL PWR PLURISM...PSY SOC.
PAGE 9 B0177
MUNIC
GEN/METH
DECISION
B61

BRADY R.A.,ORGANIZATION, AUTOMATION, AND SOCIETY.
USA+45 AGRI COM/IND DIST/IND MARKET CREATE
...DECISION MGT 20. PAGE 14 B0296
TEC/DEV
INDUS
AUTOMAT
ADMIN
B61

CHAPPLE E.D.,THE MEASURE OF MANAGEMENT. USA+45
WORKER ADMIN GP/REL EFFICIENCY...DECISION
ORG/CHARTS SIMUL 20. PAGE 20 B0412
MGT
OP/RES
PLAN
METH/CNCPT
B61

PROCEEDINGS OF THE CONFERENCE ON BUSINESS GAMES AS
TEACHING DEVICES. PROB/SOLV ECO/TAC CONFER ADMIN
TASK...MGT ANTHOL 20. PAGE 29 B0593
GAME
DECISION
EDU/PROP
EFFICIENCY
B61

DUBIN R.,HUMAN RELATIONS IN ADMINISTRATION. USA+45
INDUS LABOR LG/CO EX/STRUC GP/REL DRIVE PWR
...DECISION SOC CHARTS ANTHOL 20. PAGE 31 B0623
PERS/REL
MGT
ADMIN
EXEC
B61

GARCIA E.,LA ADMINISTRACION ESPANOLA. SPAIN GOV/REL
...CONCPT METH/COMP 20. PAGE 39 B0780
ADMIN
NAT/G
LOC/G
DECISION
B61

GORDON R.A.,BUSINESS LEADERSHIP IN THE LARGE
CORPORATION. USA+45 SOCIETY EX/STRUC ADMIN CONTROL
ROUTINE GP/REL PWR...MGT 20. PAGE 41 B0831
LG/CO
LEAD
DECISION
LOBBY
B61

GORDON W.J.J.,SYNECTICS; THE DEVELOPMENT OF
CREATIVE CAPACITY. USA+45 PLAN TEC/DEV KNOWL WEALTH
...DECISION MGT 20. PAGE 41 B0832
CREATE
PROB/SOLV
ACT/RES
TOP/EX
B61

GRIFFITH E.S.,CONGRESS: ITS CONTEMPORARY ROLE.
CONSTN POL/PAR CHIEF PLAN BUDGET DIPLOM CONFER
ADMIN LOBBY...DECISION CONGRESS. PAGE 43 B0878
PARL/PROC
EX/STRUC
TOP/EX
LEGIS
B61

HAIRE M.,MODERN ORGANIZATION THEORY. LABOR ROUTINE
PERS/REL

MAJORITY...CONCPT MODAL OBS CONT/OBS. PAGE 45 B0919 GP/REL
MGT
DECISION

B61
KRUPP S.,PATTERN IN ORGANIZATIONAL ANALYSIS: A MGT
CRITICAL EXAMINATION. INGP/REL PERS/REL RATIONAL CONTROL
ATTIT AUTHORIT DRIVE PWR...DECISION PHIL/SCI SOC CONCPT
IDEA/COMP. PAGE 61 B1239 METH/CNCPT

B61
MAYNE A.,DESIGNING AND ADMINISTERING A REGIONAL ECO/UNDEV
ECONOMIC DEVELOPMENT PLAN WITH SPECIFIC REFERENCE PLAN
TO PUERTO RICO (PAMPHLET). PUERT/RICO SOCIETY NAT/G CREATE
DELIB/GP REGION...DECISION 20. PAGE 71 B1435 ADMIN

B61
MONAS S.,THE THIRD SECTION: POLICE AND SOCIETY IN ORD/FREE
RUSSIA UNDER NICHOLAS I. MOD/EUR RUSSIA ELITES COM
STRUCT NAT/G EX/STRUC ADMIN CONTROL PWR CONSERVE FORCES
...DECISION 19 NICHOLAS/I. PAGE 74 B1499 COERCE

B61
ROWAT D.C.,BASIC ISSUES IN PUBLIC ADMINISTRATION. NAT/G
STRUCT EX/STRUC PWR CONSERVE...MAJORIT DECISION MGT ADJUD
T 20 BUREAUCRCY. PAGE 91 B1839 ADMIN

B61
SINGER J.D.,FINANCING INTERNATIONAL ORGANIZATION: INT/ORG
THE UNITED NATIONS BUDGET PROCESS. WOR+45 FINAN MGT
ACT/RES CREATE PLAN BUDGET ECO/TAC ADMIN ROUTINE
ATTIT KNOWL...DECISION METH/CNCPT TIME/SEQ UN 20.
PAGE 97 B1964

B61
TANNENBAUM R.,LEADERSHIP AND ORGANIZATION. STRUCT LEAD
ADMIN INGP/REL ATTIT PERCEPT...DECISION METH/CNCPT MGT
OBS CHARTS BIBLIOG. PAGE 103 B2075 RESPECT
ROLE

B61
TRECKER H.B.,NEW UNDERSTANDING OF ADMINISTRATION. VOL/ASSN
NEIGH DELIB/GP CONTROL LEAD GP/REL INGP/REL PROF/ORG
...POLICY DECISION BIBLIOG. PAGE 105 B2126 ADMIN
PARTIC

L61
COHEN K.J.,"THE ROLE OF MANAGEMENT GAMES IN SOCIETY
EDUCATION AND RESEARCH." INTELL ECO/DEV FINAN GAME
ACT/RES ECO/TAC DECISION. PAGE 22 B0444 MGT
EDU/PROP

S61
CYERT R.M.,"TWO EXPERIMENTS ON BIAS AND CONFLICT IN LAB/EXP
ORGANIZATIONAL ESTIMATION." WORKER PROB/SOLV ROUTINE
EFFICIENCY...MGT PSY STAT CHARTS. PAGE 25 B0518 ADMIN
DECISION

S61
DEUTSCH K.W.,"A NOTE ON THE APPEARANCE OF WISDOM IN ADMIN
LARGE BUREAUCRATIC ORGANIZATIONS." ROUTINE PERSON PROBABIL
KNOWL SKILL...DECISION STAT. PAGE 28 B0577 PROB/SOLV
SIMUL

S61
DYKMAN J.W.,"REVIEW ARTICLE* PLANNING AND DECISION DECISION
THEORY." ELITES LOC/G MUNIC CONSULT ADMIN...POLICY PLAN
MGT. PAGE 31 B0640 RATIONAL

S61
EHRMANN H.W.,"FRENCH BUREAUCRACY AND ORGANIZED ADMIN
INTERESTS" (BMR)" FRANCE NAT/G DELIB/GP ROUTINE DECISION
...INT 20 BUREAUCRCY CIVIL/SERV. PAGE 32 B0657 PLURISM
LOBBY

S61
ROBINSON J.A.,"PROCESS SATISFACTION AND POLICY GOV/REL
APPROVAL IN STATE DEPARTMENT - CONGRESSIONAL EX/STRUC
RELATIONS." ELITES CHIEF LEGIS CONFER DEBATE ADMIN POL/PAR
FEEDBACK ROLE...CHARTS 20 CONGRESS PRESIDENT DECISION
DEPT/STATE. PAGE 89 B1802

S61
SHERBENOU E.L.,"CLASS, PARTICIPATION, AND THE REPRESENT
COUNCIL-MANAGER PLAN." ELITES STRUCT LEAD GP/REL MUNIC
ATTIT PWR DECISION. PAGE 96 B1942 EXEC

B62
BAILEY S.D.,THE SECRETARIAT OF THE UNITED NATIONS. INT/ORG
FUT WOR+45 DELIB/GP PLAN BAL/PWR DOMIN EDU/PROP EXEC
ADMIN PEACE ATTIT PWR...DECISION CONCPT TREND DIPLOM
CON/ANAL CHARTS UN VAL/FREE COLD/WAR 20. PAGE 8
B0162

B62
CHANDLER A.D.,STRATEGY AND STRUCTURE: CHAPTERS IN LG/CO
THE HISTORY OF THE INDUSTRIAL ENTERPRISE. USA+45 PLAN
USA-45 ECO/DEV EX/STRUC ECO/TAC EXEC...DECISION 20. ADMIN
PAGE 20 B0403 FINAN

B62
DUCKWORTH W.E.,A GUIDE TO OPERATIONAL RESEARCH. OP/RES
INDUS PLAN PROB/SOLV EXEC EFFICIENCY PRODUC KNOWL GAME
...MGT MATH STAT SIMUL METH 20 MONTECARLO. PAGE 31 DECISION
B0624 ADMIN

B62
FOSS P.O.,REORGANIZATION AND REASSIGNMENT IN THE FORCES
CALIFORNIA HIGHWAY PATROL (PAMPHLET). USA+45 STRUCT ADMIN
WORKER EDU/PROP CONTROL COERCE INGP/REL ORD/FREE PROVS
PWR...DECISION 20 CALIFORNIA. PAGE 37 B0744 PLAN

B62
HADWEN J.G.,HOW UNITED NATIONS DECISIONS ARE MADE. INT/ORG
WOR+45 LAW EDU/PROP LEGIT ADMIN PWR...DECISION ROUTINE

SELF/OBS GEN/LAWS UN 20. PAGE 45 B0912

B62
KAMMERER G.M.,CITY MANAGERS IN POLITICS: AN MUNIC
ANALYSIS OF MANAGER TENURE AND TERMINATION. POL/PAR LEAD
LEGIS PARTIC CHOOSE PWR...DECISION GEOG METH/CNCPT. EXEC
PAGE 57 B1161

B62
MAILICK S.,CONCEPTS AND ISSUES IN ADMINISTRATIVE DECISION
BEHAVIOR. EX/STRUC TOP/EX ROUTINE INGP/REL MGT
EFFICIENCY. PAGE 68 B1380 EXEC
PROB/SOLV

B62
MARS D.,SUGGESTED LIBRARY IN PUBLIC ADMINISTRATION. BIBLIOG
FINAN DELIB/GP EX/STRUC WORKER COMPUTER ADJUD ADMIN
...DECISION PSY SOC METH/COMP 20. PAGE 69 B1403 METH
MGT

B62
NATIONAL BUREAU ECONOMIC RES,THE RATE AND DIRECTION DECISION
OF INVENTIVE ACTIVITY: ECONOMIC AND SOCIAL FACTORS. PROB/SOLV
STRUCT INDUS MARKET R+D CREATE OP/RES TEC/DEV MGT
EFFICIENCY PRODUC RATIONAL UTIL...WELF/ST PHIL/SCI
METH/CNCPT TIME. PAGE 77 B1562

B62
PRESS C.,STATE MANUALS, BLUE BOOKS AND ELECTION BIBLIOG
RESULTS. LAW LOC/G MUNIC LEGIS WRITING FEDERAL PROVS
SOVEREIGN...DECISION STAT CHARTS 20. PAGE 84 B1700 ADMIN
CHOOSE

B62
SCALAPINO R.A.,PARTIES AND POLITICS IN CONTEMPORARY POL/PAR
JAPAN. EX/STRUC DIPLOM CHOOSE NAT/LISM ATTIT PARL/PROC
...POLICY 20 CHINJAP. PAGE 93 B1876 ELITES
DECISION

B62
SNYDER R.C.,FOREIGN POLICY DECISION-MAKING. FUT TEC/DEV
KOREA WOR+45 R+D CREATE ADMIN ROUTINE PWR HYPO/EXP
...DECISION PSY SOC CONCPT METH/CNCPT CON/ANAL DIPLOM
CHARTS GEN/METH METH 20. PAGE 99 B1992

B62
THIERRY S.S.,LE VATICAN SECRET. CHRIST-17C EUR+WWI ADMIN
MOD/EUR VATICAN NAT/G SECT DELIB/GP DOMIN LEGIT EX/STRUC
SOVEREIGN. PAGE 104 B2096 CATHISM
DECISION

B62
US ADVISORY COMN INTERGOV REL,STATE CONSTITUTIONAL LOC/G
AND STATUTORY RESTRICTIONS UPON THE STRUCTURAL, CONSTN
FUNCTIONAL, AND PERSONAL POWERS OF LOCAL GOV'T. PROVS
EX/STRUC ACT/RES DOMIN GOV/REL PWR...POLICY LAW
DECISION 17/20. PAGE 108 B2172

B62
US SENATE COMM GOVT OPERATIONS,ADMINISTRATION OF ORD/FREE
NATIONAL SECURITY. USA+45 CHIEF PLAN PROB/SOLV ADMIN
TEC/DEV DIPLOM ATTIT...POLICY DECISION 20 NAT/G
KENNEDY/JF RUSK/D MCNAMARA/R BUNDY/M HERTER/C. CONTROL
PAGE 110 B2212

B62
WEDDING N.,ADVERTISING MANAGEMENT. USA+45 ECO/DEV ECO/TAC
BUDGET CAP/ISM PRODUC PROFIT ATTIT...DECISION MGT COM/IND
PSY 20. PAGE 114 B2308 PLAN
EDU/PROP

L62
ERDMANN H.H.,"ADMINISTRATIVE LAW AND FARM AGRI
ECONOMICS." USA+45 LOC/G NAT/G PLAN PROB/SOLV LOBBY ADMIN
...DECISION ANTHOL 20. PAGE 33 B0680 ADJUD
POLICY

S62
BERNTHAL W.F.,"VALUE PERSPECTIVES IN MANAGEMENT MGT
DECISIONS." LG/CO OP/RES SUPEGO MORAL. PAGE 11 PROB/SOLV
B0229 DECISION

S62
BOOTH D.A.,"POWER STRUCTURE AND COMMUNITY CHANGE: A MUNIC
REPLICATION STUDY OF COMMUNITY A." STRATA LABOR ELITES
LEAD PARTIC REPRESENT...DECISION MGT TIME. PAGE 14 PWR
B0275

S62
DUFTY N.F.,"THE IMPLEMENTATION OF A DECISION." DECISION
STRATA ACT/RES...MGT CHARTS SOC/EXP ORG/CHARTS. CREATE
PAGE 31 B0627 METH/CNCPT
SOC

S62
IKLE F.C.,"POLITICAL NEGOTIATION AS A PROCESS OF ROUTINE
MODIFYING UTILITIES." WOR+45 FACE/GP LABOR NAT/G DECISION
FORCES ACT/RES EDU/PROP DETER PERCEPT ALL/VALS DIPLOM
...PSY NEW/IDEA HYPO/EXP GEN/METH 20. PAGE 53 B1076

S62
LOCKARD D.,"THE CITY MANAGER, ADMINISTRATIVE THEORY MUNIC
AND POLITICAL POWER." LEGIS ADMIN REPRESENT GP/REL EXEC
PWR. PAGE 66 B1333 LEAD
DECISION

S62
MCCLELLAND C.A.,"DECISIONAL OPPORTUNITY AND ACT/RES
POLITICAL CONTROVERSY." USA+45 NAT/G POL/PAR FORCES PERCEPT
TOP/EX DOMIN ADMIN PEACE DRIVE ORD/FREE PWR DIPLOM
...DECISION SIMUL 20. PAGE 72 B1444

S62
NORTH R.C.,"DECISION MAKING IN CRISIS: AN INT/ORG
INTRODUCTION." WOR+45 WOR-45 NAT/G CONSULT DELIB/GP ROUTINE

TEC/DEV PERCEPT KNOWL...POLICY DECISION PSY
METH/CNCPT CONT/OBS TREND VAL/FREE 20. PAGE 79
B1590
    DIPLOM

N62

US ADVISORY COMN INTERGOV REL.ALTERNATIVE
APPROACHES TO GOVERNMENTAL REORGANIZATION IN
METROPOLITAN AREAS (PAMPHLET). EX/STRUC LEGIS EXEC
LEAD PWR...DECISION GEN/METH. PAGE 107 B2171
    MUNIC
    REGION
    PLAN
    GOV/REL

B63

BANFIELD E.C.,CITY POLITICS. CULTURE LABOR LOC/G
POL/PAR LEGIS EXEC LEAD CHOOSE...DECISION NEGRO.
PAGE 9 B0178
    MUNIC
    RIGID/FLEX
    ATTIT

B63

BONINI C.P.,SIMULATION OF INFORMATION AND DECISION
SYSTEMS IN THE FIRM. MARKET BUDGET DOMIN EDU/PROP
ADMIN COST ATTIT HABITAT PERCEPT PWR...CONCPT
PROBABIL QUANT PREDICT HYPO/EXP BIBLIOG. PAGE 13
B0273
    INDUS
    SIMUL
    DECISION
    MGT

B63

BURSK E.C.,NEW DECISION-MAKING TOOLS FOR MANAGERS.
COMPUTER PLAN PROB/SOLV ROUTINE COST. PAGE 18 B0357
    DECISION
    MGT
    MATH
    RIGID/FLEX

B63

CORLEY R.N.,THE LEGAL ENVIRONMENT OF BUSINESS.
CONSTN LEGIS TAX ADMIN CT/SYS DISCRIM ATTIT PWR
...TREND 18/20. PAGE 23 B0477
    NAT/G
    INDUS
    JURID
    DECISION

B63

COSTELLO T.W.,PSYCHOLOGY IN ADMINISTRATION: A
RESEARCH ORIENTATION. CREATE PROB/SOLV PERS/REL
ADJUST ANOMIE ATTIT DRIVE PERCEPT ROLE...DECISION
BIBLIOG T 20. PAGE 24 B0488
    PSY
    MGT
    EXEC
    ADMIN

B63

CROUCH W.W.,SOUTHERN CALIFORNIA METROPOLIS: A STUDY
IN DEVELOPMENT OF GOVERNMENT FOR A METROPOLITAN
AREA. USA+45 USA-45 PROB/SOLV ADMIN LOBBY PARTIC
CENTRAL ORD/FREE PWR...BIBLIOG 20 PROGRSV/M.
PAGE 25 B0510
    LOC/G
    MUNIC
    LEGIS
    DECISION

B63

DE GUZMAN R.P.,PATTERNS IN DECISION-MAKING: CASE
STUDIES IN PHILIPPINE PUBLIC ADMINISTRATION.
PHILIPPINE LAW CHIEF PROB/SOLV INGP/REL DRIVE
PERCEPT ROLE...ANTHOL T 20. PAGE 27 B0557
    ADMIN
    DECISION
    POLICY
    GOV/REL

B63

DEBRAY P.,LE PORTUGAL ENTRE DEUX REVOLUTIONS.
EUR+WWI PORTUGAL CONSTN LEGIT ADMIN ATTIT ALL/VALS
...DECISION CONCPT 20 SALAZAR/A. PAGE 28 B0567
    NAT/G
    DELIB/GP
    TOP/EX

B63

GREEN H.P.,GOVERNMENT OF THE ATOM. USA+45 LEGIS
PROB/SOLV ADMIN CONTROL PWR...POLICY DECISION 20
PRESIDENT CONGRESS. PAGE 43 B0864
    GOV/REL
    EX/STRUC
    NUC/PWR
    DELIB/GP

B63

HARGROVE M.M.,BUSINESS POLICY CASES-WITH BEHAVIORAL
SCIENCE IMPLICATIONS. LG/CO SML/CO EX/STRUC TOP/EX
PLAN PROB/SOLV CONFER ADMIN CONTROL ROUTINE
EFFICIENCY. PAGE 47 B0946
    SOC/EXP
    INDUS
    DECISION
    MGT

B63

HERNDON J.,A SELECTED BIBLIOGRAPHY OF MATERIALS IN
STATE GOVERNMENT AND POLITICS (PAMPHLET). USA+45
POL/PAR LEGIS ADMIN CHOOSE MGT. PAGE 49 B0993
    BIBLIOG
    GOV/COMP
    PROVS
    DECISION

B63

INDIAN INSTITUTE PUBLIC ADMIN.CASES IN INDIAN
ADMINISTRATION. INDIA AGRI NAT/G PROB/SOLV TEC/DEV
ECO/TAC ADMIN...ANTHOL METH 20. PAGE 53 B1083
    DECISION
    PLAN
    MGT
    ECO/UNDEV

B63

JACOB H.,GERMAN ADMINISTRATION SINCE BISMARCK:
CENTRAL AUTHORITY VERSUS LOCAL AUTONOMY. GERMANY
GERMANY/W LAW POL/PAR CONTROL CENTRAL TOTALISM
FASCISM...MAJORIT DECISION STAT CHARTS GOV/COMP
19/20 BISMARCK/O HITLER/A WEIMAR/REP. PAGE 55 B1111
    ADMIN
    NAT/G
    LOC/G
    POLICY

B63

KAMMERER G.M.,THE URBAN POLITICAL COMMUNITY:
PROFILES IN TOWN POLITICS. ELITES LOC/G LEAD
...DECISION GP/COMP. PAGE 57 B1162
    EXEC
    MUNIC
    PWR
    GOV/COMP

B63

KOGAN N.,THE POLITICS OF ITALIAN FOREIGN POLICY.
EUR+WWI LEGIS DOMIN EXEC PWR RESPECT SKILL
...POLICY DECISION HUM SOC METH/CNCPT OBS INT
CHARTS 20. PAGE 61 B1227
    NAT/G
    ROUTINE
    DIPLOM
    ITALY

B63

LINDBERG L.,POLITICAL DYNAMICS OF EUROPEAN ECONOMIC
INTEGRATION. EUR+WWI ECO/DEV INT/ORG VOL/ASSN
DELIB/GP ADMIN WEALTH...DECISION EEC 20. PAGE 65
B1313
    MARKET
    ECO/TAC

B63

MAHESHWARI B.,STUDIES IN PANCHAYATI RAJ. INDIA
POL/PAR EX/STRUC BUDGET EXEC REPRESENT CENTRAL
EFFICIENCY...DECISION 20. PAGE 68 B1378
    FEDERAL
    LOC/G
    GOV/REL
    LEAD

B63

MENZEL J.M.,THE CHINESE CIVIL SERVICE: CAREER OPEN
    ADMIN

TO TALENT? ASIA ROUTINE INGP/REL DISCRIM ATTIT ROLE
KNOWL ANTHOL. PAGE 73 B1468
    NAT/G
    DECISION
    ELITES

B63

MEYNAUD J.,PLANIFICATION ET POLITIQUE. FRANCE ITALY
FINAN LABOR DELIB/GP LEGIS ADMIN EFFICIENCY
...MAJORIT DECISION 20. PAGE 73 B1477
    PLAN
    ECO/TAC
    PROB/SOLV

B63

PEABODY R.L.,NEW PERSPECTIVES ON THE HOUSE OF
REPRESENTATIVES. AGRI FINAN SCHOOL FORCES CONFER
LEAD CHOOSE REPRESENT FEDERAL...POLICY DECISION
HOUSE/REP. PAGE 82 B1647
    NEW/IDEA
    LEGIS
    PWR
    ADMIN

B63

STEIN H.,AMERICAN CIVIL-MILITARY DECISION. USA+45
USA-45 EX/STRUC FORCES LEGIS TOP/EX PLAN DIPLOM
FOR/AID ATTIT 20 CONGRESS. PAGE 100 B2028
    CIVMIL/REL
    DECISION
    WAR
    BUDGET

B63

THOMETZ C.E.,THE DECISION-MAKERS: THE POWER
STRUCTURE OF DALLAS. USA+45 CULTURE EX/STRUC DOMIN
LEGIT GP/REL ATTIT OBJECTIVE...INT CHARTS GP/COMP.
PAGE 104 B2101
    ELITES
    MUNIC
    PWR
    DECISION

B63

THORELLI H.B.,INTOP: INTERNATIONAL OPERATIONS
SIMULATION: PLAYER'S MANUAL. BRAZIL FINAN OP/RES
ADMIN GP/REL INGP/REL PRODUC PERCEPT...DECISION MGT
EEC. PAGE 104 B2108
    GAME
    INT/TRADE
    EDU/PROP
    LG/CO

B63

TSOU T.,AMERICA'S FAILURE IN CHINA, 1941-1950.
USA+45 USA-45 NAT/G ACT/RES PLAN DOMIN EDU/PROP
ADMIN ROUTINE ATTIT PERSON ORD/FREE...DECISION
CONCPT MYTH TIME/SEQ TREND STERTYP 20. PAGE 105
B2132
    ASIA
    PERCEPT
    DIPLOM

B63

US SENATE COMM ON JUDICIARY,ADMINISTERED PRICES.
USA+45 RATION ADJUD CONTROL LOBBY...POLICY 20
SENATE MONOPOLY. PAGE 110 B2229
    LG/CO
    PRICE
    ADMIN
    DECISION

S63

BACHRACH P.,"DECISIONS AND NONDECISIONS: AN
ANALYTICAL FRAMEWORK." UNIV SOCIETY CREATE LEGIT
ADMIN EXEC COERCE...DECISION PSY CONCPT CHARTS.
PAGE 8 B0156
    PWR
    HYPO/EXP

S63

BOWIE R.,"STRATEGY AND THE ATLANTIC ALLIANCE."
EUR+WWI VOL/ASSN BAL/PWR COERCE NUC/PWR ATTIT
ORD/FREE PWR...DECISION GEN/LAWS NATO COLD/WAR 20.
PAGE 14 B0287
    FORCES
    ROUTINE

S63

JENNINGS M.K.,"PUBLIC ADMINISTRATORS AND COMMUNITY
DECISION-MAKING." ELITES LOC/G LEAD...GP/COMP
GOV/COMP. PAGE 56 B1134
    ADMIN
    MUNIC
    DECISION
    PWR

S63

WINGFIELD C.J.,"POWER STRUCTURE AND DECISION-MAKING
IN CITY PLANNING." EDU/PROP ADMIN LEAD PARTIC
GP/REL ATTIT. PAGE 117 B2365
    MUNIC
    PLAN
    DECISION
    PWR

B64

BLACKSTOCK P.W.,THE STRATEGY OF SUBVERSION. USA+45
FORCES EDU/PROP ADMIN COERCE GOV/REL...DECISION MGT
20 DEPT/DEFEN CIA DEPT/STATE. PAGE 12 B0247
    ORD/FREE
    DIPLOM
    CONTROL

B64

BRIGHT J.R.,RESEARCH, DEVELOPMENT AND TECHNOLOGICAL
INNOVATION. CULTURE R+D CREATE PLAN PROB/SOLV
AUTOMAT RISK PERSON...DECISION CONCPT PREDICT
BIBLIOG. PAGE 15 B0308
    TEC/DEV
    NEW/IDEA
    INDUS
    MGT

B64

COLLINS B.E.,A SOCIAL PSYCHOLOGY OF GROUP PROCESSES
FOR DECISION-MAKING. PROB/SOLV ROUTINE...SOC CHARTS
HYPO/EXP. PAGE 22 B0453
    FACE/GP
    DECISION
    NAT/G
    INDUS

B64

GORE W.J.,ADMINISTRATIVE DECISION-MAKING: A
HEURISTIC MODEL. EX/STRUC ADMIN LEAD ROUTINE
PERS/REL...METH/CNCPT ORG/CHARTS. PAGE 41 B0834
    DECISION
    MGT
    SIMUL
    GEN/METH

B64

KEEFE W.J.,THE AMERICAN LEGISLATIVE PROCESS:
CONGRESS AND THE STATES. USA+45 LAW POL/PAR
DELIB/GP DEBATE ADMIN LOBBY REPRESENT CONGRESS
PRESIDENT. PAGE 59 B1187
    LEGIS
    DECISION
    PWR
    PROVS

B64

KIMBROUGH R.B.,POLITICAL POWER AND EDUCATIONAL
DECISION-MAKING. USA+45 FINAN ADMIN LEAD GP/REL
ATTIT PWR PROG/TEAC. PAGE 60 B1207
    EDU/PROP
    PROB/SOLV
    DECISION
    SCHOOL

B64

NELSON D.H.,ADMINISTRATIVE AGENCIES OF THE USA:
THEIR DECISIONS AND AUTHORITY. USA+45 NAT/G CONTROL
CT/SYS REPRESENT...DECISION 20. PAGE 78 B1568
    ADMIN
    EX/STRUC
    ADJUD
    LAW

B64

RIES J.C.,THE MANAGEMENT OF DEFENSE: ORGANIZATION
AND CONTROL OF THE US ARMED SERVICES. PROF/ORG
DELIB/GP EX/STRUC LEGIS GOV/REL PERS/REL CENTRAL
    FORCES
    ACT/RES
    DECISION

RATIONAL PWR...POLICY TREND GOV/COMP BIBLIOG.
PAGE 88 B1782
CONTROL

B64
TINBERGEN J.,CENTRAL PLANNING. COM INTELL ECO/DEV
ECO/UNDEV FINAN INT/ORG PROB/SOLV ECO/TAC CONTROL
EXEC ROUTINE DECISION. PAGE 104 B2111
PLAN
INDUS
MGT
CENTRAL

B64
US SENATE COMM GOVT OPERATIONS,ADMINISTRATION OF
NATIONAL SECURITY. USA+45 CHIEF TOP/EX PLAN DIPLOM
CONTROL PEACE...POLICY DECISION 20 PRESIDENT
CONGRESS. PAGE 110 B2216
ADMIN
FORCES
ORD/FREE
NAT/G

L64
PRUITT D.G.,"PROBLEM SOLVING IN THE DEPARTMENT OF
STATE." USA+45 NAT/G CONSULT PROB/SOLV EXEC PWR
...DECISION INT ORG/CHARTS 20. PAGE 85 B1713
ROUTINE
MGT
DIPLOM

S64
CASE H.L.,"GORDON R. CLAPP: THE ROLE OF FAITH,
PURPOSES AND PEOPLE IN ADMINISTRATION." INDUS MUNIC
PROVS...POLICY 20. PAGE 19 B0391
ADMIN
BIOG
EX/STRUC
DECISION

S64
KAMMERER G.M.,"URBAN LEADERSHIP DURING CHANGE."
LEAD PARTIC REPRESENT GP/REL PLURISM...DECISION
GP/COMP. PAGE 58 B1164
MUNIC
PWR
ELITES
EXEC

S64
KHAN M.Z.,"THE PRESIDENT OF THE GENERAL ASSEMBLY."
WOR+45 CONSTN DELIB/GP EDU/PROP LEGIT ROUTINE PWR
RESPECT SKILL...DECISION SOC BIOG TREND UN 20.
PAGE 59 B1202
INT/ORG
TOP/EX

S64
RUSK D.,"THE MAKING OF FOREIGN POLICY" USA+45 CHIEF
DELIB/GP WORKER PROB/SOLV ADMIN ATTIT PWR
...DECISION 20 DEPT/STATE RUSK/D GOLDMAN/E. PAGE 92
B1856
DIPLOM
INT
POLICY

S64
SALISBURY R.H.,"URBAN POLITICS: THE NEW CONVERGENCE
OF POWER." STRATA POL/PAR EX/STRUC PARTIC GP/REL
DECISION. PAGE 92 B1863
MUNIC
PWR
LEAD

S64
STONE P.A.,"DECISION TECHNIQUES FOR TOWN
DEVELOPMENT." PLAN COST PROFIT...DECISION MGT
CON/ANAL CHARTS METH/COMP BIBLIOG 20. PAGE 101
B2048
OP/RES
MUNIC
ADMIN
PROB/SOLV

N64
US SENATE COMM GOVT OPERATIONS,METROPOLITAN
AMERICA: A SELECTED BIBLIOGRAPHY (PAMPHLET). USA+45
DIST/IND FINAN LOC/G EDU/PROP ADMIN HEALTH 20.
PAGE 110 B2214
BIBLIOG/A
MUNIC
GOV/REL
DECISION

B65
ANTHONY R.N.,PLANNING AND CONTROL SYSTEMS. UNIV
OP/RES...DECISION MGT LING. PAGE 6 B0114
CONTROL
PLAN
METH
HYPO/EXP

B65
BUECHNER J.C.,DIFFERENCES IN ROLE PERCEPTIONS IN
COLORADO COUNCIL-MANAGER CITIES. USA+45 ADMIN
ROUTINE GP/REL CONSEN PERCEPT PERSON ROLE
...DECISION MGT STAT INT QU CHARTS 20 COLORADO
CITY/MGT. PAGE 17 B0338
MUNIC
CONSULT
LOC/G
IDEA/COMP

B65
CAVERS D.F.,THE CHOICE-OF-LAW PROCESS. PROB/SOLV
ADJUD CT/SYS CHOOSE RATIONAL...IDEA/COMP 16/20
TREATY. PAGE 19 B0396
JURID
DECISION
METH/COMP
ADMIN

B65
DYER F.C.,BUREAUCRACY VS CREATIVITY. UNIV CONTROL
LEAD INGP/REL EFFICIENCY MGT. PAGE 31 B0639
ADMIN
DECISION
METH/COMP
CREATE

B65
FOLTZ W.J.,FROM FRENCH WEST AFRICA TO THE MALI
FEDERATION. AFR FRANCE MALI ADMIN CONTROL FEDERAL
...DECISION 20. PAGE 36 B0734
EXEC
TOP/EX
ELITES
LEAD

B65
FRIEDMAN L.,SOUTHERN JUSTICE. USA+45 PUB/INST LEGIT
ADMIN CT/SYS DISCRIM...DECISION ANTHOL 20 NEGRO
SOUTH/US CIV/RIGHTS. PAGE 37 B0758
ADJUD
LAW
CONSTN
RACE/REL

B65
HICKMAN B.G.,QUANTITATIVE PLANNING OF ECONOMIC
POLICY. FRANCE NETHERLAND OP/RES PRICE ROUTINE UTIL
...POLICY DECISION ECOMETRIC METH/CNCPT STAT STYLE
CHINJAP. PAGE 50 B1004
PROB/SOLV
PLAN
QUANT

B65
KWEDER J.B.,THE ROLES OF THE MANAGER, MAYOR, AND
COUNCILMEN IN POLICYMAKING. LEGIS PERS/REL ATTIT
ROLE PWR GP/COMP. PAGE 62 B1246
MUNIC
EXEC
LEAD
DECISION

B65
MACDONALD R.W.,THE LEAGUE OF ARAB STATES: A STUDY
IN THE DYNAMICS OF REGIONAL ORGANIZATION. ISRAEL
UAR USSR FINAN INT/ORG DELIB/GP ECO/TAC AGREE
NEUTRAL ORD/FREE PWR...DECISION BIBLIOG 20 TREATY
ISLAM
REGION
DIPLOM
ADMIN

UN. PAGE 67 B1358

B65
MARTIN R.,PUBLIC ADMINISTRATION AND DEMOCRACY.
ELITES NAT/G ADMIN EXEC ROUTINE INGP/REL. PAGE 70
B1412
EX/STRUC
DECISION
REPRESENT
GP/REL

B65
PRESTHUS R.,BEHAVIORAL APPROACHES TO PUBLIC
ADMINISTRATION. UK STRATA LG/CO PUB/INST VOL/ASSN
EX/STRUC TOP/EX EFFICIENCY HEALTH. PAGE 84 B1704
GEN/METH
DECISION
ADMIN
R+D

B65
RUBINSTEIN A.Z.,THE CHALLENGE OF POLITICS: IDEAS
AND ISSUES (2ND ED.). UNIV ELITES SOCIETY EX/STRUC
BAL/PWR PARL/PROC AUTHORIT...DECISION ANTHOL 20.
PAGE 92 B1852
NAT/G
DIPLOM
GP/REL
ORD/FREE

B65
SINGER J.D.,HUMAN BEHAVIOR AND INTERNATIONAL
POLITICS* CONTRIBUTIONS FROM THE SOCIAL-
PSYCHOLOGICAL SCIENCES. ACT/RES PLAN EDU/PROP ADMIN
KNOWL...DECISION PSY SOC NET/THEORY HYPO/EXP
LAB/EXP SOC/EXP GEN/METH ANTHOL BIBLIOG. PAGE 97
B1965
DIPLOM
PHIL/SCI
QUANT
SIMUL

B65
STANLEY D.T.,CHANGING ADMINISTRATIONS. USA+45
POL/PAR DELIB/GP TOP/EX BUDGET GOV/REL GP/REL
PERS/REL PWR...MAJORIT DECISION MGT 20 PRESIDENT
SUCCESSION DEPT/STATE DEPT/DEFEN DEPT/HEW. PAGE 100
B2021
NAT/G
CHIEF
ADMIN
EX/STRUC

B65
STARR M.K.,EXECUTIVE READINGS IN MANAGEMENT
SCIENCE. TOP/EX WORKER EDU/PROP ADMIN...DECISION
GEN/LAWS ANTHOL METH T 20. PAGE 100 B2023
MGT
EX/STRUC
PLAN
LG/CO

B65
TYBOUT R.A.,ECONOMICS OF RESEARCH AND DEVELOPMENT.
ECO/DEV ECO/UNDEV INDUS PROFIT DECISION. PAGE 106
B2141
R+D
FORCES
ADMIN
DIPLOM

B65
UNIVERSAL REFERENCE SYSTEM,INTERNATIONAL AFFAIRS:
VOLUME I IN THE POLITICAL SCIENCE, GOVERNMENT, AND
PUBLIC POLICY SERIES...DECISION ECOMETRIC GEOG
INT/LAW JURID MGT PHIL/SCI PSY SOC. PAGE 107 B2163
BIBLIOG/A
GEN/METH
COMPUT/IR
DIPLOM

B65
VEINOTT A.F. JR.,MATHEMATICAL STUDIES IN MANAGEMENT
SCIENCE. UNIV INDUS COMPUTER ADMIN...DECISION
NET/THEORY SIMUL 20. PAGE 112 B2257
MATH
MGT
PLAN
PRODUC

B65
WALTON R.E.,A BEHAVIORAL THEORY OF LABOR
NEGOTIATIONS: AN ANALYSIS OF A SOCIAL INTERACTION
SYSTEM. USA+45 FINAN PROB/SOLV ECO/TAC GP/REL
INGP/REL...DECISION BIBLIOG. PAGE 113 B2285
SOC
LABOR
BARGAIN
ADMIN

S65
AMLUND C.A.,"EXECUTIVE-LEGISLATIVE IMBALANCE:
TRUMAN TO KENNEDY." USA+45 NAT/G GOV/REL PWR.
PAGE 4 B0090
LEGIS
EXEC
DECISION

S65
GRENIEWSKI H.,"INTENTION AND PERFORMANCE: A PRIMER
OF CYBERNETICS OF PLANNING." EFFICIENCY OPTIMAL
KNOWL SKILL...DECISION MGT EQULIB. PAGE 43 B0873
SIMUL
GAME
GEN/METH
PLAN

S65
HAMMOND P.Y.,"FOREIGN POLICY-MAKING AND
ADMINISTRATIVE POLITICS." CREATE ADMIN COST
...DECISION CONCPT GAME CONGRESS PRESIDENT. PAGE 46
B0935
DIPLOM
STRUCT
IDEA/COMP
OP/RES

S65
HOLSTI O.R.,"THE 1914 CASE." MOD/EUR COMPUTER
DIPLOM EDU/PROP EXEC...DECISION PSY PROBABIL STAT
COMPUT/IR SOC/EXP TIME. PAGE 51 B1036
CON/ANAL
PERCEPT
WAR

S65
POSVAR W.W.,"NATIONAL SECURITY POLICY* THE REALM OF
OBSCURITY." CREATE PLAN PROB/SOLV ADMIN LEAD GP/REL
CONSERVE...DECISION GEOG. PAGE 84 B1694
DIPLOM
USA+45
RECORD

S65
QUADE Q.L.,"THE TRUMAN ADMINISTRATION AND THE
SEPARATION OF POWERS: THE CASE OF THE MARSHALL
PLAN." SOCIETY INT/ORG NAT/G CONSULT DELIB/GP LEGIS
PLAN ECO/TAC ROUTINE DRIVE PERCEPT RIGID/FLEX
ORD/FREE PWR WEALTH...DECISION GEOG NEW/IDEA TREND
20 TRUMAN/HS. PAGE 85 B1726
USA+45
ECO/UNDEV
DIPLOM

S65
SIMON H.A.,"ADMINISTRATIVE DECISION-MAKING." USA+45
INGP/REL 20. PAGE 97 B1960
ADMIN
DECISION
EX/STRUC
METH/CNCPT

B66
AMER ENTERPRISE INST PUB POL,CONGRESS: THE FIRST
BRANCH OF GOVERNMENT. EX/STRUC FEEDBACK REPRESENT
INGP/REL PWR...DECISION METH/CNCPT PREDICT. PAGE 4
B0081
EFFICIENCY
LEGIS
DELIB/GP
CONTROL

B66
BROWN R.E.,JUDGMENT IN ADMINISTRATION. DRIVE PERSON
KNOWL...DECISION 20. PAGE 16 B0326
ADMIN
EXEC

FABRYCKY W.J.,OPERATIONS ECONOMY INDUSTRIAL APPLICATIONS OF OPERATIONS RESEARCH. INDUS PLAN ECO/TAC PRODUC...MATH PROBABIL STAT CHARTS 20. PAGE 34 B0695
SKILL
PROB/SOLV
B66
OP/RES
MGT
SIMUL
DECISION
B66

FENN DH J.R.,BUSINESS DECISION MAKING AND GOVERNMENT POLICY. SERV/IND LEGIS LICENSE ADMIN CONTROL GP/REL INGP/REL 20 CASEBOOK. PAGE 35 B0711
DECISION
PLAN
NAT/G
LG/CO
B66

FOX K.A.,THE THEORY OF QUANTITATIVE ECONOMIC POLICY WITH APPLICATIONS TO ECONOMIC GROWTH AND STABILIZATION. ECO/DEV AGRI NAT/G PLAN ADMIN RISK ...DECISION IDEA/COMP SIMUL T. PAGE 37 B0746
ECO/TAC
ECOMETRIC
EQUILIB
GEN/LAWS
B66

HASTINGS P.G.,THE MANAGEMENT OF BUSINESS FINANCE. ECO/DEV PLAN BUDGET CONTROL COST...DECISION CHARTS BIBLIOG T 20. PAGE 48 B0966
FINAN
MGT
INDUS
ECO/TAC
B66

OWEN G.,INDUSTRY IN THE UNITED STATES. UK USA+45 NAT/G WEALTH...DECISION NAT/COMP 20. PAGE 80 B1620
METH/COMP
INDUS
MGT
PROB/SOLV
B66

RUBENSTEIN R.,THE SHARING OF POWER IN A PSYCHIATRIC HOSPITAL. CLIENT PROF/ORG PUB/INST INGP/REL ATTIT PWR...DECISION OBS RECORD. PAGE 91 B1847
ADMIN
PARTIC
HEALTH
CONCPT
B66

SAPIN B.M.,THE MAKING OF UNITED STATES FOREIGN POLICY. USA+45 INT/ORG DELIB/GP FORCES PLAN ECO/TAC CIVMIL/REL PRESIDENT. PAGE 92 B1868
DIPLOM
EX/STRUC
DECISION
NAT/G
B66

SCHMIDT K.M.,AMERICAN STATE AND LOCAL GOVERNMENT IN ACTION. USA+45 CONSTN LOC/G POL/PAR CHIEF LEGIS PROB/SOLV ADJUD LOBBY GOV/REL...DECISION ANTHOL 20 GOVERNOR MAYOR URBAN/RNWL. PAGE 94 B1896
PROVS
ADMIN
MUNIC
PLAN
B66

YOUNG S.,MANAGEMENT: A SYSTEMS ANALYSIS. DELIB/GP EX/STRUC ECO/TAC CONTROL EFFICIENCY...NET/THEORY 20. PAGE 119 B2394
PROB/SOLV
MGT
DECISION
SIMUL
L66

CRAIN R.L.,"STRUCTURE AND VALUES IN LOCAL POLITICAL SYSTEMS: THE CASE OF FLUORIDATION DECISIONS." EX/STRUC LEGIS LEAD PARTIC REPRESENT PWR...DECISION GOV/COMP. PAGE 25 B0501
MUNIC
EDU/PROP
LOC/G
ATTIT
S66

AUSLAND J.C.,"CRISIS MANAGEMENT* BERLIN, CYPRUS, LAOS." CYPRUS LAOS FORCES CREATE PLAN EDU/PROP TASK CENTRAL PERSON RIGID/FLEX...DECISION MGT 20 BERLIN KENNEDY/JF MCNAMARA/R RUSK. PAGE 7 B0148
OP/RES
DIPLOM
RISK
ADMIN
S66

BALDWIN D.A.,"CONGRESSIONAL INITIATIVE IN FOREIGN POLICY." NAT/G BARGAIN DIPLOM FOR/AID RENT GIVE ...DECISION CONGRESS. PAGE 8 B0171
EXEC
TOP/EX
GOV/REL
S66

MARKSHAK J.,"ECONOMIC PLANNING AND THE COST OF THINKING." COM MARKET EX/STRUC...DECISION GEN/LAWS. PAGE 69 B1400
ECO/UNDEV
ECO/TAC
PLAN
ECO/DEV
C66

JACOB H.,"DIMENSIONS OF STATE POLITICS HEARD A. ED. STATE LEGIWLATURES IN AMERICAN POLITICS." CULTURE STRATA POL/PAR BUDGET TAX LOBBY ROUTINE GOV/REL ...TRADIT DECISION GEOG. PAGE 55 B1112
PROVS
LEGIS
ROLE
REPRESENT
C66

SHERMAN H.,"IT ALL DEPENDS." USA+45 FINAN MARKET PLAN PROB/SOLV EXEC PARTIC INGP/REL SUPEGO ...DECISION BIBLIOG 20. PAGE 96 B1944
LG/CO
MGT
ADMIN
POLICY
B67

ENKE S.,DEFENSE MANAGEMENT. USA+45 R+D FORCES WORKER PLAN ECO/TAC ADMIN NUC/PWR BAL/PAY UTIL WEALTH...MGT DEPT/DEFEN. PAGE 33 B0675
DECISION
DELIB/GP
EFFICIENCY
BUDGET
B67

GITTELL M.,PARTICIPANTS AND PARTICIPATION: A STUDY OF SCHOOL POLICY IN NEW YORK. USA+45 MUNIC EX/STRUC BUDGET PAY ATTIT...POLICY 20 NEWYORK/C. PAGE 40 B0806
SCHOOL
DECISION
PARTIC
ADMIN
B67

GREENE L.S.,AMERICAN GOVERNMENT POLICIES AND FUNCTIONS. USA+45 LAW AGRI DIST/IND LABOR MUNIC BUDGET DIPLOM EDU/PROP ORD/FREE...BIBLIOG T 20. PAGE 43 B0867
POLICY
NAT/G
ADMIN
DECISION
B67

KRISLOV S.,THE NEGRO IN FEDERAL EMPLOYMENT. LAW STRATA LOC/G CREATE PROB/SOLV INSPECT GOV/REL DISCRIM ROLE...DECISION INT TREND 20 NEGRO WWI CIVIL/SERV. PAGE 61 B1238
WORKER
NAT/G
ADMIN
RACE/REL

ROBINSON R.D., INTERNATIONAL MANAGEMENT USA+45 FINAN R+D PLAN PRODUC...DECISION T. PAGE 67 B1352
B67
INT/TRADE
MGT
INT/LAW
MARKET
B67

TOMA P.A.,THE POLITICS OF FOOD FOR PEACE: EXECUTIVE-LEGISLATIVE INTERACTION. USA+45 ECO/UNDEV POL/PAR DEBATE EXEC LOBBY CHOOSE PEACE...DECISION CHARTS. PAGE 104 B2113
FOR/AID
POLICY
LEGIS
AGRI
L67

CAHIERS P.,"LE RECOURS EN CONSTATATION DE MANQUEMENTS DES ETATS MEMBRES DEVANT LA COUR DES COMMUNAUTES EUROPEENNES." LAW PROB/SOLV DIPLOM ADMIN CT/SYS SANCTION ATTIT...POLICY DECISION JURID ECSC EEC. PAGE 18 B0362
INT/ORG
CONSTN
ROUTINE
ADJUD
L67

TRAVERS H. JR.,"AN EXAMINATION OF THE CAB'S MERGER POLICY." USA+45 USA-45 LAW NAT/G LEGIS PLAN ADMIN ...DECISION 20 CONGRESS. PAGE 105 B2125
ADJUD
LG/CO
POLICY
DIST/IND
S67

BRADY R.H.,"COMPUTERS IN TOP-LEVEL DECISION MAKING" FUT WOR+45 CONTROL...PREDICT CHARTS. PAGE 15 B0297
COMPUTER
MGT
DECISION
TEC/DEV
S67

BURKE E.M.,"THE SEARCH FOR AUTHORITY IN PLANNING." MUNIC NEIGH CREATE PROB/SOLV LEGIT ADMIN CONTROL EFFICIENCY PWR...METH/COMP SIMUL 20. PAGE 17 B0352
DECISION
PLAN
LOC/G
METH
S67

CARIAS B.,"EL CONTROL DE LAS EMPRESAS PUBLICAS POR GRUPOS DE INTERESES DE LA COMUNIDAD." FRANCE UK VENEZUELA INDUS NAT/G CONTROL OWN PWR...DECISION NAT/COMP 20. PAGE 18 B0377
WORKER
REPRESENT
MGT
SOCISM
S67

CONWAY J.E.,"MAKING RESEARCH EFFECTIVE IN LEGISLATION." LAW R+D CONSULT EX/STRUC PLAN CONFER ADMIN LEAD ROUTINE TASK INGP/REL DECISION. PAGE 23 B0469
ACT/RES
POLICY
LEGIS
PROB/SOLV
S67

CROCKETT D.G.,"THE MP AND HIS CONSTITUENTS." UK POL/PAR...DECISION 20. PAGE 25 B0506
EXEC
NAT/G
PERS/REL
REPRESENT
S67

DIXON O.F.,"A SOCIAL SYSTEMS APPROACH TO MARKETING." ECO/DEV ECO/TAC CONTROL EFFICIENCY ...DECISION 20. PAGE 29 B0599
MARKET
SOCIETY
GP/REL
MGT
S67

DODSON D.W.,"NEW FORCES OPERATING IN EDUCATIONAL DECISION-MAKING." USA+45 NEIGH EDU/PROP ADMIN SUPEGO DECISION. PAGE 30 B0602
PROB/SOLV
SCHOOL
PERS/REL
PWR
S67

DROR Y.,"POLICY ANALYSTS." USA+45 COMPUTER OP/RES ECO/TAC ADMIN ROUTINE...ECOMETRIC METH/COMP SIMUL 20. PAGE 30 B0618
NAT/G
POLICY
PLAN
DECISION
S67

DRYDEN S.,"LOCAL GOVERNMENT IN TANZANIA PART II" TANZANIA LAW NAT/G POL/PAR CONTROL PARTIC REPRESENT ...DECISION 20. PAGE 31 B0622
LOC/G
GOV/REL
ADMIN
STRUCT
S67

GITTELL M.,"PROFESSIONALISM AND PUBLIC PARTICIPATION IN EDUCATIONAL POLICY MAKING." STRUCT ADMIN GP/REL ATTIT PWR 20. PAGE 40 B0805
DECISION
PLAN
EDU/PROP
MUNIC
S67

GOLIGHTLY H.O.,"THE AIRLINES: A CASE STUDY IN MANAGEMENT INNOVATION." USA+45 AIR FINAN INDUS TOP/EX CREATE PLAN PROB/SOLV ADMIN EXEC PROFIT ...DECISION 20. PAGE 40 B0820
DIST/IND
MARKET
MGT
TEC/DEV
S67

GORHAM W.,"NOTES OF A PRACTITIONER." USA+45 BUDGET ADMIN COST...CON/ANAL METH/COMP 20 JOHNSON/LB. PAGE 41 B0836
DECISION
NAT/G
DELIB/GP
EFFICIENCY
S67

JAVITS J.K.,"THE USE OF AMERICAN PLURALISM." USA+45 ECO/DEV BUDGET ADMIN ALL/IDEOS...DECISION TREND. PAGE 56 B1127
CENTRAL
ATTIT
POLICY
NAT/G
S67

JONES G.S.,"STRATEGIC PLANNING." USA+45 EX/STRUC FORCES DETER WAR 20 PRESIDENT. PAGE 57 B1150
PLAN
DECISION
DELIB/GP
POLICY
S67

KRARUP O.,"JUDICIAL REVIEW OF ADMINISTRATIVE ACTION IN DENMARK." DENMARK LAW CT/SYS...JURID CONCPT 19/20. PAGE 61 B1234
ADJUD
CONTROL
EXEC
DECISION

LEES J.P.,"LEGISLATIVE REVIEW AND BUREAUCRATIC
RESPONSIBILITY." USA+45 FINAN NAT/G DELIB/GP PLAN
PROB/SOLV CONFER CONTROL GP/REL DEMAND...DECISION
20 CONGRESS PRESIDENT HOUSE/REP BUREAUCRCY. PAGE 63
B1281
SUPEGO
BUDGET
LEGIS
EXEC
S67

LEVCIK B.,"WAGES AND EMPLOYMENT PROBLEMS IN THE NEW
SYSTEM OF PLANNED MANAGEMENT IN CZECHOSLOVAKIA."
CZECHOSLVK EUR+WWI NAT/G OP/RES PLAN ADMIN ROUTINE
INGP/REL CENTRAL EFFICIENCY PRODUC DECISION.
PAGE 64 B1300
MARXISM
WORKER
MGT
PAY
S67

LINEBERRY R.L.,"REFORMISM AND PUBLIC POLICIES IN
AMERICAN CITIES." USA+45 POL/PAR EX/STRUC LEGIS
BUDGET TAX GP/REL...STAT CHARTS. PAGE 65 B1317
DECISION
POLICY
MUNIC
LOC/G
S67

LLOYD K.,"URBAN RACE RIOTS V EFFECTIVE ANTI-
DISCRIMINATION AGENCIES* AN END OR A BEGINNING?"
USA+45 STRATA ACT/RES ADMIN ADJUST ORD/FREE RESPECT
...PLURIST DECISION SOC SOC/WK. PAGE 66 B1332
GP/REL
DISCRIM
LOC/G
CROWD
S67

MACDONALD G.J.F.,"SCIENCE AND SPACE POLICY* HOW
DOES IT GET PLANNED?" R+D CREATE TEC/DEV BUDGET
ADMIN ROUTINE...DECISION NASA. PAGE 67 B1357
SPACE
PLAN
MGT
EX/STRUC
S67

SPACKMAN A.,"THE SENATE OF TRINIDAD AND TOBAGO."
L/A+17C TRINIDAD WEST/IND NAT/G POL/PAR DELIB/GP
OP/RES PROB/SOLV EDU/PROP EXEC LOBBY ROUTINE
REPRESENT GP/REL 20. PAGE 99 B2002
ELITES
EFFICIENCY
LEGIS
DECISION
S67

TATU M.,"URSS: LES FLOTTEMENTS DE LA DIRECTION
COLLEGIALE." UAR USSR CHIEF LEAD INGP/REL
EFFICIENCY...DECISION TREND 20 MID/EAST. PAGE 103
B2082
POLICY
NAT/G
EX/STRUC
DIPLOM
S67

TIVEY L.,"THE POLITICAL CONSEQUENCES OF ECONOMIC
PLANNING." UK CONSTN INDUS ACT/RES ADMIN CONTROL
LOBBY REPRESENT EFFICIENCY SUPEGO SOVEREIGN
...DECISION 20. PAGE 104 B2112
PLAN
POLICY
NAT/G
S67

VERGIN R.C.,"COMPUTER INDUCED ORGANIZATION
CHANGES." FUT USA+45 R+D CREATE OP/RES TEC/DEV
ADJUST CENTRAL...MGT INT CON/ANAL COMPUT/IR.
PAGE 112 B2260
COMPUTER
DECISION
AUTOMAT
EX/STRUC
S67

WEIL G.L.,"THE MERGER OF THE INSTITUTIONS OF THE
EUROPEAN COMMUNITIES" EUR+WWI ECO/DEV INT/TRADE
CONSEN PLURISM...DECISION MGT 20 EEC EURATOM ECSC
TREATY. PAGE 115 B2313
ECO/TAC
INT/ORG
CENTRAL
INT/LAW
S67

WRIGHT F.K.,"INVESTMENT CRITERIA AND THE COST OF
CAPITAL." FINAN PLAN BUDGET OPTIMAL PRODUC...POLICY
DECISION 20. PAGE 118 B2380
COST
PROFIT
INDUS
MGT
S67

GRAM H.A.,"BUSINESS ETHICS AND THE CORPORATION."
LG/CO SECT PROB/SOLV CONTROL EXEC GP/REL INGP/REL
PERS/REL ROLE MORAL PWR...DECISION 20. PAGE 42
B0850
POLICY
ADMIN
MGT
S68

PEARSON A.W.,"RESOURCE ALLOCATION." PLAN PROB/SOLV
BUDGET ADMIN CONTROL CHOOSE EFFICIENCY...DECISION
MGT 20. PAGE 82 B1649
PROFIT
OPTIMAL
COST
INDUS
S68

DECISION-MAKING, DISIPLINE....SEE DECISION

DECISION-MAKING, INDIVIDUAL....SEE PROB/SOLV, PWR

DECISION-MAKING, PROCEDURAL....SEE PROB/SOLV

DECISION-MAKING, THEORY....SEE GAME

DECLAR/IND....DECLARATION OF INDEPENDENCE (U.S.)

DEEP/INT....DEPTH INTERVIEWS

MANNONI D.O.,"PROSPERO AND CALIBAN: THE PSYCHOLOGY
OF COLONIZATION. AFR EUR+WWI FAM KIN MUNIC SECT
DOMIN ADMIN ATTIT DRIVE LOVE PWR RESPECT...PSY SOC
CONCPT MYTH OBS DEEP/INT BIOG GEN/METH MALAGASY 20.
PAGE 69 B1394
CULTURE
COLONIAL
B56

EVANS R.H.,"COEXISTENCE: COMMUNISM AND ITS PRACTICE
IN BOLOGNA, 1945-1965. ITALY CAP/ISM ADMIN CHOOSE
PEACE ORD/FREE...SOC STAT DEEP/INT SAMP CHARTS
BIBLIOG 20. PAGE 34 B0690
MARXISM
CULTURE
MUNIC
POL/PAR
B67

DEEP/QU....DEPTH QUESTIONNAIRES

BUREAU OF NAT'L AFFAIRS INC.,A CURRENT LOOK AT:
DISCRIM
N19

(1) THE NEGRO AND TITLE VII, (2) SEX AND TITLE VII
(PAMPHLET). LAW LG/CO SML/CO RACE/REL...POLICY SOC
STAT DEEP/QU TREND CON/ANAL CHARTS 20 NEGRO
CIV/RIGHTS. PAGE 17 B0350
SEX
WORKER
MGT

MACIVER R.M.,THE NATIONS AND THE UN. WOR+45 NAT/G
CONSULT ADJUD ADMIN ALL/VALS...CONCPT DEEP/QU UN
TOT/POP UNESCO 20. PAGE 67 B1362
INT/ORG
ATTIT
DIPLOM
B59

WARNER W.L.,THE AMERICAN FEDERAL EXECUTIVE. USA+45
USA-45 CONSULT EX/STRUC GP/REL DRIVE ALL/VALS...PSY
DEEP/QU CHARTS 19/20 PRESIDENT. PAGE 114 B2295
ELITES
NAT/G
TOP/EX
ADMIN
B63

PERROW C.,ORGANIZATION FOR TREATMENT: A COMPARATIVE
STUDY OF INSTITUTIONS FOR DELINQUENTS. LAW
PROB/SOLV ADMIN CRIME PERSON MORAL...SOC/WK OBS
DEEP/QU CHARTS SOC/INTEG 20. PAGE 82 B1661
AGE/Y
PSY
PUB/INST
B66

BURACK E.H.,"INDUSTRIAL MANAGEMENT IN ADVANCED
PRODUCTION SYSTEMS: SOME THEORETICAL CONCEPTS AND
PRELIMINARY FINDINGS." INDUS CREATE PLAN PRODUC
ROLE...OBS STAND/INT DEEP/QU HYPO/EXP ORG/CHARTS
20. PAGE 17 B0346
ADMIN
MGT
TEC/DEV
EX/STRUC
S67

DEES J.W. B0568

DEFENSE....SEE DETER, PLAN, FORCES, WAR, COERCE

DEFENSE DEPARTMENT....SEE DEPT/DEFEN

DEFINETT/B....BRUNO DEFINETTI

DEFLATION....DEFLATION

DEGAULLE/C....CHARLES DE GAULLE

FURNISS E.S.,FRANCE, TROUBLED ALLY. EUR+WWI FUT
CULTURE SOCIETY BAL/PWR ADMIN ATTIT DRIVE PWR
...TREND TOT/POP 20 DEGAULLE/C. PAGE 38 B0767
NAT/G
FRANCE
B60

VIORST M.,HOSTILE ALLIES: FDR AND DE GAULLE.
EUR+WWI USA+45 ELITES NAT/G VOL/ASSN FORCES LEGIS
PLAN LEGIT ADMIN COERCE PERSON...BIOG TIME/SEQ 20
ROOSEVLT/F DEGAULLE/C. PAGE 112 B2263
TOP/EX
PWR
WAR
FRANCE
B65

DEGRAS J. B0569

DEGROVE J.M. B1164

DEITY....DEITY: GOD AND GODS

DE-STALINIZATION....SEE DESTALIN

DEKAT A.D.A. B0570

DELANEY W. B1120

DELANY V.T.H. B0571

DELAWARE....DELAWARE

SCHERMER G.,MEETING SOCIAL NEEDS IN THE PENJERDEL
REGION. SOCIETY FINAN ACT/RES EDU/PROP ADMIN
GOV/REL...SOC/WK 45 20 PENNSYLVAN DELAWARE
NEW/JERSEY. PAGE 93 B1887
PLAN
REGION
HEALTH
WEALTH
B64

DELEGATION OF POWER....SEE EX/STRUC

DELIB/GP....CONFERENCES, COMMITTEES, BOARDS, CABINETS

CONGRESSIONAL MONITOR. CONSULT DELIB/GP PROB/SOLV
PRESS DEBATE ROUTINE...POLICY CONGRESS. PAGE 1
B0002
BIBLIOG
LEGIS
REPRESENT
USA+45
N

UNITED NATIONS,OFFICIAL RECORDS OF THE UNITED
NATIONS' GENERAL ASSEMBLY. WOR+45 BUDGET DIPLOM
ADMIN 20 UN. PAGE 107 B2159
INT/ORG
DELIB/GP
INT/LAW
WRITING
N

GRIFFIN A.P.C.,LIST OF BOOKS ON THE CABINETS OF
ENGLAND AND AMERICA (PAMPHLET). MOD/EUR UK USA-45
CONSTN NAT/G CONSULT EX/STRUC 19/20. PAGE 43 B0875
BIBLIOG/A
GOV/COMP
ADMIN
DELIB/GP
B03

MEYER H.H.B.,SELECT LIST OF REFERENCES ON
COMMISSION GOVERNMENT FOR CITIES (PAMPHLET). USA-45
EX/STRUC ADMIN 20. PAGE 73 B1473
BIBLIOG
LOC/G
MUNIC
DELIB/GP
B13

HARLOW R.V.,THE HISTORY OF LEGISLATIVE METHODS IN
THE PERIOD BEFORE 1825. USA-45 EX/STRUC ADMIN
LEGIS
DELIB/GP
B17

COLONIAL LEAD PARL/PROC ROUTINE...GP/COMP GOV/COMP
HOUSE/REP. PAGE 47 B0948

PROVS
POL/PAR
B19

LOS ANGELES BD CIV SERV COMNRS,ANNUAL REPORT: LOS
ANGELES CALIFORNIA: 1919-1936. USA-45 LAW GOV/REL
PRODUC...STAT 20. PAGE 66 B1340

DELIB/GP
ADMIN
LOC/G
MUNIC
N19

ANDERSON J.,THE ORGANIZATION OF ECONOMIC STUDIES IN
RELATION TO THE PROBLEMS OF GOVERNMENT (PAMPHLET).
UK FINAN INDUS DELIB/GP PLAN PROB/SOLV ADMIN 20.
PAGE 5 B0093

ECO/TAC
ACT/RES
NAT/G
CENTRAL
N19

CANADA CIVIL SERV COMM,THE ANALYSIS OF ORGANIZATION
IN THE GOVERNMENT OF CANADA (PAMPHLET). CANADA
CONSTN EX/STRUC LEGIS TOP/EX CREATE PLAN CONTROL
GP/REL 20. PAGE 18 B0372

NAT/G
MGT
ADMIN
DELIB/GP
N19

FOLSOM M.B.,BETTER MANAGEMENT OF THE PUBLIC'S
BUSINESS (PAMPHLET). USA+45 DELIB/GP PAY CONFER
CONTROL REGION GP/REL...METH/COMP ANTHOL 20.
PAGE 36 B0733

ADMIN
NAT/G
MGT
PROB/SOLV
B20

HALDANE R.B.,BEFORE THE WAR. MOD/EUR SOCIETY
INT/ORG NAT/G DELIB/GP PLAN DOMIN EDU/PROP LEGIT
ADMIN COERCE ATTIT DRIVE MORAL ORD/FREE PWR...SOC
CONCPT SELF/OBS RECORD BIOG TIME/SEQ. PAGE 45 B0921

POLICY
DIPLOM
UK

C20

BLACHLY F.F.,"THE GOVERNMENT AND ADMINISTRATION OF
GERMANY." GERMANY CONSTN LOC/G PROVS DELIB/GP
EX/STRUC FORCES LEGIS TOP/EX CT/SYS...BIBLIOG/A
19/20. PAGE 12 B0246

NAT/G
GOV/REL
ADMIN
PHIL/SCI
B24

BAGEHOT W.,THE ENGLISH CONSTITUTION AND OTHER
POLITICAL ESSAYS. UK DELIB/GP BAL/PWR ADMIN CONTROL
EXEC ROUTINE CONSERVE...METH PARLIAMENT 19/20.
PAGE 8 B0160

NAT/G
STRUCT
CONCPT
B31

HILL N.,INTERNATIONAL ADMINISTRATION. WOR-45
DELIB/GP DIPLOM EDU/PROP ALL/VALS...MGT TIME/SEQ
LEAGUE/NAT TOT/POP VAL/FREE 20. PAGE 50 B1011

INT/ORG
ADMIN

B33

DANGERFIELD R.,IN DEFENSE OF THE SENATE. USA-45
CONSTN NAT/G EX/STRUC TOP/EX ATTIT KNOWL
...METH/CNCPT STAT TIME/SEQ TREND CON/ANAL CHARTS
CONGRESS 20 TREATY. PAGE 26 B0528

LEGIS
DELIB/GP
DIPLOM

L34

GOSNELL H.F.,"BRITISH ROYAL COMMISSIONS OF INQUIRY"
UK CONSTN LEGIS PRESS ADMIN PARL/PROC...DECISION 20
PARLIAMENT. PAGE 41 B0839

DELIB/GP
INSPECT
POLICY
NAT/G
B37

CLOKIE H.M.,ROYAL COMMISSIONS OF INQUIRY; THE
SIGNIFICANCE OF INVESTIGATIONS IN BRITISH POLITICS.
UK POL/PAR CONFER ROUTINE...POLICY DECISION
TIME/SEQ 16/20. PAGE 22 B0439

NAT/G
DELIB/GP
INSPECT

B39

MACMAHON A.W.,FEDERAL ADMINISTRATORS: A
BIOGRAPHICAL APPROACH TO THE PROBLEM OF
DEPARTMENTAL MANAGEMENT. USA-45 DELIB/GP EX/STRUC
WORKER LEAD...TIME/SEQ 19/20. PAGE 68 B1366

BIOG
ADMIN
NAT/G
MGT
B39

ZIMMERN A.,MODERN POLITICAL DOCTRINE. WOR-45
CULTURE SOCIETY ECO/UNDEV DELIB/GP EX/STRUC CREATE
DOMIN COERCE NAT/LISM ATTIT RIGID/FLEX ORD/FREE PWR
WEALTH...POLICY CONCPT OBS TIME/SEQ TREND TOT/POP
LEAGUE/NAT 20. PAGE 119 B2402

NAT/G
ECO/TAC
BAL/PWR
INT/TRADE
B40

GAUS J.M.,PUBLIC ADMINISTRATION AND THE UNITED
STATES DEPARTMENT OF AGRICULTURE. USA-45 STRUCT
DIST/IND FINAN MARKET EX/STRUC PROB/SOLV GIVE
PRODUC...POLICY GEOG CHARTS 20 DEPT/AGRI. PAGE 39
B0786

ADMIN
AGRI
DELIB/GP
OP/RES
B40

MCHENRY D.E.,HIS MAJESTY'S OPPOSITION: STRUCTURE
AND PROBLEMS OF THE BRITISH LABOUR PARTY 1931-1938.
UK FINAN LABOR LOC/G DELIB/GP LEGIS EDU/PROP LEAD
PARTIC CHOOSE GP/REL SOCISM...TREND 20 LABOR/PAR.
PAGE 72 B1450

POL/PAR
MGT
NAT/G
POLICY

S40

PERKINS J.A.,"CONGRESSIONAL INVESTIGATIONS OF
MATTERS OF INTERNATIONAL IMPORT." DELIB/GP DIPLOM
ADMIN CONTROL 20 CONGRESS. PAGE 82 B1656

POL/PAR
DECISION
PARL/PROC
GOV/REL
B41

BURTON M.E.,THE ASSEMBLY OF THE LEAGUE OF NATIONS.
WOR-45 CONSTN SOCIETY STRUCT INT/ORG NAT/G CREATE
ATTIT RIGID/FLEX PWR...POLICY TIME/SEQ LEAGUE/NAT
20. PAGE 18 B0359

DELIB/GP
EX/STRUC
DIPLOM

B42

DENNISON E.,THE SENATE FOREIGN RELATIONS COMMITTEE.
USA-45 NAT/G DELIB/GP ROUTINE CHOOSE PWR CONGRESS
20. PAGE 28 B0574

LEGIS
ACT/RES
DIPLOM
S42

HUZAR E.,"LEGISLATIVE CONTROL OVER ADMINISTRATION:
CONGRESS AND WPA" USA-45 FINAN DELIB/GP LOBBY

ADMIN
EX/STRUC

GOV/REL EFFICIENCY ATTIT...POLICY CONGRESS. PAGE 53
B1069

CONTROL
LEGIS
B43

YOUNG R.,THIS IS CONGRESS. FUT SENIOR ADMIN GP/REL
PWR...DECISION REFORMERS CONGRESS. PAGE 119 B2393

LEGIS
DELIB/GP
CHIEF
ROUTINE
L43

MACMAHON A.W.,"CONGRESSIONAL OVERSIGHT OF
ADMINISTRATION: THE POWER OF THE PURSE." USA-45
BUDGET ROUTINE GOV/REL PWR...POLICY CONGRESS.
PAGE 68 B1368

LEGIS
DELIB/GP
ADMIN
CONTROL
S43

GOLDEN C.S.,"NEW PATTERNS OF DEMOCRACY." NEIGH
DELIB/GP EDU/PROP EXEC PARTIC...MGT METH/CNCPT OBS
TREND. PAGE 40 B0815

LABOR
REPRESENT
LG/CO
GP/REL
B45

MILLIS H.A.,ORGANIZED LABOR (FIRST ED.). LAW STRUCT
DELIB/GP WORKER ECO/TAC ADJUD CONTROL REPRESENT
INGP/REL INCOME MGT. PAGE 74 B1485

LABOR
POLICY
ROUTINE
GP/REL
B45

PASTUHOV V.D.,A GUIDE TO THE PRACTICE OF
INTERNATIONAL CONFERENCES. WOR+45 PLAN LEGIT
ORD/FREE...MGT OBS RECORD VAL/FREE ILO LEAGUE/NAT
20. PAGE 81 B1640

INT/ORG
DELIB/GP

B45

RANSHOFFEN-WERTHEIMER EF,THE INTERNATIONAL
SECRETARIAT: A GREAT EXPERIMENT IN INTERNATIONAL
ADMINISTRATION. EUR+WWI FUT CONSTN FACE/GP CONSULT
DELIB/GP ACT/RES ADMIN ROUTINE PEACE ORD/FREE...MGT
RECORD ORG/CHARTS LEAGUE/NAT WORK 20. PAGE 86 B1731

INT/ORG
EXEC

S45

WHITE L.D.,"CONGRESSIONAL CONTROL OF THE PUBLIC
SERVICE." USA-45 NAT/G CONSULT DELIB/GP PLAN SENIOR
CONGRESS. PAGE 116 B2335

LEGIS
EXEC
POLICY
CONTROL
C45

MCDIARMID J.,"THE MOBILIZATION OF SOCIAL
SCIENTISTS," IN L. WHITE'S CIVIL CIVIL SERVICE IN
WARTIME." USA-45 TEC/DEV CENTRAL...SOC 20
CIVIL/SERV. PAGE 72 B1447

INTELL
WAR
DELIB/GP
ADMIN
B47

KEFAUVER E.,A TWENTIETH-CENTURY CONGRESS. POL/PAR
EX/STRUC SENIOR ADMIN CONTROL EXEC LOBBY CHOOSE
EFFICIENCY PWR. PAGE 59 B1189

LEGIS
DELIB/GP
ROUTINE
TOP/EX
B47

MILLETT J.D.,THE PROCESS AND ORGANIZATION OF
GOVERNMENT PLANNING. USA+45 DELIB/GP ACT/RES LEAD
LOBBY TASK...POLICY GEOG TIME 20 RESOURCE/N.
PAGE 73 B1482

ADMIN
NAT/G
PLAN
CONSULT
B47

PATTERSON C.P.,PRESIDENTIAL GOVERNMENT IN THE
UNITED STATES - THE UNWRITTEN CONSTITUTION. USA+45
DELIB/GP EX/STRUC ADJUD ADMIN EXEC...DECISION
PRESIDENT. PAGE 81 B1643

CHIEF
NAT/G
CONSTN
POL/PAR
S47

CALDWELL L.K.,"STRENGTHENING STATE LEGISLATURES"
FUT DELIB/GP WEALTH REFORMERS. PAGE 18 B0364

PROVS
LEGIS
ROUTINE
BUDGET
B48

HART J.,THE AMERICAN PRESIDENCY IN ACTION 1789: A
STUDY IN CONSTITUTIONAL HISTORY. USA-45 POL/PAR
DELIB/GP FORCES LEGIS ADJUD ADMIN LEAD GP/REL
PERS/REL 18 PRESIDENT CONGRESS. PAGE 47 B0959

NAT/G
CONSTN
CHIEF
EX/STRUC
B48

HULL C.,THE MEMOIRS OF CORDELL HULL (VOLUME ONE).
USA-45 WOR-45 CONSTN FAM LOC/G NAT/G PROVS DELIB/GP
FORCES LEGIS TOP/EX BAL/PWR LEGIT ADMIN EXEC WAR
ATTIT ORD/FREE PWR...MAJORIT SELF/OBS TIME/SEQ
TREND NAZI 20. PAGE 52 B1062

BIOG
DIPLOM

B48

STEWART I.,ORGANIZING SCIENTIFIC RESEARCH FOR WAR:
ADMINISTRATIVE HISTORY OF OFFICE OF SCIENTIFIC
RESEARCH AND DEVELOPMENT. USA-45 INTELL R+D LABOR
WORKER CREATE BUDGET WEAPON CIVMIL/REL GP/REL
EFFICIENCY...POLICY 20. PAGE 101 B2037

DELIB/GP
ADMIN
WAR
TEC/DEV

B48

US LIBRARY OF CONGRESS,BRAZIL: A GUIDE TO THE
OFFICIAL PUBLICATIONS OF BRAZIL. BRAZIL L/A+17C
CONSULT DELIB/GP LEGIS CT/SYS 19/20. PAGE 109 B2203

BIBLIOG/A
NAT/G
ADMIN
TOP/EX
B48

WHITE L.D.,THE FEDERALISTS: A STUDY IN
ADMINISTRATIVE HISTORY. STRUCT DELIB/GP LEGIS
BUDGET ROUTINE GOV/REL GP/REL PERS/REL PWR...BIOG
18/19 PRESIDENT CONGRESS WASHINGT/G JEFFERSN/T
HAMILTON/A. PAGE 116 B2337

ADMIN
NAT/G
POLICY
PROB/SOLV

B49

MCLEAN J.M.,THE PUBLIC SERVICE AND UNIVERSITY
EDUCATION. UK USA-45 DELIB/GP EX/STRUC TOP/EX ADMIN
...GOV/COMP METH/COMP NAT/COMP ANTHOL 20. PAGE 72
B1455

ACADEM
NAT/G
EXEC
EDU/PROP

B56

US HOUSE RULES COMM,HEARINGS BEFORE A SPECIAL
SUBCOMMITTEE: ESTABLISHMENT OF A STANDING COMMITTEE
ON ADMINISTRATIVE PROCEDURE, PRACTICE. USA+45 LAW
EX/STRUC ADJUD CONTROL EXEC GOV/REL EFFICIENCY PWR
...POLICY INT 20 CONGRESS. PAGE 109 B2199

ADJUD
ADMIN
DOMIN
DELIB/GP
NAT/G

B56

WIGGINS J.R.,FREEDOM OR SECRECY. USA+45 USA-45
DELIB/GP EX/STRUC FORCES ADJUD SANCTION KNOWL PWR
...AUD/VIS CONGRESS 20. PAGE 116 B2344

ORD/FREE
PRESS
NAT/G
CONTROL

S56

CUTLER R.,"THE DEVELOPMENT OF THE NATIONAL SECURITY
COUNCIL." USA+45 INTELL CONSULT EX/STRUC DIPLOM
LEAD 20 TRUMAN/HS EISNHWR/DD NSC. PAGE 25 B0514

ORD/FREE
DELIB/GP
PROB/SOLV
NAT/G

S56

EMMERICH H.,"COOPERATION AMONG ADMINISTRATIVE
AGENCIES." USA+45 NAT/G EX/STRUC ADMIN 20. PAGE 33
B0673

DELIB/GP
REPRESENT
GOV/REL
EXEC

S56

HEADY F.,"THE MICHIGAN DEPARTMENT OF
ADMINISTRATION; A CASE STUDY IN THE POLITICS OF
ADMINISTRATION" (BMR)" USA+45 POL/PAR PROVS CHIEF
LEGIS GP/REL ATTIT 20 MICHIGAN. PAGE 48 B0980

ADMIN
DELIB/GP
LOC/G

B57

COOPER F.E.,THE LAWYER AND ADMINISTRATIVE AGENCIES.
USA+45 CLIENT LAW PROB/SOLV CT/SYS PERSON ROLE.
PAGE 23 B0473

CONSULT
ADMIN
ADJUD
DELIB/GP

B57

JENNINGS I.,PARLIAMENT. UK FINAN INDUS POL/PAR
DELIB/GP EX/STRUC PLAN CONTROL...MAJORIT JURID
PARLIAMENT. PAGE 56 B1133

PARL/PROC
TOP/EX
MGT
LEGIS

B57

MURRAY J.N.,THE UNITED NATIONS TRUSTEESHIP SYSTEM.
AFR WOR+45 CONSTN CONSULT LEGIS EDU/PROP LEGIT EXEC
ROUTINE...INT TIME/SEQ SOMALI UN 20. PAGE 77 B1547

INT/ORG
ADMIN
DELIB/GP

B57

UDY S.H. JR.,THE ORGANIZATION OF PRODUCTION IN
NONINDUSTRIAL CULTURE. VOL/ASSN DELIB/GP TEC/DEV
...CHARTS BIBLIOG. PAGE 106 B2143

METH/COMP
ECO/UNDEV
PRODUC
ADMIN

L57

HAAS E.B.,"REGIONAL INTEGRATION AND NATIONAL
POLICY." WOR+45 VOL/ASSN DELIB/GP EX/STRUC ECO/TAC
DOMIN EDU/PROP LEGIT COERCE ATTIT PERCEPT KNOWL
...TIME/SEQ COLD/WAR 20 UN. PAGE 45 B0908

INT/ORG
ORD/FREE
REGION

S57

COTTER C.P.,"ADMINISTRATIVE ACCOUNTABILITY;
REPORTING TO CONGRESS." USA+45 CONSULT DELIB/GP
PARL/PROC PARTIC GOV/REL ATTIT PWR DECISION.
PAGE 24 B0490

LEGIS
EX/STRUC
REPRESENT
CONTROL

S57

FESLER J.W.,"ADMINISTRATIVE LITERATURE AND THE
SECOND HOOVER COMMISSION REPORTS" (BMR)" USA+45
EX/STRUC LEGIS WRITING...DECISION METH 20. PAGE 35
B0713

ADMIN
NAT/G
OP/RES
DELIB/GP

B58

CHARLES R.,LA JUSTICE EN FRANCE. FRANCE LAW CONSTN
DELIB/GP CRIME 20. PAGE 20 B0413

JURID
ADMIN
CT/SYS
ADJUD

B58

CONSERVATIVE POLITICAL CENTRE,A WORLD SECURITY
AUTHORITY? WOR+45 CONSTN ELITES FINAN DELIB/GP PLAN
PROB/SOLV ADMIN CONTROL NUC/PWR GP/REL...IDEA/COMP
20. PAGE 23 B0468

ORD/FREE
CONSERVE
FORCES
ARMS/CONT

B58

KRAINES O.,CONGRESS AND THE CHALLENGE OF BIG
GOVERNMENT. USA-45 EX/STRUC CONFER DEBATE
EFFICIENCY. PAGE 61 B1232

LEGIS
DELIB/GP
ADMIN

B58

REDFIELD C.E.,COMMUNICATION IN MANAGEMENT. DELIB/GP
EX/STRUC WRITING LEAD PERS/REL...PSY INT METH 20.
PAGE 87 B1750

COM/IND
MGT
LG/CO
ADMIN

B58

REDFORD E.S.,IDEAL AND PRACTICE IN PUBLIC
ADMINISTRATION. CONSTN ELITES NAT/G CONSULT
DELIB/GP LEAD UTOPIA ATTIT POPULISM...DECISION
METH/COMP 20. PAGE 87 B1756

POLICY
EX/STRUC
PLAN
ADMIN

B58

SCOTT D.J.R.,RUSSIAN POLITICAL INSTITUTIONS. RUSSIA
USSR CONSTN AGRI DELIB/GP PLAN EDU/PROP CONTROL
CHOOSE EFFICIENCY ATTIT MARXISM...BIBLIOG/A 13/20.
PAGE 95 B1919

NAT/G
POL/PAR
ADMIN
DECISION

B58

SHARMA M.P.,PUBLIC ADMINISTRATION IN THEORY AND
PRACTICE. INDIA UK USA+45 USA-45 EX/STRUC ADJUD
...POLICY CONCPT NAT/COMP 20. PAGE 96 B1935

MGT
ADMIN
DELIB/GP
JURID

B58

SPITZ D.,DEMOCRACY AND THE CHALLANGE OF POWER. FUT
USA+45 USA-45 LAW SOCIETY STRUCT LOC/G POL/PAR
PROVS DELIB/GP EX/STRUC LEGIS TOP/EX ACT/RES CREATE
DOMIN EDU/PROP LEGIT ADJUD ADMIN ATTIT DRIVE MORAL
ORD/FREE TOT/POP. PAGE 99 B2010

NAT/G
PWR

B58

STEWART J.D.,BRITISH PRESSURE GROUPS: THEIR ROLE IN
RELATION TO THE HOUSE OF COMMONS. UK CONSULT
DELIB/GP ADMIN ROUTINE CHOOSE REPRESENT ATTIT ROLE
20 HOUSE/CMNS PARLIAMENT. PAGE 101 B2038

LOBBY
LEGIS
PLAN
PARL/PROC

B58

TAYLOR H.,THE STATESMAN. MOD/EUR FACE/GP FAM NAT/G
POL/PAR DELIB/GP LEGIS ATTIT PERSON PWR...POLICY
CONCPT OBS GEN/LAWS. PAGE 103 B2086

EXEC
STRUCT

B58

US HOUSE COMM ON COMMERCE,ADMINISTRATIVE PROCESS
AND ETHICAL QUESTIONS. USA+45 LAW LEGIS INT/TRADE
CONTROL 20 CONGRESS. PAGE 109 B2192

POLICY
ADMIN
DELIB/GP
ADJUD

B58

US HOUSE COMM ON POST OFFICE,TO PROVIDE AN
EFFECTIVE SYSTEM OF PERSONNEL ADMINISTRATION.
USA+45 DELIB/GP CONTROL EFFICIENCY 20 CONGRESS
PRESIDENT CIVIL/SERV POSTAL/SYS. PAGE 109 B2194

ADMIN
NAT/G
EX/STRUC
LAW

B58

US HOUSE COMM POST OFFICE,MANPOWER UTILIZATION IN
THE FEDERAL GOVERNMENT. USA+45 DIST/IND EX/STRUC
LEGIS CONFER EFFICIENCY 20 CONGRESS CIVIL/SERV.
PAGE 109 B2195

ADMIN
WORKER
DELIB/GP
NAT/G

B58

US HOUSE COMM POST OFFICE,MANPOWER UTILIZATION IN
THE FEDERAL GOVERNMENT. USA+45 DIST/IND EX/STRUC
LEGIS CONFER EFFICIENCY 20 CONGRESS CIVIL/SERV.
PAGE 109 B2196

ADMIN
WORKER
DELIB/GP
NAT/G

B58

US HOUSE COMM POST OFFICE,TRAINING OF FEDERAL
EMPLOYEES. USA+45 DIST/IND NAT/G EX/STRUC EDU/PROP
CONFER GOV/REL EFFICIENCY SKILL 20 CONGRESS
CIVIL/SERV. PAGE 109 B2197

LEGIS
DELIB/GP
WORKER
ADMIN

B58

VAN RIPER P.P.,HISTORY OF THE UNITED STATES CIVIL
SERVICE. USA+45 USA-45 LABOR LOC/G DELIB/GP LEGIS
PROB/SOLV LOBBY GOV/REL GP/REL INCOME...POLICY
18/20 PRESIDENT CIVIL/SERV. PAGE 111 B2251

ADMIN
WORKER
NAT/G

B58

WHITE L.D.,THE REPUBLICAN ERA: 1869-1901, A STUDY
IN ADMINISTRATIVE HISTORY. USA-45 FINAN PLAN
NEUTRAL CRIME GP/REL MORAL LAISSEZ PRESIDENT
REFORMERS 19 CONGRESS CIVIL/SERV. PAGE 116 B2340

MGT
PWR
DELIB/GP
ADMIN

L58

HAVILAND H.F.,"FOREIGN AID AND THE POLICY PROCESS:
1957." USA+45 FACE/GP POL/PAR VOL/ASSN CHIEF
DELIB/GP ACT/RES LEGIT EXEC GOV/REL ATTIT DRIVE PWR
...POLICY TESTS CONGRESS 20. PAGE 48 B0971

LEGIS
PLAN
FOR/AID

S58

ELKIN A.B.,"OEEC-ITS STRUCTURE AND POWERS." EUR+WWI
CONSTN INDUS INT/ORG NAT/G VOL/ASSN DELIB/GP
ACT/RES PLAN ORD/FREE WEALTH...CHARTS ORG/CHARTS
OEEC 20. PAGE 33 B0666

ECO/DEV
EX/STRUC

B59

DAVIS K.C.,ADMINISTRATIVE LAW TEXT. USA+45 NAT/G
DELIB/GP EX/STRUC CONTROL ORD/FREE...T 20
SUPREME/CT. PAGE 27 B0542

ADJUD
ADMIN
JURID
CT/SYS

B59

DESMITH S.A.,JUDICIAL REVIEW OF ADMINISTRATIVE
ACTION. UK LOC/G CONSULT DELIB/GP ADMIN PWR
...DECISION JURID 20 ENGLSH/LAW. PAGE 28 B0576

ADJUD
NAT/G
PROB/SOLV
CT/SYS

B59

DIEBOLD W. JR.,THE SCHUMAN PLAN: A STUDY IN
ECONOMIC COOPERATION, 1950-1959. EUR+WWI FRANCE
GERMANY USA+45 EXTR/IND CONSULT DELIB/GP PLAN
DIPLOM ECO/TAC INT/TRADE ROUTINE ORD/FREE WEALTH
...METH/CNCPT STAT CONT/OBS INT TIME/SEQ ECSC 20.
PAGE 29 B0591

INT/ORG
REGION

B59

GORDENKER L.,THE UNITED NATIONS AND THE PEACEFUL
UNIFICATION OF KOREA. ASIA LAW LOC/G CONSULT
ACT/RES DIPLOM DOMIN LEGIT ADJUD ADMIN ORD/FREE
SOVEREIGN...INT GEN/METH UN COLD/WAR 20. PAGE 41
B0829

DELIB/GP
KOREA
INT/ORG

B59

JENNINGS W.I.,CABINET GOVERNMENT (3RD ED.). UK
POL/PAR CHIEF BUDGET ADMIN CHOOSE GP/REL 20.
PAGE 56 B1137

DELIB/GP
NAT/G
CONSTN
OP/RES

B59

MILLETT J.D.,GOVERNMENT AND PUBLIC ADMINISTRATION;
THE QUEST FOR RESPONSIBLE PERFORMANCE. USA+45 NAT/G
DELIB/GP LEGIS CT/SYS EXEC...DECISION MGT. PAGE 73
B1483

ADMIN
PWR
CONSTN
ROLE

B59

MOOS M.,THE CAMPUS AND THE STATE. LAW FINAN
DELIB/GP LEGIS EXEC LOBBY GP/REL PWR...POLICY

EDU/PROP
ACADEM

BIBLIOG. PAGE 75 B1517 — PROVS CONTROL

B59
SAYER W.S.,AN AGENDA FOR RESEARCH IN PUBLIC PERSONNEL ADMINISTRATION. FUT USA+45 ACADEM LABOR LOC/G NAT/G POL/PAR DELIB/GP MGT. PAGE 93 B1872 — WORKER ADMIN ACT/RES CONSULT

B59
WEBER W.,DER DEUTSCHE BEAMTE HEUTE. GERMANY/W NAT/G DELIB/GP LEGIS CONFER ATTIT SUPEGO...JURID 20 CIVIL/SERV. PAGE 114 B2306 — MGT EFFICIENCY ELITES GP/REL

L59
RHODE W.E.,"COMMITTEE CLEARANCE OF ADMINISTRATIVE DECISIONS." DELIB/GP LEGIS BUDGET DOMIN CIVMIL/REL 20 CONGRESS. PAGE 87 B1768 — DECISION ADMIN OP/RES NAT/G

S59
HARVEY M.F.,"THE PALESTINE REFUGEE PROBLEM: ELEMENTS OF A SOLUTION." ISLAM LAW INT/ORG DELIB/GP TOP/EX ECO/TAC ROUTINE DRIVE HEALTH LOVE ORD/FREE PWR WEALTH...MAJORIT FAO 20. PAGE 48 B0964 — ACT/RES LEGIT PEACE ISRAEL

S59
HILSMAN R.,"THE FOREIGN-POLICY CONSENSUS: AN INTERIM RESEARCH REPORT." USA+45 INT/ORG LEGIS TEC/DEV EXEC WAR CONSEN KNOWL...DECISION COLD/WAR. PAGE 50 B1013 — PROB/SOLV NAT/G DELIB/GP DIPLOM

S59
HOFFMANN S.,"IMPLEMENTATION OF INTERNATIONAL INSTRUMENTS ON HUMAN RIGHTS." WOR+45 VOL/ASSN DELIB/GP JUDGE EDU/PROP LEGIT ROUTINE PEACE COLD/WAR 20. PAGE 51 B1029 — INT/ORG MORAL

S59
JEWELL M.R.,"THE SENATE REPUBLICAN POLICY COMMITTEE AND FOREIGN POLICY." PLAN ADMIN CONTROL LEAD LOBBY EFFICIENCY PRESIDENT 20 REPUBLICAN. PAGE 56 B1139 — POL/PAR NAT/G DELIB/GP POLICY

S59
KISSINGER H.A.,"THE POLICYMAKER AND THE INTELLECTUAL." USA+45 CONSULT DELIB/GP ACT/RES ADMIN ATTIT DRIVE RIGID/FLEX KNOWL PWR...POLICY PLURIST MGT METH/CNCPT GEN/LAWS GEN/METH 20. PAGE 60 B1216 — INTELL CREATE

S59
ROBINSON J.A.,"THE ROLE OF THE RULES COMMITTEE IN ARRANGING THE PROGRAM OF THE UNITED STATES HOUSE OF REPRESENTATIVES." USA+45 DEBATE CONTROL AUTHORIT HOUSE/REP. PAGE 89 B1801 — PARL/PROC DELIB/GP ROUTINE LEGIS

S59
STOESSINGER J.G.,"THE INTERNATIONAL ATOMIC ENERGY AGENCY: THE FIRST PHASE." FUT WOR+45 NAT/G VOL/ASSN DELIB/GP BAL/PWR LEGIT ADMIN ROUTINE PWR...OBS CON/ANAL GEN/LAWS VAL/FREE 20 IAEA. PAGE 101 B2040 — INT/ORG ECO/DEV FOR/AID NUC/PWR

B60
ARGAL R.,MUNICIPAL GOVERNMENT IN INDIA. INDIA BUDGET TAX ADMIN EXEC 19/20. PAGE 6 B0126 — LOC/G MUNIC DELIB/GP CONTROL

B60
BASS B.M.,LEADERSHIP, PSYCHOLOGY, AND ORGANIZATIONAL BEHAVIOR. DOMIN CHOOSE DRIVE PERSON PWR RESPECT SKILL...SOC METH/CNCPT OBS. PAGE 9 B0193 — UNIV FACE/GP DELIB/GP ROUTINE

B60
BHAMBHRI C.P.,PARLIAMENTARY CONTROL OVER STATE ENTERPRISE IN INDIA. INDIA DELIB/GP ADMIN CONTROL INGP/REL EFFICIENCY 20 PARLIAMENT. PAGE 11 B0235 — NAT/G OWN INDUS PARL/PROC

B60
CORSON J.J.,GOVERNANCE OF COLLEGES AND UNIVERSITIES. STRUCT FINAN DELIB/GP DOMIN EDU/PROP LEAD CHOOSE GP/REL CENTRAL COST PRIVIL SUPEGO ORD/FREE PWR...DECISION BIBLIOG. PAGE 24 B0481 — ADMIN EXEC ACADEM HABITAT

B60
GRAHAM G.A.,AMERICA'S CAPACITY TO GOVERN: SOME PRELIMINARY THOUGHTS FOR PROSPECTIVE ADMINISTRATORS. USA+45 SOCIETY DELIB/GP TOP/EX CREATE PROB/SOLV RATIONAL 20. PAGE 42 B0849 — MGT LEAD CHOOSE ADMIN

B60
HAYNES G.H.,THE SENATE OF THE UNITED STATES: ITS HISTORY AND PRACTICE. CONSTN EX/STRUC TOP/EX CONFER DEBATE LEAD LOBBY PARL/PROC CHOOSE PWR SENATE CONGRESS. PAGE 48 B0977 — LEGIS DELIB/GP

B60
INDIAN INST OF PUBLIC ADMIN,STATE UNDERTAKINGS: REPORT OF A CONFERENCE, DECEMBER 19-20, 1959 (PAMPHLET). INDIA LG/CO DELIB/GP CONFER PARL/PROC EFFICIENCY OWN...MGT 20. PAGE 53 B1081 — GOV/REL ADMIN NAT/G LEGIS

B60
MARSHALL A.H.,FINANCIAL ADMINISTRATION IN LOCAL GOVERNMENT. UK DELIB/GP CONFER COST INCOME PERSON ...JURID 20. PAGE 70 B1408 — FINAN LOC/G BUDGET ADMIN

B60
MATTOD P.K.,A STUDY OF LOCAL SELF GOVERNMENT IN URBAN INDIA. INDIA FINAN DELIB/GP LEGIS BUDGET TAX — MUNIC CONSTN

SOVEREIGN...MGT GP/COMP 20. PAGE 71 B1432 — LOC/G ADMIN

B60
MORISON E.E.,TURMOIL AND TRADITION: A STUDY OF THE LIFE AND TIMES OF HENRY L. STIMSON. USA+45 USA-45 POL/PAR CHIEF DELIB/GP FORCES BAL/PWR DIPLOM ARMS/CONT WAR PEACE 19/20 STIMSON/HL ROOSEVLT/F TAFT/WH HOOVER/H REPUBLICAN. PAGE 75 B1525 — BIOG NAT/G EX/STRUC

B60
MUNRO L.,UNITED NATIONS, HOPE FOR A DIVIDED WORLD. FUT WOR+45 CONSTN DELIB/GP CREATE TEC/DEV DIPLOM EDU/PROP LEGIT PEACE ATTIT HEALTH ORD/FREE PWR ...CONCPT TREND UN VAL/FREE 20. PAGE 76 B1540 — INT/ORG ROUTINE

B60
POOLEY B.J.,THE EVOLUTION OF BRITISH PLANNING LEGISLATION. UK ECO/DEV LOC/G CONSULT DELIB/GP ADMIN 20 URBAN/RNWL. PAGE 84 B1691 — PLAN MUNIC LEGIS PROB/SOLV

B60
ROBINSON E.A.G.,ECONOMIC CONSEQUENCES OF THE SIZE OF NATIONS. AGRI INDUS DELIB/GP FOR/AID ADMIN EFFICIENCY...METH/COMP 20. PAGE 89 B1799 — CONCPT INT/ORG NAT/COMP

B60
ROY N.C.,THE CIVIL SERVICE IN INDIA. INDIA POL/PAR ECO/TAC INCOME...JURID MGT 20 CIVIL/SERV. PAGE 91 B1843 — ADMIN NAT/G DELIB/GP CONFER

B60
SAYRE W.S.,GOVERNING NEW YORK CITY; POLITICS IN THE METROPOLIS. POL/PAR CHIEF DELIB/GP LEGIS PLAN CT/SYS LEAD PARTIC CHOOSE...DECISION CHARTS BIBLIOG 20 NEWYORK/C BUREAUCRCY. PAGE 93 B1875 — MUNIC ADMIN PROB/SOLV

B60
SCHUBERT G.,THE PUBLIC INTEREST. USA+45 CONSULT PLAN PROB/SOLV ADJUD ADMIN GP/REL PWR ALL/IDEOS 20. PAGE 94 B1903 — POLICY DELIB/GP REPRESENT POL/PAR

B60
US LIBRARY OF CONGRESS,INDEX TO LATIN AMERICAN LEGISLATION: 1950-1960 (2 VOLS.). NAT/G DELIB/GP ADMIN PARL/PROC 20. PAGE 109 B2205 — BIBLIOG/A LEGIS L/A+17C JURID

S60
BOYER W.W.,"POLICY MAKING BY GOVERNMENT AGENCIES." USA+45 WOR+45 R+D DELIB/GP TOP/EX EDU/PROP ROUTINE ATTIT BIO/SOC DRIVE...CONCPT TREND TOT/POP 20. PAGE 14 B0293 — NAT/G DIPLOM

S60
GROSSMAN G.,"SOVIET GROWTH: ROUTINE, INERTIA, AND PRESSURE." COM STRATA NAT/G DELIB/GP PLAN TEC/DEV ECO/TAC EDU/PROP ADMIN ROUTINE DRIVE WEALTH COLD/WAR 20. PAGE 44 B0891 — POL/PAR ECO/DEV USSR

S60
HERRERA F.,"THE INTER-AMERICAN DEVELOPMENT BANK." USA+45 ECO/UNDEV INT/ORG CONSULT DELIB/GP PLAN ECO/TAC INT/TRADE ROUTINE WEALTH...STAT 20. PAGE 49 B0994 — L/A+17C FINAN FOR/AID REGION

S60
HUNTINGTON S.P.,"STRATEGIC PLANNING AND THE POLITICAL PROCESS." USA+45 NAT/G DELIB/GP LEGIS ACT/RES ECO/TAC LEGIT ROUTINE CHOOSE RIGID/FLEX PWR ...POLICY MAJORIT MGT 20. PAGE 53 B1066 — EXEC FORCES NUC/PWR WAR

S60
MORA J.A.,"THE ORGANIZATION OF AMERICAN STATES." USA+45 ECO/UNDEV VOL/ASSN DELIB/GP PLAN BAL/PWR EDU/PROP ADMIN DRIVE RIGID/FLEX ORD/FREE WEALTH ...TIME/SEQ GEN/LAWS OAS 20. PAGE 75 B1518 — L/A+17C INT/ORG REGION

S60
ROURKE F.E.,"ADMINISTRATIVE SECRECY: A CONGRESSIONAL DILEMMA." DELIB/GP CT/SYS ATTIT ...MAJORIT DECISION JURID. PAGE 91 B1837 — LEGIS EXEC ORD/FREE POLICY

S60
SCHER S.,"CONGRESSIONAL COMMITTEE MEMBERS AND INDEPENDENT AGENCY OVERSEERS: A CASE STUDY." DELIB/GP EX/STRUC JUDGE TOP/EX DOMIN ADMIN CONTROL PWR...SOC/EXP HOUSE/REP CONGRESS. PAGE 93 B1886 — LEGIS GOV/REL LABOR ADJUD

B61
AUERBACH C.A.,THE LEGAL PROCESS. USA+45 DELIB/GP JUDGE CONFER ADJUD CONTROL...DECISION 20 SUPREME/CT. PAGE 7 B0146 — JURID ADMIN LEGIS CT/SYS

B61
AVERY M.W.,GOVERNMENT OF WASHINGTON STATE. USA+45 MUNIC DELIB/GP EX/STRUC LEGIS GIVE CT/SYS PARTIC REGION EFFICIENCY 20 WASHINGT/G GOVERNOR. PAGE 7 B0151 — PROVS LOC/G ADMIN GOV/REL

B61
BARNES W.,THE FOREIGN SERVICE OF THE UNITED STATES. USA+45 USA-45 CONSTN INT/ORG POL/PAR CONSULT DELIB/GP LEGIS DOMIN EDU/PROP EXEC ATTIT RIGID/FLEX ORD/FREE PWR...POLICY CONCPT STAT OBS RECORD BIOG TIME/SEQ TREND. PAGE 9 B0188 — NAT/G MGT DIPLOM

B61
BENOIT E.,EUROPE AT SIXES AND SEVENS: THE COMMON MARKET, THE FREE TRADE ASSOCIATION AND THE UNITED — FINAN ECO/DEV

STATES. EUR+WWI FUT USA+45 INDUS CONSULT DELIB/GP
EX/STRUC TOP/EX ACT/RES ECO/TAC EDU/PROP ROUTINE
CHOOSE PERCEPT WEALTH...MGT TREND EEC TOT/POP 20
EFTA. PAGE 11 B0217
VOL/ASSN
B61

BISHOP D.G.,THE ADMINISTRATION OF BRITISH FOREIGN
RELATIONS. EUR+WWI MOD/EUR INT/ORG NAT/G POL/PAR
DELIB/GP LEGIS TOP/EX ECO/TAC DOMIN EDU/PROP ADMIN
COERCE 20. PAGE 12 B0243
ROUTINE
PWR
DIPLOM
UK
B61

CONFREY E.A.,ADMINISTRATION OF COMMUNITY HEALTH
SERVICES. USA+45 R+D PUB/INST DELIB/GP PLAN BUDGET
ROUTINE AGE/C HEALTH...MGT SOC/WK METH/COMP 20.
PAGE 23 B0461
HEAL
ADMIN
MUNIC
BIO/SOC
B61

DARRAH E.L.,FIFTY STATE GOVERNMENTS: A COMPILATION
OF EXECUTIVE ORGANIZATION CHARTS. USA+45 LOC/G
DELIB/GP LEGIS ADJUD LEAD PWR 20 GOVERNOR. PAGE 26
B0530
EX/STRUC
ADMIN
ORG/CHARTS
PROVS
B61

HARRISON S.,INDIA AND THE UNITED STATES. FUT S/ASIA
USA+45 WOR+45 INTELL ECO/DEV ECO/UNDEV AGRI INDUS
INT/ORG NAT/G CONSULT EX/STRUC TOP/EX PLAN ECO/TAC
NEUTRAL ALL/VALS...MGT TOT/POP 20. PAGE 47 B0956
DELIB/GP
ACT/RES
FOR/AID
INDIA
B61

INTL UNION LOCAL AUTHORITIES,LOCAL GOVERNMENT IN
THE USA. USA+45 PUB/INST DELIB/GP CONFER AUTOMAT
GP/REL POPULISM...ANTHOL 20 CITY/MGT. PAGE 54 B1101
LOC/G
MUNIC
ADMIN
GOV/REL
B61

MARKMANN C.L.,JOHN F. KENNEDY: A SENSE OF PURPOSE.
USA+45 INTELL FAM CONSULT DELIB/GP LEGIS PERSON
SKILL 20 KENNEDY/JF EISENHWR/DD ROOSEVLT/F
NEW/FRONTR PRESIDENT. PAGE 69 B1399
CHIEF
TOP/EX
ADMIN
BIOG
B61

MAYNE A.,DESIGNING AND ADMINISTERING A REGIONAL
ECONOMIC DEVELOPMENT PLAN WITH SPECIFIC REFERENCE
TO PUERTO RICO (PAMPHLET). PUERT/RICO SOCIETY NAT/G
DELIB/GP REGION...DECISION 20. PAGE 71 B1435
ECO/UNDEV
PLAN
CREATE
ADMIN
B61

PAGE T.,STATE PERSONNEL REORGANIZATION IN ILLINOIS.
USA+45 POL/PAR CHIEF TEC/DEV LEAD ADJUST 20.
PAGE 80 B1625
ADMIN
PROVS
WORKER
DELIB/GP
B61

PEASLEE A.J.,INTERNATIONAL GOVERNMENT
ORGANIZATIONS, CONSTITUTIONAL DOCUMENTS. WOR+45
WOR+45 CONSTN VOL/ASSN DELIB/GP EX/STRUC ROUTINE
KNOWL TOT/POP 20. PAGE 82 B1650
INT/ORG
STRUCT
B61

QURESHI S.,INCENTIVES IN AMERICAN EMPLOYMENT
(THESIS, UNIVERSITY OF PENNSYLVANIA). DELIB/GP
TOP/EX BUDGET ROUTINE SANCTION COST TECHRACY MGT.
PAGE 85 B1727
SERV/IND
ADMIN
PAY
EX/STRUC
B61

ROSE D.L.,THE VIETNAMESE CIVIL SERVICE. VIETNAM
CONSULT DELIB/GP GIVE PAY EDU/PROP COLONIAL GOV/REL
UTIL...CHARTS 20. PAGE 90 B1819
ADMIN
EFFICIENCY
STAT
NAT/G
B61

SHARMA T.R.,THE WORKING OF STATE ENTERPRISES IN
INDIA. INDIA DELIB/GP LEGIS WORKER BUDGET PRICE
CONTROL GP/REL OWN ATTIT...MGT CHARTS 20. PAGE 96
B1938
NAT/G
INDUS
ADMIN
SOCISM
B61

SHARP W.R.,FIELD ADMINISTRATION IN THE UNITED
NATION SYSTEM: THE CONDUCT OF INTERNATIONAL
ECONOMIC AND SOCIAL PROGRAMS. FUT WOR+45 CONSTN
SOCIETY ECO/UNDEV R+D DELIB/GP ACT/RES PLAN TEC/DEV
EDU/PROP EXEC ROUTINE HEALTH WEALTH...HUM CONCPT
CHARTS METH ILO UNESCO VAL/FREE UN 20. PAGE 96
B1939
INT/ORG
CONSULT
B61

STRAUSS E.,THE RULING SERVANTS. FRANCE UK USSR
WOR+45 WOR-45 NAT/G CONSULT DELIB/GP EX/STRUC
TOP/EX DOMIN EDU/PROP LEGIT ROUTINE...MGT TIME/SEQ
STERTYP 20. PAGE 101 B2051
ADMIN
PWR
ELITES
B61

TANZER L.,THE KENNEDY CIRCLE. INTELL CONSULT
DELIB/GP TOP/EX CONTROL EXEC INGP/REL PERS/REL PWR
...BIOG IDEA/COMP ANTHOL 20 KENNEDY/JF PRESIDENT
DEMOCRAT MCNAMARA/R RUSK/D. PAGE 103 B2077
EX/STRUC
NAT/G
CHIEF
B61

THAYER L.O.,ADMINISTRATIVE COMMUNICATION. DELIB/GP
ADMIN ROUTINE PERS/REL 20. PAGE 104 B2093
GP/REL
PSY
LG/CO
MGT
B61

TRECKER H.B.,NEW UNDERSTANDING OF ADMINISTRATION.
NEIGH DELIB/GP CONTROL LEAD GP/REL INGP/REL
...POLICY DECISION BIBLIOG. PAGE 105 B2126
VOL/ASSN
PROF/ORG
ADMIN
PARTIC
B61

WARD R.E.,JAPANESE POLITICAL SCIENCE: A GUIDE TO
JAPANESE REFERENCE AND RESEARCH MATERIALS (2ND
ED.). LAW CONSTN STRATA NAT/G POL/PAR DELIB/GP
BIBLIOG/A
PHIL/SCI

LEGIS ADMIN CHOOSE GP/REL...INT/LAW 19/20 CHINJAP.
PAGE 113 B2290
B61

WILLOUGHBY W.R.,THE ST LAWRENCE WATERWAY: A STUDY
IN POLITICS AND DIPLOMACY. USA+45 ECO/DEV COM/IND
INT/ORG CONSULT DELIB/GP ACT/RES TEC/DEV DIPLOM
ECO/TAC ROUTINE...TIME/SEQ 20. PAGE 117 B2357
LEGIS
INT/TRADE
CANADA
DIST/IND
S61

ABLARD C.D.,"EX PARTE CONTACTS WITH FEDERAL
ADMINISTRATIVE AGENCIES." USA+45 CLIENT NAT/G
DELIB/GP ADMIN PWR 20. PAGE 3 B0055
EXEC
ADJUD
LOBBY
REPRESENT
S61

ALGER C.F.,"NON-RESOLUTION CONSEQUENCES OF THE
UNITED NATIONS AND THEIR EFFECT ON INTERNATIONAL
CONFLICT." WOR+45 CONSTN ECO/DEV NAT/G CONSULT
DELIB/GP TOP/EX ACT/RES PLAN DIPLOM EDU/PROP
ROUTINE ATTIT ALL/VALS...INT/LAW TOT/POP UN 20.
PAGE 4 B0075
INT/ORG
DRIVE
BAL/PWR
S61

ANGLIN D.,"UNITED STATES OPPOSITION TO CANADIAN
MEMBERSHIP IN THE PAN AMERICAN UNION: A CANADIAN
VIEW." L/A+17C UK USA+45 VOL/ASSN DELIB/GP EX/STRUC
PLAN DIPLOM DOMIN REGION ATTIT RIGID/FLEX PWR
...RELATIV CONCPT STERTYP CMN/WLTH OAS 20. PAGE 5
B0112
INT/ORG
CANADA
S61

EHRMANN H.W.,"FRENCH BUREAUCRACY AND ORGANIZED
INTERESTS" (BMR)" FRANCE NAT/G DELIB/GP ROUTINE
...INT 20 BUREAUCRCY CIVIL/SERV. PAGE 32 B0657
ADMIN
DECISION
PLURISM
LOBBY
S61

HALPERIN M.H.,"THE GAITHER COMMITTEE AND THE POLICY
PROCESS." USA+45 NAT/G TOP/EX ACT/RES LEGIT ADMIN
BAL/PAY PERCEPT...CONCPT TOT/POP 20. PAGE 46 B0928
PLAN
POLICY
NUC/PWR
DELIB/GP
S61

JUVILER P.H.,"INTERPARLIAMENTARY CONTACTS IN SOVIET
FOREIGN POLICY." COM FUT WOR+45 WOR-45 SOCIETY
CONSULT ACT/RES DIPLOM ADMIN PEACE ATTIT RIGID/FLEX
WEALTH...WELF/ST SOC TOT/POP CONGRESS 19/20.
PAGE 57 B1156
INT/ORG
DELIB/GP
USSR
S61

LANFALUSSY A.,"EUROPE'S PROGRESS: DUE TO COMMON
MARKET." EUR+WWI ECC/DEV DELIB/GP PLAN ECO/TAC
ROUTINE WEALTH...GEOG TREND EEC 20. PAGE 62 B1257
INT/ORG
MARKET
S61

RUDOLPH S.,"CONSENSUS AND CONFLICT IN INDIAN
POLITICS." S/ASIA WOR+45 NAT/G DELIB/GP DIPLOM
EDU/PROP ADMIN CONSEN PERSON ALL/VALS...OBS TREND
TOT/POP VAL/FREE 20. PAGE 92 B1854
POL/PAR
PERCEPT
INDIA
S61

TOMASIC D.,"POLITICAL LEADERSHIP IN CONTEMPORARY
POLAND." COM EUR+WWI GERMANY NAT/G POL/PAR SECT
DELIB/GP PLAN ECO/TAC DOMIN EDU/PROP PWR MARXISM
...MARXIST GEOG MGT CONCPT TIME/SEQ STERTYP 20.
PAGE 105 B2114
SOCIETY
ROUTINE
USSR
POLAND
B62

ANDREWS W.G.,FRENCH POLITICS AND ALGERIA: THE
PROCESS OF POLICY FORMATION 1954-1962. ALGERIA
FRANCE CONSTN ELITES POL/PAR CHIEF DELIB/GP LEGIS
DIPLOM PRESS CHOOSE 20. PAGE 5 B0105
GOV/COMP
EXEC
COLONIAL
B62

BAILEY S.D.,THE SECRETARIAT OF THE UNITED NATIONS.
FUT WOR+45 DELIB/GP PLAN BAL/PWR DOMIN EDU/PROP
ADMIN PEACE ATTIT PWR...DECISION CONCPT TREND
CON/ANAL CHARTS UN VAL/FREE COLD/WAR 20. PAGE 8
B0162
INT/ORG
EXEC
DIPLOM
B62

BENSON E.T.,CROSS FIRE: THE EIGHT YEARS WITH
EISENHOWER. USA+45 DIPLOM LEAD ATTIT PERSON
CONSERVE...TRADIT BIOG 20 EISNHWR/DD PRESIDENT
TAFT/RA DULLES/JF NIXON/RM. PAGE 11 B0218
ADMIN
POLICY
DELIB/GP
TOP/EX
B62

CHERNICK J.,THE SELECTION OF TRAINEES UNDER MDTA.
USA+45 NAT/G LEGIS PERSON...CENSUS 20 CIVIL/SERV
MDTA. PAGE 20 B0418
EDU/PROP
WORKER
ADMIN
DELIB/GP
B62

DODDS H.W.,THE ACADEMIC PRESIDENT "EDUCATOR OR
CARETAKER? FINAN DELIB/GP EDU/PROP PARTIC ATTIT
ROLE PWR...POLICY RECORD INT. PAGE 30 B0601
ACADEM
ADMIN
LEAD
CONTROL
B62

GOVERNORS CONF STATE PLANNING,STATE PLANNING: A
POLICY STATEMENT (PAMPHLET). USA+45 LOC/G NAT/G
DELIB/GP LEGIS EXEC 20 GOVERNOR. PAGE 42 B0847
GOV/REL
PLAN
ADMIN
PROVS
B62

GROGAN V.,ADMINISTRATIVE TRIBUNALS IN THE PUBLIC
SERVICE. IRELAND UK NAT/G CONTROL CT/SYS...JURID
GOV/COMP 20. PAGE 44 B0884
ADMIN
LAW
ADJUD
DELIB/GP
B62

GROVE J.W.,GOVERNMENT AND INDUSTRY IN BRITAIN. UK
FINAN LOC/G CONSULT DELIB/GP INT/TRADE ADMIN
ECO/TAC
INDUS

CONTROL...BIBLIOG 20. PAGE 44 B0894   NAT/G
                                                       GP/REL
                                                              B62
HANSON A.H.,MANAGERIAL PROBLEMS IN PUBLIC   MGT
ENTERPRISE. INDIA DELIB/GP GP/REL INGP/REL   NAT/G
EFFICIENCY 20 PARLIAMENT. PAGE 46 B0940   INDUS
                                                       PROB/SOLV
                                                              B62
HSUEH S.-S.,GOVERNMENT AND ADMINISTRATION OF HONG   ADMIN
KONG. CHIEF DELIB/GP LEGIS CT/SYS REPRESENT GOV/REL   LOC/G
20 HONG/KONG CITY/MGT CIVIL/SERV GOVERNOR. PAGE 52   COLONIAL
B1055   EX/STRUC
                                                              B62
INTERNATIONAL LABOR OFFICE,WORKERS' MANAGEMENT IN   WORKER
YUGOSLAVIA. COM YUGOSLAVIA LABOR DELIB/GP EX/STRUC   CONTROL
PROB/SOLV ADMIN PWR MARXISM...CHARTS ORG/CHARTS   MGT
BIBLIOG 20. PAGE 54 B1098   INDUS
                                                              B62
JEWELL M.E.,SENATORIAL POLITICS AND FOREIGN POLICY.   USA+45
NAT/G POL/PAR CHIEF DELIB/GP TOP/EX FOR/AID   LEGIS
EDU/PROP ROUTINE ATTIT PWR SKILL...MAJORIT   DIPLOM
METH/CNCPT TIME/SEQ CONGRESS 20 PRESIDENT. PAGE 56
B1138
                                                              B62
LAWSON R.,INTERNATIONAL REGIONAL ORGANIZATIONS.   INT/ORG
WOR+45 NAT/G VOL/ASSN CONSULT LEGIS EDU/PROP LEGIT   DELIB/GP
ADMIN EXEC ROUTINE HEALTH PWR WEALTH...JURID EEC   REGION
COLD/WAR 20 UN. PAGE 63 B1277
                                                              B62
MARS D.,SUGGESTED LIBRARY IN PUBLIC ADMINISTRATION.   BIBLIOG
FINAN DELIB/GP EX/STRUC WORKER COMPUTER ADJUD   ADMIN
...DECISION PSY SOC METH/COMP 20. PAGE 69 B1403   METH
                                                       MGT
                                                              B62
MODELSKI G.,A THEORY OF FOREIGN POLICY. WOR+45   PLAN
WOR-45 NAT/G DELIB/GP EX/STRUC TOP/EX EDU/PROP   PWR
LEGIT ROUTINE...POLICY CONCPT TOT/POP COLD/WAR 20.   DIPLOM
PAGE 74 B1494
                                                              B62
MULLEY F.W.,THE POLITICS OF WESTERN DEFENSE.   INT/ORG
EUR+WWI USA-45 WOR+45 VOL/ASSN EX/STRUC FORCES   DELIB/GP
COERCE DETER PEACE ATTIT ORD/FREE PWR...RECORD   NUC/PWR
TIME/SEQ CHARTS COLD/WAR 20 NATO. PAGE 76 B1537
                                                              B62
MUNICIPAL MANPOWER COMMISSION,GOVERNMENTAL MANPOWER   LOC/G
FOR TOMORROW'S CITIES: A REPORT. USA+45 DELIB/GP   MUNIC
EX/STRUC PROB/SOLV TEC/DEV EDU/PROP ADMIN LEAD   LABOR
HABITAT. PAGE 76 B1539   GOV/REL
                                                              B62
RUDOLPH F.,THE AMERICAN COLLEGE AND UNIVERSITY.   ACADEM
CLIENT FINAN PUB/INST DELIB/GP EDU/PROP CONTROL   INGP/REL
EXEC CONSEN ATTIT POLICY. PAGE 92 B1853   PWR
                                                       ADMIN
                                                              B62
SCHILLING W.R.,STRATEGY, POLITICS, AND DEFENSE   ROUTINE
BUDGETS. USA+45 R+D CONSULT DELIB/GP FORCES   POLICY
LEGIS ACT/RES PLAN BAL/PWR LEGIT EXEC NUC/PWR
RIGID/FLEX PWR...TREND COLD/WAR CONGRESS 20
EISNHWR/DD. PAGE 93 B1890
                                                              B62
THIERRY S.S.,LE VATICAN SECRET. CHRIST-17C EUR+WWI   ADMIN
MOD/EUR VATICAN NAT/G SECT DELIB/GP DOMIN LEGIT   EX/STRUC
SOVEREIGN. PAGE 104 B2096   CATHISM
                                                       DECISION
                                                              B62
US ADMINISTRATIVE CONFERENCE,FINAL REPORT OF THE   ADMIN
ADMINISTRATIVE CONFERENCE OF THE US: SUGGESTIONS   NAT/G
FOR IMPROVING PROCESSES - ADMIN. AGENCIES. USA+45   DELIB/GP
INGP/REL EFFICIENCY RATIONAL ORD/FREE...GP/COMP   GOV/REL
METH/COMP 20. PAGE 107 B2170
                                                              L62
MALINOWSKI W.R.,"CENTRALIZATION AND DE-   CREATE
CENTRALIZATION IN THE UNITED NATIONS' ECONOMIC AND   GEN/LAWS
SOCIAL ACTIVITIES." WOR+45 CONSTN ECO/UNDEV INT/ORG
VOL/ASSN DELIB/GP ECO/TAC EDU/PROP ADMIN RIGID/FLEX
...OBS CHARTS UNESCO UN EEC OAS OEEC 20. PAGE 69
B1385
                                                              L62
NEIBURG H.L.,"THE EISENHOWER AEC AND CONGRESS: A   CHIEF
STUDY IN EXECUTIVE-LEGISLATIVE RELATIONS." USA+45   LEGIS
NAT/G POL/PAR DELIB/GP EX/STRUC TOP/EX ADMIN EXEC   GOV/REL
LEAD ROUTINE PWR...POLICY COLD/WAR CONGRESS   NUC/PWR
PRESIDENT AEC. PAGE 77 B1567
                                                              S62
GIDWANI K.A.,"LEADER BEHAVIOUR IN ELECTED AND NON-   LEAD
ELECTED GROUPS." DELIB/GP ROUTINE TASK HAPPINESS   INGP/REL
AUTHORIT...SOC STAT CHARTS SOC/EXP. PAGE 39 B0796   GP/COMP
                                                       CHOOSE
                                                              S62
HUDSON G.F.,"SOVIET FEARS OF THE WEST." COM USA+45   ATTIT
SOCIETY DELIB/GP EX/STRUC TOP/EX ACT/RES CREATE   MYTH
DOMIN EDU/PROP LEGIT ADMIN ROUTINE DRIVE PERSON   GERMANY
RIGID/FLEX PWR...RECORD TIME/SEQ TOT/POP 20   USSR
STALIN/J. PAGE 52 B1057
                                                              S62
JACOBSON H.K.,"THE UNITED NATIONS AND COLONIALISM: INT/ORG

A TENTATIVE APPRAISAL." AFR FUT S/ASIA USA+45 USSR   CONCPT
WOR+45 NAT/G DELIB/GP PLAN DIPLOM ECO/TAC DOMIN   COLONIAL
ADMIN ROUTINE COERCE ATTIT RIGID/FLEX ORD/FREE PWR
...OBS STERTYP UN 20. PAGE 55 B1115
                                                              S62
MANGIN G.,"LES ACCORDS DE COOPERATION EN MATIERE DE   INT/ORG
JUSTICE ENTRE LA FRANCE ET LES ETATS AFRICAINS ET   LAW
MALGACHE." AFR ISLAM WOR+45 STRUCT ECO/UNDEV NAT/G   FRANCE
DELIB/GP PERCEPT ALL/VALS...JURID MGT TIME/SEQ 20.
PAGE 69 B1386
                                                              S62
NORTH R.C.,"DECISION MAKING IN CRISIS: AN   INT/ORG
INTRODUCTION." WOR+45 WOR-45 NAT/G CONSULT DELIB/GP   ROUTINE
TEC/DEV PERCEPT KNOWL...POLICY DECISION PSY   DIPLOM
METH/CNCPT CONT/OBS TREND VAL/FREE 20. PAGE 79
B1590
                                                              S62
OLLERENSHAW K.,"SHARING RESPONSIBLITY." UK DELIB/GP   REPRESENT
EDU/PROP EFFICIENCY 20. PAGE 80 B1607   GP/REL
                                                       ADMIN
                                                       EX/STRUC
                                                              S62
PIQUEMAL M.,"LES PROBLEMES DES UNIONS D'ETATS EN   AFR
AFRIQUE NOIRE." FRANCE SOCIETY INT/ORG NAT/G   ECO/UNDEV
DELIB/GP PLAN LEGIT ADMIN COLONIAL ROUTINE ATTIT   REGION
ORD/FREE PWR...GEOG METH/CNCPT 20. PAGE 83 B1678
                                                              B63
BADI J.,THE GOVERNMENT OF THE STATE OF ISRAEL: A   NAT/G
CRITICAL ACCOUNT OF ITS PARLIAMENT, EXECUTIVE, AND   CONSTN
JUDICIARY. ISRAEL ECO/DEV CHIEF DELIB/GP LEGIS   EX/STRUC
DIPLOM CT/SYS INGP/REL PEACE ORD/FREE...BIBLIOG 20   POL/PAR
PARLIAMENT ARABS MIGRATION. PAGE 8 B0157
                                                              B63
BOWETT D.W.,THE LAW OF INTERNATIONAL INSTITUTIONS.   INT/ORG
WOR+45 WOR-45 CONSTN DELIB/GP EX/STRUC JUDGE   ADJUD
EDU/PROP LEGIT CT/SYS EXEC ROUTINE RIGID/FLEX   DIPLOM
ORD/FREE...JURID CONCPT ORG/CHARTS GEN/METH
LEAGUE/NAT OAS OEEC 20 UN. PAGE 14 B0286
                                                              B63
COUNCIL STATE GOVERNMENTS,HANDBOOK FOR LEGISLATIVE   LEGIS
COMMITTEES. USA+45 LAW DELIB/GP EX/STRUC TOP/EX   PARL/PROC
CHOOSE PWR...METH/COMP 20. PAGE 24 B0496   PROVS
                                                       ADJUD
                                                              B63
DE VRIES E.,SOCIAL ASPECTS OF ECONOMIC DEVELOPMENT   L/A+17C
IN LATIN AMERICA. CULTURE SOCIETY STRATA FINAN   ECO/UNDEV
INDUS INT/ORG DELIB/GP ACT/RES ECO/TAC EDU/PROP
ADMIN ATTIT SUPEGO HEALTH KNOWL ORD/FREE...SOC STAT
TREND ANTHOL TOT/POP VAL/FREE. PAGE 28 B0562
                                                              B63
DEAN A.L.,FEDERAL AGENCY APPROACHES TO FIELD   ADMIN
MANAGEMENT (PAMPHLET). R+D DELIB/GP EX/STRUC   MGT
PROB/SOLV GOV/REL...CLASSIF BIBLIOG 20 FAA NASA   NAT/G
DEPT/HEW POSTAL/SYS IRS. PAGE 28 B0563   OP/RES
                                                              B63
DEBRAY P.,LE PORTUGAL ENTRE DEUX REVOLUTIONS.   NAT/G
EUR+WWI PORTUGAL CONSTN LEGIT ADMIN ALL/VALS   DELIB/GP
...DECISION CONCPT 20 SALAZAR/A. PAGE 28 B0567   TOP/EX
                                                              B63
DOUGLASS H.R.,MODERN ADMINISTRATION OF SECONDARY   EDU/PROP
SCHOOLS. CLIENT DELIB/GP WORKER REPRESENT INGP/REL   ADMIN
AUTHORIT...TREND BIBLIOG. PAGE 30 B0613   SCHOOL
                                                       MGT
                                                              B63
GREEN H.P.,GOVERNMENT OF THE ATOM. USA+45 LEGIS   GOV/REL
PROB/SOLV ADMIN CONTROL PWR...POLICY DECISION 20   EX/STRUC
PRESIDENT CONGRESS. PAGE 43 B0864   NUC/PWR
                                                       DELIB/GP
                                                              B63
HANSON A.H.,NATIONALIZATION: A BOOK OF READINGS.   NAT/G
WOR+45 FINAN DELIB/GP LEGIS WORKER BUDGET ADMIN   OWN
GP/REL EFFICIENCY SOCISM...MGT ANTHOL. PAGE 46   INDUS
B0941   CONTROL
                                                              B63
HEUSSLER R.,YESTERDAY'S RULERS: THE MAKING OF THE   EX/STRUC
BRITISH COLONIAL SERVICE. AFR EUR+WWI UK STRATA   MORAL
SECT DELIB/GP PLAN DOMIN EDU/PROP ATTIT PERCEPT   ELITES
PERSON SUPEGO KNOWL ORD/FREE PWR...MGT SOC OBS INT
TIME/SEQ 20 CMN/WLTH. PAGE 49 B1000
                                                              B63
JOHNS R.,CONFRONTING ORGANIZATIONAL CHANGE. NEIGH   SOC/WK
DELIB/GP CREATE OP/RES ADMIN GP/REL DRIVE...WELF/ST   WEALTH
SOC RECORD BIBLIOG. PAGE 56 B1142   LEAD
                                                       VOL/ASSN
                                                              B63
KARL B.D.,EXECUTIVE REORGANIZATION AND REFORM IN   BIOG
THE NEW DEAL. ECO/DEV INDUS DELIB/GP EX/STRUC PLAN   EXEC
BUDGET ADMIN EFFICIENCY PWR POPULISM...POLICY 20   CREATE
PRESIDENT ROOSEVLT/F WILSON/W NEW/DEAL. PAGE 58   CONTROL
B1174
                                                              B63
KULZ H.R.,STAATSBURGER UND STAATSGEWALT (2 VOLS.).   ADMIN
GERMANY SWITZERLND UK USSR CONSTN DELIB/GP TARIFFS   ADJUD
TAX...JURID 20. PAGE 61 B1242   CT/SYS
                                                       NAT/COMP

B63

LANGROD G.,THE INTERNATIONAL CIVIL SERVICE: ITS
ORIGINS, ITS NATURE, ITS EVALUATION. FUT WOR+45
WOR-45 DELIB/GP ACT/RES DOMIN LEGIT ATTIT
RIGID/FLEX SUPEGO ALL/VALS...MGT CONCPT STAT
TIME/SEQ ILO LEAGUE/NAT VAL/FREE 20 UN. PAGE 62
B1259

INT/ORG
ADMIN

B63

LINDBERG L.,POLITICAL DYNAMICS OF EUROPEAN ECONOMIC
INTEGRATION. EUR+WWI ECO/DEV INT/ORG VOL/ASSN
DELIB/GP ADMIN WEALTH...DECISION EEC 20. PAGE 65
B1313

MARKET
ECO/TAC

B63

MACNEIL N.,FORGE OF DEMOCRACY: THE HOUSE OF
REPRESENTATIVES. POL/PAR EX/STRUC TOP/EX DEBATE
LEAD PARL/PROC CHOOSE GOV/REL PWR...OBS HOUSE/REP.
PAGE 68 B1374

LEGIS
DELIB/GP

B63

MAYNE R.,THE COMMUNITY OF EUROPE. UK CONSTN NAT/G
CONSULT DELIB/GP CREATE PLAN ECO/TAC LEGIT ADMIN
ROUTINE ORD/FREE PWR WEALTH...CONCPT TIME/SEQ EEC
EURATOM 20. PAGE 71 B1436

EUR+WWI
INT/ORG
REGION

B63

MEYNAUD J.,PLANIFICATION ET POLITIQUE. FRANCE ITALY
FINAN LABOR DELIB/GP LEGIS ADMIN EFFICIENCY
...MAJORIT DECISION 20. PAGE 73 B1477

PLAN
ECO/TAC
PROB/SOLV

B63

RICHARDS P.G.,PATRONAGE IN BRITISH GOVERNMENT.
ELITES DELIB/GP TOP/EX PROB/SOLV CONTROL CT/SYS
EXEC PWR. PAGE 88 B1774

EX/STRUC
REPRESENT
POL/PAR
ADMIN

B63

ROETTER C.,THE DIPLOMATIC ART. USSR INT/ORG NAT/G
DELIB/GP ROUTINE NUC/PWR PEACE...POLICY 20. PAGE 90
B1812

DIPLOM
ELITES
TOP/EX

B63

SIDEY H.,JOHN F. KENNEDY, PRESIDENT. USA+45 INTELL
FAM CONSULT DELIB/GP LEGIS ADMIN LEAD 20 KENNEDY/JF
PRESIDENT. PAGE 97 B1951

BIOG
TOP/EX
SKILL
PERSON

B63

SINGH M.M.,MUNICIPAL GOVERNMENT IN THE CALCUTTA
METROPOLITAN DISTRICT A PRELIMINARY SURVEY. FINAN
LG/CO DELIB/GP BUDGET TAX ADMIN GP/REL 20 CALCUTTA.
PAGE 97 B1969

LOC/G
HEALTH
MUNIC
JURID

B63

SWERDLOW I.,DEVELOPMENT ADMINISTRATION: CONCEPTS
AND PROBLEMS. WOR+45 CULTURE SOCIETY STRATA
DELIB/GP EX/STRUC ACT/RES PLAN ECO/TAC DOMIN LEGIT
ATTIT RIGID/FLEX SUPEGO HEALTH PWR...MGT CONCPT
ANTHOL VAL/FREE. PAGE 102 B2062

ECO/UNDEV
ADMIN

B63

US CONGRESS: SENATE,HEARINGS OF THE COMMITTEE ON
THE JUDICIARY. USA+45 CONSTN NAT/G ADMIN GOV/REL 20
CONGRESS. PAGE 108 B2179

LEGIS
LAW
ORD/FREE
DELIB/GP

B63

US HOUSE COM ON ED AND LABOR,ADMINISTRATION OF
AGING. USA+45 R+D EX/STRUC PLAN BUDGET PAY EDU/PROP
ROUTINE COST CONGRESS. PAGE 108 B2187

AGE/O
ADMIN
DELIB/GP
GIVE

B63

US SENATE COMM GOVT OPERATIONS,ADMINISTRATION OF
NATIONAL SECURITY (9 PARTS). ADMIN...INT REC/INT
CHARTS 20 SENATE CONGRESS. PAGE 110 B2213

DELIB/GP
NAT/G
OP/RES
ORD/FREE

L63

SPITZ A.A.,"DEVELOPMENT ADMINISTRATION: AN
ANNOTATED BIBLIOGRAPHY." WOR+45 CULTURE SOCIETY
STRATA DELIB/GP EX/STRUC TOP/EX ACT/RES ECO/TAC
DOMIN EDU/PROP LEGIT COERCE ATTIT ALL/VALS...MGT
VAL/FREE. PAGE 99 B2009

ADMIN
ECO/UNDEV

S63

BECHHOEFER B.G.,"UNITED NATIONS PROCEDURES IN CASE
OF VIOLATIONS OF DISARMAMENT AGREEMENTS." COM
USA+45 USSR LAW CONSTN NAT/G EX/STRUC FORCES LEGIS
BAL/PWR EDU/PROP CT/SYS ARMS/CONT ORD/FREE PWR
...POLICY STERTYP UN VAL/FREE 20. PAGE 10 B0204

INT/ORG
DELIB/GP

S63

HARRIS R.L.,"A COMPARATIVE ANALYSIS OF THE
ADMINISTRATIVE SYSTEMS OF CANADA AND CEYLON."
S/ASIA CULTURE SOCIETY STRATA TOP/EX ACT/RES DOMIN
EDU/PROP LEGIT COERCE ATTIT SUPEGO ALL/VALS...MGT
CHARTS GEN/LAWS VAL/FREE 20. PAGE 47 B0955

DELIB/GP
EX/STRUC
CANADA
CEYLON

S63

HAVILAND H.F.,"BUILDING A POLITICAL COMMUNITY."
EUR+WWI FUT UK USA+45 ECO/DEV ECO/UNDEV INT/ORG
NAT/G DELIB/GP BAL/PWR ECO/TAC NEUTRAL ROUTINE
ATTIT PWR WEALTH...CONCPT COLD/WAR TOT/POP 20.
PAGE 48 B0972

VOL/ASSN
DIPLOM

S63

JOELSON M.R.,"THE DISMISSAL OF CIVIL SERVANTS IN
THE INTERESTS OF NATIONAL SECURITY." EUR+WWI LAW
DELIB/GP ROUTINE ORD/FREE...MGT VAL/FREE 20.
PAGE 56 B1141

USA+45
NAT/G
UK
FRANCE

S63

NYE J.S. JR.,"EAST AFRICAN ECONOMIC INTEGRATION."
AFR UGANDA PROVS DELIB/GP PLAN ECO/TAC INT/TRADE
ADMIN ROUTINE ORD/FREE PWR WEALTH...OBS TIME/SEQ
VAL/FREE 20. PAGE 79 B1597

ECO/UNDEV
INT/ORG

S63

SCHMITT H.A.,"THE EUROPEAN COMMUNITIES." EUR+WWI
FRANCE DELIB/GP EX/STRUC TOP/EX CREATE TEC/DEV
ECO/TAC LEGIT REGION COERCE DRIVE ALL/VALS
...METH/CNCPT EEC 20. PAGE 94 B1897

VOL/ASSN
ECO/DEV

S63

USEEM J.,"MEN IN THE MIDDLE OF THE THIRD CULTURE:
THE ROLES OF AMERICAN AND NON-WESTERN PEOPLE IN
CROSS-CULTURAL ADMINIS-." FUT WOR+45 DELIB/GP
EX/STRUC LEGIS ATTIT ALL/VALS...MGT INT TIME/SEQ
GEN/LAWS VAL/FREE. PAGE 111 B2247

ADMIN
SOCIETY
PERSON

S63

WAGRET M.,"L'ASCENSION POLITIQUE DE L'U.D.D.I.A.
(CONGO) ET SA PRISE DU POUVOIR (1956-1959)." AFR
WOR+45 NAT/G POL/PAR CONSULT DELIB/GP LEGIS PERCEPT
ALL/VALS SOVEREIGN...TIME/SEQ CONGO. PAGE 113 B2274

EX/STRUC
CHOOSE
FRANCE

B64

APTER D.E.,IDEOLOGY AND DISCONTENT. FUT WOR+45
CONSTN CULTURE INTELL SOCIETY STRUCT INT/ORG NAT/G
DELIB/GP LEGIS CREATE PLAN TEC/DEV EDU/PROP EXEC
PERCEPT PERSON RIGID/FLEX ALL/VALS...POLICY
TOT/POP. PAGE 6 B0122

ACT/RES
ATTIT

B64

AVASTHI A.,ASPECTS OF ADMINISTRATION. INDIA UK
USA+45 FINAN ACADEM DELIB/GP LEGIS RECEIVE
PARL/PROC PRIVIL...NAT/COMP 20. PAGE 7 B0150

MGT
ADMIN
SOC/WK
ORD/FREE

B64

BENNETT H.A.,THE COMMISSION AND THE COMMON LAW: A
STUDY IN ADMINISTRATIVE ADJUDICATION. LAW ADMIN
CT/SYS LOBBY SANCTION GOV/REL 20 COMMON/LAW.
PAGE 10 B0212

ADJUD
DELIB/GP
DIST/IND
POLICY

B64

BLAKE R.R.,MANAGING INTERGROUP CONFLICT IN
INDUSTRY. INDUS DELIB/GP EX/STRUC GP/REL PERS/REL
GAME. PAGE 12 B0250

CREATE
PROB/SOLV
OP/RES
ADJUD

B64

CLARK J.S.,CONGRESS: THE SAPLESS BRANCH. DELIB/GP
SENIOR ATTIT CONGRESS. PAGE 21 B0432

LEGIS
ROUTINE
ADMIN
POL/PAR

B64

COMMITTEE ECONOMIC DEVELOPMENT,IMPROVING EXECUTIVE
MANAGEMENT IN THE FEDERAL GOVERNMENT. USA+45 CHIEF
DELIB/GP WORKER PLAN PAY SENIOR ADMIN EFFICIENCY 20
PRESIDENT. PAGE 22 B0457

EXEC
MGT
TOP/EX
NAT/G

B64

CONNECTICUT U INST PUBLIC SERV,SUMMARY OF CHARTER
PROVISIONS IN CONNECTICUT LOCAL GOVERNMENT
(PAMPHLET). USA+45 DELIB/GP LEGIS TOP/EX CHOOSE
REPRESENT 20 CONNECTICT CITY/MGT MAYOR. PAGE 23
B0462

CONSTN
MUNIC
LOC/G
EX/STRUC

B64

COTTER C.P.,POLITICS WITHOUT POWER: THE NATIONAL
PARTY COMMITTEES. USA+45 FINAN NAT/G LOBBY ROUTINE
GP/REL ATTIT ROLE SUPEGO PWR 20. PAGE 24 B0491

CHOOSE
POL/PAR
REPRESENT
DELIB/GP

B64

COTTRELL A.J.,THE POLITICS OF THE ATLANTIC
ALLIANCE. EUR+WWI USA+45 INT/ORG NAT/G DELIB/GP
EX/STRUC BAL/PWR DIPLOM REGION DETER ATTIT ORD/FREE
...CONCPT RECORD GEN/LAWS GEN/METH NATO 20. PAGE 24
B0493

VOL/ASSN
FORCES

B64

EATON H.,PRESIDENTIAL TIMBER: A HISTORY OF
NOMINATING CONVENTIONS, 1868-1960. USA+45 USA-45
POL/PAR EX/STRUC DEBATE LOBBY ATTIT PERSON ALL/VALS
...MYTH 19/20 PRESIDENT. PAGE 32 B0646

DELIB/GP
CHOOSE
CHIEF
NAT/G

B64

FONTENEAU J.,LE CONSEIL MUNICIPAL: LE MAIRE-LES
ADJOINTS. FRANCE FINAN DELIB/GP EX/STRUC BUDGET TAX
TASK COST INCOME ROLE SUPEGO 20 MAYOR. PAGE 36
B0735

MUNIC
NEIGH
ADMIN
TOP/EX

B64

GUTTSMAN W.L.,THE BRITISH POLITICAL ELITE. EUR+WWI
MOD/EUR STRATA FAM LABOR POL/PAR SCHOOL VOL/ASSN
DELIB/GP LEGIS LEGIT EXEC CHOOSE ATTIT ALL/VALS
...STAT BIOG TIME/SEQ CHARTS VAL/FREE. PAGE 45
B0905

NAT/G
SOC
UK
ELITES

B64

KAHNG T.J.,LAW, POLITICS, AND THE SECURITY COUNCIL*
AN INQUIRY INTO THE HANDLING OF LEGAL QUESTIONS.
LAW CONSTN NAT/G ACT/RES OP/RES CT/SYS TASK PWR
...INT/LAW BIBLIOG UN. PAGE 57 B1160

DELIB/GP
ADJUD
ROUTINE

B64

KEEFE W.J.,THE AMERICAN LEGISLATIVE PROCESS:
CONGRESS AND THE STATES. USA+45 LAW POL/PAR
DELIB/GP DEBATE ADMIN LOBBY REPRESENT CONGRESS
PRESIDENT. PAGE 59 B1187

LEGIS
DECISION
PWR
PROVS

PINNICK A.W.,COUNTRY PLANNERS IN ACTION. UK FINAN MUNIC
SERV/IND NAT/G CONSULT DELIB/GP PRICE CONTROL PLAN
ROUTINE LEISURE AGE/C...GEOG 20 URBAN/RNWL. PAGE 83 INDUS
B1674   ATTIT
                                                  B64

RIDDLE D.H.,THE TRUMAN COMMITTEE: A STUDY IN LEGIS
CONGRESSIONAL RESPONSIBILITY. INDUS FORCES OP/RES DELIB/GP
DOMIN ADMIN LEAD PARL/PROC WAR PRODUC SUPEGO CONFER
...BIBLIOG CONGRESS. PAGE 88 B1778
                                                  B64

RIES J.C.,THE MANAGEMENT OF DEFENSE: ORGANIZATION FORCES
AND CONTROL OF THE US ARMED SERVICES. PROF/ORG ACT/RES
DELIB/GP EX/STRUC LEGIS GOV/REL PERS/REL CENTRAL DECISION
RATIONAL PWR...POLICY TREND GOV/COMP BIBLIOG. CONTROL
PAGE 88 B1782
                                                  B64

RIGGS R.E.,THE MOVEMENT FOR ADMINISTRATIVE ADMIN
REORGANIZATION IN ARIZONA. USA+45 LAW POL/PAR PROVS
DELIB/GP LEGIS PROB/SOLV CONTROL RIGID/FLEX PWR CREATE
...ORG/CHARTS 2U ARIZONA DEMOCRAT REPUBLICAN. PLAN
PAGE 88 B1786
                                                  B64

ROCHE J.P.,THE CONGRESS. EX/STRUC BAL/PWR DIPLOM INGP/REL
DEBATE ADJUD LEAD PWR. PAGE 89 B1809 LEGIS
                                     DELIB/GP
                                     SENIOR
                                                  B64

US SENATE COMM GOVT OPERATIONS,THE SECRETARY OF DIPLOM
STATE AND THE AMBASSADOR. USA+45 CHIEF CONSULT DELIB/GP
EX/STRUC FORCES PLAN ADMIN EXEC INGP/REL ROLE NAT/G
...ANTHOL 20 PRESIDENT DEPT/STATE. PAGE 110 B2215
                                                  B64

WILSON L.,THE ACADEMIC MAN. STRUCT FINAN PROF/ORG ACADEM
OP/RES ADMIN AUTHORIT ROLE RESPECT...SOC STAT. INGP/REL
PAGE 117 B2360 STRATA
               DELIB/GP

HAAS E.B.,"ECONOMICS AND DIFFERENTIAL PATTERNS OF L/A+17C
POLITICAL INTEGRATION: PROJECTIONS ABOUT UNITY IN INT/ORG
LATIN AMERICA." SOCIETY NAT/G DELIB/GP ACT/RES MARKET
CREATE PLAN ECO/TAC REGION ROUTINE ATTIT DRIVE PWR
WEALTH...CONCPT TREND CHARTS LAFTA 20. PAGE 45
B0910
                                                  L64

RIPLEY R.B.,"INTERAGENCY COMMITTEES AND EXEC
INCREMENTALISM: THE CASE OF AID TO INDIA." INDIA MGT
USA+45 INTELL NAT/G DELIB/GP ACT/RES DIPLOM ROUTINE FOR/AID
NAT/LISM ATTIT PWR...SOC CONCPT NEW/IDEA TIME/SEQ
CON/ANAL VAL/FREE 20. PAGE 89 B1790
                                                  S64

GALTUNE J.,"BALANCE OF POWER AND THE PROBLEM OF PWR
PERCEPTION, A LOGICAL ANALYSIS." WOR+45 CONSTN PSY
SOCIETY NAT/G DELIB/GP EX/STRUC LEGIS DOMIN ADMIN ARMS/CONT
COERCE DRIVE ORD/FREE...POLICY CONCPT OBS TREND WAR
GEN/LAWS. PAGE 38 B0778
                                                  S64

GROSS J.A.,"WHITEHALL AND THE COMMONWEALTH." EX/STRUC
EUR+WWI MOD/EUR INT/ORG NAT/G CONSULT DELIB/GP ATTIT
LEGIS DOMIN ADMIN COLONIAL ROUTINE PWR CMN/WLTH TREND
19/20. PAGE 44 B0890
                                                  S64

HUELIN D.,"ECONOMIC INTEGRATION IN LATIN AMERICAN: MARKET
PROGRESS AND PROBLEMS." L/A+17C ECO/DEV AGRI ECO/UNDEV
DIST/IND FINAN INDUS NAT/G VOL/ASSN CONSULT INT/TRADE
DELIB/GP EX/STRUC ACT/RES PLAN TEC/DEV ECO/TAC
ROUTINE BAL/PAY WEALTH WORK 20. PAGE 52 B1058
                                                  S64

KHAN M.Z.,"THE PRESIDENT OF THE GENERAL ASSEMBLY." INT/ORG
WOR+45 CONSTN DELIB/GP EDU/PROP LEGIT ROUTINE PWR TOP/EX
RESPECT SKILL...DECISION SOC BIOG TREND UN 20.
PAGE 59 B1202
                                                  S64

ROGOW A.A.,"CONGRESSIONAL GOVERNMENT: LEGISLATIVE PWR
POWER V. DOMESTIC PROCESSES." USA+45 CHIEF DELIB/GP DIPLOM
ADMIN GOV/REL CONGRESS. PAGE 90 B1815 LEGIS
                                       POLICY
                                                  S64

RUSK D.,"THE MAKING OF FOREIGN POLICY" USA+45 CHIEF DIPLOM
DELIB/GP WORKER PROB/SOLV ADMIN ATTIT PWR INT
...DECISION 20 DEPT/STATE RUSK/D GOLDMAN/E. PAGE 92 POLICY
B1856
                                                  S64

SWEARER H.R.,"AFTER KHRUSHCHEV: WHAT NEXT." COM FUT EX/STRUC
USSR CONSTN ELITES NAT/G POL/PAR CHIEF DELIB/GP PWR
LEGIS DOMIN LEAD...RECORD TREND STERTYP GEN/METH
20. PAGE 102 B2058
                                                  B65

BOXER C.R.,PORTUGUESE SOCIETY IN THE TROPICS - THE MUNIC
MUNICIPAL COUNCILS OF GAO, MACAO, BAHIA, AND ADMIN
LUANDA, 1510-1800. EUR+WWI MOD/EUR PORTUGAL CONSTN COLONIAL
EX/STRUC DOMIN CONTROL ROUTINE REPRESENT PRIVIL DELIB/GP
...BIBLIOG/A 16/19 GENACCOUNT MACAO BAHIA LUANDA.
PAGE 14 B0290
                                                  B65

CAMPBELL G.A.,THE CIVIL SERVICE IN BRITAIN (2ND ADMIN

ED.). UK DELIB/GP FORCES WORKER CREATE PLAN LEGIS
...POLICY AUD/VIS 19/20 CIVIL/SERV. PAGE 18 B0370 NAT/G
                                                  FINAN
                                                  B65

COHN H.J.,THE GOVERNMENT OF THE RHINE PALATINATE IN PROVS
THE FIFTEENTH CENTURY. GERMANY FINAN LOC/G DELIB/GP JURID
LEGIS CT/SYS CHOOSE CATHISM 14/15 PALATINATE. GP/REL
PAGE 22 B0449 ADMIN
                                                  B65

FORGAC A.A.,NEW DIPLOMACY AND THE UNITED NATIONS. DIPLOM
FRANCE GERMANY UK USSR INT/ORG DELIB/GP EX/STRUC ETIQUET
PEACE...INT/LAW CONCPT UN. PAGE 36 B0740 NAT/G
                                                  B65

GOPAL S.,BRITISH POLICY IN INDIA 1858-1905. INDIA COLONIAL
UK ELITES CHIEF DELIB/GP ECO/TAC GP/REL DISCRIM ADMIN
ATTIT...IDEA/COMP NAT/COMP PERS/COMP BIBLIOG/A POL/PAR
19/20. PAGE 41 B0828 ECO/UNDEV
                                                  B65

GT BRIT ADMIN STAFF COLLEGE,THE ACCOUNTABILITY OF LG/CO
PUBLIC CORPORATIONS (REV. ED.). UK ECO/DEV FINAN NAT/G
DELIB/GP EX/STRUC BUDGET CAP/ISM CONFER PRICE ADMIN
PARL/PROC 20. PAGE 44 B0899 CONTROL
                                                  B65

HAINES R.M.,THE ADMINISTRATION OF THE DIOCESE OF ADMIN
WORCESTER IN THE FIRST HALF OF THE FOURTEENTH EX/STRUC
CENTURY. UK CATHISM...METH/COMP 13/15. PAGE 45 SECT
B0918 DELIB/GP
                                                  B65

INST INTL DES CIVILISATION DIF,THE CONSTITUTIONS CONSTN
AND ADMINISTRATIVE INSTITUTIONS OF THE NEW STATES. ADMIN
AFR ISLAM S/ASIA NAT/G POL/PAR DELIB/GP EX/STRUC ADJUD
CONFER EFFICIENCY NAT/LISM...JURID SOC 20. PAGE 54 ECO/UNDEV
B1088
                                                  B65

LATHAM E.,THE GROUP BASIS OF POLITICS: A STUDY IN LEGIS
BASING-POINT LEGISLATION. INDUS MARKET POL/PAR GP/COMP
DELIB/GP EX/STRUC DEBATE ADJUD...CHARTS PRESIDENT. GP/REL
PAGE 63 B1274
                                                  B65

MACDONALD R.W.,THE LEAGUE OF ARAB STATES: A STUDY ISLAM
IN THE POLITICS OF REGIONAL ORGANIZATION. ISRAEL REGION
UAR USSR FINAN INT/ORG DELIB/GP ECO/TAC AGREE DIPLOM
NEUTRAL ORD/FREE PWR...DECISION BIBLIOG 20 TREATY ADMIN
UN. PAGE 67 B1358
                                                  B65

MASTERS N.A.,COMMITTEE ASSIGNMENTS IN THE HOUSE OF LEAD
REPRESENTATIVES (BMR). USA+45 ELITES POL/PAR LEGIS
EX/STRUC PARTIC REPRESENT GP/REL PERS/REL ATTIT PWR CHOOSE
...STAT CHARTS 20 HOUSE/REP. PAGE 71 B1425 DELIB/GP
                                                  B65

MORGENTHAU H.,MORGENTHAU DIARY (CHINA) (2 VOLS.). DIPLOM
ASIA USA+45 USA-45 LAW DELIB/GP EX/STRUC PLAN ADMIN
FOR/AID INT/TRADE CONFER WAR MARXISM 20 CHINJAP.
PAGE 75 B1523
                                                  B65

SHARMA S.A.,PARLIAMENTARY GOVERNMENT IN INDIA. NAT/G
INDIA FINAN LOC/G PROVS DELIB/GP PLAN ADMIN CT/SYS CONSTN
FEDERAL...JURID 20. PAGE 96 B1936 PARL/PROC
                                     LEGIS
                                                  B65

STANLEY D.T.,CHANGING ADMINISTRATIONS. USA+45 NAT/G
POL/PAR DELIB/GP TOP/EX BUDGET GOV/REL GP/REL CHIEF
PERS/REL PWR...MAJORIT DECISION MGT 20 PRESIDENT ADMIN
SUCCESSION DEPT/STATE DEPT/DEFEN DEPT/HEW. PAGE 100 EX/STRUC
B2021
                                                  B65

US HOUSE COMM EDUC AND LABOR,ADMINISTRATION OF THE ADMIN
NATIONAL LABOR RELATIONS ACT. USA+45 DELIB/GP LABOR
WORKER PROB/SOLV BARGAIN PAY CONTROL 20 NLRB GP/REL
CONGRESS. PAGE 108 B2188 INDUS
                                                  B65

US SENATE COMM GOVT OPERATIONS,ADMINISTRATION OF NAT/G
NATIONAL SECURITY. USA+45 DELIB/GP ADMIN ROLE ORD/FREE
...POLICY CHARTS SENATE. PAGE 110 B2218 DIPLOM
                                        PROB/SOLV
                                                  B65

US SENATE COMM ON JUDICIARY,HEARINGS BEFORE ROUTINE
SUBCOMMITTEE ON ADMINISTRATIVE PRACTICE AND DELIB/GP
PROCEDURE ABOUT ADMINISTRATIVE PROCEDURE ACT 1965. ADMIN
USA+45 LEGIS EDU/PROP ADJUD GOV/REL INGP/REL NAT/G
EFFICIENCY...POLICY INT 20 CONGRESS. PAGE 110 B2232
                                                  L65

RUBIN A.P.,"UNITED STATES CONTEMPORARY PRACTICE LAW
RELATING TO INTERNATIONAL LAW." USA+45 WOR+45 LEGIT
CONSTN INT/ORG NAT/G DELIB/GP EX/STRUC DIPLOM DOMIN INT/LAW
CT/SYS ROUTINE ORD/FREE...CONCPT COLD/WAR 20.
PAGE 91 B1848
                                                  S65

ALEXANDER T.,"SYNECTICS: INVENTING BY THE MADNESS PROB/SOLV
METHOD." DELIB/GP TOP/EX ACT/RES TEC/DEV EXEC TASK OP/RES
KNOWL...MGT METH/COMP 20. PAGE 4 B0073 CREATE
                                        CONSULT
                                                  S65

QUADE Q.L.,"THE TRUMAN ADMINISTRATION AND THE USA+45
SEPARATION OF POWERS: THE CASE OF THE MARSHALL ECO/UNDEV
PLAN." SOCIETY INT/ORG NAT/G CONSULT DELIB/GP LEGIS DIPLOM

PLAN ECO/TAC ROUTINE DRIVE PERCEPT RIGID/FLEX
ORD/FREE PWR WEALTH...DECISION GEOG NEW/IDEA TREND
20 TRUMAN/HS. PAGE 85 B1726
S65

TABORSKY E.,"CHANGE IN CZECHOSLOVAKIA." COM USSR ECO/DEV
ELITES INTELL AGRI INDUS NAT/G DELIB/GP EX/STRUC PLAN
ECO/TAC TOTALISM ATTIT RIGID/FLEX SOCISM...MGT CZECHOSLVK
CONCPT TREND 20. PAGE 102 B2067
B66

ADAMS J.C.,THE GOVERNMENT OF REPUBLICAN ITALY (2ND NAT/G
ED.). ITALY LOC/G POL/PAR DELIB/GP LEGIS WORKER CHOOSE
ADMIN CT/SYS FASCISM...CHARTS BIBLIOG 20 EX/STRUC
PARLIAMENT. PAGE 3 B0057 CONSTN
B66

AMER ENTERPRISE INST PUB POL,CONGRESS: THE FIRST EFFICIENCY
BRANCH OF GOVERNMENT. EX/STRUC FEEDBACK REPRESENT LEGIS
INGP/REL PWR...DECISION METH/CNCPT PREDICT. PAGE 4 DELIB/GP
B0081 CONTROL
B66

DAHLBERG J.S.,THE NEW YORK BUREAU OF MUNICIPAL PROVS
RESEARCH: PIONEER IN GOVERNMENT ADMINISTRATION. MUNIC
CONSTN R+D BUDGET EDU/PROP PARTIC REPRESENT DELIB/GP
EFFICIENCY ORD/FREE...BIBLIOG METH 20 NEW/YORK ADMIN
NIPA. PAGE 26 B0522
B66

DAVIS J.A.,SOUTHERN AFRICA IN TRANSITION. SOUTH/AFR AFR
USA+45 FINAN NAT/G DELIB/GP EDU/PROP ADMIN COLONIAL ADJUST
REGION RACE/REL ATTIT SOVEREIGN...ANTHOL 20 CONSTN
RESOURCE/N. PAGE 26 B0538
B66

GHOSH P.K.,THE CONSTITUTION OF INDIA: HOW IT HAS CONSTN
BEEN FRAMED. INDIA LOC/G DELIB/GP EX/STRUC NAT/G
PROB/SOLV BUDGET INT/TRADE CT/SYS CHOOSE...LING 20. LEGIS
PAGE 39 B0795 FEDERAL
B66

INTERPARLIAMENTARY UNION,PARLIAMENTS: COMPARATIVE PARL/PROC
STUDY ON STRUCTURE AND FUNCTIONING OF LEGIS
REPRESENTATIVE INSTITUTIONS IN FIFTY-FIVE GOV/COMP
COUNTRIES. WOR+45 POL/PAR DELIB/GP BUDGET ADMIN EX/STRUC
CONTROL CHOOSE. PAGE 54 B1099
B66

JOHNSON N.,PARLIAMENT AND ADMINISTRATION: THE LEGIS
ESTIMATES COMMITTEE 1945-65. FUT UK NAT/G EX/STRUC ADMIN
PLAN BUDGET ORD/FREE...T 20 PARLIAMENT HOUSE/CMNS. FINAN
PAGE 57 B1147 DELIB/GP
B66

MANGONE G.J.,UN ADMINISTRATION OF ECONOMIC AND ADMIN
AOCIAL PROGRAMS. CONSULT BUDGET INT/TRADE REGION 20 MGT
UN. PAGE 69 B1391 ECO/TAC
DELIB/GP
B66

MONTEIRO J.B.,CORRUPTION: CONTROL OF CONTROL
MALADMINISTRATION. EUR+WWI INDIA USA+45 USSR NAT/G CRIME
DELIB/GP ADMIN...GP/COMP 20 OMBUDSMAN. PAGE 74 PROB/SOLV
B1503
B66

O'NEILL C.E.,CHURCH AND STATE IN FRENCH COLONIAL COLONIAL
LOUISIANA: POLICY AND POLITICS TO 1732. PROVS NAT/G
VOL/ASSN DELIB/GP ADJUD ADMIN GP/REL ATTIT DRIVE SECT
...POLICY BIBLIOG 17/18 LOUISIANA CHURCH/STA. PWR
PAGE 79 B1601
B66

ONYEMELUKWE C.C.,PROBLEMS OF INDUSTRIAL PLANNING ECO/UNDEV
AND MANAGEMENT IN NIGERIA. AFR FINAN LABOR DELIB/GP ECO/TAC
TEC/DEV ADJUST...MGT TREND BIBLIOG. PAGE 80 B1610 INDUS
PLAN
B66

ROSHOLT R.L.,AN ADMINISTRATIVE HISTORY OF NASA, ADMIN
1958-1963. SPACE USA+45 FINAN LEAD...MGT CHARTS EX/STRUC
BIBLIOG 20 NASA. PAGE 90 B1824 ADJUST
DELIB/GP
B66

SAPIN B.M.,THE MAKING OF UNITED STATES FOREIGN DIPLOM
POLICY. USA+45 INT/ORG DELIB/GP FORCES PLAN ECO/TAC EX/STRUC
CIVMIL/REL PRESIDENT. PAGE 92 B1868 DECISION
NAT/G
B66

US SENATE COMM GOVT OPERATIONS,INTERGOVERNMENTAL ADMIN
PERSONNEL ACT OF 1966. USA+45 NAT/G CONSULT LEGIS
DELIB/GP WORKER TEC/DEV PAY AUTOMAT UTIL 20 EFFICIENCY
CONGRESS. PAGE 110 B2219 EDU/PROP
B66

WADIA M.,THE NATURE AND SCOPE OF MANAGEMENT. MGT
DELIB/GP EX/STRUC CREATE AUTOMAT CONTROL EFFICIENCY PROB/SOLV
...ANTHOL 20. PAGE 112 B2271 IDEA/COMP
ECO/TAC
B66

WASHINGTON S.H.,BIBLIOGRAPHY: LABOR-MANAGEMENT BIBLIOG
RELATIONS ACT, 1947 AS AMENDED BY LABOR-MANAGEMENT LAW
REPORTING AND DISCLOSURE ACT, 1959. USA+45 CONSTN LABOR
INDUS DELIB/GP LEGIS WORKER BARGAIN ECO/TAC ADJUD MGT
GP/REL NEW/LIB...JURID CONGRESS. PAGE 114 B2298
B66

WHITNAH D.R.,SAFER SKYWAYS. DIST/IND DELIB/GP ADMIN
FORCES TOP/EX WORKER TEC/DEV ROUTINE WAR CIVMIL/REL NAT/G
COST...TIME/SEQ 20 FAA CAB. PAGE 116 B2342 AIR

GOV/REL
B66

YOUNG S.,MANAGEMENT: A SYSTEMS ANALYSIS. DELIB/GP PROB/SOLV
EX/STRUC ECO/TAC CONTROL EFFICIENCY...NET/THEORY MGT
20. PAGE 119 B2394 DECISION
SIMUL
S66

MATTHEWS D.G.,"ETHIOPIAN OUTLINE: A BIBLIOGRAPHIC BIBLIOG
RESEARCH GUIDE." ETHIOPIA LAW STRUCT ECO/UNDEV AGRI NAT/G
LABOR SECT CHIEF DELIB/GP EX/STRUC ADMIN...LING DIPLOM
ORG/CHARTS 20. PAGE 71 B1429 POL/PAR
C66

TACHERON D.G.,"THE JOB OF THE CONGRESSMAN: AN LEGIS
INTRODUCTION TO SERVICES IN THE US HOUSE OF PARL/PROC
REPRESENTATIVES." DELIB/GP EX/STRUC PRESS SENIOR ADMIN
CT/SYS LOBBY CHOOSE GOV/REL...BIBLIOG 20 CONGRESS POL/PAR
HOUSE/REP SENATE. PAGE 102 B2068
B67

ENKE S.,DEFENSE MANAGEMENT. USA+45 R+D FORCES DECISION
WORKER PLAN ECO/TAC ADMIN NUC/PWR BAL/PAY UTIL DELIB/GP
WEALTH...MGT DEPT/DEFEN. PAGE 33 B0675 EFFICIENCY
BUDGET
B67

FARNSWORTH B.,WILLIAM C. BULLITT AND THE SOVIET DIPLOM
UNION. COM USA+45 USSR NAT/G CHIEF CONSULT DELIB/GP BIOG
EX/STRUC WAR REPRESENT MARXISM 20 WILSON/W POLICY
ROOSEVLT/F STALIN/J BULLITT/WC. PAGE 35 B0705
B67

US SENATE COMM ON FOREIGN REL,HUMAN RIGHTS LEGIS
CONVENTIONS. USA+45 LABOR VOL/ASSN DELIB/GP DOMIN ORD/FREE
ADJUD REPRESENT...INT/LAW MGT CONGRESS. PAGE 110 WORKER
B2225 LOBBY
B67

ZELERMYER W.,BUSINESS LAW: NEW PERSPECTIVES IN LABOR
BUSINESS ECONOMICS. USA+45 LAW INDUS DELIB/GP CAP/ISM
...JURID MGT ANTHOL BIBLIOG 20 NLRB. PAGE 119 B2400 LG/CO
L67

CARMICHAEL D.M.,"FORTY YEARS OF WATER POLLUTION HEALTH
CONTROL IN WISCONSIN: A CASE STUDY." LAW EXTR/IND CONTROL
INDUS MUNIC DELIB/GP PLAN PROB/SOLV SANCTION ADMIN
...CENSUS CHARTS 20 WISCONSIN. PAGE 19 B0382 ADJUD
S67

ANDERSON L.G.,"ADMINISTERING A GOVERNMENT SOCIAL ADMIN
SERVICE" NEW/ZEALND EX/STRUC TASK ROLE 20. PAGE 5 NAT/G
B0094 DELIB/GP
SOC/WK
S67

BRADLEY A.W.,"CONSTITUTION-MAKING IN UGANDA." NAT/G
UGANDA LAW CHIEF DELIB/GP LEGIS ADMIN EXEC CREATE
PARL/PROC RACE/REL ORD/FREE...GOV/COMP 20. PAGE 14 CONSTN
B0295 FEDERAL
S67

DOERN G.B.,"THE ROYAL COMMISSIONS IN THE GENERAL R+D
POLICY PROCESS AND IN FEDERAL-PROVINCIAL EX/STRUC
RELATIONS." CANADA CONSTN ACADEM PROVS CONSULT GOV/REL
DELIB/GP LEGIS ACT/RES PROB/SOLV CONFER CONTROL NAT/G
EFFICIENCY...METH/COMP 20 SENATE ROYAL/COMM.
PAGE 30 B0603
S67

GORHAM W.,"NOTES OF A PRACTITIONER." USA+45 BUDGET DECISION
ADMIN COST...CON/ANAL METH/COMP 20 JOHNSON/LB. NAT/G
PAGE 41 B0836 DELIB/GP
EFFICIENCY
S67

JONES G.S.,"STRATEGIC PLANNING." USA+45 EX/STRUC PLAN
FORCES DETER WAR 20 PRESIDENT. PAGE 57 B1150 DECISION
DELIB/GP
POLICY
S67

LEES J.P.,"LEGISLATIVE REVIEW AND BUREAUCRATIC SUPEGO
RESPONSIBILITY." USA+45 FINAN NAT/G DELIB/GP PLAN BUDGET
PROB/SOLV CONFER CONTROL GP/REL DEMAND...DECISION LEGIS
20 CONGRESS PRESIDENT HOUSE/REP BUREAUCRCY. PAGE 63 EXEC
B1281
S67

PAYNE W.A.,"LOCAL GOVERNMENT STUDY COMMISSIONS: LOC/G
ORGANIZATION FOR ACTION." USA+45 LEGIS PWR...CHARTS DELIB/GP
20. PAGE 81 B1646 PROB/SOLV
ADMIN
S67

PRATT R.C.,"THE ADMINISTRATION OF ECONOMIC PLANNING NAT/G
IN A NEWLY INDEPENDENT STATE* THE TANZANIAN DELIB/GP
EXPERIENCE 1963-1966." AFR TANZANIA ECO/UNDEV PLAN ADMIN
CONTROL ROUTINE TASK EFFICIENCY 20. PAGE 84 B1699 TEC/DEV
S67

SPACKMAN A.,"THE SENATE OF TRINIDAD AND TOBAGO." ELITES
L/A+17C TRINIDAD WEST/IND NAT/G POL/PAR DELIB/GP EFFICIENCY
OP/RES PROB/SOLV EDU/PROP EXEC LOBBY ROUTINE LEGIS
REPRESENT GP/REL 20. PAGE 99 B2002 DECISION
S67

ZASLOW M.,"RECENT CONSTITUTIONAL DEVELOPMENTS IN GOV/REL
CANADA'S NORTHERN TERRITORIES." CANADA LOC/G REGION
DELIB/GP EX/STRUC LEGIS ADMIN ORD/FREE...TREND 20. CONSTN
PAGE 119 B2398 FEDERAL
N67

NATIONAL COMN COMMUNITY HEALTH,ACTION - PLANNING PLAN

FOR COMMUNITY HEALTH SERVICES (PAMPHLET). USA+45   MUNIC
PROF/ORG DELIB/GP BUDGET ROUTINE GP/REL ATTIT   HEALTH
...HEAL SOC SOC/WK CHARTS TIME 20. PAGE 77 B1563   ADJUST

DELLIN L.A.D. B0572

DEMAND....ECONOMIC DEMAND

INTERNATIONAL BIBLIOGRAPHY OF ECONOMICS. WOR+45   N
FINAN MARKET ADMIN DEMAND INCOME PRODUC...POLICY   BIBLIOG
IDEA/COMP METH. PAGE 1 B0003   ECO/DEV
                                                     ECO/UNDEV
                                                     INT/TRADE
                                                          NCO
STOLPER W.."SOCIAL FACTORS IN ECONOMIC PLANNING,   ECO/UNDEV
WITH SPECIAL REFERENCE TO NIGERIA" AFR NIGER   PLAN
CULTURE FAM SECT RECEIVE ETIQUET ADMIN DEMAND 20.   ADJUST
PAGE 101 B2045   RISK
                                                          B19
DUNN A..SCIENTIFIC SELLING AND ADVERTISING. CLIENT   LG/CO
ADMIN DEMAND EFFICIENCY 20. PAGE 31 B0632   PERCEPT
                                                     PERS/REL
                                                     TASK
                                                          B28
CALKINS E.E..BUSINESS THE CIVILIZER. INDUS MARKET   LAISSEZ
WORKER TAX PAY ROUTINE COST DEMAND MORAL 19/20.   POLICY
PAGE 18 B0367   WEALTH
                                                     PROFIT
                                                          B40
BURT F.A..AMERICAN ADVERTISING AGENCIES. BARGAIN   LG/CO
BUDGET LICENSE WRITING PRICE PERS/REL COST DEMAND   COM/IND
...ORG/CHARTS BIBLIOG 20. PAGE 18 B0358   ADMIN
                                                     EFFICIENCY
                                                          B51
PETERSON F..SURVEY OF LABOR ECONOMICS (REV. ED.).   WORKER
STRATA ECO/DEV LABOR INSPECT BARGAIN PAY PRICE EXEC DEMAND
ROUTINE GP/REL ALL/VALS ORD/FREE 20 AFL/CIO   IDEA/COMP
DEPT/LABOR. PAGE 82 B1662   T
                                                          B53
MAJUMDAR B.B..PROBLEMS OF PUBLIC ADMINISTRATION IN   ECO/UNDEV
INDIA. INDIA INDUS PLAN BUDGET ADJUD CENTRAL DEMAND GOV/REL
WEALTH...WELF/ST ANTHOL 20 CIVIL/SERV. PAGE 68   ADMIN
B1384   MUNIC
                                                          B58
CHANG C..THE INFLATIONARY SPIRAL: THE EXPERIENCE IN FINAN
CHINA 1939-50. CHINA/COM BUDGET INT/TRADE PRICE   ECO/TAC
ADMIN CONTROL WAR DEMAND...POLICY CHARTS 20.   BAL/PAY
PAGE 20 B0406   GOV/REL
                                                          B58
WARNER A.W..CONCEPTS AND CASES IN ECONOMIC   ECO/TAC
ANALYSIS. PROB/SOLV BARGAIN CONTROL INCOME PRODUC   DEMAND
...ECOMETRIC MGT CONCPT CLASSIF CHARTS 20   EQUILIB
KEYNES/JM. PAGE 114 B2292   COST
                                                          S58
DIAMANT A.."A CASE STUDY OF ADMINISTRATIVE   ADMIN
AUTONOMY: CONTROLS AND TENSIONS IN FRENCH   CONTROL
ADMINISTRATION." FRANCE ADJUD LOBBY DEMAND   LEGIS
EFFICIENCY 20. PAGE 29 B0585   EXEC
                                                          B61
BARRASH J..LABOR'S GRASS ROOTS: A STUDY OF THE   LABOR
LOCAL UNION. STRATA BARGAIN LEAD REPRESENT DEMAND   USA+45
ATTIT PWR. PAGE 9 B0190   INGP/REL
                                                     EXEC
                                                          B61
MACMAHON A.W..DELEGATION AND AUTONOMY. INDIA STRUCT ADMIN
LEGIS BARGAIN BUDGET ECO/TAC LEGIT EXEC REPRESENT   PLAN
GOV/REL CENTRAL DEMAND EFFICIENCY PRODUC. PAGE 68   FEDERAL
B1373
                                                          B62
FORD A.G..THE GOLD STANDARD 1880-1914: BRITAIN AND   FINAN
ARGENTINA. UK ECO/UNDEV INT/TRADE ADMIN GOV/REL   ECO/TAC
DEMAND EFFICIENCY...STAT CHARTS 19/20 ARGEN   BUDGET
GOLD/STAND. PAGE 36 B0737   BAL/PAY
                                                          B62
GRANICK D..THE EUROPEAN EXECUTIVE. BELGIUM FRANCE   MGT
GERMANY/W UK INDUS LABOR LG/CO SML/CO EX/STRUC PLAN ECO/DEV
TEC/DEV CAP/ISM COST DEMAND...POLICY CHARTS 20.   ECO/TAC
PAGE 42 B0852   EXEC
                                                          B63
OLSON M. JR..THE ECONOMICS OF WARTIME SHORTAGE.   WAR
FRANCE GERMANY MOD/EUR UK AGRI PROB/SOLV ADMIN   ADJUST
DEMAND WEALTH...POLICY OLD/LIB 17/20. PAGE 80 B1608 ECO/TAC
                                                     NAT/COMP
                                                          B64
GARFIELD PJ   LOVEJOY WF.PUBLIC UTILITY   T
ECONOMICS. DIST/IND FINAN MARKET MUNIC ADMIN COST   ECO/TAC
DEMAND...TECHNIC JURID 20 MONOPOLY. PAGE 39 B0782   OWN
                                                     SERV/IND
                                                          B64
MARRIS R..THE ECONOMIC THEORY OF "MANAGERIAL"   CAP/ISM
CAPITALISM. USA+45 ECO/DEV LG/CO ECO/TAC DEMAND   MGT
...CHARTS BIBLIOG 20. PAGE 69 B1402   CONTROL
                                                     OP/RES
                                                          B64
WERNETTE J.P..GOVERNMENT AND BUSINESS. LABOR   NAT/G
CAP/ISM ECO/TAC INT/TRADE TAX ADMIN AUTOMAT NUC/PWR FINAN

CIVMIL/REL DEMAND...MGT 20 MONOPOLY. PAGE 115 B2323 ECO/DEV
                                                     CONTROL
                                                          B65
EDELMAN M..THE POLITICS OF WAGE-PRICE DECISIONS.   GOV/COMP
GERMANY ITALY NETHERLAND UK INDUS LABOR POL/PAR   CONTROL
PROB/SOLV BARGAIN PRICE ROUTINE BAL/PAY COST DEMAND ECO/TAC
20. PAGE 32 B0654   PLAN
                                                          B65
MUSOLF L.D..PROMOTING THE GENERAL WELFARE: ECO/TAC
GOVERNMENT AND THE ECONOMY. USA+45 ECO/DEV CAP/ISM   NAT/G
DEMAND OPTIMAL 20. PAGE 77 B1550   EX/STRUC
                                                     NEW/LIB
                                                          B65
ORG FOR ECO COOP AND DEVEL,THE MEDITERRANEAN   EDU/PROP
REGIONAL PROJECT: YUGOSLAVIA; EDUCATION AND   ACADEM
DEVELOPMENT. YUGOSLAVIA SOCIETY FINAN PROF/ORG PLAN SCHOOL
ADMIN COST DEMAND MARXISM...STAT TREND CHARTS METH   ECO/UNDEV
20 OECD. PAGE 80 B1615   N65
NJ DIVISION STATE-REGION PLAN,UTILIZATION OF NEW   UTIL
JERSEY'S DELAWARE RIVER WATERFRONT (PAMPHLET). FUT   PLAN
ADMIN REGION LEISURE GOV/REL DEMAND WEALTH...CHARTS ECO/TAC
20 NEW/JERSEY. PAGE 78 B1586   PROVS
                                                          B66
SCHMIDT F..PUBLIC RELATIONS IN HEALTH AND WELFARE.   PROF/ORG
USA+45 ACADEM RECEIVE PRESS FEEDBACK GOV/REL   EDU/PROP
PERS/REL DEMAND EFFICIENCY ATTIT PERCEPT WEALTH 20   ADMIN
PUBLIC/REL. PAGE 94 B1895   HEALTH
                                                          L66
AMERICAN ECONOMIC REVIEW,"SIXTY-THIRD LIST OF   BIBLIOG/A
DOCTORAL DISSERTATIONS IN POLITICAL ECONOMY IN   CONCPT
AMERICAN UNIVERSITIES AND COLLEGES." ECO/DEV AGRI   ACADEM
FINAN LABOR WORKER PLAN BUDGET INT/TRADE ADMIN
DEMAND...MGT STAT 20. PAGE 4 B0084   B67
ANDERSON C.W..POLITICS AND ECONOMIC CHANGE IN LATIN ECO/UNDEV
AMERICA. L/A+17C INDUS NAT/G OP/RES ADMIN DEMAND   PROB/SOLV
...POLICY STAT CHARTS NAT/COMP 20. PAGE 4 B0091   PLAN
                                                     ECO/TAC
                                                          B67
GROSSMAN G..ECONOMIC SYSTEMS. USA+45 USA-45 USSR   ECO/DEV
YUGOSLAVIA WORKER CAP/ISM PRICE GP/REL EQUILIB   PLAN
WEALTH MARXISM SOCISM...MGT METH/COMP 19/20.   TEC/DEV
PAGE 44 B0892   DEMAND
                                                          B67
HIRSCHMAN A.O..DEVELOPMENT PROJECTS OBSERVED. INDUS ECO/UNDEV
INT/ORG CONSULT EX/STRUC CREATE OP/RES ECO/TAC   R+D
DEMAND...POLICY MGT METH/COMP 20 WORLD/BANK.   FINAN
PAGE 50 B1016   PLAN
                                                          B67
NARVER J.C..CONGLOMERATE MERGERS AND MARKET   DEMAND
COMPETITION. USA+45 LAW STRUCT ADMIN LEAD RISK COST LG/CO
PROFIT WEALTH...POLICY CHARTS BIBLIOG. PAGE 77   MARKET
B1555   MGT
                                                          L67
PASLEY R.S.."ORGANIZATIONAL CONFLICTS OF INTEREST   NAT/G
IN GOVERNMENT CONTRACTS." ELITES R+D ROUTINE   ECO/TAC
NUC/PWR DEMAND EFFICIENCY 20. PAGE 81 B1639   RATION
                                                     CONTROL
                                                          S67
BRIMMER A.F.."INITIATIVE AND INNOVATION IN CENTRAL   FINAN
BANKING." USA+45 ECO/DEV MARKET ECO/TAC TAX CONTROL CREATE
DEMAND...MGT CHARTS FED/RESERV. PAGE 15 B0309   NAT/G
                                                     POLICY
                                                          S67
JOHNSON L.B.."BULLETS DO NOT DISCRIMINATE-LANDLORDS NAT/G
DO." PROB/SOLV EXEC LOBBY DEMAND...REALPOL SOC 20.   DISCRIM
PAGE 57 B1145   POLICY
                                                          S67
LEES J.P.."LEGISLATIVE REVIEW AND BUREAUCRATIC   SUPEGO
RESPONSIBILITY." USA+45 FINAN NAT/G DELIB/GP PLAN   BUDGET
PROB/SOLV CONFER CONTROL GP/REL DEMAND...DECISION   LEGIS
20 CONGRESS PRESIDENT HOUSE/REP BUREAUCRCY. PAGE 63 EXEC
B1281
                                                          S67
LERNER A.P.."EMPLOYMENT THEORY AND EMPLOYMENT   CAP/ISM
POLICY." ECO/DEV INDUS LABOR LG/CO BUDGET ADMIN   WORKER
DEMAND PROFIT WEALTH LAISSEZ METH/COMP. PAGE 64   CONCPT
B1296
                                                          S67
MORTON J.A.."A SYSTEMS APPROACH TO THE INNOVATION   TEC/DEV
PROCESS: ITS USE IN THE BELL SYSTEM." USA+45 INTELL GEN/METH
INDUS LG/CO CONSULT WORKER COMPUTER AUTOMAT DEMAND   R+D
...MGT CHARTS 20. PAGE 76 B1531   COM/IND
                                                          N67
US CONGRESS JT COMM ECO GOVT,BACKGROUND MATERIAL ON BUDGET
ECONOMY IN GOVERNMENT 1967 (PAMPHLET). WOR+45   COST
ECO/DEV BARGAIN PRICE DEMAND OPTIMAL...STAT   MGT
DEPT/DEFEN. PAGE 108 B2178   NAT/G

DEMOCRACY....SEE MAJORIT, REPRESENT, CHOOSE, PWR
     POPULISM, NEW/LIB, ET AL.

DEMOCRAT....DEMOCRATIC PARTY (ALL NATIONS)

B61
TANZER L.,THE KENNEDY CIRCLE. INTELL CONSULT EX/STRUC
DELIB/GP TOP/EX CONTROL EXEC INGP/REL PERS/REL PWR NAT/G
...BIOG IDEA/COMP ANTHOL 20 KENNEDY/JF PRESIDENT CHIEF
DEMOCRAT MCNAMARA/R RUSK/D. PAGE 103 B2077

B64
RIGGS R.E.,THE MOVEMENT FOR ADMINISTRATIVE ADMIN
REORGANIZATION IN ARIZONA. USA+45 LAW POL/PAR PROVS
DELIB/GP LEGIS PROB/SOLV CONTROL RIGID/FLEX PWR CREATE
...ORG/CHARTS 20 ARIZONA DEMOCRAT REPUBLICAN. PLAN
PAGE 88 B1786

B66
CARALEY D.,PARTY POLITICS AND NATIONAL ELECTIONS. POL/PAR
USA+45 STRATA LOC/G PROVS EX/STRUC BARGAIN ADMIN CHOOSE
SANCTION GP/REL ATTIT 20 DEMOCRAT REPUBLICAN. REPRESENT
PAGE 18 B0375 NAT/G

DEMOGRAPHY....SEE GEOG

DENMARK....SEE ALSO APPROPRIATE TIME/SPACE/CULTURE INDEX

B57
MEYER P.,ADMINISTRATIVE ORGANIZATION: A COMPARATIVE ADMIN
STUDY OF THE ORGANIZATION OF PUBLIC ADMINISTRATION. METH/COMP
DENMARK FRANCE NORWAY SWEDEN UK USA+45 ELITES LOC/G NAT/G
CONSULT LEGIS ADJUD CONTROL LEAD PWR SKILL CENTRAL
DECISION. PAGE 73 B1475

B64
ANDREN N.,GOVERNMENT AND POLITICS IN THE NORDIC CONSTN
COUNTRIES: DENMARK, FINLAND, ICELAND, NORWAY, NAT/G
SWEDEN. DENMARK FINLAND ICELAND NORWAY SWEDEN CULTURE
POL/PAR CHIEF LEGIS ADMIN REGION REPRESENT ATTIT GOV/COMP
CONSERVE...CHARTS BIBLIOG/A 20. PAGE 5 B0102

B64
HALLER W.,DER SCHWEDISCHE JUSTITIEOMBUDSMAN. JURID
DENMARK FINLAND NORWAY SWEDEN LEGIS ADJUD CONTROL PARL/PROC
PERSON ORD/FREE...NAT/COMP 20 OMBUDSMAN. PAGE 46 ADMIN
B0926 CHIEF

B65
ROWAT D.C.,THE OMBUDSMAN: CITIZEN'S DEFENDER. INSPECT
DENMARK FINLAND NEW/ZEALND NORWAY SWEDEN CONSULT CONSTN
PROB/SOLV FEEDBACK PARTIC GP/REL...SOC CONCPT REPRESENT
NEW/IDEA METH/COMP ANTHOL BIBLIOG 20. PAGE 91 B1840 ADMIN

B65
SMITH C.,THE OMBUDSMAN: A BIBLIOGRAPHY (PAMPHLET). BIBLIOG
DENMARK SWEDEN USA+45 LAW LEGIS JUDGE GOV/REL ADMIN
GP/REL...JURID 20. PAGE 98 B1980 CT/SYS
ADJUD

B66
AARON T.J.,THE CONTROL OF POLICE DISCRETION: THE CONTROL
DANISH EXPERIENCE. DENMARK LAW CREATE ADMIN FORCES
INGP/REL SUPEGO PWR 20 OMBUDSMAN. PAGE 2 B0049 REPRESENT
PROB/SOLV

S67
KRARUP O.,"JUDICIAL REVIEW OF ADMINISTRATIVE ACTION ADJUD
IN DENMARK." DENMARK LAW CT/SYS...JURID CONCPT CONTROL
19/20. PAGE 61 B1234 EXEC
DECISION

DENNING A. B0573

DENNISON E. B0574

DENVER....DENVER, COLORADO

DEPARTMENT HEADS...SEE EX/STRUC, TOP/EX

DEPORT....DEPORTATION

DEPRESSION....ECONOMIC DEPRESSION; SEE ALSO ECO

B60
BERNSTEIN I.,THE LEAN YEARS. SOCIETY STRATA PARTIC WORKER
GP/REL ATTIT...SOC 20 DEPRESSION. PAGE 11 B0227 LABOR
WEALTH
MGT

DEPT/AGRI....U.S. DEPARTMENT OF AGRICULTURE

B40
GAUS J.M.,PUBLIC ADMINISTRATION AND THE UNITED ADMIN
STATES DEPARTMENT OF AGRICULTURE. USA-45 STRUCT AGRI
DIST/IND FINAN MARKET EX/STRUC PROB/SOLV GIVE DELIB/GP
PRODUC...POLICY GEOG CHARTS 20 DEPT/AGRI. PAGE 39 OP/RES
B0786

B63
SELF P.,THE STATE AND THE FARMER. UK ECO/DEV MARKET AGRI
WORKER PRICE CONTROL GP/REL...WELF/ST 20 DEPT/AGRI. NAT/G
PAGE 95 B1926 ADMIN
VOL/ASSN

L65
HAMMOND A.,"COMPREHENSIVE VERSUS INCREMENTAL TOP/EX
BUDGETING IN THE DEPARTMENT OF AGRICULTURE" USA+45 EX/STRUC
GP/REL ATTIT...PSY INT 20 DEPT/AGRI. PAGE 46 B0934 AGRI
BUDGET

DEPT/COM....U.S. DEPARTMENT OF COMMERCE

DEPT/DEFEN....U.S. DEPARTMENT OF DEFENSE

B57
US HOUSE COMM ON POST OFFICE,MANPOWER UTILIZATION NAT/G
IN THE FEDERAL GOVERNMENT. USA+45 FORCES WORKER ADMIN
CREATE PLAN EFFICIENCY UTIL 20 CONGRESS CIVIL/SERV LABOR
POSTAL/SYS DEPT/DEFEN. PAGE 109 B2193 EX/STRUC

B60
WEBSTER J.A.,A GENERAL STUDY OF THE DEPARTMENT OF ORD/FREE
DEFENSE INTERNAL SECURITY PROGRAM. USA+45 WORKER PLAN
TEC/DEV ADJUD CONTROL CT/SYS EXEC GOV/REL COST ADMIN
...POLICY DECISION MGT 20 DEPT/DEFEN SUPREME/CT. NAT/G
PAGE 114 B2307

B62
INTERNAT CONGRESS OF JURISTS,EXECUTIVE ACTION AND JURID
THE RULE OF RULE: REPORTION PROCEEDINGS OF INT'T EXEC
CONGRESS OF JURISTS,-RIO DE JANEIRO, BRAZIL. WOR+45 ORD/FREE
ACADEM CONSULT JUDGE EDU/PROP ADJUD CT/SYS INGP/REL CONTROL
PERSON DEPT/DEFEN. PAGE 54 B1094

B64
BLACKSTOCK P.W.,THE STRATEGY OF SUBVERSION. USA+45 ORD/FREE
FORCES EDU/PROP ADMIN COERCE GOV/REL...DECISION MGT DIPLOM
20 DEPT/DEFEN CIA DEPT/STATE. PAGE 12 B0247 CONTROL

B65
STANLEY D.T.,CHANGING ADMINISTRATIONS. USA+45 NAT/G
POL/PAR DELIB/GP TOP/EX BUDGET GOV/REL GP/REL CHIEF
PERS/REL PWR...MAJORIT DECISION MGT 20 PRESIDENT ADMIN
SUCCESSION DEPT/STATE DEPT/DEFEN DEPT/HEW. PAGE 100 EX/STRUC
B2021

B67
ENKE S.,DEFENSE MANAGEMENT. USA+45 R+D FORCES DECISION
WORKER PLAN ECO/TAC ADMIN NUC/PWR BAL/PAY UTIL DELIB/GP
WEALTH...MGT DEPT/DEFEN. PAGE 33 B0675 EFFICIENCY
BUDGET

N67
US CONGRESS JT COMM ECO GOVT,BACKGROUND MATERIAL ON BUDGET
ECONOMY IN GOVERNMENT 1967 (PAMPHLET). WOR+45 COST
ECO/DEV BARGAIN PRICE DEMAND OPTIMAL...STAT MGT
DEPT/DEFEN. PAGE 108 B2178 NAT/G

N67
US SENATE COMM AERO SPACE SCI,AERONAUTICAL RESEARCH DIST/IND
AND DEVELOPMENT POLICY; HEARINGS, COMM ON SPACE
AERONAUTICAL AND SPACE SCIENCES...1967 (PAMPHLET). NAT/G
R+D PROB/SOLV EXEC GOV/REL 20 DEPT/DEFEN FAA NASA PLAN
CONGRESS. PAGE 109 B2210

DEPT/HEW....U.S. DEPARTMENT OF HEALTH, EDUCATION,
    AND WELFARE

B63
DEAN A.L.,FEDERAL AGENCY APPROACHES TO FIELD ADMIN
MANAGEMENT (PAMPHLET). R+D DELIB/GP EX/STRUC MGT
PROB/SOLV GOV/REL...CLASSIF BIBLIOG 20 FAA NASA NAT/G
DEPT/HEW POSTAL/SYS IRS. PAGE 28 B0563 OP/RES

B65
STANLEY D.T.,CHANGING ADMINISTRATIONS. USA+45 NAT/G
POL/PAR DELIB/GP TOP/EX BUDGET GOV/REL GP/REL CHIEF
PERS/REL PWR...MAJORIT DECISION MGT 20 PRESIDENT ADMIN
SUCCESSION DEPT/STATE DEPT/DEFEN DEPT/HEW. PAGE 100 EX/STRUC
B2021

B67
US DEPARTMENT HEALTH EDUC WELF,NEW PROGRAMS IN ADMIN
HEALTH, EDUCATION, WELFARE, HOUSING AND URBAN HEALTH
DEVELOPMENT FOR PERSONS AND FAMILIES -LOW, MOD' SCHOOL
INCOME. USA+45 MUNIC NAT/G EDU/PROP GOV/REL HABITAT
INGP/REL ORD/FREE 20 DEPT/HEW DEPT/HUD. PAGE 108
B2180

DEPT/HUD....U.S. DEPARTMENT OF HOUSING AND URBAN DEVELOPMENT

B67
US DEPARTMENT HEALTH EDUC WELF,NEW PROGRAMS IN ADMIN
HEALTH, EDUCATION, WELFARE, HOUSING AND URBAN HEALTH
DEVELOPMENT FOR PERSONS AND FAMILIES -LOW, MOD' SCHOOL
INCOME. USA+45 MUNIC NAT/G EDU/PROP GOV/REL HABITAT
INGP/REL ORD/FREE 20 DEPT/HEW DEPT/HUD. PAGE 108
B2180

DEPT/INTER....U.S. DEPARTMENT OF THE INTERIOR

DEPT/JUST....U.S. DEPARTMENT OF JUSTICE

DEPT/LABOR....U.S. DEPARTMENT OF LABOR AND INDUSTRY

B51
PETERSON F.,SURVEY OF LABOR ECONOMICS (REV. ED.). WORKER
STRATA ECO/DEV LABOR INSPECT BARGAIN PAY PRICE EXEC DEMAND
ROUTINE GP/REL ALL/VALS ORD/FREE 20 AFL/CIO IDEA/COMP
DEPT/LABOR. PAGE 82 B1662 T

S57
ROURKE F.E.,"THE POLITICS OF ADMINISTRATIVE POLICY
ORGANIZATION: A CASE HISTORY." USA+45 LABOR WORKER ATTIT
PLAN ADMIN TASK EFFICIENCY 20 DEPT/LABOR CONGRESS. MGT
PAGE 91 B1836 GP/COMP

DEPT/STATE....U.S. DEPARTMENT OF STATE

B48
CHILDS J.R.,AMERICAN FOREIGN SERVICE. USA+45   DIPLOM
SOCIETY NAT/G ROUTINE GOV/REL 20 DEPT/STATE   ADMIN
CIVIL/SERV. PAGE 21 B0423   GP/REL

B50
KOENIG L.W.,THE SALE OF THE TANKERS. USA+45 SEA   NAT/G
DIST/IND POL/PAR DIPLOM ADMIN CIVMIL/REL ATTIT   POLICY
...DECISION 20 PRESIDENT DEPT/STATE. PAGE 60 B1223   PLAN
   GOV/REL

S61
ROBINSON J.A.,"PROCESS SATISFACTION AND POLICY   GOV/REL
APPROVAL IN STATE DEPARTMENT - CONGRESSIONAL   EX/STRUC
RELATIONS." ELITES CHIEF LEGIS CONFER DEBATE ADMIN   POL/PAR
FEEDBACK ROLE...CHARTS 20 CONGRESS PRESIDENT   DECISION
DEPT/STATE. PAGE 89 B1802

B62
US SENATE COMM ON JUDICIARY,STATE DEPARTMENT   CONTROL
SECURITY. USA+45 CHIEF TEC/DEV DOMIN ADMIN EXEC   WORKER
ATTIT ORD/FREE...POLICY CONGRESS DEPT/STATE   NAT/G
PRESIDENT KENNEDY/JF KENNEDY/JF SENATE 20. PAGE 110   GOV/REL
B2228

B64
BLACKSTOCK P.W.,THE STRATEGY OF SUBVERSION. USA+45   ORD/FREE
FORCES EDU/PROP ADMIN COERCE GOV/REL...DECISION MGT   DIPLOM
20 DEPT/DEFEN CIA DEPT/STATE. PAGE 12 B0247   CONTROL

B64
US SENATE COMM GOVT OPERATIONS,THE SECRETARY OF   DIPLOM
STATE AND THE AMBASSADOR. USA+45 CHIEF CONSULT   DELIB/GP
EX/STRUC FORCES PLAN ADMIN EXEC INGP/REL ROLE   NAT/G
...ANTHOL 20 PRESIDENT DEPT/STATE. PAGE 110 B2215

S64
RUSK D.,"THE MAKING OF FOREIGN POLICY" USA+45 CHIEF   DIPLOM
DELIB/GP WORKER PROB/SOLV ADMIN ATTIT PWR   INT
...DECISION 20 DEPT/STATE RUSK/D GOLDMAN/E. PAGE 92   POLICY
B1856

B65
STANLEY D.T.,CHANGING ADMINISTRATIONS. USA+45   NAT/G
POL/PAR DELIB/GP TOP/EX BUDGET GOV/REL GP/REL   CHIEF
PERS/REL PWR...MAJORIT DECISION MGT 20 PRESIDENT   ADMIN
SUCCESSION DEPT/STATE DEPT/DEFEN DEPT/HEW. PAGE 100   EX/STRUC
B2021

L67
"RESTRICTIVE SOVEREIGN IMMUNITY, THE STATE   SOVEREIGN
DEPARTMENT, AND THE COURTS." USA+45 USA-45 EX/STRUC   ORD/FREE
DIPLOM ADJUD CONTROL GOV/REL 19/20 DEPT/STATE   PRIVIL
SUPREME/CT. PAGE 2 B0047   CT/SYS

DEPT/TREAS....U.S. DEPARTMENT OF THE TREASURY

N19
ARNOW K.,SELF-INSURANCE IN THE TREASURY (PAMPHLET).   ADMIN
USA+45 LAW RIGID/FLEX...POLICY METH/COMP 20   PLAN
DEPT/TREAS. PAGE 7 B0135   EFFICIENCY
   NAT/G

DERGE D.R. B0575

DESCARTE/R....RENE DESCARTES

DESEGREGATION....SEE NEGRO, SOUTH/US, RACE/REL, SOC/INTEG,
    CIV/RIGHTS, DISCRIM, MISCEGEN, ISOLAT, SCHOOL, STRANGE

DESMITH S.A. B0576

DESSALIN/J....JEAN-JACQUES DESSALINES

DESTALIN....DE-STALINIZATION

DETER....DETERRENCE; SEE ALSO PWR, PLAN

B49
BUSH V.,MODERN ARMS AND FREE MEN. WOR-45 SOCIETY   TEC/DEV
NAT/G ECO/TAC DOMIN LEGIT EXEC COERCE DETER ATTIT   FORCES
DRIVE ORD/FREE PWR...CONCPT MYTH COLD/WAR 20   NUC/PWR
COLD/WAR. PAGE 18 B0361   WAR

B57
ARON R.,FRANCE DEFEATS EDC. EUR+WWI GERMANY LEGIS   INT/ORG
DIPLOM DOMIN EDU/PROP ADMIN...HIST/WRIT 20. PAGE 7   FORCES
B0136   DETER
   FRANCE

S59
SOHN L.B.,"THE DEFINITION OF AGGRESSION." FUT LAW   INT/ORG
FORCES LEGIT ADJUD ROUTINE COERCE ORD/FREE PWR   CT/SYS
...MAJORIT JURID QUANT COLD/WAR 20. PAGE 99 B1995   DETER
   SOVEREIGN

L60
BRENNAN D.G.,"SETTING AND GOALS OF ARMS CONTROL."   FORCES
FUT USA+45 USSR WOR+45 INTELL INT/ORG NAT/G   COERCE
VOL/ASSN CONSULT PLAN DIPLOM ECO/TAC ADMIN KNOWL   ARMS/CONT
PWR...POLICY CONCPT TREND COLD/WAR 20. PAGE 15   DETER
B0305

S61
DEVINS J.H.,"THE INITIATIVE." COM USA+45 USA-45   FORCES
USSR SOCIETY NAT/G ACT/RES CREATE BAL/PWR ROUTINE   CONCPT

COERCE DETER RIGID/FLEX SKILL...STERTYP COLD/WAR   WAR
20. PAGE 29 B0582

S61
LEWY G.,"SUPERIOR ORDERS, NUCLEAR WARFARE AND THE   DETER
DICTATES OF CONSCIENCE: THE DILEMMA OF MILITARY   INT/ORG
OBEDIENCE IN THE ATOMIC." FUT UNIV WOR+45 INTELL   LAW
SOCIETY FORCES TOP/EX ACT/RES ADMIN ROUTINE NUC/PWR   INT/LAW
PERCEPT RIGID/FLEX ALL/VALS...POLICY CONCPT 20.
PAGE 65 B1308

B62
MULLEY F.W.,THE POLITICS OF WESTERN DEFENSE.   INT/ORG
EUR+WWI USA-45 WOR+45 VOL/ASSN EX/STRUC FORCES   DELIB/GP
COERCE DETER PEACE ATTIT ORD/FREE PWR...RECORD   NUC/PWR
TIME/SEQ CHARTS COLD/WAR 20 NATO. PAGE 76 B1537

S62
IKLE F.C.,"POLITICAL NEGOTIATION AS A PROCESS OF   ROUTINE
MODIFYING UTILITIES." WOR+45 FACE/GP LABOR NAT/G   DECISION
FORCES ACT/RES EDU/PROP DETER PERCEPT ALL/VALS   DIPLOM
...PSY NEW/IDEA HYPO/EXP GEN/METH 20. PAGE 53 B1076

B63
KAST F.E.,SCIENCE, TECHNOLOGY, AND MANAGEMENT.   MGT
SPACE USA+45 FORCES CONFER DETER NUC/PWR...PHIL/SCI   PLAN
CHARTS ANTHOL BIBLIOG 20 NASA. PAGE 58 B1179   TEC/DEV
   PROB/SOLV

S63
MORGENTHAU H.J.,"THE POLITICAL CONDITIONS FOR AN   INT/ORG
INTERNATIONAL POLICE FORCE." FUT WOR+45 CREATE   FORCES
LEGIT ADMIN PEACE ORD/FREE 20. PAGE 75 B1524   ARMS/CONT
   DETER

B64
COTTRELL A.J.,THE POLITICS OF THE ATLANTIC   VOL/ASSN
ALLIANCE. EUR+WWI USA+45 INT/ORG NAT/G DELIB/GP   FORCES
EX/STRUC BAL/PWR DIPLOM REGION DETER ATTIT ORD/FREE
...CONCPT RECORD GEN/LAWS GEN/METH NATO 20. PAGE 24
B0493

B64
RAYMOND J.,POWER AT THE PENTAGON (1ST ED.). ELITES   PWR
NAT/G PLAN EDU/PROP ARMS/CONT DETER WAR WEAPON   CIVMIL/REL
...TIME/SEQ 20 PENTAGON MCNAMARA/R. PAGE 86 B1746   EX/STRUC
   FORCES

B66
BEAUFRE A.,NATO AND EUROPE. WOR+45 PLAN CONFER EXEC   INT/ORG
NUC/PWR ATTIT...POLICY 20 NATO EUROPE. PAGE 10   DETER
B0203   DIPLOM
   ADMIN

B66
US SENATE COMM ON FOREIGN REL,HEARINGS ON S 2859   FOR/AID
AND S 2861. USA+45 WOR+45 FORCES BUDGET CAP/ISM   DIPLOM
ADMIN DETER WEAPON TOTALISM...NAT/COMP 20 UN   ORD/FREE
CONGRESS. PAGE 110 B2221   ECO/UNDEV

S66
ZUCKERT E.M.,"THE SERVICE SECRETARY* HAS HE A   OBS
USEFUL ROLE?" USA+45 TOP/EX PLAN ADMIN EXEC DETER   OP/RES
NUC/PWR WEAPON...MGT RECORD MCNAMARA/R. PAGE 119   DIPLOM
B2407   FORCES

B67
AMERICAN FRIENDS SERVICE COMM,IN PLACE OF WAR.   PEACE
NAT/G ACT/RES DIPLOM ADMIN NUC/PWR EFFICIENCY   PACIFISM
...POLICY 20. PAGE 4 B0085   WAR
   DETER

S67
JONES G.S.,"STRATEGIC PLANNING." USA+45 EX/STRUC   PLAN
FORCES DETER WAR 20 PRESIDENT. PAGE 57 B1150   DECISION
   DELIB/GP
   POLICY

S67
LALL B.G.,"GAPS IN THE ABM DEBATE." NAT/G DIPLOM   NUC/PWR
DETER CIVMIL/REL 20. PAGE 62 B1251   ARMS/CONT
   EX/STRUC
   FORCES

DETERRENCE....SEE DETER

DETROIT....DETROIT, MICHIGAN

DEUTSCH K.W. B0577

DEUTSCHE BIBLIOTH FRANKF A M B0578

DEUTSCHE BUCHEREI B0579,B0580,B0581

DEV/ASSIST....DEVELOPMENT AND ASSISTANCE COMMITTEE

DEVELOPMENT....SEE CREATE+ECO/UNDEV

DEVELOPMENT AND ASSISTANCE COMMITTEE....SEE DEV/ASSIST

DEVELOPMNT....HUMAN DEVELOPMENTAL CHANGE, PSYCHOLOGICAL
    AND PHYSIOLOGICAL

DEVIANT BEHAVIOR....SEE ANOMIE, CRIME

DEVINS J.H. B0582

DEVLIN P. B0583

DEWEY/JOHN....JOHN DEWEY

DEWEY/THOM....THOMAS DEWEY

DEXTER L.A. B0584

DIAGRAMS....SEE CHARTS

DIAMANT A. B0585

DIAZ/P....PORFIRIO DIAZ

DICKINSON J. B0586

DICKSON P.G.M. B0587

DICKSON W.J. B0588

DICTIONARY....DICTIONARY

    BIENSTOCK G.,MANAGEMENT IN RUSSIAN INDUSTRY AND AGRICULTURE. USSR CONSULT WORKER LEAD COST PROFIT ATTIT DRIVE PWR...MGT METH/COMP DICTIONARY 20. PAGE 12 B0236 — B44 ADMIN MARXISM SML/CO AGRI

    JANSE R.S.,SOVIET TRANSPORTATION AND COMMUNICATIONS: A BIBLIOGRAPHY. COM USSR PLAN ...DICTIONARY 20. PAGE 56 B1124 — B52 BIBLIOG/A COM/IND LEGIS ADMIN

    HEATH S.,CITADEL, MARKET, AND ALTAR: EMERGING SOCIETY. SOCIETY ADMIN OPTIMAL OWN RATIONAL ORD/FREE...SOC LOG PREDICT GEN/LAWS DICTIONARY 20. PAGE 49 B0985 — B57 NEW/IDEA STRUCT UTOPIA CREATE

    WILDING N.,"AN ENCYCLOPEDIA OF PARLIAMENT." UK LAW CONSTN CHIEF PROB/SOLV DIPLOM DEBATE WAR INGP/REL PRIVIL...BIBLIOG DICTIONARY 13/20 CMN/WLTH PARLIAMENT. PAGE 116 B2350 — C58 PARL/PROC POL/PAR NAT/G ADMIN

    MARSH R.M.,THE MANDARINS: THE CIRCULATION OF ELITES IN CHINA, 1600-1900. ASIA STRUCT PROF/ORG...SOC CHARTS BIBLIOG DICTIONARY 17/20. PAGE 70 B1406 — B61 ELITES ADMIN FAM STRATA

    INAYATULLAH,BUREAUCRACY AND DEVELOPMENT IN PAKISTAN. PAKISTAN ECO/UNDEV EDU/PROP CONFER ...ANTHOL DICTIONARY 20 BUREAUCRCY. PAGE 53 B1078 — B62 EX/STRUC ADMIN NAT/G LOC/G

    HOUGHTELING J.L. JR.,THE LEGAL ENVIRONMENT OF BUSINESS. LG/CO NAT/G CONSULT AGREE CONTROL ...DICTIONARY T 20. PAGE 52 B1047 — B63 LAW MGT ADJUD JURID

    RAWLINSON J.L.,CHINA'S STRUGGLE FOR NAVAL DEVELOPMENT 1839-1895. ASIA DIPLOM ADMIN WAR ...BIBLIOG DICTIONARY 19 CHINJAP. PAGE 86 B1745 — B67 SEA FORCES PWR

    ROFF W.R.,THE ORIGINS OF MALAY NATIONALISM. MALAYSIA INTELL NAT/G ADMIN COLONIAL...BIBLIOG DICTIONARY 20 CMN/WLTH. PAGE 90 B1813 — B67 NAT/LISM ELITES VOL/ASSN SOCIETY

DIDEROT/D....DENIS DIDEROT

DIEBOLD J. B0589,B0590

DIEBOLD W. B0591

DIEM....NGO DINH DIEM

DIESNER H.J. B0592

DILL W.R. B0516

DILLEY M.R. B0594

DIMOCK G.O. B0596

DIMOCK M.E. B0430,B0595,B0596,B0597,B0598,B0785

DINERMAN B. B0510

DIPLOM....DIPLOMACY

    DEUTSCHE BIBLIOTH FRANKF A M,DEUTSCHE BIBLIOGRAPHIE. EUR+WWI GERMANY ECO/DEV FORCES DIPLOM LEAD...POLICY PHIL/SCI SOC 20. PAGE 28 B0578 — B BIBLIOG LAW ADMIN NAT/G

    AMERICAN POLITICAL SCIENCE REVIEW. USA+45 USA-45 WOR+45 WOR-45 INT/ORG ADMIN...INT/LAW PHIL/SCI CONCPT METH 20 UN. PAGE 1 B0001 — N BIBLIOG/A DIPLOM NAT/G

    INTERNATIONAL REVIEW OF ADMINISTRATIVE SCIENCES. WOR+45 WOR-45 STRATA ECO/DEV ECO/UNDEV CREATE PLAN PROB/SOLV DIPLOM CONTROL REPRESENT...MGT 20. PAGE 1 B0004 — GOV/COMP N BIBLIOG/A ADMIN INT/ORG NAT/G

    JOURNAL OF POLITICS. USA+45 USA-45 CONSTN POL/PAR EX/STRUC LEGIS PROB/SOLV DIPLOM CT/SYS CHOOSE RACE/REL 20. PAGE 1 B0005 — N BIBLIOG/A NAT/G LAW LOC/G

    REVIEW OF POLITICS. WOR+45 WOR-45 CONSTN LEGIS PROB/SOLV ADMIN LEAD ALL/IDEOS...PHIL/SCI 20. PAGE 1 B0006 — N BIBLIOG/A DIPLOM INT/ORG NAT/G

    BIBLIO, CATALOGUE DES OUVRAGES PARUS EN LANGUE FRANCAISE DANS LE MONDE ENTIER. FRANCE WOR+45 ADMIN LEAD PERSON...SOC 20. PAGE 1 B0008 — N BIBLIOG NAT/G DIPLOM ECO/DEV

    BULLETIN OF THE PUBLIC AFFAIRS INFORMATION SERVICE. WOR+45 WOR-45 ECO/UNDEV FINAN LABOR LOC/G PROVS TEC/DEV DIPLOM EDU/PROP SOC. PAGE 1 B0010 — N BIBLIOG NAT/G ECO/DEV ADMIN

    CUMULATIVE BOOK INDEX. WOR+45 WOR-45 ADMIN PERSON ALL/VALS ALL/IDEOS...HUM PHIL/SCI SOC LING 19/20. PAGE 1 B0012 — N INDEX NAT/G DIPLOM

    DEUTSCHE BIBLIOGRAPHIE, HALBJAHRESVERZEICHNIS. WOR+45 LAW ADMIN PERSON. PAGE 1 B0013 — N BIBLIOG NAT/G DIPLOM

    HANDBOOK OF LATIN AMERICAN STUDIES. LAW CULTURE ECO/UNDEV POL/PAR ADMIN LEAD...SOC 20. PAGE 1 B0014 — N BIBLIOG/A L/A+17C NAT/G DIPLOM

    PUBLISHERS' TRADE LIST ANNUAL. LAW POL/PAR ADMIN PERSON ALL/IDEOS...HUM SOC 19/20. PAGE 1 B0020 — N BIBLIOG NAT/G DIPLOM POLICY

    READERS GUIDE TO PERIODICAL LITERATURE. WOR+45 WOR-45 LAW ADMIN ATTIT PERSON...HUM PSY SOC 20. PAGE 1 B0021 — N BIBLIOG WRITING DIPLOM NAT/G

    REVUE FRANCAISE DE SCIENCE POLITIQUE. FRANCE UK ...BIBLIOG/A 20. PAGE 1 B0022 — N NAT/G DIPLOM CONCPT ROUTINE

    SUBJECT GUIDE TO BOOKS IN PRINT: AN INDEX TO THE PUBLISHERS' TRADE LIST ANNUAL. UNIV LAW LOC/G DIPLOM WRITING ADMIN LEAD PERSON...MGT SOC. PAGE 1 B0023 — N BIBLIOG ECO/DEV POL/PAR NAT/G

    THE JAPAN SCIENCE REVIEW: LAW AND POLITICS: LIST OF BOOKS AND ARTICLES ON LAW AND POLITICS. CONSTN AGRI INDUS LABOR DIPLOM TAX ADMIN CRIME...INT/LAW SOC 20 CHINJAP. PAGE 1 B0025 — N BIBLIOG LAW S/ASIA PHIL/SCI

    NEUE POLITISCHE LITERATUR; BERICHTE UBER DAS INTERNATIONALE SCHRIFTTUM ZUR POLITIK. WOR+45 LAW CONSTN POL/PAR ADMIN LEAD GOV/REL...POLICY IDEA/COMP. PAGE 2 B0027 — N BIBLIOG/A DIPLOM NAT/G NAT/COMP

    SUBJECT GUIDE TO BOOKS IN PRINT; AN INDEX TO THE PUBLISHERS' TRADE LIST ANNUAL. WOR+45 WOR-45 LAW CULTURE ADMIN LEAD PERSON...HUM MGT SOC. PAGE 2 B0029 — N BIBLIOG NAT/G DIPLOM

    DEUTSCHE BUCHEREI,JAHRESVERZEICHNIS DES DEUTSCHEN SCHRIFTUMS. AUSTRIA EUR+WWI GERMANY SWITZERLND LAW LOC/G DIPLOM ADMIN...MGT SOC 19/20. PAGE 29 B0580 — N BIBLIOG WRITING NAT/G

    DEUTSCHE BUCHEREI,DEUTSCHES BUCHERVERZEICHNIS. GERMANY LAW CULTURE POL/PAR ADMIN LEAD ATTIT PERSON ...SOC 20. PAGE 29 B0581 — N BIBLIOG NAT/G DIPLOM ECO/DEV

    DOHERTY D.K.,PRELIMINARY BIBLIOGRAPHY OF COLONIZATION AND SETTLEMENT IN LATIN AMERICA AND ANGLO-AMERICA. L/A+17C PRE/AMER USA-45 ECO/UNDEV NAT/G 15/20. PAGE 30 B0604 — N BIBLIOG COLONIAL ADMIN DIPLOM

    MINISTERE DE L'EDUC NATIONALE,CATALOGUE DES THESES DE DOCTORAT SOUTENNES DEVANT LES UNIVERSITAIRES FRANCAISES. FRANCE LAW DIPLOM ADMIN...HUM SOC 20. PAGE 74 B1490 — N BIBLIOG ACADEM KNOWL NAT/G

    UNESCO,INTERNATIONAL BIBLIOGRAPHY OF POLITICAL SCIENCE (VOLUMES 1-8). WOR+45 LAW NAT/G EX/STRUC — N BIBLIOG CONCPT

LEGIS PROB/SOLV DIPLOM ADMIN GOV/REL 20 UNESCO. PAGE 107 B2153
IDEA/COMP

N
UNITED NATIONS,OFFICIAL RECORDS OF THE UNITED NATIONS' GENERAL ASSEMBLY. WOR+45 BUDGET DIPLOM ADMIN 20 UN. PAGE 107 B2159
INT/ORG DELIB/GP INT/LAW WRITING

N
UNITED NATIONS,UNITED NATIONS PUBLICATIONS. WOR+45 ECO/UNDEV AGRI FINAN FORCES ADMIN LEAD WAR PEACE ...POLICY INT/LAW 20 UN. PAGE 107 B2160
BIBLIOG INT/ORG DIPLOM

N
UNIVERSITY MICROFILMS INC,DISSERTATION ABSTRACTS: ABSTRACTS OF DISSERTATIONS AND MONOGRAPHS IN MICROFILM. CANADA DIPLOM ADMIN...INDEX 20. PAGE 107 B2166
BIBLIOG/A ACADEM PRESS WRITING

N
US SUPERINTENDENT OF DOCUMENTS,TRANSPORTATION: HIGHWAYS, ROADS, AND POSTAL SERVICE (PRICE LIST 25). PANAMA USA+45 LAW FORCES DIPLOM ADMIN GOV/REL HEALTH MGT. PAGE 111 B2243
BIBLIOG/A DIST/IND SERV/IND NAT/G

N
WORLD PEACE FOUNDATION,DOCUMENTS OF INTERNATIONAL ORGANIZATIONS: A SELECTED BIBLIOGRAPHY. WOR+45 WOR-45 AGRI FINAN ACT/RES OP/RES INT/TRADE ADMIN ...CON/ANAL 20 UN UNESCO LEAGUE/NAT. PAGE 118 B2374
BIBLIOG DIPLOM INT/ORG REGION

B00
SANDERSON E.,AFRICA IN THE NINETEENTH CENTURY. FRANCE UK EXTR/IND FORCES LEGIS ADMIN WAR DISCRIM ORD/FREE...GEOG GP/COMP SOC/INTEG 19. PAGE 92 B1867
COLONIAL AFR DIPLOM

B02
MOREL E.D.,AFFAIRS OF WEST AFRICA. UK FINAN INDUS FAM KIN SECT CHIEF WORKER DIPLOM RACE/REL LITERACY HEALTH...CHARTS 18/20 AFRICA/W NEGRO. PAGE 75 B1521
COLONIAL ADMIN AFR

B17
CORWIN E.S.,THE PRESIDENT'S CONTROL OF FOREIGN RELATIONS. FUT USA-45 CONSTN STRATA NAT/G CHIEF EX/STRUC LEGIS KNOWL RESPECT...JURID CONCPT TREND CONGRESS VAL/FREE 20 PRESIDENT. PAGE 24 B0483
TOP/EX PWR DIPLOM

B18
US LIBRARY OF CONGRESS,LIST OF REFERENCES ON A LEAGUE OF NATIONS. DIPLOM WAR PEACE 20 LEAGUE/NAT. PAGE 109 B2201
BIBLIOG INT/ORG ADMIN EX/STRUC

B19
SUTHERLAND G.,CONSTITUTIONAL POWER AND WORLD AFFAIRS. CONSTN STRUCT INT/ORG NAT/G CHIEF LEGIS ACT/RES PLAN GOV/REL ALL/VALS...OBS TIME/SEQ CONGRESS VAL/FREE 20 PRESIDENT. PAGE 102 B2056
USA-45 EXEC DIPLOM

N19
HIGGINS R.,THE ADMINISTRATION OF UNITED KINGDOM FOREIGN POLICY THROUGH THE UNITED NATIONS (PAMPHLET). UK NAT/G ADMIN GOV/REL...CHARTS 20 UN PARLIAMENT. PAGE 50 B1009
DIPLOM POLICY INT/ORG

N19
JACKSON R.G.A.,THE CASE FOR AN INTERNATIONAL DEVELOPMENT AUTHORITY (PAMPHLET). WOR+45 ECO/DEV DIPLOM GIVE CONTROL GP/REL EFFICIENCY NAT/LISM SOVEREIGN 20. PAGE 55 B1108
FOR/AID INT/ORG ECO/UNDEV ADMIN

N19
KUWAIT ARABIA,KUWAIT FUND FOR ARAB ECONOMIC DEVELOPMENT (PAMPHLET). ISLAM KUWAIT UAR ECO/UNDEV LEGIS ECO/TAC WEALTH 20. PAGE 62 B1245
FOR/AID DIPLOM FINAN ADMIN

B20
HALDANE R.B.,BEFORE THE WAR. MOD/EUR SOCIETY INT/ORG NAT/G DELIB/GP PLAN DOMIN EDU/PROP LEGIT ADMIN COERCE ATTIT DRIVE MORAL ORD/FREE PWR...SOC CONCPT SELF/OBS RECORD BIOG TIME/SEQ. PAGE 45 B0921
POLICY DIPLOM UK

B24
POOLE D.C.,THE CONDUCT OF FOREIGN RELATIONS UNDER MODERN DEMOCRATIC CONDITIONS. EUR+WWI USA-45 INT/ORG PLAN LEGIT ADMIN KNOWL PWR...MAJORIT OBS/ENVIR HIST/WRIT GEN/LAWS 20. PAGE 84 B1689
NAT/G EDU/PROP DIPLOM

B26
INTERNATIONAL BIBLIOGRAPHY OF POLITICAL SCIENCE. WOR+45 NAT/G POL/PAR EX/STRUC LEGIS CT/SYS LEAD CHOOSE GOV/REL ATTIT...PHIL/SCI 20. PAGE 2 B0034
BIBLIOG DIPLOM CONCPT ADMIN

B26
MOON P.T.,IMPERIALISM AND WORLD POLITICS. AFR ASIA ISLAM MOD/EUR S/ASIA USA-45 SOCIETY NAT/G EX/STRUC BAL/PWR DOMIN COLONIAL NAT/LISM ATTIT DRIVE PWR ...GEOG SOC 20. PAGE 75 B1510
WEALTH TIME/SEQ CAP/ISM DIPLOM

B27
ANGELL N.,THE PUBLIC MIND. USA-45 SOCIETY EDU/PROP ROUTINE SUPEGO KNOWL...POLICY CONCPT MYTH OBS/ENVIR EUR+WWI TOT/POP 20. PAGE 5 B0109
PERCEPT ATTIT DIPLOM NAT/LISM

B28
HALL W.P.,EMPIRE TO COMMONWEALTH. FUT WOR-45 CONSTN ECO/DEV ECO/UNDEV INT/ORG PROVS PLAN DIPLOM EDU/PROP ADMIN COLONIAL PEACE PERSON ALL/VALS ...POLICY GEOG SOC OBS RECORD TREND CMN/WLTH PARLIAMENT 19/20. PAGE 46 B0925
VOL/ASSN NAT/G UK

B29
BOUDET P.,BIBLIOGRAPHIE DE L'INDOCHINE FRANCAISE. S/ASIA VIETNAM SECT...GEOG LING 20. PAGE 14 B0282
BIBLIOG ADMIN COLONIAL DIPLOM

B29
BUELL R.,INTERNATIONAL RELATIONS. WOR+45 WOR-45 CONSTN STRATA FORCES TOP/EX ADMIN ATTIT DRIVE SUPEGO MORAL ORD/FREE PWR SOVEREIGN...JURID SOC CONCPT 20. PAGE 17 B0340
INT/ORG BAL/PWR DIPLOM

B31
HILL N.,INTERNATIONAL ADMINISTRATION. WOR-45 DELIB/GP DIPLOM EDU/PROP ALL/VALS...MGT TIME/SEQ LEAGUE/NAT TOT/POP VAL/FREE 20. PAGE 50 B1011
INT/ORG ADMIN

B32
CARDINALL AW,A BIBLIOGRAPHY OF THE GOLD COAST. AFR UK NAT/G EX/STRUC ATTIT...POLICY 19/20. PAGE 18 B0376
BIBLIOG ADMIN COLONIAL DIPLOM

B33
DANGERFIELD R.,IN DEFENSE OF THE SENATE. USA-45 CONSTN NAT/G EX/STRUC TOP/EX ATTIT KNOWL ...METH/CNCPT STAT TIME/SEQ TREND CON/ANAL CHARTS CONGRESS 20 TREATY. PAGE 26 B0528
LEGIS DELIB/GP DIPLOM

B34
US TARIFF COMMISSION,THE TARIFF; A BIBLIOGRAPHY: A SELECT LIST OF REFERENCES. USA-45 LAW DIPLOM TAX ADMIN...POLICY TREATY 20. PAGE 111 B2246
BIBLIOG/A TARIFFS ECO/TAC

B37
GALLOWAY G.B.,AMERICAN PAMPHLET LITERATURE OF PUBLIC AFFAIRS (PAMPHLET). USA-45 ECO/DEV LABOR ADMIN...MGT 20. PAGE 38 B0776
BIBLIOG/A PLAN DIPLOM NAT/G

B37
UNION OF SOUTH AFRICA,REPORT CONCERNING ADMINISTRATION OF SOUTH WEST AFRICA (6 VOLS.). SOUTH/AFR INDUS PUB/INST FORCES LEGIS BUDGET DIPLOM EDU/PROP ADJUD CT/SYS...GEOG CHARTS 20 AFRICA/SW LEAGUE/NAT. PAGE 107 B2158
NAT/G ADMIN COLONIAL CONSTN

B38
HARPER S.N.,THE GOVERNMENT OF THE SOVIET UNION. COM USSR LAW CONSTN ECO/DEV PLAN TEC/DEV DIPLOM INT/TRADE ADMIN REV NAT/LISM...POLICY 20. PAGE 47 B0952
MARXISM NAT/G LEAD POL/PAR

B39
HITLER A.,MEIN KAMPF. EUR+WWI FUT MOD/EUR STRUCT INT/ORG LABOR NAT/G POL/PAR FORCES CREATE PLAN BAL/PWR DIPLOM ECO/TAC DOMIN EDU/PROP ADMIN COERCE ATTIT...SOCIALIST BIOG TREND NAZI. PAGE 50 B1020
PWR NEW/IDEA WAR

C39
REISCHAUER R.,"JAPAN'S GOVERNMENT--POLITICS." CONSTN STRATA POL/PAR FORCES LEGIS DIPLOM ADMIN EXEC CENTRAL...POLICY BIBLIOG 20 CHINJAP. PAGE 87 B1764
NAT/G S/ASIA CONCPT ROUTINE

S40
PERKINS J.A.,"CONGRESSIONAL INVESTIGATIONS OF MATTERS OF INTERNATIONAL IMPORT." DELIB/GP DIPLOM ADMIN CONTROL 20 CONGRESS. PAGE 82 B1656
POL/PAR DECISION PARL/PROC GOV/REL

C40
FAHS C.B.,"GOVERNMENT IN JAPAN." FINAN FORCES LEGIS TOP/EX BUDGET INT/TRADE EDU/PROP SOVEREIGN ...CON/ANAL BIBLIOG/A 20 CHINJAP. PAGE 34 B0698
ASIA DIPLOM NAT/G ADMIN

B41
BURTON M.E.,THE ASSEMBLY OF THE LEAGUE OF NATIONS. WOR-45 CONSTN SOCIETY STRUCT INT/ORG NAT/G CREATE ATTIT RIGID/FLEX PWR...POLICY TIME/SEQ LEAGUE/NAT 20. PAGE 18 B0359
DELIB/GP EX/STRUC DIPLOM

B41
CHILDS J.B.,A GUIDE TO THE OFFICIAL PUBLICATIONS OF THE OTHER AMERICAN REPUBLICS: ARGENTINA. CHIEF DIPLOM GOV/REL...BIBLIOG 18/19 ARGEN. PAGE 21 B0422
NAT/G EX/STRUC METH/CNCPT LEGIS

B41
PERHAM M.,AFRICANS AND BRITISH RULE. AFR UK ECO/TAC CONTROL GP/REL ATTIT 20. PAGE 82 B1654
DIPLOM COLONIAL ADMIN ECO/UNDEV

S41
ABEL T.,"THE ELEMENT OF DECISION IN THE PATTERN OF WAR." EUR+WWI FUT NAT/G TOP/EX DIPLOM ROUTINE COERCE DISPL PERCEPT PWR...SOC METH/CNCPT HIST/WRIT TREND GEN/LAWS 20. PAGE 2 B0051
TEC/DEV FORCES WAR

B42
DENNISON E.,THE SENATE FOREIGN RELATIONS COMMITTEE. USA-45 NAT/G DELIB/GP ROUTINE CHOOSE PWR CONGRESS 20. PAGE 28 B0574
LEGIS ACT/RES DIPLOM

B42
SIMOES DOS REIS A.,BIBLIOGRAFIA DAS BIBLIOGRAFIAS BRASILEIRAS. BRAZIL ADMIN COLONIAL 20. PAGE 97 B1954
BIBLIOG NAT/G DIPLOM L/A+17C

B42
US STATE DEPT.,PEACE AND WAR: UNITED STATES FOREIGN POLICY, 1931-41. CULTURE FORCES ROUTINE CHOOSE
DIPLOM USA-45

ATTIT DRIVE PERSON 20. PAGE 111 B2237 — PLAN

B43
CARLO A.M.,ENSAYO DE UNA BIBLIOGRAFIA DE — BIBLIOG
BIBLIOGRAFIAS MEXICANAS. ECO/UNDEV LOC/G ADMIN LEAD — L/A+17C
20 MEXIC/AMER. PAGE 19 B0381 — NAT/G
DIPLOM

B43
LEWIN E.,ROYAL EMPIRE SOCIETY BIBLIOGRAPHIES NO. 9: — BIBLIOG
SUB-SAHARA AFRICA. ECO/UNDEV TEC/DEV DIPLOM ADMIN — AFR
COLONIAL LEAD 20. PAGE 64 B1303 — NAT/G
SOCIETY

L44
HAILEY,"THE FUTURE OF COLONIAL PEOPLES." WOR-45 — PLAN
CONSTN CULTURE ECO/UNDEV AGRI MARKET INT/ORG NAT/G — CONCPT
SECT CONSULT ECO/TAC LEGIT ADMIN NAT/LISM ALL/VALS — DIPLOM
...SOC OBS TREND STERTYP CMN/WLTH LEAGUE/NAT — UK
PARLIAMENT 20. PAGE 45 B0916

S44
COLEGROVE K.W.,"THE ROLE OF CONGRESS AND PUBLIC — EX/STRUC
OPINION IN FORMULATING FOREIGN POLICY." USA+45 WAR — DIPLOM
...DECISION UN CONGRESS. PAGE 22 B0451 — LEGIS
PWR

B45
CLAPP G.R.,NEW HORIZONS IN PUBLIC ADMINISTRATION: A — ADMIN
SYMPOSIUM. USA-45 LEGIS PLAN DIPLOM REGION — EX/STRUC
EFFICIENCY 20. PAGE 21 B0430 — MGT
NAT/G

B45
CONOVER H.F.,THE GOVERNMENTS OF THE MAJOR FOREIGN — BIBLIOG
POWERS: A BIBLIOGRAPHY. FRANCE GERMANY ITALY UK — NAT/G
USSR CONSTN LOC/G POL/PAR EX/STRUC FORCES ADMIN — DIPLOM
CT/SYS CIVMIL/REL TOTALISM...POLICY 19/20. PAGE 23
B0464

B45
ROGERS W.C.,INTERNATIONAL ADMINISTRATION: A — BIBLIOG/A
BIBLIOGRAPHY (PUBLICATION NO 92: A PAMPHLET). — ADMIN
WOR-45 INT/ORG LOC/G NAT/G CENTRAL 20. PAGE 90 — MGT
B1814 — DIPLOM

B46
BIBLIOGRAFIIA DISSERTATSII: DOKTORSKIE DISSERTATSII — BIBLIOG
ZA 19411944 (2 VOLS.). COM USSR LAW POL/PAR DIPLOM — ACADEM
ADMIN LEAD...PHIL/SCI SOC 20. PAGE 2 B0035 — KNOWL
MARXIST

B46
GRIFFIN G.G.,A GUIDE TO MANUSCRIPTS RELATING TO — BIBLIOG/A
AMERICAN HISTORY IN BRITISH DEPOSITORIES. CANADA — ALL/VALS
IRELAND MOD/EUR UK USA-45 LAW DIPLOM ADMIN COLONIAL — NAT/G
WAR NAT/LISM SOVEREIGN...GEOG INT/LAW 15/19
CMN/WLTH. PAGE 43 B0876

C46
GOODRICH L.M.,"CHARTER OF THE UNITED NATIONS: — CONSTN
COMMENTARY AND DOCUMENTS." EX/STRUC ADMIN...INT/LAW — INT/ORG
CON/ANAL BIBLIOG 20 UN. PAGE 41 B0826 — DIPLOM

B47
BORGESE G.,COMMON CAUSE. LAW CONSTN SOCIETY STRATA — WOR+45
ECO/DEV INT/ORG POL/PAR FORCES LEGIS TOP/EX CAP/ISM — NAT/G
DIPLOM ADMIN EXEC ATTIT PWR 20. PAGE 14 B0279 — SOVEREIGN
REGION

B47
CONOVER H.F.,NON-SELF-GOVERNING AREAS. BELGIUM — BIBLIOG/A
FRANCE ITALY UK WOR+45 CULTURE ECO/UNDEV INT/ORG — COLONIAL
LOC/G NAT/G ECO/TAC INT/TRADE ADMIN HEALTH...SOC — DIPLOM
UN. PAGE 23 B0465

B47
HIRSHBERG H.S.,SUBJECT GUIDE TO UNITED STATES — BIBLIOG
GOVERNMENT PUBLICATIONS. USA+45 USA-45 LAW ADMIN — NAT/G
...SOC 20. PAGE 50 B1017 — DIPLOM
LOC/G

B47
PUBLIC ADMINISTRATION SERVICE,CURRENT RESEARCH — BIBLIOG
PROJECTS IN PUBLIC ADMINISTRATION (PAMPHLET). LAW — R+D
CONSTN COM/IND LABOR LOC/G MUNIC PROVS ACT/RES — MGT
DIPLOM RECEIVE EDU/PROP WAR 20. PAGE 85 B1716 — ADMIN

B48
CHILDS J.R.,AMERICAN FOREIGN SERVICE. USA+45 — DIPLOM
SOCIETY NAT/G ROUTINE GOV/REL 20 DEPT/STATE — ADMIN
CIVIL/SERV. PAGE 21 B0423 — GP/REL

B48
HULL C.,THE MEMOIRS OF CORDELL HULL (VOLUME ONE). — BIOG
USA-45 WOR-45 CONSTN FAM LOC/G NAT/G PROVS DELIB/GP — DIPLOM
FORCES LEGIS TOP/EX BAL/PWR LEGIT ADMIN EXEC WAR
ATTIT ORD/FREE PWR...MAJORIT SELF/OBS TIME/SEQ
TREND NAZI 20. PAGE 52 B1062

B48
SHERWOOD R.E.,ROOSEVELT AND HOPKINS. UK USA+45 USSR — TOP/EX
NAT/G EX/STRUC FORCES ADMIN ROUTINE PERSON PWR — BIOG
...TIME/SEQ 20 ROOSEVLT/F HOPKINS/H. PAGE 96 B1946 — DIPLOM
WAR

B48
STOKES W.S.,BIBLIOGRAPHY OF STANDARD AND CLASSICAL — BIBLIOG
WORKS IN THE FIELDS OF AMERICAN POLITICAL SCIENCE. — NAT/G
USA+45 USA-45 POL/PAR PROVS FORCES DIPLOM ADMIN — LOC/G
CT/SYS APPORT 20 CONGRESS PRESIDENT. PAGE 101 B2043 — CONSTN

B49
BORBA DE MORAES R.,MANUAL BIBLIOGRAFICO DE ESTUDOS — BIBLIOG
BRASILEIROS. BRAZIL DIPLOM ADMIN LEAD...SOC 20. — L/A+17C

PAGE 14 B0276 — NAT/G
ECO/UNDEV

B49
HEADLAM-MORLEY,BIBLIOGRAPHY IN POLITICS FOR THE — BIBLIOG
HONOUR SCHOOL OF PHILOSOPHY, POLITICS AND ECONOMICS — NAT/G
(PAMPHLET). UK CONSTN LABOR MUNIC DIPLOM ADMIN — PHIL/SCI
19/20. PAGE 48 B0979 — GOV/REL

B49
KENT S.,STRATEGIC INTELLIGENCE FOR AMERICAN WORLD — ACT/RES
POLICY. FUT USA+45 NAT/G ATTIT PERCEPT ORD/FREE — EX/STRUC
...OBS 20. PAGE 59 B1195 — DIPLOM

B49
ROSENHAUPT H.W.,HOW TO WAGE PEACE. USA+45 SOCIETY — INTELL
STRATA STRUCT R+D INT/ORG POL/PAR LEGIS ACT/RES — CONCPT
CREATE PLAN EDU/PROP ADMIN EXEC ATTIT ALL/VALS — DIPLOM
...TIME/SEQ TREND COLD/WAR 20. PAGE 90 B1822

B49
STEIN H.,THE FOREIGN SERVICE ACT OF 1946. USA+45 — DIPLOM
ELITES EX/STRUC PLAN PROB/SOLV LOBBY GOV/REL — LAW
PERS/REL RIGID/FLEX...POLICY IDEA/COMP 20 CONGRESS — NAT/G
BUR/BUDGET. PAGE 100 B2027 — ADMIN

L49
BROOKINGS INST.,"GOVERNMENT MECHANISM FOR CONDUCT — EXEC
OF US FOREIGN RELATIONS." USA+45 CONSTN NAT/G LEGIS — STRUCT
CT/SYS...MGT TIME/SEQ CONGRESS TOT/POP 20. PAGE 15 — DIPLOM
B0316

S49
STEINMETZ H.,"THE PROBLEMS OF THE LANDRAT: A STUDY — LOC/G
OF COUNTY GOVERNMENT IN THE US ZONE OF GERMANY." — COLONIAL
GERMANY/W USA+45 INDUS PLAN DIPLOM EDU/PROP CONTROL — MGT
WAR GOV/REL FEDERAL WEALTH PLURISM...GOV/COMP 20 — TOP/EX
LANDRAT. PAGE 100 B2031

B50
BROWN E.S.,MANUAL OF GOVERNMENT PUBLICATIONS. — BIBLIOG/A
WOR+45 WOR-45 CONSTN INT/ORG MUNIC PROVS DIPLOM — NAT/G
ADMIN 20. PAGE 16 B0322 — LAW

B50
FIGANIERE J.C.,BIBLIOTHECA HISTORICA PORTUGUEZA. — BIBLIOG
BRAZIL PORTUGAL SECT ADMIN. PAGE 35 B0717 — NAT/G
DIPLOM
COLONIAL

B50
KOENIG L.W.,THE SALE OF THE TANKERS. USA+45 SEA — NAT/G
DIST/IND POL/PAR DIPLOM ADMIN CIVMIL/REL ATTIT — POLICY
...DECISION 20 PRESIDENT DEPT/STATE. PAGE 60 B1223 — PLAN
GOV/REL

B50
MCCAMY J.,THE ADMINISTRATION OF AMERICAN FOREIGN — EXEC
AFFAIRS. USA+45 SOCIETY INT/ORG NAT/G ACT/RES PLAN — STRUCT
INT/TRADE EDU/PROP ADJUD ALL/VALS...METH/CNCPT — DIPLOM
TIME/SEQ CONGRESS 20. PAGE 71 B1441

B50
MONPIED E.,BIBLIOGRAPHIE FEDERALISTE: OUVRAGES — BIBLIOG/A
CHOISIS (VOL. I. MIMEOGRAPHED PAPER). EUR+WWI — FEDERAL
DIPLOM ADMIN REGION ATTIT PACIFISM SOCISM...INT/LAW — CENTRAL
19/20. PAGE 74 B1502 — INT/ORG

B50
WELCH S.R.,PORTUGUESE RULE AND SPANISH CROWN IN — DIPLOM
SOUTH AFRICA 1581-1640. PORTUGAL SOUTH/AFR SPAIN — COLONIAL
SOCIETY KIN NEIGH SECT INT/TRADE ADMIN 16/17 — WAR
MISSION. PAGE 115 B2317 — PEACE

S50
WITTFOGEL K.A.,"RUSSIA AND ASIA: PROBLEMS OF — ECO/DEV
CONTEMPORARY AREA STUDIES AND INTERNATIONAL — ADMIN
RELATIONS." ASIA COM USA+45 SOCIETY NAT/G DIPLOM — RUSSIA
ECO/TAC FOR/AID EDU/PROP KNOWL...HIST/WRIT TOT/POP — USSR
20. PAGE 117 B2369

B51
CHRISTENSEN A.N.,THE EVOLUTION OF LATIN AMERICAN — NAT/G
GOVERNMENT: A BOOK OF READINGS. ECO/UNDEV INDUS — CONSTN
LOC/G POL/PAR EX/STRUC LEGIS FOR/AID CT/SYS — DIPLOM
...SOC/WK 20 SOUTH/AMER. PAGE 21 B0428 — L/A+17C

B51
NIELANDER W.A.,PUBLIC RELATIONS. USA+45 COM/IND — PERS/REL
LOC/G NAT/G VOL/ASSN EX/STRUC DIPLOM EDU/PROP PRESS — GP/REL
TV...METH/CNCPT T 20. PAGE 78 B1583 — LG/CO
ROUTINE

B51
SWISHER C.B.,THE THEORY AND PRACTICE OF AMERICAN — CONSTN
NATIONAL GOVERNMENT. CULTURE LEGIS DIPLOM ADJUD — NAT/G
ADMIN WAR PEACE ORD/FREE...MAJORIT 17/20. PAGE 102 — GOV/REL
B2063 — GEN/LAWS

B51
US LIBRARY OF CONGRESS,EAST EUROPEAN ACCESSIONS — BIBLIOG/A
LIST (VOL. I). POL/PAR DIPLOM ADMIN LEAD 20. — COM
PAGE 109 B2204 — SOCIETY
NAT/G

S51
LERNER D.,"THE POLICY SCIENCES: RECENT DEVELOPMENTS — CONSULT
IN SCOPE AND METHODS." R+D SERV/IND CREATE DIPLOM — SOC
ROUTINE PWR...METH/CNCPT TREND GEN/LAWS METH 20.
PAGE 64 B1297

C51
MOORE B.,"SOVIET POLITICS - THE DILEMMA OF POWER: — ATTIT
THE ROLE OF IDEAS IN SOCIAL CHANGE." USSR PROB/SOLV — PWR
DIPLOM EDU/PROP ADMIN LEAD ROUTINE REV...POLICY — CONCPT

DECISION BIBLIOG 20. PAGE 75 B1512
MARXISM

B52

ELLIOTT W.,UNITED STATES FOREIGN POLICY, ITS
ORGANIZATION AND CONTROL. USA+45 USA-45 CONSTN
NAT/G FORCES TOP/EX PEACE...TIME/SEQ CONGRESS
LEAGUE/NAT 20. PAGE 33 B0670
LEGIS
EX/STRUC
DIPLOM

B52

UNESCO,THESES DE SCIENCES SOCIALES: CATALOGUE
ANALYTIQUE INTERNATIONAL DE THESES INEDITES DE
DOCTORAT, 1940-1950. INT/ORG DIPLOM EDU/PROP...GEOG
INT/LAW MGT PSY SOC 20. PAGE 107 B2155
BIBLIOG
ACADEM
WRITING

B52

US DEPARTMENT OF STATE,RESEARCH ON EASTERN EUROPE
(EXCLUDING USSR). EUR+WWI LAW ECO/DEV NAT/G
PROB/SOLV DIPLOM ADMIN LEAD MARXISM...TREND 19/20.
PAGE 108 B2182
BIBLIOG
R+D
ACT/RES
COM

L52

WRIGHT Q.,"CONGRESS AND THE TREATY-MAKING POWER."
USA+45 WOR+45 CONSTN INTELL NAT/G CHIEF CONSULT
EX/STRUC LEGIS TOP/EX CREATE GOV/REL DISPL DRIVE
RIGID/FLEX...TREND TOT/POP CONGRESS CONGRESS 20
TREATY. PAGE 118 B2384
ROUTINE
DIPLOM
INT/LAW
DELIB/GP

B53

GREENE K.R.C.,INSTITUTIONS AND INDIVIDUALS: AN
ANNOTATED LIST OF DIRECTORIES USEFUL IN
INTERNATIONAL ADMINISTRATION. USA+45 NAT/G VOL/ASSN
...INDEX 20. PAGE 43 B0865
BIBLIOG
INT/ORG
ADMIN
DIPLOM

B53

LARSEN K.,NATIONAL BIBLIOGRAPHIC SERVICES: THEIR
CREATION AND OPERATION. WOR+45 COM/IND CREATE PLAN
DIPLOM PRESS ADMIN ROUTINE...MGT UNESCO. PAGE 62
B1262
BIBLIOG/A
INT/ORG
WRITING

B53

MACMAHON A.W.,ADMINISTRATION IN FOREIGN AFFAIRS.
USA+45 NAT/G CONSULT DELIB/GP LEGIS ACT/RES CREATE ADMIN
EXEC RIGID/FLEX PWR...METH/CNCPT TIME/SEQ TOT/POP
VAL/FREE 20. PAGE 68 B1369
USA+45
ROUTINE
FOR/AID
DIPLOM

B53

ROBINSON E.A.G.,THE STRUCTURE OF COMPETITIVE
INDUSTRY. UK ECO/DEV DIST/IND MARKET TEC/DEV DIPLOM
EDU/PROP ADMIN EFFICIENCY WEALTH...MGT 19/20.
PAGE 89 B1798
INDUS
PRODUC
WORKER
OPTIMAL

B53

STOUT H.M.,BRITISH GOVERNMENT. UK FINAN LOC/G
POL/PAR DELIB/GP DIPLOM ADMIN COLONIAL CHOOSE
ORD/FREE...JURID BIBLIOG 20 COMMONWLTH. PAGE 101
B2049
NAT/G
PARL/PROC
CONSTN
NEW/LIB

S53

MORRIS B.S.,"THE COMINFORM: A FIVE YEAR
PERSPECTIVE." COM UNIV USSR WOR+45 ECO/DEV POL/PAR
TOP/EX PLAN DOMIN TOTALISM ATTIT ALL/VALS
...CONCPT TIME/SEQ TREND CON/ANAL WORK VAL/FREE 20.
PAGE 76 B1527
VOL/ASSN
EDU/PROP
DIPLOM

B54

BINANI G.D.,INDIA AT A GLANCE (REV. ED.). INDIA
COM/IND FINAN INDUS LABOR PROVS SCHOOL PLAN DIPLOM
INT/TRADE ADMIN...JURID 20. PAGE 12 B0238
INDEX
CON/ANAL
NAT/G
ECO/UNDEV

B54

TOTOK W.,HANDBUCH DER BIBLIOGRAPHISCHEN
NACHSCHLAGEWERKE. GERMANY LAW CULTURE ADMIN...SOC
20. PAGE 105 B2121
BIBLIOG/A
NAT/G
DIPLOM
POLICY

B54

US SENATE COMM ON FOREIGN REL,REVIEW OF THE UNITED
NATIONS CHARTER: A COLLECTION OF DOCUMENTS. LEGIS
DIPLOM ADMIN ARMS/CONT WAR REPRESENT SOVEREIGN
...INT/LAW 20 UN. PAGE 110 B2220
BIBLIOG
CONSTN
INT/ORG
DEBATE

L54

FURNISS E.S.,"WEAKNESSES IN FRENCH FOREIGN POLICY-
MAKING." EUR+WWI LEGIS LEGIT EXEC ATTIT RIGID/FLEX
ORD/FREE...SOC CONCPT METH/CNCPT OBS 20. PAGE 38
B0766
NAT/G
STRUCT
DIPLOM
FRANCE

L54

ROSTOW W.W.,"ASIAN LEADERSHIP AND FREE-WORLD
ALLIANCE." ASIA COM USA+45 CULTURE ELITES INTELL
NAT/G TEC/DEV ECO/TAC EDU/PROP COLONIAL PARL/PROC
ROUTINE COERCE DRIVE ORD/FREE MARXISM...PSY CONCPT.
PAGE 90 B1829
ATTIT
LEGIT
DIPLOM

S54

WOLFERS A.,"COLLECTIVE SECURITY AND THE WAR IN
KOREA." ASIA KOREA USA+45 INT/ORG DIPLOM ROUTINE
...GEN/LAWS UN COLD/WAR 20. PAGE 117 B2370
ACT/RES
LEGIT

B55

CRAIG J.,BIBLIOGRAPHY OF PUBLIC ADMINISTRATION IN
AUSTRALIA. CONSTN FINAN EX/STRUC LEGIS PLAN DIPLOM
RECEIVE ADJUD ROUTINE...HEAL 19/20 AUSTRAL
PARLIAMENT. PAGE 24 B0500
BIBLIOG
GOV/REL
ADMIN
NAT/G

B55

JAPAN MOMBUSHO DAIGAKU GAKIYUT,BIBLIOGRAPHY OF THE
STUDIES ON LAW AND POLITICS (PAMPHLET). CONSTN
INDUS LABOR DIPLOM TAX ADMIN...CRIMLGY INT/LAW 20
CHINJAP. PAGE 56 B1126
BIBLIOG
LAW
PHIL/SCI

B55

STEPHENS O.,FACTS TO A CANDID WORLD. USA+45 WOR+45
COM/IND EX/STRUC PRESS ROUTINE EFFICIENCY ATTIT
EDU/PROP
PHIL/SCI

...PSY 20. PAGE 100 B2033
NAT/G
DIPLOM

B55

UN HEADQUARTERS LIBRARY,BIBLIOGRAPHIE DE LA CHARTE
DES NATIONS UNIES. CHINA/COM KOREA WOR+45 VOL/ASSN
CONFER ADMIN COERCE PEACE ATTIT ORD/FREE SOVEREIGN
...INT/LAW 20 UNESCO UN. PAGE 106 B2149
BIBLIOG/A
INT/ORG
DIPLOM

L55

KISER M.,"ORGANIZATION OF AMERICAN STATES." L/A+17C
USA+45 ECO/UNDEV INT/ORG NAT/G PLAN TEC/DEV DIPLOM
ECO/TAC INT/TRADE EDU/PROP ADMIN ALL/VALS...POLICY
MGT RECORD ORG/CHARTS OAS 20. PAGE 60 B1215
VOL/ASSN
ECO/DEV
REGION

S55

ANGELL R.,"GOVERNMENTS AND PEOPLES AS A FOCI FOR
PEACE-ORIENTED RESEARCH." WOR+45 CULTURE SOCIETY
FACE/GP ACT/RES CREATE PLAN DIPLOM EDU/PROP ROUTINE
ATTIT PERCEPT SKILL...POLICY CONCPT OBS TREND
GEN/METH 20. PAGE 5 B0110
FUT
SOC
PEACE

S55

TORRE M.,"PSYCHIATRIC OBSERVATIONS OF INTERNATIONAL
CONFERENCES." WOR+45 INT/ORG PROF/ORG VOL/ASSN
CONSULT EDU/PROP ROUTINE ATTIT DRIVE KNOWL...PSY
METH/CNCPT OBS/ENVIR STERTYP 20. PAGE 105 B2119
DELIB/GP
OBS
DIPLOM

B56

DEGRAS J.,THE COMMUNIST INTERNATIONAL, 1919-1943:
DOCUMENTS (3 VOLS.). EX/STRUC...ANTHOL BIBLIOG 20.
PAGE 28 B0569
COM
DIPLOM
POLICY
POL/PAR

B56

GARDNER R.N.,STERLING-DOLLAR DIPLOMACY. EUR+WWI
USA+45 INT/ORG NAT/G PLAN INT/TRADE EDU/PROP ADMIN
KNOWL PWR WEALTH...POLICY SOC METH/CNCPT STAT
CHARTS SIMUL GEN/LAWS 20. PAGE 39 B0781
ECO/DEV
DIPLOM

B56

IRIKURA J.K.,SOUTHEAST ASIA: SELECTED ANNOTATED
BIBLIOGRAPHY OF JAPANESE PUBLICATIONS. CULTURE
ADMIN RACE/REL 20 CHINJAP. PAGE 55 B1104
BIBLIOG/A
S/ASIA
DIPLOM

B56

KAUFMANN W.W.,MILITARY POLICY AND NATIONAL
SECURITY. USA+45 ELITES INTELL NAT/G TOP/EX PLAN
BAL/PWR DIPLOM ROUTINE COERCE NUC/PWR ATTIT
ORD/FREE PWR 20 COLD/WAR. PAGE 58 B1182
FORCES
CREATE

B56

KIRK G.,THE CHANGING ENVIRONMENT OF INTERNATIONAL
RELATIONS. ASIA S/ASIA USA+45 WOR+45 ECO/UNDEV
INT/ORG NAT/G FOR/AID EDU/PROP PEACE KNOWL
...PLURIST COLD/WAR TOT/POP 20. PAGE 60 B1214
FUT
EXEC
DIPLOM

B56

KOENIG L.W.,THE TRUMAN ADMINISTRATION: ITS
PRINCIPLES AND PRACTICE. USA+45 POL/PAR CHIEF LEGIS
DIPLOM DEATH NUC/PWR WAR CIVMIL/REL PEACE
...DECISION 20 TRUMAN/HS PRESIDENT TREATY. PAGE 61
B1224
ADMIN
POLICY
EX/STRUC
GOV/REL

B56

WILSON P.,GOVERNMENT AND POLITICS OF INDIA AND
PAKISTAN: 1885-1955; A BIBLIOGRAPHY OF WORKS IN
WESTERN LANGUAGES. INDIA PAKISTAN CONSTN LOC/G
POL/PAR FORCES DIPLOM ADMIN WAR CHOOSE...BIOG
CON/ANAL 19/20. PAGE 117 B2361
BIBLIOG
COLONIAL
NAT/G
S/ASIA

B56

WU E.,LEADERS OF TWENTIETH-CENTURY CHINA; AN
ANNOTATED BIBLIOGRAPHY OF SELECTED CHINESE
BIOGRAPHICAL WORKS IN HOOVER LIBRARY. ASIA INDUS
POL/PAR DIPLOM ADMIN REV WAR...HUM MGT 20. PAGE 118
B2386
BIBLIOG/A
BIOG
INTELL
CHIEF

S56

CUTLER R.,"THE DEVELOPMENT OF THE NATIONAL SECURITY
COUNCIL." USA+45 INTELL CONSULT EX/STRUC DIPLOM
LEAD 20 TRUMAN/HS EISNHWR/DD NSC. PAGE 25 B0514
ORD/FREE
DELIB/GP
PROB/SOLV
NAT/G

B57

ARON R.,FRANCE DEFEATS EDC. EUR+WWI GERMANY LEGIS
DIPLOM DOMIN EDU/PROP ADMIN...HIST/WRIT 20. PAGE 7
B0136
INT/ORG
FORCES
DETER
FRANCE

B57

BEAL J.R.,JOHN FOSTER DULLES, A BIOGRAPHY. USA+45
USSR WOR+45 CONSTN INT/ORG NAT/G EX/STRUC LEGIT
ADMIN NUC/PWR DISPL PERSON ORD/FREE PWR SKILL
...POLICY PSY OBS RECORD COLD/WAR UN 20 DULLES/JF.
PAGE 10 B0200
BIOG
DIPLOM

B57

BISHOP O.B.,PUBLICATIONS OF THE GOVERNMENTS OF NOVA
SCOTIA, PRINCE EDWARD ISLAND, NEW BRUNSWICK
1758-1952. CANADA UK ADMIN COLONIAL LEAD...POLICY
18/20. PAGE 12 B0245
BIBLIOG
NAT/G
DIPLOM

B57

FULLER C.D.,TRAINING OF SPECIALISTS IN
INTERNATIONAL RELATIONS. FUT USA+45 USA-45 INTELL
INT/ORG...MGT METH/CNCPT INT QU GEN/METH 20.
PAGE 38 B0765
KNOWL
DIPLOM

B57

KAPLAN M.A.,SYSTEM AND PROCESS OF INTERNATIONAL
POLITICS. FUT WOR+45 WOR-45 SOCIETY PLAN BAL/PWR
ADMIN ATTIT PERSON RIGID/FLEX PWR SOVEREIGN
...DECISION TREND VAL/FREE. PAGE 58 B1168
INT/ORG
DIPLOM

B57
PYE L.W.,THE POLICY IMPLICATIONS OF SOCIAL CHANGE   SOCIETY
IN NON-WESTERN SOCIETIES. ASIA USA+45 CULTURE   ORD/FREE
STRUCT NAT/G ECO/TAC ADMIN ROLE...POLICY SOC.   ECO/UNDEV
PAGE 85 B1723   DIPLOM

B57
SCHLOCHAUER H.J.,OFFENTLICHES RECHT. GERMANY/W   CONSTN
FINAN EX/STRUC LEGIS DIPLOM FEDERAL ORD/FREE   JURID
...INT/LAW 20. PAGE 94 B1892   ADMIN
                                                       CT/SYS

C57
TANG P.S.H.,"COMMUNIST CHINA TODAY: DOMESTIC AND   POL/PAR
FOREIGN POLICIES." CHINA/COM COM S/ASIA USSR STRATA   LEAD
FORCES DIPLOM EDU/PROP COERCE GOV/REL...POLICY   ADMIN
MAJORIT BIBLIOG 20. PAGE 102 B2071   CONSTN

N57
MACMAHON A.W.,ADMINISTRATION AND FOREIGN POLICY   DIPLOM
(PAMPHLET). USA+45 CHIEF OP/RES ADMIN 20. PAGE 68   EX/STRUC
B1372   DECISION
                                                       CONFER

B58
ISLAM R.,INTERNATIONAL ECONOMIC COOPERATION AND THE   INT/ORG
UNITED NATIONS. FINAN PLAN EXEC TASK WAR PEACE   DIPLOM
...SOC METH/CNCPT 20 UN LEAGUE/NAT. PAGE 55 B1105   ADMIN

B58
KINTNER W.R.,ORGANIZING FOR CONFLICT: A PROPOSAL.   USA+45
USSR STRUCT NAT/G LEGIS ADMIN EXEC PEACE ORD/FREE   PLAN
PWR...CONCPT OBS TREND NAT/COMP VAL/FREE COLD/WAR   DIPLOM
20. PAGE 60 B1211

B58
MASON J.B.,THAILAND BIBLIOGRAPHY. S/ASIA THAILAND   BIBLIOG/A
CULTURE EDU/PROP ADMIN...GEOG SOC LING 20. PAGE 70   ECO/UNDEV
B1423   DIPLOM
                                                       NAT/G

B58
NEAL F.W.,TITOISM IN ACTION. COM YUGOSLAVIA AGRI   MARXISM
LOC/G DIPLOM TOTALISM...BIBLIOG 20 TITO/MARSH.   POL/PAR
PAGE 77 B1564   CHIEF
                                                       ADMIN

B58
PAN AMERICAN UNION,REPERTORIO DE PUBLICACIONES   BIBLIOG
PERIODICAS ACTUALES LATINO-AMERICANAS. CULTURE   L/A+17C
ECO/UNDEV ADMIN LEAD GOV/REL 20 OAS. PAGE 81 B1630   NAT/G
                                                       DIPLOM

B58
UNESCO,UNESCO PUBLICATIONS: CHECK LIST (2ND REV.   BIBLIOG
ED.). WOR+45 DIPLOM FOR/AID WEALTH...POLICY SOC   INT/ORG
UNESCO. PAGE 107 B2156   ECO/UNDEV
                                                       ADMIN

B58
US HOUSE COMM GOVT OPERATIONS,HEARINGS BEFORE A   FOR/AID
SUBCOMMITTEE OF THE COMMITTEE ON GOVERNMENT   DIPLOM
OPERATIONS. CAMBODIA PHILIPPINE USA+45 CONSTRUC   ORD/FREE
TEC/DEV ADMIN CONTROL WEAPON EFFICIENCY HOUSE/REP.   ECO/UNDEV
PAGE 108 B2189

S58
JORDAN A.,"MILITARY ASSISTANCE AND NATIONAL   FORCES
POLICY." ASIA FUT USA+45 WOR+45 ECO/DEV ECO/UNDEV   POLICY
INT/ORG NAT/G PLAN ECO/TAC ROUTINE WEAPON ATTIT   FOR/AID
RIGID/FLEX PWR...CONCPT TREND 20. PAGE 57 B1153   DIPLOM

C58
GOLAY J.F.,"THE FOUNDING OF THE FEDERAL REPUBLIC OF   FEDERAL
GERMANY." GERMANY/W CONSTN EX/STRUC DIPLOM ADMIN   NAT/G
CHOOSE...DECISION BIBLIOG 20. PAGE 40 B0814   PARL/PROC
                                                       POL/PAR

C58
WILDING N.,"AN ENCYCLOPEDIA OF PARLIAMENT." UK LAW   PARL/PROC
CONSTN CHIEF PROB/SOLV DIPLOM DELIB/GP DEBATE WAR INGP/REL POL/PAR
PRIVIL...BIBLIOG DICTIONARY 13/20 CMN/WLTH   NAT/G
PARLIAMENT. PAGE 116 B2350   ADMIN

B59
BOWLES C.,THE COMING POLITICAL BREAKTHROUGH. USA+45   DIPLOM
ECO/DEV EX/STRUC ATTIT...CONCPT OBS 20. PAGE 14   CHOOSE
B0288   PREDICT
                                                       POL/PAR

B59
DIEBOLD W. JR.,THE SCHUMAN PLAN: A STUDY IN   INT/ORG
ECONOMIC COOPERATION, 1950-1959. EUR+WWI FRANCE   REGION
GERMANY USA+45 EXTR/IND CONSULT DELIB/GP PLAN
DIPLOM ECO/TAC INT/TRADE ROUTINE ORD/FREE WEALTH
...METH/CNCPT STAT CONT/OBS INT TIME/SEQ ECSC 20.
PAGE 29 B0591

B59
GORDENKER L.,THE UNITED NATIONS AND THE PEACEFUL   DELIB/GP
UNIFICATION OF KOREA. ASIA LAW LOC/G CONSULT   KOREA
ACT/RES DIPLOM DOMIN LEGIT ADJUD ADMIN ORD/FREE   INT/ORG
SOVEREIGN...INT GEN/METH UN COLD/WAR 20. PAGE 41
B0829

B59
GRABER D.,CRISIS DIPLOMACY. L/A+17C USA+45 USA-45   ROUTINE
NAT/G TOP/EX ECO/TAC COERCE ATTIT ORD/FREE...CONCPT   MORAL
MYTH TIME/SEQ COLD/WAR 20. PAGE 42 B0848   DIPLOM

B59
INTERAMERICAN CULTURAL COUN,LISTA DE LIBROS   BIBLIOG/A
REPRESENTAVOS DE AMERICA. CULTURE DIPLOM ADMIN 20.   NAT/G
PAGE 54 B1093   L/A+17C

SOC
B59
JANOWITZ M.,SOCIOLOGY AND THE MILITARY   FORCES
ESTABLISHMENT. USA+45 WOR+45 CULTURE SOCIETY   SOC
PROF/ORG CONSULT EX/STRUC PLAN TEC/DEV DIPLOM DOMIN
COERCE DRIVE RIGID/FLEX ORD/FREE PWR SKILL COLD/WAR
20. PAGE 55 B1121

B59
MACIVER R.M.,THE NATIONS AND THE UN. WOR+45 NAT/G   INT/ORG
CONSULT ADJUD ADMIN ALL/VALS...CONCPT DEEP/QU UN   ATTIT
TOT/POP UNESCO 20. PAGE 67 B1362   DIPLOM

B59
SCHURZ W.L.,AMERICAN FOREIGN AFFAIRS: A GUIDE TO   INT/ORG
INTERNATIONAL AFFAIRS. USA+45 WOR+45 WOR-45 NAT/G   SOCIETY
FORCES LEGIS TOP/EX PLAN EDU/PROP LEGIT ADMIN   DIPLOM
ROUTINE ATTIT ORD/FREE PWR...SOC CONCPT STAT
SAMP/SIZ CHARTS STERTYP 20. PAGE 95 B1910

B59
U OF MICHIGAN LAW SCHOOL,ATOMS AND THE LAW. USA+45   NUC/PWR
PROVS WORKER PROB/SOLV DIPLOM ADMIN GOV/REL ANTHOL.   NAT/G
PAGE 106 B2142   CONTROL
                                                       LAW

B59
US PRES COMM STUDY MIL ASSIST,COMPOSITE REPORT.   FOR/AID
USA+45 ECO/UNDEV PLAN BUDGET DIPLOM EFFICIENCY   FORCES
...POLICY MGT 20. PAGE 109 B2208   WEAPON
                                                       ORD/FREE

B59
WELTON H.,THE THIRD WORLD WAR: TRADE AND INDUSTRY,   INT/TRADE
THE NEW BATTLEGROUND. WOR+45 ECO/DEV INDUS MARKET   PLAN
TASK...MGT IDEA/COMP COLD/WAR. PAGE 115 B2321   DIPLOM

S59
HILSMAN R.,"THE FOREIGN-POLICY CONSENSUS: AN   PROB/SOLV
INTERIM RESEARCH REPORT." USA+45 INT/ORG LEGIS   NAT/G
TEC/DEV EXEC WAR CONSEN KNOWL...DECISION COLD/WAR.   DELIB/GP
PAGE 50 B1013   DIPLOM

B60
)B JUNZ A.J.,PRESENT TRENDS IN AMERICAN NATIONAL   POL/PAR
GOVERNMENT. LEGIS DIPLOM ADMIN CT/SYS ORD/FREE   CHOOSE
...CONCPT ANTHOL 20 CONGRESS PRESIDENT SUPREME/CT.   CONSTN
PAGE 2 B0048   NAT/G

B60
ASPREMONT-LYNDEN H.,RAPPORT SUR L'ADMINISTRATION   AFR
BELGE DU RUANDA-URUNDI PENDANT L'ANNEE 1959.   COLONIAL
BELGIUM RWANDA AGRI INDUS DIPLOM ECO/TAC INT/TRADE   ECO/UNDEV
DOMIN ADMIN RACE/REL...GEOG CENSUS 20 UN. PAGE 7   INT/ORG
B0143

B60
BROOKINGS INSTITUTION,UNITED STATES FOREIGN POLICY: DIPLOM
STUDY NO 9: THE FORMULATION AND ADMINISTRATION OF   INT/ORG
UNITED STATES FOREIGN POLICY. USA+45 WOR+45   CREATE
EX/STRUC LEGIS BAL/PWR FOR/AID EDU/PROP CIVMIL/REL
GOV/REL...INT COLD/WAR. PAGE 16 B0317

B60
FLORES R.H.,CATALOGO DE TESIS DOCTORALES DE LAS   BIBLIOG
FACULTADES DE LA UNIVERSIDAD DE EL SALVADOR.   ACADEM
EL/SALVADR LAW DIPLOM ADMIN LEAD GOV/REL...SOC   L/A+17C
19/20. PAGE 36 B0730   NAT/G

B60
HYDE L.K.G.,THE US AND THE UN. WOR+45 STRUCT   USA+45
ECO/DEV ECO/UNDEV NAT/G ACT/RES PLAN DIPLOM   INT/ORG
EDU/PROP ADMIN ALL/VALS...CONCPT TIME/SEQ GEN/LAWS   FOR/AID
UN VAL/FREE 20. PAGE 53 B1070

B60
KINGSTON-MCCLOUG E.,DEFENSE: POLICY AND STRATEGY.   FORCES
UK SEA AIR TEC/DEV DIPLOM ADMIN LEAD WAR ORD/FREE   PLAN
...CHARTS 20. PAGE 60 B1209   POLICY
                                                       DECISION

B60
LEWIS P.R.,LITERATURE OF THE SOCIAL SCIENCES: AN   BIBLIOG/A
INTRODUCTORY SURVEY AND GUIDE. UK LAW INDUS DIPLOM   SOC
INT/TRADE ADMIN...MGT 19/20. PAGE 65 B1306

B60
LISKA G.,THE NEW STATECRAFT. WOR+45 WOR-45 LEGIS   ECO/TAC
DIPLOM ADMIN ATTIT PWR WEALTH...HIST/WRIT TREND   CONCPT
COLD/WAR 20. PAGE 66 B1323   FOR/AID

B60
MEEHAN E.J.,THE BRITISH LEFT WING AND FOREIGN   ACT/RES
POLICY: A STUDY OF THE INFLUENCE OF IDEOLOGY. FUT   ATTIT
UK UNIV WOR+45 INTELL TOP/EX PLAN ADMIN ROUTINE   DIPLOM
DRIVE...OBS TIME/SEQ GEN/LAWS PARLIAMENT 20.
PAGE 72 B1461

B60
MEYRIAT J.,LA SCIENCE POLITIQUE EN FRANCE,   BIBLIOG/A
1945-1958: BIBLIOGRAPHIES FRANCAISES DE SCIENCES   NAT/G
SOCIALES (VOL. I). EUR+WWI FRANCE POL/PAR DIPLOM   CONCPT
ADMIN CHOOSE ATTIT...IDEA/COMP METH/COMP NAT/COMP   PHIL/SCI
20. PAGE 73 B1478

B60
MORISON E.E.,TURMOIL AND TRADITION: A STUDY OF THE   BIOG
LIFE AND TIMES OF HENRY L. STIMSON. USA+45 USA-45   NAT/G
POL/PAR CHIEF DELIB/GP FORCES BAL/PWR DIPLOM   EX/STRUC
ARMS/CONT WAR PEACE 19/20 STIMSON/HL ROOSEVLT/F
TAFT/WH HOOVER/H REPUBLICAN. PAGE 75 B1525

B60
MUNRO L.,UNITED NATIONS, HOPE FOR A DIVIDED WORLD.   INT/ORG

FUT WOR+45 CONSIN DELIB/GP CREATE TEC/DEV DIPLOM — ROUTINE
EDU/PROP LEGIT PEACE ATTIT HEALTH ORD/FREE PWR
...CONCPT TREND UN VAL/FREE. PAGE 76 B1540

B60
PENTONY D.E.,UNITED STATES FOREIGN AID. INDIA LAOS — FOR/AID
USA+45 ECO/UNDEV INT/TRADE ADMIN PEACE ATTIT — DIPLOM
...POLICY METH/COMP ANTHOL 20. PAGE 82 B1653 — ECO/TAC

B60
RAO V.K.R.,INTERNATIONAL AID FOR ECONOMIC — FOR/AID
DEVELOPMENT - POSSIBILITIES AND LIMITATIONS. FINAN — DIPLOM
PLAN TEC/DEV ADMIN TASK EFFICIENCY...POLICY SOC — INT/ORG
METH/CNCPT CHARTS 20 UN. PAGE 86 B1734 — ECO/UNDEV

B60
STANFORD RESEARCH INSTITUTE,AFRICAN DEVELOPMENT: A — FOR/AID
TEST FOR INTERNATIONAL COOPERATION. AFR USA+45 — ECO/UNDEV
WOR+45 FINAN INT/ORG PLAN PROB/SOLV ECO/TAC — ATTIT
INT/TRADE ADMIN...CHARTS 20. PAGE 100 B2018 — DIPLOM

B60
WHEARE K.C.,THE CONSTITUTIONAL STRUCTURE OF THE — CONSTN
COMMONWEALTH. UK EX/STRUC DIPLOM DOMIN ADMIN — INT/ORG
COLONIAL CONTROL LEAD INGP/REL SUPEGO 20 CMN/WLTH. — VOL/ASSN
PAGE 115 B2330 — SOVEREIGN

B60
WORLEY P.,ASIA TODAY (REV. ED.) (PAMPHLET). COM — BIBLIOG/A
ECO/UNDEV AGRI FINAN INDUS POL/PAR FOR/AID ADMIN — ASIA
MARXISM 20. PAGE 118 B2376 — DIPLOM
— NAT/G

L60
BRENNAN D.G.,"SETTING AND GOALS OF ARMS CONTROL." — FORCES
FUT USA+45 USSR WOR+45 INTELL INT/ORG NAT/G — COERCE
VOL/ASSN CONSULT PLAN DIPLOM ECO/TAC ADMIN KNOWL — ARMS/CONT
PWR...POLICY CONCPT TREND COLD/WAR 20. PAGE 15 — DETER
B0305

L60
MACPHERSON C.,"TECHNICAL CHANGE AND POLITICAL — TEC/DEV
DECISION." WOR+45 NAT/G CREATE CAP/ISM DIPLOM — ADMIN
ROUTINE RIGID/FLEX...CONCPT OBS GEN/METH 20.
PAGE 68 B1375

S60
BOGARDUS E.S.,"THE SOCIOLOGY OF A STRUCTURED — INT/ORG
PEACE." FUT SOCIETY CREATE DIPLOM EDU/PROP ADJUD — SOC
ROUTINE ATTIT RIGID/FLEX KNOWL ORD/FREE RESPECT — NAT/LISM
...POLICY INT/LAW JURID NEW/IDEA SELF/OBS TOT/POP — PEACE
20 UN. PAGE 13 B0264

S60
BOYER W.W.,"POLICY MAKING BY GOVERNMENT AGENCIES." — NAT/G
USA+45 WOR+45 R+D DELIB/GP TOP/EX EDU/PROP ROUTINE — DIPLOM
ATTIT BIO/SOC DRIVE...CONCPT TREND TOT/POP 20.
PAGE 14 B0293

S60
HALPERIN M.H.,"IS THE SENATE'S FOREIGN RELATIONS — PLAN
RESEARCH WORTHWHILE." COM FUT USA+45 USSR ACT/RES — DIPLOM
BAL/PWR EDU/PROP ADMIN ALL/VALS CONGRESS VAL/FREE
20 COLD/WAR. PAGE 46 B0927

S60
HUTCHINSON C.E.,"AN INSTITUTE FOR NATIONAL SECURITY — POLICY
AFFAIRS." USA+45 R+D NAT/G CONSULT TOP/EX ACT/RES — METH/CNCPT
CREATE PLAN TEC/DEV EDU/PROP ROUTINE NUC/PWR ATTIT — ELITES
ORD/FREE PWR...DECISION MGT PHIL/SCI CONCPT RECORD — DIPLOM
GEN/LAWS GEN/METH 20. PAGE 53 B1068

S60
MODELSKI G.,"AUSTRALIA AND SEATO." S/ASIA USA+45 — INT/ORG
CULTURE INTELL ECO/DEV NAT/G PLAN DIPLOM ADMIN — ACT/RES
ROUTINE ATTIT SKILL...MGT TIME/SEQ AUSTRAL 20
SEATO. PAGE 74 B1493

S60
NELSON R.H.,"LEGISLATIVE PARTICIPATION IN THE — LEGIS
TREATY AND AGREEMENT MAKING PROCESS." CONSTN — PEACE
POL/PAR PLAN EXEC PWR FAO UN CONGRESS. PAGE 78 — DECISION
B1569 — DIPLOM

S60
REISELBACH L.N.,"THE BASIS OF ISOLATIONIST — ATTIT
BEHAVIOR." USA+45 USA-45 CULTURE ECO/DEV LOC/G — DIPLOM
NAT/G ADMIN ROUTINE CHOOSE BIO/SOC DRIVE RIGID/FLEX — ECO/TAC
...CENSUS SAMP TREND CHARTS TOT/POP 20. PAGE 87
B1765

S60
RIESELBACH Z.N.,"QUANTITATIVE TECHNIQUES FOR — QUANT
STUDYING VOTING BEHAVIOR IN THE UNITED NATIONS — CHOOSE
GENERAL ASSEMBLY." FUT S/ASIA USA+45 INT/ORG
BAL/PWR DIPLOM ECO/TAC FOR/AID ADMIN PWR...POLICY
METH/CNCPT METH UN 20. PAGE 88 B1783

S60
THOMPSON K.W.,"MORAL PURPOSE IN FOREIGN POLICY: — MORAL
REALITIES AND ILLUSIONS." WOR+45 WOR-45 LAW CULTURE — JURID
SOCIETY INT/ORG PLAN ADJUD ADMIN COERCE RIGID/FLEX — DIPLOM
SUPEGO KNOWL ORD/FREE PWR...SOC TREND SOC/EXP
TOT/POP 20. PAGE 104 B2104

C60
FITZSIMMONS T.,"USSR: ITS PEOPLE, ITS SOCIETY, ITS — CULTURE
CULTURE." USSR FAM SECT DIPLOM EDU/PROP ADMIN — STRUCT
RACE/REL ATTIT...POLICY CHARTS BIBLIOG 20. PAGE 36 — SOCIETY
B0728 — COM

B61
BAINS J.S.,STUDIES IN POLITICAL SCIENCE. INDIA — DIPLOM
WOR+45 WOR-45 CONSTN BAL/PWR ADJUD ADMIN PARL/PROC — INT/LAW

SOVEREIGN...SOC METH/COMP ANTHOL 17/20 UN. PAGE 8 — NAT/G
B0165

B61
BARNES W.,THE FOREIGN SERVICE OF THE UNITED STATES. — NAT/G
USA+45 USA-45 CONSTN INT/ORG POL/PAR CONSULT — MGT
DELIB/GP LEGIS DOMIN EDU/PROP EXEC ATTIT RIGID/FLEX — DIPLOM
ORD/FREE PWR...POLICY CONCPT STAT OBS RECORD BIOG
TIME/SEQ TREND. PAGE 9 B0188

B61
BISHOP D.G.,THE ADMINISTRATION OF BRITISH FOREIGN — ROUTINE
RELATIONS. EUR+WWI MOD/EUR INT/ORG NAT/G POL/PAR — PWR
DELIB/GP LEGIS TOP/EX ECO/TAC DOMIN EDU/PROP ADMIN — DIPLOM
COERCE 20. PAGE 12 B0243 — UK

B61
BURDETTE F.L.,POLITICAL SCIENCE: A SELECTED — BIBLIOG/A
BIBLIOGRAPHY OF BOOKS IN PRINT, WITH ANNOTATIONS — GOV/COMP
(PAMPHLET). LAW LOC/G NAT/G POL/PAR PROVS DIPLOM — CONCPT
EDU/PROP ADMIN CHOOSE ATTIT 20. PAGE 17 B0347 — ROUTINE

B61
GRIFFITH E.S.,CONGRESS: ITS CONTEMPORARY ROLE. — PARL/PROC
CONSTN POL/PAR CHIEF PLAN BUDGET DIPLOM CONFER — EX/STRUC
ADMIN LOBBY...DECISION CONGRESS. PAGE 43 B0878 — TOP/EX
— LEGIS

B61
HAYTER W.,THE DIPLOMACY OF THE GREAT POWERS. FRANCE — DIPLOM
UK USSR WOR+45 EX/STRUC TOP/EX NUC/PWR PEACE...OBS — POLICY
20. PAGE 48 B0978 — NAT/G

B61
KERTESZ S.D.,AMERICAN DIPLOMACY IN A NEW ERA. COM — ANTHOL
S/ASIA UK USA+45 FORCES PROB/SOLV BAL/PWR ECO/TAC — DIPLOM
ADMIN COLONIAL WAR PEACE ORD/FREE 20 NATO CONGRESS — TREND
UN COLD/WAR. PAGE 59 B1199

B61
MOLLAU G.,INTERNATIONAL COMMUNISM AND WORLD — COM
REVOLUTION: HISTORY AND METHODS. RUSSIA USSR — REV
INT/ORG NAT/G POL/PAR VOL/ASSN FORCES BAL/PWR
DIPLOM EXEC REGION WAR ATTIT PWR MARXISM...CONCPT
TIME/SEQ COLD/WAR 19/20. PAGE 74 B1498

B61
SHAPP W.R.,FIELD ADMINISTRATION IN THE UNITED — INT/ORG
NATIONS SYSTEM. FINAN PROB/SOLV INSPECT DIPLOM EXEC — ADMIN
REGION ROUTINE EFFICIENCY ROLE...INT CHARTS 20 UN. — GP/REL
PAGE 96 B1933 — FOR/AID

B61
US GENERAL ACCOUNTING OFFICE,EXAMINATION OF — FOR/AID
ECONOMIC AND TECHNICAL ASSISTANCE PROGRAM FOR IRAN. — ADMIN
IRAN USA+45 AGRI INDUS DIPLOM CONTROL COST 20. — TEC/DEV
PAGE 108 B2186 — ECO/UNDEV

B61
WILLOUGHBY W.R.,THE ST LAWRENCE WATERWAY: A STUDY — LEGIS
IN POLITICS AND DIPLOMACY. USA+45 ECO/DEV COM/IND — INT/TRADE
INT/ORG CONSULT DELIB/GP ACT/RES TEC/DEV DIPLOM — CANADA
ECO/TAC ROUTINE...TIME/SEQ 20. PAGE 117 B2357 — DIST/IND

S61
ALGER C.F.,"NON-RESOLUTION CONSEQUENCES OF THE — INT/ORG
UNITED NATIONS AND THEIR EFFECT ON INTERNATIONAL — DRIVE
CONFLICT." WOR+45 CONSTN ECO/DEV NAT/G CONSULT — BAL/PWR
DELIB/GP TOP/EX ACT/RES PLAN DIPLOM EDU/PROP
ROUTINE ATTIT ALL/VALS...INT/LAW TOT/POP UN 20.
PAGE 4 B0075

S61
ANGLIN D.,"UNITED STATES OPPOSITION TO CANADIAN — INT/ORG
MEMBERSHIP IN THE PAN AMERICAN UNION: A CANADIAN — CANADA
VIEW." L/A+17C UK USA+45 VOL/ASSN DELIB/GP EX/STRUC
PLAN DIPLOM DOMIN REGION ATTIT RIGID/FLEX PWR
...RELATIV CONCPT STERTYP CMN/WLTH OAS 20. PAGE 5
B0112

S61
CARLETON W.G.,"AMERICAN FOREIGN POLICY: MYTHS AND — PLAN
REALITIES." FUT USA+45 WOR+45 ECO/UNDEV INT/ORG — MYTH
EX/STRUC ARMS/CONT NUC/PWR WAR ATTIT...POLICY — DIPLOM
CONCPT CONT/OBS GEN/METH COLD/WAR TOT/POP 20.
PAGE 19 B0378

S61
GORDON L.,"ECONOMIC REGIONALISM RECONSIDERED." FUT — ECO/DEV
USA+45 WOR+45 INDUS NAT/G TEC/DEV DIPLOM ROUTINE — ATTIT
PERCEPT WEALTH...WELF/ST METH/CNCPT WORK 20. — CAP/ISM
PAGE 41 B0830 — REGION

S61
JUVILER P.H.,"INTERPARLIAMENTARY CONTACTS IN SOVIET — INT/ORG
FOREIGN POLICY." COM FUT WOR+45 WOR-45 SOCIETY — DELIB/GP
CONSULT ACT/RES DIPLOM ADMIN PEACE ATTIT RIGID/FLEX — USSR
WEALTH...WELF/ST SCC TOT/POP CONGRESS 19/20.
PAGE 57 B1156

S61
PADOVER S.K.,"PSYCHOLOGICAL WARFARE AND FOREIGN — ROUTINE
POLICY." FUT UNIV USA+45 INTELL SOCIETY CREATE — DIPLOM
EDU/PROP ADMIN WAR PEACE PERCEPT...POLICY
METH/CNCPT TESTS TIME/SEQ 20. PAGE 80 B1623

S61
RUDOLPH S.,"CONSENSUS AND CONFLICT IN INDIAN — POL/PAR
POLITICS." S/ASIA WOR+45 NAT/G DELIB/GP DIPLOM — PERCEPT
EDU/PROP ADMIN CONSEN PERSON ALL/VALS...OBS TREND — INDIA
TOT/POP VAL/FREE 20. PAGE 92 B1854

S61
VIRALLY M.,"VERS UNE REFORME DU SECRETARIAT DES — INT/ORG

NATIONS UNIES." FUT WOR+45 CONSTN ECO/DEV TOP/EX   INTELL
BAL/PWR ADMIN ALL/VALS...CONCPT BIOG UN VAL/FREE   DIPLOM
20. PAGE 112 B2264

                                                              C61
MOODIE G.C.."THE GOVERNMENT OF GREAT BRITAIN." UK   NAT/G
LAW STRUCT LOC/G POL/PAR DIPLOM RECEIVE ADMIN   SOCIETY
COLONIAL CHOOSE...BIBLIOG 20 PARLIAMENT. PAGE 75   PARL/PROC
B1508   GOV/COMP

                                                              B62
ANDREWS W.G..FRENCH POLITICS AND ALGERIA: THE   GOV/COMP
PROCESS OF POLICY FORMATION 1954-1962. ALGERIA   EXEC
FRANCE CONSTN ELITES POL/PAR CHIEF DELIB/GP LEGIS   COLONIAL
DIPLOM PRESS CHOOSE 20. PAGE 5 B0105

                                                              B62
BAILEY S.D..THE SECRETARIAT OF THE UNITED NATIONS.   INT/ORG
FUT WOR+45 DELIB/GP PLAN BAL/PWR DOMIN EDU/PROP   EXEC
ADMIN PEACE ATTIT PWR...DECISION CONCPT TREND   DIPLOM
CON/ANAL CHARTS UN VAL/FREE COLD/WAR 20. PAGE 8
B0162

                                                              B62
BENSON E.T..CROSS FIRE: THE EIGHT YEARS WITH   ADMIN
EISENHOWER. USA+45 DIPLOM LEAD ATTIT PERSON   POLICY
CONSERVE...TRADIT BIOG 20 EISNHWR/DD PRESIDENT   DELIB/GP
TAFT/RA DULLES/JF NIXON/RM. PAGE 11 B0218   TOP/EX

                                                              B62
BRIMMER B..A GUIDE TO THE USE OF UNITED NATIONS   BIBLIOG/A
DOCUMENTS. WOR+45 ECO/UNDEV AGRI EX/STRUC FORCES   INT/ORG
PROB/SOLV ADMIN WAR PEACE WEALTH...POLICY UN.   DIPLOM
PAGE 15 B0310

                                                              B62
BROWN L.C..LATIN AMERICA, A BIBLIOGRAPHY. EX/STRUC   BIBLIOG
ADMIN LEAD ATTIT...POLICY 20. PAGE 16 B0323   L/A+17C
                                                      DIPLOM
                                                      NAT/G
                                                              B62
CARTER G.M..THE GOVERNMENT OF THE SOVIET UNION.   NAT/G
USSR CULTURE LOC/G DIPLOM ECO/TAC ADJUD CT/SYS LEAD   MARXISM
WEALTH...CHARTS T 20 COM/PARTY. PAGE 19 B0390   POL/PAR
                                                      EX/STRUC
                                                              B62
COSTA RICA UNIVERSIDAD BIBL.LISTA DE TESIS DE GRADO BIBLIOG/A
DE LA UNIVERSIDAD DE COSTA RICA. COSTA/RICA LAW   NAT/G
LOC/G ADMIN LEAD...SOC 20. PAGE 24 B0487   DIPLOM
                                                      ECO/UNDEV
                                                              B62
EVANS M.S..THE FRINGE ON TOP. USSR EX/STRUC FORCES   NAT/G
DIPLOM ECO/TAC PEACE CONSERVE SOCISM...TREND 20   PWR
KENNEDY/JF. PAGE 34 B0689   CENTRAL
                                                      POLICY
                                                              B62
FRIEDMANN W..METHODS AND POLICIES OF PRINCIPAL   INT/ORG
DONOR COUNTRIES IN PUBLIC INTERNATIONAL DEVELOPMENT   FOR/AID
FINANCING: PRELIMINARY APPRAISAL. FRANCE GERMANY/W   NAT/COMP
UK USA+45 USSR WOR+45 FINAN ECO/DEV CAP/ISM DIPLOM   ADMIN
ECO/TAC ATTIT 20 EEC. PAGE 37 B0759

                                                              B62
GRAY R.K..EIGHTEEN ACRES UNDER GLASS. ELITES   CHIEF
CONSULT EX/STRUC DIPLOM PRESS CONFER WAR PERS/REL   ADMIN
PERSON 20 EISNHWR/DD TRUMAN/HS CABINET. PAGE 43   TOP/EX
B0860   NAT/G
                                                              B62
HARARI M..GOVERNMENT AND POLITICS OF THE MIDDLE   DIPLOM
EAST. ISLAM USA+45 NAT/G SECT CHIEF ADMIN ORD/FREE   ECO/UNDEV
20. PAGE 47 B0943   TEC/DEV
                                                      POLICY
                                                              B62
INGHAM K..A HISTORY OF EAST AFRICA. NAT/G DIPLOM   AFR
ADMIN WAR NAT/LISM...SOC BIOG BIBLIOG. PAGE 54   CONSTN
B1085   COLONIAL
                                                              B62
JEWELL M.E..SENATORIAL POLITICS AND FOREIGN POLICY. USA+45
NAT/G POL/PAR CHIEF DELIB/GP TOP/EX FOR/AID   LEGIS
EDU/PROP ROUTINE ATTIT PWR SKILL...MAJORIT   DIPLOM
METH/CNCPT TIME/SEQ CONGRESS 20 PRESIDENT. PAGE 56
B1138
                                                              B62
KENNEDY J.F..TO TURN THE TIDE. SPACE AGRI INT/ORG   DIPLOM
FORCES TEC/DEV ADMIN NUC/PWR PEACE WEALTH...ANTHOL   CHIEF
20 KENNEDY/JF CIV/RIGHTS. PAGE 59 B1193   POLICY
                                                      NAT/G
                                                              B62
LOWI T.J..LEGISLATIVE POLITICS U.S.A. LAW LEGIS   PARL/PROC
DIPLOM EXEC LOBBY CHOOSE SUFF FEDERAL PWR 19/20   REPRESENT
CONGRESS. PAGE 67 B1345   POLICY
                                                      ROUTINE
                                                              B62
MODELSKI G..A THEORY OF FOREIGN POLICY. WOR+45   PLAN
WOR-45 NAT/G DELIB/GP EX/STRUC TOP/EX EDU/PROP   PWR
LEGIT ROUTINE...POLICY CONCPT TOT/POP COLD/WAR 20.   DIPLOM
PAGE 74 B1494
                                                              B62
MORTON L..STRATEGY AND COMMAND: THE FIRST TWO   WAR
YEARS. USA-45 NAT/G CONTROL EXEC LEAD WEAPON   FORCES
CIVMIL/REL PWR...POLICY AUD/VIS CHARTS 20 CHINJAP.   PLAN
PAGE 76 B1532   DIPLOM

                                                              B62
SAMPSON A..ANATOMY OF BRITAIN. UK LAW COM/IND FINAN ELITES
INDUS MARKET MUNIC POL/PAR EX/STRUC TOP/EX DIPLOM   PWR
LEAD REPRESENT PERSON PARLIAMENT WORSHIP. PAGE 92   STRUCT
B1866   FORCES
                                                              B62
SCALAPINO R.A..PARTIES AND POLITICS IN CONTEMPORARY POL/PAR
JAPAN. EX/STRUC DIPLOM CHOOSE NAT/LISM ATTIT   PARL/PROC
...POLICY 20 CHINJAP. PAGE 93 B1876   ELITES
                                                      DECISION
                                                              B62
SHAPIRO D..A SELECT BIBLIOGRAPHY OF WORKS IN   BIBLIOG
ENGLISH ON RUSSIAN HISTORY, 1801-1917. COM USSR   DIPLOM
STRATA FORCES EDU/PROP ADMIN REV RACE/REL ATTIT   COLONIAL
19/20. PAGE 96 B1932
                                                              B62
SNYDER R.C..FOREIGN POLICY DECISION-MAKING. FUT   TEC/DEV
KOREA WOR+45 R+D CREATE ADMIN ROUTINE PWR   HYPO/EXP
...DECISION PSY SOC CONCPT METH/CNCPT CON/ANAL   DIPLOM
CHARTS GEN/METH METH 20. PAGE 99 B1992
                                                              B62
TAYLOR D..THE BRITISH IN AFRICA. UK CULTURE   AFR
ECO/UNDEV INDUS DIPLOM INT/TRADE ADMIN WAR RACE/REL   COLONIAL
ORD/FREE SOVEREIGN...POLICY BIBLIOG 15/20 CMN/WLTH.   DOMIN
PAGE 103 B2084
                                                              B62
US LIBRARY OF CONGRESS.A LIST OF AMERICAN DOCTORAL   BIBLIOG
DISSERTATIONS ON AFRICA. SOCIETY SECT DIPLOM   AFR
EDU/PROP ADMIN...GEOG 19/20. PAGE 109 B2206   ACADEM
                                                      CULTURE
                                                              B62
US SENATE COMM GOVT OPERATIONS.ADMINISTRATION OF   ORD/FREE
NATIONAL SECURITY. USA+45 CHIEF PLAN PROB/SOLV   ADMIN
TEC/DEV DIPLOM ATTIT...POLICY DECISION 20   NAT/G
KENNEDY/JF RUSK/D MCNAMARA/R BUNDY/M HERTER/C.   CONTROL
PAGE 110 B2212
                                                              B62
WELLEQUET J..LE CONGO BELGE ET LA WELTPOLITIK   ADMIN
(1894-1914. GERMANY DOMIN EDU/PROP WAR ATTIT   DIPLOM
...BIBLIOG T CONGO/LEOP. PAGE 115 B2318   GP/REL
                                                      COLONIAL
                                                              S62
ALGER C.F..."THE EXTERNAL BUREAUCRACY IN UNITED   ADMIN
STATES FOREIGN AFFAIRS." USA+45 WOR+45 SOCIETY   ATTIT
COM/IND INT/ORG NAT/G CONSULT EX/STRUC ACT/RES   DIPLOM
...MGT SOC CONCPT TREND 20. PAGE 4 B0076
                                                              S62
IKLE F.C.."POLITICAL NEGOTIATION AS A PROCESS OF   ROUTINE
MODIFYING UTILITIES." WOR+45 FACE/GP LABOR NAT/G   DECISION
FORCES ACT/RES EDU/PROP DETER PERCEPT ALL/VALS   DIPLOM
...PSY NEW/IDEA HYPO/EXP GEN/METH 20. PAGE 53 B1076
                                                              S62
JACOBSON H.K.."THE UNITED NATIONS AND COLONIALISM: INT/ORG
A TENTATIVE APPRAISAL." AFR FUT S/ASIA USA+45 USSR   CONCPT
WOR+45 NAT/G DELIB/GP PLAN DIPLOM ECO/TAC DOMIN   COLONIAL
ADMIN ROUTINE COERCE ATTIT RIGID/FLEX ORD/FREE PWR
...OBS STERTYP UN 20. PAGE 55 B1115
                                                              S62
MCCLELLAND C.A.."DECISIONAL OPPORTUNITY AND   ACT/RES
POLITICAL CONTROVERSY." USA+45 NAT/G POL/PAR FORCES   PERCEPT
TOP/EX DOMIN ADMIN PEACE DRIVE ORD/FREE PWR   DIPLOM
...DECISION SIMUL 20. PAGE 72 B1444
                                                              S62
NORTH R.C.."DECISION MAKING IN CRISIS: AN   INT/ORG
INTRODUCTION." WOR+45 WOR-45 NAT/G CONSULT DELIB/GP   ROUTINE
TEC/DEV PERCEPT KNOWL...POLICY DECISION PSY   DIPLOM
METH/CNCPT CONT/OBS TREND VAL/FREE 20. PAGE 79
B1590
                                                              S62
SCHILLING W.R.."SCIENTISTS, FOREIGN POLICY AND   NAT/G
POLITICS." WOR+45 WOR-45 INTELL INT/ORG CONSULT   TEC/DEV
TOP/EX ACT/RES PLAN ADMIN KNOWL...CONCPT OBS TREND   DIPLOM
LEAGUE/NAT 20. PAGE 93 B1889   NUC/PWR
                                                              S62
TRUMAN D.."THE DOMESTIC POLITICS OF FOREIGN AID."   ROUTINE
USA+45 WOR+45 NAT/G POL/PAR LEGIS DIPLOM ECO/TAC   FOR/AID
EDU/PROP ADMIN CHOOSE ATTIT PWR CONGRESS 20
CONGRESS. PAGE 105 B2129
                                                              B63
BADI J..THE GOVERNMENT OF THE STATE OF ISRAEL: A   NAT/G
CRITICAL ACCOUNT OF ITS PARLIAMENT, EXECUTIVE, AND   CONSTN
JUDICIARY. ISRAEL ECO/DEV CHIEF DELIB/GP LEGIS   EX/STRUC
DIPLOM CT/SYS INGP/REL PEACE ORD/FREE...BIBLIOG 20   POL/PAR
PARLIAMENT ARABS MIGRATION. PAGE 8 B0157
                                                              B63
BOISSIER P..HISTORIE DU COMITE INTERNATIONAL DE LA   INT/ORG
CROIX ROUGE. MOD/EUR WOR-45 CONSULT FORCES PLAN   HEALTH
DIPLOM EDU/PROP ADMIN MORAL ORD/FREE...SOC CONCPT   ARMS/CONT
RECORD TIME/SEQ GEN/LAWS TOT/POP VAL/FREE 19/20.   WAR
PAGE 13 B0267
                                                              B63
BOWETT D.W..THE LAW OF INTERNATIONAL INSTITUTIONS.   INT/ORG
WOR+45 WOR-45 CONSULT DELIB/GP EX/STRUC JUDGE   ADJUD
EDU/PROP LEGIT CT/SYS EXEC ROUTINE RIGID/FLEX   DIPLOM
ORD/FREE PWR...JURID CONCPT ORG/CHARTS GEN/METH
LEAGUE/NAT OAS OEEC 20 UN. PAGE 14 B0286

B63
BROGAN D.W.,POLITICAL PATTERNS IN TODAY'S WORLD.   NAT/COMP
FRANCE USA+45 USSR WOR+45 CONSTN STRUCT PLAN DIPLOM   NEW/LIB
ADMIN LEAD ROLE SUPEGO...PHIL/SCI 20. PAGE 15 B0313   COM
                                                       TOTALISM
                                                               B63
COMISION DE HISTORIO,GUIA DE LOS DOCUMENTOS   BIBLIOG
MICROFOTOGRAFIADOS POR LA UNIDAD MOVIL DE LA   NAT/G
UNESCO. SOCIETY ECO/UNDEV INT/ORG ADMIN...SOC 20   L/A+17C
UNESCO. PAGE 22 B0456   DIPLOM
                                                               B63
CONF ON FUTURE OF COMMONWEALTH,THE FUTURE OF THE   DIPLOM
COMMONWEALTH. UK ECO/UNDEV AGRI EDU/PROP ADMIN   RACE/REL
SOC/INTEG 20 COMMONWLTH. PAGE 23 B0460   ORD/FREE
                                                       TEC/DEV
                                                               B63
CROZIER B.,THE MORNING AFTER: A STUDY OF   SOVEREIGN
INDEPENDENCE. WOR+45 EX/STRUC PLAN BAL/PWR COLONIAL   NAT/LISM
GP/REL 20 COLD/WAR. PAGE 25 B0511   NAT/G
                                                       DIPLOM
                                                               B63
HONORD S.,PUBLIC RELATIONS IN ADMINISTRATION.   PRESS
WOR+45 NAT/G...SOC/WK BIBLIOG 20. PAGE 51 B1039   DIPLOM
                                                       MGT
                                                       METH/COMP
                                                               B63
KOGAN N.,THE POLITICS OF ITALIAN FOREIGN POLICY.   NAT/G
EUR+WWI LEGIS DOMIN LEGIT EXEC PWR RESPECT SKILL   ROUTINE
...POLICY DECISION HUM SOC METH/CNCPT OBS INT   DIPLOM
CHARTS 20. PAGE 61 B1227   ITALY
                                                               B63
MONTER W.,THE GOVERNMENT OF GENEVA, 1536-1605   SECT
(DOCTORAL THESIS). SWITZERLND DIPLOM LEAD ORD/FREE   FINAN
SOVEREIGN 16/17 CALVIN/J ROME. PAGE 74 B1504   LOC/G
                                                       ADMIN
                                                               B63
ROETTER C.,THE DIPLOMATIC ART. USSR INT/ORG NAT/G   DIPLOM
DELIB/GP ROUTINE NUC/PWR PEACE...POLICY 20. PAGE 90   ELITES
B1812   TOP/EX
                                                               B63
SCHRADER R.,SCIENCE AND POLICY. WOR+45 ECO/DEV   TEC/DEV
ECO/UNDEV R+D FORCES PLAN DIPLOM GOV/REL TECHRACY   NAT/G
BIBLIOG. PAGE 94 B1900   POLICY
                                                       ADMIN
                                                               B63
STEIN H.,AMERICAN CIVIL-MILITARY DECISION. USA+45   CIVMIL/REL
USA-45 EX/STRUC FORCES LEGIS TOP/EX PLAN DIPLOM   DECISION
FOR/AID ATTIT 20 CONGRESS. PAGE 100 B2028   WAR
                                                       BUDGET
                                                               B63
TSOU T.,AMERICA'S FAILURE IN CHINA, 1941-1950.   ASIA
USA+45 USA-45 NAT/G ACT/RES PLAN DOMIN EDU/PROP   PERCEPT
ADMIN ROUTINE ATTIT PERSON ORD/FREE...DECISION   DIPLOM
CONCPT MYTH TIME/SEQ TREND STERTYP 20. PAGE 105
B2132
                                                               B63
TUCKER R.C.,THE SOVIET POLITICAL MIND. WOR+45   COM
ELITES INT/ORG NAT/G POL/PAR PLAN DIPLOM ECO/TAC   TOP/EX
DOMIN ADMIN NUC/PWR REV DRIVE PERSON SUPEGO PWR   USSR
WEALTH...POLICY MGT PSY CONCPT OBS BIOG TREND
COLD/WAR MARX/KARL 20. PAGE 106 B2134
                                                               B63
US SENATE COMM APPROPRIATIONS,PERSONNEL   ADMIN
ADMINISTRATION AND OPERATIONS OF AGENCY FOR   FOR/AID
INTERNATIONAL DEVELOPMENT: SPECIAL HEARING. FINAN   EFFICIENCY
LEAD COST UTIL SKILL...CHARTS 20 CONGRESS AID   DIPLOM
CIVIL/SERV. PAGE 109 B2211
                                                               B63
VAN SLYCK P.,PEACE: THE CONTROL OF NATIONAL POWER.   ARMS/CONT
CUBA WOR+45 FINAN NAT/G FORCES PROB/SOLV TEC/DEV   PEACE
BAL/PWR ADMIN CONTROL ORD/FREE...POLICY INT/LAW UN   INT/ORG
COLD/WAR TREATY. PAGE 112 B2253   DIPLOM
                                                               B63
WALKER A.A.,OFFICIAL PUBLICATIONS OF SIERRA LEONE   BIBLIOG
AND GAMBIA. GAMBIA SIER/LEONE UK LAW CONSTN LEGIS   NAT/G
PLAN BUDGET DIPLOM...SOC SAMP CON/ANAL 20. PAGE 113   COLONIAL
B2278   ADMIN
                                                               L63
BEGUIN H.,"ASPECTS GEOGRAPHIQUE DE LA   ECO/UNDEV
POLARISATION." FUT WOR+45 SOCIETY STRUCT ECO/DEV   GEOG
R+D BAL/PWR ADMIN ATTIT RIGID/FLEX HEALTH WEALTH   DIPLOM
...CHARTS 20. PAGE 10 B0206
                                                               L63
FREUND G.,"ADENAUER AND THE FUTURE OF GERMANY."   NAT/G
EUR+WWI FUT GERMANY/W FORCES LEGIT ADMIN ROUTINE   BIOG
ATTIT DRIVE PERSON PWR...POLICY TIME/SEQ TREND   DIPLOM
VAL/FREE 20 ADENAUER/K. PAGE 37 B0753   GERMANY
                                                               S63
ANTHON C.G.,"THE END OF THE ADENAUER ERA." EUR+WWI   NAT/G
GERMANY/W CONSTN EX/STRUC CREATE DIPLOM LEGIT ATTIT   TOP/EX
PERSON ALL/VALS...RECORD 20 ADENAUER/K. PAGE 6   BAL/PWR
B0113   GERMANY
                                                               S63
CLEMHOUT S.,"PRODUCTION FUNCTION ANALYSIS APPLIED   ECO/DEV
TO THE LEONTIEF SCARCE-FACTOR PARADOX OF   ECO/TAC
INTERNATIONAL TRADE." EUR+WWI USA+45 DIST/IND NAT/G

PLAN TEC/DEV DIPLOM PWR WEALTH...MGT METH/CNCPT
CONT/OBS CON/ANAL CHARTS SIMUL GEN/LAWS 20. PAGE 21
B0436
                                                               S63
HAVILAND H.F.,"BUILDING A POLITICAL COMMUNITY."   VOL/ASSN
EUR+WWI FUT UK USA+45 ECO/DEV ECO/UNDEV INT/ORG   DIPLOM
NAT/G DELIB/GP BAL/PWR ECO/TAC NEUTRAL ROUTINE
ATTIT PWR WEALTH...CONCPT COLD/WAR TOT/POP 20.
PAGE 48 B0972
                                                               S63
MANGONE G.,"THE UNITED NATIONS AND UNITED STATES   INT/ORG
FOREIGN POLICY." USA+45 WOR+45 ECO/UNDEV NAT/G   ECO/TAC
DIPLOM LEGIT ROUTINE ATTIT DRIVE...TIME/SEQ UN   FOR/AID
COLD/WAR 20. PAGE 69 B1390
                                                               S63
MODELSKI G.,"STUDY OF ALLIANCES." WOR+45 WOR-45   VOL/ASSN
INT/ORG NAT/G FORCES LEGIT ADMIN CHOOSE ALL/VALS   CON/ANAL
PWR SKILL...INT/LAW CONCPT GEN/LAWS 20 TREATY.   DIPLOM
PAGE 74 B1495
                                                               C63
BLUM J.M.,"THE NATIONAL EXPERIENCE." USA+45 USA-45   ADMIN
ECO/DEV DIPLOM WAR NAT/LISM...POLICY CHARTS BIBLIOG   NAT/G
T 16/20 CONGRESS PRESIDENT COLD/WAR. PAGE 13 B0258   LEGIS
                                                       CHIEF
                                                               B64
ADAMS V.,THE PEACE CORPS IN ACTION. USA+45 VOL/ASSN   DIPLOM
EX/STRUC GOV/REL PERCEPT ORD/FREE...OBS 20   FOR/AID
KENNEDY/JF PEACE/CORP. PAGE 3 B0058   PERSON
                                                       DRIVE
                                                               B64
BLACKSTOCK P.W.,THE STRATEGY OF SUBVERSION. USA+45   ORD/FREE
FORCES EDU/PROP ADMIN COERCE GOV/REL...DECISION MGT   DIPLOM
20 DEPT/DEFEN CIA DEPT/STATE. PAGE 12 B0247   CONTROL
                                                               B64
COTTRELL A.J.,THE POLITICS OF THE ATLANTIC   VOL/ASSN
ALLIANCE. EUR+WWI USA+45 INT/ORG NAT/G DELIB/GP   FORCES
EX/STRUC BAL/PWR DIPLOM REGION DETER ATTIT ORD/FREE
...CONCPT RECORD GEN/LAWS GEN/METH NATO 20. PAGE 24
B0493
                                                               B64
DAS M.N.,INDIA UNDER MORLEY AND MINTO. INDIA UK   GOV/REL
ECO/UNDEV MUNIC PROVS EX/STRUC LEGIS DIPLOM CONTROL   COLONIAL
REV 20 MORLEY/J. PAGE 26 B0531   POLICY
                                                       ADMIN
                                                               B64
DUROSELLE J.B.,POLITIQUES NATIONALES ENVERS LES   DIPLOM
JEUNES ETATS. FRANCE ISRAEL ITALY UK USA+45 USSR   ECO/UNDEV
YUGOSLAVIA ECO/DEV FINAN ECO/TAC INT/TRADE ADMIN   COLONIAL
PWR 20. PAGE 31 B0634   DOMIN
                                                               B64
FATOUROS A.A.,CANADA'S OVERSEAS AID. CANADA WOR+45   FOR/AID
ECO/DEV FINAN NAT/G BUDGET ECO/TAC CONFER ADMIN 20.   DIPLOM
PAGE 35 B0707   ECO/UNDEV
                                                       POLICY
                                                               B64
FORBES A.H.,CURRENT RESEARCH IN BRITISH STUDIES. UK   BIBLIOG
CONSTN CULTURE POL/PAR SECT DIPLOM ADMIN...JURID   PERSON
BIOG WORSHIP 20. PAGE 36 B0736   NAT/G
                                                       PARL/PROC
                                                               B64
GJUPANOVIC H.,LEGAL SOURCES AND BIBLIOGRAPHY OF   BIBLIOG/A
YUGOSLAVIA. COM YUGOSLAVIA LAW LEGIS DIPLOM ADMIN   JURID
PARL/PROC REGION CRIME CENTRAL 20. PAGE 40 B0807   CONSTN
                                                       ADJUD
                                                               B64
GRZYBOWSKI K.,THE SOCIALIST COMMONWEALTH OF   INT/LAW
NATIONS: ORGANIZATIONS AND INSTITUTIONS. FORCES   COM
DIPLOM INT/TRADE ADJUD ADMIN LEAD WAR MARXISM   REGION
SOCISM...BIBLIOG 20 COMECON WARSAW/P. PAGE 44 B0898   INT/ORG
                                                               B64
HARMON R.B.,BIBLIOGRAPHY OF BIBLIOGRAPHIES IN   BIBLIOG
POLITICAL SCIENCE (MIMEOGRAPHED PAPER: LIMITED   NAT/G
EDITION). WOR+45 WOR-45 INT/ORG POL/PAR GOV/REL   DIPLOM
ALL/IDEOS...INT/LAW JURID MGT 19/20. PAGE 47 B0949   LOC/G
                                                               B64
IBERO-AMERICAN INSTITUTES,IBEROAMERICANA. STRUCT   BIBLIOG
ADMIN SOC. PAGE 53 B1073   L/A+17C
                                                       NAT/G
                                                       DIPLOM
                                                               B64
JACKSON H.M.,THE SECRETARY OF STATE AND THE   GOV/REL
AMBASSADOR* JACKSON SUBCOMMITTEE PAPERS ON THE   DIPLOM
CONDUCT OF AMERICAN FOREIGN POLICY. USA+45 NAT/G   ADMIN
FORCES ACT/RES OP/RES EDU/PROP CENTRAL EFFICIENCY   EX/STRUC
ORD/FREE...OBS RECORD ANTHOL CONGRESS PRESIDENT.
PAGE 55 B1107
                                                               B64
JACKSON W.V.,LIBRARY GUIDE FOR BRAZILIAN STUDIES.   BIBLIOG
BRAZIL USA+45 STRUCT DIPLOM ADMIN...SOC 20. PAGE 55   L/A+17C
B1110   NAT/G
                                                       LOC/G
                                                               B64
KNOX V.H.,PUBLIC FINANCE: INFORMATION SOURCES.   BIBLIOG/A
USA+45 DIPLOM ADMIN GOV/REL COST...POLICY 20.   FINAN
PAGE 60 B1221   TAX
                                                       BUDGET

B64

LITTLE I.M.D.,AID TO AFRICA. AFR UK TEC/DEV DIPLOM
ECO/TAC INCOME WEALTH 20. PAGE 66 B1326

FOR/AID
ECO/UNDEV
ADMIN
POLICY

B64

MAHAR J.M.,INDIA: A CRITICAL BIBLIOGRAPHY. INDIA
PAKISTAN CULTURE ECO/UNDEV LOC/G POL/PAR SECT
PROB/SOLV DIPLOM ADMIN COLONIAL PARL/PROC ATTIT 20.
PAGE 68 B1377

BIBLIOG/A
S/ASIA
NAT/G
LEAD

B64

MERILLAT H.C.L.,LEGAL ADVISERS AND FOREIGN AFFAIRS.
WOR+45 WOR-45 ELITES INTELL NAT/G LEGIT ADMIN
PERCEPT ALL/VALS...MGT NEW/IDEA RECORD 20. PAGE 73
B1469

CONSULT
EX/STRUC
DIPLOM

B64

MUSSO AMBROSI L.A.,BIBLIOGRAFIA DE BIBLIOGRAFIAS
URUGUAYAS. URUGUAY DIPLOM ADMIN ATTIT...SOC 20.
PAGE 77 B1551

BIBLIOG
NAT/G
L/A+17C
PRESS

B64

RICHARDSON I.L.,BIBLIOGRAFIA BRASILEIRA DE
ADMINISTRACAO PUBLICA E ASSUNTOS CORRELATOS. BRAZIL
CONSTN FINAN LOC/G NAT/G POL/PAR PLAN DIPLOM
RECEIVE ATTIT...METH 20. PAGE 88 B1776

BIBLIOG
MGT
ADMIN
LAW

B64

ROCHE J.P.,THE CONGRESS. EX/STRUC BAL/PWR DIPLOM
DEBATE ADJUD LEAD PWR. PAGE 89 B1809

INGP/REL
LEGIS
DELIB/GP
SENIOR

B64

ROCHE J.P.,THE PRESIDENCY. USA+45 USA-45 CONSTN
NAT/G CHIEF BAL/PWR DIPLOM GP/REL 18/20 PRESIDENT.
PAGE 90 B1810

EX/STRUC
PWR

B64

RUSSELL R.B.,UNITED NATIONS EXPERIENCE WITH
MILITARY FORCES: POLITICAL AND LEGAL ASPECTS. AFR
KOREA WOR+45 LEGIS PROB/SOLV ADMIN CONTROL
EFFICIENCY PEACE...POLICY INT/LAW BIBLIOG UN.
PAGE 92 B1857

FORCES
DIPLOM
SANCTION
ORD/FREE

B64

RUSSET B.M.,WORLD HANDBOOK OF POLITICAL AND SOCIAL
INDICATORS. WOR+45 COM/IND ADMIN WEALTH...GEOG 20.
PAGE 92 B1858

DIPLOM
STAT
NAT/G
NAT/COMP

B64

SARROS P.P.,CONGRESS AND THE NEW DIPLOMACY: THE
FORMULATION OF MUTUAL SECURITY POLICY: 1953-60
(THESIS). USA+45 CHIEF EX/STRUC REGION ROUTINE
CHOOSE GOV/REL PEACE ROLE...POLICY 20 PRESIDENT
CONGRESS. PAGE 92 B1869

DIPLOM
POL/PAR
NAT/G

B64

SCHECHTER A.H.,INTERPRETATION OF AMBIGUOUS
DOCUMENTS BY INTERNATIONAL ADMINISTRATIVE
TRIBUNALS. WOR+45 EX/STRUC INT/TRADE CT/SYS
SOVEREIGN 20 UN ILO EURCT/JUST. PAGE 93 B1884

INT/LAW
DIPLOM
INT/ORG
ADJUD

B64

SEGUNDO-SANCHEZ M.,OBRAS (2 VOLS.). VENEZUELA
EX/STRUC DIPLOM ADMIN 19/20. PAGE 95 B1924

BIBLIOG
LEAD
NAT/G
L/A+17C

B64

TILMAN R.O.,BUREAUCRATIC TRANSITION IN MALAYA.
MALAYSIA S/ASIA UK NAT/G EX/STRUC DIPLOM...CHARTS
BIBLIOG 20. PAGE 104 B2110

ADMIN
COLONIAL
SOVEREIGN
EFFICIENCY

B64

TULLY A.,WHERE DID YOUR MONEY GO. USA+45 USSR
ECO/UNDEV ADMIN EFFICIENCY WEALTH...METH/COMP 20.
PAGE 106 B2136

FOR/AID
DIPLOM
CONTROL

B64

TURNER M.C.,LIBROS EN VENTA EN HISPANOAMERICA Y
ESPANA. SPAIN LAW CONSTN CULTURE ADMIN LEAD...HUM
SOC 20. PAGE 106 B2139

BIBLIOG
L/A+17C
NAT/G
DIPLOM

B64

US SENATE COMM GOVT OPERATIONS,THE SECRETARY OF
STATE AND THE AMBASSADOR. USA+45 CHIEF CONSULT
EX/STRUC FORCES PLAN ADMIN EXEC INGP/REL ROLE
...ANTHOL 20 PRESIDENT DEPT/STATE. PAGE 110 B2215

DIPLOM
DELIB/GP
NAT/G

B64

US SENATE COMM GOVT OPERATIONS,ADMINISTRATION OF
NATIONAL SECURITY. USA+45 CHIEF TOP/EX PLAN DIPLOM
CONTROL PEACE...POLICY DECISION 20 PRESIDENT
CONGRESS. PAGE 110 B2216

ADMIN
FORCES
ORD/FREE
NAT/G

B64

VECCHIO G.D.,L'ETAT ET LE DROIT. ITALY CONSTN
EX/STRUC LEGIS DIPLOM CT/SYS...JURID 20 UN.
PAGE 112 B2256

NAT/G
SOVEREIGN
CONCPT
INT/LAW

L64

MACKINTOSH J.P.,"NIGERIA'S EXTERNAL AFFAIRS." UK
CULTURE ECO/UNDEV NAT/G VOL/ASSN EDU/PROP LEGIT
ADMIN ATTIT ORD/FREE PWR 20. PAGE 68 B1365

AFR
DIPLOM
NIGERIA

L64

PRUITT D.G.,"PROBLEM SOLVING IN THE DEPARTMENT OF

ROUTINE

STATE." USA+45 NAT/G CONSULT PROB/SOLV EXEC PWR
...DECISION INT ORG/CHARTS 20. PAGE 85 B1713

MGT
DIPLOM

L64

RIPLEY R.B.,"INTERAGENCY COMMITTEES AND
INCREMENTALISM: THE CASE OF AID TO INDIA." INDIA
USA+45 INTELL NAT/G DELIB/GP ACT/RES DIPLOM ROUTINE
NAT/LISM ATTIT PWR...SOC CONCPT NEW/IDEA TIME/SEQ
CON/ANAL VAL/FREE 20. PAGE 89 B1790

EXEC
MGT
FOR/AID

S64

HORECKY P.L.,"LIBRARY OF CONGRESS PUBLICATIONS IN
AID OF USSR AND EAST EUROPEAN RESEARCH." BULGARIA
CZECHOSLVK POLAND USSR YUGOSLAVIA NAT/G POL/PAR
DIPLOM ADMIN GOV/REL...CLASSIF 20. PAGE 51 B1042

BIBLIOG/A
COM
MARXISM

S64

KENNAN G.F.,"POLYCENTRISM AND WESTERN POLICY." ASIA
CHINA/COM COM FUT USA+45 USSR NAT/G ACT/RES DOMIN
EDU/PROP EXEC COERCE DISPL PERCEPT...POLICY
COLD/WAR 20. PAGE 59 B1192

RIGID/FLEX
ATTIT
DIPLOM

S64

LOW D.A.,"LION RAMPANT." EUR+WWI MOD/EUR S/ASIA
ECO/UNDEV NAT/G FORCES TEC/DEV ECO/TAC LEGIT ADMIN
COLONIAL COERCE ORD/FREE RESPECT 19/20. PAGE 67
B1344

AFR
DOMIN
UK

S64

ROGOW A.A.,"CONGRESSIONAL GOVERNMENT: LEGISLATIVE
POWER V. DOMESTIC PROCESSES." USA+45 CHIEF DELIB/GP
ADMIN GOV/REL CONGRESS. PAGE 90 B1815

PWR
DIPLOM
LEGIS
POLICY

S64

RUSK D.,"THE MAKING OF FOREIGN POLICY" USA+45 CHIEF
DELIB/GP WORKER PROB/SOLV ADMIN ATTIT PWR
...DECISION 20 DEPT/STATE RUSK/D GOLDMAN/E. PAGE 92
B1856

DIPLOM
INT
POLICY

B65

AIYAR S.P.,STUDIES IN INDIAN DEMOCRACY. INDIA
STRATA ECO/UNDEV LABOR POL/PAR LEGIS DIPLOM LOBBY
REGION CHOOSE ATTIT SOCISM...ANTHOL 20. PAGE 3
B0067

ORD/FREE
REPRESENT
ADMIN
NAT/G

B65

BARNETT V.M. JR.,THE REPRESENTATION OF THE UNITED
STATES ABROAD* REVISED EDITION. ECO/UNDEV ACADEM
INT/ORG FORCES ACT/RES CREATE OP/RES FOR/AID REGION
CENTRAL...CLASSIF ANTHOL. PAGE 9 B0189

USA+45
DIPLOM
ADMIN

B65

CHANDA A.,FEDERALISM IN INDIA. INDIA UK ELITES
FINAN NAT/G POL/PAR EX/STRUC LEGIS DIPLOM TAX
GOV/REL POPULISM...POLICY 20. PAGE 20 B0402

CONSTN
CENTRAL
FEDERAL

B65

CUTLIP S.M.,A PUBLIC RELATIONS BIBLIOGRAPHY. INDUS
LABOR NAT/G PROF/ORG SCHOOL DIPLOM PRESS TV GOV/REL
GP/REL...PSY SOC/WK 20. PAGE 25 B0515

BIBLIOG/A
MGT
COM/IND
ADMIN

B65

DAVISON W.P.,INTERNATIONAL POLITICAL COMMUNICATION.
COM USA+45 WOR+45 CULTURE ECO/UNDEV NAT/G PROB/SOLV
PRESS TV ADMIN 20 FILM. PAGE 27 B0545

EDU/PROP
DIPLOM
PERS/REL
COM/IND

B65

DOWD L.P.,PRINCIPLES OF WORLD BUSINESS. SERV/IND
NAT/G DIPLOM ECO/TAC TARIFFS...INT/LAW JURID 20.
PAGE 30 B0614

INT/TRADE
MGT
FINAN
MARKET

B65

ELDER R.E.,OVERSEAS REPRESENTATION AND SERVICES FOR
FEDERAL DOMESTIC AGENCIES. USA+45 NAT/G ACT/RES
FOR/AID EDU/PROP SENIOR ROUTINE TASK ADJUST...MGT
ORG/CHARTS. PAGE 33 B0663

OP/RES
DIPLOM
GOV/REL
ADMIN

B65

FORGAC A.A.,NEW DIPLOMACY AND THE UNITED NATIONS.
FRANCE GERMANY UK USSR INT/ORG DELIB/GP EX/STRUC
PEACE...INT/LAW CONCPT UN. PAGE 36 B0740

DIPLOM
ETIQUET
NAT/G

B65

HAIGHT D.E.,THE PRESIDENT: ROLES AND POWERS. USA+45
USA-45 POL/PAR PLAN DIPLOM CHOOSE PERS/REL PWR
18/20 PRESIDENT CONGRESS. PAGE 45 B0915

CHIEF
LEGIS
TOP/EX
EX/STRUC

B65

HARMON R.B.,POLITICAL SCIENCE: A BIBLIOGRAPHICAL
GUIDE TO THE LITERATURE. WOR+45 WOR-45 R+D INT/ORG
LOC/G NAT/G DIPLOM ADMIN...CONCPT METH. PAGE 47
B0950

BIBLIOG
POL/PAR
LAW
GOV/COMP

B65

HARR J.E.,THE DEVELOPMENT OF CAREERS IN THE FOREIGN
SERVICE. CREATE SENIOR EXEC FEEDBACK GOV/REL
EFFICIENCY ATTIT RESPECT ORG/CHARTS. PAGE 47 B0953

OP/RES
MGT
ADMIN
DIPLOM

B65

HISPANIC SOCIETY OF AMERICA,CATALOGUE (10 VOLS.).
PORTUGAL PRE/AMER SPAIN NAT/G ADMIN...POLICY SOC
15/20. PAGE 50 B1018

BIBLIOG
L/A+17C
COLONIAL
DIPLOM

B65

JONES A.G.,THE EVOLUTION OF PERSONNEL SYSTEMS FOR
US FOREIGN AFFAIRS* A HISTORY OF REFORM EFFORTS.
USA+45 USA-45 ACADEM OP/RES GOV/REL...MGT CONGRESS.
PAGE 57 B1149

DIPLOM
ADMIN
ACT/RES
EFFICIENCY

KOUSOULAS D.G.,REVOLUTION AND DEFEAT; THE STORY OF THE GREEK COMMUNIST PARTY. GREECE INT/ORG EX/STRUC DIPLOM FOR/AID EDU/PROP PARL/PROC ADJUST ATTIT 20 COM/PARTY. PAGE 61 B1230
REV MARXISM POL/PAR ORD/FREE
B65

MACDONALD R.W.,THE LEAGUE OF ARAB STATES: A STUDY IN THE DYNAMICS OF REGIONAL ORGANIZATION. ISRAEL UAR USSR FINAN INT/ORG DELIB/GP ECO/TAC AGREE NEUTRAL ORD/FREE PWR...DECISION BIBLIOG 20 TREATY UN. PAGE 67 B1358
ISLAM REGION DIPLOM ADMIN
B65

MORGENTHAU H.,MORGENTHAU DIARY (CHINA) (2 VOLS.). ASIA USA+45 USA-45 LAW DELIB/GP EX/STRUC PLAN FOR/AID INT/TRADE CONFER WAR MARXISM 20 CHINJAP. PAGE 75 B1523
DIPLOM ADMIN
B65

NATIONAL BOOK CENTRE PAKISTAN,BOOKS ON PAKISTAN: A BIBLIOGRAPHY. PAKISTAN CULTURE DIPLOM ADMIN ATTIT ...MAJORIT SOC CONCPT 20. PAGE 77 B1560
BIBLIOG CONSTN S/ASIA NAT/G
B65

PENNICK JL J.R.,THE POLITICS OF AMERICAN SCIENCE, 1939 TO THE PRESENT. USA+45 USA-45 INTELL TEC/DEV DIPLOM NEW/LIB...ANTHOL 20 COLD/WAR. PAGE 82 B1651
POLICY ADMIN PHIL/SCI NAT/G
B65

PHELPS-FETHERS I.,SOVIET INTERNATIONAL FRONT ORGANIZATIONS* A CONCISE HANDBOOK. DIPLOM DOMIN LEGIT ADMIN EXEC GP/REL PEACE MARXISM...TIME/SEQ GP/COMP. PAGE 83 B1668
USSR EDU/PROP ASIA COM
B65

PYLEE M.V.,CONSTITUTIONAL GOVERNMENT IN INDIA (2ND REV. ED.). INDIA POL/PAR EX/STRUC DIPLOM COLONIAL CT/SYS PARL/PROC PRIVIL...JURID 16/20. PAGE 85 B1725
CONSTN NAT/G PROVS FEDERAL
B65

REDFORD D.R.,POLITICS AND GOVERNMENT IN THE UNITED STATES. USA+45 USA-45 LOC/G PROVS FORCES DIPLOM CT/SYS LOBBY...JURID SUPREME/CT PRESIDENT. PAGE 87 B1751
NAT/G POL/PAR EX/STRUC LEGIS
B65

ROTBERG R.I.,A POLITICAL HISTORY OF TROPICAL AFRICA. EX/STRUC DIPLOM INT/TRADE DOMIN ADMIN RACE/REL NAT/LISM PWR SOVEREIGN...GEOG TIME/SEQ BIBLIOG 1/20. PAGE 91 B1832
AFR CULTURE COLONIAL
B65

RUBINSTEIN A.Z.,THE CHALLENGE OF POLITICS: IDEAS AND ISSUES (2ND ED.). UNIV ELITES SOCIETY EX/STRUC BAL/PWR PARL/PROC AUTHORIT...DECISION ANTHOL 20. PAGE 92 B1852
NAT/G DIPLOM GP/REL ORD/FREE
B65

SCOTT A.M.,THE REVOLUTION IN STATECRAFT: INFORMAL PENETRATION. WOR+45 WOR-45 CULTURE INT/ORG FORCES ECO/TAC ROUTINE...BIBLIOG 20. PAGE 95 B1918
DIPLOM EDU/PROP FOR/AID
B65

SINGER J.D.,HUMAN BEHAVIOR AND INTERNATIONAL POLITICS* CONTRIBUTIONS FROM THE SOCIAL-PSYCHOLOGICAL SCIENCES. ACT/RES PLAN EDU/PROP ADMIN KNOWL...DECISION PSY SOC NET/THEORY HYPO/EXP LAB/EXP SOC/EXP GEN/METH ANTHOL BIBLIOG. PAGE 97 B1965
DIPLOM PHIL/SCI QUANT SIMUL
B65

SPEECKAERT G.P.,SELECT BIBLIOGRAPHY ON INTERNATIONAL ORGANIZATION, 1885-1964. WOR+45 WOR-45 EX/STRUC DIPLOM ADMIN REGION 19/20 UN. PAGE 99 B2004
BIBLIOG INT/ORG GEN/LAWS STRATA
B65

TYBOUT R.A.,ECONOMICS OF RESEARCH AND DEVELOPMENT. ECO/DEV ECO/UNDEV INDUS PROFIT DECISION. PAGE 106 B2141
R+D FORCES ADMIN DIPLOM
B65

UNIVERSAL REFERENCE SYSTEM,INTERNATIONAL AFFAIRS: VOLUME I IN THE POLITICAL SCIENCE, GOVERNMENT, AND PUBLIC POLICY SERIES....DECISION ECOMETRIC GEOG INT/LAW JURID MGT PHIL/SCI PSY SOC. PAGE 107 B2163
BIBLIOG/A GEN/METH COMPUT/IR DIPLOM
B65

US SENATE COMM GOVT OPERATIONS,ORGANIZATION OF FEDERAL EXECUTIVE DEPARTMENTS AND AGENCIES: REPORT OF MARCH 23, 1965. USA+45 FORCES LEGIS DIPLOM ROUTINE CIVMIL/REL EFFICIENCY FEDERAL...MGT STAT. PAGE 110 B2217
ADMIN EX/STRUC GOV/REL ORG/CHARTS
B65

US SENATE COMM GOVT OPERATIONS,ADMINISTRATION OF NATIONAL SECURITY. USA+45 DELIB/GP ADMIN ROLE ...POLICY CHARTS SENATE. PAGE 110 B2218
NAT/G ORD/FREE DIPLOM PROB/SOLV
B65

WHITE J.,GERMAN AID. GERMANY/W FINAN PLAN TEC/DEV INT/TRADE ADMIN ATTIT...POLICY 20. PAGE 116 B2334
FOR/AID ECO/UNDEV DIPLOM ECO/TAC
B65

WITHERELL J.W.,MADAGASCAR AND ADJACENT ISLANDS; A GUIDE TO OFFICIAL PUBLICATIONS (PAMPHLET). FRANCE
BIBLIOG COLONIAL

MADAGASCAR S/ASIA UK LAW OP/RES PLAN DIPLOM ...POLICY CON/ANAL 19/20. PAGE 117 B2368
LOC/G ADMIN
L65

LASSWELL H.D.,"THE POLICY SCIENCES OF DEVELOPMENT." CULTURE SOCIETY EX/STRUC CREATE ADMIN ATTIT KNOWL ...SOC CONCPT SIMUL GEN/METH. PAGE 63 B1273
PWR METH/CNCPT DIPLOM
L65

MATTHEWS D.G.,"A CURRENT BIBLIOGRAPHY ON ETHIOPIAN AFFAIRS: A SELECT BIBLIOGRAPHY FROM 1950-1964." ETHIOPIA LAW CULTURE ECO/UNDEV INDUS LABOR SECT FORCES DIPLOM CIVMIL/REL RACE/REL...LING STAT 20. PAGE 71 B1428
BIBLIOG/A ADMIN POL/PAR NAT/G
L65

RUBIN A.P.,"UNITED STATES CONTEMPORARY PRACTICE RELATING TO INTERNATIONAL LAW." USA+45 WOR+45 CONSTN INT/ORG NAT/G DELIB/GP EX/STRUC DIPLOM DOMIN CT/SYS ROUTINE ORD/FREE...CONCPT COLD/WAR 20. PAGE 91 B1848
LAW LEGIT INT/LAW
L65

"FURTHER READING." INDIA ADMIN COLONIAL WAR GOV/REL ATTIT 20. PAGE 2 B0044
BIBLIOG DIPLOM NAT/G POLICY
S65

BROWN S.,"AN ALTERNATIVE TO THE GRAND DESIGN." EUR+WWI FUT USA+45 INT/ORG NAT/G EX/STRUC FORCES CREATE BAL/PWR DOMIN RIGID/FLEX ORD/FREE PWR ...NEW/IDEA RECORD EEC NATO 20. PAGE 16 B0327
VOL/ASSN CONCPT DIPLOM
S65

HAMMOND P.Y.,"FOREIGN POLICY-MAKING AND ADMINISTRATIVE POLITICS." CREATE ADMIN COST ...DECISION CONCPT GAME CONGRESS PRESIDENT. PAGE 46 B0935
DIPLOM STRUCT IDEA/COMP OP/RES
S65

HOLSTI O.R.,"THE 1914 CASE." MOD/EUR COMPUTER DIPLOM EDU/PROP EXEC...DECISION PSY PROBABIL STAT COMPUT/IR SOC/EXP TIME. PAGE 51 B1036
CON/ANAL PERCEPT WAR
S65

OSTGAARD E.,"FACTORS INFLUENCING THE FLOW OF NEWS." COM/IND BUDGET DIPLOM EXEC GP/REL COST ATTIT SAMP. PAGE 80 B1618
EDU/PROP PERCEPT RECORD
S65

POSVAR W.W.,"NATIONAL SECURITY POLICY* THE REALM OF OBSCURITY." CREATE PLAN PROB/SOLV ADMIN LEAD GP/REL CONSERVE...DECISION GEOG. PAGE 84 B1694
DIPLOM USA+45 RECORD
S65

QUADE Q.L.,"THE TRUMAN ADMINISTRATION AND THE SEPARATION OF POWERS: THE CASE OF THE MARSHALL PLAN." SOCIETY INT/ORG NAT/G CONSULT DELIB/GP LEGIS PLAN ECO/TAC ROUTINE DRIVE PERCEPT RIGID/FLEX ORD/FREE PWR WEALTH...DECISION GEOG NEW/IDEA TREND 20 TRUMAN/HS. PAGE 85 B1726
USA+45 ECO/UNDEV DIPLOM
S65

HUNTINGTON S.P.,"CONGRESSIONAL RESPONSES TO THE TWENTIETH CENTURY IN D. TRUMAN, ED. THE CONGRESS AND AMERICA'S FUTURE." USA+45 USA-45 DIPLOM SENIOR ADMIN EXEC PWR...SOC 20 CONGRESS. PAGE 53 B1067
FUT LEAD NAT/G LEGIS
C65

ALEXANDER Y.,INTERNATIONAL TECHNICAL ASSISTANCE EXPERTS* A CASE STUDY OF THE U.N. EXPERIENCE. ECO/UNDEV CONSULT EX/STRUC CREATE PLAN DIPLOM FOR/AID TASK EFFICIENCY...ORG/CHARTS UN. PAGE 4 B0074
ECO/TAC INT/ORG ADMIN MGT
B66

BALDWIN D.A.,FOREIGN AID AND AMERICAN FOREIGN POLICY; A DOCUMENTARY ANALYSIS. USA+45 ECO/UNDEV ADMIN....ECOMETRIC STAT STYLE CHARTS PROG/TEAC GEN/LAWS ANTHOL. PAGE 8 B0172
FOR/AID DIPLOM IDEA/COMP
B66

BEAUFRE A.,NATO AND EUROPE. WOR+45 PLAN CONFER EXEC NUC/PWR ATTIT...POLICY 20 NATO EUROPE. PAGE 10 B0203
INT/ORG DETER DIPLOM ADMIN
B66

EPSTEIN F.T.,THE AMERICAN BIBLIOGRAPHY OF RUSSIAN AND EAST EUROPEAN STUDIES FOR 1964. USSR LOC/G NAT/G POL/PAR FORCES ADMIN ARMS/CONT...JURID CONCPT 20 UN. PAGE 33 B0678
BIBLIOG COM MARXISM DIPLOM
B66

FABAR R.,THE VISION AND THE NEED: LATE VICTORIAN IMPERIALIST AIMS. MOD/EUR UK WOR-45 CULTURE NAT/G DIPLOM...TIME/SEQ METH/COMP 19 KIPLING/R COMMONWLTH. PAGE 34 B0693
COLONIAL CONCPT ADMIN ATTIT
B66

FINNISH POLITICAL SCIENCE ASSN,SCANDINAVIAN POLITICAL STUDIES (VOL. I). FINLAND DIPLOM ADMIN LOBBY PARL/PROC...CHARTS BIBLIOG 20 SCANDINAV. PAGE 36 B0721
ATTIT POL/PAR ACT/RES CHOOSE
B66

GLAZER M.,THE FEDERAL GOVERNMENT AND THE UNIVERSITY. CHILE PROB/SOLV DIPLOM GIVE ADMIN WAR ...POLICY SOC 20. PAGE 40 B0810
BIBLIOG/A NAT/G PLAN ACADEM
B66

HARMON R.B.,SOURCES AND PROBLEMS OF BIBLIOGRAPHY IN POLITICAL SCIENCE (PAMPHLET). INT/ORG LOC/G MUNIC
BIBLIOG DIPLOM

POL/PAR ADMIN GOV/REL ALL/IDEOS...JURID MGT CONCPT 19/20. PAGE 47 B0951 — INT/LAW NAT/G

B66

LEE L.T.,VIENNA CONVENTION ON CONSULAR RELATIONS. WOR+45 LAW INT/ORG CONFER GP/REL PRIVIL...INT/LAW 20 TREATY VIENNA/CNV. PAGE 63 B1279 — AGREE DIPLOM ADMIN

B66

MACFARQUHAR R.,CHINA UNDER MAO: POLITICS TAKES COMMAND. CHINA/COM COM AGRI INDUS CHIEF FORCES DIPLOM INT/TRADE EDU/PROP TASK REV ADJUST...ANTHOL 20 MAO. PAGE 67 B1359 — ECO/UNDEV TEC/DEV ECO/TAC ADMIN

B66

MARTIN L.W.,DIPLOMACY IN MODERN EUROPEAN HISTORY. EUR+WWI MOD/EUR INT/ORG NAT/G EX/STRUC ROUTINE WAR PEACE TOTALISM PWR 15/20 COLD/WAR EUROPE/W. PAGE 70 B1411 — DIPLOM POLICY

B66

MOOMAW I.W.,THE CHALLENGE OF HUNGER. USA+45 PLAN ADMIN EATING 20. PAGE 75 B1509 — FOR/AID DIPLOM ECO/UNDEV ECO/TAC

B66

NEUMANN R.G.,THE GOVERNMENT OF THE GERMAN FEDERAL REPUBLIC. EUR+WWI GERMANY/W LOC/G EX/STRUC LEGIS CT/SYS INGP/REL PWR...BIBLIOG 20 ADENAUER/K. PAGE 78 B1573 — NAT/G POL/PAR DIPLOM CONSTN

B66

OHLIN G.,AID AND INDEBTEDNESS. AUSTRIA FINAN INT/ORG PLAN DIPLOM GIVE...POLICY MATH CHARTS 20. PAGE 79 B1604 — FOR/AID ECO/UNDEV ADMIN WEALTH

B66

SAPIN B.M.,THE MAKING OF UNITED STATES FOREIGN POLICY. USA+45 INT/ORG DELIB/GP FORCES PLAN ECO/TAC CIVMIL/REL PRESIDENT. PAGE 92 B1868 — DIPLOM EX/STRUC DECISION NAT/G

B66

SPICER K.,A SAMARITAN STATE? AFR CANADA INDIA PAKISTAN UK USA+45 FINAN INDUS PRODUC...CHARTS 20 NATO. PAGE 99 B2006 — DIPLOM FOR/AID ECO/DEV ADMIN

B66

US DEPARTMENT OF THE ARMY,COMMUNIST CHINA: A STRATEGIC SURVEY: A BIBLIOGRAPHY (PAMPHLET NO. 20-67). CHINA/COM COM INDIA USSR NAT/G POL/PAR EX/STRUC FORCES NUC/PWR REV ATTIT...POLICY GEOG CHARTS. PAGE 108 B2184 — BIBLIOG/A MARXISM S/ASIA DIPLOM

B66

US LIBRARY OF CONGRESS,NIGERIA: A GUIDE TO OFFICIAL PUBLICATIONS. CAMEROON NIGERIA UK DIPLOM...POLICY 19/20 UN LEAGUE/NAT. PAGE 109 B2207 — BIBLIOG ADMIN NAT/G COLONIAL

B66

US SENATE COMM ON FOREIGN REL,HEARINGS ON S 2859 AND S 2861. USA+45 WOR+45 FORCES BUDGET CAP/ISM ADMIN DETER WEAPON TOTALISM...NAT/COMP 20 UN CONGRESS. PAGE 110 B2221 — FOR/AID DIPLOM ORD/FREE ECO/UNDEV

B66

WALL E.H.,THE COURT OF JUSTICE IN THE EUROPEAN COMMUNITIES: JURISDICTION AND PROCEDURE. EUR+WWI DIPLOM ADJUD ADMIN ROUTINE TASK...CONCPT LING 20. PAGE 113 B2281 — CT/SYS INT/ORG LAW OP/RES

B66

WARBURG J.P.,THE UNITED STATES IN THE POSTWAR WORLD. USA+45 ECO/TAC...POLICY 20 COLD/WAR. PAGE 113 B2287 — FOR/AID DIPLOM PLAN ADMIN

B66

WILSON G.,CASES AND MATERIALS ON CONSTITUTIONAL AND ADMINISTRATIVE LAW. UK LAW NAT/G EX/STRUC LEGIS BAL/PWR BUDGET DIPLOM ADJUD CONTROL CT/SYS GOV/REL ORD/FREE 20 PARLIAMENT ENGLSH/LAW. PAGE 117 B2359 — JURID ADMIN CONSTN PWR

B66

YOUNG W.,EXISTING MECHANISMS OF ARMS CONTROL. PROC/MFG OP/RES DIPLOM TASK CENTRAL...MGT TREATY. PAGE 119 B2395 — ARMS/CONT ADMIN NUC/PWR ROUTINE

S66

AUSLAND J.C.,"CRISIS MANAGEMENT* BERLIN, CYPRUS, LAOS." CYPRUS LAOS FORCES CREATE PLAN EDU/PROP TASK CENTRAL PERSON RIGID/FLEX...DECISION MGT 20 BERLIN KENNEDY/JF MCNAMARA/R RUSK. PAGE 7 B0148 — OP/RES DIPLOM RISK ADMIN

S66

BALDWIN D.A.,"CONGRESSIONAL INITIATIVE IN FOREIGN POLICY." NAT/G BARGAIN DIPLOM FOR/AID RENT GIVE ...DECISION CONGRESS. PAGE 8 B0171 — EXEC TOP/EX GOV/REL

S66

DIEBOLD J.,"COMPUTERS, PROGRAM MANAGEMENT AND FOREIGN AFFAIRS." USA+45 INDUS OP/RES TEC/DEV...MGT GP/COMP GEN/LAWS. PAGE 29 B0590 — COMPUTER DIPLOM ROUTINE ACT/RES

S66

MATTHEWS D.G.,"ETHIOPIAN OUTLINE: A BIBLIOGRAPHIC RESEARCH GUIDE." ETHIOPIA LAW STRUCT ECO/UNDEV AGRI LABOR SECT CHIEF DELIB/GP EX/STRUC ADMIN...LING ORG/CHARTS 20. PAGE 71 B1429 — BIBLIOG NAT/G DIPLOM POL/PAR

S66

ZUCKERT E.M.,"THE SERVICE SECRETARY* HAS HE A USEFUL ROLE?" USA+45 TOP/EX PLAN ADMIN EXEC DETER NUC/PWR WEAPON...MGT RECORD MCNAMARA/R. PAGE 119 B2407 — OBS OP/RES DIPLOM FORCES

B67

AMERICAN FRIENDS SERVICE COMM,IN PLACE OF WAR. NAT/G ACT/RES DIPLOM ADMIN NUC/PWR EFFICIENCY ...POLICY 20. PAGE 4 B0085 — PEACE PACIFISM WAR DETER

B67

BRAYMAN H.,CORPORATE MANAGEMENT IN A WORLD OF POLITICS. USA+45 ELITES MARKET CREATE BARGAIN DIPLOM INT/TRADE ATTIT SKILL 20. PAGE 15 B0302 — MGT ECO/DEV CAP/ISM INDUS

B67

BRZEZINSKI Z.K.,IDEOLOGY AND POWER IN SOVIET POLITICS. USSR NAT/G POL/PAR PWR...GEN/LAWS 19/20. PAGE 16 B0335 — DIPLOM EX/STRUC MARXISM

B67

BRZEZINSKI Z.K.,THE SOVIET BLOC: UNITY AND CONFLICT (2ND ED., REV., ENLARGED). COM POLAND USSR INTELL CHIEF EX/STRUC CONTROL EXEC GOV/REL PWR MARXISM ...TREND IDEA/COMP 20 LENIN/VI MARX/KARL STALIN/J. PAGE 16 B0336 — NAT/G DIPLOM

B67

CECIL L.,ALBERT BALLIN; BUSINESS AND POLITICS IN IMPERIAL GERMANY 1888-1918. GERMANY UK INT/TRADE LEAD WAR PERS/REL ADJUST PWR WEALTH...MGT BIBLIOG 19/20. PAGE 19 B0397 — DIPLOM CONSTN ECO/DEV TOP/EX

B67

DOSSICK J.J.,DOCTORAL RESEARCH ON PUERTO RICO AND PUERTO RICANS. PUERT/RICO USA+45 USA-45 ADMIN 20. PAGE 30 B0609 — BIBLIOG CONSTN POL/PAR DIPLOM

B67

FARNSWORTH B.,WILLIAM C. BULLITT AND THE SOVIET UNION. COM USA-45 USSR NAT/G CHIEF CONSULT DELIB/GP EX/STRUC WAR REPRESENT MARXISM 20 WILSON/W ROOSEVLT/F STALIN/J BULLITT/WC. PAGE 35 B0705 — DIPLOM BIOG POLICY

B67

GIFFORD P.,BRITAIN AND GERMANY IN AFRICA. AFR GERMANY UK ECO/UNDEV LEAD WAR NAT/LISM ATTIT ...POLICY HIST/WRIT METH/COMP ANTHOL BIBLIOG 19/20 WWI. PAGE 39 B0797 — COLONIAL ADMIN DIPLOM NAT/COMP

B67

GREENE L.S.,AMERICAN GOVERNMENT POLICIES AND FUNCTIONS. USA+45 LAW AGRI DIST/IND LABOR MUNIC BUDGET DIPLOM EDU/PROP ORD/FREE...BIBLIOG T 20. PAGE 43 B0867 — POLICY NAT/G ADMIN DECISION

B67

MILNE R.S.,GOVERNMENT AND POLITICS IN MALAYSIA. INDONESIA MALAYSIA LOC/G EX/STRUC FORCES DIPLOM GP/REL 20 SINGAPORE. PAGE 74 B1489 — NAT/G LEGIS ADMIN

B67

OVERSEAS DEVELOPMENT INSTIT,EFFECTIVE AID. WOR+45 INT/ORG TEC/DEV DIPLOM INT/TRADE ADMIN. PAGE 80 B1619 — FOR/AID ECO/UNDEV ECO/TAC NAT/COMP

B67

PLANO J.C.,FORGING WORLD ORDER: THE POLITICS OF INTERNATIONAL ORGANIZATION. PROB/SOLV DIPLOM CONTROL CENTRAL RATIONAL ORD/FREE...INT/LAW CHARTS BIBLIOG 20 UN LEAGUE/NAT. PAGE 83 B1679 — INT/ORG ADMIN JURID

B67

PYE L.W.,SOUTHEAST ASIA'S POLITICAL SYSTEMS. ASIA S/ASIA STRUCT ECO/UNDEV EX/STRUC CAP/ISM DIPLOM ALL/IDEOS...TREND CHARTS. PAGE 85 B1724 — NAT/G POL/PAR GOV/COMP

B67

RALSTON D.B.,THE ARMY OF THE REPUBLIC; THE PLACE OF THE MILITARY IN THE POLITICAL EVOLUTION OF FRANCE 1871-1914. FRANCE MOD/EUR EX/STRUC LEGIS TOP/EX DIPLOM ADMIN WAR GP/REL ROLE...BIBLIOG 19/20. PAGE 86 B1730 — FORCES NAT/G CIVMIL/REL POLICY

B67

RAWLINSON J.L.,CHINA'S STRUGGLE FOR NAVAL DEVELOPMENT 1839-1895. ASIA DIPLOM ADMIN WAR ...BIBLIOG DICTIONARY 19 CHINJAP. PAGE 86 B1745 — SEA FORCES PWR

B67

SABLE M.H.,A GUIDE TO LATIN AMERICAN STUDIES (2 VOLS). CONSTN FINAN INT/ORG LABOR MUNIC POL/PAR FORCES CAP/ISM FOR/AID ADMIN MARXISM SOCISM OAS. PAGE 92 B1861 — BIBLIOG/A L/A+17C DIPLOM NAT/LISM

B67

SCHEINMAN L.,EURATOM* NUCLEAR INTEGRATION IN EUROPE. EX/STRUC LEAD 20 EURATOM. PAGE 93 B1885 — INT/ORG NAT/LISM NUC/PWR DIPLOM

B67

UNITED NATIONS,UNITED NATIONS PUBLICATIONS: 1945-1966. WOR+45 COM/IND DIST/IND FINAN TEC/DEV ADMIN...POLICY INT/LAW MGT CHARTS 20 UN UNESCO. PAGE 107 B2162 — BIBLIOG/A INT/ORG DIPLOM WRITING

B67

US DEPARTMENT OF THE ARMY,CIVILIAN IN PEACE, SOLDIER IN WAR: A BIBLIOGRAPHIC SURVEY OF THE ARMY — BIBLIOG/A FORCES

S66

AND AIR NATIONAL GUARD (PAMPHLET, NOS. 130-2). POLE
USA+45 USA-45 LOC/G NAT/G PROVS LEGIS PLAN ADMIN DIPLOM
ATTIT ORD/FREE...POLICY 19/20. PAGE 108 B2185
                                                                B67
US HOUSE COMM SCI ASTRONAUT,GOVERNMENT, SCIENCE, ADMIN
AND INTERNATIONAL POLICY. R+D OP/RES PLAN 20. PHIL/SCI
PAGE 109 B2198   ACT/RES
                                                      DIPLOM
                                                                B67
WARREN S.,THE AMERICAN PRESIDENT. POL/PAR FORCES CHIEF
LEGIS DIPLOM ECO/TAC ADMIN EXEC PWR...ANTHOL 18/20 LEAD
ROOSEVLT/F KENNEDY/JF JOHNSON/LB TRUMAN/HS NAT/G
WILSON/W. PAGE 114 B2297   CONSTN
                                                                B67
WATERS M.,THE UNITED NATIONS* INTERNATIONAL CONSTN
ORGANIZATION AND ADMINISTRATION. WOR+45 EX/STRUC INT/ORG
FORCES DIPLOM LEAD REGION ARMS/CONT REPRESENT ADMIN
INGP/REL ROLE...METH/COMP ANTHOL 20 UN LEAGUE/NAT. ADJUD
PAGE 114 B2301
                                                                L67
"RESTRICTIVE SOVEREIGN IMMUNITY, THE STATE SOVEREIGN
DEPARTMENT, AND THE COURTS." USA+45 USA-45 EX/STRUC ORD/FREE
DIPLOM ADJUD CONTROL GOV/REL 19/20 DEPT/STATE PRIVIL
SUPREME/CT. PAGE 2 B0047   CT/SYS
                                                                L67
CAHIERS P.,"LE RECOURS EN CONSTATATION DE INT/ORG
MANQUEMENTS DES ETATS MEMBRES DEVANT LA COUR DES CONSTN
COMMUNAUTES EUROPEENNES." LAW PROB/SOLV DIPLOM ROUTINE
ADMIN CT/SYS SANCTION ATTIT...POLICY DECISION JURID ADJUD
ECSC EEC. PAGE 18 B0362
                                                                L67
COHEN M.,"THE DEMISE OF UNEF." CONSTN DIPLOM ADMIN INT/ORG
AGREE LEAD COERCE 20 UNEF U/THANT HAMMARSK/D. FORCES
PAGE 22 B0445   PEACE
                                                      POLICY
                                                                S67
BERRODIN E.F.,"AT THE BARGAINING TABLE." LABOR PROVS
DIPLOM ECO/TAC ADMIN...MGT 20 MICHIGAN. PAGE 11 WORKER
B0230   LAW
                                                      BARGAIN
                                                                S67
BREGMAN A.,"WHITHER RUSSIA?" COM RUSSIA INTELL MARXISM
POL/PAR DIPLOM PARTIC NAT/LISM TOTALISM ATTIT ELITES
ORD/FREE 20. PAGE 15 B0304   ADMIN
                                                      CREATE
                                                                S67
FABREGA J.,"ANTECEDENTES EXTRANJEROS EN LA CONSTN
CONSTITUCION PANAMENA." CUBA L/A+17C PANAMA URUGUAY JURID
EX/STRUC LEGIS DIPLOM ORD/FREE 19/20 COLOMB NAT/G
MEXIC/AMER. PAGE 34 B0694   PARL/PROC
                                                                S67
LALL B.G.,"GAPS IN THE ABM DEBATE." NAT/G DIPLOM NUC/PWR
DETER CIVMIL/REL 20. PAGE 62 B1251   ARMS/CONT
                                                      EX/STRUC
                                                      FORCES
                                                                S67
NEUCHTERLEIN D.E.,"THAILAND* ANOTHER VIETNAM?" WAR
THAILAND ECO/UNDEV DIPLOM ADMIN REGION CENTRAL GUERRILLA
NAT/LISM...POLICY 20. PAGE 78 B1571   S/ASIA
                                                      NAT/G
                                                                S67
ROTBERG R.I.,"COLONIALISM AND AFTER: THE POLITICAL BIBLIOG/A
LITERATURE OF CENTRAL AFRICA - A BIBLIOGRAPHIC COLONIAL
ESSAY." AFR CHIEF EX/STRUC REV INGP/REL RACE/REL DIPLOM
SOVEREIGN 20. PAGE 91 B1833   NAT/G
                                                                S67
SHOEMAKER R.L.,"JAPANESE ARMY AND THE WEST." ASIA FORCES
ELITES EX/STRUC DIPLOM DOMIN EDU/PROP COERCE ATTIT TEC/DEV
AUTHORIT PWR 1/20 CHINJAP. PAGE 96 B1950   WAR
                                                      TOTALISM
                                                                S67
TACKABERRY R.B.,"ORGANIZING AND TRAINING PEACE- PEACE
KEEPING FORCES* THE CANADIAN VIEW." CANADA PLAN FORCES
DIPLOM CONFER ADJUD ADMIN CIVMIL/REL 20 UN. INT/ORG
PAGE 102 B2069   CONSULT
                                                                S67
TATU M.,"URSS: LES FLOTTEMENTS DE LA DIRECTION POLICY
COLLEGIALE." UAR USSR CHIEF LEAD INGP/REL NAT/G
EFFICIENCY...DECISION TREND 20 MID/EAST. PAGE 103 EX/STRUC
B2082   DIPLOM
                                                                S67
TOURNELLE G.,"DIPLOMATIE D' HIER ET D'AUJOURD' DIPLOM
HUI." CONFER ADMIN ROUTINE PEACE. PAGE 105 B2123 ROLE
                                                      INT/ORG
                                                                N67
US SUPERINTENDENT OF DOCUMENTS,SPACE: MISSILES, THE BIBLIOG/A
MOON, NASA, AND SATELLITES (PRICE LIST 79A). USA+45 SPACE
COM/IND R+D NAT/G DIPLOM EDU/PROP ADMIN CONTROL TEC/DEV
HEALTH...POLICY SIMUL NASA CONGRESS. PAGE 111 B2244 PEACE
                                                                N67
US SENATE COMM ON FOREIGN REL,ARMS SALES AND ARMS/CONT
FOREIGN POLICY (PAMPHLET). FINAN FOR/AID CONTROL ADMIN
20. PAGE 110 B2222   OP/RES
                                                      DIPLOM
                                                                N67
US SENATE COMM ON FOREIGN REL,THE UNITED NATIONS AT INT/ORG

TWENTY-ONE (PAMPHLET). WOR+45 BUDGET ADMIN SENATE DIPLOM
UN. PAGE 110 B2223   PEACE
                                                                N67
US SENATE COMM ON FOREIGN REL,THE UNITED NATIONS INT/ORG
PEACEKEEPING DILEMMA (PAMPHLET). ISLAM WOR+45 DIPLOM
PROB/SOLV BUDGET ADMIN SENATE UN. PAGE 110 B2224 PEACE
                                                                B82
POOLE W.F.,INDEX TO PERIODICAL LITERATURE. LOC/G BIBLIOG
NAT/G DIPLOM ADMIN...HUM PHIL/SCI SOC 19. PAGE 84 USA-45
B1690   ALL/VALS
                                                      SOCIETY
                                                                B95
LATIMER E.W.,EUROPE IN AFRICA IN THE NINETEENTH AFR
CENTURY. ECO/UNDEV KIN SECT DIPLOM DOMIN ADMIN COLONIAL
DISCRIM 17/18. PAGE 63 B1275   WAR
                                                      FINAN

DIPLOMACY.....SEE DIPLOM

DIRECT/NAT.....DIRECTORY NATIONAL (IRELAND)

DIRECTORY NATIONAL (IRELAND).....SEE DIRECT/NAT

DIRKSEN/E.....EVERETT DIRKSEN

                                                                B62
CARPER E.T.,ILLINOIS GOES TO CONGRESS FOR ARMY ADMIN
LAND. USA+45 LAW EXTR/IND PROVS REGION CIVMIL/REL LOBBY
GOV/REL FEDERAL ATTIT 20 ILLINOIS SENATE CONGRESS GEOG
DIRKSEN/E DOUGLAS/P. PAGE 19 B0385   LEGIS

DISARMAMENT.....SEE ARMS/CONT

DISCIPLINE.....SEE EDU/PROP, CONTROL

DISCRIM.....DISCRIMINATION; SEE ALSO GP/REL, RACE/REL,
   ISOLAT

                                                                B00
SANDERSON E.,AFRICA IN THE NINETEENTH CENTURY. COLONIAL
FRANCE UK EXTR/IND FORCES LEGIS ADMIN WAR DISCRIM AFR
ORD/FREE...GEOG GP/COMP SOC/INTEG 19. PAGE 92 B1867 DIPLOM
                                                                N19
BUREAU OF NAT'L AFFAIRS INC.,A CURRENT LOOK AT: DISCRIM
(1) THE NEGRO AND TITLE VII. (2) SEX AND TITLE VII SEX
(PAMPHLET). LAW LG/CO SML/CO RACE/REL...POLICY SOC WORKER
STAT DEEP/QU TREND CON/ANAL CHARTS 20 NEGRO MGT
CIV/RIGHTS. PAGE 17 B0350
                                                                B43
LEVY H.P.,A STUDY IN PUBLIC RELATIONS: CASE HISTORY ATTIT
OF THE RELATIONS MAINTAINED BETWEEN A DEPT OF RECEIVE
PUBLIC ASSISTANCE AND PEOPLE. USA-45 NAT/G PRESS WEALTH
ADMIN LOBBY GP/REL DISCRIM...SOC/WK LING AUD/VIS 20 SERV/IND
PENNSYLVAN. PAGE 64 B1302
                                                                B48
KESSELMAN L.C.,THE SOCIAL POLITICS OF THE FEPC. POLICY
INDUS WORKER EDU/PROP GP/REL RACE/REL 20 NEGRO JEWS NAT/G
FEPC. PAGE 59 B1200   ADMIN
                                                      DISCRIM
                                                                B52
MILLER M.,THE JUDGES AND THE JUDGED. USA+45 LG/CO COM/IND
ACT/RES TV ROUTINE SANCTION NAT/LISM ATTIT ORD/FREE DISCRIM
...POLICY ACLU. PAGE 73 B1481   EDU/PROP
                                                      MARXISM
                                                                B53
WAGLEY C.,AMAZON TOWN: A STUDY OF MAN IN THE SOC
TROPICS. BRAZIL L/A+17C STRATA STRUCT ECO/UNDEV NEIGH
AGRI EX/STRUC RACE/REL DISCRIM HABITAT WEALTH...OBS CULTURE
SOC/EXP 20. PAGE 113 B2273   INGP/REL
                                                                B54
ALLPORT G.W.,THE NATURE OF PREJUDICE. USA+45 WOR+45 CULTURE
STRATA FACE/GP KIN NEIGH SECT ADMIN GP/REL DISCRIM PERSON
ATTIT DRIVE LOVE RESPECT...PSY SOC MYTH QU/SEMANT RACE/REL
20. PAGE 4 B0078
                                                                B57
DE GRAZIA A.,GRASS ROOTS PRIVATE WELFARE. LOC/G NEW/LIB
SCHOOL ACT/RES EDU/PROP ROUTINE CROWD GP/REL HEALTH
DISCRIM HAPPINESS ILLEGIT AGE HABITAT. PAGE 27 MUNIC
B0554   VOL/ASSN
                                                                S57
HAILEY,"TOMORROW IN AFRICA." CONSTN SOCIETY LOC/G AFR
NAT/G DOMIN ADJUD ADMIN GP/REL DISCRIM NAT/LISM PERSON
ATTIT MORAL ORD/FREE...PSY SOC CONCPT OBS RECORD ELITES
TREND GEN/LAWS CMN/WLTH 20. PAGE 45 B0917   RACE/REL
                                                                B58
LAW COMMISSION OF INDIA,REFORM OF JUDICIAL CT/SYS
ADMINISTRATION. INDIA TOP/EX ADMIN DISCRIM ADJUD
EFFICIENCY...METH/COMP 20. PAGE 63 B1276   GOV/REL
                                                      CONTROL
                                                                S59
DWYER R.J.,"THE ADMINISTRATIVE ROLE IN ADMIN
DESEGREGATION." USA+45 LAW PROB/SOLV LEAD RACE/REL SCHOOL
ISOLAT STRANGE ROLE...POLICY SOC/INTEG MISSOURI DISCRIM
NEGRO CIV/RIGHTS. PAGE 31 B0638   ATTIT
                                                                B60
HAYEK F.A.,THE CONSTITUTION OF LIBERTY. UNIV LAW ORD/FREE

CONSTN WORKER TAX EDU/PROP ADMIN CT/SYS COERCE
DISCRIM...IDEA/COMP 20. PAGE 48 B0974
CHOOSE
NAT/G
CONCPT

B60
SOUTH AFRICAN CONGRESS OF DEM,FACE THE FUTURE.
SOUTH/AFR ELITES LEGIS ADMIN REGION COERCE PEACE
ATTIT 20. PAGE 99 B1999
RACE/REL
DISCRIM
CONSTN
NAT/G

B61
MUNGER E.S.,AFRICAN FIELD REPORTS 1952-1961.
SOUTH/AFR SOCIETY ECO/UNDEV NAT/G POL/PAR COLONIAL
EXEC PARL/PROC GUERRILLA RACE/REL ALL/IDEOS...SOC
AUD/VIS 20. PAGE 76 B1538
AFR
DISCRIM
RECORD

B63
CORLEY R.N.,THE LEGAL ENVIRONMENT OF BUSINESS.
CONSTN LEGIS TAX ADMIN CT/SYS DISCRIM ATTIT PWR
...TREND 18/20. PAGE 23 B0477
NAT/G
INDUS
JURID
DECISION

B63
GALBRAITH J.S.,RELUCTANT EMPIRE: BRITISH POLICY OF
THE SOUTH AFRICAN FRONTIER, 1834-1854. AFR
SOUTH/AFR UK GP/REL RACE/REL DISCRIM...CHARTS
BIBLIOG 19 MISSION. PAGE 38 B0774
COLONIAL
ADMIN
POLICY
SECT

B63
MENZEL J.M.,THE CHINESE CIVIL SERVICE: CAREER OPEN
TO TALENT? ASIA ROUTINE INGP/REL DISCRIM ATTIT ROLE
KNOWL ANTHOL. PAGE 73 B1468
ADMIN
NAT/G
DECISION
ELITES

B63
SINGH H.L.,PROBLEMS AND POLICIES OF THE BRITISH IN
INDIA, 1885-1898. INDIA UK NAT/G FORCES LEGIS
PROB/SOLV CONTROL RACE/REL ADJUST DISCRIM NAT/LISM
RIGID/FLEX...MGT 19 CIVIL/SERV. PAGE 97 B1968
COLONIAL
PWR
POLICY
ADMIN

B64
BANTON M.,THE POLICEMAN IN THE COMMUNITY. UK USA+45
STRUCT PROF/ORG WORKER LOBBY ROUTINE COERCE CROWD
GP/REL ADJUST DISCRIM PERCEPT 20. PAGE 9 B0181
FORCES
ADMIN
ROLE
RACE/REL

C64
NORGREN P.H.,"TOWARD FAIR EMPLOYMENT." USA+45 LAW
STRATA LABOR NAT/G FORCES ACT/RES ADMIN ATTIT
...POLICY BIBLIOG 20 NEGRO. PAGE 79 B1588
RACE/REL
DISCRIM
WORKER
MGT

B65
FRIEDMAN L.,SOUTHERN JUSTICE. USA+45 PUB/INST LEGIT
ADMIN CT/SYS DISCRIM...DECISION ANTHOL 20 NEGRO
SOUTH/US CIV/RIGHTS. PAGE 37 B0758
ADJUD
LAW
CONSTN
RACE/REL

B65
GOPAL S.,BRITISH POLICY IN INDIA 1858-1905. INDIA
UK ELITES CHIEF DELIB/GP ECO/TAC GP/REL DISCRIM
ATTIT...IDEA/COMP NAT/COMP PERS/COMP BIBLIOG/A
19/20. PAGE 41 B0828
COLONIAL
ADMIN
POL/PAR
ECO/UNDEV

S66
JACOBSON J.,"COALITIONISM: FROM PROTEST TO
POLITICKING" USA+45 ELITES NAT/G POL/PAR PROB/SOLV
ADMIN LEAD DISCRIM ORD/FREE PWR CONSERVE 20 NEGRO
AFL/CIO CIV/RIGHTS BLACK/PWR. PAGE 55 B1116
RACE/REL
LABOR
SOCIALIST
VOL/ASSN

B67
JAKUBAUSKAS E.B.,HUMAN RESOURCES DEVELOPMENT.
USA+45 AGRI INDUS SERV/IND ACT/RES PLAN ADMIN
RACE/REL DISCRIM...TREND GEN/LAWS. PAGE 55 B1119
PROB/SOLV
ECO/TAC
EDU/PROP
WORKER

B67
KRISLOV S.,THE NEGRO IN FEDERAL EMPLOYMENT. LAW
STRATA LOC/G CREATE PROB/SOLV INSPECT GOV/REL
DISCRIM ROLE...DECISION INT TREND 20 NEGRO WWI
CIVIL/SERV. PAGE 61 B1238
WORKER
NAT/G
ADMIN
RACE/REL

B67
WEINBERG M.,SCHOOL INTEGRATION: A COMPREHENSIVE
CLASSIFIED BIBLIOGRAPHY OF 3,100 REFERENCES. USA+45
LAW NAT/G NEIGH SECT PLAN ROUTINE AGE/C WEALTH
SOC/INTEG INDIAN/AM. PAGE 115 B2314
BIBLIOG
SCHOOL
DISCRIM
RACE/REL

S67
JOHNSON L.B.,"BULLETS DO NOT DISCRIMINATE-LANDLORDS
DO." PROB/SOLV EXEC LOBBY DEMAND...REALPOL SOC 20.
PAGE 57 B1145
NAT/G
DISCRIM
POLICY

S67
LANDES W.M.,"THE EFFECT OF STATE FAIR EMPLOYMENT
LAWS ON THE ECONOMIC POSITION OF NONWHITES." USA+45
PROVS SECT LEGIS ADMIN GP/REL RACE/REL...JURID
CONCPT CHARTS HYPO/EXP NEGRO. PAGE 62 B1255
DISCRIM
LAW
WORKER

S67
LLOYD K.,"URBAN RACE RIOTS V EFFECTIVE ANTI-
DISCRIMINATION AGENCIES* AN END OR A BEGINNING?"
USA+45 STRATA ACT/RES ADMIN ADJUST ORD/FREE RESPECT
...PLURIST DECISION SOC SOC/WK. PAGE 66 B1332
GP/REL
DISCRIM
LOC/G
CROWD

S67
ROSENBERG B.,"ETHNIC LIBERALISM AND EMPLOYMENT
DISCRIMINATION IN THE NORTH." USA+45 TOP/EX
PROB/SOLV ADMIN REGION PERS/REL DISCRIM...INT
IDEA/COMP. PAGE 90 B1820
RACE/REL
ATTIT
WORKER
EXEC

B95
LATIMER E.W.,EUROPE IN AFRICA IN THE NINETEENTH
CENTURY. ECO/UNDEV KIN SECT DIPLOM DOMIN ADMIN
DISCRIM 17/18. PAGE 63 B1275
AFR
COLONIAL
WAR

FINAN
B98
THOMPSON H.C.,RHODESIA AND ITS GOVERNMENT. AFR
RHODESIA ECO/UNDEV INDUS KIN WORKER INT/TRADE
DISCRIM LITERACY ORD/FREE 19. PAGE 104 B2102
COLONIAL
ADMIN
POLICY
ELITES

DISCRIMINATION....SEE DISCRIM

DISEASE....SEE HEALTH

DISPL....DISPLACEMENT AND PROJECTION

S41
ABEL T.,"THE ELEMENT OF DECISION IN THE PATTERN OF
WAR." EUR+WWI FUT NAT/G TOP/EX DIPLOM ROUTINE
COERCE DISPL PERCEPT PWR...SOC METH/CNCPT HIST/WRIT
TREND GEN/LAWS 20. PAGE 2 B0051
TEC/DEV
FORCES
WAR

L52
WRIGHT Q.,"CONGRESS AND THE TREATY-MAKING POWER."
USA+45 WOR+45 CONSTN INTELL NAT/G CHIEF CONSULT
EX/STRUC LEGIS TOP/EX CREATE GOV/REL DISPL DRIVE
RIGID/FLEX...TREND TOT/POP CONGRESS CONGRESS 20
TREATY. PAGE 118 B2384
ROUTINE
DIPLOM
INT/LAW
DELIB/GP

B53
MEYER P.,THE JEWS IN THE SOVIET SATELLITES.
CZECHOSLVK POLAND SOCIETY STRATA NAT/G BAL/PWR
ECO/TAC EDU/PROP LEGIT ADMIN COERCE ATTIT DISPL
PERCEPT HEALTH PWR RESPECT WEALTH...METH/CNCPT JEWS
VAL/FREE NAZI 20. PAGE 73 B1474
COM
SECT
TOTALISM
USSR

B54
MILLARD E.L.,FREEDOM IN A FEDERAL WORLD. FUT WOR+45
VOL/ASSN TOP/EX LEGIT ROUTINE FEDERAL PEACE ATTIT
DISPL ORD/FREE PWR...MAJORIT INT/LAW JURID TREND
COLD/WAR 20. PAGE 73 B1479
INT/ORG
CREATE
ADJUD
BAL/PWR

B56
WHYTE W.H. JR.,THE ORGANIZATION MAN. CULTURE FINAN
VOL/ASSN DOMIN EDU/PROP EXEC DISPL HABITAT ROLE
...PERS/TEST STERTYP. PAGE 116 B2343
ADMIN
LG/CO
PERSON
CONSEN

B57
BEAL J.R.,JOHN FOSTER DULLES, A BIOGRAPHY. USA+45
USSR WOR+45 CONSTN INT/ORG NAT/G EX/STRUC LEGIT
ADMIN NUC/PWR DISPL PERSON ORD/FREE PWR SKILL
...POLICY PSY OBS RECORD COLD/WAR UN 20 DULLES/JF.
PAGE 10 B0200
BIOG
DIPLOM

B61
LASSWELL H.D.,PSYCOPATHOLOGY AND POLITICS. WOR-45
CULTURE SOCIETY FACE/GP NAT/G CONSULT CREATE
EDU/PROP EXEC ROUTINE DISPL DRIVE PERSON PWR
RESPECT...PSY CONCPT METH/CNCPT METH. PAGE 63 B1272
ATTIT
GEN/METH

B61
STONE J.,QUEST FOR SURVIVAL. WOR+45 NAT/G VOL/ASSN
LEGIT ADMIN ARMS/CONT COERCE DISPL ORD/FREE PWR
...POLICY INT/LAW JURID COLD/WAR 20. PAGE 101 B2047
INT/ORG
ADJUD
SOVEREIGN

S64
KENNAN G.F.,"POLYCENTRISM AND WESTERN POLICY." ASIA
CHINA/COM COM FUT USA+45 USSR NAT/G ACT/RES DOMIN
EDU/PROP EXEC COERCE DISPL PERCEPT...POLICY
COLD/WAR 20. PAGE 59 B1192
RIGID/FLEX
ATTIT
DIPLOM

DISPLACEMENT....SEE DISPL

DISPUTE, RESOLUTION OF....SEE ADJUD

DISRAELI/B....BENJAMIN DISRAELI

DIST/IND....DISTRIBUTIVE SYSTEM

N
MARKETING INFORMATION GUIDE. USA+45 ECO/DEV FINAN
ADMIN GP/REL. PAGE 1 B0018
BIBLIOG/A
DIST/IND
MARKET
ECO/TAC

N
US SUPERINTENDENT OF DOCUMENTS,INTERSTATE COMMERCE
(PRICE LIST 59). USA+45 LAW LOC/G NAT/G LEGIS
TARIFFS TAX ADMIN CONTROL HEALTH DECISION. PAGE 111
B2239
BIBLIOG/A
DIST/IND
GOV/REL
PROVS

N
US SUPERINTENDENT OF DOCUMENTS,TRANSPORTATION:
HIGHWAYS, ROADS, AND POSTAL SERVICE (PRICE LIST
25). PANAMA USA+45 LAW FORCES DIPLOM ADMIN GOV/REL
HEALTH MGT. PAGE 111 B2243
BIBLIOG/A
DIST/IND
SERV/IND
NAT/G

N19
DOTSON A.,PRODUCTION PLANNING IN THE PATENT OFFICE
(PAMPHLET). USA+45 DIST/IND PROB/SOLV PRODUC...MGT
PHIL/SCI 20 BUR/BUDGET PATENT/OFF. PAGE 30 B0610
EFFICIENCY
PLAN
NAT/G
ADMIN

B40
GAUS J.M.,PUBLIC ADMINISTRATION AND THE UNITED
STATES DEPARTMENT OF AGRICULTURE. USA-45 STRUCT
DIST/IND FINAN MARKET EX/STRUC PROB/SOLV GIVE
PRODUC...POLICY GEOG CHARTS 20 DEPT/AGRI. PAGE 39
B0786
ADMIN
AGRI
DELIB/GP
OP/RES

B47

REDFORD E.S.,FIELD ADMINISTRATION OF WARTIME   ADMIN
RATIONING. USA-45 CONSTN ELITES DIST/IND WORKER   NAT/G
CONTROL WAR GOV/REL ADJUST RIGID/FLEX 20 OPA.   PROB/SOLV
PAGE 87 B1752   RATION

S47

TURNER R.H.,"THE NAVY DISBURSING OFFICER AS A   FORCES
BUREAUCRAT" (BMR)" USA-45 LAW STRATA DIST/IND WAR   ADMIN
PWR...SOC 20 BUREAUCRCY. PAGE 106 B2140   PERSON
  ROLE

B50

KOENIG L.W.,THE SALE OF THE TANKERS. USA+45 SEA   NAT/G
DIST/IND POL/PAR DIPLOM ADMIN CIVMIL/REL ATTIT   POLICY
...DECISION 20 PRESIDENT DEPT/STATE. PAGE 60 B1223   PLAN
  GOV/REL

B51

BERTON P.A.,MANCHURIA: AN ANNOTATED BIBLIOGRAPHY.   BIBLIOG/A
ASIA DIST/IND ADMIN...SOC 20. PAGE 11 B0231   MARXISM
  ECO/UNDEV
  COLONIAL

B53

ROBINSON E.A.G.,THE STRUCTURE OF COMPETITIVE   INDUS
INDUSTRY. UK ECO/DEV DIST/IND MARKET TEC/DEV DIPLOM   PRODUC
EDU/PROP ADMIN EFFICIENCY WEALTH...MGT 19/20.   WORKER
PAGE 89 B1798   OPTIMAL

B54

LOCKLIN D.P.,ECONOMICS OF TRANSPORTATION (4TH ED.).   ECO/DEV
USA+45 SEA AIR LAW FINAN LG/CO EX/STRUC   DIST/IND
ADMIN CONTROL...STAT CHARTS 19/20 RAILROAD   ECO/TAC
PUB/TRANS. PAGE 66 B1335   TEC/DEV

B56

ALEXANDER R.S.,INDUSTRIAL MARKETING. USA+45 ECO/DEV   INDUS
DIST/IND FINAN NAT/G ACT/RES CAP/ISM PRICE CONTROL   MARKET
...POLICY MGT 20. PAGE 4 B0072   ECO/TAC
  PLAN

B58

OPERATIONS RESEARCH SOCIETY,A COMPREHENSIVE   BIBLIOG/A
BIBLIOGRAPHY ON OPERATIONS RESEARCH; THROUGH 1956   COMPUT/IR
WITH SUPPLEMENT FOR 1957. COM/IND DIST/IND INDUS   OP/RES
ADMIN...DECISION MATH STAT METH 20. PAGE 80 B1612   MGT

B58

US HOUSE COMM POST OFFICE,MANPOWER UTILIZATION IN   ADMIN
THE FEDERAL GOVERNMENT. USA+45 DIST/IND EX/STRUC   WORKER
LEGIS CONFER EFFICIENCY 20 CONGRESS CIVIL/SERV.   DELIB/GP
PAGE 109 B2195   NAT/G

B58

US HOUSE COMM POST OFFICE,MANPOWER UTILIZATION IN   ADMIN
THE FEDERAL GOVERNMENT. USA+45 DIST/IND EX/STRUC   WORKER
LEGIS CONFER EFFICIENCY 20 CONGRESS CIVIL/SERV.   DELIB/GP
PAGE 109 B2196   NAT/G

B58

US HOUSE COMM POST OFFICE,TRAINING OF FEDERAL   LEGIS
EMPLOYEES. USA+45 DIST/IND NAT/G EX/STRUC EDU/PROP   DELIB/GP
CONFER GOV/REL EFFICIENCY SKILL 20 CONGRESS   WORKER
CIVIL/SERV. PAGE 109 B2197   ADMIN

B59

YALE UNIV BUR OF HIGHWAY TRAF,URBAN TRANSPORTATION   ADMIN
ADMINISTRATION. FUT USA+45 CONSTRUC ACT/RES BUDGET   DIST/IND
...CENSUS 20 PUB/TRANS. PAGE 118 B2388   LOC/G
  PLAN

B60

CAMPBELL R.W.,SOVIET ECONOMIC POWER. COM USA+45   ECO/DEV
DIST/IND MARKET TOP/EX ACT/RES CAP/ISM ECO/TAC   PLAN
DOMIN EDU/PROP ADMIN ROUTINE DRIVE...MATH TIME/SEQ   SOCISM
CHARTS WORK 20. PAGE 18 B0371   USSR

B60

HOVING W.,THE DISTRIBUTION REVOLUTION. WOR+45   DIST/IND
ECO/DEV FINAN SERV/IND PRESS PRICE INCOME PRODUC   MARKET
...MGT 20. PAGE 52 B1049   ECO/TAC
  TASK

S60

"THE EMERGING COMMON MARKETS IN LATIN AMERICA." FUT   FINAN
L/A+17C STRATA DIST/IND INDUS LABOR NAT/G LEGIS   ECO/UNDEV
ECO/TAC ADMIN RIGID/FLEX HEALTH...NEW/IDEA TIME/SEQ   INT/TRADE
OAS. PAGE 2 B0039

S60

MORALES C.J.,"TRADE AND ECONOMIC INTEGRATION IN   FINAN
LATIN AMERICA." FUT L/A+17C LAW STRATA ECO/UNDEV   INT/TRADE
DIST/IND INDUS LABOR NAT/G LEGIS ECO/TAC ADMIN   REGION
RIGID/FLEX WEALTH...CONCPT NEW/IDEA CONT/OBS
TIME/SEQ WORK 20. PAGE 75 B1519

B61

BRADY R.A.,ORGANIZATION, AUTOMATION, AND SOCIETY.   TEC/DEV
USA+45 AGRI COM/IND DIST/IND MARKET CREATE   INDUS
...DECISION MGT 20. PAGE 14 B0296   AUTOMAT
  ADMIN

B61

FRIEDMANN W.G.,JOINT INTERNATIONAL BUSINESS   ECO/UNDEV
VENTURES. ASIA ISLAM L/A+17C ECO/DEV DIST/IND FINAN   INT/TRADE
PROC/MFG FACE/GP LG/CO NAT/G VOL/ASSN CONSULT
EX/STRUC PLAN ADMIN ROUTINE WEALTH...OLD/LIB WORK
20. PAGE 37 B0760

B61

HALL M.,DISTRIBUTION IN GREAT BRITAIN AND NORTH   DIST/IND
AMERICA. CANADA UK USA+45 ECO/DEV INDUS MARKET   PRODUC
EFFICIENCY PROFIT...MGT CHARTS 20. PAGE 46 B0924   ECO/TAC

CAP/ISM
B61

JACOBS J.,THE DEATH AND LIFE OF GREAT AMERICAN   MUNIC
CITIES. USA+45 SOCIETY DIST/IND CREATE PROB/SOLV   PLAN
ADMIN...GEOG SOC CENSUS 20 URBAN/RNWL. PAGE 55   ADJUST
B1113   HABITAT

B61

LAHAYE R.,LES ENTREPRISES PUBLIQUES AU MAROC.   NAT/G
FRANCE MOROCCO LAW DIST/IND EXTR/IND FINAN CONSULT   INDUS
PLAN TEC/DEV ADMIN AGREE CONTROL OWN...POLICY 20.   ECO/UNDEV
PAGE 62 B1250   ECO/TAC

B61

WILLOUGHBY W.R.,THE ST LAWRENCE WATERWAY: A STUDY   LEGIS
IN POLITICS AND DIPLOMACY. USA+45 ECO/DEV COM/IND   INT/TRADE
INT/ORG CONSULT DELIB/GP ACT/RES TEC/DEV DIPLOM   CANADA
ECO/TAC ROUTINE...TIME/SEQ 20. PAGE 117 B2357   DIST/IND

B62

BECKMAN T.N.,MARKETING (7TH ED.). USA+45 SOCIETY   MARKET
ECO/DEV NAT/G PRICE EFFICIENCY INCOME ATTIT WEALTH   ECO/TAC
...MGT BIBLIOG 20. PAGE 10 B0205   DIST/IND
  POLICY

B62

FARBER W.O.,GOVERNMENT OF SOUTH DAKOTA. USA+45   PROVS
DIST/IND POL/PAR CHIEF EX/STRUC LEGIS ECO/TAC GIVE   LOC/G
EDU/PROP CT/SYS PARTIC...T 20 SOUTH/DAK GOVERNOR.   ADMIN
PAGE 35 B0704   CONSTN

B62

INSTITUTE OF PUBLIC ADMIN,A SHORT HISTORY OF THE   ADMIN
PUBLIC SERVICE IN IRELAND. IRELAND UK DIST/IND   WORKER
INGP/REL FEDERAL 13/20 CIVIL/SERV. PAGE 54 B1091   GOV/REL
  NAT/G

L62

WATERSTON A.,"PLANNING IN MOROCCO, ORGANIZATION AND   NAT/G
IMPLEMENTATION. BALTIMORE: HOPKINS ECON. DEVELOP.   PLAN
INT. BANK FOR." ISLAM ECO/DEV AGRI DIST/IND INDUS   MOROCCO
PROC/MFG SERV/IND LOC/G EX/STRUC ECO/TAC PWR WEALTH
TOT/POP VAL/FREE 20. PAGE 114 B2302

S63

BARZANSKI S.,"REGIONAL UNDERDEVELOPMENT IN THE   ECO/UNDEV
EUROPEAN ECONOMIC COMMUNITY." EUR+WWI ELITES   PLAN
DIST/IND MARKET VOL/ASSN CONSULT EX/STRUC ECO/TAC
RIGID/FLEX WEALTH EEC OEEC 20. PAGE 9 B0192

S63

CLEMHOUT S.,"PRODUCTION FUNCTION ANALYSIS APPLIED   ECO/DEV
TO THE LEONTIEF SCARCE-FACTOR PARADOX OF   ECO/TAC
INTERNATIONAL TRADE." EUR+WWI USA+45 DIST/IND NAT/G
PLAN TEC/DEV DIPLOM PWR WEALTH...MGT METH/CNCPT
CONT/OBS CON/ANAL CHARTS SIMUL GEN/LAWS 20. PAGE 21
B0436

S63

DUCROS B.,"MOBILISATION DES RESSOURCES PRODUCTIVES   ECO/UNDEV
ET DEVELOPPEMENT." FUT INTELL SOCIETY COM/IND   TEC/DEV
DIST/IND EXTR/IND FINAN INDUS ROUTINE WEALTH
...METH/CNCPT OBS 20. PAGE 31 B0625

B64

BENNETT H.A.,THE COMMISSION AND THE COMMON LAW: A   ADJUD
STUDY IN ADMINISTRATIVE ADJUDICATION. LAW ADMIN   DELIB/GP
CT/SYS LOBBY SANCTION GOV/REL 20 COMMON/LAW.   DIST/IND
PAGE 10 B0212   POLICY

B64

CHANDLER A.D. JR.,GIANT ENTERPRISE: FORD, GENERAL   LG/CO
MOTORS, AND THE AUTOMOBILE INDUSTRY; SOURCES AND   DIST/IND
READINGS. USA+45 USA-45 FINAN MARKET CREATE   LABOR
...TIME/SEQ ANTHOL 20 AUTOMOBILE. PAGE 20 B0404   MGT

B64

FISK W.M.,ADMINISTRATIVE PROCEDURE IN A REGULATORY   SERV/IND
AGENCY: THE CAB AND THE NEW YORK-CHICAGO CASE   ECO/DEV
(PAMPHLET). USA+45 DIST/IND ADMIN CONTROL LOBBY   AIR
GP/REL ROLE ORD/FREE NEWYORK/C CHICAGO CAB. PAGE 36   JURID
B0727

B64

GARFIELD PJ   LOVEJOY WF.PUBLIC UTILITY   T
ECONOMICS. DIST/IND FINAN MARKET MUNIC ADMIN COST   ECO/TAC
DEMAND...TECHNIC JURID 20 MONOPOLY. PAGE 39 B0782   OWN
  SERV/IND

S64

HUELIN D.,"ECONOMIC INTEGRATION IN LATIN AMERICAN: MARKET
PROGRESS AND PROBLEMS." L/A+17C ECO/DEV AGRI   ECO/UNDEV
DIST/IND FINAN INDUS NAT/G VOL/ASSN CONSULT   INT/TRADE
DELIB/GP EX/STRUC ACT/RES PLAN TEC/DEV ECO/TAC
ROUTINE BAL/PAY WEALTH WORK 20. PAGE 52 B1058

N64

US SENATE COMM GOVT OPERATIONS,METROPOLITAN   BIBLIOG/A
AMERICA: A SELECTED BIBLIOGRAPHY (PAMPHLET). USA+45   MUNIC
DIST/IND FINAN LOC/G EDU/PROP ADMIN HEALTH 20.   GOV/REL
PAGE 110 B2214   DECISION

B65

KELLEY E.J.,MARKETING: STRATEGY AND FUNCTIONS.   MARKET
ECO/DEV INDUS PLAN PRICE CONTROL ROUTINE...MGT   DIST/IND
BIBLIOG 20. PAGE 59 B1191   POLICY
  ECO/TAC

B65

LEYS C.T.,FEDERATION IN EAST AFRICA. LAW AGRI   FEDERAL
DIST/IND FINAN INT/ORG LABOR INT/TRADE CONFER ADMIN   REGION
CONTROL GP/REL...ANTHOL 20 AFRICA/E. PAGE 65 B1310   ECO/UNDEV
  PLAN

B66
GREENE L.E.,GOVERNMENT IN TENNESSEE (2ND ED.).   PROVS
USA+45 DIST/IND INDUS POL/PAR EX/STRUC LEGIS PLAN   LOC/G
BUDGET GIVE CT/SYS...MGT T 20 TENNESSEE. PAGE 43   CONSTN
B0866   ADMIN

B66
GRETHER E.T.,MARKETING AND PUBLIC POLICY. USA+45   MARKET
ECO/DEV DIST/IND NAT/G PLAN CAP/ISM PRICE CONTROL   PROB/SOLV
...GEOG MGT 20. PAGE 43 B0874   ECO/TAC
                                                        POLICY

B66
WHITNAH D.R.,SAFER SKYWAYS. DIST/IND DELIB/GP   ADMIN
FORCES TOP/EX WORKER TEC/DEV ROUTINE WAR CIVMIL/REL   NAT/G
COST...TIME/SEQ 20 FAA CAB. PAGE 116 B2342   AIR
                                                        GOV/REL

B67
BUDER S.,PULLMAN: AN EXPERIMENT IN INDUSTRIAL ORDER   DIST/IND
AND COMMUNITY PLANNING, 1880-1930. USA-45 SOCIETY   INDUS
LABOR LG/CO CREATE PROB/SOLV CONTROL GP/REL   MUNIC
EFFICIENCY ATTIT...MGT BIBLIOG 19/20 PULLMAN.   PLAN
PAGE 17 B0337

B67
FARRIS M.T.,MODERN TRANSPORTATION: SELECTED   DIST/IND
READINGS. UNIV CONTROL...POLICY ANTHOL T 20.   MGT
PAGE 35 B0706   COST

B67
GREENE L.S.,AMERICAN GOVERNMENT POLICIES AND   POLICY
FUNCTIONS. USA+45 LAW AGRI DIST/IND LABOR MUNIC   NAT/G
BUDGET DIPLOM EDU/PROP ORD/FREE...BIBLIOG T 20.   ADMIN
PAGE 43 B0867   DECISION

B67
NORTHRUP H.R.,RESTRICTIVE LABOR PRACTICES IN THE   DIST/IND
SUPERMARKET INDUSTRY. USA+45 INDUS WORKER TEC/DEV   MARKET
BARGAIN PAY CONTROL GP/REL COST...STAT CHARTS NLRB.   LABOR
PAGE 79 B1592   MGT

B67
UNITED NATIONS,UNITED NATIONS PUBLICATIONS: BIBLIOG/A
1945-1966. WOR+45 COM/IND DIST/IND FINAN TEC/DEV   INT/ORG
ADMIN...POLICY INT/LAW MGT CHARTS 20 UN UNESCO.   DIPLOM
PAGE 107 B2162   WRITING

L67
TRAVERS H. JR.,"AN EXAMINATION OF THE CAB'S MERGER   ADJUD
POLICY." USA+45 USA-45 LAW NAT/G LEGIS PLAN ADMIN   LG/CO
...DECISION 20 CONGRESS. PAGE 105 B2125   POLICY
                                                        DIST/IND

S67
FOX R.G.,"FAMILY, CASTE, AND COMMERCE IN A NORTH   CULTURE
INDIAN MARKET TOWN." INDIA STRATA AGRI FACE/GP FAM   GP/REL
NEIGH OP/RES BARGAIN ADMIN ROUTINE WEALTH...SOC   ECO/UNDEV
CHARTS 20. PAGE 37 B0747   DIST/IND

S67
GOLIGHTLY H.O.,"THE AIRLINES: A CASE STUDY IN   DIST/IND
MANAGEMENT INNOVATION." USA+45 AIR FINAN INDUS   MARKET
TOP/EX CREATE PLAN PROB/SOLV ADMIN EXEC PROFIT   MGT
...DECISION 20. PAGE 40 B0820   TEC/DEV

N67
US SENATE COMM AERO SPACE SCI,AERONAUTICAL RESEARCH   DIST/IND
AND DEVELOPMENT POLICY; HEARINGS, COMM ON   SPACE
AERONAUTICAL AND SPACE SCIENCES...1967 (PAMPHLET).   NAT/G
R+D PROB/SOLV EXEC GOV/REL 20 DEPT/DEFEN FAA NASA   PLAN
CONGRESS. PAGE 109 B2210

DISTRIBUTIVE SYSTEM....SEE DIST/IND

DISTRICT COURTS....SEE COURT/DIST

DISTRICT OF COLUMBIA....SEE WASHING/DC

DISTRICTING...SEE APPORT

DIVORCE....DIVORCE

DIXON D.F. B0599

DIXON/YATE....DIXON-YATES BILL

DJILAS M. B0600

DOC/ANAL....CONVENTIONAL CONTENT ANALYSIS

DODD/TJ....SENATOR THOMAS J. DODD

DODDS H.W. B0601

DODSON D.W. B0602

DOERN G.B. B0603

DOHERTY D.K. B0604

DOMIN....DOMINATION THROUGH USE OF ESTABLISHED POWER

B00
MORRIS H.C.,THE HISTORY OF COLONIZATION. WOR+45   DOMIN
WOR-45 ECO/DEV ECO/UNDEV INT/ORG ACT/RES PLAN   SOVEREIGN
ECO/TAC LEGIT ROUTINE COERCE ATTIT DRIVE ALL/VALS   COLONIAL

...GEOG TREND 19. PAGE 76 B1528

B16
TREITSCHKE H.,POLITICS. UNIV SOCIETY STRATA NAT/G   EXEC
EX/STRUC LEGIS DOMIN EDU/PROP ATTIT PWR RESPECT   ELITES
...CONCPT TIME/SEQ GEN/LAWS TOT/POP 20. PAGE 105   GERMANY
B2127

B20
HALDANE R.B.,BEFORE THE WAR. MOD/EUR SOCIETY   POLICY
INT/ORG NAT/G DELIB/GP PLAN DOMIN EDU/PROP LEGIT   DIPLOM
ADMIN COERCE ATTIT DRIVE MORAL ORD/FREE PWR...SOC   UK
CONCPT SELF/OBS RECORD BIOG TIME/SEQ. PAGE 45 B0921

B23
FRANK T.,A HISTORY OF ROME. MEDIT-7 INTELL SOCIETY   EXEC
LOC/G NAT/G POL/PAR FORCES DOMIN LEGIT   STRUCT
ALL/VALS...POLICY CONCPT TIME/SEQ GEN/LAWS ROM/EMP   ELITES
ROM/EMP. PAGE 37 B0749

L23
DOUGLAS P.H.,"OCCUPATIONAL V PROPORTIONAL   REPRESENT
REPRESENTATION." INDUS NAT/G PLAN ROUTINE SUFF   PROF/ORG
CONSEN DRIVE...CONCPT CLASSIF. PAGE 30 B0612   DOMIN
                                                        INGP/REL

B26
MOON P.T.,IMPERIALISM AND WORLD POLITICS. AFR ASIA   WEALTH
ISLAM MOD/EUR S/ASIA USA-45 SOCIETY NAT/G EX/STRUC   TIME/SEQ
BAL/PWR DOMIN COLONIAL NAT/LISM ATTIT DRIVE PWR   CAP/ISM
...GEOG SOC 20. PAGE 75 B1510   DIPLOM

B27
DICKINSON J.,ADMINISTRATIVE JUSTICE AND THE   CT/SYS
SUPREMACY OF LAW IN THE UNITED STATES. USA-45 LAW   ADJUD
INDUS DOMIN EDU/PROP CONTROL EXEC GP/REL ORD/FREE   ADMIN
...POLICY JURID 19/20. PAGE 29 B0586   NAT/G

B28
HARDMAN J.B.,AMERICAN LABOR DYNAMICS. WORKER   LABOR
ECO/TAC DOMIN ADJUD LEAD LOBBY PWR...POLICY MGT.   INGP/REL
PAGE 47 B0944   ATTIT
                                                        GP/REL

B29
ROBERTS S.H.,HISTORY OF FRENCH COLONIAL POLICY. AFR   INT/ORG
ASIA L/A+17C S/ASIA CULTURE ECO/DEV ECO/UNDEV FINAN   ACT/RES
NAT/G PLAN ECO/TAC DOMIN ROUTINE SOVEREIGN...OBS   FRANCE
HIST/WRIT TREND CHARTS VAL/FREE 19/20. PAGE 89   COLONIAL
B1796

B30
ZINK H.,CITY BOSSES IN THE UNITED STATES: A STUDY   LOC/G
OF TWENTY MUNICIPAL BOSSES. USA-45 INDUS MUNIC   DOMIN
NEIGH POL/PAR ADMIN CRIME INGP/REL PERS/REL PWR   BIOG
...PERS/COMP 20 BOSSISM. PAGE 119 B2403   LEAD

B31
DEKAT A.D.A.,COLONIAL POLICY. S/ASIA CULTURE   DRIVE
EX/STRUC ECO/TAC DOMIN ADMIN COLONIAL ROUTINE   PWR
SOVEREIGN WEALTH...POLICY MGT RECORD KNO/TEST SAMP.   INDONESIA
PAGE 28 B0570   NETHERLAND

B36
ROBINSON H.,DEVELOPMENT OF THE BRITISH EMPIRE.   NAT/G
WOR-45 CULTURE SOCIETY STRUCT ECO/DEV ECO/UNDEV   HIST/WRIT
INT/ORG VOL/ASSN FORCES CREATE PLAN DOMIN EDU/PROP   UK
ADMIN COLONIAL PWR WEALTH...POLICY GEOG CHARTS
CMN/WLTH 16/20. PAGE 89 B1800

B39
HITLER A.,MEIN KAMPF. EUR+WWI FUT MOD/EUR STRUCT   PWR
INT/ORG LABOR NAT/G POL/PAR FORCES CREATE PLAN   NEW/IDEA
BAL/PWR DIPLOM ECO/TAC DOMIN EDU/PROP ADMIN COERCE   WAR
ATTIT...SOCIALIST BIOG TREND NAZI. PAGE 50 B1020

B39
ZIMMERN A.,MODERN POLITICAL DOCTRINE. WOR-45   NAT/G
CULTURE SOCIETY ECO/UNDEV DELIB/GP EX/STRUC CREATE   ECO/TAC
DOMIN COERCE NAT/LISM ATTIT RIGID/FLEX ORD/FREE PWR   BAL/PWR
WEALTH...POLICY CONCPT OBS TIME/SEQ TREND TOT/POP   INT/TRADE
LEAGUE/NAT 20. PAGE 119 B2402

S40
GERTH H.,"THE NAZI PARTY: ITS LEADERSHIP AND   POL/PAR
COMPOSITION" (BMR)" GERMANY ELITES STRATA STRUCT   DOMIN
EX/STRUC FORCES ECO/TAC CT/SYS CHOOSE TOTALISM   LEAD
AGE/Y AUTHORIT PWR 20. PAGE 39 B0792   ADMIN

B43
CLARKE M.P.,PARLIAMENTARY PRIVILEGE IN THE AMERICAN   LEGIS
COLONIES. PROVS DOMIN ADMIN REPRESENT GOV/REL   PWR
ORD/FREE...BIBLIOG/A 17/18. PAGE 21 B0433   COLONIAL
                                                        PARL/PROC

B44
DAVIS H.E.,PIONEERS IN WORLD ORDER. WOR-45 CONSTN   INT/ORG
ECO/TAC DOMIN EDU/PROP LEGIT ADJUD ADMIN ARMS/CONT   ROUTINE
CHOOSE KNOWL ORD/FREE...POLICY JURID SOC STAT OBS
CENSUS TIME/SEQ ANTHOL LEAGUE/NAT 20. PAGE 26 B0537

B47
FLYNN E.J.,YOU'RE THE BOSS. USA-45 ELITES TOP/EX   LOC/G
DOMIN CONTROL EXEC LEAD REPRESENT 19/20 NEWYORK/C   MUNIC
ROOSEVLT/F FLYNN/BOSS BOSSISM. PAGE 36 B0732   BIOG
                                                        POL/PAR

B49
BUSH V.,MODERN ARMS AND FREE MEN. WOR-45 SOCIETY   TEC/DEV
NAT/G ECO/TAC DOMIN LEGIT EXEC COERCE DETER ATTIT   FORCES
DRIVE ORD/FREE PWR...CONCPT MYTH COLD/WAR 20   NUC/PWR
COLD/WAR. PAGE 18 B0361   WAR

L49
FAINSED M.,"RECENT DEVELOPMENTS IN SOVIET PUBLIC   DOMIN

ADMINISTRATION." USSR EXEC 20. PAGE 34 B0699
CONTROL
CENTRAL
EX/STRUC
L49

MARX C.M.,"ADMINISTRATIVE ETHICS AND THE RULE OF
LAW." USA+45 ELITES ACT/RES DOMIN NEUTRAL ROUTINE
INGP/REL ORD/FREE...JURID IDEA/COMP. PAGE 70 B1417
ADMIN
LAW

B50
PERHAM M.,COLONIAL GOVERNMENT: ANNOTATED READING
LIST ON BRITISH COLONIAL GOVERNMENT. UK WOR+45
WOR-45 ECO/UNDEV INT/ORG LEGIS FOR/AID INT/TRADE
DOMIN ADMIN REV 20. PAGE 82 B1655
BIBLIOG/A
COLONIAL
GOV/REL
NAT/G

B50
WADE E.C.S.,CONSTITUTIONAL LAW: AN OUTLINE OF THE
LAW AND PRACTICE OF THE CONSTITUTION. UK LEGIS
DOMIN ADMIN GP/REL 16/20 CMN/WLTH PARLIAMENT
ENGLSH/LAW. PAGE 112 B2269
CONSTN
NAT/G
PARL/PROC
LAW

C50
SIMON H.A.,"PUBLIC ADMINISTRATION." LG/CO SML/CO
PLAN DOMIN LEAD GP/REL DRIVE PERCEPT ALL/VALS
...POLICY BIBLIOG/A 20. PAGE 97 B1957
MGT
ADMIN
DECISION
EX/STRUC

C50
WAGER P.W.,"COUNTY GOVERNMENT ACROSS THE NATION."
USA+45 CONSTN COM/IND FINAN SCHOOL DOMIN CT/SYS
LEAD GOV/REL...STAT BIBLIOG 20. PAGE 112 B2272
LOC/G
PROVS
ADMIN
ROUTINE

B51
DIMOCK M.E.,FREE ENTERPRISE AND THE ADMINISTRATIVE
STATE. FINAN LG/CO BARGAIN BUDGET DOMIN CONTROL
INGP/REL EFFICIENCY 20. PAGE 29 B0595
CAP/ISM
ADMIN
MGT
MARKET

B51
LASSWELL H.D.,THE POLITICAL WRITINGS OF HAROLD D
LASSWELL. UNIV DOMIN EXEC LEAD RATIONAL ATTIT DRIVE
ROLE ALL/VALS...OBS BIOG 20. PAGE 63 B1269
PERSON
PSY
INGP/REL
CONCPT

B51
LEITES N.,THE OPERATIONAL CODE OF THE POLITBURO.
COM USSR CREATE PLAN DOMIN LEGIT COERCE ALL/VALS
...SOC CONCPT MYTH TREND CON/ANAL GEN/LAWS 20
LENIN/VI STALIN/J. PAGE 64 B1284
DELIB/GP
ADMIN
SOCISM

S51
SHILS E.A.,"THE LEGISLATOR AND HIS ENVIRONMENT."
EX/STRUC DOMIN CONFER EFFICIENCY PWR MAJORIT.
PAGE 96 B1947
LEGIS
TOP/EX
ADMIN
DELIB/GP

S51
STEWART D.D.,"THE PLACE OF VOLUNTEER PARTICIPATION
IN BUREAUCRATIC ORGANIZATION." NAT/G DELIB/GP
OP/RES DOMIN LOBBY WAR ATTIT ROLE PWR. PAGE 101
B2035
ADMIN
PARTIC
VOL/ASSN
FORCES

B52
EGLE W.P.,ECONOMIC STABILIZATION. USA+45 SOCIETY
FINAN MARKET PLAN ECO/TAC DOMIN EDU/PROP LEGIT EXEC
WEALTH...CONCPT METH/CNCPT TREND HYPO/EXP GEN/METH
TOT/POP VAL/FREE 20. PAGE 32 B0656
NAT/G
ECO/DEV
CAP/ISM

B52
SELZNICK P.,THE ORGANIZATIONAL WEAPON: A STUDY OF
BOLSHEVIK STRATEGY AND TACTICS. USSR SOCIETY STRATA
LABOR DOMIN EDU/PROP PARTIC REV ATTIT PWR...POLICY
MGT CONCPT 20 BOLSHEVISM. PAGE 95 B1929
MARXISM
POL/PAR
LEAD
TOTALISM

C52
LASSWELL H.D.,"THE COMPARATIVE STUDY OF ELITES: AN
INTRODUCTION AND BIBLIOGRAPHY." STRATA POL/PAR
EDU/PROP ADMIN LOBBY COERCE ATTIT PERSON PWR
...BIBLIOG 20. PAGE 63 B1270
ELITES
LEAD
CONCPT
DOMIN

S53
MORRIS B.S.,"THE COMINFORM: A FIVE YEAR
PERSPECTIVE." COM UNIV USSR WOR+45 ECO/DEV POL/PAR
TOP/EX PLAN DOMIN ADMIN TOTALISM ATTIT ALL/VALS
...CONCPT TIME/SEQ TREND CON/ANAL WORK VAL/FREE 20.
PAGE 76 B1527
VOL/ASSN
EDU/PROP
DIPLOM

B54
COMBS C.H.,DECISION PROCESSES. INTELL SOCIETY
DELIB/GP CREATE TEC/DEV DOMIN LEGIT EXEC CHOOSE
DRIVE RIGID/FLEX KNOWL PWR...PHIL/SCI SOC
METH/CNCPT CONT/OBS REC/INT PERS/TEST SAMP/SIZ BIOG
SOC/EXP WORK. PAGE 22 B0455
MATH
DECISION

B54
GOULDNER A.W.,PATTERNS OF INDUSTRIAL BUREAUCRACY.
DOMIN ATTIT DRIVE...BIBLIOG 20 BUREAUCRCY. PAGE 42
B0844
ADMIN
INDUS
OP/RES
WORKER

B55
CHOWDHURI R.N.,INTERNATIONAL MANDATES AND
TRUSTEESHIP SYSTEMS. WOR+45 STRUCT ECO/UNDEV
INT/ORG LEGIS DOMIN EDU/PROP LEGIT ADJUD EXEC PWR
...CONCPT TIME/SEQ UN 20. PAGE 21 B0427
DELIB/GP
PLAN
SOVEREIGN

B56
MANNONI D.O.,PROSPERO AND CALIBAN: THE PSYCHOLOGY
OF COLONIZATION. AFR EUR+WWI FAM KIN MUNIC SECT
DOMIN ADMIN ATTIT DRIVE LOVE PWR RESPECT...PSY SOC
CONCPT MYTH OBS DEEP/INT BIOG GEN/METH MALAGASY 20.
PAGE 69 B1394
CULTURE
COLONIAL

B56
US HOUSE RULES COMM.,HEARINGS BEFORE A SPECIAL
SUBCOMMITTEE: ESTABLISHMENT OF A STANDING COMMITTEE
ON ADMINISTRATIVE PROCEDURE. PRACTICE. USA+45 LAW
EX/STRUC ADJUD CONTROL EXEC GOV/REL EFFICIENCY PWR
...POLICY INT 20 CONGRESS. PAGE 109 B2199
ADMIN
DOMIN
DELIB/GP
NAT/G

B56
WHYTE W.H. JR.,THE ORGANIZATION MAN. CULTURE FINAN
VOL/ASSN DOMIN EDU/PROP EXEC DISPL HABITAT ROLE
...PERS/TEST STERTYP. PAGE 116 B2343
ADMIN
LG/CO
PERSON
CONSEN

S56
CLEVELAND H.,"THE EXECUTIVE AND THE PUBLIC
INTEREST." USA+45 DOMIN ADMIN PWR...POLICY 20.
PAGE 21 B0437
LOBBY
REPRESENT
CHIEF
EXEC

C56
FALL B.B.,"THE VIET-MINH REGIME." VIETNAM LAW
ECO/UNDEV POL/PAR FORCES DOMIN WAR ATTIT MARXISM
...BIOG PREDICT BIBLIOG/A 20. PAGE 35 B0703
NAT/G
ADMIN
EX/STRUC
LEAD

C56
NEUMANN S.,"MODERN POLITICAL PARTIES: APPROACHES TO
COMPARATIVE POLITIC." FRANCE UK EX/STRUC DOMIN ADMIN
LEAD REPRESENT TOTALISM ATTIT...POLICY TREND
METH/COMP ANTHOL BIBLIOG/A 20 CMN/WLTH. PAGE 78
B1574
POL/PAR
GOV/COMP
ELITES
MAJORIT

B57
ARON R.,FRANCE DEFEATS EDC. EUR+WWI GERMANY LEGIS
DIPLOM DOMIN EDU/PROP ADMIN...HIST/WRIT 20. PAGE 7
B0136
INT/ORG
FORCES
DETER
FRANCE

B57
DJILAS M.,THE NEW CLASS: AN ANALYSIS OF THE
COMMUNIST SYSTEM. STRATA CAP/ISM ECO/TAC DOMIN
EDU/PROP LEGIT EXEC COERCE ATTIT PWR MARXISM
...MARXIST MGT CONCPT TIME/SEQ GEN/LAWS 20. PAGE 29
B0600
COM
POL/PAR
USSR
YUGOSLAVIA

B57
HUNTINGTON S.P.,THE SOLDIER AND THE STATE: THE
THEORY AND POLITICS OF CIVIL-MILITARY RELATIONS.
USA+45 USA-45 NAT/G PROF/ORG CONSULT DOMIN LEGIT
ROUTINE ATTIT PWR...CONCPT TIME/SEQ COLD/WAR 20.
PAGE 53 B1065
ACT/RES
FORCES

B57
LOEWENSTEIN K.,POLITICAL POWER AND THE GOVERNMENTAL
PROCESS. WOR+45 WOR-45 CONSTN NAT/G POL/PAR
EX/STRUC LEGIS TOP/EX DOMIN EDU/PROP LEGIT ADMIN
REGION CHOOSE ATTIT...JURID STERTYP GEN/LAWS 20.
PAGE 66 B1336
PWR
CONCPT

L57
HAAS E.B.,"REGIONAL INTEGRATION AND NATIONAL
POLICY." WOR+45 VOL/ASSN DELIB/GP EX/STRUC ECO/TAC
DOMIN EDU/PROP LEGIT COERCE ATTIT PERCEPT KNOWL
...TIME/SEQ COLD/WAR 20 UN. PAGE 45 B0908
INT/ORG
ORD/FREE
REGION

S57
HAILEY,"TOMORROW IN AFRICA." CONSTN SOCIETY LOC/G
NAT/G DOMIN ADJUD ADMIN GP/REL DISCRIM NAT/LISM
ATTIT MORAL ORD/FREE...PSY SOC CONCPT OBS RECORD
TREND GEN/LAWS CMN/WLTH 20. PAGE 45 B0917
AFR
PERSON
ELITES
RACE/REL

S57
RAPAPORT R.N.,"'DEMOCRATIZATION' AND AUTHORITY IN A
THERAPEUTIC COMMUNITY." OP/RES ADMIN PARTIC CENTRAL
ATTIT...POLICY DECISION. PAGE 86 B1735
PUB/INST
HEALTH
DOMIN
CLIENT

B58
BROWNE C.G.,THE CONCEPT OF LEADERSHIP. UNIV FACE/GP
DOMIN EDU/PROP LEGIT LEAD DRIVE PERSON PWR...MGT
SOC OBS SELF/OBS CONT/OBS INT PERS/TEST STERTYP
GEN/LAWS. PAGE 16 B0328
EXEC
CONCPT

B58
COLEMAN J.S.,NIGERIA: BACKGROUND TO NATIONALISM.
AFR SOCIETY ECO/DEV KIN LOC/G POL/PAR TEC/DEV DOMIN
ADMIN DRIVE PWR RESPECT...TRADIT SOC INT SAMP
TIME/SEQ 20. PAGE 22 B0452
NAT/G
NAT/LISM
NIGERIA

B58
MILLS C.W.,THE CAUSES OF WORLD WAR THREE. FUT
USA+45 INTELL NAT/G DOMIN EDU/PROP ADMIN WAR ATTIT
SOC. PAGE 74 B1487
CONSULT
PWR
ELITES
PEACE

B58
SKINNER G.W.,LEADERSHIP AND POWER IN THE CHINESE
COMMUNITY OF THAILAND. ASIA S/ASIA STRATA FACE/GP
KIN PROF/ORG VOL/ASSN EX/STRUC DOMIN PERSON RESPECT
...METH/CNCPT STAT INT QU BIOG CHARTS 20. PAGE 98
B1974
SOC
ELITES
THAILAND

B58
SPITZ D.,DEMOCRACY AND THE CHALLENGE OF POWER. FUT
USA+45 USA-45 LAW SOCIETY STRUCT LOC/G POL/PAR
PROVS DELIB/GP EX/STRUC LEGIS TOP/EX ACT/RES CREATE
DOMIN EDU/PROP LEGIT ADJUD ADMIN ATTIT DRIVE MORAL
ORD/FREE TOT/POP. PAGE 99 B2010
NAT/G
PWR

S58
BLAISDELL D.C.,"PRESSURE GROUPS, FOREIGN POLICIES,
AND INTERNATIONAL POLITICS." USA+45 WOR+45 INT/ORG
PLAN DOMIN EDU/PROP LEGIT ADMIN ROUTINE CHOOSE
PROF/ORG
PWR

...DECISION MGT METH/CNCPT CON/ANAL 20. PAGE 12
B0249

S58
DAHL R.A.,"A CRITIQUE OF THE RULING ELITE MODEL." CONCPT
USA+45 LOC/G MUNIC NAT/G POL/PAR PROVS DOMIN LEGIT STERTYP
ADMIN...METH/CNCPT HYPO/EXP. PAGE 25 B0520 ELITES

S58
DAVENPORT J.,"ARMS AND THE WELFARE STATE." INTELL USA+45
STRUCT FORCES CREATE ECO/TAC FOR/AID DOMIN LEGIT NAT/G
ADMIN WAR ORD/FREE PWR...POLICY SOC CONCPT MYTH OBS USSR
TREND COLD/WAR IOT/POP 20. PAGE 26 B0533

B59
GORDENKER L.,THE UNITED NATIONS AND THE PEACEFUL DELIB/GP
UNIFICATION OF KOREA. ASIA LAW LOC/G CONSULT KOREA
ACT/RES DIPLOM DOMIN LEGIT ADJUD ADMIN ORD/FREE INT/ORG
SOVEREIGN...INT GEN/METH UN COLD/WAR 20. PAGE 41
B0829

B59
JANOWITZ M.,SOCIOLOGY AND THE MILITARY FORCES
ESTABLISHMENT. USA+45 WOR+45 CULTURE SOCIETY SOC
PROF/ORG CONSULT EX/STRUC PLAN TEC/DEV DIPLOM DOMIN
COERCE DRIVE RIGID/FLEX ORD/FREE PWR SKILL COLD/WAR
20. PAGE 55 B1121

B59
MAYNTZ R.,PARTEIGRUPPEN IN DER GROSSSTADT. GERMANY MUNIC
STRATA STRUCT DOMIN CHOOSE 20. PAGE 71 B1437 MGT
POL/PAR
ATTIT

B59
YANG C.K.,A CHINESE VILLAGE IN EARLY COMMUNIST ASIA
TRANSITION. ECO/UNDEV AGRI FAM KIN MUNIC FORCES ROUTINE
PLAN ECO/TAC DOMIN EDU/PROP ATTIT DRIVE PWR RESPECT SOCISM
...SOC CONCPT METH/CNCPT OBS RECORD CON/ANAL CHARTS
WORK 20. PAGE 118 B2389

L59
BENNIS W.G.,"LEADERSHIP THEORY AND ADMINISTRATIVE LEAD
BEHAVIOR: THE PROBLEM OF AUTHORITY." ROUTINE...MGT ADMIN
HYPO/EXP. PAGE 10 B0214 DOMIN
PERS/REL

L59
RHODE W.E.,"COMMITTEE CLEARANCE OF ADMINISTRATIVE DECISION
DECISIONS." DELIB/GP LEGIS BUDGET DOMIN CIVMIL/REL ADMIN
20 CONGRESS. PAGE 87 B1768 OP/RES
NAT/G

S59
JANOWITZ M.,"CHANGING PATTERNS OF ORGANIZATIONAL FORCES
AUTHORITY: THE MILITARY ESTABLISHMENT" (BMR)" AUTHORIT
USA+45 ELITES STRUCT EX/STRUC PLAN DOMIN AUTOMAT ADMIN
NUC/PWR WEAPON 20. PAGE 55 B1122 TEC/DEV

S59
SIMPSON R.L.,"VERTICAL AND HORIZONTAL COMMUNICATION PERS/REL
IN FORMAL ORGANIZATION" USA+45 LG/CO EX/STRUC DOMIN AUTOMAT
CONTROL TASK INGP/REL TIME 20. PAGE 97 B1963 INDUS
WORKER

S59
SUTTON F.X.,"REPRESENTATION AND THE NATURE OF NAT/G
POLITICAL SYSTEMS." UNIV WOR-45 CULTURE SOCIETY CONCPT
STRATA INT/ORG FORCES JUDGE DOMIN LEGIT EXEC REGION
REPRESENT ATTIT ORD/FREE RESPECT...SOC HIST/WRIT
TIME/SEQ. PAGE 102 B2057

B60
ASPREMONT-LYNDEN H.,RAPPORT SUR L'ADMINISTRATION AFR
BELGE DU RUANDA-URUNDI PENDANT L'ANNEE 1959. COLONIAL
BELGIUM RWANDA AGRI INDUS DIPLOM ECO/TAC INT/TRADE ECO/UNDEV
DOMIN ADMIN RACE/REL...GEOG CENSUS 20 UN. PAGE 7 INT/ORG
B0143

B60
BASS B.M.,LEADERSHIP, PSYCHOLOGY, AND UNIV
ORGANIZATIONAL BEHAVIOR. DOMIN CHOOSE DRIVE PERSON FACE/GP
PWR RESPECT SKILL...SOC METH/CNCPT OBS. PAGE 9 DELIB/GP
B0193 ROUTINE

B60
CAMPBELL R.W.,SOVIET ECONOMIC POWER. COM USA+45 ECO/DEV
DIST/IND MARKET TOP/EX ACT/RES CAP/ISM ECO/TAC PLAN
DOMIN EDU/PROP ADMIN ROUTINE DRIVE...MATH TIME/SEQ SOCISM
CHARTS WORK 20. PAGE 18 B0371 USSR

B60
CORSON J.J.,GOVERNANCE OF COLLEGES AND ADMIN
UNIVERSITIES. STRUCT FINAN DELIB/GP DOMIN EDU/PROP EXEC
LEAD CHOOSE GP/REL CENTRAL COST PRIVIL SUPEGO ACADEM
ORD/FREE PWR...DECISION BIBLIOG. PAGE 24 B0481 HABITAT

B60
DRAPER T.,AMERICAN COMMUNISM AND SOVIET RUSSIA. COM
EUR+WWI USA+45 USSR INTELL AGRI COM/IND FINAN INDUS POL/PAR
LABOR PROF/ORG VOL/ASSN PLAN TEC/DEV DOMIN EDU/PROP
ADMIN COERCE REV PERSON PWR...POLICY CONCPT MYTH
19/20. PAGE 30 B0617

B60
GRUNDLICH T.,DIE TECHNIK DER DIKTATUR. ADMIN COERCE
TOTALISM ATTIT PWR...MGT CONCPT ARISTOTLE. PAGE 44 DOMIN
B0896 ORD/FREE
WAR

B60
LINDSAY K.,EUROPEAN ASSEMBLIES: THE EXPERIMENTAL VOL/ASSN
PERIOD 1949-1959. EUR+WWI ECO/DEV NAT/G POL/PAR INT/ORG
LEGIS TOP/EX ACT/RES PLAN ECO/TAC DOMIN LEGIT REGION

ROUTINE ATTIT DRIVE ORD/FREE PWR SKILL...SOC CONCPT
TREND CHARTS GEN/LAWS VAL/FREE. PAGE 65 B1315

B60
PIERCE R.A.,RUSSIAN CENTRAL ASIA, 1867-1917. ASIA COLONIAL
RUSSIA CULTURE AGRI INDUS EDU/PROP REV NAT/LISM DOMIN
...CHARTS BIBLIOG 19/20 BOLSHEVISM INTERVENT. ADMIN
PAGE 83 B1672 ECO/UNDEV

B60
WHEARE K.C.,THE CONSTITUTIONAL STRUCTURE OF THE CONSTN
COMMONWEALTH. UK EX/STRUC DIPLOM DOMIN ADMIN INT/ORG
COLONIAL CONTROL LEAD INGP/REL SUPEGO 20 CMN/WLTH. VOL/ASSN
PAGE 115 B2330 SOVEREIGN

S60
HERZ J.H.,"EAST GERMANY: PROGRESS AND PROSPECTS." POL/PAR
COM AGRI FINAN INDUS LOC/G NAT/G FORCES PLAN STRUCT
TEC/DEV DOMIN ADMIN COERCE DRIVE PERCEPT RIGID/FLEX GERMANY
MORAL ORD/FREE PWR...MARXIST PSY SOC RECORD STERTYP
WORK. PAGE 49 B0997

S60
NORTH R.C.,"DIE DISKREPANZ ZWISCHEN REALITAT UND SOCIETY
WUNSCHBILD ALS INNENPOLITISCHER FAKTOR." ASIA ECO/TAC
CHINA/COM COM FUT ECO/UNDEV NAT/G PLAN DOMIN ADMIN
COERCE PERCEPT...SOC MYTH GEN/METH WORK TOT/POP 20.
PAGE 79 B1589

S60
SCHACHTER O.,"THE ENFORCEMENT OF INTERNATIONAL INT/ORG
JUDICIAL AND ARBITRAL DECISIONS." WOR+45 NAT/G ADJUD
ECO/TAC DOMIN LEGIT ROUTINE COERCE ATTIT DRIVE INT/LAW
ALL/VALS PWR...METH/CNCPT TREND TOT/POP 20 UN.
PAGE 93 B1878

S60
SCHER S.,"CONGRESSIONAL COMMITTEE MEMBERS AND LEGIS
INDEPENDENT AGENCY OVERSEERS: A CASE STUDY." GOV/REL
DELIB/GP EX/STRUC JUDGE TOP/EX DOMIN ADMIN CONTROL LABOR
PWR...SOC/EXP HOUSE/REP CONGRESS. PAGE 93 B1886 ADJUD

C60
MCCLEERY R.,"COMMUNICATION PATTERNS AS BASES OF PERS/REL
SYSTEMS OF AUTHORITY AND POWER" IN THEORETICAL PUB/INST
STUDIES IN SOCIAL ORGAN. OF PRISON-BMR." USA+45 PWR
SOCIETY STRUCT EDU/PROP ADMIN CONTROL COERCE CRIME DOMIN
GP/REL AUTHORIT...SOC 20. PAGE 71 B1443

C60
SCHAPIRO L.B.,"THE COMMUNIST PARTY OF THE SOVIET POL/PAR
UNION." USSR INTELL CHIEF EX/STRUC FORCES DOMIN COM
ADMIN LEAD WAR ATTIT SOVEREIGN...POLICY BIBLIOG 20. REV
PAGE 93 B1881

B61
BARNES W.,THE FOREIGN SERVICE OF THE UNITED STATES. NAT/G
USA+45 USA-45 CONSTN INT/ORG POL/PAR CONSULT MGT
DELIB/GP LEGIS DOMIN EDU/PROP EXEC ATTIT RIGID/FLEX DIPLOM
ORD/FREE PWR...POLICY CONCPT STAT OBS RECORD BIOG
TIME/SEQ TREND. PAGE 9 B0188

B61
BISHOP D.G.,THE ADMINISTRATION OF BRITISH FOREIGN ROUTINE
RELATIONS. EUR+WWI MOD/EUR INT/ORG NAT/G POL/PAR PWR
DELIB/GP LEGIS TOP/EX ECO/TAC DOMIN EDU/PROP ADMIN DIPLOM
COERCE 20. PAGE 12 B0243 UK

B61
CARNEY D.E.,GOVERNMENT AND ECONOMY IN BRITISH WEST METH/COMP
AFRICA. GAMBIA GHANA NIGERIA SIER/LEONE DOMIN ADMIN COLONIAL
GOV/REL SOVEREIGN WEALTH LAISSEZ...BIBLIOG 20 ECO/TAC
CMN/WLTH. PAGE 19 B0384 ECO/UNDEV

B61
COHN B.S.,DEVELOPMENT AND IMPACT OF BRITISH BIBLIOG/A
ADMINISTRATION IN INDIA: A BIBLIOGRAPHIC ESSAY. COLONIAL
INDIA UK ECO/UNDEV NAT/G DOMIN...POLICY MGT SOC S/ASIA
19/20. PAGE 22 B0448 ADMIN

B61
HOUN F.W.,TO CHANGE A NATION: PROPAGANDA AND DOMIN
INDOCTRINATION IN COMMUNIST CHINA. CHINA/COM COM EDU/PROP
ACT/RES PLAN PRESS ADMIN FEEDBACK CENTRAL TOTALISM
EFFICIENCY ATTIT...PSY SOC 20. PAGE 52 B1048 MARXISM

B61
KOESTLER A.,THE LOTUS AND THE ROBOT. ASIA INDIA SECT
S/ASIA SOCIETY STRATA ECO/DEV AGRI INDUS FAM CREATE ECO/UNDEV
DOMIN EDU/PROP ADMIN COERCE ATTIT DRIVE SUPEGO
ORD/FREE PWR RESPECT WEALTH...MYTH OBS 20 CHINJAP.
PAGE 61 B1226

B61
MARVICK D.,POLITICAL DECISION-MAKERS. INTELL STRATA TOP/EX
NAT/G POL/PAR EX/STRUC LEGIS DOMIN EDU/PROP ATTIT BIOG
PERSON PWR...PSY STAT OBS CONT/OBS STAND/INT ELITES
UNPLAN/INT TIME/SEQ CHARTS STERTYP VAL/FREE.
PAGE 70 B1416

B61
PETRULLO L.,LEADERSHIP AND INTERPERSONAL BEHAVIOR. PERSON
FACE/GP FAM PROF/ORG EX/STRUC FORCES DOMIN WAR ATTIT
GP/REL PERS/REL EFFICIENCY PRODUC PWR...MGT PSY. LEAD
PAGE 82 B1663 HABITAT

B61
STRAUSS E.,THE RULING SERVANTS. FRANCE UK USSR ADMIN
WOR+45 WOR-45 NAT/G CONSULT DELIB/GP EX/STRUC PWR
TOP/EX DOMIN EDU/PROP LEGIT ROUTINE...MGT TIME/SEQ ELITES
STERTYP 20. PAGE 101 B2051

B61
WEST F.J.,POLITICAL ADVANCEMENT IN THE SOUTH S/ASIA

PACIFIC. CONSTN CULTURE POL/PAR LEGIS DOMIN ADMIN CHOOSE SOVEREIGN VAL/FREE 20 FIJI TAHITI SAMOA. PAGE 115 B2325 — LOC/G COLONIAL

S61
ANGLIN D.,"UNITED STATES OPPOSITION TO CANADIAN MEMBERSHIP IN THE PAN AMERICAN UNION: A CANADIAN VIEW." L/A+17C UK USA+45 VOL/ASSN DELIB/GP EX/STRUC PLAN DIPLOM DOMIN REGION ATTIT RIGID/FLEX PWR ...RELATIV CONCPT STERTYP CMN/WLTH OAS 20. PAGE 5 B0112 — INT/ORG CANADA

S61
LIEBENOW J.G.,"LEGITIMACY OF ALIEN RELATIONSHIP: THE NYATURU OF TANGANYIKA" (BMR)" AFR UK ADMIN LEAD CHOOSE 20 NYATURU TANGANYIKA. PAGE 65 B1312 — COLONIAL DOMIN LEGIT PWR

S61
TOMASIC D.,"POLITICAL LEADERSHIP IN CONTEMPORARY POLAND." COM EUR+WWI GERMANY NAT/G POL/PAR SECT DELIB/GP PLAN ECO/TAC DOMIN EDU/PROP PWR MARXISM ...MARXIST GEOG MGT CONCPT TIME/SEQ STERTYP 20. PAGE 105 B2114 — SOCIETY ROUTINE USSR POLAND

C61
VERBA S.,"SMALL GROUPS AND POLITICAL BEHAVIOR: A STUDY OF LEADERSHIP" DOMIN PARTIC ROUTINE GP/REL ATTIT DRIVE ALL/VALS...CONCPT IDEA/COMP LAB/EXP BIBLIOG METH. PAGE 112 B2259 — LEAD ELITES FACE/GP

B62
BAILEY S.D.,THE SECRETARIAT OF THE UNITED NATIONS. FUT WOR+45 DELIB/GP PLAN BAL/PWR DOMIN EDU/PROP ADMIN PEACE ATTIT PWR...DECISION CONCPT TREND CON/ANAL CHARTS UN VAL/FREE COLD/WAR 20. PAGE 8 B0162 — INT/ORG EXEC DIPLOM

B62
SIMON Y.R.,A GENERAL THEORY OF AUTHORITY. DOMIN ADMIN RATIONAL UTOPIA KNOWL MORAL PWR SOVEREIGN ...HUM CONCPT NEW/IDEA 20. PAGE 97 B1962 — PERS/REL PERSON SOCIETY ORD/FREE

B62
TAYLOR D.,THE BRITISH IN AFRICA. UK CULTURE ECO/UNDEV INDUS DIPLOM INT/TRADE ADMIN WAR RACE/REL ORD/FREE SOVEREIGN...POLICY BIBLIOG 15/20 CMN/WLTH. PAGE 103 B2084 — AFR COLONIAL DOMIN

B62
THIERRY S.S.,LE VATICAN SECRET. CHRIST-17C EUR+WWI MOD/EUR VATICAN NAT/G SECT DELIB/GP DOMIN LEGIT SOVEREIGN. PAGE 104 B2096 — ADMIN EX/STRUC CATHISM DECISION

B62
US ADVISORY COMN INTERGOV REL,STATE CONSTITUTIONAL AND STATUTORY RESTRICTIONS UPON THE STRUCTURAL, FUNCTIONAL, AND PERSONAL POWERS OF LOCAL GOV'T. EX/STRUC ACT/RES DOMIN GOV/REL PWR...POLICY DECISION 17/20. PAGE 108 B2172 — LOC/G CONSTN PROVS LAW

B62
US SENATE COMM ON JUDICIARY,STATE DEPARTMENT SECURITY. USA+45 CHIEF TEC/DEV DOMIN ADMIN EXEC ATTIT ORD/FREE...POLICY CONGRESS DEPT/STATE PRESIDENT KENNEDY/JF KENNEDY/JF SENATE 20. PAGE 110 B2228 — CONTROL WORKER NAT/G GOV/REL

B62
WELLEQUET J.,LE CONGO BELGE ET LA WELTPOLITIK (1894-1914. GERMANY DOMIN EDU/PROP WAR ATTIT ...BIBLIOG T CONGO/LEOP. PAGE 115 B2318 — ADMIN DIPLOM GP/REL COLONIAL

S62
BRZEZINSKI Z.K.,"DEVIATION CONTROL: A STUDY IN THE DYNAMICS OF DOCTRINAL CONFLICT." WOR+45 WOR-45 VOL/ASSN CREATE BAL/PWR DOMIN EXEC DRIVE PERCEPT PWR...METH/CNCPT TIME/SEQ TREND 20. PAGE 16 B0333 — RIGID/FLEX ATTIT

S62
FESLER J.W.,"FRENCH FIELD ADMINISTRATION: THE BEGINNINGS." CHRIST-17C CULTURE SOCIETY STRATA NAT/G ECO/TAC DOMIN EDU/PROP LEGIT ADJUD COERCE ATTIT ALL/VALS...TIME/SEQ CON/ANAL GEN/METH VAL/FREE 13/15. PAGE 35 B0714 — EX/STRUC FRANCE

S62
HUDSON G.F.,"SOVIET FEARS OF THE WEST." COM USA+45 SOCIETY DELIB/GP EX/STRUC TOP/EX ACT/RES CREATE DOMIN EDU/PROP LEGIT ADMIN ROUTINE DRIVE PERSON RIGID/FLEX PWR...RECORD TIME/SEQ TOT/POP 20 STALIN/J. PAGE 52 B1057 — ATTIT MYTH GERMANY USSR

S62
JACOBSON H.K.,"THE UNITED NATIONS AND COLONIALISM: A TENTATIVE APPRAISAL." AFR FUT S/ASIA USA+45 USSR WOR+45 NAT/G DELIB/GP ECO/TAC DOMIN ADMIN ROUTINE COERCE ATTIT RIGID/FLEX ORD/FREE PWR ...OBS STERTYP UN 20. PAGE 55 B1115 — INT/ORG CONCPT COLONIAL

S62
MARTIN L.W.,"POLITICAL SETTLEMENTS AND ARMS CONTROL." COM EUR+WWI GERMANY USA+45 PROVS FORCES TOP/EX ACT/RES CREATE DOMIN LEGIT ROUTINE COERCE ATTIT RIGID/FLEX ORD/FREE PWR...METH/CNCPT RECORD GEN/LAWS 20. PAGE 70 B1410 — CONCPT ARMS/CONT

S62
MCCLELLAND C.A.,"DECISIONAL OPPORTUNITY AND POLITICAL CONTROVERSY." USA+45 NAT/G POL/PAR FORCES — ACT/RES PERCEPT

TOP/EX DOMIN ADMIN PEACE DRIVE ORD/FREE PWR ...DECISION SIMUL 20. PAGE 72 B1444 — DIPLOM

S62
READ W.H.,"UPWARD COMMUNICATION IN INDUSTRIAL HIERARCHIES." LG/CO TOP/EX PROB/SOLV DOMIN EXEC PERS/REL ATTIT DRIVE PERCEPT...CORREL STAT CHARTS 20. PAGE 86 B1747 — ADMIN INGP/REL PSY MGT

S62
TANNENBAUM A.S.,"CONTROL IN ORGANIZATIONS: INDIVIDUAL ADJUSTMENT AND ORGANIZATIONAL PERFORMANCE." DOMIN PARTIC REPRESENT INGP/REL PRODUC ATTIT DRIVE PWR...PSY CORREL. PAGE 102 B2073 — ADMIN MGT STRUCT CONTROL

B63
BLONDEL J.,VOTERS, PARTIES, AND LEADERS. UK ELITES LOC/G NAT/G PROVS ACT/RES DOMIN REPRESENT GP/REL INGP/REL...SOC BIBLIOG 20. PAGE 12 B0255 — POL/PAR STRATA LEGIS ADMIN

B63
BONINI C.P.,SIMULATION OF INFORMATION AND DECISION SYSTEMS IN THE FIRM. MARKET BUDGET DOMIN EDU/PROP ADMIN COST ATTIT HABITAT PERCEPT PWR...CONCPT PROBABIL QUANT PREDICT HYPO/EXP BIBLIOG. PAGE 13 B0273 — INDUS SIMUL DECISION MGT

B63
DIESNER H.J.,KIRCHE UND STAAT IM SPATROMISCHEN REICH. ROMAN/EMP EX/STRUC COLONIAL COERCE ATTIT CATHISM 4/5 AFRICA/N CHURCH/STA. PAGE 29 B0592 — SECT GP/REL DOMIN JURID

B63
FISHER S.N.,THE MILITARY IN THE MIDDLE EAST: PROBLEMS IN SOCIETY AND GOVERNMENT. ISLAM USA+45 NAT/G DOMIN LEGIT COERCE ORD/FREE PWR...TIME/SEQ VAL/FREE 20. PAGE 36 B0725 — EX/STRUC FORCES

B63
HEUSSLER R.,YESTERDAY'S RULERS: THE MAKING OF THE BRITISH COLONIAL SERVICE. AFR EUR+WWI UK STRATA SECT DELIB/GP PLAN DOMIN EDU/PROP ATTIT PERCEPT PERSON SUPEGO KNOWL ORD/FREE PWR...MGT SOC OBS INT TIME/SEQ 20 CMN/WLTH. PAGE 49 B1000 — EX/STRUC MORAL ELITES

B63
KOGAN N.,THE POLITICS OF ITALIAN FOREIGN POLICY. EUR+WWI LEGIS DOMIN LEGIT EXEC PWR RESPECT SKILL ...POLICY DECISION HUM SOC METH/CNCPT OBS INT CHARTS 20. PAGE 61 B1227 — NAT/G ROUTINE DIPLOM ITALY

B63
LANGROD G.,THE INTERNATIONAL CIVIL SERVICE: ITS ORIGINS, ITS NATURE, ITS EVALUATION. FUT WOR+45 WOR-45 DELIB/GP ACT/RES DOMIN LEGIT ATTIT RIGID/FLEX SUPEGO ALL/VALS...MGT CONCPT STAT TIME/SEQ ILO LEAGUE/NAT VAL/FREE 20 UN. PAGE 62 B1259 — INT/ORG ADMIN

B63
LEWIS J.W.,LEADERSHIP IN COMMUNIST CHINA. ASIA INTELL ECO/UNDEV LOC/G MUNIC NAT/G PROVS ECO/TAC EDU/PROP LEGIT ADMIN COERCE ATTIT ORD/FREE PWR ...INT TIME/SEQ CHARTS TOT/POP VAL/FREE. PAGE 65 B1304 — POL/PAR DOMIN ELITES

B63
LITTERER J.A.,ORGANIZATIONS: STRUCTURE AND BEHAVIOR. PLAN DOMIN CONTROL LEAD ROUTINE SANCTION INGP/REL EFFICIENCY PRODUC DRIVE RIGID/FLEX PWR. PAGE 66 B1325 — ADMIN CREATE MGT ADJUST

B63
NORTH R.C.,CONTENT ANALYSIS: A HANDBOOK WITH APPLICATIONS FOR THE STUDY OF INTERNATIONAL CRISIS. ASIA COM EUR+WWI MOD/EUR INT/ORG TEC/DEV DOMIN EDU/PROP ROUTINE COERCE PERCEPT RIGID/FLEX ALL/VALS ...QUANT TESTS CON/ANAL SIMUL GEN/LAWS VAL/FREE. PAGE 79 B1591 — METH/CNCPT COMPUT/IR USSR

B63
ROBINSON K.,ESSAYS IN IMPERIAL GOVERNMENT. CAMEROON NIGERIA UK CONSTN LOC/G LEGIS ADMIN GOV/REL PWR ...POLICY ANTHOL BIBLIOG 17/20 PURHAM/M. PAGE 89 B1803 — COLONIAL AFR DOMIN

B63
SWERDLOW I.,DEVELOPMENT ADMINISTRATION: CONCEPTS AND PROBLEMS. WOR+45 CULTURE SOCIETY STRATA DELIB/GP EX/STRUC ACT/RES PLAN ECO/TAC DOMIN LEGIT ATTIT RIGID/FLEX SUPEGO HEALTH PWR...MGT CONCPT ANTHOL VAL/FREE. PAGE 102 B2062 — ECO/UNDEV ADMIN

B63
THOMETZ C.E.,THE DECISION-MAKERS: THE POWER STRUCTURE OF DALLAS. USA+45 CULTURE EX/STRUC DOMIN LEGIT GP/REL ATTIT OBJECTIVE...INT CHARTS GP/COMP. PAGE 104 B2101 — ELITES MUNIC PWR DECISION

B63
TSOU T.,AMERICA'S FAILURE IN CHINA, 1941-1950. ASIA USA+45 USA-45 NAT/G ACT/RES PLAN DOMIN EDU/PROP ADMIN ROUTINE ATTIT PERSON ORD/FREE...DECISION CONCPT MYTH TIME/SEQ TREND STERTYP 20. PAGE 105 B2132 — ASIA PERCEPT DIPLOM

B63
TUCKER R.C.,THE SOVIET POLITICAL MIND. WOR+45 ELITES INT/ORG NAT/G POL/PAR PLAN DIPLOM ECO/TAC DOMIN ADMIN NUC/PWR REV DRIVE PERSON SUPEGO PWR WEALTH...POLICY MGT PSY CONCPT OBS BIOG TREND — COM TOP/EX USSR

COLD/WAR MARX/KARL 20. PAGE 106 B2134

L63

EMERSON R.,"POLITICAL MODERNIZATION." WOR+45
CULTURE ECO/UNDEV NAT/G FORCES ECO/TAC DOMIN
EDU/PROP LEGIT COERCE ALL/VALS...CONCPT TIME/SEQ
VAL/FREE 20. PAGE 33 B0672
POL/PAR
ADMIN

L63

SPITZ A.A.,"DEVELOPMENT ADMINISTRATION: AN
ANNOTATED BIBLIOGRAPHY." WOR+45 CULTURE SOCIETY
STRATA DELIB/GP EX/STRUC TOP/EX ACT/RES ECO/TAC
DOMIN EDU/PROP LEGIT COERCE ATTIT ALL/VALS...MGT
VAL/FREE. PAGE 99 B2009
ADMIN
ECO/UNDEV

S63

BRZEZINSKI Z.K.,"CINCINNATUS AND THE APPARATCHIK."
COM USA+45 USA-45 ELITES LOC/G NAT/G PROVS CONSULT
LEGIS DOMIN LEGIT EXEC ROUTINE CHOOSE DRIVE PWR
SKILL...CONCPT CHARTS VAL/FREE COLD/WAR 20. PAGE 16
B0334
POL/PAR
USSR

S63

HARRIS R.L.,"A COMPARATIVE ANALYSIS OF THE
ADMINISTRATIVE SYSTEMS OF CANADA AND CEYLON."
S/ASIA CULTURE SOCIETY STRATA TOP/EX ACT/RES DOMIN
EDU/PROP LEGIT COERCE ATTIT SUPEGO ALL/VALS...MGT
CHARTS GEN/LAWS VAL/FREE 20. PAGE 47 B0955
DELIB/GP
EX/STRUC
CANADA
CEYLON

S63

RUSTOW D.A.,"THE MILITARY IN MIDDLE EASTERN SOCIETY
AND POLITICS." FUT ISLAM CONSTN SOCIETY FACE/GP
NAT/G POL/PAR PROF/GP CONSULT DOMIN ADMIN EXEC
REGION COERCE NAT/LISM ATTIT DRIVE PERSON ORD/FREE
PWR...POLICY CONCPT OBS STERTYP 20. PAGE 92 B1860
FORCES
ELITES

S63

SHIMKIN D.B.,"STRUCTURE OF SOVIET POWER." COM FUT
USA+45 USSR WOR+45 NAT/G FORCES ECO/TAC DOMIN EXEC
COERCE CHOOSE ATTIT WEALTH...TIME/SEQ COLD/WAR
TOT/POP VAL/FREE 20. PAGE 96 B1948
PWR

B64

ALDERFER H.O.,LOCAL GOVERNMENT IN DEVELOPING
COUNTRIES. ASIA COM L/A+17C S/ASIA AGRI LOC/G MUNIC
PROVS DOMIN CHOOSE PWR...POLICY MGT CONCPT 20.
PAGE 3 B0070
ADMIN
ROUTINE

B64

DUROSELLE J.B.,POLITIQUES NATIONALES ENVERS LES
JEUNES ETATS. FRANCE ISRAEL ITALY UK USA+45 USSR
YUGOSLAVIA ECO/DEV FINAN ECO/TAC INT/TRADE ADMIN
PWR 20. PAGE 31 B0634
DIPLOM
ECO/UNDEV
COLONIAL
DOMIN

B64

ETZIONI A.,MODERN ORGANIZATIONS. CLIENT STRUCT
DOMIN CONTROL LEAD PERS/REL AUTHORIT...CLASSIF
BUREAUCRCY. PAGE 34 B0685
MGT
ADMIN
PLAN
CULTURE

B64

PIPES R.,THE FORMATION OF THE SOVIET UNION. EUR+WWI
MOD/EUR STRUCT ECO/UNDEV NAT/G LEGIS DOMIN LEGIT
CT/SYS EXEC COERCE ALL/VALS...POLICY RELATIV
HIST/WRIT TIME/SEQ TOT/POP 19/20. PAGE 83 B1677
COM
USSR
RUSSIA

B64

RIDDLE D.H.,THE TRUMAN COMMITTEE: A STUDY IN
CONGRESSIONAL RESPONSIBILITY. INDUS FORCES OP/RES
DOMIN ADMIN LEAD PARL/PROC WAR PRODUC SUPEGO
...BIBLIOG CONGRESS. PAGE 88 B1778
LEGIS
DELIB/GP
CONFER

B64

ROBSON W.A.,THE GOVERNORS AND THE GOVERNED. USA+45
PROB/SOLV DOMIN ADMIN CONTROL CHOOSE...POLICY
PRESIDENT. PAGE 89 B1808
EX/STRUC
ATTIT
PARTIC
LEAD

B64

WAINHOUSE D.W.,REMNANTS OF EMPIRE: THE UNITED
NATIONS AND THE END OF COLONIALISM. FUT PORTUGAL
WOR+45 NAT/G CONSULT DOMIN LEGIT ADMIN ROUTINE
ATTIT ORD/FREE...POLICY JURID RECORD INT TIME/SEQ
UN CMN/WLTH 20. PAGE 113 B2275
INT/ORG
TREND
COLONIAL

L64

ROTBERG R.,"THE FEDERATION MOVEMENT IN BRITISH EAST
AND CENTRAL AFRICA." AFR RHODESIA UGANDA ECO/UNDEV
NAT/G POL/PAR FORCES DOMIN LEGIT ADMIN COERCE ATTIT
...CONCPT TREND 20 TANGANYIKA. PAGE 91 B1831
VOL/ASSN
PWR
REGION

S64

CLIGNET R.,"POTENTIAL ELITES IN GHANA AND THE IVORY
COAST: A PRELIMINARY SURVEY." AFR CULTURE ELITES
STRATA KIN NAT/G SECT DOMIN EXEC ORD/FREE RESPECT
SKILL...POLICY RELATIV GP/COMP NAT/COMP 20. PAGE 21
B0438
PWR
LEGIT
IVORY/CST
GHANA

S64

GALTUNE J.,"BALANCE OF POWER AND THE PROBLEM OF
PERCEPTION, A LOGICAL ANALYSIS." WOR+45 CONSTN
SOCIETY NAT/G DELIB/GP EX/STRUC LEGIS DOMIN ADMIN
COERCE DRIVE ORD/FREE...POLICY CONCPT OBS TREND
GEN/LAWS. PAGE 38 B0778
PWR
PSY
ARMS/CONT
WAR

S64

GROSS J.A.,"WHITEHALL AND THE COMMONWEALTH."
EUR+WWI MOD/EUR INT/ORG NAT/G CONSULT DELIB/GP
LEGIS DOMIN ADMIN COLONIAL ROUTINE PWR CMN/WLTH
19/20. PAGE 44 B0890
EX/STRUC
ATTIT
TREND

S64

KASSOF A.,"THE ADMINISTERED SOCIETY:
TOTALITARIANISM WITHOUT TERROR." COM USSR STRATA
SOCIETY
DOMIN

AGRI INDUS NAT/G PERF/ART SCHOOL TOP/EX EDU/PROP
ADMIN ORD/FREE PWR...POLICY SOC TIME/SEQ GEN/LAWS
VAL/FREE 20. PAGE 58 B1178
TOTALISM

S64

KENNAN G.F.,"POLYCENTRISM AND WESTERN POLICY." ASIA
CHINA/COM COM FUT USA+45 USSR NAT/G ACT/RES DOMIN
EDU/PROP EXEC COERCE DISPL PERCEPT...POLICY
COLD/WAR 20. PAGE 59 B1192
RIGID/FLEX
ATTIT
DIPLOM

S64

LOW D.A.,"LION RAMPANT." EUR+WWI MOD/EUR S/ASIA
ECO/UNDEV NAT/G FORCES TEC/DEV ECO/TAC LEGIT ADMIN
COLONIAL COERCE ORD/FREE RESPECT 19/20. PAGE 67
B1344
AFR
DOMIN
DIPLOM
UK

S64

RIGBY T.H.,"TRADITIONAL, MARKET, AND ORGANIZATIONAL
SOCIETIES AND THE USSR." COM ECO/DEV NAT/G POL/PAR
ECO/TAC DOMIN ORD/FREE PWR WEALTH...TIME/SEQ
GEN/LAWS VAL/FREE 20 STALIN/J. PAGE 88 B1784
MARKET
ADMIN
USSR

S64

SWEARER H.R.,"AFTER KHRUSHCHEV: WHAT NEXT." COM FUT
USSR CONSTN ELITES NAT/G POL/PAR CHIEF DELIB/GP
LEGIS DOMIN LEAD...RECORD TREND STERTYP GEN/METH
20. PAGE 102 B2058
EX/STRUC
PWR

S64

THOMPSON V.A.,"ADMINISTRATIVE OBJECTIVES FOR
DEVELOPMENT ADMINISTRATION." WOR+45 CREATE PLAN
DOMIN EDU/PROP EXEC ROUTINE ATTIT ORD/FREE PWR
...POLICY GEN/LAWS VAL/FREE. PAGE 104 B2107
ECO/UNDEV
MGT

B65

BERNDT R.M.,ABORIGINAL MAN IN AUSTRALIA. LAW DOMIN
ADMIN COLONIAL MARRIAGE HABITAT ORD/FREE...LING
CHARTS ANTHOL BIBLIOG WORSHIP 20 AUSTRAL ABORIGINES
MUSIC ELKIN/AP. PAGE 11 B0225
SOC
CULTURE
SOCIETY
STRUCT

B65

BOXER C.R.,PORTUGUESE SOCIETY IN THE TROPICS - THE
MUNICIPAL COUNCILS OF GAO, MACAO, BAHIA, AND
LUANDA, 1510-1800. EUR+WWI MOD/EUR PORTUGAL CONSTN
EX/STRUC DOMIN CONTROL ROUTINE REPRESENT PRIVIL
...BIBLIOG/A 16/19 GENACCOUNT MACAO BAHIA LUANDA.
PAGE 14 B0290
MUNIC
ADMIN
COLONIAL
DELIB/GP

B65

DE GRAZIA A.,REPUBLIC IN CRISIS: CONGRESS AGAINST
THE EXECUTIVE FORCE. USA+45 USA-45 SOCIETY POL/PAR
CHIEF DOMIN ROLE ORD/FREE PWR...CONCPT MYTH BIBLIOG
20 CONGRESS. PAGE 27 B0556
LEGIS
EXEC
GOV/REL
CONTROL

B65

LEMAY G.H.,BRITISH SUPREMACY IN SOUTH AFRICA
1899-1907. SOUTH/AFR UK ADMIN CONTROL LEAD GP/REL
ORD/FREE 19/20. PAGE 64 B1286
WAR
COLONIAL
DOMIN
POLICY

B65

NORDEN A.,WAR AND NAZI CRIMINALS IN WEST GERMANY:
STATE, ECONOMY, ADMINISTRATION, ARMY, JUSTICE,
SCIENCE. GERMANY GERMANY/W MOD/EUR ECO/DEV ACADEM
EX/STRUC FORCES DOMIN ADMIN CT/SYS...POLICY MAJORIT
PACIFIST 20. PAGE 78 B1587
FASCIST
WAR
NAT/G
TOP/EX

B65

PHELPS-FETHERS I.,SOVIET INTERNATIONAL FRONT
ORGANIZATIONS* A CONCISE HANDBOOK. DIPLOM DOMIN
LEGIT ADMIN EXEC GP/REL PEACE MARXISM...TIME/SEQ
GP/COMP. PAGE 83 B1668
USSR
EDU/PROP
ASIA
COM

B65

REISS A.J. JR.,SCHOOLS IN A CHANGING SOCIETY.
CULTURE PROB/SOLV INSPECT DOMIN CONFER INGP/REL
RACE/REL AGE/C AGE/Y ALL/VALS...ANTHOL SOC/INTEG 20
NEWYORK/C. PAGE 87 B1766
SCHOOL
EX/STRUC
ADJUST
ADMIN

B65

ROTBERG R.I.,A POLITICAL HISTORY OF TROPICAL
AFRICA. EX/STRUC DIPLOM INT/TRADE DOMIN ADMIN
RACE/REL NAT/LISM PWR SOVEREIGN...GEOG TIME/SEQ
BIBLIOG 1/20. PAGE 91 B1832
AFR
CULTURE
COLONIAL

L65

RUBIN A.P.,"UNITED STATES CONTEMPORARY PRACTICE
RELATING TO INTERNATIONAL LAW." USA+45 WOR+45
CONSTN INT/ORG NAT/G DELIB/GP EX/STRUC DIPLOM DOMIN
CT/SYS ROUTINE ORD/FREE...CONCPT COLD/WAR 20.
PAGE 91 B1848
LAW
LEGIT
INT/LAW

S65

BROWN S.,"AN ALTERNATIVE TO THE GRAND DESIGN."
EUR+WWI FUT USA+45 INT/ORG NAT/G EX/STRUC FORCES
CREATE BAL/PWR DOMIN RIGID/FLEX ORD/FREE PWR
...NEW/IDEA RECORD EEC NATO 20. PAGE 16 B0327
VOL/ASSN
CONCPT
DIPLOM

B66

LIVINGSTON J.C.,THE CONSENT OF THE GOVERNED. USA+45
EX/STRUC BAL/PWR DOMIN CENTRAL PERSON PWR...POLICY
CONCPT OBS IDEA/COMP 20 CONGRESS. PAGE 66 B1331
NAT/G
LOBBY
MAJORIT
PARTIC

B66

TOTTEN G.O.,THE SOCIAL DEMOCRATIC MOVEMENT IN
PREWAR JAPAN. ASIA CHIEF EX/STRUC LEGIS DOMIN LEAD
ROUTINE WAR 20 CHINJAP. PAGE 105 B2122
POL/PAR
SOCISM
PARTIC
STRATA

C66

TARLING N.,"A CONCISE HISTORY OF SOUTHEAST ASIA."
BURMA CAMBODIA LAOS S/ASIA THAILAND VIETNAM
ECO/UNDEV POL/PAR FORCES ADMIN REV WAR CIVMIL/REL
COLONIAL
DOMIN
INT/TRADE

ORD/FREE MARXISM SOCISM 13/20. PAGE 103 B2080   NAT/LISM

                                             B67

BROWN L.N.,FRENCH ADMINISTRATIVE LAW. FRANCE UK   EX/STRUC
CONSTN NAT/G LEGIS DOMIN CONTROL EXEC PARL/PROC PWR   LAW
...JURID METH/COMP GEN/METH. PAGE 16 B0324   IDEA/COMP
                                             CT/SYS

                                             B67

MCCONNELL G.,THE MODERN PRESIDENCY. USA+45 CONSTN   NAT/G
TOP/EX DOMIN EXEC CHOOSE PWR...MGT 20. PAGE 72   CHIEF
B1446   EX/STRUC

                                             B67

US SENATE COMM ON FOREIGN REL.HUMAN RIGHTS   LEGIS
CONVENTIONS. USA+45 LABOR VOL/ASSN DELIB/GP DOMIN   ORD/FREE
ADJUD REPRESENT...INT/LAW MGT CONGRESS. PAGE 110   WORKER
B2225   LOBBY

                                             B67

WESSON R.G.,THE IMPERIAL ORDER. WOR-45 STRUCT SECT   PWR
DOMIN ADMIN COLONIAL LEAD CONSERVE...CONCPT BIBLIOG   CHIEF
20. PAGE 115 B2324   CONTROL
                                             SOCIETY

                                             L67

TAMBIAH S.J.,"THE POLITICS OF LANGUAGE IN INDIA AND   POL/PAR
CEYLON." CEYLON INDIA NAT/G DOMIN ADMIN...SOC 20.   LING
PAGE 102 B2070   NAT/LISM
                                             REGION

                                             S67

BASTID M.,"ORIGINES ET DEVELOPMENT DE LA REVOLUTION   REV
CULTURELLE." CHINA/COM DOMIN ADMIN CONTROL LEAD   CULTURE
COERCE CROWD ATTIT DRIVE MARXISM...POLICY 20.   ACADEM
PAGE 10 B0195   WORKER

                                             S67

BEASLEY W.G.,"POLITICS AND THE SAMURAI CLASS   ELITES
STRUCTURE IN SATSUMA, 18581868." STRATA FORCES   STRUCT
DOMIN LEGIT ADMIN LEAD 19 CHINJAP. PAGE 10 B0202   ATTIT
                                             PRIVIL

                                             S67

EDWARDS H.T.,"POWER STRUCTURE AND ITS COMMUNICATION   ELITES
IN SAN JOSE, COSTA RICA." COSTA/RICA L/A+17C STRATA   INGP/REL
FACE/GP POL/PAR EX/STRUC PROB/SOLV ADMIN LEAD   MUNIC
GP/REL PWR...STAT INT 20. PAGE 32 B0655   DOMIN

                                             S67

GORMAN W.,"ELLUL - A PROPHETIC VOICE." WOR+45   CREATE
ELITES SOCIETY ACT/RES PLAN BAL/PWR DOMIN CONTROL   ORD/FREE
PARTIC TOTALSM PWR 20. PAGE 41 B0837   EX/STRUC
                                             UTOPIA

                                             S67

GRUNDY K.W.,"THE POLITICAL USES OF IMAGINATION."   NAT/LISM
GHANA ELITES SOCIETY NAT/G DOMIN EDU/PROP COLONIAL   EX/STRUC
REGION REPRESENT GP/REL CENTRAL PWR MARXISM 20.   AFR
PAGE 44 B0897   LEAD

                                             S67

HALL B.,"THE COALITION AGAINST DISHWASHERS." USA+45   LABOR
POL/PAR PROB/SOLV BARGAIN LEAD CHOOSE REPRESENT   ADMIN
GP/REL ORD/FREE PWR...POLICY 20. PAGE 46 B0923   DOMIN
                                             WORKER

                                             S67

LEWIS P.H.,"LEADERSHIP AND CONFLICT WITHIN   POL/PAR
FEBRERISTA PARTY OF PARAGUAY." L/A+17C PARAGUAY   ELITES
EX/STRUC DOMIN SENIOR CONTROL INGP/REL CENTRAL   LEAD
FEDERAL ATTIT 20. PAGE 65 B1305

                                             S67

SHOEMAKER R.L.,"JAPANESE ARMY AND THE WEST." ASIA   FORCES
ELITES EX/STRUC DIPLOM DOMIN EDU/PROP COERCE ATTIT   TEC/DEV
AUTHORIT PWR 1/20 CHINJAP. PAGE 96 B1950   WAR
                                             TOTALISM

                                             S67

WALLER D.J.,"CHINA: RED OR EXPERT." CHINA/COM   CONTROL
INTELL DOMIN REV ATTIT MARXISM 20. PAGE 113 B2283   FORCES
                                             ADMIN
                                             POL/PAR

                                             B95

LATIMER E.W.,EUROPE IN AFRICA IN THE NINETEENTH   AFR
CENTURY. ECO/UNDEV KIN SECT DIPLOM DOMIN ADMIN   COLONIAL
DISCRIM 17/18. PAGE 63 B1275   WAR
                                             FINAN

DOMIN/REP....DOMINICAN REPUBLIC; SEE ALSO L/A + 17C

                                             S67

TURNER F.C. JR.,"EXPERIMENT IN INTER-AMERICAN   FORCES
PEACE-KEEPING." DOMIN/REP ADMIN ROUTINE REV   ADJUD
ORD/FREE OAS 20. PAGE 106 B2137   PEACE

DOMINATION....SEE DOMIN

DOMINICAN REPUBLIC....SEE DOMIN/REP

DOMINO....THE DOMINO THEORY

DONHAM W.B. B0605

DONNELL J.C. B0606

DONNELLY D. B0607

DONNELLY/I....IGNATIUS DONNELLY

DONOGHUE J. B2247

DORNBUSCH S.M. B1921

DORWART R.A. B0608

DOSSICK J.J. B0609

DOSTOYEV/F....FYODOR DOSTOYEVSKY

DOTSON A. B0610,B0611

DOUGHERTY J.E. B0493

DOUGLAS P.H. B0612

DOUGLAS/P....PAUL DOUGLAS

                                             B62

CARPER E.T.,ILLINOIS GOES TO CONGRESS FOR ARMY   ADMIN
LAND. USA+45 LAW EXTR/IND PROVS REGION CIVMIL/REL   LOBBY
GOV/REL FEDERAL ATTIT 20 ILLINOIS SENATE CONGRESS   GEOG
DIRKSEN/E DOUGLAS/P. PAGE 19 B0385   LEGIS

DOUGLAS/WO....WILLIAM O. DOUGLAS

DOUGLASS H.R. B0613

DOWD L.P. B0614

DRAGNICH A.N. B0615

DRAPER A.P. B0616

DRAPER T. B0617

DRAPER/HAL....HAL DRAPER

DREAM....DREAMING

DREYFUS/A....ALFRED DREYFUS OR DREYFUS AFFAIR

DRIVE....DRIVE AND MORALE

                                             B00

MORRIS H.C.,THE HISTORY OF COLONIZATION. WOR+45   DOMIN
WOR-45 ECO/DEV ECO/UNDEV INT/ORG ACT/RES PLAN   SOVEREIGN
ECO/TAC LEGIT ROUTINE COERCE ATTIT DRIVE ALL/VALS   COLONIAL
...GEOG TREND 19. PAGE 76 B1528

                                             B05

MACHIAVELLI N.,THE ART OF WAR. CHRIST-17C TOP/EX   NAT/G
DRIVE ORD/FREE PWR SKILL...MGT CHARTS. PAGE 67   FORCES
B1360   WAR
                                             ITALY

                                             N19

GRIFFITH W.,THE PUBLIC SERVICE (PAMPHLET). UK LAW   ADMIN
LOC/G NAT/G PARTIC CHOOSE DRIVE ROLE SKILL...CHARTS   EFFICIENCY
20 CIVIL/SERV. PAGE 44 B0880   EDU/PROP
                                             GOV/REL

                                             B20

HALDANE R.B.,BEFORE THE WAR. MOD/EUR SOCIETY   POLICY
INT/ORG NAT/G DELIB/GP PLAN DOMIN EDU/PROP LEGIT   DIPLOM
ADMIN COERCE ATTIT DRIVE MORAL ORD/FREE PWR...SOC   UK
CONCPT SELF/OBS RECORD BIOG TIME/SEQ. PAGE 45 B0921

                                             L23

DOUGLAS P.H.,"OCCUPATIONAL V PROPORTIONAL   REPRESENT
REPRESENTATION." INDUS NAT/G PLAN ROUTINE SUFF   PROF/ORG
CONSEN DRIVE...CONCPT CLASSIF. PAGE 30 B0612   DOMIN
                                             INGP/REL

                                             B26

MOON P.T.,IMPERIALISM AND WORLD POLITICS. AFR ASIA   WEALTH
ISLAM MOD/EUR S/ASIA USA-45 SOCIETY NAT/G EX/STRUC   TIME/SEQ
BAL/PWR DOMIN COLONIAL NAT/LISM ATTIT DRIVE PWR   CAP/ISM
...GEOG SOC 20. PAGE 75 B1510   DIPLOM

                                             B28

SOROKIN P.,CONTEMPORARY SOCIOLOGICAL THEORIES.   CULTURE
MOD/EUR UNIV SOCIETY R+D SCHOOL ECO/TAC EDU/PROP   SOC
ROUTINE ATTIT DRIVE...PSY CONCPT TIME/SEQ TREND   WAR
GEN/LAWS 20. PAGE 99 B1997

                                             B29

BUELL R.,INTERNATIONAL RELATIONS. WOR+45 WOR-45   INT/ORG
CONSTN STRATA FORCES TOP/EX ADMIN ATTIT DRIVE   BAL/PWR
SUPEGO MORAL ORD/FREE PWR SOVEREIGN...JURID SOC   DIPLOM
CONCPT 20. PAGE 17 B0340

                                             B30

MURCHISON C.,PSYCHOLOGIES OF 1930. UNIV USA-45   CREATE
CULTURE INTELL SOCIETY STRATA FAM ROUTINE BIO/SOC   PERSON
DRIVE RIGID/FLEX SUPEGO...NEW/IDEA OBS SELF/OBS
CONT/OBS 20. PAGE 76 B1543

                                             B31

DEKAT A.D.A.,COLONIAL POLICY. S/ASIA CULTURE   DRIVE
EX/STRUC ECO/TAC DOMIN ADMIN COLONIAL ROUTINE   PWR
SOVEREIGN WEALTH...POLICY MGT RECORD KNO/TEST SAMP.   INDONESIA
PAGE 28 B0570   NETHERLAND

                                             B35

GREER S.,BIBLIOGRAPHY ON CIVIL SERVICE AND   BIBLIOG/A

PERSONNEL ADMINISTRATION. USA-45 LOC/G PROVS WORKER ADMIN
PRICE SENIOR DRIVE...MGT 20. PAGE 43 B0870 NAT/G
ROUTINE
B38

SALTER J.T.,THE AMERICAN POLITICIAN. USA-45 LABOR BIOG
POL/PAR EDU/PROP ADMIN CHOOSE ATTIT DRIVE PERSON LEAD
PWR...POLICY ANTHOL 20 THOMAS/N LEWIS/JL LAGUARD/F PROVS
GOVERNOR MAYOR. PAGE 92 B1865 LOC/G
S39

MARX F.M.,"POLICY FORMULATION AND THE ADMIN
ADMINISTRATIVE PROCESS" ROUTINE ADJUST EFFICIENCY LEAD
OPTIMAL PRIVIL DRIVE PERSON OBJECTIVE...DECISION INGP/REL
OBS GEN/METH. PAGE 70 B1418 MGT
B42

US STATE DEPT.,PEACE AND WAR: UNITED STATES FOREIGN DIPLOM
POLICY, 1931-41. CULTURE FORCES ROUTINE CHOOSE USA-45
ATTIT DRIVE PERSON 20. PAGE 111 B2237 PLAN
B44

BIENSTOCK G.,MANAGEMENT IN RUSSIAN INDUSTRY AND ADMIN
AGRICULTURE. USSR CONSULT WORKER LEAD COST PROFIT MARXISM
ATTIT DRIVE PWR...MGT METH/COMP DICTIONARY 20. SML/CO
PAGE 12 B0236 AGRI
B47

BARNARD C.,THE FUNCTIONS OF THE EXECUTIVE. USA+45 EXEC
ELITES INTELL LEGIT ATTIT DRIVE PERSON SKILL...PSY EX/STRUC
SOC METH/CNCPT SOC/EXP GEN/METH VAL/FREE 20. PAGE 9 ROUTINE
B0187
B47

WHITEHEAD T.N.,LEADERSHIP IN A FREE SOCIETY; A INDUS
STUDY IN HUMAN RELATIONS BASED ON AN ANALYSIS OF LEAD
PRESENT-DAY INDUSTRIAL CIVILIZATION. WOR-45 STRUCT ORD/FREE
R+D LABOR LG/CO SML/CO WORKER PLAN PROB/SOLV SOCIETY
TEC/DEV DRIVE...MGT 20. PAGE 116 B2341
S48

KNICKERBOCKER I.,"LEADERSHIP: A CONCEPTION AND SOME LEAD
IMPLICATIONS." INDUS OP/RES REPRESENT INGP/REL CONCPT
DRIVE...MGT CLASSIF. PAGE 60 B1220 PERSON
ROLE
B49

BUSH V.,MODERN ARMS AND FREE MEN. WOR-45 SOCIETY TEC/DEV
NAT/G ECO/TAC DOMIN LEGIT EXEC COERCE DETER ATTIT FORCES
DRIVE ORD/FREE PWR...CONCPT MYTH COLD/WAR 20 NUC/PWR
COLD/WAR. PAGE 18 B0361 WAR
B49

DE GRAZIA A.,HUMAN RELATIONS IN PUBLIC BIBLIOG/A
ADMINISTRATION. INDUS ACT/RES CREATE PLAN PROB/SOLV ADMIN
TEC/DEV INGP/REL PERS/REL DRIVE...POLICY SOC 20. PHIL/SCI
PAGE 27 B0552 OP/RES
B49

SINGER K.,THE IDEA OF CONFLICT. UNIV INTELL INT/ORG ACT/RES
NAT/G PLAN ROUTINE ATTIT DRIVE ALL/VALS...POLICY SOC
CONCPT TIME/SEQ. PAGE 97 B1966
B50

MANNHEIM K.,FREEDOM, POWER, AND DEMOCRATIC TEC/DEV
PLANNING. FUT USSR WOR+45 ELITES INTELL SOCIETY PLAN
NAT/G EDU/PROP ROUTINE ATTIT DRIVE SUPEGO SKILL CAP/ISM
...POLICY PSY CONCPT TREND GEN/LAWS 20. PAGE 69 UK
B1393
C50

SIMON H.A.,"PUBLIC ADMINISTRATION." LG/CO SML/CO MGT
PLAN DOMIN LEAD GP/REL DRIVE PERCEPT ALL/VALS ADMIN
...POLICY BIBLIOG/A 20. PAGE 97 B1957 DECISION
EX/STRUC
B51

LASSWELL H.D.,THE POLITICAL WRITINGS OF HAROLD D PERSON
LASSWELL. UNIV DOMIN EXEC LEAD RATIONAL ATTIT DRIVE PSY
ROLE ALL/VALS...OBS BIOG 20. PAGE 63 B1269 INGP/REL
CONCPT
C51

HOMANS G.C.,"THE WESTERN ELECTRIC RESEARCHES" IN S. OP/RES
HOSLETT, ED., HUMAN FACTORS IN MANAGEMENT (BMR)" EFFICIENCY
ACT/RES GP/REL HAPPINESS PRODUC DRIVE...MGT OBS 20. SOC/EXP
PAGE 51 B1037 WORKER
B52

BRINTON C.,THE ANATOMY OF REVOLUTION. FRANCE UK SOCIETY
USA-45 USSR WOR-45 ELITES INTELL ECO/DEV NAT/G CONCPT
EX/STRUC COERCE DRIVE ORD/FREE PWR SOVEREIGN REV
...MYTH HIST/WRIT GEN/LAWS. PAGE 15 B0311
B52

MAIER N.R.F.,PRINCIPLES OF HUMAN RELATIONS. WOR+45 INDUS
WOR-45 CULTURE SOCIETY ROUTINE ATTIT DRIVE PERCEPT
PERSON RIGID/FLEX SUPEGO PWR...PSY CONT/OBS RECORD
TOT/POP VAL/FREE 20. PAGE 68 B1379
B52

ULAM A.B.,TITOISM AND THE COMINFORM. USSR WOR+45 COM
STRUCT INT/ORG NAT/G ACT/RES PLAN EXEC ATTIT DRIVE POL/PAR
ALL/VALS...CONCPT OBS VAL/FREE 20 COMINTERN TOTALISM
TITO/MARSH. PAGE 106 B2145 YUGOSLAVIA
L52

WRIGHT Q.,"CONGRESS AND THE TREATY-MAKING POWER." ROUTINE
USA+45 WOR+45 CONSTN INTELL NAT/G CHIEF CONSULT DIPLOM
EX/STRUC LEGIS TOP/EX CREATE GOV/REL DISPL DRIVE INT/LAW
RIGID/FLEX...TREND TOT/POP CONGRESS CONGRESS 20 DELIB/GP
TREATY. PAGE 118 B2384
S52

JOSEPHSON E.,"IRRATIONAL LEADERSHIP IN FORMAL ADMIN

ORGANIZATIONS." EX/STRUC PLAN LEAD GP/REL INGP/REL RATIONAL
EFFICIENCY AUTHORIT DRIVE PSY. PAGE 57 B1154 CONCPT
PERSON
B54

ALLPORT G.W.,THE NATURE OF PREJUDICE. USA+45 WOR+45 CULTURE
STRATA FACE/GP KIN NEIGH SECT ADMIN GP/REL DISCRIM PERSON
ATTIT DRIVE LOVE RESPECT...PSY SOC MYTH QU/SEMANT RACE/REL
20. PAGE 4 B0078
B54

COMBS C.H.,DECISION PROCESSES. INTELL SOCIETY MATH
DELIB/GP CREATE TEC/DEV DOMIN LEGIT EXEC CHOOSE DECISION
DRIVE RIGID/FLEX KNOWL PWR...PHIL/SCI SOC
METH/CNCPT CONT/OBS REC/INT PERS/TEST SAMP/SIZ BIOG
SOC/EXP WORK. PAGE 22 B0455
B54

DUVERGER M.,POLITICAL PARTIES: THEIR ORGANIZATION POL/PAR
AND ACTIVITY IN THE MODERN STATE. EUR+WWI MOD/EUR EX/STRUC
USA-45 EDU/PROP ADMIN ROUTINE ATTIT DRIVE ELITES
ORD/FREE PWR...SOC CONCPT MATH STAT TIME/SEQ
TOT/POP 19/20. PAGE 31 B0635
B54

GOULDNER A.W.,PATTERNS OF INDUSTRIAL BUREAUCRACY. ADMIN
DOMIN ATTIT DRIVE...BIBLIOG 20 BUREAUCRCY. PAGE 42 INDUS
B0844 OP/RES
WORKER
B54

LAPIERRE R.T.,A THEORY OF SOCIAL CONTROL. STRUCT CONTROL
ADMIN ROUTINE SANCTION ANOMIE AUTHORIT DRIVE PERSON VOL/ASSN
PWR...MAJORIT CONCPT CLASSIF. PAGE 62 B1260 CULTURE
B54

MATTHEWS D.R.,THE SOCIAL BACKGROUND OF POLITICAL DECISION
DECISION-MAKERS. CULTURE SOCIETY STRATA FAM BIOG
EX/STRUC LEAD ATTIT BIO/SOC DRIVE PERSON ALL/VALS SOC
HIST/WRIT. PAGE 71 B1431
L54

ROSTOW W.W.,"ASIAN LEADERSHIP AND FREE-WORLD ATTIT
ALLIANCE." ASIA COM USA+45 CULTURE ELITES INTELL LEGIT
NAT/G TEC/DEV ECO/TAC EDU/PROP COLONIAL PARL/PROC DIPLOM
ROUTINE COERCE DRIVE ORD/FREE MARXISM...PSY CONCPT.
PAGE 90 B1829
C54

GOULDNER A.W.,"PATTERNS OF INDUSTRIAL BUREAUCRACY." ADMIN
GP/REL CONSEN ATTIT DRIVE...BIBLIOG 20. PAGE 42 INDUS
B0843 OP/RES
WORKER
S55

TORRE M.,"PSYCHIATRIC OBSERVATIONS OF INTERNATIONAL DELIB/GP
CONFERENCES." WOR+45 INT/ORG PROF/ORG VOL/ASSN OBS
CONSULT EDU/PROP ROUTINE ATTIT DRIVE KNOWL...PSY DIPLOM
METH/CNCPT OBS/ENVIR STERTYP 20. PAGE 105 B2119
B56

BARBASH J.,THE PRACTICE OF UNIONISM. ECO/TAC LEAD LABOR
LOBBY GP/REL INGP/REL DRIVE MARXISM BIBLIOG. PAGE 9 REPRESENT
B0182 CONTROL
ADMIN
B56

DUNNILL F.,THE CIVIL SERVICE. UK LAW PLAN ADMIN PERSON
EFFICIENCY DRIVE NEW/LIB...STAT CHARTS 20 WORKER
PARLIAMENT CIVIL/SERV. PAGE 31 B0633 STRATA
SOC/WK
B56

LOVEDAY A.,REFLECTIONS ON INTERNATIONAL INT/ORG
ADMINISTRATION. WOR+45 WOR-45 DELIB/GP ACT/RES MGT
ADMIN EXEC ROUTINE DRIVE...METH/CNCPT TIME/SEQ
CON/ANAL SIMUL TOT/POP 20. PAGE 67 B1342
B56

MANNONI D.O.,PROSPERO AND CALIBAN: THE PSYCHOLOGY CULTURE
OF COLONIZATION. AFR EUR+WWI FAM KIN MUNIC SECT COLONIAL
DOMIN ADMIN ATTIT DRIVE LOVE PWR RESPECT...PSY SOC
CONCPT MYTH OBS DEEP/INT BIOG GEN/METH MALAGASY 20.
PAGE 69 B1394
B57

MORSTEIN-MARX F.,THE ADMINISTRATIVE STATE: AN EXEC
INTRODUCTION TO BUREAUCRACY. EUR+WWI FUT MOD/EUR MGT
USA+45 USA-45 NAT/G CONSULT ADMIN ROUTINE TOTALISM CAP/ISM
DRIVE SKILL...TREND 19/20. PAGE 76 B1530 ELITES
B57

SIMON H.A.,MODELS OF MAN, SOCIAL AND RATIONAL: MATH
MATHEMATICAL ESSAYS ON RATIONAL HUMAN BEHAVIOR IN A SIMUL
SOCIAL SETTING. UNIV LAW SOCIETY FACE/GP VOL/ASSN
CONSULT EX/STRUC LEGIS CREATE ADMIN ROUTINE ATTIT
DRIVE PWR...SOC CONCPT METH/CNCPT QUANT STAT
TOT/POP VAL/FREE 20. PAGE 97 B1959
B57

BAUER R.A.,"BRAINWASHING: PSYCHOLOGY OR EDU/PROP
DEMONOLOGY." ASIA CHINA/COM COM POL/PAR ECO/TAC PSY
ADMIN COERCE ATTIT DRIVE ORD/FREE...CONCPT MYTH 20. TOTALISM
PAGE 10 B0196
B58

BROWNE C.G.,THE CONCEPT OF LEADERSHIP. UNIV FACE/GP EXEC
DOMIN EDU/PROP LEGIT LEAD DRIVE PERSON PWR...MGT CONCPT
SOC OBS SELF/OBS CONT/OBS INT PERS/TEST STERTYP
GEN/LAWS. PAGE 16 B0328
B58

COLEMAN J.S.,NIGERIA: BACKGROUND TO NATIONALISM. NAT/G
AFR SOCIETY ECO/DEV KIN LOC/G POL/PAR TEC/DEV DOMIN NAT/LISM

ADMIN DRIVE PWR RESPECT...TRADIT SOC INT SAMP NIGERIA
TIME/SEQ 20. PAGE 22 B0452

B58
LAQUER W.Z.,THE MIDDLE EAST IN TRANSITION. COM USSR ISLAM
ECO/UNDEV NAT/G VOL/ASSN EDU/PROP EXEC ATTIT DRIVE TREND
PWR MARXISM COLD/WAR TOT/POP 20. PAGE 62 B1261 NAT/LISM

B58
MARCH J.G.,ORGANIZATIONS. USA+45 CREATE OP/RES PLAN MGT
PROB/SOLV PARTIC ROUTINE RATIONAL ATTIT PERCEPT PERSON
...DECISION BIBLIOG. PAGE 69 B1397 DRIVE
CONCPT

B58
SPITZ D.,DEMOCRACY AND THE CHALLANGE OF POWER. FUT NAT/G
USA+45 USA-45 LAW SOCIETY STRUCT LOC/G POL/PAR PWR
PROVS DELIB/GP EX/STRUC LEGIS TOP/EX ACT/RES CREATE
DOMIN EDU/PROP LEGIT ADJUD ADMIN ATTIT DRIVE MORAL
ORD/FREE TOT/POP. PAGE 99 B2010

L58
HAVILAND H.F.,"FOREIGN AID AND THE POLICY PROCESS: LEGIS
1957." USA+45 FACE/GP PLAN TEC/DEV NAT/ASSN CHIEF PLAN
DELIB/GP ACT/RES LEGIT EXEC GOV/REL ATTIT DRIVE PWR FOR/AID
...POLICY TESTS CONGRESS 20. PAGE 48 B0971

S58
MITCHELL W.C.,"OCCUPATIONAL ROLE STRAINS: THE ANOMIE
AMERICAN ELECTIVE PUBLIC OFFICIAL." CONTROL DRIVE
RIGID/FLEX SUPEGO HEALTH ORD/FREE...SOC INT QU. ROUTINE
PAGE 74 B1492 PERSON

B59
GREENEWALT C.H.,THE UNCOMMON MAN. UNIV ECO/DEV TASK
ADMIN PERS/REL PERSON SUPEGO WEALTH 20. PAGE 43 ORD/FREE
B0868 DRIVE
EFFICIENCY

B59
INDIAN INSTITUTE PUBLIC ADMIN.MORALE IN THE PUBLIC HAPPINESS
SERVICES: REPORT OF A CONFERENCE JAN., 3-4, 1959. ADMIN
INDIA S/ASIA ECO/UNDEV PROVS PLAN EDU/PROP CONFER WORKER
GOV/REL EFFICIENCY DRIVE ROLE 20 CIVIL/SERV. INGP/REL
PAGE 53 B1082

B59
JANOWITZ M.,SOCIOLOGY AND THE MILITARY FORCES
ESTABLISHMENT. USA+45 WOR+45 CULTURE SOCIETY SOC
PROF/ORG CONSULT EX/STRUC PLAN TEC/DEV DIPLOM DOMIN
COERCE DRIVE RIGID/FLEX ORD/FREE PWR SKILL COLD/WAR
20. PAGE 55 B1121

B59
YANG C.K.,A CHINESE VILLAGE IN EARLY COMMUNIST ASIA
TRANSITION. ECO/UNDEV AGRI FAM KIN MUNIC FORCES ROUTINE
PLAN ECO/TAC DOMIN EDU/PROP ATTIT DRIVE PWR RESPECT SOCISM
...SOC CONCPT METH/CNCPT OBS RECORD CON/ANAL CHARTS
WORK 20. PAGE 118 B2389

S59
HARVEY M.F.,"THE PALESTINE REFUGEE PROBLEM: ACT/RES
ELEMENTS OF A SOLUTION." ISLAM LAW INT/ORG DELIB/GP LEGIT
TOP/EX ECO/TAC CREATE DRIVE HEALTH LOVE ORD/FREE PEACE
PWR WEALTH...MAJORIT FAO 20. PAGE 48 B0964 ISRAEL

S59
KISSINGER H.A.,"THE POLICYMAKER AND THE INTELL
INTELLECTUAL." USA+45 CONSULT DELIB/GP ACT/RES CREATE
ADMIN ATTIT DRIVE RIGID/FLEX KNOWL PWR...POLICY
PLURIST MGT METH/CNCPT GEN/LAWS GEN/METH 20.
PAGE 60 B1216

C59
DAHL R.A.,"SOCIAL SCIENCE RESEARCH ON BUSINESS: MGT
PRODUCT AND POTENTIAL" INDUS MARKET OP/RES CAP/ISM EFFICIENCY
ADMIN LOBBY DRIVE...PSY CONCPT BIBLIOG/A 20. PROB/SOLV
PAGE 26 B0521 EX/STRUC

B60
BASS B.M.,LEADERSHIP, PSYCHOLOGY, AND UNIV
ORGANIZATIONAL BEHAVIOR. DOMIN CHOOSE DRIVE PERSON FACE/GP
PWR RESPECT SKILL...SOC METH/CNCPT OBS. PAGE 9 DELIB/GP
B0193 ROUTINE

B60
CAMPBELL R.W.,SOVIET ECONOMIC POWER. COM USA+45 ECO/DEV
DIST/IND MARKET TOP/EX ACT/RES CAP/ISM ECO/TAC PLAN
DOMIN EDU/PROP ADMIN ROUTINE DRIVE...MATH TIME/SEQ SOCISM
CHARTS WORK 20. PAGE 18 B0371 USSR

B60
FURNISS E.S.,FRANCE, TROUBLED ALLY. EUR+WWI FUT NAT/G
CULTURE SOCIETY BAL/PWR ADMIN ATTIT DRIVE PWR FRANCE
...TREND TOT/POP 20 DEGAULLE/C. PAGE 38 B0767

B60
GRANICK D.,THE RED EXECUTIVE. COM USA+45 SOCIETY PWR
ECO/DEV INDUS NAT/G POL/PAR EX/STRUC PLAN ECO/TAC STRATA
EDU/PROP ADMIN EXEC ATTIT DRIVE...GP/COMP 20. USSR
PAGE 42 B0851 ELITES

B60
LINDSAY K.,EUROPEAN ASSEMBLIES: THE EXPERIMENTAL VOL/ASSN
PERIOD 1949-1959. EUR+WWI ECO/DEV NAT/G POL/PAR INT/ORG
LEGIS TOP/EX ACT/RES PLAN ECO/TAC DOMIN LEGIT REGION
ROUTINE ATTIT DRIVE ORD/FREE PWR SKILL...SOC CONCPT
TREND CHARTS GEN/LAWS VAL/FREE. PAGE 65 B1315

B60
LINDVEIT E.N.,SCIENTISTS IN GOVERNMENT. USA+45 PAY TEC/DEV
EDU/PROP ADMIN DRIVE HABITAT ROLE...TECHNIC BIBLIOG ECO/TAC
20. PAGE 65 B1316 PHIL/SCI
GOV/REL

B60
MEEHAN E.J.,THE BRITISH LEFT WING AND FOREIGN ACT/RES
POLICY: A STUDY OF THE INFLUENCE OF IDEOLOGY. FUT ATTIT
UK UNIV WOR+45 INTELL TOP/EX PLAN ADMIN ROUTINE DIPLOM
DRIVE...OBS TIME/SEQ GEN/LAWS PARLIAMENT 20.
PAGE 72 B1461

B60
ROEPKE W.,A HUMANE ECONOMY: THE SOCIAL FRAMEWORK OF DRIVE
THE FREE MARKET. FUT USSR WOR+45 CULTURE SOCIETY EDU/PROP
ECO/DEV PLAN ECO/TAC ADMIN ATTIT PERSON RIGID/FLEX CAP/ISM
SUPEGO MORAL WEALTH SOCISM...POLICY OLD/LIB CONCPT
TREND GEN/LAWS 20. PAGE 90 B1811

S60
BOYER W.W.,"POLICY MAKING BY GOVERNMENT AGENCIES." NAT/G
USA+45 WOR+45 R+D DELIB/GP TOP/EX EDU/PROP ROUTINE DIPLOM
ATTIT BIO/SOC DRIVE...CONCPT TREND TOT/POP 20.
PAGE 14 B0293

S60
FRANKEL S.H.,"ECONOMIC ASPECTS OF POLITICAL NAT/G
INDEPENDENCE IN AFRICA." AFR FUT SOCIETY ECO/UNDEV FOR/AID
COM/IND FINAN LEGIS PLAN TEC/DEV CAP/ISM ECO/TAC
INT/TRADE ADMIN ATTIT DRIVE RIGID/FLEX PWR WEALTH
...MGT NEW/IDEA MATH TIME/SEQ VAL/FREE 20. PAGE 37
B0751

S60
GARNICK D.H.,"ON THE ECONOMIC FEASIBILITY OF A MARKET
MIDDLE EASTERN COMMON MARKET." AFR ISLAM CULTURE INT/TRADE
INDUS NAT/G PLAN TEC/DEV ECO/TAC ADMIN ATTIT DRIVE
RIGID/FLEX...PLURIST STAT TREND GEN/LAWS 20.
PAGE 39 B0784

S60
GROSSMAN G.,"SOVIET GROWTH: ROUTINE, INERTIA, AND POL/PAR
PRESSURE." COM STRATA NAT/G DELIB/GP PLAN TEC/DEV ECO/DEV
ECO/TAC EDU/PROP ADMIN ROUTINE DRIVE WEALTH USSR
COLD/WAR 20. PAGE 44 B0891

S60
HERZ J.H.,"EAST GERMANY: PROGRESS AND PROSPECTS." POL/PAR
COM AGRI FINAN INDUS LOC/G NAT/G FORCES PLAN STRUCT
TEC/DEV DOMIN ADMIN COERCE DRIVE PERCEPT RIGID/FLEX GERMANY
MORAL ORD/FREE PWR...MARXIST PSY SOC RECORD STERTYP
WORK. PAGE 49 B0997

S60
MORA J.A.,"THE ORGANIZATION OF AMERICAN STATES." L/A+17C
USA+45 LAW ECO/UNDEV VOL/ASSN DELIB/GP PLAN BAL/PWR INT/ORG
EDU/PROP ADMIN DRIVE RIGID/FLEX ORD/FREE WEALTH REGION
...TIME/SEQ GEN/LAWS OAS 20. PAGE 75 B1518

S60
REISELBACH L.N.,"THE BASIS OF ISOLATIONIST ATTIT
BEHAVIOR." USA+45 USA-45 CULTURE ECO/DEV LOC/G DIPLOM
NAT/G ADMIN ROUTINE CHOOSE BIO/SOC DRIVE RIGID/FLEX ECO/TAC
...CENSUS SAMP TREND CHARTS TOT/POP 20. PAGE 87
B1765

S60
SCHACHTER O.,"THE ENFORCEMENT OF INTERNATIONAL INT/ORG
JUDICIAL AND ARBITRAL DECISIONS." WOR+45 NAT/G ADJUD
ECO/TAC DOMIN LEGIT ROUTINE COERCE ATTIT DRIVE INT/LAW
ALL/VALS PWR...METH/CNCPT TREND TOT/POP 20 UN.
PAGE 93 B1878

B61
DUBIN R.,HUMAN RELATIONS IN ADMINISTRATION. USA+45 PERS/REL
INDUS LABOR LG/CO EX/STRUC GP/REL DRIVE PWR MGT
...DECISION SOC CHARTS ANTHOL 20. PAGE 31 B0623 ADMIN
EXEC

B61
HASAN H.S.,PAKISTAN AND THE UN. ISLAM WOR+45 INT/ORG
ECO/DEV ECO/UNDEV NAT/G TOP/EX ECO/TAC FOR/AID ATTIT
EDU/PROP ADMIN DRIVE PERCEPT...OBS TIME/SEQ UN 20. PAKISTAN
PAGE 48 B0965

B61
KOESTLER A.,THE LOTUS AND THE ROBOT. ASIA INDIA SECT
S/ASIA SOCIETY STRATA ECO/DEV AGRI INDUS FAM CREATE ECO/UNDEV
DOMIN EDU/PROP ADMIN COERCE ATTIT DRIVE SUPEGO
ORD/FREE PWR RESPECT WEALTH...MYTH OBS 20 CHINJAP.
PAGE 61 B1226

B61
KRUPP S.,PATTERN IN ORGANIZATIONAL ANALYSIS: A MGT
CRITICAL EXAMINATION. INGP/REL PERS/REL RATIONAL CONTROL
ATTIT AUTHORIT DRIVE PWR...DECISION PHIL/SCI SOC CONCPT
IDEA/COMP. PAGE 61 B1239 METH/CNCPT

B61
LASSWELL H.D.,PSYCOPATHOLOGY AND POLITICS. WOR-45 ATTIT
CULTURE SOCIETY FACE/GP NAT/G CONSULT CREATE GEN/METH
EDU/PROP EXEC ROUTINE DISPL DRIVE PERSON PWR
RESPECT...PSY CONCPT METH/CNCPT METH. PAGE 63 B1272

B61
MARX K.,THE COMMUNIST MANIFESTO. IN (MENDEL A. COM
ESSENTIAL WORKS OF MARXISM, NEW YORK: BANTAM. FUT NEW/IDEA
MOD/EUR CULTURE ECO/DEV ECO/UNDEV AGRI FINAN INDUS CAP/ISM
MARKET PROC/MFG LABOR POL/PAR CONSULT FORCES REV
CREATE PLAN ADMIN ATTIT DRIVE RIGID/FLEX ORD/FREE
PWR RESPECT MARX/KARL WORK. PAGE 70 B1421

S61
ALGER C.F.,"NON-RESOLUTION CONSEQUENCES OF THE INT/ORG
UNITED NATIONS AND THEIR EFFECT ON INTERNATIONAL DRIVE
CONFLICT." WOR+45 CONSTN ECO/DEV NAT/G CONSULT BAL/PWR
DELIB/GP TOP/EX ACT/RES PLAN DIPLOM EDU/PROP

ROUTINE ATTIT ALL/VALS...INT/LAW TOT/POP UN 20.
PAGE 4 B0075
                                                    S61
HAAS E.B.,"INTERNATIONAL INTEGRATION: THE EUROPEAN   INT/ORG
AND THE UNIVERSAL PROCESS." EUR+WWI FUT WOR+45   TREND
NAT/G EX/STRUC ATTIT DRIVE ORD/FREE PWR...CONCPT   REGION
GEN/LAWS OEEC 20 NATO COUNCL/EUR. PAGE 45 B0909
                                                    S61
MILLER E.,"LEGAL ASPECTS OF UN ACTION IN THE   INT/ORG
CONGO." AFR CULTURE ADMIN PEACE DRIVE RIGID/FLEX   LEGIT
ORD/FREE...WELF/ST JURID OBS UN CONGO 20. PAGE 73
B1480
                                                    S61
TAUBENFELD H.J.,"OUTER SPACE--PAST POLITICS AND   PLAN
FUTURE POLICY." FUT USA+45 USA-45 WOR+45 AIR INTELL SPACE
STRUCT ECO/DEV NAT/G TOP/EX ACT/RES ADMIN ROUTINE   INT/ORG
NUC/PWR ATTIT DRIVE...CONCPT TIME/SEQ TREND TOT/POP
20. PAGE 103 B2083
                                                    C61
ETZIONI A.,"A COMPARATIVE ANALYSIS OF COMPLEX   CON/ANAL
ORGANIZATIONS: ON POWER, INVOLVEMENT AND THEIR   SOC
CORRELATES." ELITES CREATE OP/RES ROUTINE INGP/REL   LEAD
PERS/REL CONSEN ATTIT DRIVE PWR...CONCPT BIBLIOG.   CONTROL
PAGE 34 B0684
                                                    C61
VERBA S.,"SMALL GROUPS AND POLITICAL BEHAVIOR: A   LEAD
STUDY OF LEADERSHIP" DOMIN PARTIC ROUTINE GP/REL   ELITES
ATTIT DRIVE ALL/VALS...CONCPT IDEA/COMP LAB/EXP   FACE/GP
BIBLIOG METH. PAGE 112 B2259
                                                    B62
CHICAGO U CTR PROG GOVT ADMIN,EDUCATION FOR   EDU/PROP
INNOVATIVE BEHAVIOR IN EXECUTIVES. UNIV ELITES   CREATE
ADMIN EFFICIENCY DRIVE PERSON...MGT APT/TEST   EXEC
PERS/TEST CHARTS LAB/EXP BIBLIOG 20. PAGE 21 B0420   STAT
                                                    B62
JENNINGS E.E.,THE EXECUTIVE: AUTOCRAT, BUREAUCRAT,   EX/STRUC
DEMOCRAT. LEAD EFFICIENCY DRIVE 20. PAGE 56 B1131   INGP/REL
                                                    TOP/EX
                                                    CONTROL
                                                    B62
PACKARD V.,THE PYRAMID CLIMBERS. USA+45 ELITES   INDUS
SOCIETY CREATE PROB/SOLV EFFICIENCY ATTIT...MGT 20. TOP/EX
PAGE 80 B1621   PERS/REL
                                                    DRIVE
                                                    B62
PRESTHUS R.,THE ORGANIZATIONAL SOCIETY. USA+45   LG/CO
STRUCT ECO/DEV ADMIN ATTIT ALL/VALS...PSY SOC 20.   WORKER
PAGE 84 B1703   PERS/REL
                                                    DRIVE
                                                    B62
WANGSNESS P.H.,THE POWER OF THE CITY MANAGER.   PWR
USA+45 EX/STRUC BAL/PWR BUDGET TAX ADMIN REPRESENT   TOP/EX
CENTRAL EFFICIENCY DRIVE ROLE...POLICY 20 CITY/MGT. MUNIC
PAGE 113 B2286   LOC/G
                                                    S62
BRZEZINSKI Z.K.,"DEVIATION CONTROL: A STUDY IN THE   RIGID/FLEX
DYNAMICS OF DOCTRINAL CONFLICT." WOR+45 WOR-45   ATTIT
VOL/ASSN CREATE BAL/PWR DOMIN EXEC DRIVE PERCEPT
PWR...METH/CNCPT TIME/SEQ TREND 20. PAGE 16 B0333
                                                    S62
GUYOT J.F.,"GOVERNMENT BUREAUCRATS ARE DIFFERENT."   ATTIT
USA+45 REPRESENT PWR 20. PAGE 45 B0906   DRIVE
                                                    TOP/EX
                                                    ADMIN
                                                    S62
HUDSON G.F.,"SOVIET FEARS OF THE WEST." COM USA+45   ATTIT
SOCIETY DELIB/GP EX/STRUC TOP/EX ACT/RES CREATE   MYTH
DOMIN EDU/PROP LEGIT ADMIN ROUTINE DRIVE PERSON   GERMANY
RIGID/FLEX PWR...RECORD TIME/SEQ TOT/POP 20   USSR
STALIN/J. PAGE 52 B1057
                                                    S62
MCCLELLAND C.A.,"DECISIONAL OPPORTUNITY AND   ACT/RES
POLITICAL CONTROVERSY." USA+45 NAT/G POL/PAR FORCES PERCEPT
TOP/EX DOMIN ADMIN PEACE DRIVE ORD/FREE PWR   DIPLOM
...DECISION SIMUL 20. PAGE 72 B1444
                                                    S62
READ W.H.,"UPWARD COMMUNICATION IN INDUSTRIAL   ADMIN
HIERARCHIES." LG/CO TOP/EX PROB/SOLV DOMIN EXEC   INGP/REL
PERS/REL ATTIT DRIVE PERCEPT...CORREL STAT CHARTS   PSY
20. PAGE 86 B1747   MGT
                                                    S62
SPRINGER H.W.,"FEDERATION IN THE CARIBBEAN: AN   VOL/ASSN
ATTEMPT THAT FAILED." L/A+17C ECO/UNDEV INT/ORG   NAT/G
POL/PAR PROVS LEGIS CREATE PLAN LEGIT ADMIN FEDERAL REGION
ATTIT DRIVE PERSON ORD/FREE PWR...POLICY GEOG PSY
CONCPT OBS CARIBBEAN CMN/WLTH 20. PAGE 100 B2013
                                                    S62
TANNENBAUM A.S.,"CONTROL IN ORGANIZATIONS: ADMIN
INDIVIDUAL ADJUSTMENT AND ORGANIZATIONAL   MGT
PERFORMANCE." DOMIN PARTIC REPRESENT INGP/REL   STRUCT
PRODUC ATTIT DRIVE PWR...PSY CORREL. PAGE 102 B2073 CONTROL
                                                    B63
BERNE E.,THE STRUCTURE AND DYNAMICS OF   INGP/REL
ORGANIZATIONS AND GROUPS. CLIENT PARTIC DRIVE   AUTHORIT
HEALTH...MGT PSY ORG/CHARTS. PAGE 11 B0226   ROUTINE
                                                    CLASSIF

                                                    B63
COSTELLO T.W.,PSYCHOLOGY IN ADMINISTRATION: A   PSY
RESEARCH ORIENTATION. CREATE PROB/SOLV PERS/REL   MGT
ADJUST ANOMIE ATTIT DRIVE PERCEPT ROLE...DECISION   EXEC
BIBLIOG T 20. PAGE 24 B0488   ADMIN
                                                    B63
DE GUZMAN R.P.,PATTERNS IN DECISION-MAKING: CASE   ADMIN
STUDIES IN PHILIPPINE PUBLIC ADMINISTRATION.   DECISION
PHILIPPINE LAW CHIEF PROB/SOLV MGT/REL DRIVE   POLICY
PERCEPT ROLE...ANTHOL T 20. PAGE 27 B0557   GOV/REL
                                                    B63
HOWER R.M.,MANAGERS AND SCIENTISTS. EX/STRUC CREATE R+D
ADMIN REPRESENT ATTIT DRIVE ROLE PWR SKILL...SOC   MGT
INT. PAGE 52 B1052   PERS/REL
                                                    INGP/REL
                                                    B63
JOHNS R.,CONFRONTING ORGANIZATIONAL CHANGE. NEIGH   SOC/WK
DELIB/GP CREATE OP/RES ADMIN GP/REL DRIVE...WELF/ST WEALTH
SOC RECORD BIBLIOG. PAGE 56 B1142   LEAD
                                                    VOL/ASSN
                                                    B63
LITTERER J.A.,ORGANIZATIONS: STRUCTURE AND   ADMIN
BEHAVIOR. PLAN DOMIN CONTROL LEAD ROUTINE SANCTION   CREATE
INGP/REL EFFICIENCY PRODUC DRIVE RIGID/FLEX PWR.   MGT
PAGE 66 B1325   ADJUST
                                                    B63
MCKIE R.,MALAYSIA IN FOCUS. INDONESIA WOR+45   S/ASIA
ECO/UNDEV FINAN NAT/G POL/PAR SECT FORCES PLAN   NAT/LISM
ADMIN COLONIAL COERCE DRIVE ALL/VALS...POLICY   MALAYSIA
RECORD CENSUS TIME/SEQ CMN/WLTH 20. PAGE 72 B1453
                                                    B63
TUCKER R.C.,THE SOVIET POLITICAL MIND. WOR+45   COM
ELITES INT/ORG NAT/G POL/PAR PLAN DIPLOM ECO/TAC   TOP/EX
DOMIN ADMIN NUC/PWR REV DRIVE PERSON SUPEGO PWR   USSR
WEALTH...POLICY MGT PSY CONCPT OBS BIOG TREND
COLD/WAR MARX/KARL 20. PAGE 106 B2134
                                                    B63
WARNER W.L.,THE AMERICAN FEDERAL EXECUTIVE. USA+45   ELITES
USA-45 CONSULT EX/STRUC GP/REL DRIVE ALL/VALS...PSY NAT/G
DEEP/QU CHARTS 19/20 PRESIDENT. PAGE 114 B2295   TOP/EX
                                                    ADMIN
                                                    L63
FREUND G.,"ADENAUER AND THE FUTURE OF GERMANY."   NAT/G
EUR+WWI FUT GERMANY/W FORCES LEGIT ADMIN ROUTINE   BIOG
ATTIT DRIVE PERSON PWR...POLICY TIME/SEQ TREND   DIPLOM
VAL/FREE 20 ADENAUER/K. PAGE 37 B0753   GERMANY
                                                    S63
BRZEZINSKI Z.K.,"CINCINNATUS AND THE APPARATCHIK."   POL/PAR
COM USA+45 USA-45 ELITES LOC/G NAT/G PROVS CONSULT   USSR
LEGIS DOMIN LEGIT EXEC ROUTINE CHOOSE DRIVE PWR
SKILL...CONCPT CHARTS VAL/FREE COLD/WAR 20. PAGE 16
B0334
                                                    S63
MANGONE G.,"THE UNITED NATIONS AND UNITED STATES   INT/ORG
FOREIGN POLICY." USA+45 WOR+45 ECO/UNDEV NAT/G   ECO/TAC
DIPLOM LEGIT ROUTINE ATTIT DRIVE...TIME/SEQ UN   FOR/AID
COLD/WAR 20. PAGE 69 B1390
                                                    S63
RUSTOW D.A.,"THE MILITARY IN MIDDLE EASTERN SOCIETY FORCES
AND POLITICS." FUT ISLAM CONSTN SOCIETY FACE/GP   ELITES
NAT/G POL/PAR PROF/ORG CONSULT DOMIN ADMIN EXEC
REGION COERCE NAT/LISM ATTIT DRIVE PERSON ORD/FREE
PWR...POLICY CONCPT OBS STERTYP 20. PAGE 92 B1860
                                                    S63
SCHMITT H.A.,"THE EUROPEAN COMMUNITIES." EUR+WWI   VOL/ASSN
FRANCE DELIB/GP EX/STRUC TOP/EX CREATE TEC/DEV   ECO/DEV
ECO/TAC LEGIT REGION COERCE DRIVE ALL/VALS
...METH/CNCPT EEC 20. PAGE 94 B1897
                                                    S63
SCHURMANN F.,"ECONOMIC POLICY AND POLITICAL POWER   PLAN
IN COMMUNIST CHINA." ASIA CHINA/COM USSR SOCIETY   ECO/TAC
ECO/UNDEV AGRI INDUS CREATE ADMIN ROUTINE ATTIT
DRIVE RIGID/FLEX PWR WEALTH...HIST/WRIT TREND
CHARTS WORK 20. PAGE 94 B1908
                                                    B64
ADAMS V.,THE PEACE CORPS IN ACTION. USA+45 VOL/ASSN DIPLOM
EX/STRUC GOV/REL PERCEPT ORD/FREE...OBS 20   FOR/AID
KENNEDY/JF PEACE/CORP. PAGE 3 B0058   PERSON
                                                    DRIVE
                                                    B64
ARGYRIS C.,INTEGRATING THE INDIVIDUAL AND THE   ADMIN
ORGANIZATION. WORKER PROB/SOLV LEAD SANCTION   PERS/REL
REPRESENT ADJUST EFFICIENCY DRIVE PERSON...PSY   VOL/ASSN
METH/CNCPT ORG/CHARTS. PAGE 6 B0132   PARTIC
                                                    B64
KARIEL H.S.,IN SEARCH OF AUTHORITY: TWENTIETH-   CONSTN
CENTURY POLITICAL THOUGHT. WOR+45 WOR-45 NAT/G   CONCPT
EX/STRUC TOTALISM DRIVE PWR...MGT PHIL/SCI GEN/LAWS ORD/FREE
19/20 NIETZSCH/F FREUD/S WEBER/MAX NIEBUHR/R   IDEA/COMP
MARITAIN/J. PAGE 58 B1173
                                                    B64
PEABODY R.L.,ORGANIZATIONAL AUTHORITY. SCHOOL   ADMIN
WORKER PLAN SENIOR GOV/REL UTIL DRIVE PWR...PSY   EFFICIENCY
CHARTS BIBLIOG 20. PAGE 82 B1648   TASK
                                                    GP/REL

SULLIVAN G.,THE STORY OF THE PEACE CORPS. USA+45   B64
WOR+45 INTELL FACE/GP NAT/G SCHOOL VOL/ASSN CONSULT   INT/ORG
EX/STRUC PLAN EDU/PROP ADMIN ATTIT DRIVE ALL/VALS   ECO/UNDEV
...POLICY HEAL SOC CONCPT INT QU BIOG TREND SOC/EXP   FOR/AID
WORK. PAGE 102 B2054   PEACE

WILLIAMSON O.E.,THE ECONOMICS OF DISCRETIONARY   B64
BEHAVIOR: MANAGERIAL OBJECTIVES IN A THEORY OF THE   EFFICIENCY
FIRM. MARKET BUDGET CAP/ISM PRODUC DRIVE PERSON   MGT
...STAT CHARTS BIBLIOG METH 20. PAGE 117 B2354   ECO/TAC
                                                          CHOOSE

HAAS E.B.,"ECONOMICS AND DIFFERENTIAL PATTERNS OF   L64
POLITICAL INTEGRATION: PROJECTIONS ABOUT UNITY IN   L/A+17C
LATIN AMERICA." SOCIETY NAT/G DELIB/GP ACT/RES   INT/ORG
CREATE PLAN ECO/TAC REGION ROUTINE ATTIT DRIVE PWR   MARKET
WEALTH...CONCPT TREND CHARTS LAFTA 20. PAGE 45
B0910

MILLIS W.,"THE DEMILITARIZED WORLD." COM USA+45   L64
USSR WOR+45 CONSTN NAT/G EX/STRUC PLAN LEGIT ATTIT   FUT
DRIVE...CONCPT TIME/SEQ STERTYP TOT/POP COLD/WAR   INT/ORG
20. PAGE 74 B1486   BAL/PWR
                                                          PEACE

GALTUNE J.,"BALANCE OF POWER AND THE PROBLEM OF   S64
PERCEPTION, A LOGICAL ANALYSIS." WOR+45 CONSTN   PWR
SOCIETY NAT/G DELIB/GP EX/STRUC LEGIS DOMIN ADMIN   PSY
COERCE DRIVE ORD/FREE...POLICY CONCPT OBS TREND   ARMS/CONT
GEN/LAWS. PAGE 38 B0778   WAR

SCOTT R.E.,"MEXICAN GOVERNMENT IN TRANSITION (REV   C64
ED)" CULTURE STRUCT POL/PAR CHIEF ADMIN LOBBY REV   NAT/G
CHOOSE GP/REL DRIVE...BIBLIOG METH 20 MEXIC/AMER.   L/A+17C
PAGE 95 B1920   ROUTINE
                                                          CONSTN

CANADA NATL JT COUN PUB SERV,THE CANADA NATIONAL   N64
JOINT COUNCIL OF THE PUBLIC SERVICE 1944-1964   GP/REL
(PAMPHLET). CANADA EX/STRUC PERS/REL DRIVE...MGT 20   NAT/G
PEARSON/L. PAGE 18 B0373   LABOR
                                                          EFFICIENCY

ECCLES H.E.,MILITARY CONCEPTS AND PHILOSOPHY.   B65
USA+45 STRUCT EXEC ROUTINE COERCE WAR CIVMIL/REL   PLAN
COST...OBS GEN/LAWS COLD/WAR. PAGE 32 B0648   DRIVE
                                                          LEAD
                                                          FORCES

QUADE Q.L.,"THE TRUMAN ADMINISTRATION AND THE   S65
SEPARATION OF POWERS: THE CASE OF THE MARSHALL   USA+45
PLAN." SOCIETY INT/ORG NAT/G CONSULT DELIB/GP LEGIS   ECO/UNDEV
PLAN ECO/TAC ROUTINE DRIVE PERCEPT RIGID/FLEX   DIPLOM
ORD/FREE PWR WEALTH...DECISION GEOG NEW/IDEA TREND
20 TRUMAN/HS. PAGE 85 B1726

BROWN R.E.,JUDGMENT IN ADMINISTRATION. DRIVE PERSON   B66
KNOWL...DECISION 20. PAGE 16 B0326   ADMIN
                                                          EXEC
                                                          SKILL
                                                          PROB/SOLV

O'NEILL C.E.,CHURCH AND STATE IN FRENCH COLONIAL   B66
LOUISIANA: POLICY AND POLITICS TO 1732. PROVS   COLONIAL
VOL/ASSN DELIB/GP ADJUD ADMIN GP/REL ATTIT DRIVE   NAT/G
...POLICY BIBLIOG 17/18 LOUISIANA CHURCH/STA.   SECT
PAGE 79 B1601   PWR

ALPANDER G.G.,"ENTREPRENEURS AND PRIVATE ENTERPRISE   S67
IN TURKEY." TURKEY INDUS PROC/MFG EDU/PROP ATTIT   ECO/UNDEV
DRIVE WEALTH...GEOG MGT SOC STAT TREND CHARTS 20.   LG/CO
PAGE 4 B0080   NAT/G
                                                          POLICY

BASTID M.,"ORIGINES ET DEVELOPMENT DE LA REVOLUTION   S67
CULTURELLE." CHINA/COM DOMIN ADMIN CONTROL LEAD   REV
COERCE CROWD ATTIT DRIVE MARXISM...POLICY 20.   CULTURE
PAGE 10 B0195   ACADEM
                                                          WORKER

BERLINER J.S.,"RUSSIA'S BUREAUCRATS - WHY THEY'RE   S67
REACTIONARY." USSR NAT/G OP/RES PROB/SOLV TEC/DEV   CREATE
CONTROL SANCTION EFFICIENCY DRIVE PERSON...TECHNIC   ADMIN
SOC 20. PAGE 11 B0223   INDUS
                                                          PRODUC

DONNELL J.C.,"PACIFICATION REASSESSED." VIETNAM/S   S67
NAT/LISM DRIVE SUPEGO ORD/FREE...SOC/WK 20. PAGE 30   ADMIN
B0606   GP/REL
                                                          EFFICIENCY
                                                          MUNIC

SCOTT W.R.,"ORGANIZATIONAL EVALUATION AND   S67
AUTHORITY." CONTROL SANCTION PERS/REL ATTIT DRIVE   EXEC
...SOC CONCPT OBS CHARTS IDEA/COMP 20. PAGE 95   WORKER
B1921   INSPECT
                                                          EX/STRUC

SUBRAMANIAM V.,"REPRESENTATIVE BUREAUCRACY: A   S67
REASSESSMENT." USA+45 ELITES LOC/G NAT/G ADMIN   STRATA
GOV/REL PRIVIL DRIVE ROLE...POLICY CENSUS 20   GP/REL
CIVIL/SERV BUREAUCRCY. PAGE 101 B2053   MGT
                                                          GOV/COMP

DROR Y. B0618

DRUCKER P.F. B0619,B0620

DRUG ADDICTION....SEE BIO/SOC, ANOMIE, CRIME

DRURY J.W. B0621

DRYDEN S. B0622

DUBCEK/A....ALEXANDER DUBCEK

DUBIN R. B0623

DUBOIS/J....JULES DUBOIS

DUBOIS/WEB....W.E.B. DUBOIS

DUCKWORTH W.E. B0624

DUCROS B. B0625

DUE J.F. B0626

DUFTY N.F. B0627

DUGGAR G.S. B0628

DUGGAR J.W. B0629

DUGUIT/L....LEON DUGUIT

DUHRING/E....EUGEN DUHRING

DULLES/JF....JOHN FOSTER DULLES

                                                               B57
BEAL J.R.,JOHN FOSTER DULLES, A BIOGRAPHY. USA+45   BIOG
USSR WOR+45 CONSTN INT/ORG NAT/G EX/STRUC LEGIT   DIPLOM
ADMIN NUC/PWR DISPL PERSON ORD/FREE PWR SKILL
...POLICY PSY OBS RECORD COLD/WAR UN 20 DULLES/JF.
PAGE 10 B0200
                                                               B62
BENSON E.T.,CROSS FIRE: THE EIGHT YEARS WITH   ADMIN
EISENHOWER. USA+45 DIPLOM LEAD ATTIT PERSON   POLICY
CONSERVE...TRADIT BIOG 20 EISNHWR/DD PRESIDENT   DELIB/GP
TAFT/RA DULLES/JF NIXON/RM. PAGE 11 B0218   TOP/EX

DUN J.L. B0630

DUNCOMBE H.S. B0631

DUNN A. B0632

DUNNILL F. B0633

DUPONT....DUPONT CORPORATION (E.I. DUPONT DE NEMOURS)

DURKHEIM/E....EMIL DURKHEIM

DUROSELLE J.B. B0634

DUTY....SEE SUPEGO

DUVERGER M. B0635,B0636

DUVERGER/M....MAURICE DUVERGER

DWARKADAS R. B0637

DWYER R.J. B0638

DYER F.C. B0639

DYER J.M. B0639

DYKMAN J.W. B0640

E

EACM....EAST AFRICAN COMMON MARKET

EAKIN T.C. B0641

EAST J.P. B0642

EAST AFRICA....SEE AFRICA/E

EAST GERMANY....SEE GERMANY/E

EAST KENTUCKY REGIONAL PLAN B0643,B0644

EASTERN EUROPE....SEE EUROPE/E

EASTIN R. B1894

EASTON S.C. B0645

EATING....EATING, CUISINE

B58
SHAW S.J.,THE FINANCIAL AND ADMINISTRATIVE
ORGANIZATION AND DEVELOPMENT OF OTTOMAN EGYPT
1517-1798. UAR LOC/G FORCES BUDGET INT/TRADE TAX
EATING INCOME WEALTH...CHARTS BIBLIOG 16/18 OTTOMAN
NAPOLEON/B. PAGE 96 B1940
FINAN
ADMIN
GOV/REL
CULTURE

B66
MOOMAW I.W.,THE CHALLENGE OF HUNGER. USA+45 PLAN
ADMIN EATING 20. PAGE 75 B1509
FOR/AID
DIPLOM
ECO/UNDEV
ECO/TAC

EATON H. B0646

EATON J.W. B0647

ECCLES H.E. B0648

ECHAVARRIA J.M. B0562

ECHR....EUROPEAN CONVENTION ON HUMAN RIGHTS

S64
SCHWELB E.,"OPERATION OF THE EUROPEAN CONVENTION ON
HUMAN RIGHTS." EUR+WWI LAW SOCIETY CREATE EDU/PROP
ADJUD ADMIN PEACE ATTIT ORD/FREE PWR...POLICY
INT/LAW CONCPT OBS GEN/LAWS UN VAL/FREE ILO 20
ECHR. PAGE 95 B1916
INT/ORG
MORAL

ECKHOFF T. B0649

ECO....ECONOMICS

ECO/DEV....ECONOMIC SYSTEM IN DEVELOPED COUNTRIES

ECO/TAC....ECONOMIC MEASURES

N
MARKETING INFORMATION GUIDE. USA+45 ECO/DEV FINAN
ADMIN GP/REL. PAGE 1 B0018
BIBLIOG/A
DIST/IND
MARKET
ECO/TAC

B00
MORRIS H.C.,THE HISTORY OF COLONIZATION. WOR+45
WOR-45 ECO/DEV ECO/UNDEV INT/ORG ACT/RES PLAN
ECO/TAC LEGIT ROUTINE COERCE ATTIT DRIVE ALL/VALS
...GEOG TREND 19. PAGE 76 B1528
DOMIN
SOVEREIGN
COLONIAL

N19
ANDERSON J.,THE ORGANIZATION OF ECONOMIC STUDIES IN
RELATION TO THE PROBLEMS OF GOVERNMENT (PAMPHLET).
UK FINAN INDUS DELIB/GP PLAN PROB/SOLV ADMIN 20.
PAGE 5 B0093
ECO/TAC
ACT/RES
NAT/G
CENTRAL

N19
BURRUS B.R.,INVESTIGATION AND DISCOVERY IN STATE
ANTITRUST (PAMPHLET). USA+45 USA-45 LEGIS ECO/TAC
ADMIN CONTROL CT/SYS CRIME GOV/REL PWR...JURID
CHARTS 19/20 FTC MONOPOLY. PAGE 17 B0355
NAT/G
PROVS
LAW
INSPECT

N19
GORWALA A.D.,THE ADMINISTRATIVE JUNGLE (PAMPHLET).
INDIA NAT/G LEGIS ECO/TAC CONTROL GOV/REL
...METH/COMP 20. PAGE 41 B0838
ADMIN
POLICY
PLAN
ECO/UNDEV

N19
KUWAIT ARABIA,KUWAIT FUND FOR ARAB ECONOMIC
DEVELOPMENT (PAMPHLET). ISLAM KUWAIT UAR ECO/UNDEV
LEGIS ECO/TAC WEALTH 20. PAGE 62 B1245
FOR/AID
DIPLOM
FINAN
ADMIN

B25
THOMAS F.,THE ENVIRONMENTAL BASIS OF SOCIETY.
USA-45 WOR-45 STRATA ECO/DEV EXTR/IND CONSULT
ECO/TAC ROUTINE ATTIT ALL/VALS...SOC TIME/SEQ.
PAGE 104 B2098
SOCIETY
GEOG

B28
BUELL R.,THE NATIVE PROBLEM IN AFRICA. KIN LABOR
LOC/G ECO/TAC ROUTINE ORD/FREE...REC/INT KNO/TEST
CENSUS TREND CHARTS SOC/EXP STERTYP 20. PAGE 17
B0339
AFR
CULTURE

B28
HARDMAN J.B.,AMERICAN LABOR DYNAMICS. WORKER
ECO/TAC DOMIN ADJUD LEAD LOBBY PWR...POLICY MGT.
PAGE 47 B0944
LABOR
INGP/REL
ATTIT
GP/REL

B28
SOROKIN P.,CONTEMPORARY SOCIOLOGICAL THEORIES.
MOD/EUR UNIV SOCIETY R+D SCHOOL ECO/TAC EDU/PROP
ROUTINE ATTIT DRIVE...PSY CONCPT TIME/SEQ TREND
GEN/LAWS 20. PAGE 99 B1997
CULTURE
SOC
WAR

B29
ROBERTS S.H.,HISTORY OF FRENCH COLONIAL POLICY. AFR
ASIA L/A+17C S/ASIA CULTURE ECO/DEV ECO/UNDEV FINAN
NAT/G PLAN ECO/TAC DOMIN ROUTINE SOVEREIGN...OBS
HIST/WRIT TREND CHARTS VAL/FREE 19/20. PAGE 89
B1796
INT/ORG
ACT/RES
FRANCE
COLONIAL

B31
DEKAT A.D.A.,COLONIAL POLICY. S/ASIA CULTURE
EX/STRUC ECO/TAC DOMIN ADMIN COLONIAL ROUTINE
DRIVE
PWR

SOVEREIGN WEALTH...POLICY MGT RECORD KNO/TEST SAMP.
PAGE 28 B0570
INDONESIA
NETHERLAND
B32

WRIGHT Q.,GOLD AND MONETARY STABILIZATION. FUT
USA-45 WOR-45 INTELL ECO/DEV INT/ORG NAT/G CONSULT
PLAN ECO/TAC ADMIN ATTIT WEALTH...CONCPT TREND 20.
PAGE 118 B2383
FINAN
POLICY

B33
HETTINGER H.S.,A DECADE OF RADIO ADVERTISING.
USA-45 ECO/DEV CAP/ISM PRICE...CHARTS 20. PAGE 49
B0999
EDU/PROP
COM/IND
ECO/TAC
ROUTINE

B34
US TARIFF COMMISSION,THE TARIFF: A BIBLIOGRAPHY: A
SELECT LIST OF REFERENCES. USA-45 LAW DIPLOM TAX
ADMIN...POLICY TREATY 20. PAGE 111 B2246
BIBLIOG/A
TARIFFS
ECO/TAC

B37
PARSONS T.,THE STRUCTURE OF SOCIAL ACTION. UNIV
INTELL SOCIETY INDUS MARKET ECO/TAC ROUTINE CHOOSE
ALL/VALS...CONCPT OBS BIOG TREND GEN/LAWS 20.
PAGE 81 B1636
CULTURE
ATTIT
CAP/ISM

B37
ROBBINS L.,ECONOMIC PLANNING AND INTERNATIONAL
ORDER. WOR-45 SOCIETY FINAN INDUS NAT/G ECO/TAC
ROUTINE WEALTH...SOC TIME/SEQ GEN/METH WORK 20
KEYNES/JM. PAGE 89 B1791
INT/ORG
PLAN
INT/TRADE

B37
ROYAL INST. INT. AFF.,THE COLONIAL PROBLEM. WOR-45
LAW ECO/DEV ECO/UNDEV NAT/G PLAN ECO/TAC EDU/PROP
ADMIN ATTIT ALL/VALS...CONCPT 20. PAGE 91 B1844
INT/ORG
ACT/RES
SOVEREIGN
COLONIAL

B38
DAY C.,A HISTORY OF COMMERCE. CHRIST-17C EUR+WWI
ISLAM MEDIT-7 MOD/EUR USA-45 ECO/DEV FINAN NAT/G
ECO/TAC EXEC ROUTINE PWR WEALTH HIST/WRIT. PAGE 27
B0546
MARKET
INT/TRADE

B38
LANGE O.,ON THE ECONOMIC THEORY OF SOCIALISM. UNIV
ECO/DEV FINAN INDUS INT/ORG PUB/INST ROUTINE ATTIT
ALL/VALS...SOC CONCPT STAT TREND 20. PAGE 62 B1258
MARKET
ECO/TAC
INT/TRADE
SOCISM

B39
HITLER A.,MEIN KAMPF. EUR+WWI FUT MOD/EUR STRUCT
INT/ORG LABOR NAT/G POL/PAR FORCES CREATE PLAN
BAL/PWR DIPLOM ECO/TAC DOMIN EDU/PROP ADMIN COERCE
ATTIT...SOCIALIST BIOG TREND NAZI. PAGE 50 B1020
PWR
NEW/IDEA
WAR

B39
ZIMMERN A.,MODERN POLITICAL DOCTRINE. WOR-45
CULTURE SOCIETY ECO/UNDEV DELIB/GP STRUC CREATE
DOMIN COERCE NAT/LISM ATTIT RIGID/FLEX ORD/FREE PWR
WEALTH...POLICY CONCPT OBS TIME/SEQ TREND TOT/POP
LEAGUE/NAT 20. PAGE 119 B2402
NAT/G
ECO/TAC
BAL/PWR
INT/TRADE

S40
GERTH H.,"THE NAZI PARTY: ITS LEADERSHIP AND
COMPOSITION" (BMR)" GERMANY ELITES STRATA STRUCT
EX/STRUC FORCES ECO/TAC CT/SYS CHOOSE TOTALISM
AGE/Y AUTHORIT PWR 20. PAGE 39 B0792
POL/PAR
DOMIN
LEAD
ADMIN

B41
PERHAM M.,AFRICANS AND BRITISH RULE. AFR UK ECO/TAC
CONTROL GP/REL ATTIT 20. PAGE 82 B1654
DIPLOM
COLONIAL
ADMIN
ECO/UNDEV

B42
HARLOW R.F.,PUBLIC RELATIONS IN WAR AND PEACE. FUT
USA-45 ECO/DEV ECO/TAC ROUTINE 20. PAGE 47 B0947
WAR
ATTIT
SOCIETY
INGP/REL

B42
WRIGHT D.M.,THE CREATION OF PURCHASING POWER.
USA-45 NAT/G PRICE ADMIN WAR INCOME PRODUC...POLICY
CONCPT IDEA/COMP BIBLIOG 20 MONEY. PAGE 118 B2378
FINAN
ECO/TAC
ECO/DEV
CREATE

B44
DAVIS H.E.,PIONEERS IN WORLD ORDER. WOR-45 CONSTN
ECO/TAC DOMIN EDU/PROP LEGIT ADJUD ADMIN ARMS/CONT
CHOOSE KNOWL ORD/FREE...POLICY JURID SOC STAT OBS
CENSUS TIME/SEQ ANTHOL LEAGUE/NAT 20. PAGE 26 B0537
INT/ORG
ROUTINE

L44
HAILEY,"THE FUTURE OF COLONIAL PEOPLES." WOR-45
CONSTN CULTURE ECO/UNDEV AGRI MARKET INT/ORG NAT/G
SECT CONSULT ECO/TAC LEGIT ADMIN NAT/LISM ALL/VALS
...SOC OBS TREND STERTYP CMN/WLTH LEAGUE/NAT
PARLIAMENT 20. PAGE 45 B0916
PLAN
CONCPT
DIPLOM
UK

B45
MILLIS H.A.,ORGANIZED LABOR (FIRST ED.). LAW STRUCT
DELIB/GP WORKER ECO/TAC ADJUD CONTROL REPRESENT
INGP/REL INCOME MGT. PAGE 74 B1485
LABOR
POLICY
ROUTINE
GP/REL

B46
CLOUGH S.B.,ECONOMIC HISTORY OF EUROPE. CHRIST-17C
EUR+WWI MOD/EUR WOR-45 SOCIETY EXEC ATTIT WEALTH
...CONCPT GEN/LAWS WORK TOT/POP VAL/FREE 7/20.
PAGE 22 B0440
ECO/TAC
CAP/ISM

B47
CONOVER H.F.,NON-SELF-GOVERNING AREAS. BELGIUM
FRANCE ITALY UK WOR+45 CULTURE ECO/UNDEV INT/ORG
BIBLIOG/A
COLONIAL

LOC/G NAT/G ECO/TAC INT/TRADE ADMIN HEALTH...SOC
UN. PAGE 23 B0465

DIPLOM

B47

WARNER W.L..THE SOCIAL SYSTEM OF THE MODERN
FACTORY; THE STRIKE: AN ANALYSIS. USA-45 STRATA
WORKER ECO/TAC GP/REL INGP/REL...MGT SOC CHARTS 20
YANKEE/C. PAGE 114 B2293

ROLE
STRUCT
LABOR
PROC/MFG

B48

DAY P..CRISIS IN SOUTH AFRICA. SOUTH/AFR UK KIN
MUNIC ECO/TAC RECEIVE 20 SMUTS/JAN MIGRATION.
PAGE 27 B0548

RACE/REL
COLONIAL
ADMIN
EXTR/IND

B48

HOOVER E.M..THE LOCATION OF ECONOMIC ACTIVITY.
WOR+45 MARKET MUNIC WORKER PROB/SOLV INT/TRADE
ADMIN COST...POLICY CHARTS T 20. PAGE 51 B1041

HABITAT
INDUS
ECO/TAC
GEOG

B49

BUSH V..MODERN ARMS AND FREE MEN. WOR-45 SOCIETY
NAT/G ECO/TAC DOMIN LEGIT EXEC COERCE DETER ATTIT
DRIVE ORD/FREE PWR...CONCPT MYTH COLD/WAR 20
COLD/WAR. PAGE 18 B0361

TEC/DEV
FORCES
NUC/PWR
WAR

B49

SCHULTZ W.J..AMERICAN PUBLIC FINANCE. USA+45
ECO/TAC TAX ADMIN GOV/REL GP/REL INCOME 20. PAGE 94
B1906

FINAN
POLICY
ECO/DEV
NAT/G

B50

HARTLAND P.C..BALANCE OF INTERREGIONAL PAYMENTS OF
NEW ENGLAND. USA+45 TEC/DEV ECO/TAC LEGIT ROUTINE
BAL/PAY PROFIT 20 NEW/ENGLND FED/RESERV. PAGE 47
B0962

ECO/DEV
FINAN
REGION
PLAN

S50

WITTFOGEL K.A.."RUSSIA AND ASIA: PROBLEMS OF
CONTEMPORARY AREA STUDIES AND INTERNATIONAL
RELATIONS." ASIA COM USA+45 SOCIETY NAT/G DIPLOM
ECO/TAC FOR/AID EDU/PROP KNOWL...HIST/WRIT TOT/POP
20. PAGE 117 B2369

ECO/DEV
ADMIN
RUSSIA
USSR

B51

WHITE L.D..THE JEFFERSONIANS: A STUDY IN
ADMINISTRATIVE HISTORY 18011829. USA-45 DELIB/GP
LEGIS TOP/EX PROB/SOLV BUDGET ECO/TAC GP/REL
FEDERAL...BIOG IDEA/COMP 19 PRESIDENT CONGRESS
JEFFERSN/T. PAGE 116 B2338

ADMIN
NAT/G
POLICY
POL/PAR

B52

EGLE W.P..ECONOMIC STABILIZATION. USA+45 SOCIETY
FINAN MARKET PLAN ECO/TAC DOMIN EDU/PROP LEGIT EXEC
WEALTH...CONCPT METH/CNCPT TREND HYPO/EXP GEN/METH
TOT/POP VAL/FREE 20. PAGE 32 B0656

NAT/G
ECO/DEV
CAP/ISM

S52

BRUEGEL J.W.."DIE INTERNAZIONALE
GEWERKSCHAFTSBEWEGUNG." COM EUR+WWI USA+45 WOR+45
DELIB/GP EX/STRUC ECO/TAC EDU/PROP ATTIT PWR
RESPECT SKILL WEALTH WORK 20. PAGE 16 B0330

VOL/ASSN
LABOR
TOTALISM

B53

MACK R.T..RAISING THE WORLDS STANDARD OF LIVING.
IRAN INT/ORG VOL/ASSN EX/STRUC ECO/TAC WEALTH...MGT
METH/CNCPT STAT CONT/OBS INT TOT/POP VAL/FREE 20
UN. PAGE 67 B1363

WOR+45
FOR/AID
INT/TRADE

B53

MEYER P..THE JEWS IN THE SOVIET SATELLITES.
CZECHOSLVK POLAND SOCIETY STRATA NAT/G BAL/PWR
ECO/TAC EDU/PROP LEGIT ADMIN COERCE ATTIT DISPL
PERCEPT HEALTH PWR RESPECT WEALTH...METH/CNCPT JEWS
VAL/FREE NAZI 20. PAGE 73 B1474

COM
SECT
TOTALISM
USSR

B53

MILLIKAN M.F..INCOME STABILIZATION FOR A DEVELOPING
DEMOCRACY. USA+45 ECO/DEV LABOR BUDGET ECO/TAC TAX
ADMIN ADJUST PRODUC WEALTH...POLICY TREND 20.
PAGE 73 B1484

ANTHOL
MARKET
EQUILIB
EFFICIENCY

S53

BLOUGH R.."THE ROLE OF THE ECONOMIST IN FEDERAL
POLICY MAKING." USA+45 ELITES INTELL ECO/DEV NAT/G
CONSULT EX/STRUC ACT/RES PLAN INT/TRADE BAL/PAY
WEALTH...POLICY CONGRESS 20. PAGE 13 B0256

DELIB/GP
ECO/TAC

B54

HOBBS E.H..BEHIND THE PRESIDENT - A STUDY OF
EXECUTIVE OFFICE AGENCIES. USA+45 NAT/G PLAN BUDGET
ECO/TAC EXEC ORD/FREE 20 BUR/BUDGET. PAGE 50 B1022

EX/STRUC
DELIB/GP
CONFER
CONSULT

B54

LOCKLIN D.P..ECONOMICS OF TRANSPORTATION (4TH ED.).
USA+45 ECO/TAC SEA AIR LAW FINAN LG/CO EX/STRUC
ADMIN CONTROL...STAT CHARTS 19/20 RAILROAD
PUB/TRANS. PAGE 66 B1335

ECO/DEV
DIST/IND
ECO/TAC
TEC/DEV

B54

RECK D..GOVERNMENT PURCHASING AND COMPETITION.
USA+45 LEGIS CAP/ISM ECO/TAC GOV/REL CENTRAL
...POLICY 20 CONGRESS. PAGE 87 B1749

NAT/G
FINAN
MGT
COST

B54

WHITE L.D..THE JACKSONIANS: A STUDY IN
ADMINISTRATIVE HISTORY 1829-1861. USA+45 CONSTN
POL/PAR CHIEF DELIB/GP LEGIS CREATE PROB/SOLV
ECO/TAC LEAD REGION GP/REL 19 PRESIDENT CONGRESS
JACKSON/A. PAGE 116 B2339

NAT/G
ADMIN
POLICY

ROSTOW W.W.."ASIAN LEADERSHIP AND FREE-WORLD
ALLIANCE." ASIA COM USA+45 CULTURE ELITES INTELL
NAT/G TEC/DEV ECO/TAC EDU/PROP COLONIAL PARL/PROC
ROUTINE COERCE DRIVE ORD/FREE MARXISM...PSY CONCPT.
PAGE 90 B1829

L54

ATTIT
LEGIT
DIPLOM

B55

BRAUN K..LABOR DISPUTES AND THEIR SETTLEMENT.
ECO/TAC ROUTINE TASK GP/REL...DECISION GEN/LAWS.
PAGE 15 B0301

INDUS
LABOR
BARGAIN
ADJUD

B55

RUSTOW D.A..THE POLITICS OF COMPROMISE. SWEDEN
LABOR EX/STRUC LEGIS PLAN REPRESENT SOCISM...SOC
19/20. PAGE 92 B1859

POL/PAR
NAT/G
POLICY
ECO/TAC

L55

KISER M.."ORGANIZATION OF AMERICAN STATES." L/A+17C
USA+45 ECO/UNDEV INT/ORG NAT/G PLAN TEC/DEV DIPLOM
ECO/TAC INT/TRADE EDU/PROP ADMIN ALL/VALS...POLICY
MGT RECORD ORG/CHARTS OAS 20. PAGE 60 B1215

VOL/ASSN
ECO/DEV
REGION

B56

ALEXANDER R.S..INDUSTRIAL MARKETING. USA+45 ECO/DEV
DIST/IND FINAN NAT/G ACT/RES CAP/ISM PRICE CONTROL
...POLICY MGT 20. PAGE 4 B0072

INDUS
MARKET
ECO/TAC
PLAN

B56

BARBASH J..THE PRACTICE OF UNIONISM. ECO/TAC LEAD
LOBBY GP/REL INGP/REL DRIVE MARXISM BIBLIOG. PAGE 9
B0182

LABOR
REPRESENT
CONTROL
ADMIN

B56

HICKMAN C.A..INDIVIDUALS, GROUPS, AND ECONOMIC
BEHAVIOR. WORKER PAY CONTROL EXEC GP/REL INGP/REL
PERSON ROLE...PSY SOC PERS/COMP METH 20. PAGE 50
B1005

MGT
ADMIN
ECO/TAC
PLAN

B56

JENNINGS W.I..THE APPROACH TO SELF-GOVERNMENT.
CEYLON INDIA PAKISTAN S/ASIA UK SOCIETY POL/PAR
DELIB/GP LEGIS ECO/TAC EDU/PROP ADMIN EXEC CHOOSE
ATTIT ALL/VALS...JURID CONCPT GEN/METH TOT/POP 20.
PAGE 56 B1136

NAT/G
CONSTN
COLONIAL

B57

DJILAS M..THE NEW CLASS: AN ANALYSIS OF THE
COMMUNIST SYSTEM. STRATA CAP/ISM ECO/TAC DOMIN
EDU/PROP LEGIT EXEC COERCE ATTIT PWR MARXISM
...MARXIST MGT CONCPT TIME/SEQ GEN/LAWS 20. PAGE 29
B0600

COM
POL/PAR
USSR
YUGOSLAVIA

B57

PYE L.W..THE POLICY IMPLICATIONS OF SOCIAL CHANGE
IN NON-WESTERN SOCIETIES. ASIA USA+45 CULTURE
STRUCT NAT/G ECO/TAC ADMIN ROLE...POLICY SOC.
PAGE 85 B1723

SOCIETY
ORD/FREE
ECO/UNDEV
DIPLOM

L57

HAAS E.B.."REGIONAL INTEGRATION AND NATIONAL
POLICY." WOR+45 VOL/ASSN DELIB/GP EX/STRUC ECO/TAC
DOMIN EDU/PROP LEGIT COERCE ATTIT PERCEPT KNOWL
...TIME/SEQ COLD/WAR 20 UN. PAGE 45 B0908

INT/ORG
ORD/FREE
REGION

S57

BAUER R.A.."BRAINWASHING: PSYCHOLOGY OR
DEMONOLOGY." ASIA CHINA/COM COM POL/PAR ECO/TAC
ADMIN COERCE ATTIT DRIVE ORD/FREE...CONCPT MYTH 20.
PAGE 10 B0196

EDU/PROP
PSY
TOTALISM

B58

ATOMIC INDUSTRIAL FORUM.MANAGEMENT AND ATOMIC
ENERGY. WOR+45 SEA LAW MARKET NAT/G TEC/DEV INSPECT
INT/TRADE CONFER PEACE HEALTH...ANTHOL 20. PAGE 7
B0145

NUC/PWR
INDUS
MGT
ECO/TAC

B58

CHANG C..THE INFLATIONARY SPIRAL: THE EXPERIENCE IN
CHINA 1939-50. CHINA/COM BUDGET INT/TRADE PRICE
ADMIN CONTROL WAR DEMAND...POLICY CHARTS 20.
PAGE 20 B0406

FINAN
ECO/TAC
BAL/PAY
GOV/REL

B58

GROSSMAN J..BIBLIOGRAPHY ON PUBLIC ADMINISTRATION
IN LATIN AMERICA. ECO/UNDEV FINAN PLAN BUDGET
ECO/TAC TARIFFS TAX...STAT 20. PAGE 44 B0893

BIBLIOG
L/A+17C
NAT/G
ADMIN

B58

LOVEJOY D.S..RHODE ISLAND POLITICS AND THE AMERICAN
REVOLUTION 1760-1776. UK USA+45 ELITES EX/STRUC TAX
LEAD REPRESENT GOV/REL GP/REL ATTIT 18 RHODE/ISL.
PAGE 67 B1343

REV
COLONIAL
ECO/TAC
SOVEREIGN

B58

WARNER A.W..CONCEPTS AND CASES IN ECONOMIC
ANALYSIS. PROB/SOLV BARGAIN CONTROL INCOME PRODUC
...ECOMETRIC MGT CONCPT CLASSIF CHARTS 20
KEYNES/JM. PAGE 114 B2292

ECO/TAC
DEMAND
EQUILIB
COST

S58

DAVENPORT J.."ARMS AND THE WELFARE STATE." INTELL
STRUCT FORCES CREATE ECO/TAC FOR/AID DOMIN LEGIT
ADMIN WAR ORD/FREE PWR...POLICY SOC CONCPT MYTH OBS
TREND COLD/WAR TOT/POP 20. PAGE 26 B0533

USA+45
NAT/G
USSR

S58

JORDAN A.."MILITARY ASSISTANCE AND NATIONAL
POLICY." ASIA FUT USA+45 WOR+45 ECO/DEV ECO/UNDEV

FORCES
POLICY

INT/ORG NAT/G PLAN ECO/TAC ROUTINE WEAPON ATTIT FOR/AID
RIGID/FLEX PWR...CONCPT TREND 20. PAGE 57 B1153 DIPLOM
S58

STAAR R.F.."ELECTIONS IN COMMUNIST POLAND." EUR+WWI COM
SOCIETY INT/ORG NAT/G POL/PAR LEGIS ACT/RES ECO/TAC CHOOSE
EDU/PROP ADJUD ADMIN ROUTINE COERCE TOTALISM ATTIT POLAND
ORD/FREE PWR 20. PAGE 100 B2015
B59

CHRISTENSON R.M..THE BRANNAN PLAN: FARM POLITICS AGRI
AND POLICY. USA+45 ECO/DEV CONSULT PLAN PAY GOV/REL NAT/G
...POLICY 20. PAGE 21 B0429 ADMIN
ECO/TAC
B59

DIEBOLD W. JR..THE SCHUMAN PLAN: A STUDY IN INT/ORG
ECONOMIC COOPERATION, 1950-1959. EUR+WWI FRANCE REGION
GERMANY USA+45 EXTR/IND CONSULT DELIB/GP PLAN
DIPLOM ECO/TAC INT/TRADE ROUTINE ORD/FREE WEALTH
...METH/CNCPT STAT CONT/OBS INT TIME/SEQ ECSC 20.
PAGE 29 B0591
B59

GINSBURG M..LAW AND OPINION IN ENGLAND. UK CULTURE JURID
KIN LABOR LEGIS EDU/PROP ADMIN CT/SYS CRIME OWN POLICY
HEALTH...ANTHOL 20 ENGLSH/LAW. PAGE 40 B0802 ECO/TAC
B59

GRABER D..CRISIS DIPLOMACY. L/A+17C USA+45 USA-45 ROUTINE
NAT/G TOP/EX ECO/TAC COERCE ATTIT ORD/FREE...CONCPT MORAL
MYTH TIME/SEQ COLD/WAR 20. PAGE 42 B0848 DIPLOM
B59

WASSERMAN P..MEASUREMENT AND ANALYSIS OF BIBLIOG/A
ORGANIZATIONAL PERFORMANCE. FINAN MARKET EX/STRUC ECO/TAC
TEC/DEV EDU/PROP CONTROL ROUTINE TASK...MGT 20. OP/RES
PAGE 114 B2300 EFFICIENCY
B59

YANG C.K..A CHINESE VILLAGE IN EARLY COMMUNIST ASIA
TRANSITION. ECO/UNDEV AGRI FAM KIN MUNIC FORCES ROUTINE
PLAN ECO/TAC DOMIN EDU/PROP ATTIT DRIVE PWR RESPECT SOCISM
...SOC CONCPT METH/CNCPT OBS RECORD CON/ANAL CHARTS
WORK 20. PAGE 118 B2389
S59

HARVEY M.F.."THE PALESTINE REFUGEE PROBLEM: ACT/RES
ELEMENTS OF A SOLUTION." ISLAM LAW INT/ORG DELIB/GP LEGIT
TOP/EX ECO/TAC ROUTINE DRIVE HEALTH LOVE ORD/FREE PEACE
PWR WEALTH...MAJORIT FAO 20. PAGE 48 B0964 ISRAEL
S59

STINCHCOMBE A.L.."BUREAUCRATIC AND CRAFT CONSTRUC
ADMINISTRATION OF PRODUCTION: A COMPARATIVE STUDY" PROC/MFG
(BMR)" USA+45 STRUCT EX/STRUC ECO/TAC GP/REL ADMIN
...CLASSIF GP/COMP IDEA/COMP GEN/LAWS 20 WEBER/MAX. PLAN
PAGE 101 B2039
S59

ZAUBERMAN A.."SOVIET BLOC ECONOMIC INTEGRATION." MARKET
COM CULTURE INTELL ECO/DEV INDUS TOP/EX ACT/RES INT/ORG
PLAN ECO/TAC INT/TRADE ROUTINE CHOOSE ATTIT USSR
...TIME/SEQ 20. PAGE 119 B2399 TOTALISM
B60

ANGERS F.A..ESSAI SUR LA CENTRALISATION: ANALYSE CENTRAL
DES PRINCIPES ET PERSPECTIVES CANADIENNES. CANADA ADMIN
ECO/TAC CONTROL...SOC IDEA/COMP BIBLIOG 20. PAGE 5
B0111
B60

ASPREMONT-LYNDEN H..RAPPORT SUR L'ADMINISTRATION AFR
BELGE DU RUANDA-URUNDI PENDANT L'ANNEE 1959. COLONIAL
BELGIUM RWANDA AGRI INDUS DIPLOM ECO/TAC INT/TRADE ECO/UNDEV
DOMIN ADMIN RACE/REL...GEOG CENSUS 20 UN. PAGE 7 INT/ORG
B0143
B60

BAERWALD F..ECONOMIC SYSTEM ANALYSIS: CONCEPTS AND ACT/RES
PERSPECTIVES. USA+45 ECO/DEV NAT/G COMPUTER EQUILIB ECO/TAC
INCOME ATTIT...DECISION CONCPT IDEA/COMP. PAGE 8 ROUTINE
B0159 FINAN
B60

BRISTOL L.H. JR..DEVELOPING THE CORPORATE IMAGE. LG/CO
USA+45 SOCIETY ECO/DEV COM/IND SCHOOL EDU/PROP ATTIT
PRESS TV...AUD/VIS ANTHOL. PAGE 15 B0312 MGT
ECO/TAC
B60

CAMPBELL R.W..SOVIET ECONOMIC POWER. COM USA+45 ECO/DEV
DIST/IND MARKET TOP/EX ACT/RES CAP/ISM ECO/TAC PLAN
DOMIN EDU/PROP ADMIN ROUTINE DRIVE...MATH TIME/SEQ SOCISM
CHARTS WORK 20. PAGE 18 B0371 USSR
B60

EASTON S.C..THE TWILIGHT OF EUROPEAN COLONIALISM. FINAN
AFR S/ASIA CONSTN SOCIETY STRUCT ECO/UNDEV INDUS ADMIN
NAT/G FORCES ECO/TAC COLONIAL CT/SYS ATTIT KNOWL
ORD/FREE PWR...SOCIALIST TIME/SEQ TREND CON/ANAL
20. PAGE 32 B0645
B60

GILMORE D.R..DEVELOPING THE "LITTLE" ECONOMIES. ECO/TAC
USA+45 FINAN LG/CO PROF/ORG VOL/ASSN CREATE ADMIN. LOC/G
PAGE 40 B0801 PROVS
PLAN
B60

GRANICK D..THE RED EXECUTIVE. COM USA+45 SOCIETY PWR
ECO/DEV INDUS NAT/G POL/PAR EX/STRUC PLAN ECO/TAC STRATA
EDU/PROP ADMIN EXEC ATTIT DRIVE...GP/COMP 20. USSR
PAGE 42 B0851 ELITES

B60
HOVING W..THE DISTRIBUTION REVOLUTION. WOR+45 DIST/IND
ECO/DEV FINAN SERV/IND PRESS PRICE INCOME PRODUC MARKET
...MGT 20. PAGE 52 B1049 ECO/TAC
TASK
B60

LENCZOWSKI G..OIL AND STATE IN THE MIDDLE EAST. FUT ISLAM
IRAN LAW ECO/UNDEV EXTR/IND NAT/G TOP/EX PLAN INDUS
TEC/DEV ECO/TAC LEGIT ADMIN COERCE ATTIT ALL/VALS NAT/LISM
PWR...CHARTS 20. PAGE 64 B1288
B60

LERNER A.P..THE ECONOMICS OF CONTROL. USA+45 ECO/DEV
ECO/UNDEV INT/ORG ACT/RES PLAN CAP/ISM INT/TRADE ROUTINE
ATTIT WEALTH...SOC MATH STAT GEN/LAWS INDEX 20. ECO/TAC
PAGE 64 B1295 SOCISM
B60

LINDSAY K..EUROPEAN ASSEMBLIES: THE EXPERIMENTAL VOL/ASSN
PERIOD 1949-1959. EUR+WWI NAT/G POL/PAR INT/ORG
LEGIS TOP/EX ACT/RES PLAN ECO/TAC DOMIN LEGIT REGION
ROUTINE ATTIT DRIVE ORD/FREE PWR SKILL...SOC CONCPT
TREND CHARTS GEN/LAWS VAL/FREE. PAGE 65 B1315
B60

LINDVEIT E.N..SCIENTISTS IN GOVERNMENT. USA+45 PAY TEC/DEV
EDU/PROP ADMIN DRIVE HABITAT ROLE...TECHNIC BIBLIOG ECO/TAC
20. PAGE 65 B1316 PHIL/SCI
GOV/REL
B60

LISKA G..THE NEW STATECRAFT. WOR+45 WOR-45 LEGIS ECO/TAC
DIPLOM ADMIN ATTIT PWR WEALTH...HIST/WRIT TREND CONCPT
COLD/WAR 20. PAGE 66 B1323 FOR/AID
B60

PENTONY D.E..UNITED STATES FOREIGN AID. INDIA LAOS FOR/AID
USA+45 ECO/UNDEV INT/TRADE ADMIN PEACE ATTIT DIPLOM
...POLICY METH/COMP ANTHOL 20. PAGE 82 B1653 ECO/TAC
B60

ROEPKE W..A HUMANE ECONOMY: THE SOCIAL FRAMEWORK OF DRIVE
THE FREE MARKET. FUT USSR WOR+45 CULTURE SOCIETY EDU/PROP
ECO/DEV PLAN ECO/TAC ADMIN ATTIT PERSON RIGID/FLEX CAP/ISM
SUPEGO MORAL WEALTH SOCISM...POLICY OLD/LIB CONCPT
TREND GEN/LAWS 20. PAGE 90 B1811
B60

ROY N.C..THE CIVIL SERVICE IN INDIA. INDIA POL/PAR ADMIN
ECO/TAC INCOME...JURID MGT 20 CIVIL/SERV. PAGE 91 NAT/G
B1843 DELIB/GP
CONFER
B60

STANFORD RESEARCH INSTITUTE..AFRICAN DEVELOPMENT: A FOR/AID
TEST FOR INTERNATIONAL COOPERATION. AFR USA+45 ECO/UNDEV
WOR+45 FINAN INT/ORG PLAN PROB/SOLV ECO/TAC ATTIT
INT/TRADE ADMIN...CHARTS 20. PAGE 100 B2018 DIPLOM
L60

BRENNAN D.G.."SETTING AND GOALS OF ARMS CONTROL." FORCES
FUT USA+45 USSR WOR+45 INTELL INT/ORG NAT/G COERCE
VOL/ASSN CONSULT PLAN DIPLOM ECO/TAC ADMIN KNOWL ARMS/CONT
PWR...POLICY CONCPT TREND COLD/WAR 20. PAGE 15 DETER
B0305
L60

STEIN E.."LEGAL REMEDIES OF ENTERPRISES IN THE MARKET
EUROPEAN ECONOMIC COMMUNITY." EUR+WWI FUT ECO/DEV ADJUD
INDUS LABOR PLAN ECO/TAC ADMIN PWR...MGT MATH STAT TREND
CON/ANAL EEC 20. PAGE 100 B2026
S60

"THE EMERGING COMMON MARKETS IN LATIN AMERICA." FUT FINAN
L/A+17C STRATA DIST/IND INDUS LABOR NAT/G LEGIS ECO/UNDEV
ECO/TAC ADMIN RIGID/FLEX HEALTH...NEW/IDEA TIME/SEQ INT/TRADE
OAS 20. PAGE 2 B0039
S60

EMERSON R.."THE EROSION OF DEMOCRACY." AFR FUT LAW S/ASIA
CULTURE INTELL SOCIETY ECO/UNDEV FAM LOC/G NAT/G POL/PAR
FORCES PLAN TEC/DEV ECO/TAC ADMIN CT/SYS ATTIT
ORD/FREE PWR...SOCIALIST SOC CONCPT STAND/INT
TIME/SEQ WORK 20. PAGE 33 B0671
S60

FRANKEL S.H.."ECONOMIC ASPECTS OF POLITICAL NAT/G
INDEPENDENCE IN AFRICA." AFR FUT SOCIETY ECO/UNDEV FOR/AID
COM/IND FINAN LEGIS PLAN TEC/DEV CAP/ISM ECO/TAC
INT/TRADE ADMIN ATTIT DRIVE RIGID/FLEX PWR WEALTH
...MGT NEW/IDEA MATH TIME/SEQ VAL/FREE 20. PAGE 37
B0751
S60

GARNICK D.H.."ON THE ECONOMIC FEASIBILITY OF A MARKET
MIDDLE EASTERN COMMON MARKET." AFR ISLAM CULTURE INT/TRADE
INDUS NAT/G TEC/DEV ECO/TAC ADMIN ATTIT DRIVE
RIGID/FLEX...PLURIST STAT TREND GEN/LAWS 20.
PAGE 39 B0784
S60

GROSSMAN G.."SOVIET GROWTH: ROUTINE, INERTIA, AND POL/PAR
PRESSURE." COM STRATA NAT/G DELIB/GP PLAN TEC/DEV ECO/DEV
ECO/TAC EDU/PROP ADMIN ROUTINE DRIVE WEALTH USSR
COLD/WAR 20. PAGE 44 B0891
S60

HERRERA F.."THE INTER-AMERICAN DEVELOPMENT BANK." L/A+17C
USA+45 ECO/UNDEV INT/ORG CONSULT DELIB/GP PLAN FINAN
ECO/TAC INT/TRADE ROUTINE WEALTH...STAT 20. PAGE 49 FOR/AID
B0994 REGION

HUNTINGTON S.P.,"STRATEGIC PLANNING AND THE
POLITICAL PROCESS." USA+45 NAT/G DELIB/GP LEGIS
ACT/RES ECO/TAC LEGIT ROUTINE CHOOSE RIGID/FLEX PWR
...POLICY MAJORIT MGT 20. PAGE 53 B1066
S60 EXEC FORCES NUC/PWR WAR

MORALES C.J.,"TRADE AND ECONOMIC INTEGRATION IN
LATIN AMERICA." FUT L/A+17C LAW STRATA ECO/UNDEV
DIST/IND INDUS LABOR NAT/G LEGIS ECO/TAC ADMIN
RIGID/FLEX WEALTH...CONCPT NEW/IDEA CONT/OBS
TIME/SEQ WORK 20. PAGE 75 B1519
S60 FINAN INT/TRADE REGION

NORTH R.C.,"DIE DISKREPANZ ZWISCHEN REALITAT UND
WUNSCHBILD ALS INNENPOLITISCHER FAKTOR." ASIA
CHINA/COM COM FUT ECO/UNDEV NAT/G PLAN DOMIN ADMIN
COERCE PERCEPT...SOC MYTH GEN/METH WORK TOT/POP 20.
PAGE 79 B1589
S60 SOCIETY ECO/TAC

REISELBACH L.N.,"THE BASIS OF ISOLATIONIST
BEHAVIOR." USA+45 USA-45 CULTURE ECO/DEV LOC/G
NAT/G ADMIN ROUTINE CHOOSE BIO/SOC DRIVE RIGID/FLEX
...CENSUS SAMP TREND CHARTS TOT/POP 20. PAGE 87
B1765
S60 ATTIT DIPLOM ECO/TAC

RIESELBACH Z.N.,"QUANTITATIVE TECHNIQUES FOR
STUDYING VOTING BEHAVIOR IN THE UNITED NATIONS
GENERAL ASSEMBLY." FUT S/ASIA USA+45 INT/ORG
BAL/PWR DIPLOM ECO/TAC FOR/AID ADMIN PWR...POLICY
METH/CNCPT METH UN 20. PAGE 88 B1783
S60 QUANT CHOOSE

SCHACHTER O.,"THE ENFORCEMENT OF INTERNATIONAL
JUDICIAL AND ARBITRAL DECISIONS." WOR+45 NAT/G
ECO/TAC DOMIN LEGIT ROUTINE COERCE ATTIT DRIVE
ALL/VALS PWR...METH/CNCPT TREND TOT/POP 20 UN.
PAGE 93 B1878
S60 INT/ORG ADJUD INT/LAW

SCHATZ S.P.,"THE INFLENCE OF PLANNING ON
DEVELOPMENT: THE NIGERIAN EXPERIENCE." AFR FUT
FINAN INDUS NAT/G EX/STRUC ECO/TAC ADMIN ATTIT
PERCEPT ORD/FREE PWR...MATH TREND CON/ANAL SIMUL
VAL/FREE 20. PAGE 93 B1883
S60 ECO/UNDEV PLAN NIGERIA

BENOIT E.,EUROPE AT SIXES AND SEVENS: THE COMMON
MARKET, THE FREE TRADE ASSOCIATION AND THE UNITED
STATES. EUR+WWI FUT USA+45 INDUS CONSULT DELIB/GP
EX/STRUC TOP/EX ACT/RES ECO/TAC EDU/PROP ROUTINE
CHOOSE PERCEPT WEALTH...MGT TREND EEC TOT/POP 20
EFTA. PAGE 11 B0217
B61 FINAN ECO/DEV VOL/ASSN

BISHOP D.G.,THE ADMINISTRATION OF BRITISH FOREIGN
RELATIONS. EUR+WWI MOD/EUR INT/ORG NAT/G POL/PAR
DELIB/GP LEGIS TOP/EX ECO/TAC DOMIN EDU/PROP ADMIN
COERCE 20. PAGE 12 B0243
B61 ROUTINE PWR DIPLOM UK

BULLIS H.A.,MANIFESTO FOR AMERICANS. USA+45 AGRI
LABOR NAT/G NEIGH FOR/AID INT/TRADE TAX EDU/PROP
CHOOSE...POLICY MGT 20 UN UNESCO. PAGE 17 B0342
B61 ECO/TAC SOCIETY INDUS CAP/ISM

CARNEY D.E.,GOVERNMENT AND ECONOMY IN BRITISH WEST
AFRICA. GAMBIA GHANA NIGERIA SIER/LEONE DOMIN ADMIN
GOV/REL SOVEREIGN WEALTH LAISSEZ...BIBLIOG 20
CMN/WLTH. PAGE 19 B0384
B61 METH/COMP COLONIAL ECO/TAC ECO/UNDEV

PROCEEDINGS OF THE CONFERENCE ON BUSINESS GAMES AS
TEACHING DEVICES. PROB/SOLV ECO/TAC CONFER ADMIN
TASK...MGT ANTHOL 20. PAGE 29 B0593
B61 GAME DECISION EDU/PROP EFFICIENCY

HALL M.,DISTRIBUTION IN GREAT BRITAIN AND NORTH
AMERICA. CANADA UK USA+45 ECO/DEV INDUS MARKET
EFFICIENCY PROFIT...MGT CHARTS 20. PAGE 46 B0924
B61 DIST/IND PRODUC ECO/TAC CAP/ISM

HARRISON S.,INDIA AND THE UNITED STATES. FUT S/ASIA
USA+45 WOR+45 INTELL ECO/DEV ECO/UNDEV AGRI INDUS
INT/ORG NAT/G CONSULT EX/STRUC TOP/EX PLAN ECO/TAC
NEUTRAL ALL/VALS...MGT TOT/POP 20. PAGE 47 B0956
B61 DELIB/GP ACT/RES FOR/AID INDIA

HASAN H.S.,PAKISTAN AND THE UN. ISLAM WOR+45
ECO/DEV ECO/UNDEV NAT/G TOP/EX ECO/TAC FOR/AID
EDU/PROP ADMIN DRIVE PERCEPT...OBS TIME/SEQ UN 20.
PAGE 48 B0965
B61 INT/ORG ATTIT PAKISTAN

HORVATH B.,THE CHARACTERISTICS OF YUGOSLAV ECONOMIC
DEVELOPMENT. COM ECO/UNDEV AGRI INDUS PLAN CAP/ISM
ECO/TAC ROUTINE WEALTH...SOCIALIST STAT CHARTS
STERTYP WORK 20. PAGE 52 B1045
B61 ACT/RES YUGOSLAVIA

KEE R.,REFUGEE WORLD. AUSTRIA EUR+WWI GERMANY NEIGH
EX/STRUC WORKER PROB/SOLV ECO/TAC RENT EDU/PROP
INGP/REL COST LITERACY HABITAT 20 MIGRATION.
PAGE 59 B1186
B61 NAT/G GIVE WEALTH STRANGE

KERTESZ S.D.,AMERICAN DIPLOMACY IN A NEW ERA. COM
S/ASIA UK USA+45 FORCES PROB/SOLV BAL/PWR ECO/TAC
B61 ANTHOL DIPLOM

ADMIN COLONIAL WAR PEACE ORD/FREE 20 NATO CONGRESS
UN COLD/WAR. PAGE 59 B1199
TREND

LAHAYE R.,LES ENTREPRISES PUBLIQUES AU MAROC.
FRANCE MOROCCO LAW DIST/IND EXTR/IND FINAN CONSULT
PLAN TEC/DEV ADMIN AGREE CONTROL OWN...POLICY 20.
PAGE 62 B1250
B61 NAT/G INDUS ECO/UNDEV ECO/TAC

LENIN V.I.,WHAT IS TO BE DONE? (1902). RUSSIA LABOR
NAT/G POL/PAR WORKER CAP/ISM ECO/TAC ADMIN PARTIC
...MARXIST IDEA/COMP GEN/LAWS 19/20. PAGE 64 B1292
B61 EDU/PROP PRESS MARXISM METH/COMP

MACMAHON A.W.,DELEGATION AND AUTONOMY. INDIA STRUCT
LEGIS BARGAIN BUDGET ECO/TAC LEGIT EXEC REPRESENT
GOV/REL CENTRAL DEMAND EFFICIENCY PRODUC. PAGE 68
B1373
B61 ADMIN PLAN FEDERAL

NOVE A.,THE SOVIET ECONOMY. USSR ECO/DEV FINAN
NAT/G ECO/TAC PRICE ADMIN EFFICIENCY MARXISM
...TREND BIBLIOG 20. PAGE 79 B1594
B61 PLAN PRODUC POLICY

SINGER J.D.,FINANCING INTERNATIONAL ORGANIZATION:
THE UNITED NATIONS BUDGET PROCESS. WOR+45 FINAN
ACT/RES CREATE PLAN BUDGET ECO/TAC ADMIN ROUTINE
ATTIT KNOWL...DECISION METH/CNCPT TIME/SEQ UN 20.
PAGE 97 B1964
B61 INT/ORG MGT

WILLOUGHBY W.R.,THE ST LAWRENCE WATERWAY: A STUDY
IN POLITICS AND DIPLOMACY. USA+45 ECO/DEV COM/IND
INT/ORG CONSULT DELIB/GP ACT/RES TEC/DEV DIPLOM
ECO/TAC ROUTINE...TIME/SEQ 20. PAGE 117 B2357
B61 LEGIS INT/TRADE CANADA DIST/IND

COHEN K.J.,"THE ROLE OF MANAGEMENT GAMES IN
EDUCATION AND RESEARCH." INTELL ECO/DEV FINAN
ACT/RES ECO/TAC DECISION. PAGE 22 B0444
L61 SOCIETY GAME MGT EDU/PROP

LANFALUSSY A.,"EUROPE'S PROGRESS: DUE TO COMMON
MARKET." EUR+WWI ECO/DEV DELIB/GP PLAN ECO/TAC
ROUTINE WEALTH...GEOG TREND EEC 20. PAGE 62 B1257
S61 INT/ORG MARKET

TOMASIC D.,"POLITICAL LEADERSHIP IN CONTEMPORARY
POLAND." COM EUR+WWI GERMANY NAT/G POL/PAR SECT
DELIB/GP PLAN ECO/TAC DOMIN EDU/PROP PWR MARXISM
...MARXIST GEOG MGT CONCPT TIME/SEQ STERTYP 20.
PAGE 105 B2114
S61 SOCIETY ROUTINE USSR POLAND

VINER J.,"ECONOMIC FOREIGN POLICY ON THE NEW
FRONTIER." USA+45 ECO/UNDEV AGRI FINAN INDUS MARKET
INT/ORG NAT/G FOR/AID INT/TRADE ADMIN ATTIT PWR 20
KENNEDY/JF. PAGE 112 B2262
S61 TOP/EX ECO/TAC BAL/PAY TARIFFS

BECKMAN T.N.,MARKETING (7TH ED.). USA+45 SOCIETY
ECO/DEV NAT/G PRICE EFFICIENCY INCOME ATTIT WEALTH
...MGT BIBLIOG 20. PAGE 10 B0205
B62 MARKET ECO/TAC DIST/IND POLICY

CAIRNCROSS A.K.,FACTORS IN ECONOMIC DEVELOPMENT.
WOR+45 ECO/UNDEV INDUS R+D LG/CO NAT/G EX/STRUC
PLAN TEC/DEV ECO/TAC ATTIT HEALTH KNOWL PWR WEALTH
...TIME/SEQ GEN/LAWS TOT/POP VAL/FREE 20. PAGE 18
B0363
B62 MARKET ECO/DEV

CARTER G.M.,THE GOVERNMENT OF THE SOVIET UNION.
USSR CULTURE LOC/G DIPLOM ECO/TAC ADJUD CT/SYS LEAD
WEALTH...CHARTS T 20 COM/PARTY. PAGE 19 B0390
B62 NAT/G MARXISM POL/PAR EX/STRUC

CHANDLER A.D.,STRATEGY AND STRUCTURE: CHAPTERS IN
THE HISTORY OF THE INDUSTRIAL ENTERPRISE. USA+45
USA-45 ECO/DEV EX/STRUC ECO/TAC EXEC...DECISION 20.
PAGE 20 B0403
B62 LG/CO PLAN ADMIN FINAN

DIMOCK M.E.,THE NEW AMERICAN POLITICAL ECONOMY: A
SYNTHESIS OF POLITICS AND ECONOMICS. USA+45 FINAN
LG/CO PLAN ADMIN REGION GP/REL CENTRAL MORAL 20.
PAGE 29 B0598
B62 FEDERAL ECO/TAC NAT/G PARTIC

EVANS M.S.,THE FRINGE ON TOP. USSR EX/STRUC FORCES
DIPLOM ECO/TAC PEACE CONSERVE SOCISM...TREND 20
KENNEDY/JF. PAGE 34 B0689
B62 NAT/G PWR CENTRAL POLICY

FARBER W.O.,GOVERNMENT OF SOUTH DAKOTA. USA+45
DIST/IND POL/PAR CHIEF EX/STRUC LEGIS ECO/TAC GIVE
EDU/PROP CT/SYS PARTIC...T 20 SOUTH/DAK GOVERNOR.
PAGE 35 B0704
B62 PROVS LOC/G ADMIN CONSTN

FORD A.G.,THE GOLD STANDARD 1880-1914: BRITAIN AND
ARGENTINA. UK ECO/UNDEV INT/TRADE ADMIN GOV/REL
DEMAND EFFICIENCY...STAT CHARTS 19/20 ARGEN
GOLD/STAND. PAGE 36 B0737
B62 FINAN ECO/TAC BUDGET BAL/PAY

FRIEDMANN W.,METHODS AND POLICIES OF PRINCIPAL
DONOR COUNTRIES IN PUBLIC INTERNATIONAL DEVELOPMENT
B62 INT/ORG FOR/AID

FINANCING: PRELIMINARY APPRAISAL. FRANCE GERMANY/W | NAT/COMP
UK USA+45 USSR WOR+45 FINAN TEC/DEV CAP/ISM DIPLOM | ADMIN
ECO/TAC ATTIT 20 EEC. PAGE 37 B0759

B62

GRANICK D.,THE EUROPEAN EXECUTIVE. BELGIUM FRANCE | MGT
GERMANY/W UK INDUS LABOR LG/CO SML/CO EX/STRUC PLAN | ECO/DEV
TEC/DEV CAP/ISM COST DEMAND...POLICY CHARTS 20. | ECO/TAC
PAGE 42 B0852 | EXEC

B62

GROVE J.W.,GOVERNMENT AND INDUSTRY IN BRITAIN. UK | ECO/TAC
FINAN LOC/G CONSULT DELIB/GP INT/TRADE ADMIN | INDUS
CONTROL...BIBLIOG 20. PAGE 44 B0894 | NAT/G
| GP/REL

B62

KUHN T.E.,PUBLIC ENTERPRISES. PROJECT PLANNING AND | ECO/DEV
ECONOMIC DEVELOPMENT (PAMPHLET). ECO/UNDEV FINAN | ECO/TAC
PLAN ADMIN EFFICIENCY OWN...MGT STAT CHARTS ANTHOL | LG/CO
20. PAGE 61 B1240 | NAT/G

B62

WEDDING N.,ADVERTISING MANAGEMENT. USA+45 ECO/DEV | ECO/TAC
BUDGET CAP/ISM PRODUC PROFIT ATTIT...DECISION MGT | COM/IND
PSY 20. PAGE 114 B2308 | PLAN
| EDU/PROP

L62

BELSHAW D.G.R.,"PUBLIC INVESTMENT IN AGRICULTURE | ECO/UNDEV
AND ECONOMIC DEVELOPMENT OF UGANDA" UGANDA AGRI | PLAN
INDUS R+D ECO/TAC RATION TAX PAY COLONIAL 20 | ADMIN
WORLD/BANK. PAGE 10 B0209 | CENTRAL

L62

GALBRAITH J.K.,"ECONOMIC DEVELOPMENT IN | ECO/UNDEV
PERSPECTIVE." CAP/ISM ECO/TAC ROUTINE ATTIT WEALTH | PLAN
...TREND CHARTS SOC/EXP WORK 20. PAGE 38 B0773

L62

HOFFHERR R.,"LE PROBLEME DE L'ENCADREMENT DANS LES | AFR
JEUNES ETATS DE LANGUE FRANCAISE EN AFRIQUE | STRUCT
CENTRALE ET A MADAGASCAR." FUT ECO/UNDEV CONSULT | FRANCE
PLAN ECO/TAC COLONIAL ATTIT...MGT TIME/SEQ VAL/FREE
20. PAGE 51 B1028

L62

MALINOWSKI W.R.,"CENTRALIZATION AND DE- | CREATE
CENTRALIZATION IN THE UNITED NATIONS' ECONOMIC AND | GEN/LAWS
SOCIAL ACTIVITIES." WOR+45 CONSTN ECO/UNDEV INT/ORG
VOL/ASSN DELIB/GP ECO/TAC EDU/PROP ADMIN RIGID/FLEX
...OBS CHARTS UNESCO UN EEC OAS OEEC 20. PAGE 69
B1385

L62

WATERSTON A.,"PLANNING IN MOROCCO, ORGANIZATION AND | NAT/G
IMPLEMENTATION. BALTIMORE: HOPKINS ECON. DEVELOP. | PLAN
INT. BANK FOR." ISLAM ECO/DEV AGRI DIST/IND INDUS | MOROCCO
PROC/MFG SERV/IND LOC/G EX/STRUC ECO/TAC PWR WEALTH
TOT/POP VAL/FREE 20. PAGE 114 B2302

S62

ALBONETTI A.,"IL SECONDO PROGRAMMA QUINQUENNALE | R+D
1963-67 ED IL BILANCIO RICERCHE ED INVESTIMENTI PER | PLAN
IL 1963 DELL'ERATOM." EUR+WWI FUT ITALY WOR+45 | NUC/PWR
ECO/DEV SERV/IND INT/ORG TEC/DEV ECO/TAC ATTIT
SKILL WEALTH...MGT TIME/SEQ OEEC 20. PAGE 3 B0069

S62

FESLER J.W.,"FRENCH FIELD ADMINISTRATION: THE | EX/STRUC
BEGINNINGS." CHRIST-17C CULTURE SOCIETY STRATA | FRANCE
NAT/G ECO/TAC DOMIN EDU/PROP LEGIT ADJUD COERCE
ATTIT ALL/VALS...TIME/SEQ CON/ANAL GEN/METH
VAL/FREE 13/15. PAGE 35 B0714

S62

IOVTCHOUK M.T.,"ON SOME THEORETICAL PRINCIPLES AND | COM
METHODS OF SOCIOLOGICAL INVESTIGATIONS (IN | ECO/DEV
RUSSIAN)." FUT USA+45 STRATA R+D NAT/G POL/PAR | CAP/ISM
TOP/EX ACT/RES PLAN ECO/TAC EDU/PROP ROUTINE ATTIT | USSR
RIGID/FLEX MARXISM SOCISM...MARXIST METH/CNCPT OBS
TREND NAT/COMP GEN/LAWS 20. PAGE 54 B1102

S62

JACOBSON H.K.,"THE UNITED NATIONS AND COLONIALISM: | INT/ORG
A TENTATIVE APPRAISAL." AFR FUT S/ASIA USA+45 USSR | CONCPT
WOR+45 NAT/G DELIB/GP PLAN DIPLOM ECO/TAC ADMIN | COLONIAL
ADMIN ROUTINE COERCE ATTIT RIGID/FLEX ORD/FREE PWR
...OBS STERTYP UN 20. PAGE 55 B1115

S62

JOHNSON H.,"CANADA IN A CHANGING WORLD." EUR+WWI | ECO/DEV
USA+45 NAT/G CAP/ISM ECO/TAC ADMIN ATTIT WEALTH | PLAN
...TREND TOT/POP 20 EEC. PAGE 57 B1143 | CANADA

S62

TRUMAN D.,"THE DOMESTIC POLITICS OF FOREIGN AID." | ROUTINE
USA+45 WOR+45 NAT/G POL/PAR LEGIS DIPLOM ECO/TAC | FOR/AID
EDU/PROP ADMIN CHOOSE ATTIT PWR CONGRESS 20
CONGRESS. PAGE 105 B2129

B63

BRAIBANTI R.J.D.,ADMINISTRATION AND ECONOMIC | ECO/UNDEV
DEVELOPMENT IN INDIA. INDIA S/ASIA SOCIETY STRATA | ADMIN
ECO/TAC PERSON WEALTH...MGT GEN/LAWS TOT/POP
VAL/FREE 20. PAGE 15 B0300

B63

CHARLES S.,MINISTER OF RELIEF: HARRY HOPKINS AND | ADMIN
THE DEPRESSION. EX/STRUC PROB/SOLV RATION PARL/PROC | ECO/TAC
PERS/REL ALL/VALS 20 HOPKINS/H NRA. PAGE 20 B0414 | PLAN
| BIOG

B63

DE VRIES E.,SOCIAL ASPECTS OF ECONOMIC DEVELOPMENT | L/A+17C
IN LATIN AMERICA. CULTURE SOCIETY STRATA FINAN | ECO/UNDEV
INDUS INT/ORG DELIB/GP ACT/RES ECO/TAC EDU/PROP
ADMIN ATTIT SUPEGO HEALTH KNOWL ORD/FREE...SOC STAT
TREND ANTHOL TOT/POP VAL/FREE. PAGE 28 B0562

B63

INDIAN INSTITUTE PUBLIC ADMIN.CASES IN INDIAN | DECISION
ADMINISTRATION. INDIA AGRI NAT/G PROB/SOLV TEC/DEV | PLAN
ECO/TAC ADMIN...ANTHOL METH 20. PAGE 53 B1083 | MGT
| ECO/UNDEV

B63

KAPP W.K.,HINDU CULTURE: ECONOMIC DEVELOPMENT AND | SECT
ECONOMIC PLANNING IN INDIA. INDIA S/ASIA CULTURE | ECO/UNDEV
ECO/TAC EDU/PROP ADMIN ALL/VALS...POLICY MGT
TIME/SEQ VAL/FREE 20. PAGE 58 B1171

B63

LEWIS J.W.,LEADERSHIP IN COMMUNIST CHINA. ASIA | POL/PAR
INTELL ECO/UNDEV LOC/G MUNIC NAT/G PROVS ECO/TAC | DOMIN
EDU/PROP LEGIT ADMIN COERCE ATTIT ORD/FREE PWR | ELITES
...INT TIME/SEQ CHARTS TOT/POP VAL/FREE. PAGE 65
B1304

B63

LINDBERG L.,POLITICAL DYNAMICS OF EUROPEAN ECONOMIC | MARKET
INTEGRATION. EUR+WWI ECO/DEV INT/ORG VOL/ASSN | ECO/TAC
DELIB/GP ADMIN WEALTH...DECISION EEC 20. PAGE 65
B1313

B63

MAYNE R.,THE COMMUNITY OF EUROPE. UK CONSTN NAT/G | EUR+WWI
CONSULT DELIB/GP CREATE PLAN ECO/TAC LEGIT ADMIN | INT/ORG
ROUTINE ORD/FREE PWR WEALTH...CONCPT TIME/SEQ EEC | REGION
EURATOM 20. PAGE 71 B1436

B63

MEYNAUD J.,PLANIFICATION ET POLITIQUE. FRANCE ITALY | PLAN
FINAN LABOR DELIB/GP LEGIS ADMIN EFFICIENCY | ECO/TAC
...MAJORIT DECISION 20. PAGE 73 B1477 | PROB/SOLV

B63

NASA,CONFERENCE ON SPACE, SCIENCE, AND URBAN LIFE. | MUNIC
USA+45 SOCIETY INDUS ACADEM ACT/RES ECO/TAC ADMIN | SPACE
20. PAGE 77 B1556 | TEC/DEV
| PROB/SOLV

B63

OLSON M. JR.,THE ECONOMICS OF WARTIME SHORTAGE. | WAR
FRANCE GERMANY MOD/EUR UK AGRI PROB/SOLV ADMIN | ADJUST
DEMAND WEALTH...POLICY OLD/LIB 17/20. PAGE 80 B1608 | ECO/TAC
| NAT/COMP

B63

PREST A.R.,PUBLIC FINANCE IN UNDERDEVELOPED | FINAN
COUNTRIES. UK WOR+45 WOR-45 SOCIETY INT/ORG NAT/G | ECO/UNDEV
LEGIS ACT/RES PLAN ECO/TAC ADMIN ROUTINE...CHARTS | NIGERIA
20. PAGE 84 B1702

B63

RAUDSEPP E.,MANAGING CREATIVE SCIENTISTS AND | MGT
ENGINEERS. USA+45 ECO/DEV LG/CO GP/REL PERS/REL | CREATE
PRODUC. PAGE 86 B1742 | R+D
| ECO/TAC

B63

SCHOECK H.,THE NEW ARGUMENT IN ECONOMICS. UK USA+45 | WELF/ST
INDUS MARKET LABOR NAT/G ECO/TAC ADMIN ROUTINE | FOR/AID
BAL/PAY PWR...POLICY BOLIV. PAGE 94 B1899 | ECO/DEV
| ALL/IDEOS

B63

SHANKS M.,THE LESSONS OF PUBLIC ENTERPRISE. UK | SOCISM
LEGIS WORKER ECO/TAC ADMIN PARL/PROC GOV/REL ATTIT | OWN
...POLICY MGT METH/COMP NAT/COMP ANTHOL 20 | NAT/G
PARLIAMENT. PAGE 96 B1931 | INDUS

B63

SWERDLOW I.,DEVELOPMENT ADMINISTRATION: CONCEPTS | ECO/UNDEV
AND PROBLEMS. WOR+45 CULTURE SOCIETY STRATA | ADMIN
DELIB/GP EX/STRUC ACT/RES PLAN ECO/TAC DOMIN LEGIT
ATTIT RIGID/FLEX SUPEGO HEALTH PWR...MGT CONCPT
ANTHOL VAL/FREE. PAGE 102 B2062

B63

TUCKER R.C.,THE SOVIET POLITICAL MIND. WOR+45 | COM
ELITES INT/ORG NAT/G POL/PAR PLAN DIPLOM ECO/TAC | TOP/EX
DOMIN ADMIN NUC/PWR REV DRIVE PERSON SUPEGO PWR | USSR
WEALTH...POLICY MGT PSY CONCPT OBS BIOG TREND
COLD/WAR MARX/KARL 20. PAGE 106 B2134

B63

UN SECRETARY GENERAL,PLANNING FOR ECONOMIC | PLAN
DEVELOPMENT. ECO/UNDEV FINAN BUDGET INT/TRADE | ECO/TAC
TARIFFS TAX ADMIN 20 UN. PAGE 106 B2151 | MGT
| NAT/COMP

L63

EMERSON R.,"POLITICAL MODERNIZATION." WOR+45 | POL/PAR
CULTURE ECO/UNDEV NAT/G FORCES ECO/TAC DOMIN | ADMIN
EDU/PROP LEGIT COERCE ALL/VALS...CONCPT TIME/SEQ
VAL/FREE 20. PAGE 33 B0672

L63

LIVERNASH E.R.,"THE RELATION OF POWER TO THE | LABOR
STRUCTURE AND PROCESS OF COLLECTIVE BARGAINING." | GP/REL
ADJUD ORD/FREE...POLICY MGT CLASSIF GP/COMP. | PWR
PAGE 66 B1330 | ECO/TAC

L63

SPITZ A.A.,"DEVELOPMENT ADMINISTRATION: AN | ADMIN
ANNOTATED BIBLIOGRAPHY." WOR+45 CULTURE SOCIETY | ECO/UNDEV

STRATA DELIB/GP EX/STRUC TOP/EX ACT/RES ECO/TAC
DOMIN EDU/PROP LEGIT COERCE ATTIT ALL/VALS...MGT
VAL/FREE. PAGE 99 B2009

S63
BANFIELD J.,"FEDERATION IN EAST-AFRICA." AFR UGANDA EX/STRUC
ELITES INT/ORG NAT/G VOL/ASSN LEGIS ECO/TAC FEDERAL PWR
ATTIT SOVEREIGN TOT/POP 20 TANGANYIKA. PAGE 9 B0180 REGION

S63
BARZANSKI S.,"REGIONAL UNDERDEVELOPMENT IN THE   ECO/UNDEV
EUROPEAN ECONOMIC COMMUNITY." EUR+WWI ELITES   PLAN
DIST/IND MARKET VOL/ASSN CONSULT EX/STRUC ECO/TAC
RIGID/FLEX WEALTH EEC OEEC 20. PAGE 9 B0192

S63
CLEMHOUT S.,"PRODUCTION FUNCTION ANALYSIS APPLIED   ECO/DEV
TO THE LEONTIEF SCARCE-FACTOR PARADOX OF   ECO/TAC
INTERNATIONAL TRADE." EUR+WWI USA+45 DIST/IND NAT/G
PLAN TEC/DEV DIPLOM PWR WEALTH...MGT METH/CNCPT
CONT/OBS CON/ANAL CHARTS SIMUL GEN/LAWS 20. PAGE 21
B0436

S63
ETIENNE G.,"'LOIS OBJECTIVES' ET PROBLEMES DE   TOTALISM
DEVELOPPEMENT DANS LE CONTEXTE CHINE-URSS." ASIA   USSR
CHINA/COM COM FUT STRUCT INT/ORG VOL/ASSN TOP/EX
TEC/DEV ECO/TAC ATTIT RIGID/FLEX...GEOG MGT
TIME/SEQ TOT/POP 20. PAGE 34 B0682

S63
HAVILAND H.F.,"BUILDING A POLITICAL COMMUNITY."   VOL/ASSN
EUR+WWI FUT UK USA+45 ECO/DEV ECO/UNDEV INT/ORG   DIPLOM
NAT/G DELIB/GP BAL/PWR ECO/TAC NEUTRAL ROUTINE
ATTIT PWR WEALTH...CONCPT COLD/WAR TOT/POP 20.
PAGE 48 B0972

S63
MANGONE G.,"THE UNITED NATIONS AND UNITED STATES   INT/ORG
FOREIGN POLICY." USA+45 WOR+45 ECO/UNDEV NAT/G   ECO/TAC
DIPLOM LEGIT ROUTINE ATTIT DRIVE...TIME/SEQ UN   FOR/AID
COLD/WAR 20. PAGE 69 B1390

S63
NADLER E.B.,"SOME ECONOMIC DISADVANTAGES OF THE   ECO/DEV
ARMS RACE." USA+45 INDUS R+D FORCES PLAN TEC/DEV   MGT
ECO/TAC FOR/AID EDU/PROP PWR WEALTH...TREND   BAL/PAY
COLD/WAR 20. PAGE 77 B1552

S63
NYE J.S. JR.,"EAST AFRICAN ECONOMIC INTEGRATION."   ECO/UNDEV
AFR UGANDA PROVS DELIB/GP PLAN ECO/TAC INT/TRADE   INT/ORG
ADMIN ROUTINE ORD/FREE PWR WEALTH...OBS TIME/SEQ
VAL/FREE 20. PAGE 79 B1597

S63
SCHMITT H.A.,"THE EUROPEAN COMMUNITIES." EUR+WWI   VOL/ASSN
FRANCE DELIB/GP EX/STRUC TOP/EX CREATE TEC/DEV   ECO/DEV
ECO/TAC LEGIT REGION COERCE DRIVE ALL/VALS
...METH/CNCPT EEC 20. PAGE 94 B1897

S63
SCHURMANN F.,"ECONOMIC POLICY AND POLITICAL POWER   PLAN
IN COMMUNIST CHINA." ASIA CHINA/COM USSR SOCIETY   ECO/TAC
ECO/UNDEV AGRI INDUS CREATE ADMIN ROUTINE ATTIT
DRIVE RIGID/FLEX PWR WEALTH...HIST/WRIT TREND
CHARTS WORK 20. PAGE 94 B1908

S63
SHIMKIN D.B.,"STRUCTURE OF SOVIET POWER." COM FUT   PWR
USA+45 USSR WOR+45 NAT/G FORCES ECO/TAC DOMIN EXEC
COERCE CHOOSE ATTIT WEALTH...TIME/SEQ COLD/WAR
TOT/POP VAL/FREE 20. PAGE 96 B1948

N63
GREAT BRITAIN DEPT TECH COOP,PUBLIC ADMINISTRATION: BIBLIOG/A
A SELECT BIBLIOGRAPHY (PAMPHLET). WOR+45 AGRI FINAN ADMIN
INDUS EX/STRUC OP/RES ECO/TAC...MGT METH/COMP   NAT/G
NAT/COMP. PAGE 43 B0861   LOC/G

B64
COX R.,THEORY IN MARKETING. FUT USA+45 SOCIETY   MARKET
ECO/DEV PROB/SOLV PRICE RISK PRODUC ATTIT...ANTHOL   ECO/TAC
20. PAGE 24 B0499   PHIL/SCI
                                                     MGT
B64
DIEBOLD J.,BEYOND AUTOMATION: MANAGERIAL PROBLEMS   FUT
OF AN EXPLODING TECHNOLOGY. SOCIETY ECO/DEV CREATE   INDUS
ECO/TAC AUTOMAT SKILL...TECHNIC MGT WORK. PAGE 29   PROVS
B0589   NAT/G

B64
DUROSELLE J.B.,POLITIQUES NATIONALES ENVERS LES   DIPLOM
JEUNES ETATS. FRANCE ISRAEL ITALY UK USA+45 USSR   ECO/UNDEV
YUGOSLAVIA ECO/DEV FINAN ECO/TAC INT/TRADE ADMIN   COLONIAL
PWR 20. PAGE 31 B0634   DOMIN

B64
FATOUROS A.A.,CANADA'S OVERSEAS AID. CANADA WOR+45   FOR/AID
ECO/DEV FINAN NAT/G BUDGET ECO/TAC CONFER ADMIN 20. DIPLOM
PAGE 35 B0707   ECO/UNDEV
                                                     POLICY
B64
GARFIELD PJ   LOVEJOY WF,PUBLIC UTILITY   T
ECONOMICS. DIST/IND FINAN MARKET MUNIC ADMIN COST   ECO/TAC
DEMAND...TECHNIC JURID 20 MONOPOLY. PAGE 39 B0782   OWN
                                                     SERV/IND
B64
GROSS B.M.,THE MANAGING OF ORGANIZATIONS (VOL. I).   ECO/TAC
USA+45 ECO/DEV LG/CO CAP/ISM EFFICIENCY ROLE...MGT   ADMIN
20. PAGE 44 B0886   INDUS

POLICY
B64
GROSS B.M.,THE MANAGING OF ORGANIZATIONS (VOL. II). ECO/TAC
FUT USA+45 ECO/DEV EDU/PROP EFFICIENCY...MGT   ADMIN
BIBLIOG/A 20. PAGE 44 B0887   INDUS
                                                     POLICY
B64
HAMBRIDGE G.,DYNAMICS OF DEVELOPMENT. AGRI FINAN   ECO/UNDEV
INDUS LABOR INT/TRADE EDU/PROP ADMIN LEAD OWN   ECO/TAC
HEALTH...ANTHOL BIBLIOG 20. PAGE 46 B0930   OP/RES
                                                     ACT/RES
B64
LI C.M.,INDUSTRIAL DEVELOPMENT IN COMMUNIST CHINA.   ASIA
CHINA/COM ECO/DEV ECO/UNDEV AGRI FINAN INDUS MARKET TEC/DEV
LABOR NAT/G ECO/TAC INT/TRADE EXEC ALL/VALS
...POLICY RELATIV TREND WORK TOT/POP VAL/FREE 20.
PAGE 65 B1311

B64
LITTLE I.M.D.,AID TO AFRICA. AFR UK TEC/DEV DIPLOM   FOR/AID
ECO/TAC INCOME WEALTH 20. PAGE 66 B1326   ECO/UNDEV
                                                     ADMIN
                                                     POLICY
B64
MARRIS R.,THE ECONOMIC THEORY OF "MANAGERIAL"   CAP/ISM
CAPITALISM. USA+45 ECO/DEV LG/CO ECO/TAC DEMAND   MGT
...CHARTS BIBLIOG 20. PAGE 69 B1402   CONTROL
                                                     OP/RES
B64
PLISCHKE E.,SYSTEMS OF INTEGRATING THE   INT/ORG
INTERNATIONAL COMMUNITY. WOR+45 NAT/G VOL/ASSN   EX/STRUC
ECO/TAC LEGIT PWR WEALTH...TIME/SEQ ANTHOL UN   REGION
TOT/POP 20. PAGE 83 B1684

B64
REDLICH F.,THE GERMAN MILITARY ENTERPRISER AND HIS   EX/STRUC
WORK FORCE. CHRIST-17C GERMANY ELITES SOCIETY FINAN FORCES
ECO/TAC CIVMIL/REL GP/REL INGP/REL...HIST/WRIT   PROFIT
METH/COMP 14/17. PAGE 87 B1760   WORKER

B64
RIGGS F.W.,ADMINISTRATION IN DEVELOPING COUNTRIES.   ECO/UNDEV
FUT WOR+45 STRUCT AGRI INDUS NAT/G PLAN TEC/DEV   ADMIN
ECO/TAC EDU/PROP RIGID/FLEX KNOWL WEALTH...POLICY
MGT CONCPT METH/CNCPT TREND 20. PAGE 88 B1785

B64
TINBERGEN J.,CENTRAL PLANNING. COM INTELL ECO/DEV   PLAN
ECO/UNDEV FINAN INT/ORG PROB/SOLV ECO/TAC CONTROL   INDUS
EXEC ROUTINE DECISION. PAGE 104 B2111   MGT
                                                     CENTRAL

UN PUB. INFORM. ORGAN.,EVERY MAN'S UNITED NATIONS.   INT/ORG
UNIV WOR+45 CONSTN CULTURE SOCIETY ECO/DEV   ROUTINE
ECO/UNDEV NAT/G ACT/RES PLAN ECO/TAC INT/TRADE
EDU/PROP LEGIT PEACE ATTIT ALL/VALS...POLICY HUM
INT/LAW CONCPT CHARTS UN TOT/POP 20. PAGE 106 B2150

B64
WERNETTE J.P.,GOVERNMENT AND BUSINESS. LABOR   NAT/G
CAP/ISM ECO/TAC INT/TRADE TAX ADMIN AUTOMAT NUC/PWR FINAN
CIVMIL/REL DEMAND...MGT 20 MONOPOLY. PAGE 115 B2323 ECO/DEV
                                                     CONTROL
B64
WILLIAMSON O.E.,THE ECONOMICS OF DISCRETIONARY   EFFICIENCY
BEHAVIOR: MANAGERIAL OBJECTIVES IN A THEORY OF THE   MGT
FIRM. MARKET BUDGET CAP/ISM PRODUC DRIVE PERSON   ECO/TAC
...STAT CHARTS BIBLIOG METH 20. PAGE 117 B2354   CHOOSE

L64
HAAS E.B.,"ECONOMICS AND DIFFERENTIAL PATTERNS OF   L/A+17C
POLITICAL INTEGRATION: PROJECTIONS ABOUT UNITY IN   INT/ORG
LATIN AMERICA." SOCIETY NAT/G DELIB/GP ACT/RES   MARKET
CREATE PLAN ECO/TAC REGION ROUTINE ATTIT DRIVE PWR
WEALTH...CONCPT TREND CHARTS LAFTA 20. PAGE 45
B0910

L64
WORLD PEACE FOUNDATION.,"INTERNATIONAL   INT/ORG
ORGANIZATIONS: SUMMARY OF ACTIVITIES." INDIA   ROUTINE
PAKISTAN TURKEY WOR+45 CONSTN CONSULT EX/STRUC
ECO/TAC EDU/PROP LEGIT ORD/FREE...JURID SOC UN 20
CYPRESS. PAGE 118 B2375

S64
CARNEGIE ENDOWMENT INT. PEACE.,"ADMINISTRATION AND   INT/ORG
BUDGET (ISSUES BEFORE THE NINETEENTH GENERAL   ADMIN
ASSEMBLY)." WOR+45 FINAN BUDGET ECO/TAC ROUTINE
COST...STAT RECORD UN. PAGE 19 B0383

S64
FLORINSKY M.T.,"TRENDS IN THE SOVIET ECONOMY." COM   ECO/DEV
USA+45 USSR INDUS LABOR NAT/G PLAN TEC/DEV ECO/TAC   AGRI
ALL/VALS SOCISM...METH/CNCPT STYLE CON/ANAL
GEN/METH WORK 20. PAGE 36 B0731

S64
HUELIN D.,"ECONOMIC INTEGRATION IN LATIN AMERICAN: MARKET
PROGRESS AND PROBLEMS." L/A+17C ECO/DEV AGRI   ECO/UNDEV
DIST/IND FINAN INDUS NAT/G VOL/ASSN CONSULT   INT/TRADE
DELIB/GP EX/STRUC ACT/RES PLAN TEC/DEV ECO/TAC
ROUTINE BAL/PAY WEALTH WORK 20. PAGE 52 B1058

S64
LOW D.A.,"LION RAMPANT." EUR+WWI MOD/EUR S/ASIA   AFR
ECO/UNDEV NAT/G FORCES TEC/DEV ECO/TAC LEGIT ADMIN   DOMIN
COLONIAL COERCE ORD/FREE RESPECT 19/20. PAGE 67   DIPLOM

B1344   UK
                                                          S64
MOWER A.G.,"THE OFFICIAL PRESSURE GROUP OF THE   INT/ORG
COUNCIL OF EUROPE'S CONSULATIVE ASSEMBLY." EUR+WWI   EDU/PROP
SOCIETY STRUCT FINAN CONSULT ECO/TAC ADMIN ROUTINE
ATTIT PWR WEALTH...STAT CHARTS 20 COUNCL/EUR.
PAGE 76 B1535

                                                          S64
RIGBY T.H.,"TRADITIONAL, MARKET, AND ORGANIZATIONAL   MARKET
SOCIETIES AND THE USSR." COM ECO/DEV NAT/G POL/PAR   ADMIN
ECO/TAC DOMIN ORD/FREE PWR WEALTH...TIME/SEQ   USSR
GEN/LAWS VAL/FREE 20 STALIN/J. PAGE 88 B1784

                                                          B65
AMERICAN ECONOMIC ASSOCIATION,INDEX OF ECONOMIC   BIBLIOG
JOURNALS 1886-1965 (7 VOLS.). UK USA+45 USA-45 AGRI   WRITING
FINAN PLAN ECO/TAC INT/TRADE ADMIN...STAT CENSUS   INDUS
19/20. PAGE 4 B0083

                                                          B65
CHEN T.H.,THE CHINESE COMMUNIST REGIME: A   MARXISM
DOCUMENTARY STUDY (2 VOLS.). CHINA/COM LAW CONSTN   POL/PAR
ELITES ECO/UNDEV LEGIS ECO/TAC ADMIN CONTROL PWR   NAT/G
...SOC 20. PAGE 20 B0417

                                                          B65
DOWD L.P.,PRINCIPLES OF WORLD BUSINESS. SERV/IND   INT/TRADE
NAT/G DIPLOM ECO/TAC TARIFFS...INT/LAW JURID 20.   MGT
PAGE 30 B0614   FINAN
                                                       MARKET
                                                          B65
EDELMAN M.,THE POLITICS OF WAGE-PRICE DECISIONS.   GOV/COMP
GERMANY ITALY NETHERLAND UK INDUS LABOR POL/PAR   CONTROL
PROB/SOLV BARGAIN PRICE ROUTINE BAL/PAY COST DEMAND   ECO/TAC
20. PAGE 32 B0654   PLAN
                                                          B65
ETZIONI A.,POLITICAL UNIFICATION* A COMPARATIVE   INT/ORG
STUDY OF LEADERS AND FORCES. EUR+WWI ISLAM L/A+17C   FORCES
WOR+45 ELITES STRATA EXEC WEALTH...TIME/SEQ TREND   ECO/TAC
SOC/EXP. PAGE 34 B0686   REGION
                                                          B65
GOPAL S.,BRITISH POLICY IN INDIA 1858-1905. INDIA   COLONIAL
UK ELITES CHIEF DELIB/GP ECO/TAC GP/REL DISCRIM   ADMIN
ATTIT...IDEA/COMP NAT/COMP PERS/COMP BIBLIOG/A   POL/PAR
19/20. PAGE 41 B0828   ECO/UNDEV
                                                          B65
INT. BANK RECONSTR. DEVELOP.,ECONOMIC DEVELOPMENT   INDUS
OF KUWAIT. ISLAM KUWAIT AGRI FINAN MARKET EX/STRUC   NAT/G
TEC/DEV ECO/TAC ADMIN WEALTH...OBS CON/ANAL CHARTS
20. PAGE 54 B1092

                                                          B65
KELLEY E.J.,MARKETING: STRATEGY AND FUNCTIONS.   MARKET
ECO/DEV INDUS PLAN PRICE CONTROL ROUTINE...MGT   DIST/IND
BIBLIOG 20. PAGE 59 B1191   POLICY
                                                       ECO/TAC
                                                          B65
MACDONALD R.W.,THE LEAGUE OF ARAB STATES: A STUDY   ISLAM
IN THE DYNAMICS OF REGIONAL ORGANIZATION. ISRAEL   REGION
UAR USSR FINAN INT/ORG DELIB/GP ECO/TAC AGREE   DIPLOM
NEUTRAL ORD/FREE PWR...DECISION BIBLIOG 20 TREATY   ADMIN
UN. PAGE 67 B1358

                                                          B65
MELMANS S.,OUR DEPLETED SOCIETY. SPACE USA+45   CIVMIL/REL
ECO/DEV FORCES BUDGET ECO/TAC ADMIN WEAPON   INDUS
EFFICIENCY 20 COLD/WAR. PAGE 73 B1465   EDU/PROP
                                                       CONTROL
                                                          B65
MUSOLF L.D.,PROMOTING THE GENERAL WELFARE: ECO/TAC
GOVERNMENT AND THE ECONOMY. USA+45 ECO/DEV CAP/ISM   NAT/G
DEMAND OPTIMAL 20. PAGE 77 B1550   EX/STRUC
                                                       NEW/LIB
                                                          B65
ROMASCO A.U.,THE POVERTY OF ABUNDANCE: HOOVER, THE   ECO/TAC
NATION, THE DEPRESSION. USA-45 AGRI LEGIS WORKER   ADMIN
GIVE PRESS LEAD 20 HOOVER/H. PAGE 90 B1817   NAT/G
                                                       FINAN
                                                          B65
ROSS P.,THE GOVERNMENT AS A SOURCE OF UNION POWER.   LABOR
USA+45 LAW ECO/DEV PROB/SOLV ECO/TAC LEAD GP/REL   BARGAIN
...MGT 20. PAGE 90 B1826   POLICY
                                                       NAT/G
                                                          B65
SCOTT A.M.,THE REVOLUTION IN STATECRAFT: INFORMAL   DIPLOM
PENETRATION. WOR+45 WOR-45 CULTURE INT/ORG FORCES   EDU/PROP
ECO/TAC ROUTINE...BIBLIOG 20. PAGE 95 B1918   FOR/AID
                                                          B65
WALTON R.E.,A BEHAVIORAL THEORY OF LABOR   SOC
NEGOTIATIONS: AN ANALYSIS OF A SOCIAL INTERACTION   LABOR
SYSTEM. USA+45 FINAN PROB/SOLV ECO/TAC GP/REL   BARGAIN
INGP/REL...DECISION BIBLIOG. PAGE 113 B2285   ADMIN
                                                          B65
WATERSTON A.,DEVELOPMENT PLANNING* LESSONS OF   ECO/UNDEV
EXPERIENCE. ECO/TAC CENTRAL...MGT QUANT BIBLIOG.   CREATE
PAGE 114 B2303   PLAN
                                                       ADMIN
                                                          B65
WHITE J.,GERMAN AID. GERMANY/W FINAN PLAN TEC/DEV   FOR/AID
INT/TRADE ADMIN ATTIT...POLICY 20. PAGE 116 B2334   ECO/UNDEV
                                                       DIPLOM

                                                       ECO/TAC
                                                          L65
WILLIAMS S.,"NEGOTIATING INVESTMENT IN EMERGING   FINAN
COUNTRIES." USA+45 WOR+45 INDUS MARKET NAT/G TOP/EX   ECO/UNDEV
TEC/DEV CAP/ISM ECO/TAC ADMIN SKILL WEALTH...POLICY
RELATIV MGT WORK 20. PAGE 117 B2353

                                                          S65
QUADE Q.L.,"THE TRUMAN ADMINISTRATION AND THE   USA+45
SEPARATION OF POWERS: THE CASE OF THE MARSHALL   ECO/UNDEV
PLAN." SOCIETY INT/ORG NAT/G CONSULT DELIB/GP LEGIS   DIPLOM
PLAN ECO/TAC ROUTINE DRIVE PERCEPT RIGID/FLEX
ORD/FREE PWR WEALTH...DECISION GEOG NEW/IDEA TREND
20 TRUMAN/HS. PAGE 85 B1726

                                                          S65
TABORSKY E.,"CHANGE IN CZECHOSLOVAKIA." COM USSR   ECO/DEV
ELITES INTELL AGRI INDUS NAT/G DELIB/GP EX/STRUC   PLAN
ECO/TAC TOTALISM ATTIT RIGID/FLEX SOCISM...MGT   CZECHOSLVK
CONCPT TREND 20. PAGE 102 B2067

                                                          N65
NJ DIVISION STATE-REGION PLAN,UTILIZATION OF NEW   UTIL
JERSEY'S DELAWARE RIVER WATERFRONT (PAMPHLET). FUT   PLAN
ADMIN REGION LEISURE GOV/REL DEMAND WEALTH...CHARTS   ECO/TAC
20 NEW/JERSEY. PAGE 78 B1586   PROVS

                                                          B66
ALEXANDER Y.,INTERNATIONAL TECHNICAL ASSISTANCE   ECO/TAC
EXPERTS* A CASE STUDY OF THE U.N. EXPERIENCE.   INT/ORG
ECO/UNDEV CONSULT EX/STRUC CREATE PLAN DIPLOM   ADMIN
FOR/AID TASK EFFICIENCY...ORG/CHARTS UN. PAGE 4   MGT
B0074

                                                          B66
ANDREWS K.R.,THE EFFECTIVENESS OF UNIVERSITY   ECO/DEV
MANAGEMENT DEVELOPMENT PROGRAMS. FUT USA+45 ECO/TAC   ACADEM
ADMIN...MGT QU METH/COMP 20. PAGE 5 B0103   TOP/EX
                                                       ATTIT
                                                          B66
BAKKE E.W.,MUTUAL SURVIVAL; THE GOAL OF UNION AND   MGT
MANAGEMENT (2ND ED.). USA+45 ECO/DEV ECO/TAC LABOR   LABOR
CONFER ADMIN REPRESENT GP/REL INGP/REL ATTIT   BARGAIN
...GP/COMP 20. PAGE 8 B0170   INDUS
                                                          B66
BIRKHEAD G.S.,ADMINISTRATIVE PROBLEMS IN PAKISTAN.   ADMIN
PAKISTAN AGRI FINAN INDUS LG/CO ECO/TAC CONTROL PWR   NAT/G
...CHARTS ANTHOL 20. PAGE 12 B0241   ORD/FREE
                                                       ECO/UNDEV
                                                          B66
CLEGG R.K.,THE ADMINISTRATOR IN PUBLIC WELFARE.   ADMIN
USA+45 STRUCT NAT/G PROVS PROB/SOLV BUDGET ECO/TAC   GIVE
GP/REL ROLE...SOC/WK 20 PUBLIC/REL. PAGE 21 B0434   GOV/REL
                                                       OP/RES
                                                          B66
COOK P.W. JR.,PROBLEMS OF CORPORATE POWER. WOR+45   ADMIN
FINAN INDUS BARGAIN GP/REL...MGT ANTHOL. PAGE 23   LG/CO
B0471   PWR
                                                       ECO/TAC
                                                          B66
DAVIS R.G.,PLANNING HUMAN RESOURCE DEVELOPMENT,   PLAN
EDUCATIONAL MODELS AND SCHEMATA. WORKER OP/RES   EFFICIENCY
ECO/TAC EDU/PROP CONTROL COST PRODUC...GEOG STAT   SIMUL
CHARTS 20. PAGE 27 B0544   ROUTINE
                                                          B66
FABRYCKY W.J.,OPERATIONS ECONOMY INDUSTRIAL   OP/RES
APPLICATIONS OF OPERATIONS RESEARCH. INDUS PLAN   MGT
ECO/TAC PRODUC...MATH PROBABIL STAT CHARTS 20.   SIMUL
PAGE 34 B0695   DECISION
                                                          B66
FOX K.A.,THE THEORY OF QUANTITATIVE ECONOMIC POLICY   ECO/TAC
WITH APPLICATIONS TO ECONOMIC GROWTH AND   ECOMETRIC
STABILIZATION. ECO/DEV AGRI NAT/G PLAN ADMIN RISK   EQUILIB
...DECISION IDEA/COMP SIMUL T. PAGE 37 B0746   GEN/LAWS
                                                          B66
GRETHER E.T.,MARKETING AND PUBLIC POLICY. USA+45   MARKET
ECO/DEV DIST/IND NAT/G PLAN CAP/ISM PRICE CONTROL   PROB/SOLV
...GEOG MGT 20. PAGE 43 B0874   ECO/TAC
                                                       POLICY
                                                          B66
GROSS H.,MAKE OR BUY. USA+45 FINAN INDUS CREATE   ECO/TAC
PRICE PRODUC 20. PAGE 44 B0889   PLAN
                                                       MGT
                                                       COST
                                                          B66
HASTINGS P.G.,THE MANAGEMENT OF BUSINESS FINANCE.   FINAN
ECO/DEV PLAN BUDGET CONTROL COST...DECISION CHARTS   MGT
BIBLIOG T 20. PAGE 48 B0966   INDUS
                                                       ECO/TAC
                                                          B66
KAESTNER K.,GESAMTWIRTSCHAFTLICHE PLANUNG IN EINER   ECO/TAC
GEMISCHTEN WIRTSCHAFTSORDNUNG   PLAN
(WIRTSCHAFTSPOLITISCHE STUDIEN 5). GERMANY/W WOR+45   POLICY
WOR-45 INDUS MARKET NAT/G ACT/RES GP/REL INGP/REL   PREDICT
PRODUC...ECOMETRIC MGT BIBLIOG 20. PAGE 57 B1159
                                                          B66
KAUNDA K.,ZAMBIA: INDEPENDENCE AND BEYOND: THE   ORD/FREE
SPEECHES OF KENNETH KAUNDA. AFR FUT ZAMBIA SOCIETY   COLONIAL
ECO/UNDEV NAT/G PROB/SOLV ECO/TAC ADMIN RACE/REL   CONSTN
SOVEREIGN 20. PAGE 59 B1183   LEAD

KURAKOV I.G.,SCIENCE, TECHNOLOGY AND COMMUNISM; SOME QUESTIONS OF DEVELOPMENT (TRANS. BY CARIN DEDIJER). USSR INDUS PLAN PROB/SOLV COST PRODUC ...MGT MATH CHARTS METH 20. PAGE 61 B1243 — B66 CREATE TEC/DEV MARXISM ECO/TAC

MACFARQUHAR R.,CHINA UNDER MAO: POLITICS TAKES COMMAND. CHINA/COM COM AGRI INDUS CHIEF FORCES DIPLOM INT/TRADE EDU/PROP TASK REV ADJUST...ANTHOL 20 MAO. PAGE 67 B1359 — B66 ECO/UNDEV TEC/DEV ECO/TAC ADMIN

MANGONE G.J.,UN ADMINISTRATION OF ECONOMIC AND AOCIAL PROGRAMS. CONSULT BUDGET INT/TRADE REGION 20 UN. PAGE 69 B1391 — B66 ADMIN MGT ECO/TAC DELIB/GP

MANSFIELD E.,MANAGERIAL ECONOMICS AND OPERATIONS RESEARCH; A NONMATHEMATICAL INTRODUCTION. USA+45 ELITES ECO/DEV CONSULT EX/STRUC PROB/SOLV ROUTINE EFFICIENCY OPTIMAL...GAME T 20. PAGE 69 B1396 — B66 ECO/TAC OP/RES MGT COMPUTER

MONTGOMERY J.D.,APPROACHES TO DEVELOPMENT: POLITICS, ADMINISTRATION AND CHANGE. USA+45 AGRI FOR/AID ORD/FREE...CONCPT IDEA/COMP METH/COMP ANTHOL. PAGE 75 B1507 — B66 ECO/UNDEV ADMIN POLICY ECO/TAC

MOOMAW I.W.,THE CHALLENGE OF HUNGER. USA+45 PLAN ADMIN EATING 20. PAGE 75 B1509 — B66 FOR/AID DIPLOM ECO/UNDEV ECO/TAC

ONYEMELUKWE C.C.,PROBLEMS OF INDUSTRIAL PLANNING AND MANAGEMENT IN NIGERIA. AFR FINAN LABOR DELIB/GP TEC/DEV ADJUST...MGT TREND BIBLIOG. PAGE 80 B1610 — B66 ECO/UNDEV ECO/TAC INDUS PLAN

REDFORD E.S.,THE ROLE OF GOVERNMENT IN THE AMERICAN ECONOMY. USA+45 USA-45 FINAN INDUS LG/CO PROB/SOLV ADMIN INGP/REL INCOME PRODUC 18/20. PAGE 87 B1759 — B66 NAT/G ECO/DEV CAP/ISM ECO/TAC

SAPIN B.M.,THE MAKING OF UNITED STATES FOREIGN POLICY. USA+45 INT/ORG DELIB/GP FORCES PLAN ECO/TAC CIVMIL/REL PRESIDENT. PAGE 92 B1868 — B66 DIPLOM EX/STRUC DECISION NAT/G

SCHURMANN F.,IDEOLOGY AND ORGANIZATION IN COMMUNIST CHINA. CHINA/COM LOC/G MUNIC POL/PAR ECO/TAC CONTROL ATTIT...MGT STERTYP 20 COM/PARTY. PAGE 94 B1909 — B66 MARXISM STRUCT ADMIN NAT/G

SPINELLI A.,THE EUROCRATS; CONFLICT AND CRISIS IN THE EUROPEAN COMMUNITY (TRANS. BY C. GROVE HAINES). EUR+WWI MARKET POL/PAR ECO/TAC PARL/PROC EEC OEEC ECSC EURATOM. PAGE 99 B2007 — B66 INT/ORG INGP/REL CONSTN ADMIN

WADIA M.,THE NATURE AND SCOPE OF MANAGEMENT. DELIB/GP EX/STRUC CREATE AUTOMAT CONTROL EFFICIENCY ...ANTHOL 20. PAGE 112 B2271 — B66 MGT PROB/SOLV IDEA/COMP ECO/TAC

WARBURG J.P.,THE UNITED STATES IN THE POSTWAR WORLD. USA+45 ECO/TAC...POLICY 20 COLD/WAR. PAGE 113 B2287 — B66 FOR/AID DIPLOM PLAN ADMIN

WASHINGTON S.H.,BIBLIOGRAPHY: LABOR-MANAGEMENT RELATIONS ACT, 1947 AS AMENDED BY LABOR-MANAGEMENT REPORTING AND DISCLOSURE ACT, 1959. USA+45 CONSTN INDUS DELIB/GP LEGIS WORKER BARGAIN ECO/TAC ADJUD GP/REL NEW/LIB...JURID CONGRESS. PAGE 114 B2298 — B66 BIBLIOG LAW LABOR MGT

YOUNG S.,MANAGEMENT: A SYSTEMS ANALYSIS. DELIB/GP EX/STRUC ECO/TAC CONTROL EFFICIENCY...NET/THEORY 20. PAGE 119 B2394 — B66 PROB/SOLV MGT DECISION SIMUL

ZINKIN T.,CHALLENGES IN INDIA. INDIA PAKISTAN LAW AGRI FINAN INDUS TOP/EX TEC/DEV CONTROL ROUTINE ORD/FREE PWR 20 NEHRU/J SHASTRI/LB CIVIL/SERV. PAGE 119 B2404 — B66 NAT/G ECO/TAC POLICY ADMIN

MARKSHAK J.,"ECONOMIC PLANNING AND THE COST OF THINKING." COM MARKET EX/STRUC...DECISION GEN/LAWS. PAGE 69 B1400 — S66 ECO/UNDEV ECO/TAC PLAN ECO/DEV

PALMER M.,"THE UNITED ARAB REPUBLIC* AN ASSESSMENT OF ITS FAILURE." ELITES ECO/UNDEV POL/PAR FORCES ECO/TAC RUMOR ADMIN EXEC EFFICIENCY ATTIT SOCISM ...INT NASSER/G. PAGE 81 B1628 — S66 UAR SYRIA REGION FEDERAL

PRINCETON U INDUSTRIAL REL SEC,RECENT MATERIAL ON COLLECTIVE BARGAINING IN GOVERNMENT (PAMPHLET NO. 130). USA+45 ECO/DEV LABOR WORKER ECO/TAC GOV/REL ...MGT 20. PAGE 85 B1710 — N66 BIBLIOG/A BARGAIN NAT/G GP/REL

ANDERSON C.W.,POLITICS AND ECONOMIC CHANGE IN LATIN AMERICA. L/A+17C INDUS NAT/G OP/RES ADMIN DEMAND ...POLICY STAT CHARTS NAT/COMP 20. PAGE 4 B0091 — B67 ECO/UNDEV PROB/SOLV PLAN ECO/TAC

ENKE S.,DEFENSE MANAGEMENT. USA+45 R+D FORCES WORKER PLAN ECO/TAC ADMIN NUC/PWR BAL/PAY UTIL WEALTH...MGT DEPT/DEFEN. PAGE 33 B0675 — B67 DECISION DELIB/GP EFFICIENCY BUDGET

GABRIEL P.P.,THE INTERNATIONAL TRANSFER OF CORPORATE SKILLS: MANAGEMENT CONTRACTS IN LESS DEVELOPED COUNTRIES. CLIENT INDUS LG/CO PLAN PROB/SOLV CAP/ISM ECO/TAC FOR/AID INT/TRADE RENT ADMIN SKILL 20. PAGE 38 B0771 — B67 ECO/UNDEV AGREE MGT CONSULT

HIRSCHMAN A.O.,DEVELOPMENT PROJECTS OBSERVED. INDUS INT/ORG CONSULT EX/STRUC CREATE OP/RES ECO/TAC DEMAND...POLICY MGT METH/COMP 20 WORLD/BANK. PAGE 50 B1016 — B67 ECO/UNDEV R+D FINAN PLAN

JAKUBAUSKAS E.B.,HUMAN RESOURCES DEVELOPMENT. USA+45 AGRI INDUS SERV/IND ACT/RES PLAN ADMIN RACE/REL DISCRIM...TREND GEN/LAWS. PAGE 55 B1119 — B67 PROB/SOLV ECO/TAC EDU/PROP WORKER

KARDOUCHE G.K.,THE UAR IN DEVELOPMENT. UAR ECO/TAC INT/TRADE BAL/PAY...STAT CHARTS BIBLIOG 20. PAGE 58 B1172 — B67 FINAN MGT CAP/ISM ECO/UNDEV

KONCZACKI Z.A.,PUBLIC FINANCE AND ECONOMIC DEVELOPMENT OF NATAL 1893-1910. TAX ADMIN COLONIAL ...STAT CHARTS BIBLIOG 19/20 NATAL. PAGE 61 B1228 — B67 ECO/TAC FINAN NAT/G ECO/UNDEV

OVERSEAS DEVELOPMENT INSTIT,EFFECTIVE AID. WOR+45 INT/ORG TEC/DEV DIPLOM INT/TRADE ADMIN. PAGE 80 B1619 — B67 FOR/AID ECO/UNDEV ECO/TAC NAT/COMP

POSNER M.V.,ITALIAN PUBLIC ENTERPRISE. ITALY ECO/DEV FINAN INDUS CREATE ECO/TAC ADMIN CONTROL EFFICIENCY PRODUC...TREND CHARTS 20. PAGE 84 B1693 — B67 NAT/G PLAN CAP/ISM SOCISM

SALMOND J.A.,THE CIVILIAN CONSERVATION CORPS, 1933-1942. USA-45 NAT/G CREATE EXEC EFFICIENCY WEALTH...BIBLIOG 20 ROOSEVLT/F. PAGE 92 B1864 — B67 ADMIN ECO/TAC TASK AGRI

SKIDMORE T.E.,POLITICS IN BRAZIL 1930-1964. BRAZIL L/A+17C INDUS NAT/G PROB/SOLV ATTIT 20. PAGE 98 B1973 — B67 CONSTN ECO/TAC ADMIN

WARREN S.,THE AMERICAN PRESIDENT. POL/PAR FORCES LEGIS DIPLOM ECO/TAC ADMIN EXEC PWR...ANTHOL 18/20 ROOSEVLT/F KENNEDY/JF JOHNSON/LB TRUMAN/HS WILSON/W. PAGE 114 B2297 — B67 CHIEF LEAD NAT/G CONSTN

"A PROPOS DES INCITATIONS FINANCIERES AUX GROUPEMENTS DES COMMUNES: ESSAI D'INTERPRETATION." FRANCE NAT/G LEGIS ADMIN GOV/REL CENTRAL 20. PAGE 2 B0004 — L67 LOC/G ECO/TAC APPORT ADJUD

GOULD W.B.,"THE STATUS OF UNAUTHORIZED AND 'WILDCAT' STRIKES UNDER THE NATIONAL LABOR RELATIONS ACT." USA+45 ACT/RES BARGAIN ECO/TAC LEGIT ADJUD ADMIN GP/REL MGT. PAGE 42 B0842 — L67 ECO/DEV INDUS LABOR POLICY

PASLEY R.S.,"ORGANIZATIONAL CONFLICTS OF INTEREST IN GOVERNMENT CONTRACTS." ELITES R+D ROUTINE NUC/PWR DEMAND EFFICIENCY 20. PAGE 81 B1639 — L67 NAT/G ECO/TAC RATION CONTROL

BERRODIN E.F.,"AT THE BARGAINING TABLE." LABOR DIPLOM ECO/TAC ADMIN...MGT 20 MICHIGAN. PAGE 11 B0230 — S67 PROVS WORKER LAW BARGAIN

BRIMMER A.F.,"INITIATIVE AND INNOVATION IN CENTRAL BANKING." USA+45 ECO/DEV MARKET ECO/TAC TAX CONTROL DEMAND...MGT CHARTS FED/RESERV. PAGE 15 B0309 — S67 FINAN CREATE NAT/G POLICY

DIXON O.F.,"A SOCIAL SYSTEMS APPROACH TO MARKETING." ECO/DEV ECO/TAC CONTROL EFFICIENCY ...DECISION 20. PAGE 29 B0599 — S67 MARKET SOCIETY GP/REL MGT

DROR Y.,"POLICY ANALYSTS." USA+45 COMPUTER OP/RES ECO/TAC ADMIN ROUTINE...ECOMETRIC METH/COMP SIMUL 20. PAGE 30 B0618 — S67 NAT/G POLICY PLAN DECISION

HILL F.G.,"VEBLEN, BERLE AND THE MODERN
CORPORATION." FINAN ECO/TAC CONTROL OWN...MGT 20.
PAGE 50 B1010

S67
LG/CO
ROLE
INDUS
ECO/DEV

KURON J.,"AN OPEN LETTER TO THE PARTY." CONSTN
WORKER BUDGET EDU/PROP ADMIN REPRESENT SUFF OWN
...SOCIALIST 20. PAGE 62 B1244

S67
ELITES
STRUCT
POL/PAR
ECO/TAC

SPEAR P.,"NEHRU." INDIA NAT/G POL/PAR ECO/TAC ADJUD
GOV/REL CENTRAL RIGID/FLEX 20 NEHRU/J. PAGE 99
B2003

S67
CHIEF
ATTIT
ADMIN
CREATE

WEIL G.L.,"THE MERGER OF THE INSTITUTIONS OF THE
EUROPEAN COMMUNITIES" EUR+WWI ECO/DEV INT/TRADE
CONSEN PLURISM...DECISION MGT 20 EEC EURATOM ECSC
TREATY. PAGE 115 B2313

S67
ECO/TAC
INT/ORG
CENTRAL
INT/LAW

GUZZARDI W. JR.,"THE SECOND BATTLE OF BRITAIN." UK
STRATA LABOR WORKER CREATE PROB/SOLV EDU/PROP ADMIN
LEAD LOBBY...MGT SOC 20 GOLD/STAND. PAGE 45 B0907

S68
FINAN
ECO/TAC
ECO/DEV
STRUCT

ECO/UNDEV....ECONOMIC SYSTEM IN DEVELOPING COUNTRIES

CONOVER H.F.,MADAGASCAR: A SELECTED LIST OF
REFERENCES. MADAGASCAR STRUCT ECO/UNDEV NAT/G ADMIN
...SOC 19/20. PAGE 23 B0463

N
BIBLIOG/A
SOCIETY
CULTURE
COLONIAL

VENKATESAN S.L.,BIBLIOGRAPHY ON PUBLIC ENTERPRISES
IN INDIA. INDIA S/ASIA FINAN LG/CO LOC/G PLAN
BUDGET SOCISM...MGT 20. PAGE 112 B2258

N
BIBLIOG/A
ADMIN
ECO/UNDEV
INDUS

INTERNATIONAL BIBLIOGRAPHY OF ECONOMICS. WOR+45
FINAN MARKET ADMIN DEMAND INCOME PRODUC...POLICY
IDEA/COMP METH. PAGE 1 B0003

N
BIBLIOG
ECO/DEV
ECO/UNDEV
INT/TRADE

INTERNATIONAL REVIEW OF ADMINISTRATIVE SCIENCES.
WOR+45 WOR-45 STRATA ECO/DEV ECO/UNDEV CREATE PLAN
PROB/SOLV DIPLOM CONTROL REPRESENT...MGT 20. PAGE 1
B0004

N
BIBLIOG/A
ADMIN
INT/ORG
NAT/G

BULLETIN OF THE PUBLIC AFFAIRS INFORMATION SERVICE.
WOR+45 WOR-45 ECO/UNDEV FINAN LABOR LOC/G PROVS
TEC/DEV DIPLOM EDU/PROP SOC. PAGE 1 B0010

N
BIBLIOG
NAT/G
ECO/DEV
ADMIN

HANDBOOK OF LATIN AMERICAN STUDIES. LAW CULTURE
ECO/UNDEV POL/PAR ADMIN LEAD...SOC 20. PAGE 1 B0014

N
BIBLIOG/A
L/A+17C
NAT/G
DIPLOM

PUBLIC ADMINISTRATION ABSTRACTS AND INDEX OF
ARTICLES. WOR+45 PLAN PROB/SOLV...POLICY 20. PAGE 1
B0019

N
BIBLIOG/A
ADMIN
ECO/UNDEV
NAT/G

DOHERTY D.K.,PRELIMINARY BIBLIOGRAPHY OF
COLONIZATION AND SETTLEMENT IN LATIN AMERICA AND
ANGLO-AMERICA. L/A+17C PRE/AMER USA-45 ECO/UNDEV
NAT/G 15/20. PAGE 30 B0604

N
BIBLIOG
COLONIAL
ADMIN
DIPLOM

UNITED NATIONS,UNITED NATIONS PUBLICATIONS. WOR+45
ECO/UNDEV AGRI FINAN FORCES ADMIN LEAD WAR PEACE
...POLICY INT/LAW 20 UN. PAGE 107 B2160

N
BIBLIOG
INT/ORG
DIPLOM

UNIVERSITY OF FLORIDA,CARIBBEAN ACQUISITIONS:
MATERIALS ACQUIRED BY THE UNIVERSITY OF FLORIDA
1957-1960. L/A+17C...ART/METH GEOG MGT 20. PAGE 107
B2167

N
BIBLIOG
ECO/UNDEV
EDU/PROP
JURID

STOLPER W.,"SOCIAL FACTORS IN ECONOMIC PLANNING,
WITH SPECIAL REFERENCE TO NIGERIA" AFR NIGER
CULTURE FAM SECT RECEIVE ETIQUET ADMIN DEMAND 20.
PAGE 101 B2045

NCO
ECO/UNDEV
PLAN
ADJUST
RISK

MORRIS H.C.,THE HISTORY OF COLONIZATION. WOR+45
WOR-45 ECO/DEV ECO/UNDEV INT/ORG ACT/RES PLAN
ECO/TAC LEGIT ROUTINE COERCE ATTIT DRIVE ALL/VALS
...GEOG TREND 19. PAGE 76 B1528

B00
DOMIN
SOVEREIGN
COLONIAL

EAST KENTUCKY REGIONAL PLAN,PROGRAM 60: A DECADE OF
ACTION FOR PROGRESS IN EASTERN KENTUCKY (PAMPHLET).
USA+45 AGRI CONSTRUC INDUS CONSULT ACT/RES
PROB/SOLV EDU/PROP GOV/REL HEALTH KENTUCKY. PAGE 32
B0643

N19
REGION
ADMIN
PLAN
ECO/UNDEV

EAST KENTUCKY REGIONAL PLAN,PROGRAM 60 REPORT:
ACTION FOR PORGRESS IN EASTERN KENTUCKY (PAMPHLET).

N19
REGION
PLAN

USA+45 CONSTRUC INDUS ACT/RES PROB/SOLV EDU/PROP
ADMIN GOV/REL KENTUCKY. PAGE 32 B0644

ECO/UNDEV
CONSULT

GORWALA A.D.,THE ADMINISTRATIVE JUNGLE (PAMPHLET).
INDIA NAT/G LEGIS ECO/TAC CONTROL GOV/REL
...METH/COMP 20. PAGE 41 B0838

N19
ADMIN
POLICY
PLAN
ECO/UNDEV

JACKSON R.G.A.,THE CASE FOR AN INTERNATIONAL
DEVELOPMENT AUTHORITY (PAMPHLET). WOR+45 ECO/DEV
DIPLOM GIVE CONTROL GP/REL EFFICIENCY NAT/LISM
SOVEREIGN 20. PAGE 55 B1108

N19
FOR/AID
INT/ORG
ECO/UNDEV
ADMIN

KUWAIT ARABIA,KUWAIT FUND FOR ARAB ECONOMIC
DEVELOPMENT (PAMPHLET). ISLAM KUWAIT UAR ECO/UNDEV
LEGIS ECO/TAC WEALTH 20. PAGE 62 B1245

N19
FOR/AID
DIPLOM
FINAN
ADMIN

LA PALOMBARA J.G.,ALTERNATIVE STRATEGIES FOR
DEVELOPING ADMINISTRATIVE CAPABILITIES IN EMERGING
NATIONS (PAMPHLET). POL/PAR EX/STRUC PROB/SOLV
PLURISM...POLICY METH/COMP. PAGE 62 B1248

N19
ECO/UNDEV
MGT
EXEC
ADMIN

HALL W.P.,EMPIRE TO COMMONWEALTH. FUT WOR-45 CONSTN
ECO/DEV ECO/UNDEV INT/ORG PROVS PLAN DIPLOM
EDU/PROP ADMIN COLONIAL PEACE PERSON ALL/VALS
...POLICY GEOG SOC OBS RECORD TREND CMN/WLTH
PARLIAMENT 19/20. PAGE 46 B0925

B28
VOL/ASSN
NAT/G
UK

ROBERTS S.H.,HISTORY OF FRENCH COLONIAL POLICY. AFR
ASIA L/A+17C S/ASIA CULTURE ECO/DEV ECO/UNDEV FINAN
NAT/G PLAN ECO/TAC DOMIN ROUTINE SOVEREIGN...OBS
HIST/WRIT TREND CHARTS VAL/FREE 19/20. PAGE 89
B1796

B29
INT/ORG
ACT/RES
FRANCE
COLONIAL

ROBINSON H.,DEVELOPMENT OF THE BRITISH EMPIRE.
WOR-45 CULTURE SOCIETY STRUCT ECO/DEV ECO/UNDEV
INT/ORG VOL/ASSN FORCES CREATE PLAN DOMIN EDU/PROP
ADMIN COLONIAL PWR WEALTH...POLICY GEOG CHARTS
CMN/WLTH 16/20. PAGE 89 B1800

B36
NAT/G
HIST/WRIT
UK

ROYAL INST. INT. AFF.,THE COLONIAL PROBLEM. WOR-45
LAW ECO/DEV ECO/UNDEV NAT/G PLAN ECO/TAC EDU/PROP
ADMIN ATTIT ALL/VALS...CONCPT 20. PAGE 91 B1844

B37
INT/ORG
ACT/RES
SOVEREIGN
COLONIAL

ZIMMERN A.,MODERN POLITICAL DOCTRINE. WOR-45
CULTURE SOCIETY ECO/UNDEV DELIB/GP EX/STRUC CREATE
DOMIN COERCE NAT/LISM ATTIT RIGID/FLEX ORD/FREE PWR
WEALTH...POLICY CONCPT OBS TIME/SEQ TREND TOT/POP
LEAGUE/NAT 20. PAGE 119 B2402

B39
NAT/G
ECO/TAC
BAL/PWR
INT/TRADE

PERHAM M.,AFRICANS AND BRITISH RULE. AFR UK ECO/TAC
CONTROL GP/REL ATTIT 20. PAGE 82 B1654

B41
DIPLOM
COLONIAL
ADMIN
ECO/UNDEV

CARLO A.M.,ENSAYO DE UNA BIBLIOGRAFIA DE
BIBLIOGRAFIAS MEXICANAS. ECO/UNDEV LOC/G ADMIN LEAD
20 MEXIC/AMER. PAGE 19 B0381

B43
BIBLIOG
L/A+17C
NAT/G
DIPLOM

LEWIN E.,ROYAL EMPIRE SOCIETY BIBLIOGRAPHIES NO. 9:
SUB-SAHARA AFRICA. ECO/UNDEV TEC/DEV DIPLOM ADMIN
COLONIAL LEAD 20. PAGE 64 B1303

B43
BIBLIOG
AFR
NAT/G
SOCIETY

HAILEY,"THE FUTURE OF COLONIAL PEOPLES." WOR-45
CONSTN CULTURE ECO/UNDEV AGRI MARKET INT/ORG NAT/G
SECT CONSULT ECO/TAC LEGIT ADMIN NAT/LISM ALL/VALS
...SOC OBS TREND STERTYP CMN/WLTH LEAGUE/NAT
PARLIAMENT 20. PAGE 45 B0916

L44
PLAN
CONCPT
DIPLOM
UK

CONOVER H.F.,NON-SELF-GOVERNING AREAS. BELGIUM
FRANCE ITALY UK WOR+45 CULTURE ECO/UNDEV INT/ORG
LOC/G NAT/G ECO/TAC INT/TRADE ADMIN HEALTH...SOC
UN. PAGE 23 B0465

B47
BIBLIOG/A
COLONIAL
DIPLOM

MEEK C.K.,COLONIAL LAW; A BIBLIOGRAPHY WITH SPECIAL
REFERENCE TO NATIVE AFRICAN SYSTEMS OF LAW AND LAND
TENURE. AFR ECO/UNDEV AGRI CT/SYS...JURID SOC 20.
PAGE 72 B1462

B48
COLONIAL
ADMIN
LAW
CONSTN

BORBA DE MORAES R.,MANUAL BIBLIOGRAFICO DE ESTUDOS
BRASILEIROS. BRAZIL DIPLOM ADMIN LEAD...SOC 20.
PAGE 14 B0276

B49
BIBLIOG
L/A+17C
NAT/G
ECO/UNDEV

PERHAM M.,COLONIAL GOVERNMENT: ANNOTATED READING
LIST ON BRITISH COLONIAL GOVERNMENT. UK WOR+45
WOR-45 ECO/UNDEV INT/ORG LEGIS FOR/AID INT/TRADE
DOMIN ADMIN REV 20. PAGE 82 B1655

B50
BIBLIOG/A
COLONIAL
GOV/REL
NAT/G

US SENATE COMM. GOVT. OPER.,"REVISION OF THE UN
CHARTER." FUT USA+45 WOR+45 CONSTN ECO/DEV
ECO/UNDEV NAT/G DELIB/GP ACT/RES CREATE PLAN EXEC

L50
INT/ORG
LEGIS
PEACE

ROUTINE CHOOSE ALL/VALS...POLICY CONCPT CONGRESS UN
TOT/POP 20 COLD/WAR. PAGE 111 B2235
B51
BERTON P.A.,MANCHURIA: AN ANNOTATED BIBLIOGRAPHY.   BIBLIOG/A
ASIA DIST/IND ADMIN...SOC 20. PAGE 11 B0231   MARXISM
                                                      ECO/UNDEV
                                                      COLONIAL
B51
CHRISTENSEN A.N.,THE EVOLUTION OF LATIN AMERICAN   NAT/G
GOVERNMENT: A BOOK OF READINGS. ECO/UNDEV INDUS   CONSTN
LOC/G POL/PAR EX/STRUC LEGIS FOR/AID CT/SYS   DIPLOM
...SOC/WK 20 SOUTH/AMER. PAGE 21 B0428   L/A+17C
B53
MAJUMDAR B.B.,PROBLEMS OF PUBLIC ADMINISTRATION IN   ECO/UNDEV
INDIA. INDIA INDUS PLAN BUDGET ADJUD CENTRAL DEMAND   GOV/REL
WEALTH...WELF/ST ANTHOL 20 CIVIL/SERV. PAGE 68   ADMIN
B1384   MUNIC
B53
WAGLEY C.,AMAZON TOWN: A STUDY OF MAN IN THE   SOC
TROPICS. BRAZIL L/A+17C STRATA STRUCT ECO/UNDEV   NEIGH
AGRI EX/STRUC RACE/REL DISCRIM HABITAT WEALTH...OBS   CULTURE
SOC/EXP 20. PAGE 113 B2273   INGP/REL
B54
BINANI G.D.,INDIA AT A GLANCE (REV. ED.). INDIA   INDEX
COM/IND FINAN INDUS LABOR PROVS SCHOOL PLAN DIPLOM   CON/ANAL
INT/TRADE ADMIN...JURID 20. PAGE 12 B0238   NAT/G
                                                      ECO/UNDEV
B54
MOSK S.A.,INDUSTRIAL REVOLUTION IN MEXICO. MARKET   INDUS
LABOR CREATE CAP/ISM ADMIN ATTIT SOCISM...POLICY 20   TEC/DEV
MEXIC/AMER. PAGE 76 B1533   ECO/UNDEV
                                                      NAT/G
B55
APTER D.E.,THE GOLD COAST IN TRANSITION. FUT CONSTN   AFR
CULTURE SOCIETY ECO/UNDEV FAM KIN LOC/G NAT/G   SOVEREIGN
POL/PAR LEGIS TOP/EX EDU/PROP LEGIT ADMIN ATTIT
PERSON PWR...CONCPT STAT INT CENSUS TOT/POP
VAL/FREE. PAGE 6 B0120
B55
CHOWDHURI R.N.,INTERNATIONAL MANDATES AND   DELIB/GP
TRUSTEESHIP SYSTEMS. WOR+45 STRUCT ECO/UNDEV   PLAN
INT/ORG LEGIS DOMIN EDU/PROP LEGIT ADJUD EXEC PWR   SOVEREIGN
...CONCPT TIME/SEQ UN 20. PAGE 21 B0427
L55
KISER M.,"ORGANIZATION OF AMERICAN STATES." L/A+17C   VOL/ASSN
USA+45 ECO/UNDEV INT/ORG NAT/G PLAN TEC/DEV DIPLOM   ECO/DEV
ECO/TAC INT/TRADE EDU/PROP ADMIN ALL/VALS...POLICY   REGION
MGT RECORD ORG/CHARTS OAS 20. PAGE 60 B1215
B56
KIRK G.,THE CHANGING ENVIRONMENT OF INTERNATIONAL   FUT
RELATIONS. ASIA S/ASIA USA+45 WOR+45 ECO/UNDEV   EXEC
INT/ORG NAT/G FOR/AID EDU/PROP PEACE KNOWL   DIPLOM
...PLURIST COLD/WAR. TOT/POP 20. PAGE 60 B1214
B56
UNITED NATIONS,BIBLIOGRAPHY ON INDUSTRIALIZATION IN   BIBLIOG
UNDER-DEVELOPED COUNTRIES. WOR+45 R+D INT/ORG NAT/G   ECO/UNDEV
FOR/AID ADMIN LEAD 20 UN. PAGE 107 B2161   INDUS
                                                      TEC/DEV
C56
FALL B.B.,"THE VIET-MINH REGIME." VIETNAM LAW   NAT/G
ECO/UNDEV POL/PAR FORCES DOMIN WAR ATTIT MARXISM   ADMIN
...BIOG PREDICT BIBLIOG/A 20. PAGE 35 B0703   EX/STRUC
                                                      LEAD
B57
ASHER R.E.,THE UNITED NATIONS AND THE PROMOTION OF   INT/ORG
THE GENERAL WELFARE. WOR+45 WOR-45 ECO/UNDEV   CONSULT
EX/STRUC ACT/RES PLAN EDU/PROP ROUTINE HEALTH...HUM
CONCPT CHARTS UNESCO UN ILO 20. PAGE 7 B0139
B57
CENTRAL ASIAN RESEARCH CENTRE,BIBLIOGRAPHY OF   BIBLIOG/A
RECENT SOVIET SOURCE MATERIAL ON SOVIET CENTRAL   COM
ASIA AND THE BORDERLANDS. AFGHANISTN INDIA PAKISTAN   CULTURE
UAR USSR ECO/UNDEV AGRI EXTR/IND INDUS ACADEM ADMIN   NAT/G
...HEAL HUM LING CON/ANAL 20. PAGE 19 B0399
B57
PYE L.W.,THE POLICY IMPLICATIONS OF SOCIAL CHANGE   SOCIETY
IN NON-WESTERN SOCIETIES. ASIA USA+45 CULTURE   ORD/FREE
STRUCT NAT/G ECO/TAC ADMIN ROLE...POLICY SOC.   ECO/UNDEV
PAGE 85 B1723   DIPLOM
B57
UDY S.H. JR.,THE ORGANIZATION OF PRODUCTION IN   METH/COMP
NONINDUSTRIAL CULTURE. VOL/ASSN DELIB/GP TEC/DEV   ECO/UNDEV
...CHARTS BIBLIOG. PAGE 106 B2143   PRODUC
                                                      ADMIN
B58
LIST OF PUBLICATIONS (PERIODICAL OR AD HOC) ISSUED   BIBLIOG
BY VARIOUS MINISTRIES OF THE GOVERNMENT OF INDIA   NAT/G
(3RD ED.). INDIA ECO/UNDEV PLAN...POLICY MGT 20.   ADMIN
PAGE 2 B0037
B58
DWARKADAS R.,ROLE OF HIGHER CIVIL SERVICE IN INDIA.   ADMIN
INDIA ECO/UNDEV LEGIS PROB/SOLV GP/REL PERS/REL   NAT/G
...POLICY WELF/ST DECISION ORG/CHARTS BIBLIOG 20   ROLE
CIVIL/SERV INTRVN/ECO. PAGE 31 B0637   PLAN
B58
GROSSMAN J.,BIBLIOGRAPHY ON PUBLIC ADMINISTRATION   BIBLIOG

IN LATIN AMERICA. ECO/UNDEV FINAN PLAN BUDGET   L/A+17C
ECO/TAC TARIFFS TAX...STAT 20. PAGE 44 B0893   NAT/G
                                                      ADMIN
B58
INDIAN INST OF PUBLIC ADMIN,IMPROVING CITY   LOC/G
GOVERNMENT. INDIA ECO/UNDEV PLAN BUDGET PARTIC   MUNIC
GP/REL 20. PAGE 53 B1080   PROB/SOLV
                                                      ADMIN
B58
LAQUER W.Z.,THE MIDDLE EAST IN TRANSITION. COM USSR   ISLAM
ECO/UNDEV NAT/G VOL/ASSN EDU/PROP EXEC ATTIT DRIVE   TREND
PWR MARXISM COLD/WAR TOT/POP 20. PAGE 62 B1261   NAT/LISM
B58
MASON J.B.,THAILAND BIBLIOGRAPHY. S/ASIA THAILAND   BIBLIOG/A
CULTURE EDU/PROP ADMIN...GEOG SOC LING 20. PAGE 70   ECO/UNDEV
B1423   DIPLOM
                                                      NAT/G
B58
PAN AMERICAN UNION,REPERTORIO DE PUBLICACIONES   BIBLIOG
PERIODICAS ACTUALES LATINO-AMERICANAS. CULTURE   L/A+17C
ECO/UNDEV ADMIN LEAD GOV/REL 20 OAS. PAGE 81 B1630   NAT/G
                                                      DIPLOM
B58
UNESCO,UNESCO PUBLICATIONS: CHECK LIST (2ND REV.   BIBLIOG
ED.). WOR+45 DIPLOM FOR/AID WEALTH...POLICY SOC   INT/ORG
UNESCO. PAGE 107 B2156   ECO/UNDEV
                                                      ADMIN
B58
US HOUSE COMM GOVT OPERATIONS,HEARINGS BEFORE A   FOR/AID
SUBCOMMITTEE OF THE COMMITTEE ON GOVERNMENT   DIPLOM
OPERATIONS. CAMBODIA PHILIPPINE USA+45 CONSTRUC   ORD/FREE
TEC/DEV ADMIN CONTROL WEAPON EFFICIENCY HOUSE/REP.   ECO/UNDEV
PAGE 108 B2189
S58
JORDAN A.,"MILITARY ASSISTANCE AND NATIONAL   FORCES
POLICY." ASIA FUT USA+45 WOR+45 ECO/DEV ECO/UNDEV   POLICY
INT/ORG NAT/G PLAN ECO/TAC ROUTINE WEAPON ATTIT   FOR/AID
RIGID/FLEX PWR...CONCPT TREND 20. PAGE 57 B1153   DIPLOM
S58
MAIR L.P.,"REPRESENTATIVE LOCAL GOVERNMENT AS A   AFR
PROBLEM IN SOCIAL CHANGE." ECO/UNDEV KIN LOC/G   PWR
NAT/G SCHOOL JUDGE ADMIN ROUTINE REPRESENT   ELITES
RIGID/FLEX RESPECT...CONCPT STERTYP CMN/WLTH 20.
PAGE 68 B1383
B59
INDIAN INSTITUTE PUBLIC ADMIN,MORALE IN THE PUBLIC   HAPPINESS
SERVICES: REPORT OF A CONFERENCE JAN., 3-4, 1959.   ADMIN
INDIA S/ASIA ECO/UNDEV PROVS PLAN EDU/PROP CONFER   WORKER
GOV/REL EFFICIENCY DRIVE ROLE 20 CIVIL/SERV.   INGP/REL
PAGE 53 B1082
B59
MAYDA J.,ATOMIC ENERGY AND LAW. ECO/UNDEV FINAN   NUC/PWR
TEC/DEV FOR/AID EFFICIENCY PRODUC WEALTH...POLICY   L/A+17C
TECHNIC 20. PAGE 71 B1433   LAW
                                                      ADMIN
B59
PARK R.L.,LEADERSHIP AND POLITICAL INSTITUTIONS IN   NAT/G
INDIA. S/ASIA CULTURE ECO/UNDEV LOC/G MUNIC PROVS   EXEC
LEGIS PLAN ADMIN LEAD ORD/FREE WEALTH...GEOG SOC   INDIA
BIOG TOT/POP VAL/FREE 20. PAGE 81 B1633
B59
US HOUSE COMM GOVT OPERATIONS,UNITED STATES AID   FOR/AID
OPERATIONS IN LAOS. LAOS USA+45 PLAN INSPECT   ADMIN
HOUSE/REP. PAGE 108 B2190   FORCES
                                                      ECO/UNDEV
B59
US PRES COMM STUDY MIL ASSIST,COMPOSITE REPORT.   FOR/AID
USA+45 ECO/UNDEV PLAN BUDGET DIPLOM EFFICIENCY   FORCES
...POLICY MGT 20. PAGE 109 B2208   WEAPON
                                                      ORD/FREE
B59
YANG C.K.,A CHINESE VILLAGE IN EARLY COMMUNIST   ASIA
TRANSITION. ECO/UNDEV AGRI FAM KIN MUNIC FORCES   ROUTINE
PLAN ECO/TAC DOMIN EDU/PROP ATTIT DRIVE PWR RESPECT   SOCISM
...SOC CONCPT METH/CNCPT OBS RECORD CON/ANAL CHARTS
WORK 20. PAGE 118 B2389
S59
PADELFORD N.J.,"REGIONAL COOPERATION IN THE SOUTH   INT/ORG
PACIFIC: THE SOUTH PACIFIC COMMISSION." FUT   ADMIN
NEW/ZEALND UK WOR+45 CULTURE ECO/UNDEV LOC/G
VOL/ASSN...OBS CON/ANAL UNESCO VAL/FREE AUSTRAL 20.
PAGE 80 B1622
B60
ASPREMONT-LYNDEN H.,RAPPORT SUR L'ADMINISTRATION   AFR
BELGE DU RUANDA-URUNDI PENDANT L'ANNEE 1959.   COLONIAL
BELGIUM RWANDA AGRI INDUS DIPLOM ECO/TAC INT/TRADE   ECO/UNDEV
DOMIN ADMIN RACE/REL...GEOG CENSUS 20 UN. PAGE 7   INT/ORG
B0143
B60
EASTON S.C.,THE TWILIGHT OF EUROPEAN COLONIALISM.   FINAN
AFR S/ASIA CONSTN SOCIETY STRUCT ECO/UNDEV INDUS   ADMIN
NAT/G FORCES ECO/TAC COLONIAL CT/SYS ATTIT KNOWL
ORD/FREE PWR...SOCIALIST TIME/SEQ TREND CON/ANAL
20. PAGE 32 B0645
B60
HYDE L.K.G.,THE US AND THE UN. WOR+45 STRUCT   USA+45

ECO/DEV ECO/UNDEV NAT/G ACT/RES PLAN DIPLOM
EDU/PROP ADMIN ALL/VALS...CONCPT TIME/SEQ GEN/LAWS
UN VAL/FREE 20. PAGE 53 B1070
INT/ORG
FOR/AID

B60
KERR C.,INDUSTRIALISM AND INDUSTRIAL MAN. CULTURE
SOCIETY ECO/UNDEV NAT/G ADMIN PRODUC WEALTH
...PREDICT TREND NAT/COMP 19/20. PAGE 59 B1197
WORKER
MGT
ECO/DEV
INDUS

B60
LENCZOWSKI G.,OIL AND STATE IN THE MIDDLE EAST. FUT
IRAN LAW ECO/UNDEV EXTR/IND NAT/G TOP/EX PLAN
TEC/DEV ECO/TAC LEGIT ADMIN COERCE ATTIT ALL/VALS
PWR...CHARTS 20. PAGE 64 B1288
ISLAM
INDUS
NAT/LISM

B60
LERNER A.P.,THE ECONOMICS OF CONTROL. USA+45
ECO/UNDEV INT/ORG ACT/RES PLAN CAP/ISM INT/TRADE
ATTIT WEALTH...SOC MATH STAT GEN/LAWS INDEX 20.
PAGE 64 B1295
ECO/DEV
ROUTINE
ECO/TAC
SOCISM

B60
LEYDER J.,BIBLIOGRAPHIE DE L'ENSEIGNEMENT SUPERIEUR
ET DE LA RECHERCHE SCIENTIFIQUE EN AFRIQUE
INTERTROPICALE (2 VOLS.). AFR CULTURE ECO/UNDEV
AGRI PLAN EDU/PROP ADMIN COLONIAL...GEOG SOC/INTEG
20 NEGRO. PAGE 65 B1309
BIBLIOG/A
ACT/RES
ACADEM
R+D

B60
LIPSET S.M.,POLITICAL MAN. AFR COM EUR+WWI L/A+17C
MOD/EUR S/ASIA USA+45 USA-45 STRUCT ECO/DEV
ECO/UNDEV POL/PAR SECT ADMIN WEALTH...CONCPT WORK
TOT/POP 20. PAGE 65 B1320
PWR
SOC

B60
MOORE W.E.,LABOR COMMITMENT AND SOCIAL CHANGE IN
DEVELOPING AREAS. SOCIETY STRATA ECO/UNDEV MARKET
VOL/ASSN WORKER AUTHORIT SKILL...MGT NAT/COMP
SOC/INTEG 20. PAGE 75 B1514
LABOR
ORD/FREE
ATTIT
INDUS

B60
PENTONY D.E.,UNITED STATES FOREIGN AID. INDIA LAOS
USA+45 ECO/UNDEV INT/TRADE PEACE ATTIT
...POLICY METH/COMP ANTHOL 20. PAGE 82 B1653
FOR/AID
DIPLOM
ECO/TAC

B60
PIERCE R.A.,RUSSIAN CENTRAL ASIA, 1867-1917. ASIA
RUSSIA CULTURE AGRI INDUS EDU/PROP REV NAT/LISM
...CHARTS BIBLIOG 19/20 BOLSHEVISM INTERVENT.
PAGE 83 B1672
COLONIAL
DOMIN
ADMIN
ECO/UNDEV

B60
RAO V.K.R.,INTERNATIONAL AID FOR ECONOMIC
DEVELOPMENT - POSSIBILITIES AND LIMITATIONS. FINAN
PLAN TEC/DEV ADMIN TASK EFFICIENCY...POLICY SOC
METH/CNCPT CHARTS 20 UN. PAGE 86 B1734
FOR/AID
DIPLOM
INT/ORG
ECO/UNDEV

B60
SMITH M.G.,GOVERNMENT IN ZAZZAU 1800-1950. NIGERIA
UK CULTURE SOCIETY LOC/G ADMIN COLONIAL
...METH/CNCPT NEW/IDEA METH 19/20. PAGE 98 B1983
REGION
CONSTN
KIN
ECO/UNDEV

B60
STANFORD RESEARCH INSTITUTE,AFRICAN DEVELOPMENT: A
TEST FOR INTERNATIONAL COOPERATION. AFR USA+45
WOR+45 FINAN INT/ORG PLAN PROB/SOLV ECO/TAC
INT/TRADE ADMIN...CHARTS 20. PAGE 100 B2018
FOR/AID
ECO/UNDEV
ATTIT
DIPLOM

B60
WORLEY P.,ASIA TODAY (REV. ED.) (PAMPHLET). COM
ECO/UNDEV AGRI FINAN INDUS POL/PAR FOR/AID ADMIN
MARXISM 20. PAGE 118 B2376
BIBLIOG/A
ASIA
DIPLOM
NAT/G

S60
"THE EMERGING COMMON MARKETS IN LATIN AMERICA." FUT
L/A+17C STRATA DIST/IND INDUS LABOR NAT/G LEGIS
ECO/TAC ADMIN RIGID/FLEX HEALTH...NEW/IDEA TIME/SEQ
OAS 20. PAGE 2 B0039
FINAN
ECO/UNDEV
INT/TRADE

S60
EMERSON R.,"THE EROSION OF DEMOCRACY." AFR FUT LAW
CULTURE INTELL SOCIETY ECO/UNDEV FAM LOC/G NAT/G
FORCES PLAN TEC/DEV ECO/TAC ADMIN CT/SYS ATTIT
ORD/FREE PWR...SOCIALIST SOC CONCPT STAND/INT
TIME/SEQ WORK 20. PAGE 33 B0671
S/ASIA
POL/PAR

S60
FRANKEL S.H.,"ECONOMIC ASPECTS OF POLITICAL
INDEPENDENCE IN AFRICA." AFR FUT SOCIETY ECO/UNDEV
COM/IND FINAN LEGIS PLAN TEC/DEV CAP/ISM ECO/TAC
INT/TRADE ADMIN ATTIT DRIVE RIGID/FLEX PWR WEALTH
...MGT NEW/IDEA MATH TIME/SEQ VAL/FREE 20. PAGE 37
B0751
NAT/G
FOR/AID

S60
HERRERA F.,"THE INTER-AMERICAN DEVELOPMENT BANK."
USA+45 ECO/UNDEV INT/ORG CONSULT DELIB/GP PLAN
ECO/TAC INT/TRADE ROUTINE WEALTH...STAT 20. PAGE 49
B0994
L/A+17C
FINAN
FOR/AID
REGION

S60
MORA J.A.,"THE ORGANIZATION OF AMERICAN STATES."
USA+45 LAW ECO/UNDEV VOL/ASSN DELIB/GP PLAN BAL/PWR
EDU/PROP ADMIN DRIVE RIGID/FLEX ORD/FREE WEALTH
...TIME/SEQ GEN/LAWS OAS 20. PAGE 75 B1518
L/A+17C
INT/ORG
REGION

S60
MORALES C.J.,"TRADE AND ECONOMIC INTEGRATION IN
LATIN AMERICA." FUT L/A+17C LAW STRATA ECO/UNDEV
DIST/IND INDUS LABOR NAT/G LEGIS ECO/TAC ADMIN
RIGID/FLEX WEALTH...CONCPT NEW/IDEA CONT/OBS
FINAN
INT/TRADE
REGION

TIME/SEQ WORK 20. PAGE 75 B1519

S60
NORTH R.C.,"DIE DISKREPANZ ZWISCHEN REALITAT UND
WUNSCHBILD ALS INNENPOLITISCHER FAKTOR." ASIA
CHINA/COM COM FUT ECO/UNDEV NAT/G PLAN DOMIN ADMIN
COERCE PERCEPT...SOC MYTH GEN/METH WORK TOT/POP 20.
PAGE 79 B1589
SOCIETY
ECO/TAC

S60
SCHATZ S.P.,"THE INFLENCE OF PLANNING ON
DEVELOPMENT: THE NIGERIAN EXPERIENCE." AFR FUT
FINAN INDUS NAT/G EX/STRUC ECO/TAC ADMIN ATTIT
PERCEPT ORD/FREE PWR...MATH TREND CON/ANAL SIMUL
VAL/FREE 20. PAGE 93 B1883
ECO/UNDEV
PLAN
NIGERIA

C60
SMITH T.E.,"ELECTIONS IN DEVELOPING COUNTRIES: A
STUDY OF ELECTORAL PROCEDURES USED IN TOPICAL
AFRICA, SOUTH-EAST ASIA..." AFR S/ASIA UK ROUTINE
GOV/REL RACE/REL...GOV/COMP BIBLIOG 20. PAGE 98
B1985
ECO/UNDEV
CHOOSE
REPRESENT
ADMIN

N60
RHODESIA-NYASA NATL ARCHIVES,A SELECT BIBLIOGRAPHY
OF RECENT PUBLICATIONS CONCERNING THE FEDERATION OF
RHODESIA AND NYASALAND (PAMPHLET). MALAWI RHODESIA
LAW CULTURE STRUCT ECO/UNDEV LEGIS...GEOG 20.
PAGE 88 B1770
BIBLIOG
ADMIN
ORD/FREE
NAT/G

B61
AGARWAL R.C.,STATE ENTERPRISE IN INDIA. FUT INDIA
UK FINAN INDUS ADMIN CONTROL OWN...POLICY CHARTS
BIBLIOG 20 RAILROAD. PAGE 3 B0064
ECO/UNDEV
SOCISM
GOV/REL
LG/CO

B61
CARNEY D.E.,GOVERNMENT AND ECONOMY IN BRITISH WEST
AFRICA. GAMBIA GHANA NIGERIA SIER/LEONE DOMIN ADMIN
GOV/REL SOVEREIGN WEALTH LAISSEZ...BIBLIOG 20
CMN/WLTH. PAGE 19 B0384
METH/COMP
COLONIAL
ECO/TAC
ECO/UNDEV

B61
COHN B.S.,DEVELOPMENT AND IMPACT OF BRITISH
ADMINISTRATION IN INDIA: A BIBLIOGRAPHIC ESSAY.
INDIA UK ECO/UNDEV NAT/G DOMIN...POLICY MGT SOC
19/20. PAGE 22 B0440
BIBLIOG/A
COLONIAL
S/ASIA
ADMIN

B61
FRIEDMANN W.G.,JOINT INTERNATIONAL BUSINESS
VENTURES. ASIA ISLAM L/A+17C ECO/DEV DIST/IND FINAN
PROC/MFG FACE/GP LG/CO NAT/G VOL/ASSN CONSULT
EX/STRUC PLAN ADMIN ROUTINE WEALTH...OLD/LIB WORK
20. PAGE 37 B0760
ECO/UNDEV
INT/TRADE

B61
HARRISON S.,INDIA AND THE UNITED STATES. FUT S/ASIA
USA+45 WOR+45 INTELL ECO/DEV ECO/UNDEV AGRI INDUS
INT/ORG NAT/G CONSULT EX/STRUC TOP/EX PLAN ECO/TAC
NEUTRAL ALL/VALS...MGT TOT/POP 20. PAGE 47 B0956
DELIB/GP
ACT/RES
FOR/AID
INDIA

B61
HASAN H.S.,PAKISTAN AND THE UN. ISLAM WOR+45
ECO/DEV ECO/UNDEV NAT/G TOP/EX ECO/TAC FOR/AID
EDU/PROP ADMIN DRIVE PERCEPT...OBS TIME/SEQ UN 20.
PAGE 48 B0965
INT/ORG
ATTIT
PAKISTAN

B61
HICKS U.K.,DEVELOPMENT FROM BELOW. UK INDUS ADMIN
COLONIAL ROUTINE GOV/REL...POLICY METH/CNCPT CHARTS
19/20 CMN/WLTH. PAGE 50 B1006
ECO/UNDEV
LOC/G
GOV/COMP
METH/COMP

B61
HORVATH B.,THE CHARACTERISTICS OF YUGOSLAV ECONOMIC
DEVELOPMENT. COM ECO/UNDEV AGRI INDUS PLAN CAP/ISM
ECO/TAC ROUTINE WEALTH...SOCIALIST STAT CHARTS
STERTYP WORK 20. PAGE 52 B1045
ACT/RES
YUGOSLAVIA

B61
KOESTLER A.,THE LOTUS AND THE ROBOT. ASIA INDIA
S/ASIA SOCIETY STRATA ECO/DEV AGRI INDUS FAM CREATE
DOMIN EDU/PROP ADMIN COERCE ATTIT DRIVE SUPEGO
ORD/FREE PWR RESPECT WEALTH...MYTH OBS 20 CHINJAP.
PAGE 61 B1226
SECT
ECO/UNDEV

B61
LAHAYE R.,LES ENTREPRISES PUBLIQUES AU MAROC.
FRANCE MOROCCO LAW DIST/IND EXTR/IND FINAN CONSULT
PLAN TEC/DEV ADMIN AGREE CONTROL OWN...POLICY 20.
PAGE 62 B1250
NAT/G
INDUS
ECO/UNDEV
ECO/TAC

B61
MARX K.,THE COMMUNIST MANIFESTO. IN (MENDEL A.
ESSENTIAL WORKS OF MARXISM, NEW YORK: BANTAM. FUT
MOD/EUR CULTURE ECO/DEV ECO/UNDEV AGRI FINAN INDUS
MARKET PROC/MFG LABOR MUNIC POL/PAR CONSULT FORCES
CREATE PLAN ADMIN ATTIT DRIVE RIGID/FLEX ORD/FREE
PWR RESPECT MARX/KARL WORK. PAGE 70 B1421
COM
NEW/IDEA
CAP/ISM
REV

B61
MAYNE A.,DESIGNING AND ADMINISTERING A REGIONAL
ECONOMIC DEVELOPMENT PLAN WITH SPECIFIC REFERENCE
TO PUERTO RICO (PAMPHLET). PUERT/RICO SOCIETY NAT/G
DELIB/GP REGION...DECISION 20. PAGE 71 B1435
ECO/UNDEV
PLAN
CREATE
ADMIN

B61
MUNGER E.S.,AFRICAN FIELD REPORTS 1952-1961.
SOUTH/AFR SOCIETY ECO/UNDEV NAT/G POL/PAR COLONIAL
EXEC PARL/PROC GUERRILLA RACE/REL ALL/IDEOS...SOC
AUD/VIS 20. PAGE 76 B1538
AFR
DISCRIM
RECORD

B61
SHARP W.R.,FIELD ADMINISTRATION IN THE UNITED
INT/ORG

NATION SYSTEM: THE CONDUCT OF INTERNATIONAL ECONOMIC AND SOCIAL PROGRAMS. FUT WOR+45 CONSTN SOCIETY ECO/UNDEV R+D DELIB/GP ACT/RES PLAN TEC/DEV EDU/PROP EXEC ROUTINE HEALTH WEALTH...HUM CONCPT CHARTS METH ILO UNESCO VAL/FREE UN 20. PAGE 96 B1939
`CONSULT`

B61
US GENERAL ACCOUNTING OFFICE,EXAMINATION OF ECONOMIC AND TECHNICAL ASSISTANCE PROGRAM FOR IRAN. IRAN USA+45 AGRI INDUS DIPLOM CONTROL COST 20. PAGE 108 B2186
`FOR/AID` `ADMIN` `TEC/DEV` `ECO/UNDEV`

S61
CARLETON W.G.,"AMERICAN FOREIGN POLICY: MYTHS AND REALITIES." FUT USA+45 WOR+45 ECO/UNDEV INT/ORG EX/STRUC ARMS/CONT NUC/PWR WAR ATTIT...POLICY CONCPT CONT/OBS GEN/METH COLD/WAR TOT/POP 20. PAGE 19 B0378
`PLAN` `MYTH` `DIPLOM`

S61
MARSH R.M.,"FORMAL ORGANIZATION AND PROMOTION IN A PRE-INDUSTRIAL SOCIETY" (BMR)" ASIA FAM EX/STRUC LEAD...SOC CHARTS 19 WEBER/MAX. PAGE 70 B1407
`ADMIN` `STRUCT` `ECO/UNDEV` `STRATA`

S61
NOVE A.,"THE SOVIET MODEL AND UNDERDEVELOPED COUNTRIES." COM FUT USSR WOR+45 CULTURE ECO/DEV POL/PAR FOR/AID EDU/PROP ADMIN MORAL WEALTH ...POLICY RECORD HIST/WRIT 20. PAGE 79 B1593
`ECO/UNDEV` `PLAN`

S61
VINER J.,"ECONOMIC FOREIGN POLICY ON THE NEW FRONTIER." USA+45 ECO/UNDEV AGRI FINAN INDUS MARKET INT/ORG NAT/G FOR/AID INT/TRADE ADMIN ATTIT PWR 20 KENNEDY/JF. PAGE 112 B2262
`TOP/EX` `ECO/TAC` `BAL/PAY` `TARIFFS`

B62
BRIMMER B.,A GUIDE TO THE USE OF UNITED NATIONS DOCUMENTS. WOR+45 ECO/UNDEV AGRI EX/STRUC FORCES PROB/SOLV ADMIN WAR PEACE WEALTH...POLICY UN. PAGE 15 B0310
`BIBLIOG/A` `INT/ORG` `DIPLOM`

B62
CAIRNCROSS A.K.,FACTORS IN ECONOMIC DEVELOPMENT. WOR+45 ECO/UNDEV INDUS R+D LG/CO NAT/G EX/STRUC PLAN TEC/DEV ECO/TAC ATTIT HEALTH KNOWL PWR WEALTH ...TIME/SEQ GEN/LAWS TOT/POP VAL/FREE 20. PAGE 18 B0363
`MARKET` `ECO/DEV`

B62
CARSON P.,MATERIALS FOR WEST AFRICAN HISTORY IN THE ARCHIVES OF BELGIUM AND HOLLAND. CLIENT INDUS INT/TRADE ADMIN 17/19. PAGE 19 B0387
`BIBLIOG/A` `COLONIAL` `AFR` `ECO/UNDEV`

B62
COSTA RICA UNIVERSIDAD BIBL,LISTA DE TESIS DE GRADO DE LA UNIVERSIDAD DE COSTA RICA. COSTA/RICA LAW LOC/G ADMIN LEAD...SOC 20. PAGE 24 B0487
`BIBLIOG/A` `NAT/G` `DIPLOM` `ECO/UNDEV`

B62
FORD A.G.,THE GOLD STANDARD 1880-1914: BRITAIN AND ARGENTINA. UK ECO/UNDEV INT/TRADE ADMIN GOV/REL DEMAND EFFICIENCY...STAT CHARTS 19/20 ARGEN GOLD/STAND. PAGE 36 B0737
`FINAN` `ECO/TAC` `BUDGET` `BAL/PAY`

B62
GALENSON W.,LABOR IN DEVELOPING COUNTRIES. BRAZIL INDONESIA ISRAEL PAKISTAN TURKEY AGRI INDUS WORKER PAY PRICE GP/REL WEALTH...MGT CHARTS METH/COMP NAT/COMP 20. PAGE 38 B0775
`LABOR` `ECO/UNDEV` `BARGAIN` `POL/PAR`

B62
HARARI M.,GOVERNMENT AND POLITICS OF THE MIDDLE EAST. ISLAM USA+45 NAT/G SECT CHIEF ADMIN ORD/FREE 20. PAGE 47 B0943
`DIPLOM` `ECO/UNDEV` `TEC/DEV` `POLICY`

B62
INAYATULLAH,BUREAUCRACY AND DEVELOPMENT IN PAKISTAN. PAKISTAN ECO/UNDEV EDU/PROP CONFER ...ANTHOL DICTIONARY 20 BUREAUCRCY. PAGE 53 B1078
`EX/STRUC` `ADMIN` `NAT/G` `LOC/G`

B62
KUHN T.E.,PUBLIC ENTERPRISES, PROJECT PLANNING AND ECONOMIC DEVELOPMENT (PAMPHLET). ECO/UNDEV FINAN PLAN ADMIN EFFICIENCY OWN...MGT STAT CHARTS ANTHOL 20. PAGE 61 B1240
`ECO/DEV` `ECO/TAC` `LG/CO` `NAT/G`

B62
MORE S.S.,REMODELLING OF DEMOCRACY FOR AFRO-ASIAN NATIONS. AFR INDIA S/ASIA SOUTH/AFR CONSTN EX/STRUC COLONIAL CHOOSE TOTALISM SOVEREIGN NEW/LIB SOCISM ...SOC/WK 20. PAGE 75 B1520
`ORD/FREE` `ECO/UNDEV` `ADMIN` `LEGIS`

B62
PRAKASH O.M.,THE THEORY AND WORKING OF STATE CORPORATIONS: WITH SPECIAL REFERENCE TO INDIA. INDIA UK USA+45 TOP/EX PRICE ADMIN EFFICIENCY...MGT METH/COMP 20 TVA. PAGE 84 B1698
`LG/CO` `ECO/UNDEV` `GOV/REL` `SOCISM`

B62
TAYLOR D.,THE BRITISH IN AFRICA. UK CULTURE ECO/UNDEV INDUS DIPLOM INT/TRADE ADMIN WAR RACE/REL ORD/FREE SOVEREIGN...POLICY BIBLIOG 15/20 CMN/WLTH. PAGE 103 B2084
`AFR` `COLONIAL` `DOMIN`

B62
UNECA LIBRARY,NEW ACQUISITIONS IN THE UNECA LIBRARY. LAW NAT/G PLAN PROB/SOLV TEC/DEV ADMIN
`BIBLIOG` `AFR`

REGION...GEOG SOC 20 UN. PAGE 106 B2152
`ECO/UNDEV` `INT/ORG`

L62
BELSHAW D.G.R.,"PUBLIC INVESTMENT IN AGRICULTURE AND ECONOMIC DEVELOPMENT OF UGANDA" UGANDA AGRI INDUS R+D ECO/TAC RATION TAX PAY COLONIAL 20 WORLD/BANK. PAGE 10 B0209
`ECO/UNDEV` `PLAN` `ADMIN` `CENTRAL`

L62
GALBRAITH J.K.,"ECONOMIC DEVELOPMENT IN PERSPECTIVE." CAP/ISM ECO/TAC ROUTINE ATTIT WEALTH ...TREND CHARTS SOC/EXP WORK 20. PAGE 38 B0773
`ECO/UNDEV` `PLAN`

L62
HOFFHERR R.,"LE PROBLEME DE L'ENCADREMENT DANS LES JEUNES ETATS DE LANGUE FRANCAISE EN AFRIQUE CENTRALE ET A MADAGASCAR." FUT ECO/UNDEV CONSULT PLAN ECO/TAC COLONIAL ATTIT...MGT TIME/SEQ VAL/FREE 20. PAGE 51 B1028
`AFR` `STRUCT` `FRANCE`

L62
MALINOWSKI W.R.,"CENTRALIZATION AND DE-CENTRALIZATION IN THE UNITED NATIONS' ECONOMIC AND SOCIAL ACTIVITIES." WOR+45 CONSTN ECO/UNDEV INT/ORG VOL/ASSN DELIB/GP ECO/TAC EDU/PROP ADMIN RIGID/FLEX ...OBS CHARTS UNESCO UN EEC OAS OEEC 20. PAGE 69 B1385
`CREATE` `GEN/LAWS`

L62
MANGIN G.,"L'ORGANIZATION JUDICIAIRE DES ETATS D'AFRIQUE ET DE MADAGASCAR." ISLAM WOR+45 STRATA STRUCT ECO/UNDEV NAT/G LEGIT EXEC...JURID TIME/SEQ TOT/POP 20 SUPREME/CT. PAGE 69 B1387
`AFR` `LEGIS` `COLONIAL` `MADAGASCAR`

S62
GEORGE P.,"MATERIAUX ET REFLEXIONS POUR UNE POLITIQUE URBAINE RATIONNELLE DANS LES PAYS EN COURS DE DEVELOPPEMENT." FUT INTELL SOCIETY SERV/IND MUNIC ACT/RES WEALTH...MGT 20. PAGE 39 B0790
`ECO/UNDEV` `PLAN`

S62
MANGIN G.,"LES ACCORDS DE COOPERATION EN MATIERE DE JUSTICE ENTRE LA FRANCE ET LES ETATS AFRICAINS ET MALGACHE." AFR ISLAM WOR+45 STRUCT ECO/UNDEV NAT/G DELIB/GP PERCEPT ALL/VALS...JURID MGT TIME/SEQ 20. PAGE 69 B1386
`INT/ORG` `LAW` `FRANCE`

S62
MURACCIOLE L.,"LES MODIFICATIONS DE LA CONSTITUTION MALGACHE." AFR WOR+45 ECO/UNDEV LEGIT EXEC ALL/VALS ...JURID 20. PAGE 76 B1542
`NAT/G` `STRUCT` `SOVEREIGN` `MADAGASCAR`

S62
PIQUEMAL M.,"LES PROBLEMES DES UNIONS D'ETATS EN AFRIQUE NOIRE." FRANCE SOCIETY INT/ORG NAT/G DELIB/GP PLAN LEGIT ADMIN COLONIAL ROUTINE ATTIT ORD/FREE PWR...GEOG METH/CNCPT 20. PAGE 83 B1678
`AFR` `ECO/UNDEV` `REGION`

S62
SPRINGER H.W.,"FEDERATION IN THE CARIBBEAN: AN ATTEMPT THAT FAILED." L/A+17C ECO/UNDEV INT/ORG POL/PAR PROVS LEGIS CREATE PLAN LEGIT ADMIN FEDERAL ATTIT DRIVE PERSON ORD/FREE PWR...POLICY GEOG PSY CONCPT OBS CARIBBEAN CMN/WLTH 20. PAGE 100 B2013
`VOL/ASSN` `NAT/G` `REGION`

B63
BRAIBANTI R.J.D.,ADMINISTRATION AND ECONOMIC DEVELOPMENT IN INDIA. INDIA S/ASIA SOCIETY STRATA ECO/TAC PERSON WEALTH...MGT GEN/LAWS TOT/POP VAL/FREE 20. PAGE 15 B0300
`ECO/UNDEV` `ADMIN`

B63
COMISION DE HISTORIO,GUIA DE LOS DOCUMENTOS MICROFOTOGRAFIADOS POR LA UNIDAD MOVIL DE LA UNESCO. SOCIETY ECO/UNDEV INT/ORG ADMIN...SOC 20 UNESCO. PAGE 22 B0456
`BIBLIOG` `NAT/G` `L/A+17C` `DIPLOM`

B63
CONF ON FUTURE OF COMMONWEALTH,THE FUTURE OF THE COMMONWEALTH. UK ECO/UNDEV AGRI EDU/PROP ADMIN SOC/INTEG 20 COMMONWLTH. PAGE 23 B0460
`DIPLOM` `RACE/REL` `ORD/FREE` `TEC/DEV`

B63
DALAND R.T.,PERSPECTIVES OF BRAZILIAN PUBLIC ADMINISTRATION (VOL. I). BRAZIL LAW ECO/UNDEV SCHOOL CHIEF TEC/DEV CONFER CONTROL GP/REL ATTIT ROLE PWR...ANTHOL 20. PAGE 26 B0525
`ADMIN` `NAT/G` `PLAN` `GOV/REL`

B63
DE VRIES E.,SOCIAL ASPECTS OF ECONOMIC DEVELOPMENT IN LATIN AMERICA. CULTURE SOCIETY STRATA FINAN INDUS INT/ORG DELIB/GP ACT/RES ECO/TAC EDU/PROP ADMIN ATTIT SUPEGO HEALTH KNOWL ORD/FREE...SOC STAT TREND ANTHOL TOT/POP VAL/FREE. PAGE 28 B0562
`L/A+17C` `ECO/UNDEV`

B63
GANGULY D.S.,PUBLIC CORPORATIONS IN A NATIONAL ECONOMY. INDIA WOR+45 FINAN INDUS TOP/EX PRICE EFFICIENCY...MGT STAT CHARTS BIBLIOG 20. PAGE 38 B0779
`ECO/UNDEV` `LG/CO` `SOCISM` `GOV/REL`

B63
HAUSMAN W.H.,MANAGING ECONOMIC DEVELOPMENT IN AFRICA. AFR USA+45 LAW FINAN WORKER TEC/DEV WEALTH ...ANTHOL 20. PAGE 48 B0970
`ECO/UNDEV` `PLAN` `FOR/AID` `MGT`

B63
INDIAN INSTITUTE PUBLIC ADMIN,CASES IN INDIAN ADMINISTRATION. INDIA AGRI NAT/G PROB/SOLV TEC/DEV
`DECISION` `PLAN`

ECO/TAC ADMIN...ANTHOL METH 20. PAGE 53 B1083

MGT
ECO/UNDEV
B63

KAPP W.K..HINDU CULTURE: ECONOMIC DEVELOPMENT AND
ECONOMIC PLANNING IN INDIA. INDIA S/ASIA CULTURE
ECO/TAC EDU/PROP ADMIN ALL/VALS...POLICY MGT
TIME/SEQ VAL/FREE 20. PAGE 58 B1171

SECT
ECO/UNDEV

B63

LEWIS J.W..LEADERSHIP IN COMMUNIST CHINA. ASIA
INTELL ECO/UNDEV LOC/G MUNIC NAT/G PROVS ECO/TAC
EDU/PROP LEGIT ADMIN COERCE ATTIT ORD/FREE PWR
...INT TIME/SEQ CHARTS TOT/POP VAL/FREE. PAGE 65
B1304

POL/PAR
DOMIN
ELITES

B63

MCKIE R..MALAYSIA IN FOCUS. INDONESIA WOR+45
ECO/UNDEV FINAN NAT/G POL/PAR SECT FORCES PLAN
ADMIN COLONIAL COERCE DRIVE ALL/VALS...POLICY
RECORD CENSUS TIME/SEQ CMN/WLTH 20. PAGE 72 B1453

S/ASIA
NAT/LISM
MALAYSIA

B63

PREST A.R..PUBLIC FINANCE IN UNDERDEVELOPED
COUNTRIES. UK WOR+45 WOR-45 SOCIETY INT/ORG NAT/G
LEGIS ACT/RES PLAN ECO/TAC ADMIN ROUTINE...CHARTS
20. PAGE 84 B1702

FINAN
ECO/UNDEV
NIGERIA

B63

SCHRADER R..SCIENCE AND POLICY. WOR+45 ECO/DEV
ECO/UNDEV R+D FORCES PLAN DIPLOM GOV/REL TECHRACY
BIBLIOG. PAGE 94 B1900

TEC/DEV
NAT/G
POLICY
ADMIN
B63

SWERDLOW I..DEVELOPMENT ADMINISTRATION: CONCEPTS
AND PROBLEMS. WOR+45 CULTURE SOCIETY STRATA
DELIB/GP EX/STRUC ACT/RES PLAN ECO/TAC DOMIN LEGIT
ATTIT RIGID/FLEX SUPEGO HEALTH PWR...MGT CONCPT
ANTHOL VAL/FREE. PAGE 102 B2062

ECO/UNDEV
ADMIN

B63

UN SECRETARY GENERAL.PLANNING FOR ECONOMIC
DEVELOPMENT. ECO/UNDEV FINAN BUDGET INT/TRADE
TARIFFS TAX ADMIN 20 UN. PAGE 106 B2151

PLAN
ECO/TAC
MGT
NAT/COMP
B63

WEINER M..POLITICAL CHANGE IN SOUTH ASIA. CEYLON
INDIA PAKISTAN S/ASIA CULTURE ELITES ECO/UNDEV
EX/STRUC ADMIN CONTROL CHOOSE CONSERVE...GOV/COMP
ANTHOL 20. PAGE 115 B2315

NAT/G
CONSTN
TEC/DEV

L63

BEGUIN H.."ASPECTS GEOGRAPHIQUE DE LA
POLARISATION." FUT WOR+45 SOCIETY STRUCT ECO/DEV
R+D ADMIN PWR ATTIT RIGID/FLEX HEALTH WEALTH
...CHARTS 20. PAGE 10 B0206

ECO/UNDEV
GEOG
DIPLOM

L63

EMERSON R.."POLITICAL MODERNIZATION." WOR+45
CULTURE ECO/UNDEV NAT/G FORCES ECO/TAC DOMIN
EDU/PROP LEGIT COERCE ALL/VALS...CONCPT TIME/SEQ
VAL/FREE 20. PAGE 33 B0672

POL/PAR
ADMIN

L63

SPITZ A.A.."DEVELOPMENT ADMINISTRATION: AN
ANNOTATED BIBLIOGRAPHY." WOR+45 CULTURE SOCIETY
STRATA DELIB/GP EX/STRUC TOP/EX ACT/RES ECO/TAC
DOMIN EDU/PROP LEGIT COERCE ATTIT ALL/VALS...MGT
VAL/FREE. PAGE 99 B2009

ADMIN
ECO/UNDEV

S63

BARZANSKI S.."REGIONAL UNDERDEVELOPMENT IN THE
EUROPEAN ECONOMIC COMMUNITY." EUR+WWI ELITES
DIST/IND MARKET VOL/ASSN CONSULT EX/STRUC ECO/TAC
RIGID/FLEX WEALTH EEC OEEC 20. PAGE 9 B0192

ECO/UNDEV
PLAN

S63

COUTY P.."L'ASSISTANCE POUR LE DEVELOPPEMENT: POINT
DE VUE SCANDINAVES." EUR+WWI FINLAND FUT SWEDEN
WOR+45 ECO/DEV ECO/UNDEV COM/IND LABOR NAT/G
PROF/ORG ACT/RES SKILL WEALTH TOT/POP 20. PAGE 24
B0497

FINAN
ROUTINE
FOR/AID

S63

DUCROS B.."MOBILISATION DES RESSOURCES PRODUCTIVES
ET DEVELOPPEMENT." FUT INTELL SOCIETY COM/IND
DIST/IND EXTR/IND FINAN INDUS ROUTINE WEALTH
...METH/CNCPT OBS 20. PAGE 31 B0625

ECO/UNDEV
TEC/DEV

S63

HAVILAND H.F.."BUILDING A POLITICAL COMMUNITY."
EUR+WWI FUT UK USA+45 ECO/DEV ECO/UNDEV INT/ORG
NAT/G DELIB/GP BAL/PWR ECO/TAC NEUTRAL ROUTINE
ATTIT PWR WEALTH...CONCPT COLD/WAR TOT/POP 20.
PAGE 48 B0972

VOL/ASSN
DIPLOM

S63

MANGONE G.."THE UNITED NATIONS AND UNITED STATES
FOREIGN POLICY." USA+45 WOR+45 ECO/UNDEV NAT/G
DIPLOM LEGIT ROUTINE ATTIT DRIVE...TIME/SEQ UN
COLD/WAR 20. PAGE 69 B1390

INT/ORG
ECO/TAC
FOR/AID

S63

NYE J.S. JR.."EAST AFRICAN ECONOMIC INTEGRATION."
AFR UGANDA PROVS DELIB/GP PLAN ECO/TAC INT/TRADE
ADMIN ROUTINE ORD/FREE PWR WEALTH...OBS TIME/SEQ
VAL/FREE 20. PAGE 79 B1597

ECO/UNDEV
INT/ORG

S63

ROUGEMONT D.."LES NOUVELLES CHANCES DE L'EUROPE."
EUR+WWI FUT ECO/DEV INT/ORG NAT/G ACT/RES PLAN
TEC/DEV EDU/PROP ADMIN COLONIAL FEDERAL ATTIT PWR

ECO/UNDEV
PERCEPT

SKILL...TREND 20. PAGE 91 B1835

S63

SCHURMANN F.."ECONOMIC POLICY AND POLITICAL POWER
IN COMMUNIST CHINA." ASIA CHINA/COM USSR SOCIETY
ECO/UNDEV AGRI INDUS CREATE ADMIN ROUTINE ATTIT
DRIVE RIGID/FLEX PWR WEALTH...HIST/WRIT TREND
CHARTS WORK 20. PAGE 94 B1908

PLAN
ECO/TAC

B64

THE SPECIAL COMMONWEALTH AFRICAN ASSISTANCE PLAN.
AFR CANADA INDIA NIGERIA UK FINAN SCHOOL...CHARTS
20 COMMONWLTH. PAGE 2 B0041

ECO/UNDEV
TREND
FOR/AID
ADMIN
B64

AHMAD M..THE CIVIL SERVANT IN PAKISTAN. PAKISTAN
ECO/UNDEV COLONIAL INGP/REL...SOC CHARTS BIBLIOG 20
CIVIL/SERV. PAGE 3 B0065

WELF/ST
ADMIN
ATTIT
STRATA
B64

BOTTOMORE T.B..ELITES AND SOCIETY. INTELL STRATA
ECO/DEV ECO/UNDEV ADMIN GP/REL ORD/FREE...CONCPT
BIBLIOG 20. PAGE 14 B0281

ELITES
IDEA/COMP
SOCIETY
SOC
B64

BROWN C.V..GOVERNMENT AND BANKING IN WESTERN
NIGERIA. AFR NIGERIA GOV/REL GP/REL...POLICY 20.
PAGE 16 B0321

ADMIN
ECO/UNDEV
FINAN
NAT/G
B64

DAS M.N..INDIA UNDER MORLEY AND MINTO. INDIA UK
ECO/UNDEV MUNIC PROVS EX/STRUC LEGIS DIPLOM CONTROL
REV 20 MORLEY/J. PAGE 26 B0531

GOV/REL
COLONIAL
POLICY
ADMIN
B64

DUROSELLE J.B..POLITIQUES NATIONALES ENVERS LES
JEUNES ETATS. FRANCE ISRAEL ITALY UK USA+45 USSR
YUGOSLAVIA ECO/DEV FINAN ECO/TAC INT/TRADE ADMIN
PWR 20. PAGE 31 B0634

DIPLOM
ECO/UNDEV
COLONIAL
DOMIN

B64

FATOUROS A.A..CANADA'S OVERSEAS AID. CANADA WOR+45
ECO/DEV FINAN NAT/G BUDGET ECO/TAC CONFER ADMIN 20.
PAGE 35 B0707

FOR/AID
DIPLOM
ECO/UNDEV
POLICY
B64

FLORENCE P.S..ECONOMICS AND SOCIOLOGY OF INDUSTRY;
A REALISTIC ANALYSIS OF DEVELOPMENT. ECO/UNDEV
LG/CO NAT/G PLAN...GEOG MGT BIBLIOG 20. PAGE 36
B0729

INDUS
SOC
ADMIN

B64

GOODNOW H.F..THE CIVIL SERVICE OF PAKISTAN:
BUREAUCRACY IN A NEW NATION. INDIA PAKISTAN S/ASIA
ECO/UNDEV PROVS CHIEF PARTIC CHOOSE EFFICIENCY PWR
...BIBLIOG 20. PAGE 41 B0824

ADMIN
GOV/REL
LAW
NAT/G
B64

HAMBRIDGE G..DYNAMICS OF DEVELOPMENT. AGRI FINAN
INDUS LABOR INT/TRADE EDU/PROP ADMIN LEAD OWN
HEALTH...ANTHOL BIBLIOG 20. PAGE 46 B0930

ECO/UNDEV
ECO/TAC
OP/RES
ACT/RES
B64

HAMILTON B.L.S..PROBLEMS OF ADMINISTRATION IN AN
EMERGENT NATION: CASE STUDY OF JAMAICA. JAMAICA UK
WOR+45 MUNIC COLONIAL HABITAT...CHARTS BIBLIOG 20
CIVIL/SERV. PAGE 46 B0932

ADMIN
ECO/UNDEV
GOV/REL
NAT/G
B64

HANNA W.J..INDEPENDENT BLACK AFRICA: THE POLITICS
OF FREEDOM. ELITES INDUS KIN CHIEF COLONIAL CHOOSE
GOV/REL RACE/REL NAT/LISM ATTIT PERSON 20 NEGRO.
PAGE 46 B0938

AFR
ECO/UNDEV
ADMIN
PROB/SOLV
B64

HERSKOVITS M.J..ECONOMIC TRANSITION IN AFRICA. FUT
INT/ORG NAT/G WORKER PROB/SOLV TEC/DEV INT/TRADE
EQUILIB INCOME...ANTHOL 20. PAGE 49 B0996

AFR
ECO/UNDEV
PLAN
ADMIN
B64

LI C.M..INDUSTRIAL DEVELOPMENT IN COMMUNIST CHINA.
CHINA/COM ECO/DEV ECO/UNDEV AGRI FINAN INDUS MARKET
LABOR NAT/G ECO/TAC INT/TRADE EXEC ALL/VALS
...POLICY RELATIV TREND WORK TOT/POP VAL/FREE 20.
PAGE 65 B1311

ASIA
TEC/DEV

B64

LITTLE I.M.D..AID TO AFRICA. AFR UK TEC/DEV DIPLOM
ECO/TAC INCOME WEALTH 20. PAGE 66 B1326

FOR/AID
ECO/UNDEV
ADMIN
POLICY
B64

MAHAR J.M..INDIA: A CRITICAL BIBLIOGRAPHY. INDIA
PAKISTAN CULTURE ECO/UNDEV LOC/G POL/PAR SECT
PROB/SOLV DIPLOM ADMIN COLONIAL PARL/PROC ATTIT 20.
PAGE 68 B1377

BIBLIOG/A
S/ASIA
NAT/G
LEAD
B64

OECD SEMINAR REGIONAL DEV.REGIONAL DEVELOPMENT IN
ISRAEL. ISRAEL STRUCT ECO/UNDEV NAT/G REGION...GEOG
20. PAGE 79 B1603

ADMIN
PROVS
PLAN
METH/COMP
B64

PIPES R..THE FORMATION OF THE SOVIET UNION. EUR+WWI
MOD/EUR STRUCT ECO/UNDEV NAT/G LEGIS DOMIN LEGIT

COM
USSR

CT/SYS EXEC COERCE ALL/VALS...POLICY RELATIV
HIST/WRIT TIME/SEQ TOT/POP 19/20. PAGE 83 B1677
RUSSIA

B64
RIGGS F.W.,ADMINISTRATION IN DEVELOPING COUNTRIES.
FUT WOR+45 STRUCT AGRI INDUS NAT/G PLAN TEC/DEV
ECO/TAC EDU/PROP RIGID/FLEX KNOWL WEALTH...POLICY
MGT CONCPT METH/CNCPT TREND 20. PAGE 88 B1785
ECO/UNDEV
ADMIN

B64
SINGER M.R.,THE EMERGING ELITE: A STUDY OF
POLITICAL LEADERSHIP IN CEYLON. S/ASIA ECO/UNDEV
AGRI KIN NAT/G SECT EX/STRUC LEGIT ATTIT PWR
RESPECT...SOC STAT CHARTS 20. PAGE 97 B1967
TOP/EX
STRATA
NAT/LISM
CEYLON

B64
SULLIVAN G.,THE STORY OF THE PEACE CORPS. USA+45
WOR+45 INTELL FACE/GP NAT/G SCHOOL VOL/ASSN CONSULT
EX/STRUC PLAN EDU/PROP ADMIN ATTIT DRIVE ALL/VALS
...POLICY HEAL SOC CONCPT INT QU BIOG TREND SOC/EXP
WORK. PAGE 102 B2054
INT/ORG
ECO/UNDEV
FOR/AID
PEACE

B64
TINBERGEN J.,CENTRAL PLANNING. COM INTELL ECO/DEV
ECO/UNDEV FINAN INT/ORG PROB/SOLV ECO/TAC CONTROL
EXEC ROUTINE DECISION. PAGE 104 B2111
PLAN
INDUS
MGT
CENTRAL

B64
TULLY A.,WHERE DID YOUR MONEY GO. USA+45 USSR
ECO/UNDEV ADMIN EFFICIENCY WEALTH...METH/COMP 20.
PAGE 106 B2136
FOR/AID
DIPLOM
CONTROL

B64
UN PUB. INFORM. ORGAN.,EVERY MAN'S UNITED NATIONS.
UNIV WOR+45 CONSTN CULTURE SOCIETY ECO/DEV
ECO/UNDEV NAT/G ACT/RES PLAN ECO/TAC INT/TRADE
EDU/PROP LEGIT PEACE ATTIT ALL/VALS...POLICY HUM
INT/LAW CONCPT CHARTS UN TOT/POP 20. PAGE 106 B2150
INT/ORG
ROUTINE

B64
WITHERELL J.W.,OFFICIAL PUBLICATIONS OF FRENCH
EQUATORIAL AFRICA, FRENCH CAMEROONS, AND TOGO,
1946-1958 (PAMPHLET). CAMEROON CHAD FRANCE GABON
TOGO LAW ECO/UNDEV EXTR/IND INT/TRADE...GEOG HEAL
20. PAGE 117 B2367
BIBLIOG/A
AFR
NAT/G
ADMIN

B64
WRAITH R.,CORRUPTION IN DEVELOPING COUNTRIES.
NIGERIA UK LAW ELITES STRATA INDUS LOC/G NAT/G SECT
FORCES EDU/PROP ADMIN PWR WEALTH 18/20. PAGE 118
B2377
ECO/UNDEV
CRIME
SANCTION
ATTIT

L64
MACKINTOSH J.P.,"NIGERIA'S EXTERNAL AFFAIRS." UK
CULTURE ECO/UNDEV NAT/G VOL/ASSN EDU/PROP LEGIT
ADMIN ATTIT ORD/FREE PWR 20. PAGE 68 B1365
AFR
DIPLOM
NIGERIA

L64
ROTBERG R.,"THE FEDERATION MOVEMENT IN BRITISH EAST
AND CENTRAL AFRICA." AFR RHODESIA UGANDA ECO/UNDEV
NAT/G POL/PAR FORCES DOMIN LEGIT ADMIN COERCE ATTIT
...CONCPT TREND 20 TANGANYIKA. PAGE 91 B1831
VOL/ASSN
PWR
REGION

S64
HUELIN D.,"ECONOMIC INTEGRATION IN LATIN AMERICAN:
PROGRESS AND PROBLEMS." L/A+17C ECO/DEV AGRI
DIST/IND FINAN INDUS NAT/G VOL/ASSN CONSULT
DELIB/GP EX/STRUC ACT/RES PLAN TEC/DEV ECO/TAC
ROUTINE BAL/PAY WEALTH WORK 20. PAGE 52 B1058
MARKET
ECO/UNDEV
INT/TRADE

S64
LOW D.A.,"LION RAMPANT." EUR+WWI MOD/EUR S/ASIA
ECO/UNDEV NAT/G FORCES TEC/DEV ECO/TAC LEGIT ADMIN
COLONIAL COERCE ORD/FREE RESPECT 19/20. PAGE 67
B1344
AFR
DOMIN
DIPLOM
UK

S64
NASH M.,"SOCIAL PREREQUISITES TO ECONOMIC GROWTH IN
LATIN AMERICA AND SOUTHEAST ASIA." L/A+17C S/ASIA
CULTURE SOCIETY ECO/UNDEV AGRI INDUS NAT/G PLAN
TEC/DEV EDU/PROP ROUTINE ALL/VALS...POLICY RELATIV
SOC NAT/COMP WORK TOT/POP 20. PAGE 77 B1558
ECO/DEV
PERCEPT

S64
NEWLYN W.T.,"MONETARY SYSTEMS AND INTEGRATION" AFR
BUDGET ADMIN FEDERAL PRODUC PROFIT UTIL...CHARTS 20
AFRICA/E. PAGE 78 B1578
ECO/UNDEV
REGION
METH/COMP
FINAN

S64
THOMPSON V.A.,"ADMINISTRATIVE OBJECTIVES FOR
DEVELOPMENT ADMINISTRATION." WOR+45 CREATE PLAN
DOMIN EDU/PROP EXEC ROUTINE ATTIT ORD/FREE PWR
...POLICY GEN/LAWS VAL/FREE. PAGE 104 B2107
ECO/UNDEV
MGT

B65
ADU A.L.,THE CIVIL SERVICE IN NEW AFRICAN STATES.
AFR GHANA FINAN SOVEREIGN...POLICY 20 CIVIL/SERV
AFRICA/E AFRICA/W. PAGE 3 B0062
ECO/UNDEV
ADMIN
COLONIAL
NAT/G

B65
AIYAR S.P.,STUDIES IN INDIAN DEMOCRACY. INDIA
STRATA ECO/UNDEV LABOR POL/PAR LEGIS DIPLOM LOBBY
REGION CHOOSE ATTIT SOCISM...ANTHOL 20. PAGE 3
B0067
ORD/FREE
REPRESENT
ADMIN
NAT/G

B65
BARISH N.N.,MANAGEMENT SCIENCES IN THE EMERGING
COUNTRIES. AFR CHINA/COM WOR+45 FINAN INDUS PLAN
PRODUC HABITAT...ANTHOL 20. PAGE 9 B0184
ECO/UNDEV
OP/RES
MGT
TEC/DEV

B65
BARNETT V.M. JR.,THE REPRESENTATION OF THE UNITED
STATES ABROAD* REVISED EDITION. ECO/UNDEV ACADEM
INT/ORG FORCES ACT/RES CREATE OP/RES FOR/AID REGION
CENTRAL...CLASSIF ANTHOL. PAGE 9 B0189
USA+45
DIPLOM
ADMIN

B65
CHEN T.H.,THE CHINESE COMMUNIST REGIME: A
DOCUMENTARY STUDY (2 VOLS.). CHINA/COM LAW CONSTN
ELITES ECO/UNDEV LEGIS ECO/TAC ADMIN CONTROL PWR
...SOC 20. PAGE 20 B0417
MARXISM
POL/PAR
NAT/G

B65
DAVISON W.P.,INTERNATIONAL POLITICAL COMMUNICATION.
COM USA+45 WOR+45 CULTURE ECO/UNDEV NAT/G PROB/SOLV
PRESS TV ADMIN 20 FILM. PAGE 27 B0545
EDU/PROP
DIPLOM
PERS/REL
COM/IND

B65
GOODSELL C.T.,ADMINISTRATION OF A REVOLUTION.
PUERT/RICO ECO/UNDEV FINAN MUNIC POL/PAR PROVS
LEGIS PLAN BUDGET RECEIVE ADMIN COLONIAL LEAD 20
ROOSEVLT/F. PAGE 41 B0827
EXEC
SOC

B65
GOPAL S.,BRITISH POLICY IN INDIA 1858-1905. INDIA
UK ELITES CHIEF DELIB/GP ECO/TAC GP/REL DISCRIM
ATTIT...IDEA/COMP NAT/COMP PERS/COMP BIBLIOG/A
19/20. PAGE 41 B0828
COLONIAL
ADMIN
POL/PAR
ECO/UNDEV

B65
INST INTL DES CIVILISATION DIF,THE CONSTITUTIONS
AND ADMINISTRATIVE INSTITUTIONS OF THE NEW STATES.
AFR ISLAM S/ASIA NAT/G POL/PAR DELIB/GP EX/STRUC
CONFER EFFICIENCY NAT/LISM...JURID SOC 20. PAGE 54
B1088
CONSTN
ADMIN
ADJUD
ECO/UNDEV

B65
KRIESBERG M.,PUBLIC ADMINISTRATION IN DEVELOPING
COUNTRIES: PROCEEDINGS OF AN INTERNATIONAL
CONFERENCE HELD IN BOGOTA, COLUMBIA,1963. FUT
EDU/PROP ORD/FREE...MGT 20 CIVIL/SERV. PAGE 61
B1237
NAT/G
ECO/UNDEV
SOCIETY
ADMIN

B65
LEYS C.T.,FEDERATION IN EAST AFRICA. LAW AGRI
DIST/IND FINAN INT/ORG LABOR INT/TRADE CONFER ADMIN
CONTROL GP/REL...ANTHOL 20 AFRICA/E. PAGE 65 B1310
FEDERAL
REGION
ECO/UNDEV
PLAN

B65
MOORE W.E.,THE IMPACT OF INDUSTRY. CULTURE STRUCT
ORD/FREE...TREND 20. PAGE 75 B1516
INDUS
MGT
TEC/DEV
ECO/UNDEV

B65
OECD,MEDITERRANEAN REGIONAL PROJECT: TURKEY;
EDUCATION AND DEVELOPMENT. FUT TURKEY SOCIETY
STRATA FINAN NAT/G PROF/ORG PLAN PROB/SOLV ADMIN
COST...STAT CHARTS 20 OECD. PAGE 79 B1602
EDU/PROP
ACADEM
SCHOOL
ECO/UNDEV

B65
ORG FOR ECO COOP AND DEVEL,THE MEDITERRANEAN
REGIONAL PROJECT: AN EXPERIMENT IN PLANNING BY SIX
COUNTRIES. FUT GREECE SPAIN TURKEY YUGOSLAVIA
SOCIETY FINAN NAT/G PROF/ORG EDU/PROP ADMIN REGION
COST...POLICY STAT CHARTS 20 OECD. PAGE 80 B1614
PLAN
ECO/UNDEV
ACADEM
SCHOOL

B65
ORG FOR ECO COOP AND DEVEL,THE MEDITERRANEAN
REGIONAL PROJECT: YUGOSLAVIA; EDUCATION AND
DEVELOPMENT. YUGOSLAVIA SOCIETY FINAN PROF/ORG PLAN
ADMIN COST DEMAND MARXISM...STAT TREND CHARTS METH
20 OECD. PAGE 80 B1615
EDU/PROP
ACADEM
SCHOOL
ECO/UNDEV

B65
PURCELL V.,THE MEMOIRS OF A MALAYAN OFFICIAL.
MALAYSIA UK ECO/UNDEV INDUS LABOR EDU/PROP COLONIAL
CT/SYS WAR NAT/LISM TOTALISM ORD/FREE SOVEREIGN 20
UN CIVIL/SERV. PAGE 85 B1721
BIOG
ADMIN
JURID
FORCES

B65
SNYDER F.G.,ONE-PARTY GOVERNMENT IN MALI:
TRANSITION TOWARD CONTROL. MALI STRATA STRUCT SOC.
PAGE 99 B1991
ECO/UNDEV
POL/PAR
EX/STRUC
ADMIN

B65
TYBOUT R.A.,ECONOMICS OF RESEARCH AND DEVELOPMENT.
ECO/DEV ECO/UNDEV INDUS PROFIT DECISION. PAGE 106
B2141
R+D
FORCES
ADMIN
DIPLOM

B65
WARD W.E.,GOVERNMENT IN WEST AFRICA. WOR+45 POL/PAR
EX/STRUC PLAN PARTIC GP/REL SOVEREIGN 20 AFRICA/W.
PAGE 114 B2291
GOV/COMP
CONSTN
COLONIAL
ECO/UNDEV

B65
WATERSTON A.,DEVELOPMENT PLANNING* LESSONS OF
EXPERIENCE. ECO/TAC CENTRAL...MGT QUANT BIBLIOG.
PAGE 114 B2303
ECO/UNDEV
CREATE
PLAN
ADMIN

B65
WHITE J.,GERMAN AID. GERMANY/W FINAN PLAN TEC/DEV
INT/TRADE ADMIN ATTIT...POLICY 20. PAGE 116 B2334
FOR/AID
ECO/UNDEV
DIPLOM
ECO/TAC

L65
MATTHEWS D.G.,"A CURRENT BIBLIOGRAPHY ON ETHIOPIAN
BIBLIOG/A

AFFAIRS: A SELECT BIBLIOGRAPHY FROM 1950-1964." ETHIOPIA LAW CULTURE ECO/UNDEV INDUS LABOR SECT FORCES DIPLOM CIVMIL/REL RACE/REL...LING STAT 20. PAGE 71 B1428
ADMIN POL/PAR NAT/G
L65

WILLIAMS S.,"NEGOTIATING INVESTMENT IN EMERGING COUNTRIES." USA+45 WOR+45 INDUS MARKET NAT/G TOP/EX TEC/DEV CAP/ISM ECO/TAC ADMIN SKILL WEALTH...POLICY RELATIV MGT WORK 20. PAGE 117 B2353
FINAN ECO/UNDEV
S65

"FURTHER READING." INDIA STRUCT FINAN WORKER ADMIN COST 20. PAGE 2 B0042
BIBLIOG MGT ECO/UNDEV EFFICIENCY
S65

QUADE Q.L.,"THE TRUMAN ADMINISTRATION AND THE SEPARATION OF POWERS: THE CASE OF THE MARSHALL PLAN." SOCIETY INT/ORG NAT/G CONSULT DELIB/GP LEGIS PLAN ECO/TAC ROUTINE DRIVE PERCEPT RIGID/FLEX ORD/FREE PWR WEALTH...DECISION GEOG NEW/IDEA TREND 20 TRUMAN/HS. PAGE 85 B1726
USA+45 ECO/UNDEV DIPLOM
B66

ALEXANDER Y.,INTERNATIONAL TECHNICAL ASSISTANCE EXPERTS* A CASE STUDY OF THE U.N. EXPERIENCE. ECO/UNDEV CONSULT EX/STRUC CREATE PLAN DIPLOM FOR/AID TASK EFFICIENCY...ORG/CHARTS UN. PAGE 4 B0074
ECO/TAC INT/ORG ADMIN MGT
B66

ALI S.,PLANNING, DEVELOPMENT AND CHANGE: AN ANNOTATED BIBLIOGRAPHY ON DEVELOPMENTAL ADMINISTRATION. PAKISTAN SOCIETY ORD/FREE 20. PAGE 4 B0077
BIBLIOG/A ADMIN ECO/UNDEV PLAN
B66

ASHRAF A.,THE CITY GOVERNMENT OF CALCUTTA: A STUDY OF INERTIA. INDIA ELITES INDUS NAT/G EX/STRUC ACT/RES PLAN PROB/SOLV LEAD HABITAT...BIBLIOG 20 CALCUTTA. PAGE 7 B0141
LOC/G MUNIC ADMIN ECO/UNDEV
B66

BALDWIN D.A.,FOREIGN AID AND AMERICAN FOREIGN POLICY; A DOCUMENTARY ANALYSIS. USA+45 ECO/UNDEV ADMIN...ECOMETRIC STAT STYLE CHARTS PROG/TEAC GEN/LAWS ANTHOL. PAGE 8 B0172
FOR/AID DIPLOM IDEA/COMP
B66

BARBER W.F.,INTERNAL SECURITY AND MILITARY POWER* COUNTERINSURGENCY AND CIVIC ACTION IN LATIN AMERICA. ECO/UNDEV CREATE ADMIN REV ATTIT RIGID/FLEX MARXISM...INT BIBLIOG OAS. PAGE 9 B0183
L/A+17C FORCES ORD/FREE TASK
B66

BIRKHEAD G.S.,ADMINISTRATIVE PROBLEMS IN PAKISTAN. PAKISTAN AGRI FINAN INDUS LG/CO ECO/TAC CONTROL PWR ...CHARTS ANTHOL 20. PAGE 12 B0241
ADMIN NAT/G ORD/FREE ECO/UNDEV
B66

BOYD H.W.,MARKETING MANAGEMENT: CASES FROM EMERGING COUNTRIES. BRAZIL GHANA ISRAEL WOR+45 ADMIN PERS/REL ATTIT HABITAT WEALTH...ANTHOL 20 ARGEN CASEBOOK. PAGE 14 B0292
MGT ECO/UNDEV PROB/SOLV MARKET
B66

DEBENKO E.,RESEARCH SOURCES FOR SOUTH ASIAN STUDIES IN ECONOMIC DEVELOPMENT: A SELECT BIBLIOGRAPHY OF SERIAL PUBLICATIONS. CEYLON INDIA NEPAL PAKISTAN PROB/SOLV ADMIN...POLICY 20. PAGE 28 B0566
BIBLIOG ECO/UNDEV S/ASIA PLAN
B66

FISK E.K.,NEW GUINEA ON THE THRESHOLD; ASPECTS OF SOCIAL, POLITICAL, AND ECONOMIC DEVELOPMENT. AGRI NAT/G INT/TRADE ADMIN ADJUST LITERACY ROLE...CHARTS ANTHOL 20 NEW/GUINEA. PAGE 36 B0726
ECO/UNDEV SOCIETY
B66

HANKE L.,HANDBOOK OF LATIN AMERICAN STUDIES. ECO/UNDEV ADMIN LEAD...HUM SOC 20. PAGE 46 B0937
BIBLIOG/A L/A+17C INDEX NAT/G
B66

HAYER T.,FRENCH AID. AFR FRANCE AGRI FINAN BUDGET ADMIN WAR PRODUC...CHARTS 18/20 THIRD/WRLD OVRSEA/DEV. PAGE 48 B0975
TEC/DEV COLONIAL FOR/AID ECO/UNDEV
B66

HEADY F.,PUBLIC ADMINISTRATION: A COMPARATIVE PERSPECTIVE. ECO/DEV ECO/UNDEV...GOV/COMP 20 BUREAUCRCY. PAGE 48 B0982
ADMIN NAT/COMP NAT/G CIVMIL/REL
B66

KAUNDA K.,ZAMBIA: INDEPENDENCE AND BEYOND: THE SPEECHES OF KENNETH KAUNDA. AFR FUT ZAMBIA SOCIETY ECO/UNDEV NAT/G PROB/SOLV ECO/TAC ADMIN RACE/REL SOVEREIGN 20. PAGE 59 B1183
ORD/FREE COLONIAL CONSTN LEAD
B66

KIRDAR U.,THE STRUCTURE OF UNITED NATIONS ECONOMIC AID TO UNDERDEVELOPED COUNTRIES. AGRI FINAN INDUS NAT/G EX/STRUC PLAN GIVE TASK...POLICY 20 UN. PAGE 60 B1213
INT/ORG FOR/AID ECO/UNDEV ADMIN
B66

MACFARQUHAR R.,CHINA UNDER MAO: POLITICS TAKES COMMAND. CHINA/COM COM AGRI INDUS CHIEF FORCES DIPLOM INT/TRADE EDU/PROP TASK REV ADJUST...ANTHOL
ECO/UNDEV TEC/DEV ECO/TAC

20 MAO. PAGE 67 B1359
ADMIN
B66

MONTGOMERY J.D.,APPROACHES TO DEVELOPMENT: POLITICS, ADMINISTRATION AND CHANGE. USA+45 AGRI FOR/AID ORD/FREE...CONCPT IDEA/COMP METH/COMP ANTHOL. PAGE 75 B1507
ECO/UNDEV ADMIN POLICY ECO/TAC
B66

MOOMAW I.W.,THE CHALLENGE OF HUNGER. USA+45 PLAN ADMIN EATING 20. PAGE 75 B1509
FOR/AID DIPLOM ECO/UNDEV ECO/TAC
B66

OHLIN G.,AID AND INDEBTEDNESS. AUSTRIA FINAN INT/ORG PLAN DIPLOM GIVE...POLICY MATH CHARTS 20. PAGE 79 B1604
FOR/AID ECO/UNDEV ADMIN WEALTH
B66

ONYEMELUKWE C.C.,PROBLEMS OF INDUSTRIAL PLANNING AND MANAGEMENT IN NIGERIA. AFR FINAN LABOR DELIB/GP TEC/DEV ADJUST...MGT TREND BIBLIOG. PAGE 80 B1610
ECO/UNDEV ECO/TAC INDUS PLAN
B66

US HOUSE COMM GOVT OPERATIONS,AN INVESTIGATION OF THE US ECONOMIC AND MILITARY ASSISTANCE PROGRAMS IN VIETNAM. USA+45 VIETNAM/S SOCIETY CONSTRUC FINAN FORCES BUDGET INT/TRADE PEACE HEALTH...MGT HOUSE/REP AID. PAGE 108 B2191
FOR/AID ECO/UNDEV WAR INSPECT
B66

US SENATE COMM ON FOREIGN REL,HEARINGS ON S 2859 AND S 2861. USA+45 WOR+45 FORCES BUDGET CAP/ISM ADMIN DETER WEAPON TOTALISM...NAT/COMP 20 UN CONGRESS. PAGE 110 B2221
FOR/AID DIPLOM ORD/FREE ECO/UNDEV
B66

WILLNER A.R.,THE NEOTRADITIONAL ACCOMMODATION TO POLITICAL INDEPENDENCE* THE CASE OF INDONESIA * RESEARCH MONOGRAPH NO. 26. CULTURE ECO/UNDEV CREATE PROB/SOLV FOR/AID LEGIT COLONIAL EFFICIENCY NAT/LISM ALL/VALS SOC. PAGE 117 B2355
INDONESIA CONSERVE ELITES ADMIN
S66

"FURTHER READING." INDIA LOC/G NAT/G PLAN ADMIN WEALTH...GEOG SOC CONCPT CENSUS 20. PAGE 2 B0045
BIBLIOG ECO/UNDEV TEC/DEV PROVS
S66

MARKSHAK J.,"ECONOMIC PLANNING AND THE COST OF THINKING." COM MARKET EX/STRUC...DECISION GEN/LAWS. PAGE 69 B1400
ECO/UNDEV ECO/TAC PLAN ECO/DEV
S66

MATTHEWS D.G.,"ETHIOPIAN OUTLINE: A BIBLIOGRAPHIC RESEARCH GUIDE." ETHIOPIA LAW STRUCT ECO/UNDEV AGRI LABOR SECT CHIEF DELIB/GP EX/STRUC ADMIN...LING ORG/CHARTS 20. PAGE 71 B1429
BIBLIOG NAT/G DIPLOM POL/PAR
S66

PALMER M.,"THE UNITED ARAB REPUBLIC* AN ASSESSMENT OF ITS FAILURE." ELITES ECO/UNDEV POL/PAR FORCES ECO/TAC RUMOR ADMIN EXEC EFFICIENCY ATTIT SOCISM ...INT NASSER/G. PAGE 81 B1628
UAR SYRIA REGION FEDERAL
C66

TARLING N.,"A CONCISE HISTORY OF SOUTHEAST ASIA." BURMA CAMBODIA LAOS S/ASIA THAILAND VIETNAM ECO/UNDEV POL/PAR FORCES ADMIN REV WAR CIVMIL/REL ORD/FREE MARXISM SOCISM 13/20. PAGE 103 B2080
COLONIAL DOMIN INT/TRADE NAT/LISM
B67

ANDERSON C.W.,POLITICS AND ECONOMIC CHANGE IN LATIN AMERICA. L/A+17C INDUS NAT/G OP/RES ADMIN DEMAND ...POLICY STAT CHARTS NAT/COMP 20. PAGE 4 B0091
ECO/UNDEV PROB/SOLV PLAN ECO/TAC
B67

BALDWIN G.B.,PLANNING AND DEVELOPMENT IN IRAN. IRAN AGRI INDUS CONSULT WORKER EDU/PROP BAL/PAY...CHARTS 20. PAGE 8 B0173
PLAN ECO/UNDEV ADMIN PROB/SOLV
B67

COHEN R.,COMPARATIVE POLITICAL SYSTEMS: STUDIES IN THE POLITICS OF PRE-INDUSTRIAL SOCIETIES. WOR+45 WOR-45 CULTURE FAM KIN LOC/G NEIGH ADMIN LEAD MARRIAGE...BIBLIOG 20. PAGE 22 B0447
ECO/UNDEV STRUCT SOCIETY GP/COMP
B67

GABRIEL P.P.,THE INTERNATIONAL TRANSFER OF CORPORATE SKILLS: MANAGEMENT CONTRACTS IN LESS DEVELOPED COUNTRIES. CLIENT INDUS LG/CO PLAN PROB/SOLV CAP/ISM ECO/TAC FOR/AID INT/TRADE RENT ADMIN SKILL 20. PAGE 38 B0771
ECO/UNDEV AGREE MGT CONSULT
B67

GIFFORD P.,BRITAIN AND GERMANY IN AFRICA. AFR GERMANY UK ECO/UNDEV LEAD WAR NAT/LISM ATTIT ...POLICY HIST/WRIT METH/COMP ANTHOL BIBLIOG 19/20 WWI. PAGE 39 B0797
COLONIAL ADMIN DIPLOM NAT/COMP
B67

HIRSCHMAN A.O.,DEVELOPMENT PROJECTS OBSERVED. INDUS INT/ORG CONSULT EX/STRUC CREATE OP/RES ECO/TAC DEMAND...POLICY MGT METH/COMP 20 WORLD/BANK. PAGE 50 B1016
ECO/UNDEV R+D FINAN PLAN
B67

KARDOUCHE G.K.,THE UAR IN DEVELOPMENT. UAR ECO/TAC FINAN

INT/TRADE BAL/PAY...STAT CHARTS BIBLIOG 20. PAGE 58 MGT
B1172
CAP/ISM
ECO/UNDEV
B67

KONCZACKI Z.A.,PUBLIC FINANCE AND ECONOMIC
DEVELOPMENT OF NATAL 1893-1910. TAX ADMIN COLONIAL
...STAT CHARTS BIBLIOG 19/20 NATAL. PAGE 61 B1228
ECO/TAC
FINAN
NAT/G
ECO/UNDEV
B67

OVERSEAS DEVELOPMENT INSTIT,EFFECTIVE AID. WOR+45
INT/ORG TEC/DEV DIPLOM INT/TRADE ADMIN. PAGE 80
B1619
FOR/AID
ECO/UNDEV
ECO/TAC
NAT/COMP
B67

PYE L.W.,SOUTHEAST ASIA'S POLITICAL SYSTEMS. ASIA
S/ASIA STRUCT ECO/UNDEV EX/STRUC CAP/ISM DIPLOM
ALL/IDEOS...TREND CHARTS. PAGE 85 B1724
NAT/G
POL/PAR
GOV/COMP
B67

RAVKIN A.,THE NEW STATES OF AFRICA (HEADLINE
SERIES, NO. 183((PAMPHLET). CULTURE STRUCT INDUS
COLONIAL NAT/LISM...SOC 20. PAGE 86 B1744
AFR
ECO/UNDEV
SOCIETY
ADMIN
B67

TANSKY L.,US AND USSR AID TO DEVELOPING COUNTRIES.
INDIA TURKEY UAR USA+45 USSR FINAN PLAN TEC/DEV
ADMIN WEALTH...TREND METH/COMP 20. PAGE 103 B2076
FOR/AID
ECO/UNDEV
MARXISM
CAP/ISM
B67

TOMA P.A.,THE POLITICS OF FOOD FOR PEACE;
EXECUTIVE-LEGISLATIVE INTERACTION. USA+45 ECO/UNDEV
POL/PAR DEBATE EXEC LOBBY CHOOSE PEACE...DECISION
CHARTS. PAGE 104 B2113
FOR/AID
POLICY
LEGIS
AGRI
B67

ZONDAG C.H.,THE BOLIVIAN ECONOMY 1952-65. L/A+17C
TEC/DEV FOR/AID ADMIN...OBS TREND CHARTS BIBLIOG 20
BOLIV. PAGE 119 B2406
ECO/UNDEV
INDUS
PRODUC
S67

ALPANDER G.G.,"ENTREPRENEURS AND PRIVATE ENTERPRISE
IN TURKEY." TURKEY INDUS PROC/MFG EDU/PROP ATTIT
DRIVE WEALTH...GEOG MGT SOC STAT TREND CHARTS 20.
PAGE 4 B0080
ECO/UNDEV
LG/CO
NAT/G
POLICY
S67

DUGGAR J.W.,"THE DEVELOPMENT OF MONEY SUPPLY IN
ETHIOPIA." ETHIOPIA ISLAM CONSULT OP/RES BUDGET
CONTROL ROUTINE EFFICIENCY EQUILIB WEALTH...MGT 20.
PAGE 31 B0629
ECO/UNDEV
FINAN
BAL/PAY
ECOMETRIC
S67

FOX R.G.,"FAMILY, CASTE, AND COMMERCE IN A NORTH
INDIAN MARKET TOWN." INDIA STRATA AGRI FACE/GP FAM
NEIGH OP/RES BARGAIN ADMIN ROUTINE WEALTH...SOC
CHARTS 20. PAGE 37 B0747
CULTURE
GP/REL
ECO/UNDEV
DIST/IND
S67

FRYKENBURG R.E.,"STUDIES OF LAND CONTROL IN INDIAN
HISTORY: REVIEW ARTICLE." INDIA UK STRATA AGRI
MUNIC OP/RES COLONIAL REGION EFFICIENCY OWN HABITAT
...CONCPT 16/20. PAGE 38 B0763
ECO/UNDEV
CONTROL
ADMIN
S67

HUGON P.,"BLOCAGES ET DESEQUILIBRES DE LA
CROISSANCE ECONOMIQUE EN AFRIQUE NOIRE." AFR KIN
MUNIC CREATE PLAN INT/TRADE REGION ADJUST CENTRAL
EQUILIB NAT/LISM ORD/FREE 20. PAGE 52 B1060
ECO/UNDEV
COLONIAL
STRUCT
ADMIN
S67

IDENBURG P.J.,"POLITICAL STRUCTURAL DEVELOPMENT IN
TROPICAL AFRICA." UK ECO/UNDEV KIN POL/PAR CHIEF
EX/STRUC CREATE COLONIAL CONTROL REPRESENT RACE/REL
...MAJORIT TREND 20. PAGE 53 B1074
AFR
CONSTN
NAT/G
GOV/COMP
S67

MCNAMARA R.L.,"THE NEED FOR INNOVATIVENESS IN
DEVELOPING SOCIETIES." L/A+17C EDU/PROP ADMIN LEAD
WEALTH...POLICY PSY SOC METH 20 COLOMB. PAGE 72
B1456
PROB/SOLV
PLAN
ECO/UNDEV
NEW/IDEA
S67

NEUCHTERLEIN D.E.,"THAILAND* ANOTHER VIETNAM?"
THAILAND ECO/UNDEV DIPLOM ADMIN REGION CENTRAL
NAT/LISM...POLICY 20. PAGE 78 B1571
WAR
GUERRILLA
S/ASIA
NAT/G
S67

NYE J.S.,"CORRUPTION AND POLITICAL DEVELOPMENT: A
COST-BENEFIT ANALYSIS." WOR+45 SOCIETY TRIBUTE
ADMIN CONTROL COST...CHARTS 20. PAGE 79 B1598
ECO/UNDEV
NAT/G
CRIME
ACT/RES
S67

PRATT R.C.,"THE ADMINISTRATION OF ECONOMIC PLANNING
IN A NEWLY INDEPEND ENT STATE* THE TANZANIAN
EXPERIENCE 1963-1966." AFR TANZANIA ECO/UNDEV PLAN
CONTROL ROUTINE TASK EFFICIENCY 20. PAGE 84 B1699
NAT/G
DELIB/GP
ADMIN
TEC/DEV
B95

LATIMER E.W.,EUROPE IN AFRICA IN THE NINETEENTH
CENTURY. ECO/UNDEV KIN SECT DIPLOM DOMIN ADMIN
DISCRIM 17/18. PAGE 63 B1275
AFR
COLONIAL
WAR
FINAN
B98

THOMPSON H.C.,RHODESIA AND ITS GOVERNMENT. AFR
RHODESIA ECO/UNDEV INDUS KIN WORKER INT/TRADE
DISCRIM LITERACY ORD/FREE 19. PAGE 104 B2102
COLONIAL
ADMIN
POLICY
ELITES

ECOLE NATIONALE D'ADMIN B0650,B0651

ECOLOGY....SEE HABITAT

ECOMETRIC....MATHEMATICAL ECONOMICS, ECONOMETRICS

B57
PARKINSON C.N.,PARKINSON'S LAW. UNIV EX/STRUC PLAN
ATTIT PERSON TIME. PAGE 81 B1634
ADMIN
EXEC
FINAN
ECOMETRIC
B58

WARNER A.W.,CONCEPTS AND CASES IN ECONOMIC
ANALYSIS. PROB/SOLV BARGAIN CONTROL INCOME PRODUC
...ECOMETRIC MGT CONCPT CLASSIF CHARTS 20
KEYNES/JM. PAGE 114 B2292
ECO/TAC
DEMAND
EQUILIB
COST
B60

RUBENSTEIN A.H.,SOME THEORIES OF ORGANIZATION.
ROUTINE ATTIT...DECISION ECOMETRIC. PAGE 91 B1846
SOCIETY
ECO/DEV
INDUS
TOP/EX
B65

HICKMAN B.G.,QUANTITATIVE PLANNING OF ECONOMIC
POLICY. FRANCE NETHERLAND OP/RES PRICE ROUTINE UTIL
...POLICY DECISION ECOMETRIC METH/CNCPT STAT STYLE
CHINJAP. PAGE 50 B1004
PROB/SOLV
PLAN
QUANT
B65

UNIVERSAL REFERENCE SYSTEM,INTERNATIONAL AFFAIRS:
VOLUME I IN THE POLITICAL SCIENCE, GOVERNMENT, AND
PUBLIC POLICY SERIES....DECISION ECOMETRIC GEOG
INT/LAW JURID MGT PHIL/SCI PSY SOC. PAGE 107 B2163
BIBLIOG/A
GEN/METH
COMPUT/IR
DIPLOM
B66

BALDWIN D.A.,FOREIGN AID AND AMERICAN FOREIGN
POLICY; A DOCUMENTARY ANALYSIS. USA+45 ECO/UNDEV
ADMIN...ECOMETRIC STAT STYLE CHARTS PROG/TEAC
GEN/LAWS ANTHOL. PAGE 8 B0172
FOR/AID
DIPLOM
IDEA/COMP
B66

FOX K.A.,THE THEORY OF QUANTITATIVE ECONOMIC POLICY
WITH APPLICATIONS TO ECONOMIC GROWTH AND
STABILIZATION. ECO/DEV AGRI NAT/G PLAN ADMIN RISK
...DECISION IDEA/COMP SIMUL T. PAGE 37 B0746
ECO/TAC
ECOMETRIC
EQUILIB
GEN/LAWS
B66

KAESTNER K.,GESAMTWIRTSCHAFTLICHE PLANUNG IN EINER
GEMISCHTEN WIRTSCHAFTSORDNUNG
(WIRTSCHAFTSPOLITISCHE STUDIEN 5). GERMANY/W WOR+45
WOR-45 INDUS MARKET NAT/G ACT/RES GP/REL INGP/REL
PRODUC...ECOMETRIC MGT BIBLIOG 20. PAGE 57 B1159
ECO/TAC
PLAN
POLICY
PREDICT
S67

DROR Y.,"POLICY ANALYSTS." USA+45 COMPUTER OP/RES
ECO/TAC ADMIN ROUTINE...ECOMETRIC METH/COMP SIMUL
20. PAGE 30 B0618
NAT/G
POLICY
PLAN
DECISION
S67

DUGGAR J.W.,"THE DEVELOPMENT OF MONEY SUPPLY IN
ETHIOPIA." ETHIOPIA ISLAM CONSULT OP/RES BUDGET
CONTROL ROUTINE EFFICIENCY EQUILIB WEALTH...MGT 20.
PAGE 31 B0629
ECO/UNDEV
FINAN
BAL/PAY
ECOMETRIC

ECONOMIC DATA....SEE ECO

ECONOMIC DETERMINISM....SEE GEN/LAWS

ECONOMIC WARFARE....SEE ECO/TAC

ECONOMICS....SEE ECO

ECOSOC....UNITED NATIONS ECONOMIC AND SOCIAL COUNCIL

ECSC....EUROPEAN COAL AND STEEL COMMUNITY, SEE ALSO VOL/ASSN,
INT/ORG

B59
DIEBOLD W. JR.,THE SCHUMAN PLAN: A STUDY IN
ECONOMIC COOPERATION, 1950-1959. EUR+WWI FRANCE
GERMANY USA+45 EXTR/IND CONSULT DELIB/GP PLAN
DIPLOM ECO/TAC INT/TRADE ROUTINE ORD/FREE WEALTH
...METH/CNCPT STAT CONT/OBS INT TIME/SEQ ECSC 20.
PAGE 29 B0591
INT/ORG
REGION
B64

KAPP E.,THE MERGER OF THE EXECUTIVES OF THE
EUROPEAN COMMUNITIES. LAW CONSTN STRUCT ACT/RES
PLAN PROB/SOLV ADMIN REGION TASK...INT/LAW MGT ECSC
EEC. PAGE 58 B1170
CENTRAL
EX/STRUC
B66

SPINELLI A.,THE EUROCRATS; CONFLICT AND CRISIS IN
THE EUROPEAN COMMUNITY (TRANS. BY C. GROVE HAINES).
EUR+WWI MARKET POL/PAR ECO/TAC PARL/PROC EEC OEEC
ECSC EURATOM. PAGE 99 B2007
INT/ORG
INGP/REL
CONSTN
ADMIN
L67

CAHIERS P.,"LE RECOURS EN CONSTATATION DE
MANQUEMENTS DES ETATS MEMBRES DEVANT LA COUR DES
COMMUNAUTES EUROPEENNES." LAW PROB/SOLV DIPLOM
ADMIN CT/SYS SANCTION ATTIT...POLICY DECISION JURID
ECSC EEC. PAGE 18 B0362
INT/ORG
CONSTN
ROUTINE
ADJUD

S67

WEIL G.L.,"THE MERGER OF THE INSTITUTIONS OF THE EUROPEAN COMMUNITIES" EUR+WWI ECO/DEV INT/TRADE CONSEN PLURISM...DECISION MGT 20 EEC EURATOM ECSC TREATY. PAGE 115 B2313
ECO/TAC INT/ORG CENTRAL INT/LAW

ECUADOR....SEE ALSO L/A+17C

ECUMENIC....ECUMENICAL MOVEMENT OF CHURCHES

EDDING F. B1287

EDELMAN M. B0652,B0653,B0654

EDEN/A....ANTHONY EDEN

EDGEWORTH

EDSEL....EDSEL (AUTOMOBILE)

EDU/PROP....EDUCATION, PROPAGANDA, PERSUASION

N

SOVIET-EAST EUROPEAN RES SERV,SOVIET SOCIETY. USSR LABOR POL/PAR PRESS MARXISM...MARXIST 20. PAGE 99 B2001
BIBLIOG/A EDU/PROP ADMIN SOC

N

BULLETIN OF THE PUBLIC AFFAIRS INFORMATION SERVICE. WOR+45 WOR-45 ECO/UNDEV FINAN LABOR LOC/G PROVS TEC/DEV DIPLOM EDU/PROP SOC. PAGE 1 B0010
BIBLIOG NAT/G ECO/DEV ADMIN

N

KENTUCKY STATE ARCHIVES,CHECKLIST OF KENTUCKY STATE PUBLICATIONS AND STATE DIRECTORY. USA+45 LAW ACADEM EX/STRUC LEGIS EDU/PROP LEAD...JURID 20. PAGE 59 B1196
BIBLIOG/A PROVS PUB/INST ADMIN

N

UNIVERSITY OF FLORIDA,CARIBBEAN ACQUISITIONS: MATERIALS ACQUIRED BY THE UNIVERSITY OF FLORIDA 1957-1960. L/A+17C...ART/METH GEOG MGT 20. PAGE 107 B2167
BIBLIOG ECO/UNDEV EDU/PROP JURID

N

US SUPERINTENDENT OF DOCUMENTS,EDUCATION (PRICE LIST 31). USA+45 LAW FINAN LOC/G NAT/G DEBATE ADMIN LEAD RACE/REL FEDERAL HEALTH POLICY. PAGE 111 B2238
BIBLIOG/A EDU/PROP ACADEM SCHOOL

B16

TREITSCHKE H.,POLITICS. UNIV SOCIETY STRATA NAT/G EX/STRUC LEGIS DOMIN EDU/PROP ATTIT PWR RESPECT ...CONCPT TIME/SEQ GEN/LAWS TOT/POP 20. PAGE 105 B2127
EXEC ELITES GERMANY

B19

NATHAN M.,THE SOUTH AFRICAN COMMONWEALTH: CONSTITUTION, PROBLEMS, SOCIAL CONDITIONS. SOUTH/AFR UK CULTURE INDUS EX/STRUC LEGIS BUDGET EDU/PROP ADMIN CT/SYS GP/REL RACE/REL...LING 19/20 CMN/WLTH. PAGE 77 B1559
CONSTN NAT/G POL/PAR SOCIETY

N19

EAST KENTUCKY REGIONAL PLAN,PROGRAM 60: A DECADE OF ACTION FOR PROGRESS IN EASTERN KENTUCKY (PAMPHLET). USA+45 AGRI CONSTRUC INDUS CONSULT ACT/RES PROB/SOLV EDU/PROP GOV/REL HEALTH KENTUCKY. PAGE 32 B0643
REGION ADMIN PLAN ECO/UNDEV

N19

EAST KENTUCKY REGIONAL PLAN,PROGRAM 60 REPORT: ACTION FOR PORGRESS IN EASTERN KENTUCKY (PAMPHLET). USA+45 CONSTRUC INDUS ACT/RES PROB/SOLV EDU/PROP ADMIN GOV/REL KENTUCKY. PAGE 32 B0644
REGION PLAN ECO/UNDEV CONSULT

N19

FIKS M.,PUBLIC ADMINISTRATION IN ISRAEL (PAMPHLET). ISRAEL SCHOOL EX/STRUC BUDGET PAY INGP/REL ...DECISION 20 CIVIL/SERV. PAGE 35 B0718
EDU/PROP NAT/G ADMIN WORKER

N19

FIRMALINO T.,THE DISTRICT SCHOOL SUPERVISOR VS. TEACHERS AND PARENTS: A PHILIPPINE CASE STUDY (PAMPHLET) (BMR). PHILIPPINE LOC/G PLAN EDU/PROP LOBBY REGION PERS/REL 20. PAGE 36 B0722
RIGID/FLEX SCHOOL ADMIN CREATE

N19

GINZBERG E.,MANPOWER FOR GOVERNMENT (PAMPHLET). USA+45 FORCES PLAN PROB/SOLV PAY EDU/PROP ADMIN GP/REL COST...MGT PREDICT TREND 20 CIVIL/SERV. PAGE 40 B0803
WORKER CONSULT NAT/G LOC/G

N19

GRIFFITH W.,THE PUBLIC SERVICE (PAMPHLET). UK LAW LOC/G NAT/G PARTIC CHOOSE DRIVE ROLE SKILL...CHARTS 20 CIVIL/SERV. PAGE 44 B0880
ADMIN EFFICIENCY EDU/PROP GOV/REL

N19

PERREN G.E.,LANGUAGE AND COMMUNICATION IN THE COMMONWEALTH (PAMPHLET). FUT UK LAW ECO/DEV PRESS TV WRITING ADJUD ADMIN COLONIAL CONTROL 20 CMN/WLTH. PAGE 82 B1660
EDU/PROP LING GOV/REL COM/IND

B20

HALDANE R.B.,BEFORE THE WAR. MOD/EUR SOCIETY
POLICY

INT/ORG NAT/G DELIB/GP PLAN DOMIN EDU/PROP LEGIT ADMIN COERCE ATTIT DRIVE MORAL ORD/FREE PWR...SOC CONCPT SELF/OBS RECORD BIOG TIME/SEQ. PAGE 45 B0921
DIPLOM UK

B24

MERRIAM C.E.,A HISTORY OF POLITICAL THEORIES - RECENT TIMES. USA-45 WOR-45 CULTURE SOCIETY ECO/DEV R+D EDU/PROP ROUTINE CHOOSE ATTIT PERSON ALL/VALS ...POLICY SOC CONCPT METH/CNCPT OBS HIST/WRIT TIME/SEQ TREND. PAGE 73 B1471
UNIV INTELL

B24

POOLE D.C.,THE CONDUCT OF FOREIGN RELATIONS UNDER MODERN DEMOCRATIC CONDITIONS. EUR+WWI USA-45 INT/ORG PLAN LEGIT ADMIN KNOWL PWR...MAJORIT OBS/ENVIR HIST/WRIT GEN/LAWS 20. PAGE 84 B1689
NAT/G EDU/PROP DIPLOM

B27

ANGELL N.,THE PUBLIC MIND. USA-45 SOCIETY EDU/PROP ROUTINE SUPEGO KNOWL...POLICY CONCPT MYTH OBS/ENVIR EUR+WW1 TOT/POP 20. PAGE 5 B0109
PERCEPT ATTIT DIPLOM NAT/LISM

B27

DICKINSON J.,ADMINISTRATIVE JUSTICE AND THE SUPREMACY OF LAW IN THE UNITED STATES. USA-45 LAW INDUS DOMIN EDU/PROP CONTROL EXEC GP/REL ORD/FREE ...POLICY JURID 19/20. PAGE 29 B0586
CT/SYS ADJUD ADMIN NAT/G

B28

HALL W.P.,EMPIRE TO COMMONWEALTH. FUT WOR-45 CONSTN ECO/DEV ECO/UNDEV INT/ORG PROVS PLAN DIPLOM EDU/PROP ADMIN COLONIAL PEACE PERSON ALL/VALS ...POLICY GEOG SOC OBS RECORD TREND CMN/WLTH PARLIAMENT 19/20. PAGE 46 B0925
VOL/ASSN NAT/G UK

B28

SOROKIN P.,CONTEMPORARY SOCIOLOGICAL THEORIES. MOD/EUR UNIV SOCIETY R+D SCHOOL ECO/TAC EDU/PROP ROUTINE ATTIT DRIVE...PSY CONCPT TIME/SEQ TREND GEN/LAWS 20. PAGE 99 B1997
CULTURE SOC WAR

B31

HILL N.,INTERNATIONAL ADMINISTRATION. WOR-45 DELIB/GP DIPLOM EDU/PROP ALL/VALS...MGT TIME/SEQ LEAGUE/NAT TOT/POP VAL/FREE 20. PAGE 50 B1011
INT/ORG ADMIN

B33

HETTINGER H.S.,A DECADE OF RADIO ADVERTISING. USA-45 ECO/DEV CAP/ISM PRICE...CHARTS 20. PAGE 49 B0999
EDU/PROP COM/IND ECO/TAC ROUTINE

B36

ROBINSON H.,DEVELOPMENT OF THE BRITISH EMPIRE. WOR-45 CULTURE SOCIETY STRUCT ECO/DEV ECO/UNDEV INT/ORG VOL/ASSN FORCES CREATE PLAN DOMIN EDU/PROP ADMIN COLONIAL PWR WEALTH...POLICY GEOG CHARTS CMN/WLTH 16/20. PAGE 89 B1800
NAT/G HIST/WRIT UK

B37

BROOKS R.R.,WHEN LABOR ORGANIZES. FINAN EDU/PROP ADMIN LOBBY PARTIC REPRESENT WEALTH TREND. PAGE 16 B0318
LABOR GP/REL POLICY

B37

ROYAL INST. INT. AFF.,THE COLONIAL PROBLEM. WOR-45 LAW ECO/DEV ECO/UNDEV NAT/G PLAN ECO/TAC EDU/PROP ADMIN ATTIT ALL/VALS...CONCPT 20. PAGE 91 B1844
INT/ORG ACT/RES SOVEREIGN COLONIAL

B37

UNION OF SOUTH AFRICA,REPORT CONCERNING ADMINISTRATION OF SOUTH WEST AFRICA (6 VOLS.). SOUTH/AFR INDUS PUB/INST FORCES LEGIS BUDGET DIPLOM EDU/PROP ADJUD CT/SYS...GEOG CHARTS 20 AFRICA/SW LEAGUE/NAT. PAGE 107 B2158
NAT/G ADMIN COLONIAL CONSTN

B38

PETTEE G.S.,THE PROCESS OF REVOLUTION. COM FRANCE ITALY MOD/EUR RUSSIA SPAIN WOR-45 ELITES INTELL SOCIETY STRATA STRUCT INT/ORG NAT/G POL/PAR ACT/RES PLAN EDU/PROP LEGIT EXEC...SOC MYTH TIME/SEQ TOT/POP 18/20. PAGE 82 B1664
COERCE CONCPT REV

B38

RAPPARD W.E.,THE CRISIS OF DEMOCRACY. EUR+WWI UNIV WOR-45 CULTURE SOCIETY ECO/DEV INT/ORG POL/PAR ACT/RES EDU/PROP EXEC CHOOSE ATTIT ALL/VALS...SOC OBS HIST/WRIT TIME/SEQ LEAGUE/NAT NAZI TOT/POP 20. PAGE 86 B1741
NAT/G CONCPT

B38

SALTER J.T.,THE AMERICAN POLITICIAN. USA-45 LABOR POL/PAR EDU/PROP ADMIN CHOOSE ATTIT DRIVE PERSON PWR...POLICY ANTHOL 20 THOMAS/N LEWIS/JL LAGUARD/F GOVERNOR MAYOR. PAGE 92 B1865
BIOG LEAD PROVS LOC/G

B39

BAKER G.,THE COUNTY AGENT. USA-45 LOC/G NAT/G PROB/SOLV ADMIN...POLICY 20 ROOSEVLT/F NEW/DEAL COUNTY/AGT. PAGE 8 B0166
AGRI CONSULT GOV/REL EDU/PROP

B39

HITLER A.,MEIN KAMPF. EUR+WWI FUT MOD/EUR STRUCT INT/ORG LABOR NAT/G POL/PAR FORCES CREATE PLAN BAL/PWR DIPLOM ECO/TAC DOMIN EDU/PROP ADMIN COERCE ATTIT...SOCIALIST BIOG TREND NAZI. PAGE 50 B1020
PWR NEW/IDEA WAR

B39

MCCAMY J.L.,GOVERNMENT PUBLICITY: ITS PRACTICE IN FEDERAL ADMINISTRATION. USA-45 COM/IND ADMIN CONTROL EXEC PARTIC INGP/REL...SOC 20. PAGE 71
EDU/PROP NAT/G PLAN

B1442   ATTIT
                                                        B40
MCHENRY D.E.,HIS MAJESTY'S OPPOSITION: STRUCTURE   POL/PAR
AND PROBLEMS OF THE BRITISH LABOUR PARTY 1931-1938.   MGT
UK FINAN LABOR LOC/G DELIB/GP LEGIS EDU/PROP LEAD   NAT/G
PARTIC CHOOSE GP/REL SOCISM...TREND 20 LABOR/PAR.   POLICY
PAGE 72 B1450
                                                        C40
FAHS C.B.,"GOVERNMENT IN JAPAN." FINAN FORCES LEGIS   ASIA
TOP/EX BUDGET INT/TRADE EDU/PROP SOVEREIGN   DIPLOM
...CON/ANAL BIBLIOG/A 20 CHINJAP. PAGE 34 B0698   NAT/G
                                                        ADMIN
                                                        S41
STOKE H.W.,"EXECUTIVE LEADERSHIP AND THE GROWTH OF   EXEC
PROPAGANDA." USA-45 NAT/G EX/STRUC LEGIS TOP/EX   LEAD
PARL/PROC REPRESENT ORD/FREE PWR...MAJORIT 20.   EDU/PROP
PAGE 101 B2042   ADMIN
                                                        B42
NEUBURGER O.,OFFICIAL PUBLICATIONS OF PRESENT-DAY   BIBLIOG/A
GERMANY: GOVERNMENT, CORPORATE ORGANIZATIONS, AND   FASCISM
NATIONAL SOCIALIST PARTY. GERMANY CONSTN COM/IND   NAT/G
POL/PAR EDU/PROP PRESS 20 NAZI. PAGE 78 B1570   ADMIN
                                                        B42
SINGTON D.,THE GOEBBELS EXPERIMENT. GERMANY MOD/EUR   FASCISM
NAT/G EX/STRUC FORCES CONTROL ROUTINE WAR TOTALISM   EDU/PROP
PWR...ART/METH HUM 20 NAZI GOEBBELS/J. PAGE 97   ATTIT
B1970   COM/IND
                                                        S43
GOLDEN C.S.,"NEW PATTERNS OF DEMOCRACY." NEIGH   LABOR
DELIB/GP EDU/PROP EXEC PARTIC...MGT METH/CNCPT OBS   REPRESENT
TREND. PAGE 40 B0815   LG/CO
                                                        GP/REL
                                                        B44
DAVIS H.E.,PIONEERS IN WORLD ORDER. WOR-45 CONSTN   INT/ORG
ECO/TAC DOMIN EDU/PROP LEGIT ADJUD ADMIN ARMS/CONT   ROUTINE
CHOOSE KNOWL ORD/FREE...POLICY JURID SOC STAT OBS
CENSUS TIME/SEQ ANTHOL LEAGUE/NAT 20. PAGE 26 B0537
                                                        B45
BUSH V.,SCIENCE, THE ENDLESS FRONTIER. FUT USA-45   R+D
INTELL STRATA ACT/RES CREATE PLAN EDU/PROP ADMIN   NAT/G
NUC/PWR PEACE ATTIT HEALTH KNOWL...MAJORIT HEAL MGT
PHIL/SCI CONCPT OBS TREND 20. PAGE 18 B0360
                                                        S45
KRIESBERG M.,"WHAT CONGRESSMEN AND ADMINISTRATORS   LEGIS
THINK OF THE POLLS." USA-45 CONTROL PWR...INT QU.   ATTIT
PAGE 61 B1236   EDU/PROP
                                                        ADMIN
                                                        B47
DE NOIA J.,GUIDE TO OFFICIAL PUBLICATIONS OF THE   BIBLIOG/A
OTHER AMERICAN REPUBLICS: EL SALVADOR. EL/SALVADR   CONSTN
LAW LEGIS EDU/PROP CT/SYS 20. PAGE 27 B0558   NAT/G
                                                        ADMIN
                                                        B47
DE NOIA J.,GUIDE TO OFFICIAL PUBLICATIONS OF THE   BIBLIOG/A
OTHER AMERICAN REPUBLICS: NICARAGUA (VOL. XIV).   EDU/PROP
NICARAGUA LAW LEGIS ADMIN CT/SYS...JURID 19/20.   NAT/G
PAGE 27 B0559   CONSTN
                                                        B47
DE NOIA J.,GUIDE TO OFFICIAL PUBLICATIONS OF THE   BIBLIOG/A
OTHER AMERICAN REPUBLICS: PANAMA (VOL. XV). PANAMA   CONSTN
LAW LEGIS EDU/PROP CT/SYS 20. PAGE 27 B0560   ADMIN
                                                        NAT/G
                                                        B47
LASSWELL H.D.,THE ANALYSIS OF POLITICAL BEHAVIOUR: R+D
AN EMPIRICAL APPROACH. WOR+45 CULTURE NAT/G FORCES   ACT/RES
EDU/PROP ADMIN ATTIT PERCEPT KNOWL...PHIL/SCI PSY   ELITES
SOC NEW/IDEA OBS INT GEN/METH NAZI 20. PAGE 63
B1267
                                                        B47
PUBLIC ADMINISTRATION SERVICE,CURRENT RESEARCH   BIBLIOG
PROJECTS IN PUBLIC ADMINISTRATION (PAMPHLET). LAW   R+D
CONSTN COM/IND LABOR LOC/G MUNIC PROVS ACT/RES   MGT
DIPLOM RECEIVE EDU/PROP WAR 20. PAGE 85 B1716   ADMIN
                                                        B48
DE NOIA J.,GUIDE TO OFFICIAL PUBLICATIONS OF OTHER   BIBLIOG/A
AMERICAN REPUBLICS: PERU (VOL. XVII). PERU LAW   CONSTN
LEGIS ADMIN CT/SYS...JURID 19/20. PAGE 28 B0561   NAT/G
                                                        EDU/PROP
                                                        B48
KESSELMAN L.C.,THE SOCIAL POLITICS OF THE FEPC.   POLICY
INDUS WORKER EDU/PROP GP/REL RACE/REL 20 NEGRO JEWS   NAT/G
FEPC. PAGE 59 B1200   ADMIN
                                                        DISCRIM
                                                        B48
PUBLIC ADMINISTRATION SERVICE,SOURCE MATERIALS IN   BIBLIOG/A
PUBLIC ADMINISTRATION: A SELECTED BIBLIOGRAPHY (PAS   GOV/REL
PUBLICATION NO. 102). USA+45 LAW FINAN LOC/G MUNIC   MGT
NAT/G PLAN RECEIVE EDU/PROP CT/SYS CHOOSE HEALTH   ADMIN
20. PAGE 85 B1717
                                                        B49
BOYD A.M.,UNITED STATES GOVERNMENT PUBLICATIONS   BIBLIOG/A
(3RD ED.). USA+45 EX/STRUC LEGIS ADMIN...JURID   PRESS
CHARTS 20. PAGE 14 B0291   NAT/G
                                                        EDU/PROP
                                                        B49
FORD FOUNDATION,REPORT OF THE STUDY FOR THE FORD   WEALTH

FOUNDATION ON POLICY AND PROGRAM. SOCIETY R+D   GEN/LAWS
ACT/RES CAP/ISM FOR/AID EDU/PROP ADMIN KNOWL
...POLICY PSY SOC 20. PAGE 36 B0739
                                                        B49
MCLEAN J.M.,THE PUBLIC SERVICE AND UNIVERSITY   ACADEM
EDUCATION. UK USA-45 DELIB/GP EX/STRUC TOP/EX ADMIN   NAT/G
...GOV/COMP METH/COMP NAT/COMP ANTHOL 20. PAGE 72   EXEC
B1455   EDU/PROP
                                                        B49
ROSENHAUPT H.W.,HOW TO WAGE PEACE. USA+45 SOCIETY   INTELL
STRATA STRUCT R+D INT/ORG POL/PAR LEGIS ACT/RES   CONCPT
CREATE PLAN EDU/PROP ADMIN EXEC ATTIT ALL/VALS   DIPLOM
...TIME/SEQ TREND COLD/WAR 20. PAGE 90 B1822
                                                        B49
WRIGHT J.H.,PUBLIC RELATIONS IN MANAGEMENT. USA+45   MGT
USA-45 ECO/DEV LG/CO SML/CO CONSULT EXEC TASK   PLAN
PROFIT ATTIT ROLE 20. PAGE 118 B2382   EDU/PROP
                                                        PARTIC
                                                        S49
STEINMETZ H.,"THE PROBLEMS OF THE LANDRAT: A STUDY   LOC/G
OF COUNTY GOVERNMENT IN THE US ZONE OF GERMANY."   COLONIAL
GERMANY/W USA+45 INDUS PLAN DIPLOM EDU/PROP CONTROL   MGT
WAR GOV/REL FEDERAL WEALTH PLURISM...GOV/COMP 20   TOP/EX
LANDRAT. PAGE 100 B2031
                                                        B50
MANNHEIM K.,FREEDOM, POWER, AND DEMOCRATIC   TEC/DEV
PLANNING. FUT USSR WOR+45 ELITES INTELL SOCIETY   PLAN
NAT/G EDU/PROP ROUTINE ATTIT DRIVE SUPEGO SKILL   CAP/ISM
...POLICY PSY CONCPT TREND GEN/LAWS 20. PAGE 69   UK
B1393
                                                        B50
MCCAMY J.,THE ADMINISTRATION OF AMERICAN FOREIGN   EXEC
AFFAIRS. USA+45 NAT/G INT/ORG NAT/G PLAN   STRUCT
INT/TRADE EDU/PROP ADJUD ALL/VALS...METH/CNCPT   DIPLOM
TIME/SEQ CONGRESS 20. PAGE 71 B1441
                                                        S50
WITTFOGEL K.A.,"RUSSIA AND ASIA: PROBLEMS OF   ECO/DEV
CONTEMPORARY AREA STUDIES AND INTERNATIONAL   ADMIN
RELATIONS." ASIA COM USA+45 SOCIETY NAT/G DIPLOM   RUSSIA
ECO/TAC FOR/AID EDU/PROP KNOWL...HIST/WRIT TOT/POP   USSR
20. PAGE 117 B2369
                                                        C50
STEWART F.M.,"A HALF CENTURY OF MUNICIPAL REFORM."   LOC/G
USA+45 CONSTN FINAN SCHOOL EX/STRUC PLAN PROB/SOLV   VOL/ASSN
EDU/PROP ADMIN CHOOSE GOV/REL BIBLIOG. PAGE 101   MUNIC
B2036   POLICY
                                                        B51
ANDERSON W.,GOVERNMENT IN THE FIFTY STATES. LAW   LOC/G
CONSTN FINAN POL/PAR LEGIS EDU/PROP ADJUD ADMIN   PROVS
CT/SYS CHOOSE...CHARTS 20. PAGE 5 B0101   GOV/REL
                                                        B51
GUETZKOW H.,GROUPS, LEADERSHIP, AND MEN. FACE/GP   ATTIT
SECT EDU/PROP EXEC PERSON RESPECT...PERS/TEST   SOC
GEN/METH 20. PAGE 44 B0901   ELITES
                                                        B51
HARDMAN J.B.,THE HOUSE OF LABOR. LAW R+D NEIGH   LABOR
EDU/PROP LEAD ROUTINE REPRESENT GP/REL...POLICY   LOBBY
STAT. PAGE 47 B0945   ADMIN
                                                        PRESS
                                                        B51
NIELANDER W.A.,PUBLIC RELATIONS. USA+45 COM/IND   PERS/REL
LOC/G NAT/G VOL/ASSN EX/STRUC DIPLOM EDU/PROP PRESS   GP/REL
TV...METH/CNCPT T 20. PAGE 78 B1583   LG/CO
                                                        ROUTINE
                                                        S51
SCHRAMM W.,"COMMUNICATION IN THE SOVIETIZED STATE,   ATTIT
AS DEMONSTRATED IN KOREA." ASIA COM KOREA COM/IND   EDU/PROP
FACE/GP POL/PAR SCHOOL FORCES ADMIN PWR MARXISM   TOTALISM
...SOC CONCPT MYTH INT BIOG TOT/POP 20. PAGE 94
B1901
                                                        C51
MOORE B.,"SOVIET POLITICS - THE DILEMMA OF POWER: ATTIT
THE ROLE OF IDEAS IN SOCIAL CHANGE." USSR PROB/SOLV   PWR
DIPLOM EDU/PROP ADMIN LEAD ROUTINE REV...POLICY   CONCPT
DECISION BIBLIOG 20. PAGE 75 B1512   MARXISM
                                                        B52
DAY E.E.,EDUCATION FOR FREEDOM AND RESPONSIBILITY.   SCHOOL
FUT USA+45 CULTURE CONSULT EDU/PROP ATTIT SKILL   KNOWL
...MGT CONCPT OBS GEN/LAWS COLD/WAR 20. PAGE 27
B0547
                                                        B52
EGLE W.P.,ECONOMIC STABILIZATION. USA+45 SOCIETY   NAT/G
FINAN MARKET PLAN ECO/TAC DOMIN EDU/PROP LEGIT EXEC   ECO/DEV
WEALTH...CONCPT METH/CNCPT TREND HYPO/EXP GEN/METH   CAP/ISM
TOT/POP VAL/FREE 20. PAGE 32 B0656
                                                        B52
HIMMELFARB G.,LORD ACTON: A STUDY IN CONSCIENCE AND   PWR
POLITICS. MOD/EUR NAT/G POL/PAR SECT LEGIS TOP/EX   BIOG
EDU/PROP ADMIN NAT/LISM ATTIT PERSON SUPEGO MORAL
ORD/FREE...CONCPT PARLIAMENT 19 ACTON/LORD. PAGE 50
B1014
                                                        B52
MILLER M.,THE JUDGES AND THE JUDGED. USA+45 LG/CO   COM/IND
ACT/RES TV ROUTINE SANCTION NAT/LISM ATTIT ORD/FREE   DISCRIM
...POLICY ACLU. PAGE 73 B1481   EDU/PROP
                                                        MARXISM

B52

SELZNICK P.,THE ORGANIZATIONAL WEAPON: A STUDY OF   MARXISM
BOLSHEVIK STRATEGY AND TACTICS. USSR SOCIETY STRATA   POL/PAR
LABOR DOMIN EDU/PROP PARTIC REV ATTIT PWR...POLICY   LEAD
MGT CONCPT 20 BOLSHEVISM. PAGE 95 B1929   TOTALISM

B52

UNESCO,THESES DE SCIENCES SOCIALES: CATALOGUE   BIBLIOG
ANALYTIQUE INTERNATIONAL DE THESES INEDITES DE   ACADEM
DOCTORAT, 1940-1950. INT/ORG DIPLOM EDU/PROP...GEOG   WRITING
INT/LAW MGT PSY SOC 20. PAGE 107 B2155

B52

VANDENBOSCH A.,THE UN: BACKGROUND, ORGANIZATION,   DELIB/GP
FUNCTIONS, ACTIVITIES. WOR+45 LAW CONSTN STRUCT   TIME/SEQ
INT/ORG CONSULT BAL/PWR EDU/PROP EXEC ALL/VALS   PEACE
...POLICY CONCPT UN 20. PAGE 112 B2254

S52

BRUEGEL J.W.,"DIE INTERNAZIONALE   VOL/ASSN
GEWERKSCHAFTSBEWEGUNG." COM EUR+WWI USA+45 WOR+45   LABOR
DELIB/GP EX/STRUC ECO/TAC EDU/PROP ATTIT PWR   TOTALISM
RESPECT SKILL WEALTH WORK 20. PAGE 16 B0330

C52

LASSWELL H.D.,"THE COMPARATIVE STUDY OF ELITES: AN   ELITES
INTRODUCTION AND BIBLIOGRAPHY." STRATA POL/PAR   LEAD
EDU/PROP ADMIN LOBBY COERCE ATTIT PERSON PWR   CONCPT
...BIBLIOG 20. PAGE 63 B1270   DOMIN

B53

GROSS B.M.,THE LEGISLATIVE STRUGGLE: A STUDY IN   LEGIS
SOCIAL COMBAT. STRUCT LOC/G POL/PAR JUDGE EDU/PROP   DECISION
DEBATE ETIQUET ADMIN LOBBY CHOOSE GOV/REL INGP/REL   PERSON
HEREDITY ALL/VALS...SOC PRESIDENT. PAGE 44 B0885   LEAD

B53

MEYER P.,THE JEWS IN THE SOVIET SATELLITES.   COM
CZECHOSLVK POLAND SOCIETY STRATA NAT/G BAL/PWR   SECT
ECO/TAC EDU/PROP LEGIT ADMIN COERCE ATTIT DISPL   TOTALISM
PERCEPT HEALTH PWR RESPECT WEALTH...METH/CNCPT JEWS   USSR
VAL/FREE NAZI 20. PAGE 73 B1474

B53

PIERCE R.A.,RUSSIAN CENTRAL ASIA, 1867-1917: A   BIBLIOG
SELECTED BIBLIOGRAPHY (PAMPHLET). USSR LAW CULTURE   COLONIAL
NAT/G EDU/PROP WAR...GEOG SOC 19/20. PAGE 83 B1671   ADMIN
                                                         COM

B53

ROBINSON E.A.G.,THE STRUCTURE OF COMPETITIVE   INDUS
INDUSTRY. UK ECO/DEV DIST/IND MARKET TEC/DEV DIPLOM   PRODUC
EDU/PROP ADMIN EFFICIENCY WEALTH...MGT 19/20.   WORKER
PAGE 89 B1798   OPTIMAL

B53

THOMAS S.B.,GOVERNMENT AND ADMINISTRATION IN   PWR
COMMUNIST CHINA (MONOGRAPH). CHINA/COM PROB/SOLV   EX/STRUC
EDU/PROP 20. PAGE 104 B2100   REPRESENT
                                                         ELITES

S53

CORY R.H. JR.,"FORGING A PUBLIC INFORMATION POLICY   INT/ORG
FOR THE UNITED NATIONS." FUT WOR+45 SOCIETY ADMIN   EDU/PROP
PEACE ATTIT PERSON SKILL...CONCPT 20 UN. PAGE 24   BAL/PWR
B0486

S53

GABLE R.W.,"NAM: INFLUENTIAL LOBBY OR KISS OF   LOBBY
DEATH?" (BMR)" USA+45 LAW INSPECT EDU/PROP ADMIN   LEGIS
CONTROL INGP/REL EFFICIENCY PWR 20 CONGRESS NAM   INDUS
TAFT/HART. PAGE 38 B0769   LG/CO

S53

MORRIS B.S.,"THE COMINFORM: A FIVE YEAR   VOL/ASSN
PERSPECTIVE." COM UNIV USSR WOR+45 ECO/DEV POL/PAR   EDU/PROP
TOP/EX PLAN DOMIN ADMIN TOTALISM ATTIT ALL/VALS   DIPLOM
...CONCPT TIME/SEQ TREND CON/ANAL WORK VAL/FREE 20.
PAGE 76 B1527

B54

DUVERGER M.,POLITICAL PARTIES: THEIR ORGANIZATION   POL/PAR
AND ACTIVITY IN THE MODERN STATE. EUR+WWI MOD/EUR   EX/STRUC
USA+45 USA-45 EDU/PROP ADMIN ROUTINE ATTIT DRIVE   ELITES
ORD/FREE PWR...SOC CONCPT MATH STAT TIME/SEQ
TOT/POP 19/20. PAGE 31 B0635

L54

ROSTOW W.W.,"ASIAN LEADERSHIP AND FREE-WORLD   ATTIT
ALLIANCE." ASIA COM USA+45 CULTURE ELITES INTELL   LEGIT
NAT/G TEC/DEV ECO/TAC EDU/PROP COLONIAL PARL/PROC   DIPLOM
ROUTINE COERCE DRIVE ORD/FREE MARXISM...PSY CONCPT.
PAGE 90 B1829

B55

APTER D.E.,THE GOLD COAST IN TRANSITION. FUT CONSTN   AFR
CULTURE SOCIETY ECO/UNDEV FAM KIN LOC/G NAT/G   SOVEREIGN
POL/PAR LEGIS TOP/EX EDU/PROP LEGIT ADMIN ATTIT
PERSON PWR...CONCPT STAT INT CENSUS TOT/POP
VAL/FREE. PAGE 6 B0120

B55

CHOWDHURI R.N.,INTERNATIONAL MANDATES AND   DELIB/GP
TRUSTEESHIP SYSTEMS. WOR+45 STRUCT ECO/UNDEV   PLAN
INT/ORG LEGIS DOMIN EDU/PROP LEGIT ADJUD EXEC PWR   SOVEREIGN
...CONCPT TIME/SEQ UN 20. PAGE 21 B0427

B55

PULLEN W.R.,A CHECK LIST OF LEGISLATIVE JOURNALS   BIBLIOG
ISSUED SINCE 1937 BY THE STATES OF THE UNITED   PROVS
STATES OF AMERICA (PAMPHLET). USA+45 USA-45 LAW   EDU/PROP
WRITING ADJUD ADMIN...JURID 20. PAGE 85 B1720   LEGIS

B55

STEPHENS O.,FACTS TO A CANDID WORLD. USA+45 WOR+45   EDU/PROP
COM/IND EX/STRUC PRESS ROUTINE EFFICIENCY ATTIT   PHIL/SCI
...PSY 20. PAGE 100 B2033   NAT/G
                                                         DIPLOM

B55

UN ECONOMIC AND SOCIAL COUNCIL,BIBLIOGRAPHY OF   BIBLIOG/A
PUBLICATIONS OF THE UN AND SPECIALIZED AGENCIES IN   SOC/WK
THE SOCIAL WELFARE FIELD, 1946-1952. WOR+45 FAM   ADMIN
INT/ORG MUNIC ACT/RES PLAN PROB/SOLV EDU/PROP AGE/C   WEALTH
AGE/Y HABITAT...HEAL UN. PAGE 106 B2148

B55

ZABEL O.H.,GOD AND CAESAR IN NEBRASKA: A STUDY OF   SECT
LEGAL RELATIONSHIP OF CHURCH AND STATE, 1854-1954.   PROVS
TAX GIVE ADMIN CONTROL GP/REL ROLE...GP/COMP 19/20   LAW
NEBRASKA. PAGE 119 B2396   EDU/PROP

L55

KISER M.,"ORGANIZATION OF AMERICAN STATES." L/A+17C   VOL/ASSN
USA+45 ECO/UNDEV INT/ORG NAT/G PLAN TEC/DEV DIPLOM   ECO/DEV
ECO/TAC INT/TRADE EDU/PROP ADMIN ALL/VALS...POLICY   REGION
MGT RECORD ORG/CHARTS OAS 20. PAGE 60 B1215

S55

ANGELL R.,"GOVERNMENTS AND PEOPLES AS A FOCI FOR   FUT
PEACE-ORIENTED RESEARCH." WOR+45 CULTURE SOCIETY   SOC
FACE/GP ACT/RES CREATE PLAN DIPLOM EDU/PROP ROUTINE   PEACE
ATTIT PERCEPT SKILL...POLICY CONCPT OBS TREND
GEN/METH 20. PAGE 5 B0110

S55

STAHL O.G.,"DEMOCRACY AND PUBLIC EMPLOYEE   REPRESENT
MORALITY." USA+45 NAT/G EDU/PROP EXEC ROLE 20.   POLICY
PAGE 100 B2016   ADMIN

S55

TORRE M.,"PSYCHIATRIC OBSERVATIONS OF INTERNATIONAL   DELIB/GP
CONFERENCES." WOR+45 INT/ORG PROF/ORG VOL/ASSN   OBS
CONSULT EDU/PROP ROUTINE ATTIT DRIVE KNOWL...PSY   DIPLOM
METH/CNCPT OBS/ENVIR STERTYP 20. PAGE 105 B2119

S55

WRIGHT Q.,"THE PEACEFUL ADJUSTMENT OF INTERNATIONAL   R+D
RELATIONS: PROBLEMS AND RESEARCH APPROACHES." UNIV   METH/CNCPT
INTELL EDU/PROP ADJUD ROUTINE KNOWL SKILL...INT/LAW   PEACE
JURID PHIL/SCI CLASSIF 20. PAGE 118 B2385

B56

BLAU P.M.,BUREAUCRACY IN MODERN SOCIETY. STRUCT   SOC
INDUS LABOR LG/CO LOC/G NAT/G FORCES EDU/PROP   EX/STRUC
ROUTINE ORD/FREE 20 BUREAUCRCY. PAGE 12 B0252   ADMIN
                                                        EFFICIENCY

B56

ECOLE NAT'L D'ADMINISTRATION,RECRUITMENT AND   ADMIN
TRAINING FOR THE HIGHER CIVIL SERVICE IN FRANCE.   MGT
FRANCE EX/STRUC PLAN EDU/PROP CONTROL ROUTINE TASK   EXEC
COST...METH 20 CIVIL/SERV. PAGE 32 B0650   ACADEM

B56

GARDNER R.N.,STERLING-DOLLAR DIPLOMACY. EUR+WWI   ECO/DEV
USA+45 INT/ORG NAT/G PLAN INT/TRADE EDU/PROP ADMIN   DIPLOM
KNOWL PWR WEALTH...POLICY SOC METH/CNCPT STAT
CHARTS SIMUL GEN/LAWS 20. PAGE 39 B0781

B56

INTERNATIONAL AFRICAN INST,SELECT ANNOTATED   BIBLIOG/A
BIBLIOGRAPHY OF TROPICAL AFRICA. NAT/G EDU/PROP   AFR
ADMIN HEALTH. PAGE 54 B1095   SOC
                                                        HABITAT

B56

JENNINGS W.I.,THE APPROACH TO SELF-GOVERNMENT.   NAT/G
CEYLON INDIA PAKISTAN S/ASIA UK SOCIETY POL/PAR   CONSTN
DELIB/GP LEGIS ECO/TAC EDU/PROP ADMIN EXEC CHOOSE   COLONIAL
ATTIT ALL/VALS...JURID CONCPT GEN/METH TOT/POP 20.
PAGE 56 B1136

B56

KIRK G.,THE CHANGING ENVIRONMENT OF INTERNATIONAL   FUT
RELATIONS. ASIA S/ASIA USA+45 WOR+45 ECO/UNDEV   EXEC
INT/ORG NAT/G FOR/AID EDU/PROP PEACE KNOWL   DIPLOM
...PLURIST COLD/WAR TOT/POP 20. PAGE 60 B1214

B56

WASSERMAN P.,INFORMATION FOR ADMINISTRATORS: A   BIBLIOG
GUIDE TO PUBLICATIONS AND SERVICES FOR MANAGEMENT   MGT
IN BUSINESS AND GOVERNMENT. R+D LOC/G NAT/G   KNOWL
PROF/ORG VOL/ASSN PRESS...PSY SOC STAT 20. PAGE 114   EDU/PROP
B2299

B56

WHYTE W.H. JR.,THE ORGANIZATION MAN. CULTURE FINAN   ADMIN
VOL/ASSN DOMIN EDU/PROP EXEC DISPL HABITAT ROLE   LG/CO
...PERS/TEST STERTYP. PAGE 116 B2343   PERSON
                                                        CONSEN

B57

ARON R.,FRANCE DEFEATS EDC. EUR+WWI GERMANY LEGIS   INT/ORG
DIPLOM DOMIN EDU/PROP ADMIN...HIST/WRIT 20. PAGE 7   FORCES
B0136   DETER
                                                        FRANCE

B57

ASHER R.E.,THE UNITED NATIONS AND THE PROMOTION OF   INT/ORG
THE GENERAL WELFARE. WOR+45 WOR-45 ECO/UNDEV   CONSULT
EX/STRUC ACT/RES PLAN EDU/PROP ROUTINE HEALTH...HUM
CONCPT CHARTS UNESCO UN ILO 20. PAGE 7 B0139

B57

DE GRAZIA A.,GRASS ROOTS PRIVATE WELFARE. LOC/G   NEW/LIB
SCHOOL ACT/RES EDU/PROP ROUTINE CROWD GP/REL   HEALTH

DISCRIM HAPPINESS ILLEGIT AGE HABITAT. PAGE 27   MUNIC
B0554   VOL/ASSN
                                                                    B57
DJILAS M.,THE NEW CLASS: AN ANALYSIS OF THE   COM
COMMUNIST SYSTEM. STRATA CAP/ISM ECO/TAC DOMIN   POL/PAR
EDU/PROP LEGIT EXEC COERCE ATTIT PWR MARXISM   USSR
...MARXIST MGT CONCPT TIME/SEQ GEN/LAWS 20. PAGE 29 YUGOSLAVIA
B0600
                                                                    B57
HOLCOMBE A.N.,STRENGTHENING THE UNITED NATIONS.   INT/ORG
USA+45 ACT/RES CREATE PLAN EDU/PROP ATTIT PERCEPT   ROUTINE
PWR...METH/CNCPT CONT/OBS RECORD UN COLD/WAR 20.
PAGE 51 B1032
                                                                    B57
KNEIER C.M.,CITY GOVERNMENT IN THE UNITED STATES   MUNIC
(3RD ED.). USA-45 FINAN NAT/G POL/PAR LEGIS   LOC/G
EDU/PROP LEAD APPORT REPRESENT ATTIT...MGT 20   ADMIN
CITY/MGT. PAGE 60 B1219   GOV/REL
                                                                    B57
LOEWENSTEIN K.,POLITICAL POWER AND THE GOVERNMENTAL PWR
PROCESS. WOR+45 WOR-45 CONSTN NAT/G POL/PAR   CONCPT
EX/STRUC LEGIS TOP/EX DOMIN EDU/PROP LEGIT ADMIN
REGION CHOOSE ATTIT...JURID STERTYP GEN/LAWS 20.
PAGE 66 B1336
                                                                    B57
MURRAY J.N.,THE UNITED NATIONS TRUSTEESHIP SYSTEM.   INT/ORG
AFR WOR+45 CONSTN CONSULT LEGIS EDU/PROP LEGIT EXEC   DELIB/GP
ROUTINE...INT TIME/SEQ SOMALI UN 20. PAGE 77 B1547
                                                                    L57
HAAS E.B.,"REGIONAL INTEGRATION AND NATIONAL   INT/ORG
POLICY." WOR+45 VOL/ASSN DELIB/GP EX/STRUC ECO/TAC   ORD/FREE
DOMIN EDU/PROP LEGIT COERCE ATTIT PERCEPT KNOWL   REGION
...TIME/SEQ COLD/WAR 20 UN. PAGE 45 B0908
                                                                    S57
BAUER R.A.,"BRAINWASHING: PSYCHOLOGY OR   EDU/PROP
DEMONOLOGY." ASIA CHINA/COM COM POL/PAR ECO/TAC   PSY
ADMIN COERCE ATTIT DRIVE ORD/FREE...CONCPT MYTH 20.   TOTALISM
PAGE 10 B0196
                                                                    C57
TANG P.S.H.,"COMMUNIST CHINA TODAY: DOMESTIC AND   POL/PAR
FOREIGN POLICIES." CHINA/COM COM S/ASIA USSR STRATA   LEAD
FORCES DIPLOM EDU/PROP COERCE GOV/REL...POLICY   ADMIN
MAJORIT BIBLIOG 20. PAGE 102 B2071   CONSTN
                                                                    B58
BROWNE C.G.,THE CONCEPT OF LEADERSHIP. UNIV FACE/GP   EXEC
DOMIN EDU/PROP LEGIT LEAD DRIVE PERSON PWR...MGT   CONCPT
SOC OBS SELF/OBS CONT/OBS INT PERS/TEST STERTYP
GEN/LAWS. PAGE 16 B0328
                                                                    B58
CLEMENTS R.V.,MANAGERS - A STUDY OF THEIR CAREERS   MGT
IN INDUSTRY. STRATA INDUS TASK PERSON SKILL 20.   ELITES
PAGE 21 B0435   EDU/PROP
                                                        TOP/EX
                                                                    B58
HENKIN L.,ARMS CONTROL AND INSPECTION IN AMERICAN   USA+45
LAW. LAW CONSTN INT/ORG LOC/G MUNIC NAT/G PROVS   JURID
EDU/PROP LEGIT EXEC NUC/PWR KNOWL ORD/FREE...OBS   ARMS/CONT
TOT/POP CONGRESS 20. PAGE 49 B0990
                                                                    B58
LAQUER W.Z.,THE MIDDLE EAST IN TRANSITION. COM USSR   ISLAM
ECO/UNDEV NAT/G VOL/ASSN EDU/PROP EXEC DRIVE   TREND
PWR MARXISM COLD/WAR TOT/POP 20. PAGE 62 B1261   NAT/LISM
                                                                    B58
MASON J.B.,THAILAND BIBLIOGRAPHY. S/ASIA THAILAND   BIBLIOG/A
CULTURE EDU/PROP ADMIN...GEOG SOC LING 20. PAGE 70   ECO/UNDEV
B1423   DIPLOM
                                                        NAT/G
                                                                    B58
MILLS C.W.,THE CAUSES OF WORLD WAR THREE. FUT   CONSULT
USA+45 INTELL NAT/G DOMIN EDU/PROP ADMIN WAR ATTIT   PWR
SOC. PAGE 74 B1487   ELITES
                                                        PEACE
                                                                    B58
ORTIZ R.P.,ANNUARIO BIBLIOGRAFICO COLOMBIANO,   BIBLIOG
1951-1956. LAW RECEIVE EDU/PROP ADMIN...LING STAT   SOC
20 COLOMB. PAGE 80 B1617
                                                                    B58
SCOTT D.J.R.,RUSSIAN POLITICAL INSTITUTIONS. RUSSIA   NAT/G
USSR CONSTN AGRI DELIB/GP PLAN EDU/PROP CONTROL   POL/PAR
CHOOSE EFFICIENCY ATTIT MARXISM...BIBLIOG/A 13/20.   ADMIN
PAGE 95 B1919   DECISION
                                                                    B58
SHERWOOD F.P.,SUPERVISORY METHODS IN MUNICIPAL   EX/STRUC
ADMINISTRATION. USA+45 MUNIC WORKER EDU/PROP PARTIC   LEAD
INGP/REL PERS/REL 20 CITY/MGT. PAGE 96 B1945   ADMIN
                                                        LOC/G
                                                                    B58
SPITZ D.,DEMOCRACY AND THE CHALLANGE OF POWER. FUT   NAT/G
USA+45 USA-45 LAW SOCIETY STRUCT LOC/G POL/PAR   PWR
PROVS DELIB/GP EX/STRUC LEGIS TOP/EX ACT/RES CREATE
DOMIN EDU/PROP LEGIT ADJUD ADMIN ATTIT DRIVE MORAL
ORD/FREE TOT/POP. PAGE 99 B2010
                                                                    B58
SWEENEY S.B.,EDUCATION FOR ADMINISTRATIVE CAREERS   EDU/PROP
IN GOVERNMENT SERVICE. USA+45 ACADEM CONSULT CREATE   ADMIN
PLAN CONFER SKILL...TREND IDEA/COMP METH 20   NAT/G

CIVIL/SERV. PAGE 102 B2059   LOC/G
                                                                    B58
US HOUSE COMM POST OFFICE,TRAINING OF FEDERAL   LEGIS
EMPLOYEES. USA+45 DIST/IND NAT/G EX/STRUC EDU/PROP   DELIB/GP
CONFER GOV/REL EFFICIENCY SKILL 20 CONGRESS   WORKER
CIVIL/SERV. PAGE 109 B2197   ADMIN
                                                                    B58
VASEY W.,GOVERNMENT AND SOCIAL WELFARE: ROLES OF   REPRESENT
FEDERAL , STATE AND LOCAL GOVERNMENTS IN   ADMIN
ADMINISTERING WELFARE SERVICES. USA+45 EDU/PROP 20.   EX/STRUC
PAGE 112 B2255   SOC/WK
                                                                    S58
BLAISDELL D.C.,"PRESSURE GROUPS, FOREIGN POLICIES,   PROF/ORG
AND INTERNATIONAL POLITICS." USA+45 WOR+45 INT/ORG   PWR
PLAN DOMIN EDU/PROP LEGIT ADMIN ROUTINE CHOOSE
...DECISION MGT METH/CNCPT CON/ANAL 20. PAGE 12
B0249
                                                                    S58
STAAR R.F.,"ELECTIONS IN COMMUNIST POLAND." EUR+WWI   COM
SOCIETY INT/ORG NAT/G POL/PAR LEGIS ACT/RES ECO/TAC   CHOOSE
EDU/PROP ADJUD ADMIN ROUTINE COERCE TOTALISM ATTIT   POLAND
ORD/FREE PWR 20. PAGE 100 B2015
                                                                    B59
BONNETT C.E.,LABOR-MANAGEMENT RELATIONS. USA+45   MGT
OP/RES PROB/SOLV EDU/PROP...AUD/VIS CHARTS 20.   LABOR
PAGE 13 B0274   INDUS
                                                        GP/REL
                                                                    B59
CHINA INSTITUTE OF AMERICA.,CHINA AND THE UNITED   ASIA
NATIONS. CHINA/COM FUT STRUCT EDU/PROP LEGIT ADMIN   INT/ORG
ATTIT KNOWL ORD/FREE PWR...OBS RECORD STAND/INT
TIME/SEQ UN LEAGUE/NAT UNESCO 20. PAGE 21 B0425
                                                                    B59
EPSTEIN F.T.,EAST GERMANY: A SELECTED BIBLIOGRAPHY   BIBLIOG/A
(PAMPHLET). COM GERMANY/E LAW AGRI FINAN INDUS   INTELL
LABOR POL/PAR EDU/PROP ADMIN AGE/Y 20. PAGE 33   MARXISM
B0677   NAT/G
                                                                    B59
GINSBURG M.,LAW AND OPINION IN ENGLAND. UK CULTURE   JURID
KIN LABOR LEGIS EDU/PROP ADMIN CT/SYS CRIME OWN   POLICY
HEALTH...ANTHOL 20 ENGLSH/LAW. PAGE 40 B0802   ECO/TAC
                                                                    B59
INDIAN INSTITUTE PUBLIC ADMIN.,MORALE IN THE PUBLIC   HAPPINESS
SERVICES: REPORT OF A CONFERENCE JAN., 3-4, 1959.   ADMIN
INDIA S/ASIA ECO/UNDEV PROVS PLAN EDU/PROP CONFER   WORKER
GOV/REL EFFICIENCY DRIVE ROLE 20 CIVIL/SERV.   INGP/REL
PAGE 53 B1082
                                                                    B59
MOOS M.,THE CAMPUS AND THE STATE. LAW FINAN   EDU/PROP
DELIB/GP LEGIS EXEC LOBBY GP/REL PWR...POLICY   ACADEM
BIBLIOG. PAGE 75 B1517   PROVS
                                                        CONTROL
                                                                    B59
SCHURZ W.L.,AMERICAN FOREIGN AFFAIRS: A GUIDE TO   INT/ORG
INTERNATIONAL AFFAIRS. USA+45 WOR+45 WOR-45 NAT/G   SOCIETY
FORCES LEGIS TOP/EX PLAN EDU/PROP LEGIT ADMIN   DIPLOM
ROUTINE ATTIT ORD/FREE PWR...SOC CONCPT STAT
SAMP/SIZ CHARTS STERTYP 20. PAGE 95 B1910
                                                                    B59
WASSERMAN P.,MEASUREMENT AND ANALYSIS OF   BIBLIOG/A
ORGANIZATIONAL PERFORMANCE. FINAN MARKET EX/STRUC   ECO/TAC
TEC/DEV EDU/PROP CONTROL ROUTINE TASK...MGT 20.   OP/RES
PAGE 114 B2300   EFFICIENCY
                                                                    B59
YANG C.K.,A CHINESE VILLAGE IN EARLY COMMUNIST   ASIA
TRANSITION. ECO/UNDEV AGRI FAM KIN MUNIC FORCES   ROUTINE
PLAN ECO/TAC DOMIN EDU/PROP ATTIT DRIVE PWR RESPECT   SOCISM
...SOC CONCPT METH/CNCPT OBS RECORD CON/ANAL CHARTS
WORK 20. PAGE 118 B2389
                                                                    S59
HOFFMANN S.,"IMPLEMENTATION OF INTERNATIONAL   INT/ORG
INSTRUMENTS ON HUMAN RIGHTS." WOR+45 VOL/ASSN   MORAL
DELIB/GP JUDGE EDU/PROP LEGIT ROUTINE PEACE
COLD/WAR 20. PAGE 51 B1029
                                                                    S59
LASSWELL H.D.,"UNIVERSALITY IN PERSPECTIVE." FUT   INT/ORG
UNIV SOCIETY CONSULT TOP/EX PLAN EDU/PROP ADJUD   JURID
ROUTINE ARMS/CONT COERCE PEACE ATTIT PERSON   TOTALISM
ALL/VALS. PAGE 63 B1271
                                                                    B60
BRISTOL L.H. JR.,DEVELOPING THE CORPORATE IMAGE.   LG/CO
USA+45 SOCIETY ECO/DEV COM/IND SCHOOL EDU/PROP   ATTIT
PRESS TV...AUD/VIS ANTHOL. PAGE 15 B0312   MGT
                                                        ECO/TAC
                                                                    B60
BROOKINGS INSTITUTION.UNITED STATES FOREIGN POLICY: DIPLOM
STUDY NO 9: THE FORMULATION AND ADMINISTRATION OF   INT/ORG
UNITED STATES FOREIGN POLICY. USA+45 WOR+45   CREATE
EX/STRUC LEGIS BAL/PWR FOR/AID EDU/PROP CIVMIL/REL
GOV/REL...INT COLD/WAR. PAGE 16 B0317
                                                                    B60
CAMPBELL R.W.,SOVIET ECONOMIC POWER. COM USA+45   ECO/DEV
DIST/IND MARKET TOP/EX ACT/RES CAP/ISM ECO/TAC   PLAN
DOMIN EDU/PROP ADMIN ROUTINE DRIVE...MATH TIME/SEQ   SOCISM
CHARTS WORK 20. PAGE 18 B0371   USSR

B60

CORSON J.J.,GOVERNANCE OF COLLEGES AND
UNIVERSITIES. STRUCT FINAN DELIB/GP DOMIN EDU/PROP
LEAD CHOOSE GP/REL CENTRAL COST PRIVIL SUPEGO
ORD/FREE PWR...DECISION BIBLIOG. PAGE 24 B0481
ADMIN
EXEC
ACADEM
HABITAT

B60

DRAPER T.,AMERICAN COMMUNISM AND SOVIET RUSSIA.
EUR+WWI USA+45 USSR INTELL AGRI COM/IND FINAN INDUS
LABOR PROF/ORG VOL/ASSN PLAN TEC/DEV DOMIN EDU/PROP
ADMIN COERCE REV PERSON PWR...POLICY CONCPT MYTH
19/20. PAGE 30 B0617
COM
POL/PAR

B60

GRANICK D.,THE RED EXECUTIVE. COM USA+45 SOCIETY
ECO/DEV INDUS NAT/G POL/PAR EX/STRUC PLAN ECO/TAC
EDU/PROP ADMIN EXEC ATTIT DRIVE...GP/COMP 20.
PAGE 42 B0851
PWR
STRATA
USSR
ELITES

B60

HAYEK F.A.,THE CONSTITUTION OF LIBERTY. UNIV LAW
CONSTN WORKER TAX EDU/PROP ADMIN CT/SYS COERCE
DISCRIM...IDEA/COMP 20. PAGE 48 B0974
ORD/FREE
CHOOSE
NAT/G
CONCPT

B60

HYDE L.K.G.,THE US AND THE UN. WOR+45 STRUCT
ECO/DEV ECO/UNDEV NAT/G ACT/RES PLAN DIPLOM
EDU/PROP ADMIN ALL/VALS...CONCPT TIME/SEQ GEN/LAWS
UN VAL/FREE 20. PAGE 53 B1070
USA+45
INT/ORG
FOR/AID

B60

JONES V.,METROPOLITAN COMMUNITIES: A BIBLIOGRAPHY
WITH SPECIAL EMPHASIS UPON GOVERNMENT AND POLITICS,
1955-1957. STRUCT ECO/DEV FINAN FORCES PLAN
PROB/SOLV RECEIVE EDU/PROP CT/SYS...GEOG HEAL 20.
PAGE 57 B1152
BIBLIOG
LOC/G
MUNIC
ADMIN

B60

LEYDER J.,BIBLIOGRAPHIE DE L'ENSEIGNEMENT SUPERIEUR
ET DE LA RECHERCHE SCIENTIFIQUE EN AFRIQUE
INTERTROPICALE (2 VOLS.). AFR CULTURE ECO/UNDEV
AGRI PLAN EDU/PROP ADMIN COLONIAL...GEOG SOC/INTEG
20 NEGRO. PAGE 65 B1309
BIBLIOG/A
ACT/RES
ACADEM
R+D

B60

LINDVEIT E.N.,SCIENTISTS IN GOVERNMENT. USA+45 PAY
EDU/PROP ADMIN DRIVE HABITAT ROLE...TECHNIC BIBLIOG
20. PAGE 65 B1316
TEC/DEV
ECO/TAC
PHIL/SCI
GOV/REL

B60

MCGREGOR D.,THE HUMAN SIDE OF ENTERPRISE. USA+45
LEAD ROUTINE GP/REL INGP/REL...CONCPT GEN/LAWS 20.
PAGE 72 B1449
MGT
ATTIT
SKILL
EDU/PROP

B60

MUNRO L.,UNITED NATIONS, HOPE FOR A DIVIDED WORLD.
FUT WOR+45 CONSTN DELIB/GP CREATE TEC/DEV DIPLOM
EDU/PROP LEGIT PEACE ATTIT HEALTH ORD/FREE PWR
...CONCPT TREND UN VAL/FREE 20. PAGE 76 B1540
INT/ORG
ROUTINE

B60

PIERCE R.A.,RUSSIAN CENTRAL ASIA, 1867-1917. ASIA
RUSSIA CULTURE AGRI INDUS EDU/PROP REV NAT/LISM
...CHARTS BIBLIOG 19/20 BOLSHEVISM INTERVENT.
PAGE 83 B1672
COLONIAL
DOMIN
ADMIN
ECO/UNDEV

B60

ROEPKE W.,A HUMANE ECONOMY: THE SOCIAL FRAMEWORK OF
THE FREE MARKET. FUT USSR WOR+45 CULTURE SOCIETY
ECO/DEV PLAN ECO/TAC ADMIN ATTIT PERSON RIGID/FLEX
SUPEGO MORAL WEALTH SOCISM...POLICY OLD/LIB CONCPT
TREND GEN/LAWS 20. PAGE 90 B1811
DRIVE
EDU/PROP
CAP/ISM

S60

BOGARDUS E.S.,"THE SOCIOLOGY OF A STRUCTURED
PEACE." FUT SOCIETY CREATE DIPLOM EDU/PROP ADJUD
ROUTINE ATTIT RIGID/FLEX KNOWL ORD/FREE RESPECT
...POLICY INT/LAW JURID NEW/IDEA SELF/OBS TOT/POP
20 UN. PAGE 13 B0264
INT/ORG
SOC
NAT/LISM
PEACE

S60

BOYER W.W.,"POLICY MAKING BY GOVERNMENT AGENCIES."
USA+45 WOR+45 R+D DELIB/GP TOP/EX EDU/PROP ROUTINE
ATTIT BIO/SOC DRIVE...CONCPT TREND TOT/POP 20.
PAGE 14 B0293
NAT/G
DIPLOM

S60

GROSSMAN G.,"SOVIET GROWTH: ROUTINE, INERTIA, AND
PRESSURE." COM STRATA NAT/G DELIB/GP PLAN TEC/DEV
ECO/TAC EDU/PROP ADMIN ROUTINE DRIVE WEALTH
COLD/WAR 20. PAGE 44 B0891
POL/PAR
ECO/DEV
USSR

S60

HALPERIN M.H.,"IS THE SENATE'S FOREIGN RELATIONS
RESEARCH WORTHWHILE." COM FUT USA+45 USSR ACT/RES
BAL/PWR EDU/PROP ADMIN ALL/VALS CONGRESS VAL/FREE
20 COLD/WAR. PAGE 46 B0927
PLAN
DIPLOM

S60

HUTCHINSON C.E.,"AN INSTITUTE FOR NATIONAL SECURITY
AFFAIRS." USA+45 R+D NAT/G CONSULT TOP/EX ACT/RES
CREATE PLAN TEC/DEV EDU/PROP ROUTINE NUC/PWR ATTIT
ORD/FREE PWR...DECISION MGT PHIL/SCI CONCPT RECORD
GEN/LAWS GEN/METH 20. PAGE 53 B1068
POLICY
METH/CNCPT
ELITES
DIPLOM

S60

MORA J.A.,"THE ORGANIZATION OF AMERICAN STATES."
USA+45 LAW ECO/UNDEV VOL/ASSN DELIB/GP PLAN BAL/PWR
EDU/PROP ADMIN DRIVE RIGID/FLEX ORD/FREE WEALTH
...TIME/SEQ GEN/LAWS OAS 20. PAGE 75 B1518
L/A+17C
INT/ORG
REGION

C60

FITZSIMMONS T.,"USSR: ITS PEOPLE, ITS SOCIETY, ITS
CULTURE." USSR FAM SECT DIPLOM EDU/PROP ADMIN
RACE/REL ATTIT...POLICY CHARTS BIBLIOG 20. PAGE 36
B0728
CULTURE
STRUCT
SOCIETY
COM

C60

MCCLEERY R.,"COMMUNICATION PATTERNS AS BASES OF
SYSTEMS OF AUTHORITY AND POWER" IN THEORETICAL
STUDIES IN SOCIAL ORGAN. OF PRISON-BMR. USA+45
SOCIETY STRUCT EDU/PROP ADMIN CONTROL COERCE CRIME
GP/REL AUTHORIT...SOC 20. PAGE 71 B1443
PERS/REL
PUB/INST
PWR
DOMIN

C60

SCHRAMM W.,"MASS COMMUNICATIONS: A BOOK OF READINGS
(2ND ED.)" LG/CO PRESS ADMIN CONTROL ROUTINE ATTIT
ROLE SUPEGO...CHARTS ANTHOL BIBLIOG 20. PAGE 94
B1902
COM/IND
EDU/PROP
CROWD
MAJORIT

B61

BARNES W.,THE FOREIGN SERVICE OF THE UNITED STATES.
USA+45 USA-45 CONSTN INT/ORG POL/PAR CONSULT
DELIB/GP LEGIS DOMIN EDU/PROP EXEC ATTIT RIGID/FLEX
ORD/FREE PWR...POLICY CONCPT STAT OBS RECORD BIOG
TIME/SEQ TREND. PAGE 9 B0188
NAT/G
MGT
DIPLOM

B61

BENOIT E.,EUROPE AT SIXES AND SEVENS: THE COMMON
MARKET, THE FREE TRADE ASSOCIATION AND THE UNITED
STATES. EUR+WWI FUT USA+45 INDUS CONSULT DELIB/GP
EX/STRUC TOP/EX ACT/RES ECO/TAC EDU/PROP ROUTINE
CHOOSE PERCEPT WEALTH...MGT TREND EEC TOT/POP 20
EFTA. PAGE 11 B0217
FINAN
ECO/DEV
VOL/ASSN

B61

BISHOP D.G.,THE ADMINISTRATION OF BRITISH FOREIGN
RELATIONS. EUR+WWI MOD/EUR INT/ORG NAT/G POL/PAR
DELIB/GP LEGIS TOP/EX ECO/TAC DOMIN EDU/PROP ADMIN
COERCE 20. PAGE 12 B0243
ROUTINE
PWR
DIPLOM
UK

B61

BULLIS H.A.,MANIFESTO FOR AMERICANS. USA+45 AGRI
LABOR NAT/G NEIGH FOR/AID INT/TRADE TAX EDU/PROP
CHOOSE...POLICY MGT 20 UN UNESCO. PAGE 17 B0342
ECO/TAC
SOCIETY
INDUS
CAP/ISM

B61

BURDETTE F.L.,POLITICAL SCIENCE: A SELECTED
BIBLIOGRAPHY OF BOOKS IN PRINT, WITH ANNOTATIONS
(PAMPHLET). LAW LOC/G NAT/G POL/PAR PROVS DIPLOM
EDU/PROP ADMIN CHOOSE ATTIT 20. PAGE 17 B0347
BIBLIOG/A
GOV/COMP
CONCPT
ROUTINE

B61

PROCEEDINGS OF THE CONFERENCE ON BUSINESS GAMES AS
TEACHING DEVICES. PROB/SOLV ECO/TAC CONFER ADMIN
TASK...MGT ANTHOL 20. PAGE 29 B0593
GAME
DECISION
EDU/PROP
EFFICIENCY

B61

HAMILTON A.,THE FEDERALIST. USA-45 NAT/G VOL/ASSN
LEGIS TOP/EX EDU/PROP LEGIT CHOOSE ATTIT RIGID/FLEX
ORD/FREE PWR...MAJORIT JURID CONCPT ANTHOL. PAGE 46
B0931
EX/STRUC
CONSTN

B61

HASAN H.S.,PAKISTAN AND THE UN. ISLAM WOR+45
ECO/DEV ECO/UNDEV NAT/G TOP/EX ECO/TAC FOR/AID
EDU/PROP ADMIN DRIVE PERCEPT...OBS TIME/SEQ UN 20.
PAGE 48 B0965
INT/ORG
ATTIT
PAKISTAN

B61

HOUN F.W.,TO CHANGE A NATION; PROPAGANDA AND
INDOCTRINATION IN COMMUNIST CHINA. CHINA/COM COM
ACT/RES PLAN PRESS ADMIN FEEDBACK CENTRAL
EFFICIENCY ATTIT...PSY SOC 20. PAGE 52 B1048
DOMIN
EDU/PROP
TOTALISM
MARXISM

B61

KEE R.,REFUGEE WORLD. AUSTRIA EUR+WWI GERMANY NEIGH
EX/STRUC WORKER PROB/SOLV ECO/TAC RENT EDU/PROP
INGP/REL COST LITERACY HABITAT 20 MIGRATION.
PAGE 59 B1186
NAT/G
GIVE
WEALTH
STRANGE

B61

KOESTLER A.,THE LOTUS AND THE ROBOT. ASIA INDIA
S/ASIA SOCIETY STRATA ECO/DEV AGRI INDUS FAM CREATE
DOMIN EDU/PROP ADMIN COERCE ATTIT DRIVE SUPEGO
ORD/FREE PWR RESPECT WEALTH...MYTH OBS 20 CHINJAP.
PAGE 61 B1226
SECT
ECO/UNDEV

B61

LASSWELL H.D.,PSYCOPATHOLOGY AND POLITICS. WOR-45
CULTURE SOCIETY FACE/GP NAT/G CONSULT CREATE
EDU/PROP EXEC ROUTINE DISPL DRIVE PERSON PWR
RESPECT...PSY CONCPT METH/CNCPT METH. PAGE 63 B1272
ATTIT
GEN/METH

B61

LENIN V.I.,WHAT IS TO BE DONE? (1902). RUSSIA LABOR
NAT/G POL/PAR WORKER CAP/ISM ECO/TAC ADMIN PARTIC
...MARXIST IDEA/COMP GEN/LAWS 19/20. PAGE 64 B1292
EDU/PROP
PRESS
MARXISM
METH/COMP

B61

LOSCHELDER W.,AUSBILDUNG UND AUSLESE DER BEAMTEN.
GERMANY/W ELITES NAT/G ADMIN GP/REL ATTIT...JURID
20 CIVIL/SERV. PAGE 67 B1341
PROF/ORG
EDU/PROP
EX/STRUC
CHOOSE

B61

MACRIDIS R.C.,COMPARATIVE POLITICS: NOTES AND
READINGS. WOR+45 LOC/G MUNIC NAT/G PROVS VOL/ASSN
EDU/PROP ADMIN ATTIT PERSON ORD/FREE...SOC CONCPT
OBS RECORD TREND 20. PAGE 68 B1376
POL/PAR
CHOOSE

B61
MARVICK D.,POLITICAL DECISION-MAKERS. INTELL STRATA TOP/EX
NAT/G POL/PAR EX/STRUC LEGIS DOMIN EDU/PROP ATTIT BIOG
PERSON PWR...PSY STAT OBS CONT/OBS STAND/INT ELITES
UNPLAN/INT TIME/SEQ CHARTS STERTYP VAL/FREE.
PAGE 70 B1416

B61
NARAIN J.P.,SWARAJ FOR THE PEOPLE. INDIA CONSTN NAT/G
LOC/G MUNIC POL/PAR CHOOSE REPRESENT EFFICIENCY ORD/FREE
ATTIT PWR SOVEREIGN 20. PAGE 77 B1553 EDU/PROP
EX/STRUC

B61
ROBINSON M.E.,EDUCATION FOR SOCIAL CHANGE: FOR/AID
ESTABLISHING INSTITUTES OF PUBLIC AND BUSINESS EDU/PROP
ADMINISTRATION ABROAD (PAMPHLET). WOR+45 SOCIETY MGT
ACADEM CONFER INGP/REL ROLE...SOC CHARTS BIBLIOG 20 ADJUST
ICA. PAGE 89 B1805

B61
ROSE D.L.,THE VIETNAMESE CIVIL SERVICE. VIETNAM ADMIN
CONSULT DELIB/GP GIVE PAY EDU/PROP COLONIAL GOV/REL EFFICIENCY
UTIL...CHARTS 20. PAGE 90 B1819 STAT
NAT/G

B61
SCHMECKEBIER L.,GOVERNMENT PUBLICATIONS AND THEIR BIBLIOG/A
USE. USA+45 LEGIS ACT/RES CT/SYS EXEC INGP/REL 20. EDU/PROP
PAGE 94 B1894 NAT/G
ADMIN

SHARP W.R.,FIELD ADMINISTRATION IN THE UNITED INT/ORG
NATION SYSTEM: THE CONDUCT OF INTERNATIONAL CONSULT
ECONOMIC AND SOCIAL PROGRAMS. FUT WOR+45 CONSTN
SOCIETY ECO/UNDEV R+D DELIB/GP ACT/RES PLAN TEC/DEV
EDU/PROP EXEC ROUTINE HEALTH WEALTH...HUM CONCPT
CHARTS METH ILO UNESCO VAL/FREE UN 20. PAGE 96
B1939

B61
STRAUSS E.,THE RULING SERVANTS. FRANCE UK USSR ADMIN
WOR+45 WOR-45 NAT/G CONSULT DELIB/GP EX/STRUC PWR
TOP/EX DOMIN EDU/PROP LEGIT ROUTINE...MGT TIME/SEQ ELITES
STERTYP 20. PAGE 101 B2051

L61
COHEN K.J.,"THE ROLE OF MANAGEMENT GAMES IN SOCIETY
EDUCATION AND RESEARCH." INTELL ECO/DEV FINAN GAME
ACT/RES ECO/TAC DECISION. PAGE 22 B0444 MGT
EDU/PROP

S61
ALGER C.F.,"NON-RESOLUTION CONSEQUENCES OF THE INT/ORG
UNITED NATIONS AND THEIR EFFECT ON INTERNATIONAL DRIVE
CONFLICT." WOR+45 CONSTN ECO/DEV NAT/G CONSULT BAL/PWR
DELIB/GP TOP/EX ACT/RES PLAN DIPLOM EDU/PROP
ROUTINE ATTIT ALL/VALS...INT/LAW TOT/POP UN 20.
PAGE 4 B0075

S61
BROWN M.,"THE DEMISE OF STATE DEPARTMENT PUBLIC EDU/PROP
OPINION POLLS: A STUDY IN LEGISLATIVE OVERSIGHT." NAT/G
PWR...POLICY PSY SAMP. PAGE 16 B0325 LEGIS
ADMIN

S61
NOVE A.,"THE SOVIET MODEL AND UNDERDEVELOPED ECO/UNDEV
COUNTRIES." COM FUT USSR WOR+45 CULTURE ECO/DEV PLAN
POL/PAR FOR/AID EDU/PROP ADMIN MORAL WEALTH
...POLICY RECORD HIST/WRIT 20. PAGE 79 B1593

S61
PADOVER S.K.,"PSYCHOLOGICAL WARFARE AND FOREIGN ROUTINE
POLICY." FUT UNIV USA+45 INTELL SOCIETY CREATE DIPLOM
EDU/PROP ADMIN WAR PEACE PERCEPT...POLICY
METH/CNCPT TESTS TIME/SEQ 20. PAGE 80 B1623

S61
RUDOLPH S.,"CONSENSUS AND CONFLICT IN INDIAN POL/PAR
POLITICS." S/ASIA WOR+45 NAT/G DELIB/GP DIPLOM PERCEPT
EDU/PROP ADMIN CONSEN PERSON ALL/VALS...OBS TREND INDIA
TOT/POP VAL/FREE 20. PAGE 92 B1854

S61
TOMASIC D.,"POLITICAL LEADERSHIP IN CONTEMPORARY SOCIETY
POLAND." COM EUR+WWI GERMANY NAT/G POL/PAR SECT ROUTINE
DELIB/GP PLAN ECO/TAC DOMIN EDU/PROP PWR MARXISM USSR
...MARXIST GEOG MGT CONCPT TIME/SEQ STERTYP 20. POLAND
PAGE 105 B2114

B62
ARGYRIS C.,INTERPERSONAL COMPETENCE AND EX/STRUC
ORGANIZATIONAL EFFECTIVENESS. CREATE PLAN PROB/SOLV ADMIN
EDU/PROP INGP/REL PERS/REL PRODUC...OBS INT SIMUL CONSULT
20. PAGE 6 B0131 EFFICIENCY

B62
BAILEY S.D.,THE SECRETARIAT OF THE UNITED NATIONS. INT/ORG
FUT WOR+45 DELIB/GP PLAN BAL/PWR DOMIN EDU/PROP EXEC
ADMIN PEACE ATTIT PWR...DECISION CONCPT TREND DIPLOM
CON/ANAL CHARTS UN VAL/FREE COLD/WAR 20. PAGE 8
B0162

B62
BOCK E.A.,CASE STUDIES IN AMERICAN GOVERNMENT. POLICY
USA+45 ECO/DEV CHIEF EDU/PROP CT/SYS RACE/REL LEGIS
ORD/FREE...JURID MGT PHIL/SCI PRESIDENT CASEBOOK. IDEA/COMP
PAGE 13 B0262 NAT/G

B62
CHERNICK J.,THE SELECTION OF TRAINEES UNDER MDTA. EDU/PROP

B61
USA+45 NAT/G LEGIS PERSON...CENSUS 20 CIVIL/SERV WORKER
MDTA. PAGE 20 B0418 ADMIN
DELIB/GP

B62
CHICAGO U CTR PROG GOVT ADMIN,EDUCATION FOR EDU/PROP
INNOVATIVE BEHAVIOR IN EXECUTIVES. UNIV ELITES CREATE
ADMIN EFFICIENCY DRIVE PERSON...MGT APT/TEST EXEC
PERS/TEST CHARTS LAB/EXP BIBLIOG 20. PAGE 21 B0420 STAT

B62
DODDS H.W.,THE ACADEMIC PRESIDENT "EDUCATOR OR ACADEM
CARETAKER? FINAN DELIB/GP EDU/PROP PARTIC ATTIT ADMIN
ROLE PWR...POLICY RECORD INT. PAGE 30 B0601 LEAD
CONTROL

B62
EATON J.W.,STONE WALLS NOT A PRISON MAKE: THE CRIMLGY
ANATOMY OF PLANNED ADMINISTRATIVE CHANGE. USA+45 ADMIN
PROVS EDU/PROP 20. PAGE 32 B0647 EXEC
POLICY

B62
FARBER W.O.,GOVERNMENT OF SOUTH DAKOTA. USA+45 PROVS
DIST/IND POL/PAR CHIEF EX/STRUC LEGIS ECO/TAC GIVE LOC/G
EDU/PROP CT/SYS PARTIC...T 20 SOUTH/DAK GOVERNOR. ADMIN
PAGE 35 B0704 CONSTN

B62
FOSS P.O.,REORGANIZATION AND REASSIGNMENT IN THE FORCES
CALIFORNIA HIGHWAY PATROL (PAMPHLET). USA+45 STRUCT ADMIN
WORKER EDU/PROP CONTROL COERCE INGP/REL ORD/FREE PROVS
PWR...DECISION 20 CALIFORNIA. PAGE 37 B0744 PLAN

B62
HADWEN J.G.,HOW UNITED NATIONS DECISIONS ARE MADE. INT/ORG
WOR+45 LAW EDU/PROP LEGIT ADMIN PWR...DECISION ROUTINE
SELF/OBS GEN/LAWS UN 20. PAGE 45 B0912

B62
INAYATULLAH,BUREAUCRACY AND DEVELOPMENT IN EX/STRUC
PAKISTAN. PAKISTAN ECO/UNDEV EDU/PROP CONFER ADMIN
...ANTHOL DICTIONARY 20 BUREAUCRCY. PAGE 53 B1078 NAT/G
LOC/G

B62
INTERNAT CONGRESS OF JURISTS,EXECUTIVE ACTION AND JURID
THE RULE OF RULE: REPORTION PROCEEDINGS OF INT'T EXEC
CONGRESS OF JURISTS.,RIO DE JANEIRO, BRAZIL. WOR+45 ORD/FREE
ACADEM CONSULT JUDGE EDU/PROP ADJUD CT/SYS INGP/REL CONTROL
PERSON DEPT/DEFEN. PAGE 54 B1094

B62
JEWELL M.E.,SENATORIAL POLITICS AND FOREIGN POLICY. USA+45
NAT/G POL/PAR CHIEF DELIB/GP TOP/EX FOR/AID LEGIS
EDU/PROP ROUTINE ATTIT PWR SKILL...MAJORIT DIPLOM
METH/CNCPT TIME/SEQ CONGRESS 20 PRESIDENT. PAGE 56
B1138

B62
LAWSON R.,INTERNATIONAL REGIONAL ORGANIZATIONS. INT/ORG
WOR+45 NAT/G VOL/ASSN CONSULT LEGIS EDU/PROP LEGIT DELIB/GP
ADMIN EXEC ROUTINE HEALTH PWR WEALTH...JURID EEC REGION
COLD/WAR 20 UN. PAGE 63 B1277

B62
MARTIN R.C.,GOVERNMENT AND THE SUBURBAN SCHOOL. SCHOOL
USA+45 FINAN EDU/PROP ADMIN HABITAT...TREND GP/COMP LOC/G
20. PAGE 70 B1414 EX/STRUC
ISOLAT

B62
MODELSKI G.,A THEORY OF FOREIGN POLICY. WOR+45 PLAN
WOR-45 NAT/G DELIB/GP EX/STRUC TOP/EX EDU/PROP PWR
LEGIT ROUTINE...POLICY CONCPT TOT/POP COLD/WAR 20. DIPLOM
PAGE 74 B1494

B62
MUKERJI S.N.,ADMINISTRATION OF EDUCATION IN INDIA. SCHOOL
ACADEM LOC/G PROVS ROUTINE...POLICY STAT CHARTS 20. ADMIN
PAGE 76 B1536 NAT/G
EDU/PROP

B62
MUNICIPAL MANPOWER COMMISSION,GOVERNMENTAL MANPOWER LOC/G
FOR TOMORROW'S CITIES: A REPORT. USA+45 DELIB/GP MUNIC
EX/STRUC PROB/SOLV TEC/DEV EDU/PROP ADMIN LEAD LABOR
HABITAT. PAGE 76 B1539 GOV/REL

B62
NEVINS A.,THE STATE UNIVERSITIES AND DEMOCRACY. ACADEM
AGRI FINAN SCHOOL ADMIN EXEC EFFICIENCY ATTIT. PROVS
PAGE 78 B1576 EDU/PROP
POLICY

B62
RUDOLPH F.,THE AMERICAN COLLEGE AND UNIVERSITY. ACADEM
CLIENT FINAN PUB/INST DELIB/GP EDU/PROP CONTROL INGP/REL
EXEC CONSEN ATTIT POLICY. PAGE 92 B1853 PWR
ADMIN

B62
SHAPIRO D.,A SELECT BIBLIOGRAPHY OF WORKS IN BIBLIOG
ENGLISH ON RUSSIAN HISTORY, 1801-1917. COM USSR DIPLOM
STRATA FORCES EDU/PROP ADMIN REV RACE/REL ATTIT COLONIAL
19/20. PAGE 96 B1932

B62
TAYLOR J.K.L.,ATTITUDES AND METHODS OF WORKER
COMMUNICATION AND CONSULTATION BETWEEN EMPLOYERS ADMIN
AND WORKERS AT INDIVIDUAL FIRM LEVEL. WOR+45 STRUCT ATTIT
INDUS LABOR CONFER TASK GP/REL EFFICIENCY...MGT EDU/PROP
BIBLIOG METH 20 OECD. PAGE 103 B2087

US LIBRARY OF CONGRESS,A LIST OF AMERICAN DOCTORAL
DISSERTATIONS ON AFRICA. SOCIETY SECT DIPLOM
EDU/PROP ADMIN...GEOG 19/20. PAGE 109 B2206

B62
BIBLIOG
AFR
ACADEM
CULTURE

WEDDING N.,ADVERTISING MANAGEMENT. USA+45 ECO/DEV
BUDGET CAP/ISM PRODUC PROFIT ATTIT...DECISION MGT
PSY 20. PAGE 114 B2308

B62
ECO/TAC
COM/IND
PLAN
EDU/PROP

WELLEQUET J.,LE CONGO BELGE ET LA WELTPOLITIK
(1894-1914. GERMANY DOMIN EDU/PROP WAR ATTIT
...BIBLIOG T CONGO/LEOP. PAGE 115 B2318

B62
ADMIN
DIPLOM
GP/REL
COLONIAL

MALINOWSKI W.R.,"CENTRALIZATION AND DE-
CENTRALIZATION IN THE UNITED NATIONS' ECONOMIC AND
SOCIAL ACTIVITIES." WOR+45 CONSTN ECO/UNDEV INT/ORG
VOL/ASSN DELIB/GP ECO/TAC EDU/PROP ADMIN RIGID/FLEX
...OBS CHARTS UNESCO UN EEC OAS OEEC 20. PAGE 69
B1385

L62
CREATE
GEN/LAWS

BUENO M.,"ASPECTOS SOCIOLOGICOS DE LA EDUCACION."
FUT UNIV INTELL R+D SERV/IND SCHOOL CONSULT
EX/STRUC ACT/RES PLAN...METH/CNCPT OBS 20. PAGE 17
B0341

S62
SOCIETY
EDU/PROP
PERSON

DAKIN R.E.,"VARIATIONS IN POWER STRUCTURES AND
ORGANIZING EFFICIENCY: A COMPARATIVE STUDY OF FOUR
AREAS." STRATA EDU/PROP ADMIN LEAD GP/REL GOV/COMP.
PAGE 26 B0524

S62
MUNIC
STRUCT
PWR

FESLER J.W.,"FRENCH FIELD ADMINISTRATION: THE
BEGINNINGS." CHRIST-17C CULTURE SOCIETY STRATA
NAT/G ECO/TAC DOMIN EDU/PROP LEGIT ADJUD COERCE
ATTIT ALL/VALS...TIME/SEQ CON/ANAL GEN/METH
VAL/FREE 13/15. PAGE 35 B0714

S62
EX/STRUC
FRANCE

HUDSON G.F.,"SOVIET FEARS OF THE WEST." COM USA+45
SOCIETY DELIB/GP EX/STRUC TOP/EX ACT/RES CREATE
DOMIN EDU/PROP LEGIT ADMIN ROUTINE DRIVE PERSON
RIGID/FLEX PWR...RECORD TIME/SEQ TOT/POP 20
STALIN/J. PAGE 52 B1057

S62
ATTIT
MYTH
GERMANY
USSR

IKLE F.C.,"POLITICAL NEGOTIATION AS A PROCESS OF
MODIFYING UTILITIES." WOR+45 FACE/GP LABOR NAT/G
FORCES ACT/RES EDU/PROP DETER PERCEPT ALL/VALS
...PSY NEW/IDEA HYPO/EXP GEN/METH 20. PAGE 53 B1076

S62
ROUTINE
DECISION
DIPLOM

IOVTCHOUK M.T.,"ON SOME THEORETICAL PRINCIPLES AND
METHODS OF SOCIOLOGICAL INVESTIGATIONS (IN
RUSSIAN)." FUT USA+45 STRATA R+D NAT/G POL/PAR
TOP/EX ACT/RES PLAN ECO/TAC EDU/PROP ROUTINE ATTIT
RIGID/FLEX MARXISM SOCISM...MARXIST METH/CNCPT OBS
TREND NAT/COMP GEN/LAWS 20. PAGE 54 B1102

S62
COM
ECO/DEV
CAP/ISM
USSR

OLLERENSHAW K.,"SHARING RESPONSIBLITY." UK DELIB/GP
EDU/PROP EFFICIENCY 20. PAGE 80 B1607

S62
REPRESENT
GP/REL
ADMIN
EX/STRUC

TRUMAN D.,"THE DOMESTIC POLITICS OF FOREIGN AID."
USA+45 WOR+45 NAT/G POL/PAR LEGIS DIPLOM ECO/TAC
EDU/PROP ADMIN CHOOSE ATTIT PWR CONGRESS 20
CONGRESS. PAGE 105 B2129

S62
ROUTINE
FOR/AID

TRUMAN D.B.,"THE GOVERNMENTAL PROCESS: POLITICAL
INTERESTS AND PUBLIC OPINION." POL/PAR ADJUD ADMIN
EXEC LEAD ROUTINE CHOOSE REPRESENT GOV/REL
RIGID/FLEX...POLICY BIBLIOG/A 20. PAGE 105 B2131

C62
LOBBY
EDU/PROP
GP/REL
LEGIS

BOISSIER P.,HISTORIE DU COMITE INTERNATIONAL DE LA
CROIX ROUGE. MOD/EUR WOR-45 CONSULT FORCES PLAN
DIPLOM EDU/PROP ADMIN MORAL ORD/FREE...SOC CONCPT
RECORD TIME/SEQ GEN/LAWS TOT/POP VAL/FREE 19/20.
PAGE 13 B0267

B63
INT/ORG
HEALTH
ARMS/CONT
WAR

BONINI C.P.,SIMULATION OF INFORMATION AND DECISION
SYSTEMS IN THE FIRM. MARKET BUDGET DOMIN EDU/PROP
ADMIN COST ATTIT HABITAT PERCEPT PWR...CONCPT
PROBABIL QUANT PREDICT HYPO/EXP BIBLIOG. PAGE 13
B0273

B63
INDUS
SIMUL
DECISION
MGT

BOWETT D.W.,THE LAW OF INTERNATIONAL INSTITUTIONS.
WOR+45 WOR-45 CONSTN DELIB/GP EX/STRUC JUDGE
EDU/PROP LEGIT CT/SYS EXEC ROUTINE RIGID/FLEX
ORD/FREE PWR...JURID CONCPT ORG/CHARTS GEN/METH
LEAGUE/NAT OAS OEEC 20 UN. PAGE 14 B0286

B63
INT/ORG
ADJUD
DIPLOM

CHOJNACKI S.,REGISTER ON CURRENT RESEARCH ON
ETHIOPIA AND THE HORN OF AFRICA. ETHIOPIA LAW
CULTURE AGRI SECT EDU/PROP ADMIN...GEOG HEAL LING
20. PAGE 21 B0426

B63
BIBLIOG
ACT/RES
INTELL
ACADEM

CONF ON FUTURE OF COMMONWEALTH,THE FUTURE OF THE

B63
DIPLOM

COMMONWEALTH. UK ECO/UNDEV AGRI EDU/PROP ADMIN
SOC/INTEG 20 COMMONWLTH. PAGE 23 B0460

RACE/REL
ORD/FREE
TEC/DEV

DE VRIES E.,SOCIAL ASPECTS OF ECONOMIC DEVELOPMENT
IN LATIN AMERICA. CULTURE SOCIETY STRATA FINAN
INDUS INT/ORG DELIB/GP ACT/RES ECO/TAC EDU/PROP
ADMIN ATTIT SUPEGO HEALTH KNOWL ORD/FREE...SOC STAT
TREND ANTHOL TOT/POP VAL/FREE. PAGE 28 B0562

B63
L/A+17C
ECO/UNDEV

DOUGLASS H.R.,MODERN ADMINISTRATION OF SECONDARY
SCHOOLS. CLIENT DELIB/GP WORKER REPRESENT INGP/REL
AUTHORIT...TREND BIBLIOG. PAGE 30 B0613

B63
EDU/PROP
ADMIN
SCHOOL
MGT

GRANT D.R.,STATE AND LOCAL GOVERNMENT IN AMERICA.
USA+45 FINAN LOC/G MUNIC EX/STRUC FORCES EDU/PROP
ADMIN CHOOSE FEDERAL ATTIT...JURID 20. PAGE 42
B0853

B63
PROVS
POL/PAR
LEGIS
CONSTN

HEUSSLER R.,YESTERDAY'S RULERS: THE MAKING OF THE
BRITISH COLONIAL SERVICE. AFR EUR+WWI UK STRATA
SECT DELIB/GP PLAN DOMIN EDU/PROP ATTIT PERCEPT
PERSON SUPEGO KNOWL ORD/FREE PWR...MGT SOC OBS INT
TIME/SEQ 20 CMN/WLTH. PAGE 49 B1000

B63
EX/STRUC
MORAL
ELITES

INTL INST ADMIN SCIENCES,EDUCATION IN PUBLIC
ADMINISTRATION: A SYMPOSIUM ON TEACHING METHODS AND
MATERIALS. WOR+45 SCHOOL CONSULT CREATE CONFER
SKILL...OBS TREND IDEA/COMP METH/COMP 20. PAGE 54
B1100

B63
EDU/PROP
METH
ADMIN
ACADEM

KAPP W.K.,HINDU CULTURE: ECONOMIC DEVELOPMENT AND
ECONOMIC PLANNING IN INDIA. INDIA S/ASIA CULTURE
ECO/TAC EDU/PROP ADMIN ALL/VALS...POLICY MGT
TIME/SEQ VAL/FREE 20. PAGE 58 B1171

B63
SECT
ECO/UNDEV

LEWIS J.W.,LEADERSHIP IN COMMUNIST CHINA. ASIA
INTELL ECO/UNDEV LOC/G MUNIC NAT/G PROVS ECO/TAC
EDU/PROP LEGIT ADMIN COERCE ATTIT ORD/FREE PWR
...INT TIME/SEQ CHARTS TOT/POP VAL/FREE. PAGE 65
B1304

B63
POL/PAR
DOMIN
ELITES

NORTH R.C.,CONTENT ANALYSIS: A HANDBOOK WITH
APPLICATIONS FOR THE STUDY OF INTERNATIONAL CRISIS.
ASIA COM EUR+WWI MOD/EUR INT/ORG TEC/DEV DOMIN
EDU/PROP ROUTINE COERCE PERCEPT RIGID/FLEX ALL/VALS
...QUANT TESTS CON/ANAL SIMUL GEN/LAWS VAL/FREE.
PAGE 79 B1591

B63
METH/CNCPT
COMPUT/IR
USSR

RUITENBEER H.M.,THE DILEMMA OF ORGANIZATIONAL
SOCIETY. CULTURE ECO/DEV MUNIC SECT TEC/DEV
EDU/PROP NAT/LISM ORD/FREE...NAT/COMP 20 RIESMAN/D
WHYTE/WF MERTON/R MEAD/MARG JASPERS/K. PAGE 92
B1855

B63
PERSON
ROLE
ADMIN
WORKER

THORELLI H.B.,INTOP: INTERNATIONAL OPERATIONS
SIMULATION: PLAYER'S MANUAL. BRAZIL FINAN OP/RES
ADMIN GP/REL INGP/REL PRODUC PERCEPT...DECISION MGT
EEC. PAGE 104 B2108

B63
GAME
INT/TRADE
EDU/PROP
LG/CO

TSOU T.,AMERICA'S FAILURE IN CHINA, 1941-1950.
USA+45 USA-45 NAT/G ACT/RES PLAN DOMIN EDU/PROP
ADMIN ROUTINE ATTIT PERSON ORD/FREE...DECISION
CONCPT MYTH TIME/SEQ TREND STERTYP 20. PAGE 105
B2132

B63
ASIA
PERCEPT
DIPLOM

TUCKER R.C.,THE SOVIET POLITICAL MIND. COM INTELL
NAT/G TOP/EX EDU/PROP ADMIN COERCE TOTALISM ATTIT
PWR MARXISM...PSY MYTH HYPO/EXP 20. PAGE 106 B2135

B63
STRUCT
RIGID/FLEX
ELITES
USSR

US HOUSE COM ON ED AND LABOR,ADMINISTRATION OF
AGING. USA+45 R+D EX/STRUC PLAN BUDGET PAY EDU/PROP
ROUTINE COST CONGRESS. PAGE 108 B2187

B63
AGE/O
ADMIN
DELIB/GP
GIVE

EMERSON R.,"POLITICAL MODERNIZATION." WOR+45
CULTURE ECO/UNDEV NAT/G FORCES ECO/TAC DOMIN
EDU/PROP LEGIT COERCE ALL/VALS...CONCPT TIME/SEQ
VAL/FREE 20. PAGE 33 B0672

L63
POL/PAR
ADMIN

SPITZ A.A.,"DEVELOPMENT ADMINISTRATION: AN
ANNOTATED BIBLIOGRAPHY." WOR+45 CULTURE SOCIETY
STRATA DELIB/GP EX/STRUC TOP/EX ACT/RES ECO/TAC
DOMIN EDU/PROP LEGIT COERCE ATTIT ALL/VALS...MGT
VAL/FREE. PAGE 99 B2009

L63
ADMIN
ECO/UNDEV

ARASTEH R.,"THE ROLE OF INTELLECTUALS IN
ADMINISTRATIVE DEVELOPMENT AND SOCIAL CHANGE IN
MODERN IRAN." ISLAM CULTURE NAT/G CONSULT ACT/RES
EDU/PROP EXEC ATTIT BIO/SOC PERCEPT SUPEGO ALL/VALS
...POLICY MGT PSY SOC CONCPT 20. PAGE 6 B0123

S63
INTELL
ADMIN
IRAN

BECHHOEFER B.G.,"UNITED NATIONS PROCEDURES IN CASE
OF VIOLATIONS OF DISARMAMENT AGREEMENTS." COM

S63
INT/ORG
DELIB/GP

USA+45 USSR LAW CONSTN NAT/G EX/STRUC FORCES LEGIS
BAL/PWR EDU/PROP CT/SYS ARMS/CONT ORD/FREE PWR
...POLICY STERTYP UN VAL/FREE 20. PAGE 10 B0204

S63
HARRIS R.L.,"A COMPARATIVE ANALYSIS OF THE   DELIB/GP
ADMINISTRATIVE SYSTEMS OF CANADA AND CEYLON."   EX/STRUC
S/ASIA CULTURE SOCIETY STRATA TOP/EX ACT/RES DOMIN CANADA
EDU/PROP LEGIT COERCE ATTIT SUPEGO ALL/VALS...MGT   CEYLON
CHARTS GEN/LAWS VAL/FREE 20. PAGE 47 B0955

S63
MASSART L.,"L'ORGANISATION DE LA RECHERCHE   R+D
SCIENTIFIQUE EN EUROPE." EUR+WWI WOR+45 ACT/RES   CREATE
PLAN TEC/DEV EDU/PROP EXEC KNOWL...METH/CNCPT EEC
20. PAGE 70 B1424

S63
NADLER E.B.,"SOME ECONOMIC DISADVANTAGES OF THE   ECO/DEV
ARMS RACE." USA+45 INDUS R+D FORCES PLAN TEC/DEV   MGT
ECO/TAC FOR/AID EDU/PROP PWR WEALTH...TREND   BAL/PAY
COLD/WAR 20. PAGE 77 B1552

S63
ROUGEMONT D.,"LES NOUVELLES CHANCES DE L'EUROPE."   ECO/UNDEV
EUR+WWI FUT ECO/DEV INT/ORG NAT/G ACT/RES PLAN   PERCEPT
TEC/DEV EDU/PROP ADMIN COLONIAL FEDERAL ATTIT PWR
SKILL...TREND 20. PAGE 91 B1835

S63
WINGFIELD C.J.,"POWER STRUCTURE AND DECISION-MAKING MUNIC
IN CITY PLANNING." EDU/PROP ADMIN LEAD PARTIC   PLAN
GP/REL ATTIT. PAGE 117 B2365   DECISION
                                                    PWR

N63
INTERNATIONAL CITY MGRS ASSN,POST-ENTRY TRAINING IN LOC/G
THE LOCAL PUBLIC SERVICE (PAMPHLET). SCHOOL PLAN   WORKER
PROB/SOLV TEC/DEV ADMIN EFFICIENCY SKILL...POLICY   EDU/PROP
AUD/VIS CHARTS BIBLIOG 20 CITY/MGT. PAGE 54 B1096   METH/COMP

B64
RECENT PUBLICATIONS ON GOVERNMENTAL PROBLEMS. FINAN BIBLIOG
INDUS ACADEM PLAN PROB/SOLV EDU/PROP ADJUD ADMIN   AUTOMAT
BIO/SOC...MGT SOC. PAGE 2 B0040   LEGIS
                                                    JURID

B64
APTER D.E.,IDEOLOGY AND DISCONTENT. FUT WOR+45   ACT/RES
CONSTN CULTURE INTELL SOCIETY STRUCT INT/ORG NAT/G ATTIT
DELIB/GP LEGIS CREATE PLAN TEC/DEV EDU/PROP EXEC
PERCEPT PERSON RIGID/FLEX ALL/VALS...POLICY
TOT/POP. PAGE 6 B0122

B64
BLACKSTOCK P.W.,THE STRATEGY OF SUBVERSION. USA+45 ORD/FREE
FORCES EDU/PROP ADMIN COERCE GOV/REL...DECISION MGT DIPLOM
20 DEPT/DEFEN CIA DEPT/STATE. PAGE 12 B0247   CONTROL

B64
ELDREDGE H.W.,THE SECOND AMERICAN REVOLUTION.   ELITES
EDU/PROP NAT/LISM RATIONAL TOTALISM FASCISM MARXISM ORD/FREE
SOCISM. PAGE 33 B0664   ADMIN
                                                    PLAN

B64
GOODMAN W.,THE TWO-PARTY SYSTEM IN THE UNITED   POL/PAR
STATES. USA+45 USA-45 STRATA LOC/G CHIEF EDU/PROP   REPRESENT
ADMIN COST PWR POPULISM...PLURIST 18/20 PRESIDENT. CHOOSE
PAGE 41 B0821   NAT/G

B64
GROSS B.M.,THE MANAGING OF ORGANIZATIONS (VOL. II). ECO/TAC
FUT USA+45 ECO/DEV EDU/PROP EFFICIENCY...MGT   ADMIN
BIBLIOG/A 20. PAGE 44 B0887   INDUS
                                                    POLICY

B64
HAMBRIDGE G.,DYNAMICS OF DEVELOPMENT. AGRI FINAN   ECO/UNDEV
INDUS LABOR INT/TRADE EDU/PROP ADMIN LEAD OWN   ECO/TAC
HEALTH...ANTHOL BIBLIOG 20. PAGE 46 B0930   OP/RES
                                                    ACT/RES

B64
JACKSON H.M.,THE SECRETARY OF STATE AND THE   GOV/REL
AMBASSADOR* JACKSON SUBCOMMITTEE PAPERS ON THE   DIPLOM
CONDUCT OF AMERICAN FOREIGN POLICY. USA+45 NAT/G   ADMIN
FORCES ACT/RES OP/RES EDU/PROP CENTRAL EFFICIENCY   EX/STRUC
ORD/FREE...OBS RECORD ANTHOL CONGRESS PRESIDENT.
PAGE 55 B1107

B64
JACKSON R.M.,THE MACHINERY OF JUSTICE IN ENGLAND.   CT/SYS
UK EDU/PROP CONTROL COST ORD/FREE...MGT 20   ADJUD
ENGLSH/LAW. PAGE 55 B1109   JUDGE
                                                    JURID

B64
KIMBROUGH R.B.,POLITICAL POWER AND EDUCATIONAL   EDU/PROP
DECISION-MAKING. USA+45 FINAN ADMIN LEAD GP/REL   PROB/SOLV
ATTIT PWR PROG/TEAC. PAGE 60 B1207   DECISION
                                                    SCHOOL

B64
NEUSTADT R.,PRESIDENTIAL POWER. USA+45 CONSTN NAT/G TOP/EX
CHIEF LEGIS CREATE EDU/PROP LEGIT ADMIN EXEC COERCE SKILL
ATTIT PERSON RIGID/FLEX PWR CONGRESS 20 PRESIDENT
TRUMAN/HS EISNHWR/DD. PAGE 78 B1575

B64
PIERCE T.M.,FEDERAL, STATE, AND LOCAL GOVERNMENT IN NAT/G
EDUCATION. FINAN LOC/G PROVS LEGIS PLAN EDU/PROP   POLICY
ADMIN CONTROL CENTRAL COST KNOWL 20. PAGE 83 B1673 SCHOOL
                                                    GOV/REL

B64
RAPHAEL M.,PENSIONS AND PUBLIC SERVANTS. UK PLAN   ADMIN
EDU/PROP PARTIC GOV/REL HEALTH...POLICY CHARTS   SENIOR
17/20 CIVIL/SERV. PAGE 86 B1737   PAY
                                                    AGE/O

B64
RAYMOND J.,POWER AT THE PENTAGON (1ST ED.). ELITES PWR
NAT/G PLAN EDU/PROP ARMS/CONT DETER WAR WEAPON   CIVMIL/REL
...TIME/SEQ 20 PENTAGON MCNAMARA/R. PAGE 86 B1746   EX/STRUC
                                                    FORCES

B64
RIGGS F.W.,ADMINISTRATION IN DEVELOPING COUNTRIES. ECO/UNDEV
FUT WOR+45 STRUCT AGRI INDUS NAT/G PLAN TEC/DEV   ADMIN
ECO/TAC EDU/PROP RIGID/FLEX KNOWL WEALTH...POLICY
MGT CONCPT METH/CNCPT TREND 20. PAGE 88 B1785

B64
SCHERMER G.,MEETING SOCIAL NEEDS IN THE PENJERDEL   PLAN
REGION. SOCIETY FINAN ACT/RES EDU/PROP ADMIN   REGION
GOV/REL...SOC/WK 45 20 PENNSYLVAN DELAWARE   HEALTH
NEW/JERSEY. PAGE 93 B1887   WEALTH

B64
SULLIVAN G.,THE STORY OF THE PEACE CORPS. USA+45   INT/ORG
WOR+45 INTELL FACE/GP NAT/G SCHOOL VOL/ASSN CONSULT ECO/UNDEV
EX/STRUC PLAN EDU/PROP ADMIN ATTIT DRIVE ALL/VALS   FOR/AID
...POLICY HEAL SOC CONCPT INT QU BIOG TREND SOC/EXP PEACE
WORK. PAGE 102 B2054

B64
UN PUB. INFORM. ORGAN.,EVERY MAN'S UNITED NATIONS. INT/ORG
UNIV WOR+45 CONSTN CULTURE SOCIETY ECO/DEV   ROUTINE
ECO/UNDEV NAT/G ACT/RES PLAN ECO/TAC INT/TRADE
EDU/PROP LEGIT PEACE ATTIT ALL/VALS...POLICY HUM
INT/LAW CONCPT CHARTS UN TOT/POP 20. PAGE 106 B2150

B64
WRAITH R.,CORRUPTION IN DEVELOPING COUNTRIES.   ECO/UNDEV
NIGERIA UK LAW ELITES STRATA INDUS LOC/G NAT/G SECT CRIME
FORCES EDU/PROP ADMIN PWR WEALTH 18/20. PAGE 118   SANCTION
B2377   ATTIT

L64
MACKINTOSH J.P.,"NIGERIA'S EXTERNAL AFFAIRS." UK   AFR
CULTURE ECO/UNDEV NAT/G VOL/ASSN EDU/PROP LEGIT   DIPLOM
ADMIN ATTIT ORD/FREE PWR 20. PAGE 68 B1365   NIGERIA

L64
SYMONDS R.,"REFLECTIONS IN LOCALISATION." AFR   ADMIN
S/ASIA UK STRATA INT/ORG NAT/G SCHOOL EDU/PROP   MGT
LEGIT KNOWL ORD/FREE PWR RESPECT CMN/WLTH 20.   COLONIAL
PAGE 102 B2064

L64
WORLD PEACE FOUNDATION,"INTERNATIONAL   INT/ORG
ORGANIZATIONS: SUMMARY OF ACTIVITIES." INDIA   ROUTINE
PAKISTAN TURKEY WOR+45 CONSTN CONSULT EX/STRUC
ECO/TAC EDU/PROP LEGIT ORD/FREE...JURID SOC UN 20
CYPRESS. PAGE 118 B2375

S64
HOSCH L.G.,"PUBLIC ADMINISTRATION ON THE   INT/ORG
INTERNATIONAL FRONTIER." WOR+45 R+D NAT/G EDU/PROP MGT
EXEC KNOWL ORD/FREE VAL/FREE 20 UN. PAGE 52 B1046

S64
JOHNSON K.F.,"CAUSAL FACTORS IN LATIN AMERICAN   L/A+17C
POLITICAL INSTABILITY." CULTURE NAT/G VOL/ASSN   PERCEPT
EX/STRUC FORCES EDU/PROP LEGIT ADMIN COERCE REV   ELITES
ATTIT KNOWL PWR...STYLE RECORD CHARTS WORK 20.
PAGE 57 B1144

S64
KASSOF A.,"THE ADMINISTERED SOCIETY: SOCIETY
TOTALITARIANISM WITHOUT TERROR." COM USSR STRATA   DOMIN
AGRI INDUS NAT/G PERF/ART SCHOOL TOP/EX EDU/PROP   TOTALISM
ADMIN ORD/FREE PWR...POLICY SOC TIME/SEQ GEN/LAWS
VAL/FREE 20. PAGE 58 B1178

S64
KENNAN G.F.,"POLYCENTRISM AND WESTERN POLICY." ASIA RIGID/FLEX
CHINA/COM COM FUT USA+45 USSR NAT/G ACT/RES DOMIN   ATTIT
EDU/PROP EXEC COERCE DISPL PERCEPT...POLICY   DIPLOM
COLD/WAR 20. PAGE 59 B1192

S64
KHAN M.Z.,"THE PRESIDENT OF THE GENERAL ASSEMBLY." INT/ORG
WOR+45 CONSTN DELIB/GP EDU/PROP LEGIT ROUTINE PWR   TOP/EX
RESPECT SKILL...DECISION SOC BIOG TREND UN 20.
PAGE 59 B1202

S64
MOWER A.G.,"THE OFFICIAL PRESSURE GROUP OF THE   INT/ORG
COUNCIL OF EUROPE'S CONSULATIVE ASSEMBLY." EUR+WWI EDU/PROP
SOCIETY STRUCT FINAN CONSULT ECO/TAC ADMIN ROUTINE
ATTIT PWR WEALTH...STAT CHARTS 20 COUNCL/EUR.
PAGE 76 B1535

S64
MURRAY D.,"CHINESE EDUCATION IN SOUTH-EAST ASIA."   S/ASIA
SOCIETY NEIGH EDU/PROP ROUTINE PERSON KNOWL   SCHOOL
...OBS/ENVIR STERTYP. PAGE 76 B1546   REGION
                                                    ASIA

S64
NASH M.,"SOCIAL PREREQUISITES TO ECONOMIC GROWTH IN ECO/DEV
LATIN AMERICA AND SOUTHEAST ASIA." L/A+17C S/ASIA   PERCEPT
CULTURE SOCIETY ECO/UNDEV AGRI INDUS NAT/G PLAN
TEC/DEV EDU/PROP ROUTINE ALL/VALS...POLICY RELATIV
SOC NAT/COMP WORK TOT/POP 20. PAGE 77 B1558

NEEDHAM T.,"SCIENCE AND SOCIETY IN EAST AND WEST." ASIA
INTELL STRATA R+D LOC/G NAT/G PROVS CONSULT ACT/RES STRUCT
CREATE PLAN TEC/DEV EDU/PROP ADMIN ATTIT ALL/VALS
...POLICY RELATIV MGT CONCPT NEW/IDEA TIME/SEQ WORK
WORK. PAGE 77 B1565
S64

PARSONS T.,"EVOLUTIONARY UNIVERSALS IN SOCIETY." SOC
UNIV SOCIETY STRATA MARKET EDU/PROP LEGIT ADJUD CONCPT
ADMIN ALL/VALS...JURID OBS GEN/LAWS VAL/FREE 20.
PAGE 81 B1638
S64

SCHWELB E.,"OPERATION OF THE EUROPEAN CONVENTION ON INT/ORG
HUMAN RIGHTS." EUR+WWI LAW SOCIETY CREATE EDU/PROP MORAL
ADJUD ADMIN PEACE ATTIT ORD/FREE PWR...POLICY
INT/LAW CONCPT OBS GEN/LAWS UN VAL/FREE ILO 20.
ECHR. PAGE 95 B1916
S64

THOMPSON V.A.,"ADMINISTRATIVE OBJECTIVES FOR ECO/UNDEV
DEVELOPMENT ADMINISTRATION." WOR+45 CREATE PLAN MGT
DOMIN EDU/PROP EXEC ROUTINE ATTIT ORD/FREE PWR
...POLICY GEN/LAWS VAL/FREE. PAGE 104 B2107
N64

US SENATE COMM GOVT OPERATIONS.METROPOLITAN BIBLIOG/A
AMERICA: A SELECTED BIBLIOGRAPHY (PAMPHLET). USA+45 MUNIC
DIST/IND FINAN LOC/G EDU/PROP ADMIN HEALTH 20. GOV/REL
PAGE 110 B2214 DECISION
B65

ALDERSON W.,DYNAMIC MARKETING BEHAVIOR. USA+45 MGT
FINAN CREATE TEC/DEV EDU/PROP PRICE COST 20. PAGE 3 MARKET
B0071 ATTIT
CAP/ISM
B65

CRAMER J.F.,CONTEMPORARY EDUCATION: A COMPARATIVE EDU/PROP
STUDY OF NATIONAL SYSTEMS (2ND ED.). CHINA/COM NAT/COMP
EUR+WWI INDIA USA+45 FINAN PROB/SOLV ADMIN CONTROL SCHOOL
ATTIT...IDEA/COMP METH/COMP 20 CHINJAP. PAGE 25 ACADEM
B0502
B65

DAVISON W.P.,INTERNATIONAL POLITICAL COMMUNICATION. EDU/PROP
COM USA+45 WOR+45 CULTURE ECO/UNDEV NAT/G PROB/SOLV DIPLOM
PRESS TV ADMIN 20 FILM. PAGE 27 B0545 PERS/REL
COM/IND
B65

ELDER R.E.,OVERSEAS REPRESENTATION AND SERVICES FOR OP/RES
FEDERAL DOMESTIC AGENCIES. USA+45 NAT/G ACT/RES DIPLOM
FOR/AID EDU/PROP SENIOR ROUTINE TASK ADJUST...MGT GOV/REL
ORG/CHARTS. PAGE 33 B0663 ADMIN
B65

EVERETT R.O.,URBAN PROBLEMS AND PROSPECTS. USA+45 MUNIC
CREATE TEC/DEV EDU/PROP ADJUD ADMIN GOV/REL ATTIT PLAN
...ANTHOL 20 URBAN/RNWL. PAGE 34 B0691 PROB/SOLV
NEIGH
B65

FISCHER F.C.,THE GOVERNMENT OF MICHIGAN. USA+45 PROVS
NAT/G PUB/INST EX/STRUC LEGIS BUDGET GIVE EDU/PROP LOC/G
CT/SYS CHOOSE GOV/REL...T MICHIGAN. PAGE 36 B0723 ADMIN
CONSTN
B65

GOULDNER A.W.,STUDIES IN LEADERSHIP. LABOR EDU/PROP LEAD
CONTROL PARTIC...CONCPT CLASSIF. PAGE 42 B0845 ADMIN
AUTHORIT
B65

HOWE R.,THE STORY OF SCOTLAND YARD: A HISTORY OF CRIMLGY
THE CID FROM THE EARLIEST TIMES TO THE PRESENT DAY. CRIME
UK MUNIC EDU/PROP 6/20 SCOT/YARD. PAGE 52 B1051 FORCES
ADMIN
B65

HUGHES J.M.,EDUCATION IN AMERICA (2ND ED.). USA+45 EDU/PROP
USA-45 GP/REL INGP/REL AGE/C AGE/Y ROLE...IDEA/COMP SCHOOL
BIBLIOG T 20. PAGE 52 B1059 ADMIN
METH/COMP
B65

KOUSOULAS D.G.,REVOLUTION AND DEFEAT; THE STORY OF REV
THE GREEK COMMUNIST PARTY. GREECE INT/ORG EX/STRUC MARXISM
DIPLOM FOR/AID EDU/PROP PARL/PROC ADJUST ATTIT 20 POL/PAR
COM/PARTY. PAGE 61 B1230 ORD/FREE
B65

KRIESBERG M.,PUBLIC ADMINISTRATION IN DEVELOPING NAT/G
COUNTRIES: PROCEEDINGS OF AN INTERNATIONAL ECO/UNDEV
CONFERENCE HELD IN BOGOTA, COLUMBIA,1963. FUT SOCIETY
EDU/PROP ORD/FREE...MGT 20 CIVIL/SERV. PAGE 61 ADMIN
B1237
B65

LIPSET S.M.,THE BERKELEY STUDENT REVOLT: FACTS AND CROWD
INTERPRETATIONS. USA+45 INTELL VOL/ASSN CONSULT ACADEM
EDU/PROP PRESS DEBATE ADMIN REV HAPPINESS ATTIT
RIGID/FLEX MAJORIT. PAGE 65 B1322 GP/REL
B65

MATRAS J.,SOCIAL CHANGE IN ISRAEL. ISRAEL STRATA SECT
FAM ACT/RES EDU/PROP ADMIN CHOOSE...STAT CENSUS NAT/LISM
19/20 JEWS. PAGE 71 B1427 GEOG
STRUCT
B65

MELMANS S.,OUR DEPLETED SOCIETY. SPACE USA+45 CIVMIL/REL
ECO/DEV FORCES BUDGET ECO/TAC ADMIN WEAPON INDUS

EFFICIENCY 20 COLD/WAR. PAGE 73 B1465 EDU/PROP
CONTROL
B65

MEYERHOFF A.E.,THE STRATEGY OF PERSUASION. USA+45 EDU/PROP
COM/IND CONSULT FOR/AID CONTROL COERCE COST ATTIT EFFICIENCY
PERCEPT MARXISM 20 COLD/WAR. PAGE 73 B1476 OP/RES
ADMIN
B65

OECD.MEDITERRANEAN REGIONAL PROJECT: TURKEY; EDU/PROP
EDUCATION AND DEVELOPMENT. FUT TURKEY SOCIETY ACADEM
STRATA FINAN NAT/G PROF/ORG PLAN PROB/SOLV ADMIN SCHOOL
COST...STAT CHARTS 20 OECD. PAGE 79 B1602 ECO/UNDEV
B65

ORG FOR ECO COOP AND DEVEL,THE MEDITERRANEAN PLAN
REGIONAL PROJECT: AN EXPERIMENT IN PLANNING BY SIX ECO/UNDEV
COUNTRIES. FUT GREECE SPAIN TURKEY YUGOSLAVIA ACADEM
SOCIETY FINAN NAT/G PROF/ORG EDU/PROP ADMIN REGION SCHOOL
COST...POLICY STAT CHARTS 20 OECD. PAGE 80 B1614
B65

ORG FOR ECO COOP AND DEVEL,THE MEDITERRANEAN EDU/PROP
REGIONAL PROJECT: YUGOSLAVIA; EDUCATION AND ACADEM
DEVELOPMENT. YUGOSLAVIA SOCIETY FINAN PROF/ORG PLAN SCHOOL
ADMIN COST DEMAND MARXISM...STAT TREND CHARTS METH ECO/UNDEV
20 OECD. PAGE 80 B1615
B65

PARRISH W.E.,MISSOURI UNDER RADICAL RULE 1865-1870. PROVS
USA-45 SOCIETY INDUS LOC/G POL/PAR WORKER EDU/PROP ADMIN
SUFF INGP/REL ATTIT...BIBLIOG 19 NEGRO MISSOURI. RACE/REL
PAGE 81 B1635 ORD/FREE
B65

PERLOFF H.S.,URBAN RESEARCH AND EDUCATION IN THE MUNIC
NEW YORK METROPOLITAN REGION (VOL. II). FUT USA+45 PLAN
NEIGH PROF/ORG ACT/RES PROB/SOLV EDU/PROP ADMIN ACADEM
...STAT BIBLIOG 20 NEWYORK/C. PAGE 82 B1659 GP/REL
B65

PHELPS-FETHERS I.,SOVIET INTERNATIONAL FRONT USSR
ORGANIZATIONS* A CONCISE HANDBOOK. DIPLOM DOMIN EDU/PROP
LEGIT ADMIN EXEC GP/REL PEACE MARXISM...TIME/SEQ ASIA
GP/COMP. PAGE 83 B1668 COM
B65

PURCELL V.,THE MEMOIRS OF A MALAYAN OFFICIAL. BIOG
MALAYSIA UK ECO/UNDEV INDUS LABOR EDU/PROP COLONIAL ADMIN
CT/SYS WAR NAT/LISM TOTALISM ORD/FREE SOVEREIGN 20 JURID
UN CIVIL/SERV. PAGE 85 B1721 FORCES
B65

PUSTAY J.S.,COUNTER-INSURGENCY WARFARE. COM USA+45 FORCES
LOC/G NAT/G ACT/RES EDU/PROP ADMIN COERCE ATTIT PWR
...CONCPT MARX/KARL 20. PAGE 85 B1722 GUERRILLA
B65

SCOTT A.M.,THE REVOLUTION IN STATECRAFT: INFORMAL DIPLOM
PENETRATION. WOR+45 WOR-45 CULTURE INT/ORG FORCES EDU/PROP
ECO/TAC ROUTINE...BIBLIOG 20. PAGE 95 B1918 FOR/AID
B65

SINGER J.D.,HUMAN BEHAVIOR AND INTERNATINAL DIPLOM
POLITICS* CONTRIBUTIONS FROM THE SOCIAL- PHIL/SCI
PSYCHOLOGICAL SCIENCES. ACT/RES PLAN EDU/PROP ADMIN QUANT
KNOWL...DECISION PSY SOC NET/THEORY HYPO/EXP SIMUL
LAB/EXP SOC/EXP GEN/METH ANTHOL BIBLIOG. PAGE 97
B1965
B65

STARR M.K.,EXECUTIVE READINGS IN MANAGEMENT MGT
SCIENCE. TOP/EX WORKER EDU/PROP ADMIN...DECISION EX/STRUC
GEN/LAWS ANTHOL METH T 20. PAGE 100 B2023 PLAN
LG/CO
B65

US SENATE COMM ON JUDICIARY,HEARINGS BEFORE ROUTINE
SUBCOMMITTEE ON ADMINISTRATIVE PRACTICE AND DELIB/GP
PROCEDURE ABOUT ADMINISTRATIVE PROCEDURE ACT 1965. ADMIN
USA+45 LEGIS EDU/PROP ADJUD GOV/REL INGP/REL NAT/G
EFFICIENCY...POLICY INT 20 CONGRESS. PAGE 110 B2232
L65

SHARKANSKY I.,"FOUR AGENCIES AND AN APPROPRIATIONS ADMIN
SUBCOMMITTEE: A COMPARATIVE STUDY OF BDUGET EDU/PROP
STRATEGIES." USA+45 EX/STRUC TOP/EX PROB/SOLV NAT/G
CONTROL ROUTINE CONGRESS. PAGE 96 B1934 LFGIS
S65

"FURTHER READING." INDIA NAT/G ADMIN 20. PAGE 2 BIBLIOG
B0043 EDU/PROP
SCHOOL
ACADEM
S65

HOLSTI O.R.,"THE 1914 CASE." MOD/EUR COMPUTER CON/ANAL
DIPLOM EDU/PROP MARX...DECISION PSY PROBABIL STAT PERCEPT
COMPUT/IR SOC/EXP TIME. PAGE 51 B1036 WAR
S65

OSTGAARD E.,"FACTORS INFLUENCING THE FLOW OF NEWS." EDU/PROP
COM/IND BUDGET DIPLOM EXEC GP/REL COST ATTIT SAMP. PERCEPT
PAGE 80 B1618 RECORD
S65

POLK W.R.,"PROBLEMS OF GOVERNMENT UTILIZATION OF ACT/RES
SCHOLARLY RESEARCH IN INTERNATIONAL AFFAIRS." FINAN ACADEM
NAT/G EDU/PROP CONTROL TASK GP/REL ATTIT PERCEPT PLAN
KNOWL...POLICY TIME. PAGE 83 B1685 ADMIN
S65

THOMAS F.C. JR.,"THE PEACE CORPS IN MOROCCO." MOROCCO
CULTURE MUNIC PROVS CREATE ROUTINE TASK ADJUST FRANCE

STRANGE...OBS PEACE/CORP. PAGE 104 B2099 — FOR/AID EDU/PROP

B66
ANDERSON D.L.,MUNICIPAL PUBLIC RELATIONS (1ST ED.). USA+45 SOCIETY CONSULT FORCES PRESS ADMIN...CHARTS BIBLIOG/A 20. PAGE 4 B0092 — MUNIC INGP/REL EDU/PROP ATTIT

B66
DAHLBERG J.S.,THE NEW YORK BUREAU OF MUNICIPAL RESEARCH: PIONEER IN GOVERNMENT ADMINISTRATION. CONSTN R+D BUDGET EDU/PROP PARTIC REPRESENT EFFICIENCY ORD/FREE...BIBLIOG METH 20 NEW/YORK NIPA. PAGE 26 B0522 — PROVS MUNIC DELIB/GP ADMIN

B66
DAVIS J.A.,SOUTHERN AFRICA IN TRANSITION. SOUTH/AFR USA+45 FINAN NAT/G DELIB/GP EDU/PROP ADMIN COLONIAL REGION RACE/REL ATTIT SOVEREIGN...ANTHOL 20 RESOURCE/N. PAGE 26 B0538 — AFR ADJUST CONSTN

B66
DAVIS R.G.,PLANNING HUMAN RESOURCE DEVELOPMENT, EDUCATIONAL MODELS AND SCHEMATA. WORKER OP/RES ECO/TAC EDU/PROP CONTROL COST PRODUC...GEOG STAT CHARTS 20. PAGE 27 B0544 — PLAN EFFICIENCY SIMUL ROUTINE

B66
FINK M.,A SELECTIVE BIBLIOGRAPHY ON STATE CONSTITUTIONAL REVISION (PAMPHLET). USA+45 FINAN EX/STRUC LEGIS EDU/PROP ADMIN CT/SYS APPORT CHOOSE GOV/REL 20. PAGE 35 B0720 — BIBLIOG PROVS LOC/G CONSTN

B66
HALPIN A.W.,THEORY AND RESEARCH IN ADMINISTRATION. ACT/RES LEAD...MGT IDEA/COMP METH/COMP. PAGE 46 B0929 — GEN/LAWS EDU/PROP ADMIN PHIL/SCI

B66
HAWLEY C.E.,ADMINISTRATIVE QUESTIONS AND POLITICAL ANSWERS. USA+45 STRUCT WORKER EDU/PROP...GP/COMP ANTHOL 20. PAGE 48 B0973 — ADMIN GEN/LAWS GP/REL

B66
MACFARQUHAR R.,CHINA UNDER MAO: POLITICS TAKES COMMAND. CHINA/COM COM AGRI INDUS CHIEF FORCES DIPLOM INT/TRADE EDU/PROP TASK REV ADJUST...ANTHOL 20 MAO. PAGE 67 B1359 — ECO/UNDEV TEC/DEV ECO/TAC ADMIN

B66
NYC TEMPORARY COMM CITY FINAN,MUNICIPAL COLLECTIVE BARGAINING (NO. 8). USA+45 PLAN PROB/SOLV BARGAIN BUDGET TAX EDU/PROP GOV/REL COST...MGT 20 NEWYORK/C. PAGE 79 B1596 — MUNIC FINAN ADMIN LOC/G

B66
RAEFF M.,ORIGINS OF THE RUSSIAN INTELLIGENTSIA: THE EIGHTEENTH-CENTURY NOBILITY. RUSSIA FAM NAT/G EDU/PROP ADMIN PERS/REL ATTIT...HUM BIOG 18. PAGE 85 B1728 — INTELL ELITES STRATA CONSERVE

B66
ROSS R.M.,STATE AND LOCAL GOVERNMENT AND ADMINISTRATION. USA+45 CONSTN POL/PAR EX/STRUC LEGIS BUDGET EDU/PROP CONTROL CT/SYS CHOOSE GOV/REL T. PAGE 90 B1827 — LOC/G PROVS MUNIC ADMIN

B66
SCHMIDT F.,PUBLIC RELATIONS IN HEALTH AND WELFARE. USA+45 ACADEM RECEIVE PRESS FEEDBACK GOV/REL PERS/REL DEMAND EFFICIENCY ATTIT PERCEPT WEALTH 20 PUBLIC/REL. PAGE 94 B1895 — PROF/ORG EDU/PROP ADMIN HEALTH

B66
UN ECAFE,ADMINISTRATIVE ASPECTS OF FAMILY PLANNING PROGRAMMES (PAMPHLET). ASIA THAILAND WOR+45 VOL/ASSN PROB/SOLV BUDGET FOR/AID EDU/PROP CONFER CONTROL GOV/REL TIME 20 UN BIRTH/CON. PAGE 106 B2147 — PLAN CENSUS FAM ADMIN

B66
US SENATE COMM GOVT OPERATIONS,INTERGOVERNMENTAL PERSONNEL ACT OF 1966. USA+45 NAT/G CONSULT DELIB/GP WORKER TEC/DEV PAY AUTOMAT UTIL 20 CONGRESS. PAGE 110 B2219 — ADMIN LEGIS EFFICIENCY EDU/PROP

B66
VON HOFFMAN N.,THE MULTIVERSITY; A PERSONAL REPORT ON WHAT HAPPENS TO TODAY'S STUDENTS AT AMERICAN UNIVERSITIES. USA+45 SOCIETY ROUTINE ANOMIE ROLE MORAL ORD/FREE SKILL...INT 20. PAGE 112 B2266 — EDU/PROP ACADEM ATTIT STRANGE

L66
CRAIN R.L.,"STRUCTURE AND VALUES IN LOCAL POLITICAL SYSTEMS: THE CASE OF FLUORIDATION DECISIONS." EX/STRUC LEGIS LEAD PARTIC REPRESENT PWR...DECISION GOV/COMP. PAGE 25 B0501 — MUNIC EDU/PROP LOC/G ATTIT

S66
AUSLAND J.C.,"CRISIS MANAGEMENT* BERLIN, CYPRUS, LAOS." CYPRUS LAOS FORCES CREATE PLAN EDU/PROP TASK CENTRAL PERSON RIGID/FLEX...DECISION MGT 20 BERLIN KENNEDY/JF MCNAMARA/R RUSK. PAGE 7 B0148 — OP/RES DIPLOM RISK ADMIN

N66
AMERICAN SOCIETY PUBLIC ADMIN,PUBLIC ADMINISTRATION AND THE WAR ON POVERTY (PAMPHLET). USA+45 SOCIETY ECO/DEV FINAN LOC/G LEGIS CREATE EDU/PROP CONFER GOV/REL GP/REL ROLE 20 POVRTY/WAR. PAGE 4 B0089 — WEALTH NAT/G PLAN ADMIN

B67
BALDWIN G.B.,PLANNING AND DEVELOPMENT IN IRAN. IRAN AGRI INDUS CONSULT WORKER EDU/PROP BAL/PAY...CHARTS — PLAN ECO/UNDEV

20. PAGE 8 B0173 — ADMIN PROB/SOLV

B67
DE BLIJ H.J.,SYSTEMATIC POLITICAL GEOGRAPHY. WOR+45 STRUCT INT/ORG NAT/G EDU/PROP ADMIN COLONIAL ROUTINE ORD/FREE PWR...IDEA/COMP T 20. PAGE 27 B0550 — GEOG CONCPT METH

B67
GREENE L.S.,AMERICAN GOVERNMENT POLICIES AND FUNCTIONS. USA+45 LAW AGRI DIST/IND LABOR MUNIC BUDGET DIPLOM EDU/PROP ORD/FREE...BIBLIOG T 20. PAGE 43 B0867 — POLICY NAT/G ADMIN DECISION

B67
EDUCATION, INTERACTION, AND SOCIAL CHANGE. STRATA MUNIC SCHOOL ADMIN RIGID/FLEX ROLE 20. PAGE 49 B0991 — EDU/PROP ADJUST SOC ACT/RES

B67
IANNACCONE L.,POLITICS IN EDUCATION. USA+45 LOC/G PROF/ORG BAL/PWR ADMIN...CHARTS SIMUL. PAGE 53 B1072 — EDU/PROP GEN/LAWS PROVS

B67
ILLINOIS COMMISSION,IMPROVING THE STATE LEGISLATURE. USA+45 LAW CONSTN NAT/G PROB/SOLV EDU/PROP ADMIN TASK CHOOSE INGP/REL EFFICIENCY ILLINOIS. PAGE 53 B1077 — PROVS LEGIS REPRESENT PLAN

B67
JAKUBAUSKAS E.B.,HUMAN RESOURCES DEVELOPMENT. USA+45 AGRI INDUS SERV/IND ACT/RES PLAN ADMIN RACE/REL DISCRIM...TREND GEN/LAWS. PAGE 55 B1119 — PROB/SOLV ECO/TAC EDU/PROP WORKER

B67
PAULSEN F.R.,AMERICAN EDUCATION: CHALLENGES AND IMAGES. FUT USA+45 ADMIN AGE/C AGE/Y SUPEGO HEALTH ...ANTHOL 20. PAGE 81 B1644 — EDU/PROP SCHOOL ORD/FREE GOV/REL

B67
PRINCE C.E.,NEW JERSEY'S JEFFERSONIAN REPUBLICANS; THE GENESIS OF AN EARLY PARTY MACHINE (1789-1817). USA-45 LOC/G EDU/PROP PRESS CONTROL CHOOSE...CHARTS 18/19 NEW/JERSEY REPUBLICAN. PAGE 84 B1707 — POL/PAR CONSTN ADMIN PROVS

B67
ROBINSON D.W.,PROMISING PRACTICES IN CIVIC EDUCATION. FUT USA+45 CONTROL PARTIC GOV/REL...OBS AUD/VIS 20. PAGE 89 B1797 — EDU/PROP NAT/G ADJUST ADMIN

B67
US DEPARTMENT HEALTH EDUC WELF,NEW PROGRAMS IN HEALTH, EDUCATION, WELFARE, HOUSING AND URBAN DEVELOPMENT FOR PERSONS AND FAMILIES -LOW, MOD' INCOME. USA+45 MUNIC NAT/G EDU/PROP GOV/REL INGP/REL ORD/FREE 20 DEPT/HEW DEPT/HUD. PAGE 108 B2180 — ADMIN HEALTH SCHOOL HABITAT

B67
US DEPARTMENT OF JUSTICE,ANNUAL REPORT OF THE OFFICE OF ADMINISTRATIVE PROCEDURE. USA+45 PROB/SOLV EDU/PROP EXEC INGP/REL EFFICIENCY KNOWL ...POLICY STAT 20. PAGE 108 B2181 — ADMIN NAT/G ROUTINE GOV/REL

S67
ALPANDER G.G.,"ENTREPRENEURS AND PRIVATE ENTERPRISE IN TURKEY." TURKEY INDUS PROC/MFG EDU/PROP ATTIT DRIVE WEALTH...GEOG MGT SOC STAT TREND CHARTS 20. PAGE 4 B0080 — ECO/UNDEV LG/CO NAT/G POLICY

S67
BAUM R.D.,"IDEOLOGY REDIVIVUS." CHINA/COM NAT/G EDU/PROP ADMIN 20. PAGE 10 B0197 — REV MARXISM CREATE TEC/DEV

S67
DODSON D.W.,"NEW FORCES OPERATING IN EDUCATIONAL DECISION-MAKING." USA+45 NEIGH EDU/PROP ADMIN SUPEGO DECISION. PAGE 30 B0602 — PROB/SOLV SCHOOL PERS/REL PWR

S67
GITTELL M.,"PROFESSIONALISM AND PUBLIC PARTICIPATION IN EDUCATIONAL POLICY MAKING." STRUCT ADMIN GP/REL ATTIT PWR 20. PAGE 40 B0805 — DECISION PLAN EDU/PROP MUNIC

S67
GRUNDY K.W.,"THE POLITICAL USES OF IMAGINATION." GHANA ELITES SOCIETY NAT/G DOMIN EDU/PROP COLONIAL REGION REPRESENT GP/REL CENTRAL PWR MARXISM 20. PAGE 44 B0897 — NAT/LISM EX/STRUC AFR LEAD

S67
HAIRE M.,"MANAGING MANAGEMENT MANPOWER." EX/STRUC OP/RES PAY EDU/PROP COST EFFICIENCY...PREDICT SIMUL 20. PAGE 45 B0920 — MGT EXEC LEAD INDUS

S67
HSUEH C.T.,"THE CULTURAL REVOLUTION AND LEADERSHIP CRISIS IN COMMUNIST CHINA." CHINA/COM POL/PAR EX/STRUC FORCES EDU/PROP ATTIT PWR...POLICY 20. PAGE 52 B1054 — LEAD REV CULTURE MARXISM

S67
KURON J.,"AN OPEN LETTER TO THE PARTY." CONSTN WORKER BUDGET EDU/PROP ADMIN REPRESENT SUFF OWN — ELITES STRUCT

...SOCIALIST 20. PAGE 62 B1244 — POL/PAR ECO/TAC

S67
MCNAMARA R.L.,"THE NEED FOR INNOVATIVENESS IN DEVELOPING SOCIETIES." L/A+17C EDU/PROP ADMIN LEAD WEALTH...POLICY PSY SOC METH 20 COLOMB. PAGE 72 B1456 — PROB/SOLV PLAN ECO/UNDEV NEW/IDEA

S67
MONEYPENNY P.,"UNIVERSITY PURPOSE, DISCIPLINE, AND DUE PROCESS." USA+45 EDU/PROP ADJUD LEISURE ORD/FREE. PAGE 74 B1500 — ACADEM AGE/Y CONTROL ADMIN

S67
RUBIN R.I.,"THE LEGISLATIVE-EXECUTIVE RELATIONS OF THE UNITED STATES INFORMATION AGENCY." USA+45 EDU/PROP TASK INGP/REL EFFICIENCY ISOLAT ATTIT ROLE USIA CONGRESS. PAGE 91 B1850 — LEGIS EX/STRUC GP/REL PROF/ORG

S67
SHOEMAKER R.L.,"JAPANESE ARMY AND THE WEST." ASIA ELITES EX/STRUC DIPLOM DOMIN EDU/PROP COERCE ATTIT AUTHORIT PWR 1/20 CHINJAP. PAGE 96 B1950 — FORCES TEC/DEV WAR TOTALISM

S67
SMITH W.H.T.,"THE IMPLICATIONS OF THE AMERICAN BAR ASSOCIATION ADVISORY COMMITTEE RECOMMENDATIONS FOR POLICE ADMINISTRATION." ADMIN...JURID 20 ABA. PAGE 98 B1986 — EDU/PROP CONTROL GP/REL ORD/FREE

S67
SPACKMAN A.,"THE SENATE OF TRINIDAD AND TOBAGO." L/A+17C TRINIDAD WEST/IND NAT/G PAR DELIB/GP OP/RES PROB/SOLV EDU/PROP EXEC LOBBY ROUTINE REPRESENT GP/REL 20. PAGE 99 B2002 — ELITES EFFICIENCY LEGIS DECISION

N67
US SUPERINTENDENT OF DOCUMENTS,SPACE: MISSILES, THE MOON, NASA, AND SATELLITES (PRICE LIST 79A). USA+45 COM/IND R+D NAT/G DIPLOM EDU/PROP ADMIN CONTROL HEALTH...POLICY SIMUL NASA CONGRESS. PAGE 111 B2244 — BIBLIOG/A SPACE TEC/DEV PEACE

S68
GUZZARDI W. JR.,"THE SECOND BATTLE OF BRITAIN." UK STRATA LABOR WORKER CREATE PROB/SOLV EDU/PROP ADMIN LEAD LOBBY...MGT SOC 20 GOLD/STAND. PAGE 45 B0907 — FINAN ECO/TAC ECO/DEV STRUCT

B82
MACDONALD D.,AFRICANA; OR, THE HEART OF HEATHEN AFRICA, VOL. II: MISSION LIFE. SOCIETY STRATA KIN CREATE EDU/PROP ADMIN COERCE LITERACY HEALTH...MYTH WORSHIP 19 LIVNGSTN/D MISSION NEGRO. PAGE 67 B1355 — SECT AFR CULTURE ORD/FREE

EDUCATION....SEE EDU/PROP

EDUCATIONAL INSTITUTIONS....SEE ACADEM, SCHOOL

EDWARDS H.T. B0655

EEC....EUROPEAN ECONOMIC COMMUNITY; SEE ALSO VOL/ASSN, INT/ORG

N
MONPIED E.,BIBLIOGRAPHIE FEDERALISTE: ARTICLES ET DOCUMENTS PUBLIES DANS LES PERIODIQUES PARUS EN FRANCE NOV. 1945-OCT. 1950. EUR+WWI WOR+45 ADMIN REGION ATTIT MARXISM PACIFISM 20 EEC. PAGE 74 B1501 — BIBLIOG/A FEDERAL CENTRAL INT/ORG

L60
STEIN E.,"LEGAL REMEDIES OF ENTERPRISES IN THE EUROPEAN ECONOMIC COMMUNITY." EUR+WWI FUT ECO/DEV INDUS PLAN ECO/TAC ADMIN PWR...MGT MATH STAT TREND CON/ANAL EEC 20. PAGE 100 B2026 — MARKET ADJUD

B61
BENOIT E.,EUROPE AT SIXES AND SEVENS: THE COMMON MARKET, THE FREE TRADE ASSOCIATION AND THE UNITED STATES. EUR+WWI FUT USA+45 INDUS CONSULT DELIB/GP EX/STRUC TOP/EX ACT/RES ECO/TAC EDU/PROP ROUTINE CHOOSE PERCEPT WEALTH...MGT TREND EEC TOT/POP 20 EFTA. PAGE 11 B0217 — FINAN ECO/DEV VOL/ASSN

S61
LANFALUSSY A.,"EUROPE'S PROGRESS: DUE TO COMMON MARKET." EUR+WWI ECO/DEV DELIB/GP PLAN ECO/TAC ROUTINE WEALTH...GEOG TREND EEC 20. PAGE 62 B1257 — INT/ORG MARKET

B62
FRIEDMANN W.,METHODS AND POLICIES OF PRINCIPAL DONOR COUNTRIES IN PUBLIC INTERNATIONAL DEVELOPMENT FINANCING: PRELIMINARY APPRAISAL. FRANCE GERMANY/W UK USA+45 USSR WOR+45 FINAN TEC/DEV CAP/ISM DIPLOM ECO/TAC ATTIT 20 EEC. PAGE 37 B0759 — INT/ORG FOR/AID NAT/COMP ADMIN

B62
LAWSON R.,INTERNATIONAL REGIONAL ORGANIZATIONS. WOR+45 NAT/G VOL/ASSN CONSULT LEGIS EDU/PROP LEGIT ADMIN EXEC ROUTINE HEALTH PWR WEALTH...JURID EEC COLD/WAR 20 UN. PAGE 63 B1277 — INT/ORG DELIB/GP REGION

L62
MALINOWSKI W.R.,"CENTRALIZATION AND DE-CENTRALIZATION IN THE UNITED NATIONS' ECONOMIC AND SOCIAL ACTIVITIES." WOR+45 CONSTN ECO/UNDEV INT/ORG VOL/ASSN DELIB/GP ECO/TAC EDU/PROP ADMIN RIGID/FLEX ...OBS CHARTS UNESCO UN EEC OAS OEEC 20. PAGE 69 B1385 — CREATE GEN/LAWS

S62
JOHNSON H.,"CANADA IN A CHANGING WORLD." EUR+WWI USA+45 NAT/G CAP/ISM ECO/TAC ADMIN ATTIT WEALTH ...TREND TOT/POP 20 EEC. PAGE 57 B1143 — ECO/DEV PLAN CANADA

B63
LINDBERG L.,POLITICAL DYNAMICS OF EUROPEAN ECONOMIC INTEGRATION. EUR+WWI ECO/DEV INT/ORG VOL/ASSN DELIB/GP ADMIN WEALTH...DECISION EEC 20. PAGE 65 B1313 — MARKET ECO/TAC

B63
MAYNE R.,THE COMMUNITY OF EUROPE. UK CONSTN NAT/G CONSULT DELIB/GP CREATE PLAN ECO/TAC LEGIT ADMIN ROUTINE ORD/FREE PWR WEALTH...CONCPT TIME/SEQ EEC EURATOM 20. PAGE 71 B1436 — EUR+WWI INT/ORG REGION

B63
THORELLI H.B.,INTOP: INTERNATIONAL OPERATIONS SIMULATION: PLAYER'S MANUAL. BRAZIL FINAN OP/RES ADMIN GP/REL INGP/REL PRODUC PERCEPT...DECISION MGT EEC. PAGE 104 B2108 — GAME INT/TRADE EDU/PROP LG/CO

S63
BARZANSKI S.,"REGIONAL UNDERDEVELOPMENT IN THE EUROPEAN ECONOMIC COMMUNITY." EUR+WWI ELITES DIST/IND MARKET VOL/ASSN CONSULT EX/STRUC ECO/TAC RIGID/FLEX WEALTH EEC OEEC 20. PAGE 9 B0192 — ECO/UNDEV PLAN

S63
MASSART L.,"L'ORGANISATION DE LA RECHERCHE SCIENTIFIQUE EN EUROPE." EUR+WWI WOR+45 ACT/RES PLAN TEC/DEV EDU/PROP EXEC KNOWL...METH/CNCPT EEC 20. PAGE 70 B1424 — R+D CREATE

S63
SCHMITT H.A.,"THE EUROPEAN COMMUNITIES." EUR+WWI FRANCE DELIB/GP EX/STRUC TOP/EX CREATE TEC/DEV ECO/TAC LEGIT REGION COERCE DRIVE ALL/VALS ...METH/CNCPT EEC 20. PAGE 94 B1897 — VOL/ASSN ECO/DEV

B64
KAPP E.,THE MERGER OF THE EXECUTIVES OF THE EUROPEAN COMMUNITIES. LAW CONSTN STRUCT ACT/RES PLAN PROB/SOLV ADMIN REGION TASK...INT/LAW MGT ECSC EEC. PAGE 58 B1170 — CENTRAL EX/STRUC

S65
BROWN S.,"AN ALTERNATIVE TO THE GRAND DESIGN." EUR+WWI FUT USA+45 INT/ORG NAT/G EX/STRUC FORCES CREATE BAL/PWR DOMIN RIGID/FLEX ORD/FREE PWR ...NEW/IDEA RECORD EEC NATO 20. PAGE 16 B0327 — VOL/ASSN CONCPT DIPLOM

B66
SPINELLI A.,THE EUROCRATS: CONFLICT AND CRISIS IN THE EUROPEAN COMMUNITY (TRANS. BY C. GROVE HAINES). EUR+WWI MARKET POL/PAR ECO/TAC PARL/PROC EEC OEEC ECSC EURATOM. PAGE 99 B2007 — INT/ORG INGP/REL CONSTN ADMIN

L67
CAHIERS P.,"LE RECOURS EN CONSTATATION DE MANQUEMENTS DES ETATS MEMBRES DEVANT LA COUR DES COMMUNAUTES EUROPEENNES." LAW PROB/SOLV DIPLOM ADMIN CT/SYS SANCTION ATTIT...POLICY DECISION JURID ECSC EEC. PAGE 18 B0362 — INT/ORG CONSTN ROUTINE ADJUD

S67
WEIL G.L.,"THE MERGER OF THE INSTITUTIONS OF THE EUROPEAN COMMUNITIES" EUR+WWI ECO/DEV INT/TRADE CONSEN PLURISM...DECISION MGT 20 EEC EURATOM ECSC TREATY. PAGE 115 B2313 — ECO/TAC INT/ORG CENTRAL INT/LAW

EFFECTIVENESS....SEE EFFICIENCY, PRODUC

EFFICIENCY....EFFECTIVENESS

N
US CIVIL SERVICE COMMISSION,A BIBLIOGRAPHY OF PUBLIC PERSONNEL ADMINISTRATION LITERATURE. WOR+45 EFFICIENCY...POLICY MGT. PAGE 108 B2175 — BIBLIOG ADMIN WORKER PLAN

B19
DUNN A.,SCIENTIFIC SELLING AND ADVERTISING. CLIENT ADMIN DEMAND EFFICIENCY 20. PAGE 31 B0632 — LG/CO PERCEPT PERS/REL TASK

N19
ABERNATHY B.R.,SOME PERSISTING QUESTIONS CONCERNING THE CONSTITUTIONAL STATE EXECUTIVE (PAMPHLET). CONSTN TOP/EX TEC/DEV GOV/REL EFFICIENCY TIME 20 GOVERNOR. PAGE 3 B0054 — PROVS EX/STRUC PROB/SOLV PWR

N19
ANDERSON W.,THE UNITS OF GOVERNMENT IN THE UNITED STATES (PAMPHLET). USA-45 NAT/G PROVS EFFICIENCY ...CHARTS 20. PAGE 5 B0098 — LOC/G CENSUS ADMIN GOV/REL

N19
ARNOW K.,SELF-INSURANCE IN THE TREASURY (PAMPHLET). USA+45 LAW RIGID/FLEX...POLICY METH/COMP 20 DEPT/TREAS. PAGE 7 B0135 — ADMIN PLAN EFFICIENCY NAT/G

N19
DOTSON A.,PRODUCTION PLANNING IN THE PATENT OFFICE (PAMPHLET). USA+45 DIST/IND PROB/SOLV PRODUC...MGT PHIL/SCI 20 BUR/BUDGET PATENT/OFF. PAGE 30 B0610 — EFFICIENCY PLAN NAT/G ADMIN

S52

SOMERS H.M.,"THE PRESIDENT AS ADMINISTRATOR."
USA+45 NAT/G ADMIN REPRESENT GOV/REL 20 PRESIDENT.
PAGE 99 B1996

CONTROL
EFFICIENCY
EX/STRUC
EXEC

S52

TAYLOR D.W.,"TWENTY QUESTIONS: EFFICIENCY IN
PROBLEM SOLVING AS A FUNCTION OF SIZE OF GROUP"
WOR+45 CONFER ROUTINE INGP/REL...PSY GP/COMP 20.
PAGE 103 B2085

PROB/SOLV
EFFICIENCY
SKILL
PERCEPT

B53

HOBBS E.H.,EXECUTIVE REORGANIZATION IN THE NATIONAL
GOVERNMENT. USA+45 USA-45 NAT/G. PAGE 50 B1021

EFFICIENCY
EX/STRUC
ADMIN
TOP/EX

B53

MILLIKAN M.F.,INCOME STABILIZATION FOR A DEVELOPING
DEMOCRACY. USA+45 ECO/DEV LABOR BUDGET ECO/TAC TAX
ADMIN ADJUST PRODUC WEALTH...POLICY TREND 20.
PAGE 73 B1484

ANTHOL
MARKET
EQUILIB
EFFICIENCY

B53

ROBINSON E.A.G.,THE STRUCTURE OF COMPETITIVE
INDUSTRY. UK ECO/DEV DIST/IND MARKET TEC/DEV DIPLOM
EDU/PROP ADMIN EFFICIENCY WEALTH...MGT 19/20.
PAGE 89 B1798

INDUS
PRODUC
WORKER
OPTIMAL

S53

GABLE R.W.,"NAM: INFLUENTIAL LOBBY OR KISS OF
DEATH?" (BMR)" USA+45 LAW INSPECT EDU/PROP ADMIN
CONTROL INGP/REL EFFICIENCY PWR 20 CONGRESS NAM
TAFT/HART. PAGE 38 B0769

LOBBY
LEGIS
INDUS
LG/CO

S54

STONE E.O.,"ADMINISTRATIVE INTEGRATION." USA+45
NAT/G ADMIN CONTROL CENTRAL 20. PAGE 101 B2046

REPRESENT
EFFICIENCY
LOBBY
EX/STRUC

B55

GALLOWAY G.B.,CONGRESS AND PARLIAMENT: THEIR
ORGANIZATION AND OPERATION IN THE US AND THE UK:
PLANNING PAMPHLET NO. 93. POL/PAR EX/STRUC DEBATE
CONTROL LEAD ROUTINE EFFICIENCY PWR...POLICY
CONGRESS PARLIAMENT. PAGE 38 B0777

DELIB/GP
LEGIS
PARL/PROC
GOV/COMP

B55

SMITHIES A.,THE BUDGETARY PROCESS IN THE UNITED
STATES. ECO/DEV AGRI EX/STRUC FORCES LEGIS
PROB/SOLV TAX ROUTINE EFFICIENCY...MGT CONGRESS
PRESIDENT. PAGE 98 B1987

NAT/G
ADMIN
BUDGET
GOV/REL

B55

STEPHENS O.,FACTS TO A CANDID WORLD. USA+45 WOR+45
COM/IND EX/STRUC PRESS ROUTINE EFFICIENCY ATTIT
...PSY 20. PAGE 100 B2033

EDU/PROP
PHIL/SCI
NAT/G
DIPLOM

B55

WHEARE K.C.,GOVERNMENT BY COMMITTEE; AN ESSAY ON
THE BRITISH CONSTITUTION. UK NAT/G LEGIS INSPECT
CONFER ADJUD ADMIN CONTROL TASK EFFICIENCY ROLE
POPULISM 20. PAGE 115 B2329

DELIB/GP
CONSTN
LEAD
GP/COMP

B56

BLAU P.M.,BUREAUCRACY IN MODERN SOCIETY. STRUCT
INDUS LABOR LG/CO LOC/G NAT/G FORCES EDU/PROP
ROUTINE ORD/FREE 20 BUREAUCRCY. PAGE 12 B0252

SOC
EX/STRUC
ADMIN
EFFICIENCY

B56

DUNNILL F.,THE CIVIL SERVICE. UK LAW PLAN ADMIN
EFFICIENCY DRIVE NEW/LIB...STAT CHARTS 20
PARLIAMENT CIVIL/SERV. PAGE 31 B0633

PERSON
WORKER
STRATA
SOC/WK

B56

GLADDEN E.N.,CIVIL SERVICE OR BUREAUCRACY? UK LAW
STRATA LABOR TOP/EX PLAN SENIOR AUTOMAT CONTROL
PARTIC CHOOSE HAPPINESS...CHARTS 19/20 CIVIL/SERV
BUREAUCRCY. PAGE 40 B0808

ADMIN
GOV/REL
EFFICIENCY
PROVS

B56

US HOUSE RULES COMM,HEARINGS BEFORE A SPECIAL
SUBCOMMITTEE: ESTABLISHMENT OF A STANDING COMMITTEE
ON ADMINISTRATIVE PROCEDURE, PRACTICE. USA+45 LAW
EX/STRUC ADJUD CONTROL EXEC GOV/REL EFFICIENCY PWR
...POLICY INT 20 CONGRESS. PAGE 109 B2199

ADMIN
DOMIN
DELIB/GP
NAT/G

L56

LITCHFIELD E.H.,"NOTES ON A GENERAL THEORY OF
ADMINISTRATION." USA+45 OP/RES PROB/SOLV EFFICIENCY
IDEA/COMP. PAGE 66 B1324

ADMIN
ROUTINE
MGT

S56

MARGOLIS J.,"ON MUNICIPAL LAND POLICY FOR FISCAL
GAINS." USA+45 MUNIC PLAN TAX COST EFFICIENCY
HABITAT KNOWL...MGT 20. PAGE 69 B1398

BUDGET
POLICY
GEOG
LOC/G

B57

SELZNICK,LEADERSHIP IN ADMINISTRATION: A
SOCIOLOGICAL INTERPRETATION. CREATE PROB/SOLV EXEC
ROUTINE EFFICIENCY RATIONAL KNOWL...POLICY PSY.
PAGE 95 B1927

LEAD
ADMIN
DECISION
NAT/G

B57

US HOUSE COMM ON POST OFFICE,MANPOWER UTILIZATION
IN THE FEDERAL GOVERNMENT. USA+45 FORCES WORKER
CREATE PLAN EFFICIENCY UTIL 20 CONGRESS CIVIL/SERV
POSTAL/SYS DEPT/DEFEN. PAGE 109 B2193

NAT/G
ADMIN
LABOR
EX/STRUC

S57

HARRIS J.P.,"LEGISLATIVE CONTROL OF ADMINISTRATION:
SOME COMPARISONS OF AMERICAN AND EUROPEAN
PRACTICES." DEBATE PARL/PROC ROUTINE GOV/REL
EFFICIENCY SUPEGO DECISION. PAGE 47 B0954

LEGIS
CONTROL
EX/STRUC
REPRESENT

S57

HODGETTS J.E.,"THE CIVIL SERVICE AND POLICY
FORMATION." CANADA NAT/G EX/STRUC ROUTINE GOV/REL
20. PAGE 50 B1023

ADMIN
DECISION
EFFICIENCY
POLICY

S57

ROURKE F.E.,"THE POLITICS OF ADMINISTRATIVE
ORGANIZATION: A CASE HISTORY." USA+45 LABOR WORKER
PLAN ADMIN TASK EFFICIENCY 20 DEPT/LABOR CONGRESS.
PAGE 91 B1836

POLICY
ATTIT
MGT
GP/COMP

B58

AMERICAN SOCIETY PUBLIC ADMIN,STRENGTHENING
MANAGEMENT FOR DEMOCRATIC GOVERNMENT. USA+45 ACADEM
EX/STRUC WORKER PLAN BUDGET CONFER CT/SYS
EFFICIENCY ANTHOL. PAGE 4 B0088

ADMIN
NAT/G
EXEC
MGT

B58

CHEEK G.,ECONOMIC AND SOCIAL IMPLICATIONS OF
AUTOMATION: A BIBLIOGRAPHIC REVIEW (PAMPHLET).
USA+45 LG/CO WORKER CREATE PLAN CONTROL ROUTINE
PERS/REL EFFICIENCY PRODUC...METH/COMP 20. PAGE 20
B0416

BIBLIOG/A
SOCIETY
INDUS
AUTOMAT

B58

DEVLIN P.,THE CRIMINAL PROSECUTION IN ENGLAND. UK
NAT/G ADMIN ROUTINE EFFICIENCY...JURID SOC 20.
PAGE 29 B0583

CRIME
LAW
METH
CT/SYS

B58

KRAINES O.,CONGRESS AND THE CHALLENGE OF BIG
GOVERNMENT. USA-45 EX/STRUC CONFER DEBATE
EFFICIENCY. PAGE 61 B1232

LEGIS
DELIB/GP
ADMIN

B58

LAW COMMISSION OF INDIA,REFORM OF JUDICIAL
ADMINISTRATION. INDIA TOP/EX ADMIN DISCRIM
EFFICIENCY...METH/COMP 20. PAGE 63 B1276

CT/SYS
ADJUD
GOV/REL
CONTROL

B58

SCOTT D.J.R.,RUSSIAN POLITICAL INSTITUTIONS. RUSSIA
USSR CONSTN AGRI DELIB/GP PLAN EDU/PROP CONTROL
CHOOSE EFFICIENCY ATTIT MARXISM...BIBLIOG/A 13/20.
PAGE 95 B1919

NAT/G
POL/PAR
ADMIN
DECISION

B58

US HOUSE COMM GOVT OPERATIONS,HEARINGS BEFORE A
SUBCOMMITTEE OF THE COMMITTEE ON GOVERNMENT
OPERATIONS. CAMBODIA PHILIPPINE USA+45 CONSTRUC
TEC/DEV ADMIN CONTROL WEAPON EFFICIENCY HOUSE/REP.
PAGE 108 B2189

FOR/AID
DIPLOM
ORD/FREE
ECO/UNDEV

B58

US HOUSE COMM ON POST OFFICE,TO PROVIDE AN
EFFECTIVE SYSTEM OF PERSONNEL ADMINISTRATION.
USA+45 DELIB/GP CONTROL EFFICIENCY 20 CONGRESS
PRESIDENT CIVIL/SERV POSTAL/SYS. PAGE 109 B2194

ADMIN
NAT/G
EX/STRUC
LAW

B58

US HOUSE COMM POST OFFICE,MANPOWER UTILIZATION IN
THE FEDERAL GOVERNMENT. USA+45 DIST/IND EX/STRUC
LEGIS CONFER EFFICIENCY 20 CONGRESS CIVIL/SERV.
PAGE 109 B2195

ADMIN
WORKER
DELIB/GP
NAT/G

B58

US HOUSE COMM POST OFFICE,MANPOWER UTILIZATION IN
THE FEDERAL GOVERNMENT. USA+45 DIST/IND EX/STRUC
LEGIS CONFER EFFICIENCY 20 CONGRESS CIVIL/SERV.
PAGE 109 B2196

ADMIN
WORKER
DELIB/GP
NAT/G

B58

US HOUSE COMM POST OFFICE,TRAINING OF FEDERAL
EMPLOYEES. USA+45 DIST/IND NAT/G EX/STRUC EDU/PROP
CONFER GOV/REL EFFICIENCY SKILL 20 CONGRESS
CIVIL/SERV. PAGE 109 B2197

LEGIS
DELIB/GP
WORKER
ADMIN

S58

DIAMANT A.,"A CASE STUDY OF ADMINISTRATIVE
AUTONOMY: CONTROLS AND TENSIONS IN FRENCH
ADMINISTRATION." FRANCE ADJUD LOBBY DEMAND
EFFICIENCY 20. PAGE 29 B0585

ADMIN
CONTROL
LEGIS
EXEC

S58

MANSFIELD E.,"A STUDY OF DECISION-MAKING WITHIN THE
FIRM." LG/CO WORKER INGP/REL COST EFFICIENCY PRODUC
...CHARTS 20. PAGE 69 B1395

OP/RES
PROB/SOLV
AUTOMAT
ROUTINE

B59

ELLIOTT S.D.,IMPROVING OUR COURTS. LAW EX/STRUC
PLAN PROB/SOLV ADJUD ADMIN TASK CRIME EFFICIENCY
ORD/FREE 20. PAGE 33 B0669

CT/SYS
JURID
GOV/REL
NAT/G

B59

GREENEWALT C.H.,THE UNCOMMON MAN. UNIV ECO/DEV
ADMIN PERS/REL PERSON SUPEGO WEALTH 20. PAGE 43
B0868

TASK
ORD/FREE
DRIVE
EFFICIENCY

B59

HANSON A.H.,THE STRUCTURE AND CONTROL OF STATE
ENTERPRISES IN TURKEY. TURKEY LAW ADMIN GOV/REL
EFFICIENCY...CHARTS 20. PAGE 46 B0939

NAT/G
LG/CO
OWN
CONTROL

INDIAN INSTITUTE PUBLIC ADMIN.,MORALE IN THE PUBLIC SERVICES: REPORT OF A CONFERENCE JAN., 3-4, 1959. INDIA S/ASIA ECO/UNDEV PROVS PLAN EDU/PROP CONFER GOV/REL EFFICIENCY DRIVE ROLE 20 CIVIL/SERV. PAGE 53 B1082
B59 HAPPINESS ADMIN WORKER INGP/REL

MAYDA J.,ATOMIC ENERGY AND LAW. ECO/UNDEV FINAN TEC/DEV FOR/AID EFFICIENCY PRODUC WEALTH...POLICY TECHNIC 20. PAGE 71 B1433
B59 NUC/PWR L/A+17C LAW ADMIN

REDFORD E.S.,NATIONAL REGULATORY COMMISSIONS: NEED FOR A NEW LOOK (PAMPHLET). USA+45 CLIENT PROB/SOLV ADJUD LOBBY EFFICIENCY...POLICY 20. PAGE 87 B1757
B59 REPRESENT CONTROL EXEC NAT/G

SISSON C.H.,THE SPIRIT OF BRITISH ADMINISTRATION AND SOME EUROPEAN COMPARISONS. FRANCE GERMANY/W SWEDEN UK LAW EX/STRUC INGP/REL EFFICIENCY ORD/FREE ...DECISION 20. PAGE 98 B1972
B59 GOV/COMP ADMIN ELITES ATTIT

US PRES COMM STUDY MIL ASSIST,COMPOSITE REPORT. USA+45 ECO/UNDEV PLAN BUDGET DIPLOM EFFICIENCY ...POLICY MGT 20. PAGE 109 B2208
B59 FOR/AID FORCES WEAPON ORD/FREE

US SENATE COMM ON POST OFFICE,TO PROVIDE FOR AN EFFECTIVE SYSTEM OF PERSONNEL ADMINISTRATION. EFFICIENCY...MGT 20 CONGRESS CIVIL/SERV POSTAL/SYS YARBROGH/R. PAGE 111 B2233
B59 ADMIN NAT/G EX/STRUC LAW

WASSERMAN P.,MEASUREMENT AND ANALYSIS OF ORGANIZATIONAL PERFORMANCE. FINAN MARKET EX/STRUC TEC/DEV EDU/PROP CONTROL ROUTINE TASK...MGT 20. PAGE 114 B2300
B59 BIBLIOG/A ECO/TAC OP/RES EFFICIENCY

WEBER W.,DER DEUTSCHE BEAMTE HEUTE. GERMANY/W NAT/G DELIB/GP LEGIS CONFER ATTIT SUPEGO...JURID 20 CIVIL/SERV. PAGE 114 B2306
B59 MGT EFFICIENCY ELITES GP/REL

TARKOWSKI Z.M.,"SCIENTISTS VERSUS ADMINISTRATORS: AN APPROACH TOWARD ACHIEVING GREATER UNDERSTANDING." UK EXEC EFFICIENCY 20. PAGE 103 B2079
L59 INGP/REL GP/REL ADMIN EX/STRUC

BENDIX R.,"INDUSTRIALIZATION, IDEOLOGIES, AND SOCIAL STRUCTURE" (BMR)" UK USA-45 USSR STRUCT WORKER GP/REL EFFICIENCY...IDEA/COMP 20. PAGE 10 B0210
S59 INDUS ATTIT MGT ADMIN

JEWELL M.R.,"THE SENATE REPUBLICAN POLICY COMMITTEE AND FOREIGN POLICY." PLAN ADMIN CONTROL LEAD LOBBY EFFICIENCY PRESIDENT 20 REPUBLICAN. PAGE 56 B1139
S59 POL/PAR NAT/G DELIB/GP POLICY

DAHL R.A.,"SOCIAL SCIENCE RESEARCH ON BUSINESS: PRODUCT AND POTENTIAL" INDUS MARKET OP/RES CAP/ISM ADMIN LOBBY DRIVE...PSY CONCPT BIBLIOG/A 20. PAGE 26 B0521
C59 MGT EFFICIENCY PROB/SOLV EX/STRUC

BHAMBHRI C.P.,PARLIAMENTARY CONTROL OVER STATE ENTERPRISE IN INDIA. INDIA DELIB/GP ADMIN CONTROL INGP/REL EFFICIENCY 20 PARLIAMENT. PAGE 11 B0235
B60 NAT/G OWN INDUS PARL/PROC

FRYE R.J.,GOVERNMENT AND LABOR: THE ALABAMA PROGRAM. USA+45 INDUS R+D LABOR WORKER BUDGET EFFICIENCY AGE/Y HEALTH...CHARTS 20 ALABAMA. PAGE 38 B0761
B60 ADMIN LEGIS LOC/G PROVS

HODGETTS J.E.,CANADIAN PUBLIC ADMINISTRATION. CANADA CONTROL LOBBY EFFICIENCY 20. PAGE 50 B1024
B60 REPRESENT ADMIN EX/STRUC ADJUD

INDIAN INST OF PUBLIC ADMIN,STATE UNDERTAKINGS: REPORT OF A CONFERENCE, DECEMBER 19-20, 1959 (PAMPHLET). INDIA LG/CO DELIB/GP CONFER PARL/PROC EFFICIENCY OWN...MGT 20. PAGE 53 B1081
B60 GOV/REL ADMIN NAT/G LEGIS

KERSELL J.E.,PARLIAMENTARY SUPERVISION OF DELEGATED LEGISLATION. UK EFFICIENCY PWR...POLICY CHARTS BIBLIOG METH 20 PARLIAMENT. PAGE 59 B1198
B60 LEGIS CONTROL NAT/G EX/STRUC

PENNSYLVANIA ECONOMY LEAGUE,URBAN RENEWAL IMPACT STUDY: ADMINISTRATIVE-LEGAL-FISCAL. USA+45 FINAN LOC/G NEIGH ADMIN EFFICIENCY...CENSUS CHARTS 20 PENNSYLVAN. PAGE 82 B1652
B60 PLAN BUDGET MUNIC ADJUD

RAO V.K.R.,INTERNATIONAL AID FOR ECONOMIC DEVELOPMENT - POSSIBILITIES AND LIMITATIONS. FINAN PLAN TEC/DEV ADMIN TASK EFFICIENCY...POLICY SOC METH/CNCPT CHARTS 20 UN. PAGE 86 B1734
B60 FOR/AID DIPLOM INT/ORG ECO/UNDEV

ROBINSON E.A.G.,ECONOMIC CONSEQUENCES OF THE SIZE OF NATIONS. AGRI INDUS DELIB/GP FOR/AID ADMIN EFFICIENCY...METH/COMP 20. PAGE 89 B1799
B60 CONCPT INT/ORG NAT/COMP

US DEPARTMENT OF THE ARMY,SELECT BIBLIOGRAPHY ON ADMINISTRATIVE ORGANIZATION(PAMPHLET). USA+45 INDUS NAT/G EX/STRUC OP/RES CIVMIL/REL EFFICIENCY ORD/FREE. PAGE 108 B2183
B60 BIBLIOG/A ADMIN CONCPT FORCES

FUCHS R.F.,"FAIRNESS AND EFFECTIVENESS IN ADMINISTRATIVE AGENCY ORGANIZATION AND PROCEDURES." USA+45 ADJUD ADMIN REPRESENT. PAGE 38 B0764
L60 EFFICIENCY EX/STRUC EXEC POLICY

SMIGEL E.O.,"THE IMPACT OF RECRUITMENT ON THE ORGANIZATION OF THE LARGE LAW FIRM" (BMR)" USA+45 STRUCT CONSULT PLAN GP/REL EFFICIENCY JURID. PAGE 98 B1979
S60 LG/CO ADMIN LAW WORKER

AVERY M.W.,GOVERNMENT OF WASHINGTON STATE. USA+45 MUNIC DELIB/GP EX/STRUC LEGIS GIVE CT/SYS PARTIC REGION EFFICIENCY 20 WASHINGT/G GOVERNOR. PAGE 7 B0151
B61 PROVS LOC/G ADMIN GOV/REL

CHAPPLE E.D.,THE MEASURE OF MANAGEMENT. USA+45 WORKER ADMIN GP/REL EFFICIENCY...DECISION ORG/CHARTS SIMUL 20. PAGE 20 B0412
B61 MGT OP/RES PLAN METH/CNCPT

PROCEEDINGS OF THE CONFERENCE ON BUSINESS GAMES AS TEACHING DEVICES. PROB/SOLV ECO/TAC CONFER ADMIN TASK...MGT ANTHOL 20. PAGE 29 B0593
B61 GAME DECISION EDU/PROP EFFICIENCY

GLADDEN E.N.,BRITISH PUBLIC SERVICE ADMINISTRATION. UK...CHARTS 20. PAGE 40 B0809
B61 EFFICIENCY ADMIN EX/STRUC EXEC

HALL M.,DISTRIBUTION IN GREAT BRITAIN AND NORTH AMERICA. CANADA UK USA+45 ECO/DEV INDUS MARKET EFFICIENCY PROFIT...MGT CHARTS 20. PAGE 46 B0924
B61 DIST/IND PRODUC ECO/TAC CAP/ISM

HART H.C.,ADMINISTRATIVE ASPECTS OF RIVER VALLEY DEVELOPMENT. INDIA USA+45 INDUS CONTROL EFFICIENCY OPTIMAL PRODUC 20 TVA. PAGE 47 B0957
B61 ADMIN PLAN METH/COMP AGRI

HOUN F.W.,TO CHANGE A NATION; PROPAGANDA AND INDOCTRINATION IN COMMUNIST CHINA. CHINA/COM COM ACT/RES PLAN PRESS ADMIN FEEDBACK CENTRAL EFFICIENCY...PSY SOC 20. PAGE 52 B1048
B61 DOMIN EDU/PROP TOTALISM MARXISM

MACMAHON A.W.,DELEGATION AND AUTONOMY. INDIA STRUCT LEGIS BARGAIN BUDGET ECO/TAC LEGIT EXEC REPRESENT GOV/REL CENTRAL DEMAND EFFICIENCY PRODUC. PAGE 68 B1373
B61 ADMIN PLAN FEDERAL

NARAIN J.P.,SWARAJ FOR THE PEOPLE. INDIA CONSTN LOC/G MUNIC POL/PAR CHOOSE REPRESENT EFFICIENCY ATTIT PWR SOVEREIGN 20. PAGE 77 B1553
B61 NAT/G ORD/FREE EDU/PROP EX/STRUC

NARASIMHAN V.K.,THE PRESS, THE PUBLIC AND THE ADMINISTRATION (PAMPHLET). INDIA COM/IND CONTROL REPRESENT GOV/REL EFFICIENCY...ANTHOL 20. PAGE 77 B1554
B61 NAT/G ADMIN PRESS NEW/LIB

NOVE A.,THE SOVIET ECONOMY. USSR ECO/DEV FINAN NAT/G ECO/TAC PRICE ADMIN EFFICIENCY MARXISM ...TREND BIBLIOG 20. PAGE 79 B1594
B61 PLAN PRODUC POLICY

PETRULLO L.,LEADERSHIP AND INTERPERSONAL BEHAVIOR. FACE/GP FAM PROF/ORG EX/STRUC FORCES DOMIN WAR GP/REL PERS/REL EFFICIENCY PRODUC PWR...MGT PSY. PAGE 82 B1663
B61 PERSON ATTIT LEAD HABITAT

ROSE D.L.,THE VIETNAMESE CIVIL SERVICE. VIETNAM CONSULT DELIB/GP GIVE PAY EDU/PROP COLONIAL GOV/REL UTIL...CHARTS 20. PAGE 90 B1819
B61 ADMIN EFFICIENCY STAT NAT/G

SHAPP W.R.,FIELD ADMINISTRATION IN THE UNITED NATIONS SYSTEM. FINAN PROB/SOLV INSPECT DIPLOM EXEC REGION ROUTINE EFFICIENCY ROLE...INT CHARTS 20 UN. PAGE 96 B1933
B61 INT/ORG ADMIN GP/REL FOR/AID

THOMPSON V.A.,MODERN ORGANIZATION. REPRESENT EFFICIENCY. PAGE 104 B2105
B61 ADMIN EX/STRUC EXEC

WALKER N.,MORALE IN THE CIVIL SERVICE. UK EXEC LEAD INGP/REL EFFICIENCY HAPPINESS 20. PAGE 113 B2280
B61 ATTIT WORKER ADMIN

CYERT R.M.,"TWO EXPERIMENTS ON BIAS AND CONFLICT IN ORGANIZATIONAL ESTIMATION." WORKER PROB/SOLV EFFICIENCY...MGT PSY STAT CHARTS. PAGE 25 B0518
PSY
S61
LAB/EXP
ROUTINE
ADMIN
DECISION

EVAN W.M.,"A LABORATORY EXPERIMENT ON BUREAUCRATIC AUTHORITY" WORKER CONTROL EXEC PRODUC ATTIT PERSON ...PSY SOC CHARTS SIMUL 20 WEBER/MAX. PAGE 34 B0687
S61
ADMIN
LEGIT
LAB/EXP
EFFICIENCY

TANNENBAUM A.S.,"CONTROL AND EFFECTIVENESS IN A VOLUNTARY ORGANIZATION." USA+45 ADMIN...CORREL MATH REGRESS STAT TESTS SAMP/SIZ CHARTS SOC/EXP INDEX 20 LEAGUE/WV. PAGE 102 B2072
S61
EFFICIENCY
VOL/ASSN
CONTROL
INGP/REL

ARGYRIS C.,INTERPERSONAL COMPETENCE AND ORGANIZATIONAL EFFECTIVENESS. CREATE PLAN PROB/SOLV EDU/PROP INGP/REL PERS/REL PRODUC...OBS INT SIMUL 20. PAGE 6 B0131
B62
EX/STRUC
ADMIN
CONSULT
EFFICIENCY

BECKMAN T.N.,MARKETING (7TH ED.). USA+45 SOCIETY ECO/DEV NAT/G PRICE EFFICIENCY INCOME ATTIT WEALTH ...MGT BIBLIOG 20. PAGE 10 B0205
B62
MARKET
ECO/TAC
DIST/IND
POLICY

BRIEFS H.W.,PRICING POWER AND "ADMINISTRATIVE" INFLATION (PAMPHLET). USA+45 PROC/MFG CONTROL EFFICIENCY MONEY GOLD/STAND. PAGE 15 B0306
B62
ECO/DEV
PRICE
POLICY
EXEC

CHICAGO U CTR PROG GOVT ADMIN,EDUCATION FOR INNOVATIVE BEHAVIOR IN EXECUTIVES. UNIV ELITES ADMIN EFFICIENCY DRIVE PERSON...MGT APT/TEST PERS/TEST CHARTS LAB/EXP BIBLIOG 20. PAGE 21 B0420
B62
EDU/PROP
CREATE
EXEC
STAT

DUCKWORTH W.E.,A GUIDE TO OPERATIONAL RESEARCH. INDUS PLAN PROB/SOLV EXEC EFFICIENCY PRODUC KNOWL ...MGT MATH STAT SIMUL METH 20 MONTECARLO. PAGE 31 B0624
B62
OP/RES
GAME
DECISION
ADMIN

FORD A.G.,THE GOLD STANDARD 1880-1914: BRITAIN AND ARGENTINA. UK ECO/UNDEV INT/TRADE ADMIN GOV/REL DEMAND EFFICIENCY...STAT CHARTS 19/20 ARGEN GOLD/STAND. PAGE 36 B0737
B62
FINAN
ECO/TAC
BUDGET
BAL/PAY

HANSON A.H.,MANAGERIAL PROBLEMS IN PUBLIC ENTERPRISE. INDIA DELIB/GP GP/REL INGP/REL EFFICIENCY 20 PARLIAMENT. PAGE 46 B0940
B62
MGT
NAT/G
INDUS
PROB/SOLV

HATTERY L.H.,INFORMATION RETRIEVAL MANAGEMENT. CLIENT INDUS TOP/EX COMPUTER OP/RES TEC/DEV ROUTINE COST EFFICIENCY RIGID/FLEX...METH/COMP ANTHOL 20. PAGE 48 B0968
B62
R+D
COMPUT/IR
MGT
CREATE

JENNINGS E.E.,THE EXECUTIVE: AUTOCRAT, BUREAUCRAT, DEMOCRAT. LEAD EFFICIENCY DRIVE 20. PAGE 56 B1131
B62
EX/STRUC
INGP/REL
TOP/EX
CONTROL

KARNJAHAPRAKORN C.,MUNICIPAL GOVERNMENT IN THAILAND AS AN INSTITUTION AND PROCESS OF SELF-GOVERNMENT. THAILAND CULTURE FINAN EX/STRUC LEGIS PLAN CONTROL GOV/REL EFFICIENCY ATTIT...POLICY 20. PAGE 58 B1176
B62
LOC/G
MUNIC
ORD/FREE
ADMIN

KUHN T.E.,PUBLIC ENTERPRISES, PROJECT PLANNING AND ECONOMIC DEVELOPMENT (PAMPHLET). ECO/UNDEV FINAN PLAN ADMIN EFFICIENCY OWN...MGT STAT CHARTS ANTHOL 20. PAGE 61 B1240
B62
ECO/DEV
ECO/TAC
LG/CO
NAT/G

MAILICK S.,CONCEPTS AND ISSUES IN ADMINISTRATIVE BEHAVIOR. EX/STRUC TOP/EX ROUTINE INGP/REL EFFICIENCY. PAGE 68 B1380
B62
DECISION
MGT
EXEC
PROB/SOLV

NATIONAL BUREAU ECONOMIC RES,THE RATE AND DIRECTION OF INVENTIVE ACTIVITY: ECONOMIC AND SOCIAL FACTORS. STRUCT INDUS MARKET R+D CREATE OP/RES TEC/DEV EFFICIENCY PRODUC RATIONAL UTIL...WELF/ST PHIL/SCI METH/CNCPT TIME. PAGE 77 B1562
B62
DECISION
PROB/SOLV
MGT

NEVINS A.,THE STATE UNIVERSITIES AND DEMOCRACY. AGRI FINAN SCHOOL ADMIN EXEC EFFICIENCY ATTIT. PAGE 78 B1576
B62
ACADEM
PROVS
EDU/PROP
POLICY

PACKARD V.,THE PYRAMID CLIMBERS. USA+45 ELITES SOCIETY CREATE PROB/SOLV EFFICIENCY ATTIT...MGT 20. PAGE 80 B1621
B62
INDUS
TOP/EX
PERS/REL
DRIVE

PRAKASH O.M.,THE THEORY AND WORKING OF STATE CORPORATIONS: WITH SPECIAL REFERENCE TO INDIA. INDIA UK USA+45 TOP/EX PRICE ADMIN EFFICIENCY...MGT
B62
LG/CO
ECO/UNDEV
GOV/REL

METH/COMP 20 TVA. PAGE 84 B1698
SOCISM
B62

ROBINSON M.,THE COMING OF AGE OF THE LANGLEY PORTER CLINIC (PAMPHLET). USA+45 PROF/ORG PROVS PLAN...MGT PSY 20 CALIFORNIA LANGLEY. PAGE 89 B1804
PUB/INST
ADMIN
EFFICIENCY
HEAL

SRIVASTAVA G.L.,COLLECTIVE BARGAINING AND LABOR-MANAGEMENT RELATIONS IN INDIA. INDIA UK USA+45 INDUS LEGIS WORKER ADJUD EFFICIENCY PRODUC ...METH/COMP 20. PAGE 100 B2014
B62
LABOR
MGT
BARGAIN
GP/REL

TAYLOR J.K.L.,ATTITUDES AND METHODS OF COMMUNICATION AND CONSULTATION BETWEEN EMPLOYERS AND WORKERS AT INDIVIDUAL FIRM LEVEL. WOR+45 STRUCT INDUS LABOR CONFER TASK GP/REL EFFICIENCY...MGT BIBLIOG METH 20 OECD. PAGE 103 B2087
B62
WORKER
ADMIN
ATTIT
EDU/PROP

US ADMINISTRATIVE CONFERENCE,FINAL REPORT OF THE ADMINISTRATIVE CONFERENCE OF THE US: SUGGESTIONS FOR IMPROVING PROCESSES - ADMIN. AGENCIES. USA+45 INGP/REL EFFICIENCY RATIONAL ORD/FREE...GP/COMP METH/COMP 20. PAGE 107 B2170
B62
ADMIN
NAT/G
DELIB/GP
GOV/REL

WANGSNESS P.H.,THE POWER OF THE CITY MANAGER. USA+45 EX/STRUC BAL/PWR BUDGET TAX ADMIN REPRESENT CENTRAL EFFICIENCY DRIVE ROLE...POLICY 20 CITY/MGT. PAGE 113 B2286
B62
PWR
TOP/EX
MUNIC
LOC/G

DONNELLY D.,"THE POLITICS AND ADMINISTRATION OF PLANNING." UK ROUTINE FEDERAL 20. PAGE 30 B0607
S62
GOV/REL
EFFICIENCY
ADMIN
EX/STRUC

OLLERENSHAW K.,"SHARING RESPONSIBLITY." UK DELIB/GP EDU/PROP EFFICIENCY 20. PAGE 80 B1607
S62
REPRESENT
GP/REL
ADMIN
EX/STRUC

UNIVERSITY PITT INST LOC GOVT,THE COUNCIL-MANAGER FORM OF GOVERNMENT IN PENNSYLVANIA (PAMPHLET). PROVS EX/STRUC REPRESENT GOV/REL EFFICIENCY ...CHARTS SIMUL 20 PENNSYLVAN CITY/MGT. PAGE 107 B2169
N62
LOC/G
TOP/EX
MUNIC
PWR

CORSON J.J.,PUBLIC ADMINISTRATION IN MODERN SOCIETY. INDUS FORCES CONTROL CENTRAL EFFICIENCY 20. PAGE 24 B0482
B63
MGT
NAT/G
PROB/SOLV
INGP/REL

DUE J.F.,STATE SALES TAX ADMINISTRATION. OP/RES BUDGET PAY ADMIN EXEC ROUTINE COST EFFICIENCY PROFIT...CHARTS METH/COMP 20. PAGE 31 B0626
B63
PROVS
TAX
STAT
GOV/COMP

FRIED R.C.,THE ITALIAN PREFECTS. ITALY STRATA ECO/DEV NAT/LISM ALL/IDEOS...TREND CHARTS METH/COMP BIBLIOG 17/20 PREFECT. PAGE 37 B0755
B63
ADMIN
NAT/G
EFFICIENCY

GANGULY D.S.,PUBLIC CORPORATIONS IN A NATIONAL ECONOMY. INDIA WOR+45 FINAN INDUS TOP/EX PRICE EFFICIENCY...MGT STAT CHARTS BIBLIOG 20. PAGE 38 B0779
B63
ECO/UNDEV
LG/CO
SOCISM
GOV/REL

HANSON A.H.,NATIONALIZATION: A BOOK OF READINGS. WOR+45 FINAN DELIB/GP LEGIS WORKER BUDGET ADMIN GP/REL EFFICIENCY SOCISM...MGT ANTHOL. PAGE 46 B0941
B63
NAT/G
OWN
INDUS
CONTROL

HARGROVE M.M.,BUSINESS POLICY CASES-WITH BEHAVIORAL SCIENCE IMPLICATIONS. LG/CO SML/CO EX/STRUC TOP/EX PLAN PROB/SOLV CONFER ADMIN CONTROL ROUTINE EFFICIENCY. PAGE 47 B0946
B63
SOC/EXP
INDUS
DECISION
MGT

KARL B.D.,EXECUTIVE REORGANIZATION AND REFORM IN THE NEW DEAL. ECO/DEV INDUS DELIB/GP EX/STRUC PLAN BUDGET ADMIN EFFICIENCY PWR POPULISM...POLICY 20 PRESIDENT ROOSEVLT/F WILSON/W NEW/DEAL. PAGE 58 B1174
B63
BIOG
EXEC
CREATE
CONTROL

KLEIN F.J.,JUDICIAL ADMINISTRATION AND THE LEGAL PROFESSION. USA+45 ADMIN CONTROL EFFICIENCY ...POLICY 20. PAGE 60 B1217
B63
BIBLIOG/A
CT/SYS
ADJUD
JUDGE

LITTERER J.A.,ORGANIZATIONS: STRUCTURE AND BEHAVIOR. PLAN DOMIN CONTROL LEAD ROUTINE SANCTION INGP/REL EFFICIENCY PRODUC DRIVE RIGID/FLEX PWR. PAGE 66 B1325
B63
ADMIN
CREATE
MGT
ADJUST

MAHESHWARI B.,STUDIES IN PANCHAYATI RAJ. INDIA POL/PAR EX/STRUC BUDGET EXEC REPRESENT CENTRAL EFFICIENCY...DECISION 20. PAGE 68 B1378
B63
FEDERAL
LOC/G
GOV/REL
LEAD

MCDONOUGH A.M.,INFORMATION ECONOMICS AND MANAGEMENT
B63
COMPUT/IR

SYSTEMS. ECO/DEV OP/RES AUTOMAT EFFICIENCY 20. MGT CONCPT COMPUTER
PAGE 72 B1448

B63
MEYNAUD J.,PLANIFICATION ET POLITIQUE. FRANCE ITALY PLAN FINAN LABOR DELIB/GP LEGIS ADMIN EFFICIENCY ...MAJORIT DECISION 20. PAGE 73 B1477 ECO/TAC PROB/SOLV

B63
US SENATE COMM APPROPRIATIONS,PERSONNEL ADMINISTRATION AND OPERATIONS OF AGENCY FOR INTERNATIONAL DEVELOPMENT: SPECIAL HEARING. FINAN LEAD COST UTIL SKILL...CHARTS 20 CONGRESS AID CIVIL/SERV. PAGE 109 B2211 ADMIN FOR/AID EFFICIENCY DIPLOM

B63
VAN RIPER P.P.,THE MERIT SYSTEM: FOUNDATION FOR RESPONSIBLE PUBLIC MANAGEMENT (PAMPHLET). USA+45 EX/STRUC 20. PAGE 112 B2252 EFFICIENCY ADMIN INGP/REL MGT

B63
WOLL P.,ADMINISTRATIVE LAW: THE INFORMAL PROCESS. USA+45 NAT/G CONTROL EFFICIENCY 20. PAGE 118 B2373 ADMIN ADJUD REPRESENT EX/STRUC

S63
BAKER R.J.,"DISCUSSION AND DECISION-MAKING IN THE CIVIL SERVICE." UK CONTROL REPRESENT INGP/REL PERS/REL EFFICIENCY 20. PAGE 8 B0168 EXEC EX/STRUC PROB/SOLV ADMIN

N63
INTERNATIONAL CITY MGRS ASSN,POST-ENTRY TRAINING IN THE LOCAL PUBLIC SERVICE (PAMPHLET). SCHOOL PLAN PROB/SOLV TEC/DEV ADMIN EFFICIENCY SKILL...POLICY AUD/VIS CHARTS BIBLIOG 20 CITY/MGT. PAGE 54 B1096 LOC/G WORKER EDU/PROP METH/COMP

B64
ARGYRIS C.,INTEGRATING THE INDIVIDUAL AND THE ORGANIZATION. WORKER PROB/SOLV LEAD SANCTION REPRESENT ADJUST EFFICIENCY DRIVE PERSON...PSY METH/CNCPT ORG/CHARTS. PAGE 6 B0132 ADMIN PERS/REL VOL/ASSN PARTIC

B64
COMMITTEE ECONOMIC DEVELOPMENT,IMPROVING EXECUTIVE MANAGEMENT IN THE FEDERAL GOVERNMENT. USA+45 CHIEF DELIB/GP WORKER PLAN PAY SENIOR ADMIN EFFICIENCY 20 PRESIDENT. PAGE 22 B0457 EXEC MGT TOP/EX NAT/G

B64
EWING D.W.,THE MANAGERIAL MIND. SOCIETY STRUCT INDUS PERSON KNOWL 20. PAGE 34 B0692 MGT ATTIT CREATE EFFICIENCY

B64
GOLDWIN R.A.,POLITICAL PARTIES. USA. USA+45 USA-45 LOC/G ADMIN LEAD EFFICIENCY ATTIT PWR...POLICY STAT ANTHOL 18/20 CONGRESS. PAGE 40 B0818 POL/PAR PARTIC NAT/G CONSTN

B64
GOODNOW H.F.,THE CIVIL SERVICE OF PAKISTAN: BUREAUCRACY IN A NEW NATION. INDIA PAKISTAN S/ASIA ECO/UNDEV PROVS CHIEF PARTIC CHOOSE EFFICIENCY PWR ...BIBLIOG 20. PAGE 41 B0824 ADMIN GOV/REL LAW NAT/G

B64
GROSS B.M.,THE MANAGING OF ORGANIZATIONS (VOL. I). USA+45 ECO/DEV LG/CO CAP/ISM EFFICIENCY ROLE...MGT 20. PAGE 44 B0886 ECO/TAC ADMIN INDUS POLICY

B64
GROSS B.M.,THE MANAGING OF ORGANIZATIONS (VOL. II). FUT USA+45 ECO/DEV EDU/PROP EFFICIENCY...MGT BIBLIOG/A 20. PAGE 44 B0887 ECO/TAC ADMIN INDUS POLICY

B64
JACKSON H.M.,THE SECRETARY OF STATE AND THE AMBASSADOR* JACKSON SUBCOMMITTEE PAPERS ON THE CONDUCT OF AMERICAN FOREIGN POLICY. USA+45 NAT/G FORCES ACT/RES OP/RES EDU/PROP CENTRAL EFFICIENCY ORD/FREE...OBS RECORD ANTHOL CONGRESS PRESIDENT. PAGE 55 B1107 GOV/REL DIPLOM ADMIN EX/STRUC

B64
MAYER C.S.,INTERVIEWING COSTS IN SURVEY RESEARCH. USA+45 PLAN COST...MGT REC/INT SAMP METH/COMP HYPO/EXP METH 20. PAGE 71 B1434 SIMUL INT R+D EFFICIENCY

B64
NUQUIST A.E.,TOWN GOVERNMENT IN VERMONT. USA+45 FINAN TOP/EX PROB/SOLV BUDGET TAX REPRESENT SUFF EFFICIENCY...OBS INT 20 VERMONT. PAGE 79 B1595 LOC/G MUNIC POPULISM ADMIN

B64
PEABODY R.L.,ORGANIZATIONAL AUTHORITY. SCHOOL WORKER PLAN SENIOR GOV/REL UTIL DRIVE PWR...PSY CHARTS BIBLIOG 20. PAGE 82 B1648 ADMIN EFFICIENCY TASK GP/REL

B64
POTTER D.C.,GOVERNMENT IN RURAL INDIA. INDIA LEGIT INGP/REL EFFICIENCY ATTIT 20. PAGE 84 B1695 LOC/G ADMIN TAX PROB/SOLV

RIDLEY F.,PUBLIC ADMINISTRATION IN FRANCE. FRANCE UK EX/STRUC CONTROL PARTIC EFFICIENCY 20. PAGE 88 B1781 B64
ADMIN REPRESENT GOV/COMP PWR

B64
RUSSELL R.B.,UNITED NATIONS EXPERIENCE WITH MILITARY FORCES: POLITICAL AND LEGAL ASPECTS. AFR KOREA WOR+45 LEGIS PROB/SOLV ADMIN CONTROL EFFICIENCY PEACE...POLICY INT/LAW BIBLIOG UN. PAGE 92 B1857 FORCES DIPLOM SANCTION ORD/FREE

B64
STANLEY D.T.,THE HIGHER CIVIL SERVICE: AN EVALUATION OF FEDERAL PERSONNEL PRACTICES. USA+45 CREATE EXEC ROUTINE CENTRAL...MGT SAMP IDEA/COMP METH/COMP 20 CIVIL/SERV. PAGE 100 B2020 NAT/G ADMIN CONTROL EFFICIENCY

B64
TILMAN R.O.,BUREAUCRATIC TRANSITION IN MALAYA. MALAYSIA S/ASIA UK NAT/G EX/STRUC DIPLOM...CHARTS BIBLIOG 20. PAGE 104 B2110 ADMIN COLONIAL SOVEREIGN EFFICIENCY

B64
TULLY A.,WHERE DID YOUR MONEY GO. USA+45 USSR ECO/UNDEV ADMIN EFFICIENCY WEALTH...METH/COMP 20. PAGE 106 B2136 FOR/AID DIPLOM CONTROL

B64
WELLISZ S.,THE ECONOMICS OF THE SOVIET BLOC. COM USSR INDUS WORKER PLAN BUDGET INT/TRADE TAX PRICE PRODUC WEALTH MARXISM...METH/COMP 20. PAGE 115 B2319 EFFICIENCY ADMIN MARKET

B64
WILLIAMSON O.E.,THE ECONOMICS OF DISCRETIONARY BEHAVIOR: MANAGERIAL OBJECTIVES IN A THEORY OF THE FIRM. MARKET BUDGET CAP/ISM PRODUC DRIVE PERSON ...STAT CHARTS BIBLIOG METH 20. PAGE 117 B2354 EFFICIENCY MGT ECO/TAC CHOOSE

S64
STANLEY D.T.,"EXCELLENCE IN PUBLIC SERVICE - HOW DO YOU REALLY KNOW?" EXEC 20. PAGE 100 B2019 EFFICIENCY EX/STRUC ADMIN CONTROL

N64
CANADA NATL JT COUN PUB SERV,THE CANADA NATIONAL JOINT COUNCIL OF THE PUBLIC SERVICE 1944-1964 (PAMPHLET). CANADA EX/STRUC PERS/REL DRIVE...MGT 20 PEARSON/L. PAGE 18 B0373 GP/REL NAT/G LABOR EFFICIENCY

B65
DYER F.C.,BUREAUCRACY VS CREATIVITY. UNIV CONTROL LEAD INGP/REL EFFICIENCY MGT. PAGE 31 B0639 ADMIN DECISION METH/COMP CREATE

B65
HARR J.E.,THE DEVELOPMENT OF CAREERS IN THE FOREIGN SERVICE. CREATE SENIOR EXEC FEEDBACK GOV/REL EFFICIENCY ATTIT RESPECT ORG/CHARTS. PAGE 47 B0953 OP/RES MGT ADMIN DIPLOM

B65
INST INTL DES CIVILISATION DIF,THE CONSTITUTIONS AND ADMINISTRATIVE INSTITUTIONS OF THE NEW STATES. AFR ISLAM S/ASIA NAT/G POL/PAR DELIB/GP EX/STRUC CONFER EFFICIENCY NAT/LISM...JURID SOC 20. PAGE 54 B1088 CONSTN ADMIN ADJUD ECO/UNDEV

B65
JONES A.G.,THE EVOLUTION OF PERSONNEL SYSTEMS FOR US FOREIGN AFFAIRS* A HISTORY OF REFORM EFFORTS. USA+45 USA-45 ACADEM OP/RES GOV/REL...MGT CONGRESS. PAGE 57 B1149 DIPLOM ADMIN ACT/RES EFFICIENCY

B65
MELMANS S.,OUR DEPLETED SOCIETY. SPACE USA+45 ECO/DEV FORCES BUDGET ECO/TAC ADMIN WEAPON EFFICIENCY 20 COLD/WAR. PAGE 73 B1465 CIVMIL/REL INDUS EDU/PROP CONTROL

B65
MEYERHOFF A.E.,THE STRATEGY OF PERSUASION. USA+45 COM/IND CONSULT FOR/AID CONTROL COERCE COST ATTIT PERCEPT MARXISM 20 COLD/WAR. PAGE 73 B1476 EDU/PROP EFFICIENCY OP/RES ADMIN

B65
PRESTHUS R.,BEHAVIORAL APPROACHES TO PUBLIC ADMINISTRATION. UK STRATA LG/CO PUB/INST VOL/ASSN EX/STRUC TOP/EX EFFICIENCY HEALTH. PAGE 84 B1704 GEN/METH DECISION ADMIN R+D

B65
ROURKE F.E.,BUREAUCRATIC POWER IN NATIONAL POLITICS. ADMIN CONTROL EXEC GOV/REL INGP/REL 20. PAGE 91 B1838 EX/STRUC EFFICIENCY REPRESENT PWR

B65
US SENATE COMM GOVT OPERATIONS,ORGANIZATION OF FEDERAL EXECUTIVE DEPARTMENTS AND AGENCIES: REPORT OF MARCH 23, 1965. USA+45 FORCES LEGIS DIPLOM ROUTINE CIVMIL/REL EFFICIENCY FEDERAL...MGT STAT. PAGE 110 B2217 ADMIN EX/STRUC GOV/REL ORG/CHARTS

B65
US SENATE COMM ON JUDICIARY,HEARINGS BEFORE SUBCOMMITTEE ON ADMINISTRATIVE PRACTICE AND PROCEDURE ABOUT ADMINISTRATIVE PROCEDURE ACT 1965. ROUTINE DELIB/GP ADMIN

USA+45 LEGIS EDU/PROP ADJUD GOV/REL INGP/REL — NAT/G
EFFICIENCY...POLICY INT 20 CONGRESS. PAGE 110 B2232

B65
WARD R.,BACKGROUND MATERIAL ON ECONOMIC IMPACT OF — ECO/DEV
FEDERAL PROCUREMENT - 1965: FOR JOINT ECONOMIC — NAT/G
COMMITTEE US CONGRESS. FINAN ROUTINE WEAPON — OWN
CIVMIL/REL EFFICIENCY...STAT CHARTS 20 CONGRESS. — GOV/REL
PAGE 113 B2288

S65
"FURTHER READING." INDIA STRUCT FINAN WORKER ADMIN — BIBLIOG
COST 20. PAGE 2 B0042 — MGT
ECO/UNDEV
EFFICIENCY
S65
BALDWIN H.,"SLOW-DOWN IN THE PENTAGON." USA+45 — RECORD
CREATE PLAN GOV/REL CENTRAL COST EFFICIENCY PWR — R+D
...MGT MCNAMARA/R. PAGE 9 B0174 — WEAPON
ADMIN
S65
GRENIEWSKI H.,"INTENTION AND PERFORMANCE: A PRIMER — SIMUL
OF CYBERNETICS OF PLANNING." EFFICIENCY OPTIMAL — GAME
KNOWL SKILL...DECISION MGT EQULIB. PAGE 43 B0873 — GEN/METH
PLAN
B66
ALEXANDER Y.,INTERNATIONAL TECHNICAL ASSISTANCE — ECO/TAC
EXPERTS* A CASE STUDY OF THE U.N. EXPERIENCE. — INT/ORG
ECO/UNDEV CONSULT EX/STRUC CREATE PLAN DIPLOM — ADMIN
FOR/AID TASK EFFICIENCY...ORG/CHARTS UN. PAGE 4 — MGT
B0074

B66
AMER ENTERPRISE INST PUB POL,CONGRESS: THE FIRST — EFFICIENCY
BRANCH OF GOVERNMENT. EX/STRUC FEEDBACK REPRESENT — LEGIS
INGP/REL PWR...DECISION METH/CNCPT PREDICT. PAGE 4 — DELIB/GP
B0081 — CONTROL
B66
BURNS A.C.,PARLIAMENT AS AN EXPORT. WOR+45 CONSTN — PARL/PROC
BARGAIN DEBATE ROUTINE GOV/REL EFFICIENCY...ANTHOL — POL/PAR
COMMONWLTH PARLIAMENT. PAGE 17 B0353 — CT/SYS
CHIEF
B66
DAHLBERG J.S.,THE NEW YORK BUREAU OF MUNICIPAL — PROVS
RESEARCH: PIONEER IN GOVERNMENT ADMINISTRATION. — MUNIC
CONSTN R+D BUDGET EDU/PROP PARTIC REPRESENT — DELIB/GP
EFFICIENCY ORD/FREE...BIBLIOG METH 20 NEW/YORK — ADMIN
NIPA. PAGE 26 B0522
B66
DAVIS R.G.,PLANNING HUMAN RESOURCE DEVELOPMENT. — PLAN
EDUCATIONAL MODELS AND SCHEMATA. WORKER OP/RES — EFFICIENCY
ECO/TAC EDU/PROP CONTROL COST PRODUC...GEOG STAT — SIMUL
CHARTS 20. PAGE 27 B0544 — ROUTINE
B66
HESSLER I.O.,29 WAYS TO GOVERN A CITY. EX/STRUC — MUNIC
TOP/EX PROB/SOLV PARTIC CHOOSE REPRESENT EFFICIENCY — GOV/COMP
...CHARTS 20 CITY/MGT MAYOR. PAGE 49 B0998 — LOC/G
ADMIN
B66
MANSFIELD E.,MANAGERIAL ECONOMICS AND OPERATIONS — ECO/TAC
RESEARCH; A NONMATHEMATICAL INTRODUCTION. USA+45 — OP/RES
ELITES ECO/UNDEV CONSULT EX/STRUC PROB/SOLV ROUTINE — MGT
EFFICIENCY OPTIMAL...GAME T 20. PAGE 69 B1396 — COMPUTER
B66
PERKINS J.A.,THE UNIVERSITY IN TRANSITION. USA+45 — ACADEM
SOCIETY FINAN INDUS NAT/G EX/STRUC ADMIN INGP/REL — ORD/FREE
COST EFFICIENCY ATTIT 20. PAGE 82 B1658 — CREATE
ROLE
B66
RAPHAEL J.S.,GOVERNMENTAL REGULATION OF BUSINESS. — LG/CO
USA+45 LAW CONSTN TAX ADJUD ADMIN EFFICIENCY PWR — GOV/REL
20. PAGE 86 B1736 — CONTROL
ECO/DEV
B66
SCHLESSINGER P.J.,ELEMENTS OF CALIFORNIA GOVERNMENT — LOC/G
(2ND ED.). USA+45 LAW ADJUD ADMIN CONTROL CT/SYS — PROVS
EFFICIENCY...BIBLIOG T CALIFORNIA. PAGE 94 B1891 — GOV/REL
LEGIS
B66
SCHMIDT F.,PUBLIC RELATIONS IN HEALTH AND WELFARE. — PROF/ORG
USA+45 ACADEM RECEIVE PRESS FEEDBACK GOV/REL — EDU/PROP
PERS/REL DEMAND EFFICIENCY ATTIT PERCEPT WEALTH 20 — ADMIN
PUBLIC/REL. PAGE 94 B1895 — HEALTH
B66
US SENATE COMM GOVT OPERATIONS,INTERGOVERNMENTAL — ADMIN
PERSONNEL ACT OF 1966. USA+45 NAT/G CONSULT — LEGIS
DELIB/GP WORKER TEC/DEV PAY AUTOMAT UTIL 20 — EFFICIENCY
CONGRESS. PAGE 110 B2219 — EDU/PROP
B66
WADIA M.,THE NATURE AND SCOPE OF MANAGEMENT. — MGT
DELIB/GP EX/STRUC CREATE AUTOMAT CONTROL EFFICIENCY — PROB/SOLV
...ANTHOL 20. PAGE 112 B2271 — IDEA/COMP
ECO/TAC
B66
WESTON J.F.,THE SCOPE AND METHODOLOGY OF FINANCE. — FINAN
PLAN TEC/DEV CONTROL EFFICIENCY INCOME UTIL...MGT — ECO/DEV
CONCPT MATH STAT TREND METH 20. PAGE 115 B2327 — POLICY
PRICE

B66
WILLNER A.R.,THE NEOTRADITIONAL ACCOMMODATION TO — INDONESIA
POLITICAL INDEPENDENCE* THE CASE OF INDONESIA * — CONSERVE
RESEARCH MONOGRAPH NO. 26. CULTURE ECO/UNDEV CREATE — ELITES
PROB/SOLV FOR/AID LEGIT COLONIAL EFFICIENCY — ADMIN
NAT/LISM ALL/VALS SOC. PAGE 117 B2355
B66
YOUNG S.,MANAGEMENT: A SYSTEMS ANALYSIS. DELIB/GP — PROB/SOLV
EX/STRUC ECO/TAC CONTROL EFFICIENCY...NET/THEORY — MGT
20. PAGE 119 B2394 — DECISION
SIMUL
S66
PALMER M.,"THE UNITED ARAB REPUBLIC* AN ASSESSMENT — UAR
OF ITS FAILURE." ELITES ECO/UNDEV POL/PAR FORCES — SYRIA
ECO/TAC RUMOR ADMIN EXEC EFFICIENCY ATTIT SOCISM — REGION
...INT NASSER/G. PAGE 81 B1628 — FEDERAL
B67
AMERICAN FRIENDS SERVICE COMM,IN PLACE OF WAR. — PEACE
NAT/G ACT/RES DIPLOM ADMIN NUC/PWR EFFICIENCY — PACIFISM
...POLICY 20. PAGE 4 B0085 — WAR
DETER
B67
BUDER S.,PULLMAN: AN EXPERIMENT IN INDUSTRIAL ORDER — DIST/IND
AND COMMUNITY PLANNING, 1880-1930. USA-45 SOCIETY — INDUS
LABOR LG/CO CREATE PROB/SOLV CONTROL GP/REL — MUNIC
EFFICIENCY ATTIT...MGT BIBLIOG 19/20 PULLMAN. — PLAN
PAGE 17 B0337
B67
ENKE S.,DEFENSE MANAGEMENT. USA+45 R+D FORCES — DECISION
WORKER PLAN ECO/TAC ADMIN NUC/PWR BAL/PAY UTIL — DELIB/GP
WEALTH...MGT DEPT/DEFEN. PAGE 33 B0675 — EFFICIENCY
BUDGET
B67
ILLINOIS COMMISSION,IMPROVING THE STATE — PROVS
LEGISLATURE. USA+45 LAW CONSTN NAT/G PROB/SOLV — LEGIS
EDU/PROP ADMIN TASK CHOOSE INGP/REL EFFICIENCY — REPRESENT
ILLINOIS. PAGE 53 B1077 — PLAN
B67
MARRIS P.,DILEMMAS OF SOCIAL REFORM: POVERTY AND — STRUCT
COMMUNITY ACTION IN THE UNITED STATES. USA+45 NAT/G — MUNIC
OP/RES ADMIN PARTIC EFFICIENCY WEALTH...SOC — PROB/SOLV
METH/COMP T 20 REFORMERS. PAGE 69 B1401 — COST
B67
MINTZ M.,BY PRESCRIPTION ONLY. USA+45 NAT/G — BIO/SOC
EX/STRUC PLAN TEC/DEV EXEC EFFICIENCY HEALTH...MGT — PROC/MFG
SOC/WK 20. PAGE 74 B1491 — CONTROL
POLICY
B67
POSNER M.V.,ITALIAN PUBLIC ENTERPRISE. ITALY — NAT/G
ECO/DEV FINAN INDUS CREATE ECO/TAC ADMIN CONTROL — PLAN
EFFICIENCY PRODUC...TREND CHARTS 20. PAGE 84 B1693 — CAP/ISM
SOCISM
B67
SALMOND J.A.,THE CIVILIAN CONSERVATION CORPS, — ADMIN
1933-1942. USA-45 NAT/G CREATE EXEC EFFICIENCY — ECO/TAC
WEALTH...BIBLIOG 20 ROOSEVLT/F. PAGE 92 B1864 — TASK
AGRI
B67
US DEPARTMENT OF JUSTICE,ANNUAL REPORT OF THE — ADMIN
OFFICE OF ADMINISTRATIVE PROCEDURE. USA+45 — NAT/G
PROB/SOLV EDU/PROP EXEC INGP/REL EFFICIENCY KNOWL — ROUTINE
...POLICY STAT 20. PAGE 108 B2181 — GOV/REL
L67
BESCOBY I.,"A COLONIAL ADMINISTRATION* AN ANALYSIS — ADMIN
OF ADMINISTRATION IN BRITISH COLUMBIA 1869-1871." — CANADA
UK STRATA EX/STRUC LEGIS TASK GOV/REL EFFICIENCY — COLONIAL
ROLE...MGT CHARTS 19. PAGE 11 B0232 — LEAD
L67
PASLEY R.S.,"ORGANIZATIONAL CONFLICTS OF INTEREST — NAT/G
IN GOVERNMENT CONTRACTS." ELITES R+D ROUTINE — ECO/TAC
NUC/PWR DEMAND EFFICIENCY 20. PAGE 81 B1639 — RATION
CONTROL
S67
ATKIN J.M.,"THE FEDERAL GOVERNMENT, BIG BUSINESS, — SCHOOL
AND COLLEGES OF EDUCATION." PROF/ORG CONSULT CREATE — ACADEM
PLAN PROB/SOLV ADMIN EFFICIENCY. PAGE 7 B0144 — NAT/G
INDUS
S67
BERLINER J.S.,"RUSSIA'S PUREAUCRATS - WHY THEY'RE — CREATE
REACTIONARY." USSR NAT/G OP/RES PROB/SOLV TEC/DEV — ADMIN
CONTROL SANCTION EFFICIENCY DRIVE PERSON...TECHNIC — INDUS
SOC 20. PAGE 11 B0223 — PRODUC
S67
BURKE E.M.,"THE SEARCH FOR AUTHORITY IN PLANNING." — DECISION
MUNIC NEIGH CREATE PROB/SOLV LEGIT ADMIN CONTROL — PLAN
EFFICIENCY PWR...METH/COMP SIMUL 20. PAGE 17 B0352 — LOC/G
METH
S67
CHAMBERLAIN N.W.,"STRIKES IN CONTEMPORARY CONTEXT." — LABOR
LAW INDUS NAT/G CHIEF CONFER COST ATTIT ORD/FREE — BARGAIN
...POLICY MGT 20. PAGE 20 B0400 — EFFICIENCY
PROB/SOLV
S67
DIXON O.F.,"A SOCIAL SYSTEMS APPROACH TO — MARKET
MARKETING." ECO/DEV ECO/TAC CONTROL EFFICIENCY — SOCIETY
...DECISION 20. PAGE 29 B0599 — GP/REL

MGT
S67
DOERN G.B., "THE ROYAL COMMISSIONS IN THE GENERAL   R+D
POLICY PROCESS AND IN FEDERAL-PROVINCIAL   EX/STRUC
RELATIONS." CANADA CONSTN ACADEM PROVS CONSULT   GOV/REL
DELIB/GP LEGIS ACT/RES PROB/SOLV CONFER CONTROL   NAT/G
EFFICIENCY...METH/COMP 20 SENATE ROYAL/COMM.
PAGE 30 B0603
S67
DONNELL J.C., "PACIFICATION REASSESSED." VIETNAM/S   ADMIN
NAT/LISM DRIVE SUPEGO ORD/FREE...SOC/WK 20. PAGE 30   GP/REL
B0606   EFFICIENCY
MUNIC
S67
DUGGAR J.W., "THE DEVELOPMENT OF MONEY SUPPLY IN   ECO/UNDEV
ETHIOPIA." ETHIOPIA ISLAM CONSULT OP/RES BUDGET   FINAN
CONTROL ROUTINE EFFICIENCY EQUILIB WEALTH...MGT 20.   BAL/PAY
PAGE 31 B0629   ECOMETRIC
S67
FRYKENBURG R.E., "STUDIES OF LAND CONTROL IN INDIAN   ECO/UNDEV
HISTORY: REVIEW ARTICLE." INDIA UK STRATA AGRI   CONTROL
MUNIC OP/RES COLONIAL REGION EFFICIENCY OWN HABITAT   ADMIN
...CONCPT 16/20. PAGE 38 B0763
S67
GORHAM W., "NOTES OF A PRACTITIONER." USA+45 BUDGET   DECISION
ADMIN COST...CON/ANAL METH/COMP 20 JOHNSON/LB.   NAT/G
PAGE 41 B0836   DELIB/GP
EFFICIENCY
S67
GRINYER P.H., "THE SYSTEMATIC EVALUATION OF METHODS   OP/RES
OF WAGE PAYMENT." UK INDUS WORKER ADMIN EFFICIENCY   COST
...MGT METH/COMP 20. PAGE 44 B0882   PAY
PRODUC
S67
HAIRE M., "MANAGING MANAGEMENT MANPOWER." EX/STRUC   MGT
OP/RES PAY EDU/PROP COST EFFICIENCY...PREDICT SIMUL   EXEC
20. PAGE 45 B0920   LEAD
INDUS
S67
KAYSEN C., "DATA BANKS AND DOSSIERS." FUT USA+45   CENTRAL
COM/IND NAT/G PLAN PROB/SOLV TEC/DEV BUDGET ADMIN   EFFICIENCY
ROUTINE. PAGE 59 B1185   CENSUS
ACT/RES
S67
LENDVAI P., "HUNGARY* CHANGE VS. IMMOBILISM."   ECO/DEV
HUNGARY LABOR NAT/G PLAN DEBATE ADMIN ROUTINE   MGT
CENTRAL EFFICIENCY MARXISM PLURISM...PREDICT 20.   CHOOSE
PAGE 64 B1289
S67
LEVCIK B., "WAGES AND EMPLOYMENT PROBLEMS IN THE NEW   MARXISM
SYSTEM OF PLANNED MANAGEMENT IN CZECHOSLOVAKIA."   WORKER
CZECHOSLVK EUR+WWI NAT/G OP/RES PLAN ADMIN ROUTINE   MGT
INGP/REL CENTRAL EFFICIENCY PRODUC DECISION.   PAY
PAGE 64 B1300
S67
MAINZER L.C., "HONOR IN THE BUREAUCRATIC LIFE."   ADMIN
REPRESENT EFFICIENCY 20. PAGE 68 B1382   MORAL
EX/STRUC
EXEC
S67
MERON T., "THE UN'S 'COMMON SYSTEM' OF SALARY,   ADMIN
ALLOWANCE, AND BENEFITS: CRITICAL APPR*SAL OF COORD   EX/STRUC
IN PERSONNEL MATTERS." VOL/ASSN PAY EFFICIENCY   INT/ORG
...CHARTS 20 UN. PAGE 73 B1470   BUDGET
S67
MOOR E.J., "THE INTERNATIONAL IMPACT OF AUTOMATION."   TEC/DEV
WOR+45 ACT/RES COMPUTER CREATE PLAN CAP/ISM ROUTINE   OP/RES
EFFICIENCY PREDICT. PAGE 75 B1511   AUTOMAT
INDUS
S67
PRATT R.C., "THE ADMINISTRATION OF ECONOMIC PLANNING   NAT/G
IN A NEWLY INDEPEND ENT STATE* THE TANZANIAN   DELIB/GP
EXPERIENCE 1963-1966." AFR TANZANIA ECO/UNDEV PLAN   ADMIN
CONTROL ROUTINE TASK EFFICIENCY 20. PAGE 84 B1699   TEC/DEV
S67
ROBERTS E.B., "THE PROBLEM OF AGING ORGANIZATIONS."   INDUS
INTELL PROB/SOLV ADMIN EXEC FEEDBACK EFFICIENCY   R+D
PRODUC...GEN/LAWS 20. PAGE 89 B1794   MGT
PLAN
S67
ROSENZWEIG J.E., "MANAGERS AND MANAGEMENT SCIENTISTS   EFFICIENCY
(TWO CULTURES)" INDUS CREATE TEC/DEV OPTIMAL   MGT
...NEW/IDEA 20. PAGE 90 B1823   INTELL
METH/COMP
S67
ROWAT D.C., "RECENT DEVELOPMENTS IN OMBUDSMANSHIP* A   CANADA
REVIEW ARTICLE." UK USA+45 STRUCT CONSULT INSPECT   ADMIN
TASK EFFICIENCY...NEW/IDEA 20. PAGE 91 B1841   LOC/G
NAT/G
S67
RUBIN R.I., "THE LEGISLATIVE-EXECUTIVE RELATIONS OF   LEGIS
THE UNITED STATES INFORMATION AGENCY." USA+45   EX/STRUC
EDU/PROP TASK INGP/REL EFFICIENCY ISOLAT ATTIT ROLE   GP/REL
USIA CONGRESS. PAGE 91 B1850   PROF/ORG
S67
SKOLNIKOFF E.B., "MAKING FOREIGN POLICY" PROB/SOLV   TEC/DEV

EFFICIENCY PERCEPT PWR...MGT METH/CNCPT CLASSIF 20.   CONTROL
PAGE 98 B1976   USA+45
NAT/G
S67
SPACKMAN A., "THE SENATE OF TRINIDAD AND TOBAGO."   ELITES
L/A+17C TRINIDAD WEST/IND NAT/G POL/PAR DELIB/GP   EFFICIENCY
OP/RES PROB/SOLV EDU/PROP EXEC LOBBY ROUTINE   LEGIS
REPRESENT GP/REL 20. PAGE 99 B2002   DECISION
S67
TATU M., "URSS: LES FLOTTEMENTS DE LA DIRECTION   POLICY
COLLEGIALE." UAR USSR CHIEF LEAD INGP/REL   NAT/G
EFFICIENCY...DECISION TREND 20 MID/EAST. PAGE 103   EX/STRUC
B2082   DIPLOM
S67
TIVEY L., "THE POLITICAL CONSEQUENCES OF ECONOMIC   PLAN
PLANNING." UK CONSTN INDUS ACT/RES ADMIN CONTROL   POLICY
LOBBY REPRESENT EFFICIENCY SUPEGO SOVEREIGN   NAT/G
...DECISION 20. PAGE 104 B2112
S67
ZOETEWEIJ B., "INCOME POLICIES ABROAD: AN INTERIM   METH/COMP
REPORT." NAT/G PROB/SOLV BARGAIN BUDGET PRICE RISK   INCOME
CENTRAL EFFICIENCY EQUILIB...MGT NAT/COMP 20.   POLICY
PAGE 119 B2405   LABOR
S68
PEARSON A.W., "RESOURCE ALLOCATION." PLAN PROB/SOLV   PROFIT
BUDGET ADMIN CONTROL CHOOSE EFFICIENCY...DECISION   OPTIMAL
MGT 20. PAGE 82 B1649   COST
INDUS

EFTA....EUROPEAN FREE TRADE ASSOCIATION

B61
BENOIT E., EUROPE AT SIXES AND SEVENS: THE COMMON   FINAN
MARKET, THE FREE TRADE ASSOCIATION AND THE UNITED   ECO/DEV
STATES. EUR+WWI FUT USA+45 INDUS CONSULT DELIB/GP   VOL/ASSN
EX/STRUC TOP/EX ACT/RES ECO/TAC EDU/PROP ROUTINE
CHOOSE PERCEPT WEALTH...MGT TREND EEC TOT/POP 20
EFTA. PAGE 11 B0217

EGLE W.P. B0656

EGYPT....SEE ALSO ISLAM, UAR, EGYPT/ANC

EGYPT/ANC....ANCIENT EGYPT

EHRMANN H.W. B0657

EIB....EUROPEAN INVESTMENT BANK

EICHMANN/A....ADOLF EICHMANN

EINSTEIN/A....ALBERT EINSTEIN

EISENSTADT S.N. B0658,B0659,B0661

EISNHWR/DD....PRESIDENT DWIGHT DAVID EISENHOWER

S56
CUTLER R., "THE DEVELOPMENT OF THE NATIONAL SECURITY   ORD/FREE
COUNCIL." USA+45 INTELL CONSULT EX/STRUC DIPLOM   DELIB/GP
LEAD 20 TRUMAN/HS EISNHWR/DD NSC. PAGE 25 B0514   PROB/SOLV
NAT/G
B61
MARKMANN C.L., JOHN F. KENNEDY: A SENSE OF PURPOSE.   CHIEF
USA+45 INTELL FAM CONSULT DELIB/DD/GP LEGIS PERSON   TOP/EX
SKILL 20 KENNEDY/JF EISNHWR/DD ROOSEVLT/F   ADMIN
NEW/FRONTR PRESIDENT. PAGE 69 B1399   BIOG
B62
BENSON E.T., CROSS FIRE: THE EIGHT YEARS WITH   ADMIN
EISENHOWER. USA+45 DIPLOM LEAD ATTIT PERSON   POLICY
CONSERVE...TRADIT BIOG 20 EISNHWR/DD PRESIDENT   DELIB/GP
TAFT/RA DULLES/JF NIXON/RM. PAGE 11 B0218   TOP/EX
B62
GRAY R.K., EIGHTEEN ACRES UNDER GLASS. ELITES   CHIEF
CONSULT EX/STRUC DIPLOM PRESS CONFER WAR PERS/REL   ADMIN
PERSON 20 EISNHWR/DD TRUMAN/HS CABINET. PAGE 43   TOP/EX
B0860   NAT/G
B62
SCHILLING W.R., STRATEGY, POLITICS, AND DEFENSE   ROUTINE
BUDGETS." USA+45 R+D NAT/G CONSULT DELIB/GP FORCES   POLICY
LEGIS ACT/RES PLAN BAL/PWR LEGIT EXEC NUC/PWR
RIGID/FLEX PWR...TREND COLD/WAR CONGRESS 20
EISNHWR/DD. PAGE 93 B1890
B64
NEUSTADT R., PRESIDENTIAL POWER. USA+45 CONSTN NAT/G   TOP/EX
CHIEF LEGIS CREATE EDU/PROP LEGIT ADMIN EXEC COERCE   SKILL
ATTIT PERSON RIGID/FLEX PWR CONGRESS 20 PRESIDENT
TRUMAN/HS EISNHWR/DD. PAGE 78 B1575

EL/SALVADR....EL SALVADOR; SEE ALSO L/A+17C

B47
DE NOIA J., GUIDE TO OFFICIAL PUBLICATIONS OF THE   BIBLIOG/A
OTHER AMERICAN REPUBLICS: EL SALVADOR. EL/SALVADR   CONSTN

LAW LEGIS EDU/PROP CT/SYS 20. PAGE 27 B0558
   NAT/G
   ADMIN

      B60
FLORES R.H.,CATALOGO DE TESIS DOCTORALES DE LAS
FACULTADES DE LA UNIVERSIDAD DE EL SALVADOR.
EL/SALVADR LAW DIPLOM ADMIN LEAD GOV/REL...SOC
19/20. PAGE 36 B0730
   BIBLIOG
   ACADEM
   L/A+17C
   NAT/G

ELAZAR D.J. B0662

ELDER R.E. B0663

ELDREDGE H.W. B0664

ELECT/COLL....ELECTORAL COLLEGE

ELECTIONS....SEE CHOOSE

ELECTORAL COLLEGE....SEE ELECT/COLL

ELIAS T.O. B0665

ELITES....POWER-DOMINANT GROUPINGS OF A SOCIETY

      B16
TREITSCHKE H.,POLITICS. UNIV SOCIETY STRATA NAT/G
EX/STRUC LEGIS DOMIN EDU/PROP ATTIT PWR RESPECT
...CONCPT TIME/SEQ GEN/LAWS TOT/POP 20. PAGE 105
B2127
   EXEC
   ELITES
   GERMANY

      N19
ADMINISTRATIVE STAFF COLLEGE,THE ACCOUNTABILITY OF
GOVERNMENT DEPARTMENTS (PAMPHLET) (REV. ED.). UK
CONSTN FINAN NAT/G CONSULT ADMIN INGP/REL CONSEN
PRIVIL 20 PARLIAMENT. PAGE 3 B0059
   PARL/PROC
   ELITES
   SANCTION
   PROB/SOLV

      N19
BOHLKE R.H.,BUREAUCRATS AND INTELLECTUALS: A
CRITIQUE OF C. WRIGHT MILLS (PAMPHLET). ADMIN
SOCISM. PAGE 13 B0266
   PERSON
   SOC
   ELITES
   ACADEM

      B23
FRANK T.,A HISTORY OF ROME. MEDIT-7 INTELL SOCIETY
LOC/G NAT/G POL/PAR FORCES LEGIS DOMIN LEGIT
ALL/VALS...CONCPT TIME/SEQ GEN/LAWS ROM/EMP
ROM/EMP. PAGE 37 B0749
   EXEC
   STRUCT
   ELITES

      B32
MCKISACK M.,THE PARLIAMENTARY REPRESENTATION OF THE
ENGLISH BOROUGHS DURING THE MIDDLE AGES. UK CONSTN
CULTURE ELITES EX/STRUC TAX PAY ADJUD PARL/PROC
APPORT FEDERAL...POLICY 13/15 PARLIAMENT. PAGE 72
B1454
   NAT/G
   MUNIC
   LEGIS
   CHOOSE

      B36
GAUS J.M.,THE FRONTIERS OF PUBLIC ADMINISTRATION.
EFFICIENCY PERCEPT RIGID/FLEX ORD/FREE 20. PAGE 39
B0785
   ROUTINE
   GOV/REL
   ELITES
   PROB/SOLV

      S37
LASSWELL H.D.,"GOVERNMENTAL AND PARTY LEADERS IN
FASCIST ITALY." ITALY CRIME SKILL...BIOG CHARTS
GP/COMP 20. PAGE 63 B1266
   ELITES
   FASCISM
   ADMIN

      B38
PETTEE G.S.,THE PROCESS OF REVOLUTION. COM FRANCE
ITALY MOD/EUR RUSSIA SPAIN WOR+45 ELITES INTELL
SOCIETY STRATA STRUCT INT/ORG NAT/G POL/PAR ACT/RES
PLAN EDU/PROP LEGIT EXEC...SOC MYTH TIME/SEQ
TOT/POP 18/20. PAGE 82 B1664
   COERCE
   CONCPT
   REV

      S40
FAHS C.B.,"POLITICAL GROUPS IN THE JAPANESE HOUSE
OF PEERS." ELITES NAT/G ADMIN GP/REL...TREND
CHINJAP. PAGE 34 B0697
   ROUTINE
   POL/PAR
   LEGIS

      S40
GERTH H.,"THE NAZI PARTY: ITS LEADERSHIP AND
COMPOSITION" (BMR)" GERMANY ELITES STRATA STRUCT
EX/STRUC FORCES ECO/TAC CT/SYS CHOOSE TOTALISM
AGE/Y AUTHORIT PWR 20. PAGE 39 B0792
   POL/PAR
   DOMIN
   LEAD
   ADMIN

      L46
FORRESTAL J.,"THE NAVY: A STUDY IN ADMINISTRATION."
ELITES FACE/GP EX/STRUC PROB/SOLV REPRESENT
EFFICIENCY PRODUC. PAGE 37 B0741
   FORCES
   INGP/REL
   ROUTINE
   EXEC

      B47
BARNARD C.,THE FUNCTIONS OF THE EXECUTIVE. USA+45
ELITES INTELL LEGIT ATTIT DRIVE PERSON SKILL...PSY
SOC METH/CNCPT SOC/EXP GEN/METH VAL/FREE 20. PAGE 9
B0187
   EXEC
   EX/STRUC
   ROUTINE

      B47
FLYNN E.J.,YOU'RE THE BOSS. USA-45 ELITES TOP/EX
DOMIN CONTROL EXEC LEAD REPRESENT 19/20 NEWYORK/C
ROOSEVLT/F FLYNN/BOSS BOSSISM. PAGE 36 B0732
   LOC/G
   MUNIC
   BIOG
   POL/PAR

      B47
LASSWELL H.D.,THE ANALYSIS OF POLITICAL BEHAVIOUR:
AN EMPIRICAL APPROACH. WOR+45 CULTURE NAT/G FORCES
EDU/PROP ADMIN ATTIT PERCEPT KNOWL...PHIL/SCI PSY
SOC NEW/IDEA OBS INT GEN/METH NAZI 20. PAGE 63
B1267
   R+D
   ACT/RES
   ELITES

      B47
REDFORD E.S.,FIELD ADMINISTRATION OF WARTIME
RATIONING. USA-45 CONSTN ELITES DIST/IND WORKER
CONTROL WAR GOV/REL ADJUST RIGID/FLEX 20 OPA.
PAGE 87 B1752
   ADMIN
   NAT/G
   PROB/SOLV
   RATION

      B48
TOWSTER J.,POLITICAL POWER IN THE USSR: 1917-1947.
USSR CONSTN CULTURE ELITES CREATE PLAN COERCE
CENTRAL ATTIT RIGID/FLEX ORD/FREE...BIBLIOG
SOC/INTEG 20 LENIN/VI STALIN/J. PAGE 105 B2124
   EX/STRUC
   NAT/G
   MARXISM
   PWR

      B49
ASPINALL A.,POLITICS AND THE PRESS 1780-1850. UK
LAW ELITES FINAN PROF/ORG LEGIS ADMIN ATTIT
...POLICY 18/19. PAGE 7 B0142
   PRESS
   CONTROL
   POL/PAR
   ORD/FREE

      B49
GLOVER J.D.,THE ADMINISTRATOR. ELITES LG/CO
EX/STRUC ACT/RES CONTROL GP/REL INGP/REL PERS/REL
AUTHORIT...POLICY CONCPT HIST/WRIT. PAGE 40 B0811
   ADMIN
   MGT
   ATTIT
   PROF/ORG

      B49
STEIN H.,THE FOREIGN SERVICE ACT OF 1946. USA+45
ELITES EX/STRUC PLAN PROB/SOLV LOBBY GOV/REL
PERS/REL RIGID/FLEX...POLICY IDEA/COMP 20 CONGRESS
BUR/BUDGET. PAGE 100 B2027
   DIPLOM
   LAW
   NAT/G
   ADMIN

      L49
MARX C.M.,"ADMINISTRATIVE ETHICS AND THE RULE OF
LAW." USA+45 ELITES ACT/RES DOMIN NEUTRAL ROUTINE
INGP/REL ORD/FREE...JURID IDEA/COMP. PAGE 70 B1417
   ADMIN
   LAW

      B50
MANNHEIM K.,FREEDOM, POWER, AND DEMOCRATIC
PLANNING. FUT USSR WOR+45 ELITES INTELL SOCIETY
NAT/G EDU/PROP ROUTINE ATTIT DRIVE SUPEGO SKILL
...POLICY PSY CONCPT TREND GEN/LAWS 20. PAGE 69
B1393
   TEC/DEV
   PLAN
   CAP/ISM
   UK

      B50
MONTGOMERY H.,CRACKER PARTIES. CULTURE EX/STRUC
LEAD PWR POPULISM...TIME/SEQ 19 GEORGIA CALHOUN/JC
COBB/HOWLL JACKSON/A. PAGE 74 B1505
   POL/PAR
   PROVS
   ELITES
   BIOG

      S50
DALTON M.,"CONFLICTS BETWEEN STAFF AND LINE
MANAGERIAL OFFICERS" (BMR). USA+45 USA-45 ELITES
LG/CO WORKER PROB/SOLV ADMIN EXEC EFFICIENCY PRODUC
...GP/COMP 20. PAGE 26 B0526
   MGT
   ATTIT
   GP/REL
   INDUS

      B51
GUETZKOW H.,GROUPS, LEADERSHIP, AND MEN. FACE/GP
SECT EDU/PROP EXEC PERSON RESPECT...PERS/TEST
GEN/METH 20. PAGE 44 B0901
   ATTIT
   SOC
   ELITES

      B52
BRINTON C.,THE ANATOMY OF REVOLUTION. FRANCE UK
USA-45 USSR WOR+45 ELITES INTELL ECO/DEV NAT/G
EX/STRUC FORCES COERCE DRIVE ORD/FREE PWR SOVEREIGN
...MYTH HIST/WRIT GEN/LAWS. PAGE 15 B0311
   SOCIETY
   CONCPT
   REV

      S52
LIPSET S.M.,"DEMOCRACY IN PRIVATE GOVERNMENT: (A
CASE STUDY OF THE INTERNATIONAL TYPOGRAPHICAL
UNION)" (BMR)" POL/PAR CONTROL LEAD INGP/REL PWR
...MAJORIT DECISION PREDICT 20. PAGE 65 B1319
   LABOR
   ADMIN
   ELITES
   REPRESENT

      C52
LASSWELL H.D.,"THE COMPARATIVE STUDY OF ELITES: AN
INTRODUCTION AND BIBLIOGRAPHY." STRATA POL/PAR
EDU/PROP ADMIN LOBBY COERCE ATTIT PERSON PWR
...BIBLIOG 20. PAGE 63 B1270
   ELITES
   LEAD
   CONCPT
   DOMIN

      B53
THOMAS S.B.,GOVERNMENT AND ADMINISTRATION IN
COMMUNIST CHINA (MONOGRAPH). CHINA/COM PROB/SOLV
EDU/PROP 20. PAGE 104 B2100
   PWR
   EX/STRUC
   REPRESENT
   ELITES

      S53
BLOUGH R.,"THE ROLE OF THE ECONOMIST IN FEDERAL
POLICY MAKING." USA+45 ELITES INTELL ECO/DEV NAT/G
CONSULT EX/STRUC ACT/RES PLAN INT/TRADE BAL/PAY
WEALTH...POLICY CONGRESS 20. PAGE 13 B0256
   DELIB/GP
   ECO/TAC

      B54
DUVERGER M.,POLITICAL PARTIES: THEIR ORGANIZATION
AND ACTIVITY IN THE MODERN STATE. EUR+WWI MOD/EUR
USA+45 USA-45 EDU/PROP ADMIN ROUTINE ATTIT DRIVE
ORD/FREE PWR...SOC CONCPT MATH STAT TIME/SEQ
TOT/POP 19/20. PAGE 31 B0635
   POL/PAR
   EX/STRUC
   ELITES

      L54
ROSTOW W.W.,"ASIAN LEADERSHIP AND FREE-WORLD
ALLIANCE." ASIA COM USA+45 CULTURE ELITES INTELL
NAT/G TEC/DEV ECO/TAC EDU/PROP COLONIAL PARL/PROC
ROUTINE COERCE DRIVE ORD/FREE MARXISM...PSY CONCPT.
PAGE 90 B1829
   ATTIT
   LEGIT
   DIPLOM

      B55
POOL I.,SATELLITE GENERALS: A STUDY OF MILITARY
ELITES IN THE SOVIET SPHERE. ASIA CHINA/COM COM
CZECHOSLVK FUT HUNGARY POLAND ROMANIA USSR ELITES
STRATA ADMIN ATTIT PWR SKILL...METH/CNCPT BIOG 20.
PAGE 84 B1688
   FORCES
   CHOOSE

      B56
KAUFMANN W.W.,MILITARY POLICY AND NATIONAL
SECURITY. USA+45 ELITES INTELL NAT/G TOP/EX PLAN
BAL/PWR DIPLOM ROUTINE COERCE NUC/PWR ATTIT
   FORCES
   CREATE

ORD/FREE PWR 20 COLD/WAR. PAGE 58 B1182

S56
KHAMA T.,"POLITICAL CHANGE IN AFRICAN SOCIETY." AFR
CONSTN SOCIETY LOC/G NAT/G POL/PAR EX/STRUC LEGIS ELITES
LEGIT ADMIN CHOOSE REPRESENT NAT/LISM MORAL
ORD/FREE PWR...CONCPT OBS TREND GEN/METH CMN/WLTH
17/20. PAGE 59 B1201

C56
NEUMANN S.,"MODERN POLITICAL PARTIES: APPROACHES TO POL/PAR
COMPARATIVE POLITIC. FRANCE UK EX/STRUC DOMIN ADMIN GOV/COMP
LEAD REPRESENT TOTALISM ATTIT...POLICY TREND ELITES
METH/COMP ANTHOL BIBLIOG/A 20 CMN/WLTH. PAGE 78 MAJORIT
B1574

B57
CHANDRA S.,PARTIES AND POLITICS AT THE MUGHAL POL/PAR
COURT: 1707-1740. INDIA CULTURE EX/STRUC CREATE ELITES
PLAN PWR...BIBLIOG/A 18. PAGE 20 B0405 NAT/G

B57
DAVID P.T.,EXECUTIVES FOR THE GOVERNMENT: CENTRAL EX/STRUC
ISSUES OF FEDERAL PERSONNEL ADMINISTRATION. USA+45 TOP/EX
ELITES...GOV/COMP 20. PAGE 26 B0534 ADMIN

B57
MEYER P.,ADMINISTRATIVE ORGANIZATION: A COMPARATIVE ADMIN
STUDY OF THE ORGANIZATION OF PUBLIC ADMINISTRATION. METH/COMP
DENMARK FRANCE NORWAY SWEDEN UK USA+45 ELITES LOC/G NAT/G
CONSULT LEGIS ADJUD CONTROL LEAD PWR SKILL CENTRAL
DECISION. PAGE 73 B1475

B57
MORSTEIN-MARX F.,THE ADMINISTRATIVE STATE: AN EXEC
INTRODUCTION TO BUREAUCRACY. EUR+WWI FUT MOD/EUR MGT
USA+45 USA-45 NAT/G CONSULT ADMIN ROUTINE TOTALISM CAP/ISM
DRIVE SKILL...TREND 19/20. PAGE 76 B1530 ELITES

S57
HAILEY,"TOMORROW IN AFRICA." CONSTN SOCIETY LOC/G AFR
NAT/G DOMIN ADJUD ADMIN GP/REL DISCRIM NAT/LISM PERSON
ATTIT MORAL ORD/FREE...PSY SOC CONCPT OBS RECORD ELITES
TREND GEN/LAWS CMN/WLTH 20. PAGE 45 B0917 RACE/REL

S57
TAYLOR P.S.,"THE RELATION OF RESEARCH TO DECISION
LEGISLATIVE AND ADMINISTRATIVE DECISIONS." ELITES LEGIS
ACT/RES PLAN PROB/SOLV CONFER CHOOSE POLICY. MGT
PAGE 103 B2089 PWR

B58
CLEMENTS R.V.,MANAGERS - A STUDY OF THEIR CAREERS MGT
IN INDUSTRY. STRATA INDUS TASK PERSON SKILL 20. ELITES
PAGE 21 B0435 EDU/PROP
TOP/EX

B58
CONSERVATIVE POLITICAL CENTRE,A WORLD SECURITY ORD/FREE
AUTHORITY? WOR+45 CONSTN ELITES FINAN DELIB/GP PLAN CONSERVE
PROB/SOLV ADMIN CONTROL NUC/PWR GP/REL...IDEA/COMP FORCES
20. PAGE 23 B0468 ARMS/CONT

B58
LOVEJOY D.S.,RHODE ISLAND POLITICS AND THE AMERICAN REV
REVOLUTION 1760-1776. UK USA-45 ELITES EX/STRUC TAX COLONIAL
LEAD REPRESENT GOV/REL GP/REL ATTIT 18 RHODE/ISL. ECO/TAC
PAGE 67 B1343 SOVEREIGN

B58
MILLS C.W.,THE CAUSES OF WORLD WAR THREE. FUT CONSULT
USA+45 INTELL NAT/G DOMIN EDU/PROP ADMIN WAR ATTIT PWR
SOC. PAGE 74 B1487 ELITES
PEACE

B58
REDFORD E.S.,IDEAL AND PRACTICE IN PUBLIC POLICY
ADMINISTRATION. CONSTN ELITES NAT/G CONSULT EX/STRUC
DELIB/GP LEAD UTOPIA ATTIT POPULISM...DECISION PLAN
METH/COMP 20. PAGE 87 B1756 ADMIN

B58
SKINNER G.W.,LEADERSHIP AND POWER IN THE CHINESE SOC
COMMUNITY OF THAILAND. ASIA S/ASIA STRATA FACE/GP ELITES
KIN PROF/ORG VOL/ASSN EX/STRUC DOMIN PERSON RESPECT THAILAND
...METH/CNCPT STAT INT QU BIOG CHARTS 20. PAGE 98
B1974

B58
WILENSKY H.L.,INDUSTRIAL SOCIETY AND SOCIAL INDUS
WELFARE: IMPACT OF INDUSTRIALIZATION ON SUPPLY AND ECO/DEV
ORGANIZATION OF SOC WELF SERVICES. ELITES SOCIETY RECEIVE
STRATA SERV/IND FAM MUNIC PUB/INST CONSULT WORKER PROF/ORG
ADMIN AUTOMAT ANOMIE 20. PAGE 117 B2352

L58
JONAS F.H.,"BIBLIOGRAPHY ON WESTERN POLITICS." BIBLIOG/A
USA+45 USA-45 ELITES MUNIC POL/PAR LEGIS ADJUD LOC/G
ADMIN 20. PAGE 57 B1148 NAT/G
LAW

S58
DAHL R.A.,"A CRITIQUE OF THE RULING ELITE MODEL." CONCPT
USA+45 LOC/G MUNIC NAT/G POL/PAR PROVS DOMIN LEGIT STERTYP
ADMIN...METH/CNCPT HYPO/EXP. PAGE 25 B0520 ELITES

S58
EISENSTADT S.N.,"INTERNAL CONTRADICTIONS IN ELITES
BUREAUCRATIC POLITICS." ADMIN EXEC CENTRAL. PAGE 32 LEAD
B0658 PWR
EX/STRUC

S58
KEISER N.F.,"PUBLIC RESPONSIBILITY AND FEDERAL REPRESENT
ADVISORY GROUPS: A CASE STUDY." NAT/G ADMIN CONTROL ELITES

LOBBY...POLICY 20. PAGE 59 B1190 GP/REL
EX/STRUC

S58
MAIR L.P.,"REPRESENTATIVE LOCAL GOVERNMENT AS A AFR
PROBLEM IN SOCIAL CHANGE." ECO/UNDEV KIN LOC/G PWR
NAT/G SCHOOL JUDGE ADMIN ROUTINE REPRESENT ELITES
RIGID/FLEX RESPECT...CONCPT STERTYP CMN/WLTH 20.
PAGE 68 B1383

B59
SISSON C.H.,THE SPIRIT OF BRITISH ADMINISTRATION GOV/COMP
AND SOME EUROPEAN COMPARISONS. FRANCE GERMANY/W ADMIN
SWEDEN UK LAW EX/STRUC INGP/REL EFFICIENCY ORD/FREE ELITES
...DECISION 20. PAGE 98 B1972 ATTIT

B59
WARNER W.L.,INDUSTRIAL MAN. USA+45 USA-45 ELITES EXEC
INDUS LABOR TOP/EX WORKER ADMIN INGP/REL PERS/REL LEAD
...CHARTS ANTHOL 20. PAGE 114 B2294 PERSON
MGT

B59
WEBER W.,DER DEUTSCHE BEAMTE HEUTE. GERMANY/W NAT/G MGT
DELIB/GP LEGIS CONFER ATTIT SUPEGO...JURID 20 EFFICIENCY
CIVIL/SERV. PAGE 114 B2306 ELITES
GP/REL

S59
JANOWITZ M.,"CHANGING PATTERNS OF ORGANIZATIONAL FORCES
AUTHORITY: THE MILITARY ESTABLISHMENT" (BMR)" AUTHORIT
USA+45 ELITES STRUCT EX/STRUC PLAN DOMIN AUTOMAT ADMIN
NUC/PWR WEAPON 20. PAGE 55 B1122 TEC/DEV

B60
ECKHOFF T.,RATIONALITY AND RESPONSIBILITY IN ADMIN
ADMINISTRATIVE AND JUDICIAL DECISION-MAKING. ELITES PROB/SOLV
LEAD INGP/REL ATTIT PWR...MGT METH/COMP GAME 20. DECISION
PAGE 32 B0649 METH/CNCPT

B60
GRANICK D.,THE RED EXECUTIVE. COM USA+45 SOCIETY PWR
ECO/DEV INDUS NAT/G POL/PAR EX/STRUC PLAN ECO/TAC STRATA
EDU/PROP ADMIN EXEC ATTIT DRIVE...GP/COMP 20. USSR
PAGE 42 B0851 ELITES

B60
PINTO F.B.M.,ENRIQUECIMENTO ILICITO NO EXERCICIO DE ADMIN
CARGOS PUBLICOS. BRAZIL L/A+17C USA+45 ELITES NAT/G
TRIBUTE CONTROL INGP/REL ORD/FREE PWR...NAT/COMP CRIME
20. PAGE 83 B1675 LAW

B60
SOUTH AFRICAN CONGRESS OF DEM,FACE THE FUTURE. RACE/REL
SOUTH/AFR ELITES LEGIS ADMIN REGION COERCE PEACE DISCRIM
ATTIT 20. PAGE 99 B1999 CONSTN
NAT/G

S60
HUTCHINSON C.E.,"AN INSTITUTE FOR NATIONAL SECURITY POLICY
AFFAIRS." USA+45 R+D NAT/G CONSULT TOP/EX ACT/RES METH/CNCPT
CREATE PLAN TEC/DEV EDU/PROP ROUTINE NUC/PWR ATTIT ELITES
ORD/FREE PWR...DECISION MGT PHIL/SCI CONCPT RECORD DIPLOM
GEN/LAWS GEN/METH 20. PAGE 53 B1068

S60
SCHWARTZ B.,"THE INTELLIGENTSIA IN COMMUNIST CHINA: INTELL
A TENTATIVE COMPARISON." ASIA CHINA/COM COM RUSSIA RIGID/FLEX
ELITES SOCIETY STRATA POL/PAR VOL/ASSN CREATE ADMIN REV
COERCE NAT/LISM TOTALISM...POLICY TREND 20. PAGE 95
B1914

B61
AYLMER G.,THE KING'S SERVANTS. UK ELITES CHIEF PAY ADMIN
CT/SYS WEALTH 17 CROMWELL/O CHARLES/I. PAGE 7 B0153 ROUTINE
EX/STRUC
NAT/G

B61
BANFIELD E.C.,URBAN GOVERNMENT; A READER IN MUNIC
POLITICS AND ADMINISTRATION. ELITES LABOR POL/PAR GEN/METH
EXEC CHOOSE REPRESENT GP/REL PWR PLURISM...PSY SOC. DECISION
PAGE 9 B0177

B61
LOSCHELDER W.,AUSBILDUNG UND AUSLESE DER BEAMTEN. PROF/ORG
GERMANY/W ELITES NAT/G ADMIN GP/REL ATTIT...JURID EDU/PROP
20 CIVIL/SERV. PAGE 67 B1341 EX/STRUC
CHOOSE

B61
MARSH R.M.,THE MANDARINS: THE CIRCULATION OF ELITES ELITES
IN CHINA, 1600-1900. ASIA STRUCT PROF/ORG...SOC ADMIN
CHARTS BIBLIOG DICTIONARY 17/20. PAGE 70 B1406 FAM
STRATA

B61
MARVICK D.,POLITICAL DECISION-MAKERS. INTELL STRATA TOP/EX
NAT/G POL/PAR EX/STRUC LEGIS DOMIN EDU/PROP ATTIT BIOG
PERSON PWR...PSY STAT OBS CONT/OBS STAND/INT ELITES
UNPLAN/INT TIME/SEQ CHARTS STERTYP VAL/FREE.
PAGE 70 B1416

B61
MONAS S.,THE THIRD SECTION: POLICE AND SOCIETY IN ORD/FREE
RUSSIA UNDER NICHOLAS I. MOD/EUR RUSSIA ELITES COM
STRUCT NAT/G EX/STRUC ADMIN CONTROL PWR CONSERVE FORCES
...DECISION 19 NICHOLAS/I. PAGE 74 B1499 COERCE

B61
OPOTOWSKY S.,THE KENNEDY GOVERNMENT. NAT/G CONSULT ADMIN
EX/STRUC LEAD PERSON...POLICY 20 KENNEDY/JF BIOG
CONGRESS CABINET. PAGE 80 B1613 ELITES
TOP/EX

ELITES

STRAUSS E.,THE RULING SERVANTS. FRANCE UK USSR
WOR+45 WOR-45 NAT/G CONSULT DELIB/GP EX/STRUC
TOP/EX DOMIN EDU/PROP LEGIT ROUTINE...MGT TIME/SEQ
STERTYP 20. PAGE 101 B2051
ADMIN
PWR
ELITES
B61

DYKMAN J.W.,"REVIEW ARTICLE* PLANNING AND DECISION
THEORY." ELITES LOC/G MUNIC CONSULT ADMIN...POLICY
MGT. PAGE 31 B0640
DECISION
PLAN
RATIONAL
S61

ROBINSON J.A.,"PROCESS SATISFACTION AND POLICY
APPROVAL IN STATE DEPARTMENT - CONGRESSIONAL
RELATIONS." ELITES CHIEF LEGIS CONFER DEBATE ADMIN
FEEDBACK ROLE...CHARTS 20 CONGRESS PRESIDENT
DEPT/STATE. PAGE 89 B1802
GOV/REL
EX/STRUC
POL/PAR
DECISION
S61

SHERBENOU E.L.,"CLASS, PARTICIPATION, AND THE
COUNCIL-MANAGER PLAN." ELITES STRUCT LEAD GP/REL
ATTIT PWR DECISION. PAGE 96 B1942
REPRESENT
MUNIC
EXEC
C61

ETZIONI A.,"A COMPARATIVE ANALYSIS OF COMPLEX
ORGANIZATIONS: ON POWER, INVOLVEMENT AND THEIR
CORRELATES." ELITES CREATE OP/RES ROUTINE INGP/REL
PERS/REL CONSEN ATTIT DRIVE PWR...CONCPT BIBLIOG.
PAGE 34 B0684
CON/ANAL
SOC
LEAD
CONTROL
C61

VERBA S.,"SMALL GROUPS AND POLITICAL BEHAVIOR: A
STUDY OF LEADERSHIP" DOMIN PARTIC ROUTINE GP/REL
ATTIT DRIVE ALL/VALS...CONCPT IDEA/COMP LAB/EXP
BIBLIOG METH. PAGE 112 B2259
LEAD
ELITES
FACE/GP
B62

ANDREWS W.G.,FRENCH POLITICS AND ALGERIA: THE
PROCESS OF POLICY FORMATION 1954-1962. ALGERIA
FRANCE CONSTN ELITES POL/PAR CHIEF DELIB/GP LEGIS
DIPLOM PRESS CHOOSE 20. PAGE 5 B0105
GOV/COMP
EXEC
COLONIAL
B62

CHICAGO U CTR PROG GOVT ADMIN.EDUCATION FOR
INNOVATIVE BEHAVIOR IN EXECUTIVES. UNIV ELITES
ADMIN EFFICIENCY DRIVE PERSON...MGT APT/TEST
PERS/TEST CHARTS LAB/EXP BIBLIOG 20. PAGE 21 B0420
EDU/PROP
CREATE
EXEC
STAT
B62

ESCUELA SUPERIOR DE ADMIN PUBL.INFORME DEL
SEMINARIO SOBRE SERVICIO CIVIL O CARRERA
ADMINISTRATIVA. L/A+17C ELITES STRATA CONFER
CONTROL GOV/REL INGP/REL SUPEGO 20 CENTRAL/AM
CIVIL/SERV. PAGE 33 B0681
ADMIN
NAT/G
PROB/SOLV
ATTIT
B62

GRAY R.K.,EIGHTEEN ACRES UNDER GLASS. ELITES
CONSULT EX/STRUC DIPLOM PRESS CONFER WAR PERS/REL
PERSON 20 EISNHWR/DD TRUMAN/HS CABINET. PAGE 43
B0860
CHIEF
ADMIN
TOP/EX
NAT/G
B62

INST TRAINING MUNICIPAL ADMIN.MUNICIPAL FINANCE
ADMINISTRATION (6TH ED.). USA+45 ELITES ECO/DEV
LEGIS PLAN BUDGET TAX GP/REL BAL/PAY COST...POLICY
20 CITY/MGT. PAGE 54 B1089
MUNIC
ADMIN
FINAN
LOC/G
B62

PACKARD V.,THE PYRAMID CLIMBERS. USA+45 ELITES
SOCIETY CREATE PROB/SOLV EFFICIENCY ATTIT...MGT 20.
PAGE 80 B1621
INDUS
TOP/EX
PERS/REL
DRIVE
B62

SAMPSON A.,ANATOMY OF BRITAIN. UK LAW COM/IND FINAN
INDUS MARKET MUNIC POL/PAR EX/STRUC TOP/EX DIPLOM
LEAD REPRESENT PERSON PARLIAMENT WORSHIP. PAGE 92
B1866
ELITES
PWR
STRUCT
FORCES
B62

SCALAPINO R.A.,PARTIES AND POLITICS IN CONTEMPORARY
JAPAN. EX/STRUC DIPLOM CHOOSE NAT/LISM ATTIT
...POLICY 20 CHINJAP. PAGE 93 B1876
POL/PAR
PARL/PROC
ELITES
DECISION
S62

BOOTH D.A.,"POWER STRUCTURE AND COMMUNITY CHANGE: A
REPLICATION STUDY OF COMMUNITY A." STRATA LABOR
LEAD PARTIC REPRESENT...DECISION MGT TIME. PAGE 14
B0275
MUNIC
ELITES
PWR
S62

MAINZER L.C.,"INJUSTICE AND BUREAUCRACY." ELITES
STRATA STRUCT EX/STRUC SENIOR CONTROL EXEC LEAD
ROUTINE INGP/REL ORD/FREE...CONCPT 20 BUREAUCRCY.
PAGE 68 B1381
MORAL
MGT
ADMIN
B63

BLONDEL J.,VOTERS, PARTIES, AND LEADERS. UK ELITES
LOC/G NAT/G PROVS ACT/RES DOMIN REPRESENT GP/REL
INGP/REL...SOC BIBLIOG 20. PAGE 12 B0255
POL/PAR
STRATA
LEGIS
ADMIN
B63

HEUSSLER R.,YESTERDAY'S RULERS: THE MAKING OF THE
BRITISH COLONIAL SERVICE. AFR EUR+WWI UK STRATA
SECT DELIB/GP PLAN DOMIN EDU/PROP ATTIT PERCEPT
PERSON SUPEGO KNOWL ORD/FREE PWR...MGT SOC OBS INT
TIME/SEQ 20 CMN/WLTH. PAGE 49 B1000
EX/STRUC
MORAL
ELITES
B63

KAMMERER G.M.,THE URBAN POLITICAL COMMUNITY:
PROFILES IN TOWN POLITICS. ELITES LOC/G LEAD
...DECISION GP/COMP. PAGE 57 B1162
EXEC
MUNIC
PWR
B63

GOV/COMP

LEWIS J.W.,LEADERSHIP IN COMMUNIST CHINA. ASIA
INTELL ECO/UNDEV LOC/G MUNIC NAT/G PROVS ECO/TAC
EDU/PROP LEGIT ADMIN COERCE ATTIT ORD/FREE PWR
...INT TIME/SEQ CHARTS TOT/POP VAL/FREE. PAGE 65
B1304
POL/PAR
DOMIN
ELITES
B63

MENZEL J.M.,THE CHINESE CIVIL SERVICE: CAREER OPEN
TO TALENT? ASIA ROUTINE INGP/REL DISCRIM ATTIT ROLE
KNOWL ANTHOL. PAGE 73 B1468
ADMIN
NAT/G
DECISION
ELITES
B63

RICHARDS P.G.,PATRONAGE IN BRITISH GOVERNMENT.
ELITES DELIB/GP TOP/EX PROB/SOLV CONTROL CT/SYS
EXEC PWR. PAGE 88 B1774
EX/STRUC
REPRESENT
POL/PAR
ADMIN
B63

ROETTER C.,THE DIPLOMATIC ART. USSR INT/ORG NAT/G
DELIB/GP ROUTINE NUC/PWR PEACE...POLICY 20. PAGE 90
B1812
DIPLOM
ELITES
TOP/EX
B63

SPRING D.,THE ENGLISH LANDED ESTATE IN THE
NINETEENTH CENTURY: ITS ADMINISTRATION. UK ELITES
STRUCT AGRI NAT/G GP/REL OWN PWR WEALTH...BIBLIOG
19 HOUSE/LORD. PAGE 99 B2012
STRATA
PERS/REL
MGT
B63

THOMETZ C.E.,THE DECISION-MAKERS: THE POWER
STRUCTURE OF DALLAS. USA+45 CULTURE EX/STRUC DOMIN
LEGIT GP/REL ATTIT OBJECTIVE...INT CHARTS GP/COMP.
PAGE 104 B2101
ELITES
MUNIC
PWR
DECISION
B63

TUCKER R.C.,THE SOVIET POLITICAL MIND. WOR+45
ELITES INT/ORG NAT/G POL/PAR PLAN DIPLOM ECO/TAC
DOMIN ADMIN NUC/PWR REV DRIVE PERSON SUPEGO PWR
WEALTH...POLICY MGT PSY CONCPT OBS BIOG TREND
COLD/WAR MARX/KARL 20. PAGE 106 B2134
COM
TOP/EX
USSR
B63

TUCKER R.C.,THE SOVIET POLITICAL MIND. COM INTELL
NAT/G TOP/EX EDU/PROP ADMIN COERCE TOTALISM ATTIT
PWR MARXISM...PSY MYTH HYPO/EXP 20. PAGE 106 B2135
STRUCT
RIGID/FLEX
ELITES
USSR
B63

WARNER W.L.,THE AMERICAN FEDERAL EXECUTIVE. USA+45
USA-45 CONSULT EX/STRUC GP/REL DRIVE ALL/VALS...PSY
DEEP/QU CHARTS 19/20 PRESIDENT. PAGE 114 B2295
ELITES
NAT/G
TOP/EX
ADMIN
B63

WEINER M.,POLITICAL CHANGE IN SOUTH ASIA. CEYLON
INDIA PAKISTAN S/ASIA CULTURE ELITES ECO/UNDEV
EX/STRUC ADMIN CONTROL CHOOSE CONSERVE...GOV/COMP
ANTHOL 20. PAGE 115 B2315
NAT/G
CONSTN
TEC/DEV
S63

BANFIELD J.,"FEDERATION IN EAST-AFRICA." AFR UGANDA
ELITES INT/ORG NAT/G VOL/ASSN LEGIS ECO/TAC FEDERAL
ATTIT SOVEREIGN TOT/POP 20 TANGANYIKA. PAGE 9 B0180
EX/STRUC
PWR
REGION
S63

BARZANSKI S.,"REGIONAL UNDERDEVELOPMENT IN THE
EUROPEAN ECONOMIC COMMUNITY." EUR+WWI EUR-WWI
DIST/IND MARKET VOL/ASSN CONSULT EX/STRUC ECO/TAC
RIGID/FLEX WEALTH EEC OEEC 20. PAGE 9 B0192
ECO/UNDEV
PLAN
S63

BRZEZINSKI Z.K.,"CINCINNATUS AND THE APPARATCHIK."
COM USA+45 USA-45 ELITES LOC/G NAT/G PROVS CONSULT
LEGIS DOMIN LEGIT EXEC ROUTINE CHOOSE DRIVE PWR
SKILL...CONCPT CHARTS VAL/FREE COLD/WAR 20. PAGE 16
B0334
POL/PAR
USSR
S63

JENNINGS M.K.,"PUBLIC ADMINISTRATORS AND COMMUNITY
DECISION-MAKING." ELITES LOC/G LEAD...GP/COMP
GOV/COMP. PAGE 56 B1134
ADMIN
MUNIC
DECISION
PWR
S63

RUSTOW D.A.,"THE MILITARY IN MIDDLE EASTERN SOCIETY
AND POLITICS." FUT ISLAM CONSTN SOCIETY FACE/GP
NAT/G POL/PAR PROF/ORG CONSULT DOMIN ADMIN EXEC
REGION COERCE NAT/LISM ATTIT DRIVE PERSON ORD/FREE
PWR...POLICY CONCPT OBS STERTYP 20. PAGE 92 B1860
FORCES
ELITES
S63

STANLEY T.W.,"DECENTRALIZING NUCLEAR CONTROL IN
NATO." EUR+WWI USA+45 ELITES FORCES ACT/RES ATTIT
ORD/FREE PWR...NEW/IDEA HYPO/EXP TOT/POP 20 NATO.
PAGE 100 B2022
INT/ORG
EX/STRUC
NUC/PWR
B64

BOTTOMORE T.B.,ELITES AND SOCIETY. INTELL STRATA
ECO/DEV ECO/UNDEV ADMIN GP/REL ORD/FREE...CONCPT
BIBLIOG 20. PAGE 14 B0281
ELITES
IDEA/COMP
SOCIETY
SOC
B64

EDELMAN M.,THE SYMBOLIC USES OF POWER. USA+45
EX/STRUC CONTROL GP/REL INGP/REL...MGT T. PAGE 32
B0653
CLIENT
PWR
EXEC
ELITES
B64

ELDREDGE H.W.,THE SECOND AMERICAN REVOLUTION.
EDU/PROP NAT/LISM RATIONAL TOTALISM FASCISM MARXISM
ELITES
ORD/FREE

SOCISM. PAGE 33 B0664 ADMIN
  PLAN
    B64

GUTTSMAN W.L.,THE BRITISH POLITICAL ELITE. EUR+WWI NAT/G
MOD/EUR STRATA FAM LABOR POL/PAR SCHOOL VOL/ASSN SOC
DELIB/GP LEGIS LEGIT EXEC CHOOSE ATTIT ALL/VALS UK
...STAT BIOG TIME/SEQ CHARTS VAL/FREE. PAGE 45 ELITES
B0905
    B64

HANNA W.J.,INDEPENDENT BLACK AFRICA: THE POLITICS AFR
OF FREEDOM. ELITES FAM INDUS KIN CHIEF COLONIAL CHOOSE ECO/UNDEV
GOV/REL RACE/REL NAT/LISM ATTIT PERSON 20 NEGRO. ADMIN
PAGE 46 B0938 PROB/SOLV
    B64

MERILLAT H.C.L.,LEGAL ADVISERS AND FOREIGN AFFAIRS. CONSULT
WOR+45 WOR-45 ELITES INTELL NAT/G LEGIT ADMIN EX/STRUC
PERCEPT ALL/VALS...MGT NEW/IDEA RECORD 20. PAGE 73 DIPLOM
B1469
    B64

RAYMOND J.,POWER AT THE PENTAGON (1ST ED.). ELITES PWR
NAT/G PLAN EDU/PROP ARMS/CONT DETER WAR WEAPON CIVMIL/REL
...TIME/SEQ 20 PENTAGON MCNAMARA/R. PAGE 86 B1746 EX/STRUC
  FORCES
    B64

REDLICH F.,THE GERMAN MILITARY ENTERPRISER AND HIS EX/STRUC
WORK FORCE. CHRIST-17C GERMANY ELITES SOCIETY FINAN FORCES
ECO/TAC CIVMIL/REL GP/REL INGP/REL...HIST/WRIT PROFIT
METH/COMP 14/17. PAGE 87 B1760 WORKER
    B64

WILDAVSKY A.,LEADERSHIP IN A SMALL TOWN. USA+45 LEAD
STRUCT PROB/SOLV EXEC PARTIC RACE/REL PWR PLURISM MUNIC
...SOC 20 NEGRO WATER CIV/RIGHTS OBERLIN CITY/MGT. ELITES
PAGE 116 B2348
    B64

WRAITH R.,CORRUPTION IN DEVELOPING COUNTRIES. ECO/UNDEV
NIGERIA UK LAW ELITES STRATA INDUS LOC/G NAT/G SECT CRIME
FORCES EDU/PROP ADMIN PWR WEALTH 18/20. PAGE 118 SANCTION
B2377 ATTIT
    L64

FOX G.H.,"PERCEPTIONS OF THE VIETNAMESE PUBLIC ADMIN
ADMINISTRATION SYSTEM" VIETNAM ELITES CONTROL EXEC EX/STRUC
LEAD PWR...INT 20. PAGE 37 B0745 INGP/REL
  ROLE
    L64

GILBERT C.E.,"NATIONAL POLITICAL ALIGNMENTS AND THE MUNIC
POLITICS OF LARGE CITIES." ELITES LOC/G NAT/G LEGIS CHOOSE
EXEC LEAD PLURISM GOV/COMP. PAGE 39 B0800 POL/PAR
  PWR
    S64

CLIGNET R.,"POTENTIAL ELITES IN GHANA AND THE IVORY PWR
COAST: A PRELIMINARY SURVEY." AFR CULTURE ELITES LEGIT
STRATA KIN NAT/G SECT DOMIN EXEC ORD/FREE RESPECT IVORY/CST
SKILL...POLICY RELATIV GP/COMP NAT/COMP 20. PAGE 21 GHANA
B0438
    S64

JOHNSON K.F.,"CAUSAL FACTORS IN LATIN AMERICAN L/A+17C
POLITICAL INSTABILITY." CULTURE NAT/G VOL/ASSN PERCEPT
EX/STRUC FORCES EDU/PROP LEGIT ADMIN COERCE REV ELITES
ATTIT KNOWL PWR...STYLE RECORD CHARTS WORK 20.
PAGE 57 B1144
    S64

KAMMERER G.M.,"URBAN LEADERSHIP DURING CHANGE." MUNIC
LEAD PARTIC REPRESENT GP/REL PLURISM...DECISION PWR
GP/COMP. PAGE 58 B1164 ELITES
  EXEC
    S64

LIPSET S.M.,"SOCIOLOGY AND POLITICAL SCIENCE: A BIBLIOG/A
BIBLIOGRAPHICAL NOTE." WOR+45 ELITES LEGIS ADJUD SOC
ADMIN ATTIT IDEA/COMP. PAGE 65 B1321 METH/COMP
    S64

SWEARER H.R.,"AFTER KHRUSHCHEV: WHAT NEXT." COM FUT EX/STRUC
USSR CONSTN ELITES NAT/G POL/PAR CHIEF DELIB/GP PWR
LEGIS DOMIN LEAD...RECORD TREND STERTYP GEN/METH
20. PAGE 102 B2058
    B65

CHANDA A.,FEDERALISM IN INDIA. INDIA UK ELITES CONSTN
FINAN NAT/G POL/PAR EX/STRUC LEGIS DIPLOM TAX CENTRAL
GOV/REL POPULISM...POLICY 20. PAGE 20 B0402 FEDERAL
    B65

CHEN T.H.,THE CHINESE COMMUNIST REGIME: A MARXISM
DOCUMENTARY STUDY (2 VOLS.). CHINA/COM LAW CONSTN POL/PAR
ELITES ECO/UNDEV LEGIS ECO/TAC ADMIN CONTROL PWR NAT/G
...SOC 20. PAGE 20 B0417
    B65

ETZIONI A.,POLITICAL UNIFICATION* A COMPARATIVE INT/ORG
STUDY OF LEADERS AND FORCES. EUR+WWI ISLAM L/A+17C FORCES
WOR+45 ELITES STRATA EXEC WEALTH...TIME/SEQ TREND ECO/TAC
SOC/EXP. PAGE 34 B0686 REGION
    B65

FOLTZ W.J.,FROM FRENCH WEST AFRICA TO THE MALI EXEC
FEDERATION. AFR FRANCE MALI ADMIN CONTROL FEDERAL TOP/EX
...DECISION 20. PAGE 36 B0734 ELITES
  LEAD
    B65

GOPAL S.,BRITISH POLICY IN INDIA 1858-1905. INDIA COLONIAL
UK ELITES CHIEF DELIB/GP ECO/TAC GP/REL DISCRIM ADMIN

ATTIT...IDEA/COMP NAT/COMP PERS/COMP BIBLIOG/A POL/PAR
19/20. PAGE 41 B0828 ECO/UNDEV
    B65

MARTIN R.,PUBLIC ADMINISTRATION AND DEMOCRACY. EX/STRUC
ELITES NAT/G ADMIN EXEC ROUTINE INGP/REL. PAGE 70 DECISION
B1412 REPRESENT
  GP/REL
    B65

MASTERS N.A.,COMMITTEE ASSIGNMENTS IN THE HOUSE OF LEAD
REPRESENTATIVES (BMR). USA+45 ELITES POL/PAR LEGIS
EX/STRUC PARTIC REPRESENT GP/REL PERS/REL ATTIT PWR CHOOSE
...STAT CHARTS 20 HOUSE/REP. PAGE 71 B1425 DELIB/GP
    B65

MEISEL J.H.,PARETO & MOSCA. ITALY STRUCT ADMIN PWR
...SOC CON/ANAL ANTHOL BIBLIOG 19/20. PAGE 72 B1463 ELITES
  CONTROL
  LAISSEZ
    B65

MOORE C.H.,TUNISIA SINCE INDEPENDENCE. ELITES LOC/G NAT/G
POL/PAR ADMIN COLONIAL CONTROL EXEC GOV/REL EX/STRUC
TOTALISM MARXISM...INT 20 TUNIS. PAGE 75 B1513 SOCISM
    B65

RUBINSTEIN A.Z.,THE CHALLENGE OF POLITICS: IDEAS NAT/G
AND ISSUES (2ND ED.). UNIV ELITES SOCIETY EX/STRUC DIPLOM
BAL/PWR PARL/PROC AUTHORIT...DECISION ANTHOL 20. GP/REL
PAGE 92 B1852 ORD/FREE
    B65

STEINER G.A.,THE CREATIVE ORGANIZATION. ELITES CREATE
LG/CO PLAN PROB/SOLV TEC/DEV INSPECT CAP/ISM MGT
CONTROL EXEC PERSON...METH/COMP HYPO/EXP 20. ADMIN
PAGE 100 B2029 SOC
    B65

VIORST M.,HOSTILE ALLIES: FDR AND DE GAULLE. TOP/EX
EUR+WWI USA+45 ELITES NAT/G VOL/ASSN FORCES LEGIS PWR
PLAN LEGIT ADMIN COERCE PERSON...BIOG TIME/SEQ 20 WAR
ROOSEVLT/F DEGAULLE/C. PAGE 112 B2263 FRANCE
    B65

YOUNG C.,POLITICS IN THE CONGO* DECOLONIZATION AND BELGIUM
INDEPENDENCE. ELITES STRATA FORCES ADMIN REV COLONIAL
RACE/REL FEDERAL SOVEREIGN...OBS INT CHARTS NAT/LISM
CONGO/LEOP. PAGE 118 B2391
    L65

HOOK S.,"SECOND THOUGHTS ON BERKELEY" USA+45 ELITES ACADEM
INTELL LEGIT ADMIN COERCE REPRESENT GP/REL INGP/REL ORD/FREE
TOTALISM AGE/Y MARXISM 20 BERKELEY FREE/SPEE POLICY
STUDNT/PWR. PAGE 51 B1040 CREATE
    S65

TABORSKY E.,"CHANGE IN CZECHOSLOVAKIA." COM USSR ECO/DEV
ELITES INTELL AGRI INDUS NAT/G DELIB/GP EX/STRUC PLAN
ECO/TAC TOTALISM ATTIT RIGID/FLEX SOCISM...MGT CZECHOSLVK
CONCPT TREND 20. PAGE 102 B2067
    B66

ASHRAF A.,THE CITY GOVERNMENT OF CALCUTTA: A STUDY LOC/G
OF INERTIA. INDIA ELITES INDUS NAT/G EX/STRUC MUNIC
ACT/RES PLAN PROB/SOLV LEAD HABITAT...BIBLIOG 20 ADMIN
CALCUTTA. PAGE 7 B0141 ECO/UNDEV
    B66

BAKKE E.W.,MUTUAL SURVIVAL; THE GOAL OF UNION AND MGT
MANAGEMENT (2ND ED.). USA+45 ELITES ECO/DEV ECO/TAC LABOR
CONFER ADMIN REPRESENT GP/REL INGP/REL ATTIT BARGAIN
...GP/COMP 20. PAGE 8 B0170 INDUS
    B66

MANSFIELD E.,MANAGERIAL ECONOMICS AND OPERATIONS ECO/TAC
RESEARCH; A NONMATHEMATICAL INTRODUCTION. USA+45 OP/RES
ELITES ECO/DEV CONSULT EX/STRUC PROB/SOLV ROUTINE MGT
EFFICIENCY OPTIMAL...GAME T 20. PAGE 69 B1396 COMPUTER
    B66

RAEFF M.,ORIGINS OF THE RUSSIAN INTELLIGENTSIA: THE INTELL
EIGHTEENTH-CENTURY NOBILITY. RUSSIA FAM NAT/G ELITES
EDU/PROP ADMIN PERS/REL ATTIT...HUM BIOG 18. STRATA
PAGE 85 B1728 CONSERVE
    B66

SILBERMAN B.S.,MODERN JAPANESE LEADERSHIP; LEAD
TRANSITION AND CHANGE. NAT/G POL/PAR CHIEF ADMIN CULTURE
REPRESENT GP/REL ADJUST RIGID/FLEX...SOC METH/COMP ELITES
ANTHOL 19/20 CHINJAP CHRISTIAN. PAGE 97 B1952 MUNIC
    B66

THOENES P.,THE ELITE IN THE WELFARE STATE ,TRANS. ADMIN
BY J BINGHAM; ED. BY. STRATA NAT/G GP/REL HAPPINESS ELITES
INCOME OPTIMAL MORAL PWR WEALTH...POLICY CONCPT. MGT
PAGE 104 B2097 WELF/ST
    B66

WILLNER A.R.,THE NEOTRADITIONAL ACCOMMODATION TO INDONESIA
POLITICAL INDEPENDENCE* THE CASE OF INDONESIA * CONSERVE
RESEARCH MONOGRAPH NO. 26. CULTURE ECO/UNDEV CREATE ELITES
PROB/SOLV FOR/AID LEGIT COLONIAL EFFICIENCY ADMIN
NAT/LISM ALL/VALS SOC. PAGE 117 B2355
    B66

ZALEZNIK A.,HUMAN DILEMMAS OF LEADERSHIP. ELITES LEAD
INDUS EX/STRUC INGP/REL ATTIT...PSY 20. PAGE 119 PERSON
B2397 EXEC
  MGT
    L66

LEMARCHAND R.,"SOCIAL CHANGE AND POLITICAL NAT/G
MODERNISATION IN BURUNDI." AFR BURUNDI STRATA CHIEF STRUCT
EX/STRUC RIGID/FLEX PWR...SOC 20. PAGE 64 B1285 ELITES

MCAUSLAN J.P.W.,"CONSTITUTIONAL INNOVATION AND POLITICAL STABILITY IN TANZANIA: A PRELIMINARY ASSESSMENT." AFR TANZANIA ELITES CHIEF EX/STRUC RIGID/FLEX PWR 20 PRESIDENT BUREAUCRCY. PAGE 71 B1440
CONSERVE
L66
CONSTN
NAT/G
EXEC
POL/PAR

JACOBSON J.,"COALITIONISM: FROM PROTEST TO POLITICKING" USA+45 ELITES NAT/G POL/PAR PROB/SOLV ADMIN LEAD DISCRIM ORD/FREE PWR CONSERVE 20 NEGRO AFL/CIO CIV/RIGHTS BLACK/PWR. PAGE 55 B1116
S66
RACE/REL
LABOR
SOCIALIST
VOL/ASSN

PALMER M.,"THE UNITED ARAB REPUBLIC* AN ASSESSMENT OF ITS FAILURE." ELITES ECO/UNDEV POL/PAR FORCES ECO/TAC RUMOR ADMIN EXEC EFFICIENCY ATTIT SOCISM ...INT NASSER/G. PAGE 81 B1628
S66
UAR
SYRIA
REGION
FEDERAL

BRAYMAN H.,CORPORATE MANAGEMENT IN A WORLD OF POLITICS. USA+45 ELITES MARKET CREATE BARGAIN DIPLOM INT/TRADE ATTIT SKILL 20. PAGE 15 B0302
B67
MGT
ECO/DEV
CAP/ISM
INDUS

BULPITT J.G.,PARTY POLITICS IN ENGLISH LOCAL GOVERNMENT. UK CONSTN ACT/RES TAX CONTROL CHOOSE REPRESENT GOV/REL KNOWL 20. PAGE 17 B0344
B67
POL/PAR
LOC/G
ELITES
EX/STRUC

ROFF W.R.,THE ORIGINS OF MALAY NATIONALISM. MALAYSIA INTELL NAT/G ADMIN COLONIAL...BIBLIOG DICTIONARY 20 CMN/WLTH. PAGE 90 B1813
B67
NAT/LISM
ELITES
VOL/ASSN
SOCIETY

MANNE H.G.,"OUR TWO CORPORATION SYSTEMS* LAW AND ECONOMICS." LAW CONTROL SANCTION GP/REL...JURID 20. PAGE 69 B1392
L67
INDUS
ELITES
CAP/ISM
ADMIN

PASLEY R.S.,"ORGANIZATIONAL CONFLICTS OF INTEREST IN GOVERNMENT CONTRACTS." ELITES R+D ROUTINE NUC/PWR DEMAND EFFICIENCY 20. PAGE 81 B1639
L67
NAT/G
ECO/TAC
RATION
CONTROL

BEASLEY W.G.,"POLITICS AND THE SAMURAI CLASS STRUCTURE IN SATSUMA, 18581868." STRATA FORCES DOMIN LEGIT ADMIN LEAD 19 CHINJAP. PAGE 10 B0202
S67
ELITES
STRUCT
ATTIT
PRIVIL

BREGMAN A.,"WHITHER RUSSIA?" COM RUSSIA INTELL POL/PAR DIPLOM PARTIC NAT/LISM TOTALISM ATTIT ORD/FREE 20. PAGE 15 B0304
S67
MARXISM
ELITES
ADMIN
CREATE

DRAPER A.P.,"UNIONS AND THE WAR IN VIETNAM." USA+45 LABOR CONFER ADMIN LEAD WAR ORD/FREE PACIFIST 20. PAGE 30 B0616
S67
PACIFISM
ATTIT
ELITES

EDWARDS H.T.,"POWER STRUCTURE AND ITS COMMUNICATION IN SAN JOSE, COSTA RICA." COSTA/RICA L/A+17C STRATA FACE/GP POL/PAR EX/STRUC PROB/SOLV ADMIN LEAD GP/REL PWR...STAT INT 20. PAGE 32 B0655
S67
ELITES
INGP/REL
MUNIC
DOMIN

GORMAN W.,"ELLUL - A PROPHETIC VOICE." WOR+45 ELITES SOCIETY ACT/RES PLAN BAL/PWR DOMIN CONTROL PARTIC TOTALISM PWR 20. PAGE 41 B0837
S67
CREATE
ORD/FREE
EX/STRUC
UTOPIA

GRUNDY K.W.,"THE POLITICAL USES OF IMAGINATION." GHANA ELITES SOCIETY NAT/G DOMIN EDU/PROP COLONIAL REGION REPRESENT GP/REL CENTRAL PWR MARXISM 20. PAGE 44 B0897
S67
NAT/LISM
EX/STRUC
AFR
LEAD

KURON J.,"AN OPEN LETTER TO THE PARTY." CONSTN WORKER BUDGET EDU/PROP ADMIN REPRESENT SUFF OWN ...SOCIALIST 20. PAGE 62 B1244
S67
ELITES
STRUCT
POL/PAR
ECO/TAC

LEWIS P.H.,"LEADERSHIP AND CONFLICT WITHIN FEBRERISTA PARTY OF PARAGUAY." L/A+17C PARAGUAY EX/STRUC DOMIN SENIOR CONTROL INGP/REL CENTRAL FEDERAL ATTIT 20. PAGE 65 B1305
S67
POL/PAR
ELITES
LEAD

SHOEMAKER R.L.,"JAPANESE ARMY AND THE WEST." ASIA ELITES EX/STRUC DIPLOM DOMIN EDU/PROP COERCE ATTIT AUTHORIT PWR 1/20 CHINJAP. PAGE 96 B1950
S67
FORCES
TEC/DEV
WAR
TOTALISM

SPACKMAN A.,"THE SENATE OF TRINIDAD AND TOBAGO." L/A+17C TRINIDAD WEST/IND NAT/G POL/PAR DELIB/GP OP/RES PROB/SOLV EDU/PROP EXEC LOBBY ROUTINE REPRESENT GP/REL 20. PAGE 99 B2002
S67
ELITES
EFFICIENCY
LEGIS
DECISION

SUBRAMANIAM V.,"REPRESENTATIVE BUREAUCRACY: A REASSESSMENT." USA+45 ELITES LOC/G NAT/G ADMIN GOV/REL PRIVIL DRIVE ROLE...POLICY CENSUS 20
S67
STRATA
GP/REL
MGT

CIVIL/SERV BUREAUCRCY. PAGE 101 B2053
GOV/COMP
B98

THOMPSON H.C.,RHODESIA AND ITS GOVERNMENT. AFR RHODESIA ECO/UNDEV INDUS KIN WORKER INT/TRADE DISCRIM LITERACY ORD/FREE 19. PAGE 104 B2102
COLONIAL
ADMIN
POLICY
ELITES

ELIZABTH/I....ELIZABETH I OF ENGLAND

ELKIN A.B. B0666

ELKIN/AP....A.P. ELKIN
B65

BERNDT R.M.,ABORIGINAL MAN IN AUSTRALIA. LAW DOMIN ADMIN COLONIAL MARRIAGE HABITAT ORD/FREE...LING CHARTS ANTHOL BIBLIOG WORSHIP 20 AUSTRAL ABORIGINES MUSIC ELKIN/AP. PAGE 11 B0225
SOC
CULTURE
SOCIETY
STRUCT

ELKOURI E.A. B0667

ELKOURI F. B0667

ELLIOTT O. B0668

ELLIOTT S.D. B0669

ELLIOTT W. B0670

EMERGENCY....SEE DECISION

EMERSON R. B0671,B0672

EMMERICH H. B0673

EMPLOYMENT....SEE WORKER

ENDACOTT G.B. B0674

ENG/CIV/WR....ENGLISH CIVIL WAR

ENGELS F. B1421

ENGELS/F....FRIEDRICH ENGELS

ENGLAND, BANK OF....SEE BANK/ENGL

ENGLAND....SEE UK. ALSO APPROPRIATE TIME/SPACE/CULTURE
    INDEX

ENGLISH CIVIL WAR....SEE ENG/CIV/WR

ENGLSH/LAW....ENGLISH LAW
B24

HOLDSWORTH W.S.,A HISTORY OF ENGLISH LAW; THE COMMON LAW AND ITS RIVALS (VOL. V). UK SEA EX/STRUC WRITING ADMIN...INT/LAW JURID CONCPT IDEA/COMP WORSHIP 16/17 PARLIAMENT ENGLSH/LAW COMMON/LAW. PAGE 51 B1033
LAW
LEGIS
ADJUD
CT/SYS
B24

HOLDSWORTH W.S.,A HISTORY OF ENGLISH LAW; THE COMMON LAW AND ITS RIVALS (VOL. VI). UK STRATA EX/STRUC ADJUD ADMIN CONTROL CT/SYS...JURID CONCPT GEN/LAWS 17 COMMONWLTH PARLIAMENT ENGLSH/LAW COMMON/LAW. PAGE 51 B1034
LAW
CONSTN
LEGIS
CHIEF
B48

SLESSER H.,THE ADMINISTRATION OF THE LAW. UK CONSTN EX/STRUC OP/RES PROB/SOLV CRIME ROLE...DECISION METH/COMP 20 CIVIL/LAW ENGLSH/LAW CIVIL/LAW. PAGE 98 B1977
LAW
CT/SYS
ADJUD
B49

DENNING A.,FREEDOM UNDER THE LAW. MOD/EUR UK LAW SOCIETY CHIEF EX/STRUC LEGIS ADJUD CT/SYS PERS/REL PERSON 17/20 ENGLSH/LAW. PAGE 28 B0573
ORD/FREE
JURID
NAT/G
B50

WADE E.C.S.,CONSTITUTIONAL LAW; AN OUTLINE OF THE LAW AND PRACTICE OF THE CONSTITUTION. UK LEGIS DOMIN ADMIN GP/REL 16/20 CMN/WLTH PARLIAMENT ENGLSH/LAW. PAGE 112 B2269
CONSTN
NAT/G
PARL/PROC
LAW
B54

SCHWARTZ B.,FRENCH ADMINISTRATIVE LAW AND THE COMMON-LAW WORLD. FRANCE CULTURE LOC/G NAT/G PROVS DELIB/GP EX/STRUC LEGIS PROB/SOLV GOV/REL IDEA/COMP ENGLSH/LAW. PAGE 95 B1912
JURID
LAW
METH/COMP
ADJUD
B59

DESMITH S.A.,JUDICIAL REVIEW OF ADMINISTRATIVE ACTION. UK LOC/G CONSULT DELIB/GP ADMIN PWR ...DECISION JURID 20 ENGLSH/LAW. PAGE 28 B0576
ADJUD
NAT/G
PROB/SOLV
CT/SYS
B59

GINSBURG M.,LAW AND OPINION IN ENGLAND. UK CULTURE KIN LABOR LEGIS EDU/PROP ADMIN CT/SYS CRIME OWN HEALTH...ANTHOL 20 ENGLSH/LAW. PAGE 40 B0802
JURID
POLICY
ECO/TAC
B60

HANBURY H.G.,ENGLISH COURTS OF LAW. UK EX/STRUC
JURID

LEGIS CRIME ROLE 12/20 COMMON/LAW ENGLSH/LAW.   CT/SYS
PAGE 46 B0936   CONSTN
                                                      GOV/REL
                                                            B63
ELIAS T.O.,THE NIGERIAN LEGAL SYSTEM. NIGERIA LAW   CT/SYS
FAM KIN SECT ADMIN NAT/LISM...JURID 18/20   ADJUD
ENGLSH/LAW COMMON/LAW. PAGE 33 B0665   COLONIAL
                                                      PROF/ORG
                                                            B63
WADE H.W.R.,TOWARDS ADMINISTRATIVE JUSTICE. UK   ADJUD
USA+45 CONSTN CONSULT PROB/SOLV CT/SYS PARL/PROC   IDEA/COMP
...POLICY JURID METH/COMP 20 ENGLSH/LAW. PAGE 112   ADMIN
B2270
                                                            B64
JACKSON R.M.,THE MACHINERY OF JUSTICE IN ENGLAND.   CT/SYS
UK EDU/PROP CONTROL COST ORD/FREE...MGT 20   ADJUD
ENGLSH/LAW. PAGE 55 B1109   JUDGE
                                                      JURID
                                                            B66
WILSON G.,CASES AND MATERIALS ON CONSTITUTIONAL AND   JURID
ADMINISTRATIVE LAW. UK LAW NAT/G EX/STRUC LEGIS   ADMIN
BAL/PWR BUDGET DIPLOM ADJUD CONTROL CT/SYS GOV/REL   CONSTN
ORD/FREE 20 PARLIAMENT ENGLSH/LAW. PAGE 117 B2359   PWR

ENKE S. B0675

ENLIGHTNMT....THE ENLIGHTENMENT

ENSOR R.C.K. B0676

ENTREPRENEURSHIP....SEE OWN, INDUS, CAP/ISM

ENVY....SEE WEALTH, LOVE, AND VALUES INDEX

EPIST....EPISTEMOLOGY, SOCIOLOGY OF KNOWLEDGE

                                                            B54
BENTLEY A.F.,INQUIRY INTO INQUIRIES: ESSAYS IN   EPIST
SOCIAL THEORY. UNIV LEGIS ADJUD ADMIN LOBBY   SOC
...PHIL/SCI PSY NEW/IDEA LING METH 20. PAGE 11   CONCPT
B0220

EPISTEMOLOGY....SEE EPIST

EPSTEIN F.T. B0677,B0678

EPSTEIN L.D. B0679

EPTA....EXPANDED PROGRAM OF TECHNICAL ASSISTANCE

EQUILIB....EQUILIBRIUM; SEE ALSO BAL/PWR

                                                            B47
SIMON H.A.,ADMINISTRATIVE BEHAVIOR: A STUDY OF   DECISION
DECISION-MAKING PROCESSES IN ADMINISTRATIVE   NEW/IDEA
ORGANIZATION. STRUCT COM/IND OP/RES PROB/SOLV   ADMIN
EFFICIENCY EQUILIB UTIL...PHIL/SCI PSY STYLE.   RATIONAL
PAGE 97 B1956
                                                            C50
HOLCOMBE A.,"OUR MORE PERFECT UNION." USA+45 USA-45   CONSTN
POL/PAR JUDGE CT/SYS EQUILIB FEDERAL PWR...MAJORIT   NAT/G
TREND BIBLIOG 18/20 CONGRESS PRESIDENT. PAGE 51   ADMIN
B1031   PLAN
                                                            B52
REDFORD E.S.,ADMINISTRATION OF NATIONAL ECONOMIC   ADMIN
CONTROL. ECO/DEV DELIB/GP ADJUD CONTROL EQUILIB 20.   ROUTINE
PAGE 87 B1753   GOV/REL
                                                      LOBBY
                                                            B53
MILLIKAN M.F.,INCOME STABILIZATION FOR A DEVELOPING   ANTHOL
DEMOCRACY. USA+45 ECO/DEV LABOR BUDGET ECO/TAC TAX   MARKET
ADMIN ADJUST PRODUC WEALTH...POLICY TREND 20.   EQUILIB
PAGE 73 B1484   EFFICIENCY
                                                            B58
WARNER A.W.,CONCEPTS AND CASES IN ECONOMIC   ECO/TAC
ANALYSIS. PROB/SOLV BARGAIN CONTROL INCOME PRODUC   DEMAND
...ECOMETRIC MGT CONCPT CLASSIF CHARTS 20   EQUILIB
KEYNES/JM. PAGE 114 B2292   COST
                                                            B60
BAERWALD F.,ECONOMIC SYSTEM ANALYSIS: CONCEPTS AND   ACT/RES
PERSPECTIVES. USA+45 ECO/DEV NAT/G COMPUTER EQUILIB   ECO/TAC
INCOME ATTIT...DECISION CONCPT IDEA/COMP. PAGE 8   ROUTINE
B0159   FINAN
                                                            B64
HERSKOVITS M.J.,ECONOMIC TRANSITION IN AFRICA. FUT   AFR
INT/ORG NAT/G WORKER PROB/SOLV TEC/DEV INT/TRADE   ECO/UNDEV
EQUILIB INCOME...ANTHOL 20. PAGE 49 B0996   PLAN
                                                      ADMIN
                                                            S65
GRENIEWSKI H.,"INTENTION AND PERFORMANCE: A PRIMER   SIMUL
OF CYBERNETICS OF PLANNING." EFFICIENCY OPTIMAL   GAME
KNOWL SKILL...MGT EQULIB. PAGE 43 B0873   GEN/METH
                                                      PLAN
                                                            B66
FOX K.A.,THE THEORY OF QUANTITATIVE ECONOMIC POLICY   ECO/TAC

WITH APPLICATIONS TO ECONOMIC GROWTH AND   ECOMETRIC
STABILIZATION. AGRI PLAN ADMIN RISK...IDEA/COMP   EQUILIB
SIMUL T. PAGE 37 B0746   GEN/LAWS
                                                            B67
GROSSMAN G.,ECONOMIC SYSTEMS. USA+45 USA-45 USSR   PLAN
YUGOSLAVIA WORKER CAP/ISM PRICE GP/REL EQUILIB   TEC/DEV
WEALTH MARXISM SOCISM...MGT METH/COMP 19/20.   DEMAND
PAGE 44 B0892
                                                            S67
DUGGAR J.W.,"THE DEVELOPMENT OF MONEY SUPPLY IN   ECO/UNDEV
ETHIOPIA." ETHIOPIA ISLAM CONSULT OP/RES BUDGET   FINAN
CONTROL ROUTINE EFFICIENCY EQUILIB WEALTH...MGT 20.   BAL/PAY
PAGE 31 B0629   ECOMETRIC
                                                            S67
HUGON P.,"BLOCAGES ET DESEQUILIBRES DE LA   ECO/UNDEV
CROISSANCE ECONOMIQUE EN AFRIQUE NOIRE." AFR KIN   COLONIAL
CREATE PLAN INT/TRADE REGION ADJUST CENTRAL EQUILIB   STRUCT
NAT/LISM ORD/FREE MUNICH 20. PAGE 52 B1060   ADMIN
                                                            S67
ZOETEWEIJ B.,"INCOME POLICIES ABROAD: AN INTERIM   METH/COMP
REPORT." PROB/SOLV BARGAIN BUDGET PRICE RISK   INCOME
CENTRAL EFFICIENCY EQUILIB...MGT NAT/COMP 20.   POLICY
PAGE 119 B2405   LABOR

ERDEMLI....ERDEMLI, TURKEY

ERDMANN H.H. B0680

ESCUELA SUPERIOR DE ADMIN PUBL B0681

ESPIONAGE....ESPIONAGE

ESTIMATION....SEE COST

ESTONIA....SEE ALSO USSR

                                                            B63
KLESMENT J.,LEGAL SOURCES AND BIBLIOGRAPHY OF THE   BIBLIOG/A
BALTIC STATES (ESTONIA, LATVIA, LITHUANIA). COM   JURID
ESTONIA LATVIA LITHUANIA LAW FINAN ADJUD CT/SYS   CONSTN
REGION CENTRAL MARXISM 19/20. PAGE 60 B1218   ADMIN

ESTRANGEMENT....SEE STRANGE

ETHIC....PERSONAL ETHICS

ETHIOPIA....SEE ALSO AFR

                                                            B63
CHOJNACKI S.,REGISTER ON CURRENT RESEARCH ON   BIBLIOG
ETHIOPIA AND THE HORN OF AFRICA. ETHIOPIA LAW   ACT/RES
CULTURE AGRI SECT EDU/PROP ADMIN...GEOG HEAL LING   INTELL
20. PAGE 21 B0426   ACADEM
                                                            L65
MATTHEWS D.G.,"A CURRENT BIBLIOGRAPHY ON ETHIOPIAN   BIBLIOG/A
AFFAIRS: A SELECT BIBLIOGRAPHY FROM 1950-1964."   ADMIN
ETHIOPIA LAW CULTURE ECO/UNDEV INDUS LABOR SECT   POL/PAR
FORCES DIPLOM CIVMIL/REL RACE/REL...LING STAT 20.   NAT/G
PAGE 71 B1428
                                                            S66
MATTHEWS D.G.,"ETHIOPIAN OUTLINE: A BIBLIOGRAPHIC   BIBLIOG
RESEARCH GUIDE." ETHIOPIA LAW STRUCT ECO/UNDEV AGRI NAT/G
LABOR SECT CHIEF DELIB/GP EX/STRUC ADMIN...LING   DIPLOM
ORG/CHARTS 20. PAGE 71 B1429   POL/PAR
                                                            S67
DUGGAR J.W.,"THE DEVELOPMENT OF MONEY SUPPLY IN   ECO/UNDEV
ETHIOPIA." ETHIOPIA ISLAM CONSULT OP/RES BUDGET   FINAN
CONTROL ROUTINE EFFICIENCY EQUILIB WEALTH...MGT 20. BAL/PAY
PAGE 31 B0629   ECOMETRIC

ETHNICITY....SEE RACE/REL, CULTURE

ETHNOGRAPHY....SEE CULTURE

ETIENNE G. B0682

ETIQUET....ETIQUETTE, STYLING, FASHION, MANNERS

                                                            NCO
STOLPER W.,"SOCIAL FACTORS IN ECONOMIC PLANNING,   ECO/UNDEV
WITH SPECIAL REFERENCE TO NIGERIA" AFR NIGER   PLAN
CULTURE FAM SECT RECEIVE ETIQUET ADMIN DEMAND 20.   ADJUST
PAGE 101 B2045   RISK
                                                            B53
GROSS B.M.,THE LEGISLATIVE STRUGGLE: A STUDY IN   LEGIS
SOCIAL COMBAT. STRUCT LOC/G POL/PAR JUDGE EDU/PROP   DECISION
DEBATE ETIQUET ADMIN LOBBY CHOOSE GOV/REL INGP/REL   PERSON
HEREDITY ALL/VALS...SOC PRESIDENT. PAGE 44 B0885   LEAD
                                                            S57
HUITT R.K.,"THE MORSE COMMITTEE ASSIGNMENT   LEGIS
CONTROVERSY: A STUDY IN SENATE NORMS." USA+45   ETIQUET
USA-45 POL/PAR SENIOR ROLE SUPEGO SENATE. PAGE 52   PWR

B1061   ROUTINE
                                                                  B65
FORGAC A.A.,NEW DIPLOMACY AND THE UNITED NATIONS.   DIPLOM
FRANCE GERMANY UK USSR INT/ORG DELIB/GP EX/STRUC   ETIQUET
PEACE...INT/LAW CONCPT UN. PAGE 36 B0740   NAT/G

ETZIONI A. B0683,B0684,B0685,B0686

EUGENICS....SEE BIO/SOC+GEOG

EUGENIE....EMPRESS EUGENIE (FRANCE)

EUR+WWI....EUROPE SINCE WORLD WAR I

EUR+WW1

                                                                  B27
ANGELL N.,THE PUBLIC MIND. USA-45 SOCIETY EDU/PROP   PERCEPT
ROUTINE SUPEGO KNOWL...POLICY CONCPT MYTH OBS/ENVIR   ATTIT
EUR+WW1 TOT/POP 20. PAGE 5 B0109   DIPLOM
                                                      NAT/LISM

EURATOM....EUROPEAN ATOMIC ENERGY COMMUNITY

                                                                  B63
MAYNE R.,THE COMMUNITY OF EUROPE. UK CONSTN NAT/G   EUR+WWI
CONSULT DELIB/GP CREATE PLAN ECO/TAC LEGIT ADMIN   INT/ORG
ROUTINE ORD/FREE PWR WEALTH...CONCPT TIME/SEQ EEC   REGION
EURATOM 20. PAGE 71 B1436
                                                                  B66
SPINELLI A.,THE EUROCRATS; CONFLICT AND CRISIS IN   INT/ORG
THE EUROPEAN COMMUNITY (TRANS. BY C. GROVE HAINES).   INGP/REL
EUR+WWI MARKET POL/PAR ECO/TAC PARL/PROC EEC OEEC   CONSTN
ECSC EURATOM. PAGE 99 B2007   ADMIN
                                                                  B67
SCHEINMAN L.,EURATOM* NUCLEAR INTEGRATION IN   INT/ORG
EUROPE. EX/STRUC LEAD 20 EURATOM. PAGE 93 B1885   NAT/LISM
                                                      NUC/PWR
                                                      DIPLOM
                                                                  S67
WEIL G.L.,"THE MERGER OF THE INSTITUTIONS OF THE   ECO/TAC
EUROPEAN COMMUNITIES" EUR+WWI ECO/DEV INT/TRADE   INT/ORG
CONSEN PLURISM...DECISION MGT 20 EEC EURATOM ECSC   CENTRAL
TREATY. PAGE 115 B2313   INT/LAW

EURCOALSTL....EUROPEAN COAL AND STEEL COMMUNITY; SEE ALSO
     VOL/ASSN, INT/ORG

EURCT/JUST....EUROPEAN COURT OF JUSTICE

                                                                  B64
SCHECHTER A.H.,INTERPRETATION OF AMBIGUOUS   INT/LAW
DOCUMENTS BY INTERNATIONAL ADMINISTRATIVE   DIPLOM
TRIBUNALS. WOR+45 EX/STRUC INT/TRADE CT/SYS   INT/ORG
SOVEREIGN 20 UN ILO EURCT/JUST. PAGE 93 B1884   ADJUD

EUROPE....SEE EUR+WWI, MOD/EUR

                                                                  B66
BEAUFRE A.,NATO AND EUROPE. WOR+45 PLAN CONFER EXEC   INT/ORG
NUC/PWR ATTIT...POLICY 20 NATO EUROPE. PAGE 10   DETER
B0203   DIPLOM
                                                      ADMIN

EUROPE/E....EASTERN EUROPE (ALL EUROPEAN COMMUNIST NATIONS)

                                                                  L63
BOLGAR V.,"THE PUBLIC INTEREST: A JURISPRUDENTIAL   CONCPT
AND COMPARATIVE OVERVIEW OF SYMPOSIUM ON   ORD/FREE
FUNDAMENTAL CONCEPTS OF PUBLIC LAW" COM FRANCE   CONTROL
GERMANY SWITZERLND LAW ADJUD ADMIN AGREE LAISSEZ   NAT/COMP
...JURID GEN/LAWS 20 EUROPE/E. PAGE 13 B0268

EUROPE/W....WESTERN EUROPE (NON-COMMUNIST EUROPE, EXCLUDING
     GREECE, TURKEY, SCANDINAVIA, AND THE BRITISH ISLES)

                                                                  B66
MARTIN L.W.,DIPLOMACY IN MODERN EUROPEAN HISTORY.   DIPLOM
EUR+WWI MOD/EUR INT/ORG NAT/G EX/STRUC ROUTINE WAR   POLICY
PEACE TOTALISM PWR 15/20 COLD/WAR EUROPE/W. PAGE 70
B1411

EUROPEAN ATOMIC ENERGY COMMUNITY....SEE EURATOM

EUROPEAN COAL AND STEEL COMMUNITY....SEE EURCOALSTL

EUROPEAN CONVENTION ON HUMAN RIGHTS....SEE ECHR

EUROPEAN COURT OF JUSTICE....SEE EURCT/JUST

EUROPEAN ECONOMIC COMMUNITY....SEE EEC

EUROPEAN FREE TRADE ASSOCIATION....SEE EFTA

EUROPEAN INVESTMENT BANK....SEE EIB

EVAN W.M. B0687

EVANS L.H. B0688

EVANS M.S. B0689

EVANS R.H. B0690

EVERETT R.O. B0691

EVERS/MED....MEDGAR EVERS

EWING D.W. B0692

EX POST FACTO LAWS....SEE EXPOSTFACT

EX/IM/BANK....EXPORT-IMPORT BANK

EX/STRUC....EXECUTIVE ESTABLISHMENTS

                                                                  N
JOURNAL OF POLITICS. USA+45 USA-45 CONSTN POL/PAR   BIBLIOG/A
EX/STRUC LEGIS PROB/SOLV DIPLOM CT/SYS CHOOSE   NAT/G
RACE/REL 20. PAGE 1 B0005   LAW
                                                      LOC/G
                                                                  N
THE MANAGEMENT REVIEW. FINAN EX/STRUC PROFIT   LABOR
BIBLIOG/A. PAGE 1 B0017   MGT
                                                      ADMIN
                                                      MARKET
                                                                  N
PERSONNEL ADMINISTRATION: THE JOURNAL OF THE   WORKER
SOCIETY FOR PERSONNEL ADMINISTRATION. USA+45 INDUS   MGT
LG/CO SML/CO...BIBLIOG/A 20. PAGE 2 B0028   ADMIN
                                                      EX/STRUC

KENTUCKY STATE ARCHIVES,CHECKLIST OF KENTUCKY STATE   BIBLIOG/A
PUBLICATIONS AND STATE DIRECTORY. USA+45 LAW ACADEM   PROVS
EX/STRUC LEGIS EDU/PROP LEAD...JURID 20. PAGE 59   PUB/INST
B1196   ADMIN
                                                                  N
PRINCETON UNIVERSITY,SELECTED REFERENCES: BIBLIOG/A
INDUSTRIAL RELATIONS SECTION. USA+45 EX/STRUC   LABOR
WORKER TEC/DEV...MGT 20. PAGE 85 B1712   INDUS
                                                      GP/REL
                                                                  N
UNESCO,INTERNATIONAL BIBLIOGRAPHY OF POLITICAL   BIBLIOG
SCIENCE (VOLUMES 1-8). WOR+45 LAW NAT/G EX/STRUC   CONCPT
LEGIS PROB/SOLV DIPLOM ADMIN GOV/REL 20 UNESCO.   IDEA/COMP
PAGE 107 B2153
                                                                  N
US SUPERINTENDENT OF DOCUMENTS,POLITICAL SCIENCE: BIBLIOG/A
GOVERNMENT, CRIME, DISTRICT OF COLUMBIA (PRICE LIST   NAT/G
54). USA+45 LAW CONSTN EX/STRUC WORKER ADJUD ADMIN   CRIME
CT/SYS CHOOSE INGP/REL RACE/REL CONGPESS PRESIDENT.
PAGE 111 B2241
                                                                  B03
GRIFFIN A.P.C.,LIST OF BOOKS ON THE CABINETS OF   BIBLIOG/A
ENGLAND AND AMERICA (PAMPHLET). MOD/EUR UK USA-45   GOV/COMP
CONSTN NAT/G CONSULT EX/STRUC 19/20. PAGE 43 B0875   ADMIN
                                                      DELIB/GP
                                                                  B05
GOODNOW F.J.,THE PRINCIPLES OF THE ADMINISTRATIVE   ADMIN
LAW OF THE UNITED STATES. USA-45 LAW STRUCT   NAT/G
EX/STRUC LEGIS BAL/PWR CONTROL GOV/REL PWR...JURID   PROVS
19/20 CIVIL/SERV. PAGE 41 B0822   LOC/G
                                                                  B08
THE GOVERNMENT OF SOUTH AFRICA (VOL. II). SOUTH/AFR   CONSTN
STRATA EXTR/IND EX/STRUC TOP/EX BUDGET ADJUD ADMIN   FINAN
CT/SYS PRODUC...CORREL CENSUS 19 RAILROAD   LEGIS
CIVIL/SERV POSTAL/SYS. PAGE 2 B0033   NAT/G
                                                                  B13
MEYER H.H.B.,SELECT LIST OF REFERENCES ON   BIBLIOG
COMMISSION GOVERNMENT FOR CITIES (PAMPHLET). USA-45   LOC/G
EX/STRUC ADMIN 20. PAGE 73 B1473   MUNIC
                                                      DELIB/GP
                                                                  B16
TREITSCHKE H.,POLITICS. UNIV SOCIETY STRATA NAT/G   EXEC
EX/STRUC LEGIS DOMIN EDU/PROP ATTIT PWR RESPECT   ELITES
...CONCPT TIME/SEQ GEN/LAWS TOT/POP 20. PAGE 105   GERMANY
B2127
                                                                  B17
CORWIN E.S.,THE PRESIDENT'S CONTROL OF FOREIGN   TOP/EX
RELATIONS. FUT USA-45 CONSTN STRATA NAT/G CHIEF   PWR
EX/STRUC LEGIS KNOWL RESPECT...JURID CONCPT TREND   DIPLOM
CONGRESS VAL/FREE 20 PRESIDENT. PAGE 24 B0483
                                                                  B17
HARLOW R.V.,THE HISTORY OF LEGISLATIVE METHODS IN   LEGIS
THE PERIOD BEFORE 1825. USA-45 EX/STRUC ADMIN   DELIB/GP
COLONIAL LEAD PARL/PROC ROUTINE...GP/COMP GOV/COMP   PROVS
HOUSE/REP. PAGE 47 B0948   POL/PAR
                                                                  B18
US LIBRARY OF CONGRESS,LIST OF REFERENCES ON A   BIBLIOG
LEAGUE OF NATIONS. DIPLOM WAR PEACE 20 LEAGUE/NAT.   INT/ORG
PAGE 109 B2201   ADMIN
                                                      EX/STRUC

WILSON W.,THE STATE: ELEMENTS OF HISTORICAL AND
PRACTICAL POLITICS. FRANCE GERMANY ITALY UK USSR
CONSTN EX/STRUC LEGIS CT/SYS WAR PWR...POLICY
GOV/COMP 20. PAGE 117 B2363
NAT/G JURID CONCPT NAT/COMP
B18

NATHAN M.,THE SOUTH AFRICAN COMMONWEALTH:
CONSTITUTION, PROBLEMS, SOCIAL CONDITIONS.
SOUTH/AFR UK CULTURE INDUS EX/STRUC LEGIS BUDGET
EDU/PROP ADMIN CT/SYS GP/REL RACE/REL...LING 19/20
CMN/WLTH. PAGE 77 B1559
CONSTN NAT/G POL/PAR SOCIETY
B19

ABBOT F.C.,THE CAMBRIDGE CITY MANAGER (PAMPHLET).
PROB/SOLV ADMIN PERS/REL RIGID/FLEX PWR...MGT 20
MASSACHU CITY/MGT. PAGE 2 B0050
MUNIC EX/STRUC TOP/EX GP/REL
N19

ABERNATHY B.R.,SOME PERSISTING QUESTIONS CONCERNING
THE CONSTITUTIONAL STATE EXECUTIVE (PAMPHLET).
CONSTN TOP/EX TEC/DEV GOV/REL EFFICIENCY TIME 20
GOVERNOR. PAGE 3 B0054
PROVS EX/STRUC PROB/SOLV PWR
N19

CANADA CIVIL SERV COMM,THE ANALYSIS OF ORGANIZATION
IN THE GOVERNMENT OF CANADA (PAMPHLET). CANADA
CONSTN EX/STRUC LEGIS TOP/EX CREATE PLAN CONTROL
GP/REL 20. PAGE 18 B0372
NAT/G MGT ADMIN DELIB/GP
N19

FIKS M.,PUBLIC ADMINISTRATION IN ISRAEL (PAMPHLET).
ISRAEL SCHOOL EX/STRUC BUDGET PAY INGP/REL
...DECISION 20 CIVIL/SERV. PAGE 35 B0718
EDU/PROP NAT/G ADMIN WORKER
N19

LA PALOMBARA J.G.,ALTERNATIVE STRATEGIES FOR
DEVELOPING ADMINISTRATIVE CAPABILITIES IN EMERGING
NATIONS (PAMPHLET). POL/PAR EX/STRUC PROB/SOLV
PLURISM...POLICY METH/COMP. PAGE 62 B1248
ECO/UNDEV MGT EXEC ADMIN
N19

MARSH J.F. JR.,THE FBI RETIREMENT BILL (PAMPHLET).
USA+45 EX/STRUC WORKER PLAN PROB/SOLV BUDGET LEAD
LOBBY PARL/PROC PERS/REL RIGID/FLEX...POLICY 20 FBI
PRESIDENT BUR/BUDGET. PAGE 70 B1405
ADMIN SENIOR GOV/REL
C20

BLACHLY F.F.,"THE GOVERNMENT AND ADMINISTRATION OF
GERMANY." GERMANY CONSTN LOC/G PROVS DELIB/GP
EX/STRUC FORCES LEGIS TOP/EX CT/SYS...BIBLIOG/A
19/20. PAGE 12 B0246
NAT/G GOV/REL ADMIN PHIL/SCI
B21

BRYCE J.,MODERN DEMOCRACIES. FUT NEW/ZEALND USA-45
LAW CONSTN POL/PAR PROVS VOL/ASSN EX/STRUC LEGIS
LEGIT CT/SYS EXEC KNOWL CONGRESS AUSTRAL 20.
PAGE 16 B0332
NAT/G TREND
B24

HOLDSWORTH W.S.,A HISTORY OF ENGLISH LAW; THE
COMMON LAW AND ITS RIVALS (VOL. V). UK SEA EX/STRUC
WRITING ADMIN...INT/LAW JURID CONCPT IDEA/COMP
WORSHIP 16/17 PARLIAMENT ENGLSH/LAW COMMON/LAW.
PAGE 51 B1033
LAW LEGIS ADJUD CT/SYS
B24

HOLDSWORTH W.S.,A HISTORY OF ENGLISH LAW; THE
COMMON LAW AND ITS RIVALS (VOL. VI). UK STRATA
EX/STRUC ADJUD ADMIN CONTROL CT/SYS...JURID CONCPT
GEN/LAWS 17 COMMONWLTH PARLIAMENT ENGLSH/LAW
COMMON/LAW. PAGE 51 B1034
LAW CONSTN LEGIS CHIEF
B24

KENT F.R.,THE GREAT GAME OF POLITICS. USA-45 LOC/G
NAT/G POL/PAR EX/STRUC PROB/SOLV BUDGET CHOOSE
GOV/REL 20. PAGE 59 B1194
ADMIN OP/RES STRUCT
B25

MATHEWS J.M.,AMERICAN STATE GOVERNMENT. USA-45
LOC/G CHIEF EX/STRUC LEGIS ADJUD CONTROL CT/SYS
ROUTINE GOV/REL PWR 20 GOVERNOR. PAGE 71 B1426
PROVS ADMIN FEDERAL CONSTN
B26

INTERNATIONAL BIBLIOGRAPHY OF POLITICAL SCIENCE.
WOR+45 NAT/G POL/PAR EX/STRUC LEGIS CT/SYS LEAD
CHOOSE GOV/REL ATTIT...PHIL/SCI 20. PAGE 2 B0034
BIBLIOG DIPLOM CONCPT ADMIN
B26

MOON P.T.,IMPERIALISM AND WORLD POLITICS. AFR ASIA
ISLAM MOD/EUR S/ASIA USA-45 SOCIETY NAT/G EX/STRUC
BAL/PWR DOMIN COLONIAL NAT/LISM ATTIT DRIVE PWR
...GEOG SOC 20. PAGE 75 B1510
WEALTH TIME/SEQ CAP/ISM DIPLOM
B27

WILLOUGHBY W.F.,PRINCIPLES OF PUBLIC ADMINISTRATION
WITH SPECIAL REFERENCE TO THE NATIONAL AND STATE
GOVERNMENTS OF THE UNITED STATES. FINAN PROVS CHIEF
CONSULT LEGIS CREATE BUDGET EXEC ROUTINE GOV/REL
CENTRAL...MGT 20 BUR/BUDGET CONGRESS PRESIDENT.
PAGE 117 B2356
NAT/G EX/STRUC OP/RES ADMIN
B29

MOLEY R.,POLITICS AND CRIMINAL PROSECUTION. USA-45
POL/PAR EX/STRUC LEGIT CONTROL LEAD ROUTINE CHOOSE
INGP/REL...JURID CHARTS 20. PAGE 74 B1497
PWR CT/SYS CRIME ADJUD
B31

DEKAT A.D.A.,COLONIAL POLICY. S/ASIA CULTURE
DRIVE

EX/STRUC ECO/TAC DOMIN ADMIN COLONIAL ROUTINE
SOVEREIGN WEALTH...POLICY MGT RECORD KNO/TEST SAMP.
PAGE 28 B0570
PWR INDONESIA NETHERLAND
B32

CARDINALL AW.,A BIBLIOGRAPHY OF THE GOLD COAST. AFR
UK NAT/G EX/STRUC ATTIT...POLICY 19/20. PAGE 18
B0376
BIBLIOG ADMIN COLONIAL DIPLOM
B32

MCKISACK M.,THE PARLIAMENTARY REPRESENTATION OF THE
ENGLISH BOROUGHS DURING THE MIDDLE AGES. UK CONSTN
CULTURE ELITES EX/STRUC TAX PAY ADJUD PARL/PROC
APPORT FEDERAL...POLICY 13/15 PARLIAMENT. PAGE 72
B1454
NAT/G MUNIC LEGIS CHOOSE
B33

DANGERFIELD R.,IN DEFENSE OF THE SENATE. USA-45
CONSTN NAT/G EX/STRUC TOP/EX ATTIT KNOWL
...METH/CNCPT STAT TIME/SEQ TREND CON/ANAL CHARTS
CONGRESS 20 TREATY. PAGE 26 B0528
LEGIS DELIB/GP DIPLOM
B33

ENSOR R.C.K.,COURTS AND JUDGES IN FRANCE, GERMANY,
AND ENGLAND. FRANCE GERMANY UK LAW PROB/SOLV ADMIN
ROUTINE CRIME ROLE...METH/COMP 20 CIVIL/LAW.
PAGE 33 B0676
CT/SYS EX/STRUC ADJUD NAT/COMP
B33

GREER S.,A BIBLIOGRAPHY OF PUBLIC ADMINISTRATION.
WOR-45 CONSTN LOC/G MUNIC EX/STRUC LEGIS...CONCPT
20. PAGE 43 B0869
BIBLIOG/A ADMIN MGT NAT/G
B34

RIDLEY C.E.,THE CITY-MANAGER PROFESSION. CHIEF PLAN
ADMIN CONTROL ROUTINE CHOOSE...TECHNIC CHARTS
GOV/COMP BIBLIOG 20. PAGE 88 B1780
MUNIC EX/STRUC LOC/G EXEC
B35

HOLECOMBE A.N.,GOVERNMENT IN A PLANNED DEMOCRACY.
USA+45 NAT/G EX/STRUC 20. PAGE 51 B1035
ADMIN REPRESENT LOBBY PLURISM
B36

GRAVES W.B.,AMERICAN STATE GOVERNMENT. CONSTN FINAN
EX/STRUC FORCES LEGIS BUDGET TAX CT/SYS REPRESENT
GOV/REL...BIBLIOG/A 19/20. PAGE 42 B0855
NAT/G PROVS ADMIN FEDERAL
B37

GOSNELL H.F.,MACHINE POLITICS: CHICAGO MODEL.
COM/IND FACE/GP LOC/G EX/STRUC LEAD ROUTINE
SANCTION REPRESENT GOV/REL PWR...POLICY MATH OBS
INT CHARTS. PAGE 41 B0840
POL/PAR MUNIC ADMIN CHOOSE
B38

FIELD G.L.,THE SYNDICAL AND CORPORATIVE
INSTITUTIONS OF ITALIAN FASCISM. ITALY CONSTN
STRATA LABOR EX/STRUC TOP/EX ADJUD ADMIN LEAD
TOTALISM AUTHORIT...MGT 20 MUSSOLIN/B. PAGE 35
B0716
FASCISM INDUS NAT/G WORKER
B39

MACMAHON A.W.,FEDERAL ADMINISTRATORS: A
BIOGRAPHICAL APPROACH TO THE PROBLEM OF
DEPARTMENTAL MANAGEMENT. USA-45 DELIB/GP EX/STRUC
WORKER LEAD...TIME/SEQ 19/20. PAGE 68 B1366
BIOG ADMIN NAT/G MGT
B39

ZIMMERN A.,MODERN POLITICAL DOCTRINE. WOR-45
CULTURE SOCIETY ECO/UNDEV DELIB/GP EX/STRUC CREATE
DOMIN COERCE NAT/LISM ATTIT RIGID/FLEX ORD/FREE PWR
WEALTH...POLICY CONCPT OBS TIME/SEQ TREND TOT/POP
LEAGUE/NAT 20. PAGE 119 B2402
NAT/G ECO/TAC BAL/PWR INT/TRADE
B40

GAUS J.M.,PUBLIC ADMINISTRATION AND THE UNITED
STATES DEPARTMENT OF AGRICULTURE. USA-45 STRUCT
DIST/IND FINAN MARKET EX/STRUC PROB/SOLV GIVE
PRODUC...POLICY GEOG CHARTS 20 DEPT/AGRI. PAGE 39
B0786
ADMIN AGRI DELIB/GP OP/RES
B40

HART J.,AN INTRODUCTION TO ADMINISTRATIVE LAW, WITH
SELECTED CASES. USA+45 CONSTN SOCIETY NAT/G
EX/STRUC ADJUD CT/SYS LEAD CRIME ORD/FREE
...DECISION JURID 20 CASEBOOK. PAGE 47 B0958
LAW ADMIN LEGIS PWR
B40

PATTERSON C.P.,STATE AND LOCAL GOVERNMENT IN TEXAS
(3RD ED.). USA-45 EX/STRUC LEGIS CT/SYS CHOOSE 20
TEXAS. PAGE 81 B1642
CONSTN PROVS GOV/REL LOC/G
S40

GERTH H.,"THE NAZI PARTY: ITS LEADERSHIP AND
COMPOSITION" (BMR)" GERMANY ELITES STRATA STRUCT
EX/STRUC FORCES ECO/TAC CT/SYS CHOOSE TOTALISM
AGE/Y AUTHORIT PWR 20. PAGE 39 B0792
POL/PAR DOMIN LEAD ADMIN
B41

BURTON M.E.,THE ASSEMBLY OF THE LEAGUE OF NATIONS.
WOR-45 CONSTN SOCIETY STRUCT INT/ORG NAT/G CREATE
ATTIT RIGID/FLEX PWR...POLICY TIME/SEQ LEAGUE/NAT
20. PAGE 18 B0359
DELIB/GP EX/STRUC DIPLOM
B41

CHILDS J.B.,A GUIDE TO THE OFFICIAL PUBLICATIONS OF
THE OTHER AMERICAN REPUBLICS: ARGENTINA. CHIEF
DIPLOM GOV/REL...BIBLIOG 18/19 ARGEN. PAGE 21 B0422
NAT/G EX/STRUC METH/CNCPT

LEGIS
B41

GELLHORN W.,FEDERAL ADMINISTRATIVE PROCEEDINGS. EX/STRUC
USA+45 CLIENT FACE/GP NAT/G LOBBY REPRESENT PWR 20. LAW
PAGE 39 B0788 ADJUD
POLICY
B41

MACMAHON A.W.,THE ADMINISTRATION OF FEDERAL WORK ADMIN
RELIEF. USA-45 EX/STRUC WORKER BUDGET EFFICIENCY NAT/G
...CONT/OBS CHARTS 20 WPA. PAGE 68 B1367 MGT
GIVE
S41

STOKE H.W.,"EXECUTIVE LEADERSHIP AND THE GROWTH OF EXEC
PROPAGANDA." USA-45 NAT/G EX/STRUC LEGIS TOP/EX LEAD
PARL/PROC REPRESENT ORD/FREE PWR...MAJORIT 20. EDU/PROP
PAGE 101 B2042 ADMIN
B42

LEISERSON A.,ADMINISTRATIVE REGULATION: A STUDY IN LOBBY
REPRESENTATION OF INTERESTS. NAT/G EX/STRUC ADMIN
PROB/SOLV BARGAIN CONFER ROUTINE REPRESENT PERS/REL GP/REL
UTIL PWR POLICY. PAGE 63 B1283 GOV/REL
B42

SINGTON D.,THE GOEBBELS EXPERIMENT. GERMANY MOD/EUR FASCISM
NAT/G EX/STRUC FORCES CONTROL ROUTINE WAR TOTALISM EDU/PROP
PWR...ART/METH HUM 20 NAZI GOEBBELS/J. PAGE 97 ATTIT
B1970 COM/IND
S42

HUZAR E.,"LEGISLATIVE CONTROL OVER ADMINISTRATION: ADMIN
CONGRESS AND WPA" USA-45 FINAN DELIB/GP LOBBY EX/STRUC
GOV/REL EFFICIENCY ATTIT...POLICY CONGRESS. PAGE 53 CONTROL
B1069 LEGIS
S43

PRICE D.K.,"THE PARLIAMENTARY AND PRESIDENTIAL LEGIS
SYSTEMS" (BMR)" USA-45 NAT/G EX/STRUC PARL/PROC REPRESENT
GOV/REL PWR 20 PRESIDENT CONGRESS PARLIAMENT. ADMIN
PAGE 84 B1706 GOV/COMP
S43

SELZNICK P.,"AN APPROACH TO A THEORY OF ROUTINE
BUREAUCRACY." INDUS WORKER CONTROL LEAD EFFICIENCY ADMIN
OPTIMAL...SOC METH 20 BARNARD/C BUREAUCRCY MGT
WEBER/MAX FRIEDRCH/C MICHELS/R. PAGE 95 B1928 EX/STRUC
B44

BARKER E.,THE DEVELOPMENT OF PUBLIC SERVICES IN GOV/COMP
WESTERN WUROPE: 1660-1930. FRANCE GERMANY UK SCHOOL ADMIN
CONTROL REPRESENT ROLE...WELF/ST 17/20. PAGE 9 EX/STRUC
B0185
B44

KINGSLEY J.D.,REPRESENTATIVE BUREAUCRACY. UK...MGT ADMIN
20. PAGE 60 B1208 REPRESENT
EX/STRUC
L44

CORWIN E.S.,"THE CONSTITUTION AND WORLD INT/ORG
ORGANIZATION." FUT USA+45 USA-45 NAT/G EX/STRUC CONSTN
LEGIS PEACE KNOWL...CON/ANAL UN 20. PAGE 24 B0484 SOVEREIGN
S44

COLEGROVE K.W.,"THE ROLE OF CONGRESS AND PUBLIC EX/STRUC
OPINION IN FORMULATING FOREIGN POLICY." USA+45 WAR DIPLOM
...DECISION UN CONGRESS. PAGE 22 B0451 LEGIS
PWR
B45

CLAPP G.R.,NEW HORIZONS IN PUBLIC ADMINISTRATION: A ADMIN
SYMPOSIUM. USA-45 LEGIS PLAN DIPLOM REGION EX/STRUC
EFFICIENCY 20. PAGE 21 B0430 MGT
NAT/G
B45

CONOVER H.F.,THE GOVERNMENTS OF THE MAJOR FOREIGN BIBLIOG
POWERS: A BIBLIOGRAPHY. FRANCE GERMANY ITALY UK NAT/G
USSR CONSTN LOC/G POL/PAR EX/STRUC FORCES ADMIN DIPLOM
CT/SYS CIVMIL/REL TOTALISM...POLICY 19/20. PAGE 23
B0464
B45

PLATO,THE REPUBLIC. MEDIT-7 UNIV SOCIETY STRUCT PERSON
EX/STRUC FORCES UTOPIA ATTIT PERCEPT HEALTH KNOWL PHIL/SCI
ORD/FREE PWR...HUM CONCPT STERTYP TOT/POP. PAGE 83
B1681
S45

TRUMAN D.B.,"PUBLIC OPINION RESEARCH AS A TOOL OF REPRESENT
PUBLIC ADMINISTRATION" ADMIN PARTIC ROLE...DECISION METH/CNCPT
20. PAGE 105 B2130 ATTIT
EX/STRUC
B46

CORRY J.A.,DEMOCRATIC GOVERNMENT AND POLITICS. NAT/G
WOR-45 EX/STRUC LOBBY TOTALISM...MAJORIT CONCPT CONSTN
METH/COMP NAT/COMP 20. PAGE 24 B0479 POL/PAR
JURID
B46

DAVIES E.,NATIONAL ENTERPRISE: THE DEVELOPMENT OF ADMIN
THE PUBLIC CORPORATION. UK LG/CO EX/STRUC WORKER NAT/G
PROB/SOLV COST ATTIT SOCISM 20. PAGE 26 B0536 CONTROL
INDUS
L46

FORRESTAL J.,"THE NAVY: A STUDY IN ADMINISTRATION." FORCES
ELITES FACE/GP EX/STRUC PROB/SOLV REPRESENT INGP/REL
EFFICIENCY PRODUC. PAGE 37 B0741 ROUTINE
EXEC

S46

CAMPBELL A.,"THE USES OF INTERVIEW SURVEYS IN INT
FEDERAL ADMNISTRATION" PROB/SOLV EXEC PARTIC ADMIN
DECISION. PAGE 18 B0369 EX/STRUC
REPRESENT
C46

GOODRICH L.M.,"CHARTER OF THE UNITED NATIONS: CONSTN
COMMENTARY AND DOCUMENTS." EX/STRUC ADMIN...INT/LAW INT/ORG
CON/ANAL BIBLIOG 20 UN. PAGE 41 B0826 DIPLOM
B47

BARNARD C.,THE FUNCTIONS OF THE EXECUTIVE. USA+45 EXEC
ELITES INTELL LEGIT ATTIT DRIVE PERSON SKILL...PSY EX/STRUC
SOC METH/CNCPT SOC/EXP GEN/METH VAL/FREE 20. PAGE 9 ROUTINE
B0187
B47

GAUS J.M.,REFLECTIONS ON PUBLIC ADMINISTRATION. MGT
USA+45 CONTROL GOV/REL CENTRAL FEDERAL ATTIT WEALTH POLICY
...DECISION 20. PAGE 39 B0787 EX/STRUC
ADMIN
B47

KEFAUVER E.,A TWENTIETH-CENTURY CONGRESS. POL/PAR LEGIS
EX/STRUC SENIOR ADMIN CONTROL EXEC LOBBY CHOOSE DELIB/GP
EFFICIENCY PWR. PAGE 59 B1189 ROUTINE
TOP/EX
B47

MARX F.M.,THE PRESIDENT AND HIS STAFF SERVICES CONSTN
PUBLIC ADMINISTRATION SERVICES NUMBER 98 CHIEF
(PAMPHLET). FINAN ADMIN CT/SYS REPRESENT PWR 20 NAT/G
PRESIDENT. PAGE 70 B1419 EX/STRUC
B47

PATTERSON C.P.,PRESIDENTIAL GOVERNMENT IN THE CHIEF
UNITED STATES - THE UNWRITTEN CONSTITUTION. USA+45 NAT/G
DELIB/GP EX/STRUC ADJUD ADMIN EXEC...DECISION CONSTN
PRESIDENT. PAGE 81 B1643 POL/PAR
B47

TAPPAN P.W.,DELINQUENT GIRLS IN COURT. USA-45 MUNIC CT/SYS
EX/STRUC FORCES ADMIN EXEC ADJUST SEX RESPECT AGE/Y
...JURID SOC/WK 20 NEWYORK/C FEMALE/SEX. PAGE 103 CRIME
B2078 ADJUD
B48

BISHOP H.M.,BASIC ISSUES OF AMERICAN DEMOCRACY. NAT/G
USA+45 USA-45 POL/PAR EX/STRUC LEGIS ADJUD FEDERAL PARL/PROC
...BIBLIOG 18/20. PAGE 12 B0244 CONSTN
B48

HART J.,THE AMERICAN PRESIDENCY IN ACTION 1789: A NAT/G
STUDY IN CONSTITUTIONAL HISTORY. USA-45 POL/PAR CONSTN
DELIB/GP FORCES LEGIS ADJUD ADMIN LEAD GP/REL CHIEF
PERS/REL 18 PRESIDENT CONGRESS. PAGE 47 B0959 EX/STRUC
B48

ROSSITER C.L.,CONSTITUTIONAL DICTATORSHIP: CRISIS NAT/G
GOVERNMENT IN THE MODERN DEMOCRACIES. FRANCE AUTHORIT
GERMANY UK USA-45 WOR-45 EX/STRUC BAL/PWR CONTROL CONSTN
COERCE WAR CENTRAL ORD/FREE...DECISION 19/20. TOTALISM
PAGE 90 B1828
B48

SHERWOOD R.E.,ROOSEVELT AND HOPKINS. UK USA+45 USSR TOP/EX
NAT/G EX/STRUC FORCES ADMIN ROUTINE PERSON PWR BIOG
...TIME/SEQ 20 ROOSEVLT/F HOPKINS/H. PAGE 96 B1946 DIPLOM
WAR
B48

SLESSER H.,THE ADMINISTRATION OF THE LAW. UK CONSTN LAW
EX/STRUC OP/RES PROB/SOLV CRIME ROLE...DECISION CT/SYS
METH/COMP 20 CIVIL/LAW ENGLSH/LAW CIVIL/LAW. ADJUD
PAGE 98 B1977
B48

SPERO S.D.,GOVERNMENT AS EMPLOYER. USA+45 NAT/G SOVEREIGN
EX/STRUC ADMIN CONTROL EXEC 20. PAGE 99 B2005 INGP/REL
REPRESENT
CONFER
B48

TOWSTER J.,POLITICAL POWER IN THE USSR: 1917-1947. EX/STRUC
USSR CONSTN CULTURE ELITES CREATE PLAN COERCE NAT/G
CENTRAL ATTIT RIGID/FLEX ORD/FREE...BIBLIOG MARXISM
SOC/INTEG 20 LENIN/VI STALIN/J. PAGE 105 B2124 PWR
B48

WHITE L.D.,INTRODUCTION OT THE STUDY OF PUBLIC ADMIN
ADMINISTRATION. STRUCT PLAN PROB/SOLV EXEC ROUTINE MGT
GOV/REL EFFICIENCY PWR CHARTS. PAGE 116 B2336 EX/STRUC
NAT/G
C48

WALKER H.,"THE LEGISLATIVE PROCESS; LAWMAKING IN PARL/PROC
THE UNITED STATES." NAT/G POL/PAR PROVS EX/STRUC LEGIS
OP/RES PROB/SOLV CT/SYS LOBBY GOV/REL...CHARTS LAW
BIBLIOG T 18/20 CONGRESS. PAGE 113 B2279 CONSTN
B49

BOYD A.M.,UNITED STATES GOVERNMENT PUBLICATIONS BIBLIOG/A
(3RD ED.). USA+45 EX/STRUC LEGIS ADMIN...JURID PRESS
CHARTS 20. PAGE 14 B0291 NAT/G
EDU/PROP
B49

DENNING A.,FREEDOM UNDER THE LAW. MOD/EUR UK LAW ORD/FREE
SOCIETY CHIEF EX/STRUC LEGIS ADJUD CT/SYS PERS/REL JURID
PERSON 17/20 ENGLSH/LAW. PAGE 28 B0573 NAT/G
B49

GLOVER J.D.,THE ADMINISTRATOR. ELITES LG/CO ADMIN
EX/STRUC ACT/RES CONTROL GP/REL INGP/REL PERS/REL MGT

AUTHORIT...POLICY CONCPT HIST/WRIT. PAGE 40 B0811 ATTIT PROF/ORG

B49
GRAVES W.B.,BASIC INFORMATION ON THE REORGANIZATION BIBLIOG/A OF THE EXECUTIVE BRANCH: 1912-1948. USA-45 BUDGET EX/STRUC ADMIN CONTROL GP/REL EFFICIENCY...MGT CHARTS NAT/G ORG/CHARTS 20 PRESIDENT. PAGE 42 B0857 CHIEF

B49
KENT S.,STRATEGIC INTELLIGENCE FOR AMERICAN WORLD ACT/RES POLICY. FUT USA+45 NAT/G ATTIT PERCEPT ORD/FREE EX/STRUC ...OBS 20. PAGE 59 B1195 DIPLOM

B49
LEPAWSKY A.,ADMINISTRATION. FINAN INDUS LG/CO ADMIN SML/CO INGP/REL PERS/REL COST EFFICIENCY OPTIMAL MGT SKILL 20. PAGE 64 B1294 WORKER EX/STRUC

B49
MCLEAN J.M.,THE PUBLIC SERVICE AND UNIVERSITY ACADEM EDUCATION. UK USA-45 DELIB/GP EX/STRUC TOP/EX ADMIN NAT/G ...GOV/COMP METH/COMP NAT/COMP ANTHOL 20. PAGE 72 EXEC B1455 EDU/PROP

B49
RIDDICK F.M.,THE UNITED STATES CONGRESS LEGIS ORGANIZATION AND PROCEDURE. POL/PAR DELIB/GP PARL/PROC PROB/SOLV DEBATE CONTROL EXEC LEAD INGP/REL PWR CHIEF ...MAJORIT DECISION CONGRESS PRESIDENT. PAGE 88 EX/STRUC B1777

B49
SCHWARTZ B.,LAW AND THE EXECUTIVE IN BRITAIN: A ADMIN COMPARATIVE STUDY. UK USA+45 LAW EX/STRUC PWR EXEC ...GOV/COMP 20. PAGE 95 B1911 CONTROL REPRESENT

B49
STEIN H.,THE FOREIGN SERVICE ACT OF 1946. USA+45 DIPLOM ELITES EX/STRUC PLAN PROB/SOLV LOBBY GOV/REL LAW PERS/REL RIGID/FLEX...POLICY IDEA/COMP 20 CONGRESS NAT/G BUR/BUDGET. PAGE 100 B2027 ADMIN

L49
FAINSED M.,"RECENT DEVELOPMENTS IN SOVIET PUBLIC DOMIN ADMINISTRATION." USSR EXEC 20. PAGE 34 B0699 CONTROL CENTRAL EX/STRUC

N49
UN DEPARTMENT PUBLIC INF,SELECTED BIBLIOGRAPHY OF BIBLIOG THE SPECIALIZED AGENCIES RELATED TO THE UNITED INT/ORG NATIONS (PAMPHLET). USA+45 ROLE 20 UN. PAGE 106 EX/STRUC B2146 ADMIN

B50
GREAT BRITAIN TREASURY,PUBLIC ADMINISTRATION: A BIBLIOG BIBLIOGRAPHY FOR ORGANISATION AND METHODS PLAN (PAMPHLET). LOC/G NAT/G CONSULT EX/STRUC CONFER CONTROL ROUTINE TASK EFFICIENCY...MGT 20. PAGE 43 B0862 ADMIN

B50
HYNEMAN C.S.,BUREAUCRACY IN A DEMOCRACY. CHIEF NAT/G LEGIS ADMIN CONTROL LEAD ROUTINE PERS/REL COST CENTRAL EFFICIENCY UTIL ATTIT AUTHORIT PERSON MORAL. EX/STRUC PAGE 53 B1071 MYTH

B50
MCHENRY D.E.,THE THIRD FORCE IN CANADA: THE POL/PAR COOPERATIVE COMMONWEALTH FEDERATION, 1932-1948. ADMIN CANADA EX/STRUC LEGIS REPRESENT 20 LABOR/PAR. CHOOSE PAGE 72 B1451 POLICY

B50
MONTGOMERY H.,CRACKER PARTIES. CULTURE EX/STRUC POL/PAR LEAD PWR POPULISM...TIME/SEQ 19 GEORGIA CALHOUN/JC PROVS COBB/HOWLL JACKSON/A. PAGE 74 B1505 ELITES BIOG

C50
SIMON H.A.,"PUBLIC ADMINISTRATION." LG/CO SML/CO MGT PLAN DOMIN LEAD GP/REL DRIVE PERCEPT ALL/VALS ADMIN ...POLICY BIBLIOG/A 20. PAGE 97 B1957 DECISION EX/STRUC

C50
STEWART F.M.,"A HALF CENTURY OF MUNICIPAL REFORM." LOC/G USA+45 CONSTN FINAN SCHOOL EX/STRUC PLAN PROB/SOLV VOL/ASSN EDU/PROP ADMIN CHOOSE GOV/REL BIBLIOG. PAGE 101 MUNIC B2036 POLICY

B51
ANDERSON W.,STATE AND LOCAL GOVERNMENT IN THE LOC/G UNITED STATES. USA+45 CONSTN POL/PAR EX/STRUC LEGIS MUNIC BUDGET TAX ADJUD CT/SYS CHOOSE...CHARTS T 20. PROVS PAGE 5 B0100 GOV/REL

B51
CHRISTENSEN A.N.,THE EVOLUTION OF LATIN AMERICAN NAT/G GOVERNMENT: A BOOK OF READINGS. ECO/UNDEV INDUS CONSTN LOC/G POL/PAR EX/STRUC LEGIS FOR/AID CT/SYS DIPLOM ...SOC/WK 20 SOUTH/AMER. PAGE 21 B0428 L/A+17C

B51
DAVIS K.C.,ADMINISTRATIVE LAW. USA+45 USA-45 NAT/G ADMIN PROB/SOLV BAL/PWR CONTROL ORD/FREE...POLICY 20 JURID SUPREME/CT. PAGE 26 B0539 EX/STRUC ADJUD

B51
NIELANDER W.A.,PUBLIC RELATIONS. USA+45 COM/IND PERS/REL LOC/G NAT/G VOL/ASSN EX/STRUC DIPLOM EDU/PROP PRESS GP/REL TV...METH/CNCPT T 20. PAGE 78 B1583 LG/CO

ROUTINE
S51
SHILS E.A.,"THE LEGISLATOR AND HIS ENVIRONMENT." LEGIS EX/STRUC DOMIN CONFER EFFICIENCY PWR MAJORIT. TOP/EX PAGE 96 B1947 ADMIN DELIB/GP

B52
APPLEBY P.H.,MORALITY AND ADMINISTRATION IN REPRESENT DEMOCRATIC GOVERNMENT. USA+45 CLIENT NAT/G EXEC LOBBY EFFICIENCY 20. PAGE 6 B0117 ADMIN EX/STRUC

B52
BRINTON C.,THE ANATOMY OF REVOLUTION. FRANCE UK SOCIETY USA-45 USSR WOR-45 ELITES INTELL ECO/DEV NAT/G CONCPT EX/STRUC FORCES COERCE DRIVE ORD/FREE PWR SOVEREIGN REV ...MYTH HIST/WRIT GEN/LAWS. PAGE 15 B0311

B52
CORSON J.J.,EXECUTIVES FOR THE FEDERAL SERVICE. LOBBY USA+45 CHIEF...MGT 20. PAGE 24 B0480 ADMIN EX/STRUC PERS/REL

B52
DONHAM W.B.,ADMINISTRATION AND BLIND SPOTS. LG/CO ADMIN EX/STRUC BARGAIN ADJUD ROUTINE ROLE SUPEGO 20. TOP/EX PAGE 30 B0605 DECISION POLICY

B52
ELLIOTT W.,UNITED STATES FOREIGN POLICY, ITS LEGIS ORGANIZATION AND CONTROL. USA+45 USA-45 CONSTN EX/STRUC NAT/G FORCES TOP/EX PEACE...TIME/SEQ CONGRESS DIPLOM LEAGUE/NAT 20. PAGE 33 B0670

B52
GOLDSTEIN J.,THE GOVERNMENT OF BRITISH TRADE LABOR UNIONS. UK ECO/DEV EX/STRUC INGP/REL...BIBLIOG 20. PARTIC PAGE 40 B0817

B52
NASH B.D.,STAFFING THE PRESIDENCY: PLANNING EX/STRUC PAMPHLET NO. 80 (PAMPHLET). NAT/G CHIEF CONSULT EXEC DELIB/GP CONFER ADMIN 20 PRESIDENT. PAGE 77 B1557 TOP/EX ROLE

L52
WRIGHT Q.,"CONGRESS AND THE TREATY-MAKING POWER." ROUTINE USA+45 WOR+45 CONSTN INTELL NAT/G CHIEF CONSULT DIPLOM EX/STRUC LEGIS TOP/EX CREATE GOV/REL DISPL DRIVE INT/LAW RIGID/FLEX...TREND TOT/POP CONGRESS CONGRESS 20 DELIB/GP TREATY. PAGE 118 B2384

S52
BRUEGEL J.W.,"DIE INTERNAZIONALE VOL/ASSN GEWERKSCHAFTSBEWEGUNG." COM EUR+WWI USA+45 WOR+45 LABOR DELIB/GP EX/STRUC ECO/TAC EDU/PROP ATTIT PWR TOTALISM RESPECT SKILL WEALTH WORK 20. PAGE 16 B0330

S52
EDELMAN M.,"GOVERNMENTAL ORGANIZATION AND PUBLIC ADMIN POLICY." DELIB/GP ADJUD DECISION. PAGE 32 B0652 PLURIST LOBBY EX/STRUC

S52
JOSEPHSON E.,"IRRATIONAL LEADERSHIP IN FORMAL ADMIN ORGANIZATIONS." EX/STRUC PLAN LEAD GP/REL INGP/REL RATIONAL EFFICIENCY AUTHORIT DRIVE PSY. PAGE 57 B1154 CONCPT PERSON

S52
MASLAND J.W.,"THE NATIONAL WAR COLLEGE AND THE CIVMIL/REL ADMINISTRATION OF FOREIGN AFFAIRS." USA+45 NAT/G EX/STRUC FORCES EXEC 20. PAGE 70 B1422 REPRESENT PROB/SOLV

S52
RICH B.M.,"ADMINISTRATION REORGANIZATION IN NEW ADMIN JERSEY" (BMR) USA+45 DELIB/GP EX/STRUC WORKER CONSTN OP/RES BUDGET 20 NEW/JERSEY. PAGE 88 B1772 PROB/SOLV PROVS

S52
SNIDER C.F.,"AMERICAN COUNTY GOVERNMENT: A MID- LOC/G CENTURY REVIEW" (BMR)" USA+45 USA-45 PROVS DELIB/GP ADMIN EX/STRUC BUDGET TAX PWR 20. PAGE 98 B1988 GOV/REL REGION

S52
SOMERS H.M.,"THE PRESIDENT AS ADMINISTRATOR." CONTROL USA+45 NAT/G ADMIN REPRESENT GOV/REL 20 PRESIDENT. EFFICIENCY PAGE 99 B1996 EX/STRUC EXEC

B53
APPLEBY P.H.,PUBLIC ADMINISTRATION IN INDIA: REPORT ADMIN OF A SURVEY. INDIA LOC/G OP/RES ATTIT ORD/FREE 20. NAT/G PAGE 6 B0118 EX/STRUC GOV/REL

B53
ARGYRIS C.,EXECUTIVE LEADERSHIP: AN APPRAISAL OF A MGT MANAGER IN ACTION. TOP/EX ADMIN LEAD ADJUST ATTIT EX/STRUC ...METH 20. PAGE 6 B0127 WORKER PERS/REL

B53
HOBBS E.H.,EXECUTIVE REORGANIZATION IN THE NATIONAL EFFICIENCY GOVERNMENT. USA+45 USA-45 NAT/G. PAGE 50 B1021 EX/STRUC ADMIN TOP/EX

MACK R.T.,RAISING THE WORLDS STANDARD OF LIVING.   WOR+45
IRAN INT/ORG VOL/ASSN EX/STRUC ECO/TAC WEALTH...MGT   FOR/AID
METH/CNCPT STAT CONT/OBS INT TOT/POP VAL/FREE 20   INT/TRADE
UN. PAGE 67 B1363

B53

STENE E.O.,ABANDONMENTS OF THE MANAGER PLAN. LEGIS   MUNIC
LEAD GP/REL PWR DECISION. PAGE 100 B2032   EX/STRUC
                                                         REPRESENT
                                                         ADMIN
B53

THOMAS S.B.,GOVERNMENT AND ADMINISTRATION IN   PWR
COMMUNIST CHINA (MONOGRAPH). CHINA/COM PROB/SOLV   EX/STRUC
EDU/PROP 20. PAGE 104 B2100   REPRESENT
                                                         ELITES
B53

WAGLEY C.,AMAZON TOWN: A STUDY OF MAN IN THE   SOC
TROPICS. BRAZIL L/A+17C STRATA STRUCT ECO/UNDEV   NEIGH
AGRI EX/STRUC RACE/REL DISCRIM HABITAT WEALTH...OBS   CULTURE
SOC/EXP 20. PAGE 113 B2273   INGP/REL
L53

NEWMAN F.C.,"CONGRESS AND THE FAITHFUL EXECUTION OF   REPRESENT
LAWS - SHOULD LEGISLATORS SUPERVISE   CONTROL
ADMINISTRATORS." USA+45 NAT/G EX/STRUC EXEC PWR   ADMIN
POLICY. PAGE 78 B1579   LEGIS

BLOUGH R.,"THE ROLE OF THE ECONOMIST IN FEDERAL   DELIB/GP
POLICY MAKING." USA+45 ELITES INTELL ECO/DEV NAT/G   ECO/TAC
CONSULT EX/STRUC ACT/RES PLAN INT/TRADE BAL/PAY
WEALTH...POLICY CONGRESS 20. PAGE 13 B0256
S53

PERKINS J.A.,"ADMINISTRATION OF THE NATIONAL   CONTROL
SECURITY PROGRAM." USA+45 EX/STRUC FORCES ADMIN   GP/REL
CIVMIL/REL ORD/FREE 20. PAGE 82 B1657   REPRESENT
                                                         PROB/SOLV
B54

BIESANZ J.,MODERN SOCIETY: AN INTRODUCTION TO   SOCIETY
SOCIAL SCIENCE. COM CONSTN STRUCT FAM MUNIC NAT/G   PROB/SOLV
SECT EX/STRUC LEGIS GP/REL PERSON...SOC 20. PAGE 12   CULTURE
B0237
B54

CHICAGO JOINT REFERENCE LIB,FEDERAL-STATE-LOCAL   BIBLIOG
RELATIONS; A SELECTED BIBLIOGRAPHY. USA+45 AGRI   FEDERAL
LABOR LOC/G MUNIC EX/STRUC ADMIN REGION HEALTH   GOV/REL
CON/ANAL. PAGE 21 B0419
B54

CONWAY O.B. JR.,LEGISLATIVE-EXECUTIVE RELATIONS IN   BAL/PWR
THE GOVERNMENT OF THE UNITED STATES (PAMPHLET).   FEDERAL
BUDGET ATTIT PERCEPT...DECISION 20. PAGE 23 B0470   GOV/REL
                                                         EX/STRUC
B54

DUVERGER M.,POLITICAL PARTIES: THEIR ORGANIZATION   POL/PAR
AND ACTIVITY IN THE MODERN STATE. EUR+WWI MOD/EUR   EX/STRUC
USA+45 USA-45 EDU/PROP ADMIN ROUTINE ATTIT DRIVE   ELITES
ORD/FREE PWR...SOC CONCPT MATH STAT TIME/SEQ
TOT/POP 19/20. PAGE 31 B0635
B54

HOBBS E.H.,BEHIND THE PRESIDENT - A STUDY OF   EX/STRUC
EXECUTIVE OFFICE AGENCIES. USA+45 NAT/G PLAN BUDGET   DELIB/GP
ECO/TAC EXEC ORD/FREE 20 BUR/BUDGET. PAGE 50 B1022   CONFER
                                                         CONSULT
B54

LOCKLIN D.P.,ECONOMICS OF TRANSPORTATION (4TH ED.).   ECO/DEV
USA-45 USA-45 SEA AIR LAW FINAN LG/CO EX/STRUC   DIST/IND
ADMIN CONTROL...STAT CHARTS 19/20 RAILROAD   ECO/TAC
PUB/TRANS. PAGE 66 B1335   TEC/DEV
B54

MATTHEWS D.R.,THE SOCIAL BACKGROUND OF POLITICAL   DECISION
DECISION-MAKERS. CULTURE SOCIETY STRATA FAM   BIOG
EX/STRUC LEAD ATTIT BIO/SOC DRIVE PERSON ALL/VALS   SOC
HIST/WRIT. PAGE 71 B1431
B54

SCHWARTZ B.,FRENCH ADMINISTRATIVE LAW AND THE   JURID
COMMON-LAW WORLD. FRANCE CULTURE LOC/G NAT/G PROVS   LAW
DELIB/GP EX/STRUC LEGIS PROB/SOLV CT/SYS EXEC   METH/COMP
GOV/REL...IDEA/COMP ENGLSH/LAW. PAGE 95 B1912   ADJUD
S54

APPLEBY P.H.,"BUREAUCRACY AND THE FUTURE." USA+45   EX/STRUC
NAT/G CONTROL EXEC...MAJORIT 20. PAGE 6 B0119   LOBBY
                                                         REPRESENT
                                                         ADMIN
S54

CHILDS R.S.,"CITIZEN ORGANIZATION FOR CONTROL OF   CHOOSE
GOVERNMENT." USA+45 POL/PAR CONTROL LOBBY...MAJORIT   REPRESENT
20. PAGE 21 B0424   ADMIN
                                                         EX/STRUC
S54

COLE T.,"LESSONS FROM RECENT EUROPEAN EXPERIENCE."   GOV/COMP
EUR+WWI EX/STRUC 20. PAGE 22 B0450   ADMIN
                                                         REPRESENT
S54

COOPER L.,"ADMINISTRATIVE JUSTICE." UK ADMIN   LAW
REPRESENT PWR...POLICY 20. PAGE 23 B0475   ADJUD
                                                         CONTROL
                                                         EX/STRUC

GILBERT C.E.,"LEGISLATIVE CONTROL OF THE   CONTROL
BUREAUCRACY." USA+45 NAT/G ADMIN EXEC 20. PAGE 39   EX/STRUC
B0798   REPRESENT
                                                         GOV/REL
S54

LANE E.,"INTEREST GROUPS AND BUREAUCRACY." NAT/G   EX/STRUC
ADMIN GP/REL INGP/REL 20. PAGE 62 B1256   LOBBY
                                                         REPRESENT
                                                         PWR
S54

LONG N.E.,"PUBLIC POLICY AND ADMINISTRATION: THE   PROB/SOLV
GOALS OF RATIONALITY AND RESPONSIBILITY." EX/STRUC   EXEC
ADMIN LEAD 20. PAGE 66 B1338   REPRESENT
S54

STONE E.O.,"ADMINISTRATIVE INTEGRATION." USA+45   REPRESENT
NAT/G ADMIN CONTROL CENTRAL 20. PAGE 101 B2046   EFFICIENCY
                                                         LOBBY
                                                         EX/STRUC
C54

CALDWELL L.K.,"THE GOVERNMENT AND ADMINISTRATION OF   PROVS
NEW YORK." LOC/G MUNIC POL/PAR SCHOOL CHIEF LEGIS   ADMIN
PLAN TAX CT/SYS...MGT SOC/WK BIBLIOG 20 NEWYORK/C.   CONSTN
PAGE 18 B0366   EX/STRUC
C54

ROBSON W.A.,"GREAT CITIES OF THE WORLD: THEIR   LOC/G
GOVERNMENT, POLITICS, AND PLANNING." CONSTN FINAN   MUNIC
EX/STRUC ADMIN EXEC CHOOSE GOV/REL...STAT TREND   PLAN
ANTHOL BIBLIOG 20. PAGE 89 B1806   PROB/SOLV
C54

ZELLER B.,"AMERICAN STATE LEGISLATURES: REPORT ON   REPRESENT
THE COMMITTEE ON AMERICAN LEGISLATURES." CONSTN   LEGIS
POL/PAR EX/STRUC CONFER ADMIN CONTROL EXEC LOBBY   PROVS
ROUTINE GOV/REL...POLICY BIBLIOG 20. PAGE 119 B2401   APPORT
B55

BLAU P.M.,THE DYNAMICS OF BUREAUCRACY: A STUDY OF   CLIENT
INTERPERSONAL RELATIONS IN TWO GOVERNMENT AGENCIES.   ADMIN
USA+45 EX/STRUC REPRESENT INGP/REL PERS/REL.   EXEC
PAGE 12 B0251   ROUTINE
B55

CHAPMAN B.,THE PREFECTS AND PROVINCIAL FRANCE.   ADMIN
FRANCE DELIB/GP WORKER ROLE PWR 19/20 PREFECT.   PROVS
PAGE 20 B0408   EX/STRUC
                                                         LOC/G
B55

CRAIG J.,BIBLIOGRAPHY OF PUBLIC ADMINISTRATION IN   BIBLIOG
AUSTRALIA. CONSTN FINAN EX/STRUC LEGIS PLAN DIPLOM   GOV/REL
RECEIVE ADJUD ROUTINE...HEAL 19/20 AUSTRAL   ADMIN
PARLIAMENT. PAGE 24 B0500   NAT/G
B55

CUSHMAN R.E.,LEADING CONSTITUTIONAL DECISIONS.   CONSTN
USA+45 USA-45 NAT/G EX/STRUC LEGIS JUDGE TAX   PROB/SOLV
FEDERAL...DECISION 20 SUPREME/CT CASEBOOK. PAGE 25   JURID
B0513   CT/SYS
B55

DE ARAGAO J.G.,LA JURIDICTION ADMINISTRATIVE AU   EX/STRUC
BRESIL. BRAZIL ADJUD COLONIAL CT/SYS REV FEDERAL   ADMIN
ORD/FREE...BIBLIOG 19/20. PAGE 27 B0549   NAT/G
B55

GALLOWAY G.B.,CONGRESS AND PARLIAMENT: THEIR   DELIB/GP
ORGANIZATION AND OPERATION IN THE US AND THE UK: LEGIS
PLANNING PAMPHLET NO. 93. POL/PAR EX/STRUC DEBATE   PARL/PROC
CONTROL LEAD ROUTINE EFFICIENCY PWR...POLICY   GOV/COMP
CONGRESS PARLIAMENT. PAGE 38 B0777
B55

MAZZINI J.,THE DUTIES OF MAN. MOD/EUR LAW SOCIETY   SUPEGO
FAM NAT/G POL/PAR SECT VOL/ASSN EX/STRUC ACT/RES   CONCPT
CREATE REV PEACE ATTIT ALL/VALS...GEN/LAWS WORK 19.   NAT/LISM
PAGE 71 B1439
B55

RUSTOW D.A.,THE POLITICS OF COMPROMISE. SWEDEN   POL/PAR
LABOR EX/STRUC LEGIS PLAN REPRESENT SOCISM...SOC   NAT/G
19/20. PAGE 92 B1859   POLICY
                                                         ECO/TAC
B55

SMITHIES A.,THE BUDGETARY PROCESS IN THE UNITED   NAT/G
STATES. ECO/DEV AGRI EX/STRUC FORCES LEGIS   ADMIN
PROB/SOLV TAX ROUTINE EFFICIENCY...MGT CONGRESS   BUDGET
PRESIDENT. PAGE 98 B1987   GOV/REL
B55

STEPHENS O.,FACTS TO A CANDID WORLD. USA+45 WOR+45   EDU/PROP
COM/IND EX/STRUC PRESS ROUTINE EFFICIENCY ATTIT   PHIL/SCI
...PSY 20. PAGE 100 B2033   NAT/G
                                                         DIPLOM
S55

SCHWARTZ B.,"LEGISLATIVE CONTROL OF ADMINISTRATIVE   CONTROL
RULES AND REGULATIONS THE AMERICAN EXPERIENCE."   ADMIN
USA+45 GOV/REL...GOV/COMP 20. PAGE 95 B1913   EX/STRUC
                                                         LEGIS
C55

GRASSMUCK G.L.,"A MANUAL OF LEBANESE   ADMIN
ADMINISTRATION." LEBANON PLAN...CHARTS BIBLIOG/A   NAT/G
20. PAGE 42 B0854   ISLAM
                                                         EX/STRUC
B56

BLAU P.M.,BUREAUCRACY IN MODERN SOCIETY. STRUCT   SOC

INDUS LABOR LG/CO LOC/G NAT/G FORCES EDU/PROP
ROUTINE ORD/FREE 20 BUREAUCRCY. PAGE 12 B0252

EX/STRUC
ADMIN
EFFICIENCY
B56

CARTER B.E.,THE OFFICE OF THE PRIME MINISTER. UK
ADMIN REPRESENT PARLIAMENT 20. PAGE 19 B0388

GOV/REL
CHIEF
EX/STRUC
LEAD
B56

DEGRAS J.,THE COMMUNIST INTERNATIONAL, 1919-1943:
DOCUMENTS (3 VOLS.). EX/STRUC...ANTHOL BIBLIOG 20.
PAGE 28 B0569

COM
DIPLOM
POLICY
POL/PAR
B56

ECOLE NAT'L D'ADMINISTRATION,RECRUITMENT AND
TRAINING FOR THE HIGHER CIVIL SERVICE IN FRANCE.
FRANCE EX/STRUC PLAN EDU/PROP CONTROL ROUTINE TASK
COST...METH 20 CIVIL/SERV. PAGE 32 B0650

ADMIN
MGT
EXEC
ACADEM
B56

KOENIG L.W.,THE TRUMAN ADMINISTRATION: ITS
PRINCIPLES AND PRACTICE. USA+45 POL/PAR CHIEF LEGIS
DIPLOM DEATH NUC/PWR WAR CIVMIL/REL PEACE
...DECISION 20 TRUMAN/HS PRESIDENT TREATY. PAGE 61
B1224

ADMIN
POLICY
EX/STRUC
GOV/REL
B56

RANSONE C.B.,THE OFFICE OF GOVERNOR IN THE UNITED
STATES. USA+45 ADMIN...MGT INT CHARTS 20 GOVERNOR.
PAGE 86 B1732

PROVS
TOP/EX
POL/PAR
EX/STRUC
B56

REDFORD E.S.,PUBLIC ADMINISTRATION AND POLICY
FORMATION: STUDIES IN OIL, GAS, BANKING, RIVER
DEVELOPMENT AND CORPORATE INVESTIGATIONS. USA+45
CLIENT NAT/G ADMIN LOBBY REPRESENT GOV/REL INGP/REL
20. PAGE 87 B1754

EX/STRUC
PROB/SOLV
CONTROL
EXEC
B56

US HOUSE RULES COMM,HEARINGS BEFORE A SPECIAL
SUBCOMMITTEE: ESTABLISHMENT OF A STANDING COMMITTEE
ON ADMINISTRATIVE PROCEDURE, PRACTICE. USA+45 LAW
EX/STRUC ADJUD CONTROL EXEC GOV/REL EFFICIENCY PWR
...POLICY INT 20 CONGRESS. PAGE 109 B2199

ADMIN
DOMIN
DELIB/GP
NAT/G
B56

WAUGH E.W.,SECOND CONSUL. USA+45 USA-45 CONSTN
POL/PAR PROB/SOLV PARL/PROC CHOOSE PERS/REL ATTIT
...BIBLIOG 18/20 VICE/PRES. PAGE 114 B2304

NAT/G
EX/STRUC
PWR
CHIEF
B56

WIGGINS J.R.,FREEDOM OR SECRECY. USA+45 USA-45
DELIB/GP EX/STRUC FORCES ADJUD SANCTION KNOWL PWR
...AUD/VIS CONGRESS 20. PAGE 116 B2344

ORD/FREE
PRESS
NAT/G
CONTROL
L56

PARSONS T.,"SUGGESTIONS FOR A SOCIOLOGICAL APPROACH
TO THE THEORY OF ORGANIZATIONS - I" (BMR)" FINAN
EX/STRUC LEGIT ALL/VALS...POLICY DECISION 20.
PAGE 81 B1637

SOC
CONCPT
ADMIN
STRUCT
S56

COTTER C.P.,"ADMINISTRATIVE ACCOUNTABILITY TO
CONGRESS: THE CONCURRENT RESOLUTION." USA+45 NAT/G
EXEC REPRESENT PWR 20. PAGE 24 B0489

CONTROL
GOV/REL
LEGIS
EX/STRUC
S56

CUTLER R.,"THE DEVELOPMENT OF THE NATIONAL SECURITY
COUNCIL." USA+45 INTELL CONSULT EX/STRUC DIPLOM
LEAD 20 TRUMAN/HS EISNHWR/DD NSC. PAGE 25 B0514

ORD/FREE
DELIB/GP
PROB/SOLV
NAT/G
S56

EMMERICH H.,"COOPERATION AMONG ADMINISTRATIVE
AGENCIES." USA+45 NAT/G EX/STRUC ADMIN 20. PAGE 33
B0673

DELIB/GP
REPRESENT
GOV/REL
EXEC
S56

KAUFMAN H.,"EMERGING CONFLICTS IN THE DOCTRINES OF
PUBLIC ADMINISTRATION" (BMR)" USA+45 USA-45 NAT/G
EX/STRUC LEGIS CONTROL NEUTRAL ATTIT PWR...TREND
20. PAGE 58 B1181

ADMIN
ORD/FREE
REPRESENT
LEAD
S56

KHAMA T.,"POLITICAL CHANGE IN AFRICAN SOCIETY."
CONSTN SOCIETY LOC/G NAT/G POL/PAR EX/STRUC LEGIS
LEGIT ADMIN CHOOSE REPRESENT NAT/LISM MORAL
ORD/FREE PWR...CONCPT OBS TREND GEN/METH CMN/WLTH
17/20. PAGE 59 B1201

AFR
ELITES
S56

MILNE R.S.,"CONTROL OF GOVERNMENT CORPORATIONS IN
THE UNITED STATES." USA+45 NAT/G CHIEF LEGIS BUDGET
20 GENACCOUNT. PAGE 74 B1488

CONTROL
EX/STRUC
GOV/REL
PWR
S56

TSUJI K.,"THE CABINET, ADMINISTRATIVE ORGANIZATION
AND THE BUREAUCRACY." EXEC 19/20 CHINJAP. PAGE 106
B2133

GOV/REL
EX/STRUC
ADMIN
REPRESENT
C56

FALL B.B.,"THE VIET-MINH REGIME." VIETNAM LAW
ECO/UNDEV POL/PAR FORCES DOMIN WAR ATTIT MARXISM
...BIOG PREDICT BIBLIOG/A 20. PAGE 35 B0703

NAT/G
ADMIN
EX/STRUC

LEAD
C56

NEUMANN S.,"MODERN POLITICAL PARTIES: APPROACHES TO
COMPARATIVE POLITIC. FRANCE UK EX/STRUC DOMIN ADMIN
LEAD REPRESENT TOTALISM ATTIT...POLICY TREND
METH/COMP ANTHOL BIBLIOG/A 20 CMN/WLTH. PAGE 78
B1574

POL/PAR
GOV/COMP
ELITES
MAJORIT
B57

ASHER R.E.,THE UNITED NATIONS AND THE PROMOTION OF
THE GENERAL WELFARE. WOR+45 WOR-45 ECO/UNDEV
EX/STRUC ACT/RES PLAN EDU/PROP ROUTINE HEALTH...HUM
CONCPT CHARTS UNESCO UN ILO 20. PAGE 7 B0139

INT/ORG
CONSULT

B57

BABCOCK R.S.,STATE & LOCAL GOVERNMENT AND POLITICS.
USA+45 CONSTN POL/PAR EX/STRUC LEGIS BUDGET LOBBY
CHOOSE SUFF...CHARTS BIBLIOG T 20. PAGE 8 B0154

PROVS
LOC/G
GOV/REL
B57

BEAL J.R.,JOHN FOSTER DULLES, A BIOGRAPHY. USA+45
USSR WOR+45 CONSTN INT/ORG NAT/G EX/STRUC LEGIT
ADMIN NUC/PWR DISPL PERSON ORD/FREE PWR SKILL
...POLICY PSY OBS RECORD COLD/WAR UN 20 DULLES/JF.
PAGE 10 B0200

BIOG
DIPLOM

B57

CHANDRA S.,PARTIES AND POLITICS AT THE MUGHAL
COURT: 1707-1740. INDIA CULTURE EX/STRUC CREATE
PLAN PWR...BIBLIOG/A 18. PAGE 20 B0405

POL/PAR
ELITES
NAT/G
B57

DAVID P.T.,EXECUTIVES FOR THE GOVERNMENT: CENTRAL
ISSUES OF FEDERAL PERSONNEL ADMINISTRATION. USA+45
ELITES...GOV/COMP 20. PAGE 26 B0534

EX/STRUC
TOP/EX
ADMIN
B57

JENNINGS I.,PARLIAMENT. UK FINAN INDUS POL/PAR
DELIB/GP EX/STRUC PLAN CONTROL...MAJORIT JURID
PARLIAMENT. PAGE 56 B1133

PARL/PROC
TOP/EX
MGT
LEGIS
B57

LOEWENSTEIN K.,POLITICAL POWER AND THE GOVERNMENTAL
PROCESS. WOR+45 WOR-45 CONSTN NAT/G POL/PAR
EX/STRUC LEGIS TOP/EX DOMIN EDU/PROP LEGIT ADMIN
REGION CHOOSE ATTIT...JURID STERTYP GEN/LAWS 20.
PAGE 66 B1336

PWR
CONCPT

B57

PARKINSON C.N.,PARKINSON'S LAW. UNIV EX/STRUC PLAN
ATTIT PERSON TIME. PAGE 81 B1634

ADMIN
EXEC
FINAN
ECOMETRIC
B57

SCARROW H.A.,THE HIGHER PUBLIC SERVICE OF THE
COMMONWEALTH OF AUSTRALIA. LAW SENIOR LOBBY ROLE 20
AUSTRAL CIVIL/SERV COMMONWLTH. PAGE 93 B1877

ADMIN
NAT/G
EX/STRUC
GOV/COMP
B57

SCHLOCHAUER H.J.,OFFENTLICHES RECHT. GERMANY/W
FINAN EX/STRUC LEGIS DIPLOM FEDERAL ORD/FREE
...INT/LAW 20. PAGE 94 B1892

CONSTN
JURID
ADMIN
CT/SYS
B57

SIMON H.A.,MODELS OF MAN, SOCIAL AND RATIONAL:
MATHEMATICAL ESSAYS ON RATIONAL HUMAN BEHAVIOR IN A
SOCIAL SETTING. UNIV LAW SOCIETY FACE/GP VOL/ASSN
CONSULT EX/STRUC LEGIS CREATE ADMIN ROUTINE ATTIT
DRIVE PWR...SOC CONCPT METH/CNCPT QUANT STAT
TOT/POP VAL/FREE 20. PAGE 97 B1959

MATH
SIMUL

B57

US CIVIL SERVICE COMMISSION,DISSERTATIONS AND
THESES RELATING TO PERSONNEL ADMINISTRATION
(PAMPHLET). USA+45 COM/IND LABOR EX/STRUC GP/REL
INGP/REL DECISION. PAGE 108 B2176

BIBLIOG
ADMIN
MGT
WORKER
B57

US HOUSE COMM ON POST OFFICE,MANPOWER UTILIZATION
IN THE FEDERAL GOVERNMENT. USA+45 FORCES WORKER
CREATE PLAN EFFICIENCY UTIL 20 CONGRESS CIVIL/SERV
POSTAL/SYS DEPT/DEFEN. PAGE 109 B2193

NAT/G
ADMIN
LABOR
EX/STRUC
B57

WEIDLUND J.,COMPARATIVE PUBLIC ADMINISTRATION.
EX/STRUC METH/COMP. PAGE 114 B2310

ADMIN
NAT/G
GOV/COMP
BIBLIOG/A
L57

HAAS E.B.,"REGIONAL INTEGRATION AND NATIONAL
POLICY." WOR+45 VOL/ASSN DELIB/GP EX/STRUC ECO/TAC
DOMIN EDU/PROP LEGIT COERCE ATTIT PERCEPT KNOWL
...TIME/SEQ COLD/WAR 20 UN. PAGE 45 B0908

INT/ORG
ORD/FREE
REGION

S57

COTTER C.P.,"ADMINISTRATIVE ACCOUNTABILITY:
REPORTING TO CONGRESS." USA+45 CONSULT DELIB/GP
PARL/PROC PARTIC GOV/REL ATTIT PWR DECISION.
PAGE 24 B0490

LEGIS
EX/STRUC
REPRESENT
CONTROL
S57

COTTER C.R.,"ADMINISTRATIVE RESPONSIBILITY:
CONGRESSIONAL PRESCRIPTION OF INTERAGENCY
RELATIONSHIPS." USA+45 NAT/G ADMIN 20. PAGE 24
B0492

GOV/REL
LEGIS
REPRESENT
EX/STRUC
S57

FESLER J.W.,"ADMINISTRATIVE LITERATURE AND THE
SECOND HOOVER COMMISSION REPORTS" (BMR)" USA+45

ADMIN
NAT/G

EX/STRUC LEGIS WRITING...DECISION METH 20. PAGE 35   OP/RES
B0713   DELIB/GP
                                                            S57
HARRIS J.P.,"LEGISLATIVE CONTROL OF ADMINISTRATION: LEGIS
SOME COMPARISONS OF AMERICAN AND EUROPEAN   CONTROL
PRACTICES." DEBATE PARL/PROC ROUTINE GOV/REL   EX/STRUC
EFFICIENCY SUPEGO DECISION. PAGE 47 B0954   REPRESENT
                                                            S57
HODGETTS J.E.,"THE CIVIL SERVICE AND POLICY   ADMIN
FORMATION." CANADA NAT/G EX/STRUC ROUTINE GOV/REL   DECISION
20. PAGE 50 B1023   EFFICIENCY
                                                       POLICY
                                                            S57
HONEY J.C.,"RESEARCH IN PUBLIC ADMINISTRATION: A   ADMIN
FURTHER NOTE." EX/STRUC 20. PAGE 51 B1038   EXEC
                                                       METH/COMP
                                                       METH/CNCPT
                                                            S57
JANOWITZ M.,"THE BUREAUCRAT AND THE PUBLIC: A STUDY   REPRESENT
OF INFORMATIONAL PERSPECTIVES." USA+45 PROB/SOLV   ADMIN
ATTIT 20. PAGE 55 B1120   EX/STRUC
                                                       CLIENT
                                                            S57
ROBSON W.A.,"TWO-LEVEL GOVERNMENT FOR METROPOLITAN   REGION
AREAS." MUNIC EX/STRUC LEGIS PARTIC REPRESENT   LOC/G
MAJORITY. PAGE 89 B1807   PLAN
                                                       GOV/REL
                                                            S57
SCHUBERT G.A.,"'THE PUBLIC INTEREST' IN   ADMIN
ADMINISTRATIVE DECISION-MAKING: THEOREM, THEOSOPHY   DECISION
OR THEORY" USA+45 EX/STRUC PROB/SOLV...METH/CNCPT   POLICY
STAT. PAGE 94 B1904   EXEC
                                                            N57
MACMAHON A.W.,ADMINISTRATION AND FOREIGN POLICY   DIPLOM
(PAMPHLET). USA+45 CHIEF OP/RES ADMIN 20. PAGE 68   EX/STRUC
B1372   DECISION
                                                       CONFER
                                                            B58
AMERICAN SOCIETY PUBLIC ADMIN,STRENGTHENING   ADMIN
MANAGEMENT FOR DEMOCRATIC GOVERNMENT. USA+45 ACADEM   NAT/G
EX/STRUC WORKER PLAN BUDGET CONFER CT/SYS   EXEC
EFFICIENCY ANTHOL. PAGE 4 B0088   MGT
                                                            B58
BLAIR L.,THE COMMONWEALTH PUBLIC SERVICE. LAW   ADMIN
WORKER...MGT CHARTS GOV/COMP 20 COMMONWLTH AUSTRAL   NAT/G
CIVIL/SERV. PAGE 12 B0248   EX/STRUC
                                                       INGP/REL
                                                            B58
DAVIS K.C.,ADMINISTRATIVE LAW TREATISE (VOLS. I AND   ADMIN
IV). NAT/G JUDGE PROB/SOLV ADJUD GP/REL 20   JURID
SUPREME/CT. PAGE 26 B0540   CT/SYS
                                                       EX/STRUC
                                                            B58
KRAINES O.,CONGRESS AND THE CHALLENGE OF BIG   LEGIS
GOVERNMENT. USA-45 EX/STRUC CONFER DEBATE   DELIB/GP
EFFICIENCY. PAGE 61 B1232   ADMIN
                                                            B58
LOVEJOY D.S.,RHODE ISLAND POLITICS AND THE AMERICAN   REV
REVOLUTION 1760-1776. UK USA-45 ELITES EX/STRUC TAX   COLONIAL
LEAD REPRESENT GOV/REL GP/REL ATTIT 18 RHODE/ISL.   ECO/TAC
PAGE 67 B1343   SOVEREIGN
                                                            B58
MELMAN S.,DECISION-MAKING AND PRODUCTIVITY. INDUS   LABOR
EX/STRUC WORKER OP/RES PROB/SOLV TEC/DEV ADMIN   PRODUC
ROUTINE RIGID/FLEX GP/COMP. PAGE 73 B1464   DECISION
                                                       MGT
                                                            B58
REDFIELD C.E.,COMMUNICATION IN MANAGEMENT. DELIB/GP   COM/IND
EX/STRUC WRITING LEAD PERS/REL...PSY INT METH 20.   MGT
PAGE 87 B1750   LG/CO
                                                       ADMIN
                                                            B58
REDFORD E.S.,IDEAL AND PRACTICE IN PUBLIC   POLICY
ADMINISTRATION. CONSTN ELITES NAT/G CONSULT   EX/STRUC
DELIB/GP LEAD UTOPIA ATTIT POPULISM...DECISION   PLAN
METH/COMP 20. PAGE 87 B1756   ADMIN
                                                            B58
SHARMA M.P.,PUBLIC ADMINISTRATION IN THEORY AND   MGT
PRACTICE. INDIA UK USA+45 USA-45 EX/STRUC ADJUD   ADMIN
...POLICY CONCPT NAT/COMP 20. PAGE 96 B1935   DELIB/GP
                                                       JURID
                                                            B58
SHERWOOD F.P.,SUPERVISORY METHODS IN MUNICIPAL   EX/STRUC
ADMINISTRATION. USA+45 MUNIC WORKER EDU/PROP PARTIC   LEAD
INGP/REL PERS/REL 20 CITY/MGT. PAGE 96 B1945   ADMIN
                                                       LOC/G
                                                            B58
SKINNER G.W.,LEADERSHIP AND POWER IN THE CHINESE   SOC
COMMUNITY OF THAILAND. ASIA S/ASIA STRATA FACE/GP   ELITES
KIN PROF/ORG VOL/ASSN EX/STRUC DOMIN PERSON RESPECT   THAILAND
...METH/CNCPT STAT INT QU BIOG CHARTS 20. PAGE 98
B1974
                                                            B58
SPITZ D.,DEMOCRACY AND THE CHALLANGE OF POWER. FUT   NAT/G
USA+45 USA-45 LAW SOCIETY STRUCT LOC/G POL/PAR   PWR
PROVS DELIB/GP EX/STRUC LEGIS TOP/EX ACT/RES CREATE

DOMIN EDU/PROP LEGIT ADJUD ADMIN ATTIT DRIVE MORAL
ORD/FREE TOT/POP. PAGE 99 B2010
                                                            B58
US HOUSE COMM ON POST OFFICE,TO PROVIDE AN   ADMIN
EFFECTIVE SYSTEM OF PERSONNEL ADMINISTRATION.   NAT/G
USA+45 DELIB/GP CONTROL EFFICIENCY 20 CONGRESS   EX/STRUC
PRESIDENT CIVIL/SERV POSTAL/SYS. PAGE 109 B2194   LAW
                                                            B58
US HOUSE COMM POST OFFICE,MANPOWER UTILIZATION IN   ADMIN
THE FEDERAL GOVERNMENT. USA+45 DIST/IND EX/STRUC   WORKER
LEGIS CONFER EFFICIENCY 20 CONGRESS CIVIL/SERV.   DELIB/GP
PAGE 109 B2195   NAT/G
                                                            B58
US HOUSE COMM POST OFFICE,MANPOWER UTILIZATION IN   ADMIN
THE FEDERAL GOVERNMENT. USA+45 DIST/IND EX/STRUC   WORKER
LEGIS CONFER EFFICIENCY 20 CONGRESS CIVIL/SERV.   DELIB/GP
PAGE 109 B2196   NAT/G
                                                            B58
US HOUSE COMM POST OFFICE,TRAINING OF FEDERAL   LEGIS
EMPLOYEES. USA+45 DIST/IND NAT/G EX/STRUC EDU/PROP   DELIB/GP
CONFER GOV/REL EFFICIENCY SKILL 20 CONGRESS   WORKER
CIVIL/SERV. PAGE 109 B2197   ADMIN
                                                            B58
US SENATE COMM POST OFFICE,TO PROVIDE AN EFFECTIVE   INT
SYSTEM OF PERSONNEL ADMINISTRATION. USA+45 NAT/G   LEGIS
EX/STRUC PARL/PROC GOV/REL...JURID 20 SENATE   CONFER
CIVIL/SERV. PAGE 111 B2234   ADMIN
                                                            B58
VASEY W.,GOVERNMENT AND SOCIAL WELFARE: ROLES OF   REPRESENT
FEDERAL , STATE AND LOCAL GOVERNMENTS IN   ADMIN
ADMINISTERING WELFARE SERVICES. USA+45 EDU/PROP 20.   EX/STRUC
PAGE 112 B2255   SOC/WK
                                                            S58
ALMOND G.A.,"COMPARATIVE STUDY OF INTEREST GROUPS."   LOBBY
USA+45 EX/STRUC PWR 20. PAGE 4 B0079   REPRESENT
                                                       ADMIN
                                                       VOL/ASSN
                                                            S58
ARGYRIS C.,"SOME PROBLEMS IN CONCEPTUALIZING   FINAN
ORGANIZATIONAL CLIMATE: A CASE STUDY OF A BANK"   CONCPT
(BMR)" USA+45 EX/STRUC ADMIN PERS/REL ADJUST PERSON   LG/CO
...POLICY HYPO/EXP SIMUL 20. PAGE 6 B0129   INGP/REL
                                                            S58
EISENSTADT S.N.,"INTERNAL CONTRADICTIONS IN   ELITES
BUREAUCRATIC POLITICS." ADMIN EXEC CENTRAL. PAGE 32   LEAD
B0658   PWR
                                                       EX/STRUC
                                                            S58
ELKIN A.B.,"OEEC-ITS STRUCTURE AND POWERS." EUR+WWI   ECO/DEV
CONSTN INDUS INT/ORG NAT/G VOL/ASSN DELIB/GP   EX/STRUC
ACT/RES PLAN ORD/FREE WEALTH...CHARTS ORG/CHARTS
OEEC 20. PAGE 33 B0666
                                                            S58
FREEMAN J.L.,"THE BUREAUCRACY IN PRESSURE   CONTROL
POLITICS." USA+45 NAT/G CHIEF ADMIN EXEC 20.   EX/STRUC
PAGE 37 B0752   REPRESENT
                                                       LOBBY
                                                            S58
KAMPELMAN M.M.,"CONGRESSIONAL CONTROL VS EXECUTIVE   CIVMIL/REL
FLEXIBILITY." USA+45 NAT/G 20. PAGE 58 B1165   ADMIN
                                                       EX/STRUC
                                                       CONTROL
                                                            S58
KEISER N.F.,"PUBLIC RESPONSIBILITY AND FEDERAL   REPRESENT
ADVISORY GROUPS: A CASE STUDY." NAT/G ADMIN CONTROL   ELITES
LOBBY...POLICY 20. PAGE 59 B1190   GP/REL
                                                       EX/STRUC
                                                            S58
SALETAN E.N.,"ADMINISTRATIVE TRUSTIFICATION." NAT/G   LOBBY
EX/STRUC ADMIN 20. PAGE 92 B1862   PWR
                                                       CONTROL
                                                       REPRESENT
                                                            C58
GOLAY J.F.,"THE FOUNDING OF THE FEDERAL REPUBLIC OF   FEDERAL
GERMANY." GERMANY/W CONSTN EX/STRUC DIPLOM ADMIN   NAT/G
CHOOSE...DECISION BIBLIOG 20. PAGE 40 B0814   PARL/PROC
                                                       POL/PAR
                                                            B59
BHAMBHRI C.P.,SUBSTANCE OF HINDU POLITY. INDIA   GOV/REL
S/ASIA LAW EX/STRUC JUDGE TAX COERCE GP/REL   WRITING
POPULISM 20 HINDU. PAGE 11 B0234   SECT
                                                       PROVS
                                                            B59
BOWLES C.,THE COMING POLITICAL BREAKTHROUGH. USA+45   DIPLOM
ECO/DEV EX/STRUC ATTIT...CONCPT OBS 20. PAGE 14   CHOOSE
B0288   PREDICT
                                                       POL/PAR
                                                            B59
CHAPMAN B.,THE PROFESSION OF GOVERNMENT: THE PUBLIC   ADMIN
SERVICE IN EUROPE. MOD/EUR LABOR CT/SYS...T 20   CONTROL
CIVIL/SERV. PAGE 20 B0409   ROUTINE
                                                       EX/STRUC
                                                            B59
DAVIS K.C.,ADMINISTRATIVE LAW TEXT. USA+45 NAT/G   ADJUD
DELIB/GP EX/STRUC CONTROL ORD/FREE...T 20   ADMIN
SUPREME/CT. PAGE 27 B0542   JURID

DIMOCK M.E.,ADMINISTRATIVE VITALITY: THE CONFLICT WITH BUREAUCRACY. PROB/SOLV EXEC 20. PAGE 29 B0597
CT/SYS
REPRESENT
ADMIN
EX/STRUC
ROUTINE
B59

DUVERGER M.,LA CINQUIEME REPUBLIQUE. FRANCE WOR+45 POL/PAR CHIEF EX/STRUC LOBBY. PAGE 31 B0636
NAT/G
CONSTN
GOV/REL
PARL/PROC
B59

ELLIOTT O.,MEN AT THE TOP. USA+45 CULTURE EX/STRUC PRESS GOV/REL ATTIT ALL/VALS...OBS INT QU 20. PAGE 33 B0668
TOP/EX
PERSON
LEAD
POLICY
B59

ELLIOTT S.D.,IMPROVING OUR COURTS. LAW EX/STRUC PLAN PROB/SOLV ADJUD ADMIN TASK CRIME EFFICIENCY ORD/FREE 20. PAGE 33 B0669
CT/SYS
JURID
GOV/REL
NAT/G
B59

JANOWITZ M.,SOCIOLOGY AND THE MILITARY ESTABLISHMENT. USA+45 WOR+45 CULTURE SOCIETY PROF/ORG CONSULT EX/STRUC PLAN TEC/DEV DIPLOM DOMIN COERCE DRIVE RIGID/FLEX ORD/FREE PWR SKILL COLD/WAR 20. PAGE 55 B1121
FORCES
SOC
B59

JOYCE J.A.,RED CROSS INTERNATIONAL AND THE STRATEGY OF PEACE. WOR+45 WOR-45 EX/STRUC SUPEGO ALL/VALS ...CONCPT GEN/LAWS TOT/POP 19/20 RED/CROSS. PAGE 57 B1155
VOL/ASSN
HEALTH
B59

LOEWENSTEIN K.,VERFASSUNGSRECHT UND VERFASSUNGSPRAXIS DER VEREINIGTEN STAATEN. USA+45 USA-45 COLONIAL CT/SYS GP/REL RACE/REL ORD/FREE ...JURID 18/20 SUPREME/CT CONGRESS PRESIDENT BILL/RIGHT CIVIL/LIB. PAGE 66 B1337
CONSTN
POL/PAR
EX/STRUC
NAT/G
B59

MAASS A.,AREA AND POWER: A THEORY OF LOCAL GOVERNMENT. MUNIC PROVS EX/STRUC LEGIS CT/SYS CHOOSE PWR 20. PAGE 67 B1354
LOC/G
FEDERAL
BAL/PWR
GOV/REL
B59

MONTGOMERY J.D.,CASES IN VIETNAMESE ADMINISTRATION. VIETNAM/S EX/STRUC 20. PAGE 75 B1506
ADMIN
DECISION
PROB/SOLV
LEAD
B59

SINHA H.N.,OUTLINES OF POLITICAL SCIENCE. NAT/G POL/PAR EX/STRUC LEGIS CT/SYS CHOOSE REPRESENT 20. PAGE 98 B1971
JURID
CONCPT
ORD/FREE
SOVEREIGN
B59

SISSON C.H.,THE SPIRIT OF BRITISH ADMINISTRATION AND SOME EUROPEAN COMPARISONS. FRANCE GERMANY/W SWEDEN UK LAW EX/STRUC INGP/REL EFFICIENCY ORD/FREE ...DECISION 20. PAGE 98 B1972
GOV/COMP
ADMIN
ELITES
ATTIT
B59

THARAMATHAJ C.,A STUDY OF THE COMPOSITION OF THE THAI CIVIL SERVICE (PAPER). THAILAND PAY ROLE ...CHARTS 20 CIVIL/SERV FEMALE/SEX. PAGE 103 B2092
ADMIN
EX/STRUC
STRATA
INGP/REL
B59

US SENATE COMM ON POST OFFICE,TO PROVIDE FOR AN EFFECTIVE SYSTEM OF PERSONNEL ADMINISTRATION. EFFICIENCY...MGT 20 CONGRESS CIVIL/SERV POSTAL/SYS YARBROGH/R. PAGE 111 B2233
ADMIN
NAT/G
EX/STRUC
LAW
B59

WASSERMAN P.,MEASUREMENT AND ANALYSIS OF ORGANIZATIONAL PERFORMANCE. FINAN MARKET EX/STRUC TEC/DEV EDU/PROP CONTROL ROUTINE TASK...MGT 20. PAGE 114 B2300
BIBLIOG/A
ECO/TAC
OP/RES
EFFICIENCY
L59

GILBERT C.E.,"THE FRAMEWORK OF ADMINISTRATIVE RESPONSIBILITY." USA+45 20. PAGE 39 B0799
REPRESENT
EXEC
EX/STRUC
CONTROL
L59

HECTOR L.J.,"GOVERNMENT BY ANONYMITY: WHO WRITES OUR REGULATORY OPINIONS?" USA+45 NAT/G TOP/EX CONTROL EXEC. PAGE 49 B0987
ADJUD
REPRESENT
EX/STRUC
ADMIN
L59

TARKOWSKI Z.M.,"SCIENTISTS VERSUS ADMINISTRATORS: AN APPROACH TOWARD ACHIEVING GREATER UNDERSTANDING." UK EXEC EFFICIENCY 20. PAGE 103 B2079
INGP/REL
GP/REL
ADMIN
EX/STRUC
S59

CALKINS R.D.,"THE DECISION PROCESS IN ADMINISTRATION." EX/STRUC PROB/SOLV ROUTINE MGT. PAGE 18 B0368
ADMIN
OP/RES
DECISION
CON/ANAL
S59

GABLE R.W.,"CULTURE AND ADMINISTRATION IN IRAN." IRAN EXEC PARTIC REPRESENT PWR. PAGE 38 B0770
ADMIN
CULTURE

JANOWITZ M.,"CHANGING PATTERNS OF ORGANIZATIONAL AUTHORITY: THE MILITARY ESTABLISHMENT" (BMR)" USA+45 ELITES STRUCT EX/STRUC PLAN DOMIN AUTOMAT NUC/PWR WEAPON 20. PAGE 55 B1122
EX/STRUC
INGP/REL
S59
FORCES
AUTHORIT
ADMIN
TEC/DEV
S59

PRESTHUS R.V.,"BEHAVIOR AND BUREAUCRACY IN MANY CULTURES." EXEC INGP/REL 20. PAGE 84 B1705
ADMIN
EX/STRUC
GOV/COMP
METH/CNCPT
S59

SEIDMAN H.,"THE GOVERNMENT CORPORATION IN THE UNITED STATES." USA+45 LEGIS ADMIN PLURISM 20. PAGE 95 B1925
CONTROL
GOV/REL
EX/STRUC
EXEC
S59

SIMPSON R.L.,"VERTICAL AND HORIZONTAL COMMUNICATION IN FORMAL ORGANIZATION" USA+45 LG/CO EX/STRUC DOMIN CONTROL TASK INGP/REL TIME 20. PAGE 97 B1963
PERS/REL
AUTOMAT
INDUS
WORKER
S59

STINCHCOMBE A.L.,"BUREAUCRATIC AND CRAFT ADMINISTRATION OF PRODUCTION: A COMPARATIVE STUDY" (BMR)" USA+45 STRUCT EX/STRUC ECO/TAC GP/REL ...CLASSIF GP/COMP IDEA/COMP GEN/LAWS 20 WEBER/MAX. PAGE 101 B2039
CONSTRUC
PROC/MFG
ADMIN
PLAN
C59

DAHL R.A.,"SOCIAL SCIENCE RESEARCH ON BUSINESS: PRODUCT AND POTENTIAL" INDUS MARKET OP/RES CAP/ISM ADMIN LOBBY DRIVE...PSY CONCPT BIBLIOG/A 20. PAGE 26 B0521
MGT
EFFICIENCY
PROB/SOLV
EX/STRUC
B60

AYEARST M.,THE BRITISH WEST INDIES: THE SEARCH FOR SELF-GOVERNMENT. FUT WEST/IND LOC/G POL/PAR EX/STRUC LEGIS CHOOSE FEDERAL...NAT/COMP BIBLIOG 17/20. PAGE 7 B0152
CONSTN
COLONIAL
REPRESENT
NAT/G
B60

BROOKINGS INSTITUTION.UNITED STATES FOREIGN POLICY: STUDY NO 9: THE FORMULATION AND ADMINISTRATION OF UNITED STATES FOREIGN POLICY. USA+45 WOR+45 EX/STRUC LEGIS BAL/PWR FOR/AID EDU/PROP CIVMIL/REL GOV/REL...INT COLD/WAR. PAGE 16 B0317
DIPLOM
INT/ORG
CREATE
B60

DAVIS K.C.,ADMINISTRATIVE LAW AND GOVERNMENT. USA+45 EX/STRUC PROB/SOLV ADJUD GP/REL PWR...POLICY 20 SUPREME/CT. PAGE 27 B0543
ADMIN
JURID
CT/SYS
NAT/G
B60

FOSS P.,POLITICS AND GRASS: THE ADMINISTRATION OF GRAZING ON THE PUBLIC DOMAIN. USA+45 LEGIS TOP/EX EXEC...DECISION 20. PAGE 37 B0743
REPRESENT
ADMIN
LOBBY
EX/STRUC
B60

GLOVER J.D.,A CASE STUDY OF HIGH LEVEL ADMINISTRATION IN A LARGE ORGANIZATION. EX/STRUC EXEC LEAD ROUTINE INGP/REL OPTIMAL ATTIT PERSON ...POLICY DECISION INT QU. PAGE 40 B0812
ADMIN
TOP/EX
FORCES
NAT/G
B60

GRANICK D.,THE RED EXECUTIVE. COM USA+45 SOCIETY ECO/DEV INDUS NAT/G POL/PAR EX/STRUC PLAN ECO/TAC EDU/PROP ADMIN EXEC ATTIT DRIVE...GP/COMP 20. PAGE 42 B0851
PWR
STRATA
USSR
ELITES
B60

HANBURY H.G.,ENGLISH COURTS OF LAW. UK EX/STRUC LEGIS CRIME ROLE 12/20 COMMON/LAW ENGLSH/LAW. PAGE 46 B0936
JURID
CT/SYS
CONSTN
GOV/REL
B60

HAYNES G.H.,THE SENATE OF THE UNITED STATES: ITS HISTORY AND PRACTICE. CONSTN EX/STRUC TOP/EX CONFER DEBATE LEAD LOBBY PARL/PROC CHOOSE PWR SENATE CONGRESS. PAGE 48 B0977
LEGIS
DELIB/GP
B60

HODGETTS J.E.,CANADIAN PUBLIC ADMINISTRATION. CANADA CONTROL LOBBY EFFICIENCY 20. PAGE 50 B1024
REPRESENT
ADMIN
EX/STRUC
ADJUD
B60

KERSELL J.E.,PARLIAMENTARY SUPERVISION OF DELEGATED LEGISLATION. UK EFFICIENCY PWR...POLICY CHARTS BIBLIOG METH 20 PARLIAMENT. PAGE 59 B1198
LEGIS
CONTROL
NAT/G
EX/STRUC
B60

MORISON E.E.,TURMOIL AND TRADITION: A STUDY OF THE LIFE AND TIMES OF HENRY L. STIMSON. USA+45 USA-45 POL/PAR CHIEF DELIB/GP FORCES BAL/PWR DIPLOM ARMS/CONT WAR PEACE 19/20 STIMSON/HL ROOSEVLT/F TAFT/WH HOOVER/H REPUBLICAN. PAGE 75 B1525
BIOG
NAT/G
EX/STRUC
B60

US DEPARTMENT OF THE ARMY.SELECT BIBLIOGRAPHY ON ADMINISTRATIVE ORGANIZATION(PAMPHLET). USA+45 INDUS NAT/G EX/STRUC OP/RES CIVMIL/REL EFFICIENCY ORD/FREE. PAGE 108 B2183
BIBLIOG/A
ADMIN
CONCPT
FORCES

B60
WEIDNER E.W.,INTERGOVERNMENTAL RELATIONS AS SEEN BY ATTIT
PUBLIC OFFICIALS. USA+45 PROVS EX/STRUC EXEC GP/REL
FEDERAL...QU 20. PAGE 115 B2311 GOV/REL
ADMIN

B60
WHEARE K.C.,THE CONSTITUTIONAL STRUCTURE OF THE CONSTN
COMMONWEALTH. UK EX/STRUC DIPLOM DOMIN ADMIN INT/ORG
COLONIAL CONTROL LEAD INGP/REL SUPEGO 20 CMN/WLTH. VOL/ASSN
PAGE 115 B2330 SOVEREIGN

L60
FUCHS R.F.,"FAIRNESS AND EFFECTIVENESS IN EFFICIENCY
ADMINISTRATIVE AGENCY ORGANIZATION AND PROCEDURES." EX/STRUC
USA+45 ADJUD ADMIN REPRESENT. PAGE 38 B0764 EXEC
POLICY

S60
HEADY F.,"RECENT LITERATURE ON COMPARATIVE PUBLIC GOV/COMP
ADMINISTRATION." EXEC 20. PAGE 48 B0981 ADMIN
EX/STRUC
BIBLIOG

S60
RAPHAELI N.,"SELECTED ARTICLES AND DOCUMENTS ON BIBLIOG
COMPARATIVE PUBLIC ADMINISTRATION." USA+45 FINAN MGT
LOC/G TOP/EX TEC/DEV EXEC GP/REL INGP/REL...GP/COMP ADMIN
GOV/COMP METH/COMP. PAGE 86 B1738 EX/STRUC

S60
RAPP W.F.,"MANAGEMENT ANALYSIS AT THE HEADQUARTERS INGP/REL
OF FEDERAL AGENCIES." USA+45 NAT/G 20. PAGE 86 ADMIN
B1740 EX/STRUC
MGT

S60
SCHATZ S.P.,"THE INFLENCE OF PLANNING ON ECO/UNDEV
DEVELOPMENT: THE NIGERIAN EXPERIENCE." AFR FUT PLAN
FINAN INDUS NAT/G EX/STRUC ECO/TAC ADMIN ATTIT NIGERIA
PERCEPT ORD/FREE PWR...MATH TREND CON/ANAL SIMUL
VAL/FREE 20. PAGE 93 B1883

S60
SCHER S.,"CONGRESSIONAL COMMITTEE MEMBERS AND LEGIS
INDEPENDENT AGENCY OVERSEERS: A CASE STUDY." GOV/REL
DELIB/GP EX/STRUC JUDGE TOP/EX DOMIN ADMIN CONTROL LABOR
PWR...SOC/EXP HOUSE/REP CONGRESS. PAGE 93 B1886 ADJUD

C60
SCHAPIRO L.B.,"THE COMMUNIST PARTY OF THE SOVIET POL/PAR
UNION." USSR INTELL CHIEF EX/STRUC FORCES DOMIN COM
ADMIN LEAD WAR ATTIT SOVEREIGN...POLICY BIBLIOG 20. REV
PAGE 93 B1881

B61
ARMSTRONG J.A.,AN ESSAY ON SOURCES FOR THE STUDY OF BIBLIOG/A
THE COMMUNIST PARTY OF THE SOVIET UNION, 1934-1960 COM
(EXTERNAL RESEARCH PAPER 137). USSR EX/STRUC ADMIN POL/PAR
LEAD REV 20. PAGE 7 B0134 MARXISM

B61
AVERY M.W.,GOVERNMENT OF WASHINGTON STATE. USA+45 PROVS
MUNIC DELIB/GP EX/STRUC LEGIS GIVE CT/SYS PARTIC LOC/G
REGION EFFICIENCY 20 WASHINGT/G GOVERNOR. PAGE 7 ADMIN
B0151 GOV/REL

B61
AYLMER G.,THE KING'S SERVANTS. UK ELITES CHIEF PAY ADMIN
CT/SYS WEALTH 17 CROMWELL/O CHARLES/I. PAGE 7 B0153 ROUTINE
EX/STRUC
NAT/G

B61
BENOIT E.,EUROPE AT SIXES AND SEVENS: THE COMMON FINAN
MARKET, THE FREE TRADE ASSOCIATION AND THE UNITED ECO/DEV
STATES. EUR+WWI FUT USA+45 INDUS CONSULT DELIB/GP VOL/ASSN
EX/STRUC TOP/EX ACT/RES ECO/TAC EDU/PROP ROUTINE
CHOOSE PERCEPT WEALTH...MGT TREND EEC TOT/POP 20
EFTA. PAGE 11 B0217

B61
DARRAH E.L.,FIFTY STATE GOVERNMENTS: A COMPILATION EX/STRUC
OF EXECUTIVE ORGANIZATION CHARTS. USA+45 LOC/G ADMIN
DELIB/GP LEGIS ADJUD LEAD PWR 20 GOVERNOR. PAGE 26 ORG/CHARTS
B0530 PROVS

B61
DRAGNICH A.N.,MAJOR EUROPEAN GOVERNMENTS. FRANCE NAT/G
GERMANY/W UK USSR LOC/G EX/STRUC CT/SYS PARL/PROC LEGIS
ATTIT MARXISM...JURID MGT NAT/COMP 19/20. PAGE 30 CONSTN
B0615 POL/PAR

B61
DUBIN R.,HUMAN RELATIONS IN ADMINISTRATION. USA+45 PERS/REL
INDUS LABOR LG/CO EX/STRUC GP/REL DRIVE PWR MGT
...DECISION SOC CHARTS ANTHOL 20. PAGE 31 B0623 ADMIN
EXEC

B61
FRIEDMANN W.G.,JOINT INTERNATIONAL BUSINESS ECO/UNDEV
VENTURES. ASIA ISLAM L/A+17C ECO/DEV DIST/IND FINAN INT/TRADE
PROC/MFG FACE/GP LG/CO NAT/G VOL/ASSN CONSULT
EX/STRUC PLAN ADMIN ROUTINE WEALTH...OLD/LIB WORK
20. PAGE 37 B0760

B61
GLADDEN E.N.,BRITISH PUBLIC SERVICE ADMINISTRATION. EFFICIENCY
UK...CHARTS 20. PAGE 40 B0809 ADMIN
EX/STRUC
EXEC

B61
GORDON R.A.,BUSINESS LEADERSHIP IN THE LARGE LG/CO

CORPORATION. USA+45 SOCIETY EX/STRUC ADMIN CONTROL LEAD
ROUTINE GP/REL PWR...MGT 20. PAGE 41 B0831 DECISION
LOBBY

B61
GRIFFITH E.S.,CONGRESS: ITS CONTEMPORARY ROLE. PARL/PROC
CONSTN POL/PAR CHIEF PLAN BUDGET DIPLOM CONFER EX/STRUC
ADMIN LOBBY...DECISION CONGRESS. PAGE 43 B0878 TOP/EX
LEGIS

B61
HAMILTON A.,THE FEDERALIST. USA-45 NAT/G VOL/ASSN EX/STRUC
LEGIS TOP/EX EDU/PROP LEGIT CHOOSE ATTIT RIGID/FLEX CONSTN
ORD/FREE PWR...MAJORIT JURID CONCPT ANTHOL. PAGE 46
B0931

B61
HARRISON S.,INDIA AND THE UNITED STATES. FUT S/ASIA DELIB/GP
USA+45 WOR+45 INTELL ECO/DEV ECO/UNDEV AGRI INDUS ACT/RES
INT/ORG NAT/G CONSULT EX/STRUC TOP/EX PLAN ECO/TAC FOR/AID
NEUTRAL ALL/VALS...MGT TOT/POP 20. PAGE 47 B0956 INDIA

B61
HART W.R.,COLLECTIVE BARGAINING IN THE FEDERAL INGP/REL
CIVIL SERVICE. NAT/G EX/STRUC ADMIN EXEC 20. MGT
PAGE 47 B0961 REPRESENT
LABOR

B61
HAYTER W.,THE DIPLOMACY OF THE GREAT POWERS. FRANCE DIPLOM
UK USSR WOR+45 EX/STRUC TOP/EX NUC/PWR PEACE...OBS POLICY
20. PAGE 48 B0978 NAT/G

B61
KEE R.,REFUGEE WORLD. AUSTRIA EUR+WWI GERMANY NEIGH NAT/G
EX/STRUC WORKER PROB/SOLV ECO/TAC RENT EDU/PROP GIVE
INGP/REL COST LITERACY HABITAT 20 MIGRATION. WEALTH
PAGE 59 B1186 STRANGE

B61
LOSCHELDER W.,AUSBILDUNG UND AUSLESE DER BEAMTEN. PROF/ORG
GERMANY/W ELITES NAT/G ADMIN GP/REL ATTIT...JURID EDU/PROP
20 CIVIL/SERV. PAGE 67 B1341 EX/STRUC
CHOOSE

B61
MARVICK D.,POLITICAL DECISION-MAKERS. INTELL STRATA TOP/EX
NAT/G POL/PAR EX/STRUC LEGIS DOMIN EDU/PROP ATTIT BIOG
PERSON PWR...PSY STAT OBS CONT/OBS STAND/INT ELITES
UNPLAN/INT TIME/SEQ CHARTS STERTYP VAL/FREE.
PAGE 70 B1416

B61
MONAS S.,THE THIRD SECTION: POLICE AND SOCIETY IN ORD/FREE
RUSSIA UNDER NICHOLAS I. MOD/EUR RUSSIA ELITES COM
STRUCT NAT/G EX/STRUC ADMIN CONTROL PWR CONSERVE FORCES
...DECISION 19 NICHOLAS/I. PAGE 74 B1499 COERCE

B61
NARAIN J.P.,SWARAJ FOR THE PEOPLE. INDIA CONSTN NAT/G
LOC/G MUNIC POL/PAR CHOOSE REPRESENT EFFICIENCY ORD/FREE
ATTIT PWR SOVEREIGN 20. PAGE 77 B1553 EDU/PROP
EX/STRUC

B61
OPOTOWSKY S.,THE KENNEDY GOVERNMENT. NAT/G CONSULT ADMIN
EX/STRUC LEAD PERSON...POLICY 20 KENNEDY/JF BIOG
CONGRESS CABINET. PAGE 80 B1613 ELITES
TOP/EX

B61
PEASLEE A.J.,INTERNATIONAL GOVERNMENT INT/ORG
ORGANIZATIONS, CONSTITUTIONAL DOCUMENTS. WOR+45 STRUCT
WOR-45 CONSTN VOL/ASSN DELIB/GP EX/STRUC ROUTINE
KNOWL TOT/POP 20. PAGE 82 B1650

B61
PETRULLO L.,LEADERSHIP AND INTERPERSONAL BEHAVIOR. PERSON
FACE/GP FAM PROF/ORG EX/STRUC FORCES DOMIN WAR ATTIT
GP/REL PERS/REL EFFICIENCY PRODUC PWR...MGT PSY. LEAD
PAGE 82 B1663 HABITAT

B61
QURESHI S.,INCENTIVES IN AMERICAN EMPLOYMENT SERV/IND
(THESIS, UNIVERSITY OF PENNSYLVANIA). DELIB/GP ADMIN
TOP/EX BUDGET ROUTINE SANCTION COST TECHRACY MGT. PAY
PAGE 85 B1727 EX/STRUC

B61
RAO K.V.,PARLIAMENTARY DEMOCRACY OF INDIA. INDIA CONSTN
EX/STRUC TOP/EX COLONIAL CT/SYS PARL/PROC ORD/FREE ADJUD
...POLICY CONCPT TREND 20 PARLIAMENT. PAGE 86 B1733 NAT/G
FEDERAL

B61
ROWAT D.C.,BASIC ISSUES IN PUBLIC ADMINISTRATION. NAT/G
STRUCT EX/STRUC PWR CONSERVE...MAJORIT DECISION MGT ADJUD
T 20 BUREAUCRCY. PAGE 91 B1839 ADMIN

B61
STRAUSS E.,THE RULING SERVANTS. FRANCE UK USSR ADMIN
WOR+45 WOR-45 NAT/G CONSULT DELIB/GP EX/STRUC PWR
TOP/EX DOMIN EDU/PROP LEGIT ROUTINE...MGT TIME/SEQ ELITES
STERTYP 20. PAGE 101 B2051

B61
TANZER L.,THE KENNEDY CIRCLE. INTELL CONSULT EX/STRUC
DELIB/GP TOP/EX CONTROL EXEC INGP/REL PERS/REL PWR NAT/G
...BIOG IDEA/COMP ANTHOL 20 KENNEDY/JF PRESIDENT CHIEF
DEMOCRAT MCNAMARA/R RUSK/D. PAGE 103 B2077

B61
THOMPSON V.A.,MODERN ORGANIZATION. REPRESENT ADMIN
EFFICIENCY. PAGE 104 B2105 EX/STRUC
EXEC

B61

TOMPKINS D.C.,CONFLICT OF INTEREST IN THE FEDERAL BIBLIOG
GOVERNMENT: A BIBLIOGRAPHY. USA+45 EX/STRUC LEGIS ROLE
ADJUD ADMIN CRIME CONGRESS PRESIDENT. PAGE 105 NAT/G
B2117 LAW

L61

KRAMER R.,"EXECUTIVE PRIVILEGE - A STUDY OF THE REPRESENT
PERIOD 1953-1960." NAT/G CHIEF EX/STRUC LEGIS PWR. LEAD
PAGE 61 B1233 EXEC
GOV/REL

L61

THOMPSON V.A.,"HIERARACHY, SPECIALIZATION, AND PERS/REL
ORGANIZATIONAL CONFLICT" (BMR) WOR+45 STRATA PROB/SOLV
STRUCT WORKER TEC/DEV GP/REL INGP/REL ATTIT ADMIN
AUTHORIT 20 BUREAUCRCY. PAGE 104 B2106 EX/STRUC

S61

ANGLIN D.,"UNITED STATES OPPOSITION TO CANADIAN INT/ORG
MEMBERSHIP IN THE PAN AMERICAN UNION: A CANADIAN CANADA
VIEW." L/A+17C UK USA+45 VOL/ASSN DELIB/GP EX/STRUC
PLAN DIPLOM DOMIN REGION ATTIT RIGID/FLEX PWR
...RELATIV CONCPT STERTYP CMN/WLTH OAS 20. PAGE 5
B0112

S61

BARTLEY H.J.,"COMMAND EXPERIENCE." USA+45 EX/STRUC CONCPT
FORCES LEGIT ROUTINE SKILL...POLICY OBS HYPO/EXP TREND
GEN/LAWS 20. PAGE 9 B0191

S61

CARLETON W.G.,"AMERICAN FOREIGN POLICY: MYTHS AND PLAN
REALITIES." FUT USA+45 WOR+45 ECO/UNDEV INT/ORG MYTH
EX/STRUC ARMS/CONT NUC/PWR WAR ATTIT...POLICY DIPLOM
CONCPT CONT/OBS GEN/METH COLD/WAR TOT/POP 20.
PAGE 19 B0378

S61

DEXTER L.A.,"HAS THE PUBLIC OFFICIAL ON OBLIGATION ADMIN
TO RESTRICT HIS FRIENDSHIPS?" NAT/G EX/STRUC TOP/EX ATTIT
20. PAGE 29 B0584 REPRESENT
POLICY

S61

HAAS E.B.,"INTERNATIONAL INTEGRATION: THE EUROPEAN INT/ORG
AND THE UNIVERSAL PROCESS." EUR+WWI FUT WOR+45 TREND
NAT/G EX/STRUC ATTIT DRIVE ORD/FREE PWR...CONCPT REGION
GEN/LAWS OEEC 20 NATO COUNCL/EUR. PAGE 45 B0909

S61

JOHNSON N.,"PARLIAMENTARY QUESTIONS AND THE CONDUCT CONTROL
OF ADMINISTRATION." UK REPRESENT PARLIAMENT 20. EXEC
PAGE 57 B1146 EX/STRUC

S61

KUIC V.,"THEORY AND PRACTICE OF THE AMERICAN EXEC
PRESIDENCY." USA+45 USA-45 NAT/G ADMIN REPRESENT EX/STRUC
...PLURIST 20 PRESIDENT. PAGE 61 B1241 PWR
CHIEF

S61

LYONS G.M.,"THE NEW CIVIL-MILITARY RELATIONS." CIVMIL/REL
USA+45 NAT/G EX/STRUC TOP/EX PROB/SOLV ADMIN EXEC PWR
PARTIC 20. PAGE 67 B1350 REPRESENT

S61

MARSH R.M.,"FORMAL ORGANIZATION AND PROMOTION IN A ADMIN
PRE-INDUSTRIAL SOCIETY" (BMR)" ASIA FAM EX/STRUC STRUCT
LEAD...SOC CHARTS 19 WEBER/MAX. PAGE 70 B1407 ECO/UNDEV
STRATA

S61

REAGAN M.O.,"THE POLITICAL STRUCTURE OF THE FEDERAL PWR
RESERVE SYSTEM." USA+45 FINAN NAT/G ADMIN 20. EX/STRUC
PAGE 87 B1748 EXEC
LEAD

S61

ROBINSON J.A.,"PROCESS SATISFACTION AND POLICY GOV/REL
APPROVAL IN STATE DEPARTMENT - CONGRESSIONAL EX/STRUC
RELATIONS." ELITES CHIEF LEGIS CONFER DEBATE ADMIN POL/PAR
FEEDBACK ROLE...CHARTS 20 CONGRESS PRESIDENT DECISION
DEPT/STATE. PAGE 89 B1802

B62

ANDREWS W.G.,EUROPEAN POLITICAL INSTITUTIONS. NAT/COMP
FRANCE GERMANY UK USSR TOP/EX LEAD PARL/PROC CHOOSE POL/PAR
20. PAGE 5 B0104 EX/STRUC
LEGIS

B62

ARGYRIS C.,INTERPERSONAL COMPETENCE AND EX/STRUC
ORGANIZATIONAL EFFECTIVENESS. CREATE PLAN PROB/SOLV ADMIN
EDU/PROP INGP/REL PERS/REL PRODUC...OBS INT SIMUL CONSULT
20. PAGE 6 B0131 EFFICIENCY

B62

BRIMMER B.,A GUIDE TO THE USE OF UNITED NATIONS BIBLIOG/A
DOCUMENTS. WOR+45 ECO/UNDEV AGRI EX/STRUC FORCES INT/ORG
PROB/SOLV ADMIN WAR PEACE WEALTH...POLICY UN. DIPLOM
PAGE 15 B0310

B62

BROWN B.E.,NEW DIRECTIONS IN COMPARATIVE POLITICS. NAT/COMP
AUSTRIA FRANCE GERMANY UK WOR+45 EX/STRUC LEGIS METH
ORD/FREE 20. PAGE 16 B0320 POL/PAR
FORCES

B62

BROWN L.C.,LATIN AMERICA, A BIBLIOGRAPHY. EX/STRUC BIBLIOG
ADMIN LEAD ATTIT...POLICY 20. PAGE 16 B0323 L/A+17C
DIPLOM
NAT/G

B62

CAIRNCROSS A.K.,FACTORS IN ECONOMIC DEVELOPMENT. MARKET
WOR+45 ECO/UNDEV INDUS R+D LG/CO NAT/G EX/STRUC ECO/DEV
PLAN TEC/DEV ECO/TAC ATTIT HEALTH KNOWL PWR WEALTH
...TIME/SEQ GEN/LAWS TOT/POP VAL/FREE 20. PAGE 18
B0363

B62

CARTER G.M.,THE GOVERNMENT OF THE SOVIET UNION. NAT/G
USSR CULTURE LOC/G DIPLOM ECO/TAC ADJUD CT/SYS LEAD MARXISM
WEALTH...CHARTS T 20 COM/PARTY. PAGE 19 B0390 POL/PAR
EX/STRUC

B62

CHANDLER A.D.,STRATEGY AND STRUCTURE: CHAPTERS IN LG/CO
THE HISTORY OF THE INDUSTRIAL ENTERPRISE. USA+45 PLAN
USA-45 ECO/DEV EX/STRUC ECO/TAC EXEC...DECISION 20. ADMIN
PAGE 20 B0403 FINAN

B62

EVANS M.S.,THE FRINGE ON TOP. USSR EX/STRUC FORCES NAT/G
DIPLOM ECO/TAC PEACE CONSERVE SOCISM...TREND 20 PWR
KENNEDY/JF. PAGE 34 B0689 CENTRAL
POLICY

B62

FARBER W.O.,GOVERNMENT OF SOUTH DAKOTA. USA+45 PROVS
DIST/IND POL/PAR CHIEF EX/STRUC LEGIS ECO/TAC GIVE LOC/G
EDU/PROP CT/SYS PARTIC...T 20 SOUTH/DAK GOVERNOR. ADMIN
PAGE 35 B0704 CONSTN

B62

GRANICK D.,THE EUROPEAN EXECUTIVE. BELGIUM FRANCE MGT
GERMANY/W UK INDUS LABOR LG/CO SML/CO EX/STRUC PLAN ECO/DEV
TEC/DEV CAP/ISM COST DEMAND...POLICY CHARTS 20. ECO/TAC
PAGE 42 B0852 EXEC

B62

GRAY R.K.,EIGHTEEN ACRES UNDER GLASS. ELITES CHIEF
CONSULT EX/STRUC DIPLOM PRESS CONFER WAR PERS/REL ADMIN
PERSON 20 EISNHWR/DD TRUMAN/HS CABINET. PAGE 43 TOP/EX
B0860 NAT/G

B62

HSUEH S.-.S.,GOVERNMENT AND ADMINISTRATION OF HONG ADMIN
KONG. CHIEF DELIB/GP LEGIS CT/SYS REPRESENT GOV/REL LOC/G
20 HONG/KONG CITY/MGT CIVIL/SERV GOVERNOR. PAGE 52 COLONIAL
B1055 EX/STRUC

B62

INAYATULLAH,BUREAUCRACY AND DEVELOPMENT IN EX/STRUC
PAKISTAN. PAKISTAN ECO/UNDEV EDU/PROP CONFER ADMIN
...ANTHOL DICTIONARY 20 BUREAUCRCY. PAGE 53 B1078 NAT/G
LOC/G

B62

INTERNATIONAL LABOR OFFICE,WORKERS' MANAGEMENT IN WORKER
YUGOSLAVIA. COM YUGOSLAVIA LABOR DELIB/GP EX/STRUC CONTROL
PROB/SOLV ADMIN PWR MARXISM...CHARTS ORG/CHARTS MGT
BIBLIOG 20. PAGE 54 B1098 INDUS

B62

JENNINGS E.E.,THE EXECUTIVE: AUTOCRAT, BUREAUCRAT, EX/STRUC
DEMOCRAT. LEAD EFFICIENCY DRIVE 20. PAGE 56 B1131 INGP/REL
TOP/EX
CONTROL

B62

KARNJAHAPRAKORN C.,MUNICIPAL GOVERNMENT IN THAILAND LOC/G
AS AN INSTITUTION AND PROCESS OF SELF-GOVERNMENT. MUNIC
THAILAND CULTURE FINAN EX/STRUC LEGIS PLAN CONTROL ORD/FREE
GOV/REL EFFICIENCY ATTIT...POLICY 20. PAGE 58 B1176 ADMIN

B62

MAILICK S.,CONCEPTS AND ISSUES IN ADMINISTRATIVE DECISION
BEHAVIOR. EX/STRUC TOP/EX ROUTINE INGP/REL MGT
EFFICIENCY. PAGE 68 B1380 EXEC
PROB/SOLV

B62

MARS D.,SUGGESTED LIBRARY IN PUBLIC ADMINISTRATION. BIBLIOG
FINAN DELIB/GP EX/STRUC WORKER COMPUTER ADJUD ADMIN
...DECISION PSY SOC METH/COMP 20. PAGE 69 B1403 METH
MGT

B62

MARTIN R.C.,GOVERNMENT AND THE SUBURBAN SCHOOL. SCHOOL
USA+45 FINAN EDU/PROP ADMIN HABITAT...TREND GP/COMP LOC/G
20. PAGE 70 B1414 EX/STRUC
ISOLAT

B62

MODELSKI G.,A THEORY OF FOREIGN POLICY. WOR+45 PLAN
WOR-45 NAT/G DELIB/GP EX/STRUC TOP/EX EDU/PROP PWR
LEGIT ROUTINE...POLICY CONCPT TOT/POP COLD/WAR 20. DIPLOM
PAGE 74 B1494

B62

MORE S.S.,REMODELLING OF DEMOCRACY FOR AFRO-ASIAN ORD/FREE
NATIONS. AFR INDIA S/ASIA SOUTH/AFR EX/STRUC ECO/UNDEV
COLONIAL CHOOSE TOTALISM SOVEREIGN NEW/LIB SOCISM ADMIN
...SOC/WK 20. PAGE 75 B1520 LEGIS

B62

MULLEY F.W.,THE POLITICS OF WESTERN DEFENSE. INT/ORG
EUR+WWI USA-45 WOR+45 VOL/ASSN EX/STRUC FORCES DELIB/GP
COERCE DETER PEACE ATTIT ORD/FREE PWR...RECORD NUC/PWR
TIME/SEQ CHARTS COLD/WAR 20 NATO. PAGE 76 B1537

B62

MUNICIPAL MANPOWER COMMISSION,GOVERNMENTAL MANPOWER LOC/G
FOR TOMORROW'S CITIES: A REPORT. USA+45 DELIB/GP MUNIC
EX/STRUC PROB/SOLV TEC/DEV EDU/PROP ADMIN LEAD LABOR
HABITAT. PAGE 76 B1539 GOV/REL

B62
NEW ZEALAND COMM OF ST SERVICE,THE STATE SERVICES   ADMIN
IN NEW ZEALAND. NEW/ZEALND CONSULT EX/STRUC ACT/RES   WORKER
...BIBLIOG 20. PAGE 78 B1577   TEC/DEV
                                                     NAT/G
                                                      B62
NICHOLAS H.G.,THE UNITED NATIONS AS A POLITICAL   INT/ORG
INSTITUTION. WOR+45 CONSTN EX/STRUC ACT/RES LEGIT   ROUTINE
PERCEPT KNOWL PWR...CONCPT TIME/SEQ CON/ANAL
ORG/CHARTS UN 20. PAGE 78 B1580
                                                      B62
PHILLIPS O.H.,CONSTITUTIONAL AND ADMINISTRATIVE LAW JURID
(3RD ED.). UK INT/ORG LOC/G CHIEF EX/STRUC LEGIS   ADMIN
BAL/PWR ADJUD COLONIAL CT/SYS PWR...CHARTS 20.   CONSTN
PAGE 83 B1670   NAT/G
                                                      B62
REICH C.A.,BUREAUCRACY AND THE FORESTS (PAMPHLET).   ADMIN
USA+45 LOBBY...POLICY MGT 20. PAGE 87 B1762   CONTROL
                                                     EX/STRUC
                                                     REPRESENT
                                                      B62
SAMPSON A.,ANATOMY OF BRITAIN. UK LAW COM/IND FINAN ELITES
INDUS MARKET MUNIC POL/PAR EX/STRUC TOP/EX DIPLOM   PWR
LEAD REPRESENT PERSON PARLIAMENT WORSHIP. PAGE 92   STRUCT
B1866   FORCES
                                                      B62
SCALAPINO R.A.,PARTIES AND POLITICS IN CONTEMPORARY POL/PAR
JAPAN. EX/STRUC DIPLOM CHOOSE NAT/LISM ATTIT   PARL/PROC
...POLICY 20 CHINJAP. PAGE 93 B1876   ELITES
                                                     DECISION
                                                      B62
STAHL O.G.,PUBLIC PERSONNEL ADMINISTRATION. LOC/G   ADMIN
TOP/EX CREATE PLAN ROUTINE...TECHNIC MGT T.   WORKER
PAGE 100 B2017   EX/STRUC
                                                     NAT/G
                                                      B62
THIERRY S.S.,LE VATICAN SECRET. CHRIST-17C EUR+WWI   ADMIN
MOD/EUR VATICAN NAT/G SECT DELIB/GP DOMIN LEGIT   EX/STRUC
SOVEREIGN. PAGE 104 B2096   CATHISM
                                                     DECISION
                                                      B62
US ADVISORY COMN INTERGOV REL,STATE CONSTITUTIONAL   LOC/G
AND STATUTORY RESTRICTIONS UPON THE STRUCTURAL,   CONSTN
FUNCTIONAL, AND PERSONAL POWERS OF LOCAL GOV'T.   PROVS
EX/STRUC ACT/RES DOMIN GOV/REL PWR...POLICY   LAW
DECISION 17/20. PAGE 108 B2172
                                                      B62
WANGSNESS P.H.,THE POWER OF THE CITY MANAGER.   PWR
USA+45 EX/STRUC BAL/PWR BUDGET TAX ADMIN REPRESENT   TOP/EX
CENTRAL EFFICIENCY DRIVE ROLE...POLICY 20 CITY/MGT. MUNIC
PAGE 113 B2286   LOC/G
                                                      L62
ABERLE D.F.,"CHAHAR AND DAGOR MONGOL BUREAUCRATIC   EX/STRUC
ADMINISTRATION: 19621945." ASIA MUNIC TOP/EX PWR   STRATA
...MGT OBS INT MONGOL 20. PAGE 3 B0053
                                                      L62
NEIBURG H.L.,"THE EISENHOWER AEC AND CONGRESS: A   CHIEF
STUDY IN EXECUTIVE-LEGISLATIVE RELATIONS." USA+45   LEGIS
NAT/G POL/PAR DELIB/GP EX/STRUC TOP/EX ADMIN EXEC   GOV/REL
LEAD ROUTINE PWR...POLICY COLD/WAR CONGRESS   NUC/PWR
PRESIDENT AEC. PAGE 77 B1567
                                                      L62
WATERSTON A.,"PLANNING IN MOROCCO, ORGANIZATION AND NAT/G
IMPLEMENTATION. BALTIMORE: HOPKINS ECON. DEVELOP.   PLAN
INT. BANK FOR." ISLAM ECO/DEV AGRI DIST/IND INDUS   MOROCCO
PROC/MFG SERV/IND LOC/G EX/STRUC ECO/TAC PWR WEALTH
TOT/POP VAL/FREE 20. PAGE 114 B2302
                                                      S62
ALGER C.F.,"THE EXTERNAL BUREAUCRACY IN UNITED   ADMIN
STATES FOREIGN AFFAIRS." USA+45 WOR+45 SOCIETY   ATTIT
COM/IND INT/ORG NAT/G CONSULT EX/STRUC ACT/RES   DIPLOM
...MGT SOC CONCPT TREND 20. PAGE 4 B0076
                                                      S62
BUENO M.,"ASPECTOS SOCIOLOGICOS DE LA EDUCACION."   SOCIETY
FUT UNIV INTELL R+D SERV/IND SCHOOL CONSULT   EDU/PROP
EX/STRUC ACT/RES PLAN...METH/CNCPT OBS 20. PAGE 17   PERSON
B0341
                                                      S62
DONNELLY D.,"THE POLITICS AND ADMINISTRATION OF   GOV/REL
PLANNING." UK ROUTINE FEDERAL 20. PAGE 30 B0607   EFFICIENCY
                                                     ADMIN
                                                     EX/STRUC
                                                      S62
FESLER J.W.,"FRENCH FIELD ADMINISTRATION: THE   EX/STRUC
BEGINNINGS." CHRIST-17C CULTURE SOCIETY STRATA   FRANCE
NAT/G ECO/TAC DOMIN EDU/PROP LEGIT ADJUD COERCE
ATTIT ALL/VALS...TIME/SEQ CON/ANAL GEN/METH
VAL/FREE 13/15. PAGE 35 B0714
                                                      S62
HUDSON G.F.,"SOVIET FEARS OF THE WEST." COM USA+45   ATTIT
SOCIETY DELIB/GP EX/STRUC TOP/EX ACT/RES CREATE   MYTH
DOMIN EDU/PROP LEGIT ADMIN ROUTINE DRIVE PERSON   GERMANY
RIGID/FLEX PWR...RECORD TIME/SEQ TOT/POP 20   USSR
STALIN/J. PAGE 52 B1057
                                                      S62
MAINZER L.C.,"INJUSTICE AND BUREAUCRACY." ELITES   MORAL

STRATA STRUCT EX/STRUC SENIOR CONTROL EXEC LEAD   MGT
ROUTINE INGP/REL ORD/FREE...CONCPT 20 BUREAUCRCY.   ADMIN
PAGE 68 B1381
                                                      S62
OLLERENSHAW K.,"SHARING RESPONSIBLITY." UK DELIB/GP REPRESENT
EDU/PROP EFFICIENCY 20. PAGE 80 B1607   GP/REL
                                                     ADMIN
                                                     EX/STRUC
                                                      N62
UNIVERSITY PITT INST LOC GOVT,THE COUNCIL-MANAGER   LOC/G
FORM OF GOVERNMENT IN PENNSYLVANIA (PAMPHLET).   TOP/EX
PROVS EX/STRUC REPRESENT GOV/REL EFFICIENCY   MUNIC
...CHARTS SIMUL 20 PENNSYLVAN CITY/MGT. PAGE 107   PWR
B2169
                                                      N62
US ADVISORY COMN INTERGOV REL,ALTERNATIVE   MUNIC
APPROACHES TO GOVERNMENTAL REORGANIZATION IN   REGION
METROPOLITAN AREAS (PAMPHLET). EX/STRUC LEGIS EXEC   PLAN
LEAD PWR...DECISION GEN/METH. PAGE 107 B2171   GOV/REL
                                                      B63
ADRIAN C.R.,GOVERNING OVER FIFTY STATES AND THEIR   PROVS
COMMUNITIES. USA+45 CONSTN FINAN MUNIC NAT/G   LOC/G
POL/PAR EX/STRUC LEGIS ADMIN CONTROL CT/SYS   GOV/REL
...CHARTS 20. PAGE 3 B0061   GOV/COMP
                                                      B63
BADI J.,THE GOVERNMENT OF THE STATE OF ISRAEL: A   NAT/G
CRITICAL ACCOUNT OF ITS PARLIAMENT, EXECUTIVE, AND   CONSTN
JUDICIARY. ISRAEL ECO/DEV CHIEF DELIB/GP LEGIS   EX/STRUC
DIPLOM CT/SYS INGP/REL PEACE ORD/FREE...BIBLIOG 20   POL/PAR
PARLIAMENT ARABS MIGRATION. PAGE 8 B0157
                                                      B63
BLUM H.L.,PUBLIC ADMINISTRATION - A PUBLIC HEALTH   REPRESENT
VIEWPOINT. USA+45 NAT/G 20. PAGE 13 B0257   EX/STRUC
                                                     EXEC
                                                     ADMIN
                                                      B63
BOWETT D.W.,THE LAW OF INTERNATIONAL INSTITUTIONS.   INT/ORG
WOR+45 WOR-45 CONSTN DELIB/GP EX/STRUC JUDGE   ADJUD
EDU/PROP LEGIT CT/SYS EXEC ROUTINE RIGID/FLEX   DIPLOM
ORD/FREE PWR...JURID CONCPT ORG/CHARTS GEN/METH
LEAGUE/NAT OAS OEEC 20 UN. PAGE 14 B0286
                                                      B63
BURRUS B.R.,ADMINSTRATIVE LAW AND LOCAL GOVERNMENT. EX/STRUC
USA+45 PROVS LEGIS LICENSE ADJUD ORD/FREE 20.   LOC/G
PAGE 17 B0356   JURID
                                                     CONSTN
                                                      B63
CHARLES S.,MINISTER OF RELIEF: HARRY HOPKINS AND   ADMIN
THE DEPRESSION. EX/STRUC PROB/SOLV RATION PARL/PROC ECO/TAC
PERS/REL ALL/VALS 20 HOPKINS/H NRA. PAGE 20 B0414   PLAN
                                                     BIOG
                                                      B63
COUNCIL STATE GOVERNMENTS,HANDBOOK FOR LEGISLATIVE   LEGIS
COMMITTEES. USA+45 LAW DELIB/GP EX/STRUC TOP/EX   PARL/PROC
CHOOSE PWR...METH/COMP 20. PAGE 24 B0496   PROVS
                                                     ADJUD
                                                      B63
CROZIER B.,THE MORNING AFTER: A STUDY OF   SOVEREIGN
INDEPENDENCE. WOR+45 EX/STRUC PLAN BAL/PWR COLONIAL NAT/LISM
GP/REL 20 COLD/WAR. PAGE 25 B0511   NAT/G
                                                     DIPLOM
                                                      B63
DEAN A.L.,FEDERAL AGENCY APPROACHES TO FIELD   ADMIN
MANAGEMENT (PAMPHLET). R+D DELIB/GP EX/STRUC   MGT
PROB/SOLV GOV/REL...CLASSIF BIBLIOG 20 FAA NASA   NAT/G
DEPT/HEW POSTAL/SYS IRS. PAGE 28 B0563   OP/RES
                                                      B63
DIESNER H.J.,KIRCHE UND STAAT IM SPATROMISCHEN   SECT
REICH. ROMAN/EMP EX/STRUC COLONIAL COERCE ATTIT   GP/REL
CATHISM 4/5 AFRICA/N CHURCH/STA. PAGE 29 B0592   DOMIN
                                                     JURID
                                                      B63
ECOLE NATIONALE D'ADMIN,BIBLIOGRAPHIE SELECTIVE   BIBLIOG
D'OUVRAGES DE LANGUE FRANCAISE TRAITANT DES   AFR
PROBLEMES GOUVERNEMENTAUX ET ADMINISTRATIFS. NAT/G   ADMIN
FORCES ACT/RES OP/RES PLAN PROB/SOLV BUDGET ADJUD   EX/STRUC
COLONIAL LEAD 20. PAGE 32 B0651
                                                      B63
FISHER S.N.,THE MILITARY IN THE MIDDLE EAST: EX/STRUC
PROBLEMS IN SOCIETY AND GOVERNMENT. ISLAM USA+45   FORCES
NAT/G DOMIN LEGIT COERCE ORD/FREE PWR...TIME/SEQ
VAL/FREE 20. PAGE 36 B0725
                                                      B63
GARNER J.F.,ADMINISTRATIVE LAW. UK LAW LOC/G NAT/G   ADMIN
EX/STRUC LEGIS JUDGE BAL/PWR BUDGET ADJUD CONTROL   JURID
CT/SYS...BIBLIOG 20. PAGE 39 B0783   PWR
                                                     GOV/REL
                                                      B63
GOURNAY B.,PUBLIC ADMINISTRATION. FRANCE LAW CONSTN BIBLIOG/A
AGRI FINAN LABOR SCHOOL EX/STRUC CHOOSE...MGT   ADMIN
METH/COMP 20. PAGE 42 B0846   NAT/G
                                                     LOC/G
                                                      B63
GRANT D.R.,STATE AND LOCAL GOVERNMENT IN AMERICA.   PROVS
USA+45 FINAN LOC/G MUNIC EX/STRUC FORCES EDU/PROP   POL/PAR
ADMIN CHOOSE FEDERAL ATTIT...JURID 20. PAGE 42   LEGIS

B0853

GREEN H.P..GOVERNMENT OF THE ATOM. USA+45 LEGIS
PROB/SOLV ADMIN CONTROL PWR...POLICY DECISION 20
PRESIDENT CONGRESS. PAGE 43 B0864

CONSTN
                                                                            B63
GOV/REL
EX/STRUC
NUC/PWR
DELIB/GP
                                                                            B63

GRIFFITH J.A.G..PRINCIPLES OF ADMINISTRATIVE LAW
(3RD ED.). UK CONSTN EX/STRUC LEGIS ADJUD CONTROL
CT/SYS PWR...CHARTS 20. PAGE 43 B0879

JURID
ADMIN
NAT/G
BAL/PWR
                                                                            B63

HARGROVE M.M..BUSINESS POLICY CASES-WITH BEHAVIORAL
SCIENCE IMPLICATIONS. LG/CO SML/CO EX/STRUC TOP/EX
PLAN PROB/SOLV CONFER ADMIN CONTROL ROUTINE
EFFICIENCY. PAGE 47 B0946

SOC/EXP
INDUS
DECISION
MGT
                                                                            B63

HATHAWAY D.A..GOVERNMENT AND AGRICULTURE: PUBLIC
POLICY IN A DEMOCRATIC SOCIETY. USA+45 LEGIS ADMIN
EXEC LOBBY REPRESENT PWR 20. PAGE 48 B0967

AGRI
GOV/REL
PROB/SOLV
EX/STRUC
                                                                            B63

HEUSSLER R..YESTERDAY'S RULERS: THE MAKING OF THE
BRITISH COLONIAL SERVICE. AFR EUR+WWI UK STRATA
SECT DELIB/GP PLAN DOMIN EDU/PROP ATTIT PERCEPT
PERSON SUPEGO KNOWL ORD/FREE PWR...MGT SOC OBS INT
TIME/SEQ 20 CMN/WLTH. PAGE 49 B1000

EX/STRUC
MORAL
ELITES
                                                                            B63

HOWER R.M..MANAGERS AND SCIENTISTS. EX/STRUC CREATE
ADMIN REPRESENT ATTIT DRIVE ROLE PWR SKILL...SOC
INT. PAGE 52 B1052

R+D
MGT
PERS/REL
INGP/REL
                                                                            B63

KARL B.D..EXECUTIVE REORGANIZATION AND REFORM IN
THE NEW DEAL. ECO/DEV INDUS DELIB/GP EX/STRUC PLAN
BUDGET ADMIN EFFICIENCY PWR POPULISM...POLICY 20
PRESIDENT ROOSEVLT/F WILSON/W NEW/DEAL. PAGE 58
B1174

BIOG
EXEC
CREATE
CONTROL
                                                                            B63

LOCKARD D..THE POLITICS OF STATE AND LOCAL
GOVERNMENT. USA+45 CONSTN EX/STRUC LEGIS CT/SYS
FEDERAL...CHARTS BIBLIOG 20. PAGE 66 B1334

LOC/G
PROVS
OP/RES
ADMIN
                                                                            B63

MACNEIL N..FORGE OF DEMOCRACY: THE HOUSE OF
REPRESENTATIVES. POL/PAR EX/STRUC TOP/EX DEBATE
LEAD PARL/PROC CHOOSE GOV/REL PWR...OBS HOUSE/REP.
PAGE 68 B1374

LEGIS
DELIB/GP
                                                                            B63

MAHESHWARI B..STUDIES IN PANCHAYATI RAJ. INDIA
POL/PAR EX/STRUC BUDGET EXEC REPRESENT CENTRAL
EFFICIENCY...DECISION 20. PAGE 68 B1378

FEDERAL
LOC/G
GOV/REL
LEAD
                                                                            B63

PLANTEY A..TRAITE PRATIQUE DE LA FONCTION PUBLIQUE
(2ND ED., 2 VOLS.). FRANCE FINAN EX/STRUC PROB/SOLV
GP/REL ATTIT...SOC 20 CIVIL/SERV. PAGE 83 B1680

ADMIN
SUPEGO
JURID
                                                                            B63

RICHARDS P.G..PATRONAGE IN BRITISH GOVERNMENT.
ELITES DELIB/GP TOP/EX PROB/SOLV CONTROL CT/SYS
EXEC PWR. PAGE 88 B1774

EX/STRUC
REPRESENT
POL/PAR
ADMIN
                                                                            B63

RICHARDSON H.G..THE ADMINISTRATION OF IRELAND
1172-1377. IRELAND CONSTN EX/STRUC LEGIS JUDGE
CT/SYS PARL/PROC...CHARTS BIBLIOG 12/14. PAGE 88
B1775

ADMIN
NAT/G
PWR
                                                                            B63

ROBERT J..LA MONARCHIE MAROCAINE. MOROCCO LABOR
MUNIC POL/PAR EX/STRUC ORD/FREE PWR...JURID TREND T
20. PAGE 89 B1793

CHIEF
CONSERVE
ADMIN
CONSTN
                                                                            B63

SMITH R.M..STATE GOVERNMENT IN TRANSITION. USA+45
POL/PAR LEGIS PARL/PROC GOV/REL 20 PENNSYLVAN
GOVERNOR. PAGE 98 B1984

PROVS
POLICY
EX/STRUC
PLAN
                                                                            B63

STEIN H..AMERICAN CIVIL-MILITARY DECISION. USA+45
USA-45 EX/STRUC FORCES LEGIS TOP/EX PLAN DIPLOM
FOR/AID ATTIT 20 CONGRESS. PAGE 100 B2028

CIVMIL/REL
DECISION
WAR
BUDGET
                                                                            B63

STEVENSON A.E..LOOKING OUTWARD: YEARS OF CRISIS AT
THE UNITED NATIONS. COM CUBA USA+45 WOR+45 SOCIETY
NAT/G EX/STRUC ACT/RES LEGIT COLONIAL ATTIT PERSON
SUPEGO ALL/VALS...POLICY HUM UN COLD/WAR CONGO 20.
PAGE 100 B2034

INT/ORG
CONCPT
ARMS/CONT
                                                                            B63

SWERDLOW I..DEVELOPMENT ADMINISTRATION: CONCEPTS
AND PROBLEMS. WOR+45 CULTURE SOCIETY STRATA
DELIB/GP EX/STRUC ACT/RES PLAN ECO/TAC DOMIN LEGIT
ATTIT RIGID/FLEX SUPEGO HEALTH PWR...MGT CONCPT
ANTHOL VAL/FREE. PAGE 102 B2062

ECO/UNDEV
ADMIN
                                                                            B63

THOMETZ C.E..THE DECISION-MAKERS: THE POWER

ELITES

STRUCTURE OF DALLAS. USA+45 CULTURE EX/STRUC DOMIN
LEGIT GP/REL ATTIT OBJECTIVE...INT CHARTS GP/COMP.
PAGE 104 B2101

MUNIC
PWR
DECISION
                                                                            B63

US HOUSE COM ON ED AND LABOR.ADMINISTRATION OF
AGING. USA+45 R+D EX/STRUC PLAN BUDGET PAY EDU/PROP
ROUTINE COST CONGRESS. PAGE 108 B2187

AGE/O
ADMIN
DELIB/GP
GIVE
                                                                            B63

VAN RIPER P.P..THE MERIT SYSTEM: FOUNDATION FOR
RESPONSIBLE PUBLIC MANAGEMENT (PAMPHLET). USA+45
EX/STRUC 20. PAGE 112 B2252

EFFICIENCY
ADMIN
INGP/REL
MGT
                                                                            B63

WARNER W.L..THE AMERICAN FEDERAL EXECUTIVE. USA+45
USA-45 CONSULT EX/STRUC GP/REL DRIVE ALL/VALS...PSY
DEEP/QU CHARTS 19/20 PRESIDENT. PAGE 114 B2295

ELITES
NAT/G
TOP/EX
ADMIN
                                                                            B63

WEINER M..POLITICAL CHANGE IN SOUTH ASIA. CEYLON
INDIA PAKISTAN S/ASIA CULTURE ELITES ECO/UNDEV
EX/STRUC ADMIN CONTROL CHOOSE CONSERVE...GOV/COMP
ANTHOL 20. PAGE 115 B2315

NAT/G
CONSTN
TEC/DEV
                                                                            B63

WOLL P..AMERICAN BUREAUCRACY. USA+45 USA-45 CONSTN
NAT/G ADJUD PWR OBJECTIVE...MGT GP/COMP. PAGE 118
B2372

LEGIS
EX/STRUC
ADMIN
GP/REL
                                                                            B63

WOLL P..ADMINISTRATIVE LAW: THE INFORMAL PROCESS.
USA+45 NAT/G CONTROL EFFICIENCY 20. PAGE 118 B2373

ADMIN
ADJUD
REPRESENT
EX/STRUC
                                                                            L63

SPITZ A.A.."DEVELOPMENT ADMINISTRATION: AN
ANNOTATED BIBLIOGRAPHY." WOR+45 CULTURE SOCIETY
STRATA DELIB/GP EX/STRUC TOP/EX ACT/RES ECO/TAC
DOMIN EDU/PROP LEGIT COERCE ATTIT ALL/VALS...MGT
VAL/FREE. PAGE 99 B2009

ADMIN
ECO/UNDEV
                                                                            S63

ANTHON C.G.."THE END OF THE ADENAUER ERA." EUR+WWI
GERMANY/W CONSTN EX/STRUC CREATE DIPLOM LEGIT ATTIT
PERSON ALL/VALS...RECORD 20 ADENAUER/K. PAGE 6
B0113

NAT/G
TOP/EX
BAL/PWR
GERMANY
                                                                            S63

BAKER R.J.."DISCUSSION AND DECISION-MAKING IN THE
CIVIL SERVICE." UK CONTROL REPRESENT INGP/REL
PERS/REL EFFICIENCY 20. PAGE 8 B0168

EXEC
EX/STRUC
PROB/SOLV
ADMIN
                                                                            S63

BANFIELD J.."FEDERATION IN EAST-AFRICA." AFR UGANDA
ELITES INT/ORG NAT/G VOL/ASSN LEGIS ECO/TAC FEDERAL
ATTIT SOVEREIGN TOT/POP 20 TANGANYIKA. PAGE 9 B0180

EX/STRUC
PWR
REGION
                                                                            S63

BARZANSKI S.."REGIONAL UNDERDEVELOPMENT IN THE
EUROPEAN ECONOMIC COMMUNITY." EUR+WWI ELITES
DIST/IND MARKET VOL/ASSN CONSULT EX/STRUC ECO/TAC
RIGID/FLEX WEALTH EEC OEEC 20. PAGE 9 B0192

ECO/UNDEV
PLAN
                                                                            S63

BECHHOEFER B.G.."UNITED NATIONS PROCEDURES IN CASE
OF VIOLATIONS OF DISARMAMENT AGREEMENTS." COM
USA+45 USSR LAW CONSTN NAT/G EX/STRUC FORCES LEGIS
BAL/PWR EDU/PROP CT/SYS ARMS/CONT ORD/FREE PWR
...POLICY STERTYP UN VAL/FREE 20. PAGE 10 B0204

INT/ORG
DELIB/GP
                                                                            S63

DELLIN L.A.D.."BULGARIA UNDER SOVIET LEADERSHIP."
BULGARIA COM USA+45 USSR ECO/DEV INDUS POL/PAR
EX/STRUC TOP/EX COERCE ATTIT RIGID/FLEX...POLICY
TIME/SEQ 20. PAGE 28 B0572

AGRI
NAT/G
TOTALISM
                                                                            S63

EVANS L.H.."SOME MANAGEMENT PROBLEMS OF UNESCO."
WOR+45 EX/STRUC LEGIS PWR UNESCO VAL/FREE 20.
PAGE 34 B0688

INT/ORG
MGT
                                                                            S63

HARRIS R.L.."A COMPARATIVE ANALYSIS OF THE
ADMINISTRATIVE SYSTEMS OF CANADA AND CEYLON."
S/ASIA CULTURE SOCIETY STRATA TOP/EX ACT/RES DOMIN
EDU/PROP LEGIT COERCE ATTIT SUPEGO ALL/VALS...MGT
CHARTS GEN/LAWS VAL/FREE 20. PAGE 47 B0955

DELIB/GP
EX/STRUC
CANADA
CEYLON
                                                                            S63

PIPER D.C.."THE ROLE OF INTER-GOVERNMENTAL
MACHINERY IN CANADIANAMERICAN RELATIONS." CANADA
USA+45 PROB/SOLV REPRESENT 20. PAGE 83 B1676

GOV/REL
ADMIN
EX/STRUC
CONFER
                                                                            S63

SCHMITT H.A.."THE EUROPEAN COMMUNITIES." EUR+WWI
FRANCE DELIB/GP EX/STRUC TOP/EX CREATE TEC/DEV
ECO/TAC LEGIT REGION COERCE DRIVE ALL/VALS
...METH/CNCPT EEC 20. PAGE 94 B1897

VOL/ASSN
ECO/DEV
                                                                            S63

STANLEY T.W.."DECENTRALIZING NUCLEAR CONTROL IN
NATO." EUR+WWI USA+45 ELITES FORCES ACT/RES ATTIT
ORD/FREE PWR...NEW/IDEA HYPO/EXP TOT/POP 20 NATO.
PAGE 100 B2022

INT/ORG
EX/STRUC
NUC/PWR
                                                                            S63

USEEM J.."MEN IN THE MIDDLE OF THE THIRD CULTURE:

ADMIN

THE ROLES OF AMERICAN AND NON-WESTERN PEOPLE IN CROSS-CULTURAL ADMINIS-." FUT WOR+45 DELIB/GP EX/STRUC LEGIS ATTIT ALL/VALS...MGT INT TIME/SEQ GEN/LAWS VAL/FREE. PAGE 111 B2247
SOCIETY PERSON
S63

WAGRET M.."L'ASCENSION POLITIQUE DE L'U.D.D.I.A. (CONGO) ET SA PRISE DU POUVOIR (1956-1959)." AFR WOR+45 NAT/G POL/PAR CONSULT DELIB/GP LEGIS PERCEPT ALL/VALS SOVEREIGN...TIME/SEQ CONGO. PAGE 113 B2274
EX/STRUC CHOOSE FRANCE
N63

GREAT BRITAIN DEPT TECH COOP,PUBLIC ADMINISTRATION: A SELECT BIBLIOGRAPHY (PAMPHLET). WOR+45 AGRI FINAN INDUS EX/STRUC OP/RES ECO/TAC...MGT METH/COMP NAT/COMP. PAGE 43 B0861
BIBLIOG/A ADMIN NAT/G LOC/G
B64

ADAMS V.,THE PEACE CORPS IN ACTION. USA+45 VOL/ASSN EX/STRUC GOV/REL PERCEPT ORD/FREE...OBS 20 KENNEDY/JF PEACE/CORP. PAGE 3 B0058
DIPLOM FOR/AID PERSON DRIVE
B64

BLAKE R.R.,MANAGING INTERGROUP CONFLICT IN INDUSTRY. INDUS DELIB/GP EX/STRUC GP/REL PERS/REL GAME. PAGE 12 B0250
CREATE PROB/SOLV OP/RES ADJUD
B64

BOYER W.W.,BUREAUCRACY ON TRIAL: POLICY MAKING BY GOVERNMENT AGENCIES. USA+45 NAT/G REPRESENT 20. PAGE 14 B0294
ADMIN LOBBY EXEC EX/STRUC
B64

CAPLOW T.,PRINCIPLES OF ORGANIZATION. UNIV CULTURE STRUCT CREATE INGP/REL UTOPIA...GEN/LAWS TIME. PAGE 18 B0374
VOL/ASSN CONCPT SIMUL EX/STRUC
B64

CATER D.,POWER IN WASHINGTON: A CRITICAL LOOK AT TODAY'S STRUGGLE TO GOVERN IN THE NATION'S CAPITAL. USA+45 NAT/G LEGIS ADMIN EXEC LOBBY PLURISM 20. PAGE 19 B0392
REPRESENT GOV/REL INGP/REL EX/STRUC
B64

CONNECTICUT U INST PUBLIC SERV,SUMMARY OF CHARTER PROVISIONS IN CONNECTICUT LOCAL GOVERNMENT (PAMPHLET). USA+45 DELIB/GP LEGIS TOP/EX CHOOSE REPRESENT 20 CONNECTICT CITY/MGT MAYOR. PAGE 23 B0462
CONSTN MUNIC LOC/G EX/STRUC
B64

COTTRELL A.J.,THE POLITICS OF THE ATLANTIC ALLIANCE. EUR+WWI USA+45 INT/ORG NAT/G DELIB/GP EX/STRUC BAL/PWR DIPLOM REGION DETER ATTIT ORD/FREE ...CONCPT RECORD GEN/LAWS GEN/METH NATO 20. PAGE 24 B0493
VOL/ASSN FORCES
B64

DAS M.N.,INDIA UNDER MORLEY AND MINTO. INDIA UK ECO/UNDEV MUNIC PROVS EX/STRUC LEGIS DIPLOM CONTROL REV 20 MORLEY/J. PAGE 26 B0531
GOV/REL COLONIAL POLICY ADMIN
B64

EATON H.,PRESIDENTIAL TIMBER: A HISTORY OF NOMINATING CONVENTIONS, 1868-1960. USA+45 USA-45 POL/PAR EX/STRUC DEBATE LOBBY ATTIT PERSON ALL/VALS ...MYTH 19/20 PRESIDENT. PAGE 32 B0646
DELIB/GP CHOOSE CHIEF NAT/G
B64

EDELMAN M.,THE SYMBOLIC USES OF POWER. USA+45 EX/STRUC CONTROL GP/REL INGP/REL...MGT T. PAGE 32 B0653
CLIENT PWR EXEC ELITES
B64

FAINSOD M.,HOW RUSSIA IS RULED (REV. ED.). RUSSIA USSR AGRI PROC/MFG LABOR POL/PAR EX/STRUC CONTROL PWR...POLICY BIBLIOG 19/20 KHRUSH/N COM/PARTY. PAGE 34 B0700
NAT/G REV MARXISM
B64

FONTENEAU J.,LE CONSEIL MUNICIPAL: LE MAIRE-LES ADJOINTS. FRANCE FINAN DELIB/GP EX/STRUC BUDGET TAX TASK COST INCOME ROLE SUPEGO 20 MAYOR. PAGE 36 B0735
MUNIC NEIGH ADMIN TOP/EX
B64

GORE W.J.,ADMINISTRATIVE DECISION-MAKING* A HEURISTIC MODEL. EX/STRUC ADMIN LEAD ROUTINE PERS/REL...METH/CNCPT ORG/CHARTS. PAGE 41 B0834
DECISION MGT SIMUL GEN/METH
B64

JACKSON H.M.,THE SECRETARY OF STATE AND THE AMBASSADOR* JACKSON SUBCOMMITTEE PAPERS ON THE CONDUCT OF AMERICAN FOREIGN POLICY. USA+45 NAT/G FORCES ACT/RES OP/RES EDU/PROP CENTRAL EFFICIENCY ORD/FREE...OBS RECORD ANTHOL CONGRESS PRESIDENT. PAGE 55 B1107
GOV/REL DIPLOM ADMIN EX/STRUC
B64

KAPP E.,THE MERGER OF THE EXECUTIVES OF THE EUROPEAN COMMUNITIES. LAW CONSTN STRUCT ACT/RES PLAN PROB/SOLV ADMIN REGION TASK...INT/LAW MGT ECSC EEC. PAGE 58 B1170
CENTRAL EX/STRUC
B64

KARIEL H.S.,IN SEARCH OF AUTHORITY: TWENTIETH-CENTURY POLITICAL THOUGHT. WOR+45 WOR-45 NAT/G
CONSTN CONCPT

EX/STRUC TOTALISM DRIVE PWR...MGT PHIL/SCI GEN/LAWS 19/20 NIETZSCH/F FREUD/S WEBER/MAX NIEBUHR/R MARITAIN/J. PAGE 58 B1173
ORD/FREE IDEA/COMP
B64

KILPATRICKFP,SOURCE BOOK OF OCCUPATIONAL VALUES AND THE IMAGE OF THE FEDERAL SERVICE. USA+45 EX/STRUC ...POLICY MGT INT METH/COMP 20. PAGE 60 B1205
NAT/G ATTIT ADMIN WORKER
B64

KILPATRICKFP,THE IMAGE OF THE FEDERAL SERVICE. USA+45 EX/STRUC...POLICY MGT INT METH/COMP 20. PAGE 60 B1206
NAT/G ATTIT ADMIN WORKER
B64

LOWI T.J.,AT THE PLEASURE OF THE MAYOR. EX/STRUC PROB/SOLV BAL/PWR ADMIN PARTIC CHOOSE GP/REL ...CONT/OBS NET/THEORY CHARTS 20 NEWYORK/C MAYOR. PAGE 67 B1346
LOBBY LOC/G PWR MUNIC
B64

MERILLAT H.C.L.,LEGAL ADVISERS AND FOREIGN AFFAIRS. WOR+45 WOR-45 ELITES INTELL NAT/G LEGIT ADMIN PERCEPT ALL/VALS...MGT NEW/IDEA RECORD 20. PAGE 73 B1469
CONSULT EX/STRUC DIPLOM
B64

NELSON D.H.,ADMINISTRATIVE AGENCIES OF THE USA: THEIR DECISIONS AND AUTHORITY. USA+45 NAT/G CONTROL CT/SYS REPRESENT...DECISION 20. PAGE 78 B1568
ADMIN EX/STRUC ADJUD LAW
B64

O'HEARN P.J.T.,PEACE, ORDER AND GOOD GOVERNMENT; A NEW CONSTITUTION FOR CANADA. CANADA EX/STRUC LEGIS CT/SYS PARL/PROC...BIBLIOG 20. PAGE 79 B1600
NAT/G CONSTN LAW CREATE
B64

PLISCHKE E.,SYSTEMS OF INTEGRATING THE INTERNATIONAL COMMUNITY. WOR+45 NAT/G VOL/ASSN ECO/TAC LEGIT PWR WEALTH...TIME/SEQ ANTHOL UN TOT/POP 20. PAGE 83 B1684
INT/ORG EX/STRUC REGION
B64

PRESS C.,A BIBLIOGRAPHIC INTRODUCTION TO AMERICAN STATE GOVERNMENT AND POLITICS (PAMPHLET). USA+45 USA-45 EX/STRUC ADJUD INGP/REL FEDERAL ORD/FREE 20. PAGE 84 B1701
BIBLIOG LEGIS LOC/G POL/PAR
B64

RAYMOND J.,POWER AT THE PENTAGON (1ST ED.). ELITES NAT/G PLAN EDU/PROP ARMS/CONT DETER WAR WEAPON ...TIME/SEQ 20 PENTAGON MCNAMARA/R. PAGE 86 B1746
PWR CIVMIL/REL EX/STRUC FORCES
B64

REDLICH F.,THE GERMAN MILITARY ENTERPRISER AND HIS WORK FORCE. CHRIST-17C GERMANY ELITES SOCIETY FINAN ECO/TAC CIVMIL/REL GP/REL INGP/REL...HIST/WRIT METH/COMP 14/17. PAGE 87 B1760
EX/STRUC FORCES PROFIT WORKER
B64

RIDLEY F.,PUBLIC ADMINISTRATION IN FRANCE. FRANCE UK EX/STRUC CONTROL PARTIC EFFICIENCY 20. PAGE 88 B1781
ADMIN REPRESENT GOV/COMP PWR
B64

RIES J.C.,THE MANAGEMENT OF DEFENSE: ORGANIZATION AND CONTROL OF THE US ARMED SERVICES. PROF/ORG DELIB/GP EX/STRUC LEGIS GOV/REL PERS/REL CENTRAL RATIONAL PWR...POLICY TREND GOV/COMP BIBLIOG. PAGE 88 B1782
FORCES ACT/RES DECISION CONTROL
B64

ROBSON W.A.,THE GOVERNORS AND THE GOVERNED. USA+45 PROB/SOLV DOMIN ADMIN CONTROL CHOOSE...POLICY PRESIDENT. PAGE 89 B1808
EX/STRUC ATTIT PARTIC LEAD
B64

ROCHE J.P.,THE CONGRESS. EX/STRUC BAL/PWR DIPLOM DEBATE ADJUD LEAD PWR. PAGE 89 B1809
INGP/REL LEGIS DELIB/GP SENIOR
B64

ROCHE J.P.,THE PRESIDENCY. USA+45 USA-45 CONSTN NAT/G CHIEF BAL/PWR DIPLOM GP/REL 18/20 PRESIDENT. PAGE 90 B1810
EX/STRUC PWR
B64

SARROS P.P.,CONGRESS AND THE NEW DIPLOMACY: THE FORMULATION OF MUTUAL SECURITY POLICY: 1953-60 (THESIS). USA+45 CHIEF EX/STRUC REGION ROUTINE CHOOSE GOV/REL PEACE ROLE...POLICY 20 PRESIDENT CONGRESS. PAGE 92 B1869
DIPLOM POL/PAR NAT/G
B64

SAYLES L.R.,MANAGERIAL BEHAVIOR: ADMINISTRATION IN COMPLEX ORGANIZATIONS. INDUS LG/CO PROB/SOLV CONTROL EXEC INGP/REL PERS/REL SKILL...MGT OBS PREDICT GEN/LAWS 20. PAGE 93 B1874
CONCPT ADMIN TOP/EX EX/STRUC
B64

SCHECHTER A.H.,INTERPRETATION OF AMBIGUOUS DOCUMENTS BY INTERNATIONAL ADMINISTRATIVE TRIBUNALS. WOR+45 EX/STRUC INT/TRADE CT/SYS SOVEREIGN 20 UN ILO EURCT/JUST. PAGE 93 B1884
INT/LAW DIPLOM INT/ORG ADJUD
B64

SEGUNDO-SANCHEZ M.,OBRAS (2 VOLS.). VENEZUELA
BIBLIOG

EX/STRUC DIPLOM ADMIN 19/20. PAGE 95 B1924
LEAD
NAT/G
L/A+17C
B64

SINGER M.R.,THE EMERGING ELITE: A STUDY OF
POLITICAL LEADERSHIP IN CEYLON. S/ASIA ECO/UNDEV
AGRI KIN NAT/G SECT EX/STRUC LEGIT ATTIT PWR
RESPECT...SOC STAT CHARTS 20. PAGE 97 B1967
TOP/EX
STRATA
NAT/LISM
CEYLON
B64

SULLIVAN G.,THE STORY OF THE PEACE CORPS. USA+45
WOR+45 INTELL FACE/GP NAT/G SCHOOL VOL/ASSN CONSULT
EX/STRUC PLAN EDU/PROP ADMIN ATTIT DRIVE ALL/VALS
...POLICY HEAL SOC CONCPT INT QU BIOG TREND SOC/EXP
WORK. PAGE 102 B2054
INT/ORG
ECO/UNDEV
FOR/AID
PEACE
B64

TILMAN R.O.,BUREAUCRATIC TRANSITION IN MALAYA.
MALAYSIA S/ASIA UK NAT/G EX/STRUC DIPLOM...CHARTS
BIBLIOG 20. PAGE 104 B2110
ADMIN
COLONIAL
SOVEREIGN
EFFICIENCY
B64

TURNER H.A.,THE GOVERNMENT AND POLITICS OF
CALIFORNIA (2ND ED.). LAW FINAN MUNIC POL/PAR
SCHOOL EX/STRUC LEGIS LOBBY CHOOSE...CHARTS T 20
CALIFORNIA. PAGE 106 B2138
PROVS
ADMIN
LOC/G
CONSTN
B64

US SENATE COMM GOVT OPERATIONS,THE SECRETARY OF
STATE AND THE AMBASSADOR. USA+45 CHIEF CONSULT
EX/STRUC FORCES PLAN ADMIN EXEC INGP/REL ROLE
...ANTHOL 20 PRESIDENT DEPT/STATE. PAGE 110 B2215
DIPLOM
DELIB/GP
NAT/G
B64

VECCHIO G.D.,L'ETAT ET LE DROIT. ITALY CONSTN
EX/STRUC LEGIS DIPLOM CT/SYS...JURID 20 UN.
PAGE 112 B2256
NAT/G
SOVEREIGN
CONCPT
INT/LAW
B64

WEIDENBAUM M.L.,CONGRESS AND THE FEDERAL BUDGET:
FEDERAL BUDGETING AND THE RESPONSIBLE USE OF POWER.
LOC/G PLAN TAX CONGRESS. PAGE 114 B2309
LEGIS
EX/STRUC
BUDGET
ADMIN
B64

WHEARE K.C.,FEDERAL GOVERNMENT (4TH ED.). WOR+45
WOR-45 POL/PAR LEGIS BAL/PWR CT/SYS...POLICY JURID
CONCPT GOV/COMP 17/20. PAGE 116 B2331
FEDERAL
CONSTN
EX/STRUC
NAT/COMP
L64

FOX G.H.,"PERCEPTIONS OF THE VIETNAMESE PUBLIC
ADMINISTRATION SYSTEM" VIETNAM ELITES CONTROL EXEC
LEAD PWR...INT 20. PAGE 37 B0745
ADMIN
EX/STRUC
INGP/REL
ROLE
L64

MILLIS W.,"THE DEMILITARIZED WORLD." COM USA+45
USSR WOR+45 CONSTN NAT/G EX/STRUC PLAN LEGIT ATTIT
DRIVE...CONCPT TIME/SEQ STERTYP TOT/POP COLD/WAR
20. PAGE 74 B1486
FUT
INT/ORG
BAL/PWR
PEACE
L64

WORLD PEACE FOUNDATION,"INTERNATIONAL
ORGANIZATIONS: SUMMARY OF ACTIVITIES." INDIA
PAKISTAN TURKEY WOR+45 CONSTN CONSULT EX/STRUC
ECO/TAC EDU/PROP LEGIT ORD/FREE...JURID SOC UN 20
CYPRESS. PAGE 118 B2375
INT/ORG
ROUTINE
S64

CASE H.L.,"GORDON R. CLAPP: THE ROLE OF FAITH,
PURPOSES AND PEOPLE IN ADMINISTRATION." INDUS MUNIC
PROVS...POLICY 20. PAGE 19 B0391
ADMIN
BIOG
EX/STRUC
DECISION
S64

GALTUNE J.,"BALANCE OF POWER AND THE PROBLEM OF
PERCEPTION, A LOGICAL ANALYSIS." WOR+45 CONSTN
SOCIETY NAT/G DELIB/GP EX/STRUC LEGIS DOMIN ADMIN
COERCE DRIVE ORD/FREE...POLICY CONCPT OBS TREND
GEN/LAWS. PAGE 38 B0778
PWR
PSY
ARMS/CONT
WAR
S64

GROSS J.A.,"WHITEHALL AND THE COMMONWEALTH."
EUR+WWI MOD/EUR INT/ORG NAT/G CONSULT DELIB/GP
LEGIS DOMIN ADMIN COLONIAL ROUTINE PWR CMN/WLTH
19/20. PAGE 44 B0890
EX/STRUC
ATTIT
TREND
S64

HUELIN D.,"ECONOMIC INTEGRATION IN LATIN AMERICAN:
PROGRESS AND PROBLEMS." L/A+17C ECO/DEV AGRI
DIST/IND FINAN INDUS NAT/G VOL/ASSN CONSULT
DELIB/GP EX/STRUC ACT/RES PLAN TEC/DEV ECO/TAC
ROUTINE BAL/PAY WEALTH WORK 20. PAGE 52 B1058
MARKET
ECO/UNDEV
INT/TRADE
S64

JOHNSON K.F.,"CAUSAL FACTORS IN LATIN AMERICAN
POLITICAL INSTABILITY." CULTURE NAT/G VOL/ASSN
EX/STRUC FORCES EDU/PROP LEGIT ADMIN COERCE REV
ATTIT KNOWL PWR...STYLE RECORD CHARTS WORK 20.
PAGE 57 B1144
L/A+17C
PERCEPT
ELITES
S64

KAPLAN N.,"RESEARCH ADMINISTRATION AND THE
ADMINISTRATOR: USSR AND US." COM USA+45 INTELL
EX/STRUC KNOWL...MGT 20. PAGE 58 B1169
R+D
ADMIN
USSR
S64

REDFORD E.S.,"THE PROTECTION OF THE PUBLIC INTEREST
WITH SPECIAL REFERENCE TO ADMINISTRATIVE
REGULATION." POL/PAR LEGIS PRESS PARL/PROC. PAGE 87
ADMIN
VOL/ASSN
EX/STRUC

B1758
GP/REL
S64

SALISBURY R.H.,"URBAN POLITICS: THE NEW CONVERGENCE
OF POWER." STRATA POL/PAR EX/STRUC PARTIC GP/REL
DECISION. PAGE 92 B1863
MUNIC
PWR
LEAD
S64

STANLEY D.T.,"EXCELLENCE IN PUBLIC SERVICE - HOW DO
YOU REALLY KNOW?" EXEC 20. PAGE 100 B2019
EFFICIENCY
EX/STRUC
ADMIN
CONTROL
S64

SWEARER H.R.,"AFTER KHRUSHCHEV: WHAT NEXT." COM FUT
USSR CONSTN ELITES NAT/G POL/PAR CHIEF DELIB/GP
LEGIS DOMIN LEAD...RECORD TREND STERTYP GEN/METH
20. PAGE 102 B2058
EX/STRUC
PWR
N64

CANADA NATL JT COUN PUB SERV,THE CANADA NATIONAL
JOINT COUNCIL OF THE PUBLIC SERVICE 1944-1964
(PAMPHLET). CANADA EX/STRUC PERS/REL DRIVE...MGT 20
PEARSON/L. PAGE 18 B0373
GP/REL
NAT/G
LABOR
EFFICIENCY
B65

AMERICAN ASSEMBLY COLUMBIA U,THE FEDERAL GOVERNMENT
SERVICE. USA+45 POL/PAR EX/STRUC EXEC 20. PAGE 4
B0082
ADMIN
MGT
NAT/G
INGP/REL
B65

BOCK E.,GOVERNMENT REGULATION OF BUSINESS. USA+45
LAW EX/STRUC LEGIS EXEC ORD/FREE PWR...ANTHOL
CONGRESS. PAGE 13 B0261
MGT
ADMIN
NAT/G
CONTROL
B65

BOXER C.R.,PORTUGUESE SOCIETY IN THE TROPICS - THE
MUNICIPAL COUNCILS OF GAO, MACAO, BAHIA, AND
LUANDA, 1510-1800. EUR+WWI MOD/EUR PORTUGAL CONSTN
EX/STRUC DOMIN CONTROL ROUTINE REPRESENT PRIVIL
...BIBLIOG/A 16/19 GENACCOUNT MACAO BAHIA LUANDA.
PAGE 14 B0290
MUNIC
ADMIN
COLONIAL
DELIB/GP
B65

CHANDA A.,FEDERALISM IN INDIA. INDIA UK ELITES
FINAN NAT/G POL/PAR EX/STRUC LEGIS DIPLOM TAX
GOV/REL POPULISM...POLICY 20. PAGE 20 B0402
CONSTN
CENTRAL
FEDERAL
B65

COHEN H.,THE DEMONICS OF BUREAUCRACY: PROBLEMS OF
CHANGE IN A GOVERNMENT AGENCY. USA+45 CLIENT
ROUTINE REPRESENT 20. PAGE 22 B0443
EXEC
EX/STRUC
INGP/REL
ADMIN
B65

EAST J.P.,COUNCIL-MANAGER GOVERNMENT: THE POLITICAL
THOUGHT OF ITS FOUNDER, RICHARD S. CHILDS. USA+45
CREATE ADMIN CHOOSE...BIOG GEN/LAWS BIBLIOG 20
CHILDS/RS CITY/MGT. PAGE 32 B0642
SIMUL
LOC/G
MUNIC
EX/STRUC
B65

FEERICK J.D.,FROM FAILING HANDS: THE STUDY OF
PRESIDENTIAL SUCCESSION. CONSTN NAT/G PROB/SOLV
LEAD PARL/PROC MURDER CHOOSE...NEW/IDEA BIBLIOG 20
KENNEDY/JF JOHNSON/LB PRESIDENT PRE/US/AM
VICE/PRES. PAGE 35 B0710
EX/STRUC
CHIEF
LAW
LEGIS
B65

FISCHER F.C.,THE GOVERNMENT OF MICHIGAN. USA+45
NAT/G PUB/INST EX/STRUC LEGIS BUDGET GIVE EDU/PROP
CT/SYS CHOOSE GOV/REL...T MICHIGAN. PAGE 36 B0723
PROVS
LOC/G
ADMIN
CONSTN
B65

FORGAC A.A.,NEW DIPLOMACY AND THE UNITED NATIONS.
FRANCE GERMANY UK USSR INT/ORG DELIB/GP EX/STRUC
PEACE...INT/LAW CONCPT UN. PAGE 36 B0740
DIPLOM
ETIQUET
NAT/G
B65

GOLEMBIEWSKI R.T.,MEN, MANAGEMENT, AND MORALITY:
TOWARD A NEW ORGANIZATIONAL ETHIC. CONSTN EX/STRUC
CREATE ADMIN CONTROL INGP/REL PERSON SUPEGO MORAL
PWR...GOV/COMP METH/COMP 20 BUREAUCRCY. PAGE 40
B0819
LG/CO
MGT
PROB/SOLV
B65

GREGG J.L.,POLITICAL PARTIES AND PARTY SYSTEMS IN
GUATEMALA, 1944-1963. GUATEMALA L/A+17C EX/STRUC
FORCES CREATE CONTROL REV CHOOSE PWR...TREND
IDEA/COMP 20. PAGE 43 B0872
LEAD
POL/PAR
NAT/G
CHIEF
B65

GT BRIT ADMIN STAFF COLLEGE,THE ACCOUNTABILITY OF
PUBLIC CORPORATIONS (REV. ED.). UK ECO/DEV FINAN
DELIB/GP EX/STRUC BUDGET CAP/ISM CONFER PRICE
PARL/PROC 20. PAGE 44 B0899
LG/CO
NAT/G
ADMIN
CONTROL
B65

HAIGHT D.E.,THE PRESIDENT: ROLES AND POWERS. USA+45
USA-45 POL/PAR PLAN DIPLOM CHOOSE PERS/REL PWR
18/20 PRESIDENT CONGRESS. PAGE 45 B0915
CHIEF
LEGIS
TOP/EX
EX/STRUC
B65

HAINES R.M.,THE ADMINISTRATION OF THE DIOCESE OF
WORCESTER IN THE FIRST HALF OF THE FOURTEENTH
CENTURY. UK CATHISM...METH/COMP 13/15. PAGE 45
B0918
ADMIN
EX/STRUC
SECT
DELIB/GP
B65

INST INTL DES CIVILISATION DIF,THE CONSTITUTIONS
AND ADMINISTRATIVE INSTITUTIONS OF THE NEW STATES.
AFR ISLAM S/ASIA NAT/G POL/PAR DELIB/GP EX/STRUC
CONSTN
ADMIN
ADJUD

CONFER EFFICIENCY NAT/LISM...JURID SOC 20. PAGE 54
B1088

INT. BANK RECONSTR. DEVELOP.,ECONOMIC DEVELOPMENT
OF KUWAIT. ISLAM KUWAIT AGRI FINAN MARKET EX/STRUC
TEC/DEV ECO/TAC ADMIN WEALTH...OBS CON/ANAL CHARTS
20. PAGE 54 B1092

ECO/UNDEV

INDUS
NAT/G

B65

KOENIG C.W.,OFFICIAL MAKERS OF PUBLIC POLICY:
CONGRESS AND THE PRESIDENT. USA+45 USA-45 NAT/G
EX/STRUC PROB/SOLV PWR. PAGE 60 B1222

CHIEF
LEGIS
GOV/REL
PLURISM

B65

KOENIG L.W.,OFFICIAL MAKERS OF PUBLIC POLICY:
CONGRESS AND THE PRESIDENT. USA+45 USA-45 EX/STRUC
ADMIN CONTROL GOV/REL PWR 18/20 CONGRESS PRESIDENT.
PAGE 61 B1225

POLICY
LEGIS
CHIEF
NAT/G

B65

KOUSOULAS D.G.,REVOLUTION AND DEFEAT; THE STORY OF
THE GREEK COMMUNIST PARTY. GREECE INT/ORG EX/STRUC
DIPLOM FOR/AID EDU/PROP PARL/PROC ADJUST ATTIT 20
COM/PARTY. PAGE 61 B1230

REV
MARXISM
POL/PAR
ORD/FREE

B65

LATHAM E.,THE GROUP BASIS OF POLITICS: A STUDY IN
BASING-POINT LEGISLATION. INDUS MARKET POL/PAR
DELIB/GP EX/STRUC DEBATE ADJUD...CHARTS PRESIDENT.
PAGE 63 B1274

LEGIS
GP/COMP
GP/REL

B65

MARTIN R.,PUBLIC ADMINISTRATION AND DEMOCRACY.
ELITES NAT/G ADMIN EXEC ROUTINE INGP/REL. PAGE 70
B1412

EX/STRUC
DECISION
REPRESENT
GP/REL

B65

MASTERS N.A.,COMMITTEE ASSIGNMENTS IN THE HOUSE OF
REPRESENTATIVES (BMR). USA+45 ELITES POL/PAR
EX/STRUC PARTIC REPRESENT GP/REL PERS/REL ATTIT PWR
...STAT CHARTS 20 HOUSE/REP. PAGE 71 B1425

LEAD
LEGIS
CHOOSE
DELIB/GP

B65

MOORE C.H.,TUNISIA SINCE INDEPENDENCE. ELITES LOC/G
POL/PAR ADMIN COLONIAL CONTROL EXEC GOV/REL
TOTALISM MARXISM...INT 20 TUNIS. PAGE 75 B1513

NAT/G
EX/STRUC
SOCISM

B65

MORGENTHAU H.,MORGENTHAU DIARY (CHINA) (2 VOLS.).
ASIA USA+45 USA-45 LAW DELIB/GP EX/STRUC PLAN
FOR/AID INT/TRADE CONFER WAR MARXISM 20 CHINJAP.
PAGE 75 B1523

DIPLOM
ADMIN

B65

MUSOLF L.D.,PROMOTING THE GENERAL WELFARE:
GOVERNMENT AND THE ECONOMY. USA+45 ECO/DEV CAP/ISM
DEMAND OPTIMAL 20. PAGE 77 B1550

ECO/TAC
NAT/G
EX/STRUC
NEW/LIB

B65

NORDEN A.,WAR AND NAZI CRIMINALS IN WEST GERMANY:
STATE. ECONOMY, ADMINISTRATION, ARMY, JUSTICE,
SCIENCE. GERMANY GERMANY/W MOD/EUR ECO/DEV ACADEM
EX/STRUC FORCES DOMIN ADMIN CT/SYS...POLICY MAJORIT
PACIFIST 20. PAGE 78 B1587

FASCIST
WAR
NAT/G
TOP/EX

B65

PANJABI K.L.,THE CIVIL SERVANT IN INDIA. INDIA UK
NAT/G CONSULT EX/STRUC REGION GP/REL RACE/REL 20.
PAGE 81 B1631

ADMIN
WORKER
BIOG
COLONIAL

B65

PAYNE J.L.,LABOR AND POLITICS IN PERU; THE SYSTEM
OF POLITICAL BARGAINING. PERU CONSTN VOL/ASSN
EX/STRUC LEAD PWR...CHARTS 20. PAGE 81 B1645

LABOR
POL/PAR
BARGAIN
GP/REL

B65

PRESTHUS R.,BEHAVIORAL APPROACHES TO PUBLIC
ADMINISTRATION. UK STRATA LG/CO PUB/INST VOL/ASSN
EX/STRUC TOP/EX EFFICIENCY HEALTH. PAGE 84 B1704

GEN/METH
DECISION
ADMIN
R+D

B65

PYLEE M.V.,CONSTITUTIONAL GOVERNMENT IN INDIA (2ND
REV. ED.). INDIA POL/PAR EX/STRUC DIPLOM COLONIAL
CT/SYS PARL/PROC PRIVIL...JURID 16/20. PAGE 85
B1725

CONSTN
NAT/G
PROVS
FEDERAL

B65

REDFORD D.R.,POLITICS AND GOVERNMENT IN THE UNITED
STATES. USA+45 USA-45 LOC/G PROVS FORCES DIPLOM
CT/SYS LOBBY...JURID SUPREME/CT PRESIDENT. PAGE 87
B1751

NAT/G
POL/PAR
EX/STRUC
LEGIS

B65

REISS A.J. JR.,SCHOOLS IN A CHANGING SOCIETY.
CULTURE PROB/SOLV INSPECT DOMIN CONFER INGP/REL
RACE/REL AGE/C AGE/Y ALL/VALS...ANTHOL SOC/INTEG 20
NEWYORK/C. PAGE 87 B1766

SCHOOL
EX/STRUC
ADJUST
ADMIN

B65

ROTBERG R.I.,A POLITICAL HISTORY OF TROPICAL
AFRICA. EX/STRUC DIPLOM INT/TRADE DOMIN ADMIN
RACE/REL NAT/LISM PWR SOVEREIGN...GEOG TIME/SEQ
BIBLIOG 1/20. PAGE 91 B1832

AFR
CULTURE
COLONIAL

B65

ROURKE F.E.,BUREAUCRATIC POWER IN NATIONAL
POLITICS. ADMIN CONTROL EXEC GOV/REL INGP/REL 20.
PAGE 91 B1838

EX/STRUC
EFFICIENCY
REPRESENT

PWR
B65

ROWE J.Z.,THE PUBLIC-PRIVATE CHARACTER OF UNITED
STATES CENTRAL BANKING. USA+45 NAT/G EX/STRUC
...BIBLIOG 20 FED/RESERV. PAGE 91 B1842

FINAN
PLAN
FEDERAL
LAW

B65

RUBINSTEIN A.Z.,THE CHALLENGE OF POLITICS: IDEAS
AND ISSUES (2ND ED.). UNIV ELITES SOCIETY EX/STRUC
BAL/PWR PARL/PROC AUTHORIT...DECISION ANTHOL 20.
PAGE 92 B1852

NAT/G
DIPLOM
GP/REL
ORD/FREE

B65

SNIDER C.F.,AMERICAN STATE AND LOCAL GOVERNMENT.
USA+45 FINAN CHIEF EX/STRUC TAX ADMIN CONTROL SUFF
INGP/REL PWR 20. PAGE 98 B1989

GOV/REL
MUNIC
PROVS
LOC/G

B65

SNYDER F.G.,ONE-PARTY GOVERNMENT IN MALI:
TRANSITION TOWARD CONTROL. MALI STRATA STRUCT SOC.
PAGE 99 B1991

ECO/UNDEV
POL/PAR
EX/STRUC
ADMIN

B65

SPEECKAERT G.P.,SELECT BIBLIOGRAPHY ON
INTERNATIONAL ORGANIZATION, 1885-1964. WOR+45
WOR-45 EX/STRUC DIPLOM ADMIN REGION 19/20 UN.
PAGE 99 B2004

BIBLIOG
INT/ORG
GEN/LAWS
STRATA

B65

STANLEY D.T.,CHANGING ADMINISTRATIONS. USA+45
POL/PAR DELIB/GP TOP/EX BUDGET GOV/REL GP/REL
PERS/REL PWR...MAJORIT DECISION MGT 20 PRESIDENT
SUCCESSION DEPT/STATE DEPT/DEFEN DEPT/HEW. PAGE 100
B2021

NAT/G
CHIEF
ADMIN
EX/STRUC

B65

STARR M.K.,EXECUTIVE READINGS IN MANAGEMENT
SCIENCE. TOP/EX WORKER EDU/PROP ADMIN...DECISION
GEN/LAWS ANTHOL METH T 20. PAGE 100 B2023

MGT
EX/STRUC
PLAN
LG/CO

B65

US SENATE COMM GOVT OPERATIONS,ORGANIZATION OF
FEDERAL EXECUTIVE DEPARTMENTS AND AGENCIES: REPORT
OF MARCH 23, 1965. USA+45 FORCES LEGIS DIPLOM
ROUTINE CIVMIL/REL EFFICIENCY FEDERAL...MGT STAT.
PAGE 110 B2217

ADMIN
EX/STRUC
GOV/REL
ORG/CHARTS

B65

WARD W.E.,GOVERNMENT IN WEST AFRICA. WOR+45 POL/PAR
EX/STRUC PLAN PARTIC GP/REL SOVEREIGN 20 AFRICA/W.
PAGE 114 B2291

GOV/COMP
CONSTN
COLONIAL
ECO/UNDEV

B65

WILDER B.E.,BIBLIOGRAPHY OF THE OFFICIAL
PUBLICATIONS OF KANSAS, 1854-1958. USA+45 USA-45
ECO/DEV POL/PAR EX/STRUC LEGIS ADJUD ATTIT 19/20.
PAGE 116 B2349

BIBLIOG
PROVS
GOV/REL
ADMIN

L65

HAMMOND A.,"COMPREHENSIVE VERSUS INCREMENTAL
BUDGETING IN THE DEPARTMENT OF AGRICULTURE" USA+45
GP/REL ATTIT...PSY INT 20 DEPT/AGRI. PAGE 46 B0934

TOP/EX
EX/STRUC
AGRI
BUDGET

L65

LASSWELL H.D.,"THE POLICY SCIENCES OF DEVELOPMENT."
CULTURE SOCIETY EX/STRUC CREATE ADMIN ATTIT KNOWL
...SOC CONCPT SIMUL GEN/METH. PAGE 63 B1273

PWR
METH/CNCPT
DIPLOM

L65

RUBIN A.P.,"UNITED STATES CONTEMPORARY PRACTICE
RELATING TO INTERNATIONAL LAW." USA+45 WOR+45
CONSTN INT/ORG NAT/G DELIB/GP EX/STRUC DIPLOM DOMIN
CT/SYS ROUTINE ORD/FREE...CONCPT COLD/WAR 20.
PAGE 91 B1848

LAW
LEGIT
INT/LAW

L65

SHARKANSKY I.,"FOUR AGENCIES AND AN APPROPRIATIONS
SUBCOMMITTEE: A COMPARATIVE STUDY OF BDUGET
STRATEGIES." USA+45 EX/STRUC TOP/EX PROB/SOLV
CONTROL ROUTINE CONGRESS. PAGE 96 B1934

ADMIN
EDU/PROP
NAT/G
LEGIS

S65

ANDERSON T.J.,"PRESSURE GROUPS AND
INTERGOVERNMENTAL RELATIONS." USA+45 NAT/G ROLE 20.
PAGE 5 B0097

ADMIN
EX/STRUC
LOBBY
GOV/REL

S65

ASHFORD D.E.,"BUREAUCRATS AND CITIZENS." MOROCCO
PAKISTAN PARTIC 20 TUNIS. PAGE 7 B0140

GOV/COMP
ADMIN
EX/STRUC
ROLE

S65

BROWN S.,"AN ALTERNATIVE TO THE GRAND DESIGN."
EUR+WWI FUT USA+45 INT/ORG NAT/G EX/STRUC FORCES
CREATE BAL/PWR DOMIN RIGID/FLEX ORD/FREE PWR
...NEW/IDEA RECORD EEC NATO 20. PAGE 16 B0327

VOL/ASSN
CONCPT
DIPLOM

S65

LONG T.G.,"THE ADMINISTRATIVE PROCESS: AGONIZING
REAPPRAISAL IN THE FTC." NAT/G REPRESENT 20 FTC.
PAGE 66 B1339

ADJUD
LOBBY
ADMIN
EX/STRUC

S65

RUBINSTEIN A.Z.,"YUGOSLAVIA'S OPENING SOCIETY." COM
USSR INTELL NAT/G LEGIS TOP/EX LEGIT CT/SYS

CONSTN
EX/STRUC

RIGID/FLEX ALL/VALS SOCISM...HUM TIME/SEQ TREND 20. YUGOSLAVIA
PAGE 92 B1851

S65

SIMON H.A.,"ADMINISTRATIVE DECISION-MAKING." USA+45 ADMIN
INGP/REL 20. PAGE 97 B1960
DECISION
EX/STRUC
METH/CNCPT

S65

TABORSKY E.,"CHANGE IN CZECHOSLOVAKIA." COM USSR ECO/DEV
ELITES INTELL AGRI INDUS NAT/G DELIB/GP EX/STRUC PLAN
ECO/TAC TOTALISM ATTIT RIGID/FLEX SOCISM...MGT CZECHOSLVK
CONCPT TREND 20. PAGE 102 B2067

B66

ADAMS J.C.,THE GOVERNMENT OF REPUBLICAN ITALY (2ND NAT/G
ED.). ITALY LOC/G POL/PAR DELIB/GP LEGIS WORKER CHOOSE
ADMIN CT/SYS FASCISM...CHARTS BIBLIOG 20 EX/STRUC
PARLIAMENT. PAGE 3 B0057 CONSTN

B66

ALEXANDER Y.,INTERNATIONAL TECHNICAL ASSISTANCE ECO/TAC
EXPERTS* A CASE STUDY OF THE U.N. EXPERIENCE. INT/ORG
ECO/UNDEV CONSULT EX/STRUC CREATE PLAN DIPLOM ADMIN
FOR/AID TASK EFFICIENCY...ORG/CHARTS UN. PAGE 4 MGT
B0074

B66

AMER ENTERPRISE INST PUB POL,CONGRESS: THE FIRST EFFICIENCY
BRANCH OF GOVERNMENT. EX/STRUC FEEDBACK REPRESENT LEGIS
INGP/REL PWR...DECISION METH/CNCPT PREDICT. PAGE 4 DELIB/GP
B0081 CONTROL

B66

ASHRAF A.,THE CITY GOVERNMENT OF CALCUTTA: A STUDY LOC/G
OF INERTIA. INDIA ELITES INDUS NAT/G EX/STRUC MUNIC
ACT/RES PLAN PROB/SOLV LEAD HABITAT...BIBLIOG 20 ADMIN
CALCUTTA. PAGE 7 B0141 ECO/UNDEV

B66

BHALERAO C.N.,PUBLIC SERVICE COMMISSIONS OF INDIA: NAT/G
A STUDY. INDIA SERV/IND EX/STRUC ROUTINE CHOOSE OP/RES
GOV/REL INGP/REL...KNO/TEST EXHIBIT 20. PAGE 11 LOC/G
B0233 ADMIN

B66

CARALEY D.,PARTY POLITICS AND NATIONAL ELECTIONS. POL/PAR
USA+45 STRATA LOC/G PROVS EX/STRUC BARGAIN ADMIN CHOOSE
SANCTION GP/REL ATTIT 20 DEMOCRAT REPUBLICAN. REPRESENT
PAGE 18 B0375 NAT/G

B66

CHAPMAN B.,THE PROFESSION OF GOVERNMENT: THE PUBLIC BIBLIOG
SERVICE IN EUROPE. CONSTN NAT/G POL/PAR EX/STRUC ADMIN
LEGIS TOP/EX PROB/SOLV DEBATE EXEC PARL/PROC PARTIC LEGIS
20. PAGE 20 B0411 GOV/COMP

B66

CORNWELL E.E. JR.,THE AMERICAN PRESIDENCY: VITAL CHIEF
CENTER. USA+45 USA-45 POL/PAR LEGIS PROB/SOLV EX/STRUC
CONTROL PARTIC GOV/REL 18/20 PRESIDENT. PAGE 23 NAT/G
B0478 ADMIN

B66

FINK M.,A SELECTIVE BIBLIOGRAPHY ON STATE BIBLIOG
CONSTITUTIONAL REVISION (PAMPHLET). USA+45 FINAN PROVS
EX/STRUC LEGIS EDU/PROP ADMIN CT/SYS APPORT CHOOSE LOC/G
GOV/REL 20. PAGE 35 B0720 CONSTN

B66

GERBERDING W.P.,UNITED STATES FOREIGN POLICY: PROB/SOLV
PERSPECTIVES AND ANALYSIS. USA+45 LEGIS EXEC LEAD CHIEF
REPRESENT PWR 20. PAGE 39 B0791 EX/STRUC
CONTROL

B66

GHOSH P.K.,THE CONSTITUTION OF INDIA: HOW IT HAS CONSTN
BEEN FRAMED. INDIA LOC/G DELIB/GP EX/STRUC NAT/G
PROB/SOLV BUDGET INT/TRADE CT/SYS CHOOSE...LING 20. LEGIS
PAGE 39 B0795 FEDERAL

B66

GREENE L.E.,GOVERNMENT IN TENNESSEE (2ND ED.). PROVS
USA+45 DIST/IND INDUS POL/PAR EX/STRUC LEGIS PLAN LOC/G
BUDGET GIVE CT/SYS...MGT T 20 TENNESSEE. PAGE 43 CONSTN
B0866 ADMIN

B66

HESSLER I.O.,29 WAYS TO GOVERN A CITY. EX/STRUC MUNIC
TOP/EX PROB/SOLV PARTIC CHOOSE REPRESENT EFFICIENCY GOV/COMP
...CHARTS 20 CITY/MGT MAYOR. PAGE 49 B0998 LOC/G
ADMIN

B66

HIDAYATULLAH M.,DEMOCRACY IN INDIA AND THE JUDICIAL NAT/G
PROCESS. INDIA EX/STRUC LEGIS LEAD GOV/REL ATTIT CT/SYS
ORD/FREE...MAJORIT CONCPT 20 NEHRU/J. PAGE 50 B1007 CONSTN
JURID

B66

INTERPARLIAMENTARY UNION,PARLIAMENTS: COMPARATIVE PARL/PROC
STUDY ON STRUCTURE AND FUNCTIONING OF LEGIS
REPRESENTATIVE INSTITUTIONS IN FIFTY-FIVE GOV/COMP
COUNTRIES. WOR+45 POL/PAR DELIB/GP BUDGET ADMIN EX/STRUC
CONTROL CHOOSE. PAGE 54 B1099

B66

JOHNSON N.,PARLIAMENT AND ADMINISTRATION: THE LEGIS
ESTIMATES COMMITTEE 1945-65. FUT UK NAT/G EX/STRUC ADMIN
PLAN BUDGET ORD/FREE...T 20 PARLIAMENT HOUSE/CMNS. FINAN
PAGE 57 B1147 DELIB/GP

B66

KIRDAR U.,THE STRUCTURE OF UNITED NATIONS ECONOMIC INT/ORG

AID TO UNDERDEVELOPED COUNTRIES. AGRI FINAN INDUS FOR/AID
NAT/G EX/STRUC PLAN GIVE TASK...POLICY 20 UN. ECO/UNDEV
PAGE 60 B1213 ADMIN

B66

LIVINGSTON J.C.,THE CONSENT OF THE GOVERNED. USA+45 NAT/G
EX/STRUC BAL/PWR DOMIN CENTRAL PERSON PWR...POLICY LOBBY
CONCPT OBS IDEA/COMP 20 CONGRESS. PAGE 66 B1331 MAJORIT
PARTIC

B66

MANSFIELD E.,MANAGERIAL ECONOMICS AND OPERATIONS ECO/TAC
RESEARCH: A NONMATHEMATICAL INTRODUCTION. USA+45 OP/RES
ELITES ECO/DEV CONSULT EX/STRUC PROB/SOLV ROUTINE MGT
EFFICIENCY OPTIMAL...GAME T 20. PAGE 69 B1396 COMPUTER

B66

MARTIN L.W.,DIPLOMACY IN MODERN EUROPEAN HISTORY. DIPLOM
EUR+WWI MOD/EUR INT/ORG NAT/G EX/STRUC ROUTINE WAR POLICY
PEACE TOTALISM PWR 15/20 COLD/WAR EUROPE/W. PAGE 70
B1411

B66

NEUMANN R.G.,THE GOVERNMENT OF THE GERMAN FEDERAL NAT/G
REPUBLIC. EUR+WWI GERMANY/W LOC/G EX/STRUC LEGIS POL/PAR
CT/SYS INGP/REL PWR...BIBLIOG 20 ADENAUER/K. DIPLOM
PAGE 78 B1573 CONSTN

B66

NIEBURG H.L.,IN THE NAME OF SCIENCE. USA+45 NAT/G
EX/STRUC LEGIS TEC/DEV BUDGET PAY AUTOMAT LOBBY PWR INDUS
...OBS 20. PAGE 78 B1581 TECHRACY

B66

PERKINS J.A.,THE UNIVERSITY IN TRANSITION. USA+45 ACADEM
SOCIETY FINAN INDUS NAT/G EX/STRUC ADMIN INGP/REL ORD/FREE
COST EFFICIENCY ATTIT 20. PAGE 82 B1658 CREATE
ROLE

B66

RICHARD J.B.,GOVERNMENT AND POLITICS OF WYOMING. PROVS
USA+45 POL/PAR EX/STRUC LEGIS CT/SYS LOBBY APPORT LOC/G
CHOOSE REPRESENT 20 WYOMING GOVERNOR. PAGE 88 B1773 ADMIN

B66

ROSHOLT R.L.,AN ADMINISTRATIVE HISTORY OF NASA, ADMIN
1958-1963. SPACE USA+45 FINAN LEAD...MGT CHARTS EX/STRUC
BIBLIOG 20 NASA. PAGE 90 B1824 ADJUST
DELIB/GP

B66

ROSS R.M.,STATE AND LOCAL GOVERNMENT AND LOC/G
ADMINISTRATION. USA+45 CONSTN POL/PAR EX/STRUC PROVS
LEGIS BUDGET EDU/PROP CONTROL CT/SYS CHOOSE GOV/REL MUNIC
T. PAGE 90 B1827 ADMIN

B66

SAPIN B.M.,THE MAKING OF UNITED STATES FOREIGN DIPLOM
POLICY. USA+45 INT/ORG DELIB/GP FORCES PLAN ECO/TAC EX/STRUC
CIVMIL/REL PRESIDENT. PAGE 92 B1868 DECISION
NAT/G

B66

TOTTEN G.O.,THE SOCIAL DEMOCRATIC MOVEMENT IN POL/PAR
PREWAR JAPAN. ASIA CHIEF EX/STRUC LEGIS DOMIN LEAD SOCISM
ROUTINE WAR 20 CHINJAP. PAGE 105 B2122 PARTIC
STRATA

B66

US DEPARTMENT OF THE ARMY,COMMUNIST CHINA: A BIBLIOG/A
STRATEGIC SURVEY: A BIBLIOGRAPHY (PAMPHLET NO. MARXISM
20-67). CHINA/COM COM INDIA USSR NAT/G POL/PAR S/ASIA
EX/STRUC FORCES NUC/PWR REV ATTIT...POLICY GEOG DIPLOM
CHARTS. PAGE 108 B2184

B66

WADIA M.,THE NATURE AND SCOPE OF MANAGEMENT. MGT
DELIB/GP EX/STRUC CREATE AUTOMAT CONTROL EFFICIENCY PROB/SOLV
...ANTHOL 20. PAGE 112 B2271 IDEA/COMP
ECO/TAC

B66

WARREN R.O.,GOVERNMENT IN METROPOLITAN REGIONS: A LOC/G
REAPPRAISAL OF FRACTIONATED POLITICAL ORGANIZATION. MUNIC
USA+45 ACT/RES PROB/SOLV REGION...CHARTS METH/COMP EX/STRUC
BIBLIOG CITY/MGT. PAGE 114 B2296 PLAN

B66

WILSON G.,CASES AND MATERIALS ON CONSTITUTIONAL AND JURID
ADMINISTRATIVE LAW. UK LAW NAT/G EX/STRUC LEGIS ADMIN
BAL/PWR BUDGET DIPLOM ADJUD CONTROL CT/SYS GOV/REL CONSTN
ORD/FREE 20 PARLIAMENT ENGLSH/LAW. PAGE 117 B2359 PWR

B66

YOUNG S.,MANAGEMENT: A SYSTEMS ANALYSIS. DELIB/GP PROB/SOLV
EX/STRUC ECO/TAC CONTROL EFFICIENCY...NET/THEORY MGT
20. PAGE 119 B2394 DECISION
SIMUL

B66

ZALEZNIK A.,HUMAN DILEMMAS OF LEADERSHIP. ELITES LEAD
INDUS EX/STRUC INGP/REL ATTIT...PSY 20. PAGE 119 PERSON
B2397 EXEC
MGT

L66

CRAIN R.L.,"STRUCTURE AND VALUES IN LOCAL POLITICAL MUNIC
SYSTEMS: THE CASE OF FLUORIDATION DECISIONS." EDU/PROP
EX/STRUC LEGIS LEAD PARTIC REPRESENT PWR...DECISION LOC/G
GOV/COMP. PAGE 25 B0501 ATTIT

L66

LEMARCHAND R.,"SOCIAL CHANGE AND POLITICAL NAT/G
MODERNISATION IN BURUNDI." AFR BURUNDI STRATA CHIEF STRUCT
EX/STRUC RIGID/FLEX PWR...SOC 20. PAGE 64 B1285 ELITES

CONSERVE
L66
MCAUSLAN J.P.W.,"CONSTITUTIONAL INNOVATION AND
POLITICAL STABILITY IN TANZANIA: A PRELIMINARY
ASSESSMENT." AFR TANZANIA ELITES CHIEF EX/STRUC
RIGID/FLEX PWR 20 PRESIDENT BUREAUCRCY. PAGE 71
B1440
CONSTN
NAT/G
EXEC
POL/PAR

S66
MARKSHAK J.,"ECONOMIC PLANNING AND THE COST OF
THINKING." COM MARKET EX/STRUC...DECISION GEN/LAWS.
PAGE 69 B1400
ECO/UNDEV
ECO/TAC
PLAN
ECO/DEV

S66
MATTHEWS D.G.,"ETHIOPIAN OUTLINE: A BIBLIOGRAPHIC
RESEARCH GUIDE." ETHIOPIA LAW STRUCT ECO/UNDEV AGRI
LABOR SECT CHIEF DELIB/GP EX/STRUC ADMIN...LING
ORG/CHARTS 20. PAGE 71 B1429
BIBLIOG
NAT/G
DIPLOM
POL/PAR

S66
WOLFINGER R.E.,"POLITICAL ETHOS AND THE STRUCTURE
OF CITY GOVERNMENT." POL/PAR EX/STRUC REPRESENT
GP/REL PERS/REL RIGID/FLEX PWR. PAGE 118 B2371
MUNIC
ATTIT
STRATA
GOV/COMP

C66
TACHERON D.G.,"THE JOB OF THE CONGRESSMAN: AN
INTRODUCTION TO SERVICES IN THE US HOUSE OF
REPRESENTATIVES." DELIB/GP EX/STRUC PRESS SENIOR
CT/SYS LOBBY CHOOSE GOV/REL...BIBLIOG 20 CONGRESS
HOUSE/REP SENATE. PAGE 102 B2068
LEGIS
PARL/PROC
ADMIN
POL/PAR

B67
BROWN L.N.,FRENCH ADMINISTRATIVE LAW. FRANCE UK
CONSTN NAT/G LEGIS DOMIN CONTROL EXEC PARL/PROC PWR
...JURID METH/COMP GEN/METH. PAGE 16 B0324
EX/STRUC
LAW
IDEA/COMP
CT/SYS

B67
BRZEZINSKI Z.K.,IDEOLOGY AND POWER IN SOVIET
POLITICS. USSR NAT/G POL/PAR PWR...GEN/LAWS 19/20.
PAGE 16 B0335
DIPLOM
EX/STRUC
MARXISM

B67
BRZEZINSKI Z.K.,THE SOVIET BLOC: UNITY AND CONFLICT
(2ND ED., REV., ENLARGED). COM POLAND USSR INTELL
CHIEF EX/STRUC CONTROL EXEC GOV/REL PWR MARXISM
...TREND IDEA/COMP 20 LENIN/VI MARX/KARL STALIN/J.
PAGE 16 B0336
NAT/G
DIPLOM

B67
BULPITT J.G.,PARTY POLITICS IN ENGLISH LOCAL
GOVERNMENT. UK CONSTN ACT/RES TAX CONTROL CHOOSE
REPRESENT GOV/REL KNOWL 20. PAGE 17 B0344
POL/PAR
LOC/G
ELITES
EX/STRUC

B67
BUREAU GOVERNMENT RES AND SERV.COUNTY GOVERNMENT
REORGANIZATION - A SELECTED ANNOTATED BIBLIOGRAPHY
(PAPER). USA+45 USA-45 LAW CONSTN MUNIC PROVS
EX/STRUC CREATE PLAN PROB/SOLV REPRESENT GOV/REL
20. PAGE 17 B0349
BIBLIOG/A
APPORT
LOC/G
ADMIN

B67
FARNSWORTH B.,WILLIAM C. BULLITT AND THE SOVIET
UNION. COM USA-45 USSR NAT/G CHIEF CONSULT DELIB/GP
EX/STRUC WAR REPRESENT MARXISM 20 WILSON/W
ROOSEVLT/F STALIN/J BULLITT/WC. PAGE 35 B0705
DIPLOM
BIOG
POLICY

B67
FINCHER F.,THE GOVERNMENT OF THE UNITED STATES.
USA+45 USA-45 POL/PAR CHIEF CT/SYS LOBBY GP/REL
INGP/REL...CONCPT CHARTS BIBLIOG T 18/20 PRESIDENT
CONGRESS SUPREME/CT. PAGE 35 B0719
NAT/G
EX/STRUC
LEGIS
OP/RES

B67
GITTELL M.,PARTICIPANTS AND PARTICIPATION: A STUDY
OF SCHOOL POLICY IN NEW YORK. USA+45 MUNIC EX/STRUC
BUDGET PAY ATTIT...POLICY 20 NEWYORK/C. PAGE 40
B0806
SCHOOL
DECISION
PARTIC
ADMIN

B67
HIRSCHMAN A.O.,DEVELOPMENT PROJECTS OBSERVED. INDUS
INT/ORG CONSULT EX/STRUC CREATE OP/RES ECO/TAC
DEMAND...POLICY MGT METH/COMP 20 WORLD/BANK.
PAGE 50 B1016
ECO/UNDEV
R+D
FINAN
PLAN

B67
MCCONNELL G.,THE MODERN PRESIDENCY. USA+45 CONSTN
TOP/EX DOMIN EXEC CHOOSE PWR...MGT 20. PAGE 72
B1446
NAT/G
CHIEF
EX/STRUC

B67
MILNE R.S.,GOVERNMENT AND POLITICS IN MALAYSIA.
INDONESIA MALAYSIA LOC/G EX/STRUC FORCES DIPLOM
GP/REL 20 SINGAPORE. PAGE 74 B1489
NAT/G
LEGIS
ADMIN

B67
MINTZ M.,BY PRESCRIPTION ONLY. USA+45 NAT/G
EX/STRUC PLAN TEC/DEV EXEC EFFICIENCY HEALTH...MGT
SOC/WK 20. PAGE 74 B1491
BIO/SOC
PROC/MFG
CONTROL
POLICY

B67
NIVEN R.,NIGERIA. NIGERIA CONSTN INDUS EX/STRUC
COLONIAL REV NAT/LISM...CHARTS 19/20. PAGE 78 B1584
NAT/G
REGION
CHOOSE
GP/REL

B67
PYE L.W.,SOUTHEAST ASIA'S POLITICAL SYSTEMS. ASIA
S/ASIA STRUCT ECO/UNDEV EX/STRUC CAP/ISM DIPLOM
ALL/IDEOS...TREND CHARTS. PAGE 85 B1724
NAT/G
POL/PAR
GOV/COMP

B67
RALSTON D.B.,THE ARMY OF THE REPUBLIC; THE PLACE OF
THE MILITARY IN THE POLITICAL EVOLUTION OF FRANCE
1871-1914. FRANCE MOD/EUR EX/STRUC LEGIS TOP/EX
DIPLOM ADMIN WAR GP/REL ROLE...BIBLIOG 19/20.
PAGE 86 B1730
FORCES
NAT/G
CIVMIL/REL
POLICY

B67
SCHEINMAN L.,EURATOM* NUCLEAR INTEGRATION IN
EUROPE. EX/STRUC LEAD 20 EURATOM. PAGE 93 B1885
INT/ORG
NAT/LISM
NUC/PWR
DIPLOM

B67
TOTMAN C.,POLITICS IN THE TOKUGAWA BAKUFU,
1600-1843. EX/STRUC...GOV/COMP 17/19 CHINJAP.
PAGE 105 B2120
NAT/G
ADMIN
LEAD

B67
WATERS M.,THE UNITED NATIONS* INTERNATIONAL
ORGANIZATION AND ADMINISTRATION. WOR+45 EX/STRUC
FORCES DIPLOM LEAD REGION ARMS/CONT REPRESENT
INGP/REL ROLE...METH/COMP ANTHOL 20 UN LEAGUE/NAT.
PAGE 114 B2301
CONSTN
INT/ORG
ADMIN
ADJUD

B67
WESTON P.B.,THE ADMINISTRATION OF JUSTICE. USA+45
CONSTN MUNIC NAT/G PROVS EX/STRUC JUDGE ADMIN
CONTROL SANCTION ORD/FREE...CHARTS 20. PAGE 115
B2328
CRIME
CT/SYS
JURID
ADJUD

L67
"RESTRICTIVE SOVEREIGN IMMUNITY, THE STATE
DEPARTMENT, AND THE COURTS." USA+45 USA-45 EX/STRUC
DIPLOM ADJUD CONTROL GOV/REL 19/20 DEPT/STATE
SUPREME/CT. PAGE 2 B0047
SOVEREIGN
ORD/FREE
PRIVIL
CT/SYS

L67
BESCOBY I.,"A COLONIAL ADMINISTRATION* AN ANALYSIS
OF ADMINISTRATION IN BRITISH COLUMBIA 1869-1871."
UK STRATA EX/STRUC LEGIS TASK GOV/REL EFFICIENCY
ROLE...MGT CHARTS 19. PAGE 11 B0232
ADMIN
CANADA
COLONIAL
LEAD

S67
ANDERSON L.G.,"ADMINISTERING A GOVERNMENT SOCIAL
SERVICE" NEW/ZEALND EX/STRUC TASK ROLE 20. PAGE 5
B0094
ADMIN
NAT/G
DELIB/GP
SOC/WK

S67
ANDERSON M.,"THE FRENCH PARLIAMENT." EUR+WWI FRANCE
MOD/EUR CONSTN POL/PAR CHIEF LEGIS LOBBY ATTIT ROLE
PWR 19/20. PAGE 5 B0095
PARL/PROC
LEAD
GOV/COMP
EX/STRUC

S67
BURACK E.H.,"INDUSTRIAL MANAGEMENT IN ADVANCED
PRODUCTION SYSTEMS: SOME THEORETICAL CONCEPTS AND
PRELIMINARY FINDINGS." INDUS CREATE PLAN PRODUC
ROLE...OBS STAND/INT DEEP/QU HYPO/EXP ORG/CHARTS
20. PAGE 17 B0346
ADMIN
MGT
TEC/DEV
EX/STRUC

S67
CONWAY J.E.,"MAKING RESEARCH EFFECTIVE IN
LEGISLATION." LAW R+D CONSULT EX/STRUC PLAN CONFER
ADMIN LEAD ROUTINE TASK INGP/REL DECISION. PAGE 23
B0469
ACT/RES
POLICY
LEGIS
PROB/SOLV

S67
DOERN G.B.,"THE ROYAL COMMISSIONS IN THE GENERAL
POLICY PROCESS AND IN FEDERAL-PROVINCIAL
RELATIONS." CANADA CONSTN ACADEM PROVS CONSULT
DELIB/GP LEGIS ACT/RES PROB/SOLV CONFER CONTROL
EFFICIENCY...METH/COMP 20 SENATE ROYAL/COMM.
PAGE 30 B0603
R+D
EX/STRUC
GOV/REL
NAT/G

S67
EDWARDS H.T.,"POWER STRUCTURE AND ITS COMMUNICATION
IN SAN JOSE, COSTA RICA." COSTA/RICA L/A+17C STRATA
FACE/GP POL/PAR EX/STRUC PROB/SOLV ADMIN LEAD
GP/REL PWR...STAT INT 20. PAGE 32 B0655
ELITES
INGP/REL
MUNIC
DOMIN

S67
FABREGA J.,"ANTECEDENTES EXTRANJEROS EN LA
CONSTITUCION PANAMENA." CUBA L/A+17C PANAMA URUGUAY
EX/STRUC LEGIS DIPLOM ORD/FREE 19/20 COLOMB
MEXIC/AMER. PAGE 34 B0694
CONSTN
JURID
NAT/G
PARL/PROC

S67
GORMAN W.,"ELLUL - A PROPHETIC VOICE." WOR+45
ELITES SOCIETY ACT/RES PLAN BAL/PWR DOMIN CONTROL
PARTIC TOTALISM PWR 20. PAGE 41 B0837
CREATE
ORD/FREE
EX/STRUC
UTOPIA

S67
GRUNDY K.W.,"THE POLITICAL USES OF IMAGINATION."
GHANA ELITES SOCIETY NAT/G DOMIN EDU/PROP COLONIAL
REGION REPRESENT GP/REL CENTRAL PWR MARXISM 20.
PAGE 44 B0897
NAT/LISM
EX/STRUC
AFR
LEAD

S67
HAIRE M.,"MANAGING MANAGEMENT MANPOWER." EX/STRUC
OP/RES PAY EDU/PROP COST EFFICIENCY...PREDICT SIMUL
20. PAGE 45 B0920
MGT
EXEC
LEAD
INDUS

S67
HSUEH C.T.,"THE CULTURAL REVOLUTION AND LEADERSHIP
CRISIS IN COMMUNIST CHINA." CHINA/COM POL/PAR
EX/STRUC FORCES EDU/PROP ATTIT PWR...POLICY 20.
PAGE 52 B1054
LEAD
REV
CULTURE
MARXISM

S67
IDENBURG P.J.,"POLITICAL STRUCTURAL DEVELOPMENT IN
AFR

TROPICAL AFRICA." UK ECO/UNDEV KIN POL/PAR CHIEF   CONSTN
EX/STRUC CREATE COLONIAL CONTROL REPRESENT RACE/REL   NAT/G
...MAJORIT TREND 20. PAGE 53 B1074   GOV/COMP
  S67

JONES G.S.,"STRATEGIC PLANNING." USA+45 EX/STRUC   PLAN
FORCES DETER WAR 20 PRESIDENT. PAGE 57 B1150   DECISION
  DELIB/GP
  POLICY
  S67

LALL B.G.,"GAPS IN THE ABM DEBATE." NAT/G DIPLOM   NUC/PWR
DETER CIVMIL/REL 20. PAGE 62 B1251   ARMS/CONT
  EX/STRUC
  FORCES
  S67

LEWIS P.H.,"LEADERSHIP AND CONFLICT WITHIN   POL/PAR
FEBRERISTA PARTY OF PARAGUAY." L/A+17C PARAGUAY   ELITES
EX/STRUC DOMIN SENIOR CONTROL INGP/REL CENTRAL   LEAD
FEDERAL ATTIT 20. PAGE 65 B1305   S67

LINEBERRY R.L.,"REFORMISM AND PUBLIC POLICIES IN   DECISION
AMERICAN CITIES." USA+45 POL/PAR EX/STRUC LEGIS   POLICY
BUDGET TAX GP/REL...STAT CHARTS. PAGE 65 B1317   MUNIC
  LOC/G
  S67

MACDONALD G.J.F.,"SCIENCE AND SPACE POLICY* HOW   SPACE
DOES IT GET PLANNED?" R+D CREATE TEC/DEV BUDGET   PLAN
ADMIN ROUTINE...DECISION NASA. PAGE 67 B1357   MGT
  EX/STRUC
  S67

MAINZER L.C.,"HONOR IN THE BUREAUCRATIC LIFE."   ADMIN
REPRESENT EFFICIENCY 20. PAGE 68 B1382   MORAL
  EX/STRUC
  EXEC
  S67

MERON T.,"THE UN'S 'COMMON SYSTEM' OF SALARY,   ADMIN
ALLOWANCE, AND BENEFITS: CRITICAL APPR'SAL OF COORD   EX/STRUC
IN PERSONNEL MATTERS." VOL/ASSN PAY EFFICIENCY   INT/ORG
...CHARTS 20 UN. PAGE 73 B1470   BUDGET
  S67

RAUM O.,"THE MODERN LEADERSHIP GROUP AMONG THE   RACE/REL
SOUTH AFRICAN XHOSA." SOUTH/AFR SOCIETY SECT   KIN
EX/STRUC REPRESENT GP/REL INGP/REL PERSON   LEAD
...METH/COMP 17/20 XHOSA NEGRO. PAGE 86 B1743   CULTURE
  S67

ROSE A.M.,"CONFIDENCE AND THE CORPORATION." LG/CO   INDUS
CONTROL CRIME INCOME PROFIT 20. PAGE 90 B1818   EX/STRUC
  VOL/ASSN
  RESPECT
  S67

ROTBERG R.I.,"COLONIALISM AND AFTER: THE POLITICAL   BIBLIOG/A
LITERATURE OF CENTRAL AFRICA - A BIBLIOGRAPHIC   COLONIAL
ESSAY." AFR CHIEF EX/STRUC REV INGP/REL RACE/REL   DIPLOM
SOVEREIGN 20. PAGE 91 B1833   NAT/G
  S67

RUBIN R.I.,"THE LEGISLATIVE-EXECUTIVE RELATIONS OF   LEGIS
THE UNITED STATES INFORMATION AGENCY." USA+45   EX/STRUC
EDU/PROP TASK INGP/REL EFFICIENCY ISOLAT ATTIT ROLE   GP/REL
USIA CONGRESS. PAGE 91 B1850   PROF/ORG
  S67

SCOTT W.R.,"ORGANIZATIONAL EVALUATION AND   EXEC
AUTHORITY." CONTROL SANCTION PERS/REL ATTIT DRIVE   WORKER
...SOC CONCPT OBS CHARTS IDEA/COMP 20. PAGE 95   INSPECT
B1921   EX/STRUC
  S67

SHOEMAKER R.L.,"JAPANESE ARMY AND THE WEST." ASIA   FORCES
ELITES EX/STRUC DIPLOM DOMIN EDU/PROP COERCE ATTIT   TEC/DEV
AUTHORIT PWR 1/20 CHINJAP. PAGE 96 B1950   WAR
  TOTALISM
  S67

TATU M.,"URSS: LES FLOTTEMENTS DE LA DIRECTION   POLICY
COLLEGIALE." UAR USSR CHIEF LEAD INGP/REL   NAT/G
EFFICIENCY...DECISION TREND 20 MID/EAST. PAGE 103   EX/STRUC
B2082   DIPLOM
  S67

VERGIN R.C.,"COMPUTER INDUCED ORGANIZATION   COMPUTER
CHANGES." FUT USA+45 R+D CREATE OP/RES TEC/DEV   DECISION
ADJUST CENTRAL...MGT INT CON/ANAL COMPUT/IR.   AUTOMAT
PAGE 112 B2260   EX/STRUC
  S67

ZASLOW M.,"RECENT CONSTITUTIONAL DEVELOPMENTS IN   GOV/REL
CANADA'S NORTHERN TERRITORIES." CANADA LOC/G   REGION
DELIB/GP EX/STRUC LEGIS ADMIN ORD/FREE...TREND 20.   CONSTN
PAGE 119 B2398   FEDERAL
  B86

BOLINSBROKE H ST J.,A DISSERTATION UPON PARTIES   CONSERVE
(1729). UK LEGIS CHOOSE GOV/REL SOVEREIGN...TRADIT   POL/PAR
18 PARLIAMENT. PAGE 13 B0269   CHIEF
  EX/STRUC
  B87

KINNEAR J.B.,PRINCIPLES OF CIVIL GOVERNMENT.   POL/PAR
MOD/EUR USA+45 CONSTN LOC/G EX/STRUC ADMIN   NAT/G
PARL/PROC RACE/REL...CONCPT 18/19. PAGE 60 B1210   GOV/COMP
  REPRESENT

EXEC....EXECUTIVE PROCESS

RIORDAN W.L.,PLUNKITT OF TAMMANY HALL. USA-45   B05
SOCIETY PROB/SOLV EXEC LEAD TASK CHOOSE ALL/VALS   POL/PAR
...RECORD ANTHOL 20 REFORMERS TAMMANY NEWYORK/C   MUNIC
PLUNKITT/G. PAGE 88 B1789   CHIEF
  ATTIT
  B08

WILSON W.,CONSTITUTIONAL GOVERNMENT IN THE UNITED   NAT/G
STATES. USA-45 LAW POL/PAR PROVS CHIEF LEGIS   GOV/REL
BAL/PWR ADJUD EXEC FEDERAL PWR 18/20 SUPREME/CT   CONSTN
HOUSE/REP SENATE. PAGE 117 B2362   PARL/PROC
  B16

TREITSCHKE H.,POLITICS. UNIV SOCIETY STRATA NAT/G   EXEC
EX/STRUC LEGIS DOMIN EDU/PROP ATTIT PWR RESPECT   ELITES
...CONCPT TIME/SEQ GEN/LAWS TOT/POP 20. PAGE 105   GERMANY
B2127   B19

SUTHERLAND G.,CONSTITUTIONAL POWER AND WORLD   USA-45
AFFAIRS. CONSTN STRUCT INT/ORG NAT/G CHIEF LEGIS   EXEC
ACT/RES PLAN GOV/REL ALL/VALS...OBS TIME/SEQ   DIPLOM
CONGRESS VAL/FREE 20 PRESIDENT. PAGE 102 B2056   N19

LA PALOMBARA J.G.,ALTERNATIVE STRATEGIES FOR   ECO/UNDEV
DEVELOPING ADMINISTRATIVE CAPABILITIES IN EMERGING   MGT
NATIONS (PAMPHLET). POL/PAR EX/STRUC PROB/SOLV   EXEC
PLURISM...POLICY METH/COMP. PAGE 62 B1248   ADMIN
  N19

OPERATIONS AND POLICY RESEARCH,PERU ELECTION   CHOOSE
MEMORANDA (PAMPHLET). L/A+17C PERU POL/PAR LEGIS   CONSTN
EXEC APPORT REPRESENT 20. PAGE 80 B1611   SUFF
  NAT/G
  N19

TREVELYAN G.M.,THE TWO-PARTY SYSTEM IN ENGLISH   PARL/PROC
POLITICAL HISTORY (PAMPHLET). UK CHIEF LEGIS   POL/PAR
COLONIAL EXEC REV CHOOSE 17/19. PAGE 105 B2128   NAT/G
  PWR
  B21

BRYCE J.,MODERN DEMOCRACIES. FUT NEW/ZEALND USA-45   NAT/G
LAW CONSTN POL/PAR PROVS VOL/ASSN EX/STRUC LEGIS   TREND
LEGIT CT/SYS EXEC KNOWL CONGRESS AUSTRAL 20.
PAGE 16 B0332   B23

FRANK T.,A HISTORY OF ROME. MEDIT-7 INTELL SOCIETY   EXEC
LOC/G NAT/G POL/PAR FORCES LEGIS DOMIN LEGIT   STRUCT
ALL/VALS...POLICY CONCPT TIME/SEQ GEN/LAWS ROM/EMP   ELITES
ROM/EMP. PAGE 37 B0749   B24

BAGEHOT W.,THE ENGLISH CONSTITUTION AND OTHER   NAT/G
POLITICAL ESSAYS. UK DELIB/GP BAL/PWR ADMIN CONTROL   STRUCT
EXEC ROUTINE CONSERVE...METH PARLIAMENT 19/20.   CONCPT
PAGE 8 B0160   B27

DICKINSON J.,ADMINISTRATIVE JUSTICE AND THE   CT/SYS
SUPREMACY OF LAW IN THE UNITED STATES. USA-45 LAW   ADJUD
INDUS DOMIN EDU/PROP CONTROL EXEC GP/REL ORD/FREE   ADMIN
...POLICY JURID 19/20. PAGE 29 B0586   NAT/G
  B27

WILLOUGHBY W.F.,PRINCIPLES OF PUBLIC ADMINISTRATION   NAT/G
WITH SPECIAL REFERENCE TO THE NATIONAL AND STATE   EX/STRUC
GOVERNMENTS OF THE UNITED STATES. FINAN PROVS CHIEF   OP/RES
CONSULT LEGIS CREATE BUDGET EXEC ROUTINE GOV/REL   ADMIN
CENTRAL...MGT 20 BUR/BUDGET CONGRESS PRESIDENT.
PAGE 117 B2356   S30

CRAWFORD F.G.,"THE EXECUTIVE BUDGET DECISION IN NEW   LEAD
YORK." LEGIS EXEC PWR NEW/YORK. PAGE 25 B0504   BUDGET
  PROVS
  PROB/SOLV
  B34

RIDLEY C.E.,THE CITY-MANAGER PROFESSION. CHIEF PLAN   MUNIC
ADMIN CONTROL ROUTINE CHOOSE...TECHNIC CHARTS   EX/STRUC
GOV/COMP BIBLIOG 20. PAGE 88 B1780   LOC/G
  EXEC
  B38

DAY C.,A HISTORY OF COMMERCE. CHRIST-17C EUR+WWI   MARKET
ISLAM MEDIT-7 MOD/EUR USA-45 ECO/DEV FINAN NAT/G   INT/TRADE
ECO/TAC EXEC ROUTINE PWR WEALTH HIST/WRIT. PAGE 27
B0546   B38

PETTEE G.S.,THE PROCESS OF REVOLUTION. COM FRANCE   COERCE
ITALY MOD/EUR RUSSIA SPAIN WOR-45 ELITES INTELL   CONCPT
SOCIETY STRATA STRUCT INT/ORG NAT/G POL/PAR ACT/RES   REV
PLAN EDU/PROP LEGIT EXEC...SOC MYTH TIME/SEQ
TOT/POP 18/20. PAGE 82 B1664   B38

RAPPARD W.E.,THE CRISIS OF DEMOCRACY. EUR+WWI UNIV   NAT/G
WOR-45 CULTURE SOCIETY ECO/DEV INT/ORG POL/PAR   CONCPT
ACT/RES EDU/PROP EXEC CHOOSE ATTIT ALL/VALS...SOC
OBS HIST/WRIT TIME/SEQ LEAGUE/NAT NAZI TOT/POP 20.
PAGE 86 B1741   B39

MCCAMY J.L.,GOVERNMENT PUBLICITY: ITS PRACTICE IN   EDU/PROP
FEDERAL ADMINISTRATION. USA-45 COM/IND ADMIN   NAT/G
CONTROL EXEC PARTIC INGP/REL...SOC 20. PAGE 71   PLAN
B1442   ATTIT
  C39

REISCHAUER R.,"JAPAN'S GOVERNMENT--POLITICS."   NAT/G

CONSTN STRATA POL/PAR FORCES LEGIS DIPLOM ADMIN
EXEC CENTRAL...POLICY BIBLIOG 20 CHINJAP. PAGE 87
B1764
S/ASIA
CONCPT
ROUTINE

B41
YOUNG G.,FEDERALISM AND FREEDOM. EUR+WWI MOD/EUR
RUSSIA USA-45 WOR-45 SOCIETY STRUCT ECO/DEV INT/ORG
EXEC FEDERAL ATTIT PERSON ALL/VALS...OLD/LIB CONCPT
OBS TREND LEAGUE/NAT TOT/POP. PAGE 119 B2392
NAT/G
WAR

S41
STOKE H.W.,"EXECUTIVE LEADERSHIP AND THE GROWTH OF
PROPAGANDA." USA-45 NAT/G EX/STRUC LEGIS TOP/EX
PARL/PROC REPRESENT ORD/FREE PWR...MAJORIT 20.
PAGE 101 B2042
EXEC
LEAD
EDU/PROP
ADMIN

S43
GOLDEN C.S.,"NEW PATTERNS OF DEMOCRACY." NEIGH
DELIB/GP EDU/PROP EXEC PARTIC...MGT METH/CNCPT OBS
TREND. PAGE 40 B0815
LABOR
REPRESENT
LG/CO
GP/REL

S44
KEFAUVER E.,"THE NEED FOR BETTER EXECUTIVE-
LEGISLATIVE TEAMWORK IN THE NATIONAL GOVERNMENT."
USA-45 CONSTN NAT/G ROUTINE...TRADIT CONGRESS
REFORMERS. PAGE 59 B1188
LEGIS
EXEC
CONFER
LEAD

B45
RANSHOFFEN-WERTHEIMER EF,THE INTERNATIONAL
SECRETARIAT: A GREAT EXPERIMENT IN INTERNATIONAL
ADMINISTRATION. EUR+WWI FUT CONSTN FACE/GP CONSULT
DELIB/GP ACT/RES ADMIN ROUTINE PEACE ORD/FREE...MGT
RECORD ORG/CHARTS LEAGUE/NAT WORK 20. PAGE 86 B1731
INT/ORG
EXEC

S45
WHITE L.D.,"CONGRESSIONAL CONTROL OF THE PUBLIC
SERVICE." USA-45 NAT/G CONSULT DELIB/GP PLAN SENIOR
CONGRESS. PAGE 116 B2335
LEGIS
EXEC
POLICY
CONTROL

B46
CLOUGH S.B.,ECONOMIC HISTORY OF EUROPE. CHRIST-17C
EUR+WWI MOD/EUR WOR-45 SOCIETY EXEC ATTIT WEALTH
...CONCPT GEN/LAWS WORK TOT/POP VAL/FREE 7/20.
PAGE 22 B0440
ECO/TAC
CAP/ISM

L46
FORRESTAL J.,"THE NAVY: A STUDY IN ADMINISTRATION."
ELITES FACE/GP EX/STRUC PROB/SOLV REPRESENT
EFFICIENCY PRODUC. PAGE 37 B0741
FORCES
INGP/REL
ROUTINE
EXEC

S46
CAMPBELL A.,"THE USES OF INTERVIEW SURVEYS IN
FEDERAL ADMINISTRATION" PROB/SOLV EXEC PARTIC
DECISION. PAGE 18 B0369
INT
ADMIN
EX/STRUC
REPRESENT

B47
BARNARD C.,THE FUNCTIONS OF THE EXECUTIVE. USA+45
ELITES INTELL LEGIT ATTIT DRIVE PERSON SKILL...PSY
SOC METH/CNCPT SOC/EXP GEN/METH VAL/FREE 20. PAGE 9
B0187
EXEC
EX/STRUC
ROUTINE

B47
BORGESE G.,COMMON CAUSE. LAW CONSTN SOCIETY STRATA
ECO/DEV INT/ORG POL/PAR FORCES LEGIS TOP/EX CAP/ISM
DIPLOM ADMIN EXEC ATTIT PWR 20. PAGE 14 B0279
WOR+45
NAT/G
SOVEREIGN
REGION

B47
FLYNN E.J.,YOU'RE THE BOSS. USA-45 ELITES TOP/EX
DOMIN CONTROL EXEC LEAD REPRESENT 19/20 NEWYORK/C
ROOSEVLT/F FLYNN/BOSS BOSSISM. PAGE 36 B0732
LOC/G
MUNIC
BIOG
POL/PAR

B47
KEFAUVER E.,A TWENTIETH-CENTURY CONGRESS. POL/PAR
EX/STRUC SENIOR ADMIN CONTROL EXEC LOBBY CHOOSE
EFFICIENCY PWR. PAGE 59 B1189
LEGIS
DELIB/GP
ROUTINE
TOP/EX

B47
PATTERSON C.P.,PRESIDENTIAL GOVERNMENT IN THE
UNITED STATES - THE UNWRITTEN CONSTITUTION. USA+45
DELIB/GP EX/STRUC ADJUD ADMIN EXEC...DECISION
PRESIDENT. PAGE 81 B1643
CHIEF
NAT/G
CONSTN
POL/PAR

B47
TAPPAN P.W.,DELINQUENT GIRLS IN COURT. USA-45 MUNIC
EX/STRUC FORCES ADMIN EXEC ADJUST SEX RESPECT
...JURID SOC/WK 20 NEWYORK/C FEMALE/SEX. PAGE 103
B2078
CT/SYS
AGE/Y
CRIME
ADJUD

B48
HULL C.,THE MEMOIRS OF CORDELL HULL (VOLUME ONE).
USA-45 WOR-45 CONSTN FAM LOC/G NAT/G PROVS DELIB/GP
FORCES LEGIS TOP/EX BAL/PWR LEGIT ADMIN EXEC WAR
ATTIT ORD/FREE PWR...MAJORIT SELF/OBS TIME/SEQ
TREND NAZI 20. PAGE 52 B1062
BIOG
DIPLOM

B48
SPERO S.D.,GOVERNMENT AS EMPLOYER. USA+45 NAT/G
EX/STRUC ADMIN CONTROL EXEC 20. PAGE 99 B2005
SOVEREIGN
INGP/REL
REPRESENT
CONFER

B48
WHITE L.D.,INTRODUCTION OT THE STUDY OF PUBLIC
ADMINISTRATION. STRUCT PLAN PROB/SOLV EXEC ROUTINE
GOV/REL EFFICIENCY PWR CHARTS. PAGE 116 B2336
ADMIN
MGT
EX/STRUC
NAT/G

B49
APPLEBY P.H.,POLICY AND ADMINISTRATION. USA+45
NAT/G LOBBY PWR 20. PAGE 6 B0116
REPRESENT
EXEC
ADMIN
CLIENT

B49
BURNS J.M.,CONGRESS ON TRIAL: THE LEGISLATIVE
PROCESS AND THE ADMINISTRATIVE STATE. USA+45 NAT/G
ADMIN ROUTINE REPRESENT...PREDICT TREND. PAGE 17
B0354
LEGIS
EXEC
GP/REL
PWR

B49
BUSH V.,MODERN ARMS AND FREE MEN. WOR-45 SOCIETY
NAT/G ECO/TAC DOMIN LEGIT EXEC COERCE DETER ATTIT
DRIVE ORD/FREE PWR...CONCPT MYTH COLD/WAR 20
COLD/WAR. PAGE 18 B0361
TEC/DEV
FORCES
NUC/PWR
WAR

B49
MCLEAN J.M.,THE PUBLIC SERVICE AND UNIVERSITY
EDUCATION. UK USA-45 DELIB/GP EX/STRUC TOP/EX ADMIN
...GOV/COMP METH/COMP NAT/COMP ANTHOL 20. PAGE 72
B1455
ACADEM
NAT/G
EXEC
EDU/PROP

B49
RIDDICK F.M.,THE UNITED STATES CONGRESS
ORGANIZATION AND PROCEDURE. POL/PAR DELIB/GP
PROB/SOLV DEBATE CONTROL EXEC LEAD INGP/REL PWR
...MAJORIT DECISION CONGRESS PRESIDENT. PAGE 88
B1777
LEGIS
PARL/PROC
CHIEF
EX/STRUC

B49
ROSENHAUPT H.W.,HOW TO WAGE PEACE. USA+45 SOCIETY
STRATA STRUCT R+D INT/ORG POL/PAR LEGIS ACT/RES
CREATE PLAN EDU/PROP ADMIN EXEC ATTIT ALL/VALS
...TIME/SEQ TREND COLD/WAR 20. PAGE 90 B1822
INTELL
CONCPT
DIPLOM

B49
SCHWARTZ B.,LAW AND THE EXECUTIVE IN BRITAIN: A
COMPARATIVE STUDY. UK USA+45 LAW EX/STRUC PWR
...GOV/COMP 20. PAGE 95 B1911
ADMIN
EXEC
CONTROL
REPRESENT

B49
SHISTER J.,ECONOMICS OF THE LABOR MARKET. LOC/G
NAT/G WORKER TEC/DEV BARGAIN PAY PRICE EXEC GP/REL
INCOME...MGT T 20. PAGE 96 B1949
MARKET
LABOR
INDUS

B49
WRIGHT J.H.,PUBLIC RELATIONS IN MANAGEMENT. USA+45
USA+45 ECO/DEV LG/CO SML/CO CONSULT EXEC TASK
PROFIT ATTIT ROLE 20. PAGE 118 B2382
MGT
PLAN
EDU/PROP
PARTIC

L49
BROOKINGS INST.,"GOVERNMENT MECHANISM FOR CONDUCT
OF US FOREIGN RELATIONS." USA+45 CONSTN NAT/G LEGIS
CT/SYS...MGT TIME/SEQ CONGRESS TOT/POP 20. PAGE 15
B0316
EXEC
STRUCT
DIPLOM

L49
FAINSED M.,"RECENT DEVELOPMENTS IN SOVIET PUBLIC
ADMINISTRATION." USSR EXEC 20. PAGE 34 B0699
DOMIN
CONTROL
CENTRAL
EX/STRUC

S49
CORWIN E.S.,"THE PRESIDENCY IN PERSPECTIVE." USA+45
USA-45 NAT/G LEAD 20 PRESIDENT. PAGE 24 B0485
CHIEF
PWR
REPRESENT
EXEC

B50
MCCAMY J.,THE ADMINISTRATION OF AMERICAN FOREIGN
AFFAIRS. USA+45 SOCIETY INT/ORG NAT/G ACT/RES PLAN
INT/TRADE EDU/PROP ADJUD ALL/VALS...METH/CNCPT
TIME/SEQ CONGRESS 20. PAGE 71 B1441
EXEC
STRUCT
DIPLOM

L50
US SENATE COMM. GOVT. OPER.,"REVISION OF THE UN
CHARTER." FUT USA+45 WOR+45 CONSTN ECO/DEV
ECO/UNDEV NAT/G DELIB/GP ACT/RES CREATE PLAN EXEC
ROUTINE CHOOSE ALL/VALS...POLICY CONCPT CONGRESS UN
TOT/POP 20 COLD/WAR. PAGE 111 B2235
INT/ORG
LEGIS
PEACE

S50
DALTON M.,"CONFLICTS BETWEEN STAFF AND LINE
MANAGERIAL OFFICERS" (BMR). USA+45 USA-45 ELITES
LG/CO WORKER PROB/SOLV ADMIN EXEC EFFICIENCY PRODUC
...GP/COMP 20. PAGE 26 B0526
MGT
ATTIT
GP/REL
INDUS

B51
GUETZKOW H.,GROUPS, LEADERSHIP, AND MEN. FACE/GP
SECT EDU/PROP EXEC PERSON RESPECT...PERS/TEST
GEN/METH 20. PAGE 44 B0901
ATTIT
SOC
ELITES

B51
LASSWELL H.D.,THE POLITICAL WRITINGS OF HAROLD D
LASSWELL. UNIV DOMIN EXEC LEAD RATIONAL ATTIT DRIVE
ROLE ALL/VALS...OBS BIOG 20. PAGE 63 B1269
PERSON
PSY
INGP/REL
CONCPT

B51
MAASS A.,MUDDY WATERS: THE ARMY ENGINEERS AND THE
NATIONS RIVERS. USA-45 PROF/ORG CONSULT LEGIS ADMIN
EXEC ROLE PWR...SOC PRESIDENT 20. PAGE 67 B1353
FORCES
GP/REL
LOBBY
CONSTRUC

B51
PETERSON F.,SURVEY OF LABOR ECONOMICS (REV. ED.).
STRATA ECO/DEV LABOR INSPECT BARGAIN PAY PRICE EXEC
ROUTINE GP/REL ALL/VALS ORD/FREE 20 AFL/CIO
DEPT/LABOR. PAGE 82 B1662
WORKER
DEMAND
IDEA/COMP
T

B51

SMITH L.,AMERICAN DEMOCRACY AND MILITARY POWER. FORCES
USA+45 USA-45 CONSTN STRATA NAT/G LEGIS ACT/RES STRUCT
LEGIT ADMIN EXEC GOV/REL ALL/VALS...CONCPT WAR
HIST/WRIT CONGRESS 20. PAGE 98 B1982

B52

APPLEBY P.H.,MORALITY AND ADMINISTRATION IN REPRESENT
DEMOCRATIC GOVERNMENT. USA+45 CLIENT NAT/G EXEC LOBBY
EFFICIENCY 20. PAGE 6 B0117 ADMIN
EX/STRUC

B52

EGLE W.P.,ECONOMIC STABILIZATION. USA+45 SOCIETY NAT/G
FINAN MARKET PLAN ECO/TAC DOMIN EDU/PROP LEGIT EXEC ECO/DEV
WEALTH...CONCPT METH/CNCPT TREND HYPO/EXP GEN/METH CAP/ISM
TOT/POP VAL/FREE 20. PAGE 32 B0656

B52

NASH B.D.,STAFFING THE PRESIDENCY: PLANNING EX/STRUC
PAMPHLET NO. 80 (PAMPHLET). NAT/G CHIEF CONSULT EXEC
DELIB/GP CONFER ADMIN 20 PRESIDENT. PAGE 77 B1557 TOP/EX
ROLE

B52

ULAM A.B.,TITOISM AND THE COMINFORM. USSR WOR+45 COM
STRUCT INT/ORG NAT/G ACT/RES PLAN EXEC ATTIT DRIVE POL/PAR
ALL/VALS...CONCPT OBS VAL/FREE 20 COMINTERN TOTALISM
TITO/MARSH. PAGE 106 B2145 YUGOSLAVIA

B52

VANDENBOSCH A.,THE UN: BACKGROUND, ORGANIZATION, DELIB/GP
FUNCTIONS, ACTIVITIES. WOR+45 LAW CONSTN STRUCT TIME/SEQ
INT/ORG CONSULT BAL/PWR EDU/PROP EXEC ALL/VALS PEACE
...POLICY CONCPT UN 20. PAGE 112 B2254

S52

MASLAND J.W.,"THE NATIONAL WAR COLLEGE AND THE CIVMIL/REL
ADMINISTRATION OF FOREIGN AFFAIRS." USA+45 NAT/G EX/STRUC
FORCES EXEC 20. PAGE 70 B1422 REPRESENT
PROB/SOLV

S52

SOMERS H.M.,"THE PRESIDENT AS ADMINISTRATOR." CONTROL
USA+45 NAT/G ADMIN REPRESENT GOV/REL 20 PRESIDENT. EFFICIENCY
PAGE 99 B1996 EX/STRUC
EXEC

B53

MACMAHON A.W.,ADMINISTRATION IN FOREIGN AFFAIRS. USA+45
NAT/G CONSULT DELIB/GP LEGIS ACT/RES CREATE ADMIN ROUTINE
EXEC RIGID/FLEX PWR...METH/CNCPT TIME/SEQ TOT/POP FOR/AID
VAL/FREE 20. PAGE 68 B1369 DIPLOM

L53

NEWMAN F.C.,"CONGRESS AND THE FAITHFUL EXECUTION OF REPRESENT
LAWS - SHOULD LEGISLATORS SUPERVISE CONTROL
ADMINISTRATORS." USA+45 NAT/G EX/STRUC EXEC PWR ADMIN
POLICY. PAGE 78 B1579 LEGIS

S53

BOSWORTH K.A.,"THE POLITICS OF MANAGEMENT PWR
IMPROVEMENT IN THE STATES" USA+45 POLICY. PAGE 14 PROVS
B0280 LEGIS
EXEC

B54

COMBS C.H.,DECISION PROCESSES. INTELL SOCIETY MATH
DELIB/GP CREATE TEC/DEV DOMIN LEGIT EXEC CHOOSE DECISION
DRIVE RIGID/FLEX KNOWL PWR...PHIL/SCI SOC
METH/CNCPT CONT/OBS REC/INT PERS/TEST SAMP/SIZ BIOG
SOC/EXP WORK. PAGE 22 B0455

B54

HOBBS E.H.,BEHIND THE PRESIDENT - A STUDY OF EX/STRUC
EXECUTIVE OFFICE AGENCIES. USA+45 NAT/G PLAN BUDGET DELIB/GP
ECO/TAC EXEC ORD/FREE 20 BUR/BUDGET. PAGE 50 B1022 CONFER
CONSULT

B54

SCHWARTZ B.,FRENCH ADMINISTRATIVE LAW AND THE JURID
COMMON-LAW WORLD. FRANCE CULTURE LOC/G NAT/G PROVS LAW
DELIB/GP EX/STRUC LEGIS PROB/SOLV CT/SYS EXEC METH/COMP
GOV/REL...IDEA/COMP ENGLSH/LAW. PAGE 95 B1912 ADJUD

L54

FURNISS E.S.,"WEAKNESSES IN FRENCH FOREIGN POLICY- NAT/G
MAKING." EUR+WWI LEGIS LEGIT EXEC ATTIT RIGID/FLEX STRUCT
ORD/FREE...SOC CONCPT METH/CNCPT OBS 20. PAGE 38 DIPLOM
B0766 FRANCE

S54

APPLEBY P.H.,"BUREAUCRACY AND THE FUTURE." USA+45 EX/STRUC
NAT/G CONTROL EXEC...MAJORIT 20. PAGE 6 B0119 LOBBY
REPRESENT
ADMIN

S54

GILBERT C.E.,"LEGISLATIVE CONTROL OF THE CONTROL
BUREAUCRACY." USA+45 NAT/G ADMIN EXEC 20. PAGE 39 EX/STRUC
B0798 REPRESENT
GOV/REL

S54

LONG N.E.,"PUBLIC POLICY AND ADMINISTRATION: THE PROB/SOLV
GOALS OF RATIONALITY AND RESPONSIBILITY." EX/STRUC EXEC
ADMIN LEAD 20. PAGE 66 B1338 REPRESENT

C54

ROBSON W.A.,"GREAT CITIES OF THE WORLD: THEIR LOC/G
GOVERNMENT, POLITICS, AND PLANNING." CONSTN FINAN MUNIC
EX/STRUC ADMIN EXEC CHOOSE GOV/REL...STAT TREND PLAN
ANTHOL BIBLIOG 20. PAGE 89 B1806 PROB/SOLV

C54

ZELLER B.,"AMERICAN STATE LEGISLATURES: REPORT ON REPRESENT
THE COMMITTEE ON AMERICAN LEGISLATURES." CONSTN LEGIS
POL/PAR EX/STRUC CONFER ADMIN CONTROL EXEC LOBBY PROVS
ROUTINE GOV/REL...POLICY BIBLIOG 20. PAGE 119 B2401 APPORT

B55

BLAU P.M.,THE DYNAMICS OF BUREAUCRACY: A STUDY OF CLIENT
INTERPERSONAL RELATIONS IN TWO GOVERNMENT AGENCIES. ADMIN
USA+45 EX/STRUC REPRESENT INGP/REL PERS/REL. EXEC
PAGE 12 B0251 ROUTINE

B55

CHOWDHURI R.N.,INTERNATIONAL MANDATES AND DELIB/GP
TRUSTEESHIP SYSTEMS. WOR+45 STRUCT ECO/UNDEV PLAN
INT/ORG LEGIS DOMIN EDU/PROP LEGIT ADJUD EXEC PWR SOVEREIGN
...CONCPT TIME/SEQ UN 20. PAGE 21 B0427

S55

MARTIN R.C.,"ADMINISTRATIVE LEADERSHIP IN TOP/EX
GOVERNMENT." NAT/G PARTIC ROUTINE INGP/REL...MGT ADMIN
20. PAGE 70 B1413 EXEC
REPRESENT

S55

STAHL O.G.,"DEMOCRACY AND PUBLIC EMPLOYEE REPRESENT
MORALITY." USA+45 NAT/G EDU/PROP EXEC ROLE 20. POLICY
PAGE 100 B2016 ADMIN

S55

WEISS R.S.,"A METHOD FOR THE ANALYSIS OF THE PROF/ORG
STRUCTURE OF COMPLEX ORGANIZATIONS." WOR+45 INDUS SOC/EXP
LG/CO NAT/G EXEC ROUTINE ORD/FREE PWR SKILL...MGT
PSY SOC NEW/IDEA STAT INT REC/INT STAND/INT CHARTS
WORK. PAGE 115 B2316

B56

ECOLE NAT'L D'ADMINISTRATION,RECRUITMENT AND ADMIN
TRAINING FOR THE HIGHER CIVIL SERVICE IN FRANCE. MGT
FRANCE EX/STRUC PLAN EDU/PROP CONTROL ROUTINE TASK EXEC
COST...METH 20 CIVIL/SERV. PAGE 32 B0650 ACADEM

B56

FRANCIS R.G.,SERVICE AND PROCEDURE IN BUREAUCRACY. CLIENT
EXEC LEAD ROUTINE...QU 20. PAGE 37 B0748 ADMIN
INGP/REL
REPRESENT

B56

HICKMAN C.A.,INDIVIDUALS, GROUPS, AND ECONOMIC MGT
BEHAVIOR. WORKER PAY CONTROL EXEC GP/REL INGP/REL ADMIN
PERSON ROLE...PSY SOC PERS/COMP METH 20. PAGE 50 ECO/TAC
B1005 PLAN

B56

JENNINGS W.I.,THE APPROACH TO SELF-GOVERNMENT. NAT/G
CEYLON INDIA PAKISTAN S/ASIA UK SOCIETY POL/PAR CONSTN
DELIB/GP LEGIS ECO/TAC EDU/PROP ADMIN EXEC CHOOSE COLONIAL
ATTIT ALL/VALS...JURID CONCPT GEN/METH TOT/POP 20.
PAGE 56 B1136

B56

KIRK G.,THE CHANGING ENVIRONMENT OF INTERNATIONAL FUT
RELATIONS. ASIA S/ASIA USA+45 WOR+45 ECO/UNDEV EXEC
INT/ORG NAT/G FOR/AID EDU/PROP PEACE KNOWL DIPLOM
...PLURIST COLD/WAR TOT/POP 20. PAGE 60 B1214

B56

LOVEDAY A.,REFLECTIONS ON INTERNATIONAL INT/ORG
ADMINISTRATION. WOR+45 WOR-45 DELIB/GP ACT/RES MGT
ADMIN EXEC ROUTINE DRIVE...METH/CNCPT TIME/SEQ
CON/ANAL SIMUL TOT/POP 20. PAGE 67 B1342

B56

REDFORD E.S.,PUBLIC ADMINISTRATION AND POLICY EX/STRUC
FORMATION: STUDIES IN OIL, GAS, BANKING, RIVER PROB/SOLV
DEVELOPMENT AND CORPORATE INVESTIGATIONS. USA+45 CONTROL
CLIENT NAT/G ADMIN LOBBY REPRESENT GOV/REL INGP/REL EXEC
20. PAGE 87 B1754

B56

SOHN L.B.,BASIC DOCUMENTS OF THE UNITED NATIONS. DELIB/GP
WOR+45 LAW INT/ORG EXEC ROUTINE CHOOSE PWR CONSTN
...JURID CONCPT GEN/LAWS ANTHOL UN TOT/POP OAS FAO
ILO 20. PAGE 99 B1993

B56

US HOUSE RULES COMM,HEARINGS BEFORE A SPECIAL ADMIN
SUBCOMMITTEE: ESTABLISHMENT OF A STANDING COMMITTEE DOMIN
ON ADMINISTRATIVE PROCEDURE, PRACTICE. USA+45 LAW DELIB/GP
EX/STRUC ADJUD CONTROL EXEC GOV/REL EFFICIENCY PWR NAT/G
...POLICY INT 20 CONGRESS. PAGE 109 B2199

B56

WHYTE W.H. JR.,THE ORGANIZATION MAN. CULTURE FINAN ADMIN
VOL/ASSN DOMIN EDU/PROP EXEC DISPL HABITAT ROLE LG/CO
...PERS/TEST STERTYP. PAGE 116 B2343 PERSON
CONSEN

B56

WILSON W.,CONGRESSIONAL GOVERNMENT. USA-45 NAT/G LEGIS
ADMIN EXEC PARL/PROC GP/REL MAJORITY ATTIT 19 CHIEF
SENATE HOUSE/REP. PAGE 117 B2364 CONSTN
PWR

S56

CLEVELAND H.,"THE EXECUTIVE AND THE PUBLIC LOBBY
INTEREST." USA+45 DOMIN ADMIN PWR...POLICY 20. REPRESENT
PAGE 21 B0437 CHIEF
EXEC

S56

COTTER C.P.,"ADMINISTRATIVE ACCOUNTABILITY TO CONTROL
CONGRESS: THE CONCURRENT RESOLUTION." USA+45 NAT/G GOV/REL

EXEC REPRESENT PWR 20. PAGE 24 B0489
LEGIS
EX/STRUC
S56

EMMERICH H.,"COOPERATION AMONG ADMINISTRATIVE
AGENCIES." USA+45 NAT/G EX/STRUC ADMIN 20. PAGE 33
B0673
DELIB/GP
REPRESENT
GOV/REL
EXEC
S56

TSUJI K.,"THE CABINET, ADMINISTRATIVE ORGANIZATION,
AND THE BUREAUCRACY." EXEC 19/20 CHINJAP. PAGE 106
B2133
GOV/REL
EX/STRUC
ADMIN
REPRESENT
B57

BERGER M.,BUREAUCRACY AND SOCIETY IN MODERN EGYPT;
A STUDY OF THE HIGHER CIVIL SERVICE. UAR REPRESENT
...QU 20. PAGE 11 B0221
ATTIT
EXEC
ADMIN
ROUTINE
B57

DJILAS M.,THE NEW CLASS: AN ANALYSIS OF THE
COMMUNIST SYSTEM. STRATA CAP/ISM ECO/TAC DOMIN
EDU/PROP LEGIT EXEC COERCE ATTIT PWR MARXISM
...MARXIST MGT CONCPT TIME/SEQ GEN/LAWS 20. PAGE 29
B0600
COM
POL/PAR
USSR
YUGOSLAVIA
B57

MORSTEIN-MARX F.,THE ADMINISTRATIVE STATE: AN
INTRODUCTION TO BUREAUCRACY. EUR+WWI FUT MOD/EUR
USA+45 USA-45 NAT/G CONSULT ADMIN ROUTINE TOTALISM
DRIVE SKILL...TREND 19/20. PAGE 76 B1530
EXEC
MGT
CAP/ISM
ELITES
B57

MURRAY J.N.,THE UNITED NATIONS TRUSTEESHIP SYSTEM.
AFR WOR+45 CONSTN CONSULT LEGIS EDU/PROP LEGIT EXEC
ROUTINE...INT TIME/SEQ SOMALI UN 20. PAGE 77 B1547
INT/ORG
DELIB/GP
B57

PARKINSON C.N.,PARKINSON'S LAW. UNIV EX/STRUC PLAN
ATTIT PERSON TIME. PAGE 81 B1634
ADMIN
EXEC
FINAN
ECOMETRIC
B57

SELZNICK,LEADERSHIP IN ADMINISTRATION: A
SOCIOLOGICAL INTERPRETATION. CREATE PROB/SOLV EXEC
ROUTINE EFFICIENCY RATIONAL KNOWL...POLICY PSY.
PAGE 95 B1927
LEAD
ADMIN
DECISION
NAT/G
B57

SHARMA S.R.,SOME ASPECTS OF THE INDIAN
ADMINISTRATIVE SYSTEM. INDIA WOR+45 TEC/DEV BUDGET
LEGIT ROUTINE ATTIT. PAGE 96 B1937
EXEC
DECISION
ADMIN
INGP/REL
L57

DOTSON A.,"FUNDAMENTAL APPROACHES TO
RESPONSIBILITY." USA+45 NAT/G PWR 20. PAGE 30 B0611
ADMIN
REPRESENT
EXEC
CONTROL
S57

BAUMGARTEL H.,"LEADERSHIP STYLE AS A VARIABLE IN
RESEARCH ADMINISTRATION." USA+45 ADMIN REPRESENT
PERS/REL 20. PAGE 10 B0198
LEAD
EXEC
MGT
INGP/REL
S57

GULICK L.,"METROPOLITAN ORGANIZATION." LEGIS EXEC
PARTIC CHOOSE REPRESENT GOV/REL...MAJORIT DECISION.
PAGE 45 B0904
REGION
LOC/G
MUNIC
S57

HONEY J.C.,"RESEARCH IN PUBLIC ADMINISTRATION: A
FURTHER NOTE." EX/STRUC 20. PAGE 51 B1038
ADMIN
EXEC
METH/COMP
METH/CNCPT
S57

SCHUBERT G.A.,"'THE PUBLIC INTEREST' IN
ADMINISTRATIVE DECISION-MAKING: THEOREM, THEOSOPHY
OR THEORY" USA+45 EX/STRUC PROB/SOLV...METH/CNCPT
STAT. PAGE 94 B1904
ADMIN
DECISION
POLICY
EXEC
B58

AMERICAN SOCIETY PUBLIC ADMIN,STRENGTHENING
MANAGEMENT FOR DEMOCRATIC GOVERNMENT. USA+45 ACADEM
EX/STRUC WORKER PLAN BUDGET CONFER CT/SYS
EFFICIENCY ANTHOL. PAGE 4 B0088
ADMIN
NAT/G
EXEC
MGT
B58

BERNSTEIN M.H.,THE JOB OF THE FEDERAL EXECUTIVE.
POL/PAR CHIEF LEGIS ADMIN EXEC LOBBY CHOOSE GOV/REL
ORD/FREE PWR...MGT TREND. PAGE 11 B0228
NAT/G
TOP/EX
PERS/COMP
B58

BROWNE C.G.,THE CONCEPT OF LEADERSHIP. UNIV FACE/GP
DOMIN EDU/PROP LEGIT LEAD DRIVE PERSON PWR...MGT
SOC OBS SELF/OBS CONT/OBS INT PERS/TEST STERTYP
GEN/LAWS. PAGE 16 B0328
EXEC
CONCPT
B58

HENKIN L.,ARMS CONTROL AND INSPECTION IN AMERICAN
LAW. LAW CONSTN INT/ORG LOC/G MUNIC NAT/G PROVS
EDU/PROP LEGIT EXEC NUC/PWR KNOWL ORD/FREE...OBS
TOT/POP CONGRESS 20. PAGE 49 B0990
USA+45
JURID
ARMS/CONT
B58

ISLAM R.,INTERNATIONAL ECONOMIC COOPERATION AND THE
UNITED NATIONS. FINAN PLAN EXEC TASK WAR PEACE
...SOC METH/CNCPT 20 UN LEAGUE/NAT. PAGE 55 B1105
INT/ORG
DIPLOM
ADMIN
B58

KINTNER W.R.,ORGANIZING FOR CONFLICT: A PROPOSAL.
USA+45

USSR STRUCT NAT/G LEGIS ADMIN EXEC PEACE ORD/FREE
PWR...CONCPT OBS TREND NAT/COMP VAL/FREE COLD/WAR
20. PAGE 60 B1211
PLAN
DIPLOM
B58

LAQUER W.Z.,THE MIDDLE EAST IN TRANSITION. COM USSR
ECO/UNDEV NAT/G VOL/ASSN EDU/PROP EXEC ATTIT DRIVE
PWR MARXISM COLD/WAR TOT/POP 20. PAGE 62 B1261
ISLAM
TREND
NAT/LISM
B58

TAYLOR H.,THE STATESMAN. MOD/EUR FACE/GP FAM NAT/G
POL/PAR DELIB/GP LEGIS ATTIT PERSON PWR...POLICY
CONCPT OBS GEN/LAWS. PAGE 103 B2086
EXEC
STRUCT
B58

WESTIN A.F.,THE ANATOMY OF A CONSTITUTIONAL LAW
CASE. USA+45 LAW LEGIS ADMIN EXEC...DECISION MGT
SOC RECORD 20 SUPREME/CT. PAGE 115 B2326
CT/SYS
INDUS
ADJUD
CONSTN
L58

CYERT R.M.,"THE ROLE OF EXPECTATIONS IN BUSINESS
DECISION-MAKING." PROB/SOLV PRICE RIGID/FLEX.
PAGE 25 B0516
LG/CO
DECISION
ROUTINE
EXEC
L58

HAVILAND H.F.,"FOREIGN AID AND THE POLICY PROCESS:
1957." USA+45 FACE/GP POL/PAR VOL/ASSN CHIEF
DELIB/GP ACT/RES LEGIT EXEC GOV/REL ATTIT DRIVE PWR
...POLICY TESTS CONGRESS 20. PAGE 48 B0971
LEGIS
PLAN
FOR/AID
S58

DIAMANT A.,"A CASE STUDY OF ADMINISTRATIVE
AUTONOMY: CONTROLS AND TENSIONS IN FRENCH
ADMINISTRATION." FRANCE ADJUD LOBBY DEMAND
EFFICIENCY 20. PAGE 29 B0585
ADMIN
CONTROL
LEGIS
EXEC
S58

EISENSTADT S.N.,"INTERNAL CONTRADICTIONS IN
BUREAUCRATIC POLITICS." ADMIN EXEC CENTRAL. PAGE 32
B0658
ELITES
LEAD
PWR
EX/STRUC
S58

FREEMAN J.L.,"THE BUREAUCRACY IN PRESSURE
POLITICS." USA+45 NAT/G CHIEF ADMIN EXEC 20.
PAGE 37 B0752
CONTROL
EX/STRUC
REPRESENT
LOBBY
B59

DIMOCK M.E.,ADMINISTRATIVE VITALITY: THE CONFLICT
WITH BUREAUCRACY. PROB/SOLV EXEC 20. PAGE 29 B0597
REPRESENT
ADMIN
EX/STRUC
ROUTINE
B59

MILLETT J.D.,GOVERNMENT AND PUBLIC ADMINISTRATION;
THE QUEST FOR RESPONSIBLE PERFORMANCE. USA+45 NAT/G
DELIB/GP LEGIS CT/SYS EXEC...DECISION MGT. PAGE 73
B1483
ADMIN
PWR
CONSTN
ROLE
B59

MOOS M.,THE CAMPUS AND THE STATE. LAW FINAN
DELIB/GP LEGIS EXEC LOBBY GP/REL PWR...POLICY
BIBLIOG. PAGE 75 B1517
EDU/PROP
ACADEM
PROVS
CONTROL
B59

PARK R.L.,LEADERSHIP AND POLITICAL INSTITUTIONS IN
INDIA. S/ASIA CULTURE ECO/UNDEV LOC/G MUNIC PROVS
LEGIS PLAN ADMIN LEAD ORD/FREE WEALTH...GEOG SOC
BIOG TOT/POP VAL/FREE 20. PAGE 81 B1633
NAT/G
EXEC
INDIA
B59

REDFORD E.S.,NATIONAL REGULATORY COMMISSIONS: NEED
FOR A NEW LOOK (PAMPHLET). USA+45 CLIENT PROB/SOLV
ADJUD LOBBY EFFICIENCY...POLICY 20. PAGE 87 B1757
REPRESENT
CONTROL
EXEC
NAT/G
B59

WARNER W.L.,INDUSTRIAL MAN. USA+45 USA-45 ELITES
INDUS LABOR TOP/EX WORKER ADMIN INGP/REL PERS/REL
...CHARTS ANTHOL 20. PAGE 114 B2294
EXEC
LEAD
PERSON
MGT
L59

GILBERT C.E.,"THE FRAMEWORK OF ADMINISTRATIVE
RESPONSIBILITY." USA+45 20. PAGE 39 B0799
REPRESENT
EXEC
EX/STRUC
CONTROL
L59

HECTOR L.J.,"GOVERNMENT BY ANONYMITY: WHO WRITES
OUR REGULATORY OPINIONS?" USA+45 NAT/G TOP/EX
CONTROL EXEC. PAGE 49 B0987
ADJUD
REPRESENT
EX/STRUC
ADMIN
L59

TARKOWSKI Z.M.,"SCIENTISTS VERSUS ADMINISTRATORS:
AN APPROACH TOWARD ACHIEVING GREATER
UNDERSTANDING." UK EXEC EFFICIENCY 20. PAGE 103
B2079
INGP/REL
GP/REL
ADMIN
EX/STRUC
S59

GABLE R.W.,"CULTURE AND ADMINISTRATION IN IRAN."
IRAN EXEC PARTIC REPRESENT PWR. PAGE 38 B0770
ADMIN
CULTURE
EX/STRUC
INGP/REL
S59

HILSMAN R.,"THE FOREIGN-POLICY CONSENSUS: AN
INTERIM RESEARCH REPORT." USA+45 INT/ORG LEGIS
TEC/DEV EXEC WAR CONSEN KNOWL...DECISION COLD/WAR.
PAGE 50 B1013
PROB/SOLV
NAT/G
DELIB/GP
DIPLOM

S59

LENGYEL P.,"SOME TRENDS IN THE INTERNATIONAL CIVIL   ADMIN
SERVICE." FUT WOR+45 INT/ORG CONSULT ATTIT...MGT   EXEC
OBS TREND CON/ANAL LEAGUE/NAT UNESCO 20. PAGE 64
B1291

S59

PRESTHUS R.V.,"BEHAVIOR AND BUREAUCRACY IN MANY   ADMIN
CULTURES." EXEC INGP/REL 20. PAGE 84 B1705   EX/STRUC
                                                       GOV/COMP
                                                       METH/CNCPT
S59

SEIDMAN H.,"THE GOVERNMENT CORPORATION IN THE   CONTROL
UNITED STATES." USA+45 LEGIS ADMIN PLURISM 20.   GOV/REL
PAGE 95 B1925   EX/STRUC
                                                       EXEC
S59

SUTTON F.X.,"REPRESENTATION AND THE NATURE OF   NAT/G
POLITICAL SYSTEMS." UNIV WOR-45 CULTURE SOCIETY   CONCPT
STRATA INT/ORG FORCES JUDGE DOMIN LEGIT EXEC REGION
REPRESENT ATTIT ORD/FREE RESPECT...SOC HIST/WRIT
TIME/SEQ. PAGE 102 B2057

B60

ADRIAN C.R.,STATE AND LOCAL GOVERNMENTS: A STUDY IN LOC/G
THE POLITICAL PROCESS. USA+45 LAW FINAN MUNIC   PROVS
POL/PAR LEGIS ADJUD EXEC CHOOSE REPRESENT. PAGE 3   GOV/REL
B0060   ATTIT

B60

ALBI F.,TRATADO DE LOS MODOS DE GESTION DE LAS   LOC/G
CORPORACIONES LOCALES. SPAIN FINAN NAT/G BUDGET   LAW
CONTROL EXEC ROUTINE GOV/REL ORD/FREE SOVEREIGN   ADMIN
...MGT 20. PAGE 3 B0068   MUNIC

B60

ARGAL R.,MUNICIPAL GOVERNMENT IN INDIA. INDIA   LOC/G
BUDGET TAX ADMIN EXEC 19/20. PAGE 6 B0126   MUNIC
                                                       DELIB/GP
                                                       CONTROL
B60

BELL J.,THE SPLENDID MISERY: THE STORY OF THE   EXEC
PRESIDENCY AND POWER POLITICS AT CLOSE RANGE.   TOP/EX
USA+45 USA-45 PRESS ADMIN LEAD LOBBY GP/REL   LEGIS
PERS/REL PERSON PRESIDENT. PAGE 10 B0208

B60

CORSON J.J.,GOVERNANCE OF COLLEGES AND   ADMIN
UNIVERSITIES. STRUCT FINAN DELIB/GP DOMIN EDU/PROP   EXEC
LEAD CHOOSE GP/REL CENTRAL COST PRIVIL SUPEGO   ACADEM
ORD/FREE PWR...DECISION BIBLIOG. PAGE 24 B0481   HABITAT

B60

FOSS P.,POLITICS AND GRASS: THE ADMINISTRATION OF   REPRESENT
GRAZING ON THE PUBLIC DOMAIN. USA+45 LEGIS TOP/EX   ADMIN
EXEC...DECISION 20. PAGE 37 B0743   LOBBY
                                                       EX/STRUC
B60

GLOVER J.D.,A CASE STUDY OF HIGH LEVEL   ADMIN
ADMINISTRATION IN A LARGE ORGANIZATION. EX/STRUC   TOP/EX
EXEC LEAD ROUTINE INGP/REL OPTIMAL ATTIT PERSON   FORCES
...POLICY DECISION INT QU. PAGE 40 B0812   NAT/G

B60

GRANICK D.,THE RED EXECUTIVE. COM USA+45 SOCIETY   PWR
ECO/DEV INDUS NAT/G POL/PAR EX/STRUC PLAN ECO/TAC   STRATA
EDU/PROP ADMIN EXEC ATTIT DRIVE...GP/COMP 20.   USSR
PAGE 42 B0851   ELITES

B60

PAGE T.,THE PUBLIC PERSONNEL AGENCY AND THE CHIEF   WORKER
EXECUTIVE (REPORT NO. 601). USA+45 LOC/G NAT/G   EXEC
GP/REL PERS/REL...ANTHOL 20. PAGE 80 B1624   ADMIN
                                                       MGT
B60

PFIFFNER J.M.,PUBLIC ADMINISTRATION. USA+45 FINAN   ADMIN
WORKER PLAN PROB/SOLV ADJUD CONTROL EXEC...T 20.   NAT/G
PAGE 82 B1666   LOC/G
                                                       MGT
B60

US SENATE COMM. GOVT. OPER.,ORGANIZING FOR NATIONAL   CONSULT
SECURITY. USA+45 USA-45 INTELL STRUCT SML/CO   EXEC
ACT/RES ADMIN ATTIT PERSON PWR SKILL...DECISION 20.
PAGE 111 B2236

B60

WEBSTER J.A.,A GENERAL STUDY OF THE DEPARTMENT OF   ORD/FREE
DEFENSE INTERNAL SECURITY PROGRAM. USA+45 WORKER   PLAN
TEC/DEV ADJUD CONTROL CT/SYS EXEC GOV/REL COST   ADMIN
...POLICY DECISION MGT 20 DEPT/DEFEN SUPREME/CT.   NAT/G
PAGE 114 B2307

B60

WEIDNER E.W.,INTERGOVERNMENTAL RELATIONS AS SEEN BY   ATTIT
PUBLIC OFFICIALS. USA+45 PROVS EX/STRUC EXEC   GP/REL
FEDERAL...QU 20. PAGE 115 B2311   GOV/REL
                                                       ADMIN
L60

FUCHS R.F.,"FAIRNESS AND EFFECTIVENESS IN   EFFICIENCY
ADMINISTRATIVE AGENCY ORGANIZATION AND PROCEDURES."   EX/STRUC
USA+45 ADJUD ADMIN REPRESENT. PAGE 38 B0764   EXEC
                                                       POLICY
S60

HEADY F.,"RECENT LITERATURE ON COMPARATIVE PUBLIC   GOV/COMP
ADMINISTRATION." EXEC 20. PAGE 48 B0981   ADMIN
                                                       EX/STRUC

BIBLIOG
S60

HUNTINGTON S.P.,"STRATEGIC PLANNING AND THE   EXEC
POLITICAL PROCESS." USA+45 NAT/G DELIB/GP LEGIS   FORCES
ACT/RES ECO/TAC LEGIT ROUTINE CHOOSE RIGID/FLEX PWR   NUC/PWR
...POLICY MAJORIT MGT 20. PAGE 53 B1066   WAR

S60

MARSHALL G.,"POLICE RESPONSIBILITY." UK LOC/G ADJUD   CONTROL
ADMIN EXEC 20. PAGE 70 B1409   REPRESENT
                                                       LAW
                                                       FORCES
S60

NELSON R.H.,"LEGISLATIVE PARTICIPATION IN THE   LEGIS
TREATY AND AGREEMENT MAKING PROCESS." CONSTN   PEACE
POL/PAR PLAN EXEC PWR FAO UN CONGRESS. PAGE 78   DECISION
B1569   DIPLOM

S60

RAPHAELI N.,"SELECTED ARTICLES AND DOCUMENTS ON   BIBLIOG
COMPARATIVE PUBLIC ADMINISTRATION." USA+45 FINAN   MGT
LOC/G TOP/EX TEC/DEV EXEC GP/REL INGP/REL...GP/COMP   ADMIN
GOV/COMP METH/COMP. PAGE 86 B1738   EX/STRUC

S60

ROURKE F.E.,"ADMINISTRATIVE SECRECY: A   LEGIS
CONGRESSIONAL DILEMMA." DELIB/GP CT/SYS ATTIT   EXEC
...MAJORIT DECISION JURID. PAGE 91 B1837   ORD/FREE
                                                       POLICY
B61

AMERICAN MANAGEMENT ASSN.SUPERIOR-SUBORDINATE   MGT
COMMUNICATION IN MANAGEMENT. STRATA FINAN INDUS   ACT/RES
SML/CO WORKER CONTROL EXEC ATTIT 20. PAGE 4 B0086   PERS/REL
                                                       LG/CO
B61

BANFIELD E.C.,URBAN GOVERNMENT; A READER IN   MUNIC
POLITICS AND ADMINISTRATION. ELITES LABOR POL/PAR   GEN/METH
EXEC CHOOSE REPRESENT GP/REL PWR PLURISM...PSY SOC.   DECISION
PAGE 9 B0177

B61

BARNES W.,THE FOREIGN SERVICE OF THE UNITED STATES.   NAT/G
USA+45 USA-45 CONSTN INT/ORG POL/PAR CONSULT   MGT
DELIB/GP LEGIS DOMIN EDU/PROP EXEC ATTIT RIGID/FLEX   DIPLOM
ORD/FREE PWR...POLICY CONCPT STAT OBS RECORD BIOG
TIME/SEQ TREND. PAGE 9 B0188

B61

BARRASH J.,LABOR'S GRASS ROOTS; A STUDY OF THE   LABOR
LOCAL UNION. STRATA BARGAIN LEAD REPRESENT DEMAND   USA+45
ATTIT PWR. PAGE 9 B0190   INGP/REL
                                                       EXEC
B61

DUBIN R.,HUMAN RELATIONS IN ADMINISTRATION. USA+45   PERS/REL
INDUS LABOR LG/CO EX/STRUC GP/REL DRIVE PWR   MGT
...DECISION SOC CHARTS ANTHOL 20. PAGE 31 B0623   ADMIN
                                                       EXEC
B61

GLADDEN E.N.,BRITISH PUBLIC SERVICE ADMINISTRATION.   EFFICIENCY
UK...CHARTS 20. PAGE 40 B0809   ADMIN
                                                       EX/STRUC
                                                       EXEC
B61

HART W.R.,COLLECTIVE BARGAINING IN THE FEDERAL   INGP/REL
CIVIL SERVICE. NAT/G EX/STRUC ADMIN EXEC 20.   MGT
PAGE 47 B0961   REPRESENT
                                                       LABOR
B61

LASSWELL H.D.,PSYCOPATHOLOGY AND POLITICS. WOR-45   ATTIT
CULTURE SOCIETY FACE/GP NAT/G CONSULT CREATE   GEN/METH
EDU/PROP EXEC ROUTINE DISPL DRIVE PERSON PWR
RESPECT...PSY CONCPT METH/CNCPT METH. PAGE 63 B1272

B61

MACMAHON A.W.,DELEGATION AND AUTONOMY. INDIA STRUCT   ADMIN
LEGIS BARGAIN BUDGET ECO/TAC LEGIT EXEC REPRESENT   PLAN
GOV/REL CENTRAL DEMAND EFFICIENCY PRODUC. PAGE 68   FEDERAL
B1373

B61

MOLLAU G.,INTERNATIONAL COMMUNISM AND WORLD   COM
REVOLUTION: HISTORY AND METHODS. RUSSIA USSR   REV
INT/ORG NAT/G POL/PAR VOL/ASSN FORCES BAL/PWR
DIPLOM EXEC REGION WAR ATTIT PWR MARXISM...CONCPT
TIME/SEQ COLD/WAR 19/20. PAGE 74 B1498

B61

MUNGER E.S.,AFRICAN FIELD REPORTS 1952-1961.   AFR
SOUTH/AFR SOCIETY ECO/UNDEV NAT/G POL/PAR COLONIAL   DISCRIM
EXEC PARL/PROC RACE/REL ALL/IDEOS...SOC   RECORD
AUD/VIS 20. PAGE 76 B1538

B61

SCHMECKEBIER L.,GOVERNMENT PUBLICATIONS AND THEIR   BIBLIOG/A
USE. USA+45 LEGIS ACT/RES CT/SYS EXEC INGP/REL 20.   EDU/PROP
PAGE 94 B1894   NAT/G
                                                       ADMIN
B61

SHAPP W.R.,FIELD ADMINISTRATION IN THE UNITED   INT/ORG
NATIONS SYSTEM. FINAN PROB/SOLV INSPECT DIPLOM EXEC   ADMIN
REGION ROUTINE EFFICIENCY ROLE...INT CHARTS 20 UN.   GP/REL
PAGE 96 B1933   FOR/AID
B61

SHARP W.R.,FIELD ADMINISTRATION IN THE UNITED   INT/ORG
NATION SYSTEM: THE CONDUCT OF INTERNATIONAL   CONSULT

ECONOMIC AND SOCIAL PROGRAMS. FUT WOR+45 CONSTN SOCIETY ECO/UNDEV R+D DELIB/GP ACT/RES PLAN TEC/DEV EDU/PROP EXEC ROUTINE HEALTH WEALTH...HUM CONCPT CHARTS METH ILO UNESCO VAL/FREE UN 20. PAGE 96 B1939
B61

TANZER L.,THE KENNEDY CIRCLE. INTELL CONSULT DELIB/GP TOP/EX CONTROL EXEC INGP/REL PERS/REL PWR ...BIOG IDEA/COMP ANTHOL 20 KENNEDY/JF PRESIDENT DEMOCRAT MCNAMARA/R RUSK/D. PAGE 103 B2077 — EX/STRUC NAT/G CHIEF
B61

THOMPSON V.A.,MODERN ORGANIZATION. REPRESENT EFFICIENCY. PAGE 104 B2105 — ADMIN EX/STRUC EXEC
B61

WALKER N.,MORALE IN THE CIVIL SERVICE. UK EXEC LEAD INGP/REL EFFICIENCY HAPPINESS 20. PAGE 113 B2280 — ATTIT WORKER ADMIN PSY
L61

KRAMER R.,"EXECUTIVE PRIVILEGE - A STUDY OF THE PERIOD 1953-1960." NAT/G CHIEF EX/STRUC LEGIS PWR. PAGE 61 B1233 — REPRESENT LEAD EXEC GOV/REL
S61

ABLARD C.D.,"EX PARTE CONTACTS WITH FEDERAL ADMINISTRATIVE AGENCIES." USA+45 CLIENT NAT/G DELIB/GP ADMIN PWR 20. PAGE 3 B0055 — EXEC ADJUD LOBBY REPRESENT
S61

EVAN W.M.,"A LABORATORY EXPERIMENT ON BUREAUCRATIC AUTHORITY" WORKER CONTROL EXEC PRODUC ATTIT PERSON ...PSY SOC CHARTS SIMUL 20 WEBER/MAX. PAGE 34 B0687 — ADMIN LEGIT LAB/EXP EFFICIENCY
S61

JACKSON E.,"CONSTITUTIONAL DEVELOPMENTS OF THE UNITED NATIONS: THE GROWTH OF ITS EXECUTIVE CAPACITY." FUT WOR+45 CONSTN STRUCT ACT/RES PLAN ALL/VALS...NEW/IDEA OBS COLD/WAR UN 20. PAGE 55 B1106 — INT/ORG EXEC
S61

JOHNSON N.,"PARLIAMENTARY QUESTIONS AND THE CONDUCT OF ADMINISTRATION." UK REPRESENT PARLIAMENT 20. PAGE 57 B1146 — CONTROL EXEC EX/STRUC
S61

KUIC V.,"THEORY AND PRACTICE OF THE AMERICAN PRESIDENCY." USA+45 USA-45 NAT/G ADMIN REPRESENT ...PLURIST 20 PRESIDENT. PAGE 61 B1241 — EXEC EX/STRUC PWR CHIEF
S61

LYONS G.M.,"THE NEW CIVIL-MILITARY RELATIONS." USA+45 NAT/G EX/STRUC TOP/EX PROB/SOLV ADMIN EXEC PARTIC 20. PAGE 67 B1350 — CIVMIL/REL PWR REPRESENT
S61

REAGAN M.O.,"THE POLITICAL STRUCTURE OF THE FEDERAL RESERVE SYSTEM." USA+45 FINAN NAT/G ADMIN 20. PAGE 87 B1748 — PWR EX/STRUC EXEC LEAD
S61

SHERBENOU E.L.,"CLASS, PARTICIPATION, AND THE COUNCIL-MANAGER PLAN." ELITES STRUCT LEAD GP/REL ATTIT PWR DECISION. PAGE 96 B1942 — REPRESENT MUNIC EXEC
B62

ANDREWS W.G.,FRENCH POLITICS AND ALGERIA: THE PROCESS OF POLICY FORMATION 1954-1962. ALGERIA FRANCE CONSTN ELITES POL/PAR CHIEF DELIB/GP LEGIS DIPLOM PRESS CHOOSE 20. PAGE 5 B0105 — GOV/COMP EXEC COLONIAL
B62

BAILEY S.D.,THE SECRETARIAT OF THE UNITED NATIONS. FUT WOR+45 DELIB/GP PLAN BAL/PWR DOMIN EDU/PROP ADMIN PEACE ATTIT PWR...DECISION CONCPT TREND CON/ANAL CHARTS UN VAL/FREE COLD/WAR 20. PAGE 8 B0162 — INT/ORG EXEC DIPLOM
B62

BRIEFS H.W.,PRICING POWER AND "ADMINISTRATIVE" INFLATION (PAMPHLET). USA+45 PROC/MFG CONTROL EFFICIENCY MONEY GOLD/STAND. PAGE 15 B0306 — ECO/DEV PRICE POLICY EXEC
B62

CHANDLER A.D.,STRATEGY AND STRUCTURE: CHAPTERS IN THE HISTORY OF THE INDUSTRIAL ENTERPRISE. USA+45 USA-45 ECO/DEV EX/STRUC ECO/TAC EXEC...DECISION 20. PAGE 20 B0403 — LG/CO PLAN ADMIN FINAN
B62

CHICAGO U CTR PROG GOVT ADMIN,EDUCATION FOR INNOVATIVE BEHAVIOR IN EXECUTIVES. UNIV ELITES ADMIN EFFICIENCY DRIVE PERSON...MGT APT/TEST PERS/TEST CHARTS LAB/EXP BIBLIOG 20. PAGE 21 B0420 — EDU/PROP CREATE EXEC STAT
B62

DUCKWORTH W.E.,A GUIDE TO OPERATIONAL RESEARCH. INDUS PLAN PROB/SOLV EXEC EFFICIENCY PRODUC KNOWL ...MGT MATH STAT SIMUL METH 20 MONTECARLO. PAGE 31 B0624 — OP/RES GAME DECISION ADMIN
B62

EATON J.W.,STONE WALLS NOT A PRISON MAKE: THE ANATOMY OF PLANNED ADMINISTRATIVE CHANGE. USA+45 — CRIMLGY ADMIN

PROVS EDU/PROP 20. PAGE 32 B0647 — EXEC POLICY
B62

GOVERNORS CONF STATE PLANNING,STATE PLANNING: A POLICY STATEMENT (PAMPHLET). USA+45 LOC/G NAT/G DELIB/GP LEGIS EXEC 20 GOVERNOR. PAGE 42 B0847 — GOV/REL PLAN ADMIN PROVS
B62

GRANICK D.,THE EUROPEAN EXECUTIVE. BELGIUM FRANCE GERMANY/W UK INDUS LABOR LG/CO SML/CO EX/STRUC PLAN TEC/DEV CAP/ISM COST DEMAND...POLICY CHARTS 20. PAGE 42 B0852 — MGT ECO/DEV ECO/TAC EXEC
B62

HITCHNER D.G.,MODERN GOVERNMENT: A SURVEY OF POLITICAL SCIENCE. WOR+45 INT/ORG LEGIS ADMIN CT/SYS EXEC CHOOSE TOTALISM POPULISM...INT/LAW PHIL/SCI METH 20. PAGE 50 B1019 — CONCPT NAT/G STRUCT
B62

INTERNAT CONGRESS OF JURISTS,EXECUTIVE ACTION AND THE RULE OF RULE: REPORTION PROCEEDINGS OF INT'T CONGRESS OF JURISTS,--RIO DE JANEIRO, BRAZIL. WOR+45 ACADEM CONSULT JUDGE EDU/PROP ADJUD CT/SYS INGP/REL PERSON DEPT/DEFEN. PAGE 54 B1094 — JURID EXEC ORD/FREE CONTROL
B62

KAMMERER G.M.,CITY MANAGERS IN POLITICS: AN ANALYSIS OF MANAGER TENURE AND TERMINATION. POL/PAR LEGIS PARTIC CHOOSE PWR...DECISION GEOG METH/CNCPT. PAGE 57 B1161 — MUNIC LEAD EXEC
B62

LAWSON R.,INTERNATIONAL REGIONAL ORGANIZATIONS. WOR+45 NAT/G VOL/ASSN CONSULT LEGIS EDU/PROP LEGIT ADMIN EXEC ROUTINE HEALTH PWR WEALTH...JURID EEC COLD/WAR 20 UN. PAGE 63 B1277 — INT/ORG DELIB/GP REGION
B62

LOWI T.J.,LEGISLATIVE POLITICS U.S.A. LAW LEGIS DIPLOM EXEC LOBBY CHOOSE SUFF FEDERAL PWR 19/20 CONGRESS. PAGE 67 B1345 — PARL/PROC REPRESENT POLICY ROUTINE
B62

MAILICK S.,CONCEPTS AND ISSUES IN ADMINISTRATIVE BEHAVIOR. EX/STRUC TOP/EX ROUTINE INGP/REL EFFICIENCY. PAGE 68 B1380 — DECISION MGT EXEC PROB/SOLV
B62

MORTON L.,STRATEGY AND COMMAND: THE FIRST TWO YEARS. USA-45 NAT/G CONTROL EXEC LEAD WEAPON CIVMIL/REL PWR...POLICY AUD/VIS CHARTS 20 CHINJAP. PAGE 76 B1532 — WAR FORCES PLAN DIPLOM
B62

NEVINS A.,THE STATE UNIVERSITIES AND DEMOCRACY. AGRI FINAN SCHOOL ADMIN EXEC EFFICIENCY ATTIT. PAGE 78 B1576 — ACADEM PROVS EDU/PROP POLICY
B62

RUDOLPH F.,THE AMERICAN COLLEGE AND UNIVERSITY. CLIENT FINAN PUB/INST DELIB/GP EDU/PROP CONTROL EXEC CONSEN ATTIT POLICY. PAGE 92 B1853 — ACADEM INGP/REL PWR ADMIN
B62

SCHILLING W.R.,STRATEGY, POLITICS, AND DEFENSE BUDGETS. USA+45 R+D NAT/G CONSULT DELIB/GP FORCES LEGIS ACT/RES PLAN BAL/PWR LEGIT EXEC NUC/PWR RIGID/FLEX PWR...TREND COLD/WAR CONGRESS 20 EISNHWR/DD. PAGE 93 B1890 — ROUTINE POLICY
B62

US SENATE COMM ON JUDICIARY,STATE DEPARTMENT SECURITY. USA+45 CHIEF TEC/DEV DOMIN ADMIN EXEC ATTIT ORD/FREE...POLICY CONGRESS DEPT/STATE PRESIDENT KENNEDY/JF KENNEDY/JF SENATE 20. PAGE 110 B2228 — CONTROL WORKER NAT/G GOV/REL
L62

BAILEY S.D.,"THE TROIKA AND THE FUTURE OF THE UN." CONSTN CREATE LEGIT EXEC CHOOSE ORD/FREE PWR ...CONCPT NEW/IDEA UN COLD/WAR 20. PAGE 8 B0163 — FUT INT/ORG USSR
L62

BORCHARDT K.,"CONGRESSIONAL USE OF ADMINISTRATIVE ORGANIZATION AND PROCEDURE FOR POLICY-MAKING PURPOSES." USA+45 NAT/G EXEC LOBBY. PAGE 14 B0278 — ADMIN LEGIS REPRESENT CONTROL
L62

CAVERS D.F.,"ADMINISTRATIVE DECISION-MAKING IN NUCLEAR FACILITIES LICENSING." USA+45 CLIENT ADMIN EXEC 20 AEC. PAGE 19 B0395 — REPRESENT LOBBY PWR CONTROL
L62

MANGIN G.,"L'ORGANIZATION JUDICIAIRE DES ETATS D'AFRIQUE ET DE MADAGASCAR." ISLAM WOR+45 STRATA STRUCT ECO/UNDEV NAT/G LEGIT EXEC...JURID TIME/SEQ TOT/POP 20 SUPREME/CT. PAGE 69 B1387 — AFR LEGIS COLONIAL MADAGASCAR
L62

NEIBURG H.L.,"THE EISENHOWER AEC AND CONGRESS: A STUDY IN EXECUTIVE-LEGISLATIVE RELATIONS." USA+45 NAT/G POL/PAR DELIB/GP EX/STRUC TOP/EX ADMIN EXEC LEAD ROUTINE PWR...POLICY COLD/WAR CONGRESS PRESIDENT AEC. PAGE 77 B1567 — CHIEF LEGIS GOV/REL NUC/PWR

BRZEZINSKI Z.K.,"DEVIATION CONTROL: A STUDY IN THE   RIGID/FLEX
DYNAMICS OF DOCTRINAL CONFLICT." WOR+45 WOR-45   ATTIT
VOL/ASSN CREATE BAL/PWR DOMIN EXEC DRIVE PERCEPT
PWR...METH/CNCPT TIME/SEQ TREND 20. PAGE 16 B0333
S62

LARSON R.L.,"HOW TO DEFINE ADMINISTRATIVE   UNIV
PROBLEMS." ROUTINE PERCEPT KNOWL SKILL...MGT   FACE/GP
METH/CNCPT CHARTS TOT/POP. PAGE 63 B1263   INDUS
EXEC
S62

LOCKARD D.,"THE CITY MANAGER. ADMINISTRATIVE THEORY   MUNIC
AND POLITICAL POWER." LEGIS ADMIN REPRESENT GP/REL   EXEC
PWR. PAGE 66 B1333   LEAD
DECISION
S62

MAINZER L.C.,"INJUSTICE AND BUREAUCRACY." ELITES   MORAL
STRATA STRUCT EX/STRUC SENIOR CONTROL EXEC LEAD   MGT
ROUTINE INGP/REL ORD/FREE...CONCPT 20 BUREAUCRCY.   ADMIN
PAGE 68 B1381
S62

MURACCIOLE L.,"LES CONSTITUTIONS DES ETATS   NAT/G
AFRICAINS D'EXPRESSION FRANCAISE: LA CONSTITUTION   CONSTN
DU 16 AVRIL 1962 DE LA REPUBLIQUE DU" AFR CHAD
CHIEF LEGIS LEGIT COLONIAL EXEC ROUTINE ORD/FREE
SOVEREIGN...SOC CONCPT 20. PAGE 76 B1541
S62

MURACCIOLE L.,"LES MODIFICATIONS DE LA CONSTITUTION   NAT/G
MALGACHE." AFR WOR+45 ECO/UNDEV LEGIT EXEC ALL/VALS   STRUCT
...JURID 20. PAGE 76 B1542   SOVEREIGN
MADAGASCAR
S62

READ W.H.,"UPWARD COMMUNICATION IN INDUSTRIAL   ADMIN
HIERARCHIES." LG/CO TOP/EX PROB/SOLV DOMIN EXEC   INGP/REL
PERS/REL ATTIT DRIVE PERCEPT...CORREL STAT CHARTS   PSY
20. PAGE 86 B1747   MGT
C62

TRUMAN D.B.,"THE GOVERNMENTAL PROCESS: POLITICAL   LOBBY
INTERESTS AND PUBLIC OPINION." POL/PAR ADJUD ADMIN   EDU/PROP
EXEC LEAD ROUTINE CHOOSE REPRESENT GOV/REL   GP/REL
RIGID/FLEX...POLICY BIBLIOG/A 20. PAGE 105 B2131   LEGIS
N62

US ADVISORY COMN INTERGOV REL,ALTERNATIVE   MUNIC
APPROACHES TO GOVERNMENTAL REORGANIZATION IN   REGION
METROPOLITAN AREAS (PAMPHLET). EX/STRUC LEGIS EXEC   PLAN
LEAD PWR...DECISION GEN/METH. PAGE 107 B2171   GOV/REL
B63

BANFIELD E.C.,CITY POLITICS. CULTURE LABOR LOC/G   MUNIC
POL/PAR LEGIS EXEC LEAD CHOOSE...DECISION NEGRO.   RIGID/FLEX
PAGE 9 B0178   ATTIT
B63

BLUM H.L.,PUBLIC ADMINISTRATION - A PUBLIC HEALTH   REPRESENT
VIEWPOINT. USA+45 NAT/G 20. PAGE 13 B0257   EX/STRUC
EXEC
ADMIN
B63

BOWETT D.W.,THE LAW OF INTERNATIONAL INSTITUTIONS.   INT/ORG
WOR+45 WOR-45 CONSTN DELIB/GP EX/STRUC JUDGE   ADJUD
EDU/PROP LEGIT CT/SYS EXEC ROUTINE RIGID/FLEX   DIPLOM
ORD/FREE PWR...JURID CONCPT ORG/CHARTS GEN/METH
LEAGUE/NAT OAS OEEC 20 UN. PAGE 14 B0286
B63

COSTELLO T.W.,PSYCHOLOGY IN ADMINISTRATION: A   PSY
RESEARCH ORIENTATION. CREATE PROB/SOLV PERS/REL   MGT
ADJUST ANOMIE ATTIT DRIVE PERCEPT ROLE...DECISION   EXEC
BIBLIOG T 20. PAGE 24 B0488   ADMIN
B63

DUE J.F.,STATE SALES TAX ADMINISTRATION. OP/RES   PROVS
BUDGET PAY ADMIN EXEC ROUTINE COST EFFICIENCY   TAX
PROFIT...CHARTS METH/COMP 20. PAGE 31 B0626   STAT
GOV/COMP
B63

HATHAWAY D.A.,GOVERNMENT AND AGRICULTURE: PUBLIC   AGRI
POLICY IN A DEMOCRATIC SOCIETY. USA+45 LEGIS ADMIN   GOV/REL
EXEC LOBBY REPRESENT PWR 20. PAGE 48 B0967   PROB/SOLV
EX/STRUC
B63

HAYMAN D.,POLITICAL ACTIVITY RESTRICTION; AN   CONTROL
ANALYSIS WITH RECOMMENDATIONS (PAMPHLET). USA+45   ADMIN
EXEC PARTIC ROLE PWR 20. PAGE 48 B0976   INGP/REL
REPRESENT
B63

HERMAN H.,NEW YORK STATE AND THE METROPOLITAN   GOV/REL
PROBLEM. USA+45 ECO/DEV PUB/INST SCHOOL LEGIS PLAN   PROVS
TAX EXEC PARL/PROC PARTIC...HEAL 20 NEW/YORK.   LOC/G
PAGE 49 B0992   POLICY
B63

KAMMERER G.M.,THE URBAN POLITICAL COMMUNITY: EXEC
PROFILES IN TOWN POLITICS. ELITES LOC/G LEAD   MUNIC
...DECISION GP/COMP. PAGE 57 B1162   PWR
GOV/COMP
B63

KARL B.D.,EXECUTIVE REORGANIZATION AND REFORM IN   BIOG
THE NEW DEAL. ECO/DEV INDUS DELIB/GP EX/STRUC PLAN   EXEC
BUDGET ADMIN EFFICIENCY PWR POPULISM...POLICY 20   CREATE
PRESIDENT ROOSEVLT/F WILSON/W NEW/DEAL. PAGE 58   CONTROL

B1174

KOGAN N.,THE POLITICS OF ITALIAN FOREIGN POLICY.   NAT/G
EUR+WWI LEGIS DOMIN LEGIT EXEC PWR RESPECT SKILL   ROUTINE
...POLICY DECISION HUM SOC METH/CNCPT OBS INT   DIPLOM
CHARTS 20. PAGE 61 B1227   ITALY
B63

MAHESHWARI B.,STUDIES IN PANCHAYATI RAJ. INDIA   FEDERAL
POL/PAR EX/STRUC BUDGET EXEC REPRESENT CENTRAL   LOC/G
EFFICIENCY...DECISION 20. PAGE 68 B1378   GOV/REL
LEAD
B63

RICHARDS P.G.,PATRONAGE IN BRITISH GOVERNMENT.   EX/STRUC
ELITES DELIB/GP TOP/EX PROB/SOLV CONTROL CT/SYS   REPRESENT
EXEC PWR. PAGE 88 B1774   POL/PAR
ADMIN
L63

ROBERT J.,"LES ELECTIONS LEGISLATIVES DU 17 MAI   CHOOSE
1963 ET L'EVOLUTION POLITIQUE INTERNE DU MAROC."   MOROCCO
ISLAM WOR+45 NAT/G POL/PAR EXEC ALL/VALS 20.
PAGE 89 B1792
S63

ARASTEH R.,"THE ROLE OF INTELLECTUALS IN   INTELL
ADMINISTRATIVE DEVELOPMENT AND SOCIAL CHANGE IN   ADMIN
MODERN IRAN." ISLAM CULTURE NAT/G CONSULT ACT/RES   IRAN
EDU/PROP EXEC ATTIT BIO/SOC PERCEPT SUPEGO ALL/VALS
...POLICY MGT PSY SOC CONCPT 20. PAGE 6 B0123
S63

BACHRACH P.,"DECISIONS AND NONDECISIONS: AN   PWR
ANALYTICAL FRAMEWORK." UNIV SOCIETY CREATE LEGIT   HYPO/EXP
ADMIN EXEC COERCE...DECISION PSY CONCPT CHARTS.
PAGE 8 B0156
S63

BAKER R.J.,"DISCUSSION AND DECISION-MAKING IN THE   EXEC
CIVIL SERVICE." UK CONTROL REPRESENT INGP/REL   EX/STRUC
PERS/REL EFFICIENCY 20. PAGE 8 B0168   PROB/SOLV
ADMIN
S63

BRZEZINSKI Z.K.,"CINCINNATUS AND THE APPARATCHIK."   POL/PAR
COM USA+45 USA-45 ELITES LOC/G NAT/G PROVS CONSULT   USSR
LEGIS DOMIN LEGIT EXEC ROUTINE CHOOSE DRIVE PWR
SKILL...CONCPT CHARTS VAL/FREE COLD/WAR 20. PAGE 16
B0334
S63

GITTELL M.,"METROPOLITAN MAYOR: DEAD END." LOC/G   MUNIC
PARTIC REGION ATTIT PWR GP/COMP. PAGE 40 B0804   LEAD
EXEC
S63

HILLS R.J.,"THE REPRESENTATIVE FUNCTION: NEGLECTED   LEAD
DIMENSION OF LEADERSHIP BEHAVIOR" USA+45 CLIENT   ADMIN
STRUCT SCHOOL PERS/REL...STAT QU SAMP LAB/EXP 20.   EXEC
PAGE 50 B1012   ACT/RES
S63

MASSART L.,"L'ORGANISATION DE LA RECHERCHE   R+D
SCIENTIFIQUE EN EUROPE." EUR+WWI WOR+45 ACT/RES   CREATE
PLAN TEC/DEV EDU/PROP EXEC KNOWL...METH/CNCPT EEC
20. PAGE 70 B1424
S63

RUSTOW D.A.,"THE MILITARY IN MIDDLE EASTERN SOCIETY   FORCES
AND POLITICS." FUT ISLAM CONSTN SOCIETY FACE/GP   ELITES
NAT/G POL/PAR PROF/ORG CONSULT DOMIN ADMIN EXEC
REGION COERCE NAT/LISM ATTIT DRIVE PERSON ORD/FREE
PWR...POLICY CONCPT OBS STERTYP 20. PAGE 92 B1860
S63

SHIMKIN D.B.,"STRUCTURE OF SOVIET POWER." COM FUT   PWR
USA+45 USSR WOR+45 NAT/G FORCES ECO/TAC DOMIN EXEC
COERCE CHOOSE ATTIT WEALTH...TIME/SEQ COLD/WAR
TOT/POP VAL/FREE 20. PAGE 96 B1948
B64

APTER D.E.,IDEOLOGY AND DISCONTENT. FUT WOR+45   ACT/RES
CONSTN CULTURE INTELL SOCIETY STRUCT INT/ORG NAT/G   ATTIT
DELIB/GP LEGIS CREATE PLAN TEC/DEV EDU/PROP EXEC
PERCEPT PERSON RIGID/FLEX ALL/VALS...POLICY
TOT/POP. PAGE 6 B0122
B64

BOYER W.W.,BUREAUCRACY ON TRIAL: POLICY MAKING BY   ADMIN
GOVERNMENT AGENCIES. USA+45 NAT/G REPRESENT 20.   LOBBY
PAGE 14 B0294   EXEC
EX/STRUC
B64

CATER D.,POWER IN WASHINGTON: A CRITICAL LOOK AT   REPRESENT
TODAY'S STRUGGLE TO GOVERN IN THE NATION'S CAPITAL.   GOV/REL
USA+45 NAT/G LEGIS ADMIN EXEC LOBBY PLURISM 20.   INGP/REL
PAGE 19 B0392   EX/STRUC
B64

COMMITTEE ECONOMIC DEVELOPMENT,IMPROVING EXECUTIVE   EXEC
MANAGEMENT IN THE FEDERAL GOVERNMENT. USA+45 CHIEF   MGT
DELIB/GP WORKER PLAN PAY SENIOR ADMIN EFFICIENCY 20   TOP/EX
PRESIDENT. PAGE 22 B0457   NAT/G
B64

EDELMAN M.,THE SYMBOLIC USES OF POWER. USA+45   CLIENT
EX/STRUC CONTROL GP/REL INGP/REL...MGT T. PAGE 32   PWR
B0653   EXEC
ELITES
B64

GUTTSMAN W.L.,THE BRITISH POLITICAL ELITE. EUR+WWI   NAT/G

MOD/EUR STRATA FAM LABOR POL/PAR SCHOOL VOL/ASSN   SOC
DELIB/GP LEGIS LEGIT EXEC CHOOSE ATTIT ALL/VALS   UK
...STAT BIOG TIME/SEQ CHARTS VAL/FREE. PAGE 45   ELITES
B0905
                                                     B64
LI C.M.,INDUSTRIAL DEVELOPMENT IN COMMUNIST CHINA.   ASIA
CHINA/COM ECO/DEV ECO/UNDEV AGRI FINAN INDUS MARKET TEC/DEV
LABOR NAT/G ECO/TAC INT/TRADE EXEC ALL/VALS
...POLICY RELATIV TREND WORK TOT/POP VAL/FREE 20.
PAGE 65 B1311
                                                     B64
NEUSTADT R.,PRESIDENTIAL POWER. USA+45 CONSTN NAT/G TOP/EX
CHIEF LEGIS CREATE EDU/PROP LEGIT ADMIN EXEC COERCE SKILL
ATTIT PERSON RIGID/FLEX PWR CONGRESS 20 PRESIDENT
TRUMAN/HS EISNHWR/DD. PAGE 78 B1575
                                                     B64
PIPES R.,THE FORMATION OF THE SOVIET UNION. EUR+WWI COM
MOD/EUR STRUCT ECO/UNDEV NAT/G LEGIS DOMIN LEGIT   USSR
CT/SYS EXEC COERCE ALL/VALS...POLICY RELATIV   RUSSIA
HIST/WRIT TIME/SEQ TOT/POP 19/20. PAGE 83 B1677
                                                     B64
SAYLES L.R.,MANAGERIAL BEHAVIOR: ADMINISTRATION IN   CONCPT
COMPLEX ORGANIZATIONS. INDUS LG/CO PROB/SOLV   ADMIN
CONTROL EXEC INGP/REL PERS/REL SKILL...MGT OBS   TOP/EX
PREDICT GEN/LAWS 20. PAGE 93 B1874   EX/STRUC
                                                     B64
STANLEY D.T.,THE HIGHER CIVIL SERVICE: AN   NAT/G
EVALUATION OF FEDERAL PERSONNEL PRACTICES. USA+45   ADMIN
CREATE EXEC ROUTINE CENTRAL...MGT SAMP IDEA/COMP   CONTROL
METH/COMP 20 CIVIL/SERV. PAGE 100 B2020   EFFICIENCY
                                                     B64
TINBERGEN J.,CENTRAL PLANNING. COM INTELL ECO/DEV   PLAN
ECO/UNDEV FINAN INT/ORG PROB/SOLV ECO/TAC CONTROL   INDUS
EXEC ROUTINE DECISION. PAGE 104 B2111   MGT
                                                     CENTRAL
                                                     B64
US SENATE COMM GOVT OPERATIONS,THE SECRETARY OF   DIPLOM
STATE AND THE AMBASSADOR. USA+45 CHIEF CONSULT   DELIB/GP
EX/STRUC FORCES PLAN ADMIN EXEC INGP/REL ROLE   NAT/G
...ANTHOL 20 PRESIDENT DEPT/STATE. PAGE 110 B2215
                                                     B64
WILDAVSKY A.,LEADERSHIP IN A SMALL TOWN. USA+45   LEAD
STRUCT PROB/SOLV EXEC PARTIC RACE/REL PWR PLURISM   MUNIC
...SOC 20 NEGRO WATER CIV/RIGHTS OBERLIN CITY/MGT.   ELITES
PAGE 116 B2348
                                                     L64
FOX G.H.,"PERCEPTIONS OF THE VIETNAMESE PUBLIC   ADMIN
ADMINISTRATION SYSTEM" VIETNAM ELITES CONTROL EXEC   EX/STRUC
LEAD PWR...INT 20. PAGE 37 B0745   INGP/REL
                                                     ROLE
                                                     L64
GILBERT C.E.,"NATIONAL POLITICAL ALIGNMENTS AND THE MUNIC
POLITICS OF LARGE CITIES." ELITES LOC/G NAT/G LEGIS CHOOSE
EXEC LEAD PLURISM GOV/COMP. PAGE 39 B0800   POL/PAR
                                                     PWR
                                                     L64
PRUITT D.G.,"PROBLEM SOLVING IN THE DEPARTMENT OF   ROUTINE
STATE." USA+45 NAT/G CONSULT PROB/SOLV EXEC PWR   MGT
...DECISION INT ORG/CHARTS 20. PAGE 85 B1713   DIPLOM
                                                     L64
RIPLEY R.B.,"INTERAGENCY COMMITTEES AND   EXEC
INCREMENTALISM: THE CASE OF AID TO INDIA." INDIA   MGT
USA+45 INTELL NAT/G DELIB/GP ACT/RES DIPLOM ROUTINE FOR/AID
NAT/LISM ATTIT PWR...SOC CONCPT NEW/IDEA TIME/SEQ
CON/ANAL VAL/FREE 20. PAGE 89 B1790
                                                     S64
CLIGNET R.,"POTENTIAL ELITES IN GHANA AND THE IVORY PWR
COAST: A PRELIMINARY SURVEY." AFR CULTURE ELITES   LEGIT
STRATA KIN NAT/G SECT DOMIN EXEC ORD/FREE RESPECT   IVORY/CST
SKILL...POLICY RELATIV GP/COMP NAT/COMP 20. PAGE 21 GHANA
B0438
                                                     S64
HOSCH L.G.,"PUBLIC ADMINISTRATION ON THE   INT/ORG
INTERNATIONAL FRONTIER." WOR+45 R+D NAT/G EDU/PROP   MGT
EXEC KNOWL ORD/FREE VAL/FREE 20 UN. PAGE 52 B1046
                                                     S64
KAMMERER G.M.,"ROLE DIVERSITY OF CITY MANAGERS."   MUNIC
LOC/G ADMIN LEAD PERCEPT PWR GP/COMP. PAGE 57 B1163 EXEC
                                                     ATTIT
                                                     ROLE
                                                     S64
KAMMERER G.M.,"URBAN LEADERSHIP DURING CHANGE."   MUNIC
LEAD PARTIC REPRESENT GP/REL PLURISM...DECISION   PWR
GP/COMP. PAGE 58 B1164   ELITES
                                                     EXEC
                                                     S64
KENNAN G.F.,"POLYCENTRISM AND WESTERN POLICY." ASIA RIGID/FLEX
CHINA/COM COM FUT USA+45 USSR NAT/G ACT/RES DOMIN   ATTIT
EDU/PROP EXEC COERCE DISPL PERCEPT...POLICY   DIPLOM
COLD/WAR 20. PAGE 59 B1192
                                                     S64
STANLEY D.T.,"EXCELLENCE IN PUBLIC SERVICE - HOW DO EFFICIENCY
YOU REALLY KNOW?" EXEC 20. PAGE 100 B2019   EX/STRUC
                                                     ADMIN
                                                     CONTROL

THOMPSON V.A.,"ADMINISTRATIVE OBJECTIVES FOR   S64
DEVELOPMENT ADMINISTRATION." WOR+45 CREATE PLAN   ECO/UNDEV
DOMIN EDU/PROP EXEC ROUTINE ATTIT ORD/FREE PWR   MGT
...POLICY GEN/LAWS VAL/FREE. PAGE 104 B2107
                                                     B65
AMERICAN ASSEMBLY COLUMBIA U,THE FEDERAL GOVERNMENT ADMIN
SERVICE. USA+45 POL/PAR EX/STRUC EXEC 20. PAGE 4   MGT
B0082   NAT/G
                                                     INGP/REL
                                                     B65
BOCK E.,GOVERNMENT REGULATION OF BUSINESS. USA+45   MGT
LAW EX/STRUC LEGIS EXEC ORD/FREE PWR...ANTHOL   ADMIN
CONGRESS. PAGE 13 B0261   NAT/G
                                                     CONTROL
                                                     B65
COHEN H.,THE DEMONICS OF BUREAUCRACY: PROBLEMS OF   EXEC
CHANGE IN A GOVERNMENT AGENCY. USA+45 CLIENT   EX/STRUC
ROUTINE REPRESENT 20. PAGE 22 B0443   INGP/REL
                                                     ADMIN
                                                     B65
DE GRAZIA A.,REPUBLIC IN CRISIS: CONGRESS AGAINST   LEGIS
THE EXECUTIVE FORCE. USA+45 USA-45 SOCIETY POL/PAR   EXEC
CHIEF DOMIN ROLE ORD/FREE PWR...CONCPT MYTH BIBLIOG GOV/REL
20 CONGRESS. PAGE 27 B0556   CONTROL
                                                     B65
ECCLES H.E.,MILITARY CONCEPTS AND PHILOSOPHY.   PLAN
USA+45 STRUCT EXEC ROUTINE COERCE WAR CIVMIL/REL   DRIVE
COST...OBS GEN/LAWS COLD/WAR. PAGE 32 B0648   LEAD
                                                     FORCES
                                                     B65
ETZIONI A.,POLITICAL UNIFICATION* A COMPARATIVE   INT/ORG
STUDY OF LEADERS AND FORCES. EUR+WWI ISLAM L/A+17C   FORCES
WOR+45 ELITES STRATA EXEC WEALTH...TIME/SEQ TREND   ECO/TAC
SOC/EXP. PAGE 34 B0686   REGION
                                                     B65
FOLTZ W.J.,FROM FRENCH WEST AFRICA TO THE MALI   EXEC
FEDERATION. AFR FRANCE MALI ADMIN CONTROL FEDERAL   TOP/EX
...DECISION 20. PAGE 36 B0734   ELITES
                                                     LEAD
                                                     B65
GOODSELL C.T.,ADMINISTRATION OF A REVOLUTION.   EXEC
PUERT/RICO ECO/UNDEV FINAN MUNIC POL/PAR PROVS   SOC
LEGIS PLAN BUDGET RECEIVE ADMIN COLONIAL LEAD 20
ROOSEVLT/F. PAGE 41 B0827
                                                     B65
HARR J.E.,THE DEVELOPMENT OF CAREERS IN THE FOREIGN OP/RES
SERVICE. CREATE SENIOR EXEC FEEDBACK GOV/REL   MGT
EFFICIENCY ATTIT RESPECT ORG/CHARTS. PAGE 47 B0953   ADMIN
                                                     DIPLOM
                                                     B65
HODGSON R.C.,THE EXECUTIVE ROLE CONSTELLATION: AN   LG/CO
ANALYSIS OF PERSONALITY AND ROLE RELATIONS IN   ADMIN
MANAGEMENT. USA+45 PUB/INST EXEC PERS/REL PERSON   TOP/EX
...PSY PERS/COMP HYPO/EXP 20. PAGE 51 B1027   ROLE
                                                     B65
KWEDER J.B.,THE ROLES OF THE MANAGER, MAYOR, AND   MUNIC
COUNCILMEN IN POLICYMAKING. LEGIS PERS/REL ATTIT   EXEC
ROLE PWR GP/COMP. PAGE 62 B1246   LEAD
                                                     DECISION
                                                     B65
MARTIN R.,PUBLIC ADMINISTRATION AND DEMOCRACY.   EX/STRUC
ELITES NAT/G ADMIN EXEC ROUTINE INGP/REL. PAGE 70   DECISION
B1412   REPRESENT
                                                     GP/REL
                                                     B65
MOORE C.H.,TUNISIA SINCE INDEPENDENCE. ELITES LOC/G NAT/G
POL/PAR ADMIN COLONIAL CONTROL EXEC GOV/REL   EX/STRUC
TOTALISM MARXISM...INT 20 TUNIS. PAGE 75 B1513   SOCISM
                                                     B65
PHELPS-FETHERS I.,SOVIET INTERNATIONAL FRONT   USSR
ORGANIZATIONS* A CONCISE HANDBOOK. DIPLOM DOMIN   EDU/PROP
LEGIT ADMIN EXEC GP/REL PEACE MARXISM...TIME/SEQ   ASIA
GP/COMP. PAGE 83 B1668   COM
                                                     B65
ROURKE F.E.,BUREAUCRATIC POWER IN NATIONAL   EX/STRUC
POLITICS. ADMIN CONTROL EXEC GOV/REL INGP/REL 20.   EFFICIENCY
PAGE 91 B1838   REPRESENT
                                                     PWR
                                                     B65
STEINER G.A.,THE CREATIVE ORGANIZATION. ELITES   CREATE
LG/CO PLAN PROB/SOLV TEC/DEV INSPECT CAP/ISM   MGT
CONTROL EXEC PERSON...METH/COMP HYPO/EXP 20.   ADMIN
PAGE 100 B2029   SOC
                                                     B65
VONGLAHN G.,LAW AMONG NATIONS: AN INTRODUCTION TO   CONSTN
PUBLIC INTERNATIONAL LAW. UNIV WOR+45 LAW INT/ORG   JURID
NAT/G LEGIT EXEC RIGID/FLEX...CONCPT TIME/SEQ   INT/LAW
GEN/LAWS UN TOT/POP 20. PAGE 112 B2267
                                                     S65
ALEXANDER T.,"SYNECTICS: INVENTING BY THE MADNESS   PROB/SOLV
METHOD." DELIB/GP TOP/EX ACT/RES TEC/DEV EXEC TASK   OP/RES
KNOWL...MGT METH/COMP 20. PAGE 4 B0073   CREATE
                                                     CONSULT
                                                     S65
AMLUND C.A.,"EXECUTIVE-LEGISLATIVE IMBALANCE: LEGIS

TRUMAN TO KENNEDY." USA+45 NAT/G GOV/REL PWR. EXEC DECISION
PAGE 4 B0090

S65

HOLSTI O.R.,"THE 1914 CASE." MOD/EUR COMPUTER CON/ANAL
DIPLOM EDU/PROP EXEC...DECISION PSY PROBABIL STAT PERCEPT
COMPUT/IR SOC/EXP TIME. PAGE 51 B1036 WAR

S65

OSTGAARD E.,"FACTORS INFLUENCING THE FLOW OF NEWS." EDU/PROP
COM/IND BUDGET DIPLOM EXEC GP/REL COST ATTIT SAMP. PERCEPT
PAGE 80 B1618 RECORD

C65

HUNTINGTON S.P.,"CONGRESSIONAL RESPONSES TO THE FUT
TWENTIETH CENTURY IN D. TRUMAN. ED. THE CONGRESS LEAD
AND AMERICA'S FUTURE." USA+45 USA+45 DIPLOM SENIOR NAT/G
ADMIN EXEC PWR...SOC 20 CONGRESS. PAGE 53 B1067 LEGIS

B66

BEAUFRE A.,NATO AND EUROPE. WOR+45 PLAN CONFER EXEC INT/ORG
NUC/PWR ATTIT...POLICY 20 NATO EUROPE. PAGE 10 DETER
B0203 DIPLOM
ADMIN

B66

BROWN R.E.,JUDGMENT IN ADMINISTRATION. DRIVE PERSON ADMIN
KNOWL...DECISION 20. PAGE 16 B0326 EXEC
SKILL
PROB/SOLV

B66

CHAPMAN B.,THE PROFESSION OF GOVERNMENT: THE PUBLIC BIBLIOG
SERVICE IN EUROPE. CONSTN NAT/G POL/PAR EX/STRUC ADMIN
LEGIS TOP/EX PROB/SOLV DEBATE EXEC PARL/PROC PARTIC EUR+WWI
20. PAGE 20 B0411 GOV/COMP

B66

GERBERDING W.P.,UNITED STATES FOREIGN POLICY: PROB/SOLV
PERSPECTIVES AND ANALYSIS. USA+45 LEGIS EXEC LEAD CHIEF
REPRESENT PWR 20. PAGE 39 B0791 EX/STRUC
CONTROL

B66

ZALEZNIK A.,HUMAN DILEMMAS OF LEADERSHIP. ELITES LEAD
INDUS EX/STRUC INGP/REL ATTIT...PSY 20. PAGE 119 PERSON
B2397 EXEC
MGT

L66

MCAUSLAN J.P.W.,"CONSTITUTIONAL INNOVATION AND CONSTN
POLITICAL STABILITY IN TANZANIA: A PRELIMINARY NAT/G
ASSESSMENT." AFR TANZANIA ELITES CHIEF EX/STRUC EXEC
RIGID/FLEX PWR 20 PRESIDENT BUREAUCRCY. PAGE 71 POL/PAR
B1440

S66

BALDWIN D.A.,"CONGRESSIONAL INITIATIVE IN FOREIGN EXEC
POLICY." NAT/G BARGAIN DIPLOM FOR/AID RENT GIVE TOP/EX
...DECISION CONGRESS. PAGE 8 B0171 GOV/REL

S66

BURDETTE F.L.,"SELECTED ARTICLES AND DOCUMENTS ON BIBLIOG
AMERICAN GOVERNMENT AND POLITICS." LAW LOC/G MUNIC USA+45
NAT/G POL/PAR PROVS LEGIS BAL/PWR ADMIN EXEC JURID
REPRESENT MGT. PAGE 17 B0348 CONSTN

S66

PALMER M.,"THE UNITED ARAB REPUBLIC* AN ASSESSMENT UAR
OF ITS FAILURE." ELITES ECO/UNDEV POL/PAR FORCES SYRIA
ECO/TAC RUMOR ADMIN EXEC EFFICIENCY ATTIT SOCISM REGION
...INT NASSER/G. PAGE 81 B1628 FEDERAL

S66

ZUCKERT E.M.,"THE SERVICE SECRETARY* HAS HE A OBS
USEFUL ROLE?" USA+45 TOP/EX PLAN ADMIN EXEC DETER OP/RES
NUC/PWR WEAPON...MGT RECORD MCNAMARA/R. PAGE 119 DIPLOM
B2407 FORCES

C66

SHERMAN H.,"IT ALL DEPENDS." USA+45 FINAN MARKET LG/CO
PLAN PROB/SOLV EXEC PARTIC INGP/REL SUPEGO MGT
...DECISION BIBLIOG 20. PAGE 96 B1944 ADMIN
POLICY

B67

ANGEL D.D.,ROMNEY. LABOR LG/CO NAT/G EXEC WAR BIOG
RACE/REL PERSON ORD/FREE...MGT WORSHIP 20 CHIEF
ROMNEY/GEO CIV/RIGHTS MORMON GOVERNOR. PAGE 5 B0108 PROVS
POLICY

B67

BROWN L.N.,FRENCH ADMINISTRATIVE LAW. FRANCE UK EX/STRUC
CONSTN NAT/G LEGIS DOMIN CONTROL EXEC PARL/PROC PWR LAW
...JURID METH/COMP GEN/METH. PAGE 16 B0324 IDEA/COMP
CT/SYS

B67

BRZEZINSKI Z.K.,THE SOVIET BLOC: UNITY AND CONFLICT NAT/G
(2ND ED., REV., ENLARGED). COM POLAND USSR INTELL DIPLOM
CHIEF EX/STRUC CONTROL EXEC GOV/REL PWR MARXISM
...TREND IDEA/COMP 20 LENIN/VI MARX/KARL STALIN/J.
PAGE 16 B0336

B67

HOROWITZ I.L.,THE RISE AND FALL OF PROJECT CAMELOT: NAT/G
STUDIES IN THE RELATIONSHIP BETWEEN SOCIAL SCIENCE ACADEM
AND PRACTICAL POLITICS. USA+45 WOR+45 CULTURE ACT/RES
FORCES LEGIS EXEC CIVMIL/REL KNOWL...POLICY SOC GP/REL
METH/CNCPT 20. PAGE 51 B1043

B67

LEACH R.H.,GOVERNING THE AMERICAN NATION. FUT NAT/G
USA+45 USA+45 CONSTN POL/PAR PLAN ADJUD EXEC CONSEN LEGIS
CONGRESS PRESIDENT. PAGE 63 B1278 PWR

B67

MCCONNELL G.,THE MODERN PRESIDENCY. USA+45 CONSTN NAT/G
TOP/EX DOMIN EXEC CHOOSE PWR...MGT 20. PAGE 72 CHIEF
B1446 EX/STRUC

B67

MINTZ M.,BY PRESCRIPTION ONLY. USA+45 NAT/G BIO/SOC
EX/STRUC PLAN TEC/DEV EXEC EFFICIENCY HEALTH...MGT PROC/MFG
SOC/WK 20. PAGE 74 B1491 CONTROL
POLICY

B67

SALMOND J.A.,THE CIVILIAN CONSERVATION CORPS, ADMIN
1933-1942. USA-45 NAT/G CREATE EXEC EFFICIENCY ECO/TAC
WEALTH...BIBLIOG 20 ROOSEVLT/F. PAGE 92 B1864 TASK
AGRI

B67

TOMA P.A.,THE POLITICS OF FOOD FOR PEACE: FOR/AID
EXECUTIVE-LEGISLATIVE INTERACTION. USA+45 ECO/UNDEV POLICY
POL/PAR DEBATE EXEC LOBBY CHOOSE PEACE...DECISION LEGIS
CHARTS. PAGE 104 B2113 AGRI

B67

US DEPARTMENT OF JUSTICE,ANNUAL REPORT OF THE ADMIN
OFFICE OF ADMINISTRATIVE PROCEDURE. USA+45 NAT/G
PROB/SOLV EDU/PROP EXEC EFFICIENCY KNOWL ROUTINE
...POLICY STAT 20. PAGE 108 B2181 GOV/REL

B67

WARREN S.,THE AMERICAN PRESIDENT. POL/PAR FORCES CHIEF
LEGIS DIPLOM ECO/TAC ADMIN EXEC PWR...ANTHOL 18/20 LEAD
ROOSEVLT/F KENNEDY/JF JOHNSON/LB TRUMAN/HS NAT/G
WILSON/W. PAGE 114 B2297 CONSTN

S67

BRADLEY A.W.,"CONSTITUTION-MAKING IN UGANDA." NAT/G
UGANDA LAW CHIEF DELIB/GP LEGIS ADMIN EXEC CREATE
PARL/PROC RACE/REL ORD/FREE...GOV/COMP 20. PAGE 14 CONSTN
B0295 FEDERAL

S67

CROCKETT D.G.,"THE MP AND HIS CONSTITUENTS." UK EXEC
POL/PAR...DECISION 20. PAGE 25 B0506 NAT/G
PERS/REL
REPRESENT

S67

GOLIGHTLY H.O.,"THE AIRLINES: A CASE STUDY IN DIST/IND
MANAGEMENT INNOVATION." USA+45 AIR FINAN INDUS MARKET
TOP/EX CREATE PLAN PROB/SOLV ADMIN EXEC PROFIT MGT
...DECISION 20. PAGE 40 B0820 TEC/DEV

S67

HAIRE M.,"MANAGING MANAGEMENT MANPOWER." EX/STRUC MGT
OP/RES PAY EDU/PROP COST EFFICIENCY...PREDICT SIMUL EXEC
20. PAGE 45 B0920 LEAD
INDUS

S67

JOHNSON L.B.,"BULLETS DO NOT DISCRIMINATE-LANDLORDS NAT/G
DO." PROB/SOLV EXEC LOBBY DEMAND...REALPOL SOC 20. DISCRIM
PAGE 57 B1145 POLICY

S67

KRARUP O.,"JUDICIAL REVIEW OF ADMINISTRATIVE ACTION ADJUD
IN DENMARK." DENMARK LAW CT/SYS...JURID CONCPT CONTROL
19/20. PAGE 61 B1234 EXEC
DECISION

S67

LEES J.P.,"LEGISLATIVE REVIEW AND BUREAUCRATIC SUPEGO
RESPONSIBILITY." USA+45 FINAN NAT/G DELIB/GP PLAN BUDGET
PROB/SOLV CONFER CONTROL GP/REL DEMAND...DECISION LEGIS
20 CONGRESS PRESIDENT HOUSE/REP BUREAUCRCY. PAGE 63 EXEC
B1281

S67

MAINZER L.C.,"HONOR IN THE BUREAUCRATIC LIFE." ADMIN
REPRESENT EFFICIENCY 20. PAGE 68 B1382 MORAL
EX/STRUC
EXEC

S67

O'DELL J.H.,"THE JULY REBELLIONS AND THE 'MILITARY PWR
STATE'." USA+45 VIETNAM STRATA CHIEF WORKER NAT/G
COLONIAL EXEC CROWD CIVMIL/REL RACE/REL TOTALISM COERCE
...WELF/ST PACIFIST 20 NEGRO JOHNSON/LB PRESIDENT FORCES
CIV/RIGHTS. PAGE 79 B1599

S67

ROBERTS E.B.,"THE PROBLEM OF AGING ORGANIZATIONS." INDUS
INTELL PROB/SOLV ADMIN EXEC FEEDBACK EFFICIENCY R+D
PRODUC...GEN/LAWS 20. PAGE 89 B1794 MGT
PLAN

S67

ROSENBERG B.,"ETHNIC LIBERALISM AND EMPLOYMENT RACE/REL
DISCRIMINATION IN THE NORTH." USA+45 TOP/EX ATTIT
PROB/SOLV ADMIN REGION PERS/REL DISCRIM...INT WORKER
IDEA/COMP. PAGE 90 B1820 EXEC

S67

SCOTT W.R.,"ORGANIZATIONAL EVALUATION AND EXEC
AUTHORITY." CONTROL SANCTION PERS/REL ATTIT DRIVE WORKER
...SOC CONCPT OBS CHARTS IDEA/COMP 20. PAGE 95 INSPECT
B1921 EX/STRUC

S67

SPACKMAN A.,"THE SENATE OF TRINIDAD AND TOBAGO." ELITES
L/A+17C TRINIDAD WEST/IND NAT/G POL/PAR DELIB/GP EFFICIENCY
OP/RES PROB/SOLV EDU/PROP EXEC LOBBY ROUTINE LEGIS
REPRESENT GP/REL 20. PAGE 99 B2002 DECISION

US SENATE COMM AERO SPACE SCI,AERONAUTICAL RESEARCH
AND DEVELOPMENT POLICY: HEARINGS, COMM ON
AERONAUTICAL AND SPACE SCIENCES...1967 (PAMPHLET).
R+D PROB/SOLV EXEC GOV/REL 20 DEPT/DEFEN FAA NASA
CONGRESS. PAGE 109 B2210
DIST/IND SPACE NAT/G PLAN
N67

GRAM H.A.,"BUSINESS ETHICS AND THE CORPORATION."
LG/CO SECT PROB/SOLV CONTROL EXEC GP/REL INGP/REL
PERS/REL ROLE MORAL PWR...DECISION 20. PAGE 42
B0850
POLICY ADMIN MGT
S68

EXECUTIVE....SEE TOP/EX

EXECUTIVE ESTABLISHMENTS....SEE EX/STRUC

EXECUTIVE PROCESS....SEE EXEC

EXHIBIT....DISPLAY

EXPECTATIONS....SEE PROBABIL, SUPEGO, PREDICT

EXPERIMENTATION....SEE EXPERIMENTATION INDEX, P. XIV

EXPOSTFACT....EX POST FACTO LAWS

EXPROPRIAT....EXPROPRIATION

EXTR/IND....EXTRACTIVE INDUSTRY (FISHING, LUMBERING, ETC.)

KYRIAK T.E.,EAST EUROPE: BIBLIOGRAPHY--INDEX TO US
JPRS RESEARCH TRANSLATIONS. ALBANIA BULGARIA COM
CZECHOSLVK HUNGARY POLAND ROMANIA AGRI EXTR/IND
FINAN SERV/IND INT/TRADE WEAPON...GEOG MGT SOC 20.
PAGE 62 B1247
BIBLIOG/A PRESS MARXISM INDUS
N

SANDERSON E.,AFRICA IN THE NINETEENTH CENTURY.
FRANCE UK EXTR/IND FORCES LEGIS ADMIN WAR DISCRIM
ORD/FREE...GEOG GP/COMP SOC/INTEG 19. PAGE 92 B1867
COLONIAL AFR DIPLOM
B00

THE GOVERNMENT OF SOUTH AFRICA (VOL. II). SOUTH/AFR
STRATA EXTR/IND EX/STRUC TOP/EX BUDGET ADJUD ADMIN
CT/SYS PRODUC...CORREL CENSUS 19 RAILROAD
CIVIL/SERV POSTAL/SYS. PAGE 2 B0033
CONSTN FINAN LEGIS NAT/G
B08

THOMAS F.,THE ENVIRONMENTAL BASIS OF SOCIETY.
USA-45 WOR-45 STRATA ECO/DEV EXTR/IND CONSULT
ECO/TAC ROUTINE ATTIT ALL/VALS...SOC TIME/SEQ.
PAGE 104 B2098
SOCIETY GEOG
B25

DAY P.,CRISIS IN SOUTH AFRICA. SOUTH/AFR UK KIN
MUNIC ECO/TAC RECEIVE 20 SMUTS/JAN MIGRATION.
PAGE 27 B0548
RACE/REL COLONIAL ADMIN EXTR/IND
B48

US TARIFF COMMISSION,LIST OF PUBLICATIONS OF THE
TARIFF COMMISSION (PAMPHLET). USA+45 USA-45 AGRI
EXTR/IND INDUS INT/TRADE...STAT 20. PAGE 111 B2245
BIBLIOG TARIFFS NAT/G ADMIN
B51

CENTRAL ASIAN RESEARCH CENTRE,BIBLIOGRAPHY OF
RECENT SOVIET SOURCE MATERIAL ON SOVIET CENTRAL
ASIA AND THE BORDERLANDS. AFGHANISTN INDIA PAKISTAN
UAR USSR ECO/UNDEV AGRI EXTR/IND INDUS ACADEM ADMIN
...HEAL HUM LING CON/ANAL 20. PAGE 19 B0399
BIBLIOG/A COM CULTURE NAT/G
B57

DIEBOLD W. JR.,THE SCHUMAN PLAN: A STUDY IN
ECONOMIC COOPERATION, 1950-1959. EUR+WWI FRANCE
GERMANY USA+45 EXTR/IND CONSULT DELIB/GP PLAN
DIPLOM ECO/TAC INT/TRADE ROUTINE ORD/FREE WEALTH
...METH/CNCPT STAT CONT/OBS INT TIME/SEQ ECSC 20.
PAGE 29 B0591
INT/ORG REGION
B59

LENCZOWSKI G.,OIL AND STATE IN THE MIDDLE EAST. FUT
IRAN LAW ECO/UNDEV EXTR/IND NAT/G TOP/EX PLAN
TEC/DEV ECO/TAC LEGIT ADMIN COERCE ATTIT ALL/VALS
PWR...CHARTS 20. PAGE 64 B1288
ISLAM INDUS NAT/LISM
B60

LAHAYE R.,LES ENTREPRISES PUBLIQUES AU MAROC.
FRANCE MOROCCO LAW DIST/IND EXTR/IND FINAN CONSULT
PLAN TEC/DEV ADMIN AGREE CONTROL OWN...POLICY 20.
PAGE 62 B1250
NAT/G INDUS ECO/UNDEV ECO/TAC
B61

CARPER E.T.,ILLINOIS GOES TO CONGRESS FOR ARMY
LAND. USA+45 LAW EXTR/IND PROVS REGION CIVMIL/REL
GOV/REL FEDERAL ATTIT 20 ILLINOIS SENATE CONGRESS
DIRKSEN/E DOUGLAS/P. PAGE 19 B0385
ADMIN LOBBY GEOG LEGIS
B62

DUCROS B.,"MOBILISATION DES RESSOURCES PRODUCTIVES
ET DEVELOPPEMENT." FUT INTELL SOCIETY COM/IND
DIST/IND EXTR/IND FINAN INDUS ROUTINE WEALTH
...METH/CNCPT OBS 20. PAGE 31 B0625
ECO/UNDEV TEC/DEV
S63

WITHERELL J.W.,OFFICIAL PUBLICATIONS OF FRENCH
EQUATORIAL AFRICA, FRENCH CAMEROONS, AND TOGO,
BIBLIOG/A AFR
B64

1946-1958 (PAMPHLET). CAMEROON CHAD FRANCE GABON
TOGO LAW ECO/UNDEV EXTR/IND INT/TRADE...GEOG HEAL
20. PAGE 117 B2367
NAT/G ADMIN

CARMICHAEL D.M.,"FORTY YEARS OF WATER POLLUTION
CONTROL IN WISCONSIN: A CASE STUDY." LAW EXTR/IND
INDUS MUNIC DELIB/GP PLAN PROB/SOLV SANCTION
...CENSUS CHARTS 20 WISCONSIN. PAGE 19 B0382
HEALTH CONTROL ADMIN ADJUD
L67

JENCKS C.E.,"SOCIAL STATUS OF COAL MINERS IN
BRITAIN SINCE NATIONALIZATION." UK STRATA STRUCT
LABOR RECEIVE GP/REL INCOME OWN ATTIT HABITAT...MGT
T 20. PAGE 56 B1128
EXTR/IND WORKER CONTROL NAT/G
S67

EXTRACTIVE INDUSTRY....SEE EXTR/IND

F

FAA....U.S. FEDERAL AVIATION AGENCY

DEAN A.L.,FEDERAL AGENCY APPROACHES TO FIELD
MANAGEMENT (PAMPHLET). R+D DELIB/GP EX/STRUC
PROB/SOLV GOV/REL...CLASSIF BIBLIOG 20 FAA NASA
DEPT/HEW POSTAL/SYS IRS. PAGE 28 B0563
ADMIN MGT NAT/G OP/RES
B63

WHITNAH D.R.,SAFER SKYWAYS. DIST/IND DELIB/GP
FORCES TOP/EX WORKER TEC/DEV ROUTINE WAR CIVMIL/REL
COST...TIME/SEQ 20 FAA CAB. PAGE 116 B2342
ADMIN NAT/G AIR GOV/REL
B66

US SENATE COMM AERO SPACE SCI,AERONAUTICAL RESEARCH
AND DEVELOPMENT POLICY: HEARINGS, COMM ON
AERONAUTICAL AND SPACE SCIENCES...1967 (PAMPHLET).
R+D PROB/SOLV EXEC GOV/REL 20 DEPT/DEFEN FAA NASA
CONGRESS. PAGE 109 B2210
DIST/IND SPACE NAT/G PLAN
N67

FABAR R. B0693

FABIAN....FABIANS: MEMBERS AND/OR SUPPORTERS OF FABIAN
SOCIETY

FABREGA J. B0694

FABRYCKY W.J. B0695

FACE/GP....ACQUAINTANCE GROUP

GOSNELL H.F.,MACHINE POLITICS: CHICAGO MODEL.
COM/IND FACE/GP LOC/G EX/STRUC LEAD ROUTINE
SANCTION REPRESENT GOV/REL PWR...POLICY MATH OBS
INT CHARTS. PAGE 41 B0840
POL/PAR MUNIC ADMIN CHOOSE
B37

GELLHORN W.,FEDERAL ADMINISTRATIVE PROCEEDINGS.
USA+45 CLIENT FACE/GP NAT/G LOBBY REPRESENT PWR 20.
PAGE 39 B0788
EX/STRUC LAW ADJUD POLICY
B41

RANSHOFFEN-WERTHEIMER EF,THE INTERNATIONAL
SECRETARIAT: A GREAT EXPERIMENT IN INTERNATIONAL
ADMINISTRATION. EUR+WWI FUT CONSTN FACE/GP CONSULT
DELIB/GP ACT/RES ADMIN ROUTINE PEACE ORD/FREE...MGT
RECORD ORG/CHARTS LEAGUE/NAT WORK 20. PAGE 86 B1731
INT/ORG EXEC
B45

FORRESTAL J.,"THE NAVY: A STUDY IN ADMINISTRATION."
ELITES FACE/GP EX/STRUC PROB/SOLV REPRESENT
EFFICIENCY PRODUC. PAGE 37 B0741
FORCES INGP/REL ROUTINE EXEC
L46

LASSWELL H.D.,NATIONAL SECURITY AND INDIVIDUAL
FREEDOM. USA+45 R+D NAT/G VOL/ASSN CONSULT DELIB/GP
LEGIT ADMIN KNOWL ORD/FREE PWR...PLURIST TOT/POP
COLD/WAR 20. PAGE 63 B1268
FACE/GP ROUTINE BAL/PWR
B50

GUETZKOW H.,GROUPS, LEADERSHIP, AND MEN. FACE/GP
SECT EDU/PROP EXEC PERSON RESPECT...PERS/TEST
GEN/METH 20. PAGE 44 B0901
ATTIT SOC ELITES
B51

SCHRAMM W.,"COMMUNICATION IN THE SOVIETIZED STATE,
AS DEMONSTRATED IN KOREA." ASIA COM KOREA COM/IND
FACE/GP POL/PAR SCHOOL FORCES ADMIN PWR MARXISM
...SOC CONCPT MYTH INT BIOG TOT/POP 20. PAGE 94
B1901
ATTIT EDU/PROP TOTALISM
S51

ALLPORT G.W.,THE NATURE OF PREJUDICE. USA+45 WOR+45
STRATA FACE/GP KIN NEIGH SECT ADMIN GP/REL DISCRIM
ATTIT DRIVE LOVE RESPECT...PSY SOC MYTH QU/SEMANT
20. PAGE 4 B0078
CULTURE PERSON RACE/REL
B54

ANGELL R.,"GOVERNMENTS AND PEOPLES AS A FOCI FOR
PEACE-ORIENTED RESEARCH." WOR+45 CULTURE SOCIETY
FACE/GP ACT/RES CREATE PLAN DIPLOM EDU/PROP ROUTINE
ATTIT PERCEPT SKILL...POLICY CONCPT OBS TREND
GEN/METH 20. PAGE 5 B0110
FUT SOC PEACE
S55

SIMON H.A.,MODELS OF MAN, SOCIAL AND RATIONAL:
MATHEMATICAL ESSAYS ON RATIONAL HUMAN BEHAVIOR IN A
MATH SIMUL
B57

SOCIAL SETTING. UNIV LAW SOCIETY FACE/GP VOL/ASSN
CONSULT EX/STRUC LEGIS CREATE ADMIN ROUTINE ATTIT
DRIVE PWR...SOC CONCPT METH/CNCPT QUANT STAT
TOT/POP VAL/FREE 20. PAGE 97 B1959
                                                          B58

BROWNE C.G.,THE CONCEPT OF LEADERSHIP. UNIV FACE/GP   EXEC
DOMIN EDU/PROP LEGIT LEAD DRIVE PERSON PWR...MGT   CONCPT
SOC OBS SELF/OBS CONT/OBS INT PERS/TEST STERTYP
GEN/LAWS. PAGE 16 B0328
                                                          B58

SKINNER G.W.,LEADERSHIP AND POWER IN THE CHINESE   SOC
COMMUNITY OF THAILAND. ASIA S/ASIA STRATA FACE/GP   ELITES
KIN PROF/ORG VOL/ASSN EX/STRUC DOMIN PERSON RESPECT   THAILAND
...METH/CNCPT STAT INT QU BIOG CHARTS 20. PAGE 98
B1974
                                                          B58

TAYLOR H.,THE STATESMAN. MOD/EUR FACE/GP FAM NAT/G   EXEC
POL/PAR DELIB/GP LEGIS ATTIT PERSON PWR...POLICY   STRUCT
CONCPT OBS GEN/LAWS. PAGE 103 B2086
                                                          L58

HAVILAND H.F.,"FOREIGN AID AND THE POLICY PROCESS: LEGIS
1957." USA+45 FACE/GP POL/PAR VOL/ASSN CHIEF   PLAN
DELIB/GP ACT/RES LEGIT EXEC GOV/REL ATTIT DRIVE PWR   FOR/AID
...POLICY TESTS CONGRESS 20. PAGE 48 B0971
                                                          B60

BASS B.M.,LEADERSHIP, PSYCHOLOGY, AND   UNIV
ORGANIZATIONAL BEHAVIOR. DOMIN CHOOSE DRIVE PERSON   FACE/GP
PWR RESPECT SKILL...SOC METH/CNCPT OBS. PAGE 9   DELIB/GP
B0193   ROUTINE

FRIEDMANN W.G.,JOINT INTERNATIONAL BUSINESS   ECO/UNDEV
VENTURES. ASIA ISLAM L/A+17C ECO/DEV DIST/IND FINAN   INT/TRADE
PROC/MFG FACE/GP LG/CO NAT/G VOL/ASSN CONSULT
EX/STRUC PLAN ADMIN ROUTINE WEALTH...OLD/LIB WORK
20. PAGE 37 B0760
                                                          B61

LASSWELL H.D.,PSYCOPATHOLOGY AND POLITICS. WOR-45   ATTIT
CULTURE SOCIETY FACE/GP NAT/G CONSULT CREATE   GEN/METH
EDU/PROP EXEC ROUTINE DISPL DRIVE PERSON PWR
RESPECT...PSY CONCPT METH/CNCPT METH. PAGE 63 B1272
                                                          B61

PETRULLO L.,LEADERSHIP AND INTERPERSONAL BEHAVIOR.   PERSON
FACE/GP FAM PROF/ORG EX/STRUC FORCES DOMIN WAR   ATTIT
GP/REL PERS/REL EFFICIENCY PRODUC PWR...MGT PSY.   LEAD
PAGE 82 B1663   HABITAT
                                                          C61

VERBA S.,"SMALL GROUPS AND POLITICAL BEHAVIOR: A   LEAD
STUDY OF LEADERSHIP" DOMIN PARTIC ROUTINE GP/REL   ELITES
ATTIT DRIVE ALL/VALS...CONCPT IDEA/COMP LAB/EXP   FACE/GP
BIBLIOG METH. PAGE 112 B2259
                                                          S62

IKLE F.C.,"POLITICAL NEGOTIATION AS A PROCESS OF   ROUTINE
MODIFYING UTILITIES." WOR+45 FACE/GP LABOR NAT/G   DECISION
FORCES ACT/RES EDU/PROP DETER PERCEPT ALL/VALS   DIPLOM
...PSY NEW/IDEA HYPO/EXP GEN/METH 20. PAGE 53 B1076
                                                          S62

LARSON R.L.,"HOW TO DEFINE ADMINISTRATIVE   UNIV
PROBLEMS." ROUTINE PERCEPT KNOWL SKILL...MGT   FACE/GP
METH/CNCPT CHARTS TOT/POP. PAGE 63 B1263   INDUS
                                                     EXEC
                                                          S63

RUSTOW D.A.,"THE MILITARY IN MIDDLE EASTERN SOCIETY   FORCES
AND POLITICS." FUT ISLAM CONSTN SOCIETY FACE/GP   ELITES
NAT/G POL/PAR PROF/ORG CONSULT DOMIN ADMIN EXEC
REGION COERCE NAT/LISM ATTIT DRIVE PERSON ORD/FREE
PWR...POLICY CONCPT OBS STERTYP 20. PAGE 92 B1860
                                                          B64

COLLINS B.E.,A SOCIAL PSYCHOLOGY OF GROUP PROCESSES   FACE/GP
FOR DECISION-MAKING. PROB/SOLV ROUTINE...SOC CHARTS   DECISION
HYPO/EXP. PAGE 22 B0453   NAT/G
                                                      INDUS
                                                          B64

SULLIVAN G.,THE STORY OF THE PEACE CORPS. USA+45   INT/ORG
WOR+45 INTELL FACE/GP NAT/G SCHOOL VOL/ASSN CONSULT   ECO/UNDEV
EX/STRUC PLAN EDU/PROP ADMIN ATTIT DRIVE ALL/VALS   FOR/AID
...POLICY HEAL SOC CONCPT INT QU BIOG TREND SOC/EXP   PEACE
WORK. PAGE 102 B2054
                                                          S67

EDWARDS H.T.,"POWER STRUCTURE AND ITS COMMUNICATION   ELITES
IN SAN JOSE, COSTA RICA." COSTA/RICA L/A+17C STRATA   INGP/REL
FACE/GP POL/PAR EX/STRUC PROB/SOLV ADMIN LEAD   MUNIC
GP/REL PWR...STAT INT 20. PAGE 32 B0655   DOMIN
                                                          S67

FOX R.G.,"FAMILY, CASTE, AND COMMERCE IN A NORTH   CULTURE
INDIAN MARKET TOWN." INDIA STRATA AGRI FACE/GP FAM   GP/REL
NEIGH OP/RES BARGAIN ADMIN ROUTINE WEALTH...SOC   ECO/UNDEV
CHARTS 20. PAGE 37 B0747   DIST/IND

FACTION....FACTION

FACTOR ANALYSIS....SEE CON/ANAL

FAHRNKOPF N. B0696

FAHS C.B. B0697,B0698

FAINSOD M. B0699,B0700

FAIR EMPLOYMENT PRACTICES COMMISSION....SEE FEPC

FAIR/LABOR....FAIR LABOR STANDARD ACT

FAIRLIE J.A. B0701

FAIRNESS, JUSTICE....SEE VALUES INDEX

FALANGE....FALANGE PARTY (SPAIN)

FALK L.A. B0702

FALKLAND/I....FALKLAND ISLANDS

FALL B.B. B0703

FAM....FAMILY

                                                          NCO

STOLPER W.,"SOCIAL FACTORS IN ECONOMIC PLANNING,   ECO/UNDEV
WITH SPECIAL REFERENCE TO NIGERIA" AFR NIGER   PLAN
CULTURE FAM SECT RECEIVE ETIQUET ADMIN DEMAND 20.   ADJUST
PAGE 101 B2045   RISK
                                                          B02

MOREL E.D.,AFFAIRS OF WEST AFRICA. UK FINAN INDUS   COLONIAL
FAM KIN SECT CHIEF WORKER DIPLOM RACE/REL LITERACY   ADMIN
HEALTH...CHARTS 18/20 AFRICA/W NEGRO. PAGE 75 B1521   AFR
                                                          B30

MURCHISON C.,PSYCHOLOGIES OF 1930. UNIV USA-45   CREATE
CULTURE INTELL SOCIETY STRATA FAM ROUTINE BIO/SOC   PERSON
DRIVE RIGID/FLEX SUPEGO...NEW/IDEA OBS SELF/OBS
CONT/OBS 20. PAGE 76 B1543
                                                          B44

DAHL D.,SICKNESS BENEFITS AND GROUP PURCHASE OF   BIBLIOG/A
MEDICAL CARE FOR INDUSTRIAL EMPLOYEES. FAM LABOR   INDUS
NAT/G PLAN...POLICY MGT SOC STAT 20. PAGE 25 B0519   WORKER
                                                      HEAL
                                                          B48

HULL C.,THE MEMOIRS OF CORDELL HULL (VOLUME ONE).   BIOG
USA-45 WOR-45 CONSTN FAM LOC/G NAT/G PROVS DELIB/GP   DIPLOM
FORCES LEGIS TOP/EX BAL/PWR LEGIT ADMIN EXEC WAR
ATTIT ORD/FREE PWR...MAJORIT SELF/OBS TIME/SEQ
TREND NAZI 20. PAGE 52 B1062
                                                          B54

BIESANZ J.,MODERN SOCIETY: AN INTRODUCTION TO   SOCIETY
SOCIAL SCIENCE. COM CONSTN STRUCT FAM MUNIC NAT/G   PROB/SOLV
SECT EX/STRUC LEGIS GP/REL PERSON...SOC 20. PAGE 12   CULTURE
B0237
                                                          B54

MATTHEWS D.R.,THE SOCIAL BACKGROUND OF POLITICAL   DECISION
DECISION-MAKERS. CULTURE SOCIETY STRATA FAM   BIOG
EX/STRUC LEAD ATTIT BIO/SOC DRIVE PERSON ALL/VALS   SOC
HIST/WRIT. PAGE 71 B1431
                                                          B55

APTER D.E.,THE GOLD COAST IN TRANSITION. FUT CONSTN   AFR
CULTURE SOCIETY ECO/UNDEV FAM KIN LOC/G NAT/G   SOVEREIGN
POL/PAR LEGIS TOP/EX EDU/PROP LEGIT ADMIN ATTIT
PERSON PWR...CONCPT STAT INT CENSUS TOT/POP
VAL/FREE. PAGE 6 B0120
                                                          B55

MAZZINI J.,THE DUTIES OF MAN. MOD/EUR LAW SOCIETY   SUPEGO
FAM NAT/G POL/PAR SECT VOL/ASSN EX/STRUC ACT/RES   CONCPT
CREATE REV PEACE ATTIT ALL/VALS...GEN/LAWS WORK 19.   NAT/LISM
PAGE 71 B1439
                                                          B55

UN ECONOMIC AND SOCIAL COUNCIL,BIBLIOGRAPHY OF   BIBLIOG/A
PUBLICATIONS OF THE UN AND SPECIALIZED AGENCIES IN   SOC/WK
THE SOCIAL WELFARE FIELD, 1946-1952. WOR+45 FAM   ADMIN
INT/ORG MUNIC ACT/RES PLAN PROB/SOLV EDU/PROP AGE/C   WEALTH
AGE/Y HABITAT...HEAL UN. PAGE 106 B2148
                                                          C55

BONER H.A.,"HUNGRY GENERATIONS." UK WOR+45 WOR-45   ECO/DEV
STRATA INDUS FAM LABOR CAP/ISM...MGT BIBLIOG 19/20.   PHIL/SCI
PAGE 13 B0272   CONCPT
                                                      WEALTH
                                                          B56

MANNONI D.O.,PROSPERO AND CALIBAN: THE PSYCHOLOGY   CULTURE
OF COLONIZATION. AFR EUR+WWI FAM KIN MUNIC SECT   COLONIAL
DOMIN ADMIN ATTIT DRIVE LOVE PWR RESPECT...PSY SOC
CONCPT MYTH OBS DEEP/INT BIOG GEN/METH MALAGASY 20.
PAGE 69 B1394
                                                          B57

IKE N.,JAPANESE POLITICS. INTELL STRUCT AGRI INDUS   NAT/G
FAM KIN LABOR PRESS CHOOSE ATTIT...DECISION BIBLIOG   ADMIN
19/20 CHINJAP. PAGE 53 B1075   POL/PAR
                                                      CULTURE
                                                          B58

TAYLOR H.,THE STATESMAN. MOD/EUR FACE/GP FAM NAT/G   EXEC
POL/PAR DELIB/GP LEGIS ATTIT PERSON PWR...POLICY   STRUCT
CONCPT OBS GEN/LAWS. PAGE 103 B2086
                                                          B58

WILENSKY H.L.,INDUSTRIAL SOCIETY AND SOCIAL   INDUS

WELFARE: IMPACT OF INDUSTRIALIZATION ON SUPPLY AND ORGANIZATION OF SOC WELF SERVICES. ELITES SOCIETY STRATA SERV/IND FAM MUNIC PUB/INST CONSULT WORKER ADMIN AUTOMAT ANOMIE 20. PAGE 117 B2352 — ECO/DEV RECEIVE PROF/ORG
B59

YANG C.K.,A CHINESE VILLAGE IN EARLY COMMUNIST TRANSITION. ECO/UNDEV AGRI FAM KIN MUNIC FORCES PLAN ECO/TAC DOMIN EDU/PROP ATTIT DRIVE PWR RESPECT ...SOC CONCPT METH/CNCPT OBS RECORD CON/ANAL CHARTS WORK 20. PAGE 118 B2389 — ASIA ROUTINE SOCISM
S60

EMERSON R.,"THE EROSION OF DEMOCRACY." AFR FUT LAW CULTURE INTELL SOCIETY ECO/UNDEV FAM LOC/G NAT/G FORCES PLAN TEC/DEV ECO/TAC ADMIN CT/SYS ATTIT ORD/FREE PWR...SOCIALIST SOC CONCPT STAND/INT TIME/SEQ WORK 20. PAGE 33 B0671 — S/ASIA POL/PAR
C60

FITZSIMMONS T.,"USSR: ITS PEOPLE, ITS SOCIETY, ITS CULTURE." USSR FAM SECT DIPLOM EDU/PROP ADMIN RACE/REL ATTIT...POLICY CHARTS BIBLIOG 20. PAGE 36 B0728 — CULTURE STRUCT SOCIETY COM
B61

KOESTLER A.,THE LOTUS AND THE ROBOT. ASIA INDIA S/ASIA SOCIETY STRATA ECO/DEV AGRI INDUS FAM CREATE DOMIN EDU/PROP ADMIN COERCE ATTIT DRIVE SUPEGO ORD/FREE PWR RESPECT WEALTH...MYTH OBS 20 CHINJAP. PAGE 61 B1226 — SECT ECO/UNDEV
B61

MARKMANN C.L.,JOHN F. KENNEDY: A SENSE OF PURPOSE. USA+45 INTELL FAM CONSULT DELIB/GP LEGIS PERSON SKILL 20 KENNEDY/JF EISNHWR/DD ROOSEVLT/F NEW/FRONTR PRESIDENT. PAGE 69 B1399 — CHIEF TOP/EX ADMIN BIOG
B61

MARSH R.M.,THE MANDARINS: THE CIRCULATION OF ELITES IN CHINA, 1600-1900. ASIA STRUCT PROF/ORG...SOC CHARTS BIBLIOG DICTIONARY 17/20. PAGE 70 B1406 — ELITES ADMIN FAM STRATA
B61

PETRULLO L.,LEADERSHIP AND INTERPERSONAL BEHAVIOR. FACE/GP FAM PROF/ORG EX/STRUC FORCES DOMIN WAR GP/REL PERS/REL EFFICIENCY PRODUC PWR...MGT PSY. PAGE 82 B1663 — PERSON ATTIT LEAD HABITAT
S61

MARSH R.M.,"FORMAL ORGANIZATION AND PROMOTION IN A PRE-INDUSTRIAL SOCIETY" (BMR)" ASIA FAM EX/STRUC LEAD...SOC CHARTS 19 WEBER/MAX. PAGE 70 B1407 — ADMIN STRUCT ECO/UNDEV STRATA
B63

ELIAS T.O.,THE NIGERIAN LEGAL SYSTEM. NIGERIA LAW FAM KIN SECT ADMIN NAT/LISM...JURID 18/20 ENGLSH/LAW COMMON/LAW. PAGE 33 B0665 — CT/SYS ADJUD COLONIAL PROF/ORG
B63

MOORE W.E.,MAN, TIME, AND SOCIETY. UNIV STRUCT FAM MUNIC VOL/ASSN ADMIN...SOC NEW/IDEA TIME/SEQ TREND TIME 20. PAGE 75 B1515 — CONCPT SOCIETY CONTROL
B63

SIDEY H.,JOHN F. KENNEDY, PRESIDENT. USA+45 INTELL FAM CONSULT DELIB/GP LEGIS ADMIN LEAD 20 KENNEDY/JF PRESIDENT. PAGE 97 B1951 — BIOG TOP/EX SKILL PERSON
B64

GUTTSMAN W.L.,THE BRITISH POLITICAL ELITE. EUR+WWI MOD/EUR STRATA FAM LABOR POL/PAR SCHOOL VOL/ASSN DELIB/GP LEGIS LEGIT EXEC CHOOSE ATTIT ALL/VALS ...STAT BIOG TIME/SEQ CHARTS VAL/FREE. PAGE 45 B0905 — NAT/G SOC UK ELITES
B64

HICKEY G.C.,VILLAGE IN VIETNAM. USA+45 VIETNAM LAW AGRI FAM SECT ADMIN ATTIT...SOC CHARTS WORSHIP 20. PAGE 49 B1003 — CULTURE SOCIETY STRUCT S/ASIA
B65

LAMBIRI I.,SOCIAL CHANGE IN A GREEK COUNTRY TOWN. GREECE FAM PROB/SOLV ROUTINE TASK LEISURE INGP/REL CONSEN ORD/FREE...SOC INT QU CHARTS 20. PAGE 62 B1252 — INDUS WORKER CULTURE NEIGH
B65

MATRAS J.,SOCIAL CHANGE IN ISRAEL. ISRAEL STRATA FAM ACT/RES EDU/PROP ADMIN CHOOSE...STAT CENSUS 19/20 JEWS. PAGE 71 B1427 — SECT NAT/LISM GEOG STRUCT
B66

RAEFF M.,ORIGINS OF THE RUSSIAN INTELLIGENTSIA: THE EIGHTEENTH-CENTURY NOBILITY. RUSSIA FAM NAT/G EDU/PROP ADMIN PERS/REL ATTIT...HUM BIOG 18. PAGE 85 B1728 — INTELL ELITES STRATA CONSERVE
B66

SZLADITS C.,A BIBLIOGRAPHY ON FOREIGN AND COMPARATIVE LAW (SUPPLEMENT 1964). FINAN FAM LABOR LG/CO LEGIS JUDGE ADMIN CRIME...CRIMLGY 20. PAGE 102 B2066 — BIBLIOG/A CT/SYS INT/LAW
B66

UN ECAFE,ADMINISTRATIVE ASPECTS OF FAMILY PLANNING PROGRAMMES (PAMPHLET). ASIA THAILAND WOR+45 VOL/ASSN PROB/SOLV BUDGET FOR/AID EDU/PROP CONFER — PLAN CENSUS FAM

CONTROL GOV/REL TIME 20 UN BIRTH/CON. PAGE 106 B2147 — ADMIN
B67

BENNETT J.W.,HUTTERIAN BRETHREN: THE AGRICULTURAL ECONOMY AND SOCIAL ORGANIZATION OF A COMMUNAL PEOPLE. USA+45 SOCIETY FAM KIN TEC/DEV ADJUST...MGT AUD/VIS GP/COMP 20. PAGE 10 B0213 — SECT AGRI STRUCT GP/REL
B67

COHEN R.,COMPARATIVE POLITICAL SYSTEMS: STUDIES IN THE POLITICS OF PRE-INDUSTRIAL SOCIETIES. WOR+45 WOR-45 CULTURE FAM KIN LOC/G NEIGH ADMIN LEAD MARRIAGE...BIBLIOG 20. PAGE 22 B0447 — ECO/UNDEV STRUCT SOCIETY GP/COMP
B67

DUN J.L.,THE ESSENCE OF CHINESE CIVILIZATION. ASIA FAM NAT/G TEC/DEV ADMIN SANCTION WAR HABITAT ...ANTHOL WORSHIP. PAGE 31 B0630 — CULTURE SOCIETY
S67

FOX R.G.,"FAMILY, CASTE, AND COMMERCE IN A NORTH INDIAN MARKET TOWN." INDIA STRATA AGRI FACE/GP FAM NEIGH OP/RES BARGAIN ADMIN ROUTINE WEALTH...SOC CHARTS 20. PAGE 37 B0747 — CULTURE GP/REL ECO/UNDEV DIST/IND

FAMILY....SEE FAM

FAMINE....SEE AGRI, HEALTH

FAO....FOOD AND AGRICULTURE ORGANIZATION; SEE ALSO UN, INT/ORG

B56

SOHN L.B.,BASIC DOCUMENTS OF THE UNITED NATIONS. WOR+45 LAW INT/ORG LEGIT EXEC ROUTINE CHOOSE PWR ...JURID CONCPT GEN/LAWS ANTHOL UN TOT/POP OAS FAO ILO 20. PAGE 99 B1993 — DELIB/GP CONSTN
S59

HARVEY M.F.,"THE PALESTINE REFUGEE PROBLEM: ELEMENTS OF A SOLUTION." ISLAM LAW INT/ORG DELIB/GP TOP/EX ECO/TAC ROUTINE DRIVE HEALTH LOVE ORD/FREE PWR WEALTH...MAJORIT FAO 20. PAGE 48 B0964 — ACT/RES LEGIT PEACE ISRAEL
S60

NELSON R.H.,"LEGISLATIVE PARTICIPATION IN THE TREATY AND AGREEMENT MAKING PROCESS." CONSTN POL/PAR PLAN EXEC PWR FAO UN CONGRESS. PAGE 78 B1569 — LEGIS PEACE DECISION DIPLOM

FARBER W.O. B0704

FARM/BUR....FARM BUREAU

FARMING....SEE AGRI

FARNSWORTH B. B0705

FARRIS C.D. B1162

FARRIS M.T. B0706

FASCISM....FASCISM; SEE ALSO TOTALISM, FASCIST

S37

LASSWELL H.D.,"GOVERNMENTAL AND PARTY LEADERS IN FASCIST ITALY." ITALY CRIME SKILL...BIOG CHARTS GP/COMP 20. PAGE 63 B1266 — ELITES FASCISM ADMIN
B38

FIELD G.L.,THE SYNDICAL AND CORPORATIVE INSTITUTIONS OF ITALIAN FASCISM. ITALY CONSTN STRATA LABOR EX/STRUC TOP/EX ADJUD ADMIN LEAD TOTALISM AUTHORIT...MGT 20 MUSSOLIN/B. PAGE 35 B0716 — FASCISM INDUS NAT/G WORKER
B38

REICH N.,LABOR RELATIONS IN REPUBLICAN GERMANY. GERMANY CONSTN ECO/DEV INDUS NAT/G ADMIN CONTROL GP/REL FASCISM POPULISM 20 WEIMAR/REP. PAGE 87 B1763 — WORKER MGT LABOR BARGAIN
B42

NEUBURGER O.,OFFICIAL PUBLICATIONS OF PRESENT-DAY GERMANY: GOVERNMENT, CORPORATE ORGANIZATIONS, AND NATIONAL SOCIALIST PARTY. GERMANY CONSTN COM/IND POL/PAR EDU/PROP PRESS 20 NAZI. PAGE 78 B1570 — BIBLIOG/A FASCISM NAT/G ADMIN
B42

SINGTON D.,THE GOEBBELS EXPERIMENT. GERMANY MOD/EUR NAT/G EX/STRUC FORCES CONTROL ROUTINE WAR TOTALISM PWR...ART/METH HUM 20 NAZI GOEBBELS/J. PAGE 97 B1970 — FASCISM EDU/PROP ATTIT COM/IND
B63

JACOB H.,GERMAN ADMINISTRATION SINCE BISMARCK: CENTRAL AUTHORITY VERSUS LOCAL AUTONOMY. GERMANY GERMANY/W LAW POL/PAR CONTROL CENTRAL TOTALISM FASCISM...MAJORIT DECISION STAT CHARTS GOV/COMP 19/20 BISMARCK/O HITLER/A WEIMAR/REP. PAGE 55 B1111 — ADMIN NAT/G LOC/G POLICY
B64

ELDREDGE H.W.,THE SECOND AMERICAN REVOLUTION. EDU/PROP NAT/LISM RATIONAL TOTALISM FASCISM MARXISM SOCISM. PAGE 33 B0664 — ELITES ORD/FREE ADMIN PLAN

B64

WHEELER-BENNETT J.W.,THE NEMESIS OF POWER (2ND
ED.). EUR+WWI GERMANY TOP/EX TEC/DEV ADMIN WAR
PERS/REL RIGID/FLEX ROLE ORD/FREE PWR FASCISM 20
HITLER/A. PAGE 116 B2332

FORCES
NAT/G
GP/REL
STRUCT

B66

ADAMS J.C.,THE GOVERNMENT OF REPUBLICAN ITALY (2ND
ED.). ITALY LOC/G POL/PAR DELIB/GP LEGIS WORKER
ADMIN CT/SYS FASCISM...CHARTS BIBLIOG 20
PARLIAMENT. PAGE 3 B0057

NAT/G
CHOOSE
EX/STRUC
CONSTN

FASCIST....FASCIST

B65

NORDEN A.,WAR AND NAZI CRIMINALS IN WEST GERMANY:
STATE. ECONOMY, ADMINISTRATION, ARMY, JUSTICE,
SCIENCE. GERMANY GERMANY/W MOD/EUR ECO/DEV ACADEM
EX/STRUC FORCES DOMIN ADMIN CT/SYS...POLICY MAJORIT
PACIFIST 20. PAGE 78 B1587

FASCIST
WAR
NAT/G
TOP/EX

FASHION....SEE ETIQUET, MODAL

FATHER/DIV....FATHER DIVINE AND HIS FOLLOWERS

FATIGUE....SEE SLEEP

FATOUROS A.A. B0707

FAUNT J.R. B0708

FAUST W.L. B2085

FAYERWEATHER J. B0709

FBI....U.S. FEDERAL BUREAU OF INVESTIGATION

N19

MARSH J.F. JR.,THE FBI RETIREMENT BILL (PAMPHLET).
USA+45 EX/STRUC WORKER PLAN PROB/SOLV BUDGET LEAD
LOBBY PARL/PROC PERS/REL RIGID/FLEX...POLICY 20 FBI
PRESIDENT BUR/BUDGET. PAGE 70 B1405

ADMIN
NAT/G
SENIOR
GOV/REL

FCC....U.S. FEDERAL COMMUNICATIONS COMMISSION

FDA....U.S. FOOD AND DRUG ADMINISTRATION

FDR....FRANKLIN D. ROOSEVELT

FEARS....SEE ANOMIE

FECHNER/GT....GUSTAV THEODOR FECHNER

FED/OPNMKT....FEDERAL OPEN MARKET COMMITTEE

FED/RESERV....U.S. FEDERAL RESERVE SYSTEM (INCLUDES FEDERAL
RESERVE BANK)

B50

HARTLAND P.C.,BALANCE OF INTERREGIONAL PAYMENTS OF
NEW ENGLAND. USA+45 TEC/DEV ECO/TAC LEGIT ROUTINE
BAL/PAY PROFIT 20 NEW/ENGLND FED/RESERV. PAGE 47
B0962

ECO/DEV
FINAN
REGION
PLAN

B65

ROWE J.Z.,THE PUBLIC-PRIVATE CHARACTER OF UNITED
STATES CENTRAL BANKING. USA+45 NAT/G EX/STRUC
...BIBLIOG 20 FED/RESERV. PAGE 91 B1842

FINAN
PLAN
FEDERAL
LAW

S67

BRIMMER A.F.,"INITIATIVE AND INNOVATION IN CENTRAL
BANKING." USA+45 ECO/DEV MARKET ECO/TAC TAX CONTROL
DEMAND...MGT CHARTS FED/RESERV. PAGE 15 B0309

FINAN
CREATE
NAT/G
POLICY

FEDERAL AVIATION AGENCY....SEE FAA

FEDERAL BUREAU OF INVESTIGATION....SEE FBI

FEDERAL COMMUNICATIONS COMMISSION....SEE FCC

FEDERAL COUNCIL FOR SCIENCE + TECHNOLOGY....SEE FEDSCI/TEC

FEDERAL HOUSING ADMINISTRATION....SEE FHA

FEDERAL RESERVE SYSTEM....SEE FED/RESERV

FEDERAL TRADE COMMISSION....SEE FTC

FEDERAL....FEDERALISM

N

MONPIED E.,BIBLIOGRAPHIE FEDERALISTE: ARTICLES ET
DOCUMENTS PUBLIES DANS LES PERIODIQUES PARUS EN
FRANCE NOV. 1945-OCT. 1950. EUR+WWI WOR+45 ADMIN
REGION ATTIT MARXISM PACIFISM 20 EEC. PAGE 74 B1501

BIBLIOG/A
FEDERAL
CENTRAL
INT/ORG

N

US SUPERINTENDENT OF DOCUMENTS.EDUCATION (PRICE

BIBLIOG/A

LIST 31). USA+45 LAW FINAN LOC/G NAT/G DEBATE ADMIN
LEAD RACE/REL FEDERAL HEALTH POLICY. PAGE 111 B2238

EDU/PROP
ACADEM
SCHOOL

B08

WILSON W.,CONSTITUTIONAL GOVERNMENT IN THE UNITED
STATES. USA-45 LAW POL/PAR PROVS CHIEF LEGIS
BAL/PWR ADJUD EXEC FEDERAL PWR 18/20 SUPREME/CT
HOUSE/REP SENATE. PAGE 117 B2362

NAT/G
GOV/REL
CONSTN
PARL/PROC

B25

MATHEWS J.M.,AMERICAN STATE GOVERNMENT. USA-45
LOC/G CHIEF EX/STRUC LEGIS ADJUD CONTROL CT/SYS
ROUTINE GOV/REL PWR 20 GOVERNOR. PAGE 71 B1426

PROVS
ADMIN
FEDERAL
CONSTN

B32

MCKISACK M.,THE PARLIAMENTARY REPRESENTATION OF THE
ENGLISH BOROUGHS DURING THE MIDDLE AGES. UK CONSTN
CULTURE ELITES EX/STRUC TAX PAY ADJUD PARL/PROC
APPORT FEDERAL...POLICY 13/15 PARLIAMENT. PAGE 72
B1454

NAT/G
MUNIC
LEGIS
CHOOSE

B36

GRAVES W.B.,AMERICAN STATE GOVERNMENT. CONSTN FINAN
EX/STRUC FORCES LEGIS BUDGET TAX CT/SYS REPRESENT
GOV/REL...BIBLIOG/A 19/20. PAGE 42 B0855

NAT/G
PROVS
ADMIN
FEDERAL

B41

YOUNG G.,FEDERALISM AND FREEDOM. EUR+WWI MOD/EUR
RUSSIA USA-45 WOR-45 SOCIETY STRUCT ECO/DEV INT/ORG
EXEC FEDERAL ATTIT PERSON ALL/VALS...OLD/LIB CONCPT
OBS TREND LEAGUE/NAT TOT/POP. PAGE 119 B2392

NAT/G
WAR

B42

BROWN A.D.,LIST OF REFERENCES ON THE CIVIL SERVICE
AND PERSONNEL ADMINISTRATION IN THE UNITED STATES
(2ND MIMEOGRAPHED SUPPLEMENT). USA+45 LOC/G POL/PAR
PROVS FEDERAL...TESTS 20. PAGE 16 B0319

BIBLIOG
ADMIN
MGT
NAT/G

B45

BRECHT A.,FEDERALISM AND REGIONALISM IN GERMANY;
THE DIVISION OF PRUSSIA. GERMANY PRUSSIA WOR-45
CREATE ADMIN WAR TOTALISM PWR...CHARTS 20 HITLER/A.
PAGE 15 B0303

FEDERAL
REGION
PROB/SOLV
CONSTN

B47

GAUS J.M.,REFLECTIONS ON PUBLIC ADMINISTRATION.
USA+45 CONTROL GOV/REL CENTRAL FEDERAL ATTIT WEALTH
...DECISION 20. PAGE 39 B0787

MGT
POLICY
EX/STRUC
ADMIN

B48

BISHOP H.M.,BASIC ISSUES OF AMERICAN DEMOCRACY.
USA+45 USA-45 POL/PAR EX/STRUC LEGIS ADJUD FEDERAL
...BIBLIOG 18/20. PAGE 12 B0244

NAT/G
PARL/PROC
CONSTN

S49

STEINMETZ H.,"THE PROBLEMS OF THE LANDRAT: A STUDY
OF COUNTY GOVERNMENT IN THE US ZONE OF GERMANY."
GERMANY/W USA+45 INDUS PLAN DIPLOM EDU/PROP CONTROL
WAR GOV/REL FEDERAL WEALTH PLURISM...GOV/COMP 20
LANDRAT. PAGE 100 B2031

LOC/G
COLONIAL
MGT
TOP/EX

B50

MONPIED E.,BIBLIOGRAPHIE FEDERALISTE: OUVRAGES
CHOISIS (VOL. I, MIMEOGRAPHED PAPER). EUR+WWI
DIPLOM ADMIN REGION ATTIT PACIFISM SOCISM...INT/LAW
19/20. PAGE 74 B1502

BIBLIOG/A
FEDERAL
CENTRAL
INT/ORG

C50

HOLCOMBE A.,"OUR MORE PERFECT UNION." USA+45 USA-45
POL/PAR JUDGE CT/SYS EQUILIB FEDERAL PWR...MAJORIT
TREND BIBLIOG 18/20 CONGRESS PRESIDENT. PAGE 51
B1031

CONSTN
NAT/G
ADMIN
PLAN

B51

WHITE L.D.,THE JEFFERSONIANS: A STUDY IN
ADMINISTRATIVE HISTORY 18011829. USA+45 DELIB/GP
LEGIS TOP/EX PROB/SOLV BUDGET ECO/TAC GP/REL
FEDERAL...BIOG IDEA/COMP 19 PRESIDENT CONGRESS
JEFFERSN/T. PAGE 116 B2338

ADMIN
NAT/G
POLICY
POL/PAR

B52

DE GRAZIA A.,POLITICAL ORGANIZATION. CONSTN LOC/G
MUNIC NAT/G CHIEF LEGIS TOP/EX ADJUD CT/SYS
PERS/REL...INT/LAW MYTH UN. PAGE 27 B0553

FEDERAL
LAW
ADMIN

B54

CHICAGO JOINT REFERENCE LIB,FEDERAL-STATE-LOCAL
RELATIONS; A SELECTED BIBLIOGRAPHY. USA+45 AGRI
LABOR LOC/G MUNIC EX/STRUC ADMIN REGION HEALTH
CON/ANAL. PAGE 21 B0419

BIBLIOG
FEDERAL
GOV/REL

B54

CONWAY O.B. JR.,LEGISLATIVE-EXECUTIVE RELATIONS IN
THE GOVERNMENT OF THE UNITED STATES (PAMPHLET).
BUDGET ATTIT PERCEPT...DECISION 20. PAGE 23 B0470

BAL/PWR
FEDERAL
GOV/REL
EX/STRUC

B54

MILLARD E.L.,FREEDOM IN A FEDERAL WORLD. FUT WOR+45
VOL/ASSN TOP/EX LEGIT ROUTINE FEDERAL PEACE ATTIT
DISPL ORD/FREE PWR...MAJORIT INT/LAW JURID TREND
COLD/WAR 20. PAGE 73 B1479

INT/ORG
CREATE
ADJUD
BAL/PWR

S54

HART J.,"ADMINISTRATION AND THE COURTS." USA+45
NAT/G REPRESENT 20. PAGE 47 B0960

ADMIN
GOV/REL
CT/SYS
FEDERAL

B55

CUSHMAN R.E.,LEADING CONSTITUTIONAL DECISIONS.

CONSTN

USA+45 USA-45 NAT/G EX/STRUC LEGIS JUDGE TAX
FEDERAL...DECISION 20 SUPREME/CT CASEBOOK. PAGE 25
B0513
PROB/SOLV
JURID
CT/SYS

B55

DE ARAGAO J.G.,LA JURIDICTION ADMINISTRATIVE AU
BRESIL. BRAZIL ADJUD COLONIAL CT/SYS REV FEDERAL
ORD/FREE...BIBLIOG 19/20. PAGE 27 B0549
EX/STRUC
ADMIN
NAT/G

B55

MACMAHON A.W.,FEDERALISM: MATURE AND EMERGENT.
EUR+WWI FUT WOR+45 WOR-45 INT/ORG NAT/G REPRESENT
FEDERAL...POLICY MGT RECORD TREND GEN/LAWS 20.
PAGE 68 B1370
STRUCT
CONCPT

S56

GORE W.J.,"ADMINISTRATIVE DECISION-MAKING IN
FEDERAL FIELD OFFICES." USA+45 PROVS PWR CONT/OBS.
PAGE 41 B0833
DECISION
PROB/SOLV
FEDERAL
ADMIN

B57

SCHLOCHAUER H.J.,OFFENTLICHES RECHT. GERMANY/W
FINAN EX/STRUC LEGIS DIPLOM FEDERAL ORD/FREE
...INT/LAW 20. PAGE 94 B1892
CONSTN
JURID
ADMIN
CT/SYS

B58

CARTER G.M.,TRANSITION IN AFRICA; STUDIES IN
POLITICAL ADAPTATION. AFR CENTRL/AFR GHANA NIGERIA
CONSTN LOC/G POL/PAR ADMIN GP/REL FEDERAL...MAJORIT
BIBLIOG 20. PAGE 19 B0389
NAT/COMP
PWR
CONTROL
NAT/G

B58

DAVIS K.C.,ADMINISTRATIVE LAW; CASES, TEXT,
PROBLEMS. LAW LOC/G NAT/G TOP/EX PAY CONTROL
GOV/REL INGP/REL FEDERAL 20 SUPREME/CT. PAGE 27
B0541
ADJUD
JURID
CT/SYS
ADMIN

C58

GOLAY J.F.,"THE FOUNDING OF THE FEDERAL REPUBLIC OF
GERMANY." GERMANY/W CONSTN EX/STRUC DIPLOM ADMIN
CHOOSE...DECISION BIBLIOG 20. PAGE 40 B0814
FEDERAL
NAT/G
PARL/PROC
POL/PAR

B59

ELAZAR D.J.,INTERGOVERNMENTAL RELATIONS IN
NINETEENTH CENTURY AMERICAN FEDERALISM (DOCTORAL
THESIS). USA-45 FINAN LOC/G NAT/G GP/REL 18/19.
PAGE 33 B0662
FEDERAL
ADMIN
PROVS
GOV/REL

B59

MAASS A.,AREA AND POWER: A THEORY OF LOCAL
GOVERNMENT. MUNIC PROVS EX/STRUC LEGIS CT/SYS
CHOOSE PWR 20. PAGE 67 B1354
LOC/G
FEDERAL
BAL/PWR
GOV/REL

B60

AYEARST M.,THE BRITISH WEST INDIES: THE SEARCH FOR
SELF-GOVERNMENT. FUT WEST/IND LOC/G POL/PAR
EX/STRUC LEGIS CHOOSE...NAT/COMP BIBLIOG
17/20. PAGE 7 B0152
CONSTN
COLONIAL
REPRESENT
NAT/G

B60

WEIDNER E.W.,INTERGOVERNMENTAL RELATIONS AS SEEN BY
PUBLIC OFFICIALS. USA+45 PROVS EX/STRUC EXEC
FEDERAL...QU 20. PAGE 115 B2311
ATTIT
GP/REL
GOV/REL
ADMIN

L60

GRODZINS M.,"AMERICAN POLITICAL PARTIES AND THE
AMERICAN SYSTEM" (BMR)" USA+45 LOC/G NAT/G LEGIS
BAL/PWR ADMIN ROLE PWR...DECISION 20. PAGE 44 B0883
POL/PAR
FEDERAL
CENTRAL
GOV/REL

B61

MACMAHON A.W.,DELEGATION AND AUTONOMY. INDIA STRUCT
LEGIS BARGAIN BUDGET ECO/TAC LEGIT EXEC REPRESENT
GOV/REL CENTRAL DEMAND EFFICIENCY PRODUC. PAGE 68
B1373
ADMIN
PLAN
FEDERAL

B61

RAO K.V.,PARLIAMENTARY DEMOCRACY OF INDIA. INDIA
EX/STRUC TOP/EX COLONIAL CT/SYS PARL/PROC ORD/FREE
...POLICY CONCPT TREND 20 PARLIAMENT. PAGE 86 B1733
CONSTN
ADJUD
NAT/G
FEDERAL

L61

GERWIG R.,"PUBLIC AUTHORITIES IN THE UNITED
STATES." LAW CONSTN PROVS TAX ADMIN FEDERAL.
PAGE 39 B0793
LOC/G
MUNIC
GOV/REL
PWR

B62

CARPER E.T.,ILLINOIS GOES TO CONGRESS FOR ARMY
LAND. USA+45 LAW EXTR/IND PROVS REGION CIVMIL/REL
GOV/REL FEDERAL ATTIT 20 ILLINOIS SENATE CONGRESS
DIRKSEN/E DOUGLAS/P. PAGE 19 B0385
ADMIN
LOBBY
GEOG
LEGIS

B62

DIMOCK M.E.,THE NEW AMERICAN POLITICAL ECONOMY: A
SYNTHESIS OF POLITICS AND ECONOMICS. USA+45 FINAN
LG/CO PLAN ADMIN REGION GP/REL CENTRAL MORAL 20.
PAGE 29 B0598
FEDERAL
ECO/TAC
NAT/G
PARTIC

B62

INSTITUTE OF PUBLIC ADMIN,A SHORT HISTORY OF THE
PUBLIC SERVICE IN IRELAND. IRELAND UK DIST/IND
INGP/REL FEDERAL 13/20 CIVIL/SERV. PAGE 54 B1091
ADMIN
WORKER
GOV/REL
NAT/G

B62

LOWI T.J.,LEGISLATIVE POLITICS U.S.A. LAW LEGIS
DIPLOM EXEC LOBBY CHOOSE SUFF FEDERAL PWR 19/20
CONGRESS. PAGE 67 B1345
PARL/PROC
REPRESENT
POLICY

ROUTINE

B62

PRESS C.,STATE MANUALS, BLUE BOOKS AND ELECTION
RESULTS. LAW LOC/G MUNIC LEGIS WRITING FEDERAL
SOVEREIGN...DECISION STAT CHARTS 20. PAGE 84 B1700
BIBLIOG
PROVS
ADMIN
CHOOSE

S62

DONNELLY D.,"THE POLITICS AND ADMINISTRATION OF
PLANNING." UK ROUTINE FEDERAL 20. PAGE 30 B0607
GOV/REL
EFFICIENCY
ADMIN
EX/STRUC

S62

SPRINGER H.W.,"FEDERATION IN THE CARIBBEAN: AN
ATTEMPT THAT FAILED." L/A+17C ECO/UNDEV INT/ORG
POL/PAR PROVS LEGIS CREATE PLAN LEGIT ADMIN FEDERAL
ATTIT DRIVE PERSON ORD/FREE PWR...POLICY GEOG PSY
CONCPT OBS CARIBBEAN CMN/WLTH 20. PAGE 100 B2013
VOL/ASSN
NAT/G
REGION

B63

GRANT D.R.,STATE AND LOCAL GOVERNMENT IN AMERICA.
USA+45 FINAN LOC/G MUNIC EX/STRUC FORCES EDU/PROP
ADMIN CHOOSE FEDERAL ATTIT...JURID 20. PAGE 42
B0853
PROVS
POL/PAR
LEGIS
CONSTN

B63

LEONARD T.J.,THE FEDERAL SYSTEM OF INDIA. INDIA
MUNIC NAT/G PROVS ADMIN SOVEREIGN...IDEA/COMP 20.
PAGE 64 B1293
FEDERAL
MGT
NAT/COMP
METH/COMP

B63

LOCKARD D.,THE POLITICS OF STATE AND LOCAL
GOVERNMENT. USA+45 CONSTN EX/STRUC LEGIS CT/SYS
FEDERAL...CHARTS BIBLIOG 20. PAGE 66 B1334
LOC/G
PROVS
OP/RES
ADMIN

B63

MAHESHWARI B.,STUDIES IN PANCHAYATI RAJ. INDIA
POL/PAR EX/STRUC BUDGET EXEC REPRESENT CENTRAL
EFFICIENCY...DECISION 20. PAGE 68 B1378
FEDERAL
LOC/G
GOV/REL
LEAD

B63

PEABODY R.L.,NEW PERSPECTIVES ON THE HOUSE OF
REPRESENTATIVES. AGRI FINAN SCHOOL FORCES CONFER
LEAD CHOOSE REPRESENT FEDERAL...POLICY DECISION
HOUSE/REP. PAGE 82 B1647
NEW/IDEA
LEGIS
PWR
ADMIN

S63

BANFIELD J.,"FEDERATION IN EAST-AFRICA." AFR UGANDA
ELITES INT/ORG NAT/G VOL/ASSN LEGIS ECO/TAC FEDERAL
ATTIT SOVEREIGN TOT/POP 20 TANGANYIKA. PAGE 9 B0180
EX/STRUC
PWR
REGION

S63

ROUGEMONT D.,"LES NOUVELLES CHANCES DE L'EUROPE."
EUR+WWI FUT ECO/DEV INT/ORG NAT/G ACT/RES PLAN
TEC/DEV EDU/PROP ADMIN COLONIAL FEDERAL ATTIT PWR
SKILL...TREND 20. PAGE 91 B1835
ECO/UNDEV
PERCEPT

B64

PRESS C.,A BIBLIOGRAPHIC INTRODUCTION TO AMERICAN
STATE GOVERNMENT AND POLITICS (PAMPHLET). USA+45
USA-45 EX/STRUC ADJUD INGP/REL FEDERAL ORD/FREE 20.
PAGE 84 B1701
BIBLIOG
LEGIS
LOC/G
POL/PAR

B64

RIKER W.H.,FEDERALISM. WOR+45 WOR-45 CONSTN CHIEF
LEGIS ADMIN COLONIAL CONTROL CT/SYS PWR...BIBLIOG/A
18/20. PAGE 88 B1787
FEDERAL
NAT/G
ORD/FREE
CENTRAL

B64

WHEARE K.C.,FEDERAL GOVERNMENT (4TH ED.). WOR+45
WOR-45 POL/PAR LEGIS BAL/PWR CT/SYS...POLICY JURID
CONCPT GOV/COMP 17/20. PAGE 116 B2331
FEDERAL
CONSTN
EX/STRUC
NAT/COMP

S64

NEWLYN W.T.,"MONETARY SYSTEMS AND INTEGRATION" AFR
BUDGET ADMIN FEDERAL PRODUC PROFIT UTIL...CHARTS 20
AFRICA/E. PAGE 78 B1578
ECO/UNDEV
REGION
METH/COMP
FINAN

B65

CHANDA A.,FEDERALISM IN INDIA. INDIA UK ELITES
FINAN NAT/G POL/PAR EX/STRUC LEGIS DIPLOM TAX
GOV/REL POPULISM...POLICY 20. PAGE 20 B0402
CONSTN
CENTRAL
FEDERAL

B65

COOPER F.E.,STATE ADMINISTRATIVE LAW (2 VOLS.). LAW
LEGIS PLAN TAX ADJUD CT/SYS FEDERAL PWR...CONCPT
20. PAGE 23 B0474
JURID
CONSTN
ADMIN
PROVS

B65

FOLTZ W.J.,FROM FRENCH WEST AFRICA TO THE MALI
FEDERATION. AFR FRANCE MALI ADMIN CONTROL FEDERAL
...DECISION 20. PAGE 36 B0734
EXEC
TOP/EX
ELITES
LEAD

B65

LEYS C.T.,FEDERATION IN EAST AFRICA. LAW AGRI
DIST/IND FINAN INT/ORG LABOR INT/TRADE CONFER ADMIN
CONTROL GP/REL...ANTHOL 20 AFRICA/E. PAGE 65 B1310
FEDERAL
REGION
ECO/UNDEV
PLAN

B65

PYLEE M.V.,CONSTITUTIONAL GOVERNMENT IN INDIA (2ND
REV. ED.). INDIA POL/PAR EX/STRUC DIPLOM COLONIAL
CT/SYS PARL/PROC PRIVIL...JURID 16/20. PAGE 85
B1725
CONSTN
NAT/G
PROVS
FEDERAL

B65
ROWE J.Z.,THE PUBLIC-PRIVATE CHARACTER OF UNITED   FINAN
STATES CENTRAL BANKING. USA+45 NAT/G EX/STRUC   PLAN
...BIBLIOG 20 FED/RESERV. PAGE 91 B1842   FEDERAL
                                                       LAW
                                                       B65
SHARMA S.A.,PARLIAMENTARY GOVERNMENT IN INDIA.   NAT/G
INDIA FINAN LOC/G PROVS DELIB/GP PLAN ADMIN CT/SYS   CONSTN
FEDERAL...JURID 20. PAGE 96 B1936   PARL/PROC
                                                       LEGIS
                                                       B65
US SENATE COMM GOVT OPERATIONS.ORGANIZATION OF   ADMIN
FEDERAL EXECUTIVE DEPARTMENTS AND AGENCIES: REPORT   EX/STRUC
OF MARCH 23, 1965. USA+45 FORCES LEGIS DIPLOM   GOV/REL
ROUTINE CIVMIL/REL EFFICIENCY FEDERAL...MGT STAT.   ORG/CHARTS
PAGE 110 B2217
                                                       B65
YOUNG C.,POLITICS IN THE CONGO* DECOLONIZATION AND   BELGIUM
INDEPENDENCE. ELITES STRATA FORCES ADMIN REV   COLONIAL
RACE/REL FEDERAL SOVEREIGN...OBS INT CHARTS   NAT/LISM
CONGO/LEOP. PAGE 118 B2391
                                                       B66
GHOSH P.K.,THE CONSTITUTION OF INDIA: HOW IT HAS   CONSTN
BEEN FRAMED. INDIA LOC/G DELIB/GP EX/STRUC   NAT/G
PROB/SOLV BUDGET INT/TRADE CT/SYS CHOOSE...LING 20.   LEGIS
PAGE 39 B0795   FEDERAL
                                                       S66
PALMER M.,"THE UNITED ARAB REPUBLIC* AN ASSESSMENT   UAR
OF ITS FAILURE." ELITES ECO/UNDEV POL/PAR FORCES   SYRIA
ECO/TAC RUMOR ADMIN EXEC EFFICIENCY ATTIT SOCISM   REGION
...INT NASSER/G. PAGE 81 B1628   FEDERAL
                                                       N66
BACHELDER G.L.,THE LITERATURE OF FEDERALISM: A   BIBLIOG
SELECTED BIBLIOGRAPHY (REV ED) (A PAMPHLET). USA+45   FEDERAL
USA-45 WOR+45 WOR-45 LAW CONSTN PROVS ADMIN CT/SYS   NAT/G
GOV/REL ROLE...CONCPT 19/20. PAGE 8 B0155   LOC/G
                                                       B67
FESLER J.W.,THE FIFTY STATES AND THEIR LOCAL   PROVS
GOVERNMENTS. FUT USA+45 POL/PAR LEGIS PROB/SOLV   LOC/G
ADMIN CT/SYS CHOOSE GOV/REL FEDERAL...POLICY CHARTS
20 SUPREME/CT. PAGE 35 B0715
                                                       B67
KAPLAN H.,URBAN POLITICAL SYSTEMS: A FUNCTIONAL   GEN/LAWS
ANALYSIS OF METRO TORONTO. CANADA STRUCT NEIGH PLAN   MUNIC
ADMIN...POLICY METH 20 TORONTO. PAGE 58 B1166   LOC/G
                                                       FEDERAL
                                                       S67
BRADLEY A.W.,"CONSTITUTION-MAKING IN UGANDA."   NAT/G
UGANDA LAW CHIEF DELIB/GP LEGIS ADMIN EXEC   CREATE
PARL/PROC RACE/REL ORD/FREE...GOV/COMP 20. PAGE 14   CONSTN
B0295   FEDERAL
                                                       S67
GOBER J.L.,"FEDERALISM AT WORK." USA+45 NAT/G   MUNIC
CONSULT ACT/RES PLAN CONFER ADMIN LEAD PARTIC   TEC/DEV
FEDERAL ATTIT. PAGE 40 B0813   R+D
                                                       GOV/REL
                                                       S67
HOFMANN W.,"THE PUBLIC INTEREST PRESSURE GROUP: THE   LOC/G
CASE OF THE DEUTSCHE STADTETAG." GERMANY GERMANY/W   VOL/ASSN
CONSTN STRUCT NAT/G CENTRAL FEDERAL PWR...TIME/SEQ   LOBBY
20. PAGE 51 B1030   ADMIN
                                                       S67
HUMPHREY H.,"A MORE PERFECT UNION." USA+45 LOC/G   GOV/REL
NAT/G ACT/RES BUDGET RECEIVE CENTRAL CONGRESS.   FEDERAL
PAGE 52 B1063   ADMIN
                                                       PROB/SOLV
                                                       S67
LEWIS P.H.,"LEADERSHIP AND CONFLICT WITHIN   POL/PAR
FEBRERISTA PARTY OF PARAGUAY." L/A+17C PARAGUAY   ELITES
EX/STRUC DOMIN SENIOR CONTROL INGP/REL CENTRAL   LEAD
FEDERAL ATTIT 20. PAGE 65 B1305
                                                       S67
ZASLOW M.,"RECENT CONSTITUTIONAL DEVELOPMENTS IN   GOV/REL
CANADA'S NORTHERN TERRITORIES." CANADA LOC/G   REGION
DELIB/GP EX/STRUC LEGIS ADMIN ORD/FREE...TREND 20.   CONSTN
PAGE 119 B2398   FEDERAL

FEDERALIST....FEDERALIST PARTY (ALL NATIONS)

FEDSCI/TEC....FEDERAL COUNCIL FOR SCIENCE AND TECHNOLOGY

FEEDBACK....FEEDBACK PHENOMENA

                                                       B60
ARGYRIS C.,UNDERSTANDING ORGANIZATIONAL BEHAVIOR.   LG/CO
OP/RES FEEDBACK...MGT PSY METH/CNCPT OBS INT SIMUL   PERSON
20. PAGE 6 B0130   ADMIN
                                                       ROUTINE
                                                       B61
HOUN F.W.,TO CHANGE A NATION: PROPAGANDA AND   DOMIN
INDOCTRINATION IN COMMUNIST CHINA. CHINA/COM COM   EDU/PROP
ACT/RES PLAN PRESS ADMIN FEEDBACK CENTRAL   TOTALISM
EFFICIENCY ATTIT...PSY SOC 20. PAGE 52 B1048   MARXISM
                                                       S61
ROBINSON J.A.,"PROCESS SATISFACTION AND POLICY   GOV/REL
APPROVAL IN STATE DEPARTMENT - CONGRESSIONAL   EX/STRUC

RELATIONS." ELITES CHIEF LEGIS CONFER DEBATE ADMIN   POL/PAR
FEEDBACK ROLE...CHARTS 20 CONGRESS PRESIDENT   DECISION
DEPT/STATE. PAGE 89 B1802
                                                       B65
HARR J.E.,THE DEVELOPMENT OF CAREERS IN THE FOREIGN   OP/RES
SERVICE. CREATE SENIOR EXEC FEEDBACK GOV/REL   MGT
EFFICIENCY ATTIT RESPECT ORG/CHARTS. PAGE 47 B0953   ADMIN
                                                       DIPLOM
                                                       B65
ROWAT D.C.,THE OMBUDSMAN: CITIZEN'S DEFENDER.   INSPECT
DENMARK FINLAND NEW/ZEALND NORWAY SWEDEN CONSULT   CONSTN
PROB/SOLV FEEDBACK PARTIC GP/REL...SOC CONCPT   NAT/G
NEW/IDEA METH/COMP ANTHOL BIBLIOG 20. PAGE 91 B1840   ADMIN
                                                       B66
AMER ENTERPRISE INST PUB POL.CONGRESS: THE FIRST   EFFICIENCY
BRANCH OF GOVERNMENT. EX/STRUC FEEDBACK REPRESENT   LEGIS
INGP/REL PWR...DECISION METH/CNCPT PREDICT. PAGE 4   DELIB/GP
B0081   CONTROL
                                                       B66
SCHMIDT F.,PUBLIC RELATIONS IN HEALTH AND WELFARE.   PROF/ORG
USA+45 ACADEM RECEIVE PRESS FEEDBACK GOV/REL   EDU/PROP
PERS/REL DEMAND EFFICIENCY ATTIT PERCEPT WEALTH 20   ADMIN
PUBLIC/REL. PAGE 94 B1895   HEALTH
                                                       B67
VOOS H.,ORGANIZATIONAL COMMUNICATION: A   BIBLIOG/A
BIBLIOGRAPHY. WOR+45 STRATA R+D PROB/SOLV FEEDBACK   INDUS
COERCE...MGT PSY NET/THEORY HYPO/EXP. PAGE 112   COM/IND
B2268   VOL/ASSN
                                                       S67
ROBERTS E.B.,"THE PROBLEM OF AGING ORGANIZATIONS."   INDUS
INTELL PROB/SOLV ADMIN EXEC FEEDBACK EFFICIENCY   R+D
PRODUC...GEN/LAWS 20. PAGE 89 B1794   MGT
                                                       PLAN

FEERICK J.D. B0710

FEIGENBAUM E.A. B0517

FELD B. B2055

FELDMAN A.S. B1514

FEMALE/SEX....FEMALE SEX

                                                       B47
TAPPAN P.W.,DELINQUENT GIRLS IN COURT. USA-45 MUNIC   CT/SYS
EX/STRUC FORCES ADMIN EXEC ADJUST SEX RESPECT   AGE/Y
...JURID SOC/WK 20 NEWYORK/C FEMALE/SEX. PAGE 103   CRIME
B2078   ADJUD
                                                       B59
THARAMATHAJ C.,A STUDY OF THE COMPOSITION OF THE   ADMIN
THAI CIVIL SERVICE (PAPER). THAILAND PAY ROLE   EX/STRUC
...CHARTS 20 CIVIL/SERV FEMALE/SEX. PAGE 103 B2092   STRATA
                                                       INGP/REL

FENN DH J.R. B0711

FEPC....FAIR EMPLOYMENT PRACTICES COMMISSION

                                                       B48
KESSELMAN L.C.,THE SOCIAL POLITICS OF THE FEPC.   POLICY
INDUS WORKER EDU/PROP GP/REL RACE/REL 20 NEGRO JEWS   NAT/G
FEPC. PAGE 59 B1200   ADMIN
                                                       DISCRIM

FERGUSON H. B0712

FESLER J.W. B0713,B0714,B0715

FEUDALISM....FEUDALISM

FHA....U.S. FEDERAL HOUSING ADMINISTRATION

FICHTE/JG....JOHANN GOTTLIEB FICHTE

FICTIONS....SEE MYTH

FIELD G.L. B0716

FIELD J.O. B2371

FIELD/S....STEVEN FIELD

FIGANIERE J.C. B0717

FIJI

                                                       B61
WEST F.J.,POLITICAL ADVANCEMENT IN THE SOUTH   S/ASIA
PACIFIC. CONSTN CULTURE POL/PAR LEGIS DOMIN ADMIN   LOC/G
CHOOSE SOVEREIGN VAL/FREE 20 FIJI TAHITI SAMOA.   COLONIAL
PAGE 115 B2325

FIKS M. B0718

FILLMORE/M....PRESIDENT MILLARD FILLMORE

FILM....FILM AND CINEMA

B65
DAVISON W.P.,INTERNATIONAL POLITICAL COMMUNICATION. EDU/PROP
COM USA+45 WOR+45 CULTURE ECO/UNDEV NAT/G PROB/SOLV DIPLOM
PRESS TV ADMIN 20 FILM. PAGE 27 B0545 PERS/REL
COM/IND

FINAN....FINANCIAL SERVICE, BANKS, INSURANCE SYSTEMS,
SECURITIES, EXCHANGES

N
VENKATESAN S.L.,BIBLIOGRAPHY ON PUBLIC ENTERPRISES BIBLIOG/A
IN INDIA. INDIA S/ASIA FINAN LG/CO LOC/G PLAN ADMIN
BUDGET SOCISM...MGT 20. PAGE 112 B2258 ECO/UNDEV
INDUS

N
INTERNATIONAL BIBLIOGRAPHY OF ECONOMICS. WOR+45 BIBLIOG
FINAN MARKET ADMIN DEMAND INCOME PRODUC...POLICY ECO/DEV
IDEA/COMP METH. PAGE 1 B0003 ECO/UNDEV
INT/TRADE

N
BULLETIN OF THE PUBLIC AFFAIRS INFORMATION SERVICE. BIBLIOG
WOR+45 WOR-45 ECO/UNDEV FINAN LABOR LOC/G PROVS NAT/G
TEC/DEV DIPLOM EDU/PROP SOC. PAGE 1 B0010 ECO/DEV
ADMIN

N
THE MANAGEMENT REVIEW. FINAN EX/STRUC PROFIT LABOR
BIBLIOG/A. PAGE 1 B0017 MGT
ADMIN
MARKET

N
MARKETING INFORMATION GUIDE. USA+45 ECO/DEV FINAN BIBLIOG/A
ADMIN GP/REL. PAGE 1 B0018 DIST/IND
MARKET
ECO/TAC

N
ECONOMIC LIBRARY SELECTIONS. AGRI INDUS MARKET BIBLIOG/A
ADMIN...STAT NAT/COMP 20. PAGE 2 B0026 WRITING
FINAN

N
BUSINESS LITERATURE. WOR+45 MARKET ADMIN MGT. BIBLIOG/A
PAGE 2 B0031 INDUS
FINAN
POLICY

N
FINANCIAL INDEX. CANADA UK USA+45 ECO/DEV LG/CO BIBLIOG
ADMIN 20. PAGE 2 B0032 INDUS
FINAN
PRESS

N
CATHERINE R.,LA REVUE ADMINISTRATIVE. FRANCE LAW ADMIN
NAT/G LEGIS...JURID BIBLIOG/A 20. PAGE 19 B0393 MGT
FINAN
METH/COMP

N
KYRIAK T.E.,EAST EUROPE: BIBLIOGRAPHY--INDEX TO US BIBLIOG/A
JPRS RESEARCH TRANSLATIONS. ALBANIA BULGARIA COM PRESS
CZECHOSLVK HUNGARY POLAND ROMANIA AGRI EXTR/IND MARXISM
FINAN SERV/IND INT/TRADE WEAPON...GEOG MGT SOC 20. INDUS
PAGE 62 B1247

N
STATE OF ILLINOIS,PUBLICATIONS OF THE STATE OF BIBLIOG
ILLINOIS. USA+45 FINAN POL/PAR ADMIN LEAD 20 PROVS
ILLINOIS. PAGE 100 B2024 LOC/G
GOV/REL

N
UNITED NATIONS,UNITED NATIONS PUBLICATIONS. WOR+45 BIBLIOG
ECO/UNDEV AGRI FINAN FORCES ADMIN LEAD WAR PEACE INT/ORG
...POLICY INT/LAW 20 UN. PAGE 107 B2160 DIPLOM

N
US SUPERINTENDENT OF DOCUMENTS,EDUCATION (PRICE BIBLIOG/A
LIST 31). USA+45 LAW FINAN LOC/G NAT/G DEBATE ADMIN EDU/PROP
LEAD RACE/REL FEDERAL HEALTH POLICY. PAGE 111 B2238 ACADEM
SCHOOL

N
WORLD PEACE FOUNDATION,DOCUMENTS OF INTERNATIONAL BIBLIOG
ORGANIZATIONS: A SELECTED BIBLIOGRAPHY. WOR+45 DIPLOM
WOR-45 FINAN ACT/RES OP/RES INT/TRADE ADMIN INT/ORG
...CON/ANAL 20 UN UNESCO LEAGUE/NAT. PAGE 118 B2374 REGION

B02
MOREL E.D.,AFFAIRS OF WEST AFRICA. UK FINAN INDUS COLONIAL
FAM KIN SECT CHIEF WORKER DIPLOM RACE/REL LITERACY ADMIN
HEALTH...CHARTS 18/20 AFRICA/W NEGRO. PAGE 75 B1521 AFR

B08
THE GOVERNMENT OF SOUTH AFRICA (VOL. II). SOUTH/AFR CONSTN
STRATA EXTR/IND EX/STRUC TOP/EX BUDGET ADJUD ADMIN FINAN
CT/SYS PRODUC...CORREL CENSUS 19 RAILROAD LEGIS
CIVIL/SERV POSTAL/SYS. PAGE 2 B0033 NAT/G

B15
SAWYER R.A.,A LIST OF WORKS ON COUNTY GOVERNMENT. BIBLIOG/A
LAW FINAN MUNIC TOP/EX ROUTINE CRIME...CLASSIF LOC/G
RECORD 19/20. PAGE 93 B1871 GOV/REL
ADMIN

N19
ADMINISTRATIVE STAFF COLLEGE,THE ACCOUNTABILITY OF PARL/PROC

GOVERNMENT DEPARTMENTS (PAMPHLET) (REV. ED.). UK ELITES
CONSTN FINAN NAT/G CONSULT ADMIN INGP/REL CONSEN SANCTION
PRIVIL 20 PARLIAMENT. PAGE 3 B0059 PROB/SOLV
N19
ANDERSON J.,THE ORGANIZATION OF ECONOMIC STUDIES IN ECO/TAC
RELATION TO THE PROBLEMS OF GOVERNMENT (PAMPHLET). ACT/RES
UK FINAN INDUS DELIB/GP PLAN PROB/SOLV ADMIN 20. NAT/G
PAGE 5 B0093 CENTRAL
N19
KUWAIT ARABIA,KUWAIT FUND FOR ARAB ECONOMIC FOR/AID
DEVELOPMENT (PAMPHLET). ISLAM KUWAIT UAR ECO/UNDEV DIPLOM
LEGIS ECO/TAC WEALTH 20. PAGE 62 B1245 FINAN
ADMIN
N19
RIDLEY C.E.,MEASURING MUNICIPAL ACTIVITIES MGT
(PAMPHLET). FINAN SERV/IND FORCES RECEIVE INGP/REL HEALTH
HABITAT...POLICY SOC/WK 20. PAGE 88 B1779 WEALTH
LOC/G
B26
LUCE R.,CONGRESS: AN EXPLANATION. USA-45 CONSTN DECISION
FINAN ADMIN LEAD. PAGE 67 B1347 LEGIS
CREATE
REPRESENT
B27
WILLOUGHBY W.F.,PRINCIPLES OF PUBLIC ADMINISTRATION NAT/G
WITH SPECIAL REFERENCE TO THE NATIONAL AND STATE EX/STRUC
GOVERNMENTS OF THE UNITED STATES. FINAN PROVS CHIEF OP/RES
CONSULT LEGIS CREATE BUDGET EXEC ROUTINE GOV/REL ADMIN
CENTRAL...MGT 20 BUR/BUDGET CONGRESS PRESIDENT.
PAGE 117 B2356
B29
ROBERTS S.H.,HISTORY OF FRENCH COLONIAL POLICY. AFR INT/ORG
ASIA L/A+17C S/ASIA CULTURE ECO/DEV ECO/UNDEV FINAN ACT/RES
NAT/G PLAN ECO/TAC DOMIN ROUTINE SOVEREIGN...OBS FRANCE
HIST/WRIT TREND CHARTS VAL/FREE 19/20. PAGE 89 COLONIAL
B1796
B31
BORCHARD E.H.,GUIDE TO THE LAW AND LEGAL LITERATURE BIBLIOG/A
OF FRANCE. FRANCE FINAN INDUS LABOR SECT LEGIS LAW
ADMIN COLONIAL CRIME OWN...INT/LAW 20. PAGE 14 CONSTN
B0277 METH
B32
WRIGHT Q.,GOLD AND MONETARY STABILIZATION. FUT FINAN
USA-45 WOR-45 INTELL ECO/DEV INT/ORG NAT/G CONSULT POLICY
PLAN ECO/TAC ADMIN ATTIT WEALTH...CONCPT TREND 20.
PAGE 118 B2383
B36
GRAVES W.B.,AMERICAN STATE GOVERNMENT. CONSTN FINAN NAT/G
EX/STRUC FORCES LEGIS BUDGET TAX CT/SYS REPRESENT PROVS
GOV/REL...BIBLIOG/A 19/20. PAGE 42 B0855 ADMIN
FEDERAL
B37
BROOKS R.R.,WHEN LABOR ORGANIZES. FINAN EDU/PROP LABOR
ADMIN LOBBY PARTIC REPRESENT WEALTH TREND. PAGE 16 GP/REL
B0318 POLICY
B37
ROBBINS L.,ECONOMIC PLANNING AND INTERNATIONAL INT/ORG
ORDER. WOR-45 SOCIETY FINAN INDUS NAT/G ECO/TAC PLAN
ROUTINE WEALTH...SOC TIME/SEQ GEN/METH WORK 20 INT/TRADE
KEYNES/JM. PAGE 89 B1791
B38
DAY C.,A HISTORY OF COMMERCE. CHRIST-17C EUR+WWI MARKET
ISLAM MEDIT-7 MOD/EUR USA-45 ECO/DEV FINAN NAT/G INT/TRADE
ECO/TAC EXEC ROUTINE PWR WEALTH HIST/WRIT. PAGE 27
B0546
B38
LANGE O.,ON THE ECONOMIC THEORY OF SOCIALISM. UNIV MARKET
ECO/DEV FINAN INDUS INT/ORG PUB/INST ROUTINE ATTIT ECO/TAC
ALL/VALS...SOC CONCPT STAT TREND 20. PAGE 62 B1258 INT/TRADE
SOCISM
B40
GAUS J.M.,PUBLIC ADMINISTRATION AND THE UNITED ADMIN
STATES DEPARTMENT OF AGRICULTURE. USA-45 STRUCT AGRI
DIST/IND FINAN MARKET EX/STRUC PROB/SOLV GIVE DELIB/GP
PRODUC...POLICY GEOG CHARTS 20 DEPT/AGRI. PAGE 39 OP/RES
B0786
B40
MCHENRY D.E.,HIS MAJESTY'S OPPOSITION: STRUCTURE POL/PAR
AND PROBLEMS OF THE BRITISH LABOUR PARTY 1931-1938. MGT
UK FINAN LABOR LOC/G DELIB/GP LEGIS EDU/PROP LEAD NAT/G
PARTIC CHOOSE GP/REL SOCISM...TREND 20 LABOR/PAR. POLICY
PAGE 72 B1450
B40
WILCOX J.K.,MANUAL ON THE USE OF STATE BIBLIOG/A
PUBLICATIONS. USA-45 FINAN LEGIS TAX GOV/REL PROVS
...CHARTS 20. PAGE 116 B2346 ADMIN
LAW
C40
FAHS C.B.,"GOVERNMENT IN JAPAN." FINAN FORCES LEGIS ASIA
TOP/EX BUDGET INT/TRADE EDU/PROP SOVEREIGN DIPLOM
...CON/ANAL BIBLIOG/A 20 CHINJAP. PAGE 34 B0698 NAT/G
ADMIN
B41
STATIST REICHSAMTE,BIBLIOGRAPHIE DER STAATS- UND BIBLIOG
WIRSCHAFTSWISSENSCHAFTEN. EUR+WWI GERMANY FINAN ECO/DEV
ADMIN. PAGE 100 B2025 NAT/G

POLICY
B41

THE TAX FOUNDATION,STUDIES IN ECONOMY AND   BIBLIOG
EFFICIENCY IN GOVERNMENT. FINAN R+D OP/RES BUDGET   ADMIN
TAX 20. PAGE 104 B2095   EFFICIENCY
                                                           NAT/G
B42

WRIGHT D.M.,THE CREATION OF PURCHASING POWER.   FINAN
USA-45 NAT/G PRICE ADMIN WAR INCOME PRODUC...POLICY   ECO/TAC
CONCPT IDEA/COMP BIBLIOG 20 MONEY. PAGE 118 B2378   ECO/DEV
                                                          CREATE
S42

HUZAR E.,"LEGISLATIVE CONTROL OVER ADMINISTRATION: ADMIN
CONGRESS AND WPA" USA-45 FINAN DELIB/GP LOBBY   EX/STRUC
GOV/REL EFFICIENCY ATTIT...POLICY CONGRESS. PAGE 53   CONTROL
B1069   LEGIS
B44

PUBLIC ADMINISTRATION SERVICE,YOUR BUSINESS OF   BIBLIOG
GOVERNMENT: A CATALOG OF PUBLICATIONS IN THE FIELD   ADMIN
OF PUBLIC ADMINISTRATION (PAMPHLET). FINAN R+D   NAT/G
LOC/G ACT/RES OP/RES PLAN 20. PAGE 85 B1715   MUNIC
B44

WRIGHT H.R.,SOCIAL SERVICE IN WARTIME. FINAN NAT/G   GIVE
VOL/ASSN PLAN GP/REL ROLE. PAGE 118 B2381   WAR
                                                          SOC/WK
                                                          ADMIN
S44

GRIFFITH E.S.,"THE CHANGING PATTERN OF PUBLIC   LAW
POLICY FORMATION." MOD/EUR WOR+45 FINAN CHIEF   POLICY
CONFER ADMIN LEAD CONSERVE SOCISM TECHRACY...SOC   TEC/DEV
CHARTS CONGRESS. PAGE 43 B0877
B47

MARX F.M.,THE PRESIDENT AND HIS STAFF SERVICES   CONSTN
PUBLIC ADMINISTRATION SERVICES NUMBER 98   CHIEF
(PAMPHLET). FINAN ADMIN CT/SYS REPRESENT PWR 20   NAT/G
PRESIDENT. PAGE 70 B1419   EX/STRUC
B48

PUBLIC ADMINISTRATION SERVICE,SOURCE MATERIALS IN   BIBLIOG/A
PUBLIC ADMINISTRATION: A SELECTED BIBLIOGRAPHY (PAS   GOV/REL
PUBLICATION NO. 102). USA+45 LAW FINAN LOC/G MUNIC   MGT
NAT/G PLAN RECEIVE EDU/PROP CT/SYS CHOOSE HEALTH   ADMIN
20. PAGE 85 B1717
B49

ASPINALL A.,POLITICS AND THE PRESS 1780-1850. UK   PRESS
LAW ELITES FINAN PROF/ORG LEGIS ADMIN ATTIT   CONTROL
...POLICY 18/19. PAGE 7 B0142   POL/PAR
                                                          ORD/FREE
B49

LEPAWSKY A.,ADMINISTRATION. FINAN INDUS LG/CO   ADMIN
SML/CO INGP/REL PERS/REL COST EFFICIENCY OPTIMAL   MGT
SKILL 20. PAGE 64 B1294   WORKER
                                                          EX/STRUC
B49

SCHULTZ W.J.,AMERICAN PUBLIC FINANCE. USA+45   FINAN
ECO/TAC TAX ADMIN GOV/REL GP/REL INCOME 20. PAGE 94   POLICY
B1906   ECO/DEV
                                                          NAT/G
B50

BAKKE E.W.,BONDS OF ORGANIZATION (2ND ED.). USA+45   ECO/DEV
COM/IND FINAN ADMIN LEAD PERS/REL...INT SOC/INTEG   MGT
20. PAGE 8 B0169   LABOR
                                                          GP/REL
B50

GRAVES W.B.,PUBLIC ADMINISTRATION: A COMPREHENSIVE   BIBLIOG
BIBLIOGRAPHY ON PUBLIC ADMINISTRATION IN THE UNITED   FINAN
STATES (PAMPHLET). USA+45 USA-45 LOC/G NAT/G LEGIS   CONTROL
ADJUD INGP/REL...MGT 20. PAGE 42 B0858   ADMIN
B50

HARTLAND P.C.,BALANCE OF INTERREGIONAL PAYMENTS OF   ECO/DEV
NEW ENGLAND. USA+45 TEC/DEV ECO/TAC LEGIT ROUTINE   FINAN
BAL/PAY PROFIT 20 NEW/ENGLND FED/RESERV. PAGE 47   REGION
B0962   PLAN
C50

MORLAN R.L.,"INTERGOVERNMENTAL RELATIONS IN   SCHOOL
EDUCATION." USA+45 FINAN LOC/G MUNIC NAT/G FORCES   GOV/REL
PROB/SOLV RECEIVE ADMIN RACE/REL COST...BIBLIOG   ACADEM
INDIAN/AM. PAGE 76 B1526   POLICY
C50

STEWART F.M.,"A HALF CENTURY OF MUNICIPAL REFORM."   LOC/G
USA+45 CONSTN FINAN SCHOOL EX/STRUC PLAN PROB/SOLV   VOL/ASSN
EDU/PROP ADMIN CHOOSE GOV/REL BIBLIOG. PAGE 101   MUNIC
B2036   POLICY
C50

WAGER P.W.,"COUNTY GOVERNMENT ACROSS THE NATION."   LOC/G
USA+45 CONSTN COM/IND FINAN SCHOOL DOMIN CT/SYS   PROVS
LEAD GOV/REL...STAT BIBLIOG 20. PAGE 112 B2272   ADMIN
                                                          ROUTINE
B51

ANDERSON W.,GOVERNMENT IN THE FIFTY STATES. LAW   LOC/G
CONSTN FINAN POL/PAR LEGIS EDU/PROP ADJUD ADMIN   PROVS
CT/SYS CHOOSE...CHARTS 20. PAGE 5 B0101   GOV/REL
B51

DIMOCK M.E.,FREE ENTERPRISE AND THE ADMINISTRATIVE   CAP/ISM
STATE. FINAN LG/CO BARGAIN BUDGET DOMIN CONTROL   ADMIN
INGP/REL EFFICIENCY 20. PAGE 29 B0595   MGT
                                                          MARKET

B52

EGLE W.P.,ECONOMIC STABILIZATION. USA+45 SOCIETY   NAT/G
FINAN MARKET PLAN ECO/TAC DOMIN EDU/PROP LEGIT EXEC   ECO/DEV
WEALTH...CONCPT METH/CNCPT TREND HYPO/EXP GEN/METH   CAP/ISM
TOT/POP VAL/FREE 20. PAGE 32 B0656
B53

DIMOCK M.E.,PUBLIC ADMINISTRATION. USA+45 FINAN   ADMIN
WORKER BUDGET CONTROL CHOOSE...T 20. PAGE 29 B0596   STRUCT
                                                          OP/RES
                                                          POLICY
B53

STOUT H.M.,BRITISH GOVERNMENT. UK FINAN LOC/G   NAT/G
POL/PAR DELIB/GP DIPLOM ADMIN COLONIAL CHOOSE   PARL/PROC
ORD/FREE...JURID BIBLIOG 20 COMMONWLTH. PAGE 101   CONSTN
B2049   NEW/LIB
B54

BINANI G.D.,INDIA AT A GLANCE (REV. ED.). INDIA   INDEX
COM/IND FINAN INDUS LABOR PROVS SCHOOL PLAN DIPLOM   CON/ANAL
INT/TRADE ADMIN...JURID 20. PAGE 12 B0238   NAT/G
                                                          ECO/UNDEV
B54

LOCKLIN D.P.,ECONOMICS OF TRANSPORTATION (4TH ED.).   ECO/DEV
USA+45 USA-45 SEA AIR LAW FINAN LG/CO EX/STRUC   DIST/IND
ADMIN CONTROL...STAT CHARTS 19/20 RAILROAD   ECO/TAC
PUB/TRANS. PAGE 66 B1335   TEC/DEV
B54

RECK D.,GOVERNMENT PURCHASING AND COMPETITION.   NAT/G
USA+45 LEGIS CAP/ISM ECO/TAC GOV/REL CENTRAL   FINAN
...POLICY 20 CONGRESS. PAGE 87 B1749   MGT
                                                          COST
C54

ROBSON W.A.,"GREAT CITIES OF THE WORLD: THEIR   LOC/G
GOVERNMENT, POLITICS, AND PLANNING." CONSTN FINAN   MUNIC
EX/STRUC ADMIN EXEC CHOOSE GOV/REL...STAT TREND   PLAN
ANTHOL BIBLIOG 20. PAGE 89 B1806   PROB/SOLV
C55

CRAIG J.,BIBLIOGRAPHY OF PUBLIC ADMINISTRATION IN   BIBLIOG
AUSTRALIA. CONSTN FINAN EX/STRUC LEGIS PLAN DIPLOM   GOV/REL
RECEIVE ADJUD ROUTINE...HEAL 19/20 AUSTRAL   ADMIN
PARLIAMENT. PAGE 24 B0500   NAT/G
B56

ALEXANDER R.S.,INDUSTRIAL MARKETING. USA+45 ECO/DEV   INDUS
DIST/IND FINAN NAT/G ACT/RES CAP/ISM PRICE CONTROL   MARKET
...POLICY MGT 20. PAGE 4 B0072   ECO/TAC
                                                          PLAN
B56

WHYTE W.H. JR.,THE ORGANIZATION MAN. CULTURE FINAN   ADMIN
VOL/ASSN DOMIN EDU/PROP EXEC DISPL HABITAT ROLE   LG/CO
...PERS/TEST STERTYP. PAGE 116 B2343   PERSON
                                                          CONSEN
L56

PARSONS T.,"SUGGESTIONS FOR A SOCIOLOGICAL APPROACH   SOC
TO THE THEORY OF ORGANIZATIONS - I" (BMR)" FINAN   CONCPT
EX/STRUC LEGIT ALL/VALS...POLICY DECISION 20.   ADMIN
PAGE 81 B1637   STRUCT
B57

JENNINGS I.,PARLIAMENT. UK FINAN INDUS POL/PAR   PARL/PROC
DELIB/GP EX/STRUC PLAN CONTROL...MAJORIT JURID   TOP/EX
PARLIAMENT. PAGE 56 B1133   MGT
                                                          LEGIS
B57

KNEIER C.M.,CITY GOVERNMENT IN THE UNITED STATES   MUNIC
(3RD ED.). USA-45 FINAN NAT/G POL/PAR LEGIS   LOC/G
EDU/PROP LEAD APPORT REPRESENT ATTIT...MGT 20   ADMIN
CITY/MGT. PAGE 60 B1219   GOV/REL
B57

PARKINSON C.N.,PARKINSON'S LAW. UNIV EX/STRUC PLAN   ADMIN
ATTIT PERSON TIME. PAGE 81 B1634   EXEC
                                                          FINAN
                                                          ECOMETRIC
B57

SCHLOCHAUER H.J.,OFFENTLICHES RECHT. GERMANY/W   CONSTN
FINAN EX/STRUC LEGIS DIPLOM FEDERAL ORD/FREE   JURID
...INT/LAW 20. PAGE 94 B1892   ADMIN
                                                          CT/SYS
B58

CHANG C.,THE INFLATIONARY SPIRAL: THE EXPERIENCE IN   FINAN
CHINA 1939-50. CHINA/COM BUDGET INT/TRADE PRICE   ECO/TAC
ADMIN CONTROL WAR DEMAND...POLICY CHARTS 20.   BAL/PAY
PAGE 20 B0406   GOV/REL
B58

CONSERVATIVE POLITICAL CENTRE,A WORLD SECURITY   ORD/FREE
AUTHORITY? WOR+45 CONSTN ELITES FINAN DELIB/GP PLAN   CONSERVE
PROB/SOLV ADMIN CONTROL NUC/PWR GP/REL...IDEA/COMP   FORCES
20. PAGE 23 B0468   ARMS/CONT
B58

GROSSMAN J.,BIBLIOGRAPHY ON PUBLIC ADMINISTRATION   BIBLIOG
IN LATIN AMERICA. ECO/UNDEV FINAN PLAN BUDGET   L/A+17C
ECO/TAC TARIFFS TAX...STAT 20. PAGE 44 B0893   NAT/G
                                                          ADMIN
B58

ISLAM R.,INTERNATIONAL ECONOMIC COOPERATION AND THE   INT/ORG
UNITED NATIONS. FINAN PLAN EXEC TASK WAR PEACE   DIPLOM
...SOC METH/CNCPT 20 UN LEAGUE/NAT. PAGE 55 B1105   ADMIN
B58

SHAW S.J.,THE FINANCIAL AND ADMINISTRATIVE   FINAN

ORGANIZATION AND DEVELOPMENT OF OTTOMAN EGYPT 1517-1798. UAR LOC/G FORCES BUDGET INT/TRADE TAX EATING INCOME WEALTH...CHARTS BIBLIOG 16/18 OTTOMAN NAPOLEON/B. PAGE 96 B1940 — ADMIN GOV/REL CULTURE

B58
WHITE L.D.,THE REPUBLICAN ERA: 1869-1901, A STUDY IN ADMINISTRATIVE HISTORY. USA-45 FINAN PLAN NEUTRAL CRIME GP/REL MORAL LAISSEZ PRESIDENT REFORMERS 19 CONGRESS CIVIL/SERV. PAGE 116 B2340 — MGT PWR DELIB/GP ADMIN

S58
ARGYRIS C.,"SOME PROBLEMS IN CONCEPTUALIZING ORGANIZATIONAL CLIMATE: A CASE STUDY OF A BANK" (BMR)" USA+45 EX/STRUC ADMIN PERS/REL ADJUST PERSON ...POLICY HYPO/EXP SIMUL 20. PAGE 6 B0129 — FINAN CONCPT LG/CO INGP/REL

B59
CONOVER H.F.,NIGERIAN OFFICIAL PUBLICATIONS, 1869-1959: A GUIDE. NIGER CONSTN FINAN ACADEM SCHOOL FORCES PRESS ADMIN COLONIAL...HIST/WRIT 19/20. PAGE 23 B0466 — BIBLIOG NAT/G CON/ANAL

B59
ELAZAR D.J.,INTERGOVERNMENTAL RELATIONS IN NINETEENTH CENTURY AMERICAN FEDERALISM (DOCTORAL THESIS). USA-45 FINAN LOC/G NAT/G GP/REL 18/19. PAGE 33 B0662 — FEDERAL ADMIN PROVS GOV/REL

B59
EPSTEIN F.T.,EAST GERMANY: A SELECTED BIBLIOGRAPHY (PAMPHLET). COM GERMANY/E LAW AGRI FINAN INDUS LABOR POL/PAR EDU/PROP ADMIN AGE/Y 20. PAGE 33 B0677 — BIBLIOG/A INTELL MARXISM NAT/G

B59
IPSEN H.P.,HAMBURGISCHES STAATS- UND VERWALTUNGSRECHT. CONSTN LOC/G FORCES BUDGET CT/SYS ...JURID 20 HAMBURG. PAGE 54 B1103 — ADMIN PROVS LEGIS FINAN

B59
MAYDA J.,ATOMIC ENERGY AND LAW. ECO/UNDEV FINAN TEC/DEV FOR/AID EFFICIENCY PRODUC WEALTH...POLICY TECHNIC 20. PAGE 71 B1433 — NUC/PWR L/A+17C LAW ADMIN

B59
MOOS M.,THE CAMPUS AND THE STATE. LAW FINAN DELIB/GP LEGIS EXEC LOBBY GP/REL PWR...POLICY BIBLIOG. PAGE 75 B1517 — EDU/PROP ACADEM PROVS CONTROL

B59
WASSERMAN P.,MEASUREMENT AND ANALYSIS OF ORGANIZATIONAL PERFORMANCE. FINAN MARKET EX/STRUC TEC/DEV EDU/PROP CONTROL ROUTINE TASK...MGT 20. PAGE 114 B2300 — BIBLIOG/A ECO/TAC OP/RES EFFICIENCY

B60
ADRIAN C.R.,STATE AND LOCAL GOVERNMENTS: A STUDY IN THE POLITICAL PROCESS. USA+45 LAW FINAN MUNIC POL/PAR LEGIS ADJUD EXEC CHOOSE REPRESENT. PAGE 3 B0060 — LOC/G PROVS GOV/REL ATTIT

B60
ALBI F.,TRATADO DE LOS MODOS DE GESTION DE LAS CORPORACIONES LOCALES. SPAIN FINAN NAT/G BUDGET CONTROL EXEC ROUTINE GOV/REL ORD/FREE SOVEREIGN ...MGT 20. PAGE 3 B0068 — LOC/G LAW ADMIN MUNIC

B60
BAERWALD F.,ECONOMIC SYSTEM ANALYSIS: CONCEPTS AND PERSPECTIVES. USA+45 ECO/DEV NAT/G COMPUTER EQUILIB INCOME ATTIT...DECISION CONCPT IDEA/COMP. PAGE 8 B0159 — ACT/RES ECO/TAC ROUTINE FINAN

B60
CORSON J.J.,GOVERNANCE OF COLLEGES AND UNIVERSITIES. STRUCT FINAN DELIB/GP DOMIN EDU/PROP LEAD CHOOSE GP/REL CENTRAL COST PRIVIL SUPEGO ORD/FREE PWR...DECISION BIBLIOG. PAGE 24 B0481 — ADMIN EXEC ACADEM HABITAT

B60
CRAUMER L.V.,BUSINESS PERIODICALS INDEX (8VOLS.). USA+45 LABOR TAX 20. PAGE 25 B0503 — BIBLIOG/A FINAN FCO/DEV MGT

B60
DRAPER T.,AMERICAN COMMUNISM AND SOVIET RUSSIA. EUR+WWI USA+45 USSR INTELL AGRI COM/IND FINAN INDUS LABOR PROF/ORG VOL/ASSN PLAN TEC/DEV DOMIN EDU/PROP ADMIN COERCE REV PERSON PWR...POLICY CONCPT MYTH 19/20. PAGE 30 B0617 — COM POL/PAR

B60
EASTON S.C.,THE TWILIGHT OF EUROPEAN COLONIALISM. AFR S/ASIA CONSTN SOCIETY STRUCT ECO/UNDEV INDUS NAT/G FORCES ECO/TAC COLONIAL CT/SYS ATTIT KNOWL ORD/FREE PWR...SOCIALIST TIME/SEQ TREND CON/ANAL 20. PAGE 32 B0645 — FINAN ADMIN

B60
GILMORE D.R.,DEVELOPING THE "LITTLE" ECONOMIES. USA+45 FINAN LG/CO PROF/ORG VOL/ASSN CREATE ADMIN. PAGE 40 B0801 — ECO/TAC LOC/G PROVS PLAN

B60
HOVING W.,THE DISTRIBUTION REVOLUTION. WOR+45 ECO/DEV FINAN SERV/IND PRESS PRICE INCOME PRODUC ...MGT 20. PAGE 52 B1049 — DIST/IND MARKET ECO/TAC TASK

B60
JONES V.,METROPOLITAN COMMUNITIES: A BIBLIOGRAPHY WITH SPECIAL EMPHASIS UPON GOVERNMENT AND POLITICS, 1955-1957. STRUCT ECO/DEV FINAN FORCES PLAN PROB/SOLV RECEIVE EDU/PROP CT/SYS...GEOG HEAL 20. PAGE 57 B1152 — BIBLIOG LOC/G MUNIC ADMIN

B60
MARSHALL A.H.,FINANCIAL ADMINISTRATION IN LOCAL GOVERNMENT. UK DELIB/GP CONFER COST INCOME PERSON ...JURID 20. PAGE 70 B1408 — FINAN LOC/G BUDGET ADMIN

B60
MATTOD P.K.,A STUDY OF LOCAL SELF GOVERNMENT IN URBAN INDIA. INDIA FINAN DELIB/GP LEGIS BUDGET TAX SOVEREIGN...MGT GP/COMP 20. PAGE 71 B1432 — MUNIC CONSTN LOC/G ADMIN

B60
PENNSYLVANIA ECONOMY LEAGUE,URBAN RENEWAL IMPACT STUDY: ADMINISTRATIVE-LEGAL-FISCAL. USA+45 FINAN LOC/G NEIGH ADMIN EFFICIENCY...CENSUS CHARTS 20 PENNSYLVAN. PAGE 82 B1652 — PLAN BUDGET MUNIC ADJUD

B60
PFIFFNER J.M.,PUBLIC ADMINISTRATION. USA+45 FINAN WORKER PLAN PROB/SOLV ADJUD CONTROL EXEC...T 20. PAGE 82 B1666 — ADMIN NAT/G LOC/G MGT

B60
PHILLIPS J.C.,MUNICIPAL GOVERNMENT AND ADMINISTRATION IN AMERICA. USA+45 LAW CONSTN FINAN FORCES PLAN RECEIVE OWN ORD/FREE 20 CIVIL/LIB. PAGE 83 B1669 — MUNIC GOV/REL LOC/G ADMIN

B60
RAO V.K.R.,INTERNATIONAL AID FOR ECONOMIC DEVELOPMENT - POSSIBILITIES AND LIMITATIONS. FINAN PLAN TEC/DEV ADMIN TASK EFFICIENCY...POLICY SOC METH/CNCPT CHARTS 20 UN. PAGE 86 B1734 — FOR/AID DIPLOM INT/ORG ECO/UNDEV

B60
STANFORD RESEARCH INSTITUTE,AFRICAN DEVELOPMENT: A TEST FOR INTERNATIONAL COOPERATION. AFR USA+45 WOR+45 FINAN INT/ORG PLAN PROB/SOLV ECO/TAC INT/TRADE ADMIN...CHARTS 20. PAGE 100 B2018 — FOR/AID ECO/UNDEV ATTIT DIPLOM

B60
WALDO D.,THE RESEARCH FUNCTION OF UNIVERSITY BUREAUS AND INSTITUTES FOR GOVERNMENTAL-RELATED RESEARCH. FINAN ACADEM NAT/G INGP/REL ROLE...POLICY CLASSIF GOV/COMP. PAGE 113 B2276 — ADMIN R+D MUNIC

B60
WORLEY P.,ASIA TODAY (REV. ED.) (PAMPHLET). COM ECO/UNDEV AGRI FINAN INDUS POL/PAR FOR/AID ADMIN MARXISM 20. PAGE 118 B2376 — BIBLIOG/A ASIA DIPLOM NAT/G

S60
"THE EMERGING COMMON MARKETS IN LATIN AMERICA." FUT L/A+17C STRATA DIST/IND INDUS LABOR NAT/G LEGIS ECO/TAC ADMIN RIGID/FLEX HEALTH...NEW/IDEA TIME/SEQ OAS 20. PAGE 2 B0039 — FINAN ECO/UNDEV INT/TRADE

S60
FRANKEL S.H.,"ECONOMIC ASPECTS OF POLITICAL INDEPENDENCE IN AFRICA." AFR FUT SOCIETY ECO/UNDEV COM/IND FINAN LEGIS PLAN TEC/DEV CAP/ISM ECO/TAC INT/TRADE ADMIN ATTIT DRIVE RIGID/FLEX PWR WEALTH ...MGT NEW/IDEA MATH TIME/SEQ VAL/FREE 20. PAGE 37 B0751 — NAT/G FOR/AID

S60
HERRERA F.,"THE INTER-AMERICAN DEVELOPMENT BANK." USA+45 ECO/UNDEV INT/ORG CONSULT DELIB/GP PLAN ECO/TAC INT/TRADE ROUTINE WEALTH...STAT 20. PAGE 49 B0994 — L/A+17C FINAN FOR/AID REGION

S60
HERZ J.H.,"EAST GERMANY: PROGRESS AND PROSPECTS." COM AGRI FINAN INDUS LOC/G NAT/G FORCES PLAN TEC/DEV DOMIN ADMIN COERCE DRIVE PERCEPT RIGID/FLEX MORAL ORD/FREE PWR...MARXIST PSY SOC RECORD STERTYP WORK. PAGE 49 B0997 — POL/PAR STRUCT GERMANY

S60
MORALES C.J.,"TRADE AND ECONOMIC INTEGRATION IN LATIN AMERICA." FUT L/A+17C LAW STRATA ECO/UNDEV DIST/IND INDUS LABOR NAT/G LEGIS ECO/TAC ADMIN RIGID/FLEX WEALTH...CONCPT NEW/IDEA CONT/OBS TIME/SEQ WORK 20. PAGE 75 B1519 — FINAN INT/TRADE REGION

S60
RAPHAELI N.,"SELECTED ARTICLES AND DOCUMENTS ON COMPARATIVE PUBLIC ADMINISTRATION." USA+45 FINAN LOC/G TOP/EX TEC/DEV EXEC GP/REL INGP/REL...GP/COMP GOV/COMP METH/COMP. PAGE 86 B1738 — BIBLIOG MGT ADMIN EX/STRUC

S60
SCHATZ S.P.,"THE INFLENCE OF PLANNING ON DEVELOPMENT: THE NIGERIAN EXPERIENCE." AFR FUT FINAN INDUS NAT/G EX/STRUC ECO/TAC ADMIN ATTIT PERCEPT ORD/FREE PWR...MATH TREND CON/ANAL SIMUL VAL/FREE 20. PAGE 93 B1883 — ECO/UNDEV PLAN NIGERIA

B61
AGARWAL R.C.,STATE ENTERPRISE IN INDIA. FUT INDIA UK FINAN INDUS ADMIN CONTROL OWN...POLICY CHARTS BIBLIOG 20 RAILROAD. PAGE 3 B0064 — ECO/UNDEV SOCISM GOV/REL LG/CO

B61

AMERICAN MANAGEMENT ASSN.,SUPERIOR-SUBORDINATE   MGT
COMMUNICATION IN MANAGEMENT. STRATA FINAN INDUS   ACT/RES
SML/CO WORKER CONTROL EXEC ATTIT 20. PAGE 4 B0086   PERS/REL
                                                        LG/CO

B61

BEASLEY K.E.,STATE SUPERVISION OF MUNICIPAL DEBT IN   MUNIC
KANSAS - A CASE STUDY. USA+45 USA-45 FINAN PROVS   LOC/G
BUDGET TAX ADJUD ADMIN CONTROL SUPEGO. PAGE 10   LEGIS
B0201   JURID

B61

BENOIT E.,EUROPE AT SIXES AND SEVENS: THE COMMON   FINAN
MARKET. THE FREE TRADE ASSOCIATION AND THE UNITED   ECO/DEV
STATES. EUR+WWI FUT USA+45 INDUS CONSULT DELIB/GP   VOL/ASSN
EX/STRUC TOP/EX ACT/RES ECO/TAC EDU/PROP ROUTINE
CHOOSE PERCEPT WEALTH...MGT TREND EEC TOT/POP 20
EFTA. PAGE 11 B0217

B61

FRIEDMANN W.G.,JOINT INTERNATIONAL BUSINESS   ECO/UNDEV
VENTURES. ASIA ISLAM L/A+17C ECO/DEV DIST/IND FINAN   INT/TRADE
PROC/MFG FACE/GP LG/CO NAT/G VOL/ASSN CONSULT
EX/STRUC PLAN ADMIN ROUTINE WEALTH...OLD/LIB WORK
20. PAGE 37 B0760

B61

LAHAYE R.,LES ENTREPRISES PUBLIQUES AU MAROC.   NAT/G
FRANCE MOROCCO LAW DIST/IND EXTR/IND FINAN CONSULT   INDUS
PLAN TEC/DEV ADMIN AGREE CONTROL OWN...POLICY 20.   ECO/UNDEV
PAGE 62 B1250   ECO/TAC

B61

LEE R.R.,ENGINEERING-ECONOMIC PLANNING   BIBLIOG/A
MISCELLANEOUS SUBJECTS: A SELECTED BIBLIOGRAPHY   PLAN
(MIMEOGRAPHED). FINAN LOC/G MUNIC NEIGH ADMIN   REGION
CONTROL INGP/REL HABITAT...GEOG MGT SOC/WK 20
RESOURCE/N. PAGE 63 B1280

B61

MARX K.,THE COMMUNIST MANIFESTO. IN (MENDEL A.   COM
ESSENTIAL WORKS OF MARXISM. NEW YORK: BANTAM. FUT   NEW/IDEA
MOD/EUR CULTURE ECO/DEV ECO/UNDEV AGRI FINAN INDUS   CAP/ISM
MARKET PROC/MFG LABOR MUNIC POL/PAR CONSULT FORCES   REV
CREATE PLAN ADMIN ATTIT DRIVE RIGID/FLEX ORD/FREE
PWR RESPECT MARX/KARL WORK. PAGE 70 B1421

B61

NOVE A.,THE SOVIET ECONOMY. USSR ECO/DEV FINAN   PLAN
NAT/G ECO/TAC PRICE ADMIN EFFICIENCY MARXISM   PRODUC
...TREND BIBLIOG 20. PAGE 79 B1594   POLICY

B61

SHAPP W.R.,FIELD ADMINISTRATION IN THE UNITED   INT/ORG
NATIONS SYSTEM. FINAN PROB/SOLV INSPECT DIPLOM EXEC   ADMIN
REGION ROUTINE EFFICIENCY ROLE...INT CHARTS 20 UN.   GP/REL
PAGE 96 B1933   FOR/AID

B61

SINGER J.D.,FINANCING INTERNATIONAL ORGANIZATION: INT/ORG
THE UNITED NATIONS BUDGET PROCESS. WOR+45 FINAN   MGT
ACT/RES CREATE PLAN BUDGET ECO/TAC ADMIN ROUTINE
ATTIT KNOWL...DECISION METH/CNCPT TIME/SEQ UN 20.
PAGE 97 B1964

L61

COHEN K.J.,"THE ROLE OF MANAGEMENT GAMES IN   SOCIETY
EDUCATION AND RESEARCH." INTELL ECO/DEV FINAN   GAME
ACT/RES ECO/TAC DECISION. PAGE 22 B0444   MGT
                                                        EDU/PROP

S61

REAGAN M.O.,"THE POLITICAL STRUCTURE OF THE FEDERAL   PWR
RESERVE SYSTEM." USA+45 FINAN NAT/G ADMIN 20.   EX/STRUC
PAGE 87 B1748   EXEC
                                                        LEAD

S61

VINER J.,"ECONOMIC FOREIGN POLICY ON THE NEW   TOP/EX
FRONTIER." USA+45 ECO/UNDEV AGRI FINAN INDUS MARKET   ECO/TAC
INT/ORG NAT/G FOR/AID INT/TRADE ADMIN ATTIT PWR 20   BAL/PAY
KENNEDY/JF. PAGE 112 B2262   TARIFFS

B62

BOWEN W.G.,THE FEDERAL GOVERNMENT AND PRINCETON   NAT/G
UNIVERSITY. USA+45 FINAN ACT/RES PROB/SOLV ADMIN   ACADEM
CONTROL COST...POLICY 20 PRINCETN/U. PAGE 14 B0285   GP/REL
                                                        OP/RES

B62

CHANDLER A.D.,STRATEGY AND STRUCTURE: CHAPTERS IN   LG/CO
THE HISTORY OF THE INDUSTRIAL ENTERPRISE. USA+45   PLAN
USA-45 ECO/DEV EX/STRUC ECO/TAC EXEC...DECISION 20.   ADMIN
PAGE 20 B0403   FINAN

B62

DELANY V.T.H.,THE ADMINISTRATION OF JUSTICE IN   ADMIN
IRELAND. IRELAND CONSTN FINAN JUDGE COLONIAL CRIME   JURID
...CRIMLGY 19/20. PAGE 28 B0571   CT/SYS
                                                        ADJUD

B62

DIMOCK M.E.,THE NEW AMERICAN POLITICAL ECONOMY: A   FEDERAL
SYNTHESIS OF POLITICS AND ECONOMICS. USA+45 FINAN   ECO/TAC
LG/CO PLAN ADMIN REGION GP/REL CENTRAL MORAL 20.   NAT/G
PAGE 29 B0598   PARTIC

B62

DODDS H.W.,THE ACADEMIC PRESIDENT "EDUCATOR OR   ACADEM
CARETAKER? FINAN DELIB/GP EDU/PROP PARTIC ATTIT   ADMIN
ROLE PWR...POLICY RECORD INT. PAGE 30 B0601   LEAD
                                                        CONTROL

B62

FORD A.G.,THE GOLD STANDARD 1880-1914: BRITAIN AND   FINAN
ARGENTINA. UK ECO/UNDEV INT/TRADE ADMIN GOV/REL   ECO/TAC
DEMAND EFFICIENCY...STAT CHARTS 19/20 ARGEN   BUDGET
GOLD/STAND. PAGE 36 B0737   BAL/PAY

B62

FRIEDLANDER W.A.,INDIVIDUALISM AND SOCIAL WELFARE.   GIVE
FRANCE ACADEM OP/RES ADMIN AGE/Y AGE/A ORD/FREE 20.   SOC/WK
PAGE 37 B0756   SOC/EXP
                                                        FINAN

B62

FRIEDMANN W.,METHODS AND POLICIES OF PRINCIPAL   INT/ORG
DONOR COUNTRIES IN PUBLIC INTERNATIONAL DEVELOPMENT   FOR/AID
FINANCING: PRELIMINARY APPRAISAL. FRANCE GERMANY/W   NAT/COMP
UK USA+45 USSR WOR+45 FINAN TEC/DEV CAP/ISM DIPLOM   ADMIN
ECO/TAC ATTIT 20 EEC. PAGE 37 B0759

B62

GROVE J.W.,GOVERNMENT AND INDUSTRY IN BRITAIN. UK   ECO/TAC
FINAN LOC/G CONSULT DELIB/GP INT/TRADE ADMIN   INDUS
CONTROL...BIBLIOG 20. PAGE 44 B0894   NAT/G
                                                        GP/REL

B62

INST TRAINING MUNICIPAL ADMIN.,MUNICIPAL FINANCE   MUNIC
ADMINISTRATION (6TH ED.). USA+45 ELITES ECO/DEV   ADMIN
LEGIS PLAN BUDGET TAX GP/REL BAL/PAY COST...POLICY   FINAN
20 CITY/MGT. PAGE 54 B1089   LOC/G

B62

KARNJAHAPRAKORN C.,MUNICIPAL GOVERNMENT IN THAILAND   LOC/G
AS AN INSTITUTION AND PROCESS OF SELF-GOVERNMENT.   MUNIC
THAILAND CULTURE FINAN EX/STRUC LEGIS PLAN CONTROL   ORD/FREE
GOV/REL EFFICIENCY ATTIT...POLICY 20. PAGE 58 B1176   ADMIN

B62

KUHN T.E.,PUBLIC ENTERPRISES, PROJECT PLANNING AND   ECO/DEV
ECONOMIC DEVELOPMENT (PAMPHLET). ECO/UNDEV FINAN   ECO/TAC
PLAN ADMIN EFFICIENCY OWN...MGT STAT CHARTS ANTHOL   LG/CO
20. PAGE 61 B1240   NAT/G

B62

MARS D.,SUGGESTED LIBRARY IN PUBLIC ADMINISTRATION.   BIBLIOG
FINAN DELIB/GP EX/STRUC WORKER COMPUTER ADJUD   ADMIN
...DECISION PSY SOC METH/COMP 20. PAGE 69 B1403   METH
                                                        MGT

B62

MARTIN R.C.,GOVERNMENT AND THE SUBURBAN SCHOOL.   SCHOOL
USA+45 FINAN EDU/PROP ADMIN HABITAT...TREND GP/COMP   LOC/G
20. PAGE 70 B1414   EX/STRUC
                                                        ISOLAT

B62

NEVINS A.,THE STATE UNIVERSITIES AND DEMOCRACY.   ACADEM
AGRI FINAN SCHOOL ADMIN EXEC EFFICIENCY ATTIT.   PROVS
PAGE 78 B1576   EDU/PROP
                                                        POLICY

B62

RUDOLPH F.,THE AMERICAN COLLEGE AND UNIVERSITY.   ACADEM
CLIENT FINAN PUB/INST DELIB/GP EDU/PROP CONTROL   INGP/REL
EXEC CONSEN ATTIT POLICY. PAGE 92 B1853   PWR
                                                        ADMIN

B62

SAMPSON A.,ANATOMY OF BRITAIN. UK LAW COM/IND FINAN   ELITES
INDUS MARKET MUNIC POL/PAR EX/STRUC TOP/EX DIPLOM   PWR
LEAD REPRESENT PERSON PARLIAMENT WORSHIP. PAGE 92   STRUCT
B1866   FORCES

B63

ADRIAN C.R.,GOVERNING OVER FIFTY STATES AND THEIR   PROVS
COMMUNITIES. USA+45 CONSTN FINAN MUNIC NAT/G   LOC/G
POL/PAR EX/STRUC LEGIS ADMIN CONTROL CT/SYS   GOV/REL
...CHARTS 20. PAGE 3 B0061   GOV/COMP

B63

BASS M.E.,SELECTIVE BIBLIOGRAPHY ON MUNICIPAL   BIBLIOG
GOVERNMENT FROM THE FILES OF THE MUNICIPAL   LOC/G
TECHNICAL ADVISORY SERVICE. USA+45 FINAN SERV/IND   ADMIN
PLAN 20. PAGE 9 B0194   MUNIC

B63

BOCK E.A.,STATE AND LOCAL GOVERNMENT: A CASE BOOK.   PROVS
USA+45 FINAN CHIEF PROB/SOLV TAX ATTIT...POLICY 20   LOC/G
CASEBOOK. PAGE 13 B0263   ADMIN
                                                        GOV/REL

B63

DE VRIES E.,SOCIAL ASPECTS OF ECONOMIC DEVELOPMENT   L/A+17C
IN LATIN AMERICA. CULTURE SOCIETY STRATA FINAN   ECO/UNDEV
INDUS INT/ORG DELIB/GP ACT/RES ECO/TAC EDU/PROP
ADMIN ATTIT SUPEGO HEALTH KNOWL ORD/FREE...SOC STAT
TREND ANTHOL TOT/POP VAL/FREE. PAGE 28 B0562

B63

GANGULY D.S.,PUBLIC CORPORATIONS IN A NATIONAL   ECO/UNDEV
ECONOMY. INDIA WOR+45 FINAN INDUS TOP/EX PRICE   LG/CO
EFFICIENCY...MGT STAT CHARTS BIBLIOG 20. PAGE 38   SOCISM
B0779   GOV/REL

B63

GOURNAY B.,PUBLIC ADMINISTRATION. FRANCE LAW CONSTN   BIBLIOG/A
AGRI FINAN LABOR SCHOOL EX/STRUC CHOOSE...MGT   ADMIN
METH/COMP 20. PAGE 42 B0846   NAT/G
                                                        LOC/G

B63

GRANT D.R.,STATE AND LOCAL GOVERNMENT IN AMERICA.   PROVS
USA+45 FINAN LOC/G MUNIC EX/STRUC FORCES EDU/PROP   POL/PAR
ADMIN CHOOSE FEDERAL ATTIT...JURID 20. PAGE 42   LEGIS

B0853   CONSTN
                                                   B63
HANSON A.H.,NATIONALIZATION: A BOOK OF READINGS.   NAT/G
WOR+45 FINAN DELIB/GP LEGIS WORKER BUDGET ADMIN   OWN
GP/REL EFFICIENCY SOCISM...MGT ANTHOL. PAGE 46   INDUS
B0941   CONTROL
                                                   B63
HAUSMAN W.H.,MANAGING ECONOMIC DEVELOPMENT IN   ECO/UNDEV
AFRICA. AFR USA+45 LAW FINAN WORKER TEC/DEV WEALTH PLAN
...ANTHOL 20. PAGE 48 B0970   FOR/AID
                                                 MGT
                                                   B63
HEYEL C.,THE ENCYCLOPEDIA OF MANAGEMENT. WOR+45   MGT
MARKET TOP/EX TEC/DEV AUTOMAT LEAD ADJUST...STAT   INDUS
CHARTS GAME ANTHOL BIBLIOG. PAGE 49 B1002   ADMIN
                                                 FINAN
                                                   B63
KLESMENT J.,LEGAL SOURCES AND BIBLIOGRAPHY OF THE BIBLIOG/A
BALTIC STATES (ESTONIA, LATVIA, LITHUANIA). COM   JURID
ESTONIA LATVIA LITHUANIA LAW FINAN ADJUD CT/SYS   CONSTN
REGION CENTRAL MARXISM 19/20. PAGE 60 B1218   ADMIN
                                                   B63
MCKIE R.,MALAYSIA IN FOCUS. INDONESIA WOR+45   S/ASIA
ECO/UNDEV FINAN NAT/G POL/PAR SECT FORCES PLAN   NAT/LISM
ADMIN COLONIAL COERCE DRIVE ALL/VALS...POLICY   MALAYSIA
RECORD CENSUS TIME/SEQ CMN/WLTH 20. PAGE 72 B1453
                                                   B63
MEYNAUD J.,PLANIFICATION ET POLITIQUE. FRANCE ITALY PLAN
FINAN LABOR DELIB/GP LEGIS ADMIN EFFICIENCY   ECO/TAC
...MAJORIT DECISION 20. PAGE 73 B1477   PROB/SOLV
                                                   B63
MONTER W.,THE GOVERNMENT OF GENEVA, 1536-1605   SECT
(DOCTORAL THESIS). SWITZERLND DIPLOM LEAD ORD/FREE FINAN
SOVEREIGN 16/17 CALVIN/J ROME. PAGE 74 B1504   LOC/G
                                                 ADMIN
                                                   B63
PALOTAI O.C.,PUBLICATIONS OF THE INSTITUTE OF   BIBLIOG/A
GOVERNMENT, 1930-1962. LAW PROVS SCHOOL WORKER   ADMIN
ACT/RES OP/RES CT/SYS GOV/REL...CRIMLGY SOC/WK.   LOC/G
PAGE 81 B1629   FINAN
                                                   B63
PEABODY R.L.,NEW PERSPECTIVES ON THE HOUSE OF   NEW/IDEA
REPRESENTATIVES. AGRI FINAN SCHOOL FORCES CONFER   LEGIS
LEAD CHOOSE REPRESENT FEDERAL...POLICY DECISION   PWR
HOUSE/REP. PAGE 82 B1647   ADMIN
                                                   B63
PLANTEY A.,TRAITE PRATIQUE DE LA FONCTION PUBLIQUE ADMIN
(2ND ED., 2 VOLS.). FRANCE FINAN EX/STRUC PROB/SOLV SUPEGO
GP/REL ATTIT...SOC 20 CIVIL/SERV. PAGE 83 B1680   JURID
                                                   B63
PREST A.R.,PUBLIC FINANCE IN UNDERDEVELOPED   FINAN
COUNTRIES. UK WOR+45 WOR-45 SOCIETY INT/ORG NAT/G ECO/UNDEV
LEGIS ACT/RES PLAN ECO/TAC ADMIN ROUTINE...CHARTS NIGERIA
20. PAGE 84 B1702
                                                   B63
ROYAL INSTITUTE PUBLIC ADMIN,BRITISH PUBLIC   BIBLIOG
ADMINISTRATION. UK LAW FINAN INDUS LOC/G POL/PAR   ADMIN
LEGIS LOBBY PARL/PROC CHOOSE JURID. PAGE 91 B1845 MGT
                                                 NAT/G
                                                   B63
SINGH M.M.,MUNICIPAL GOVERNMENT IN THE CALCUTTA   LOC/G
METROPOLITAN DISTRICT A PRELIMINARY SURVEY. FINAN   HEALTH
LG/CO DELIB/GP BUDGET TAX ADMIN GP/REL 20 CALCUTTA. MUNIC
PAGE 97 B1969   JURID
                                                   B63
THORELLI H.B.,INTOP: INTERNATIONAL OPERATIONS   GAME
SIMULATION: PLAYER'S MANUAL. BRAZIL FINAN OP/RES   INT/TRADE
ADMIN GP/REL INGP/REL PRODUC PERCEPT...DECISION MGT EDU/PROP
EEC. PAGE 104 B2108   LG/CO
                                                   B63
UN SECRETARY GENERAL,PLANNING FOR ECONOMIC   PLAN
DEVELOPMENT. ECO/UNDEV FINAN BUDGET INT/TRADE   ECO/TAC
TARIFFS TAX ADMIN 20 UN. PAGE 106 B2151   MGT
                                                 NAT/COMP
                                                   B63
US SENATE COMM APPROPRIATIONS,PERSONNEL   ADMIN
ADMINISTRATION AND OPERATIONS OF AGENCY FOR   FOR/AID
INTERNATIONAL DEVELOPMENT: SPECIAL HEARING. FINAN EFFICIENCY
LEAD COST UTIL SKILL...CHARTS 20 CONGRESS AID   DIPLOM
CIVIL/SERV. PAGE 109 B2211
                                                   B63
VAN SLYCK P.,PEACE: THE CONTROL OF NATIONAL POWER. ARMS/CONT
CUBA WOR+45 FINAN NAT/G FORCES PROB/SOLV TEC/DEV   PEACE
BAL/PWR ADMIN CONTROL ORD/FREE...POLICY INT/LAW UN INT/ORG
COLD/WAR TREATY. PAGE 112 B2253   DIPLOM
                                                   S63
COUTY P.,"L'ASSISTANCE POUR LE DEVELOPPEMENT: POINT FINAN
DE VUE SCANDINAVES." EUR+WWI FINLAND FUT SWEDEN   ROUTINE
WOR+45 ECO/DEV ECO/UNDEV COM/IND LABOR NAT/G   FOR/AID
PROF/ORG ACT/RES SKILL WEALTH TOT/POP 20. PAGE 24
B0497
                                                   S63
DAVEE R.,"POUR UN FONDS DE DEVELOPPEMENT SOCIAL."   INT/ORG
FUT WOR+45 INTELL SOCIETY ECO/DEV FINAN TEC/DEV   SOC
ROUTINE WEALTH...TREND TOT/POP VAL/FREE UN 20.   FOR/AID
PAGE 26 B0532

                                                   S63
DUCROS B.,"MOBILISATION DES RESSOURCES PRODUCTIVES ECO/UNDEV
ET DEVELOPPEMENT." FUT INTELL SOCIETY COM/IND   TEC/DEV
DIST/IND EXTR/IND FINAN INDUS ROUTINE WEALTH
...METH/CNCPT OBS 20. PAGE 31 B0625
                                                   N63
GREAT BRITAIN DEPT TECH COOP,PUBLIC ADMINISTRATION: BIBLIOG/A
A SELECT BIBLIOGRAPHY (PAMPHLET). WOR+45 AGRI FINAN ADMIN
INDUS EX/STRUC OP/RES ECO/TAC...MGT METH/COMP   NAT/G
NAT/COMP. PAGE 43 B0861   LOC/G
                                                 B64
RECENT PUBLICATIONS ON GOVERNMENTAL PROBLEMS. FINAN BIBLIOG
INDUS ACADEM PLAN PROB/SOLV EDU/PROP ADJUD ADMIN   AUTOMAT
BIO/SOC...MGT SOC. PAGE 2 B0040   LEGIS
                                                 JURID
                                                 B64
THE SPECIAL COMMONWEALTH AFRICAN ASSISTANCE PLAN.   ECO/UNDEV
AFR CANADA INDIA NIGERIA UK FINAN SCHOOL...CHARTS   TREND
20 COMMONWLTH. PAGE 2 B0041   FOR/AID
                                                 ADMIN
                                                 B64
AVASTHI A.,ASPECTS OF ADMINISTRATION. INDIA UK   MGT
USA+45 FINAN ACADEM DELIB/GP LEGIS RECEIVE   ADMIN
PARL/PROC PRIVIL...NAT/COMP 20. PAGE 7 B0150   SOC/WK
                                                 ORD/FREE
                                                 B64
BROWN C.V.,GOVERNMENT AND BANKING IN WESTERN   ADMIN
NIGERIA. AFR NIGERIA GOV/REL GP/REL...POLICY 20.   ECO/UNDEV
PAGE 16 B0321   FINAN
                                                 NAT/G
                                                 B64
CHANDLER A.D. JR.,GIANT ENTERPRISE: FORD, GENERAL   LG/CO
MOTORS, AND THE AUTOMOBILE INDUSTRY; SOURCES AND   DIST/IND
READINGS. USA+45 USA-45 FINAN MARKET CREATE ADMIN   LABOR
...TIME/SEQ ANTHOL 20 AUTOMOBILE. PAGE 20 B0404   MGT
                                                 B64
COTTER C.P.,POLITICS WITHOUT POWER: THE NATIONAL   CHOOSE
PARTY COMMITTEES. USA+45 FINAN NAT/G LOBBY ROUTINE POL/PAR
GP/REL ATTIT ROLE SUPEGO PWR 20. PAGE 24 B0491   REPRESENT
                                                 DELIB/GP
                                                 B64
DUROSELLE J.B.,POLITIQUES NATIONALES ENVERS LES   DIPLOM
JEUNES ETATS. FRANCE ISRAEL ITALY UK USA+45 USSR   ECO/UNDEV
YUGOSLAVIA ECO/DEV FINAN ECO/TAC INT/TRADE ADMIN   COLONIAL
PWR 20. PAGE 31 B0634   DOMIN
                                                 B64
FALK L.A.,ADMINISTRATIVE ASPECTS OF GROUP PRACTICE. BIBLIOG/A
USA+45 FINAN PROF/ORG PLAN MGT. PAGE 35 B0702   HEAL
                                                 ADMIN
                                                 SERV/IND
                                                 B64
FATOUROS A.A.,CANADA'S OVERSEAS AID. CANADA WOR+45 FOR/AID
ECO/DEV FINAN NAT/G BUDGET ECO/TAC CONFER ADMIN 20. DIPLOM
PAGE 35 B0707   ECO/UNDEV
                                                 POLICY
                                                 B64
FONTENEAU J.,LE CONSEIL MUNICIPAL: LE MAIRE-LES   MUNIC
ADJOINTS. FRANCE FINAN DELIB/GP EX/STRUC BUDGET TAX NEIGH
TASK COST INCOME ROLE SUPEGO 20 MAYOR. PAGE 36   ADMIN
B0735   TOP/EX
                                                 B64
GARFIELD PJ   LOVEJOY WF,PUBLIC UTILITY   T
ECONOMICS. DIST/IND FINAN MARKET MUNIC ADMIN COST   ECO/TAC
DEMAND...TECHNIC JURID 20 MONOPOLY. PAGE 39 B0782   OWN
                                                 SERV/IND
                                                 B64
GESELLSCHAFT RECHTSVERGLEICH,BIBLIOGRAPHIE DES   BIBLIOG/A
DEUTSCHEN RECHTS (BIBLIOGRAPHY OF GERMAN LAW,   JURID
TRANS. BY COURTLAND PETERSON). GERMANY FINAN INDUS CONSTN
LABOR SECT FORCES CT/SYS PARL/PROC CRIME...INT/LAW ADMIN
SOC NAT/COMP 20. PAGE 39 B0794
                                                 B64
HAMBRIDGE G.,DYNAMICS OF DEVELOPMENT. AGRI FINAN   ECO/UNDEV
INDUS LABOR INT/TRADE EDU/PROP ADMIN LEAD OWN   ECO/TAC
HEALTH...ANTHOL BIBLIOG 20. PAGE 46 B0930   OP/RES
                                                 ACT/RES
                                                 B64
KIESER P.J.,THE COST OF ADMINISTRATION, SUPERVISION AFR
AND SERVICES IN URBAN BANTU TOWNSHIPS. SOUTH/AFR   MGT
SERV/IND MUNIC PROVS ADMIN COST...OBS QU CHARTS 20 FINAN
BANTU. PAGE 60 B1203
                                                 B64
KIMBROUGH R.B.,POLITICAL POWER AND EDUCATIONAL   EDU/PROP
DECISION-MAKING. USA+45 FINAN ADMIN LEAD GP/REL   PROB/SOLV
ATTIT PWR PROG/TEAC. PAGE 60 B1207   DECISION
                                                 SCHOOL
                                                 B64
KNOX V.H.,PUBLIC FINANCE: INFORMATION SOURCES.   BIBLIOG/A
USA+45 DIPLOM ADMIN GOV/REL COST...POLICY 20.   FINAN
PAGE 60 B1221   TAX
                                                 BUDGET
                                                 B64
LI C.M.,INDUSTRIAL DEVELOPMENT IN COMMUNIST CHINA. ASIA
CHINA/COM COM ECO/DEV ECO/UNDEV AGRI FINAN INDUS MARKET TEC/DEV
LABOR NAT/G ECO/TAC INT/TRADE EXEC ALL/VALS
...POLICY RELATIV TREND WORK TOT/POP VAL/FREE 20.

PAGE 65 B1311

B64
NUQUIST A.E.,TOWN GOVERNMENT IN VERMONT. USA+45   LOC/G
FINAN TOP/EX PROB/SOLV BUDGET TAX REPRESENT SUFF   MUNIC
EFFICIENCY...OBS INT 20 VERMONT. PAGE 79 B1595   POPULISM
  ADMIN
B64
ORTH C.D.,ADMINISTERING RESEARCH AND DEVELOPMENT.   MGT
FINAN PLAN PROB/SOLV ADMIN ROUTINE...METH/CNCPT   R+D
STAT CHARTS METH 20. PAGE 80 B1616   LG/CO
  INDUS
B64
PIERCE T.M.,FEDERAL, STATE, AND LOCAL GOVERNMENT IN   NAT/G
EDUCATION. FINAN LOC/G PROVS LEGIS PLAN EDU/PROP   POLICY
ADMIN CONTROL CENTRAL COST KNOWL 20. PAGE 83 B1673   SCHOOL
  GOV/REL
B64
PINNICK A.W.,COUNTRY PLANNERS IN ACTION. UK FINAN   MUNIC
SERV/IND NAT/G CONSULT DELIB/GP PRICE CONTROL   PLAN
ROUTINE LEISURE AGE/C...GEOG 20 URBAN/RNWL. PAGE 83   INDUS
B1674   ATTIT
B64
REDLICH F.,THE GERMAN MILITARY ENTERPRISER AND HIS   EX/STRUC
WORK FORCE. CHRIST-17C GERMANY ELITES SOCIETY FINAN   FORCES
ECO/TAC CIVMIL/REL GP/REL INGP/REL...HIST/WRIT   PROFIT
METH/COMP 14/17. PAGE 87 B1760   WORKER
B64
RICHARDSON I.L.,BIBLIOGRAFIA BRASILEIRA DE   BIBLIOG
ADMINISTRACAO PUBLICA E ASSUNTOS CORRELATOS. BRAZIL   MGT
CONSTN FINAN LOC/G NAT/G POL/PAR PLAN DIPLOM   ADMIN
RECEIVE ATTIT...METH 20. PAGE 88 B1776   LAW
B64
SCHERMER G.,MEETING SOCIAL NEEDS IN THE PENJERDEL   PLAN
REGION. SOCIETY FINAN ACT/RES EDU/PROP ADMIN   REGION
GOV/REL...SOC/WK 45 20 PENNSYLVAN DELAWARE   HEALTH
NEW/JERSEY. PAGE 93 B1887   WEALTH
B64
STOICOIU V.,LEGAL SOURCES AND BIBLIOGRAPHY OF   BIBLIOG/A
ROMANIA. COM ROMANIA LAW FINAN POL/PAR LEGIS JUDGE   JURID
ADJUD CT/SYS PARL/PROC MARXISM 20. PAGE 101 B2041   CONSTN
  ADMIN
B64
SZLADITS C.,BIBLIOGRAPHY ON FOREIGN AND COMPARATIVE   BIBLIOG/A
LAW: BOOKS AND ARTICLES IN ENGLISH (SUPPLEMENT   JURID
1962). FINAN INDUS JUDGE LICENSE ADMIN CT/SYS   ADJUD
PARL/PROC OWN...INT/LAW CLASSIF METH/COMP NAT/COMP   LAW
20. PAGE 102 B2065
B64
THE BRITISH COUNCIL,PUBLIC ADMINISTRATION: A SELECT   BIBLIOG
LIST OF BOOKS AND PERIODICALS. LAW CONSTN FINAN   ADMIN
POL/PAR SCHOOL CHOOSE...HEAL MGT METH/COMP 19/20   LOC/G
CMN/WLTH. PAGE 104 B2094   INDUS
B64
TINBERGEN J.,CENTRAL PLANNING. COM INTELL ECO/DEV   PLAN
ECO/UNDEV FINAN INT/ORG PROB/SOLV ECO/TAC CONTROL   INDUS
EXEC ROUTINE DECISION. PAGE 104 B2111   MGT
  CENTRAL
B64
TURNER H.A.,THE GOVERNMENT AND POLITICS OF   PROVS
CALIFORNIA (2ND ED.). LAW FINAN MUNIC POL/PAR   ADMIN
SCHOOL EX/STRUC LEGIS LOBBY CHOOSE...CHARTS T 20   LOC/G
CALIFORNIA. PAGE 106 B2138   CONSTN
B64
WERNETTE J.P.,GOVERNMENT AND BUSINESS. LABOR   NAT/G
CAP/ISM ECO/TAC INT/TRADE TAX ADMIN AUTOMAT NUC/PWR   FINAN
CIVMIL/REL DEMAND...MGT 20 MONOPOLY. PAGE 115 B2323   ECO/DEV
  CONTROL
B64
WILSON L.,THE ACADEMIC MAN. STRUCT FINAN PROF/ORG   ACADEM
OP/RES ADMIN AUTHORIT ROLE RESPECT...SOC STAT.   INGP/REL
PAGE 117 B2360   STRATA
  DELIB/GP
S64
CARNEGIE ENDOWMENT INT. PEACE,"ADMINISTRATION AND   INT/ORG
BUDGET (ISSUES BEFORE THE NINETEENTH GENERAL   ADMIN
ASSEMBLY)." WOR+45 FINAN BUDGET ECO/TAC ROUTINE
COST...STAT RECORD UN. PAGE 19 B0383
S64
HUELIN D.,"ECONOMIC INTEGRATION IN LATIN AMERICAN: MARKET
PROGRESS AND PROBLEMS." L/A+17C ECO/DEV AGRI   ECO/UNDEV
DIST/IND FINAN INDUS NAT/G VOL/ASSN CONSULT   INT/TRADE
DELIB/GP EX/STRUC ACT/RES PLAN TEC/DEV ECO/TAC
ROUTINE BAL/PAY WEALTH WORK 20. PAGE 52 B1058
S64
MOWER A.G.,"THE OFFICIAL PRESSURE GROUP OF THE   INT/ORG
COUNCIL OF EUROPE'S CONSULATIVE ASSEMBLY." EUR+WWI   EDU/PROP
SOCIETY STRUCT FINAN CONSULT ECO/TAC ADMIN ROUTINE
ATTIT PWR WEALTH...STAT CHARTS 20 COUNCL/EUR.
PAGE 76 B1535
S64
NEWLYN W.T.,"MONETARY SYSTEMS AND INTEGRATION" AFR   ECO/UNDEV
BUDGET ADMIN FEDERAL PRODUC PROFIT UTIL...CHARTS 20   REGION
AFRICA/E. PAGE 78 B1578   METH/COMP
  FINAN
N64
US BOARD GOVERNORS FEDL RESRV,SELECTED BIBLIOGRAPHY   BIBLIOG

ON MONETARY POLICY AND MANAGEMENT OF THE PUBLIC   FINAN
DEBT 1947-1960 AND 1961-1963 SUPPLEMENT (PAMPH.).   NAT/G
USA+45 PLAN...POLICY MGT 20. PAGE 108 B2173
N64
US SENATE COMM GOVT OPERATIONS,METROPOLITAN   BIBLIOG/A
AMERICA: A SELECTED BIBLIOGRAPHY (PAMPHLET). USA+45   MUNIC
DIST/IND FINAN LOC/G EDU/PROP ADMIN HEALTH 20.   GOV/REL
PAGE 110 B2214   DECISION
B65
ADU A.L.,THE CIVIL SERVICE IN NEW AFRICAN STATES.   ECO/UNDEV
AFR GHANA FINAN SOVEREIGN...POLICY 20 CIVIL/SERV   ADMIN
AFRICA/E AFRICA/W. PAGE 3 B0062   COLONIAL
  NAT/G
B65
ALDERSON W.,DYNAMIC MARKETING BEHAVIOR. USA+45   MGT
FINAN CREATE TEC/DEV EDU/PROP PRICE COST 20. PAGE 3   MARKET
B0071   ATTIT
  CAP/ISM
B65
AMERICAN ECONOMIC ASSOCIATION,INDEX OF ECONOMIC   BIBLIOG
JOURNALS 1886-1965 (7 VOLS.). UK USA+45 USA-45 AGRI   WRITING
FINAN PLAN ECO/TAC INT/TRADE ADMIN...STAT CENSUS   INDUS
19/20. PAGE 4 B0083
B65
ARTHUR D LITTLE INC,SAN FRANCISCO COMMUNITY RENEWAL   HABITAT
PROGRAM. USA+45 FINAN PROVS ADMIN INCOME...CHARTS   MUNIC
20 CALIFORNIA SAN/FRAN URBAN/RNWL. PAGE 7 B0138   PLAN
  PROB/SOLV
B65
BARISH N.N.,MANAGEMENT SCIENCES IN THE EMERGING   ECO/UNDEV
COUNTRIES. AFR CHINA/COM WOR+45 FINAN INDUS PLAN   OP/RES
PRODUC HABITAT...ANTHOL 20. PAGE 9 B0184   MGT
  TEC/DEV
B65
CAMPBELL G.A.,THE CIVIL SERVICE IN BRITAIN (2ND   ADMIN
ED.). UK DELIB/GP FORCES WORKER CREATE PLAN   LEGIS
...POLICY AUD/VIS 19/20 CIVIL/SERV. PAGE 18 B0370   NAT/G
  FINAN
B65
CHANDA A.,FEDERALISM IN INDIA. INDIA UK ELITES   CONSTN
FINAN NAT/G POL/PAR EX/STRUC LEGIS DIPLOM TAX   CENTRAL
GOV/REL POPULISM...POLICY 20. PAGE 20 B0402   FEDERAL
B65
COHN H.J.,THE GOVERNMENT OF THE RHINE PALATINATE IN   PROVS
THE FIFTEENTH CENTURY. GERMANY FINAN LOC/G DELIB/GP   JURID
LEGIS CT/SYS CHOOSE CATHISM 14/15 PALATINATE.   GP/REL
PAGE 22 B0449   ADMIN
B65
COPELAND M.A.,OUR FREE ENTERPRISE ECONOMY. USA+45   CAP/ISM
INDUS LABOR ADMIN CONTROL GP/REL MGT. PAGE 23 B0476   PLAN
  FINAN
  ECO/DEV
B65
CRAMER J.F.,CONTEMPORARY EDUCATION: A COMPARATIVE   EDU/PROP
STUDY OF NATIONAL SYSTEMS (2ND ED.). CHINA/COM   NAT/COMP
EUR+WWI INDIA USA+45 FINAN PROB/SOLV ADMIN CONTROL   SCHOOL
ATTIT...IDEA/COMP METH/COMP 20 CHINJAP. PAGE 25   ACADEM
B0502
B65
DOWD L.P.,PRINCIPLES OF WORLD BUSINESS. SERV/IND   INT/TRADE
NAT/G DIPLOM ECO/TAC TARIFFS...INT/LAW JURID 20.   MGT
PAGE 30 B0614   FINAN
  MARKET
B65
GOODSELL C.T.,ADMINISTRATION OF A REVOLUTION.   EXEC
PUERT/RICO ECO/UNDEV FINAN MUNIC POL/PAR PROVS   SOC
LEGIS PLAN BUDGET RECEIVE ADMIN COLONIAL LEAD 20
ROOSEVLT/F. PAGE 41 B0827
B65
GT BRIT ADMIN STAFF COLLEGE,THE ACCOUNTABILITY OF   LG/CO
PUBLIC CORPORATIONS (REV. ED.). UK ECO/DEV FINAN   NAT/G
DELIB/GP EX/STRUC BUDGET CAP/ISM CONFER PRICE   ADMIN
PARL/PROC 20. PAGE 44 B0899   CONTROL
B65
INT. BANK RECONSTR. DEVELOP.,ECONOMIC DEVELOPMENT   INDUS
OF KUWAIT. ISLAM KUWAIT AGRI FINAN MARKET EX/STRUC   NAT/G
TEC/DEV ECO/TAC ADMIN WEALTH...OBS CON/ANAL CHARTS
20. PAGE 54 B1092
B65
LEYS C.T.,FEDERATION IN EAST AFRICA. LAW AGRI   FEDERAL
DIST/IND FINAN INT/ORG LABOR INT/TRADE CONFER ADMIN   REGION
CONTROL GP/REL...ANTHOL 20 AFRICA/E. PAGE 65 B1310   ECO/UNDEV
  PLAN
B65
LYONS G.M.,SCHOOLS FOR STRATEGY* EDUCATION AND   ACADEM
RESEARCH IN NATIONAL SECURITY AFFAIRS. USA+45 FINAN   ACT/RES
NAT/G VOL/ASSN FORCES TEC/DEV ADMIN WAR...GP/COMP   INTELL
IDEA/COMP PERS/COMP COLD/WAR. PAGE 67 B1351
B65
MACDONALD R.W.,THE LEAGUE OF ARAB STATES: A STUDY   ISLAM
IN THE DYNAMICS OF REGIONAL ORGANIZATION. ISRAEL   REGION
UAR USSR FINAN INT/ORG DELIB/GP ECO/TAC AGREE   DIPLOM
NEUTRAL ORD/FREE PWR...DECISION BIBLIOG 20 TREATY   ADMIN
UN. PAGE 67 B1358
B65
OECD,MEDITERRANEAN REGIONAL PROJECT: TURKEY;   EDU/PROP

EDUCATION AND DEVELOPMENT. FUT TURKEY SOCIETY
STRATA FINAN NAT/G PROF/ORG PLAN PROB/SOLV ADMIN
COST...STAT CHARTS 20 OECD. PAGE 79 B1602 — ACADEM SCHOOL ECO/UNDEV
B65

OLSON M. JR.,DROIT PUBLIC. FRANCE NAT/G LEGIS SUFF
GP/REL PRIVIL...TREND 18/20. PAGE 80 B1609 — CONSTN FINAN ADMIN ORD/FREE
B65

ORG FOR ECO COOP AND DEVEL,THE MEDITERRANEAN
REGIONAL PROJECT: AN EXPERIMENT IN PLANNING BY SIX
COUNTRIES. FUT GREECE SPAIN TURKEY YUGOSLAVIA
SOCIETY FINAN NAT/G PROF/ORG EDU/PROP ADMIN REGION
COST...POLICY STAT CHARTS 20 OECD. PAGE 80 B1614 — PLAN ECO/UNDEV ACADEM SCHOOL
B65

ORG FOR ECO COOP AND DEVEL,THE MEDITERRANEAN
REGIONAL PROJECT: YUGOSLAVIA; EDUCATION AND
DEVELOPMENT. YUGOSLAVIA SOCIETY FINAN PROF/ORG PLAN
ADMIN COST DEMAND MARXISM...STAT TREND CHARTS METH
20 OECD. PAGE 80 B1615 — EDU/PROP ACADEM SCHOOL ECO/UNDEV
B65

RHODES G.,PUBLIC SECTOR PENSIONS. UK FINAN LEGIS
BUDGET TAX PAY INCOME...CHARTS 20 CIVIL/SERV.
PAGE 88 B1769 — ADMIN RECEIVE AGE/O WORKER
B65

ROMASCO A.U.,THE POVERTY OF ABUNDANCE: HOOVER, THE
NATION, THE DEPRESSION. USA-45 AGRI LEGIS WORKER
GIVE PRESS LEAD 20 HOOVER/H. PAGE 90 B1817 — ECO/TAC ADMIN NAT/G FINAN
B65

ROWE J.Z.,THE PUBLIC-PRIVATE CHARACTER OF UNITED
STATES CENTRAL BANKING. USA+45 NAT/G EX/STRUC
...BIBLIOG 20 FED/RESERV. PAGE 91 B1842 — FINAN PLAN FEDERAL LAW
B65

SHARMA S.A.,PARLIAMENTARY GOVERNMENT IN INDIA.
INDIA FINAN LOC/G PROVS DELIB/GP PLAN ADMIN CT/SYS
FEDERAL...JURID 20. PAGE 96 B1936 — NAT/G CONSTN PARL/PROC LEGIS
B65

SNIDER C.F.,AMERICAN STATE AND LOCAL GOVERNMENT.
USA+45 FINAN CHIEF EX/STRUC TAX ADMIN CONTROL SUFF
INGP/REL PWR 20. PAGE 98 B1989 — GOV/REL MUNIC PROVS LOC/G
B65

WALTON R.E.,A BEHAVIORAL THEORY OF LABOR
NEGOTIATIONS: AN ANALYSIS OF A SOCIAL INTERACTION
SYSTEM. USA+45 FINAN PROB/SOLV ECO/TAC GP/REL
INGP/REL...DECISION BIBLIOG. PAGE 113 B2285 — SOC LABOR BARGAIN ADMIN
B65

WARD R.,BACKGROUND MATERIAL ON ECONOMIC IMPACT OF
FEDERAL PROCUREMENT - 1965: FOR JOINT ECONOMIC
COMMITTEE US CONGRESS. FINAN ROUTINE WEAPON
CIVMIL/REL EFFICIENCY...STAT CHARTS 20 CONGRESS.
PAGE 113 B2288 — ECO/DEV NAT/G OWN GOV/REL
B65

WHITE J.,GERMAN AID. GERMANY/W FINAN PLAN TEC/DEV
INT/TRADE ADMIN ATTIT...POLICY 20. PAGE 116 B2334 — FOR/AID ECO/UNDEV DIPLOM ECO/TAC
L65

WILLIAMS S.,"NEGOTIATING INVESTMENT IN EMERGING
COUNTRIES." USA+45 WOR+45 INDUS MARKET NAT/G TOP/EX
TEC/DEV CAP/ISM ECO/TAC ADMIN SKILL WEALTH...POLICY
RELATIV MGT WORK 20. PAGE 117 B2353 — FINAN ECO/UNDEV
S65

"FURTHER READING." INDIA STRUCT FINAN WORKER ADMIN
COST 20. PAGE 2 B0042 — BIBLIOG MGT ECO/UNDEV EFFICIENCY
S65

POLK W.R.,"PROBLEMS OF GOVERNMENT UTILIZATION OF
SCHOLARLY RESEARCH IN INTERNATIONAL AFFAIRS." FINAN
NAT/G EDU/PROP CONTROL TASK GP/REL ATTIT PERCEPT
KNOWL...POLICY TIME. PAGE 83 B1685 — ACT/RES ACADEM PLAN ADMIN
S65

RAPHAELI N.,"SELECTED ARTICLES AND DOCUMENTS ON
COMPARATIVE PUBLIC ADMINISTRATION." USA+45 FINAN
LOC/G WORKER TEC/DEV CONTROL LEAD...SOC/WK GOV/COMP
METH/COMP. PAGE 86 B1739 — BIBLIOG ADMIN NAT/G MGT
S65

SILVERT K.H.,"AMERICAN ACADEMIC ETHICS AND SOCIAL
RESEARCH ABROAD* THE LESSON OF PROJECT CAMELOT."
CHILE L/A+17C USA+45 FINAN ADMIN...PHIL/SCI SOC
GEN/LAWS CAMELOT. PAGE 97 B1953 — ACADEM NAT/G ACT/RES POLICY
B66

BIRKHEAD G.S.,ADMINISTRATIVE PROBLEMS IN PAKISTAN.
PAKISTAN AGRI FINAN INDUS LG/CO ECO/TAC CONTROL PWR
...CHARTS ANTHOL 20. PAGE 12 B0241 — ADMIN NAT/G ORD/FREE ECO/UNDEV
B66

COOK P.W. JR.,PROBLEMS OF CORPORATE POWER. WOR+45
FINAN INDUS BARGAIN GP/REL...MGT ANTHOL. PAGE 23
B0471 — ADMIN LG/CO PWR ECO/TAC

B66
DAVIS J.A.,SOUTHERN AFRICA IN TRANSITION. SOUTH/AFR
USA+45 FINAN NAT/G DELIB/GP EDU/PROP ADMIN COLONIAL
REGION RACE/REL ATTIT SOVEREIGN...ANTHOL 20
RESOURCE/N. PAGE 26 B0538 — AFR ADJUST CONSTN
B66

DUNCOMBE H.S.,COUNTY GOVERNMENT IN AMERICA. USA+45
FINAN MUNIC ADMIN ROUTINE GOV/REL...GOV/COMP 20.
PAGE 31 B0631 — LOC/G PROVS CT/SYS TOP/EX
B66

FINK M.,A SELECTIVE BIBLIOGRAPHY ON STATE
CONSTITUTIONAL REVISION (PAMPHLET). USA+45 FINAN
EX/STRUC LEGIS EDU/PROP GOV/REL 20. PAGE 35 B0720 — BIBLIOG PROVS LOC/G CT/SYS APPORT CHOOSE CONSTN
B66

GROSS H.,MAKE OR BUY. USA+45 FINAN INDUS CREATE
PRICE PRODUC 20. PAGE 44 B0889 — ECO/TAC PLAN MGT COST
B66

HASTINGS P.G.,THE MANAGEMENT OF BUSINESS FINANCE.
ECO/DEV PLAN BUDGET CONTROL COST...DECISION CHARTS
BIBLIOG T 20. PAGE 48 B0966 — FINAN MGT INDUS ECO/TAC
B66

HAYER T.,FRENCH AID. AFR FRANCE AGRI FINAN BUDGET
ADMIN WAR PRODUC...CHARTS 18/20 THIRD/WRLD
OVRSEA/DEV. PAGE 48 B0975 — TEC/DEV COLONIAL FOR/AID ECO/UNDEV
B66

JOHNSON N.,PARLIAMENT AND ADMINISTRATION: THE
ESTIMATES COMMITTEE 1945-65. FUT UK NAT/G EX/STRUC
PLAN BUDGET ORD/FREE...T 20 PARLIAMENT HOUSE/CMNS.
PAGE 57 B1147 — LEGIS ADMIN FINAN DELIB/GP
B66

KIRDAR U.,THE STRUCTURE OF UNITED NATIONS ECONOMIC
AID TO UNDERDEVELOPED COUNTRIES. AGRI FINAN INDUS
NAT/G EX/STRUC PLAN GIVE TASK...POLICY 20 UN.
PAGE 60 B1213 — INT/ORG FOR/AID ECO/UNDEV ADMIN
B66

LEWIS W.A.,DEVELOPMENT PLANNING; THE ESSENTIALS OF
ECONOMIC POLICY. USA+45 FINAN INDUS NAT/G WORKER
FOR/AID INT/TRADE ADMIN ROUTINE WEALTH...CONCPT
STAT. PAGE 65 B1307 — PLAN ECO/DEV POLICY CREATE
B66

LINDFORS G.V.,INTERCOLLEGIATE BIBLIOGRAPHY; CASES
IN BUSINESS ADMINISTRATION (VOL. X). FINAN MARKET
LABOR CONSULT PLAN GP/REL PRODUC 20. PAGE 65 B1314 — BIBLIOG/A ADMIN MGT OP/RES
B66

MURDOCK J.C.,RESEARCH AND REGIONS. AGRI FINAN INDUS
LOC/G MUNIC NAT/G PROB/SOLV TEC/DEV ADMIN REGION
20. PAGE 76 B1545 — BIBLIOG ECO/DEV COMPUT/IR R+D
B66

NYC TEMPORARY COMM CITY FINAN,MUNICIPAL COLLECTIVE
BARGAINING (NO. 8). USA+45 PLAN PROB/SOLV BARGAIN
BUDGET TAX EDU/PROP GOV/REL COST...MGT 20
NEWYORK/C. PAGE 79 B1596 — MUNIC FINAN ADMIN LOC/G
B66

OHLIN G.,AID AND INDEBTEDNESS. AUSTRIA FINAN
INT/ORG PLAN DIPLOM GIVE...POLICY MATH CHARTS 20.
PAGE 79 B1604 — FOR/AID ECO/UNDEV ADMIN WEALTH
B66

ONYEMELUKWE C.C.,PROBLEMS OF INDUSTRIAL PLANNING
AND MANAGEMENT IN NIGERIA. AFR FINAN LABOR DELIB/GP
TEC/DEV ADJUST...MGT TREND BIBLIOG. PAGE 80 B1610 — ECO/UNDEV ECO/TAC INDUS PLAN
B66

PERKINS J.A.,THE UNIVERSITY IN TRANSITION. USA+45
SOCIETY FINAN INDUS NAT/G EX/STRUC ADMIN INGP/REL
COST EFFICIENCY ATTIT 20. PAGE 82 B1658 — ACADEM ORD/FREE CREATE ROLE
B66

REDFORD E.S.,THE ROLE OF GOVERNMENT IN THE AMERICAN
ECONOMY. USA+45 USA-45 FINAN INDUS LG/CO PROB/SOLV
ADMIN INGP/REL INCOME PRODUC 18/20. PAGE 87 B1759 — NAT/G ECO/DEV CAP/ISM ECO/TAC
B66

ROSHOLT R.L.,AN ADMINISTRATIVE HISTORY OF NASA,
1958-1963. SPACE USA+45 FINAN LEAD...MGT CHARTS
BIBLIOG 20 NASA. PAGE 90 B1824 — ADMIN EX/STRUC ADJUST DELIB/GP
B66

SEASHOLES B.,VOTING, INTEREST GROUPS, AND PARTIES.
USA+45 FINAN LOC/G NAT/G ADMIN LEAD GP/REL INGP/REL
ROLE...CHARTS ANTHOL 20. PAGE 95 B1922 — CHOOSE POL/PAR LOBBY PARTIC
B66

SMITH H.E.,READINGS IN ECONOMIC DEVELOPMENT AND
ADMINISTRATION IN TANZANIA. TANZANIA FINAN INDUS
LABOR NAT/G PLAN PROB/SOLV INT/TRADE COLONIAL
REGION...ANTHOL BIBLIOG 20 AFRICA/E. PAGE 98 B1981 — TEC/DEV ADMIN GOV/REL

SPICER K.,A SAMARITAN STATE? AFR CANADA INDIA | DIPLOM
PAKISTAN UK USA+45 FINAN INDUS PRODUC...CHARTS 20 | FOR/AID
NATO. PAGE 99 B2006 | ECO/DEV
| ADMIN
B66

SZLADITS C.,A BIBLIOGRAPHY ON FOREIGN AND | BIBLIOG/A
COMPARATIVE LAW (SUPPLEMENT 1964). FINAN FAM LABOR | CT/SYS
LG/CO LEGIS JUDGE ADMIN CRIME...CRIMLGY 20. | INT/LAW
PAGE 102 B2066
B66

US HOUSE COMM GOVT OPERATIONS,AN INVESTIGATION OF | FOR/AID
THE US ECONOMIC AND MILITARY ASSISTANCE PROGRAMS IN | ECO/UNDEV
VIETNAM. USA+45 VIETNAM/S SOCIETY CONSTRUC FINAN | WAR
FORCES BUDGET INT/TRADE PEACE HEALTH...MGT | INSPECT
HOUSE/REP AID. PAGE 108 B2191
B66

WESTON J.F.,THE SCOPE AND METHODOLOGY OF FINANCE. | FINAN
PLAN TEC/DEV CONTROL EFFICIENCY INCOME UTIL...MGT | ECO/DEV
CONCPT MATH STAT TREND METH 20. PAGE 115 B2327 | POLICY
| PRICE
B66

ZINKIN T.,CHALLENGES IN INDIA. INDIA PAKISTAN LAW | NAT/G
AGRI FINAN INDUS TOP/EX TEC/DEV CONTROL ROUTINE | ECO/TAC
ORD/FREE PWR 20 NEHRU/J SHASTRI/LB CIVIL/SERV. | POLICY
PAGE 119 B2404 | ADMIN
L66

AMERICAN ECONOMIC REVIEW,"SIXTY-THIRD LIST OF | BIBLIOG/A
DOCTORAL DISSERTATIONS IN POLITICAL ECONOMY IN | CONCPT
AMERICAN UNIVERSITIES AND COLLEGES." ECO/DEV AGRI | ACADEM
FINAN LABOR WORKER PLAN BUDGET INT/TRADE ADMIN
DEMAND...MGT STAT 20. PAGE 4 B0084
S66

JACOBS P.,"RE-RADICALIZING THE DE-RADICALIZED." | NAT/G
USA+45 SOCIETY STRUCT FINAN PLAN PROB/SOLV CAP/ISM | POLICY
WEALTH CONSERVE NEW/LIB 20. PAGE 55 B1114 | MARXIST
| ADMIN
C66

SHERMAN H.,"IT ALL DEPENDS." USA+45 FINAN MARKET | LG/CO
PLAN PROB/SOLV EXEC PARTIC INGP/REL SUPEGO | MGT
...DECISION BIBLIOG 20. PAGE 96 B1944 | ADMIN
| POLICY
N66

AMERICAN SOCIETY PUBLIC ADMIN,PUBLIC ADMINISTRATION | WEALTH
AND THE WAR ON POVERTY (PAMPHLET). USA+45 SOCIETY | NAT/G
ECO/DEV FINAN LOC/G LEGIS CREATE EDU/PROP CONFER | PLAN
GOV/REL GP/REL ROLE 20 POVRTY/WAR. PAGE 4 B0089 | ADMIN
B67

DICKSON P.G.M.,THE FINANCIAL REVOLUTION IN ENGLAND. | ECO/DEV
UK NAT/G TEC/DEV ADMIN GOV/REL...SOC METH/CNCPT | FINAN
CHARTS GP/COMP BIBLIOG 17/18. PAGE 29 B0587 | CAP/ISM
| MGT
B67

HIRSCHMAN A.O.,DEVELOPMENT PROJECTS OBSERVED. INDUS | ECO/UNDEV
INT/ORG CONSULT EX/STRUC CREATE OP/RES ECO/TAC | R+D
DEMAND...POLICY MGT METH/COMP 20 WORLD/BANK. | FINAN
PAGE 50 B1016 | PLAN
B67

JAIN R.K.,MANAGEMENT OF STATE ENTERPRISES. INDIA | NAT/G
SOCIETY FINAN WORKER BUDGET ADMIN CONTROL OWN 20. | SOCISM
PAGE 55 B1118 | INDUS
| MGT
B67

KARDOUCHE G.K.,THE UAR IN DEVELOPMENT. UAR ECO/TAC | FINAN
INT/TRADE BAL/PAY...STAT CHARTS BIBLIOG 20. PAGE 58 | MGT
B1172 | CAP/ISM
| ECO/UNDEV
B67

KONCZACKI Z.A.,PUBLIC FINANCE AND ECONOMIC | ECO/TAC
DEVELOPMENT OF NATAL 1893-1910. TAX ADMIN COLONIAL | FINAN
...STAT CHARTS BIBLIOG 19/20 NATAL. PAGE 61 B1228 | NAT/G
| ECO/UNDEV
B67

ROBINSON R.D., INTERNATIONAL MANAGEMENT. USA&45 | INT/TRADE
FINAN R+D PLAN PRODUC...DECISION T. PAGE 67 B1352 | MGT
| INT/LAW
| MARKET
B67

POSNER M.V.,ITALIAN PUBLIC ENTERPRISE. ITALY | NAT/G
ECO/DEV FINAN INDUS CREATE ECO/TAC ADMIN CONTROL | PLAN
EFFICIENCY PRODUC...TREND CHARTS 20. PAGE 84 B1693 | CAP/ISM
| SOCISM
B67

SABLE M.H.,A GUIDE TO LATIN AMERICAN STUDIES (2 | BIBLIOG/A
VOLS). CONSTN FINAN INT/ORG LABOR MUNIC POL/PAR | L/A+17C
FORCES CAP/ISM FOR/AID ADMIN MARXISM SOCISM OAS. | DIPLOM
PAGE 92 B1861 | NAT/LISM
B67

TANSKY L.,US AND USSR AID TO DEVELOPING COUNTRIES. | FOR/AID
INDIA TURKEY UAR USA+45 USSR FINAN PLAN TEC/DEV | ECO/UNDEV
ADMIN WEALTH...TREND METH/COMP 20. PAGE 103 B2076 | MARXISM
| CAP/ISM
B67

UNITED NATIONS,UNITED NATIONS PUBLICATIONS: | BIBLIOG/A
1945-1966. WOR+45 COM/IND DIST/IND FINAN TEC/DEV | INT/ORG
ADMIN...POLICY INT/LAW MGT CHARTS 20 UN UNESCO. | DIPLOM

PAGE 107 B2162 | WRITING
S67

BRIMMER A.F.,"INITIATIVE AND INNOVATION IN CENTRAL | FINAN
BANKING." USA+45 ECO/DEV MARKET ECO/TAC TAX CONTROL | CREATE
DEMAND...MGT CHARTS FED/RESERV. PAGE 15 B0309 | NAT/G
| POLICY
S67

DUGGAR J.W.,"THE DEVELOPMENT OF MONEY SUPPLY IN | ECO/UNDEV
ETHIOPIA." ETHIOPIA ISLAM CONSULT OP/RES BUDGET | FINAN
CONTROL ROUTINE EFFICIENCY EQUILIB WEALTH...MGT 20. | BAL/PAY
PAGE 31 B0629 | ECOMETRIC
S67

GOLIGHTLY H.O.,"THE AIRLINES: A CASE STUDY IN | DIST/IND
MANAGEMENT INNOVATION." USA+45 AIR FINAN INDUS | MARKET
TOP/EX CREATE PLAN PROB/SOLV ADMIN EXEC PROFIT | MGT
...DECISION 20. PAGE 40 B0820 | TEC/DEV
S67

HILL F.G.,"VEBLEN, BERLE AND THE MODERN | LG/CO
CORPORATION." FINAN ECO/TAC CONTROL OWN...MGT 20. | ROLE
PAGE 50 B1010 | INDUS
| ECO/DEV
S67

LEES J.P.,"LEGISLATIVE REVIEW AND BUREAUCRATIC | SUPEGO
RESPONSIBILITY." USA+45 FINAN NAT/G DELIB/GP PLAN | BUDGET
PROB/SOLV CONFER CONTROL GP/REL DEMAND...DECISION | LEGIS
20 CONGRESS PRESIDENT HOUSE/REP BUREAUCRCY. PAGE 63 | EXEC
B1281
S67

WRIGHT F.K.,"INVESTMENT CRITERIA AND THE COST OF | COST
CAPITAL." FINAN PLAN BUDGET OPTIMAL PRODUC...POLICY | PROFIT
DECISION 20. PAGE 118 B2380 | INDUS
| MGT
N67

US SENATE COMM ON FOREIGN REL,ARMS SALES AND | ARMS/CONT
FOREIGN POLICY (PAMPHLET). FINAN FOR/AID CONTROL | ADMIN
20. PAGE 110 B2222 | OP/RES
| DIPLOM
S68

GUZZARDI W. JR.,"THE SECOND BATTLE OF BRITAIN." UK | FINAN
STRATA LABOR WORKER CREATE PROB/SOLV EDU/PROP ADMIN | ECO/TAC
LEAD LOBBY...MGT SOC 20 GOLD/STAND. PAGE 45 B0907 | ECO/DEV
| STRUCT
B95

LATIMER E.W.,EUROPE IN AFRICA IN THE NINETEENTH | AFR
CENTURY. ECO/UNDEV KIN SECT DIPLOM DOMIN ADMIN | COLONIAL
DISCRIM 17/18. PAGE 63 B1275 | WAR
| FINAN

FINANCE....SEE FINAN

FINCH/D....DANIEL FINCH

FINCH/ER....E.R. FINCH

FINCHER F. B0719

FINE ARTS....SEE ART/METH

FINK M. B0720

FINLAND....SEE ALSO APPROPRIATE TIME/SPACE/CULTURE INDEX
S63

COUTY P.,"L'ASSISTANCE POUR LE DEVELOPPEMENT: POINT | FINAN
DE VUE SCANDINAVES." EUR+WWI FINLAND FUT SWEDEN | ROUTINE
WOR+45 ECO/DEV ECO/UNDEV COM/IND LABOR NAT/G | FOR/AID
PROF/ORG ACT/RES SKILL WEALTH TOT/POP 20. PAGE 24
B0497
B64

ANDREN N.,GOVERNMENT AND POLITICS IN THE NORDIC | CONSTN
COUNTRIES: DENMARK, FINLAND, ICELAND, NORWAY, | NAT/G
SWEDEN. DENMARK FINLAND ICELAND NORWAY SWEDEN | CULTURE
POL/PAR CHIEF LEGIS ADMIN REGION REPRESENT ATTIT | GOV/COMP
CONSERVE...CHARTS BIBLIOG/A 20. PAGE 5 B0102
B64

HALLER W.,DER SCHWEDISCHE JUSTITIEOMBUDSMAN. | JURID
DENMARK FINLAND NORWAY SWEDEN LEGIS ADJUD CONTROL | PARL/PROC
PERSON ORD/FREE...NAT/COMP 20 OMBUDSMAN. PAGE 46 | ADMIN
B0926 | CHIEF
B65

ROWAT D.C.,THE OMBUDSMAN: CITIZEN'S DEFENDER. | INSPECT
DENMARK FINLAND NEW/ZEALND NORWAY SWEDEN CONSULT | CONSTN
PROB/SOLV FEEDBACK PARTIC GP/REL...SOC CONCPT | NAT/G
NEW/IDEA METH/COMP ANTHOL BIBLIOG 20. PAGE 91 B1840 | ADMIN
B66

FINNISH POLITICAL SCIENCE ASSN,SCANDINAVIAN | ATTIT
POLITICAL STUDIES (VOL. I). FINLAND DIPLOM ADMIN | POL/PAR
LOBBY PARL/PROC...CHARTS BIBLIOG 20 SCANDINAV. | ACT/RES
PAGE 36 B0721 | CHOOSE

FINNISH POLITICAL SCIENCE ASSN B0721

FIRM....SEE INDUS

FIRMALINO T. B0722

FISCAL POLICY....SEE ECO, NAT/G, BUDGET

FISCHER F.C. B0723

FISHER M.J. B0724

FISHER S.N. B0725

FISHING INDUSTRY....SEE EXTR/IND

FISK E.K. B0726

FISK W.M. B0727

FITZSIMMONS T. B0728

FLANDERS....FLANDERS

FLEISCHER G.A. B1280

FLEMING R.W. B0654

FLETCHER W.I. B1690

FLORENCE P.S. B0729

FLORENCE....MEDIEVAL AND RENAISSANCE

FLORES R.H. B0730

FLORIDA....FLORIDA

> B53
> A BIBLIOGRAPHY AND SUBJECT INDEX OF PUBLICATIONS OF   BIBLIOG
> FLORIDA STATE AGENCIES. USA+45 LOC/G LEAD ATTIT 20   PROVS
> FLORIDA. PAGE 2 B0036   GOV/REL
>   ADMIN

FLORINSKY M.T. B0731

FLORO G.K. B2032

FLYNN E.J. B0732

FLYNN/BOSS....BOSS FLYNN

> B47
> FLYNN E.J.,YOU'RE THE BOSS. USA-45 ELITES TOP/EX   LOC/G
> DOMIN CONTROL EXEC LEAD REPRESENT 19/20 NEWYORK/C   MUNIC
> ROOSEVLT/F FLYNN/BOSS BOSSISM. PAGE 36 B0732   BIOG
>   POL/PAR

FNMA....FEDERAL NATIONAL MORTGAGE ASSOCIATION

FOCH/F....FERDINAND FOCH

FOINER C.A. B0745

FOLKLORE....SEE MYTH

FOLSOM M.B. B0733

FOLTZ W.J. B0734

FONTANE/T....THEODORE FONTANE

FONTENEAU J. B0735

FOOD....SEE AGRI, ALSO EATING

FOOD AND AGRICULTURAL ORGANIZATION....SEE FAO

FOOD AND DRUG ADMINISTRATION....SEE FDA

FOOD/PEACE....OFFICE OF FOOD FOR PEACE

FOR/AID....FOREIGN AID

> N19
> JACKSON R.G.A.,THE CASE FOR AN INTERNATIONAL   FOR/AID
> DEVELOPMENT AUTHORITY (PAMPHLET). WOR+45 ECO/DEV   INT/ORG
> DIPLOM GIVE CONTROL GP/REL EFFICIENCY NAT/LISM   ECO/UNDEV
> SOVEREIGN 20. PAGE 55 B1108   ADMIN
> N19
> KUWAIT ARABIA,KUWAIT FUND FOR ARAB ECONOMIC   FOR/AID
> DEVELOPMENT (PAMPHLET). ISLAM KUWAIT UAR ECO/UNDEV   DIPLOM
> LEGIS ECO/TAC WEALTH 20. PAGE 62 B1245   FINAN
>   ADMIN
> B49
> FORD FOUNDATION,REPORT OF THE STUDY FOR THE FORD   WEALTH
> FOUNDATION ON POLICY AND PROGRAM. SOCIETY R+D   GEN/LAWS
> ACT/RES CAP/ISM FOR/AID EDU/PROP ADMIN KNOWL
> ...POLICY PSY SOC 20. PAGE 36 B0739
> B50
> PERHAM M.,COLONIAL GOVERNMENT: ANNOTATED READING   BIBLIOG/A
> LIST ON BRITISH COLONIAL GOVERNMENT. UK WOR+45   COLONIAL

WOR-45 ECO/UNDEV INT/ORG LEGIS FOR/AID INT/TRADE   GOV/REL
DOMIN ADMIN REV 20. PAGE 82 B1655   NAT/G
  S50
WITTFOGEL K.A.,"RUSSIA AND ASIA: PROBLEMS OF   ECO/DEV
CONTEMPORARY AREA STUDIES AND INTERNATIONAL   ADMIN
RELATIONS." ASIA COM USA+45 SOCIETY NAT/G DIPLOM   RUSSIA
ECO/TAC FOR/AID EDU/PROP KNOWL...HIST/WRIT TOT/POP   USSR
20. PAGE 117 B2369
  B51
CHRISTENSEN A.N.,THE EVOLUTION OF LATIN AMERICAN   NAT/G
GOVERNMENT: A BOOK OF READINGS. ECO/UNDEV INDUS   CONSTN
LOC/G POL/PAR EX/STRUC LEGIS FOR/AID CT/SYS   DIPLOM
...SOC/WK 20 SOUTH/AMER. PAGE 21 B0428   L/A+17C
  B53
MACK R.T.,RAISING THE WORLDS STANDARD OF LIVING.   WOR+45
IRAN INT/ORG VOL/ASSN EX/STRUC ECO/TAC WEALTH...MGT   FOR/AID
METH/CNCPT STAT CONT/OBS INT TOT/POP VAL/FREE 20   INT/TRADE
UN. PAGE 67 B1363
  B53
MACMAHON A.W.,ADMINISTRATION IN FOREIGN AFFAIRS.   USA+45
NAT/G CONSULT DELIB/GP LEGIS ACT/RES CREATE ADMIN   ROUTINE
EXEC RIGID/FLEX PWR...METH/CNCPT TIME/SEQ TOT/POP   FOR/AID
VAL/FREE 20. PAGE 68 B1369   DIPLOM
  B56
KIRK G.,THE CHANGING ENVIRONMENT OF INTERNATIONAL   FUT
RELATIONS. ASIA S/ASIA USA+45 WOR+45 ECO/UNDEV   EXEC
INT/ORG NAT/G FOR/AID EDU/PROP PEACE KNOWL   DIPLOM
...PLURIST COLD/WAR TOT/POP 20. PAGE 60 B1214
  B56
UNITED NATIONS,BIBLIOGRAPHY ON INDUSTRIALIZATION IN   BIBLIOG
UNDER-DEVELOPED COUNTRIES. WOR+45 R+D INT/ORG NAT/G   ECO/UNDEV
FOR/AID ADMIN LEAD 20 UN. PAGE 107 B2161   INDUS
  TEC/DEV
  B58
UNESCO,UNESCO PUBLICATIONS: CHECK LIST (2ND REV.   BIBLIOG
ED.). WOR+45 DIPLOM FOR/AID WEALTH...POLICY SOC   INT/ORG
UNESCO. PAGE 107 B2156   ECO/UNDEV
  ADMIN
  B58
US HOUSE COMM GOVT OPERATIONS,HEARINGS BEFORE A   FOR/AID
SUBCOMMITTEE OF THE COMMITTEE ON GOVERNMENT   DIPLOM
OPERATIONS. CAMBODIA PHILIPPINE USA+45 CONSTRUC   ORD/FREE
TEC/DEV ADMIN CONTROL WEAPON EFFICIENCY HOUSE/REP.   ECO/UNDEV
PAGE 108 B2189
  L58
HAVILAND H.F.,"FOREIGN AID AND THE POLICY PROCESS: LEGIS
1957." USA+45 FACE/GP POL/PAR VOL/ASSN CHIEF   PLAN
DELIB/GP ACT/RES LEGIT EXEC GOV/REL ATTIT DRIVE PWR   FOR/AID
...POLICY TESTS CONGRESS 20. PAGE 48 B0971
  S58
DAVENPORT J.,"ARMS AND THE WELFARE STATE." INTELL   USA+45
STRUCT FORCES CREATE ECO/TAC FOR/AID DOMIN LEGIT   NAT/G
ADMIN WAR ORD/FREE PWR...POLICY SOC CONCPT MYTH OBS   USSR
TREND COLD/WAR TOT/POP 20. PAGE 26 B0533
  S58
JORDAN A.,"MILITARY ASSISTANCE AND NATIONAL   FORCES
POLICY." ASIA FUT USA+45 WOR+45 ECO/DEV ECO/UNDEV   POLICY
INT/ORG NAT/G PLAN ECO/TAC ROUTINE WEAPON ATTIT   FOR/AID
RIGID/FLEX PWR...CONCPT TREND 20. PAGE 57 B1153   DIPLOM
  B59
MAYDA J.,ATOMIC ENERGY AND LAW. ECO/UNDEV FINAN   NUC/PWR
TEC/DEV FOR/AID EFFICIENCY PRODUC WEALTH...POLICY   L/A+17C
TECHNIC 20. PAGE 71 B1433   LAW
  ADMIN
  B59
US HOUSE COMM GOVT OPERATIONS,UNITED STATES AID   FOR/AID
OPERATIONS IN LAOS. LAOS USA+45 PLAN INSPECT   ADMIN
HOUSE/REP. PAGE 108 B2190   FORCES
  ECO/UNDEV
  B59
US PRES COMM STUDY MIL ASSIST,COMPOSITE REPORT.   FOR/AID
USA+45 ECO/UNDEV PLAN BUDGET DIPLOM EFFICIENCY   FORCES
...POLICY MGT 20. PAGE 109 B2208   WEAPON
  ORD/FREE
  S59
STOESSINGER J.G.,"THE INTERNATIONAL ATOMIC ENERGY   INT/ORG
AGENCY: THE FIRST PHASE." FUT WOR+45 NAT/G VOL/ASSN   ECO/DEV
DELIB/GP BAL/PWR LEGIT ADMIN ROUTINE PWR...OBS   FOR/AID
CON/ANAL GEN/LAWS VAL/FREE 20 IAEA. PAGE 101 B2040   NUC/PWR
  B60
BROOKINGS INSTITUTION,UNITED STATES FOREIGN POLICY: DIPLOM
STUDY NO 9: THE FORMULATION AND ADMINISTRATION OF   INT/ORG
UNITED STATES FOREIGN POLICY. USA+45 WOR+45   CREATE
EX/STRUC LEGIS BAL/PWR FOR/AID EDU/PROP CIVMIL/REL
GOV/REL...INT COLD/WAR. PAGE 16 B0317
  B60
HYDE L.K.G.,THE US AND THE UN. WOR+45 STRUCT   USA+45
ECO/DEV ECO/UNDEV NAT/G ACT/RES PLAN DIPLOM   INT/ORG
EDU/PROP ADMIN ALL/VALS...CONCPT TIME/SEQ GEN/LAWS   FOR/AID
UN VAL/FREE 20. PAGE 53 B1070
  B60
LISKA G.,THE NEW STATECRAFT. WOR+45 WOR-45 LEGIS   ECO/TAC
DIPLOM ADMIN ATTIT PWR WEALTH...HIST/WRIT TREND   CONCPT
COLD/WAR 20. PAGE 66 B1323   FOR/AID
  B60
PENTONY D.E.,UNITED STATES FOREIGN AID. INDIA LAOS   FOR/AID

USA+45 ECO/UNDEV INT/TRADE ADMIN PEACE ATTIT
...POLICY METH/COMP ANTHOL 20. PAGE 82 B1653
DIPLOM
ECO/TAC

B60
RAO V.K.R.,INTERNATIONAL AID FOR ECONOMIC
DEVELOPMENT - POSSIBILITIES AND LIMITATIONS. FINAN
PLAN TEC/DEV ADMIN TASK EFFICIENCY...POLICY SOC
METH/CNCPT CHARTS 20 UN. PAGE 86 B1734
FOR/AID
DIPLOM
INT/ORG
ECO/UNDEV

B60
ROBINSON E.A.G.,ECONOMIC CONSEQUENCES OF THE SIZE
OF NATIONS. AGRI INDUS DELIB/GP FOR/AID ADMIN
EFFICIENCY...METH/COMP 20. PAGE 89 B1799
CONCPT
INT/ORG
NAT/COMP

B60
STANFORD RESEARCH INSTITUTE,AFRICAN DEVELOPMENT: A
TEST FOR INTERNATIONAL COOPERATION. AFR USA+45
WOR+45 FINAN INT/ORG PLAN PROB/SOLV ECO/TAC
INT/TRADE ADMIN...CHARTS 20. PAGE 100 B2018
FOR/AID
ECO/UNDEV
ATTIT
DIPLOM

B60
WORLEY P.,ASIA TODAY (REV. ED.) (PAMPHLET). COM
ECO/UNDEV AGRI FINAN INDUS POL/PAR FOR/AID ADMIN
MARXISM 20. PAGE 118 B2376
BIBLIOG/A
ASIA
DIPLOM
NAT/G

S60
FRANKEL S.H.,"ECONOMIC ASPECTS OF POLITICAL
INDEPENDENCE IN AFRICA." AFR FUT SOCIETY ECO/UNDEV
COM/IND FINAN LEGIS PLAN TEC/DEV CAP/ISM ECO/TAC
INT/TRADE ADMIN ATTIT DRIVE RIGID/FLEX PWR WEALTH
...MGT NEW/IDEA MATH TIME/SEQ VAL/FREE 20. PAGE 37
B0751
NAT/G
FOR/AID

S60
HERRERA F.,"THE INTER-AMERICAN DEVELOPMENT BANK."
USA+45 ECO/UNDEV INT/ORG CONSULT DELIB/GP PLAN
ECO/TAC INT/TRADE ROUTINE WEALTH...STAT 20. PAGE 49
B0994
L/A+17C
FINAN
FOR/AID
REGION

S60
RIESELBACH Z.N.,"QUANTITATIVE TECHNIQUES FOR
STUDYING VOTING BEHAVIOR IN THE UNITED NATIONS
GENERAL ASSEMBLY." FUT S/ASIA USA+45 INT/ORG
BAL/PWR DIPLOM ECO/TAC FOR/AID ADMIN PWR...POLICY
METH/CNCPT METH UN 20. PAGE 88 B1783
QUANT
CHOOSE

B61
BULLIS H.A.,MANIFESTO FOR AMERICANS. USA+45 AGRI
LABOR NAT/G NEIGH FOR/AID INT/TRADE TAX EDU/PROP
CHOOSE...POLICY MGT 20 UN UNESCO. PAGE 17 B0342
ECO/TAC
SOCIETY
INDUS
CAP/ISM

B61
HARRISON S.,INDIA AND THE UNITED STATES. FUT S/ASIA
USA+45 WOR+45 INTELL ECO/DEV ECO/UNDEV AGRI INDUS
INT/ORG NAT/G CONSULT EX/STRUC TOP/EX PLAN ECO/TAC
NEUTRAL ALL/VALS...MGT TOT/POP 20. PAGE 47 B0956
DELIB/GP
ACT/RES
FOR/AID
INDIA

B61
HASAN H.S.,PAKISTAN AND THE UN. ISLAM WOR+45
ECO/DEV ECO/UNDEV NAT/G TOP/EX ECO/TAC FOR/AID
EDU/PROP ADMIN DRIVE PERCEPT...OBS TIME/SEQ UN 20.
PAGE 48 B0965
INT/ORG
ATTIT
PAKISTAN

B61
ROBINSON M.E.,EDUCATION FOR SOCIAL CHANGE:
ESTABLISHING INSTITUTES OF PUBLIC AND BUSINESS
ADMINISTRATION ABROAD (PAMPHLET). WOR+45 SOCIETY
ACADEM CONFER INGP/REL ROLE...SOC CHARTS BIBLIOG 20
ICA. PAGE 89 B1805
FOR/AID
EDU/PROP
MGT
ADJUST

B61
SHAPP W.R.,FIELD ADMINISTRATION IN THE UNITED
NATIONS SYSTEM. FINAN PROB/SOLV INSPECT DIPLOM EXEC
REGION ROUTINE EFFICIENCY ROLE...INT CHARTS 20 UN.
PAGE 96 B1933
INT/ORG
ADMIN
GP/REL
FOR/AID

B61
US GENERAL ACCOUNTING OFFICE,EXAMINATION OF
ECONOMIC AND TECHNICAL ASSISTANCE PROGRAM FOR IRAN.
IRAN USA+45 AGRI INDUS DIPLOM CONTROL COST 20.
PAGE 108 B2186
FOR/AID
ADMIN
TEC/DEV
ECO/UNDEV

S61
NOVE A.,"THE SOVIET MODEL AND UNDERDEVELOPED
COUNTRIES." COM FUT USSR WOR+45 CULTURE ECO/DEV
POL/PAR FOR/AID EDU/PROP ADMIN MORAL WEALTH
...POLICY RECORD HIST/WRIT 20. PAGE 79 B1593
ECO/UNDEV
PLAN

S61
VINER J.,"ECONOMIC FOREIGN POLICY ON THE NEW
FRONTIER." USA+45 ECO/UNDEV AGRI FINAN INDUS MARKET
INT/ORG NAT/G FOR/AID INT/TRADE ADMIN ATTIT PWR 20
KENNEDY/JF. PAGE 112 B2262
TOP/EX
ECO/TAC
BAL/PAY
TARIFFS

B62
FRIEDMANN W.,METHODS AND POLICIES OF PRINCIPAL
DONOR COUNTRIES IN PUBLIC INTERNATIONAL DEVELOPMENT
FINANCING: PRELIMINARY APPRAISAL. FRANCE GERMANY/W
UK USA+45 USSR WOR+45 FINAN TEC/DEV CAP/ISM DIPLOM
ECO/TAC ATTIT 20 EEC. PAGE 37 B0759
INT/ORG
FOR/AID
NAT/COMP
ADMIN

B62
JEWELL M.E.,SENATORIAL POLITICS AND FOREIGN POLICY.
USA+45 NAT/G POL/PAR CHIEF DELIB/GP TOP/EX FOR/AID
EDU/PROP ROUTINE ATTIT PWR SKILL...MAJORIT
METH/CNCPT TIME/SEQ CONGRESS 20 PRESIDENT. PAGE 56
B1138
USA+45
LEGIS
DIPLOM

S62
TRUMAN D.,"THE DOMESTIC POLITICS OF FOREIGN AID."
USA+45 WOR+45 NAT/G POL/PAR LEGIS DIPLOM ECO/TAC
EDU/PROP ADMIN CHOOSE ATTIT PWR CONGRESS 20
ROUTINE
FOR/AID

CONGRESS. PAGE 105 B2129

B63
HAUSMAN W.H.,MANAGING ECONOMIC DEVELOPMENT IN
AFRICA. AFR USA+45 LAW FINAN WORKER TEC/DEV WEALTH
...ANTHOL 20. PAGE 48 B0970
ECO/UNDEV
PLAN
FOR/AID
MGT

B63
SCHOECK H.,THE NEW ARGUMENT IN ECONOMICS. UK USA+45
INDUS MARKET LABOR NAT/G ECO/TAC ADMIN ROUTINE
BAL/PAY PWR...POLICY BOLIV. PAGE 94 B1899
WELF/ST
FOR/AID
ECO/DEV
ALL/IDEOS

B63
STEIN H.,AMERICAN CIVIL-MILITARY DECISION. USA+45
USA-45 EX/STRUC FORCES LEGIS TOP/EX PLAN DIPLOM
FOR/AID ATTIT 20 CONGRESS. PAGE 100 B2028
CIVMIL/REL
DECISION
WAR
BUDGET

B63
US SENATE COMM APPROPRIATIONS,PERSONNEL
ADMINISTRATION AND OPERATIONS OF AGENCY FOR
INTERNATIONAL DEVELOPMENT: SPECIAL HEARING. FINAN
LEAD COST UTIL SKILL...CHARTS 20 CONGRESS AID
CIVIL/SERV. PAGE 109 B2211
ADMIN
FOR/AID
EFFICIENCY
DIPLOM

S63
COUTY P.,"L'ASSISTANCE POUR LE DEVELOPPEMENT: POINT
DE VUE SCANDINAVES." EUR+WWI FINLAND FUT SWEDEN
WOR+45 ECO/DEV ECO/UNDEV COM/IND LABOR NAT/G
PROF/ORG ACT/RES SKILL WEALTH TOT/POP 20. PAGE 24
B0497
FINAN
ROUTINE
FOR/AID

S63
DAVEE R.,"POUR UN FONDS DE DEVELOPPEMENT SOCIAL."
FUT WOR+45 INTELL SOCIETY ECO/DEV FINAN TEC/DEV
ROUTINE WEALTH...TREND TOT/POP VAL/FREE UN 20.
PAGE 26 B0532
INT/ORG
SOC
FOR/AID

S63
MANGONE G.,"THE UNITED NATIONS AND UNITED STATES
FOREIGN POLICY." FUT WOR+45 ECO/UNDEV NAT/G
DIPLOM LEGIT ROUTINE ATTIT DRIVE...TIME/SEQ UN
COLD/WAR 20. PAGE 69 B1390
INT/ORG
ECO/TAC
FOR/AID

S63
NADLER E.B.,"SOME ECONOMIC DISADVANTAGES OF THE
ARMS RACE." USA+45 INDUS R+D FORCES PLAN TEC/DEV
ECO/TAC FOR/AID EDU/PROP PWR WEALTH...TREND
COLD/WAR 20. PAGE 77 B1552
ECO/DEV
MGT
BAL/PAY

B64
THE SPECIAL COMMONWEALTH AFRICAN ASSISTANCE PLAN.
AFR CANADA INDIA NIGERIA UK FINAN SCHOOL...CHARTS
20 COMMONWLTH. PAGE 2 B0041
ECO/UNDEV
TREND
FOR/AID
ADMIN

B64
ADAMS V.,THE PEACE CORPS IN ACTION. USA+45 VOL/ASSN
EX/STRUC GOV/REL PERCEPT ORD/FREE...OBS 20
KENNEDY/JF PEACE/CORP. PAGE 3 B0058
DIPLOM
FOR/AID
PERSON
DRIVE

B64
FATOUROS A.A.,CANADA'S OVERSEAS AID. CANADA WOR+45
ECO/DEV FINAN NAT/G BUDGET ECO/TAC CONFER ADMIN 20.
PAGE 35 B0707
FOR/AID
DIPLOM
ECO/UNDEV
POLICY

B64
LITTLE I.M.D.,AID TO AFRICA. AFR UK TEC/DEV DIPLOM
ECO/TAC INCOME WEALTH 20. PAGE 66 B1326
FOR/AID
ECO/UNDEV
ADMIN
POLICY

B64
SULLIVAN G.,THE STORY OF THE PEACE CORPS. USA+45
WOR+45 INTELL FACE/GP NAT/G SCHOOL VOL/ASSN CONSULT
EX/STRUC PLAN EDU/PROP ADMIN ATTIT DRIVE ALL/VALS
...POLICY HEAL SOC CONCPT INT QU BIOG TREND SOC/EXP
WORK. PAGE 102 B2054
INT/ORG
ECO/UNDEV
FOR/AID
PEACE

B64
TULLY A.,WHERE DID YOUR MONEY GO. USA+45 USSR
ECO/UNDEV ADMIN EFFICIENCY WEALTH...METH/COMP 20.
PAGE 106 B2136
FOR/AID
DIPLOM
CONTROL

L64
RIPLEY R.B.,"INTERAGENCY COMMITTEES AND
INCREMENTALISM: THE CASE OF AID TO INDIA." INDIA
USA+45 INTELL NAT/G DELIB/GP ACT/RES DIPLOM ROUTINE
NAT/LISM ATTIT PWR...SOC CONCPT NEW/IDEA TIME/SEQ
CON/ANAL VAL/FREE 20. PAGE 89 B1790
EXEC
MGT
FOR/AID

B65
BARNETT V.M. JR.,THE REPRESENTATION OF THE UNITED
STATES ABROAD* REVISED EDITION. ECO/UNDEV ACADEM
INT/ORG FORCES ACT/RES CREATE OP/RES FOR/AID REGION
CENTRAL...CLASSIF ANTHOL. PAGE 9 B0189
USA+45
DIPLOM
ADMIN

B65
ELDER R.E.,OVERSEAS REPRESENTATION AND SERVICES FOR
FEDERAL DOMESTIC AGENCIES. USA+45 NAT/G ACT/RES
FOR/AID EDU/PROP SENIOR ROUTINE TASK ADJUST...MGT
ORG/CHARTS. PAGE 33 B0663
OP/RES
DIPLOM
GOV/REL
ADMIN

B65
KOUSOULAS D.G.,REVOLUTION AND DEFEAT; THE STORY OF
THE GREEK COMMUNIST PARTY. GREECE INT/ORG EX/STRUC
DIPLOM FOR/AID EDU/PROP PARL/PROC ADJUST ATTIT 20
COM/PARTY. PAGE 61 B1230
REV
MARXISM
POL/PAR
ORD/FREE

B65
MEYERHOFF A.E.,THE STRATEGY OF PERSUASION. USA+45
EDU/PROP

COM/IND CONSULT FOR/AID CONTROL COERCE COST ATTIT PERCEPT MARXISM 20 COLD/WAR. PAGE 73 B1476
EFFICIENCY
OP/RES
ADMIN

B65
MORGENTHAU H.,MORGENTHAU DIARY (CHINA) (2 VOLS.). ASIA USA+45 USA-45 LAW DELIB/GP EX/STRUC PLAN FOR/AID INT/TRADE CONFER WAR MARXISM 20 CHINJAP. PAGE 75 B1523
DIPLOM
ADMIN

B65
SCOTT A.M.,THE REVOLUTION IN STATECRAFT: INFORMAL PENETRATION. WOR+45 WOR-45 CULTURE INT/ORG FORCES ECO/TAC ROUTINE...BIBLIOG 20. PAGE 95 B1918
DIPLOM
EDU/PROP
FOR/AID

B65
WHITE J.,GERMAN AID. GERMANY/W FINAN PLAN TEC/DEV INT/TRADE ADMIN ATTIT...POLICY 20. PAGE 116 B2334
FOR/AID
ECO/UNDEV
DIPLOM
ECO/TAC

S65
THOMAS F.C. JR.,"THE PEACE CORPS IN MOROCCO." CULTURE MUNIC PROVS CREATE ROUTINE TASK ADJUST STRANGE...OBS PEACE/CORP. PAGE 104 B2099
MOROCCO
FRANCE
FOR/AID
EDU/PROP

B66
ALEXANDER Y.,INTERNATIONAL TECHNICAL ASSISTANCE EXPERTS* A CASE STUDY OF THE U.N. EXPERIENCE. ECO/UNDEV CONSULT EX/STRUC CREATE PLAN DIPLOM FOR/AID TASK EFFICIENCY...ORG/CHARTS UN. PAGE 4 B0074
ECO/TAC
INT/ORG
ADMIN
MGT

B66
BALDWIN D.A.,FOREIGN AID AND AMERICAN FOREIGN POLICY: A DOCUMENTARY ANALYSIS. USA+45 ECO/UNDEV ADMIN...ECOMETRIC STAT STYLE CHARTS PROG/TEAC GEN/LAWS ANTHOL. PAGE 8 B0172
FOR/AID
DIPLOM
IDEA/COMP

B66
HAYER T.,FRENCH AID. AFR FRANCE AGRI FINAN BUDGET ADMIN WAR PRODUC...CHARTS 18/20 THIRD/WRLD OVRSEA/DEV. PAGE 48 B0975
TEC/DEV
COLONIAL
FOR/AID
ECO/UNDEV

B66
KIRDAR U.,THE STRUCTURE OF UNITED NATIONS ECONOMIC AID TO UNDERDEVELOPED COUNTRIES. AGRI FINAN INDUS NAT/G EX/STRUC PLAN GIVE TASK...POLICY 20 UN. PAGE 60 B1213
INT/ORG
FOR/AID
ECO/UNDEV
ADMIN

B66
LEWIS W.A.,DEVELOPMENT PLANNING: THE ESSENTIALS OF ECONOMIC POLICY. USA+45 FINAN INDUS NAT/G WORKER FOR/AID INT/TRADE ADMIN ROUTINE WEALTH...CONCPT STAT. PAGE 65 B1307
PLAN
ECO/DEV
POLICY
CREATE

B66
MONTGOMERY J.D.,APPROACHES TO DEVELOPMENT: POLITICS, ADMINISTRATION AND CHANGE. USA+45 AGRI FOR/AID ORD/FREE...CONCPT IDEA/COMP METH/COMP ANTHOL. PAGE 75 B1507
ECO/UNDEV
ADMIN
POLICY
ECO/TAC

B66
MOOMAW I.W.,THE CHALLENGE OF HUNGER. USA+45 PLAN ADMIN EATING 20. PAGE 75 B1509
FOR/AID
DIPLOM
ECO/UNDEV
ECO/TAC

B66
OHLIN G.,AID AND INDEBTEDNESS. AUSTRIA FINAN INT/ORG PLAN DIPLOM GIVE...POLICY MATH CHARTS 20. PAGE 79 B1604
FOR/AID
ECO/UNDEV
ADMIN
WEALTH

B66
SPICER K.,A SAMARITAN STATE? AFR CANADA INDIA PAKISTAN UK USA+45 FINAN INDUS PRODUC...CHARTS 20 NATO. PAGE 99 B2006
DIPLOM
FOR/AID
ECO/DEV
ADMIN

B66
UN ECAFE,ADMINISTRATIVE ASPECTS OF FAMILY PLANNING PROGRAMMES (PAMPHLET). ASIA THAILAND WOR+45 VOL/ASSN PROB/SOLV BUDGET FOR/AID EDU/PROP CONFER CONTROL GOV/REL TIME 20 UN BIRTH/CON. PAGE 106 B2147
PLAN
CENSUS
FAM
ADMIN

B66
US HOUSE COMM GOVT OPERATIONS,AN INVESTIGATION OF THE US ECONOMIC AND MILITARY ASSISTANCE PROGRAMS IN VIETNAM. USA+45 VIETNAM/S SOCIETY CONSTRUC FINAN FORCES BUDGET INT/TRADE PEACE HEALTH...MGT HOUSE/REP AID. PAGE 108 B2191
FOR/AID
ECO/UNDEV
WAR
INSPECT

B66
US SENATE COMM ON FOREIGN REL,HEARINGS ON S 2859 AND S 2861. USA+45 WOR+45 FORCES BUDGET CAP/ISM ADMIN DETER WEAPON TOTALISM...NAT/COMP 20 UN CONGRESS. PAGE 110 B2221
FOR/AID
DIPLOM
ORD/FREE
ECO/UNDEV

B66
WARBURG J.P.,THE UNITED STATES IN THE POSTWAR WORLD. USA+45 ECO/TAC...POLICY 20 COLD/WAR. PAGE 113 B2287
FOR/AID
DIPLOM
PLAN
ADMIN

B66
WILLNER A.R.,THE NEOTRADITIONAL ACCOMMODATION TO POLITICAL INDEPENDENCE* THE CASE OF INDONESIA * RESEARCH MONOGRAPH NO. 26. CULTURE ECO/UNDEV CREATE PROB/SOLV FOR/AID LEGIT COLONIAL EFFICIENCY NAT/LISM ALL/VALS SOC. PAGE 117 B2355
INDONESIA
CONSERVE
ELITES
ADMIN

S66
AFRICAN BIBLIOGRAPHIC CENTER,"A CURRENT VIEW OF AFRICANA: A SELECT AND ANNOTATED BIBLIOGRAPHICAL PUBLISHING GUIDE, 1965-1966." AFR CULTURE INDUS LABOR SECT FOR/AID ADMIN COLONIAL REV RACE/REL SOCISM...LING 20. PAGE 3 B0063
BIBLIOG/A
NAT/G
TEC/DEV
POL/PAR

S66
BALDWIN D.A.,"CONGRESSIONAL INITIATIVE IN FOREIGN POLICY." NAT/G BARGAIN DIPLOM FOR/AID RENT GIVE ...DECISION CONGRESS. PAGE 8 B0171
EXEC
TOP/EX
GOV/REL

B67
GABRIEL P.P.,THE INTERNATIONAL TRANSFER OF CORPORATE SKILLS: MANAGEMENT CONTRACTS IN LESS DEVELOPED COUNTRIES. CLIENT INDUS LG/CO PLAN PROB/SOLV CAP/ISM ECO/TAC FOR/AID INT/TRADE RENT ADMIN SKILL 20. PAGE 38 B0771
ECO/UNDEV
AGREE
MGT
CONSULT

B67
OVERSEAS DEVELOPMENT INSTIT,EFFECTIVE AID. WOR+45 INT/ORG TEC/DEV DIPLOM INT/TRADE ADMIN. PAGE 80 B1619
FOR/AID
ECO/UNDEV
ECO/TAC
NAT/COMP

B67
SABLE M.H.,A GUIDE TO LATIN AMERICAN STUDIES (2 VOLS). CONSTN FINAN INT/ORG LABOR MUNIC POL/PAR FORCES CAP/ISM FOR/AID ADMIN MARXISM SOCISM OAS. PAGE 92 B1861
BIBLIOG/A
L/A+17C
DIPLOM
NAT/LISM

B67
TANSKY L.,US AND USSR AID TO DEVELOPING COUNTRIES. INDIA TURKEY UAR USA+45 USSR FINAN PLAN TEC/DEV ADMIN WEALTH...TREND METH/COMP 20. PAGE 103 B2076
FOR/AID
ECO/UNDEV
MARXISM
CAP/ISM

B67
TOMA P.A.,THE POLITICS OF FOOD FOR PEACE: EXECUTIVE-LEGISLATIVE INTERACTION. USA+45 ECO/UNDEV POL/PAR DEBATE EXEC LOBBY CHOOSE PEACE...DECISION CHARTS. PAGE 104 B2113
FOR/AID
POLICY
LEGIS
AGRI

B67
ZONDAG C.H.,THE BOLIVIAN ECONOMY 1952-65. L/A+17C TEC/DEV FOR/AID ADMIN...OBS TREND CHARTS BIBLIOG 20 BOLIV. PAGE 119 B2406
ECO/UNDEV
INDUS
PRODUC

N67
US SENATE COMM ON FOREIGN REL,ARMS SALES AND FOREIGN POLICY (PAMPHLET). FINAN FOR/AID CONTROL 20. PAGE 110 B2222
ARMS/CONT
ADMIN
OP/RES
DIPLOM

FORBES A.H. B0736

FORCE AND VIOLENCE....SEE COERCE

FORCES....ARMED FORCES AND POLICE

N
WEIGLEY R.F.,HISTORY OF THE UNITED STATES ARMY. USA+45 USA-45 SOCIETY NAT/G LEAD WAR GP/REL PWR ...SOC METH/COMP COLD/WAR. PAGE 115 B2312
FORCES
ADMIN
ROLE
CIVMIL/REL

B
DEUTSCHE BIBLIOTH FRANKF A M,DEUTSCHE BIBLIOGRAPHIE. EUR+WWI GERMANY ECO/DEV FORCES DIPLOM LEAD...POLICY PHIL/SCI SOC 20. PAGE 28 B0578
BIBLIOG
LAW
ADMIN
NAT/G

N
UNITED NATIONS,UNITED NATIONS PUBLICATIONS. WOR+45 ECO/UNDEV AGRI FINAN FORCES ADMIN LEAD WAR PEACE ...POLICY INT/LAW 20 UN. PAGE 107 B2160
BIBLIOG
INT/ORG
DIPLOM

N
US SUPERINTENDENT OF DOCUMENTS,TRANSPORTATION: HIGHWAYS, ROADS, AND POSTAL SERVICE (PRICE LIST 25). PANAMA USA+45 LAW FORCES DIPLOM ADMIN GOV/REL HEALTH MGT. PAGE 111 B2243
BIBLIOG/A
DIST/IND
SERV/IND
NAT/G

B00
SANDERSON E.,AFRICA IN THE NINETEENTH CENTURY. FRANCE UK EXTR/IND FORCES LEGIS ADMIN WAR DISCRIM ORD/FREE...GEOG GP/COMP SOC/INTEG 19. PAGE 92 B1867
COLONIAL
AFR
DIPLOM

B05
MACHIAVELLI N.,THE ART OF WAR. CHRIST-17C TOP/EX DRIVE ORD/FREE PWR SKILL...MGT CHARTS. PAGE 67 B1360
NAT/G
FORCES
WAR
ITALY

N19
GINZBERG E.,MANPOWER FOR GOVERNMENT (PAMPHLET). USA+45 FORCES PLAN PROB/SOLV PAY EDU/PROP ADMIN GP/REL COST...MGT PREDICT TREND 20 CIVIL/SERV. PAGE 40 B0803
WORKER
CONSULT
NAT/G
LOC/G

N19
RIDLEY C.E.,MEASURING MUNICIPAL ACTIVITIES (PAMPHLET). FINAN SERV/IND FORCES RECEIVE INGP/REL HABITAT...POLICY SOC/WK 20. PAGE 88 B1779
MGT
HEALTH
WEALTH
LOC/G

N19
SOUTH AFRICA COMMISSION ON FUT,INTERIM AND FINAL REPORTS ON FUTURE FORM OF GOVERNMENT IN THE SOUTH-WEST AFRICAN PROTECTORATE (PAMPHLET). SOUTH/AFR NAT/G FORCES CONFER COLONIAL CONTROL 20 AFRICA/SW. PAGE 99 B1998
CONSTN
REPRESENT
ADMIN
PROB/SOLV

BLACHLY F.F.,"THE GOVERNMENT AND ADMINISTRATION OF | NAT/G
GERMANY." GERMANY CONSTN LOC/G PROVS DELIB/GP | GOV/REL
EX/STRUC FORCES LEGIS TOP/EX CT/SYS...BIBLIOG/A | ADMIN
19/20. PAGE 12 B0246 | PHIL/SCI
                                                              C20
                                                              B23

FRANK T.,A HISTORY OF ROME. MEDIT-7 INTELL SOCIETY | EXEC
LOC/G NAT/G POL/PAR FORCES LEGIS DOMIN LEGIT | STRUCT
ALL/VALS...POLICY CONCPT TIME/SEQ GEN/LAWS ROM/EMP | ELITES
ROM/EMP. PAGE 37 B0749
                                                              B29

BUELL R.,INTERNATIONAL RELATIONS. WOR+45 WOR-45 | INT/ORG
CONSTN STRATA FORCES TOP/EX ADMIN ATTIT DRIVE | BAL/PWR
SUPEGO MORAL ORD/FREE PWR SOVEREIGN...JURID SOC | DIPLOM
CONCPT 20. PAGE 17 B0340
                                                              B30

FAIRLIE J.A.,COUNTY GOVERNMENT AND ADMINISTRATION. | ADMIN
UK USA-45 NAT/G SCHOOL FORCES BUDGET TAX CT/SYS | GOV/REL
CHOOSE...JURID BIBLIOG 11/20. PAGE 35 B0701 | LOC/G
                                                              MUNIC
                                                              B35

GORER G.,AFRICA DANCES: A BOOK ABOUT WEST AFRICAN | AFR
NEGROES. STRUCT LOC/G SECT FORCES TAX ADMIN | ATTIT
COLONIAL...ART/METH MYTH WORSHIP 20 NEGRO AFRICA/W | CULTURE
CHRISTIAN RITUAL. PAGE 41 B0835 | SOCIETY
                                                              B36

GRAVES W.B.,AMERICAN STATE GOVERNMENT. CONSTN FINAN | NAT/G
EX/STRUC FORCES LEGIS BUDGET TAX CT/SYS REPRESENT | PROVS
GOV/REL...BIBLIOG/A 19/20. PAGE 42 B0855 | ADMIN
                                                              FEDERAL
                                                              B36

ROBINSON H.,DEVELOPMENT OF THE BRITISH EMPIRE. | NAT/G
WOR-45 CULTURE SOCIETY STRUCT ECO/DEV ECO/UNDEV | HIST/WRIT
INT/ORG VOL/ASSN FORCES CREATE PLAN DOMIN EDU/PROP | UK
ADMIN COLONIAL PWR WEALTH...POLICY GEOG CHARTS
CMN/WLTH 16/20. PAGE 89 B1800
                                                              B37

UNION OF SOUTH AFRICA,REPORT CONCERNING | NAT/G
ADMINISTRATION OF SOUTH WEST AFRICA (6 VOLS.). | ADMIN
SOUTH/AFR INDUS PUB/INST FORCES LEGIS BUDGET DIPLOM | COLONIAL
EDU/PROP ADJUD CT/SYS...GEOG CHARTS 20 AFRICA/SW | CONSTN
LEAGUE/NAT. PAGE 107 B2158
                                                              B39

HITLER A.,MEIN KAMPF. EUR+WWI FUT MOD/EUR STRUCT | PWR
INT/ORG LABOR NAT/G POL/PAR FORCES CREATE PLAN | NEW/IDEA
BAL/PWR DIPLOM ECO/TAC DOMIN EDU/PROP ADMIN COERCE | WAR
ATTIT...SOCIALIST BIOG TREND NAZI. PAGE 50 B1020
                                                              C39

REISCHAUER R.,"JAPAN'S GOVERNMENT--POLITICS." | NAT/G
CONSTN STRATA POL/PAR FORCES LEGIS DIPLOM ADMIN | S/ASIA
EXEC CENTRAL...POLICY BIBLIOG 20 CHINJAP. PAGE 87 | CONCPT
B1764 | ROUTINE
                                                              S40

GERTH H.,"THE NAZI PARTY: ITS LEADERSHIP AND | POL/PAR
COMPOSITION" (BMR)" GERMANY ELITES STRATA STRUCT | DOMIN
EX/STRUC FORCES ECO/TAC CT/SYS CHOOSE TOTALISM | LEAD
AGE/Y AUTHORIT PWR 20. PAGE 39 B0792 | ADMIN
                                                              C40

FAHS C.B.,"GOVERNMENT IN JAPAN." FINAN FORCES LEGIS | ASIA
TOP/EX BUDGET INT/TRADE EDU/PROP SOVEREIGN | DIPLOM
...CON/ANAL BIBLIOG/A 20 CHINJAP. PAGE 34 B0698 | NAT/G
                                                              ADMIN
                                                              B41

PALMER J.M.,AMERICA IN ARMS: THE EXPERIENCE OF THE | FORCES
UNITED STATES WITH MILITARY ORGANIZATION. FUT | NAT/G
USA-45 LEAD REV PWR 18/20 WASHINGT/G KNOX/HENRY | ADMIN
PRE/US/AM. PAGE 81 B1627 | WAR
                                                              S41

ABEL T.,"THE ELEMENT OF DECISION IN THE PATTERN OF | TEC/DEV
WAR." EUR+WWI FUT NAT/G TOP/EX DIPLOM ROUTINE | FORCES
COERCE DISPL PERCEPT PWR...SOC METH/CNCPT HIST/WRIT | WAR
TREND GEN/LAWS 20. PAGE 2 B0051
                                                              B42

SINGTON D.,THE GOEBBELS EXPERIMENT. GERMANY MOD/EUR | FASCISM
NAT/G EX/STRUC FORCES CONTROL ROUTINE WAR TOTALISM | EDU/PROP
PWR...ART/METH HUM 20 NAZI GOEBBELS/J. PAGE 97 | ATTIT
B1970 | COM/IND
                                                              B42

US STATE DEPT.,PEACE AND WAR: UNITED STATES FOREIGN | DIPLOM
POLICY, 1931-41. CULTURE FORCES ROUTINE CHOOSE | USA-45
ATTIT DRIVE PERSON 20. PAGE 111 B2237 | PLAN
                                                              B45

CONOVER H.F.,THE GOVERNMENTS OF THE MAJOR FOREIGN | BIBLIOG
POWERS: A BIBLIOGRAPHY. FRANCE GERMANY ITALY UK | NAT/G
USSR CONSTN LOC/G POL/PAR EX/STRUC FORCES ADMIN | DIPLOM
CT/SYS CIVMIL/REL TOTALISM...POLICY 19/20. PAGE 23
B0464
                                                              B45

PLATO,THE REPUBLIC. MEDIT-7 UNIV SOCIETY STRUCT | PERSON
EX/STRUC FORCES UTOPIA ATTIT PERCEPT HEALTH KNOWL | PHIL/SCI
ORD/FREE PWR...HUM CONCPT STERTYP TOT/POP. PAGE 83
B1681
                                                              B46

WILCOX J.K.,OFFICIAL DEFENSE PUBLICATIONS, | BIBLIOG/A
1941-1945 (NINE VOLS.). USA-45 AGRI INDUS R+D LABOR | WAR
FORCES TEC/DEV EFFICIENCY PRODUC SKILL WEALTH 20. | CIVMIL/REL

PAGE 116 B2347 | ADMIN
                                                              L46

FORRESTAL J.,"THE NAVY: A STUDY IN ADMINISTRATION." | FORCES
ELITES FACE/GP EX/STRUC PROB/SOLV REPRESENT | INGP/REL
EFFICIENCY PRODUC. PAGE 37 B0741 | ROUTINE
                                                              EXEC
                                                              B47

BORGESE G.,COMMON CAUSE. LAW CONSTN SOCIETY STRATA | WOR+45
ECO/DEV INT/ORG POL/PAR FORCES LEGIS TOP/EX CAP/ISM | NAT/G
DIPLOM ADMIN EXEC ATTIT PWR 20. PAGE 14 B0279 | SOVEREIGN
                                                              REGION
                                                              B47

LASSWELL H.D.,THE ANALYSIS OF POLITICAL BEHAVIOUR: | R+D
AN EMPIRICAL APPROACH. WOR+45 CULTURE NAT/G FORCES | ACT/RES
EDU/PROP ADMIN ATTIT PERCEPT KNOWL...PHIL/SCI PSY | ELITES
SOC NEW/IDEA OBS INT GEN/METH NAZI 20. PAGE 63
B1267
                                                              B47

TAPPAN P.W.,DELINQUENT GIRLS IN COURT. USA-45 MUNIC | CT/SYS
EX/STRUC FORCES ADMIN EXEC ADJUST SEX RESPECT | AGE/Y
...JURID SOC/WK 20 NEWYORK/C FEMALE/SEX. PAGE 103 | CRIME
B2078 | ADJUD
                                                              S47

TURNER R.H.,"THE NAVY DISBURSING OFFICER AS A | FORCES
BUREAUCRAT" (BMR)" USA-45 LAW STRATA DIST/IND WAR | ADMIN
PWR...SOC 20 BUREAUCRCY. PAGE 106 B2140 | PERSON
                                                              ROLE
                                                              B48

BONAPARTE M.,MYTHS OF WAR. GERMANY WOR+45 WOR-45 | ROUTINE
CULTURE SOCIETY NAT/G FORCES LEGIT ATTIT ALL/VALS | MYTH
...CONCPT HIST/WRIT TIME/SEQ 20 JEWS. PAGE 13 B0271 | WAR
                                                              B48

HART J.,THE AMERICAN PRESIDENCY IN ACTION 1789: A | NAT/G
STUDY IN CONSTITUTIONAL HISTORY. USA-45 POL/PAR | CONSTN
DELIB/GP FORCES LEGIS ADJUD ADMIN LEAD GP/REL | CHIEF
PERS/REL 18 PRESIDENT CONGRESS. PAGE 47 B0959 | EX/STRUC
                                                              B48

HULL C.,THE MEMOIRS OF CORDELL HULL (VOLUME ONE). | BIOG
USA-45 WOR+45 CONSTN FAM LOC/G NAT/G PROVS DELIB/GP | DIPLOM
FORCES LEGIS TOP/EX BAL/PWR LEGIT ADMIN EXEC WAR
ATTIT ORD/FREE PWR...MAJORIT SELF/OBS TIME/SEQ
TREND NAZI 20. PAGE 52 B1062
                                                              B48

SHERWOOD R.E.,ROOSEVELT AND HOPKINS. UK USA+45 USSR | TOP/EX
NAT/G EX/STRUC FORCES ADMIN ROUTINE PERSON PWR | BIOG
...TIME/SEQ 20 ROOSEVLT/F HOPKINS/H. PAGE 96 B1946 | DIPLOM
                                                              WAR
                                                              B48

STOKES W.S.,BIBLIOGRAPHY OF STANDARD AND CLASSICAL | BIBLIOG
WORKS IN THE FIELDS OF AMERICAN POLITICAL SCIENCE. | NAT/G
USA+45 USA-45 POL/PAR PROVS FORCES DIPLOM ADMIN | LOC/G
CT/SYS APPORT 20 CONGRESS PRESIDENT. PAGE 101 B2043 | CONSTN
                                                              B49

BUSH V.,MODERN ARMS AND FREE MEN. WOR-45 SOCIETY | TEC/DEV
NAT/G ECO/TAC DOMIN LEGIT EXEC COERCE DETER ATTIT | FORCES
DRIVE ORD/FREE PWR...CONCPT MYTH COLD/WAR 20 | NUC/PWR
COLD/WAR. PAGE 18 B0361 | WAR
                                                              C50

MORLAN R.L.,"INTERGOVERNMENTAL RELATIONS IN | SCHOOL
EDUCATION." USA+45 FINAN LOC/G MUNIC NAT/G FORCES | GOV/REL
PROB/SOLV RECEIVE ADMIN RACE/REL COST...BIBLIOG | ACADEM
INDIAN/AM. PAGE 76 B1526 | POLICY
                                                              B51

MAASS A.,MUDDY WATERS: THE ARMY ENGINEERS AND THE | FORCES
NATIONS RIVERS. USA-45 PROF/ORG CONSULT LEGIS ADMIN | GP/REL
EXEC ROLE PWR...SOC PRESIDENT 20. PAGE 67 B1353 | LOBBY
                                                              CONSTRUC
                                                              B51

SMITH L.,AMERICAN DEMOCRACY AND MILITARY POWER. | FORCES
USA+45 USA-45 CONSTN STRATA NAT/G LEGIS ACT/RES | STRUCT
LEGIT ADMIN EXEC GOV/REL ALL/VALS...CONCPT | WAR
HIST/WRIT CONGRESS 20. PAGE 98 B1982
                                                              S51

SCHRAMM W.,"COMMUNICATION IN THE SOVIETIZED STATE, | ATTIT
AS DEMONSTRATED IN KOREA." ASIA COM KOREA COM/IND | EDU/PROP
FACE/GP POL/PAR SCHOOL FORCES ADMIN PWR MARXISM | TOTALISM
...SOC CONCPT MYTH INT BIOG TOT/POP 20. PAGE 94
B1901
                                                              S51

STEWART D.D.,"THE PLACE OF VOLUNTEER PARTICIPATION | ADMIN
IN BUREAUCRATIC ORGANIZATION." NAT/G DELIB/GP | PARTIC
OP/RES DOMIN LOBBY WAR ATTIT ROLE PWR. PAGE 101 | VOL/ASSN
B2035 | FORCES
                                                              B52

BRINTON C.,THE ANATOMY OF REVOLUTION. FRANCE UK | SOCIETY
USA-45 USSR WOR-45 ELITES INTELL ECO/DEV NAT/G | CONCPT
EX/STRUC FORCES COERCE DRIVE ORD/FREE PWR SOVEREIGN | REV
...MYTH HIST/WRIT GEN/LAWS. PAGE 15 B0311
                                                              B52

ELLIOTT W.,UNITED STATES FOREIGN POLICY, ITS | LEGIS
ORGANIZATION AND CONTROL. USA+45 USA-45 CONSTN | EX/STRUC
NAT/G FORCES TOP/EX PEACE...TIME/SEQ CONGRESS | DIPLOM
LEAGUE/NAT 20. PAGE 33 B0670
                                                              B52

POOL I.,SYMBOLS OF DEMOCRACY. WOR+45 WOR-45 POL/PAR | INTELL
FORCES ADMIN PERSON PWR...CONCPT 20. PAGE 83 B1687 | SOCIETY

MASLAND J.W.,"THE NATIONAL WAR COLLEGE AND THE ADMINISTRATION OF FOREIGN AFFAIRS." USA+45 NAT/G FORCES EXEC 20. PAGE 70 B1422
USSR
S52
CIVMIL/REL
EX/STRUC
REPRESENT
PROB/SOLV

LANCASTER L.W.,"GOVERNMENT IN RURAL AMERICA." USA+45 ECO/DEV AGRI SCHOOL FORCES LEGIS JUDGE BUDGET TAX CT/SYS...CHARTS BIBLIOG. PAGE 62 B1253
C52
GOV/REL
LOC/G
MUNIC
ADMIN

PERKINS J.A.,"ADMINISTRATION OF THE NATIONAL SECURITY PROGRAM." USA+45 EX/STRUC FORCES ADMIN CIVMIL/REL ORD/FREE 20. PAGE 82 B1657
S53
CONTROL
GP/REL
REPRESENT
PROB/SOLV

POOL I.,SATELLITE GENERALS: A STUDY OF MILITARY ELITES IN THE SOVIET SPHERE. ASIA CHINA/COM COM CZECHOSLVK FUT HUNGARY POLAND ROMANIA USSR ELITES STRATA ADMIN ATTIT PWR SKILL...METH/CNCPT BIOG 20. PAGE 84 B1688
B55
FORCES
CHOOSE

SMITHIES A.,THE BUDGETARY PROCESS IN THE UNITED STATES. ECO/DEV AGRI EX/STRUC FORCES LEGIS PROB/SOLV TAX ROUTINE EFFICIENCY...MGT CONGRESS PRESIDENT. PAGE 98 B1987
B55
NAT/G
ADMIN
BUDGET
GOV/REL

BLAU P.M.,BUREAUCRACY IN MODERN SOCIETY. STRUCT INDUS LABOR LG/CO LOC/G NAT/G FORCES EDU/PROP ROUTINE ORD/FREE 20 BUREAUCRCY. PAGE 12 B0252
B56
SOC
EX/STRUC
ADMIN
EFFICIENCY

BROWNE D.G.,THE RISE OF SCOTLAND YARD: A HISTORY OF THE METROPOLITAN POLICE. UK MUNIC CHIEF ADMIN CRIME GP/REL 19/20. PAGE 16 B0329
B56
CRIMLGY
LEGIS
CONTROL
FORCES

KAUFMANN W.W.,MILITARY POLICY AND NATIONAL SECURITY. USA+45 ELITES INTELL NAT/G TOP/EX PLAN BAL/PWR DIPLOM ROUTINE COERCE NUC/PWR ATTIT ORD/FREE PWR 20 COLD/WAR. PAGE 58 B1182
B56
FORCES
CREATE

WIGGINS J.R.,FREEDOM OR SECRECY. USA+45 USA-45 DELIB/GP EX/STRUC FORCES ADJUD SANCTION KNOWL PWR ...AUD/VIS CONGRESS 20. PAGE 116 B2344
B56
ORD/FREE
PRESS
NAT/G
CONTROL

WILSON P.,GOVERNMENT AND POLITICS OF INDIA AND PAKISTAN: 1885-1955; A BIBLIOGRAPHY OF WORKS IN WESTERN LANGUAGES. INDIA PAKISTAN CONSTN LOC/G POL/PAR FORCES DIPLOM ADMIN WAR CHOOSE...BIOG CON/ANAL 19/20. PAGE 117 B2361
B56
BIBLIOG
COLONIAL
NAT/G
S/ASIA

FALL B.B.,"THE VIET-MINH REGIME." VIETNAM LAW ECO/UNDEV POL/PAR FORCES DOMIN WAR ATTIT MARXISM ...BIOG PREDICT BIBLIOG/A 20. PAGE 35 B0703
C56
NAT/G
ADMIN
EX/STRUC
LEAD

ARON R.,FRANCE DEFEATS EDC. EUR+WWI GERMANY LEGIS DIPLOM DOMIN EDU/PROP ADMIN...HIST/WRIT 20. PAGE 7 B0136
B57
INT/ORG
FORCES
DETER
FRANCE

HUNTINGTON S.P.,THE SOLDIER AND THE STATE: THE THEORY AND POLITICS OF CIVIL-MILITARY RELATIONS. USA+45 USA-45 NAT/G PROF/ORG CONSULT DOMIN LEGIT ROUTINE ATTIT PWR...CONCPT TIME/SEQ COLD/WAR 20. PAGE 53 B1065
B57
ACT/RES
FORCES

US HOUSE COMM ON POST OFFICE,MANPOWER UTILIZATION IN THE FEDERAL GOVERNMENT. USA+45 FORCES WORKER CREATE PLAN EFFICIENCY UTIL 20 CONGRESS CIVIL/SERV POSTAL/SYS DEPT/DEFEN. PAGE 109 B2193
B57
NAT/G
ADMIN
LABOR
EX/STRUC

TANG P.S.H.,"COMMUNIST CHINA TODAY: DOMESTIC AND FOREIGN POLICIES." CHINA/COM COM S/ASIA USSR STRATA FORCES DIPLOM EDU/PROP COERCE GOV/REL...POLICY MAJORIT BIBLIOG 20. PAGE 102 B2071
C57
POL/PAR
LEAD
ADMIN
CONSTN

CONSERVATIVE POLITICAL CENTRE,A WORLD SECURITY AUTHORITY? WOR+45 CONSTN ELITES FINAN DELIB/GP PLAN PROB/SOLV ADMIN CONTROL NUC/PWR GP/REL...IDEA/COMP 20. PAGE 23 B0468
B58
ORD/FREE
CONSERVE
FORCES
ARMS/CONT

JAPAN MINISTRY OF JUSTICE,CRIMINAL JUSTICE IN JAPAN. LAW PROF/ORG PUB/INST FORCES CONTROL CT/SYS PARL/PROC 20 CHINJAP. PAGE 56 B1125
B58
CONSTN
CRIME
JURID
ADMIN

SHAW S.J.,THE FINANCIAL AND ADMINISTRATIVE ORGANIZATION AND DEVELOPMENT OF OTTOMAN EGYPT 1517-1798. UAR LOC/G FORCES BUDGET INT/TRADE TAX EATING INCOME WEALTH...CHARTS BIBLIOG 16/18 OTTOMAN NAPOLEON/B. PAGE 96 B1940
B58
FINAN
ADMIN
GOV/REL
CULTURE

DAVENPORT J.,"ARMS AND THE WELFARE STATE." INTELL STRUCT FORCES CREATE ECO/TAC FOR/AID DOMIN LEGIT ADMIN WAR ORD/FREE PWR...POLICY SOC CONCPT MYTH OBS TREND COLD/WAR TOT/POP 20. PAGE 26 B0533
S58
USA+45
NAT/G
USSR

JORDAN A.,"MILITARY ASSISTANCE AND NATIONAL POLICY." ASIA FUT USA+45 WOR+45 ECO/DEV ECO/UNDEV INT/ORG NAT/G PLAN ECO/TAC ROUTINE WEAPON ATTIT RIGID/FLEX PWR...CONCPT TREND 20. PAGE 57 B1153
S58
FORCES
POLICY
FOR/AID
DIPLOM

CONOVER H.F.,NIGERIAN OFFICIAL PUBLICATIONS, 1869-1959: A GUIDE. NIGER CONSTN FINAN ACADEM SCHOOL FORCES PRESS ADMIN COLONIAL...HIST/WRIT 19/20. PAGE 23 B0466
B59
BIBLIOG
NAT/G
CON/ANAL

IPSEN H.P.,HAMBURGISCHES STAATS- UND VERWALTUNGSRECHT. CONSTN LOC/G FORCES BUDGET CT/SYS ...JURID 20 HAMBURG. PAGE 54 B1103
B59
ADMIN
PROVS
LEGIS
FINAN

JANOWITZ M.,SOCIOLOGY AND THE MILITARY ESTABLISHMENT. USA+45 WOR+45 CULTURE SOCIETY PROF/ORG CONSULT EX/STRUC PLAN TEC/DEV DIPLOM DOMIN COERCE DRIVE RIGID/FLEX ORD/FREE PWR SKILL COLD/WAR 20. PAGE 55 B1121
B59
FORCES
SOC

SCHURZ W.L.,AMERICAN FOREIGN AFFAIRS: A GUIDE TO INTERNATIONAL AFFAIRS. USA+45 WOR+45 NAT/G FORCES LEGIS TOP/EX PLAN EDU/PROP LEGIT ADMIN ROUTINE ATTIT ORD/FREE PWR...SOC CONCPT STAT SAMP/SIZ CHARTS STERTYP 20. PAGE 95 B1910
B59
INT/ORG
SOCIETY
DIPLOM

US HOUSE COMM GOVT OPERATIONS,UNITED STATES AID OPERATIONS IN LAOS. LAOS USA+45 PLAN INSPECT HOUSE/REP. PAGE 108 B2190
B59
FOR/AID
ADMIN
FORCES
ECO/UNDEV

US PRES COMM STUDY MIL ASSIST,COMPOSITE REPORT. USA+45 ECO/UNDEV PLAN BUDGET DIPLOM EFFICIENCY ...POLICY MGT 20. PAGE 109 B2208
B59
FOR/AID
FORCES
WEAPON
ORD/FREE

YANG C.K.,A CHINESE VILLAGE IN EARLY COMMUNIST TRANSITION. ECO/UNDEV AGRI FAM KIN MUNIC FORCES PLAN ECO/TAC DOMIN EDU/PROP ATTIT DRIVE PWR RESPECT ...SOC CONCPT METH/CNCPT OBS RECORD CON/ANAL CHARTS WORK 20. PAGE 118 B2389
B59
ASIA
ROUTINE
SOCISM

JANOWITZ M.,"CHANGING PATTERNS OF ORGANIZATIONAL AUTHORITY: THE MILITARY ESTABLISHMENT" (BMR)" USA+45 ELITES STRUCT EX/STRUC PLAN DOMIN AUTOMAT NUC/PWR WEAPON 20. PAGE 55 B1122
S59
FORCES
AUTHORIT
ADMIN
TEC/DEV

SOHN L.B.,"THE DEFINITION OF AGGRESSION." FUT LAW FORCES LEGIT ADJUD ROUTINE COERCE ORD/FREE PWR ...MAJORIT JURID QUANT COLD/WAR 20. PAGE 99 B1995
S59
INT/ORG
CT/SYS
DETER
SOVEREIGN

SUTTON F.X.,"REPRESENTATION AND THE NATURE OF POLITICAL SYSTEMS." UNIV WOR-45 CULTURE SOCIETY STRATA INT/ORG FORCES JUDGE DOMIN LEGIT EXEC REGION REPRESENT ATTIT ORD/FREE RESPECT...SOC HIST/WRIT TIME/SEQ. PAGE 102 B2057
S59
NAT/G
CONCPT

EASTON S.C.,THE TWILIGHT OF EUROPEAN COLONIALISM. AFR S/ASIA CONSTN SOCIETY STRUCT ECO/UNDEV INDUS NAT/G FORCES ECO/TAC COLONIAL CT/SYS ATTIT KNOWL ORD/FREE PWR...SOCIALIST TIME/SEQ TREND CON/ANAL 20. PAGE 32 B0645
B60
FINAN
ADMIN

GLOVER J.D.,A CASE STUDY OF HIGH LEVEL ADMINISTRATION IN A LARGE ORGANIZATION. EX/STRUC EXEC LEAD ROUTINE INGP/REL OPTIMAL ATTIT PERSON ...POLICY DECISION INT QU. PAGE 40 B0812
B60
ADMIN
TOP/EX
FORCES
NAT/G

JONES V.,METROPOLITAN COMMUNITIES: A BIBLIOGRAPHY WITH SPECIAL EMPHASIS UPON GOVERNMENT AND POLITICS, 1955-1957. STRUCT ECO/DEV FINAN FORCES PLAN PROB/SOLV RECEIVE EDU/PROP CT/SYS...GEOG HEAL 20. PAGE 57 B1152
B60
BIBLIOG
LOC/G
MUNIC
ADMIN

KINGSTON-MCCLOUG E.,DEFENSE; POLICY AND STRATEGY. UK SEA AIR TEC/DEV DIPLOM ADMIN LEAD WAR ORD/FREE ...CHARTS 20. PAGE 60 B1209
B60
FORCES
PLAN
POLICY
DECISION

MORISON E.E.,TURMOIL AND TRADITION: A STUDY OF THE LIFE AND TIMES OF HENRY L. STIMSON. USA+45 USA-45 POL/PAR CHIEF DELIB/GP FORCES BAL/PWR DIPLOM ARMS/CONT WAR PEACE 19/20 STIMSON/HL ROOSEVLT/F TAFT/WH HOOVER/H REPUBLICAN. PAGE 75 B1525
B60
BIOG
NAT/G
EX/STRUC

PHILLIPS J.C.,MUNICIPAL GOVERNMENT AND ADMINISTRATION IN AMERICA. USA+45 LAW CONSTN FINAN FORCES PLAN RECEIVE OWN ORD/FREE 20 CIVIL/LIB.
B60
MUNIC
GOV/REL
LOC/G

PAGE 83 B1669

ADMIN
B60

US DEPARTMENT OF THE ARMY.SELECT BIBLIOGRAPHY ON ADMINISTRATIVE ORGANIZATION(PAMPHLET). USA+45 INDUS NAT/G EX/STRUC OP/RES CIVMIL/REL EFFICIENCY ORD/FREE. PAGE 108 B2183

BIBLIOG/A
ADMIN
CONCPT
FORCES

L60

BRENNAN D.G.,"SETTING AND GOALS OF ARMS CONTROL." FUT USA+45 USSR WOR+45 INTELL INT/ORG NAT/G VOL/ASSN CONSULT PLAN DIPLOM ECO/TAC ADMIN KNOWL PWR...POLICY CONCPT TREND COLD/WAR 20. PAGE 15 B0305

FORCES
COERCE
ARMS/CONT
DETER

S60

EMERSON R.,"THE EROSION OF DEMOCRACY." AFR FUT LAW CULTURE INTELL SOCIETY ECO/UNDEV FAM LOC/G NAT/G FORCES PLAN TEC/DEV ECO/TAC ADMIN CT/SYS ATTIT ORD/FREE PWR...SOCIALIST SOC CONCPT STAND/INT TIME/SEQ WORK 20. PAGE 33 B0671

S/ASIA
POL/PAR

S60

HERZ J.H.,"EAST GERMANY: PROGRESS AND PROSPECTS." COM AGRI FINAN INDUS LOC/G NAT/G FORCES PLAN TEC/DEV DOMIN ADMIN COERCE DRIVE PERCEPT RIGID/FLEX MORAL ORD/FREE PWR...MARXIST PSY SOC RECORD STERTYP WORK. PAGE 49 B0997

POL/PAR
STRUCT
GERMANY

S60

HUNTINGTON S.P.,"STRATEGIC PLANNING AND THE POLITICAL PROCESS." USA+45 NAT/G DELIB/GP LEGIS ACT/RES ECO/TAC LEGIT ROUTINE CHOOSE RIGID/FLEX PWR ...POLICY MAJORIT MGT 20. PAGE 53 B1066

EXEC
FORCES
NUC/PWR
WAR

S60

MARSHALL G.,"POLICE RESPONSIBILITY." UK LOC/G ADJUD ADMIN EXEC 20. PAGE 70 B1409

CONTROL
REPRESENT
LAW
FORCES

C60

SCHAPIRO L.B.,"THE COMMUNIST PARTY OF THE SOVIET UNION." USSR INTELL CHIEF EX/STRUC FORCES DOMIN ADMIN LEAD WAR ATTIT SOVEREIGN...POLICY BIBLIOG 20. PAGE 93 B1881

POL/PAR
COM
REV

B61

KERTESZ S.D.,AMERICAN DIPLOMACY IN A NEW ERA. COM S/ASIA UK USA+45 FORCES PROB/SOLV BAL/PWR ECO/TAC ADMIN COLONIAL WAR PEACE ORD/FREE 20 NATO CONGRESS UN COLD/WAR. PAGE 59 B1199

ANTHOL
DIPLOM
TREND

B61

MARX K.,THE COMMUNIST MANIFESTO. IN (MENDEL A. ESSENTIAL WORKS OF MARXISM. NEW YORK: BANTAM. FUT MOD/EUR CULTURE ECO/DEV ECO/UNDEV AGRI FINAN INDUS MARKET PROC/MFG LABOR MUNIC POL/PAR CONSULT FORCES CREATE PLAN ADMIN ATTIT DRIVE RIGID/FLEX ORD/FREE PWR RESPECT MARX/KARL WORK. PAGE 70 B1421

COM
NEW/IDEA
CAP/ISM
REV

B61

MOLLAU G.,INTERNATIONAL COMMUNISM AND WORLD REVOLUTION: HISTORY AND METHODS. RUSSIA USSR INT/ORG NAT/G POL/PAR VOL/ASSN FORCES BAL/PWR DIPLOM EXEC REGION WAR ATTIT PWR MARXISM...CONCPT TIME/SEQ COLD/WAR 19/20. PAGE 74 B1498

COM
REV

B61

MONAS S.,THE THIRD SECTION: POLICE AND SOCIETY IN RUSSIA UNDER NICHOLAS I. MOD/EUR RUSSIA ELITES STRUCT NAT/G EX/STRUC ADMIN CONTROL PWR CONSERVE ...DECISION 19 NICHOLAS/I. PAGE 74 B1499

ORD/FREE
COM
FORCES
COERCE

B61

PETRULLO L.,LEADERSHIP AND INTERPERSONAL BEHAVIOR. FACE/GP FAM PROF/ORG EX/STRUC FORCES DOMIN WAR GP/REL PERS/REL EFFICIENCY PRODUC PWR...MGT PSY. PAGE 82 B1663

PERSON
ATTIT
LEAD
HABITAT

B61

BARTLEY H.J.,"COMMAND EXPERIENCE." USA+45 EX/STRUC FORCES LEGIT ROUTINE SKILL...POLICY OBS HYPO/EXP GEN/LAWS 20. PAGE 9 B0191

CONCPT
TREND

S61

DEVINS J.H.,"THE INITIATIVE." COM USA+45 USA-45 USSR SOCIETY NAT/G ACT/RES CREATE BAL/PWR ROUTINE COERCE DETER RIGID/FLEX SKILL...STERTYP COLD/WAR 20. PAGE 29 B0582

FORCES
CONCPT
WAR

S61

LEWY G.,"SUPERIOR ORDERS, NUCLEAR WARFARE AND THE DICTATES OF CONSCIENCE: THE DILEMMA OF MILITARY OBEDIENCE IN THE ATOMIC." FUT UNIV WOR+45 INTELL SOCIETY FORCES TOP/EX ACT/RES ADMIN ROUTINE NUC/PWR PERCEPT RIGID/FLEX ALL/VALS...POLICY CONCPT 20. PAGE 65 B1308

DETER
INT/ORG
LAW
INT/LAW

B62

BRIMMER B.,A GUIDE TO THE USE OF UNITED NATIONS DOCUMENTS. WOR+45 ECO/UNDEV AGRI EX/STRUC FORCES PROB/SOLV ADMIN WAR PEACE WEALTH...POLICY UN. PAGE 15 B0310

BIBLIOG/A
INT/ORG
DIPLOM

B62

BROWN B.E.,NEW DIRECTIONS IN COMPARATIVE POLITICS. AUSTRIA FRANCE GERMANY UK WOR+45 EX/STRUC LEGIS ORD/FREE 20. PAGE 16 B0320

NAT/COMP
METH
POL/PAR
FORCES

B62

EVANS M.S.,THE FRINGE ON TOP. USSR EX/STRUC FORCES DIPLOM ECO/TAC PEACE CONSERVE SOCISM...TREND 20

NAT/G
PWR

KENNEDY/JF. PAGE 34 B0689

CENTRAL
POLICY
B62

FOSS P.O.,REORGANIZATION AND REASSIGNMENT IN THE CALIFORNIA HIGHWAY PATROL (PAMPHLET). USA+45 STRUCT WORKER EDU/PROP CONTROL COERCE INGP/REL ORD/FREE PWR...DECISION 20 CALIFORNIA. PAGE 37 B0744

FORCES
ADMIN
PROVS
PLAN

B62

KENNEDY J.F.,TO TURN THE TIDE. SPACE AGRI INT/ORG FORCES TEC/DEV ADMIN NUC/PWR PEACE WEALTH...ANTHOL 20 KENNEDY/JF CIV/RIGHTS. PAGE 59 B1193

DIPLOM
CHIEF
POLICY
NAT/G

B62

MORTON L.,STRATEGY AND COMMAND: THE FIRST TWO YEARS. USA-45 NAT/G CONTROL EXEC LEAD WEAPON CIVMIL/REL PWR...POLICY AUD/VIS CHARTS 20 CHINJAP. PAGE 76 B1532

WAR
FORCES
PLAN
DIPLOM

B62

MULLEY F.W.,THE POLITICS OF WESTERN DEFENSE. EUR+WWI USA-45 WOR+45 VOL/ASSN EX/STRUC FORCES COERCE DETER PEACE ATTIT ORD/FREE PWR...RECORD TIME/SEQ CHARTS COLD/WAR 20 NATO. PAGE 76 B1537

INT/ORG
DELIB/GP
NUC/PWR

B62

SAMPSON A.,ANATOMY OF BRITAIN. UK LAW COM/IND FINAN INDUS MARKET MUNIC POL/PAR EX/STRUC TOP/EX DIPLOM LEAD REPRESENT PERSON PARLIAMENT WORSHIP. PAGE 92 B1866

ELITES
PWR
STRUCT
FORCES

B62

SCHILLING W.R.,STRATEGY, POLITICS, AND DEFENSE BUDGETS. USA+45 R+D NAT/G CONSULT DELIB/GP FORCES LEGIS ACT/RES PLAN BAL/PWR LEGIT EXEC NUC/PWR RIGID/FLEX PWR...TREND COLD/WAR CONGRESS 20 EISNHWR/DD. PAGE 93 B1890

ROUTINE
POLICY

B62

SHAPIRO D.,A SELECT BIBLIOGRAPHY OF WORKS IN ENGLISH ON RUSSIAN HISTORY, 1801-1917. COM USSR STRATA FORCES EDU/PROP ADMIN REV RACE/REL ATTIT 19/20. PAGE 96 B1932

BIBLIOG
DIPLOM
COLONIAL

S62

IKLE F.C.,"POLITICAL NEGOTIATION AS A PROCESS OF MODIFYING UTILITIES." WOR+45 FACE/GP LABOR NAT/G FORCES ACT/RES EDU/PROP DETER PERCEPT ALL/VALS ...PSY NEW/IDEA HYPO/EXP GEN/METH 20. PAGE 53 B1076

ROUTINE
DECISION
DIPLOM

S62

MARTIN L.W.,"POLITICAL SETTLEMENTS AND ARMS CONTROL." COM EUR+WWI GERMANY USA+45 PROVS FORCES TOP/EX ACT/RES CREATE DOMIN LEGIT ROUTINE COERCE ATTIT RIGID/FLEX ORD/FREE PWR...METH/CNCPT RECORD GEN/LAWS 20. PAGE 70 B1410

CONCPT
ARMS/CONT

S62

MCCLELLAND C.A.,"DECISIONAL OPPORTUNITY AND POLITICAL CONTROVERSY." USA+45 NAT/G POL/PAR FORCES TOP/EX DOMIN ADMIN PEACE DRIVE ORD/FREE PWR ...DECISION SIMUL 20. PAGE 72 B1444

ACT/RES
PERCEPT
DIPLOM

B63

BOISSIER P.,HISTORIE DU COMITE INTERNATIONAL DE LA CROIX ROUGE. MOD/EUR WOR-45 CONSULT FORCES PLAN DIPLOM EDU/PROP ADMIN MORAL ORD/FREE...SOC CONCPT RECORD TIME/SEQ GEN/LAWS TOT/POP VAL/FREE 19/20. PAGE 13 B0267

INT/ORG
HEALTH
ARMS/CONT
WAR

B63

CORSON J.J.,PUBLIC ADMINISTRATION IN MODERN SOCIETY. INDUS FORCES CONTROL CENTRAL EFFICIENCY 20. PAGE 24 B0482

MGT
NAT/G
PROB/SOLV
INGP/REL

B63

ECOLE NATIONALE D'ADMIN.BIBLIOGRAPHIE SELECTIVE D'OUVRAGES DE LANGUE FRANCAISE TRAITANT DES PROBLEMES GOUVERNEMENTAUX ET ADMINISTRATIFS. NAT/G FORCES ACT/RES OP/RES PLAN PROB/SOLV BUDGET ADJUD COLONIAL LEAD 20. PAGE 32 B0651

BIBLIOG
AFR
ADMIN
EX/STRUC

B63

FISHER S.N.,THE MILITARY IN THE MIDDLE EAST: PROBLEMS IN SOCIETY AND GOVERNMENT. ISLAM USA+45 NAT/G DOMIN LEGIT COERCE ORD/FREE PWR...TIME/SEQ VAL/FREE 20. PAGE 36 B0725

EX/STRUC
FORCES

B63

GRANT D.R.,STATE AND LOCAL GOVERNMENT IN AMERICA. USA+45 FINAN LOC/G MUNIC EX/STRUC FORCES EDU/PROP ADMIN CHOOSE FEDERAL ATTIT...JURID 20. PAGE 42 B0853

PROVS
POL/PAR
LEGIS
CONSTN

B63

HIGA M.,POLITICS AND PARTIES IN POSTWAR OKINAWA. USA+45 VOL/ASSN LEGIS CONTROL LOBBY CHOOSE NAT/LISM PWR SOVEREIGN MARXISM SOCISM 20 OKINAWA CHINJAP. PAGE 50 B1008

GOV/REL
POL/PAR
ADMIN
FORCES

B63

KAST F.E.,SCIENCE, TECHNOLOGY, AND MANAGEMENT. SPACE USA+45 FORCES CONFER DETER NUC/PWR...PHIL/SCI CHARTS ANTHOL BIBLIOG 20 NASA. PAGE 58 B1179

MGT
PLAN
TEC/DEV
PROB/SOLV

B63

MCKIE R.,MALAYSIA IN FOCUS. INDONESIA WOR+45 ECO/UNDEV FINAN NAT/G POL/PAR SECT FORCES PLAN ADMIN COLONIAL COERCE DRIVE ALL/VALS...POLICY RECORD CENSUS TIME/SEQ CMN/WLTH 20. PAGE 72 B1453

S/ASIA
NAT/LISM
MALAYSIA

PEABODY R.L.,NEW PERSPECTIVES ON THE HOUSE OF
REPRESENTATIVES. AGRI FINAN SCHOOL FORCES CONFER
LEAD CHOOSE REPRESENT FEDERAL...POLICY DECISION
HOUSE/REP. PAGE 82 B1647
NEW/IDEA
LEGIS
PWR
ADMIN
B63

SCHRADER R.,SCIENCE AND POLICY. WOR+45 ECO/DEV
ECO/UNDEV R+D FORCES PLAN DIPLOM GOV/REL TECHRACY
BIBLIOG. PAGE 94 B1900
TEC/DEV
NAT/G
POLICY
ADMIN
B63

SINGH H.L.,PROBLEMS AND POLICIES OF THE BRITISH IN
INDIA, 1885-1898. INDIA UK NAT/G FORCES LEGIS
PROB/SOLV CONTROL RACE/REL ADJUST DISCRIM NAT/LISM
RIGID/FLEX...MGT 19 CIVIL/SERV. PAGE 97 B1968
COLONIAL
PWR
POLICY
ADMIN
B63

STEIN H.,AMERICAN CIVIL-MILITARY DECISION. USA+45
USA-45 EX/STRUC FORCES LEGIS TOP/EX PLAN DIPLOM
FOR/AID ATTIT 20 CONGRESS. PAGE 100 B2028
CIVMIL/REL
DECISION
WAR
BUDGET
B63

VAN SLYCK P.,PEACE: THE CONTROL OF NATIONAL POWER.
CUBA WOR+45 FINAN NAT/G FORCES PROB/SOLV TEC/DEV
BAL/PWR ADMIN CONTROL ORD/FREE...POLICY INT/LAW UN
COLD/WAR TREATY. PAGE 112 B2253
ARMS/CONT
PEACE
INT/ORG
DIPLOM
B63

EMERSON R.,"POLITICAL MODERNIZATION." WOR+45
CULTURE ECO/UNDEV NAT/G FORCES ECO/TAC DOMIN
EDU/PROP LEGIT COERCE ALL/VALS...CONCPT TIME/SEQ
VAL/FREE 20. PAGE 33 B0672
POL/PAR
ADMIN
L63

FREUND G.,"ADENAUER AND THE FUTURE OF GERMANY."
EUR+WWI FUT GERMANY/W FORCES LEGIT ADMIN ROUTINE
ATTIT DRIVE PERSON PWR...POLICY TIME/SEQ TREND
VAL/FREE 20 ADENAUER/K. PAGE 37 B0753
NAT/G
BIOG
DIPLOM
GERMANY
L63

BECHHOEFER B.G.,"UNITED NATIONS PROCEDURES IN CASE
OF VIOLATIONS OF DISARMAMENT AGREEMENTS." COM
USA+45 USSR NAT/G FORCES EX/STRUC FORCES LEGIS
BAL/PWR EDU/PROP CT/SYS ARMS/CONT ORD/FREE PWR
...POLICY STERTYP UN VAL/FREE 20. PAGE 10 B0204
INT/ORG
DELIB/GP
S63

BOWIE R.,"STRATEGY AND THE ATLANTIC ALLIANCE."
EUR+WWI VOL/ASSN BAL/PWR COERCE NUC/PWR ATTIT
ORD/FREE PWR...DECISION GEN/LAWS NATO COLD/WAR 20.
PAGE 14 B0287
FORCES
ROUTINE
S63

MODELSKI G.,"STUDY OF ALLIANCES." WOR+45 WOR-45
INT/ORG NAT/G FORCES LEGIT ADMIN CHOOSE ALL/VALS
PWR SKILL...INT/LAW CONCPT GEN/LAWS 20 TREATY.
PAGE 74 B1495
VOL/ASSN
CON/ANAL
DIPLOM
S63

MORGENTHAU H.J.,"THE POLITICAL CONDITIONS FOR AN
INTERNATIONAL POLICE FORCE." FUT WOR+45 CREATE
LEGIT ADMIN PEACE ORD/FREE 20. PAGE 75 B1524
INT/ORG
FORCES
ARMS/CONT
DETER
S63

NADLER E.B.,"SOME ECONOMIC DISADVANTAGES OF THE
ARMS RACE." USA+45 INDUS R+D FORCES PLAN TEC/DEV
ECO/TAC FOR/AID EDU/PROP PWR WEALTH...TREND
COLD/WAR 20. PAGE 77 B1552
ECO/DEV
MGT
BAL/PAY
S63

RUSTOW D.A.,"THE MILITARY IN MIDDLE EASTERN SOCIETY
AND POLITICS." FUT ISLAM CONSTN SOCIETY FACE/GP
NAT/G POL/PAR PROF/ORG CONSULT DOMIN ADMIN EXEC
REGION COERCE NAT/LISM ATTIT DRIVE PERSON ORD/FREE
PWR...POLICY CONCPT OBS STERTYP 20. PAGE 92 B1860
FORCES
ELITES
S63

SHIMKIN D.B.,"STRUCTURE OF SOVIET POWER." COM FUT
USA+45 USSR WOR+45 NAT/G FORCES ECO/DEV DOMIN EXEC
COERCE CHOOSE ATTIT WEALTH...TIME/SEQ COLD/WAR
TOT/POP VAL/FREE 20. PAGE 96 B1948
PWR
S63

STANLEY T.W.,"DECENTRALIZING NUCLEAR CONTROL IN
NATO." EUR+WWI USA+45 ELITES FORCES ACT/RES ATTIT
ORD/FREE PWR...NEW/IDEA HYPO/EXP TOT/POP 20 NATO.
PAGE 100 B2022
INT/ORG
EX/STRUC
NUC/PWR
B64

BANTON M.,THE POLICEMAN IN THE COMMUNITY. UK USA+45
STRUCT PROF/ORG WORKER LOBBY ROUTINE COERCE CROWD
GP/REL ADJUST DISCRIM PERCEPT 20. PAGE 9 B0181
FORCES
ADMIN
ROLE
RACE/REL
B64

BLACKSTOCK P.W.,THE STRATEGY OF SUBVERSION. USA+45
FORCES EDU/PROP ADMIN COERCE GOV/REL...DECISION MGT
20 DEPT/DEFEN CIA DEPT/STATE. PAGE 12 B0247
ORD/FREE
DIPLOM
CONTROL
B64

COTTRELL A.J.,THE POLITICS OF THE ATLANTIC
ALLIANCE. EUR+WWI USA+45 INT/ORG NAT/G DELIB/GP
EX/STRUC BAL/PWR DIPLOM REGION DETER ATTIT ORD/FREE
...CONCPT RECORD GEN/LAWS GEN/METH NATO 20. PAGE 24
B0493
VOL/ASSN
FORCES
B64

GESELLSCHAFT RECHTSVERGLEICH,BIBLIOGRAPHIE DES
DEUTSCHEN RECHTS (BIBLIOGRAPHY OF GERMAN LAW,
TRANS. BY COURTLAND PETERSON). GERMANY FINAN INDUS
BIBLIOG/A
JURID
CONSTN

LABOR SECT FORCES CT/SYS PARL/PROC CRIME...INT/LAW
SOC NAT/COMP 20. PAGE 39 B0794
ADMIN
B64

GRZYBOWSKI K.,THE SOCIALIST COMMONWEALTH OF
NATIONS: ORGANIZATIONS AND INSTITUTIONS. FORCES
DIPLOM INT/TRADE ADJUD ADMIN LEAD WAR MARXISM
SOCISM...BIBLIOG 20 COMECON WARSAW/P. PAGE 44 B0898
INT/LAW
COM
REGION
INT/ORG
B64

JACKSON H.M.,THE SECRETARY OF STATE AND THE
AMBASSADOR* JACKSON SUBCOMMITTEE PAPERS ON THE
CONDUCT OF AMERICAN FOREIGN POLICY. USA+45 NAT/G
FORCES ACT/RES OP/RES EDU/PROP CENTRAL EFFICIENCY
ORD/FREE...OBS RECORD ANTHOL CONGRESS PRESIDENT.
PAGE 55 B1107
GOV/REL
DIPLOM
ADMIN
EX/STRUC
B64

PARET P.,FRENCH REVOLUTIONARY WARFARE FROM
INDOCHINA TO ALGERIA* THE ANALYSIS OF A POLITICAL
AND MILITARY DOCTRINE. ALGERIA VIETNAM FORCES
OP/RES TEC/DEV ROUTINE REV ATTIT...PSY BIBLIOG.
PAGE 81 B1632
FRANCE
GUERRILLA
GEN/LAWS
B64

RAYMOND J.,POWER AT THE PENTAGON (1ST ED.). ELITES
NAT/G PLAN EDU/PROP ARMS/CONT DETER WAR WEAPON
...TIME/SEQ 20 PENTAGON MCNAMARA/R. PAGE 86 B1746
PWR
CIVMIL/REL
EX/STRUC
FORCES
B64

REDLICH F.,THE GERMAN MILITARY ENTERPRISER AND HIS
WORK FORCE. CHRIST-17C GERMANY ELITES SOCIETY FINAN
ECO/TAC CIVMIL/REL GP/REL INGP/REL...HIST/WRIT
METH/COMP 14/17. PAGE 87 B1760
EX/STRUC
FORCES
PROFIT
WORKER
B64

RIDDLE D.H.,THE TRUMAN COMMITTEE: A STUDY IN
CONGRESSIONAL RESPONSIBILITY. INDUS FORCES OP/RES
DOMIN ADMIN LEAD PARL/PROC WAR PRODUC SUPEGO
...BIBLIOG CONGRESS. PAGE 88 B1778
LEGIS
DELIB/GP
CONFER
B64

RIES J.C.,THE MANAGEMENT OF DEFENSE: ORGANIZATION
AND CONTROL OF THE US ARMED SERVICES. PROF/ORG
DELIB/GP EX/STRUC LEGIS GOV/REL PERS/REL CENTRAL
RATIONAL PWR...POLICY TREND GOV/COMP BIBLIOG.
PAGE 88 B1782
FORCES
ACT/RES
DECISION
CONTROL
B64

RUSSELL R.B.,UNITED NATIONS EXPERIENCE WITH
MILITARY FORCES: POLITICAL AND LEGAL ASPECTS. AFR
KOREA WOR+45 LEGIS PROB/SOLV ADMIN CONTROL
EFFICIENCY PEACE...POLICY INT/LAW BIBLIOG UN.
PAGE 92 B1857
FORCES
DIPLOM
SANCTION
ORD/FREE
B64

TOMPKINS D.C.,PROBATION SINCE WORLD WAR II. USA+45
FORCES ADMIN ROUTINE PERS/REL AGE...CRIMLGY HEAL
20. PAGE 105 B2118
BIBLIOG
PUB/INST
ORD/FREE
CRIME
B64

US SENATE COMM GOVT OPERATIONS,THE SECRETARY OF
STATE AND THE AMBASSADOR. USA+45 CHIEF CONSULT
EX/STRUC FORCES PLAN ADMIN EXEC INGP/REL ROLE
...ANTHOL 20 PRESIDENT DEPT/STATE. PAGE 110 B2215
DIPLOM
DELIB/GP
NAT/G
B64

US SENATE COMM GOVT OPERATIONS,ADMINISTRATION OF
NATIONAL SECURITY. USA+45 CHIEF TOP/EX PLAN DIPLOM
CONTROL PEACE...POLICY DECISION 20 PRESIDENT
CONGRESS. PAGE 110 B2216
ADMIN
FORCES
ORD/FREE
NAT/G
B64

WHEELER-BENNETT J.W.,THE NEMESIS OF POWER (2ND
ED.). EUR+WWI GERMANY TOP/EX TEC/DEV ADMIN WAR
PERS/REL RIGID/FLEX ROLE ORD/FREE PWR FASCISM 20
HITLER/A. PAGE 116 B2332
FORCES
NAT/G
GP/REL
STRUCT
B64

WRAITH R.,CORRUPTION IN DEVELOPING COUNTRIES.
NIGERIA UK LAW ELITES STRATA INDUS LOC/G NAT/G SECT
FORCES EDU/PROP ADMIN PWR WEALTH 18/20. PAGE 118
B2377
ECO/UNDEV
CRIME
SANCTION
ATTIT
B64

ROTBERG R.,"THE FEDERATION MOVEMENT IN BRITISH EAST
AND CENTRAL AFRICA." AFR RHODESIA UGANDA ECO/UNDEV
NAT/G POL/PAR FORCES DOMIN LEGIT ADMIN COERCE ATTIT
...CONCPT TREND 20 TANGANYIKA. PAGE 91 B1831
VOL/ASSN
PWR
REGION
L64

JOHNSON K.F.,"CAUSAL FACTORS IN LATIN AMERICAN
POLITICAL INSTABILITY." CULTURE NAT/G VOL/ASSN
EX/STRUC FORCES EDU/PROP LEGIT ADMIN COERCE REV
ATTIT KNOWL PWR...STYLE RECORD CHARTS WORK 20.
PAGE 57 B1144
L/A+17C
PERCEPT
ELITES
S64

LOW D.A.,"LION RAMPANT." EUR+WWI MOD/EUR S/ASIA
ECO/UNDEV NAT/G FORCES TEC/DEV ECO/TAC LEGIT ADMIN
COLONIAL COERCE ORD/FREE RESPECT 19/20. PAGE 67
B1344
AFR
DOMIN
DIPLOM
UK
S64

NORGREN P.H.,"TOWARD FAIR EMPLOYMENT." USA+45 LAW
STRATA LABOR NAT/G FORCES ACT/RES ADMIN ATTIT
...POLICY BIBLIOG 20 NEGRO. PAGE 79 B1588
RACE/REL
DISCRIM
WORKER
MGT
C64

BARNETT V.M. JR.,THE REPRESENTATION OF THE UNITED
STATES ABROAD* REVISED EDITION. ECO/UNDEV ACADEM
USA+45
DIPLOM
B65

INT/ORG FORCES ACT/RES CREATE OP/RES FOR/AID REGION ADMIN
CENTRAL...CLASSIF ANTHOL. PAGE 9 B0189
B65

CAMPBELL G.A.,THE CIVIL SERVICE IN BRITAIN (2ND   ADMIN
ED.). UK DELIB/GP FORCES WORKER CREATE PLAN   LEGIS
...POLICY AUD/VIS 19/20 CIVIL/SERV. PAGE 18 B0370   NAT/G
  FINAN
B65

ECCLES H.E.,MILITARY CONCEPTS AND PHILOSOPHY.   PLAN
USA+45 STRUCT EXEC ROUTINE COERCE WAR CIVMIL/REL   DRIVE
COST...OBS GEN/LAWS COLD/WAR. PAGE 32 B0648   LEAD
  FORCES
B65

ETZIONI A.,POLITICAL UNIFICATION* A COMPARATIVE   INT/ORG
STUDY OF LEADERS AND FORCES. EUR+WWI ISLAM L/A+17C   FORCES
WOR+45 ELITES STRATA EXEC WEALTH...TIME/SEQ TREND   ECO/TAC
SOC/EXP. PAGE 34 B0686   REGION
B65

GREGG J.L.,POLITICAL PARTIES AND PARTY SYSTEMS IN   LEAD
GUATEMALA, 1944-1963. GUATEMALA L/A+17C EX/STRUC   POL/PAR
FORCES CREATE CONTROL REV CHOOSE PWR...TREND   NAT/G
IDEA/COMP 20. PAGE 43 B0872   CHIEF
B65

HOWE R.,THE STORY OF SCOTLAND YARD: A HISTORY OF   CRIMLGY
THE CID FROM THE EARLIEST TIMES TO THE PRESENT DAY.   CRIME
UK MUNIC EDU/PROP 6/20 SCOT/YARD. PAGE 52 B1051   FORCES
  ADMIN
B65

LYONS G.M.,SCHOOLS FOR STRATEGY* EDUCATION AND   ACADEM
RESEARCH IN NATIONAL SECURITY AFFAIRS. USA+45 FINAN   ACT/RES
NAT/G VOL/ASSN FORCES TEC/DEV ADMIN WAR...GP/COMP   INTELL
IDEA/COMP PERS/COMP COLD/WAR. PAGE 67 B1351
B65

MELMANS S.,OUR DEPLETED SOCIETY. SPACE USA+45   CIVMIL/REL
ECO/DEV FORCES BUDGET ECO/TAC ADMIN WEAPON   INDUS
EFFICIENCY 20 COLD/WAR. PAGE 73 B1465   EDU/PROP
  CONTROL
B65

NORDEN A.,WAR AND NAZI CRIMINALS IN WEST GERMANY: FASCIST
STATE, ECONOMY, ADMINISTRATION, ARMY, JUSTICE,   WAR
SCIENCE. GERMANY GERMANY/W MOD/EUR ECO/DEV ACADEM   NAT/G
EX/STRUC FORCES DOMIN ADMIN CT/SYS...POLICY MAJORIT   TOP/EX
PACIFIST 20. PAGE 78 B1587
B65

PURCELL V.,THE MEMOIRS OF A MALAYAN OFFICIAL.   BIOG
MALAYSIA UK ECO/UNDEV INDUS LABOR EDU/PROP COLONIAL   ADMIN
CT/SYS WAR NAT/LISM TOTALISM ORD/FREE SOVEREIGN 20   JURID
UN CIVIL/SERV. PAGE 85 B1721   FORCES
B65

PUSTAY J.S.,COUNTER-INSURGENCY WARFARE. COM USA+45   FORCES
LOC/G NAT/G ACT/RES EDU/PROP ADMIN COERCE ATTIT   PWR
...CONCPT MARX/KARL 20. PAGE 85 B1722   GUERRILLA
B65

REDFORD D.R.,POLITICS AND GOVERNMENT IN THE UNITED   NAT/G
STATES. USA+45 USA-45 LOC/G PROVS FORCES DIPLOM   POL/PAR
CT/SYS LOBBY...JURID SUPREME/CT PRESIDENT. PAGE 87   EX/STRUC
B1751   LEGIS
B65

SCOTT A.M.,THE REVOLUTION IN STATECRAFT: INFORMAL   DIPLOM
PENETRATION. WOR+45 WOR-45 CULTURE INT/ORG FORCES   EDU/PROP
ECO/TAC ROUTINE...BIBLIOG 20. PAGE 95 B1918   FOR/AID
B65

TYBOUT R.A.,ECONOMICS OF RESEARCH AND DEVELOPMENT.   R+D
ECO/DEV ECO/UNDEV INDUS PROFIT DECISION. PAGE 106   FORCES
B2141   ADMIN
  DIPLOM
B65

US SENATE COMM GOVT OPERATIONS,ORGANIZATION OF   ADMIN
FEDERAL EXECUTIVE DEPARTMENTS AND AGENCIES: REPORT   EX/STRUC
OF MARCH 23, 1965. USA+45 FORCES LEGIS DIPLOM   GOV/REL
ROUTINE CIVMIL/REL EFFICIENCY FEDERAL...MGT STAT.   ORG/CHARTS
PAGE 110 B2217
B65

VIORST M.,HOSTILE ALLIES: FDR AND DE GAULLE.   TOP/EX
EUR+WWI USA-45 ELITES NAT/G VOL/ASSN FORCES LEGIS   PWR
PLAN LEGIT ADMIN COERCE PERSON...BIOG TIME/SEQ 20   WAR
ROOSEVLT/F DEGAULLE/C. PAGE 112 B2263   FRANCE
B65

YOUNG C.,POLITICS IN THE CONGO* DECOLONIZATION AND   BELGIUM
INDEPENDENCE. ELITES STRATA FORCES ADMIN REV   COLONIAL
RACE/REL FEDERAL SOVEREIGN...OBS INT CHARTS   NAT/LISM
CONGO/LEOP. PAGE 118 B2391
L65

MATTHEWS D.G.,"A CURRENT BIBLIOGRAPHY ON ETHIOPIAN   BIBLIOG/A
AFFAIRS: A SELECT BIBLIOGRAPHY FROM 1950-1964."   ADMIN
ETHIOPIA LAW CULTURE ECO/UNDEV INDUS LABOR SECT   POL/PAR
FORCES DIPLOM CIVMIL/REL RACE/REL...LING STAT 20.   NAT/G
PAGE 71 B1428
S65

BROWN S.,"AN ALTERNATIVE TO THE GRAND DESIGN."   VOL/ASSN
EUR+WWI FUT USA+45 INT/ORG NAT/G EX/STRUC FORCES   CONCPT
CREATE BAL/PWR DOMIN RIGID/FLEX ORD/FREE PWR   DIPLOM
...NEW/IDEA RECORD EEC NATO 20. PAGE 16 B0327
B66

AARON T.J.,THE CONTROL OF POLICE DISCRETION: THE   CONTROL
DANISH EXPERIENCE. DENMARK LAW CREATE ADMIN   FORCES

INGP/REL SUPEGO PWR 20 OMBUDSMAN. PAGE 2 B0049   REPRESENT
  PROB/SOLV
B66

ANDERSON D.L.,MUNICIPAL PUBLIC RELATIONS (1ST ED.).   MUNIC
USA+45 SOCIETY CONSULT FORCES PRESS ADMIN...CHARTS   INGP/REL
BIBLIOG/A 20. PAGE 4 B0092   EDU/PROP
  ATTIT
B66

BARBER W.F.,INTERNAL SECURITY AND MILITARY POWER*   L/A+17C
COUNTERINSURGENCY AND CIVIC ACTION IN LATIN   FORCES
AMERICA. ECO/UNDEV CREATE ADMIN REV ATTIT   ORD/FREE
RIGID/FLEX MARXISM...INT BIBLIOG OAS. PAGE 9 B0183   TASK
B66

EPSTEIN F.T.,THE AMERICAN BIBLIOGRAPHY OF RUSSIAN   BIBLIOG
AND EAST EUROPEAN STUDIES FOR 1964. USSR LOC/G   COM
NAT/G POL/PAR FORCES ADMIN ARMS/CONT...JURID CONCPT   MARXISM
20 UN. PAGE 33 B0678   DIPLOM
B66

MACFARQUHAR R.,CHINA UNDER MAO: POLITICS TAKES   ECO/UNDEV
COMMAND. CHINA/COM COM AGRI INDUS CHIEF FORCES   TEC/DEV
DIPLOM INT/TRADE EDU/PROP TASK REV ADJUST...ANTHOL   ECO/TAC
20 MAO. PAGE 67 B1359   ADMIN
B66

SAPIN B.M.,THE MAKING OF UNITED STATES FOREIGN   DIPLOM
POLICY. USA+45 INT/ORG DELIB/GP FORCES PLAN ECO/TAC   EX/STRUC
CIVMIL/REL PRESIDENT. PAGE 92 B1868   DECISION
  NAT/G
B66

US DEPARTMENT OF THE ARMY,COMMUNIST CHINA: A   BIBLIOG/A
STRATEGIC SURVEY: A BIBLIOGRAPHY (PAMPHLET NO.   MARXISM
20-67). CHINA/COM COM INDIA USSR NAT/G POL/PAR   S/ASIA
EX/STRUC FORCES NUC/PWR REV ATTIT...POLICY GEOG   DIPLOM
CHARTS. PAGE 108 B2184
B66

US HOUSE COMM GOVT OPERATIONS,AN INVESTIGATION OF   FOR/AID
THE US ECONOMIC AND MILITARY ASSISTANCE PROGRAMS IN   ECO/UNDEV
VIETNAM. USA+45 VIETNAM/S SOCIETY CONSTRUC FINAN   WAR
FORCES BUDGET INT/TRADE PEACE HEALTH...MGT   INSPECT
HOUSE/REP AID. PAGE 108 B2191
B66

US SENATE COMM ON FOREIGN REL,HEARINGS ON S 2859   FOR/AID
AND S 2861. USA+45 WOR+45 FORCES BUDGET CAP/ISM   DIPLOM
ADMIN DETER WEAPON TOTALISM...NAT/COMP 20 UN   ORD/FREE
CONGRESS. PAGE 110 B2221   ECO/UNDEV
B66

WHITNAH D.R.,SAFER SKYWAYS. DIST/IND DELIB/GP   ADMIN
FORCES TOP/EX WORKER TEC/DEV ROUTINE WAR CIVMIL/REL   NAT/G
COST...TIME/SEQ 20 FAA CAB. PAGE 116 B2342   AIR
  GOV/REL
S66

AUSLAND J.C.,"CRISIS MANAGEMENT* BERLIN, CYPRUS,   OP/RES
LAOS." CYPRUS LAOS FORCES CREATE PLAN EDU/PROP TASK   DIPLOM
CENTRAL PERSON RIGID/FLEX...DECISION MGT 20 BERLIN   RISK
KENNEDY/JF MCNAMARA/R RUSK. PAGE 7 B0148   ADMIN
S66

PALMER M.,"THE UNITED ARAB REPUBLIC* AN ASSESSMENT   UAR
OF ITS FAILURE." ELITES ECO/UNDEV POL/PAR FORCES   SYRIA
ECO/TAC RUMOR ADMIN EXEC EFFICIENCY ATTIT SOCISM   REGION
...INT NASSER/G. PAGE 81 B1628   FEDERAL
S66

ZUCKERT E.M.,"THE SERVICE SECRETARY* HAS HE A   OBS
USEFUL ROLE?" USA+45 TOP/EX PLAN ADMIN EXEC DETER   OP/RES
NUC/PWR WEAPON...MGT RECORD MCNAMARA/R. PAGE 119   DIPLOM
B2407   FORCES
C66

TARLING N.,"A CONCISE HISTORY OF SOUTHEAST ASIA."   COLONIAL
BURMA CAMBODIA LAOS S/ASIA THAILAND VIETNAM   DOMIN
ECO/UNDEV POL/PAR FORCES ADMIN REV WAR CIVMIL/REL   INT/TRADE
ORD/FREE MARXISM SOCISM 13/20. PAGE 103 B2080   NAT/LISM
B67

BLUMBERG A.S.,CRIMINAL JUSTICE. USA+45 CLIENT LAW   JURID
LOC/G FORCES JUDGE ACT/RES LEGIT ADMIN RATIONAL   CT/SYS
MYTH. PAGE 13 B0259   PROF/ORG
  CRIME
B67

ENKE S.,DEFENSE MANAGEMENT. USA+45 R+D FORCES   DECISION
WORKER PLAN ECO/TAC ADMIN NUC/PWR BAL/PAY UTIL   DELIB/GP
WEALTH...MGT DEPT/DEFEN. PAGE 33 B0675   EFFICIENCY
  BUDGET
B67

HEWITT W.H.,ADMINISTRATION OF CRIMINAL JUSTICE IN   CRIME
NEW YORK. LAW PROB/SOLV ADJUD ADMIN...CRIMLGY   ROLE
CHARTS T 20 NEW/YORK. PAGE 49 B1001   CT/SYS
  FORCES
B67

HOROWITZ I.L.,THE RISE AND FALL OF PROJECT CAMELOT: NAT/G
STUDIES IN THE RELATIONSHIP BETWEEN SOCIAL SCIENCE   ACADEM
AND PRACTICAL POLITICS. USA+45 WOR+45 CULTURE   ACT/RES
FORCES LEGIS EXEC CIVMIL/REL KNOWL...POLICY SOC   GP/REL
METH/CNCPT 20. PAGE 51 B1043
B67

LENG S.C.,JUSTICE IN COMMUNIST CHINA: A SURVEY OF   CT/SYS
THE JUDICIAL SYSTEM OF THE CHINESE PEOPLE'S   ADJUD
REPUBLIC. CHINA/COM LAW CONSTN LOC/G NAT/G PROF/ORG   JURID
CONSULT FORCES ADMIN CRIME ORD/FREE...BIBLIOG 20   MARXISM
MAO. PAGE 64 B1290

MACKINTOSH J.M.,JUGGERNAUT. USSR NAT/G POL/PAR ADMIN LEAD CIVMIL/REL COST TOTALISM PWR MARXISM ...GOV/COMP 20. PAGE 68 B1364
WAR FORCES COM PROF/ORG
B67

MILNE R.S.,GOVERNMENT AND POLITICS IN MALAYSIA. INDONESIA MALAYSIA LOC/G EX/STRUC FORCES DIPLOM GP/REL 20 SINGAPORE. PAGE 74 B1489
NAT/G LEGIS ADMIN
B67

NIEDERHOFFER A.,BEHIND THE SHIELD; THE POLICE IN URBAN SOCIETY. USA+45 LEGIT ADJUD ROUTINE COERCE CRIME ADJUST...INT CHARTS 20 NEWYORK/C. PAGE 78 B1582
FORCES PERSON SOCIETY ATTIT
B67

RALSTON D.B.,THE ARMY OF THE REPUBLIC; THE PLACE OF THE MILITARY IN THE POLITICAL EVOLUTION OF FRANCE 1871-1914. FRANCE MOD/EUR EX/STRUC LEGIS TOP/EX DIPLOM ADMIN WAR GP/REL ROLE...BIBLIOG 19/20. PAGE 86 B1730
FORCES NAT/G CIVMIL/REL POLICY
B67

RAWLINSON J.L.,CHINA'S STRUGGLE FOR NAVAL DEVELOPMENT 1839-1895. ASIA DIPLOM ADMIN WAR ...BIBLIOG DICTIONARY 19 CHINJAP. PAGE 86 B1745
SEA FORCES PWR
B67

SABLE M.H.,A GUIDE TO LATIN AMERICAN STUDIES (2 VOLS). CONSTN FINAN INT/ORG LABOR MUNIC POL/PAR FORCES CAP/ISM FOR/AID ADMIN MARXISM SOCISM OAS. PAGE 92 B1861
BIBLIOG/A L/A+17C DIPLOM NAT/LISM
B67

SCHAEFER W.V.,THE SUSPECT AND SOCIETY: CRIMINAL PROCEDURE AND CONVERGING CONSTITUTIONAL DOCTRINES. USA+45 TEC/DEV LOBBY ROUTINE SANCTION...INT 20. PAGE 93 B1879
CRIME FORCES CONSTN JURID
B67

US DEPARTMENT OF THE ARMY,CIVILIAN IN PEACE, SOLDIER IN WAR: A BIBLIOGRAPHIC SURVEY OF THE ARMY AND AIR NATIONAL GUARD (PAMPHLET, NOS. 130-2). USA+45 USA-45 LOC/G NAT/G PROVS LEGIS PLAN ADMIN ATTIT ORD/FREE...POLICY 19/20. PAGE 108 B2185
BIBLIOG/A FORCES ROLE DIPLOM
B67

WARREN S.,THE AMERICAN PRESIDENT. POL/PAR FORCES LEGIS DIPLOM ECO/TAC ADMIN EXEC PWR...ANTHOL 18/20 ROOSEVLT/F KENNEDY/JF JOHNSON/LB TRUMAN/HS WILSON/W. PAGE 114 B2297
CHIEF LEAD NAT/G CONSTN
B67

WATERS M.,THE UNITED NATIONS* INTERNATIONAL ORGANIZATION AND ADMINISTRATION. WOR+45 EX/STRUC FORCES DIPLOM LEAD REGION ARMS/CONT REPRESENT INGP/REL ROLE...METH/COMP ANTHOL 20 UN LEAGUE/NAT. PAGE 114 B2301
CONSTN INT/ORG ADMIN ADJUD
L67

COHEN M.,"THE DEMISE OF UNEF." CONSTN DIPLOM ADMIN AGREE LEAD COERCE 20 UNEF U/THANT HAMMARSK/D. PAGE 22 B0445
INT/ORG FORCES PEACE POLICY
S67

BEASLEY W.G.,"POLITICS AND THE SAMURAI CLASS STRUCTURE IN SATSUMA, 18581868." STRATA FORCES DOMIN LEGIT ADMIN LEAD 19 CHINJAP. PAGE 10 B0202
ELITES STRUCT ATTIT PRIVIL
S67

HSUEH C.T.,"THE CULTURAL REVOLUTION AND LEADERSHIP CRISIS IN COMMUNIST CHINA." CHINA/COM POL/PAR EX/STRUC FORCES EDU/PROP ATTIT PWR...POLICY 20. PAGE 52 B1054
LEAD REV CULTURE MARXISM
S67

JONES G.S.,"STRATEGIC PLANNING." USA+45 EX/STRUC FORCES DETER WAR 20 PRESIDENT. PAGE 57 B1150
PLAN DECISION DELIB/GP POLICY
S67

LALL B.G.,"GAPS IN THE ABM DEBATE." NAT/G DIPLOM DETER CIVMIL/REL 20. PAGE 62 B1251
NUC/PWR ARMS/CONT EX/STRUC FORCES
S67

O'DELL J.H.,"THE JULY REBELLIONS AND THE 'MILITARY STATE'." USA+45 VIETNAM STRATA CHIEF WORKER COLONIAL EXEC CROWD CIVMIL/REL RACE/REL TOTALISM ...WELF/ST PACIFIST 20 NEGRO JOHNSON/LB PRESIDENT CIV/RIGHTS. PAGE 79 B1599
PWR NAT/G COERCE FORCES
S67

RAI H.,"DISTRICT MAGISTRATE AND POLICE SUPERINTENDENT IN INDIA: THE CONTROVERSY OF DUAL CONTROL" INDIA LAW PROVS ADMIN PWR 19/20. PAGE 86 B1729
STRUCT CONTROL ROLE FORCES
S67

SHOEMAKER R.L.,"JAPANESE ARMY AND THE WEST." ASIA ELITES EX/STRUC DIPLOM DOMIN EDU/PROP COERCE ATTIT AUTHORIT PWR 1/20 CHINJAP. PAGE 96 B1950
FORCES TEC/DEV WAR TOTALISM
S67

TACKABERRY R.B.,"ORGANIZING AND TRAINING PEACE-KEEPING FORCES* THE CANADIAN VIEW." CANADA PLAN DIPLOM CONFER ADJUD ADMIN CIVMIL/REL 20 UN.
PEACE FORCES INT/ORG

PAGE 102 B2069
CONSULT
S67

TURNER F.C. JR.,"EXPERIMENT IN INTER-AMERICAN PEACE-KEEPING." DOMIN/REP ADMIN ROUTINE REV ORD/FREE OAS 20. PAGE 106 B2137
FORCES ADJUD PEACE
S67

WALLER D.J.,"CHINA: RED OR EXPERT." CHINA/COM INTELL DOMIN REV ATTIT MARXISM 20. PAGE 113 B2283
CONTROL FORCES ADMIN POL/PAR

FORD A.G. B0737

FORD FOUNDATION....SEE FORD/FOUND

FORD FOUNDATION B0739

FORD/FOUND....FORD FOUNDATION

FOREIGN AID....SEE FOR/AID

FOREIGN TRADE....SEE INT/TRADE

FOREIGNREL....UNITED STATES SENATE COMMITTEE ON FOREIGN RELATIONS

FORGAC A.A. B0740

FORGN/SERV....FOREIGN SERVICE

FORMOSA....FORMOSA, PRE-1949; FOR POST-1949, SEE TAIWAN; SEE ALSO ASIA, CHINA

FORRESTAL J. B0741

FORTES A.B. B0742

FORTRAN....FORTRAN - COMPUTER LANGUAGE

FOSS P. B0743

FOSS P.O. B0744

FOSTER P. B0438

FOSTER/G....G. FOSTER

FOURIER/FM....FRANCOIS MARIE CHARLES FOURIER

FOWLER E.P. B1317

FOX G.H. B0745

FOX K.A. B0746

FOX R.G. B0747

FOX/CJ....CHARLES J. FOX

FOX/INDIAN....FOX INDIANS

FPC....U.S. FEDERAL POWER COMMISSION

FRANCE....SEE ALSO APPROPRIATE TIME/SPACE/CULTURE INDEX

BIBLIO, CATALOGUE DES OUVRAGES PARUS EN LANGUE FRANCAISE DANS LE MONDE ENTIER. FRANCE WOR+45 ADMIN LEAD PERSON...SOC 20. PAGE 1 B0008
BIBLIOG NAT/G DIPLOM ECO/DEV
N

REVUE FRANCAISE DE SCIENCE POLITIQUE. FRANCE UK ...BIBLIOG/A 20. PAGE 1 B0022
NAT/G DIPLOM CONCPT ROUTINE
N

CATHERINE R.,LA REVUE ADMINISTRATIVE. FRANCE LAW NAT/G LEGIS...JURID BIBLIOG/A 20. PAGE 19 B0393
ADMIN MGT FINAN METH/COMP
N

MINISTERE DE L'EDUC NATIONALE,CATALOGUE DES THESES DE DOCTORAT SOUTENNES DEVANT LES UNIVERSITAIRES FRANCAISES. FRANCE LAW DIPLOM ADMIN...HUM SOC 20. PAGE 74 B1490
BIBLIOG ACADEM KNOWL NAT/G
B00

SANDERSON E.,AFRICA IN THE NINETEENTH CENTURY. FRANCE UK EXTR/IND FORCES LEGIS ADMIN WAR DISCRIM ORD/FREE...GEOG GP/COMP SOC/INTEG 19. PAGE 92 B1867
COLONIAL AFR DIPLOM
B18

WILSON W.,THE STATE: ELEMENTS OF HISTORICAL AND PRACTICAL POLITICS. FRANCE GERMANY ITALY UK USSR CONSTN EX/STRUC LEGIS CT/SYS WAR PWR...POLICY GOV/COMP 20. PAGE 117 B2363
NAT/G JURID CONCPT NAT/COMP
B29

ROBERTS S.H.,HISTORY OF FRENCH COLONIAL POLICY. AFR
INT/ORG

ASIA L/A+17C S/ASIA CULTURE ECO/DEV ECO/UNDEV FINAN ACT/RES
NAT/G PLAN ECO/TAC DOMIN ROUTINE SOVEREIGN...OBS FRANCE
HIST/WRIT TREND CHARTS VAL/FREE 19/20. PAGE 89 COLONIAL
B1796

B31
BORCHARD E.H.,GUIDE TO THE LAW AND LEGAL LITERATURE BIBLIOG/A
OF FRANCE. FRANCE FINAN INDUS LABOR SECT LEGIS LAW
ADMIN COLONIAL CRIME OWN...INT/LAW 20. PAGE 14 CONSTN
B0277 METH

B33
ENSOR R.C.K.,COURTS AND JUDGES IN FRANCE, GERMANY, CT/SYS
AND ENGLAND. FRANCE GERMANY UK LAW PROB/SOLV ADMIN EX/STRUC
ROUTINE CRIME ROLE...METH/COMP 20 CIVIL/LAW. ADJUD
PAGE 33 B0676 NAT/COMP

B34
DE CENIVAL P.,BIBLIOGRAPHIE MAROCAINE: 1923-1933. BIBLIOG/A
FRANCE MOROCCO SECT ADMIN LEAD GP/REL ATTIT...LING ISLAM
20. PAGE 27 B0551 NAT/G
COLONIAL

B38
PETTEE G.S.,THE PROCESS OF REVOLUTION. COM FRANCE COERCE
ITALY MOD/EUR RUSSIA SPAIN WOR-45 ELITES INTELL CONCPT
SOCIETY STRATA STRUCT INT/ORG NAT/G POL/PAR ACT/RES REV
PLAN EDU/PROP LEGIT EXEC...SOC MYTH TIME/SEQ
TOT/POP 18/20. PAGE 82 B1664

B39
ANDERSON W.,LOCAL GOVERNMENT IN EUROPE. FRANCE GOV/COMP
GERMANY ITALY UK USSR MUNIC PROVS ADMIN GOV/REL NAT/COMP
CENTRAL SOVEREIGN 20. PAGE 5 B0099 LOC/G
CONSTN

B44
BARKER E.,THE DEVELOPMENT OF PUBLIC SERVICES IN GOV/COMP
WESTERN WUROPE: 1660-1930. FRANCE GERMANY UK SCHOOL ADMIN
CONTROL REPRESENT ROLE...WELF/ST 17/20. PAGE 9 EX/STRUC
B0185

B45
CONOVER H.F.,THE GOVERNMENTS OF THE MAJOR FOREIGN BIBLIOG
POWERS: A BIBLIOGRAPHY. FRANCE GERMANY ITALY UK NAT/G
USSR CONSTN LOC/G POL/PAR EX/STRUC FORCES ADMIN DIPLOM
CT/SYS CIVMIL/REL TOTALISM...POLICY 19/20. PAGE 23
B0464

B47
CONOVER H.F.,NON-SELF-GOVERNING AREAS. BELGIUM BIBLIOG/A
FRANCE ITALY UK WOR+45 CULTURE ECO/UNDEV INT/ORG COLONIAL
LOC/G NAT/G ECO/TAC INT/TRADE ADMIN HEALTH...SOC DIPLOM
UN. PAGE 23 B0465

B47
CROCKER W.R.,ON GOVERNING COLONIES: BEING AN COLONIAL
OUTLINE OF THE REAL ISSUES AND A COMPARISON OF THE POLICY
BRITISH, FRENCH, AND BELGIAN... AFR BELGIUM FRANCE GOV/COMP
UK CULTURE SOVEREIGN...OBS 20. PAGE 25 B0505 ADMIN

B48
ROSSITER C.L.,CONSTITUTIONAL DICTATORSHIP; CRISIS NAT/G
GOVERNMENT IN THE MODERN DEMOCRACIES. FRANCE AUTHORIT
GERMANY USA-45 WOR-45 EX/STRUC BAL/PWR CONTROL CONSTN
COERCE WAR CENTRAL ORD/FREE...DECISION 19/20. TOTALISM
PAGE 90 B1828

B49
WALINE M.,LE CONTROLE JURIDICTIONNEL DE JURID
L'ADMINISTRATION. BELGIUM FRANCE UAR JUDGE BAL/PWR ADMIN
ADJUD CONTROL CT/SYS...GP/COMP 20. PAGE 113 B2277 PWR
ORD/FREE

B51
UNESCO,REPERTOIRE DES BIBLIOTHEQUES DE FRANCE: BIBLIOG
CENTRES ET SERVICES DE DOCUMENTATION DE FRANCE. ADMIN
FRANCE INDUS ACADEM NAT/G INT/TRADE 20 UNESCO.
PAGE 107 B2154

B52
BRINTON C.,THE ANATOMY OF REVOLUTION. FRANCE UK SOCIETY
USA+45 USSR WOR-45 ELITES INTELL ECO/DEV NAT/G CONCPT
EX/STRUC FORCES COERCE DRIVE ORD/FREE PWR SOVEREIGN REV
...MYTH HIST/WRIT GEN/LAWS. PAGE 15 B0311

B54
SCHWARTZ B.,FRENCH ADMINISTRATIVE LAW AND THE JURID
COMMON-LAW WORLD. FRANCE CULTURE LOC/G NAT/G PROVS LAW
DELIB/GP EX/STRUC LEGIS PROB/SOLV CT/SYS EXEC METH/COMP
GOV/REL...IDEA/COMP ENGLSH/LAW. PAGE 95 B1912 ADJUD

L54
FURNISS E.S.,"WEAKNESSES IN FRENCH FOREIGN POLICY- NAT/G
MAKING." EUR+WWI LEGIS LEGIT EXEC ATTIT RIGID/FLEX STRUCT
ORD/FREE...SOC CONCPT METH/CNCPT OBS 20. PAGE 38 DIPLOM
B0766 FRANCE

B55
CHAPMAN B.,THE PREFECTS AND PROVINCIAL FRANCE. ADMIN
FRANCE DELIB/GP WORKER ROLE PWR 19/20 PREFECT. PROVS
PAGE 20 B0408 EX/STRUC
LOC/G

B56
ECOLE NAT'L D'ADMINISTRATION,RECRUITMENT AND ADMIN
TRAINING FOR THE HIGHER CIVIL SERVICE IN FRANCE. MGT
FRANCE EX/STRUC PLAN EDU/PROP CONTROL ROUTINE TASK EXEC
COST...METH 20 CIVIL/SERV. PAGE 32 B0650 ACADEM

C56
NEUMANN S.,"MODERN POLITICAL PARTIES: APPROACHES TO POL/PAR
COMPARATIVE POLITIC. FRANCE UK EX/STRUC DOMIN ADMIN GOV/COMP
LEAD REPRESENT TOTALISM ATTIT...POLICY TREND ELITES

METH/COMP ANTHOL BIBLIOG/A 20 CMN/WLTH. PAGE 78 MAJORIT
B1574

B57
ARON R.,FRANCE DEFEATS EDC. EUR+WWI GERMANY LEGIS INT/ORG
DIPLOM DOMIN EDU/PROP ADMIN...HIST/WRIT 20. PAGE 7 FORCES
B0136 DETER
FRANCE

B57
MEYER P.,ADMINISTRATIVE ORGANIZATION: A COMPARATIVE ADMIN
STUDY OF THE ORGANIZATION OF PUBLIC ADMINISTRATION. METH/COMP
DENMARK FRANCE NORWAY SWEDEN UK USA+45 ELITES LOC/G NAT/G
CONSULT LEGIS ADJUD CONTROL LEAD PWR SKILL CENTRAL
DECISION. PAGE 73 B1475

B57
MURDESHWAR A.K.,ADMINISTRATIVE PROBLEMS RELATING TO NAT/G
NATIONALISATION: WITH SPECIAL REFERENCE TO INDIAN OWN
STATE ENTERPRISES. CZECHOSLVK FRANCE INDIA UK INDUS
USA+45 LEGIS WORKER PROB/SOLV BUDGET PRICE CONTROL ADMIN
...MGT GEN/LAWS 20 PARLIAMENT. PAGE 76 B1544

B58
CHARLES R.,LA JUSTICE EN FRANCE. FRANCE LAW CONSTN JURID
DELIB/GP CRIME 20. PAGE 20 B0413 ADMIN
CT/SYS
ADJUD

B58
COWAN L.G.,LOCAL GOVERNMENT IN WEST AFRICA. AFR LOC/G
FRANCE UK CULTURE KIN POL/PAR CHIEF LEGIS CREATE COLONIAL
ADMIN PARTIC GOV/REL GP/REL...METH/COMP 20. PAGE 24 SOVEREIGN
B0498 REPRESENT

S58
DIAMANT A.,"A CASE STUDY OF ADMINISTRATIVE ADMIN
AUTONOMY: CONTROLS AND TENSIONS IN FRENCH CONTROL
ADMINISTRATION." FRANCE ADJUD LOBBY DEMAND LEGIS
EFFICIENCY 20. PAGE 29 B0585 EXEC

B59
DIEBOLD W. JR.,THE SCHUMAN PLAN: A STUDY IN INT/ORG
ECONOMIC COOPERATION, 1950-1959. EUR+WWI FRANCE REGION
GERMANY USA+45 EXTR/IND CONSULT DELIB/GP PLAN
DIPLOM ECO/TAC INT/TRADE ORD/FREE WEALTH
...METH/CNCPT STAT CONT/OBS INT TIME/SEQ ECSC 20.
PAGE 29 B0591

B59
DUVERGER M.,LA CINQUIEME REPUBLIQUE. FRANCE WOR+45 NAT/G
POL/PAR CHIEF EX/STRUC LOBBY. PAGE 31 B0636 CONSTN
GOV/REL
PARL/PROC

B59
SISSON C.H.,THE SPIRIT OF BRITISH ADMINISTRATION GOV/COMP
AND SOME EUROPEAN COMPARISONS. FRANCE GERMANY/W ADMIN
SWEDEN UK LAW EX/STRUC INGP/REL EFFICIENCY ORD/FREE ELITES
...DECISION 20. PAGE 98 B1972 ATTIT

S59
CHAPMAN B.,"THE FRENCH CONSEIL D'ETAT." FRANCE ADMIN
NAT/G CONSULT OP/RES PROB/SOLV PWR...OBS 20. LAW
PAGE 20 B0410 CT/SYS
LEGIS

B60
FURNISS E.S.,FRANCE, TROUBLED ALLY. EUR+WWI FUT NAT/G
CULTURE SOCIETY BAL/PWR ADMIN ATTIT DRIVE PWR FRANCE
...TREND TOT/POP 20 DEGAULLE/C. PAGE 38 B0767

B60
MEYRIAT J.,LA SCIENCE POLITIQUE EN FRANCE, BIBLIOG/A
1945-1958; BIBLIOGRAPHIES FRANCAISES DE SCIENCES NAT/G
SOCIALES (VOL. I). EUR+WWI FRANCE POL/PAR DIPLOM CONCPT
ADMIN CHOOSE ATTIT...IDEA/COMP METH/COMP NAT/COMP PHIL/SCI
20. PAGE 73 B1478

B61
CATHERINE R.,LE FONCTIONNAIRE FRANCAIS. FRANCE ADMIN
NAT/G INGP/REL ATTIT MORAL ORD/FREE...T CIVIL/SERV. GP/REL
PAGE 19 B0394 LEAD
SUPEGO

B61
DRAGNICH A.N.,MAJOR EUROPEAN GOVERNMENTS. FRANCE NAT/G
GERMANY/W UK USSR LOC/G EX/STRUC CT/SYS PARL/PROC LEGIS
ATTIT MARXISM...JURID MGT NAT/COMP 19/20. PAGE 30 CONSTN
B0615 POL/PAR

B61
HAYTER W.,THE DIPLOMACY OF THE GREAT POWERS. FRANCE DIPLOM
UK USSR WOR+45 EX/STRUC TOP/EX NUC/PWR PEACE...OBS POLICY
20. PAGE 48 B0978 NAT/G

B61
LAHAYE R.,LES ENTREPRISES PUBLIQUES AU MAROC. NAT/G
FRANCE MOROCCO LAW DIST/IND EXTR/IND FINAN CONSULT INDUS
PLAN TEC/DEV ADMIN AGREE CONTROL OWN...POLICY 20. ECO/UNDEV
PAGE 62 B1250 ECO/TAC

B61
STRAUSS E.,THE RULING SERVANTS. FRANCE UK USSR ADMIN
WOR+45 WOR-45 NAT/G CONSULT DELIB/GP EX/STRUC PWR
TOP/EX DOMIN EDU/PROP LEGIT ROUTINE...MGT TIME/SEQ ELITES
STERTYP 20. PAGE 101 B2051

S61
EHRMANN H.W.,"FRENCH BUREAUCRACY AND ORGANIZED ADMIN
INTERESTS" (BMR)" FRANCE NAT/G DELIB/GP ROUTINE DECISION
...INT 20 BUREAUCRCY CIVIL/SERV. PAGE 32 B0657 PLURISM
LOBBY

ANDREWS W.G.,EUROPEAN POLITICAL INSTITUTIONS.
FRANCE GERMANY UK USSR TOP/EX LEAD PARL/PROC CHOOSE
20. PAGE 5 B0104
B62
NAT/COMP
POL/PAR
EX/STRUC
LEGIS

ANDREWS W.G.,FRENCH POLITICS AND ALGERIA: THE
PROCESS OF POLICY FORMATION 1954-1962. ALGERIA
FRANCE CONSTN ELITES POL/PAR CHIEF DELIB/GP LEGIS
DIPLOM PRESS CHOOSE 20. PAGE 5 B0105
B62
GOV/COMP
EXEC
COLONIAL

BROWN B.E.,NEW DIRECTIONS IN COMPARATIVE POLITICS.
AUSTRIA FRANCE GERMANY UK WOR+45 EX/STRUC LEGIS
ORD/FREE 20. PAGE 16 B0320
B62
NAT/COMP
METH
POL/PAR
FORCES

FRIEDLANDER W.A.,INDIVIDUALISM AND SOCIAL WELFARE.
FRANCE ACADEM OP/RES ADMIN AGE/Y AGE/A ORD/FREE 20.
PAGE 37 B0756
B62
GIVE
SOC/WK
SOC/EXP
FINAN

FRIEDMANN W.,METHODS AND POLICIES OF PRINCIPAL
DONOR COUNTRIES IN PUBLIC INTERNATIONAL DEVELOPMENT
FINANCING: PRELIMINARY APPRAISAL. FRANCE GERMANY/W
UK USA+45 USSR WOR+45 FINAN TEC/DEV CAP/ISM DIPLOM
ECO/TAC ATTIT 20 EEC. PAGE 37 B0759
B62
INT/ORG
FOR/AID
NAT/COMP
ADMIN

GRANICK D.,THE EUROPEAN EXECUTIVE. BELGIUM FRANCE
GERMANY/W UK INDUS LABOR LG/CO SML/CO EX/STRUC PLAN
TEC/DEV CAP/ISM COST DEMAND...POLICY CHARTS 20.
PAGE 42 B0852
B62
MGT
ECO/DEV
ECO/TAC
EXEC

OLLE-LAPRUNE J.,LA STABILITE DES MINISTRES SOUS LA
TROISIEME REPUBLIQUE, 1879-1940. FRANCE CONSTN
POL/PAR LEAD WAR INGP/REL RIGID/FLEX PWR...POLICY
CHARTS 19/20. PAGE 79 B1606
B62
LEGIS
NAT/G
ADMIN
PERSON

HOFFHERR R.,"LE PROBLEME DE L'ENCADREMENT DANS LES
JEUNES ETATS DE LANGUE FRANCAISE EN AFRIQUE
CENTRALE ET A MADAGASCAR." FUT ECO/UNDEV CONSULT
PLAN ECO/TAC COLONIAL ATTIT...MGT TIME/SEQ VAL/FREE
20. PAGE 51 B1028
L62
AFR
STRUCT
FRANCE

FESLER J.W.,"FRENCH FIELD ADMINISTRATION: THE
BEGINNINGS." CHRIST-17C CULTURE SOCIETY STRATA
NAT/G ECO/TAC DOMIN EDU/PROP LEGIT ADJUD COERCE
ATTIT ALL/VALS...TIME/SEQ CON/ANAL GEN/METH
VAL/FREE 13/15. PAGE 35 B0714
S62
EX/STRUC
FRANCE

MANGIN G.,"LES ACCORDS DE COOPERATION EN MATIERE DE
JUSTICE ENTRE LA FRANCE ET LES ETATS AFRICAINS ET
MALGACHE." AFR ISLAM WOR+45 STRUCT ECO/UNDEV NAT/G
DELIB/GP PERCEPT ALL/VALS...JURID MGT TIME/SEQ 20.
PAGE 69 B1386
S62
INT/ORG
LAW
FRANCE

PIQUEMAL M.,"LES PROBLEMES DES UNIONS D'ETATS EN
AFRIQUE NOIRE." FRANCE SOCIETY INT/ORG NAT/G
DELIB/GP PLAN LEGIT ADMIN COLONIAL ROUTINE ATTIT
ORD/FREE PWR...GEOG METH/CNCPT 20. PAGE 83 B1678
S62
AFR
ECO/UNDEV
REGION

BROGAN D.W.,POLITICAL PATTERNS IN TODAY'S WORLD.
FRANCE USA+45 USSR WOR+45 CONSTN STRUCT PLAN DIPLOM
ADMIN LEAD ROLE SUPEGO...PHIL/SCI 20. PAGE 15 B0313
B63
NAT/COMP
NEW/LIB
COM
TOTALISM

GOURNAY B.,PUBLIC ADMINISTRATION. FRANCE LAW CONSTN
AGRI FINAN LABOR SCHOOL EX/STRUC CHOOSE...MGT
METH/COMP 20. PAGE 42 B0846
B63
BIBLIOG/A
ADMIN
NAT/G
LOC/G

MEYNAUD J.,PLANIFICATION ET POLITIQUE. FRANCE ITALY
FINAN LABOR DELIB/GP LEGIS ADMIN EFFICIENCY
...MAJORIT DECISION 20. PAGE 73 B1477
B63
PLAN
ECO/TAC
PROB/SOLV

OLSON M. JR.,THE ECONOMICS OF WARTIME SHORTAGE.
FRANCE GERMANY MOD/EUR UK AGRI PROB/SOLV ADMIN
DEMAND WEALTH...POLICY OLD/LIB 17/20. PAGE 80 B1608
B63
WAR
ADJUST
ECO/TAC
NAT/COMP

PLANTEY A.,TRAITE PRATIQUE DE LA FONCTION PUBLIQUE
(2ND ED., 2 VOLS.). FRANCE FINAN EX/STRUC PROB/SOLV
GP/REL ATTIT...SOC 20 CIVIL/SERV. PAGE 83 B1680
B63
ADMIN
SUPEGO
JURID

BOLGAR V.,"THE PUBLIC INTEREST: A JURISPRUDENTIAL
AND COMPARATIVE OVERVIEW OF SYMPOSIUM ON
FUNDAMENTAL CONCEPTS OF PUBLIC LAW" COM FRANCE
GERMANY SWITZERLND LAW ADJUD ADMIN AGREE LAISSEZ
...JURID GEN/LAWS 20 EUROPE/E. PAGE 13 B0268
L63
CONCPT
ORD/FREE
CONTROL
NAT/COMP

JOELSON M.R.,"THE DISMISSAL OF CIVIL SERVANTS IN
THE INTERESTS OF NATIONAL SECURITY." EUR+WWI LAW
DELIB/GP ROUTINE ORD/FREE...MGT VAL/FREE 20.
PAGE 56 B1141
S63
USA+45
NAT/G
UK
FRANCE

SCHMITT H.A.,"THE EUROPEAN COMMUNITIES." EUR+WWI
FRANCE DELIB/GP EX/STRUC TOP/EX CREATE TEC/DEV
S63
VOL/ASSN
ECO/DEV

ECO/TAC LEGIT REGION COERCE DRIVE ALL/VALS
...METH/CNCPT EEC 20. PAGE 94 B1897

WAGRET M.,"L'ASCENSION POLITIQUE DE L'U.D.D.I.A.
(CONGO) ET SA PRISE DU POUVOIR (1956-1959)." AFR
WOR+45 NAT/G POL/PAR CONSULT DELIB/GP LEGIS PERCEPT
ALL/VALS SOVEREIGN...TIME/SEQ CONGO. PAGE 113 B2274
S63
EX/STRUC
CHOOSE
FRANCE

BOUVIER-AJAM M.,MANUEL TECHNIQUE ET PRATIQUE DU
MAIRE ET DES ELUS ET AGENTS COMMUNAUX. FRANCE LOC/G
BUDGET CHOOSE GP/REL SUPEGO...JURID BIBLIOG 20
MAYOR COMMUNES. PAGE 14 B0284
B64
MUNIC
ADMIN
CHIEF
NEIGH

DUROSELLE J.B.,POLITIQUES NATIONALES ENVERS LES
JEUNES ETATS. FRANCE ISRAEL ITALY UK USA+45 USSR
YUGOSLAVIA ECO/DEV FINAN ECO/TAC INT/TRADE ADMIN
PWR 20. PAGE 31 B0634
B64
DIPLOM
ECO/UNDEV
COLONIAL
DOMIN

FONTENEAU J.,LE CONSEIL MUNICIPAL: LE MAIRE-LES
ADJOINTS. FRANCE FINAN DELIB/GP EX/STRUC BUDGET TAX
TASK COST INCOME ROLE SUPEGO 20 MAYOR. PAGE 36
B0735
B64
MUNIC
NEIGH
ADMIN
TOP/EX

GRAVIER J.F.,AMENAGEMENT DU TERRITOIRE ET L'AVENIR
DES REGIONS FRANCAISES. FRANCE ECO/DEV AGRI INDUS
CREATE...GEOG CHARTS 20. PAGE 42 B0859
B64
PLAN
MUNIC
NEIGH
ADMIN

INST D'ETUDE POL L'U GRENOBLE,ADMINISTRATION
TRADITIONELLE ET PLANIFICATION REGIONALE. FRANCE
LAW POL/PAR PROB/SOLV ADJUST RIGID/FLEX...CHARTS
ANTHOL BIBLIOG T 20 REFORMERS. PAGE 54 B1087
B64
ADMIN
MUNIC
PLAN
CREATE

PARET P.,FRENCH REVOLUTIONARY WARFARE FROM
INDOCHINA TO ALGERIA* THE ANALYSIS OF A POLITICAL
AND MILITARY DOCTRINE. ALGERIA VIETNAM FORCES
OP/RES TEC/DEV ROUTINE REV ATTIT...PSY BIBLIOG.
PAGE 81 B1632
B64
FRANCE
GUERRILLA
GEN/LAWS

RIDLEY F.,PUBLIC ADMINISTRATION IN FRANCE. FRANCE
UK EX/STRUC CONTROL PARTIC EFFICIENCY 20. PAGE 88
B1781
B64
ADMIN
REPRESENT
GOV/COMP
PWR

WITHERELL J.W.,OFFICIAL PUBLICATIONS OF FRENCH
EQUATORIAL AFRICA, FRENCH CAMEROONS, AND TOGO,
1946-1958 (PAMPHLET). CAMEROON CHAD FRANCE GABON
TOGO LAW ECO/UNDEV EXTR/IND INT/TRADE...GEOG HEAL
20. PAGE 117 B2367
B64
BIBLIOG/A
AFR
NAT/G
ADMIN

FOLTZ W.J.,FROM FRENCH WEST AFRICA TO THE MALI
FEDERATION. AFR FRANCE MALI ADMIN CONTROL FEDERAL
...DECISION 20. PAGE 36 B0734
B65
EXEC
TOP/EX
ELITES
LEAD

FORGAC A.A.,NEW DIPLOMACY AND THE UNITED NATIONS.
FRANCE GERMANY UK USSR INT/ORG DELIB/GP EX/STRUC
PEACE...INT/LAW CONCPT UN. PAGE 36 B0740
B65
DIPLOM
ETIQUET
NAT/G

HICKMAN B.G.,QUANTITATIVE PLANNING OF ECONOMIC
POLICY. FRANCE NETHERLAND OP/RES PRICE ROUTINE UTIL
...POLICY DECISION ECOMETRIC METH/CNCPT STAT STYLE
CHINJAP. PAGE 50 B1004
B65
PROB/SOLV
PLAN
QUANT

LUTZ V.,FRENCH PLANNING. FRANCE TEC/DEV RIGID/FLEX
ORD/FREE 20. PAGE 67 B1348
B65
PLAN
ADMIN
FUT

OLSON M. JR.,DROIT PUBLIC. FRANCE NAT/G LEGIS SUFF
GP/REL PRIVIL...TREND 18/20. PAGE 80 B1609
B65
CONSTN
FINAN
ADMIN
ORD/FREE

VIORST M.,HOSTILE ALLIES: FDR AND DE GAULLE.
EUR+WWI USA-45 ELITES NAT/G VOL/ASSN FORCES LEGIS
PLAN LEGIT ADMIN COERCE PERSON...BIOG TIME/SEQ 20
ROOSEVLT/F DEGAULLE/C. PAGE 112 B2263
B65
TOP/EX
PWR
WAR
FRANCE

WITHERELL J.W.,MADAGASCAR AND ADJACENT ISLANDS: A
GUIDE TO OFFICIAL PUBLICATIONS (PAMPHLET). FRANCE
MADAGASCAR S/ASIA UK LAW OP/RES PLAN DIPLOM
...POLICY CON/ANAL 19/20. PAGE 117 B2368
B65
BIBLIOG
COLONIAL
LOC/G
ADMIN

THOMAS F.C. JR.,"THE PEACE CORPS IN MOROCCO."
CULTURE MUNIC PROVS CREATE ROUTINE TASK ADJUST
STRANGE...OBS PEACE/CORP. PAGE 104 B2099
S65
MOROCCO
FRANCE
FOR/AID
EDU/PROP

HAYER T.,FRENCH AID. AFR FRANCE AGRI FINAN BUDGET
ADMIN WAR PRODUC...CHARTS 18/20 THIRD/WRLD
OVRSEA/DEV. PAGE 48 B0975
B66
TEC/DEV
COLONIAL
FOR/AID
ECO/UNDEV

BROWN L.N.,FRENCH ADMINISTRATIVE LAW. FRANCE UK
CONSTN NAT/G LEGIS DOMIN CONTROL EXEC PARL/PROC PWR
...JURID METH/COMP GEN/METH. PAGE 16 B0324
B67
EX/STRUC
LAW
IDEA/COMP

RALSTON D.B.,THE ARMY OF THE REPUBLIC; THE PLACE OF THE MILITARY IN THE POLITICAL EVOLUTION OF FRANCE 1871-1914. FRANCE MOD/EUR EX/STRUC LEGIS TOP/EX DIPLOM ADMIN WAR GP/REL ROLE...BIBLIOG 19/20. PAGE 86 B1730
CT/SYS B67 FORCES NAT/G CIVMIL/REL POLICY

"A PROPOS DES INCITATIONS FINANCIERES AUX GROUPEMENTS DES COMMUNES: ESSAI D'INTERPRETATION." FRANCE NAT/G LEGIS ADMIN GOV/REL CENTRAL 20. PAGE 2 B0046
L67 LOC/G ECO/TAC APPORT ADJUD

ANDERSON M.,"THE FRENCH PARLIAMENT." EUR+WWI FRANCE MOD/EUR CONSTN POL/PAR CHIEF LEGIS LOBBY ATTIT ROLE PWR 19/20. PAGE 5 B0095
S67 PARL/PROC LEAD GOV/COMP EX/STRUC

CARIAS B.,"EL CONTROL DE LAS EMPRESAS PUBLICAS POR GRUPOS DE INTERESES DE LA COMUNIDAD." FRANCE UK VENEZUELA INDUS NAT/G CONTROL OWN PWR...DECISION NAT/COMP 20. PAGE 18 B0377
S67 WORKER REPRESENT MGT SOCISM

GOODNOW F.J.,"AN EXECUTIVE AND THE COURTS: JUDICIAL REMEDIES AGAINST ADMINISTRATIVE ACTION" FRANCE UK USA-45 WOR-45 LAW CONSTN SANCTION ORD/FREE 19. PAGE 41 B0823
L86 CT/SYS GOV/REL ADMIN ADJUD

FRANCHISE....FRANCHISE

FRANCIS R.G. B0748

FRANCO/F....FRANCISCO FRANCO

FRANCO-PRUSSIAN WAR....SEE FRNCO/PRUS

FRANK T. B0749

FRANK/PARL....FRANKFURT PARLIAMENT

FRANKE W. B0750

FRANKEL S.H. B0751

FRANKFUR/F....FELIX FRANKFURTER

FRANKFURT PARLIAMENT....SEE FRANK/PARL

FRANKLIN/B....BENJAMIN FRANKLIN

FREDERICK....FREDERICK THE GREAT

FREDRKSBRG....FREDERICKSBURG, VIRGINIA

FREE CHINA....SEE TAIWAN

FREE/SOIL....FREE-SOIL DEBATE (U.S.)

FREE/SPEE....FREE SPEECH MOVEMENT; SEE ALSO AMEND/I

HOOK S.,"SECOND THOUGHTS ON BERKELEY" USA+45 ELITES INTELL LEGIT ADMIN COERCE REPRESENT GP/REL INGP/REL TOTALISM AGE/Y MARXISM 20 BERKELEY FREE/SPEE STUDNT/PWR. PAGE 51 B1040
L65 ACADEM ORD/FREE POLICY CREATE

FREEDOM....SEE ORD/FREE

FREEDOM/HS....FREEDOM HOUSE

FREEMAN J.L. B0752

FRELIMO....MOZAMBIQUE LIBERATION FRONT

FRENCH J.R.P. B0441

FRENCH CIVIL CODE....SEE CIVIL/CODE

FRENCH/CAN....FRENCH CANADA

FREUD/S....SIGMUND FREUD

KARIEL H.S.,IN SEARCH OF AUTHORITY: TWENTIETH-CENTURY POLITICAL THOUGHT. WOR+45 WOR-45 NAT/G EX/STRUC TOTALISM DRIVE PWR...MGT PHIL/SCI GEN/LAWS 19/20 NIETZSCH/F FREUD/S WEBER/MAX NIEBUHR/R MARITAIN/J. PAGE 58 B1173
B64 CONSTN CONCPT ORD/FREE IDEA/COMP

FREUND G. B0753

FREYRE G. B0754

FRIED R.C. B0755

FRIEDLANDER W.A. B0756

FRIEDMAN L. B0757,B0758

FRIEDMANN W. B0759

FRIEDMANN W.G. B0760

FRIEDRCH/C

SELZNICK P.,"AN APPROACH TO A THEORY OF BUREAUCRACY." INDUS WORKER CONTROL LEAD EFFICIENCY OPTIMAL...SOC METH 20 BARNARD/C BUREAUCRCY WEBER/MAX FRIEDRCH/C MICHELS/R. PAGE 95 B1928
S43 ROUTINE ADMIN MGT EX/STRUC

FRIENDSHIP....SEE LOVE

FRNCO/PRUS....FRANCO-PRUSSIAN WAR

FROMM/E....ERICH FROMM

FRONTIER....FRONTIER

FRUSTRATION....SEE BIO/SOC, ANOMIE, DRIVE

FRYE R.J. B0761,B0762

FRYKENBURG R.E. B0763

FTC....FEDERAL TRADE COMMISSION

BURRUS B.R.,INVESTIGATION AND DISCOVERY IN STATE ANTITRUST (PAMPHLET). USA+45 USA-45 LEGIS ECO/TAC ADMIN CONTROL CT/SYS CRIME GOV/REL PWR...JURID CHARTS 19/20 FTC MONOPOLY. PAGE 17 B0355
N19 NAT/G PROVS LAW INSPECT

LONG T.G.,"THE ADMINISTRATIVE PROCESS: AGONIZING REAPPRAISAL IN THE FTC." NAT/G REPRESENT 20 FTC. PAGE 66 B1339
S65 ADJUD LOBBY ADMIN EX/STRUC

FUCHS R.F. B0764

FUCHS V.R. B2292

FULBRGHT/J....J. WILLIAM FULBRIGHT

FULLER C.D. B0765

FULLER/MW....MELVILLE WESTON FULLER

FUNCK-BRETANO C. B0551

FUNCTIONAL ANALYSIS....SEE OP/RES

FUNCTIONALISM (THEORY)....SEE GEN/LAWS

FURNISS E.S. B0766,B0767

FURNIVAL/J....J.S. FURNIVAL

FUT....FUTURE (PAST AND PRESENT ATTEMPTS TO DEPICT IT)

CORWIN E.S.,THE PRESIDENT'S CONTROL OF FOREIGN RELATIONS. FUT USA-45 CONSTN STRATA NAT/G CHIEF EX/STRUC LEGIS KNOWL RESPECT...JURID CONCPT TREND CONGRESS VAL/FREE 20 PRESIDENT. PAGE 24 B0483
B17 TOP/EX PWR DIPLOM

PERREN G.E.,LANGUAGE AND COMMUNICATION IN THE COMMONWEALTH (PAMPHLET). FUT UK LAW ECO/DEV PRESS TV WRITING ADJUD ADMIN COLONIAL CONTROL 20 CMN/WLTH. PAGE 82 B1660
N19 EDU/PROP LING GOV/REL COM/IND

BRYCE J.,MODERN DEMOCRACIES. FUT NEW/ZEALND USA-45 LAW CONSTN POL/PAR PROVS VOL/ASSN EX/STRUC LEGIS LEGIT CT/SYS EXEC KNOWL CONGRESS AUSTRAL 20. PAGE 16 B0332
B21 NAT/G TREND

HALL W.P.,EMPIRE TO COMMONWEALTH. FUT WOR-45 CONSTN ECO/DEV ECO/UNDEV INT/ORG PROVS PLAN DIPLOM EDU/PROP ADMIN COLONIAL PEACE PERSON ALL/VALS ...POLICY GEOG SOC OBS RECORD TREND CMN/WLTH PARLIAMENT 19/20. PAGE 46 B0925
B28 VOL/ASSN NAT/G UK

WRIGHT Q.,GOLD AND MONETARY STABILIZATION. FUT USA-45 WOR-45 INTELL ECO/DEV INT/ORG NAT/G CONSULT PLAN ECO/TAC ADMIN ATTIT WEALTH...CONCPT TREND 20. PAGE 118 B2383
B32 FINAN POLICY

HITLER A.,MEIN KAMPF. EUR+WWI FUT MOD/EUR STRUCT INT/ORG LABOR NAT/G POL/PAR FORCES CREATE PLAN BAL/PWR DIPLOM ECO/TAC DOMIN EDU/PROP ADMIN COERCE ATTIT...SOCIALIST BIOG TREND NAZI. PAGE 50 B1020
B39 PWR NEW/IDEA WAR

PALMER J.M.,AMERICA IN ARMS: THE EXPERIENCE OF THE
B41 FORCES

S41

UNITED STATES WITH MILITARY ORGANIZATION. FUT
USA-45 LEAD REV PWR 18/20 WASHINGT/G KNOX/HENRY
PRE/US/AM. PAGE 81 B1627

NAT/G
ADMIN
WAR

ABEL T.,"THE ELEMENT OF DECISION IN THE PATTERN OF
WAR." EUR+WWI FUT NAT/G TOP/EX DIPLOM ROUTINE
COERCE DISPL PERCEPT PWR...SOC METH/CNCPT HIST/WRIT
TREND GEN/LAWS 20. PAGE 2 B0051

TEC/DEV
FORCES
WAR

B42

HARLOW R.F.,PUBLIC RELATIONS IN WAR AND PEACE. FUT
USA-45 ECO/DEV ECO/TAC ROUTINE 20. PAGE 47 B0947

WAR
ATTIT
SOCIETY
INGP/REL

B43

YOUNG R.,THIS IS CONGRESS. FUT SENIOR ADMIN GP/REL
PWR...DECISION REFORMERS CONGRESS. PAGE 119 B2393

LEGIS
DELIB/GP
CHIEF
ROUTINE

L44

CORWIN E.S.,"THE CONSTITUTION AND WORLD
ORGANIZATION." FUT USA+45 USA-45 NAT/G EX/STRUC
LEGIS PEACE KNOWL...CON/ANAL UN 20. PAGE 24 B0484

INT/ORG
CONSTN
SOVEREIGN

B45

BUSH V.,SCIENCE, THE ENDLESS FRONTIER. FUT USA-45
INTELL STRATA ACT/RES CREATE PLAN EDU/PROP ADMIN
NUC/PWR PEACE ATTIT HEALTH KNOWL...MAJORIT HEAL MGT
PHIL/SCI CONCPT OBS TREND 20. PAGE 18 B0360

R+D
NAT/G

B45

RANSHOFFEN-WERTHEIMER EF,THE INTERNATIONAL
SECRETARIAT: A GREAT EXPERIMENT IN INTERNATIONAL
ADMINISTRATION. EUR+WWI FUT CONSTN FACE/GP CONSULT
DELIB/GP ACT/RES ADMIN ROUTINE PEACE ORD/FREE...MGT
RECORD ORG/CHARTS LEAGUE/NAT WORK 20. PAGE 86 B1731

INT/ORG
EXEC

S47

CALDWELL L.K.,"STRENGTHENING STATE LEGISLATURES"
FUT DELIB/GP WEALTH REFORMERS. PAGE 18 B0364

PROVS
LEGIS
ROUTINE
BUDGET

B49

KENT S.,STRATEGIC INTELLIGENCE FOR AMERICAN WORLD
POLICY. FUT USA+45 NAT/G ATTIT PERCEPT ORD/FREE
...OBS 20. PAGE 59 B1195

ACT/RES
EX/STRUC
DIPLOM

B50

MANNHEIM K.,FREEDOM, POWER, AND DEMOCRATIC
PLANNING. FUT USSR WOR+45 ELITES INTELL SOCIETY
NAT/G EDU/PROP ROUTINE ATTIT DRIVE SUPEGO SKILL
...POLICY PSY CONCPT TREND GEN/LAWS 20. PAGE 69
B1393

TEC/DEV
PLAN
CAP/ISM
UK

L50

US SENATE COMM. GOVT. OPER.,"REVISION OF THE UN
CHARTER." FUT USA+45 WOR+45 CONSTN ECO/DEV
ECO/UNDEV NAT/G DELIB/GP ACT/RES CREATE PLAN EXEC
ROUTINE CHOOSE ALL/VALS...POLICY CONCPT CONGRESS UN
TOT/POP 20 COLD/WAR. PAGE 111 B2235

INT/ORG
LEGIS
PEACE

L51

MANGONE G.,"THE IDEA AND PRACTICE OF WORLD
GOVERNMENT." FUT WOR+45 WOR-45 ECO/DEV LEGIS CREATE
LEGIT ROUTINE ATTIT MORAL PWR WEALTH...CONCPT
GEN/LAWS 20. PAGE 69 B1388

INT/ORG
SOCIETY
INT/LAW

B52

DAY E.E.,EDUCATION FOR FREEDOM AND RESPONSIBILITY.
FUT USA+45 CULTURE CONSULT EDU/PROP ATTIT SKILL
...MGT CONCPT OBS GEN/LAWS COLD/WAR 20. PAGE 27
B0547

SCHOOL
KNOWL

S52

SCHWEBEL S.M.,"THE SECRETARY-GENERAL OF THE UN."
FUT INTELL CONSULT DELIB/GP ADMIN PEACE ATTIT
...JURID MGT CONCPT TREND UN CONGRESS 20. PAGE 95
B1915

INT/ORG
TOP/EX

S53

CORY R.H. JR.,"FORGING A PUBLIC INFORMATION POLICY
FOR THE UNITED NATIONS." FUT WOR+45 SOCIETY ADMIN
PEACE ATTIT PERSON SKILL...CONCPT 20 UN. PAGE 24
B0486

INT/ORG
EDU/PROP
BAL/PWR

B54

MILLARD E.L.,FREEDOM IN A FEDERAL WORLD. FUT WOR+45
VOL/ASSN TOP/EX LEGIT ROUTINE FEDERAL PEACE ATTIT
DISPL ORD/FREE PWR...MAJORIT INT/LAW JURID TREND
COLD/WAR 20. PAGE 73 B1479

INT/ORG
CREATE
ADJUD
BAL/PWR

B55

APTER D.E.,THE GOLD COAST IN TRANSITION. FUT CONSTN
CULTURE SOCIETY ECO/UNDEV FAM KIN LOC/G NAT/G
POL/PAR LEGIS TOP/EX EDU/PROP LEGIT ADMIN ATTIT
PERSON PWR...CONCPT STAT INT CENSUS TOT/POP
VAL/FREE. PAGE 6 B0120

AFR
SOVEREIGN

B55

MACMAHON A.W.,FEDERALISM: MATURE AND EMERGENT.
EUR+WWI FUT WOR+45 WOR-45 INT/ORG NAT/G REPRESENT
FEDERAL...POLICY MGT RECORD TREND GEN/LAWS 20.
PAGE 68 B1370

STRUCT
CONCPT

B55

POOL I.,SATELLITE GENERALS: A STUDY OF MILITARY
ELITES IN THE SOVIET SPHERE. ASIA CHINA/COM COM
CZECHOSLVK FUT HUNGARY POLAND ROMANIA USSR ELITES
STRATA ADMIN ATTIT PWR SKILL...METH/CNCPT BIOG 20.
PAGE 84 B1688

FORCES
CHOOSE

S55

ANGELL R.,"GOVERNMENTS AND PEOPLES AS A FOCI FOR
PEACE-ORIENTED RESEARCH." WOR+45 CULTURE SOCIETY
FACE/GP ACT/RES CREATE PLAN DIPLOM EDU/PROP ROUTINE
ATTIT PERCEPT SKILL...POLICY CONCPT OBS TREND
GEN/METH 20. PAGE 5 B0110

FUT
SOC
PEACE

S55

KAUTSKY J.H.,"THE NEW STRATEGY OF INTERNATIONAL
COMMUNISM." ASIA CHINA/COM FUT WOR+45 WOR-45 ADMIN
ROUTINE PERSON MARXISM SOCISM...TREND IDEA/COMP 20
LENIN/VI MAO. PAGE 59 B1184

COM
POL/PAR
TOTALISM
USSR

B56

KIRK G.,THE CHANGING ENVIRONMENT OF INTERNATIONAL
RELATIONS. ASIA S/ASIA USA+45 WOR+45 ECO/UNDEV
INT/ORG NAT/G FOR/AID EDU/PROP PEACE KNOWL
...PLURIST COLD/WAR TOT/POP 20. PAGE 60 B1214

FUT
EXEC
DIPLOM

B57

FULLER C.D.,TRAINING OF SPECIALISTS IN
INTERNATIONAL RELATIONS. FUT USA+45 USA-45 INTELL
INT/ORG...MGT METH/CNCPT INT QU GEN/METH 20.
PAGE 38 B0765

KNOWL
DIPLOM

B57

KAPLAN M.A.,SYSTEM AND PROCESS OF INTERNATIONAL
POLITICS. FUT WOR+45 WOR-45 SOCIETY PLAN BAL/PWR
ADMIN ATTIT PERSON RIGID/FLEX PWR SOVEREIGN
...DECISION TREND VAL/FREE. PAGE 58 B1168

INT/ORG
DIPLOM

B57

MORSTEIN-MARX F.,THE ADMINISTRATIVE STATE: AN
INTRODUCTION TO BUREAUCRACY. EUR+WWI FUT MOD/EUR
USA+45 USA-45 NAT/G CONSULT ADMIN ROUTINE TOTALISM
DRIVE SKILL...TREND 19/20. PAGE 76 B1530

EXEC
MGT
CAP/ISM
ELITES

B58

MILLS C.W.,THE CAUSES OF WORLD WAR THREE. FUT
USA+45 INTELL NAT/G DOMIN EDU/PROP ADMIN WAR ATTIT
SOC. PAGE 74 B1487

CONSULT
PWR
ELITES
PEACE

B58

SPITZ D.,DEMOCRACY AND THE CHALLANGE OF POWER. FUT
USA+45 USA-45 LAW SOCIETY STRUCT LOC/G POL/PAR
PROVS DELIB/GP EX/STRUC LEGIS TOP/EX ACT/RES CREATE
DOMIN EDU/PROP LEGIT ADJUD ADMIN ATTIT DRIVE MORAL
ORD/FREE TOT/POP. PAGE 99 B2010

NAT/G
PWR

S58

JORDAN A.,"MILITARY ASSISTANCE AND NATIONAL
POLICY." ASIA FUT USA+45 WOR+45 ECO/DEV ECO/UNDEV
INT/ORG NAT/G PLAN ECO/TAC ROUTINE WEAPON ATTIT
RIGID/FLEX PWR...CONCPT TREND 20. PAGE 57 B1153

FORCES
POLICY
FOR/AID
DIPLOM

B59

CHINA INSTITUTE OF AMERICA.,CHINA AND THE UNITED
NATIONS. CHINA/COM FUT STRUCT EDU/PROP LEGIT ADMIN
ATTIT KNOWL ORD/FREE PWR...OBS RECORD STAND/INT
TIME/SEQ UN LEAGUE/NAT UNESCO 20. PAGE 21 B0425

ASIA
INT/ORG

B59

SAYER W.S.,AN AGENDA FOR RESEARCH IN PUBLIC
PERSONNEL ADMINISTRATION. FUT USA+45 ACADEM LABOR
LOC/G NAT/G POL/PAR DELIB/GP MGT. PAGE 93 B1872

WORKER
ADMIN
ACT/RES
CONSULT

B59

SPIRO H.J.,GOVERNMENT BY CONSTITUTIONS: THE
POLITICAL SYSTEMS OF DEMOCRACY. CANADA EUR+WWI FUT
USA+45 WOR+45 WOR-45 LEGIS TOP/EX LEGIT ADMIN
CT/SYS ORD/FREE PWR...TREND TOT/POP VAL/FREE 20.
PAGE 99 B2008

NAT/G
CONSTN

B59

YALE UNIV BUR OF HIGHWAY TRAF,URBAN TRANSPORTATION
ADMINISTRATION. FUT USA+45 CONSTRUC ACT/PES BUDGET
...CENSUS 20 PUB/TRANS. PAGE 118 B2388

ADMIN
DIST/IND
LOC/G
PLAN

S59

BAILEY S.D.,"THE FUTURE COMPOSITION OF THE
TRUSTEESHIP COUNCIL." FUT WOR+45 CONSTN VOL/ASSN
ADMIN ATTIT PWR...OBS TREND CON/ANAL VAL/FREE UN
20. PAGE 8 B0161

INT/ORG
NAT/LISM
SOVEREIGN

S59

LASSWELL H.D.,"UNIVERSALITY IN PERSPECTIVE." FUT
UNIV SOCIETY CONSULT TOP/EX PLAN EDU/PROP ADJUD
ROUTINE ARMS/CONT COERCE PEACE ATTIT PERSON
ALL/VALS. PAGE 63 B1271

INT/ORG
JURID
TOTALISM

S59

LENGYEL P.,"SOME TRENDS IN THE INTERNATIONAL CIVIL
SERVICE." FUT WOR+45 INT/ORG CONSULT ATTIT...MGT
OBS TREND CON/ANAL LEAGUE/NAT UNESCO 20. PAGE 64
B1291

ADMIN
EXEC

S59

PADELFORD N.J.,"REGIONAL COOPERATION IN THE SOUTH
PACIFIC: THE SOUTH PACIFIC COMMISSION." FUT
NEW/ZEALND UK WOR+45 CULTURE ECO/UNDEV LOC/G
VOL/ASSN...OBS CON/ANAL UNESCO VAL/FREE AUSTRAL 20.
PAGE 80 B1622

INT/ORG
ADMIN

S59

SOHN L.B.,"THE DEFINITION OF AGGRESSION." FUT LAW
FORCES LEGIT ADJUD ROUTINE COERCE ORD/FREE PWR
...MAJORIT JURID QUANT COLD/WAR 20. PAGE 99 B1995

INT/ORG
CT/SYS
DETER
SOVEREIGN

S59

STOESSINGER J.G.,"THE INTERNATIONAL ATOMIC ENERGY

INT/ORG

AGENCY: THE FIRST PHASE." FUT WOR+45 NAT/G VOL/ASSN ECO/DEV
DELIB/GP BAL/PWR LEGIT ADMIN ROUTINE PWR...OBS FOR/AID
CON/ANAL GEN/LAWS VAL/FREE 20 IAEA. PAGE 101 B2040 NUC/PWR

B60
AYEARST M..THE BRITISH WEST INDIES: THE SEARCH FOR CONSTN
SELF-GOVERNMENT. FUT WEST/IND LOC/G POL/PAR COLONIAL
EX/STRUC LEGIS CHOOSE FEDERAL...NAT/COMP BIBLIOG REPRESENT
17/20. PAGE 7 B0152 NAT/G

B60
FURNISS E.S..FRANCE, TROUBLED ALLY. EUR+WWI FUT NAT/G
CULTURE SOCIETY BAL/PWR ADMIN ATTIT DRIVE PWR FRANCE
...TREND TOT/POP 20 DEGAULLE/C. PAGE 38 B0767

B60
LENCZOWSKI G..OIL AND STATE IN THE MIDDLE EAST. FUT ISLAM
IRAN LAW ECO/UNDEV EXTR/IND NAT/G TOP/EX PLAN INDUS
TEC/DEV ECO/TAC LEGIT ADMIN COERCE ATTIT ALL/VALS NAT/LISM
PWR...CHARTS 20. PAGE 64 B1288

B60
MEEHAN E.J..THE BRITISH LEFT WING AND FOREIGN ACT/RES
POLICY: A STUDY OF THE INFLUENCE OF IDEOLOGY. FUT ATTIT
UK WOR+45 INTELL TOP/EX PLAN ADMIN ROUTINE DIPLOM
DRIVE...OBS TIME/SEQ GEN/LAWS PARLIAMENT 20.
PAGE 72 B1461

B60
MUNRO L..UNITED NATIONS, HOPE FOR A DIVIDED WORLD. INT/ORG
FUT WOR+45 CONSTN DELIB/GP CREATE TEC/DEV DIPLOM ROUTINE
EDU/PROP LEGIT PEACE ATTIT HEALTH ORD/FREE PWR
...CONCPT TREND UN VAL/FREE 20. PAGE 76 B1540

B60
ROEPKE W..A HUMANE ECONOMY: THE SOCIAL FRAMEWORK OF DRIVE
THE FREE MARKET. FUT USSR WOR+45 CULTURE SOCIETY EDU/PROP
ECO/DEV PLAN ECO/TAC ADMIN ATTIT PERSON RIGID/FLEX CAP/ISM
SUPEGO MORAL WEALTH SOCISM...POLICY OLD/LIB CONCPT
TREND GEN/LAWS 20. PAGE 90 B1811

L60
BRENNAN D.G.."SETTING AND GOALS OF ARMS CONTROL." FORCES
FUT USA+45 USSR WOR+45 INTELL INT/ORG NAT/G COERCE
VOL/ASSN CONSULT PLAN DIPLOM ECO/TAC ADMIN KNOWL ARMS/CONT
PWR...POLICY CONCPT TREND COLD/WAR 20. PAGE 15 DETER
B0305

L60
DEAN A.W.."SECOND GENEVA CONFERENCE OF THE LAW OF INT/ORG
THE SEA: THE FIGHT FOR FREEDOM OF THE SEAS." FUT JURID
USA+45 USSR WOR-45 SEA CONSTN STRUCT PLAN INT/LAW
INT/TRADE ADJUD ADMIN ORD/FREE...DECISION RECORD
TREND GEN/LAWS 20 TREATY. PAGE 28 B0564

L60
STEIN E.."LEGAL REMEDIES OF ENTERPRISES IN THE MARKET
EUROPEAN ECONOMIC COMMUNITY." EUR+WWI FUT ECO/DEV ADJUD
INDUS PLAN ECO/TAC ADMIN PWR...MGT MATH STAT TREND
CON/ANAL EEC 20. PAGE 100 B2026

S60
"THE EMERGING COMMON MARKETS IN LATIN AMERICA." FUT FINAN
L/A+17C STRATA DIST/IND INDUS LABOR NAT/G LEGIS ECO/UNDEV
ECO/TAC ADMIN RIGID/FLEX HEALTH...NEW/IDEA TIME/SEQ INT/TRADE
OAS 20. PAGE 2 B0039

S60
BOGARDUS E.S.."THE SOCIOLOGY OF A STRUCTURED INT/ORG
PEACE." FUT SOCIETY CREATE DIPLOM EDU/PROP ADJUD SOC
ROUTINE ATTIT RIGID/FLEX KNOWL ORD/FREE RESPECT NAT/LISM
...POLICY INT/LAW JURID NEW/IDEA SELF/OBS TOT/POP PEACE
20 UN. PAGE 13 B0264

S60
EMERSON R.."THE EROSION OF DEMOCRACY." AFR FUT LAW S/ASIA
CULTURE INTELL SOCIETY ECO/UNDEV FAM LOC/G NAT/G POL/PAR
FORCES PLAN TEC/DEV ECO/TAC ADMIN CT/SYS ATTIT
ORD/FREE PWR...SOCIALIST SOC CONCPT STAND/INT
TIME/SEQ WORK 20. PAGE 33 B0671

S60
FRANKEL S.H.."ECONOMIC ASPECTS OF POLITICAL NAT/G
INDEPENDENCE IN AFRICA." AFR FUT SOCIETY ECO/UNDEV FOR/AID
COM/IND FINAN LEGIS PLAN TEC/DEV CAP/ISM ECO/TAC
INT/TRADE ADMIN ATTIT DRIVE RIGID/FLEX PWR WEALTH
...MGT NEW/IDEA MATH TIME/SEQ VAL/FREE 20. PAGE 37
B0751

S60
HALPERIN M.H.."IS THE SENATE'S FOREIGN RELATIONS PLAN
RESEARCH WORTHWHILE." COM FUT USA+45 USSR ACT/RES DIPLOM
BAL/PWR EDU/PROP ADMIN ALL/VALS CONGRESS VAL/FREE
20 COLD/WAR. PAGE 46 B0927

S60
MORALES C.J.."TRADE AND ECONOMIC INTEGRATION IN FINAN
LATIN AMERICA." FUT L/A+17C LAW STRATA ECO/UNDEV INT/TRADE
DIST/IND INDUS LABOR NAT/G LEGIS ECO/TAC ADMIN REGION
RIGID/FLEX WEALTH...CONCPT NEW/IDEA CONT/OBS
TIME/SEQ WORK 20. PAGE 75 B1519

S60
NORTH R.C.."DIE DISKREPANZ ZWISCHEN REALITAT UND SOCIETY
WUNSCHBILD ALS INNENPOLITISCHER FAKTOR." ASIA ECO/TAC
CHINA/COM COM FUT ECO/UNDEV NAT/G PLAN DOMIN ADMIN
COERCE PERCEPT...SOC MYTH GEN/METH WORK TOT/POP 20.
PAGE 79 B1589

S60
RIESELBACH Z.N.."QUANTITATIVE TECHNIQUES FOR QUANT
STUDYING VOTING BEHAVIOR IN THE UNITED NATIONS CHOOSE
GENERAL ASSEMBLY." FUT S/ASIA USA+45 INT/ORG

BAL/PWR DIPLOM ECO/TAC FOR/AID ADMIN PWR...POLICY
METH/CNCPT METH UN 20. PAGE 88 B1783

S60
SCHATZ S.P.."THE INFLENCE OF PLANNING ON ECO/UNDEV
DEVELOPMENT: THE NIGERIAN EXPERIENCE." AFR FUT PLAN
FINAN INDUS NAT/G EX/STRUC ECO/TAC ADMIN ATTIT NIGERIA
PERCEPT ORD/FREE PWR...MATH TREND CON/ANAL SIMUL
VAL/FREE 20. PAGE 93 B1883

B61
AGARWAL R.C..STATE ENTERPRISE IN INDIA. FUT INDIA ECO/UNDEV
UK FINAN INDUS ADMIN CONTROL OWN...POLICY CHARTS SOCISM
BIBLIOG 20 RAILROAD. PAGE 3 B0064 GOV/REL
LG/CO

B61
BENOIT E..EUROPE AT SIXES AND SEVENS: THE COMMON FINAN
MARKET, THE FREE TRADE ASSOCIATION AND THE UNITED ECO/DEV
STATES. EUR+WWI FUT USA+45 INDUS CONSULT DELIB/GP VOL/ASSN
EX/STRUC TOP/EX ACT/RES ECO/TAC EDU/PROP ROUTINE
CHOOSE PERCEPT WEALTH...MGT TREND EEC TOT/POP 20
EFTA. PAGE 11 B0217

B61
HARRISON S..INDIA AND THE UNITED STATES. FUT S/ASIA DELIB/GP
USA+45 WOR+45 INTELL ECO/DEV ECO/UNDEV AGRI INDUS ACT/RES
INT/ORG NAT/G CONSULT EX/STRUC TOP/EX PLAN ECO/TAC FOR/AID
NEUTRAL ALL/VALS...MGT TOT/POP 20. PAGE 47 B0956 INDIA

B61
MARX K..THE COMMUNIST MANIFESTO. IN (MENDEL A. COM
ESSENTIAL WORKS OF MARXISM, NEW YORK: BANTAM. FUT NEW/IDEA
MOD/EUR CULTURE ECO/DEV ECO/UNDEV AGRI FINAN INDUS CAP/ISM
MARKET PROC/MFG LABOR MUNIC POL/PAR CONSULT FORCES REV
CREATE PLAN ADMIN ATTIT DRIVE RIGID/FLEX ORD/FREE
PWR RESPECT MARX/KARL WORK. PAGE 70 B1421

B61
SHARP W.R..FIELD ADMINISTRATION IN THE UNITED INT/ORG
NATION SYSTEM: THE CONDUCT OF INTERNATIONAL CONSULT
ECONOMIC AND SOCIAL PROGRAMS. FUT WOR+45 CONSTN
SOCIETY ECO/UNDEV R+D DELIB/GP ACT/RES PLAN TEC/DEV
EDU/PROP EXEC ROUTINE HEALTH WEALTH...HUM CONCPT
CHARTS METH ILO UNESCO VAL/FREE UN 20. PAGE 96
B1939

S61
CARLETON W.G.."AMERICAN FOREIGN POLICY: MYTHS AND PLAN
REALITIES." FUT USA+45 WOR+45 ECO/UNDEV INT/ORG MYTH
EX/STRUC ARMS/CONT NUC/PWR WAR ATTIT...POLICY DIPLOM
CONCPT CONT/OBS GEN/METH COLD/WAR TOT/POP 20.
PAGE 19 B0378

S61
GORDON L.."ECONOMIC REGIONALISM RECONSIDERED." FUT ECO/DEV
USA+45 WOR+45 INDUS NAT/G TEC/DEV DIPLOM ROUTINE ATTIT
PERCEPT WEALTH...WELF/ST METH/CNCPT WORK 20. CAP/ISM
PAGE 41 B0830 REGION

S61
HAAS E.B..INTERNATIONAL INTEGRATION: THE EUROPEAN INT/ORG
AND THE UNIVERSAL PROCESS." EUR+WWI FUT WOR+45 TREND
NAT/G EX/STRUC ATTIT DRIVE ORD/FREE PWR...CONCPT REGION
GEN/LAWS OEEC 20 NATO COUNCL/EUR. PAGE 45 B0909

S61
JACKSON E.."CONSTITUTIONAL DEVELOPMENTS OF THE INT/ORG
UNITED NATIONS: THE GROWTH OF ITS EXECUTIVE EXEC
CAPACITY." FUT WOR+45 CONSTN STRUCT ACT/RES PLAN
ALL/VALS...NEW/IDEA OBS COLD/WAR UN 20. PAGE 55
B1106

S61
JUVILER P.H.."INTERPARLIAMENTARY CONTACTS IN SOVIET INT/ORG
FOREIGN POLICY." COM FUT WOR+45 WOR-45 SOCIETY DELIB/GP
CONSULT ACT/RES DIPLOM ADMIN PEACE ATTIT RIGID/FLEX USSR
WEALTH...WELF/ST SOC TOT/POP CONGRESS 19/20.
PAGE 57 B1156

S61
LEWY G.."SUPERIOR ORDERS, NUCLEAR WARFARE AND THE DETER
DICTATES OF CONSCIENCE: THE DILEMMA OF MILITARY INT/ORG
OBEDIENCE IN THE ATOMIC." FUT UNIV WOR+45 INTELL LAW
SOCIETY FORCES TOP/EX ACT/RES ADMIN ROUTINE NUC/PWR INT/LAW
PERCEPT RIGID/FLEX ALL/VALS...POLICY CONCPT 20.
PAGE 65 B1308

S61
NOVE A.."THE SOVIET MODEL AND UNDERDEVELOPED ECO/UNDEV
COUNTRIES." COM FUT USSR WOR+45 CULTURE ECO/DEV PLAN
POL/PAR FOR/AID EDU/PROP ADMIN MORAL WEALTH
...POLICY RECORD HIST/WRIT 20. PAGE 79 B1593

S61
PADOVER S.K.."PSYCHOLOGICAL WARFARE AND FOREIGN ROUTINE
POLICY." FUT UNIV USA+45 INTELL SOCIETY CREATE DIPLOM
EDU/PROP ADMIN WAR PEACE PERCEPT...POLICY
METH/CNCPT TESTS TIME/SEQ 20. PAGE 80 B1623

S61
SCHILLING W.R.."THE H-BOMB: HOW TO DECIDE WITHOUT PERSON
ACTUALLY CHOOSING." FUT USA+45 INTELL CONSULT ADMIN LEGIT
CT/SYS MORAL...JURID OBS 20 TRUMAN/HS. PAGE 93 NUC/PWR
B1888

S61
TAUBENFELD H.J.."OUTER SPACE--PAST POLITICS AND PLAN
FUTURE POLICY." FUT USA+45 USA-45 WOR+45 AIR INTELL SPACE
STRUCT ECO/DEV NAT/G TOP/EX ACT/RES ADMIN ROUTINE INT/ORG
NUC/PWR ATTIT DRIVE...CONCPT TIME/SEQ TREND TOT/POP
20. PAGE 103 B2083

VIRALLY M.,"VERS UNE REFORME DU SECRETARIAT DES
NATIONS UNIES." FUT WOR+45 CONSTN ECO/DEV TOP/EX
BAL/PWR ADMIN ALL/VALS...CONCPT BIOG UN VAL/FREE
20. PAGE 112 B2264
> S61
> INT/ORG
> INTELL
> DIPLOM

BAILEY S.D.,THE SECRETARIAT OF THE UNITED NATIONS.
FUT WOR+45 DELIB/GP PLAN BAL/PWR DOMIN EDU/PROP
ADMIN PEACE ATTIT PWR...DECISION CONCPT TREND
CON/ANAL CHARTS UN VAL/FREE COLD/WAR 20. PAGE 8
B0162
> B62
> INT/ORG
> EXEC
> DIPLOM

SNYDER R.C.,FOREIGN POLICY DECISION-MAKING. FUT
KOREA WOR+45 R+D CREATE ADMIN ROUTINE PWR
...DECISION PSY SOC CONCPT METH/CNCPT CON/ANAL
CHARTS GEN/METH METH 20. PAGE 99 B1992
> B62
> TEC/DEV
> HYPO/EXP
> DIPLOM

BAILEY S.D.,"THE TROIKA AND THE FUTURE OF THE UN."
CONSTN CREATE LEGIT EXEC CHOOSE ORD/FREE PWR
...CONCPT NEW/IDEA UN COLD/WAR 20. PAGE 8 B0163
> L62
> FUT
> INT/ORG
> USSR

HOFFHERR R.,"LE PROBLEME DE L'ENCADREMENT DANS LES
JEUNES ETATS DE LANGUE FRANCAISE EN AFRIQUE
CENTRALE ET A MADAGASCAR." FUT ECO/UNDEV CONSULT
PLAN ECO/TAC COLONIAL ATTIT...MGT TIME/SEQ VAL/FREE
20. PAGE 51 B1028
> L62
> AFR
> STRUCT
> FRANCE

ALBONETTI A.,"IL SECONDO PROGRAMMA QUINQUENNALE
1963-67 ED IL BILANCIO RICERCHE ED INVESTIMENTI PER
IL 1963 DELL'ERATOM." EUR+WWI FUT ITALY USA+45
ECO/DEV SERV/IND INT/ORG TEC/DEV ECO/TAC ATTIT
SKILL WEALTH...MGT TIME/SEQ OEEC 20. PAGE 3 B0069
> S62
> R+D
> PLAN
> NUC/PWR

BUENO M.,"ASPECTOS SOCIOLOGICOS DE LA EDUCACION."
FUT UNIV INTELL R+D SERV/IND SCHOOL CONSULT
EX/STRUC ACT/RES PLAN...METH/CNCPT OBS 20. PAGE 17
B0341
> S62
> SOCIETY
> EDU/PROP
> PERSON

GEORGE P.,"MATERIAUX ET REFLEXIONS POUR UNE
POLITIQUE URBAINE RATIONNELLE DANS LES PAYS EN
COURS DE DEVELOPPEMENT." FUT INTELL SOCIETY
SERV/IND MUNIC ACT/RES WEALTH...MGT 20. PAGE 39
B0790
> S62
> ECO/UNDEV
> PLAN

IOVTCHOUK M.T.,"ON SOME THEORETICAL PRINCIPLES AND
METHODS OF SOCIOLOGICAL INVESTIGATIONS (IN
RUSSIAN)." FUT USA+45 STRATA R+D NAT/G POL/PAR
TOP/EX ACT/RES PLAN ECO/TAC EDU/PROP ROUTINE ATTIT
RIGID/FLEX MARXISM SOCISM...MARXIST METH/CNCPT OBS
TREND NAT/COMP GEN/LAWS 20. PAGE 54 B1102
> S62
> COM
> ECO/DEV
> CAP/ISM
> USSR

JACOBSON H.K.,"THE UNITED NATIONS AND COLONIALISM:
A TENTATIVE APPRAISAL." AFR FUT S/ASIA USA+45 USSR
WOR+45 NAT/G DELIB/GP PLAN DIPLOM ECO/TAC DOMIN
ADMIN ROUTINE COERCE ATTIT RIGID/FLEX ORD/FREE PWR
...OBS STERTYP UN 20. PAGE 55 B1115
> S62
> INT/ORG
> CONCPT
> COLONIAL

LANGROD G.,THE INTERNATIONAL CIVIL SERVICE: ITS
ORIGINS, ITS NATURE, ITS EVALUATION. FUT WOR+45
WOR+45 DELIB/GP ACT/RES DOMIN LEGIT ATTIT
RIGID/FLEX SUPEGO ALL/VALS...MGT CONCPT STAT
TIME/SEQ ILO LEAGUE/NAT VAL/FREE 20 UN. PAGE 62
B1259
> B63
> INT/ORG
> ADMIN

SWEENEY S.B.,ACHIEVING EXCELLENCE IN PUBLIC
SERVICE. FUT USA+45 NAT/G ACT/RES GOV/REL...POLICY
ANTHOL 20 CIVIL/SERV. PAGE 102 B2060
> ADMIN
> WORKER
> TASK
> PLAN

BEGUIN H.,"ASPECTS GEOGRAPHIQUE DE LA
POLARISATION." FUT WOR+45 SOCIETY STRUCT ECO/DEV
R+D BAL/PWR ADMIN ATTIT RIGID/FLEX HEALTH WEALTH
...CHARTS 20. PAGE 10 B0206
> L63
> ECO/UNDEV
> GEOG
> DIPLOM

FREUND G.,"ADENAUER AND THE FUTURE OF GERMANY."
EUR+WWI FUT GERMANY/W FORCES LEGIT ADMIN ROUTINE
ATTIT DRIVE PERSON PWR...POLICY TIME/SEQ TREND
VAL/FREE 20 ADENAUER/K. PAGE 37 B0753
> L63
> NAT/G
> BIOG
> DIPLOM
> GERMANY

COUTY P.,"L'ASSISTANCE POUR LE DEVELOPPEMENT: POINT
DE VUE SCANDINAVES." EUR+WWI FINLAND FUT SWEDEN
WOR+45 ECO/DEV ECO/UNDEV COM/IND LABOR NAT/G
PROF/ORG ACT/RES SKILL WEALTH TOT/POP 20. PAGE 24
B0497
> S63
> FINAN
> ROUTINE
> FOR/AID

DAVEE R.,"POUR UN FONDS DE DEVELOPPEMENT SOCIAL."
FUT WOR+45 INTELL SOCIETY ECO/DEV FINAN TEC/DEV
ROUTINE WEALTH...TREND TOT/POP VAL/FREE UN 20.
PAGE 26 B0532
> S63
> INT/ORG
> SOC
> FOR/AID

DUCROS B.,"MOBILISATION DES RESSOURCES PRODUCTIVES
ET DEVELOPPEMENT." FUT INTELL SOCIETY COM/IND
DIST/IND EXTR/IND FINAN INDUS ROUTINE WEALTH
...METH/CNCPT OBS 20. PAGE 31 B0625
> S63
> ECO/UNDEV
> TEC/DEV

ETIENNE G.,"'LOIS OBJECTIVES' ET PROBLEMES DE
> S63
> TOTALISM

DEVELOPPEMENT DANS LE CONTEXTE CHINE-URSS." ASIA
CHINA/COM COM FUT STRUCT INT/ORG VOL/ASSN TOP/EX
TEC/DEV ECO/TAC ATTIT RIGID/FLEX...GEOG MGT
TIME/SEQ TOT/POP 20. PAGE 34 B0682
> USSR

HAVILAND H.F.,"BUILDING A POLITICAL COMMUNITY."
EUR+WWI FUT UK USA+45 ECO/DEV ECO/UNDEV INT/ORG
NAT/G BAL/PWR ECO/TAC NEUTRAL ROUTINE
ATTIT PWR WEALTH...CONCPT COLD/WAR TOT/POP 20.
PAGE 48 B0972
> S63
> VOL/ASSN
> DIPLOM

MORGENTHAU H.J.,"THE POLITICAL CONDITIONS FOR AN
INTERNATIONAL POLICE FORCE." FUT WOR+45 CREATE
LEGIT ADMIN PEACE ORD/FREE 20. PAGE 75 B1524
> S63
> INT/ORG
> FORCES
> ARMS/CONT
> DETER

ROUGEMONT D.,"LES NOUVELLES CHANCES DE L'EUROPE."
EUR+WWI FUT ECO/DEV INT/ORG NAT/G ACT/RES PLAN
TEC/DEV ECO/TAC ADMIN COLONIAL FEDERAL ATTIT PWR
SKILL...TREND 20. PAGE 91 B1835
> S63
> ECO/UNDEV
> PERCEPT

RUSTOW D.A.,"THE MILITARY IN MIDDLE EASTERN SOCIETY
AND POLITICS." FUT ISLAM CONSTN SOCIETY FACE/GP
NAT/G POL/PAR PROF/ORG CONSULT DOMIN ADMIN EXEC
REGION COERCE NAT/LISM ATTIT DRIVE PERSON ORD/FREE
PWR...POLICY CONCPT OBS STERTYP 20. PAGE 92 B1860
> S63
> FORCES
> ELITES

SHIMKIN D.B.,"STRUCTURE OF SOVIET POWER." COM FUT
USA+45 USSR WOR+45 NAT/G FORCES ECO/TAC DOMIN EXEC
COERCE CHOOSE ATTIT WEALTH...TIME/SEQ COLD/WAR
TOT/POP VAL/FREE 20. PAGE 96 B1948
> S63
> PWR

USEEM J.,"MEN IN THE MIDDLE OF THE THIRD CULTURE:
THE ROLES OF AMERICAN AND NON-WESTERN PEOPLE IN
CROSS-CULTURAL ADMINIS-." FUT WOR+45 DELIB/GP
EX/STRUC LEGIS ATTIT ALL/VALS...MGT INT TIME/SEQ
GEN/LAWS VAL/FREE. PAGE 111 B2247
> S63
> ADMIN
> SOCIETY
> PERSON

APTER D.E.,IDEOLOGY AND DISCONTENT. FUT WOR+45
CONSTN CULTURE INTELL SOCIETY STRUCT INT/ORG NAT/G
DELIB/GP LEGIS CREATE PLAN TEC/DEV EDU/PROP EXEC
PERCEPT PERSON RIGID/FLEX ALL/VALS...POLICY
TOT/POP. PAGE 6 B0122
> B64
> ACT/RES
> ATTIT

COX R.,THEORY IN MARKETING. FUT USA+45 SOCIETY
ECO/DEV PROB/SOLV PRICE RISK PRODUC ATTIT...ANTHOL
20. PAGE 24 B0499
> B64
> MARKET
> ECO/TAC
> PHIL/SCI
> MGT

DIEBOLD J.,BEYOND AUTOMATION: MANAGERIAL PROBLEMS
OF AN EXPLODING TECHNOLOGY. SOCIETY ECO/DEV CREATE
ECO/TAC AUTOMAT SKILL...TECHNIC MGT WORK. PAGE 29
B0589
> B64
> FUT
> INDUS
> PROVS
> NAT/G

GROSS B.M.,THE MANAGING OF ORGANIZATIONS (VOL. II).
FUT USA+45 ECO/DEV EDU/PROP EFFICIENCY...MGT
BIBLIOG/A 20. PAGE 44 B0887
> B64
> ECO/TAC
> ADMIN
> INDUS
> POLICY

HERSKOVITS M.J.,ECONOMIC TRANSITION IN AFRICA. FUT
INT/ORG NAT/G WORKER PROB/SOLV TEC/DEV INT/TRADE
EQUILIB INCOME...ANTHOL 20. PAGE 49 B0996
> B64
> AFR
> ECO/UNDEV
> PLAN
> ADMIN

RIGGS F.W.,ADMINISTRATION IN DEVELOPING COUNTRIES.
FUT WOR+45 STRUCT AGRI INDUS NAT/G PLAN TEC/DEV
ECO/TAC EDU/PROP RIGID/FLEX KNOWL WEALTH...POLICY
MGT CONCPT METH/CNCPT TREND 20. PAGE 88 B1785
> B64
> ECO/UNDEV
> ADMIN

WAINHOUSE D.W.,REMNANTS OF EMPIRE: THE UNITED
NATIONS AND THE END OF COLONIALISM. FUT PORTUGAL
WOR+45 NAT/G CONSULT DOMIN LEGIT ADMIN ROUTINE
ATTIT ORD/FREE...POLICY JURID RECORD INT TIME/SEQ
UN CMN/WLTH 20. PAGE 113 B2275
> B64
> INT/ORG
> TREND
> COLONIAL

MILLIS W.,"THE DEMILITARIZED WORLD." COM USA+45
USSR WOR+45 CONSTN NAT/G EX/STRUC PLAN LEGIT ATTIT
DRIVE...CONCPT TIME/SEQ STERTYP TOT/POP COLD/WAR
20. PAGE 74 B1486
> L64
> FUT
> INT/ORG
> BAL/PWR
> PEACE

KENNAN G.F.,"POLYCENTRISM AND WESTERN POLICY." ASIA
CHINA/COM COM FUT USA+45 USSR NAT/G ACT/RES DOMIN
EDU/PROP EXEC COERCE DISPL PERCEPT...POLICY
COLD/WAR 20. PAGE 59 B1192
> S64
> RIGID/FLEX
> ATTIT
> DIPLOM

SWEARER H.R.,"AFTER KHRUSHCHEV: WHAT NEXT." COM FUT
USSR CONSTN ELITES NAT/G POL/PAR CHIEF DELIB/GP
LEGIS DOMIN LEAD...RECORD TREND STERTYP GEN/METH
20. PAGE 102 B2058
> S64
> EX/STRUC
> PWR

KRIESBERG M.,PUBLIC ADMINISTRATION IN DEVELOPING
COUNTRIES: PROCEEDINGS OF AN INTERNATIONAL
CONFERENCE HELD IN BOGOTA, COLUMBIA,1963. FUT
EDU/PROP ORD/FREE...MGT 20 CIVIL/SERV. PAGE 61
B1237
> B65
> NAT/G
> ECO/UNDEV
> SOCIETY
> ADMIN

LUTZ V.,FRENCH PLANNING. FRANCE TEC/DEV RIGID/FLEX
ORD/FREE 20. PAGE 67 B1348
B65
PLAN
ADMIN
FUT

OECD,MEDITERRANEAN REGIONAL PROJECT: TURKEY;
EDUCATION AND DEVELOPMENT. FUT TURKEY SOCIETY
STRATA FINAN NAT/G PLAN PROB/SOLV ADMIN
COST...STAT CHARTS 20 OECD. PAGE 79 B1602
B65
EDU/PROP
ACADEM
SCHOOL
ECO/UNDEV

ORG FOR ECO COOP AND DEVEL,THE MEDITERRANEAN
REGIONAL PROJECT: AN EXPERIMENT IN PLANNING BY SIX
COUNTRIES. FUT GREECE SPAIN TURKEY YUGOSLAVIA
SOCIETY FINAN NAT/G PROF/ORG EDU/PROP ADMIN REGION
COST...POLICY STAT CHARTS 20 OECD. PAGE 80 B1614
B65
PLAN
ECO/UNDEV
ACADEM
SCHOOL

PERLOFF H.S.,URBAN RESEARCH AND EDUCATION IN THE
NEW YORK METROPOLITAN REGION (VOL. II). FUT USA+45
NEIGH PROF/ORG ACT/RES PROB/SOLV EDU/PROP ADMIN
...STAT BIBLIOG 20 NEWYORK/C. PAGE 82 B1659
B65
MUNIC
PLAN
ACADEM
GP/REL

BROWN S.,"AN ALTERNATIVE TO THE GRAND DESIGN."
EUR+WWI FUT USA+45 INT/ORG NAT/G EX/STRUC FORCES
CREATE BAL/PWR DOMIN RIGID/FLEX ORD/FREE PWR
...NEW/IDEA RECORD EEC NATO 20. PAGE 16 B0327
S65
VOL/ASSN
CONCPT
DIPLOM

HUNTINGTON S.P.,"CONGRESSIONAL RESPONSES TO THE
TWENTIETH CENTURY IN D. TRUMAN, ED. THE CONGRESS
AND AMERICA'S FUTURE." USA+45 USA-45 DIPLOM SENIOR
ADMIN EXEC PWR...SOC 20 CONGRESS. PAGE 53 B1067
C65
FUT
LEAD
NAT/G
LEGIS

NJ DIVISION STATE-REGION PLAN,UTILIZATION OF NEW
JERSEY'S DELAWARE RIVER WATERFRONT (PAMPHLET). FUT
ADMIN REGION LEISURE GOV/REL DEMAND WEALTH...CHARTS
20 NEW/JERSEY. PAGE 78 B1586
N65
UTIL
PLAN
ECO/TAC
PROVS

ANDREWS K.R.,THE EFFECTIVENESS OF UNIVERSITY
MANAGEMENT DEVELOPMENT PROGRAMS. FUT USA+45 ECO/TAC
ADMIN...MGT GU METH/COMP 20. PAGE 5 B0103
B66
ECO/DEV
ACADEM
TOP/EX
ATTIT

JOHNSON N.,PARLIAMENT AND ADMINISTRATION: THE
ESTIMATES COMMITTEE 1945-65. FUT UK NAT/G EX/STRUC
PLAN BUDGET ORD/FREE...T 20 PARLIAMENT HOUSE/CMNS.
PAGE 57 B1147
B66
LEGIS
ADMIN
FINAN
DELIB/GP

KAUNDA K.,ZAMBIA: INDEPENDENCE AND BEYOND: THE
SPEECHES OF KENNETH KAUNDA. AFR FUT ZAMBIA SOCIETY
ECO/UNDEV NAT/G PROB/SOLV ECO/TAC ADMIN RACE/REL
SOVEREIGN 20. PAGE 59 B1183
B66
ORD/FREE
COLONIAL
CONSTN
LEAD

FESLER J.W.,THE FIFTY STATES AND THEIR LOCAL
GOVERNMENTS. FUT USA+45 POL/PAR LEGIS PROB/SOLV
ADMIN CT/SYS CHOOSE GOV/REL FEDERAL...POLICY CHARTS
20 SUPREME/CT. PAGE 35 B0715
B67
PROVS
LOC/G

LEACH R.H.,GOVERNING THE AMERICAN NATION. FUT
USA+45 USA-45 CONSTN POL/PAR PLAN ADJUD EXEC CONSEN
CONGRESS PRESIDENT. PAGE 63 B1278
B67
NAT/G
LEGIS
PWR

PAULSEN F.R.,AMERICAN EDUCATION: CHALLENGES AND
IMAGES. FUT USA+45 ADMIN AGE/C AGE/Y SUPEGO HEALTH
...ANTHOL 20. PAGE 81 B1644
B67
EDU/PROP
SCHOOL
ORD/FREE
GOV/REL

ROBINSON D.W.,PROMISING PRACTICES IN CIVIC
EDUCATION. FUT USA+45 CONTROL PARTIC GOV/REL...OBS
AUD/VIS 20. PAGE 89 B1797
B67
EDU/PROP
NAT/G
ADJUST
ADMIN

UNIVERSAL REFERENCE SYSTEM,PUBLIC POLICY AND THE
MANAGEMENT OF SCIENCE (VOLUME IX). FUT SPACE WOR+45
LAW NAT/G TEC/DEV CONTROL NUC/PWR GOV/REL
...COMPUT/IR METH. PAGE 107 B2165
B67
BIBLIOG/A
POLICY
MGT
PHIL/SCI

BRADY R.H.,"COMPUTERS IN TOP-LEVEL DECISION MAKING"
FUT WOR+45 CONTROL...PREDICT CHARTS. PAGE 15 B0297
S67
COMPUTER
MGT
DECISION
TEC/DEV

KAYSEN C.,"DATA BANKS AND DOSSIERS." FUT USA+45
COM/IND NAT/G PLAN PROB/SOLV TEC/DEV BUDGET ADMIN
ROUTINE. PAGE 59 B1185
S67
CENTRAL
EFFICIENCY
CENSUS
ACT/RES

LEVIN M.R.,"PLANNERS AND METROPOLITAN PLANNING."
FUT USA+45 SOCIETY NAT/G PROVS PROB/SOLV LEAD
PARTIC GOV/REL RACE/REL HABITAT ROLE. PAGE 64 B1301
S67
PLAN
MUNIC
R+D
ADMIN

VERGIN R.C.,"COMPUTER INDUCED ORGANIZATION
CHANGES." FUT USA+45 R+D CREATE OP/RES TEC/DEV
ADJUST CENTRAL...MGT INT CON/ANAL COMPUT/IR.
PAGE 112 B2260
S67
COMPUTER
DECISION
AUTOMAT
EX/STRUC

WINTHROP H.,"THE MEANING OF DECENTRALIZATION FOR
S67
ADMIN

TWENTIETH-CENTURY MAN." FUT WOR+45 SOCIETY TEC/DEV.
PAGE 117 B2366
STRUCT
CENTRAL
PROB/SOLV

FUTURE....SEE FUT

FYFE H. B0768

GABLE R.W. B0769,B0770

GABON....SEE ALSO AFR

WITHERELL J.W.,OFFICIAL PUBLICATIONS OF FRENCH
EQUATORIAL AFRICA, FRENCH CAMEROONS, AND TOGO,
1946-1958 (PAMPHLET). CAMEROON CHAD FRANCE GABON
TOGO LAW ECO/UNDEV EXTR/IND INT/TRADE...GEOG HEAL
20. PAGE 117 B2367
B64
BIBLIOG/A
AFR
NAT/G
ADMIN

GABRIEL P.P. B0771

GAINES J.E. B0772

GALBRAITH J.K. B0773

GALBRAITH J.S. B0774

GALBRAITH, JOHN KENNETH....SEE GALBRTH/JK

GALBRTH/JK....JOHN KENNETH GALBRAITH

GALENSON W. B0775

GALLOWAY G.B. B0776,B0777

GALTUNG J. B0778

GAMBIA....SEE ALSO AFR

CARNEY D.E.,GOVERNMENT AND ECONOMY IN BRITISH WEST
AFRICA. GAMBIA GHANA NIGERIA SIER/LEONE DOMIN ADMIN
GOV/REL SOVEREIGN WEALTH LAISSEZ...BIBLIOG 20
CMN/WLTH. PAGE 19 B0384
B61
METH/COMP
COLONIAL
ECO/TAC
ECO/UNDEV

WALKER A.A.,OFFICIAL PUBLICATIONS OF SIERRA LEONE
AND GAMBIA. GAMBIA SIER/LEONE UK LAW CONSTN LEGIS
PLAN BUDGET DIPLOM...SOC SAMP CON/ANAL 20. PAGE 113
B2278
B63
BIBLIOG
NAT/G
COLONIAL
ADMIN

GAMBLE....SPECULATION ON AN UNCERTAIN EVENT

GAMBLING....SEE RISK, GAMBLE

GAME....GAME THEORY AND DECISION THEORY IN MODELS

BAILEY S.K.,RESEARCH FRONTIERS IN POLITICS AND
GOVERNMENT. CONSTN LEGIS ADMIN REV CHOOSE...CONCPT
IDEA/COMP GAME ANTHOL 20. PAGE 8 B0164
B55
R+D
METH
NAT/G

HELMER O.,"THE PROSPECTS OF A UNIFIED THEORY OF
ORGANIZATIONS" UNIV ACT/RES ADMIN...CONCPT HYPO/EXP
METH. PAGE 49 B0989
S58
SIMUL
LG/CO
METH/CNCPT
GAME

CYERT R.M.,"MODELS IN A BEHAVIORAL THEORY OF THE
FIRM." ROUTINE...DECISION MGT METH/CNCPT MATH.
PAGE 25 B0517
S59
SIMUL
GAME
PREDICT
INDUS

ARROW K.J.,MATHEMATICAL METHODS IN THE SOCIAL
SCIENCES, 1959. TEC/DEV CHOOSE UTIL GAME
...KNO/TEST GAME SIMUL ANTHOL. PAGE 7 B0137
B60
MATH
PSY
MGT

ECKHOFF T.,RATIONALITY AND RESPONSIBILITY IN
ADMINISTRATIVE AND JUDICIAL DECISION-MAKING. ELITES
LEAD INGP/REL ATTIT PWR...MGT METH/COMP GAME 20.
PAGE 32 B0649
B60
ADMIN
PROB/SOLV
DECISION
METH/CNCPT

MORRIS W.T.,ENGINEERING ECONOMY. AUTOMAT RISK
RATIONAL...PROBABIL STAT CHARTS GAME SIMUL BIBLIOG
T 20. PAGE 76 B1529
B60
OP/RES
DECISION
MGT
PROB/SOLV

FRIEDMAN L.,"DECISION MAKING IN COMPETITIVE
SITUATIONS" OP/RES...MGT PROBABIL METH/COMP SIMUL
20. PAGE 37 B0757
S60
DECISION
UTIL
OPTIMAL
GAME

PROCEEDINGS OF THE CONFERENCE ON BUSINESS GAMES AS
TEACHING DEVICES. PROB/SOLV ECO/TAC CONFER ADMIN
TASK...MGT ANTHOL 20. PAGE 29 B0593
B61
GAME
DECISION
EDU/PROP
EFFICIENCY

COHEN K.J.,"THE ROLE OF MANAGEMENT GAMES IN
L61
SOCIETY

EDUCATION AND RESEARCH." INTELL ECO/DEV FINAN
ACT/RES ECO/TAC DECISION. PAGE 22 B0444
GAME
MGT
EDU/PROP
B62

DUCKWORTH W.E.,A GUIDE TO OPERATIONAL RESEARCH.
INDUS PLAN PROB/SOLV EXEC EFFICIENCY PRODUC KNOWL
...MGT MATH STAT SIMUL METH 20 MONTECARLO. PAGE 31
B0624
OP/RES
GAME
DECISION
ADMIN
B63

HEYEL C.,THE ENCYCLOPEDIA OF MANAGEMENT. WOR+45
MARKET TOP/EX TEC/DEV AUTOMAT LEAD ADJUST...STAT
CHARTS GAME ANTHOL BIBLIOG. PAGE 49 B1002
MGT
INDUS
ADMIN
FINAN
B63

THORELLI H.B.,INTOP: INTERNATIONAL OPERATIONS
SIMULATION: PLAYER'S MANUAL. BRAZIL FINAN OP/RES
ADMIN GP/REL INGP/REL PRODUC PERCEPT...DECISION MGT
EEC. PAGE 104 B2108
GAME
INT/TRADE
EDU/PROP
LG/CO
B64

BLAKE R.R.,MANAGING INTERGROUP CONFLICT IN
INDUSTRY. INDUS DELIB/GP EX/STRUC GP/REL PERS/REL
GAME. PAGE 12 B0250
CREATE
PROB/SOLV
OP/RES
ADJUD
S65

GRENIEWSKI H.,"INTENTION AND PERFORMANCE: A PRIMER
OF CYBERNETICS OF PLANNING." EFFICIENCY OPTIMAL
KNOWL SKILL...DECISION MGT EQULIB. PAGE 43 B0873
SIMUL
GAME
GEN/METH
PLAN
S65

HAMMOND P.Y.,"FOREIGN POLICY-MAKING AND
ADMINISTRATIVE POLITICS." CREATE ADMIN COST
...DECISION CONCPT GAME CONGRESS PRESIDENT. PAGE 46
B0935
DIPLOM
STRUCT
IDEA/COMP
OP/RES
B66

MANSFIELD E.,MANAGERIAL ECONOMICS AND OPERATIONS
RESEARCH; A NONMATHEMATICAL INTRODUCTION. USA+45
ELITES ECO/DEV CONSULT EX/STRUC PROB/SOLV ROUTINE
EFFICIENCY OPTIMAL...GAME T 20. PAGE 69 B1396
ECO/TAC
OP/RES
MGT
COMPUTER

GANDHI/I....MME. INDIRA GANDHI

GANDHI/M....MAHATMA GANDHI

GANGULY D.S. B0779

GAO....THE EMPIRE OF GAO

GARCIA E. B0780

GARDNER R.N. B0781

GARFIELD PJ   LOVEJOY WF B0782

GARFIELD/J....PRESIDENT JAMES A. GARFIELD

GARIBALD/G....GUISEPPE GARIBALDI

GARNER J.F. B0324

GARNER U.F. B0783

GARNICK D.H. B0784

GARRISON L.K. B0146

GARY....GARY, INDIANA

GAS/NATURL....GAS, NATURAL

GATT....GENERAL AGREEMENT ON TARIFFS AND TRADE; SEE ALSO
     VOL/ASSN, INT/ORG

US SUPERINTENDENT OF DOCUMENTS,TARIFF AND TAXATION
(PRICE LIST 37). USA+45 LAW INT/TRADE ADJUD ADMIN
CT/SYS INCOME OWN...DECISION GATT. PAGE 111 B2242
BIBLIOG/A
TAX
TARIFFS
NAT/G

GAUS J.M. B0785,B0786,B0787

GEARY T.C. B0704

GEARY....GEARY ACT

GELLHORN W. B0788,B0789

GEN/DYNMCS....GENERAL DYNAMICS CORPORATION

GEN/ELCTRC....GENERAL ELECTRIC CO.

GEN/LAWS....SYSTEMS AND APPROACHES BASED ON SUBSTANTIVE
     RELATIONS

GEN/METH....SYSTEMS BASED ON METHODOLGY

GEN/MOTORS....GENERAL MOTORS CORPORATION

GENACCOUNT....GENERAL ACCOUNTING OFFICE

S56

MILNE R.S.,"CONTROL OF GOVERNMENT CORPORATIONS IN
THE UNITED STATES." USA+45 NAT/G CHIEF LEGIS BUDGET
20 GENACCOUNT. PAGE 74 B1488
CONTROL
EX/STRUC
GOV/REL
PWR
B65

BOXER C.R.,PORTUGUESE SOCIETY IN THE TROPICS - THE
MUNICIPAL COUNCILS OF GAO, MACAO, BAHIA, AND
LUANDA, 1510-1800. EUR+WWI MOD/EUR PORTUGAL CONSTN
EX/STRUC DOMIN CONTROL ROUTINE REPRESENT PRIVIL
...BIBLIOG/A 16/19 GENACCOUNT MACAO BAHIA LUANDA.
PAGE 14 B0290
MUNIC
ADMIN
COLONIAL
DELIB/GP

GENERAL ACCOUNTING OFFICE....SEE GENACCOUNT

GENERAL AGREEMENT ON TARIFFS AND TRADE....SEE GATT

GENERAL AND COMPLETE DISARMAMENT....SEE ARMS/CONT

GENERAL ASSEMBLY....SEE UN+LEGIS

GENERAL DYNAMICS CORPORATION....SEE GEN/DYNMCS

GENERAL ELECTRIC COMPANY....SEE GEN/ELCTRC

GENERAL MOTORS CORPORATION....SEE GEN/MOTORS

GENEVA/CON....GENEVA CONFERENCES (ANY OR ALL)

GEOG....DEMOGRAPHY AND GEOGRAPHY

N

KYRIAK T.E.,EAST EUROPE: BIBLIOGRAPHY--INDEX TO US
JPRS RESEARCH TRANSLATIONS. ALBANIA BULGARIA COM
CZECHOSLVK HUNGARY POLAND ROMANIA AGRI EXTR/IND
FINAN SERV/IND INT/TRADE WEAPON...GEOG MGT SOC 20.
PAGE 62 B1247
BIBLIOG/A
PRESS
MARXISM
INDUS

N

UNIVERSITY OF FLORIDA,CARIBBEAN ACQUISITIONS:
MATERIALS ACQUIRED BY THE UNIVERSITY OF FLORIDA
1957-1960. L/A+17C...ART/METH GEOG MGT 20. PAGE 107
B2167
BIBLIOG
ECO/UNDEV
EDU/PROP
JURID
B00

MORRIS H.C.,THE HISTORY OF COLONIZATION. WOR+45
WOR-45 ECO/DEV ECO/UNDEV INT/ORG ACT/RES PLAN
ECO/TAC LEGIT ROUTINE COERCE ATTIT DRIVE ALL/VALS
...GEOG TREND 19. PAGE 76 B1528
DOMIN
SOVEREIGN
COLONIAL
B00

SANDERSON E.,AFRICA IN THE NINETEENTH CENTURY.
FRANCE UK EXTR/IND FORCES LEGIS ADMIN WAR DISCRIM
ORD/FREE...GEOG GP/COMP SOC/INTEG 19. PAGE 92 B1867
COLONIAL
AFR
DIPLOM
B25

THOMAS F.,THE ENVIRONMENTAL BASIS OF SOCIETY.
USA+45 WOR-45 STRATA ECO/DEV EXTR/IND CONSULT
ECO/TAC ROUTINE ATTIT ALL/VALS...SOC TIME/SEQ.
PAGE 104 B2098
SOCIETY
GEOG
B26

MOON P.T.,IMPERIALISM AND WORLD POLITICS. AFR ASIA
ISLAM MOD/EUR S/ASIA USA+45 SOCIETY NAT/G EX/STRUC
BAL/PWR DOMIN COLONIAL NAT/LISM ATTIT DRIVE PWR
...GEOG SOC 20. PAGE 75 B1510
WEALTH
TIME/SEQ
CAP/ISM
DIPLOM
B28

HALL W.P.,EMPIRE TO COMMONWEALTH. FUT WOR-45 CONSTN
ECO/DEV ECO/UNDEV INT/ORG PROVS PLAN DIPLOM
EDU/PROP ADMIN COLONIAL PEACE PERSON ALL/VALS
...POLICY GEOG SOC OBS RECORD TREND CMN/WLTH
PARLIAMENT 19/20. PAGE 46 B0925
VOL/ASSN
NAT/G
UK
B29

BOUDET P.,BIBLIOGRAPHIE DE L'INDOCHINE FRANCAISE.
S/ASIA VIETNAM SECT...GEOG LING 20. PAGE 14 B0282
BIBLIOG
ADMIN
COLONIAL
DIPLOM
B36

ROBINSON H.,DEVELOPMENT OF THE BRITISH EMPIRE.
WOR-45 CULTURE SOCIETY STRUCT ECO/DEV ECO/UNDEV
INT/ORG VOL/ASSN FORCES CREATE PLAN DOMIN EDU/PROP
ADMIN COLONIAL PWR WEALTH...POLICY GEOG CHARTS
CMN/WLTH 16/20. PAGE 89 B1800
NAT/G
HIST/WRIT
UK
B37

UNION OF SOUTH AFRICA,REPORT CONCERNING
ADMINISTRATION OF SOUTH WEST AFRICA (6 VOLS.).
SOUTH/AFR INDUS PUB/INST FORCES LEGIS BUDGET DIPLOM
EDU/PROP ADJUD CT/SYS...GEOG CHARTS 20 AFRICA/SW
LEAGUE/NAT. PAGE 107 B2158
NAT/G
ADMIN
COLONIAL
CONSTN
B40

GAUS J.M.,PUBLIC ADMINISTRATION AND THE UNITED
STATES DEPARTMENT OF AGRICULTURE. USA-45 STRUCT
DIST/IND FINAN MARKET EX/STRUC PROB/SOLV GIVE
PRODUC...POLICY GEOG CHARTS 20 DEPT/AGRI. PAGE 39
B0786
ADMIN
AGRI
DELIB/GP
OP/RES
B46

GRIFFIN G.G.,A GUIDE TO MANUSCRIPTS RELATING TO
AMERICAN HISTORY IN BRITISH DEPOSITORIES. CANADA
IRELAND MOD/EUR UK USA-45 LAW DIPLOM ADMIN COLONIAL
BIBLIOG/A
ALL/VALS
NAT/G

WAR NAT/LISM SOVEREIGN...GEOG INT/LAW 15/19
CMN/WLTH. PAGE 43 B0876

B47
MILLETT J.D.,THE PROCESS AND ORGANIZATION OF   ADMIN
GOVERNMENT PLANNING. USA+45 DELIB/GP ACT/RES LEAD   NAT/G
LOBBY TASK...POLICY GEOG TIME 20 RESOURCE/N.   PLAN
PAGE 73 B1482   CONSULT

B48
HOOVER E.M.,THE LOCATION OF ECONOMIC ACTIVITY.   HABITAT
WOR+45 MARKET MUNIC WORKER PROB/SOLV INT/TRADE   INDUS
ADMIN COST...POLICY CHARTS T 20. PAGE 51 B1041   ECO/TAC
                                                      GEOG

C50
STOKES W.S.,"HONDURAS: AN AREA STUDY IN   CONSTN
GOVERNMENT." HONDURAS NAT/G POL/PAR COLONIAL CT/SYS   LAW
ROUTINE CHOOSE REPRESENT...GEOG RECORD BIBLIOG   L/A+17C
19/20. PAGE 101 B2044   ADMIN

B52
UNESCO,THESES DE SCIENCES SOCIALES: CATALOGUE   BIBLIOG
ANALYTIQUE INTERNATIONAL DE THESES INEDITES DE   ACADEM
DOCTORAT. 1940-1950. INT/ORG DIPLOM EDU/PROP...GEOG   WRITING
INT/LAW MGT PSY SOC 20. PAGE 107 B2155

B53
PIERCE R.A.,RUSSIAN CENTRAL ASIA, 1867-1917: A   BIBLIOG
SELECTED BIBLIOGRAPHY (PAMPHLET). USSR LAW CULTURE   COLONIAL
NAT/G EDU/PROP WAR...GEOG SOC 19/20. PAGE 83 B1671   ADMIN
                                                      COM

S56
MARGOLIS J.,"ON MUNICIPAL LAND POLICY FOR FISCAL   BUDGET
GAINS." USA+45 MUNIC PLAN TAX COST EFFICIENCY   POLICY
HABITAT KNOWL...MGT 20. PAGE 69 B1398   GEOG
                                                      LOC/G

B58
MASON J.B.,THAILAND BIBLIOGRAPHY. S/ASIA THAILAND   BIBLIOG/A
CULTURE EDU/PROP ADMIN...GEOG SOC LING 20. PAGE 70   ECO/UNDEV
B1423   DIPLOM
                                                      NAT/G

B59
PARK R.L.,LEADERSHIP AND POLITICAL INSTITUTIONS IN   NAT/G
INDIA. S/ASIA CULTURE ECO/UNDEV LOC/G MUNIC PROVS   EXEC
LEGIS PLAN ADMIN LEAD ORD/FREE WEALTH...GEOG SOC   INDIA
BIOG TOT/POP VAL/FREE 20. PAGE 81 B1633

B60
ASPREMONT-LYNDEN H.,RAPPORT SUR L'ADMINISTRATION   AFR
BELGE DU RUANDA-URUNDI PENDANT L'ANNEE 1959.   COLONIAL
BELGIUM RWANDA AGRI INDUS DIPLOM ECO/TAC INT/TRADE   ECO/UNDEV
DOMIN ADMIN RACE/REL...GEOG CENSUS 20 UN. PAGE 7   INT/ORG
B0143

B60
JONES V.,METROPOLITAN COMMUNITIES: A BIBLIOGRAPHY   BIBLIOG
WITH SPECIAL EMPHASIS UPON GOVERNMENT AND POLITICS,   LOC/G
1955-1957. STRUCT ECO/DEV FINAN FORCES PLAN   MUNIC
PROB/SOLV RECEIVE EDU/PROP CT/SYS...GEOG HEAL 20.   ADMIN
PAGE 57 B1152

B60
LEYDER J.,BIBLIOGRAPHIE DE L'ENSEIGNEMENT SUPERIEUR   BIBLIOG/A
ET DE LA RECHERCHE SCIENTIFIQUE EN AFRIQUE   ACT/RES
INTERTROPICALE (2 VOLS.). AFR CULTURE ECO/UNDEV   ACADEM
AGRI PLAN EDU/PROP ADMIN COLONIAL...GEOG SOC/INTEG   R+D
20 NEGRO. PAGE 65 B1309

N60
RHODESIA-NYASA NATL ARCHIVES,A SELECT BIBLIOGRAPHY   BIBLIOG
OF RECENT PUBLICATIONS CONCERNING THE FEDERATION OF   ADMIN
RHODESIA AND NYASALAND (PAMPHLET). MALAWI RHODESIA   ORD/FREE
LAW CULTURE STRUCT ECO/UNDEV LEGIS...GEOG 20.   NAT/G
PAGE 88 B1770

B61
JACOBS J.,THE DEATH AND LIFE OF GREAT AMERICAN   MUNIC
CITIES. USA+45 SOCIETY DIST/IND CREATE PROB/SOLV   PLAN
ADMIN...GEOG SOC CENSUS 20 URBAN/RNWL. PAGE 55   ADJUST
B1113   HABITAT

B61
LEE R.R.,ENGINEERING-ECONOMIC PLANNING   BIBLIOG/A
MISCELLANEOUS SUBJECTS: A SELECTED BIBLIOGRAPHY   PLAN
(MIMEOGRAPHED). FINAN LOC/G MUNIC NEIGH ADMIN   REGION
CONTROL INGP/REL HABITAT...GEOG MGT SOC/WK 20
RESOURCE/N. PAGE 63 B1280

S61
LANFALUSSY A.,"EUROPE'S PROGRESS: DUE TO COMMON   INT/ORG
MARKET." EUR+WWI ECO/DEV DELIB/GP PLAN ECO/TAC   MARKET
ROUTINE WEALTH...GEOG TREND EEC 20. PAGE 62 B1257

S61
TOMASIC D.,"POLITICAL LEADERSHIP IN CONTEMPORARY   SOCIETY
POLAND." COM EUR+WWI GERMANY NAT/G POL/PAR SECT   ROUTINE
DELIB/GP PLAN ECO/TAC DOMIN EDU/PROP PWR MARXISM   USSR
...MARXIST GEOG MGT CONCPT TIME/SEQ STERTYP 20.   POLAND
PAGE 105 B2114

B62
CARPER E.T.,ILLINOIS GOES TO CONGRESS FOR ARMY   ADMIN
LAND. USA+45 LAW EXTR/IND PROVS REGION CIVMIL/REL   LOBBY
GOV/REL FEDERAL ATTIT 20 ILLINOIS SENATE CONGRESS   GEOG
DIRKSEN/E DOUGLAS/P. PAGE 19 B0385   LEGIS

B62
KAMMERER G.M.,CITY MANAGERS IN POLITICS: AN   MUNIC
ANALYSIS OF MANAGER TENURE AND TERMINATION. POL/PAR   LEAD
LEGIS PARTIC CHOOSE PWR...DECISION GEOG METH/CNCPT.   EXEC

PAGE 57 B1161

B62
UNECA LIBRARY,NEW ACQUISITIONS IN THE UNECA   BIBLIOG
LIBRARY. LAW NAT/G PLAN PROB/SOLV TEC/DEV ADMIN   AFR
REGION...GEOG SOC 20 UN. PAGE 106 B2152   ECO/UNDEV
                                                      INT/ORG

B62
US LIBRARY OF CONGRESS,A LIST OF AMERICAN DOCTORAL   BIBLIOG
DISSERTATIONS ON AFRICA. SOCIETY SECT DIPLOM   AFR
EDU/PROP ADMIN...GEOG 19/20. PAGE 109 B2206   ACADEM
                                                      CULTURE

S62
PIQUEMAL M.,"LES PROBLEMES DES UNIONS D'ETATS EN   AFR
AFRIQUE NOIRE." FRANCE SOCIETY INT/ORG NAT/G   ECO/UNDEV
DELIB/GP PLAN LEGIT ADMIN COLONIAL ROUTINE ATTIT   REGION
ORD/FREE PWR...GEOG METH/CNCPT 20. PAGE 83 B1678

S62
SPRINGER H.W.,"FEDERATION IN THE CARIBBEAN: AN   VOL/ASSN
ATTEMPT THAT FAILED." L/A+17C ECO/UNDEV INT/ORG   NAT/G
POL/PAR PROVS LEGIS CREATE PLAN LEGIT ADMIN FEDERAL   REGION
ATTIT DRIVE PERSON ORD/FREE PWR...POLICY GEOG PSY
CONCPT OBS CARIBBEAN CMN/WLTH 20. PAGE 100 B2013

B63
CHOJNACKI S.,REGISTER ON CURRENT RESEARCH ON   BIBLIOG
ETHIOPIA AND THE HORN OF AFRICA. ETHIOPIA LAW   ACT/RES
CULTURE AGRI SECT EDU/PROP ADMIN...GEOG HEAL LING   INTELL
20. PAGE 21 B0426   ACADEM

L63
BEGUIN H.,"ASPECTS GEOGRAPHIQUE DE LA   ECO/UNDEV
POLARISATION." FUT WOR+45 SOCIETY STRUCT ECO/DEV   GEOG
R+D BAL/PWR ADMIN ATTIT RIGID/FLEX HEALTH WEALTH   DIPLOM
...CHARTS 20. PAGE 10 B0206

S63
ETIENNE G.,"'LOIS OBJECTIVES' ET PROBLEMES DE   TOTALISM
DEVELOPPEMENT DANS LE CONTEXTE CHINE-URSS." ASIA   USSR
CHINA/COM COM FUT STRUCT INT/ORG VOL/ASSN TOP/EX
TEC/DEV ECO/TAC ATTIT RIGID/FLEX...GEOG MGT
TIME/SEQ TOT/POP 20. PAGE 34 B0682

B64
CULLINGWORTH J.B.,TOWN AND COUNTRY PLANNING IN   MUNIC
ENGLAND AND WALES. UK LAW SOCIETY CONSULT ACT/RES   PLAN
ADMIN ROUTINE LEISURE INGP/REL ADJUST PWR...GEOG 20   NAT/G
OPEN/SPACE URBAN/RNWL. PAGE 25 B0512   PROB/SOLV

B64
FLORENCE P.S.,ECONOMICS AND SOCIOLOGY OF INDUSTRY;   INDUS
A REALISTIC ANALYSIS OF DEVELOPMENT. ECO/UNDEV   SOC
LG/CO NAT/G PLAN...GEOG MGT BIBLIOG 20. PAGE 36   ADMIN
B0729

B64
GRAVIER J.F.,AMENAGEMENT DU TERRITOIRE ET L'AVENIR   PLAN
DES REGIONS FRANCAISES. FRANCE ECO/DEV AGRI INDUS   MUNIC
CREATE...GEOG CHARTS 20. PAGE 42 B0859   NEIGH
                                                      ADMIN

B64
OECD SEMINAR REGIONAL DEV,REGIONAL DEVELOPMENT IN   ADMIN
ISRAEL. ISRAEL STRUCT ECO/UNDEV NAT/G REGION...GEOG   PROVS
20. PAGE 79 B1603   PLAN
                                                      METH/COMP

B64
PINNICK A.W.,COUNTRY PLANNERS IN ACTION. UK FINAN   MUNIC
SERV/IND NAT/G CONSULT DELIB/GP PRICE CONTROL   PLAN
ROUTINE LEISURE AGE/C...GEOG 20 URBAN/RNWL. PAGE 83   INDUS
B1674   ATTIT

B64
RUSSET B.M.,WORLD HANDBOOK OF POLITICAL AND SOCIAL   DIPLOM
INDICATORS. WOR+45 COM/IND ADMIN WEALTH...GEOG 20.   STAT
PAGE 92 B1858   NAT/G
                                                      NAT/COMP

B64
WITHERELL J.W.,OFFICIAL PUBLICATIONS OF FRENCH   BIBLIOG/A
EQUATORIAL AFRICA, FRENCH CAMEROONS, AND TOGO,   AFR
1946-1958 (PAMPHLET). CAMEROON CHAD FRANCE GABON   NAT/G
TOGO LAW ECO/UNDEV EXTR/IND INT/TRADE...GEOG HEAL   ADMIN
20. PAGE 117 B2367

S64
HADY T.F.,"CONGRESSIONAL TOWNSHIPS AS INCORPORATED   MUNIC
MUNICIPALITIES." NEIGH ADMIN REPRESENT ATTIT GEOG.   REGION
PAGE 45 B0914   LOC/G
                                                      GOV/COMP

B65
BANFIELD E.C.,BIG CITY POLITICS. USA+45 CONSTN   METH/COMP
POL/PAR ADMIN LOBBY CHOOSE SUFF INGP/REL PWR...GEOG   MUNIC
20. PAGE 9 B0179   STRUCT

B65
MATRAS J.,SOCIAL CHANGE IN ISRAEL. ISRAEL STRATA   SECT
FAM ACT/RES EDU/PROP ADMIN CHOOSE...STAT CENSUS   NAT/LISM
19/20 JEWS. PAGE 71 B1427   GEOG
                                                      STRUCT

B65
ROTBERG R.I.,A POLITICAL HISTORY OF TROPICAL   AFR
AFRICA. EX/STRUC DIPLOM INT/TRADE DOMIN ADMIN   CULTURE
RACE/REL NAT/LISM PWR SOVEREIGN...GEOG TIME/SEQ   COLONIAL
BIBLIOG 1/20. PAGE 91 B1832

B65
UNESCO,INTERNATIONAL ORGANIZATIONS IN THE SOCIAL   INT/ORG
SCIENCES(REV. ED.). LAW ADMIN ATTIT...CRIMLGY GEOG   R+D

INT/LAW PSY SOC STAT 20 UNESCO. PAGE 107 B2157   PROF/ORG
                                                        ACT/RES
                                                             B65
UNIVERSAL REFERENCE SYSTEM,INTERNATIONAL AFFAIRS: BIBLIOG/A
VOLUME I IN THE POLITICAL SCIENCE, GOVERNMENT, AND   GEN/METH
PUBLIC POLICY SERIES....DECISION ECOMETRIC GEOG   COMPUT/IR
INT/LAW JURID MGT PHIL/SCI PSY SOC. PAGE 107 B2163   DIPLOM
                                                             S65
POSVAR W.W.,"NATIONAL SECURITY POLICY* THE REALM OF   DIPLOM
OBSCURITY." CREATE PLAN PROB/SOLV ADMIN LEAD GP/REL   USA+45
CONSERVE...DECISION GEOG. PAGE 84 B1694   RECORD
                                                             S65
QUADE Q.L.,"THE TRUMAN ADMINISTRATION AND THE   USA+45
SEPARATION OF POWERS: THE CASE OF THE MARSHALL   ECO/UNDEV
PLAN." SOCIETY INT/ORG NAT/G CONSULT DELIB/GP LEGIS   DIPLOM
PLAN ECO/TAC ROUTINE DRIVE PERCEPT RIGID/FLEX
ORD/FREE PWR WEALTH...DECISION GEOG NEW/IDEA TREND
20 TRUMAN/HS. PAGE 85 B1726
                                                             B66
DAVIS R.G.,PLANNING HUMAN RESOURCE DEVELOPMENT.   PLAN
EDUCATIONAL MODELS AND SCHEMATA. WORKER OP/RES   EFFICIENCY
ECO/TAC EDU/PROP CONTROL COST PRODUC...GEOG STAT   SIMUL
CHARTS 20 B0544   ROUTINE
                                                             B66
GRETHER E.T.,MARKETING AND PUBLIC POLICY. USA+45   MARKET
ECO/DEV DIST/IND NAT/G PLAN CAP/ISM PRICE CONTROL   PROB/SOLV
...GEOG MGT 20. PAGE 43 B0874   ECO/TAC
                                                        POLICY
                                                             B66
US DEPARTMENT OF THE ARMY,COMMUNIST CHINA: A   BIBLIOG/A
STRATEGIC SURVEY: A BIBLIOGRAPHY (PAMPHLET NO.   MARXISM
20-67). CHINA/COM COM INDIA USSR NAT/G POL/PAR   S/ASIA
EX/STRUC FORCES NUC/PWR REV ATTIT...POLICY GEOG   DIPLOM
CHARTS. PAGE 108 B2184
                                                             S66
"FURTHER READING." INDIA LOC/G NAT/G PLAN ADMIN   BIBLIOG
WEALTH...GEOG SOC CONCPT CENSUS 20. PAGE 2 B0045   ECO/UNDEV
                                                        TEC/DEV
                                                        PROVS
                                                             C66
JACOB H.,"DIMENSIONS OF STATE POLITICS HEARD A. ED.   PROVS
STATE LEGIWLATURES IN AMERICAN POLITICS." CULTURE   LEGIS
STRATA POL/PAR BUDGET TAX LOBBY ROUTINE GOV/REL   ROLE
...TRADIT DECISION GEOG. PAGE 55 B1112   REPRESENT
                                                             B67
DE BLIJ H.J.,SYSTEMATIC POLITICAL GEOGRAPHY. WOR+45   GEOG
STRUCT INT/ORG NAT/G EDU/PROP ADMIN COLONIAL   CONCPT
ROUTINE ORD/FREE PWR...IDEA/COMP T 20. PAGE 27   METH
B0550
                                                             S67
ALPANDER G.G.,"ENTREPRENEURS AND PRIVATE ENTERPRISE   ECO/UNDEV
IN TURKEY." TURKEY INDUS PROC/MFG EDU/PROP ATTIT   LG/CO
DRIVE WEALTH...GEOG MGT SOC STAT TREND CHARTS 20.   NAT/G
PAGE 4 B0080   POLICY

GEOGRAPHY....SEE GEOG

GEOPOLITIC....GEOPOLITICS

GEOPOLITICS....SEE GEOG+POL, GEOPOLITIC

GEORGE P. B0790

GEORGE/DL....DAVID LLOYD GEORGE

GEORGE/III....GEORGE THE THIRD OF ENGLAND

GEORGIA....GEORGIA
                                                             B50
MONTGOMERY H.,CRACKER PARTIES. CULTURE EX/STRUC   POL/PAR
LEAD PWR POPULISM...TIME/SEQ 19 GEORGIA CALHOUN/JC   PROVS
COBB/HOWLL JACKSON/A. PAGE 74 B1505   ELITES
                                                        BIOG

GER/CONFED....GERMAN CONFEDERATION

GERBERDING W.P. B0791

GERMAN CONFEDERATION....SEE GER/CONFED

GERMAN/AM....GERMAN-AMERICANS

GERMANS/PA....GERMANS IN PENNSYLVANIA

GERMANY....GERMANY IN GENERAL; SEE ALSO APPROPRIATE TIME/
    SPACE/CULTURE INDEX
                                                             B
DEUTSCHE BIBLIOTH FRANKF A M,DEUTSCHE   BIBLIOG
BIBLIOGRAPHIE. EUR+WWI GERMANY ECO/DEV FORCES   LAW
DIPLOM LEAD...POLICY PHIL/SCI SOC 20. PAGE 28 B0578   ADMIN
                                                        NAT/G
                                                             N
DEUTSCHE BUCHEREI,JAHRESVERZEICHNIS DER DEUTSCHEN   BIBLIOG
HOCHSCHULSCHRIFTEN. EUR+WWI GERMANY LAW ADMIN   WRITING

PERSON...MGT SOC 19/20. PAGE 28 B0579   ACADEM
                                                        INTELL
                                                             N
DEUTSCHE BUCHEREI,JAHRESVERZEICHNIS DES DEUTSCHEN   BIBLIOG
SCHRIFTUMS. AUSTRIA EUR+WWI GERMANY SWITZERLND LAW   WRITING
LOC/G DIPLOM ADMIN...MGT SOC 19/20. PAGE 29 B0580   NAT/G
                                                             N
DEUTSCHE BUCHEREI,DEUTSCHES BUCHERVERZEICHNIS.   BIBLIOG
GERMANY LAW CULTURE POL/PAR ADMIN LEAD ATTIT PERSON   NAT/G
...SOC 20. PAGE 29 B0581   DIPLOM
                                                        ECO/DEV
                                                             B16
TREITSCHKE H.,POLITICS. UNIV SOCIETY STRATA NAT/G   EXEC
EX/STRUC LEGIS DOMIN EDU/PROP ATTIT PWR RESPECT   ELITES
...CONCPT TIME/SEQ GEN/LAWS TOT/POP 20. PAGE 105   GERMANY
B2127
                                                             B18
WILSON W.,THE STATE: ELEMENTS OF HISTORICAL AND   NAT/G
PRACTICAL POLITICS. FRANCE GERMANY ITALY UK USSR   JURID
CONSTN EX/STRUC LEGIS CT/SYS WAR PWR...POLICY   CONCPT
GOV/COMP 20. PAGE 117 B2363   NAT/COMP
                                                             C20
BLACHLY F.F.,"THE GOVERNMENT AND ADMINISTRATION OF   NAT/G
GERMANY." GERMANY CONSTN LOC/G PROVS DELIB/GP   GOV/REL
EX/STRUC FORCES LEGIS TOP/EX CT/SYS...BIBLIOG/A   ADMIN
19/20. PAGE 12 B0246   PHIL/SCI
                                                             B33
ENSOR R.C.K.,COURTS AND JUDGES IN FRANCE, GERMANY,   CT/SYS
AND ENGLAND. FRANCE GERMANY UK LAW PROB/SOLV ADMIN   EX/STRUC
ROUTINE CRIME ROLE...METH/COMP 20 CIVIL/LAW.   ADJUD
PAGE 33 B0676   NAT/COMP
                                                             B38
REICH N.,LABOR RELATIONS IN REPUBLICAN GERMANY.   WORKER
GERMANY CONSTN ECO/DEV INDUS NAT/G ADMIN CONTROL   MGT
GP/REL FASCISM POPULISM 20 WEIMAR/REP. PAGE 87   LABOR
B1763   BARGAIN
                                                             B39
ANDERSON W.,LOCAL GOVERNMENT IN EUROPE. FRANCE   GOV/COMP
GERMANY ITALY UK USSR MUNIC PROVS ADMIN GOV/REL   NAT/COMP
CENTRAL SOVEREIGN 20. PAGE 5 B0099   LOC/G
                                                        CONSTN
                                                             S40
GERTH H.,"THE NAZI PARTY: ITS LEADERSHIP AND   POL/PAR
COMPOSITION" (BMR)" GERMANY ELITES STRATA STRUCT   DOMIN
EX/STRUC FORCES ECO/TAC CT/SYS CHOOSE TOTALISM   LEAD
AGE/Y AUTHORIT PWR 20. PAGE 39 B0792   ADMIN
                                                             B41
STATIST REICHSAMTE,BIBLIOGRAPHIE DER STAATS- UND   BIBLIOG
WIRSCHAFTSWISSENSCHAFTEN. EUR+WWI GERMANY FINAN   ECO/DEV
ADMIN. PAGE 100 B2025   NAT/G
                                                        POLICY
                                                             B42
CHAMBERLIN W.,INDUSTRIAL RELATIONS IN GERMANY   BIBLIOG/A
1914-1939. GERMANY 20. PAGE 20 B0401   LABOR
                                                        MGT
                                                        GP/REL
                                                             B42
NEUBURGER O.,OFFICIAL PUBLICATIONS OF PRESENT-DAY   BIBLIOG/A
GERMANY: GOVERNMENT, CORPORATE ORGANIZATIONS, AND   FASCISM
NATIONAL SOCIALIST PARTY. GERMANY CONSTN COM/IND   NAT/G
POL/PAR EDU/PROP PRESS 20 NAZI. PAGE 78 B1570   ADMIN
                                                             B42
SINGTON D.,THE GOEBBELS EXPERIMENT. GERMANY MOD/EUR   FASCISM
NAT/G EX/STRUC FORCES CONTROL ROUTINE WAR TOTALISM   EDU/PROP
PWR...ART/METH HUM 20 NAZI GOEBBELS/J. PAGE 97   ATTIT
B1970   COM/IND
                                                             B44
BARKER E.,THE DEVELOPMENT OF PUBLIC SERVICES IN   GOV/COMP
WESTERN WUROPE: 1660-1930. FRANCE GERMANY UK SCHOOL   ADMIN
CONTROL REPRESENT ROLE...WELF/ST 17/20. PAGE 9   EX/STRUC
B0185
                                                             B45
BRECHT A.,FEDERALISM AND REGIONALISM IN GERMANY;   FEDERAL
THE DIVISION OF PRUSSIA. GERMANY PRUSSIA WOR-45   REGION
CREATE ADMIN WAR TOTALISM PWR...CHARTS 20 HITLER/A.   PROB/SOLV
PAGE 15 B0303   CONSTN
                                                             B45
CONOVER H.F.,THE GOVERNMENTS OF THE MAJOR FOREIGN   BIBLIOG
POWERS: A BIBLIOGRAPHY. FRANCE GERMANY ITALY UK   NAT/G
USSR CONSTN LOC/G POL/PAR EX/STRUC FORCES ADMIN   DIPLOM
CT/SYS CIVMIL/REL TOTALISM...POLICY 19/20. PAGE 23
B0464
                                                             B48
BONAPARTE M.,MYTHS OF WAR. GERMANY WOR+45 WOR-45   ROUTINE
CULTURE SOCIETY NAT/G FORCES LEGIT ATTIT ALL/VALS   MYTH
...CONCPT HIST/WRIT TIME/SEQ 20 JEWS. PAGE 13 B0271   WAR
                                                             B48
ROSSITER C.L.,CONSTITUTIONAL DICTATORSHIP; CRISIS   NAT/G
GOVERNMENT IN THE MODERN DEMOCRACIES. FRANCE   AUTHORIT
GERMANY UK USA-45 WOR-45 EX/STRUC BAL/PWR CONTROL   CONSTN
COERCE WAR CENTRAL ORD/FREE...DECISION 19/20.   TOTALISM
PAGE 90 B1828
                                                             C53
DORWART R.A.,"THE ADMINISTRATIVE REFORMS OF   ADMIN
FREDRICK WILLIAM I OF PRUSSIA. GERMANY MOD/EUR   NAT/G
CHIEF CONTROL PWR...BIBLIOG 16/18. PAGE 30 B0608   CENTRAL

TOTOK W.,HANDBUCH DER BIBLIOGRAPHISCHEN
NACHSCHLAGEWERKE. GERMANY LAW CULTURE ADMIN...SOC
20. PAGE 105 B2121

GOV/REL
      B54
BIBLIOG/A
NAT/G
DIPLOM
POLICY

ARON R.,FRANCE DEFEATS EDC. EUR+WWI GERMANY LEGIS
DIPLOM DOMIN EDU/PROP ADMIN...HIST/WRIT 20. PAGE 7
B0136

      B57
INT/ORG
FORCES
DETER
FRANCE

DIEBOLD W. JR.,THE SCHUMAN PLAN: A STUDY IN
ECONOMIC COOPERATION, 1950-1959. EUR+WWI FRANCE
GERMANY USA+45 EXTR/IND CONSULT DELIB/GP PLAN
DIPLOM ECO/TAC INT/TRADE ROUTINE ORD/FREE WEALTH
...METH/CNCPT STAT CONT/OBS INT TIME/SEQ ECSC 20.
PAGE 29 B0591

      B59
INT/ORG
REGION

MAYNTZ R.,PARTEIGRUPPEN IN DER GROSSSTADT. GERMANY
STRATA STRUCT DOMIN CHOOSE 20. PAGE 71 B1437

      B59
MUNIC
MGT
POL/PAR
ATTIT

HERZ J.H.,"EAST GERMANY: PROGRESS AND PROSPECTS."
COM AGRI FINAN INDUS LOC/G NAT/G FORCES PLAN
TEC/DEV DOMIN ADMIN COERCE DRIVE PERCEPT RIGID/FLEX
MORAL ORD/FREE PWR...MARXIST PSY SOC RECORD STERTYP
WORK. PAGE 49 B0997

      S60
POL/PAR
STRUCT
GERMANY

KEE R.,REFUGEE WORLD. AUSTRIA EUR+WWI GERMANY NEIGH
EX/STRUC WORKER PROB/SOLV ECO/TAC RENT EDU/PROP
INGP/REL COST LITERACY HABITAT 20 MIGRATION.
PAGE 59 B1186

      B61
NAT/G
GIVE
WEALTH
STRANGE

TOMASIC D.,"POLITICAL LEADERSHIP IN CONTEMPORARY
POLAND." COM EUR+WWI GERMANY NAT/G POL/PAR SECT
DELIB/GP PLAN ECO/TAC DOMIN EDU/PROP PWR MARXISM
...MARXIST GEOG MGT CONCPT TIME/SEQ STERTYP 20.
PAGE 105 B2114

      S61
SOCIETY
ROUTINE
USSR
POLAND

ANDREWS W.G.,EUROPEAN POLITICAL INSTITUTIONS.
FRANCE GERMANY UK USSR TOP/EX LEAD PARL/PROC CHOOSE
20. PAGE 5 B0104

      B62
NAT/COMP
POL/PAR
EX/STRUC
LEGIS

BROWN B.E.,NEW DIRECTIONS IN COMPARATIVE POLITICS.
AUSTRIA FRANCE GERMANY UK WOR+45 EX/STRUC LEGIS
ORD/FREE 20. PAGE 16 B0320

      B62
NAT/COMP
METH
POL/PAR
FORCES

WELLEQUET J.,LE CONGO BELGE ET LA WELTPOLITIK
(1894-1914. GERMANY DOMIN EDU/PROP WAR ATTIT
...BIBLIOG T CONGO/LEOP. PAGE 115 B2318

      B62
ADMIN
DIPLOM
GP/REL
COLONIAL

HUDSON G.F.,"SOVIET FEARS OF THE WEST." COM USA+45
SOCIETY DELIB/GP EX/STRUC TOP/EX ACT/RES CREATE
DOMIN EDU/PROP LEGIT ADMIN ROUTINE DRIVE PERSON
RIGID/FLEX PWR...RECORD TIME/SEQ TOT/POP 20
STALIN/J. PAGE 52 B1057

      S62
ATTIT
MYTH
GERMANY
USSR

MARTIN L.W.,"POLITICAL SETTLEMENTS AND ARMS
CONTROL." COM EUR+WWI GERMANY USA+45 PROVS FORCES
TOP/EX ACT/RES CREATE DOMIN LEGIT ROUTINE COERCE
ATTIT RIGID/FLEX ORD/FREE PWR...METH/CNCPT RECORD
GEN/LAWS 20. PAGE 70 B1410

      S62
CONCPT
ARMS/CONT

JACOB H.,GERMAN ADMINISTRATION SINCE BISMARCK:
CENTRAL AUTHORITY VERSUS LOCAL AUTONOMY. GERMANY
GERMANY/W LAW POL/PAR CONTROL CENTRAL TOTALISM
FASCISM...MAJORIT DECISION STAT CHARTS GOV/COMP
19/20 BISMARCK/O HITLER/A WEIMAR/REP. PAGE 55 B1111

      B63
ADMIN
NAT/G
LOC/G
POLICY

KULZ H.R.,STAATSBURGER UND STAATSGEWALT (2 VOLS.).
GERMANY SWITZERLND UK USSR CONSTN DELIB/GP TARIFFS
TAX...JURID 20. PAGE 61 B1242

      B63
ADMIN
ADJUD
CT/SYS
NAT/COMP

OLSON M. JR.,THE ECONOMICS OF WARTIME SHORTAGE.
FRANCE GERMANY MOD/EUR UK AGRI PROB/SOLV ADMIN
DEMAND WEALTH...POLICY OLD/LIB 17/20. PAGE 80 B1608

      B63
WAR
ADJUST
ECO/TAC
NAT/COMP

PLISCHKE E.,GOVERNMENT AND POLITICS OF CONTEMPORARY
BERLIN. GERMANY LAW CONSTN POL/PAR LEGIS WAR CHOOSE
REPRESENT GOV/REL...CHARTS BIBLIOG 20 BERLIN.
PAGE 83 B1683

      B63
MUNIC
LOC/G
POLICY
ADMIN

BOLGAR V.,"THE PUBLIC INTEREST: A JURISPRUDENTIAL
AND COMPARATIVE OVERVIEW OF SYMPOSIUM ON
FUNDAMENTAL CONCEPTS OF PUBLIC LAW" COM FRANCE
GERMANY SWITZERLND LAW ADJUD ADMIN AGREE LAISSEZ
...JURID GEN/LAWS 20 EUROPE/E. PAGE 13 B0268

      L63
CONCPT
ORD/FREE
CONTROL
NAT/COMP

FREUND G.,"ADENAUER AND THE FUTURE OF GERMANY."

      L63
NAT/G

EUR+WWI FUT GERMANY/W FORCES LEGIT ADMIN ROUTINE
ATTIT DRIVE PERSON PWR...POLICY TIME/SEQ TREND
VAL/FREE 20 ADENAUER/K. PAGE 37 B0753

BIOG
DIPLOM
GERMANY
      S63

ANTHON C.G.,"THE END OF THE ADENAUER ERA." EUR+WWI
GERMANY/W CONSTN EX/STRUC CREATE DIPLOM LEGIT ATTIT
PERSON ALL/VALS...RECORD 20 ADENAUER/K. PAGE 6
B0113

NAT/G
TOP/EX
BAL/PWR
GERMANY
      B64

GESELLSCHAFT RECHTSVERGLEICH,BIBLIOGRAPHIE DES
DEUTSCHEN RECHTS (BIBLIOGRAPHY OF GERMAN LAW.
TRANS. BY COURTLAND PETERSON). GERMANY FINAN INDUS
LABOR SECT FORCES CT/SYS PARL/PROC CRIME...INT/LAW
SOC NAT/COMP 20. PAGE 39 B0794

BIBLIOG/A
JURID
CONSTN
ADMIN
      B64

REDLICH F.,THE GERMAN MILITARY ENTERPRISER AND HIS
WORK FORCE. CHRIST-17C GERMANY ELITES SOCIETY FINAN
ECO/TAC CIVMIL/REL GP/REL INGP/REL...HIST/WRIT
METH/COMP 14/17. PAGE 87 B1760

EX/STRUC
FORCES
PROFIT
WORKER
      B64

WHEELER-BENNETT J.W.,THE NEMESIS OF POWER (2ND
ED.). EUR+WWI GERMANY TOP/EX TEC/DEV ADMIN WAR
PERS/REL RIGID/FLEX ROLE ORD/FREE PWR FASCISM 20
HITLER/A. PAGE 116 B2332

FORCES
NAT/G
GP/REL
STRUCT
      B65

COHN H.J.,THE GOVERNMENT OF THE RHINE PALATINATE IN
THE FIFTEENTH CENTURY. GERMANY FINAN LOC/G DELIB/GP
LEGIS CT/SYS CHOOSE CATHISM 14/15 PALATINATE.
PAGE 22 B0449

PROVS
JURID
GP/REL
ADMIN
      B65

EDELMAN M.,THE POLITICS OF WAGE-PRICE DECISIONS.
GERMANY ITALY NETHERLAND UK INDUS LABOR POL/PAR
PROB/SOLV BARGAIN PRICE ROUTINE BAL/PAY COST DEMAND
20. PAGE 32 B0654

GOV/COMP
CONTROL
ECO/TAC
PLAN
      B65

FORGAC A.A.,NEW DIPLOMACY AND THE UNITED NATIONS.
FRANCE GERMANY UK USSR INT/ORG DELIB/GP EX/STRUC
PEACE...INT/LAW CONCPT UN. PAGE 36 B0740

DIPLOM
ETIQUET
NAT/G
      B65

NORDEN A.,WAR AND NAZI CRIMINALS IN WEST GERMANY:
STATE, ECONOMY, ADMINISTRATION, ARMY, JUSTICE,
SCIENCE. GERMANY GERMANY/W MOD/EUR ECO/DEV ACADEM
EX/STRUC FORCES DOMIN ADMIN CT/SYS...POLICY MAJORIT
PACIFIST 20. PAGE 78 B1587

FASCIST
WAR
NAT/G
TOP/EX
      B67

CECIL L.,ALBERT BALLIN; BUSINESS AND POLITICS IN
IMPERIAL GERMANY 1888-1918. GERMANY UK INT/TRADE
LEAD WAR PERS/REL ADJUST PWR WEALTH...MGT BIBLIOG
19/20. PAGE 19 B0397

DIPLOM
CONSTN
ECO/DEV
TOP/EX
      B67

GIFFORD P.,BRITAIN AND GERMANY IN AFRICA. AFR
GERMANY UK ECO/UNDEV LEAD WAR NAT/LISM ATTIT
...POLICY HIST/WRIT METH/COMP ANTHOL BIBLIOG 19/20
WWI. PAGE 39 B0797

COLONIAL
ADMIN
DIPLOM
NAT/COMP
      S67

HOFMANN W.,"THE PUBLIC INTEREST PRESSURE GROUP: THE
CASE OF THE DEUTSCHE STADTETAG." GERMANY GERMANY/W
CONSTN STRUCT NAT/G CENTRAL FEDERAL PWR...TIME/SEQ
20. PAGE 51 B1030

LOC/G
VOL/ASSN
LOBBY
ADMIN

GERMANY/E....EAST GERMANY; SEE ALSO COM

EPSTEIN F.T.,EAST GERMANY: A SELECTED BIBLIOGRAPHY
(PAMPHLET). COM GERMANY/E LAW AGRI FINAN INDUS
LABOR POL/PAR EDU/PROP ADMIN AGE/Y 20. PAGE 33
B0677

      B59
BIBLIOG/A
INTELL
MARXISM
NAT/G

GERMANY/W....WEST GERMANY

STEINMETZ H.,"THE PROBLEMS OF THE LANDRAT: A STUDY
OF COUNTY GOVERNMENT IN THE US ZONE OF GERMANY."
GERMANY/W USA+45 INDUS PLAN DIPLOM EDU/PROP CONTROL
WAR GOV/REL FEDERAL WEALTH PLURISM...GOV/COMP 20
LANDRAT. PAGE 100 B2031

      S49
LOC/G
COLONIAL
MGT
TOP/EX

HINDERLING A.,DIE REFORMATORISCHE
VERWALTUNGSGERICHTSBARKEIT. GERMANY/W PROB/SOLV
ADJUD SUPEGO PWR...CONCPT 20. PAGE 50 B1015

      B57
ADMIN
CT/SYS
JURID
CONTROL

SCHLOCHAUER H.J.,OFFENTLICHES RECHT. GERMANY/W
FINAN EX/STRUC LEGIS DIPLOM FEDERAL ORD/FREE
...INT/LAW 20. PAGE 94 B1892

      B57
CONSTN
JURID
ADMIN
CT/SYS

GOLAY J.F.,"THE FOUNDING OF THE FEDERAL REPUBLIC OF
GERMANY." GERMANY/W CONSTN EX/STRUC DIPLOM ADMIN
CHOOSE...DECISION BIBLIOG 20. PAGE 40 B0814

      C58
FEDERAL
NAT/G
PARL/PROC
POL/PAR

LEMBERG E.,DIE VERTRIEBENEN IN WESTDEUTSCHLAND (3
VOLS.). GERMANY/W CULTURE STRUCT AGRI PROVS ADMIN
...JURID 20 MIGRATION. PAGE 64 B1287

      B59
GP/REL
INGP/REL
SOCIETY

B59

SISSON C.H.,THE SPIRIT OF BRITISH ADMINISTRATION
AND SOME EUROPEAN COMPARISONS. FRANCE GERMANY/W
SWEDEN UK LAW EX/STRUC INGP/REL EFFICIENCY ORD/FREE
...DECISION 20. PAGE 98 B1972

GOV/COMP
ADMIN
ELITES
ATTIT

B59

WEBER W.,DER DEUTSCHE BEAMTE HEUTE. GERMANY/W NAT/G
DELIB/GP LEGIS CONFER ATTIT SUPEGO...JURID 20
CIVIL/SERV. PAGE 114 B2306

MGT
EFFICIENCY
ELITES
GP/REL

B61

DRAGNICH A.N.,MAJOR EUROPEAN GOVERNMENTS. FRANCE
GERMANY/W UK USSR LOC/G EX/STRUC CT/SYS PARL/PROC
ATTIT MARXISM...JURID MGT NAT/COMP 19/20. PAGE 30
B0615

NAT/G
LEGIS
CONSTN
POL/PAR

B61

LOSCHELDER W.,AUSBILDUNG UND AUSLESE DER BEAMTEN.
GERMANY/W ELITES NAT/G ADMIN GP/REL ATTIT...JURID
20 CIVIL/SERV. PAGE 67 B1341

PROF/ORG
EDU/PROP
EX/STRUC
CHOOSE

B62

FRIEDMANN W.,METHODS AND POLICIES OF PRINCIPAL
DONOR COUNTRIES IN PUBLIC INTERNATIONAL DEVELOPMENT
FINANCING: PRELIMINARY APPRAISAL. FRANCE GERMANY/W
UK USA+45 USSR WOR+45 FINAN TEC/DEV CAP/ISM DIPLOM
ECO/TAC ATTIT 20 EEC. PAGE 37 B0759

INT/ORG
FOR/AID
NAT/COMP
ADMIN

B62

GRANICK D.,THE EUROPEAN EXECUTIVE. BELGIUM FRANCE
GERMANY/W UK INDUS LABOR LG/CO SML/CO EX/STRUC PLAN
TEC/DEV CAP/ISM COST DEMAND...POLICY CHARTS 20.
PAGE 42 B0852

MGT
ECO/DEV
ECO/TAC
EXEC

B62

WENDT P.F.,HOUSING POLICY - THE SEARCH FOR
SOLUTIONS. GERMANY/W SWEDEN UK USA+45 OP/RES
HABITAT WEALTH...SOC/WK CHARTS 20. PAGE 115 B2322

PLAN
ADMIN
METH/COMP
NAT/G

B63

JACOB H.,GERMAN ADMINISTRATION SINCE BISMARCK:
CENTRAL AUTHORITY VERSUS LOCAL AUTONOMY. GERMANY
GERMANY/W LAW POL/PAR CONTROL CENTRAL TOTALISM
FASCISM...MAJORIT DECISION STAT CHARTS GOV/COMP
19/20 BISMARCK/O HITLER/A WEIMAR/REP. PAGE 55 B1111

ADMIN
NAT/G
LOC/G
POLICY

L63

FREUND G.,"ADENAUER AND THE FUTURE OF GERMANY."
EUR+WWI FUT GERMANY/W FORCES LEGIT ROUTINE
ATTIT DRIVE PERSON PWR...POLICY TIME/SEQ TREND
VAL/FREE 20 ADENAUER/K. PAGE 37 B0753

NAT/G
BIOG
DIPLOM
GERMANY

S63

ANTHON C.G.,"THE END OF THE ADENAUER ERA." EUR+WWI
GERMANY/W CONSTN EX/STRUC CREATE DIPLOM LEGIT ATTIT
PERSON ALL/VALS...RECORD 20 ADENAUER/K. PAGE 6
B0113

NAT/G
TOP/EX
BAL/PWR
GERMANY

B64

KAACK H.,DIE PARTEIEN IN DER
VERFASSUNGSWIRKLICHKEIT DER BUNDESREPUBLIK.
GERMANY/W ADMIN PARL/PROC CHOOSE...JURID 20.
PAGE 57 B1157

POL/PAR
PROVS
NAT/G

B65

NORDEN A.,WAR AND NAZI CRIMINALS IN WEST GERMANY:
STATE, ECONOMY, ADMINISTRATION, ARMY, JUSTICE,
SCIENCE. GERMANY GERMANY/W MOD/EUR ECO/DEV ACADEM
EX/STRUC FORCES DOMIN ADMIN CT/SYS...POLICY MAJORIT
PACIFIST 20. PAGE 78 B1587

FASCIST
WAR
NAT/G
TOP/EX

B65

WHITE J.,GERMAN AID. GERMANY/W FINAN PLAN TEC/DEV
INT/TRADE ADMIN ATTIT...POLICY 20. PAGE 116 B2334

FOR/AID
ECO/UNDEV
DIPLOM
ECO/TAC

B66

KAESTNER K.,GESAMTWIRTSCHAFTLICHE PLANUNG IN EINER
GEMISCHTEN WIRTSCHAFTORDNUNG
(WIRTSCHAFTSPOLITISCHE STUDIEN 5). GERMANY/W WOR+45
WOR-45 INDUS MARKET NAT/G ACT/RES GP/REL INGP/REL
PRODUC...ECOMETRIC MGT BIBLIOG 20. PAGE 57 B1159

ECO/TAC
PLAN
POLICY
PREDICT

B66

NEUMANN R.G.,THE GOVERNMENT OF THE GERMAN FEDERAL
REPUBLIC. EUR+WWI GERMANY/W LOC/G EX/STRUC LEGIS
CT/SYS INGP/REL PWR...BIBLIOG 20 ADENAUER/K.
PAGE 78 B1573

NAT/G
POL/PAR
DIPLOM
CONSTN

S67

HOFMANN W.,"THE PUBLIC INTEREST PRESSURE GROUP: THE
CASE OF THE DEUTSCHE STADTETAG." GERMANY GERMANY/W
CONSTN STRUCT NAT/G CENTRAL FEDERAL PWR...TIME/SEQ
20. PAGE 51 B1030

LOC/G
VOL/ASSN
LOBBY
ADMIN

S67

HUDDLESTON J.,"TRADE UNIONS IN THE GERMAN FEDERAL
REPUBLIC." EUR+WWI GERMANY/W UK LAW INDUS WORKER
CREATE CENTRAL...MGT GP/COMP 20. PAGE 52 B1056

LABOR
GP/REL
SCHOOL
ROLE

GERTH H. B0792

GERWIG R. B0793

GESELLSCHAFT RECHTSVERGLEICH B0794

GETTYSBURG....BATTLE OF GETTYSBURG

GHAI Y.P. B1440

GHANA....SEE ALSO AFR

B58

CARTER G.M.,TRANSITION IN AFRICA: STUDIES IN
POLITICAL ADAPTATION. AFR CENTRL/AFR GHANA NIGERIA
CONSTN LOC/G POL/PAR ADMIN GP/REL FEDERAL...MAJORIT
BIBLIOG 20. PAGE 19 B0389

NAT/COMP
PWR
CONTROL
NAT/G

S60

APTER D.E.,"THE ROLE OF TRADITIONALISM IN THE
POLITICAL MODERNIZATION OF GHANA AND UGANDA" (BMR)"
AFR GHANA UGANDA CULTURE NAT/G POL/PAR NAT/LISM
...CON/ANAL 20. PAGE 6 B0121

CONSERVE
ADMIN
GOV/COMP
PROB/SOLV

B61

CARNEY D.E.,GOVERNMENT AND ECONOMY IN BRITISH WEST
AFRICA. GAMBIA GHANA NIGERIA SIER/LEONE DOMIN ADMIN
GOV/REL SOVEREIGN WEALTH LAISSEZ...BIBLIOG 20
CMN/WLTH. PAGE 19 B0384

METH/COMP
COLONIAL
ECO/TAC
ECO/UNDEV

S64

CLIGNET R.,"POTENTIAL ELITES IN GHANA AND THE IVORY
COAST: A PRELIMINARY SURVEY." AFR CULTURE ELITES
STRATA KIN NAT/G SECT DOMIN EXEC ORD/FREE RESPECT
SKILL...POLICY RELATIV GP/COMP NAT/COMP 20. PAGE 21
B0438

PWR
LEGIT
IVORY/CST
GHANA

B65

ADU A.L.,THE CIVIL SERVICE IN NEW AFRICAN STATES.
AFR GHANA FINAN SOVEREIGN...POLICY 20 CIVIL/SERV
AFRICA/E AFRICA/W. PAGE 3 B0062

ECO/UNDEV
ADMIN
COLONIAL
NAT/G

B66

BOYD H.W.,MARKETING MANAGEMENT: CASES FROM EMERGING
COUNTRIES. BRAZIL GHANA ISRAEL WOR+45 ADMIN
PERS/REL ATTIT HABITAT WEALTH...ANTHOL 20 ARGEN
CASEBOOK. PAGE 14 B0292

MGT
ECO/UNDEV
PROB/SOLV
MARKET

S67

GRUNDY K.W.,"THE POLITICAL USES OF IMAGINATION."
GHANA ELITES SOCIETY NAT/G DOMIN EDU/PROP COLONIAL
REGION REPRESENT GP/REL CENTRAL PWR MARXISM 20.
PAGE 44 B0897

NAT/LISM
EX/STRUC
AFR
LEAD

S67

MURRAY R.,"SECOND THOUGHTS ON GHANA." AFR GHANA
NAT/G POL/PAR ADMIN REV GP/REL CENTRAL...SOCIALIST
CONCPT METH 20. PAGE 77 B1548

COLONIAL
CONTROL
REGION
SOCISM

GHOSH P.K. B0795

GIBBON/EDW....EDWARD GIBBON

GIBRALTAR....SEE UK

GIBSON D.M.T. B0292

GIDWANI K.A. B0796

GIFFORD P. B0797

GILBERT C.E. B0798,B0799,B0800

GILCHRIST M. B2390

GILMORE D.R. B0801

GINSBURG M. B0802

GINZBERG E. B0803

GITTELL M. B0804,B0805,B0806

GIVE....GIVING, PHILANTHROPY

N19

JACKSON R.G.A.,THE CASE FOR AN INTERNATIONAL
DEVELOPMENT AUTHORITY (PAMPHLET). WOR+45 ECO/DEV
DIPLOM GIVE CONTROL GP/REL EFFICIENCY NAT/LISM
SOVEREIGN 20. PAGE 55 B1108

FOR/AID
INT/ORG
ECO/UNDEV
ADMIN

B40

GAUS J.M.,PUBLIC ADMINISTRATION AND THE UNITED
STATES DEPARTMENT OF AGRICULTURE. USA-45 STRUCT
DIST/IND FINAN MARKET EX/STRUC PROB/SOLV GIVE
PRODUC...POLICY GEOG CHARTS 20 DEPT/AGRI. PAGE 39
B0786

ADMIN
AGRI
DELIB/GP
OP/RES

B41

MACMAHON A.W.,THE ADMINISTRATION OF FEDERAL WORK
RELIEF. USA-45 EX/STRUC WORKER BUDGET EFFICIENCY
...CONT/OBS CHARTS 20 WPA. PAGE 68 B1367

ADMIN
NAT/G
MGT
GIVE

B44

WRIGHT H.R.,SOCIAL SERVICE IN WARTIME. FINAN NAT/G
VOL/ASSN PLAN GP/REL ROLE. PAGE 118 B2381

GIVE
WAR
SOC/WK
ADMIN

ZABEL O.H.,GOD AND CAESAR IN NEBRASKA: A STUDY OF | B55 | SECT
LEGAL RELATIONSHIP OF CHURCH AND STATE, 1854-1954. | | PROVS
TAX GIVE ADMIN CONTROL GP/REL ROLE...GP/COMP 19/20 | | LAW
NEBRASKA. PAGE 119 B2396 | | EDU/PROP

KIETH-LUCAS A.,DECISIONS ABOUT PEOPLE IN NEED. A | B57 | ADMIN
STUDY OF ADMINISTRATIVE RESPONSIVENESS IN PUBLIC | | RIGID/FLEX
ASSISTANCE. USA+45 GIVE RECEIVE INGP/REL PERS/REL | | SOC/WK
MORAL RESPECT WEALTH...SOC OBS BIBLIOG 20. PAGE 60 | | DECISION
B1204

AVERY M.W.,GOVERNMENT OF WASHINGTON STATE. USA+45 | B61 | PROVS
MUNIC DELIB/GP EX/STRUC LEGIS GIVE CT/SYS PARTIC | | LOC/G
REGION EFFICIENCY 20 WASHINGT/G GOVERNOR. PAGE 7 | | ADMIN
B0151 | | GOV/REL

DRURY J.W.,THE GOVERNMENT OF KANSAS. USA+45 AGRI | B61 | PROVS
INDUS CHIEF LEGIS WORKER PLAN BUDGET GIVE CT/SYS | | CONSTN
GOV/REL...T 20 KANSAS GOVERNOR CITY/MGT. PAGE 31 | | ADMIN
B0621 | | LOC/G

KEE R.,REFUGEE WORLD. AUSTRIA EUR+WWI GERMANY NEIGH | B61 | NAT/G
EX/STRUC WORKER PROB/SOLV ECO/TAC RENT EDU/PROP | | GIVE
INGP/REL COST LITERACY HABITAT 20 MIGRATION. | | WEALTH
PAGE 59 B1186 | | STRANGE

ROMANO F.,CIVIL SERVICE AND PUBLIC EMPLOYEE LAW IN | B61 | ADMIN
NEW JERSEY. CONSTN MUNIC WORKER GIVE PAY CHOOSE | | PROVS
UTIL 20. PAGE 90 B1816 | | ADJUD
| | LOC/G

ROSE D.L.,THE VIETNAMESE CIVIL SERVICE. VIETNAM | B61 | ADMIN
CONSULT DELIB/GP GIVE PAY EDU/PROP COLONIAL GOV/REL | | EFFICIENCY
UTIL...CHARTS 20. PAGE 90 B1819 | | STAT
| | NAT/G

FARBER W.O.,GOVERNMENT OF SOUTH DAKOTA. USA+45 | B62 | PROVS
DIST/IND POL/PAR CHIEF EX/STRUC LEGIS ECO/TAC GIVE | | LOC/G
EDU/PROP CT/SYS PARTIC...T 20 SOUTH/DAK GOVERNOR. | | ADMIN
PAGE 35 B0704 | | CONSTN

FRIEDLANDER W.A.,INDIVIDUALISM AND SOCIAL WELFARE. | B62 | GIVE
FRANCE ACADEM OP/RES ADMIN AGE/Y AGE/A ORD/FREE 20. | | SOC/WK
PAGE 37 B0756 | | SOC/EXP
| | FINAN

US HOUSE COM ON ED AND LABOR,ADMINISTRATION OF | B63 | AGE/O
AGING. USA+45 R+D EX/STRUC PLAN BUDGET PAY EDU/PROP | | ADMIN
ROUTINE COST CONGRESS. PAGE 108 B2187 | | DELIB/GP
| | GIVE

FISCHER F.C.,THE GOVERNMENT OF MICHIGAN. USA+45 | B65 | PROVS
NAT/G PUB/INST EX/STRUC LEGIS BUDGET GIVE EDU/PROP | | LOC/G
CT/SYS CHOOSE GOV/REL...T MICHIGAN. PAGE 36 B0723 | | ADMIN
| | CONSTN

ROMASCO A.U.,THE POVERTY OF ABUNDANCE: HOOVER, THE | B65 | ECO/TAC
NATION, THE DEPRESSION. USA-45 AGRI LEGIS WORKER | | ADMIN
GIVE PRESS LEAD 20 HOOVER/H. PAGE 90 B1817 | | NAT/G
| | FINAN

CLEGG R.K.,THE ADMINISTRATOR IN PUBLIC WELFARE. | B66 | ADMIN
USA+45 STRUCT NAT/G PROVS PROB/SOLV BUDGET ECO/TAC | | GIVE
GP/REL ROLE...SOC/WK 20 PUBLIC/REL. PAGE 21 B0434 | | GOV/REL
| | OP/RES

GLAZER M.,THE FEDERAL GOVERNMENT AND THE | B66 | BIBLIOG/A
UNIVERSITY. CHILE PROB/SOLV DIPLOM GIVE ADMIN WAR | | NAT/G
...POLICY SOC 20. PAGE 40 B0810 | | PLAN
| | ACADEM

GREENE L.E.,GOVERNMENT IN TENNESSEE (2ND ED.). | B66 | PROVS
USA+45 DIST/IND INDUS POL/PAR EX/STRUC LEGIS PLAN | | LOC/G
BUDGET GIVE CT/SYS...MGT T 20 TENNESSEE. PAGE 43 | | CONSTN
B0866 | | ADMIN

KIRDAR U.,THE STRUCTURE OF UNITED NATIONS ECONOMIC | B66 | INT/ORG
AID TO UNDERDEVELOPED COUNTRIES. AGRI FINAN INDUS | | FOR/AID
NAT/G EX/STRUC PLAN GIVE TASK...POLICY 20 UN. | | ECO/UNDEV
PAGE 60 B1213 | | ADMIN

OHLIN G.,AID AND INDEBTEDNESS. AUSTRIA FINAN | B66 | FOR/AID
INT/ORG PLAN DIPLOM GIVE...POLICY MATH CHARTS 20. | | ECO/UNDEV
PAGE 79 B1604 | | ADMIN
| | WEALTH

BALDWIN D.A.,"CONGRESSIONAL INITIATIVE IN FOREIGN | S66 | EXEC
POLICY." NAT/G BARGAIN DIPLOM FOR/AID RENT GIVE | | TOP/EX
...DECISION CONGRESS. PAGE 8 B0171 | | GOV/REL

GJUPANOVIC H. B0807

GLADDEN E.N. B0808,B0809

GLADSTON/W....WILLIAM GLADSTONE

GLAZER M. B0810

GLESER G.C. B0508

GLOVER J.D. B0811,B0812

GMP/REG....GOOD MANUFACTURING PRACTICE REGULATIONS

GOBER J.L. B0813

GOEBBELS/J....JOSEPH GOEBBELS

SINGTON D.,THE GOEBBELS EXPERIMENT. GERMANY MOD/EUR | B42 | FASCISM
NAT/G EX/STRUC FORCES CONTROL ROUTINE WAR TOTALSM | | EDU/PROP
PWR...ART/METH HUM 20 NAZI GOEBBELS/J. PAGE 97 | | ATTIT
B1970 | | COM/IND

GOETHE/J....JOHANN WOLFGANG VON GOETHE

GOLAY J.F. B0814

GOLD....GOLD

GOLD/COAST....GOLD COAST (PRE-GHANA)

GOLD/STAND....GOLD STANDARD

BRIEFS H.W.,PRICING POWER AND "ADMINISTRATIVE" | B62 | ECO/DEV
INFLATION (PAMPHLET). USA+45 PROC/MFG CONTROL | | PRICE
EFFICIENCY MONEY GOLD/STAND. PAGE 15 B0306 | | POLICY
| | EXEC

FORD A.G.,THE GOLD STANDARD 1880-1914: BRITAIN AND | B62 | FINAN
ARGENTINA. UK ECO/UNDEV INT/TRADE ADMIN GOV/REL | | ECO/TAC
DEMAND EFFICIENCY...STAT CHARTS 19/20 ARGEN | | BUDGET
GOLD/STAND. PAGE 36 B0737 | | BAL/PAY

GUZZARDI W. JR.,"THE SECOND BATTLE OF BRITAIN." UK | S68 | FINAN
STRATA LABOR WORKER CREATE PROB/SOLV EDU/PROP ADMIN | | ECO/TAC
LEAD LOBBY...MGT SOC 20 GOLD/STAND. PAGE 45 B0907 | | ECO/DEV
| | STRUCT

GOLDEN C.S. B0815

GOLDMAN/E....ERIC GOLDMAN

RUSK D.,"THE MAKING OF FOREIGN POLICY" USA+45 CHIEF | S64 | DIPLOM
DELIB/GP WORKER PROB/SOLV ADMIN ATTIT PWR | | INT
...DECISION 20 DEPT/STATE RUSK/D GOLDMAN/E. PAGE 92 | | POLICY
B1856

GOLDSTEIN J. B0817,B1180

GOLDWATR/B....BARRY GOLDWATER

GOLDWIN R.A. B0818

GOLEMBIEWSKI R.T. B0819

GOLIGHTLY H.O. B0820

GOMILLN/CG....C.G. GOMILLION

GOOD MANUFACTURING PRACTICE REGULATIONS....SEE GMP/REG

GOODALL M.C. B0124

GOODMAN W. B0821

GOODNOW F.J. B0822,B0823

GOODNOW H.F. B0824

GOODRICH L. B0825

GOODRICH L.M. B0826

GOODSELL C.T. B0827

GOPAL S. B0828

GORDENKER L. B0829

GORDON L. B0830

GORDON R.A. B0831

GORDON W.J.J. B0832

GORDON/K....K. GORDON

GORDON/W....WILLIAM GORDON

GORE W.J. B0833,B0834

GORER G. B0835

GORHAM W. B0836

GORMAN W. B0837

GORWALA A.D. B0838

GOSNELL H.F. B0839,B0840

GOTLIEB A. B0841

GOULD W.B. B0842

GOULDNER A.W. B0816,B0843,B0844,B0845

GOURNAY B. B0846

GOV/COMP....COMPARISON OF GOVERNMENTS

AMERICAN POLITICAL SCIENCE REVIEW. USA+45 USA-45 WOR+45 WOR-45 INT/ORG ADMIN...INT/LAW PHIL/SCI CONCPT METH 20 UN. PAGE 1 B0001
BIBLIOG/A DIPLOM NAT/G GOV/COMP
N

GRIFFIN A.P.C.,LIST OF BOOKS ON THE CABINETS OF ENGLAND AND AMERICA (PAMPHLET). MOD/EUR UK USA-45 CONSTN NAT/G CONSULT EX/STRUC 19/20. PAGE 43 B0875
BIBLIOG/A GOV/COMP ADMIN DELIB/GP
B03

HARLOW R.V.,THE HISTORY OF LEGISLATIVE METHODS IN THE PERIOD BEFORE 1825. USA-45 EX/STRUC ADMIN COLONIAL LEAD PARL/PROC ROUTINE...GP/COMP GOV/COMP HOUSE/REP. PAGE 47 B0948
LEGIS DELIB/GP PROVS POL/PAR
B17

WILSON W.,THE STATE: ELEMENTS OF HISTORICAL AND PRACTICAL POLITICS. FRANCE GERMANY ITALY UK USSR CONSTN EX/STRUC LEGIS CT/SYS WAR PWR...POLICY GOV/COMP 20. PAGE 117 B2363
NAT/G JURID CONCPT NAT/COMP
B18

RIDLEY C.E.,THE CITY-MANAGER PROFESSION. CHIEF PLAN ADMIN CONTROL ROUTINE CHOOSE...TECHNIC CHARTS GOV/COMP BIBLIOG 20. PAGE 88 B1780
MUNIC EX/STRUC LOC/G EXEC
B34

ANDERSON W.,LOCAL GOVERNMENT IN EUROPE. FRANCE GERMANY ITALY UK USSR MUNIC PROVS ADMIN GOV/REL CENTRAL SOVEREIGN 20. PAGE 5 B0099
GOV/COMP NAT/COMP LOC/G CONSTN
B39

PRICE D.K.,"THE PARLIAMENTARY AND PRESIDENTIAL SYSTEMS" USA-45 NAT/G EX/STRUC PARL/PROC GOV/REL PWR 20 PRESIDENT CONGRESS PARLIAMENT. PAGE 84 B1706
LEGIS REPRESENT ADMIN GOV/COMP
S43

BARKER E.,THE DEVELOPMENT OF PUBLIC SERVICES IN WESTERN WUROPE: 1660-1930. FRANCE GERMANY UK SCHOOL CONTROL REPRESENT ROLE...WELF/ST 17/20. PAGE 9 B0185
GOV/COMP ADMIN EX/STRUC
B44

CROCKER W.R.,ON GOVERNING COLONIES: BEING AN OUTLINE OF THE REAL ISSUES AND A COMPARISON OF THE BRITISH, FRENCH, AND BELGIAN... AFR BELGIUM FRANCE UK CULTURE SOVEREIGN...OBS 20. PAGE 25 B0505
COLONIAL POLICY GOV/COMP ADMIN
B47

MCLEAN J.M.,THE PUBLIC SERVICE AND UNIVERSITY EDUCATION. UK USA-45 DELIB/GP EX/STRUC TOP/EX ADMIN ...GOV/COMP METH/COMP NAT/COMP ANTHOL 20. PAGE 72 B1455
ACADEM NAT/G EXEC EDU/PROP
B49

SCHWARTZ B.,LAW AND THE EXECUTIVE IN BRITAIN: A COMPARATIVE STUDY. UK USA+45 LAW EX/STRUC PWR ...GOV/COMP 20. PAGE 95 B1911
ADMIN EXEC CONTROL REPRESENT
B49

STEINMETZ H.,"THE PROBLEMS OF THE LANDRAT: A STUDY OF COUNTY GOVERNMENT IN THE US ZONE OF GERMANY." GERMANY/W USA+45 INDUS PLAN DIPLOM EDU/PROP CONTROL WAR GOV/REL FEDERAL WEALTH PLURISM...GOV/COMP 20 LANDRAT. PAGE 100 B2031
LOC/G COLONIAL MGT TOP/EX
S49

COLE T.,"LESSONS FROM RECENT EUROPEAN EXPERIENCE." EUR+WWI EX/STRUC 20. PAGE 22 B0450
GOV/COMP ADMIN REPRESENT
S54

GALLOWAY G.B.,CONGRESS AND PARLIAMENT: THEIR ORGANIZATION AND OPERATION IN THE US AND THE UK: PLANNING PAMPHLET NO. 93. POL/PAR EX/STRUC DEBATE CONTROL LEAD ROUTINE EFFICIENCY PWR...POLICY
DELIB/GP LEGIS PARL/PROC GOV/COMP
B55

CONGRESS PARLIAMENT. PAGE 38 B0777

ROSTOW W.W.,"RUSSIA AND CHINA UNDER COMMUNISM." CHINA/COM USSR INTELL STRUCT INT/ORG NAT/G POL/PAR TOP/EX ACT/RES PLAN ADMIN ATTIT ALL/VALS MARXISM ...CONCPT OBS TIME/SEQ TREND GOV/COMP VAL/FREE 20. PAGE 91 B1830
L55
COM ASIA

SCHWARTZ B.,"LEGISLATIVE CONTROL OF ADMINISTRATIVE RULES AND REGULATIONS THE AMERICAN EXPERIENCE." USA+45 GOV/REL...GOV/COMP 20. PAGE 95 B1913
S55
CONTROL ADMIN EX/STRUC LEGIS

NEUMANN S.,"MODERN POLITICAL PARTIES: APPROACHES TO COMPARATIVE POLITIC. FRANCE UK EX/STRUC DOMIN ADMIN LEAD REPRESENT TOTALISM ATTIT...POLICY TREND METH/COMP ANTHOL BIBLIOG/A 20 CMN/WLTH. PAGE 78 B1574
C56
POL/PAR GOV/COMP ELITES MAJORIT

DAVID P.T.,EXECUTIVES FOR THE GOVERNMENT: CENTRAL ISSUES OF FEDERAL PERSONNEL ADMINISTRATION. USA+45 ELITES...GOV/COMP 20. PAGE 26 B0534
B57
EX/STRUC TOP/EX ADMIN

SCARROW H.A.,THE HIGHER PUBLIC SERVICE OF THE COMMONWEALTH OF AUSTRALIA. LAW SENIOR LOBBY ROLE 20 AUSTRAL CIVIL/SERV COMMONWLTH. PAGE 93 B1877
B57
ADMIN NAT/G EX/STRUC GOV/COMP

WEIDLUND J.,COMPARATIVE PUBLIC ADMINISTRATION. EX/STRUC METH/COMP. PAGE 114 B2310
B57
ADMIN NAT/G GOV/COMP BIBLIOG/A

BLAIR L.,THE COMMONWEALTH PUBLIC SERVICE. LAW WORKER...MGT CHARTS GOV/COMP 20 COMMONWLTH AUSTRAL CIVIL/SERV. PAGE 12 B0248
B58
ADMIN NAT/G EX/STRUC INGP/REL

SISSON C.H.,THE SPIRIT OF BRITISH ADMINISTRATION AND SOME EUROPEAN COMPARISONS. FRANCE GERMANY/W SWEDEN UK LAW EX/STRUC INGP/REL EFFICIENCY ORD/FREE ...DECISION 20. PAGE 98 B1972
B59
GOV/COMP ADMIN ELITES ATTIT

PRESTHUS R.V.,"BEHAVIOR AND BUREAUCRACY IN MANY CULTURES." EXEC INGP/REL 20. PAGE 84 B1705
S59
ADMIN EX/STRUC GOV/COMP METH/CNCPT

WALDO D.,THE RESEARCH FUNCTION OF UNIVERSITY BUREAUS AND INSTITUTES FOR GOVERNMENTAL-RELATED RESEARCH. FINAN ACADEM NAT/G INGP/REL ROLE...POLICY CLASSIF GOV/COMP. PAGE 113 B2276
B60
ADMIN R+D MUNIC

APTER D.E.,"THE ROLE OF TRADITIONALISM IN THE POLITICAL MODERNIZATION OF GHANA AND UGANDA" (BMR)" AFR GHANA UGANDA CULTURE NAT/G POL/PAR NAT/LISM ...CON/ANAL 20. PAGE 6 B0121
S60
CONSERVE ADMIN GOV/COMP PROB/SOLV

BANFIELD E.C.,"THE POLITICAL IMPLICATIONS OF METROPOLITAN GROWTH" (BMR)" UK USA+45 LOC/G PROB/SOLV ADMIN GP/REL...METH/COMP NAT/COMP 20. PAGE 9 B0176
S60
TASK MUNIC GOV/COMP CENSUS

HEADY F.,"RECENT LITERATURE ON COMPARATIVE PUBLIC ADMINISTRATION." EXEC 20. PAGE 48 B0981
S60
GOV/COMP ADMIN EX/STRUC BIBLIOG

RAPHAELI N.,"SELECTED ARTICLES AND DOCUMENTS ON COMPARATIVE PUBLIC ADMINISTRATION." USA+45 FINAN LOC/G TOP/EX TEC/DEV EXEC GP/REL INGP/REL...GP/COMP GOV/COMP METH/COMP. PAGE 86 B1738
S60
BIBLIOG MGT ADMIN EX/STRUC

SMITH T.E.,"ELECTIONS IN DEVELOPING COUNTRIES: A STUDY OF ELECTORAL PROCEDURES USED IN TOPICAL AFRICA, SOUTH-EAST ASIA..." AFR S/ASIA UK ROUTINE GOV/REL RACE/REL...GOV/COMP BIBLIOG 20. PAGE 98 B1985
C60
ECO/UNDEV CHOOSE REPRESENT ADMIN

BURDETTE F.L.,POLITICAL SCIENCE: A SELECTED BIBLIOGRAPHY OF BOOKS IN PRINT, WITH ANNOTATIONS (PAMPHLET). LAW LOC/G NAT/G POL/PAR PROVS DIPLOM EDU/PROP ADMIN CHOOSE ATTIT 20. PAGE 17 B0347
B61
BIBLIOG/A GOV/COMP CONCPT ROUTINE

HICKS U.K.,DEVELOPMENT FROM BELOW. UK INDUS ADMIN COLONIAL ROUTINE GOV/REL...POLICY METH/CNCPT CHARTS 19/20 CMN/WLTH. PAGE 50 B1006
B61
ECO/UNDEV LOC/G GOV/COMP METH/COMP

MOODIE G.C.,"THE GOVERNMENT OF GREAT BRITAIN." UK LAW STRUCT LOC/G POL/PAR DIPLOM RECEIVE ADMIN COLONIAL CHOOSE...BIBLIOG 20 PARLIAMENT. PAGE 75 B1508
C61
NAT/G SOCIETY PARL/PROC GOV/COMP

ANDREWS W.G.,FRENCH POLITICS AND ALGERIA: THE PROCESS OF POLICY FORMATION 1954-1962. ALGERIA
B62
GOV/COMP EXEC

FRANCE CONSTN ELITES POL/PAR CHIEF DELIB/GP LEGIS   COLONIAL
DIPLOM PRESS CHOOSE 20. PAGE 5 B0105
                                                              B62
GROGAN V.,ADMINISTRATIVE TRIBUNALS IN THE PUBLIC   ADMIN
SERVICE. IRELAND UK NAT/G CONTROL CT/SYS...JURID   LAW
GOV/COMP 20. PAGE 44 B0884   ADJUD
                                                      DELIB/GP
                                                              S62
BRAIBANTI R.,"REFLECTIONS ON BUREAUCRATIC   CONTROL
CORRPUTION." LAW REPRESENT 20. PAGE 15 B0298   MORAL
                                                      ADMIN
                                                      GOV/COMP
                                                              S62
DAKIN R.E.,"VARIATIONS IN POWER STRUCTURES AND   MUNIC
ORGANIZING EFFICIENCY: A COMPARATIVE STUDY OF FOUR   STRUCT
AREAS." STRATA EDU/PROP ADMIN LEAD GP/REL GOV/COMP.   PWR
PAGE 26 B0524
                                                              B63
ADRIAN C.R.,GOVERNING OVER FIFTY STATES AND THEIR   PROVS
COMMUNITIES. USA+45 CONSTN FINAN MUNIC NAT/G   LOC/G
POL/PAR EX/STRUC LEGIS ADMIN CONTROL CT/SYS   GOV/REL
...CHARTS 20. PAGE 3 B0061   GOV/COMP
                                                              B63
DUE J.F.,STATE SALES TAX ADMINISTRATION. OP/RES   PROVS
BUDGET PAY ADMIN EXEC ROUTINE COST EFFICIENCY   TAX
PROFIT...CHARTS METH/COMP 20. PAGE 31 B0626   STAT
                                                      GOV/COMP
                                                              B63
HERNDON J.,A SELECTED BIBLIOGRAPHY OF MATERIALS IN   BIBLIOG
STATE GOVERNMENT AND POLITICS (PAMPHLET). USA+45   GOV/COMP
POL/PAR LEGIS ADMIN CHOOSE MGT. PAGE 49 B0993   PROVS
                                                      DECISION
                                                              B63
JACOB H.,GERMAN ADMINISTRATION SINCE BISMARCK: ADMIN
CENTRAL AUTHORITY VERSUS LOCAL AUTONOMY. GERMANY   NAT/G
GERMANY/W LAW POL/PAR CONTROL CENTRAL TOTALISM   LOC/G
FASCISM...MAJORIT DECISION STAT CHARTS GOV/COMP   POLICY
19/20 BISMARCK/O HITLER/A WEIMAR/REP. PAGE 55 B1111
                                                              B63
KAMMERER G.M.,THE URBAN POLITICAL COMMUNITY: EXEC
PROFILES IN TOWN POLITICS. ELITES LOC/G LEAD   MUNIC
...DECISION GP/COMP. PAGE 57 B1162   PWR
                                                      GOV/COMP
                                                              B63
WEINER M.,POLITICAL CHANGE IN SOUTH ASIA. CEYLON   NAT/G
INDIA PAKISTAN S/ASIA CULTURE ELITES ECO/UNDEV   CONSTN
EX/STRUC ADMIN CONTROL CHOOSE CONSERVE...GOV/COMP   TEC/DEV
ANTHOL 20. PAGE 115 B2315
                                                              S63
JENNINGS M.K.,"PUBLIC ADMINISTRATORS AND COMMUNITY   ADMIN
DECISION-MAKING." ELITES LOC/G LEAD...GP/COMP   MUNIC
GOV/COMP. PAGE 56 B1134   DECISION
                                                      PWR
                                                              B64
ANDREN N.,GOVERNMENT AND POLITICS IN THE NORDIC   CONSTN
COUNTRIES: DENMARK, FINLAND, ICELAND, NORWAY,   NAT/G
SWEDEN. DENMARK FINLAND ICELAND NORWAY SWEDEN   CULTURE
POL/PAR CHIEF LEGIS ADMIN REGION REPRESENT ATTIT   GOV/COMP
CONSERVE...CHARTS BIBLIOG/A 20. PAGE 5 B0102
                                                              B64
RIDLEY F.,PUBLIC ADMINISTRATION IN FRANCE. FRANCE   ADMIN
UK EX/STRUC CONTROL PARTIC EFFICIENCY 20. PAGE 88   REPRESENT
B1781   GOV/COMP
                                                      PWR
                                                              B64
RIES J.C.,THE MANAGEMENT OF DEFENSE: ORGANIZATION   FORCES
AND CONTROL OF THE US ARMED SERVICES. PROF/ORG   ACT/RES
DELIB/GP EX/STRUC LEGIS GOV/REL PERS/REL CENTRAL   DECISION
RATIONAL PWR...POLICY TREND GOV/COMP BIBLIOG.   CONTROL
PAGE 88 B1782
                                                              B64
WHEARE K.C.,FEDERAL GOVERNMENT (4TH ED.). WOR+45   FEDERAL
WOR-45 POL/PAR LEGIS BAL/PWR CT/SYS...POLICY JURID   CONSTN
CONCPT GOV/COMP 17/20. PAGE 116 B2331   EX/STRUC
                                                      NAT/COMP
                                                              L64
GILBERT C.E.,"NATIONAL POLITICAL ALIGNMENTS AND THE   MUNIC
POLITICS OF LARGE CITIES." ELITES LOC/G NAT/G LEGIS   CHOOSE
EXEC LEAD PLURISM GOV/COMP. PAGE 39 B0800   POL/PAR
                                                      PWR
                                                              S64
HADY T.F.,"CONGRESSIONAL TOWNSHIPS AS INCORPORATED   MUNIC
MUNICIPALITIES." NEIGH ADMIN REPRESENT ATTIT GEOG.   REGION
PAGE 45 B0914   LOC/G
                                                      GOV/COMP
                                                              B65
EDELMAN M.,THE POLITICS OF WAGE-PRICE DECISIONS.   GOV/COMP
GERMANY ITALY NETHERLAND UK INDUS LABOR POL/PAR   CONTROL
PROB/SOLV BARGAIN PRICE ROUTINE BAL/PAY COST DEMAND   ECO/TAC
20. PAGE 32 B0654   PLAN
                                                              B65
GOLEMBIEWSKI R.T.,MEN, MANAGEMENT, AND MORALITY;   LG/CO
TOWARD A NEW ORGANIZATIONAL ETHIC. CONSTN EX/STRUC   MGT
CREATE ADMIN CONTROL INGP/REL PERSON SUPEGO MORAL   PROB/SOLV
PWR...GOV/COMP METH/COMP 20 BUREAUCRCY. PAGE 40
B0819

HARMON R.B.,POLITICAL SCIENCE: A BIBLIOGRAPHICAL   BIBLIOG
GUIDE TO THE LITERATURE. WOR+45 WOR-45 R+D INT/ORG   POL/PAR
LOC/G NAT/G DIPLOM ADMIN...CONCPT METH. PAGE 47   LAW
B0950   GOV/COMP
                                                              B65
WARD W.E.,GOVERNMENT IN WEST AFRICA. WOR+45 POL/PAR   GOV/COMP
EX/STRUC PLAN PARTIC GP/REL SOVEREIGN 20 AFRICA/W.   CONSTN
PAGE 114 B2291   COLONIAL
                                                      ECO/UNDEV
                                                              S65
ASHFORD D.E.,"BUREAUCRATS AND CITIZENS." MOROCCO   GOV/COMP
PAKISTAN PARTIC 20 TUNIS. PAGE 7 B0140   ADMIN
                                                      EX/STRUC
                                                      ROLE
                                                              S65
RAPHAELI N.,"SELECTED ARTICLES AND DOCUMENTS ON   BIBLIOG
COMPARATIVE PUBLIC ADMINISTRATION." USA+45 FINAN   ADMIN
LOC/G WORKER TEC/DEV CONTROL LEAD...SOC/WK GOV/COMP   NAT/G
METH/COMP. PAGE 86 B1739   MGT
                                                              B66
CHAPMAN B.,THE PROFESSION OF GOVERNMENT: THE PUBLIC   BIBLIOG
SERVICE IN EUROPE. CONSTN NAT/G POL/PAR EX/STRUC   ADMIN
LEGIS TOP/EX PROB/SOLV DEBATE EXEC PARL/PROC PARTIC   EUR+WWI
20. PAGE 20 B0411   GOV/COMP
                                                              B66
DUNCOMBE H.S.,COUNTY GOVERNMENT IN AMERICA. USA+45   LOC/G
FINAN MUNIC ADMIN ROUTINE GOV/REL...GOV/COMP 20.   PROVS
PAGE 31 B0631   CT/SYS
                                                      TOP/EX
                                                              B66
HEADY F.,PUBLIC ADMINISTRATION: A COMPARATIVE   ADMIN
PERSPECTIVE. ECO/DEV ECO/UNDEV...GOV/COMP 20   NAT/COMP
BUREAUCRCY. PAGE 48 B0982   NAT/G
                                                      CIVMIL/REL
                                                              B66
HESSLER I.O.,29 WAYS TO GOVERN A CITY. EX/STRUC   MUNIC
TOP/EX PROB/SOLV PARTIC CHOOSE REPRESENT EFFICIENCY   GOV/COMP
...CHARTS 20 CITY/MGT MAYOR. PAGE 49 B0998   LOC/G
                                                      ADMIN
                                                              B66
INTERPARLIAMENTARY UNION,PARLIAMENTS: COMPARATIVE   PARL/PROC
STUDY ON STRUCTURE AND FUNCTIONING OF   LEGIS
REPRESENTATIVE INSTITUTIONS IN FIFTY-FIVE   GOV/COMP
COUNTRIES. WOR+45 POL/PAR DELIB/GP BUDGET ADMIN   EX/STRUC
CONTROL CHOOSE. PAGE 54 B1099
                                                              L66
CRAIN R.L.,"STRUCTURE AND VALUES IN LOCAL POLITICAL   MUNIC
SYSTEMS: THE CASE OF FLUORIDATION DECISIONS."   EDU/PROP
EX/STRUC LEGIS LEAD PARTIC REPRESENT PWR...DECISION   LOC/G
GOV/COMP. PAGE 25 B0501   ATTIT
                                                              L66
SEYLER W.C.,"DOCTORAL DISSERTATIONS IN POLITICAL   BIBLIOG
SCIENCE IN UNIVERSITIES OF THE UNITED STATES AND   LAW
CANADA." INT/ORG LOC/G ADMIN...INT/LAW MGT   NAT/G
GOV/COMP. PAGE 96 B1930
                                                              S66
WOLFINGER R.E.,"POLITICAL ETHOS AND THE STRUCTURE   MUNIC
OF CITY GOVERNMENT." POL/PAR EX/STRUC REPRESENT   ATTIT
GP/REL PERS/REL RIGID/FLEX PWR. PAGE 118 B2371   STRATA
                                                      GOV/COMP
                                                              B67
MACKINTOSH J.M.,JUGGERNAUT. USSR NAT/G POL/PAR   WAR
ADMIN LEAD CIVMIL/REL COST TOTALISM PWR MARXISM   FORCES
...GOV/COMP 20. PAGE 68 B1364   COM
                                                      PROF/ORG
                                                              B67
PYE L.W.,SOUTHEAST ASIA'S POLITICAL SYSTEMS. ASIA   NAT/G
S/ASIA STRUCT ECO/UNDEV EX/STRUC CAP/ISM DIPLOM   POL/PAR
ALL/IDEOS...TREND CHARTS. PAGE 85 B1724   GOV/COMP
                                                              B67
TOTMAN C.,POLITICS IN THE TOKUGAWA BAKUFU,   NAT/G
1600-1843. EX/STRUC...GOV/COMP 17/19 CHINJAP.   ADMIN
PAGE 105 B2120   LEAD
                                                              S67
ANDERSON M.,"THE FRENCH PARLIAMENT." EUR+WWI FRANCE   PARL/PROC
MOD/EUR CONSTN POL/PAR CHIEF LEGIS LOBBY ATTIT ROLE   LEAD
PWR 19/20. PAGE 5 B0095   GOV/COMP
                                                      EX/STRUC
                                                              S67
BRADLEY A.W.,"CONSTITUTION-MAKING IN UGANDA."   NAT/G
UGANDA LAW CHIEF DELIB/GP LEGIS ADMIN EXEC   CREATE
PARL/PROC RACE/REL ORD/FREE...GOV/COMP 20. PAGE 14   CONSTN
B0295   FEDERAL
                                                              S67
IDENBURG P.J.,"POLITICAL STRUCTURAL DEVELOPMENT IN   AFR
TROPICAL AFRICA." UK ECO/UNDEV KIN POL/PAR CHIEF   CONSTN
EX/STRUC CREATE COLONIAL CONTROL REPRESENT RACE/REL   NAT/G
...MAJORIT TREND 20. PAGE 53 B1074   GOV/COMP
                                                              S67
SUBRAMANIAM V.,"REPRESENTATIVE BUREAUCRACY: A   STRATA
REASSESSMENT." USA+45 ELITES LOC/G NAT/G ADMIN   GP/REL
GOV/REL PRIVIL DRIVE ROLE...POLICY CENSUS 20   MGT
CIVIL/SERV BUREAUCRCY. PAGE 101 B2053   GOV/COMP
                                                              B87
KINNEAR J.B.,PRINCIPLES OF CIVIL GOVERNMENT.   POL/PAR

MOD/EUR USA-45 CONSTN LOC/G EX/STRUC ADMIN
PARL/PROC RACE/REL...CONCPT 18/19. PAGE 60 B1210
NAT/G
GOV/COMP
REPRESENT

GOV/REL....RELATIONS BETWEEN GOVERNMENTS

N
THE AMERICAN CITY. INDUS PROF/ORG PLAN GOV/REL
...MGT 20. PAGE 1 B0007
BIBLIOG/A
ADMIN
TEC/DEV
MUNIC

N
LOCAL GOVERNMENT SERVICE....SOC BIBLIOG/A 20.
PAGE 1 B0016
LOC/G
ADMIN
MUNIC
GOV/REL

N
NEUE POLITISCHE LITERATUR; BERICHTE UBER DAS
INTERNATIONALE SCHRIFTTUM ZUR POLITIK. WOR+45 LAW
CONSTN POL/PAR ADMIN LEAD GOV/REL...POLICY
IDEA/COMP. PAGE 2 B0027
BIBLIOG/A
DIPLOM
NAT/G
NAT/COMP

PERSONNEL. USA+45 LAW LABOR LG/CO WORKER CREATE
GOV/REL PERS/REL ATTIT WEALTH. PAGE 2 B0030
BIBLIOG/A
ADMIN
MGT
GP/REL

N
FAUNT J.R.,A CHECKLIST OF SOUTH CAROLINA STATE
PUBLICATIONS. USA+45 CONSTN LEGIS ADMIN ATTIT 20.
PAGE 35 B0708
BIBLIOG
PROVS
LOC/G
GOV/REL

N
MARTIN W.O. JR.,STATE OF LOUISIANA OFFICIAL
PUBLICATIONS. USA+45 USA-45 LEGIS ADMIN LEAD 19/20.
PAGE 70 B1415
BIBLIOG
PROVS
GOV/REL

STATE OF ILLINOIS,PUBLICATIONS OF THE STATE OF
ILLINOIS. USA+45 FINAN POL/PAR ADMIN LEAD 20
ILLINOIS. PAGE 100 B2024
BIBLIOG
PROVS
LOC/G
GOV/REL

N
UNESCO,INTERNATIONAL BIBLIOGRAPHY OF POLITICAL
SCIENCE (VOLUMES 1-8). WOR+45 LAW NAT/G EX/STRUC
LEGIS PROB/SOLV DIPLOM ADMIN GOV/REL 20 UNESCO.
PAGE 107 B2153
BIBLIOG
CONCPT
IDEA/COMP

N
US LIBRARY OF CONGRESS,CATALOG OF THE PUBLIC
DOCUMENTS OF THE UNITED STATES, 18931940. USA-45
LAW ECO/DEV AGRI PLAN PROB/SOLV ADMIN LEAD GOV/REL
ATTIT 19/20. PAGE 109 B2200
BIBLIOG
NAT/G
POLICY
LOC/G

N
US SUPERINTENDENT OF DOCUMENTS,INTERSTATE COMMERCE
(PRICE LIST 59). USA+45 LAW LOC/G NAT/G LEGIS
TARIFFS TAX ADMIN CONTROL HEALTH DECISION. PAGE 111
B2239
BIBLIOG/A
DIST/IND
GOV/REL
PROVS

N
US SUPERINTENDENT OF DOCUMENTS,TRANSPORTATION:
HIGHWAYS, ROADS, AND POSTAL SERVICE (PRICE LIST
25). PANAMA USA+45 LAW FORCES DIPLOM ADMIN GOV/REL
HEALTH MGT. PAGE 111 B2243
BIBLIOG/A
DIST/IND
SERV/IND
NAT/G

N
VIRGINIA STATE LIBRARY,CHECK-LIST OF VIRGINIA STATE
PUBLICATIONS. USA+45 USA-45 ECO/DEV POL/PAR LEGIS
ADJUD LEAD 18/20. PAGE 112 B2265
BIBLIOG/A
PROVS
ADMIN
GOV/REL

B05
GOODNOW F.J.,THE PRINCIPLES OF THE ADMINISTRATIVE
LAW OF THE UNITED STATES. USA-45 LAW STRUCT
EX/STRUC LEGIS BAL/PWR CONTROL GOV/REL PWR...JURID
19/20 CIVIL/SERV. PAGE 41 B0822
ADMIN
NAT/G
PROVS
LOC/G

B07
HAASE A.R.,INDEX OF ECONOMIC MATERIAL IN DOCUMENTS
OF STATES OF THE UNITED STATES (13 VOLS.). USA-45
NAT/G GOV/REL...POLICY 18/20. PAGE 45 B0911
BIBLIOG
ECO/DEV
PROVS
ADMIN

B08
WILSON W.,CONSTITUTIONAL GOVERNMENT IN THE UNITED
STATES. USA-45 LAW POL/PAR PROVS CHIEF LEGIS
BAL/PWR ADJUD EXEC FEDERAL PWR 18/20 SUPREME/CT
HOUSE/REP SENATE. PAGE 117 B2362
NAT/G
GOV/REL
CONSTN
PARL/PROC

B15
SAWYER R.A.,A LIST OF WORKS ON COUNTY GOVERNMENT.
LAW FINAN MUNIC TOP/EX ROUTINE CRIME...CLASSIF
RECORD 19/20. PAGE 93 B1871
BIBLIOG/A
LOC/G
GOV/REL
ADMIN

B19
LOS ANGELES BD CIV SERV COMNRS,ANNUAL REPORT: LOS
ANGELES CALIFORNIA: 1919-1936. USA-45 LAW GOV/REL
PRODUC...STAT 20. PAGE 66 B1340
DELIB/GP
ADMIN
LOC/G
MUNIC

B19
SUTHERLAND G.,CONSTITUTIONAL POWER AND WORLD
AFFAIRS. CONSTN STRUCT INT/ORG NAT/G CHIEF LEGIS
ACT/RES PLAN GOV/REL ALL/VALS...OBS TIME/SEQ
CONGRESS VAL/FREE 20 PRESIDENT. PAGE 102 B2056
USA-45
EXEC
DIPLOM

N19
ABERNATHY B.R.,SOME PERSISTING QUESTIONS CONCERNING
THE CONSTITUTIONAL STATE EXECUTIVE (PAMPHLET).
CONSTN TOP/EX TEC/DEV GOV/REL EFFICIENCY TIME 20
GOVERNOR. PAGE 3 B0054
PROVS
EX/STRUC
PROB/SOLV
PWR

N19
ANDERSON W.,THE UNITS OF GOVERNMENT IN THE UNITED
STATES (PAMPHLET). USA-45 NAT/G PROVS EFFICIENCY
...CHARTS 20. PAGE 5 B0098
LOC/G
CENSUS
ADMIN
GOV/REL

N19
BURRUS B.R.,INVESTIGATION AND DISCOVERY IN STATE
ANTITRUST (PAMPHLET). USA+45 USA-45 LEGIS ECO/TAC
ADMIN CONTROL CT/SYS CRIME GOV/REL PWR...JURID
CHARTS 19/20 FTC MONOPOLY. PAGE 17 B0355
NAT/G
PROVS
LAW
INSPECT

N19
EAST KENTUCKY REGIONAL PLAN,PROGRAM 60: A DECADE OF
ACTION FOR PROGRESS IN EASTERN KENTUCKY (PAMPHLET).
USA+45 AGRI CONSTRUC INDUS CONSULT ACT/RES
PROB/SOLV EDU/PROP GOV/REL HEALTH KENTUCKY. PAGE 32
B0643
REGION
ADMIN
PLAN
ECO/UNDEV

N19
EAST KENTUCKY REGIONAL PLAN,PROGRAM 60 REPORT:
ACTION FOR PORGRESS IN EASTERN KENTUCKY (PAMPHLET).
USA+45 CONSTRUC INDUS ACT/RES PROB/SOLV EDU/PROP
ADMIN GOV/REL KENTUCKY. PAGE 32 B0644
REGION
PLAN
ECO/UNDEV
CONSULT

N19
FAHRNKOPF N.,STATE AND LOCAL GOVERNMENT IN ILLINOIS
(PAMPHLET). CONSTN ADMIN PARTIC CHOOSE REPRESENT
GOV/REL...JURID MGT 20 ILLINOIS. PAGE 34 B0696
BIBLIOG
LOC/G
LEGIS
CT/SYS

N19
GORWALA A.D.,THE ADMINISTRATIVE JUNGLE (PAMPHLET).
INDIA NAT/G LEGIS ECO/TAC CONTROL GOV/REL
...METH/COMP 20. PAGE 41 B0838
ADMIN
POLICY
PLAN
ECO/UNDEV

N19
GRIFFITH W.,THE PUBLIC SERVICE (PAMPHLET). UK LAW
LOC/G NAT/G PARTIC CHOOSE DRIVE ROLE SKILL...CHARTS
20 CIVIL/SERV. PAGE 44 B0880
ADMIN
EFFICIENCY
EDU/PROP
GOV/REL

N19
HIGGINS R.,THE ADMINISTRATION OF UNITED KINGDOM
FOREIGN POLICY THROUGH THE UNITED NATIONS
(PAMPHLET). UK NAT/G ADMIN GOV/REL...CHARTS 20 UN
PARLIAMENT. PAGE 50 B1009
DIPLOM
POLICY
INT/ORG

N19
KRIESBERG M.,CANCELLATION OF THE RATION STAMPS
(PAMPHLET). USA+45 USA-45 MARKET PROB/SOLV PRICE
GOV/REL RIGID/FLEX 20 OPA. PAGE 61 B1235
RATION
DECISION
ADMIN
NAT/G

N19
MARSH J.F. JR.,THE FBI RETIREMENT BILL (PAMPHLET).
USA+45 EX/STRUC WORKER PLAN PROB/SOLV BUDGET LEAD
LOBBY PARL/PROC PERS/REL RIGID/FLEX...POLICY 20 FBI
PRESIDENT BUR/BUDGET. PAGE 70 B1405
ADMIN
NAT/G
SENIOR
GOV/REL

N19
PERREN G.E.,LANGUAGE AND COMMUNICATION IN THE
COMMONWEALTH (PAMPHLET). FUT UK LAW ECO/DEV PRESS
TV WRITING ADJUD ADMIN COLONIAL CONTROL 20
CMN/WLTH. PAGE 82 B1660
EDU/PROP
LING
GOV/REL
COM/IND

C20
BLACHLY F.F.,"THE GOVERNMENT AND ADMINISTRATION OF
GERMANY." GERMANY CONSTN LOC/G PROVS DELIB/GP
EX/STRUC FORCES LEGIS TOP/EX CT/SYS...BIBLIOG/A
19/20. PAGE 12 B0246
NAT/G
GOV/REL
ADMIN
PHIL/SCI

B24
KENT F.R.,THE GREAT GAME OF POLITICS. USA-45 LOC/G
NAT/G POL/PAR EX/STRUC PROB/SOLV BUDGET CHOOSE
GOV/REL 20. PAGE 59 B1194
ADMIN
OP/RES
STRUCT

B25
MATHEWS J.M.,AMERICAN STATE GOVERNMENT. USA-45
LOC/G CHIEF EX/STRUC LEGIS ADJUD CONTROL CT/SYS
ROUTINE GOV/REL PWR 20 GOVERNOR. PAGE 71 B1426
PROVS
ADMIN
FEDERAL
CONSTN

B26
INTERNATIONAL BIBLIOGRAPHY OF POLITICAL SCIENCE.
WOR+45 NAT/G POL/PAR EX/STRUC LEGIS CT/SYS LEAD
CHOOSE GOV/REL ATTIT...PHIL/SCI 20. PAGE 2 B0034
BIBLIOG
DIPLOM
CONCPT
ADMIN

B27
WILLOUGHBY W.F.,PRINCIPLES OF PUBLIC ADMINISTRATION
WITH SPECIAL REFERENCE TO THE NATIONAL AND STATE
GOVERNMENTS OF THE UNITED STATES. FINAN PROVS CHIEF
CONSULT LEGIS CREATE BUDGET EXEC ROUTINE GOV/REL
CENTRAL...MGT 20 BUR/BUDGET CONGRESS PRESIDENT.
PAGE 117 B2356
NAT/G
EX/STRUC
OP/RES
ADMIN

B30
FAIRLIE J.A.,COUNTY GOVERNMENT AND ADMINISTRATION.
UK USA-45 NAT/G SCHOOL FORCES BUDGET TAX CT/SYS
CHOOSE...JURID BIBLIOG 11/20. PAGE 35 B0701
ADMIN
GOV/REL
LOC/G
MUNIC

B33
BROMAGE A.W.,AMERICAN COUNTY GOVERNMENT. USA-45
NAT/G LEAD GOV/REL CENTRAL PWR...MGT BIBLIOG 18/20.
PAGE 15 B0314
LOC/G
CREATE
ADMIN

GAUS J.M.,THE FRONTIERS OF PUBLIC ADMINISTRATION. EFFICIENCY PERCEPT RIGID/FLEX ORD/FREE 20. PAGE 39 B0785 — MUNIC / ROUTINE / GOV/REL / ELITES / PROB/SOLV — B36

GRAVES W.B.,AMERICAN STATE GOVERNMENT. CONSTN FINAN EX/STRUC FORCES LEGIS BUDGET TAX CT/SYS REPRESENT GOV/REL...BIBLIOG/A 19/20. PAGE 42 B0855 — NAT/G / PROVS / ADMIN / FEDERAL — B36

GOSNELL H.F.,MACHINE POLITICS: CHICAGO MODEL. COM/IND FACE/GP LOC/G EX/STRUC LEAD ROUTINE SANCTION REPRESENT GOV/REL PWR...POLICY MATH OBS INT CHARTS. PAGE 41 B0840 — POL/PAR / MUNIC / ADMIN / CHOOSE — B37

MACDONALD G.E.,CHECK LIST OF LEGISLATIVE JOURNALS OF THE STATES OF THE UNITED STATES OF AMERICA. USA-45 ADMIN GOV/REL ATTIT...POLICY 18/20. PAGE 67 B1356 — BIBLIOG / PROVS / LEGIS / LOC/G — B38

ANDERSON W.,LOCAL GOVERNMENT IN EUROPE. FRANCE GERMANY ITALY UK USSR MUNIC PROVS ADMIN GOV/REL CENTRAL SOVEREIGN 20. PAGE 5 B0099 — GOV/COMP / NAT/COMP / LOC/G / CONSTN — B39

BAKER G.,THE COUNTY AGENT. USA-45 LOC/G NAT/G PROB/SOLV ADMIN...POLICY 20 ROOSEVLT/F NEW/DEAL COUNTY/AGT. PAGE 8 B0166 — AGRI / CONSULT / GOV/REL / EDU/PROP — B39

PATTERSON C.P.,STATE AND LOCAL GOVERNMENT IN TEXAS (3RD ED.). USA-45 EX/STRUC LEGIS CT/SYS CHOOSE 20 TEXAS. PAGE 81 B1642 — CONSTN / PROVS / GOV/REL / LOC/G — B40

WILCOX J.K.,MANUAL ON THE USE OF STATE PUBLICATIONS. USA-45 FINAN LEGIS TAX GOV/REL ...CHARTS 20. PAGE 116 B2346 — BIBLIOG/A / PROVS / ADMIN / LAW — B40

PERKINS J.A.,"CONGRESSIONAL INVESTIGATIONS OF MATTERS OF INTERNATIONAL IMPORT." DELIB/GP DIPLOM ADMIN CONTROL 20 CONGRESS. PAGE 82 B1656 — POL/PAR / DECISION / PARL/PROC / GOV/REL — S40

CHILDS J.B.,A GUIDE TO THE OFFICIAL PUBLICATIONS OF THE OTHER AMERICAN REPUBLICS: ARGENTINA. CHIEF DIPLOM GOV/REL...BIBLIOG 18/19 ARGEN. PAGE 21 B0422 — NAT/G / EX/STRUC / METH/CNCPT / LEGIS — B41

COHEN E.W.,THE GROWTH OF THE BRITISH CIVIL SERVICE 1780-1939. UK NAT/G SENIOR ROUTINE GOV/REL...MGT METH/COMP BIBLIOG 18/20. PAGE 22 B0442 — OP/RES / TIME/SEQ / CENTRAL / ADMIN — B41

LEISERSON A.,ADMINISTRATIVE REGULATION: A STUDY IN REPRESENTATION OF INTERESTS. NAT/G EX/STRUC PROB/SOLV BARGAIN CONFER ROUTINE REPRESENT PERS/REL UTIL PWR POLICY. PAGE 63 B1283 — LOBBY / ADMIN / GP/REL / GOV/REL — B42

HUZAR E.,"LEGISLATIVE CONTROL OVER ADMINISTRATION: CONGRESS AND WPA" USA-45 FINAN DELIB/GP LOBBY GOV/REL EFFICIENCY ATTIT...POLICY CONGRESS. PAGE 53 B1069 — ADMIN / EX/STRUC / CONTROL / LEGIS — S42

CLARKE M.P.,PARLIAMENTARY PRIVILEGE IN THE AMERICAN COLONIES. PROVS DOMIN ADMIN REPRESENT GOV/REL ORD/FREE...BIBLIOG/A 17/18. PAGE 21 B0433 — LEGIS / PWR / COLONIAL / PARL/PROC — B43

MACMAHON A.W.,"CONGRESSIONAL OVERSIGHT OF ADMINISTRATION: THE POWER OF THE PURSE." USA-45 BUDGET ROUTINE GOV/REL PWR...POLICY CONGRESS. PAGE 68 B1368 — LEGIS / DELIB/GP / ADMIN / CONTROL — L43

PRICE D.K.,"THE PARLIAMENTARY AND PRESIDENTIAL SYSTEMS" (BMR) USA-45 NAT/G EX/STRUC PARL/PROC GOV/REL PWR 20 PRESIDENT CONGRESS PARLIAMENT. PAGE 84 B1706 — LEGIS / REPRESENT / ADMIN / GOV/COMP — S43

GAUS J.M.,REFLECTIONS ON PUBLIC ADMINISTRATION. USA+45 CONTROL GOV/REL CENTRAL FEDERAL ATTIT WEALTH ...DECISION 20. PAGE 39 B0787 — MGT / POLICY / EX/STRUC / ADMIN — B47

JENKINS W.S.,COLLECTED PUBLIC DOCUMENTS OF THE STATES: A CHECK LIST. USA-45 ECO/DEV NAT/G ADMIN GOV/REL 20. PAGE 56 B1129 — BIBLIOG / PROVS / LEGIS / TOP/EX — B47

REDFORD E.S.,FIELD ADMINISTRATION OF WARTIME RATIONING. USA-45 CONSTN ELITES DIST/IND WORKER CONTROL WAR GOV/REL ADJUST RIGID/FLEX 20 OPA. PAGE 87 B1752 — ADMIN / NAT/G / PROB/SOLV / RATION — B47

CHILDS J.R.,AMERICAN FOREIGN SERVICE. USA+45 SOCIETY NAT/G ROUTINE GOV/REL 20 DEPT/STATE CIVIL/SERV. PAGE 21 B0423 — DIPLOM / ADMIN / GP/REL — B48

PUBLIC ADMINISTRATION SERVICE,SOURCE MATERIALS IN PUBLIC ADMINISTRATION: A SELECTED BIBLIOGRAPHY (PAS PUBLICATION NO. 102). USA+45 LAW FINAN LOC/G MUNIC NAT/G PLAN RECEIVE EDU/PROP CT/SYS CHOOSE HEALTH 20. PAGE 85 B1717 — BIBLIOG/A / GOV/REL / MGT / ADMIN — B48

WHITE L.D.,INTRODUCTION OT THE STUDY OF PUBLIC ADMINISTRATION. STRUCT PLAN PROB/SOLV EXEC ROUTINE GOV/REL EFFICIENCY PWR CHARTS. PAGE 116 B2336 — ADMIN / MGT / EX/STRUC / NAT/G — B48

WHITE L.D.,THE FEDERALISTS: A STUDY IN ADMINISTRATIVE HISTORY. STRUCT DELIB/GP LEGIS BUDGET ROUTINE GOV/REL GP/REL PERS/REL PWR...BIOG 18/19 PRESIDENT CONGRESS WASHINGT/G JEFFERSN/T HAMILTON/A. PAGE 116 B2337 — ADMIN / NAT/G / POLICY / PROB/SOLV — B48

BOLLENS J.C.,"THE PROBLEM OF GOVERNMENT IN THE SAN FRANCISCO BAY REGION." INDUS PROVS ADMIN GOV/REL ...SOC CHARTS BIBLIOG 20. PAGE 13 B0270 — USA+45 / MUNIC / LOC/G / PROB/SOLV — C48

WALKER H.,"THE LEGISLATIVE PROCESS; LAWMAKING IN THE UNITED STATES." NAT/G POL/PAR PROVS EX/STRUC OP/RES PROB/SOLV CT/SYS LOBBY GOV/REL...CHARTS BIBLIOG T 18/20 CONGRESS. PAGE 113 B2279 — PARL/PROC / LEGIS / LAW / CONSTN — C48

HEADLAM-MORLEY,BIBLIOGRAPHY IN POLITICS FOR THE HONOUR SCHOOL OF PHILOSOPHY, POLITICS AND ECONOMICS (PAMPHLET). UK CONSTN LABOR MUNIC DIPLOM ADMIN 19/20. PAGE 48 B0979 — BIBLIOG / NAT/G / PHIL/SCI / GOV/REL — B49

SCHULTZ W.J.,AMERICAN PUBLIC FINANCE. USA+45 ECO/TAC TAX ADMIN GOV/REL GP/REL INCOME 20. PAGE 94 B1906 — FINAN / POLICY / ECO/DEV / NAT/G — B49

STEIN H.,THE FOREIGN SERVICE ACT OF 1946. USA+45 ELITES ADMIN PLAN PROB/SOLV LOBBY GOV/REL PERS/REL RIGID/FLEX...POLICY IDEA/COMP 20 CONGRESS BUR/BUDGET. PAGE 100 B2027 — DIPLOM / LAW / NAT/G / ADMIN — B49

STEINMETZ H.,"THE PROBLEMS OF THE LANDRAT: A STUDY OF COUNTY GOVERNMENT IN THE US ZONE OF GERMANY." GERMANY/W USA+45 INDUS PLAN DIPLOM EDU/PROP CONTROL WAR GOV/REL FEDERAL WEALTH PLURISM...GOV/COMP 20 LANDRAT. PAGE 100 B2031 — LOC/G / COLONIAL / MGT / TOP/EX — S49

KOENIG L.W.,THE SALE OF THE TANKERS. USA+45 SEA DIST/IND POL/PAR DIPLOM ADMIN CIVMIL/REL ATTIT ...DECISION 20 PRESIDENT DEPT/STATE. PAGE 60 B1223 — NAT/G / POLICY / PLAN / GOV/REL — B50

LITTLE HOOVER COMM,HOW TO ACHIEVE GREATER EFFICIENCY AND ECONOMY IN MINNESOTA'S GOVERNMENT (PAMPHLET). PLAN BUDGET ADMIN CHOOSE EFFICIENCY ALL/VALS 20 MINNESOTA. PAGE 66 B1327 — TOP/EX / LOC/G / GOV/REL / PROVS — B50

PERHAM M.,COLONIAL GOVERNMENT: ANNOTATED READING LIST ON BRITISH COLONIAL GOVERNMENT. UK WOR+45 WOR-45 ECO/UNDEV INT/ORG LEGIS FOR/AID INT/TRADE DOMIN ADMIN REV 20. PAGE 82 B1655 — BIBLIOG/A / COLONIAL / GOV/REL / NAT/G — B50

MORLAN R.L.,"INTERGOVERNMENTAL RELATIONS IN EDUCATION." USA+45 FINAN LOC/G MUNIC NAT/G FORCES PROB/SOLV RECEIVE ADMIN RACE/REL COST...BIBLIOG INDIAN/AM. PAGE 76 B1526 — SCHOOL / GOV/REL / ACADEM / POLICY — C50

STEWART F.M.,"A HALF CENTURY OF MUNICIPAL REFORM." USA+45 CONSTN FINAN SCHOOL EX/STRUC PLAN PROB/SOLV EDU/PROP ADMIN CHOOSE GOV/REL BIBLIOG. PAGE 101 B2036 — LOC/G / VOL/ASSN / MUNIC / POLICY — C50

WAGER P.W.,"COUNTY GOVERNMENT ACROSS THE NATION." USA+45 CONSTN COM/IND FINAN SCHOOL DOMIN CT/SYS LEAD GOV/REL...STAT BIBLIOG 20. PAGE 112 B2272 — LOC/G / PROVS / ADMIN / ROUTINE — C50

ANDERSON W.,STATE AND LOCAL GOVERNMENT IN THE UNITED STATES. USA+45 CONSTN POL/PAR EX/STRUC LEGIS BUDGET TAX ADJUD CT/SYS CHOOSE...CHARTS T 20. PAGE 5 B0100 — LOC/G / MUNIC / PROVS / GOV/REL — B51

ANDERSON W.,GOVERNMENT IN THE FIFTY STATES. LAW CONSTN FINAN POL/PAR LEGIS EDU/PROP ADJUD ADMIN CT/SYS CHOOSE...CHARTS 20. PAGE 5 B0101 — LOC/G / PROVS / GOV/REL — B51

SMITH L.,AMERICAN DEMOCRACY AND MILITARY POWER. USA+45 USA+45 CONSTN STRATA NAT/G LEGIS ACT/RES LEGIT ADMIN EXEC GOV/REL ALL/VALS...CONCPT HIST/WRIT CONGRESS 20. PAGE 98 B1982 — FORCES / STRUCT / WAR — B51

B51

SWISHER C.B.,THE THEORY AND PRACTICE OF AMERICAN
NATIONAL GOVERNMENT. CULTURE LEGIS DIPLOM ADJUD
ADMIN WAR PEACE ORD/FREE...MAJORIT 17/20. PAGE 102
B2063

CONSTN
NAT/G
GOV/REL
GEN/LAWS

S51

MARX F.M.,"SIGNIFICANCE FOR THE ADMINISTRATIVE
PROCESS." POL/PAR LEAD PARL/PROC GOV/REL EFFICIENCY
SUPEGO...POLICY CONGRESS. PAGE 70 B1420

LEGIS
ADMIN
CHIEF

B52

REDFORD E.S.,ADMINISTRATION OF NATIONAL ECONOMIC
CONTROL. ECO/DEV DELIB/GP ADJUD CONTROL EQUILIB 20.
PAGE 87 B1753

ADMIN
ROUTINE
GOV/REL
LOBBY

B52

SWENSON R.J.,FEDERAL ADMINISTRATIVE LAW: A STUDY OF
THE GROWTH, NATURE, AND CONTROL OF ADMINISTRATIVE
ACTION. USA-45 JUDGE ADMIN GOV/REL EFFICIENCY
PRIVIL ATTIT NEW/LIB SUPREME/CT. PAGE 102 B2061

JURID
CONSTN
LEGIS
ADJUD

L52

WRIGHT Q.,"CONGRESS AND THE TREATY-MAKING POWER."
USA+45 WOR+45 CONSTN INTELL NAT/G CHIEF CONSULT
EX/STRUC LEGIS TOP/EX CREATE GOV/REL DISPL DRIVE
RIGID/FLEX...TREND TOT/POP CONGRESS CONGRESS 20
TREATY. PAGE 118 B2384

ROUTINE
DIPLOM
INT/LAW
DELIB/GP

S52

SNIDER C.F.,"AMERICAN COUNTY GOVERNMENT: A MID-
CENTURY REVIEW" (BMR)" USA+45 USA-45 PROVS DELIB/GP
EX/STRUC BUDGET TAX PWR 20. PAGE 98 B1988

LOC/G
ADMIN
GOV/REL
REGION

S52

SOMERS H.M.,"THE PRESIDENT AS ADMINISTRATOR."
USA+45 NAT/G ADMIN REPRESENT GOV/REL 20 PRESIDENT.
PAGE 99 B1996

CONTROL
EFFICIENCY
EX/STRUC
EXEC

C52

LANCASTER L.W.,"GOVERNMENT IN RURAL AMERICA."
USA+45 ECO/DEV AGRI SCHOOL FORCES LEGIS JUDGE
BUDGET TAX CT/SYS...CHARTS BIBLIOG. PAGE 62 B1253

GOV/REL
LOC/G
MUNIC
ADMIN

B53

A BIBLIOGRAPHY AND SUBJECT INDEX OF PUBLICATIONS OF
FLORIDA STATE AGENCIES. USA+45 LOC/G LEAD ATTIT 20
FLORIDA. PAGE 2 B0036

BIBLIOG
PROVS
GOV/REL
ADMIN

B53

APPLEBY P.H.,PUBLIC ADMINISTRATION IN INDIA: REPORT
OF A SURVEY. INDIA LOC/G OP/RES ATTIT ORD/FREE 20.
PAGE 6 B0118

ADMIN
NAT/G
EX/STRUC
GOV/REL

B53

GROSS B.M.,THE LEGISLATIVE STRUGGLE: A STUDY IN
SOCIAL COMBAT. STRUCT LOC/G POL/PAR JUDGE EDU/PROP
DEBATE ETIQUET ADMIN LOBBY CHOOSE GOV/REL INGP/REL
HEREDITY ALL/VALS...SOC PRESIDENT. PAGE 44 B0885

LEGIS
DECISION
PERSON
LEAD

B53

MAJUMDAR B.B.,PROBLEMS OF PUBLIC ADMINISTRATION IN
INDIA. INDIA INDUS PLAN BUDGET ADJUD CENTRAL DEMAND
WEALTH...WELF/ST ANTHOL 20 CIVIL/SERV. PAGE 68
B1384

ECO/UNDEV
GOV/REL
ADMIN
MUNIC

B53

SECKLER-HUDSON C.,BIBLIOGRAPHY ON PUBLIC
ADMINISTRATION (4TH ED.). USA+45 LAW POL/PAR
DELIB/GP BUDGET ADJUD LOBBY GOV/REL GP/REL ATTIT
...JURID 20. PAGE 95 B1923

BIBLIOG/A
ADMIN
NAT/G
MGT

C53

DORWART R.A.,"THE ADMINISTRATIVE REFORMS OF
FREDRICK WILLIAM I OF PRUSSIA. GERMANY MOD/EUR
CHIEF CONTROL PWR...BIBLIOG 16/18. PAGE 30 B0608

ADMIN
NAT/G
CENTRAL
GOV/REL

B54

CHICAGO JOINT REFERENCE LIB,FEDERAL-STATE-LOCAL
RELATIONS: A SELECTED BIBLIOGRAPHY. USA+45 AGRI
LABOR LOC/G MUNIC EX/STRUC ADMIN REGION HEALTH
CON/ANAL. PAGE 21 B0419

BIBLIOG
FEDERAL
GOV/REL

B54

CONWAY O.B. JR.,LEGISLATIVE-EXECUTIVE RELATIONS IN
THE GOVERNMENT OF THE UNITED STATES (PAMPHLET).
BUDGET ATTIT PERCEPT...DECISION 20. PAGE 23 B0470

BAL/PWR
FEDERAL
GOV/REL
EX/STRUC

B54

RECK D.,GOVERNMENT PURCHASING AND COMPETITION.
USA+45 LEGIS CAP/ISM ECO/TAC GOV/REL CENTRAL
...POLICY 20 CONGRESS. PAGE 87 B1749

NAT/G
FINAN
MGT
COST

B54

SCHWARTZ B.,FRENCH ADMINISTRATIVE LAW AND THE
COMMON-LAW WORLD. FRANCE CULTURE LOC/G NAT/G PROVS
DELIB/GP EX/STRUC LEGIS PROB/SOLV CT/SYS EXEC
GOV/REL...IDEA/COMP ENGLSH/LAW. PAGE 95 B1912

JURID
LAW
METH/COMP
ADJUD

B54

SHELTON W.L.,CHECKLIST OF NEW MEXICO PUBLICATIONS,
1850-1953. USA+45 USA-45 LEGIS ADMIN LEAD 19/20.
PAGE 96 B1941

BIBLIOG
PROVS
GOV/REL

B54

THORNTON M.L.,OFFICIAL PUBLICATIONS OF THE COLONY

BIBLIOG

AND STATE OF NORTH CAROLINA, 1749-1939. USA+45
USA-45 LEGIS LEAD GOV/REL ATTIT 18/20. PAGE 104
B2109

ADMIN
PROVS
ACADEM

S54

GILBERT C.E.,"LEGISLATIVE CONTROL OF THE
BUREAUCRACY." USA+45 NAT/G ADMIN EXEC 20. PAGE 39
B0798

CONTROL
EX/STRUC
REPRESENT
GOV/REL

S54

HART J.,"ADMINISTRATION AND THE COURTS." USA+45
NAT/G REPRESENT 20. PAGE 47 B0960

ADMIN
GOV/REL
CT/SYS
FEDERAL

C54

ROBSON W.A.,"GREAT CITIES OF THE WORLD: THEIR
GOVERNMENT, POLITICS, AND PLANNING." CONSTN FINAN
EX/STRUC ADMIN EXEC CHOOSE GOV/REL...STAT TREND
ANTHOL BIBLIOG 20. PAGE 89 B1806

LOC/G
MUNIC
PLAN
PROB/SOLV

C54

ZELLER B.,"AMERICAN STATE LEGISLATURES: REPORT ON
THE COMMITTEE ON AMERICAN LEGISLATURES." CONSTN
POL/PAR EX/STRUC CONFER ADMIN CONTROL EXEC LOBBY
ROUTINE GOV/REL...POLICY BIBLIOG 20. PAGE 119 B2401

REPRESENT
LEGIS
PROVS
APPORT

B55

CRAIG J.,BIBLIOGRAPHY OF PUBLIC ADMINISTRATION IN
AUSTRALIA. CONSTN FINAN EX/STRUC LEGIS PLAN DIPLOM
RECEIVE ADJUD ROUTINE...HEAL 19/20 AUSTRAL
PARLIAMENT. PAGE 24 B0500

BIBLIOG
GOV/REL
ADMIN
NAT/G

B55

GUAITA A.,BIBLIOGRAFIA ESPANOLA DE DERECHO
ADMINISTRATIVO (PAMPHLET). SPAIN LOC/G MUNIC NAT/G
PROVS JUDGE BAL/PWR GOV/REL OWN...JURID 18/19.
PAGE 44 B0900

BIBLIOG
ADMIN
CONSTN
PWR

B55

SMITHIES A.,THE BUDGETARY PROCESS IN THE UNITED
STATES. ECO/DEV AGRI EX/STRUC FORCES LEGIS
PROB/SOLV TAX ROUTINE EFFICIENCY...MGT CONGRESS
PRESIDENT. PAGE 98 B1987

NAT/G
ADMIN
BUDGET
GOV/REL

S55

SCHWARTZ B.,"LEGISLATIVE CONTROL OF ADMINISTRATIVE
RULES AND REGULATIONS THE AMERICAN EXPERIENCE."
USA+45 GOV/REL...GOV/COMP 20. PAGE 95 B1913

CONTROL
ADMIN
EX/STRUC
LEGIS

B56

CARTER B.E.,THE OFFICE OF THE PRIME MINISTER. UK
ADMIN REPRESENT PARLIAMENT 20. PAGE 19 B0388

GOV/REL
CHIEF
EX/STRUC
LEAD

B56

GLADDEN E.N.,CIVIL SERVICE OR BUREAUCRACY? UK LAW
STRATA LABOR TOP/EX PLAN SENIOR AUTOMAT CONTROL
PARTIC CHOOSE HAPPINESS...CHARTS 19/20 CIVIL/SERV
BUREAUCRCY. PAGE 40 B0808

ADMIN
GOV/REL
EFFICIENCY
PROVS

B56

HOWARD L.V.,TULANE STUDIES IN POLITICAL SCIENCE:
CIVIL SERVICE DEVELOPMENT IN LOUISIANA VOLUME 3.
LAW POL/PAR LEGIS CT/SYS ADJUST ORD/FREE...STAT
CHARTS 19/20 LOUISIANA CIVIL/SERV. PAGE 52 B1050

ADMIN
GOV/REL
PROVS
POLICY

B56

KOENIG L.W.,THE TRUMAN ADMINISTRATION: ITS
PRINCIPLES AND PRACTICE. USA+45 POL/PAR CHIEF LEGIS
DIPLOM DEATH NUC/PWR WAR CIVMIL/REL PEACE
...DECISION 20 TRUMAN/HS PRESIDENT TREATY. PAGE 61
B1224

ADMIN
POLICY
EX/STRUC
GOV/REL

B56

REDFORD E.S.,PUBLIC ADMINISTRATION AND POLICY
FORMATION: STUDIES IN OIL, GAS, BANKING, RIVER
DEVELOPMENT AND CORPORATE INVESTIGATIONS. USA+45
CLIENT NAT/G ADMIN LOBBY REPRESENT GOV/REL INGP/REL
20. PAGE 87 B1754

EX/STRUC
PROB/SOLV
CONTROL
EXEC

B56

US HOUSE RULES COMM,HEARINGS BEFORE A SPECIAL
SUBCOMMITTEE: ESTABLISHMENT OF A STANDING COMMITTEE
ON ADMINISTRATIVE PROCEDURE, PRACTICE. USA+45 LAW
EX/STRUC ADJUD CONTROL EXEC GOV/REL EFFICIENCY PWR
...POLICY INT 20 CONGRESS. PAGE 109 B2199

ADMIN
DOMIN
DELIB/GP
NAT/G

S56

COTTER C.P.,"ADMINISTRATIVE ACCOUNTABILITY TO
CONGRESS: THE CONCURRENT RESOLUTION." USA+45 NAT/G
EXEC REPRESENT PWR 20. PAGE 24 B0489

CONTROL
GOV/REL
LEGIS
EX/STRUC

S56

EMMERICH H.,"COOPERATION AMONG ADMINISTRATIVE
AGENCIES." USA+45 NAT/G EX/STRUC ADMIN 20. PAGE 33
B0673

DELIB/GP
REPRESENT
GOV/REL
EXEC

S56

MILNE R.S.,"CONTROL OF GOVERNMENT CORPORATIONS IN
THE UNITED STATES." USA+45 NAT/G CHIEF LEGIS BUDGET
20 GENACCOUNT. PAGE 74 B1488

CONTROL
EX/STRUC
GOV/REL
PWR

S56

TSUJI K.,"THE CABINET, ADMINISTRATIVE ORGANIZATION,
AND THE BUREAUCRACY." EXEC 19/20 CHINJAP. PAGE 106
B2133

GOV/REL
EX/STRUC
ADMIN
REPRESENT

B57

BABCOCK R.S.,STATE & LOCAL GOVERNMENT AND POLITICS. PROVS
USA+45 CONSTN POL/PAR EX/STRUC LEGIS BUDGET LOBBY   LOC/G
CHOOSE SUFF...CHARTS BIBLIOG T 20. PAGE 8 B0154   GOV/REL

B57

CHICAGO U LAW SCHOOL,CONFERENCE ON JUDICIAL   CT/SYS
ADMINISTRATION. LOC/G MUNIC NAT/G PROVS...ANTHOL   ADJUD
20. PAGE 21 B0421   ADMIN
                                                     GOV/REL
B57

KNEIER C.M.,CITY GOVERNMENT IN THE UNITED STATES   MUNIC
(3RD ED.). USA-45 FINAN NAT/G POL/PAR LEGIS   LOC/G
EDU/PROP LEAD APPORT REPRESENT ATTIT...MGT 20   ADMIN
CITY/MGT. PAGE 60 B1219   GOV/REL
S57

COTTER C.P.,"ADMINISTRATIVE ACCOUNTABILITY: LEGIS
REPORTING TO CONGRESS." USA+45 CONSULT DELIB/GP   EX/STRUC
PARL/PROC PARTIC GOV/REL ATTIT PWR DECISION.   REPRESENT
PAGE 24 B0490   CONTROL
S57

COTTER C.R.,"ADMINISTRATIVE RESPONSIBILITY: GOV/REL
CONGRESSIONAL PRESCRIPTION OF INTERAGENCY   LEGIS
RELATIONSHIPS." USA+45 NAT/G ADMIN 20. PAGE 24   REPRESENT
B0492   EX/STRUC
S57

GULICK L.,"METROPOLITAN ORGANIZATION." LEGIS EXEC   REGION
PARTIC CHOOSE REPRESENT GOV/REL...MAJORIT DECISION. LOC/G
PAGE 45 B0904   MUNIC
S57

HARRIS J.P.,"LEGISLATIVE CONTROL OF ADMINISTRATION: LEGIS
SOME COMPARISONS OF AMERICAN AND EUROPEAN   CONTROL
PRACTICES." DEBATE PARL/PROC ROUTINE GOV/REL   EX/STRUC
EFFICIENCY SUPEGO DECISION. PAGE 47 B0954   REPRESENT
S57

HODGETTS J.E.,"THE CIVIL SERVICE AND POLICY   ADMIN
FORMATION." CANADA NAT/G EX/STRUC ROUTINE GOV/REL   DECISION
20. PAGE 50 B1023   EFFICIENCY
                                                     POLICY
S57

ROBSON W.A.,"TWO-LEVEL GOVERNMENT FOR METROPOLITAN   REGION
AREAS." MUNIC EX/STRUC LEGIS PARTIC REPRESENT   LOC/G
MAJORITY. PAGE 89 B1807   PLAN
                                                     GOV/REL
C57

TANG P.S.H.,"COMMUNIST CHINA TODAY: DOMESTIC AND   POL/PAR
FOREIGN POLICIES." CHINA/COM COM S/ASIA USSR STRATA LEAD
FORCES DIPLOM EDU/PROP COERCE GOV/REL...POLICY   ADMIN
MAJORIT BIBLIOG 20. PAGE 102 B2071   CONSTN
B58

BERNSTEIN M.H.,THE JOB OF THE FEDERAL EXECUTIVE.   NAT/G
POL/PAR CHIEF LEGIS ADMIN EXEC LOBBY CHOOSE GOV/REL TOP/EX
ORD/FREE PWR...MGT TREND. PAGE 11 B0228   PERS/COMP
B58

CHANG C.,THE INFLATIONARY SPIRAL: THE EXPERIENCE IN FINAN
CHINA 1939-50. CHINA/COM BUDGET INT/TRADE PRICE   ECO/TAC
ADMIN CONTROL WAR DEMAND...POLICY CHARTS 20.   BAL/PAY
PAGE 20 B0406   GOV/REL
B58

COWAN L.G.,LOCAL GOVERNMENT IN WEST AFRICA. AFR   LOC/G
FRANCE UK CULTURE KIN POL/PAR CHIEF LEGIS CREATE   COLONIAL
ADMIN PARTIC GOV/REL GP/REL...METH/COMP 20. PAGE 24 SOVEREIGN
B0498   REPRESENT
B58

DAVIS K.C.,ADMINISTRATIVE LAW: CASES, TEXT,   ADJUD
PROBLEMS. LAW LOC/G NAT/G TOP/EX PAY CONTROL   JURID
GOV/REL INGP/REL FEDERAL 20 SUPREME/CT. PAGE 27   CT/SYS
B0541   ADMIN
B58

KAPLAN H.E.,THE LAW OF CIVIL SERVICE. USA+45 LAW   ADJUD
POL/PAR CT/SYS CRIME GOV/REL...POLICY JURID 20.   NAT/G
PAGE 58 B1167   ADMIN
                                                     CONSTN
B58

LAW COMMISSION OF INDIA,REFORM OF JUDICIAL   CT/SYS
ADMINISTRATION. INDIA TOP/EX ADMIN DISCRIM   ADJUD
EFFICIENCY...METH/COMP 20. PAGE 63 B1276   GOV/REL
                                                     CONTROL
B58

LOVEJOY D.S.,RHODE ISLAND POLITICS AND THE AMERICAN REV
REVOLUTION 1760-1776. UK USA-45 ELITES EX/STRUC TAX COLONIAL
LEAD REPRESENT GOV/REL GP/REL ATTIT 18 RHODE/ISL.   ECO/TAC
PAGE 67 B1343   SOVEREIGN
B58

PAN AMERICAN UNION,REPERTORIO DE PUBLICACIONES   BIBLIOG
PERIODICAS ACTUALES LATINO-AMERICANAS. CULTURE   L/A+17C
ECO/UNDEV ADMIN LEAD GOV/REL 20 OAS. PAGE 81 B1630   NAT/G
                                                     DIPLOM
B58

SHAW S.J.,THE FINANCIAL AND ADMINISTRATIVE   FINAN
ORGANIZATION AND DEVELOPMENT OF OTTOMAN EGYPT   ADMIN
1517-1798. UAR LOC/G FORCES BUDGET INT/TRADE TAX   GOV/REL
EATING INCOME WEALTH...CHARTS BIBLIOG 16/18 OTTOMAN CULTURE
NAPOLEON/B. PAGE 96 B1940
B58

US HOUSE COMM POST OFFICE,TRAINING OF FEDERAL   LEGIS
EMPLOYEES. USA+45 DIST/IND NAT/G EX/STRUC EDU/PROP   DELIB/GP

CONFER GOV/REL EFFICIENCY SKILL 20 CONGRESS   WORKER
CIVIL/SERV. PAGE 109 B2197   ADMIN
B58

US SENATE COMM POST OFFICE,TO PROVIDE AN EFFECTIVE   INT
SYSTEM OF PERSONNEL ADMINISTRATION. USA+45 NAT/G   LEGIS
EX/STRUC PARL/PROC GOV/REL...JURID 20 SENATE   CONFER
CIVIL/SERV. PAGE 111 B2234   ADMIN
B58

VAN RIPER P.P.,HISTORY OF THE UNITED STATES CIVIL   ADMIN
SERVICE. USA+45 USA-45 LABOR LOC/G DELIB/GP LEGIS   WORKER
PROB/SOLV LOBBY GOV/REL GP/REL INCOME...POLICY   NAT/G
18/20 PRESIDENT CIVIL/SERV. PAGE 111 B2251
L58

EISENSTADT S.N.,"BUREAUCRACY AND   ADMIN
BUREAUCRATIZATION." WOR+45 ECO/DEV INDUS R+D PLAN   OP/RES
GOV/REL...WELF/ST TREND BIBLIOG/A 20. PAGE 32 B0659 MGT
                                                     PHIL/SCI
L58

HAVILAND H.F.,"FOREIGN AID AND THE POLICY PROCESS: LEGIS
1957." USA+45 FACE/GP POL/PAR VOL/ASSN CHIEF   PLAN
DELIB/GP ACT/RES LEGIT EXEC GOV/REL ATTIT DRIVE PWR FOR/AID
...POLICY TESTS CONGRESS 20. PAGE 48 B0971
S58

DERGE D.R.,"METROPOLITAN AND OUTSTATE ALIGNMENTS IN LEGIS
ILLINOIS AND MISSOURI LEGISLATIVE DELEGATIONS"   MUNIC
(BMR)" USA+45 ADMIN PARTIC GOV/REL...MYTH CHARTS 20 PROVS
ILLINOIS MISSOURI. PAGE 28 B0575   POL/PAR
B59

BHAMBHRI C.P.,SUBSTANCE OF HINDU POLITY. INDIA   GOV/REL
S/ASIA LAW EX/STRUC JUDGE TAX COERCE GP/REL   WRITING
POPULISM 20 HINDU. PAGE 11 B0234   SECT
                                                     PROVS
B59

CHRISTENSON R.M.,THE BRANNAN PLAN: FARM POLITICS   AGRI
AND POLICY. USA+45 ECO/DEV CONSULT PLAN PAY GOV/REL NAT/G
...POLICY 20. PAGE 21 B0429   ADMIN
                                                     ECO/TAC
B59

DUVERGER M.,LA CINQUIEME REPUBLIQUE. FRANCE WOR+45   NAT/G
POL/PAR CHIEF EX/STRUC LOBBY. PAGE 31 B0636   CONSTN
                                                     GOV/REL
                                                     PARL/PROC
B59

ELAZAR D.J.,INTERGOVERNMENTAL RELATIONS IN   FEDERAL
NINETEENTH CENTURY AMERICAN FEDERALISM (DOCTORAL   ADMIN
THESIS). USA-45 FINAN LOC/G NAT/G GP/REL 18/19.   PROVS
PAGE 33 B0662   GOV/REL
B59

ELLIOTT O.,MEN AT THE TOP. USA+45 CULTURE EX/STRUC   TOP/EX
PRESS GOV/REL ATTIT ALL/VALS...OBS INT QU 20.   PERSON
PAGE 33 B0668   LEAD
                                                     POLICY
B59

ELLIOTT S.D.,IMPROVING OUR COURTS. LAW EX/STRUC   CT/SYS
PLAN PROB/SOLV ADJUD ADMIN TASK CRIME EFFICIENCY   JURID
ORD/FREE 20. PAGE 33 B0669   GOV/REL
                                                     NAT/G
B59

HANSON A.H.,THE STRUCTURE AND CONTROL OF STATE   NAT/G
ENTERPRISES IN TURKEY. TURKEY LAW ADMIN GOV/REL   LG/CO
EFFICIENCY...CHARTS 20. PAGE 46 B0939   OWN
                                                     CONTROL
B59

INDIAN INSTITUTE PUBLIC ADMIN,MORALE IN THE PUBLIC   HAPPINESS
SERVICES: REPORT OF A CONFERENCE JAN., 3-4, 1959.   ADMIN
INDIA S/ASIA ECO/UNDEV PROVS PLAN EDU/PROP CONFER   WORKER
GOV/REL EFFICIENCY DRIVE ROLE 20 CIVIL/SERV.   INGP/REL
PAGE 53 B1082
B59

MAASS A.,AREA AND POWER: A THEORY OF LOCAL   LOC/G
GOVERNMENT. MUNIC PROVS EX/STRUC LEGIS CT/SYS   FEDERAL
CHOOSE PWR 20. PAGE 67 B1354   BAL/PWR
                                                     GOV/REL
B59

ROSOLIO D.,TEN YEARS OF THE CIVIL SERVICE IN ISRAEL ADMIN
(1948-1958) (PAMPHLET). ISRAEL NAT/G RECEIVE 20.   WORKER
PAGE 90 B1825   GOV/REL
                                                     PAY
B59

U OF MICHIGAN LAW SCHOOL,ATOMS AND THE LAW. USA+45   NUC/PWR
PROVS WORKER PROB/SOLV DIPLOM ADMIN GOV/REL ANTHOL. NAT/G
PAGE 106 B2142   CONTROL
                                                     LAW
S59

SEIDMAN H.,"THE GOVERNMENT CORPORATION IN THE   CONTROL
UNITED STATES." USA+45 LEGIS ADMIN PLURISM 20.   GOV/REL
PAGE 95 B1925   EX/STRUC
                                                     EXEC
B60

ADRIAN C.R.,STATE AND LOCAL GOVERNMENTS: A STUDY IN LOC/G
THE POLITICAL PROCESS. USA+45 LAW FINAN MUNIC   PROVS
POL/PAR LEGIS ADJUD EXEC CHOOSE REPRESENT. PAGE 3   GOV/REL
B0060   ATTIT
B60

ALBI F.,TRATADO DE LOS MODOS DE GESTION DE LAS   LOC/G
CORPORACIONES LOCALES. SPAIN FINAN NAT/G BUDGET   LAW

CONTROL EXEC ROUTINE GOV/REL ORD/FREE SOVEREIGN
...MGT 20. PAGE 3 B0068

ADMIN
MUNIC

B60
BROOKINGS INSTITUTION,UNITED STATES FOREIGN POLICY:
STUDY NO 9: THE FORMULATION AND ADMINISTRATION OF
UNITED STATES FOREIGN POLICY. USA+45 WOR+45
EX/STRUC LEGIS BAL/PWR FOR/AID EDU/PROP CIVMIL/REL
GOV/REL...INT COLD/WAR. PAGE 16 B0317

DIPLOM
INT/ORG
CREATE

B60
FLORES R.H.,CATALOGO DE TESIS DOCTORALES DE LAS
FACULTADES DE LA UNIVERSIDAD DE EL SALVADOR.
EL/SALVADR LAW DIPLOM ADMIN LEAD GOV/REL...SOC
19/20. PAGE 36 B0730

BIBLIOG
ACADEM
L/A+17C
NAT/G

B60
HANBURY H.G.,ENGLISH COURTS OF LAW. UK EX/STRUC
LEGIS CRIME ROLE 12/20 COMMON/LAW ENGLSH/LAW.
PAGE 46 B0936

JURID
CT/SYS
CONSTN
GOV/REL

B60
INDIAN INST OF PUBLIC ADMIN,STATE UNDERTAKINGS:
REPORT OF A CONFERENCE, DECEMBER 19-20, 1959
(PAMPHLET). INDIA LG/CO DELIB/GP CONFER PARL/PROC
EFFICIENCY OWN...MGT 20. PAGE 53 B1081

GOV/REL
ADMIN
NAT/G
LEGIS

B60
LINDVEIT E.N.,SCIENTISTS IN GOVERNMENT. USA+45 PAY
EDU/PROP ADMIN DRIVE HABITAT ROLE...TECHNIC BIBLIOG
20. PAGE 65 B1316

TEC/DEV
ECO/TAC
PHIL/SCI
GOV/REL

B60
PHILLIPS J.C.,MUNICIPAL GOVERNMENT AND
ADMINISTRATION IN AMERICA. USA+45 LAW CONSTN FINAN
FORCES PLAN RECEIVE OWN ORD/FREE 20 CIVIL/LIB.
PAGE 83 B1669

MUNIC
GOV/REL
LOC/G
ADMIN

B60
US SENATE COMM ON JUDICIARY,FEDERAL ADMINISTRATIVE
PROCEDURE. USA+45 CONSTN NAT/G PROB/SOLV CONFER
GOV/REL...JURID INT 20 SENATE. PAGE 110 B2226

PARL/PROC
LEGIS
ADMIN
LAW

B60
US SENATE COMM ON JUDICIARY,ADMINISTRATIVE
PROCEDURE LEGISLATION. USA+45 CONSTN NAT/G
PROB/SOLV CONFER ROUTINE GOV/REL...INT 20 SENATE.
PAGE 110 B2227

PARL/PROC
LEGIS
ADMIN
JURID

B60
WEBSTER J.A.,A GENERAL STUDY OF THE DEPARTMENT OF
DEFENSE INTERNAL SECURITY PROGRAM. USA+45 WORKER
TEC/DEV ADJUD CONTROL CT/SYS EXEC GOV/REL COST
...POLICY DECISION MGT 20 DEPT/DEFEN SUPREME/CT.
PAGE 114 B2307

ORD/FREE
PLAN
ADMIN
NAT/G

B60
WEIDNER E.W.,INTERGOVERNMENTAL RELATIONS AS SEEN BY
PUBLIC OFFICIALS. USA+45 PROVS EX/STRUC EXEC
FEDERAL...QU 20. PAGE 115 B2311

ATTIT
GP/REL
GOV/REL
ADMIN

L60
GRODZINS M.,"AMERICAN POLITICAL PARTIES AND THE
AMERICAN SYSTEM" (BMR)" USA+45 LOC/G NAT/G LEGIS
BAL/PWR ADMIN ROLE PWR...DECISION 20. PAGE 44 B0883

POL/PAR
FEDERAL
CENTRAL
GOV/REL

S60
SCHER S.,"CONGRESSIONAL COMMITTEE MEMBERS AND
INDEPENDENT AGENCY OVERSEERS: A CASE STUDY."
DELIB/GP EX/STRUC JUDGE TOP/EX DOMIN ADMIN CONTROL
PWR...SOC/EXP HOUSE/REP CONGRESS. PAGE 93 B1886

LEGIS
GOV/REL
LABOR
ADJUD

C60
SMITH T.E.,"ELECTIONS IN DEVELOPING COUNTRIES: A
STUDY OF ELECTORAL PROCEDURES USED IN TOPICAL
AFRICA, SOUTH-EAST ASIA..." AFR S/ASIA UK ROUTINE
GOV/REL RACE/REL...GOV/COMP BIBLIOG 20. PAGE 98
B1985

ECO/UNDEV
CHOOSE
REPRESENT
ADMIN

B61
AGARWAL R.C.,STATE ENTERPRISE IN INDIA. FUT INDIA
UK FINAN INDUS ADMIN CONTROL OWN...POLICY CHARTS
BIBLIOG 20 RAILROAD. PAGE 3 B0064

ECO/UNDEV
SOCISM
GOV/REL
LG/CO

B61
AVERY M.W.,GOVERNMENT OF WASHINGTON STATE. USA+45
MUNIC DELIB/GP EX/STRUC LEGIS GIVE CT/SYS PARTIC
REGION EFFICIENCY 20 WASHINGT/G GOVERNOR. PAGE 7
B0151

PROVS
LOC/G
ADMIN
GOV/REL

B61
CARNEY D.E.,GOVERNMENT AND ECONOMY IN BRITISH WEST
AFRICA. GAMBIA GHANA NIGERIA SIER/LEONE DOMIN ADMIN
GOV/REL SOVEREIGN WEALTH LAISSEZ...BIBLIOG 20
CMN/WLTH. PAGE 19 B0384

METH/COMP
COLONIAL
ECO/TAC
ECO/UNDEV

B61
DRURY J.W.,THE GOVERNMENT OF KANSAS. USA+45 AGRI
INDUS CHIEF LEGIS WORKER PLAN BUDGET GIVE CT/SYS
GOV/REL...T 20 KANSAS GOVERNOR CITY/MGT. PAGE 31
B0621

PROVS
CONSTN
ADMIN
LOC/G

B61
GARCIA E.,LA ADMINISTRACION ESPANOLA. SPAIN GOV/REL
...CONCPT METH/COMP 20. PAGE 39 B0780

ADMIN
NAT/G
LOC/G
DECISION

B61
HICKS U.K.,DEVELOPMENT FROM BELOW. UK INDUS ADMIN
COLONIAL ROUTINE GOV/REL...POLICY METH/CNCPT CHARTS
19/20 CMN/WLTH. PAGE 50 B1006

ECO/UNDEV
LOC/G
GOV/COMP
METH/COMP

B61
INTL UNION LOCAL AUTHORITIES,LOCAL GOVERNMENT IN
THE USA. USA+45 PUB/INST DELIB/GP CONFER AUTOMAT
GP/REL POPULISM...ANTHOL 20 CITY/MGT. PAGE 54 B1101

LOC/G
MUNIC
ADMIN
GOV/REL

B61
MACMAHON A.W.,DELEGATION AND AUTONOMY. INDIA STRUCT
LEGIS BARGAIN BUDGET ECO/TAC LEGIT EXEC REPRESENT
GOV/REL CENTRAL DEMAND EFFICIENCY PRODUC. PAGE 68
B1373

ADMIN
PLAN
FEDERAL

B61
NARASIMHAN V.K.,THE PRESS, THE PUBLIC AND THE
ADMINISTRATION (PAMPHLET). INDIA COM/IND CONTROL
REPRESENT GOV/REL EFFICIENCY...ANTHOL 20. PAGE 77
B1554

NAT/G
ADMIN
PRESS
NEW/LIB

B61
ROSE D.L.,THE VIETNAMESE CIVIL SERVICE. VIETNAM
CONSULT DELIB/GP GIVE PAY EDU/PROP COLONIAL GOV/REL
UTIL...CHARTS 20. PAGE 90 B1819

ADMIN
EFFICIENCY
STAT
NAT/G

L61
GERWIG R.,"PUBLIC AUTHORITIES IN THE UNITED
STATES." LAW CONSTN PROVS TAX ADMIN FEDERAL.
PAGE 39 B0793

LOC/G
MUNIC
GOV/REL
PWR

L61
KRAMER R.,"EXECUTIVE PRIVILEGE - A STUDY OF THE
PERIOD 1953-1960." NAT/G CHIEF EX/STRUC LEGIS PWR.
PAGE 61 B1233

REPRESENT
LEAD
EXEC
GOV/REL

S61
ROBINSON J.A.,"PROCESS SATISFACTION AND POLICY
APPROVAL IN STATE DEPARTMENT - CONGRESSIONAL
RELATIONS." ELITES CHIEF LEGIS CONFER DEBATE ADMIN
FEEDBACK ROLE...CHARTS 20 CONGRESS PRESIDENT
DEPT/STATE. PAGE 89 B1802

GOV/REL
EX/STRUC
POL/PAR
DECISION

B62
CARPER E.T.,ILLINOIS GOES TO CONGRESS FOR ARMY
LAND. USA+45 LAW EXTR/IND PROVS REGION CIVMIL/REL
GOV/REL FEDERAL ATTIT 20 ILLINOIS SENATE CONGRESS
DIRKSEN/E DOUGLAS/P. PAGE 19 B0385

ADMIN
LOBBY
GEOG
LEGIS

B62
ESCUELA SUPERIOR DE ADMIN PUBL,INFORME DEL
SEMINARIO SOBRE SERVICIO CIVIL O CARRERA
ADMINISTRATIVA. L/A+17C ELITES STRATA CONFER
CONTROL GOV/REL INGP/REL SUPEGO 20 CENTRAL/AM
CIVIL/SERV. PAGE 33 B0681

ADMIN
NAT/G
PROB/SOLV
ATTIT

B62
FORD A.G.,THE GOLD STANDARD 1880-1914: BRITAIN AND
ARGENTINA. UK ECO/UNDEV INT/TRADE ADMIN GOV/REL
DEMAND EFFICIENCY...STAT CHARTS 19/20 ARGEN
GOLD/STAND. PAGE 36 B0737

FINAN
ECO/TAC
BUDGET
BAL/PAY

B62
GOVERNORS CONF STATE PLANNING,STATE PLANNING: A
POLICY STATEMENT (PAMPHLET). USA+45 LOC/G NAT/G
DELIB/GP LEGIS EXEC 20 GOVERNOR. PAGE 42 B0847

GOV/REL
PLAN
ADMIN
PROVS

B62
HSUEH S.-.S.,GOVERNMENT AND ADMINISTRATION OF HONG
KONG. CHIEF DELIB/GP LEGIS CT/SYS REPRESENT GOV/REL
20 HONG/KONG CITY/MGT CIVIL/SERV GOVERNOR. PAGE 52
B1055

ADMIN
LOC/G
COLONIAL
EX/STRUC

B62
INSTITUTE JUDICIAL ADMIN,JUDGES: THEIR TEMPORARY
APPOINTMENT, ASSIGNMENT AND TRANSFER: SURVEY OF FED
AND STATE CONSTN'S STATUTES, ROLES OF CT. USA+45
CONSTN PROVS CT/SYS GOV/REL PWR JURID. PAGE 54
B1090

NAT/G
LOC/G
JUDGE
ADMIN

B62
INSTITUTE OF PUBLIC ADMIN,A SHORT HISTORY OF THE
PUBLIC SERVICE IN IRELAND. IRELAND UK DIST/IND
INGP/REL FEDERAL 13/20 CIVIL/SERV. PAGE 54 B1091

ADMIN
WORKER
GOV/REL
NAT/G

B62
KARNJAHAPRAKORN C.,MUNICIPAL GOVERNMENT IN THAILAND
AS AN INSTITUTION AND PROCESS OF SELF-GOVERNMENT.
THAILAND CULTURE FINAN EX/STRUC LEGIS PLAN CONTROL
GOV/REL EFFICIENCY ATTIT...POLICY 20. PAGE 58 B1176

LOC/G
MUNIC
ORD/FREE
ADMIN

B62
MUNICIPAL MANPOWER COMMISSION,GOVERNMENTAL MANPOWER
FOR TOMORROW'S CITIES: A REPORT. USA+45 DELIB/GP
EX/STRUC PROB/SOLV TEC/DEV EDU/PROP ADMIN LEAD
HABITAT. PAGE 76 B1539

LOC/G
MUNIC
LABOR
GOV/REL

B62
PRAKASH O.M.,THE THEORY AND WORKING OF STATE
CORPORATIONS: WITH SPECIAL REFERENCE TO INDIA.
INDIA UK USA+45 TOP/EX PRICE ADMIN EFFICIENCY...MGT
METH/COMP 20 TVA. PAGE 84 B1698

LG/CO
ECO/UNDEV
GOV/REL
SOCISM

B62
US ADMINISTRATIVE CONFERENCE,FINAL REPORT OF THE
ADMINISTRATIVE CONFERENCE OF THE US; SUGGESTIONS

ADMIN
NAT/G

FOR IMPROVING PROCESSES - ADMIN. AGENCIES. USA+45   DELIB/GP
INGP/REL EFFICIENCY RATIONAL ORD/FREE...GP/COMP   GOV/REL
METH/COMP 20. PAGE 107 B2170
                                                              B62
US ADVISORY COMN INTERGOV REL,STATE CONSTITUTIONAL   LOC/G
AND STATUTORY RESTRICTIONS UPON THE STRUCTURAL,   CONSTN
FUNCTIONAL, AND PERSONAL POWERS OF LOCAL GOV'T.   PROVS
EX/STRUC ACT/RES DOMIN GOV/REL PWR...POLICY   LAW
DECISION 17/20. PAGE 108 B2172
                                                              B62
US SENATE COMM ON JUDICIARY,STATE DEPARTMENT   CONTROL
SECURITY. USA+45 CHIEF TEC/DEV DOMIN ADMIN EXEC   WORKER
ATTIT ORD/FREE...POLICY CONGRESS DEPT/STATE   NAT/G
PRESIDENT KENNEDY/JF KENNEDY/JF SENATE 20. PAGE 110   GOV/REL
B2228
                                                              L62
NEIBURG H.L.,"THE EISENHOWER AEC AND CONGRESS: A   CHIEF
STUDY IN EXECUTIVE-LEGISLATIVE RELATIONS." USA+45   LEGIS
NAT/G POL/PAR DELIB/GP EX/STRUC TOP/EX ADMIN EXEC   GOV/REL
LEAD ROUTINE PWR...POLICY COLD/WAR CONGRESS   NUC/PWR
PRESIDENT AEC. PAGE 77 B1567
                                                              S62
DONNELLY D.,"THE POLITICS AND ADMINISTRATION OF   GOV/REL
PLANNING." UK ROUTINE FEDERAL 20. PAGE 30 B0607   EFFICIENCY
                                                      ADMIN
                                                      EX/STRUC
                                                              C62
TRUMAN D.B.,"THE GOVERNMENTAL PROCESS: POLITICAL   LOBBY
INTERESTS AND PUBLIC OPINION." POL/PAR ADJUD ADMIN   EDU/PROP
EXEC LEAD ROUTINE CHOOSE REPRESENT GOV/REL   GP/REL
RIGID/FLEX...POLICY BIBLIOG/A 20. PAGE 105 B2131   LEGIS
                                                              C62
VAN DER SPRENKEL S.,"LEGAL INSTITUTIONS IN MANCHU   LAW
CHINA." ASIA STRUCT CT/SYS ROUTINE GOV/REL GP/REL   JURID
...CONCPT BIBLIOG 17/20. PAGE 111 B2250   ADMIN
                                                      ADJUD
                                                              N62
UNIVERSITY PITT INST LOC GOVT,THE COUNCIL-MANAGER   LOC/G
FORM OF GOVERNMENT IN PENNSYLVANIA (PAMPHLET).   TOP/EX
PROVS EX/STRUC REPRESENT GOV/REL EFFICIENCY   MUNIC
...CHARTS SIMUL 20 PENNSYLVAN CITY/MGT. PAGE 107   PWR
B2169
                                                              N62
US ADVISORY COMN INTERGOV REL,ALTERNATIVE   MUNIC
APPROACHES TO GOVERNMENTAL REORGANIZATION IN   REGION
METROPOLITAN AREAS (PAMPHLET). EX/STRUC LEGIS EXEC   PLAN
LEAD PWR...DECISION GEN/METH. PAGE 107 B2171   GOV/REL
                                                              B63
ADRIAN C.R.,GOVERNING OVER FIFTY STATES AND THEIR   PROVS
COMMUNITIES. USA+45 CONSTN FINAN MUNIC NAT/G   LOC/G
POL/PAR EX/STRUC LEGIS ADMIN CONTROL CT/SYS   GOV/REL
...CHARTS 20. PAGE 3 B0061   GOV/COMP
                                                              B63
BOCK E.A.,STATE AND LOCAL GOVERNMENT: A CASE BOOK.   PROVS
USA+45 FINAN CHIEF PROB/SOLV TAX ATTIT...POLICY 20   LOC/G
CASEBOOK. PAGE 13 B0263   ADMIN
                                                      GOV/REL
                                                              B63
DALAND R.T.,PERSPECTIVES OF BRAZILIAN PUBLIC   ADMIN
ADMINISTRATION (VOL. I). BRAZIL LAW ECO/UNDEV   NAT/G
SCHOOL CHIEF TEC/DEV CONFER CONTROL GP/REL ATTIT   PLAN
ROLE PWR...ANTHOL 20. PAGE 26 B0525   GOV/REL
                                                              B63
DE GUZMAN R.P.,PATTERNS IN DECISION-MAKING: CASE   ADMIN
STUDIES IN PHILIPPINE PUBLIC ADMINISTRATION.   DECISION
PHILIPPINE LAW CHIEF PROB/SOLV INGP/REL DRIVE   POLICY
PERCEPT ROLE...ANTHOL T 20. PAGE 27 B0557   GOV/REL
                                                              B63
DEAN A.L.,FEDERAL AGENCY APPROACHES TO FIELD   ADMIN
MANAGEMENT (PAMPHLET). R+D DELIB/GP EX/STRUC   MGT
PROB/SOLV GOV/REL...CLASSIF BIBLIOG 20 FAA NASA   NAT/G
DEPT/HEW POSTAL/SYS IRS. PAGE 28 B0563   OP/RES
                                                              B63
GANGULY D.S.,PUBLIC CORPORATIONS IN A NATIONAL   ECO/UNDEV
ECONOMY. INDIA WOR+45 FINAN INDUS TOP/EX PRICE   LG/CO
EFFICIENCY...MGT STAT CHARTS BIBLIOG 20. PAGE 38   SOCISM
B0779   GOV/REL
                                                              B63
GARNER U.F.,ADMINISTRATIVE LAW. UK LAW LOC/G NAT/G   ADMIN
EX/STRUC LEGIS JUDGE BAL/PWR BUDGET ADJUD CONTROL   JURID
CT/SYS...BIBLIOG 20. PAGE 39 B0783   PWR
                                                      GOV/REL
                                                              B63
GREEN H.P.,GOVERNMENT OF THE ATOM. USA+45 LEGIS   GOV/REL
PROB/SOLV ADMIN CONTROL PWR...POLICY DECISION 20   EX/STRUC
PRESIDENT CONGRESS. PAGE 43 B0864   NUC/PWR
                                                      DELIB/GP
                                                              B63
HATHAWAY D.A.,GOVERNMENT AND AGRICULTURE: PUBLIC   AGRI
POLICY IN A DEMOCRATIC SOCIETY. USA+45 LEGIS ADMIN   GOV/REL
EXEC LOBBY REPRESENT PWR 20. PAGE 48 B0967   PROB/SOLV
                                                      EX/STRUC
                                                              B63
HERMAN H.,NEW YORK STATE AND THE METROPOLITAN   GOV/REL
PROBLEM. USA+45 ECO/DEV PUB/INST SCHOOL LEGIS PLAN   PROVS
TAX EXEC PARL/PROC PARTIC...HEAL 20 NEW/YORK.   LOC/G

PAGE 49 B0992   POLICY
                                                              B63
HIGA M.,POLITICS AND PARTIES IN POSTWAR OKINAWA.   GOV/REL
USA+45 VOL/ASSN LEGIS CONTROL LOBBY CHOOSE NAT/LISM   POL/PAR
PWR SOVEREIGN MARXISM SOCISM 20 OKINAWA CHINJAP.   ADMIN
PAGE 50 B1008   FORCES
                                                              B63
MACNEIL N.,FORGE OF DEMOCRACY: THE HOUSE OF   LEGIS
REPRESENTATIVES. POL/PAR EX/STRUC TOP/EX DEBATE   DELIB/GP
LEAD PARL/PROC CHOOSE GOV/REL PWR...OBS HOUSE/REP.
PAGE 68 B1374
                                                              B63
MAHESHWARI B.,STUDIES IN PANCHAYATI RAJ. INDIA   FEDERAL
POL/PAR EX/STRUC BUDGET EXEC REPRESENT CENTRAL   LOC/G
EFFICIENCY...DECISION 20. PAGE 68 B1378   GOV/REL
                                                      LEAD
                                                              B63
PALOTAI O.C.,PUBLICATIONS OF THE INSTITUTE OF   BIBLIOG/A
GOVERNMENT, 1930-1962. LAW PROVS SCHOOL WORKER   ADMIN
ACT/RES OP/RES CT/SYS GOV/REL...CRIMLGY SOC/WK.   LOC/G
PAGE 81 B1629   FINAN
                                                              B63
PLISCHKE E.,GOVERNMENT AND POLITICS OF CONTEMPORARY   MUNIC
BERLIN. GERMANY LAW CONSTN POL/PAR LEGIS WAR CHOOSE   LOC/G
REPRESENT GOV/REL...CHARTS BIBLIOG 20 BERLIN.   POLICY
PAGE 83 B1683   ADMIN
                                                              B63
ROBINSON K.,ESSAYS IN IMPERIAL GOVERNMENT. CAMEROON   COLONIAL
NIGERIA UK CONSTN LOC/G LEGIS ADMIN GOV/REL PWR   AFR
...POLICY ANTHOL BIBLIOG 17/20 PURHAM/M. PAGE 89   DOMIN
B1803
                                                              B63
SCHRADER R.,SCIENCE AND POLICY. WOR+45 ECO/DEV   TEC/DEV
ECO/UNDEV R+D FORCES PLAN DIPLOM GOV/REL TECHRACY   NAT/G
BIBLIOG. PAGE 94 B1900   POLICY
                                                      ADMIN
                                                              B63
SHANKS M.,THE LESSONS OF PUBLIC ENTERPRISE. UK   SOCISM
LEGIS WORKER ECO/TAC ADMIN PARL/PROC GOV/REL ATTIT   OWN
...POLICY MGT METH/COMP NAT/COMP ANTHOL 20   NAT/G
PARLIAMENT. PAGE 96 B1931   INDUS
                                                              B63
SMITH R.M.,STATE GOVERNMENT IN TRANSITION. USA+45   PROVS
POL/PAR LEGIS PARL/PROC GOV/REL 20 PENNSYLVAN   POLICY
GOVERNOR. PAGE 98 B1984   EX/STRUC
                                                      PLAN
                                                              B63
SWEENEY S.B.,ACHIEVING EXCELLENCE IN PUBLIC   ADMIN
SERVICE. FUT USA+45 NAT/G ACT/RES GOV/REL...POLICY   WORKER
ANTHOL 20 CIVIL/SERV. PAGE 102 B2060   TASK
                                                      PLAN
                                                              B63
US CONGRESS: SENATE,HEARINGS OF THE COMMITTEE ON   LEGIS
THE JUDICIARY. USA+45 CONSTN NAT/G ADMIN GOV/REL 20   LAW
CONGRESS. PAGE 108 B2179   ORD/FREE
                                                      DELIB/GP
                                                              B63
US SENATE COMM ON JUDICIARY,ADMINISTRATIVE   PARL/PROC
CONFERENCE OF THE UNITED STATES. USA+45 CONSTN   JURID
NAT/G PROB/SOLV CONFER GOV/REL...INT 20 SENATE.   ADMIN
PAGE 110 B2230   LEGIS
                                                              S63
MEDALIA N.Z.,"POSITION AND PROSPECTS OF   NAT/G
SOCIOLOGISTS IN FEDERAL EMPLOYMENT." USA+45 CONSULT   WORKER
PAY SENIOR ADMIN GOV/REL...TREND CHARTS 20   SOC
CIVIL/SERV. PAGE 72 B1460   SKILL
                                                              S63
PIPER D.C.,"THE ROLE OF INTER-GOVERNMENTAL   GOV/REL
MACHINERY IN CANADIANAMERICAN RELATIONS." CANADA   ADMIN
USA+45 PROB/SOLV REPRESENT 20. PAGE 83 B1676   EX/STRUC
                                                      CONFER
                                                              B64
ADAMS V.,THE PEACE CORPS IN ACTION. USA+45 VOL/ASSN   DIPLOM
EX/STRUC GOV/REL PERCEPT ORD/FREE...OBS 20   FOR/AID
KENNEDY/JF PEACE/CORP. PAGE 3 B0058   PERSON
                                                      DRIVE
                                                              B64
BENNETT H.A.,THE COMMISSION AND THE COMMON LAW: A   ADJUD
STUDY IN ADMINISTRATIVE ADJUDICATION. LAW ADMIN   DELIB/GP
CT/SYS LOBBY SANCTION GOV/REL 20 COMMON/LAW.   DIST/IND
PAGE 10 B0212   POLICY
                                                              B64
BLACKSTOCK P.W.,THE STRATEGY OF SUBVERSION. USA+45   ORD/FREE
FORCES EDU/PROP ADMIN COERCE GOV/REL...DECISION MGT   DIPLOM
20 DEPT/DEFEN CIA DEPT/STATE. PAGE 12 B0247   CONTROL
                                                              B64
BROWN C.V.,GOVERNMENT AND BANKING IN WESTERN   ADMIN
NIGERIA. AFR NIGERIA GOV/REL GP/REL...POLICY 20.   ECO/UNDEV
PAGE 16 B0321   FINAN
                                                      NAT/G
                                                              B64
CATER D.,POWER IN WASHINGTON: A CRITICAL LOOK AT   REPRESENT
TODAY'S STRUGGLE TO GOVERN IN THE NATION'S CAPITAL.   GOV/REL
USA+45 NAT/G LEGIS ADMIN EXEC LOBBY PLURISM 20.   INGP/REL
PAGE 19 B0392   EX/STRUC

B64

DAS M.N.,INDIA UNDER MORLEY AND MINTO. INDIA UK
ECO/UNDEV MUNIC PROVS EX/STRUC LEGIS DIPLOM CONTROL
REV 20 MORLEY/J. PAGE 26 B0531
GOV/REL
COLONIAL
POLICY
ADMIN

B64

GOODNOW H.F.,THE CIVIL SERVICE OF PAKISTAN:
BUREAUCRACY IN A NEW NATION. INDIA PAKISTAN S/ASIA
ECO/UNDEV PROVS CHIEF PARTIC CHOOSE EFFICIENCY PWR
...BIBLIOG 20. PAGE 41 B0824
ADMIN
GOV/REL
LAW
NAT/G

B64

HAMILTON B.L.S.,PROBLEMS OF ADMINISTRATION IN AN
EMERGENT NATION: CASE STUDY OF JAMAICA. JAMAICA UK
WOR+45 MUNIC COLONIAL HABITAT...CHARTS BIBLIOG 20
CIVIL/SERV. PAGE 46 B0932
ADMIN
ECO/UNDEV
GOV/REL
NAT/G

B64

HANNA W.J.,INDEPENDENT BLACK AFRICA: THE POLITICS
OF FREEDOM. ELITES INDUS KIN CHIEF COLONIAL CHOOSE
GOV/REL RACE/REL NAT/LISM ATTIT PERSON 20 NEGRO.
PAGE 46 B0938
AFR
ECO/UNDEV
ADMIN
PROB/SOLV

B64

HARMON R.B.,BIBLIOGRAPHY OF BIBLIOGRAPHIES IN
POLITICAL SCIENCE (MIMEOGRAPHED PAPER: LIMITED
EDITION). WOR+45 WOR-45 INT/ORG POL/PAR GOV/REL
ALL/IDEOS...INT/LAW JURID MGT 19/20. PAGE 47 B0949
BIBLIOG
NAT/G
DIPLOM
LOC/G

B64

INDIAN COMM PREVENTION CORRUPT,REPORT, 1964. INDIA
NAT/G GOV/REL ATTIT ORD/FREE...CRIMLGY METH 20.
PAGE 53 B1079
CRIME
ADMIN
LEGIS
LOC/G

B64

JACKSON H.M.,THE SECRETARY OF STATE AND THE
AMBASSADOR* JACKSON SUBCOMMITTEE PAPERS ON THE
CONDUCT OF AMERICAN FOREIGN POLICY. USA+45 NAT/G
FORCES ACT/RES OP/RES EDU/PROP CENTRAL EFFICIENCY
ORD/FREE...OBS RECORD ANTHOL CONGRESS PRESIDENT.
PAGE 55 B1107
GOV/REL
DIPLOM
ADMIN
EX/STRUC

B64

KARLEN D.,THE CITIZEN IN COURT. USA+45 LAW ADMIN
ROUTINE CRIME GP/REL...JURID 20. PAGE 58 B1175
CT/SYS
ADJUD
GOV/REL
JUDGE

B64

KNOX V.H.,PUBLIC FINANCE: INFORMATION SOURCES.
USA+45 DIPLOM ADMIN GOV/REL COST...POLICY 20.
PAGE 60 B1221
BIBLIOG/A
FINAN
TAX
BUDGET

B64

PEABODY R.L.,ORGANIZATIONAL AUTHORITY. SCHOOL
WORKER PLAN SENIOR GOV/REL UTIL DRIVE PWR...PSY
CHARTS BIBLIOG 20. PAGE 82 B1648
ADMIN
EFFICIENCY
TASK
GP/REL

B64

PIERCE T.M.,FEDERAL, STATE, AND LOCAL GOVERNMENT IN
EDUCATION. FINAN LOC/G PROVS LEGIS PLAN EDU/PROP
ADMIN CONTROL CENTRAL COST KNOWL 20. PAGE 83 B1673
NAT/G
POLICY
SCHOOL
GOV/REL

B64

RAPHAEL M.,PENSIONS AND PUBLIC SERVANTS. UK PLAN
EDU/PROP PARTIC GOV/REL HEALTH...POLICY CHARTS
17/20 CIVIL/SERV. PAGE 86 B1737
ADMIN
SENIOR
PAY
AGE/O

B64

RIES J.C.,THE MANAGEMENT OF DEFENSE: ORGANIZATION
AND CONTROL OF THE US ARMED SERVICES. PROF/ORG
DELIB/GP EX/STRUC LEGIS GOV/REL PERS/REL CENTRAL
RATIONAL PWR...POLICY TREND GOV/COMP BIBLIOG.
PAGE 88 B1782
FORCES
ACT/RES
DECISION
CONTROL

B64

SARROS P.P.,CONGRESS AND THE NEW DIPLOMACY: THE
FORMULATION OF MUTUAL SECURITY POLICY: 1953-60
(THESIS). USA+45 CHIEF EX/STRUC REGION ROUTINE
CHOOSE GOV/REL PEACE ROLE...POLICY 20 PRESIDENT
CONGRESS. PAGE 92 B1869
DIPLOM
POL/PAR
NAT/G

B64

SCHERMER G.,MEETING SOCIAL NEEDS IN THE PENJERDEL
REGION. SOCIETY FINAN ACT/RES EDU/PROP ADMIN
GOV/REL...SOC/WK 45 20 PENNSYLVAN DELAWARE
NEW/JERSEY. PAGE 93 B1887
PLAN
REGION
HEALTH
WEALTH

B64

US SENATE COMM ON JUDICIARY,ADMINISTRATIVE
PROCEDURE ACT. USA+45 CONSTN NAT/G PROB/SOLV CONFER
GOV/REL PWR...INT 20 SENATE. PAGE 110 B2231
PARL/PROC
LEGIS
JURID
ADMIN

S64

HORECKY P.L.,"LIBRARY OF CONGRESS PUBLICATIONS IN
AID OF USSR AND EAST EUROPEAN RESEARCH." BULGARIA
CZECHOSLVK POLAND USSR YUGOSLAVIA NAT/G POL/PAR
DIPLOM ADMIN GOV/REL...CLASSIF 20. PAGE 51 B1042
BIBLIOG/A
COM
MARXISM

S64

ROGOW A.A.,"CONGRESSIONAL GOVERNMENT: LEGISLATIVE
POWER V. DOMESTIC PROCESSES." USA+45 CHIEF DELIB/GP
ADMIN GOV/REL CONGRESS. PAGE 90 B1815
PWR
DIPLOM
LEGIS
POLICY

N64

US SENATE COMM GOVT OPERATIONS,METROPOLITAN
BIBLIOG/A

AMERICA: A SELECTED BIBLIOGRAPHY (PAMPHLET). USA+45
DIST/IND FINAN LOC/G EDU/PROP ADMIN HEALTH 20.
PAGE 110 B2214
MUNIC
GOV/REL
DECISION

B65

CHANDA A.,FEDERALISM IN INDIA. INDIA UK ELITES
FINAN NAT/G POL/PAR EX/STRUC LEGIS DIPLOM TAX
GOV/REL POPULISM...POLICY 20. PAGE 20 B0402
CONSTN
CENTRAL
FEDERAL

B65

CUTLIP S.M.,A PUBLIC RELATIONS BIBLIOGRAPHY. INDUS
LABOR NAT/G PROF/ORG SCHOOL DIPLOM PRESS TV GOV/REL
GP/REL...PSY SOC/WK 20. PAGE 25 B0515
BIBLIOG/A
MGT
COM/IND
ADMIN

B65

DE GRAZIA A.,REPUBLIC IN CRISIS: CONGRESS AGAINST
THE EXECUTIVE FORCE. USA+45 USA-45 SOCIETY POL/PAR
CHIEF DOMIN ROLE ORD/FREE PWR...CONCPT MYTH BIBLIOG
20 CONGRESS. PAGE 27 B0556
LEGIS
EXEC
GOV/REL
CONTROL

B65

DUGGAR G.S.,RENEWAL OF TOWN AND VILLAGE I: A WORLD-
WIDE SURVEY OF LOCAL GOVERNMENT EXPERIENCE. WOR+45
CONSTRUC INDUS CREATE BUDGET REGION GOV/REL...QU
NAT/COMP 20 URBAN/RNWL. PAGE 31 B0628
MUNIC
NEIGH
PLAN
ADMIN

B65

ELDER R.E.,OVERSEAS REPRESENTATION AND SERVICES FOR
FEDERAL DOMESTIC AGENCIES. USA+45 NAT/G ACT/RES
FOR/AID EDU/PROP SENIOR ROUTINE TASK ADJUST...MGT
ORG/CHARTS. PAGE 33 B0663
OP/RES
DIPLOM
GOV/REL
ADMIN

B65

EVERETT R.O.,URBAN PROBLEMS AND PROSPECTS. USA+45
CREATE TEC/DEV EDU/PROP ADJUD ADMIN GOV/REL ATTIT
...ANTHOL 20 URBAN/RNWL. PAGE 34 B0691
MUNIC
PLAN
PROB/SOLV
NEIGH

B65

FISCHER F.C.,THE GOVERNMENT OF MICHIGAN. USA+45
NAT/G PUB/INST EX/STRUC LEGIS BUDGET GIVE EDU/PROP
CT/SYS CHOOSE GOV/REL...T MICHIGAN. PAGE 36 B0723
PROVS
LOC/G
ADMIN
CONSTN

B65

FRYE R.J.,HOUSING AND URBAN RENEWAL IN ALABAMA.
USA+45 NEIGH LEGIS BUDGET ADJUD ADMIN PARTIC...MGT
20 ALABAMA URBAN/RNWL. PAGE 38 B0762
MUNIC
PROB/SOLV
PLAN
GOV/REL

B65

GREER S.,URBAN RENEWAL AND AMERICAN CITIES: THE
DILEMMA OF DEMOCRATIC INTERVENTION. USA+45 R+D
LOC/G VOL/ASSN ACT/RES BUDGET ADMIN GOV/REL...SOC
INT SAMP 20 BOSTON CHICAGO MIAMI URBAN/RNWL.
PAGE 43 B0871
MUNIC
PROB/SOLV
PLAN
NAT/G

B65

HARR J.E.,THE DEVELOPMENT OF CAREERS IN THE FOREIGN
SERVICE. CREATE SENIOR EXEC FEEDBACK GOV/REL
EFFICIENCY ATTIT RESPECT ORG/CHARTS. PAGE 47 B0953
OP/RES
MGT
ADMIN
DIPLOM

B65

INTERNATIONAL CITY MGRS ASSN,COUNCIL-MANAGER
GOVERNMENT, 1940-64: AN ANNOTATED BIBLIOGRAPHY.
USA+45 ADMIN GOV/REL ROLE...MGT 20. PAGE 54 B1097
BIBLIOG/A
MUNIC
CONSULT
PLAN

B65

JONES A.G.,THE EVOLUTION OF PERSONNEL SYSTEMS FOR
US FOREIGN AFFAIRS* A HISTORY OF REFORM EFFORTS.
USA+45 USA-45 ACADEM OP/RES GOV/REL...MGT CONGRESS.
PAGE 57 B1149
DIPLOM
ADMIN
ACT/RES
EFFICIENCY

B65

KOENIG C.W.,OFFICIAL MAKERS OF PUBLIC POLICY:
CONGRESS AND THE PRESIDENT. USA+45 USA-45 NAT/G
EX/STRUC PROB/SOLV PWR. PAGE 60 B1222
CHIEF
LEGIS
GOV/REL
PLURISM

B65

KOENIG L.W.,OFFICIAL MAKERS OF PUBLIC POLICY:
CONGRESS AND THE PRESIDENT. USA+45 USA-45 EX/STRUC
ADMIN CONTROL GOV/REL PWR 18/20 CONGRESS PRESIDENT.
PAGE 61 B1225
POLICY
LEGIS
CHIEF
NAT/G

B65

MOORE C.H.,TUNISIA SINCE INDEPENDENCE. ELITES LOC/G
POL/PAR ADMIN COLONIAL CONTROL EXEC GOV/REL
TOTALISM MARXISM...INT 20 TUNIS. PAGE 75 B1513
NAT/G
EX/STRUC
SOCISM

B65

MUSHKIN S.J.,STATE PROGRAMMING. USA+45 PLAN BUDGET
TAX ADMIN REGION GOV/REL...BIBLIOG 20. PAGE 77
B1549
PROVS
POLICY
CREATE
ECO/DEV

B65

ROURKE F.E.,BUREAUCRATIC POWER IN NATIONAL
POLITICS. ADMIN CONTROL EXEC GOV/REL INGP/REL 20.
PAGE 91 B1838
EX/STRUC
EFFICIENCY
REPRESENT
PWR

B65

SCHAPIRO L.,THE GOVERNMENT AND POLITICS OF THE
SOVIET UNION. USSR WOR+45 WOR-45 ADMIN PARTIC REV
CHOOSE REPRESENT PWR...POLICY IDEA/COMP 20. PAGE 93
B1880
MARXISM
GOV/REL
NAT/G
LOC/G

B65

SMITH C.,THE OMBUDSMAN: A BIBLIOGRAPHY (PAMPHLET).
DENMARK SWEDEN USA+45 LAW LEGIS JUDGE GOV/REL
GP/REL...JURID 20. PAGE 98 B1980
BIBLIOG
ADMIN
CT/SYS

SNIDER C.F.,AMERICAN STATE AND LOCAL GOVERNMENT.
USA+45 FINAN CHIEF EX/STRUC TAX ADMIN CONTROL SUFF
INGP/REL PWR 20. PAGE 98 B1989

ADJUD
GOV/REL
MUNIC
PROVS
LOC/G

B65

STANLEY D.T.,CHANGING ADMINISTRATIONS. USA+45
POL/PAR DELIB/GP TOP/EX BUDGET GOV/REL GP/REL
PERS/REL PWR...MAJORIT DECISION MGT 20 PRESIDENT
SUCCESSION DEPT/STATE DEPT/DEFEN DEPT/HEW. PAGE 100
B2021

NAT/G
CHIEF
ADMIN
EX/STRUC

B65

US SENATE COMM GOVT OPERATIONS,ORGANIZATION OF
FEDERAL EXECUTIVE DEPARTMENTS AND AGENCIES: REPORT
OF MARCH 23, 1965. USA+45 FORCES LEGIS DIPLOM
ROUTINE CIVMIL/REL EFFICIENCY FEDERAL...MGT STAT.
PAGE 110 B2217

ADMIN
EX/STRUC
GOV/REL
ORG/CHARTS

B65

US SENATE COMM ON JUDICIARY,HEARINGS BEFORE
SUBCOMMITTEE ON ADMINISTRATIVE PRACTICE AND
PROCEDURE ABOUT ADMINISTRATIVE PROCEDURE ACT 1965.
USA+45 LEGIS EDU/PROP ADJUD GOV/REL INGP/REL
EFFICIENCY...POLICY INT 20 CONGRESS. PAGE 110 B2232

ROUTINE
DELIB/GP
ADMIN
NAT/G

B65

WARD R.,BACKGROUND MATERIAL ON ECONOMIC IMPACT OF
FEDERAL PROCUREMENT - 1965: FOR JOINT ECONOMIC
COMMITTEE US CONGRESS. FINAN ROUTINE WEAPON
CIVMIL/REL EFFICIENCY...STAT CHARTS 20 CONGRESS.
PAGE 113 B2288

ECO/DEV
NAT/G
OWN
GOV/REL

B65

WILDER B.E.,BIBLIOGRAPHY OF THE OFFICIAL
PUBLICATIONS OF KANSAS, 1854-1958. USA+45 USA-45
ECO/DEV POL/PAR EX/STRUC LEGIS ADJUD ATTIT 19/20.
PAGE 116 B2349

BIBLIOG
PROVS
GOV/REL
ADMIN

S65

"FURTHER READING." INDIA ADMIN COLONIAL WAR GOV/REL
ATTIT 20. PAGE 2 B0044

BIBLIOG
DIPLOM
NAT/G
POLICY

S65

AMLUND C.A.,"EXECUTIVE-LEGISLATIVE IMBALANCE:
TRUMAN TO KENNEDY." USA+45 NAT/G GOV/REL PWR.
PAGE 4 B0090

LEGIS
EXEC
DECISION

S65

ANDERSON T.J.,"PRESSURE GROUPS AND
INTERGOVERNMENTAL RELATIONS." USA+45 NAT/G ROLE 20.
PAGE 5 B0097

ADMIN
EX/STRUC
LOBBY
GOV/REL

S65

BALDWIN H.,"SLOW-DOWN IN THE PENTAGON." USA+45
CREATE PLAN GOV/REL CENTRAL COST EFFICIENCY PWR
...MGT MCNAMARA/R. PAGE 9 B0174

RECORD
R+D
WEAPON
ADMIN

N65

MOTE M.E.,SOVIET LOCAL AND REPUBLIC ELECTIONS. COM
USSR NAT/G PLAN PARTIC GOV/REL TOTALISM PWR
...CHARTS 20. PAGE 76 B1534

CHOOSE
ADMIN
CONTROL
LOC/G

N65

NJ DIVISION STATE-REGION PLAN,UTILIZATION OF NEW
JERSEY'S DELAWARE RIVER WATERFRONT (PAMPHLET). FUT
ADMIN REGION LEISURE GOV/REL DEMAND WEALTH...CHARTS
20 NEW/JERSEY. PAGE 78 B1586

UTIL
PLAN
ECO/TAC
PROVS

B66

BHALERAO C.N.,PUBLIC SERVICE COMMISSIONS OF INDIA:
A STUDY. INDIA SERV/IND EX/STRUC ROUTINE CHOOSE
GOV/REL INGP/REL...KNO/TEST EXHIBIT 20. PAGE 11
B0233

NAT/G
OP/RES
LOC/G
ADMIN

B66

BURNS A.C.,PARLIAMENT AS AN EXPORT. WOR+45 CONSTN
BARGAIN DEBATE ROUTINE GOV/REL EFFICIENCY...ANTHOL
COMMONWLTH PARLIAMENT. PAGE 17 B0353

PARL/PROC
POL/PAR
CT/SYS
CHIEF

B66

CLEGG R.K.,THE ADMINISTRATOR IN PUBLIC WELFARE.
USA+45 STRUCT NAT/G PROVS PROB/SOLV BUDGET ECO/TAC
GP/REL ROLE...SOC/WK 20 PUBLIC/REL. PAGE 21 B0434

ADMIN
GIVE
GOV/REL
OP/RES

B66

CORNWELL E.E. JR.,THE AMERICAN PRESIDENCY: VITAL
CENTER. USA+45 USA-45 POL/PAR LEGIS PROB/SOLV
CONTROL PARTIC GOV/REL 18/20 PRESIDENT. PAGE 23
B0478

CHIEF
EX/STRUC
NAT/G
ADMIN

B66

DAVIDSON R.H.,CONGRESS IN CRISIS: POLITICS AND
CONGRESSIONAL REFORM. USA+45 SOCIETY POL/PAR
CONTROL LEAD ROUTINE GOV/REL ATTIT PWR...POLICY 20
CONGRESS. PAGE 26 B0535

LEGIS
PARL/PROC
PROB/SOLV
NAT/G

B66

DUNCOMBE H.S.,COUNTY GOVERNMENT IN AMERICA. USA+45
FINAN MUNIC ADMIN ROUTINE GOV/REL...GOV/COMP 20.
PAGE 31 B0631

LOC/G
PROVS
CT/SYS
TOP/EX

B66

FINK M.,A SELECTIVE BIBLIOGRAPHY ON STATE

BIBLIOG

CONSTITUTIONAL REVISION (PAMPHLET). USA+45 FINAN
EX/STRUC LEGIS EDU/PROP ADMIN CT/SYS APPORT CHOOSE
GOV/REL 20. PAGE 35 B0720

PROVS
LOC/G
CONSTN

B66

HARMON R.B.,SOURCES AND PROBLEMS OF BIBLIOGRAPHY IN
POLITICAL SCIENCE (PAMPHLET). INT/ORG LOC/G MUNIC
POL/PAR ADMIN GOV/REL ALL/IDEOS...JURID MGT CONCPT
19/20. PAGE 47 B0951

BIBLIOG
DIPLOM
INT/LAW
NAT/G

B66

HIDAYATULLAH M.,DEMOCRACY IN INDIA AND THE JUDICIAL
PROCESS. INDIA EX/STRUC LEGIS LEAD GOV/REL ATTIT
ORD/FREE...MAJORIT CONCPT 20 NEHRU/J. PAGE 50 B1007

NAT/G
CT/SYS
CONSTN
JURID

B66

NYC TEMPORARY COMM CITY FINAN,MUNICIPAL COLLECTIVE
BARGAINING (NO. 8). USA+45 PLAN PROB/SOLV BARGAIN
BUDGET TAX EDU/PROP GOV/REL COST...MGT 20
NEWYORK/C. PAGE 79 B1596

MUNIC
FINAN
ADMIN
LOC/G

B66

RAPHAEL J.S.,GOVERNMENTAL REGULATION OF BUSINESS.
USA+45 LAW CONSTN TAX ADJUD ADMIN EFFICIENCY PWR
20. PAGE 86 B1736

LG/CO
GOV/REL
CONTROL
ECO/DEV

B66

ROSS R.M.,STATE AND LOCAL GOVERNMENT AND
ADMINISTRATION. USA+45 CONSTN POL/PAR EX/STRUC
LEGIS BUDGET EDU/PROP CONTROL CT/SYS CHOOSE GOV/REL
T. PAGE 90 B1827

LOC/G
PROVS
MUNIC
ADMIN

B66

SCHLESSINGER P.J.,ELEMENTS OF CALIFORNIA GOVERNMENT
(2ND ED.). USA+45 LAW ADJUD ADMIN CONTROL CT/SYS
EFFICIENCY...BIBLIOG T CALIFORNIA. PAGE 94 B1891

LOC/G
PROVS
GOV/REL
LEGIS

B66

SCHMIDT F.,PUBLIC RELATIONS IN HEALTH AND WELFARE.
USA+45 ACADEM RECEIVE PRESS FEEDBACK GOV/REL
PERS/REL DEMAND EFFICIENCY ATTIT PERCEPT WEALTH 20
PUBLIC/REL. PAGE 94 B1895

PROF/ORG
EDU/PROP
ADMIN
HEALTH

B66

SCHMIDT K.M.,AMERICAN STATE AND LOCAL GOVERNMENT IN
ACTION. USA+45 CONSTN LOC/G POL/PAR CHIEF LEGIS
PROB/SOLV ADJUD LOBBY GOV/REL...DECISION ANTHOL 20
GOVERNOR MAYOR URBAN/RNWL. PAGE 94 B1896

PROVS
ADMIN
MUNIC
PLAN

B66

SMITH H.E.,READINGS IN ECONOMIC DEVELOPMENT AND
ADMINISTRATION IN TANZANIA. TANZANIA FINAN INDUS
LABOR NAT/G PLAN PROB/SOLV INT/TRADE COLONIAL
REGION...ANTHOL BIBLIOG 20 AFRICA/E. PAGE 98 B1981

TEC/DEV
ADMIN
GOV/REL

B66

UN ECAFE,ADMINISTRATIVE ASPECTS OF FAMILY PLANNING
PROGRAMMES (PAMPHLET). ASIA THAILAND WOR+45
VOL/ASSN PROB/SOLV BUDGET FOR/AID EDU/PROP CONFER
CONTROL GOV/REL TIME 20 UN BIRTH/CON. PAGE 106
B2147

PLAN
CENSUS
FAM
ADMIN

B66

WHITNAH D.R.,SAFER SKYWAYS. DIST/IND DELIB/GP
FORCES TOP/EX WORKER TEC/DEV ROUTINE WAR CIVMIL/REL
COST...TIME/SEQ 20 FAA CAB. PAGE 116 B2342

ADMIN
NAT/G
AIR
GOV/REL

B66

WILSON G.,CASES AND MATERIALS ON CONSTITUTIONAL AND
ADMINISTRATIVE LAW. UK LAW NAT/G EX/STRUC LEGIS
BAL/PWR BUDGET DIPLOM ADJUD CONTROL CT/SYS GOV/REL
ORD/FREE 20 PARLIAMENT ENGLSH/LAW. PAGE 117 B2359

JURID
ADMIN
CONSTN
PWR

S66

BALDWIN D.A.,"CONGRESSIONAL INITIATIVE IN FOREIGN
POLICY." NAT/G BARGAIN DIPLOM FOR/AID RENT GIVE
...DECISION CONGRESS. PAGE 8 B0171

EXEC
TOP/EX
GOV/REL

S66

MATTHEWS D.G.,"PRELUDE-COUP D'ETAT-MILITARY
GOVERNMENT: A BIBLIOGRAPHICAL AND RESEARCH GUIDE TO
NIGERIAN POL AND GOVT, JAN, 1965-66." AFR NIGER LAW
CONSTN POL/PAR LEGIS CIVMIL/REL GOV/REL...STAT 20.
PAGE 71 B1430

BIBLIOG
NAT/G
ADMIN
CHOOSE

C66

JACOB H.,"DIMENSIONS OF STATE POLITICS HEARD A, ED.
STATE LEGIWLATURES IN AMERICAN POLITICS." CULTURE
STRATA POL/PAR BUDGET TAX LOBBY ROUTINE GOV/REL
...TRADIT DECISION GEOG. PAGE 55 B1112

PROVS
LEGIS
ROLE
REPRESENT

C66

TACHERON D.G.,"THE JOB OF THE CONGRESSMAN: AN
INTRODUCTION TO SERVICES IN THE US HOUSE OF
REPRESENTATIVES." DELIB/GP EX/STRUC PRESS SENIOR
CT/SYS LOBBY CHOOSE GOV/REL...BIBLIOG 20 CONGRESS
HOUSE/REP SENATE. PAGE 102 B2068

LEGIS
PARL/PROC
ADMIN
POL/PAR

N66

AMERICAN SOCIETY PUBLIC ADMIN,PUBLIC ADMINISTRATION
AND THE WAR ON POVERTY (PAMPHLET). USA+45 SOCIETY
ECO/DEV FINAN LOC/G LEGIS CREATE EDU/PROP CONFER
GOV/REL GP/REL ROLE 20 POVRTY/WAR. PAGE 4 B0089

WEALTH
NAT/G
PLAN
ADMIN

N66

BACHELDER G.L.,THE LITERATURE OF FEDERALISM: A
SELECTED BIBLIOGRAPHY (REV ED) (A PAMPHLET). USA+45
USA-45 WOR+45 WOR-45 LAW CONSTN PROVS ADMIN CT/SYS
GOV/REL ROLE...CONCPT 19/20. PAGE 8 B0155

BIBLIOG
FEDERAL
NAT/G
LOC/G

N66
PRINCETON U INDUSTRIAL REL SEC.OUTSTANDING BOOKS ON | BIBLIOG/A
INDUSTRIAL RELATIONS, 1965 (PAMPHLET NO. 128). | INDUS
WOR+45 LABOR BARGAIN GOV/REL RACE/REL HEALTH PWR | GP/REL
...MGT 20. PAGE 85 B1709 | POLICY

N66
PRINCETON U INDUSTRIAL REL SEC.RECENT MATERIAL ON | BIBLIOG/A
COLLECTIVE BARGAINING IN GOVERNMENT (PAMPHLET NO. | BARGAIN
130). USA+45 ECO/DEV LABOR WORKER ECO/TAC GOV/REL | NAT/G
...MGT 20. PAGE 85 B1710 | GP/REL

B67
BRZEZINSKI Z.K.,THE SOVIET BLOC: UNITY AND CONFLICT | NAT/G
(2ND ED., REV., ENLARGED). COM POLAND USSR INTELL | DIPLOM
CHIEF EX/STRUC CONTROL EXEC GOV/REL PWR MARXISM
...TREND IDEA/COMP 20 LENIN/VI MARX/KARL STALIN/J.
PAGE 16 B0336

B67
BULPITT J.G.,PARTY POLITICS IN ENGLISH LOCAL | POL/PAR
GOVERNMENT. UK CONSTN ACT/RES TAX CONTROL CHOOSE | LOC/G
REPRESENT GOV/REL KNOWL 20. PAGE 17 B0344 | ELITES
| EX/STRUC

B67
BUREAU GOVERNMENT RES AND SERV.COUNTY GOVERNMENT | BIBLIOG/A
REORGANIZATION - A SELECTED ANNOTATED BIBLIOGRAPHY | APPORT
(PAPER). USA+45 USA-45 LAW CONSTN MUNIC PROVS | LOC/G
EX/STRUC CREATE PLAN PROB/SOLV REPRESENT GOV/REL | ADMIN
20. PAGE 17 B0349

B67
DICKSON P.G.M.,THE FINANCIAL REVOLUTION IN ENGLAND. | ECO/DEV
UK NAT/G TEC/DEV ADMIN GOV/REL...SOC METH/CNCPT | FINAN
CHARTS GP/COMP BIBLIOG 17/18. PAGE 29 B0587 | CAP/ISM
| MGT

B67
FESLER J.W.,THE FIFTY STATES AND THEIR LOCAL | PROVS
GOVERNMENTS. FUT USA+45 POL/PAR LEGIS PROB/SOLV | LOC/G
ADMIN CT/SYS CHOOSE GOV/REL FEDERAL...POLICY CHARTS
20 SUPREME/CT. PAGE 35 B0715

B67
KRISLOV S.,THE NEGRO IN FEDERAL EMPLOYMENT. LAW | WORKER
STRATA LOC/G CREATE PROB/SOLV INSPECT GOV/REL | NAT/G
DISCRIM ROLE...DECISION INT TREND 20 NEGRO WWI | ADMIN
CIVIL/SERV. PAGE 61 B1238 | RACE/REL

B67
PAULSEN F.R.,AMERICAN EDUCATION: CHALLENGES AND | EDU/PROP
IMAGES. FUT USA+45 ADMIN AGE/C AGE/Y SUPEGO HEALTH | SCHOOL
...ANTHOL 20. PAGE 81 B1644 | ORD/FREE
| GOV/REL

B67
ROBINSON D.W.,PROMISING PRACTICES IN CIVIC | EDU/PROP
EDUCATION. FUT USA+45 CONTROL PARTIC GOV/REL...OBS | NAT/G
AUD/VIS 20. PAGE 89 B1797 | ADJUST
| ADMIN

B67
UNIVERSAL REFERENCE SYSTEM.ADMINISTRATIVE | BIBLIOG/A
MANAGEMENT: PUBLIC AND PRIVATE BUREAUCRACY (VOLUME | MGT
IV). WOR+45 WOR-45 ECO/DEV LG/CO LOC/G PUB/INST | ADMIN
VOL/ASSN GOV/REL...COMPUT/IR GEN/METH. PAGE 107 | NAT/G
B2164

B67
UNIVERSAL REFERENCE SYSTEM.PUBLIC POLICY AND THE | BIBLIOG/A
MANAGEMENT OF SCIENCE (VOLUME IX). FUT SPACE WOR+45 | POLICY
LAW NAT/G TEC/DEV CONTROL NUC/PWR GOV/REL | MGT
...COMPUT/IR GEN/METH. PAGE 107 B2165 | PHIL/SCI

B67
US DEPARTMENT HEALTH EDUC WELF.NEW PROGRAMS IN | ADMIN
HEALTH, EDUCATION, WELFARE, HOUSING AND URBAN | HEALTH
DEVELOPMENT FOR PERSONS AND FAMILIES -LOW, MOD' | SCHOOL
INCOME. USA+45 MUNIC NAT/G EDU/PROP GOV/REL | HABITAT
INGP/REL ORD/FREE 20 DEPT/HEW DEPT/HUD. PAGE 108
B2180

B67
US DEPARTMENT OF JUSTICE.ANNUAL REPORT OF THE | ADMIN
OFFICE OF ADMINISTRATIVE PROCEDURE. USA+45 | NAT/G
PROB/SOLV EDU/PROP EXEC INGP/REL EFFICIENCY KNOWL | ROUTINE
...POLICY STAT 20. PAGE 108 B2181 | GOV/REL

L67
"A PROPOS DES INCITATIONS FINANCIERES AUX | LOC/G
GROUPEMENTS DES COMMUNES: ESSAI D'INTERPRETATION." | ECO/TAC
FRANCE NAT/G LEGIS ADMIN GOV/REL CENTRAL 20. PAGE 2 | APPORT
B0046 | ADJUD

L67
"RESTRICTIVE SOVEREIGN IMMUNITY, THE STATE | SOVEREIGN
DEPARTMENT, AND THE COURTS." USA+45 USA-45 EX/STRUC | ORD/FREE
DIPLOM ADJUD CONTROL GOV/REL 19/20 DEPT/STATE | PRIVIL
SUPREME/CT. PAGE 2 B0047 | CT/SYS

L67
BESCOBY I.,"A COLONIAL ADMINISTRATION* AN ANALYSIS | ADMIN
OF ADMINISTRATION IN BRITISH COLUMBIA 1869-1871." | CANADA
UK STRATA EX/STRUC LEGIS TASK GOV/REL EFFICIENCY | COLONIAL
ROLE...MGT CHARTS 19. PAGE 11 B0232 | LEAD

S67
DOERN G.B.,"THE ROYAL COMMISSIONS IN THE GENERAL | R+D
POLICY PROCESS AND IN FEDERAL-PROVINCIAL | EX/STRUC
RELATIONS." CANADA CONSTN ACADEM PROVS CONSULT | GOV/REL
DELIB/GP LEGIS ACT/RES PROB/SOLV CONFER CONTROL | NAT/G
EFFICIENCY...METH/COMP 20 SENATE ROYAL/COMM.

PAGE 30 B0603

S67
DRYDEN S.,"LOCAL GOVERNMENT IN TANZANIA PART II" | LOC/G
TANZANIA LAW NAT/G POL/PAR CONTROL PARTIC REPRESENT | GOV/REL
...DECISION 20. PAGE 31 B0622 | ADMIN
| STRUCT

S67
GOBER J.L.,"FEDERALISM AT WORK." USA+45 NAT/G | MUNIC
CONSULT ACT/RES PLAN CONFER ADMIN LEAD PARTIC | TEC/DEV
FEDERAL ATTIT. PAGE 40 B0813 | R+D
| GOV/REL

S67
HUMPHREY H.,"A MORE PERFECT UNION." USA+45 LOC/G | GOV/REL
NAT/G ACT/RES BUDGET RECEIVE CENTRAL CONGRESS. | FEDERAL
PAGE 52 B1063 | ADMIN
| PROB/SOLV

S67
LEVIN M.R.,"PLANNERS AND METROPOLITAN PLANNING." | PLAN
FUT USA+45 SOCIETY NAT/G PROVS PROB/SOLV LEAD | MUNIC
PARTIC GOV/REL RACE/REL HABITAT ROLE. PAGE 64 B1301 | R+D
| ADMIN

S67
SPEAR P.,"NEHRU." INDIA NAT/G POL/PAR ECO/TAC ADJUD | CHIEF
GOV/REL CENTRAL RIGID/FLEX 20 NEHRU/J. PAGE 99 | ATTIT
B2003 | ADMIN
| CREATE

S67
SUBRAMANIAM V.,"REPRESENTATIVE BUREAUCRACY: A | STRATA
REASSESSMENT." USA+45 ELITES LOC/G NAT/G ADMIN | GP/REL
GOV/REL PRIVIL DRIVE ROLE...POLICY CENSUS 20 | MGT
CIVIL/SERV BUREAUCRCY. PAGE 101 B2053 | GOV/COMP

S67
ZASLOW M.,"RECENT CONSTITUTIONAL DEVELOPMENTS IN | GOV/REL
CANADA'S NORTHERN TERRITORIES." CANADA LOC/G | REGION
DELIB/GP EX/STRUC LEGIS ADMIN ORD/FREE...TREND 20. | CONSTN
PAGE 119 B2398 | FEDERAL

N67
US SENATE COMM AERO SPACE SCI.AERONAUTICAL RESEARCH | DIST/IND
AND DEVELOPMENT POLICY; HEARINGS, COMM ON | SPACE
AERONAUTICAL AND SPACE SCIENCES...1967 (PAMPHLET). | NAT/G
R+D PROB/SOLV EXEC GOV/REL 20 DEPT/DEFEN FAA NASA | PLAN
CONGRESS. PAGE 109 B2210

B86
BOLINSBROKE H ST J.,A DISSERTATION UPON PARTIES | CONSERVE
(1729). UK LEGIS CHOOSE GOV/REL SOVEREIGN...TRADIT | POL/PAR
18 PARLIAMENT. PAGE 13 B0269 | CHIEF
| EX/STRUC

L86
GOODNOW F.J.,"AN EXECUTIVE AND THE COURTS: JUDICIAL | CT/SYS
REMEDIES AGAINST ADMINISTRATIVE ACTION" FRANCE UK | GOV/REL
USA-45 WOR+45 LAW CONSTN SANCTION ORD/FREE 19. | ADMIN
PAGE 41 B0823 | ADJUD

GOVERNMENT....SEE NAT/G, LOC/G

GOVERNOR....GOVERNOR; SEE ALSO PROVS, CHIEF, LEAD

N19
ABERNATHY B.R.,SOME PERSISTING QUESTIONS CONCERNING | PROVS
THE CONSTITUTIONAL STATE EXECUTIVE (PAMPHLET). | EX/STRUC
CONSTN TOP/EX TEC/DEV GOV/REL EFFICIENCY TIME 20 | PROB/SOLV
GOVERNOR. PAGE 3 B0054 | PWR

B25
MATHEWS J.M.,AMERICAN STATE GOVERNMENT. USA-45 | PROVS
LOC/G CHIEF EX/STRUC LEGIS ADJUD CONTROL CT/SYS | ADMIN
ROUTINE GOV/REL PWR 20 GOVERNOR. PAGE 71 B1426 | FEDERAL
| CONSTN

B38
SALTER J.T.,THE AMERICAN POLITICIAN. USA-45 LABOR | BIOG
POL/PAR EDU/PROP ADMIN CHOOSE ATTIT DRIVE PERSON | LEAD
PWR...POLICY ANTHOL 20 THOMAS/N LEWIS/JL LAGUARD/F | PROVS
GOVERNOR MAYOR. PAGE 92 B1865 | LOC/G

B56
RANSONE C.B.,THE OFFICE OF GOVERNOR IN THE UNITED | PROVS
STATES. USA+45 ADMIN...MGT INT CHARTS 20 GOVERNOR. | TOP/EX
PAGE 86 B1732 | POL/PAR
| EX/STRUC

B61
AVERY M.W.,GOVERNMENT OF WASHINGTON STATE. USA+45 | PROVS
MUNIC DELIB/GP EX/STRUC LEGIS GIVE CT/SYS PARTIC | LOC/G
REGION EFFICIENCY 20 WASHINGT/G GOVERNOR. PAGE 7 | ADMIN
B0151 | GOV/REL

B61
DARRAH E.L.,FIFTY STATE GOVERNMENTS: A COMPILATION | EX/STRUC
OF EXECUTIVE ORGANIZATION CHARTS. USA+45 LOC/G | ADMIN
DELIB/GP LEGIS ADJUD LEAD PWR 20 GOVERNOR. PAGE 26 | ORG/CHARTS
B0530 | PROVS

B61
DRURY J.W.,THE GOVERNMENT OF KANSAS. USA+45 AGRI | PROVS
INDUS CHIEF LEGIS WORKER PLAN BUDGET GIVE CT/SYS | CONSTN
GOV/REL...T 20 KANSAS GOVERNOR CITY/MGT. PAGE 31 | ADMIN
B0621 | LOC/G

B62
FARBER W.O.,GOVERNMENT OF SOUTH DAKOTA. USA+45 | PROVS
DIST/IND POL/PAR CHIEF EX/STRUC LEGIS ECO/TAC GIVE | LOC/G
EDU/PROP CT/SYS PARTIC...T 20 SOUTH/DAK GOVERNOR. | ADMIN

PAGE 35 B0704   CONSTN

                                                          B62
GOVERNORS CONF STATE PLANNING,STATE PLANNING: A   GOV/REL
POLICY STATEMENT (PAMPHLET). USA+45 LOC/G NAT/G   PLAN
DELIB/GP LEGIS EXEC 20 GOVERNOR. PAGE 42 B0847   ADMIN
                                                     PROVS
                                                          B62
HSUEH S.--S.,GOVERNMENT AND ADMINISTRATION OF HONG   ADMIN
KONG. CHIEF DELIB/GP LEGIS CT/SYS REPRESENT GOV/REL LOC/G
20 HONG/KONG CITY/MGT CIVIL/SERV GOVERNOR. PAGE 52   COLONIAL
B1055   EX/STRUC
                                                          B63
BOCK E.A., STATE AND LOCAL GOVERNMENT: A CASE BOOK. LOC/G
USA+45 MUNIC PROVS CONSULT GP/REL ATTIT...MGT 20   ADMIN
CASEBOOK GOVERNOR MAYOR. PAGE 12 B0254   PROB/SOLV
                                                     CHIEF
                                                          B63
SMITH R.M.,STATE GOVERNMENT IN TRANSITION. USA+45   PROVS
POL/PAR LEGIS PARL/PROC GOV/REL 20 PENNSYLVAN   POLICY
GOVERNOR. PAGE 98 B1984   EX/STRUC
                                                     PLAN
                                                          B66
RICHARD J.B.,GOVERNMENT AND POLITICS OF WYOMING.   PROVS
USA+45 POL/PAR EX/STRUC LEGIS CT/SYS LOBBY APPORT   LOC/G
CHOOSE REPRESENT 20 WYOMING GOVERNOR. PAGE 88 B1773 ADMIN
                                                          B66
SCHMIDT K.M.,AMERICAN STATE AND LOCAL GOVERNMENT IN PROVS
ACTION. USA+45 CONSTN LOC/G POL/PAR CHIEF LEGIS   ADMIN
PROB/SOLV ADJUD LOBBY GOV/REL...DECISION ANTHOL 20   MUNIC
GOVERNOR MAYOR URBAN/RNWL. PAGE 94 B1896   PLAN
                                                          B67
ANGEL D.D.,ROMNEY. LABOR LG/CO NAT/G EXEC WAR   BIOG
RACE/REL PERSON ORD/FREE...MGT WORSHIP 20   CHIEF
ROMNEY/GEO CIV/RIGHTS MORMON GOVERNOR. PAGE 5 B0108 PROVS
                                                     POLICY

GOVERNORS CONF STATE PLANNING B0847

GP/COMP....COMPARISON OF GROUPS

                                                          B00
SANDERSON E.,AFRICA IN THE NINETEENTH CENTURY.   COLONIAL
FRANCE UK EXTR/IND FORCES LEGIS ADMIN WAR DISCRIM   AFR
ORD/FREE...GEOG GP/COMP SOC/INTEG 19. PAGE 92 B1867 DIPLOM
                                                          B17
HARLOW R.V.,THE HISTORY OF LEGISLATIVE METHODS IN   LEGIS
THE PERIOD BEFORE 1825. USA-45 EX/STRUC ADMIN   DELIB/GP
COLONIAL LEAD PARL/PROC ROUTINE...GP/COMP GOV/COMP   PROVS
HOUSE/REP. PAGE 47 B0948   POL/PAR
                                                          S37
LASSWELL H.D.,"GOVERNMENTAL AND PARTY LEADERS IN   ELITES
FASCIST ITALY." ITALY CRIME SKILL...BIOG CHARTS   FASCISM
GP/COMP 20. PAGE 63 B1266   ADMIN
                                                          B49
WALINE M.,LE CONTROLE JURIDICTIONNEL DE   JURID
L'ADMINISTRATION. BELGIUM FRANCE UAR JUDGE BAL/PWR   ADMIN
ADJUD CONTROL CT/SYS...GP/COMP 20. PAGE 113 B2277   PWR
                                                     ORD/FREE
                                                          S50
DALTON M.,"CONFLICTS BETWEEN STAFF AND LINE   MGT
MANAGERIAL OFFICERS" (BMR). USA+45 USA-45 ELITES   ATTIT
LG/CO WORKER PROB/SOLV ADMIN EXEC EFFICIENCY PRODUC GP/REL
...GP/COMP 20. PAGE 26 B0526   INDUS
                                                          S52
TAYLOR D.W.,"TWENTY QUESTIONS: EFFICIENCY IN   PROB/SOLV
PROBLEM SOLVING AS A FUNCTION OF SIZE OF GROUP"   EFFICIENCY
WOR+45 CONFER ROUTINE INGP/REL...PSY GP/COMP 20.   SKILL
PAGE 103 B2085   PERCEPT
                                                          B55
WHEARE K.C.,GOVERNMENT BY COMMITTEE; AN ESSAY ON   DELIB/GP
THE BRITISH CONSTITUTION. UK NAT/G LEGIS INSPECT   CONSTN
CONFER ADJUD ADMIN CONTROL TASK EFFICIENCY ROLE   LEAD
POPULISM 20. PAGE 115 B2329   GP/COMP
                                                          B55
ZABEL O.H.,GOD AND CAESAR IN NEBRASKA: A STUDY OF   SECT
LEGAL RELATIONSHIP OF CHURCH AND STATE, 1854-1954.   PROVS
TAX GIVE ADMIN CONTROL GP/REL ROLE...GP/COMP 19/20   LAW
NEBRASKA. PAGE 119 B2396   EDU/PROP
                                                          S57
ROURKE F.E.,"THE POLITICS OF ADMINISTRATIVE   POLICY
ORGANIZATION: A CASE HISTORY." USA+45 LABOR WORKER   ATTIT
PLAN ADMIN TASK EFFICIENCY 20 DEPT/LABOR CONGRESS.   MGT
PAGE 91 B1836   GP/COMP
                                                          B58
MELMAN S.,DECISION-MAKING AND PRODUCTIVITY. INDUS   LABOR
EX/STRUC WORKER OP/RES PROB/SOLV TEC/DEV ADMIN   PRODUC
ROUTINE RIGID/FLEX GP/COMP. PAGE 73 B1464   DECISION
                                                     MGT
                                                          S59
STINCHCOMBE A.L.,"BUREAUCRATIC AND CRAFT   CONSTRUC
ADMINISTRATION OF PRODUCTION: A COMPARATIVE STUDY"   PROC/MFG
(BMR)" USA+45 STRUCT EX/STRUC ECO/TAC GP/REL   ADMIN
...CLASSIF GP/COMP IDEA/COMP GEN/LAWS 20 WEBER/MAX. PLAN
PAGE 101 B2039
                                                          B60
GRANICK D.,THE RED EXECUTIVE. COM USA+45 SOCIETY   PWR

ECO/DEV INDUS NAT/G POL/PAR EX/STRUC PLAN ECO/TAC   STRATA
EDU/PROP ADMIN EXEC ATTIT DRIVE...GP/COMP 20.   USSR
PAGE 42 B0851   ELITES
                                                          B60
MATTOD P.K.,A STUDY OF LOCAL SELF GOVERNMENT IN   MUNIC
URBAN INDIA. INDIA FINAN DELIB/GP LEGIS BUDGET TAX   CONSTN
SOVEREIGN...MGT GP/COMP 20. PAGE 71 B1432   LOC/G
                                                     ADMIN
                                                          S60
RAPHAELI N.,"SELECTED ARTICLES AND DOCUMENTS ON   BIBLIOG
COMPARATIVE PUBLIC ADMINISTRATION." USA+45 FINAN   MGT
LOC/G TOP/EX TEC/DEV EXEC GP/REL INGP/REL...GP/COMP ADMIN
GOV/COMP METH/COMP. PAGE 86 B1738   EX/STRUC
                                                          S60
THOMPSON J.D.,"ORGANIZATIONAL MANAGEMENT OF   PROB/SOLV
CONFLICT" (BMR)" WOR+45 STRUCT LABOR LG/CO WORKER   PERS/REL
TEC/DEV INGP/REL ATTIT GP/COMP. PAGE 104 B2103   ADMIN
                                                     MGT
                                                          B62
MARTIN R.C.,GOVERNMENT AND THE SUBURBAN SCHOOL.   SCHOOL
USA+45 FINAN EDU/PROP ADMIN HABITAT...TREND GP/COMP LOC/G
20. PAGE 70 B1414   EX/STRUC
                                                     ISOLAT
                                                          B62
US ADMINISTRATIVE CONFERENCE,FINAL REPORT OF THE   ADMIN
ADMINISTRATIVE CONFERENCE OF THE US: SUGGESTIONS   NAT/G
FOR IMPROVING PROCESSES - ADMIN. AGENCIES. USA+45   DELIB/GP
INGP/REL EFFICIENCY RATIONAL ORD/FREE...GP/COMP   GOV/REL
METH/COMP 20. PAGE 107 B2170
                                                          S62
GIDWANI K.A.,"LEADER BEHAVIOUR IN ELECTED AND NON-   LEAD
ELECTED GROUPS." DELIB/GP ROUTINE TASK HAPPINESS   INGP/REL
AUTHORIT...SOC STAT CHARTS SOC/EXP. PAGE 39 B0796   GP/COMP
                                                     CHOOSE
                                                          B63
KAMMERER G.M.,THE URBAN POLITICAL COMMUNITY: EXEC
PROFILES IN TOWN POLITICS. ELITES LOC/G LEAD   MUNIC
...DECISION GP/COMP. PAGE 57 B1162   PWR
                                                     GOV/COMP
                                                          B63
THOMETZ C.E.,THE DECISION-MAKERS: THE POWER   ELITES
STRUCTURE OF DALLAS. USA+45 CULTURE EX/STRUC DOMIN   MUNIC
LEGIT GP/REL ATTIT OBJECTIVE...INT CHARTS GP/COMP.   PWR
PAGE 104 B2101   DECISION
                                                          B63
WOLL P.,AMERICAN BUREAUCRACY. USA+45 USA-45 CONSTN   LEGIS
NAT/G ADJUD PWR OBJECTIVE...MGT GP/COMP. PAGE 118   EX/STRUC
B2372   ADMIN
                                                     GP/REL
                                                          L63
BENNIS W.G.,"A NEW ROLE FOR THE BEHAVIORAL   METH/CNCPT
SCIENCES: EFFECTING ORGANIZATIONAL CHANGE." ACT/RES CREATE
...MGT GP/COMP PERS/COMP SOC/EXP ORG/CHARTS.   STRUCT
PAGE 11 B0216   SOC
                                                          L63
LIVERNASH E.R.,"THE RELATION OF POWER TO THE   LABOR
STRUCTURE AND PROCESS OF COLLECTIVE BARGAINING."   GP/REL
ADJUD ORD/FREE...POLICY MGT CLASSIF GP/COMP.   PWR
PAGE 66 B1330   ECO/TAC
                                                          S63
GITTELL M.,"METROPOLITAN MAYOR: DEAD END." LOC/G   MUNIC
PARTIC REGION ATTIT PWR GP/COMP. PAGE 40 B0804   LEAD
                                                     EXEC
                                                          S63
JENNINGS M.K.,"PUBLIC ADMINISTRATORS AND COMMUNITY   ADMIN
DECISION-MAKING." ELITES LOC/G LEAD...GP/COMP   MUNIC
GOV/COMP. PAGE 56 B1134   DECISION
                                                     PWR
                                                          S64
CLIGNET R.,"POTENTIAL ELITES IN GHANA AND THE IVORY PWR
COAST: A PRELIMINARY SURVEY." AFR CULTURE ELITES   LEGIT
STRATA KIN NAT/G SECT DOMIN EXEC ORD/FREE RESPECT   IVORY/CST
SKILL...POLICY RELATIV GP/COMP NAT/COMP 20. PAGE 21 GHANA
B0438
                                                          S64
KAMMERER G.M.,"ROLE DIVERSITY OF CITY MANAGERS."   MUNIC
LOC/G ADMIN LEAD PERCEPT PWR GP/COMP. PAGE 57 B1163 EXEC
                                                     ATTIT
                                                     ROLE
                                                          S64
KAMMERER G.M.,"URBAN LEADERSHIP DURING CHANGE."   MUNIC
LEAD PARTIC REPRESENT GP/REL PLURISM...DECISION   PWR
GP/COMP. PAGE 58 B1164   ELITES
                                                     EXEC
                                                          B65
KWEDER J.B.,THE ROLES OF THE MANAGER, MAYOR, AND   MUNIC
COUNCILMEN IN POLICYMAKING. LEGIS PERS/REL ATTIT   EXEC
ROLE PWR GP/COMP. PAGE 62 B1246   LEAD
                                                     DECISION
                                                          B65
LATHAM E.,THE GROUP BASIS OF POLITICS: A STUDY IN   LEGIS
BASING-POINT LEGISLATION. INDUS MARKET POL/PAR   GP/COMP
DELIB/GP EX/STRUC DEBATE ADJUD...CHARTS PRESIDENT.   GP/REL
PAGE 63 B1274
                                                          B65
LYONS G.M.,SCHOOLS FOR STRATEGY* EDUCATION AND   ACADEM

RESEARCH IN NATIONAL SECURITY AFFAIRS. USA+45 FINAN ACT/RES
NAT/G VOL/ASSN FORCES TEC/DEV ADMIN WAR...GP/COMP INTELL
IDEA/COMP PERS/COMP COLD/WAR. PAGE 67 B1351
B65

PHELPS-FETHERS I.,SOVIET INTERNATIONAL FRONT USSR
ORGANIZATIONS* A CONCISE HANDBOOK. DIPLOM DOMIN EDU/PROP
LEGIT ADMIN EXEC GP/REL PEACE MARXISM...TIME/SEQ ASIA
GP/COMP. PAGE 83 B1668 COM
B66

BAKKE E.W.,MUTUAL SURVIVAL; THE GOAL OF UNION AND MGT
MANAGEMENT (2ND ED.). USA+45 ELITES ECO/DEV ECO/TAC LABOR
CONFER ADMIN REPRESENT GP/REL INGP/REL ATTIT BARGAIN
...GP/COMP 20. PAGE 8 B0170 INDUS
B66

HAWLEY C.E.,ADMINISTRATIVE QUESTIONS AND POLITICAL ADMIN
ANSWERS. USA+45 STRUCT WORKER EDU/PROP...GP/COMP GEN/LAWS
ANTHOL 20. PAGE 48 B0973 GP/REL
B66

MONTEIRO J.B.,CORRUPTION: CONTROL OF CONTROL
MALADMINISTRATION (2ND ED.). EUR+WWI INDIA USA+45 USSR NAT/G CRIME
DELIB/GP ADMIN...GP/COMP 20 OMBUDSMAN. PAGE 74 PROB/SOLV
B1503
B66

STREET D.,ORGANIZATION FOR TREATMENT. CLIENT PROVS GP/COMP
PUB/INST PLAN CONTROL PARTIC REPRESENT ATTIT PWR AGE/Y
...POLICY BIBLIOG. PAGE 101 B2052 ADMIN
VOL/ASSN
S66

DIEBOLD J.,"COMPUTERS, PROGRAM MANAGEMENT AND COMPUTER
FOREIGN AFFAIRS." USA+45 INDUS OP/RES TEC/DEV...MGT DIPLOM
GP/COMP GEN/LAWS. PAGE 29 B0590 ROUTINE
ACT/RES
B67

BENNETT J.W.,HUTTERIAN BRETHREN; THE AGRICULTURAL SECT
ECONOMY AND SOCIAL ORGANIZATION OF A COMMUNAL AGRI
PEOPLE. USA+45 SOCIETY FAM KIN TEC/DEV ADJUST...MGT STRUCT
AUD/VIS GP/COMP 20. PAGE 10 B0213 GP/REL
B67

COHEN R.,COMPARATIVE POLITICAL SYSTEMS: STUDIES IN ECO/UNDEV
THE POLITICS OF PRE-INDUSTRIAL SOCIETIES. WOR+45 STRUCT
WOR-45 CULTURE FAM KIN LOC/G NEIGH ADMIN LEAD SOCIETY
MARRIAGE...BIBLIOG 20. PAGE 22 B0447 GP/COMP
B67

DICKSON P.G.M.,THE FINANCIAL REVOLUTION IN ENGLAND. ECO/DEV
UK NAT/G TEC/DEV ADMIN GOV/REL...SOC METH/CNCPT FINAN
CHARTS GP/COMP BIBLIOG 17/18. PAGE 29 B0587 CAP/ISM
MGT
S67

HUDDLESTON J.,"TRADE UNIONS IN THE GERMAN FEDERAL LABOR
REPUBLIC." EUR+WWI GERMANY/W UK LAW INDUS WORKER GP/REL
CREATE CENTRAL...MGT GP/COMP 20. PAGE 52 B1056 SCHOOL
ROLE
S67

LASLETT J.H.M.,"SOCIALISM AND THE AMERICAN LABOR LABOR
MOVEMENT* SOME NEW REFLECTIONS." USA-45 VOL/ASSN ROUTINE
LOBBY PARTIC CENTRAL ALL/VALS SOCISM...GP/COMP 20. ATTIT
PAGE 63 B1265 GP/REL

GP/REL....RELATIONS AMONG GROUPS

N
PRINCETON U INDUSTRIAL REL SEC,SELECTED REFERENCES BIBLIOG/A
OF THE INDUSTRIAL RELATIONS SECTION OF PRINCETON, INDUS
NEW JERSEY. LG/CO NAT/G LEGIS WORKER PLAN PROB/SOLV LABOR
PAY ADMIN ROUTINE TASK GP/REL...PSY 20. PAGE 84 MGT
B1708
N

WEIGLEY R.F.,HISTORY OF THE UNITED STATES ARMY. FORCES
USA+45 USA-45 SOCIETY NAT/G LEAD WAR GP/REL PWR ADMIN
...SOC METH/COMP COLD/WAR. PAGE 115 B2312 ROLE
CIVMIL/REL
N

JOURNAL OF PUBLIC ADMINISTRATION: JOURNAL OF THE BIBLIOG/A
ROYAL INSTITUTE OF PUBLIC ADMINISTRATION. UK PLAN ADMIN
GP/REL INGP/REL 20. PAGE 1 B0015 NAT/G
MGT
N

MARKETING INFORMATION GUIDE. USA+45 ECO/DEV FINAN BIBLIOG/A
ADMIN GP/REL. PAGE 1 B0018 DIST/IND
MARKET
ECO/TAC
N

PERSONNEL. USA+45 LAW LABOR LG/CO WORKER CREATE BIBLIOG/A
GOV/REL PERS/REL ATTIT WEALTH. PAGE 2 B0030 ADMIN
MGT
GP/REL
N

PRINCETON UNIVERSITY,SELECTED REFERENCES: BIBLIOG/A
INDUSTRIAL RELATIONS SECTION. USA+45 EX/STRUC LABOR
WORKER TEC/DEV...MGT 20. PAGE 85 B1712 INDUS
GP/REL
B19

NATHAN M.,THE SOUTH AFRICAN COMMONWEALTH: CONSTN
CONSTITUTION, PROBLEMS, SOCIAL CONDITIONS. NAT/G
SOUTH/AFR UK CULTURE INDUS EX/STRUC LEGIS BUDGET POL/PAR
EDU/PROP ADMIN CT/SYS GP/REL RACE/REL...LING 19/20 SOCIETY

CMN/WLTH. PAGE 77 B1559
N19

ABBOT F.C.,THE CAMBRIDGE CITY MANAGER (PAMPHLET). MUNIC
PROB/SOLV ADMIN PERS/REL RIGID/FLEX PWR...MGT 20 EX/STRUC
MASSACHU CITY/MGT. PAGE 2 B0050 TOP/EX
GP/REL
N19

CANADA CIVIL SERV COMM,THE ANALYSIS OF ORGANIZATION NAT/G
IN THE GOVERNMENT OF CANADA (PAMPHLET). CANADA MGT
CONSTN EX/STRUC LEGIS TOP/EX CREATE PLAN CONTROL ADMIN
GP/REL 20. PAGE 18 B0372 DELIB/GP
N19

FOLSOM M.B.,BETTER MANAGEMENT OF THE PUBLIC'S ADMIN
BUSINESS (PAMPHLET). USA+45 DELIB/GP PAY CONFER NAT/G
CONTROL REGION GP/REL...METH/COMP ANTHOL 20. MGT
PAGE 36 B0733 PROB/SOLV
N19

GINZBERG E.,MANPOWER FOR GOVERNMENT (PAMPHLET). WORKER
USA+45 FORCES PLAN PROB/SOLV PAY EDU/PROP ADMIN CONSULT
GP/REL COST...MGT PREDICT TREND 20 CIVIL/SERV. NAT/G
PAGE 40 B0803 LOC/G
N19

JACKSON R.G.A.,THE CASE FOR AN INTERNATIONAL FOR/AID
DEVELOPMENT AUTHORITY (PAMPHLET). WOR+45 ECO/DEV INT/ORG
DIPLOM GIVE CONTROL GP/REL EFFICIENCY NAT/LISM ECO/UNDEV
SOVEREIGN 20. PAGE 55 B1108 ADMIN
N19

WALL N.L.,MUNICIPAL REPORTING TO THE PUBLIC METH
(PAMPHLET). LOC/G PLAN WRITING ADMIN REPRESENT MUNIC
EFFICIENCY...AUD/VIS CHARTS 20. PAGE 113 B2282 GP/REL
COM/IND
B27

DICKINSON J.,ADMINISTRATIVE JUSTICE AND THE CT/SYS
SUPREMACY OF LAW IN THE UNITED STATES. USA-45 LAW ADJUD
INDUS DOMIN EDU/PROP CONTROL EXEC GP/REL ORD/FREE ADMIN
...POLICY JURID 19/20. PAGE 29 B0586 NAT/G
B28

FYFE H.,THE BRITISH LIBERAL PARTY. UK SECT ADMIN POL/PAR
LEAD CHOOSE GP/REL PWR SOCISM...MAJORIT TIME/SEQ NAT/G
19/20 LIB/PARTY CONSRV/PAR. PAGE 38 B0768 REPRESENT
POPULISM
B28

HARDMAN J.B.,AMERICAN LABOR DYNAMICS. WORKER LABOR
ECO/TAC DOMIN ADJUD LEAD LOBBY PWR...POLICY MGT. INGP/REL
PAGE 47 B0944 ATTIT
GP/REL
B29

MERRIAM C.E.,CHICAGO: A MORE INTIMATE VIEW OF URBAN STRUCT
POLITICS. USA-45 CONSTN POL/PAR LEGIS ADMIN CRIME GP/REL
INGP/REL 18/20 CHICAGO. PAGE 73 B1472 MUNIC
B34

DE CENIVAL P.,BIBLIOGRAPHIE MAROCAINE: 1923-1933. BIBLIOG/A
FRANCE MOROCCO SECT ADMIN LEAD GP/REL ATTIT...LING ISLAM
20. PAGE 27 B0551 NAT/G
COLONIAL
B36

HERRING E.P.,PUBLIC ADMINISTRATION AND THE PUBLIC GP/REL
INTEREST. LABOR NAT/G PARTIC EFFICIENCY 20. PAGE 49 DECISION
B0995 PROB/SOLV
ADMIN
B37

BROOKS R.R.,WHEN LABOR ORGANIZES. FINAN EDU/PROP LABOR
ADMIN LOBBY PARTIC REPRESENT WEALTH TREND. PAGE 16 GP/REL
B0318 POLICY
B38

BALDWIN R.N.,CIVIL LIBERTIES AND INDUSTRIAL LABOR
CONFLICT. USA+45 STRATA WORKER INGP/REL...MGT 20 LG/CO
ACLU CIVIL/LIB. PAGE 9 B0175 INDUS
GP/REL
B38

REICH N.,LABOR RELATIONS IN REPUBLICAN GERMANY. WORKER
GERMANY CONSTN ECO/DEV INDUS NAT/G ADMIN CONTROL MGT
GP/REL FASCISM POPULISM 20 WEIMAR/REP. PAGE 87 LABOR
B1763 BARGAIN
B39

JENNINGS W.I.,PARLIAMENT. UK POL/PAR OP/RES BUDGET PARL/PROC
LEAD CHOOSE GP/REL...MGT 20 PARLIAMENT HOUSE/LORD LEGIS
HOUSE/CMNS. PAGE 56 B1135 CONSTN
NAT/G
B40

MCHENRY D.E.,HIS MAJESTY'S OPPOSITION: STRUCTURE POL/PAR
AND PROBLEMS OF THE BRITISH LABOUR PARTY 1931-1938. MGT
UK FINAN LABOR LOC/G DELIB/GP LEGIS EDU/PROP LEAD NAT/G
PARTIC CHOOSE GP/REL SOCISM...TREND 20 LABOR/PAR. POLICY
PAGE 72 B1450
S40

FAHS C.B.,"POLITICAL GROUPS IN THE JAPANESE HOUSE ROUTINE
OF PEERS." ELITES NAT/G ADMIN GP/REL...TREND POL/PAR
CHINJAP. PAGE 34 B0697 LEGIS
B41

PERHAM M.,AFRICANS AND BRITISH RULE. AFR UK ECO/TAC DIPLOM
CONTROL GP/REL ATTIT 20. PAGE 82 B1654 COLONIAL
ADMIN
ECO/UNDEV
B41

SLICHTER S.H.,UNION POLICIES AND INDUSTRIAL BARGAIN

MANAGEMENT. USA-45 INDUS TEC/DEV PAY GP/REL INGP/REL COST EFFICIENCY PRODUC...POLICY 20. PAGE 98 B1978
LABOR MGT WORKER

B42
CHAMBERLIN W.,INDUSTRIAL RELATIONS IN GERMANY 1914-1939. GERMANY 20. PAGE 20 B0401
BIBLIOG/A LABOR MGT GP/REL

B42
LEISERSON A.,ADMINISTRATIVE REGULATION: A STUDY IN REPRESENTATION OF INTERESTS. NAT/G EX/STRUC PROB/SOLV BARGAIN CONFER ROUTINE REPRESENT PERS/REL UTIL PWR POLICY. PAGE 63 B1283
LOBBY ADMIN GP/REL GOV/REL

B43
LEVY H.P.,A STUDY IN PUBLIC RELATIONS: CASE HISTORY OF THE RELATIONS MAINTAINED BETWEEN A DEPT OF PUBLIC ASSISTANCE AND PEOPLE. USA-45 NAT/G PRESS ADMIN LOBBY GP/REL DISCRIM...SOC/WK LING AUD/VIS 20 PENNSYLVAN. PAGE 64 B1302
ATTIT RECEIVE WEALTH SERV/IND

B43
YOUNG R.,THIS IS CONGRESS. FUT SENIOR ADMIN GP/REL PWR...DECISION REFORMERS CONGRESS. PAGE 119 B2393
LEGIS DELIB/GP CHIEF ROUTINE

S43
GOLDEN C.S.,"NEW PATTERNS OF DEMOCRACY." NEIGH DELIB/GP EDU/PROP EXEC PARTIC...MGT METH/CNCPT OBS TREND. PAGE 40 B0815
LABOR REPRESENT LG/CO GP/REL

B44
WRIGHT H.R.,SOCIAL SERVICE IN WARTIME. FINAN NAT/G VOL/ASSN PLAN GP/REL ROLE. PAGE 118 B2381
GIVE WAR SOC/WK ADMIN

B45
MAYO E.,THE SOCIAL PROBLEMS OF AN INDUSTRIAL CIVILIZATION. USA+45 SOCIETY LABOR CROWD PERS/REL LAISSEZ. PAGE 71 B1438
INDUS GP/REL MGT WORKER

B45
MILLIS H.A.,ORGANIZED LABOR (FIRST ED.). LAW STRUCT DELIB/GP WORKER ECO/TAC ADJUD CONTROL REPRESENT INGP/REL INCOME MGT. PAGE 74 B1485
LABOR POLICY ROUTINE GP/REL

B47
BAERWALD F.,FUNDAMENTALS OF LABOR ECONOMICS. LAW INDUS LABOR LG/CO CONTROL GP/REL INCOME TOTALISM ...MGT CHARTS GEN/LAWS BIBLIOG 20. PAGE 8 B0158
ECO/DEV WORKER MARKET

B47
WARNER W.L.,THE SOCIAL SYSTEM OF THE MODERN FACTORY; THE STRIKE: AN ANALYSIS. USA-45 STRATA WORKER ECO/TAC GP/REL INGP/REL...MGT SOC CHARTS 20 YANKEE/C. PAGE 114 B2293
ROLE STRUCT LABOR PROC/MFG

B48
CHILDS J.R.,AMERICAN FOREIGN SERVICE. USA+45 SOCIETY NAT/G ROUTINE GOV/REL 20 DEPT/STATE CIVIL/SERV. PAGE 21 B0423
DIPLOM ADMIN GP/REL

B48
HART J.,THE AMERICAN PRESIDENCY IN ACTION 1789: A STUDY IN CONSTITUTIONAL HISTORY. USA-45 POL/PAR DELIB/GP FORCES LEGIS ADJUD ADMIN LEAD GP/REL PERS/REL 18 PRESIDENT CONGRESS. PAGE 47 B0959
NAT/G CONSTN CHIEF EX/STRUC

B48
KESSELMAN L.C.,THE SOCIAL POLITICS OF THE FEPC. INDUS WORKER EDU/PROP GP/REL RACE/REL 20 NEGRO JEWS FEPC. PAGE 59 B1200
POLICY NAT/G ADMIN DISCRIM

B48
STEWART I.,ORGANIZING SCIENTIFIC RESEARCH FOR WAR: ADMINISTRATIVE HISTORY OF OFFICE OF SCIENTIFIC RESEARCH AND DEVELOPMENT. USA-45 INTELL R+D LABOR WORKER CREATE BUDGET WEAPON CIVMIL/REL GP/REL EFFICIENCY...POLICY 20. PAGE 101 B2037
DELIB/GP ADMIN WAR TEC/DEV

B48
WHITE L.D.,THE FEDERALISTS: A STUDY IN ADMINISTRATIVE HISTORY. STRUCT DELIB/GP LEGIS BUDGET ROUTINE GOV/REL GP/REL PERS/REL PWR...BIOG 18/19 PRESIDENT CONGRESS WASHINGT/G JEFFERSN/T HAMILTON/A. PAGE 116 B2337
ADMIN NAT/G POLICY PROB/SOLV

S48
COCH L.,"OVERCOMING RESISTANCE TO CHANGE" (BMR)" USA+45 CONSULT ADMIN ROUTINE GP/REL EFFICIENCY PRODUC PERCEPT SKILL...CHARTS SOC/EXP 20. PAGE 22 B0441
WORKER OP/RES PROC/MFG RIGID/FLEX

B49
BURNS J.M.,CONGRESS ON TRIAL: THE LEGISLATIVE PROCESS AND THE ADMINISTRATIVE STATE. USA+45 NAT/G ADMIN ROUTINE REPRESENT...PREDICT TREND. PAGE 17 B0354
LEGIS EXEC GP/REL PWR

B49
GLOVER J.D.,THE ADMINISTRATOR. ELITES LG/CO EX/STRUC ACT/RES CONTROL GP/REL INGP/REL PERS/REL AUTHORIT...POLICY CONCPT HIST/WRIT. PAGE 40 B0811
ADMIN MGT ATTIT PROF/ORG

B49
GRAVES W.B.,BASIC INFORMATION ON THE REORGANIZATION OF THE EXECUTIVE BRANCH: 1912-1948. USA-45 BUDGET ADMIN CONTROL GP/REL EFFICIENCY...MGT CHARTS ORG/CHARTS 20 PRESIDENT. PAGE 42 B0857
BIBLIOG/A EX/STRUC NAT/G CHIEF

B49
SCHULTZ W.J.,AMERICAN PUBLIC FINANCE. USA+45 ECO/TAC TAX ADMIN GOV/REL GP/REL INCOME 20. PAGE 94 B1906
FINAN POLICY ECO/DEV NAT/G

B49
SHISTER J.,ECONOMICS OF THE LABOR MARKET. LOC/G NAT/G WORKER TEC/DEV BARGAIN PAY PRICE EXEC GP/REL INCOME...MGT T 20. PAGE 96 B1949
MARKET LABOR INDUS

B50
BAKKE E.W.,BONDS OF ORGANIZATION (2ND ED.). USA+45 COM/IND FINAN ADMIN LEAD PERS/REL...INT SOC/INTEG 20. PAGE 8 B0169
ECO/DEV MGT LABOR GP/REL

B50
WADE E.C.S.,CONSTITUTIONAL LAW; AN OUTLINE OF THE LAW AND PRACTICE OF THE CONSTITUTION. UK LEGIS DOMIN ADMIN GP/REL 16/20 CMN/WLTH PARLIAMENT ENGLSH/LAW. PAGE 112 B2269
CONSTN NAT/G PARL/PROC LAW

S50
DALTON M.,"CONFLICTS BETWEEN STAFF AND LINE MANAGERIAL OFFICERS" (BMR). USA+45 USA-45 ELITES LG/CO WORKER PROB/SOLV ADMIN EXEC EFFICIENCY PRODUC ...GP/COMP 20. PAGE 26 B0526
MGT ATTIT GP/REL INDUS

C50
SIMON H.A.,"PUBLIC ADMINISTRATION." LG/CO SML/CO PLAN DOMIN LEAD GP/REL DRIVE PERCEPT ALL/VALS ...POLICY BIBLIOG/A 20. PAGE 97 B1957
MGT ADMIN DECISION EX/STRUC

B51
HARDMAN J.B.,THE HOUSE OF LABOR. LAW R+D NEIGH EDU/PROP LEAD ROUTINE REPRESENT GP/REL...POLICY STAT. PAGE 47 B0945
LABOR LOBBY ADMIN PRESS

B51
MAASS A.,MUDDY WATERS: THE ARMY ENGINEERS AND THE NATIONS RIVERS. USA-45 PROF/ORG CONSULT LEGIS ADMIN EXEC ROLE PWR...SOC PRESIDENT 20. PAGE 67 B1353
FORCES GP/REL LOBBY CONSTRUC

B51
NIELANDER W.A.,PUBLIC RELATIONS. USA+45 COM/IND LOC/G NAT/G VOL/ASSN EX/STRUC DIPLOM EDU/PROP PRESS TV...METH/CNCPT T 20. PAGE 78 B1583
PERS/REL GP/REL LG/CO ROUTINE

B51
PETERSON F.,SURVEY OF LABOR ECONOMICS (REV. ED.). STRATA ECO/DEV LABOR INSPECT BARGAIN PAY PRICE EXEC ROUTINE GP/REL ALL/VALS ORD/FREE 20 AFL/CIO DEPT/LABOR. PAGE 82 B1662
WORKER DEMAND IDEA/COMP T

B51
WHITE L.D.,THE JEFFERSONIANS: A STUDY IN ADMINISTRATIVE HISTORY 18011829. USA-45 DELIB/GP LEGIS TOP/EX PROB/SOLV BUDGET ECO/TAC GP/REL FEDERAL...BIOG IDEA/COMP 19 PRESIDENT CONGRESS JEFFERSN/T. PAGE 116 B2338
ADMIN NAT/G POLICY POL/PAR

C51
HOMANS G.C.,"THE WESTERN ELECTRIC RESEARCHES" IN S. HOSLETT, ED., HUMAN FACTORS IN MANAGEMENT (BMR)" ACT/RES GP/REL HAPPINESS PRODUC DRIVE...MGT OBS 20. PAGE 51 B1037
OP/RES EFFICIENCY SOC/EXP WORKER

S52
JOSEPHSON E.,"IRRATIONAL LEADERSHIP IN FORMAL ORGANIZATIONS." EX/STRUC PLAN LEAD GP/REL INGP/REL EFFICIENCY AUTHORIT DRIVE PSY. PAGE 57 B1154
ADMIN RATIONAL CONCPT PERSON

B53
SAYLES L.R.,THE LOCAL UNION. CONSTN CULTURE DELIB/GP PARTIC CHOOSE GP/REL INGP/REL ATTIT ROLE ...MAJORIT DECISION MGT. PAGE 93 B1873
LABOR LEAD ADJUD ROUTINE

B53
SECKLER-HUDSON C.,BIBLIOGRAPHY ON PUBLIC ADMINISTRATION (4TH ED.). USA+45 LAW POL/PAR DELIB/GP BUDGET ADJUD LOBBY GOV/REL GP/REL ATTIT ...JURID 20. PAGE 95 B1923
BIBLIOG/A ADMIN NAT/G MGT

B53
STENE E.O.,ABANDONMENTS OF THE MANAGER PLAN. LEGIS LEAD GP/REL PWR DECISION. PAGE 100 B2032
MUNIC EX/STRUC REPRESENT ADMIN

S53
PERKINS J.A.,"ADMINISTRATION OF THE NATIONAL SECURITY PROGRAM." USA+45 EX/STRUC FORCES ADMIN CIVMIL/REL ORD/FREE 20. PAGE 82 B1657
CONTROL GP/REL REPRESENT PROB/SOLV

C53
BULNER-THOMAS I.,"THE PARTY SYSTEM IN GREAT BRITAIN." UK CONSTN SECT PRESS CONFER GP/REL ATTIT ...POLICY TREND BIBLIOG 19/20 PARLIAMENT. PAGE 17 B0343
NAT/G POL/PAR ADMIN ROUTINE

C53
KRACKE E.A. JR.,"CIVIL SERVICE IN EARLY SUNG CHINA, 960-1067." ASIA GP/REL...BIBLIOG/A 10/11. PAGE 61
ADMIN NAT/G

B1231   WORKER
                                               CONTROL
                                                    B54
ALLPORT G.W.,THE NATURE OF PREJUDICE. USA+45 WOR+45   CULTURE
STRATA FACE/GP KIN NEIGH SECT ADMIN GP/REL DISCRIM   PERSON
ATTIT DRIVE LOVE RESPECT...PSY SOC MYTH QU/SEMANT   RACE/REL
20. PAGE 4 B0078
                                                    B54
BIESANZ J.,MODERN SOCIETY: AN INTRODUCTION TO   SOCIETY
SOCIAL SCIENCE. COM CONSTN STRUCT FAM MUNIC NAT/G   PROB/SOLV
SECT EX/STRUC LEGIS GP/REL PERSON...SOC 20. PAGE 12   CULTURE
B0237
                                                    B54
GOLDNER A.W.,WILDCAT STRIKE. LABOR TEC/DEV PAY   INDUS
ADMIN LEAD PERS/REL ATTIT RIGID/FLEX PWR...MGT   WORKER
CONCPT. PAGE 40 B0816   GP/REL
                                                      SOC
                                                    B54
WHITE L.D.,THE JACKSONIANS: A STUDY IN   NAT/G
ADMINISTRATIVE HISTORY 1829-1861. USA-45 CONSTN   ADMIN
POL/PAR CHIEF DELIB/GP LEGIS CREATE PROB/SOLV   POLICY
ECO/TAC LEAD REGION GP/REL 19 PRESIDENT CONGRESS
JACKSON/A. PAGE 116 B2339
                                                    S54
LANE E.,"INTEREST GROUPS AND BUREAUCRACY." NAT/G   EX/STRUC
ADMIN GP/REL INGP/REL 20. PAGE 62 B1256   LOBBY
                                                      REPRESENT
                                                      PWR
                                                    C54
GOULDNER A.W.,"PATTERNS OF INDUSTRIAL BUREAUCRACY."   ADMIN
GP/REL CONSEN ATTIT DRIVE...BIBLIOG 20. PAGE 42   INDUS
B0843   OP/RES
                                                      WORKER
                                                    B55
BERNAYS E.L.,THE ENGINEERING OF CONSENT. VOL/ASSN   GP/REL
OP/RES ROUTINE INGP/REL ATTIT RESPECT...POLICY   PLAN
METH/CNCPT METH/COMP 20. PAGE 11 B0224   ACT/RES
                                                      ADJUST
                                                    B55
BRAUN K.,LABOR DISPUTES AND THEIR SETTLEMENT.   INDUS
ECO/TAC ROUTINE TASK GP/REL...DECISION GEN/LAWS.   LABOR
PAGE 15 B0301   BARGAIN
                                                      ADJUD
                                                    B55
HOROWITZ M.,INCENTIVE WAGE SYSTEMS. INDUS LG/CO   BIBLIOG/A
WORKER CONTROL GP/REL...MGT PSY 20. PAGE 51 B1044   PAY
                                                      PLAN
                                                      TASK
                                                    B55
ZABEL O.H.,GOD AND CAESAR IN NEBRASKA: A STUDY OF   SECT
LEGAL RELATIONSHIP OF CHURCH AND STATE, 1854-1954.   PROVS
TAX GIVE ADMIN CONTROL GP/REL ROLE...GP/COMP 19/20   LAW
NEBRASKA. PAGE 119 B2396   EDU/PROP
                                                    S55
BUNZEL J.H.,"THE GENERAL IDEOLOGY OF AMERICAN SMALL   ALL/IDEOS
BUSINESS"(BMR)" USA+45 USA-45 AGRI GP/REL INGP/REL   ATTIT
PERSON...MGT IDEA/COMP 18/20. PAGE 17 B0345   SML/CO
                                                      INDUS
                                                    S55
TERRIEN F.W.,"THE EFFECT OF CHANGING SIZE UPON THE   SOC
INTERNAL STRUCTURE OF ORGANIZATIONS" (BMR)" WOR+45   ADMIN
WOR-45 CHARTS. PAGE 103 B2091   GP/REL
                                                      METH
                                                    B56
BARBASH J.,THE PRACTICE OF UNIONISM. ECO/TAC LEAD   LABOR
LOBBY GP/REL INGP/REL DRIVE MARXISM BIBLIOG. PAGE 9   REPRESENT
B0182   CONTROL
                                                      ADMIN
                                                    B56
BROWNE D.G.,THE RISE OF SCOTLAND YARD: A HISTORY OF   CRIMLGY
THE METROPOLITAN POLICE. UK MUNIC CHIEF ADMIN CRIME   LEGIS
GP/REL 19/20. PAGE 16 B0329   CONTROL
                                                      FORCES
                                                    B56
CENTRAL AFRICAN ARCHIVES,A GUIDE TO THE PUBLIC   BIBLIOG/A
RECORDS OF SOUTHERN RHODESIA UNDER THE REGIME OF   COLONIAL
THE BRITISH SOUTH AFRICA COMPANY, 1890-1923. UK   ADMIN
STRUCT NAT/G WRITING GP/REL 19/20. PAGE 19 B0398   AFR
                                                    B56
CONAWAY O.B.,DEMOCRACY IN FEDERAL ADMINISTRATION   ADMIN
(PAMPHLET). USA+45 LEGIS PARTIC ATTIT...TREND   SERV/IND
ANTHOL 20. PAGE 23 B0459   NAT/G
                                                      GP/REL
                                                    B56
HICKMAN C.A.,INDIVIDUALS, GROUPS, AND ECONOMIC   MGT
BEHAVIOR. WORKER PAY CONTROL EXEC GP/REL INGP/REL   ADMIN
PERSON ROLE...PSY SOC PERS/COMP METH 20. PAGE 50   ECO/TAC
B1005   PLAN
                                                    B56
POWELL N.J.,PERSONNEL ADMINISTRATION IN GOVERNMENT.   ADMIN
COM/IND POL/PAR LEGIS PAY CT/SYS ROUTINE GP/REL   WORKER
PERS/REL...POLICY METH 20 CIVIL/SERV. PAGE 84 B1697   LOC/G
                                                      NAT/G
                                                    B56
WILSON W.,CONGRESSIONAL GOVERNMENT. USA-45 NAT/G   LEGIS
ADMIN EXEC PARL/PROC GP/REL MAJORITY ATTIT 19   CHIEF

SENATE HOUSE/REP. PAGE 117 B2364   CONSTN
                                                      PWR
                                                    S56
HEADY F.,"THE MICHIGAN DEPARTMENT OF   ADMIN
ADMINISTRATION; A CASE STUDY IN THE POLITICS OF   DELIB/GP
ADMINISTRATION" (BMR) USA+45 POL/PAR PROVS CHIEF   LOC/G
LEGIS GP/REL ATTIT 20 MICHIGAN. PAGE 48 B0980
                                                    B57
DE GRAZIA A.,GRASS ROOTS PRIVATE WELFARE. LOC/G   NEW/LIB
SCHOOL ACT/RES EDU/PROP ROUTINE CROWD GP/REL   HEALTH
DISCRIM HAPPINESS ILLEGIT AGE HABITAT. PAGE 27   MUNIC
B0554   VOL/ASSN
                                                    B57
INDUSTRIAL RELATIONS RES ASSN,RESEARCH IN   INDUS
INDUSTRIAL HUMAN RELATIONS. INTELL ACT/RES OP/RES   MGT
ADMIN 20. PAGE 54 B1084   LABOR
                                                     GP/REL
                                                    B57
SCHNEIDER E.V.,INDUSTRIAL SOCIOLOGY: THE SOCIAL   LABOR
RELATIONS OF INDUSTRY AND COMMUNITY. STRATA INDUS   MGT
NAT/G NEIGH CREATE ADMIN PARTIC GP/REL RACE/REL   INGP/REL
ROLE PWR...POLICY BIBLIOG. PAGE 94 B1898   STRUCT
                                                    B57
US CIVIL SERVICE COMMISSION,DISSERTATIONS AND   BIBLIOG
THESES RELATING TO PERSONNEL ADMINISTRATION   ADMIN
(PAMPHLET). USA+45 COM/IND LABOR EX/STRUC GP/REL   MGT
INGP/REL DECISION. PAGE 108 B2176   WORKER
                                                    S57
DANIELSON L.E.,"SUPERVISORY PROBLEMS IN DECISION   PROB/SOLV
MAKING." WORKER ADMIN ROUTINE TASK MGT. PAGE 26   DECISION
B0529   CONTROL
                                                     GP/REL
                                                    S57
HAILEY,"TOMORROW IN AFRICA." CONSTN SOCIETY LOC/G   AFR
NAT/G DOMIN ADJUD ADMIN GP/REL DISCRIM NAT/LISM   PERSON
ATTIT MORAL ORD/FREE...PSY SOC CONCPT OBS RECORD   ELITES
TREND GEN/LAWS CMN/WLTH 20. PAGE 45 B0917   RACE/REL
                                                    B58
CARTER G.M.,TRANSITION IN AFRICA; STUDIES IN   NAT/COMP
POLITICAL ADAPTATION. AFR CENTRL/AFR GHANA NIGERIA   PWR
CONSTN LOC/G POL/PAR ADMIN GP/REL FEDERAL...MAJORIT CONTROL
BIBLIOG 20. PAGE 19 B0389   NAT/G
                                                    B58
CONSERVATIVE POLITICAL CENTRE,A WORLD SECURITY   ORD/FREE
AUTHORITY? WOR+45 CONSTN ELITES FINAN DELIB/GP PLAN CONSERVE
PROB/SOLV ADMIN CONTROL NUC/PWR GP/REL...IDEA/COMP   FORCES
20. PAGE 23 B0468   ARMS/CONT
                                                    B58
COWAN L.G.,LOCAL GOVERNMENT IN WEST AFRICA. AFR   LOC/G
FRANCE UK CULTURE KIN POL/PAR CHIEF LEGIS CREATE   COLONIAL
ADMIN PARTIC GOV/REL GP/REL...METH/COMP 20. PAGE 24 SOVEREIGN
B0498   REPRESENT
                                                    B58
DAVIS K.C.,ADMINISTRATIVE LAW TREATISE (VOLS. I AND ADMIN
IV). NAT/G JUDGE PROB/SOLV ADJUD GP/REL 20   JURID
SUPREME/CT. PAGE 26 B0540   CT/SYS
                                                     EX/STRUC
                                                    B58
DWARKADAS R.,ROLE OF HIGHER CIVIL SERVICE IN INDIA. ADMIN
INDIA ECO/UNDEV LEGIS PROB/SOLV GP/REL PERS/REL   NAT/G
...POLICY WELF/ST DECISION ORG/CHARTS BIBLIOG 20   ROLE
CIVIL/SERV INTRVN/ECO. PAGE 31 B0637   PLAN
                                                    B58
INDIAN INST OF PUBLIC ADMIN,IMPROVING CITY   LOC/G
GOVERNMENT. INDIA ECO/UNDEV PLAN BUDGET PARTIC   MUNIC
GP/REL 20. PAGE 53 B1080   PROB/SOLV
                                                     ADMIN
                                                    B58
LESTER R.A.,AS UNIONS MATURE. POL/PAR BARGAIN LEAD   LABOR
PARTIC GP/REL CENTRAL...MAJORIT TIME/SEQ METH/COMP. INDUS
PAGE 64 B1299   POLICY
                                                     MGT
                                                    B58
LOVEJOY D.S.,RHODE ISLAND POLITICS AND THE AMERICAN REV
REVOLUTION 1760-1776. UK USA-45 ELITES EX/STRUC TAX COLONIAL
LEAD REPRESENT GOV/REL GP/REL ATTIT 18 RHODE/ISL.   ECO/TAC
PAGE 67 B1343   SOVEREIGN
                                                    B58
MOEN N.W.,THE GOVERNMENT OF SCOTLAND 1603 - 1625.   CHIEF
UK JUDGE ADMIN GP/REL PWR 17 SCOTLAND COMMON/LAW.   JURID
PAGE 74 B1496   CONTROL
                                                     PARL/PROC
                                                    B58
VAN RIPER P.P.,HISTORY OF THE UNITED STATES CIVIL   ADMIN
SERVICE. USA+45 USA-45 LABOR LOC/G DELIB/GP LEGIS   WORKER
PROB/SOLV LOBBY GOV/REL GP/REL ADMIN...POLICY   NAT/G
18/20 PRESIDENT CIVIL/SERV. PAGE 111 B2251
                                                    B58
WHITE L.D.,THE REPUBLICAN ERA: 1869-1901, A STUDY   MGT
IN ADMINISTRATIVE HISTORY. USA-45 FINAN PLAN   PWR
NEUTRAL CRIME GP/REL MORAL LAISSEZ PRESIDENT   DELIB/GP
REFORMERS 19 CONGRESS CIVIL/SERV. PAGE 116 B2340   ADMIN
                                                    S58
KEISER N.F.,"PUBLIC RESPONSIBILITY AND FEDERAL   REPRESENT
ADVISORY GROUPS: A CASE STUDY." NAT/G ADMIN CONTROL ELITES
LOBBY...POLICY 20. PAGE 59 B1190   GP/REL

EX/STRUC
C58
REDFORD E.S.,"THE NEVER-ENDING SEARCH FOR THE   LOBBY
PUBLIC INTEREST" IN E. REDFORD. IDEALS AND PRACTICE   POLICY
IN PUBLIC ADMINISTRATION (BMR)" USA+45 USA-45   ADMIN
SOCIETY PARTIC GP/REL ATTIT PLURISM...DECISION SOC   MAJORIT
20. PAGE 87 B1755
B59
BHAMBHRI C.P.,SUBSTANCE OF HINDU POLITY. INDIA   GOV/REL
S/ASIA LAW EX/STRUC JUDGE TAX COERCE GP/REL   WRITING
POPULISM 20 HINDU. PAGE 11 B0234   SECT
PROVS
B59
BONNETT C.E.,LABOR-MANAGEMENT RELATIONS. USA+45   MGT
OP/RES PROB/SOLV EDU/PROP...AUD/VIS CHARTS 20.   LABOR
PAGE 13 B0274   INDUS
GP/REL
B59
DAHRENDORF R.,CLASS AND CLASS CONFLICT IN   VOL/ASSN
INDUSTRIAL SOCIETY. LABOR NAT/G COERCE ROLE PLURISM   STRUCT
...POLICY MGT CONCPT CLASSIF. PAGE 26 B0523   SOC
GP/REL
B59
ELAZAR D.J.,INTERGOVERNMENTAL RELATIONS IN   FEDERAL
NINETEENTH CENTURY AMERICAN FEDERALISM (DOCTORAL   ADMIN
THESIS). USA-45 FINAN LOC/G NAT/G GP/REL 18/19.   PROVS
PAGE 33 B0662   GOV/REL
B59
JENNINGS W.I.,CABINET GOVERNMENT (3RD ED.). UK   DELIB/GP
POL/PAR CHIEF BUDGET ADMIN CHOOSE GP/REL 20.   NAT/G
PAGE 56 B1137   CONSTN
OP/RES
B59
LEMBERG E.,DIE VERTRIEBENEN IN WESTDEUTSCHLAND (3   GP/REL
VOLS.). GERMANY/W CULTURE STRUCT AGRI PROVS ADMIN   INGP/REL
...JURID 20 MIGRATION. PAGE 64 B1287   SOCIETY
B59
LOEWENSTEIN K.,VERFASSUNGSRECHT UND   CONSTN
VERFASSUNGSPRAXIS DER VEREINIGTEN STAATEN. USA+45   POL/PAR
USA-45 COLONIAL CT/SYS GP/REL RACE/REL ORD/FREE   EX/STRUC
...JURID 18/20 SUPREME/CT CONGRESS PRESIDENT   NAT/G
BILL/RIGHT CIVIL/LIB. PAGE 66 B1337
B59
MOOS M.,THE CAMPUS AND THE STATE. LAW FINAN   EDU/PROP
DELIB/GP LEGIS EXEC LOBBY GP/REL PWR...POLICY   ACADEM
BIBLIOG. PAGE 75 B1517   PROVS
CONTROL
B59
WEBER W.,DER DEUTSCHE BEAMTE HEUTE. GERMANY/W NAT/G   MGT
DELIB/GP LEGIS CONFER ATTIT SUPEGO...JURID 20   EFFICIENCY
CIVIL/SERV. PAGE 114 B2306   ELITES
GP/REL
L59
"A BIBLIOGRAPHICAL ESSAY ON DECISION MAKING."   BIBLIOG/A
WOR+45 WOR-45 STRUCT OP/RES GP/REL...CONCPT   DECISION
IDEA/COMP METH 20. PAGE 2 B0038   ADMIN
LEAD
L59
TARKOWSKI Z.M.,"SCIENTISTS VERSUS ADMINISTRATORS: INGP/REL
AN APPROACH TOWARD ACHIEVING GREATER   GP/REL
UNDERSTANDING." UK EXEC EFFICIENCY 20. PAGE 103   ADMIN
B2079   EX/STRUC
S59
BENDIX R.,"INDUSTRIALIZATION, IDEOLOGIES, AND   INDUS
SOCIAL STRUCTURE" (BMR)" UK USA-45 USSR STRUCT   ATTIT
WORKER GP/REL EFFICIENCY...IDEA/COMP 20. PAGE 10   MGT
B0210   ADMIN
S59
STINCHCOMBE A.L.,"BUREAUCRATIC AND CRAFT   CONSTRUC
ADMINISTRATION OF PRODUCTION: A COMPARATIVE STUDY"   PROC/MFG
(BMR)" USA+45 STRUCT EX/STRUC ECO/TAC GP/REL   ADMIN
...CLASSIF GP/COMP IDEA/COMP GEN/LAWS 20 WEBER/MAX.   PLAN
PAGE 101 B2039
B60
BELL J.,THE SPLENDID MISERY: THE STORY OF THE   EXEC
PRESIDENCY AND POWER POLITICS AT CLOSE RANGE.   TOP/EX
USA+45 USA-45 PRESS ADMIN LEAD LOBBY GP/REL   LEGIS
PERS/REL PERSON PRESIDENT. PAGE 10 B0208
B60
BERNSTEIN I.,THE LEAN YEARS. SOCIETY STRATA PARTIC   WORKER
GP/REL ATTIT...SOC 20 DEPRESSION. PAGE 11 B0227   LABOR
WEALTH
MGT
B60
CORSON J.J.,GOVERNANCE OF COLLEGES AND   ADMIN
UNIVERSITIES. STRUCT FINAN DELIB/GP DOMIN EDU/PROP   EXEC
LEAD CHOOSE GP/REL CENTRAL COST PRIVIL SUPEGO   ACADEM
ORD/FREE PWR...DECISION BIBLIOG. PAGE 24 B0481   HABITAT
B60
DAVIS K.C.,ADMINISTRATIVE LAW AND GOVERNMENT.   ADMIN
USA+45 EX/STRUC PROB/SOLV ADJUD GP/REL PWR...POLICY   JURID
20 SUPREME/CT. PAGE 27 B0543   CT/SYS
NAT/G
B60
ELKOURI F.,HOW ARBITRATION WORKS (REV. ED.). LAW   MGT
INDUS BARGAIN 20. PAGE 33 B0667   LABOR

ADJUD
GP/REL
B60
MCGREGOR D.,THE HUMAN SIDE OF ENTERPRISE. USA+45   MGT
LEAD ROUTINE GP/REL INGP/REL...CONCPT GEN/LAWS 20.   ATTIT
PAGE 72 B1449   SKILL
EDU/PROP
B60
PAGE T.,THE PUBLIC PERSONNEL AGENCY AND THE CHIEF   WORKER
EXECUTIVE (REPORT NO. 601). USA+45 LOC/G NAT/G   EXEC
GP/REL PERS/REL...ANTHOL 20. PAGE 80 B1624   ADMIN
MGT
B60
SCHUBERT G.,THE PUBLIC INTEREST. USA+45 CONSULT   POLICY
PLAN PROB/SOLV ADJUD ADMIN GP/REL PWR ALL/IDEOS 20.   DELIB/GP
PAGE 94 B1903   REPRESENT
POL/PAR
B60
WEIDNER E.W.,INTERGOVERNMENTAL RELATIONS AS SEEN BY   ATTIT
PUBLIC OFFICIALS. USA+45 PROVS EX/STRUC EXEC   GP/REL
FEDERAL...QU 20. PAGE 115 B2311   GOV/REL
ADMIN
S60
BANFIELD E.C.,"THE POLITICAL IMPLICATIONS OF   TASK
METROPOLITAN GROWTH" (BMR)" UK USA+45 LOC/G   MUNIC
PROB/SOLV ADMIN GP/REL...METH/COMP NAT/COMP 20.   GOV/COMP
PAGE 9 B0176   CENSUS
S60
RAPHAELI N.,"SELECTED ARTICLES AND DOCUMENTS ON   BIBLIOG
COMPARATIVE PUBLIC ADMINISTRATION." USA+45 FINAN   MGT
LOC/G TOP/EX TEC/DEV EXEC GP/REL INGP/REL...GP/COMP   ADMIN
GOV/COMP METH/COMP. PAGE 86 B1738   EX/STRUC
S60
SMIGEL E.O.,"THE IMPACT OF RECRUITMENT ON THE   LG/CO
ORGANIZATION OF THE LARGE LAW FIRM" (BMR)" USA+45   ADMIN
STRUCT CONSULT PLAN GP/REL EFFICIENCY JURID.   LAW
PAGE 98 B1979   WORKER
S60
TAYLOR M.G.,"THE ROLE OF THE MEDICAL PROFESSION IN   PROF/ORG
THE FORMULATION AND EXECUTION OF PUBLIC POLICY"   HEALTH
(BMR)" CANADA NAT/G CONSULT ADMIN REPRESENT GP/REL   LOBBY
ROLE SOVEREIGN...DECISION 20 CMA. PAGE 103 B2088   POLICY
C60
MCCLEERY R.,"COMMUNICATION PATTERNS AS BASES OF   PERS/REL
SYSTEMS OF AUTHORITY AND POWER" IN THEORETICAL   PUB/INST
STUDIES IN SOCIAL ORGAN. OF PRISON-BMR. USA+45   PWR
SOCIETY STRUCT EDU/PROP ADMIN CONTROL COERCE CRIME   DOMIN
GP/REL AUTHORIT...SOC 20. PAGE 71 B1443
B61
BANFIELD E.C.,URBAN GOVERNMENT; A READER IN   MUNIC
POLITICS AND ADMINISTRATION. ELITES LABOR POL/PAR   GEN/METH
EXEC CHOOSE REPRESENT GP/REL PWR PLURISM...PSY SOC.   DECISION
PAGE 9 B0177
B61
CARROTHERS A.W.R.,LABOR ARBITRATION IN CANADA.   LABOR
CANADA LAW NAT/G CONSULT LEGIS WORKER ADJUD ADMIN   MGT
CT/SYS 20. PAGE 19 B0386   GP/REL
BARGAIN
B61
CATHERINE R.,LE FONCTIONNAIRE FRANCAIS. FRANCE   ADMIN
NAT/G INGP/REL ATTIT MORAL ORD/FREE...T CIVIL/SERV.   GP/REL
PAGE 19 B0394   LEAD
SUPEGO
B61
CHAPPLE E.D.,THE MEASURE OF MANAGEMENT. USA+45   MGT
WORKER ADMIN GP/REL EFFICIENCY...DECISION   OP/RES
ORG/CHARTS SIMUL 20. PAGE 20 B0412   PLAN
METH/CNCPT
B61
DUBIN R.,HUMAN RELATIONS IN ADMINISTRATION. USA+45   PERS/REL
INDUS LABOR LG/CO EX/STRUC GP/REL DRIVE PWR   MGT
...DECISION SOC CHARTS ANTHOL 20. PAGE 31 B0623   ADMIN
EXEC
B61
FREYRE G.,THE PORTUGUESE AND THE TROPICS. L/A+17C   COLONIAL
PORTUGAL SOCIETY PERF/ART ADMIN TASK GP/REL   METH
...ART/METH CONCPT SOC/INTEG 20. PAGE 37 B0754   PLAN
CULTURE
B61
GORDON R.A.,BUSINESS LEADERSHIP IN THE LARGE   LG/CO
CORPORATION. USA+45 SOCIETY EX/STRUC ADMIN CONTROL   LEAD
ROUTINE GP/REL PWR...MGT 20. PAGE 41 B0831   DECISION
LOBBY
B61
HAIRE M.,MODERN ORGANIZATION THEORY. LABOR ROUTINE   PERS/REL
MAJORITY...CONCPT MODAL OBS CONT/OBS. PAGE 45 B0919   GP/REL
MGT
DECISION
B61
INTL UNION LOCAL AUTHORITIES,LOCAL GOVERNMENT IN   LOC/G
THE USA. USA+45 PUB/INST DELIB/GP CONFER AUTOMAT   MUNIC
GP/REL POPULISM...ANTHOL 20 CITY/MGT. PAGE 54 B1101   ADMIN
GOV/REL
B61
LOSCHELDER W.,AUSBILDUNG UND AUSLESE DER BEAMTEN.   PROF/ORG
GERMANY/W ELITES NAT/G ADMIN GP/REL ATTIT...JURID   EDU/PROP

20 CIVIL/SERV. PAGE 67 B1341   EX/STRUC
                                                      CHOOSE
                                                             B61
PETRULLO L.,LEADERSHIP AND INTERPERSONAL BEHAVIOR.   PERSON
FACE/GP FAM PROF/ORG EX/STRUC FORCES DOMIN WAR   ATTIT
GP/REL PERS/REL EFFICIENCY PRODUC PWR...MGT PSY.   LEAD
PAGE 82 B1663   HABITAT
                                                             B61
SHAPP W.R.,FIELD ADMINISTRATION IN THE UNITED   INT/ORG
NATIONS SYSTEM. FINAN PROB/SOLV INSPECT DIPLOM EXEC   ADMIN
REGION ROUTINE EFFICIENCY ROLE...INT CHARTS 20 UN.   GP/REL
PAGE 96 B1933   FOR/AID
                                                             B61
SHARMA T.R.,THE WORKING OF STATE ENTERPRISES IN   NAT/G
INDIA. INDIA DELIB/GP LEGIS WORKER BUDGET PRICE   INDUS
CONTROL GP/REL OWN ATTIT...MGT CHARTS 20. PAGE 96   ADMIN
B1938   SOCISM
                                                             B61
THAYER L.O.,ADMINISTRATIVE COMMUNICATION. DELIB/GP   GP/REL
ADMIN ROUTINE PERS/REL 20. PAGE 104 B2093   PSY
                                                      LG/CO
                                                      MGT
                                                             B61
TRECKER H.B.,NEW UNDERSTANDING OF ADMINISTRATION.   VOL/ASSN
NEIGH DELIB/GP CONTROL LEAD GP/REL INGP/REL   PROF/ORG
...POLICY DECISION BIBLIOG. PAGE 105 B2126   ADMIN
                                                      PARTIC
                                                             B61
WARD R.E.,JAPANESE POLITICAL SCIENCE: A GUIDE TO   BIBLIOG/A
JAPANESE REFERENCE AND RESEARCH MATERIALS (2ND   PHIL/SCI
ED.). LAW CONSTN STRATA NAT/G POL/PAR DELIB/GP
LEGIS ADMIN CHOOSE GP/REL...INT/LAW 19/20 CHINJAP.
PAGE 113 B2290
                                                             L61
THOMPSON V.A.,"HIERARCHY, SPECIALIZATION, AND   PERS/REL
ORGANIZATIONAL CONFLICT" (BMR)" WOR+45 STRATA   PROB/SOLV
STRUCT WORKER TEC/DEV GP/REL INGP/REL ATTIT   ADMIN
AUTHORIT 20 BUREAUCRCY. PAGE 104 B2106   EX/STRUC
                                                             S61
SHERBENOU E.L.,"CLASS, PARTICIPATION, AND THE   REPRESENT
COUNCIL-MANAGER PLAN." ELITES STRUCT LEAD GP/REL   MUNIC
ATTIT PWR DECISION. PAGE 96 B1942   EXEC
                                                             C61
VERBA S.,"SMALL GROUPS AND POLITICAL BEHAVIOR: A   LEAD
STUDY OF LEADERSHIP" DOMIN PARTIC ROUTINE GP/REL   ELITES
ATTIT DRIVE ALL/VALS...CONCPT IDEA/COMP LAB/EXP   FACE/GP
BIBLIOG METH. PAGE 112 B2259
                                                             B62
BINDER L.,IRAN: POLITICAL DEVELOPMENT IN A CHANGING LEGIT
SOCIETY. IRAN OP/RES REV GP/REL CENTRAL RATIONAL   NAT/G
PWR...PHIL/SCI NAT/COMP GEN/LAWS 20. PAGE 12 B0239   ADMIN
                                                      STRUCT
                                                             B62
BOWEN W.G.,THE FEDERAL GOVERNMENT AND PRINCETON   NAT/G
UNIVERSITY. USA+45 FINAN ACT/RES PROB/SOLV ADMIN   ACADEM
CONTROL COST...POLICY 20 PRINCETN/U. PAGE 14 B0285   GP/REL
                                                      OP/RES
                                                             B62
DIMOCK M.E.,THE NEW AMERICAN POLITICAL ECONOMY: A   FEDERAL
SYNTHESIS OF POLITICS AND ECONOMICS. USA+45 FINAN   ECO/TAC
LG/CO PLAN ADMIN REGION GP/REL CENTRAL MORAL 20.   NAT/G
PAGE 29 B0598   PARTIC
                                                             B62
GALENSON W.,LABOR IN DEVELOPING COUNTRIES. BRAZIL   LABOR
INDONESIA ISRAEL PAKISTAN TURKEY AGRI INDUS WORKER   ECO/UNDEV
PAY PRICE GP/REL WEALTH...MGT CHARTS METH/COMP   BARGAIN
NAT/COMP 20. PAGE 38 B0775   POL/PAR
                                                             B62
GROVE J.W.,GOVERNMENT AND INDUSTRY IN BRITAIN. UK   ECO/TAC
FINAN LOC/G CONSULT DELIB/GP INT/TRADE ADMIN   INDUS
CONTROL...BIBLIOG 20. PAGE 44 B0894   NAT/G
                                                      GP/REL
                                                             B62
HANSON A.H.,MANAGERIAL PROBLEMS IN PUBLIC   MGT
ENTERPRISE. INDIA DELIB/GP GP/REL INGP/REL   NAT/G
EFFICIENCY 20 PARLIAMENT. PAGE 46 B0940   INDUS
                                                      PROB/SOLV
                                                             B62
INST TRAINING MUNICIPAL ADMIN,MUNICIPAL FINANCE   MUNIC
ADMINISTRATION (6TH ED.). USA+45 ELITES ECO/DEV   ADMIN
LEGIS PLAN BUDGET TAX GP/REL BAL/PAY COST...POLICY   FINAN
20 CITY/MGT. PAGE 54 B1089   LOC/G
                                                             B62
LITTLEFIELD N.,METROPOLITAN AREA PROBLEMS AND   LOC/G
MUNICIPAL HOME RULE. USA+45 PROVS ADMIN CONTROL   SOVEREIGN
GP/REL PWR. PAGE 66 B1328   JURID
                                                      LEGIS
                                                             B62
SRIVASTAVA G.L.,COLLECTIVE BARGAINING AND LABOR-   LABOR
MANAGEMENT RELATIONS IN INDIA. INDIA UK USA+45   MGT
INDUS LEGIS WORKER ADJUD EFFICIENCY PRODUC   BARGAIN
...METH/COMP 20. PAGE 100 B2014   GP/REL
                                                             B62
TAYLOR J.K.L.,ATTITUDES AND METHODS OF   WORKER
COMMUNICATION AND CONSULTATION BETWEEN EMPLOYERS   ADMIN
AND WORKERS AT INDIVIDUAL FIRM LEVEL. WOR+45 STRUCT   ATTIT

INDUS LABOR CONFER TASK GP/REL EFFICIENCY...MGT   EDU/PROP
BIBLIOG METH 20 OECD. PAGE 103 B2087
                                                             B62
WELLEQUET J.,LE CONGO BELGE ET LA WELTPOLITIK   ADMIN
(1894-1914. GERMANY DOMIN EDU/PROP WAR ATTIT   DIPLOM
...BIBLIOG T CONGO/LEOP. PAGE 115 B2318   GP/REL
                                                      COLONIAL
                                                             S62
DAKIN R.E.,"VARIATIONS IN POWER STRUCTURES AND   MUNIC
ORGANIZING EFFICIENCY: A COMPARATIVE STUDY OF FOUR   STRUCT
AREAS." STRATA EDU/PROP ADMIN LEAD GP/REL GOV/COMP.   PWR
PAGE 26 B0524
                                                             S62
LOCKARD D.,"THE CITY MANAGER, ADMINISTRATIVE THEORY MUNIC
AND POLITICAL POWER." LEGIS ADMIN REPRESENT GP/REL   EXEC
PWR. PAGE 66 B1333   LEAD
                                                      DECISION
                                                             S62
OLLERENSHAW K.,"SHARING RESPONSIBLITY." UK DELIB/GP REPRESENT
EDU/PROP EFFICIENCY 20. PAGE 80 B1607   GP/REL
                                                      ADMIN
                                                      EX/STRUC
                                                             C62
BLAU P.M.,"FORMAL ORGANIZATIONS." WOR+45 SOCIETY   ADMIN
STRUCT ECO/DEV GP/REL ATTIT...METH/CNCPT BIBLIOG   SOC
20. PAGE 12 B0253   GEN/METH
                                                      INGP/REL
                                                             C62
TRUMAN D.B.,"THE GOVERNMENTAL PROCESS: POLITICAL   LOBBY
INTERESTS AND PUBLIC OPINION." POL/PAR ADJUD ADMIN   EDU/PROP
EXEC LEAD ROUTINE CHOOSE REPRESENT GOV/REL   GP/REL
RIGID/FLEX...POLICY BIBLIOG/A 20. PAGE 105 B2131   LEGIS
                                                             C62
VAN DER SPRENKEL S.,"LEGAL INSTITUTIONS IN MANCHU   LAW
CHINA." ASIA STRUCT CT/SYS ROUTINE GOV/REL GP/REL   JURID
...CONCPT BIBLIOG 17/20. PAGE 111 B2250   ADMIN
                                                      ADJUD
                                                             B63
ACKOFF R.L.,A MANAGER'S GUIDE TO OPERATIONS   OP/RES
RESEARCH. STRUCT INDUS PROB/SOLV ROUTINE 20. PAGE 3   MGT
B0056   GP/REL
                                                      ADMIN
                                                             B63
BOCK E.A., STATE AND LOCAL GOVERNMENT: A CASE BOOK. LOC/G
USA+45 MUNIC PROVS CONSULT GP/REL ATTIT...MGT 20   ADMIN
CASEBOOK GOVERNOR MAYOR. PAGE 12 B0254   PROB/SOLV
                                                      CHIEF
                                                             B63
BLONDEL J.,VOTERS, PARTIES, AND LEADERS. UK ELITES   POL/PAR
LOC/G NAT/G PROVS ACT/RES DOMIN REPRESENT GP/REL   STRATA
INGP/REL...SOC BIBLIOG 20. PAGE 12 B0255   LEGIS
                                                      ADMIN
                                                             B63
CROZIER B.,THE MORNING AFTER: A STUDY OF   SOVEREIGN
INDEPENDENCE. WOR+45 EX/STRUC PLAN BAL/PWR COLONIAL   NAT/LISM
GP/REL 20 COLD/WAR. PAGE 25 B0511   NAT/G
                                                      DIPLOM
                                                             B63
DALAND R.T.,PERSPECTIVES OF BRAZILIAN PUBLIC   ADMIN
ADMINISTRATION (VOL. I). BRAZIL LAW ECO/UNDEV   NAT/G
SCHOOL CHIEF TEC/DEV CONFER CONTROL GP/REL ATTIT   PLAN
ROLE PWR...ANTHOL 20. PAGE 26 B0525   GOV/REL
                                                             B63
DIESNER H.J.,KIRCHE UND STAAT IM SPATROMISCHEN   SECT
REICH. ROMAN/EMP EX/STRUC COLONIAL COERCE ATTIT   GP/REL
CATHISM 4/5 AFRICA/N CHURCH/STA. PAGE 29 B0592   DOMIN
                                                      JURID
                                                             B63
GALBRAITH J.S.,RELUCTANT EMPIRE: BRITISH POLICY OF   COLONIAL
THE SOUTH AFRICAN FRONTIER, 1834-1854. AFR   ADMIN
SOUTH/AFR UK GP/REL RACE/REL DISCRIM...CHARTS   POLICY
BIBLIOG 19 MISSION. PAGE 38 B0774   SECT
                                                             B63
HANSON A.H.,NATIONALIZATION: A BOOK OF READINGS.   NAT/G
WOR+45 FINAN DELIB/GP LEGIS WORKER BUDGET ADMIN   OWN
GP/REL EFFICIENCY SOCISM...MGT ANTHOL. PAGE 46   INDUS
B0941   CONTROL
                                                             B63
JOHNS R.,CONFRONTING ORGANIZATIONAL CHANGE. NEIGH   SOC/WK
DELIB/GP CREATE OP/RES ADMIN GP/REL DRIVE...WELF/ST   WEALTH
SOC RECORD BIBLIOG. PAGE 56 B1142   LEAD
                                                      VOL/ASSN
                                                             B63
KORNHAUSER W.,SCIENTISTS IN INDUSTRY: CONFLICT AND   CREATE
ACCOMMODATION. USA+45 R+D LG/CO NAT/G TEC/DEV   INDUS
CONTROL ADJUST ATTIT...MGT STAT INT BIBLIOG 20.   PROF/ORG
PAGE 61 B1229   GP/REL
                                                             B63
PLANTEY A.,TRAITE PRATIQUE DE LA FONCTION PUBLIQUE   ADMIN
(2ND ED., 2 VOLS.). FRANCE FINAN EX/STRUC PROB/SOLV   SUPEGO
GP/REL ATTIT...SOC 20 CIVIL/SERV. PAGE 83 B1680   JURID
                                                             B63
RAUDSEPP E.,MANAGING CREATIVE SCIENTISTS AND   MGT
ENGINEERS. USA+45 ECO/DEV LG/CO GP/REL PERS/REL   CREATE
PRODUC. PAGE 86 B1742   R+D
                                                      ECO/TAC

B63

SELF P.,THE STATE AND THE FARMER. UK ECO/DEV MARKET AGRI
WORKER PRICE CONTROL GP/REL...WELF/ST 20 DEPT/AGRI. NAT/G
PAGE 95 B1926   ADMIN
                                                             VOL/ASSN

B63

SINGH M.M.,MUNICIPAL GOVERNMENT IN THE CALCUTTA   LOC/G
METROPOLITAN DISTRICT A PRELIMINARY SURVEY. FINAN   HEALTH
LG/CO DELIB/GP BUDGET TAX ADMIN GP/REL 20 CALCUTTA.   MUNIC
PAGE 97 B1969   JURID

B63

SPRING D.,THE ENGLISH LANDED ESTATE IN THE   STRATA
NINETEENTH CENTURY: ITS ADMINISTRATION. UK ELITES   PERS/REL
STRUCT AGRI NAT/G GP/REL OWN PWR WEALTH...BIBLIOG   MGT
19 HOUSE/LORD. PAGE 99 B2012

B63

THOMETZ C.E.,THE DECISION-MAKERS: THE POWER   ELITES
STRUCTURE OF DALLAS. USA+45 CULTURE EX/STRUC DOMIN   MUNIC
LEGIT GP/REL ATTIT OBJECTIVE...INT CHARTS GP/COMP.   PWR
PAGE 104 B2101   DECISION

B63

THORELLI H.B.,INTOP: INTERNATIONAL OPERATIONS   GAME
SIMULATION: PLAYER'S MANUAL. BRAZIL FINAN OP/RES   INT/TRADE
ADMIN GP/REL INGP/REL PRODUC PERCEPT...DECISION MGT   EDU/PROP
EEC. PAGE 104 B2108   LG/CO

B63

WARNER W.L.,THE AMERICAN FEDERAL EXECUTIVE. USA+45   ELITES
USA-45 CONSULT EX/STRUC GP/REL DRIVE ALL/VALS...PSY   NAT/G
DEEP/QU CHARTS 19/20 PRESIDENT. PAGE 114 B2295   TOP/EX
                                                        ADMIN

B63

WOLL P.,AMERICAN BUREAUCRACY. USA+45 USA-45 CONSTN   LEGIS
NAT/G ADJUD PWR OBJECTIVE...MGT GP/COMP. PAGE 118   EX/STRUC
B2372   ADMIN
                                                        GP/REL

L63

LIVERNASH E.R.,"THE RELATION OF POWER TO THE   LABOR
STRUCTURE AND PROCESS OF COLLECTIVE BARGAINING."   GP/REL
ADJUD ORD/FREE...POLICY MGT CLASSIF GP/COMP.   PWR
PAGE 66 B1330   ECO/TAC

S63

REES A.,"THE EFFECTS OF UNIONS ON RESOURCE   LABOR
ALLOCATION." USA+45 WORKER PRICE CONTROL GP/REL   BARGAIN
...MGT METH/COMP 20. PAGE 87 B1761   RATION
                                                       INCOME

S63

WINGFIELD C.J.,"POWER STRUCTURE AND DECISION-MAKING   MUNIC
IN CITY PLANNING." EDU/PROP ADMIN LEAD PARTIC   PLAN
GP/REL ATTIT. PAGE 117 B2365   DECISION
                                                        PWR

B64

BANTON M.,THE POLICEMAN IN THE COMMUNITY. UK USA+45   FORCES
STRUCT PROF/ORG WORKER LOBBY ROUTINE COERCE CROWD   ADMIN
GP/REL ADJUST DISCRIM PERCEPT 20. PAGE 9 B0181   ROLE
                                                        RACE/REL

B64

BLAKE R.R.,MANAGING INTERGROUP CONFLICT IN   CREATE
INDUSTRY. INDUS DELIB/GP EX/STRUC GP/REL PERS/REL   PROB/SOLV
GAME. PAGE 12 B0250   OP/RES
                                                        ADJUD

B64

BOTTOMORE T.B.,ELITES AND SOCIETY. INTELL STRATA   ELITES
ECO/DEV ECO/UNDEV ADMIN GP/REL ORD/FREE...CONCPT   IDEA/COMP
BIBLIOG 20. PAGE 14 B0281   SOCIETY
                                                        SOC

B64

BOUVIER-AJAM M.,MANUEL TECHNIQUE ET PRATIQUE DU   MUNIC
MAIRE ET DES ELUS ET AGENTS COMMUNAUX. FRANCE LOC/G   ADMIN
BUDGET CHOOSE GP/REL SUPEGO...JURID BIBLIOG 20   CHIEF
MAYOR COMMUNES. PAGE 14 B0284   NEIGH

B64

BROWN C.V.,GOVERNMENT AND BANKING IN WESTERN   ADMIN
NIGERIA. AFR NIGERIA GOV/REL GP/REL...POLICY 20.   ECO/UNDEV
PAGE 16 B0321   FINAN
                                                        NAT/G

B64

COTTER C.P.,POLITICS WITHOUT POWER: THE NATIONAL   CHOOSE
PARTY COMMITTEES. USA+45 FINAN NAT/G LOBBY ROUTINE   POL/PAR
GP/REL ATTIT ROLE SUPEGO PWR 20. PAGE 24 B0491   REPRESENT
                                                        DELIB/GP

B64

EDELMAN M.,THE SYMBOLIC USES OF POWER. USA+45   CLIENT
EX/STRUC CONTROL GP/REL INGP/REL...MGT T. PAGE 32   PWR
B0653   EXEC
                                                        ELITES

B64

FISK W.M.,ADMINISTRATIVE PROCEDURE IN A REGULATORY   SERV/IND
AGENCY: THE CAB AND THE NEW YORK-CHICAGO CASE   ECO/DEV
(PAMPHLET). USA+45 DIST/IND ADMIN CONTROL LOBBY   AIR
GP/REL ROLE ORD/FREE NEWYORK/C CHICAGO CAB. PAGE 36   JURID
B0727

B64

KARLEN D.,THE CITIZEN IN COURT. USA+45 LAW ADMIN   CT/SYS
ROUTINE CRIME GP/REL...JURID 20. PAGE 58 B1175   ADJUD
                                                        GOV/REL
                                                        JUDGE

B64

KIMBROUGH R.B.,POLITICAL POWER AND EDUCATIONAL   EDU/PROP
DECISION-MAKING. USA+45 FINAN ADMIN LEAD GP/REL   PROB/SOLV
ATTIT PWR PROG/TEAC. PAGE 60 B1207   DECISION
                                                        SCHOOL

B64

LOWI T.J.,AT THE PLEASURE OF THE MAYOR. EX/STRUC   LOBBY
PROB/SOLV BAL/PWR ADMIN PARTIC CHOOSE GP/REL   LOC/G
...CONT/OBS NET/THEORY CHARTS 20 NEWYORK/C MAYOR.   PWR
PAGE 67 B1346   MUNIC

B64

PEABODY R.L.,ORGANIZATIONAL AUTHORITY. SCHOOL   ADMIN
WORKER PLAN SENIOR GOV/REL UTIL DRIVE PWR...PSY   EFFICIENCY
CHARTS BIBLIOG 20. PAGE 82 B1648   TASK
                                                       GP/REL

B64

REDLICH F.,THE GERMAN MILITARY ENTERPRISER AND HIS   EX/STRUC
WORK FORCE. CHRIST-17C GERMANY ELITES SOCIETY FINAN   FORCES
ECO/TAC CIVMIL/REL GP/REL INGP/REL...HIST/WRIT   PROFIT
METH/COMP 14/17. PAGE 87 B1760   WORKER

B64

ROCHE J.P.,THE PRESIDENCY. USA+45 USA-45 CONSTN   EX/STRUC
NAT/G CHIEF BAL/PWR DIPLOM GP/REL 18/20 PRESIDENT.   PWR
PAGE 90 B1810

B64

WHEELER-BENNETT J.W.,THE NEMESIS OF POWER (2ND   FORCES
ED.). EUR+WWI GERMANY TOP/EX TEC/DEV ADMIN WAR   NAT/G
PERS/REL RIGID/FLEX ROLE ORD/FREE PWR FASCISM 20   GP/REL
HITLER/A. PAGE 116 B2332   STRUCT

S64

KAMMERER G.M.,"URBAN LEADERSHIP DURING CHANGE."   MUNIC
LEAD PARTIC REPRESENT GP/REL PLURISM...DECISION   PWR
GP/COMP. PAGE 58 B1164   ELITES
                                                       EXEC

S64

REDFORD E.S.,"THE PROTECTION OF THE PUBLIC INTEREST   ADMIN
WITH SPECIAL REFERENCE TO ADMINISTRATIVE   VOL/ASSN
REGULATION." POL/PAR LEGIS PRESS PARL/PROC. PAGE 87   EX/STRUC
B1758   GP/REL

S64

SALISBURY R.H.,"URBAN POLITICS: THE NEW CONVERGENCE   MUNIC
OF POWER." STRATA POL/PAR EX/STRUC PARTIC GP/REL   PWR
DECISION. PAGE 92 B1863   LEAD

C64

SCOTT R.E.,"MEXICAN GOVERNMENT IN TRANSITION (REV   NAT/G
ED)" CULTURE STRUCT POL/PAR CHIEF ADMIN LOBBY REV   L/A+17C
CHOOSE GP/REL DRIVE...BIBLIOG METH 20 MEXIC/AMER.   ROUTINE
PAGE 95 B1920   CONSTN

N64

CANADA NATL JT COUN PUB SERV.THE CANADA NATIONAL   GP/REL
JOINT COUNCIL OF THE PUBLIC SERVICE 1944-1964   NAT/G
(PAMPHLET). CANADA EX/STRUC PERS/REL DRIVE...MGT 20   LABOR
PEARSON/L. PAGE 18 B0373   EFFICIENCY

B65

BUECHNER J.C.,DIFFERENCES IN ROLE PERCEPTIONS IN   MUNIC
COLORADO COUNCIL-MANAGER CITIES. USA+45 ADMIN   CONSULT
ROUTINE GP/REL CONSEN PERCEPT PERSON ROLE   LOC/G
...DECISION MGT STAT INT QU CHARTS 20 COLORADO   IDEA/COMP
CITY/MGT. PAGE 17 B0338

B65

COHN H.J.,THE GOVERNMENT OF THE RHINE PALATINATE IN   PROVS
THE FIFTEENTH CENTURY. GERMANY FINAN LOC/G DELIB/GP   JURID
LEGIS CT/SYS CHOOSE CATHISM 14/15 PALATINATE.   GP/REL
PAGE 22 B0449   ADMIN

B65

COPELAND M.A.,OUR FREE ENTERPRISE ECONOMY. USA+45   CAP/ISM
INDUS LABOR ADMIN CONTROL GP/REL MGT. PAGE 23 B0476   PLAN
                                                       FINAN
                                                       ECO/DEV

B65

CUTLIP S.M.,A PUBLIC RELATIONS BIBLIOGRAPHY. INDUS   BIBLIOG/A
LABOR NAT/G PROF/ORG SCHOOL DIPLOM PRESS TV GOV/REL   MGT
GP/REL...PSY SOC/WK 20. PAGE 25 B0515   COM/IND
                                                       ADMIN

B65

GOPAL S.,BRITISH POLICY IN INDIA 1858-1905. INDIA   COLONIAL
UK ELITES CHIEF DELIB/GP ECO/TAC GP/REL DISCRIM   ADMIN
ATTIT...IDEA/COMP NAT/COMP PERS/COMP BIBLIOG/A   POL/PAR
19/20. PAGE 41 B0828   ECO/UNDEV

B65

HADWIGER D.F.,PRESSURES AND PROTEST. NAT/G LEGIS   AGRI
PLAN LEAD PARTIC ROUTINE ATTIT POLICY. PAGE 45   GP/REL
B0913   LOBBY
                                                       CHOOSE

B65

HUGHES J.M.,EDUCATION IN AMERICA (2ND ED.). USA+45   EDU/PROP
USA-45 GP/REL INGP/REL AGE/C AGE/Y ROLE...IDEA/COMP   SCHOOL
BIBLIOG T 20. PAGE 52 B1059   ADMIN
                                                       METH/COMP

B65

KAAS L.,DIE GEISTLICHE GERICHTSBARKEIT DER   JURID
KATHOLISCHEN KIRCHE IN PREUSSEN (2 VOLS.). PRUSSIA   CATHISM
CONSTN NAT/G PROVS SECT ADJUD ADMIN ATTIT 16/20.   GP/REL
PAGE 57 B1158   CT/SYS

B65

LATHAM E.,THE GROUP BASIS OF POLITICS: A STUDY IN   LEGIS

BASING-POINT LEGISLATION. INDUS MARKET POL/PAR
DELIB/GP EX/STRUC DEBATE ADJUD...CHARTS PRESIDENT.
PAGE 63 B1274
GP/COMP
GP/REL

B65
LEMAY G.H.,BRITISH SUPREMACY IN SOUTH AFRICA
1899-1907. SOUTH/AFR UK ADMIN CONTROL LEAD GP/REL
ORD/FREE 19/20. PAGE 64 B1286
WAR
COLONIAL
DOMIN
POLICY

B65
LEYS C.T.,FEDERATION IN EAST AFRICA. LAW AGRI
DIST/IND FINAN INT/ORG LABOR INT/TRADE CONFER ADMIN
CONTROL GP/REL...ANTHOL 20 AFRICA/E. PAGE 65 B1310
FEDERAL
REGION
ECO/UNDEV
PLAN

B65
LIPSET S.M.,THE BERKELEY STUDENT REVOLT: FACTS AND
INTERPRETATIONS. USA+45 INTELL VOL/ASSN CONSULT
EDU/PROP PRESS DEBATE ADMIN REV HAPPINESS
RIGID/FLEX MAJORIT. PAGE 65 B1322
CROWD
ACADEM
ATTIT
GP/REL

B65
MARTIN R.,PUBLIC ADMINISTRATION AND DEMOCRACY.
ELITES NAT/G ADMIN EXEC ROUTINE INGP/REL. PAGE 70
B1412
EX/STRUC
DECISION
REPRESENT
GP/REL

B65
MASTERS N.A.,COMMITTEE ASSIGNMENTS IN THE HOUSE OF
REPRESENTATIVES (BMR). USA+45 ELITES POL/PAR
EX/STRUC PARTIC REPRESENT GP/REL PERS/REL ATTIT PWR
...STAT CHARTS 20 HOUSE/REP. PAGE 71 B1425
LEAD
LEGIS
CHOOSE
DELIB/GP

B65
OLSON M. JR.,DROIT PUBLIC. FRANCE NAT/G LEGIS SUFF
GP/REL PRIVIL...TREND 18/20. PAGE 80 B1609
CONSTN
FINAN
ADMIN
ORD/FREE

B65
PANJABI K.L.,THE CIVIL SERVANT IN INDIA. INDIA UK
NAT/G CONSULT EX/STRUC REGION GP/REL RACE/REL 20.
PAGE 81 B1631
ADMIN
WORKER
BIOG
COLONIAL

B65
PAYNE J.L.,LABOR AND POLITICS IN PERU; THE SYSTEM
OF POLITICAL BARGAINING. PERU CONSTN VOL/ASSN
EX/STRUC LEAD PWR...CHARTS 20. PAGE 81 B1645
LABOR
POL/PAR
BARGAIN
GP/REL

B65
PERLOFF H.S.,URBAN RESEARCH AND EDUCATION IN THE
NEW YORK METROPOLITAN REGION (VOL. II). FUT USA+45
NEIGH PROF/ORG ACT/RES PROB/SOLV EDU/PROP ADMIN
...STAT BIBLIOG 20 NEWYORK/C. PAGE 82 B1659
MUNIC
PLAN
ACADEM
GP/REL

B65
PHELPS-FETHERS I.,SOVIET INTERNATIONAL FRONT
ORGANIZATIONS* A CONCISE HANDBOOK. DIPLOM DOMIN
LEGIT ADMIN EXEC GP/REL PEACE MARXISM...TIME/SEQ
GP/COMP. PAGE 83 B1668
USSR
EDU/PROP
ASIA
COM

B65
ROSS P.,THE GOVERNMENT AS A SOURCE OF UNION POWER.
USA+45 LAW ECO/DEV PROB/SOLV ECO/TAC LEAD GP/REL
...MGT 20. PAGE 90 B1826
LABOR
BARGAIN
POLICY
NAT/G

B65
ROWAT D.C.,THE OMBUDSMAN: CITIZEN'S DEFENDER.
DENMARK FINLAND NEW/ZEALND NORWAY SWEDEN CONSULT
PROB/SOLV FEEDBACK PARTIC GP/REL...SOC CONCPT
NEW/IDEA METH/COMP ANTHOL BIBLIOG 20. PAGE 91 B1840
INSPECT
CONSTN
NAT/G
ADMIN

B65
RUBINSTEIN A.Z.,THE CHALLENGE OF POLITICS: IDEAS
AND ISSUES (2ND ED.). UNIV ELITES SOCIETY EX/STRUC
BAL/PWR PARL/PROC AUTHORIT...DECISION ANTHOL 20.
PAGE 92 B1852
NAT/G
DIPLOM
GP/REL
ORD/FREE

B65
SMITH C.,THE OMBUDSMAN: A BIBLIOGRAPHY (PAMPHLET).
DENMARK SWEDEN USA+45 LAW LEGIS JUDGE GOV/REL
GP/REL...JURID 20. PAGE 98 B1980
BIBLIOG
ADMIN
CT/SYS
ADJUD

B65
STANLEY D.T.,CHANGING ADMINISTRATIONS. USA+45
POL/PAR DELIB/GP TOP/EX BUDGET GOV/REL GP/REL
PERS/REL PWR...MAJORIT DECISION MGT 20 PRESIDENT
SUCCESSION DEPT/STATE DEPT/DEFEN DEPT/HEW. PAGE 100
B2021
NAT/G
CHIEF
ADMIN
EX/STRUC

B65
US HOUSE COMM EDUC AND LABOR,ADMINISTRATION OF THE
NATIONAL LABOR RELATIONS ACT. USA+45 DELIB/GP
WORKER PROB/SOLV BARGAIN PAY CONTROL 20 NLRB
CONGRESS. PAGE 108 B2188
ADMIN
LABOR
GP/REL
INDUS

B65
VAID K.N.,STATE AND LABOR IN INDIA. INDIA INDUS
WORKER PAY PRICE ADJUD CONTROL PARL/PROC GP/REL
ORD/FREE 20. PAGE 111 B2248
LAW
LABOR
MGT
NEW/LIB

B65
WALTON R.E.,A BEHAVIORAL THEORY OF LABOR
NEGOTIATIONS: AN ANALYSIS OF A SOCIAL INTERACTION
SYSTEM. USA+45 FINAN PROB/SOLV ECO/TAC GP/REL
INGP/REL...DECISION BIBLIOG. PAGE 113 B2285
SOC
LABOR
BARGAIN
ADMIN

B65
WARD W.E.,GOVERNMENT IN WEST AFRICA. WOR+45 POL/PAR GOV/COMP

EX/STRUC PLAN PARTIC GP/REL SOVEREIGN 20 AFRICA/W.
PAGE 114 B2291
CONSTN
COLONIAL
ECO/UNDEV

L65
HAMMOND A.,"COMPREHENSIVE VERSUS INCREMENTAL
BUDGETING IN THE DEPARTMENT OF AGRICULTURE" USA+45
GP/REL ATTIT...PSY INT 20 DEPT/AGRI. PAGE 46 B0934
TOP/EX
EX/STRUC
AGRI
BUDGET

L65
HOOK S.,"SECOND THOUGHTS ON BERKELEY" USA+45 ELITES
INTELL LEGIT ADMIN COERCE REPRESENT GP/REL INGP/REL
TOTALISM AGE/Y MARXISM 20 BERKELEY FREE/SPEE
STUDNT/PWR. PAGE 51 B1040
ACADEM
ORD/FREE
POLICY
CREATE

S65
OSTGAARD E.,"FACTORS AFFECTING THE FLOW OF NEWS."
COM/IND BUDGET DIPLOM EXEC GP/REL COST ATTIT SAMP.
PAGE 80 B1618
EDU/PROP
PERCEPT
RECORD

S65
POLK W.R.,"PROBLEMS OF GOVERNMENT UTILIZATION OF
SCHOLARLY RESEARCH IN INTERNATIONAL AFFAIRS." FINAN
NAT/G EDU/PROP CONTROL TASK GP/REL ATTIT PERCEPT
KNOWL...POLICY TIME. PAGE 83 B1685
ACT/RES
ACADEM
PLAN
ADMIN

S65
POSVAR W.W.,"NATIONAL SECURITY POLICY* THE REALM OF
OBSCURITY." CREATE PLAN PROB/SOLV ADMIN LEAD GP/REL
CONSERVE...DECISION GEOG. PAGE 84 B1694
DIPLOM
USA+45
RECORD

B66
BAKKE E.W.,MUTUAL SURVIVAL; THE GOAL OF UNION AND
MANAGEMENT (2ND ED.). USA+45 ELITES ECO/DEV ECO/TAC
CONFER ADMIN REPRESENT GP/REL INGP/REL ATTIT
...GP/COMP 20. PAGE 8 B0170
MGT
LABOR
BARGAIN
INDUS

B66
CARALEY D.,PARTY POLITICS AND NATIONAL ELECTIONS.
USA+45 STRATA LOC/G PROVS EX/STRUC BARGAIN ADMIN
SANCTION GP/REL ATTIT 20 DEMOCRAT REPUBLICAN.
PAGE 18 B0375
POL/PAR
CHOOSE
REPRESENT
NAT/G

B66
CLEGG R.K.,THE ADMINISTRATOR IN PUBLIC WELFARE.
USA+45 STRUCT NAT/G PROVS PROB/SOLV BUDGET ECO/TAC
GP/REL ROLE...SOC/WK 20 PUBLIC/REL. PAGE 21 B0434
ADMIN
GIVE
GOV/REL
OP/RES

B66
COOK P.W. JR.,PROBLEMS OF CORPORATE POWER. WOR+45
FINAN INDUS BARGAIN GP/REL...MGT ANTHOL. PAGE 23
B0471
ADMIN
LG/CO
PWR
ECO/TAC

B66
DILLEY M.R.,BRITISH POLICY IN KENYA COLONY (2ND
ED.). AFR INDIA UK LABOR BUDGET TAX ADMIN PARL/PROC
GP/REL...BIBLIOG 20 PARLIAMENT. PAGE 29 B0594
COLONIAL
REPRESENT
SOVEREIGN

B66
FENN DH J.R.,BUSINESS DECISION MAKING AND
GOVERNMENT POLICY. SERV/IND LEGIS LICENSE ADMIN
CONTROL GP/REL INGP/REL 20 CASEBOOK. PAGE 35 B0711
DECISION
PLAN
NAT/G
LG/CO

B66
HAWLEY C.E.,ADMINISTRATIVE QUESTIONS AND POLITICAL
ANSWERS. USA+45 STRUCT WORKER EDU/PROP...GP/COMP
ANTHOL 20. PAGE 48 B0973
ADMIN
GEN/LAWS
GP/REL

B66
KAESTNER K.,GESAMTWIRTSCHAFTLICHE PLANUNG IN EINER
GEMISCHTEN WIRTSCHAFTSORDNUNG
(WIRTSCHAFTSPOLITISCHE STUDIEN 5). GERMANY/W WOR+45
WOR-45 INDUS MARKET NAT/G ACT/RES GP/REL INGP/REL
PRODUC...ECOMETRIC MGT BIBLIOG 20. PAGE 57 B1159
ECO/TAC
PLAN
POLICY
PREDICT

B66
LEE L.T.,VIENNA CONVENTION ON CONSULAR RELATIONS.
WOR+45 LAW INT/ORG CONFER GP/REL PRIVIL...INT/LAW
20 TREATY VIENNA/CNV. PAGE 63 B1279
AGREE
DIPLOM
ADMIN

B66
LINDFORS G.V.,INTERCOLLEGIATE BIBLIOGRAPHY; CASES
IN BUSINESS ADMINISTRATION (VOL. X). FINAN MARKET
LABOR CONSULT PLAN GP/REL PRODUC 20. PAGE 65 B1314
BIBLIOG/A
ADMIN
MGT
OP/RES

B66
O'NEILL C.E.,CHURCH AND STATE IN FRENCH COLONIAL
LOUISIANA: POLICY AND POLITICS TO 1732. PROVS
VOL/ASSN DELIB/GP ADJUD ADMIN GP/REL ATTIT DRIVE
...POLICY BIBLIOG 17/18 LOUISIANA CHURCH/STA.
PAGE 79 B1601
COLONIAL
NAT/G
SECT
PWR

B66
SEASHOLES B.,VOTING, INTEREST GROUPS, AND PARTIES.
USA+45 FINAN LOC/G NAT/G ADMIN LEAD GP/REL INGP/REL
ROLE...CHARTS ANTHOL 20. PAGE 95 B1922
CHOOSE
POL/PAR
LOBBY
PARTIC

B66
SILBERMAN B.S.,MODERN JAPANESE LEADERSHIP;
TRANSITION AND CHANGE. NAT/G POL/PAR CHIEF ADMIN
REPRESENT GP/REL ADJUST RIGID/FLEX...SOC METH/COMP
ANTHOL 19/20 CHINJAP CHRISTIAN. PAGE 97 B1952
LEAD
CULTURE
ELITES
MUNIC

B66
SIMON R.,PERSPECTIVES IN PUBLIC RELATIONS. USA+45
INDUS ACT/RES PLAN ADMIN ATTIT MGT. PAGE 97 B1961
GP/REL
PERS/REL
COM/IND
SOCIETY

THOENES P.,THE ELITE IN THE WELFARE STATE ,TRANS. ADMIN
BY J BINGHAM; ED. BY. STRATA NAT/G GP/REL HAPPINESS ELITES
INCOME OPTIMAL MORAL PWR WEALTH...POLICY CONCPT. MGT
PAGE 104 B2097 WELF/ST
B66

US BUREAU OF THE BUDGET,THE ADMINISTRATION OF ACT/RES
GOVERNMENT SUPPORTED RESEARCH AT UNIVERSITIES NAT/G
(PAMPHLET). USA+45 CONSULT TOP/EX ADMIN INCOME ACADEM
WEALTH...MGT PHIL/SCI INT. PAGE 108 B2174 GP/REL
B66

WASHINGTON S.H.,BIBLIOGRAPHY: LABOR-MANAGEMENT BIBLIOG
RELATIONS ACT, 1947 AS AMENDED BY LABOR-MANAGEMENT LAW
REPORTING AND DISCLOSURE ACT, 1959. USA+45 CONSTN LABOR
INDUS DELIB/GP LEGIS WORKER BARGAIN ECO/TAC ADJUD MGT
GP/REL NEW/LIB...JURID CONGRESS. PAGE 114 B2298
B66

WYLIE C.M.,RESEARCH IN PUBLIC HEALTH BIBLIOG/A
ADMINISTRATION; SELECTED RECENT ABSTRACTS IV R+D
(PAMPHLET). USA+45 MUNIC PUB/INST ACT/RES CREATE HEAL
OP/RES TEC/DEV GP/REL ROLE...MGT PHIL/SCI STAT. ADMIN
PAGE 118 B2387
S66

WOLFINGER R.E.,"POLITICAL ETHOS AND THE STRUCTURE MUNIC
OF CITY GOVERNMENT." POL/PAR EX/STRUC REPRESENT ATTIT
GP/REL PERS/REL RIGID/FLEX PWR. PAGE 118 B2371 STRATA
GOV/COMP
N66

AMERICAN SOCIETY PUBLIC ADMIN.PUBLIC ADMINISTRATION WEALTH
AND THE WAR ON POVERTY (PAMPHLET). USA+45 SOCIETY NAT/G
ECO/DEV FINAN LOC/G LEGIS CREATE EDU/PROP CONFER PLAN
GOV/REL GP/REL ROLE 20 POVRTY/WAR. PAGE 4 B0089 ADMIN
N66

PRINCETON U INDUSTRIAL REL SEC.OUTSTANDING BOOKS ON BIBLIOG/A
INDUSTRIAL RELATIONS, 1965 (PAMPHLET NO. 128). INDUS
WOR+45 LABOR BARGAIN GOV/REL RACE/REL HEALTH PWR GP/REL
...MGT 20. PAGE 85 B1709 POLICY
N66

PRINCETON U INDUSTRIAL REL SEC.RECENT MATERIAL ON BIBLIOG/A
COLLECTIVE BARGAINING IN GOVERNMENT (PAMPHLET NO. BARGAIN
130). USA+45 ECO/DEV LABOR WORKER ECO/TAC GOV/REL NAT/G
...MGT 20. PAGE 85 B1710 GP/REL
B67

BENNETT J.W.,HUTTERIAN BRETHREN; THE AGRICULTURAL SECT
ECONOMY AND SOCIAL ORGANIZATION OF A COMMUNAL AGRI
PEOPLE. USA+45 SOCIETY FAM KIN TEC/DEV ADJUST...MGT STRUCT
AUD/VIS GP/COMP 20. PAGE 10 B0213 GP/REL
B67

BUDER S.,PULLMAN: AN EXPERIMENT IN INDUSTRIAL ORDER DIST/IND
AND COMMUNITY PLANNING, 1880-1930. USA+45 SOCIETY INDUS
LABOR LG/CO CREATE PROB/SOLV CONTROL GP/REL MUNIC
EFFICIENCY ATTIT...MGT BIBLIOG 19/20 PULLMAN. PLAN
PAGE 17 B0337
B67

CROTTY W.J.,APPROACHES TO THE STUDY OF PARTY POL/PAR
ORGANIZATION. USA+45 SOCIETY GP/REL...ANTHOL 20. STRUCT
PAGE 25 B0509 GEN/LAWS
ADMIN
B67

FINCHER F.,THE GOVERNMENT OF THE UNITED STATES. NAT/G
USA+45 USA-45 POL/PAR CHIEF CT/SYS LOBBY GP/REL EX/STRUC
INGP/REL...CONCPT CHARTS BIBLIOG T 18/20 PRESIDENT LEGIS
CONGRESS SUPREME/CT. PAGE 35 B0719 OP/RES
B67

GROSSMAN G.,ECONOMIC SYSTEMS. USA+45 USA-45 USSR ECO/DEV
YUGOSLAVIA WORKER CAP/ISM PRICE GP/REL EQUILIB PLAN
WEALTH MARXISM SOCISM...MGT METH/COMP 19/20. TEC/DEV
PAGE 44 B0892 DEMAND
B67

GRUBER H.,INTERNATIONAL COMMUNISM IN THE ERA OF MARXISM
LENIN. COM ADMIN REV GP/REL 20. PAGE 44 B0895 HIST/WRIT
POL/PAR
B67

HOROWITZ I.L.,THE RISE AND FALL OF PROJECT CAMELOT: NAT/G
STUDIES IN THE RELATIONSHIP BETWEEN SOCIAL SCIENCE ACADEM
AND PRACTICAL POLITICS. USA+45 WOR+45 CULTURE ACT/RES
FORCES LEGIS EXEC CIVMIL/REL KNOWL...POLICY SOC GP/REL
METH/CNCPT 20. PAGE 51 B1043
B67

MILNE R.S.,GOVERNMENT AND POLITICS IN MALAYSIA. NAT/G
INDONESIA MALAYSIA LOC/G EX/STRUC FORCES DIPLOM LEGIS
GP/REL 20 SINGAPORE. PAGE 74 B1489 ADMIN
B67

NIVEN R.,NIGERIA. NIGERIA CONSTN INDUS EX/STRUC NAT/G
COLONIAL REV NAT/LISM...CHARTS 19/20. PAGE 78 B1584 REGION
CHOOSE
GP/REL
B67

NORTHRUP H.R.,RESTRICTIVE LABOR PRACTICES IN THE DIST/IND
SUPERMARKET INDUSTRY. USA+45 INDUS WORKER TEC/DEV MARKET
BARGAIN PAY CONTROL GP/REL COST...STAT CHARTS NLRB. LABOR
PAGE 79 B1592 MGT
B67

RALSTON D.B.,THE ARMY OF THE REPUBLIC; THE PLACE OF FORCES
THE MILITARY IN THE POLITICAL EVOLUTION OF FRANCE NAT/G
1871-1914. FRANCE MOD/EUR EX/STRUC LEGIS TOP/EX CIVMIL/REL

DIPLOM ADMIN WAR GP/REL ROLE...BIBLIOG 19/20. POLICY
PAGE 86 B1730
B67

SCHLOSSBERG S.I.,ORGANIZING AND THE LAW. USA+45 LABOR
WORKER PLAN LEGIT REPRESENT GP/REL...JURID MGT 20 CONSULT
NLRB. PAGE 94 B1893 BARGAIN
PRIVIL
L67

BLUMBERG A.S.,"THE PRACTICE OF LAW AS CONFIDENCE CT/SYS
GAME; ORGANIZATIONAL COOPTATION OF A PROFESSION." ADJUD
USA+45 CLIENT SOCIETY CONSULT ROLE JURID. PAGE 13 GP/REL
B0260 ADMIN
L67

GOULD W.B.,"THE STATUS OF UNAUTHORIZED AND ECO/DEV
'WILDCAT' STRIKES UNDER THE NATIONAL LABOR INDUS
RELATIONS ACT." USA+45 ACT/RES BARGAIN ECO/TAC LABOR
LEGIT ADJUD ADMIN GP/REL MGT. PAGE 42 B0842 POLICY
L67

MANNE H.G.,"OUR TWO CORPORATION SYSTEMS* LAW AND INDUS
ECONOMICS." LAW CONTROL SANCTION GP/REL...JURID 20. ELITES
PAGE 69 B1392 CAP/ISM
ADMIN
S67

DIXON O.F.,"A SOCIAL SYSTEMS APPROACH TO MARKET
MARKETING." ECO/DEV ECO/TAC CONTROL EFFICIENCY SOCIETY
...DECISION 20. PAGE 29 B0599 GP/REL
MGT
S67

DONNELL J.C.,"PACIFICATION REASSESSED." VIETNAM/S ADMIN
NAT/LISM DRIVE SUPEGO ORD/FREE...SOC/WK 20. PAGE 30 GP/REL
B0606 EFFICIENCY
MUNIC
S67

EDWARDS H.T.,"POWER STRUCTURE AND ITS COMMUNICATION ELITES
IN SAN JOSE, COSTA RICA." COSTA/RICA L/A+17C STRATA INGP/REL
FACE/GP POL/PAR EX/STRUC PROB/SOLV ADMIN LEAD MUNIC
GP/REL PWR...STAT INT 20. PAGE 32 B0655 DOMIN
S67

FOX R.G.,"FAMILY, CASTE, AND COMMERCE IN A NORTH CULTURE
INDIAN MARKET TOWN." INDIA STRATA AGRI FACE/GP FAM GP/REL
NEIGH OP/RES BARGAIN ADMIN ROUTINE WEALTH...SOC ECO/UNDEV
CHARTS 20. PAGE 37 B0747 DIST/IND
S67

GITTELL M.,"PROFESSIONALISM AND PUBLIC DECISION
PARTICIPATION IN EDUCATIONAL POLICY MAKING." STRUCT PLAN
ADMIN GP/REL ATTIT PWR 20. PAGE 40 B0805 EDU/PROP
MUNIC
S67

GRUNDY K.W.,"THE POLITICAL USES OF IMAGINATION." NAT/LISM
GHANA ELITES SOCIETY NAT/G DOMIN EDU/PROP COLONIAL EX/STRUC
REGION REPRESENT GP/REL CENTRAL PWR MARXISM 20. AFR
PAGE 44 B0897 LEAD
S67

HALL B.,"THE COALITION AGAINST DISHWASHERS." USA+45 LABOR
POL/PAR PROB/SOLV BARGAIN LEAD CHOOSE REPRESENT ADMIN
GP/REL ORD/FREE PWR...POLICY 20. PAGE 46 B0923 DOMIN
WORKER
S67

HUDDLESTON J.,"TRADE UNIONS IN THE GERMAN FEDERAL LABOR
REPUBLIC." EUR+WWI GERMANY/W UK LAW INDUS WORKER GP/REL
CREATE CENTRAL...MGT GP/COMP 20. PAGE 52 B1056 SCHOOL
ROLE
S67

JENCKS C.E.,"SOCIAL STATUS OF COAL MINERS IN EXTR/IND
BRITAIN SINCE NATIONALIZATION." UK STRATA STRUCT WORKER
LABOR RECEIVE GP/REL INCOME OWN ATTIT HABITAT...MGT CONTROL
T 20. PAGE 56 B1128 NAT/G
S67

LA PORTE T.,"DIFFUSION AND DISCONTINUITY IN INTELL
SCIENCE, TECHNOLOGY AND PUBLIC AFFAIRS: RESULTS OF ADMIN
A SEARCH IN THE FIELD." USA+45 ACT/RES TEC/DEV ACADEM
PERS/REL ATTIT PHIL/SCI. PAGE 62 B1249 GP/REL
S67

LANDES W.M.,"THE EFFECT OF STATE FAIR EMPLOYMENT DISCRIM
LAWS ON THE ECONOMIC POSITION OF NONWHITES." USA+45 LAW
PROVS SECT LEGIS ADMIN GP/REL RACE/REL...JURID WORKER
CONCPT CHARTS HYPO/EXP NEGRO. PAGE 62 B1255
S67

LASLETT J.H.M.,"SOCIALISM AND THE AMERICAN LABOR LABOR
MOVEMENT* SOME NEW REFLECTIONS." USA-45 VOL/ASSN ROUTINE
LOBBY PARTIC CENTRAL ALL/VALS SOCISM...GP/COMP 20. ATTIT
PAGE 63 B1265 GP/REL
S67

LEES J.P.,"LEGISLATIVE REVIEW AND BUREAUCRATIC SUPEGO
RESPONSIBILITY." USA+45 FINAN NAT/G DELIB/GP PLAN BUDGET
PROB/SOLV CONFER CONTROL GP/REL DEMAND...DECISION LEGIS
20 CONGRESS PRESIDENT HOUSE/REP BUREAUCRCY. PAGE 63 EXEC
B1281
S67

LINEBERRY R.L.,"REFORMISM AND PUBLIC POLICIES IN DECISION
AMERICAN CITIES." USA+45 POL/PAR EX/STRUC LEGIS POLICY
BUDGET TAX GP/REL...STAT CHARTS. PAGE 65 B1317 MUNIC
LOC/G
S67

LLOYD K.,"URBAN RACE RIOTS V EFFECTIVE ANTI- GP/REL
DISCRIMINATION AGENCIES* AN END OR A BEGINNING?" DISCRIM

USA+45 STRATA ACT/RES ADMIN ADJUST ORD/FREE RESPECT LOC/G
...PLURIST DECISION SOC SOC/WK. PAGE 66 B1332
CROWD
S67

MURRAY R.,"SECOND THOUGHTS ON GHANA." AFR GHANA COLONIAL
NAT/G POL/PAR ADMIN REV GP/REL CENTRAL...SOCIALIST CONTROL
CONCPT METH 20. PAGE 77 B1548
REGION
SOCISM
S67

RAUM O.,"THE MODERN LEADERSHIP GROUP AMONG THE RACE/REL
SOUTH AFRICAN XHOSA." SOUTH/AFR SOCIETY SECT KIN
EX/STRUC REPRESENT GP/REL INGP/REL PERSON LEAD
...METH/COMP 17/20 XHOSA NEGRO. PAGE 86 B1743
CULTURE
S67

RUBIN R.I.,"THE LEGISLATIVE-EXECUTIVE RELATIONS OF LEGIS
THE UNITED STATES INFORMATION AGENCY." USA+45 EX/STRUC
EDU/PROP TASK INGP/REL EFFICIENCY ISOLAT ATTIT ROLE GP/REL
USIA CONGRESS. PAGE 91 B1850
PROF/ORG
S67

SMITH W.H.T.,"THE IMPLICATIONS OF THE AMERICAN BAR EDU/PROP
ASSOCIATION ADVISORY COMMITTEE RECOMMENDATIONS FOR CONTROL
POLICE ADMINISTRATION." ADMIN...JURID 20 ABA. GP/REL
PAGE 98 B1986
ORD/FREE
S67

SPACKMAN A.,"THE SENATE OF TRINIDAD AND TOBAGO." ELITES
L/A+17C TRINIDAD WEST/IND NAT/G POL/PAR DELIB/GP EFFICIENCY
OP/RES PROB/SOLV EDU/PROP EXEC LOBBY ROUTINE LEGIS
REPRESENT GP/REL 20. PAGE 99 B2002
DECISION
S67

SUBRAMANIAM V.,"REPRESENTATIVE BUREAUCRACY: A STRATA
REASSESSMENT." USA+45 ELITES LOC/G NAT/G ADMIN GP/REL
GOV/REL PRIVIL DRIVE ROLE...POLICY CENSUS 20 MGT
CIVIL/SERV BUREAUCRCY. PAGE 101 B2053
GOV/COMP
N67

NATIONAL COMN COMMUNITY HEALTH,ACTION - PLANNING PLAN
FOR COMMUNITY HEALTH SERVICES (PAMPHLET). USA+45 MUNIC
PROF/ORG DELIB/GP BUDGET ROUTINE GP/REL ATTIT HEALTH
...HEAL SOC SOC/WK CHARTS TIME 20. PAGE 77 B1563
ADJUST
N67

PRINCETON U INDUSTRIAL REL SEC,OUTSTANDING BOOKS ON BIBLIOG/A
INDUSTRIAL RELATIONS, 1966 (PAMPHLET NO. 134). INDUS
WOR+45 LABOR WORKER PLAN PRICE CONTROL INCOME...MGT GP/REL
20. PAGE 85 B1711
POLICY
S68

GRAM H.A.,"BUSINESS ETHICS AND THE CORPORATION." POLICY
LG/CO SECT PROB/SOLV CONTROL EXEC GP/REL INGP/REL ADMIN
PERS/REL ROLE MORAL PWR...DECISION 20. PAGE 42 MGT
B0850

GRABER D. B0848

GRAFT....SEE TRIBUTE

GRAHAM G.A. B0849

GRAM H.A. B0850

GRAND/JURY....GRAND JURIES

GRANGE....GRANGE AND GRANGERS

GRANICK D. B0851,B0852

GRANT D.R. B0853

GRANT/US....PRESIDENT ULYSSES S. GRANT

GRANTS....SEE GIVE+FOR/AID

GRAPHIC PRESENTATION....SEE CHARTS

GRASSMUCK G.L. B0854

GRAVES J. B1545

GRAVES R.L. B2108

GRAVES W.B. B0855,B0856,B0857,B0858

GRAVIER J.F. B0859

GRAY R.K. B0860

GREAT BRITAIN....SEE UK

GREAT BRITAIN DEPT TECH COOP B0861

GREAT BRITAIN TREASURY B0862

GREAT/SOC....GREAT SOCIETY

GREBLER L. B0863

GRECO/ROMN....GRECO-ROMAN CIVILIZATION

GREECE....MODERN GREECE

KOUSOULAS D.G.,REVOLUTION AND DEFEAT; THE STORY OF REV
THE GREEK COMMUNIST PARTY. GREECE INT/ORG EX/STRUC MARXISM
DIPLOM FOR/AID EDU/PROP PARL/PROC ADJUST ATTIT 20 POL/PAR
COM/PARTY. PAGE 61 B1230
ORD/FREE
B65

LAMBIRI I.,SOCIAL CHANGE IN A GREEK COUNTRY TOWN. INDUS
GREECE FAM PROB/SOLV ROUTINE TASK LEISURE INGP/REL WORKER
CONSEN ORD/FREE...SOC INT QU CHARTS 20. PAGE 62 CULTURE
B1252
NEIGH
B65

ORG FOR ECO COOP AND DEVEL,THE MEDITERRANEAN PLAN
REGIONAL PROJECT: AN EXPERIMENT IN PLANNING BY SIX ECO/UNDEV
COUNTRIES. FUT GREECE SPAIN TURKEY YUGOSLAVIA ACADEM
SOCIETY FINAN NAT/G PROF/ORG EDU/PROP ADMIN REGION SCHOOL
COST...POLICY STAT CHARTS 20 OECD. PAGE 80 B1614

GREECE/ANC....ANCIENT GREECE

GREEK ORTHODOX CATHOLIC....SEE ORTHO/GK

GREEN H.P. B0864

GREEN/TH....T.H. GREEN

GREENBACK....GREENBACK PARTY

GREENE K.R.C. B0865

GREENE L.S. B0866,B0867

GREENEWALT C.H. B0868

GREENWICH VILLAGE....SEE GRNWCH/VIL

GREENWICH....GREENWICH, ENGLAND

GREER S. B0869,B0870,B0871

GREGG J.L. B0872

GRENADA....GRENADA (WEST INDIES)

GRENIEWSKI H. B0873

GRENVILLES....GRENVILLES - ENGLISH FAMILY; SEE ALSO UK

GRESHAM-YANG TREATY....SEE GRESHMYANG

GRESHAM'S LAW....SEE GRESHM/LAW

GRESHM/LAW....GRESHAM'S LAW

GRESHMYANG....GRESHAM-YANG TREATY

GRETHER E.T. B0874

GRIFFIN A.P.C. B0875

GRIFFIN G.G. B0876

GRIFFITH E.S. B0877,B0878

GRIFFITH J.A.G. B0879

GRIFFITH W. B0880

GRINYER P.H. B0882

GRNWCH/VIL....GREENWICH VILLAGE

GRODZINS M. B0883

GROGAN V. B0884

GROSS B.M. B0885,B0886,B0887

GROSS C. B0888

GROSS H. B0889

GROSS J.A. B0890

GROSS NATIONAL PRODUCT....WEALTH+ECO+PRODUC

GROSSMAN G. B0891,B0892

GROSSMAN J. B0893

GROUP RELATIONS....SEE GP/REL

GROVE J.W. B0894

GROWTH....SEE CREATE,CREATE+ECO/UNDEV

GRUBER H. B0895

GRUNDLICH T. B0896

GRUNDY K.W. B0897

GRUNEWALD D. B0711

GRZYBOWSKI K. B0898

GT BRIT ADMIN STAFF COLLEGE B0899

GUAITA A. B0900

GUAM....GUAM

B59
COUNCIL OF STATE GOVERNORS,AMERICAN LEGISLATURES: LEGIS
STRUCTURE AND PROCEDURES. SUMMARY AND TABULATIONS CHARTS
OF A 1959 SURVEY. PUERT/RICO USA+45 PAY ADJUD ADMIN PROVS
APPORT...IDEA/COMP 20 GUAM VIRGIN/ISL. PAGE 24 REPRESENT
B0495

GUATEMALA....SEE ALSO L/A+17C

B65
GREGG J.L.,POLITICAL PARTIES AND PARTY SYSTEMS IN LEAD
GUATEMALA, 1944-1963. GUATEMALA L/A+17C EX/STRUC POL/PAR
FORCES CREATE CONTROL REV CHOOSE PWR...TREND NAT/G
IDEA/COMP 20. PAGE 43 B0872 CHIEF

GUEMES/M....MARTIN GUEMES

GUERRILLA....GUERRILLA WARFARE

B61
MUNGER E.S.,AFRICAN FIELD REPORTS 1952-1961. AFR
SOUTH/AFR SOCIETY ECO/UNDEV NAT/G POL/PAR COLONIAL DISCRIM
EXEC PARL/PROC GUERRILLA RACE/REL ALL/IDEOS...SOC RECORD
AUD/VIS 20. PAGE 76 B1538

B64
PARET P.,FRENCH REVOLUTIONARY WARFARE FROM FRANCE
INDOCHINA TO ALGERIA* THE ANALYSIS OF A POLITICAL GUERRILLA
AND MILITARY DOCTRINE. ALGERIA VIETNAM FORCES GEN/LAWS
OP/RES TEC/DEV ROUTINE REV ATTIT...PSY BIBLIOG.
PAGE 81 B1632

B65
PUSTAY J.S.,COUNTER-INSURGENCY WARFARE. COM USA+45 FORCES
LOC/G NAT/G ACT/RES EDU/PROP ADMIN COERCE ATTIT PWR
...CONCPT MARX/KARL 20. PAGE 85 B1722 GUERRILLA

S67
NEUCHTERLEIN D.E.,"THAILAND* ANOTHER VIETNAM?" WAR
THAILAND ECO/UNDEV DIPLOM ADMIN REGION CENTRAL GUERRILLA
NAT/LISM...POLICY 20. PAGE 78 B1571 S/ASIA
NAT/G

GUETZKOW H. B0453,B0901,B1397

GUEVARA/E....ERNESTO GUEVARA

GUIANA/BR....BRITISH GUIANA; SEE ALSO GUYANA

GUIANA/FR....FRENCH GUIANA

GUILDS....SEE PROF/ORG

GUINEA....SEE ALSO AFR

GUJARAT....GUJARAT (STATE OF INDIA)

GULICK C.A. B0902

GULICK L. B0903,B0904

GUNTER E. B2252

GUTTMAN/L....LOUIS GUTTMAN (AND GUTTMAN SCALE)

GUTTSMAN W.L. B0905

GUYANA....GUYANA; SEE ALSO GUIANA/BR, L/A+17C

GUYOT J.F. B0906

GUZZARDI W. B0907

───────────────H───────────────

HAAS E.B. B0908,B0909,B0910

HAASE A.R. B0911

HABERST C.T. B1846

HABITAT....ECOLOGY

N19
RIDLEY C.E.,MEASURING MUNICIPAL ACTIVITIES MGT

(PAMPHLET). FINAN SERV/IND FORCES RECEIVE INGP/REL HEALTH
HABITAT...POLICY SOC/WK 20. PAGE 88 B1779 WEALTH
LOC/G

N19
VERNON R.,THE MYTH AND REALITY OF OUR URBAN PLAN
PROBLEMS (PAMPHLET). USA+45 SOCIETY LOC/G ADMIN MUNIC
COST 20 PRINCETN/U INTERVENT URBAN/RNWL. PAGE 112 HABITAT
B2261 PROB/SOLV

B37
GULICK L.,PAPERS ON THE SCIENCE OF ADMINISTRATION. OP/RES
INDUS PROB/SOLV TEC/DEV COST EFFICIENCY PRODUC CONTROL
HABITAT...PHIL/SCI METH/COMP 20. PAGE 45 B0903 ADMIN
MGT

B42
JONES V.,METROPOLITAN GOVERNMENT. HABITAT ALL/VALS LOC/G
...MGT SOC CHARTS. PAGE 57 B1151 MUNIC
ADMIN
TECHRACY

B48
HOOVER E.M.,THE LOCATION OF ECONOMIC ACTIVITY. HABITAT
WOR+45 MARKET MUNIC WORKER PROB/SOLV INT/TRADE INDUS
ADMIN COST...POLICY CHARTS T 20. PAGE 51 B1041 ECO/TAC
GEOG

B50
DEES J.W. JR.,URBAN SOCIOLOGY AND THE EMERGING PLAN
ATOMIC MEGALOPOLIS. PART I. USA+45 TEC/DEV ADMIN NEIGH
NUC/PWR HABITAT...SOC AUD/VIS CHARTS GEN/LAWS 20 MUNIC
WATER. PAGE 28 B0568 PROB/SOLV

B53
WAGLEY C.,AMAZON TOWN: A STUDY OF MAN IN THE SOC
TROPICS. BRAZIL L/A+17C STRATA STRUCT ECO/UNDEV NEIGH
AGRI EX/STRUC RACE/REL DISCRIM HABITAT WEALTH...OBS CULTURE
SOC/EXP 20. PAGE 113 B2273 INGP/REL

B55
UN ECONOMIC AND SOCIAL COUNCIL,BIBLIOGRAPHY OF BIBLIOG/A
PUBLICATIONS OF THE UN AND SPECIALIZED AGENCIES IN SOC/WK
THE SOCIAL WELFARE FIELD, 1946-1952. WOR+45 FAM ADMIN
INT/ORG MUNIC ACT/RES PLAN PROB/SOLV EDU/PROP AGE/C WEALTH
AGE/Y HABITAT...HEAL UN. PAGE 106 B2148

B56
INTERNATIONAL AFRICAN INST,SELECT ANNOTATED BIBLIOG/A
BIBLIOGRAPHY OF TROPICAL AFRICA. NAT/G EDU/PROP AFR
ADMIN HEALTH. PAGE 54 B1095 SOC
HABITAT

B56
WHYTE W.H. JR.,THE ORGANIZATION MAN. CULTURE FINAN ADMIN
VOL/ASSN DOMIN EDU/PROP EXEC DISPL HABITAT ROLE LG/CO
...PERS/TEST STERTYP. PAGE 116 B2343 PERSON
CONSEN

S56
MARGOLIS J.,"ON MUNICIPAL LAND POLICY FOR FISCAL BUDGET
GAINS." USA+45 MUNIC PLAN TAX COST EFFICIENCY POLICY
HABITAT KNOWL...MGT 20. PAGE 69 B1398 GEOG
LOC/G

B57
DE GRAZIA A.,GRASS ROOTS PRIVATE WELFARE. LOC/G NEW/LIB
SCHOOL ACT/RES EDU/PROP ROUTINE CROWD GP/REL HEALTH
DISCRIM HAPPINESS ILLEGIT AGE HABITAT. PAGE 27 MUNIC
B0554 VOL/ASSN

B60
CORSON J.J.,GOVERNANCE OF COLLEGES AND ADMIN
UNIVERSITIES. STRUCT FINAN DELIB/GP DOMIN EDU/PROP EXEC
LEAD CHOOSE GP/REL CENTRAL COST PRIVIL SUPEGO ACADEM
ORD/FREE PWR...DECISION BIBLIOG. PAGE 24 B0481 HABITAT

B60
LINDVEIT E.N.,SCIENTISTS IN GOVERNMENT. USA+45 PAY TEC/DEV
EDU/PROP ADMIN DRIVE HABITAT ROLE...TECHNIC BIBLIOG ECO/TAC
20. PAGE 65 B1316 PHIL/SCI
GOV/REL

B61
JACOBS J.,THE DEATH AND LIFE OF GREAT AMERICAN MUNIC
CITIES. USA+45 SOCIETY DIST/IND CREATE PROB/SOLV PLAN
ADMIN...GEOG SOC CENSUS 20 URBAN/RNWL. PAGE 55 ADJUST
B1113 HABITAT

B61
KEE R.,REFUGEE WORLD. AUSTRIA EUR+WWI GERMANY NEIGH NAT/G
EX/STRUC WORKER PROB/SOLV ECO/TAC RENT EDU/PROP GIVE
INGP/REL COST LITERACY HABITAT 20 MIGRATION. WEALTH
PAGE 59 B1186 STRANGE

B61
LEE R.R.,ENGINEERING-ECONOMIC PLANNING BIBLIOG/A
MISCELLANEOUS SUBJECTS: A SELECTED BIBLIOGRAPHY PLAN
(MIMEOGRAPHED). FINAN LOC/G MUNIC NEIGH ADMIN REGION
CONTROL INGP/REL HABITAT...GEOG MGT SOC/WK 20
RESOURCE/N. PAGE 63 B1280

B61
PETRULLO L.,LEADERSHIP AND INTERPERSONAL BEHAVIOR. PERSON
FACE/GP FAM PROF/ORG EX/STRUC FORCES DOMIN WAR ATTIT
GP/REL PERS/REL EFFICIENCY PRODUC PWR...MGT PSY. LEAD
PAGE 82 B1663 HABITAT

B62
MARTIN R.C.,GOVERNMENT AND THE SUBURBAN SCHOOL. SCHOOL
USA+45 FINAN EDU/PROP ADMIN HABITAT...TREND GP/COMP LOC/G
20. PAGE 70 B1414 EX/STRUC
ISOLAT

B62

MUNICIPAL MANPOWER COMMISSION,GOVERNMENTAL MANPOWER LOC/G
FOR TOMORROW'S CITIES: A REPORT. USA+45 DELIB/GP MUNIC
EX/STRUC PROB/SOLV TEC/DEV EDU/PROP ADMIN LEAD LABOR
HABITAT. PAGE 76 B1539 GOV/REL

B62

WENDT P.F.,HOUSING POLICY - THE SEARCH FOR PLAN
SOLUTIONS. GERMANY/W SWEDEN UK USA+45 OP/RES ADMIN
HABITAT WEALTH...SOC/WK CHARTS 20. PAGE 115 B2322 METH/COMP
NAT/G

B63

BONINI C.P.,SIMULATION OF INFORMATION AND DECISION INDUS
SYSTEMS IN THE FIRM. MARKET BUDGET DOMIN EDU/PROP SIMUL
ADMIN COST ATTIT HABITAT PERCEPT PWR...CONCPT DECISION
PROBABIL QUANT PREDICT HYPO/EXP BIBLIOG. PAGE 13 MGT
B0273

B64

HAMILTON B.L.S.,PROBLEMS OF ADMINISTRATION IN AN ADMIN
EMERGENT NATION: CASE STUDY OF JAMAICA. JAMAICA UK ECO/UNDEV
WOR+45 MUNIC COLONIAL HABITAT...CHARTS BIBLIOG 20 GOV/REL
CIVIL/SERV. PAGE 46 B0932 NAT/G

B65

ARTHUR D LITTLE INC,SAN FRANCISCO COMMUNITY RENEWAL HABITAT
PROGRAM. USA+45 FINAN PROVS ADMIN INCOME...CHARTS MUNIC
20 CALIFORNIA SAN/FRAN URBAN/RNWL. PAGE 7 B0138 PLAN
PROB/SOLV

B65

BARISH N.N.,MANAGEMENT SCIENCES IN THE EMERGING ECO/UNDEV
COUNTRIES. AFR CHINA/COM WOR+45 FINAN INDUS PLAN OP/RES
PRODUC HABITAT...ANTHOL 20. PAGE 9 B0184 MGT
TEC/DEV

B65

BERNDT R.M.,ABORIGINAL MAN IN AUSTRALIA. LAW DOMIN SOC
ADMIN COLONIAL MARRIAGE HABITAT ORD/FREE...LING CULTURE
CHARTS ANTHOL BIBLIOG WORSHIP 20 AUSTRAL ABORIGINES SOCIETY
MUSIC ELKIN/AP. PAGE 11 B0225 STRUCT

B66

ASHRAF A.,THE CITY GOVERNMENT OF CALCUTTA: A STUDY LOC/G
OF INERTIA. INDIA ELITES INDUS NAT/G EX/STRUC MUNIC
ACT/RES PLAN PROB/SOLV LEAD HABITAT...BIBLIOG 20 ADMIN
CALCUTTA. PAGE 7 B0141 ECO/UNDEV

B66

BOYD H.W.,MARKETING MANAGEMENT: CASES FROM EMERGING MGT
COUNTRIES. BRAZIL GHANA ISRAEL WOR+45 ADMIN ECO/UNDEV
PERS/REL ATTIT HABITAT WEALTH...ANTHOL 20 ARGEN PROB/SOLV
CASEBOOK. PAGE 14 B0292 MARKET

B66

BRAIBANTI R.,RESEARCH ON THE BUREAUCRACY OF HABITAT
PAKISTAN. PAKISTAN LAW CULTURE INTELL ACADEM LOC/G NAT/G
SECT PRESS CT/SYS...LING CHARTS 20 BUREAUCRCY. ADMIN
PAGE 15 B0299 CONSTN

B67

DUN J.L.,THE ESSENCE OF CHINESE CIVILIZATION. ASIA CULTURE
FAM NAT/G TEC/DEV ADMIN SANCTION WAR HABITAT SOCIETY
...ANTHOL WORSHIP. PAGE 31 B0630

B67

US DEPARTMENT HEALTH EDUC WELF,NEW PROGRAMS IN ADMIN
HEALTH, EDUCATION, WELFARE, HOUSING AND URBAN HEALTH
DEVELOPMENT FOR PERSONS AND FAMILIES -LOW, MOD' SCHOOL
INCOME. USA+45 MUNIC NAT/G EDU/PROP GOV/REL HABITAT
INGP/REL ORD/FREE 20 DEPT/HEW DEPT/HUD. PAGE 108
B2180

S67

FRYKENBURG R.E.,"STUDIES OF LAND CONTROL IN INDIAN ECO/UNDEV
HISTORY: REVIEW ARTICLE." INDIA UK STRATA AGRI CONTROL
MUNIC OP/RES COLONIAL REGION EFFICIENCY OWN HABITAT ADMIN
...CONCPT 16/20. PAGE 38 B0763

S67

JENCKS C.E.,"SOCIAL STATUS OF COAL MINERS IN EXTR/IND
BRITAIN SINCE NATIONALIZATION." UK STRATA STRUCT WORKER
LABOR RECEIVE GP/REL INCOME OWN ATTIT HABITAT...MGT CONTROL
T 20. PAGE 56 B1128 NAT/G

S67

LEVIN M.R.,"PLANNERS AND METROPOLITAN PLANNING." PLAN
FUT USA+45 SOCIETY NAT/G PROVS PROB/SOLV LEAD MUNIC
PARTIC GOV/REL RACE/REL HABITAT ROLE. PAGE 64 B1301 R+D
ADMIN

HADWEN J.G. B0912

HADWIGER D.F. B0913

HADY T.F. B0914

HAGUE/F....FRANK HAGUE

HAIGHT D.E. B0915

HAILEY B0916,B0917

HAINES R.M. B0918

HAIRE M. B0521,B0919,B0920

HAITI....SEE ALSO L/A+17C

HAKLUYT/R....RICHARD HAKLUYT

HALDANE R.B. B0921

HALL B. B0922,B0923

HALL M. B0924

HALL W.P. B0925

HALLECK/C....CHARLES HALLECK

HALLER W. B0926

HALPERIN M.H. B0927,B0928

HALPIN A.W. B0929

HAMBRIDGE G. B0930

HAMBRO E. B0826

HAMBURG....HAMBURG, GERMANY

B59

IPSEN H.P.,HAMBURGISCHES STAATS- UND ADMIN
VERWALTUNGSRECHT. CONSTN LOC/G FORCES BUDGET CT/SYS PROVS
...JURID 20 HAMBURG. PAGE 54 B1103 LEGIS
FINAN

HAMILTON A. B0931

HAMILTON B.L.S. B0932

HAMILTON R.F. B0933

HAMILTON/A....ALEXANDER HAMILTON

B48

WHITE L.D.,THE FEDERALISTS: A STUDY IN ADMIN
ADMINISTRATIVE HISTORY. STRUCT DELIB/GP LEGIS NAT/G
BUDGET ROUTINE GOV/REL GP/REL PERS/REL PWR...BIOG POLICY
18/19 PRESIDENT CONGRESS WASHINGT/G JEFFERSN/T PROB/SOLV
HAMILTON/A. PAGE 116 B2337

HAMMARSK/D....DAG HAMMARSKJOLD

L67

COHEN M.,"THE DEMISE OF UNEF." CONSTN DIPLOM ADMIN INT/ORG
AGREE LEAD COERCE 20 UNEF U/THANT HAMMARSK/D. FORCES
PAGE 22 B0445 PEACE
POLICY

HAMMARSKJOLD, DAG....SEE HAMMARSK/D

HAMMOND A. B0934

HAMMOND P.Y. B0935,B1890

HANBURY H.G. B0936

HANKE L. B0937

HANNA W.J. B0938

HANNA/MARK....MARK HANNA

HANSON A.H. B0939,B0940,B0941,B0942

HAPPINESS.... HAPPINESS AS A CONDITION (UNHAPPINESS)

C51

HOMANS G.C.,"THE WESTERN ELECTRIC RESEARCHES" IN S. OP/RES
HOSLETT, ED., HUMAN FACTORS IN MANAGEMENT (BMR)" EFFICIENCY
ACT/RES GP/REL HAPPINESS PRODUC DRIVE...MGT OBS 20. SOC/EXP
PAGE 51 B1037 WORKER

B56

GLADDEN E.N.,CIVIL SERVICE OR BUREAUCRACY? UK LAW ADMIN
STRATA LABOR TOP/EX PLAN SENIOR AUTOMAT CONTROL GOV/REL
PARTIC CHOOSE HAPPINESS...CHARTS 19/20 CIVIL/SERV EFFICIENCY
BUREAUCRCY. PAGE 40 B0808 PROVS

B57

DE GRAZIA A.,GRASS ROOTS PRIVATE WELFARE. LOC/G NEW/LIB
SCHOOL ACT/RES EDU/PROP ROUTINE CROWD GP/REL HEALTH
DISCRIM HAPPINESS ILLEGIT AGE HABITAT. PAGE 27 MUNIC
B0554 VOL/ASSN

B59

INDIAN INSTITUTE PUBLIC ADMIN,MORALE IN THE PUBLIC HAPPINESS
SERVICES: REPORT OF A CONFERENCE JAN., 3-4, 1959. ADMIN
INDIA S/ASIA ECO/UNDEV PROVS PLAN EDU/PROP CONFER WORKER
GOV/REL EFFICIENCY DRIVE ROLE 20 CIVIL/SERV. INGP/REL
PAGE 53 B1082

B61

BIRNBACH B.,NEO-FREUDIAN SOCIAL PHILOSOPHY. TEC/DEV SOCIETY
INGP/REL ADJUST HAPPINESS SUPEGO HEALTH...CONCPT PSY
GEN/LAWS BIBLIOG 20. PAGE 12 B0242 PERSON

WALKER N.,MORALE IN THE CIVIL SERVICE. UK EXEC LEAD INGP/REL EFFICIENCY HAPPINESS 20. PAGE 113 B2280
ADMIN
B61
ATTIT
WORKER
ADMIN
PSY

GIDWANI K.A.,"LEADER BEHAVIOUR IN ELECTED AND NON-ELECTED GROUPS." DELIB/GP ROUTINE TASK HAPPINESS AUTHORIT...SOC STAT CHARTS SOC/EXP. PAGE 39 B0796
S62
LEAD
INGP/REL
GP/COMP
CHOOSE

LIPSET S.M.,THE BERKELEY STUDENT REVOLT: FACTS AND INTERPRETATIONS. USA+45 INTELL VOL/ASSN CONSULT EDU/PROP PRESS DEBATE ADMIN REV HAPPINESS RIGID/FLEX MAJORIT. PAGE 65 B1322
B65
CROWD
ACADEM
ATTIT
GP/REL

DICKSON W.J.,COUNSELING IN AN ORGANIZATION: A SEQUEL TO THE HAWTHORNE RESEARCHES. CLIENT VOL/ASSN ACT/RES PROB/SOLV AUTOMAT ROUTINE PERS/REL HAPPINESS ANOMIE ROLE...OBS CHARTS 20 AT+T. PAGE 29 B0588
B66
INDUS
WORKER
PSY
MGT

THOENES P.,THE ELITE IN THE WELFARE STATE ,TRANS. BY J BINGHAM; ED. BY. STRATA NAT/G GP/REL HAPPINESS INCOME OPTIMAL MORAL PWR WEALTH...POLICY CONCPT. PAGE 104 B2097
B66
ADMIN
ELITES
MGT
WELF/ST

HAPSBURG....HAPSBURG MONARCHY

HAPTHEKER....HAPTHEKER THEORY

HARARI M. B0943

HARBOLD W.H. B1019

HARDING/WG....PRESIDENT WARREN G. HARDING

HARDMAN J.B. B0944,B0945

HARGIS/BJ....BILLY JAMES HARGIS

HARGROVE M.M. B0946

HARLAN/JM....JOHN MARSHALL HARLAN

HARLEM....HARLEM

HARLOW R.F. B0947

HARLOW R.V. B0948

HARMON R.B. B0949,B0950,B0951

HAROOTUNIAN H.D. B1952

HARPER S.N. B0952

HARR J.E. B0953

HARRIMAN/A....AVERILL HARRIMAN

HARRIS C.L. B1906

HARRIS J.P. B0482,B0954

HARRIS R.L. B0955

HARRISN/WH....PRESIDENT WILLIAM HENRY HARRISON

HARRISON I.H. B0946

HARRISON R. B0131

HARRISON S. B0956

HARRISON/B....PRESIDENT BENJAMIN HARRISON

HART H.C. B0957

HART J. B0958,B0959,B0960

HART W.R. B0961

HARTLAND P.C. B0962

HARVARD UNIVERSITY LAW LIBRARY B0963

HARVARD/U....HARVARD UNIVERSITY

HARVEY M.F. B0964

HARWITZ M. B0996

HASAN H.S. B0965

HASTINGS P.G. B0966

HATCHER/R....RICHARD HATCHER

HATHAWAY D.A. B0967

HATRED....SEE LOVE

HATTERY L.H. B0968

HAUSER O. B0969

HAUSMAN W.H. B0970

HAVILAND H.F. B0971,B0972

HAWAII....HAWAII

HAWLEY C.E. B0973

HAY P. B2026

HAYEK/V.... FRIEDRICH AUGUST VON HAYEK

HAYER T. B0975

HAYES/RB....PRESIDENT RUTHERFORD B. HAYES

HAYMAN D. B0976

HAYNES G.H. B0977

HAYTER W. B0978

HEAD/START....THE "HEAD START" PROGRAM

HEADLAM-MORLEY B0979

HEADY F. B0980,B0981,B0982

HEAL....HEALTH SCIENCES

AUSTRALIAN NATIONAL RES COUN,AUSTRALIAN SOCIAL SCIENCE ABSTRACTS. NEW/ZEALND CULTURE SOCIETY LOC/G CT/SYS PARL/PROC...HEAL JURID PSY SOC 20 AUSTRAL. PAGE 7 B0149
N
BIBLIOG/A
POLICY
NAT/G
ADMIN

HODGSON J.G.,THE OFFICIAL PUBLICATIONS OF AMERICAN COUNTIES: A UNION LIST. SCHOOL BUDGET...HEAL MGT SOC/WK 19/20. PAGE 51 B1026
B37
BIBLIOG
LOC/G
PUB/INST

DAHL D.,SICKNESS BENEFITS AND GROUP PURCHASE OF MEDICAL CARE FOR INDUSTRIAL EMPLOYEES. FAM LABOR NAT/G PLAN...POLICY MGT SOC STAT 20. PAGE 25 B0519
B44
BIBLIOG/A
INDUS
WORKER
HEAL

BUSH V.,SCIENCE, THE ENDLESS FRONTIER. FUT USA-45 INTELL STRATA ACT/RES CREATE PLAN EDU/PROP ADMIN NUC/PWR PEACE ATTIT HEALTH KNOWL...MAJORIT HEAL MGT PHIL/SCI CONCPT OBS TREND 20. PAGE 18 B0360
B45
R+D
NAT/G

CRAIG J.,BIBLIOGRAPHY OF PUBLIC ADMINISTRATION IN AUSTRALIA. CONSTN FINAN EX/STRUC LEGIS PLAN DIPLOM RECEIVE ADJUD ROUTINE...HEAL 19/20 AUSTRAL PARLIAMENT. PAGE 24 B0500
B55
BIBLIOG
GOV/REL
ADMIN
NAT/G

PALMER A.M.,ADMINISTRATION OF MEDICAL AND PHARMACEUTICAL PATENTS (PAMPHLET). USA+45 PROF/ORG ADMIN PHIL/SCI. PAGE 80 B1626
B55
HEAL
ACADEM
LAW
LICENSE

UN ECONOMIC AND SOCIAL COUNCIL,BIBLIOGRAPHY OF PUBLICATIONS OF THE UN AND SPECIALIZED AGENCIES IN THE SOCIAL WELFARE FIELD, 1946-1952. WOR+45 FAM INT/ORG MUNIC ACT/RES PLAN PROB/SOLV EDU/PROP AGE/C AGE/Y HABITAT...HEAL UN. PAGE 106 B2148
B55
BIBLIOG/A
SOC/WK
ADMIN
WEALTH

CENTRAL ASIAN RESEARCH CENTRE,BIBLIOGRAPHY OF RECENT SOVIET SOURCE MATERIAL ON SOVIET CENTRAL ASIA AND THE BORDERLANDS. AFGHANISTN INDIA PAKISTAN UAR USSR ECO/UNDEV AGRI EXTR/IND INDUS ACADEM ADMIN ...HEAL HUM LING CON/ANAL 20. PAGE 19 B0399
B57
BIBLIOG/A
COM
CULTURE
NAT/G

COUNCIL OF STATE GOVERNMENTS,STATE GOVERNMENT: AN ANNOTATED BIBLIOGRAPHY (PAMPHLET). USA+45 LAW AGRI INDUS WORKER PLAN TAX ADJUST AGE/Y ORD/FREE...HEAL MGT 20. PAGE 24 B0494
B59
BIBLIOG/A
PROVS
LOC/G
ADMIN

JONES V.,METROPOLITAN COMMUNITIES: A BIBLIOGRAPHY WITH SPECIAL EMPHASIS UPON GOVERNMENT AND POLITICS, 1955-1957. STRUCT ECO/DEV FORCES PLAN PROB/SOLV RECEIVE EDU/PROP CT/SYS...GEOG HEAL 20. PAGE 57 B1152
B60
BIBLIOG
LOC/G
MUNIC
ADMIN

B61
CONFREY E.A.,ADMINISTRATION OF COMMUNITY HEALTH
SERVICES. USA+45 R+D PUB/INST DELIB/GP PLAN BUDGET
ROUTINE AGE/C HEALTH...MGT SOC/WK METH/COMP 20.
PAGE 23 B0461

HEAL
ADMIN
MUNIC
BIO/SOC

B62
ROBINSON M.,THE COMING OF AGE OF THE LANGLEY PORTER
CLINIC (PAMPHLET). USA+45 PROF/ORG PROVS PLAN...MGT
PSY 20 CALIFORNIA LANGLEY. PAGE 89 B1804

PUB/INST
ADMIN
EFFICIENCY
HEAL

B63
CHOJNACKI S.,REGISTER ON CURRENT RESEARCH ON
ETHIOPIA AND THE HORN OF AFRICA. ETHIOPIA LAW
CULTURE AGRI SECT EDU/PROP ADMIN...GEOG HEAL LING
20. PAGE 21 B0426

BIBLIOG
ACT/RES
INTELL
ACADEM

B63
HERMAN H.,NEW YORK STATE AND THE METROPOLITAN
PROBLEM. USA+45 ECO/DEV PUB/INST SCHOOL LEGIS PLAN
TAX EXEC PARL/PROC PARTIC...HEAL 20 NEW/YORK.
PAGE 49 B0992

GOV/REL
PROVS
LOC/G
POLICY

B64
FALK L.A.,ADMINISTRATIVE ASPECTS OF GROUP PRACTICE.
USA+45 FINAN PROF/ORG PLAN MGT. PAGE 35 B0702

BIBLIOG/A
HEAL
ADMIN
SERV/IND

B64
SULLIVAN G.,THE STORY OF THE PEACE CORPS. USA+45
WOR+45 INTELL FACE/GP SCHOOL VOL/ASSN CONSULT
EX/STRUC PLAN EDU/PROP ADMIN ATTIT DRIVE ALL/VALS
...POLICY HEAL SOC CONCPT INT QU BIOG TREND SOC/EXP
WORK. PAGE 102 B2054

INT/ORG
ECO/UNDEV
FOR/AID
PEACE

B64
THE BRITISH COUNCIL,PUBLIC ADMINISTRATION: A SELECT
LIST OF BOOKS AND PERIODICALS. LAW CONSTN FINAN
POL/PAR SCHOOL CHOOSE...HEAL MGT METH/COMP 19/20
CMN/WLTH. PAGE 104 B2094

BIBLIOG
ADMIN
LOC/G
INDUS

B64
TOMPKINS D.C.,PROBATION SINCE WORLD WAR II. USA+45
FORCES ADMIN ROUTINE PERS/REL AGE...CRIMLGY HEAL
20. PAGE 105 B2118

BIBLIOG
PUB/INST
ORD/FREE
CRIME

B64
WITHERELL J.W.,OFFICIAL PUBLICATIONS OF FRENCH
EQUATORIAL AFRICA, FRENCH CAMEROONS, AND TOGO,
1946-1958 (PAMPHLET). CAMEROON CHAD FRANCE GABON
TOGO LAW ECO/UNDEV EXTR/IND INT/TRADE...GEOG HEAL
20. PAGE 117 B2367

BIBLIOG/A
AFR
NAT/G
ADMIN

B66
WYLIE C.M.,RESEARCH IN PUBLIC HEALTH
ADMINISTRATION; SELECTED RECENT ABSTRACTS IV
(PAMPHLET). USA+45 MUNIC PUB/INST ACT/RES CREATE
OP/RES TEC/DEV GP/REL ROLE...MGT PHIL/SCI STAT.
PAGE 118 B2387

BIBLIOG/A
R+D
HEAL
ADMIN

L67
ROBERTS J.C.,"CIVIL RESTRAINT, MENTAL ILLNESS, AND
THE RIGHT TO TREATMENT." PROB/SOLV ADMIN PERSON
HEAL. PAGE 89 B1795

HEALTH
ORD/FREE
COERCE
LAW

N67
NATIONAL COMN COMMUNITY HEALTH,ACTION - PLANNING
FOR COMMUNITY HEALTH SERVICES (PAMPHLET). USA+45
PROF/ORG DELIB/GP BUDGET ROUTINE GP/REL ATTIT
...HEAL SOC SOC/WK CHARTS TIME 20. PAGE 77 B1563

PLAN
MUNIC
HEALTH
ADJUST

HEALEY/D...DOROTHY HEALEY

HEALTH....WELL-BEING, BODILY AND PSYCHIC INTEGRITY

N
US SUPERINTENDENT OF DOCUMENTS,EDUCATION (PRICE
LIST 31). USA+45 LAW FINAN LOC/G NAT/G DEBATE ADMIN
LEAD RACE/REL FEDERAL HEALTH POLICY. PAGE 111 B2238

BIBLIOG/A
EDU/PROP
ACADEM
SCHOOL

N
US SUPERINTENDENT OF DOCUMENTS,INTERSTATE COMMERCE
(PRICE LIST 59). USA+45 LAW LOC/G NAT/G LEGIS
TARIFFS TAX ADMIN CONTROL HEALTH DECISION. PAGE 111
B2239

BIBLIOG/A
DIST/IND
GOV/REL
PROVS

N
US SUPERINTENDENT OF DOCUMENTS,TRANSPORTATION:
HIGHWAYS, ROADS, AND POSTAL SERVICE (PRICE LIST
25). PANAMA USA+45 LAW FORCES DIPLOM ADMIN GOV/REL
HEALTH MGT. PAGE 111 B2243

BIBLIOG/A
DIST/IND
SERV/IND
NAT/G

B02
MOREL E.D.,AFFAIRS OF WEST AFRICA. UK FINAN INDUS
FAM KIN SECT CHIEF WORKER DIPLOM RACE/REL LITERACY
HEALTH...CHARTS 18/20 AFRICA/W NEGRO. PAGE 75 B1521

COLONIAL
ADMIN
AFR

N19
EAST KENTUCKY REGIONAL PLAN,PROGRAM 60: A DECADE OF
ACTION FOR PROGRESS IN EASTERN KENTUCKY (PAMPHLET).
USA+45 AGRI CONSTRUC INDUS CONSULT ACT/RES
PROB/SOLV EDU/PROP GOV/REL HEALTH KENTUCKY. PAGE 32
B0643

REGION
ADMIN
PLAN
ECO/UNDEV

N19
RIDLEY C.E.,MEASURING MUNICIPAL ACTIVITIES
(PAMPHLET). FINAN SERV/IND FORCES RECEIVE INGP/REL

MGT
HEALTH

HABITAT...POLICY SOC/WK 20. PAGE 88 B1779

WEALTH
LOC/G

B45
BUSH V.,SCIENCE, THE ENDLESS FRONTIER. FUT USA-45
INTELL STRATA ACT/RES CREATE PLAN EDU/PROP ADMIN
NUC/PWR PEACE ATTIT HEALTH KNOWL...MAJORIT HEAL MGT
PHIL/SCI CONCPT OBS TREND 20. PAGE 18 B0360

R+D
NAT/G

B45
PLATO,THE REPUBLIC. MEDIT-7 UNIV SOCIETY STRUCT
EX/STRUC FORCES UTOPIA ATTIT PERCEPT HEALTH KNOWL
ORD/FREE PWR...HUM CONCPT STERTYP TOT/POP. PAGE 83
B1681

PERSON
PHIL/SCI

B47
CONOVER H.F.,NON-SELF-GOVERNING AREAS. BELGIUM
FRANCE ITALY UK WOR+45 CULTURE ECO/UNDEV INT/ORG
LOC/G NAT/G ECO/TAC INT/TRADE ADMIN HEALTH...SOC
UN. PAGE 23 B0465

BIBLIOG/A
COLONIAL
DIPLOM

B48
PUBLIC ADMINISTRATION SERVICE,SOURCE MATERIALS IN
PUBLIC ADMINISTRATION: A SELECTED BIBLIOGRAPHY (PAS
PUBLICATION NO. 102). USA+45 LAW FINAN LOC/G MUNIC
NAT/G PLAN RECEIVE EDU/PROP CT/SYS CHOOSE HEALTH
20. PAGE 85 B1717

BIBLIOG/A
GOV/REL
MGT
ADMIN

B53
MEYER P.,THE JEWS IN THE SOVIET SATELLITES.
CZECHOSLVK POLAND SOCIETY STRATA NAT/G BAL/PWR
ECO/TAC EDU/PROP LEGIT ADMIN COERCE ATTIT DISPL
PERCEPT HEALTH PWR RESPECT WEALTH...METH/CNCPT JEWS
VAL/FREE NAZI 20. PAGE 73 B1474

COM
SECT
TOTALISM
USSR

B54
CHICAGO JOINT REFERENCE LIB,FEDERAL-STATE-LOCAL
RELATIONS: A SELECTED BIBLIOGRAPHY. USA+45 AGRI
LABOR LOC/G MUNIC EX/STRUC ADMIN REGION HEALTH
CON/ANAL. PAGE 21 B0419

BIBLIOG
FEDERAL
GOV/REL

B56
INTERNATIONAL AFRICAN INST,SELECT ANNOTATED
BIBLIOGRAPHY OF TROPICAL AFRICA. NAT/G EDU/PROP
ADMIN HEALTH. PAGE 54 B1095

BIBLIOG/A
AFR
SOC
HABITAT

B57
ASHER R.E.,THE UNITED NATIONS AND THE PROMOTION OF
THE GENERAL WELFARE. WOR+45 WOR-45 ECO/UNDEV
EX/STRUC ACT/RES PLAN EDU/PROP ROUTINE HEALTH...HUM
CONCPT CHARTS UNESCO UN ILO 20. PAGE 7 B0139

INT/ORG
CONSULT

B57
DE GRAZIA A.,GRASS ROOTS PRIVATE WELFARE. LOC/G
SCHOOL ACT/RES EDU/PROP ROUTINE CROWD GP/REL
DISCRIM HAPPINESS ILLEGIT AGE HABITAT. PAGE 27
B0554

NEW/LIB
HEALTH
MUNIC
VOL/ASSN

S57
RAPAPORT R.N.,"'DEMOCRATIZATION' AND AUTHORITY IN A
THERAPEUTIC COMMUNITY." OP/RES ADMIN PARTIC CENTRAL
ATTIT...POLICY DECISION. PAGE 86 B1735

PUB/INST
HEALTH
DOMIN
CLIENT

B58
ATOMIC INDUSTRIAL FORUM,MANAGEMENT AND ATOMIC
ENERGY. WOR+45 SEA LAW MARKET NAT/G TEC/DEV INSPECT
INT/TRADE CONFER PEACE HEALTH...ANTHOL 20. PAGE 7
B0145

NUC/PWR
INDUS
MGT
ECO/TAC

S58
MITCHELL W.C.,"OCCUPATIONAL ROLE STRAINS: THE
AMERICAN ELECTIVE PUBLIC OFFICIAL." CONTROL
RIGID/FLEX SUPEGO HEALTH ORD/FREE...SOC INT QU.
PAGE 74 B1492

ANOMIE
DRIVE
ROUTINE
PERSON

B59
GINSBURG M.,LAW AND OPINION IN ENGLAND. UK CULTURE
KIN LABOR LEGIS EDU/PROP ADMIN CT/SYS CRIME OWN
HEALTH...ANTHOL 20 ENGLSH/LAW. PAGE 40 B0802

JURID
POLICY
ECO/TAC

B59
JOYCE J.A.,RED CROSS INTERNATIONAL AND THE STRATEGY
OF PEACE. WOR+45 WOR-45 EX/STRUC SUPEGO ALL/VALS
...CONCPT GEN/LAWS TOT/POP 19/20 RED/CROSS. PAGE 57
B1155

VOL/ASSN
HEALTH

S59
HARVEY M.F.,"THE PALESTINE REFUGEE PROBLEM:
ELEMENTS OF A SOLUTION." ISLAM LEGIS INT/ORG DELIB/GP
TOP/EX ECO/TAC ROUTINE DRIVE HEALTH LOVE ORD/FREE
PWR WEALTH...MAJORIT FAO 20. PAGE 48 B0964

ACT/RES
LEGIT
PEACE
ISRAEL

B60
FRYE R.J.,GOVERNMENT AND LABOR: THE ALABAMA
PROGRAM. USA+45 INDUS R+D LABOR WORKER BUDGET
EFFICIENCY AGE/Y HEALTH...CHARTS 20 ALABAMA.
PAGE 38 B0761

ADMIN
LEGIS
LOC/G
PROVS

B60
MUNRO L.,UNITED NATIONS, HOPE FOR A DIVIDED WORLD.
FUT WOR+45 CONSTN DELIB/GP CREATE TEC/DEV DIPLOM
EDU/PROP LEGIT PEACE ATTIT HEALTH ORD/FREE PWR
...CONCPT TREND UN VAL/FREE 20. PAGE 76 B1540

INT/ORG
ROUTINE

S60
"THE EMERGING COMMON MARKETS IN LATIN AMERICA." FUT
L/A+17C STRATA DIST/IND INDUS LABOR NAT/G LEGIS
ECO/TAC ADMIN RIGID/FLEX HEALTH...NEW/IDEA TIME/SEQ
OAS 20. PAGE 2 B0039

FINAN
ECO/UNDEV
INT/TRADE

S60
TAYLOR M.G.,"THE ROLE OF THE MEDICAL PROFESSION IN
THE FORMULATION AND EXECUTION OF PUBLIC POLICY"

PROF/ORG
HEALTH

(BMR)" CANADA NAT/G CONSULT ADMIN REPRESENT GP/REL LOBBY
ROLE SOVEREIGN...DECISION 20 CMA. PAGE 103 B2088 POLICY
B61

BIRNBACH B.,NEO-FREUDIAN SOCIAL PHILOSOPHY. TEC/DEV SOCIETY
INGP/REL ADJUST HAPPINESS SUPEGO HEALTH...CONCPT PSY
GEN/LAWS BIBLIOG 20. PAGE 12 B0242 PERSON
ADMIN
B61

CONFREY E.A.,ADMINISTRATION OF COMMUNITY HEALTH HEAL
SERVICES. USA+45 R+D PUB/INST DELIB/GP PLAN BUDGET ADMIN
ROUTINE AGE/C HEALTH...MGT SOC/WK METH/COMP 20. MUNIC
PAGE 23 B0461 BIO/SOC
B61

SHARP W.R.,FIELD ADMINISTRATION IN THE UNITED INT/ORG
NATION SYSTEM: THE CONDUCT OF INTERNATIONAL CONSULT
ECONOMIC AND SOCIAL PROGRAMS. FUT WOR+45 CONSTN
SOCIETY ECO/UNDEV R+D DELIB/GP ACT/RES PLAN TEC/DEV
EDU/PROP EXEC ROUTINE HEALTH WEALTH...HUM CONCPT
CHARTS METH ILO UNESCO VAL/FREE UN 20. PAGE 96
B1939
B62

CAIRNCROSS A.K.,FACTORS IN ECONOMIC DEVELOPMENT. MARKET
WOR+45 ECO/UNDEV INDUS R+D LG/CO NAT/G EX/STRUC ECO/DEV
PLAN TEC/DEV ECO/TAC ATTIT HEALTH KNOWL PWR WEALTH
...TIME/SEQ GEN/LAWS TOT/POP VAL/FREE 20. PAGE 18
B0363
B62

LAWSON R.,INTERNATIONAL REGIONAL ORGANIZATIONS. INT/ORG
WOR+45 NAT/G VOL/ASSN CONSULT LEGIS EDU/PROP LEGIT DELIB/GP
ADMIN EXEC ROUTINE HEALTH PWR WEALTH...JURID EEC REGION
COLD/WAR 20 UN. PAGE 63 B1277
B63

BERNE E.,THE STRUCTURE AND DYNAMICS OF INGP/REL
ORGANIZATIONS AND GROUPS. CLIENT PARTIC DRIVE AUTHORIT
HEALTH...MGT PSY ORG/CHARTS. PAGE 11 B0226 ROUTINE
CLASSIF
B63

BOISSIER P.,HISTORIE DU COMITE INTERNATIONAL DE LA INT/ORG
CROIX ROUGE. MOD/EUR WOR-45 CONSULT FORCES DIAN HEALTH
DIPLOM EDU/PROP ADMIN MORAL ORD/FREE...SOC CONCPT ARMS/CONT
RECORD TIME/SEQ GEN/LAWS TOT/POP VAL/FREE 19/20. WAR
PAGE 13 B0267
B63

DE VRIES E.,SOCIAL ASPECTS OF ECONOMIC DEVELOPMENT L/A+17C
IN LATIN AMERICA. CULTURE SOCIETY STRATA FINAN ECO/UNDEV
INDUS INT/ORG DELIB/GP ACT/RES ECO/TAC EDU/PROP
ADMIN ATTIT SUPEGO HEALTH KNOWL ORD/FREE...SOC STAT
TREND ANTHOL TOT/POP VAL/FREE. PAGE 28 B0562
B63

SINGH M.M.,MUNICIPAL GOVERNMENT IN THE CALCUTTA LOC/G
METROPOLITAN DISTRICT A PRELIMINARY SURVEY. FINAN HEALTH
LG/CO DELIB/GP BUDGET TAX ADMIN GP/REL 20 CALCUTTA. MUNIC
PAGE 97 B1969 JURID
B63

SWERDLOW I.,DEVELOPMENT ADMINISTRATION: CONCEPTS ECO/UNDEV
AND PROBLEMS. WOR+45 CULTURE SOCIETY STRATA ADMIN
DELIB/GP EX/STRUC ACT/RES PLAN ECO/TAC DOMIN LEGIT
ATTIT RIGID/FLEX SUPEGO HEALTH PWR...MGT CONCPT
ANTHOL VAL/FREE. PAGE 102 B2062
L63

BEGUIN H.,"ASPECTS GEOGRAPHIQUE DE LA ECO/UNDEV
POLARISATION." FUT WOR+45 SOCIETY STRUCT ECO/DEV GEOG
R+D BAL/PWR ADMIN ATTIT RIGID/FLEX HEALTH WEALTH DIPLOM
...CHARTS 20. PAGE 10 B0206
B64

HAMBRIDGE G.,DYNAMICS OF DEVELOPMENT. AGRI FINAN ECO/UNDEV
INDUS LABOR INT/TRADE EDU/PROP ADMIN LEAD OWN ECO/TAC
HEALTH...ANTHOL BIBLIOG 20. PAGE 46 B0930 OP/RES
ACT/RES
B64

RAPHAEL M.,PENSIONS AND PUBLIC SERVANTS. UK PLAN ADMIN
EDU/PROP PARTIC GOV/REL HEALTH...POLICY CHARTS SENIOR
17/20 CIVIL/SERV. PAGE 86 B1737 PAY
AGE/O
B64

SCHERMER G.,MEETING SOCIAL NEEDS IN THE PENJERDEL PLAN
REGION. SOCIETY FINAN ACT/RES EDU/PROP ADMIN REGION
GOV/REL...SOC/WK 45 20 PENNSYLVAN DELAWARE HEALTH
NEW/JERSEY. PAGE 93 B1887 WEALTH
N64

US SENATE COMM GOVT OPERATIONS,METROPOLITAN BIBLIOG/A
AMERICA: A SELECTED BIBLIOGRAPHY (PAMPHLET). USA+45 MUNIC
DIST/IND FINAN LOC/G EDU/PROP ADMIN HEALTH 20. GOV/REL
PAGE 110 B2214 DECISION
B65

PRESTHUS R.,BEHAVIORAL APPROACHES TO PUBLIC GEN/METH
ADMINISTRATION. UK STRATA LG/CO PUB/INST VOL/ASSN DECISION
EX/STRUC TOP/EX EFFICIENCY HEALTH. PAGE 84 B1704 ADMIN
R+D
B66

RUBENSTEIN R.,THE SHARING OF POWER IN A PSYCHIATRIC ADMIN
HOSPITAL. CLIENT PROF/ORG PUB/INST INGP/REL ATTIT PARTIC
PWR...DECISION OBS RECORD. PAGE 91 B1847 HEALTH
CONCPT
B66

SCHMIDT F.,PUBLIC RELATIONS IN HEALTH AND WELFARE. PROF/ORG

USA+45 ACADEM RECEIVE PRESS FEEDBACK GOV/REL EDU/PROP
PERS/REL DEMAND EFFICIENCY ATTIT PERCEPT WEALTH 20 ADMIN
PUBLIC/REL. PAGE 94 B1895 HEALTH
B66

US HOUSE COMM GOVT OPERATIONS,AN INVESTIGATION OF FOR/AID
THE US ECONOMIC AND MILITARY ASSISTANCE PROGRAMS IN ECO/UNDEV
VIETNAM. USA+45 VIETNAM/S SOCIETY CONSTRUC FINAN WAR
FORCES BUDGET INT/TRADE PEACE HEALTH...MGT INSPECT
HOUSE/REP AID. PAGE 108 B2191
N66

PRINCETON U INDUSTRIAL REL SEC,OUTSTANDING BOOKS ON BIBLIOG/A
INDUSTRIAL RELATIONS, 1965 (PAMPHLET NO. 128). INDUS
WOR+45 LABOR BARGAIN GOV/REL RACE/REL HEALTH PWR GP/REL
...MGT 20. PAGE 85 B1709 POLICY
B67

KATZ J.,PSYCHOANALYSIS, PSYCHIATRY, AND LAW. USA+45 LAW
LOC/G NAT/G PUB/INST PROB/SOLV ADMIN HEALTH PSY
...CRIMLGY CONCPT SAMP/SIZ IDEA/COMP. PAGE 58 B1180 CT/SYS
ADJUD
B67

MINTZ M.,BY PRESCRIPTION ONLY. USA+45 NAT/G BIO/SOC
EX/STRUC PLAN TEC/DEV EXEC EFFICIENCY HEALTH...MGT PROC/MFG
SOC/WK 20. PAGE 74 B1491 CONTROL
POLICY
B67

PAULSEN F.R.,AMERICAN EDUCATION: CHALLENGES AND EDU/PROP
IMAGES. FUT USA+45 ADMIN AGE/C AGE/Y SUPEGO HEALTH SCHOOL
...ANTHOL 20. PAGE 81 B1644 ORD/FREE
GOV/REL
B67

US DEPARTMENT HEALTH EDUC WELF,NEW PROGRAMS IN ADMIN
HEALTH, EDUCATION, WELFARE, HOUSING AND URBAN HEALTH
DEVELOPMENT FOR PERSONS AND FAMILIES -LOW, MOD' SCHOOL
INCOME. USA+45 MUNIC NAT/G EDU/PROP GOV/REL HABITAT
INGP/PEL ORD/FREE 20 DEPT/HEW DEPT/HUD. PAGE 108
B2180
L67

CARMICHAEL D.M.,"FORTY YEARS OF WATER POLLUTION HEALTH
CONTROL IN WISCONSIN: A CASE STUDY." LAW EXTR/IND CONTROL
INDUS MUNIC DELIB/GP PLAN PROB/SOLV SANCTION ADMIN
...CENSUS CHARTS 20 WISCONSIN. PAGE 19 B0382 ADJUD
L67

ROBERTS J.C.,"CIVIL RESTRAINT, MENTAL ILLNESS, AND HEALTH
THE RIGHT TO TREATMENT." PROB/SOLV ADMIN PERSON ORD/FREE
HEAL. PAGE 89 B1795 COERCE
LAW
N67

US SUPERINTENDENT OF DOCUMENTS,SPACE: MISSILES, THE BIBLIOG/A
MOON, NASA, AND SATELLITES (PRICE LIST 79A). USA+45 SPACE
COM/IND R+D NAT/G DIPLOM EDU/PROP ADMIN CONTROL TEC/DEV
HEALTH...POLICY SIMUL NASA CONGRESS. PAGE 111 B2244 PEACE
N67

NATIONAL COMN COMMUNITY HEALTH,ACTION - PLANNING PLAN
FOR COMMUNITY HEALTH SERVICES (PAMPHLET). USA+45 MUNIC
PROF/ORG DELIB/GP BUDGET ROUTINE GP/REL ATTIT HEALTH
...HEAL SOC SOC/WK CHARTS TIME 20. PAGE 77 B1563 ADJUST
B82

MACDONALD D.,AFRICANA; OR, THE HEART OF HEATHEN SECT
AFRICA, VOL. II: MISSION LIFE. SOCIETY STRATA KIN AFR
CREATE EDU/PROP ADMIN COERCE LITERACY HEALTH...MYTH CULTURE
WORSHIP 19 LIVNGSTN/D MISSION NEGRO. PAGE 67 B1355 ORD/FREE

B53

GROSS B.M.,THE LEGISLATIVE STRUGGLE: A STUDY IN LEGIS
SOCIAL COMBAT. STRUCT LOC/G POL/PAR JUDGE EDU/PROP DECISION
DEBATE ETIQUET ADMIN LOBBY CHOOSE GOV/REL INGP/REL PERSON
HEREDITY ALL/VALS...SOC PRESIDENT. PAGE 44 B0885 LEAD

HERMAN H. B0992

HERNDON J. B0993

HERRERA F. B0994

HERRING E.P. B0995

HERSKOVITS M.J. B0996

HERTER/C

	B62
US SENATE COMM GOVT OPERATIONS,ADMINISTRATION OF NATIONAL SECURITY. USA+45 CHIEF PLAN PROB/SOLV TEC/DEV DIPLOM ATTIT...POLICY DECISION 20 KENNEDY/JF RUSK/D MCNAMARA/R BUNDY/M HERTER/C. PAGE 110 B2212	ORD/FREE ADMIN NAT/G CONTROL

HERZ J.H. B0997

HESSLER I.O. B0998

HESTER G.C. B1642

HETTINGER H.S. B0999

HEUSSLER R. B1000

HEWITT W.H. B1001

HEYEL C. B1002

HICKEY G.C. B1003

HICKMAN B.G. B1004

HICKMAN C.A. B1005

HICKS U.K. B1006

HIDAYATULLAH M. B1007

HIESTAND/F....FRED J. HIESTAND

HIGA M. B1008

HIGGINS R. B1009

HIGGINS/G....GODFREY HIGGINS

HIGHWAY PLANNING AND DEVELOPMENT....SEE HIGHWAY

HIGHWAY....HIGHWAY PLANNING AND DEVELOPMENT

HILL F.G. B1010

HILL N. B1011

HILL S.E. B1588

HILLS R.J. B1012

HILSMAN R. B1013

HIMMELFARB G. B1014

HINDERLING A. B1015

HINDU....HINDUISM AND HINDU PEOPLE

	B59
BHAMBHRI C.P.,SUBSTANCE OF HINDU POLITY. INDIA S/ASIA LAW EX/STRUC JUDGE TAX COERCE GP/REL POPULISM 20 HINDU. PAGE 11 B0234	GOV/REL WRITING SECT PROVS

HIROSHIMA....SEE WAR, NUC/PWR, PLAN, PROB/SOLV, CONSULT

HIRSCHMAN A.O. B1016

HIRSHBERG H.S. B1017

HISPANIC SOCIETY OF AMERICA B1018

HISS/ALGER....ALGER HISS

HIST....HISTORY, INCLUDING CURRENT EVENTS

HIST/WRIT....HISTORIOGRAPHY

	B24
MERRIAM C.E.,A HISTORY OF POLITICAL THEORIES - RECENT TIMES. USA-45 WOR-45 CULTURE SOCIETY ECO/DEV R+D EDU/PROP ROUTINE CHOOSE ATTIT PERSON ALL/VALS ...POLICY SOC CONCPT METH/CNCPT OBS HIST/WRIT	UNIV INTELL

TIME/SEQ TREND. PAGE 73 B1471

	B24
POOLE D.C.,THE CONDUCT OF FOREIGN RELATIONS UNDER MODERN DEMOCRATIC CONDITIONS. EUR+WWI USA-45 INT/ORG PLAN LEGIT ADMIN KNOWL PWR...MAJORIT OBS/ENVIR HIST/WRIT GEN/LAWS 20. PAGE 84 B1689	NAT/G EDU/PROP DIPLOM

	B29
ROBERTS S.H.,HISTORY OF FRENCH COLONIAL POLICY. AFR ASIA L/A+17C S/ASIA CULTURE ECO/DEV ECO/UNDEV FINAN NAT/G PLAN ECO/TAC DOMIN ROUTINE SOVEREIGN...OBS HIST/WRIT TREND CHARTS VAL/FREE 19/20. PAGE 89 B1796	INT/ORG ACT/RES FRANCE COLONIAL

	B36
ROBINSON H.,DEVELOPMENT OF THE BRITISH EMPIRE. WOR-45 CULTURE SOCIETY STRUCT ECO/DEV ECO/UNDEV INT/ORG VOL/ASSN FORCES CREATE PLAN DOMIN EDU/PROP ADMIN COLONIAL PWR WEALTH...POLICY GEOG CHARTS CMN/WLTH 16/20. PAGE 89 B1800	NAT/G HIST/WRIT UK

	B38
DAY C.,A HISTORY OF COMMERCE. CHRIST-17C EUR+WWI ISLAM MEDIT-7 MOD/EUR USA-45 ECO/DEV FINAN NAT/G ECO/TAC EXEC ROUTINE PWR WEALTH HIST/WRIT. PAGE 27 B0546	MARKET INT/TRADE

	B38
RAPPARD W.E.,THE CRISIS OF DEMOCRACY. EUR+WWI UNIV WOR-45 CULTURE SOCIETY ECO/DEV INT/ORG POL/PAR ACT/RES EDU/PROP EXEC CHOOSE ATTIT ALL/VALS...SOC OBS HIST/WRIT TIME/SEQ LEAGUE/NAT NAZI TOT/POP 20. PAGE 86 B1741	NAT/G CONCPT

	S41
ABEL T.,"THE ELEMENT OF DECISION IN THE PATTERN OF WAR." EUR+WWI FUT NAT/G TOP/EX DIPLOM ROUTINE COERCE DISPL PERCEPT PWR...SOC METH/CNCPT HIST/WRIT TREND GEN/LAWS 20. PAGE 2 B0051	TEC/DEV FORCES WAR

	B48
BONAPARTE M.,MYTHS OF WAR. GERMANY WOR+45 WOR-45 CULTURE SOCIETY NAT/G FORCES LEGIT NAT/VALS ...CONCPT HIST/WRIT TIME/SEQ 20 JEWS. PAGE 13 B0271	ROUTINE MYTH WAR

	B49
GLOVER J.D.,THE ADMINISTRATOR. ELITES LG/CO EX/STRUC ACT/RES CONTROL GP/REL INGP/REL PERS/REL AUTHORIT...POLICY CONCPT HIST/WRIT. PAGE 40 B0811	ADMIN MGT ATTIT PROF/ORG

	S50
WITTFOGEL K.A.,"RUSSIA AND ASIA: PROBLEMS OF CONTEMPORARY AREA STUDIES AND INTERNATIONAL RELATIONS." ASIA COM USA+45 SOCIETY NAT/G DIPLOM ECO/TAC FOR/AID EDU/PROP KNOWL...HIST/WRIT TOT/POP 20. PAGE 117 B2369	ECO/DEV ADMIN RUSSIA USSR

	B51
SMITH L.,AMERICAN DEMOCRACY AND MILITARY POWER. USA+45 USA-45 CONSTN STRATA NAT/G LEGIS ACT/RES LEGIT ADMIN EXEC GOV/REL ALL/VALS...CONCPT HIST/WRIT CONGRESS 20. PAGE 98 B1982	FORCES STRUCT WAR

	B52
BRINTON C.,THE ANATOMY OF REVOLUTION. FRANCE UK USA-45 USSR WOR-45 ELITES INTELL ECO/DEV NAT/G EX/STRUC FORCES COERCE DRIVE ORD/FREE PWR SOVEREIGN ...MYTH HIST/WRIT GEN/LAWS. PAGE 15 B0311	SOCIETY CONCPT REV

	B54
MATTHEWS D.R.,THE SOCIAL BACKGROUND OF POLITICAL DECISION-MAKERS. CULTURE SOCIETY STRATA FAM EX/STRUC LEAD ATTIT BIO/SOC DRIVE PERSON ALL/VALS HIST/WRIT. PAGE 71 B1431	DECISION BIOG SOC

	L56
MACMAHON A.W.,"WOODROW WILSON AS LEGISLATIVE LEADER AND ADMINISTRATOR." CONSTN POL/PAR ADMIN...POLICY HIST/WRIT WILSON/W PRESIDENT. PAGE 68 B1371	LEGIS CHIEF LEAD BIOG

	B57
ARON R.,FRANCE DEFEATS EDC. EUR+WWI GERMANY LEGIS DIPLOM DOMIN EDU/PROP ADMIN...HIST/WRIT 20. PAGE 7 B0136	INT/ORG FORCES DETER FRANCE

	B59
CONOVER H.F.,NIGERIAN OFFICIAL PUBLICATIONS, 1869-1959: A GUIDE. NIGER CONSTN FINAN ACADEM SCHOOL FORCES PRESS ADMIN COLONIAL...HIST/WRIT 19/20. PAGE 23 B0466	BIBLIOG NAT/G CON/ANAL

	S59
SUTTON F.X.,"REPRESENTATION AND THE NATURE OF POLITICAL SYSTEMS." UNIV WOR-45 CULTURE SOCIETY STRATA INT/ORG FORCES JUDGE DOMIN LEGIT EXEC REGION REPRESENT ATTIT ORD/FREE RESPECT...SOC HIST/WRIT TIME/SEQ. PAGE 102 B2057	NAT/G CONCPT

	B60
LISKA G.,THE NEW STATECRAFT. WOR+45 WOR-45 LEGIS DIPLOM ADMIN ATTIT PWR WEALTH...HIST/WRIT TREND COLD/WAR 20. PAGE 66 B1323	ECO/TAC CONCPT FOR/AID

	S61
NOVE A.,"THE SOVIET MODEL AND UNDERDEVELOPED COUNTRIES." COM FUT USSR WOR+45 CULTURE ECO/DEV POL/PAR FOR/AID EDU/PROP ADMIN MORAL WEALTH ...POLICY RECORD HIST/WRIT 20. PAGE 79 B1593	ECO/UNDEV PLAN

	S63
SCHURMANN F.,"ECONOMIC POLICY AND POLITICAL POWER	PLAN

IN COMMUNIST CHINA." ASIA CHINA/COM USSR SOCIETY   ECO/TAC
ECO/UNDEV AGRI INDUS CREATE ADMIN ROUTINE ATTIT
DRIVE RIGID/FLEX PWR WEALTH...HIST/WRIT TREND
CHARTS WORK 20. PAGE 94 B1908
                                                                        B64

PIPES R.,THE FORMATION OF THE SOVIET UNION. EUR+WWI COM
MOD/EUR STRUCT ECO/UNDEV NAT/G LEGIS DOMIN LEGIT   USSR
CT/SYS EXEC COERCE ALL/VALS...POLICY RELATIV   RUSSIA
HIST/WRIT TIME/SEQ TOT/POP 19/20. PAGE 83 B1677
                                                                        B64

REDLICH F.,THE GERMAN MILITARY ENTERPRISER AND HIS   EX/STRUC
WORK FORCE. CHRIST-17C GERMANY ELITES SOCIETY FINAN   FORCES
ECO/TAC CIVMIL/REL GP/REL INGP/REL...HIST/WRIT   PROFIT
METH/COMP 14/17. PAGE 87 B1760   WORKER
                                                                        B67

GIFFORD P.,BRITAIN AND GERMANY IN AFRICA. AFR   COLONIAL
GERMANY UK ECO/UNDEV LEAD WAR NAT/LISM ATTIT   ADMIN
...POLICY HIST/WRIT METH/COMP ANTHOL BIBLIOG 19/20   DIPLOM
WWI. PAGE 39 B0797   NAT/COMP
                                                                        B67

GRUBER H.,INTERNATIONAL COMMUNISM IN THE ERA OF   MARXISM
LENIN. COM ADMIN REV GP/REL 20. PAGE 44 B0895   HIST/WRIT
                                                         POL/PAR

HITCHNER D.G. B1019

HITLER A. B1020

HITLER/A....ADOLF HITLER
                                                                        B45
BRECHT A.,FEDERALISM AND REGIONALISM IN GERMANY;   FEDERAL
THE DIVISION OF PRUSSIA. GERMANY PRUSSIA WOR-45   REGION
CREATE ADMIN WAR TOTALISM PWR...CHARTS 20 HITLER/A.   PROB/SOLV
PAGE 15 B0303   CONSTN
                                                                        B63
JACOB H.,GERMAN ADMINISTRATION SINCE BISMARCK: ADMIN
CENTRAL AUTHORITY VERSUS LOCAL AUTONOMY. GERMANY   NAT/G
GERMANY/W LAW POL/PAR CONTROL CENTRAL TOTALISM   LOC/G
FASCISM...MAJORIT DECISION STAT CHARTS GOV/COMP   POLICY
19/20 BISMARCK/O HITLER/A WEIMAR/REP. PAGE 55 B1111
                                                                        B64
WHEELER-BENNETT J.W.,THE NEMESIS OF POWER (2ND   FORCES
ED.). EUR+WWI GERMANY TOP/EX TEC/DEV ADMIN WAR   NAT/G
PERS/REL RIGID/FLEX ROLE ORD/FREE PWR FASCISM 20   GP/REL
HITLER/A. PAGE 116 B2332   STRUCT

HO/CHI/MIN....HO CHI MINH

HOBBES/T....THOMAS HOBBES

HOBBS E.H. B1021,B1022

HOC V.V. B1819

HODGETTS J.E. B1023,B1024,B1025

HODGSON J.G. B1026

HODGSON R.C. B1027

HOFFA/J....JAMES HOFFA

HOFFHERR R. B1028

HOFFMANN S. B1029

HOFMANN W. B1030

HOGAN W.N. B2254

HOLCOMBE A. B1031

HOLCOMBE A.N. B1032

HOLDSWORTH W.S. B1033,B1034

HOLECOMBE A.N. B1035

HOLIFLD/C....CHET HOLIFIELD

HOLLAND....SEE NETHERLAND

HOLLOWAY M.F. B1660

HOLMES/OW....OLIVER WENDELL HOLMES

HOLMES/OWJ....OLIVER WENDELL HOLMES, JR.

HOLSTI O.R. B1036

HOLSTI/KJ....K.J. HOLSTI

HOMANS G.C. B1037

HOMEOSTASIS....SEE FEEDBACK

HOMER....HOMER

HOMEST/ACT....HOMESTEAD ACT OF 1862

HOMESTEAD ACT OF 1862....SEE HOMEST/ACT

HOMICIDE....SEE MURDER

HOMOSEXUAL....HOMOSEXUALITY; SEE ALSO BIO/SOC, CRIME, SEX

HOMOSEXUALITY....SEE BIO/SOC, SEX, CRIME, HOMOSEXUAL

HONDURAS....SEE ALSO L/A+17C
                                                                        C50
STOKES W.S.,"HONDURAS: AN AREA STUDY IN   CONSTN
GOVERNMENT." HONDURAS NAT/G POL/PAR COLONIAL CT/SYS   LAW
ROUTINE CHOOSE REPRESENT...GEOG RECORD BIBLIOG   L/A+17C
19/20. PAGE 101 B2044   ADMIN

HONEY J.C. B1038

HONG/KONG....HONG KONG
                                                                        B62
HSUEH S.-.S.,GOVERNMENT AND ADMINISTRATION OF HONG   ADMIN
KONG. CHIEF DELIB/GP LEGIS CT/SYS REPRESENT GOV/REL   LOC/G
20 HONG/KONG CITY/MGT CIVIL/SERV GOVERNOR. PAGE 52   COLONIAL
B1055   EX/STRUC
                                                                        B64
ENDACOTT G.B.,GOVERNMENT AND PEOPLE IN HONG KONG   CONSTN
1841-1962: A CONSTITUTIONAL HISTORY. UK LEGIS ADJUD   COLONIAL
REPRESENT ATTIT 19/20 HONG/KONG. PAGE 33 B0674   CONTROL
                                                        ADMIN

HONORD S. B1039

HOOK S. B1040

HOOVER E.M. B1041

HOOVER/H....HERBERT HOOVER
                                                                        B60
MORISON E.E.,TURMOIL AND TRADITION: A STUDY OF THE   BIOG
LIFE AND TIMES OF HENRY L. STIMSON. USA+45 USA-45   NAT/G
POL/PAR CHIEF DELIB/GP FORCES BAL/PWP DIPLOM   EX/STRUC
ARMS/CONT WAR PEACE 19/20 STIMSON/HL ROOSEVLT/F
TAFT/WH HOOVER/H REPUBLICAN. PAGE 75 B1525
                                                                        B65
ROMASCO A.U.,THE POVERTY OF ABUNDANCE: HOOVER, THE   ECO/TAC
NATION, THE DEPRESSION. USA-45 AGRI LEGIS WORKER   ADMIN
GIVE PRESS LEAD 20 HOOVER/H. PAGE 90 B1817   NAT/G
                                                        FINAN

HOPI....HOPI INDIANS

HOPKINS/H....HARRY HOPKINS
                                                                        B48
SHERWOOD R.E.,ROOSEVELT AND HOPKINS. UK USA+45 USSR   TOP/EX
NAT/G EX/STRUC FORCES ADMIN ROUTINE PERSON PWR   BIOG
...TIME/SEQ 20 ROOSEVLT/F HOPKINS/H. PAGE 96 B1946   DIPLOM
                                                        WAR
                                                                        B63
CHARLES S.,MINISTER OF RELIEF: HARRY HOPKINS AND   ADMIN
THE DEPRESSION. EX/STRUC PROB/SOLV RATION PARL/PROC   ECO/TAC
PERS/REL ALL/VALS 20 HOPKINS/H NRA. PAGE 20 B0414   PLAN
                                                        BIOG

HORECKY P.L. B1042

HOROWITZ I.L. B1043

HOROWITZ M. B1044

HORVATH B. B1045

HOSCH L.G. B1046

HOSPITALS....SEE PUB/INST

HOUGHTELING J.L. B1047

HOUN F.W. B1048

HOUSE COMMITTEE ON SCIENCE AND ASTRONAUTICS....SEE
   HS/SCIASTR

HOUSE OF REPRESENTATIVES....SEE HOUSE/REP

HOUSE RULES COMMITTEE....SEE RULES/COMM, HOUSE/REP

HOUSE UNAMERICAN ACTIVITIES COMMITTEE....SEE HUAC

HOUSE/CMNS....HOUSE OF COMMONS (ALL NATIONS)

B39
JENNINGS W.I.,PARLIAMENT. UK POL/PAR OP/RES BUDGET PARL/PROC
LEAD CHOOSE GP/REL...MGT 20 PARLIAMENT HOUSE/LORD LEGIS
HOUSE/CMNS. PAGE 56 B1135 CONSTN
NAT/G

B58
STEWART J.D.,BRITISH PRESSURE GROUPS: THEIR ROLE IN LOBBY
RELATION TO THE HOUSE OF COMMONS. UK CONSULT LEGIS
DELIB/GP ADMIN ROUTINE CHOOSE REPRESENT ATTIT ROLE PLAN
20 HOUSE/CMNS PARLIAMENT. PAGE 101 B2038 PARL/PROC

B66
JOHNSON N.,PARLIAMENT AND ADMINISTRATION: THE LEGIS
ESTIMATES COMMITTEE 1945-65. FUT UK NAT/G EX/STRUC ADMIN
PLAN BUDGET ORD/FREE...T 20 PARLIAMENT HOUSE/CMNS. FINAN
PAGE 57 B1147 DELIB/GP

HOUSE/LORD....HOUSE OF LORDS (ALL NATIONS)

B39
JENNINGS W.I.,PARLIAMENT. UK POL/PAR OP/RES BUDGET PARL/PROC
LEAD CHOOSE GP/REL...MGT 20 PARLIAMENT HOUSE/LORD LEGIS
HOUSE/CMNS. PAGE 56 B1135 CONSTN
NAT/G

B63
SPRING D.,THE ENGLISH LANDED ESTATE IN THE STRATA
NINETEENTH CENTURY: ITS ADMINISTRATION. UK ELITES PERS/REL
STRUCT AGRI NAT/G GP/REL OWN PWR WEALTH...BIBLIOG MGT
19 HOUSE/LORD. PAGE 99 B2012

HOUSE/REP....HOUSE OF REPRESENTATIVES (ALL NATIONS)L SEE
ALSO CONGRESS, LEGIS

B08
WILSON W.,CONSTITUTIONAL GOVERNMENT IN THE UNITED NAT/G
STATES. USA-45 LAW POL/PAR PROVS CHIEF LEGIS GOV/REL
BAL/PWR ADJUD EXEC FEDERAL PWR 18/20 SUPREME/CT CONSTN
HOUSE/REP SENATE. PAGE 117 B2362 PARL/PROC

B17
HARLOW R.V.,THE HISTORY OF LEGISLATIVE METHODS IN LEGIS
THE PERIOD BEFORE 1825. USA-45 EX/STRUC ADMIN DELIB/GP
COLONIAL LEAD PARL/PROC ROUTINE...GP/COMP GOV/COMP PROVS
HOUSE/REP. PAGE 47 B0948 POL/PAR

B56
WILSON W.,CONGRESSIONAL GOVERNMENT. USA-45 NAT/G LEGIS
ADMIN EXEC PARL/PROC GP/REL MAJORITY ATTIT 19 CHIEF
SENATE HOUSE/REP. PAGE 117 B2364 CONSTN
PWR

B58
US HOUSE COMM GOVT OPERATIONS,HEARINGS BEFORE A FOR/AID
SUBCOMMITTEE OF THE COMMITTEE ON GOVERNMENT DIPLOM
OPERATIONS. CAMBODIA PHILIPPINE USA+45 CONSTRUC ORD/FREE
TEC/DEV ADMIN CONTROL WEAPON EFFICIENCY HOUSE/REP. ECO/UNDEV
PAGE 108 B2189

B59
US HOUSE COMM GOVT OPERATIONS,UNITED STATES AID FOR/AID
OPERATIONS IN LAOS. LAOS USA+45 PLAN INSPECT ADMIN
HOUSE/REP. PAGE 108 B2190 FORCES
ECO/UNDEV

S59
ROBINSON J.A.,"THE ROLE OF THE RULES COMMITTEE IN PARL/PROC
ARRANGING THE PROGRAM OF THE UNITED STATES HOUSE OF DELIB/GP
REPRESENTATIVES." USA+45 DEBATE CONTROL AUTHORIT ROUTINE
HOUSE/REP. PAGE 89 B1801 LEGIS

S60
SCHER S.,"CONGRESSIONAL COMMITTEE MEMBERS AND LEGIS
INDEPENDENT AGENCY OVERSEERS: A CASE STUDY." GOV/REL
DELIB/GP EX/STRUC JUDGE TOP/EX DOMIN ADMIN CONTROL LABOR
PWR...SOC/EXP HOUSE/REP CONGRESS. PAGE 93 B1886 ADJUD

B63
MACNEIL N.,FORGE OF DEMOCRACY: THE HOUSE OF LEGIS
REPRESENTATIVES. POL/PAR EX/STRUC TOP/EX DEBATE DELIB/GP
LEAD PARL/PROC CHOOSE GOV/REL PWR...OBS HOUSE/REP.
PAGE 68 B1374

B63
PEABODY R.L.,NEW PERSPECTIVES ON THE HOUSE OF NEW/IDEA
REPRESENTATIVES. AGRI FINAN SCHOOL FORCES CONFER LEGIS
LEAD CHOOSE REPRESENT FEDERAL...POLICY DECISION PWR
HOUSE/REP. PAGE 82 B1647 ADMIN

B65
MASTERS N.A.,COMMITTEE ASSIGNMENTS IN THE HOUSE OF LEAD
REPRESENTATIVES (BMR). USA+45 ELITES POL/PAR LEGIS
EX/STRUC PARTIC REPRESENT GP/REL PERS/REL ATTIT PWR CHOOSE
...STAT CHARTS 20 HOUSE/REP. PAGE 71 B1425 DELIB/GP

B66
US HOUSE COMM GOVT OPERATIONS,AN INVESTIGATION OF FOR/AID
THE US ECONOMIC AND MILITARY ASSISTANCE PROGRAMS IN ECO/UNDEV
VIETNAM. USA+45 VIETNAM/S SOCIETY CONSTRUC FINAN WAR
FORCES BUDGET INT/TRADE PEACE HEALTH...MGT INSPECT
HOUSE/REP AID. PAGE 108 B2191

C66
TACHERON D.G.,"THE JOB OF THE CONGRESSMAN: AN LEGIS
INTRODUCTION TO SERVICES IN THE US HOUSE OF PARL/PROC
REPRESENTATIVES." DELIB/GP EX/STRUC PRESS SENIOR ADMIN
CT/SYS LOBBY CHOOSE GOV/REL...BIBLIOG 20 CONGRESS POL/PAR
HOUSE/REP SENATE. PAGE 102 B2068

S67
LEES J.P.,"LEGISLATIVE REVIEW AND BUREAUCRATIC SUPEGO
RESPONSIBILITY." USA+45 FINAN NAT/G DELIB/GP PLAN BUDGET
PROB/SOLV CONFER CONTROL GP/REL DEMAND...DECISION LEGIS
20 CONGRESS PRESIDENT HOUSE/REP BUREAUCRCY. PAGE 63 EXEC
B1281

HOUSTON....HOUSTON, TEXAS

HOVING W. B1049

HOWARD L.V. B1050

HOWE R. B1051

HOWELLS L.T. B2108

HOWER R.M. B0811,B1052

HOWTON F.W. B1820

HS/SCIASTR....HOUSE COMMITTEE ON SCIENCE AND ASTRONAUTICS

HSIAO K.C. B1053

HSUEH C.T. B1054

HSUEH S-S. B1055

HU/FENG....HU FENG

HUAC....HOUSE UNAMERICAN ACTIVITIES COMMITTEE

HUDDLESTON J. B1056

HUDSON B. B1152

HUDSON G.F. B1057

HUELIN D. B1058

HUGHES J.M. B1059

HUGON P. B1060

HUITT R.K. B1061

HUKS....HUKS (PHILIPPINES)

HULL C. B1062

HUM....METHODS OF HUMANITIES, LITERARY ANALYSIS

N
WELLS A.J.,THE BRITISH NATIONAL BIBLIOGRAPHY BIBLIOG
CUMULATED SUBJECT CATALOGUE, 1951-1954. UK WOR+45 NAT/G
LAW ADMIN LEAD...HUM SOC 20. PAGE 115 B2320

N
WHITAKER'S CUMULATIVE BOOKLIST. UK ADMIN...HUM SOC BIBLIOG/A
20. PAGE 1 B0009 WRITING
CON/ANAL

N
CUMULATIVE BOOK INDEX. WOR+45 WOR-45 ADMIN PERSON INDEX
ALL/VALS ALL/IDEOS...HUM PHIL/SCI SOC LING 19/20. NAT/G
PAGE 1 B0012 DIPLOM

N
PUBLISHERS' TRADE LIST ANNUAL. LAW POL/PAR ADMIN BIBLIOG
PERSON ALL/IDEOS...HUM SOC 19/20. PAGE 1 B0020 NAT/G
DIPLOM
POLICY

N
READERS GUIDE TO PERIODICAL LITERATURE. WOR+45 BIBLIOG
WOR-45 LAW ADMIN ATTIT PERSON...HUM PSY SOC 20. WRITING
PAGE 1 B0021 DIPLOM
NAT/G

N
SUBJECT GUIDE TO BOOKS IN PRINT; AN INDEX TO THE BIBLIOG
PUBLISHERS' TRADE LIST ANNUAL. WOR+45 WOR-45 LAW NAT/G
CULTURE ADMIN LEAD PERSON...HUM MGT SOC. PAGE 2 DIPLOM
B0029

N
MINISTERE DE L'EDUC NATIONALE,CATALOGUE DES THESES BIBLIOG
DE DOCTORAT SOUTENNES DEVANT LES UNIVERSITAIRES ACADEM
FRANCAISES. FRANCE LAW DIPLOM ADMIN...HUM SOC 20. KNOWL
PAGE 74 B1490 NAT/G

B42
SINGTON D.,THE GOEBBELS EXPERIMENT. GERMANY MOD/EUR FASCISM
NAT/G EX/STRUC FORCES CONTROL ROUTINE WAR TOTALISM EDU/PROP
PWR...ART/METH HUM 20 NAZI GOEBBELS/J. PAGE 97 ATTIT
B1970 COM/IND

B45
PLATO,THE REPUBLIC. MEDIT-7 UNIV SOCIETY STRUCT PERSON
EX/STRUC FORCES UTOPIA ATTIT PERCEPT HEALTH KNOWL PHIL/SCI
ORD/FREE PWR...HUM CONCPT STERTYP TOT/POP. PAGE 83
B1681

WU E.,LEADERS OF TWENTIETH-CENTURY CHINA: AN   BIBLIOG/A
ANNOTATED BIBLIOGRAPHY OF SELECTED CHINESE   BIOG
BIOGRAPHICAL WORKS IN HOOVER LIBRARY. ASIA INDUS   INTELL
POL/PAR DIPLOM ADMIN REV WAR...HUM MGT 20. PAGE 118 CHIEF
B2386   B56

ASHER R.E.,THE UNITED NATIONS AND THE PROMOTION OF INT/ORG
THE GENERAL WELFARE. WOR+45 WOR-45 ECO/UNDEV   CONSULT
EX/STRUC ACT/RES PLAN EDU/PROP ROUTINE HEALTH...HUM
CONCPT CHARTS UNESCO UN ILO 20. PAGE 7 B0139   B57

CENTRAL ASIAN RESEARCH CENTRE,BIBLIOGRAPHY OF   BIBLIOG/A
RECENT SOVIET SOURCE MATERIAL ON SOVIET CENTRAL COM
ASIA AND THE BORDERLANDS. AFGHANISTN INDIA PAKISTAN CULTURE
UAR USSR ECO/UNDEV AGRI EXTR/IND INDUS ACADEM ADMIN NAT/G
...HEAL HUM LING CON/ANAL 20. PAGE 19 B0399   B57

SHARP W.R.,FIELD ADMINISTRATION IN THE UNITED   INT/ORG
NATION SYSTEM: THE CONDUCT OF INTERNATIONAL   CONSULT
ECONOMIC AND SOCIAL PROGRAMS. FUT WOR+45 CONSTN
SOCIETY ECO/UNDEV R+D DELIB/GP ACT/RES TEC/DEV
EDU/PROP EXEC ROUTINE HEALTH WEALTH...HUM CONCPT
CHARTS METH ILO UNESCO VAL/FREE UN 20. PAGE 96
B1939   B61

SIMON Y.R.,A GENERAL THEORY OF AUTHORITY. DOMIN PERS/REL
ADMIN RATIONAL UTOPIA KNOWL MORAL PWR SOVEREIGN PERSON
...HUM CONCPT NEW/IDEA 20. PAGE 97 B1962   SOCIETY
                              ORD/FREE
                              B62

KOGAN N.,THE POLITICS OF ITALIAN FOREIGN POLICY. NAT/G
EUR+WWI LEGIS DOMIN LEGIT EXEC PWR RESPECT SKILL ROUTINE
...POLICY DECISION HUM SOC METH/CNCPT OBS INT   DIPLOM
CHARTS 20. PAGE 61 B1227   ITALY
                              B63

STEVENSON A.E.,LOOKING OUTWARD: YEARS OF CRISIS AT INT/ORG
THE UNITED NATIONS. COM CUBA USA+45 WOR+45 SOCIETY CONCPT
NAT/G EX/STRUC ACT/RES LEGIT COLONIAL ATTIT PERSON ARMS/CONT
SUPEGO ALL/VALS...POLICY HUM UN COLD/WAR CONGO 20.
PAGE 100 B2034   B63

TURNER M.C.,LIBROS EN VENTA EN HISPANOAMERICA Y BIBLIOG
ESPANA. SPAIN LAW CONSTN CULTURE ADMIN LEAD...HUM L/A+17C
SOC 20. PAGE 106 B2139   NAT/G
                              DIPLOM
                              B64

UN PUB. INFORM. ORGAN.,EVERY MAN'S UNITED NATIONS. INT/ORG
UNIV WOR+45 CONSTN CULTURE SOCIETY ECO/DEV   ROUTINE
ECO/UNDEV NAT/G ACT/RES PLAN ECO/TAC INT/TRADE
EDU/PROP LEGIT PEACE ATTIT ALL/VALS...POLICY HUM
INT/LAW CONCPT CHARTS UN TOT/POP 20. PAGE 106 B2150 B64

RUBINSTEIN A.Z.,"YUGOSLAVIA'S OPENING SOCIETY." COM CONSTN
USSR INTELL NAT/G LEGIS TOP/EX LEGIT CT/SYS   EX/STRUC
RIGID/FLEX ALL/VALS SOCISM...HUM TIME/SEQ TREND 20. YUGOSLAVIA
PAGE 92 B1851   S65

HANKE L.,HANDBOOK OF LATIN AMERICAN STUDIES.   BIBLIOG/A
ECO/UNDEV ADMIN LEAD...HUM SOC 20. PAGE 46 B0937 L/A+17C
                              INDEX
                              NAT/G
                              B66

RAEFF M.,ORIGINS OF THE RUSSIAN INTELLIGENTSIA: THE INTELL
EIGHTEENTH-CENTURY NOBILITY. RUSSIA FAM NAT/G   ELITES
EDU/PROP ADMIN PERS/REL ATTIT...HUM BIOG 18.   STRATA
PAGE 85 B1728   CONSERVE
                              B66

POOLE W.F.,INDEX TO PERIODICAL LITERATURE. LOC/G BIBLIOG
NAT/G DIPLOM ADMIN...HUM PHIL/SCI SOC 19. PAGE 84 USA-45
B1690   ALL/VALS
                              SOCIETY

HUM/RIGHTS....HUMAN RIGHTS, DECLARATIONS OF HUMAN RIGHTS,
    AND HUMAN RIGHTS COMMISSIONS (OFFICIAL ORGANIZATIONS)

HUMAN DEVELOPMENTAL CHANGE....SEE DEVELOPMNT

HUMAN NATURE....SEE PERSON

HUMAN RELATIONS....SEE RELATIONS INDEX

HUMAN RIGHTS, DECLARATIONS OF HUMAN RIGHTS, AND HUMAN
    RIGHTS COMMISSIONS (OFFICIAL ORGANIZATIONS)....SEE
    HUM/RIGHTS

HUMANISM....HUMANISM AND HUMANISTS

HUMANITARIANISM....SEE HUMANISM

HUMANITIES....SEE HUM

HUME/D....DAVID HUME

HUMPHREY H.H. B1063,B1064

HUMPHREY/H....HUBERT HORATIO HUMPHREY

HUNGARY....SEE ALSO COM

KYRIAK T.E.,EAST EUROPE: BIBLIOGRAPHY--INDEX TO US BIBLIOG/A
JPRS RESEARCH TRANSLATIONS. ALBANIA BULGARIA COM PRESS
CZECHOSLVK HUNGARY POLAND ROMANIA AGRI EXTR/IND MARXISM
FINAN SERV/IND INT/TRADE WEAPON...GEOG MGT SOC 20. INDUS
PAGE 62 B1247   N

POOL I.,SATELLITE GENERALS: A STUDY OF MILITARY FORCES
ELITES IN THE SOVIET SPHERE. ASIA CHINA/COM COM CHOOSE
CZECHOSLVK FUT HUNGARY POLAND ROMANIA USSR ELITES
STRATA ADMIN ATTIT PWR SKILL...METH/CNCPT BIOG 20.
PAGE 84 B1688   B55

LENDVAI P.,"HUNGARY* CHANGE VS. IMMOBILISM."   ECO/DEV
HUNGARY LABOR NAT/G PLAN DEBATE ADMIN ROUTINE   MGT
CENTRAL EFFICIENCY MARXISM PLURISM...PREDICT 20. CHOOSE
PAGE 64 B1289   S67

HUNTINGTON S.P. B0334,B1065,B1066,B1067

HUNTNGTN/S....SAMUEL P. HUNTINGTON

HUNTON/P....PHILIP HUNTON

HURLEY/PJ....PATRICK J. HURLEY

HUSSEIN....KING HUSSEIN I, KING OF JORDAN

HUTCHINS/R....ROBERT HUTCHINS

HUTCHINSON C.E. B1068

HUZAR E. B1069

HYDE L.K.G. B1070

HYNEMAN C.S. B1071

HYPO/EXP....INTELLECTUAL CONSTRUCTS

EGLE W.P.,ECONOMIC STABILIZATION. USA+45 SOCIETY NAT/G
FINAN MARKET PLAN ECO/TAC DOMIN EDU/PROP LEGIT EXEC ECO/DEV
WEALTH...CONCPT METH/CNCPT TREND HYPO/EXP GEN/METH CAP/ISM
TOT/POP VAL/FREE 20. PAGE 32 B0656   B52

DRUCKER P.F.,"'MANAGEMENT SCIENCE' AND THE   MGT
MANAGER." PLAN ROUTINE RIGID/FLEX...METH/CNCPT LOG STRUCT
HYPO/EXP. PAGE 30 B0620   DECISION
                            RATIONAL
                            S55

ARGYRIS C.,"SOME PROBLEMS IN CONCEPTUALIZING   FINAN
ORGANIZATIONAL CLIMATE: A CASE STUDY OF A BANK" CONCPT
(BMR)" USA+45 EX/STRUC ADMIN PERS/REL ADJUST PERSON LG/CO
...POLICY HYPO/EXP SIMUL 20. PAGE 6 B0129   INGP/REL
                            S58

DAHL R.A.,"A CRITIQUE OF THE RULING ELITE MODEL." CONCPT
USA+45 LOC/G MUNIC NAT/G POL/PAR PROVS DOMIN LEGIT STERTYP
ADMIN...METH/CNCPT HYPO/EXP. PAGE 25 B0520   ELITES
                            S58

HELMER O.,"THE PROSPECTS OF A UNIFIED THEORY OF SIMUL
ORGANIZATIONS" UNIV ACT/RES ADMIN...CONCPT HYPO/EXP LG/CO
METH. PAGE 49 B0989   METH/CNCPT
                            GAME
                            L59

BENNIS W.G.,"LEADERSHIP THEORY AND ADMINISTRATIVE LEAD
BEHAVIOR: THE PROBLEM OF AUTHORITY." ROUTINE...MGT ADMIN
HYPO/EXP. PAGE 10 B0214   DOMIN
                            PERS/REL
                            S61

BARTLEY H.J.,"COMMAND EXPERIENCE." USA+45 EX/STRUC CONCPT
FORCES LEGIT ROUTINE SKILL...POLICY OBS HYPO/EXP TREND
GEN/LAWS 20. PAGE 9 B0191   S61

BENNIS W.G.,"REVISIONIST THEORY OF LEADERSHIP"   LEAD
MUNIC ACT/RES TEC/DEV...SIMUL 20. PAGE 11 B0215 ADMIN
                            PERS/REL
                            HYPO/EXP
                            B62

SNYDER R.C.,FOREIGN POLICY DECISION-MAKING. FUT TEC/DEV
KOREA WOR+45 R+D CREATE ADMIN ROUTINE PWR   HYPO/EXP
...DECISION PSY SOC CONCPT METH/CNCPT CON/ANAL DIPLOM
CHARTS GEN/METH METH 20. PAGE 99 B1992   S62

IKLE F.C.,"POLITICAL NEGOTIATION AS A PROCESS OF ROUTINE
MODIFYING UTILITIES." WOR+45 FACE/GP LABOR NAT/G DECISION
FORCES ACT/RES EDU/PROP DETER PERCEPT ALL/VALS   DIPLOM
...PSY NEW/IDEA HYPO/EXP GEN/METH 20. PAGE 53 B1076
                            B63

BONINI C.P.,SIMULATION OF INFORMATION AND DECISION INDUS

SYSTEMS IN THE FIRM. MARKET BUDGET DOMIN EDU/PROP   SIMUL
ADMIN COST ATTIT HABITAT PERCEPT PWR...CONCPT   DECISION
PROBABIL QUANT PREDICT HYPO/EXP BIBLIOG. PAGE 13   MGT
B0273
                                                     B63
TUCKER R.C.,THE SOVIET POLITICAL MIND. COM INTELL   STRUCT
NAT/G TOP/EX EDU/PROP ADMIN COERCE TOTALSM ATTIT   RIGID/FLEX
PWR MARXISM...PSY MYTH HYPO/EXP 20. PAGE 106 B2135   ELITES
                                                     USSR
                                                     S63
BACHRACH P.,"DECISIONS AND NONDECISIONS: AN   PWR
ANALYTICAL FRAMEWORK." UNIV SOCIETY CREATE LEGIT   HYPO/EXP
ADMIN EXEC COERCE...DECISION PSY CONCPT CHARTS.
PAGE 8 B0156
                                                     S63
STANLEY T.W.,"DECENTRALIZING NUCLEAR CONTROL IN   INT/ORG
NATO." EUR+WWI USA+45 ELITES FORCES ACT/RES ATTIT   EX/STRUC
ORD/FREE PWR...NEW/IDEA HYPO/EXP TOT/POP 20 NATO.   NUC/PWR
PAGE 100 B2022
                                                     B64
COLLINS B.E.,A SOCIAL PSYCHOLOGY OF GROUP PROCESSES FACE/GP
FOR DECISION-MAKING. PROB/SOLV ROUTINE...SOC CHARTS DECISION
HYPO/EXP. PAGE 22 B0453   NAT/G
                                                     INDUS
                                                     B64
MAYER C.S.,INTERVIEWING COSTS IN SURVEY RESEARCH.   SIMUL
USA+45 PLAN COST...MGT REC/INT SAMP METH/COMP   INT
HYPO/EXP METH 20. PAGE 71 B1434   R+D
                                                     EFFICIENCY
                                                     B65
ANTHONY R.N.,PLANNING AND CONTROL SYSTEMS. UNIV   CONTROL
OP/RES...DECISION MGT LING. PAGE 6 B0114   PLAN
                                                     METH
                                                     HYPO/EXP
                                                     B65
HODGSON R.C.,THE EXECUTIVE ROLE CONSTELLATION: AN   LG/CO
ANALYSIS OF PERSONALITY AND ROLE RELATIONS IN   ADMIN
MANAGEMENT. USA+45 PUB/INST EXEC PERS/REL PERSON   TOP/EX
...PSY PERS/COMP HYPO/EXP 20. PAGE 51 B1027   ROLE
                                                     B65
SINGER J.D.,HUMAN BEHAVIOR AND INTERNATIONAL   DIPLOM
POLITICS* CONTRIBUTIONS FROM THE SOCIAL-   PHIL/SCI
PSYCHOLOGICAL SCIENCES. ACT/RES PLAN EDU/PROP ADMIN QUANT
KNOWL...DECISION PSY SOC NET/THEORY HYPO/EXP   SIMUL
LAB/EXP SOC/EXP GEN/METH ANTHOL BIBLIOG. PAGE 97
B1965
                                                     B65
STEINER G.A.,THE CREATIVE ORGANIZATION. ELITES   CREATE
LG/CO PLAN PROB/SOLV TEC/DEV INSPECT CAP/ISM   MGT
CONTROL EXEC PERSON...METH/COMP HYPO/EXP 20.   ADMIN
PAGE 100 B2029   SOC
                                                     B67
VOOS H.,ORGANIZATIONAL COMMUNICATION: A   BIBLIOG/A
BIBLIOGRAPHY. WOR+45 STRATA R+D PROB/SOLV FEEDBACK   INDUS
COERCE...MGT PSY NET/THEORY HYPO/EXP. PAGE 112   COM/IND
B2268   VOL/ASSN
                                                     S67
BURACK E.H.,"INDUSTRIAL MANAGEMENT IN ADVANCED   ADMIN
PRODUCTION SYSTEMS: SOME THEORETICAL CONCEPTS AND   MGT
PRELIMINARY FINDINGS." INDUS CREATE PLAN PRODUC   TEC/DEV
ROLE...OBS STAND/INT DEEP/QU HYPO/EXP ORG/CHARTS   EX/STRUC
20. PAGE 17 B0346
                                                     S67
LANDES W.M.,"THE EFFECT OF STATE FAIR EMPLOYMENT   DISCRIM
LAWS ON THE ECONOMIC POSITION OF NONWHITES." USA+45 LAW
PROVS SECT LEGIS ADMIN GP/REL RACE/REL...JURID   WORKER
CONCPT CHARTS HYPO/EXP NEGRO. PAGE 62 B1255

HYPOTHETICAL EXPERIMENTS....SEE HYPO/EXP

IADB....INTER-ASIAN DEVELOPMENT BANK

IAEA....INTERNATIONAL ATOMIC ENERGY AGENCY

                                                     S59
STOESSINGER J.G.,"THE INTERNATIONAL ATOMIC ENERGY   INT/ORG
AGENCY: THE FIRST PHASE." FUT WOR+45 NAT/G VOL/ASSN ECO/DEV
DELIB/GP BAL/PWR LEGIT ADMIN ROUTINE PWR...OBS   FOR/AID
CON/ANAL GEN/LAWS VAL/FREE 20 IAEA. PAGE 101 B2040   NUC/PWR

IANNACCONE L. B1072

IBERO-AMERICAN INSTITUTES B1073

IBO....IBO TRIBE

IBRD....INTERNATIONAL BANK FOR RECONSTRUCTION AND
   DEVELOPMENT

ICA....INTERNATIONAL COOPERATION ADMINISTRATION

                                                     B61
ROBINSON M.E.,EDUCATION FOR SOCIAL CHANGE: FOR/AID
ESTABLISHING INSTITUTES OF PUBLIC AND BUSINESS   EDU/PROP
ADMINISTRATION ABROAD (PAMPHLET). WOR+45 SOCIETY   MGT
ACADEM CONFER INGP/REL ROLE...SOC CHARTS BIBLIOG 20 ADJUST

ICA. PAGE 89 B1805

ICC....U.S. INTERSTATE COMMERCE COMMISSION

ICELAND....ICELAND

                                                     B64
ANDREN N.,GOVERNMENT AND POLITICS IN THE NORDIC   CONSTN
COUNTRIES: DENMARK, FINLAND, ICELAND, NORWAY,   NAT/G
SWEDEN. DENMARK FINLAND ICELAND NORWAY SWEDEN   CULTURE
POL/PAR CHIEF LEGIS ADMIN REGION REPRESENT ATTIT   GOV/COMP
CONSERVE...CHARTS BIBLIOG/A 20. PAGE 5 B0102

ICJ....INTERNATIONAL COURT OF JUSTICE; SEE ALSO WORLD/CT

ICSU....INTERNATIONAL COUNCIL OF SCIENTIFIC UNIONS

IDA....INTERNATIONAL DEVELOPMENT ASSOCIATION

IDAHO....IDAHO

IDEA....SEE NEW/IDEA

IDEA/COMP....COMPARISON OF IDEAS

                                                     N
INTERNATIONAL BIBLIOGRAPHY OF ECONOMICS. WOR+45   BIBLIOG
FINAN MARKET ADMIN DEMAND INCOME PRODUC...POLICY   ECO/DEV
IDEA/COMP METH. PAGE 1 B0003   ECO/UNDEV
                                                     INT/TRADE
                                                     N
NEUE POLITISCHE LITERATUR; BERICHTE UBER DAS   BIBLIOG/A
INTERNATIONALE SCHRIFTTUM ZUR POLITIK. WOR+45 LAW   DIPLOM
CONSTN POL/PAR ADMIN LEAD GOV/REL...POLICY   NAT/G
IDEA/COMP. PAGE 2 B0027   NAT/COMP
                                                     N
UNESCO,INTERNATIONAL BIBLIOGRAPHY OF POLITICAL   BIBLIOG
SCIENCE (VOLUMES 1-8). WOR+45 LAW NAT/G EX/STRUC   CONCPT
LEGIS PROB/SOLV DIPLOM ADMIN GOV/REL 20 UNESCO.   IDEA/COMP
PAGE 107 B2153
                                                     B24
HOLDSWORTH W.S.,A HISTORY OF ENGLISH LAW; THE   LAW
COMMON LAW AND ITS RIVALS (VOL. V). UK SEA EX/STRUC LEGIS
WRITING ADMIN...INT/LAW JURID CONCPT IDEA/COMP   ADJUD
WORSHIP 16/17 PARLIAMENT ENGLSH/LAW COMMON/LAW.   CT/SYS
PAGE 51 B1033
                                                     B42
WRIGHT D.M.,THE CREATION OF PURCHASING POWER.   FINAN
USA-45 NAT/G PRICE ADMIN WAR INCOME PRODUC...POLICY ECO/TAC
CONCPT IDEA/COMP BIBLIOG 20 MONEY. PAGE 118 B2378   ECO/DEV
                                                     CREATE
                                                     B49
STEIN H.,THE FOREIGN SERVICE ACT OF 1946. USA+45   DIPLOM
ELITES EX/STRUC PLAN PROB/SOLV LOBBY GOV/REL   LAW
PERS/REL RIGID/FLEX...POLICY IDEA/COMP 20 CONGRESS   NAT/G
BUR/BUDGET. PAGE 100 B2027   ADMIN
                                                     L49
MARX C.M.,"ADMINISTRATIVE ETHICS AND THE RULE OF   ADMIN
LAW." USA+45 ELITES ACT/RES DOMIN NEUTRAL ROUTINE   LAW
INGP/REL ORD/FREE...JURID IDEA/COMP. PAGE 70 B1417
                                                     S49
REISSMAN L.,"A STUDY OF ROLE CONCEPTIONS IN   ADMIN
BUREAUCRACY" (BMR)" PERS/REL ROLE...SOC CONCPT   METH/CNCPT
NEW/IDEA IDEA/COMP SOC/EXP 20 BUREAUCRCY. PAGE 87   GEN/LAWS
B1767   PROB/SOLV
                                                     S50
NEUMANN F.L.,"APPROACHES TO THE STUDY OF POLITICAL   PWR
POWER." POL/PAR TOP/EX ADMIN LEAD ATTIT ORD/FREE   IDEA/COMP
CONSERVE LAISSEZ MARXISM...PSY SOC. PAGE 78 B1572   CONCPT
                                                     B51
PETERSON F.,SURVEY OF LABOR ECONOMICS (REV. ED.).   WORKER
STRATA ECO/DEV LABOR INSPECT BARGAIN PAY PRICE EXEC DEMAND
ROUTINE GP/REL ALL/VALS ORD/FREE 20 AFL/CIO   IDEA/COMP
DEPT/LABOR. PAGE 82 B1662   T
                                                     B51
WHITE L.D.,THE JEFFERSONIANS: A STUDY IN   ADMIN
ADMINISTRATIVE HISTORY 18011829. USA-45 DELIB/GP   NAT/G
LEGIS TOP/EX PROB/SOLV BUDGET ECO/TAC GP/REL   POLICY
FEDERAL...BIOG IDEA/COMP 19 PRESIDENT CONGRESS   POL/PAR
JEFFERSN/T. PAGE 116 B2338
                                                     S52
TAYLOR R.W.,"ARTHUR F. BENTLEY'S POLITICAL SCIENCE" GEN/LAWS
(BMR)" USA+45 INTELL NAT/G...DECISION CLASSIF   POLICY
IDEA/COMP 20 BENTLEY/AF. PAGE 103 B2090   ADMIN
                                                     B54
SCHWARTZ B.,FRENCH ADMINISTRATIVE LAW AND THE   JURID
COMMON-LAW WORLD. FRANCE CULTURE LOC/G NAT/G PROVS   LAW
DELIB/GP EX/STRUC LEGIS PROB/SOLV CT/SYS EXEC   METH/COMP
GOV/REL...IDEA/COMP ENGLSH/LAW. PAGE 95 B1912   ADJUD
                                                     B55
BAILEY S.K.,RESEARCH FRONTIERS IN POLITICS AND   R+D
GOVERNMENT. CONSTN LEGIS ADMIN REV CHOOSE...CONCPT   METH
IDEA/COMP GAME ANTHOL 20. PAGE 8 B0164   NAT/G
                                                     S55
BUNZEL J.H.,"THE GENERAL IDEOLOGY OF AMERICAN SMALL ALL/IDEOS
BUSINESS"(BMR)" USA+45 USA-45 AGRI GP/REL INGP/REL   ATTIT

PERSON...MGT IDEA/COMP 18/20. PAGE 17 B0345
SML/CO
INDUS
S55

KAUTSKY J.H.,"THE NEW STRATEGY OF INTERNATIONAL
COMMUNISM." ASIA CHINA/COM FUT WOR+45 WOR-45 ADMIN
ROUTINE PERSON MARXISM SOCISM...TREND IDEA/COMP 20
LENIN/VI MAO. PAGE 59 B1184
COM
POL/PAR
TOTALISM
USSR
L56

LITCHFIELD E.H.,"NOTES ON A GENERAL THEORY OF
ADMINISTRATION." USA+45 OP/RES PROB/SOLV EFFICIENCY
IDEA/COMP. PAGE 66 B1324
ADMIN
ROUTINE
MGT
B58

CONSERVATIVE POLITICAL CENTRE,A WORLD SECURITY
AUTHORITY? WOR+45 CONSTN ELITES FINAN DELIB/GP PLAN
PROB/SOLV ADMIN CONTROL NUC/PWR GP/REL...IDEA/COMP
20. PAGE 23 B0468
ORD/FREE
CONSERVE
FORCES
ARMS/CONT
B58

SWEENEY S.B.,EDUCATION FOR ADMINISTRATIVE CAREERS
IN GOVERNMENT SERVICE. USA+45 ACADEM CONSULT CREATE
PLAN CONFER SKILL...TREND IDEA/COMP METH 20
CIVIL/SERV. PAGE 102 B2059
EDU/PROP
ADMIN
NAT/G
LOC/G
B59

COUNCIL OF STATE GOVERNORS,AMERICAN LEGISLATURES:
STRUCTURE AND PROCEDURES. SUMMARY AND TABULATIONS
OF A 1959 SURVEY. PUERT/RICO USA+45 PAY ADJUD ADMIN
APPORT...IDEA/COMP 20 GUAM VIRGIN/ISL. PAGE 24
B0495
LEGIS
CHARTS
PROVS
REPRESENT
B59

WELTON H.,THE THIRD WORLD WAR; TRADE AND INDUSTRY,
THE NEW BATTLEGROUND. WOR+45 ECO/DEV INDUS MARKET
TASK...MGT IDEA/COMP COLD/WAR. PAGE 115 B2321
INT/TRADE
PLAN
DIPLOM
L59

"A BIBLIOGRAPHICAL ESSAY ON DECISION MAKING."
WOR+45 WOR-45 STRUCT OP/RES GP/REL...CONCPT
IDEA/COMP METH 20. PAGE 2 B0038
BIBLIOG/A
DECISION
ADMIN
LEAD
S59

BENDIX R.,"INDUSTRIALIZATION, IDEOLOGIES, AND
SOCIAL STRUCTURE" (BMR)" UK USA-45 USSR STRUCT
WORKER GP/REL EFFICIENCY...IDEA/COMP 20. PAGE 10
B0210
INDUS
ATTIT
MGT
ADMIN
S59

STINCHCOMBE A.L.,"BUREAUCRATIC AND CRAFT
ADMINISTRATION OF PRODUCTION: A COMPARATIVE STUDY"
(BMR)" USA+45 STRUCT EX/STRUC ECO/TAC GP/REL
...CLASSIF GP/COMP IDEA/COMP GEN/LAWS 20 WEBER/MAX.
PAGE 101 B2039
CONSTRUC
PROC/MFG
ADMIN
PLAN
B60

ANGERS F.A.,ESSAI SUR LA CENTRALISATION: ANALYSE
DES PRINCIPES ET PERSPECTIVES CANADIENNES. CANADA
ECO/TAC CONTROL...SOC IDEA/COMP BIBLIOG 20. PAGE 5
B0111
CENTRAL
ADMIN
B60

BAERWALD F.,ECONOMIC SYSTEM ANALYSIS: CONCEPTS AND
PERSPECTIVES. USA+45 ECO/DEV NAT/G COMPUTER EQUILIB
INCOME ATTIT...DECISION CONCPT IDEA/COMP. PAGE 8
B0159
ACT/RES
ECO/TAC
ROUTINE
FINAN
B60

HAYEK F.A.,THE CONSTITUTION OF LIBERTY. UNIV LAW
CONSTN WORKER TAX EDU/PROP ADMIN CT/SYS COERCE
DISCRIM...IDEA/COMP 20. PAGE 48 B0974
ORD/FREE
CHOOSE
NAT/G
CONCPT
B60

MEYRIAT J.,LA SCIENCE POLITIQUE EN FRANCE,
1945-1958; BIBLIOGRAPHIES FRANCAISES DE SCIENCES
SOCIALES (VOL. I). EUR+WWI FRANCE POL/PAR DIPLOM
ADMIN CHOOSE ATTIT...IDEA/COMP METH/COMP NAT/COMP
20. PAGE 73 B1478
BIBLIOG/A
NAT/G
CONCPT
PHIL/SCI
S60

PFIFFNER J.M.,"ADMINISTRATIVE RATIONALITY" (BMR)"
UNIV CONTROL...POLICY IDEA/COMP SIMUL. PAGE 83
B1667
ADMIN
DECISION
RATIONAL
B61

KRUPP S.,PATTERN IN ORGANIZATIONAL ANALYSIS: A
CRITICAL EXAMINATION. INGP/REL PERS/REL RATIONAL
ATTIT AUTHORIT DRIVE PWR...DECISION PHIL/SCI SOC
IDEA/COMP. PAGE 61 B1239
MGT
CONTROL
CONCPT
METH/CNCPT
B61

LENIN V.I.,WHAT IS TO BE DONE? (1902). RUSSIA LABOR
NAT/G POL/PAR WORKER CAP/ISM ECO/TAC ADMIN PARTIC
...MARXIST IDEA/COMP GEN/LAWS 19/20. PAGE 64 B1292
EDU/PROP
PRESS
MARXISM
METH/COMP
B61

TANZER L.,THE KENNEDY CIRCLE. INTELL CONSULT
DELIB/GP TOP/EX CONTROL EXEC INGP/REL PERS/REL PWR
...BIOG IDEA/COMP ANTHOL 20 KENNEDY/JF PRESIDENT
DEMOCRAT MCNAMARA/R RUSK/D. PAGE 103 B2077
EX/STRUC
NAT/G
CHIEF
C61

VERBA S.,"SMALL GROUPS AND POLITICAL BEHAVIOR: A
STUDY OF LEADERSHIP" DOMIN PARTIC ROUTINE GP/REL
ATTIT DRIVE ALL/VALS...CONCPT IDEA/COMP LAB/EXP
BIBLIOG METH. PAGE 112 B2259
LEAD
ELITES
FACE/GP
B62

BOCK E.A.,CASE STUDIES IN AMERICAN GOVERNMENT.
USA+45 ECO/DEV CHIEF EDU/PROP CT/SYS RACE/REL
ORD/FREE...JURID MGT PHIL/SCI PRESIDENT CASEBOOK.
POLICY
LEGIS
IDEA/COMP

PAGE 13 B0262
NAT/G
B62

LIPPMANN W.,PREFACE TO POLITICS. LABOR CHIEF
CONTROL LEAD...MYTH IDEA/COMP 19/20 ROOSEVLT/T
TAMMANY WILSON/H SANTAYAN/G BERGSON/H. PAGE 65
B1318
PARTIC
ATTIT
ADMIN
B62

MEANS G.C.,THE CORPORATE REVOLUTION IN AMERICA:
ECONOMIC REALITY VS. ECONOMIC THEORY. USA+45 USA-45
INDUS WORKER PLAN CAP/ISM ADMIN...IDEA/COMP 20.
PAGE 72 B1459
LG/CO
MARKET
CONTROL
PRICE
B63

INTL INST ADMIN SCIENCES,EDUCATION IN PUBLIC
ADMINISTRATION: A SYMPOSIUM ON TEACHING METHODS AND
MATERIALS. WOR+45 SCHOOL CONSULT CREATE CONFER
SKILL...OBS TREND IDEA/COMP METH/COMP 20. PAGE 54
B1100
EDU/PROP
METH
ADMIN
ACADEM
B63

LEONARD T.J.,THE FEDERAL SYSTEM OF INDIA. INDIA
MUNIC NAT/G PROVS ADMIN SOVEREIGN...IDEA/COMP 20.
PAGE 64 B1293
FEDERAL
MGT
NAT/COMP
METH/COMP
B63

WADE H.W.R.,TOWARDS ADMINISTRATIVE JUSTICE. UK
USA+45 CONSTN CONSULT PROB/SOLV CT/SYS PARL/PROC
...POLICY JURID METH/COMP 20 ENGLSH/LAW. PAGE 112
B2270
ADJUD
IDEA/COMP
ADMIN
B64

BOTTOMORE T.B.,ELITES AND SOCIETY. INTELL STRATA
ECO/DEV ECO/UNDEV ADMIN GP/REL ORD/FREE...CONCPT
BIBLIOG 20. PAGE 14 B0281
ELITES
IDEA/COMP
SOCIETY
SOC
B64

HODGETTS J.E.,ADMINISTERING THE ATOM FOR PEACE.
OP/RES TEC/DEV ADMIN...IDEA/COMP METH/COMP 20.
PAGE 50 B1025
PROB/SOLV
NUC/PWR
PEACE
MGT
B64

KARIEL H.S.,IN SEARCH OF AUTHORITY: TWENTIETH-
CENTURY POLITICAL THOUGHT. WOR+45 WOR-45 NAT/G
EX/STRUC TOTALISM DRIVE PWR...MGT PHIL/SCI GEN/LAWS
19/20 NIETZSCH/F FREUD/S WEBER/MAX NIEBUHR/R
MARITAIN/J. PAGE 58 B1173
CONSTN
CONCPT
ORD/FREE
IDEA/COMP
B64

STANLEY D.T.,THE HIGHER CIVIL SERVICE: AN
EVALUATION OF FEDERAL PERSONNEL PRACTICES. USA+45
CREATE EXEC ROUTINE CENTRAL...MGT SAMP IDEA/COMP
METH/COMP 20 CIVIL/SERV. PAGE 100 B2020
NAT/G
ADMIN
CONTROL
EFFICIENCY
S64

LIPSET S.M.,"SOCIOLOGY AND POLITICAL SCIENCE: A
BIBLIOGRAPHICAL NOTE." WOR+45 ELITES LEGIS ADJUD
ADMIN ATTIT IDEA/COMP. PAGE 65 B1321
BIBLIOG/A
SOC
METH/COMP
B65

BOGUSLAW R.,THE NEW UTOPIANS. OP/RES ADMIN CONTROL
PWR...IDEA/COMP SIMUL 20. PAGE 13 B0265
UTOPIA
AUTOMAT
COMPUTER
PLAN
B65

BUECHNER J.C.,DIFFERENCES IN ROLE PERCEPTIONS IN
COLORADO COUNCIL-MANAGER CITIES. USA+45 ADMIN
ROUTINE GP/REL CONSEN PERCEPT PERSON ROLE
...DECISION MGT STAT INT QU CHARTS 20 COLORADO
CITY/MGT. PAGE 17 B0338
MUNIC
CONSULT
LOC/G
IDEA/COMP
B65

CAVERS D.F.,THE CHOICE-OF-LAW PROCESS. PROB/SOLV
ADJUD CT/SYS CHOOSE RATIONAL...IDEA/COMP 16/20
TREATY. PAGE 19 B0396
JURID
DECISION
METH/COMP
ADMIN
B65

CRAMER J.F.,CONTEMPORARY EDUCATION: A COMPARATIVE
STUDY OF NATIONAL SYSTEMS (2ND ED.). CHINA/COM
EUR+WWI INDIA USA+45 FINAN PROB/SOLV ADMIN CONTROL
ATTIT...IDEA/COMP METH/COMP 20 CHINJAP. PAGE 25
B0502
EDU/PROP
NAT/COMP
SCHOOL
ACADEM
B65

GOPAL S.,BRITISH POLICY IN INDIA 1858-1905. INDIA
UK ELITES CHIEF DELIB/GP ECO/TAC GP/REL DISCRIM
ATTIT...IDEA/COMP NAT/COMP PERS/COMP BIBLIOG/A
19/20. PAGE 41 B0828
COLONIAL
ADMIN
POL/PAR
ECO/UNDEV
B65

GOTLIEB A.,DISARMAMENT AND INTERNATIONAL LAW* A
STUDY OF THE ROLE OF LAW IN THE DISARMAMENT
PROCESS. USA+45 USSR PROB/SOLV CONFER ADMIN ROUTINE
NUC/PWR ORD/FREE SOVEREIGN UN TREATY. PAGE 42 B0841
INT/LAW
INT/ORG
ARMS/CONT
IDEA/COMP
B65

GREGG J.L.,POLITICAL PARTIES AND PARTY SYSTEMS IN
GUATEMALA, 1944-1963. GUATEMALA L/A+17C EX/STRUC
FORCES CREATE CONTROL REV CHOOSE PWR...TREND
IDEA/COMP 20. PAGE 43 B0872
LEAD
POL/PAR
NAT/G
CHIEF
B65

HUGHES J.M.,EDUCATION IN AMERICA (2ND ED.). USA+45
USA-45 GP/REL INGP/REL AGE/C AGE/Y ROLE...IDEA/COMP
BIBLIOG T 20. PAGE 52 B1059
EDU/PROP
SCHOOL
ADMIN
METH/COMP
B65

LYONS G.M.,SCHOOLS FOR STRATEGY* EDUCATION AND
ACADEM

RESEARCH IN NATIONAL SECURITY AFFAIRS. USA+45 FINAN   ACT/RES
NAT/G VOL/ASSN FORCES TEC/DEV ADMIN WAR...GP/COMP   INTELL
IDEA/COMP PERS/COMP COLD/WAR. PAGE 67 B1351

                                                      B65
SCHAPIRO L.,THE GOVERNMENT AND POLITICS OF THE   MARXISM
SOVIET UNION. USSR WOR+45 WOR-45 ADMIN PARTIC REV   GOV/REL
CHOOSE REPRESENT PWR...POLICY IDEA/COMP 20. PAGE 93   NAT/G
B1880   LOC/G

                                                      S65
HAMMOND P.Y.,"FOREIGN POLICY-MAKING AND   DIPLOM
ADMINISTRATIVE POLITICS." CREATE ADMIN COST   STRUCT
...DECISION CONCPT GAME CONGRESS PRESIDENT. PAGE 46   IDEA/COMP
B0935   OP/RES

                                                      B66
ANDERSON S.V.,CANADIAN OMBUDSMAN PROPOSALS. CANADA   NAT/G
LEGIS DEBATE PARL/PROC...MAJORIT JURID TIME/SEQ   CREATE
IDEA/COMP 20 OMBUDSMAN PARLIAMENT. PAGE 5 B0096   ADMIN
                                                      POL/PAR

                                                      B66
BALDWIN D.A.,FOREIGN AID AND AMERICAN FOREIGN   FOR/AID
POLICY: A DOCUMENTARY ANALYSIS. USA+45 ECO/UNDEV   DIPLOM
ADMIN...ECOMETRIC STAT STYLE CHARTS PROG/TEAC   IDEA/COMP
GEN/LAWS ANTHOL. PAGE 8 B0172

                                                      B66
FOX K.A.,THE THEORY OF QUANTITATIVE ECONOMIC POLICY   ECO/TAC
WITH APPLICATIONS TO ECONOMIC GROWTH AND   ECOMETRIC
STABILIZATION. ECO/DEV AGRI NAT/G PLAN ADMIN RISK   EQUILIB
...DECISION IDEA/COMP SIMUL T. PAGE 37 B0746   GEN/LAWS

                                                      B66
HALPIN A.W.,THEORY AND RESEARCH IN ADMINISTRATION.   GEN/LAWS
ACT/RES LEAD...MGT IDEA/COMP METH/COMP. PAGE 46   EDU/PROP
B0929   ADMIN
                                                      PHIL/SCI

                                                      B66
LIVINGSTON J.C.,THE CONSENT OF THE GOVERNED. USA+45   NAT/G
EX/STRUC BAL/PWR DOMIN CENTRAL PERSON PWR...POLICY   LOBBY
CONCPT OBS IDEA/COMP 20 CONGRESS. PAGE 66 B1331   MAJORIT
                                                      PARTIC

                                                      B66
MONTGOMERY J.D.,APPROACHES TO DEVELOPMENT: ECO/UNDEV
POLITICS, ADMINISTRATION AND CHANGE. USA+45 AGRI   ADMIN
FOR/AID ORD/FREE...CONCPT IDEA/COMP METH/COMP   POLICY
ANTHOL. PAGE 75 B1507   ECO/TAC

                                                      B66
WADIA M.,THE NATURE AND SCOPE OF MANAGEMENT.   MGT
DELIB/GP EX/STRUC CREATE AUTOMAT CONTROL EFFICIENCY   PROB/SOLV
...ANTHOL 20. PAGE 112 B2271   IDEA/COMP
                                                      ECO/TAC

                                                      B67
BROWN L.N.,FRENCH ADMINISTRATIVE LAW. FRANCE UK   EX/STRUC
CONSTN NAT/G LEGIS DOMIN CONTROL EXEC PARL/PROC PWR   LAW
...JURID METH/COMP GEN/METH. PAGE 16 B0324   IDEA/COMP
                                                      CT/SYS

                                                      B67
BRZEZINSKI Z.K.,THE SOVIET BLOC: UNITY AND CONFLICT   NAT/G
(2ND ED., REV., ENLARGED). COM POLAND USSR INTELL   DIPLOM
CHIEF EX/STRUC CONTROL EXEC GOV/REL PWR MARXISM
...TREND IDEA/COMP 20 LENIN/VI MARX/KARL STALIN/J.
PAGE 16 B0336

                                                      B67
DE BLIJ H.J.,SYSTEMATIC POLITICAL GEOGRAPHY. WOR+45   GEOG
STRUCT INT/ORG NAT/G EDU/PROP ADMIN COLONIAL   CONCPT
ROUTINE ORD/FREE PWR...IDEA/COMP T 20. PAGE 27   METH
B0550

                                                      B67
KATZ J.,PSYCHOANALYSIS, PSYCHIATRY, AND LAW. USA+45   LAW
LOC/G NAT/G PUB/INST PROB/SOLV ADMIN HEALTH   PSY
...CRIMLGY CONCPT SAMP/SIZ IDEA/COMP. PAGE 58 B1180   CT/SYS
                                                      ADJUD

                                                      S67
ROSENBERG B.,"ETHNIC LIBERALISM AND EMPLOYMENT   RACE/REL
DISCRIMINATION IN THE NORTH." USA+45 TOP/EX   ATTIT
PROB/SOLV ADMIN REGION PERS/REL DISCRIM...INT   WORKER
IDEA/COMP. PAGE 90 B1820   EXEC

                                                      S67
SCOTT W.R.,"ORGANIZATIONAL EVALUATION AND   EXEC
AUTHORITY." CONTROL SANCTION PERS/REL ATTIT DRIVE   WORKER
...SOC CONCPT OBS CHARTS IDEA/COMP 20. PAGE 95   INSPECT
B1921   EX/STRUC

IDENBURG P.J. B1074

IDEOLOGY....SEE ATTIT, STERTYP, ALSO IDEOLOGICAL TOPIC
     INDEX, P. XIII

IFC....INTERNATIONAL FINANCE CORPORATION

IFFLAND C.P. B0292

IGNORANCE....SEE KNOWL

IGY....INTERNATIONAL GEOPHYSICAL YEAR

IKE N. B1075

IKLE F.C. B1076

ILLEGIT....BASTARDY

                                                      B57
DE GRAZIA A.,GRASS ROOTS PRIVATE WELFARE. LOC/G   NEW/LIB
SCHOOL ACT/RES EDU/PROP ROUTINE CROWD GP/REL   HEALTH
DISCRIM HAPPINESS ILLEGIT AGE HABITAT. PAGE 27   MUNIC
B0554   VOL/ASSN

ILLEGITIMACY....SEE ILLEGIT
ILLINOIS, STATE OF B2024
ILLINOIS....ILLINOIS

                                                      N
STATE OF ILLINOIS,PUBLICATIONS OF THE STATE OF   BIBLIOG
ILLINOIS. USA+45 FINAN POL/PAR ADMIN LEAD 20   PROVS
ILLINOIS. PAGE 100 B2024   LOC/G
                                                      GOV/REL

                                                      N19
FAHRNKOPF N.,STATE AND LOCAL GOVERNMENT IN ILLINOIS   BIBLIOG
(PAMPHLET). CONSTN ADMIN PARTIC CHOOSE REPRESENT   LOC/G
GOV/REL...JURID MGT 20 ILLINOIS. PAGE 34 B0696   LEGIS
                                                      CT/SYS

                                                      S58
DERGE D.R.,"METROPOLITAN AND OUTSTATE ALIGNMENTS IN   LEGIS
ILLINOIS AND MISSOURI LEGISLATIVE DELEGATIONS"   MUNIC
(BMR)" USA+45 ADMIN PARTIC GOV/REL...MYTH CHARTS 20   PROVS
ILLINOIS MISSOURI. PAGE 28 B0575   POL/PAR

                                                      B62
CARPER E.T.,ILLINOIS GOES TO CONGRESS FOR ARMY   ADMIN
LAND. USA+45 LAW EXTR/IND PROVS REGION CIVMIL/REL   LOBBY
GOV/REL FEDERAL ATTIT 20 ILLINOIS SENATE CONGRESS   GEOG
DIRKSEN/E DOUGLAS/P. PAGE 19 B0385   LEGIS

                                                      B67
ILLINOIS COMMISSION,IMPROVING THE STATE   PROVS
LEGISLATURE. USA+45 LAW CONSTN NAT/G PROB/SOLV   LEGIS
EDU/PROP ADMIN TASK CHOOSE INGP/REL EFFICIENCY   REPRESENT
ILLINOIS. PAGE 53 B1077   PLAN

ILLINOIS COMMISSION B1077

ILO....INTERNATIONAL LABOR ORGANIZATION; SEE ALSO INT/ORG

                                                      B45
PASTUHOV V.D.,A GUIDE TO THE PRACTICE OF   INT/ORG
INTERNATIONAL CONFERENCES. WOR+45 PLAN LEGIT   DELIB/GP
ORD/FREE...MGT OBS RECORD VAL/FREE ILO LEAGUE/NAT
20. PAGE 81 B1640

                                                      B56
SOHN L.B.,BASIC DOCUMENTS OF THE UNITED NATIONS.   DELIB/GP
WOR+45 LAW INT/ORG LEGIT EXEC ROUTINE CHOOSE PWR   CONSTN
...JURID CONCPT GEN/LAWS ANTHOL UN TOT/POP OAS FAO
ILO 20. PAGE 99 B1993

                                                      B57
ASHER R.E.,THE UNITED NATIONS AND THE PROMOTION OF   INT/ORG
THE GENERAL WELFARE. WOR+45 WOR-45 ECO/UNDEV   CONSULT
EX/STRUC ACT/RES PLAN EDU/PROP ROUTINE HEALTH...HUM
CONCPT CHARTS UNESCO UN ILO 20. PAGE 7 B0139

                                                      B61
SHARP W.R.,FIELD ADMINISTRATION IN THE UNITED   INT/ORG
NATION SYSTEM: THE CONDUCT OF INTERNATIONAL   CONSULT
ECONOMIC AND SOCIAL PROGRAMS. FUT WOR+45 CONSTN
SOCIETY ECO/UNDEV R+D DELIB/GP ACT/RES PLAN TEC/DEV
EDU/PROP EXEC ROUTINE HEALTH WEALTH...HUM CONCPT
CHARTS METH ILO UNESCO VAL/FREE UN 20. PAGE 96
B1939

                                                      S62
TATOMIR N.,"ORGANIZATIA INTERNATIONALA A MUNCII: INT/ORG
ASPECTE NOI ALE PROBLEMEI IMBUNATATIRII   INT/TRADE
MECANISMULUI EI." EUR+WWI ECO/DEV VOL/ASSN ADMIN
...METH/CNCPT WORK ILO 20. PAGE 103 B2081

                                                      B63
LANGROD G.,THE INTERNATIONAL CIVIL SERVICE: ITS   INT/ORG
ORIGINS, ITS NATURE, ITS EVALUATION. FUT WOR+45   ADMIN
WOR-45 DELIB/GP ACT/RES DOMIN LEGIT ATTIT
RIGID/FLEX SUPEGO ALL/VALS...MGT CONCPT STAT
TIME/SEQ ILO LEAGUE/NAT VAL/FREE 20 UN. PAGE 62
B1259

                                                      B64
SCHECHTER A.H.,INTERPRETATION OF AMBIGUOUS   INT/LAW
DOCUMENTS BY INTERNATIONAL ADMINISTRATIVE   DIPLOM
TRIBUNALS. WOR+45 EX/STRUC INT/TRADE CT/SYS   INT/ORG
SOVEREIGN 20 UN ILO EURCT/JUST. PAGE 93 B1884   ADJUD

                                                      S64
SCHWELB E.,"OPERATION OF THE EUROPEAN CONVENTION ON   INT/ORG
HUMAN RIGHTS." EUR+WWI LAW SOCIETY CREATE EDU/PROP   MORAL
ADJUD ADMIN PEACE ATTIT ORD/FREE PWR...POLICY
INT/LAW CONCPT OBS GEN/LAWS UN VAL/FREE ILO 20
ECHR. PAGE 95 B1916

IMF....INTERNATIONAL MONETARY FUND

IMITATION....SEE NEW/IDEA, CONSEN, CREATE

IMMUNITY....SEE PRIVIL

IMPERIALISM....SEE COLONIAL, SOVEREIGN, DOMIN

IMPERSONALITY....SEE STRANGE

IMPROMPTU INTERVIEW....SEE UNPLAN/INT

INAUGURATE....INAUGURATIONS AND CORONATIONS

INAYATULLAH B1078

INCOME....SEE ALSO FINAN, WEALTH

INTERNATIONAL BIBLIOGRAPHY OF ECONOMICS. WOR+45 FINAN MARKET ADMIN DEMAND INCOME PRODUC...POLICY IDEA/COMP METH. PAGE 1 B0003	N BIBLIOG ECO/DEV ECO/UNDEV INT/TRADE
US SUPERINTENDENT OF DOCUMENTS,TARIFF AND TAXATION (PRICE LIST 37). USA+45 LAW INT/TRADE ADJUD ADMIN CT/SYS INCOME OWN...DECISION GATT. PAGE 111 B2242	N BIBLIOG/A TAX TARIFFS NAT/G
	B41
LESTER R.A.,ECONOMICS OF LABOR. UK USA-45 TEC/DEV BARGAIN PAY INGP/REL INCOME...MGT 19/20. PAGE 64 B1298	LABOR ECO/DEV INDUS WORKER
	B42
WRIGHT D.M.,THE CREATION OF PURCHASING POWER. USA-45 NAT/G PRICE ADMIN WAR INCOME PRODUC...POLICY CONCPT IDEA/COMP BIBLIOG 20 MONEY. PAGE 118 B2378	FINAN ECO/TAC ECO/DEV CREATE
	B45
MILLIS H.A.,ORGANIZED LABOR (FIRST ED.). LAW STRUCT DELIB/GP WORKER ECO/TAC ADJUD CONTROL REPRESENT INGP/REL INCOME MGT. PAGE 74 B1485	LABOR POLICY ROUTINE GP/REL
	B47
BAERWALD F.,FUNDAMENTALS OF LABOR ECONOMICS. LAW INDUS LABOR LG/CO CONTROL GP/REL INCOME TOTALISM ...MGT CHARTS GEN/LAWS BIBLIOG 20. PAGE 8 B0158	ECO/DEV WORKER MARKET
	B49
SCHULTZ W.J.,AMERICAN PUBLIC FINANCE. USA+45 ECO/TAC TAX ADMIN GOV/REL GP/REL INCOME 20. PAGE 94 B1906	FINAN POLICY ECO/DEV NAT/G
	B49
SHISTER J.,ECONOMICS OF THE LABOR MARKET. LOC/G NAT/G WORKER TEC/DEV BARGAIN PAY PRICE EXEC GP/REL INCOME...MGT T 20. PAGE 96 B1949	MARKET LABOR INDUS
	B58
SHAW S.J.,THE FINANCIAL AND ADMINISTRATIVE ORGANIZATION AND DEVELOPMENT OF OTTOMAN EGYPT 1517-1798. UAR LOC/G FORCES BUDGET INT/TRADE TAX EATING INCOME WEALTH...CHARTS BIBLIOG 16/18 OTTOMAN NAPOLEON/B. PAGE 96 B1940	FINAN ADMIN GOV/REL CULTURE
	B58
VAN RIPER P.P.,HISTORY OF THE UNITED STATES CIVIL SERVICE. USA+45 USA-45 LABOR LOC/G DELIB/GP LEGIS PROB/SOLV LOBBY GOV/REL GP/REL INCOME...POLICY 18/20 PRESIDENT CIVIL/SERV. PAGE 111 B2251	ADMIN WORKER NAT/G
	B58
WARNER A.W.,CONCEPTS AND CASES IN ECONOMIC ANALYSIS. PROB/SOLV BARGAIN CONTROL INCOME PRODUC ...ECOMETRIC MGT CONCPT CLASSIF CHARTS 20 KEYNES/JM. PAGE 114 B2292	ECO/TAC DEMAND EQUILIB COST
	B60
BAERWALD F.,ECONOMIC SYSTEM ANALYSIS: CONCEPTS AND PERSPECTIVES. USA+45 ECO/DEV NAT/G COMPUTER EQUILIB INCOME ATTIT...DECISION CONCPT IDEA/COMP. PAGE 8 B0159	ACT/RES ECO/TAC ROUTINE FINAN
	B60
HOVING W.,THE DISTRIBUTION REVOLUTION. WOR+45 ECO/DEV FINAN SERV/IND PRESS PRICE INCOME PRODUC ...MGT 20. PAGE 52 B1049	DIST/IND MARKET ECO/TAC TASK
	B60
MARSHALL A.H.,FINANCIAL ADMINISTRATION IN LOCAL GOVERNMENT. UK DELIB/GP CONFER COST INCOME PERSON ...JURID 20. PAGE 70 B1408	FINAN LOC/G BUDGET ADMIN
	B60
ROY N.C.,THE CIVIL SERVICE IN INDIA. INDIA POL/PAR ECO/TAC INCOME...JURID MGT 20 CIVIL/SERV. PAGE 91 B1843	ADMIN NAT/G DELIB/GP CONFER
	B62
BECKMAN T.N.,MARKETING (7TH ED.). USA+45 SOCIETY ECO/DEV NAT/G PRICE EFFICIENCY INCOME ATTIT WEALTH ...MGT BIBLIOG 20. PAGE 10 B0205	MARKET ECO/TAC DIST/IND POLICY
	S63
REES A.,"THE EFFECTS OF UNIONS ON RESOURCE ALLOCATION." USA+45 WORKER PRICE CONTROL GP/REL ...MGT METH/COMP 20. PAGE 87 B1761	LABOR BARGAIN RATION INCOME
	B64
FONTENEAU J.,LE CONSEIL MUNICIPAL: LE MAIRE-LES	MUNIC

ADJOINTS. FRANCE FINAN DELIB/GP EX/STRUC BUDGET TAX TASK COST INCOME ROLE SUPEGO 20 MAYOR. PAGE 36 B0735	NEIGH ADMIN TOP/EX
	B64
HERSKOVITS M.J.,ECONOMIC TRANSITION IN AFRICA. FUT INT/ORG NAT/G WORKER PROB/SOLV TEC/DEV INT/TRADE EQUILIB INCOME...ANTHOL 20. PAGE 49 B0996	AFR ECO/UNDEV PLAN ADMIN
	B64
LITTLE I.M.D.,AID TO AFRICA. AFR UK TEC/DEV DIPLOM ECO/TAC INCOME WEALTH 20. PAGE 66 B1326	FOR/AID ECO/UNDEV ADMIN POLICY
	B65
ARTHUR D LITTLE INC,SAN FRANCISCO COMMUNITY RENEWAL PROGRAM. USA+45 FINAN PROVS ADMIN INCOME...CHARTS 20 CALIFORNIA SAN/FRAN URBAN/RNWL. PAGE 7 B0138	HABITAT MUNIC PLAN PROB/SOLV
	B65
RHODES G.,PUBLIC SECTOR PENSIONS. UK FINAN LEGIS BUDGET TAX PAY INCOME...CHARTS 20 CIVIL/SERV. PAGE 88 B1769	ADMIN RECEIVE AGE/O WORKER
	B66
REDFORD E.S.,THE ROLE OF GOVERNMENT IN THE AMERICAN ECONOMY. USA+45 USA-45 FINAN INDUS LG/CO PROB/SOLV ADMIN INGP/REL INCOME PRODUC 18/20. PAGE 87 B1759	NAT/G ECO/DEV CAP/ISM ECO/TAC
	B66
THOENES P.,THE ELITE IN THE WELFARE STATE ,TRANS. BY J BINGHAM; ED. BY. STRATA NAT/G GP/REL HAPPINESS INCOME OPTIMAL MORAL PWR WEALTH...POLICY CONCPT. PAGE 104 B2097	ADMIN ELITES MGT WELF/ST
	B66
US BUREAU OF THE BUDGET,THE ADMINISTRATION OF GOVERNMENT SUPPORTED RESEARCH AT UNIVERSITIES (PAMPHLET). USA+45 CONSULT TOP/EX ADMIN INCOME WEALTH...MGT PHIL/SCI INT. PAGE 108 B2174	ACT/RES NAT/G ACADEM GP/REL
	B66
WESTON J.F.,THE SCOPE AND METHODOLOGY OF FINANCE. PLAN TEC/DEV CONTROL EFFICIENCY INCOME UTIL...MGT CONCPT MATH STAT TREND METH 20. PAGE 115 B2327	FINAN ECO/DEV POLICY PRICE
	S67
JENCKS C.E.,"SOCIAL STATUS OF COAL MINERS IN BRITAIN SINCE NATIONALIZATION." UK STRATA STRUCT LABOR RECEIVE GP/REL INCOME OWN ATTIT HABITAT...MGT T 20. PAGE 56 B1128	EXTR/IND WORKER CONTROL NAT/G
	S67
ROSE A.M.,"CONFIDENCE AND THE CORPORATION." LG/CO CONTROL CRIME INCOME PROFIT 20. PAGE 90 B1818	INDUS EX/STRUC VOL/ASSN RESPECT
	S67
ZOETEWEIJ B.,"INCOME POLICIES ABROAD: AN INTERIM REPORT." NAT/G PROB/SOLV BARGAIN BUDGET PRICE RISK CENTRAL EFFICIENCY EQUILIB...MGT NAT/COMP 20. PAGE 119 B2405	METH/COMP INCOME POLICY LABOR
	N67
PRINCETON U INDUSTRIAL REL SEC,OUTSTANDING BOOKS ON INDUSTRIAL RELATIONS, 1966 (PAMPHLET NO. 134). WOR+45 LABOR WORKER PLAN PRICE CONTROL INCOME...MGT 20. PAGE 85 B1711	BIBLIOG/A INDUS GP/REL POLICY

INCOMPETENCE....SEE SKILL

IND/WRK/AF....INDUSTRIAL AND WORKERS' COMMERCIAL UNION OF AFRICA

INDEX....INDEX SYSTEM

CUMULATIVE BOOK INDEX. WOR+45 WOR-45 ADMIN PERSON ALL/VALS ALL/IDEOS...HUM PHIL/SCI SOC LING 19/20. PAGE 1 B0012	N INDEX NAT/G DIPLOM
UNIVERSITY MICROFILMS INC,DISSERTATION ABSTRACTS: ABSTRACTS OF DISSERTATIONS AND MONOGRAPHS IN MICROFILM. CANADA DIPLOM ADMIN...INDEX 20. PAGE 107 B2166	N BIBLIOG/A ACADEM PRESS WRITING
	B53
GREENE K.R.C.,INSTITUTIONS AND INDIVIDUALS: AN ANNOTATED LIST OF DIRECTORIES USEFUL IN INTERNATIONAL ADMINISTRATION. USA+45 NAT/G VOL/ASSN ...INDEX 20. PAGE 43 B0865	BIBLIOG INT/ORG ADMIN DIPLOM
	B54
BINANI G.D.,INDIA AT A GLANCE (REV. ED.). INDIA COM/IND FINAN INDUS LABOR PROVS SCHOOL PLAN DIPLOM INT/TRADE ADMIN...JURID 20. PAGE 12 B0238	INDEX CON/ANAL NAT/G ECO/UNDEV
	B54
PUBLIC ADMIN CLEARING HOUSE,PUBLIC ADMINISTRATIONS ORGANIZATIONS: A DIRECTORY, 1954. USA+45 R+D PROVS ACT/RES...MGT 20. PAGE 85 B1714	INDEX VOL/ASSN NAT/G ADMIN

B60
LERNER A.P.,THE ECONOMICS OF CONTROL. USA+45
ECO/UNDEV INT/ORG ACT/RES PLAN CAP/ISM INT/TRADE
ATTIT WEALTH...SOC MATH STAT GEN/LAWS INDEX 20.
PAGE 64 B1295

ECO/DEV
POUTINE
ECO/TAC
SOCISM

S61
TANNENBAUM A.S.,"CONTROL AND EFFECTIVENESS IN A
VOLUNTARY ORGANIZATION." USA+45 ADMIN...CORREL MATH
REGRESS STAT TESTS SAMP/SIZ CHARTS SOC/EXP INDEX 20
LEAGUE/WV. PAGE 102 B2072

EFFICIENCY
VOL/ASSN
CONTROL
INGP/REL

B66
HANKE L.,HANDBOOK OF LATIN AMERICAN STUDIES.
ECO/UNDEV ADMIN LEAD...HUM SOC 20. PAGE 46 B0937

BIBLIOG/A
L/A+17C
INDEX
NAT/G

INDIA....SEE ALSO S/ASIA

N
VENKATESAN S.L.,BIBLIOGRAPHY ON PUBLIC ENTERPRISES
IN INDIA. INDIA S/ASIA FINAN LG/CO LOC/G PLAN
BUDGET SOCISM...MGT 20. PAGE 112 B2258

BIBLIOG/A
ADMIN
ECO/UNDEV
INDUS

N19
GORWALA A.D.,THE ADMINISTRATIVE JUNGLE (PAMPHLET).
INDIA NAT/G LEGIS ECO/TAC CONTROL GOV/REL
...METH/COMP 20. PAGE 41 B0838

ADMIN
POLICY
PLAN
ECO/UNDEV

B53
APPLEBY P.H.,PUBLIC ADMINISTRATION IN INDIA: REPORT
OF A SURVEY. INDIA LOC/G OP/RES ATTIT ORD/FREE 20.
PAGE 6 B0118

ADMIN
NAT/G
EX/STRUC
GOV/REL

B53
MAJUMDAR B.B.,PROBLEMS OF PUBLIC ADMINISTRATION IN
INDIA. INDIA INDUS PLAN BUDGET ADJUD CENTRAL DEMAND
WEALTH...WELF/ST ANTHOL 20 CIVIL/SERV. PAGE 68
B1384

ECO/UNDEV
GOV/REL
ADMIN
MUNIC

B54
BINANI G.D.,INDIA AT A GLANCE (REV. ED.). INDIA
COM/IND FINAN INDUS LABOR PROVS SCHOOL PLAN DIPLOM
INT/TRADE ADMIN...JURID 20. PAGE 12 B0238

INDEX
CON/ANAL
NAT/G
ECO/UNDEV

B56
JENNINGS W.I.,THE APPROACH TO SELF-GOVERNMENT.
CEYLON INDIA PAKISTAN S/ASIA UK SOCIETY POL/PAR
DELIB/GP LEGIS ECO/TAC EDU/PROP ADMIN EXEC CHOOSE
ATTIT ALL/VALS...JURID CONCPT GEN/METH TOT/POP 20.
PAGE 56 B1136

NAT/G
CONSTN
COLONIAL

B56
WILSON P.,GOVERNMENT AND POLITICS OF INDIA AND
PAKISTAN: 1885-1955; A BIBLIOGRAPHY OF WORKS IN
WESTERN LANGUAGES. INDIA PAKISTAN CONSTN LOC/G
POL/PAR FORCES DIPLOM ADMIN WAR CHOOSE...BIOG
CON/ANAL 19/20. PAGE 117 B2361

BIBLIOG
COLONIAL
NAT/G
S/ASIA

B57
CENTRAL ASIAN RESEARCH CENTRE,BIBLIOGRAPHY OF
RECENT SOVIET SOURCE MATERIAL ON SOVIET CENTRAL
ASIA AND THE BORDERLANDS. AFGHANISTN INDIA PAKISTAN
UAR USSR ECO/UNDEV AGRI EXTR/IND INDUS ACADEM ADMIN
...HEAL HUM LING CON/ANAL 20. PAGE 19 B0399

BIBLIOG/A
COM
CULTURE
NAT/G

B57
CHANDRA S.,PARTIES AND POLITICS AT THE MUGHAL
COURT: 1707-1740. INDIA CULTURE EX/STRUC CREATE
PLAN PWR...BIBLIOG/A 18. PAGE 20 B0405

POL/PAR
ELITES
NAT/G

B57
MURDESHWAR A.K.,ADMINISTRATIVE PROBLEMS RELATING TO
NATIONALISATION: WITH SPECIAL REFERENCE TO INDIAN
STATE ENTERPRISES. CZECHOSLVK FRANCE INDIA UK
USA+45 LEGIS WORKER PROB/SOLV BUDGET PRICE CONTROL
...MGT GEN/LAWS 20 PARLIAMENT. PAGE 76 B1544

NAT/G
OWN
INDUS
ADMIN

B57
SHARMA S.R.,SOME ASPECTS OF THE INDIAN
ADMINISTRATIVE SYSTEM. INDIA WOR+45 TEC/DEV BUDGET
LEGIT ROUTINE ATTIT. PAGE 96 B1937

EXEC
DECISION
ADMIN
INGP/REL

B58
LIST OF PUBLICATIONS (PERIODICAL OR AD HOC) ISSUED
BY VARIOUS MINISTRIES OF THE GOVERNMENT OF INDIA
(3RD ED.). INDIA ECO/UNDEV PLAN...POLICY MGT 20.
PAGE 2 B0037

BIBLIOG
NAT/G
ADMIN

B58
DWARKADAS R.,ROLE OF HIGHER CIVIL SERVICE IN INDIA.
INDIA ECO/UNDEV LEGIS PROB/SOLV GP/REL PERS/REL
...POLICY WELF/ST DECISION ORG/CHARTS BIBLIOG 20
CIVIL/SERV INTRVN/ECO. PAGE 31 B0637

ADMIN
NAT/G
ROLE
PLAN

B58
INDIAN INST OF PUBLIC ADMIN,IMPROVING CITY
GOVERNMENT. INDIA ECO/UNDEV PLAN BUDGET PARTIC
GP/REL 20. PAGE 53 B1080

LOC/G
MUNIC
PROB/SOLV
ADMIN

B58
LAW COMMISSION OF INDIA,REFORM OF JUDICIAL
ADMINISTRATION. INDIA TOP/EX ADMIN DISCRIM
EFFICIENCY...METH/COMP 20. PAGE 63 B1276

CT/SYS
ADJUD
GOV/REL
CONTROL

B58
SHARMA M.P.,PUBLIC ADMINISTRATION IN THEORY AND
PRACTICE. INDIA UK USA+45 USA-45 EX/STRUC ADJUD
...POLICY CONCPT NAT/COMP 20. PAGE 96 B1935

MGT
ADMIN
DELIB/GP
JURID

B59
BHAMBHRI C.P.,SUBSTANCE OF HINDU POLITY. INDIA
S/ASIA LAW EX/STRUC JUDGE TAX COERCE GP/REL
POPULISM 20 HINDU. PAGE 11 B0234

GOV/REL
WRITING
SECT
PROVS

B59
INDIAN INSTITUTE PUBLIC ADMIN,MORALE IN THE PUBLIC
SERVICES: REPORT OF A CONFERENCE JAN., 3-4, 1959.
INDIA S/ASIA ECO/UNDEV PROVS PLAN EDU/PROP CONFER
GOV/REL EFFICIENCY DRIVE ROLE 20 CIVIL/SERV.
PAGE 53 B1082

HAPPINESS
ADMIN
WORKER
INGP/REL

B59
PARK R.L.,LEADERSHIP AND POLITICAL INSTITUTIONS IN
INDIA. S/ASIA CULTURE ECO/UNDEV LOC/G MUNIC PROVS
LEGIS PLAN ADMIN LEAD ORD/FREE WEALTH...GEOG SOC
BIOG TOT/POP VAL/FREE 20. PAGE 81 B1633

NAT/G
EXEC
INDIA

B60
ARGAL R.,MUNICIPAL GOVERNMENT IN INDIA. INDIA
BUDGET TAX ADMIN EXEC 19/20. PAGE 6 B0126

LOC/G
MUNIC
DELIB/GP
CONTROL

B60
BHAMBHRI C.P.,PARLIAMENTARY CONTROL OVER STATE
ENTERPRISE IN INDIA. INDIA DELIB/GP ADMIN CONTROL
INGP/REL EFFICIENCY 20 PARLIAMENT. PAGE 11 B0235

NAT/G
OWN
INDUS
PARL/PROC

B60
INDIAN INST OF PUBLIC ADMIN,STATE UNDERTAKINGS:
REPORT OF A CONFERENCE, DECEMBER 19-20, 1959
(PAMPHLET). INDIA LG/CO DELIB/GP CONFER PARL/PROC
EFFICIENCY OWN...MGT 20. PAGE 53 B1081

GOV/REL
ADMIN
NAT/G
LEGIS

B60
MATTOD P.K.,A STUDY OF LOCAL SELF GOVERNMENT IN
URBAN INDIA. INDIA FINAN DELIB/GP LEGIS BUDGET TAX
SOVEREIGN...MGT GP/COMP 20. PAGE 71 B1432

MUNIC
CONSTN
LOC/G
ADMIN

B60
PENTONY D.E.,UNITED STATES FOREIGN AID. INDIA LAOS
USA+45 ECO/UNDEV INT/TRADE ADMIN PEACE ATTIT
...POLICY METH/COMP ANTHOL 20. PAGE 82 B1653

FOR/AID
DIPLOM
ECO/TAC

B60
ROY N.C.,THE CIVIL SERVICE IN INDIA. INDIA POL/PAR
ECO/TAC INCOME...JURID MGT 20 CIVIL/SERV. PAGE 91
B1843

ADMIN
NAT/G
DELIB/GP
CONFER

B61
AGARWAL R.C.,STATE ENTERPRISE IN INDIA. FUT INDIA
UK FINAN INDUS ADMIN CONTROL OWN...POLICY CHARTS
BIBLIOG 20 RAILROAD. PAGE 3 B0064

ECO/UNDEV
SOCISM
GOV/REL
LG/CO

B61
BAINS J.S.,STUDIES IN POLITICAL SCIENCE. INDIA
WOR+45 WOR-45 CONSTN BAL/PWR ADJUD ADMIN PARL/PROC
SOVEREIGN...SOC METH/COMP ANTHOL 17/20 UN. PAGE 8
B0165

DIPLOM
INT/LAW
NAT/G

B61
COHN B.S.,DEVELOPMENT AND IMPACT OF BRITISH
ADMINISTRATION IN INDIA: A BIBLIOGRAPHIC ESSAY.
INDIA UK ECO/UNDEV NAT/G DOMIN...POLICY MGT SOC
19/20. PAGE 22 B0448

BIBLIOG/A
COLONIAL
S/ASIA
ADMIN

B61
HARRISON S.,INDIA AND THE UNITED STATES. FUT S/ASIA
USA+45 WOR+45 INTELL ECO/DEV ECO/UNDEV AGRI INDUS
INT/ORG NAT/G CONSULT EX/STRUC TOP/EX PLAN ECO/TAC
NEUTRAL ALL/VALS...MGT TOT/POP 20. PAGE 47 B0956

DELIB/GP
ACT/RES
FOR/AID
INDIA

B61
HART H.C.,ADMINISTRATIVE ASPECTS OF RIVER VALLEY
DEVELOPMENT. INDIA USA+45 INDUS CONTROL EFFICIENCY
OPTIMAL PRODUC 20 TVA. PAGE 47 B0957

ADMIN
PLAN
METH/COMP
AGRI

B61
KOESTLER A.,THE LOTUS AND THE ROBOT. ASIA INDIA
S/ASIA SOCIETY STRATA ECO/DEV AGRI INDUS FAM CREATE
DOMIN EDU/PROP ADMIN COERCE ATTIT DRIVE SUPEGO
ORD/FREE PWR RESPECT WEALTH...MYTH OBS 20 CHINJAP.
PAGE 61 B1226

SECT
ECO/UNDEV

B61
MACMAHON A.W.,DELEGATION AND AUTONOMY. INDIA STRUCT
LEGIS BARGAIN BUDGET ECO/TAC LEGIT EXEC REPRESENT
GOV/REL CENTRAL DEMAND EFFICIENCY PRODUC. PAGE 68
B1373

ADMIN
PLAN
FEDERAL

B61
NARAIN J.P.,SWARAJ FOR THE PEOPLE. INDIA CONSTN
LOC/G MUNIC POL/PAR CHOOSE REPRESENT EFFICIENCY
ATTIT PWR SOVEREIGN 20. PAGE 77 B1553

NAT/G
ORD/FREE
EDU/PROP
EX/STRUC

B61
NARASIMHAN V.K.,THE PRESS, THE PUBLIC AND THE
ADMINISTRATION (PAMPHLET). INDIA COM/IND CONTROL
REPRESENT GOV/REL EFFICIENCY...ANTHOL 20. PAGE 77
B1554

NAT/G
ADMIN
PRESS
NEW/LIB

B61
RAO K.V.,PARLIAMENTARY DEMOCRACY OF INDIA. INDIA   CONSTN
EX/STRUC TOP/EX COLONIAL CT/SYS PARL/PROC ORD/FREE   ADJUD
...POLICY CONCPT TREND 20 PARLIAMENT. PAGE 86 B1733   NAT/G
                                                          FEDERAL
                                                               B61
SHARMA T.R.,THE WORKING OF STATE ENTERPRISES IN   NAT/G
INDIA. INDIA DELIB/GP LEGIS WORKER BUDGET PRICE   INDUS
CONTROL GP/REL OWN ATTIT...MGT CHARTS 20. PAGE 96   ADMIN
B1938   SOCISM
                                                               S61
RUDOLPH S.,"CONSENSUS AND CONFLICT IN INDIAN   POL/PAR
POLITICS." S/ASIA WOR+45 NAT/G DELIB/GP DIPLOM   PERCEPT
EDU/PROP ADMIN CONSEN PERSON ALL/VALS...OBS TREND   INDIA
TOT/POP VAL/FREE 20. PAGE 92 B1854
                                                               B62
HANSON A.H.,MANAGERIAL PROBLEMS IN PUBLIC   MGT
ENTERPRISE. INDIA DELIB/GP GP/REL INGP/REL   NAT/G
EFFICIENCY 20 PARLIAMENT. PAGE 46 B0940   INDUS
                                                          PROB/SOLV
                                                               B62
MORE S.S.,REMODELLING OF DEMOCRACY FOR AFRO-ASIAN   ORD/FREE
NATIONS. AFR INDIA S/ASIA SOUTH/AFR CONSTN EX/STRUC   ECO/UNDEV
COLONIAL CHOOSE TOTALISM SOVEREIGN NEW/LIB SOCISM   ADMIN
...SOC/WK 20. PAGE 75 B1520   LEGIS
                                                               B62
PRAKASH O.M.,THE THEORY AND WORKING OF STATE   LG/CO
CORPORATIONS: WITH SPECIAL REFERENCE TO INDIA.   ECO/UNDEV
INDIA UK USA+45 TOP/EX PRICE ADMIN EFFICIENCY...MGT   GOV/REL
METH/COMP 20 TVA. PAGE 84 B1698   SOCISM
                                                               B62
SRIVASTAVA G.L.,COLLECTIVE BARGAINING AND LABOR-   LABOR
MANAGEMENT RELATIONS IN INDIA. INDIA USA+45   MGT
INDUS LEGIS WORKER ADJUD EFFICIENCY PRODUC   BARGAIN
...METH/COMP 20. PAGE 100 B2014   GP/REL
                                                               B63
BRAIBANTI R.J.D.,ADMINISTRATION AND ECONOMIC   ECO/UNDEV
DEVELOPMENT IN INDIA. INDIA S/ASIA SOCIETY STRATA   ADMIN
ECO/TAC PERSON WEALTH...MGT GEN/LAWS TOT/POP
VAL/FREE 20. PAGE 15 B0300
                                                               B63
GANGULY D.S.,PUBLIC CORPORATIONS IN A NATIONAL   ECO/UNDEV
ECONOMY. INDIA WOR+45 FINAN INDUS TOP/EX PRICE   LG/CO
EFFICIENCY...MGT STAT CHARTS BIBLIOG 20. PAGE 38   SOCISM
B0779   GOV/REL
                                                               B63
INDIAN INSTITUTE PUBLIC ADMIN,CASES IN INDIAN   DECISION
ADMINISTRATION. INDIA AGRI NAT/G PROB/SOLV TEC/DEV   PLAN
ECO/TAC ADMIN...ANTHOL METH 20. PAGE 53 B1083   MGT
                                                          ECO/UNDEV
                                                               B63
KAPP W.K.,HINDU CULTURE: ECONOMIC DEVELOPMENT AND   SECT
ECONOMIC PLANNING IN INDIA. INDIA S/ASIA CULTURE   ECO/UNDEV
ECO/TAC EDU/PROP ADMIN ALL/VALS...POLICY MGT
TIME/SEQ VAL/FREE 20. PAGE 58 B1171
                                                               B63
LEONARD T.J.,THE FEDERAL SYSTEM OF INDIA. INDIA   FEDERAL
MUNIC NAT/G PROVS ADMIN SOVEREIGN...IDEA/COMP 20.   MGT
PAGE 64 B1293   NAT/COMP
                                                          METH/COMP
                                                               B63
MAHESHWARI B.,STUDIES IN PANCHAYATI RAJ. INDIA   FEDERAL
POL/PAR EX/STRUC BUDGET EXEC REPRESENT CENTRAL   LOC/G
EFFICIENCY...DECISION 20. PAGE 68 B1378   GOV/REL
                                                          LEAD
PATRA A.C.,THE ADMINISTRATION OF JUSTICE UNDER THE   ADMIN
EAST INDIA COMPANY IN BENGAL, BIHAR AND ORISSA.   JURID
INDIA UK LG/CO CAP/ISM INT/TRADE ADJUD COLONIAL   CONCPT
CONTROL CT/SYS...POLICY 20. PAGE 81 B1641
                                                               B63
SINGH H.L.,PROBLEMS AND POLICIES OF THE BRITISH IN   COLONIAL
INDIA, 1885-1898. INDIA UK NAT/G FORCES LEGIS   PWR
PROB/SOLV CONTROL RACE/REL ADJUST DISCRIM NAT/LISM   POLICY
RIGID/FLEX...MGT 19 CIVIL/SERV. PAGE 97 B1968   ADMIN
                                                               B63
WEINER M.,POLITICAL CHANGE IN SOUTH ASIA. CEYLON   NAT/G
INDIA PAKISTAN S/ASIA CULTURE ELITES ECO/UNDEV   CONSTN
EX/STRUC ADMIN CONTROL CHOOSE CONSERVE...GOV/COMP   TEC/DEV
ANTHOL 20. PAGE 115 B2315
                                                               B64
THE SPECIAL COMMONWEALTH AFRICAN ASSISTANCE PLAN.   ECO/UNDEV
AFR CANADA INDIA NIGERIA UK FINAN SCHOOL...CHARTS   TREND
20 COMMONWLTH. PAGE 2 B0041   FOR/AID
                                                          ADMIN
                                                               B64
AVASTHI A.,ASPECTS OF ADMINISTRATION. INDIA UK   MGT
USA+45 FINAN ACADEM DELIB/GP LEGIS RECEIVE   ADMIN
PARL/PROC PRIVIL...NAT/COMP 20. PAGE 7 B0150   SOC/WK
                                                          ORD/FREE
                                                               B64
DAS M.N.,INDIA UNDER MORLEY AND MINTO. INDIA UK   GOV/REL
ECO/UNDEV MUNIC PROVS EX/STRUC LEGIS DIPLOM CONTROL   COLONIAL
REV 20 MORLEY/J. PAGE 26 B0531   POLICY
                                                          ADMIN

                                                               B64
GOODNOW H.F.,THE CIVIL SERVICE OF PAKISTAN: ADMIN
BUREAUCRACY IN A NEW NATION. INDIA PAKISTAN S/ASIA   GOV/REL
ECO/UNDEV PROVS CHIEF PARTIC CHOOSE EFFICIENCY PWR   LAW
...BIBLIOG 20. PAGE 41 B0824   NAT/G
                                                               B64
INDIAN COMM PREVENTION CORRUPT,REPORT, 1964. INDIA   CRIME
NAT/G GOV/REL ATTIT ORD/FREE...CRIMLGY METH 20.   ADMIN
PAGE 53 B1079   LEGIS
                                                          LOC/G
                                                               B64
MAHAR J.M.,INDIA: A CRITICAL BIBLIOGRAPHY. INDIA   BIBLIOG/A
PAKISTAN CULTURE ECO/UNDEV LOC/G POL/PAR SECT   S/ASIA
PROB/SOLV DIPLOM ADMIN COLONIAL PARL/PROC ATTIT 20.   NAT/G
PAGE 68 B1377   LEAD
                                                               B64
POTTER D.C.,GOVERNMENT IN RURAL INDIA. INDIA LEGIT   LOC/G
INGP/REL EFFICIENCY ATTIT 20. PAGE 84 B1695   ADMIN
                                                          TAX
                                                          PROB/SOLV
                                                               L64
RIPLEY R.B.,"INTERAGENCY COMMITTEES AND   EXEC
INCREMENTALISM: THE CASE OF AID TO INDIA." INDIA   MGT
USA+45 INTELL NAT/G DELIB/GP ACT/RES DIPLOM ROUTINE   FOR/AID
NAT/LISM ATTIT PWR...SOC CONCPT NEW/IDEA TIME/SEQ
CON/ANAL VAL/FREE 20. PAGE 89 B1790
                                                               L64
WORLD PEACE FOUNDATION,"INTERNATIONAL   INT/ORG
ORGANIZATIONS: SUMMARY OF ACTIVITIES." INDIA   ROUTINE
PAKISTAN TURKEY WOR+45 CONSTN CONSULT EX/STRUC
ECO/TAC EDU/PROP LEGIT ORD/FREE...JURID SOC UN 20
CYPRESS. PAGE 118 B2375
                                                               B65
AIYAR S.P.,STUDIES IN INDIAN DEMOCRACY. INDIA   ORD/FREE
STRATA ECO/UNDEV LABOR POL/PAR LEGIS DIPLOM LOBBY   REPRESENT
REGION CHOOSE ATTIT SOCISM...ANTHOL 20. PAGE 3   ADMIN
B0067   NAT/G
                                                               B65
CHANDA A.,FEDERALISM IN INDIA. INDIA UK ELITES   CONSTN
FINAN NAT/G POL/PAR EX/STRUC LEGIS DIPLOM TAX   CENTRAL
GOV/REL POPULISM...POLICY 20. PAGE 20 B0402   FEDERAL
                                                               B65
CRAMER J.F.,CONTEMPORARY EDUCATION: A COMPARATIVE   EDU/PROP
STUDY OF NATIONAL SYSTEMS (2ND ED.). CHINA/COM   NAT/COMP
EUR+WWI INDIA USA+45 FINAN PROB/SOLV ADMIN CONTROL   SCHOOL
ATTIT...IDEA/COMP METH/COMP 20 CHINJAP. PAGE 25   ACADEM
B0502
                                                               B65
GOPAL S.,BRITISH POLICY IN INDIA 1858-1905. INDIA   COLONIAL
UK ELITES CHIEF DELIB/GP ECO/TAC GP/REL DISCRIM   ADMIN
ATTIT...IDEA/COMP NAT/COMP PERS/COMP BIBLIOG/A   POL/PAR
19/20. PAGE 41 B0828   ECO/UNDEV
                                                               B65
PANJABI K.L.,THE CIVIL SERVANT IN INDIA. INDIA UK   ADMIN
NAT/G CONSULT EX/STRUC REGION GP/REL RACE/REL 20.   WORKER
PAGE 81 B1631   BIOG
                                                          COLONIAL
                                                               B65
PYLEE M.V.,CONSTITUTIONAL GOVERNMENT IN INDIA (2ND   CONSTN
REV. ED.). INDIA POL/PAR EX/STRUC DIPLOM COLONIAL   NAT/G
CT/SYS PARL/PROC PRIVIL...JURID 16/20. PAGE 85   PROVS
B1725   FEDERAL
                                                               B65
SHARMA S.A.,PARLIAMENTARY GOVERNMENT IN INDIA.   NAT/G
INDIA FINAN LOC/G PROVS DELIB/GP PLAN ADMIN CT/SYS   CONSTN
FEDERAL...JURID 20. PAGE 96 B1936   PARL/PROC
                                                          LEGIS
                                                               B65
VAID K.N.,STATE AND LABOR IN INDIA. INDIA INDUS   LAW
WORKER PAY PRICE ADJUD CONTROL PARL/PROC GP/REL   LABOR
ORD/FREE 20. PAGE 111 B2248   MGT
                                                          NEW/LIB
                                                               S65
"FURTHER READING." INDIA STRUCT FINAN WORKER ADMIN   BIBLIOG
COST 20. PAGE 2 B0042   MGT
                                                          ECO/UNDEV
                                                          EFFICIENCY
                                                               S65
"FURTHER READING." INDIA NAT/G ADMIN 20. PAGE 2   BIBLIOG
B0043   EDU/PROP
                                                          SCHOOL
                                                          ACADEM
                                                               S65
"FURTHER READING." INDIA ADMIN COLONIAL WAR GOV/REL   BIBLIOG
ATTIT 20. PAGE 2 B0044   DIPLOM
                                                          NAT/G
                                                          POLICY
                                                               B66
ASHRAF A.,THE CITY GOVERNMENT OF CALCUTTA: A STUDY   LOC/G
OF INERTIA. INDIA ELITES INDUS NAT/G EX/STRUC   MUNIC
ACT/RES PLAN PROB/SOLV LEAD HABITAT...BIBLIOG 20   ADMIN
CALCUTTA. PAGE 7 B0141   ECO/UNDEV
                                                               B66
BHALERAO C.N.,PUBLIC SERVICE COMMISSIONS OF INDIA: NAT/G
A STUDY. INDIA SERV/IND EX/STRUC ROUTINE CHOOSE   OP/RES
GOV/REL INGP/REL...KNO/TEST EXHIBIT 20. PAGE 11   LOC/G

B0233   ADMIN
                                                           B66
DEBENKO E.,RESEARCH SOURCES FOR SOUTH ASIAN STUDIES   BIBLIOG
IN ECONOMIC DEVELOPMENT: A SELECT BIBLIOGRAPHY OF   ECO/UNDEV
SERIAL PUBLICATIONS. CEYLON INDIA NEPAL PAKISTAN   S/ASIA
PROB/SOLV ADMIN...POLICY 20. PAGE 28 B0566   PLAN
                                                           B66
DILLEY M.R.,BRITISH POLICY IN KENYA COLONY (2ND   COLONIAL
ED.). AFR INDIA UK LABOR BUDGET TAX ADMIN PARL/PROC   REPRESENT
GP/REL...BIBLIOG 20 PARLIAMENT. PAGE 29 B0594   SOVEREIGN
                                                           B66
GHOSH P.K.,THE CONSTITUTION OF INDIA: HOW IT HAS   CONSTN
BEEN FRAMED. INDIA LOC/G DELIB/GP EX/STRUC   NAT/G
PROB/SOLV BUDGET INT/TRADE CT/SYS CHOOSE...LING 20.   LEGIS
PAGE 39 B0795   FEDERAL
                                                           B66
HIDAYATULLAH M.,DEMOCRACY IN INDIA AND THE JUDICIAL   NAT/G
PROCESS. INDIA EX/STRUC LEGIS LEAD GOV/REL ATTIT   CT/SYS
ORD/FREE...MAJORIT CONCPT 20 NEHRU/J. PAGE 50 B1007   CONSTN
                                                     JURID
                                                           B66
MONTEIRO J.B.,CORRUPTION: CONTROL OF   CONTROL
MALADMINISTRATION. EUR+WWI INDIA USA+45 USSR NAT/G   CRIME
DELIB/GP ADMIN...GP/COMP 20 OMBUDSMAN. PAGE 74   PROB/SOLV
B1503
                                                           B66
SPICER K.,A SAMARITAN STATE? AFR CANADA INDIA   DIPLOM
PAKISTAN UK USA+45 FINAN INDUS PRODUC...CHARTS 20   FOR/AID
NATO. PAGE 99 B2006   ECO/DEV
                                                     ADMIN
                                                           B66
US DEPARTMENT OF THE ARMY,COMMUNIST CHINA: A   BIBLIOG/A
STRATEGIC SURVEY: A BIBLIOGRAPHY (PAMPHLET NO.   MARXISM
20-67). CHINA/COM COM INDIA USSR NAT/G POL/PAR   S/ASIA
EX/STRUC FORCES NUC/PWR REV ATTIT...POLICY GEOG   DIPLOM
CHARTS. PAGE 108 B2184
                                                           B66
ZINKIN T.,CHALLENGES IN INDIA. INDIA PAKISTAN LAW   NAT/G
AGRI FINAN INDUS TOP/EX TEC/DEV CONTROL ROUTINE   ECO/TAC
ORD/FREE PWR 20 NEHRU/J SHASTRI/LB CIVIL/SERV.   POLICY
PAGE 119 B2404   ADMIN
                                                           S66
"FURTHER READING." INDIA LOC/G NAT/G PLAN ADMIN   BIBLIOG
WEALTH...GEOG SOC CONCPT CENSUS 20. PAGE 2 B0045   ECO/UNDEV
                                                     TEC/DEV
                                                     PROVS
                                                           B67
JAIN R.K.,MANAGEMENT OF STATE ENTERPRISES. INDIA   NAT/G
SOCIETY FINAN WORKER BUDGET ADMIN CONTROL OWN 20.   SOCISM
PAGE 55 B1118   INDUS
                                                     MGT
                                                           B67
JHANGIANI M.A.,JANA SANGH AND SWATANTRA: A PROFILE   POL/PAR
OF THE RIGHTIST PARTIES IN INDIA. INDIA ADMIN   LAISSEZ
CHOOSE MARXISM SOCISM...INT CHARTS BIBLIOG 20.   NAT/LISM
PAGE 56 B1140   ATTIT
                                                           B67
TANSKY L.,US AND USSR AID TO DEVELOPING COUNTRIES.   FOR/AID
INDIA TURKEY UAR USA+45 USSR FINAN PLAN TEC/DEV   ECO/UNDEV
ADMIN WEALTH...TREND METH/COMP 20. PAGE 103 B2076   MARXISM
                                                     CAP/ISM
                                                           L67
TAMBIAH S.J.,"THE POLITICS OF LANGUAGE IN INDIA AND   POL/PAR
CEYLON." CEYLON INDIA NAT/G DOMIN ADMIN...SOC 20.   LING
PAGE 102 B2070   NAT/LISM
                                                     REGION
                                                           S67
FOX R.G.,"FAMILY, CASTE, AND COMMERCE IN A NORTH   CULTURE
INDIAN MARKET TOWN." INDIA STRATA AGRI FACE/GP FAM   GP/REL
NEIGH OP/RES BARGAIN ADMIN ROUTINE WEALTH...SOC   ECO/UNDEV
CHARTS 20. PAGE 37 B0747   DIST/IND
                                                           S67
FRYKENBURG R.E.,"STUDIES OF LAND CONTROL IN INDIAN   ECO/UNDEV
HISTORY: REVIEW ARTICLE." INDIA UK STRATA AGRI   CONTROL
MUNIC OP/RES COLONIAL REGION EFFICIENCY OWN HABITAT   ADMIN
...CONCPT 16/20. PAGE 38 B0763
                                                           S67
RAI H.,"DISTRICT MAGISTRATE AND POLICE   STRUCT
SUPERINTENDENT IN INDIA: THE CONTROVERSY OF DUAL   CONTROL
CONTROL" INDIA LAW PROVS ADMIN PWR 19/20. PAGE 86   ROLE
B1729   FORCES
                                                           S67
SPEAR P.,"NEHRU." INDIA NAT/G POL/PAR ECO/TAC ADJUD   CHIEF
GOV/REL CENTRAL RIGID/FLEX 20 NEHRU/J. PAGE 99   ATTIT
B2003   ADMIN
                                                     CREATE

INDIAN COMM PREVENTION CORRUPT B1079

INDIAN INST OF PUBLIC ADMIN B1080,B1081

INDIAN INSTITUTE PUBLIC ADMIN B1082,B1083

INDIAN/AM....AMERICAN INDIANS

                                                           C50
MORLAN R.L.,"INTERGOVERNMENTAL RELATIONS IN   SCHOOL
EDUCATION." USA+45 FINAN LOC/G MUNIC NAT/G FORCES   GOV/REL
PROB/SOLV RECEIVE ADMIN RACE/REL COST...BIBLIOG   ACADEM
INDIAN/AM. PAGE 76 B1526   POLICY
                                                           B67
WEINBERG M.,SCHOOL INTEGRATION: A COMPREHENSIVE   BIBLIOG
CLASSIFIED BIBLIOGRAPHY OF 3,100 REFERENCES. USA+45   SCHOOL
LAW NAT/G NEIGH SECT PLAN ROUTINE AGE/C WEALTH   DISCRIM
SOC/INTEG INDIAN/AM. PAGE 115 B2314   RACE/REL

INDIANA....INDIANA

INDICATOR....NUMERICAL INDICES AND INDICATORS

INDIK B.P. B0418

INDIVIDUAL....SEE PERSON

INDOCTRINATION....SEE EDU/PROP

INDONESIA....SEE ALSO S/ASIA

                                                           B31
DEKAT A.D.A.,COLONIAL POLICY. S/ASIA CULTURE   DRIVE
EX/STRUC ECO/TAC DOMIN ADMIN COLONIAL ROUTINE   PWR
SOVEREIGN WEALTH...POLICY MGT RECORD KNO/TEST SAMP.   INDONESIA
PAGE 28 B0570   NETHERLAND
                                                           B62
GALENSON W.,LABOR IN DEVELOPING COUNTRIES. BRAZIL   LABOR
INDONESIA ISRAEL PAKISTAN TURKEY AGRI INDUS WORKER   ECO/UNDEV
PAY PRICE GP/REL WEALTH...MGT CHARTS METH/COMP   BARGAIN
NAT/COMP 20. PAGE 38 B0775   POL/PAR
                                                           B63
MCKIE R.,MALAYSIA IN FOCUS. INDONESIA WOR+45   S/ASIA
ECO/UNDEV FINAN POL/PAR SECT FORCES PLAN   NAT/LISM
ADMIN COLONIAL COERCE DRIVE ALL/VALS...POLICY   MALAYSIA
RECORD CENSUS TIME/SEQ CMN/WLTH 20. PAGE 72 B1453
                                                           B66
WILLNER A.R.,THE NEOTRADITIONAL ACCOMMODATION TO   INDONESIA
POLITICAL INDEPENDENCE* THE CASE OF INDONESIA *   CONSERVE
RESEARCH MONOGRAPH NO. 26. CULTURE ECO/UNDEV CREATE   ELITES
PROB/SOLV FOR/AID LEGIT COLONIAL EFFICIENCY   ADMIN
NAT/LISM ALL/VALS SOC. PAGE 117 B2355
                                                           B67
MILNE R.S.,GOVERNMENT AND POLITICS IN MALAYSIA.   NAT/G
INDONESIA MALAYSIA LOC/G EX/STRUC FORCES DIPLOM   LEGIS
GP/REL 20 SINGAPORE. PAGE 74 B1489   ADMIN

INDUS....ALL OR MOST INDUSTRY; SEE ALSO SPECIFIC
         INDUSTRIES, INSTITUTIONAL INDEX, PART C, P. XII

                                                           N
PRINCETON U INDUSTRIAL REL SEC,SELECTED REFERENCES   BIBLIOG/A
OF THE INDUSTRIAL RELATIONS SECTION OF PRINCETON,   INDUS
NEW JERSEY. LG/CO NAT/G LEGIS WORKER PLAN PROB/SOLV   LABOR
PAY ADMIN ROUTINE TASK GP/REL...PSY 20. PAGE 84   MGT
B1708
                                                           N
VENKATESAN S.L.,BIBLIOGRAPHY ON PUBLIC ENTERPRISES   BIBLIOG/A
IN INDIA. INDIA S/ASIA FINAN LG/CO LOC/G PLAN   ADMIN
BUDGET SOCISM...MGT 20. PAGE 112 B2258   ECO/UNDEV
                                                     INDUS
                                                           N
THE AMERICAN CITY. INDUS PROF/ORG PLAN GOV/REL   BIBLIOG/A
...MGT 20. PAGE 1 B0007   ADMIN
                                                     TEC/DEV
                                                     MUNIC
                                                           N
THE JAPAN SCIENCE REVIEW: LAW AND POLITICS: LIST OF   BIBLIOG
BOOKS AND ARTICLES ON LAW AND POLITICS. CONSTN AGRI   LAW
INDUS LABOR DIPLOM TAX ADMIN CRIME...INT/LAW SOC 20   S/ASIA
CHINJAP. PAGE 1 B0025   PHIL/SCI
                                                           N
ECONOMIC LIBRARY SELECTIONS. AGRI INDUS MARKET   BIBLIOG/A
ADMIN...STAT NAT/COMP 20. PAGE 2 B0026   WRITING
                                                     FINAN
                                                           N
PERSONNEL ADMINISTRATION: THE JOURNAL OF THE   WORKER
SOCIETY FOR PERSONNEL ADMINISTRATION. USA+45 INDUS   MGT
LG/CO SML/CO...BIBLIOG/A 20. PAGE 2 B0028   ADMIN
                                                     EX/STRUC
                                                           N
BUSINESS LITERATURE. WOR+45 MARKET ADMIN MGT.   BIBLIOG/A
PAGE 2 B0031   INDUS
                                                     FINAN
                                                     POLICY
                                                           N
FINANCIAL INDEX. CANADA UK USA+45 ECO/DEV LG/CO   BIBLIOG
ADMIN 20. PAGE 2 B0032   INDUS
                                                     FINAN
                                                     PRESS
                                                           N
KYRIAK T.E.,EAST EUROPE: BIBLIOGRAPHY--INDEX TO US   BIBLIOG/A
JPRS RESEARCH TRANSLATIONS. ALBANIA BULGARIA COM   PRESS
CZECHOSLVK HUNGARY POLAND ROMANIA AGRI EXTR/IND   MARXISM

FINAN SERV/IND INT/TRADE WEAPON...GEOG MGT SOC 20.   INDUS
PAGE 62 B1247

N

PRINCETON UNIVERSITY.SELECTED REFERENCES: BIBLIOG/A
INDUSTRIAL RELATIONS SECTION. USA+45 EX/STRUC   LABOR
WORKER TEC/DEV...MGT 20. PAGE 85 B1712   INDUS
                                                        GP/REL

N

US SUPERINTENDENT OF DOCUMENTS.LABOR (PRICE LIST   BIBLIOG/A
33). USA+45 LAW AGRI CONSTRUC INDUS NAT/G BARGAIN   WORKER
PRICE ADMIN AUTOMAT PRODUC MGT. PAGE 111 B2240   LABOR
                                                        LEGIS

B02

MOREL E.D.,AFFAIRS OF WEST AFRICA. UK FINAN INDUS   COLONIAL
FAM KIN SECT CHIEF WORKER DIPLOM RACE/REL LITERACY   ADMIN
HEALTH...CHARTS 18/20 AFRICA/W NEGRO. PAGE 75 B1521   AFR

B19

NATHAN M.,THE SOUTH AFRICAN COMMONWEALTH: CONSTN
CONSTITUTION, PROBLEMS, SOCIAL CONDITIONS.   NAT/G
SOUTH/AFR UK CULTURE INDUS EX/STRUC LEGIS BUDGET   POL/PAR
EDU/PROP ADMIN CT/SYS GP/REL RACE/REL...LING 19/20   SOCIETY
CMN/WLTH. PAGE 77 B1559

N19

ANDERSON J.,THE ORGANIZATION OF ECONOMIC STUDIES IN   ECO/TAC
RELATION TO THE PROBLEMS OF GOVERNMENT (PAMPHLET).   ACT/RES
UK FINAN INDUS DELIB/GP PLAN PROB/SOLV ADMIN 20.   NAT/G
PAGE 5 B0093   CENTRAL

N19

EAST KENTUCKY REGIONAL PLAN,PROGRAM 60: A DECADE OF   REGION
ACTION FOR PROGRESS IN EASTERN KENTUCKY (PAMPHLET).   ADMIN
USA+45 AGRI CONSTRUC INDUS CONSULT ACT/RES   PLAN
PROB/SOLV EDU/PROP GOV/REL HEALTH KENTUCKY. PAGE 32   ECO/UNDEV
B0643

N19

EAST KENTUCKY REGIONAL PLAN,PROGRAM 60 REPORT: REGION
ACTION FOR PORGRESS IN EASTERN KENTUCKY (PAMPHLET).   PLAN
USA+45 CONSTRUC INDUS ACT/RES PROB/SOLV EDU/PROP   ECO/UNDEV
ADMIN GOV/REL KENTUCKY. PAGE 32 B0644   CONSULT

L23

DOUGLAS P.H.,"OCCUPATIONAL V PROPORTIONAL   REPRESENT
REPRESENTATION." INDUS NAT/G PLAN ROUTINE SUFF   PROF/ORG
CONSEN DRIVE...CONCPT CLASSIF. PAGE 30 B0612   DOMIN
                                                        INGP/REL

B27

DICKINSON J.,ADMINISTRATIVE JUSTICE AND THE   CT/SYS
SUPREMACY OF LAW IN THE UNITED STATES. USA-45 LAW   ADJUD
INDUS DOMIN EDU/PROP CONTROL EXEC GP/REL ORD/FREE   ADMIN
...POLICY JURID 19/20. PAGE 29 B0586   NAT/G

B28

CALKINS E.E.,BUSINESS THE CIVILIZER. INDUS MARKET   LAISSEZ
WORKER TAX PAY ROUTINE COST DEMAND MORAL 19/20.   POLICY
PAGE 18 B0367   WEALTH
                                                        PROFIT

B30

ZINK H.,CITY BOSSES IN THE UNITED STATES: A STUDY   LOC/G
OF TWENTY MUNICIPAL BOSSES. USA-45 INDUS MUNIC   DOMIN
NEIGH POL/PAR ADMIN CRIME INGP/REL PERS/REL PWR   BIOG
...PERS/COMP 20 BOSSISM. PAGE 119 B2403   LEAD

B31

BORCHARD E.H.,GUIDE TO THE LAW AND LEGAL LITERATURE   BIBLIOG/A
OF FRANCE. FRANCE FINAN INDUS LABOR SECT LEGIS   LAW
ADMIN COLONIAL CRIME OWN...INT/LAW 20. PAGE 14   CONSTN
B0277   METH

B37

GULICK L.,PAPERS ON THE SCIENCE OF ADMINISTRATION.   OP/RES
INDUS PROB/SOLV TEC/DEV COST EFFICIENCY PRODUC   CONTROL
HABITAT...PHIL/SCI METH/COMP 20. PAGE 45 B0903   ADMIN
                                                        MGT

B37

PARSONS T.,THE STRUCTURE OF SOCIAL ACTION. UNIV   CULTURE
INTELL SOCIETY INDUS MARKET ECO/TAC ROUTINE CHOOSE   ATTIT
ALL/VALS...CONCPT OBS BIOG TREND GEN/LAWS 20.   CAP/ISM
PAGE 81 B1636

B37

ROBBINS L.,ECONOMIC PLANNING AND INTERNATIONAL   INT/ORG
ORDER. WOR-45 SOCIETY FINAN INDUS NAT/G ECO/TAC   PLAN
ROUTINE WEALTH...SOC TIME/SEQ GEN/METH WORK 20   INT/TRADE
KEYNES/JM. PAGE 89 B1791

B37

UNION OF SOUTH AFRICA,REPORT CONCERNING   NAT/G
ADMINISTRATION OF SOUTH WEST AFRICA (6 VOLS.).   ADMIN
SOUTH/AFR INDUS PUB/INST FORCES LEGIS BUDGET DIPLOM   COLONIAL
EDU/PROP ADJUD CT/SYS...GEOG CHARTS 20 AFRICA/SW   CONSTN
LEAGUE/NAT. PAGE 107 B2158

B38

BALDWIN R.N.,CIVIL LIBERTIES AND INDUSTRIAL   LABOR
CONFLICT. USA+45 STRATA WORKER INGP/REL...MGT 20   LG/CO
ACLU CIVIL/LIB. PAGE 9 B0175   INDUS
                                                        GP/REL

B38

FIELD G.L.,THE SYNDICAL AND CORPORATIVE   FASCISM
INSTITUTIONS OF ITALIAN FASCISM. ITALY CONSTN   INDUS
STRATA LABOR EX/STRUC TOP/EX ADJUD ADMIN LEAD   NAT/G
TOTALISM AUTHORIT...MGT 20 MUSSOLIN/B. PAGE 35   WORKER
B0716

B38

LANGE O.,ON THE ECONOMIC THEORY OF SOCIALISM. UNIV   MARKET
ECO/DEV FINAN INDUS INT/ORG PUB/INST ROUTINE ATTIT   ECO/TAC
ALL/VALS...SOC CONCPT STAT TREND 20. PAGE 62 B1258   INT/TRADE
                                                        SOCISM

B38

REICH N.,LABOR RELATIONS IN REPUBLICAN GERMANY.   WORKER
GERMANY CONSTN ECO/DEV INDUS NAT/G ADMIN CONTROL   MGT
GP/REL FASCISM POPULISM 20 WEIMAR/REP. PAGE 87   LABOR
B1763   BARGAIN

B41

LESTER R.A.,ECONOMICS OF LABOR. UK USA-45 TEC/DEV   LABOR
BARGAIN PAY INGP/REL INCOME...MGT 19/20. PAGE 64   ECO/DEV
B1298   INDUS
                                                        WORKER

B41

SLICHTER S.H.,UNION POLICIES AND INDUSTRIAL   BARGAIN
MANAGEMENT. USA-45 INDUS TEC/DEV PAY GP/REL   LABOR
INGP/REL COST EFFICIENCY PRODUC...POLICY 20.   MGT
PAGE 98 B1978   WORKER

S43

SELZNICK P.,"AN APPROACH TO A THEORY OF   ROUTINE
BUREAUCRACY." INDUS WORKER CONTROL LEAD EFFICIENCY   ADMIN
OPTIMAL...SOC METH 20 BARNARD/C BUREAUCRCY   MGT
WEBER/MAX FRIEDRCH/C MICHELS/R. PAGE 95 B1928   EX/STRUC

B44

DAHL D.,SICKNESS BENEFITS AND GROUP PURCHASE OF   BIBLIOG/A
MEDICAL CARE FOR INDUSTRIAL EMPLOYEES. FAM LABOR   INDUS
NAT/G PLAN...POLICY MGT SOC STAT 20. PAGE 25 B0519   WORKER
                                                        HEAL

B45

BAKER H.,PROBLEMS OF REEMPLOYMENT AND RETRAINING OF   BIBLIOG/A
MANPOWER DURING THE TRANSITION FROM WAR TO PEACE.   ADJUST
USA+45 INDUS LABOR LG/CO NAT/G PLAN ADMIN PEACE   WAR
...POLICY MGT 20. PAGE 8 B0167   PROB/SOLV

B45

BENJAMIN H.C.,EMPLOYMENT TESTS IN INDUSTRY AND   BIBLIOG/A
BUSINESS. LG/CO WORKER ROUTINE...MGT PSY SOC   METH
CLASSIF PROBABIL STAT APT/TEST KNO/TEST PERS/TEST   TESTS
20. PAGE 10 B0211   INDUS

B45

MAYO E.,THE SOCIAL PROBLEMS OF AN INDUSTRIAL   INDUS
CIVILIZATION. USA+45 SOCIETY LABOR CROWD PERS/REL   GP/REL
LAISSFZ. PAGE 71 B1438   MGT
                                                        WORKER

B46

DAVIES E.,NATIONAL ENTERPRISE: THE DEVELOPMENT OF   ADMIN
THE PUBLIC CORPORATION. UK LG/CO EX/STRUC WORKER   NAT/G
PROB/SOLV COST ATTIT SOCISM 20. PAGE 26 B0536   CONTROL
                                                        INDUS

B46

WILCOX J.K.,OFFICIAL DEFENSE PUBLICATIONS,   BIBLIOG/A
1941-1945 (NINE VOLS.). USA-45 AGRI INDUS R+D LABOR   WAR
FORCES TEC/DEV EFFICIENCY PRODUC SKILL WEALTH 20.   CIVMIL/REL
PAGE 116 B2347   ADMIN

B47

BAERWALD F.,FUNDAMENTALS OF LABOR ECONOMICS. LAW   ECO/DEV
INDUS LABOR LG/CO CONTROL GP/REL INCOME TOTALISM   WORKER
...MGT CHARTS GEN/LAWS BIBLIOG 20. PAGE 8 B0158   MARKET

B47

WHITEHEAD T.N.,LEADERSHIP IN A FREE SOCIETY; A   INDUS
STUDY IN HUMAN RELATIONS BASED ON AN ANALYSIS OF   LEAD
PRESENT-DAY INDUSTRIAL CIVILIZATION. WOR-45 STRUCT   ORD/FREE
R+D LABOR LG/CO SML/CO WORKER PLAN PROB/SOLV   SOCIETY
TEC/DEV DRIVE...MGT 20. PAGE 116 B2341

B48

HOOVER E.M.,THE LOCATION OF ECONOMIC ACTIVITY.   HABITAT
WOR+45 MARKET MUNIC WORKER PROB/SOLV INT/TRADE   INDUS
ADMIN COST...POLICY CHARTS T 20. PAGE 51 B1041   ECO/TAC
                                                        GEOG

B48

KESSELMAN L.C.,THE SOCIAL POLITICS OF THE FEPC.   POLICY
INDUS WORKER EDU/PROP GP/REL RACE/REL 20 NEGRO JEWS   NAT/G
FEPC. PAGE 59 B1200   ADMIN
                                                        DISCRIM

B48

ROSENFARB J.,FREEDOM AND THE ADMINISTRATIVE STATE.   ECO/DEV
NAT/G ROUTINE EFFICIENCY PRODUC RATIONAL UTIL   INDUS
...TECHNIC WELF/ST MGT 20 BUREAUCRCY. PAGE 90 B1821   PLAN
                                                        WEALTH

S48

KNICKERBOCKER I.,"LEADERSHIP: A CONCEPTION AND SOME   LEAD
IMPLICATIONS." INDUS OP/RES REPRESENT INGP/REL   CONCPT
DRIVE...MGT CLASSIF. PAGE 60 B1220   PERSON
                                                        ROLE

C48

BOLLENS J.C.,"THE PROBLEM OF GOVERNMENT IN THE SAN   USA+45
FRANCISCO BAY REGION." INDUS PROVS ADMIN GOV/REL   MUNIC
...SOC CHARTS BIBLIOG 20. PAGE 13 B0270   LOC/G
                                                        PROB/SOLV

B49

DE GRAZIA A.,HUMAN RELATIONS IN PUBLIC   BIBLIOG/A
ADMINISTRATION. INDUS ACT/RES CREATE PLAN PROB/SOLV   ADMIN
TEC/DEV INGP/REL PERS/REL DRIVE...POLICY SOC 20.   PHIL/SCI
PAGE 27 B0552   OP/RES

B49

LEPAWSKY A.,ADMINISTRATION. FINAN INDUS LG/CO
SML/CO INGP/REL PERS/REL COST EFFICIENCY OPTIMAL
SKILL 20. PAGE 64 B1294

ADMIN
MGT
WORKER
EX/STRUC

B49

SHISTER J.,ECONOMICS OF THE LABOR MARKET. LOC/G
NAT/G WORKER TEC/DEV BARGAIN PAY PRICE EXEC GP/REL
INCOME...MGT T 20. PAGE 96 B1949

MARKET
LABOR
INDUS

S49

STEINMETZ H.,"THE PROBLEMS OF THE LANDRAT: A STUDY
OF COUNTY GOVERNMENT IN THE US ZONE OF GERMANY."
GERMANY/W USA+45 INDUS PLAN DIPLOM EDU/PROP CONTROL
WAR GOV/REL FEDERAL WEALTH PLURISM...GOV/COMP 20
LANDRAT. PAGE 100 B2031

LOC/G
COLONIAL
MGT
TOP/EX

B50

COMMONS J.R.,THE ECONOMICS OF COLLECTIVE ACTION.
USA+45 AGRI INDUS LABOR NAT/G LEGIS ADMIN
EFFICIENCY...MGT METH/COMP BIBLIOG 20. PAGE 22
B0458

ECO/DEV
CAP/ISM
ACT/RES
CONCPT

S50

DALTON M.,"CONFLICTS BETWEEN STAFF AND LINE
MANAGERIAL OFFICERS" (BMR). USA+45 USA-45 ELITES
LG/CO WORKER PROB/SOLV ADMIN EXEC EFFICIENCY PRODUC
...GP/COMP 20 B0526

MGT
ATTIT
GP/REL
INDUS

S50

TANNENBAUM R.,"PARTICIPATION BY SUBORDINATES IN THE
MANAGERIAL DECISIONMAKING PROCESS" (BMR)" WOR+45
INDUS SML/CO WORKER INGP/REL...CONCPT GEN/LAWS 20.
PAGE 103 B2074

PARTIC
DECISION
MGT
LG/CO

B51

CHRISTENSEN A.N.,THE EVOLUTION OF LATIN AMERICAN
GOVERNMENT: A BOOK OF READINGS. ECO/UNDEV INDUS
LOC/G POL/PAR EX/STRUC LEGIS FOR/AID CT/SYS
...SOC/WK 20 SOUTH/AMER. PAGE 21 B0428

NAT/G
CONSTN
DIPLOM
L/A+17C

B51

UNESCO,REPERTOIRE DES BIBLIOTHEQUES DE FRANCE:
CENTRES ET SERVICES DE DOCUMENTATION DE FRANCE.
FRANCE INDUS ACADEM NAT/G INT/TRADE 20 UNESCO.
PAGE 107 B2154

BIBLIOG
ADMIN

B51

US TARIFF COMMISSION,LIST OF PUBLICATIONS OF THE
TARIFF COMMISSION (PAMPHLET). USA+45 USA-45 AGRI
EXTR/IND INDUS INT/TRADE...STAT 20. PAGE 111 B2245

BIBLIOG
TARIFFS
NAT/G
ADMIN

B52

MAIER N.R.F.,PRINCIPLES OF HUMAN RELATIONS. WOR+45
WOR-45 CULTURE SOCIETY ROUTINE ATTIT DRIVE PERCEPT
PERSON RIGID/FLEX SUPEGO PWR...PSY CONT/OBS RECORD
TOT/POP VAL/FREE 20. PAGE 68 B1379

INDUS

B53

MAJUMDAR B.B.,PROBLEMS OF PUBLIC ADMINISTRATION IN
INDIA. INDIA INDUS PLAN BUDGET ADJUD CENTRAL DEMAND
WEALTH...WELF/ST ANTHOL 20 CIVIL/SERV. PAGE 68
B1384

ECO/UNDEV
GOV/REL
ADMIN
MUNIC

B53

ROBINSON E.A.G.,THE STRUCTURE OF COMPETITIVE
INDUSTRY. UK ECO/DEV DIST/IND MARKET TEC/DEV DIPLOM
EDU/PROP ADMIN EFFICIENCY WEALTH...MGT 19/20.
PAGE 89 B1798

INDUS
PRODUC
WORKER
OPTIMAL

S53

GABLE R.W.,"NAM: INFLUENTIAL LOBBY OR KISS OF
DEATH?" (BMR)" USA+45 LAW INSPECT EDU/PROP ADMIN
CONTROL INGP/REL EFFICIENCY PWR 20 CONGRESS NAM
TAFT/HART. PAGE 38 B0769

LOBBY
LEGIS
INDUS
LG/CO

B54

BINANI G.D.,INDIA AT A GLANCE (REV. ED.). INDIA
COM/IND FINAN INDUS LABOR PROVS SCHOOL PLAN DIPLOM
INT/TRADE ADMIN...JURID 20. PAGE 12 B0238

INDEX
CON/ANAL
NAT/G
ECO/UNDEV

B54

GOULDNER A.W.,WILDCAT STRIKE. LABOR TEC/DEV PAY
ADMIN LEAD PERS/REL ATTIT RIGID/FLEX PWR...MGT
CONCPT. PAGE 40 B0816

INDUS
WORKER
GP/REL
SOC

B54

GOULDNER A.W.,PATTERNS OF INDUSTRIAL BUREAUCRACY.
DOMIN ATTIT DRIVE...BIBLIOG 20 BUREAUCRCY. PAGE 42
B0844

ADMIN
INDUS
OP/RES
WORKER

B54

MOSK S.A.,INDUSTRIAL REVOLUTION IN MEXICO. MARKET
LABOR CREATE CAP/ISM ADMIN ATTIT SOCISM...POLICY 20
MEXIC/AMER. PAGE 76 B1533

INDUS
TEC/DEV
ECO/UNDEV
NAT/G

B54

WILENSKY H.L.,SYLLABUS OF INDUSTRIAL RELATIONS: A
GUIDE TO READING AND RESEARCH. USA+45 MUNIC ADMIN
INGP/REL...POLICY MGT PHIL/SCI 20. PAGE 117 B2351

BIBLIOG
INDUS
LABOR
WORKER

C54

GOULDNER A.W.,"PATTERNS OF INDUSTRIAL BUREAUCRACY."
GP/REL CONSEN ATTIT DRIVE...BIBLIOG 20. PAGE 42
B0843

ADMIN
INDUS
OP/RES
WORKER

B55

BRAUN K.,LABOR DISPUTES AND THEIR SETTLEMENT.
ECO/TAC ROUTINE TASK GP/REL...DECISION GEN/LAWS.
PAGE 15 B0301

INDUS
LABOR
BARGAIN
ADJUD

B55

HOROWITZ M.,INCENTIVE WAGE SYSTEMS. INDUS LG/CO
WORKER CONTROL GP/REL...MGT PSY 20. PAGE 51 B1044

BIBLIOG/A
PAY
PLAN
TASK

B55

JAPAN MOMBUSHO DAIGAKU GAKIYUT,BIBLIOGRAPHY OF THE
STUDIES ON LAW AND POLITICS (PAMPHLET). CONSTN
INDUS LABOR DIPLOM TAX ADMIN...CRIMLGY INT/LAW 20
CHINJAP. PAGE 56 B1126

BIBLIOG
LAW
PHIL/SCI

S55

BUNZEL J.H.,"THE GENERAL IDEOLOGY OF AMERICAN SMALL
BUSINESS"(BMR)" USA+45 USA-45 AGRI GP/REL INGP/REL
PERSON...MGT IDEA/COMP 18/20. PAGE 17 B0345

ALL/IDEOS
ATTIT
SML/CO
INDUS

S55

WEISS R.S.,"A METHOD FOR THE ANALYSIS OF THE
STRUCTURE OF COMPLEX ORGANIZATIONS." WOR+45 INDUS
LG/CO NAT/G ROUTINE ORD/FREE PWR SKILL...MGT
PSY SOC NEW/IDEA STAT INT REC/INT STAND/INT CHARTS
WORK. PAGE 115 B2316

PROF/ORG
SOC/EXP

C55

BONER H.A.,"HUNGRY GENERATIONS." UK WOR+45 WOR-45
STRATA INDUS FAM LABOR CAP/ISM...MGT BIBLIOG 19/20.
PAGE 13 B0272

ECO/DEV
PHIL/SCI
CONCPT
WEALTH

B56

ALEXANDER R.S.,INDUSTRIAL MARKETING. USA+45 ECO/DEV
DIST/IND FINAN NAT/G ACT/RES CAP/ISM PRICE CONTROL
...POLICY MGT 20. PAGE 4 B0072

INDUS
MARKET
ECO/TAC
PLAN

B56

BLAU P.M.,BUREAUCRACY IN MODERN SOCIETY. STRUCT
INDUS LABOR LG/CO LOC/G NAT/G FORCES EDU/PROP
ROUTINE ORD/FREE 20 BUREAUCRCY. PAGE 12 B0252

SOC
EX/STRUC
ADMIN
EFFICIENCY

B56

UNITED NATIONS,BIBLIOGRAPHY ON INDUSTRIALIZATION IN
UNDER-DEVELOPED COUNTRIES. WOR+45 R+D INT/ORG NAT/G
FOR/AID ADMIN LEAD 20 UN. PAGE 107 B2161

BIBLIOG
ECO/UNDEV
INDUS
TEC/DEV

B56

WU E.,LEADERS OF TWENTIETH-CENTURY CHINA; AN
ANNOTATED BIBLIOGRAPHY OF SELECTED CHINESE
BIOGRAPHICAL WORKS IN HOOVER LIBRARY. ASIA INDUS
POL/PAR DIPLOM ADMIN REV WAR...HUM MGT 20. PAGE 118
B2386

BIBLIOG/A
BIOG
INTELL
CHIEF

B57

CENTRAL ASIAN RESEARCH CENTRE,BIBLIOGRAPHY OF
RECENT SOVIET SOURCE MATERIAL ON SOVIET CENTRAL
ASIA AND THE BORDERLANDS. AFGHANISTN INDIA PAKISTAN
UAR USSR ECO/UNDEV AGRI EXTR/IND INDUS ACADEM ADMIN
...HEAL HUM LING CON/ANAL 20. PAGE 19 B0399

BIBLIOG/A
COM
CULTURE
NAT/G

B57

IKE N.,JAPANESE POLITICS. INTELL STRUCT AGRI INDUS
FAM KIN LABOR PRESS CHOOSE ATTIT...DECISION BIBLIOG
19/20 CHINJAP. PAGE 53 B1075

NAT/G
ADMIN
POL/PAR
CULTURE

B57

INDUSTRIAL RELATIONS RES ASSN,RESEARCH IN
INDUSTRIAL HUMAN RELATIONS. INTELL ACT/RES OP/RES
ADMIN 20. PAGE 54 B1084

INDUS
MGT
LABOR
GP/REL

B57

JENNINGS I.,PARLIAMENT. UK FINAN INDUS POL/PAR
DELIB/GP EX/STRUC PLAN CONTROL...MAJORIT JURID
PARLIAMENT. PAGE 56 B1133

PARL/PROC
TOP/EX
MGT
LEGIS

B57

MURDESHWAR A.K.,ADMINISTRATIVE PROBLEMS RELATING TO
NATIONALISATION: WITH SPECIAL REFERENCE TO INDIAN
STATE ENTERPRISES. CZECHOSLVK FRANCE INDIA UK
USA+45 LEGIS WORKER PROB/SOLV BUDGET PRICE CONTROL
...MGT GEN/LAWS 20 PARLIAMENT. PAGE 76 B1544

NAT/G
OWN
INDUS
ADMIN

SCHNEIDER E.V.,INDUSTRIAL SOCIOLOGY: THE SOCIAL
RELATIONS OF INDUSTRY AND COMMUNITY. STRATA INDUS
NAT/G NEIGH CREATE ADMIN PARTIC GP/REL RACE/REL
ROLE PWR...POLICY BIBLIOG. PAGE 94 B1898

LABOR
MGT
INGP/REL
STRUCT

B58

ATOMIC INDUSTRIAL FORUM,MANAGEMENT AND ATOMIC
ENERGY. WOR+45 SEA LAW MARKET NAT/G TEC/DEV INSPECT
INT/TRADE CONFER PEACE HEALTH...ANTHOL 20. PAGE 7
B0145

NUC/PWR
INDUS
MGT
ECO/TAC

B58

BRIGHT J.R.,AUTOMATION AND MANAGEMENT. INDUS LABOR
WORKER OP/RES TEC/DEV INSPECT 20. PAGE 15 B0307

AUTOMAT
COMPUTER
PLAN
MGT

B58

CHEEK G.,ECONOMIC AND SOCIAL IMPLICATIONS OF

BIBLIOG/A

AUTOMATION: A BIBLIOGRAPHIC REVIEW (PAMPHLET).
USA+45 LG/CO WORKER CREATE PLAN CONTROL ROUTINE
PERS/REL EFFICIENCY PRODUC...METH/COMP 20. PAGE 20
B0416
SOCIETY
INDUS
AUTOMAT

B58

CLEMENTS R.V.,MANAGERS - A STUDY OF THEIR CAREERS
IN INDUSTRY. STRATA INDUS TASK PERSON SKILL 20.
PAGE 21 B0435
MGT
ELITES
EDU/PROP
TOP/EX

B58

LESTER R.A.,AS UNIONS MATURE. POL/PAR BARGAIN LEAD
PARTIC GP/REL CENTRAL...MAJORIT TIME/SEQ METH/COMP.
PAGE 64 B1299
LABOR
INDUS
POLICY
MGT

B58

MELMAN S.,DECISION-MAKING AND PRODUCTIVITY. INDUS
EX/STRUC WORKER OP/RES PROB/SOLV TEC/DEV ADMIN
ROUTINE RIGID/FLEX GP/COMP. PAGE 73 B1464
LABOR
PRODUC
DECISION
MGT

B58

OPERATIONS RESEARCH SOCIETY,A COMPREHENSIVE
BIBLIOGRAPHY ON OPERATIONS RESEARCH: THROUGH 1956
WITH SUPPLEMENT FOR 1957. COM/IND DIST/IND INDUS
ADMIN...DECISION MATH STAT METH 20. PAGE 80 B1612
BIBLIOG/A
COMPUT/IR
OP/RES
MGT

B58

WESTIN A.F.,THE ANATOMY OF A CONSTITUTIONAL LAW
CASE. USA+45 LAW LEGIS ADMIN EXEC...DECISION MGT
SOC RECORD 20 SUPREME/CT. PAGE 115 B2326
CT/SYS
INDUS
ADJUD
CONSTN

B58

WILENSKY H.L.,INDUSTRIAL SOCIETY AND SOCIAL
WELFARE: IMPACT OF INDUSTRIALIZATION ON SUPPLY AND
ORGANIZATION OF SOC WELF SERVICES. ELITES SOCIETY
STRATA SERV/IND FAM MUNIC PUB/INST CONSULT WORKER
ADMIN AUTOMAT ANOMIE 20. PAGE 117 B2352
INDUS
ECO/DEV
RECEIVE
PROF/ORG

L58

EISENSTADT S.N.,"BUREAUCRACY AND
BUREAUCRATIZATION." WOR+45 ECO/DEV INDUS R+D PLAN
GOV/REL...WELF/ST TREND BIBLIOG/A 20. PAGE 32 B0659
ADMIN
OP/RES
MGT
PHIL/SCI

S58

ELKIN A.B.,"OEEC-ITS STRUCTURE AND POWERS." EUR+WWI
CONSTN INDUS INT/ORG NAT/G VOL/ASSN DELIB/GP
ACT/RES PLAN ORD/FREE WEALTH...CHARTS ORG/CHARTS
OEEC 20. PAGE 33 B0666
ECO/DEV
EX/STRUC

B59

BONNETT C.E.,LABOR-MANAGEMENT RELATIONS. USA+45
OP/RES PROB/SOLV EDU/PROP...AUD/VIS CHARTS 20.
PAGE 13 B0274
MGT
LABOR
INDUS
GP/REL

B59

COUNCIL OF STATE GOVERNMENTS,STATE GOVERNMENT: AN
ANNOTATED BIBLIOGRAPHY (PAMPHLET). USA+45 LAW AGRI
INDUS WORKER PLAN TAX ADJUST AGE/Y ORD/FREE...HEAL
MGT 20. PAGE 24 B0494
BIBLIOG/A
PROVS
LOC/G
ADMIN

B59

EPSTEIN F.T.,EAST GERMANY: A SELECTED BIBLIOGRAPHY
(PAMPHLET). COM GERMANY/E LAW AGRI FINAN INDUS
LABOR POL/PAR EDU/PROP ADMIN AGE/Y 20. PAGE 33
B0677
BIBLIOG/A
INTELL
MARXISM
NAT/G

B59

WARNER W.L.,INDUSTRIAL MAN. USA+45 USA-45 ELITES
INDUS LABOR TOP/EX WORKER ADMIN INGP/REL PERS/REL
...CHARTS ANTHOL 20. PAGE 114 B2294
EXEC
LEAD
PERSON
MGT

B59

WELTON H.,THE THIRD WORLD WAR: TRADE AND INDUSTRY,
THE NEW BATTLEGROUND. WOR+45 ECO/DEV INDUS MARKET
TASK...MGT IDEA/COMP COLD/WAR. PAGE 115 B2321
INT/TRADE
PLAN
DIPLOM

S59

BENDIX R.,"INDUSTRIALIZATION, IDEOLOGIES, AND
SOCIAL STRUCTURE" (BMR)" UK USA-45 USSR STRUCT
WORKER GP/REL EFFICIENCY...IDEA/COMP 20. PAGE 10
B0210
INDUS
ATTIT
MGT
ADMIN

S59

CYERT R.M.,"MODELS IN A BEHAVIORAL THEORY OF THE
FIRM." ROUTINE...DECISION MGT METH/CNCPT MATH.
PAGE 25 B0517
SIMUL
GAME
PREDICT
INDUS

S59

SIMPSON R.L.,"VERTICAL AND HORIZONTAL COMMUNICATION
IN FORMAL ORGANIZATION" USA+45 LG/CO EX/STRUC DOMIN
CONTROL TASK INGP/REL TIME 20. PAGE 97 B1963
PERS/REL
AUTOMAT
INDUS
WORKER

S59

UDY S.H. JR.,"'BUREAUCRACY' AND 'RATIONALITY' IN
WEBER'S ORGANIZATION THEORY: AN EMPIRICAL STUDY"
(BMR)" UNIV STRUCT INDUS LG/CO SML/CO VOL/ASSN
...SOC SIMUL 20 WEBER/MAX BUREAUCRCY. PAGE 106
B2144
GEN/LAWS
METH/CNCPT
ADMIN
RATIONAL

S59

ZAUBERMAN A.,"SOVIET BLOC ECONOMIC INTEGRATION."
COM CULTURE INTELL ECO/DEV INDUS TOP/EX ACT/RES
PLAN ECO/TAC INT/TRADE ROUTINE CHOOSE ATTIT
...TIME/SEQ 20. PAGE 119 B2399
MARKET
INT/ORG
USSR
TOTALISM

C59

DAHL R.A.,"SOCIAL SCIENCE RESEARCH ON BUSINESS:
PRODUCT AND POTENTIAL" INDUS MARKET OP/RES CAP/ISM
ADMIN LOBBY DRIVE...PSY CONCPT BIBLIOG/A 20.
PAGE 26 B0521
MGT
EFFICIENCY
PROB/SOLV
EX/STRUC

B60

ASPREMONT-LYNDEN H.,RAPPORT SUR L'ADMINISTRATION
BELGE DU RUANDA-URUNDI PENDANT L'ANNEE 1959.
BELGIUM RWANDA AGRI INDUS DIPLOM ECO/TAC INT/TRADE
DOMIN ADMIN RACE/REL...GEOG CENSUS 20 UN. PAGE 7
B0143
AFR
COLONIAL
ECO/UNDEV
INT/ORG

B60

BHAMBHRI C.P.,PARLIAMENTARY CONTROL OVER STATE
ENTERPRISE IN INDIA. INDIA DELIB/GP ADMIN CONTROL
INGP/REL EFFICIENCY 20 PARLIAMENT. PAGE 11 B0235
NAT/G
OWN
INDUS
PARL/PROC

B60

DRAPER T.,AMERICAN COMMUNISM AND SOVIET RUSSIA.
EUR+WWI USA+45 USSR INTELL AGRI COM/IND INDUS
LABOR PROF/ORG VOL/ASSN PLAN TEC/DEV DOMIN EDU/PROP
ADMIN COERCE REV PERSON PWR...POLICY CONCPT MYTH
19/20. PAGE 30 B0617
COM
POL/PAR

B60

EASTON S.C.,THE TWILIGHT OF EUROPEAN COLONIALISM.
AFR S/ASIA CONSTN SOCIETY STRUCT ECO/UNDEV INDUS
NAT/G FORCES ECO/TAC COLONIAL CT/SYS ATTIT KNOWL
ORD/FREE PWR...SOCIALIST TIME/SEQ TREND CON/ANAL
20. PAGE 32 B0645
FINAN
ADMIN

B60

ELKOURI F.,HOW ARBITRATION WORKS (REV. ED.). LAW
INDUS BARGAIN 20. PAGE 33 B0667
MGT
LABOR
ADJUD
GP/REL

B60

FRYE R.J.,GOVERNMENT AND LABOR: THE ALABAMA
PROGRAM. USA+45 INDUS R+D LABOR WORKER BUDGET
EFFICIENCY AGE/Y HEALTH...CHARTS 20 ALABAMA.
PAGE 38 B0761
ADMIN
LEGIS
LOC/G
PROVS

B60

GRANICK D.,THE RED EXECUTIVE. COM USA+45 SOCIETY
ECO/DEV INDUS NAT/G POL/PAR EX/STRUC PLAN ECO/TAC
EDU/PROP ADMIN EXEC ATTIT DRIVE...GP/COMP 20.
PAGE 42 B0851
PWR
STRATA
USSR
ELITES

B60

KERR C.,INDUSTRIALISM AND INDUSTRIAL MAN. CULTURE
SOCIETY ECO/UNDEV NAT/G ADMIN PRODUC WEALTH
...PREDICT TREND NAT/COMP 19/20. PAGE 59 B1197
WORKER
MGT
ECO/DEV
INDUS

B60

LENCZOWSKI G.,OIL AND STATE IN THE MIDDLE EAST. FUT
IRAN LAW ECO/UNDEV EXTR/IND NAT/G TOP/EX PLAN
TEC/DEV ECO/TAC LEGIT ADMIN COERCE ATTIT ALL/VALS
PWR...CHARTS 20. PAGE 64 B1288
ISLAM
INDUS
NAT/LISM

B60

LEWIS P.R.,LITERATURE OF THE SOCIAL SCIENCES: AN
INTRODUCTORY SURVEY AND GUIDE. UK LAW INDUS DIPLOM
INT/TRADE ADMIN...MGT 19/20. PAGE 65 B1306
BIBLIOG/A
SOC

B60

MOORE W.E.,LABOR COMMITMENT AND SOCIAL CHANGE IN
DEVELOPING AREAS. SOCIETY STRATA ECO/UNDEV MARKET
VOL/ASSN WORKER AUTHORIT SKILL...MGT NAT/COMP
SOC/INTEG 20. PAGE 75 B1514
LABOR
ORD/FREE
ATTIT
INDUS

B60

PIERCE R.A.,RUSSIAN CENTRAL ASIA, 1867-1917. ASIA
RUSSIA CULTURE AGRI INDUS EDU/PROP REV NAT/LISM
...CHARTS BIBLIOG 19/20 BOLSHEVISM INTERVENT.
PAGE 83 B1672
COLONIAL
DOMIN
ADMIN
ECO/UNDEV

B60

ROBINSON E.A.G.,ECONOMIC CONSEQUENCES OF THE SIZE
OF NATIONS. AGRI INDUS DELIB/GP FOR/AID ADMIN
EFFICIENCY...METH/COMP 20. PAGE 89 B1799
CONCPT
INT/ORG
NAT/COMP

B60

RUBENSTEIN A.H.,SOME THEORIES OF ORGANIZATION.
ROUTINE ATTIT...DECISION ECOMETRIC. PAGE 91 B1846
SOCIETY
ECO/DEV
INDUS
TOP/EX

B60

US DEPARTMENT OF THE ARMY,SELECT BIBLIOGRAPHY ON
ADMINISTRATIVE ORGANIZATION(PAMPHLET). USA+45 INDUS
NAT/G EX/STRUC OP/RES CIVMIL/REL EFFICIENCY
ORD/FREE. PAGE 108 B2183
BIBLIOG/A
ADMIN
CONCPT
FORCES

B60

WORLEY P.,ASIA TODAY (REV. ED.) (PAMPHLET). COM
ECO/UNDEV AGRI FINAN INDUS POL/PAR FOR/AID ADMIN
MARXISM 20. PAGE 118 B2376
BIBLIOG/A
ASIA
DIPLOM
NAT/G

L60

STEIN E.,"LEGAL REMEDIES OF ENTERPRISES IN THE
EUROPEAN ECONOMIC COMMUNITY." EUR+WWI FUT ECO/DEV
INDUS PLAN ECO/TAC ADMIN PWR...MGT MATH STAT TREND
CON/ANAL EEC 20. PAGE 100 B2026
MARKET
ADJUD

S60

"THE EMERGING COMMON MARKETS IN LATIN AMERICA." FUT
L/A+17C STRATA DIST/IND INDUS LABOR NAT/G LEGIS
ECO/TAC ADMIN RIGID/FLEX HEALTH...NEW/IDEA TIME/SEQ
OAS 20. PAGE 2 B0039
FINAN
ECO/UNDEV
INT/TRADE

GARNICK D.H.,"ON THE ECONOMIC FEASIBILITY OF A
MIDDLE EASTERN COMMON MARKET." AFR ISLAM CULTURE
INDUS NAT/G PLAN TEC/DEV ECO/TAC ADMIN ATTIT DRIVE
RIGID/FLEX...PLURIST STAT TREND GEN/LAWS 20.
PAGE 39 B0784
S60
MARKET
INT/TRADE

HERZ J.H.,"EAST GERMANY: PROGRESS AND PROSPECTS."
COM AGRI FINAN INDUS LOC/G NAT/G FORCES PLAN
TEC/DEV DOMIN ADMIN COERCE DRIVE PERCEPT RIGID/FLEX
MORAL ORD/FREE PWR...MARXIST PSY SOC RECORD STERTYP
WORK. PAGE 49 B0997
S60
POL/PAR
STRUCT
GERMANY

MORALES C.J.,"TRADE AND ECONOMIC INTEGRATION IN
LATIN AMERICA." FUT L/A+17C LAW STRATA ECO/UNDEV
DIST/IND INDUS LABOR NAT/G LEGIS ECO/TAC ADMIN
RIGID/FLEX WEALTH...CONCPT NEW/IDEA CONT/OBS
TIME/SEQ WORK 20. PAGE 75 B1519
S60
FINAN
INT/TRADE
REGION

SCHATZ S.P.,"THE INFLENCE OF PLANNING ON
DEVELOPMENT: THE NIGERIAN EXPERIENCE." AFR FUT
FINAN INDUS NAT/G EX/STRUC ECO/TAC ADMIN ATTIT
PERCEPT ORD/FREE PWR...MATH TREND CON/ANAL SIMUL
VAL/FREE 20. PAGE 93 B1883
S60
ECO/UNDEV
PLAN
NIGERIA

AGARWAL R.C.,STATE ENTERPRISE IN INDIA. FUT INDIA
UK FINAN INDUS ADMIN CONTROL OWN...POLICY CHARTS
BIBLIOG 20 RAILROAD. PAGE 3 B0064
B61
ECO/UNDEV
SOCISM
GOV/REL
LG/CO

AMERICAN MANAGEMENT ASSN,SUPERIOR-SUBORDINATE
COMMUNICATION IN MANAGEMENT. STRATA FINAN INDUS
SML/CO WORKER CONTROL EXEC ATTIT 20. PAGE 4 B0086
B61
MGT
ACT/RES
PERS/REL
LG/CO

BENOIT E.,EUROPE AT SIXES AND SEVENS: THE COMMON
MARKET, THE FREE TRADE ASSOCIATION AND THE UNITED
STATES. EUR+WWI FUT USA+45 INDUS CONSULT DELIB/GP
EX/STRUC TOP/EX ACT/RES ECO/TAC EDU/PROP ROUTINE
CHOOSE PERCEPT WEALTH...MGT TREND EEC TOT/POP 20
EFTA. PAGE 11 B0217
B61
FINAN
ECO/DEV
VOL/ASSN

BRADY R.A.,ORGANIZATION, AUTOMATION, AND SOCIETY.
USA+45 AGRI COM/IND DIST/IND MARKET CREATE
...DECISION MGT 20. PAGE 14 B0296
B61
TEC/DEV
INDUS
AUTOMAT
ADMIN

BULLIS H.A.,MANIFESTO FOR AMERICANS. USA+45 AGRI
LABOR NAT/G NEIGH FOR/AID INT/TRADE TAX EDU/PROP
CHOOSE...POLICY MGT 20 UN UNESCO. PAGE 17 B0342
B61
ECO/TAC
SOCIETY
INDUS
CAP/ISM

DRURY J.W.,THE GOVERNMENT OF KANSAS. USA+45 AGRI
INDUS CHIEF LEGIS WORKER PLAN BUDGET GIVE CT/SYS
GOV/REL...T 20 KANSAS GOVERNOR CITY/MGT. PAGE 31
B0621
B61
PROVS
CONSTN
ADMIN
LOC/G

DUBIN R.,HUMAN RELATIONS IN ADMINISTRATION. USA+45
INDUS LABOR LG/CO EX/STRUC GP/REL DRIVE PWR
...DECISION SOC CHARTS ANTHOL 20. PAGE 31 B0623
B61
PERS/REL
MGT
ADMIN
EXEC

HALL M.,DISTRIBUTION IN GREAT BRITAIN AND NORTH
AMERICA. CANADA UK USA+45 ECO/DEV INDUS MARKET
EFFICIENCY PROFIT...MGT CHARTS 20. PAGE 46 B0924
B61
DIST/IND
PRODUC
ECO/TAC
CAP/ISM

HARRISON S.,INDIA AND THE UNITED STATES. FUT S/ASIA
USA+45 WOR+45 INTELL ECO/DEV ECO/UNDEV AGRI INDUS
INT/ORG NAT/G CONSULT EX/STRUC TOP/EX PLAN ECO/TAC
NEUTRAL ALL/VALS...MGT TOT/POP 20. PAGE 47 B0956
B61
DELIB/GP
ACT/RES
FOR/AID
INDIA

HART H.C.,ADMINISTRATIVE ASPECTS OF RIVER VALLEY
DEVELOPMENT. INDIA USA+45 INDUS CONTROL EFFICIENCY
OPTIMAL PRODUC 20 TVA. PAGE 47 B0957
B61
ADMIN
PLAN
METH/COMP
AGRI

HICKS U.K.,DEVELOPMENT FROM BELOW. UK INDUS ADMIN
COLONIAL ROUTINE GOV/REL...POLICY METH/CNCPT CHARTS
19/20 CMN/WLTH. PAGE 50 B1006
B61
ECO/UNDEV
LOC/G
GOV/COMP
METH/COMP

HORVATH B.,THE CHARACTERISTICS OF YUGOSLAV ECONOMIC
DEVELOPMENT. COM ECO/UNDEV AGRI INDUS PLAN CAP/ISM
ECO/TAC ROUTINE WEALTH...SOCIALIST STAT CHARTS
STERTYP WORK 20. PAGE 52 B1045
B61
ACT/RES
YUGOSLAVIA

JANOWITZ M.,COMMUNITY POLITICAL SYSTEMS. USA+45
SOCIETY INDUS VOL/ASSN TEC/DEV ADMIN LEAD CHOOSE
...SOC SOC/WK 20. PAGE 56 B1123
B61
MUNIC
STRUCT
POL/PAR

KOESTLER A.,THE LOTUS AND THE ROBOT. ASIA INDIA
S/ASIA SOCIETY STRATA ECO/DEV AGRI INDUS FAM CREATE
DOMIN EDU/PROP ADMIN COERCE ATTIT DRIVE SUPEGO
ORD/FREE PWR RESPECT WEALTH...MYTH OBS 20 CHINJAP.
PAGE 61 B1226
B61
SECT
ECO/UNDEV

LAHAYE R.,LES ENTREPRISES PUBLIQUES AU MAROC.
FRANCE MOROCCO LAW DIST/IND EXTR/IND FINAN CONSULT
PLAN TEC/DEV ADMIN AGREE CONTROL OWN...POLICY 20.
PAGE 62 B1250
B61
NAT/G
INDUS
ECO/UNDEV
ECO/TAC

MARX K.,THE COMMUNIST MANIFESTO. IN (MENDEL A.
ESSENTIAL WORKS OF MARXISM, NEW YORK: BANTAM. FUT
MOD/EUR CULTURE ECO/DEV ECO/UNDEV AGRI FINAN INDUS
MARKET PROC/MFG LABOR MUNIC POL/PAR CONSULT FORCES
CREATE PLAN ADMIN ATTIT DRIVE RIGID/FLEX ORD/FREE
PWR RESPECT MARX/KARL WORK. PAGE 70 B1421
B61
COM
NEW/IDEA
CAP/ISM
REV

SHARMA T.R.,THE WORKING OF STATE ENTERPRISES IN
INDIA. INDIA DELIB/GP LEGIS WORKER BUDGET PRICE
CONTROL GP/REL OWN ATTIT...MGT CHARTS 20. PAGE 96
B1938
B61
NAT/G
INDUS
ADMIN
SOCISM

US GENERAL ACCOUNTING OFFICE,EXAMINATION OF
ECONOMIC AND TECHNICAL ASSISTANCE PROGRAM FOR IRAN.
IRAN USA+45 AGRI INDUS DIPLOM CONTROL COST 20.
PAGE 108 B2186
B61
FOR/AID
ADMIN
TEC/DEV
ECO/UNDEV

GORDON L.,"ECONOMIC REGIONALISM RECONSIDERED." FUT
USA+45 WOR+45 INDUS NAT/G TEC/DEV DIPLOM ROUTINE
PERCEPT WEALTH...WELF/ST METH/CNCPT WORK 20.
PAGE 41 B0830
S61
ECO/DEV
ATTIT
CAP/ISM
REGION

VINER J.,"ECONOMIC FOREIGN POLICY ON THE NEW
FRONTIER." USA+45 ECO/UNDEV AGRI FINAN INDUS MARKET
INT/ORG NAT/G FOR/AID INT/TRADE ADMIN ATTIT PWR 20
KENNEDY/JF. PAGE 112 B2262
S61
TOP/EX
ECO/TAC
BAL/PAY
TARIFFS

CAIRNCROSS A.K.,FACTORS IN ECONOMIC DEVELOPMENT.
WOR+45 ECO/UNDEV INDUS R+D LG/CO NAT/G EX/STRUC
PLAN TEC/DEV ECO/TAC ATTIT HEALTH KNOWL PWR WEALTH
...TIME/SEQ GEN/LAWS TOT/POP VAL/FREE 20. PAGE 18
B0363
B62
MARKET
ECO/DEV

CARSON P.,MATERIALS FOR WEST AFRICAN HISTORY IN THE
ARCHIVES OF BELGIUM AND HOLLAND. CLIENT INDUS
INT/TRADE ADMIN 17/19. PAGE 19 B0387
B62
BIBLIOG/A
COLONIAL
AFR
ECO/UNDEV

DUCKWORTH W.E.,A GUIDE TO OPERATIONAL RESEARCH.
INDUS PLAN PROB/SOLV EXEC EFFICIENCY PRODUC KNOWL
...MGT MATH STAT SIMUL METH 20 MONTECARLO. PAGE 31
B0624
B62
OP/RES
GAME
DECISION
ADMIN

GALENSON W.,LABOR IN DEVELOPING COUNTRIES. BRAZIL
INDONESIA ISRAEL PAKISTAN TURKEY AGRI INDUS WORKER
PAY PRICE GP/REL WEALTH...MGT CHARTS METH/COMP
NAT/COMP 20. PAGE 38 B0775
B62
LABOR
ECO/UNDEV
BARGAIN
POL/PAR

GRANICK D.,THE EUROPEAN EXECUTIVE. BELGIUM FRANCE
GERMANY/W UK INDUS LABOR LG/CO SML/CO EX/STRUC PLAN
TEC/DEV CAP/ISM COST DEMAND...POLICY CHARTS 20.
PAGE 42 B0852
B62
MGT
ECO/DEV
ECO/TAC
EXEC

GROVE J.W.,GOVERNMENT AND INDUSTRY IN BRITAIN. UK
FINAN LOC/G CONSULT DELIB/GP INT/TRADE ADMIN
CONTROL...BIBLIOG 20. PAGE 44 B0894
B62
ECO/TAC
INDUS
NAT/G
GP/REL

HANSON A.H.,MANAGERIAL PROBLEMS IN PUBLIC
ENTERPRISE. INDIA DELIB/GP GP/REL INGP/REL
EFFICIENCY 20 PARLIAMENT. PAGE 46 B0940
B62
MGT
NAT/G
INDUS
PROB/SOLV

HATTERY L.H.,INFORMATION RETRIEVAL MANAGEMENT.
CLIENT INDUS TOP/EX COMPUTER OP/RES TEC/DEV ROUTINE
COST EFFICIENCY RIGID/FLEX...METH/COMP ANTHOL 20.
PAGE 48 B0968
B62
R+D
COMPUT/IR
MGT
CREATE

INTERNATIONAL LABOR OFFICE,WORKERS' MANAGEMENT IN
YUGOSLAVIA. COM YUGOSLAVIA LABOR DELIB/GP EX/STRUC
PROB/SOLV ADMIN PWR MARXISM...CHARTS ORG/CHARTS
BIBLIOG 20. PAGE 54 B1098
B62
WORKER
CONTROL
MGT
INDUS

MEANS G.C.,THE CORPORATE REVOLUTION IN AMERICA:
ECONOMIC REALITY VS. ECONOMIC THEORY. USA+45 USA-45
INDUS WORKER PLAN CAP/ISM ADMIN...IDEA/COMP 20.
PAGE 72 B1459
B62
LG/CO
MARKET
CONTROL
PRICE

NATIONAL BUREAU ECONOMIC RES,THE RATE AND DIRECTION
OF INVENTIVE ACTIVITY: ECONOMIC AND SOCIAL FACTORS.
STRUCT INDUS MARKET R+D CREATE OP/RES TEC/DEV
EFFICIENCY PRODUC RATIONAL UTIL...WELF/ST PHIL/SCI
METH/CNCPT TIME. PAGE 77 B1562
B62
DECISION
PROB/SOLV
MGT

PACKARD V.,THE PYRAMID CLIMBERS. USA+45 ELITES
SOCIETY CREATE PROB/SOLV EFFICIENCY ATTIT...MGT 20.
PAGE 80 B1621
B62
INDUS
TOP/EX
PERS/REL
DRIVE

SAMPSON A.,ANATOMY OF BRITAIN. UK LAW COM/IND FINAN
B62
ELITES

INDUS MARKET MUNIC POL/PAR EX/STRUC TOP/EX DIPLOM LEAD REPRESENT PERSON PARLIAMENT WORSHIP. PAGE 92 B1866 — PWR STRUCT FORCES

B62
SRIVASTAVA G.L.,COLLECTIVE BARGAINING AND LABOR-MANAGEMENT RELATIONS IN INDIA. INDIA UK USA+45 INDUS LEGIS WORKER ADJUD EFFICIENCY PRODUC ...METH/COMP 20. PAGE 100 B2014 — LABOR MGT BARGAIN GP/REL

B62
TAYLOR D.,THE BRITISH IN AFRICA. UK CULTURE ECO/UNDEV INDUS DIPLOM INT/TRADE ADMIN WAR RACE/REL ORD/FREE SOVEREIGN...POLICY BIBLIOG 15/20 CMN/WLTH. PAGE 103 B2084 — AFR COLONIAL DOMIN

B62
TAYLOR J.K.L.,ATTITUDES AND METHODS OF COMMUNICATION AND CONSULTATION BETWEEN EMPLOYERS AND WORKERS AT INDIVIDUAL FIRM LEVEL. WOR+45 STRUCT INDUS LABOR CONFER TASK GP/REL EFFICIENCY...MGT BIBLIOG METH 20 OECD. PAGE 103 B2087 — WORKER ADMIN ATTIT EDU/PROP

L62
BELSHAW D.G.R.,"PUBLIC INVESTMENT IN AGRICULTURE AND ECONOMIC DEVELOPMENT OF UGANDA" UGANDA AGRI INDUS R+D ECO/TAC RATION TAX PAY COLONIAL 20 WORLD/BANK. PAGE 10 B0209 — ECO/UNDEV PLAN ADMIN CENTRAL

L62
WATERSTON A.,"PLANNING IN MOROCCO, ORGANIZATION AND IMPLEMENTATION. BALTIMORE: HOPKINS ECON. DEVELOP. INT. BANK FOR." ISLAM ECO/DEV AGRI DIST/IND INDUS PROC/MFG SERV/IND LOC/G EX/STRUC ECO/TAC PWR WEALTH TOT/POP VAL/FREE 20. PAGE 114 B2302 — NAT/G PLAN MOROCCO

S62
LARSON R.L.,"HOW TO DEFINE ADMINISTRATIVE PROBLEMS." ROUTINE PERCEPT KNOWL SKILL...MGT METH/CNCPT CHARTS TOT/POP. PAGE 63 B1263 — UNIV FACE/GP INDUS EXEC

B63
ACKOFF R.L.,A MANAGER'S GUIDE TO OPERATIONS RESEARCH. STRUCT INDUS PROB/SOLV ROUTINE 20. PAGE 3 B0056 — OP/RES MGT GP/REL ADMIN

B63
BONINI C.P.,SIMULATION OF INFORMATION AND DECISION SYSTEMS IN THE FIRM. MARKET BUDGET DOMIN EDU/PROP ADMIN COST ATTIT HABITAT PERCEPT PWR...CONCPT PROBABIL QUANT PREDICT HYPO/EXP BIBLIOG. PAGE 13 B0273 — INDUS SIMUL DECISION MGT

B63
CORLEY R.N.,THE LEGAL ENVIRONMENT OF BUSINESS. CONSTN LEGIS TAX ADMIN CT/SYS DISCRIM ATTIT PWR ...TREND 18/20. PAGE 23 B0477 — NAT/G INDUS JURID DECISION

B63
CORSON J.J.,PUBLIC ADMINISTRATION IN MODERN SOCIETY. INDUS FORCES CONTROL CENTRAL EFFICIENCY 20. PAGE 24 B0482 — MGT NAT/G PROB/SOLV INGP/REL

B63
DE VRIES E.,SOCIAL ASPECTS OF ECONOMIC DEVELOPMENT IN LATIN AMERICA. CULTURE SOCIETY STRATA FINAN INDUS INT/ORG DELIB/GP ACT/RES ECO/TAC EDU/PROP ADMIN ATTIT SUPEGO HEALTH KNOWL ORD/FREE...SOC STAT TREND ANTHOL TOT/POP VAL/FREE. PAGE 28 B0562 — L/A+17C ECO/UNDEV

B63
GANGULY D.S.,PUBLIC CORPORATIONS IN A NATIONAL ECONOMY. INDIA WOR+45 FINAN INDUS TOP/EX PRICE EFFICIENCY...MGT STAT CHARTS BIBLIOG 20. PAGE 38 B0779 — ECO/UNDEV LG/CO SOCISM GOV/REL

B63
HANSON A.H.,NATIONALIZATION: A BOOK OF READINGS. WOR+45 FINAN DELIB/GP LEGIS WORKER BUDGET ADMIN GP/REL EFFICIENCY SOCISM...MGT ANTHOL. PAGE 46 B0941 — NAT/G OWN INDUS CONTROL

B63
HARGROVE M.M.,BUSINESS POLICY CASES-WITH BEHAVIORAL SCIENCE IMPLICATIONS. LG/CO SML/CO EX/STRUC TOP/EX PLAN PROB/SOLV CONFER ADMIN CONTROL ROUTINE EFFICIENCY. PAGE 47 B0946 — SOC/EXP INDUS DECISION MGT

B63
HEYEL C.,THE ENCYCLOPEDIA OF MANAGEMENT. WOR+45 MARKET TOP/EX TEC/DEV AUTOMAT LEAD ADJUST...STAT CHARTS GAME ANTHOL BIBLIOG. PAGE 49 B1002 — MGT INDUS ADMIN FINAN

B63
KARL B.D.,EXECUTIVE REORGANIZATION AND REFORM IN THE NEW DEAL. ECO/DEV INDUS DELIB/GP EX/STRUC PLAN BUDGET ADMIN EFFICIENCY PWR POPULISM...POLICY 20 PRESIDENT ROOSEVLT/F WILSON/W NEW/DEAL. PAGE 58 B1174 — BIOG EXEC CREATE CONTROL

B63
KORNHAUSER W.,SCIENTISTS IN INDUSTRY: CONFLICT AND ACCOMMODATION. USA+45 R+D LG/CO NAT/G TEC/DEV CONTROL ADJUST ATTIT...MGT STAT INT BIBLIOG 20. PAGE 61 B1229 — CREATE INDUS PROF/ORG GP/REL

B63
NASA,CONFERENCE ON SPACE, SCIENCE, AND URBAN LIFE. USA+45 SOCIETY INDUS ACADEM ACT/RES ECO/TAC ADMIN — MUNIC SPACE

20. PAGE 77 B1556 — TEC/DEV PROB/SOLV

B63
ROYAL INSTITUTE PUBLIC ADMIN,BRITISH PUBLIC ADMINISTRATION. UK LAW FINAN INDUS LOC/G POL/PAR LEGIS LOBBY PARL/PROC CHOOSE JURID. PAGE 91 B1845 — BIBLIOG ADMIN MGT NAT/G

B63
SCHOECK H.,THE NEW ARGUMENT IN ECONOMICS. UK USA+45 INDUS MARKET LABOR NAT/G ECO/TAC ADMIN ROUTINE BAL/PAY PWR...POLICY BOLIV. PAGE 94 B1899 — WELF/ST FOR/AID ECO/DEV ALL/IDEOS

B63
SHANKS M.,THE LESSONS OF PUBLIC ENTERPRISE. UK LEGIS WORKER ECO/TAC ADMIN PARL/PROC GOV/REL ATTIT ...POLICY MGT METH/COMP NAT/COMP ANTHOL 20 PARLIAMENT. PAGE 96 B1931 — SOCISM OWN NAT/G INDUS

S63
DELLIN L.A.D.,"BULGARIA UNDER SOVIET LEADERSHIP." BULGARIA COM USA+45 USSR ECO/DEV INDUS POL/PAR EX/STRUC TOP/EX COERCE ATTIT RIGID/FLEX...POLICY TIME/SEQ 20. PAGE 28 B0572 — AGRI NAT/G TOTALISM

S63
DUCROS B.,"MOBILISATION DES RESSOURCES PRODUCTIVES ET DEVELOPPEMENT." FUT INTELL SOCIETY COM/IND DIST/IND EXTR/IND FINAN INDUS ROUTINE WEALTH ...METH/CNCPT OBS 20. PAGE 31 B0625 — ECO/UNDEV TEC/DEV

S63
NADLER E.B.,"SOME ECONOMIC DISADVANTAGES OF THE ARMS RACE." USA+45 INDUS R+D FORCES PLAN TEC/DEV ECO/TAC FOR/AID EDU/PROP PWR WEALTH...TREND COLD/WAR 20. PAGE 77 B1552 — ECO/DEV MGT BAL/PAY

S63
SCHURMANN F.,"ECONOMIC POLICY AND POLITICAL POWER IN COMMUNIST CHINA." ASIA CHINA/COM USSR SOCIETY ECO/UNDEV AGRI INDUS CREATE ADMIN ROUTINE ATTIT DRIVE RIGID/FLEX PWR WEALTH...HIST/WRIT TREND CHARTS WORK 20. PAGE 94 B1908 — PLAN ECO/TAC

N63
GREAT BRITAIN DEPT TECH COOP,PUBLIC ADMINISTRATION: A SELECT BIBLIOGRAPHY (PAMPHLET). WOR+45 AGRI FINAN INDUS EX/STRUC OP/RES ECO/TAC...MGT METH/COMP NAT/COMP. PAGE 43 B0861 — BIBLIOG/A ADMIN NAT/G LOC/G

B64
RECENT PUBLICATIONS ON GOVERNMENTAL PROBLEMS. FINAN INDUS ACADEM PLAN PROB/SOLV EDU/PROP ADJUD ADMIN BIO/SOC...MGT SOC. PAGE 2 B0040 — BIBLIOG AUTOMAT LEGIS JURID

B64
BLAKE R.R.,MANAGING INTERGROUP CONFLICT IN INDUSTRY. INDUS DELIB/GP EX/STRUC GP/REL PERS/REL GAME. PAGE 12 B0250 — CREATE PROB/SOLV OP/RES ADJUD

B64
BRIGHT J.R.,RESEARCH, DEVELOPMENT AND TECHNOLOGICAL INNOVATION. CULTURE R+D CREATE PLAN PROB/SOLV AUTOMAT RISK PERSON...DECISION CONCPT PREDICT BIBLIOG. PAGE 15 B0308 — TEC/DEV NEW/IDEA INDUS MGT

B64
COLLINS B.E.,A SOCIAL PSYCHOLOGY OF GROUP PROCESSES FOR DECISION-MAKING. PROB/SOLV ROUTINE...SOC CHARTS HYPO/EXP. PAGE 22 B0453 — FACE/GP DECISION NAT/G INDUS

B64
DIEBOLD J.,BEYOND AUTOMATION: MANAGERIAL PROBLEMS OF AN EXPLODING TECHNOLOGY. SOCIETY ECO/DEV CREATE ECO/TAC AUTOMAT SKILL...TECHNIC MGT WORK. PAGE 29 B0589 — FUT INDUS PROVS NAT/G

B64
EWING D.W.,THE MANAGERIAL MIND. SOCIETY STRUCT INDUS PERSON KNOWL 20. PAGE 34 B0692 — MGT ATTIT CREATE EFFICIENCY

B64
FLORENCE P.S.,ECONOMICS AND SOCIOLOGY OF INDUSTRY; A REALISTIC ANALYSIS OF DEVELOPMENT. ECO/UNDEV LG/CO NAT/G PLAN...GEOG MGT BIBLIOG 20. PAGE 36 B0729 — INDUS SOC ADMIN

B64
GESELLSCHAFT RECHTSVERGLEICH,BIBLIOGRAPHIE DES DEUTSCHEN RECHTS (BIBLIOGRAPHY OF GERMAN LAW, TRANS. BY COURTLAND PETERSON). GERMANY FINAN INDUS LABOR SECT FORCES CT/SYS PARL/PROC CRIME...INT/LAW SOC NAT/COMP 20. PAGE 39 B0794 — BIBLIOG/A JURID CONSTN ADMIN

B64
GRAVIER J.F.,AMENAGEMENT DU TERRITOIRE ET L'AVENIR DES REGIONS FRANCAISES. FRANCE ECO/DEV AGRI INDUS CREATE...GEOG CHARTS 20. PAGE 42 B0859 — PLAN MUNIC NEIGH ADMIN

B64
GROSS B.M.,THE MANAGING OF ORGANIZATIONS (VOL. I). USA+45 ECO/DEV LG/CO CAP/ISM EFFICIENCY ROLE...MGT 20. PAGE 44 B0886 — ECO/TAC ADMIN INDUS POLICY

B64
GROSS B.M.,THE MANAGING OF ORGANIZATIONS (VOL. II). — ECO/TAC

FUT USA+45 ECO/DEV EDU/PROP EFFICIENCY...MGT
BIBLIOG/A 20. PAGE 44 B0887

ADMIN
INDUS
POLICY
B64

HAMBRIDGE G.,DYNAMICS OF DEVELOPMENT. AGRI FINAN
INDUS LABOR INT/TRADE EDU/PROP ADMIN LEAD OWN
HEALTH...ANTHOL BIBLIOG 20. PAGE 46 B0930

ECO/UNDEV
ECO/TAC
OP/RES
ACT/RES
B64

HANNA W.J.,INDEPENDENT BLACK AFRICA: THE POLITICS
OF FREEDOM. ELITES INDUS KIN CHIEF COLONIAL CHOOSE
GOV/REL RACE/REL NAT/LISM ATTIT PERSON 20 NEGRO.
PAGE 46 B0938

AFR
ECO/UNDEV
ADMIN
PROB/SOLV
B64

LI C.M.,INDUSTRIAL DEVELOPMENT IN COMMUNIST CHINA.
CHINA/COM ECO/DEV ECO/UNDEV AGRI FINAN INDUS MARKET
LABOR NAT/G ECO/TAC INT/TRADE EXEC ALL/VALS
...POLICY RELATIV TREND WORK TOT/POP VAL/FREE 20.
PAGE 65 B1311

ASIA
TEC/DEV

B64

ORTH C.D.,ADMINISTERING RESEARCH AND DEVELOPMENT.
FINAN PLAN PROB/SOLV ADMIN ROUTINE...METH/CNCPT
STAT CHARTS METH 20. PAGE 80 B1616

MGT
R+D
LG/CO
INDUS
B64

PINNICK A.W.,COUNTRY PLANNERS IN ACTION. UK FINAN
SERV/IND NAT/G CONSULT DELIB/GP PRICE CONTROL
ROUTINE LEISURE AGE/C...GEOG 20 URBAN/RNWL. PAGE 83
B1674

MUNIC
PLAN
INDUS
ATTIT
B64

RIDDLE D.H.,THE TRUMAN COMMITTEE: A STUDY IN
CONGRESSIONAL RESPONSIBILITY. INDUS FORCES OP/RES
DOMIN ADMIN LEAD PARL/PROC WAR PRODUC SUPEGO
...BIBLIOG CONGRESS. PAGE 88 B1778

LEGIS
DELIB/GP
CONFER

B64

RIGGS F.W.,ADMINISTRATION IN DEVELOPING COUNTRIES.
FUT WOR+45 STRUCT AGRI INDUS NAT/G PLAN TEC/DEV
ECO/TAC EDU/PROP RIGID/FLEX KNOWL WEALTH...POLICY
MGT CONCPT METH/CNCPT TREND 20. PAGE 88 B1785

ECO/UNDEV
ADMIN

B64

SAYLES L.R.,MANAGERIAL BEHAVIOR: ADMINISTRATION IN
COMPLEX ORGANIZATIONS. INDUS LG/CO PROB/SOLV
CONTROL EXEC INGP/REL PERS/REL SKILL...MGT OBS
PREDICT GEN/LAWS 20. PAGE 93 B1874

CONCPT
ADMIN
TOP/EX
EX/STRUC
B64

SZLADITS C.,BIBLIOGRAPHY ON FOREIGN AND COMPARATIVE
LAW: BOOKS AND ARTICLES IN ENGLISH (SUPPLEMENT
1962). FINAN INDUS JUDGE LICENSE ADMIN CT/SYS
PARL/PROC OWN...INT/LAW CLASSIF METH/COMP NAT/COMP
20. PAGE 102 B2065

BIBLIOG/A
JURID
ADJUD
LAW

B64

THE BRITISH COUNCIL,PUBLIC ADMINISTRATION: A SELECT
LIST OF BOOKS AND PERIODICALS. LAW CONSTN FINAN
POL/PAR SCHOOL CHOOSE...HEAL MGT METH/COMP 19/20
CMN/WLTH. PAGE 104 B2094

BIBLIOG
ADMIN
LOC/G
INDUS

B64

TINBERGEN J.,CENTRAL PLANNING. COM INTELL ECO/DEV
ECO/UNDEV FINAN INT/ORG PROB/SOLV ECO/TAC CONTROL
EXEC ROUTINE DECISION. PAGE 104 B2111

PLAN
INDUS
MGT
CENTRAL
B64

WELLISZ S.,THE ECONOMICS OF THE SOVIET BLOC. COM
USSR INDUS WORKER PLAN BUDGET INT/TRADE TAX PRICE
PRODUC WEALTH MARXISM...METH/COMP 20. PAGE 115
B2319

EFFICIENCY
ADMIN
MARKET

B64

WRAITH R.,CORRUPTION IN DEVELOPING COUNTRIES.
NIGERIA UK LAW ELITES STRATA INDUS LOC/G NAT/G SECT
FORCES EDU/PROP ADMIN PWR WEALTH 18/20. PAGE 118
B2377

ECO/UNDEV
CRIME
SANCTION
ATTIT
S64

CASE H.L.,"GORDON R. CLAPP: THE ROLE OF FAITH,
PURPOSES AND PEOPLE IN ADMINISTRATION." INDUS MUNIC
PROVS...POLICY 20. PAGE 19 B0391

ADMIN
BIOG
EX/STRUC
DECISION
S64

FLORINSKY M.T.,"TRENDS IN THE SOVIET ECONOMY." COM
USA+45 USSR INDUS LABOR NAT/G PLAN TEC/DEV ECO/TAC
ALL/VALS SOCISM...MGT METH/CNCPT STYLE CON/ANAL
GEN/METH WORK 20. PAGE 36 B0731

ECO/DEV
AGRI

S64

HUELIN D.,"ECONOMIC INTEGRATION IN LATIN AMERICAN:
PROGRESS AND PROBLEMS." L/A+17C ECO/DEV AGRI
DIST/IND FINAN INDUS NAT/G VOL/ASSN CONSULT
DELIB/GP EX/STRUC ACT/RES PLAN TEC/DEV ECO/TAC
ROUTINE BAL/PAY WEALTH WORK 20. PAGE 52 B1058

MARKET
ECO/UNDEV
INT/TRADE

S64

KASSOF A.,"THE ADMINISTERED SOCIETY:
TOTALITARIANISM WITHOUT TERROR." COM USSR STRATA
AGRI INDUS NAT/G PERF/ART SCHOOL TOP/EX EDU/PROP
ADMIN ORD/FREE PWR...POLICY SOC TIME/SEQ GEN/LAWS
VAL/FREE 20. PAGE 58 B1178

SOCIETY
DOMIN
TOTALISM

S64

NASH M.,"SOCIAL PREREQUISITES TO ECONOMIC GROWTH IN
LATIN AMERICA AND SOUTHEAST ASIA." L/A+17C S/ASIA
CULTURE SOCIETY ECO/UNDEV AGRI INDUS NAT/G PLAN

ECO/DEV
PERCEPT

TEC/DEV EDU/PROP ROUTINE ALL/VALS...POLICY RELATIV
SOC NAT/COMP WORK TOT/POP 20. PAGE 77 B1558

B65

AMERICAN ECONOMIC ASSOCIATION,INDEX OF ECONOMIC
JOURNALS 1886-1965 (7 VOLS.). UK USA+45 USA-45 AGRI
FINAN PLAN ECO/TAC INT/TRADE ADMIN...STAT CENSUS
19/20. PAGE 4 B0083

BIBLIOG
WRITING
INDUS

B65

BARISH N.N.,MANAGEMENT SCIENCES IN THE EMERGING
COUNTRIES. AFR CHINA/COM WOR+45 FINAN INDUS PLAN
PRODUC HABITAT...ANTHOL 20. PAGE 9 B0184

ECO/UNDEV
OP/RES
MGT
TEC/DEV
B65

COPELAND M.A.,OUR FREE ENTERPRISE ECONOMY. USA+45
INDUS LABOR ADMIN CONTROL GP/REL MGT. PAGE 23 B0476

CAP/ISM
PLAN
FINAN
ECO/DEV
B65

CUTLIP S.M.,A PUBLIC RELATIONS BIBLIOGRAPHY. INDUS
LABOR NAT/G PROF/ORG SCHOOL DIPLOM PRESS TV GOV/REL
GP/REL...PSY SOC/WK 20. PAGE 25 B0515

BIBLIOG/A
MGT
COM/IND
ADMIN
B65

DUGGAR G.S.,RENEWAL OF TOWN AND VILLAGE I: A WORLD-
WIDE SURVEY OF LOCAL GOVERNMENT EXPERIENCE. WOR+45
CONSTRUC INDUS CREATE BUDGET REGION GOV/REL...QU
NAT/COMP 20 URBAN/RNWL. PAGE 31 B0628

MUNIC
NEIGH
PLAN
ADMIN
B65

EDELMAN M.,THE POLITICS OF WAGE-PRICE DECISIONS.
GERMANY ITALY NETHERLAND UK INDUS LABOR POL/PAR
PROB/SOLV BARGAIN PRICE ROUTINE BAL/PAY COST DEMAND
20. PAGE 32 B0654

GOV/COMP
CONTROL
PLAN

B65

INT. BANK RECONSTR. DEVELOP.,ECONOMIC DEVELOPMENT
OF KUWAIT. ISLAM KUWAIT AGRI FINAN MARKET EX/STRUC
TEC/DEV ECO/TAC ADMIN WEALTH...OBS CON/ANAL CHARTS
20. PAGE 54 B1092

INDUS
NAT/G

B65

KELLEY E.J.,MARKETING: STRATEGY AND FUNCTIONS.
ECO/DEV INDUS PLAN PRICE CONTROL ROUTINE...MGT
BIBLIOG 20. PAGE 59 B1191

MARKET
DIST/IND
POLICY
ECO/TAC
B65

LAMBIRI I.,SOCIAL CHANGE IN A GREEK COUNTRY TOWN.
GREECE FAM PROB/SOLV ROUTINE TASK LEISURE INGP/REL
CONSEN ORD/FREE...SOC INT QU CHARTS 20. PAGE 62
B1252

INDUS
WORKER
CULTURE
NEIGH
B65

LATHAM E.,THE GROUP BASIS OF POLITICS: A STUDY IN
BASING-POINT LEGISLATION. INDUS MARKET POL/PAR
DELIB/GP EX/STRUC DEBATE ADJUD...CHARTS PRESIDENT.
PAGE 63 B1274

LEGIS
GP/COMP
GP/REL

B65

MELMANS S.,OUR DEPLETED SOCIETY. SPACE USA+45
ECO/DEV FORCES BUDGET ECO/TAC ADMIN WEAPON
EFFICIENCY 20 COLD/WAR. PAGE 73 B1465

CIVMIL/REL
INDUS
EDU/PROP
CONTROL
B65

MOORE W.E.,THE IMPACT OF INDUSTRY. CULTURE STRUCT
ORD/FREE...TREND 20. PAGE 75 B1516

INDUS
MGT
TEC/DEV
ECO/UNDEV
B65

PARRISH W.E.,MISSOURI UNDER RADICAL RULE 1865-1870.
USA-45 SOCIETY INDUS LOC/G POL/PAR WORKER EDU/PROP
SUFF INGP/REL ATTIT...BIBLIOG 19 NEGRO MISSOURI.
PAGE 81 B1635

PROVS
ADMIN
RACE/REL
ORD/FREE
B65

PURCELL V.,THE MEMOIRS OF A MALAYAN OFFICIAL.
MALAYSIA UK ECO/UNDEV INDUS LABOR EDU/PROP COLONIAL
CT/SYS WAR NAT/LISM TOTALISM ORD/FREE SOVEREIGN 20
UN CIVIL/SERV. PAGE 85 B1721

BIOG
ADMIN
JURID
FORCES
B65

TYROUT R.A.,ECONOMICS OF RESEARCH AND DEVELOPMENT.
ECO/DEV ECO/UNDEV INDUS PROFIT DECISION. PAGE 106
B2141

R+D
FORCES
ADMIN
DIPLOM
B65

US HOUSE COMM EDUC AND LABOR,ADMINISTRATION OF THE
NATIONAL LABOR RELATIONS ACT. USA+45 DELIB/GP
WORKER PROB/SOLV BARGAIN PAY CONTROL 20 NLRB
CONGRESS. PAGE 108 B2188

ADMIN
LABOR
GP/REL
INDUS
B65

VAID K.N.,STATE AND LABOR IN INDIA. INDIA INDUS
WORKER PAY PRICE ADJUD CONTROL PARL/PROC GP/REL
ORD/FREE 20. PAGE 111 B2248

LAW
LABOR
MGT
NEW/LIB
B65

VEINOTT A.F. JR.,MATHEMATICAL STUDIES IN MANAGEMENT
SCIENCE. UNIV INDUS COMPUTER ADMIN...DECISION
NET/THEORY SIMUL 20. PAGE 112 B2257

MATH
MGT
PLAN
PRODUC
L65

MATTHEWS D.G.,"A CURRENT BIBLIOGRAPHY ON ETHIOPIAN
AFFAIRS: A SELECT BIBLIOGRAPHY FROM 1950-1964."
ETHIOPIA LAW CULTURE ECO/UNDEV INDUS LABOR SECT

BIBLIOG/A
ADMIN
POL/PAR

FORCES DIPLOM CIVMIL/REL RACE/REL...LING STAT 20. NAT/G
PAGE 71 B1428

L65

WILLIAMS S.,"NEGOTIATING INVESTMENT IN EMERGING FINAN
COUNTRIES." USA+45 WOR+45 INDUS MARKET NAT/G TOP/EX ECO/UNDEV
TEC/DEV CAP/ISM ECO/TAC ADMIN SKILL WEALTH...POLICY
RELATIV MGT WORK 20. PAGE 117 B2353

S65

TABORSKY E.,"CHANGE IN CZECHOSLOVAKIA." COM USSR ECO/DEV
ELITES INTELL AGRI INDUS NAT/G DELIB/GP EX/STRUC PLAN
ECO/TAC TOTALISM ATTIT RIGID/FLEX SOCISM...MGT CZECHOSLVK
CONCPT TREND 20. PAGE 102 B2067

B66

ASHRAF A.,THE CITY GOVERNMENT OF CALCUTTA: A STUDY LOC/G
OF INERTIA. INDIA ELITES INDUS NAT/G EX/STRUC MUNIC
ACT/RES PLAN PROB/SOLV LEAD HABITAT...BIBLIOG 20 ADMIN
CALCUTTA. PAGE 7 B0141 ECO/UNDEV

B66

BAKKE E.W.,MUTUAL SURVIVAL; THE GOAL OF UNION AND MGT
MANAGEMENT (2ND ED.). USA+45 ELITES ECO/DEV ECO/TAC LABOR
CONFER ADMIN REPRESENT GP/REL INGP/REL ATTIT BARGAIN
...GP/COMP 20. PAGE 8 B0170 INDUS

B66

BIRKHEAD G.S.,ADMINISTRATIVE PROBLEMS IN PAKISTAN. ADMIN
PAKISTAN AGRI FINAN INDUS LG/CO ECO/TAC CONTROL PWR NAT/G
...CHARTS ANTHOL 20. PAGE 12 B0241 ORD/FREE
ECO/UNDEV

B66

COOK P.W. JR.,PROBLEMS OF CORPORATE POWER. WOR+45 ADMIN
FINAN INDUS BARGAIN GP/REL...MGT ANTHOL. PAGE 23 LG/CO
B0471 PWR
ECO/TAC

B66

DICKSON W.J.,COUNSELING IN AN ORGANIZATION: A INDUS
SEQUEL TO THE HAWTHORNE RESEARCHES. CLIENT VOL/ASSN WORKER
ACT/RES PROB/SOLV AUTOMAT ROUTINE PERS/REL PSY
HAPPINESS ANOMIE ROLE...OBS CHARTS 20 AT+T. PAGE 29 MGT
B0588

B66

FABRYCKY W.J.,OPERATIONS ECONOMY INDUSTRIAL OP/RES
APPLICATIONS OF OPERATIONS RESEARCH. INDUS PLAN MGT
ECO/TAC PRODUC...MATH PROBABIL STAT CHARTS 20. SIMUL
PAGE 34 B0695 DECISION

B66

GREENE L.E.,GOVERNMENT IN TENNESSEE (2ND ED.). PROVS
USA+45 DIST/IND INDUS POL/PAR EX/STRUC LEGIS PLAN LOC/G
BUDGET GIVE CT/SYS...MGT T 20 TENNESSEE. PAGE 43 CONSTN
B0866 ADMIN

B66

GROSS H.,MAKE OR BUY. USA+45 FINAN INDUS CREATE ECO/TAC
PRICE PRODUC 20. PAGE 44 B0889 PLAN
MGT
COST

B66

HASTINGS P.G.,THE MANAGEMENT OF BUSINESS FINANCE. FINAN
ECO/DEV PLAN BUDGET CONTROL COST...DECISION CHARTS MGT
BIBLIOG T 20. PAGE 48 B0966 INDUS
ECO/TAC

B66

KAESTNER K.,GESAMTWIRTSCHAFTLICHE PLANUNG IN EINER ECO/TAC
GEMISCHTEN WIRTSCHAFTSORDNUNG PLAN
(WIRTSCHAFTSPOLITISCHE STUDIEN 5). GERMANY/W WOR+45 POLICY
WOR-45 INDUS MARKET NAT/G ACT/RES GP/REL INGP/REL PREDICT
PRODUC...ECOMETRIC MGT BIBLIOG 20. PAGE 57 B1159

B66

KIRDAR U.,THE STRUCTURE OF UNITED NATIONS ECONOMIC INT/ORG
AID TO UNDERDEVELOPED COUNTRIES. AGRI FINAN INDUS FOR/AID
NAT/G EX/STRUC PLAN GIVE TASK...POLICY 20 UN. ECO/UNDEV
PAGE 60 B1213 ADMIN

B66

KURAKOV I.G.,SCIENCE, TECHNOLOGY AND COMMUNISM; CREATE
SOME QUESTIONS OF DEVELOPMENT (TRANS. BY CARIN TEC/DEV
DEDIJER). USSR INDUS PLAN PROB/SOLV COST PRODUC MARXISM
...MGT MATH CHARTS METH 20. PAGE 61 B1243 ECO/TAC

B66

LEWIS W.A.,DEVELOPMENT PLANNING; THE ESSENTIALS OF PLAN
ECONOMIC POLICY. USA+45 FINAN INDUS NAT/G WORKER ECO/DEV
FOR/AID INT/TRADE ADMIN ROUTINE WEALTH...CONCPT POLICY
STAT. PAGE 65 B1307 CREATE

B66

MACFARQUHAR R.,CHINA UNDER MAO: POLITICS TAKES ECO/UNDEV
COMMAND. CHINA/COM COM AGRI INDUS CHIEF FORCES TEC/DEV
DIPLOM INT/TRADE EDU/PROP TASK REV ADJUST...ANTHOL ECO/TAC
20 MAO. PAGE 67 B1359 ADMIN

B66

MURDOCK J.C.,RESEARCH AND REGIONS. AGRI FINAN INDUS BIBLIOG
LOC/G MUNIC NAT/G PROB/SOLV TEC/DEV ADMIN REGION ECO/DEV
20. PAGE 76 B1545 COMPUT/IR
R+D

B66

NIEBURG H.L.,IN THE NAME OF SCIENCE. USA+45 NAT/G
EX/STRUC LEGIS TEC/DEV BUDGET PAY AUTOMAT LOBBY PWR INDUS
...OBS 20. PAGE 78 B1581 TECHRACY

B66

ONYEMELUKWE C.C.,PROBLEMS OF INDUSTRIAL PLANNING ECO/UNDEV
AND MANAGEMENT IN NIGERIA. AFR FINAN LABOR DELIB/GP ECO/TAC

TEC/DEV ADJUST...MGT TREND BIBLIOG. PAGE 80 B1610 INDUS
PLAN

B66

OWEN G.,INDUSTRY IN THE UNITED STATES. UK USA+45 METH/COMP
NAT/G WEALTH...DECISION NAT/COMP 20. PAGE 80 B1620 INDUS
MGT
PROB/SOLV

B66

PERKINS J.A.,THE UNIVERSITY IN TRANSITION. USA+45 ACADEM
SOCIETY FINAN INDUS NAT/G EX/STRUC ADMIN INGP/REL ORD/FREE
COST EFFICIENCY ATTIT 20. PAGE 82 B1658 CREATE
ROLE

B66

REDFORD E.S.,THE ROLE OF GOVERNMENT IN THE AMERICAN NAT/G
ECONOMY. USA+45 USA-45 FINAN INDUS LG/CO PROB/SOLV ECO/DEV
ADMIN INGP/REL INCOME PRODUC 18/20. PAGE 87 B1759 CAP/ISM
ECO/TAC

B66

SIMON R.,PERSPECTIVES IN PUBLIC RELATIONS. USA+45 GP/REL
INDUS ACT/RES PLAN ADMIN ATTIT MGT. PAGE 97 B1961 PERS/REL
COM/IND
SOCIETY

B66

SMITH H.E.,READINGS IN ECONOMIC DEVELOPMENT AND TEC/DEV
ADMINISTRATION IN TANZANIA. TANZANIA FINAN INDUS ADMIN
LABOR NAT/G PLAN PROB/SOLV INT/TRADE COLONIAL GOV/REL
REGION...ANTHOL BIBLIOG 20 AFRICA/E. PAGE 98 B1981

B66

SPICER K.,A SAMARITAN STATE? AFR CANADA INDIA DIPLOM
PAKISTAN UK USA+45 FINAN INDUS PRODUC...CHARTS 20 FOR/AID
NATO. PAGE 99 B2006 ECO/DEV
ADMIN

B66

WASHINGTON S.H.,BIBLIOGRAPHY: LABOR-MANAGEMENT BIBLIOG
RELATIONS ACT, 1947 AS AMENDED BY LABOR-MANAGEMENT LAW
REPORTING AND DISCLOSURE ACT, 1959. USA+45 CONSTN LABOR
INDUS DELIB/GP LEGIS WORKER BARGAIN ECO/TAC ADJUD MGT
GP/REL NEW/LIB...JURID CONGRESS. PAGE 114 B2298

B66

ZALEZNIK A.,HUMAN DILEMMAS OF LEADERSHIP. ELITES LEAD
INDUS EX/STRUC INGP/REL ATTIT...PSY 20. PAGE 119 PERSON
B2397 EXEC
MGT

B66

ZINKIN T.,CHALLENGES IN INDIA. INDIA PAKISTAN LAW NAT/G
AGRI FINAN INDUS TOP/EX TEC/DEV CONTROL ROUTINE ECO/TAC
ORD/FREE PWR 20 NEHRU/J SHASTRI/LB CIVIL/SERV. POLICY
PAGE 119 B2404 ADMIN

S66

AFRICAN BIBLIOGRAPHIC CENTER,"A CURRENT VIEW OF BIBLIOG/A
AFRICANA: A SELECT AND ANNOTATED BIBLIOGRAPHICAL NAT/G
PUBLISHING GUIDE, 1965-1966." AFR CULTURE INDUS TEC/DEV
LABOR SECT FOR/AID ADMIN COLONIAL REV RACE/REL POL/PAR
SOCISM...LING 20. PAGE 3 B0063

S66

DIEBOLD J.,"COMPUTERS, PROGRAM MANAGEMENT AND COMPUTER
FOREIGN AFFAIRS." USA+45 INDUS OP/RES TEC/DEV...MGT DIPLOM
GP/COMP GEN/LAWS. PAGE 29 B0590 ROUTINE
ACT/RES

N66

PRINCETON U INDUSTRIAL REL SEC,OUTSTANDING BOOKS ON BIBLIOG/A
INDUSTRIAL RELATIONS, 1965 (PAMPHLET NO. 128). INDUS
WOR+45 LABOR BARGAIN GOV/REL RACE/REL HEALTH PWR GP/REL
...MGT 20. PAGE 85 B1709 POLICY

B67

ANDERSON C.W.,POLITICS AND ECONOMIC CHANGE IN LATIN ECO/UNDEV
AMERICA. L/A+17C INDUS NAT/G OP/RES ADMIN DEMAND PROB/SOLV
...POLICY STAT CHARTS NAT/COMP 20. PAGE 4 B0091 PLAN
ECO/TAC

B67

BALDWIN G.B.,PLANNING AND DEVELOPMENT IN IRAN. IRAN PLAN
AGRI INDUS CONSULT WORKER EDU/PROP BAL/PAY...CHARTS ECO/UNDEV
20. PAGE 8 B0173 ADMIN
PROB/SOLV

B67

BRAYMAN H.,CORPORATE MANAGEMENT IN A WORLD OF MGT
POLITICS. USA+45 ELITES MARKET CREATE BARGAIN ECO/DEV
DIPLOM INT/TRADE ATTIT SKILL 20. PAGE 15 B0302 CAP/ISM
INDUS

B67

BUDER S.,PULLMAN: AN EXPERIMENT IN INDUSTRIAL ORDER DIST/IND
AND COMMUNITY PLANNING, 1880-1930. USA-45 SOCIETY INDUS
LABOR LG/CO CREATE PROB/SOLV CONTROL GP/REL MUNIC
EFFICIENCY ATTIT...MGT BIBLIOG 19/20 PULLMAN. PLAN
PAGE 17 B0337

B67

GABRIEL P.P.,THE INTERNATIONAL TRANSFER OF ECO/UNDEV
CORPORATE SKILLS: MANAGEMENT CONTRACTS IN LESS AGREE
DEVELOPED COUNTRIES. CLIENT INDUS LG/CO PLAN MGT
PROB/SOLV CAP/ISM ECO/TAC FOR/AID INT/TRADE RENT CONSULT
ADMIN SKILL 20. PAGE 38 B0771

B67

HIRSCHMAN A.O.,DEVELOPMENT PROJECTS OBSERVED. INDUS ECO/UNDEV
INT/ORG CONSULT EX/STRUC CREATE OP/RES ECO/TAC R+D
DEMAND...POLICY MGT METH/COMP 20 WORLD/BANK. FINAN
PAGE 50 B1016 PLAN

JAIN R.K.,MANAGEMENT OF STATE ENTERPRISES. INDIA
SOCIETY FINAN WORKER BUDGET ADMIN CONTROL OWN 20.
PAGE 55 B1118

B67
NAT/G
SOCISM
INDUS
MGT

JAKUBAUSKAS E.B.,HUMAN RESOURCES DEVELOPMENT.
USA+45 AGRI INDUS SERV/IND ACT/RES PLAN ADMIN
RACE/REL DISCRIM...TREND GEN/LAWS. PAGE 55 B1119

B67
PROB/SOLV
ECO/TAC
EDU/PROP
WORKER

NIVEN R.,NIGERIA. NIGERIA CONSTN INDUS EX/STRUC
COLONIAL REV NAT/LISM...CHARTS 19/20. PAGE 78 B1584

B67
NAT/G
REGION
CHOOSE
GP/REL

NORTHRUP H.R.,RESTRICTIVE LABOR PRACTICES IN THE
SUPERMARKET INDUSTRY. USA+45 INDUS WORKER TEC/DEV
BARGAIN PAY CONTROL GP/REL COST...STAT CHARTS NLRB.
PAGE 79 B1592

B67
DIST/IND
MARKET
LABOR
MGT

POSNER M.V.,ITALIAN PUBLIC ENTERPRISE. ITALY
ECO/DEV FINAN INDUS CREATE ECO/TAC ADMIN CONTROL
EFFICIENCY PRODUC...TREND CHARTS 20. PAGE 84 B1693

B67
NAT/G
PLAN
CAP/ISM
SOCISM

RAVKIN A.,THE NEW STATES OF AFRICA (HEADLINE
SERIES, NO. 183((PAMPHLET). CULTURE STRUCT INDUS
COLONIAL NAT/LISM...SOC 20. PAGE 86 B1744

B67
AFR
ECO/UNDEV
SOCIETY
ADMIN

SKIDMORE T.E.,POLITICS IN BRAZIL 1930-1964. BRAZIL
L/A+17C INDUS NAT/G PROB/SOLV ATTIT 20. PAGE 98
B1973

B67
CONSTN
ECO/TAC
ADMIN

VOOS H.,ORGANIZATIONAL COMMUNICATION: A
BIBLIOGRAPHY. WOR+45 STRATA R+D PROB/SOLV FEEDBACK
COERCE...MGT PSY NET/THEORY HYPO/EXP. PAGE 112
B2268

B67
BIBLIOG/A
INDUS
COM/IND
VOL/ASSN

ZELERMYER W.,BUSINESS LAW: NEW PERSPECTIVES IN
BUSINESS ECONOMICS. USA+45 LAW INDUS DELIB/GP
...JURID MGT ANTHOL BIBLIOG 20 NLRB. PAGE 119 B2400

B67
LABOR
CAP/ISM
LG/CO

ZONDAG C.H.,THE BOLIVIAN ECONOMY 1952-65. L/A+17C
TEC/DEV FOR/AID ADMIN...OBS TREND CHARTS BIBLIOG 20
BOLIV. PAGE 119 B2406

B67
ECO/UNDEV
INDUS
PRODUC

CARMICHAEL D.M.,"FORTY YEARS OF WATER POLLUTION
CONTROL IN WISCONSIN: A CASE STUDY." LAW EXTR/IND
INDUS MUNIC DELIB/GP PLAN PROB/SOLV SANCTION
...CENSUS CHARTS 20 WISCONSIN. PAGE 19 B0382

L67
HEALTH
CONTROL
ADMIN
ADJUD

GOULD W.B.,"THE STATUS OF UNAUTHORIZED AND
'WILDCAT' STRIKES UNDER THE NATIONAL LABOR
RELATIONS ACT." USA+45 ACT/RES BARGAIN ECO/TAC
LEGIT ADJUD GP/REL MGT. PAGE 42 B0842

L67
ECO/DEV
INDUS
LABOR
POLICY

MANNE H.G.,"OUR TWO CORPORATION SYSTEMS* LAW AND
ECONOMICS." LAW CONTROL SANCTION GP/REL...JURID 20.
PAGE 69 B1392

L67
INDUS
ELITES
CAP/ISM
ADMIN

ALPANDER G.G.,"ENTREPRENEURS AND PRIVATE ENTERPRISE
IN TURKEY." TURKEY INDUS PROC/MFG EDU/PROP ATTIT
DRIVE WEALTH...GEOG MGT SOC STAT TREND CHARTS 20.
PAGE 4 B0080

S67
ECO/UNDEV
LG/CO
NAT/G
POLICY

ATKIN J.M.,"THE FEDERAL GOVERNMENT, BIG BUSINESS,
AND COLLEGES OF EDUCATION." PROF/ORG CONSULT CREATE
PLAN PROB/SOLV ADMIN EFFICIENCY. PAGE 7 B0144

S67
SCHOOL
ACADEM
NAT/G
INDUS

BERLINER J.S.,"RUSSIA'S BUREAUCRATS - WHY THEY'RE
REACTIONARY." USSR NAT/G OP/RES PROB/SOLV TEC/DEV
CONTROL SANCTION EFFICIENCY DRIVE PERSON...TECHNIC
SOC 20. PAGE 11 B0223

S67
CREATE
ADMIN
INDUS
PRODUC

BURACK E.H.,"INDUSTRIAL MANAGEMENT IN ADVANCED
PRODUCTION SYSTEMS: SOME THEORETICAL CONCEPTS AND
PRELIMINARY FINDINGS." INDUS CREATE PLAN PRODUC
ROLE...OBS STAND/INT DEEP/QU HYPO/EXP ORG/CHARTS
20. PAGE 17 B0346

S67
ADMIN
MGT
TEC/DEV
EX/STRUC

CARIAS B.,"EL CONTROL DE LAS EMPRESAS PUBLICAS POR
GRUPOS DE INTERESES DE LA COMUNIDAD." FRANCE UK
VENEZUELA INDUS NAT/G CONTROL OWN PWR...DECISION
NAT/COMP 20. PAGE 18 B0377

S67
WORKER
REPRESENT
MGT
SOCISM

CHAMBERLAIN N.W.,"STRIKES IN CONTEMPORARY CONTEXT."
LAW INDUS NAT/G CHIEF CONFER COST ATTIT ORD/FREE
...POLICY MGT 20. PAGE 20 B0400

S67
LABOR
BARGAIN
EFFICIENCY
PROB/SOLV

FERGUSON H.,"3-CITY CONSOLIDATION." USA+45 CONSTN
INDUS BARGAIN BUDGET CONFER ADMIN INGP/REL COST

S67
MUNIC
CHOOSE

UTIL. PAGE 35 B0712

CREATE
PROB/SOLV

GOLIGHTLY H.O.,"THE AIRLINES: A CASE STUDY IN
MANAGEMENT INNOVATION." USA+45 AIR FINAN INDUS
TOP/EX CREATE PLAN PROB/SOLV ADMIN EXEC PROFIT
...DECISION 20. PAGE 40 B0820

S67
DIST/IND
MARKET
MGT
TEC/DEV

GRINYER P.H.,"THE SYSTEMATIC EVALUATION OF METHODS
OF WAGE PAYMENT." UK INDUS WORKER ADMIN EFFICIENCY
...MGT METH/COMP 20. PAGE 44 B0882

S67
OP/RES
COST
PAY
PRODUC

HAIRE M.,"MANAGING MANAGEMENT MANPOWER." EX/STRUC
OP/RES PAY EDU/PROP COST EFFICIENCY...PREDICT SIMUL
20. PAGE 45 B0920

S67
MGT
EXEC
LEAD
INDUS

HILL F.G.,"VEBLEN, BERLE AND THE MODERN
CORPORATION." FINAN ECO/TAC CONTROL OWN...MGT 20.
PAGE 50 B1010

S67
LG/CO
ROLE
INDUS
ECO/DEV

HUDDLESTON J.,"TRADE UNIONS IN THE GERMAN FEDERAL
REPUBLIC." EUR+WWI GERMANY/W UK LAW INDUS WORKER
CREATE CENTRAL...MGT GP/COMP 20. PAGE 52 B1056

S67
LABOR
GP/REL
SCHOOL
ROLE

LERNER A.P.,"EMPLOYMENT THEORY AND EMPLOYMENT
POLICY." ECO/DEV INDUS LABOR LG/CO BUDGET ADMIN
DEMAND PROFIT WEALTH LAISSEZ METH/COMP. PAGE 64
B1296

S67
CAP/ISM
WORKER
CONCPT

MOOR E.J.,"THE INTERNATIONAL IMPACT OF AUTOMATION."
WOR+45 ACT/RES COMPUTER CREATE PLAN CAP/ISM ROUTINE
EFFICIENCY PREDICT. PAGE 75 B1511

S67
TEC/DEV
OP/RES
AUTOMAT
INDUS

MORTON J.A.,"A SYSTEMS APPROACH TO THE INNOVATION
PROCESS: ITS USE IN THE BELL SYSTEM." USA+45 INTELL
INDUS LG/CO CONSULT WORKER COMPUTER AUTOMAT DEMAND
...MGT CHARTS 20. PAGE 76 B1531

S67
TEC/DEV
GEN/METH
R+D
COM/IND

ROBERTS E.B.,"THE PROBLEM OF AGING ORGANIZATIONS."
INTELL PROB/SOLV ADMIN EXEC FEEDBACK EFFICIENCY
PRODUC...GEN/LAWS 20. PAGE 89 B1794

S67
INDUS
R+D
MGT
PLAN

ROSE A.M.,"CONFIDENCE AND THE CORPORATION." LG/CO
CONTROL CRIME INCOME PROFIT 20. PAGE 90 B1818

S67
INDUS
EX/STRUC
VOL/ASSN
RESPECT

ROSENZWEIG J.E.,"MANAGERS AND MANAGEMENT SCIENTISTS
(TWO CULTURES)" INDUS CREATE TEC/DEV OPTIMAL
...NEW/IDEA 20. PAGE 90 B1823

S67
EFFICIENCY
MGT
INTELL
METH/COMP

TIVEY L.,"THE POLITICAL CONSEQUENCES OF ECONOMIC
PLANNING." UK CONSTN INDUS ACT/RES ADMIN CONTROL
LOBBY REPRESENT EFFICIENCY SUPEGO SOVEREIGN
...DECISION 20. PAGE 104 B2112

S67
PLAN
POLICY
NAT/G

WRIGHT F.K.,"INVESTMENT CRITERIA AND THE COST OF
CAPITAL." FINAN PLAN BUDGET OPTIMAL PRODUC...POLICY
DECISION 20. PAGE 118 B2380

S67
COST
PROFIT
INDUS
MGT

PRINCETON U INDUSTRIAL REL SEC,OUTSTANDING BOOKS ON
INDUSTRIAL RELATIONS, 1966 (PAMPHLET NO. 134).
WOR+45 LABOR WORKER PLAN PRICE CONTROL INCOME...MGT
20. PAGE 85 B1711

N67
BIBLIOG/A
INDUS
GP/REL
POLICY

PEARSON A.W.,"RESOURCE ALLOCATION." PLAN PROB/SOLV
BUDGET ADMIN CONTROL CHOOSE EFFICIENCY...DECISION
MGT 20. PAGE 82 B1649

S68
PROFIT
OPTIMAL
COST
INDUS

THOMPSON H.C.,RHODESIA AND ITS GOVERNMENT. AFR
RHODESIA ECO/UNDEV INDUS KIN WORKER INT/TRADE
DISCRIM LITERACY ORD/FREE 19. PAGE 104 B2102

B98
COLONIAL
ADMIN
POLICY
ELITES

INDUSTRY, COMMUNICATION....SEE COM/IND

INDUSTRY, CONSTRUCTION....SEE CONSTRUC

INDUSTRY, EXTRACTIVE....SEE EXTR/IND

INDUSTRY, MANUFACTURING....SEE PROC/MFG

INDUSTRY, PROCESSING....SEE PROC/MFG

INDUSTRY, SERVICE....SEE SERV/IND

INDUSTRY, TRANSPORTATION....SEE DIST/IND

INDUSTRY, WAREHOUSING....SEE DIST/IND

INFLATION....INFLATION

INFLUENCING....SEE MORE SPECIFIC FORMS, E.G., DOMIN, PWR,
    WEALTH, EDU/PROP, SKILL, CHANGE, LOBBY

INGHAM K. B1085

INGP/REL....INTRAGROUP RELATIONS

		N
CIVIL SERVICE JOURNAL. PARTIC INGP/REL PERS/REL ...MGT BIBLIOG/A 20. PAGE 1 B0011	ADMIN NAT/G SERV/IND WORKER	

		N
JOURNAL OF PUBLIC ADMINISTRATION: JOURNAL OF THE ROYAL INSTITUTE OF PUBLIC ADMINISTRATION. UK PLAN GP/REL INGP/REL 20. PAGE 1 B0015	BIBLIOG/A ADMIN NAT/G MGT	

		N
US SUPERINTENDENT OF DOCUMENTS,POLITICAL SCIENCE: GOVERNMENT, CRIME, DISTRICT OF COLUMBIA (PRICE LIST 54). USA+45 LAW CONSTN EX/STRUC WORKER ADJUD ADMIN CT/SYS CHOOSE INGP/REL RACE/REL CONGRESS PRESIDENT. PAGE 111 B2241	BIBLIOG/A NAT/G CRIME	

		N19
ADMINISTRATIVE STAFF COLLEGE,THE ACCOUNTABILITY OF GOVERNMENT DEPARTMENTS (PAMPHLET) (REV. ED.). UK CONSTN FINAN NAT/G CONSULT ADMIN INGP/REL CONSEN PRIVIL 20 PARLIAMENT. PAGE 3 B0059	PARL/PROC ELITES SANCTION PROB/SOLV	

		N19
FIKS M.,PUBLIC ADMINISTRATION IN ISRAEL (PAMPHLET). ISRAEL SCHOOL EX/STRUC BUDGET PAY INGP/REL ...DECISION 20 CIVIL/SERV. PAGE 35 B0718	EDU/PROP NAT/G ADMIN WORKER	

		N19
RIDLEY C.E.,MEASURING MUNICIPAL ACTIVITIES (PAMPHLET). FINAN SERV/IND FORCES RECEIVE INGP/REL HABITAT...POLICY SOC/WK 20. PAGE 88 B1779	MGT HEALTH WEALTH LOC/G	

		L23
DOUGLAS P.H.,"OCCUPATIONAL V PROPORTIONAL REPRESENTATION." INDUS NAT/G PLAN ROUTINE SUFF CONSEN DRIVE...CONCPT CLASSIF. PAGE 30 B0612	REPRESENT PROF/ORG DOMIN INGP/REL	

		B28
HARDMAN J.B.,AMERICAN LABOR DYNAMICS. WORKER ECO/TAC DOMIN ADJUD LEAD LOBBY PWR...POLICY MGT. PAGE 47 B0944	LABOR INGP/REL ATTIT GP/REL	

		B29
MERRIAM C.E.,CHICAGO: A MORE INTIMATE VIEW OF URBAN POLITICS. USA-45 CONSTN POL/PAR LEGIS ADMIN CRIME INGP/REL 18/20 CHICAGO. PAGE 73 B1472	STRUCT GP/REL MUNIC	

		B29
MOLEY R.,POLITICS AND CRIMINAL PROSECUTION. USA-45 POL/PAR EX/STRUC LEGIT CONTROL LEAD ROUTINE CHOOSE INGP/REL...JURID CHARTS 20. PAGE 74 B1497	PWR CT/SYS CRIME ADJUD	

		B30
ZINK H.,CITY BOSSES IN THE UNITED STATES: A STUDY OF TWENTY MUNICIPAL BOSSES. USA-45 INDUS MUNIC NEIGH POL/PAR ADMIN CRIME INGP/REL PERS/REL PWR ...PERS/COMP 20 BOSSISM. PAGE 119 B2403	LOC/G DOMIN BIOG LEAD	

		B37
BUREAU OF NATIONAL AFFAIRS,LABOR RELATIONS REFERENCE MANUAL VOL 1, 1935-1937. BARGAIN DEBATE ROUTINE INGP/REL 20 NLRB. PAGE 17 B0351	LABOR ADMIN ADJUD NAT/G	

		B38
BALDWIN R.N.,CIVIL LIBERTIES AND INDUSTRIAL CONFLICT. USA+45 STRATA WORKER INGP/REL...MGT 20 ACLU CIVIL/LIB. PAGE 9 B0175	LABOR LG/CO INDUS GP/REL	

		B39
MCCAMY J.L.,GOVERNMENT PUBLICITY: ITS PRACTICE IN FEDERAL ADMINISTRATION. USA-45 COM/IND ADMIN CONTROL EXEC PARTIC INGP/REL...SOC 20. PAGE 71 B1442	EDU/PROP NAT/G PLAN ATTIT	

		S39
MARX F.M.,"POLICY FORMULATION AND THE ADMINISTRATIVE PROCESS" ROUTINE ADJUST EFFICIENCY OPTIMAL PRIVIL DRIVE PERSON OBJECTIVE...DECISION OBS GEN/METH. PAGE 70 B1418	ADMIN LEAD INGP/REL MGT	

		B41
LESTER R.A.,ECONOMICS OF LABOR. UK USA-45 TEC/DEV BARGAIN PAY INGP/REL INCOME...MGT 19/20. PAGE 64 B1298	LABOR ECO/DEV INDUS WORKER	

		B41
SLICHTER S.H.,UNION POLICIES AND INDUSTRIAL MANAGEMENT. USA-45 INDUS TEC/DEV PAY GP/REL INGP/REL COST EFFICIENCY PRODUC...POLICY 20. PAGE 98 B1978	BARGAIN LABOR MGT WORKER	

		B42
HARLOW R.F.,PUBLIC RELATIONS IN WAR AND PEACE. FUT USA-45 ECO/DEV ECO/TAC ROUTINE 20. PAGE 47 B0947	WAR ATTIT SOCIETY INGP/REL	

		S44
SIMON H.A.,"DECISION-MAKING AND ADMINISTRATIVE ORGANIZATION" (BMR)" WOR-45 CHOOSE INGP/REL EFFICIENCY ATTIT RESPECT...MGT 20. PAGE 97 B1955	DECISION ADMIN CONTROL WORKER	

		B45
MILLIS H.A.,ORGANIZED LABOR (FIRST ED.). LAW STRUCT DELIB/GP WORKER ECO/TAC ADJUD CONTROL REPRESENT INGP/REL INCOME MGT. PAGE 74 B1485	LABOR POLICY ROUTINE GP/REL	

		L46
FORRESTAL J.,"THE NAVY: A STUDY IN ADMINISTRATION." ELITES FACE/GP EX/STRUC PROB/SOLV REPRESENT EFFICIENCY PRODUC. PAGE 37 B0741	FORCES INGP/REL ROUTINE EXEC	

		B47
WARNER W.L.,THE SOCIAL SYSTEM OF THE MODERN FACTORY; THE STRIKE: AN ANALYSIS. USA-45 STRATA WORKER ECO/TAC GP/REL INGP/REL...MGT SOC CHARTS 20 YANKEE/C. PAGE 114 B2293	ROLE STRUCT LABOR PROC/MFG	

		B48
SPERO S.D.,GOVERNMENT AS EMPLOYER. USA+45 NAT/G EX/STRUC ADMIN CONTROL EXEC 20. PAGE 99 B2005	SOVEREIGN INGP/REL REPRESENT CONFER	

		S48
KNICKERBOCKER I.,"LEADERSHIP: A CONCEPTION AND SOME IMPLICATIONS." INDUS OP/RES REPRESENT INGP/REL DRIVE...MGT CLASSIF. PAGE 60 B1220	LEAD CONCPT PERSON ROLE	

		B49
DE GRAZIA A.,HUMAN RELATIONS IN PUBLIC ADMINISTRATION. INDUS ACT/RES CREATE PLAN PROB/SOLV TEC/DEV INGP/REL PERS/REL DRIVE...POLICY SOC 20. PAGE 27 B0552	BIBLIOG/A ADMIN PHIL/SCI OP/RES	

		B49
GLOVER J.D.,THE ADMINISTRATOR. ELITES LG/CO EX/STRUC ACT/RES CONTROL GP/REL INGP/REL PERS/REL AUTHORIT...POLICY CONCPT HIST/WRIT. PAGE 40 B0811	ADMIN MGT ATTIT PROF/ORG	

		B49
LEPAWSKY A.,ADMINISTRATION. FINAN INDUS LG/CO SML/CO INGP/REL PERS/REL COST EFFICIENCY OPTIMAL SKILL 20. PAGE 64 B1294	ADMIN MGT WORKER EX/STRUC	

		B49
RIDDICK F.M.,THE UNITED STATES CONGRESS ORGANIZATION AND PROCEDURE. POL/PAR DELIB/GP PROB/SOLV DEBATE CONTROL EXEC LEAD INGP/REL PWR ...MAJORIT DECISION CONGRESS PRESIDENT. PAGE 88 B1777	LEGIS PARL/PROC CHIEF EX/STRUC	

		L49
MARX C.M.,"ADMINISTRATIVE ETHICS AND THE RULE OF LAW." USA+45 ELITES ACT/RES DOMIN NEUTRAL ROUTINE INGP/REL ORD/FREE...JURID IDEA/COMP. PAGE 70 B1417	ADMIN LAW	

		B50
GRAVES W.B.,PUBLIC ADMINISTRATION: A COMPREHENSIVE BIBLIOGRAPHY ON PUBLIC ADMINISTRATION IN THE UNITED STATES (PAMPHLET). USA+45 USA-45 LOC/G NAT/G LEGIS ADJUD INGP/REL...MGT 20. PAGE 42 B0858	BIBLIOG FINAN CONTROL ADMIN	

		S50
TANNENBAUM R.,"PARTICIPATION BY SUBORDINATES IN THE MANAGERIAL DECISIONMAKING PROCESS" (BMR)" WOR+45 INDUS SML/CO WORKER INGP/REL...CONCPT GEN/LAWS 20. PAGE 103 B2074	PARTIC DECISION MGT LG/CO	

		B51
DIMOCK M.E.,FREE ENTERPRISE AND THE ADMINISTRATIVE STATE. FINAN LG/CO BARGAIN BUDGET DOMIN CONTROL INGP/REL EFFICIENCY 20. PAGE 29 B0595	CAP/ISM ADMIN MGT MARKET	

		B51
LASSWELL H.D.,THE POLITICAL WRITINGS OF HAROLD D LASSWELL. UNIV DOMIN EXEC LEAD RATIONAL ATTIT DRIVE ROLE ALL/VALS...OBS BIOG 20. PAGE 63 B1269	PERSON PSY INGP/REL CONCPT	

B52
GOLDSTEIN J.,THE GOVERNMENT OF BRITISH TRADE   LABOR
UNIONS. UK ECO/DEV EX/STRUC INGP/REL...BIBLIOG 20.   PARTIC
PAGE 40 B0817

S52
JOSEPHSON E.,"IRRATIONAL LEADERSHIP IN FORMAL   ADMIN
ORGANIZATIONS." EX/STRUC PLAN LEAD GP/REL INGP/REL   RATIONAL
EFFICIENCY AUTHORIT DRIVE PSY. PAGE 57 B1154   CONCPT
                                                     PERSON
S52
LIPSET S.M.,"DEMOCRACY IN PRIVATE GOVERNMENT; (A   LABOR
CASE STUDY OF THE INTERNATIONAL TYPOGRAPHICAL   ADMIN
UNION)" (BMR)" POL/PAR CONTROL LEAD INGP/REL PWR   ELITES
...MAJORIT DECISION PREDICT 20. PAGE 65 B1319   REPRESENT
S52
TAYLOR D.W.,"TWENTY QUESTIONS: EFFICIENCY IN   PROB/SOLV
PROBLEM SOLVING AS A FUNCTION OF SIZE OF GROUP"   EFFICIENCY
WOR+45 CONFER ROUTINE INGP/REL...PSY GP/COMP 20.   SKILL
PAGE 103 B2085   PERCEPT
B53
GROSS B.M.,THE LEGISLATIVE STRUGGLE: A STUDY IN   LEGIS
SOCIAL COMBAT. STRUCT LOC/G POL/PAR JUDGE EDU/PROP   DECISION
DEBATE ETIQUET ADMIN LOBBY CHOOSE GOV/REL INGP/REL   PERSON
HEREDITY ALL/VALS...SOC PRESIDENT. PAGE 44 B0885   LEAD
B53
SAYLES L.R.,THE LOCAL UNION. CONSTN CULTURE   LABOR
DELIB/GP PARTIC CHOOSE GP/REL INGP/REL ATTIT ROLE   LEAD
...MAJORIT DECISION MGT. PAGE 93 B1873   ADJUD
                                                     ROUTINE
B53
WAGLEY C.,AMAZON TOWN: A STUDY OF MAN IN THE   SOC
TROPICS. BRAZIL L/A+17C STRATA STRUCT ECO/UNDEV   NEIGH
AGRI EX/STRUC RACE/REL DISCRIM HABITAT WEALTH...OBS   CULTURE
SOC/EXP 20. PAGE 113 B2273   INGP/REL
S53
GABLE R.W.,"NAM: INFLUENTIAL LOBBY OR KISS OF   LOBBY
DEATH?" (BMR)" USA+45 LAW INSPECT EDU/PROP ADMIN   LEGIS
CONTROL INGP/REL EFFICIENCY PWR 20 CONGRESS NAM   INDUS
TAFT/HART. PAGE 38 B0769   LG/CO
B54
WILENSKY H.L.,SYLLABUS OF INDUSTRIAL RELATIONS: A   BIBLIOG
GUIDE TO READING AND RESEARCH. USA+45 MUNIC ADMIN   INDUS
INGP/REL...POLICY MGT PHIL/SCI 20. PAGE 117 B2351   LABOR
                                                     WORKER
S54
LANE E.,"INTEREST GROUPS AND BUREAUCRACY." NAT/G   EX/STRUC
ADMIN GP/REL INGP/REL 20. PAGE 62 B1256   LOBBY
                                                     REPRESENT
                                                     PWR
B55
BERNAYS E.L.,THE ENGINEERING OF CONSENT. VOL/ASSN   GP/REL
OP/RES ROUTINE INGP/REL ATTIT RESPECT...POLICY   PLAN
METH/CNCPT METH/COMP 20. PAGE 11 B0224   ACT/RES
                                                     ADJUST
B55
BLAU P.M.,THE DYNAMICS OF BUREAUCRACY: A STUDY OF   CLIENT
INTERPERSONAL RELATIONS IN TWO GOVERNMENT AGENCIES.   ADMIN
USA+45 EX/STRUC REPRESENT INGP/REL PERS/REL.   EXEC
PAGE 12 B0251   ROUTINE
S55
BUNZEL J.H.,"THE GENERAL IDEOLOGY OF AMERICAN SMALL   ALL/IDEOS
BUSINESS"(BMR)" USA+45 USA-45 AGRI GP/REL INGP/REL   ATTIT
PERSON...MGT IDEA/COMP 18/20. PAGE 17 B0345   SML/CO
                                                     INDUS
S55
CHAPIN F.S.,"FORMALIZATION OBSERVED IN TEN   VOL/ASSN
VOLUNTARY ORGANIZATIONS: CONCEPTS, MORPHOLOGY,   ROUTINE
PROCESS." STRUCT INGP/REL PERS/REL...METH/CNCPT   CONTROL
CLASSIF OBS RECORD. PAGE 20 B0407   OP/RES
S55
MARTIN R.C.,"ADMINISTRATIVE LEADERSHIP IN   TOP/EX
GOVERNMENT." NAT/G PARTIC ROUTINE INGP/REL...MGT   ADMIN
20. PAGE 70 B1413.   EXEC
                                                     REPRESENT
B56
BARBASH J.,THE PRACTICE OF UNIONISM. ECO/TAC LEAD   LABOR
LOBBY GP/REL INGP/REL DRIVE MARXISM BIBLIOG. PAGE 9   REPRESENT
B0182   CONTROL
                                                     ADMIN
B56
FRANCIS R.G.,SERVICE AND PROCEDURE IN BUREAUCRACY.   CLIENT
EXEC LEAD ROUTINE...GU 20. PAGE 37 B0748   ADMIN
                                                     INGP/REL
                                                     REPRESENT
B56
HICKMAN C.A.,INDIVIDUALS, GROUPS, AND ECONOMIC   MGT
BEHAVIOR. WORKER PAY CONTROL EXEC GP/REL INGP/REL   ADMIN
PERSON ROLE...PSY SOC PERS/COMP METH 20. PAGE 50   ECO/TAC
B1005   PLAN
B56
REDFORD E.S.,PUBLIC ADMINISTRATION AND POLICY   EX/STRUC
FORMATION: STUDIES IN OIL, GAS, BANKING, RIVER   PROB/SOLV
DEVELOPMENT AND CORPORATE INVESTIGATIONS. USA+45   CONTROL
CLIENT NAT/G ADMIN LOBBY REPRESENT GOV/REL INGP/REL   EXEC
20. PAGE 87 B1754

B57
KIETH-LUCAS A.,DECISIONS ABOUT PEOPLE IN NEED, A   ADMIN
STUDY OF ADMINISTRATIVE RESPONSIVENESS IN PUBLIC   RIGID/FLEX
ASSISTANCE. USA+45 GIVE RECEIVE INGP/REL PERS/REL   SOC/WK
MORAL RESPECT WEALTH...SOC OBS BIBLIOG 20. PAGE 60   DECISION
B1204
B57
SCHNEIDER E.V.,INDUSTRIAL SOCIOLOGY: THE SOCIAL   LABOR
RELATIONS OF INDUSTRY AND COMMUNITY. STRATA INDUS   MGT
NAT/G NEIGH CREATE ADMIN PARTIC GP/REL RACE/REL   INGP/REL
ROLE PWR...POLICY BIBLIOG. PAGE 94 B1898   STRUCT
B57
SHARMA S.R.,SOME ASPECTS OF THE INDIAN   EXEC
ADMINISTRATIVE SYSTEM. INDIA WOR+45 TEC/DEV BUDGET   DECISION
LEGIT ROUTINE ATTIT. PAGE 96 B1937   ADMIN
                                                     INGP/REL
B57
US CIVIL SERVICE COMMISSION,DISSERTATIONS AND   BIBLIOG
THESES RELATING TO PERSONNEL ADMINISTRATION   ADMIN
(PAMPHLET). USA+45 COM/IND LABOR EX/STRUC GP/REL   MGT
INGP/REL DECISION. PAGE 108 B2176   WORKER
S57
ARGYRIS C.,"THE INDIVIDUAL AND ORGANIZATION: SOME   PERSON
PROBLEMS OF MUTUAL ADJUSTMENT" (BMR)" USA+45   METH
PROB/SOLV ADMIN CONTROL 20. PAGE 6 B0128   INGP/REL
                                                     TASK
S57
BAUMGARTEL H.,"LEADERSHIP STYLE AS A VARIABLE IN   LEAD
RESEARCH ADMINISTRATION." USA+45 ADMIN REPRESENT   EXEC
PERS/REL 20. PAGE 10 B0198   MGT
                                                     INGP/REL
B58
BLAIR L.,THE COMMONWEALTH PUBLIC SERVICE. LAW   ADMIN
WORKER...MGT CHARTS GOV/COMP 20 COMMONWLTH AUSTRAL   NAT/G
CIVIL/SERV. PAGE 12 B0248   EX/STRUC
                                                     INGP/REL
B58
DAVIS K.C.,ADMINISTRATIVE LAW; CASES, TEXT,   ADJUD
PROBLEMS. LAW LOC/G NAT/G TOP/EX PAY CONTROL   JURID
GOV/REL INGP/REL FEDERAL 20 SUPREME/CT. PAGE 27   CT/SYS
B0541   ADMIN
B58
SHERWOOD F.P.,SUPERVISORY METHODS IN MUNICIPAL   EX/STRUC
ADMINISTRATION. USA+45 MUNIC WORKER EDU/PROP PARTIC   LEAD
INGP/REL PERS/REL 20 CITY/MGT. PAGE 96 B1945   ADMIN
                                                     LOC/G
S58
ARGYRIS C.,"SOME PROBLEMS IN CONCEPTUALIZING   FINAN
ORGANIZATIONAL CLIMATE: A CASE STUDY OF A BANK"   CONCPT
(BMR)" USA+45 EX/STRUC ADMIN PERS/REL ADJUST PERSON   LG/CO
...POLICY HYPO/EXP SIMUL 20. PAGE 6 B0129   INGP/REL
S58
MANSFIELD E.,"A STUDY OF DECISION-MAKING WITHIN THE   OP/RES
FIRM." LG/CO WORKER INGP/REL COST EFFICIENCY PRODUC   PROB/SOLV
...CHARTS 20. PAGE 69 B1395   AUTOMAT
                                                     ROUTINE
C58
WILDING N.,"AN ENCYCLOPEDIA OF PARLIAMENT." UK LAW   PARL/PROC
CONSTN CHIEF PROB/SOLV DIPLOM DEBATE WAR INGP/REL   POL/PAR
PRIVIL...BIBLIOG DICTIONARY 13/20 CMN/WLTH   NAT/G
PARLIAMENT. PAGE 116 B2350   ADMIN
B59
INDIAN INSTITUTE PUBLIC ADMIN,MORALE IN THE PUBLIC   HAPPINESS
SERVICES: REPORT OF A CONFERENCE JAN., 3-4, 1959.   ADMIN
INDIA S/ASIA ECO/UNDEV PROVS PLAN EDU/PROP CONFER   WORKER
GOV/REL EFFICIENCY DRIVE ROLE 20 CIVIL/SERV.   INGP/REL
PAGE 53 B1082
B59
LEMBERG E.,DIE VERTRIEBENEN IN WESTDEUTSCHLAND (3   GP/REL
VOLS.). GERMANY/W CULTURE STRUCT AGRI PROVS ADMIN   INGP/REL
...JURID 20 MIGRATION. PAGE 64 B1287   SOCIETY
B59
SISSON C.H.,THE SPIRIT OF BRITISH ADMINISTRATION   GOV/COMP
AND SOME EUROPEAN COMPARISONS. FRANCE GERMANY/W   ADMIN
SWEDEN UK LAW EX/STRUC INGP/REL EFFICIENCY ORD/FREE   ELITES
...DECISION 20. PAGE 98 B1972   ATTIT
B59
THARAMATHAJ C.,A STUDY OF THE COMPOSITION OF THE   ADMIN
THAI CIVIL SERVICE (PAPER). THAILAND PAY ROLE   EX/STRUC
...CHARTS 20 CIVIL/SERV FEMALE/SEX. PAGE 103 B2092   STRATA
                                                     INGP/REL
B59
WARNER W.L.,INDUSTRIAL MAN. USA+45 USA-45 ELITES   EXEC
INDUS LABOR TOP/EX WORKER ADMIN INGP/REL PERS/REL   LEAD
...CHARTS ANTHOL 20. PAGE 114 B2294   PERSON
                                                     MGT
L59
TARKOWSKI Z.M.,"SCIENTISTS VERSUS ADMINISTRATORS: INGP/REL
AN APPROACH TOWARD ACHIEVING GREATER   GP/REL
UNDERSTANDING." UK EXEC EFFICIENCY 20. PAGE 103   ADMIN
B2079   EX/STRUC
S59
GABLE R.W.,"CULTURE AND ADMINISTRATION IN IRAN."   ADMIN
IRAN EXEC PARTIC REPRESENT PWR. PAGE 38 B0770   CULTURE
                                                     EX/STRUC
                                                     INGP/REL

S59
PRESTHUS R.V.,"BEHAVIOR AND BUREAUCRACY IN MANY   ADMIN
CULTURES." EXEC INGP/REL 20. PAGE 84 B1705   EX/STRUC
                                                        GOV/COMP
                                                        METH/CNCPT
S59
SIMPSON R.L.,"VERTICAL AND HORIZONTAL COMMUNICATION   PERS/REL
IN FORMAL ORGANIZATION" USA+45 LG/CO EX/STRUC DOMIN   AUTOMAT
CONTROL TASK INGP/REL TIME 20. PAGE 97 B1963   INDUS
                                                        WORKER
B60
BHAMBHRI C.P.,PARLIAMENTARY CONTROL OVER STATE   NAT/G
ENTERPRISE IN INDIA. INDIA DELIB/GP ADMIN CONTROL   OWN
INGP/REL EFFICIENCY 20 PARLIAMENT. PAGE 11 B0235   INDUS
                                                        PARL/PROC
B60
ECKHOFF T.,RATIONALITY AND RESPONSIBILITY IN   ADMIN
ADMINISTRATIVE AND JUDICIAL DECISION-MAKING. ELITES   PROB/SOLV
LEAD INGP/REL ATTIT PWR...MGT METH/COMP GAME 20.   DECISION
PAGE 32 B0649   METH/CNCPT
B60
GLOVER J.D.,A CASE STUDY OF HIGH LEVEL   ADMIN
ADMINISTRATION IN A LARGE ORGANIZATION. EX/STRUC   TOP/EX
EXEC LEAD ROUTINE INGP/REL OPTIMAL ATTIT PERSON   FORCES
...POLICY DECISION INT QU. PAGE 40 B0812   NAT/G
B60
MCGREGOR D.,THE HUMAN SIDE OF ENTERPRISE. USA+45   MGT
LEAD ROUTINE GP/REL INGP/REL...CONCPT GEN/LAWS 20.   ATTIT
PAGE 72 B1449   SKILL
                                                        EDU/PROP
B60
PINTO F.B.M.,ENRIQUECIMENTO ILICITO NO EXERCICIO DE   ADMIN
CARGOS PUBLICOS. BRAZIL L/A+17C USA+45 ELITES   NAT/G
TRIBUTE CONTROL INGP/REL ORD/FREE PWR...NAT/COMP   CRIME
20. PAGE 83 B1675   LAW
B60
WALDO D.,THE RESEARCH FUNCTION OF UNIVERSITY   ADMIN
BUREAUS AND INSTITUTES FOR GOVERNMENTAL-RELATED   R+D
RESEARCH. FINAN ACADEM NAT/G INGP/REL ROLE...POLICY   MUNIC
CLASSIF GOV/COMP. PAGE 113 B2276   NAT/G
B60
WHEARE K.C.,THE CONSTITUTIONAL STRUCTURE OF THE   CONSTN
COMMONWEALTH. UK EX/STRUC DIPLOM DOMIN ADMIN   INT/ORG
COLONIAL CONTROL LEAD INGP/REL SUPEGO 20 CMN/WLTH.   VOL/ASSN
PAGE 115 B2330   SOVEREIGN
S60
RAPHAELI N.,"SELECTED ARTICLES AND DOCUMENTS ON   BIBLIOG
COMPARATIVE PUBLIC ADMINISTRATION." USA+45 FINAN   MGT
LOC/G TOP/EX TEC/DEV EXEC GP/REL INGP/REL...GP/COMP   ADMIN
GOV/COMP METH/COMP. PAGE 86 B1738   EX/STRUC
S60
RAPP W.F.,"MANAGEMENT ANALYSIS AT THE HEADQUARTERS   INGP/REL
OF FEDERAL AGENCIES." USA+45 NAT/G 20. PAGE 86   ADMIN
B1740   EX/STRUC
                                                        MGT
S60
THOMPSON J.D.,"ORGANIZATIONAL MANAGEMENT OF   PROB/SOLV
CONFLICT" (BMR)" WOR+45 STRUCT LABOR LG/CO WORKER   PERS/REL
TEC/DEV INGP/REL ATTIT GP/COMP. PAGE 104 B2103   ADMIN
                                                        MGT
B61
BARRASH J.,LABOR'S GRASS ROOTS; A STUDY OF THE   LABOR
LOCAL UNION. STRATA BARGAIN LEAD REPRESENT DEMAND   USA+45
ATTIT PWR. PAGE 9 B0190   INGP/REL
                                                        EXEC
B61
BIRNBACH B.,NEO-FREUDIAN SOCIAL PHILOSOPHY. TEC/DEV   SOCIETY
INGP/REL ADJUST HAPPINESS SUPEGO HEALTH...CONCPT   PSY
GEN/LAWS BIBLIOG 20. PAGE 12 B0242   PERSON
                                                        ADMIN
B61
CATHERINE R.,LE FONCTIONNAIRE FRANCAIS. FRANCE   ADMIN
NAT/G INGP/REL ATTIT MORAL ORD/FREE...T CIVIL/SERV.   GP/REL
PAGE 19 B0394   LEAD
                                                        SUPEGO
B61
HART W.R.,COLLECTIVE BARGAINING IN THE FEDERAL   INGP/REL
CIVIL SERVICE. NAT/G EX/STRUC ADMIN EXEC 20.   MGT
PAGE 47 B0961   REPRESENT
                                                        LABOR
B61
KEE R.,REFUGEE WORLD. AUSTRIA EUR+WWI GERMANY NEIGH   NAT/G
EX/STRUC WORKER PROB/SOLV ECO/TAC RENT EDU/PROP   GIVE
INGP/REL COST LITERACY HABITAT 20 MIGRATION.   WEALTH
PAGE 59 B1186   STRANGE
B61
KRUPP S.,PATTERN IN ORGANIZATIONAL ANALYSIS: A   MGT
CRITICAL EXAMINATION. INGP/REL PERS/REL RATIONAL   CONTROL
ATTIT AUTHORIT DRIVE PWR...DECISION PHIL/SCI SOC   CONCPT
IDEA/COMP. PAGE 61 B1239   METH/CNCPT
B61
LEE R.R.,ENGINEERING-ECONOMIC PLANNING   BIBLIOG/A
MISCELLANEOUS SUBJECTS: A SELECTED BIBLIOGRAPHY   PLAN
(MIMEOGRAPHED). FINAN LOC/G MUNIC NEIGH ADMIN   REGION
CONTROL INGP/REL HABITAT...GEOG MGT SOC/WK 20
RESOURCE/N. PAGE 63 B1280

B61
ROBINSON M.E.,EDUCATION FOR SOCIAL CHANGE: FOR/AID
ESTABLISHING INSTITUTES OF PUBLIC AND BUSINESS   EDU/PROP
ADMINISTRATION ABROAD (PAMPHLET). WOR+45 SOCIETY   MGT
ACADEM CONFER INGP/REL ROLE...SOC CHARTS BIBLIOG 20   ADJUST
ICA. PAGE 89 B1805
B61
SCHMECKEBIER L.,GOVERNMENT PUBLICATIONS AND THEIR   BIBLIOG/A
USE. USA+45 LEGIS ACT/RES CT/SYS EXEC INGP/REL 20.   EDU/PROP
PAGE 94 B1894   NAT/G
                                                        ADMIN
B61
TANNENBAUM R.,LEADERSHIP AND ORGANIZATION. STRUCT   LEAD
ADMIN INGP/REL ATTIT PERCEPT...DECISION METH/CNCPT   MGT
OBS CHARTS BIBLIOG. PAGE 103 B2075   RESPECT
                                                        ROLE
B61
TANZER L.,THE KENNEDY CIRCLE. INTELL CONSULT   EX/STRUC
DELIB/GP TOP/EX CONTROL EXEC INGP/REL PERS/REL PWR   NAT/G
...BIOG IDEA/COMP ANTHOL 20 KENNEDY/JF PRESIDENT   CHIEF
DEMOCRAT MCNAMARA/R RUSK/D. PAGE 103 B2077
B61
TRECKER H.B.,NEW UNDERSTANDING OF ADMINISTRATION.   VOL/ASSN
NEIGH DELIB/GP CONTROL LEAD GP/REL INGP/REL   PROF/ORG
...POLICY DECISION BIBLIOG. PAGE 105 B2126   ADMIN
                                                        PARTIC
B61
WALKER N.,MORALE IN THE CIVIL SERVICE. UK EXEC LEAD   ATTIT
INGP/REL EFFICIENCY HAPPINESS 20. PAGE 113 B2280   WORKER
                                                        ADMIN
                                                        PSY
L61
THOMPSON V.A.,"HIERARACHY, SPECIALIZATION, AND   PERS/REL
ORGANIZATIONAL CONFLICT" (BMR)" WOR+45 STRATA   PROB/SOLV
STRUCT WORKER TEC/DEV GP/REL INGP/REL ATTIT   ADMIN
AUTHORIT 20 BUREAUCRCY. PAGE 104 B2106   EX/STRUC
S61
TANNENBAUM A.S.,"CONTROL AND EFFECTIVENESS IN A   EFFICIENCY
VOLUNTARY ORGANIZATION." USA+45 ADMIN...CORREL MATH   VOL/ASSN
REGRESS STAT TESTS SAMP/SIZ CHARTS SOC/EXP INDEX 20   CONTROL
LEAGUE/WV. PAGE 102 B2072   INGP/REL
C61
ETZIONI A.,"A COMPARATIVE ANALYSIS OF COMPLEX   CON/ANAL
ORGANIZATIONS: ON POWER, INVOLVEMENT AND THEIR   SOC
CORRELATES." ELITES CREATE OP/RES ROUTINE INGP/REL   LEAD
PERS/REL CONSEN ATTIT DRIVE PWR...CONCPT BIBLIOG.   CONTROL
PAGE 34 B0684
B62
ARGYRIS C.,INTERPERSONAL COMPETENCE AND   EX/STRUC
ORGANIZATIONAL EFFECTIVENESS. CREATE PLAN PROB/SOLV   ADMIN
EDU/PROP INGP/REL PERS/REL PRODUC...OBS INT SIMUL   CONSULT
20. PAGE 6 B0131   EFFICIENCY
B62
ESCUELA SUPERIOR DE ADMIN PUBL,INFORME DEL   ADMIN
SEMINARIO SOBRE SERVICIO CIVIL O CARRERA   NAT/G
ADMINISTRATIVA. L/A+17C ELITES STRATA CONFER   PROB/SOLV
CONTROL GOV/REL INGP/REL SUPEGO 20 CENTRAL/AM   ATTIT
CIVIL/SERV. PAGE 33 B0681
B62
FOSS P.O.,REORGANIZATION AND REASSIGNMENT IN THE   FORCES
CALIFORNIA HIGHWAY PATROL (PAMPHLET). USA+45 STRUCT   ADMIN
WORKER EDU/PROP CONTROL COERCE INGP/REL ORD/FREE   PROVS
PWR...DECISION 20 CALIFORNIA. PAGE 37 B0744   PLAN
B62
HANSON A.H.,MANAGERIAL PROBLEMS IN PUBLIC   MGT
ENTERPRISE. INDIA DELIB/GP GP/REL INGP/REL   NAT/G
EFFICIENCY 20 PARLIAMENT. PAGE 46 B0940   INDUS
                                                        PROB/SOLV
B62
INSTITUTE OF PUBLIC ADMIN,A SHORT HISTORY OF THE   ADMIN
PUBLIC SERVICE IN IRELAND. IRELAND UK DIST/IND   WORKER
INGP/REL FEDERAL 13/20 CIVIL/SERV. PAGE 54 B1091   GOV/REL
                                                        NAT/G
B62
INTERNAT CONGRESS OF JURISTS,EXECUTIVE ACTION AND   JURID
THE RULE OF RULE: REPORTION PROCEEDINGS OF INT'T   EXEC
CONGRESS OF JURISTS-RIO DE JANEIRO, BRAZIL. WOR+45   ORD/FREE
ACADEM CONSULT JUDGE EDU/PROP ADJUD CT/SYS INGP/REL   CONTROL
PERSON DEPT/DEFEN. PAGE 54 B1094
B62
JENNINGS E.E.,THE EXECUTIVE: AUTOCRAT, BUREAUCRAT,   EX/STRUC
DEMOCRAT. LEAD EFFICIENCY DRIVE 20. PAGE 56 B1131   INGP/REL
                                                        TOP/EX
                                                        CONTROL
B62
MAILICK S.,CONCEPTS AND ISSUES IN ADMINISTRATIVE   DECISION
BEHAVIOR. EX/STRUC TOP/EX ROUTINE INGP/REL   MGT
EFFICIENCY. PAGE 68 B1380   EXEC
                                                        PROB/SOLV
B62
OLLE-LAPRUNE J.,LA STABILITE DES MINISTRES SOUS LA   LEGIS
TROISIEME REPUBLIQUE, 1879-1940. FRANCE CONSTN   NAT/G
POL/PAR LEAD WAR INGP/REL RIGID/FLEX PWR...POLICY   ADMIN
CHARTS 19/20. PAGE 79 B1606   PERSON
B62
RUDOLPH F.,THE AMERICAN COLLEGE AND UNIVERSITY.   ACADEM

563

CLIENT FINAN PUB/INST DELIB/GP EDU/PROP CONTROL
EXEC CONSEN ATTIT POLICY. PAGE 92 B1853

INGP/REL
PWR
ADMIN
B62

US ADMINISTRATIVE CONFERENCE.FINAL REPORT OF THE
ADMINISTRATIVE CONFERENCE OF THE US; SUGGESTIONS
FOR IMPROVING PROCESSES - ADMIN. AGENCIES. USA+45
INGP/REL EFFICIENCY RATIONAL ORD/FREE...GP/COMP
METH/COMP 20. PAGE 107 B2170

ADMIN
NAT/G
DELIB/GP
GOV/REL

S62

GIDWANI K.A.."LEADER BEHAVIOUR IN ELECTED AND NON-
ELECTED GROUPS." DELIB/GP ROUTINE TASK HAPPINESS
AUTHORIT...SOC STAT CHARTS SOC/EXP. PAGE 39 B0796

LEAD
INGP/REL
GP/COMP
CHOOSE

S62

MAINZER L.C.."INJUSTICE AND BUREAUCRACY." ELITES
STRATA STRUC EX/STRUC SENIOR CONTROL EXEC LEAD
ROUTINE INGP/REL ORD/FREE...CONCPT 20 BUREAUCRCY.
PAGE 68 B1381

MORAL
MGT
ADMIN

S62

READ W.H.."UPWARD COMMUNICATION IN INDUSTRIAL
HIERARCHIES." LG/CO TOP/EX PROB/SOLV DOMIN EXEC
PERS/REL ATTIT DRIVE PERCEPT...CORREL STAT CHARTS
20. PAGE 86 B1747

ADMIN
INGP/REL
PSY
MGT

S62

TANNENBAUM A.S.."CONTROL IN ORGANIZATIONS:
INDIVIDUAL ADJUSTMENT AND ORGANIZATIONAL
PERFORMANCE." DOMIN PARTIC REPRESENT INGP/REL
PRODUC ATTIT DRIVE PWR...PSY CORREL. PAGE 102 B2073

ADMIN
MGT
STRUCT
CONTROL

C62

BLAU P.M.."FORMAL ORGANIZATIONS." WOR+45 SOCIETY
STRUCT ECO/DEV GP/REL ATTIT...METH/CNCPT BIBLIOG
20. PAGE 12 B0253

ADMIN
SOC
GEN/METH
INGP/REL

B63

BADI J..THE GOVERNMENT OF THE STATE OF ISRAEL: A
CRITICAL ACCOUNT OF ITS PARLIAMENT, EXECUTIVE, AND
JUDICIARY. ISRAEL ECO/DEV CHIEF DELIB/GP LEGIS
DIPLOM CT/SYS INGP/REL PEACE ORD/FREE...BIBLIOG 20
PARLIAMENT ARABS MIGRATION. PAGE 8 B0157

NAT/G
CONSTN
EX/STRUC
POL/PAR

B63

BERNE E..THE STRUCTURE AND DYNAMICS OF
ORGANIZATIONS AND GROUPS. CLIENT PARTIC DRIVE
HEALTH...MGT PSY ORG/CHARTS. PAGE 11 B0226

INGP/REL
AUTHORIT
ROUTINE
CLASSIF

B63

BLONDEL J..VOTERS, PARTIES, AND LEADERS. UK ELITES
LOC/G NAT/G PROVS ACT/RES DOMIN REPRESENT GP/REL
INGP/REL...SOC BIBLIOG 20. PAGE 12 B0255

POL/PAR
STRATA
LEGIS
ADMIN

B63

CORSON J.J..PUBLIC ADMINISTRATION IN MODERN
SOCIETY. INDUS FORCES CONTROL CENTRAL EFFICIENCY
20. PAGE 24 B0482

MGT
NAT/G
PROB/SOLV
INGP/REL

B63

DE GUZMAN R.P..PATTERNS IN DECISION-MAKING: CASE
STUDIES IN PHILIPPINE PUBLIC ADMINISTRATION.
PHILIPPINE LAW CHIEF PROB/SOLV INGP/REL DRIVE
PERCEPT ROLE...ANTHOL T 20. PAGE 27 B0557

ADMIN
DECISION
POLICY
GOV/REL

B63

DOUGLASS H.R..MODERN ADMINISTRATION OF SECONDARY
SCHOOLS. CLIENT DELIB/GP WORKER REPRESENT INGP/REL
AUTHORIT...TREND BIBLIOG. PAGE 30 B0613

EDU/PROP
ADMIN
SCHOOL
MGT

B63

HAYMAN D..POLITICAL ACTIVITY RESTRICTION; AN
ANALYSIS WITH RECOMMENDATIONS (PAMPHLET). USA+45
EXEC PARTIC ROLE PWR 20. PAGE 48 B0976

CONTROL
ADMIN
INGP/REL
REPRESENT

B63

HOWER R.M..MANAGERS AND SCIENTISTS. EX/STRUC CREATE
ADMIN REPRESENT ATTIT DRIVE ROLE PWR SKILL...SOC
INT. PAGE 52 B1052

R+D
MGT
PERS/REL
INGP/REL

B63

LITTERER J.A..ORGANIZATIONS: STRUCTURE AND
BEHAVIOR. PLAN DOMIN CONTROL LEAD ROUTINE SANCTION
INGP/REL EFFICIENCY PRODUC DRIVE RIGID/FLEX PWR.
PAGE 66 B1325

ADMIN
CREATE
MGT
ADJUST

B63

MENZEL J.M..THE CHINESE CIVIL SERVICE: CAREER OPEN
TO TALENT? ASIA ROUTINE INGP/REL DISCRIM ATTIT ROLE
KNOWL ANTHOL. PAGE 73 B1468

ADMIN
NAT/G
DECISION
ELITES

B63

THORELLI H.B..INTOP: INTERNATIONAL OPERATIONS
SIMULATION: PLAYER'S MANUAL. BRAZIL FINAN OP/RES
ADMIN GP/REL INGP/REL PRODUC PERCEPT...DECISION MGT
EEC. PAGE 104 B2108

GAME
INT/TRADE
EDU/PROP
LG/CO

B63

VAN RIPER P.P..THE MERIT SYSTEM: FOUNDATION FOR
RESPONSIBLE PUBLIC MANAGEMENT (PAMPHLET). USA+45
EX/STRUC 20. PAGE 112 B2252

EFFICIENCY
ADMIN
INGP/REL
MGT

BAKER R.J.."DISCUSSION AND DECISION-MAKING IN THE
CIVIL SERVICE." UK CONTROL REPRESENT INGP/REL
PERS/REL EFFICIENCY 20. PAGE 8 B0168

EXEC
EX/STRUC
PROB/SOLV
ADMIN
B64

AHMAD M..THE CIVIL SERVANT IN PAKISTAN. PAKISTAN
ECO/UNDEV COLONIAL INGP/REL...SOC CHARTS BIBLIOG 20
CIVIL/SERV. PAGE 3 B0065

WELF/ST
ADMIN
ATTIT
STRATA
B64

CAPLOW T..PRINCIPLES OF ORGANIZATION. UNIV CULTURE
STRUCT CREATE INGP/REL UTOPIA...GEN/LAWS TIME.
PAGE 18 B0374

VOL/ASSN
CONCPT
SIMUL
EX/STRUC
B64

CATER D..POWER IN WASHINGTON: A CRITICAL LOOK AT
TODAY'S STRUGGLE TO GOVERN IN THE NATION'S CAPITAL.
USA+45 NAT/G LEGIS ADMIN EXEC LOBBY PLURISM 20.
PAGE 19 B0392

REPRESENT
GOV/REL
INGP/REL
EX/STRUC
B64

CULLINGWORTH J.B..TOWN AND COUNTRY PLANNING IN
ENGLAND AND WALES. UK LAW SOCIETY CONSULT ACT/RES
ADMIN ROUTINE LEISURE INGP/REL ADJUST PWR...GEOG 20
OPEN/SPACE URBAN/RNWL. PAGE 25 B0512

MUNIC
PLAN
NAT/G
PROB/SOLV
B64

EDELMAN M..THE SYMBOLIC USES OF POWER. USA+45
EX/STRUC CONTROL GP/REL INGP/REL...MGT T. PAGE 32
B0653

CLIENT
PWR
EXEC
ELITES
B64

POTTER D.C..GOVERNMENT IN RURAL INDIA. INDIA LEGIT
INGP/REL EFFICIENCY ATTIT 20. PAGE 84 B1695

LOC/G
ADMIN
TAX
PROB/SOLV
B64

PRESS C..A BIBLIOGRAPHIC INTRODUCTION TO AMERICAN
STATE GOVERNMENT AND POLITICS (PAMPHLET). USA+45
USA-45 EX/STRUC ADJUD INGP/REL FEDERAL ORD/FREE 20.
PAGE 84 B1701

BIBLIOG
LEGIS
LOC/G
POL/PAR
B64

REDLICH F..THE GERMAN MILITARY ENTERPRISER AND HIS
WORK FORCE. CHRIST-17C GERMANY ELITES SOCIETY FINAN
ECO/DEV CIVMIL/REL GP/REL INGP/REL...HIST/WRIT
METH/COMP 14/17. PAGE 87 B1760

EX/STRUC
FORCES
PROFIT
WORKER
B64

ROCHE J.P..THE CONGRESS. EX/STRUC BAL/PWR DIPLOM
DEBATE ADJUD LEAD PWR. PAGE 89 B1809

INGP/REL
LEGIS
DELIB/GP
SENIOR
B64

SAYLES L.R..MANAGERIAL BEHAVIOR: ADMINISTRATION IN
COMPLEX ORGANIZATIONS. INDUS LG/CO PROB/SOLV
CONTROL EXEC INGP/REL PERS/REL SKILL...MGT OBS
PREDICT GEN/LAWS 20. PAGE 93 B1874

CONCPT
ADMIN
TOP/EX
EX/STRUC
B64

US SENATE COMM GOVT OPERATIONS.THE SECRETARY OF
STATE AND THE AMBASSADOR. USA+45 CHIEF CONSULT
EX/STRUC FORCES PLAN ADMIN EXEC INGP/REL ROLE
...ANTHOL 20 PRESIDENT DEPT/STATE. PAGE 110 B2215

DIPLOM
DELIB/GP
NAT/G

B64

VALEN H..POLITICAL PARTIES IN NORWAY. NORWAY ACADEM
PARTIC ROUTINE INGP/REL KNOWL...QU 20. PAGE 111
B2249

LOC/G
POL/PAR
PERSON
B64

WILSON L..THE ACADEMIC MAN. STRUCT FINAN PROF/ORG
OP/RES ADMIN AUTHORIT ROLE RESPECT...SOC STAT.
PAGE 117 B2360

ACADEM
INGP/REL
STRATA
DELIB/GP
L64

FOX G.H.."PERCEPTIONS OF THE VIETNAMESE PUBLIC
ADMINISTRATION SYSTEM" VIETNAM ELITES CONTROL EXEC
LEAD PWR...INT 20. PAGE 37 B0745

ADMIN
EX/STRUC
INGP/REL
ROLE

B65

AMERICAN ASSEMBLY COLUMBIA U.THE FEDERAL GOVERNMENT
SERVICE. USA+45 POL/PAR EX/STRUC EXEC 20. PAGE 4
B0082

ADMIN
MGT
NAT/G
INGP/REL
B65

BANFIELD E.C..BIG CITY POLITICS. USA+45 CONSTN
POL/PAR ADMIN LOBBY CHOOSE SUFF INGP/REL PWR...GEOG
20. PAGE 9 B0179

METH/COMP
MUNIC
STRUCT

B65

COHEN H..THE DEMONICS OF BUREAUCRACY: PROBLEMS OF
CHANGE IN A GOVERNMENT AGENCY. USA+45 CLIENT
ROUTINE REPRESENT 20. PAGE 22 B0443

EXEC
EX/STRUC
INGP/REL
ADMIN

B65

DYER F.C..BUREAUCRACY VS CREATIVITY. UNIV CONTROL
LEAD INGP/REL EFFICIENCY MGT. PAGE 31 B0639

ADMIN
DECISION
METH/COMP
CREATE
B65

GOLEMBIEWSKI R.T..MEN, MANAGEMENT, AND MORALITY;
TOWARD A NEW ORGANIZATIONAL ETHIC. CONSTN EX/STRUC

LG/CO
MGT

CREATE ADMIN CONTROL INGP/REL PERSON SUPEGO MORAL PROB/SOLV
PWR...GOV/COMP METH/COMP 20 BUREAUCRCY. PAGE 40
B0819
B65

HUGHES J.M.,EDUCATION IN AMERICA (2ND ED.). USA+45 EDU/PROP
USA-45 GP/REL INGP/REL AGE/C AGE/Y ROLE...IDEA/COMP SCHOOL
BIBLIOG T 20. PAGE 52 B1059 ADMIN
METH/COMP
B65

LAMBIRI I.,SOCIAL CHANGE IN A GREEK COUNTRY TOWN. INDUS
GREECE FAM PROB/SOLV ROUTINE TASK LEISURE INGP/REL WORKER
CONSEN ORD/FREE...SOC INT QU CHARTS 20. PAGE 62 CULTURE
B1252 NEIGH
B65

MARTIN R.,PUBLIC ADMINISTRATION AND DEMOCRACY. EX/STRUC
ELITES NAT/G ADMIN EXEC ROUTINE INGP/REL. PAGE 70 DECISION
B1412 REPRESENT
GP/REL
B65

PARRISH W.E.,MISSOURI UNDER RADICAL RULE 1865-1870. PROVS
USA-45 SOCIETY INDUS LOC/G POL/PAR WORKER EDU/PROP ADMIN
SUFF INGP/REL ATTIT...BIBLIOG 19 NEGRO MISSOURI. RACE/REL
PAGE 81 B1635 ORD/FREE
B65

REISS A.J. JR.,SCHOOLS IN A CHANGING SOCIETY. SCHOOL
CULTURE PROB/SOLV INSPECT DOMIN CONFER INGP/REL EX/STRUC
RACE/REL AGE/C AGE/Y ALL/VALS...ANTHOL SOC/INTEG 20 ADJUST
NEWYORK/C. PAGE 87 B1766 ADMIN
B65

ROURKE F.E.,BUREAUCRATIC POWER IN NATIONAL EX/STRUC
POLITICS. ADMIN CONTROL EXEC GOV/REL INGP/REL 20. EFFICIENCY
PAGE 91 B1838 REPRESENT
PWR
B65

SNIDER C.F.,AMERICAN STATE AND LOCAL GOVERNMENT. GOV/REL
USA+45 FINAN CHIEF EX/STRUC TAX ADMIN CONTROL SUFF MUNIC
INGP/REL PWR 20. PAGE 98 B1989 PROVS
LOC/G
B65

US SENATE COMM ON JUDICIARY,HEARINGS BEFORE ROUTINE
SUBCOMMITTEE ON ADMINISTRATIVE PRACTICE AND DELIB/GP
PROCEDURE ABOUT ADMINISTRATIVE PROCEDURE ACT 1965. ADMIN
USA+45 LEGIS EDU/PROP ADJUD GOV/REL INGP/REL NAT/G
EFFICIENCY...POLICY INT 20 CONGRESS. PAGE 110 B2232
B65

WALTON R.E.,A BEHAVIORAL THEORY OF LABOR SOC
NEGOTIATIONS: AN ANALYSIS OF A SOCIAL INTERACTION LABOR
SYSTEM. USA+45 FINAN PROB/SOLV ECO/TAC GP/REL BARGAIN
INGP/REL...DECISION BIBLIOG. PAGE 113 B2285 ADMIN
L65

HOOK S.,"SECOND THOUGHTS ON BERKELEY" USA+45 ELITES ACADEM
INTELL LEGIT ADMIN COERCE REPRESENT GP/REL INGP/REL ORD/FREE
TOTALISM AGE/Y MARXISM 20 BERKELEY FREE/SPEE POLICY
STUDNT/PWR. PAGE 51 B1040 CREATE
S65

SIMON H.A.,"ADMINISTRATIVE DECISION-MAKING." USA+45 ADMIN
INGP/REL 20. PAGE 97 B1960 DECISION
EX/STRUC
METH/CNCPT
B66

AARON T.J.,THE CONTROL OF POLICE DISCRETION: THE CONTROL
DANISH EXPERIENCE. DENMARK LAW CREATE ADMIN FORCES
INGP/REL SUPEGO PWR 20 OMBUDSMAN. PAGE 2 B0049 REPRESENT
PROB/SOLV
B66

AMER ENTERPRISE INST PUB POL,CONGRESS: THE FIRST EFFICIENCY
BRANCH OF GOVERNMENT. EX/STRUC FEEDBACK REPRESENT LEGIS
INGP/REL PWR...DECISION METH/CNCPT PREDICT. PAGE 4 DELIB/GP
B0081 CONTROL
B66

ANDERSON D.L.,MUNICIPAL PUBLIC RELATIONS (1ST ED.). MUNIC
USA+45 SOCIETY CONSULT FORCES PRESS ADMIN...CHARTS INGP/REL
BIBLIOG/A 20. PAGE 4 B0092 EDU/PROP
ATTIT
B66

BAKKE E.W.,MUTUAL SURVIVAL: THE GOAL OF UNION AND MGT
MANAGEMENT (2ND ED.). USA+45 ELITES ECO/DEV ECO/TAC LABOR
CONFER ADMIN REPRESENT GP/REL INGP/REL ATTIT BARGAIN
...GP/COMP 20. PAGE 8 B0170 INDUS
B66

BHALERAO C.N.,PUBLIC SERVICE COMMISSIONS OF INDIA: NAT/G
A STUDY. INDIA SERV/IND EX/STRUC ROUTINE CHOOSE OP/RES
GOV/REL INGP/REL...KNO/TEST EXHIBIT 20. PAGE 11 LOC/G
B0233 ADMIN
B66

FENN DH J.R.,BUSINESS DECISION MAKING AND DECISION
GOVERNMENT POLICY. SERV/IND LEGIS LICENSE ADMIN PLAN
CONTPOL GP/REL INGP/REL 20 CASEBOOK. PAGE 35 B0711 NAT/G
LG/CO
B66

KAESTNER K.,GESAMTWIRTSCHAFTLICHE PLANUNG IN EINER ECO/TAC
GEMISCHTEN WIRTSCHAFTSORDNUNG PLAN
(WIRTSCHAFTSPOLITISCHE STUDIEN 5). GERMANY/W WOR+45 POLICY
WOR-45 INDUS MARKET NAT/G ACT/RES GP/REL INGP/REL PREDICT
PRODUC...ECOMETRIC MGT BIBLIOG 20. PAGE 57 B1159

MCKENZIE J.L.,AUTHORITY IN THE CHURCH. STRUCT LEAD SECT
INGP/REL PERS/REL CENTRAL ANOMIE ATTIT ORD/FREE AUTHORIT
RESPECT CATH. PAGE 72 B1452 PWR
ADMIN
B66

NEUMANN R.G.,THE GOVERNMENT OF THE GERMAN FEDERAL NAT/G
REPUBLIC. EUR+WWI GERMANY/W LOC/G EX/STRUC LEGIS POL/PAR
CT/SYS INGP/REL PWR...BIBLIOG 20 ADENAUER/K. DIPLOM
PAGE 78 B1573 CONSTN
B66

PERKINS J.A.,THE UNIVERSITY IN TRANSITION. USA+45 ACADEM
SOCIETY FINAN INDUS NAT/G EX/STRUC ADMIN INGP/REL ORD/FREE
COST EFFICIENCY ATTIT 20. PAGE 82 B1658 CREATE
ROLE
B66

REDFORD E.S.,THE ROLE OF GOVERNMENT IN THE AMERICAN NAT/G
ECONOMY. USA+45 USA-45 FINAN INDUS LG/CO PROB/SOLV ECO/DEV
ADMIN INGP/REL INCOME PRODUC 18/20. PAGE 87 B1759 CAP/ISM
ECO/TAC
B66

RUBENSTEIN R.,THE SHARING OF POWER IN A PSYCHIATRIC ADMIN
HOSPITAL. CLIENT PROF/ORG PUB/INST INGP/REL ATTIT PARTIC
PWR...DECISION OBS RECORD. PAGE 91 B1847 HEALTH
CONCPT
B66

SEASHOLES B.,VOTING, INTEREST GROUPS, AND PARTIES. CHOOSE
USA+45 FINAN LOC/G NAT/G ADMIN LEAD GP/REL INGP/REL POL/PAR
ROLE...CHARTS ANTHOL 20. PAGE 95 B1922 LOBBY
PARTIC
B66

SPINELLI A.,THE EUROCRATS; CONFLICT AND CRISIS IN INT/ORG
THE EUROPEAN COMMUNITY (TRANS. BY C. GROVE HAINES). INGP/REL
EUR+WWI MARKET POL/PAR ECO/TAC PARL/PROC EEC OEEC CONSTN
ECSC EURATOM. PAGE 99 B2007 ADMIN
B66

ZALEZNIK A.,HUMAN DILEMMAS OF LEADERSHIP. ELITES LEAD
INDUS EX/STRUC INGP/REL ATTIT...PSY 20. PAGE 119 PERSON
B2397 EXEC
MGT
C66

SHERMAN H.,"IT ALL DEPENDS." USA+45 FINAN MARKET LG/CO
PLAN PROB/SOLV EXEC PARTIC INGP/REL SUPEGO MGT
...DECISION BIBLIOG 20. PAGE 96 B1944 ADMIN
POLICY
B67

FINCHER F.,THE GOVERNMENT OF THE UNITED STATES. NAT/G
USA+45 USA-45 POL/PAR CHIEF CT/SYS LOBBY GP/REL EX/STRUC
INGP/REL...CONCPT CHARTS BIBLIOG T 18/20 PRESIDENT LEGIS
CONGRESS SUPREME/CT. PAGE 35 B0719 OP/RES
B67

GELLHORN W.,OMBUDSMEN AND OTHERS: CITIZENS' NAT/COMP
PROTECTORS IN NINE COUNTRIES. WOR+45 LAW CONSTN REPRESENT
LEGIS INSPECT ADJUD ADMIN CONTROL CT/SYS CHOOSE INGP/REL
PERS/REL...STAT CHARTS 20. PAGE 39 B0789 PROB/SOLV
B67

ILLINOIS COMMISSION,IMPROVING THE STATE PROVS
LEGISLATURE. USA+45 LAW CONSTN NAT/G PROB/SOLV LEGIS
EDU/PROP ADMIN TASK CHOOSE INGP/REL EFFICIENCY REPRESENT
ILLINOIS. PAGE 53 B1077 PLAN
B67

US DEPARTMENT HEALTH EDUC WELF,NEW PROGRAMS IN ADMIN
HEALTH, EDUCATION, WELFARE, HOUSING AND URBAN HEALTH
DEVELOPMENT FOR PERSONS AND FAMILIES -LOW, MOD' SCHOOL
INCOME. USA+45 MUNIC NAT/G EDU/PROP GOV/REL HABITAT
INGP/REL ORD/FREE 20 DEPT/HEW DEPT/HUD. PAGE 108
B2180
B67

US DEPARTMENT OF JUSTICE,ANNUAL REPORT OF THE ADMIN
OFFICE OF ADMINISTRATIVE PROCEDURE. USA+45 NAT/G
PROB/SOLV EDU/PROP EXEC INGP/REL EFFICIENCY KNOWL ROUTINE
...POLICY STAT 20. PAGE 108 B2181 GOV/REL
B67

WATERS M.,THE UNITED NATIONS* INTERNATIONAL CONSTN
ORGANIZATION AND ADMINISTRATION. WOR+45 EX/STRUC INT/ORG
FORCES DIPLOM LEAD REGION ARMS/CONT REPRESENT ADMIN
INGP/REL ROLE...METH/COMP ANTHOL 20 UN LEAGUE/NAT. ADJUD
PAGE 114 B2301
L67

BERGER R.,"ADMINISTRATIVE ARBITRARINESS* A SEQUEL." LAW
USA+45 CONSTN ADJUD CT/SYS SANCTION INGP/REL LABOR
...POLICY JURID. PAGE 11 B0222 BARGAIN
ADMIN
L67

GAINES J.E.,"THE YOUTH COURT CONCEPT AND ITS CT/SYS
IMPLEMENTATION IN TOMPKINS COUNTY, NEW YORK." AGE/Y
USA+45 LAW CONSTN JUDGE WORKER ADJUD ADMIN CHOOSE INGP/REL
PERSON...JURID NEW/YORK. PAGE 38 B0772 CRIME
S67

CONWAY J.E.,"MAKING RESEARCH EFFECTIVE IN ACT/RES
LEGISLATION." LAW R+D CONSULT EX/STRUC PLAN CONFER POLICY
ADMIN LEAD ROUTINE TASK INGP/REL DECISION. PAGE 23 LEGIS
B0469 PROB/SOLV
S67

DANELSKI D.J.,"CONFLICT AND ITS RESOLUTION IN THE ROLE
SUPREME COURT." PROB/SOLV LEAD ROUTINE PERSON...PSY JURID

PERS/COMP BIBLIOG 20. PAGE 26 B0527   JUDGE INGP/REL

S67
EDWARDS H.T.,"POWER STRUCTURE AND ITS COMMUNICATION IN SAN JOSE, COSTA RICA." COSTA/RICA L/A+17C STRATA FACE/GP POL/PAR EX/STRUC PROB/SOLV ADMIN LEAD GP/REL PWR...STAT INT 20. PAGE 32 B0655   ELITES INGP/REL MUNIC DOMIN

S67
FERGUSON H.,"3-CITY CONSOLIDATION." USA+45 CONSTN INDUS BARGAIN BUDGET CONFER ADMIN INGP/REL COST UTIL. PAGE 35 B0712   MUNIC CHOOSE CREATE PROB/SOLV

S67
LEVCIK B.,"WAGES AND EMPLOYMENT PROBLEMS IN THE NEW SYSTEM OF PLANNED MANAGEMENT IN CZECHOSLOVAKIA." CZECHOSLVK EUR+WWI NAT/G OP/RES PLAN ADMIN ROUTINE INGP/REL CENTRAL EFFICIENCY PRODUC DECISION. PAGE 64 B1300   MARXISM WORKER MGT PAY

S67
LEWIS P.H.,"LEADERSHIP AND CONFLICT WITHIN FEBRERISTA PARTY OF PARAGUAY." L/A+17C PARAGUAY EX/STRUC DOMIN SENIOR CONTROL INGP/REL CENTRAL FEDERAL ATTIT 20. PAGE 65 B1305   POL/PAR ELITES LEAD

S67
RAUM O.,"THE MODERN LEADERSHIP GROUP AMONG THE SOUTH AFRICAN XHOSA." SOUTH/AFR SOCIETY SECT EX/STRUC REPRESENT GP/REL INGP/REL PERSON ...METH/COMP 17/20 XHOSA NEGRO. PAGE 86 B1743   RACE/REL KIN LEAD CULTURE

S67
ROTBERG R.I.,"COLONIALISM AND AFTER: THE POLITICAL LITERATURE OF CENTRAL AFRICA - A BIBLIOGRAPHIC ESSAY." AFR CHIEF EX/STRUC REV INGP/REL RACE/REL SOVEREIGN 20. PAGE 91 B1833   BIBLIOG/A COLONIAL DIPLOM NAT/G

S67
RUBIN R.I.,"THE LEGISLATIVE-EXECUTIVE RELATIONS OF THE UNITED STATES INFORMATION AGENCY." USA+45 EDU/PROP TASK INGP/REL EFFICIENCY ISOLAT ATTIT ROLE USIA CONGRESS. PAGE 91 B1850   LEGIS EX/STRUC GP/REL PROF/ORG

S67
TATU M.,"URSS: LES FLOTTEMENTS DE LA DIRECTION COLLEGIALE." UAR USSR CHIEF LEAD INGP/REL EFFICIENCY...DECISION TREND 20 MID/EAST. PAGE 103 B2082   POLICY NAT/G EX/STRUC DIPLOM

S68
GRAM H.A.,"BUSINESS ETHICS AND THE CORPORATION." LG/CO SECT PROB/SOLV CONTROL EXEC GP/REL INGP/REL PERS/REL ROLE MORAL PWR...DECISION 20. PAGE 42 B0850   POLICY ADMIN MGT

INKELES A. B1086

INNIS/H....HAROLD ADAMS INNIS

INNOVATION....SEE CREATE

INONU/I....ISMET INONU

INSPECT....EXAMINING FOR QUALITY, OUTPUT, LEGALITY

N19
BURRUS B.R.,INVESTIGATION AND DISCOVERY IN STATE ANTITRUST (PAMPHLET). USA+45 USA-45 LEGIS ECO/TAC ADMIN CONTROL CT/SYS CRIME GOV/REL PWR...JURID CHARTS 19/20 FTC MONOPOLY. PAGE 17 B0355   NAT/G PROVS LAW INSPECT

L34
GOSNELL H.F.,"BRITISH ROYAL COMMISSIONS OF INQUIRY" UK CONSTN LEGIS PRESS ADMIN PARL/PROC...DECISION 20 PARLIAMENT. PAGE 41 B0839   DELIB/GP INSPECT POLICY NAT/G

B37
CLOKIE H.M.,ROYAL COMMISSIONS OF INQUIRY; THE SIGNIFICANCE OF INVESTIGATIONS IN BRITISH POLITICS. UK POL/PAR CONFER ROUTINE...POLICY DECISION TIME/SEQ 16/20. PAGE 22 B0439   NAT/G DELIB/GP INSPECT

B51
PETERSON F.,SURVEY OF LABOR ECONOMICS (REV. ED.). STRATA ECO/DEV LABOR INSPECT BARGAIN PAY PRICE EXEC ROUTINE GP/REL ALL/VALS ORD/FREE 20 AFL/CIO DEPT/LABOR. PAGE 82 B1662   WORKER DEMAND IDEA/COMP T

S53
GABLE R.W.,"NAM: INFLUENTIAL LOBBY OR KISS OF DEATH?" (BMR) USA+45 LAW INSPECT EDU/PROP ADMIN CONTROL INGP/REL EFFICIENCY PWR 20 CONGRESS NAM TAFT/HART. PAGE 38 B0769   LOBBY LEGIS INDUS LG/CO

B55
WHEARE K.C.,GOVERNMENT BY COMMITTEE; AN ESSAY ON THE BRITISH CONSTITUTION. UK NAT/G LEGIS INSPECT CONFER ADJUD ADMIN CONTROL TASK EFFICIENCY ROLE POPULISM 20. PAGE 115 B2329   DELIB/GP CONSTN LEAD GP/COMP

B58
ATOMIC INDUSTRIAL FORUM,MANAGEMENT AND ATOMIC ENERGY. WOR+45 SEA LAW MARKET NAT/G TEC/DEV INSPECT INT/TRADE CONFER PEACE HEALTH...ANTHOL 20. PAGE 7 B0145   NUC/PWR INDUS MGT ECO/TAC

B58
BRIGHT J.R.,AUTOMATION AND MANAGEMENT. INDUS LABOR   AUTOMAT

WORKER OP/RES TEC/DEV INSPECT 20. PAGE 15 B0307   COMPUTER PLAN MGT

B59
US HOUSE COMM GOVT OPERATIONS,UNITED STATES AID OPERATIONS IN LAOS. LAOS USA+45 PLAN INSPECT HOUSE/REP. PAGE 108 B2190   FOR/AID ADMIN FORCES ECO/UNDEV

B61
SHAPP W.R.,FIELD ADMINISTRATION IN THE UNITED NATIONS SYSTEM. FINAN PROB/SOLV INSPECT DIPLOM EXEC REGION ROUTINE EFFICIENCY ROLE...INT CHARTS 20 UN. PAGE 96 B1933   INT/ORG ADMIN GP/REL FOR/AID

B64
MARSH D.C.,THE FUTURE OF THE WELFARE STATE. UK CONSTN NAT/G POL/PAR...POLICY WELF/ST 20. PAGE 69 B1404   NEW/LIB ADMIN CONCPT INSPECT

B65
REISS A.J. JR.,SCHOOLS IN A CHANGING SOCIETY. CULTURE PROB/SOLV INSPECT DOMIN CONFER INGP/REL RACE/RFL AGE/C AGE/Y ALL/VALS...ANTHOL SOC/INTEG 20 NEWYORK/C. PAGE 87 B1766   SCHOOL EX/STRUC ADJUST ADMIN

B65
ROWAT D.C.,THE OMBUDSMAN: CITIZEN'S DEFENDER. DENMARK FINLAND NEW/ZEALND NORWAY SWEDEN CONSULT PROB/SOLV FEEDBACK PARTIC GP/REL...SOC CONCPT NEW/IDEA METH/COMP ANTHOL BIBLIOG 20. PAGE 91 B1840   INSPECT CONSTN NAT/G ADMIN

B65
STEINER G.A.,THE CREATIVE ORGANIZATION. ELITES LG/CO PLAN PROB/SOLV TEC/DEV INSPECT CAP/ISM CONTROL EXEC PERSON...METH/COMP HYPO/EXP 20. PAGE 100 B2029   CREATE MGT ADMIN SOC

B66
US HOUSE COMM GOVT OPERATIONS,AN INVESTIGATION OF THE US ECONOMIC AND MILITARY ASSISTANCE PROGRAMS IN VIETNAM. USA+45 VIETNAM/S SOCIETY CONSTRUC FINAN FORCES BUDGET INT/TRADE PEACE HEALTH...MGT HOUSE/REP AID. PAGE 108 B2191   FOR/AID ECO/UNDEV WAR INSPECT

B67
GELLHORN W.,OMBUDSMEN AND OTHERS: CITIZENS' PROTECTORS IN NINE COUNTRIES. WOR+45 LAW CONSTN LEGIS INSPECT ADJUD ADMIN CONTROL CT/SYS CHOOSE PERS/REL...STAT CHARTS 20. PAGE 39 B0789   NAT/COMP REPRESENT INGP/REL PROB/SOLV

B67
KRISLOV S.,THE NEGRO IN FEDERAL EMPLOYMENT. LAW STRATA LOC/G CREATE PROB/SOLV INSPECT GOV/REL DISCRIM ROLE...DECISION INT TREND 20 NEGRO WWI CIVIL/SERV. PAGE 61 B1238   WORKER NAT/G ADMIN RACE/REL

S67
ROWAT D.C.,"RECENT DEVELOPMENTS IN OMBUDSMANSHIP* A REVIEW ARTICLE." UK USA+45 STRUCT CONSULT INSPECT TASK EFFICIENCY...NEW/IDEA 20. PAGE 91 B1841   CANADA ADMIN LOC/G NAT/G

S67
SCOTT W.R.,"ORGANIZATIONAL EVALUATION AND AUTHORITY." CONTROL SANCTION PERS/REL ATTIT DRIVE ...SOC CONCPT OBS CHARTS IDEA/COMP 20. PAGE 95 B1921   EXEC WORKER INSPECT EX/STRUC

INST D'ETUDE POL L'U GRENOBLE B1087

INST INTL DES CIVILISATION DIF B1088

INST TRAINING MUNICIPAL ADMIN B1089

INSTITUTE JUDICIAL ADMIN B1090

INSTITUTE OF PUBLIC ADMIN B1091

INSTITUTION, EDUCATIONAL....SEE SCHOOL, ACADEM

INSTITUTION, MENTAL....SEE PUB/INST

INSTITUTION, RELIGIOUS....SEE SECT

INSTITUTIONS....SEE DESCRIPTORS IN INSTITUTIONAL INDEX
    (TOPICAL INDEX, NO. 2)

INSURANCE....SEE FINAN, SERV/IND

INSURRECTION....SEE REV

INT....INTERVIEW; SEE ALSO INTERVIEWS INDEX, P. XIV

B37
GOSNELL H.F.,MACHINE POLITICS: CHICAGO MODEL. COM/IND FACE/GP LOC/G EX/STRUC LEAD ROUTINE SANCTION REPRESENT GOV/REL PWR...POLICY MATH OBS INT CHARTS. PAGE 41 B0840   POL/PAR MUNIC ADMIN CHOOSE

B40
PFIFFNER J.M.,RESEARCH METHODS IN PUBLIC ADMINISTRATION. USA-45 R+D...MGT STAT INT QU T 20. PAGE 82 B1665   ADMIN OP/RES METH TEC/DEV

KRIESBERG M.,"WHAT CONGRESSMEN AND ADMINISTRATORS THINK OF THE POLLS." USA-45 CONTROL PWR...INT QU. PAGE 61 B1236
S45
LEGIS
ATTIT
EDU/PROP
ADMIN

CAMPBELL A.,"THE USES OF INTERVIEW SURVEYS IN FEDERAL ADMNSTRATION" PROB/SOLV EXEC PARTIC DECISION. PAGE 18 B0369
S46
INT
ADMIN
EX/STRUC
REPRESENT

LASSWELL H.D.,THE ANALYSIS OF POLITICAL BEHAVIOUR: AN EMPIRICAL APPROACH. WOR+45 CULTURE NAT/G FORCES EDU/PROP ADMIN ATTIT PERCEPT KNOWL...PHIL/SCI PSY SOC NEW/IDEA OBS INT GEN/METH NAZI 20. PAGE 63 B1267
B47
R+D
ACT/RES
ELITES

BAKKE E.W.,BONDS OF ORGANIZATION (2ND ED.). USA+45 COM/IND FINAN ADMIN LEAD PERS/REL...INT SOC/INTEG 20. PAGE 8 B0169
B50
ECO/DEV
MGT
LABOR
GP/REL

COHEN M.B.,"PERSONALITY AS A FACTOR IN ADMINISTRATIVE DECISIONS." ADJUD PERS/REL ANOMIE SUPEGO...OBS SELF/OBS INT. PAGE 22 B0446
S51
PERSON
ADMIN
PROB/SOLV
PSY

SCHRAMM W.,"COMMUNICATION IN THE SOVIETIZED STATE, AS DEMONSTRATED IN KOREA." ASIA COM KOREA COM/IND FACE/GP POL/PAR SCHOOL FORCES ADMIN PWR MARXISM ...SOC CONCPT MYTH INT BIOG TOT/POP 20. PAGE 94 B1901
S51
ATTIT
EDU/PROP
TOTALISM

MACK R.T.,RAISING THE WORLDS STANDARD OF LIVING. IRAN INT/ORG VOL/ASSN EX/STRUC ECO/TAC WEALTH...MGT METH/CNCPT STAT CONT/OBS INT TOT/POP VAL/FREE 20 UN. PAGE 67 B1363
B53
WOR+45
FOR/AID
INT/TRADE

APTER D.E.,THE GOLD COAST IN TRANSITION. FUT CONSTN CULTURE SOCIETY ECO/UNDEV FAM KIN LOC/G NAT/G POL/PAR LEGIS TOP/EX EDU/PROP LEGIT ADMIN ATTIT PERSON PWR...CONCPT STAT INT CENSUS TOT/POP VAL/FREE. PAGE 6 B0120
B55
AFR
SOVEREIGN

WEISS R.S.,"A METHOD FOR THE ANALYSIS OF THE STRUCTURE OF COMPLEX ORGANIZATIONS." WOR+45 INDUS LG/CO NAT/G EXEC ROUTINE ORD/FREE PWR SKILL...MGT PSY SOC NEW/IDEA STAT INT REC/INT STAND/INT CHARTS WORK. PAGE 115 B2316
S55
PROF/ORG
SOC/EXP

RANSONE C.B.,THE OFFICE OF GOVERNOR IN THE UNITED STATES. USA+45 ADMIN...MGT INT CHARTS 20 GOVERNOR. PAGE 86 B1732
B56
PROVS
TOP/EX
POL/PAR
EX/STRUC

US HOUSE RULES COMM,HEARINGS BEFORE A SPECIAL SUBCOMMITTEE: ESTABLISHMENT OF A STANDING COMMITTEE ON ADMINISTRATIVE PROCEDURE, PRACTICE. USA+45 LAW EX/STRUC ADJUD CONTROL EXEC GOV/REL EFFICIENCY PWR ...POLICY INT 20 CONGRESS. PAGE 109 B2199
B56
ADMIN
DOMIN
DELIB/GP
NAT/G

FULLER C.D.,TRAINING OF SPECIALISTS IN INTERNATIONAL RELATIONS. FUT USA+45 USA-45 INTELL INT/ORG...MGT METH/CNCPT INT QU GEN/METH 20. PAGE 38 B0765
B57
KNOWL
DIPLOM

MURRAY J.N.,THE UNITED NATIONS TRUSTEESHIP SYSTEM. AFR WOR+45 CONSTN CONSULT LEGIS EDU/PROP LEGIT EXEC ROUTINE...INT TIME/SEQ SOMALI UN 20. PAGE 77 B1547
B57
INT/ORG
DELIB/GP

BROWNE C.G.,THE CONCEPT OF LEADERSHIP. UNIV FACE/GP DOMIN EDU/PROP LEGIT LEAD DRIVE PERSON PWR...MGT SOC OBS SELF/OBS CONT/OBS INT PERS/TEST STERTYP GEN/LAWS. PAGE 16 B0328
B58
EXEC
CONCPT

COLEMAN J.S.,NIGERIA: BACKGROUND TO NATIONALISM. AFR SOCIETY ECO/DEV KIN LOC/G POL/PAR TEC/DEV DOMIN ADMIN DRIVE PWR RESPECT...TRADIT SOC INT SAMP TIME/SEQ 20. PAGE 22 B0452
B58
NAT/G
NAT/LISM
NIGERIA

REDFIELD C.E.,COMMUNICATION IN MANAGEMENT. DELIB/GP EX/STRUC WRITING LEAD PERS/REL...PSY INT METH 20. PAGE 87 B1750
B58
COM/IND
MGT
LG/CO
ADMIN

SKINNER G.W.,LEADERSHIP AND POWER IN THE CHINESE COMMUNITY OF THAILAND. ASIA S/ASIA STRATA FACE/GP KIN PROF/ORG VOL/ASSN EX/STRUC DOMIN PERSON RESPECT ...METH/CNCPT STAT INT QU BIOG CHARTS 20. PAGE 98 B1974
B58
SOC
ELITES
THAILAND

US SENATE COMM POST OFFICE,TO PROVIDE AN EFFECTIVE SYSTEM OF PERSONNEL ADMINISTRATION. USA+45 NAT/G EX/STRUC PARL/PROC GOV/REL...JURID 20 SENATE CIVIL/SERV. PAGE 111 B2234
B58
INT
LEGIS
CONFER
ADMIN

MITCHELL W.C.,"OCCUPATIONAL ROLE STRAINS: THE AMERICAN ELECTIVE PUBLIC OFFICIAL." CONTROL RIGID/FLEX SUPEGO HEALTH ORD/FREE...SOC INT QU. PAGE 74 B1492
S58
ANOMIE
DRIVE
ROUTINE
PERSON

DIEBOLD W. JR.,THE SCHUMAN PLAN: A STUDY IN ECONOMIC COOPERATION, 1950-1959. EUR+WWI FRANCE GERMANY USA+45 EXTR/IND CONSULT DELIB/GP PLAN DIPLOM ECO/TAC INT/TRADE ROUTINE ORD/FREE WEALTH ...METH/CNCPT STAT CONT/OBS INT TIME/SEQ ECSC 20. PAGE 29 B0591
B59
INT/ORG
REGION

ELLIOTT O.,MEN AT THE TOP. USA+45 CULTURE EX/STRUC PRESS GOV/REL ATTIT ALL/VALS...OBS INT QU 20. PAGE 33 B0668
B59
TOP/EX
PERSON
LEAD
POLICY

GORDENKER L.,THE UNITED NATIONS AND THE PEACEFUL UNIFICATION OF KOREA. ASIA LAW LOC/G CONSULT ACT/RES DIPLOM DOMIN LEGIT ADJUD ADMIN ORD/FREE SOVEREIGN...INT GEN/METH UN COLD/WAR 20. PAGE 41 B0829
B59
DELIB/GP
KOREA
INT/ORG

ARGYRIS C.,UNDERSTANDING ORGANIZATIONAL BEHAVIOR. OP/RES FEEDBACK...MGT PSY METH/CNCPT OBS INT SIMUL 20. PAGE 6 B0130
B60
LG/CO
PERSON
ADMIN
ROUTINE

BROOKINGS INSTITUTION,UNITED STATES FOREIGN POLICY: STUDY NO 9: THE FORMULATION AND ADMINISTRATION OF UNITED STATES FOREIGN POLICY. USA+45 WOR+45 EX/STRUC LEGIS BAL/PWR FOR/AID EDU/PROP CIVMIL/REL GOV/REL...INT COLD/WAR. PAGE 16 B0317
B60
DIPLOM
INT/ORG
CREATE

GLOVER J.D.,A CASE STUDY OF HIGH LEVEL ADMINISTRATION IN A LARGE ORGANIZATION. EX/STRUC EXEC LEAD ROUTINE INGP/REL OPTIMAL ATTIT PERSON ...POLICY DECISION INT QU. PAGE 40 B0812
B60
ADMIN
TOP/EX
FORCES
NAT/G

US SENATE COMM ON JUDICIARY,FEDERAL ADMINISTRATIVE PROCEDURE. USA+45 CONSTN NAT/G PROB/SOLV CONFER GOV/REL...JURID INT 20 SENATE. PAGE 110 B2226
B60
PARL/PROC
LEGIS
ADMIN
LAW

US SENATE COMM ON JUDICIARY,ADMINISTRATIVE PROCEDURE LEGISLATION. USA+45 CONSTN NAT/G PROB/SOLV CONFER ROUTINE GOV/REL...INT 20 SENATE. PAGE 110 B2227
B60
PARL/PROC
LEGIS
ADMIN
JURID

SHAPP W.R.,FIELD ADMINISTRATION IN THE UNITED NATIONS SYSTEM. FINAN PROB/SOLV INSPECT DIPLOM EXEC REGION ROUTINE EFFICIENCY ROLE...INT CHARTS 20 UN. PAGE 96 B1933
B61
INT/ORG
ADMIN
GP/REL
FOR/AID

EHRMANN H.W.,"FRENCH BUREAUCRACY AND ORGANIZED INTERESTS" (BMR)" FRANCE NAT/G DELIB/GP ROUTINE ...INT 20 BUREAUCRCY CIVIL/SERV. PAGE 32 B0657
S61
ADMIN
DECISION
PLURISM
LOBBY

ARGYRIS C.,INTERPERSONAL COMPETENCE AND ORGANIZATIONAL EFFECTIVENESS. CREATE PLAN PROB/SOLV EDU/PROP INGP/REL PERS/REL PRODUC...OBS INT SIMUL 20. PAGE 6 B0131
B62
EX/STRUC
ADMIN
CONSULT
EFFICIENCY

DODDS H.W.,THE ACADEMIC PRESIDENT "EDUCATOR OR CARETAKER? FINAN DELIB/GP EDU/PROP PARTIC ATTIT ROLE PWR...POLICY RECORD INT. PAGE 30 B0601
B62
ACADEM
ADMIN
LEAD
CONTROL

ABERLE D.F.,"CHAHAR AND DAGOR MONGOL BUREAUCRATIC ADMINISTRATION: 19621945." ASIA MUNIC TOP/EX PWR ...MGT OBS INT MONGOL 20. PAGE 3 B0053
L62
EX/STRUC
STRATA

HEUSSLER R.,YESTERDAY'S RULERS: THE MAKING OF THE BRITISH COLONIAL SERVICE. AFR EUR+WWI UK STRATA SECT DELIB/GP PLAN DOMIN EDU/PROP ATTIT PERCEPT PERSON SUPEGO KNOWL ORD/FREE PWR...MGT SOC OBS INT TIME/SEQ 20 CMN/WLTH. PAGE 49 B1000
B63
EX/STRUC
MORAL
ELITES

HOWER R.M.,MANAGERS AND SCIENTISTS. EX/STRUC CREATE ADMIN REPRESENT ATTIT DRIVE ROLE PWR SKILL...SOC INT. PAGE 52 B1052
B63
R+D
MGT
PERS/REL
INGP/REL

KOGAN N.,THE POLITICS OF ITALIAN FOREIGN POLICY. EUR+WWI LEGIS DOMIN LEGIT EXEC PWR RESPECT SKILL ...POLICY DECISION HUM SOC METH/CNCPT OBS INT CHARTS 20. PAGE 61 B1227
B63
NAT/G
ROUTINE
DIPLOM
ITALY

KORNHAUSER W.,SCIENTISTS IN INDUSTRY: CONFLICT AND ACCOMMODATION. USA+45 R+D LG/CO NAT/G TEC/DEV CONTROL ADJUST ATTIT...MGT STAT INT BIBLIOG 20. PAGE 61 B1229
B63
CREATE
INDUS
PROF/ORG
GP/REL

LEWIS J.W.,LEADERSHIP IN COMMUNIST CHINA. ASIA
B63
POL/PAR

INTELL ECO/UNDEV LOC/G MUNIC NAT/G PROVS ECO/TAC EDU/PROP LEGIT ADMIN COERCE ATTIT ORD/FREE PWR ...INT TIME/SEQ CHARTS TOT/POP VAL/FREE. PAGE 65 B1304
DOMIN ELITES
B63

THOMETZ C.E.,THE DECISION-MAKERS: THE POWER STRUCTURE OF DALLAS. USA+45 CULTURE EX/STRUC DOMIN LEGIT GP/REL ATTIT OBJECTIVE...INT CHARTS GP/COMP. PAGE 104 B2101
ELITES MUNIC PWR DECISION
B63

US SENATE COMM GOVT OPERATIONS,ADMINISTRATION OF NATIONAL SECURITY (9 PARTS). ADMIN...INT REC/INT CHARTS 20 SENATE CONGRESS. PAGE 110 B2213
DELIB/GP NAT/G OP/RES ORD/FREE
B63

US SENATE COMM ON JUDICIARY,ADMINISTRATIVE CONFERENCE OF THE UNITED STATES. USA+45 CONSTN NAT/G PROB/SOLV CONFER GOV/REL...INT 20 SENATE. PAGE 110 B2230
PARL/PROC JURID ADMIN LEGIS
S63

USEEM J.,"MEN IN THE MIDDLE OF THE THIRD CULTURE: THE ROLES OF AMERICAN AND NON-WESTERN PEOPLE IN CROSS-CULTURAL ADMINIS-." FUT WOR+45 DELIB/GP EX/STRUC LEGIS ATTIT ALL/VALS...MGT INT TIME/SEQ GEN/LAWS VAL/FREE. PAGE 111 B2247
ADMIN SOCIETY PERSON
B64

KILPATRICKFP,SOURCE BOOK OF OCCUPATIONAL VALUES AND THE IMAGE OF THE FEDERAL SERVICE. USA+45 EX/STRUC ...POLICY MGT INT METH/COMP 20. PAGE 60 B1205
NAT/G ATTIT ADMIN WORKER
B64

KILPATRICKFP,THE IMAGE OF THE FEDERAL SERVICE. USA+45 EX/STRUC...POLICY MGT INT METH/COMP 20. PAGE 60 B1206
NAT/G ATTIT ADMIN WORKER
B64

MAYER C.S.,INTERVIEWING COSTS IN SURVEY RESEARCH. USA+45 PLAN COST...MGT REC/INT SAMP METH/COMP HYPO/EXP METH 20. PAGE 71 B1434
SIMUL INT R+D EFFICIENCY
B64

NUQUIST A.E.,TOWN GOVERNMENT IN VERMONT. USA+45 FINAN TOP/EX PROB/SOLV BUDGET TAX REPRESENT SUFF EFFICIENCY...OBS INT 20 VERMONT. PAGE 79 B1595
LOC/G MUNIC POPULISM ADMIN
B64

SULLIVAN G.,THE STORY OF THE PEACE CORPS. USA+45 WOR+45 INTELL FACE/GP NAT/G SCHOOL VOL/ASSN CONSULT EX/STRUC PLAN EDU/PROP ADMIN ATTIT DRIVE ALL/VALS ...POLICY HEAL SOC CONCPT INT QU BIOG TREND SOC/EXP WORK. PAGE 102 B2054
INT/ORG ECO/UNDEV FOR/AID PEACE
B64

US SENATE COMM ON JUDICIARY,ADMINISTRATIVE PROCEDURE ACT. USA+45 CONSTN NAT/G PROB/SOLV CONFER GOV/REL PWR...INT 20 SENATE. PAGE 110 B2231
PARL/PROC LEGIS JURID ADMIN
B64

WAINHOUSE D.W.,REMNANTS OF EMPIRE: THE UNITED NATIONS AND THE END OF COLONIALISM. FUT PORTUGAL WOR+45 NAT/G CONSULT DOMIN LEGIT ADMIN ROUTINE ATTIT ORD/FREE...POLICY JURID RECORD INT TIME/SEQ UN CMN/WLTH 20. PAGE 113 B2275
INT/ORG TREND COLONIAL
L64

FOX G.H.,"PERCEPTIONS OF THE VIETNAMESE PUBLIC ADMINISTRATION SYSTEM" VIETNAM ELITES CONTROL EXEC LEAD PWR...INT 20. PAGE 37 B0745
ADMIN EX/STRUC INGP/REL ROLE
L64

PRUITT D.G.,"PROBLEM SOLVING IN THE DEPARTMENT OF STATE." USA+45 NAT/G CONSULT PROB/SOLV EXEC PWR ...DECISION INT ORG/CHARTS 20. PAGE 85 B1713
ROUTINE MGT DIPLOM
S64

RUSK D.,"THE MAKING OF FOREIGN POLICY" USA+45 CHIEF DELIB/GP WORKER PROB/SOLV ADMIN ATTIT PWR ...DECISION 20 DEPT/STATE RUSK/D GOLDMAN/E. PAGE 92 B1856
DIPLOM INT POLICY
B65

BUECHNER J.C.,DIFFERENCES IN ROLE PERCEPTIONS IN COLORADO COUNCIL-MANAGER CITIES. USA+45 ADMIN ROUTINE GP/REL CONSEN PERCEPT PERSON ROLE ...DECISION MGT STAT INT QU CHARTS 20 COLORADO CITY/MGT. PAGE 17 B0338
MUNIC CONSULT LOC/G IDEA/COMP
B65

GREER S.,URBAN RENEWAL AND AMERICAN CITIES: THE DILEMMA OF DEMOCRATIC INTERVENTION. USA+45 R+D LOC/G VOL/ASSN ACT/RES BUDGET ADMIN GOV/REL...SOC INT SAMP 20 BOSTON CHICAGO MIAMI URBAN/RNWL. PAGE 43 B0871
MUNIC PROB/SOLV PLAN NAT/G
B65

LAMBIRI I.,SOCIAL CHANGE IN A GREEK COUNTRY TOWN. GREECE FAM PROB/SOLV ROUTINE TASK LEISURE INGP/REL CONSEN ORD/FREE...SOC INT QU CHARTS 20. PAGE 62 B1252
INDUS WORKER CULTURE NEIGH
B65

MOORE C.H.,TUNISIA SINCE INDEPENDENCE. ELITES LOC/G POL/PAR ADMIN COLONIAL CONTROL EXEC GOV/REL
NAT/G EX/STRUC

TOTALISM MARXISM...INT 20 TUNIS. PAGE 75 B1513
SOCISM
B65

US SENATE COMM ON JUDICIARY,HEARINGS BEFORE SUBCOMMITTEE ON ADMINISTRATIVE PRACTICE AND PROCEDURE ABOUT ADMINISTRATIVE PROCEDURE ACT 1965. USA+45 LEGIS EDU/PROP ADJUD GOV/REL INGP/REL EFFICIENCY...POLICY INT 20 CONGRESS. PAGE 110 B2232
ROUTINE DELIB/GP ADMIN NAT/G
B65

YOUNG C.,POLITICS IN THE CONGO* DECOLONIZATION AND INDEPENDENCE. ELITES STRATA FORCES ADMIN REV RACE/REL FEDERAL SOVEREIGN...OBS INT CHARTS CONGO/LEOP. PAGE 118 B2391
BELGIUM COLONIAL NAT/LISM
L65

HAMMOND A.,"COMPREHENSIVE VERSUS INCREMENTAL BUDGETING IN THE DEPARTMENT OF AGRICULTURE" USA+45 GP/REL ATTIT...PSY INT 20 DEPT/AGRI. PAGE 46 B0934
TOP/EX EX/STRUC AGRI BUDGET
B66

BARBER W.F.,INTERNAL SECURITY AND MILITARY POWER* COUNTERINSURGENCY AND CIVIC ACTION IN LATIN AMERICA. ECO/UNDEV CREATE ADMIN REV ATTIT RIGID/FLEX MARXISM...INT BIBLIOG OAS. PAGE 9 B0183
L/A+17C FORCES ORD/FREE TASK
B66

US BUREAU OF THE BUDGET,THE ADMINISTRATION OF GOVERNMENT SUPPORTED RESEARCH AT UNIVERSITIES (PAMPHLET). USA+45 CONSULT TOP/EX ADMIN INCOME WEALTH...MGT PHIL/SCI INT. PAGE 108 B2174
ACT/RES NAT/G ACADEM GP/REL
B66

VON HOFFMAN N.,THE MULTIVERSITY; A PERSONAL REPORT ON WHAT HAPPENS TO TODAY'S STUDENTS AT AMERICAN UNIVERSITIES. USA+45 SOCIETY ROUTINE ANOMIE ROLE MORAL ORD/FREE SKILL...INT 20. PAGE 112 B2266
EDU/PROP ACADEM ATTIT STRANGE
S66

PALMER M.,"THE UNITED ARAB REPUBLIC* AN ASSESSMENT OF ITS FAILURE." ELITES ECO/UNDEV POL/PAR FORCES ECO/TAC RUMOR ADMIN EXEC EFFICIENCY ATTIT SOCISM ...INT NASSER/G. PAGE 81 B1628
UAR SYRIA REGION FEDERAL
B67

JHANGIANI M.A.,JANA SANGH AND SWATANTRA: A PROFILE OF THE RIGHTIST PARTIES IN INDIA. INDIA ADMIN CHOOSE MARXISM SOCISM...INT CHARTS BIBLIOG 20. PAGE 56 B1140
POL/PAR LAISSEZ NAT/LISM ATTIT
B67

KRISLOV S.,THE NEGRO IN FEDERAL EMPLOYMENT. LAW STRATA LOC/G CREATE PROB/SOLV INSPECT GOV/REL DISCRIM ROLE...DECISION INT TREND 20 NEGRO WWI CIVIL/SERV. PAGE 61 B1238
WORKER NAT/G ADMIN RACE/REL
B67

NIEDERHOFFER A.,BEHIND THE SHIELD; THE POLICE IN URBAN SOCIETY. USA+45 LEGIT ADJUD ROUTINE COERCE CRIME ADJUST...INT CHARTS 20 NEWYORK/C. PAGE 78 B1582
FORCES PERSON SOCIETY ATTIT
B67

SCHAEFER W.V.,THE SUSPECT AND SOCIETY: CRIMINAL PROCEDURE AND CONVERGING CONSTITUTIONAL DOCTRINES. USA+45 TEC/DEV LOBBY ROUTINE SANCTION...INT 20. PAGE 93 B1879
CRIME FORCES CONSTN JURID
S67

EDWARDS H.T.,"POWER STRUCTURE AND ITS COMMUNICATION IN SAN JOSE, COSTA RICA." COSTA/RICA L/A+17C STRATA FACE/GP POL/PAR EX/STRUC PROB/SOLV ADMIN LEAD GP/REL PWR...STAT INT 20. PAGE 32 B0655
ELITES INGP/REL MUNIC DOMIN
S67

ROSENBERG B.,"ETHNIC LIBERALISM AND EMPLOYMENT DISCRIMINATION IN THE NORTH." USA+45 TOP/EX PROB/SOLV ADMIN REGION PERS/REL DISCRIM...INT IDEA/COMP. PAGE 90 B1820
RACE/REL ATTIT WORKER EXEC
S67

VERGIN R.C.,"COMPUTER INDUCED ORGANIZATION CHANGES." FUT USA+45 R+D CREATE OP/RES TEC/DEV ADJUST CENTRAL...MGT INT CON/ANAL COMPUT/IR. PAGE 112 B2260
COMPUTER DECISION AUTOMAT EX/STRUC

INT. BANK RECONSTR. DEVELOP. B1092

INT/AM/DEV....INTER-AMERICAN DEVELOPMENT BANK

INT/AVIATN....INTERNATIONAL CIVIL AVIATION ORGANIZATION

INT/LAW....INTERNATIONAL LAW

N

AMERICAN POLITICAL SCIENCE REVIEW. USA+45 USA-45 WOR+45 WOR-45 INT/ORG ADMIN...INT/LAW PHIL/SCI CONCPT METH 20 UN. PAGE 1 B0001
BIBLIOG/A DIPLOM NAT/G GOV/COMP
N

THE JAPAN SCIENCE REVIEW: LAW AND POLITICS: LIST OF BOOKS AND ARTICLES ON LAW AND POLITICS. CONSTN INDUS LABOR DIPLOM TAX ADMIN CRIME...INT/LAW SOC 20 CHINJAP. PAGE 1 B0025
BIBLIOG LAW AGRI S/ASIA PHIL/SCI
N

UNITED NATIONS,OFFICIAL RECORDS OF THE UNITED NATIONS' GENERAL ASSEMBLY. WOR+45 BUDGET DIPLOM ADMIN 20 UN. PAGE 107 B2159
INT/ORG DELIB/GP INT/LAW WRITING

UNITED NATIONS,UNITED NATIONS PUBLICATIONS. WOR+45 — BIBLIOG — N
ECO/UNDEV AGRI FINAN FORCES ADMIN LEAD WAR PEACE — INT/ORG
...POLICY INT/LAW 20 UN. PAGE 107 B2160 — DIPLOM

HOLDSWORTH W.S.,A HISTORY OF ENGLISH LAW; THE — LAW — B24
COMMON LAW AND ITS RIVALS (VOL. V). UK SEA EX/STRUC — LEGIS
WRITING ADMIN...INT/LAW JURID CONCPT IDEA/COMP — ADJUD
WORSHIP 16/17 PARLIAMENT ENGLSH/LAW COMMON/LAW. — CT/SYS
PAGE 51 B1033

HSIAO K.C.,"POLITICAL PLURALISM." LAW CONSTN — STRUCT — C27
POL/PAR LEGIS PLAN ADMIN CENTRAL SOVEREIGN — GEN/LAWS
...INT/LAW BIBLIOG 19/20. PAGE 52 B1053 — PLURISM

BORCHARD E.H.,GUIDE TO THE LAW AND LEGAL LITERATURE — BIBLIOG/A — B31
OF FRANCE. FRANCE FINAN INDUS LABOR SECT LEGIS — LAW
ADMIN COLONIAL CRIME OWN...INT/LAW 20. PAGE 14 — CONSTN
B0277 — METH

GRIFFIN G.G.,A GUIDE TO MANUSCRIPTS RELATING TO — BIBLIOG/A — B46
AMERICAN HISTORY IN BRITISH DEPOSITORIES. CANADA — ALL/VALS
IRELAND MOD/EUR UK USA-45 LAW DIPLOM ADMIN COLONIAL — NAT/G
WAR NAT/LISM SOVEREIGN...GEOG INT/LAW 15/19
CMN/WLTH. PAGE 43 B0876

GOODRICH L.M.,"CHARTER OF THE UNITED NATIONS: — CONSTN — C46
COMMENTARY AND DOCUMENTS." EX/STRUC ADMIN...INT/LAW — INT/ORG
CON/ANAL BIBLIOG 20 UN. PAGE 41 B0826 — DIPLOM

MONPIED E.,BIBLIOGRAPHIE FEDERALISTE: OUVRAGES — BIBLIOG/A — B50
CHOISIS (VOL. I. MIMEOGRAPHED PAPER). EUR+WWI — FEDERAL
DIPLOM ADMIN REGION ATTIT PACIFISM SOCISM...INT/LAW — CENTRAL
19/20. PAGE 74 B1502 — INT/ORG

MANGONE G.,"THE IDEA AND PRACTICE OF WORLD — INT/ORG — L51
GOVERNMENT." FUT WOR+45 WOR-45 ECO/DEV LEGIS CREATE — SOCIETY
LEGIT ROUTINE ATTIT MORAL PWR WEALTH...CONCPT — INT/LAW
GEN/LAWS 20. PAGE 69 B1388

DE GRAZIA A.,POLITICAL ORGANIZATION. CONSTN LOC/G — FEDERAL — B52
MUNIC NAT/G CHIEF LEGIS TOP/EX ADJUD CT/SYS — LAW
PERS/REL...INT/LAW MYTH UN. PAGE 27 B0553 — ADMIN

UNESCO,THESES DE SCIENCES SOCIALES: CATALOGUE — BIBLIOG — B52
ANALYTIQUE INTERNATIONAL DE THESES INEDITES DE — ACADEM
DOCTORAT, 1940-1950. INT/ORG DIPLOM EDU/PROP...GEOG — WRITING
INT/LAW MGT PSY SOC 20. PAGE 107 B2155

WRIGHT Q.,"CONGRESS AND THE TREATY-MAKING POWER." — ROUTINE — L52
USA+45 WOR+45 CONSTN INTELL NAT/G CHIEF CONSULT — DIPLOM
EX/STRUC LEGIS TOP/EX CREATE GOV/REL DISPL DRIVE — INT/LAW
RIGID/FLEX...TREND TOT/POP CONGRESS CONGRESS 20 — DELIB/GP
TREATY. PAGE 118 B2384

MANGONE G.,A SHORT HISTORY OF INTERNATIONAL — INT/ORG — B54
ORGANIZATION. MOD/EUR USA+45 USA-45 WOR+45 WOR-45 — INT/LAW
LAW LEGIS CREATE LEGIT ROUTINE RIGID/FLEX PWR
...JURID CONCPT OBS TIME/SEQ STERTYP GEN/LAWS UN
TOT/POP VAL/FREE 18/20. PAGE 69 B1389

MILLARD E.L.,FREEDOM IN A FEDERAL WORLD. FUT WOR+45 — INT/ORG — B54
VOL/ASSN TOP/EX LEGIS LEGIT ROUTINE FEDERAL PEACE ATTIT — CREATE
DISPL ORD/FREE PWR...MAJORIT INT/LAW JURID TREND — ADJUD
COLD/WAR 20. PAGE 73 B1479 — BAL/PWR

US SENATE COMM ON FOREIGN REL,REVIEW OF THE UNITED — BIBLIOG — B54
NATIONS CHARTER: A COLLECTION OF DOCUMENTS. LEGIS — CONSTN
DIPLOM ADMIN ARMS/CONT WAR REPRESENT SOVEREIGN — INT/ORG
...INT/LAW 20 UN. PAGE 110 B2220 — DEBATE

JAPAN MOMBUSHO DAIGAKU GAKIYUT,BIBLIOGRAPHY OF THE — BIBLIOG — B55
STUDIES ON LAW AND POLITICS (PAMPHLET). CONSTN — LAW
INDUS LABOR DIPLOM TAX ADMIN...CRIMLGY INT/LAW 20 — PHIL/SCI
CHINJAP. PAGE 56 B1126

UN HEADQUARTERS LIBRARY,BIBLIOQRAPHIE DE LA CHARTE — BIBLIOG/A — B55
DES NATIONS UNIES. CHINA/COM KOREA WOR+45 VOL/ASSN — INT/ORG
CONFER ADMIN COERCE PEACE ATTIT ORD/FREE SOVEREIGN — DIPLOM
...INT/LAW 20 UNESCO UN. PAGE 106 B2149

WRIGHT Q.,"THE PEACEFUL ADJUSTMENT OF INTERNATIONAL — R+D — S55
RELATIONS: PROBLEMS AND RESEARCH APPROACHES." UNIV — METH/CNCPT
INTELL EDU/PROP ADJUD ROUTINE KNOWL SKILL...INT/LAW — PEACE
JURID PHIL/SCI CLASSIF 20. PAGE 118 B2385

SOHN L.B.,CASES ON UNITED NATIONS LAW. STRUCT — INT/ORG — B56
DELIB/GP WAR PEACE ORD/FREE...DECISION ANTHOL 20 — INT/LAW
UN. PAGE 99 B1994 — ADMIN
— ADJUD

SCHLOCHAUER H.J.,OFFENTLICHES RECHT. GERMANY/W — CONSTN — B57
FINAN EX/STRUC LEGIS DIPLOM FEDERAL ORD/FREE — JURID
...INT/LAW 20. PAGE 94 B1892 — ADMIN
— CT/SYS

DEAN A.W.,"SECOND GENEVA CONFERENCE OF THE LAW OF — INT/ORG — L60
THE SEA: THE FIGHT FOR FREEDOM OF THE SEAS." FUT — JURID
USA+45 USSR WOR+45 WOR-45 SEA CONSTN STRUCT PLAN — INT/LAW
INT/TRADE ADJUD ADMIN ORD/FREE...DECISION RECORD
TREND GEN/LAWS 20 TREATY. PAGE 28 B0564

BOGARDUS E.S.,"THE SOCIOLOGY OF A STRUCTURED — INT/ORG — S60
PEACE." FUT SOCIETY CREATE DIPLOM EDU/PROP ADJUD — SOC
ROUTINE ATTIT RIGID/FLEX KNOWL ORD/FREE RESPECT — NAT/LISM
...POLICY INT/LAW JURID NEW/IDEA SELF/OBS TOT/POP — PEACE
20 UN. PAGE 13 B0264

SCHACHTER O.,"THE ENFORCEMENT OF INTERNATIONAL — INT/ORG — S60
JUDICIAL AND ARBITRAL DECISIONS." WOR+45 NAT/G — ADJUD
ECO/TAC DOMIN LEGIT ROUTINE COERCE ATTIT DRIVE — INT/LAW
ALL/VALS PWR...METH/CNCPT TREND TOT/POP 20 UN.
PAGE 93 B1878

BAINS J.S.,STUDIES IN POLITICAL SCIENCE. INDIA — DIPLOM — B61
WOR+45 WOR-45 CONSTN BAL/PWR ADJUD ADMIN PARL/PROC — INT/LAW
SOVEREIGN...SOC METH/COMP ANTHOL 17/20 UN. PAGE 8 — NAT/G
B0165

STONE J.,QUEST FOR SURVIVAL. WOR+45 NAT/G VOL/ASSN — INT/ORG — B61
LEGIT ADMIN ARMS/CONT COERCE DISPL ORD/FREE PWR — ADJUD
...POLICY INT/LAW JURID COLD/WAR 20. PAGE 101 B2047 — SOVEREIGN

WARD R.E.,JAPANESE POLITICAL SCIENCE: A GUIDE TO — BIBLIOG/A — B61
JAPANESE REFERENCE AND RESEARCH MATERIALS (2ND — PHIL/SCI
ED.). LAW CONSTN STRATA NAT/G POL/PAR DELIB/GP
LEGIS ADMIN CHOOSE GP/REL...INT/LAW 19/20 CHINJAP.
PAGE 113 B2290

ALGER C.F.,"NON-RESOLUTION CONSEQUENCES OF THE — INT/ORG — S61
UNITED NATIONS AND THEIR EFFECT ON INTERNATIONAL — DRIVE
CONFLICT." WOR+45 CONSTN ECO/DEV NAT/G CONSULT — BAL/PWR
DELIB/GP TOP/EX ACT/RES PLAN DIPLOM EDU/PROP
ROUTINE ATTIT ALL/VALS...INT/LAW TOT/POP UN 20.
PAGE 4 B0075

LEWY G.,"SUPERIOR ORDERS, NUCLEAR WARFARE AND THE — DETER — S61
DICTATES OF CONSCIENCE: THE DILEMMA OF MILITARY — INT/ORG
OBEDIENCE IN THE ATOMIC." FUT UNIV WOR+45 INTELL — LAW
SOCIETY FORCES TOP/EX ACT/RES ADMIN ROUTINE NUC/PWR — INT/LAW
PERCEPT RIGID/FLEX ALL/VALS...POLICY CONCPT 20.
PAGE 65 B1308

HITCHNER D.G.,MODERN GOVERNMENT: A SURVEY OF — CONCPT — B62
POLITICAL SCIENCE. WOR+45 INT/ORG LEGIS ADMIN — NAT/G
CT/SYS EXEC CHOOSE TOTALISM POPULISM...INT/LAW — STRUCT
PHIL/SCI METH 20. PAGE 50 B1019

SCHWERIN K.,"LAW LIBRARIES AND FOREIGN LAW — BIBLIOG — L62
COLLECTION IN THE USA." USA+45 USA-45...INT/LAW — LAW
STAT 20. PAGE 95 B1917 — ACADEM
— ADMIN

VAN SLYCK P.,PEACE: THE CONTROL OF NATIONAL POWER. — ARMS/CONT — B63
CUBA WOR+45 FINAN NAT/G FORCES PROB/SOLV TEC/DEV — PEACE
BAL/PWR ADMIN CONTROL ORD/FREE...POLICY INT/LAW UN — INT/ORG
COLD/WAR TREATY. PAGE 112 B2253 — DIPLOM

MODELSKI G.,"STUDY OF ALLIANCES." WOR+45 WOR-45 — VOL/ASSN — S63
INT/ORG NAT/G FORCES LEGIT ADMIN CHOOSE ALL/VALS — CON/ANAL
PWR SKILL...INT/LAW CONCPT GEN/LAWS 20 TREATY. — DIPLOM
PAGE 74 B1495

GESELLSCHAFT RECHTSVERGLEICH,BIBLIOGRAPHIE DES — BIBLIOG/A — B64
DEUTSCHEN RECHTS (BIBLIOGRAPHY OF GERMAN LAW, — JURID
TRANS. BY COURTLAND PETERSON). GERMANY FINAN INDUS — CONSTN
LABOR SECT FORCES CT/SYS PARL/PROC CRIME...INT/LAW — ADMIN
SOC NAT/COMP 20. PAGE 39 B0794

GRZYBOWSKI K.,THE SOCIALIST COMMONWEALTH OF — INT/LAW — B64
NATIONS: ORGANIZATIONS AND INSTITUTIONS. FORCES — COM
DIPLOM INT/TRADE ADJUD ADMIN LEAD WAR MARXISM — REGION
SOCISM...BIBLIOG 20 COMECON WARSAW/P. PAGE 44 B0898 — INT/ORG

HARMON R.B.,BIBLIOGRAPHY OF BIBLIOGRAPHIES IN — BIBLIOG — B64
POLITICAL SCIENCE (MIMEOGRAPHED PAPER: LIMITED — NAT/G
EDITION). WOR+45 WOR-45 INT/ORG POL/PAR GOV/REL — DIPLOM
ALL/IDEOS...INT/LAW JURID MGT 19/20. PAGE 47 B0949 — LOC/G

KAHNG T.J.,LAW, POLITICS, AND THE SECURITY COUNCIL* — DELIB/GP — B64
AN INQUIRY INTO THE HANDLING OF LEGAL QUESTIONS. — ADJUD
LAW CONSTN NAT/G ACT/RES OP/RES CT/SYS TASK PWR — ROUTINE
...INT/LAW BIBLIOG UN. PAGE 57 B1160

KAPP E.,THE MERGER OF THE EXECUTIVES OF THE — CENTRAL — B64
EUROPEAN COMMUNITIES. LAW CONSTN STRUCT ACT/RES — EX/STRUC
PLAN PROB/SOLV ADMIN REGION TASK...INT/LAW MGT ECSC
EEC. PAGE 58 B1170

RUSSELL R.B.,UNITED NATIONS EXPERIENCE WITH — FORCES — B64
MILITARY FORCES: POLITICAL AND LEGAL ASPECTS. AFR — DIPLOM

KOREA WOR+45 LEGIS PROB/SOLV ADMIN CONTROL
EFFICIENCY PEACE...POLICY INT/LAW BIBLIOG UN.
PAGE 92 B1857
SANCTION
ORD/FREE

SCHECHTER A.H.,INTERPRETATION OF AMBIGUOUS
DOCUMENTS BY INTERNATIONAL ADMINISTRATIVE
TRIBUNALS. WOR+45 EX/STRUC INT/TRADE CT/SYS
SOVEREIGN 20 UN ILO EURCT/JUST. PAGE 93 B1884
INT/LAW
DIPLOM
INT/ORG
ADJUD
B64

SZLADITS C.,BIBLIOGRAPHY ON FOREIGN AND COMPARATIVE
LAW: BOOKS AND ARTICLES IN ENGLISH (SUPPLEMENT
1962). FINAN INDUS JUDGE LICENSE ADMIN CT/SYS
PARL/PROC OWN...INT/LAW CLASSIF METH/COMP NAT/COMP
20. PAGE 102 B2065
BIBLIOG/A
JURID
ADJUD
LAW
B64

UN PUB. INFORM. ORGAN.,EVERY MAN'S UNITED NATIONS.
UNIV WOR+45 CONSTN CULTURE SOCIETY ECO/DEV
ECO/UNDEV NAT/G ACT/RES PLAN ECO/TAC INT/TRADE
EDU/PROP LEGIT PEACE ATTIT ALL/VALS...POLICY HUM
INT/LAW CONCPT CHARTS UN TOT/POP 20. PAGE 106 B2150
INT/ORG
ROUTINE
B64

VECCHIO G.D.,L'ETAT ET LE DROIT. ITALY CONSTN
EX/STRUC LEGIS DIPLOM CT/SYS...JURID 20 UN.
PAGE 112 B2256
NAT/G
SOVEREIGN
CONCPT
INT/LAW
S64

SCHWELB E.,"OPERATION OF THE EUROPEAN CONVENTION ON
HUMAN RIGHTS." EUR+WWI LAW SOCIETY CREATE EDU/PROP
ADJUD ADMIN PEACE ATTIT ORD/FREE PWR...POLICY
INT/LAW CONCPT OBS GEN/LAWS UN VAL/FREE ILO 20
ECHR. PAGE 95 B1916
INT/ORG
MORAL
B65

DOWD L.P.,PRINCIPLES OF WORLD BUSINESS. SERV/IND
NAT/G DIPLOM ECO/TAC TARIFFS...INT/LAW JURID 20.
PAGE 30 B0614
INT/TRADE
MGT
FINAN
MARKET
B65

FORGAC A.A.,NEW DIPLOMACY AND THE UNITED NATIONS.
FRANCE GERMANY UK USSR INT/ORG DELIB/GP EX/STRUC
PEACE...INT/LAW CONCPT UN. PAGE 36 B0740
DIPLOM
ETIQUET
NAT/G
B65

GOTLIEB A.,DISARMAMENT AND INTERNATIONAL LAW* A
STUDY OF THE ROLE OF LAW IN THE DISARMAMENT
PROCESS. USA+45 USSR PROB/SOLV CONFER ADMIN ROUTINE
NUC/PWR ORD/FREE SOVEREIGN UN TREATY. PAGE 42 B0841
INT/LAW
INT/ORG
ARMS/CONT
IDEA/COMP
B65

UNESCO,INTERNATIONAL ORGANIZATIONS IN THE SOCIAL
SCIENCES(REV. ED.). LAW ADMIN ATTIT...CRIMLGY GEOG
INT/LAW PSY SOC STAT 20 UNESCO. PAGE 107 B2157
INT/ORG
R+D
PROF/ORG
ACT/RES
B65

UNIVERSAL REFERENCE SYSTEM,INTERNATIONAL AFFAIRS:
VOLUME I IN THE POLITICAL SCIENCE, GOVERNMENT, AND
PUBLIC POLICY SERIES...DECISION ECOMETRIC GEOG
INT/LAW JURID MGT PHIL/SCI PSY SOC. PAGE 107 B2163
BIBLIOG/A
GEN/METH
COMPUT/IR
DIPLOM
B65

VONGLAHN G.,LAW AMONG NATIONS: AN INTRODUCTION TO
PUBLIC INTERNATIONAL LAW. UNIV WOR+45 LAW INT/ORG
NAT/G LEGIT EXEC RIGID/FLEX...CONCPT TIME/SEQ
GEN/LAWS UN TOT/POP 20. PAGE 112 B2267
CONSTN
JURID
INT/LAW
L65

RUBIN A.P.,"UNITED STATES CONTEMPORARY PRACTICE
RELATING TO INTERNATIONAL LAW." USA+45 WOR+45
CONSTN INT/ORG NAT/G DELIB/GP EX/STRUC DIPLOM DOMIN
CT/SYS ROUTINE ORD/FREE...CONCPT COLD/WAR 20.
PAGE 91 B1848
LAW
LEGIT
INT/LAW
B66

HARMON R.B.,SOURCES AND PROBLEMS OF BIBLIOGRAPHY IN
POLITICAL SCIENCE (PAMPHLET). INT/ORG LOC/G MUNIC
POL/PAR ADMIN GOV/REL ALL/IDEOS...JURID MGT CONCPT
19/20. PAGE 47 B0951
BIBLIOG
DIPLOM
INT/LAW
NAT/G
B66

LEE L.T.,VIENNA CONVENTION ON CONSULAR RELATIONS.
WOR+45 LAW INT/ORG CONFER GP/REL PRIVIL...INT/LAW
20 TREATY VIENNA/CNV. PAGE 63 B1279
AGREE
DIPLOM
ADMIN
B66

SZLADITS C.,A BIBLIOGRAPHY ON FOREIGN AND
COMPARATIVE LAW (SUPPLEMENT 1964). FINAN FAM LABOR
LG/CO LEGIS JUDGE ADMIN CRIME...CRIMLGY 20.
PAGE 102 B2066
BIBLIOG/A
CT/SYS
INT/LAW
L66

SEYLER W.C.,"DOCTORAL DISSERTATIONS IN POLITICAL
SCIENCE IN UNIVERSITIES OF THE UNITED STATES AND
CANADA." INT/ORG LOC/G ADMIN...INT/LAW MGT
GOV/COMP. PAGE 96 B1930
BIBLIOG
LAW
NAT/G
B67

ROBINSON R.D., INTERNATIONAL MANAGEMENT. USA&45
FINAN R+D PLAN PRODUC...DECISION T. PAGE 67 B1352
INT/TRADE
MGT
INT/LAW
MARKET
B67

PLANO J.C.,FORGING WORLD ORDER: THE POLITICS OF
INTERNATIONAL ORGANIZATION. PROB/SOLV DIPLOM
CONTROL CENTRAL RATIONAL ORD/FREE...INT/LAW CHARTS
BIBLIOG 20 UN LEAGUE/NAT. PAGE 83 B1679
INT/ORG
ADMIN
JURID

UNITED NATIONS,UNITED NATIONS PUBLICATIONS:
1945-1966. WOR+45 COM/IND DIST/IND FINAN TEC/DEV
ADMIN...POLICY INT/LAW MGT CHARTS 20 UN UNESCO.
PAGE 107 B2162
B67
BIBLIOG/A
INT/ORG
DIPLOM
WRITING

US SENATE COMM ON FOREIGN REL,HUMAN RIGHTS
CONVENTIONS. USA+45 LABOR VOL/ASSN DELIB/GP DOMIN
ADJUD REPRESENT...INT/LAW MGT CONGRESS. PAGE 110
B2225
B67
LEGIS
ORD/FREE
WORKER
LOBBY

WEIL G.L.,"THE MERGER OF THE INSTITUTIONS OF THE
EUROPEAN COMMUNITIES" EUR+WWI ECO/DEV INT/TRADE
CONSEN PLURISM...DECISION MGT 20 EEC EURATOM ECSC
TREATY. PAGE 115 B2313
S67
ECO/TAC
INT/ORG
CENTRAL
INT/LAW

INT/ORG....INTERNATIONAL ORGANIZATIONS; SEE ALSO VOL/ASSN
   AND APPROPRIATE ORGANIZATION

MONPIED E.,BIBLIOGRAPHIE FEDERALISTE: ARTICLES ET
DOCUMENTS PUBLIES DANS LES PERIODIQUES PARUS EN
FRANCE NOV. 1945-OCT. 1950. EUR+WWI WOR+45 ADMIN
REGION ATTIT MARXISM PACIFISM 20 EEC. PAGE 74 B1501
N
BIBLIOG/A
FEDERAL
CENTRAL
INT/ORG

AMERICAN POLITICAL SCIENCE REVIEW. USA+45 USA-45
WOR+45 WOR-45 INT/ORG ADMIN...INT/LAW PHIL/SCI
CONCPT METH 20 UN. PAGE 1 B0001
N
BIBLIOG/A
DIPLOM
NAT/G
GOV/COMP

INTERNATIONAL REVIEW OF ADMINISTRATIVE SCIENCES.
WOR+45 WOR-45 STRATA ECO/DEV ECO/UNDEV CREATE PLAN
PROB/SOLV DIPLOM CONTROL REPRESENT...MGT 20. PAGE 1
B0004
N
BIBLIOG/A
ADMIN
INT/ORG
NAT/G

REVIEW OF POLITICS. WOR+45 WOR-45 CONSTN LEGIS
PROB/SOLV ADMIN LEAD ALL/IDEOS...PHIL/SCI 20.
PAGE 1 B0006
N
BIBLIOG/A
DIPLOM
INT/ORG
NAT/G

UNITED NATIONS,OFFICIAL RECORDS OF THE UNITED
NATIONS' GENERAL ASSEMBLY. WOR+45 BUDGET DIPLOM
ADMIN 20 UN. PAGE 107 B2159
N
INT/ORG
DELIB/GP
INT/LAW
WRITING

UNITED NATIONS,UNITED NATIONS PUBLICATIONS. WOR+45
ECO/UNDEV AGRI FINAN FORCES ADMIN LEAD WAR PEACE
...POLICY INT/LAW 20 UN. PAGE 107 B2160
N
BIBLIOG
INT/ORG
DIPLOM

WORLD PEACE FOUNDATION,DOCUMENTS OF INTERNATIONAL
ORGANIZATIONS: A SELECTED BIBLIOGRAPHY. WOR+45
WOR-45 AGRI FINAN ACT/RES OP/RES INT/TRADE ADMIN
...CON/ANAL 20 UN LEAGUE/NAT. PAGE 118 B2374
N
BIBLIOG
DIPLOM
INT/ORG
REGION

MORRIS H.C.,THE HISTORY OF COLONIZATION. WOR+45
WOR-45 ECO/DEV ECO/UNDEV INT/ORG ACT/RES PLAN
ECO/TAC LEGIT ROUTINE COERCE ATTIT DRIVE ALL/VALS
...GEOG TREND 19. PAGE 76 B1528
B00
DOMIN
SOVEREIGN
COLONIAL

US LIBRARY OF CONGRESS,LIST OF REFERENCES ON A
LEAGUE OF NATIONS. DIPLOM WAR PEACE 20 LEAGUE/NAT.
PAGE 109 B2201
B18
BIBLIOG
INT/ORG
ADMIN
EX/STRUC

SUTHERLAND G.,CONSTITUTIONAL POWER AND WORLD
AFFAIRS. CONSTN STRUCT INT/ORG NAT/G CHIEF LEGIS
ACT/RES PLAN GOV/REL ALL/VALS...OBS TIME/SEQ
CONGRESS VAL/FREE 20 PRESIDENT. PAGE 102 B2056
B19
USA-45
EXEC
DIPLOM

HIGGINS R.,THE ADMINISTRATION OF UNITED KINGDOM
FOREIGN POLICY THROUGH THE UNITED NATIONS
(PAMPHLET). UK NAT/G ADMIN GOV/REL...CHARTS 20 UN
PARLIAMENT. PAGE 50 B1009
N19
DIPLOM
POLICY
INT/ORG

JACKSON R.G.A.,THE CASE FOR AN INTERNATIONAL
DEVELOPMENT AUTHORITY (PAMPHLET). WOR+45 ECO/DEV
DIPLOM GIVE CONTROL GP/REL EFFICIENCY NAT/LISM
SOVEREIGN 20. PAGE 55 B1108
N19
FOR/AID
INT/ORG
ECO/UNDEV
ADMIN

HALDANE R.B.,BEFORE THE WAR. MOD/EUR SOCIETY
INT/ORG NAT/G DELIB/GP PLAN DOMIN EDU/PROP LEGIT
ADMIN COERCE ATTIT DRIVE MORAL ORD/FREE PWR...SOC
CONCPT SELF/OBS RECORD BIOG TIME/SEQ. PAGE 45 B0921
B20
POLICY
DIPLOM
UK

STOWELL E.C.,INTERVENTION IN INTERNATIONAL LAW.
UNIV LAW SOCIETY INT/ORG ACT/RES PLAN LEGIT ROUTINE
WAR...JURID OBS GEN/LAWS 20. PAGE 101 B2050
B21
BAL/PWR
SOVEREIGN

POOLE D.C.,THE CONDUCT OF FOREIGN RELATIONS UNDER
MODERN DEMOCRATIC CONDITIONS. EUR+WWI USA+45
INT/ORG PLAN LEGIT ADMIN KNOWL PWR...MAJORIT
OBS/ENVIR HIST/WRIT GEN/LAWS 20. PAGE 84 B1689
B24
NAT/G
EDU/PROP
DIPLOM

HALL W.P.,EMPIRE TO COMMONWEALTH. FUT WOR-45 CONSTN
ECO/DEV ECO/UNDEV INT/ORG PROVS PLAN DIPLOM
EDU/PROP ADMIN COLONIAL PEACE PERSON ALL/VALS
B28
VOL/ASSN
NAT/G
UK

...POLICY GEOG SOC OBS RECORD TREND CMN/WLTH
PARLIAMENT 19/20. PAGE 46 B0925

B29
BUELL R..INTERNATIONAL RELATIONS. WOR+45 WOR-45   INT/ORG
CONSTN STRATA FORCES TOP/EX ADMIN ATTIT DRIVE   BAL/PWR
SUPEGO MORAL ORD/FREE PWR SOVEREIGN...JURID SOC   DIPLOM
CONCPT 20. PAGE 17 B0340

B29
ROBERTS S.H..HISTORY OF FRENCH COLONIAL POLICY. AFR   INT/ORG
ASIA L/A+17C S/ASIA CULTURE ECO/DEV ECO/UNDEV FINAN   ACT/RES
NAT/G PLAN ECO/TAC DOMIN ROUTINE SOVEREIGN...OBS   FRANCE
HIST/WRIT TREND CHARTS VAL/FREE 19/20. PAGE 89   COLONIAL
B1796

B31
HILL N..INTERNATIONAL ADMINISTRATION. WOR-45   INT/ORG
DELIB/GP DIPLOM ADMIN POL ALL/VALS...MGT TIME/SEQ   ADMIN
LEAGUE/NAT TOT/POP VAL/FREE 20. PAGE 50 B1011

B32
WRIGHT Q..GOLD AND MONETARY STABILIZATION. FUT   FINAN
USA-45 WOR-45 INTELL ECO/DEV INT/ORG NAT/G CONSULT   POLICY
PLAN ECO/TAC ADMIN ATTIT WEALTH...CONCPT TREND 20.
PAGE 118 B2383

B36
ROBINSON H..DEVELOPMENT OF THE BRITISH EMPIRE.   NAT/G
WOR-45 CULTURE SOCIETY STRUCT ECO/DEV ECO/UNDEV   HIST/WRIT
INT/ORG VOL/ASSN FORCES CREATE PLAN DOMIN EDU/PROP   UK
ADMIN COLONIAL PWR WEALTH...POLICY GEOG CHARTS
CMN/WLTH 16/20. PAGE 89 B1800

B37
ROBBINS L..ECONOMIC PLANNING AND INTERNATIONAL   INT/ORG
ORDER. WOR-45 SOCIETY FINAN INDUS NAT/G ECO/TAC   PLAN
ROUTINE WEALTH...SOC TIME/SEQ GEN/METH WORK 20   INT/TRADE
KEYNES/JM. PAGE 89 B1791

B37
ROYAL INST. INT. AFF..THE COLONIAL PROBLEM. WOR-45   INT/ORG
LAW ECO/DEV ECO/UNDEV NAT/G PLAN ECO/TAC EDU/PROP   ACT/RES
ADMIN ATTIT ALL/VALS...CONCPT 20. PAGE 91 B1844   SOVEREIGN
                                                        COLONIAL

B38
LANGE O..ON THE ECONOMIC THEORY OF SOCIALISM. UNIV   MARKET
ECO/DEV FINAN INDUS INT/ORG PUB/INST ROUTINE ATTIT   ECO/TAC
ALL/VALS...SOC CONCPT STAT TREND 20. PAGE 62 B1258   INT/TRADE
                                                        SOCISM

B38
PETTEE G.S..THE PROCESS OF REVOLUTION. COM FRANCE   COERCE
ITALY MOD/EUR RUSSIA SPAIN WOR-45 ELITES INTELL   CONCPT
SOCIETY STRATA STRUCT INT/ORG NAT/G POL/PAR ACT/RES   REV
PLAN EDU/PROP LEGIT EXEC...SOC MYTH TIME/SEQ
TOT/POP 18/20. PAGE 82 B1664

B38
RAPPARD W.E..THE CRISIS OF DEMOCRACY. EUR+WWI UNIV   NAT/G
WOR-45 CULTURE SOCIETY ECO/DEV INT/ORG POL/PAR   CONCPT
ACT/RES EDU/PROP EXEC CHOOSE ATTIT ALL/VALS...SOC
OBS HIST/WRIT TIME/SEQ LEAGUE/NAT NAZI TOT/POP 20.
PAGE 86 B1741

B39
HITLER A..MEIN KAMPF. EUR+WWI FUT MOD/EUR STRUCT   PWR
INT/ORG LABOR NAT/G POL/PAR FORCES CREATE PLAN   NEW/IDEA
BAL/PWR DIPLOM ECO/TAC DOMIN EDU/PROP ADMIN COERCE   WAR
ATTIT...SOCIALIST BIOG TREND NAZI. PAGE 50 B1020

B41
BURTON M.E..THE ASSEMBLY OF THE LEAGUE OF NATIONS.   DELIB/GP
WOR-45 CONSTN SOCIETY STRUCT INT/ORG NAT/G CREATE   EX/STRUC
ATTIT RIGID/FLEX PWR...POLICY TIME/SEQ LEAGUE/NAT   DIPLOM
20. PAGE 18 B0359

B41
YOUNG G..FEDERALISM AND FREEDOM. EUR+WWI MOD/EUR   NAT/G
RUSSIA USA-45 WOR-45 SOCIETY STRUCT ECO/DEV INT/ORG   WAR
EXEC FEDERAL ATTIT PERSON ALL/VALS...OLD/LIB CONCPT
OBS TREND LEAGUE/NAT TOT/POP. PAGE 119 B2392

B44
DAVIS H.E..PIONEERS IN WORLD ORDER. WOR-45 CONSTN   INT/ORG
ECO/TAC DOMIN EDU/PROP LEGIT ADJUD ADMIN ARMS/CONT   ROUTINE
CHOOSE KNOWL ORD/FREE...POLICY JURID SOC STAT OBS
CENSUS TIME/SEQ ANTHOL LEAGUE/NAT 20. PAGE 26 B0537

L44
CORWIN E.S.."THE CONSTITUTION AND WORLD   INT/ORG
ORGANIZATION." FUT USA+45 USA-45 NAT/G EX/STRUC   CONSTN
LEGIS PEACE KNOWL...CON/ANAL UN 20. PAGE 24 B0484   SOVEREIGN

L44
HAILEY,"THE FUTURE OF COLONIAL PEOPLES." WOR-45   PLAN
CONSTN CULTURE ECO/UNDEV AGRI MARKET INT/ORG NAT/G   CONCPT
SECT CONSULT ECO/TAC LEGIT ADMIN NAT/LISM ALL/VALS   DIPLOM
...SOC OBS TREND STERTYP CMN/WLTH LEAGUE/NAT   UK
PARLIAMENT 20. PAGE 45 B0916

B45
PASTUHOV V.D..A GUIDE TO THE PRACTICE OF   INT/ORG
INTERNATIONAL CONFERENCES. WOR+45 PLAN LEGIT   DELIB/GP
ORD/FREE...MGT OBS RECORD VAL/FREE ILO LEAGUE/NAT
20. PAGE 81 B1640

B45
RANSHOFFEN-WERTHEIMER EF.THE INTERNATIONAL   INT/ORG
SECRETARIAT: A GREAT EXPERIMENT IN INTERNATIONAL   EXEC
ADMINISTRATION. EUR+WWI FUT CONSTN FACE/GP CONSULT
DELIB/GP ACT/RES ADMIN ROUTINE PEACE ORD/FREE...MGT
RECORD ORG/CHARTS LEAGUE/NAT WORK 20. PAGE 86 B1731

B45
ROGERS W.C..INTERNATIONAL ADMINISTRATION: A   BIBLIOG/A
BIBLIOGRAPHY (PUBLICATION NO 92; A PAMPHLET).   ADMIN
WOR-45 INT/ORG LOC/G NAT/G CENTRAL 20. PAGE 90   MGT
B1814   DIPLOM

C46
GOODRICH L.M.."CHARTER OF THE UNITED NATIONS: CONSTN
COMMENTARY AND DOCUMENTS." EX/STRUC ADMIN...INT/LAW   INT/ORG
CON/ANAL BIBLIOG 20 UN. PAGE 41 B0826   DIPLOM

B47
BORGESE G..COMMON CAUSE. LAW CONSTN SOCIETY STRATA   WOR+45
ECO/DEV INT/ORG POL/PAR FORCES LEGIS TOP/EX CAP/ISM   NAT/G
DIPLOM ADMIN EXEC ATTIT PWR 20. PAGE 14 B0279   SOVEREIGN
                                                       REGION

B47
CONOVER H.F..NON-SELF-GOVERNING AREAS. BELGIUM   BIBLIOG/A
FRANCE ITALY UK WOR+45 CULTURE ECO/UNDEV INT/ORG   COLONIAL
LOC/G NAT/G ECO/TAC INT/TRADE ADMIN HEALTH...SOC   DIPLOM
UN. PAGE 23 B0465

B49
ROSENHAUPT H.W..HOW TO WAGE PEACE. USA+45 SOCIETY   INTELL
STRATA STRUCT R+D INT/ORG POL/PAR LEGIS ACT/RES   CONCPT
CREATE PLAN EDU/PROP ADMIN EXEC ATTIT ALL/VALS   DIPLOM
...TIME/SEQ TREND COLD/WAR 20. PAGE 90 B1822

B49
SINGER K..THE IDEA OF CONFLICT. UNIV INTELL INT/ORG   ACT/RES
NAT/G PLAN ROUTINE ATTIT DRIVE ALL/VALS...POLICY   SOC
CONCPT TIME/SEQ. PAGE 97 B1966

N49
UN DEPARTMENT PUBLIC INF.SELECTED BIBLIOGRAPHY OF   BIBLIOG
THE SPECIALIZED AGENCIES RELATED TO THE UNITED   INT/ORG
NATIONS (PAMPHLET). USA+45 ROLE 20 UN. PAGE 106   EX/STRUC
B2146   ADMIN

B50
BROWN E.S..MANUAL OF GOVERNMENT PUBLICATIONS.   BIBLIOG/A
WOR+45 WOR-45 CONSTN INT/ORG MUNIC PROVS DIPLOM   NAT/G
ADMIN 20. PAGE 16 B0322   LAW

B50
MCCAMY J..THE ADMINISTRATION OF AMERICAN FOREIGN   EXEC
AFFAIRS. USA+45 SOCIETY INT/ORG NAT/G ACT/RES PLAN   STRUCT
INT/TRADE EDU/PROP ADJUD ALL/VALS...METH/CNCPT   DIPLOM
TIME/SEQ CONGRESS 20. PAGE 71 B1441

B50
MONPIED E..BIBLIOGRAPHIE FEDERALISTE: OUVRAGES   BIBLIOG/A
CHOISIS (VOL. I, MIMEOGRAPHED PAPER). EUR+WWI   FEDERAL
DIPLOM ADMIN REGION ATTIT PACIFISM SOCISM...INT/LAW   CENTRAL
19/20. PAGE 74 B1502   INT/ORG

B50
PERHAM M..COLONIAL GOVERNMENT: ANNOTATED READING   BIBLIOG/A
LIST ON BRITISH COLONIAL GOVERNMENT. UK WOR+45   COLONIAL
WOR-45 ECO/UNDEV INT/ORG LEGIS FOR/AID INT/TRADE   GOV/REL
DOMIN ADMIN REV 20. PAGE 82 B1655   NAT/G

L50
US SENATE COMM. GOVT. OPER.."REVISION OF THE UN   INT/ORG
CHARTER." FUT USA+45 WOR+45 CONSTN ECO/DEV   LEGIS
ECO/UNDEV NAT/G DELIB/GP ACT/RES CREATE PLAN EXEC   PEACE
ROUTINE CHOOSE ALL/VALS...POLICY CONCPT CONGRESS UN
TOT/POP 20 COLD/WAR. PAGE 111 B2235

L51
MANGONE G.."THE IDEA AND PRACTICE OF WORLD   INT/ORG
GOVERNMENT." FUT WOR+45 WOR-45 ECO/DEV LEGIS CREATE   SOCIETY
LEGIT ROUTINE ATTIT MORAL PWR WEALTH...CONCPT   INT/LAW
GEN/LAWS 20. PAGE 69 B1388

B52
ULAM A.B..TITOISM AND THE COMINFORM. USSR WOR+45   COM
STRUCT INT/ORG NAT/G ACT/RES PLAN EXEC ATTIT DRIVE   POL/PAR
ALL/VALS...CONCPT OBS VAL/FREE 20 COMINTERN   TOTALISM
TITO/MARSH. PAGE 106 B2145   YUGOSLAVIA

B52
UNESCO.THESES DE SCIENCES SOCIALES: CATALOGUE   BIBLIOG
ANALYTIQUE INTERNATIONAL DE THESES INEDITES DE   ACADEM
DOCTORAT, 1940-1950. INT/ORG DIPLOM EDU/PROP...GEOG   WRITING
INT/LAW MGT PSY SOC 20. PAGE 107 B2155

B52
VANDENBOSCH A..THE UN: BACKGROUND, ORGANIZATION,   DELIB/GP
FUNCTIONS, ACTIVITIES. WOR+45 LAW CONSTN STRUCT   TIME/SEQ
INT/ORG CONSULT BAL/PWR EDU/PROP EXEC ALL/VALS   PEACE
...POLICY CONCPT UN 20. PAGE 112 B2254

S52
SCHWEBEL S.M.."THE SECRETARY-GENERAL OF THE UN."   INT/ORG
FUT INTELL CONSULT DELIB/GP ADMIN PEACE ATTIT   TOP/EX
...JURID MGT CONCPT TREND UN CONGRESS 20. PAGE 95
B1915

B53
GREENE K.R.C..INSTITUTIONS AND INDIVIDUALS: AN   BIBLIOG
ANNOTATED LIST OF DIRECTORIES USEFUL IN   INT/ORG
INTERNATIONAL ADMINISTRATION. USA+45 NAT/G VOL/ASSN   ADMIN
...INDEX 20. PAGE 43 B0865   DIPLOM

B53
LARSEN K..NATIONAL BIBLIOGRAPHIC SERVICES: THEIR   BIBLIOG/A
CREATION AND OPERATION. WOR+45 COM/IND CREATE PLAN   INT/ORG
DIPLOM PRESS ADMIN ROUTINE...MGT UNESCO. PAGE 62   WRITING
B1262

B53
MACK R.T..RAISING THE WORLDS STANDARD OF LIVING.   WOR+45
IRAN INT/ORG VOL/ASSN EX/STRUC ECO/TAC WEALTH...MGT   FOR/AID

METH/CNCPT STAT CONT/OBS INT TOT/POP VAL/FREE 20
UN. PAGE 67 B1363   INT/TRADE

S53
CORY R.H. JR.,"FORGING A PUBLIC INFORMATION POLICY   INT/ORG
FOR THE UNITED NATIONS." FUT WOR+45 SOCIETY ADMIN   EDU/PROP
PEACE ATTIT PERSON SKILL...CONCPT 20 UN. PAGE 24   BAL/PWR
B0486

B54
MANGONE G.,A SHORT HISTORY OF INTERNATIONAL   INT/ORG
ORGANIZATION. MOD/EUR USA+45 USA-45 WOR+45 WOR-45   INT/LAW
LAW LEGIS CREATE LEGIT ROUTINE RIGID/FLEX PWR
...JURID CONCPT OBS TIME/SEQ STERTYP GEN/LAWS UN
TOT/POP VAL/FREE 18/20. PAGE 69 B1389

B54
MILLARD E.L.,FREEDOM IN A FEDERAL WORLD. FUT WOR+45 INT/ORG
VOL/ASSN TOP/EX LEGIT ROUTINE FEDERAL PEACE ATTIT   CREATE
DISPL ORD/FREE PWR...MAJORIT INT/LAW JURID TREND   ADJUD
COLD/WAR 20. PAGE 73 B1479   BAL/PWR

B54
US SENATE COMM ON FOREIGN REL,REVIEW OF THE UNITED   BIBLIOG
NATIONS CHARTER: A COLLECTION OF DOCUMENTS. LEGIS   CONSTN
DIPLOM ADMIN ARMS/CONT WAR REPRESENT SOVEREIGN   INT/ORG
...INT/LAW 20 UN. PAGE 110 B2220   DEBATE

S54
WOLFERS A.,"COLLECTIVE SECURITY AND THE WAR IN   ACT/RES
KOREA." ASIA KOREA USA+45 INT/ORG DIPLOM ROUTINE   LEGIT
...GEN/LAWS UN COLD/WAR 20. PAGE 117 B2370

B55
CHOWDHURI R.N.,INTERNATIONAL MANDATES AND   DELIB/GP
TRUSTEESHIP SYSTEMS. WOR+45 STRUCT ECO/UNDEV   PLAN
INT/ORG LEGIS DOMIN EDU/PROP LEGIT ADJUD EXEC PWR   SOVEREIGN
...CONCPT TIME/SEQ UN 20. PAGE 21 B0427

B55
GULICK C.A.,HISTORY AND THEORIES OF WORKING-CLASS   BIBLIOG
MOVEMENTS: A SELECT BIBLIOGRAPHY. EUR+WWI MOD/EUR   WORKER
UK USA-45 INT/ORG. PAGE 44 B0902   LABOR
                                       ADMIN

B55
MACMAHON A.W.,FEDERALISM: MATURE AND EMERGENT.   STRUCT
EUR+WWI FUT WOR+45 WOR-45 INT/ORG NAT/G REPRESENT   CONCPT
FEDERAL...POLICY MGT RECORD TREND GEN/LAWS 20.
PAGE 68 B1370

B55
UN ECONOMIC AND SOCIAL COUNCIL,BIBLIOGRAPHY OF   BIBLIOG/A
PUBLICATIONS OF THE UN AND SPECIALIZED AGENCIES IN   SOC/WK
THE SOCIAL WELFARE FIELD, 1946-1952. WOR+45 FAM   ADMIN
INT/ORG MUNIC ACT/RES PLAN PROB/SOLV EDU/PROP AGE/C WEALTH
AGE/Y HABITAT...HEAL UN. PAGE 106 B2148

B55
UN HEADQUARTERS LIBRARY,BIBLIOGRAPHIE DE LA CHARTE   BIBLIOG/A
DES NATIONS UNIES. CHINA/COM KOREA WOR+45 VOL/ASSN   INT/ORG
CONFER ADMIN COERCE PEACE ATTIT ORD/FREE SOVEREIGN   DIPLOM
...INT/LAW 20 UNESCO UN. PAGE 106 B2149

L55
KISER M.,"ORGANIZATION OF AMERICAN STATES." L/A+17C VOL/ASSN
USA+45 ECO/UNDEV INT/ORG NAT/G PLAN TEC/DEV DIPLOM   ECO/DEV
ECO/TAC INT/TRADE EDU/PROP ADMIN ALL/VALS...POLICY   REGION
MGT RECORD ORG/CHARTS OAS 20. PAGE 60 B1215

L55
ROSTOW W.W.,"RUSSIA AND CHINA UNDER COMMUNISM."   COM
CHINA/COM USSR INTELL STRUCT INT/ORG NAT/G POL/PAR   ASIA
TOP/EX ACT/RES PLAN ADMIN ATTIT ALL/VALS MARXISM
...CONCPT OBS TIME/SEQ TREND GOV/COMP VAL/FREE 20.
PAGE 91 B1830

S55
TORRE M.,"PSYCHIATRIC OBSERVATIONS OF INTERNATIONAL DELIB/GP
CONFERENCES." WOR+45 INT/ORG PROF/ORG VOL/ASSN   OBS
CONSULT EDU/PROP ROUTINE ATTIT DRIVE KNOWL...PSY   DIPLOM
METH/CNCPT OBS/ENVIR STERTYP 20. PAGE 105 B2119

B56
GARDNER R.N.,STERLING-DOLLAR DIPLOMACY. EUR+WWI   ECO/DEV
USA+45 INT/ORG NAT/G PLAN INT/TRADE EDU/PROP ADMIN   DIPLOM
KNOWL PWR WEALTH...POLICY SOC METH/CNCPT STAT
CHARTS SIMUL GEN/LAWS 20. PAGE 39 B0781

B56
KIRK G.,THE CHANGING ENVIRONMENT OF INTERNATIONAL   FUT
RELATIONS. ASIA S/ASIA USA+45 WOR+45 ECO/UNDEV   EXEC
INT/ORG NAT/G FOR/AID EDU/PROP PEACE KNOWL   DIPLOM
...PLURIST COLD/WAR TOT/POP 20. PAGE 60 B1214

B56
LOVEDAY A.,REFLECTIONS ON INTERNATIONAL   INT/ORG
ADMINISTRATION. WOR+45 WOR-45 DELIB/GP ACT/RES   MGT
ADMIN EXEC ROUTINE DRIVE...METH/CNCPT TIME/SEQ
CON/ANAL SIMUL TOT/POP 20. PAGE 67 B1342

B56
SOHN L.B.,BASIC DOCUMENTS OF THE UNITED NATIONS.   DELIB/GP
WOR+45 LAW INT/ORG LEGIT EXEC ROUTINE CHOOSE PWR   CONSTN
...JURID CONCPT GEN/LAWS ANTHOL UN TOT/POP OAS FAO
ILO 20. PAGE 99 B1993

B56
SOHN L.B.,CASES ON UNITED NATIONS LAW. STRUCT   INT/ORG
DELIB/GP WAR PEACE ORD/FREE...DECISION ANTHOL 20   INT/LAW
UN. PAGE 99 B1994   ADMIN
                                       ADJUD

B56
UNITED NATIONS,BIBLIOGRAPHY ON INDUSTRIALIZATION IN BIBLIOG

UNDER-DEVELOPED COUNTRIES. WOR+45 R+D INT/ORG NAT/G ECO/UNDEV
FOR/AID ADMIN LEAD 20 UN. PAGE 107 B2161   INDUS
                                       TEC/DEV

B57
ARON R.,FRANCE DEFEATS EDC. EUR+WWI GERMANY LEGIS   INT/ORG
DIPLOM DOMIN EDU/PROP ADMIN...HIST/WRIT 20. PAGE 7   FORCES
B0136   DETER
                                       FRANCE

B57
ASHER R.E.,THE UNITED NATIONS AND THE PROMOTION OF   INT/ORG
THE GENERAL WELFARE. WOR+45 WOR-45 ECO/UNDEV   CONSULT
EX/STRUC ACT/RES PLAN EDU/PROP ROUTINE HEALTH...HUM
CONCPT CHARTS UNESCO UN ILO 20. PAGE 7 B0139

B57
BEAL J.R.,JOHN FOSTER DULLES, A BIOGRAPHY. USA+45   BIOG
USSR WOR+45 CONSTN INT/ORG NAT/G EX/STRUC LEGIT   DIPLOM
ADMIN NUC/PWR DISPL PERSON ORD/FREE PWR SKILL
...POLICY PSY OBS RECORD COLD/WAR UN 20 DULLES/JF.
PAGE 10 B0200

B57
FULLER C.D.,TRAINING OF SPECIALISTS IN   KNOWL
INTERNATIONAL RELATIONS. FUT USA+45 USA-45 INTELL   DIPLOM
INT/ORG...MGT METH/CNCPT INT QU GEN/METH 20.
PAGE 38 B0765

B57
HOLCOMBE A.N.,STRENGTHENING THE UNITED NATIONS.   INT/ORG
USA+45 ACT/RES CREATE PLAN EDU/PROP ATTIT PERCEPT   ROUTINE
PWR...METH/CNCPT CONT/OBS RECORD UN COLD/WAR 20.
PAGE 51 B1032

B57
KAPLAN M.A.,SYSTEM AND PROCESS OF INTERNATIONAL   INT/ORG
POLITICS. FUT WOR+45 WOR-45 SOCIETY PLAN BAL/PWR   DIPLOM
ADMIN ATTIT PERSON RIGID/FLEX PWR SOVEREIGN
...DECISION TREND VAL/FREE. PAGE 58 B1168

B57
MURRAY J.N.,THE UNITED NATIONS TRUSTEESHIP SYSTEM.   INT/ORG
AFR WOR+45 CONSTN CONSULT LEGIS EDU/PROP LEGIT EXEC DELIB/GP
ROUTINE...INT TIME/SEQ SOMALI UN 20. PAGE 77 B1547

L57
HAAS E.B.,"REGIONAL INTEGRATION AND NATIONAL   INT/ORG
POLICY." WOR+45 VOL/ASSN DELIB/GP EX/STRUC ECO/TAC   ORD/FREE
DOMIN EDU/PROP LEGIT COERCE ATTIT PERCEPT KNOWL   REGION
...TIME/SEQ COLD/WAR 20 UN. PAGE 45 B0908

B58
HENKIN L.,ARMS CONTROL AND INSPECTION IN AMERICAN   USA+45
LAW. LAW CONSTN INT/ORG LOC/G MUNIC NAT/G PROVS   JURID
EDU/PROP LEGIT EXEC NUC/PWR KNOWL ORD/FREE...OBS   ARMS/CONT
TOT/POP CONGRESS 20. PAGE 49 B0990

B58
ISLAM R.,INTERNATIONAL ECONOMIC COOPERATION AND THE INT/ORG
UNITED NATIONS. FINAN PLAN EXEC TASK WAR PEACE   DIPLOM
...SOC METH/CNCPT 20 UN LEAGUE/NAT. PAGE 55 B1105   ADMIN

B58
UNESCO,UNESCO PUBLICATIONS: CHECK LIST (2ND REV.   BIBLIOG
ED.). WOR+45 DIPLOM FOR/AID WEALTH...POLICY SOC   INT/ORG
UNESCO. PAGE 107 B2156   ECO/UNDEV
                                       ADMIN

S58
BLAISDELL D.C.,"PRESSURE GROUPS, FOREIGN POLICIES,   PROF/PWR
AND INTERNATIONAL POLITICS." USA+45 WOR+45 INT/ORG   PWR
PLAN DOMIN EDU/PROP LEGIT ADMIN ROUTINE CHOOSE
...DECISION MGT METH/CNCPT CON/ANAL 20. PAGE 12
B0249

S58
ELKIN A.B.,"OEEC-ITS STRUCTURE AND POWERS." EUR+WWI ECO/DEV
CONSTN INDUS INT/ORG NAT/G VOL/ASSN DELIB/GP   EX/STRUC
ACT/RES PLAN ORD/FREE WEALTH...CHARTS ORG/CHARTS
OEEC 20. PAGE 33 B0666

S58
JORDAN A.,"MILITARY ASSISTANCE AND NATIONAL   FORCES
POLICY." ASIA FUT USA+45 WOR+45 ECO/DEV ECO/UNDEV   POLICY
INT/ORG NAT/G ECO/TAC ROUTINE WEAPON ATTIT   FOR/AID
RIGID/FLEX PWR...CONCPT TREND 20. PAGE 57 B1153   DIPLOM

S58
STAAR R.F.,"ELECTIONS IN COMMUNIST POLAND." EUR+WWI COM
SOCIETY INT/ORG NAT/G POL/PAR LEGIS ACT/RES ECO/TAC CHOOSE
EDU/PROP ADJUD ADMIN ROUTINE COERCE TOTALISM ATTIT   POLAND
ORD/FREE PWR 20. PAGE 100 B2015

B59
CHINA INSTITUTE OF AMERICA,CHINA AND THE UNITED   ASIA
NATIONS. CHINA/COM FUT STRUCT EDU/PROP LEGIT ADMIN   INT/ORG
ATTIT KNOWL ORD/FREE PWR...OBS RECORD STAND/INT
TIME/SEQ UN LEAGUE/NAT UNESCO 20. PAGE 21 B0425

B59
DIEBOLD W. JR.,THE SCHUMAN PLAN: A STUDY IN   INT/ORG
ECONOMIC COOPERATION, 1950-1959. EUR+WWI FRANCE   REGION
GERMANY USA+45 EXTR/IND CONSULT DELIB/GP PLAN
DIPLOM ECO/TAC INT/TRADE ROUTINE ORD/FREE WEALTH
...METH/CNCPT STAT CONT/OBS INT TIME/SEQ ECSC 20.
PAGE 29 B0591

B59
GOODRICH L.,THE UNITED NATIONS. WOR+45 CONSTN   INT/ORG
STRUCT ACT/RES LEGIT COERCE KNOWL ORD/FREE PWR   ROUTINE
...GEN/LAWS UN 20. PAGE 41 B0825

B59
GORDENKER L.,THE UNITED NATIONS AND THE PEACEFUL   DELIB/GP

UNIFICATION OF KOREA. ASIA LAW LOC/G CONSULT   KOREA
ACT/RES DIPLOM DOMIN LEGIT ADJUD ADMIN ORD/FREE   INT/ORG
SOVEREIGN...INT GEN/METH UN COLD/WAR 20. PAGE 41
B0829
                                                        B59
MACIVER R.M.,THE NATIONS AND THE UN. WOR+45 NAT/G   INT/ORG
CONSULT ADJUD ADMIN ALL/VALS...CONCPT DEEP/QU UN   ATTIT
TOT/POP UNESCO 20. PAGE 67 B1362   DIPLOM
                                                        B59
SCHURZ W.L.,AMERICAN FOREIGN AFFAIRS: A GUIDE TO   INT/ORG
INTERNATIONAL AFFAIRS. USA+45 WOR+45 WOR-45 NAT/G   SOCIETY
FORCES LEGIS TOP/EX PLAN EDU/PROP LEGIT ADMIN   DIPLOM
ROUTINE ATTIT ORD/FREE PWR...SOC CONCPT STAT
SAMP/SIZ CHARTS STERTYP 20. PAGE 95 B1910
                                                        S59
BAILEY S.D.,"THE FUTURE COMPOSITION OF THE   INT/ORG
TRUSTEESHIP COUNCIL." FUT WOR+45 CONSTN VOL/ASSN   NAT/LISM
ADMIN ATTIT PWR...OBS TREND CON/ANAL VAL/FREE UN   SOVEREIGN
20. PAGE 8 B0161
                                                        S59
HARVEY M.F.,"THE PALESTINE REFUGEE PROBLEM: ACT/RES
ELEMENTS OF A SOLUTION." ISLAM LAW INT/ORG DELIB/GP   LEGIT
TOP/EX ECO/TAC ROUTINE DRIVE HEALTH LOVE ORD/FREE   PEACE
PWR WEALTH...MAJORIT FAO 20. PAGE 48 B0964   ISRAEL
                                                        S59
HILSMAN R.,"THE FOREIGN-POLICY CONSENSUS: AN   PROB/SOLV
INTERIM RESEARCH REPORT." USA+45 INT/ORG LEGIS   NAT/G
TEC/DEV EXEC WAR CONSEN KNOWL...DECISION COLD/WAR.   DELIB/GP
PAGE 50 B1013   DIPLOM
                                                        S59
HOFFMANN S.,"IMPLEMENTATION OF INTERNATIONAL   INT/ORG
INSTRUMENTS ON HUMAN RIGHTS." WOR+45 VOL/ASSN   MORAL
DELIB/GP JUDGE EDU/PROP LEGIT ROUTINE PEACE
COLD/WAR 20. PAGE 51 B1029
                                                        S59
LASSWELL H.D.,"UNIVERSALITY IN PERSPECTIVE." FUT   INT/ORG
UNIV SOCIETY CONSULT TOP/EX PLAN EDU/PROP ADJUD   JURID
ROUTINE ARMS/CONT COERCE PEACE ATTIT PERSON   TOTALISM
ALL/VALS. PAGE 63 B1271
                                                        S59
LENGYEL P.,"SOME TRENDS IN THE INTERNATIONAL CIVIL   ADMIN
SERVICE." FUT WOR+45 INT/ORG CONSULT ATTIT...MGT   EXEC
OBS TREND CON/ANAL LEAGUE/NAT UNESCO 20. PAGE 64
B1291
                                                        S59
PADELFORD N.J.,"REGIONAL COOPERATION IN THE SOUTH   INT/ORG
PACIFIC: THE SOUTH PACIFIC COMMISSION." FUT   ADMIN
NEW/ZEALND UK WOR+45 CULTURE ECO/UNDEV LOC/G
VOL/ASSN...OBS CON/ANAL UNESCO VAL/FREE AUSTRAL 20.
PAGE 80 B1622
                                                        S59
SOHN L.B.,"THE DEFINITION OF AGGRESSION." FUT LAW   INT/ORG
FORCES LEGIT ADJUD ROUTINE COERCE ORD/FREE PWR   CT/SYS
...MAJORIT JURID QUANT COLD/WAR 20. PAGE 99 B1995   DETER
                                                     SOVEREIGN
                                                        S59
STOESSINGER J.G.,"THE INTERNATIONAL ATOMIC ENERGY   INT/ORG
AGENCY: THE FIRST PHASE." FUT WOR+45 NAT/G VOL/ASSN   ECO/DEV
DELIB/GP BAL/PWR LEGIT ADMIN ROUTINE PWR...OBS   FOR/AID
CON/ANAL GEN/LAWS VAL/FREE 20 IAEA. PAGE 101 B2040   NUC/PWR
                                                        S59
SUTTON F.X.,"REPRESENTATION AND THE NATURE OF   NAT/G
POLITICAL SYSTEMS." UNIV WOR-45 CULTURE SOCIETY   CONCPT
STRATA INT/ORG FORCES JUDGE DOMIN LEGIT EXEC REGION
REPRESENT ATTIT ORD/FREE RESPECT...SOC HIST/WRIT
TIME/SEQ. PAGE 102 B2057
                                                        S59
ZAUBERMAN A.,"SOVIET BLOC ECONOMIC INTEGRATION."   MARKET
COM CULTURE INTELL ECO/DEV INDUS TOP/EX ACT/RES   INT/ORG
PLAN ECO/TAC INT/TRADE ROUTINE CHOOSE ATTIT   USSR
...TIME/SEQ 20. PAGE 119 B2399   TOTALISM
                                                        B60
ASPREMONT-LYNDEN H.,RAPPORT SUR L'ADMINISTRATION   AFR
BELGE DU RUANDA-URUNDI PENDANT L'ANNEE 1959.   COLONIAL
BELGIUM RWANDA AGRI INDUS DIPLOM ECO/TAC INT/TRADE   ECO/UNDEV
DOMIN ADMIN RACE/REL...GEOG CENSUS 20 UN. PAGE 7   INT/ORG
B0143
                                                        B60
BROOKINGS INSTITUTION,UNITED STATES FOREIGN POLICY: DIPLOM
STUDY NO 9: THE FORMULATION AND ADMINISTRATION OF   INT/ORG
UNITED STATES FOREIGN POLICY. USA+45 WOR+45   CREATE
EX/STRUC LEGIS BAL/PWR FOR/AID EDU/PROP CIVMIL/REL
GOV/REL...INT COLD/WAR. PAGE 16 B0317
                                                        B60
HYDE L.K.G.,THE US AND THE UN. WOR+45 STRUCT   USA+45
ECO/DEV ECO/UNDEV NAT/G ACT/RES PLAN DIPLOM   INT/ORG
EDU/PROP ADMIN ALL/VALS...CONCPT TIME/SEQ GEN/LAWS   FOR/AID
UN VAL/FREE 20. PAGE 53 B1070
                                                        B60
LERNER A.P.,THE ECONOMICS OF CONTROL. USA+45   ECO/DEV
ECO/UNDEV INT/ORG ACT/RES PLAN CAP/ISM INT/TRADE   ROUTINE
ATTIT WEALTH...SOC MATH STAT GEN/LAWS INDEX 20.   ECO/TAC
PAGE 64 B1295   SOCISM
                                                        B60
LINDSAY K.,EUROPEAN ASSEMBLIES: THE EXPERIMENTAL   VOL/ASSN
PERIOD 1949-1959. EUR+WWI ECO/DEV NAT/G POL/PAR   INT/ORG

LEGIS TOP/EX ACT/RES PLAN ECO/TAC DOMIN LEGIT   REGION
ROUTINE ATTIT DRIVE ORD/FREE PWR SKILL...SOC CONCPT
TREND CHARTS GEN/LAWS VAL/FREE. PAGE 65 B1315
                                                        B60
MUNRO L.,UNITED NATIONS, HOPE FOR A DIVIDED WORLD.   INT/ORG
FUT WOR+45 CONSTN DELIB/GP CREATE TEC/DEV DIPLOM   ROUTINE
EDU/PROP LEGIT PEACE ATTIT HEALTH ORD/FREE PWR
...CONCPT TREND UN VAL/FREE 20. PAGE 76 B1540
                                                        B60
RAO V.K.R.,INTERNATIONAL AID FOR ECONOMIC   FOR/AID
DEVELOPMENT - POSSIBILITIES AND LIMITATIONS. FINAN   DIPLOM
PLAN TEC/DEV ADMIN TASK EFFICIENCY...POLICY SOC   INT/ORG
METH/CNCPT CHARTS 20 UN. PAGE 86 B1734   ECO/UNDEV
                                                        B60
ROBINSON E.A.G.,ECONOMIC CONSEQUENCES OF THE SIZE   CONCPT
OF NATIONS. AGRI INDUS DELIB/GP FOR/AID ADMIN   INT/ORG
EFFICIENCY...METH/COMP 20. PAGE 89 B1799   NAT/COMP
                                                        B60
STANFORD RESEARCH INSTITUTE,AFRICAN DEVELOPMENT: A   FOR/AID
TEST FOR INTERNATIONAL COOPERATION. AFR USA+45   ECO/UNDEV
WOR+45 FINAN INT/ORG PLAN PROB/SOLV ECO/TAC   ATTIT
INT/TRADE ADMIN...CHARTS 20. PAGE 100 B2018   DIPLOM
                                                        B60
WHEARE K.C.,THE CONSTITUTIONAL STRUCTURE OF THE   CONSTN
COMMONWEALTH. UK EX/STRUC DIPLOM DOMIN ADMIN   INT/ORG
COLONIAL CONTROL LEAD INGP/REL SUPEGO 20 CMN/WLTH.   VOL/ASSN
PAGE 115 B2330   SOVEREIGN
                                                        L60
BRENNAN D.G.,"SETTING AND GOALS OF ARMS CONTROL."   FORCES
FUT USA+45 USSR WOR+45 INTELL INT/ORG NAT/G   COERCE
VOL/ASSN CONSULT PLAN DIPLOM ECO/TAC ADMIN KNOWL   ARMS/CONT
PWR...POLICY CONCPT TREND COLD/WAR 20. PAGE 15   DETER
B0305
                                                        L60
DEAN A.W.,"SECOND GENEVA CONFERENCE OF THE LAW OF   INT/ORG
THE SEA: THE FIGHT FOR FREEDOM OF THE SEAS." FUT   JURID
USA+45 USSR WOR+45 WOR-45 SEA CONSTN STRUCT PLAN   INT/LAW
INT/TRADE ADJUD ADMIN ORD/FREE...DECISION RECORD
TREND GEN/LAWS 20 TREATY. PAGE 28 B0564
                                                        S60
BOGARDUS E.S.,"THE SOCIOLOGY OF A STRUCTURED   INT/ORG
PEACE." FUT SOCIETY CREATE DIPLOM EDU/PROP ADJUD   SOC
ROUTINE ATTIT RIGID/FLEX KNOWL ORD/FREE RESPECT   NAT/LISM
...POLICY INT/LAW JURID NEW/IDEA SELF/OBS TOT/POP   PEACE
20 UN. PAGE 13 B0264
                                                        S60
HERRERA F.,"THE INTER-AMERICAN DEVELOPMENT BANK."   L/A+17C
USA+45 ECO/UNDEV INT/ORG CONSULT DELIB/GP PLAN   FINAN
ECO/TAC INT/TRADE ROUTINE WEALTH...STAT 20. PAGE 49   FOR/AID
B0994   REGION
                                                        S60
MODELSKI G.,"AUSTRALIA AND SEATO." S/ASIA USA+45   INT/ORG
CULTURE INTELL ECO/DEV NAT/G PLAN DIPLOM ADMIN   ACT/RES
ROUTINE ATTIT SKILL...MGT TIME/SEQ AUSTRAL 20
SEATO. PAGE 74 B1493
                                                        S60
MORA J.A.,"THE ORGANIZATION OF AMERICAN STATES."   L/A+17C
USA+45 LAW ECO/UNDEV VOL/ASSN DELIB/GP PLAN BAL/PWR   INT/ORG
EDU/PROP ADMIN DRIVE RIGID/FLEX ORD/FREE WEALTH   REGION
...TIME/SEQ GEN/LAWS OAS 20. PAGE 75 B1518
                                                        S60
RIESELBACH Z.N.,"QUANTITATIVE TECHNIQUES FOR   QUANT
STUDYING VOTING BEHAVIOR IN THE UNITED NATIONS   CHOOSE
GENERAL ASSEMBLY." FUT S/ASIA USA+45 INT/ORG
BAL/PWR DIPLOM ECO/TAC FOR/AID ADMIN PWR...POLICY
METH/CNCPT METH UN 20. PAGE 88 B1783
                                                        S60
SCHACHTER O.,"THE ENFORCEMENT OF INTERNATIONAL   INT/ORG
JUDICIAL AND ARBITRAL DECISIONS." WOR+45 NAT/G   ADJUD
ECO/TAC DOMIN LEGIT ROUTINE COERCE ATTIT DRIVE   INT/LAW
ALL/VALS PWR...METH/CNCPT TREND TOT/POP 20 UN.
PAGE 93 B1878
                                                        S60
THOMPSON K.W.,"MORAL PURPOSE IN FOREIGN POLICY: MORAL
REALITIES AND ILLUSIONS." WOR+45 WOR-45 LAW CULTURE   JURID
SOCIETY INT/ORG PLAN ADJUD ADMIN COERCE RIGID/FLEX   DIPLOM
SUPEGO KNOWL ORD/FREE PWR...SOC TREND SOC/EXP
TOT/POP 20. PAGE 104 B2104
                                                        B61
BARNES W.,THE FOREIGN SERVICE OF THE UNITED STATES.   NAT/G
USA+45 USA-45 CONSTN INT/ORG POL/PAR CONSULT   MGT
DELIB/GP LEGIS DOMIN EDU/PROP EXEC ATTIT RIGID/FLEX   DIPLOM
ORD/FREE PWR...POLICY CONCPT STAT OBS RECORD BIOG
TIME/SEQ TREND. PAGE 9 B0188
                                                        B61
BISHOP D.G.,THE ADMINISTRATION OF BRITISH FOREIGN   ROUTINE
RELATIONS. EUR+WWI MOD/EUR INT/ORG NAT/G POL/PAR   PWR
DELIB/GP LEGIS TOP/EX ECO/TAC DOMIN EDU/PROP ADMIN   DIPLOM
COERCE 20. PAGE 12 B0243   UK
                                                        B61
HARRISON S.,INDIA AND THE UNITED STATES. FUT S/ASIA   DELIB/GP
USA+45 WOR+45 INTELL ECO/DEV ECO/UNDEV AGRI INDUS   ACT/RES
INT/ORG NAT/G CONSULT EX/STRUC TOP/EX PLAN ECO/TAC   FOR/AID
NEUTRAL ALL/VALS...MGT TOT/POP 20. PAGE 47 B0956   INDIA
                                                        B61
HASAN H.S.,PAKISTAN AND THE UN. ISLAM WOR+45   INT/ORG

ECO/DEV ECO/UNDEV NAT/G TOP/EX ECO/TAC FOR/AID ATTIT
EDU/PROP ADMIN DRIVE PERCEPT...OBS TIME/SEQ UN 20. PAKISTAN
PAGE 48 B0965
B61

MOLLAU G.,INTERNATIONAL COMMUNISM AND WORLD COM
REVOLUTION: HISTORY AND METHODS. RUSSIA USSR REV
INT/ORG NAT/G POL/PAR VOL/ASSN FORCES BAL/PWR
DIPLOM EXEC REGION WAR ATTIT PWR MARXISM...CONCPT
TIME/SEQ COLD/WAR 19/20. PAGE 74 B1498
B61

PEASLEE A.J.,INTERNATIONAL GOVERNMENT INT/ORG
ORGANIZATIONS, CONSTITUTIONAL DOCUMENTS. WOR+45 STRUCT
WOR-45 CONSTN VOL/ASSN DELIB/GP EX/STRUC ROUTINE
KNOWL TOT/POP 20. PAGE 82 B1650
B61

SHAPP W.R.,FIELD ADMINISTRATION IN THE UNITED INT/ORG
NATIONS SYSTEM. FINAN PROB/SOLV INSPECT DIPLOM EXEC ADMIN
REGION ROUTINE EFFICIENCY ROLE...INT CHARTS 20 UN. GP/REL
PAGE 96 B1933 FOR/AID
B61

SHARP W.R.,FIELD ADMINISTRATION IN THE UNITED INT/ORG
NATION SYSTEM: THE CONDUCT OF INTERNATIONAL CONSULT
ECONOMIC AND SOCIAL PROGRAMS. FUT WOR+45 CONSTN
SOCIETY ECO/UNDEV R+D DELIB/GP ACT/RES PLAN TEC/DEV
EDU/PROP EXEC ROUTINE HEALTH WEALTH...HUM CONCPT
CHARTS METH ILO UNESCO VAL/FREE UN 20. PAGE 96
B1939
B61

SINGER J.D.,FINANCING INTERNATIONAL ORGANIZATION: INT/ORG
THE UNITED NATIONS BUDGET PROCESS. WOR+45 FINAN MGT
ACT/RES CREATE PLAN BUDGET ECO/TAC ADMIN ROUTINE
ATTIT KNOWL...DECISION METH/CNCPT TIME/SEQ UN 20.
PAGE 97 B1964
B61

STONE J.,QUEST FOR SURVIVAL. WOR+45 NAT/G VOL/ASSN INT/ORG
LEGIT ADMIN ARMS/CONT COERCE DISPL ORD/FREE PWR ADJUD
...POLICY INT/LAW JURID COLD/WAR 20. PAGE 101 B2047 SOVEREIGN
B61

WILLOUGHBY W.R.,THE ST LAWRENCE WATERWAY: A STUDY LEGIS
IN POLITICS AND DIPLOMACY. USA+45 ECO/DEV COM/IND INT/TRADE
INT/ORG CONSULT DELIB/GP ACT/RES TEC/DEV DIPLOM CANADA
ECO/TAC ROUTINE...TIME/SEQ 20. PAGE 117 B2357 DIST/IND
S61

ALGER C.F.,"NON-RESOLUTION CONSEQUENCES OF THE INT/ORG
UNITED NATIONS AND THEIR EFFECT ON INTERNATIONAL DRIVE
CONFLICT." WOR+45 CONSTN ECO/DEV NAT/G CONSULT BAL/PWR
DELIB/GP TOP/EX ACT/RES PLAN DIPLOM EDU/PROP
ROUTINE ATTIT ALL/VALS...INT/LAW TOT/POP UN 20.
PAGE 4 B0075
S61

ANGLIN D.,"UNITED STATES OPPOSITION TO CANADIAN INT/ORG
MEMBERSHIP IN THE PAN AMERICAN UNION: A CANADIAN CANADA
VIEW." L/A+17C UK USA+45 VOL/ASSN DELIB/GP EX/STRUC
PLAN DIPLOM DOMIN REGION ATTIT RIGID/FLEX PWR
...RELATIV CONCPT STERTYP CMN/WLTH OAS 20. PAGE 5
B0112
S61

CARLETON W.G.,"AMERICAN FOREIGN POLICY: MYTHS AND PLAN
REALITIES." FUT USA+45 WOR+45 ECO/UNDEV INT/ORG MYTH
EX/STRUC ARMS/CONT NUC/PWR WAR ATTIT...POLICY DIPLOM
CONCPT CONT/OBS GEN/METH COLD/WAR TOT/POP 20.
PAGE 19 B0378
S61

HAAS E.B.,"INTERNATIONAL INTEGRATION: THE EUROPEAN INT/ORG
AND THE UNIVERSAL PROCESS." EUR+WWI FUT WOR+45 TREND
NAT/G EX/STRUC ATTIT DRIVE ORD/FREE PWR...CONCPT REGION
GEN/LAWS OEEC 20 NATO COUNCL/EUR. PAGE 45 B0909
S61

JACKSON E.,"CONSTITUTIONAL DEVELOPMENTS OF THE INT/ORG
UNITED NATIONS: ITS GROWTH OF ITS EXECUTIVE EXEC
CAPACITY." FUT WOR+45 CONSTN STRUCT ACT/RES PLAN
ALL/VALS...NEW/IDEA OBS COLD/WAR UN 20. PAGE 55
B1106
S61

JUVILER P.H.,"INTERPARLIAMENTARY CONTACTS IN SOVIET INT/ORG
FOREIGN POLICY." COM FUT WOR+45 WOR-45 SOCIETY DELIB/GP
CONSULT ACT/RES DIPLOM ADMIN PEACE ATTIT RIGID/FLEX USSR
WEALTH...WELF/ST SOC TOT/POP CONGRESS 19/20.
PAGE 57 B1156
S61

LANFALUSSY A.,"EUROPE'S PROGRESS: DUE TO COMMON INT/ORG
MARKET." EUR+WWI ECO/DEV DELIB/GP PLAN ECO/TAC MARKET
ROUTINE WEALTH...GEOG TREND EEC 20. PAGE 62 B1257
S61

LEWY G.,"SUPERIOR ORDERS, NUCLEAR WARFARE AND THE DETER
DICTATES OF CONSCIENCE: THE DILEMMA OF MILITARY INT/ORG
OBEDIENCE IN THE ATOMIC." FUT UNIV WOR+45 INTELL LAW
SOCIETY FORCES TOP/EX ACT/RES ADMIN ROUTINE NUC/PWR INT/LAW
PERCEPT RIGID/FLEX ALL/VALS...POLICY CONCPT 20.
PAGE 65 B1308
S61

MILLER E.,"LEGAL ASPECTS OF UN ACTION IN THE INT/ORG
CONGO." AFR CULTURE ADMIN PEACE DRIVE RIGID/FLEX LEGIT
ORD/FREE...WELF/ST JURID OBS UN CONGO 20. PAGE 73
B1480

TAUBENFELD H.J.,"OUTER SPACE--PAST POLITICS AND PLAN
FUTURE POLICY." FUT USA+45 USA-45 WOR+45 AIR INTELL SPACE
STRUCT ECO/DEV NAT/G TOP/EX ACT/RES ADMIN ROUTINE INT/ORG
NUC/PWR ATTIT DRIVE...CONCPT TIME/SEQ TREND TOT/POP
20. PAGE 103 B2083
S61

VINER J.,"ECONOMIC FOREIGN POLICY ON THE NEW TOP/EX
FRONTIER." USA+45 ECO/UNDEV AGRI FINAN INDUS MARKET ECO/TAC
INT/ORG NAT/G FOR/AID INT/TRADE ADMIN ATTIT PWR 20 BAL/PAY
KENNEDY/JF. PAGE 112 B2262 TARIFFS
S61

VIRALLY M.,"VERS UNE REFORME DU SECRETARIAT DES INT/ORG
NATIONS UNIES." FUT WOR+45 CONSTN ECO/DEV TOP/EX INTELL
BAL/PWR ADMIN ALL/VALS...CONCPT BIOG UN VAL/FREE DIPLOM
20. PAGE 112 B2264
B62

BAILEY S.D.,THE SECRETARIAT OF THE UNITED NATIONS. INT/ORG
FUT WOR+45 DELIB/GP PLAN BAL/PWR DOMIN EDU/PROP EXEC
ADMIN PEACE ATTIT PWR...DECISION CONCPT TREND DIPLOM
CON/ANAL CHARTS UN VAL/FREE COLD/WAR 20. PAGE 8
B0162
B62

BRIMMER B.,A GUIDE TO THE USE OF UNITED NATIONS BIBLIOG/A
DOCUMENTS. WOR+45 ECO/UNDEV AGRI EX/STRUC FORCES INT/ORG
PROB/SOLV ADMIN WAR PEACE WEALTH...POLICY UN. DIPLOM
PAGE 15 B0310
B62

FRIEDMANN W.,METHODS AND POLICIES OF PRINCIPAL INT/ORG
DONOR COUNTRIES IN PUBLIC INTERNATIONAL DEVELOPMENT FOR/AID
FINANCING: PRELIMINARY APPRAISAL. FRANCE GERMANY/W NAT/COMP
UK USA+45 USSR WOR+45 FINAN TEC/DEV CAP/ISM DIPLOM ADMIN
ECO/TAC ATTIT 20 EEC. PAGE 37 B0759
B62

HADWEN J.G.,HOW UNITED NATIONS DECISIONS ARE MADE. INT/ORG
WOR+45 LAW EDU/PROP LEGIT ADMIN PWR...DECISION ROUTINE
SELF/OBS GEN/LAWS UN 20. PAGE 45 B0912
B62

HITCHNER D.G.,MODERN GOVERNMENT: A SURVEY OF CONCPT
POLITICAL SCIENCE. WOR+45 INT/ORG LEGIS ADMIN NAT/G
CT/SYS EXEC CHOOSE TOTALISM POPULISM...INT/LAW STRUCT
PHIL/SCI METH 20. PAGE 50 B1019
B62

KENNEDY J.F.,TO TURN THE TIDE. SPACE AGRI INT/ORG DIPLOM
FORCES TEC/DEV ADMIN NUC/PWR PEACE WEALTH...ANTHOL CHIEF
20 KENNEDY/JF CIV/RIGHTS. PAGE 59 B1193 POLICY
NAT/G
B62

LAWSON R.,INTERNATIONAL REGIONAL ORGANIZATIONS. INT/ORG
WOR+45 NAT/G VOL/ASSN CONSULT EDU/PROP LEGIT DELIB/GP
ADMIN EXEC ROUTINE HEALTH PWR WEALTH...JURID EEC REGION
COLD/WAR 20 UN. PAGE 63 B1277
B62

MULLEY F.W.,THE POLITICS OF WESTERN DEFENSE. INT/ORG
EUR+WWI WOR-45 VOL/ASSN EX/STRUC FORCES DELIB/GP
COERCE DETER PEACE ATTIT ORD/FREE PWR...RECORD NUC/PWR
TIME/SEQ CHARTS COLD/WAR 20 NATO. PAGE 76 B1537
B62

NICHOLAS H.G.,THE UNITED NATIONS AS A POLITICAL INT/ORG
INSTITUTION. WOR+45 CONSTN EX/STRUC ACT/RES LEGIT ROUTINE
PERCEPT KNOWL PWR...CONCPT TIME/SEQ CON/ANAL
ORG/CHARTS UN 20. PAGE 78 B1580
B62

PHILLIPS O.H.,CONSTITUTIONAL AND ADMINISTRATIVE LAW JURID
(3RD ED.). UK INT/ORG LOC/G CHIEF EX/STRUC LEGIS ADMIN
BAL/PWR ADJUD COLONIAL CT/SYS PWR...CHARTS 20. CONSTN
PAGE 83 B1670 NAT/G
B62

UNECA LIBRARY,NEW ACQUISITIONS IN THE UNECA BIBLIOG
LIBRARY. LAW NAT/G PLAN PROB/SOLV TEC/DEV ADMIN AFR
REGION...GEOG SOC 20 UN. PAGE 106 B2152 ECO/UNDEV
INT/ORG
L62

BAILEY S.D.,"THE TROIKA AND THE FUTURE OF THE UN." FUT
CONSTN CREATE LEGIT EXEC CHOOSE ORD/FREE PWR INT/ORG
...CONCPT NEW/IDEA UN COLD/WAR 20. PAGE 8 B0163 USSR
L62

MALINOWSKI W.R.,"CENTRALIZATION AND DE- CREATE
CENTRALIZATION IN THE UNITED NATIONS' ECONOMIC AND GEN/LAWS
SOCIAL ACTIVITIES." WOR+45 CONSTN ECO/UNDEV INT/ORG
VOL/ASSN DELIB/GP ECO/TAC EDU/PROP ADMIN RIGID/FLEX
...OBS CHARTS UNESCO UN EEC OAS OEEC 20. PAGE 69
B1385
S62

ALBONETTI A.,"IL SECONDO PROGRAMMA QUINQUENNALE R+D
1963-67 ED IL BILANCIO RICERCHE ED INVESTIMENTI PER PLAN
IL 1963 DELL'ERATOM." EUR+WWI FUT ITALY WOR+45 NUC/PWR
ECO/DEV SERV/IND INT/ORG TEC/DEV ECO/TAC ATTIT
SKILL WEALTH...MGT TIME/SEQ OEEC 20. PAGE 3 B0069
S62

ALGER C.F.,"THE EXTERNAL BUREAUCRACY IN UNITED ADMIN
STATES FOREIGN AFFAIRS." USA+45 WOR+45 SOCIETY ATTIT
COM/IND INT/ORG NAT/G CONSULT EX/STRUC ACT/RES DIPLOM
...MGT SOC CONCPT TREND 20. PAGE 4 B0076
S62

JACOBSON H.K.,"THE UNITED NATIONS AND COLONIALISM: INT/ORG

A TENTATIVE APPRAISAL." AFR FUT S/ASIA USA+45 USSR   CONCPT
WOR+45 NAT/G DELIB/GP PLAN DIPLOM ECO/TAC DOMIN   COLONIAL
ADMIN ROUTINE COERCE ATTIT RIGID/FLEX ORD/FREE PWR
...OBS STERTYP UN 20. PAGE 55 B1115

                                                        S62
MANGIN G.,"LES ACCORDS DE COOPERATION EN MATIERE DE INT/ORG
JUSTICE ENTRE LA FRANCE ET LES ETATS AFRICAINS ET   LAW
MALGACHE." AFR ISLAM WOR+45 STRUCT ECO/UNDEV NAT/G   FRANCE
DELIB/GP PERCEPT ALL/VALS...JURID MGT TIME/SEQ 20.
PAGE 69 B1386

                                                        S62
NORTH R.C.,"DECISION MAKING IN CRISIS: AN   INT/ORG
INTRODUCTION." WOR+45 WOR-45 NAT/G CONSULT DELIB/GP ROUTINE
TEC/DEV PERCEPT KNOWL...POLICY DECISION PSY   DIPLOM
METH/CNCPT CONT/OBS TREND VAL/FREE 20. PAGE 79
B1590

                                                        S62
PIQUEMAL M.,"LES PROBLEMES DES UNIONS D'ETATS EN   AFR
AFRIQUE NOIRE." FRANCE SOCIETY INT/ORG NAT/G   ECO/UNDEV
DELIB/GP PLAN LEGIT ADMIN COLONIAL ROUTINE ATTIT   REGION
ORD/FREE PWR...GEOG METH/CNCPT 20. PAGE 83 B1678

                                                        S62
SCHILLING W.R.,"SCIENTISTS, FOREIGN POLICY AND   NAT/G
POLITICS." WOR+45 INTELL INT/ORG CONSULT   TEC/DEV
TOP/EX ACT/RES PLAN ADMIN KNOWL...CONCPT OBS TREND   DIPLOM
LEAGUE/NAT 20. PAGE 93 B1889   NUC/PWR

                                                        S62
SPRINGER H.W.,"FEDERATION IN THE CARIBBEAN: AN   VOL/ASSN
ATTEMPT THAT FAILED." L/A+17C ECO/UNDEV INT/ORG   NAT/G
POL/PAR PROVS LEGIS CREATE PLAN FEDERAL ADMIN   REGION
ATTIT DRIVE PERSON ORD/FREE PWR...POLICY GEOG PSY
CONCPT OBS CARIBBEAN CMN/WLTH 20. PAGE 100 B2013

                                                        S62
TATOMIR N.,"ORGANIZATIA INTERNATIONALA A MUNCII: INT/ORG
ASPECTE NOI ALE PROBLEMEI IMBUNATATIRII   INT/TRADE
MECANISMULUI EI." EUR+45 ECO/DEV VOL/ASSN ADMIN
...METH/CNCPT WORK ILO 20. PAGE 103 B2081

                                                        B63
BOISSIER P.,HISTORIE DU COMITE INTERNATIONAL DE LA   INT/ORG
CROIX ROUGE. MOD/EUR WOR+45 CONSULT FORCES PLAN   HEALTH
DIPLOM EDU/PROP ADMIN MORAL ORD/FREE...SOC CONCPT   ARMS/CONT
RECORD TIME/SEQ GEN/LAWS TOT/POP VAL/FREE 19/20.   WAR
PAGE 13 B0267

                                                        B63
BOWETT D.W.,THE LAW OF INTERNATIONAL INSTITUTIONS.   INT/ORG
WOR+45 WOR-45 CONSTN DELIB/GP EX/STRUC JUDGE   ADJUD
EDU/PROP LEGIT CT/SYS EXEC ROUTINE RIGID/FLEX   DIPLOM
ORD/FREE PWR...JURID CONCPT ORG/CHARTS GEN/METH
LEAGUE/NAT OAS OEEC 20 UN. PAGE 14 B0286

                                                        B63
COMISION DE HISTORIO.GUIA DE LOS DOCUMENTOS   BIBLIOG
MICROFOTOGRAFIADOS POR LA UNIDAD MOVIL DE LA   NAT/G
UNESCO. SOCIETY ECO/UNDEV INT/ORG ADMIN...SOC 20   L/A+17C
UNESCO. PAGE 22 B0456   DIPLOM

                                                        B63
DE VRIES E.,SOCIAL ASPECTS OF ECONOMIC DEVELOPMENT   L/A+17C
IN LATIN AMERICA. CULTURE SOCIETY STRATA FINAN   ECO/UNDEV
INDUS INT/ORG DELIB/GP ACT/RES ECO/TAC EDU/PROP
ADMIN ATTIT SUPEGO HEALTH KNOWL ORD/FREE...SOC STAT
TREND ANTHOL TOT/POP VAL/FREE. PAGE 28 B0562

                                                        B63
LANGROD G.,THE INTERNATIONAL CIVIL SERVICE: ITS   INT/ORG
ORIGINS, ITS NATURE, ITS EVALUATION. FUT WOR+45   ADMIN
WOR-45 DELIB/GP ACT/RES DOMIN LEGIT ATTIT
RIGID/FLEX SUPEGO ALL/VALS...MGT CONCPT STAT
TIME/SEQ ILO LEAGUE/NAT VAL/FREE 20 UN. PAGE 62
B1259

                                                        B63
LINDBERG L.,POLITICAL DYNAMICS OF EUROPEAN ECONOMIC MARKET
INTEGRATION. EUR+WWI ECO/DEV INT/ORG VOL/ASSN   ECO/TAC
DELIB/GP ADMIN WEALTH...DECISION EEC 20. PAGE 65
B1313

                                                        B63
MAYNE R.,THE COMMUNITY OF EUROPE. UK CONSTN NAT/G   EUR+WWI
CONSULT DELIB/GP CREATE PLAN ECO/TAC LEGIT ADMIN   INT/ORG
ROUTINE ORD/FREE PWR WEALTH...CONCPT TIME/SEQ EEC   REGION
EURATOM 20. PAGE 71 B1436

                                                        B63
NORTH R.C.,CONTENT ANALYSIS: A HANDBOOK WITH   METH/CNCPT
APPLICATIONS FOR THE STUDY OF INTERNATIONAL CRISIS. COMPUT/IR
ASIA COM EUR+WWI MOD/EUR INT/ORG TEC/DEV DOMIN   USSR
EDU/PROP ROUTINE COERCE PERCEPT RIGID/FLEX ALL/VALS
...QUANT TESTS CON/ANAL SIMUL GEN/LAWS VAL/FREE.
PAGE 79 B1591

                                                        B63
PREST A.R.,PUBLIC FINANCE IN UNDERDEVELOPED   FINAN
COUNTRIES. UK WOR+45 WOR-45 SOCIETY INT/ORG NAT/G   ECO/UNDEV
LEGIS ACT/RES PLAN ECO/TAC ADMIN ROUTINE...CHARTS   NIGERIA
20. PAGE 84 B1702

                                                        B63
ROETTER C.,THE DIPLOMATIC ART. USSR INT/ORG NAT/G   DIPLOM
DELIB/GP ROUTINE NUC/PWR PEACE...POLICY 20. PAGE 90 ELITES
B1812   TOP/EX

                                                        B63
STEVENSON A.E.,LOOKING OUTWARD: YEARS OF CRISIS AT   INT/ORG
THE UNITED NATIONS. COM CUBA USA+45 WOR+45 SOCIETY   CONCPT

NAT/G EX/STRUC ACT/RES LEGIT COLONIAL ATTIT PERSON   ARMS/CONT
SUPEGO ALL/VALS...POLICY HUM UN COLD/WAR CONGO 20.
PAGE 100 B2034

                                                        B63
TUCKER R.C.,THE SOVIET POLITICAL MIND. WOR+45   COM
ELITES INT/ORG NAT/G POL/PAR PLAN DIPLOM ECO/TAC   TOP/EX
DOMIN ADMIN NUC/PWR REV DRIVE PERSON SUPEGO PWR   USSR
WEALTH...POLICY MGT PSY CONCPT OBS BIOG TREND
COLD/WAR MARX/KARL 20. PAGE 106 B2134

                                                        B63
VAN SLYCK P.,PEACE: THE CONTROL OF NATIONAL POWER.   ARMS/CONT
CUBA WOR+45 FINAN NAT/G FORCES PROB/SOLV TEC/DEV   PEACE
BAL/PWR ADMIN CONTROL ORD/FREE...POLICY INT/LAW UN   INT/ORG
COLD/WAR TREATY. PAGE 112 B2253   DIPLOM

                                                        S63
BANFIELD J.,"FEDERATION IN EAST-AFRICA." AFR UGANDA EX/STRUC
ELITES INT/ORG NAT/G VOL/ASSN LEGIS ECO/TAC FEDERAL PWR
ATTIT SOVEREIGN TOT/POP 20 TANGANYIKA. PAGE 9 B0180 REGION

                                                        S63
BECHHOEFER B.G.,"UNITED NATIONS PROCEDURES IN CASE   INT/ORG
OF VIOLATIONS OF DISARMAMENT AGREEMENTS." COM   DELIB/GP
USA+45 USSR LAW CONSTN NAT/G EX/STRUC FORCES LEGIS
BAL/PWR EDU/PROP CT/SYS ARMS/CONT ORD/FREE PWR
...POLICY STERTYP UN VAL/FREE 20. PAGE 10 B0204

                                                        S63
DAVEE R.,"POUR UN FONDS DE DEVELOPPEMENT SOCIAL."   INT/ORG
FUT WOR+45 INTELL SOCIETY ECO/DEV FINAN TEC/DEV   SOC
ROUTINE WEALTH...TREND TOT/POP VAL/FREE UN 20.   FOR/AID
PAGE 26 B0532

                                                        S63
ETIENNE G.,"'LOIS OBJECTIVES' ET PROBLEMES DE   TOTALISM
DEVELOPPEMENT DANS LE CONTEXTE CHINE-URSS." ASIA   USSR
CHINA/COM COM FUT STRUCT INT/ORG VOL/ASSN TOP/EX
TEC/DEV ECO/TAC ATTIT RIGID/FLEX...GEOG MGT
TIME/SEQ TOT/POP 20. PAGE 34 B0682

                                                        S63
EVANS L.H.,"SOME MANAGEMENT PROBLEMS OF UNESCO."   INT/ORG
WOR+45 EX/STRUC LEGIS PWR UNESCO VAL/FREE 20.   MGT
PAGE 34 B0688

                                                        S63
HAVILAND H.F.,"BUILDING A POLITICAL COMMUNITY."   VOL/ASSN
EUR+WWI FUT UK USA+45 ECO/DEV INT/ORG   DIPLOM
NAT/G DELIB/GP BAL/PWR ECO/TAC NEUTRAL ROUTINE
ATTIT PWR WEALTH...CONCPT COLD/WAR TOT/POP 20.
PAGE 48 B0972

                                                        S63
MANGONE G.,"THE UNITED NATIONS AND UNITED STATES   INT/ORG
FOREIGN POLICY." USA+45 WOR+45 ECO/UNDEV NAT/G   ECO/TAC
DIPLOM LEGIT ROUTINE ATTIT DRIVE...TIME/SEQ UN   FOR/AID
COLD/WAR 20. PAGE 69 B1390

                                                        S63
MODELSKI G.,"STUDY OF ALLIANCES." WOR+45 WOR-45   VOL/ASSN
INT/ORG NAT/G FORCES LEGIT ADMIN CHOOSE ALL/VALS   CON/ANAL
PWR SKILL...INT/LAW CONCPT GEN/LAWS 20 TREATY.   DIPLOM
PAGE 74 B1495

                                                        S63
MORGENTHAU H.J.,"THE POLITICAL CONDITIONS FOR AN   INT/ORG
INTERNATIONAL POLICE FORCE." FUT WOR+45 CREATE   FORCES
LEGIT ADMIN PEACE ORD/FREE 20. PAGE 75 B1524   ARMS/CONT
                                                     DETER

                                                        S63
NYE J.S. JR.,"EAST AFRICAN ECONOMIC INTEGRATION."   ECO/UNDEV
AFR UGANDA PROVS DELIB/GP PLAN ECO/TAC INT/TRADE   INT/ORG
ADMIN ROUTINE ORD/FREE PWR WEALTH...OBS TIME/SEQ
VAL/FREE 20. PAGE 79 B1597

                                                        S63
ROUGEMONT D.,"LES NOUVELLES CHANCES DE L'EUROPE."   ECO/UNDEV
EUR+WWI FUT ECO/DEV INT/ORG NAT/G ACT/RES PLAN   PERCEPT
TEC/DEV EDU/PROP ADMIN COLONIAL FEDERAL ATTIT PWR
SKILL...TREND 20. PAGE 91 B1835

                                                        S63
STANLEY T.W.,"DECENTRALIZING NUCLEAR CONTROL IN   INT/ORG
NATO." EUR+WWI USA+45 ELITES FORCES ACT/RES ATTIT   EX/STRUC
ORD/FREE PWR...NEW/IDEA HYPO/EXP TOT/POP 20 NATO.   NUC/PWR
PAGE 100 B2022

                                                        B64
APTER D.E.,IDEOLOGY AND DISCONTENT. FUT WOR+45   ACT/RES
CONSTN CULTURE INTELL SOCIETY STRUCT INT/ORG NAT/G   ATTIT
DELIB/GP LEGIS CREATE PLAN TEC/DEV EDU/PROP EXEC
PERCEPT PERSON RIGID/FLEX ALL/VALS...POLICY
TOT/POP. PAGE 6 B0122

                                                        B64
COTTRELL A.J.,THE POLITICS OF THE ATLANTIC   VOL/ASSN
ALLIANCE. EUR+WWI USA+45 INT/ORG NAT/G DELIB/GP   FORCES
EX/STRUC BAL/PWR DIPLOM REGION DETER ATTIT ORD/FREE
...CONCPT RECORD GEN/LAWS GEN/METH NATO 20. PAGE 24
B0493

                                                        B64
GRZYBOWSKI K.,THE SOCIALIST COMMONWEALTH OF   INT/LAW
NATIONS: ORGANIZATIONS AND INSTITUTIONS. FORCES   COM
DIPLOM INT/TRADE ADJUD ADMIN LEAD WAR MARXISM   REGION
SOCISM...BIBLIOG 20 COMECON WARSAW/P. PAGE 44 B0898 INT/ORG

                                                        B64
HARMON R.B.,BIBLIOGRAPHY OF BIBLIOGRAPHIES IN   BIBLIOG
POLITICAL SCIENCE (MIMEOGRAPHED PAPER: LIMITED   NAT/G
EDITION). WOR+45 WOR-45 INT/ORG POL/PAR GOV/REL   DIPLOM

ALL/IDEOS...INT/LAW JURID MGT 19/20. PAGE 47 B0949 LOC/G

B64

HERSKOVITS M.J.,ECONOMIC TRANSITION IN AFRICA. FUT AFR
INT/ORG NAT/G WORKER PROB/SOLV TEC/DEV INT/TRADE ECO/UNDEV
EQUILIB INCOME...ANTHOL 20. PAGE 49 B0996 PLAN
ADMIN

B64

PLISCHKE E.,SYSTEMS OF INTEGRATING THE INT/ORG
INTERNATIONAL COMMUNITY. WOR+45 NAT/G VOL/ASSN EX/STRUC
ECO/TAC LEGIT PWR WEALTH...TIME/SEQ ANTHOL UN REGION
TOT/POP 20. PAGE 83 B1684

B64

SCHECHTER A.H.,INTERPRETATION OF AMBIGUOUS INT/LAW
DOCUMENTS BY INTERNATIONAL ADMINISTRATIVE DIPLOM
TRIBUNALS. WOR+45 EX/STRUC INT/TRADE CT/SYS INT/ORG
SOVEREIGN 20 UN ILO EURCT/JUST. PAGE 93 B1884 ADJUD

B64

SULLIVAN G.,THE STORY OF THE PEACE CORPS. USA+45 INT/ORG
WOR+45 INTELL FACE/GP NAT/G SCHOOL VOL/ASSN CONSULT ECO/UNDEV
EX/STRUC PLAN EDU/PROP ADMIN ATTIT DRIVE ALL/VALS FOR/AID
...POLICY HEAL SOC CONCPT INT QU BIOG TREND SOC/EXP PEACE
WORK. PAGE 102 B2054

B64

TINBERGEN J.,CENTRAL PLANNING. COM INTELL ECO/DEV PLAN
ECO/UNDEV FINAN INT/ORG PROB/SOLV ECO/TAC CONTROL INDUS
EXEC ROUTINE DECISION. PAGE 104 B2111 MGT
CENTRAL

B64

UN PUB. INFORM. ORGAN.,EVERY MAN'S UNITED NATIONS. INT/ORG
UNIV WOR+45 CONSTN CULTURE SOCIETY ECO/DEV ROUTINE
ECO/UNDEV NAT/G ACT/RES PLAN ECO/TAC INT/TRADE
EDU/PROP LEGIT PEACE ATTIT ALL/VALS...POLICY HUM
INT/LAW CONCPT CHARTS UN TOT/POP 20. PAGE 106 B2150

B64

WAINHOUSE D.W.,REMNANTS OF EMPIRE: THE UNITED INT/ORG
NATIONS AND THE END OF COLONIALISM. FUT PORTUGAL TREND
WOR+45 CONSULT DOMIN LEGIT ADMIN ROUTINE COLONIAL
ATTIT ORD/FREE...POLICY JURID RECORD INT TIME/SEQ
UN CMN/WLTH 20. PAGE 113 B2275

HAAS E.B.,"ECONOMICS AND DIFFERENTIAL PATTERNS OF L/A+17C
POLITICAL INTEGRATION: PROJECTIONS ABOUT UNITY IN INT/ORG
LATIN AMERICA." SOCIETY NAT/G DELIB/GP ACT/RES MARKET
CREATE PLAN ECO/TAC REGION ROUTINE ATTIT DRIVE PWR
WEALTH...CONCPT TREND CHARTS LAFTA 20. PAGE 45
B0910

L64

MILLIS W.,"THE DEMILITARIZED WORLD." COM USA+45 FUT
USSR WOR+45 CONSTN NAT/G EX/STRUC PLAN LEGIT ATTIT INT/ORG
DRIVE...CONCPT TIME/SEQ STERTYP TOT/POP COLD/WAR BAL/PWR
20. PAGE 74 B1486 PEACE

L64

SYMONDS R.,"REFLECTIONS IN LOCALISATION." AFR ADMIN
S/ASIA UK STRATA INT/ORG NAT/G SCHOOL EDU/PROP MGT
LEGIT KNOWL ORD/FREE PWR RESPECT CMN/WLTH 20. COLONIAL
PAGE 102 B2064

L64

WORLD PEACE FOUNDATION,"INTERNATIONAL INT/ORG
ORGANIZATIONS: SUMMARY OF ACTIVITIES." INDIA ROUTINE
PAKISTAN TURKEY WOR+45 CONSTN CONSULT EX/STRUC
ECO/TAC EDU/PROP LEGIT ORD/FREE...JURID SOC UN 20
CYPRESS. PAGE 118 B2375

S64

CARNEGIE ENDOWMENT INT. PEACE,"ADMINISTRATION AND INT/ORG
BUDGET (ISSUES BEFORE THE NINETEENTH GENERAL ADMIN
ASSEMBLY)." WOR+45 FINAN BUDGET ECO/TAC ROUTINE
COST...STAT RECORD UN. PAGE 19 B0383

S64

GROSS J.A.,"WHITEHALL AND THE COMMONWEALTH." EX/STRUC
EUR+WWI MOD/EUR INT/ORG NAT/G CONSULT DELIB/GP ATTIT
LEGIS DOMIN ADMIN COLONIAL ROUTINE PWR CMN/WLTH TREND
19/20. PAGE 44 B0890

S64

HOSCH L.G.,"PUBLIC ADMINISTRATION ON THE INT/ORG
INTERNATIONAL FRONTIER." WOR+45 R+D NAT/G EDU/PROP MGT
EXEC KNOWL ORD/FREE VAL/FREE 20 UN. PAGE 52 B1046

S64

KHAN M.Z.,"THE PRESIDENT OF THE GENERAL ASSEMBLY." INT/ORG
WOR+45 CONSTN DELIB/GP EDU/PROP LEGIT ROUTINE PWR TOP/EX
RESPECT SKILL...DECISION SOC BIOG TREND UN 20.
PAGE 59 B1202

S64

MOWER A.G.,"THE OFFICIAL PRESSURE GROUP OF THE INT/ORG
COUNCIL OF EUROPE'S CONSULATIVE ASSEMBLY." EUR+WWI EDU/PROP
SOCIETY STRUCT FINAN CONSULT ECO/TAC ADMIN ROUTINE
ATTIT PWR WEALTH...STAT CHARTS 20 COUNCL/EUR.
PAGE 76 B1535

S64

SCHWELB E.,"OPERATION OF THE EUROPEAN CONVENTION ON INT/ORG
HUMAN RIGHTS." EUR+WWI LAW SOCIETY CREATE EDU/PROP MORAL
ADJUD ADMIN PEACE ATTIT ORD/FREE PWR...POLICY
INT/LAW CONCPT OBS GEN/LAWS UN VAL/FREE ILO 20
ECHR. PAGE 95 B1916

B65

BARNETT V.M. JR.,THE REPRESENTATION OF THE UNITED USA+45
STATES ABROAD* REVISED EDITION. ECO/UNDEV ACADEM DIPLOM

INT/ORG FORCES ACT/RES CREATE OP/RES FOR/AID REGION ADMIN
CENTRAL...CLASSIF ANTHOL. PAGE 9 B0189

B65

ETZIONI A.,POLITICAL UNIFICATION* A COMPARATIVE INT/ORG
STUDY OF LEADERS AND FORCES. EUR+WWI ISLAM L/A+17C FORCES
WOR+45 ELITES STRATA EXEC WEALTH...TIME/SEQ TREND ECO/TAC
SOC/EXP. PAGE 34 B0686 REGION

B65

FORGAC A.A.,NEW DIPLOMACY AND THE UNITED NATIONS. DIPLOM
FRANCE GERMANY UK USSR INT/ORG DELIB/GP EX/STRUC ETIQUET
PEACE...INT/LAW CONCPT UN. PAGE 36 B0740 NAT/G

B65

GOTLIEB A.,DISARMAMENT AND INTERNATIONAL LAW* A INT/LAW
STUDY OF THE ROLE OF LAW IN THE DISARMAMENT INT/ORG
PROCESS. USA+45 USSR PROB/SOLV CONFER ADMIN ROUTINE ARMS/CONT
NUC/PWR ORD/FREE SOVEREIGN UN TREATY. PAGE 42 B0841 IDEA/COMP

B65

HARMON R.B.,POLITICAL SCIENCE: A BIBLIOGRAPHICAL BIBLIOG
GUIDE TO THE LITERATURE. WOR+45 WOR-45 R+D INT/ORG POL/PAR
LOC/G NAT/G DIPLOM ADMIN...CONCPT METH. PAGE 47 LAW
B0950 GOV/COMP

B65

KASER M.,COMECON* INTEGRATION PROBLEMS OF THE PLAN
PLANNED ECONOMIES. INT/ORG TEC/DEV INT/TRADE PRICE ECO/DEV
ADMIN ADJUST CENTRAL...STAT TIME/SEQ ORG/CHARTS COM
COMECON. PAGE 58 B1177 REGION

B65

KOUSOULAS D.G.,REVOLUTION AND DEFEAT: THE STORY OF REV
THE GREEK COMMUNIST PARTY. GREECE INT/ORG EX/STRUC MARXISM
DIPLOM FOR/AID EDU/PROP PARL/PROC ADJUST ATTIT 20 POL/PAR
COM/PARTY. PAGE 61 B1230 ORD/FREE

B65

LEYS C.T.,FEDERATION IN EAST AFRICA. LAW AGRI FEDERAL
DIST/IND FINAN INT/ORG LABOR INT/TRADE CONFER ADMIN REGION
CONTROL GP/REL...ANTHOL 20 AFRICA/E. PAGE 65 B1310 ECO/UNDEV
PLAN

B65

MACDONALD R.W.,THE LEAGUE OF ARAB STATES: A STUDY ISLAM
IN THE DYNAMICS OF REGIONAL ORGANIZATION. ISRAEL REGION
UAR USSR FINAN INT/ORG DELIB/GP ECO/TAC AGREE DIPLOM
NEUTRAL ORD/FREE PWR...DECISION BIBLIOG 20 TREATY ADMIN
UN. PAGE 67 B1358

B65

SCOTT A.M.,THE REVOLUTION IN STATECRAFT: INFORMAL DIPLOM
PENETRATION. WOR+45 WOR-45 CULTURE INT/ORG FORCES EDU/PROP
ECO/TAC ROUTINE...BIBLIOG 20. PAGE 95 B1918 FOR/AID

B65

SPEECKAERT G.P.,SELECT BIBLIOGRAPHY ON BIBLIOG
INTERNATIONAL ORGANIZATION. 1885-1964. WOR+45 INT/ORG
WOR-45 EX/STRUC DIPLOM ADMIN REGION 19/20 UN. GEN/LAWS
PAGE 99 B2004 STRATA

B65

UNESCO,INTERNATIONAL ORGANIZATIONS IN THE SOCIAL INT/ORG
SCIENCES(REV. ED.). LAW ADMIN ATTIT...CRIMLGY GEOG R+D
INT/LAW PSY SOC STAT 20 UNESCO. PAGE 107 B2157 PROF/ORG
ACT/RES

B65

VONGLAHN G.,LAW AMONG NATIONS: AN INTRODUCTION TO CONSTN
PUBLIC INTERNATIONAL LAW. UNIV WOR+45 LAW INT/ORG JURID
NAT/G LEGIT EXEC RIGID/FLEX...CONCPT TIME/SEQ INT/LAW
GEN/LAWS UN TOT/POP 20. PAGE 112 B2267

L65

RUBIN A.P.,"UNITED STATES CONTEMPORARY PRACTICE LAW
RELATING TO INTERNATIONAL LAW." USA+45 WOR+45 LEGIT
CONSTN INT/ORG NAT/G DELIB/GP EX/STRUC DIPLOM DOMIN INT/LAW
CT/SYS ROUTINE ORD/FREE...CONCPT COLD/WAR 20.
PAGE 91 B1848

S65

BROWN S.,"AN ALTERNATIVE TO THE GRAND DESIGN." VOL/ASSN
EUR+WWI FUT USA+45 INT/ORG NAT/G EX/STRUC FORCES CONCPT
CREATE BAL/PWR DOMIN RIGID/FLEX ORD/FREE PWR DIPLOM
...NEW/IDEA RECORD EEC NATO 20. PAGE 16 B0327

S65

QUADE Q.L.,"THE TRUMAN ADMINISTRATION AND THE USA+45
SEPARATION OF POWERS: THE CASE OF THE MARSHALL ECO/UNDEV
PLAN." SOCIETY INT/ORG NAT/G CONSULT DELIB/GP LEGIS DIPLOM
PLAN ECO/TAC ROUTINE DRIVE PERCEPT RIGID/FLEX
ORD/FREE PWR WEALTH...DECISION GEOG NEW/IDEA TREND
20 TRUMAN/HS. PAGE 85 B1726

B66

ALEXANDER Y.,INTERNATIONAL TECHNICAL ASSISTANCE ECO/TAC
EXPERTS* A CASE STUDY OF THE U.N. EXPERIENCE. INT/ORG
ECO/UNDEV CONSULT EX/STRUC CREATE PLAN DIPLOM ADMIN
FOR/AID TASK EFFICIENCY...ORG/CHARTS UN. PAGE 4 MGT
B0074

B66

BEAUFRE A.,NATO AND EUROPE. WOR+45 PLAN CONFER EXEC INT/ORG
NUC/PWR ATTIT...POLICY 20 NATO EUROPE. PAGE 10 DETER
B0203 DIPLOM
ADMIN

B66

HARMON R.B.,SOURCES AND PROBLEMS OF BIBLIOGRAPHY IN BIBLIOG
POLITICAL SCIENCE (PAMPHLET). INT/ORG LOC/G MUNIC DIPLOM
POL/PAR ADMIN GOV/REL ALL/IDEOS...JURID MGT CONCPT INT/LAW
19/20. PAGE 47 B0951 NAT/G

B66
KIRDAR U.,THE STRUCTURE OF UNITED NATIONS ECONOMIC   INT/ORG
AID TO UNDERDEVELOPED COUNTRIES. AGRI FINAN INDUS   FOR/AID
NAT/G EX/STRUC PLAN GIVE TASK...POLICY 20 UN.   ECO/UNDEV
PAGE 60 B1213   ADMIN

B66
LEE L.T.,VIENNA CONVENTION ON CONSULAR RELATIONS.   AGREE
WOR+45 LAW INT/ORG CONFER GP/REL PRIVIL...INT/LAW   DIPLOM
20 TREATY VIENNA/CNV. PAGE 63 B1279   ADMIN

B66
MARTIN L.W.,DIPLOMACY IN MODERN EUROPEAN HISTORY.   DIPLOM
EUR+WWI MOD/EUR INT/ORG NAT/G EX/STRUC ROUTINE WAR   POLICY
PEACE TOTALISM PWR 15/20 COLD/WAR EUROPE/W. PAGE 70
B1411

B66
OHLIN G.,AID AND INDEBTEDNESS. AUSTRIA FINAN   FOR/AID
INT/ORG PLAN DIPLOM GIVE...POLICY MATH CHARTS 20.   ECO/UNDEV
PAGE 79 B1604   ADMIN
                                                      WEALTH

B66
SAPIN B.M.,THE MAKING OF UNITED STATES FOREIGN   DIPLOM
POLICY. USA+45 INT/ORG DELIB/GP FORCES PLAN ECO/TAC   EX/STRUC
CIVMIL/REL PRESIDENT. PAGE 92 B1868   DECISION
                                                      NAT/G

B66
SPINELLI A.,THE EUROCRATS; CONFLICT AND CRISIS IN   INT/ORG
THE EUROPEAN COMMUNITY (TRANS. BY C. GROVE HAINES).   INGP/REL
EUR+WWI MARKET POL/PAR ECO/TAC PARL/PROC EEC OEEC   CONSTN
ECSC EURATOM. PAGE 99 B2007   ADMIN

B66
WALL E.H.,THE COURT OF JUSTICE IN THE EUROPEAN   CT/SYS
COMMUNITIES: JURISDICTION AND PROCEDURE. EUR+WWI   INT/ORG
DIPLOM ADJUD ADMIN ROUTINE TASK...CONCPT LING 20.   LAW
PAGE 113 B2281   OP/RES

L66
SEYLER W.C.,"DOCTORAL DISSERTATIONS IN POLITICAL   BIBLIOG
SCIENCE IN UNIVERSITIES OF THE UNITED STATES AND   LAW
CANADA." INT/ORG LOC/G ADMIN...INT/LAW MGT   NAT/G
GOV/COMP. PAGE 96 B1930

B67
DE BLIJ H.J.,SYSTEMATIC POLITICAL GEOGRAPHY. WOR+45   GEOG
STRUCT INT/ORG NAT/G EDU/PROP ADMIN COLONIAL   CONCPT
ROUTINE ORD/FREE PWR...IDEA/COMP T 20. PAGE 27   METH
B0550

B67
HIRSCHMAN A.O.,DEVELOPMENT PROJECTS OBSERVED. INDUS   ECO/UNDEV
INT/ORG CONSULT EX/STRUC CREATE OP/RES ECO/TAC   R+D
DEMAND...POLICY MGT METH/COMP 20 WORLD/BANK.   FINAN
PAGE 50 B1016   PLAN

B67
OVERSEAS DEVELOPMENT INSTIT,EFFECTIVE AID. WOR+45   FOR/AID
INT/ORG TEC/DEV DIPLOM INT/TRADE ADMIN. PAGE 80   ECO/UNDEV
B1619   ECO/TAC
                                                      NAT/COMP

B67
PLANO J.C.,FORGING WORLD ORDER: THE POLITICS OF   INT/ORG
INTERNATIONAL ORGANIZATION. PROB/SOLV DIPLOM   ADMIN
CONTROL CENTRAL RATIONAL ORD/FREE...INT/LAW CHARTS   JURID
BIBLIOG 20 UN LEAGUE/NAT. PAGE 83 B1679

B67
SABLE M.H.,A GUIDE TO LATIN AMERICAN STUDIES (2   BIBLIOG/A
VOLS). CONSTN FINAN INT/ORG LABOR MUNIC POL/PAR   L/A+17C
FORCES CAP/ISM FOR/AID ADMIN MARXISM SOCISM OAS.   DIPLOM
PAGE 92 B1861   NAT/LISM

B67
SCHEINMAN L.,EURATOM* NUCLEAR INTEGRATION IN   INT/ORG
EUROPE. EX/STRUC LEAD 20 EURATOM. PAGE 93 B1885   NAT/LISM
                                                      NUC/PWR
                                                      DIPLOM

B67
UNITED NATIONS,UNITED NATIONS PUBLICATIONS: BIBLIOG/A
1945-1966. WOR+45 COM/IND DIST/IND FINAN TEC/DEV   INT/ORG
ADMIN...POLICY INT/LAW MGT CHARTS 20 UN UNESCO.   DIPLOM
PAGE 107 B2162   WRITING

B67
WATERS M.,THE UNITED NATIONS* INTERNATIONAL   CONSTN
ORGANIZATION AND ADMINISTRATION. WOR+45 EX/STRUC   INT/ORG
FORCES DIPLOM LEAD REGION ARMS/CONT REPRESENT   ADMIN
INGP/REL ROLE...METH/COMP ANTHOL 20 UN LEAGUE/NAT.   ADJUD
PAGE 114 B2301

L67
CAHIERS P.,"LE RECOURS EN CONSTATATION DE   INT/ORG
MANQUEMENTS DES ETATS MEMBRES DEVANT LA COUR DES   CONSTN
COMMUNAUTES EUROPEENNES." LAW PROB/SOLV DIPLOM   ROUTINE
ADMIN CT/SYS SANCTION ATTIT...POLICY DECISION JURID   ADJUD
ECSC EEC. PAGE 18 B0362

L67
COHEN M.,"THE DEMISE OF UNEF." CONSTN DIPLOM ADMIN   INT/ORG
AGREE LEAD COERCE 20 UNEF U/THANT HAMMARSK/D.   FORCES
PAGE 22 B0445   PEACE
                                                      POLICY

S67
MERON T.,"THE UN'S 'COMMON SYSTEM' OF SALARY,   ADMIN
ALLOWANCE, AND BENEFITS: CRITICAL APPR'SAL OF COORD   EX/STRUC
IN PERSONNEL MATTERS." VOL/ASSN PAY EFFICIENCY   INT/ORG
...CHARTS 20 UN. PAGE 73 B1470   BUDGET

S67
SATHYAMURTHY T.V.,"TWENTY YEARS OF UNESCO: AN   ADMIN
INTERPRETATION." SOCIETY PROB/SOLV LEAD PEACE   CONSTN
UNESCO. PAGE 92 B1870   INT/ORG
                                                      TIME/SEQ

S67
TACKABERRY R.B.,"ORGANIZING AND TRAINING PEACE-   PEACE
KEEPING FORCES* THE CANADIAN VIEW." CANADA PLAN   FORCES
DIPLOM CONFER ADJUD ADMIN CIVMIL/REL 20 UN.   INT/ORG
PAGE 102 B2069   CONSULT

S67
TOURNELLE G.,"DIPLOMATIE D' HIER ET D'AUJOURD'   DIPLOM
HUI." CONFER ADMIN ROUTINE PEACE. PAGE 105 B2123   ROLE
                                                      INT/ORG

S67
WEIL G.L.,"THE MERGER OF THE INSTITUTIONS OF THE   ECO/TAC
EUROPEAN COMMUNITIES" EUR+WWI ECO/DEV INT/TRADE   INT/ORG
CONSEN PLURISM...DECISION MGT 20 EEC EURATOM ECSC   CENTRAL
TREATY. PAGE 115 B2313   INT/LAW

N67
US SENATE COMM ON FOREIGN REL,THE UNITED NATIONS AT   INT/ORG
TWENTY-ONE (PAMPHLET). WOR+45 BUDGET ADMIN SENATE   DIPLOM
UN. PAGE 110 B2223   PEACE

N67
US SENATE COMM ON FOREIGN REL,THE UNITED NATIONS   INT/ORG
PEACEKEEPING DILEMMA (PAMPHLET). ISLAM WOR+45   DIPLOM
PROB/SOLV BUDGET ADMIN SENATE UN. PAGE 110 B2224   PEACE

INT/REL....INTERNATIONAL RELATIONS

INT/TRADE....INTERNATIONAL TRADE

N
INTERNATIONAL BIBLIOGRAPHY OF ECONOMICS. WOR+45   BIBLIOG
FINAN MARKET ADMIN DEMAND INCOME PRODUC...POLICY   ECO/DEV
IDEA/COMP METH. PAGE 1 B0003   ECO/UNDEV
                                                      INT/TRADE

N
KYRIAK T.E.,EAST EUROPE: BIBLIOGRAPHY--INDEX TO US   BIBLIOG/A
JPRS RESEARCH TRANSLATIONS. ALBANIA BULGARIA COM   PRESS
CZECHOSLVK HUNGARY POLAND ROMANIA AGRI EXTR/IND   MARXISM
FINAN SERV/IND INT/TRADE WEAPON...GEOG MGT SOC 20.   INDUS
PAGE 62 B1247

N
US SUPERINTENDENT OF DOCUMENTS,TARIFF AND TAXATION   BIBLIOG/A
(PRICE LIST 37). USA+45 LAW INT/TRADE ADJUD ADMIN   TAX
CT/SYS INCOME OWN...DECISION GATT. PAGE 111 B2242   TARIFFS
                                                      NAT/G

N
WORLD PEACE FOUNDATION,DOCUMENTS OF INTERNATIONAL   BIBLIOG
ORGANIZATIONS: A SELECTED BIBLIOGRAPHY. WOR+45   DIPLOM
WOR-45 AGRI FINAN ACT/RES OP/RES INT/TRADE ADMIN   INT/ORG
...CON/ANAL 20 UN UNESCO LEAGUE/NAT. PAGE 118 B2374   REGION

B37
ROBBINS L.,ECONOMIC PLANNING AND INTERNATIONAL   INT/ORG
ORDER. WOR+45 SOCIETY FINAN INDUS NAT/G ECO/TAC   PLAN
ROUTINE WEALTH...SOC TIME/SEQ GEN/METH WORK 20   INT/TRADE
KEYNES/JM. PAGE 89 B1791

B38
DAY C.,A HISTORY OF COMMERCE. CHRIST-17C EUR+WWI   MARKET
ISLAM MEDIT-7 MOD/EUR USA+45 ECO/DEV FINAN NAT/G   INT/TRADE
ECO/TAC EXEC ROUTINE PWR WEALTH HIST/WRIT. PAGE 27
B0546

B38
HARPER S.N.,THE GOVERNMENT OF THE SOVIET UNION. COM   MARXISM
USSR LAW CONSTN ECO/DEV PLAN TEC/DEV DIPLOM   NAT/G
INT/TRADE ADMIN REV NAT/LISM...POLICY 20. PAGE 47   LEAD
B0952   POL/PAR

B38
LANGE O.,ON THE ECONOMIC THEORY OF SOCIALISM. UNIV   MARKET
ECO/DEV FINAN INDUS INT/ORG PUB/INST ROUTINE ATTIT   ECO/TAC
ALL/VALS...SOC CONCPT STAT TREND 20. PAGE 62 B1258   INT/TRADE
                                                      SOCISM

B39
ZIMMERN A.,MODERN POLITICAL DOCTRINE. WOR-45   NAT/G
CULTURE SOCIETY ECO/UNDEV DELIB/GP EX/STRUC CREATE   ECO/TAC
DOMIN COERCE NAT/LISM ATTIT RIGID/FLEX ORD/FREE PWR   BAL/PWR
WEALTH...POLICY CONCPT OBS TIME/SEQ TREND TOT/POP   INT/TRADE
LEAGUE/NAT 20. PAGE 119 B2402

C40
FAHS C.B.,"GOVERNMENT IN JAPAN." FINAN FORCES LEGIS   ASIA
TOP/EX BUDGET INT/TRADE EDU/PROP SOVEREIGN   DIPLOM
...CON/ANAL BIBLIOG/A 20 CHINJAP. PAGE 34 B0698   NAT/G
                                                      ADMIN

B47
CONOVER H.F.,NON-SELF-GOVERNING AREAS. BELGIUM   BIBLIOG/A
FRANCE ITALY UK WOR+45 CULTURE ECO/UNDEV INT/ORG   COLONIAL
LOC/G NAT/G ECO/TAC INT/TRADE ADMIN HEALTH...SOC   DIPLOM
UN. PAGE 23 B0465

B48
HOOVER E.M.,THE LOCATION OF ECONOMIC ACTIVITY.   HABITAT
WOR+45 MARKET MUNIC WORKER PROB/SOLV INT/TRADE   INDUS
ADMIN COST...POLICY CHARTS T 20. PAGE 51 B1041   ECO/TAC
                                                      GEOG

B50
MCCAMY J.,THE ADMINISTRATION OF AMERICAN FOREIGN   EXEC

AFFAIRS. USA+45 SOCIETY INT/ORG NAT/G ACT/RES PLAN INT/TRADE EDU/PROP ADJUD ALL/VALS...METH/CNCPT TIME/SEQ CONGRESS 20. PAGE 71 B1441
STRUCT DIPLOM

B50
PERHAM M.,COLONIAL GOVERNMENT: ANNOTATED READING LIST ON BRITISH COLONIAL GOVERNMENT. UK WOR+45 WOR-45 ECO/UNDEV INT/ORG LEGIS FOR/AID INT/TRADE DOMIN ADMIN REV 20. PAGE 82 B1655
BIBLIOG/A COLONIAL GOV/REL NAT/G

B50
WELCH S.R.,PORTUGUESE RULE AND SPANISH CROWN IN SOUTH AFRICA 1581-1640. PORTUGAL SOUTH/AFR SPAIN SOCIETY KIN NEIGH SECT INT/TRADE ADMIN 16/17 MISSION. PAGE 115 B2317
DIPLOM COLONIAL WAR PEACE

B51
UNESCO,REPERTOIRE DES BIBLIOTHEQUES DE FRANCE: CENTRES ET SERVICES DE DOCUMENTATION DE FRANCE. FRANCE INDUS ACADEM NAT/G INT/TRADE 20 UNESCO. PAGE 107 B2154
BIBLIOG ADMIN

B51
US TARIFF COMMISSION,LIST OF PUBLICATIONS OF THE TARIFF COMMISSION (PAMPHLET). USA+45 USA-45 AGRI EXTR/IND INDUS INT/TRADE...STAT 20. PAGE 111 B2245
BIBLIOG TARIFFS NAT/G ADMIN

B53
MACK R.T.,RAISING THE WORLDS STANDARD OF LIVING. IRAN INT/ORG VOL/ASSN EX/STRUC ECO/TAC WEALTH...MGT METH/CNCPT STAT CONT/OBS INT TOT/POP VAL/FREE 20 UN. PAGE 67 B1363
WOR+45 FOR/AID INT/TRADE

S53
BLOUGH R.,"THE ROLE OF THE ECONOMIST IN FEDERAL POLICY MAKING." USA+45 ELITES INTELL ECO/DEV NAT/G CONSULT EX/STRUC ACT/RES PLAN INT/TRADE BAL/PAY WEALTH...POLICY CONGRESS 20. PAGE 13 B0256
DELIB/GP ECO/TAC

B54
BINANI G.D.,INDIA AT A GLANCE (REV. ED.). INDIA COM/IND FINAN INDUS LABOR PROVS SCHOOL PLAN DIPLOM INT/TRADE ADMIN...JURID 20. PAGE 12 B0238
INDEX CON/ANAL NAT/G ECO/UNDEV

L55
KISER M.,"ORGANIZATION OF AMERICAN STATES." L/A+17C USA+45 ECO/UNDEV INT/ORG NAT/G PLAN TEC/DEV DIPLOM ECO/TAC INT/TRADE EDU/PROP ADMIN ALL/VALS...POLICY MGT RECORD ORG/CHARTS OAS 20. PAGE 60 B1215
VOL/ASSN ECO/DEV REGION

B56
GARDNER R.N.,STERLING-DOLLAR DIPLOMACY. EUR+WWI USA+45 INT/ORG NAT/G PLAN INT/TRADE EDU/PROP ADMIN KNOWL PWR WEALTH...POLICY SOC METH/CNCPT STAT CHARTS SIMUL GEN/LAWS 20. PAGE 39 B0781
ECO/DEV DIPLOM

B58
ATOMIC INDUSTRIAL FORUM,MANAGEMENT AND ATOMIC ENERGY. WOR+45 SEA LAW MARKET NAT/G TEC/DEV INSPECT INT/TRADE CONFER PEACE HEALTH...ANTHOL 20. PAGE 7 B0145
NUC/PWR INDUS MGT ECO/TAC

B58
CHANG C.,THE INFLATIONARY SPIRAL: THE EXPERIENCE IN CHINA 1939-50. CHINA/COM BUDGET INT/TRADE PRICE ADMIN CONTROL WAR DEMAND...POLICY CHARTS 20. PAGE 20 B0406
FINAN ECO/TAC BAL/PAY GOV/REL

B58
SHAW S.J.,THE FINANCIAL AND ADMINISTRATIVE ORGANIZATION AND DEVELOPMENT OF OTTOMAN EGYPT 1517-1798. UAR LOC/G FORCES BUDGET INT/TRADE TAX EATING INCOME WEALTH...CHARTS BIBLIOG 16/18 OTTOMAN NAPOLEON/B. PAGE 96 B1940
FINAN ADMIN GOV/REL CULTURE

B58
US HOUSE COMM ON COMMERCE,ADMINISTRATIVE PROCESS AND ETHICAL QUESTIONS. USA+45 LAW LEGIS INT/TRADE CONTROL 20 CONGRESS. PAGE 109 B2192
POLICY ADMIN DELIB/GP ADJUD

B59
DIEBOLD W. JR.,THE SCHUMAN PLAN: A STUDY IN ECONOMIC COOPERATION, 1950-1959. EUR+WWI FRANCE GERMANY USA+45 EXTR/IND CONSULT DELIB/GP PLAN DIPLOM ECO/TAC INT/TRADE ROUTINE ORD/FREE WEALTH ...METH/CNCPT STAT CONT/OBS INT TIME/SEQ ECSC 20. PAGE 29 B0591
INT/ORG REGION

B59
FAYERWEATHER J.,THE EXECUTIVE OVERSEAS: ADMINISTRATIVE ATTITUDES AND RELATIONSHIPS IN A FOREIGN CULTURE. USA+45 WOR+45 CULTURE LG/CO SML/CO ATTIT...MGT PERS/COMP 20 MEXIC/AMER. PAGE 35 B0709
INT/TRADE TOP/EX NAT/COMP PERS/REL

B59
WELTON H.,THE THIRD WORLD WAR; TRADE AND INDUSTRY, THE NEW BATTLEGROUND. WOR+45 ECO/DEV INDUS MARKET TASK...MGT IDEA/COMP COLD/WAR. PAGE 115 B2321
INT/TRADE PLAN DIPLOM

S59
ZAUBERMAN A.,"SOVIET BLOC ECONOMIC INTEGRATION." COM CULTURE INTELL ECO/DEV INDUS TOP/EX ACT/RES PLAN ECO/TAC INT/TRADE ROUTINE CHOOSE ATTIT ...TIME/SEQ 20. PAGE 119 B2399
MARKET INT/ORG USSR TOTALISM

B60
ASPREMONT-LYNDEN H.,RAPPORT SUR L'ADMINISTRATION BELGE DU RUANDA-URUNDI PENDANT L'ANNEE 1959. BELGIUM RWANDA AGRI INDUS DIPLOM ECO/TAC INT/TRADE DOMIN ADMIN RACE/REL...GEOG CENSUS 20 UN. PAGE 7 B0143
AFR COLONIAL ECO/UNDEV INT/ORG

B60
LERNER A.P.,THE ECONOMICS OF CONTROL. USA+45 ECO/UNDEV INT/ORG ACT/RES PLAN CAP/ISM INT/TRADE ATTIT WEALTH...SOC MATH STAT GEN/LAWS INDEX 20. PAGE 64 B1295
ECO/DEV ROUTINE ECO/TAC SOCISM

B60
LEWIS P.R.,LITERATURE OF THE SOCIAL SCIENCES: AN INTRODUCTORY SURVEY AND GUIDE. UK LAW INDUS DIPLOM INT/TRADE ADMIN...MGT 19/20. PAGE 65 B1306
BIBLIOG/A SOC

B60
PENTONY D.E.,UNITED STATES FOREIGN AID. INDIA LAOS USA+45 ECO/UNDEV INT/TRADE ADMIN PEACE ATTIT ...POLICY METH/COMP ANTHOL 20. PAGE 82 B1653
FOR/AID DIPLOM ECO/TAC

B60
STANFORD RESEARCH INSTITUTE,AFRICAN DEVELOPMENT: A TEST FOR INTERNATIONAL COOPERATION. AFR USA+45 WOR+45 FINAN INT/ORG PLAN PROB/SOLV ECO/TAC INT/TRADE ADMIN...CHARTS 20. PAGE 100 B2018
FOR/AID ECO/UNDEV ATTIT DIPLOM

L60
DEAN A.W.,"SECOND GENEVA CONFERENCE OF THE LAW OF THE SEA: THE FIGHT FOR FREEDOM OF THE SEAS." FUT USA+45 USSR WOR+45 WOR-45 SEA CONSTN STRUCT PLAN INT/TRADE ADJUD ADMIN ORD/FREE...DECISION RECORD TREND GEN/LAWS 20 TREATY. PAGE 28 B0564
INT/ORG JURID INT/LAW

S60
"THE EMERGING COMMON MARKETS IN LATIN AMERICA." FUT L/A+17C STRATA DIST/IND INDUS LABOR NAT/G LEGIS ECO/TAC ADMIN RIGID/FLEX HEALTH...NEW/IDEA TIME/SEQ OAS 20. PAGE 2 B0039
FINAN ECO/UNDEV INT/TRADE

S60
FRANKEL S.H.,"ECONOMIC ASPECTS OF POLITICAL INDEPENDENCE IN AFRICA." AFR FUT SOCIETY ECO/UNDEV COM/IND FINAN LEGIS PLAN TEC/DEV CAP/ISM ECO/TAC INT/TRADE ADMIN ATTIT DRIVE RIGID/FLEX PWR WEALTH ...MGT NEW/IDEA MATH TIME/SEQ VAL/FREE 20. PAGE 37 B0751
NAT/G FOR/AID

S60
GARNICK D.H.,"ON THE ECONOMIC FEASIBILITY OF A MIDDLE EASTERN COMMON MARKET." AFR ISLAM CULTURE INDUS NAT/G PLAN TEC/DEV ECO/TAC ADMIN ATTIT DRIVE RIGID/FLEX...PLURIST STAT TREND GEN/LAWS 20. PAGE 39 B0784
MARKET INT/TRADE

S60
HERRERA F.,"THE INTER-AMERICAN DEVELOPMENT BANK." USA+45 ECO/UNDEV INT/ORG CONSULT DELIB/GP PLAN ECO/TAC INT/TRADE ROUTINE WEALTH...STAT 20. PAGE 49 B0994
L/A+17C FINAN FOR/AID REGION

S60
MORALES C.J.,"TRADE AND ECONOMIC INTEGRATION IN LATIN AMERICA." FUT L/A+17C LAW STRATA ECO/UNDEV DIST/IND INDUS LABOR NAT/G LEGIS ECO/TAC ADMIN RIGID/FLEX WEALTH...CONCPT NEW/IDEA CONT/OBS TIME/SEQ WORK 20. PAGE 75 B1519
FINAN INT/TRADE REGION

B61
BULLIS H.A.,MANIFESTO FOR AMERICANS. USA+45 AGRI LABOR NAT/G NEIGH FOR/AID INT/TRADE TAX EDU/PROP CHOOSE...POLICY MGT 20 UN UNESCO. PAGE 17 B0342
ECO/TAC SOCIETY INDUS CAP/ISM

B61
FRIEDMANN W.G.,JOINT INTERNATIONAL BUSINESS VENTURES. ASIA ISLAM L/A+17C ECO/DEV DIST/IND FINAN PROC/MFG FACE/GP LG/CO NAT/G VOL/ASSN CONSULT EX/STRUC PLAN ADMIN ROUTINE WEALTH...OLD/LIB WORK 20. PAGE 37 B0760
ECO/UNDEV INT/TRADE

B61
WILLOUGHBY W.R.,THE ST LAWRENCE WATERWAY: A STUDY IN POLITICS AND DIPLOMACY. USA+45 ECO/DEV COM/IND INT/ORG CONSULT DELIB/GP ACT/RES TEC/DEV DIPLOM ECO/TAC ROUTINE...TIME/SEQ 20. PAGE 117 B2357
LEGIS INT/TRADE CANADA DIST/IND

S61
VINER J.,"ECONOMIC FOREIGN POLICY ON THE NEW FRONTIER." USA+45 ECO/UNDEV AGRI FINAN INDUS MARKET INT/ORG NAT/G FOR/AID INT/TRADE ADMIN ATTIT PWR 20 KENNEDY/JF. PAGE 112 B2262
TOP/EX ECO/TAC BAL/PAY TARIFFS

B62
CARSON P.,MATERIALS FOR WEST AFRICAN HISTORY IN THE ARCHIVES OF BELGIUM AND HOLLAND. CLIENT INDUS INT/TRADE ADMIN 17/19. PAGE 19 B0387
BIBLIOG/A COLONIAL AFR ECO/UNDEV

B62
FORD A.G.,THE GOLD STANDARD 1880-1914: BRITAIN AND ARGENTINA. UK ECO/UNDEV INT/TRADE ADMIN GOV/REL DEMAND EFFICIENCY...STAT CHARTS 19/20 ARGEN GOLD/STAND. PAGE 36 B0737
FINAN ECO/TAC BUDGET BAL/PAY

B62
GROVE J.W.,GOVERNMENT AND INDUSTRY IN BRITAIN. UK FINAN LOC/G CONSULT DELIB/GP INT/TRADE ADMIN CONTROL...BIBLIOG 20. PAGE 44 B0894
ECO/TAC INDUS NAT/G GP/REL

B62
TAYLOR D.,THE BRITISH IN AFRICA. UK CULTURE ECO/UNDEV INDUS DIPLOM INT/TRADE ADMIN WAR RACE/REL ORD/FREE SOVEREIGN...POLICY BIBLIOG 15/20 CMN/WLTH. PAGE 103 B2084
AFR COLONIAL DOMIN

S62
TATOMIR N.,"ORGANIZATIA INTERNATIONALA A MUNCII:
INT/ORG

ASPECTE NOI ALE PROBLEMEI IMBUNATATIRII
MECANISMULUI EI." EUR+WWI ECO/DEV VOL/ASSN ADMIN
...METH/CNCPT WORK ILO 20. PAGE 103 B2081
INT/TRADE

B63
PATRA A.C.,THE ADMINISTRATION OF JUSTICE UNDER THE
EAST INDIA COMPANY IN BENGAL, BIHAR AND ORISSA.
INDIA UK LG/CO CAP/ISM INT/TRADE ADJUD COLONIAL
CONTROL CT/SYS...POLICY 20. PAGE 81 B1641
**ADMIN
JURID
CONCPT**

B63
THORELLI H.B.,INTOP: INTERNATIONAL OPERATIONS
SIMULATION: PLAYER'S MANUAL. BRAZIL FINAN OP/RES
ADMIN GP/REL INGP/REL PRODUC PERCEPT...DECISION MGT
EEC. PAGE 104 B2108
**GAME
INT/TRADE
EDU/PROP
LG/CO**

B63
UN SECRETARY GENERAL,PLANNING FOR ECONOMIC
DEVELOPMENT. ECO/UNDEV FINAN BUDGET INT/TRADE
TARIFFS TAX ADMIN 20 UN. PAGE 106 B2151
**PLAN
ECO/TAC
MGT
NAT/COMP**

S63
NYE J.S. JR.,"EAST AFRICAN ECONOMIC INTEGRATION."
AFR UGANDA PROVS DELIB/GP PLAN ECO/TAC INT/TRADE
ADMIN ROUTINE ORD/FREE PWR WEALTH...OBS TIME/SEQ
VAL/FREE 20. PAGE 79 B1597
**ECO/UNDEV
INT/ORG**

DUROSELLE J.B.,POLITIQUES NATIONALES ENVERS LES
JEUNES ETATS. FRANCE ISRAEL ITALY UK USA+45 USSR
YUGOSLAVIA ECO/DEV FINAN ECO/TAC INT/TRADE ADMIN
PWR 20. PAGE 31 B0634
**DIPLOM
ECO/UNDEV
COLONIAL
DOMIN**

B64
GRZYBOWSKI K.,THE SOCIALIST COMMONWEALTH OF
NATIONS: ORGANIZATIONS AND INSTITUTIONS. FORCES
DIPLOM INT/TRADE ADJUD ADMIN LEAD WAR MARXISM
SOCISM...BIBLIOG 20 COMECON WARSAW/P. PAGE 44 B0898
**INT/LAW
COM
REGION
INT/ORG**

B64
HAMBRIDGE G.,DYNAMICS OF DEVELOPMENT. AGRI FINAN
INDUS LABOR INT/TRADE EDU/PROP ADMIN LEAD OWN
HEALTH...ANTHOL BIBLIOG 20. PAGE 46 B0930
**ECO/UNDEV
ECO/TAC
OP/RES
ACT/RES**

B64
HERSKOVITS M.J.,ECONOMIC TRANSITION IN AFRICA. FUT
INT/ORG NAT/G WORKER PROB/SOLV TEC/DEV INT/TRADE
EQUILIB INCOME...ANTHOL 20. PAGE 49 B0996
**AFR
ECO/UNDEV
PLAN
ADMIN**

B64
LI C.M.,INDUSTRIAL DEVELOPMENT IN COMMUNIST CHINA.
CHINA/COM ECO/DEV ECO/UNDEV AGRI FINAN INDUS MARKET
LABOR NAT/G ECO/TAC INT/TRADE EXEC ALL/VALS
...POLICY RELATIV TREND WORK TOT/POP VAL/FREE 20.
PAGE 65 B1311
**ASIA
TEC/DEV**

B64
SCHECHTER A.H.,INTERPRETATION OF AMBIGUOUS
DOCUMENTS BY INTERNATIONAL ADMINISTRATIVE
TRIBUNALS. WOR+45 EX/STRUC INT/TRADE CT/SYS
SOVEREIGN 20 UN ILO EURCT/JUST. PAGE 93 B1884
**INT/LAW
DIPLOM
INT/ORG
ADJUD**

B64
UN PUB. INFORM. ORGAN.,EVERY MAN'S UNITED NATIONS.
UNIV WOR+45 CONSTN CULTURE SOCIETY ECO/DEV
ECO/UNDEV NAT/G ACT/RES PLAN ECO/TAC INT/TRADE
EDU/PROP LEGIT PEACE ATTIT ALL/VALS...POLICY HUM
INT/LAW CONCPT CHARTS UN TOT/POP 20. PAGE 106 B2150
**INT/ORG
ROUTINE**

B64
WELLISZ S.,THE ECONOMICS OF THE SOVIET BLOC. COM
USSR INDUS WORKER PLAN BUDGET INT/TRADE TAX PRICE
PRODUC WEALTH MARXISM...METH/COMP 20. PAGE 115
B2319
**EFFICIENCY
ADMIN
MARKET**

B64
WERNETTE J.P.,GOVERNMENT AND BUSINESS. LABOR
CAP/ISM ECO/TAC INT/TRADE TAX ADMIN AUTOMAT NUC/PWR
CIVMIL/REL DEMAND...MGT 20 MONOPOLY. PAGE 115 B2323
**NAT/G
FINAN
ECO/DEV
CONTROL**

B64
WITHERELL J.W.,OFFICIAL PUBLICATIONS OF FRENCH
EQUATORIAL AFRICA, FRENCH CAMEROONS, AND TOGO,
1946-1958 (PAMPHLET). CAMEROON CHAD FRANCE GABON
TOGO LAW ECO/UNDEV EXTR/IND INT/TRADE...GEOG HEAL
20. PAGE 117 B2367
**BIBLIOG/A
AFR
NAT/G
ADMIN**

S64
HUELIN D.,"ECONOMIC INTEGRATION IN LATIN AMERICAN:
PROGRESS AND PROBLEMS." L/A+17C ECO/DEV AGRI
DIST/IND FINAN INDUS NAT/G VOL/ASSN CONSULT
DELIB/GP EX/STRUC ACT/RES PLAN TEC/DEV ECO/TAC
ROUTINE BAL/PAY WEALTH WORK 20. PAGE 52 B1058
**MARKET
ECO/UNDEV
INT/TRADE**

B65
AMERICAN ECONOMIC ASSOCIATION,INDEX OF ECONOMIC
JOURNALS 1886-1965 (7 VOLS.). UK USA+45 USA-45 AGRI
FINAN PLAN ECO/TAC INT/TRADE ADMIN...STAT CENSUS
19/20. PAGE 4 B0083
**BIBLIOG
WRITING
INDUS**

B65
DOWD L.P.,PRINCIPLES OF WORLD BUSINESS. SERV/IND
NAT/G DIPLOM ECO/TAC TARIFFS...INT/LAW JURID 20.
PAGE 30 B0614
**INT/TRADE
MGT
FINAN
MARKET**

B65
KASER M.,COMECON* INTEGRATION PROBLEMS OF THE
PLANNED ECONOMIES. INT/ORG TEC/DEV INT/TRADE PRICE
ADMIN ADJUST CENTRAL...STAT TIME/SEQ ORG/CHARTS
**PLAN
ECO/DEV
COM**

COMECON. PAGE 58 B1177
REGION

B65
LEYS C.T.,FEDERATION IN EAST AFRICA. LAW AGRI
DIST/IND FINAN INT/ORG LABOR INT/TRADE CONFER ADMIN
CONTROL GP/REL...ANTHOL 20 AFRICA/E. PAGE 65 B1310
**FEDERAL
REGION
ECO/UNDEV
PLAN**

B65
MORGENTHAU H.,MORGENTHAU DIARY (CHINA) (2 VOLS.).
ASIA USA+45 USA-45 LAW DELIB/GP EX/STRUC PLAN
FOR/AID INT/TRADE CONFER WAR MARXISM 20 CHINJAP.
PAGE 75 B1523
**DIPLOM
ADMIN**

B65
ROTBERG R.I.,A POLITICAL HISTORY OF TROPICAL
AFRICA. EX/STRUC DIPLOM INT/TRADE DOMIN ADMIN
RACE/REL NAT/LISM PWR SOVEREIGN...GEOG TIME/SEQ
BIBLIOG 1/20. PAGE 91 B1832
**AFR
CULTURE
COLONIAL**

B65
WHITE J.,GERMAN AID. GERMANY/W FINAN PLAN TEC/DEV
INT/TRADE ADMIN ATTIT...POLICY 20. PAGE 116 B2334
**FOR/AID
ECO/UNDEV
DIPLOM
ECO/TAC**

B66
FISK E.K.,NEW GUINEA ON THE THRESHOLD: ASPECTS OF
SOCIAL, POLITICAL, AND ECONOMIC DEVELOPMENT. AGRI
NAT/G INT/TRADE ADMIN ADJUST LITERACY ROLE...CHARTS
ANTHOL 20 NEW/GUINEA. PAGE 36 B0726
**ECO/UNDEV
SOCIETY**

B66
GHOSH P.K.,THE CONSTITUTION OF INDIA: HOW IT HAS
BEEN FRAMED. INDIA LOC/G DELIB/GP EX/STRUC
PROB/SOLV BUDGET INT/TRADE CT/SYS CHOOSE...LING 20.
PAGE 39 B0795
**CONSTN
NAT/G
LEGIS
FEDERAL**

B66
LEWIS W.A.,DEVELOPMENT PLANNING: THE ESSENTIALS OF
ECONOMIC POLICY. USA+45 FINAN INDUS NAT/G WORKER
FOR/AID INT/TRADE ADMIN ROUTINE WEALTH...CONCPT
STAT. PAGE 65 B1307
**PLAN
ECO/DEV
POLICY
CREATE**

B66
MACFARQUHAR R.,CHINA UNDER MAO: POLITICS TAKES
COMMAND. CHINA/COM COM AGRI INDUS CHIEF FORCES
DIPLOM INT/TRADE EDU/PROP TASK REV ADJUST...ANTHOL
20 MAO. PAGE 67 B1359
**ECO/UNDEV
TEC/DEV
ECO/TAC
ADMIN**

B66
MANGONE G.J.,UN ADMINISTRATION OF ECONOMIC AND
AOCIAL PROGRAMS. CONSULT BUDGET INT/TRADE REGION 20
UN. PAGE 69 B1391
**ADMIN
MGT
ECO/TAC
DELIB/GP**

B66
SMITH H.E.,READINGS IN ECONOMIC DEVELOPMENT AND
ADMINISTRATION IN TANZANIA. TANZANIA FINAN INDUS
LABOR NAT/G PLAN PROB/SOLV INT/TRADE COLONIAL
REGION...ANTHOL BIBLIOG 20 AFRICA/E. PAGE 98 B1981
**TEC/DEV
ADMIN
GOV/REL**

B66
US HOUSE COMM GOVT OPERATIONS,AN INVESTIGATION OF
THE US ECONOMIC AND MILITARY ASSISTANCE PROGRAMS IN
VIETNAM. USA+45 VIETNAM/S SOCIETY CONSTRUC FINAN
FORCES BUDGET INT/TRADE PEACE HEALTH...MGT
HOUSE/REP AID. PAGE 108 B2191
**FOR/AID
ECO/UNDEV
WAR
INSPECT**

L66
AMERICAN ECONOMIC REVIEW,"SIXTY-THIRD LIST OF
DOCTORAL DISSERTATIONS IN POLITICAL ECONOMY IN
AMERICAN UNIVERSITIES AND COLLEGES." ECO/DEV AGRI
FINAN LABOR WORKER PLAN BUDGET INT/TRADE ADMIN
DEMAND...MGT STAT 20. PAGE 4 B0084
**BIBLIOG/A
CONCPT
ACADEM**

C66
TARLING N.,"A CONCISE HISTORY OF SOUTHEAST ASIA."
BURMA CAMBODIA LAOS S/ASIA THAILAND VIETNAM
ECO/UNDEV POL/PAR FORCES ADMIN REV WAR CIVMIL/REL
ORD/FREE MARXISM SOCISM 13/20. PAGE 103 B2080
**COLONIAL
DOMIN
INT/TRADE
NAT/LISM**

B67
BRAYMAN H.,CORPORATE MANAGEMENT IN A WORLD OF
POLITICS. USA+45 ELITES MARKET CREATE BARGAIN
DIPLOM INT/TRADE ATTIT SKILL 20. PAGE 15 B0302
**MGT
ECO/DEV
CAP/ISM
INDUS**

B67
CECIL L.,ALBERT BALLIN; BUSINESS AND POLITICS IN
IMPERIAL GERMANY 1888-1918. GERMANY UK INT/TRADE
LEAD WAR PERS/REL ADJUST PWR WEALTH...MGT BIBLIOG
19/20. PAGE 19 B0397
**DIPLOM
CONSTN
ECO/DEV
TOP/EX**

B67
GABRIEL P.P.,THE INTERNATIONAL TRANSFER OF
CORPORATE SKILLS: MANAGEMENT CONTRACTS IN LESS
DEVELOPED COUNTRIES. CLIENT INDUS LG/CO PLAN
PROB/SOLV CAP/ISM ECO/TAC FOR/AID INT/TRADE RENT
ADMIN SKILL 20. PAGE 38 B0771
**ECO/UNDEV
AGREE
MGT
CONSULT**

B67
KARDOUCHE G.K.,THE UAR IN DEVELOPMENT. UAR ECO/TAC
INT/TRADE BAL/PAY...STAT CHARTS BIBLIOG 20. PAGE 58
B1172
**FINAN
MGT
CAP/ISM
ECO/UNDEV**

B67
ROBINSON R.D., INTERNATIONAL MANAGEMENT. USA&45
FINAN R+D PLAN PRODUC...DECISION T. PAGE 67 B1352
**INT/TRADE
MGT
INT/LAW
MARKET**

B67
OVERSEAS DEVELOPMENT INSTIT,EFFECTIVE AID. WOR+45
FOR/AID

INT/ORG TEC/DEV DIPLOM INT/TRADE ADMIN. PAGE 80 B1619
ECO/UNDEV ECO/TAC NAT/COMP
S67

HUGON P.,"BLOCAGES ET DESEQUILIBRES DE LA CROISSANCE ECONOMIQUE EN AFRIQUE NOIRE." AFR KIN MUNIC CREATE PLAN INT/TRADE REGION ADJUST CENTRAL EQUILIB NAT/LISM ORD/FREE 20. PAGE 52 B1060
ECO/UNDEV COLONIAL STRUCT ADMIN
S67

WEIL G.L.,"THE MERGER OF THE INSTITUTIONS OF THE EUROPEAN COMMUNITIES" EUR+WWI ECO/DEV INT/TRADE CONSEN PLURISM...DECISION MGT 20 EEC EURATOM ECSC TREATY. PAGE 115 B2313
ECO/TAC INT/ORG CENTRAL INT/LAW
B98

THOMPSON H.C.,RHODESIA AND ITS GOVERNMENT. AFR RHODESIA ECO/UNDEV INDUS KIN WORKER INT/TRADE DISCRIM LITERACY ORD/FREE 19. PAGE 104 B2102
COLONIAL ADMIN POLICY ELITES

INTEGRATION....SEE NEGRO, SOUTH/US, RACE/REL, SOC/INTEG, CIV/RIGHTS, DISCRIM, ISOLAT, SCHOOL, STRANGE

INTEGRATION, POLITICAL+ECONOMIC....SEE REGION+INT/ORG+ VOL/ASSN+CENTRAL

INTELL....INTELLIGENTSIA

DEUTSCHE BUCHEREI,JAHRESVERZEICHNIS DER DEUTSCHEN HOCHSCHULSCHRIFTEN. EUR+WWI GERMANY LAW ADMIN PERSON...MGT SOC 19/20. PAGE 28 B0579
N
BIBLIOG WRITING ACADEM INTELL
B23

FRANK T.,A HISTORY OF ROME. MEDIT-7 INTELL SOCIETY LOC/G NAT/G POL/PAR FORCES LEGIS DOMIN LEGIT ALL/VALS...POLICY CONCPT TIME/SEQ GEN/LAWS ROM/EMP ROM/EMP. PAGE 37 B0749
EXEC STRUCT ELITES
B24

MERRIAM C.E.,A HISTORY OF POLITICAL THEORIES - RECENT TIMES. USA-45 WOR-45 CULTURE SOCIETY ECO/DEV R+D EDU/PROP ROUTINE CHOOSE ATTIT PERSON ALL/VALS ...POLICY SOC CONCPT METH/CNCPT OBS HIST/WRIT TIME/SEQ TREND. PAGE 73 B1471
UNIV INTELL
B30

MURCHISON C.,PSYCHOLOGIES OF 1930. UNIV USA-45 CULTURE INTELL SOCIETY STRATA FAM ROUTINE BIO/SOC DRIVE RIGID/FLEX SUPEGO...NEW/IDEA OBS SELF/OBS CONT/OBS 20. PAGE 76 B1543
CREATE PERSON
B32

WRIGHT Q.,GOLD AND MONETARY STABILIZATION. FUT USA-45 WOR-45 INTELL ECO/DEV INT/ORG NAT/G CONSULT PLAN ECO/TAC ADMIN ATTIT WEALTH...CONCPT TREND 20. PAGE 118 B2383
FINAN POLICY
B37

PARSONS T.,THE STRUCTURE OF SOCIAL ACTION. UNIV INTELL SOCIETY INDUS MARKET ECO/TAC ROUTINE CHOOSE ALL/VALS...CONCPT OBS BIOG TREND GEN/LAWS 20. PAGE 81 B1636
CULTURE ATTIT CAP/ISM
B38

PETTEE G.S.,THE PROCESS OF REVOLUTION. COM FRANCE ITALY MOD/EUR RUSSIA SPAIN WOR-45 ELITES INTELL SOCIETY STRATA STRUCT INT/ORG NAT/G POL/PAR ACT/RES PLAN EDU/PROP LEGIT EXEC...SOC MYTH TIME/SEQ TOT/POP 18/20. PAGE 82 B1664
COERCE CONCPT REV
B45

BUSH V.,SCIENCE, THE ENDLESS FRONTIER. FUT USA-45 INTELL STRATA ACT/RES CREATE PLAN EDU/PROP NUC/PWR PEACE ATTIT HEALTH KNOWL...MAJORIT HEAL MGT PHIL/SCI CONCPT OBS TREND 20. PAGE 18 B0360
R+D NAT/G
C45

MCDIARMID J.,"THE MOBILIZATION OF SOCIAL SCIENTISTS," IN L. WHITE'S CIVIL CIVIL SERVICE IN WARTIME." USA-45 INTELL TEC/DEV CENTRAL...SOC 20 CIVIL/SERV. PAGE 72 B1447
INTELL WAR DELIB/GP ADMIN
B47

BARNARD C.,THE FUNCTIONS OF THE EXECUTIVE. USA+45 ELITES INTELL LEGIT ATTIT DRIVE PERSON SKILL...PSY SOC METH/CNCPT SOC/EXP GEN/METH VAL/FREE 20. PAGE 9 B0187
EXEC EX/STRUC ROUTINE
B48

STEWART I.,ORGANIZING SCIENTIFIC RESEARCH FOR WAR: ADMINISTRATIVE HISTORY OF OFFICE OF SCIENTIFIC RESEARCH AND DEVELOPMENT. USA-45 INTELL R+D LABOR WORKER CREATE BUDGET WEAPON CIVMIL/REL GP/REL EFFICIENCY...POLICY 20. PAGE 101 B2037
DELIB/GP ADMIN WAR TEC/DEV
B49

ROSENHAUPT H.W.,HOW TO WAGE PEACE. USA+45 SOCIETY STRATA STRUCT R+D INT/ORG POL/PAR LEGIS ACT/RES CREATE PLAN EDU/PROP ADMIN EXEC ATTIT ALL/VALS ...TIME/SEQ TREND COLD/WAR 20. PAGE 90 B1822
INTELL CONCPT DIPLOM
B49

SINGER K.,THE IDEA OF CONFLICT. UNIV INTELL INT/ORG NAT/G PLAN ROUTINE ATTIT DRIVE ALL/VALS...POLICY CONCPT TIME/SEQ. PAGE 97 B1966
ACT/RES SOC
B50

MANNHEIM K.,FREEDOM, POWER, AND DEMOCRATIC
TEC/DEV

PLANNING. FUT USSR WOR+45 ELITES INTELL SOCIETY NAT/G EDU/PROP ROUTINE ATTIT DRIVE SUPEGO SKILL ...POLICY PSY CONCPT TREND GEN/LAWS 20. PAGE 69 B1393
PLAN CAP/ISM UK
B52

BRINTON C.,THE ANATOMY OF REVOLUTION. FRANCE UK USA-45 USSR WOR+45 ELITES INTELL ECO/DEV NAT/G EX/STRUC FORCES COERCE DRIVE ORD/FREE PWR SOVEREIGN ...MYTH HIST/WRIT GEN/LAWS. PAGE 15 B0311
SOCIETY CONCPT REV
B52

POOL I.,SYMBOLS OF DEMOCRACY. WOR+45 WOR-45 POL/PAR FORCES ADMIN PERSON PWR...CONCPT 20. PAGE 83 B1687
INTELL SOCIETY USSR
B52

SCHATTSCHNEIDER E.E.,A GUIDE TO THE STUDY OF PUBLIC AFFAIRS. LAW LOC/G NAT/G LEGIS BUDGET PRESS ADMIN LOBBY...JURID CHARTS 20. PAGE 93 B1882
ACT/RES INTELL ACADEM METH/COMP
L52

WRIGHT Q.,"CONGRESS AND THE TREATY-MAKING POWER." USA+45 WOR+45 CONSTN INTELL NAT/G CHIEF CONSULT EX/STRUC LEGIS TOP/EX CREATE GOV/REL DISPL DRIVE RIGID/FLEX...TREND TOT/POP CONGRESS CONGRESS 20 TREATY. PAGE 118 B2384
ROUTINE DIPLOM INT/LAW DELIB/GP
S52

SCHWEBEL S.M.,"THE SECRETARY-GENERAL OF THE UN." FUT INTELL CONSULT DELIB/GP ADMIN PEACE ATTIT ...JURID MGT CONCPT TREND UN CONGRESS 20. PAGE 95 B1915
INT/ORG TOP/EX
S52

TAYLOR R.W.,"ARTHUR F. BENTLEY'S POLITICAL SCIENCE" (BMR)" USA+45 INTELL NAT/G...DECISION CLASSIF IDEA/COMP 20 BENTLEY/AF. PAGE 103 B2090
GEN/LAWS POLICY ADMIN
S53

BLOUGH R.,"THE ROLE OF THE ECONOMIST IN FEDERAL POLICY MAKING." USA+45 ELITES INTELL ECO/DEV NAT/G CONSULT EX/STRUC ACT/RES PLAN INT/TRADE BAL/PAY WEALTH...POLICY CONGRESS 20. PAGE 13 B0256
DELIB/GP ECO/TAC
B54

COMBS C.H.,DECISION PROCESSES. INTELL SOCIETY DELIB/GP CREATE TEC/DEV DOMIN LEGIT EXEC CHOOSE DRIVE RIGID/FLEX KNOWL PWR...PHIL/SCI SOC METH/CNCPT CONT/OBS REC/INT PERS/TEST SAMP/SIZ BIOG SOC/EXP WORK. PAGE 22 B0455
MATH DECISION
L54

ARCIENEGAS G.,"POST-WAR SOVIET FOREIGN POLICY: A WORLD PERSPECTIVE." COM USA+45 STRUCT NAT/G POL/PAR TOP/EX PLAN ADMIN ALL/VALS...TREND COLD/WAR TOT/POP 20. PAGE 6 B0124
INTELL ACT/RES USSR
L54

ROSTOW W.W.,"ASIAN LEADERSHIP AND FREE-WORLD ALLIANCE." ASIA COM USA+45 CULTURE ELITES INTELL NAT/G TEC/DEV ECO/TAC EDU/PROP COLONIAL PARL/PROC ROUTINE COERCE DRIVE ORD/FREE MARXISM...PSY CONCPT. PAGE 90 B1829
ATTIT LEGIT DIPLOM
L55

ROSTOW W.W.,"RUSSIA AND CHINA UNDER COMMUNISM." CHINA/COM USSR INTELL STRUCT INT/ORG NAT/G POL/PAR TOP/EX ACT/RES PLAN ADMIN ATTIT ALL/VALS MARXISM ...CONCPT OBS TIME/SEQ TREND GOV/COMP VAL/FREE 20. PAGE 91 B1830
COM ASIA
S55

WRIGHT Q.,"THE PEACEFUL ADJUSTMENT OF INTERNATIONAL RELATIONS: PROBLEMS AND RESEARCH APPROACHES." UNIV INTELL EDU/PROP ADJUD ROUTINE KNOWL SKILL...INT/LAW JURID PHIL/SCI CLASSIF 20. PAGE 118 B2385
R+D METH/CNCPT PEACE
B56

KAUFMANN W.W.,MILITARY POLICY AND NATIONAL SECURITY. USA+45 ELITES INTELL NAT/G TOP/EX PLAN BAL/PWR DIPLOM ROUTINE COERCE NUC/PWR ATTIT ORD/FREE PWR 20 COLD/WAR. PAGE 58 B1182
FORCES CREATE
B56

WU E.,LEADERS OF TWENTIETH-CENTURY CHINA: AN ANNOTATED BIBLIOGRAPHY OF SELECTED CHINESE BIOGRAPHICAL WORKS IN HOOVER LIBRARY. ASIA INDUS POL/PAR DIPLOM ADMIN REV WAR...HUM MGT 20. PAGE 118 B2386
BIBLIOG/A BIOG INTELL CHIEF
S56

CUTLER R.,"THE DEVELOPMENT OF THE NATIONAL SECURITY COUNCIL." USA+45 INTELL CONSULT EX/STRUC DIPLOM LEAD 20 TRUMAN/HS EISNHWR/DD NSC. PAGE 25 B0514
ORD/FREE DELIB/GP PROB/SOLV NAT/G
B57

FULLER C.D.,TRAINING OF SPECIALISTS IN INTERNATIONAL RELATIONS. FUT USA+45 USA-45 INTELL INT/ORG...MGT METH/CNCPT INT QU GEN/METH 20. PAGE 38 B0765
KNOWL DIPLOM
B57

IKE N.,JAPANESE POLITICS. INTELL STRUCT AGRI INDUS FAM KIN LABOR PRESS CHOOSE ATTIT...DECISION BIBLIOG 19/20 CHINJAP. PAGE 53 B1075
NAT/G ADMIN POL/PAR CULTURE
B57

INDUSTRIAL RELATIONS RES ASSN,RESEARCH IN INDUSTRIAL HUMAN RELATIONS. INTELL ACT/RES OP/RES ADMIN 20. PAGE 54 B1084
INDUS MGT LABOR

MILLS C.W.,THE CAUSES OF WORLD WAR THREE. FUT
USA+45 INTELL NAT/G DOMIN EDU/PROP ADMIN WAR ATTIT
SOC. PAGE 74 B1487

GP/REL
B58
CONSULT
PWR
ELITES
PEACE

DAVENPORT J.,"ARMS AND THE WELFARE STATE." INTELL
STRUCT FORCES CREATE ECO/TAC FOR/AID DOMIN LEGIT
ADMIN WAR ORD/FREE PWR...POLICY SOC CONCPT MYTH OBS
TREND COLD/WAR TOT/POP 20. PAGE 26 B0533

S58
USA+45
NAT/G
USSR

EPSTEIN F.T.,EAST GERMANY: A SELECTED BIBLIOGRAPHY
(PAMPHLET). COM GERMANY/E LAW AGRI FINAN INDUS
LABOR POL/PAR EDU/PROP ADMIN AGE/Y 20. PAGE 33
B0677

B59
BIBLIOG/A
INTELL
MARXISM
NAT/G

KISSINGER H.A.,"THE POLICYMAKER AND THE
INTELLECTUAL." USA+45 CONSULT DELIB/GP ACT/RES
ADMIN ATTIT DRIVE RIGID/FLEX KNOWL PWR...POLICY
PLURIST MGT METH/CNCPT GEN/LAWS GEN/METH 20.
PAGE 60 B1216

S59
INTELL
CREATE

ZAUBERMAN A.,"SOVIET BLOC ECONOMIC INTEGRATION."
COM CULTURE INTELL ECO/DEV INDUS TOP/EX ACT/RES
PLAN ECO/TAC INT/TRADE ROUTINE CHOOSE ATTIT
...TIME/SEQ 20. PAGE 119 B2399

S59
MARKET
INT/ORG
USSR
TOTALISM

DRAPER T.,AMERICAN COMMUNISM AND SOVIET RUSSIA.
EUR+WWI USA+45 USSR INTELL AGRI COM/IND FINAN INDUS
LABOR PROF/ORG VOL/ASSN PLAN TEC/DEV DOMIN EDU/PROP
ADMIN COERCE REV PERSON PWR...POLICY CONCPT MYTH
19/20. PAGE 30 B0617

B60
COM
POL/PAR

MEEHAN E.J.,THE BRITISH LEFT WING AND FOREIGN
POLICY: A STUDY OF THE INFLUENCE OF IDEOLOGY. FUT
UK UNIV WOR+45 INTELL TOP/EX PLAN ADMIN ROUTINE
DRIVE...OBS TIME/SEQ GEN/LAWS PARLIAMENT 20.
PAGE 72 B1461

B60
ACT/RES
ATTIT
DIPLOM

US SENATE COMM. GOVT. OPER.,ORGANIZING FOR NATIONAL
SECURITY. USA+45 USA-45 INTELL STRUCT SML/CO
ACT/RES ADMIN ATTIT PERSON PWR SKILL...DECISION 20.
PAGE 111 B2236

B60
CONSULT
EXEC

BRENNAN D.G.,"SETTING AND GOALS OF ARMS CONTROL."
FUT USA+45 USSR WOR+45 INTELL INT/ORG NAT/G
VOL/ASSN CONSULT PLAN DIPLOM ECO/TAC ADMIN KNOWL
PWR...POLICY CONCPT TREND COLD/WAR 20. PAGE 15
B0305

L60
FORCES
COERCE
ARMS/CONT
DETER

EMERSON R.,"THE EROSION OF DEMOCRACY." AFR FUT LAW
CULTURE INTELL SOCIETY ECO/UNDEV FAM LOC/G NAT/G
FORCES PLAN TEC/DEV ECO/TAC ADMIN CT/SYS ATTIT
ORD/FREE PWR...SOCIALIST SOC CONCPT STAND/INT
TIME/SEQ WORK 20. PAGE 33 B0671

S60
S/ASIA
POL/PAR

MODELSKI G.,"AUSTRALIA AND SEATO." S/ASIA USA+45
CULTURE INTELL ECO/DEV NAT/G PLAN DIPLOM ADMIN
ROUTINE ATTIT SKILL...MGT TIME/SEQ AUSTRAL 20
SEATO. PAGE 74 B1493

S60
INT/ORG
ACT/RES

SCHWARTZ B.,"THE INTELLIGENTSIA IN COMMUNIST CHINA:
A TENTATIVE COMPARISON." ASIA CHINA/COM COM RUSSIA
ELITES SOCIETY STRATA POL/PAR VOL/ASSN CREATE ADMIN
COERCE NAT/LISM TOTALISM...POLICY TREND 20. PAGE 95
B1914

S60
INTELL
RIGID/FLEX
REV

SCHAPIRO L.B.,"THE COMMUNIST PARTY OF THE SOVIET
UNION." USSR INTELL CHIEF EX/STRUC FORCES DOMIN
ADMIN LEAD WAR ATTIT SOVEREIGN...POLICY BIBLIOG 20.
PAGE 93 B1881

C60
POL/PAR
COM
REV

HARRISON S.,INDIA AND THE UNITED STATES. FUT S/ASIA
USA+45 WOR+45 INTELL ECO/DEV ECO/UNDEV AGRI INDUS
INT/ORG NAT/G CONSULT EX/STRUC TOP/EX PLAN ECO/TAC
NEUTRAL ALL/VALS...MGT TOT/POP 20. PAGE 47 B0956

B61
DELIB/GP
ACT/RES
FOR/AID
INDIA

MARKMANN C.L.,JOHN F. KENNEDY: A SENSE OF PURPOSE.
USA+45 INTELL FAM CONSULT DELIB/GP LEGIS PERSON
SKILL 20 KENNEDY/JF EISNHWR/DD ROOSEVLT/F
NEW/FRONTR PRESIDENT. PAGE 69 B1399

B61
CHIEF
TOP/EX
ADMIN
BIOG

MARVICK D.,POLITICAL DECISION-MAKERS. INTELL STRATA
NAT/G POL/PAR EX/STRUC LEGIS DOMIN EDU/PROP ATTIT
PERSON PWR...PSY STAT OBS CONT/OBS STAND/INT
UNPLAN/INT TIME/SEQ CHARTS STERTYP VAL/FREE.
PAGE 70 B1416

B61
TOP/EX
BIOG
ELITES

TANZER L.,THE KENNEDY CIRCLE. INTELL CONSULT
DELIB/GP TOP/EX CONTROL EXEC INGP/REL PERS/REL PWR
...BIOG IDEA/COMP ANTHOL 20 KENNEDY/JF PRESIDENT
DEMOCRAT MCNAMARA/R RUSK/D. PAGE 103 B2077

B61
EX/STRUC
NAT/G
CHIEF

COHEN K.J.,"THE ROLE OF MANAGEMENT GAMES IN
EDUCATION AND RESEARCH." INTELL ECO/DEV FINAN

L61
SOCIETY
GAME

ACT/RES ECO/TAC DECISION. PAGE 22 B0444

MGT
EDU/PROP
S61

LEWY G.,"SUPERIOR ORDERS, NUCLEAR WARFARE AND THE
DICTATES OF CONSCIENCE: THE DILEMMA OF MILITARY
OBEDIENCE IN THE ATOMIC." FUT UNIV WOR+45 INTELL
SOCIETY FORCES TOP/EX ACT/RES ADMIN ROUTINE NUC/PWR
PERCEPT RIGID/FLEX ALL/VALS...POLICY CONCPT 20.
PAGE 65 B1308

DETER
INT/ORG
LAW
INT/LAW

PADOVER S.K.,"PSYCHOLOGICAL WARFARE AND FOREIGN
POLICY." FUT UNIV USA+45 INTELL SOCIETY CREATE
EDU/PROP ADMIN WAR PEACE PERCEPT...POLICY
METH/CNCPT TESTS TIME/SEQ 20. PAGE 80 B1623

S61
ROUTINE
DIPLOM

SCHILLING W.R.,"THE H-BOMB: HOW TO DECIDE WITHOUT
ACTUALLY CHOOSING." FUT USA+45 INTELL CONSULT ADMIN
CT/SYS MORAL...JURID OBS 20 TRUMAN/HS. PAGE 93
B1888

S61
PERSON
LEGIT
NUC/PWR

TAUBENFELD H.J.,"OUTER SPACE--PAST POLITICS AND
FUTURE POLICY." FUT USA+45 USA-45 WOR+45 AIR INTELL
STRUCT ECO/DEV NAT/G TOP/EX ACT/RES ADMIN ROUTINE
NUC/PWR ATTIT DRIVE...CONCPT TIME/SEQ TREND TOT/POP
20. PAGE 103 B2083

S61
PLAN
SPACE
INT/ORG

VIRALLY M.,"VERS UNE REFORME DU SECRETARIAT DES
NATIONS UNIES." FUT WOR+45 CONSTN ECO/DEV TOP/EX
BAL/PWR ADMIN ALL/VALS...CONCPT BIOG UN VAL/FREE
20. PAGE 112 B2264

S61
INT/ORG
INTELL
DIPLOM

BUENO M.,"ASPECTOS SOCIOLOGICOS DE LA EDUCACION."
FUT UNIV INTELL R+D SERV/IND SCHOOL CONSULT
EX/STRUC ACT/RES PLAN...METH/CNCPT OBS 20. PAGE 17
B0341

S62
SOCIETY
EDU/PROP
PERSON

GEORGE P.,"MATERIAUX ET REFLEXIONS POUR UNE
POLITIQUE URBAINE RATIONNELLE DANS LES PAYS EN
COURS DE DEVELOPPEMENT." FUT INTELL SOCIETY
SERV/IND MUNIC ACT/RES WEALTH...MGT 20. PAGE 39
B0790

S62
ECO/UNDEV
PLAN

SCHILLING W.R.,"SCIENTISTS, FOREIGN POLICY AND
POLITICS." WOR+45 WOR-45 INTELL INT/ORG CONSULT
TOP/EX ACT/RES PLAN ADMIN KNOWL...CONCPT OBS TREND
LEAGUE/NAT 20. PAGE 93 B1889

S62
NAT/G
TEC/DEV
DIPLOM
NUC/PWR

CHOJNACKI S.,REGISTER ON CURRENT RESEARCH ON
ETHIOPIA AND THE HORN OF AFRICA. ETHIOPIA LAW
CULTURE AGRI SECT EDU/PROP ADMIN...GEOG HEAL LING
20. PAGE 21 B0426

B63
BIBLIOG
ACT/RES
INTELL
ACADEM

LEWIS J.W.,LEADERSHIP IN COMMUNIST CHINA. ASIA
INTELL ECO/UNDEV LOC/G MUNIC NAT/G PROVS ECO/TAC
EDU/PROP LEGIT ADMIN COERCE ATTIT ORD/FREE PWR
...INT TIME/SEQ CHARTS TOT/POP VAL/FREE. PAGE 65
B1304

B63
POL/PAR
DOMIN
ELITES

SIDEY H.,JOHN F. KENNEDY, PRESIDENT. USA+45 INTELL
FAM CONSULT DELIB/GP LEGIS ADMIN LEAD 20 KENNEDY/JF
PRESIDENT. PAGE 97 B1951

B63
BIOG
TOP/EX
SKILL
PERSON

TUCKER R.C.,THE SOVIET POLITICAL MIND. COM INTELL
NAT/G TOP/EX EDU/PROP ADMIN COERCE TOTALISM ATTIT
PWR MARXISM...PSY MYTH HYPO/EXP 20. PAGE 106 B2135

B63
STRUCT
RIGID/FLEX
ELITES
USSR

ARASTEH R.,"THE ROLE OF INTELLECTUALS IN
ADMINISTRATIVE DEVELOPMENT AND SOCIAL CHANGE IN
MODERN IRAN." ISLAM CULTURE NAT/G CONSULT ACT/RES
EDU/PROP EXEC ATTIT BIO/SOC PERCEPT SUPEGO ALL/VALS
...POLICY MGT PSY SOC CONCPT 20. PAGE 6 B0123

S63
INTELL
ADMIN
IRAN

DAVEE R.,"POUR UN FONDS DE DEVELOPPEMENT SOCIAL."
FUT WOR+45 INTELL SOCIETY ECO/DEV FINAN TEC/DEV
ROUTINE WEALTH...TREND TOT/POP VAL/FREE UN 20.
PAGE 26 B0532

S63
INT/ORG
SOC
FOR/AID

DUCROS B.,"MOBILISATION DES RESSOURCES PRODUCTIVES
ET DEVELOPPEMENT." FUT INTELL SOCIETY COM/IND
DIST/IND EXTR/IND FINAN INDUS ROUTINE WEALTH
...METH/CNCPT OBS 20. PAGE 31 B0625

S63
ECO/UNDEV
TEC/DEV

APTER D.E.,IDEOLOGY AND DISCONTENT. FUT WOR+45
CONSTN CULTURE INTELL SOCIETY STRUCT INT/ORG NAT/G
DELIB/GP LEGIS CREATE PLAN TEC/DEV EDU/PROP EXEC
PERCEPT PERSON RIGID/FLEX ALL/VALS...POLICY
TOT/POP. PAGE 6 B0122

B64
ACT/RES
ATTIT

BOTTOMORE T.B.,ELITES AND SOCIETY. INTELL STRATA
ECO/DEV ECO/UNDEV ADMIN GP/REL ORD/FREE...CONCPT
BIBLIOG 20. PAGE 14 B0281

B64
ELITES
IDEA/COMP
SOCIETY
SOC

MERILLAT H.C.L.,LEGAL ADVISERS AND FOREIGN AFFAIRS. CONSULT

B64

WOR+45 WOR-45 ELITES INTELL NAT/G LEGIT ADMIN   EX/STRUC
PERCEPT ALL/VALS...MGT NEW/IDEA RECORD 20. PAGE 73   DIPLOM
B1469

B64
POPPINO R.E.,INTERNATIONAL COMMUNISM IN LATIN   MARXISM
AMERICA: A HISTORY OF THE MOVEMENT 1917-1963.   POL/PAR
CHINA/COM USSR INTELL STRATA LABOR WORKER ADMIN REV   L/A+17C
ATTIT...POLICY 20 COLD/WAR. PAGE 84 B1692

B64
SULLIVAN G.,THE STORY OF THE PEACE CORPS. USA+45   INT/ORG
WOR+45 INTELL FACE/GP NAT/G SCHOOL VOL/ASSN CONSULT   ECO/UNDEV
EX/STRUC PLAN EDU/PROP ADMIN ATTIT DRIVE ALL/VALS   FOR/AID
...POLICY HEAL SOC CONCPT INT QU BIOG TREND SOC/EXP   PEACE
WORK. PAGE 102 B2054

B64
TINBERGEN J.,CENTRAL PLANNING. COM INTELL ECO/DEV   PLAN
ECO/UNDEV FINAN INT/ORG PROB/SOLV ECO/TAC CONTROL   INDUS
EXEC ROUTINE DECISION. PAGE 104 B2111   MGT
                                                       CENTRAL

L64
RIPLEY R.B.,"INTERAGENCY COMMITTEES AND   EXEC
INCREMENTALISM: THE CASE OF AID TO INDIA." INDIA   MGT
USA+45 INTELL NAT/G DELIB/GP ACT/RES DIPLOM ROUTINE   FOR/AID
NAT/LISM ATTIT PWR...SOC CONCPT NEW/IDEA TIME/SEQ
CON/ANAL VAL/FREE 20. PAGE 89 B1790

S64
KAPLAN N.,"RESEARCH ADMINISTRATION AND THE   R+D
ADMINISTRATOR: USSR AND US." COM USA+45 INTELL   ADMIN
EX/STRUC KNOWL...MGT 20. PAGE 58 B1169   USSR

S64
NEEDHAM T.,"SCIENCE AND SOCIETY IN EAST AND WEST."   ASIA
INTELL STRATA R+D LOC/G NAT/G PROVS CONSULT ACT/RES   STRUCT
CREATE PLAN TEC/DEV EDU/PROP ADMIN ATTIT ALL/VALS
...POLICY RELATIV MGT CONCPT NEW/IDEA TIME/SEQ WORK
WORK. PAGE 77 B1565

B65
LIPSET S.M.,THE BERKELEY STUDENT REVOLT: FACTS AND   CROWD
INTERPRETATIONS. USA+45 INTELL VOL/ASSN CONSULT   ACADEM
EDU/PROP PRESS DEBATE ADMIN REV HAPPINESS   ATTIT
RIGID/FLEX MAJORIT. PAGE 65 B1322   GP/REL

B65
LYONS G.M.,SCHOOLS FOR STRATEGY* EDUCATION AND   ACADEM
RESEARCH IN NATIONAL SECURITY AFFAIRS. USA+45 FINAN   ACT/RES
NAT/G VOL/ASSN FORCES TEC/DEV ADMIN WAR...GP/COMP   INTELL
IDEA/COMP PERS/COMP COLD/WAR. PAGE 67 B1351

B65
PENNICK JL J.R.,THE POLITICS OF AMERICAN SCIENCE,   POLICY
1939 TO THE PRESENT. USA+45 USA-45 INTELL TEC/DEV   ADMIN
DIPLOM NEW/LIB...ANTHOL 20 COLD/WAR. PAGE 82 B1651   PHIL/SCI
                                                       NAT/G

L65
HOOK S.,"SECOND THOUGHTS ON BERKELEY" USA+45 ELITES   ACADEM
INTELL LEGIT ADMIN COERCE REPRESENT GP/REL INGP/REL   ORD/FREE
TOTALISM AGE/Y MARXISM 20 BERKELEY FREE/SPEE   POLICY
STUDNT/PWR. PAGE 51 B1040   CREATE

S65
RUBINSTEIN A.Z.,"YUGOSLAVIA'S OPENING SOCIETY." COM   CONSTN
USSR INTELL NAT/G LEGIS TOP/EX LEGIT CT/SYS   EX/STRUC
RIGID/FLEX ALL/VALS SOCISM...HUM TIME/SEQ TREND 20.   YUGOSLAVIA
PAGE 92 B1851

S65
TABORSKY E.,"CHANGE IN CZECHOSLOVAKIA." COM USSR   ECO/DEV
ELITES INTELL AGRI INDUS NAT/G DELIB/GP EX/STRUC   PLAN
ECO/TAC TOTALISM ATTIT RIGID/FLEX SOCISM...MGT   CZECHOSLVK
CONCPT TREND 20. PAGE 102 B2067

B66
BRAIBANTI R.,RESEARCH ON THE BUREAUCRACY OF   HABITAT
PAKISTAN. PAKISTAN LAW CULTURE INTELL ACADEM LOC/G   NAT/G
SECT PRESS CT/SYS...LING CHARTS 20 BUREAUCRCY.   ADMIN
PAGE 15 B0299   CONSTN

B66
RAEFF M.,ORIGINS OF THE RUSSIAN INTELLIGENTSIA: THE   INTELL
EIGHTEENTH-CENTURY NOBILITY. RUSSIA FAM NAT/G   FLITES
EDU/PROP ADMIN PERS/REL ATTIT...HUM BIOG 18.   STRATA
PAGE 85 B1728   CONSERVE

B67
BRZEZINSKI Z.K.,THE SOVIET BLOC: UNITY AND CONFLICT   NAT/G
(2ND ED., REV., ENLARGED). COM POLAND USSR INTELL   DIPLOM
CHIEF EX/STRUC CONTROL EXEC GOV/REL PWR MARXISM
...TREND IDEA/COMP 20 LENIN/VI MARX/KARL STALIN/J.
PAGE 16 B0336

B67
ROFF W.R.,THE ORIGINS OF MALAY NATIONALISM.   NAT/LISM
MALAYSIA INTELL NAT/G ADMIN COLONIAL...BIBLIOG   ELITES
DICTIONARY 20 CMN/WLTH. PAGE 90 B1813   VOL/ASSN
                                                       SOCIETY

S67
BREGMAN A.,"WHITHER RUSSIA?" COM RUSSIA INTELL   MARXISM
POL/PAR DIPLOM PARTIC NAT/LISM TOTALISM ATTIT   ELITES
ORD/FREE 20. PAGE 15 B0304   ADMIN
                                                       CREATE

S67
LA PORTE T.,"DIFFUSION AND DISCONTINUITY IN   INTELL
SCIENCE, TECHNOLOGY AND PUBLIC AFFAIRS: RESULTS OF   ADMIN
A SEARCH IN THE FIELD." USA+45 ACT/RES TEC/DEV   ACADEM
PERS/REL ATTIT PHIL/SCI. PAGE 62 B1249   GP/REL

S67
MORTON J.A.,"A SYSTEMS APPROACH TO THE INNOVATION   TEC/DEV
PROCESS: ITS USE IN THE BELL SYSTEM." USA+45 INTELL   GEN/METH
INDUS LG/CO CONSULT WORKER COMPUTER AUTOMAT DEMAND   R+D
...MGT CHARTS 20. PAGE 76 B1531   COM/IND

S67
ROBERTS E.B.,"THE PROBLEM OF AGING ORGANIZATIONS."   INDUS
INTELL PROB/SOLV ADMIN EXEC FEEDBACK EFFICIENCY   R+D
PRODUC...GEN/LAWS 20. PAGE 89 B1794   MGT
                                                       PLAN

S67
ROSENZWEIG J.E.,"MANAGERS AND MANAGEMENT SCIENTISTS   EFFICIENCY
(TWO CULTURES)" INDUS CREATE TEC/DEV OPTIMAL   MGT
...NEW/IDEA 20. PAGE 90 B1823   INTELL
                                                       METH/COMP

S67
WALLER D.J.,"CHINA: RED OR EXPERT." CHINA/COM   CONTROL
INTELL DOMIN REV ATTIT MARXISM 20. PAGE 113 B2283   FORCES
                                                       ADMIN
                                                       POL/PAR

N19
VERNON R.,THE MYTH AND REALITY OF OUR URBAN PLAN
PROBLEMS (PAMPHLET). USA+45 SOCIETY LOC/G ADMIN MUNIC
COST 20 PRINCETN/U INTERVENT URBAN/RNWL. PAGE 112 HABITAT
B2261 PROB/SOLV

B60
PIERCE R.A.,RUSSIAN CENTRAL ASIA, 1867-1917. ASIA COLONIAL
RUSSIA CULTURE AGRI INDUS EDU/PROP REV NAT/LISM DOMIN
...CHARTS BIBLIOG 19/20 BOLSHEVISM INTERVENT. ADMIN
PAGE 83 B1672 ECO/UNDEV

INTERVIEWING....SEE INT, REC/INT

INTERVIEWS....SEE INTERVIEWS INDEX, P. XIV

INTGOV/REL....ADVISORY COMMISSION ON INTERGOVERNMENTAL
RELATIONS

INTL INST ADMIN SCIENCES B1100

INTL UNION LOCAL AUTHORITIES B1101

INTL/DEV....INTERNATIONAL DEVELOPMENT ASSOCIATION

INTL/ECON....INTERNATIONAL ECONOMIC ASSOCIATION

INTL/FINAN....INTERNATIONAL FINANCE CORPORATION

INTRAGROUP RELATIONS....SEE INGP/REL

INTRVN/ECO....INTERVENTION (ECONOMIC) - PHILOSOPHY OF
GOVERNMENTAL INTERFERENCE IN DOMESTIC ECONOMIC AFFAIRS

B58
DWARKADAS R.,ROLE OF HIGHER CIVIL SERVICE IN INDIA. ADMIN
INDIA ECO/UNDEV LEGIS PROB/SOLV GP/REL PERS/REL NAT/G
...POLICY WELF/ST DECISION ORG/CHARTS BIBLIOG 20 ROLE
CIVIL/SERV INTRVN/ECO. PAGE 31 B0637 PLAN

INTST/CRIM....U.S. INTERSTATE COMMISSION ON CRIME

INVENTION....SEE CREATE

INVESTMENT....SEE FINAN

IOVTCHOUK M.T. B1102

IOWA....IOWA

IPSEN H.P. B1103

IRAN....SEE ALSO ISLAM

B53
MACK R.T.,RAISING THE WORLDS STANDARD OF LIVING. WOR+45
IRAN INT/ORG VOL/ASSN EX/STRUC ECO/TAC WEALTH...MGT FOR/AID
METH/CNCPT STAT CONT/OBS INT TOT/POP VAL/FREE 20 INT/TRADE
UN. PAGE 67 B1363

S59
GABLE R.W.,"CULTURE AND ADMINISTRATION IN IRAN." ADMIN
IRAN EXEC PARTIC REPRESENT PWR. PAGE 38 B0770 CULTURE
EX/STRUC
INGP/REL

B60
LENCZOWSKI G.,OIL AND STATE IN THE MIDDLE EAST. FUT ISLAM
IRAN LAW ECO/UNDEV EXTR/IND NAT/G TOP/EX PLAN INDUS
TEC/DEV ECO/TAC LEGIT ADMIN COERCE ATTIT ALL/VALS NAT/LISM
PWR...CHARTS 20. PAGE 64 B1288

B61
US GENERAL ACCOUNTING OFFICE.EXAMINATION OF FOR/AID
ECONOMIC AND TECHNICAL ASSISTANCE PROGRAM FOR IRAN. ADMIN
IRAN USA+45 AGRI INDUS DIPLOM CONTROL COST 20. TEC/DEV
PAGE 108 B2186 ECO/UNDEV

B62
BINDER L.,IRAN: POLITICAL DEVELOPMENT IN A CHANGING LEGIT
SOCIETY. IRAN OP/RES REV GP/REL CENTRAL RATIONAL NAT/G
PWR...PHIL/SCI NAT/COMP GEN/LAWS 20. PAGE 12 B0239 ADMIN
STRUCT

S63
ARASTEH R.,"THE ROLE OF INTELLECTUALS IN INTELL
ADMINISTRATIVE DEVELOPMENT AND SOCIAL CHANGE IN ADMIN
MODERN IRAN." ISLAM CULTURE NAT/G CONSULT ACT/RES IRAN
EDU/PROP EXEC ATTIT BIO/SOC PERCEPT SUPEGO ALL/VALS
...POLICY MGT PSY SOC CONCPT 20. PAGE 6 B0123

B67
BALDWIN G.B.,PLANNING AND DEVELOPMENT IN IRAN. IRAN PLAN
AGRI INDUS CONSULT WORKER EDU/PROP BAL/PAY...CHARTS ECO/UNDEV
20. PAGE 8 B0173 ADMIN
PROB/SOLV

IRAQ....SEE ALSO ISLAM

IRELAND....SEE ALSO UK

B46
GRIFFIN G.G.,A GUIDE TO MANUSCRIPTS RELATING TO BIBLIOG/A
AMERICAN HISTORY IN BRITISH DEPOSITORIES. CANADA ALL/VALS
IRELAND MOD/EUR UK USA-45 LAW DIPLOM ADMIN COLONIAL NAT/G
WAR NAT/LISM SOVEREIGN...GEOG INT/LAW 15/19
CMN/WLTH. PAGE 43 B0876

B62
DELANY V.T.H.,THE ADMINISTRATION OF JUSTICE IN ADMIN
IRELAND. IRELAND CONSTN FINAN JUDGE COLONIAL CRIME JURID
...CRIMLGY 19/20. PAGE 28 B0571 CT/SYS
ADJUD

B62
GROGAN V.,ADMINISTRATIVE TRIBUNALS IN THE PUBLIC ADMIN
SERVICE. IRELAND UK NAT/G CONTROL CT/SYS...JURID LAW
GOV/COMP 20. PAGE 44 B0884 ADJUD
DELIB/GP

B62
INSTITUTE OF PUBLIC ADMIN.A SHORT HISTORY OF THE ADMIN
PUBLIC SERVICE IN IRELAND. IRELAND UK DIST/IND WORKER
INGP/REL FEDERAL 13/20 CIVIL/SERV. PAGE 54 B1091 GOV/REL
NAT/G

B63
RICHARDSON H.G.,THE ADMINISTRATION OF IRELAND ADMIN
1172-1377. IRELAND CONSTN EX/STRUC LEGIS JUDGE NAT/G
CT/SYS PARL/PROC...CHARTS BIBLIOG 12/14. PAGE 88 PWR
B1775

IRGUN....IRGUN - PALESTINE REVOLUTIONARY ORGANIZATION

IRIKURA J.K. B1104

IRISH/AMER....IRISH AMERICANS

IRS....U.S. INTERNAL REVENUE SERVICE

B63
DEAN A.L.,FEDERAL AGENCY APPROACHES TO FIELD ADMIN
MANAGEMENT (PAMPHLET). R+D DELIB/GP EX/STRUC MGT
PROB/SOLV GOV/REL...CLASSIF BIBLIOG 20 FAA NASA NAT/G
DEPT/HEW POSTAL/SYS IRS. PAGE 28 B0563 OP/RES

ISLAM R. B1105

ISLAM....ISLAMIC WORLD; SEE ALSO APPROPRIATE NATIONS

N19
KUWAIT ARABIA,KUWAIT FUND FOR ARAB ECONOMIC FOR/AID
DEVELOPMENT (PAMPHLET). ISLAM KUWAIT UAR ECO/UNDEV DIPLOM
LEGIS ECO/TAC WEALTH 20. PAGE 62 B1245 FINAN
ADMIN

B26
MOON P.T.,IMPERIALISM AND WORLD POLITICS. AFR ASIA WEALTH
ISLAM MOD/EUR S/ASIA USA-45 SOCIETY NAT/G EX/STRUC TIME/SEQ
BAL/PWR DOMIN COLONIAL NAT/LISM ATTIT DRIVE PWR CAP/ISM
...GEOG SOC 20. PAGE 75 B1510 DIPLOM

B34
DE CENIVAL P.,BIBLIOGRAPHIE MAROCAINE: 1923-1933. BIBLIOG/A
FRANCE MOROCCO SECT ADMIN LEAD GP/REL ATTIT...LING ISLAM
20. PAGE 27 B0551 NAT/G
COLONIAL

B38
DAY C.,A HISTORY OF COMMERCE. CHRIST-17C EUR+WWI MARKET
ISLAM MEDIT-7 MOD/EUR USA-45 ECO/DEV FINAN NAT/G INT/TRADE
ECO/TAC EXEC ROUTINE PWR WEALTH HIST/WRIT. PAGE 27
B0546

C54
LANDAU J.M.,"PARLIAMENTS AND PARTIES IN EGYPT." UAR ISLAM
NAT/G SECT CONSULT LEGIS TOP/EX PROB/SOLV ADMIN NAT/LISM
COLONIAL...GEN/LAWS BIBLIOG 19/20. PAGE 62 B1254 PARL/PROC
POL/PAR

C55
GRASSMUCK G.L.,"A MANUAL OF LEBANESE ADMIN
ADMINISTRATION." LEBANON PLAN...CHARTS BIBLIOG/A NAT/G
20. PAGE 42 B0854 ISLAM
EX/STRUC

B58
LAQUER W.Z.,THE MIDDLE EAST IN TRANSITION. COM USSR ISLAM
ECO/UNDEV NAT/G VOL/ASSN EDU/PROP ATTIT DRIVE TREND
PWR MARXISM COLD/WAR TOT/POP 20. PAGE 62 B1261 NAT/LISM

S59
HARVEY M.F.,"THE PALESTINE REFUGEE PROBLEM: ACT/RES
ELEMENTS OF A SOLUTION." ISLAM LAW INT/ORG DELIB/GP LEGIT
TOP/EX ECO/TAC ROUTINE DRIVE HEALTH LOVE ORD/FREE PEACE
PWR WEALTH...MAJORIT FAO 20. PAGE 48 B0964 ISRAEL

B60
LENCZOWSKI G.,OIL AND STATE IN THE MIDDLE EAST. FUT ISLAM
IRAN LAW ECO/UNDEV EXTR/IND NAT/G TOP/EX PLAN INDUS
TEC/DEV ECO/TAC LEGIT ADMIN COERCE ATTIT ALL/VALS NAT/LISM
PWR...CHARTS 20. PAGE 64 B1288

S60
GARNICK D.H.,"ON THE ECONOMIC FEASIBILITY OF A MARKET
MIDDLE EASTERN ISLAM COMMON MARKET." AFR ISLAM CULTURE INT/TRADE
INDUS NAT/G PLAN TEC/DEV ECO/TAC ADMIN ATTIT DRIVE
RIGID/FLEX...PLURIST STAT TREND GEN/LAWS 20.
PAGE 39 B0784

B61
FRIEDMANN W.G.,JOINT INTERNATIONAL BUSINESS ECO/UNDEV
VENTURES. ASIA ISLAM L/A+17C ECO/DEV DIST/IND FINAN INT/TRADE

PROC/MFG FACE/GP LG/CO NAT/G VOL/ASSN CONSULT
EX/STRUC PLAN ADMIN ROUTINE WEALTH...OLD/LIB WORK
20. PAGE 37 B0760

B61
HASAN H.S.,PAKISTAN AND THE UN. ISLAM WOR+45   INT/ORG
ECO/DEV ECO/UNDEV NAT/G TOP/EX ECO/TAC FOR/AID   ATTIT
EDU/PROP ADMIN DRIVE PERCEPT...OBS TIME/SEQ UN 20.   PAKISTAN
PAGE 48 B0965

B62
HARARI M.,GOVERNMENT AND POLITICS OF THE MIDDLE   DIPLOM
EAST. ISLAM USA+45 NAT/G SECT CHIEF ADMIN ORD/FREE   ECO/UNDEV
20. PAGE 47 B0943   TEC/DEV
                                                     POLICY

L62
MANGIN G.,"L'ORGANIZATION JUDICIAIRE DES ETATS   AFR
D'AFRIQUE ET DE MADAGASCAR." ISLAM WOR+45 STRATA   LEGIS
STRUCT ECO/UNDEV NAT/G LEGIT EXEC...JURID TIME/SEQ   COLONIAL
TOT/POP 20 SUPREME/CT. PAGE 69 B1387   MADAGASCAR

L62
WATERSTON A.,"PLANNING IN MOROCCO, ORGANIZATION AND NAT/G
IMPLEMENTATION. BALTIMORE: HOPKINS ECON. DEVELOP.   PLAN
INT. BANK FOR." ISLAM ECO/DEV AGRI DIST/IND INDUS   MOROCCO
PROC/MFG SERV/IND LOC/G EX/STRUC ECO/TAC PWR WEALTH
TOT/POP VAL/FREE 20. PAGE 114 B2302

S62
MANGIN G.,"LES ACCORDS DE COOPERATION EN MATIERE DE INT/ORG
JUSTICE ENTRE LA FRANCE ET LES ETATS AFRICAINS ET   LAW
MALGACHE." AFR ISLAM WOR+45 STRUCT ECO/UNDEV NAT/G   FRANCE
DELIB/GP PERCEPT ALL/VALS...JURID MGT TIME/SEQ 20.
PAGE 69 B1386

B63
FISHER S.N.,THE MILITARY IN THE MIDDLE EAST: EX/STRUC
PROBLEMS IN SOCIETY AND GOVERNMENT. ISLAM USA+45   FORCES
NAT/G DOMIN LEGIT COERCE ORD/FREE PWR...TIME/SEQ
VAL/FREE 20. PAGE 36 B0725

L63
ROBERT J.,"LES ELECTIONS LEGISLATIVES DU 17 MAI   CHOOSE
1963 ET L'EVOLUTION POLITIQUE INTERNE DU MAROC."   MOROCCO
ISLAM WOR+45 NAT/G POL/PAR EXEC ALL/VALS 20.
PAGE 89 B1792

S63
ARASTEH R.,"THE ROLE OF INTELLECTUALS IN   INTELL
ADMINISTRATIVE DEVELOPMENT AND SOCIAL CHANGE IN   ADMIN
MODERN IRAN." ISLAM CULTURE NAT/G CONSULT ACT/RES   IRAN
EDU/PROP EXEC ATTIT BIO/SOC PERCEPT SUPEGO ALL/VALS
...POLICY MGT PSY SOC CONCPT 20. PAGE 6 B0123

S63
RUSTOW D.A.,"THE MILITARY IN MIDDLE EASTERN SOCIETY FORCES
AND POLITICS." FUT ISLAM CONSTN SOCIETY FACE/GP   ELITES
NAT/G POL/PAR PROF/ORG CONSULT DOMIN ADMIN EXEC
REGION COERCE NAT/LISM ATTIT DRIVE PERSON ORD/FREE
PWR...POLICY CONCPT OBS STERTYP 20. PAGE 92 B1860

B65
ETZIONI A.,POLITICAL UNIFICATION* A COMPARATIVE   INT/ORG
STUDY OF LEADERS AND FORCES. EUR+WWI ISLAM L/A+17C   FORCES
WOR+45 ELITES STRATA EXEC WEALTH...TIME/SEQ TREND   ECO/TAC
SOC/EXP. PAGE 34 B0686   REGION

B65
INST INTL DES CIVILISATION DIF,THE CONSTITUTIONS   CONSTN
AND ADMINISTRATIVE INSTITUTIONS OF THE NEW STATES.   ADMIN
AFR ISLAM S/ASIA NAT/G POL/PAR DELIB/GP EX/STRUC   ADJUD
CONFER EFFICIENCY NAT/LISM...JURID SOC 20. PAGE 54   ECO/UNDEV
B1088

B65
INT. BANK RECONSTR. DEVELOP.,ECONOMIC DEVELOPMENT   INDUS
OF KUWAIT. ISLAM KUWAIT AGRI FINAN MARKET EX/STRUC   NAT/G
TEC/DEV ECO/TAC ADMIN WEALTH...OBS CON/ANAL CHARTS
20. PAGE 54 B1092

B65
MACDONALD R.W.,THE LEAGUE OF ARAB STATES: A STUDY   ISLAM
IN THE DYNAMICS OF REGIONAL ORGANIZATION. ISRAEL   REGION
UAR USSR FINAN INT/ORG DELIB/GP ECO/TAC AGREE   DIPLOM
NEUTRAL ORD/FREE PWR...DECISION BIBLIOG 20 TREATY   ADMIN
UN. PAGE 67 B1358

S67
DUGGAR J.W.,"THE DEVELOPMENT OF MONEY SUPPLY IN   ECO/UNDEV
ETHIOPIA." ETHIOPIA ISLAM CONSULT OP/RES BUDGET   FINAN
CONTROL ROUTINE EFFICIENCY EQUILIB WEALTH...MGT 20. BAL/PAY
PAGE 31 B0629   ECOMETRIC

N67
US SENATE COMM ON FOREIGN REL,THE UNITED NATIONS   INT/ORG
PEACEKEEPING DILEMMA (PAMPHLET). ISLAM WOR+45   DIPLOM
PROB/SOLV BUDGET ADMIN SENATE UN. PAGE 110 B2224   PEACE

ISOLAT....ISOLATION AND COMMUNITY, CONDITIONS OF HIGH
     GROUP SEGREGATION

S59
DWYER R.J.,"THE ADMINISTRATIVE ROLE IN   ADMIN
DESEGREGATION." USA+45 LAW PROB/SOLV LEAD RACE/REL   SCHOOL
ISOLAT STRANGE ROLE...POLICY SOC/INTEG MISSOURI   DISCRIM
NEGRO CIV/RIGHTS. PAGE 31 B0638   ATTIT

B62
MARTIN R.C.,GOVERNMENT AND THE SUBURBAN SCHOOL.   SCHOOL
USA+45 FINAN EDU/PROP ADMIN HABITAT...TREND GP/COMP LOC/G
20. PAGE 70 B1414   EX/STRUC

ISOLAT
S67
RUBIN R.I.,"THE LEGISLATIVE-EXECUTIVE RELATIONS OF   LEGIS
THE UNITED STATES INFORMATION AGENCY." USA+45   EX/STRUC
EDU/PROP TASK INGP/REL EFFICIENCY ISOLAT ATTIT ROLE GP/REL
USIA CONGRESS. PAGE 91 B1850   PROF/ORG

ISOLATION....SEE ISOLAT

ISRAEL....SEE ALSO JEWS, ISLAM

N19
FIKS M.,PUBLIC ADMINISTRATION IN ISRAEL (PAMPHLET). EDU/PROP
ISRAEL SCHOOL EX/STRUC BUDGET PAY INGP/REL   NAT/G
...DECISION 20 CIVIL/SERV. PAGE 35 B0718   ADMIN
                                                     WORKER

B59
ROSOLIO D.,TEN YEARS OF THE CIVIL SERVICE IN ISRAEL ADMIN
(1948-1958) (PAMPHLET). ISRAEL NAT/G RECEIVE 20.   WORKER
PAGE 90 B1825   GOV/REL
                                                     PAY

S59
HARVEY M.F.,"THE PALESTINE REFUGEE PROBLEM: ACT/RES
ELEMENTS OF A SOLUTION." ISLAM LAW INT/ORG DELIB/GP LEGIT
TOP/EX ECO/TAC ROUTINE HEALTH LOVE ORD/FREE   PEACE
PWR WEALTH...MAJORIT FAO 20. PAGE 48 B0964   ISRAEL

B62
GALENSON W.,LABOR IN DEVELOPING COUNTRIES. BRAZIL   LABOR
INDONESIA ISRAEL PAKISTAN TURKEY AGRI INDUS WORKER   ECO/UNDEV
PAY PRICE GP/REL WEALTH...MGT CHARTS METH/COMP   BARGAIN
NAT/COMP 20. PAGE 38 B0775   POL/PAR

B63
BADI J.,THE GOVERNMENT OF THE STATE OF ISRAEL: A   NAT/G
CRITICAL ACCOUNT OF ITS PARLIAMENT, EXECUTIVE, AND   CONSTN
JUDICIARY. ISRAEL ECO/DEV CHIEF DELIB/GP LEGIS   EX/STRUC
DIPLOM CT/SYS INGP/REL PEACE ORD/FREE...BIBLIOG 20   POL/PAR
PARLIAMENT ARABS MIGRATION. PAGE 8 B0157

B64
DUROSELLE J.B.,POLITIQUES NATIONALES ENVERS LES   DIPLOM
JEUNES ETATS. FRANCE ISRAEL ITALY UK USA+45 USSR   ECO/UNDEV
YUGOSLAVIA ECO/DEV FINAN ECO/TAC INT/TRADE ADMIN   COLONIAL
PWR 20. PAGE 31 B0634   DOMIN

B64
OECD SEMINAR REGIONAL DEV,REGIONAL DEVELOPMENT IN   ADMIN
ISRAEL. ISRAEL STRUCT ECO/UNDEV NAT/G REGION...GEOG PROVS
20. PAGE 79 B1603   PLAN
                                                     METH/COMP

B65
MACDONALD R.W.,THE LEAGUE OF ARAB STATES: A STUDY   ISLAM
IN THE DYNAMICS OF REGIONAL ORGANIZATION. ISRAEL   REGION
UAR USSR FINAN INT/ORG DELIB/GP ECO/TAC AGREE   DIPLOM
NEUTRAL ORD/FREE PWR...DECISION BIBLIOG 20 TREATY   ADMIN
UN. PAGE 67 B1358

B65
MATRAS J.,SOCIAL CHANGE IN ISRAEL. ISRAEL STRATA   SECT
FAM ACT/RES EDU/PROP ADMIN CHOOSE...STAT CENSUS   NAT/LISM
19/20 JEWS. PAGE 71 B1427   GEOG
                                                     STRUCT

B66
BOYD H.W.,MARKETING MANAGEMENT: CASES FROM EMERGING MGT
COUNTRIES. BRAZIL GHANA ISRAEL WOR+45 ADMIN   ECO/UNDEV
PERS/REL ATTIT HABITAT WEALTH...ANTHOL 20 ARGEN   PROB/SOLV
CASEBOOK. PAGE 14 B0292   MARKET

ISSUES (CURRENT SUBJECTS OF DISCOURSE)....SEE CONCPT, POLICY

ITAL/AMER....ITALIAN-AMERICANS

ITALY....SEE ALSO APPROPRIATE TIME/SPACE/CULTURE INDEX

B05
MACHIAVELLI N.,THE ART OF WAR. CHRIST-17C TOP/EX   NAT/G
DRIVE ORD/FREE PWR SKILL...MGT CHARTS. PAGE 67   FORCES
B1360   WAR
                                                     ITALY

B18
WILSON W.,THE STATE: ELEMENTS OF HISTORICAL AND   NAT/G
PRACTICAL POLITICS. FRANCE GERMANY ITALY UK USSR   JURID
CONSTN EX/STRUC LEGIS CT/SYS WAR PWR...POLICY   CONCPT
GOV/COMP 20. PAGE 117 B2363   NAT/COMP

S37
LASSWELL H.D.,"GOVERNMENTAL AND PARTY LEADERS IN   ELITES
FASCIST ITALY." ITALY CRIME SKILL...BIOG CHARTS   FASCISM
GP/COMP 20. PAGE 63 B1266   ADMIN

B38
FIELD G.L.,THE SYNDICAL AND CORPORATIVE   FASCISM
INSTITUTIONS OF ITALIAN FASCISM. ITALY CONSTN   INDUS
STRATA LABOR EX/STRUC TOP/EX ADJUD ADMIN LEAD   NAT/G
TOTALISM AUTHORIT...MGT 20 MUSSOLIN/B. PAGE 35   WORKER
B0716

B38
PETTEE G.S.,THE PROCESS OF REVOLUTION. COM FRANCE   COERCE
ITALY MOD/EUR RUSSIA SPAIN WOR-45 ELITES INTELL   CONCPT
SOCIETY STRATA STRUCT INT/ORG NAT/G POL/PAR ACT/RES REV
PLAN EDU/PROP LEGIT EXEC...SOC MYTH TIME/SEQ
TOT/POP 18/20. PAGE 82 B1664

ANDERSON W.,LOCAL GOVERNMENT IN EUROPE. FRANCE   GOV/COMP B39
GERMANY ITALY UK USSR MUNIC PROVS ADMIN GOV/REL   NAT/COMP
CENTRAL SOVEREIGN 20. PAGE 5 B0099   LOC/G
    CONSTN

CONOVER H.F.,THE GOVERNMENTS OF THE MAJOR FOREIGN   BIBLIOG B45
POWERS: A BIBLIOGRAPHY. FRANCE GERMANY ITALY UK   NAT/G
USSR CONSTN LOC/G POL/PAR EX/STRUC FORCES ADMIN   DIPLOM
CT/SYS CIVMIL/REL TOTALISM...POLICY 19/20. PAGE 23
B0464

CONOVER H.F.,NON-SELF-GOVERNING AREAS. BELGIUM   BIBLIOG/A B47
FRANCE ITALY UK WOR+45 CULTURE ECO/UNDEV INT/ORG   COLONIAL
LOC/G NAT/G ECO/TAC INT/TRADE ADMIN HEALTH...SOC   DIPLOM
UN. PAGE 23 B0465

ALBONETTI A.,"IL SECONDO PROGRAMMA QUINQUENNALE   R+D S62
1963-67 ED IL BILANCIO RICERCHE ED INVESTIMENTI PER   PLAN
IL 1963 DELL'ERATOM." EUR+WWI FUT ITALY WOR+45   NUC/PWR
ECO/DEV SERV/IND INT/ORG TEC/DEV ECO/TAC ATTIT
SKILL WEALTH...MGT TIME/SEQ OEEC 20. PAGE 3 B0069

FRIED R.C.,THE ITALIAN PREFECTS. ITALY STRATA   ADMIN B63
ECO/DEV NAT/LISM ALL/IDEOS...TREND CHARTS METH/COMP NAT/G
BIBLIOG 17/20 PREFECT. PAGE 37 B0755   EFFICIENCY

KOGAN N.,THE POLITICS OF ITALIAN FOREIGN POLICY.   NAT/G B63
EUR+WWI LEGIS DOMIN LEGIT EXEC PWR RESPECT SKILL   ROUTINE
...POLICY DECISION HUM SOC METH/CNCPT OBS INT   DIPLOM
CHARTS 20. PAGE 61 B1227   ITALY

MEYNAUD J.,PLANIFICATION ET POLITIQUE. FRANCE ITALY PLAN B63
FINAN LABOR DELIB/GP LEGIS ADMIN EFFICIENCY   ECO/TAC
...MAJORIT DECISION 20. PAGE 73 B1477   PROB/SOLV

DUROSELLE J.B.,POLITIQUES NATIONALES ENVERS LES   DIPLOM B64
JEUNES ETATS. FRANCE ISRAEL ITALY UK USA+45 USSR   ECO/UNDEV
YUGOSLAVIA ECO/DEV FINAN ECO/TAC INT/TRADE ADMIN   COLONIAL
PWR 20. PAGE 31 B0634   DOMIN

VECCHIO G.D.,L'ETAT ET LE DROIT. ITALY CONSTN   NAT/G B64
EX/STRUC LEGIS DIPLOM CT/SYS...JURID 20 UN.   SOVEREIGN
PAGE 112 B2256   CONCPT
    INT/LAW

EDELMAN M.,THE POLITICS OF WAGE-PRICE DECISIONS.   GOV/COMP B65
GERMANY ITALY NETHERLAND UK INDUS LABOR POL/PAR   CONTROL
PROB/SOLV BARGAIN PRICE ROUTINE BAL/PAY COST DEMAND ECO/TAC
20. PAGE 32 B0654   PLAN

MEISEL J.H.,PARETO & MOSCA. ITALY STRUCT ADMIN   PWR B65
...SOC CON/ANAL ANTHOL BIBLIOG 19/20. PAGE 72 B1463 ELITES
    CONTROL
    LAISSEZ

ADAMS J.C.,THE GOVERNMENT OF REPUBLICAN ITALY (2ND   NAT/G B66
ED.). ITALY LOC/G POL/PAR DELIB/GP LEGIS WORKER   CHOOSE
ADMIN CT/SYS FASCISM...CHARTS BIBLIOG 20   EX/STRUC
PARLIAMENT. PAGE 3 B0057   CONSTN

EVANS R.H.,COEXISTENCE: COMMUNISM AND ITS PRACTICE   MARXISM B67
IN BOLOGNA, 1945-1965. ITALY CAP/ISM ADMIN CHOOSE   CULTURE
PEACE ORD/FREE...SOC STAT DEEP/INT SAMP CHARTS   MUNIC
BIBLIOG 20. PAGE 34 B0690   POL/PAR

POSNER M.V.,ITALIAN PUBLIC ENTERPRISE. ITALY   NAT/G B67
ECO/DEV FINAN INDUS CREATE ECO/TAC ADMIN CONTROL   PLAN
EFFICIENCY PRODUC...TREND CHARTS 20. PAGE 84 B1693 CAP/ISM
    SOCISM

ITO....INTERNATIONAL TRADE ORGANIZATION

ITU....INTERNATIONAL TELECOMMUNICATIONS UNION

IVORY COAST....SEE IVORY/CST

IVORY/CST....IVORY COAST; SEE ALSO AFR

CLIGNET R.,"POTENTIAL ELITES IN GHANA AND THE IVORY PWR S64
COAST: A PRELIMINARY SURVEY." AFR CULTURE ELITES   LEGIT
STRATA KIN NAT/G SECT DOMIN EXEC ORD/FREE RESPECT   IVORY/CST
SKILL...POLICY RELATIV GP/COMP NAT/COMP 20. PAGE 21 GHANA
B0438

IWW....INTERNATIONAL WORKERS OF THE WORLD

J

JACKSON E. B1106

JACKSON H.M. B1107

JACKSON J.R. B0593

JACKSON R.G.A. B1108

JACKSON R.M. B1109

JACKSON W.V. B1110

JACKSON/A....PRESIDENT ANDREW JACKSON

MONTGOMERY H.,CRACKER PARTIES. CULTURE EX/STRUC   POL/PAR B50
LEAD PWR POPULISM...TIME/SEQ 19 GEORGIA CALHOUN/JC PROVS
COBB/HOWLL JACKSON/A. PAGE 74 B1505   ELITES
    BIOG

WHITE L.D.,THE JACKSONIANS: A STUDY IN   NAT/G B54
ADMINISTRATIVE HISTORY 1829-1861. USA-45 CONSTN   ADMIN
POL/PAR CHIEF DELIB/GP LEGIS CREATE PROB/SOLV   POLICY
ECO/TAC LEAD REGION GP/REL 19 PRESIDENT CONGRESS
JACKSON/A. PAGE 116 B2339

JACKSON/RH....R.H. JACKSON

JACOB H. B1111,B1112

JACOBINISM....JACOBINISM: FRENCH DEMOCRATIC REVOLUTIONARY
    DOCTRINE, 1789

JACOBS J. B1113

JACOBS P. B1114

JACOBSEN K.D. B0649

JACOBSON E. B2316

JACOBSON H.K. B1115

JACOBSON J. B1116

JACOBY S.B. B1117

JAFFA/HU....H.U. JAFFA

JAIN R.K. B1118

JAKARTA....JAKARTA, INDONESIA

JAKUBAUSKAS E.B. B1119

JAMAICA....SEE ALSO L/A+17C

HAMILTON B.L.S.,PROBLEMS OF ADMINISTRATION IN AN   ADMIN B64
EMERGENT NATION: CASE STUDY OF JAMAICA. JAMAICA UK ECO/UNDEV
WOR+45 MUNIC COLONIAL HABITAT...CHARTS BIBLIOG 20   GOV/REL
CIVIL/SERV. PAGE 46 B0932   NAT/G

JANET/P....PIERRE JANET

JANOWITZ M. B1120,B1121,B1122,B1123

JANSE R.S. B1124

JAPAN....SEE ALSO ASIA

JAPAN MINISTRY OF JUSTICE B1125

JAPAN MOMBUSHO DAIGAKU GAKIYUT B1126

JAPANESE AMERICANS....SEE NISEI

JARMO....JARMO, A PRE- OR EARLY HISTORIC SOCIETY

JASPERS/K....KARL JASPERS

RUITENBEER H.M.,THE DILEMMA OF ORGANIZATIONAL   PERSON B63
SOCIETY. CULTURE ECO/DEV MUNIC SECT TEC/DEV   ROLE
EDU/PROP NAT/LISM ORD/FREE...NAT/COMP 20 RIESMAN/D ADMIN
WHYTE/WF MERTON/R MEAD/MARG JASPERS/K. PAGE 92   WORKER
B1855

JAT....A POLITICAL SYSTEM OF INDIA

JAURES/JL....JEAN LEON JAURES (FRENCH SOCIALIST 1859-1914)

JAVA....JAVA, INDONESIA; SEE ALSO INDONESIA

JAVITS J.K. B1127

JAY J. B0931

JEFFERSN/T....PRESIDENT THOMAS JEFFERSON

WHITE L.D.,THE FEDERALISTS: A STUDY IN   ADMIN B48
ADMINISTRATIVE HISTORY. STRUCT DELIB/GP LEGIS   NAT/G
BUDGET ROUTINE GOV/REL GP/REL PERS/REL PWR...BIOG POLICY

18/19 PRESIDENT CONGRESS WASHINGT/G JEFFERSN/T   PROB/SOLV
HAMILTON/A. PAGE 116 B2337
                                                                    B51
WHITE L.D.,THE JEFFERSONIANS: A STUDY IN   ADMIN
ADMINISTRATIVE HISTORY 18011829. USA-45 DELIB/GP   NAT/G
LEGIS TOP/EX PROB/SOLV BUDGET ECO/TAC GP/REL   POLICY
FEDERAL...BIOG IDEA/COMP 19 PRESIDENT CONGRESS   POL/PAR
JEFFERSN/T. PAGE 116 B2338

JEHOVA/WIT....JEHOVAHOS WITNESSES

JENCKS C.E. B1128

JENCKS/C....C. JENCKS

JENKINS W.S. B1129,B1130

JENNINGS E.E. B1131

JENNINGS I. B1132,B1133

JENNINGS M.K. B1134,B1205,B1206

JENNINGS W.I. B1135,B1136,B1137

JEWELL M.E. B1138,B1139

JEWS....JEWS, JUDAISM
                                                                    B48
BONAPARTE M.,MYTHS OF WAR. GERMANY WOR+45 WOR-45   ROUTINE
CULTURE SOCIETY NAT/G FORCES LEGIT ATTIT ALL/VALS   MYTH
...CONCPT HIST/WRIT TIME/SEQ 20 JEWS. PAGE 13 B0271 WAR
                                                                    B48
KESSELMAN L.C.,THE SOCIAL POLITICS OF THE FEPC.   POLICY
INDUS WORKER EDU/PROP GP/REL RACE/REL 20 NEGRO JEWS NAT/G
FEPC. PAGE 59 B1200   ADMIN
                                                    DISCRIM
                                                                    B53
MEYER P.,THE JEWS IN THE SOVIET SATELLITES.   COM
CZECHOSLVK POLAND SOCIETY STRATA NAT/G BAL/PWR   SECT
ECO/TAC EDU/PROP LEGIT ADMIN COERCE ATTIT DISPL   TOTALISM
PERCEPT HEALTH PWR RESPECT WEALTH...METH/CNCPT JEWS USSR
VAL/FREE NAZI 20. PAGE 73 B1474
                                                                    B65
MATRAS J.,SOCIAL CHANGE IN ISRAEL. ISRAEL STRATA   SECT
FAM ACT/RES EDU/PROP ADMIN CHOOSE...STAT CENSUS   NAT/LISM
19/20 JEWS. PAGE 71 B1427   GEOG
                                                    STRUCT

JHANGIANI M.A. B1140

JOELSON M.R. B1141

JOHN BIRCH SOCIETY....SEE BIRCH/SOC

JOHN/XXII....POPE JOHN XXII

JOHN/XXIII....POPE JOHN XXIII

JOHNS R. B1142

JOHNSN/ALB....ALBERT JOHNSON

JOHNSN/AND....PRESIDENT ANDREW JOHNSON

JOHNSN/LB....PRESIDENT LYNDON BAINES JOHNSON

JOHNSON H. B1143

JOHNSON K.F. B1144

JOHNSON L.B. B1145

JOHNSON N. B1146,B1147

JOHNSON/D....D. JOHNSON

JOHNSON/LB
                                                                    B65
FEERICK J.D.,FROM FAILING HANDS: THE STUDY OF   EX/STRUC
PRESIDENTIAL SUCCESSION. CONSTN NAT/G PROB/SOLV   CHIEF
LEAD PARL/PROC MURDER CHOOSE...NEW/IDEA BIBLIOG 20 LAW
KENNEDY/JF JOHNSON/LB PRESIDENT PRE/US/AM   LEGIS
VICE/PRES. PAGE 35 B0710
                                                                    B67
WARREN S.,THE AMERICAN PRESIDENT. POL/PAR FORCES   CHIEF
LEGIS DIPLOM ECO/TAC ADMIN EXEC PWR...ANTHOL 18/20 LEAD
ROOSEVLT/F KENNEDY/JF JOHNSON/LB TRUMAN/HS   NAT/G
WILSON/W. PAGE 114 B2297   CONSTN
                                                                    S67
GORHAM W.,"NOTES OF A PRACTITIONER." USA+45 BUDGET DECISION
ADMIN COST...CON/ANAL METH/COMP 20 JOHNSON/LB.   NAT/G

PAGE 41 B0836   DELIB/GP
                                                    EFFICIENCY
                                                                    S67
O'DELL J.H.,"THE JULY REBELLIONS AND THE 'MILITARY PWR
STATE'." USA+45 VIETNAM STRATA CHIEF WORKER   NAT/G
COLONIAL EXEC CROWD CIVMIL/REL RACE/REL TOTALISM   COERCE
...WELF/ST PACIFIST 20 NEGRO JOHNSON/LB PRESIDENT   FORCES
CIV/RIGHTS. PAGE 79 B1599

JOHNSTN/GD....GEORGE D. JOHNSTON

JOHNSTON L.D. B1152

JOHNSTON L.P. B0915

JONAS F.H. B1148

JONES A.G. B1149

JONES G.N. B0077

JONES G.S. B1150

JONES V. B1151,B1152,B1882

JONESVILLE....JONESVILLE: LOCATION OF W.L. WARNEROS
    "DEMOCRACY IN JONESVILLE"

JORDAN A. B1153

JORDAN....SEE ALSO ISLAM

JOSEPHSON E. B1154

JOURNALISM....SEE PRESS

JOYCE J.A. B1155

JUDGE....JUDGES; SEE ALSO ADJUD
                                                                    B09
HARVARD UNIVERSITY LAW LIBRARY,CATALOGUE OF THE   BIBLIOG/A
LIBRARY OF THE LAW SCHOOL OF HARVARD UNIVERSITY (3 LAW
VOLS.). UK USA-45 LEGIS JUDGE ADJUD CT/SYS...JURID ADMIN
CHARTS 14/20. PAGE 48 B0963
                                                                    B49
WALINE M.,LE CONTROLE JURIDICTIONNEL DE   JURID
L'ADMINISTRATION. BELGIUM FRANCE UAR JUDGE BAL/PWR ADMIN
ADJUD CONTROL CT/SYS...GP/COMP 20. PAGE 113 B2277   PWR
                                                    ORD/FREE
                                                                    C50
HOLCOMBE A.,"OUR MORE PERFECT UNION." USA+45 USA-45 CONSTN
POL/PAR JUDGE CT/SYS EQUILIB FEDERAL PWR...MAJORIT NAT/G
TREND BIBLIOG 18/20 CONGRESS PRESIDENT. PAGE 51   ADMIN
B1031   PLAN
                                                                    B52
SWENSON R.J.,FEDERAL ADMINISTRATIVE LAW: A STUDY OF JURID
THE GROWTH, NATURE, AND CONTROL OF ADMINISTRATIVE   CONSTN
ACTION. USA+45 JUDGE ADMIN GOV/REL EFFICIENCY   LEGIS
PRIVIL ATTIT NEW/LIB SUPREME/CT. PAGE 102 B2061   ADJUD
                                                                    C52
LANCASTER L.W.,"GOVERNMENT IN RURAL AMERICA."   GOV/REL
USA+45 ECO/DEV AGRI SCHOOL FORCES LEGIS JUDGE   LOC/G
BUDGET TAX CT/SYS...CHARTS BIBLIOG. PAGE 62 B1253   MUNIC
                                                    ADMIN
                                                                    B53
GROSS B.M.,THE LEGISLATIVE STRUGGLE: A STUDY IN   LEGIS
SOCIAL COMBAT. STRUCT LOC/G POL/PAR JUDGE EDU/PROP DECISION
DEBATE ETIQUET ADMIN LOBBY CHOOSE GOV/REL INGP/REL PERSON
HEREDITY ALL/VALS...SOC PRESIDENT. PAGE 44 B0885   LEAD
                                                                    B54
TOMPKINS D.C.,STATE GOVERNMENT AND ADMINISTRATION: BIBLIOG/A
A BIBLIOGRAPHY. USA+45 USA-45 CONSTN LEGIS JUDGE   LOC/G
BUDGET CT/SYS LOBBY...CHARTS 20. PAGE 105 B2116   PROVS
                                                    ADMIN
                                                                    B55
CUSHMAN R.E.,LEADING CONSTITUTIONAL DECISIONS.   CONSTN
USA+45 USA-45 NAT/G EX/STRUC LEGIS JUDGE TAX   PROB/SOLV
FEDERAL...DECISION 20 SUPREME/CT CASEBOOK. PAGE 25 JURID
B0513   CT/SYS
                                                                    B55
GUAITA A.,BIBLIOGRAFIA ESPANOLA DE DERECHO   BIBLIOG
ADMINISTRATIVO (PAMPHLET). SPAIN LOC/G MUNIC NAT/G ADMIN
PROVS JUDGE BAL/PWR GOV/REL OWN...JURID 18/19.   CONSTN
PAGE 44 B0900   PWR
                                                                    C56
AUMANN F.R.,"THE ISTRUMENTALITIES OF JUSTICE: THEIR JURID
FORMS, FUNCTIONS, AND LIMITATIONS." WOR+45 WOR-45   ADMIN
JUDGE PROB/SOLV ROUTINE ATTIT...BIBLIOG 20. PAGE 7 CT/SYS
B0147   ADJUD
                                                                    B58
DAVIS K.C.,ADMINISTRATIVE LAW TREATISE (VOLS. I AND ADMIN
IV). NAT/G JUDGE PROB/SOLV ADJUD GP/REL 20   JURID
SUPREME/CT. PAGE 26 B0540   CT/SYS
                                                    EX/STRUC

MOEN N.W.,THE GOVERNMENT OF SCOTLAND 1603 - 1625. CHIEF / JURID / CONTROL / PARL/PROC
UK JUDGE ADMIN GP/REL PWR 17 SCOTLAND COMMON/LAW.
PAGE 74 B1496
B58

MAIR L.P.,"REPRESENTATIVE LOCAL GOVERNMENT AS A AFR / PWR / ELITES
PROBLEM IN SOCIAL CHANGE." ECO/UNDEV KIN LOC/G
NAT/G SCHOOL JUDGE ADMIN ROUTINE REPRESENT
RIGID/FLEX RESPECT...CONCPT STERTYP CMN/WLTH 20.
PAGE 68 B1383
S58

BHAMBHRI C.P.,SUBSTANCE OF HINDU POLITY. INDIA GOV/REL / WRITING / SECT / PROVS
S/ASIA LAW EX/STRUC JUDGE TAX COERCE GP/REL
POPULISM 20 HINDU. PAGE 11 B0234
B59

HOFFMANN S.,"IMPLEMENTATION OF INTERNATIONAL INT/ORG / MORAL
INSTRUMENTS ON HUMAN RIGHTS." WOR+45 VOL/ASSN
DELIB/GP JUDGE EDU/PROP LEGIT ROUTINE PEACE
COLD/WAR 20. PAGE 51 B1029
S59

SUTTON F.X.,"REPRESENTATION AND THE NATURE OF NAT/G / CONCPT
POLITICAL SYSTEMS." UNIV WOR-45 CULTURE SOCIETY
STRATA INT/ORG FORCES JUDGE DOMIN LEGIT EXEC REGION
REPRESENT ATTIT ORD/FREE RESPECT...SOC HIST/WRIT
TIME/SEQ. PAGE 102 B2057
S59

SCHER S.,"CONGRESSIONAL COMMITTEE MEMBERS AND LEGIS / GOV/REL / LABOR / ADJUD
INDEPENDENT AGENCY OVERSEERS: A CASE STUDY."
DELIB/GP EX/STRUC JUDGE TOP/EX DOMIN ADMIN CONTROL
PWR...SOC/EXP HOUSE/REP CONGRESS. PAGE 93 B1886
S60

AUERBACH C.A.,THE LEGAL PROCESS. USA+45 DELIB/GP JURID / ADMIN / LEGIS / CT/SYS
JUDGE CONFER ADJUD CONTROL...DECISION 20
SUPREME/CT. PAGE 7 B0146
B61

DELANY V.T.H.,THE ADMINISTRATION OF JUSTICE IN ADMIN / JURID / CT/SYS / ADJUD
IRELAND. IRELAND CONSTN FINAN JUDGE COLONIAL CRIME
...CRIMLGY 19/20. PAGE 28 B0571
B62

INSTITUTE JUDICIAL ADMIN,JUDGES: THEIR TEMPORARY NAT/G / LOC/G / JUDGE / ADMIN
APPOINTMENT, ASSIGNMENT AND TRANSFER: SURVEY OF FED
AND STATE CONSTN'S STATUTES, ROLES OF CT. USA+45
CONSTN PROVS CT/SYS GOV/REL PWR JURID. PAGE 54
B1090
B62

INTERNAT CONGRESS OF JURISTS,EXECUTIVE ACTION AND JURID / EXEC / ORD/FREE / CONTROL
THE RULE OF RULE: REPORTION PROCEEDINGS OF INT'T
CONGRESS OF JURISTS,-RIO DE JANEIRO, BRAZIL. WOR+45
ACADEM CONSULT JUDGE EDU/PROP ADJUD CT/SYS INGP/REL
PERSON DEPT/DEFEN. PAGE 54 B1094
B62

SCHULMAN S.,TOWARD JUDICIAL REFORM IN PENNSYLVANIA; CT/SYS / ACT/RES / PROB/SOLV
A STUDY IN COURT REORGANIZATION. USA+45 CONSTN
JUDGE PLAN ADMIN LOBBY SANCTION PRIVIL PWR...JURID
20 PENNSYLVAN. PAGE 94 B1905
B62

BOWETT D.W.,THE LAW OF INTERNATIONAL INSTITUTIONS. INT/ORG / ADJUD / DIPLOM
WOR+45 WOR-45 CONSTN DELIB/GP EX/STRUC JUDGE
EDU/PROP LEGIT CT/SYS EXEC ROUTINE RIGID/FLEX
ORD/FREE PWR...JURID CONCPT ORG/CHARTS GEN/METH
LEAGUE/NAT OAS OEEC 20 UN. PAGE 14 B0286
B63

GARNER U.F.,ADMINISTRATIVE LAW. UK LAW LOC/G NAT/G ADMIN / JURID / PWR / GOV/REL
EX/STRUC LEGIS JUDGE BAL/PWR BUDGET ADJUD CONTROL
CT/SYS...BIBLIOG 20. PAGE 39 B0783
B63

KLEIN F.J.,JUDICIAL ADMINISTRATION AND THE LEGAL BIBLIOG/A / CT/SYS / ADJUD / JUDGE
PROFESSION. USA+45 ADMIN CONTROL EFFICIENCY
...POLICY 20. PAGE 60 B1217
B63

RICHARDSON H.G.,THE ADMINISTRATION OF IRELAND ADMIN / NAT/G / PWR
1172-1377. IRELAND CONSTN EX/STRUC LEGIS JUDGE
CT/SYS PARL/PROC...CHARTS BIBLIOG 12/14. PAGE 88
B1775
B64

JACKSON R.M.,THE MACHINERY OF JUSTICE IN ENGLAND. CT/SYS / ADJUD / JUDGE / JURID
UK EDU/PROP CONTROL COST ORD/FREE...MGT 20
ENGLSH/LAW. PAGE 55 B1109
B64

KARLEN D.,THE CITIZEN IN COURT. USA+45 LAW ADMIN CT/SYS / ADJUD / GOV/REL / JUDGE
ROUTINE CRIME GP/REL...JURID 20. PAGE 58 B1175
B64

STOICOIU V.,LEGAL SOURCES AND BIBLIOGRAPHY OF BIBLIOG/A / JURID / CONSTN / ADMIN
ROMANIA. COM ROMANIA LAW FINAN POL/PAR LEGIS JUDGE
ADJUD CT/SYS PARL/PROC MARXISM 20. PAGE 101 B2041
B64

SZLADITS C.,BIBLIOGRAPHY ON FOREIGN AND COMPARATIVE BIBLIOG/A / JURID / ADJUD / LAW
LAW: BOOKS AND ARTICLES IN ENGLISH (SUPPLEMENT
1962). FINAN INDUS JUDGE LICENSE ADMIN CT/SYS
PARL/PROC OWN...INT/LAW CLASSIF METH/COMP NAT/COMP
20. PAGE 102 B2065
B64

SMITH C.,THE OMBUDSMAN: A BIBLIOGRAPHY (PAMPHLET). BIBLIOG / ADMIN / CT/SYS / ADJUD
DENMARK SWEDEN USA+45 LAW LEGIS JUDGE GOV/REL
GP/REL...JURID 20. PAGE 98 B1980
B65

SZLADITS C.,A BIBLIOGRAPHY ON FOREIGN AND BIBLIOG/A / CT/SYS / INT/LAW
COMPARATIVE LAW (SUPPLEMENT 1964). FINAN FAM LABOR
LG/CO LEGIS JUDGE ADMIN CRIME...CRIMLGY 20.
PAGE 102 B2066
B66

BLUMBERG A.S.,CRIMINAL JUSTICE. USA+45 CLIENT LAW JURID / CT/SYS / PROF/ORG / CRIME
LOC/G FORCES JUDGE ACT/RES LEGIT ADMIN RATIONAL
MYTH. PAGE 13 B0259
B67

WESTON P.B.,THE ADMINISTRATION OF JUSTICE. USA+45 CRIME / CT/SYS / JURID / ADJUD
CONSTN MUNIC NAT/G PROVS EX/STRUC JUDGE ADMIN
CONTROL SANCTION ORD/FREE...CHARTS 20. PAGE 115
B2328
B67

GAINES J.E.,"THE YOUTH COURT CONCEPT AND ITS CT/SYS / AGE/Y / INGP/REL / CRIME
IMPLEMENTATION IN TOMPKINS COUNTY, NEW YORK."
USA+45 LAW CONSTN JUDGE WORKER ADJUD ADMIN CHOOSE
PERSON...JURID NEW/YORK. PAGE 38 B0772
L67

DANELSKI D.J.,"CONFLICT AND ITS RESOLUTION IN THE ROLE / JURID / JUDGE / INGP/REL
SUPREME COURT." PROB/SOLV LEAD ROUTINE PERSON...PSY
PERS/COMP BIBLIOG 20. PAGE 26 B0527
S67

JUDICIAL PROCESS....SEE ADJUD

JUGOSLAVIA....SEE YUGOSLAVIA

JUNKER ....JUNKER: REACTIONARY PRUSSIAN ARISTOCRACY
JUNZ A.J.   B0048
JURID....LAW

AUSTRALIAN NATIONAL RES COUN,AUSTRALIAN SOCIAL BIBLIOG/A / POLICY / NAT/G / ADMIN
SCIENCE ABSTRACTS. NEW/ZEALND CULTURE SOCIETY LOC/G
CT/SYS PARL/PROC...HEAL JURID PSY SOC 20 AUSTRAL.
PAGE 7 B0149
N

CATHERINE R.,LA REVUE ADMINISTRATIVE. FRANCE LAW ADMIN / MGT / FINAN / METH/COMP
NAT/G LEGIS...JURID BIBLIOG/A 20. PAGE 19 B0393
N

KENTUCKY STATE ARCHIVES,CHECKLIST OF KENTUCKY STATE BIBLIOG/A / PROVS / PUB/INST / ADMIN
PUBLICATIONS AND STATE DIRECTORY. USA+45 LAW ACADEM
EX/STRUC LEGIS EDU/PROP LEAD...JURID 20. PAGE 59
B1196
N

UNIVERSITY OF FLORIDA,CARIBBEAN ACQUISITIONS: BIBLIOG / ECO/UNDEV / EDU/PROP / JURID
MATERIALS ACQUIRED BY THE UNIVERSITY OF FLORIDA
1957-1960. L/A+17C...ART/METH GEOG MGT 20. PAGE 107
B2167
B05

GOODNOW F.J.,THE PRINCIPLES OF THE ADMINISTRATIVE ADMIN / NAT/G / PROVS / LOC/G
LAW OF THE UNITED STATES. USA-45 LAW STRUCT
EX/STRUC LEGIS BAL/PWR CONTROL GOV/REL PWR...JURID
19/20 CIVIL/SERV. PAGE 41 B0822
B09

HARVARD UNIVERSITY LAW LIBRARY,CATALOGUE OF THE BIBLIOG/A / LAW / ADMIN
LIBRARY OF THE LAW SCHOOL OF HARVARD UNIVERSITY (3
VOLS.). UK USA-45 LEGIS JUDGE ADJUD CT/SYS...JURID
CHARTS 14/20. PAGE 48 B0963
B17

CORWIN E.S.,THE PRESIDENT'S CONTROL OF FOREIGN TOP/EX / PWR / DIPLOM
RELATIONS. FUT USA-45 CONSTN STRATA NAT/G CHIEF
EX/STRUC LEGIS KNOWL RESPECT...JURID CONCPT TREND
CONGRESS VAL/FREE 20 PRESIDENT. PAGE 24 B0483
B18

WILSON W.,THE STATE: ELEMENTS OF HISTORICAL AND NAT/G / JURID / CONCPT / NAT/COMP
PRACTICAL POLITICS. FRANCE GERMANY ITALY UK USSR
CONSTN EX/STRUC LEGIS CT/SYS WAR PWR...POLICY
GOV/COMP 20. PAGE 117 B2363
N19

BURRUS B.R.,INVESTIGATION AND DISCOVERY IN STATE NAT/G / PROVS / LAW / INSPECT
ANTITRUST (PAMPHLET). USA+45 USA-45 LEGIS ECO/TAC
ADMIN CONTROL CT/SYS CRIME GOV/REL PWR...JURID
CHARTS 19/20 FTC MONOPOLY. PAGE 17 B0355
N19

FAHRNKOPF N.,STATE AND LOCAL GOVERNMENT IN ILLINOIS BIBLIOG / LOC/G / LEGIS / CT/SYS
(PAMPHLET). CONSTN ADMIN PARTIC CHOOSE REPRESENT
GOV/REL...JURID MGT 20 ILLINOIS. PAGE 34 B0696

STOWELL E.C.,INTERVENTION IN INTERNATIONAL LAW. UNIV LAW SOCIETY INT/ORG ACT/RES PLAN LEGIT ROUTINE WAR...JURID OBS GEN/LAWS 20. PAGE 101 B2050
B21
BAL/PWR
SOVEREIGN

HOLDSWORTH W.S.,A HISTORY OF ENGLISH LAW; THE COMMON LAW AND ITS RIVALS (VOL. V). UK SEA EX/STRUC WRITING ADMIN...INT/LAW JURID CONCPT IDEA/COMP WORSHIP 16/17 PARLIAMENT ENGLSH/LAW COMMON/LAW. PAGE 51 B1033
B24
LAW
LEGIS
ADJUD
CT/SYS

HOLDSWORTH W.S.,A HISTORY OF ENGLISH LAW; THE COMMON LAW AND ITS RIVALS (VOL. VI). UK STRATA EX/STRUC ADJUD ADMIN CONTROL CT/SYS...JURID CONCPT GEN/LAWS 17 COMMONWLTH PARLIAMENT ENGLSH/LAW COMMON/LAW. PAGE 51 B1034
B24
LAW
CONSTN
LEGIS
CHIEF

DICKINSON J.,ADMINISTRATIVE JUSTICE AND THE SUPREMACY OF LAW IN THE UNITED STATES. USA-45 LAW INDUS DOMIN EDU/PROP CONTROL EXEC GP/REL ORD/FREE ...POLICY JURID 19/20. PAGE 29 B0586
B27
CT/SYS
ADJUD
ADMIN
NAT/G

BUELL R.,INTERNATIONAL RELATIONS. WOR+45 WOR-45 CONSTN STRATA FORCES TOP/EX ADMIN ATTIT DRIVE SUPEGO MORAL ORD/FREE PWR SOVEREIGN...JURID SOC CONCPT 20. PAGE 17 B0340
B29
INT/ORG
BAL/PWR
DIPLOM

MOLEY R.,POLITICS AND CRIMINAL PROSECUTION. USA-45 POL/PAR EX/STRUC LEGIT CONTROL LEAD ROUTINE CHOOSE INGP/REL...JURID CHARTS 20. PAGE 74 B1497
B29
PWR
CT/SYS
CRIME
ADJUD

FAIRLIE J.A.,COUNTY GOVERNMENT AND ADMINISTRATION. UK USA-45 NAT/G SCHOOL FORCES BUDGET TAX CT/SYS CHOOSE...JURID BIBLIOG 11/20. PAGE 35 B0701
B30
ADMIN
GOV/REL
LOC/G
MUNIC

HART J.,AN INTRODUCTION TO ADMINISTRATIVE LAW, WITH SELECTED CASES. USA-45 CONSTN SOCIETY NAT/G EX/STRUC ADJUD CT/SYS LEAD CRIME ORD/FREE ...DECISION JURID 20 CASEBOOK. PAGE 47 B0958
B40
LAW
ADMIN
LEGIS
PWR

DAVIS H.E.,PIONEERS IN WORLD ORDER. WOR-45 CONSTN ECO/TAC DOMIN EDU/PROP LEGIT ADJUD ADMIN ARMS/CONT CHOOSE KNOWL ORD/FREE...POLICY JURID SOC STAT OBS CENSUS TIME/SEQ ANTHOL LEAGUE/NAT 20. PAGE 26 B0537
B44
INT/ORG
ROUTINE

CORRY J.A.,DEMOCRATIC GOVERNMENT AND POLITICS. WOR-45 EX/STRUC LOBBY TOTALISM...MAJORIT CONCPT METH/COMP NAT/COMP 20. PAGE 24 B0479
B46
NAT/G
CONSTN
POL/PAR
JURID

DE NOIA J.,GUIDE TO OFFICIAL PUBLICATIONS OF THE OTHER AMERICAN REPUBLICS: NICARAGUA (VOL. XIV). NICARAGUA LAW LEGIS ADMIN CT/SYS...JURID 19/20. PAGE 27 B0559
B47
BIBLIOG/A
EDU/PROP
NAT/G
CONSTN

TAPPAN P.W.,DELINQUENT GIRLS IN COURT. USA-45 MUNIC EX/STRUC FORCES ADMIN EXEC ADJUST SEX RESPECT ...JURID SOC/WK 20 NEWYORK/C FEMALE/SEX. PAGE 103 B2078
B47
CT/SYS
AGE/Y
CRIME
ADJUD

DE NOIA J.,GUIDE TO OFFICIAL PUBLICATIONS OF OTHER AMERICAN REPUBLICS: PERU (VOL. XVII). PERU LAW LEGIS ADMIN CT/SYS...JURID 19/20. PAGE 28 B0561
B48
BIBLIOG/A
CONSTN
NAT/G
EDU/PROP

MEEK C.K.,COLONIAL LAW; A BIBLIOGRAPHY WITH SPECIAL REFERENCE TO NATIVE AFRICAN SYSTEMS OF LAW AND LAND TENURE. AFR ECO/UNDEV AGRI CT/SYS...JURID SOC 20. PAGE 72 B1462
B48
COLONIAL
ADMIN
LAW
CONSTN

BOYD A.M.,UNITED STATES GOVERNMENT PUBLICATIONS (3RD ED.). USA+45 EX/STRUC LEGIS ADMIN...JURID CHARTS 20. PAGE 14 B0291
B49
BIBLIOG/A
PRESS
NAT/G
EDU/PROP

DENNING A.,FREEDOM UNDER THE LAW. MOD/EUR UK LAW SOCIETY CHIEF EX/STRUC LEGIS ADJUD CT/SYS PERS/REL PERSON 17/20 ENGLSH/LAW. PAGE 28 B0573
B49
ORD/FREE
JURID
NAT/G

WALINE M.,LE CONTROLE JURIDICTIONNEL DE L'ADMINISTRATION. BELGIUM FRANCE UAR JUDGE BAL/PWR ADJUD CONTROL CT/SYS...GP/COMP 20. PAGE 113 B2277
B49
JURID
ADMIN
PWR
ORD/FREE

MARX C.M.,"ADMINISTRATIVE ETHICS AND THE RULE OF LAW." USA+45 ELITES ACT/RES DOMIN NEUTRAL ROUTINE INGP/REL ORD/FREE...JURID IDEA/COMP. PAGE 70 B1417
L49
ADMIN
LAW

DAVIS K.C.,ADMINISTRATIVE LAW. USA+45 USA-45 NAT/G PROB/SOLV BAL/PWR CONTROL ORD/FREE...POLICY 20 SUPREME/CT. PAGE 26 B0539
B51
ADMIN
JURID
EX/STRUC
ADJUD

SCHATTSCHNEIDER E.E.,A GUIDE TO THE STUDY OF PUBLIC
B52
ACT/RES

AFFAIRS. LAW LOC/G NAT/G LEGIS BUDGET PRESS ADMIN LOBBY...JURID CHARTS 20. PAGE 93 B1882
INTELL
ACADEM
METH/COMP

SWENSON R.J.,FEDERAL ADMINISTRATIVE LAW: A STUDY OF THE GROWTH, NATURE, AND CONTROL OF ADMINISTRATIVE ACTION. USA-45 JUDGE ADMIN GOV/REL EFFICIENCY PRIVIL ATTIT NEW/LIB SUPREME/CT. PAGE 102 B2061
B52
JURID
CONSTN
LEGIS
ADJUD

SCHWEBEL S.M.,"THE SECRETARY-GENERAL OF THE UN." FUT INTELL CONSULT DELIB/GP ADMIN PEACE ATTIT ...JURID MGT CONCPT TREND UN CONGRESS 20. PAGE 95 B1915
S52
INT/ORG
TOP/EX

SECKLER-HUDSON C.,BIBLIOGRAPHY ON PUBLIC ADMINISTRATION (4TH ED.). USA+45 LAW POL/PAR DELIB/GP BUDGET ADJUD LOBBY GOV/REL GP/REL ATTIT ...JURID 20. PAGE 95 B1923
B53
BIBLIOG/A
ADMIN
NAT/G
MGT

STOUT H.M.,BRITISH GOVERNMENT. UK FINAN LOC/G POL/PAR DELIB/GP DIPLOM ADMIN COLONIAL CHOOSE ORD/FREE...JURID BIBLIOG 20 COMMONWLTH. PAGE 101 B2049
B53
NAT/G
PARL/PROC
CONSTN
NEW/LIB

BINANI G.D.,INDIA AT A GLANCE (REV. ED.). INDIA COM/IND FINAN INDUS LABOR PROVS SCHOOL PLAN DIPLOM INT/TRADE ADMIN...JURID 20. PAGE 12 B0238
B54
INDEX
CON/ANAL
NAT/G
ECO/UNDEV

MANGONE G.,A SHORT HISTORY OF INTERNATIONAL ORGANIZATION. MOD/EUR USA+45 USA-45 WOR+45 WOR-45 LAW LEGIS CREATE LEGIT ROUTINE RIGID/FLEX PWR ...JURID CONCPT OBS TIME/SEQ GEN/LAWS UN TOT/POP VAL/FREE 18/20. PAGE 69 B1389
B54
INT/ORG
INT/LAW

MILLARD E.L.,FREEDOM IN A FEDERAL WORLD. FUT WOR+45 VOL/ASSN TOP/EX LEGIT ROUTINE FEDERAL PEACE ATTIT DISPL ORD/FREE PWR...MAJORIT INT/LAW JURID TREND CCLD/WAR 20. PAGE 73 B1479
B54
INT/ORG
CREATE
ADJUD
BAL/PWR

SCHWARTZ B.,FRENCH ADMINISTRATIVE LAW AND THE COMMON-LAW WORLD. FRANCE CULTURE LOC/G NAT/G PROVS DELIB/GP EX/STRUC LEGIS PROB/SOLV CT/SYS EXEC GOV/REL...IDEA/COMP ENGLSH/LAW. PAGE 95 B1912
B54
JURID
LAW
METH/COMP
ADJUD

CUSHMAN R.E.,LEADING CONSTITUTIONAL DECISIONS. USA+45 USA-45 NAT/G EX/STRUC LEGIS JUDGE TAX FEDERAL...DECISION 20 SUPREME/CT CASEBOOK. PAGE 25 B0513
B55
CONSTN
PROB/SOLV
JURID
CT/SYS

GUAITA A.,BIBLIOGRAFIA ESPANOLA DE DERECHO ADMINISTRATIVO (PAMPHLET). SPAIN LOC/G MUNIC NAT/G PROVS JUDGE BAL/PWR GOV/REL OWN...JURID 18/19. PAGE 44 B0900
B55
BIBLIOG
ADMIN
CONSTN
PWR

PULLEN W.R.,A CHECK LIST OF LEGISLATIVE JOURNALS ISSUED SINCE 1937 BY THE STATES OF THE UNITED STATES OF AMERICA (PAMPHLET). USA+45 USA-45 LAW WRITING ADJUD ADMIN...JURID 20. PAGE 85 B1720
B55
BIBLIOG
PROVS
EDU/PROP
LEGIS

WRIGHT Q.,"THE PEACEFUL ADJUSTMENT OF INTERNATIONAL RELATIONS: PROBLEMS AND RESEARCH APPROACHES." UNIV INTELL EDU/PROP ADJUD ROUTINE KNOWL SKILL...INT/LAW JURID PHIL/SCI CLASSIF 20. PAGE 118 B2385
S55
R+D
METH/CNCPT
PEACE

JENNINGS W.I.,THE APPROACH TO SELF-GOVERNMENT. CEYLON INDIA PAKISTAN S/ASIA UK SOCIETY POL/PAR DELIB/GP LEGIS ECO/TAC EDU/PROP ADMIN EXEC CHOOSE ATTIT ALL/VALS...JURID CONCPT GEN/METH TOT/POP 20. PAGE 56 B1136
B56
NAT/G
CONSTN
COLONIAL

SOHN L.B.,BASIC DOCUMENTS OF THE UNITED NATIONS. WOR+45 LAW INT/ORG LEGIT EXEC ROUTINE CHOOSE PWR ...JURID CONCPT GEN/LAWS ANTHOL UN TOT/POP OAS FAO ILO 20. PAGE 99 B1993
B56
DELIB/GP
CONSTN

WEBER M.,STAATSSOZIOLOGIE. STRUCT LEGIT ADMIN PARL/PROC SUPEGO CONSERVE JURID. PAGE 114 B2305
B56
SOC
NAT/G
POL/PAR
LEAD

AUMANN F.R.,"THE ISTRUMENTALITIES OF JUSTICE: THEIR FORMS, FUNCTIONS, AND LIMITATIONS." WOR+45 WOR-45 JUDGE PROB/SOLV ROUTINE ATTIT...BIBLIOG 20. PAGE 7 B0147
C56
JURID
ADMIN
CT/SYS
ADJUD

HINDERLING A.,DIE REFORMATORISCHE VERWALTUNGSGERICHTSBARKEIT. GERMANY/W PROB/SOLV ADJUD SUPEGO PWR...CONCPT 20. PAGE 50 B1015
B57
ADMIN
CT/SYS
JURID
CONTROL

JENNINGS I.,PARLIAMENT. UK FINAN INDUS POL/PAR DELIB/GP EX/STRUC PLAN CONTROL...MAJORIT JURID PARLIAMENT. PAGE 56 B1133
B57
PARL/PROC
TOP/EX
MGT
LEGIS

LOEWENSTEIN K.,POLITICAL POWER AND THE GOVERNMENTAL PWR
PROCESS. WOR+45 WOR-45 CONSTN NAT/G POL/PAR CONCPT
EX/STRUC LEGIS TOP/EX DOMIN EDU/PROP LEGIT ADMIN
REGION CHOOSE ATTIT...JURID STERTYP GEN/LAWS 20.
PAGE 66 B1336

B57
SCHLOCHAUER H.J.,OFFENTLICHES RECHT. GERMANY/W CONSTN
FINAN EX/STRUC LEGIS DIPLOM FEDERAL ORD/FREE JURID
...INT/LAW 20. PAGE 94 B1892 ADMIN
CT/SYS

B58
CHARLES R.,LA JUSTICE EN FRANCE. FRANCE LAW CONSTN JURID
DELIB/GP CRIME 20. PAGE 20 B0413 ADMIN
CT/SYS
ADJUD

B58
DAVIS K.C.,ADMINISTRATIVE LAW TREATISE (VOLS. I AND ADMIN
IV). NAT/G JUDGE PROB/SOLV ADJUD GP/REL 20 JURID
SUPREME/CT. PAGE 26 B0540 CT/SYS
EX/STRUC

B58
DAVIS K.C.,ADMINISTRATIVE LAW; CASES, TEXT, ADJUD
PROBLEMS. LAW LOC/G NAT/G TOP/EX PAY CONTROL JURID
GOV/REL INGP/REL FEDERAL 20 SUPREME/CT. PAGE 27 CT/SYS
B0541 ADMIN

B58
DEVLIN P.,THE CRIMINAL PROSECUTION IN ENGLAND. UK CRIME
NAT/G ADMIN ROUTINE EFFICIENCY...JURID SOC 20. LAW
PAGE 29 B0583 METH
CT/SYS

B58
HENKIN L.,ARMS CONTROL AND INSPECTION IN AMERICAN USA+45
LAW. LAW CONSTN INT/ORG LOC/G MUNIC NAT/G PROVS JURID
EDU/PROP LEGIT EXEC NUC/PWR KNOWL ORD/FREE...OBS ARMS/CONT
TOT/POP CONGRESS 20. PAGE 49 B0990

B58
JAPAN MINISTRY OF JUSTICE,CRIMINAL JUSTICE IN CONSTN
JAPAN. LAW PROF/ORG PUB/INST FORCES CONTROL CT/SYS CRIME
PARL/PROC 20 CHINJAP. PAGE 56 B1125 JURID
ADMIN

B58
KAPLAN H.E.,THE LAW OF CIVIL SERVICE. USA+45 LAW ADJUD
POL/PAR CT/SYS CRIME GOV/REL...POLICY JURID 20. NAT/G
PAGE 58 B1167 ADMIN
CONSTN

B58
MOEN N.W.,THE GOVERNMENT OF SCOTLAND 1603 - 1625. CHIEF
UK JUDGE ADMIN GP/REL PWR 17 SCOTLAND COMMON/LAW. JURID
PAGE 74 B1496 CONTROL
PARL/PROC

B58
POUND R.,JUSTICE ACCORDING TO LAW. LAW SOCIETY CONCPT
CT/SYS 20. PAGE 84 B1696 JURID
ADJUD
ADMIN

B58
SHARMA M.P.,PUBLIC ADMINISTRATION IN THEORY AND MGT
PRACTICE. INDIA UK USA+45 USA-45 EX/STRUC ADJUD ADMIN
...POLICY CONCPT NAT/COMP 20. PAGE 96 B1935 DELIB/GP
JURID

B58
US SENATE COMM POST OFFICE,TO PROVIDE AN EFFECTIVE INT
SYSTEM OF PERSONNEL ADMINISTRATION. USA+45 NAT/G LEGIS
EX/STRUC PARL/PROC GOV/REL...JURID 20 SENATE CONFER
CIVIL/SERV. PAGE 111 B2234 ADMIN

B59
DAVIS K.C.,ADMINISTRATIVE LAW TEXT. USA+45 NAT/G ADJUD
DELIB/GP EX/STRUC CONTROL ORD/FREE...T 20 ADMIN
SUPREME/CT. PAGE 27 B0542 JURID
CT/SYS

B59
DESMITH S.A.,JUDICIAL REVIEW OF ADMINISTRATIVE ADJUD
ACTION. UK LOC/G CONSULT DELIB/GP ADMIN PWR NAT/G
...DECISION JURID 20 ENGLSH/LAW. PAGE 28 B0576 PROB/SOLV
CT/SYS

B59
ELLIOTT S.D.,IMPROVING OUR COURTS. LAW EX/STRUC CT/SYS
PLAN PROB/SOLV ADJUD ADMIN TASK CRIME EFFICIENCY JURID
ORD/FREE 20. PAGE 33 B0669 GOV/REL
NAT/G

B59
GINSBURG M.,LAW AND OPINION IN ENGLAND. UK CULTURE JURID
KIN LABOR LEGIS EDU/PROP ADMIN CT/SYS CRIME OWN POLICY
HEALTH...ANTHOL 20 ENGLSH/LAW. PAGE 40 B0802 ECO/TAC

B59
IPSEN H.P.,HAMBURGISCHES STAATS- UND ADMIN
VERWALTUNGSRECHT. CONSTN LOC/G FORCES BUDGET CT/SYS PROVS
...JURID 20 HAMBURG. PAGE 54 B1103 LEGIS
FINAN

B59
LEMBERG E.,DIE VERTRIEBENEN IN WESTDEUTSCHLAND (3 GP/REL
VOLS.). GERMANY/W CULTURE STRUCT AGRI PROVS ADMIN INGP/REL
...JURID 20 MIGRATION. PAGE 64 B1287 SOCIETY

B59
LOEWENSTEIN K.,VERFASSUNGSRECHT UND CONSTN

B57
VERFASSUNGSPRAXIS DER VEREINIGTEN STAATEN. USA+45 POL/PAR
USA-45 COLONIAL CT/SYS GP/REL RACE/REL ORD/FREE EX/STRUC
...JURID 18/20 SUPREME/CT CONGRESS PRESIDENT NAT/G
BILL/RIGHT CIVIL/LIB. PAGE 66 B1337

B59
SINHA H.N.,OUTLINES OF POLITICAL SCIENCE. NAT/G JURID
POL/PAR EX/STRUC LEGIS CT/SYS CHOOSE REPRESENT 20. CONCPT
PAGE 98 B1971 ORD/FREE
SOVEREIGN

B59
SURRENCY E.C.,A GUIDE TO LEGAL RESEARCH. USA+45 NAT/G
ACADEM LEGIS ACT/RES ADMIN...DECISION METH/COMP PROVS
BIBLIOG METH. PAGE 102 B2055 ADJUD
JURID

B59
WEBER W.,DER DEUTSCHE BEAMTE HEUTE. GERMANY/W NAT/G MGT
DELIB/GP LEGIS CONFER ATTIT SUPEGO...JURID 20 EFFICIENCY
CIVIL/SERV. PAGE 114 B2306 ELITES
GP/REL

S59
LASSWELL H.D.,"UNIVERSALITY IN PERSPECTIVE." FUT INT/ORG
UNIV SOCIETY CONSULT TOP/EX PLAN EDU/PROP ADJUD JURID
ROUTINE ARMS/CONT COERCE PEACE ATTIT PERSON TOTALISM
ALL/VALS. PAGE 63 B1271

S59
SOHN L.B.,"THE DEFINITION OF AGGRESSION." FUT LAW INT/ORG
FORCES LEGIT ADJUD ROUTINE COERCE ORD/FREE PWR CT/SYS
...MAJORIT JURID QUANT COLD/WAR 20. PAGE 99 B1995 DETER
SOVEREIGN

B60
DAVIS K.C.,ADMINISTRATIVE LAW AND GOVERNMENT. ADMIN
USA+45 EX/STRUC PROB/SOLV ADJUD GP/REL PWR...POLICY JURID
20 SUPREME/CT. PAGE 27 B0543 CT/SYS
NAT/G

B60
HANBURY H.G.,ENGLISH COURTS OF LAW. UK EX/STRUC JURID
LEGIS CRIME ROLE 12/20 COMMON/LAW ENGLSH/LAW. CT/SYS
PAGE 46 B0936 CONSTN
GOV/REL

B60
HEAP D.,AN OUTLINE OF PLANNING LAW (3RD ED.). UK MUNIC
LAW PROB/SOLV ADMIN CONTROL 20. PAGE 49 B0983 PLAN
JURID
LOC/G

B60
MARSHALL A.H.,FINANCIAL ADMINISTRATION IN LOCAL FINAN
GOVERNMENT. UK DELIB/GP CONFER COST INCOME PERSON LOC/G
...JURID 20. PAGE 70 B1408 BUDGET
ADMIN

B60
ROY N.C.,THE CIVIL SERVICE IN INDIA. INDIA POL/PAR ADMIN
ECO/TAC INCOME...JURID MGT 20 CIVIL/SERV. PAGE 91 NAT/G
B1843 DELIB/GP
CONFER

B60
US LIBRARY OF CONGRESS,INDEX TO LATIN AMERICAN BIBLIOG/A
LEGISLATION: 1950-1960 (2 VOLS.). NAT/G DELIB/GP LEGIS
ADMIN PARL/PROC 20. PAGE 109 B2205 L/A+17C
JURID

B60
US SENATE COMM ON JUDICIARY,FEDERAL ADMINISTRATIVE PARL/PROC
PROCEDURE. USA+45 CONSTN NAT/G PROB/SOLV CONFER LEGIS
GOV/REL...JURID INT 20 SENATE. PAGE 110 B2226 ADMIN
LAW

B60
US SENATE COMM ON JUDICIARY,ADMINISTRATIVE PARL/PROC
PROCEDURE LEGISLATION. USA+45 CONSTN NAT/G LEGIS
PROB/SOLV CONFER ROUTINE GOV/REL...INT 20 SENATE. ADMIN
PAGE 110 B2227 JURID

L60
DEAN A.W.,"SECOND GENEVA CONFERENCE OF THE LAW OF INT/ORG
THE SEA: THE FIGHT FOR FREEDOM OF THE SEAS." FUT JURID
USA+45 USSR WOR+45 WOR-45 SEA CONSTN STRUCT PLAN INT/LAW
INT/TRADE ADJUD ADMIN ORD/FREE...DECISION RECORD
TREND GEN/LAWS 20 TREATY. PAGE 28 B0564

S60
BOGARDUS E.S.,"THE SOCIOLOGY OF A STRUCTURED INT/ORG
PEACE." FUT SOCIETY CREATE DIPLOM EDU/PROP ADJUD SOC
ROUTINE ATTIT RIGID/FLEX KNOWL ORD/FREE RESPECT NAT/LISM
...POLICY INT/LAW JURID NEW/IDEA SELF/OBS TOT/POP PEACE
20 UN. PAGE 13 B0264

S60
ROURKE F.E.,"ADMINISTRATIVE SECRECY: A LEGIS
CONGRESSIONAL DILEMMA." DELIB/GP CT/SYS ATTIT EXEC
...MAJORIT DECISION JURID. PAGE 91 B1837 ORD/FREE
POLICY

S60
SMIGEL E.O.,"THE IMPACT OF RECRUITMENT ON THE LG/CO
ORGANIZATION OF THE LARGE LAW FIRM" (BMR)" USA+45 ADMIN
STRUCT CONSULT PLAN GP/REL EFFICIENCY JURID. LAW
PAGE 98 B1979 WORKER

S60
THOMPSON K.W.,"MORAL PURPOSE IN FOREIGN POLICY: MORAL
REALITIES AND ILLUSIONS." WOR+45 WOR-45 LAW CULTURE JURID
SOCIETY INT/ORG PLAN ADJUD ADMIN COERCE RIGID/FLEX DIPLOM
SUPEGO KNOWL ORD/FREE PWR...SOC TREND SOC/EXP

TOT/POP 20. PAGE 104 B2104

B61
AUERBACH C.A.,THE LEGAL PROCESS. USA+45 DELIB/GP
JUDGE CONFER ADJUD CONTROL...DECISION 20
SUPREME/CT. PAGE 7 B0146
JURID
ADMIN
LEGIS
CT/SYS

B61
BEASLEY K.E.,STATE SUPERVISION OF MUNICIPAL DEBT IN
KANSAS - A CASE STUDY. USA+45 USA-45 FINAN PROVS
BUDGET TAX ADJUD ADMIN CONTROL SUPEGO. PAGE 10
B0201
MUNIC
LOC/G
LEGIS
JURID

B61
DRAGNICH A.N.,MAJOR EUROPEAN GOVERNMENTS. FRANCE
GERMANY/W UK USSR LOC/G EX/STRUC CT/SYS PARL/PROC
ATTIT MARXISM...JURID MGT NAT/COMP 19/20. PAGE 30
B0615
NAT/G
LEGIS
CONSTN
POL/PAR

B61
HAMILTON A.,THE FEDERALIST. USA-45 NAT/G VOL/ASSN
LEGIS TOP/EX EDU/PROP LEGIT CHOOSE ATTIT RIGID/FLEX
ORD/FREE PWR...MAJORIT JURID CONCPT ANTHOL. PAGE 46
B0931
EX/STRUC
CONSTN

B61
LOSCHELDER W.,AUSBILDUNG UND AUSLESE DER BEAMTEN.
GERMANY/W ELITES NAT/G ADMIN GP/REL ATTIT...JURID
20 CIVIL/SERV. PAGE 67 B1341
PROF/ORG
EDU/PROP
EX/STRUC
CHOOSE

B61
STONE J.,QUEST FOR SURVIVAL. WOR+45 NAT/G VOL/ASSN
LEGIT ADMIN ARMS/CONT COERCE DISPL ORD/FREE PWR
...POLICY INT/LAW JURID COLD/WAR 20. PAGE 101 B2047
INT/ORG
ADJUD
SOVEREIGN

S61
MILLER E.,"LEGAL ASPECTS OF UN ACTION IN THE
CONGO." AFR CULTURE ADMIN PEACE DRIVE RIGID/FLEX
ORD/FREE...WELF/ST JURID OBS UN CONGO 20. PAGE 73
B1480
INT/ORG
LEGIT

S61
SCHILLING W.R.,"THE H-BOMB: HOW TO DECIDE WITHOUT
ACTUALLY CHOOSING." FUT USA+45 INTELL CONSULT ADMIN
CT/SYS MORAL...JURID OBS 20 TRUMAN/HS. PAGE 93
B1888
PERSON
LEGIT
NUC/PWR

B62
BOCK E.A.,CASE STUDIES IN AMERICAN GOVERNMENT.
USA+45 ECO/DEV CHIEF EDU/PROP CT/SYS RACE/REL
ORD/FREE...JURID MGT PHIL/SCI PRESIDENT CASEBOOK.
PAGE 13 B0262
POLICY
LEGIS
IDEA/COMP
NAT/G

B62
DELANY V.T.H.,THE ADMINISTRATION OF JUSTICE IN
IRELAND. IRELAND CONSTN FINAN JUDGE COLONIAL CRIME
...CRIMLGY 19/20. PAGE 28 B0571
ADMIN
JURID
CT/SYS
ADJUD

B62
GROGAN V.,ADMINISTRATIVE TRIBUNALS IN THE PUBLIC
SERVICE. IRELAND UK NAT/G CONTROL CT/SYS...JURID
GOV/COMP 20. PAGE 44 B0884
ADMIN
LAW
ADJUD
DELIB/GP

B62
INSTITUTE JUDICIAL ADMIN,JUDGES: THEIR TEMPORARY
APPOINTMENT, ASSIGNMENT AND TRANSFER: SURVEY OF FED
AND STATE CONSTN'S STATUTES, ROLES OF CT. USA+45
CONSTN PROVS CT/SYS GOV/REL PWR JURID. PAGE 54
B1090
NAT/G
LOC/G
JUDGE
ADMIN

B62
INTERNAT CONGRESS OF JURISTS,EXECUTIVE ACTION AND
THE RULE OF RULE: REPORTION PROCEEDINGS OF INT'T
CONGRESS OF JURISTS,-RIO DE JANEIRO, BRAZIL. WOR+45
ACADEM CONSULT JUDGE EDU/PROP ADJUD CT/SYS INGP/REL
PERSON DEPT/DEFEN. PAGE 54 B1094
JURID
EXEC
ORD/FREE
CONTROL

B62
LAWSON R.,INTERNATIONAL REGIONAL ORGANIZATIONS.
WOR+45 NAT/G VOL/ASSN CONSULT LEGIS EDU/PROP LEGIT
ADMIN EXEC ROUTINE HEALTH PWR WEALTH...JURID EEC
COLD/WAR 20 UN. PAGE 63 B1277
INT/ORG
DELIB/GP
REGION

B62
LITTLEFIELD N.,METROPOLITAN AREA PROBLEMS AND
MUNICIPAL HOME RULE. USA+45 PROVS ADMIN CONTROL
GP/REL PWR. PAGE 66 B1328
LOC/G
SOVEREIGN
JURID
LEGIS

B62
NJ DEPARTMENT CIVIL SERV,THE CIVIL SERVICE RULES OF
THE STATE OF NEW JERSEY. USA+45 USA-45 PAY...JURID
ANTHOL 20 CIVIL/SERV NEW/JERSEY. PAGE 78 B1585
ADMIN
PROVS
ROUTINE
WORKER

B62
PHILLIPS O.H.,CONSTITUTIONAL AND ADMINISTRATIVE LAW
(3RD ED.). UK INT/ORG LOC/G CHIEF EX/STRUC LEGIS
BAL/PWR ADJUD COLONIAL CT/SYS PWR...CHARTS 20.
PAGE 83 B1670
JURID
ADMIN
CONSTN
NAT/G

B62
SCHULMAN S.,TOWARD JUDICIAL REFORM IN PENNSYLVANIA;
A STUDY IN COURT REORGANIZATION. USA+45 CONSTN
JUDGE PLAN ADMIN LOBBY SANCTION PRIVIL PWR...JURID
20 PENNSYLVAN. PAGE 94 B1905
CT/SYS
ACT/RES
PROB/SOLV

L62
MANGIN G.,"L'ORGANIZATION JUDICIAIRE DES ETATS
D'AFRIQUE ET DE MADAGASCAR." ISLAM WOR+45 STRATA
STRUCT ECO/UNDEV NAT/G LEGIT EXEC...JURID TIME/SEQ
AFR
LEGIS
COLONIAL

TOT/POP 20 SUPREME/CT. PAGE 69 B1387

MADAGASCAR
S62
MANGIN G.,"LES ACCORDS DE COOPERATION EN MATIERE DE
JUSTICE ENTRE LA FRANCE ET LES ETATS AFRICAINS ET
MALGACHE." AFR ISLAM WOR+45 STRUCT ECO/UNDEV NAT/G
DELIB/GP PERCEPT ALL/VALS...JURID MGT TIME/SEQ 20.
PAGE 69 B1386
INT/ORG
LAW
FRANCE

S62
MURACCIOLE L.,"LES MODIFICATIONS DE LA CONSTITUTION
MALGACHE." AFR WOR+45 ECO/UNDEV LEGIT EXEC ALL/VALS
...JURID 20. PAGE 76 B1542
NAT/G
STRUCT
SOVEREIGN
MADAGASCAR

C62
VAN DER SPRENKEL S.,"LEGAL INSTITUTIONS IN MANCHU
CHINA." ASIA STRUCT CT/SYS ROUTINE GOV/REL GP/REL
...CONCPT BIBLIOG 17/20. PAGE 111 B2250
LAW
JURID
ADMIN
ADJUD

B63
BOWETT D.W.,THE LAW OF INTERNATIONAL INSTITUTIONS.
WOR+45 WOR-45 CONSTN DELIB/GP EX/STRUC JUDGE
EDU/PROP LEGIT CT/SYS EXEC ROUTINE RIGID/FLEX
ORD/FREE PWR...JURID CONCPT ORG/CHARTS GEN/METH
LEAGUE/NAT OAS OEEC 20 UN. PAGE 14 B0286
INT/ORG
ADJUD
DIPLOM

B63
BURRUS B.R.,ADMINSTRATIVE LAW AND LOCAL GOVERNMENT.
USA+45 PROVS LEGIS LICENSE ADJUD ORD/FREE 20.
PAGE 17 B0356
EX/STRUC
LOC/G
JURID
CONSTN

B63
CORLEY R.N.,THE LEGAL ENVIRONMENT OF BUSINESS.
CONSTN LEGIS TAX ADMIN CT/SYS DISCRIM ATTIT PWR
...TREND 18/20. PAGE 23 B0477
NAT/G
INDUS
JURID
DECISION

B63
DIESNER H.J.,KIRCHE UND STAAT IM SPATROMISCHEN
REICH. ROMAN/EMP EX/STRUC COLONIAL COERCE ATTIT
CATHISM 4/5 AFRICA/N CHURCH/STA. PAGE 29 B0592
SECT
GP/REL
DOMIN
JURID

B63
ELIAS T.O.,THE NIGERIAN LEGAL SYSTEM. NIGERIA LAW
FAM KIN SECT ADMIN NAT/LISM...JURID 18/20
ENGLSH/LAW COMMON/LAW. PAGE 33 B0665
CT/SYS
ADJUD
COLONIAL
PROF/ORG

B63
FORTES A.B.,HISTORIA ADMINISTRATIVA, JUDICIARIA E
ECLESIASTICA DO RIO GRANDE DO SUL. BRAZIL L/A+17C
LOC/G SECT COLONIAL CT/SYS ORD/FREE CATHISM 16/20.
PAGE 37 B0742
PROVS
ADMIN
JURID

B63
GARNER U.F.,ADMINISTRATIVE LAW. UK LAW LOC/G NAT/G
EX/STRUC LEGIS JUDGE BAL/PWR BUDGET ADJUD CONTROL
CT/SYS...BIBLIOG 20. PAGE 39 B0783
ADMIN
JURID
PWR
GOV/REL

B63
GRANT D.R.,STATE AND LOCAL GOVERNMENT IN AMERICA.
USA+45 FINAN LOC/G MUNIC EX/STRUC FORCES EDU/PROP
ADMIN CHOOSE FEDERAL ATTIT...JURID 20. PAGE 42
B0853
PROVS
POL/PAR
LEGIS
CONSTN

B63
GRIFFITH J.A.G.,PRINCIPLES OF ADMINISTRATIVE LAW
(3RD ED.). UK CONSTN EX/STRUC LEGIS ADJUD CONTROL
CT/SYS PWR...CHARTS 20. PAGE 43 B0879
JURID
ADMIN
NAT/G
BAL/PWR

B63
HOUGHTELING J.L. JR.,THE LEGAL ENVIRONMENT OF
BUSINESS. LG/CO NAT/G CONSULT AGREE CONTROL
...DICTIONARY T 20. PAGE 52 B1047
LAW
MGT
ADJUD
JURID

B63
KLESMENT J.,LEGAL SOURCES AND BIBLIOGRAPHY OF THE
BALTIC STATES (ESTONIA, LATVIA, LITHUANIA). COM
ESTONIA LATVIA LITHUANIA LAW FINAN ADJUD CT/SYS
REGION CENTRAL MARXISM 19/20. PAGE 60 B1218
BIBLIOG/A
JURID
CONSTN
ADMIN

B63
KULZ H.R.,STAATSBURGER UND STAATSGEWALT (2 VOLS.).
GERMANY SWITZERLND UK USSR CONSTN DELIB/GP TARIFFS
TAX...JURID 20. PAGE 61 B1242
ADMIN
ADJUD
CT/SYS
NAT/COMP

B63
PATRA A.C.,THE ADMINISTRATION OF JUSTICE UNDER THE
EAST INDIA COMPANY IN BENGAL, BIHAR AND ORISSA.
INDIA UK LG/CO CAP/ISM INT/TRADE ADJUD COLONIAL
CONTROL CT/SYS...POLICY 20. PAGE 81 B1641
ADMIN
JURID
CONCPT

B63
PLANTEY A.,TRAITE PRATIQUE DE LA FONCTION PUBLIQUE
(2ND ED., 2 VOLS.). FRANCE FINAN EX/STRUC PROB/SOLV
GP/REL ATTIT...SOC 20 CIVIL/SERV. PAGE 83 B1680
ADMIN
SUPEGO
JURID

B63
ROBERT J.,LA MONARCHIE MAROCAINE. MOROCCO LABOR
MUNIC POL/PAR EX/STRUC ORD/FREE PWR...JURID TREND T
20. PAGE 89 B1793
CHIEF
CONSERVE
ADMIN
CONSTN

B63
ROYAL INSTITUTE PUBLIC ADMIN,BRITISH PUBLIC
ADMINISTRATION. UK LAW FINAN INDUS LOC/G POL/PAR
LEGIS LOBBY PARL/PROC CHOOSE JURID. PAGE 91 B1845
BIBLIOG
ADMIN
MGT

SINGH M.M.,MUNICIPAL GOVERNMENT IN THE CALCUTTA METROPOLITAN DISTRICT A PRELIMINARY SURVEY. FINAN LG/CO DELIB/GP BUDGET TAX ADMIN GP/REL 20 CALCUTTA. PAGE 97 B1969
NAT/G
B63
LOC/G
HEALTH
MUNIC
JURID

US SENATE COMM ON JUDICIARY,ADMINISTRATIVE CONFERENCE OF THE UNITED STATES. USA+45 CONSTN NAT/G PROB/SOLV CONFER GOV/REL...INT 20 SENATE. PAGE 110 B2230
B63
PARL/PROC
JURID
ADMIN
LEGIS

WADE H.W.R.,TOWARDS ADMINISTRATIVE JUSTICE. UK USA+45 CONSTN CONSULT PROB/SOLV CT/SYS PARL/PROC ...POLICY JURID METH/COMP 20 ENGLSH/LAW. PAGE 112 B2270
B63
ADJUD
IDEA/COMP
ADMIN

BOLGAR V.,"THE PUBLIC INTEREST: A JURISPRUDENTIAL AND COMPARATIVE OVERVIEW OF SYMPOSIUM ON FUNDAMENTAL CONCEPTS OF PUBLIC LAW" COM FRANCE GERMANY SWITZERLND LAW ADJUD ADMIN AGREE LAISSEZ ...JURID GEN/LAWS 20 EUROPE/E. PAGE 13 B0268
L63
CONCPT
ORD/FREE
CONTROL
NAT/COMP

RECENT PUBLICATIONS ON GOVERNMENTAL PROBLEMS. FINAN INDUS ACADEM PLAN PROB/SOLV EDU/PROP ADJUD ADMIN BIO/SOC...MGT SOC. PAGE 2 B0040
B64
BIBLIOG
AUTOMAT
LEGIS
JURID

BOUVIER-AJAM M.,MANUEL TECHNIQUE ET PRATIQUE DU MAIRE ET DES ELUS ET AGENTS COMMUNAUX. FRANCE LOC/G BUDGET CHOOSE GP/REL SUPEGO...JURID BIBLIOG 20 MAYOR COMMUNES. PAGE 14 B0284
B64
MUNIC
ADMIN
CHIEF
NEIGH

FISK W.M.,ADMINISTRATIVE PROCEDURE IN A REGULATORY AGENCY: THE CAB AND THE NEW YORK-CHICAGO CASE (PAMPHLET). USA+45 DIST/IND ADMIN CONTROL LOBBY GP/REL ROLE ORD/FREE NEWYORK/C CHICAGO CAB. PAGE 36 B0727
B64
SERV/IND
ECO/DEV
AIR
JURID

FORBES A.H.,CURRENT RESEARCH IN BRITISH STUDIES. UK CONSTN CULTURE POL/PAR SECT DIPLOM ADMIN...JURID BIOG WORSHIP 20. PAGE 36 B0736
B64
BIBLIOG
PERSON
NAT/G
PARL/PROC

GARFIELD PJ   LOVEJOY WF,PUBLIC UTILITY ECONOMICS. DIST/IND FINAN MARKET MUNIC ADMIN COST DEMAND...TECHNIC JURID 20 MONOPOLY. PAGE 39 B0782
B64
T
ECO/TAC
OWN
SERV/IND

GESELLSCHAFT RECHTSVERGLEICH,BIBLIOGRAPHIE DES DEUTSCHEN RECHTS (BIBLIOGRAPHY OF GERMAN LAW, TRANS. BY COURTLAND PETERSON). GERMANY FINAN INDUS LABOR SECT FORCES CT/SYS PARL/PROC CRIME...INT/LAW SOC NAT/COMP 20. PAGE 39 B0794
B64
BIBLIOG/A
JURID
CONSTN
ADMIN

GJUPANOVIC H.,LEGAL SOURCES AND BIBLIOGRAPHY OF YUGOSLAVIA. COM YUGOSLAVIA LAW LEGIS DIPLOM ADMIN PARL/PROC REGION CRIME CENTRAL 20. PAGE 40 B0807
B64
BIBLIOG/A
JURID
CONSTN
ADJUD

HALLER W.,DER SCHWEDISCHE JUSTITIEOMBUDSMAN. DENMARK FINLAND NORWAY SWEDEN LEGIS ADJUD CONTROL PERSON ORD/FREE...NAT/COMP 20 OMBUDSMAN. PAGE 46 B0926
B64
JURID
PARL/PROC
ADMIN
CHIEF

HARMON R.B.,BIBLIOGRAPHY OF BIBLIOGRAPHIES IN POLITICAL SCIENCE (MIMEOGRAPHED PAPER: LIMITED EDITION). WOR+45 WOR-45 INT/ORG POL/PAR GOV/REL ALL/IDEOS...INT/LAW JURID MGT 19/20. PAGE 47 B0949
B64
BIBLIOG
NAT/G
DIPLOM
LOC/G

JACKSON R.M.,THE MACHINERY OF JUSTICE IN ENGLAND. UK EDU/PROP CONTROL COST ORD/FREE...MGT 20 ENGLSH/LAW. PAGE 55 B1109
B64
CT/SYS
ADJUD
JUDGE
JURID

KAACK H.,DIE PARTEIEN IN DER VERFASSUNGSWIRKLICHKEIT DER BUNDESREPUBLIK. GERMANY/W ADMIN PARL/PROC CHOOSE...JURID 20. PAGE 57 B1157
B64
POL/PAR
PROVS
NAT/G

KARLEN D.,THE CITIZEN IN COURT. USA+45 LAW ADMIN ROUTINE CRIME GP/REL...JURID 20. PAGE 58 B1175
B64
CT/SYS
ADJUD
GOV/REL
JUDGE

NATIONAL BOOK LEAGUE,THE COMMONWEALTH IN BOOKS: AN ANNOTATED LIST. CANADA UK LOC/G SECT ADMIN...SOC BIOG 20 CMN/WLTH. PAGE 77 B1561
B64
BIBLIOG/A
JURID
NAT/G

SHERIDAN R.G.,URBAN JUSTICE. USA+45 PROVS CREATE ADMIN CT/SYS ORD/FREE 20 TENNESSEE. PAGE 96 B1943
B64
LOC/G
JURID
ADJUD
MUNIC

STOICOIU V.,LEGAL SOURCES AND BIBLIOGRAPHY OF ROMANIA. COM ROMANIA LAW FINAN POL/PAR LEGIS JUDGE
B64
BIBLIOG/A
JURID

ADJUD CT/SYS PARL/PROC MARXISM 20. PAGE 101 B2041
CONSTN
ADMIN

SZLADITS C.,BIBLIOGRAPHY ON FOREIGN AND COMPARATIVE LAW: BOOKS AND ARTICLES IN ENGLISH (SUPPLEMENT 1962). FINAN INDUS JUDGE LICENSE ADMIN CT/SYS PARL/PROC OWN...INT/LAW CLASSIF METH/COMP NAT/COMP 20. PAGE 102 B2065
B64
BIBLIOG/A
JURID
ADJUD
LAW

US SENATE COMM ON JUDICIARY,ADMINISTRATIVE PROCEDURE ACT. USA+45 CONSTN NAT/G PROB/SOLV CONFER GOV/REL PWR...INT 20 SENATE. PAGE 110 B2231
B64
PARL/PROC
LEGIS
JURID
ADMIN

VECCHIO G.D.,L'ETAT ET LE DROIT. ITALY CONSTN EX/STRUC LEGIS DIPLOM CT/SYS...JURID 20 UN. PAGE 112 B2256
B64
NAT/G
SOVEREIGN
CONCPT
INT/LAW

WAINHOUSE D.W.,REMNANTS OF EMPIRE: THE UNITED NATIONS AND THE END OF COLONIALISM. FUT PORTUGAL WOR+45 NAT/G CONSULT DOMIN LEGIT ADMIN ROUTINE ATTIT ORD/FREE...POLICY JURID RECORD INT TIME/SEQ UN CMN/WLTH 20. PAGE 113 B2275
B64
INT/ORG
TREND
COLONIAL

WHEARE K.C.,FEDERAL GOVERNMENT (4TH ED.). WOR+45 WOR-45 POL/PAR LEGIS BAL/PWR CT/SYS...POLICY JURID CONCPT GOV/COMP 17/20. PAGE 116 B2331
B64
FEDERAL
CONSTN
EX/STRUC
NAT/COMP

WORLD PEACE FOUNDATION,"INTERNATIONAL ORGANIZATIONS: SUMMARY OF ACTIVITIES." INDIA PAKISTAN TURKEY WOR+45 NAT/G CONSTN CONSULT EX/STRUC ECO/TAC EDU/PROP LEGIT ORD/FREE...JURID SOC UN 20 CYPRESS. PAGE 118 B2375
L64
INT/ORG
ROUTINE

PARSONS T.,"EVOLUTIONARY UNIVERSALS IN SOCIETY." UNIV SOCIETY STRATA MARKET EDU/PROP LEGIT ADJUD ADMIN ALL/VALS...JURID OBS GEN/LAWS VAL/FREE 20. PAGE 81 B1638
S64
SOC
CONCPT

CAVERS D.F.,THE CHOICE-OF-LAW PROCESS. PROB/SOLV ADJUD CT/SYS CHOOSE RATIONAL...IDEA/COMP 16/20 TREATY. PAGE 19 B0396
B65
JURID
DECISION
METH/COMP
ADMIN

COHN H.J.,THE GOVERNMENT OF THE RHINE PALATINATE IN THE FIFTEENTH CENTURY. GERMANY FINAN LOC/G DELIB/GP LEGIS CT/SYS CHOOSE CATHISM 14/15 PALATINATE. PAGE 22 B0449
B65
PROVS
JURID
GP/REL
ADMIN

COOPER F.E.,STATE ADMINISTRATIVE LAW (2 VOLS.). LAW LEGIS PLAN TAX ADJUD CT/SYS FEDERAL PWR...CONCPT 20. PAGE 23 B0474
B65
JURID
CONSTN
ADMIN
PROVS

DOWD L.P.,PRINCIPLES OF WORLD BUSINESS. SERV/IND NAT/G DIPLOM ECO/TAC TARIFFS...INT/LAW JURID 20. PAGE 30 B0614
B65
INT/TRADE
MGT
FINAN
MARKET

INST INTL DES CIVILISATION DIF,THE CONSTITUTIONS AND ADMINISTRATIVE INSTITUTIONS OF THE NEW STATES. AFR ISLAM S/ASIA NAT/G POL/PAR DELIB/GP EX/STRUC CONFER EFFICIENCY NAT/LISM...JURID SOC 20. PAGE 54 B1088
B65
CONSTN
ADMIN
ADJUD
ECO/UNDEV

KAAS L.,DIE GEISTLICHE GERICHTSBARKEIT DER KATHOLISCHEN KIRCHE IN PREUSSEN (2 VOLS.). PRUSSIA CONSTN NAT/G PROVS SECT ADJUD ADMIN ATTIT 16/20. PAGE 57 B1158
B65
JURID
CATHISM
GP/REL
CT/SYS

PURCELL V.,THE MEMOIRS OF A MALAYAN OFFICIAL. MALAYSIA UK ECO/UNDEV INDUS LABOR EDU/PROP COLONIAL CT/SYS WAR NAT/LISM TOTALISM ORD/FREE SOVEREIGN 20 UN CIVIL/SERV. PAGE 85 B1721
B65
BIOG
ADMIN
JURID
FORCES

PYLEE M.V.,CONSTITUTIONAL GOVERNMENT IN INDIA (2ND REV. ED.). INDIA POL/PAR EX/STRUC DIPLOM COLONIAL CT/SYS PARL/PROC PRIVIL...JURID 16/20. PAGE 85 B1725
B65
CONSTN
NAT/G
PROVS
FEDERAL

REDFORD D.R.,POLITICS AND GOVERNMENT IN THE UNITED STATES. USA+45 USA-45 LOC/G PROVS FORCES DIPLOM CT/SYS LOBBY...JURID SUPREME/CT PRESIDENT. PAGE 87 B1751
B65
NAT/G
POL/PAR
EX/STRUC
LEGIS

SHARMA S.A.,PARLIAMENTARY GOVERNMENT IN INDIA. INDIA FINAN LOC/G PROVS DELIB/GP PLAN ADMIN CT/SYS FEDERAL...JURID 20. PAGE 96 B1936
B65
NAT/G
CONSTN
PARL/PROC
LEGIS

SMITH C.,THE OMBUDSMAN: A BIBLIOGRAPHY (PAMPHLET). DENMARK SWEDEN USA+45 LAW LEGIS JUDGE GOV/REL GP/REL...JURID 20. PAGE 98 B1980
B65
BIBLIOG
ADMIN
CT/SYS
ADJUD

B65

STEINER K.,LOCAL GOVERNMENT IN JAPAN. CONSTN
CULTURE NAT/G ADMIN CHOOSE...SOC STAT 20 CHINJAP.
PAGE 100 B2030

LOC/G
SOCIETY
JURID
ORD/FREE

B65

UNIVERSAL REFERENCE SYSTEM,INTERNATIONAL AFFAIRS:
VOLUME I IN THE POLITICAL SCIENCE, GOVERNMENT, AND
PUBLIC POLICY SERIES...DECISION ECOMETRIC GEOG
INT/LAW JURID MGT PHIL/SCI PSY SOC. PAGE 107 B2163

BIBLIOG/A
GEN/METH
COMPUT/IR
DIPLOM

B65

VONGLAHN G.,LAW AMONG NATIONS: AN INTRODUCTION TO
PUBLIC INTERNATIONAL LAW. UNIV WOR+45 LAW INT/ORG
NAT/G LEGIT EXEC RIGID/FLEX...CONCPT TIME/SEQ
GEN/LAWS UN TOT/POP 20. PAGE 112 B2267

CONSTN
JURID
INT/LAW

B66

ANDERSON S.V.,CANADIAN OMBUDSMAN PROPOSALS. CANADA
LEGIS DEBATE PARL/PROC...MAJORIT JURID TIME/SEQ
IDEA/COMP 20 OMBUDSMAN PARLIAMENT. PAGE 5 B0096

NAT/G
CREATE
ADMIN
POL/PAR

B66

EPSTEIN F.T.,THE AMERICAN BIBLIOGRAPHY OF RUSSIAN
AND EAST EUROPEAN STUDIES FOR 1964. USSR LOC/G
NAT/G POL/PAR FORCES ADMIN ARMS/CONT...JURID CONCPT
20 UN. PAGE 33 B0678

BIBLIOG
COM
MARXISM
DIPLOM

B66

HARMON R.B.,SOURCES AND PROBLEMS OF BIBLIOGRAPHY IN
POLITICAL SCIENCE (PAMPHLET). INT/ORG LOC/G MUNIC
POL/PAR ADMIN GOV/REL ALL/IDEOS...JURID MGT CONCPT
19/20. PAGE 47 B0951

BIBLIOG
DIPLOM
INT/LAW
NAT/G

B66

HIDAYATULLAH M.,DEMOCRACY IN INDIA AND THE JUDICIAL
PROCESS. INDIA EX/STRUC LEGIS LEAD GOV/REL ATTIT
ORD/FREE...MAJORIT CONCPT 20 NEHRU/J. PAGE 50 B1007

NAT/G
CT/SYS
CONSTN
JURID

B66

WASHINGTON S.H.,BIBLIOGRAPHY: LABOR-MANAGEMENT
RELATIONS ACT, 1947 AS AMENDED BY LABOR-MANAGEMENT
REPORTING AND DISCLOSURE ACT, 1959. USA+45 CONSTN
INDUS DELIB/GP LEGIS WORKER BARGAIN ECO/TAC ADJUD
GP/REL NEW/LIB...JURID CONGRESS. PAGE 114 B2298

BIBLIOG
LAW
LABOR
MGT

B66

WILSON G.,CASES AND MATERIALS ON CONSTITUTIONAL AND
ADMINISTRATIVE LAW. UK LAW NAT/G EX/STRUC LEGIS
BAL/PWR BUDGET DIPLOM ADJUD CONTROL CT/SYS GOV/REL
ORD/FREE 20 PARLIAMENT ENGLSH/LAW. PAGE 117 B2359

JURID
LAW
CONSTN
PWR

S66

BURDETTE F.L.,"SELECTED ARTICLES AND DOCUMENTS ON
AMERICAN GOVERNMENT AND POLITICS." LAW LOC/G MUNIC
NAT/G POL/PAR PROVS LEGIS BAL/PWR ADMIN EXEC
REPRESENT MGT. PAGE 17 B0348

BIBLIOG
USA+45
JURID
CONSTN

S66

POLSBY N.W.,"BOOKS IN THE FIELD: POLITICAL
SCIENCE." LAW CONSTN LOC/G NAT/G LEGIS ADJUD PWR 20
SUPREME/CT. PAGE 83 B1686

BIBLIOG/A
ATTIT
ADMIN
JURID

B67

BLUMBERG A.S.,CRIMINAL JUSTICE. USA+45 CLIENT LAW
LOC/G FORCES JUDGE ACT/RES LEGIT ADMIN RATIONAL
MYTH. PAGE 13 B0259

JURID
CT/SYS
PROF/ORG
CRIME

B67

BROWN L.N.,FRENCH ADMINISTRATIVE LAW. FRANCE UK
CONSTN NAT/G LEGIS DOMIN CONTROL EXEC PARL/PROC PWR
...JURID METH/COMP GEN/METH. PAGE 16 B0324

EX/STRUC
LAW
IDEA/COMP
CT/SYS

B67

LENG S.C.,JUSTICE IN COMMUNIST CHINA: A SURVEY OF
THE JUDICIAL SYSTEM OF THE CHINESE PEOPLE'S
REPUBLIC. CHINA/COM LAW CONSTN LOC/G NAT/G PROF/ORG
CONSULT FORCES ADMIN CRIME ORD/FREE...BIBLIOG 20
MAO. PAGE 64 B1290

CT/SYS
ADJUD
JURID
MARXISM

B67

PLANO J.C.,FORGING WORLD ORDER: THE POLITICS OF
INTERNATIONAL ORGANIZATION. PROB/SOLV DIPLOM
CONTROL CENTRAL RATIONAL ORD/FREE...INT/LAW CHARTS
BIBLIOG 20 UN LEAGUE/NAT. PAGE 83 B1679

INT/ORG
ADMIN
JURID

B67

SCHAEFER W.V.,THE SUSPECT AND SOCIETY: CRIMINAL
PROCEDURE AND CONVERGING CONSTITUTIONAL DOCTRINES.
USA+45 TEC/DEV LOBBY ROUTINE SANCTION...INT 20.
PAGE 93 B1879

CRIME
FORCES
CONSTN
JURID

B67

SCHLOSSBERG S.I.,ORGANIZING AND THE LAW. USA+45
WORKER PLAN LEGIT REPRESENT GP/REL...JURID MGT 20
NLRB. PAGE 94 B1893

LABOR
CONSULT
BARGAIN
PRIVIL

B67

WESTON P.B.,THE ADMINISTRATION OF JUSTICE. USA+45
CONSTN MUNIC NAT/G PROVS EX/STRUC JUDGE ADMIN
CONTROL SANCTION ORD/FREE...CHARTS 20. PAGE 115
B2328

CRIME
CT/SYS
JURID
ADJUD

B67

ZELERMYER W.,BUSINESS LAW: NEW PERSPECTIVES IN
BUSINESS ECONOMICS. USA+45 LAW INDUS DELIB/GP
...JURID MGT ANTHOL BIBLIOG 20 NLRB. PAGE 119 B2400

LABOR
CAP/ISM
LG/CO

L67

BERGER R.,"ADMINISTRATIVE ARBITRARINESS* A SEQUEL."
USA+45 CONSTN ADJUD CT/SYS SANCTION INGP/REL
...POLICY JURID. PAGE 11 B0222

LAW
LABOR
BARGAIN
ADMIN

L67

BLUMBERG A.S.,"THE PRACTICE OF LAW AS CONFIDENCE
GAME; ORGANIZATIONAL COOPTATION OF A PROFESSION."
USA+45 CLIENT SOCIETY CONSULT ROLE JURID. PAGE 13
B0260

CT/SYS
ADJUD
GP/REL
ADMIN

L67

CAHIERS P.,"LE RECOURS EN CONSTATATION DE
MANQUEMENTS DES ETATS MEMBRES DEVANT LA COUR DES
COMMUNAUTES EUROPEENNES." LAW PROB/SOLV DIPLOM
ADMIN CT/SYS SANCTION ATTIT...POLICY DECISION JURID
ECSC EEC. PAGE 18 B0362

INT/ORG
CONSTN
ROUTINE
ADJUD

L67

GAINES J.E.,"THE YOUTH COURT CONCEPT AND ITS
IMPLEMENTATION IN TOMPKINS COUNTY, NEW YORK."
USA+45 LAW CONSTN JUDGE WORKER ADJUD ADMIN CHOOSE
PERSON...JURID NEW/YORK. PAGE 38 B0772

CT/SYS
AGE/Y
INGP/REL
CRIME

L67

JACOBY S.B.,"THE 89TH CONGRESS AND GOVERNMENT
LITIGATION." USA+45 ADMIN COST...JURID 20 CONGRESS.
PAGE 55 B1117

LAW
NAT/G
ADJUD
SANCTION

L67

MANNE H.G.,"OUR TWO CORPORATION SYSTEMS* LAW AND
ECONOMICS." LAW CONTROL SANCTION GP/REL...JURID 20.
PAGE 69 B1392

INDUS
ELITES
CAP/ISM
ADMIN

S67

DANELSKI D.J.,"CONFLICT AND ITS RESOLUTION IN THE
SUPREME COURT." PROB/SOLV LEAD ROUTINE PERSON...PSY
PERS/COMP BIBLIOG 20. PAGE 26 B0527

ROLE
JURID
JUDGE
INGP/REL

S67

FABREGA J.,"ANTECEDENTES EXTRANJEROS EN LA
CONSTITUCION PANAMENA." CUBA L/A+17C PANAMA URUGUAY
EX/STRUC LEGIS DIPLOM ORD/FREE 19/20 COLOMB
MEXIC/AMER. PAGE 34 B0694

CONSTN
JURID
NAT/G
PARL/PROC

S67

KRARUP O.,"JUDICIAL REVIEW OF ADMINISTRATIVE ACTION
IN DENMARK." DENMARK LAW CT/SYS...JURID CONCPT
19/20. PAGE 61 B1234

ADJUD
CONTROL
EXEC
DECISION

S67

LANDES W.M.,"THE EFFECT OF STATE FAIR EMPLOYMENT
LAWS ON THE ECONOMIC POSITION OF NONWHITES." USA+45
PROVS SECT LEGIS ADMIN GP/REL RACE/REL...JURID
CONCPT CHARTS HYPO/EXP NEGRO. PAGE 62 B1255

DISCRIM
LAW
WORKER

S67

MELTZER B.D.,"RUMINATIONS ABOUT IDEOLOGY, LAW, AND
LABOR ARBITRATION." USA+45 ECO/DEV PROB/SOLV CONFER
MGT. PAGE 73 B1466

JURID
ADJUD
LABOR
CONSULT

S67

SMITH W.H.T.,"THE IMPLICATIONS OF THE AMERICAN BAR
ASSOCIATION ADVISORY COMMITTEE RECOMMENDATIONS FOR
POLICE ADMINISTRATION." ADMIN...JURID 20 ABA.
PAGE 98 B1986

EDU/PROP
CONTROL
GP/REL
ORD/FREE

JURISPRUDENCE....SEE LAW

JURY....JURIES AND JURY BEHAVIOR; SEE ALSO DELIB/GP, ADJUD

JUSTICE DEPARTMENT....SEE DEPT/JUST

JUVILER P.H. B1156

K

KAACK H. B1157

KAAS L. B1158

KADALIE/C....CLEMENTS KADALIE

KAESTNER K. B1159

KAHNG T.J. B1160

KAISR/ALUM....KAISER ALUMINUM

KALBUS E.C. B0741

KALMANOFF G. B0760

KAMCHATKA....KAMCHATKA, U.S.S.R.

KAMMERER G.M. B1161,B1162,B1163,B1164

KAMPELMAN M.M. B0798,B1165

KANSAS....KANSAS

B61

DRURY J.W.,THE GOVERNMENT OF KANSAS. USA+45 AGRI   PROVS

INDUS CHIEF LEGIS WORKER PLAN BUDGET GIVE CT/SYS   CONSTN
GOV/REL...T 20 KANSAS GOVERNOR CITY/MGT. PAGE 31   ADMIN
B0621   LOC/G

KANT/I....IMMANUEL KANT

KAPINGAMAR....KAPINGAMARANGI

KAPLAN H. B1166

KAPLAN H.E. B1167

KAPLAN M.A. B1168

KAPLAN N. B1169

KAPP E. B1170

KAPP W.K. B1171

KARDOUCHE G.K. B1172

KARIEL H.S. B1173

KARL B.D. B1174

KARLEN D. B1175

KARLIN S. B0137

KARNJAHAPRAKORN C. B1176

KASER M. B1177

KASHMIR....SEE ALSO S/ASIA

KASSOF A. B1178

KATANGA....SEE ALSO AFR

KATZ D. B2249

KATZ J. B1180

KATZ R.N. B0711

KAUFMAN H. B1181,B1875

KAUFMANN J. B0912

KAUFMANN W.W. B1182

KAUNDA K. B1183

KAUNDA/K....KENNETH KAUNDA, PRESIDENT OF ZAMBIA

KAUTSKY J.H. B1184

KAYSEN C. B1185

KEARNEY R.N. B0955

KEATON H.J. B1579

KEE R. B1186

KEEFE W.J. B1187

KEFAUVER E. B1188,B1189

KEFAUVER/E....ESTES KEFAUVER

KEISER N.F. B1190

KEITA/M....MOBIDO KEITA

KEL/BRIAND....KELLOGG BRIAND PEACE PACT

KELLEY E.J. B1191

KELLOG BRIAND PEACE PACT....SEE KEL/BRIAND

KELSEN/H....HANS KELSEN

KELSON R N. B0707

KENNAN G.F. B1192

KENNAN/G....GEORGE KENNAN

KENNEDY J.F. B1193

KENNEDY/JF....PRESIDENT JOHN F. KENNEDY

                                                          B61
MARKMANN C.L.,JOHN F. KENNEDY: A SENSE OF PURPOSE. CHIEF
USA+45 INTELL FAM CONSULT DELIB/GP LEGIS PERSON   TOP/EX
SKILL 20 KENNEDY/JF EISNHWR/DD ROOSEVLT/F   ADMIN
NEW/FRONTR PRESIDENT. PAGE 69 B1399   BIOG

                                                          B61
OPOTOWSKY S.,THE KENNEDY GOVERNMENT. NAT/G CONSULT ADMIN
EX/STRUC LEAD PERSON...POLICY 20 KENNEDY/JF   BIOG
CONGRESS CABINET. PAGE 80 B1613   ELITES
                                                   TOP/EX

                                                          B61
TANZER L.,THE KENNEDY CIRCLE. INTELL CONSULT   EX/STRUC
DELIB/GP TOP/EX CONTROL EXEC INGP/REL PERS/REL PWR NAT/G
...BIOG IDEA/COMP ANTHOL 20 KENNEDY/JF PRESIDENT   CHIEF
DEMOCRAT MCNAMARA/R RUSK/D. PAGE 103 B2077

                                                          S61
VINER J.,"ECONOMIC FOREIGN POLICY ON THE NEW   TOP/EX
FRONTIER." USA+45 ECO/UNDEV AGRI FINAN INDUS MARKET ECO/TAC
INT/ORG NAT/G FOR/AID INT/TRADE ADMIN ATTIT PWR 20 BAL/PAY
KENNEDY/JF. PAGE 112 B2262   TARIFFS

                                                          B62
EVANS M.S.,THE FRINGE ON TOP. USSR EX/STRUC FORCES NAT/G
DIPLOM ECO/TAC PEACE CONSERVE SOCISM...TREND 20   PWR
KENNEDY/JF. PAGE 34 B0689   CENTRAL
                                                   POLICY

                                                          B62
KENNEDY J.F.,TO TURN THE TIDE. SPACE AGRI INT/ORG   DIPLOM
FORCES TEC/DEV ADMIN NUC/PWR PEACE WEALTH...ANTHOL CHIEF
20 KENNEDY/JF CIV/RIGHTS. PAGE 59 B1193   POLICY
                                                   NAT/G

                                                          B62
US SENATE COMM GOVT OPERATIONS,ADMINISTRATION OF   ORD/FREE
NATIONAL SECURITY. USA+45 CHIEF PLAN PROB/SOLV   ADMIN
TEC/DEV DIPLOM ATTIT...POLICY DECISION 20   NAT/G
KENNEDY/JF RUSK/D MCNAMARA/R BUNDY/M HERTER/C.   CONTROL
PAGE 110 B2212

                                                          B62
US SENATE COMM ON JUDICIARY,STATE DEPARTMENT   CONTROL
SECURITY. USA+45 CHIEF TEC/DEV DOMIN ADMIN EXEC   WORKER
ATTIT ORD/FREE...POLICY CONGRESS DEPT/STATE   NAT/G
PRESIDENT KENNEDY/JF KENNEDY/JF SENATE 20. PAGE 110 GOV/REL
B2228

                                                          B62
US SENATE COMM ON JUDICIARY,STATE DEPARTMENT   CONTROL
SECURITY. USA+45 CHIEF TEC/DEV DOMIN ADMIN EXEC   WORKER
ATTIT ORD/FREE...POLICY CONGRESS DEPT/STATE   NAT/G
PRESIDENT KENNEDY/JF KENNEDY/JF SENATE 20. PAGE 110 GOV/REL
B2228

                                                          B63
SIDEY H.,JOHN F. KENNEDY, PRESIDENT. USA+45 INTELL BIOG
FAM CONSULT DELIB/GP LEGIS ADMIN LEAD 20 KENNEDY/JF TOP/EX
PRESIDENT. PAGE 97 B1951   SKILL
                                                   PERSON

                                                          B64
ADAMS V.,THE PEACE CORPS IN ACTION. USA+45 VOL/ASSN DIPLOM
EX/STRUC GOV/REL PERCEPT ORD/FREE...OBS 20   FOR/AID
KENNEDY/JF PEACE/CORP. PAGE 3 B0058   PERSON
                                                   DRIVE

                                                          B65
FEERICK J.D.,FROM FAILING HANDS: THE STUDY OF   EX/STRUC
PRESIDENTIAL SUCCESSION. CONSTN NAT/G PROB/SOLV   CHIEF
LEAD PARL/PROC MURDER CHOOSE...NEW/IDEA BIBLIOG 20 LAW
KENNEDY/JF JOHNSON/LB PRESIDENT PRE/US/AM   LEGIS
VICE/PRES. PAGE 35 B0710

                                                          S66
AUSLAND J.C.,"CRISIS MANAGEMENT* BERLIN, CYPRUS,   OP/RES
LAOS." CYPRUS LAOS FORCES CREATE PLAN EDU/PROP TASK DIPLOM
CENTRAL PERSON RIGID/FLEX...DECISION MGT 20 BERLIN RISK
KENNEDY/JF MCNAMARA/R RUSK. PAGE 7 B0148   ADMIN

                                                          B67
WARREN S.,THE AMERICAN PRESIDENT. POL/PAR FORCES   CHIEF
LEGIS DIPLOM ECO/TAC ADMIN EXEC PWR...ANTHOL 18/20 LEAD
ROOSEVLT/F KENNEDY/JF JOHNSON/LB TRUMAN/HS   NAT/G
WILSON/W. PAGE 114 B2297   CONSTN

KENNEDY/RF....ROBERT F. KENNEDY

KENT F.R. B1194

KENT S. B1195

KENTUCKY....KENTUCKY

                                                          N19
EAST KENTUCKY REGIONAL PLAN,PROGRAM 60: A DECADE OF REGION
ACTION FOR PROGRESS IN EASTERN KENTUCKY (PAMPHLET). ADMIN
USA+45 AGRI CONSTRUC INDUS CONSULT ACT/RES   PLAN
PROB/SOLV EDU/PROP GOV/REL HEALTH KENTUCKY. PAGE 32 ECO/UNDEV
B0643

                                                          N19
EAST KENTUCKY REGIONAL PLAN,PROGRAM 60 REPORT: REGION
ACTION FOR PORGRESS IN EASTERN KENTUCKY (PAMPHLET). PLAN
USA+45 CONSTRUC INDUS ACT/RES PROB/SOLV EDU/PROP   ECO/UNDEV
ADMIN GOV/REL KENTUCKY. PAGE 32 B0644   CONSULT

KENTUCKY STATE ARCHIVES B1196

KENYA....KENYA

KENYATTA....JOMO KENYATTA

KERR C. B1197

KERSELL J.E. B1198

KERTESZ S.D. B1199

KESSELMAN L.C. B1200

KESSLER S. B0882

KEYNES/G....GEOFFREY KEYNES

KEYNES/JM....JOHN MAYNARD KEYNES

B37
ROBBINS L.,ECONOMIC PLANNING AND INTERNATIONAL   INT/ORG
ORDER. WOR-45 SOCIETY FINAN INDUS NAT/G ECO/TAC   PLAN
ROUTINE WEALTH...SOC TIME/SEQ GEN/METH WORK 20   INT/TRADE
KEYNES/JM. PAGE 89 B1791
  B58
WARNER A.W.,CONCEPTS AND CASES IN ECONOMIC   ECO/TAC
ANALYSIS. PROB/SOLV BARGAIN CONTROL INCOME PRODUC   DEMAND
...ECOMETRIC MGT CONCPT CLASSIF CHARTS 20   EQUILIB
KEYNES/JM. PAGE 114 B2292   COST

KHAMA T. B1201

KHAN M.Z. B1202

KHASAS....KHASAS (ANCIENT COMMUNITY)

KHRUSH/N....NIKITA KHRUSHCHEV

B64
FAINSOD M.,HOW RUSSIA IS RULED (REV. ED.). RUSSIA   NAT/G
USSR AGRI PROC/MFG LABOR POL/PAR EX/STRUC CONTROL   REV
PWR...POLICY BIBLIOG 19/20 KHRUSH/N COM/PARTY.   MARXISM
PAGE 34 B0700

KIERKE/S....SOREN KIERKEGAARD

KIESER P.J. B1203

KIETH-LUCAS A. B1204

KILPATRICK F.P.   B1205, B1206

KIM/IL-SON....IL-SON KIM

KIMBROUGH R.B. B1207

KIN....KINSHIP (EXCEPT NUCLEAR FAMILY)

B02
MOREL E.D.,AFFAIRS OF WEST AFRICA. UK FINAN INDUS   COLONIAL
FAM KIN SECT CHIEF WORKER DIPLOM RACE/REL LITERACY   ADMIN
HEALTH...CHARTS 18/20 AFRICA/W NEGRO. PAGE 75 B1521   AFR
  B28
BUELL R.,THE NATIVE PROBLEM IN AFRICA. KIN LABOR   AFR
LOC/G ECO/TAC ROUTINE ORD/FREE...REC/INT KNO/TEST   CULTURE
CENSUS TREND CHARTS SOC/EXP STERTYP 20. PAGE 17
B0339
  B48
DAY P.,CRISIS IN SOUTH AFRICA. SOUTH/AFR UK KIN   RACE/REL
MUNIC ECO/TAC RECEIVE 20 SMUTS/JAN MIGRATION.   COLONIAL
PAGE 27 B0548   ADMIN
  EXTR/IND
  B50
WELCH S.R.,PORTUGUESE RULE AND SPANISH CROWN IN   DIPLOM
SOUTH AFRICA 1581-1640. PORTUGAL SOUTH/AFR SPAIN   COLONIAL
SOCIETY KIN NEIGH SECT INT/TRADE ADMIN 16/17   WAR
MISSION. PAGE 115 B2317   PEACE
  B54
ALLPORT G.W.,THE NATURE OF PREJUDICE. USA+45 WOR+45   CULTURE
STRATA FACE/GP KIN NEIGH SECT ADMIN GP/REL DISCRIM   PERSON
ATTIT DRIVE LOVE RESPECT...PSY SOC MYTH QU/SEMANT   RACE/REL
20. PAGE 4 B0078
  B55
APTER D.E.,THE GOLD COAST IN TRANSITION. FUT CONSTN   AFR
CULTURE SOCIETY ECO/UNDEV FAM KIN NAT/G   SOVEREIGN
POL/PAR LEGIS TOP/EX EDU/PROP LEGIT ADMIN ATTIT
PERSON PWR...CONCPT STAT INT CENSUS TOT/POP
VAL/FREE. PAGE 6 B0120
  B56
MANNONI D.O.,PROSPERO AND CALIBAN: THE PSYCHOLOGY   CULTURE
OF COLONIZATION. AFR EUR+WWI FAM KIN MUNIC SECT   COLONIAL
DOMIN ADMIN ATTIT DRIVE LOVE PWR RESPECT...PSY SOC
CONCPT MYTH OBS DEEP/INT BIOG GEN/METH MALAGASY 20.
PAGE 69 B1394
  B57
IKE N.,JAPANESE POLITICS. INTELL STRUCT AGRI INDUS   NAT/G
FAM KIN LABOR PRESS CHOOSE ATTIT...DECISION BIBLIOG   ADMIN

19/20 CHINJAP. PAGE 53 B1075   POL/PAR
  CULTURE
  B58
COLEMAN J.S.,NIGERIA: BACKGROUND TO NATIONALISM.   NAT/G
AFR SOCIETY ECO/DEV KIN LOC/G POL/PAR TEC/DEV DOMIN   NAT/LISM
ADMIN DRIVE PWR RESPECT...TRADIT SOC INT SAMP   NIGERIA
TIME/SEQ 20. PAGE 22 B0452
  B58
COWAN L.G.,LOCAL GOVERNMENT IN WEST AFRICA. AFR   LOC/G
FRANCE UK CULTURE KIN POL/PAR CHIEF LEGIS CREATE   COLONIAL
ADMIN PARTIC GOV/REL GP/REL...METH/COMP 20. PAGE 24   SOVEREIGN
B0498   REPRESENT
  B58
SKINNER G.W.,LEADERSHIP AND POWER IN THE CHINESE   SOC
COMMUNITY OF THAILAND. ASIA S/ASIA STRATA FACE/GP   ELITES
KIN PROF/ORG VOL/ASSN EX/STRUC DOMIN PERSON RESPECT   THAILAND
...METH/CNCPT STAT INT QU BIOG CHARTS 20. PAGE 98
B1974
  S58
MAIR L.P.,"REPRESENTATIVE LOCAL GOVERNMENT AS A   AFR
PROBLEM IN SOCIAL CHANGE." ECO/UNDEV KIN LOC/G   PWR
NAT/G SCHOOL JUDGE ADMIN ROUTINE REPRESENT   ELITES
RIGID/FLEX RESPECT...CONCPT STERTYP CMN/WLTH 20.
PAGE 68 B1383
  B59
GINSBURG M.,LAW AND OPINION IN ENGLAND. UK CULTURE   JURID
KIN LABOR LEGIS EDU/PROP ADMIN CT/SYS CRIME OWN   POLICY
HEALTH...ANTHOL 20 ENGLSH/LAW. PAGE 40 B0802   ECO/TAC
  B59
YANG C.K.,A CHINESE VILLAGE IN EARLY COMMUNIST   ASIA
TRANSITION. ECO/UNDEV AGRI FAM KIN MUNIC FORCES   ROUTINE
PLAN ECO/TAC DOMIN EDU/PROP ATTIT DRIVE PWR RESPECT   SOCISM
...SOC CONCPT METH/CNCPT OBS RECORD CON/ANAL CHARTS
WORK 20. PAGE 118 B2389
  B60
SMITH M.G.,GOVERNMENT IN ZAZZAU 1800-1950. NIGERIA   REGION
UK CULTURE SOCIETY LOC/G ADMIN COLONIAL   CONSTN
...METH/CNCPT NEW/IDEA METH 19/20. PAGE 98 B1983   KIN
  ECO/UNDEV
  B63
ELIAS T.O.,THE NIGERIAN LEGAL SYSTEM. NIGERIA LAW   CT/SYS
FAM KIN SECT ADMIN NAT/LISM...JURID 18/20   ADJUD
ENGLSH/LAW COMMON/LAW. PAGE 33 B0665   COLONIAL
  PROF/ORG
  B64
HANNA W.J.,INDEPENDENT BLACK AFRICA: THE POLITICS   AFR
OF FREEDOM. ELITES INDUS KIN CHIEF COLONIAL CHOOSE   ECO/UNDEV
GOV/REL RACE/REL NAT/LISM ATTIT PERSON 20 NEGRO.   ADMIN
PAGE 46 B0938   PROB/SOLV
  B64
SINGER M.R.,THE EMERGING ELITE: A STUDY OF   TOP/EX
POLITICAL LEADERSHIP IN CEYLON. S/ASIA ECO/UNDEV   STRATA
AGRI KIN NAT/G SECT EX/STRUC LEGIT ATTIT PWR   NAT/LISM
RESPECT...SOC STAT CHARTS 20. PAGE 97 B1967   CEYLON
  S64
CLIGNET R.,"POTENTIAL ELITES IN GHANA AND THE IVORY   PWR
COAST: A PRELIMINARY SURVEY." AFR CULTURE ELITES   LEGIT
STRATA KIN NAT/G SECT DOMIN EXEC ORD/FREE RESPECT   IVORY/CST
SKILL...POLICY RELATIV GP/COMP NAT/COMP 20. PAGE 21   GHANA
B0438
  B67
BENNETT J.W.,HUTTERIAN BRETHREN; THE AGRICULTURAL   SECT
ECONOMY AND SOCIAL ORGANIZATION OF A COMMUNAL   AGRI
PEOPLE. USA+45 SOCIETY FAM KIN TEC/DEV ADJUST...MGT   STRUCT
AUD/VIS GP/COMP 20. PAGE 10 B0213   GP/REL
  B67
COHEN R.,COMPARATIVE POLITICAL SYSTEMS: STUDIES IN   ECO/UNDEV
THE POLITICS OF PRE-INDUSTRIAL SOCIETIES. WOR+45   STRUCT
WOR-45 CULTURE FAM KIN LOC/G NEIGH ADMIN LEAD   SOCIETY
MARRIAGE...BIBLIOG 20. PAGE 22 B0447   GP/COMP
  S67
HUGON P.,"BLOCAGES ET DESEQUILIBRES DE LA   ECO/UNDEV
CROISSANCE ECONOMIQUE EN AFRIQUE NOIRE." AFR KIN   COLONIAL
MUNIC CREATE PLAN INT/TRADE REGION ADJUST CENTRAL   STRUCT
EQUILIB NAT/LISM ORD/FREE 20. PAGE 52 B1060   ADMIN
  S67
IDENBURG P.J.,"POLITICAL STRUCTURAL DEVELOPMENT IN   AFR
TROPICAL AFRICA." UK ECO/UNDEV KIN POL/PAR CHIEF   CONSTN
EX/STRUC CREATE COLONIAL CONTROL REPRESENT RACE/REL   NAT/G
...MAJORIT TREND 20. PAGE 53 B1074   GOV/COMP
  S67
RAUM O.,"THE MODERN LEADERSHIP GROUP AMONG THE   RACE/REL
SOUTH AFRICAN XHOSA." SOUTH/AFR SOCIETY SECT   KIN
EX/STRUC REPRESENT GP/REL INGP/REL PERSON   LEAD
...METH/COMP 17/20 XHOSA NEGRO. PAGE 86 B1743   CULTURE
  B82
MACDONALD D.,AFRICANA; OR, THE HEART OF HEATHEN   SECT
AFRICA, VOL. II: MISSION LIFE. SOCIETY STRATA KIN   AFR
CREATE EDU/PROP ADMIN COERCE LITERACY HEALTH...MYTH   CULTURE
WORSHIP 19 LIVNGSTN/D MISSION NEGRO. PAGE 67 B1355   ORD/FREE
  B95
LATIMER E.W.,EUROPE IN AFRICA IN THE NINETEENTH   AFR
CENTURY. ECO/UNDEV KIN SECT DIPLOM DOMIN ADMIN   COLONIAL
DISCRIM 17/18. PAGE 63 B1275   WAR
  FINAN

THOMPSON H.C.,RHODESIA AND ITS GOVERNMENT. AFR — COLONIAL
RHODESIA ECO/UNDEV INDUS KIN WORKER INT/TRADE — ADMIN
DISCRIM LITERACY ORD/FREE 19. PAGE 104 B2102 — POLICY
— ELITES — B98

KING....KING AND KINGSHIP; SEE ALSO CHIEF, CONSERVE, TRADIT

KING/MAR/L....REVEREND MARTIN LUTHER KING

KINGSLEY J.D. B1208

KINGSTON-MCCLOUG E. B1209

KINNEAR J.B. B1210

KINSEY/A....ALFRED KINSEY

KINTNER W.R. B1211

KIPLING/R....RUDYARD KIPLING

FABAR R.,THE VISION AND THE NEED: LATE VICTORIAN — COLONIAL
IMPERIALIST AIMS. MOD/EUR UK WOR-45 CULTURE NAT/G — CONCPT
DIPLOM...TIME/SEQ METH/COMP 19 KIPLING/R — ADMIN
COMMONWLTH. PAGE 34 B0693 — ATTIT — B66

KIRDAR U. B1213

KIRK G. B1214

KIRK/GRAY....GRAYSON KIRK

KISER M. B1215

KISSINGER H.A. B1216

KKK....KU KLUX KLAN

KLEIN F.J. B1217

KLESMENT J. B1218

KLUCKHN/C....CLYDE KLUCKHOHN

KNAPP J. B0924

KNEIER C.M. B1219

KNEIR C.M. B0701

KNICKERBOCKER I. B1220

KNO/TEST....TESTS FOR FACTUAL KNOWLEDGE

BUELL R.,THE NATIVE PROBLEM IN AFRICA. KIN LABOR — AFR
LOC/G ECO/TAC ROUTINE ORD/FREE...REC/INT KNO/TEST — CULTURE
CENSUS TREND CHARTS SOC/EXP STERTYP 20. PAGE 17 — B28
B0339

DEKAT A.D.A.,COLONIAL POLICY. S/ASIA CULTURE — DRIVE
EX/STRUC ECO/TAC DOMIN ADMIN COLONIAL ROUTINE — PWR
SOVEREIGN WEALTH...POLICY MGT RECORD KNO/TEST SAMP. — INDONESIA
PAGE 28 B0570 — NETHERLAND — B31

BENJAMIN H.C.,EMPLOYMENT TESTS IN INDUSTRY AND — BIBLIOG/A
BUSINESS. LG/CO WORKER ROUTINE...MGT PSY SOC — METH
CLASSIF PROBABIL STAT APT/TEST KNO/TEST PERS/TEST — TESTS
20. PAGE 10 B0211 — INDUS — B45

ARROW K.J.,MATHEMATICAL METHODS IN THE SOCIAL — MATH
SCIENCES, 1959. TEC/DEV CHOOSE UTIL PERCEPT — PSY
...KNO/TEST GAME SIMUL ANTHOL. PAGE 7 B0137 — MGT — B60

BHALERAO C.N.,PUBLIC SERVICE COMMISSIONS OF INDIA: — NAT/G
A STUDY. INDIA SERV/IND EX/STRUC ROUTINE CHOOSE — OP/RES
GOV/REL INGP/REL...KNO/TEST EXHIBIT 20. PAGE 11 — LOC/G
B0233 — ADMIN — B66

KNOWL....ENLIGHTENMENT, KNOWLEDGE

MINISTERE DE L'EDUC NATIONALE,CATALOGUE DES THESES — BIBLIOG
DE DOCTORAT SOUTENNES DEVANT LES UNIVERSITAIRES — ACADEM
FRANCAISES. FRANCE LAW DIPLOM ADMIN...HUM SOC 20. — KNOWL
PAGE 74 B1490 — NAT/G — N

CORWIN E.S.,THE PRESIDENT'S CONTROL OF FOREIGN — TOP/EX
RELATIONS. FUT USA-45 CONSTN STRATA NAT/G CHIEF — PWR
EX/STRUC LEGIS KNOWL RESPECT...JURID CONCPT TREND — DIPLOM
CONGRESS VAL/FREE 20 PRESIDENT. PAGE 24 B0483 — B17

BRYCE J.,MODERN DEMOCRACIES. FUT NEW/ZEALND USA-45 — NAT/G
LAW CONSTN POL/PAR PROVS VOL/ASSN EX/STRUC LEGIS — TREND — B21

LEGIT CT/SYS EXEC KNOWL CONGRESS AUSTRAL 20.
PAGE 16 B0332 — B24

POOLE D.C.,THE CONDUCT OF FOREIGN RELATIONS UNDER — NAT/G
MODERN DEMOCRATIC CONDITIONS. EUR+WWI USA-45 — EDU/PROP
INT/ORG PLAN LEGIT ADMIN KNOWL PWR...MAJORIT — DIPLOM
OBS/ENVIR HIST/WRIT GEN/LAWS 20. PAGE 84 B1689 — B27

ANGELL N.,THE PUBLIC MIND. USA-45 SOCIETY EDU/PROP — PERCEPT
ROUTINE SUPEGO KNOWL...POLICY CONCPT MYTH OBS/ENVIR — ATTIT
EUR+WW1 TOT/POP 20. PAGE 5 B0109 — DIPLOM
— NAT/LISM — B33

DANGERFIELD R.,IN DEFENSE OF THE SENATE. USA-45 — LEGIS
CONSTN NAT/G EX/STRUC TOP/EX ATTIT KNOWL — DELIB/GP
...METH/CNCPT STAT TIME/SEQ TREND CON/ANAL CHARTS — DIPLOM
CONGRESS 20 TREATY. PAGE 26 B0528 — B44

DAVIS H.E.,PIONEERS IN WORLD ORDER. WOR-45 CONSTN — INT/ORG
ECO/TAC DOMIN EDU/PROP LEGIT ADJUD ADMIN ARMS/CONT — ROUTINE
CHOOSE KNOWL ORD/FREE...POLICY JURID SOC STAT OBS
CENSUS TIME/SEQ ANTHOL LEAGUE/NAT 20. PAGE 26 B0537 — L44

CORWIN E.S.,"THE CONSTITUTION AND WORLD — INT/ORG
ORGANIZATION." FUT USA-45 USA-45 NAT/G EX/STRUC — CONSTN
LEGIS PEACE KNOWL...CON/ANAL UN 20. PAGE 24 B0484 — SOVEREIGN
— B45

BUSH V.,SCIENCE, THE ENDLESS FRONTIER. FUT USA-45 — R+D
INTELL STRATA ACT/RES CREATE PLAN EDU/PROP ADMIN — NAT/G
NUC/PWR PEACE ATTIT HEALTH KNOWL...MAJORIT HEAL MGT
PHIL/SCI CONCPT OBS TREND 20. PAGE 18 B0360 — B45

PLATO,THE REPUBLIC. MEDIT-7 UNIV SOCIETY STRUCT — PERSON
EX/STRUC FORCES UTOPIA ATTIT PERCEPT HEALTH KNOWL — PHIL/SCI
ORD/FREE PWR...HUM CONCPT STERTYP TOT/POP. PAGE 83
B1681

FISHER M.J.,"PARTIES AND POLITICS IN THE LOCAL — CHOOSE
COMMUNITY." USA-45 NAT/G SCHOOL ADMIN PARTIC — LOC/G
REPRESENT KNOWL...BIBLIOG 20. PAGE 36 B0724 — POL/PAR
— ROUTINE — C45

BIBLIOGRAFIIA DISSERTATSII: DOKTORSKIE DISSERTATSII — BIBLIOG
ZA 19411944 (2 VOLS.). COM USSR LAW POL/PAR DIPLOM — ACADEM
ADMIN LEAD...PHIL/SCI SOC 20. PAGE 2 B0035 — KNOWL
— MARXIST — B46

LASSWELL H.D.,THE ANALYSIS OF POLITICAL BEHAVIOUR: — R+D
AN EMPIRICAL APPROACH. WOR+45 CULTURE NAT/G FORCES — ACT/RES
EDU/PROP ADMIN ATTIT PERCEPT KNOWL...PHIL/SCI PSY — ELITES
SOC NEW/IDEA OBS INT GEN/METH NAZI 20. PAGE 63
B1267 — B47

FORD FOUNDATION,REPORT OF THE STUDY FOR THE FORD — WEALTH
FOUNDATION ON POLICY AND PROGRAM. SOCIETY R+D — GEN/LAWS
ACT/RES CAP/ISM FOR/AID EDU/PROP ADMIN KNOWL
...POLICY PSY SOC 20. PAGE 36 B0739 — B49

LASSWELL H.D.,NATIONAL SECURITY AND INDIVIDUAL — FACE/GP
FREEDOM. USA+45 R+D NAT/G VOL/ASSN CONSULT DELIB/GP — ROUTINE
LEGIT ADMIN KNOWL ORD/FREE PWR...PLURIST TOT/POP — BAL/PWR
COLD/WAR 20. PAGE 63 B1268 — B50

WITTFOGEL K.A.,"RUSSIA AND ASIA: PROBLEMS OF — ECO/DEV
CONTEMPORARY AREA STUDIES AND INTERNATIONAL — ADMIN
RELATIONS." ASIA COM USA+45 SOCIETY NAT/G DIPLOM — RUSSIA
ECO/TAC FOR/AID EDU/PROP KNOWL...HIST/WRIT TOT/POP — USSR
20. PAGE 117 B2369 — S50

INKELES A.,"UNDERSTANDING A FOREIGN SOCIETY: A — SOC
SOCIOLOGIST'S VIEW." SOCIETY ROUTINE KNOWL...PSY — METH/CNCPT
CONCPT GEN/METH 20. PAGE 54 B1086 — PERCEPT
— ATTIT — S51

DAY E.E.,EDUCATION FOR FREEDOM AND RESPONSIBILITY. — SCHOOL
FUT USA+45 CULTURE CONSULT EDU/PROP ATTIT SKILL — KNOWL
...MGT CONCPT OBS GEN/LAWS COLD/WAR 20. PAGE 27
B0547 — B52

CALDWELL L.K.,RESEARCH METHODS IN PUBLIC — BIBLIOG/A
ADMINISTRATION; AN OUTLINE OF TOPICS AND READINGS — METH/COMP
(PAMPHLET). LAW ACT/RES COMPUTER KNOWL...SOC STAT — ADMIN
GEN/METH 20. PAGE 18 B0365 — OP/RES — B53

COMBS C.H.,DECISION PROCESSES. INTELL SOCIETY — MATH
DELIB/GP CREATE TEC/DEV DOMIN LEGIT EXEC CHOOSE — DECISION
DRIVE RIGID/FLEX KNOWL PWR...PHIL/SCI SOC
METH/CNCPT CONT/OBS REC/INT PERS/TEST SAMP/SIZ BIOG
SOC/EXP WORK. PAGE 22 B0455 — B54

TORRE M.,"PSYCHIATRIC OBSERVATIONS OF INTERNATIONAL — DELIB/GP
CONFERENCES." WOR+45 INT/ORG PROF/ORG VOL/ASSN — OBS
CONSULT EDU/PROP ROUTINE ATTIT DRIVE KNOWL...PSY — DIPLOM
METH/CNCPT OBS/ENVIR STERTYP 20. PAGE 105 B2119 — S55

WRIGHT Q.,"THE PEACEFUL ADJUSTMENT OF INTERNATIONAL — R+D — S55

RELATIONS: PROBLEMS AND RESEARCH APPROACHES." UNIV   METH/CNCPT
INTELL EDU/PROP ADJUD ROUTINE KNOWL SKILL...INT/LAW PEACE
JURID PHIL/SCI CLASSIF 20. PAGE 118 B2385
                                                     B56
GARDNER R.N.,STERLING-DOLLAR DIPLOMACY. EUR+WWI   ECO/DEV
USA+45 INT/ORG NAT/G PLAN INT/TRADE EDU/PROP ADMIN   DIPLOM
KNOWL PWR WEALTH...POLICY SOC METH/CNCPT STAT
CHARTS SIMUL GEN/LAWS 20. PAGE 39 B0781
                                                     B56
KIRK G.,THE CHANGING ENVIRONMENT OF INTERNATIONAL   FUT
RELATIONS. ASIA S/ASIA USA+45 WOR+45 ECO/UNDEV   EXEC
INT/ORG NAT/G FOR/AID EDU/PROP PEACE KNOWL   DIPLOM
...PLURIST COLD/WAR TOT/POP 20. PAGE 60 B1214
                                                     B56
WASSERMAN P.,INFORMATION FOR ADMINISTRATORS: A   BIBLIOG
GUIDE TO PUBLICATIONS AND SERVICES FOR MANAGEMENT   MGT
IN BUSINESS AND GOVERNMENT. R+D LOC/G NAT/G   KNOWL
PROF/ORG VOL/ASSN PRESS...PSY SOC STAT 20. PAGE 114   EDU/PROP
B2299
                                                     B56
WIGGINS J.R.,FREEDOM OR SECRECY. USA+45 USA-45   ORD/FREE
DELIB/GP EX/STRUC FORCES ADJUD SANCTION KNOWL PWR   PRESS
...AUD/VIS CONGRESS 20. PAGE 116 B2344   NAT/G
                                                     CONTROL
                                                     S56
MARGOLIS J.,"ON MUNICIPAL LAND POLICY FOR FISCAL   BUDGET
GAINS." USA+45 MUNIC PLAN TAX COST EFFICIENCY   POLICY
HABITAT KNOWL...MGT 20. PAGE 69 B1398   GEOG
                                                     LOC/G
                                                     B57
FULLER C.D.,TRAINING OF SPECIALISTS IN   KNOWL
INTERNATIONAL RELATIONS. FUT USA+45 USA-45 INTELL   DIPLOM
INT/ORG...MGT METH/CNCPT INT QU GEN/METH 20.
PAGE 38 B0765
                                                     B57
SELZNICK,LEADERSHIP IN ADMINISTRATION: A   LEAD
SOCIOLOGICAL INTERPRETATION. CREATE PROB/SOLV EXEC   ADMIN
ROUTINE EFFICIENCY RATIONAL KNOWL...POLICY PSY.   DECISION
PAGE 95 B1927   NAT/G
                                                     L57
HAAS E.B.,"REGIONAL INTEGRATION AND NATIONAL   INT/ORG
POLICY." WOR+45 VOL/ASSN DELIB/GP EX/STRUC ECO/TAC   ORD/FREE
DOMIN EDU/PROP LEGIT COERCE ATTIT PERCEPT KNOWL   REGION
...TIME/SEQ COLD/WAR 20 UN. PAGE 45 B0908
                                                     B58
HENKIN L.,ARMS CONTROL AND INSPECTION IN AMERICAN   USA+45
LAW. LAW CONSTN INT/ORG LOC/G MUNIC NAT/G PROVS   JURID
EDU/PROP LEGIT EXEC NUC/PWR KNOWL ORD/FREE...OBS   ARMS/CONT
TOT/POP CONGRESS 20. PAGE 49 B0990
                                                     B59
CHINA INSTITUTE OF AMERICA,.CHINA AND THE UNITED   ASIA
NATIONS. CHINA/COM FUT STRUCT EDU/PROP LEGIT ADMIN   INT/ORG
ATTIT KNOWL ORD/FREE PWR...OBS RECORD STAND/INT
TIME/SEQ UN LEAGUE/NAT UNESCO 20. PAGE 21 B0425
                                                     B59
GOODRICH L.,THE UNITED NATIONS. WOR+45 CONSTN   INT/ORG
STRUCT ACT/RES LEGIT COERCE KNOWL ORD/FREE PWR   ROUTINE
...GEN/LAWS UN 20. PAGE 41 B0825
                                                     S59
HILSMAN R.,"THE FOREIGN-POLICY CONSENSUS: AN   PROB/SOLV
INTERIM RESEARCH REPORT." USA+45 INT/ORG LEGIS   NAT/G
TEC/DEV EXEC WAR CONSEN KNOWL...DECISION COLD/WAR.   DELIB/GP
PAGE 50 B1013   DIPLOM
                                                     S59
KISSINGER H.A.,"THE POLICYMAKER AND THE   INTELL
INTELLECTUAL." USA+45 CONSULT DELIB/GP ACT/RES   CREATE
ADMIN ATTIT DRIVE RIGID/FLEX KNOWL PWR...POLICY
PLURIST MGT METH/CNCPT GEN/LAWS GEN/METH 20.
PAGE 60 B1216
                                                     B60
EASTON S.C.,THE TWILIGHT OF EUROPEAN COLONIALISM.   FINAN
AFR S/ASIA CONSTN SOCIETY STRUCT ECO/UNDEV INDUS   ADMIN
NAT/G FORCES ECO/TAC COLONIAL CT/SYS ATTIT KNOWL
ORD/FREE PWR...SOCIALIST TIME/SEQ TREND CON/ANAL
20. PAGE 32 B0645
                                                     L60
BRENNAN D.G.,"SETTING AND GOALS OF ARMS CONTROL."   FORCES
FUT USA+45 USSR WOR+45 INTELL INT/ORG NAT/G   COERCE
VOL/ASSN CONSULT PLAN DIPLOM ECO/TAC ADMIN KNOWL   ARMS/CONT
PWR...POLICY CONCPT TREND COLD/WAR 20. PAGE 15   DETER
B0305
                                                     S60
BOGARDUS E.S.,"THE SOCIOLOGY OF A STRUCTURED   INT/ORG
PEACE." FUT SOCIETY CREATE DIPLOM EDU/PROP ADJUD   SOC
ROUTINE ATTIT RIGID/FLEX KNOWL ORD/FREE RESPECT   NAT/LISM
...POLICY INT/LAW JURID NEW/IDEA SELF/OBS TOT/POP   PEACE
20 UN. PAGE 13 B0264
                                                     S60
THOMPSON K.W.,"MORAL PURPOSE IN FOREIGN POLICY: MORAL
REALITIES AND ILLUSIONS." WOR+45 WOR-45 LAW CULTURE   JURID
SOCIETY INT/ORG PLAN ADJUD ADMIN COERCE RIGID/FLEX   DIPLOM
SUPEGO KNOWL ORD/FREE PWR...SOC TREND SOC/EXP
TOT/POP 20. PAGE 104 B2104
                                                     B61
GORDON W.J.J.,SYNECTICS; THE DEVELOPMENT OF   CREATE
CREATIVE CAPACITY. USA+45 PLAN TEC/DEV KNOWL WEALTH   PROB/SOLV

...DECISION MGT 20. PAGE 41 B0832   ACT/RES
                                                     TOP/EX
                                                     B61
PEASLEE A.J.,INTERNATIONAL GOVERNMENT   INT/ORG
ORGANIZATIONS, CONSTITUTIONAL DOCUMENTS. WOR+45   STRUCT
WOR-45 CONSTN VOL/ASSN DELIB/GP EX/STRUC ROUTINE
KNOWL TOT/POP 20. PAGE 82 B1650
                                                     B61
SINGER J.D.,FINANCING INTERNATIONAL ORGANIZATION: INT/ORG
THE UNITED NATIONS BUDGET PROCESS. WOR+45 ACT/RES   MGT
ACT/RES CREATE PLAN BUDGET ECO/TAC ADMIN ROUTINE
ATTIT KNOWL...DECISION METH/CNCPT TIME/SEQ UN 20.
PAGE 97 B1964
                                                     S61
DEUTSCH K.W.,"A NOTE ON THE APPEARANCE OF WISDOM IN ADMIN
LARGE BUREAUCRATIC ORGANIZATIONS." ROUTINE PERSON   PROBABIL
KNOWL SKILL...DECISION STAT. PAGE 28 B0577   PROB/SOLV
                                                     SIMUL
                                                     B62
CAIRNCROSS A.K.,FACTORS IN ECONOMIC DEVELOPMENT.   MARKET
WOR+45 ECO/UNDEV INDUS R+D LG/CO NAT/G EX/STRUC   ECO/DEV
PLAN TEC/DEV ECO/TAC ATTIT HEALTH KNOWL PWR WEALTH
...TIME/SEQ GEN/LAWS TOT/POP VAL/FREE 20. PAGE 18
B0363
                                                     B62
DUCKWORTH W.E.,A GUIDE TO OPERATIONAL RESEARCH.   OP/RES
INDUS PLAN PROB/SOLV EXEC EFFICIENCY PRODUC KNOWL   GAME
...MGT MATH STAT SIMUL METH 20 MONTECARLO. PAGE 31   DECISION
B0624   ADMIN
                                                     B62
NICHOLAS H.G.,THE UNITED NATIONS AS A POLITICAL   INT/ORG
INSTITUTION. WOR+45 CONSTN EX/STRUC ACT/RES LEGIT   ROUTINE
PERCEPT KNOWL PWR...CONCPT TIME/SEQ CON/ANAL
ORG/CHARTS UN 20. PAGE 78 B1580
                                                     B62
SIMON Y.R.,A GENERAL THEORY OF AUTHORITY. DOMIN   PERS/REL
ADMIN RATIONAL UTOPIA KNOWL MORAL PWR SOVEREIGN   PERSON
...HUM CONCPT NEW/IDEA 20. PAGE 97 B1962   SOCIETY
                                                     ORD/FREE
                                                     S62
LARSON R.L.,"HOW TO DEFINE ADMINISTRATIVE   UNIV
PROBLEMS." ROUTINE PERCEPT KNOWL SKILL...MGT   FACE/GP
METH/CNCPT CHARTS TOT/POP. PAGE 63 B1263   INDUS
                                                     EXEC
                                                     S62
NORTH R.C.,"DECISION MAKING IN CRISIS: AN   INT/ORG
INTRODUCTION." WOR+45 WOR-45 NAT/G CONSULT DELIB/GP   ROUTINE
TEC/DEV PERCEPT KNOWL...POLICY DECISION PSY   DIPLOM
METH/CNCPT CONT/OBS TREND VAL/FREE 20. PAGE 79
B1590
                                                     S62
SCHILLING W.R.,"SCIENTISTS, FOREIGN POLICY AND   NAT/G
POLITICS." WOR+45 INTELL INT/ORG CONSULT   TEC/DEV
TOP/EX ACT/RES PLAN ADMIN KNOWL...CONCPT OBS TREND   DIPLOM
LEAGUE/NAT 20. PAGE 93 B1889   NUC/PWR
                                                     B63
DE VRIES E.,SOCIAL ASPECTS OF ECONOMIC DEVELOPMENT   L/A+17C
IN LATIN AMERICA. CULTURE SOCIETY FINAN   ECO/UNDEV
INDUS INT/ORG DELIB/GP ACT/RES ECO/TAC EDU/PROP
ADMIN ATTIT SUPEGO HEALTH KNOWL ORD/FREE...SOC STAT
TREND ANTHOL TOT/POP VAL/FREE. PAGE 28 B0562
                                                     B63
HEUSSLER R.,YESTERDAY'S RULERS: THE MAKING OF THE   EX/STRUC
BRITISH COLONIAL SERVICE. AFR EUR+WWI UK STRATA   MORAL
SECT DELIB/GP PLAN DOMIN EDU/PROP ATTIT PERCEPT   ELITES
PERSON SUPEGO KNOWL ORD/FREE PWR...MGT SOC OBS INT
TIME/SEQ 20 CMN/WLTH. PAGE 49 B1000
                                                     B63
MENZEL J.M.,THE CHINESE CIVIL SERVICE: CAREER OPEN   ADMIN
TO TALENT? ASIA ROUTINE INGP/REL DISCRIM ATTIT ROLE NAT/G
KNOWL ANTHOL. PAGE 73 B1468   DECISION
                                                     ELITES
                                                     S63
MASSART L.,"L'ORGANISATION DE LA RECHERCHE   R+D
SCIENTIFIQUE EN EUROPE." EUR+WWI WOR+45 ACT/RES   CREATE
PLAN TEC/DEV EDU/PROP EXEC KNOWL...METH/CNCPT EEC
20. PAGE 70 B1424
                                                     B64
EWING D.W.,THE MANAGERIAL MIND. SOCIETY STRUCT   MGT
INDUS PERSON KNOWL 20. PAGE 34 B0692   ATTIT
                                                     CREATE
                                                     EFFICIENCY
                                                     B64
PIERCE T.M.,FEDERAL, STATE, AND LOCAL GOVERNMENT IN NAT/G
EDUCATION. FINAN LOC/G PROVS LEGIS PLAN EDU/PROP   POLICY
ADMIN CONTROL CENTRAL COST KNOWL 20. PAGE 83 B1673   SCHOOL
                                                     GOV/REL
                                                     B64
RIGGS F.W.,ADMINISTRATION IN DEVELOPING COUNTRIES.   ECO/UNDEV
FUT WOR+45 STRUCT AGRI INDUS NAT/G PLAN TEC/DEV   ADMIN
ECO/TAC EDU/PROP RIGID/FLEX KNOWL WEALTH...POLICY
MGT CONCPT METH/CNCPT TREND 20. PAGE 88 B1785
                                                     B64
VALEN H.,POLITICAL PARTIES IN NORWAY. NORWAY ACADEM LOC/G
PARTIC ROUTINE INGP/REL KNOWL...QU 20. PAGE 111   POL/PAR
B2249   PERSON

SYMONDS R.,"REFLECTIONS IN LOCALISATION." AFR
S/ASIA UK STRATA INT/ORG NAT/G SCHOOL EDU/PROP
LEGIT KNOWL ORD/FREE PWR RESPECT CMN/WLTH 20.
PAGE 102 B2064
— L64 — ADMIN MGT COLONIAL

HOSCH L.G.,"PUBLIC ADMINISTRATION ON THE
INTERNATIONAL FRONTIER." WOR+45 R+D NAT/G EDU/PROP
EXEC KNOWL ORD/FREE VAL/FREE 20 UN. PAGE 52 B1046
— S64 — INT/ORG MGT

JOHNSON K.F.,"CAUSAL FACTORS IN LATIN AMERICAN
POLITICAL INSTABILITY." CULTURE NAT/G VOL/ASSN
EX/STRUC FORCES EDU/PROP LEGIT ADMIN COERCE REV
ATTIT KNOWL PWR...STYLE RECORD CHARTS WORK 20.
PAGE 57 B1144
— S64 — L/A+17C PERCEPT ELITES

KAPLAN N.,"RESEARCH ADMINISTRATION AND THE
ADMINISTRATOR: USSR AND US." COM USA+45 INTELL
EX/STRUC KNOWL...MGT 20. PAGE 58 B1169
— S64 — R+D ADMIN USSR

MURRAY D.,"CHINESE EDUCATION IN SOUTH-EAST ASIA."
SOCIETY NEIGH EDU/PROP ROUTINE PERSON KNOWL
...OBS/ENVIR STERTYP. PAGE 76 B1546
— S64 — S/ASIA SCHOOL REGION ASIA

SINGER J.D.,HUMAN BEHAVIOR AND INTERNATIONAL
POLITICS* CONTRIBUTIONS FROM THE SOCIAL-
PSYCHOLOGICAL SCIENCES. ACT/RES PLAN EDU/PROP ADMIN
KNOWL...DECISION PSY SOC NET/THEORY HYPO/EXP
LAB/EXP SOC/EXP GEN/METH ANTHOL BIBLIOG. PAGE 97
B1965
— B65 — DIPLOM PHIL/SCI QUANT SIMUL

LASSWELL H.D.,"THE POLICY SCIENCES OF DEVELOPMENT." PWR
CULTURE SOCIETY EX/STRUC CREATE ADMIN ATTIT KNOWL
...SOC CONCPT SIMUL GEN/METH. PAGE 63 B1273
— L65 — PWR METH/CNCPT DIPLOM

ALEXANDER T.,"SYNECTICS: INVENTING BY THE MADNESS
METHOD." DELIB/GP TOP/EX ACT/RES TEC/DEV EXEC TASK
KNOWL...MGT METH/COMP 20. PAGE 4 B0073
— S65 — PROB/SOLV OP/RES CREATE CONSULT

GRENIEWSKI H.,"INTENTION AND PERFORMANCE: A PRIMER
OF CYBERNETICS OF PLANNING." EFFICIENCY OPTIMAL
KNOWL SKILL...DECISION MGT EQULIB. PAGE 43 B0873
— S65 — SIMUL GAME GEN/METH PLAN

POLK W.R.,"PROBLEMS OF GOVERNMENT UTILIZATION OF
SCHOLARLY RESEARCH IN INTERNATIONAL AFFAIRS." FINAN
NAT/G EDU/PROP CONTROL TASK GP/REL ATTIT PERCEPT
KNOWL...POLICY TIME. PAGE 83 B1685
— S65 — ACT/RES ACADEM PLAN ADMIN

BROWN R.E.,JUDGMENT IN ADMINISTRATION. DRIVE PERSON
KNOWL...DECISION 20. PAGE 16 B0326
— B66 — ADMIN EXEC SKILL PROB/SOLV

BULPITT J.G.,PARTY POLITICS IN ENGLISH LOCAL
GOVERNMENT. UK CONSTN ACT/RES TAX CONTROL CHOOSE
REPRESENT GOV/REL KNOWL 20. PAGE 17 B0344
— B67 — POL/PAR LOC/G ELITES EX/STRUC

HOROWITZ I.L.,THE RISE AND FALL OF PROJECT CAMELOT:
STUDIES IN THE RELATIONSHIP BETWEEN SOCIAL SCIENCE
AND PRACTICAL POLITICS. USA+45 WOR+45 CULTURE
FORCES LEGIS EXEC CIVMIL/REL KNOWL...POLICY SOC
METH/CNCPT 20. PAGE 51 B1043
— B67 — NAT/G ACADEM ACT/RES GP/REL

US DEPARTMENT OF JUSTICE,ANNUAL REPORT OF THE
OFFICE OF ADMINISTRATIVE PROCEDURE. USA+45
PROB/SOLV EDU/PROP EXEC INGP/REL EFFICIENCY KNOWL
...POLICY STAT 20. PAGE 108 B2181
— B67 — ADMIN NAT/G ROUTINE GOV/REL

KNOWLEDGE TEST....SEE KNO/TEST

KNOX V.H. B1221

KNOX/HENRY....HENRY KNOX (SECRETARY OF WAR 1789)

PALMER J.M.,AMERICA IN ARMS: THE EXPERIENCE OF THE
UNITED STATES WITH MILITARY ORGANIZATION. FUT
USA-45 LEAD REV PWR 18/20 WASHINGT/G KNOX/HENRY
PRE/US/AM. PAGE 81 B1627
— B41 — FORCES NAT/G ADMIN WAR

KOENIG L.W. B1222,B1223,B1224,B1225

KOESTLER A. B1226

KOGAN N. B1227

KOHLER/J....JOSEF KOHLER

KONCZACKI Z.A. B1228

KOREA....KOREA IN GENERAL; SEE ALSO ASIA

SCHRAMM W.,"COMMUNICATION IN THE SOVIETIZED STATE,
AS DEMONSTRATED IN KOREA." ASIA COM KOREA COM/IND
FACE/GP POL/PAR SCHOOL FORCES ADMIN PWR MARXISM
...SOC CONCPT MYTH INT BIOG TOT/POP 20. PAGE 94
B1901
— S51 — ATTIT EDU/PROP TOTALISM

WOLFERS A.,"COLLECTIVE SECURITY AND THE WAR IN
KOREA." ASIA KOREA USA+45 INT/ORG DIPLOM ROUTINE
...GEN/LAWS UN COLD/WAR 20. PAGE 117 B2370
— S54 — ACT/RES LEGIT

UN HEADQUARTERS LIBRARY,BIBLIOGRAPHIE DE LA CHARTE
DES NATIONS UNIES. CHINA/COM KOREA WOR+45 VOL/ASSN
CONFER ADMIN COERCE PEACE ATTIT ORD/FREE SOVEREIGN
...INT/LAW 20 UNESCO UN. PAGE 106 B2149
— B55 — BIBLIOG/A INT/ORG DIPLOM

GORDENKER L.,THE UNITED NATIONS AND THE PEACEFUL
UNIFICATION OF KOREA. ASIA LAW LOC/G CONSULT
ACT/RES DIPLOM DOMIN LEGIT ADJUD ADMIN ORD/FREE
SOVEREIGN...INT GEN/METH UN COLD/WAR 20. PAGE 41
B0829
— B59 — DELIB/GP KOREA INT/ORG

SNYDER R.C.,FOREIGN POLICY DECISION-MAKING. FUT
KOREA WOR+45 R+D CREATE ADMIN ROUTINE PWR
...DECISION PSY SOC CONCPT METH/CNCPT CON/ANAL
CHARTS GEN/METH METH 20. PAGE 99 B1992
— B62 — TEC/DEV HYPO/EXP DIPLOM

RUSSELL R.B.,UNITED NATIONS EXPERIENCE WITH
MILITARY FORCES: POLITICAL AND LEGAL ASPECTS. AFR
KOREA WOR+45 LEGIS PROB/SOLV ADMIN CONTROL
EFFICIENCY PEACE...POLICY INT/LAW BIBLIOG UN.
PAGE 92 B1857
— B64 — FORCES DIPLOM SANCTION ORD/FREE

KOREA/N....NORTH KOREA

KOREA/S....SOUTH KOREA

KORNHAUSER W. B1229

KORNILOV/L....LAVR GEORGIEVICH KORNILOV

KOUSOULAS D.G. B1230

KOVENOCK D.M. B0535

KRACKE E.A. B1231

KRAINES O. B1232

KRAMER R. B1233

KRARUP O. B1234

KRIESBERG M. B1235,B1236,B1237

KRISHNAN V.N. B0566

KRISLOV S. B1238

KRIVICKAS D. B1218

KRUPP S. B1239

KU KLUX KLAN....SEE KKK

KUHN M.H. B1005

KUHN T.E. B1240

KUIC V. B1241

KULZ H.R. B1242

KUOMINTANG....KUOMINTANG

KURAKOV I.G. B1243

KURON J. B1244

KUWAIT....SEE ALSO ISLAM

KUWAIT ARABIA,KUWAIT FUND FOR ARAB ECONOMIC
DEVELOPMENT (PAMPHLET). ISLAM KUWAIT UAR ECO/UNDEV
LEGIS ECO/TAC WEALTH 20. PAGE 62 B1245
— N19 — FOR/AID DIPLOM FINAN ADMIN

INT. BANK RECONSTR. DEVELOP.,ECONOMIC DEVELOPMENT
OF KUWAIT. ISLAM KUWAIT AGRI FINAN MARKET EX/STRUC
TEC/DEV ECO/TAC ADMIN WEALTH...OBS CON/ANAL CHARTS
20. PAGE 54 B1092
— B65 — INDUS NAT/G

KUWAIT ARABIA B1245

KUZNETS....KUZNETS SCALE

KWEDER J.B. B1246

KY/NGUYEN....NGUYEN KY

KYRIAK T.E. B1247

L

L/A+17C....LATIN AMERICA SINCE 1700; SEE ALSO APPROPRIATE
    NATIONS

           N

HANDBOOK OF LATIN AMERICAN STUDIES. LAW CULTURE   BIBLIOG/A
ECO/UNDEV POL/PAR ADMIN LEAD...SOC 20. PAGE 1 B0014 L/A+17C
           NAT/G
           DIPLOM
           N

DOHERTY D.K.,PRELIMINARY BIBLIOGRAPHY OF   BIBLIOG
COLONIZATION AND SETTLEMENT IN LATIN AMERICA AND COLONIAL
ANGLO-AMERICA. L/A+17C PRE/AMER USA-45 ECO/UNDEV ADMIN
NAT/G 15/20. PAGE 30 B0604   DIPLOM
           N

UNIVERSITY OF FLORIDA,CARIBBEAN ACQUISITIONS: BIBLIOG
MATERIALS ACQUIRED BY THE UNIVERSITY OF FLORIDA ECO/UNDEV
1957-1960. L/A+17C...ART/METH GEOG MGT 20. PAGE 107 EDU/PROP
B2167   JURID
           N19

OPERATIONS AND POLICY RESEARCH,PERU ELECTION CHOOSE
MEMORANDA (PAMPHLET). L/A+17C PERU POL/PAR LEGIS CONSTN
EXEC APPORT REPRESENT 20. PAGE 80 B1611 SUFF
           NAT/G
           B29

ROBERTS S.H.,HISTORY OF FRENCH COLONIAL POLICY. AFR INT/ORG
ASIA L/A+17C S/ASIA CULTURE ECO/DEV ECO/UNDEV FINAN ACT/RES
NAT/G PLAN ECO/TAC DOMIN ROUTINE SOVEREIGN...OBS FRANCE
HIST/WRIT TREND CHARTS VAL/FREE 19/20. PAGE 89 COLONIAL
B1796
           B42

SIMOES DOS REIS A.,BIBLIOGRAFIA DAS BIBLIOGRAFIAS BIBLIOG
BRASILEIRAS. BRAZIL ADMIN COLONIAL 20. PAGE 97 NAT/G
B1954   DIPLOM
           L/A+17C
           B43

CARLO A.M.,ENSAYO DE UNA BIBLIOGRAFIA DE BIBLIOG
BIBLIOGRAFIAS MEXICANAS. ECO/UNDEV LOC/G ADMIN LEAD L/A+17C
20 MEXIC/AMER. PAGE 19 B0381 NAT/G
           DIPLOM
           B48

US LIBRARY OF CONGRESS,BRAZIL: A GUIDE TO THE BIBLIOG/A
OFFICIAL PUBLICATIONS OF BRAZIL. BRAZIL L/A+17C NAT/G
CONSULT DELIB/GP LEGIS CT/SYS 19/20. PAGE 109 B2203 ADMIN
           TOP/EX
           B49

BORBA DE MORAES R.,MANUAL BIBLIOGRAFICO DE ESTUDOS BIBLIOG
BRASILEIROS. BRAZIL DIPLOM ADMIN LEAD...SOC 20. L/A+17C
PAGE 14 B0276   NAT/G
           ECO/UNDEV
           C50

STOKES W.S.,"HONDURAS: AN AREA STUDY IN CONSTN
GOVERNMENT." HONDURAS NAT/G POL/PAR COLONIAL CT/SYS LAW
ROUTINE CHOOSE REPRESENT...GEOG RECORD BIBLIOG L/A+17C
19/20. PAGE 101 B2044   ADMIN
           B51

CHRISTENSEN A.N.,THE EVOLUTION OF LATIN AMERICAN NAT/G
GOVERNMENT: A BOOK OF READINGS. ECO/UNDEV INDUS CONSTN
LOC/G POL/PAR EX/STRUC LEGIS FOR/AID CT/SYS DIPLOM
...SOC/WK 20 SOUTH/AMER. PAGE 21 B0428 L/A+17C
           B53

WAGLEY C.,AMAZON TOWN: A STUDY OF MAN IN THE SOC
TROPICS. BRAZIL L/A+17C STRATA STRUCT ECO/UNDEV NEIGH
AGRI EX/STRUC RACE/REL DISCRIM HABITAT WEALTH...OBS CULTURE
SOC/EXP 20. PAGE 113 B2273 INGP/REL
           L55

KISER M.,"ORGANIZATION OF AMERICAN STATES." L/A+17C VOL/ASSN
USA+45 ECO/UNDEV INT/ORG NAT/G PLAN TEC/DEV DIPLOM ECO/DEV
ECO/TAC INT/TRADE EDU/PROP ADMIN ALL/VALS...POLICY REGION
MGT RECORD ORG/CHARTS OAS 20. PAGE 60 B1215
           B58

GROSSMAN J.,BIBLIOGRAPHY ON PUBLIC ADMINISTRATION BIBLIOG
IN LATIN AMERICA. ECO/UNDEV FINAN PLAN BUDGET L/A+17C
ECO/TAC TARIFFS TAX...STAT 20. PAGE 44 B0893 NAT/G
           ADMIN
           B58

PAN AMERICAN UNION,REPERTORIO DE PUBLICACIONES BIBLIOG
PERIODICAS ACTUALES LATINO-AMERICANAS. CULTURE L/A+17C
ECO/UNDEV ADMIN LEAD GOV/REL 20 OAS. PAGE 81 B1630 NAT/G
           DIPLOM
           B59

GRABER D.,CRISIS DIPLOMACY. L/A+17C USA+45 USA-45 ROUTINE
NAT/G TOP/EX ECO/TAC COERCE ATTIT ORD/FREE...CONCPT MORAL
MYTH TIME/SEQ COLD/WAR 20. PAGE 42 B0848 DIPLOM
           B59

INTERAMERICAN CULTURAL COUN,LISTA DE LIBROS BIBLIOG/A
REPRESENTAVOS DE AMERICA. CULTURE DIPLOM ADMIN 20. NAT/G
PAGE 54 B1093   L/A+17C
           SOC

           B59

MAYDA J.,ATOMIC ENERGY AND LAW. ECO/UNDEV FINAN NUC/PWR
TEC/DEV FOR/AID EFFICIENCY PRODUC WEALTH...POLICY L/A+17C
TECHNIC 20. PAGE 71 B1433 LAW
           ADMIN
           B60

FLORES R.H.,CATALOGO DE TESIS DOCTORALES DE LAS BIBLIOG
FACULTADES DE LA UNIVERSIDAD DE EL SALVADOR. ACADEM
EL/SALVADR LAW DIPLOM ADMIN LEAD GOV/REL...SOC L/A+17C
19/20. PAGE 36 B0730   NAT/G
           B60

LIPSET S.M.,POLITICAL MAN. AFR COM EUR+WWI L/A+17C PWR
MOD/EUR S/ASIA USA+45 USA-45 STRUCT ECO/DEV SOC
ECO/UNDEV POL/PAR SECT ADMIN WEALTH...CONCPT WORK
TOT/POP 20. PAGE 65 B1320
           B60

PINTO F.B.M.,ENRIQUECIMENTO ILICITO NO EXERCICIO DE ADMIN
CARGOS PUBLICOS. BRAZIL L/A+17C USA+45 ELITES NAT/G
TRIBUTE CONTROL INGP/REL ORD/FREE PWR...NAT/COMP CRIME
20. PAGE 83 B1675   LAW
           B60

US LIBRARY OF CONGRESS,INDEX TO LATIN AMERICAN BIBLIOG/A
LEGISLATION: 1950-1960 (2 VOLS.). NAT/G DELIB/GP LEGIS
ADMIN PARL/PROC 20. PAGE 109 B2205 L/A+17C
           JURID
           S60

"THE EMERGING COMMON MARKETS IN LATIN AMERICA." FUT FINAN
L/A+17C STRATA DIST/IND INDUS LABOR NAT/G LEGIS ECO/UNDEV
ECO/TAC ADMIN RIGID/FLEX HEALTH...NEW/IDEA TIME/SEQ INT/TRADE
OAS 20. PAGE 2 B0039   S60

HERRERA F.,"THE INTER-AMERICAN DEVELOPMENT BANK." L/A+17C
USA+45 ECO/UNDEV INT/ORG CONSULT DELIB/GP PLAN FINAN
ECO/TAC INT/TRADE ROUTINE WEALTH...STAT 20. PAGE 49 FOR/AID
B0994   REGION
           S60

MORA J.A.,"THE ORGANIZATION OF AMERICAN STATES." L/A+17C
USA+45 LAW ECO/UNDEV VOL/ASSN DELIB/GP PLAN BAL/PWR INT/ORG
EDU/PROP ADMIN DRIVE RIGID/FLEX ORD/FREE WEALTH REGION
...TIME/SEQ GEN/LAWS OAS 20. PAGE 75 B1518
           S60

MORALES C.J.,"TRADE AND ECONOMIC INTEGRATION IN FINAN
LATIN AMERICA." FUT L/A+17C LAW STRATA ECO/UNDEV INT/TRADE
DIST/IND INDUS LABOR NAT/G LEGIS ECO/TAC ADMIN REGION
RIGID/FLEX WEALTH...CONCPT NEW/IDEA CONT/OBS
TIME/SEQ WORK 20. PAGE 75 B1519
           B61

FREYRE G.,THE PORTUGUESE AND THE TROPICS. L/A+17C COLONIAL
PORTUGAL SOCIETY PERF/ART ADMIN TASK GP/REL METH
...ART/METH CONCPT SOC/INTEG 20. PAGE 37 B0754 PLAN
           CULTURE
           B61

FRIEDMANN W.G.,JOINT INTERNATIONAL BUSINESS ECO/UNDEV
VENTURES. ASIA ISLAM L/A+17C ECO/DEV DIST/IND FINAN INT/TRADE
PROC/MFG FACE/GP LG/CO NAT/G VOL/ASSN CONSULT
EX/STRUC PLAN ADMIN ROUTINE WEALTH...OLD/LIB WORK
20. PAGE 37 B0760
           S61

ANGLIN D.,"UNITED STATES OPPOSITION TO CANADIAN INT/ORG
MEMBERSHIP IN THE PAN AMERICAN UNION: A CANADIAN CANADA
VIEW." L/A+17C UK USA+45 VOL/ASSN DELIB/GP EX/STRUC
PLAN DIPLOM DOMIN REGION ATTIT RIGID/FLEX PWR
...RELATIV CONCPT STERTYP CMN/WLTH OAS 20. PAGE 5
B0112
           S61

NEEDLER M.C.,"THE POLITICAL DEVELOPMENT OF MEXICO." L/A+17C
STRUCT NAT/G ADMIN RIGID/FLEX...TIME/SEQ TREND POL/PAR
MEXIC/AMER TOT/POP VAL/FREE 19/20. PAGE 77 B1566
           B62

BROWN L.C.,LATIN AMERICA, A BIBLIOGRAPHY. EX/STRUC BIBLIOG
ADMIN LEAD ATTIT...POLICY 20. PAGE 16 B0323 L/A+17C
           DIPLOM
           NAT/G
           B62

ESCUELA SUPERIOR DE ADMIN PUBL,INFORME DEL ADMIN
SEMINARIO SOBRE SERVICIO CIVIL O CARRERA NAT/G
ADMINISTRATIVA. L/A+17C ELITES STRATA CONFER PROB/SOLV
CONTROL GOV/REL INGP/REL SUPEGO 20 CENTRAL/AM ATTIT
CIVIL/SERV. PAGE 33 B0681
           S62

SPRINGER H.W.,"FEDERATION IN THE CARIBBEAN: AN VOL/ASSN
ATTEMPT THAT FAILED." L/A+17C ECO/UNDEV INT/ORG NAT/G
POL/PAR PROVS LEGIS CREATE PLAN LEGIT ADMIN FEDERAL REGION
ATTIT DRIVE PERSON ORD/FREE PWR...POLICY GEOG PSY
CONCPT OBS CARIBBEAN CMN/WLTH 20. PAGE 100 B2013
           B63

COMISION DE HISTORIO,GUIA DE LOS DOCUMENTOS BIBLIOG
MICROFOTOGRAFIADOS POR LA UNIDAD MOVIL DE LA NAT/G
UNESCO. SOCIETY ECO/UNDEV INT/ORG ADMIN...SOC 20 L/A+17C
UNESCO. PAGE 22 B0456   DIPLOM
           B63

DE VRIES E.,SOCIAL ASPECTS OF ECONOMIC DEVELOPMENT L/A+17C
IN LATIN AMERICA. CULTURE SOCIETY STRATA FINAN ECO/UNDEV
INDUS INT/ORG DELIB/GP ACT/RES ECO/TAC EDU/PROP
ADMIN ATTIT SUPEGO HEALTH KNOWL ORD/FREE...SOC STAT
TREND ANTHOL TOT/POP VAL/FREE. PAGE 28 B0562

FORTES A.B.,HISTORIA ADMINISTRATIVA, JUDICIARIA E   B63
ECLESIASTICA DO RIO GRANDE DO SUL. BRAZIL L/A+17C   PROVS
LOC/G SECT COLONIAL CT/SYS ORD/FREE CATHISM 16/20.   ADMIN
PAGE 37 B0742   JURID

ALDERFER H.O.,LOCAL GOVERNMENT IN DEVELOPING   B64
COUNTRIES. ASIA COM L/A+17C S/ASIA AGRI LOC/G MUNIC ADMIN
PROVS DOMIN CHOOSE PWR...POLICY MGT CONCPT 20.   ROUTINE
PAGE 3 B0070

IBERO-AMERICAN INSTITUTES,IBEROAMERICANA. STRUCT   B64
ADMIN SOC. PAGE 53 B1073   BIBLIOG
                                                     L/A+17C
                                                     NAT/G
                                                     DIPLOM

JACKSON W.V.,LIBRARY GUIDE FOR BRAZILIAN STUDIES.   B64
BRAZIL USA+45 STRUCT DIPLOM ADMIN...SOC 20. PAGE 55 BIBLIOG
B1110   L/A+17C
                                                     NAT/G
                                                     LOC/G

MUSSO AMBROSI L.A.,BIBLIOGRAFIA DE BIBLIOGRAFIAS   B64
URUGUAYAS. URUGUAY DIPLOM ADMIN ATTIT...SOC 20.   BIBLIOG
PAGE 77 B1551   NAT/G
                                                     L/A+17C
                                                     PRESS

POPPINO R.E.,INTERNATIONAL COMMUNISM IN LATIN   B64
AMERICA: A HISTORY OF THE MOVEMENT 1917-1963.   MARXISM
CHINA/COM USSR INTELL STRATA LABOR WORKER ADMIN REV POL/PAR
ATTIT...POLICY 20 COLD/WAR. PAGE 84 B1692   L/A+17C

SEGUNDO-SANCHEZ M.,OBRAS (2 VOLS.). VENEZUELA   B64
EX/STRUC DIPLOM ADMIN 19/20. PAGE 95 B1924   BIBLIOG
                                                     LEAD
                                                     NAT/G
                                                     L/A+17C

TURNER M.C.,LIBROS EN VENTA EN HISPANOAMERICA Y   B64
ESPANA. SPAIN LAW CONSTN CULTURE ADMIN LEAD...HUM   BIBLIOG
SOC 20. PAGE 106 B2139   L/A+17C
                                                     NAT/G
                                                     DIPLOM

HAAS E.B.,"ECONOMICS AND DIFFERENTIAL PATTERNS OF   L64
POLITICAL INTEGRATION: PROJECTIONS ABOUT UNITY IN   L/A+17C
LATIN AMERICA." SOCIETY NAT/G DELIB/GP ACT/RES   INT/ORG
CREATE PLAN ECO/TAC REGION ROUTINE ATTIT DRIVE PWR   MARKET
WEALTH...CONCPT TREND CHARTS LAFTA 20. PAGE 45
B0910

HUELIN D.,"ECONOMIC INTEGRATION IN LATIN AMERICAN: S64
PROGRESS AND PROBLEMS." L/A+17C ECO/DEV AGRI   MARKET
DIST/IND FINAN INDUS NAT/G VOL/ASSN CONSULT   ECO/UNDEV
DELIB/GP EX/STRUC ACT/RES PLAN TEC/DEV ECO/TAC   INT/TRADE
ROUTINE BAL/PAY WEALTH WORK 20. PAGE 52 B1058

JOHNSON K.F.,"CAUSAL FACTORS IN LATIN AMERICAN   S64
POLITICAL INSTABILITY." CULTURE NAT/G VOL/ASSN   L/A+17C
EX/STRUC FORCES EDU/PROP LEGIT ADMIN COERCE REV   PERCEPT
ATTIT KNOWL PWR...STYLE RECORD CHARTS WORK 20.   ELITES
PAGE 57 B1144

NASH M.,"SOCIAL PREREQUISITES TO ECONOMIC GROWTH IN   S64
LATIN AMERICA AND SOUTHEAST ASIA." L/A+17C S/ASIA   ECO/DEV
CULTURE SOCIETY ECO/UNDEV AGRI INDUS NAT/G PLAN   PERCEPT
TEC/DEV EDU/PROP ROUTINE ALL/VALS...POLICY RELATIV
SOC NAT/COMP WORK TOT/POP 20. PAGE 77 B1558

SCOTT R.E.,"MEXICAN GOVERNMENT IN TRANSITION (REV   C64
ED)" CULTURE STRUCT POL/PAR CHIEF ADMIN LOBBY REV   NAT/G
CHOOSE GP/REL DRIVE...BIBLIOG METH 20 MEXIC/AMER.   L/A+17C
PAGE 95 B1920   ROUTINE
                                                     CONSTN

ETZIONI A.,POLITICAL UNIFICATION* A COMPARATIVE   B65
STUDY OF LEADERS AND FORCES. EUR+WWI ISLAM L/A+17C   INT/ORG
WOR+45 ELITES STRATA EXEC WEALTH...TIME/SEQ TREND   FORCES
SOC/EXP. PAGE 34 B0686   ECO/TAC
                                                     REGION

GREGG J.L.,POLITICAL PARTIES AND PARTY SYSTEMS IN   B65
GUATEMALA 1944-1963. GUATEMALA L/A+17C EX/STRUC   LEAD
FORCES CREATE CONTROL REV CHOOSE PWR...TREND   POL/PAR
IDEA/COMP 20. PAGE 43 B0872   NAT/G
                                                     CHIEF

HISPANIC SOCIETY OF AMERICA,CATALOGUE (10 VOLS.).   B65
PORTUGAL PRE/AMER SPAIN NAT/G ADMIN...POLICY SOC   BIBLIOG
15/20. PAGE 50 B1018   L/A+17C
                                                     COLONIAL
                                                     DIPLOM

SILVERT K.H.,"AMERICAN ACADEMIC ETHICS AND SOCIAL   S65
RESEARCH ABROAD* THE LESSON OF PROJECT CAMELOT."   ACADEM
CHILE L/A+17C USA+45 FINAN ADMIN...PHIL/SCI SOC   NAT/G
GEN/LAWS CAMELOT. PAGE 97 B1953   ACT/RES
                                                     POLICY

BARBER W.F.,INTERNAL SECURITY AND MILITARY POWER*   B66
COUNTERINSURGENCY AND CIVIC ACTION IN LATIN   L/A+17C
AMERICA. ECO/UNDEV CREATE ADMIN REV ATTIT   FORCES
RIGID/FLEX MARXISM...INT BIBLIOG OAS. PAGE 9 B0183   ORD/FREE
                                                     TASK

HANKE L.,HANDBOOK OF LATIN AMERICAN STUDIES.   B66
ECO/UNDEV ADMIN LEAD...HUM SOC 20. PAGE 46 B0937   BIBLIOG/A
                                                     L/A+17C
                                                     INDEX
                                                     NAT/G

ANDERSON C.W.,POLITICS AND ECONOMIC CHANGE IN LATIN   B67
AMERICA. L/A+17C INDUS NAT/G OP/RES ADMIN DEMAND   ECO/UNDEV
...POLICY STAT CHARTS NAT/COMP 20. PAGE 4 B0091   PROB/SOLV
                                                     PLAN
                                                     ECO/TAC

SABLE M.H.,A GUIDE TO LATIN AMERICAN STUDIES (2   B67
VOLS). CONSTN FINAN INT/ORG LABOR MUNIC POL/PAR   BIBLIOG/A
FORCES CAP/ISM FOR/AID ADMIN MARXISM SOCISM OAS.   L/A+17C
PAGE 92 B1861   DIPLOM
                                                     NAT/LISM

SKIDMORE T.E.,POLITICS IN BRAZIL 1930-1964. BRAZIL   B67
L/A+17C INDUS NAT/G PROB/SOLV ATTIT 20. PAGE 98   CONSTN
B1973   ECO/TAC
                                                     ADMIN

ZONDAG C.H.,THE BOLIVIAN ECONOMY 1952-65. L/A+17C   B67
TEC/DEV FOR/AID ADMIN...OBS TREND CHARTS BIBLIOG 20 ECO/UNDEV
BOLIV. PAGE 119 B2406   INDUS
                                                     PRODUC

EDWARDS H.T.,"POWER STRUCTURE AND ITS COMMUNICATION   S67
IN SAN JOSE, COSTA RICA." COSTA/RICA L/A+17C STRATA ELITES
FACE/GP POL/PAR EX/STRUC PROB/SOLV ADMIN LEAD   INGP/REL
GP/REL PWR...STAT INT 20. PAGE 32 B0655   MUNIC
                                                     DOMIN

FABREGA J.,"ANTECEDENTES EXTRANJEROS EN LA   S67
CONSTITUCION PANAMENA." CUBA L/A+17C PANAMA URUGUAY CONSTN
EX/STRUC LEGIS DIPLOM ORD/FREE 19/20 COLOMB   JURID
MEXIC/AMER. PAGE 34 B0694   NAT/G
                                                     PARL/PROC

LEWIS P.H.,"LEADERSHIP AND CONFLICT WITHIN   S67
FEBRERISTA PARTY OF PARAGUAY." L/A+17C PARAGUAY   POL/PAR
EX/STRUC DOMIN SENIOR CONTROL INGP/REL CENTRAL   ELITES
FEDERAL ATTIT 20. PAGE 65 B1305   LEAD

MCNAMARA R.L.,"THE NEED FOR INNOVATIVENESS IN   S67
DEVELOPING SOCIETIES." L/A+17C EDU/PROP ADMIN LEAD   PROB/SOLV
WEALTH...POLICY PSY SOC METH 20 COLOMB. PAGE 72   PLAN
B1456   ECO/UNDEV
                                                     NEW/IDEA

SPACKMAN A.,"THE SENATE OF TRINIDAD AND TOBAGO."   S67
L/A+17C TRINIDAD WEST/IND NAT/G POL/PAR DELIB/GP   ELITES
OP/RES PROB/SOLV EDU/PROP EXEC LOBBY ROUTINE   EFFICIENCY
REPRESENT GP/REL 20. PAGE 99 B2002   LEGIS
                                                     DECISION

LA PALOMBARA J.G. B1248

LA PORTE T. B1249

LAB/EXP....LABORATORY EXPERIMENTS

CYERT R.M.,"TWO EXPERIMENTS ON BIAS AND CONFLICT IN   S61
ORGANIZATIONAL ESTIMATION." WORKER PROB/SOLV   LAB/EXP
EFFICIENCY...MGT PSY STAT CHARTS. PAGE 25 B0518   ROUTINE
                                                     ADMIN
                                                     DECISION

EVAN W.M.,"A LABORATORY EXPERIMENT ON BUREAUCRATIC   S61
AUTHORITY" WORKER CONTROL EXEC PRODUC ATTIT PERSON   ADMIN
...PSY SOC CHARTS SIMUL 20 WEBER/MAX. PAGE 34 B0687 LEGIT
                                                     LAB/EXP
                                                     EFFICIENCY

VERBA S.,"SMALL GROUPS AND POLITICAL BEHAVIOR: A   C61
STUDY OF LEADERSHIP" DOMIN PARTIC ROUTINE GP/REL   LEAD
ATTIT DRIVE ALL/VALS...CONCPT IDEA/COMP LAB/EXP   ELITES
BIBLIOG METH. PAGE 112 B2259   FACE/GP

CHICAGO U CTR PROG GOVT ADMIN,EDUCATION FOR   B62
INNOVATIVE BEHAVIOR IN EXECUTIVES. UNIV ELITES   EDU/PROP
ADMIN EFFICIENCY DRIVE PERSON...MGT APT/TEST   CREATE
PERS/TEST CHARTS LAB/EXP BIBLIOG 20. PAGE 21 B0420   EXEC
                                                     STAT

HILLS R.J.,"THE REPRESENTATIVE FUNCTION: NEGLECTED   S63
DIMENSION OF LEADERSHIP BEHAVIOR" USA+45 CLIENT   LEAD
STRUCT SCHOOL PERS/REL...STAT QU SAMP LAB/EXP 20.   ADMIN
PAGE 50 B1012   EXEC
                                                     ACT/RES

SINGER J.D.,HUMAN BEHAVIOR AND INTERNATINAL   B65
POLITICS* CONTRIBUTIONS FROM THE SOCIAL-   DIPLOM
PSYCHOLOGICAL SCIENCES. ACT/RES PLAN EDU/PROP ADMIN PHIL/SCI
KNOWL...DECISION PSY SOC NET/THEORY HYPO/EXP   QUANT
LAB/EXP SOC/EXP GEN/METH ANTHOL BIBLIOG. PAGE 97   SIMUL
B1965

LABOR FORCE....SEE WORKER

LABOR RELATIONS....SEE LABOR, ALSO RELATIONS INDEX

LABOR UNIONS....SEE LABOR

LABOR....LABOR UNIONS (BUT NOT GUILDS)

N

PRINCETON U INDUSTRIAL REL SEC,SELECTED REFERENCES   BIBLIOG/A
OF THE INDUSTRIAL RELATIONS SECTION OF PRINCETON,   INDUS
NEW JERSEY. LG/CO NAT/G LEGIS WORKER PLAN PROB/SOLV LABOR
PAY ADMIN ROUTINE TASK GP/REL...PSY 20. PAGE 84   MGT
B1708

N

SOVIET-EAST EUROPEAN RES SERV,SOVIET SOCIETY. USSR   BIBLIOG/A
LABOR POL/PAR PRESS MARXISM...MARXIST 20. PAGE 99   EDU/PROP
B2001   ADMIN
                                                     SOC

N

BULLETIN OF THE PUBLIC AFFAIRS INFORMATION SERVICE. BIBLIOG
WOR+45 WOR-45 ECO/UNDEV FINAN LABOR LOC/G PROVS   NAT/G
TEC/DEV DIPLOM EDU/PROP SOC. PAGE 1 B0010   ECO/DEV
                                                     ADMIN

N

THE MANAGEMENT REVIEW. FINAN EX/STRUC PROFIT   LABOR
BIBLIOG/A. PAGE 1 B0017   MGT
                                                     ADMIN
                                                     MARKET

N

THE JAPAN SCIENCE REVIEW: LAW AND POLITICS: LIST OF BIBLIOG
BOOKS AND ARTICLES ON LAW AND POLITICS. CONSTN AGRI LAW
INDUS LABOR DIPLOM TAX ADMIN CRIME...INT/LAW SOC 20 S/ASIA
CHINJAP. PAGE 1 B0025   PHIL/SCI

N

PERSONNEL. USA+45 LAW LABOR LG/CO WORKER CREATE   BIBLIOG/A
GOV/REL PERS/REL ATTIT WEALTH. PAGE 2 B0030   ADMIN
                                                     MGT
                                                     GP/REL

N

PRINCETON UNIVERSITY,SELECTED REFERENCES: BIBLIOG/A
INDUSTRIAL RELATIONS SECTION. USA+45 EX/STRUC   LABOR
WORKER TEC/DEV...MGT 20. PAGE 85 B1712   INDUS
                                                     GP/REL

N

US SUPERINTENDENT OF DOCUMENTS,LABOR (PRICE LIST   BIBLIOG/A
33). USA+45 LAW AGRI CONSTRUC INDUS NAT/G BARGAIN   WORKER
PRICE ADMIN AUTOMAT PRODUC MGT. PAGE 111 B2240   LABOR
                                                     LEGIS

B28

BUELL R.,THE NATIVE PROBLEM IN AFRICA. KIN LABOR   AFR
LOC/G ECO/TAC ROUTINE ORD/FREE...REC/INT KNO/TEST   CULTURE
CENSUS TREND CHARTS SOC/EXP STERTYP 20. PAGE 17
B0339

B28

HARDMAN J.B.,AMERICAN LABOR DYNAMICS. WORKER   LABOR
ECO/TAC DOMIN ADJUD LEAD LOBBY PWR...POLICY MGT.   INGP/REL
PAGE 47 B0944   ATTIT
                                                     GP/REL

B31

BORCHARD E.H.,GUIDE TO THE LAW AND LEGAL LITERATURE BIBLIOG/A
OF FRANCE. FRANCE FINAN INDUS LABOR SECT LEGIS   LAW
ADMIN COLONIAL CRIME OWN...INT/LAW 20. PAGE 14   CONSTN
B0277   METH

B36

HERRING E.P.,PUBLIC ADMINISTRATION AND THE PUBLIC   GP/REL
INTEREST. LABOR NAT/G PARTIC EFFICIENCY 20. PAGE 49 DECISION
B0995   PROB/SOLV
                                                     ADMIN

B37

BROOKS R.R.,WHEN LABOR ORGANIZES. FINAN EDU/PROP   LABOR
ADMIN LOBBY PARTIC REPRESENT WEALTH TREND. PAGE 16   GP/REL
B0318   POLICY

B37

BUREAU OF NATIONAL AFFAIRS,LABOR RELATIONS   LABOR
REFERENCE MANUAL VOL 1, 1935-1937. BARGAIN DEBATE   ADMIN
ROUTINE INGP/REL 20 NLRB. PAGE 17 B0351   ADJUD
                                                     NAT/G

B37

GALLOWAY G.B.,AMERICAN PAMPHLET LITERATURE OF   BIBLIOG/A
PUBLIC AFFAIRS (PAMPHLET). USA-45 ECO/DEV LABOR   PLAN
ADMIN...MGT 20. PAGE 38 B0776   DIPLOM
                                                     NAT/G

B38

BALDWIN R.N.,CIVIL LIBERTIES AND INDUSTRIAL   LABOR
CONFLICT. USA+45 STRATA WORKER INGP/REL...MGT 20   LG/CO
ACLU CIVIL/LIB. PAGE 9 B0175   INDUS
                                                     GP/REL

B38

FIELD G.L.,THE SYNDICAL AND CORPORATIVE   FASCISM
INSTITUTIONS OF ITALIAN FASCISM. ITALY CONSTN   INDUS
STRATA LABOR EX/STRUC TOP/EX ADJUD ADMIN LEAD   NAT/G
TOTALISM AUTHORIT...MGT 20 MUSSOLIN/B. PAGE 35   WORKER
B0716

B38

REICH N.,LABOR RELATIONS IN REPUBLICAN GERMANY.   WORKER
GERMANY CONSTN ECO/DEV INDUS NAT/G ADMIN CONTROL   MGT
GP/REL FASCISM POPULISM 20 WEIMAR/REP. PAGE 87   LABOR
B1763   BARGAIN

B38

SALTER J.T.,THE AMERICAN POLITICIAN. USA-45 LABOR   BIOG
POL/PAR EDU/PROP ADMIN CHOOSE ATTIT DRIVE PERSON   LEAD
PWR...POLICY ANTHOL 20 THOMAS/N LEWIS/JL LAGUARD/F   PROVS
GOVERNOR MAYOR. PAGE 92 B1865   LOC/G

B39

HITLER A.,MEIN KAMPF. EUR+WWI FUT MOD/EUR STRUCT   PWR
INT/ORG LABOR NAT/G POL/PAR FORCES CREATE PLAN   NEW/IDEA
BAL/PWR DIPLOM ECO/TAC DOMIN EDU/PROP ADMIN COERCE   WAR
ATTIT...SOCIALIST BIOG TREND NAZI. PAGE 50 B1020

B40

MCHENRY D.E.,HIS MAJESTY'S OPPOSITION: STRUCTURE   POL/PAR
AND PROBLEMS OF THE BRITISH LABOUR PARTY 1931-1938. MGT
UK FINAN LABOR LOC/G DELIB/GP LEGIS EDU/PROP LEAD   NAT/G
PARTIC CHOOSE GP/REL SOCISM...TREND 20 LABOR/PAR.   POLICY
PAGE 72 B1450

B41

LESTER R.A.,ECONOMICS OF LABOR. UK USA-45 TEC/DEV   LABOR
BARGAIN PAY INGP/REL INCOME...MGT 19/20. PAGE 64   ECO/DEV
B1298   INDUS
                                                     WORKER

B41

SLICHTER S.H.,UNION POLICIES AND INDUSTRIAL   BARGAIN
MANAGEMENT. USA-45 INDUS TEC/DEV PAY GP/REL   LABOR
INGP/REL COST EFFICIENCY PRODUC...POLICY 20.   MGT
PAGE 98 B1978   WORKER

B42

CHAMBERLIN W.,INDUSTRIAL RELATIONS IN GERMANY   BIBLIOG/A
1914-1939. GERMANY 20. PAGE 20 B0401   LABOR
                                                     MGT
                                                     GP/REL

S43

GOLDEN C.S.,"NEW PATTERNS OF DEMOCRACY." NEIGH   LABOR
DELIB/GP EDU/PROP EXEC PARTIC...MGT METH/CNCPT OBS   REPRESENT
TREND. PAGE 40 B0815   LG/CO
                                                     GP/REL

B44

DAHL D.,SICKNESS BENEFITS AND GROUP PURCHASE OF   BIBLIOG/A
MEDICAL CARE FOR INDUSTRIAL EMPLOYEES. FAM LABOR   INDUS
NAT/G PLAN...POLICY MGT SOC STAT 20. PAGE 25 B0519   WORKER
                                                     HEAL

B45

BAKER H.,PROBLEMS OF REEMPLOYMENT AND RETRAINING OF BIBLIOG/A
MANPOWER DURING THE TRANSITION FROM WAR TO PEACE.   ADJUST
USA+45 INDUS LABOR LG/CO NAT/G PLAN ADMIN PEACE   WAR
...POLICY MGT 20. PAGE 8 B0167   PROB/SOLV

B45

MAYO E.,THE SOCIAL PROBLEMS OF AN INDUSTRIAL   INDUS
CIVILIZATION. USA+45 SOCIETY LABOR CROWD PERS/REL   GP/REL
LAISSEZ. PAGE 71 B1438   MGT
                                                     WORKER

B45

MILLIS H.A.,ORGANIZED LABOR (FIRST ED.). LAW STRUCT LABOR
DELIB/GP WORKER ECO/TAC ADJUD CONTROL REPRESENT   POLICY
INGP/REL INCOME MGT. PAGE 74 B1485   ROUTINE
                                                     GP/REL

B46

WILCOX J.K.,OFFICIAL DEFENSE PUBLICATIONS,   BIBLIOG/A
1941-1945 (NINE VOLS.). USA-45 AGRI INDUS R+D LABOR WAR
FORCES TEC/DEV EFFICIENCY PRODUC SKILL WEALTH 20.   CIVMIL/REL
PAGE 116 B2347   ADMIN

B47

BAERWALD F.,FUNDAMENTALS OF LABOR ECONOMICS. LAW   ECO/DEV
INDUS LABOR LG/CO CONTROL GP/REL INCOME TOTALISM   WORKER
...MGT CHARTS GEN/LAWS BIBLIOG 20. PAGE 8 B0158   MARKET

B47

PUBLIC ADMINISTRATION SERVICE,CURRENT RESEARCH   BIBLIOG
PROJECTS IN PUBLIC ADMINISTRATION (PAMPHLET). LAW   R+D
CONSTN COM/IND LABOR LOC/G MUNIC PROVS ACT/RES   MGT
DIPLOM RECEIVE EDU/PROP WAR 20. PAGE 85 B1716   ADMIN

B47

WARNER W.L.,THE SOCIAL SYSTEM OF THE MODERN   ROLE
FACTORY; THE STRIKE: AN ANALYSIS. USA-45 STRATA   STRUCT
WORKER ECO/TAC GP/REL INGP/REL...MGT SOC CHARTS 20   LABOR
YANKEE/C. PAGE 114 B2293   PROC/MFG

B47

WHITEHEAD T.N.,LEADERSHIP IN A FREE SOCIETY; A   INDUS
STUDY IN HUMAN RELATIONS BASED ON AN ANALYSIS OF   LEAD
PRESENT-DAY INDUSTRIAL CIVILIZATION. WOR-45 STRUCT   ORD/FREE
R+D LABOR LG/CO SML/CO WORKER PLAN PROB/SOLV   SOCIETY
TEC/DEV DRIVE...MGT 20. PAGE 116 B2341

B48

STEWART I.,ORGANIZING SCIENTIFIC RESEARCH FOR WAR: DELIB/GP
ADMINISTRATIVE HISTORY OF OFFICE OF SCIENTIFIC   ADMIN
RESEARCH AND DEVELOPMENT. USA-45 INTELL R+D LABOR   WAR
WORKER CREATE BUDGET WEAPON CIVMIL/REL GP/REL   TEC/DEV
EFFICIENCY...POLICY 20. PAGE 101 B2037

B49

HEADLAM-MORLEY,BIBLIOGRAPHY IN POLITICS FOR THE   BIBLIOG
HONOUR SCHOOL OF PHILOSOPHY, POLITICS AND ECONOMICS NAT/G
(PAMPHLET). UK CONSTN LABOR MUNIC DIPLOM ADMIN   PHIL/SCI
19/20. PAGE 48 B0979   GOV/REL

B49

SHISTER J.,ECONOMICS OF THE LABOR MARKET. LOC/G   MARKET
NAT/G WORKER TEC/DEV BARGAIN PAY PRICE EXEC GP/REL   LABOR
INCOME...MGT T 20. PAGE 96 B1949   INDUS

B50

BAKKE E.W.,BONDS OF ORGANIZATION (2ND ED.). USA+45   ECO/DEV
COM/IND FINAN ADMIN LEAD PERS/REL...INT SOC/INTEG   MGT
20. PAGE 8 B0169   LABOR
                                                     GP/REL

B50
COMMONS J.R.,THE ECONOMICS OF COLLECTIVE ACTION.   ECO/DEV
USA-45 AGRI INDUS LABOR NAT/G LEGIS ADMIN   CAP/ISM
EFFICIENCY...MGT METH/COMP BIBLIOG 20. PAGE 22   ACT/RES
B0458   CONCPT

B51
HARDMAN J.B.,THE HOUSE OF LABOR. LAW R+D NEIGH   LABOR
EDU/PROP LEAD ROUTINE REPRESENT GP/REL...POLICY   LOBBY
STAT. PAGE 47 B0945   ADMIN
                                                          PRESS

B51
PETERSON F.,SURVEY OF LABOR ECONOMICS (REV. ED.).   WORKER
STRATA ECO/DEV LABOR INSPECT BARGAIN PAY PRICE EXEC   DEMAND
ROUTINE GP/REL ALL/VALS ORD/FREE 20 AFL/CIO   IDEA/COMP
DEPT/LABOR. PAGE 82 B1662   T

B52
GOLDSTEIN J.,THE GOVERNMENT OF BRITISH TRADE   LABOR
UNIONS. UK ECO/DEV EX/STRUC INGP/REL...BIBLIOG 20.   PARTIC
PAGE 40 B0817

B52
SELZNICK P.,THE ORGANIZATIONAL WEAPON: A STUDY OF   MARXISM
BOLSHEVIK STRATEGY AND TACTICS. USSR SOCIETY STRATA   POL/PAR
LABOR DOMIN EDU/PROP PARTIC REV ATTIT PWR...POLICY   LEAD
MGT CONCPT 20 BOLSHEVISM. PAGE 95 B1929   TOTALISM

S52
BRUEGEL J.W.,"DIE INTERNAZIONALE   VOL/ASSN
GEWERKSCHAFTSBEWEGUNG." COM EUR+WWI USA+45 WOR+45   LABOR
DELIB/GP EX/STRUC ECO/TAC EDU/PROP ATTIT PWR   TOTALISM
RESPECT SKILL WEALTH WORK 20. PAGE 16 B0330

S52
LIPSET S.M.,"DEMOCRACY IN PRIVATE GOVERNMENT; (A   LABOR
CASE STUDY OF THE INTERNATIONAL TYPOGRAPHICAL   ADMIN
UNION)" (BMR)" POL/PAR CONTROL LEAD INGP/REL PWR   ELITES
...MAJORIT DECISION PREDICT 20. PAGE 65 B1319   REPRESENT

B53
MILLIKAN M.F.,INCOME STABILIZATION FOR A DEVELOPING   ANTHOL
DEMOCRACY. USA+45 ECO/DEV LABOR BUDGET ECO/TAC TAX   MARKET
ADMIN ADJUST PRODUC WEALTH...POLICY TREND 20.   EQUILIB
PAGE 73 B1484   EFFICIENCY

B53
SAYLES L.R.,THE LOCAL UNION. CONSTN CULTURE   LABOR
DELIB/GP PARTIC CHOOSE GP/REL INGP/REL ATTIT ROLE   LEAD
...MAJORIT DECISION MGT. PAGE 93 B1873   ADJUD
                                                          ROUTINE

B53
TOMPKINS D.C.,CIVIL DEFENSE IN THE STATES: A   BIBLIOG
BIBLIOGRAPHY (DEFENSE BIBLIOGRAPHIES NO. 3;   WAR
PAMPHLET). USA+45 LABOR LOC/G NAT/G PROVS LEGIS.   ORD/FREE
PAGE 105 B2115   ADMIN

S53
DRUCKER P.F.,"THE EMPLOYEE SOCIETY." STRUCT BAL/PWR LABOR
PARTIC REPRESENT PWR...DECISION CONCPT. PAGE 30   MGT
B0619   WORKER
                                                          CULTURE

B54
BINANI G.D.,INDIA AT A GLANCE (REV. ED.). INDIA   INDEX
COM/IND FINAN INDUS LABOR PROVS SCHOOL PLAN DIPLOM   CON/ANAL
INT/TRADE ADMIN...JURID 20. PAGE 12 B0238   NAT/G
                                                          ECO/UNDEV

B54
CHICAGO JOINT REFERENCE LIB,FEDERAL-STATE-LOCAL   BIBLIOG
RELATIONS; A SELECTED BIBLIOGRAPHY. USA+45 AGRI   FEDERAL
LABOR LOC/G MUNIC EX/STRUC ADMIN REGION HEALTH   GOV/REL
CON/ANAL. PAGE 21 B0419

B54
GOLDNER A.W.,WILDCAT STRIKE. LABOR TEC/DEV PAY   INDUS
ADMIN LEAD PERS/REL ATTIT RIGID/FLEX PWR...MGT   WORKER
CONCPT. PAGE 40 B0816   GP/REL
                                                          SOC

B54
MOSK S.A.,INDUSTRIAL REVOLUTION IN MEXICO. MARKET   INDUS
LABOR CREATE CAP/ISM ADMIN ATTIT SOCISM...POLICY 20   TEC/DEV
MEXIC/AMER. PAGE 76 B1533   ECO/UNDEV
                                                          NAT/G

B54
WILENSKY H.L.,SYLLABUS OF INDUSTRIAL RELATIONS: A   BIBLIOG
GUIDE TO READING AND RESEARCH. USA+45 MUNIC ADMIN   INDUS
INGP/REL...POLICY MGT PHIL/SCI 20. PAGE 117 B2351   LABOR
                                                          WORKER

B55
BRAUN K.,LABOR DISPUTES AND THEIR SETTLEMENT.   INDUS
ECO/TAC ROUTINE TASK GP/REL...DECISION GEN/LAWS.   LABOR
PAGE 15 B0301   BARGAIN
                                                          ADJUD

B55
GULICK C.A.,HISTORY AND THEORIES OF WORKING-CLASS   BIBLIOG
MOVEMENTS: A SELECT BIBLIOGRAPHY. EUR+WWI MOD/EUR   WORKER
UK USA-45 INT/ORG. PAGE 44 B0902   LABOR
                                                          ADMIN

B55
JAPAN MOMBUSHO DAIGAKU GAKIYUT,BIBLIOGRAPHY OF THE   BIBLIOG
STUDIES ON LAW AND POLITICS (PAMPHLET). CONSTN   LAW
INDUS LABOR DIPLOM TAX ADMIN...CRIMLGY INT/LAW 20   PHIL/SCI
CHINJAP. PAGE 56 B1126

B55
RUSTOW D.A.,THE POLITICS OF COMPROMISE. SWEDEN   POL/PAR

LABOR EX/STRUC LEGIS PLAN REPRESENT SOCISM...SOC   NAT/G
19/20. PAGE 92 B1859   POLICY
                                                          ECO/TAC

C55
BONER H.A.,"HUNGRY GENERATIONS." UK WOR+45 WOR-45   ECO/DEV
STRATA INDUS FAM LABOR CAP/ISM...MGT BIBLIOG 19/20.   PHIL/SCI
PAGE 13 B0272   CONCPT
                                                          WEALTH

B56
BARBASH J.,THE PRACTICE OF UNIONISM. ECO/TAC LEAD   LABOR
LOBBY GP/REL INGP/REL DRIVE MARXISM BIBLIOG. PAGE 9   REPRESENT
B0182   CONTROL
                                                          ADMIN

B56
BLAU P.M.,BUREAUCRACY IN MODERN SOCIETY. STRUCT   SOC
INDUS LABOR LG/CO LOC/G NAT/G FORCES EDU/PROP   EX/STRUC
ROUTINE ORD/FREE 20 BUREAUCRCY. PAGE 12 B0252   ADMIN
                                                          EFFICIENCY

B56
GLADDEN E.N.,CIVIL SERVICE OR BUREAUCRACY? UK LAW   ADMIN
STRATA LABOR TOP/EX PLAN SENIOR AUTOMAT CONTROL   GOV/REL
PARTIC CHOOSE HAPPINESS...CHARTS 19/20 CIVIL/SERV   EFFICIENCY
BUREAUCRCY. PAGE 40 B0808   PROVS

B57
IKE N.,JAPANESE POLITICS. INTELL STRUCT AGRI INDUS   NAT/G
FAM KIN LABOR PRESS CHOOSE ATTIT...DECISION BIBLIOG   ADMIN
19/20 CHINJAP. PAGE 53 B1075   POL/PAR
                                                          CULTURE

B57
INDUSTRIAL RELATIONS RES ASSN,RESEARCH IN   INDUS
INDUSTRIAL HUMAN RELATIONS. INTELL ACT/RES OP/RES   MGT
ADMIN 20. PAGE 54 B1084   LABOR
                                                          GP/REL

B57
SCHNEIDER E.V.,INDUSTRIAL SOCIOLOGY: THE SOCIAL   LABOR
RELATIONS OF INDUSTRY AND COMMUNITY. STRATA INDUS   MGT
NAT/G NEIGH CREATE ADMIN PARTIC GP/REL RACE/REL   INGP/REL
ROLE PWR...POLICY BIBLIOG. PAGE 94 B1898   STRUCT

B57
US CIVIL SERVICE COMMISSION,DISSERTATIONS AND   BIBLIOG
THESES RELATING TO PERSONNEL ADMINISTRATION   ADMIN
(PAMPHLET). USA+45 COM/IND LABOR EX/STRUC GP/REL   MGT
INGP/REL DECISION. PAGE 108 B2176   WORKER

B57
US HOUSE COMM ON POST OFFICE,MANPOWER UTILIZATION   NAT/G
IN THE FEDERAL GOVERNMENT. USA+45 FORCES WORKER   ADMIN
CREATE PLAN EFFICIENCY UTIL 20 CONGRESS CIVIL/SERV   LABOR
POSTAL/SYS DEPT/DEFEN. PAGE 109 B2193   EX/STRUC

S57
ROURKE F.E.,"THE POLITICS OF ADMINISTRATIVE   POLICY
ORGANIZATION: A CASE HISTORY." USA+45 LABOR WORKER   ATTIT
PLAN ADMIN TASK EFFICIENCY 20 DEPT/LABOR CONGRESS.   MGT
PAGE 91 B1836   GP/COMP

B58
BRIGHT J.R.,AUTOMATION AND MANAGEMENT. INDUS LABOR   AUTOMAT
WORKER OP/RES TEC/DEV INSPECT 20. PAGE 15 B0307   COMPUTER
                                                          PLAN
                                                          MGT

B58
LESTER R.A.,AS UNIONS MATURE. POL/PAR BARGAIN LEAD   LABOR
PARTIC GP/REL CENTRAL...MAJORIT TIME/SEQ METH/COMP.   INDUS
PAGE 64 B1299   POLICY
                                                          MGT

B58
MELMAN S.,DECISION-MAKING AND PRODUCTIVITY. INDUS   LABOR
EX/STRUC WORKER OP/RES PROB/SOLV TEC/DEV ADMIN   PRODUC
ROUTINE RIGID/FLEX GP/COMP. PAGE 73 B1464   DECISION
                                                          MGT

B58
VAN RIPER P.P.,HISTORY OF THE UNITED STATES CIVIL   ADMIN
SERVICE. USA+45 USA-45 LABOR LOC/G DELIB/GP LEGIS   WORKER
PROB/SOLV LOBBY GOV/REL GP/REL INCOME...POLICY   NAT/G
18/20 PRESIDENT CIVIL/SERV. PAGE 111 B2251

B59
BONNETT C.E.,LABOR-MANAGEMENT RELATIONS. USA+45   MGT
OP/RES PROB/SOLV EDU/PROP...AUD/VIS CHARTS 20.   LABOR
PAGE 13 B0274   INDUS
                                                          GP/REL

B59
CHAPMAN B.,THE PROFESSION OF GOVERNMENT: THE PUBLIC ADMIN
SERVICE IN EUROPE. MOD/EUR LABOR CT/SYS...T 20   CONTROL
CIVIL/SERV. PAGE 20 B0409   ROUTINE
                                                          EX/STRUC

B59
DAHRENDORF R.,CLASS AND CLASS CONFLICT IN   VOL/ASSN
INDUSTRIAL SOCIETY. LABOR NAT/G COERCE ROLE PLURISM   STRUCT
...POLICY MGT CONCPT CLASSIF. PAGE 26 B0523   SOC
                                                          GP/REL

B59
EPSTEIN F.T.,EAST GERMANY: A SELECTED BIBLIOGRAPHY   BIBLIOG/A
(PAMPHLET). COM GERMANY/E LAW AGRI FINAN INDUS   INTELL
LABOR POL/PAR EDU/PROP ADMIN AGE/Y 20. PAGE 33   MARXISM
B0677   NAT/G

B59
GINSBURG M.,LAW AND OPINION IN ENGLAND. UK CULTURE   JURID
KIN LABOR LEGIS EDU/PROP ADMIN CT/SYS CRIME OWN   POLICY

HEALTH...ANTHOL 20 ENGLSH/LAW. PAGE 40 B0802   ECO/TAC
                                                      B59
SAYER W.S.,AN AGENDA FOR RESEARCH IN PUBLIC   WORKER
PERSONNEL ADMINISTRATION. FUT USA+45 ACADEM LABOR   ADMIN
LOC/G NAT/G POL/PAR DELIB/GP MGT. PAGE 93 B1872   ACT/RES
                                                      CONSULT
                                                      B59
WARNER W.L.,INDUSTRIAL MAN. USA+45 USA-45 ELITES   EXEC
INDUS LABOR TOP/EX WORKER ADMIN INGP/REL PERS/REL   LEAD
...CHARTS ANTHOL 20. PAGE 114 B2294   PERSON
                                                      MGT
                                                      B60
BERNSTEIN I.,THE LEAN YEARS. SOCIETY STRATA PARTIC   WORKER
GP/REL ATTIT...SOC 20 DEPRESSION. PAGE 11 B0227   LABOR
                                                      WEALTH
                                                      MGT
                                                      B60
CRAUMER L.V.,BUSINESS PERIODICALS INDEX (8VOLS.).   BIBLIOG/A
USA+45 LABOR TAX 20. PAGE 25 B0503   FINAN
                                                      ECO/DEV
                                                      MGT
                                                      B60
DRAPER T.,AMERICAN COMMUNISM AND SOVIET RUSSIA.   COM
EUR+WWI USA+45 USSR INTELL AGRI COM/IND FINAN INDUS   POL/PAR
LABOR PROF/ORG VOL/ASSN PLAN TEC/DEV DOMIN EDU/PROP
ADMIN COERCE REV PERSON PWR...POLICY CONCPT MYTH
19/20. PAGE 30 B0617
                                                      B60
ELKOURI F.,HOW ARBITRATION WORKS (REV. ED.). LAW   MGT
INDUS BARGAIN 20. PAGE 33 B0667   LABOR
                                                      ADJUD
                                                      GP/REL
                                                      B60
FRYE R.J.,GOVERNMENT AND LABOR: THE ALABAMA   ADMIN
PROGRAM. USA+45 INDUS R+D LABOR WORKER BUDGET   LEGIS
EFFICIENCY AGE/Y HEALTH...CHARTS 20 ALABAMA.   LOC/G
PAGE 38 B0761   PROVS
                                                      B60
MOORE W.E.,LABOR COMMITMENT AND SOCIAL CHANGE IN   LABOR
DEVELOPING AREAS. SOCIETY STRATA ECO/UNDEV MARKET   ORD/FREE
VOL/ASSN WORKER AUTHORIT SKILL...MGT NAT/COMP   ATTIT
SOC/INTEG 20. PAGE 75 B1514   INDUS
                                                      S60
"THE EMERGING COMMON MARKETS IN LATIN AMERICA." FUT   FINAN
L/A+17C STRATA DIST/IND INDUS LABOR NAT/G LEGIS   ECO/UNDEV
ECO/TAC ADMIN RIGID/FLEX HEALTH...NEW/IDEA TIME/SEQ   INT/TRADE
OAS 20. PAGE 2 B0039
                                                      S60
MORALES C.J.,"TRADE AND ECONOMIC INTEGRATION IN   FINAN
LATIN AMERICA." FUT L/A+17C LAW STRATA ECO/UNDEV   INT/TRADE
DIST/IND INDUS LABOR NAT/G LEGIS ECO/TAC ADMIN   REGION
RIGID/FLEX WEALTH...CONCPT NEW/IDEA CONT/OBS
TIME/SEQ WORK 20. PAGE 75 B1519
                                                      S60
SCHER S.,"CONGRESSIONAL COMMITTEE MEMBERS AND   LEGIS
INDEPENDENT AGENCY OVERSEERS: A CASE STUDY."   GOV/REL
DELIB/GP EX/STRUC JUDGE TOP/EX DOMIN ADMIN CONTROL   LABOR
PWR...SOC/EXP HOUSE/REP CONGRESS. PAGE 93 B1886   ADJUD
                                                      S60
THOMPSON J.D.,"ORGANIZATIONAL MANAGEMENT OF   PROB/SOLV
CONFLICT" (BMR)" WOR+45 STRUCT LABOR LG/CO WORKER   PERS/REL
TEC/DEV INGP/REL ATTIT GP/COMP. PAGE 104 B2103   ADMIN
                                                      MGT
                                                      B61
BANFIELD E.C.,URBAN GOVERNMENT; A READER IN   MUNIC
POLITICS AND ADMINISTRATION. ELITES LABOR POL/PAR   GEN/METH
EXEC CHOOSE REPRESENT GP/REL PWR PLURISM...PSY SOC.   DECISION
PAGE 9 B0177
                                                      B61
BARRASH J.,LABOR'S GRASS ROOTS; A STUDY OF THE   LABOR
LOCAL UNION. STRATA BARGAIN LEAD REPRESENT DEMAND   USA+45
ATTIT PWR. PAGE 9 B0190   INGP/REL
                                                      EXEC
                                                      B61
BULLIS H.A.,MANIFESTO FOR AMERICANS. USA+45 AGRI   ECO/TAC
LABOR NAT/G NEIGH FOR/AID INT/TRADE TAX EDU/PROP   SOCIETY
CHOOSE...POLICY MGT 20 UN UNESCO. PAGE 17 B0342   INDUS
                                                      CAP/ISM
                                                      B61
CARROTHERS A.W.R.,LABOR ARBITRATION IN CANADA.   LABOR
CANADA LAW NAT/G CONSULT LEGIS WORKER ADJUD ADMIN   MGT
CT/SYS 20. PAGE 19 B0386   GP/REL
                                                      BARGAIN
                                                      B61
DUBIN R.,HUMAN RELATIONS IN ADMINISTRATION. USA+45   PERS/REL
INDUS LABOR LG/CO EX/STRUC GP/REL DRIVE PWR   MGT
...DECISION SOC CHARTS ANTHOL 20. PAGE 31 B0623   ADMIN
                                                      EXEC
                                                      B61
HAIRE M.,MODERN ORGANIZATION THEORY. LABOR ROUTINE   PERS/REL
MAJORITY...CONCPT MODAL OBS CONT/OBS. PAGE 45 B0919   GP/REL
                                                      MGT
                                                      DECISION
                                                      B61
HART W.R.,COLLECTIVE BARGAINING IN THE FEDERAL   INGP/REL
CIVIL SERVICE. NAT/G EX/STRUC ADMIN EXEC 20.   MGT

PAGE 47 B0961   REPRESENT
                                                      LABOR
                                                      B61
LENIN V.I.,WHAT IS TO BE DONE? (1902). RUSSIA LABOR   EDU/PROP
NAT/G POL/PAR WORKER CAP/ISM ECO/TAC ADMIN PARTIC   PRESS
...MARXIST IDEA/COMP GEN/LAWS 19/20. PAGE 64 B1292   MARXISM
                                                      METH/COMP
                                                      B61
MARX K.,THE COMMUNIST MANIFESTO. IN (MENDEL A.   COM
ESSENTIAL WORKS OF MARXISM, NEW YORK: BANTAM. FUT   NEW/IDEA
MOD/EUR CULTURE ECO/DEV ECO/UNDEV AGRI FINAN INDUS   CAP/ISM
MARKET PROC/MFG LABOR MUNIC POL/PAR CONSULT FORCES   REV
CREATE PLAN ADMIN ATTIT DRIVE RIGID/FLEX ORD/FREE
PWR RESPECT MARX/KARL WORK. PAGE 70 B1421
                                                      B62
GALENSON W.,LABOR IN DEVELOPING COUNTRIES. BRAZIL   LABOR
INDONESIA ISRAEL PAKISTAN TURKEY AGRI INDUS WORKER   ECO/UNDEV
PAY PRICE GP/REL WEALTH...MGT CHARTS METH/COMP   BARGAIN
NAT/COMP 20. PAGE 38 B0775   POL/PAR
                                                      B62
GRANICK D.,THE EUROPEAN EXECUTIVE. BELGIUM FRANCE   MGT
GERMANY/W UK INDUS LABOR LG/CO SML/CO EX/STRUC PLAN   ECO/DEV
TEC/DEV CAP/ISM COST DEMAND...POLICY CHARTS 20.   ECO/TAC
PAGE 42 B0852   EXEC
                                                      B62
INTERNATIONAL LABOR OFFICE,WORKERS' MANAGEMENT IN   WORKER
YUGOSLAVIA. COM YUGOSLAVIA LABOR DELIB/GP EX/STRUC   CONTROL
PROB/SOLV ADMIN PWR MARXISM...CHARTS ORG/CHARTS   MGT
BIBLIOG 20. PAGE 54 B1098   INDUS
                                                      B62
LIPPMANN W.,PREFACE TO POLITICS. LABOR CHIEF   PARTIC
CONTROL LEAD...MYTH IDEA/COMP 19/20 ROOSEVLT/T   ATTIT
TAMMANY WILSON/H SANTAYAN/G BERGSON/H. PAGE 65   ADMIN
B1318
                                                      B62
MUNICIPAL MANPOWER COMMISSION,GOVERNMENTAL MANPOWER   LOC/G
FOR TOMORROW'S CITIES: A REPORT. USA+45 DELIB/GP   MUNIC
EX/STRUC PROB/SOLV TEC/DEV EDU/PROP ADMIN LEAD   LABOR
HABITAT. PAGE 76 B1539   GOV/REL
                                                      B62
SRIVASTAVA G.L.,COLLECTIVE BARGAINING AND LABOR-   LABOR
MANAGEMENT RELATIONS IN INDIA. INDIA UK USA+45   MGT
INDUS LEGIS WORKER ADJUD EFFICIENCY PRODUC   BARGAIN
...METH/COMP 20. PAGE 100 B2014   GP/REL
                                                      B62
TAYLOR J.K.L.,ATTITUDES AND METHODS OF   WORKER
COMMUNICATION AND CONSULTATION BETWEEN EMPLOYERS   ADMIN
AND WORKERS AT INDIVIDUAL FIRM LEVEL. WOR+45 STRUCT   ATTIT
INDUS LABOR CONFER TASK GP/REL EFFICIENCY...MGT   EDU/PROP
BIBLIOG METH 20 OECD. PAGE 103 B2087
                                                      S62
BOOTH D.A.,"POWER STRUCTURE AND COMMUNITY CHANGE: A   MUNIC
REPLICATION STUDY OF COMMUNITY A." STRATA LABOR   ELITES
LEAD PARTIC REPRESENT...DECISION MGT TIME. PAGE 14   PWR
B0275
                                                      S62
IKLE F.C.,"POLITICAL NEGOTIATION AS A PROCESS OF   ROUTINE
MODIFYING UTILITIES." WOR+45 FACE/GP LABOR NAT/G   DECISION
FORCES ACT/RES EDU/PROP DETER PERCEPT ALL/VALS   DIPLOM
...PSY NEW/IDEA HYPO/EXP GEN/METH 20. PAGE 53 B1076
                                                      B63
BANFIELD E.C.,CITY POLITICS. CULTURE LABOR LOC/G   MUNIC
POL/PAR LEGIS EXEC LEAD CHOOSE...DECISION NEGRO.   RIGID/FLEX
PAGE 9 B0178   ATTIT
                                                      B63
COM INTERNAT DES MOUVEMENTS,REPERTOIRE   BIBLIOG/A
INTERNATIONAL DES SOURCES POUR L'ETUDE DES   MARXISM
MOUVEMENTS SOCIAUX AUX XIXE ET XXE SIECLES (VOL.   POL/PAR
III). MOD/EUR ADMIN...SOC 19. PAGE 22 B0454   LABOR
                                                      B63
GOURNAY B.,PUBLIC ADMINISTRATION. FRANCE LAW CONSTN   BIBLIOG/A
AGRI FINAN LABOR SCHOOL EX/STRUC CHOOSE...MGT   ADMIN
METH/COMP 20. PAGE 42 B0846   NAT/G
                                                      LOC/G
                                                      B63
MEYNAUD J.,PLANIFICATION ET POLITIQUE. FRANCE ITALY   PLAN
FINAN LABOR DELIB/GP LEGIS ADMIN EFFICIENCY   ECO/TAC
...MAJORIT DECISION 20. PAGE 73 B1477   PROB/SOLV
                                                      B63
ROBERT J.,LA MONARCHIE MAROCAINE. MOROCCO LABOR   CHIEF
MUNIC POL/PAR EX/STRUC ORD/FREE PWR...JURID TREND T   CONSERVE
20. PAGE 89 B1793   ADMIN
                                                      CONSTN
                                                      B63
SCHOECK H.,THE NEW ARGUMENT IN ECONOMICS. UK USA+45   WELF/ST
INDUS MARKET LABOR NAT/G ECO/TAC ADMIN ROUTINE   FOR/AID
BAL/PAY PWR...POLICY BOLIV. PAGE 94 B1899   ECO/DEV
                                                      ALL/IDEOS
                                                      L63
LIVERNASH E.R.,"THE RELATION OF POWER TO THE   LABOR
STRUCTURE AND PROCESS OF COLLECTIVE BARGAINING."   GP/REL
ADJUD ORD/FREE...POLICY MGT CLASSIF GP/COMP.   PWR
PAGE 66 B1330   ECO/TAC
                                                      S63
COUTY P.,"L'ASSISTANCE POUR LE DEVELOPPEMENT: POINT   FINAN
DE VUE SCANDINAVES." EUR+WWI FINLAND FUT SWEDEN   ROUTINE

WOR+45 ECO/DEV ECO/UNDEV COM/IND LABOR NAT/G   FOR/AID
PROF/ORG ACT/RES SKILL WEALTH TOT/POP 20. PAGE 24
B0497

S63

REES A.,"THE EFFECTS OF UNIONS ON RESOURCE   LABOR
ALLOCATION." USA+45 WORKER PRICE CONTROL GP/REL   BARGAIN
...MGT METH/COMP 20. PAGE 87 B1761   RATION
                                                       INCOME

B64

CHANDLER A.D. JR.,GIANT ENTERPRISE: FORD, GENERAL   LG/CO
MOTORS, AND THE AUTOMOBILE INDUSTRY; SOURCES AND   DIST/IND
READINGS. USA+45 USA-45 FINAN MARKET CREATE ADMIN   LABOR
...TIME/SEQ ANTHOL 20 AUTOMOBILE. PAGE 20 B0404   MGT

B64

FAINSOD M.,HOW RUSSIA IS RULED (REV. ED.). RUSSIA   NAT/G
USSR AGRI PROC/MFG LABOR POL/PAR EX/STRUC CONTROL   REV
PWR...POLICY BIBLIOG 19/20 KHRUSH/N COM/PARTY.   MARXISM
PAGE 34 B0700

B64

GESELLSCHAFT RECHTSVERGLEICH,BIBLIOGRAPHIE DES   BIBLIOG/A
DEUTSCHEN RECHTS (BIBLIOGRAPHY OF GERMAN LAW,   JURID
TRANS. BY COURTLAND PETERSON). GERMANY FINAN INDUS   CONSTN
LABOR SECT FORCES CT/SYS PARL/PROC CRIME...INT/LAW   ADMIN
SOC NAT/COMP 20. PAGE 39 B0794

B64

GUTTSMAN W.L.,THE BRITISH POLITICAL ELITE. EUR+WWI   NAT/G
MOD/EUR STRATA FAM LABOR POL/PAR SCHOOL VOL/ASSN   SOC
DELIB/GP LEGIS LEGIT EXEC CHOOSE ATTIT ALL/VALS   UK
...STAT BIOG TIME/SEQ CHARTS VAL/FREE. PAGE 45   ELITES
B0905

B64

HAMBRIDGE G.,DYNAMICS OF DEVELOPMENT. AGRI FINAN   ECO/UNDEV
INDUS LABOR INT/TRADE EDU/PROP ADMIN LEAD OWN   ECO/TAC
HEALTH...ANTHOL BIBLIOG 20. PAGE 46 B0930   OP/RES
                                                       ACT/RES

B64

LI C.M.,INDUSTRIAL DEVELOPMENT IN COMMUNIST CHINA.   ASIA
CHINA/COM ECO/DEV ECO/UNDEV AGRI FINAN INDUS MARKET   TEC/DEV
LABOR NAT/G ECO/TAC INT/TRADE EXEC ALL/VALS
...POLICY RELATIV TREND WORK TOT/POP VAL/FREE 20.
PAGE 65 B1311

B64

POPPINO R.E.,INTERNATIONAL COMMUNISM IN LATIN   MARXISM
AMERICA: A HISTORY OF THE MOVEMENT 1917-1963.   POL/PAR
CHINA/COM USSR INTELL STRATA LABOR WORKER ADMIN REV   L/A+17C
ATTIT...POLICY 20 COLD/WAR. PAGE 84 B1692

B64

WERNETTE J.P.,GOVERNMENT AND BUSINESS. LABOR   NAT/G
CAP/ISM ECO/TAC INT/TRADE TAX ADMIN AUTOMAT NUC/PWR   FINAN
CIVMIL/REL DEMAND...MGT 20 MONOPOLY. PAGE 115 B2323   ECO/DEV
                                                       CONTROL

S64

FLORINSKY M.T.,"TRENDS IN THE SOVIET ECONOMY." COM   ECO/DEV
USA+45 USSR INDUS LABOR NAT/G PLAN TEC/DEV ECO/TAC   AGRI
ALL/VALS SOCISM...MGT METH/CNCPT STYLE CON/ANAL
GEN/METH WORK 20. PAGE 36 B0731

C64

NORGREN P.H.,"TOWARD FAIR EMPLOYMENT." USA+45 LAW   RACE/REL
STRATA LABOR NAT/G FORCES ACT/RES ADMIN ATTIT   DISCRIM
...POLICY BIBLIOG 20 NEGRO. PAGE 79 B1588   WORKER
                                                       MGT

N64

CANADA NATL JT COUN PUB SERV,THE CANADA NATIONAL   GP/REL
JOINT COUNCIL OF THE PUBLIC SERVICE 1944-1964   NAT/G
(PAMPHLET). CANADA EX/STRUC PERS/REL DRIVE...MGT 20   LABOR
PEARSON/L. PAGE 18 B0373   EFFICIENCY

B65

AIYAR S.P.,STUDIES IN INDIAN DEMOCRACY. INDIA   ORD/FREE
STRATA ECO/UNDEV LABOR POL/PAR LEGIS DIPLOM LOBBY   REPRESENT
REGION CHOOSE ATTIT SOCISM...ANTHOL 20. PAGE 3   ADMIN
B0067   NAT/G

B65

COPELAND M.A.,OUR FREE ENTERPRISE ECONOMY. USA+45   CAP/ISM
INDUS LABOR ADMIN CONTROL GP/REL MGT. PAGE 23 B0476   PLAN
                                                       FINAN
                                                       ECO/DEV

B65

CUTLIP S.M.,A PUBLIC RELATIONS BIBLIOGRAPHY. INDUS   BIBLIOG/A
LABOR NAT/G PROF/ORG SCHOOL DIPLOM PRESS TV GOV/REL   MGT
GP/REL...PSY SOC/WK 20. PAGE 25 B0515   COM/IND
                                                       ADMIN

B65

EDELMAN M.,THE POLITICS OF WAGE-PRICE DECISIONS.   GOV/COMP
GERMANY ITALY NETHERLAND UK INDUS LABOR POL/PAR   CONTROL
PROB/SOLV BARGAIN PRICE ROUTINE BAL/PAY COST DEMAND   ECO/TAC
20. PAGE 32 B0654   PLAN

B65

GOULDNER A.W.,STUDIES IN LEADERSHIP. LABOR EDU/PROP   LEAD
CONTROL PARTIC...CONCPT CLASSIF. PAGE 42 B0845   ADMIN
                                                       AUTHORIT

B65

LEYS C.T.,FEDERATION IN EAST AFRICA. LAW AGRI   FEDERAL
DIST/IND FINAN INT/ORG LABOR INT/TRADE CONFER ADMIN   REGION
CONTROL GP/REL...ANTHOL 20 AFRICA/E. PAGE 65 B1310   ECO/UNDEV
                                                       PLAN

B65

PAYNE J.L.,LABOR AND POLITICS IN PERU; THE SYSTEM   LABOR
OF POLITICAL BARGAINING. PERU CONSTN VOL/ASSN   POL/PAR
EX/STRUC LEAD PWR...CHARTS 20. PAGE 81 B1645   BARGAIN
                                                       GP/REL

B65

PURCELL V.,THE MEMOIRS OF A MALAYAN OFFICIAL.   BIOG
MALAYSIA UK ECO/UNDEV INDUS LABOR EDU/PROP COLONIAL   ADMIN
CT/SYS WAR NAT/LISM TOTALISM ORD/FREE SOVEREIGN 20   JURID
UN CIVIL/SERV. PAGE 85 B1721   FORCES

B65

ROSS P.,THE GOVERNMENT AS A SOURCE OF UNION POWER.   LABOR
USA+45 LAW ECO/DEV PROB/SOLV ECO/TAC LEAD GP/REL   BARGAIN
...MGT 20. PAGE 90 B1826   POLICY
                                                       NAT/G

B65

US HOUSE COMM EDUC AND LABOR,ADMINISTRATION OF THE   ADMIN
NATIONAL LABOR RELATIONS ACT. USA+45 DELIB/GP   LABOR
WORKER PROB/SOLV BARGAIN PAY CONTROL 20 NLRB   GP/REL
CONGRESS. PAGE 108 B2188   INDUS

B65

VAID K.N.,STATE AND LABOR IN INDIA. INDIA INDUS   LAW
WORKER PAY PRICE ADJUD CONTROL PARL/PROC GP/REL   LABOR
ORD/FREE 20. PAGE 111 B2248   MGT
                                                       NEW/LIB

B65

WALTON R.E.,A BEHAVIORAL THEORY OF LABOR   SOC
NEGOTIATIONS: AN ANALYSIS OF A SOCIAL INTERACTION   LABOR
SYSTEM. USA+45 FINAN PROB/SOLV ECO/TAC GP/REL   BARGAIN
INGP/REL...DECISION BIBLIOG. PAGE 113 B2285   ADMIN

L65

MATTHEWS D.G.,"A CURRENT BIBLIOGRAPHY ON ETHIOPIAN   BIBLIOG/A
AFFAIRS: A SELECT BIBLIOGRAPHY FROM 1950-1964."   ADMIN
ETHIOPIA LAW CULTURE ECO/UNDEV INDUS LABOR SECT   POL/PAR
FORCES DIPLOM CIVMIL/REL RACE/REL...LING STAT 20.   NAT/G
PAGE 71 B1428

S65

HAMILTON R.F.,"SKILL LEVEL AND POLITICS." USA+45   SKILL
CULTURE STRATA STRUCT LABOR CONSERVE NEW/LIB.   ADMIN
PAGE 46 B0933

B66

BAKKE E.W.,MUTUAL SURVIVAL; THE GOAL OF UNION AND   MGT
MANAGEMENT (2ND ED.). USA+45 ELITES ECO/DEV ECO/TAC   LABOR
CONFER ADMIN REPRESENT GP/REL INGP/REL ATTIT   BARGAIN
...GP/COMP 20. PAGE 8 B0170   INDUS

B66

DILLEY M.R.,BRITISH POLICY IN KENYA COLONY (2ND   COLONIAL
ED.). AFR INDIA UK LABOR BUDGET TAX ADMIN PARL/PROC   REPRESENT
GP/REL...BIBLIOG 20 PARLIAMENT. PAGE 29 B0594   SOVEREIGN

B66

LINDFORS G.V.,INTERCOLLEGIATE BIBLIOGRAPHY; CASES   BIBLIOG/A
IN BUSINESS ADMINISTRATION (VOL. X). FINAN MARKET   ADMIN
LABOR CONSULT PLAN GP/REL PRODUC 20. PAGE 65 B1314   MGT
                                                       OP/RES

B66

ONYEMELUKWE C.C.,PROBLEMS OF INDUSTRIAL PLANNING   ECO/UNDEV
AND MANAGEMENT IN NIGERIA. AFR FINAN LABOR DELIB/GP   ECO/TAC
TEC/DEV ADJUST...MGT TREND BIBLIOG. PAGE 80 B1610   INDUS
                                                       PLAN

B66

SMITH H.E.,READINGS IN ECONOMIC DEVELOPMENT AND   TEC/DEV
ADMINISTRATION IN TANZANIA. TANZANIA FINAN INDUS   ADMIN
LABOR NAT/G PLAN PROB/SOLV INT/TRADE COLONIAL   GOV/REL
REGION...ANTHOL BIBLIOG 20 AFRICA/E. PAGE 98 B1981

B66

SZLADITS C.,A BIBLIOGRAPHY ON FOREIGN AND   BIBLIOG/A
COMPARATIVE LAW (SUPPLEMENT 1964). FINAN FAM LABOR   CT/SYS
LG/CO LEGIS JUDGE ADMIN CRIME...CRIMLGY 20.   INT/LAW
PAGE 102 B2066

B66

WASHINGTON S.H.,BIBLIOGRAPHY: LABOR-MANAGEMENT   BIBLIOG
RELATIONS ACT, 1947 AS AMENDED BY LABOR-MANAGEMENT   LAW
REPORTING AND DISCLOSURE ACT, 1959. USA+45 CONSTN   LABOR
INDUS DELIB/GP LEGIS WORKER BARGAIN ECO/TAC ADJUD   MGT
GP/REL NEW/LIB...JURID CONGRESS. PAGE 114 B2298

L66

AMERICAN ECONOMIC REVIEW,"SIXTY-THIRD LIST OF   BIBLIOG/A
DOCTORAL DISSERTATIONS IN POLITICAL ECONOMY IN   CONCPT
AMERICAN UNIVERSITIES AND COLLEGES." ECO/DEV AGRI   ACADEM
FINAN LABOR WORKER PLAN BUDGET INT/TRADE ADMIN
DEMAND...MGT STAT 20. PAGE 4 B0084

S66

AFRICAN BIBLIOGRAPHIC CENTER,"A CURRENT VIEW OF   BIBLIOG/A
AFRICANA: A SELECT AND ANNOTATED BIBLIOGRAPHICAL   NAT/G
PUBLISHING GUIDE, 1965-1966." AFR CULTURE INDUS   TEC/DEV
LABOR SECT FOR/AID ADMIN COLONIAL REV RACE/REL   POL/PAR
SOCISM...LING 20. PAGE 3 B0063

S66

JACOBSON J.,"COALITIONISM: FROM PROTEST TO   RACE/REL
POLITICKING" USA+45 ELITES NAT/G POL/PAR PROB/SOLV   LABOR
ADMIN LEAD DISCRIM ORD/FREE PWR CONSERVE 20 NEGRO   SOCIALIST
AFL/CIO CIV/RIGHTS BLACK/PWR. PAGE 55 B1116   VOL/ASSN

S66

MATTHEWS D.G.,"ETHIOPIAN OUTLINE: A BIBLIOGRAPHIC   BIBLIOG
RESEARCH GUIDE." ETHIOPIA LAW STRUCT ECO/UNDEV AGRI   NAT/G
LABOR SECT CHIEF DELIB/GP EX/STRUC ADMIN...LING   DIPLOM

ORG/CHARTS 20. PAGE 71 B1429   POL/PAR

N66
PRINCETON U INDUSTRIAL REL SEC,OUTSTANDING BOOKS ON   BIBLIOG/A
INDUSTRIAL RELATIONS, 1965 (PAMPHLET NO. 128).   INDUS
WOR+45 LABOR BARGAIN GOV/REL RACE/REL HEALTH PWR   GP/REL
...MGT 20. PAGE 85 B1709   POLICY

N66
PRINCETON U INDUSTRIAL REL SEC,RECENT MATERIAL ON   BIBLIOG/A
COLLECTIVE BARGAINING IN GOVERNMENT (PAMPHLET NO.   BARGAIN
130). USA+45 ECO/DEV LABOR WORKER ECO/TAC GOV/REL   NAT/G
...MGT 20. PAGE 85 B1710   GP/REL

B67
ANGEL D.D.,ROMNEY. LABOR LG/CO NAT/G EXEC WAR   BIOG
RACE/REL PERSON ORD/FREE...MGT WORSHIP 20   CHIEF
ROMNEY/GEO CIV/RIGHTS MORMON GOVERNOR. PAGE 5 B0108   PROVS
                                                       POLICY

B67
BUDER S.,PULLMAN: AN EXPERIMENT IN INDUSTRIAL ORDER   DIST/IND
AND COMMUNITY PLANNING, 1880-1930. USA-45 SOCIETY   INDUS
LABOR LG/CO CREATE PROB/SOLV CONTROL GP/REL   MUNIC
EFFICIENCY ATTIT...MGT BIBLIOG 19/20 PULLMAN.   PLAN
PAGE 17 B0337

B67
GREENE L.S.,AMERICAN GOVERNMENT POLICIES AND   POLICY
FUNCTIONS. USA+45 LAW AGRI DIST/IND LABOR MUNIC   NAT/G
BUDGET DIPLOM EDU/PROP ORD/FREE...BIBLIOG T 20.   ADMIN
PAGE 43 B0867   DECISION

B67
NORTHRUP H.R.,RESTRICTIVE LABOR PRACTICES IN THE   DIST/IND
SUPERMARKET INDUSTRY. USA+45 INDUS WORKER TEC/DEV   MARKET
BARGAIN PAY CONTROL GP/REL COST...STAT CHARTS NLRB.   LABOR
PAGE 79 B1592   MGT

B67
SABLE M.H.,A GUIDE TO LATIN AMERICAN STUDIES (2   BIBLIOG/A
VOLS). CONSTN FINAN INT/ORG LABOR MUNIC POL/PAR   L/A+17C
FORCES CAP/ISM FOR/AID ADMIN MARXISM SOCISM OAS.   DIPLOM
PAGE 92 B1861   NAT/LISM

B67
SCHLOSSBERG S.I.,ORGANIZING AND THE LAW. USA+45   LABOR
WORKER PLAN LEGIT REPRESENT GP/REL...JURID MGT 20   CONSULT
NLRB. PAGE 94 B1893   BARGAIN
                                                       PRIVIL

B67
US SENATE COMM ON FOREIGN REL,HUMAN RIGHTS   LEGIS
CONVENTIONS. USA+45 LABOR VOL/ASSN DELIB/GP DOMIN   ORD/FREE
ADJUD REPRESENT...INT/LAW MGT CONGRESS. PAGE 110   WORKER
B2225   LOBBY

B67
ZELERMYER W.,BUSINESS LAW: NEW PERSPECTIVES IN   LABOR
BUSINESS ECONOMICS. USA+45 LAW INDUS DELIB/GP   CAP/ISM
...JURID MGT ANTHOL BIBLIOG 20 NLRB. PAGE 119 B2400   LG/CO

L67
BERGER R.,"ADMINISTRATIVE ARBITRARINESS* A SEQUEL."   LAW
USA+45 CONSTN ADJUD CT/SYS SANCTION INGP/REL   LABOR
...POLICY JURID. PAGE 11 B0222   BARGAIN
                                                       ADMIN

L67
GOULD W.B.,"THE STATUS OF UNAUTHORIZED AND   ECO/DEV
'WILDCAT' STRIKES UNDER THE NATIONAL LABOR   INDUS
RELATIONS ACT." USA+45 ACT/RES BARGAIN ECO/TAC   LABOR
LEGIT ADJUD ADMIN GP/REL MGT. PAGE 42 B0842   POLICY

S67
BERRODIN E.F.,"AT THE BARGAINING TABLE." LABOR   PROVS
DIPLOM ECO/TAC ADMIN...MGT 20 MICHIGAN. PAGE 11   WORKER
B0230   LAW
                                                       BARGAIN

S67
CHAMBERLAIN N.W.,"STRIKES IN CONTEMPORARY CONTEXT."   LABOR
LAW INDUS NAT/G CHIEF CONFER COST ATTIT ORD/FREE   BARGAIN
...POLICY MGT 20. PAGE 20 B0400   EFFICIENCY
                                                       PROB/SOLV

S67
DRAPER A.P.,"UNIONS AND THE WAR IN VIETNAM." USA+45   LABOR
CONFER ADMIN LEAD WAR ORD/FREE PACIFIST 20. PAGE 30   PACIFISM
B0616   ATTIT
                                                       ELITES

S67
HALL B.,"THE PAINTER'S UNION: A PARTIAL VICTORY."   LABOR
USA+45 PROB/SOLV LEGIT ADMIN REPRESENT 20. PAGE 45   CHIEF
B0922   CHOOSE
                                                       CRIME

S67
HALL B.,"THE COALITION AGAINST DISHWASHERS." USA+45   LABOR
POL/PAR PROB/SOLV BARGAIN LEAD CHOOSE REPRESENT   ADMIN
GP/REL ORD/FREE PWR...POLICY 20. PAGE 46 B0923   DOMIN
                                                       WORKER

S67
HUDDLESTON J.,"TRADE UNIONS IN THE GERMAN FEDERAL   LABOR
REPUBLIC." EUR+WWI GERMANY/W UK LAW INDUS WORKER   GP/REL
CREATE CENTRAL...MGT GP/COMP 20. PAGE 52 B1056   SCHOOL
                                                       ROLE

S67
JENCKS C.E.,"SOCIAL STATUS OF COAL MINERS IN   EXTR/IND
BRITAIN SINCE NATIONALIZATION." UK STRATA STRUCT   WORKER
LABOR RECEIVE GP/REL INCOME OWN ATTIT HABITAT...MGT   CONTROL
T 20. PAGE 56 B1128   NAT/G

S67
LASLETT J.H.M.,"SOCIALISM AND THE AMERICAN LABOR   LABOR
MOVEMENT* SOME NEW REFLECTIONS." USA-45 VOL/ASSN   ROUTINE
LOBBY PARTIC CENTRAL ALL/VALS SOCISM...GP/COMP 20.   ATTIT
PAGE 63 B1265   GP/REL

S67
LENDVAI P.,"HUNGARY* CHANGE VS. IMMOBILISM."   ECO/DEV
HUNGARY LABOR NAT/G PLAN DEBATE ADMIN ROUTINE   MGT
CENTRAL EFFICIENCY MARXISM PLURISM...PREDICT 20.   CHOOSE
PAGE 64 B1289

S67
LERNER A.P.,"EMPLOYMENT THEORY AND EMPLOYMENT   CAP/ISM
POLICY." ECO/DEV INDUS LABOR LG/CO BUDGET ADMIN   WORKER
DEMAND PROFIT WEALTH LAISSEZ METH/COMP. PAGE 64   CONCPT
B1296

S67
MELTZER B.D.,"RUMINATIONS ABOUT IDEOLOGY, LAW, AND   JURID
LABOR ARBITRATION." USA+45 ECO/DEV PROB/SOLV CONFER   ADJUD
MGT. PAGE 73 B1466   LABOR
                                                       CONSULT

S67
ZOETEWEIJ B.,"INCOME POLICIES ABROAD: AN INTERIM   METH/COMP
REPORT." NAT/G PROB/SOLV BARGAIN BUDGET PRICE RISK   INCOME
CENTRAL EFFICIENCY EQUILIB...MGT NAT/COMP 20.   POLICY
PAGE 119 B2405   LABOR

N67
PRINCETON U INDUSTRIAL REL SEC,OUTSTANDING BOOKS ON   BIBLIOG/A
INDUSTRIAL RELATIONS, 1966 (PAMPHLET NO. 134).   INDUS
WOR+45 LABOR WORKER PLAN PRICE CONTROL INCOME...MGT   GP/REL
20. PAGE 85 B1711   POLICY

S68
GUZZARDI W. JR.,"THE SECOND BATTLE OF BRITAIN." UK   FINAN
STRATA LABOR WORKER CREATE PROB/SOLV EDU/PROP ADMIN   ECO/TAC
LEAD LOBBY...MGT SOC 20 GOLD/STAND. PAGE 45 B0907   ECO/DEV
                                                       STRUCT

LABOR/PAR....LABOR PARTY (ALL NATIONS)

B40
MCHENRY D.E.,HIS MAJESTY'S OPPOSITION: STRUCTURE   POL/PAR
AND PROBLEMS OF THE BRITISH LABOUR PARTY 1931-1938.   MGT
UK FINAN LABOR LOC/G DELIB/GP LEGIS EDU/PROP LEAD   NAT/G
PARTIC CHOOSE GP/REL SOCISM...TREND 20 LABOR/PAR.   POLICY
PAGE 72 B1450

B50
MCHENRY D.E.,THE THIRD FORCE IN CANADA: THE   POL/PAR
COOPERATIVE COMMONWEALTH FEDERATION, 1932-1948.   ADMIN
CANADA EX/STRUC LEGIS REPRESENT 20 LABOR/PAR.   CHOOSE
PAGE 72 B1451   POLICY

LABORATORY EXPERIMENTS....SEE LAB/EXP

LAFTA....LATIN AMERICAN FREE TRADE ASSOCIATION; SEE ALSO
    INT/ORG, VOL/ASSN, INT/TRADE

L64
HAAS E.B.,"ECONOMICS AND DIFFERENTIAL PATTERNS OF   L/A+17C
POLITICAL INTEGRATION: PROJECTIONS ABOUT UNITY IN   INT/ORG
LATIN AMERICA." SOCIETY NAT/G DELIB/GP ACT/RES   MARKET
CREATE PLAN ECO/TAC REGION ROUTINE ATTIT DRIVE PWR
WEALTH...CONCPT TREND CHARTS LAFTA 20. PAGE 45
B0910

LAGUARD/F....FIORELLO LAGUARDIA

B38
SALTER J.T.,THE AMERICAN POLITICIAN. USA-45 LABOR   BIOG
POL/PAR EDU/PROP ADMIN CHOOSE ATTIT DRIVE PERSON   LEAD
PWR...POLICY ANTHOL 20 THOMAS/N LEWIS/JL LAGUARD/F   PROVS
GOVERNOR MAYOR. PAGE 92 B1865   LOC/G

LAHAYE R. B1250

LAISSEZ....LAISSEZ-FAIRE-ISM; SEE ALSO OLD/LIB

B28
CALKINS E.E.,BUSINESS THE CIVILIZER. INDUS MARKET   LAISSEZ
WORKER TAX PAY ROUTINE COST DEMAND MORAL 19/20.   POLICY
PAGE 18 B0367   WEALTH
                                                       PROFIT

B45
MAYO E.,THE SOCIAL PROBLEMS OF AN INDUSTRIAL   INDUS
CIVILIZATION. USA+45 SOCIETY LABOR CROWD PERS/REL   GP/REL
LAISSEZ. PAGE 71 B1438   MGT
                                                       WORKER

S50
NEUMANN F.L.,"APPROACHES TO THE STUDY OF POLITICAL   PWR
POWER." POL/PAR TOP/EX ADMIN LEAD ATTIT ORD/FREE   IDEA/COMP
CONSERVE LAISSEZ MARXISM...PSY SOC. PAGE 78 B1572   CONCPT

B58
WHITE L.D.,THE REPUBLICAN ERA: 1869-1901, A STUDY   MGT
IN ADMINISTRATIVE HISTORY. USA-45 FINAN PLAN   PWR
NEUTRAL CRIME GP/REL MORAL LAISSEZ PRESIDENT   DELIB/GP
REFORMERS 19 CONGRESS CIVIL/SERV. PAGE 116 B2340   ADMIN

B61
CARNEY D.E.,GOVERNMENT AND ECONOMY IN BRITISH WEST   METH/COMP

AFRICA. GAMBIA GHANA NIGERIA SIER/LEONE DOMIN ADMIN | COLONIAL
GOV/REL SOVEREIGN WEALTH LAISSEZ...BIBLIOG 20 | ECO/TAC
CMN/WLTH. PAGE 19 B0384 | ECO/UNDEV

L63
BOLGAR V.,"THE PUBLIC INTEREST: A JURISPRUDENTIAL | CONCPT
AND COMPARATIVE OVERVIEW OF SYMPOSIUM ON | ORD/FREE
FUNDAMENTAL CONCEPTS OF PUBLIC LAW" COM FRANCE | CONTROL
GERMANY SWITZERLND LAW ADJUD ADMIN AGREE LAISSEZ | NAT/COMP
...JURID GEN/LAWS 20 EUROPE/E. PAGE 13 B0268

B65
MEISEL J.H.,PARETO & MOSCA. ITALY STRUCT ADMIN | PWR
...SOC CON/ANAL ANTHOL BIBLIOG 19/20. PAGE 72 B1463 | ELITES
CONTROL
LAISSEZ

B67
JHANGIANI M.A.,JANA SANGH AND SWATANTRA: A PROFILE | POL/PAR
OF THE RIGHTIST PARTIES IN INDIA. INDIA ADMIN | LAISSEZ
CHOOSE MARXISM SOCISM...INT CHARTS BIBLIOG 20. | NAT/LISM
PAGE 56 B1140 | ATTIT

S67
LERNER A.P.,"EMPLOYMENT THEORY AND EMPLOYMENT | CAP/ISM
POLICY." ECO/DEV INDUS LABOR LG/CO BUDGET ADMIN | WORKER
DEMAND PROFIT WEALTH LAISSEZ METH/COMP. PAGE 64 | CONCPT
B1296

LAKEWOOD....LAKEWOOD, CALIFORNIA

LAKOFF/SA....SANFORD A. LAKOFF

LALL B.G. B1251

LAMBIRI I. B1252

LANCASTER L.W. B1253

LAND REFORM....SEE AGRI + CREATE

LAND/LEAG....LAND LEAGUE (IRELAND)

LAND/VALUE....LAND VALUE TAX

LANDAU J.M. B1254

LANDES W.M. B1255

LANDRAT....COUNTY CHIEF EXECUTIVE (GERMANY)

S49
STEINMETZ H.,"THE PROBLEMS OF THE LANDRAT: A STUDY | LOC/G
OF COUNTY GOVERNMENT IN THE US ZONE OF GERMANY." | COLONIAL
GERMANY/W USA+45 INDUS PLAN DIPLOM EDU/PROP CONTROL | MGT
WAR GOV/REL FEDERAL WEALTH PLURISM...GOV/COMP 20 | TOP/EX
LANDRAT. PAGE 100 B2031

LANDRM/GRF....LANDRUM-GRIFFIN ACT

LANDRUM-GRIFFIN ACT....SEE LANDRM/GRF

LANE E. B1256

LANFALUSSY A. B1257

LANGE O. B1258

LANGLEY....LANGLEY-PORTER NEUROPSYCHIATRIC INSTITUTE

B62
ROBINSON M.,THE COMING OF AGE OF THE LANGLEY PORTER | PUB/INST
CLINIC (PAMPHLET). USA+45 PROF/ORG PROVS PLAN...MGT | ADMIN
PSY 20 CALIFORNIA LANGLEY. PAGE 89 B1804 | EFFICIENCY
HEAL

LANGROD G. B1259

LANGUAGE....SEE LING, ALSO LOGIC, MATHEMATICS, AND
LANGUAGE INDEX, P. XIV

LANGUEDOC....LANGUEDOC, SOUTHERN FRANCE

LAO/TZU....LAO TZU

LAOS....SEE ALSO S/ASIA

B59
US HOUSE COMM GOVT OPERATIONS,UNITED STATES AID | FOR/AID
OPERATIONS IN LAOS. LAOS USA+45 PLAN INSPECT | ADMIN
HOUSE/REP. PAGE 108 B2190 | FORCES
ECO/UNDEV

B60
PENTONY D.E.,UNITED STATES FOREIGN AID. INDIA LAOS | FOR/AID
USA+45 ECO/UNDEV INT/TRADE ADMIN PEACE ATTIT | DIPLOM
...POLICY METH/COMP ANTHOL 20. PAGE 82 B1653 | ECO/TAC

S66
AUSLAND J.C.,"CRISIS MANAGEMENT* BERLIN, CYPRUS, | OP/RES
LAOS." CYPRUS LAOS FORCES CREATE PLAN EDU/PROP TASK | DIPLOM
CENTRAL PERSON RIGID/FLEX...DECISION MGT 20 BERLIN | RISK

KENNEDY/JF MCNAMARA/R RUSK. PAGE 7 B0148 | ADMIN

C66
TARLING N.,"A CONCISE HISTORY OF SOUTHEAST ASIA." | COLONIAL
BURMA CAMBODIA LAOS S/ASIA THAILAND VIETNAM | DOMIN
ECO/UNDEV POL/PAR FORCES ADMIN REV WAR CIVMIL/REL | INT/TRADE
ORD/FREE MARXISM SOCISM 13/20. PAGE 103 B2080 | NAT/LISM

LAPIERRE R.T. B1260

LAQUEUR W.Z. B1261

LARCENY....LARCENY

LARSEN K. B1262

LARSON R.L. B1263

LARTEH....LARTEH, GHANA

LASKI/H....HAROLD LASKI

LASLETT J.H.M. B1265

LASSALLE/F....FERDINAND LASSALLE

LASSWELL H.D. B1266,B1267,B1268,B1269,B1270,B1271,B1272,B1273,
B1297,B1847

LASSWELL/H....HAROLD D. LASSWELL

LATHAM E. B1274

LATIMER E.W. B1275

LATIN AMERICA....SEE L/A+17C

LATIN AMERICAN FREE TRADE ASSOCIATION....SEE LAFTA

LATVIA....SEE ALSO USSR

B63
KLESMENT J.,LEGAL SOURCES AND BIBLIOGRAPHY OF THE | BIBLIOG/A
BALTIC STATES (ESTONIA, LATVIA, LITHUANIA). COM | JURID
ESTONIA LATVIA LITHUANIA LAW FINAN ADJUD CT/SYS | CONSTN
REGION CENTRAL MARXISM 19/20. PAGE 60 B1218 | ADMIN

LAUNDY P. B2350

LAURIER/W....SIR WILFRED LAURIER

LAW....LAW, ETHICAL DIRECTIVES IN A COMMUNITY; SEE ALSO
JURID

N
WELLS A.J.,THE BRITISH NATIONAL BIBLIOGRAPHY | BIBLIOG
CUMULATED SUBJECT CATALOGUE, 1951-1954. UK WOR+45 | NAT/G
LAW ADMIN LEAD...HUM SOC 20. PAGE 115 B2320

B
DEUTSCHE BIBLIOTH FRANKF A M,DEUTSCHE | BIBLIOG
BIBLIOGRAPHIE. EUR+WWI GERMANY ECO/DEV FORCES | LAW
DIPLOM LEAD...POLICY PHIL/SCI SOC 20. PAGE 28 B0578 | ADMIN
NAT/G

N
JOURNAL OF POLITICS. USA+45 USA-45 CONSTN POL/PAR | BIBLIOG/A
EX/STRUC LEGIS PROB/SOLV DIPLOM CT/SYS CHOOSE | NAT/G
RACE/REL 20. PAGE 1 B0005 | LAW
LOC/G

N
DEUTSCHE BIBLIOGRAPHIE, HALBJAHRESVERZEICHNIS. | BIBLIOG
WOR+45 LAW ADMIN PERSON. PAGE 1 B0013 | NAT/G
DIPLOM

N
HANDBOOK OF LATIN AMERICAN STUDIES. LAW CULTURE | BIBLIOG/A
ECO/UNDEV POL/PAR ADMIN LEAD...SOC 20. PAGE 1 B0014 | L/A+17C
NAT/G
DIPLOM

N
PUBLISHERS' TRADE LIST ANNUAL. LAW POL/PAR ADMIN | BIBLIOG
PERSON ALL/IDEOS...HUM SOC 19/20. PAGE 1 B0020 | NAT/G
DIPLOM
POLICY

N
READERS GUIDE TO PERIODICAL LITERATURE. WOR+45 | BIBLIOG
WOR-45 LAW ADMIN ATTIT PERSON...HUM PSY SOC 20. | WRITING
PAGE 1 B0021 | DIPLOM
NAT/G

N
SUBJECT GUIDE TO BOOKS IN PRINT: AN INDEX TO THE | BIBLIOG
PUBLISHERS' TRADE LIST ANNUAL. UNIV LAW LOC/G | ECO/DEV
DIPLOM WRITING ADMIN LEAD PERSON...MGT SOC. PAGE 1 | POL/PAR
B0023 | NAT/G

N
SUMMARIES OF SELECTED JAPANESE MAGAZINES. LAW | BIBLIOG/A
CULTURE ADMIN LEAD 20 CHINJAP. PAGE 1 B0024 | ATTIT
NAT/G
ASIA

THE JAPAN SCIENCE REVIEW: LAW AND POLITICS: LIST OF BIBLIOG
BOOKS AND ARTICLES ON LAW AND POLITICS. CONSTN AGRI LAW
INDUS LABOR DIPLOM TAX ADMIN CRIME...INT/LAW SOC 20 S/ASIA
CHINJAP. PAGE 1 B0025   PHIL/SCI

NEUE POLITISCHE LITERATUR; BERICHTE UBER DAS   BIBLIOG/A
INTERNATIONALE SCHRIFTTUM ZUR POLITIK. WOR+45 LAW   DIPLOM
CONSTN POL/PAR ADMIN LEAD GOV/REL...POLICY   NAT/G
IDEA/COMP. PAGE 2 B0027   NAT/COMP

SUBJECT GUIDE TO BOOKS IN PRINT; AN INDEX TO THE   BIBLIOG
PUBLISHERS' TRADE LIST ANNUAL. WOR+45 WOR-45 LAW   NAT/G
CULTURE ADMIN LEAD PERSON...HUM MGT SOC. PAGE 2   DIPLOM
B0029

PERSONNEL. USA+45 LAW LABOR LG/CO WORKER CREATE   BIBLIOG/A
GOV/REL PERS/REL ATTIT WEALTH. PAGE 2 B0030   ADMIN
                                                       MGT
                                                       GP/REL

CATHERINE R.,LA REVUE ADMINISTRATIVE. FRANCE LAW   ADMIN
NAT/G LEGIS...JURID BIBLIOG/A 20. PAGE 19 B0393   MGT
                                                       FINAN
                                                       METH/COMP

DEUTSCHE BUCHEREI,JAHRESVERZEICHNIS DER DEUTSCHEN   BIBLIOG
HOCHSCHULSCHRIFTEN. EUR+WWI GERMANY LAW ADMIN   WRITING
PERSON...MGT SOC 19/20. PAGE 28 B0579   ACADEM
                                                       INTELL

DEUTSCHE BUCHEREI,JAHRESVERZEICHNIS DES DEUTSCHEN   BIBLIOG
SCHRIFTUMS. AUSTRIA EUR+WWI GERMANY SWITZERLND LAW   WRITING
LOC/G DIPLOM ADMIN...MGT SOC 19/20. PAGE 29 B0580   NAT/G

DEUTSCHE BUCHEREI,DEUTSCHES BUCHERVERZEICHNIS.   BIBLIOG
GERMANY LAW CULTURE POL/PAR ADMIN LEAD ATTIT PERSON   NAT/G
...SOC 20. PAGE 29 B0581   DIPLOM
                                                       ECO/DEV

KENTUCKY STATE ARCHIVES,CHECKLIST OF KENTUCKY STATE   BIBLIOG/A
PUBLICATIONS AND STATE DIRECTORY. USA+45 LAW ACADEM   PROVS
EX/STRUC LEGIS EDU/PROP LEAD...JURID 20. PAGE 59   PUB/INST
B1196   ADMIN

MINISTERE DE L'EDUC NATIONALE,CATALOGUE DES THESES   BIBLIOG
DE DOCTORAT SOUTENNES DEVANT LES UNIVERSITAIRES   ACADEM
FRANCAISES. FRANCE LAW DIPLOM ADMIN...HUM SOC 20.   KNOWL
PAGE 74 B1490   NAT/G

PUBLISHERS' CIRCULAR LIMITED,THE ENGLISH CATALOGUE   BIBLIOG
OF BOOKS. UK WOR+45 WOR-45 LAW CULTURE LOC/G NAT/G   ALL/VALS
ADMIN LEAD...MGT 19/20. PAGE 85 B1718   ALL/IDEOS
                                                       SOCIETY

UNESCO,INTERNATIONAL BIBLIOGRAPHY OF POLITICAL   BIBLIOG
SCIENCE (VOLUMES 1-8). WOR+45 LAW NAT/G EX/STRUC   CONCPT
LEGIS PROB/SOLV DIPLOM ADMIN GOV/REL 20 UNESCO.   IDEA/COMP
PAGE 107 B2153

US LIBRARY OF CONGRESS,CATALOG OF THE PUBLIC   BIBLIOG
DOCUMENTS OF THE UNITED STATES. 1893-1940. USA-45   NAT/G
LAW ECO/DEV AGRI PLAN PROB/SOLV ADMIN LEAD GOV/REL   POLICY
ATTIT 19/20. PAGE 109 B2200   LOC/G

US SUPERINTENDENT OF DOCUMENTS,EDUCATION (PRICE   BIBLIOG/A
LIST 31). USA+45 LAW FINAN LOC/G NAT/G DEBATE ADMIN   EDU/PROP
LEAD RACE/REL FEDERAL HEALTH POLICY. PAGE 111 B2238   ACADEM
                                                       SCHOOL

US SUPERINTENDENT OF DOCUMENTS,INTERSTATE COMMERCE   BIBLIOG/A
(PRICE LIST 59). USA+45 LAW LOC/G NAT/G LEGIS   DIST/IND
TARIFFS TAX ADMIN CONTROL HEALTH DECISION. PAGE 111   GOV/REL
B2239   PROVS

US SUPERINTENDENT OF DOCUMENTS,LABOR (PRICE LIST   BIBLIOG/A
33). USA+45 LAW AGRI CONSTRUC INDUS NAT/G BARGAIN   WORKER
PRICE ADMIN AUTOMAT PRODUC MGT. PAGE 111 B2240   LABOR
                                                       LEGIS

US SUPERINTENDENT OF DOCUMENTS,POLITICAL SCIENCE: BIBLIOG/A
GOVERNMENT, CRIME, DISTRICT OF COLUMBIA (PRICE LIST   NAT/G
54). USA+45 LAW CONSTN EX/STRUC WORKER ADJUD ADMIN   CRIME
CT/SYS CHOOSE INGP/REL RACE/REL CONGRESS PRESIDENT.
PAGE 111 B2241

US SUPERINTENDENT OF DOCUMENTS,TARIFF AND TAXATION   BIBLIOG/A
(PRICE LIST 37). USA+45 LAW INT/TRADE ADJUD ADMIN   TAX
CT/SYS INCOME OWN...DECISION GATT. PAGE 111 B2242   TARIFFS
                                                       NAT/G

US SUPERINTENDENT OF DOCUMENTS,TRANSPORTATION: BIBLIOG/A
HIGHWAYS, ROADS, AND POSTAL SERVICE (PRICE LIST   DIST/IND
25). PANAMA USA+45 LAW FORCES DIPLOM ADMIN GOV/REL   SERV/IND
HEALTH MGT. PAGE 111 B2243   NAT/G

GOODNOW F.J.,THE PRINCIPLES OF THE ADMINISTRATIVE   ADMIN
LAW OF THE UNITED STATES. USA-45 LAW STRUCT   NAT/G
EX/STRUC LEGIS BAL/PWR CONTROL GOV/REL PWR...JURID   PROVS
19/20 CIVIL/SERV. PAGE 41 B0822   LOC/G

WILSON W.,CONSTITUTIONAL GOVERNMENT IN THE UNITED   NAT/G
STATES. USA-45 LAW POL/PAR PROVS CHIEF LEGIS   GOV/REL
BAL/PWR ADJUD EXEC FEDERAL PWR 18/20 SUPREME/CT   CONSTN
HOUSE/REP SENATE. PAGE 117 B2362   PARL/PROC

HARVARD UNIVERSITY LAW LIBRARY,CATALOGUE OF THE   BIBLIOG/A
LIBRARY OF THE LAW SCHOOL OF HARVARD UNIVERSITY (3   LAW
VOLS.). UK USA-45 LEGIS JUDGE ADJUD CT/SYS...JURID   ADMIN
CHARTS 14/20. PAGE 48 B0963

SAWYER R.A.,A LIST OF WORKS ON COUNTY GOVERNMENT.   BIBLIOG/A
LAW FINAN MUNIC TOP/EX ROUTINE CRIME...CLASSIF   LOC/G
RECORD 19/20. PAGE 93 B1871   GOV/REL
                                                       ADMIN

LOS ANGELES BD CIV SERV COMNRS,ANNUAL REPORT: LOS   DELIB/GP
ANGELES CALIFORNIA: 1919-1936. USA-45 LAW GOV/REL   ADMIN
PRODUC...STAT 20. PAGE 66 B1340   LOC/G
                                                       MUNIC

ARNOW K.,SELF-INSURANCE IN THE TREASURY (PAMPHLET).   ADMIN
USA+45 LAW RIGID/FLEX...POLICY METH/COMP 20   PLAN
DEPT/TREAS. PAGE 7 B0135   EFFICIENCY
                                                       NAT/G

BUREAU OF NAT'L AFFAIRS INC.,A CURRENT LOOK AT: DISCRIM
(1) THE NEGRO AND TITLE VII, (2) SEX AND TITLE VII   SEX
(PAMPHLET). LAW LG/CO SML/CO RACE/REL...POLICY SOC   WORKER
STAT DEEP/QU TREND CON/ANAL CHARTS 20 NEGRO   MGT
CIV/RIGHTS. PAGE 17 B0350

BURRUS B.R.,INVESTIGATION AND DISCOVERY IN STATE   NAT/G
ANTITRUST (PAMPHLET). USA+45 USA-45 LEGIS ECO/TAC   PROVS
ADMIN CONTROL CT/SYS CRIME GOV/REL PWR...JURID   LAW
CHARTS 19/20 FTC MONOPOLY. PAGE 17 B0355   INSPECT

GRIFFITH W.,THE PUBLIC SERVICE (PAMPHLET). UK LAW   ADMIN
LOC/G NAT/G PARTIC CHOOSE DRIVE ROLE SKILL...CHARTS   EFFICIENCY
20 CIVIL/SERV. PAGE 44 B0880   EDU/PROP
                                                       GOV/REL

PERREN G.E.,LANGUAGE AND COMMUNICATION IN THE   EDU/PROP
COMMONWEALTH (PAMPHLET). FUT UK LAW ECO/DEV PRESS   LING
TV WRITING ADJUD ADMIN COLONIAL CONTROL 20   GOV/REL
CMN/WLTH. PAGE 82 B1660   COM/IND

BRYCE J.,MODERN DEMOCRACIES. FUT NEW/ZEALND USA-45   NAT/G
LAW CONSTN POL/PAR PROVS VOL/ASSN EX/STRUC LEGIS   TREND
LEGIT CT/SYS EXEC KNOWL CONGRESS AUSTRAL 20.
PAGE 16 B0332

STOWELL E.C.,INTERVENTION IN INTERNATIONAL LAW.   BAL/PWR
UNIV LAW SOCIETY INT/ORG ACT/RES PLAN LEGIT ROUTINE   SOVEREIGN
WAR...JURID OBS GEN/LAWS 20. PAGE 101 B2050

HOLDSWORTH W.S.,A HISTORY OF ENGLISH LAW; THE   LAW
COMMON LAW AND ITS RIVALS (VOL. V). UK SEA EX/STRUC   LEGIS
WRITING ADMIN...INT/LAW JURID CONCPT IDEA/COMP   ADJUD
WORSHIP 16/17 PARLIAMENT ENGLSH/LAW COMMON/LAW.   CT/SYS
PAGE 51 B1033

HOLDSWORTH W.S.,A HISTORY OF ENGLISH LAW; THE   LAW
COMMON LAW AND ITS RIVALS (VOL. VI). UK STRATA   CONSTN
EX/STRUC ADJUD ADMIN CONTROL CT/SYS...JURID CONCPT   LEGIS
GEN/LAWS 17 COMMONWLTH PARLIAMENT ENGLSH/LAW   CHIEF
COMMON/LAW. PAGE 51 B1034

DICKINSON J.,ADMINISTRATIVE JUSTICE AND THE   CT/SYS
SUPREMACY OF LAW IN THE UNITED STATES. USA-45 LAW   ADJUD
INDUS DOMIN EDU/PROP CONTROL EXEC GP/REL ORD/FREE   ADMIN
...POLICY JURID 19/20. PAGE 29 B0586   NAT/G

HSIAO K.C.,"POLITICAL PLURALISM." LAW CONSTN   STRUCT
POL/PAR LEGIS PLAN ADMIN CENTRAL SOVEREIGN   GEN/LAWS
...INT/LAW BIBLIOG 19/20. PAGE 52 B1053   PLURISM

BORCHARD E.H.,GUIDE TO THE LAW AND LEGAL LITERATURE   BIBLIOG/A
OF FRANCE. FRANCE FINAN INDUS LABOR SECT LEGIS   LAW
ADMIN COLONIAL CRIME OWN...INT/LAW 20. PAGE 14   CONSTN
B0277   METH

ENSOR R.C.K.,COURTS AND JUDGES IN FRANCE, GERMANY,   CT/SYS
AND ENGLAND. FRANCE GERMANY UK LAW PROB/SOLV ADMIN   EX/STRUC
ROUTINE CRIME ROLE...METH/COMP 20 CIVIL/LAW.   ADJUD
PAGE 33 B0676   NAT/COMP

US TARIFF COMMISSION,THE TARIFF; A BIBLIOGRAPHY: A   BIBLIOG/A
SELECT LIST OF REFERENCES. USA-45 LAW DIPLOM TAX   TARIFFS
ADMIN...POLICY TREATY 20. PAGE 111 B2246   ECO/TAC

B05
B08
B09
B15
B19
N19
N19
N19
N19
N19
B21
B21
B24
B24
B27
C27
B31
B33
B34

B37
ROYAL INST. INT. AFF.,THE COLONIAL PROBLEM. WOR-45   INT/ORG
LAW ECO/DEV ECO/UNDEV NAT/G PLAN ECO/TAC EDU/PROP   ACT/RES
ADMIN ATTIT ALL/VALS...CONCPT 20. PAGE 91 B1844   SOVEREIGN
                                                     COLONIAL
B38
HARPER S.N.,THE GOVERNMENT OF THE SOVIET UNION. COM MARXISM
USSR LAW CONSTN ECO/DEV PLAN TEC/DEV DIPLOM   NAT/G
INT/TRADE ADMIN REV NAT/LISM...POLICY 20. PAGE 47   LEAD
B0952   POL/PAR
B40
HART J.,AN INTRODUCTION TO ADMINISTRATIVE LAW, WITH LAW
SELECTED CASES. USA-45 CONSTN SOCIETY NAT/G   ADMIN
EX/STRUC ADJUD CT/SYS LEAD CRIME ORD/FREE   LEGIS
...DECISION JURID 20 CASEBOOK. PAGE 47 B0958   PWR
B40
WILCOX J.K.,MANUAL ON THE USE OF STATE   BIBLIOG/A
PUBLICATIONS. USA-45 FINAN LEGIS TAX GOV/REL   PROVS
...CHARTS 20. PAGE 116 B2346   ADMIN
                                                     LAW
N40
COUNTY GOVERNMENT IN THE UNITED STATES: A LIST OF   BIBLIOG/A
RECENT REFERENCES (PAMPHLET). USA-45 LAW PUB/INST   LOC/G
PLAN BUDGET CT/SYS CENTRAL 20. PAGE 49 B0988   ADMIN
                                                     MUNIC
B41
GELLHORN W.,FEDERAL ADMINISTRATIVE PROCEEDINGS.   EX/STRUC
USA+45 CLIENT FACE/GP NAT/G LOBBY REPRESENT PWR 20. LAW
PAGE 39 B0788   ADJUD
                                                     POLICY
S44
GRIFFITH E.S.,"THE CHANGING PATTERN OF PUBLIC   LAW
POLICY FORMATION." MOD/EUR WOR+45 FINAN CHIEF   POLICY
CONFER ADMIN LEAD CONSERVE SOCISM TECHRACY...SOC   TEC/DEV
CHARTS CONGRESS. PAGE 43 B0877
B45
MILLIS H.A.,ORGANIZED LABOR (FIRST ED.). LAW STRUCT LABOR
DELIB/GP WORKER ECO/TAC ADJUD CONTROL REPRESENT   POLICY
INGP/REL INCOME MGT. PAGE 74 B1485   ROUTINE
                                                     GP/REL
B46
BIBLIOGRAFIIA DISSERTATSII: DOKTORSKIE DISSERTATSII BIBLIOG
ZA 19411944 (2 VOLS.). COM USSR LAW POL/PAR DIPLOM   ACADEM
ADMIN LEAD...PHIL/SCI SOC 20. PAGE 2 B0035   KNOWL
                                                     MARXIST
B46
GRIFFIN G.G.,A GUIDE TO MANUSCRIPTS RELATING TO   BIBLIOG/A
AMERICAN HISTORY IN BRITISH DEPOSITORIES. CANADA   ALL/VALS
IRELAND MOD/EUR UK USA-45 LAW DIPLOM ADMIN COLONIAL NAT/G
WAR NAT/LISM SOVEREIGN...GEOG INT/LAW 15/19
CMN/WLTH. PAGE 43 B0876
B47
BAERWALD F.,FUNDAMENTALS OF LABOR ECONOMICS. LAW   ECO/DEV
INDUS LABOR LG/CO CONTROL GP/REL INCOME TOTALISM   WORKER
...MGT CHARTS GEN/LAWS BIBLIOG 20. PAGE 8 B0158   MARKET
B47
BORGESE G.,COMMON CAUSE. LAW CONSTN SOCIETY STRATA   WOR+45
ECO/DEV INT/ORG POL/PAR FORCES LEGIS TOP/EX CAP/ISM NAT/G
DIPLOM ADMIN EXEC ATTIT PWR 20. PAGE 14 B0279   SOVEREIGN
                                                     REGION
B47
DE NOIA J.,GUIDE TO OFFICIAL PUBLICATIONS OF THE   BIBLIOG/A
OTHER AMERICAN REPUBLICS: EL SALVADOR. EL/SALVADR   CONSTN
LAW LEGIS EDU/PROP CT/SYS 20. PAGE 27 B0558   NAT/G
                                                     ADMIN
B47
DE NOIA J.,GUIDE TO OFFICIAL PUBLICATIONS OF THE   BIBLIOG/A
OTHER AMERICAN REPUBLICS: NICARAGUA (VOL. XIV).   EDU/PROP
NICARAGUA LAW LEGIS ADMIN CT/SYS...JURID 19/20.   NAT/G
PAGE 27 B0559   CONSTN
B47
DE NOIA J.,GUIDE TO OFFICIAL PUBLICATIONS OF THE   BIBLIOG/A
OTHER AMERICAN REPUBLICS: PANAMA (VOL. XV). PANAMA   CONSTN
LAW LEGIS EDU/PROP CT/SYS 20. PAGE 27 B0560   ADMIN
                                                     NAT/G
B47
HIRSHBERG H.S.,SUBJECT GUIDE TO UNITED STATES   BIBLIOG
GOVERNMENT PUBLICATIONS. USA+45 USA-45 LAW ADMIN   NAT/G
...SOC 20. PAGE 50 B1017   DIPLOM
                                                     LOC/G
B47
PUBLIC ADMINISTRATION SERVICE,CURRENT RESEARCH   BIBLIOG
PROJECTS IN PUBLIC ADMINISTRATION (PAMPHLET). LAW   R+D
CONSTN COM/IND LABOR LOC/G MUNIC PROVS ACT/RES   MGT
DIPLOM RECEIVE EDU/PROP WAR 20. PAGE 85 B1716   ADMIN
S47
TURNER R.H.,"THE NAVY DISBURSING OFFICER AS A   FORCES
BUREAUCRAT" (BMR)" USA-45 LAW STRATA DIST/IND WAR   ADMIN
PWR...SOC 20 BUREAUCRCY. PAGE 106 B2140   PERSON
                                                     ROLE
B48
DE NOIA J.,GUIDE TO OFFICIAL PUBLICATIONS OF OTHER   BIBLIOG/A
AMERICAN REPUBLICS: PERU (VOL. XVII). PERU LAW   CONSTN
LEGIS ADMIN CT/SYS...JURID 19/20. PAGE 28 B0561   NAT/G
                                                     EDU/PROP

B48
MEEK C.K.,COLONIAL LAW: A BIBLIOGRAPHY WITH SPECIAL COLONIAL
REFERENCE TO NATIVE AFRICAN SYSTEMS OF LAW AND LAND ADMIN
TENURE. AFR ECO/UNDEV AGRI CT/SYS...JURID SOC 20.   LAW
PAGE 72 B1462   CONSTN
B48
PUBLIC ADMINISTRATION SERVICE,SOURCE MATERIALS IN   BIBLIOG/A
PUBLIC ADMINISTRATION: A SELECTED BIBLIOGRAPHY (PAS GOV/REL
PUBLICATION NO. 102). USA+45 LAW FINAN LOC/G MUNIC   MGT
NAT/G PLAN RECEIVE EDU/PROP CT/SYS CHOOSE HEALTH   ADMIN
20. PAGE 85 B1717
B48
SLESSER H.,THE ADMINISTRATION OF THE LAW. UK CONSTN LAW
EX/STRUC OP/RES PROB/SOLV CRIME ROLE...DECISION   CT/SYS
METH/COMP 20 CIVIL/LAW ENGLSH/LAW CIVIL/LAW.   ADJUD
PAGE 98 B1977
C48
WALKER H.,"THE LEGISLATIVE PROCESS: LAWMAKING IN   PARL/PROC
THE UNITED STATES." NAT/G POL/PAR PROVS EX/STRUC   LEGIS
OP/RES PROB/SOLV CT/SYS LOBBY GOV/REL...CHARTS   LAW
BIBLIOG T 18/20 CONGRESS. PAGE 113 B2279   CONSTN
B49
ASPINALL A.,POLITICS AND THE PRESS 1780-1850. UK   PRESS
LAW ELITES FINAN PROF/ORG LEGIS ADMIN ATTIT   CONTROL
...POLICY 18/19. PAGE 7 B0142   POL/PAR
                                                     ORD/FREE
B49
DENNING A.,FREEDOM UNDER THE LAW. MOD/EUR UK LAW   ORD/FREE
SOCIETY CHIEF EX/STRUC LEGIS ADJUD CT/SYS PERS/REL   JURID
PERSON 17/20 ENGLSH/LAW. PAGE 28 B0573   NAT/G
B49
SCHWARTZ B.,LAW AND THE EXECUTIVE IN BRITAIN: A   ADMIN
COMPARATIVE STUDY. UK USA+45 LAW EX/STRUC PWR   EXEC
...GOV/COMP 20. PAGE 95 B1911   CONTROL
                                                     REPRESENT
B49
STEIN H.,THE FOREIGN SERVICE ACT OF 1946. USA+45   DIPLOM
ELITES EX/STRUC PLAN PROB/SOLV LOBBY GOV/REL   LAW
PERS/REL RIGID/FLEX...POLICY IDEA/COMP 20 CONGRESS   NAT/G
BUR/BUDGET. PAGE 100 B2027   ADMIN
L49
MARX C.M.,"ADMINISTRATIVE ETHICS AND THE RULE OF   ADMIN
LAW." USA+45 ELITES ACT/RES DOMIN NEUTRAL ROUTINE   LAW
INGP/REL ORD/FREE...JURID IDEA/COMP. PAGE 70 B1417
B50
BROWN E.S.,MANUAL OF GOVERNMENT PUBLICATIONS.   BIBLIOG/A
WOR+45 WOR-45 CONSTN INT/ORG MUNIC PROVS DIPLOM   NAT/G
ADMIN 20. PAGE 16 B0322   LAW
B50
WADE E.C.S.,CONSTITUTIONAL LAW: AN OUTLINE OF THE   CONSTN
LAW AND PRACTICE OF THE CONSTITUTION. UK LEGIS   NAT/G
DOMIN ADMIN GP/REL 16/20 CMN/WLTH PARLIAMENT   PARL/PROC
ENGLSH/LAW. PAGE 112 B2269   LAW
B50
WARD R.E.,A GUIDE TO JAPANESE REFERENCE AND   BIBLIOG/A
RESEARCH MATERIALS IN THE FIELD OF POLITICAL   ASIA
SCIENCE. LAW CONSTN LOC/G PRESS ADMIN...SOC   NAT/G
CON/ANAL METH 19/20 CHINJAP. PAGE 113 B2289
C50
STOKES W.S.,"HONDURAS: AN AREA STUDY IN   CONSTN
GOVERNMENT." HONDURAS NAT/G POL/PAR COLONIAL CT/SYS LAW
ROUTINE CHOOSE REPRESENT...GEOG RECORD BIBLIOG   L/A+17C
19/20. PAGE 101 B2044   ADMIN
B51
ANDERSON W.,GOVERNMENT IN THE FIFTY STATES. LAW   LOC/G
CONSTN FINAN POL/PAR LEGIS EDU/PROP ADJUD ADMIN   PROVS
CT/SYS CHOOSE...CHARTS 20. PAGE 5 B0101   GOV/REL
B51
HARDMAN J.B.,THE HOUSE OF LABOR. LAW R+D NEIGH   LABOR
EDU/PROP LEAD ROUTINE REPRESENT GP/REL...POLICY   LOBBY
STAT. PAGE 47 B0945   ADMIN
                                                     PRESS
B52
DE GRAZIA A.,POLITICAL ORGANIZATION. CONSTN LOC/G   FEDERAL
MUNIC NAT/G CHIEF LEGIS TOP/EX ADJUD CT/SYS   LAW
PERS/REL...INT/LAW MYTH UN. PAGE 27 B0553   ADMIN
B52
SCHATTSCHNEIDER E.E.,A GUIDE TO THE STUDY OF PUBLIC ACT/RES
AFFAIRS. LAW LOC/G NAT/G LEGIS BUDGET PRESS ADMIN   INTELL
LOBBY...JURID CHARTS 20. PAGE 93 B1882   ACADEM
                                                     METH/COMP
B52
US DEPARTMENT OF STATE,RESEARCH ON EASTERN EUROPE   BIBLIOG
(EXCLUDING USSR). EUR+WWI LAW ECO/DEV NAT/G   R+D
PROB/SOLV DIPLOM ADMIN LEAD MARXISM...TREND 19/20.   ACT/RES
PAGE 108 B2182   COM
B52
VANDENBOSCH A.,THE UN: BACKGROUND, ORGANIZATION,   DELIB/GP
FUNCTIONS, ACTIVITIES. WOR+45 LAW CONSTN STRUCT   TIME/SEQ
INT/ORG CONSULT BAL/PWR EDU/PROP EXEC ALL/VALS   PEACE
...POLICY CONCPT UN 20. PAGE 112 B2254
B53
CALDWELL L.K.,RESEARCH METHODS IN PUBLIC   BIBLIOG/A
ADMINISTRATION: AN OUTLINE OF TOPICS AND READINGS   METH/COMP
(PAMPHLET). LAW ACT/RES COMPUTER KNOWL...SOC STAT   ADMIN
GEN/METH 20. PAGE 18 B0365   OP/RES

PIERCE R.A.,RUSSIAN CENTRAL ASIA, 1867-1917: A
SELECTED BIBLIOGRAPHY (PAMPHLET). USSR LAW CULTURE
NAT/G EDU/PROP WAR...GEOG SOC 19/20. PAGE 83 B1671
   B53 BIBLIOG COLONIAL ADMIN COM

SECKLER-HUDSON C.,BIBLIOGRAPHY ON PUBLIC
ADMINISTRATION (4TH ED.). USA+45 LAW POL/PAR
DELIB/GP BUDGET ADJUD LOBBY GOV/REL GP/REL ATTIT
...JURID 20. PAGE 95 B1923
   B53 BIBLIOG/A ADMIN NAT/G MGT

GABLE R.W.,"NAM: INFLUENTIAL LOBBY OR KISS OF
DEATH?" (BMR)" USA+45 LAW INSPECT EDU/PROP ADMIN
CONTROL INGP/REL EFFICIENCY PWR 20 CONGRESS NAM
TAFT/HART. PAGE 38 B0769
   S53 LOBBY LEGIS INDUS LG/CO

LOCKLIN D.P.,ECONOMICS OF TRANSPORTATION (4TH ED.).
USA+45 USA-45 SEA AIR LAW FINAN LG/CO EX/STRUC
ADMIN CONTROL...STAT CHARTS 19/20 RAILROAD
PUB/TRANS. PAGE 66 B1335
   B54 ECO/DEV DIST/IND ECO/TAC TEC/DEV

MANGONE G.,A SHORT HISTORY OF INTERNATIONAL
ORGANIZATION. MOD/EUR USA+45 USA-45 WOR+45 WOR-45
LAW LEGIS CREATE LEGIT ROUTINE RIGID/FLEX PWR
...JURID CONCPT OBS TIME/SEQ STERTYP GEN/LAWS UN
TOT/POP VAL/FREE 18/20. PAGE 69 B1389
   B54 INT/ORG INT/LAW

SCHWARTZ B.,FRENCH ADMINISTRATIVE LAW AND THE
COMMON-LAW WORLD. FRANCE CULTURE LOC/G NAT/G PROVS
DELIB/GP EX/STRUC LEGIS PROB/SOLV CT/SYS EXEC
GOV/REL...IDEA/COMP ENGLSH/LAW. PAGE 95 B1912
   B54 JURID LAW METH/COMP ADJUD

TOTOK W.,HANDBUCH DER BIBLIOGRAPHISCHEN
NACHSCHLAGEWERKE. GERMANY LAW CULTURE ADMIN...SOC
20. PAGE 105 B2121
   B54 BIBLIOG/A NAT/G DIPLOM POLICY

COOPER L.,"ADMINISTRATIVE JUSTICE." UK ADMIN
REPRESENT PWR...POLICY 20. PAGE 23 B0475
   S54 LAW ADJUD CONTROL EX/STRUC

BEISEL A.R.,CONTROL OVER ILLEGAL ENFORCEMENT OF THE
CRIMINAL LAW: ROLE OF THE SUPREME COURT. CONSTN
ROUTINE MORAL PWR...SOC 20 SUPREME/CT. PAGE 10
B0207
   B55 ORD/FREE LAW CRIME

JAPAN MOMBUSHO DAIGAKU GAKIYUT,BIBLIOGRAPHY OF THE
STUDIES ON LAW AND POLITICS (PAMPHLET). CONSTN
INDUS LABOR DIPLOM TAX ADMIN...CRIMLGY INT/LAW 20
CHINJAP. PAGE 56 B1126
   B55 BIBLIOG LAW PHIL/SCI

MAZZINI J.,THE DUTIES OF MAN. MOD/EUR LAW SOCIETY
FAM NAT/G POL/PAR SECT VOL/ASSN EX/STRUC ACT/RES
CREATE REV PEACE ATTIT ALL/VALS...GEN/LAWS WORK 19.
PAGE 71 B1439
   B55 SUPEGO CONCPT NAT/LISM

PALMER A.M.,ADMINISTRATION OF MEDICAL AND
PHARMACEUTICAL PATENTS (PAMPHLET). USA+45 PROF/ORG
ADMIN PHIL/SCI. PAGE 80 B1626
   B55 HEAL ACADEM LAW LICENSE

PULLEN W.R.,A CHECK LIST OF LEGISLATIVE JOURNALS
ISSUED SINCE 1937 BY THE STATES OF THE UNITED
STATES OF AMERICA (PAMPHLET). USA+45 USA-45 LAW
WRITING ADJUD ADMIN...JURID 20. PAGE 85 B1720
   B55 BIBLIOG PROVS EDU/PROP LEGIS

ZABEL O.H.,GOD AND CAESAR IN NEBRASKA: A STUDY OF
LEGAL RELATIONSHIP OF CHURCH AND STATE, 1854-1954.
TAX GIVE ADMIN CONTROL GP/REL ROLE...GP/COMP 19/20
NEBRASKA. PAGE 119 B2396
   B55 SECT PROVS LAW EDU/PROP

DUNNILL F.,THE CIVIL SERVICE. UK LAW PLAN ADMIN
EFFICIENCY DRIVE NEW/LIB...STAT CHARTS 20
PARLIAMENT CIVIL/SERV. PAGE 31 B0633
   B56 PERSON WORKER STRATA SOC/WK

GLADDEN E.N.,CIVIL SERVICE OR BUREAUCRACY? UK LAW
STRATA LABOR TOP/EX PLAN SENIOR AUTOMAT CONTROL
PARTIC CHOOSE HAPPINESS...CHARTS 19/20 CIVIL/SERV
BUREAUCRCY. PAGE 40 B0808
   B56 ADMIN GOV/REL EFFICIENCY PROVS

HOWARD L.V.,TULANE STUDIES IN POLITICAL SCIENCE:
CIVIL SERVICE DEVELOPMENT IN LOUISIANA VOLUME 3.
LAW POL/PAR LEGIS CT/SYS ADJUST ORD/FREE...STAT
CHARTS 19/20 LOUISIANA CIVIL/SERV. PAGE 52 B1050
   B56 ADMIN GOV/REL PROVS POLICY

SOHN L.B.,BASIC DOCUMENTS OF THE UNITED NATIONS.
WOR+45 LAW INT/ORG LEGIT EXEC ROUTINE CHOOSE PWR
...JURID CONCPT GEN/LAWS ANTHOL UN TOT/POP OAS FAO
ILO 20. PAGE 99 B1993
   B56 DELIB/GP CONSTN

US HOUSE RULES COMM,HEARINGS BEFORE A SPECIAL
SUBCOMMITTEE: ESTABLISHMENT OF A STANDING COMMITTEE
ON ADMINISTRATIVE PROCEDURE, PRACTICE. USA+45 LAW
EX/STRUC ADJUD CONTROL EXEC GOV/REL EFFICIENCY PWR
   B56 ADMIN DOMIN DELIB/GP NAT/G

...POLICY INT 20 CONGRESS. PAGE 109 B2199

FALL B.B.,"THE VIET-MINH REGIME." VIETNAM LAW
ECO/UNDEV POL/PAR FORCES DOMIN WAR ATTIT MARXISM
...BIOG PREDICT BIBLIOG/A 20. PAGE 35 B0703
   C56 NAT/G ADMIN EX/STRUC LEAD

COOPER F.E.,THE LAWYER AND ADMINISTRATIVE AGENCIES.
USA+45 CLIENT LAW PROB/SOLV CT/SYS PERSON ROLE.
PAGE 23 B0473
   B57 CONSULT ADMIN ADJUD DELIB/GP

SCARROW H.A.,THE HIGHER PUBLIC SERVICE OF THE
COMMONWEALTH OF AUSTRALIA. LAW SENIOR LOBBY ROLE 20
AUSTRAL CIVIL/SERV COMMONWLTH. PAGE 93 B1877
   B57 ADMIN NAT/G EX/STRUC GOV/COMP

SIMON H.A.,MODELS OF MAN, SOCIAL AND RATIONAL:
MATHEMATICAL ESSAYS ON RATIONAL HUMAN BEHAVIOR IN A
SOCIAL SETTING. UNIV LAW SOCIETY FACE/GP VOL/ASSN
CONSULT EX/STRUC LEGIS CREATE ADMIN ROUTINE ATTIT
DRIVE PWR...SOC CONCPT METH/CNCPT QUANT STAT
TOT/POP VAL/FREE 20. PAGE 97 B1959
   B57 MATH SIMUL

ATOMIC INDUSTRIAL FORUM,MANAGEMENT AND ATOMIC
ENERGY. WOR+45 SEA LAW MARKET NAT/G TEC/DEV INSPECT
INT/TRADE CONFER PEACE HEALTH...ANTHOL 20. PAGE 7
B0145
   B58 NUC/PWR INDUS MGT ECO/TAC

BLAIR L.,THE COMMONWEALTH PUBLIC SERVICE. LAW
WORKER...MGT CHARTS GOV/COMP 20 COMMONWLTH. AUSTRAL
CIVIL/SERV. PAGE 12 B0248
   B58 ADMIN NAT/G EX/STRUC INGP/REL

CHARLES R.,LA JUSTICE EN FRANCE. FRANCE LAW CONSTN
DELIB/GP CRIME 20. PAGE 20 B0413
   B58 JURID ADMIN CT/SYS ADJUD

DAVIS K.C.,ADMINISTRATIVE LAW: CASES, TEXT,
PROBLEMS. LAW LOC/G NAT/G TOP/EX PAY CONTROL
GOV/REL INGP/REL FEDERAL 20 SUPREME/CT. PAGE 27
B0541
   B58 ADJUD JURID CT/SYS ADMIN

DEVLIN P.,THE CRIMINAL PROSECUTION IN ENGLAND. UK
NAT/G ADMIN ROUTINE EFFICIENCY...JURID SOC 20.
PAGE 29 B0583
   B58 CRIME LAW METH CT/SYS

HENKIN L.,ARMS CONTROL AND INSPECTION IN AMERICAN
LAW. LAW CONSTN INT/ORG LOC/G MUNIC NAT/G PROVS
EDU/PROP LEGIT EXEC NUC/PWR KNOWL ORD/FREE...OBS
TOT/POP CONGRESS 20. PAGE 49 B0990
   B58 USA+45 JURID ARMS/CONT

JAPAN MINISTRY OF JUSTICE,CRIMINAL JUSTICE IN
JAPAN. LAW PROF/ORG PUB/INST FORCES CONTROL CT/SYS
PARL/PROC 20 CHINJAP. PAGE 56 B1125
   B58 CONSTN CRIME JURID ADMIN

KAPLAN H.E.,THE LAW OF CIVIL SERVICE. USA+45 LAW
POL/PAR CT/SYS CRIME GOV/REL...POLICY JURID 20.
PAGE 58 B1167
   B58 ADJUD NAT/G ADMIN CONSTN

ORTIZ R.P.,ANNUARIO BIBLIOGRAFICO COLOMBIANO,
1951-1956. LAW RECEIVE EDU/PROP ADMIN...LING STAT
20 COLOMB. PAGE 80 B1617
   B58 BIBLIOG SOC

POUND R.,JUSTICE ACCORDING TO LAW. LAW SOCIETY
CT/SYS 20. PAGE 84 B1696
   B58 CONCPT JURID ADJUD ADMIN

SPITZ D.,DEMOCRACY AND THE CHALLANGE OF POWER. FUT
USA+45 USA-45 LAW SOCIETY STRUCT LOC/G POL/PAR
PROVS DELIB/GP EX/STRUC LEGIS TOP/EX ACT/RES CREATE
DOMIN EDU/PROP LEGIT ADJUD ADMIN ATTIT DRIVE MORAL
ORD/FREE TOT/POP. PAGE 99 B2010
   B58 NAT/G PWR

UNIVERSITY OF LONDON,THE FAR EAST AND SOUTH-EAST
ASIA: A CUMULATED LIST OF PERIODICAL ARTICLES, MAY
1956-APRIL 1957. ASIA S/ASIA LAW ADMIN...LING 20.
PAGE 107 B2168
   B58 BIBLIOG SOC

US HOUSE COMM ON COMMERCE,ADMINISTRATIVE PROCESS
AND ETHICAL QUESTIONS. USA+45 LAW LEGIS INT/TRADE
CONTROL 20 CONGRESS. PAGE 109 B2192
   B58 POLICY ADMIN DELIB/GP ADJUD

US HOUSE COMM ON POST OFFICE,TO PROVIDE AN
EFFECTIVE SYSTEM OF PERSONNEL ADMINISTRATION.
USA+45 DELIB/GP CONTROL EFFICIENCY 20 CONGRESS
PRESIDENT CIVIL/SERV POSTAL/SYS. PAGE 109 B2194
   B58 ADMIN NAT/G EX/STRUC LAW

WESTIN A.F.,THE ANATOMY OF A CONSTITUTIONAL LAW
CASE. USA+45 LAW LEGIS ADMIN EXEC...DECISION MGT
   B58 CT/SYS INDUS

SOC RECORD 20 SUPREME/CT. PAGE 115 B2326 — ADJUD CONSTN

L58

JONAS F.H.,"BIBLIOGRAPHY ON WESTERN POLITICS." USA+45 USA-45 ELITES MUNIC POL/PAR LEGIS ADJUD ADMIN 20. PAGE 57 B1148 — BIBLIOG/A LOC/G NAT/G LAW

C58

WILDING N.,"AN ENCYCLOPEDIA OF PARLIAMENT." UK LAW CONSTN CHIEF PROB/SOLV DIPLOM DEBATE WAR INGP/REL PRIVIL...BIBLIOG DICTIONARY 13/20 CMN/WLTH PARLIAMENT. PAGE 116 B2350 — PARL/PROC POL/PAR NAT/G ADMIN

B59

BHAMBHRI C.P.,SUBSTANCE OF HINDU POLITY. INDIA S/ASIA LAW EX/STRUC JUDGE TAX COERCE GP/REL POPULISM 20 HINDU. PAGE 11 B0234 — GOV/REL WRITING SECT PROVS

B59

COUNCIL OF STATE GOVERNMENTS,STATE GOVERNMENT: AN ANNOTATED BIBLIOGRAPHY (PAMPHLET). USA+45 LAW AGRI INDUS WORKER PLAN TAX ADJUST AGE/Y ORD/FREE...HEAL MGT 20. PAGE 24 B0494 — BIBLIOG/A PROVS LOC/G ADMIN

B59

ELLIOTT S.D.,IMPROVING OUR COURTS. LAW EX/STRUC PLAN PROB/SOLV ADJUD ADMIN TASK CRIME EFFICIENCY ORD/FREE 20. PAGE 33 B0669 — CT/SYS JURID GOV/REL NAT/G

B59

EPSTEIN F.T.,EAST GERMANY: A SELECTED BIBLIOGRAPHY (PAMPHLET). COM GERMANY/E LAW AGRI FINAN INDUS LABOR POL/PAR EDU/PROP ADMIN AGE/Y 20. PAGE 33 B0677 — BIBLIOG/A INTELL MARXISM NAT/G

B59

GORDENKER L.,THE UNITED NATIONS AND THE PEACEFUL UNIFICATION OF KOREA. ASIA LAW LOC/G CONSULT ACT/RES DIPLOM DOMIN LEGIT ADJUD ADMIN ORD/FREE SOVEREIGN...INT GEN/METH UN COLD/WAR 20. PAGE 41 B0829 — DELIB/GP KOREA INT/ORG

B59

HANSON A.H.,THE STRUCTURE AND CONTROL OF STATE ENTERPRISES IN TURKEY. TURKEY LAW ADMIN GOV/REL EFFICIENCY...CHARTS 20. PAGE 46 B0939 — NAT/G LG/CO OWN CONTROL

B59

MAYDA J.,ATOMIC ENERGY AND LAW. ECO/UNDEV FINAN TEC/DEV FOR/AID EFFICIENCY PRODUC WEALTH...POLICY TECHNIC 20. PAGE 71 B1433 — NUC/PWR L/A+17C LAW ADMIN

B59

MOOS M.,THE CAMPUS AND THE STATE. LAW FINAN DELIB/GP LEGIS EXEC LOBBY GP/REL PWR...POLICY BIBLIOG. PAGE 75 B1517 — EDU/PROP ACADEM PROVS CONTROL

B59

SISSON C.H.,THE SPIRIT OF BRITISH ADMINISTRATION AND SOME EUROPEAN COMPARISONS. FRANCE GERMANY/W SWEDEN UK LAW EX/STRUC INGP/REL EFFICIENCY ORD/FREE ...DECISION 20. PAGE 98 B1972 — GOV/COMP ADMIN ELITES ATTIT

B59

U OF MICHIGAN LAW SCHOOL,ATOMS AND THE LAW. USA+45 PROVS WORKER PROB/SOLV DIPLOM ADMIN GOV/REL ANTHOL. PAGE 106 B2142 — NUC/PWR NAT/G CONTROL LAW

B59

US SENATE COMM ON POST OFFICE,TO PROVIDE FOR AN EFFECTIVE SYSTEM OF PERSONNEL ADMINISTRATION. EFFICIENCY...MGT 20 CONGRESS CIVIL/SERV POSTAL/SYS YARBROGH/R. PAGE 111 B2233 — ADMIN NAT/G EX/STRUC LAW

S59

CHAPMAN B.,"THE FRENCH CONSEIL D'ETAT." FRANCE NAT/G CONSULT OP/RES PROB/SOLV PWR...OBS 20. PAGE 20 B0410 — ADMIN LAW CT/SYS LEGIS

S59

DWYER R.J.,"THE ADMINISTRATIVE ROLE IN DESEGREGATION." USA+45 LAW PROB/SOLV LEAD RACE/REL ISOLAT STRANGE ROLE...POLICY SOC/INTEG MISSOURI NEGRO CIV/RIGHTS. PAGE 31 B0638 — ADMIN SCHOOL DISCRIM ATTIT

S59

HARVEY M.F.,"THE PALESTINE REFUGEE PROBLEM: ELEMENTS OF A SOLUTION." ISLAM LAW INT/ORG DELIB/GP LEGIT TOP/EX ECO/TAC ROUTINE DRIVE HEALTH LOVE ORD/FREE PWR WEALTH...MAJORIT FAO 20. PAGE 48 B0964 — ACT/RES PEACE ISRAEL

S59

SOHN L.B.,"THE DEFINITION OF AGGRESSION." FUT LAW FORCES LEGIT ADJUD ROUTINE COERCE ORD/FREE PWR ...MAJORIT JURID QUANT COLD/WAR 20. PAGE 99 B1995 — INT/ORG CT/SYS DETER SOVEREIGN

B60

ADRIAN C.R.,STATE AND LOCAL GOVERNMENTS: A STUDY IN THE POLITICAL PROCESS. USA+45 LAW FINAN MUNIC POL/PAR LEGIS ADJUD EXEC CHOOSE REPRESENT. PAGE 3 B0060 — LOC/G PROVS GOV/REL ATTIT

B60

ALBI F.,TRATADO DE LOS MODOS DE GESTION DE LAS CORPORACIONES LOCALES. SPAIN FINAN NAT/G BUDGET — LOC/G LAW

CONTROL EXEC ROUTINE GOV/REL ORD/FREE SOVEREIGN ...MGT 20. PAGE 3 B0068 — ADMIN MUNIC

B60

ELKOURI F.,HOW ARBITRATION WORKS (REV. ED.). LAW INDUS BARGAIN 20. PAGE 33 B0667 — MGT LABOR ADJUD GP/REL

B60

FLORES R.H.,CATALOGO DE TESIS DOCTORALES DE LAS FACULTADES DE LA UNIVERSIDAD DE EL SALVADOR. EL/SALVADR LAW DIPLOM ADMIN LEAD GOV/REL...SOC 19/20. PAGE 36 B0730 — BIBLIOG ACADEM L/A+17C NAT/G

B60

HAYEK F.A.,THE CONSTITUTION OF LIBERTY. UNIV LAW CONSTN WORKER TAX EDU/PROP ADMIN CT/SYS COERCE DISCRIM...IDEA/COMP 20. PAGE 48 B0974 — ORD/FREE CHOOSE NAT/G CONCPT

B60

HEAP D.,AN OUTLINE OF PLANNING LAW (3RD ED.). UK LAW PROB/SOLV ADMIN CONTROL 20. PAGE 49 B0983 — MUNIC PLAN JURID LOC/G

B60

LENCZOWSKI G.,OIL AND STATE IN THE MIDDLE EAST. FUT IRAN LAW ECO/UNDEV EXTR/IND NAT/G TOP/EX PLAN TEC/DEV ECO/TAC LEGIT ADMIN COERCE ATTIT ALL/VALS PWR...CHARTS 20. PAGE 64 B1288 — ISLAM INDUS NAT/LISM

B60

LEWIS P.R.,LITERATURE OF THE SOCIAL SCIENCES: AN INTRODUCTORY SURVEY AND GUIDE. UK LAW INDUS DIPLOM INT/TRADE ADMIN...MGT 19/20. PAGE 65 B1306 — BIBLIOG/A SOC

B60

PHILLIPS J.C.,MUNICIPAL GOVERNMENT AND ADMINISTRATION IN AMERICA. USA+45 LAW CONSTN FINAN FORCES PLAN RECEIVE OWN ORD/FREE 20 CIVIL/LIB. PAGE 83 B1669 — MUNIC GOV/REL LOC/G ADMIN

B60

PINTO F.B.M.,ENRIQUECIMENTO ILICITO NO EXERCICIO DE CARGOS PUBLICOS. BRAZIL L/A+17C USA+45 ELITES TRIBUTE CONTROL INGP/REL ORD/FREE PWR...NAT/COMP 20. PAGE 83 B1675 — ADMIN NAT/G CRIME LAW

B60

US SENATE COMM ON JUDICIARY,FEDERAL ADMINISTRATIVE PROCEDURE. USA+45 CONSTN NAT/G PROB/SOLV CONFER GOV/REL...JURID INT 20 SENATE. PAGE 110 B2226 — PARL/PROC LEGIS ADMIN LAW

S60

EMERSON R.,"THE EROSION OF DEMOCRACY." AFR FUT LAW CULTURE INTELL SOCIETY ECO/UNDEV FAM LOC/G NAT/G FORCES PLAN TEC/DEV ECO/TAC ADMIN CT/SYS ATTIT ORD/FREE PWR...SOCIALIST SOC CONCPT STAND/INT TIME/SEQ WORK 20. PAGE 33 B0671 — S/ASIA POL/PAR

S60

MARSHALL G.,"POLICE RESPONSIBILITY." UK LOC/G ADJUD ADMIN EXEC 20. PAGE 70 B1409 — CONTROL REPRESENT LAW FORCES

S60

MORA J.A.,"THE ORGANIZATION OF AMERICAN STATES." USA+45 LAW ECO/UNDEV VOL/ASSN DELIB/GP PLAN BAL/PWR EDU/PROP ADMIN DRIVE RIGID/FLEX ORD/FREE WEALTH ...TIME/SEQ GEN/LAWS OAS 20. PAGE 75 B1518 — L/A+17C INT/ORG REGION

S60

MORALES C.J.,"TRADE AND ECONOMIC INTEGRATION IN LATIN AMERICA." FUT L/A+17C LAW STRATA ECO/UNDEV DIST/IND INDUS LABOR NAT/G LEGIS ECO/TAC ADMIN RIGID/FLEX WEALTH...CONCPT NEW/IDEA CONT/OBS TIME/SEQ WORK 20. PAGE 75 B1519 — FINAN INT/TRADE REGION

S60

SMIGEL E.O.,"THE IMPACT OF RECRUITMENT ON THE ORGANIZATION OF THE LARGE LAW FIRM" (BMR)" USA+45 STRUCT CONSULT PLAN GP/REL EFFICIENCY JURID. PAGE 98 B1979 — LG/CO ADMIN LAW WORKER

S60

THOMPSON K.W.,"MORAL PURPOSE IN FOREIGN POLICY: REALITIES AND ILLUSIONS." WOR+45 WOR-45 LAW CULTURE SOCIETY INT/ORG PLAN ADJUD ADMIN COERCE RIGID/FLEX SUPEGO KNOWL ORD/FREE PWR...SOC TREND SOC/EXP TOT/POP 20. PAGE 104 B2104 — MORAL JURID DIPLOM

N60

RHODESIA-NYASA NATL ARCHIVES,A SELECT BIBLIOGRAPHY OF RECENT PUBLICATIONS CONCERNING THE FEDERATION OF RHODESIA AND NYASALAND (PAMPHLET). MALAWI RHODESIA LAW CULTURE STRUCT ECO/UNDEV LEGIS...GEOG 20. PAGE 88 B1770 — BIBLIOG ADMIN ORD/FREE NAT/G

B61

BURDETTE F.L.,POLITICAL SCIENCE: A SELECTED BIBLIOGRAPHY OF BOOKS IN PRINT, WITH ANNOTATIONS (PAMPHLET). LAW LOC/G NAT/G POL/PAR PROVS DIPLOM EDU/PROP ADMIN CHOOSE ATTIT 20. PAGE 17 B0347 — BIBLIOG/A GOV/COMP CONCPT ROUTINE

B61

CARROTHERS A.W.R.,LABOR ARBITRATION IN CANADA. CANADA LAW NAT/G CONSULT LEGIS WORKER ADJUD ADMIN CT/SYS 20. PAGE 19 B0386 — LABOR MGT GP/REL BARGAIN

LAHAYE R.,LES ENTREPRISES PUBLIQUES AU MAROC.
FRANCE MOROCCO LAW DIST/IND EXTR/IND FINAN CONSULT
PLAN TEC/DEV ADMIN AGREE CONTROL OWN...POLICY 20.
PAGE 62 B1250
B61
NAT/G
INDUS
ECO/UNDEV
ECO/TAC

PUGET H.,ESSAI DE BIBLIOGRAPHIE DES PRINCIPAUX
OUVRAGES DE DROIT PUBLIC... QUI ONT PARU HORS DE
FRANCE DE 1945 A 1958. EUR+WWI USA+45 CONSTN LOC/G
...METH 20. PAGE 85 B1719
B61
BIBLIOG
MGT
ADMIN
LAW

TOMPKINS D.C.,CONFLICT OF INTEREST IN THE FEDERAL
GOVERNMENT: A BIBLIOGRAPHY. USA+45 EX/STRUC LEGIS
ADJUD ADMIN CRIME CONGRESS PRESIDENT. PAGE 105
B2117
B61
BIBLIOG
ROLE
NAT/G
LAW

WARD R.E.,JAPANESE POLITICAL SCIENCE: A GUIDE TO
JAPANESE REFERENCE AND RESEARCH MATERIALS (2ND
ED.). LAW CONSTN STRATA NAT/G POL/PAR DELIB/GP
LEGIS CHOOSE GP/REL...INT/LAW 19/20 CHINJAP.
PAGE 113 B2290
B61
BIBLIOG/A
PHIL/SCI

GERWIG R.,"PUBLIC AUTHORITIES IN THE UNITED
STATES." LAW CONSTN PROVS TAX ADMIN FEDERAL.
PAGE 39 B0793
L61
LOC/G
MUNIC
GOV/REL
PWR

MCNAMEE B.J.,"CONFLICT OF INTEREST: STATE
GOVERNMENT EMPLUYEES." USA+45 PROVS 20. PAGE 72
B1457
L61
LAW
REPRESENT
ADMIN
CONTROL

LEWY G.,"SUPERIOR ORDERS, NUCLEAR WARFARE AND THE
DICTATES OF CONSCIENCE: THE DILEMMA OF MILITARY
OBEDIENCE IN THE ATOMIC." FUT UNIV WOR+45 INTELL
SOCIETY FORCES TOP/EX ACT/RES ADMIN ROUTINE NUC/PWR
PERCEPT RIGID/FLEX ALL/VALS...POLICY CONCPT 20.
PAGE 65 B1308
S61
DETER
INT/ORG
LAW
INT/LAW

MOODIE G.C.,"THE GOVERNMENT OF GREAT BRITAIN." UK
LAW STRUCT LOC/G POL/PAR DIPLOM RECEIVE ADMIN
COLONIAL CHOOSE...BIBLIOG 20 PARLIAMENT. PAGE 75
B1508
C61
NAT/G
SOCIETY
PARL/PROC
GOV/COMP

CARPER E.T.,ILLINOIS GOES TO CONGRESS FOR ARMY
LAND. USA+45 LAW EXTR/IND PROVS REGION CIVMIL/REL
GOV/REL FEDERAL ATTIT 20 ILLINOIS SENATE CONGRESS
DIRKSEN/E DOUGLAS/P. PAGE 19 B0385
B62
ADMIN
LOBBY
GEOG
LEGIS

COSTA RICA UNIVERSIDAD BIBL,LISTA DE TESIS DE GRADO
DE LA UNIVERSIDAD DE COSTA RICA. COSTA/RICA LAW
LOC/G ADMIN LEAD...SOC 20. PAGE 24 B0487
B62
BIBLIOG/A
NAT/G
DIPLOM
ECO/UNDEV

GROGAN V.,ADMINISTRATIVE TRIBUNALS IN THE PUBLIC
SERVICE. IRELAND UK NAT/G CONTROL CT/SYS...JURID
GOV/COMP 20. PAGE 44 B0884
B62
ADMIN
LAW
ADJUD
DELIB/GP

HADWEN J.G.,HOW UNITED NATIONS DECISIONS ARE MADE.
WOR+45 LAW EDU/PROP LEGIT ADMIN PWR...DECISION
SELF/OBS GEN/LAWS UN 20. PAGE 45 B0912
B62
INT/ORG
ROUTINE

LOWI T.J.,LEGISLATIVE POLITICS U.S.A. LAW LEGIS
DIPLOM EXEC LOBBY CHOOSE SUFF FEDERAL PWR 19/20
CONGRESS. PAGE 67 B1345
B62
PARL/PROC
REPRESENT
POLICY
ROUTINE

PRESS C.,STATE MANUALS, BLUE BOOKS AND ELECTION
RESULTS. LAW LOC/G MUNIC LEGIS WRITING FEDERAL
SOVEREIGN...DECISION STAT CHARTS 20. PAGE 84 B1700
B62
BIBLIOG
PROVS
ADMIN
CHOOSE

SAMPSON A.,ANATOMY OF BRITAIN. UK LAW COM/IND FINAN
INDUS MARKET MUNIC POL/PAR EX/STRUC TOP/EX DIPLOM
LEAD REPRESENT PERSON PARLIAMENT WORSHIP. PAGE 92
B1866
B62
ELITES
PWR
STRUCT
FORCES

UNECA LIBRARY,NEW ACQUISITIONS IN THE UNECA
LIBRARY. LAW NAT/G PLAN PROB/SOLV TEC/DEV ADMIN
REGION...GEOG SOC 20 UN. PAGE 106 B2152
B62
BIBLIOG
AFR
ECO/UNDEV
INT/ORG

US ADVISORY COMN INTERGOV REL,STATE CONSTITUTIONAL
AND STATUTORY RESTRICTIONS UPON THE STRUCTURAL,
FUNCTIONAL, AND PERSONAL POWERS OF LOCAL GOV'T.
EX/STRUC ACT/RES DOMIN GOV/REL PWR...POLICY
DECISION 17/20. PAGE 108 B2172
B62
LOC/G
CONSTN
PROVS
LAW

SCHWERIN K.,"LAW LIBRARIES AND FOREIGN LAW
COLLECTION IN THE USA." USA+45 USA-45...INT/LAW
STAT 20. PAGE 95 B1917
L62
BIBLIOG
LAW
ACADEM
ADMIN

BRAIBANTI R.,"REFLECTIONS ON BUREAUCRATIC
CORRPUTION." LAW REPRESENT 20. PAGE 15 B0298
S62
CONTROL
MORAL

ADMIN
GOV/COMP

MANGIN G.,"LES ACCORDS DE COOPERATION EN MATIERE DE
JUSTICE ENTRE LA FRANCE ET LES ETATS AFRICAINS ET
MALGACHE." AFR ISLAM WOR+45 STRUCT ECO/UNDEV NAT/G
DELIB/GP PERCEPT ALL/VALS...JURID MGT TIME/SEQ 20.
PAGE 69 B1386
S62
INT/ORG
LAW
FRANCE

MORGAN G.G.,"SOVIET ADMINISTRATIVE LEGALITY: THE
ROLE OF THE ATTORNEY GENERAL'S OFFICE." COM USSR
CONTROL ROUTINE...CONCPT BIBLIOG 18/20. PAGE 75
B1522
C62
LAW
CONSTN
LEGIS
ADMIN

VAN DER SPRENKEL S.,"LEGAL INSTITUTIONS IN MANCHU
CHINA." ASIA STRUCT CT/SYS ROUTINE GOV/REL GP/REL
...CONCPT BIBLIOG 17/20. PAGE 111 B2250
C62
LAW
JURID
ADMIN
ADJUD

CHOJNACKI S.,REGISTER ON CURRENT RESEARCH ON
ETHIOPIA AND THE HORN OF AFRICA. ETHIOPIA LAW
CULTURE AGRI SECT EDU/PROP ADMIN...GEOG HEAL LING
20. PAGE 21 B0426
B63
BIBLIOG
ACT/RES
INTELL
ACADEM

COUNCIL STATE GOVERNMENTS,HANDBOOK FOR LEGISLATIVE
COMMITTEES. USA+45 LAW DELIB/GP EX/STRUC TOP/EX
CHOOSE PWR...METH/COMP 20. PAGE 24 B0496
B63
LEGIS
PARL/PROC
PROVS
ADJUD

DALAND R.T.,PERSPECTIVES OF BRAZILIAN PUBLIC
ADMINISTRATION (VOL. I). BRAZIL LAW ECO/UNDEV
SCHOOL CHIEF TEC/DEV CONFER CONTROL GP/REL ATTIT
ROLE PWR...ANTHOL 20. PAGE 26 B0525
B63
ADMIN
NAT/G
PLAN
GOV/REL

DE GUZMAN R.P.,PATTERNS IN DECISION-MAKING: CASE
STUDIES IN PHILIPPINE PUBLIC ADMINISTRATION.
PHILIPPINE LAW CHIEF PROB/SOLV INGP/REL DRIVE
PERCEPT ROLE...ANTHOL T 20. PAGE 27 B0557
B63
ADMIN
DECISION
POLICY
GOV/REL

ELIAS T.O.,THE NIGERIAN LEGAL SYSTEM. NIGERIA LAW
FAM KIN SECT ADMIN NAT/LISM...JURID 18/20
ENGLSH/LAW COMMON/LAW. PAGE 33 B0665
B63
CT/SYS
ADJUD
COLONIAL
PROF/ORG

GARNER U.F.,ADMINISTRATIVE LAW. UK LAW LOC/G NAT/G
EX/STRUC LEGIS JUDGE BAL/PWR BUDGET ADJUD CONTROL
CT/SYS...BIBLIOG 20. PAGE 39 B0783
B63
ADMIN
JURID
PWR
GOV/REL

GOURNAY B.,PUBLIC ADMINISTRATION. FRANCE LAW CONSTN
AGRI FINAN LABOR SCHOOL EX/STRUC CHOOSE...MGT
METH/COMP 20. PAGE 42 B0846
B63
BIBLIOG/A
ADMIN
NAT/G
LOC/G

HAUSMAN W.H.,MANAGING ECONOMIC DEVELOPMENT IN
AFRICA. AFR USA+45 LAW FINAN WORKER TEC/DEV WEALTH
...ANTHOL 20. PAGE 48 B0970
B63
ECO/UNDEV
PLAN
FOR/AID
MGT

HOUGHTELING J.L. JR.,THE LEGAL ENVIRONMENT OF
BUSINESS. LG/CO NAT/G CONSULT AGREE CONTROL
...DICTIONARY T 20. PAGE 52 B1047
B63
LAW
MGT
ADJUD
JURID

JACOB H.,GERMAN ADMINISTRATION SINCE BISMARCK:
CENTRAL AUTHORITY VERSUS LOCAL AUTONOMY. GERMANY
GERMANY/W LAW POL/PAR CONTROL CENTRAL TOTALISM
FASCISM...MAJORIT DECISION STAT CHARTS GOV/COMP
19/20 BISMARCK/O HITLER/A WEIMAR/REP. PAGE 55 B1111
B63
ADMIN
NAT/G
LOC/G
POLICY

KLESMENT J.,LEGAL SOURCES AND BIBLIOGRAPHY OF THE
BALTIC STATES (ESTONIA, LATVIA, LITHUANIA). COM
ESTONIA LATVIA LITHUANIA LAW FINAN ADJUD CT/SYS
REGION CENTRAL MARXISM 19/20. PAGE 60 B1218
B63
BIBLIOG/A
JURID
CONSTN
ADMIN

PALOTAI O.C.,PUBLICATIONS OF THE INSTITUTE OF
GOVERNMENT, 1930-1962. LAW PROVS SCHOOL WORKER
ACT/RES OP/RES CT/SYS GOV/REL...CRIMLGY SOC/WK.
PAGE 81 B1629
B63
BIBLIOG/A
ADMIN
LOC/G
FINAN

PLISCHKE E.,GOVERNMENT AND POLITICS OF CONTEMPORARY
BERLIN. GERMANY LAW CONSTN POL/PAR LEGIS WAR CHOOSE
REPRESENT GOV/REL...CHARTS BIBLIOG 20 BERLIN.
PAGE 83 B1683
B63
MUNIC
LOC/G
POLICY
ADMIN

ROYAL INSTITUTE PUBLIC ADMIN,BRITISH PUBLIC
ADMINISTRATION. UK LAW FINAN INDUS LOC/G POL/PAR
LEGIS LOBBY PARL/PROC CHOOSE JURID. PAGE 91 B1845
B63
BIBLIOG
ADMIN
MGT
NAT/G

US CONGRESS: SENATE,HEARINGS OF THE COMMITTEE ON
THE JUDICIARY. USA+45 CONSTN NAT/G ADMIN GOV/REL 20
CONGRESS. PAGE 108 B2179
B63
LEGIS
LAW
ORD/FREE
DELIB/GP

WALKER A.A.,OFFICIAL PUBLICATIONS OF SIERRA LEONE
B63
BIBLIOG

AND GAMBIA. GAMBIA SIER/LEONE UK LAW CONSTN LEGIS NAT/G
PLAN BUDGET DIPLOM...SOC SAMP CON/ANAL 20. PAGE 113 COLONIAL
B2278 ADMIN

L63
BOLGAR V.,"THE PUBLIC INTEREST: A JURISPRUDENTIAL CONCPT
AND COMPARATIVE OVERVIEW OF SYMPOSIUM ON ORD/FREE
FUNDAMENTAL CONCEPTS OF PUBLIC LAW" COM FRANCE CONTROL
GERMANY SWITZERLND LAW ADJUD ADMIN AGREE LAISSEZ NAT/COMP
...JURID GEN/LAWS 20 EUROPE/E. PAGE 13 B0268

S63
BECHHOEFER B.G.,"UNITED NATIONS PROCEDURES IN CASE INT/ORG
OF VIOLATIONS OF DISARMAMENT AGREEMENTS." COM DELIB/GP
USA+45 USSR LAW CONSTN NAT/G EX/STRUC FORCES LEGIS
BAL/PWR EDU/PROP CT/SYS ARMS/CONT ORD/FREE PWR
...POLICY STERTYP UN VAL/FREE 20. PAGE 10 B0204

S63
JOELSON M.R.,"THE DISMISSAL OF CIVIL SERVANTS IN USA+45
THE INTERESTS OF NATIONAL SECURITY." EUR+WWI LAW NAT/G
DELIB/GP ROUTINE ORD/FREE...MGT VAL/FREE 20. UK
PAGE 56 B1141 FRANCE

B64
BENNETT H.A.,THE COMMISSION AND THE COMMON LAW: A ADJUD
STUDY IN ADMINISTRATIVE ADJUDICATION. LAW ADMIN DELIB/GP
CT/SYS LOBBY SANCTION GOV/REL 20 COMMON/LAW. DIST/IND
PAGE 10 B0212 POLICY

B64
CULLINGWORTH J.B.,TOWN AND COUNTRY PLANNING IN MUNIC
ENGLAND AND WALES. UK LAW SOCIETY CONSULT ACT/RES PLAN
ADMIN ROUTINE LEISURE INGP/REL ADJUST PWR...GEOG 20 NAT/G
OPEN/SPACE URBAN/RNWL. PAGE 25 B0512 PROB/SOLV

B64
GJUPANOVIC H.,LEGAL SOURCES AND BIBLIOGRAPHY OF BIBLIOG/A
YUGOSLAVIA. COM YUGOSLAVIA LAW LEGIS DIPLOM ADMIN JURID
PARL/PROC REGION CRIME CENTRAL 20. PAGE 40 B0807 CONSTN
ADJUD

B64
GOODNOW H.F.,THE CIVIL SERVICE OF PAKISTAN: ADMIN
BUREAUCRACY IN A NEW NATION. INDIA PAKISTAN S/ASIA GOV/REL
ECO/UNDEV PROVS CHIEF PARTIC CHOOSE EFFICIENCY PWR LAW
...BIBLIOG 20. PAGE 41 B0824 NAT/G

B64
HICKEY G.C.,VILLAGE IN VIETNAM. USA+45 VIETNAM LAW CULTURE
AGRI FAM SECT ADMIN ATTIT...SOC CHARTS WORSHIP 20. SOCIETY
PAGE 49 B1003 STRUCT
S/ASIA

B64
INST D'ETUDE POL L'U GRENOBLE,ADMINISTRATION ADMIN
TRADITIONELLE ET PLANIFICATION REGIONALE. FRANCE MUNIC
LAW POL/PAR PROB/SOLV ADJUST RIGID/FLEX...CHARTS PLAN
ANTHOL BIBLIOG T 20 REFORMERS. PAGE 54 B1087 CREATE

B64
KAHNG T.J.,LAW, POLITICS, AND THE SECURITY COUNCIL* DELIB/GP
AN INQUIRY INTO THE HANDLING OF LEGAL QUESTIONS. ADJUD
LAW CONSTN NAT/G ACT/RES OP/RES CT/SYS TASK PWR ROUTINE
...INT/LAW BIBLIOG UN. PAGE 57 B1160

B64
KAPP E.,THE MERGER OF THE EXECUTIVES OF THE CENTRAL
EUROPEAN COMMUNITIES. LAW CONSTN STRUCT ACT/RES EX/STRUC
PLAN PROB/SOLV ADMIN REGION TASK...INT/LAW MGT ECSC
EEC. PAGE 58 B1170

B64
KARLEN D.,THE CITIZEN IN COURT. USA+45 LAW ADMIN CT/SYS
ROUTINE CRIME GP/REL...JURID 20. PAGE 58 B1175 ADJUD
GOV/REL
JUDGE

B64
KEEFE W.J.,THE AMERICAN LEGISLATIVE PROCESS: LEGIS
CONGRESS AND THE STATES. USA+45 LAW POL/PAR DECISION
DELIB/GP DEBATE ADMIN LOBBY REPRESENT CONGRESS PWR
PRESIDENT. PAGE 59 B1187 PROVS

B64
NELSON D.H.,ADMINISTRATIVE AGENCIES OF THE USA: ADMIN
THEIR DECISIONS AND AUTHORITY. USA+45 NAT/G CONTROL EX/STRUC
CT/SYS REPRESENT...DECISION 20. PAGE 78 B1568 ADJUD
LAW

B64
O'HEARN P.J.T.,PEACE, ORDER AND GOOD GOVERNMENT; A NAT/G
NEW CONSTITUTION FOR CANADA. CANADA EX/STRUC LEGIS CONSTN
CT/SYS PARL/PROC...BIBLIOG 20. PAGE 79 B1600 LAW
CREATE

B64
RICHARDSON I.L.,BIBLIOGRAFIA BRASILEIRA DE BIBLIOG
ADMINISTRACAO PUBLICA E ASSUNTOS CORRELATOS. BRAZIL MGT
CONSTN FINAN LOC/G NAT/G POL/PAR PLAN DIPLOM ADMIN
RECEIVE ATTIT...METH 20. PAGE 88 B1776 LAW

B64
RIGGS R.E.,THE MOVEMENT FOR ADMINISTRATIVE ADMIN
REORGANIZATION IN ARIZONA. USA+45 LAW POL/PAR PROVS
DELIB/GP LEGIS PROB/SOLV CONTROL RIGID/FLEX PWR CREATE
...ORG/CHARTS 20 ARIZONA DEMOCRAT REPUBLICAN. PLAN
PAGE 88 B1786

B64
STOICOIU V.,LEGAL SOURCES AND BIBLIOGRAPHY OF BIBLIOG/A
ROMANIA. COM ROMANIA LAW FINAN POL/PAR LEGIS JUDGE JURID
ADJUD CT/SYS PARL/PROC MARXISM 20. PAGE 101 B2041 CONSTN
ADMIN

B64
SZLADITS C.,BIBLIOGRAPHY ON FOREIGN AND COMPARATIVE BIBLIOG/A
LAW: BOOKS AND ARTICLES IN ENGLISH (SUPPLEMENT JURID
1962). FINAN INDUS JUDGE LICENSE ADMIN CT/SYS ADJUD
PARL/PROC OWN...INT/LAW CLASSIF METH/COMP NAT/COMP LAW
20. PAGE 102 B2065

B64
THE BRITISH COUNCIL,PUBLIC ADMINISTRATION: A SELECT BIBLIOG
LIST OF BOOKS AND PERIODICALS. LAW CONSTN FINAN ADMIN
POL/PAR SCHOOL CHOOSE...HEAL MGT METH/COMP 19/20 LOC/G
CMN/WLTH. PAGE 104 B2094 INDUS

B64
TURNER H.A.,THE GOVERNMENT AND POLITICS OF PROVS
CALIFORNIA (2ND ED.). LAW FINAN MUNIC POL/PAR ADMIN
SCHOOL EX/STRUC LEGIS LOBBY CHOOSE...CHARTS T 20 LOC/G
CALIFORNIA. PAGE 106 B2138 CONSTN

B64
TURNER M.C.,LIBROS EN VENTA EN HISPANOAMERICA Y BIBLIOG
ESPANA. SPAIN LAW CONSTN CULTURE ADMIN LEAD...HUM L/A+17C
SOC 20. PAGE 106 B2139 NAT/G
DIPLOM

B64
WITHERELL J.W.,OFFICIAL PUBLICATIONS OF FRENCH BIBLIOG/A
EQUATORIAL AFRICA, FRENCH CAMEROONS, AND TOGO, AFR
1946-1958 (PAMPHLET). CAMEROON CHAD FRANCE GABON NAT/G
TOGO LAW ECO/UNDEV EXTR/IND INT/TRADE...GEOG HEAL ADMIN
20. PAGE 117 B2367

B64
WRAITH R.,CORRUPTION IN DEVELOPING COUNTRIES. ECO/UNDEV
NIGERIA UK LAW ELITES STRATA INDUS LOC/G NAT/G SECT CRIME
FORCES EDU/PROP ADMIN PWR WEALTH 18/20. PAGE 118 SANCTION
B2377 ATTIT

S64
SCHWELB E.,"OPERATION OF THE EUROPEAN CONVENTION ON INT/ORG
HUMAN RIGHTS." EUR+WWI LAW SOCIETY CREATE EDU/PROP MORAL
ADJUD ADMIN PEACE ATTIT ORD/FREE PWR...POLICY
INT/LAW CONCPT OBS GEN/LAWS UN VAL/FREE ILO 20
ECHR. PAGE 95 B1916

C64
NORGREN P.H.,"TOWARD FAIR EMPLOYMENT." USA+45 LAW RACE/REL
STRATA LABOR NAT/G FORCES ACT/RES ADMIN ATTIT DISCRIM
...POLICY BIBLIOG 20 NEGRO. PAGE 79 B1588 WORKER
MGT

B65
BERNDT R.M.,ABORIGINAL MAN IN AUSTRALIA. LAW DOMIN SOC
ADMIN COLONIAL MARRIAGE HABITAT ORD/FREE...LING CULTURE
CHARTS ANTHOL BIBLIOG WORSHIP 20 AUSTRAL ABORIGINES SOCIETY
MUSIC ELKIN/AP. PAGE 11 B0225 STRUCT

B65
BOCK E.,GOVERNMENT REGULATION OF BUSINESS. USA+45 MGT
LAW EX/STRUC LEGIS EXEC ORD/FREE PWR...ANTHOL ADMIN
CONGRESS. PAGE 13 B0261 NAT/G
CONTROL

B65
CHEN T.H.,THE CHINESE COMMUNIST REGIME: A MARXISM
DOCUMENTARY STUDY (2 VOLS.). CHINA/COM LAW CONSTN POL/PAR
ELITES ECO/UNDEV LEGIS ECO/TAC ADMIN CONTROL PWR NAT/G
...SOC 20. PAGE 20 B0417

B65
COOPER F.E.,STATE ADMINISTRATIVE LAW (2 VOLS.). LAW JURID
LEGIS PLAN TAX ADJUD CT/SYS FEDERAL PWR...CONCPT CONSTN
20. PAGE 23 B0474 ADMIN
PROVS

B65
FEERICK J.D.,FROM FAILING HANDS: THE STUDY OF EX/STRUC
PRESIDENTIAL SUCCESSION. CONSTN NAT/G PROB/SOLV CHIEF
LEAD PARL/PROC MURDER CHOOSE...NEW/IDEA BIBLIOG 20 LAW
KENNEDY/JF JOHNSON/LB PRESIDENT PRE/US/AM LEGIS
VICE/PRES. PAGE 35 B0710

B65
FRIEDMAN L.,SOUTHERN JUSTICE. USA+45 PUB/INST LEGIT ADJUD
ADMIN CT/SYS DISCRIM...DECISION ANTHOL 20 NEGRO LAW
SOUTH/US CIV/RIGHTS. PAGE 37 B0758 CONSTN
RACE/REL

B65
HARMON R.B.,POLITICAL SCIENCE: A BIBLIOGRAPHICAL BIBLIOG
GUIDE TO THE LITERATURE. WOR+45 WOR-45 R+D INT/ORG POL/PAR
LOC/G NAT/G DIPLOM ADMIN...CONCPT METH. PAGE 47 LAW
B0950 GOV/COMP

B65
LEYS C.T.,FEDERATION IN EAST AFRICA. LAW AGRI FEDERAL
DIST/IND FINAN INT/ORG LABOR INT/TRADE CONFER ADMIN REGION
CONTROL GP/REL...ANTHOL 20 AFRICA/E. PAGE 65 B1310 ECO/UNDEV
PLAN

B65
MORGENTHAU H.,MORGENTHAU DIARY (CHINA) (2 VOLS.). DIPLOM
ASIA USA+45 USA-45 LAW DELIB/GP EX/STRUC PLAN ADMIN
FOR/AID INT/TRADE CONFER WAR MARXISM 20 CHINJAP.
PAGE 75 B1523

B65
ROSS P.,THE GOVERNMENT AS A SOURCE OF UNION POWER. LABOR
USA+45 LAW ECO/DEV PROB/SOLV ECO/TAC LEAD GP/REL BARGAIN
...MGT 20. PAGE 90 B1826 POLICY
NAT/G

B65
ROWE J.Z.,THE PUBLIC-PRIVATE CHARACTER OF UNITED FINAN

STATES CENTRAL BANKING. USA+45 NAT/G EX/STRUC
...BIBLIOG 20 FED/RESERV. PAGE 91 B1842
PLAN
FEDERAL
LAW
B65

SMITH C.,THE OMBUDSMAN: A BIBLIOGRAPHY (PAMPHLET).
DENMARK SWEDEN USA+45 LAW LEGIS JUDGE GOV/REL
GP/REL...JURID 20. PAGE 98 B1980
BIBLIOG
ADMIN
CT/SYS
ADJUD
B65

UNESCO,INTERNATIONAL ORGANIZATIONS IN THE SOCIAL
SCIENCES(REV. ED.). LAW ADMIN ATTIT...CRIMLGY GEOG
INT/LAW PSY SOC STAT 20 UNESCO. PAGE 107 B2157
INT/ORG
R+D
PROF/ORG
ACT/RES
B65

VAID K.N.,STATE AND LABOR IN INDIA. INDIA INDUS
WORKER PAY PRICE ADJUD CONTROL PARL/PROC GP/REL
ORD/FREE 20. PAGE 111 B2248
LAW
LABOR
MGT
NEW/LIB
B65

VONGLAHN G.,LAW AMONG NATIONS: AN INTRODUCTION TO
PUBLIC INTERNATIONAL LAW. UNIV WOR+45 LAW INT/ORG
NAT/G LEGIT EXEC RIGID/FLEX...CONCPT TIME/SEQ
GEN/LAWS UN TOT/POP 20. PAGE 112 B2267
CONSTN
JURID
INT/LAW
B65

WITHERELL J.W.,MADAGASCAR AND ADJACENT ISLANDS: A
GUIDE TO OFFICIAL PUBLICATIONS (PAMPHLET). FRANCE
MADAGASCAR S/ASIA UK LAW OP/RES PLAN DIPLOM
...POLICY CON/ANAL 19/20. PAGE 117 B2368
BIBLIOG
COLONIAL
LOC/G
ADMIN
L65

MATTHEWS D.G.,"A CURRENT BIBLIOGRAPHY ON ETHIOPIAN
AFFAIRS: A SELECT BIBLIOGRAPHY FROM 1950-1964."
ETHIOPIA LAW CULTURE ECO/UNDEV INDUS LABOR SECT
FORCES DIPLOM CIVMIL/REL RACE/REL...LING STAT 20.
PAGE 71 B1428
BIBLIOG/A
ADMIN
POL/PAR
NAT/G
L65

RUBIN A.P.,"UNITED STATES CONTEMPORARY PRACTICE
RELATING TO INTERNATIONAL LAW." USA+45 WOR+45
CONSTN INT/ORG NAT/G DELIB/GP EX/STRUC DIPLOM DOMIN
CT/SYS ROUTINE ORD/FREE...CONCPT COLD/WAR 20.
PAGE 91 B1848
LAW
LEGIT
INT/LAW
B66

AARON T.J.,THE CONTROL OF POLICE DISCRETION: THE
DANISH EXPERIENCE. DENMARK LAW CREATE ADMIN
INGP/REL SUPEGO PWR 20 OMBUDSMAN. PAGE 2 B0049
CONTROL
FORCES
REPRESENT
PROB/SOLV
B66

BRAIBANTI R.,RESEARCH ON THE BUREAUCRACY OF
PAKISTAN. PAKISTAN LAW CULTURE INTELL ACADEM LOC/G
SECT PRESS CT/SYS...LING CHARTS 20 BUREAUCRCY.
PAGE 15 B0299
HABITAT
NAT/G
ADMIN
CONSTN
B66

LEE L.T.,VIENNA CONVENTION ON CONSULAR RELATIONS.
WOR+45 LAW INT/ORG CONFER GP/REL PRIVIL...INT/LAW
20 TREATY VIENNA/CNV. PAGE 63 B1279
AGREE
DIPLOM
ADMIN
B66

PERROW C.,ORGANIZATION FOR TREATMENT: A COMPARATIVE
STUDY OF INSTITUTIONS FOR DELINQUENTS. LAW
PROB/SOLV ADMIN CRIME PERSON MORAL...SOC/WK OBS
DEEP/QU CHARTS SOC/EXP SOC/INTEG 20. PAGE 82 B1661
AGE/Y
PSY
PUB/INST
B66

RAPHAEL J.S.,GOVERNMENTAL REGULATION OF BUSINESS.
USA+45 LAW CONSTN TAX ADJUD ADMIN EFFICIENCY PWR
20. PAGE 86 B1736
LG/CO
GOV/REL
CONTROL
ECO/DEV
B66

SCHLESSINGER P.J.,ELEMENTS OF CALIFORNIA GOVERNMENT
(2ND ED.). USA+45 LAW ADJUD ADMIN CONTROL CT/SYS
EFFICIENCY...BIBLIOG T CALIFORNIA. PAGE 94 B1891
LOC/G
PROVS
GOV/REL
LEGIS
B66

WALL E.H.,THE COURT OF JUSTICE IN THE EUROPEAN
COMMUNITIES: JURISDICTION AND PROCEDURE. EUR+WWI
DIPLOM ADJUD ADMIN ROUTINE TASK...CONCPT LING 20.
PAGE 113 B2281
CT/SYS
INT/ORG
LAW
OP/RES
B66

WASHINGTON S.H.,BIBLIOGRAPHY: LABOR-MANAGEMENT
RELATIONS ACT, 1947 AS AMENDED BY LABOR-MANAGEMENT
REPORTING AND DISCLOSURE ACT, 1959. USA+45 CONSTN
INDUS DELIB/GP LEGIS WORKER BARGAIN ECO/TAC ADJUD
GP/REL NEW/LIB...JURID CONGRESS. PAGE 114 B2298
BIBLIOG
LAW
LABOR
MGT
B66

WILSON G.,CASES AND MATERIALS ON CONSTITUTIONAL AND
ADMINISTRATIVE LAW. UK LAW NAT/G EX/STRUC LEGIS
BAL/PWR BUDGET DIPLOM ADJUD CONTROL CT/SYS GOV/REL
ORD/FREE 20 PARLIAMENT ENGLSH/LAW. PAGE 117 B2359
JURID
ADMIN
CONSTN
PWR
B66

ZINKIN T.,CHALLENGES IN INDIA. INDIA PAKISTAN LAW
AGRI FINAN INDUS TOP/EX TEC/DEV CONTROL ROUTINE
ORD/FREE PWR 20 NEHRU/J SHASTRI/LB CIVIL/SERV.
PAGE 119 B2404
NAT/G
ECO/TAC
POLICY
ADMIN
L66

SEYLER W.C.,"DOCTORAL DISSERTATIONS IN POLITICAL
SCIENCE IN UNIVERSITIES OF THE UNITED STATES AND
CANADA." INT/ORG LOC/G ADMIN...INT/LAW MGT
GOV/COMP. PAGE 96 B1930
BIBLIOG
LAW
NAT/G

BURDETTE F.L.,"SELECTED ARTICLES AND DOCUMENTS ON
AMERICAN GOVERNMENT AND POLITICS." LAW LOC/G MUNIC
NAT/G POL/PAR PROVS LEGIS BAL/PWR ADMIN EXEC
REPRESENT MGT. PAGE 17 B0348
S66
BIBLIOG
USA+45
JURID
CONSTN
S66

MATTHEWS D.G.,"ETHIOPIAN OUTLINE: A BIBLIOGRAPHIC
RESEARCH GUIDE." ETHIOPIA LAW STRUCT ECO/UNDEV AGRI
LABOR SECT CHIEF DELIB/GP EX/STRUC ADMIN...LING
ORG/CHARTS 20. PAGE 71 B1429
BIBLIOG
NAT/G
DIPLOM
POL/PAR
S66

MATTHEWS D.G.,"PRELUDE-COUP D'ETAT-MILITARY
GOVERNMENT: A BIBLIOGRAPHICAL AND RESEARCH GUIDE TO
NIGERIAN POL AND GOVT, JAN. 1965-66." AFR NIGER LAW
CONSTN POL/PAR LEGIS CIVMIL/REL GOV/REL...STAT 20.
PAGE 71 B1430
BIBLIOG
NAT/G
ADMIN
CHOOSE
S66

POLSBY N.W.,"BOOKS IN THE FIELD: POLITICAL
SCIENCE." LAW CONSTN LOC/G NAT/G LEGIS ADJUD PWR 20
SUPREME/CT. PAGE 83 B1686
BIBLIOG/A
ATTIT
ADMIN
JURID
N66

BACHELDER G.L.,THE LITERATURE OF FEDERALISM: A
SELECTED BIBLIOGRAPHY (REV ED) (A PAMPHLET). USA+45
USA-45 WOR+45 LAW CONSTN PROVS ADMIN CT/SYS
GOV/REL ROLE...CONCPT 19/20. PAGE 8 B0155
BIBLIOG
FEDERAL
NAT/G
LOC/G
B67

BLUMBERG A.S.,CRIMINAL JUSTICE. USA+45 CLIENT LAW
LOC/G FORCES JUDGE ACT/RES LEGIT ADMIN RATIONAL
MYTH. PAGE 13 B0259
JURID
CT/SYS
PROF/ORG
CRIME
B67

BROWN L.N.,FRENCH ADMINISTRATIVE LAW. FRANCE UK
CONSTN NAT/G LEGIS DOMIN CONTROL EXEC PARL/PROC PWR
...JURID METH/COMP GEN/METH. PAGE 16 B0324
EX/STRUC
LAW
IDEA/COMP
CT/SYS
B67

BUREAU GOVERNMENT RES AND SERV,COUNTY GOVERNMENT
REORGANIZATION - A SELECTED ANNOTATED BIBLIOGRAPHY
(PAPER). USA+45 USA-45 LAW CONSTN MUNIC PROVS
EX/STRUC CREATE PLAN PROB/SOLV REPRESENT GOV/REL
20. PAGE 17 B0349
BIBLIOG/A
APPORT
LOC/G
ADMIN
B67

GELLHORN W.,OMBUDSMEN AND OTHERS: CITIZENS'
PROTECTORS IN NINE COUNTRIES. WOR+45 LAW CONSTN
LEGIS INSPECT ADJUD ADMIN CONTROL CT/SYS CHOOSE
PERS/REL...STAT CHARTS 20. PAGE 39 B0789
NAT/COMP
REPRESENT
INGP/REL
PROB/SOLV
B67

GREENE L.S.,AMERICAN GOVERNMENT POLICIES AND
FUNCTIONS. USA+45 LAW AGRI DIST/IND LABOR MUNIC
BUDGET DIPLOM EDU/PROP ORD/FREE...BIBLIOG T 20.
PAGE 43 B0867
POLICY
NAT/G
ADMIN
DECISION
B67

HEWITT W.H.,ADMINISTRATION OF CRIMINAL JUSTICE IN
NEW YORK. LAW PROB/SOLV ADJUD ADMIN...CRIMLGY
CHARTS T 20 NEW/YORK. PAGE 49 B1001
CRIME
ROLE
CT/SYS
FORCES
B67

ILLINOIS COMMISSION,IMPROVING THE STATE
LEGISLATURE. USA+45 LAW CONSTN NAT/G PROB/SOLV
EDU/PROP ADMIN TASK CHOOSE INGP/REL EFFICIENCY
ILLINOIS. PAGE 53 B1077
PROVS
LEGIS
REPRESENT
PLAN
B67

KATZ J.,PSYCHOANALYSIS, PSYCHIATRY, AND LAW. USA+45
LOC/G NAT/G PUB/INST PROB/SOLV ADMIN HEALTH
...CRIMLGY CONCPT SAMP/SIZ IDEA/COMP. PAGE 58 B1180
LAW
PSY
CT/SYS
ADJUD
B67

KRISLOV S.,THE NEGRO IN FEDERAL EMPLOYMENT. LAW
STRATA LOC/G CREATE PROB/SOLV INSPECT GOV/REL
DISCRIM ROLE...DECISION INT TREND 20 NEGRO WWI
CIVIL/SERV. PAGE 61 B1238
WORKER
NAT/G
ADMIN
RACE/REL
B67

LENG S.C.,JUSTICE IN COMMUNIST CHINA: A SURVEY OF
THE JUDICIAL SYSTEM OF THE CHINESE PEOPLE'S
REPUBLIC. CHINA/COM LAW CONSTN LOC/G NAT/G PROF/ORG
CONSULT FORCES ADMIN CRIME ORD/FREE...BIBLIOG 20
MAO. PAGE 64 B1290
CT/SYS
ADJUD
JURID
MARXISM
B67

NARVER J.C.,CONGLOMERATE MERGERS AND MARKET
COMPETITION. USA+45 LAW STRUCT ADMIN LEAD RISK COST
PROFIT WEALTH...POLICY CHARTS BIBLIOG. PAGE 77
B1555
DEMAND
LG/CO
MARKET
MGT
B67

UNIVERSAL REFERENCE SYSTEM,PUBLIC POLICY AND THE
MANAGEMENT OF SCIENCE (VOLUME IX). FUT SPACE WOR+45
LAW NAT/G TEC/DEV CONTROL NUC/PWR GOV/REL
...COMPUT/IR GEN/METH. PAGE 107 B2165
BIBLIOG/A
POLICY
MGT
PHIL/SCI
B67

WEINBERG M.,SCHOOL INTEGRATION: A COMPREHENSIVE
CLASSIFIED BIBLIOGRAPHY OF 3,100 REFERENCES. USA+45
LAW NAT/G NEIGH SECT PLAN ROUTINE AGE/C WEALTH
SOC/INTEG INDIAN/AM. PAGE 115 B2314
BIBLIOG
SCHOOL
DISCRIM
RACE/REL
B67

ZELERMYER W.,BUSINESS LAW: NEW PERSPECTIVES IN
BUSINESS ECONOMICS. USA+45 LAW INDUS DELIB/GP
LABOR
CAP/ISM

...JURID MGT ANTHOL BIBLIOG 20 NLRB. PAGE 119 B2400 LG/CO

L67
BERGER R.,"ADMINISTRATIVE ARBITRARINESS* A SEQUEL." LAW
USA+45 CONSTN ADJUD CT/SYS SANCTION INGP/REL   LABOR
...POLICY JURID. PAGE 11 B0222   BARGAIN
                                                          ADMIN

L67
CAHIERS P.,"LE RECOURS EN CONSTATATION DE   INT/ORG
MANQUEMENTS DES ETATS MEMBRES DEVANT LA COUR DES   CONSTN
COMMUNAUTES EUROPEENNES." LAW PROB/SOLV DIPLOM   ROUTINE
ADMIN CT/SYS SANCTION ATTIT...POLICY DECISION JURID ADJUD
ECSC EEC. PAGE 18 B0362

L67
CARMICHAEL D.M.,"FORTY YEARS OF WATER POLLUTION   HEALTH
CONTROL IN WISCONSIN: A CASE STUDY." LAW EXTR/IND   CONTROL
INDUS MUNIC DELIB/GP PLAN PROB/SOLV SANCTION   ADMIN
...CENSUS CHARTS 20 WISCONSIN. PAGE 19 B0382   ADJUD

L67
GAINES J.E.,"THE YOUTH COURT CONCEPT AND ITS   CT/SYS
IMPLEMENTATION IN TOMPKINS COUNTY, NEW YORK."   AGE/Y
USA+45 LAW CONSTN JUDGE WORKER ADJUD ADMIN CHOOSE   INGP/REL
PERSON...JURID NEW/YORK. PAGE 38 B0772   CRIME

L67
JACOBY S.B.,"THE 89TH CONGRESS AND GOVERNMENT   LAW
LITIGATION." USA+45 ADMIN COST...JURID 20 CONGRESS.   NAT/G
PAGE 55 B1117   ADJUD
                                                        SANCTION

L67
MANNE H.G.,"OUR TWO CORPORATION SYSTEMS* LAW AND   INDUS
ECONOMICS." LAW CONTROL SANCTION GP/REL...JURID 20.   ELITES
PAGE 69 B1392   CAP/ISM
                                                        ADMIN

L67
ROBERTS J.C.,"CIVIL RESTRAINT, MENTAL ILLNESS, AND   HEALTH
THE RIGHT TO TREATMENT." PROB/SOLV ADMIN PERSON   ORD/FREE
HEAL. PAGE 89 B1795   COERCE
                                                        LAW

L67
TRAVERS H. JR.,"AN EXAMINATION OF THE CAB'S MERGER   ADJUD
POLICY." USA+45 USA-45 LAW NAT/G LEGIS PLAN ADMIN   LG/CO
...DECISION 20 CONGRESS. PAGE 105 B2125   POLICY
                                                        DIST/IND

S67
BERRODIN E.F.,"AT THE BARGAINING TABLE." LABOR   PROVS
DIPLOM ECO/TAC ADMIN...MGT 20 MICHIGAN. PAGE 11   WORKER
B0230   LAW
                                                        BARGAIN

S67
BRADLEY A.W.,"CONSTITUTION-MAKING IN UGANDA."   NAT/G
UGANDA LAW CHIEF DELIB/GP LEGIS ADMIN EXEC   CREATE
PARL/PROC RACE/REL ORD/FREE...GOV/COMP 20. PAGE 14   CONSTN
B0295   FEDERAL

S67
CHAMBERLAIN N.W.,"STRIKES IN CONTEMPORARY CONTEXT."   LABOR
LAW INDUS NAT/G CHIEF CONFER COST ATTIT ORD/FREE   BARGAIN
...POLICY MGT 20. PAGE 20 B0400   EFFICIENCY
                                                        PROB/SOLV

S67
CONWAY J.E.,"MAKING RESEARCH EFFECTIVE IN   ACT/RES
LEGISLATION." LAW R+D CONSULT EX/STRUC PLAN CONFER   POLICY
ADMIN LEAD ROUTINE TASK INGP/REL DECISION. PAGE 23   LEGIS
B0469   PROB/SOLV

S67
DRYDEN S.,"LOCAL GOVERNMENT IN TANZANIA PART II"   LOC/G
TANZANIA LAW NAT/G POL/PAR CONTROL PARTIC REPRESENT   GOV/REL
...DECISION 20. PAGE 31 B0622   ADMIN
                                                        STRUCT

S67
HUDDLESTON J.,"TRADE UNIONS IN THE GERMAN FEDERAL   LABOR
REPUBLIC." EUR+WWI GERMANY/W UK LAW INDUS WORKER   GP/REL
CREATE CENTRAL...MGT GP/COMP 20. PAGE 52 B1056   SCHOOL
                                                        ROLE

S67
KRARUP O.,"JUDICIAL REVIEW OF ADMINISTRATIVE ACTION   ADJUD
IN DENMARK." DENMARK LAW CT/SYS...JURID CONCPT   CONTROL
19/20. PAGE 61 B1234   EXEC
                                                        DECISION

S67
LANDES W.M.,"THE EFFECT OF STATE FAIR EMPLOYMENT   DISCRIM
LAWS ON THE ECONOMIC POSITION OF NONWHITES." USA+45 LAW
PROVS SECT LEGIS ADMIN GP/REL RACE/REL...JURID   WORKER
CONCPT CHARTS HYPO/EXP NEGRO. PAGE 62 B1255

S67
RAI H.,"DISTRICT MAGISTRATE AND POLICE   STRUCT
SUPERINTENDENT IN INDIA: THE CONTROVERSY OF DUAL   CONTROL
CONTROL" INDIA LAW PROVS ADMIN PWR 19/20. PAGE 86   ROLE
B1729   FORCES

L86
GOODNOW F.J.,"AN EXECUTIVE AND THE COURTS: JUDICIAL   CT/SYS
REMEDIES AGAINST ADMINISTRATIVE ACTION" FRANCE UK   GOV/REL
USA-45 WOR-45 LAW CONSTN SANCTION ORD/FREE 19.   ADMIN
PAGE 41 B0823   ADJUD

LAW COMMISSION OF INDIA B1276

LAW/ETHIC....ETHICS OF LAW AND COURT PROCESSES

LAWRENC/TE....THOMAS EDWARD LAWRENCE

LAWRENCE P.R. B0812

LAWSON R. B1277

LAZARSFELD P.F. B0521

LAZRSFLD/P....PAUL LAZARSFELD (AND LAZARSFELD SCALE)

LEACH R.H. B0691,B1278

LEAD....LEADING, CONTRIBUTING MORE THAN AVERAGE

N
WEIGLEY R.F.,HISTORY OF THE UNITED STATES ARMY.   FORCES
USA+45 USA-45 SOCIETY NAT/G LEAD WAR GP/REL PWR   ADMIN
...SOC METH/COMP COLD/WAR. PAGE 115 B2312   ROLE
                                                       CIVMIL/REL

N
WELLS A.J.,THE BRITISH NATIONAL BIBLIOGRAPHY   BIBLIOG
CUMULATED SUBJECT CATALOGUE, 1951-1954. UK WOR+45   NAT/G
LAW ADMIN LEAD...HUM SOC 20. PAGE 115 B2320   DIPLOM

B
DEUTSCHE BIBLIOTH FRANKF A M,DEUTSCHE   BIBLIOG
BIBLIOGRAPHIE. EUR+WWI GERMANY ECO/DEV FORCES   LAW
DIPLOM LEAD...POLICY PHIL/SCI SOC 20. PAGE 28 B0578   ADMIN
                                                       NAT/G

N
REVIEW OF POLITICS. WOR+45 WOR-45 CONSTN LEGIS   BIBLIOG/A
PROB/SOLV ADMIN LEAD ALL/IDEOS...PHIL/SCI 20.   DIPLOM
PAGE 1 B0006   INT/ORG
                                                       NAT/G

N
BIBLIO, CATALOGUE DES OUVRAGES PARUS EN LANGUE   BIBLIOG
FRANCAISE DANS LE MONDE ENTIER. FRANCE WOR+45 ADMIN   NAT/G
LEAD PERSON...SOC 20. PAGE 1 B0008   DIPLOM
                                                       ECO/DEV

N
HANDBOOK OF LATIN AMERICAN STUDIES. LAW CULTURE   BIBLIOG/A
ECO/UNDEV POL/PAR ADMIN LEAD...SOC 20. PAGE 1 B0014   L/A+17C
                                                       NAT/G
                                                       DIPLOM

N
SUBJECT GUIDE TO BOOKS IN PRINT: AN INDEX TO THE   BIBLIOG
PUBLISHERS' TRADE LIST ANNUAL. UNIV LAW LOC/G   ECO/DEV
DIPLOM WRITING ADMIN LEAD PERSON...MGT SOC. PAGE 1   POL/PAR
B0023   NAT/G

N
SUMMARIES OF SELECTED JAPANESE MAGAZINES. LAW   BIBLIOG/A
CULTURE ADMIN LEAD 20 CHINJAP. PAGE 1 B0024   ATTIT
                                                       NAT/G
                                                       ASIA

N
NEUE POLITISCHE LITERATUR; BERICHTE UBER DAS   BIBLIOG/A
INTERNATIONALE SCHRIFTTUM ZUR POLITIK. WOR+45 LAW   DIPLOM
CONSTN POL/PAR ADMIN LEAD GOV/REL...POLICY   NAT/G
IDEA/COMP. PAGE 2 B0027   NAT/COMP

N
SUBJECT GUIDE TO BOOKS IN PRINT; AN INDEX TO THE   BIBLIOG
PUBLISHERS' TRADE LIST ANNUAL. WOR+45 WOR-45 LAW   NAT/G
CULTURE ADMIN LEAD PERSON...HUM MGT SOC. PAGE 2   DIPLOM
B0029

N
DEUTSCHE BUCHEREI,DEUTSCHES BUCHERVERZEICHNIS.   BIBLIOG
GERMANY LAW CULTURE POL/PAR ADMIN LEAD ATTIT PERSON   NAT/G
...SOC 20. PAGE 29 B0581   DIPLOM
                                                       ECO/DEV

N
KENTUCKY STATE ARCHIVES,CHECKLIST OF KENTUCKY STATE BIBLIOG/A
PUBLICATIONS AND STATE DIRECTORY. USA+45 LAW ACADEM PROVS
EX/STRUC LEGIS EDU/PROP LEAD...JURID 20. PAGE 59   PUB/INST
B1196   ADMIN

N
MARTIN W.O. JR.,STATE OF LOUISIANA OFFICIAL   BIBLIOG
PUBLICATIONS. USA+45 USA-45 LEGIS ADMIN LEAD 19/20.   PROVS
PAGE 70 B1415   GOV/REL

N
PUBLISHERS' CIRCULAR LIMITED,THE ENGLISH CATALOGUE   BIBLIOG
OF BOOKS. UK WOR+45 WOR-45 LAW CULTURE LOC/G NAT/G   ALL/VALS
ADMIN LEAD...MGT 19/20. PAGE 85 B1718   ALL/IDEOS
                                                       SOCIETY

N
STATE OF ILLINOIS,PUBLICATIONS OF THE STATE OF   BIBLIOG
ILLINOIS. USA+45 FINAN POL/PAR ADMIN LEAD 20   PROVS
ILLINOIS. PAGE 100 B2024   LOC/G
                                                       GOV/REL

N
UNITED NATIONS,UNITED NATIONS PUBLICATIONS. WOR+45   BIBLIOG
ECO/UNDEV AGRI FINAN FORCES ADMIN LEAD WAR PEACE   INT/ORG
...POLICY INT/LAW 20 UN. PAGE 107 B2160   DIPLOM

N
US LIBRARY OF CONGRESS,CATALOG OF THE PUBLIC   BIBLIOG
DOCUMENTS OF THE UNITED STATES, 18931940. USA-45   NAT/G
LAW ECO/DEV AGRI PLAN PROB/SOLV ADMIN LEAD GOV/REL   POLICY
ATTIT 19/20. PAGE 109 B2200   LOC/G

US SUPERINTENDENT OF DOCUMENTS,EDUCATION (PRICE
LIST 31). USA+45 LAW FINAN LOC/G NAT/G DEBATE ADMIN
LEAD RACE/REL FEDERAL HEALTH POLICY. PAGE 111 B2238
BIBLIOG/A
EDU/PROP
ACADEM
SCHOOL

VIRGINIA STATE LIBRARY,CHECK-LIST OF VIRGINIA STATE
PUBLICATIONS. USA+45 USA-45 ECO/DEV POL/PAR LEGIS
ADJUD LEAD 18/20. PAGE 112 B2265
BIBLIOG/A
PROVS
ADMIN
GOV/REL

RIORDAN W.L.,PLUNKITT OF TAMMANY HALL. USA-45
SOCIETY PROB/SOLV EXEC LEAD TASK CHOOSE ALL/VALS
...RECORD ANTHOL 20 REFORMERS TAMMANY NEWYORK/C
PLUNKITT/G. PAGE 88 B1789
B05
POL/PAR
MUNIC
CHIEF
ATTIT

HARLOW R.V.,THE HISTORY OF LEGISLATIVE METHODS IN
THE PERIOD BEFORE 1825. USA-45 EX/STRUC ADMIN
COLONIAL LEAD PARL/PROC ROUTINE...GP/COMP GOV/COMP
HOUSE/REP. PAGE 47 B0948
B17
LEGIS
DELIB/GP
PROVS
POL/PAR

MARSH J.F. JR.,THE FBI RETIREMENT BILL (PAMPHLET).
USA+45 EX/STRUC WORKER PLAN PROB/SOLV BUDGET LEAD
LOBBY PARL/PROC PERS/REL RIGID/FLEX...POLICY 20 FBI
PRESIDENT BUR/BUDGET. PAGE 70 B1405
N19
ADMIN
NAT/G
SENIOR
GOV/REL

INTERNATIONAL BIBLIOGRAPHY OF POLITICAL SCIENCE.
WOR+45 NAT/G POL/PAR EX/STRUC LEGIS CT/SYS LEAD
CHOOSE GOV/REL ATTIT...PHIL/SCI 20. PAGE 2 B0034
B26
BIBLIOG
DIPLOM
CONCPT
ADMIN

LUCE R.,CONGRESS: AN EXPLANATION. USA-45 CONSTN
FINAN ADMIN LEAD. PAGE 67 B1347
B26
DECISION
LEGIS
CREATE
REPRESENT

FYFE H.,THE BRITISH LIBERAL PARTY. UK SECT ADMIN
LEAD CHOOSE GP/REL PWR SOCISM...MAJORIT TIME/SEQ
19/20 LIB/PARTY CONSRV/PAR. PAGE 38 B0768
B28
POL/PAR
NAT/G
REPRESENT
POPULISM

HARDMAN J.B.,AMERICAN LABOR DYNAMICS. WORKER
ECO/TAC DOMIN ADJUD LEAD LOBBY PWR...POLICY MGT.
PAGE 47 B0944
B28
LABOR
INGP/REL
ATTIT
GP/REL

MOLEY R.,POLITICS AND CRIMINAL PROSECUTION. USA-45
POL/PAR EX/STRUC LEGIT CONTROL LEAD ROUTINE CHOOSE
INGP/REL...JURID CHARTS 20. PAGE 74 B1497
B29
PWR
CT/SYS
CRIME
ADJUD

ZINK H.,CITY BOSSES IN THE UNITED STATES: A STUDY
OF TWENTY MUNICIPAL BOSSES. USA-45 INDUS MUNIC
NEIGH POL/PAR ADMIN CRIME INGP/REL PERS/REL PWR
...PERS/COMP 20 BOSSISM. PAGE 119 B2403
B30
LOC/G
DOMIN
BIOG
LEAD

CRAWFORD F.G.,"THE EXECUTIVE BUDGET DECISION IN NEW
YORK." LEGIS EXEC PWR NEW/YORK. PAGE 25 B0504
S30
LEAD
BUDGET
PROVS
PROB/SOLV

BROMAGE A.W.,AMERICAN COUNTY GOVERNMENT. USA-45
NAT/G LEAD GOV/REL CENTRAL PWR...MGT BIBLIOG 18/20.
PAGE 15 B0314
B33
LOC/G
CREATE
ADMIN
MUNIC

DE CENIVAL P.,BIBLIOGRAPHIE MAROCAINE: 1923-1933.
FRANCE MOROCCO SECT ADMIN LEAD GP/REL ATTIT...LING
20. PAGE 27 B0551
B34
BIBLIOG/A
ISLAM
NAT/G
COLONIAL

GOSNELL H.F.,MACHINE POLITICS: CHICAGO MODEL.
COM/IND FACE/GP LOC/G EX/STRUC LEAD ROUTINE
SANCTION REPRESENT GOV/REL PWR...POLICY MATH OBS
INT CHARTS. PAGE 41 B0840
B37
POL/PAR
MUNIC
ADMIN
CHOOSE

FIELD G.L.,THE SYNDICAL AND CORPORATIVE
INSTITUTIONS OF ITALIAN FASCISM. ITALY CONSTN
STRATA LABOR EX/STRUC TOP/EX ADJUD ADMIN LEAD
TOTALISM AUTHORIT...MGT 20 MUSSOLIN/B. PAGE 35
B0716
B38
FASCISM
INDUS
NAT/G
WORKER

HARPER S.N.,THE GOVERNMENT OF THE SOVIET UNION. COM
USSR LAW CONSTN ECO/DEV PLAN TEC/DEV DIPLOM
INT/TRADE ADMIN REV NAT/LISM...POLICY 20. PAGE 47
B0952
B38
MARXISM
NAT/G
LEAD
POL/PAR

SALTER J.T.,THE AMERICAN POLITICIAN. USA-45 LABOR
POL/PAR EDU/PROP ADMIN CHOOSE ATTIT DRIVE PERSON
PWR...POLICY ANTHOL 20 THOMAS/N LEWIS/JL LAGUARD/F
GOVERNOR MAYOR. PAGE 92 B1865
B38
BIOG
LEAD
PROVS
LOC/G

JENNINGS W.I.,PARLIAMENT. UK POL/PAR OP/RES BUDGET
LEAD CHOOSE GP/REL...MGT 20 PARLIAMENT HOUSE/LORD
HOUSE/CMNS. PAGE 56 B1135
B39
PARL/PROC
LEGIS
CONSTN
NAT/G

MACMAHON A.W.,FEDERAL ADMINISTRATORS: A
BIOGRAPHICAL APPROACH TO THE PROBLEM OF
DEPARTMENTAL MANAGEMENT. USA-45 DELIB/GP EX/STRUC
WORKER LEAD...TIME/SEQ 19/20. PAGE 68 B1366
B39
BIOG
ADMIN
NAT/G
MGT

MARX F.M.,"POLICY FORMULATION AND THE
ADMINISTRATIVE PROCESS" ROUTINE ADJUST EFFICIENCY
OPTIMAL PRIVIL DRIVE PERSON OBJECTIVE...DECISION
OBS GEN/METH. PAGE 70 B1418
S39
ADMIN
LEAD
INGP/REL
MGT

HART J.,AN INTRODUCTION TO ADMINISTRATIVE LAW, WITH
SELECTED CASES. USA-45 CONSTN SOCIETY NAT/G
EX/STRUC ADJUD CT/SYS LEAD CRIME ORD/FREE
...DECISION JURID 20 CASEBOOK. PAGE 47 B0958
B40
LAW
ADMIN
LEGIS
PWR

MCHENRY D.E.,HIS MAJESTY'S OPPOSITION: STRUCTURE
AND PROBLEMS OF THE BRITISH LABOUR PARTY 1931-1938.
UK FINAN LABOR LOC/G DELIB/GP LEGIS EDU/PROP LEAD
PARTIC CHOOSE GP/REL SOCISM...TREND 20 LABOR/PAR.
PAGE 72 B1450
B40
POL/PAR
MGT
NAT/G
POLICY

GERTH H.,"THE NAZI PARTY: ITS LEADERSHIP AND
COMPOSITION" (BMR)" GERMANY ELITES STRATA STRUCT
EX/STRUC FORCES ECO/TAC CT/SYS CHOOSE TOTALISM
AGE/Y AUTHORIT PWR 20. PAGE 39 B0792
S40
POL/PAR
DOMIN
LEAD
ADMIN

PALMER J.M.,AMERICA IN ARMS: THE EXPERIENCE OF THE
UNITED STATES WITH MILITARY ORGANIZATION. FUT
USA-45 LEAD REV PWR 18/20 WASHINGT/G KNOX/HENRY
PRE/US/AM. PAGE 81 B1627
B41
FORCES
NAT/G
ADMIN
WAR

STOKE H.W.,"EXECUTIVE LEADERSHIP AND THE GROWTH OF
PROPAGANDA." USA-45 NAT/G EX/STRUC LEGIS TOP/EX
PARL/PROC REPRESENT ORD/FREE PWR...MAJORIT 20.
PAGE 101 B2042
S41
EXEC
LEAD
EDU/PROP
ADMIN

CARLO A.M.,ENSAYO DE UNA BIBLIOGRAFIA DE
BIBLIOGRAFIAS MEXICANAS. ECO/UNDEV LOC/G ADMIN LEAD
20 MEXIC/AMER. PAGE 19 B0381
B43
BIBLIOG
L/A+17C
NAT/G
DIPLOM

LEWIN E.,ROYAL EMPIRE SOCIETY BIBLIOGRAPHIES NO. 9:
SUB-SAHARA AFRICA. ECO/UNDEV TEC/DEV DIPLOM ADMIN
COLONIAL LEAD 20. PAGE 64 B1303
B43
BIBLIOG
AFR
NAT/G
SOCIETY

SELZNICK P.,"AN APPROACH TO A THEORY OF
BUREAUCRACY." INDUS WORKER CONTROL LEAD EFFICIENCY
OPTIMAL...SOC METH 20 BARNARD/C BUREAUCRCY
WEBER/MAX FRIEDRCH/C MICHELS/R. PAGE 95 B1928
S43
ROUTINE
ADMIN
MGT
EX/STRUC

BIENSTOCK G.,MANAGEMENT IN RUSSIAN INDUSTRY AND
AGRICULTURE. USSR CONSULT WORKER LEAD COST PROFIT
ATTIT DRIVE PWR...MGT METH/COMP DICTIONARY 20.
PAGE 12 B0236
B44
ADMIN
MARXISM
SML/CO
AGRI

GRIFFITH E.S.,"THE CHANGING PATTERN OF PUBLIC
POLICY FORMATION." MOD/EUR WOR+45 FINAN CHIEF
CONFER ADMIN LEAD CONSERVE SOCISM TECHRACY...SOC
CHARTS CONGRESS. PAGE 43 B0877
S44
LAW
POLICY
TEC/DEV

KEFAUVER E.,"THE NEED FOR BETTER EXECUTIVE-
LEGISLATIVE TEAMWORK IN THE NATIONAL GOVERNMENT."
USA-45 CONSTN NAT/G ROUTINE...TRADIT CONGRESS
REFORMERS. PAGE 59 B1188
S44
LEGIS
EXEC
CONFER
LEAD

BIBLIOGRAFIIA DISSERTATSII: DOKTORSKIE DISSERTATSII
ZA 19411944 (2 VOLS.). COM USSR LAW POL/PAR DIPLOM
ADMIN LEAD...PHIL/SCI SOC 20. PAGE 2 B0035
B46
BIBLIOG
ACADEM
KNOWL
MARXIST

FLYNN E.J.,YOU'RE THE BOSS. USA-45 ELITES TOP/EX
DOMIN CONTROL EXEC LEAD REPRESENT 19/20 NEWYORK/C
ROOSEVLT/F FLYNN/BOSS BOSSISM. PAGE 36 B0732
B47
LOC/G
MUNIC
BIOG
POL/PAR

MILLETT J.D.,THE PROCESS AND ORGANIZATION OF
GOVERNMENT PLANNING. USA+45 DELIB/GP ACT/RES LEAD
LOBBY TASK...POLICY GEOG TIME 20 RESOURCE/N.
PAGE 73 B1482
B47
ADMIN
NAT/G
PLAN
CONSULT

WHITEHEAD T.N.,LEADERSHIP IN A FREE SOCIETY; A
STUDY IN HUMAN RELATIONS BASED ON AN ANALYSIS OF
PRESENT-DAY INDUSTRIAL CIVILIZATION. WOR-45 STRUCT
R+D LABOR LG/CO SML/CO WORKER PLAN PROB/SOLV
TEC/DEV DRIVE...MGT 20. PAGE 116 B2341
B47
INDUS
LEAD
ORD/FREE
SOCIETY

HART J.,THE AMERICAN PRESIDENCY IN ACTION 1789: A
STUDY IN CONSTITUTIONAL HISTORY. USA-45 POL/PAR
DELIB/GP FORCES LEGIS ADJUD ADMIN LEAD GP/REL
PERS/REL 18 PRESIDENT CONGRESS. PAGE 47 B0959
B48
NAT/G
CONSTN
CHIEF
EX/STRUC

KNICKERBOCKER I.,"LEADERSHIP: A CONCEPTION AND SOME
IMPLICATIONS." INDUS OP/RES REPRESENT INGP/REL
DRIVE...MGT CLASSIF. PAGE 60 B1220
S48
LEAD
CONCPT
PERSON

ROLE
B49

BORBA DE MORAES R.,MANUAL BIBLIOGRAFICO DE ESTUDOS   BIBLIOG
BRASILEIROS. BRAZIL DIPLOM ADMIN LEAD...SOC 20.   L/A+17C
PAGE 14 B0276   NAT/G
                                                      ECO/UNDEV
                                                      B49

RIDDICK F.M.,THE UNITED STATES CONGRESS   LEGIS
ORGANIZATION AND PROCEDURE. POL/PAR DELIB/GP   PARL/PROC
PROB/SOLV DEBATE CONTROL EXEC LEAD INGP/REL PWR   CHIEF
...MAJORIT DECISION CONGRESS PRESIDENT. PAGE 88   EX/STRUC
B1777
                                                      S49

CORWIN E.S.,"THE PRESIDENCY IN PERSPECTIVE." USA+45   CHIEF
USA-45 NAT/G LEAD 20 PRESIDENT. PAGE 24 B0485   PWR
                                                      REPRESENT
                                                      EXEC
                                                      B50

AMERICAN POLITICAL SCI ASSN,TOWARD A MORE   POL/PAR
RESPONSIBLE TWO-PARTY SYSTEM. USA+45 CONSTN   TASK
VOL/ASSN LEGIS LEAD CHOOSE...POLICY MGT 20. PAGE 4   PARTIC
B0087   ACT/RES
                                                      B50

BAKKE E.W.,BONDS OF ORGANIZATION (2ND ED.). USA+45   ECO/DEV
COM/IND FINAN ADMIN LEAD PERS/REL...INT SOC/INTEG   MGT
20. PAGE 8 B0169   LABOR
                                                      GP/REL
                                                      B50

HYNEMAN C.S.,BUREAUCRACY IN A DEMOCRACY. CHIEF   NAT/G
LEGIS ADMIN CONTROL LEAD ROUTINE PERS/REL COST   CENTRAL
EFFICIENCY UTIL ATTIT AUTHORIT PERSON MORAL.   EX/STRUC
PAGE 53 B1071   MYTH
                                                      B50

MONTGOMERY H.,CRACKER PARTIES. CULTURE EX/STRUC   POL/PAR
LEAD PWR POPULISM...TIME/SEQ 19 GEORGIA CALHOUN/JC   PROVS
COBB/HOWLL JACKSON/A. PAGE 74 B1505   ELITES
                                                      BIOG
                                                      S50

NEUMANN F.L.,"APPROACHES TO THE STUDY OF POLITICAL   PWR
POWER." POL/PAR TOP/EX ADMIN LEAD ATTIT ORD/FREE   IDEA/COMP
CONSERVE LAISSEZ MARXISM...PSY SOC. PAGE 78 B1572   CONCPT
                                                      C50

SIMON H.A.,"PUBLIC ADMINISTRATION." LG/CO SML/CO   MGT
PLAN DOMIN LEAD GP/REL DRIVE PERCEPT ALL/VALS   ADMIN
...POLICY BIBLIOG/A 20. PAGE 97 B1957   DECISION
                                                      EX/STRUC
                                                      C50

WAGER P.W.,"COUNTY GOVERNMENT ACROSS THE NATION."   LOC/G
USA+45 CONSTN COM/IND FINAN SCHOOL DOMIN CT/SYS   PROVS
LEAD GOV/REL...STAT BIBLIOG 20. PAGE 112 B2272   ADMIN
                                                      ROUTINE
                                                      B51

HARDMAN J.B.,THE HOUSE OF LABOR. LAW R+D NEIGH   LABOR
EDU/PROP LEAD ROUTINE REPRESENT GP/REL...POLICY   LOBBY
STAT. PAGE 47 B0945   ADMIN
                                                      PRESS
                                                      B51

LASSWELL H.D.,THE POLITICAL WRITINGS OF HAROLD D   PERSON
LASSWELL. UNIV DOMIN EXEC LEAD RATIONAL ATTIT DRIVE   PSY
ROLE ALL/VALS...OBS BIOG 20. PAGE 63 B1269   INGP/REL
                                                      CONCPT
                                                      B51

US LIBRARY OF CONGRESS,EAST EUROPEAN ACCESSIONS   BIBLIOG/A
LIST (VOL. I). POL/PAR DIPLOM ADMIN LEAD 20.   COM
PAGE 109 B2204   SOCIETY
                                                      NAT/G
                                                      S51

MARX F.M.,"SIGNIFICANCE FOR THE ADMINISTRATIVE   LEGIS
PROCESS." POL/PAR LEAD PARL/PROC GOV/REL EFFICIENCY   ADMIN
SUPEGO...POLICY CONGRESS. PAGE 70 B1420   CHIEF
                                                      C51

MOORE B.,"SOVIET POLITICS - THE DILEMMA OF POWER: ATTIT
THE ROLE OF IDEAS IN SOCIAL CHANGE." USSR PROB/SOLV   PWR
DIPLOM EDU/PROP ADMIN LEAD ROUTINE REV...POLICY   CONCPT
DECISION BIBLIOG 20. PAGE 75 B1512   MARXISM
                                                      B52

SELZNICK P.,THE ORGANIZATIONAL WEAPON: A STUDY OF   MARXISM
BOLSHEVIK STRATEGY AND TACTICS. USSR SOCIETY STRATA   POL/PAR
LABOR DOMIN EDU/PROP PARTIC REV ATTIT PWR...POLICY   LEAD
MGT CONCPT 20 BOLSHEVISM. PAGE 95 B1929   TOTALISM
                                                      B52

US DEPARTMENT OF STATE,RESEARCH ON EASTERN EUROPE   BIBLIOG
(EXCLUDING USSR). EUR+WWI LAW ECO/DEV NAT/G   R+D
PROB/SOLV DIPLOM ADMIN LEAD MARXISM...TREND 19/20.   ACT/RES
PAGE 108 B2182   COM
                                                      S52

JOSEPHSON E.,"IRRATIONAL LEADERSHIP IN FORMAL   ADMIN
ORGANIZATIONS." EX/STRUC PLAN LEAD GP/REL INGP/REL   RATIONAL
EFFICIENCY AUTHORIT DRIVE PSY. PAGE 57 B1154   CONCPT
                                                      PERSON
                                                      S52

LIPSET S.M.,"DEMOCRACY IN PRIVATE GOVERNMENT; (A   LABOR
CASE STUDY OF THE INTERNATIONAL TYPOGRAPHICAL   ADMIN
UNION)" (BMR)" POL/PAR CONTROL LEAD INGP/REL PWR   ELITES
...MAJORIT DECISION PREDICT 20. PAGE 65 B1319   REPRESENT

C52

LASSWELL H.D.,"THE COMPARATIVE STUDY OF ELITES: AN   ELITES
INTRODUCTION AND BIBLIOGRAPHY." STRATA POL/PAR   LEAD
EDU/PROP ADMIN LOBBY COERCE ATTIT PERSON PWR   CONCPT
...BIBLIOG 20. PAGE 63 B1270   DOMIN
                                                      B53

A BIBLIOGRAPHY AND SUBJECT INDEX OF PUBLICATIONS OF   BIBLIOG
FLORIDA STATE AGENCIES. USA+45 LOC/G LEAD ATTIT 20   PROVS
FLORIDA. PAGE 2 B0036   GOV/REL
                                                      ADMIN
                                                      B53

ARGYRIS C.,EXECUTIVE LEADERSHIP: AN APPRAISAL OF A   MGT
MANAGER IN ACTION. TOP/EX ADMIN LEAD ADJUST ATTIT   EX/STRUC
...METH 20. PAGE 6 B0127   WORKER
                                                      PERS/REL
                                                      B53

GROSS B.M.,THE LEGISLATIVE STRUGGLE: A STUDY IN   LEGIS
SOCIAL COMBAT. STRUCT LOC/G POL/PAR JUDGE EDU/PROP   DECISION
DEBATE ETIQUET ADMIN LOBBY CHOOSE GOV/REL INGP/REL   PERSON
HEREDITY ALL/VALS...SOC PRESIDENT. PAGE 44 B0885   LEAD
                                                      B53

SAYLES L.R.,THE LOCAL UNION. CONSTN CULTURE   LABOR
DELIB/GP PARTIC CHOOSE GP/REL INGP/REL ATTIT ROLE   LEAD
...MAJORIT DECISION MGT. PAGE 93 B1873   ADJUD
                                                      ROUTINE
                                                      B53

STENE E.O.,ABANDONMENTS OF THE MANAGER PLAN. LEGIS   MUNIC
LEAD GP/REL PWR DECISION. PAGE 100 B2032   EX/STRUC
                                                      REPRESENT
                                                      ADMIN
                                                      B54

GOLDNER A.W.,WILDCAT STRIKE. LABOR TEC/DEV PAY   INDUS
ADMIN LEAD PERS/REL ATTIT RIGID/FLEX PWR...MGT   WORKER
CONCPT. PAGE 40 B0816   GP/REL
                                                      SOC
                                                      B54

MATTHEWS D.R.,THE SOCIAL BACKGROUND OF POLITICAL   DECISION
DECISION-MAKERS. CULTURE SOCIETY STRATA FAM   BIOG
EX/STRUC LEAD ATTIT BIO/SOC DRIVE PERSON ALL/VALS   SOC
HIST/WRIT. PAGE 71 B1431
                                                      B54

SHELTON W.L.,CHECKLIST OF NEW MEXICO PUBLICATIONS,   BIBLIOG
1850-1953. USA+45 USA-45 LEGIS ADMIN LEAD 19/20.   PROVS
PAGE 96 B1941   GOV/REL
                                                      B54

THORNTON M.L.,OFFICIAL PUBLICATIONS OF THE COLONY   BIBLIOG
AND STATE OF NORTH CAROLINA. 1749-1939. USA+45   ADMIN
USA-45 LEGIS LEAD GOV/REL ATTIT 18/20. PAGE 104   PROVS
B2109   ACADEM
                                                      B54

WHITE L.D.,THE JACKSONIANS: A STUDY IN   NAT/G
ADMINISTRATIVE HISTORY 1829-1861. USA-45 CONSTN   ADMIN
POL/PAR CHIEF DELIB/GP LEGIS CREATE PROB/SOLV   POLICY
ECO/TAC LEAD REGION GP/REL 19 PRESIDENT CONGRESS
JACKSON/A. PAGE 116 B2339
                                                      S54

LONG N.E.,"PUBLIC POLICY AND ADMINISTRATION: THE   PROB/SOLV
GOALS OF RATIONALITY AND RESPONSIBILITY." EX/STRUC   EXEC
ADMIN LEAD 20. PAGE 66 B1338   REPRESENT
                                                      B55

GALLOWAY G.B.,CONGRESS AND PARLIAMENT: THEIR   DELIB/GP
ORGANIZATION AND OPERATION IN THE US AND THE UK: LEGIS
PLANNING PAMPHLET NO. 93. POL/PAR EX/STRUC DEBATE   PARL/PROC
CONTROL LEAD ROUTINE EFFICIENCY PWR...POLICY   GOV/COMP
CONGRESS PARLIAMENT. PAGE 38 B0777
                                                      B55

WHEARE K.C.,GOVERNMENT BY COMMITTEE; AN ESSAY ON   DELIB/GP
THE BRITISH CONSTITUTION. UK NAT/G LEGIS INSPECT   CONSTN
CONFER ADJUD ADMIN CONTROL TASK EFFICIENCY ROLE   LEAD
POPULISM 20. PAGE 115 B2329   GP/COMP
                                                      B56

BARBASH J.,THE PRACTICE OF UNIONISM. ECO/TAC LEAD   LABOR
LOBBY GP/REL INGP/REL DRIVE MARXISM BIBLIOG. PAGE 9   REPRESENT
B0182   CONTROL
                                                      ADMIN
                                                      B56

CARTER B.E.,THE OFFICE OF THE PRIME MINISTER. UK   GOV/REL
ADMIN REPRESENT PARLIAMENT 20. PAGE 19 B0388   CHIEF
                                                      EX/STRUC
                                                      LEAD
                                                      B56

FRANCIS R.G.,SERVICE AND PROCEDURE IN BUREAUCRACY.   CLIENT
EXEC LEAD ROUTINE...QU 20. PAGE 37 B0748   ADMIN
                                                      INGP/REL
                                                      REPRESENT
                                                      B56

UNITED NATIONS,BIBLIOGRAPHY ON INDUSTRIALIZATION IN   BIBLIOG
UNDER-DEVELOPED COUNTRIES. WOR+45 R+D INT/ORG NAT/G   ECO/UNDEV
FOR/AID ADMIN LEAD 20 UN. PAGE 107 B2161   INDUS
                                                      TEC/DEV
                                                      B56

WEBER M.,STAATSSOZIOLOGIE. STRUCT LEGIT ADMIN   SOC
PARL/PROC SUPEGO CONSERVE JURID. PAGE 114 B2305   NAT/G
                                                      POL/PAR
                                                      LEAD

L56
MACMAHON A.W.,"WOODROW WILSON AS LEGISLATIVE LEADER LEGIS
AND ADMINISTRATOR." CONSTN POL/PAR ADMIN...POLICY CHIEF
HIST/WRIT WILSON/W PRESIDENT. PAGE 68 B1371 LEAD
BIOG

S56
CUTLER R.,"THE DEVELOPMENT OF THE NATIONAL SECURITY ORD/FREE
COUNCIL." USA+45 INTELL CONSULT EX/STRUC DIPLOM DELIB/GP
LEAD 20 TRUMAN/HS EISNHWR/DD NSC. PAGE 25 B0514 PROB/SOLV
NAT/G

S56
KAUFMAN H.,"EMERGING CONFLICTS IN THE DOCTRINES OF ADMIN
PUBLIC ADMINISTRATION" (BMR) USA+45 USA-45 NAT/G ORD/FREE
EX/STRUC LEGIS CONTROL NEUTRAL ATTIT PWR...TREND REPRESENT
20. PAGE 58 B1181 LEAD

C56
FALL B.B.,"THE VIET-MINH REGIME." VIETNAM LAW NAT/G
ECO/UNDEV POL/PAR FORCES DOMIN WAR ATTIT MARXISM ADMIN
...BIOG PREDICT BIBLIOG/A 20. PAGE 35 B0703 EX/STRUC
LEAD

C56
NEUMANN S.,"MODERN POLITICAL PARTIES: APPROACHES TO POL/PAR
COMPARATIVE POLITIC. FRANCE UK EX/STRUC DOMIN ADMIN GOV/COMP
LEAD REPRESENT TOTALISM ATTIT...POLICY TREND ELITES
METH/COMP ANTHOL BIBLIOG/A 20 CMN/WLTH. PAGE 78 MAJORIT
B1574

B57
BISHOP O.B.,PUBLICATIONS OF THE GOVERNMENTS OF NOVA BIBLIOG
SCOTIA, PRINCE EDWARD ISLAND, NEW BRUNSWICK NAT/G
1758-1952. CANADA UK ADMIN COLONIAL LEAD...POLICY DIPLOM
18/20. PAGE 12 B0245

B57
KNEIER C.M.,CITY GOVERNMENT IN THE UNITED STATES MUNIC
(3RD ED.). USA-45 FINAN NAT/G POL/PAR LEGIS LOC/G
EDU/PROP LEAD APPORT REPRESENT ATTIT...MGT 20 ADMIN
CITY/MGT. PAGE 60 B1219 GOV/REL

B57
MEYER P.,ADMINISTRATIVE ORGANIZATION: A COMPARATIVE ADMIN
STUDY OF THE ORGANIZATION OF PUBLIC ADMINISTRATION. METH/COMP
DENMARK FRANCE NORWAY SWEDEN UK USA+45 ELITES LOC/G NAT/G
CONSULT LEGIS ADJUD CONTROL LEAD PWR SKILL CENTRAL
DECISION. PAGE 73 B1475

B57
SELZNICK,LEADERSHIP IN ADMINISTRATION: A LEAD
SOCIOLOGICAL INTERPRETATION. CREATE PROB/SOLV EXEC ADMIN
ROUTINE EFFICIENCY RATIONAL KNOWL...POLICY PSY. DECISION
PAGE 95 B1927 NAT/G

S57
BAUMGARTEL H.,"LEADERSHIP STYLE AS A VARIABLE IN LEAD
RESEARCH ADMINISTRATION." USA+45 ADMIN REPRESENT EXEC
PERS/REL 20. PAGE 10 B0198 MGT
INGP/REL

C57
TANG P.S.H.,"COMMUNIST CHINA TODAY: DOMESTIC AND POL/PAR
FOREIGN POLICIES." CHINA/COM COM S/ASIA USSR STRATA LEAD
FORCES DIPLOM EDU/PROP COERCE GOV/REL...POLICY ADMIN
MAJORIT BIBLIOG 20. PAGE 102 B2071 CONSTN

B58
BROWNE C.G.,THE CONCEPT OF LEADERSHIP. UNIV FACE/GP EXEC
DOMIN EDU/PROP LEGIT LEAD DRIVE PERSON PWR...MGT CONCPT
SOC OBS SELF/OBS CONT/OBS INT PERS/TEST STERTYP
GEN/LAWS. PAGE 16 B0328

B58
LESTER R.A.,AS UNIONS MATURE. POL/PAR BARGAIN LEAD LABOR
PARTIC GP/REL CENTRAL...MAJORIT TIME/SEQ METH/COMP. INDUS
PAGE 64 B1299 POLICY
MGT

B58
LOVEJOY D.S.,RHODE ISLAND POLITICS AND THE AMERICAN REV
REVOLUTION 1760-1776. UK USA-45 ELITES EX/STRUC TAX COLONIAL
LEAD REPRESENT GOV/REL GP/REL ATTIT 18 RHODE/ISL. ECO/TAC
PAGE 67 B1343 SOVEREIGN

B58
PAN AMERICAN UNION,REPERTORIO DE PUBLICACIONES BIBLIOG
PERIODICAS ACTUALES LATINO-AMERICANAS. CULTURE L/A+17C
ECO/UNDEV ADMIN LEAD GOV/REL 20 OAS. PAGE 81 B1630 NAT/G
DIPLOM

B58
REDFIELD C.E.,COMMUNICATION IN MANAGEMENT. DELIB/GP COM/IND
EX/STRUC WRITING LEAD PERS/REL...PSY INT METH 20. MGT
PAGE 87 B1750 LG/CO
ADMIN

B58
REDFORD E.S.,IDEAL AND PRACTICE IN PUBLIC POLICY
ADMINISTRATION. CONSTN ELITES NAT/G CONSULT EX/STRUC
DELIB/GP LEAD UTOPIA ATTIT POPULISM...DECISION PLAN
METH/COMP 20. PAGE 87 B1756 ADMIN

B58
SHERWOOD F.P.,SUPERVISORY METHODS IN MUNICIPAL EX/STRUC
ADMINISTRATION. USA+45 MUNIC WORKER EDU/PROP PARTIC LEAD
INGP/REL PERS/REL 20 CITY/MGT. PAGE 96 B1945 ADMIN
LOC/G

S58
EISENSTADT S.N.,"INTERNAL CONTRADICTIONS IN ELITES
BUREAUCRATIC POLITICS." ADMIN EXEC CENTRAL. PAGE 32 LEAD
B0658 PWR

EX/STRUC
B59
ELLIOTT O.,MEN AT THE TOP. USA+45 CULTURE EX/STRUC TOP/EX
PRESS GOV/REL ATTIT ALL/VALS...OBS INT QU 20. PERSON
PAGE 33 B0668 LEAD
POLICY

B59
MONTGOMERY J.D.,CASES IN VIETNAMESE ADMINISTRATION. ADMIN
VIETNAM/S EX/STRUC 20. PAGE 75 B1506 DECISION
PROB/SOLV
LEAD

B59
PARK R.L.,LEADERSHIP AND POLITICAL INSTITUTIONS IN NAT/G
INDIA. S/ASIA CULTURE ECO/UNDEV LOC/G MUNIC PROVS EXEC
LEGIS PLAN ADMIN LEAD ORD/FREE WEALTH...GEOG SOC INDIA
BIOG TOT/POP VAL/FREE 20. PAGE 81 B1633

B59
WARNER W.L.,INDUSTRIAL MAN. USA+45 USA-45 ELITES EXEC
INDUS LABOR TOP/EX WORKER ADMIN INGP/REL PERS/REL LEAD
...CHARTS ANTHOL 20. PAGE 114 B2294 PERSON
MGT

L59
"A BIBLIOGRAPHICAL ESSAY ON DECISION MAKING." BIBLIOG/A
WOR+45 WOR-45 STRUCT OP/RES GP/REL...CONCPT DECISION
IDEA/COMP METH 20. PAGE 2 B0038 ADMIN
LEAD

L59
BENNIS W.G.,"LEADERSHIP THEORY AND ADMINISTRATIVE LEAD
BEHAVIOR: THE PROBLEM OF AUTHORITY." ROUTINE...MGT ADMIN
HYPO/EXP. PAGE 10 B0214 DOMIN
PERS/REL

S59
DWYER R.J.,"THE ADMINISTRATIVE ROLE IN ADMIN
DESEGREGATION." USA+45 LAW PROB/SOLV LEAD RACE/REL SCHOOL
ISOLAT STRANGE ROLE...POLICY SOC/INTEG MISSOURI DISCRIM
NEGRO CIV/RIGHTS. PAGE 31 B0638 ATTIT

S59
JEWELL M.R.,"THE SENATE REPUBLICAN POLICY COMMITTEE POL/PAR
AND FOREIGN POLICY." PLAN ADMIN CONTROL LEAD LOBBY NAT/G
EFFICIENCY PRESIDENT 20 REPUBLICAN. PAGE 56 B1139 DELIB/GP
POLICY

B60
BELL J.,THE SPLENDID MISERY: THE STORY OF THE EXEC
PRESIDENCY AND POWER POLITICS AT CLOSE RANGE. TOP/EX
USA+45 USA-45 PRESS ADMIN LEAD LOBBY GP/REL LEGIS
PERS/REL PERSON PRESIDENT. PAGE 10 B0208

B60
CORSON J.J.,GOVERNANCE OF COLLEGES AND ADMIN
UNIVERSITIES. STRUCT FINAN DELIB/GP DOMIN EDU/PROP EXEC
LEAD CHOOSE GP/REL CENTRAL COST PRIVIL SUPEGO ACADEM
ORD/FREE PWR...DECISION BIBLIOG. PAGE 24 B0481 HABITAT

B60
ECKHOFF T.,RATIONALITY AND RESPONSIBILITY IN ADMIN
ADMINISTRATIVE AND JUDICIAL DECISION-MAKING. ELITES PROB/SOLV
LEAD INGP/REL ATTIT PWR...MGT METH/COMP GAME 20. DECISION
PAGE 32 B0649 METH/CNCPT

B60
FLORES R.H.,CATALOGO DE TESIS DOCTORALES DE LAS BIBLIOG
FACULTADES DE LA UNIVERSIDAD DE EL SALVADOR. ACADEM
EL/SALVADR LAW DIPLOM ADMIN LEAD GOV/REL...SOC L/A+17C
19/20. PAGE 36 B0730 NAT/G

B60
GLOVER J.D.,A CASE STUDY OF HIGH LEVEL ADMIN
ADMINISTRATION IN A LARGE ORGANIZATION. EX/STRUC TOP/EX
EXEC LEAD ROUTINE INGP/REL OPTIMAL ATTIT PERSON FORCES
...POLICY DECISION INT QU. PAGE 40 B0812 NAT/G

B60
GRAHAM G.A.,AMERICA'S CAPACITY TO GOVERN: SOME MGT
PRELIMINARY THOUGHTS FOR PROSPECTIVE LEAD
ADMINISTRATORS. USA+45 SOCIETY DELIB/GP TOP/EX CHOOSE
CREATE PROB/SOLV RATIONAL 20. PAGE 42 B0849 ADMIN

B60
HAYNES G.H.,THE SENATE OF THE UNITED STATES: ITS LEGIS
HISTORY AND PRACTICE. CONSTN EX/STRUC TOP/EX CONFER DELIB/GP
DEBATE LEAD LOBBY PARL/PROC CHOOSE PWR SENATE
CONGRESS. PAGE 48 B0977

B60
KINGSTON-MCCLOUG E.,DEFENSE: POLICY AND STRATEGY. FORCES
UK SEA AIR TEC/DEV DIPLOM ADMIN LEAD WAR ORD/FREE PLAN
...CHARTS 20. PAGE 60 B1209 POLICY
DECISION

B60
MCGREGOR D.,THE HUMAN SIDE OF ENTERPRISE. USA+45 MGT
LEAD ROUTINE GP/REL INGP/REL...CONCPT GEN/LAWS 20. ATTIT
PAGE 72 B1449 SKILL
EDU/PROP

B60
SAYRE W.S.,GOVERNING NEW YORK CITY: POLITICS IN THE MUNIC
METROPOLIS. POL/PAR CHIEF DELIB/GP LEGIS PLAN ADMIN
CT/SYS LEAD PARTIC CHOOSE...DECISION CHARTS BIBLIOG PROB/SOLV
20 NEWYORK/C BUREAUCRCY. PAGE 93 B1875

B60
WALTER B.,COMMUNICATIONS AND INFLUENCE: DEXISION MUNIC
MAKING IN A MUNICIPAL ADMINISTRATIVE HIERARCHY DECISION
(PH.D. DISS., UNPUBL.). LEAD CHOOSE PWR METH/CNCPT. ADMIN
PAGE 113 B2284 STRUCT

WHEARE K.C.,THE CONSTITUTIONAL STRUCTURE OF THE COMMONWEALTH. UK EX/STRUC DIPLOM DOMIN ADMIN COLONIAL CONTROL LEAD INGP/REL SUPEGO 20 CMN/WLTH. PAGE 115 B2330
CONSTN INT/ORG VOL/ASSN SOVEREIGN
B60

BAVELAS A.,"LEADERSHIP: MAN AND FUNCTION." WORKER CREATE PLAN CONTROL PERS/REL PERSON PWR...MGT 20. PAGE 10 B0199
LEAD ADMIN ROUTINE ROLE
S60

SCHAPIRO L.B.,"THE COMMUNIST PARTY OF THE SOVIET UNION." USSR INTELL CHIEF EX/STRUC FORCES DOMIN ADMIN LEAD WAR ATTIT SOVEREIGN...POLICY BIBLIOG 20. PAGE 93 B1881
POL/PAR COM REV
C60

ARMSTRONG J.A.,AN ESSAY ON SOURCES FOR THE STUDY OF THE COMMUNIST PARTY OF THE SOVIET UNION, 1934-1960 (EXTERNAL RESEARCH PAPER 137). USSR EX/STRUC ADMIN LEAD REV 20. PAGE 7 B0134
BIBLIOG/A COM POL/PAR MARXISM
B61

BARRASH J.,LABOR'S GRASS ROOTS; A STUDY OF THE LOCAL UNION. STRATA BARGAIN LEAD REPRESENT DEMAND ATTIT PWR. PAGE 9 B0190
LABOR USA+45 INGP/REL EXEC
B61

CATHERINE R.,LE FONCTIONNAIRE FRANCAIS. FRANCE NAT/G INGP/REL ATTIT MORAL ORD/FREE...T CIVIL/SERV. PAGE 19 B0394
ADMIN GP/REL LEAD SUPEGO
B61

DARRAH E.L.,FIFTY STATE GOVERNMENTS: A COMPILATION OF EXECUTIVE ORGANIZATION CHARTS. USA+45 LOC/G DELIB/GP LEGIS ADJUD LEAD PWR 20 GOVERNOR. PAGE 26 B0530
EX/STRUC ADMIN ORG/CHARTS PROVS
B61

GORDON R.A.,BUSINESS LEADERSHIP IN THE LARGE CORPORATION. USA+45 SOCIETY EX/STRUC ADMIN CONTROL ROUTINE GP/REL PWR...MGT 20. PAGE 41 B0831
LG/CO LEAD DECISION LOBBY
B61

JANOWITZ M.,COMMUNITY POLITICAL SYSTEMS. USA+45 SOCIETY INDUS VOL/ASSN TEC/DEV ADMIN LEAD CHOOSE ...SOC SOC/WK 20. PAGE 56 B1123
MUNIC STRUCT POL/PAR
B61

OPOTOWSKY S.,THE KENNEDY GOVERNMENT. NAT/G CONSULT EX/STRUC LEAD PERSON...POLICY 20 KENNEDY/JF CONGRESS CABINET. PAGE 80 B1613
ADMIN BIOG ELITES TOP/EX
B61

PAGE T.,STATE PERSONNEL REORGANIZATION IN ILLINOIS. USA+45 POL/PAR CHIEF TEC/DEV LEAD ADJUST 20. PAGE 80 B1625
ADMIN PROVS WORKER DELIB/GP
B61

PETRULLO L.,LEADERSHIP AND INTERPERSONAL BEHAVIOR. FACE/GP FAM PROF/ORG EX/STRUC FORCES DOMIN WAR GP/REL PERS/REL EFFICIENCY PRODUC PWR...MGT PSY. PAGE 82 B1663
PERSON ATTIT LEAD HABITAT
B61

TANNENBAUM R.,LEADERSHIP AND ORGANIZATION. STRUCT ADMIN INGP/REL ATTIT PERCEPT...DECISION METH/CNCPT OBS CHARTS BIBLIOG. PAGE 103 B2075
LEAD MGT RESPECT ROLE
B61

TRECKER H.B.,NEW UNDERSTANDING OF ADMINISTRATION. NEIGH DELIB/GP CONTROL LEAD GP/REL INGP/REL ...POLICY DECISION BIBLIOG. PAGE 105 B2126
VOL/ASSN PROF/ORG ADMIN PARTIC
B61

WALKER N.,MORALE IN THE CIVIL SERVICE. UK EXEC LEAD INGP/REL EFFICIENCY HAPPINESS 20. PAGE 113 B2280
ATTIT WORKER ADMIN PSY
B61

KRAMER R.,"EXECUTIVE PRIVILEGE - A STUDY OF THE PERIOD 1953-1960." NAT/G CHIEF EX/STRUC LEGIS PWR. PAGE 61 B1233
REPRESENT LEAD EXEC GOV/REL
L61

BENNIS W.G.,"REVISIONIST THEORY OF LEADERSHIP" MUNIC ACT/RES TEC/DEV...SIMUL 20. PAGE 11 B0215
LEAD ADMIN PERS/REL HYPO/EXP
S61

LIEBENOW J.G.,"LEGITIMACY OF ALIEN RELATIONSHIP: THE NYATURU OF TANGANYIKA" (BMR)" AFR UK ADMIN LEAD CHOOSE 20 NYATURU TANGANYIKA. PAGE 65 B1312
COLONIAL DOMIN LEGIT PWR
S61

MARSH R.M.,"FORMAL ORGANIZATION AND PROMOTION IN A PRE-INDUSTRIAL SOCIETY" (BMR)" ASIA FAM EX/STRUC LEAD...SOC CHARTS 19 WEBER/MAX. PAGE 70 B1407
ADMIN STRUCT ECO/UNDEV STRATA
S61

REAGAN M.O.,"THE POLITICAL STRUCTURE OF THE FEDERAL
PWR
S61

RESERVE SYSTEM." USA+45 FINAN NAT/G ADMIN 20. PAGE 87 B1748
EX/STRUC EXEC LEAD
S61

SHERBENOU E.L.,"CLASS, PARTICIPATION, AND THE COUNCIL-MANAGER PLAN." ELITES STRUCT LEAD GP/REL ATTIT PWR DECISION. PAGE 96 B1942
REPRESENT MUNIC EXEC
C61

ETZIONI A.,"A COMPARATIVE ANALYSIS OF COMPLEX ORGANIZATIONS: ON POWER, INVOLVEMENT AND THEIR CORRELATES." ELITES CREATE OP/RES ROUTINE INGP/REL PERS/REL CONSEN ATTIT DRIVE PWR...CONCPT BIBLIOG. PAGE 34 B0684
CON/ANAL SOC LEAD CONTROL
C61

VERBA S.,"SMALL GROUPS AND POLITICAL BEHAVIOR: A STUDY OF LEADERSHIP" DOMIN PARTIC ROUTINE GP/REL ATTIT DRIVE ALL/VALS...CONCPT IDEA/COMP LAB/EXP BIBLIOG METH. PAGE 112 B2259
LEAD ELITES FACE/GP
B62

ANDREWS W.G.,EUROPEAN POLITICAL INSTITUTIONS. FRANCE GERMANY UK USSR TOP/EX LEAD PARL/PROC CHOOSE 20. PAGE 5 B0104
NAT/COMP POL/PAR EX/STRUC LEGIS
B62

BENSON E.T.,CROSS FIRE: THE EIGHT YEARS WITH EISENHOWER. USA+45 DIPLOM LEAD ATTIT PERSON CONSERVE...TRADIT BIOG 20 EISNHWR/DD PRESIDENT TAFT/RA DULLES/JF NIXON/RM. PAGE 11 B0218
ADMIN POLICY DELIB/GP TOP/EX
B62

BROWN L.C.,LATIN AMERICA, A BIBLIOGRAPHY. EX/STRUC ADMIN LEAD ATTIT...POLICY 20. PAGE 16 B0323
BIBLIOG L/A+17C DIPLOM NAT/G
B62

CARTER G.M.,THE GOVERNMENT OF THE SOVIET UNION. USSR CULTURE LOC/G DIPLOM ECO/TAC ADJUD CT/SYS LEAD WEALTH...CHARTS T 20 COM/PARTY. PAGE 19 B0390
NAT/G MARXISM POL/PAR EX/STRUC
B62

COSTA RICA UNIVERSIDAD BIBL,LISTA DE TESIS DE GRADO DE LA UNIVERSIDAD DE COSTA RICA. COSTA/RICA LAW LOC/G ADMIN LEAD...SOC 20. PAGE 24 B0487
BIBLIOG/A NAT/G DIPLOM ECO/UNDEV
B62

DODDS H.W.,THE ACADEMIC PRESIDENT "EDUCATOR OR CARETAKER? FINAN DELIB/GP EDU/PROP PARTIC ATTIT ROLE PWR...POLICY RECORD INT. PAGE 30 B0601
ACADEM ADMIN LEAD CONTROL
B62

JENNINGS E.E.,THE EXECUTIVE: AUTOCRAT, BUREAUCRAT, DEMOCRAT. LEAD EFFICIENCY DRIVE 20. PAGE 56 B1131
EX/STRUC INGP/REL TOP/EX CONTROL
B62

KAMMERER G.M.,CITY MANAGERS IN POLITICS: AN ANALYSIS OF MANAGER TENURE AND TERMINATION. POL/PAR LEGIS PARTIC CHOOSE PWR...DECISION GEOG METH/CNCPT. PAGE 57 B1161
MUNIC LEAD EXEC
B62

LIPPMANN W.,PREFACE TO POLITICS. LABOR CHIEF CONTROL LEAD...MYTH IDEA/COMP 19/20 ROOSEVLT/T TAMMANY WILSON/H SANTAYAN/G BERGSON/H. PAGE 65 B1318
PARTIC ATTIT ADMIN
B62

MORTON L.,STRATEGY AND COMMAND: THE FIRST TWO YEARS. USA-45 NAT/G CONTROL EXEC LEAD WEAPON CIVMIL/REL PWR...POLICY AUD/VIS CHARTS 20 CHINJAP. PAGE 76 B1532
WAR FORCES PLAN DIPLOM
B62

MUNICIPAL MANPOWER COMMISSION,GOVERNMENTAL MANPOWER FOR TOMORROW'S CITIES: A REPORT. USA+45 DELIB/GP EX/STRUC PROB/SOLV TEC/DEV EDU/PROP ADMIN LEAD HABITAT. PAGE 76 B1539
LOC/G MUNIC LABOR GOV/REL
B62

OLLE-LAPRUNE J.,LA STABILITE DES MINISTRES SOUS LA TROISIEME REPUBLIQUE, 1879-1940. FRANCE CONSTN POL/PAR LEAD WAR INGP/REL RIGID/FLEX PWR...POLICY CHARTS 19/20. PAGE 79 B1606
LEGIS NAT/G ADMIN PERSON
B62

SAMPSON A.,ANATOMY OF BRITAIN. UK LAW COM/IND FINAN INDUS MARKET MUNIC POL/PAR EX/STRUC TOP/EX DIPLOM LEAD REPRESENT PERSON PARLIAMENT WORSHIP. PAGE 92 B1866
ELITES PWR STRUCT FORCES
B62

NEIBURG H.L.,"THE EISENHOWER AEC AND CONGRESS: A STUDY IN EXECUTIVE-LEGISLATIVE RELATIONS." USA+45 NAT/G POL/PAR DELIB/GP EX/STRUC TOP/EX ADMIN EXEC LEAD ROUTINE PWR...POLICY COLD/WAR CONGRESS PRESIDENT AEC. PAGE 77 B1567
CHIEF LEGIS GOV/REL NUC/PWR
L62

BOOTH D.A.,"POWER STRUCTURE AND COMMUNITY CHANGE: A REPLICATION STUDY OF COMMUNITY A." STRATA LABOR LEAD PARTIC REPRESENT...DECISION MGT TIME. PAGE 14 B0275
MUNIC ELITES PWR
S62

DAKIN R.E.,"VARIATIONS IN POWER STRUCTURES AND
MUNIC
S62

ORGANIZING EFFICIENCY: A COMPARATIVE STUDY OF FOUR
AREAS." STRATA EDU/PROP ADMIN LEAD GP/REL GOV/COMP.
PAGE 26 B0524
STRUCT
PWR
S62

GIDWANI K.A.,"LEADER BEHAVIOUR IN ELECTED AND NON-
ELECTED GROUPS." DELIB/GP ROUTINE TASK HAPPINESS
AUTHORIT...SOC STAT CHARTS SOC/EXP. PAGE 39 B0796
LEAD
INGP/REL
GP/COMP
CHOOSE
S62

LOCKARD D.,"THE CITY MANAGER, ADMINISTRATIVE THEORY
AND POLITICAL POWER." LEGIS ADMIN REPRESENT GP/REL
PWR. PAGE 66 B1333
MUNIC
EXEC
LEAD
DECISION
S62

MAINZER L.C.,"INJUSTICE AND BUREAUCRACY." ELITES
STRATA STRUCT EX/STRUC SENIOR CONTROL EXEC LEAD
ROUTINE INGP/REL ORD/FREE...CONCPT 20 BUREAUCRCY.
PAGE 68 B1381
MORAL
MGT
ADMIN
C62

DE GRAZIA A.,"POLITICAL BEHAVIOR (REV. ED.)" STRATA
POL/PAR LEAD LOBBY ROUTINE WAR CHOOSE REPRESENT
CONSEN ATTIT ORD/FREE BIBLIOG. PAGE 27 B0555
PHIL/SCI
OP/RES
CONCPT
C62

TRUMAN D.B.,"THE GOVERNMENTAL PROCESS: POLITICAL
INTERESTS AND PUBLIC OPINION." POL/PAR ADJUD ADMIN
EXEC LEAD ROUTINE CHOOSE REPRESENT GOV/REL
RIGID/FLEX...POLICY BIBLIOG/A 20. PAGE 105 B2131
LOBBY
EDU/PROP
GP/REL
LEGIS
N62

US ADVISORY COMN INTERGOV REL,ALTERNATIVE
APPROACHES TO GOVERNMENTAL REORGANIZATION IN
METROPOLITAN AREAS (PAMPHLET). EX/STRUC LEGIS EXEC
LEAD PWR...DECISION GEN/METH. PAGE 107 B2171
MUNIC
REGION
PLAN
GOV/REL
B63

BANFIELD E.C.,CITY POLITICS. CULTURE LABOR LOC/G
POL/PAR LEGIS EXEC LEAD CHOOSE...DECISION NEGRO.
PAGE 9 B0178
MUNIC
RIGID/FLEX
ATTIT
B63

BROGAN D.W.,POLITICAL PATTERNS IN TODAY'S WORLD.
FRANCE USA+45 USSR WOR+45 CONSTN STRUCT PLAN DIPLOM
ADMIN LEAD ROLE SUPEGO...PHIL/SCI 20. PAGE 15 B0313
NAT/COMP
NEW/LIB
COM
TOTALISM
B63

CLARK J.S.,THE SENATE ESTABLISHMENT. USA+45 NAT/G
POL/PAR ADMIN CHOOSE PERSON SENATE. PAGE 21 B0431
LEGIS
ROUTINE
LEAD
SENIOR
B63

ECOLE NATIONALE D'ADMIN,BIBLIOGRAPHIE SELECTIVE
D'OUVRAGES DE LANGUE FRANCAISE TRAITANT DES
PROBLEMES GOUVERNEMENTAUX ET ADMINISTRATIFS. NAT/G
FORCES ACT/RES OP/RES PLAN PROB/SOLV BUDGET ADJUD
COLONIAL LEAD 20. PAGE 32 B0651
BIBLIOG
AFR
ADMIN
EX/STRUC
B63

HEYEL C.,THE ENCYCLOPEDIA OF MANAGEMENT. WOR+45
MARKET TOP/EX TEC/DEV AUTOMAT LEAD ADJUST...STAT
CHARTS GAME ANTHOL BIBLIOG. PAGE 49 B1002
MGT
INDUS
ADMIN
FINAN
B63

JOHNS R.,CONFRONTING ORGANIZATIONAL CHANGE. NEIGH
DELIB/GP CREATE OP/RES ADMIN GP/REL DRIVE...WELF/ST
SOC RECORD BIBLIOG. PAGE 56 B1142
SOC/WK
WEALTH
LEAD
VOL/ASSN
B63

KAMMERER G.M.,THE URBAN POLITICAL COMMUNITY:
PROFILES IN TOWN POLITICS. ELITES LOC/G LEAD
...DECISION GP/COMP. PAGE 57 B1162
EXEC
MUNIC
PWR
GOV/COMP
B63

LITTERER J.A.,ORGANIZATIONS: STRUCTURE AND
BEHAVIOR. PLAN DOMIN CONTROL LEAD ROUTINE SANCTION
INGP/REL EFFICIENCY PRODUC DRIVE RIGID/FLEX PWR.
PAGE 66 B1325
ADMIN
CREATE
MGT
ADJUST
B63

MACNEIL N.,FORGE OF DEMOCRACY: THE HOUSE OF
REPRESENTATIVES. POL/PAR EX/STRUC TOP/EX DEBATE
LEAD PARL/PROC CHOOSE GOV/REL PWR...OBS HOUSE/REP.
PAGE 68 B1374
LEGIS
DELIB/GP
B63

MAHESHWARI B.,STUDIES IN PANCHAYATI RAJ. INDIA
POL/PAR EX/STRUC BUDGET EXEC REPRESENT CENTRAL
EFFICIENCY...DECISION 20. PAGE 68 B1378
FEDERAL
LOC/G
GOV/REL
LEAD
B63

MONTER W.,THE GOVERNMENT OF GENEVA, 1536-1605
(DOCTORAL THESIS). SWITZERLND DIPLOM LEAD ORD/FREE
SOVEREIGN 16/17 CALVIN/J ROME. PAGE 74 B1504
SECT
FINAN
LOC/G
ADMIN
B63

PEABODY R.L.,NEW PERSPECTIVES ON THE HOUSE OF
REPRESENTATIVES. AGRI FINAN SCHOOL FORCES CONFER
LEAD CHOOSE REPRESENT FEDERAL...POLICY DECISION
HOUSE/REP. PAGE 82 B1647
NEW/IDEA
LEGIS
PWR
ADMIN
B63

SIDEY H.,JOHN F. KENNEDY, PRESIDENT. USA+45 INTELL
FAM CONSULT DELIB/GP LEGIS ADMIN LEAD 20 KENNEDY/JF
PRESIDENT. PAGE 97 B1951
BIOG
TOP/EX
SKILL

PERSON
B63

US SENATE COMM APPROPRIATIONS,PERSONNEL
ADMINISTRATION AND OPERATIONS OF AGENCY FOR
INTERNATIONAL DEVELOPMENT: SPECIAL HEARING. FINAN
LEAD COST UTIL SKILL...CHARTS 20 CONGRESS AID
CIVIL/SERV. PAGE 109 B2211
ADMIN
FOR/AID
EFFICIENCY
DIPLOM
S63

GITTELL M.,"METROPOLITAN MAYOR: DEAD END." LOC/G
PARTIC REGION ATTIT PWR GP/COMP. PAGE 40 B0804
MUNIC
LEAD
EXEC
S63

HILLS R.J.,"THE REPRESENTATIVE FUNCTION: NEGLECTED
DIMENSION OF LEADERSHIP BEHAVIOR" USA+45 CLIENT
STRUCT SCHOOL PERS/REL...STAT QU SAMP LAB/EXP 20.
PAGE 50 B1012
LEAD
ADMIN
EXEC
ACT/RES
S63

JENNINGS M.K.,"PUBLIC ADMINISTRATORS AND COMMUNITY
DECISION-MAKING." ELITES LOC/G LEAD...GP/COMP
GOV/COMP. PAGE 56 B1134
ADMIN
MUNIC
DECISION
PWR
S63

WINGFIELD C.J.,"POWER STRUCTURE AND DECISION-MAKING
IN CITY PLANNING." EDU/PROP ADMIN LEAD PARTIC
GP/REL ATTIT. PAGE 117 B2365
MUNIC
PLAN
DECISION
PWR
B64

ARGYRIS C.,INTEGRATING THE INDIVIDUAL AND THE
ORGANIZATION. WORKER PROB/SOLV LEAD SANCTION
REPRESENT ADJUST EFFICIENCY DRIVE PERSON...PSY
METH/CNCPT ORG/CHARTS. PAGE 6 B0132
ADMIN
PERS/REL
VOL/ASSN
PARTIC
B64

ETZIONI A.,MODERN ORGANIZATIONS. CLIENT STRUCT
DOMIN CONTROL LEAD PERS/REL AUTHORIT...CLASSIF
BUREAUCRCY. PAGE 34 B0685
MGT
ADMIN
PLAN
CULTURE
B64

GOLDWIN R.A.,POLITICAL PARTIES, USA. USA+45 USA-45
LOC/G ADMIN LEAD EFFICIENCY ATTIT PWR...POLICY STAT
ANTHOL 18/20 CONGRESS. PAGE 40 B0818
POL/PAR
PARTIC
NAT/G
CONSTN
B64

GORE W.J.,ADMINISTRATIVE DECISION-MAKING* A
HEURISTIC MODEL. EX/STRUC ADMIN LEAD ROUTINE
PERS/REL...METH/CNCPT ORG/CHARTS. PAGE 41 B0834
DECISION
MGT
SIMUL
GEN/METH
B64

GRZYBOWSKI K.,THE SOCIALIST COMMONWEALTH OF
NATIONS: ORGANIZATIONS AND INSTITUTIONS. FORCES
DIPLOM INT/TRADE ADJUD ADMIN LEAD WAR MARXISM
SOCISM...BIBLIOG 20 COMECON WARSAW/P. PAGE 44 B0898
INT/LAW
COM
REGION
INT/ORG
B64

HAMBRIDGE G.,DYNAMICS OF DEVELOPMENT. AGRI FINAN
INDUS LABOR INT/TRADE EDU/PROP ADMIN LEAD OWN
HEALTH...ANTHOL BIBLIOG 20. PAGE 46 B0930
ECO/UNDEV
ECO/TAC
OP/RES
ACT/RES
B64

KIMBROUGH R.B.,POLITICAL POWER AND EDUCATIONAL
DECISION-MAKING. USA+45 FINAN ADMIN LEAD GP/REL
ATTIT PWR PROG/TEAC. PAGE 60 B1207
EDU/PROP
PROB/SOLV
DECISION
SCHOOL
B64

MAHAR J.M.,INDIA: A CRITICAL BIBLIOGRAPHY. INDIA
PAKISTAN CULTURE ECO/UNDEV LOC/G POL/PAR SECT
PROB/SOLV DIPLOM ADMIN COLONIAL PARL/PROC ATTIT 20.
PAGE 68 B1377
BIBLIOG/A
S/ASIA
NAT/G
LEAD
B64

RIDDLE D.H.,THE TRUMAN COMMITTEE: A STUDY IN
CONGRESSIONAL RESPONSIBILITY. INDUS FORCES OP/RES
DOMIN ADMIN LEAD PARL/PROC WAR PRODUC SUPEGO
...BIBLIOG CONGRESS. PAGE 88 B1778
LEGIS
DELIB/GP
CONFER
B64

ROBSON W.A.,THE GOVERNORS AND THE GOVERNED. USA+45
PROB/SOLV DOMIN ADMIN CONTROL CHOOSE...POLICY
PRESIDENT. PAGE 89 B1808
EX/STRUC
ATTIT
PARTIC
LEAD
B64

ROCHE J.P.,THE CONGRESS. EX/STRUC BAL/PWR DIPLOM
DEBATE ADJUD LEAD PWR. PAGE 89 B1809
INGP/REL
LEGIS
DELIB/GP
SENIOR
B64

SEGUNDO-SANCHEZ M.,OBRAS (2 VOLS.). VENEZUELA
EX/STRUC DIPLOM ADMIN 19/20. PAGE 95 B1924
BIBLIOG
LEAD
NAT/G
L/A+17C
B64

TURNER M.C.,LIBROS EN VENTA EN HISPANOAMERICA Y
ESPANA. SPAIN LAW CONSTN CULTURE ADMIN LEAD...HUM
SOC 20. PAGE 106 B2139
BIBLIOG
L/A+17C
NAT/G
DIPLOM
B64

WILDAVSKY A.,LEADERSHIP IN A SMALL TOWN. USA+45
STRUCT PROB/SOLV EXEC PARTIC RACE/REL PWR PLURISM
...SOC 20 NEGRO WATER CIV/RIGHTS OBERLIN CITY/MGT.
PAGE 116 B2348
LEAD
MUNIC
ELITES

L64

FOX G.H.,"PERCEPTIONS OF THE VIETNAMESE PUBLIC
ADMINISTRATION SYSTEM" VIETNAM ELITES CONTROL EXEC
LEAD PWR...INT 20. PAGE 37 B0745
ADMIN
EX/STRUC
INGP/REL
ROLE

L64

GILBERT C.E.,"NATIONAL POLITICAL ALIGNMENTS AND THE
POLITICS OF LARGE CITIES." ELITES LOC/G NAT/G LEGIS
EXEC LEAD PLURISM GOV/COMP. PAGE 39 B0800
MUNIC
CHOOSE
POL/PAR
PWR

S64

KAMMERER G.M.,"ROLE DIVERSITY OF CITY MANAGERS."
LOC/G ADMIN LEAD PERCEPT PWR GP/COMP. PAGE 57 B1163
MUNIC
EXEC
ATTIT
ROLE

S64

KAMMERER G.M.,"URBAN LEADERSHIP DURING CHANGE."
LEAD PARTIC REPRESENT GP/REL PLURISM...DECISION
GP/COMP. PAGE 58 B1164
MUNIC
PWR
ELITES
EXEC

S64

SALISBURY R.H.,"URBAN POLITICS: THE NEW CONVERGENCE
OF POWER." STRATA POL/PAR EX/STRUC PARTIC GP/REL
DECISION. PAGE 92 B1863
MUNIC
PWR
LEAD

S64

SWEARER H.R.,"AFTER KHRUSHCHEV: WHAT NEXT." COM FUT
USSR CONSTN ELITES NAT/G POL/PAR CHIEF DELIB/GP
LEGIS DOMIN LEAD...RECORD TREND STERTYP GEN/METH
20. PAGE 102 B2058
EX/STRUC
PWR

B65

DYER F.C.,BUREAUCRACY VS CREATIVITY. UNIV CONTROL
LEAD INGP/REL EFFICIENCY MGT. PAGE 31 B0639
ADMIN
DECISION
METH/COMP
CREATE

B65

ECCLES H.E.,MILITARY CONCEPTS AND PHILOSOPHY.
USA+45 STRUCT EXEC ROUTINE COERCE WAR CIVMIL/REL
COST...OBS GEN/LAWS COLD/WAR. PAGE 32 B0648
PLAN
DRIVE
LEAD
FORCES

B65

FEERICK J.D.,FROM FAILING HANDS: THE STUDY OF
PRESIDENTIAL SUCCESSION. CONSTN NAT/G PROB/SOLV
LEAD PARL/PROC MURDER CHOOSE...NEW/IDEA BIBLIOG 20
KENNEDY/JF JOHNSON/LB PRESIDENT PRE/US/AM
VICE/PRES. PAGE 35 B0710
EX/STRUC
CHIEF
LAW
LEGIS

B65

FOLTZ W.J.,FROM FRENCH WEST AFRICA TO THE MALI
FEDERATION. AFR FRANCE MALI ADMIN CONTROL FEDERAL
...DECISION 20. PAGE 36 B0734
EXEC
TOP/EX
ELITES
LEAD

B65

GOODSELL C.T.,ADMINISTRATION OF A REVOLUTION.
PUERT/RICO ECO/UNDEV FINAN MUNIC POL/PAR PROVS
LEGIS PLAN BUDGET RECEIVE ADMIN COLONIAL LEAD 20
ROOSEVLT/F. PAGE 41 B0827
EXEC
SOC

B65

GOULDNER A.W.,STUDIES IN LEADERSHIP. LABOR EDU/PROP
CONTROL PARTIC...CONCPT CLASSIF. PAGE 42 B0845
LEAD
ADMIN
AUTHORIT

B65

GREGG J.L.,POLITICAL PARTIES AND PARTY SYSTEMS IN
GUATEMALA, 1944-1963. GUATEMALA L/A+17C EX/STRUC
FORCES CREATE CONTROL REV CHOOSE PWR...TREND
IDEA/COMP 20. PAGE 43 B0872
LEAD
POL/PAR
NAT/G
CHIEF

B65

HADWIGER D.F.,PRESSURES AND PROTEST. NAT/G LEGIS
PLAN LEAD PARTIC ROUTINE ATTIT POLICY. PAGE 45
B0913
AGRI
GP/REL
LOBBY
CHOOSE

B65

KWEDER J.B.,THE ROLES OF THE MANAGER, MAYOR, AND
COUNCILMEN IN POLICYMAKING. LEGIS PERS/REL ATTIT
ROLE PWR GP/COMP. PAGE 62 B1246
MUNIC
EXEC
LEAD
DECISION

B65

LEMAY G.H.,BRITISH SUPREMACY IN SOUTH AFRICA
1899-1907. SOUTH/AFR UK ADMIN CONTROL LEAD GP/REL
ORD/FREE 19/20. PAGE 64 B1286
WAR
COLONIAL
DOMIN
POLICY

B65

MASTERS N.A.,COMMITTEE ASSIGNMENTS IN THE HOUSE OF
REPRESENTATIVES (BMR). USA+45 ELITES POL/PAR
EX/STRUC PARTIC REPRESENT GP/REL PERS/REL ATTIT PWR
...STAT CHARTS 20 HOUSE/REP. PAGE 71 B1425
LEAD
LEGIS
CHOOSE
DELIB/GP

B65

PAYNE J.L.,LABOR AND POLITICS IN PERU; THE SYSTEM
OF POLITICAL BARGAINING. PERU CONSTN VOL/ASSN
EX/STRUC LEAD PWR...CHARTS 20. PAGE 81 B1645
LABOR
POL/PAR
BARGAIN
GP/REL

B65

ROMASCO A.U.,THE POVERTY OF ABUNDANCE: HOOVER, THE
NATION, THE DEPRESSION. USA-45 AGRI LEGIS WORKER
GIVE PRESS LEAD 20 HOOVER/H. PAGE 90 B1817
ECO/TAC
ADMIN
NAT/G
FINAN

B65

ROSS P.,THE GOVERNMENT AS A SOURCE OF UNION POWER.
LABOR

USA+45 LAW ECO/DEV PROB/SOLV ECO/TAC LEAD GP/REL
...MGT 20. PAGE 90 B1826
BARGAIN
POLICY
NAT/G

S65

POSVAR W.W.,"NATIONAL SECURITY POLICY* THE REALM OF
OBSCURITY." CREATE PLAN PROB/SOLV ADMIN LEAD GP/REL
CONSERVE...DECISION GEOG. PAGE 84 B1694
DIPLOM
USA+45
RECORD

S65

RAPHAELI N.,"SELECTED ARTICLES AND DOCUMENTS ON
COMPARATIVE PUBLIC ADMINISTRATION." USA+45 FINAN
LOC/G WORKER TEC/DEV CONTROL LEAD...SOC/WK GOV/COMP
METH/COMP. PAGE 86 B1739
BIBLIOG
ADMIN
NAT/G
MGT

C65

HUNTINGTON S.P.,"CONGRESSIONAL RESPONSES TO THE
TWENTIETH CENTURY IN D. TRUMAN, ED. THE CONGRESS
AND AMERICA'S FUTURE." USA+45 USA-45 DIPLOM SENIOR
ADMIN EXEC PWR...SOC 20 CONGRESS. PAGE 53 B1067
FUT
LEAD
NAT/G
LEGIS

B66

ASHRAF A.,THE CITY GOVERNMENT OF CALCUTTA: A STUDY
OF INERTIA. INDIA ELITES INDUS NAT/G EX/STRUC
ACT/RES PLAN PROB/SOLV LEAD HABITAT...BIBLIOG 20
CALCUTTA. PAGE 7 B0141
LOC/G
MUNIC
ADMIN
ECO/UNDEV

B66

DAVIDSON R.H.,CONGRESS IN CRISIS: POLITICS AND
CONGRESSIONAL REFORM. USA+45 SOCIETY POL/PAR
CONTROL LEAD ROUTINE GOV/REL ATTIT PWR...POLICY 20
CONGRESS. PAGE 26 B0535
LEGIS
PARL/PROC
PROB/SOLV
NAT/G

B66

GERBERDING W.P.,UNITED STATES FOREIGN POLICY:
PERSPECTIVES AND ANALYSIS. USA+45 LEGIS EXEC LEAD
REPRESENT PWR 20. PAGE 39 B0791
PROB/SOLV
CHIEF
EX/STRUC
CONTROL

B66

HALPIN A.W.,THEORY AND RESEARCH IN ADMINISTRATION.
ACT/RES LEAD...MGT IDEA/COMP METH/COMP. PAGE 46
B0929
GEN/LAWS
EDU/PROP
ADMIN
PHIL/SCI

B66

HANKE L.,HANDBOOK OF LATIN AMERICAN STUDIES.
ECO/UNDEV ADMIN LEAD...HUM SOC 20. PAGE 46 B0937
BIBLIOG/A
L/A+17C
INDEX
NAT/G

B66

HIDAYATULLAH M.,DEMOCRACY IN INDIA AND THE JUDICIAL
PROCESS. INDIA EX/STRUC LEGIS LEAD GOV/REL ATTIT
ORD/FREE...MAJORIT CONCPT 20 NEHRU/J. PAGE 50 B1007
NAT/G
CT/SYS
CONSTN
JURID

B66

KAUNDA K.,ZAMBIA: INDEPENDENCE AND BEYOND: THE
SPEECHES OF KENNETH KAUNDA. AFR FUT ZAMBIA SOCIETY
ECO/UNDEV NAT/G PROB/SOLV ECO/TAC ADMIN RACE/REL
SOVEREIGN 20. PAGE 59 B1183
ORD/FREE
COLONIAL
CONSTN
LEAD

B66

MCKENZIE J.L.,AUTHORITY IN THE CHURCH. STRUCT LEAD
INGP/REL PERS/REL CENTRAL ANOMIE ATTIT ORD/FREE
RESPECT CATH. PAGE 72 B1452
SECT
AUTHORIT
PWR
ADMIN

B66

ROSHOLT R.L.,AN ADMINISTRATIVE HISTORY OF NASA,
1958-1963. SPACE USA+45 FINAN LEAD...MGT CHARTS
BIBLIOG 20 NASA. PAGE 90 B1824
ADMIN
EX/STRUC
ADJUST
DELIB/GP

B66

SEASHOLES B.,VOTING, INTEREST GROUPS, AND PARTIES.
USA+45 FINAN LOC/G NAT/G ADMIN LEAD GP/REL INGP/REL
ROLE...CHARTS ANTHOL 20. PAGE 95 B1922
CHOOSE
POL/PAR
LOBBY
PARTIC

B66

SILBERMAN B.S.,MODERN JAPANESE LEADERSHIP;
TRANSITION AND CHANGE. NAT/G POL/PAR CHIEF ADMIN
REPRESENT GP/REL ADJUST RIGID/FLEX...SOC METH/COMP
ANTHOL 19/20 CHINJAP CHRISTIAN. PAGE 97 B1952
LEAD
CULTURE
ELITES
MUNIC

B66

TOTTEN G.O.,THE SOCIAL DEMOCRATIC MOVEMENT IN
PREWAR JAPAN. ASIA CHIEF EX/STRUC LEGIS DOMIN LEAD
ROUTINE WAR 20 CHINJAP. PAGE 105 B2122
POL/PAR
SOCISM
PARTIC
STRATA

B66

ZALEZNIK A.,HUMAN DILEMMAS OF LEADERSHIP. ELITES
INDUS EX/STRUC INGP/REL ATTIT...PSY 20. PAGE 119
B2397
LEAD
PERSON
EXEC
MGT

L66

CRAIN R.L.,"STRUCTURE AND VALUES IN LOCAL POLITICAL
SYSTEMS: THE CASE OF FLUORIDATION DECISIONS."
EX/STRUC LEGIS LEAD PARTIC REPRESENT PWR...DECISION
GOV/COMP. PAGE 25 B0501
MUNIC
EDU/PROP
LOC/G
ATTIT

S66

JACOBSON J.,"COALITIONISM: FROM PROTEST TO
POLITICKING" USA+45 ELITES NAT/G POL/PAR PROB/SOLV
ADMIN LEAD DISCRIM ORD/FREE PWR CONSERVE 20 NEGRO
AFL/CIO CIV/RIGHTS BLACK/PWR. PAGE 55 B1116
RACE/REL
LABOR
SOCIALIST
VOL/ASSN

B67

CECIL L.,ALBERT BALLIN; BUSINESS AND POLITICS IN
IMPERIAL GERMANY 1888-1918. GERMANY UK INT/TRADE
LEAD WAR PERS/REL ADJUST PWR WEALTH...MGT BIBLIOG
DIPLOM
CONSTN
ECO/DEV

19/20. PAGE 19 B0397 — TOP/EX

B67
COHEN R.,COMPARATIVE POLITICAL SYSTEMS: STUDIES IN THE POLITICS OF PRE-INDUSTRIAL SOCIETIES. WOR+45 WOR-45 CULTURE FAM KIN LOC/G NEIGH ADMIN LEAD MARRIAGE...BIBLIOG 20. PAGE 22 B0447 — ECO/UNDEV STRUCT SOCIETY GP/COMP

B67
GIFFORD P.,BRITAIN AND GERMANY IN AFRICA. AFR GERMANY UK ECO/UNDEV LEAD WAR NAT/LISM ATTIT ...POLICY HIST/WRIT METH/COMP ANTHOL BIBLIOG 19/20 WWI. PAGE 39 B0797 — COLONIAL ADMIN DIPLOM NAT/COMP

B67
MACKINTOSH J.M.,JUGGERNAUT. USSR NAT/G POL/PAR ADMIN LEAD CIVMIL/REL COST TOTALISM PWR MARXISM ...GOV/COMP 20. PAGE 68 B1364 — WAR FORCES COM PROF/ORG

B67
NARVER J.C.,CONGLOMERATE MERGERS AND MARKET COMPETITION. USA+45 LAW STRUCT ADMIN LEAD RISK COST PROFIT WEALTH...POLICY CHARTS BIBLIOG. PAGE 77 B1555 — DEMAND LG/CO MARKET MGT

B67
SCHEINMAN L.,EURATOM* NUCLEAR INTEGRATION IN EUROPE. EX/STRUC LEAD 20 EURATOM. PAGE 93 B1885 — INT/ORG NAT/LISM NUC/PWR DIPLOM

B67
TOTMAN C.,POLITICS IN THE TOKUGAWA BAKUFU, 1600-1843. EX/STRUC...GOV/COMP 17/19 CHINJAP. PAGE 105 B2120 — NAT/G ADMIN LEAD

B67
WARREN S.,THE AMERICAN PRESIDENT. POL/PAR FORCES LEGIS DIPLOM ECO/TAC ADMIN EXEC PWR...ANTHOL 18/20 ROOSEVLT/F KENNEDY/JF JOHNSON/LB TRUMAN/HS WILSON/W. PAGE 114 B2297 — CHIEF LEAD NAT/G CONSTN

B67
WATERS M.,THE UNITED NATIONS* INTERNATIONAL ORGANIZATION AND ADMINISTRATION. WOR+45 EX/STRUC FORCES DIPLOM LEAD REGION ARMS/CONT REPRESENT INGP/REL ROLE...METH/COMP ANTHOL 20 UN LEAGUE/NAT. PAGE 114 B2301 — CONSTN INT/ORG ADMIN ADJUD

B67
WESSON R.G.,THE IMPERIAL ORDER. WOR-45 STRUCT SECT DOMIN ADMIN COLONIAL LEAD CONSERVE...CONCPT BIBLIOG 20. PAGE 115 B2324 — PWR CHIEF CONTROL SOCIETY

L67
BESCOBY I.,"A COLONIAL ADMINISTRATION* AN ANALYSIS OF ADMINISTRATION IN BRITISH COLUMBIA 1869-1871." UK STRATA EX/STRUC LEGIS TASK GOV/REL EFFICIENCY ROLE...MGT CHARTS 19. PAGE 11 B0232 — ADMIN CANADA COLONIAL LEAD

L67
COHEN M.,"THE DEMISE OF UNEF." CONSTN DIPLOM ADMIN AGREE LEAD COERCE 20 UNEF U/THANT HAMMARSK/D. PAGE 22 B0445 — INT/ORG FORCES PEACE POLICY

S67
ANDERSON M.,"THE FRENCH PARLIAMENT." EUR+WWI FRANCE MOD/EUR CONSTN POL/PAR CHIEF LEGIS LOBBY ATTIT ROLE PWR 19/20. PAGE 5 B0095 — PARL/PROC LEAD GOV/COMP EX/STRUC

S67
BASTID M.,"ORIGINES ET DEVELOPMENT DE LA REVOLUTION CULTURELLE." CHINA/COM DOMIN ADMIN CONTROL LEAD COERCE CROWD ATTIT DRIVE MARXISM...POLICY 20. PAGE 10 B0195 — REV CULTURE ACADEM WORKER

S67
BEASLEY W.G.,"POLITICS AND THE SAMURAI CLASS STRUCTURE IN SATSUMA, 18581868." STRATA FORCES DOMIN LEGIT ADMIN LEAD 19 CHINJAP. PAGE 10 B0202 — ELITES STRUCT ATTIT PRIVIL

S67
CONWAY J.E.,"MAKING RESEARCH EFFECTIVE IN LEGISLATION." LAW R+D CONSULT EX/STRUC PLAN CONFER ADMIN LEAD ROUTINE TASK INGP/REL DECISION. PAGE 23 B0469 — ACT/RES POLICY LEGIS PROB/SOLV

S67
DANELSKI D.J.,"CONFLICT AND ITS RESOLUTION IN THE SUPREME COURT." PROB/SOLV LEAD ROUTINE PERSON...PSY PERS/COMP BIBLIOG 20. PAGE 26 B0527 — ROLE JURID JUDGE INGP/REL

S67
DRAPER A.P.,"UNIONS AND THE WAR IN VIETNAM." USA+45 CONFER ADMIN LEAD WAR ORD/FREE PACIFIST 20. PAGE 30 B0616 — LABOR PACIFISM ATTIT ELITES

S67
EDWARDS H.T.,"POWER STRUCTURE AND ITS COMMUNICATION IN SAN JOSE, COSTA RICA." COSTA/RICA L/A+17C STRATA FACE/GP POL/PAR EX/STRUC PROB/SOLV ADMIN LEAD GP/REL PWR...STAT INT 20. PAGE 32 B0655 — ELITES INGP/REL MUNIC DOMIN

S67
GOBER J.L.,"FEDERALISM AT WORK." USA+45 NAT/G CONSULT ACT/RES PLAN CONFER ADMIN LEAD PARTIC FEDERAL ATTIT. PAGE 40 B0813 — MUNIC TEC/DEV R+D GOV/REL

S67
GRUNDY K.W.,"THE POLITICAL USES OF IMAGINATION." GHANA ELITES SOCIETY NAT/G DOMIN EDU/PROP COLONIAL REGION REPRESENT GP/REL CENTRAL PWR MARXISM 20. PAGE 44 B0897 — NAT/LISM EX/STRUC AFR LEAD

S67
HAIRE M.,"MANAGING MANAGEMENT MANPOWER." EX/STRUC OP/RES PAY EDU/PROP COST EFFICIENCY...PREDICT SIMUL 20. PAGE 45 B0920 — MGT EXEC LEAD INDUS

S67
HALL B.,"THE COALITION AGAINST DISHWASHERS." USA+45 POL/PAR PROB/SOLV BARGAIN LEAD CHOOSE REPRESENT GP/REL ORD/FREE PWR...POLICY 20. PAGE 46 B0923 — LABOR ADMIN DOMIN WORKER

S67
HSUEH C.T.,"THE CULTURAL REVOLUTION AND LEADERSHIP CRISIS IN COMMUNIST CHINA." CHINA/COM POL/PAR EX/STRUC FORCES EDU/PROP ATTIT PWR...POLICY 20. PAGE 52 B1054 — LEAD REV CULTURE MARXISM

S67
LEVIN M.R.,"PLANNERS AND METROPOLITAN PLANNING." FUT USA+45 SOCIETY NAT/G PROVS PROB/SOLV LEAD PARTIC GOV/REL RACE/REL HABITAT ROLE. PAGE 64 B1301 — PLAN MUNIC R+D ADMIN

S67
LEWIS P.H.,"LEADERSHIP AND CONFLICT WITHIN FEBRERISTA PARTY OF PARAGUAY." L/A+17C PARAGUAY EX/STRUC DOMIN SENIOR CONTROL INGP/REL CENTRAL FEDERAL ATTIT 20. PAGE 65 B1305 — POL/PAR ELITES LEAD

S67
MCNAMARA R.L.,"THE NEED FOR INNOVATIVENESS IN DEVELOPING SOCIETIES." L/A+17C EDU/PROP ADMIN LEAD WEALTH...POLICY PSY SOC METH 20 COLOMB. PAGE 72 B1456 — PROB/SOLV PLAN ECO/UNDEV NEW/IDEA

S67
RAUM O.,"THE MODERN LEADERSHIP GROUP AMONG THE SOUTH AFRICAN XHOSA." SOUTH/AFR SOCIETY SECT EX/STRUC REPRESENT GP/REL INGP/REL PERSON ...METH/COMP 17/20 XHOSA NEGRO. PAGE 86 B1743 — RACE/REL KIN LEAD CULTURE

S67
SATHYAMURTHY T.V.,"TWENTY YEARS OF UNESCO: AN INTERPRETATION." SOCIETY PROB/SOLV LEAD PEACE UNESCO. PAGE 92 B1870 — ADMIN CONSTN INT/ORG TIME/SEQ

S67
TATU M.,"URSS: LES FLOTTEMENTS DE LA DIRECTION COLLEGIALE." UAR USSR CHIEF LEAD INGP/REL EFFICIENCY...DECISION TREND 20 MID/EAST. PAGE 103 B2082 — POLICY NAT/G EX/STRUC DIPLOM

S68
GUZZARDI W. JR.,"THE SECOND BATTLE OF BRITAIN." UK STRATA LABOR WORKER CREATE PROB/SOLV EDU/PROP ADMIN LEAD LOBBY...MGT SOC 20 GOLD/STAND. PAGE 45 B0907 — FINAN ECO/TAC ECO/DEV STRUCT

LEADING....SEE LEAD

LEAGUE OF FREE NATIONS ASSOCIATION....SEE LFNA

LEAGUE OF WOMEN VOTERS....SEE LEAGUE/WV

LEAGUE/NAT....LEAGUE OF NATIONS; SEE ALSO INT/ORG

N
WORLD PEACE FOUNDATION,DOCUMENTS OF INTERNATIONAL ORGANIZATIONS: A SELECTED BIBLIOGRAPHY. WOR+45 WOR-45 AGRI FINAN ACT/RES OP/RES INT/TRADE ADMIN ...CON/ANAL 20 UN UNESCO LEAGUE/NAT. PAGE 118 B2374 — BIBLIOG DIPLOM INT/ORG REGION

B18
US LIBRARY OF CONGRESS,LIST OF REFERENCES ON A LEAGUE OF NATIONS. DIPLOM WAR PEACE 20 LEAGUE/NAT. PAGE 109 B2201 — BIBLIOG INT/ORG ADMIN EX/STRUC

B31
HILL N.,INTERNATIONAL ADMINISTRATION. WOR-45 DELIB/GP DIPLOM EDU/PROP ALL/VALS...MGT TIME/SEQ LEAGUE/NAT TOT/POP VAL/FREE 20. PAGE 50 B1011 — INT/ORG ADMIN

B37
UNION OF SOUTH AFRICA,REPORT CONCERNING ADMINISTRATION OF SOUTH WEST AFRICA (6 VOLS.). SOUTH/AFR INDUS PUB/INST FORCES LEGIS BUDGET DIPLOM EDU/PROP ADJUD CT/SYS...GEOG CHARTS 20 AFRICA/SW LEAGUE/NAT. PAGE 107 B2158 — NAT/G ADMIN COLONIAL CONSTN

B38
RAPPARD W.E.,THE CRISIS OF DEMOCRACY. EUR+WWI UNIV WOR-45 CULTURE SOCIETY ECO/DEV INT/ORG POL/PAR ACT/RES EDU/PROP EXEC CHOOSE ATTIT ALL/VALS...SOC OBS HIST/WRIT TIME/SEQ LEAGUE/NAT NAZI TOT/POP 20. PAGE 86 B1741 — NAT/G CONCPT

B39
ZIMMERN A.,MODERN POLITICAL DOCTRINE. WOR-45 CULTURE SOCIETY ECO/UNDEV DELIB/GP EX/STRUC CREATE DOMIN COERCE NAT/LISM ATTIT RIGID/FLEX ORD/FREE PWR WEALTH...POLICY CONCPT OBS TIME/SEQ TREND TOT/POP LEAGUE/NAT 20. PAGE 119 B2402 — NAT/G ECO/TAC BAL/PWR INT/TRADE

B41
BURTON M.E.,THE ASSEMBLY OF THE LEAGUE OF NATIONS.   DELIB/GP
WOR-45 CONSTN SOCIETY STRUCT INT/ORG NAT/G CREATE   EX/STRUC
ATTIT RIGID/FLEX PWR...POLICY TIME/SEQ LEAGUE/NAT   DIPLOM
20. PAGE 18 B0359

B41
YOUNG G.,FEDERALISM AND FREEDOM. EUR+WWI MOD/EUR   NAT/G
RUSSIA USA-45 WOR-45 SOCIETY STRUCT ECO/DEV INT/ORG   WAR
EXEC FEDERAL ATTIT PERSON ALL/VALS...OLD/LIB CONCPT
OBS TREND LEAGUE/NAT TOT/POP. PAGE 119 B2392

B44
DAVIS H.E.,PIONEERS IN WORLD ORDER. WOR-45 CONSTN   INT/ORG
ECO/TAC DOMIN EDU/PROP LEGIT ADJUD ADMIN ARMS/CONT   ROUTINE
CHOOSE KNOWL ORD/FREE...POLICY JURID SOC STAT OBS
CENSUS TIME/SEQ ANTHOL LEAGUE/NAT 20. PAGE 26 B0537

L44
HAILEY.,"THE FUTURE OF COLONIAL PEOPLES." WOR-45   PLAN
CONSTN CULTURE ECO/UNDEV AGRI MARKET INT/ORG NAT/G   CONCPT
SECT CONSULT ECO/TAC LEGIT ADMIN NAT/LISM ALL/VALS   DIPLOM
...SOC OBS TREND STERTYP CMN/WLTH LEAGUE/NAT   UK
PARLIAMENT 20. PAGE 45 B0916

B45
PASTUHOV V.D.,A GUIDE TO THE PRACTICE OF   INT/ORG
INTERNATIONAL CONFERENCES. WOR+45 PLAN LEGIT   DELIB/GP
ORD/FREE...MGT OBS RECORD VAL/FREE ILO LEAGUE/NAT
20. PAGE 81 B1640

B45
RANSHOFFEN-WERTHEIMER EF,THE INTERNATIONAL   INT/ORG
SECRETARIAT: A GREAT EXPERIMENT IN INTERNATIONAL   EXEC
ADMINISTRATION. EUR+WWI FUT CONSTN FACE/GP CONSULT
DELIB/GP ACT/RES ADMIN ROUTINE PEACE ORD/FREE...MGT
RECORD ORG/CHARTS LEAGUE/NAT WORK 20. PAGE 86 B1731

B52
ELLIOTT W.,UNITED STATES FOREIGN POLICY, ITS   LEGIS
ORGANIZATION AND CONTROL. USA+45 USA-45 CONSTN   EX/STRUC
NAT/G FORCES TOP/EX PEACE...TIME/SEQ CONGRESS   DIPLOM
LEAGUE/NAT 20. PAGE 33 B0670

B58
ISLAM R.,INTERNATIONAL ECONOMIC COOPERATION AND THE INT/ORG
UNITED NATIONS. FINAN PLAN EXEC TASK WAR PEACE   DIPLOM
...SOC METH/CNCPT 20 UN LEAGUE/NAT. PAGE 55 B1105   ADMIN

B59
CHINA INSTITUTE OF AMERICA.,CHINA AND THE UNITED   ASIA
NATIONS. CHINA/COM FUT STRUCT EDU/PROP LEGIT ADMIN   INT/ORG
ATTIT KNOWL ORD/FREE PWR...OBS RECORD STAND/INT
TIME/SEQ UN LEAGUE/NAT UNESCO 20. PAGE 21 B0425

S59
LENGYEL P.,"SOME TRENDS IN THE INTERNATIONAL CIVIL   ADMIN
SERVICE." FUT WOR+45 INT/ORG CONSULT ATTIT...MGT   EXEC
OBS TREND CON/ANAL LEAGUE/NAT UNESCO 20. PAGE 64
B1291

S62
SCHILLING W.R.,"SCIENTISTS, FOREIGN POLICY AND   NAT/G
POLITICS." WOR+45 WOR-45 INTELL INT/ORG CONSULT   TEC/DEV
TOP/EX ACT/RES PLAN ADMIN KNOWL...CONCPT OBS TREND   DIPLOM
LEAGUE/NAT 20. PAGE 93 B1889   NUC/PWR

B63
BOWETT D.W.,THE LAW OF INTERNATIONAL INSTITUTIONS.   INT/ORG
WOR+45 WOR-45 CONSTN DELIB/GP EX/STRUC JUDGE   ADJUD
EDU/PROP LEGIT CT/SYS EXEC ROUTINE RIGID/FLEX   DIPLOM
ORD/FREE PWR...JURID CONCPT ORG/CHARTS GEN/METH
LEAGUE/NAT OAS OEEC 20 UN. PAGE 14 B0286

B63
LANGROD G.,THE INTERNATIONAL CIVIL SERVICE: ITS   INT/ORG
ORIGINS, ITS NATURE, ITS EVALUATION. FUT WOR+45   ADMIN
WOR-45 DELIB/GP ACT/RES DOMIN LEGIT ATTIT
RIGID/FLEX SUPEGO ALL/VALS...MGT CONCPT STAT
TIME/SEQ ILO LEAGUE/NAT VAL/FREE 20 UN. PAGE 62
B1259

B66
US LIBRARY OF CONGRESS,NIGERIA: A GUIDE TO OFFICIAL   BIBLIOG
PUBLICATIONS. CAMEROON NIGERIA UK DIPLOM...POLICY   ADMIN
19/20 UN LEAGUE/NAT. PAGE 109 B2207   NAT/G
                                                       COLONIAL

B67
PLANO J.C.,FORGING WORLD ORDER: THE POLITICS OF   INT/ORG
INTERNATIONAL ORGANIZATION. PROB/SOLV DIPLOM   ADMIN
CONTROL CENTRAL RATIONAL ORD/FREE...INT/LAW CHARTS   JURID
BIBLIOG 20 UN LEAGUE/NAT. PAGE 83 B1679

B67
WATERS M.,THE UNITED NATIONS* INTERNATIONAL   CONSTN
ORGANIZATION AND ADMINISTRATION. WOR+45 EX/STRUC   INT/ORG
FORCES DIPLOM LEAD REGION ARMS/CONT REPRESENT   ADMIN
INGP/REL ROLE...METH/COMP ANTHOL 20 UN LEAGUE/NAT.   ADJUD
PAGE 114 B2301

LEAGUE/WV....LEAGUE OF WOMEN VOTERS

S61
TANNENBAUM A.S.,"CONTROL AND EFFECTIVENESS IN A   EFFICIENCY
VOLUNTARY ORGANIZATION." USA+45 ADMIN...CORREL MATH   VOL/ASSN
REGRESS STAT TESTS SAMP/SIZ CHARTS SOC/EXP INDEX 20   CONTROL
LEAGUE/WV. PAGE 102 B2072   INGP/REL

LEARNING....SEE PERCEPT

LEASE....SEE RENT

LEBANON....SEE ALSO ISLAM

C55
GRASSMUCK G.L.,"A MANUAL OF LEBANESE   ADMIN
ADMINISTRATION." LEBANON PLAN...CHARTS BIBLIOG/A   NAT/G
20. PAGE 42 B0854   ISLAM
                                                       EX/STRUC

LEBEAUX C.N. B2352

LEDYARD/J....JOHN LEDYARD

LEE L.T. B1279

LEE R.R. B1280

LEE/IVY....IVY LEE

LEES J.P. B1281

LEEVILLE....LEEVILLE, TEXAS

LEGAL SYSTEM....SEE LAW

LEGAL PERMIT....SEE LICENSE

LEGION OF DECENCY....SEE LEGION/DCY

LEGION/DCY....LEGION OF DECENCY

LEGIS....LEGISLATURES; SEE ALSO PARLIAMENT, CONGRESS

N
PRINCETON U INDUSTRIAL REL SEC,SELECTED REFERENCES   BIBLIOG/A
OF THE INDUSTRIAL RELATIONS SECTION OF PRINCETON,   INDUS
NEW JERSEY. LG/CO NAT/G LEGIS WORKER PLAN PROB/SOLV   LABOR
PAY ADMIN ROUTINE TASK GP/REL...PSY 20. PAGE 84   MGT
B1708

N
CONGRESSIONAL MONITOR. CONSULT DELIB/GP PROB/SOLV   BIBLIOG
PRESS DEBATE ROUTINE...POLICY CONGRESS. PAGE 1   LEGIS
B0002   REPRESENT
                                                      USA+45

N
JOURNAL OF POLITICS. USA+45 USA-45 CONSTN POL/PAR   BIBLIOG/A
EX/STRUC LEGIS PROB/SOLV DIPLOM CT/SYS CHOOSE   NAT/G
RACE/REL 20. PAGE 1 B0005   LAW
                                                     LOC/G

N
REVIEW OF POLITICS. WOR+45 WOR-45 CONSTN LEGIS   BIBLIOG/A
PROB/SOLV ADMIN LEAD ALL/IDEOS...PHIL/SCI 20.   DIPLOM
PAGE 1 B0006   INT/ORG
                                                     NAT/G

N
CARLETON UNIVERSITY LIBRARY,SELECTED LIST OF   BIBLIOG
CURRENT MATERIALS ON CANADIAN PUBLIC   ADMIN
ADMINISTRATION. CANADA LEGIS WORKER PLAN BUDGET 20.   LOC/G
PAGE 19 B0379   MUNIC

N
CATHERINE R.,LA REVUE ADMINISTRATIVE. FRANCE LAW   ADMIN
NAT/G LEGIS...JURID BIBLIOG/A 20. PAGE 19 B0393   MGT
                                                     FINAN
                                                     METH/COMP

N
FAUNT J.R.,A CHECKLIST OF SOUTH CAROLINA STATE   BIBLIOG
PUBLICATIONS. USA+45 CONSTN LEGIS ADMIN ATTIT 20.   PROVS
PAGE 35 B0708   LOC/G
                                                     GOV/REL

N
KENTUCKY STATE ARCHIVES,CHECKLIST OF KENTUCKY STATE BIBLIOG/A
PUBLICATIONS AND STATE DIRECTORY. USA+45 LAW ACADEM   PROVS
EX/STRUC LEGIS EDU/PROP LEAD...JURID 20. PAGE 59   PUB/INST
B1196   ADMIN

N
MARTIN W.O. JR.,STATE OF LOUISIANA OFFICIAL   BIBLIOG
PUBLICATIONS. USA+45 USA-45 LEGIS ADMIN LEAD 19/20.   PROVS
PAGE 70 B1415   GOV/REL

N
UNESCO,INTERNATIONAL BIBLIOGRAPHY OF POLITICAL   BIBLIOG
SCIENCE (VOLUMES 1-8). WOR+45 LAW NAT/G EX/STRUC   CONCPT
LEGIS PROB/SOLV DIPLOM ADMIN GOV/REL 20 UNESCO.   IDEA/COMP
PAGE 107 B2153

N
US SUPERINTENDENT OF DOCUMENTS,INTERSTATE COMMERCE BIBLIOG/A
(PRICE LIST 59). USA+45 LAW LOC/G NAT/G LEGIS   DIST/IND
TARIFFS TAX ADMIN CONTROL HEALTH DECISION. PAGE 111   GOV/REL
B2239   PROVS

N
US SUPERINTENDENT OF DOCUMENTS,LABOR (PRICE LIST   BIBLIOG/A
33). USA+45 LAW AGRI CONSTRUC INDUS NAT/G BARGAIN   WORKER
PRICE ADMIN AUTOMAT PRODUC MGT. PAGE 111 B2240   LABOR
                                                     LEGIS

N
VIRGINIA STATE LIBRARY,CHECK-LIST OF VIRGINIA STATE BIBLIOG/A

PUBLICATIONS. USA+45 USA-45 ECO/DEV POL/PAR LEGIS ADJUD LEAD 18/20. PAGE 112 B2265
PROVS ADMIN GOV/REL
B00

SANDERSON E.,AFRICA IN THE NINETEENTH CENTURY. FRANCE UK EXTR/IND FORCES LEGIS ADMIN WAR DISCRIM ORD/FREE...GEOG GP/COMP SOC/INTEG 19. PAGE 92 B1867
COLONIAL AFR DIPLOM
B05

GOODNOW F.J.,THE PRINCIPLES OF THE ADMINISTRATIVE LAW OF THE UNITED STATES. USA-45 LAW STRUCT EX/STRUC LEGIS BAL/PWR CONTROL GOV/REL PWR...JURID 19/20 CIVIL/SERV. PAGE 41 B0822
ADMIN NAT/G PROVS LOC/G
B08

THE GOVERNMENT OF SOUTH AFRICA (VOL. II). SOUTH/AFR STRATA EXTR/IND EX/STRUC TOP/EX BUDGET ADJUD ADMIN CT/SYS PRODUC...CORREL CENSUS 19 RAILROAD CIVIL/SERV POSTAL/SYS. PAGE 2 B0033
CONSTN FINAN LEGIS NAT/G
B08

WILSON W.,CONSTITUTIONAL GOVERNMENT IN THE UNITED STATES. USA-45 LAW POL/PAR PROVS CHIEF LEGIS BAL/PWR ADJUD EXEC FEDERAL PWR 18/20 SUPREME/CT HOUSE/REP SENATE. PAGE 117 B2362
NAT/G GOV/REL CONSTN PARL/PROC
B09

HARVARD UNIVERSITY LAW LIBRARY,CATALOGUE OF THE LIBRARY OF THE LAW SCHOOL OF HARVARD UNIVERSITY (3 VOLS.). UK USA-45 LEGIS JUDGE ADJUD CT/SYS...JURID CHARTS 14/20. PAGE 48 B0963
BIBLIOG/A LAW ADMIN
B16

TREITSCHKE H.,POLITICS. UNIV SOCIETY STRATA NAT/G EX/STRUC LEGIS DOMIN EDU/PROP ATTIT PWR RESPECT ...CONCPT TIME/SEQ GEN/LAWS TOT/POP 20. PAGE 105 B2127
EXEC ELITES GERMANY
B17

CORWIN E.S.,THE PRESIDENT'S CONTROL OF FOREIGN RELATIONS. FUT USA-45 CONSTN STRATA NAT/G CHIEF EX/STRUC LEGIS KNOWL RESPECT...JURID CONCPT TREND CONGRESS VAL/FREE 20 PRESIDENT. PAGE 24 B0483
TOP/EX PWR DIPLOM
B17

HARLOW R.V.,THE HISTORY OF LEGISLATIVE METHODS IN THE PERIOD BEFORE 1825. USA-45 EX/STRUC ADMIN COLONIAL LEAD PARL/PROC ROUTINE...GP/COMP GOV/COMP HOUSE/REP. PAGE 47 B0948
LEGIS DELIB/GP PROVS POL/PAR
B18

WILSON W.,THE STATE: ELEMENTS OF HISTORICAL AND PRACTICAL POLITICS. FRANCE GERMANY ITALY UK USSR CONSTN EX/STRUC LEGIS CT/SYS WAR PWR...POLICY GOV/COMP 20. PAGE 117 B2363
NAT/G JURID CONCPT NAT/COMP
B19

NATHAN M.,THE SOUTH AFRICAN COMMONWEALTH: CONSTITUTION, PROBLEMS, SOCIAL CONDITIONS. SOUTH/AFR UK CULTURE INDUS EX/STRUC LEGIS BUDGET EDU/PROP ADMIN CT/SYS GP/REL RACE/REL...LING 19/20 CMN/WLTH. PAGE 77 B1559
CONSTN NAT/G POL/PAR SOCIETY
B19

SUTHERLAND G.,CONSTITUTIONAL POWER AND WORLD AFFAIRS. CONSTN STRUCT INT/ORG NAT/G CHIEF LEGIS ACT/RES PLAN GOV/REL ALL/VALS...OBS TIME/SEQ CONGRESS VAL/FREE 20 PRESIDENT. PAGE 102 B2056
USA-45 EXEC DIPLOM
N19

BURRUS B.R.,INVESTIGATION AND DISCOVERY IN STATE ANTITRUST (PAMPHLET). USA-45 LEGIS ECO/TAC ADMIN CONTROL CT/SYS CRIME GOV/REL PWR...JURID CHARTS 19/20 FTC MONOPOLY. PAGE 17 B0355
NAT/G PROVS LAW INSPECT
N19

CANADA CIVIL SERV COMM,THE ANALYSIS OF ORGANIZATION IN THE GOVERNMENT OF CANADA (PAMPHLET). CANADA CONSTN EX/STRUC LEGIS TOP/EX CREATE PLAN CONTROL GP/REL 20. PAGE 18 B0372
NAT/G MGT ADMIN DELIB/GP
N19

FAHRNKOPF N.,STATE AND LOCAL GOVERNMENT IN ILLINOIS (PAMPHLET). CONSTN ADMIN PARTIC CHOOSE REPRESENT GOV/REL...JURID MGT 20 ILLINOIS. PAGE 34 B0696
BIBLIOG LOC/G LEGIS CT/SYS
N19

GORWALA A.D.,THE ADMINISTRATIVE JUNGLE (PAMPHLET). INDIA NAT/G LEGIS ECO/TAC CONTROL GOV/REL ...METH/COMP 20. PAGE 41 B0838
ADMIN POLICY PLAN ECO/UNDEV
N19

KUWAIT ARABIA,KUWAIT FUND FOR ARAB ECONOMIC DEVELOPMENT (PAMPHLET). ISLAM KUWAIT UAR ECO/UNDEV LEGIS ECO/TAC WEALTH 20. PAGE 62 B1245
FOR/AID DIPLOM FINAN ADMIN
N19

OPERATIONS AND POLICY RESEARCH,PERU ELECTION MEMORANDA (PAMPHLET). L/A+17C PERU POL/PAR LEGIS EXEC APPORT REPRESENT 20. PAGE 80 B1611
CHOOSE CONSTN SUFF NAT/G
N19

TREVELYAN G.M.,THE TWO-PARTY SYSTEM IN ENGLISH POLITICAL HISTORY (PAMPHLET). UK CHIEF LEGIS COLONIAL EXEC REV CHOOSE 17/19. PAGE 105 B2128
PARL/PROC POL/PAR NAT/G PWR
C20

BLACHLY F.F.,"THE GOVERNMENT AND ADMINISTRATION OF GERMANY." GERMANY CONSTN LOC/G PROVS DELIB/GP
NAT/G GOV/REL

EX/STRUC FORCES LEGIS TOP/EX CT/SYS...BIBLIOG/A 19/20. PAGE 12 B0246
ADMIN PHIL/SCI
B21

BRYCE J.,MODERN DEMOCRACIES. FUT NEW/ZEALND USA-45 LAW CONSTN POL/PAR PROVS VOL/ASSN EX/STRUC LEGIS LEGIT CT/SYS EXEC KNOWL CONGRESS AUSTRAL 20. PAGE 16 B0332
NAT/G TREND
B23

FRANK T.,A HISTORY OF ROME. MEDIT-7 INTELL SOCIETY LOC/G NAT/G POL/PAR FORCES LEGIS DOMIN LEGIT ALL/VALS...POLICY CONCPT TIME/SEQ GEN/LAWS ROM/EMP ROM/EMP. PAGE 37 B0749
EXEC STRUCT ELITES
B24

HOLDSWORTH W.S.,A HISTORY OF ENGLISH LAW: THE COMMON LAW AND ITS RIVALS (VOL. V). UK SEA EX/STRUC WRITING ADMIN...INT/LAW JURID CONCPT IDEA/COMP WORSHIP 16/17 PARLIAMENT ENGLSH/LAW COMMON/LAW. PAGE 51 B1033
LAW LEGIS ADJUD CT/SYS
B24

HOLDSWORTH W.S.,A HISTORY OF ENGLISH LAW: THE COMMON LAW AND ITS RIVALS (VOL. VI). UK STRATA EX/STRUC ADJUD ADMIN CONTROL CT/SYS...JURID CONCPT GEN/LAWS 17 COMMONWLTH PARLIAMENT ENGLSH/LAW COMMON/LAW. PAGE 51 B1034
LAW CONSTN LEGIS CHIEF
B25

MATHEWS J.M.,AMERICAN STATE GOVERNMENT. USA-45 LOC/G CHIEF EX/STRUC LEGIS ADJUD CONTROL CT/SYS ROUTINE GOV/REL PWR 20 GOVERNOR. PAGE 71 B1426
PROVS ADMIN FEDERAL CONSTN
B26

INTERNATIONAL BIBLIOGRAPHY OF POLITICAL SCIENCE. WOR+45 NAT/G POL/PAR EX/STRUC LEGIS CT/SYS LEAD CHOOSE GOV/REL ATTIT...PHIL/SCI 20. PAGE 2 B0034
BIBLIOG DIPLOM CONCPT ADMIN
B26

LUCE R.,CONGRESS: AN EXPLANATION. USA-45 CONSTN FINAN ADMIN LEAD. PAGE 67 B1347
DECISION LEGIS CREATE REPRESENT
B27

WILLOUGHBY W.F.,PRINCIPLES OF PUBLIC ADMINISTRATION WITH SPECIAL REFERENCE TO THE NATIONAL AND STATE GOVERNMENTS OF THE UNITED STATES. FINAN PROVS CHIEF CONSULT LEGIS CREATE BUDGET EXEC ROUTINE GOV/REL CENTRAL...MGT 20 BUR/BUDGET CONGRESS PRESIDENT. PAGE 117 B2356
NAT/G EX/STRUC OP/RES ADMIN
C27

HSIAO K.C.,"POLITICAL PLURALISM." LAW CONSTN POL/PAR LEGIS PLAN ADMIN CENTRAL SOVEREIGN ...INT/LAW BIBLIOG 19/20. PAGE 52 B1053
STRUCT GEN/LAWS PLURISM
B29

MERRIAM C.E.,CHICAGO: A MORE INTIMATE VIEW OF URBAN POLITICS. USA-45 CONSTN POL/PAR LEGIS ADMIN CRIME INGP/REL 18/20 CHICAGO. PAGE 73 B1472
STRUCT GP/REL MUNIC
S30

CRAWFORD F.G.,"THE EXECUTIVE BUDGET DECISION IN NEW YORK." LEGIS EXEC PWR NEW/YORK. PAGE 25 B0504
LEAD BUDGET PROVS PROB/SOLV
B31

BORCHARD E.H.,GUIDE TO THE LAW AND LEGAL LITERATURE OF FRANCE. FRANCE FINAN INDUS LABOR SECT LEGIS ADMIN COLONIAL CRIME OWN...INT/LAW 20. PAGE 14 B0277
BIBLIOG/A LAW CONSTN METH
B32

MCKISACK M.,THE PARLIAMENTARY REPRESENTATION OF THE ENGLISH BOROUGHS DURING THE MIDDLE AGES. UK CONSTN CULTURE ELITES EX/STRUC TAX PAY ADJUD PARL/PROC APPORT FEDERAL...POLICY 13/15 PARLIAMENT. PAGE 72 B1454
NAT/G MUNIC LEGIS CHOOSE
B33

DANGERFIELD R.,IN DEFENSE OF THE SENATE. USA-45 CONSTN NAT/G EX/STRUC TOP/EX ATTIT KNOWL ...METH/CNCPT STAT TIME/SEQ TREND CON/ANAL CHARTS CONGRESS 20 TREATY. PAGE 26 B0528
LEGIS DELIB/GP DIPLOM
B33

GREER S.,A BIBLIOGRAPHY OF PUBLIC ADMINISTRATION. WOR-45 CONSTN LOC/G MUNIC EX/STRUC LEGIS...CONCPT 20. PAGE 43 B0869
BIBLIOG/A ADMIN MGT NAT/G
B34

WILCOX J.K.,GUIDE TO THE OFFICIAL PUBLICATIONS OF THE NEW DEAL ADMINISTRATION (2 VOLS.). USA-45 CHIEF LEGIS ADMIN...POLICY 20 CONGRESS ROOSEVLT/F. PAGE 116 B2345
BIBLIOG NEW/LIB RECEIVE
L34

GOSNELL H.F.,"BRITISH ROYAL COMMISSIONS OF INQUIRY" UK CONSTN LEGIS PRESS ADMIN PARL/PROC...DECISION 20 PARLIAMENT. PAGE 41 B0839
DELIB/GP INSPECT POLICY NAT/G
B36

GRAVES W.B.,AMERICAN STATE GOVERNMENT. CONSTN FINAN EX/STRUC FORCES LEGIS BUDGET TAX CT/SYS REPRESENT GOV/REL...BIBLIOG/A 19/20. PAGE 42 B0855
NAT/G PROVS ADMIN FEDERAL

B37
UNION OF SOUTH AFRICA.REPORT CONCERNING   NAT/G
ADMINISTRATION OF SOUTH WEST AFRICA (6 VOLS.).   ADMIN
SOUTH/AFR INDUS PUB/INST FORCES LEGIS BUDGET DIPLOM   COLONIAL
EDU/PROP ADJUD CT/SYS...GEOG CHARTS 20 AFRICA/SW   CONSTN
LEAGUE/NAT. PAGE 107 B2158

B38
MACDONALD G.E.,CHECK LIST OF LEGISLATIVE JOURNALS   BIBLIOG
OF THE STATES OF THE UNITED STATES OF AMERICA.   PROVS
USA-45 ADMIN GOV/REL ATTIT...POLICY 18/20. PAGE 67   LEGIS
B1356   LOC/G

B39
JENNINGS W.I.,PARLIAMENT. UK POL/PAR OP/RES BUDGET   PARL/PROC
LEAD CHOOSE GP/REL...MGT 20 PARLIAMENT HOUSE/LORD   LEGIS
HOUSE/CMNS. PAGE 56 B1135   CONSTN
                                                      NAT/G
S39
AIKEN C.,"THE BRITISH BUREAUCRACY AND THE ORIGINS   MGT
OF PARLIAMENTARY DEMOCRACY" UK TOP/EX ADMIN. PAGE 3   NAT/G
B0066   LEGIS

C39
REISCHAUER R.,"JAPAN'S GOVERNMENT--POLITICS."   NAT/G
CONSTN STRATA POL/PAR FORCES LEGIS DIPLOM ADMIN   S/ASIA
EXEC CENTRAL...POLICY BIBLIOG 20 CHINJAP. PAGE 87   CONCPT
B1764   ROUTINE

B40
HART J.,AN INTRODUCTION TO ADMINISTRATIVE LAW, WITH   LAW
SELECTED CASES. USA-45 CONSTN SOCIETY NAT/G   ADMIN
EX/STRUC ADJUD CT/SYS LEAD CRIME ORD/FREE   LEGIS
...DECISION JURID 20 CASEBOOK. PAGE 47 B0958   PWR

B40
MCHENRY D.E.,HIS MAJESTY'S OPPOSITION: STRUCTURE   POL/PAR
AND PROBLEMS OF THE BRITISH LABOUR PARTY 1931-1938.   MGT
UK FINAN LABOR LOC/G DELIB/GP LEGIS EDU/PROP LEAD   NAT/G
PARTIC CHOOSE GP/REL SOCISM...TREND 20 LABOR/PAR.   POLICY
PAGE 72 B1450

B40
PATTERSON C.P.,STATE AND LOCAL GOVERNMENT IN TEXAS   CONSTN
(3RD ED.). USA-45 EX/STRUC LEGIS CT/SYS CHOOSE 20   PROVS
TEXAS. PAGE 81 B1642   GOV/REL
                                                      LOC/G
B40
WILCOX J.K.,MANUAL ON THE USE OF STATE   BIBLIOG/A
PUBLICATIONS. USA-45 FINAN LEGIS TAX GOV/REL   PROVS
...CHARTS 20. PAGE 116 B2346   ADMIN
                                                      LAW
S40
FAHS C.B.,"POLITICAL GROUPS IN THE JAPANESE HOUSE   ROUTINE
OF PEERS." ELITES NAT/G ADMIN GP/REL...TREND   POL/PAR
CHINJAP. PAGE 34 B0697   LEGIS

C40
FAHS C.B.,"GOVERNMENT IN JAPAN." FINAN FORCES LEGIS   ASIA
TOP/EX BUDGET INT/TRADE EDU/PROP SOVEREIGN   DIPLOM
...CON/ANAL BIBLIOG/A 20 CHINJAP. PAGE 34 B0698   NAT/G
                                                      ADMIN
B41
CHILDS J.B.,A GUIDE TO THE OFFICIAL PUBLICATIONS OF   NAT/G
THE OTHER AMERICAN REPUBLICS: ARGENTINA. CHIEF   EX/STRUC
DIPLOM GOV/REL...BIBLIOG 18/19 ARGEN. PAGE 21 B0422   METH/CNCPT
                                                      LEGIS
S41
STOKE H.W.,"EXECUTIVE LEADERSHIP AND THE GROWTH OF   EXEC
PROPAGANDA." USA-45 NAT/G EX/STRUC LEGIS TOP/EX   LEAD
PARL/PROC REPRESENT ORD/FREE PWR...MAJORIT 20.   EDU/PROP
PAGE 101 B2042   ADMIN

B42
BINGHAM A.M.,THE TECHNIQUES OF DEMOCRACY. USA-45   POPULISM
CONSTN STRUCT POL/PAR LEGIS PLAN PARTIC CHOOSE   ORD/FREE
REPRESENT NAT/LISM TOTALISM...MGT 20. PAGE 12 B0240   ADMIN
                                                      NAT/G
B42
DENNISON E.,THE SENATE FOREIGN RELATIONS COMMITTEE.   LEGIS
USA-45 NAT/G DELIB/GP ROUTINE CHOOSE PWR CONGRESS   ACT/RES
20. PAGE 28 B0574   DIPLOM

S42
HUZAR E.,"LEGISLATIVE CONTROL OVER ADMINISTRATION: ADMIN
CONGRESS AND WPA" USA-45 FINAN DELIB/GP LOBBY   EX/STRUC
GOV/REL EFFICIENCY ATTIT...POLICY CONGRESS. PAGE 53   CONTROL
B1069   LEGIS

B43
CLARKE M.P.,PARLIAMENTARY PRIVILEGE IN THE AMERICAN   LEGIS
COLONIES. PROVS DOMIN ADMIN REPRESENT GOV/REL   PWR
ORD/FREE...BIBLIOG/A 17/18. PAGE 21 B0433   COLONIAL
                                                      PARL/PROC
B43
YOUNG R.,THIS IS CONGRESS. FUT SENIOR ADMIN GP/REL   LEGIS
PWR...DECISION REFORMERS CONGRESS. PAGE 119 B2393   DELIB/GP
                                                      CHIEF
                                                      ROUTINE
L43
MACMAHON A.W.,"CONGRESSIONAL OVERSIGHT OF   LEGIS
ADMINISTRATION: THE POWER OF THE PURSE." USA-45   DELIB/GP
BUDGET ROUTINE GOV/REL PWR...POLICY CONGRESS.   ADMIN
PAGE 68 B1368   CONTROL

S43
PRICE D.K.,"THE PARLIAMENTARY AND PRESIDENTIAL   LEGIS

SYSTEMS" (BMR)" USA-45 NAT/G EX/STRUC PARL/PROC   REPRESENT
GOV/REL PWR 20 PRESIDENT CONGRESS PARLIAMENT.   ADMIN
PAGE 84 B1706   GOV/COMP

L44
CORWIN E.S.,"THE CONSTITUTION AND WORLD   INT/ORG
ORGANIZATION." FUT USA+45 USA-45 NAT/G EX/STRUC   CONSTN
LEGIS PEACE KNOWL...CON/ANAL UN 20. PAGE 24 B0484   SOVEREIGN

S44
COLEGROVE K.W.,"THE ROLE OF CONGRESS AND PUBLIC   EX/STRUC
OPINION IN FORMULATING FOREIGN POLICY." USA+45 WAR   DIPLOM
...DECISION UN CONGRESS. PAGE 22 B0451   LEGIS
                                                      PWR
S44
KEFAUVER E.,"THE NEED FOR BETTER EXECUTIVE-   LEGIS
LEGISLATIVE TEAMWORK IN THE NATIONAL GOVERNMENT."   EXEC
USA-45 CONSTN NAT/G ROUTINE...TRADIT CONGRESS   CONFER
REFORMERS. PAGE 59 B1188   LEAD

B45
CLAPP G.R.,NEW HORIZONS IN PUBLIC ADMINISTRATION: A   ADMIN
SYMPOSIUM. USA-45 LEGIS PLAN DIPLOM REGION   EX/STRUC
EFFICIENCY 20. PAGE 21 B0430   MGT
                                                      NAT/G
S45
KRIESBERG M.,"WHAT CONGRESSMEN AND ADMINISTRATORS   LEGIS
THINK OF THE POLLS." USA-45 CONTROL PWR...INT QU.   ATTIT
PAGE 61 B1236   EDU/PROP
                                                      ADMIN
S45
WHITE L.D.,"CONGRESSIONAL CONTROL OF THE PUBLIC   LEGIS
SERVICE." USA-45 NAT/G CONSULT DELIB/GP PLAN SENIOR   EXEC
CONGRESS. PAGE 116 B2335   POLICY
                                                      CONTROL
B47
BORGESE G.,COMMON CAUSE. LAW CONSTN SOCIETY STRATA   WOR+45
ECO/DEV INT/ORG POL/PAR FORCES LEGIS TOP/EX CAP/ISM   NAT/G
DIPLOM ADMIN EXEC ATTIT PWR 20. PAGE 14 B0279   SOVEREIGN
                                                      REGION
B47
DE NOIA J.,GUIDE TO OFFICIAL PUBLICATIONS OF THE   BIBLIOG/A
OTHER AMERICAN REPUBLICS: EL SALVADOR. EL/SALVADR   CONSTN
LAW LEGIS EDU/PROP CT/SYS 20. PAGE 27 B0558   NAT/G
                                                      ADMIN
B47
DE NOIA J.,GUIDE TO OFFICIAL PUBLICATIONS OF THE   BIBLIOG/A
OTHER AMERICAN REPUBLICS: NICARAGUA (VOL. XIV).   EDU/PROP
NICARAGUA LAW LEGIS ADMIN CT/SYS...JURID 19/20.   NAT/G
PAGE 27 B0559   CONSTN
                                                      B47
DE NOIA J.,GUIDE TO OFFICIAL PUBLICATIONS OF THE   BIBLIOG/A
OTHER AMERICAN REPUBLICS: PANAMA (VOL. XV). PANAMA   CONSTN
LAW LEGIS EDU/PROP CT/SYS 20. PAGE 27 B0560   ADMIN
                                                      NAT/G
B47
JENKINS W.S.,COLLECTED PUBLIC DOCUMENTS OF THE   BIBLIOG
STATES: A CHECK LIST. USA-45 ECO/DEV NAT/G ADMIN   PROVS
GOV/REL 20. PAGE 56 B1129   LEGIS
                                                      TOP/EX
B47
KEFAUVER E.,A TWENTIETH-CENTURY CONGRESS. POL/PAR   LEGIS
EX/STRUC SENIOR ADMIN CONTROL EXEC LOBBY CHOOSE   DELIB/GP
EFFICIENCY PWR. PAGE 59 B1189   ROUTINE
                                                      TOP/EX
S47
CALDWELL L.K.,"STRENGTHENING STATE LEGISLATURES"   PROVS
FUT DELIB/GP WEALTH REFORMERS. PAGE 18 B0364   LEGIS
                                                      ROUTINE
                                                      BUDGET
S47
GRAVES W.B.,"LEGISLATIVE REFERENCE SYSTEM FOR THE   LEGIS
CONGRESS OF THE UNITED STATES." ROUTINE...CLASSIF   STRUCT
TREND EXHIBIT CONGRESS. PAGE 42 B0856

B48
BISHOP H.M.,BASIC ISSUES OF AMERICAN DEMOCRACY.   NAT/G
USA+45 USA-45 POL/PAR EX/STRUC LEGIS ADJUD FEDERAL   PARL/PROC
...BIBLIOG 18/20. PAGE 12 B0244   CONSTN
                                                      B48
DE NOIA J.,GUIDE TO OFFICIAL PUBLICATIONS OF OTHER   BIBLIOG/A
AMERICAN REPUBLICS: PERU (VOL. XVII). PERU LAW   CONSTN
LEGIS ADMIN CT/SYS...JURID 19/20. PAGE 28 B0561   NAT/G
                                                      EDU/PROP
B48
HART J.,THE AMERICAN PRESIDENCY IN ACTION 1789: A   NAT/G
STUDY IN CONSTITUTIONAL HISTORY. USA-45 POL/PAR   CONSTN
DELIB/GP FORCES LEGIS ADMIN LEAD GP/REL   CHIEF
PERS/REL 18 PRESIDENT CONGRESS. PAGE 47 B0959   EX/STRUC
                                                      B48
HULL C.,THE MEMOIRS OF CORDELL HULL (VOLUME ONE).   BIOG
USA-45 WOR-45 CONSTN FAM LOC/G NAT/G PROVS DELIB/GP   DIPLOM
FORCES LEGIS TOP/EX BAL/PWR LEGIT ADMIN EXEC WAR
ATTIT ORD/FREE PWR...MAJORIT SELF/OBS TIME/SEQ
TREND NAZI 20. PAGE 52 B1062

B48
US LIBRARY OF CONGRESS,BRAZIL: A GUIDE TO THE   BIBLIOG/A
OFFICIAL PUBLICATIONS OF BRAZIL. BRAZIL L/A+17C   NAT/G
CONSULT DELIB/GP LEGIS CT/SYS 19/20. PAGE 109 B2203   ADMIN
                                                      TOP/EX

B48

WHITE L.D.,THE FEDERALISTS: A STUDY IN
ADMINISTRATIVE HISTORY. STRUCT DELIB/GP LEGIS
BUDGET ROUTINE GOV/REL GP/REL PERS/REL PWR...BIOG
18/19 PRESIDENT CONGRESS WASHINGT/G JEFFERSN/T
HAMILTON/A. PAGE 116 B2337

ADMIN
NAT/G
POLICY
PROB/SOLV

C48

WALKER H.,"THE LEGISLATIVE PROCESS; LAWMAKING IN
THE UNITED STATES." NAT/G POL/PAR PROVS EX/STRUC
OP/RES PROB/SOLV CT/SYS LOBBY GOV/REL...CHARTS
BIBLIOG T 18/20 CONGRESS. PAGE 113 B2279

PARL/PROC
LEGIS
LAW
CONSTN

B49

ASPINALL A.,POLITICS AND THE PRESS 1780-1850. UK
LAW ELITES FINAN PROF/ORG LEGIS ADMIN ATTIT
...POLICY 18/19. PAGE 7 B0142

PRESS
CONTROL
POL/PAR
ORD/FREE

B49

BOYD A.M.,UNITED STATES GOVERNMENT PUBLICATIONS
(3RD ED.). USA+45 EX/STRUC LEGIS ADMIN...JURID
CHARTS 20. PAGE 14 B0291

BIBLIOG/A
PRESS
NAT/G
EDU/PROP

B49

BURNS J.M.,CONGRESS ON TRIAL: THE LEGISLATIVE
PROCESS AND THE ADMINISTRATIVE STATE. USA+45 NAT/G
ADMIN ROUTINE REPRESENT...PREDICT TREND. PAGE 17
B0354

LEGIS
EXEC
GP/REL
PWR

B49

DENNING A.,FREEDOM UNDER THE LAW. MOD/EUR UK LAW
SOCIETY CHIEF EX/STRUC LEGIS ADJUD CT/SYS PERS/REL
PERSON 17/20 ENGLSH/LAW. PAGE 28 B0573

ORD/FREE
JURID
NAT/G

B49

RIDDICK F.M.,THE UNITED STATES CONGRESS
ORGANIZATION AND PROCEDURE. POL/PAR DELIB/GP
PROB/SOLV DEBATE CONTROL EXEC LEAD INGP/REL PWR
...MAJORIT DECISION CONGRESS PRESIDENT. PAGE 88
B1777

LEGIS
PARL/PROC
CHIEF
EX/STRUC

B49

ROSENHAUPT H.W.,HOW TO WAGE PEACE. USA+45 SOCIETY
STRATA STRUCT R+D INT/ORG POL/PAR LEGIS ACT/RES
CREATE PLAN EDU/PROP ADMIN EXEC ATTIT ALL/VALS
...TIME/SEQ TREND COLD/WAR 20. PAGE 90 B1822

INTELL
CONCPT
DIPLOM

L49

BROOKINGS INST.,"GOVERNMENT MECHANISM FOR CONDUCT
OF US FOREIGN RELATIONS." USA+45 CONSTN NAT/G LEGIS
CT/SYS...MGT TIME/SEQ CONGRESS TOT/POP 20. PAGE 15
B0316

EXEC
STRUCT
DIPLOM

B50

AMERICAN POLITICAL SCI ASSN,TOWARD A MORE
RESPONSIBLE TWO-PARTY SYSTEM. USA+45 CONSTN
VOL/ASSN LEGIS LEAD CHOOSE...POLICY MGT 20. PAGE 4
B0087

POL/PAR
TASK
PARTIC
ACT/RES

B50

COMMONS J.R.,THE ECONOMICS OF COLLECTIVE ACTION.
USA-45 AGRI INDUS LABOR NAT/G LEGIS ADMIN
EFFICIENCY...MGT METH/COMP BIBLIOG 20. PAGE 22
B0458

ECO/DEV
CAP/ISM
ACT/RES
CONCPT

B50

GRAVES W.B.,PUBLIC ADMINISTRATION: A COMPREHENSIVE
BIBLIOGRAPHY ON PUBLIC ADMINISTRATION IN THE UNITED
STATES (PAMPHLET). USA+45 USA-45 LOC/G NAT/G LEGIS
ADJUD INGP/REL...MGT 20. PAGE 42 B0858

BIBLIOG
FINAN
CONTROL
ADMIN

B50

HYNEMAN C.S.,BUREAUCRACY IN A DEMOCRACY. CHIEF
LEGIS ADMIN CONTROL LEAD ROUTINE PERS/REL COST
EFFICIENCY UTIL ATTIT AUTHORIT PERSON MORAL.
PAGE 53 B1071

NAT/G
CENTRAL
EX/STRUC
MYTH

B50

JENKINS W.S.,A GUIDE TO THE MICROFILM COLLECTION OF
EARLY STATE RECORDS. USA+45 CONSTN MUNIC LEGIS
PRESS ADMIN CT/SYS 18/20. PAGE 56 B1130

BIBLIOG
PROVS
AUD/VIS

B50

MCHENRY D.E.,THE THIRD FORCE IN CANADA: THE
COOPERATIVE COMMONWEALTH FEDERATION, 1932-1948.
CANADA EX/STRUC LEGIS REPRESENT 20 LABOR/PAR.
PAGE 72 B1451

POL/PAR
ADMIN
CHOOSE
POLICY

B50

PERHAM M.,COLONIAL GOVERNMENT: ANNOTATED READING
LIST ON BRITISH COLONIAL GOVERNMENT. UK WOR+45
WOR-45 ECO/UNDEV INT/ORG LEGIS FOR/AID INT/TRADE
DOMIN ADMIN REV 20. PAGE 82 B1655

BIBLIOG/A
COLONIAL
GOV/REL
NAT/G

B50

WADE E.C.S.,CONSTITUTIONAL LAW: AN OUTLINE OF THE
LAW AND PRACTICE OF THE CONSTITUTION. UK LEGIS
DOMIN ADMIN GP/REL 16/20 CMN/WLTH PARLIAMENT
ENGLSH/LAW. PAGE 112 B2269

CONSTN
NAT/G
PARL/PROC
LAW

L50

US SENATE COMM. GOVT. OPER.,"REVISION OF THE UN
CHARTER." FUT USA+45 WOR+45 CONSTN ECO/DEV
ECO/UNDEV NAT/G DELIB/GP ACT/RES CREATE PLAN EXEC
ROUTINE CHOOSE ALL/VALS...POLICY CONCPT CONGRESS UN
TOT/POP 20 COLD/WAR. PAGE 111 B2235

INT/ORG
LEGIS
PEACE

S50

EPSTEIN L.D.,"POLITICAL STERILIZATION OF CIVIL
SERVANTS: THE UNITED STATES AND GREAT BRITAIN." UK
USA+45 USA-45 STRUCT TOP/EX OP/RES PARTIC CHOOSE
NAT/LISM 20 CONGRESS CIVIL/SERV. PAGE 33 B0679

ADMIN
LEGIS
DECISION
POL/PAR

S50

HUMPHREY H.H.,"THE SENATE ON TRIAL." USA+45 POL/PAR
DEBATE REPRESENT EFFICIENCY ATTIT RIGID/FLEX
...TRADIT SENATE. PAGE 52 B1064

PARL/PROC
ROUTINE
PWR
LEGIS

B51

ANDERSON W.,STATE AND LOCAL GOVERNMENT IN THE
UNITED STATES. USA+45 CONSTN POL/PAR EX/STRUC LEGIS
BUDGET TAX ADJUD CT/SYS CHOOSE...CHARTS T 20.
PAGE 5 B0100

LOC/G
MUNIC
PROVS
GOV/REL

B51

ANDERSON W.,GOVERNMENT IN THE FIFTY STATES. LAW
CONSTN FINAN POL/PAR LEGIS EDU/PROP ADJUD ADMIN
CT/SYS CHOOSE...CHARTS 20. PAGE 5 B0101

LOC/G
PROVS
GOV/REL

B51

CHRISTENSEN A.N.,THE EVOLUTION OF LATIN AMERICAN
GOVERNMENT: A BOOK OF READINGS. ECO/UNDEV INDUS
LOC/G POL/PAR EX/STRUC LEGIS FOR/AID CT/SYS
...SOC/WK 20 SOUTH/AMER. PAGE 21 B0428

NAT/G
CONSTN
DIPLOM
L/A+17C

B51

MAASS A.,MUDDY WATERS: THE ARMY ENGINEERS AND THE
NATIONS RIVERS. USA-45 PROF/ORG CONSULT LEGIS ADMIN
EXEC ROLE PWR...SOC PRESIDENT 20. PAGE 67 B1353

FORCES
GP/REL
LOBBY
CONSTRUC

B51

SMITH L.,AMERICAN DEMOCRACY AND MILITARY POWER.
USA+45 USA-45 CONSTN STRATA NAT/G LEGIS ACT/RES
LEGIT ADMIN EXEC GOV/REL ALL/VALS...CONCPT
HIST/WRIT CONGRESS 20. PAGE 98 B1982

FORCES
STRUCT
WAR

B51

SWISHER C.B.,THE THEORY AND PRACTICE OF AMERICAN
NATIONAL GOVERNMENT. CULTURE LEGIS DIPLOM ADJUD
ADMIN WAR PEACE ORD/FREE...MAJORIT 17/20. PAGE 102
B2063

CONSTN
NAT/G
GOV/REL
GEN/LAWS

B51

WHITE L.D.,THE JEFFERSONIANS: A STUDY IN
ADMINISTRATIVE HISTORY 1801-1829. USA-45 DELIB/GP
LEGIS TOP/EX PROB/SOLV BUDGET ECO/TAC GP/REL
FEDERAL...BIOG IDEA/COMP 19 PRESIDENT CONGRESS
JEFFERSN/T. PAGE 116 B2338

ADMIN
NAT/G
POLICY
POL/PAR

L51

MANGONE G.,"THE IDEA AND PRACTICE OF WORLD
GOVERNMENT." FUT WOR+45 WOR-45 ECO/DEV LEGIS CREATE
LEGIT ROUTINE ATTIT MORAL PWR WEALTH...CONCPT
GEN/LAWS 20. PAGE 69 B1388

INT/ORG
SOCIETY
INT/LAW

S51

MARX F.M.,"SIGNIFICANCE FOR THE ADMINISTRATIVE
PROCESS." POL/PAR LEAD PARL/PROC GOV/REL EFFICIENCY
SUPEGO...POLICY CONGRESS. PAGE 70 B1420

LEGIS
ADMIN
CHIEF

S51

SHILS E.A.,"THE LEGISLATOR AND HIS ENVIRONMENT."
EX/STRUC DOMIN CONFER EFFICIENCY PWR MAJORIT.
PAGE 96 B1947

LEGIS
TOP/EX
ADMIN
DELIB/GP

B52

DE GRAZIA A.,POLITICAL ORGANIZATION. CONSTN LOC/G
MUNIC NAT/G CHIEF LEGIS TOP/EX ADJUD CT/SYS
PERS/REL...INT/LAW MYTH UN. PAGE 27 B0553

FEDERAL
LAW
ADMIN

B52

ELLIOTT W.,UNITED STATES FOREIGN POLICY, ITS
ORGANIZATION AND CONTROL. USA+45 USA-45 CONSTN
NAT/G FORCES TOP/EX PEACE...TIME/SEQ CONGRESS
LEAGUE/NAT 20. PAGE 33 B0670

LEGIS
EX/STRUC
DIPLOM

B52

HIMMELFARB G.,LORD ACTON: A STUDY IN CONSCIENCE AND
POLITICS. MOD/EUR NAT/G POL/PAR SECT LEGIS TOP/EX
EDU/PROP ADMIN NAT/LISM ATTIT PERSON SUPEGO MORAL
ORD/FREE...CONCPT PARLIAMENT 19 ACTON/LORD. PAGE 50
B1014

PWR
BIOG

B52

JANSE R.S.,SOVIET TRANSPORTATION AND
COMMUNICATIONS: A BIBLIOGRAPHY. COM USSR PLAN
...DICTIONARY 20. PAGE 56 B1124

BIBLIOG/A
COM/IND
LEGIS
ADMIN

B52

LEGISLATIVE REFERENCE SERVICE,PROBLEMS OF
LEGISLATIVE APPORTIONMENT ON BOTH FEDERAL AND STATE
LEVELS: SELECTED REFERENCES (PAMPHLET). USA+45
USA-45 LOC/G NAT/G LEGIS WRITING ADMIN APPORT 20
CONGRESS. PAGE 63 B1282

BIBLIOG
REPRESENT
CHOOSE
PROVS

B52

SCHATTSCHNEIDER E.E.,A GUIDE TO THE STUDY OF PUBLIC
AFFAIRS. LAW LOC/G NAT/G LEGIS BUDGET PRESS ADMIN
LOBBY...JURID CHARTS 20. PAGE 93 B1882

ACT/RES
INTELL
ACADEM
METH/COMP

B52

SWENSON R.J.,FEDERAL ADMINISTRATIVE LAW: A STUDY OF
THE GROWTH, NATURE, AND CONTROL OF ADMINISTRATIVE
ACTION. USA-45 JUDGE ADMIN GOV/REL EFFICIENCY
PRIVIL ATTIT NEW/LIB SUPREME/CT. PAGE 102 B2061

JURID
CONSTN
LEGIS
ADJUD

L52

WRIGHT Q.,"CONGRESS AND THE TREATY-MAKING POWER."
USA+45 WOR+45 CONSTN INTELL NAT/G CHIEF CONSULT
EX/STRUC LEGIS TOP/EX CREATE GOV/REL DISPL DRIVE
RIGID/FLEX...TREND TOT/POP CONGRESS CONGRESS 20
TREATY. PAGE 118 B2384

ROUTINE
DIPLOM
INT/LAW
DELIB/GP

LANCASTER L.W.,"GOVERNMENT IN RURAL AMERICA." USA+45 ECO/DEV AGRI SCHOOL FORCES LEGIS JUDGE BUDGET TAX CT/SYS...CHARTS BIBLIOG. PAGE 62 B1253
C52
GOV/REL LOC/G MUNIC ADMIN

GROSS B.M.,THE LEGISLATIVE STRUGGLE: A STUDY IN SOCIAL COMBAT. STRUCT LOC/G POL/PAR JUDGE EDU/PROP DEBATE ETIQUET ADMIN LOBBY CHOOSE GOV/REL INGP/REL HEREDITY ALL/VALS...SOC PRESIDENT. PAGE 44 B0885
B53
LEGIS DECISION PERSON LEAD

MACMAHON A.W.,ADMINISTRATION IN FOREIGN AFFAIRS. NAT/G CONSULT DELIB/GP LEGIS ACT/RES CREATE ADMIN EXEC RIGID/FLEX PWR...METH/CNCPT TIME/SEQ TOT/POP VAL/FREE 20. PAGE 68 B1369
B53
USA+45 ROUTINE FOR/AID DIPLOM

STENE E.O.,ABANDONMENTS OF THE MANAGER PLAN. LEGIS LEAD GP/REL PWR DECISION. PAGE 100 B2032
B53
MUNIC EX/STRUC REPRESENT ADMIN

TOMPKINS D.C.,CIVIL DEFENSE IN THE STATES: A BIBLIOGRAPHY (DEFENSE BIBLIOGRAPHIES NO. 3; PAMPHLET). USA+45 LABOR LOC/G NAT/G PROVS LEGIS. PAGE 105 B2115
B53
BIBLIOG WAR ORD/FREE ADMIN

NEWMAN F.C.,"CONGRESS AND THE FAITHFUL EXECUTION OF LAWS - SHOULD LEGISLATORS SUPERVISE ADMINISTRATORS." USA+45 NAT/G EX/STRUC EXEC PWR POLICY. PAGE 78 B1579
L53
REPRESENT CONTROL ADMIN LEGIS

BOSWORTH K.A.,"THE POLITICS OF MANAGEMENT IMPROVEMENT IN THE STATES" USA+45 POLICY. PAGE 14 B0280
S53
PWR PROVS LEGIS EXEC

GABLE R.W.,"NAM: INFLUENTIAL LOBBY OR KISS OF DEATH?" (BMR)" USA+45 LAW INSPECT EDU/PROP ADMIN CONTROL INGP/REL EFFICIENCY PWR 20 CONGRESS NAM TAFT/HART. PAGE 38 B0769
S53
LOBBY LEGIS INDUS LG/CO

BENTLEY A.F.,INQUIRY INTO INQUIRIES: ESSAYS IN SOCIAL THEORY. UNIV LEGIS ADJUD ADMIN LOBBY ...PHIL/SCI PSY NEW/IDEA LING METH 20. PAGE 11 B0220
B54
EPIST SOC CONCPT

BIESANZ J.,MODERN SOCIETY: AN INTRODUCTION TO SOCIAL SCIENCE. COM CONSTN STRUCT FAM MUNIC NAT/G SECT EX/STRUC LEGIS GP/REL PERSON...SOC 20. PAGE 12 B0237
B54
SOCIETY PROB/SOLV CULTURE

JENNINGS I.,THE QUEEN'S GOVERNMENT. UK POL/PAR DELIB/GP ADJUD ADMIN CT/SYS PARL/PROC REPRESENT CONSERVE 13/20 PARLIAMENT. PAGE 56 B1132
B54
NAT/G CONSTN LEGIS CHIEF

MANGONE G.,A SHORT HISTORY OF INTERNATIONAL ORGANIZATION. MOD/EUR USA+45 USA-45 WOR+45 WOR-45 LAW LEGIS CREATE LEGIT ROUTINE RIGID/FLEX PWR ...JURID CONCPT OBS TIME/SEQ STERTYP GEN/LAWS UN TOT/POP VAL/FREE 18/20. PAGE 69 B1389
B54
INT/ORG INT/LAW

RECK D.,GOVERNMENT PURCHASING AND COMPETITION. USA+45 LEGIS CAP/ISM ECO/TAC GOV/REL CENTRAL ...POLICY 20 CONGRESS. PAGE 87 B1749
B54
NAT/G FINAN MGT COST

SCHWARTZ B.,FRENCH ADMINISTRATIVE LAW AND THE COMMON-LAW WORLD. FRANCE CULTURE LOC/G NAT/G PROVS DELIB/GP EX/STRUC LEGIS PROB/SOLV CT/SYS EXEC GOV/REL...IDEA/COMP ENGLSH/LAW. PAGE 95 B1912
B54
JURID LAW METH/COMP ADJUD

SHELTON W.L.,CHECKLIST OF NEW MEXICO PUBLICATIONS, 1850-1953. USA+45 USA-45 LEGIS ADMIN LEAD 19/20. PAGE 96 B1941
B54
BIBLIOG PROVS GOV/REL

THORNTON M.L.,OFFICIAL PUBLICATIONS OF THE COLONY AND STATE OF NORTH CAROLINA, 1749-1939. USA+45 USA-45 LEGIS LEAD GOV/REL ATTIT 18/20. PAGE 104 B2109
B54
BIBLIOG ADMIN PROVS ACADEM

TOMPKINS D.C.,STATE GOVERNMENT AND ADMINISTRATION: A BIBLIOGRAPHY. USA+45 USA-45 CONSTN LEGIS JUDGE BUDGET CT/SYS LOBBY...CHARTS 20. PAGE 105 B2116
B54
BIBLIOG/A LOC/G PROVS ADMIN

US SENATE COMM ON FOREIGN REL,REVIEW OF THE UNITED NATIONS CHARTER: A COLLECTION OF DOCUMENTS. LEGIS DIPLOM ADMIN ARMS/CONT WAR REPRESENT SOVEREIGN ...INT/LAW 20 UN. PAGE 110 B2220
B54
BIBLIOG CONSTN INT/ORG DEBATE

WHITE L.D.,THE JACKSONIANS: A STUDY IN ADMINISTRATIVE HISTORY 1829-1861. USA-45 CONSTN POL/PAR CHIEF DELIB/GP LEGIS CREATE PROB/SOLV ECO/TAC LEAD REGION GP/REL 19 PRESIDENT CONGRESS JACKSON/A. PAGE 116 B2339
B54
NAT/G ADMIN POLICY

FURNISS E.S.,"WEAKNESSES IN FRENCH FOREIGN POLICY-MAKING." EUR+WWI LEGIS LEGIT EXEC ATTIT RIGID/FLEX ORD/FREE...SOC CONCPT METH/CNCPT OBS 20. PAGE 38 B0766
L54
NAT/G STRUCT DIPLOM FRANCE

CALDWELL L.K.,"THE GOVERNMENT AND ADMINISTRATION OF NEW YORK." LOC/G MUNIC POL/PAR SCHOOL CHIEF LEGIS PLAN TAX CT/SYS...MGT SOC/WK BIBLIOG 20 NEWYORK/C. PAGE 18 B0366
C54
PROVS ADMIN CONSTN EX/STRUC

LANDAU J.M.,"PARLIAMENTS AND PARTIES IN EGYPT." UAR NAT/G SECT CONSULT LEGIS TOP/EX PROB/SOLV ADMIN COLONIAL...GEN/LAWS BIBLIOG 19/20. PAGE 62 B1254
C54
ISLAM NAT/LISM PARL/PROC POL/PAR

ZELLER B.,"AMERICAN STATE LEGISLATURES: REPORT ON THE COMMITTEE ON AMERICAN LEGISLATURES." CONSTN POL/PAR EX/STRUC CONFER ADMIN CONTROL EXEC LOBBY ROUTINE GOV/REL...POLICY BIBLIOG 20. PAGE 119 B2401
C54
REPRESENT LEGIS PROVS APPORT

APTER D.E.,THE GOLD COAST IN TRANSITION. FUT CONSTN CULTURE SOCIETY ECO/UNDEV FAM KIN LOC/G NAT/G POL/PAR LEGIS TOP/EX EDU/PROP LEGIT ADMIN ATTIT PERSON PWR...CONCPT STAT INT CENSUS TOT/POP VAL/FREE. PAGE 6 B0120
B55
AFR SOVEREIGN

BAILEY S.K.,RESEARCH FRONTIERS IN POLITICS AND GOVERNMENT. CONSTN LEGIS ADMIN REV CHOOSE...CONCPT IDEA/COMP GAME ANTHOL 20. PAGE 8 B0164
B55
R+D METH NAT/G

CHOWDHURI R.N.,INTERNATIONAL MANDATES AND TRUSTEESHIP SYSTEMS. WOR+45 STRUCT ECO/UNDEV INT/ORG LEGIS DOMIN EDU/PROP LEGIT ADJUD EXEC PWR ...CONCPT TIME/SEQ UN 20. PAGE 21 B0427
B55
DELIB/GP PLAN SOVEREIGN

CRAIG J.,BIBLIOGRAPHY OF PUBLIC ADMINISTRATION IN AUSTRALIA. CONSTN FINAN EX/STRUC LEGIS PLAN DIPLOM RECEIVE ADJUD ROUTINE...HEAL 19/20 AUSTRAL PARLIAMENT. PAGE 24 B0500
B55
BIBLIOG GOV/REL ADMIN NAT/G

CUSHMAN R.E.,LEADING CONSTITUTIONAL DECISIONS. USA+45 USA-45 NAT/G EX/STRUC LEGIS JUDGE TAX FEDERAL...DECISION 20 SUPREME/CT CASEBOOK. PAGE 25 B0513
B55
CONSTN PROB/SOLV JURID CT/SYS

GALLOWAY G.B.,CONGRESS AND PARLIAMENT: THEIR ORGANIZATION AND OPERATION IN THE US AND THE UK: PLANNING PAMPHLET NO. 93. POL/PAR EX/STRUC DEBATE CONTROL LEAD ROUTINE EFFICIENCY PWR...POLICY CONGRESS PARLIAMENT. PAGE 38 B0777
B55
DELIB/GP LEGIS PARL/PROC GOV/COMP

PULLEN W.R.,A CHECK LIST OF LEGISLATIVE JOURNALS ISSUED SINCE 1937 BY THE STATES OF THE UNITED STATES OF AMERICA (PAMPHLET). USA+45 USA-45 LAW WRITING ADJUD ADMIN...JURID 20. PAGE 85 B1720
B55
BIBLIOG PROVS EDU/PROP LEGIS

RUSTOW D.A.,THE POLITICS OF COMPROMISE. SWEDEN LABOR EX/STRUC LEGIS PLAN REPRESENT SOCISM...SOC 19/20. PAGE 92 B1859
B55
POL/PAR NAT/G POLICY ECO/TAC

SMITHIES A.,THE BUDGETARY PROCESS IN THE UNITED STATES. ECO/DEV AGRI EX/STRUC FORCES LEGIS PROB/SOLV TAX ROUTINE EFFICIENCY...MGT CONGRESS PRESIDENT. PAGE 98 B1987
B55
NAT/G ADMIN BUDGET GOV/REL

WHEARE K.C.,GOVERNMENT BY COMMITTEE; AN ESSAY ON THE BRITISH CONSTITUTION. UK NAT/G LEGIS INSPECT CONFER ADJUD ADMIN CONTROL TASK EFFICIENCY ROLE POPULISM 20. PAGE 115 B2329
B55
DELIB/GP CONSTN LEAD GP/COMP

SCHWARTZ B.,"LEGISLATIVE CONTROL OF ADMINISTRATIVE RULES AND REGULATIONS THE AMERICAN EXPERIENCE." USA+45 GOV/REL...GOV/COMP 20. PAGE 95 B1913
S55
CONTROL ADMIN EX/STRUC LEGIS

BROWNE D.G.,THE RISE OF SCOTLAND YARD: A HISTORY OF THE METROPOLITAN POLICE. UK MUNIC CHIEF ADMIN CRIME GP/REL 19/20. PAGE 16 B0329
B56
CRIMLGY LEGIS CONTROL FORCES

CONAWAY O.B.,DEMOCRACY IN FEDERAL ADMINISTRATION (PAMPHLET). USA+45 LEGIS PARTIC ATTIT...TREND ANTHOL 20. PAGE 23 B0459
B56
ADMIN SERV/IND NAT/G GP/REL

HOWARD L.V.,TULANE STUDIES IN POLITICAL SCIENCE: CIVIL SERVICE DEVELOPMENT IN LOUISIANA VOLUME 3. LAW POL/PAR LEGIS CT/SYS ADJUST ORD/FREE...STAT CHARTS 19/20 LOUISIANA CIVIL/SERV. PAGE 52 B1050
B56
ADMIN GOV/REL PROVS POLICY

JENNINGS W.I.,THE APPROACH TO SELF-GOVERNMENT. CEYLON INDIA PAKISTAN S/ASIA UK SOCIETY POL/PAR DELIB/GP LEGIS ECO/TAC EDU/PROP ADMIN EXEC CHOOSE ATTIT ALL/VALS...JURID CONCPT GEN/METH TOT/POP 20.
B56
NAT/G CONSTN COLONIAL

PAGE 56 B1136

B56

KOENIG L.W.,THE TRUMAN ADMINISTRATION: ITS
PRINCIPLES AND PRACTICE. USA+45 POL/PAR CHIEF LEGIS
DIPLOM DEATH NUC/PWR WAR CIVMIL/REL PEACE
...DECISION 20 TRUMAN/HS PRESIDENT TREATY. PAGE 61
B1224

ADMIN
POLICY
EX/STRUC
GOV/REL

B56

POWELL N.J.,PERSONNEL ADMINISTRATION IN GOVERNMENT.
COM/IND POL/PAR LEGIS PAY CT/SYS ROUTINE GP/REL
PERS/REL...POLICY METH 20 CIVIL/SERV. PAGE 84 B1697

ADMIN
WORKER
LOC/G
NAT/G

B56

WILSON W.,CONGRESSIONAL GOVERNMENT. USA-45 NAT/G
ADMIN EXEC PARL/PROC GP/REL MAJORITY ATTIT 19
SENATE HOUSE/REP. PAGE 117 B2364

LEGIS
CHIEF
CONSTN
PWR

L56

MACMAHON A.W.,"WOODROW WILSON AS LEGISLATIVE LEADER
AND ADMINISTRATOR." CONSTN POL/PAR ADMIN...POLICY
HIST/WRIT WILSON/W PRESIDENT. PAGE 68 B1371

LEGIS
CHIEF
LEAD
BIOG

S56

COTTER C.P.,"ADMINISTRATIVE ACCOUNTABILITY TO
CONGRESS: THE CONCURRENT RESOLUTION." USA+45 NAT/G
EXEC REPRESENT PWR 20. PAGE 24 B0489

CONTROL
GOV/REL
LEGIS
EX/STRUC

S56

HEADY F.,"THE MICHIGAN DEPARTMENT OF
ADMINISTRATION; A CASE STUDY IN THE POLITICS OF
ADMINISTRATION" (BMR)" USA+45 POL/PAR PROVS CHIEF
LEGIS GP/REL ATTIT 20 MICHIGAN. PAGE 48 B0980

ADMIN
DELIB/GP
LOC/G

S56

KAUFMAN H.,"EMERGING CONFLICTS IN THE DOCTRINES OF
PUBLIC ADMINISTRATION" (BMR)" USA+45 USA-45 NAT/G
EX/STRUC LEGIS CONTROL NEUTRAL ATTIT PWR...TREND
20. PAGE 58 B1181

ADMIN
ORD/FREE
REPRESENT
LEAD

S56

KHAMA T.,"POLITICAL CHANGE IN AFRICAN SOCIETY."
CONSTN SOCIETY LOC/G NAT/G POL/PAR EX/STRUC LEGIS
LEGIT ADMIN CHOOSE REPRESENT NAT/LISM MORAL
ORD/FREE PWR...CONCPT OBS TREND GEN/METH CMN/WLTH
17/20. PAGE 59 B1201

AFR
ELITES

S56

MILNE R.S.,"CONTROL OF GOVERNMENT CORPORATIONS IN
THE UNITED STATES." USA+45 NAT/G CHIEF LEGIS BUDGET
20 GENACCOUNT. PAGE 74 B1488

CONTROL
EX/STRUC
GOV/REL
PWR

B57

ARON R.,FRANCE DEFEATS EDC. EUR+WWI GERMANY LEGIS
DIPLOM DOMIN EDU/PROP ADMIN...HIST/WRIT 20. PAGE 7
B0136

INT/ORG
FORCES
DETER
FRANCE

B57

BABCOCK R.S.,STATE & LOCAL GOVERNMENT AND POLITICS.
USA+45 CONSTN POL/PAR EX/STRUC LEGIS BUDGET LOBBY
CHOOSE SUFF...CHARTS BIBLIOG T 20. PAGE 8 B0154

PROVS
LOC/G
GOV/REL

B57

JENNINGS I.,PARLIAMENT. UK FINAN INDUS POL/PAR
DELIB/GP EX/STRUC PLAN CONTROL...MAJORIT JURID
PARLIAMENT. PAGE 56 B1133

PARL/PROC
TOP/EX
MGT
LEGIS

B57

KNEIER C.M.,CITY GOVERNMENT IN THE UNITED STATES
(3RD ED.). USA-45 FINAN NAT/G POL/PAR LEGIS
EDU/PROP LEAD APPORT REPRESENT ATTIT...MGT 20
CITY/MGT. PAGE 60 B1219

MUNIC
LOC/G
ADMIN
GOV/REL

B57

LOEWENSTEIN K.,POLITICAL POWER AND THE GOVERNMENTAL
PROCESS. WOR+45 WOR-45 CONSTN NAT/G POL/PAR
EX/STRUC LEGIS TOP/EX DOMIN EDU/PROP LEGIT ADMIN
REGION CHOOSE ATTIT...JURID STERTYP GEN/LAWS 20.
PAGE 66 B1336

PWR
CONCPT

B57

MEYER P.,ADMINISTRATIVE ORGANIZATION: A COMPARATIVE
STUDY OF THE ORGANIZATION OF PUBLIC ADMINISTRATION.
DENMARK FRANCE NORWAY SWEDEN UK USA+45 ELITES LOC/G
CONSULT LEGIS ADJUD CONTROL LEAD PWR SKILL
DECISION. PAGE 73 B1475

ADMIN
METH/COMP
NAT/G
CENTRAL

B57

MURDESHWAR A.K.,ADMINISTRATIVE PROBLEMS RELATING TO
NATIONALISATION: WITH SPECIAL REFERENCE TO INDIAN
STATE ENTERPRISES. CZECHOSLVK FRANCE INDIA UK
USA+45 LEGIS WORKER PROB/SOLV BUDGET PRICE CONTROL
...MGT GEN/LAWS 20 PARLIAMENT. PAGE 76 B1544

NAT/G
OWN
INDUS
ADMIN

B57

MURRAY J.N.,THE UNITED NATIONS TRUSTEESHIP SYSTEM.
AFR WOR+45 CONSTN CONSULT LEGIS EDU/PROP LEGIT EXEC
ROUTINE...INT TIME/SEQ SOMALI UN 20. PAGE 77 B1547

INT/ORG
DELIB/GP

B57

SCHLOCHAUER H.J.,OFFENTLICHES RECHT. GERMANY/W
FINAN EX/STRUC LEGIS DIPLOM FEDERAL ORD/FREE
...INT/LAW 20. PAGE 94 B1892

CONSTN
JURID
ADMIN
CT/SYS

B57

SIMON H.A.,MODELS OF MAN, SOCIAL AND RATIONAL:

MATH

MATHEMATICAL ESSAYS ON RATIONAL HUMAN BEHAVIOR IN A
SOCIAL SETTING. UNIV LAW SOCIETY FACE/GP VOL/ASSN
CONSULT EX/STRUC LEGIS CREATE ADMIN ROUTINE ATTIT
DRIVE PWR...SOC CONCPT METH/CNCPT QUANT STAT
TOT/POP VAL/FREE 20. PAGE 97 B1959

SIMUL

S57

COTTER C.P.,"ADMINISTRATIVE ACCOUNTABILITY;
REPORTING TO CONGRESS." USA+45 CONSULT DELIB/GP
PARL/PROC PARTIC GOV/REL ATTIT PWR DECISION.
PAGE 24 B0490

LEGIS
EX/STRUC
REPRESENT
CONTROL

S57

COTTER C.R.,"ADMINISTRATIVE RESPONSIBILITY:
CONGRESSIONAL PRESCRIPTION OF INTERAGENCY
RELATIONSHIPS." USA+45 NAT/G ADMIN 20. PAGE 24
B0492

GOV/REL
LEGIS
REPRESENT
EX/STRUC

S57

FESLER J.W.,"ADMINISTRATIVE LITERATURE AND THE
SECOND HOOVER COMMISSION REPORTS" (BMR)" USA+45
EX/STRUC LEGIS WRITING...DECISION METH 20. PAGE 35
B0713

ADMIN
NAT/G
OP/RES
DELIB/GP

S57

GULICK L.,"METROPOLITAN ORGANIZATION." LEGIS EXEC
PARTIC CHOOSE REPRESENT GOV/REL...MAJORIT DECISION.
PAGE 45 B0904

REGION
LOC/G
MUNIC

S57

HARRIS J.P.,"LEGISLATIVE CONTROL OF ADMINISTRATION:
SOME COMPARISONS OF AMERICAN AND EUROPEAN
PRACTICES." DEBATE PARL/PROC ROUTINE GOV/REL
EFFICIENCY SUPEGO DECISION. PAGE 47 B0954

LEGIS
CONTROL
EX/STRUC
REPRESENT

S57

HUITT R.K.,"THE MORSE COMMITTEE ASSIGNMENT
CONTROVERSY: A STUDY IN SENATE NORMS." USA+45
USA-45 POL/PAR SENIOR ROLE SUPEGO SENATE. PAGE 52
B1061

LEGIS
ETIQUET
PWR
ROUTINE

S57

ROBSON W.A.,"TWO-LEVEL GOVERNMENT FOR METROPOLITAN
AREAS." MUNIC EX/STRUC LEGIS PARTIC REPRESENT
MAJORITY. PAGE 89 B1807

REGION
LOC/G
PLAN
GOV/REL

S57

TAYLOR P.S.,"THE RELATION OF RESEARCH TO
LEGISLATIVE AND ADMINISTRATIVE DECISIONS." ELITES
ACT/RES PLAN PROB/SOLV CONFER CHOOSE POLICY.
PAGE 103 B2089

DECISION
LEGIS
MGT
PWR

B58

BERNSTEIN M.H.,THE JOB OF THE FEDERAL EXECUTIVE.
POL/PAR CHIEF LEGIS ADMIN EXEC LOBBY CHOOSE GOV/REL
ORD/FREE PWR...MGT TREND. PAGE 11 B0228

NAT/G
TOP/EX
PERS/COMP

B58

COWAN L.G.,LOCAL GOVERNMENT IN WEST AFRICA. AFR
FRANCE UK CULTURE KIN POL/PAR CHIEF LEGIS CREATE
ADMIN PARTIC GOV/REL GP/REL...METH/COMP 20. PAGE 24
B0498

LOC/G
COLONIAL
SOVEREIGN
REPRESENT

B58

DWARKADAS R.,ROLE OF HIGHER CIVIL SERVICE IN INDIA.
INDIA ECO/UNDEV LEGIS PROB/SOLV GP/REL PERS/REL
...POLICY WELF/ST DECISION ORG/CHARTS BIBLIOG 20
CIVIL/SERV INTRVN/ECO. PAGE 31 B0637

ADMIN
NAT/G
ROLE
PLAN

B58

KINTNER W.R.,ORGANIZING FOR CONFLICT: A PROPOSAL.
USSR STRUCT NAT/G LEGIS ADMIN EXEC PEACE ORD/FREE
PWR...CONCPT OBS TREND NAT/COMP VAL/FREE COLD/WAR
20. PAGE 60 B1211

USA+45
PLAN
DIPLOM

B58

KRAINES O.,CONGRESS AND THE CHALLENGE OF BIG
GOVERNMENT. USA-45 EX/STRUC CONFER DEBATE
EFFICIENCY. PAGE 61 B1232

LEGIS
DELIB/GP
ADMIN

B58

SPITZ D.,DEMOCRACY AND THE CHALLANGE OF POWER. FUT
USA+45 USA-45 LAW SOCIETY STRUCT LOC/G POL/PAR
PROVS DELIB/GP EX/STRUC LEGIS TOP/EX ACT/RES CREATE
DOMIN EDU/PROP LEGIT ADJUD ADMIN ATTIT DRIVE MORAL
ORD/FREE TOT/POP. PAGE 99 B2010

NAT/G
PWR

B58

STEWART J.D.,BRITISH PRESSURE GROUPS: THEIR ROLE IN
RELATION TO THE HOUSE OF COMMONS. UK CONSULT
DELIB/GP ADMIN ROUTINE CHOOSE REPRESENT ATTIT ROLE
20 HOUSE/CMNS PARLIAMENT. PAGE 101 B2038

LOBBY
LEGIS
PLAN
PARL/PROC

B58

TAYLOR H.,THE STATESMAN. MOD/EUR FACE/GP FAM NAT/G
POL/PAR DELIB/GP LEGIS ATTIT PERSON PWR...POLICY
CONCPT OBS GEN/LAWS. PAGE 103 B2086

EXEC
STRUCT

B58

US HOUSE COMM ON COMMERCE,ADMINISTRATIVE PROCESS
AND ETHICAL QUESTIONS. USA+45 LAW LEGIS INT/TRADE
CONTROL 20 CONGRESS. PAGE 109 B2192

POLICY
ADMIN
DELIB/GP
ADJUD

B58

US HOUSE COMM POST OFFICE,MANPOWER UTILIZATION IN
THE FEDERAL GOVERNMENT. USA+45 DIST/IND EX/STRUC
LEGIS CONFER EFFICIENCY 20 CONGRESS CIVIL/SERV.
PAGE 109 B2195

ADMIN
WORKER
DELIB/GP
NAT/G

B58

US HOUSE COMM POST OFFICE,MANPOWER UTILIZATION IN
THE FEDERAL GOVERNMENT. USA+45 DIST/IND EX/STRUC
LEGIS CONFER EFFICIENCY 20 CONGRESS CIVIL/SERV.

ADMIN
WORKER
DELIB/GP

PAGE 109 B2196   NAT/G
                                                          B58
US HOUSE COMM POST OFFICE,TRAINING OF FEDERAL   LEGIS
EMPLOYEES. USA+45 DIST/IND NAT/G EX/STRUC EDU/PROP   DELIB/GP
CONFER GOV/REL EFFICIENCY SKILL 20 CONGRESS   WORKER
CIVIL/SERV. PAGE 109 B2197   ADMIN
                                                          B58
US SENATE COMM POST OFFICE,TO PROVIDE AN EFFECTIVE   INT
SYSTEM OF PERSONNEL ADMINISTRATION. USA+45 NAT/G   LEGIS
EX/STRUC PARL/PROC GOV/REL...JURID 20 SENATE   CONFER
CIVIL/SERV. PAGE 111 B2234   ADMIN
                                                          B58
VAN RIPER P.P.,HISTORY OF THE UNITED STATES CIVIL   ADMIN
SERVICE. USA+45 USA-45 LABOR LOC/G DELIB/GP LEGIS   WORKER
PROB/SOLV LOBBY GOV/REL GP/REL INCOME...POLICY   NAT/G
18/20 PRESIDENT CIVIL/SERV. PAGE 111 B2251
                                                          B58
WESTIN A.F.,THE ANATOMY OF A CONSTITUTIONAL LAW   CT/SYS
CASE. USA+45 LAW LEGIS ADMIN EXEC...DECISION MGT   INDUS
SOC RECORD 20 SUPREME/CT. PAGE 115 B2326   ADJUD
                                                      CONSTN
                                                          L58
HAVILAND H.F.,"FOREIGN AID AND THE POLICY PROCESS: LEGIS
1957." USA+45 FACE/GP POL/PAR VOL/ASSN CHIEF   PLAN
DELIB/GP ACT/RES LEGIT EXEC GOV/REL ATTIT DRIVE PWR   FOR/AID
...POLICY TESTS CONGRESS 20. PAGE 48 B0971
                                                          L58
JONAS F.H.,"BIBLIOGRAPHY ON WESTERN POLITICS."   BIBLIOG/A
USA+45 USA-45 ELITES MUNIC POL/PAR LEGIS ADJUD   LOC/G
ADMIN 20. PAGE 57 B1148   NAT/G
                                                      LAW
                                                          S58
DERGE D.R.,"METROPOLITAN AND OUTSTATE ALIGNMENTS IN   LEGIS
ILLINOIS AND MISSOURI LEGISLATIVE DELEGATIONS"   MUNIC
(BMR)" USA+45 ADMIN PARTIC GOV/REL...MYTH CHARTS 20   PROVS
ILLINOIS MISSOURI. PAGE 28 B0575   POL/PAR
                                                          S58
DIAMANT A.,"A CASE STUDY OF ADMINISTRATIVE   ADMIN
AUTONOMY: CONTROLS AND TENSIONS IN FRENCH   CONTROL
ADMINISTRATION." FRANCE ADJUD LOBBY DEMAND   LEGIS
EFFICIENCY 20. PAGE 29 B0585   EXEC
                                                          S58
STAAR R.F.,"ELECTIONS IN COMMUNIST POLAND." EUR+WWI   COM
SOCIETY INT/ORG NAT/G POL/PAR LEGIS ACT/RES ECO/TAC   CHOOSE
EDU/PROP ADJUD ADMIN ROUTINE COERCE TOTALISM ATTIT   POLAND
ORD/FREE PWR 20. PAGE 100 B2015
                                                          B59
COUNCIL OF STATE GOVERNORS,AMERICAN LEGISLATURES: LEGIS
STRUCTURE AND PROCEDURES. SUMMARY AND TABULATIONS   CHARTS
OF A 1959 SURVEY. PUERT/RICO USA+45 PAY ADJUD ADMIN   PROVS
APPORT...IDEA/COMP 20 GUAM VIRGIN/ISL. PAGE 24   REPRESENT
B0495
                                                          B59
GINSBURG M.,LAW AND OPINION IN ENGLAND. UK CULTURE   JURID
KIN LABOR LEGIS EDU/PROP ADMIN CT/SYS CRIME OWN   POLICY
HEALTH...ANTHOL 20 ENGLSH/LAW. PAGE 40 B0802   ECO/TAC
                                                          B59
IPSEN H.P.,HAMBURGISCHES STAATS- UND   ADMIN
VERWALTUNGSRECHT. CONSTN LOC/G FORCES BUDGET CT/SYS   PROVS
...JURID 20 HAMBURG. PAGE 54 B1103   LEGIS
                                                      FINAN
                                                          B59
MAASS A.,AREA AND POWER: A THEORY OF LOCAL   LOC/G
GOVERNMENT. MUNIC PROVS EX/STRUC LEGIS CT/SYS   FEDERAL
CHOOSE PWR 20. PAGE 67 B1354   BAL/PWR
                                                      GOV/REL
                                                          B59
MILLETT J.D.,GOVERNMENT AND PUBLIC ADMINISTRATION: ADMIN
THE QUEST FOR RESPONSIBLE PERFORMANCE. USA+45 NAT/G   PWR
DELIB/GP LEGIS CT/SYS EXEC...DECISION MGT. PAGE 73   CONSTN
B1483   ROLE
                                                          B59
MOOS M.,THE CAMPUS AND THE STATE. LAW FINAN   EDU/PROP
DELIB/GP LEGIS EXEC LOBBY GP/REL PWR...POLICY   ACADEM
BIBLIOG. PAGE 75 B1517   PROVS
                                                      CONTROL
                                                          B59
PARK R.L.,LEADERSHIP AND POLITICAL INSTITUTIONS IN   NAT/G
INDIA. S/ASIA CULTURE ECO/UNDEV LOC/G MUNIC PROVS   EXEC
LEGIS PLAN ADMIN LEAD ORD/FREE WEALTH...GEOG SOC   INDIA
BIOG TOT/POP VAL/FREE 20. PAGE 81 B1633
                                                          B59
SCHURZ W.L.,AMERICAN FOREIGN AFFAIRS: A GUIDE TO   INT/ORG
INTERNATIONAL AFFAIRS. USA+45 WOR+45 WOR-45 NAT/G   SOCIETY
FORCES LEGIS TOP/EX PLAN EDU/PROP LEGIT ADMIN   DIPLOM
ROUTINE ATTIT ORD/FREE PWR...SOC CONCPT STAT
SAMP/SIZ CHARTS STERTYP 20. PAGE 95 B1910
                                                          B59
SINHA H.N.,OUTLINES OF POLITICAL SCIENCE. NAT/G   JURID
POL/PAR EX/STRUC LEGIS CT/SYS CHOOSE REPRESENT 20.   CONCPT
PAGE 98 B1971   ORD/FREE
                                                      SOVEREIGN
                                                          B59
SPIRO H.J.,GOVERNMENT BY CONSTITUTIONS: THE   NAT/G
POLITICAL SYSTEMS OF DEMOCRACY. CANADA EUR+WWI FUT   CONSTN
USA+45 WOR+45 WOR-45 LEGIS TOP/EX LEGIT ADMIN

CT/SYS ORD/FREE PWR...TREND TOT/POP VAL/FREE 20.
PAGE 99 B2008
                                                          B59
SURRENCY E.C.,A GUIDE TO LEGAL RESEARCH. USA+45   NAT/G
ACADEM LEGIS ACT/RES ADMIN...DECISION METH/COMP   PROVS
BIBLIOG METH. PAGE 102 B2055   ADJUD
                                                      JURID
                                                          B59
US CIVIL SERVICE COMMISSION,CONGRESSIONAL DOCUMENTS   BIBLIOG/A
RELATING TO CIVIL SERVICE. USA+45 USA-45 CONFER   ADMIN
19/20 CONGRESS. PAGE 108 B2177   NAT/G
                                                      LEGIS
                                                          B59
WEBER W.,DER DEUTSCHE BEAMTE HEUTE. GERMANY/W NAT/G   MGT
DELIB/GP LEGIS CONFER ATTIT SUPEGO...JURID 20   EFFICIENCY
CIVIL/SERV. PAGE 114 B2306   ELITES
                                                      GP/REL
                                                          L59
RHODE W.E.,"COMMITTEE CLEARANCE OF ADMINISTRATIVE   DECISION
DECISIONS." DELIB/GP LEGIS BUDGET DOMIN CIVMIL/REL   ADMIN
20 CONGRESS. PAGE 87 B1768   OP/RES
                                                      NAT/G
                                                          S59
CHAPMAN B.,"THE FRENCH CONSEIL D'ETAT." FRANCE   ADMIN
NAT/G CONSULT OP/RES PROB/SOLV PWR...OBS 20.   LAW
PAGE 20 B0410   CT/SYS
                                                      LEGIS
                                                          S59
HILSMAN R.,"THE FOREIGN-POLICY CONSENSUS: AN   PROB/SOLV
INTERIM RESEARCH REPORT." USA+45 INT/ORG LEGIS   NAT/G
TEC/DEV EXEC WAR CONSEN KNOWL...DECISION COLD/WAR.   DELIB/GP
PAGE 50 B1013   DIPLOM
                                                          S59
ROBINSON J.A.,"THE ROLE OF THE RULES COMMITTEE IN   PARL/PROC
ARRANGING THE PROGRAM OF THE UNITED STATES HOUSE OF   DELIB/GP
REPRESENTATIVES." USA+45 DEBATE CONTROL AUTHORIT   ROUTINE
HOUSE/REP. PAGE 89 B1801   LEGIS
                                                          S59
SEIDMAN H.,"THE GOVERNMENT CORPORATION IN THE   CONTROL
UNITED STATES." USA+45 LEGIS ADMIN PLURISM 20.   GOV/REL
PAGE 95 B1925   EX/STRUC
                                                      EXEC
                                                          B60
JUNZ A.J., PRESENT TRENDS IN AMERICAN NATIONAL   POL/PAR
GOVERNMENT. LEGIS DIPLOM ADMIN CT/SYS ORD/FREE   CHOOSE
...CONCPT ANTHOL 20 CONGRESS PRESIDENT SUPREME/CT.   CONSTN
PAGE 2 B0048   NAT/G
                                                          B60
ADRIAN C.R.,STATE AND LOCAL GOVERNMENTS: A STUDY IN   LOC/G
THE POLITICAL PROCESS. USA+45 LAW FINAN MUNIC   PROVS
POL/PAR LEGIS ADJUD EXEC CHOOSE REPRESENT. PAGE 3   GOV/REL
B0060   ATTIT
                                                          B60
AYEARST M.,THE BRITISH WEST INDIES: THE SEARCH FOR   CONSTN
SELF-GOVERNMENT. FUT WEST/IND LOC/G POL/PAR   COLONIAL
EX/STRUC LEGIS CHOOSE FEDERAL...NAT/COMP BIBLIOG   REPRESENT
17/20. PAGE 7 B0152   NAT/G
                                                          B60
BELL J.,THE SPLENDID MISERY: THE STORY OF THE   EXEC
PRESIDENCY AND POWER POLITICS AT CLOSE RANGE.   TOP/EX
USA+45 USA-45 PRESS ADMIN LEAD LOBBY GP/REL   LEGIS
PERS/REL PERSON PRESIDENT. PAGE 10 B0208
                                                          B60
BROOKINGS INSTITUTION,UNITED STATES FOREIGN POLICY: DIPLOM
STUDY NO 9: THE FORMULATION AND ADMINISTRATION OF   INT/ORG
UNITED STATES FOREIGN POLICY. USA+45 WOR+45   CREATE
EX/STRUC LEGIS BAL/PWR FOR/AID EDU/PROP CIVMIL/REL
GOV/REL...INT COLD/WAR. PAGE 16 B0317
                                                          B60
FOSS P.,POLITICS AND GRASS: THE ADMINISTRATION OF   REPRESENT
GRAZING ON THE PUBLIC DOMAIN. USA+45 LEGIS TOP/EX   ADMIN
EXEC...DECISION 20. PAGE 37 B0743   LOBBY
                                                      EX/STRUC
                                                          B60
FRYE R.J.,GOVERNMENT AND LABOR: THE ALABAMA   ADMIN
PROGRAM. USA+45 INDUS R+D LABOR WORKER BUDGET   LEGIS
EFFICIENCY AGE/Y HEALTH...CHARTS 20 ALABAMA.   LOC/G
PAGE 38 B0761   PROVS
                                                          B60
HANBURY H.G.,ENGLISH COURTS OF LAW. UK EX/STRUC   JURID
LEGIS CRIME ROLE 12/20 COMMON/LAW ENGLSH/LAW.   CT/SYS
PAGE 46 B0936   CONSTN
                                                      GOV/REL
                                                          B60
HAYNES G.H.,THE SENATE OF THE UNITED STATES: ITS   LEGIS
HISTORY AND PRACTICE. CONSTN EX/STRUC TOP/EX CONFER   DELIB/GP
DEBATE LEAD LOBBY PARL/PROC CHOOSE PWR SENATE
CONGRESS. PAGE 48 B0977
                                                          B60
INDIAN INST OF PUBLIC ADMIN,STATE UNDERTAKINGS: GOV/REL
REPORT OF A CONFERENCE, DECEMBER 19-20, 1959   ADMIN
(PAMPHLET). INDIA LG/CO DELIB/GP CONFER PARL/PROC   NAT/G
EFFICIENCY OWN...MGT 20. PAGE 53 B1081   LEGIS
                                                          B60
KERSELL J.E.,PARLIAMENTARY SUPERVISION OF DELEGATED   LEGIS
LEGISLATION. UK EFFICIENCY PWR...POLICY CHARTS   CONTROL

BIBLIOG METH 20 PARLIAMENT. PAGE 59 B1198 — NAT/G EX/STRUC

B60

LINDSAY K.,EUROPEAN ASSEMBLIES: THE EXPERIMENTAL PERIOD 1949-1959. EUR+WWI ECO/DEV NAT/G POL/PAR LEGIS TOP/EX ACT/RES PLAN ECO/TAC DOMIN LEGIT ROUTINE ATTIT DRIVE ORD/FREE PWR SKILL...SOC CONCPT TREND CHARTS GEN/LAWS VAL/FREE. PAGE 65 B1315 — VOL/ASSN INT/ORG REGION

B60

LISKA G.,THE NEW STATECRAFT. WOR+45 WOR-45 LEGIS DIPLOM ADMIN ATTIT PWR WEALTH...HIST/WRIT TREND COLD/WAR 20. PAGE 66 B1323 — ECO/TAC CONCPT FOR/AID

B60

MATTOD P.K.,A STUDY OF LOCAL SELF GOVERNMENT IN URBAN INDIA. INDIA FINAN DELIB/GP LEGIS BUDGET TAX SOVEREIGN...MGT GP/COMP 20. PAGE 71 B1432 — MUNIC CONSTN LOC/G ADMIN

B60

POOLEY B.J.,THE EVOLUTION OF BRITISH PLANNING LEGISLATION. UK ECO/DEV LOC/G CONSULT DELIB/GP ADMIN 20 URBAN/RNWL. PAGE 84 B1691 — PLAN MUNIC LEGIS PROB/SOLV

B60

SAYRE W.S.,GOVERNING NEW YORK CITY; POLITICS IN THE METROPOLIS. POL/PAR CHIEF DELIB/GP LEGIS PLAN CT/SYS LEAD PARTIC CHOOSE...DECISION CHARTS BIBLIOG 20 NEWYORK/C BUREAUCRCY. PAGE 93 B1875 — MUNIC ADMIN PROB/SOLV

B60

SOUTH AFRICAN CONGRESS OF DEM,FACE THE FUTURE. SOUTH/AFR ELITES LEGIS ADMIN REGION COERCE PEACE ATTIT 20. PAGE 99 B1999 — RACE/REL DISCRIM CONSTN NAT/G

B60

US LIBRARY OF CONGRESS,INDEX TO LATIN AMERICAN LEGISLATION: 1950-1960 (2 VOLS.). NAT/G DELIB/GP ADMIN PARL/PROC 20. PAGE 109 B2205 — BIBLIOG/A LEGIS L/A+17C JURID

B60

US SENATE COMM ON JUDICIARY,FEDERAL ADMINISTRATIVE PROCEDURE. USA+45 CONSTN NAT/G PROB/SOLV CONFER GOV/REL...JURID INT 20 SENATE. PAGE 110 B2226 — PARL/PROC LEGIS ADMIN LAW

B60

US SENATE COMM ON JUDICIARY,ADMINISTRATIVE PROCEDURE LEGISLATION. USA+45 CONSTN NAT/G PROB/SOLV CONFER ROUTINE GOV/REL...INT 20 SENATE. PAGE 110 B2227 — PARL/PROC LEGIS ADMIN JURID

L60

GRODZINS M.,"AMERICAN POLITICAL PARTIES AND THE AMERICAN SYSTEM" (BMR)" USA+45 LOC/G NAT/G LEGIS BAL/PWR ADMIN ROLE PWR...DECISION 20. PAGE 44 B0883 — POL/PAR FEDERAL CENTRAL GOV/REL

S60

"THE EMERGING COMMON MARKETS IN LATIN AMERICA." FUT L/A+17C STRATA DIST/IND INDUS LABOR NAT/G LEGIS ECO/TAC ADMIN RIGID/FLEX HEALTH...NEW/IDEA TIME/SEQ OAS 20. PAGE 2 B0039 — FINAN ECO/UNDEV INT/TRADE

S60

FRANKEL S.H.,"ECONOMIC ASPECTS OF POLITICAL INDEPENDENCE IN AFRICA." AFR FUT SOCIETY ECO/UNDEV COM/IND FINAN LEGIS PLAN TEC/DEV CAP/ISM ECO/TAC INT/TRADE ADMIN ATTIT DRIVE RIGID/FLEX PWR WEALTH ...MGT NEW/IDEA MATH TIME/SEQ VAL/FREE 20. PAGE 37 B0751 — NAT/G FOR/AID

S60

HUNTINGTON S.P.,"STRATEGIC PLANNING AND THE POLITICAL PROCESS." USA+45 NAT/G DELIB/GP LEGIS ACT/RES ECO/TAC LEGIT ROUTINE CHOOSE RIGID/FLEX PWR ...POLICY MAJORIT MGT 20. PAGE 53 B1066 — EXEC FORCES NUC/PWR WAR

S60

MORALES C.J.,"TRADE AND ECONOMIC INTEGRATION IN LATIN AMERICA." FUT L/A+17C LAW STRATA ECO/UNDEV DIST/IND INDUS LABOR NAT/G LEGIS ECO/TAC ADMIN RIGID/FLEX WEALTH...CONCPT NEW/IDEA CONT/OBS TIME/SEQ WORK 20. PAGE 75 B1519 — FINAN INT/TRADE REGION

S60

NELSON R.H.,"LEGISLATIVE PARTICIPATION IN THE TREATY AND AGREEMENT MAKING PROCESS." CONSTN POL/PAR PLAN EXEC PWR FAO UN CONGRESS. PAGE 78 B1569 — LEGIS PEACE DECISION DIPLOM

S60

ROURKE F.E.,"ADMINISTRATIVE SECRECY: A CONGRESSIONAL DILEMMA." DELIB/GP CT/SYS ATTIT ...MAJORIT DECISION JURID. PAGE 91 B1837 — LEGIS EXEC ORD/FREE POLICY

S60

SCHER S.,"CONGRESSIONAL COMMITTEE MEMBERS AND INDEPENDENT AGENCY OVERSEERS: A CASE STUDY." DELIB/GP EX/STRUC JUDGE TOP/EX DOMIN ADMIN CONTROL PWR...SOC/EXP HOUSE/REP CONGRESS. PAGE 93 B1886 — LEGIS GOV/REL LABOR ADJUD

N60

RHODESIA-NYASA NATL ARCHIVES,A SELECT BIBLIOGRAPHY OF RECENT PUBLICATIONS CONCERNING THE FEDERATION OF RHODESIA AND NYASALAND (PAMPHLET). MALAWI RHODESIA LAW CULTURE STRUCT ECO/UNDEV LEGIS...GEOG 20. PAGE 88 B1770 — BIBLIOG ADMIN ORD/FREE NAT/G

B61

AUERBACH C.A.,THE LEGAL PROCESS. USA+45 DELIB/GP JUDGE CONFER ADJUD CONTROL...DECISION 20 SUPREME/CT. PAGE 7 B0146 — JURID ADMIN LEGIS CT/SYS

B61

AVERY M.W.,GOVERNMENT OF WASHINGTON STATE. USA+45 MUNIC DELIB/GP EX/STRUC LEGIS GIVE CT/SYS PARTIC REGION EFFICIENCY 20 WASHINGT/G GOVERNOR. PAGE 7 B0151 — PROVS LOC/G ADMIN GOV/REL

B61

BARNES W.,THE FOREIGN SERVICE OF THE UNITED STATES. USA+45 USA-45 CONSTN INT/ORG POL/PAR CONSULT DELIB/GP LEGIS DOMIN EDU/PROP EXEC ATTIT RIGID/FLEX ORD/FREE PWR...POLICY CONCPT STAT OBS RECORD BIOG TIME/SEQ TREND. PAGE 9 B0188 — NAT/G MGT DIPLOM

B61

BEASLEY K.E.,STATE SUPERVISION OF MUNICIPAL DEBT IN KANSAS - A CASE STUDY. USA+45 USA-45 FINAN PROVS BUDGET TAX ADJUD ADMIN CONTROL SUPEGO. PAGE 10 B0201 — MUNIC LOC/G LEGIS JURID

B61

BISHOP D.G.,THE ADMINISTRATION OF BRITISH FOREIGN RELATIONS. EUR+WWI MOD/EUR INT/ORG NAT/G POL/PAR DELIB/GP LEGIS TOP/EX ECO/TAC DOMIN EDU/PROP ADMIN COERCE 20. PAGE 12 B0243 — ROUTINE PWR DIPLOM UK

B61

CARROTHERS A.W.R.,LABOR ARBITRATION IN CANADA. CANADA LAW NAT/G CONSULT LEGIS WORKER ADJUD ADMIN CT/SYS 20. PAGE 19 B0386 — LABOR MGT GP/REL BARGAIN

B61

DARRAH E.L.,FIFTY STATE GOVERNMENTS: A COMPILATION OF EXECUTIVE ORGANIZATION CHARTS. USA+45 LOC/G DELIB/GP LEGIS ADJUD LEAD PWR 20 GOVERNOR. PAGE 26 B0530 — EX/STRUC ADMIN ORG/CHARTS PROVS

B61

DRAGNICH A.N.,MAJOR EUROPEAN GOVERNMENTS. FRANCE GERMANY/W UK USSR LOC/G EX/STRUC CT/SYS PARL/PROC ATTIT MARXISM...JURID MGT NAT/COMP 19/20. PAGE 30 B0615 — NAT/G LEGIS CONSTN POL/PAR

B61

DRURY J.W.,THE GOVERNMENT OF KANSAS. USA+45 AGRI INDUS CHIEF LEGIS WORKER PLAN BUDGET GIVE CT/SYS GOV/REL...T 20 KANSAS GOVERNOR CITY/MGT. PAGE 31 B0621 — PROVS CONSTN ADMIN LOC/G

B61

GRIFFITH E.S.,CONGRESS: ITS CONTEMPORARY ROLE. CONSTN POL/PAR CHIEF PLAN BUDGET DIPLOM CONFER ADMIN LOBBY...DECISION CONGRESS. PAGE 43 B0878 — PARL/PROC EX/STRUC TOP/EX LEGIS

B61

HAMILTON A.,THE FEDERALIST. USA-45 NAT/G VOL/ASSN LEGIS TOP/EX EDU/PROP LEGIT CHOOSE ATTIT RIGID/FLEX ORD/FREE PWR...MAJORIT JURID CONCPT ANTHOL. PAGE 46 B0931 — EX/STRUC CONSTN

B61

MACMAHON A.W.,DELEGATION AND AUTONOMY. INDIA STRUCT LEGIS BARGAIN BUDGET ECO/TAC LEGIT EXEC REPRESENT GOV/REL CENTRAL DEMAND EFFICIENCY PRODUC. PAGE 68 B1373 — ADMIN PLAN FEDERAL

B61

MARKMANN C.L.,JOHN F. KENNEDY: A SENSE OF PURPOSE. USA+45 INTELL FAM CONSULT DELIB/GP LEGIS PERSON SKILL 20 KENNEDY/JF EISNHWR/DD ROOSEVLT/F NEW/FRONTR PRESIDENT. PAGE 69 B1399 — CHIEF TOP/EX ADMIN BIOG

B61

MARVICK D.,POLITICAL DECISION-MAKERS. INTELL STRATA NAT/G POL/PAR EX/STRUC LEGIS DOMIN EDU/PROP ATTIT PERSON PWR...PSY STAT OBS CONT/OBS STAND/INT UNPLAN/INT TIME/SEQ CHARTS STERTYP VAL/FREE. PAGE 70 B1416 — TOP/EX BIOG ELITES

B61

SCHMECKEBIER L.,GOVERNMENT PUBLICATIONS AND THEIR USE. USA+45 LEGIS ACT/RES CT/SYS EXEC INGP/REL 20. PAGE 94 B1894 — BIBLIOG/A EDU/PROP NAT/G ADMIN

B61

SHARMA T.R.,THE WORKING OF STATE ENTERPRISES IN INDIA. INDIA DELIB/GP LEGIS WORKER BUDGET PRICE CONTROL GP/REL OWN ATTIT...MGT CHARTS 20. PAGE 96 B1938 — NAT/G INDUS ADMIN SOCISM

B61

TOMPKINS D.C.,CONFLICT OF INTEREST IN THE FEDERAL GOVERNMENT: A BIBLIOGRAPHY. USA+45 EX/STRUC LEGIS ADJUD ADMIN CRIME CONGRESS PRESIDENT. PAGE 105 B2117 — BIBLIOG ROLE NAT/G LAW

B61

WARD R.E.,JAPANESE POLITICAL SCIENCE: A GUIDE TO JAPANESE REFERENCE AND RESEARCH MATERIALS (2ND ED.). LAW CONSTN STRATA NAT/G POL/PAR DELIB/GP LEGIS ADMIN CHOOSE GP/REL...INT/LAW 19/20 CHINJAP. PAGE 113 B2290 — BIBLIOG/A PHIL/SCI

B61

WEST F.J.,POLITICAL ADVANCEMENT IN THE SOUTH PACIFIC. CONSTN CULTURE POL/PAR LEGIS DOMIN ADMIN — S/ASIA LOC/G

CHOOSE SOVEREIGN VAL/FREE 20 FIJI TAHITI SAMOA. COLONIAL
PAGE 115 B2325

  B61
WILLOUGHBY W.R.,THE ST LAWRENCE WATERWAY: A STUDY LEGIS
IN POLITICS AND DIPLOMACY. USA+45 ECO/DEV COM/IND INT/TRADE
INT/ORG CONSULT DELIB/GP ACT/RES TEC/DEV DIPLOM CANADA
ECO/TAC ROUTINE...TIME/SEQ 20. PAGE 117 B2357 DIST/IND

  L61
KRAMER R.,"EXECUTIVE PRIVILEGE - A STUDY OF THE REPRESENT
PERIOD 1953-1960." NAT/G CHIEF EX/STRUC LEGIS PWR. LEAD
PAGE 61 B1233 EXEC
  GOV/REL

  S61
BROWN M.,"THE DEMISE OF STATE DEPARTMENT PUBLIC EDU/PROP
OPINION POLLS: A STUDY IN LEGISLATIVE OVERSIGHT." NAT/G
PWR...POLICY PSY SAMP. PAGE 16 B0325 LEGIS
  ADMIN

  S61
ROBINSON J.A.,"PROCESS SATISFACTION AND POLICY GOV/REL
APPROVAL IN STATE DEPARTMENT - CONGRESSIONAL EX/STRUC
RELATIONS." ELITES CHIEF LEGIS CONFER DEBATE ADMIN POL/PAR
FEEDBACK ROLE...CHARTS 20 CONGRESS PRESIDENT DECISION
DEPT/STATE. PAGE 89 B1802

  B62
ANDREWS W.G.,EUROPEAN POLITICAL INSTITUTIONS. NAT/COMP
FRANCE GERMANY UK USSR TOP/EX LEAD PARL/PROC CHOOSE POL/PAR
20. PAGE 5 B0104 EX/STRUC
  LEGIS

  B62
ANDREWS W.G.,FRENCH POLITICS AND ALGERIA: THE GOV/COMP
PROCESS OF POLICY FORMATION 1954-1962. ALGERIA EXEC
FRANCE CONSTN ELITES POL/PAR CHIEF DELIB/GP LEGIS COLONIAL
DIPLOM PRESS CHOOSE 20. PAGE 5 B0105

  B62
BOCK E.A.,CASE STUDIES IN AMERICAN GOVERNMENT. POLICY
USA+45 ECO/DEV CHIEF EDU/PROP CT/SYS RACE/REL LEGIS
ORD/FREE...JURID MGT PHIL/SCI PRESIDENT CASEBOOK. IDEA/COMP
PAGE 13 B0262 NAT/G

  B62
BROWN B.E.,NEW DIRECTIONS IN COMPARATIVE POLITICS. NAT/COMP
AUSTRIA FRANCE GERMANY UK WOR+45 EX/STRUC LEGIS METH
ORD/FREE 20. PAGE 16 B0320 POL/PAR
  FORCES

  B62
CARPER E.T.,ILLINOIS GOES TO CONGRESS FOR ARMY ADMIN
LAND. USA+45 LAW EXTR/IND PROVS REGION CIVMIL/REL LOBBY
GOV/REL FEDERAL ATTIT 20 ILLINOIS SENATE CONGRESS GEOG
DIRKSEN/E DOUGLAS/P. PAGE 19 B0385 LEGIS

  B62
CHERNICK J.,THE SELECTION OF TRAINEES UNDER MDTA. EDU/PROP
USA+45 NAT/G LEGIS PERSON...CENSUS 20 CIVIL/SERV WORKER
MDTA. PAGE 20 B0418 ADMIN
  DELIB/GP

  B62
FARBER W.O.,GOVERNMENT OF SOUTH DAKOTA. USA+45 PROVS
DIST/IND POL/PAR CHIEF EX/STRUC LEGIS ECO/TAC GIVE LOC/G
EDU/PROP CT/SYS PARTIC...T 20 SOUTH/DAK GOVERNOR. ADMIN
PAGE 35 B0704 CONSTN

  B62
GOVERNORS CONF STATE PLANNING,STATE PLANNING: A GOV/REL
POLICY STATEMENT (PAMPHLET). USA+45 LOC/G NAT/G PLAN
DELIB/GP LEGIS EXEC 20 GOVERNOR. PAGE 42 B0847 ADMIN
  PROVS

  B62
HITCHNER D.G.,MODERN GOVERNMENT: A SURVEY OF CONCPT
POLITICAL SCIENCE. WOR+45 INT/ORG LEGIS ADMIN NAT/G
CT/SYS EXEC CHOOSE TOTALISM POPULISM...INT/LAW STRUCT
PHIL/SCI METH 20. PAGE 50 B1019

  B62
HSUEH S.-.S.,GOVERNMENT AND ADMINISTRATION OF HONG ADMIN
KONG. CHIEF DELIB/GP LEGIS CT/SYS REPRESENT GOV/REL LOC/G
20 HONG/KONG CITY/MGT CIVIL/SERV GOVERNOR. PAGE 52 COLONIAL
B1055 EX/STRUC

  B62
INST TRAINING MUNICIPAL ADMIN,MUNICIPAL FINANCE MUNIC
ADMINISTRATION (6TH ED.). USA+45 ELITES ECO/DEV ADMIN
LEGIS PLAN BUDGET TAX GP/REL BAL/PAY COST...POLICY FINAN
20 CITY/MGT. PAGE 54 B1089 LOC/G

  B62
JEWELL M.E.,SENATORIAL POLITICS AND FOREIGN POLICY. USA+45
NAT/G POL/PAR CHIEF DELIB/GP TOP/EX FOR/AID LEGIS
EDU/PROP ROUTINE ATTIT PWR SKILL...MAJORIT DIPLOM
METH/CNCPT TIME/SEQ CONGRESS 20 PRESIDENT. PAGE 56
B1138

  B62
KAMMERER G.M.,CITY MANAGERS IN POLITICS: AN MUNIC
ANALYSIS OF MANAGER TENURE AND TERMINATION. POL/PAR LEAD
LEGIS PARTIC CHOOSE PWR...DECISION GEOG METH/CNCPT. EXEC
PAGE 57 B1161

  B62
KARNJAHAPRAKORN C.,MUNICIPAL GOVERNMENT IN THAILAND LOC/G
AS AN INSTITUTION AND PROCESS OF SELF-GOVERNMENT. MUNIC
THAILAND CULTURE FINAN EX/STRUC LEGIS PLAN CONTROL ORD/FREE
GOV/REL EFFICIENCY ATTIT...POLICY 20. PAGE 58 B1176 ADMIN

  B62
LAWSON R.,INTERNATIONAL REGIONAL ORGANIZATIONS. INT/ORG

WOR+45 NAT/G VOL/ASSN CONSULT LEGIS EDU/PROP LEGIT DELIB/GP
ADMIN EXEC ROUTINE HEALTH PWR WEALTH...JURID EEC REGION
COLD/WAR 20 UN. PAGE 63 B1277

  B62
LITTLEFIELD N.,METROPOLITAN AREA PROBLEMS AND LOC/G
MUNICIPAL HOME RULE. USA+45 PROVS ADMIN CONTROL SOVEREIGN
GP/REL PWR. PAGE 66 B1328 JURID
  LEGIS

  B62
LOWI T.J.,LEGISLATIVE POLITICS U.S.A. LAW LEGIS PARL/PROC
DIPLOM EXEC LOBBY CHOOSE SUFF FEDERAL PWR 19/20 REPRESENT
CONGRESS. PAGE 67 B1345 POLICY
  ROUTINE

  B62
MORE S.S.,REMODELLING OF DEMOCRACY FOR AFRO-ASIAN ORD/FREE
NATIONS. AFR INDIA S/ASIA SOUTH/AFR CONSTN EX/STRUC ECO/UNDEV
COLONIAL CHOOSE TOTALISM SOVEREIGN NEW/LIB SOCISM ADMIN
...SOC/WK 20. PAGE 75 B1520 LEGIS

  B62
OLLE-LAPRUNE J.,LA STABILITE DES MINISTRES SOUS LA LEGIS
TROISIEME REPUBLIQUE, 1879-1940. FRANCE CONSTN NAT/G
POL/PAR LEAD WAR INGP/REL RIGID/FLEX PWR...POLICY ADMIN
CHARTS 19/20. PAGE 79 B1606 PERSON

  B62
PHILLIPS O.H.,CONSTITUTIONAL AND ADMINISTRATIVE LAW JURID
(3RD ED.). UK INT/ORG LOC/G CHIEF EX/STRUC LEGIS ADMIN
BAL/PWR ADJUD COLONIAL CT/SYS PWR...CHARTS 20. CONSTN
PAGE 83 B1670 NAT/G

  B62
PRESS C.,STATE MANUALS, BLUE BOOKS AND ELECTION BIBLIOG
RESULTS. LAW LOC/G MUNIC LEGIS WRITING FEDERAL PROVS
SOVEREIGN...DECISION STAT CHARTS 20. PAGE 84 B1700 ADMIN
  CHOOSE

  B62
SCHILLING W.R.,STRATEGY, POLITICS, AND DEFENSE ROUTINE
BUDGETS. USA+45 R+D NAT/G CONSULT DELIB/GP FORCES POLICY
LEGIS ACT/RES PLAN BAL/PWR LEGIT EXEC NUC/PWR
RIGID/FLEX PWR...TREND COLD/WAR CONGRESS 20
EISNHWR/DD. PAGE 93 B1890

  B62
SRIVASTAVA G.L.,COLLECTIVE BARGAINING AND LABOR- LABOR
MANAGEMENT RELATIONS IN INDIA. INDIA UK USA+45 MGT
INDUS LEGIS WORKER ADJUD EFFICIENCY PRODUC BARGAIN
...METH/COMP 20. PAGE 100 B2014 GP/REL

  L62
BORCHARDT K.,"CONGRESSIONAL USE OF ADMINISTRATIVE ADMIN
ORGANIZATION AND PROCEDURE FOR POLICY-MAKING LEGIS
PURPOSES." USA+45 NAT/G EXEC LOBBY. PAGE 14 B0278 REPRESENT
  CONTROL

  L62
MANGIN G.,"L'ORGANIZATION JUDICIAIRE DES ETATS AFR
D'AFRIQUE ET DE MADAGASCAR." ISLAM WOR+45 STRATA LEGIS
STRUCT ECO/UNDEV NAT/G LEGIT EXEC...JURID TIME/SEQ COLONIAL
TOT/POP 20 SUPREME/CT. PAGE 69 B1387 MADAGASCAR
  L62
NEIBURG H.L.,"THE EISENHOWER AEC AND CONGRESS: A CHIEF
STUDY IN EXECUTIVE-LEGISLATIVE RELATIONS." USA+45 LEGIS
NAT/G POL/PAR DELIB/GP EX/STRUC TOP/EX ADMIN EXEC GOV/REL
LEAD ROUTINE PWR...POLICY COLD/WAR CONGRESS NUC/PWR
PRESIDENT AEC. PAGE 77 B1567

  S62
LOCKARD D.,"THE CITY MANAGER, ADMINISTRATIVE THEORY MUNIC
AND POLITICAL POWER." LEGIS ADMIN REPRESENT GP/REL EXEC
PWR. PAGE 66 B1333 LEAD
  DECISION

  S62
MURACCIOLE L.,"LES CONSTITUTIONS DES ETATS NAT/G
AFRICAINS D'EXPRESSION FRANCAISE: LA CONSTITUTION CONSTN
DU 16 AVRIL 1962 DE LA REPUBLIQUE DU" AFR CHAD
CHIEF LEGIS LEGIT COLONIAL EXEC ROUTINE ORD/FREE
SOVEREIGN...SOC CONCPT 20. PAGE 76 B1541

  S62
SPRINGER H.W.,"FEDERATION IN THE CARIBBEAN: AN VOL/ASSN
ATTEMPT THAT FAILED." L/A+17C ECO/UNDEV INT/ORG NAT/G
POL/PAR PROVS LEGIS CREATE PLAN LEGIT ADMIN FEDERAL REGION
ATTIT DRIVE PERSON ORD/FREE PWR...POLICY GEOG PSY
CONCPT OBS CARIBBEAN CMN/WLTH 20. PAGE 100 B2013

  S62
TRUMAN D.,"THE DOMESTIC POLITICS OF FOREIGN AID." ROUTINE
USA+45 WOR+45 NAT/G POL/PAR LEGIS DIPLOM ECO/TAC FOR/AID
EDU/PROP ADMIN CHOOSE ATTIT PWR CONGRESS 20
CONGRESS. PAGE 105 B2129

  C62
MORGAN G.G.,"SOVIET ADMINISTRATIVE LEGALITY: THE LAW
ROLE OF THE ATTORNEY GENERAL'S OFFICE." COM USSR CONSTN
CONTROL ROUTINE...CONCPT BIBLIOG 18/20. PAGE 75 LEGIS
B1522 ADMIN

  C62
TRUMAN D.B.,"THE GOVERNMENTAL PROCESS: POLITICAL LOBBY
INTERESTS AND PUBLIC OPINION." POL/PAR ADJUD ADMIN EDU/PROP
EXEC LEAD ROUTINE CHOOSE REPRESENT GOV/REL GP/REL
RIGID/FLEX...POLICY BIBLIOG/A 20. PAGE 105 B2131 LEGIS

  N62
US ADVISORY COMN INTERGOV REL,ALTERNATIVE MUNIC
APPROACHES TO GOVERNMENTAL REORGANIZATION IN REGION
METROPOLITAN AREAS (PAMPHLET). EX/STRUC LEGIS EXEC PLAN

LEAD PWR...DECISION GEN/METH. PAGE 107 B2171   GOV/REL
B63

ADRIAN C.R.,GOVERNING OVER FIFTY STATES AND THEIR   PROVS
COMMUNITIES. USA+45 CONSTN FINAN MUNIC NAT/G   LOC/G
POL/PAR EX/STRUC LEGIS ADMIN CONTROL CT/SYS   GOV/REL
...CHARTS 20. PAGE 3 B0061   GOV/COMP
B63

BADI J.,THE GOVERNMENT OF THE STATE OF ISRAEL: A   NAT/G
CRITICAL ACCOUNT OF ITS PARLIAMENT, EXECUTIVE, AND   CONSTN
JUDICIARY. ISRAEL ECO/DEV CHIEF DELIB/GP LEGIS   EX/STRUC
DIPLOM CT/SYS INGP/REL PEACE ORD/FREE...BIBLIOG 20   POL/PAR
PARLIAMENT ARABS MIGRATION. PAGE 8 B0157
B63

BANFIELD E.C.,CITY POLITICS. CULTURE LABOR LOC/G   MUNIC
POL/PAR LEGIS EXEC LEAD CHOOSE...DECISION NEGRO.   RIGID/FLEX
PAGE 9 B0178   ATTIT
B63

BLONDEL J.,VOTERS, PARTIES, AND LEADERS. UK ELITES   POL/PAR
LOC/G NAT/G PROVS ACT/RES DOMIN REPRESENT GP/REL   STRATA
INGP/REL...SOC BIBLIOG 20. PAGE 12 B0255   LEGIS
    ADMIN
B63

BURRUS B.R.,ADMINSTRATIVE LAW AND LOCAL GOVERNMENT.   EX/STRUC
USA+45 PROVS LEGIS LICENSE ADJUD ORD/FREE 20.   LOC/G
PAGE 17 B0356   JURID
    CONSTN
B63

CLARK J.S.,THE SENATE ESTABLISHMENT. USA+45 NAT/G   LEGIS
POL/PAR ADMIN CHOOSE PERSON SENATE. PAGE 21 B0431   ROUTINE
    LEAD
    SENIOR
B63

CORLEY R.N.,THE LEGAL ENVIRONMENT OF BUSINESS.   NAT/G
CONSTN LEGIS TAX ADMIN CT/SYS DISCRIM ATTIT PWR   INDUS
...TREND 18/20. PAGE 23 B0477   JURID
    DECISION
B63

COUNCIL STATE GOVERNMENTS,HANDBOOK FOR LEGISLATIVE   LEGIS
COMMITTEES. USA+45 LAW DELIB/GP EX/STRUC TOP/EX   PARL/PROC
CHOOSE PWR...METH/COMP 20. PAGE 24 B0496   PROVS
    ADJUD
B63

CROUCH W.W.,SOUTHERN CALIFORNIA METROPOLIS: A STUDY   LOC/G
IN DEVELOPMENT OF GOVERNMENT FOR A METROPOLITAN   MUNIC
AREA. USA+45 USA-45 PROB/SOLV ADMIN LOBBY PARTIC   LEGIS
CENTRAL ORD/FREE PWR...BIBLIOG 20 PROGRSV/M.   DECISION
PAGE 25 B0510
B63

GARNER U.F.,ADMINISTRATIVE LAW. UK LAW LOC/G NAT/G   ADMIN
EX/STRUC LEGIS JUDGE BAL/PWR BUDGET ADJUD CONTROL   JURID
CT/SYS...BIBLIOG 20. PAGE 39 B0783   PWR
    GOV/REL
B63

GRANT D.R.,STATE AND LOCAL GOVERNMENT IN AMERICA.   PROVS
USA+45 FINAN LOC/G MUNIC EX/STRUC FORCES EDU/PROP   POL/PAR
ADMIN CHOOSE FEDERAL ATTIT...JURID 20. PAGE 42   LEGIS
B0853   CONSTN
B63

GREEN H.P.,GOVERNMENT OF THE ATOM. USA+45 LEGIS   GOV/REL
PROB/SOLV ADMIN CONTROL PWR...POLICY DECISION 20   EX/STRUC
PRESIDENT CONGRESS. PAGE 43 B0864   NUC/PWR
    DELIB/GP
B63

GRIFFITH J.A.G.,PRINCIPLES OF ADMINISTRATIVE LAW   JURID
(3RD ED.). UK CONSTN EX/STRUC LEGIS ADJUD CONTROL   ADMIN
CT/SYS PWR...CHARTS 20. PAGE 43 B0879   NAT/G
    BAL/PWR
B63

HANSON A.H.,NATIONALIZATION: A BOOK OF READINGS.   NAT/G
WOR+45 FINAN DELIB/GP LEGIS WORKER BUDGET ADMIN   OWN
GP/REL EFFICIENCY SOCISM...MGT ANTHOL. PAGE 46   INDUS
B0941   CONTROL
B63

HATHAWAY D.A.,GOVERNMENT AND AGRICULTURE: PUBLIC   AGRI
POLICY IN A DEMOCRATIC SOCIETY. USA+45 LEGIS ADMIN   GOV/REL
EXEC LOBBY REPRESENT PWR 20. PAGE 48 B0967   PROB/SOLV
    EX/STRUC
B63

HERMAN H.,NEW YORK STATE AND THE METROPOLITAN   GOV/REL
PROBLEM. USA+45 ECO/DEV PUB/INST SCHOOL LEGIS PLAN   PROVS
TAX EXEC PARL/PROC PARTIC...HEAL 20 NEW/YORK.   LOC/G
PAGE 49 B0992   POLICY
B63

HERNDON J.,A SELECTED BIBLIOGRAPHY OF MATERIALS IN   BIBLIOG
STATE GOVERNMENT AND POLITICS (PAMPHLET). USA+45   GOV/COMP
POL/PAR LEGIS ADMIN CHOOSE MGT. PAGE 49 B0993   PROVS
    DECISION
B63

HIGA M.,POLITICS AND PARTIES IN POSTWAR OKINAWA.   GOV/REL
USA+45 VOL/ASSN LEGIS CONTROL LOBBY CHOOSE NAT/LISM   POL/PAR
PWR SOVEREIGN MARXISM SOCISM 20 OKINAWA CHINJAP.   ADMIN
PAGE 50 B1008   FORCES
B63

KOGAN N.,THE POLITICS OF ITALIAN FOREIGN POLICY.   NAT/G
EUR+WWI LEGIS DOMIN LEGIT EXEC PWR RESPECT SKILL   ROUTINE
...POLICY DECISION HUM SOC METH/CNCPT OBS INT   DIPLOM

CHARTS 20. PAGE 61 B1227   ITALY
B63

LOCKARD D.,THE POLITICS OF STATE AND LOCAL   LOC/G
GOVERNMENT. USA+45 CONSTN EX/STRUC LEGIS CT/SYS   PROVS
FEDERAL...CHARTS BIBLIOG 20. PAGE 66 B1334   OP/RES
    ADMIN
B63

MACNEIL N.,FORGE OF DEMOCRACY: THE HOUSE OF   LEGIS
REPRESENTATIVES. POL/PAR EX/STRUC TOP/EX DEBATE   DELIB/GP
LEAD PARL/PROC CHOOSE GOV/REL PWR...OBS HOUSE/REP.
PAGE 68 B1374
B63

MEYNAUD J.,PLANIFICATION ET POLITIQUE. FRANCE ITALY   PLAN
FINAN LABOR DELIB/GP LEGIS ADMIN EFFICIENCY   ECO/TAC
...MAJORIT DECISION 20. PAGE 73 B1477   PROB/SOLV
B63

PEABODY R.L.,NEW PERSPECTIVES ON THE HOUSE OF   NEW/IDEA
REPRESENTATIVES. AGRI FINAN SCHOOL FORCES CONFER   LEGIS
LEAD CHOOSE REPRESENT FEDERAL...POLICY DECISION   PWR
HOUSE/REP. PAGE 82 B1647   ADMIN
B63

PLISCHKE E.,GOVERNMENT AND POLITICS OF CONTEMPORARY   MUNIC
BERLIN. GERMANY LAW CONSTN POL/PAR LEGIS WAR CHOOSE   LOC/G
REPRESENT GOV/REL...CHARTS BIBLIOG 20 BERLIN.   POLICY
PAGE 83 B1683   ADMIN
B63

PREST A.R.,PUBLIC FINANCE IN UNDERDEVELOPED   FINAN
COUNTRIES. UK WOR+45 WOR-45 SOCIETY INT/ORG NAT/G   ECO/UNDEV
LEGIS ACT/RES PLAN ECO/TAC ADMIN ROUTINE...CHARTS   NIGERIA
20. PAGE 84 B1702
B63

RICHARDSON H.G.,THE ADMINISTRATION OF IRELAND   ADMIN
1172-1377. IRELAND CONSTN EX/STRUC LEGIS JUDGE   NAT/G
CT/SYS PARL/PROC...CHARTS BIBLIOG 12/14. PAGE 88   PWR
B1775
B63

ROBINSON K.,ESSAYS IN IMPERIAL GOVERNMENT. CAMEROON   COLONIAL
NIGERIA UK CONSTN LOC/G LEGIS ADMIN GOV/REL PWR   AFR
...POLICY ANTHOL BIBLIOG 17/20 PURHAM/M. PAGE 89   DOMIN
B1803
B63

ROYAL INSTITUTE PUBLIC ADMIN,BRITISH PUBLIC   BIBLIOG
ADMINISTRATION. UK LAW FINAN INDUS LOC/G POL/PAR   ADMIN
LEGIS LOBBY PARL/PROC CHOOSE JURID. PAGE 91 B1845   MGT
    NAT/G
B63

SHANKS M.,THE LESSONS OF PUBLIC ENTERPRISE. UK   SOCISM
LEGIS WORKER ECO/TAC ADMIN PARL/PROC GOV/REL ATTIT   OWN
...POLICY MGT METH/COMP NAT/COMP ANTHOL 20   NAT/G
PARLIAMENT. PAGE 96 B1931   INDUS
B63

SIDEY H.,JOHN F. KENNEDY, PRESIDENT. USA+45 INTELL   BIOG
FAM CONSULT DELIB/GP LEGIS ADMIN LEAD 20 KENNEDY/JF   TOP/EX
PRESIDENT. PAGE 97 B1951   SKILL
    PERSON
B63

SINGH H.L.,PROBLEMS AND POLICIES OF THE BRITISH IN   COLONIAL
INDIA, 1885-1898. INDIA UK NAT/G FORCES LEGIS   PWR
PROB/SOLV CONTROL RACE/REL ADJUST DISCRIM NAT/LISM   POLICY
RIGID/FLEX...MGT 19 CIVIL/SERV. PAGE 97 B1968   ADMIN
B63

SMITH R.M.,STATE GOVERNMENT IN TRANSITION. USA+45   PROVS
POL/PAR LEGIS PARL/PROC GOV/REL 20 PENNSYLVAN   POLICY
GOVERNOR. PAGE 98 B1984   EX/STRUC
    PLAN
B63

STEIN H.,AMERICAN CIVIL-MILITARY DECISION. USA+45   CIVMIL/REL
USA-45 EX/STRUC FORCES LEGIS TOP/EX PLAN DIPLOM   DECISION
FOR/AID ATTIT 20 CONGRESS. PAGE 100 B2028   WAR
    BUDGET
B63

US CONGRESS: SENATE,HEARINGS OF THE COMMITTEE ON   LEGIS
THE JUDICIARY. USA+45 CONSTN NAT/G ADMIN GOV/REL 20   LAW
CONGRESS. PAGE 108 B2179   ORD/FREE
    DELIB/GP
B63

US SENATE COMM ON JUDICIARY,ADMINISTRATIVE   PARL/PROC
CONFERENCE OF THE UNITED STATES. USA+45 CONSTN   JURID
NAT/G PROB/SOLV CONFER GOV/REL...INT 20 SENATE.   ADMIN
PAGE 110 B2230   LEGIS
B63

WALKER A.A.,OFFICIAL PUBLICATIONS OF SIERRA LEONE   BIBLIOG
AND GAMBIA. GAMBIA SIER/LEONE UK LAW CONSTN LEGIS   NAT/G
PLAN BUDGET DIPLOM...SOC SAMP CON/ANAL 20. PAGE 113   COLONIAL
B2278   ADMIN
B63

WOLL P.,AMERICAN BUREAUCRACY. USA+45 USA-45 CONSTN   LEGIS
NAT/G ADJUD PWR OBJECTIVE...MGT GP/COMP. PAGE 118   EX/STRUC
B2372   ADMIN
    GP/REL
S63

BANFIELD J.,"FEDERATION IN EAST-AFRICA." AFR UGANDA   EX/STRUC
ELITES INT/ORG NAT/G VOL/ASSN LEGIS ECO/TAC FEDERAL   PWR
ATTIT SOVEREIGN TOT/POP 20 TANGANYIKA. PAGE 9 B0180   REGION
S63

BECHHOEFER B.G.,"UNITED NATIONS PROCEDURES IN CASE   INT/ORG

OF VIOLATIONS OF DISARMAMENT AGREEMENTS." COM
USA+45 USSR LAW CONSTN NAT/G EX/STRUC FORCES LEGIS
BAL/PWR EDU/PROP CT/SYS ARMS/CONT ORD/FREE PWR
...POLICY STERTYP UN VAL/FREE 20. PAGE 10 B0204
DELIB/GP

S63
BRZEZINSKI Z.K.,"CINCINNATUS AND THE APPARATCHIK."
COM USA+45 USA-45 ELITES LOC/G NAT/G PROVS CONSULT
LEGIS DOMIN LEGIT EXEC ROUTINE CHOOSE DRIVE PWR
SKILL...CONCPT CHARTS VAL/FREE COLD/WAR 20. PAGE 16
B0334
POL/PAR
USSR

S63
EVANS L.H.,"SOME MANAGEMENT PROBLEMS OF UNESCO."
WOR+45 EX/STRUC LEGIS PWR UNESCO VAL/FREE 20.
PAGE 34 B0688
INT/ORG
MGT

S63
USEEM J.,"MEN IN THE MIDDLE OF THE THIRD CULTURE:
THE ROLES OF AMERICAN AND NON-WESTERN PEOPLE IN
CROSS-CULTURAL ADMINIS-." FUT WOR+45 DELIB/GP
EX/STRUC LEGIS ATTIT ALL/VALS...MGT INT TIME/SEQ
GEN/LAWS VAL/FREE. PAGE 111 B2247
ADMIN
SOCIETY
PERSON

S63
WAGRET M.,"L'ASCENSION POLITIQUE DE L'U.D.D.I.A.
(CONGO) ET SA PRISE DU POUVOIR (1956-1959)." AFR
WOR+45 NAT/G POL/PAR CONSULT DELIB/GP LEGIS PERCEPT
ALL/VALS SOVEREIGN...TIME/SEQ CONGO. PAGE 113 B2274
EX/STRUC
CHOOSE
FRANCE

C63
BLUM J.M.,"THE NATIONAL EXPERIENCE." USA+45 USA-45
ECO/DEV DIPLOM WAR NAT/LISM...POLICY CHARTS BIBLIOG
T 16/20 CONGRESS PRESIDENT COLD/WAR. PAGE 13 B0258
ADMIN
NAT/G
LEGIS
CHIEF

B64
RECENT PUBLICATIONS ON GOVERNMENTAL PROBLEMS. FINAN
INDUS ACADEM PLAN PROB/SOLV EDU/PROP ADJUD ADMIN
BIO/SOC...MGT SOC. PAGE 2 B0040
BIBLIOG
AUTOMAT
LEGIS
JURID

B64
ANDREN N.,GOVERNMENT AND POLITICS IN THE NORDIC
COUNTRIES: DENMARK, FINLAND, ICELAND, NORWAY,
SWEDEN. DENMARK FINLAND ICELAND NORWAY SWEDEN
POL/PAR CHIEF LEGIS ADMIN REGION REPRESENT ATTIT
CONSERVE...CHARTS BIBLIOG/A 20. PAGE 5 B0102
CONSTN
NAT/G
CULTURE
GOV/COMP

B64
APTER D.E.,IDEOLOGY AND DISCONTENT. FUT WOR+45
CONSTN CULTURE INTELL SOCIETY STRUCT INT/ORG NAT/G
DELIB/GP LEGIS CREATE PLAN TEC/DEV EDU/PROP EXEC
PERCEPT PERSON RIGID/FLEX ALL/VALS...POLICY
TOT/POP. PAGE 6 B0122
ACT/RES
ATTIT

B64
AVASTHI A.,ASPECTS OF ADMINISTRATION. INDIA UK
USA+45 FINAN ACADEM DELIB/GP LEGIS RECEIVE
PARL/PROC PRIVIL...NAT/COMP 20. PAGE 7 B0150
MGT
ADMIN
SOC/WK
ORD/FREE

B64
CATER D.,POWER IN WASHINGTON: A CRITICAL LOOK AT
TODAY'S STRUGGLE TO GOVERN IN THE NATION'S CAPITAL.
USA+45 NAT/G LEGIS ADMIN EXEC LOBBY PLURISM 20.
PAGE 19 B0392
REPRESENT
GOV/REL
INGP/REL
EX/STRUC

B64
CLARK J.S.,CONGRESS: THE SAPLESS BRANCH. DELIB/GP
SENIOR ATTIT CONGRESS. PAGE 21 B0432
LEGIS
ROUTINE
ADMIN
POL/PAR

B64
CONNECTICUT U INST PUBLIC SERV,SUMMARY OF CHARTER
PROVISIONS IN CONNECTICUT LOCAL GOVERNMENT
(PAMPHLET). USA+45 DELIB/GP LEGIS TOP/EX CHOOSE
REPRESENT 20 CONNECTICT CITY/MGT MAYOR. PAGE 23
B0462
CONSTN
MUNIC
LOC/G
EX/STRUC

B64
DAS M.N.,INDIA UNDER MORLEY AND MINTO. INDIA UK
ECO/UNDEV MUNIC PROVS EX/STRUC LEGIS DIPLOM CONTROL
REV 20 MORLEY/J. PAGE 26 B0531
GOV/REL
COLONIAL
POLICY
ADMIN

B64
ENDACOTT G.B.,GOVERNMENT AND PEOPLE IN HONG KONG
1841-1962: A CONSTITUTIONAL HISTORY. UK LEGIS ADJUD
REPRESENT ATTIT 19/20 HONG/KONG. PAGE 33 B0674
CONSTN
COLONIAL
CONTROL
ADMIN

B64
GJUPANOVIC H.,LEGAL SOURCES AND BIBLIOGRAPHY OF
YUGOSLAVIA. COM YUGOSLAVIA LAW LEGIS DIPLOM ADMIN
PARL/PROC REGION CRIME CENTRAL 20. PAGE 40 B0807
BIBLIOG/A
JURID
CONSTN
ADJUD

B64
GUTTSMAN W.L.,THE BRITISH POLITICAL ELITE. EUR+WWI
MOD/EUR STRATA FAM LABOR POL/PAR SCHOOL VOL/ASSN
DELIB/GP LEGIS LEGIT EXEC CHOOSE ATTIT ALL/VALS
...STAT BIOG TIME/SEQ CHARTS VAL/FREE. PAGE 45
B0905
NAT/G
SOC
UK
ELITES

B64
HALLER W.,DER SCHWEDISCHE JUSTITIEOMBUDSMAN.
DENMARK FINLAND NORWAY SWEDEN LEGIS ADJUD CONTROL
PERSON ORD/FREE...NAT/COMP 20 OMBUDSMAN. PAGE 46
B0926
JURID
PARL/PROC
ADMIN
CHIEF

B64
INDIAN COMM PREVENTION CORRUPT,REPORT, 1964. INDIA
CRIME

NAT/G GOV/REL ATTIT ORD/FREE...CRIMLGY METH 20.
PAGE 53 B1079
ADMIN
LEGIS
LOC/G

B64
KEEFE W.J.,THE AMERICAN LEGISLATIVE PROCESS:
CONGRESS AND THE STATES. USA+45 LAW POL/PAR
DELIB/GP DEBATE ADMIN LOBBY REPRESENT CONGRESS
PRESIDENT. PAGE 59 B1187
LEGIS
DECISION
PWR
PROVS

B64
NEUSTADT R.,PRESIDENTIAL POWER. USA+45 CONSTN NAT/G
CHIEF LEGIS CREATE EDU/PROP LEGIT ADMIN EXEC COERCE
ATTIT PERSON RIGID/FLEX PWR CONGRESS 20 PRESIDENT
TRUMAN/HS EISENHWR/DD. PAGE 78 B1575
TOP/EX
SKILL

B64
O'HEARN P.J.T.,PEACE, ORDER AND GOOD GOVERNMENT: A
NEW CONSTITUTION FOR CANADA. CANADA EX/STRUC LEGIS
CT/SYS PARL/PROC...BIBLIOG 20. PAGE 79 B1600
NAT/G
CONSTN
LAW
CREATE

B64
PIERCE T.M.,FEDERAL, STATE, AND LOCAL GOVERNMENT IN
EDUCATION. FINAN LOC/G PROVS LEGIS PLAN EDU/PROP
ADMIN CONTROL CENTRAL COST KNOWL 20. PAGE 83 B1673
NAT/G
POLICY
SCHOOL
GOV/REL

B64
PIPES R.,THE FORMATION OF THE SOVIET UNION. EUR+WWI
MOD/EUR STRUCT ECO/UNDEV NAT/G LEGIS DOMIN LEGIT
CT/SYS EXEC COERCE ALL/VALS...POLICY RELATIV
HIST/WRIT TIME/SEQ TOT/POP 19/20. PAGE 83 B1677
COM
USSR
RUSSIA

B64
PRESS C.,A BIBLIOGRAPHIC INTRODUCTION TO AMERICAN
STATE GOVERNMENT AND POLITICS (PAMPHLET). USA+45
USA-45 EX/STRUC ADJUD INGP/REL FEDERAL ORD/FREE 20.
PAGE 84 B1701
BIBLIOG
LEGIS
LOC/G
POL/PAR

B64
RIDDLE D.H.,THE TRUMAN COMMITTEE: A STUDY IN
CONGRESSIONAL RESPONSIBILITY. INDUS FORCES OP/RES
DOMIN ADMIN LEAD PARL/PROC WAR PRODUC SUPEGO
...BIBLIOG CONGRESS. PAGE 88 B1778
LEGIS
DELIB/GP
CONFER

B64
RIES J.C.,THE MANAGEMENT OF DEFENSE: ORGANIZATION
AND CONTROL OF THE US ARMED SERVICES. PROF/ORG
DELIB/GP EX/STRUC LEGIS GOV/REL PERS/REL CENTRAL
RATIONAL PWR...POLICY TREND GOV/COMP BIBLIOG.
PAGE 88 B1782
FORCES
ACT/RES
DECISION
CONTROL

B64
RIGGS R.E.,THE MOVEMENT FOR ADMINISTRATIVE
REORGANIZATION IN ARIZONA. USA+45 LAW POL/PAR
DELIB/GP LEGIS PROB/SOLV CONTROL RIGID/FLEX PWR
...ORG/CHARTS 20 ARIZONA DEMOCRAT REPUBLICAN.
PAGE 88 B1786
ADMIN
PROVS
CREATE
PLAN

B64
RIKER W.H.,FEDERALISM. WOR+45 WOR-45 CONSTN CHIEF
LEGIS ADMIN COLONIAL CONTROL CT/SYS PWR...BIBLIOG/A
18/20. PAGE 88 B1787
FEDERAL
NAT/G
ORD/FREE
CENTRAL

B64
ROCHE J.P.,THE CONGRESS. EX/STRUC BAL/PWR DIPLOM
DEBATE ADJUD LEAD PWR. PAGE 89 B1809
INGP/REL
LEGIS
DELIB/GP
SENIOR

B64
RUSSELL R.B.,UNITED NATIONS EXPERIENCE WITH
MILITARY FORCES: POLITICAL AND LEGAL ASPECTS. AFR
KOREA WOR+45 LEGIS PROB/SOLV ADMIN CONTROL
EFFICIENCY PEACE...POLICY INT/LAW BIBLIOG UN.
PAGE 92 B1857
FORCES
DIPLOM
SANCTION
ORD/FREE

B64
STOICOIU V.,LEGAL SOURCES AND BIBLIOGRAPHY OF
ROMANIA. COM ROMANIA LAW FINAN POL/PAR LEGIS JUDGE
ADJUD CT/SYS PARL/PROC MARXISM 20. PAGE 101 B2041
BIBLIOG/A
JURID
CONSTN
ADMIN

B64
TURNER H.A.,THE GOVERNMENT AND POLITICS OF
CALIFORNIA (2ND ED.). LAW FINAN MUNIC POL/PAR
SCHOOL EX/STRUC LEGIS LOBBY CHOOSE...CHARTS T 20
CALIFORNIA. PAGE 106 B2138
PROVS
ADMIN
LOC/G
CONSTN

B64
US SENATE COMM ON JUDICIARY,ADMINISTRATIVE
PROCEDURE ACT. USA+45 CONSTN NAT/G PROB/SOLV CONFER
GOV/REL PWR...INT 20 SENATE. PAGE 110 B2231
PARL/PROC
LEGIS
JURID
ADMIN

B64
VECCHIO G.D.,L'ETAT ET LE DROIT. ITALY CONSTN
EX/STRUC LEGIS DIPLOM CT/SYS...JURID 20 UN.
PAGE 112 B2256
NAT/G
SOVEREIGN
CONCPT
INT/LAW

B64
WEIDENBAUM M.L.,CONGRESS AND THE FEDERAL BUDGET:
FEDERAL BUDGETING AND THE RESPONSIBLE USE OF POWER.
LOC/G PLAN TAX CONGRESS. PAGE 114 B2309
LEGIS
EX/STRUC
BUDGET
ADMIN

B64
WHEARE K.C.,FEDERAL GOVERNMENT (4TH ED.). WOR+45
WOR-45 POL/PAR LEGIS BAL/PWR CT/SYS...POLICY JURID
CONCPT GOV/COMP 17/20. PAGE 116 B2331
FEDERAL
CONSTN
EX/STRUC
NAT/COMP

L64

GILBERT C.E.,,"NATIONAL POLITICAL ALIGNMENTS AND THE MUNIC
POLITICS OF LARGE CITIES." ELITES LOC/G NAT/G LEGIS CHOOSE
EXEC LEAD PLURISM GOV/COMP. PAGE 39 B0800   POL/PAR
                                                         PWR

S64

EAKIN T.C.,,"LEGISLATIVE POLITICS -- I AND II THE   PROVS
WESTERN STATES, 19581964" (SUPPLEMENT)" USA+45   LEGIS
POL/PAR SCHOOL CONTROL LOBBY CHOOSE AGE. PAGE 32   ROUTINE
B0641   STRUCT

S64

GALTUNE J.,"BALANCE OF POWER AND THE PROBLEM OF   PWR
PERCEPTION, A LOGICAL ANALYSIS." WOR+45 CONSTN   PSY
SOCIETY NAT/G DELIB/GP EX/STRUC LEGIS DOMIN ADMIN   ARMS/CONT
COERCE DRIVE ORD/FREE...POLICY CONCPT OBS TREND   WAR
GEN/LAWS. PAGE 38 B0778

S64

GROSS J.A.,"WHITEHALL AND THE COMMONWEALTH."   EX/STRUC
EUR+WWI MOD/EUR INT/ORG NAT/G CONSULT DELIB/GP   ATTIT
LEGIS DOMIN ADMIN COLONIAL ROUTINE PWR CMN/WLTH   TREND
19/20. PAGE 44 B0890

S64

LIPSET S.M.,"SOCIOLOGY AND POLITICAL SCIENCE: A   BIBLIOG/A
BIBLIOGRAPHICAL NOTE." WOR+45 ELITES LEGIS ADJUD   SOC
ADMIN ATTIT IDEA/COMP. PAGE 65 B1321   METH/COMP

S64

REDFORD E.S.,"THE PROTECTION OF THE PUBLIC INTEREST   ADMIN
WITH SPECIAL REFERENCE TO ADMINISTRATIVE   VOL/ASSN
REGULATION." POL/PAR LEGIS PRESS PARL/PROC. PAGE 87   EX/STRUC
B1758   GP/REL

S64

ROGOW A.A.,"CONGRESSIONAL GOVERNMENT: LEGISLATIVE   PWR
POWER V. DOMESTIC PROCESSES." USA+45 CHIEF DELIB/GP   DIPLOM
ADMIN GOV/REL CONGRESS. PAGE 90 B1815   LEGIS
                                                        POLICY

S64

SWEARER H.R.,"AFTER KHRUSHCHEV: WHAT NEXT." COM FUT   EX/STRUC
USSR CONSTN ELITES NAT/G POL/PAR CHIEF DELIB/GP   PWR
LEGIS DOMIN LEAD...RECORD TREND STERTYP GEN/METH
20. PAGE 102 B2058

B65

AIYAR S.P.,STUDIES IN INDIAN DEMOCRACY. INDIA   ORD/FREE
STRATA ECO/UNDEV LABOR POL/PAR LEGIS DIPLOM LOBBY   REPRESENT
REGION CHOOSE ATTIT SOCISM...ANTHOL 20. PAGE 3   ADMIN
B0067   NAT/G

B65

BOCK E.,GOVERNMENT REGULATION OF BUSINESS. USA+45   MGT
LAW EX/STRUC LEGIS EXEC ORD/FREE PWR...ANTHOL   ADMIN
CONGRESS. PAGE 13 B0261   NAT/G
                                                        CONTROL

B65

CAMPBELL G.A.,THE CIVIL SERVICE IN BRITAIN (2ND   ADMIN
ED.). UK DELIB/GP FORCES WORKER CREATE PLAN   LEGIS
...POLICY AUD/VIS 19/20 CIVIL/SERV. PAGE 18 B0370   NAT/G
                                                        FINAN

B65

CHANDA A.,FEDERALISM IN INDIA. INDIA UK ELITES   CONSTN
FINAN NAT/G POL/PAR EX/STRUC LEGIS DIPLOM TAX   CENTRAL
GOV/REL POPULISM...POLICY 20. PAGE 20 B0402   FEDERAL

B65

CHEN T.H.,THE CHINESE COMMUNIST REGIME: A   MARXISM
DOCUMENTARY STUDY (2 VOLS). CHINA/COM LAW CONSTN   POL/PAR
ELITES ECO/UNDEV LEGIS ECO/TAC ADMIN CONTROL PWR   NAT/G
...SOC 20. PAGE 20 B0417

B65

COHN H.J.,THE GOVERNMENT OF THE RHINE PALATINATE IN   PROVS
THE FIFTEENTH CENTURY. GERMANY FINAN LOC/G DELIB/GP   JURID
LEGIS CT/SYS CHOOSE CATHISM 14/15 PALATINATE.   GP/REL
PAGE 22 B0449   ADMIN

B65

COOPER F.E.,STATE ADMINISTRATIVE LAW (2 VOLS.). LAW   JURID
LEGIS PLAN TAX ADJUD CT/SYS FEDERAL PWR...CONCPT   CONSTN
20. PAGE 23 B0474   ADMIN
                                                        PROVS

B65

DE GRAZIA A.,REPUBLIC IN CRISIS: CONGRESS AGAINST   LEGIS
THE EXECUTIVE FORCE. USA+45 USA-45 SOCIETY POL/PAR   EXEC
CHIEF DOMIN ROLE ORD/FREE PWR...CONCPT MYTH BIBLIOG   GOV/REL
20 CONGRESS. PAGE 27 B0556   CONTROL

B65

FEERICK J.D.,FROM FAILING HANDS: THE STUDY OF   EX/STRUC
PRESIDENTIAL SUCCESSION. CONSTN NAT/G PROB/SOLV   CHIEF
LEAD PARL/PROC MURDER CHOOSE...NEW/IDEA BIBLIOG 20   LAW
KENNEDY/JF JOHNSON/LB PRESIDENT PRE/US/AM   LEGIS
VICE/PRES. PAGE 35 B0710

B65

FISCHER F.C.,THE GOVERNMENT OF MICHIGAN. USA+45   PROVS
NAT/G PUB/INST EX/STRUC LEGIS BUDGET GIVE EDU/PROP   LOC/G
CT/SYS CHOOSE GOV/REL...T MICHIGAN. PAGE 36 B0723   ADMIN
                                                        CONSTN

B65

FRYE R.J.,HOUSING AND URBAN RENEWAL IN ALABAMA.   MUNIC
USA+45 NEIGH LEGIS BUDGET ADJUD ADMIN PARTIC...MGT   PROB/SOLV
20 ALABAMA URBAN/RNWL. PAGE 38 B0762   PLAN
                                                        GOV/REL

B65

GOODSELL C.T.,ADMINISTRATION OF A REVOLUTION.   EXEC
PUERT/RICO ECO/UNDEV FINAN MUNIC POL/PAR PROVS   SOC
LEGIS PLAN BUDGET RECEIVE ADMIN COLONIAL LEAD 20
ROOSEVLT/F. PAGE 41 B0827

B65

HADWIGER D.F.,PRESSURES AND PROTEST. NAT/G LEGIS   AGRI
PLAN LEAD PARTIC ROUTINE ATTIT POLICY. PAGE 45   GP/REL
B0913   LOBBY
                                                        CHOOSE

B65

HAIGHT D.E.,THE PRESIDENT; ROLES AND POWERS. USA+45   CHIEF
USA-45 POL/PAR PLAN DIPLOM CHOOSE PERS/REL PWR   LEGIS
18/20 PRESIDENT CONGRESS. PAGE 45 B0915   TOP/EX
                                                        EX/STRUC

B65

KOENIG C.W.,OFFICIAL MAKERS OF PUBLIC POLICY: CHIEF
CONGRESS AND THE PRESIDENT. USA+45 USA-45 NAT/G   LEGIS
EX/STRUC PROB/SOLV PWR. PAGE 60 B1222   GOV/REL
                                                        PLURISM

B65

KOENIG L.W.,OFFICIAL MAKERS OF PUBLIC POLICY: POLICY
CONGRESS AND THE PRESIDENT. USA+45 USA-45 EX/STRUC   LEGIS
ADMIN CONTROL GOV/REL PWR 18/20 CONGRESS PRESIDENT.   CHIEF
PAGE 61 B1225   NAT/G

B65

KWEDER J.B.,THE ROLES OF THE MANAGER, MAYOR, AND   MUNIC
COUNCILMEN IN POLICYMAKING. LEGIS PERS/REL ATTIT   EXEC
ROLE PWR GP/COMP. PAGE 62 B1246   LEAD
                                                        DECISION

B65

LATHAM E.,THE GROUP BASIS OF POLITICS: A STUDY IN   LEGIS
BASING-POINT LEGISLATION. INDUS MARKET POL/PAR   GP/COMP
DELIB/GP EX/STRUC DEBATE ADJUD...CHARTS PRESIDENT.   GP/REL
PAGE 63 B1274

B65

MASTERS N.A.,COMMITTEE ASSIGNMENTS IN THE HOUSE OF   LEAD
REPRESENTATIVES (BMR). USA+45 ELITES POL/PAR   LEGIS
EX/STRUC PARTIC REPRESENT GP/REL PERS/REL ATTIT PWR   CHOOSE
...STAT CHARTS 20 HOUSE/REP. PAGE 71 B1425   DELIB/GP

B65

OLSON M. JR.,DROIT PUBLIC. FRANCE NAT/G LEGIS SUFF   CONSTN
GP/REL PRIVIL...TREND 18/20. PAGE 80 B1609   FINAN
                                                        ADMIN
                                                        ORD/FREE

B65

REDFORD D.R.,POLITICS AND GOVERNMENT IN THE UNITED   NAT/G
STATES. USA+45 USA-45 LOC/G PROVS FORCES DIPLOM   POL/PAR
CT/SYS LOBBY...JURID SUPREME/CT PRESIDENT. PAGE 87   EX/STRUC
B1751   LEGIS

B65

RHODES G.,PUBLIC SECTOR PENSIONS. UK FINAN LEGIS   ADMIN
BUDGET TAX PAY INCOME...CHARTS 20 CIVIL/SERV.   RECEIVE
PAGE 88 B1769   AGE/O
                                                        WORKER

B65

ROMASCO A.U.,THE POVERTY OF ABUNDANCE: HOOVER, THE   ECO/TAC
NATION, THE DEPRESSION. USA-45 AGRI LEGIS WORKER   ADMIN
GIVE PRESS LEAD 20 HOOVER/H. PAGE 90 B1817   NAT/G
                                                        FINAN

B65

SHARMA S.A.,PARLIAMENTARY GOVERNMENT IN INDIA.   NAT/G
INDIA FINAN LOC/G PROVS DELIB/GP PLAN ADMIN CT/SYS   CONSTN
FEDERAL...JURID 20. PAGE 96 B1936   PARL/PROC
                                                        LEGIS

B65

SMITH C.,THE OMBUDSMAN: A BIBLIOGRAPHY (PAMPHLET).   BIBLIOG
DENMARK SWEDEN USA+45 LAW LEGIS JUDGE GOV/REL   ADMIN
GP/REL...JURID 20. PAGE 98 B1980   CT/SYS
                                                        ADJUD

B65

US SENATE COMM GOVT OPERATIONS,ORGANIZATION OF   ADMIN
FEDERAL EXECUTIVE DEPARTMENTS AND AGENCIES: REPORT   EX/STRUC
OF MARCH 23, 1965. USA+45 FORCES LEGIS DIPLOM   GOV/REL
ROUTINE CIVML/REL EFFICIENCY FEDERAL...MGT STAT.   ORG/CHARTS
PAGE 110 B2217

B65

US SENATE COMM ON JUDICIARY,HEARINGS BEFORE   ROUTINE
SUBCOMMITTEE ON ADMINISTRATIVE PRACTICE AND   DELIB/GP
PROCEDURE ABOUT ADMINISTRATIVE PROCEDURE ACT 1965.   ADMIN
USA+45 LEGIS EDU/PROP ADJUD GOV/REL INGP/REL   NAT/G
EFFICIENCY...POLICY INT 20 CONGRESS. PAGE 110 B2232

B65

VIORST M.,HOSTILE ALLIES: FDR AND DE GAULLE.   TOP/EX
EUR+WWI USA-45 ELITES NAT/G VOL/ASSN FORCES LEGIS   PWR
PLAN LEGIT ADMIN COERCE PERSON...BIOG TIME/SEQ 20   WAR
ROOSEVLT/F DEGAULLE/C. PAGE 112 B2263   FRANCE

B65

WILDER B.E.,BIBLIOGRAPHY OF THE OFFICIAL   BIBLIOG
PUBLICATIONS OF KANSAS, 1854-1958. USA+45 USA-45   PROVS
ECO/DEV POL/PAR EX/STRUC LEGIS ADJUD ATTIT 19/20.   GOV/REL
PAGE 116 B2349   ADMIN

L65

SHARKANSKY I.,"FOUR AGENCIES AND AN APPROPRIATIONS   ADMIN
SUBCOMMITTEE: A COMPARATIVE STUDY OF BDUGET   EDU/PROP
STRATEGIES." USA+45 EX/STRUC TOP/EX PROB/SOLV   NAT/G

CONTROL ROUTINE CONGRESS. PAGE 96 B1934 — LEGIS

S65
AMLUND C.A.,"EXECUTIVE-LEGISLATIVE IMBALANCE: TRUMAN TO KENNEDY." USA+45 NAT/G GOV/REL PWR. PAGE 4 B0090 — LEGIS EXEC DECISION

S65
QUADE Q.L.,"THE TRUMAN ADMINISTRATION AND THE SEPARATION OF POWERS: THE CASE OF THE MARSHALL PLAN." SOCIETY INT/ORG NAT/G CONSULT DELIB/GP LEGIS PLAN ECO/TAC ROUTINE DRIVE PERCEPT RIGID/FLEX ORD/FREE PWR WEALTH...DECISION GEOG NEW/IDEA TREND 20 TRUMAN/HS. PAGE 85 B1726 — USA+45 ECO/UNDEV DIPLOM

S65
RUBINSTEIN A.Z.,"YUGOSLAVIA'S OPENING SOCIETY." COM USSR INTELL NAT/G LEGIS TOP/EX LEGIT CT/SYS RIGID/FLEX ALL/VALS SOCISM...HUM TIME/SEQ TREND 20. YUGOSLAVIA PAGE 92 B1851 — CONSTN EX/STRUC

C65
HUNTINGTON S.P.,"CONGRESSIONAL RESPONSES TO THE TWENTIETH CENTURY IN D. TRUMAN, ED. THE CONGRESS AND AMERICA'S FUTURE." USA+45 USA-45 DIPLOM SENIOR ADMIN EXEC PWR...SOC 20 CONGRESS. PAGE 53 B1067 — FUT LEAD NAT/G LEGIS

B66
ADAMS J.C.,THE GOVERNMENT OF REPUBLICAN ITALY (2ND ED.). ITALY LOC/G POL/PAR DELIB/GP LEGIS WORKER ADMIN CT/SYS FASCISM...CHARTS BIBLIOG 20 PARLIAMENT. PAGE 3 B0057 — NAT/G CHOOSE EX/STRUC CONSTN

B66
AMER ENTERPRISE INST PUB POL,CONGRESS: THE FIRST BRANCH OF GOVERNMENT. EX/STRUC FEEDBACK REPRESENT INGP/REL PWR...DECISION METH/CNCPT PREDICT. PAGE 4 B0081 — EFFICIENCY LEGIS DELIB/GP CONTROL

B66
ANDERSON S.V.,CANADIAN OMBUDSMAN PROPOSALS. CANADA LEGIS DEBATE PARL/PROC...MAJORIT JURID TIME/SEQ IDEA/COMP 20 OMBUDSMAN PARLIAMENT. PAGE 5 B0096 — NAT/G CREATE ADMIN POL/PAR

B66
CHAPMAN B.,THE PROFESSION OF GOVERNMENT: THE PUBLIC SERVICE IN EUROPE. CONSTN NAT/G POL/PAR EX/STRUC LEGIS TOP/EX PROB/SOLV DEBATE EXEC PARL/PROC PARTIC 20. PAGE 20 B0411 — BIBLIOG ADMIN EUR+WWI GOV/COMP

B66
CORNWELL E.E. JR.,THE AMERICAN PRESIDENCY: VITAL CENTER. USA+45 USA-45 POL/PAR LEGIS PROB/SOLV CONTROL PARTIC GOV/REL 18/20 PRESIDENT. PAGE 23 B0478 — CHIEF EX/STRUC NAT/G ADMIN

B66
DAVIDSON R.H.,CONGRESS IN CRISIS: POLITICS AND CONGRESSIONAL REFORM. USA+45 SOCIETY POL/PAR CONTROL LEAD ROUTINE GOV/REL ATTIT PWR...POLICY 20 CONGRESS. PAGE 26 B0535 — LEGIS PARL/PROC PROB/SOLV NAT/G

B66
FENN DH J.R.,BUSINESS DECISION MAKING AND GOVERNMENT POLICY. SERV/IND LEGIS LICENSE ADMIN CONTROL GP/REL INGP/REL 20 CASEBOOK. PAGE 35 B0711 — DECISION PLAN NAT/G LG/CO

B66
FINK M.,A SELECTIVE BIBLIOGRAPHY ON STATE CONSTITUTIONAL REVISION (PAMPHLET). USA+45 FINAN EX/STRUC LEGIS EDU/PROP ADMIN CT/SYS APPORT CHOOSE GOV/REL 20. PAGE 35 B0720 — BIBLIOG PROVS LOC/G CONSTN

B66
GERBERDING W.P.,UNITED STATES FOREIGN POLICY: PERSPECTIVES AND ANALYSIS. USA+45 LEGIS EXEC LEAD REPRESENT PWR 20. PAGE 39 B0791 — PROB/SOLV CHIEF EX/STRUC CONTROL

B66
GHOSH P.K.,THE CONSTITUTION OF INDIA: HOW IT HAS BEEN FRAMED. INDIA LOC/G DELIB/GP EX/STRUC PROB/SOLV BUDGET INT/TRADE CT/SYS CHOOSE...LING 20. PAGE 39 B0795 — CONSTN NAT/G LEGIS FEDERAL

B66
GREENE L.E.,GOVERNMENT IN TENNESSEE (2ND ED.). USA+45 DIST/IND INDUS POL/PAR EX/STRUC LEGIS PLAN BUDGET GIVE CT/SYS...MGT T 20 TENNESSEE. PAGE 43 B0866 — PROVS LOC/G CONSTN ADMIN

B66
HIDAYATULLAH M.,DEMOCRACY IN INDIA AND THE JUDICIAL PROCESS. INDIA EX/STRUC LEGIS LEAD GOV/REL ATTIT ORD/FREE...MAJORIT CONCPT 20 NEHRU/J. PAGE 50 B1007 — NAT/G CT/SYS CONSTN JURID

B66
INTERPARLIAMENTARY UNION,PARLIAMENTS: COMPARATIVE STUDY ON STRUCTURE AND FUNCTIONING OF REPRESENTATIVE INSTITUTIONS IN FIFTY-FIVE COUNTRIES. WOR+45 POL/PAR DELIB/GP BUDGET ADMIN CONTROL CHOOSE. PAGE 54 B1099 — PARL/PROC LEGIS GOV/COMP EX/STRUC

B66
JOHNSON N.,PARLIAMENT AND ADMINISTRATION: THE ESTIMATES COMMITTEE 1945-65. FUT UK NAT/G EX/STRUC PLAN BUDGET ORD/FREE...T 20 PARLIAMENT HOUSE/CMNS. PAGE 57 B1147 — LEGIS ADMIN FINAN DELIB/GP

B66
NEUMANN R.G.,THE GOVERNMENT OF THE GERMAN FEDERAL REPUBLIC. EUR+WWI GERMANY/W LOC/G EX/STRUC LEGIS — NAT/G POL/PAR

CT/SYS INGP/REL PWR...BIBLIOG 20 ADENAUER/K. PAGE 78 B1573 — DIPLOM CONSTN

B66
NIEBURG H.L.,IN THE NAME OF SCIENCE. USA+45 EX/STRUC LEGIS TEC/DEV BUDGET PAY AUTOMAT LOBBY PWR ...OBS 20. PAGE 78 B1581 — NAT/G INDUS TECHRACY

B66
RICHARD J.B.,GOVERNMENT AND POLITICS OF WYOMING. USA+45 POL/PAR EX/STRUC LEGIS CT/SYS LOBBY APPORT CHOOSE REPRESENT 20 WYOMING GOVERNOR. PAGE 88 B1773 — PROVS LOC/G ADMIN

B66
ROSS R.M.,STATE AND LOCAL GOVERNMENT AND ADMINISTRATION. USA+45 CONSTN POL/PAR EX/STRUC LEGIS BUDGET EDU/PROP CONTROL CT/SYS CHOOSE GOV/REL T. PAGE 90 B1827 — LOC/G PROVS MUNIC ADMIN

B66
SCHLESSINGER P.J.,ELEMENTS OF CALIFORNIA GOVERNMENT (2ND ED.). USA+45 LAW ADJUD ADMIN CONTROL CT/SYS EFFICIENCY...BIBLIOG T CALIFORNIA. PAGE 94 B1891 — LOC/G PROVS GOV/REL LEGIS

B66
SCHMIDT K.M.,AMERICAN STATE AND LOCAL GOVERNMENT IN ACTION. USA+45 CONSTN LOC/G POL/PAR CHIEF LEGIS PROB/SOLV ADJUD LOBBY GOV/REL...DECISION ANTHOL 20 GOVERNOR MAYOR URBAN/RNWL. PAGE 94 B1896 — PROVS ADMIN MUNIC PLAN

B66
SZLADITS C.,A BIBLIOGRAPHY ON FOREIGN AND COMPARATIVE LAW (SUPPLEMENT 1964). FINAN FAM LABOR LG/CO LEGIS JUDGE ADMIN CRIME...CRIMLGY 20. PAGE 102 B2066 — BIBLIOG/A CT/SYS INT/LAW

B66
TOTTEN G.O.,THE SOCIAL DEMOCRATIC MOVEMENT IN PREWAR JAPAN. ASIA CHIEF EX/STRUC LEGIS DOMIN LEAD ROUTINE WAR 20 CHINJAP. PAGE 105 B2122 — POL/PAR SOCISM PARTIC STRATA

B66
US SENATE COMM GOVT OPERATIONS,INTERGOVERNMENTAL PERSONNEL ACT OF 1966. USA+45 NAT/G CONSULT DELIB/GP WORKER TEC/DEV PAY AUTOMAT UTIL 20 CONGRESS. PAGE 110 B2219 — ADMIN LEGIS EFFICIENCY EDU/PROP

B66
WASHINGTON S.H.,BIBLIOGRAPHY: LABOR-MANAGEMENT RELATIONS ACT, 1947 AS AMENDED BY LABOR-MANAGEMENT REPORTING AND DISCLOSURE ACT, 1959. USA+45 CONSTN INDUS DELIB/GP LEGIS WORKER BARGAIN ECO/TAC ADJUD GP/REL NEW/LIB...JURID CONGRESS. PAGE 114 B2298 — BIBLIOG LAW LABOR MGT

B66
WILSON G.,CASES AND MATERIALS ON CONSTITUTIONAL AND ADMINISTRATIVE LAW. UK LAW NAT/G EX/STRUC LEGIS BAL/PWR BUDGET DIPLOM ADJUD CONTROL CT/SYS GOV/REL ORD/FREE 20 PARLIAMENT ENGLSH/LAW. PAGE 117 B2359 — JURID ADMIN CONSTN PWR

L66
CRAIN R.L.,"STRUCTURE AND VALUES IN LOCAL POLITICAL SYSTEMS: THE CASE OF FLUORIDATION DECISIONS." EX/STRUC LEGIS LEAD PARTIC REPRESENT PWR...DECISION GOV/COMP. PAGE 25 B0501 — MUNIC EDU/PROP LOC/G ATTIT

S66
BURDETTE F.L.,"SELECTED ARTICLES AND DOCUMENTS ON AMERICAN GOVERNMENT AND POLITICS." LAW LOC/G MUNIC NAT/G POL/PAR PROVS LEGIS BAL/PWR ADMIN EXEC REPRESENT MGT. PAGE 17 B0348 — BIBLIOG USA+45 JURID CONSTN

S66
MATTHEWS D.G.,"PRELUDE-COUP D'ETAT-MILITARY GOVERNMENT: A BIBLIOGRAPHICAL AND RESEARCH GUIDE TO NIGERIAN POL AND GOVT, JAN, 1965-66." AFR NIGER LAW CONSTN POL/PAR LEGIS CIVMIL/REL GOV/REL...STAT 20. PAGE 71 B1430 — BIBLIOG NAT/G ADMIN CHOOSE

S66
POLSBY N.W.,"BOOKS IN THE FIELD: POLITICAL SCIENCE." LAW CONSTN LOC/G NAT/G LEGIS ADJUD PWR 20 SUPREME/CT. PAGE 83 B1686 — BIBLIOG/A ATTIT ADMIN JURID

S66
SNOWISS L.M.,"CONGRESSIONAL RECRUITMENT AND REPRESENTATION." USA+45 LG/CO MUNIC POL/PAR ADMIN REGION CONGRESS CHICAGO. PAGE 98 B1990 — LEGIS REPRESENT CHOOSE LOC/G

C66
JACOB H.,"DIMENSIONS OF STATE POLITICS HEARD A. ED. STATE LEGIWLATURES IN AMERICAN POLITICS." CULTURE STRATA POL/PAR BUDGET TAX LOBBY ROUTINE GOV/REL ...TRADIT DECISION GEOG. PAGE 55 B1112 — PROVS LEGIS ROLE REPRESENT

C66
TACHERON D.G.,"THE JOB OF THE CONGRESSMAN: AN INTRODUCTION TO SERVICES IN THE US HOUSE OF REPRESENTATIVES." DELIB/GP EX/STRUC PRESS SENIOR CT/SYS LOBBY CHOOSE GOV/REL...BIBLIOG 20 CONGRESS HOUSE/REP SENATE. PAGE 102 B2068 — LEGIS PARL/PROC ADMIN POL/PAR

N66
AMERICAN SOCIETY PUBLIC ADMIN,PUBLIC ADMINISTRATION AND THE WAR ON POVERTY (PAMPHLET). USA+45 SOCIETY ECO/DEV FINAN LOC/G LEGIS CREATE EDU/PROP CONFER GOV/REL GP/REL ROLE 20 POVRTY/WAR. PAGE 4 B0089 — WEALTH NAT/G PLAN ADMIN

B67
BROWN L.N.,FRENCH ADMINISTRATIVE LAW. FRANCE UK CONSTN NAT/G LEGIS DOMIN CONTROL EXEC PARL/PROC PWR — EX/STRUC LAW

...JURID METH/COMP GEN/METH. PAGE 16 B0324   IDEA/COMP
                                                   CT/SYS
                                                        B67
FESLER J.W.,THE FIFTY STATES AND THEIR LOCAL   PROVS
GOVERNMENTS. FUT USA+45 POL/PAR LEGIS PROB/SOLV   LOC/G
ADMIN CT/SYS CHOOSE GOV/REL FEDERAL...POLICY CHARTS
20 SUPREME/CT. PAGE 35 B0715
                                                        B67
FINCHER F.,THE GOVERNMENT OF THE UNITED STATES.   NAT/G
USA+45 USA-45 POL/PAR CHIEF CT/SYS LOBBY GP/REL   EX/STRUC
INGP/REL...CONCPT CHARTS BIBLIOG T 18/20 PRESIDENT LEGIS
CONGRESS SUPREME/CT. PAGE 35 B0719   OP/RES
                                                        B67
GELLHORN W.,OMBUDSMEN AND OTHERS: CITIZENS'   NAT/COMP
PROTECTORS IN NINE COUNTRIES. WOR+45 LAW CONSTN   REPRESENT
LEGIS INSPECT ADJUD ADMIN CONTROL CT/SYS CHOOSE   INGP/REL
PERS/REL...STAT CHARTS 20. PAGE 39 B0789   PROB/SOLV
                                                        B67
HOROWITZ I.L.,THE RISE AND FALL OF PROJECT CAMELOT: NAT/G
STUDIES IN THE RELATIONSHIP BETWEEN SOCIAL SCIENCE ACADEM
AND PRACTICAL POLITICS. USA+45 WOR+45 CULTURE   ACT/RES
FORCES LEGIS EXEC CIVMIL/REL KNOWL...POLICY SOC   GP/REL
METH/CNCPT 20. PAGE 51 B1043
                                                        B67
ILLINOIS COMMISSION,IMPROVING THE STATE   PROVS
LEGISLATURE. USA+45 LAW CONSTN NAT/G PROB/SOLV   LEGIS
EDU/PROP ADMIN TASK CHOOSE INGP/REL EFFICIENCY   REPRESENT
ILLINOIS. PAGE 53 B1077   PLAN
                                                        B67
LEACH R.H.,GOVERNING THE AMERICAN NATION. FUT   NAT/G
USA+45 USA-45 CONSTN POL/PAR PLAN ADJUD EXEC CONSEN LEGIS
CONGRESS PRESIDENT. PAGE 63 B1278   PWR
                                                        B67
MENHENNET D.,PARLIAMENT IN PERSPECTIVE. UK ROUTINE LEGIS
REPRESENT ROLE PWR 20 PARLIAMENT. PAGE 73 B1467   PARL/PROC
                                                   CONCPT
                                                   POPULISM
                                                        B67
MILNE R.S.,GOVERNMENT AND POLITICS IN MALAYSIA.   NAT/G
INDONESIA MALAYSIA LOC/G EX/STRUC FORCES DIPLOM   LEGIS
GP/REL 20 SINGAPORE. PAGE 74 B1489   ADMIN
                                                        B67
RALSTON D.B.,THE ARMY OF THE REPUBLIC; THE PLACE OF FORCES
THE MILITARY IN THE POLITICAL EVOLUTION OF FRANCE NAT/G
1871-1914. FRANCE MOD/EUR EX/STRUC LEGIS TOP/EX   CIVMIL/REL
DIPLOM ADMIN WAR GP/REL ROLE...BIBLIOG 19/20.   POLICY
PAGE 86 B1730
                                                        B67
TOMA P.A.,THE POLITICS OF FOOD FOR PEACE;   FOR/AID
EXECUTIVE-LEGISLATIVE INTERACTION. USA+45 ECO/UNDEV POLICY
POL/PAR DEBATE EXEC LOBBY CHOOSE PEACE...DECISION LEGIS
CHARTS. PAGE 104 B2113   AGRI
                                                        B67
US DEPARTMENT OF THE ARMY,CIVILIAN IN PEACE,   BIBLIOG/A
SOLDIER IN WAR: A BIBLIOGRAPHIC SURVEY OF THE ARMY FORCES
AND AIR NATIONAL GUARD (PAMPHLET, NOS. 130-2).   ROLE
USA+45 USA-45 LOC/G NAT/G PROVS LEGIS PLAN ADMIN   DIPLOM
ATTIT ORD/FREE...POLICY 19/20. PAGE 108 B2185
                                                        B67
US SENATE COMM ON FOREIGN REL,HUMAN RIGHTS   LEGIS
CONVENTIONS. USA+45 LABOR VOL/ASSN DELIB/GP DOMIN ORD/FREE
ADJUD REPRESENT...INT/LAW MGT CONGRESS. PAGE 110   WORKER
B2225   LOBBY
                                                        B67
WARREN S.,THE AMERICAN PRESIDENT. POL/PAR FORCES   CHIEF
LEGIS DIPLOM ECO/TAC ADMIN EXEC PWR...ANTHOL 18/20 LEAD
ROOSEVLT/F KENNEDY/JF JOHNSON/LB TRUMAN/HS   NAT/G
WILSON/W. PAGE 114 B2297   CONSTN
                                                        L67
"A PROPOS DES INCITATIONS FINANCIERES AUX   LOC/G
GROUPEMENTS DES COMMUNES: ESSAI D'INTERPRETATION." ECO/TAC
FRANCE NAT/G LEGIS ADMIN GOV/REL CENTRAL 20. PAGE 2 APPORT
B0046   ADJUD
                                                        L67
BESCOBY I.,"A COLONIAL ADMINISTRATION* AN ANALYSIS ADMIN
OF ADMINISTRATION IN BRITISH COLUMBIA 1869-1871." CANADA
UK STRATA EX/STRUC LEGIS TASK GOV/REL EFFICIENCY   COLONIAL
ROLE...MGT CHARTS 19. PAGE 11 B0232   LEAD
                                                        L67
TRAVERS H. JR.,"AN EXAMINATION OF THE CAB'S MERGER ADJUD
POLICY." USA+45 USA-45 LAW NAT/G LEGIS PLAN ADMIN LG/CO
...DECISION 20 CONGRESS. PAGE 105 B2125   POLICY
                                                   DIST/IND
                                                        S67
ANDERSON M.,"THE FRENCH PARLIAMENT." EUR+WWI FRANCE PARL/PROC
MOD/EUR CONSTN POL/PAR CHIEF LEGIS LOBBY ATTIT ROLE LEAD
PWR 19/20. PAGE 5 B0095   GOV/COMP
                                                   EX/STRUC
                                                        S67
BRADLEY A.W.,"CONSTITUTION-MAKING IN UGANDA."   NAT/G
UGANDA LAW CHIEF DELIB/GP LEGIS ADMIN EXEC   CREATE
PARL/PROC RACE/REL ORD/FREE...GOV/COMP 20. PAGE 14 CONSTN
B0295   FEDERAL
                                                        S67
CONWAY J.E.,"MAKING RESEARCH EFFECTIVE IN   ACT/RES
LEGISLATION." LAW R+D CONSULT EX/STRUC PLAN CONFER POLICY

ADMIN LEAD ROUTINE TASK INGP/REL DECISION. PAGE 23 LEGIS
B0469   PROB/SOLV
                                                        S67
DOERN G.B.,"THE ROYAL COMMISSIONS IN THE GENERAL   R+D
POLICY PROCESS AND IN FEDERAL-PROVINCIAL   EX/STRUC
RELATIONS." CANADA CONSTN ACADEM PROVS CONSULT   GOV/REL
DELIB/GP LEGIS ACT/RES PROB/SOLV CONFER CONTROL   NAT/G
EFFICIENCY...METH/COMP 20 SENATE ROYAL/COMM.
PAGE 30 B0603
                                                        S67
FABREGA J.,"ANTECEDENTES EXTRANJEROS EN LA   CONSTN
CONSTITUCION PANAMENA." CUBA L/A+17C PANAMA URUGUAY JURID
EX/STRUC LEGIS DIPLOM ORD/FREE 19/20 COLOMB   NAT/G
MEXIC/AMER. PAGE 34 B0694   PARL/PROC
                                                        S67
LANDES W.M.,"THE EFFECT OF STATE FAIR EMPLOYMENT   DISCRIM
LAWS ON THE ECONOMIC POSITION OF NONWHITES." USA+45 LAW
PROVS SECT LEGIS ADMIN GP/REL RACE/REL...JURID   WORKER
CONCPT CHARTS HYPO/EXP NEGRO. PAGE 62 B1255
                                                        S67
LEES J.P.,"LEGISLATIVE REVIEW AND BUREAUCRATIC   SUPEGO
RESPONSIBILITY." USA+45 FINAN NAT/G DELIB/GP PLAN BUDGET
PROB/SOLV CONFER CONTROL GP/REL DEMAND...DECISION LEGIS
20 CONGRESS PRESIDENT HOUSE/REP BUREAUCRCY. PAGE 63 EXEC
B1281
                                                        S67
LINEBERRY R.L.,"REFORMISM AND PUBLIC POLICIES IN   DECISION
AMERICAN CITIES." USA+45 POL/PAR EX/STRUC LEGIS   POLICY
BUDGET TAX GP/REL...STAT CHARTS. PAGE 65 B1317   MUNIC
                                                   LOC/G
                                                        S67
PAYNE W.A.,"LOCAL GOVERNMENT STUDY COMMISSIONS: LOC/G
ORGANIZATION FOR ACTION." USA+45 LEGIS PWR...CHARTS DELIB/GP
20. PAGE 81 B1646   PROB/SOLV
                                                   ADMIN
                                                        S67
RUBIN R.I.,"THE LEGISLATIVE-EXECUTIVE RELATIONS OF LEGIS
THE UNITED STATES INFORMATION AGENCY." USA+45   EX/STRUC
EDU/PROP TASK INGP/REL EFFICIENCY ISOLAT ATTIT ROLE GP/REL
USIA CONGRESS. PAGE 91 B1850   PROF/ORG
                                                        S67
SPACKMAN A.,"THE SENATE OF TRINIDAD AND TOBAGO."   ELITES
L/A+17C TRINIDAD WEST/IND NAT/G POL/PAR DELIB/GP   EFFICIENCY
OP/RES PROB/SOLV EDU/PROP LEGIS LOBBY ROUTINE   LEGIS
REPRESENT GP/REL 20. PAGE 99 B2002   DECISION
                                                        S67
ZASLOW M.,"RECENT CONSTITUTIONAL DEVELOPMENTS IN   GOV/REL
CANADA'S NORTHERN TERRITORIES." CANADA LOC/G   REGION
DELIB/GP EX/STRUC LEGIS ADMIN ORD/FREE...TREND 20. CONSTN
PAGE 119 B2398   FEDERAL
                                                        B86
BOLINSBROKE H ST J.,A DISSERTATION UPON PARTIES   CONSERVE
(1729). UK LEGIS CHOOSE GOV/REL SOVEREIGN...TRADIT POL/PAR
18 PARLIAMENT. PAGE 13 B0269   CHIEF
                                                   EX/STRUC

LEGISLATION....SEE CONGRESS, LEGIS, SENATE, HOUSE/REP

LEGISLATIVE REFERENCE SERVICE B1282

LEGISLATIVE APPORTIONMENT....SEE APPORT

LEGISLATURES....SEE LEGIS

LEGIT....LEGITIMACY

                                                        B00
MORRIS H.C.,THE HISTORY OF COLONIZATION. WOR+45   DOMIN
WOR-45 ECO/DEV ECO/UNDEV INT/ORG ACT/RES PLAN   SOVEREIGN
ECO/TAC LEGIT ROUTINE COERCE ATTIT DRIVE ALL/VALS COLONIAL
...GEOG TREND 19. PAGE 76 B1528
                                                        B20
HALDANE R.B.,BEFORE THE WAR. MOD/EUR SOCIETY   POLICY
INT/ORG NAT/G DELIB/GP PLAN DOMIN EDU/PROP LEGIT   DIPLOM
ADMIN COERCE ATTIT DRIVE MORAL ORD/FREE PWR...SOC UK
CONCPT SELF/OBS RECORD BIOG TIME/SEQ. PAGE 45 B0921
                                                        B21
BRYCE J.,MODERN DEMOCRACIES. FUT NEW/ZEALND USA-45 NAT/G
LAW CONSTN POL/PAR PROVS VOL/ASSN EX/STRUC LEGIS   TREND
LEGIT CT/SYS EXEC KNOWL CONGRESS AUSTRAL 20.
PAGE 16 B0332
                                                        B21
STOWELL E.C.,INTERVENTION IN INTERNATIONAL LAW.   BAL/PWR
UNIV LAW SOCIETY INT/ORG ACT/RES PLAN LEGIT ROUTINE SOVEREIGN
WAR...JURID OBS GEN/LAWS 20. PAGE 101 B2050
                                                        B23
FRANK T.,A HISTORY OF ROME. MEDIT-7 INTELL SOCIETY EXEC
LOC/G NAT/G POL/PAR FORCES LEGIS DOMIN LEGIT   STRUCT
ALL/VALS...POLICY CONCPT TIME/SEQ GEN/LAWS ROM/EMP ELITES
ROM/EMP. PAGE 37 B0749
                                                        B24
POOLE D.C.,THE CONDUCT OF FOREIGN RELATIONS UNDER NAT/G
MODERN DEMOCRATIC CONDITIONS. EUR+WWI USA-45   EDU/PROP
INT/ORG PLAN LEGIT ADMIN KNOWL PWR...MAJORIT   DIPLOM
OBS/ENVIR HIST/WRIT GEN/LAWS 20. PAGE 84 B1689

B29
MOLEY R.,POLITICS AND CRIMINAL PROSECUTION. USA-45 PWR
POL/PAR EX/STRUC LEGIT CONTROL LEAD ROUTINE CHOOSE CT/SYS
INGP/REL...JURID CHARTS 20. PAGE 74 B1497 CRIME
ADJUD

B38
PETTEE G.S.,THE PROCESS OF REVOLUTION. COM FRANCE COERCE
ITALY MOD/EUR RUSSIA SPAIN WOR-45 ELITES INTELL CONCPT
SOCIETY STRATA STRUCT INT/ORG NAT/G POL/PAR ACT/RES REV
PLAN EDU/PROP LEGIT EXEC...SOC MYTH TIME/SEQ
TOT/POP 18/20. PAGE 82 B1664

B44
DAVIS H.E.,PIONEERS IN WORLD ORDER. WOR-45 CONSTN INT/ORG
ECO/TAC DOMIN EDU/PROP LEGIT ADJUD ADMIN ARMS/CONT ROUTINE
CHOOSE KNOWL ORD/FREE...POLICY JURID SOC STAT OBS
CENSUS TIME/SEQ ANTHOL LEAGUE/NAT 20. PAGE 26 B0537

L44
HAILEY,"THE FUTURE OF COLONIAL PEOPLES." WOR+45 PLAN
CONSTN CULTURE ECO/UNDEV AGRI MARKET INT/ORG NAT/G CONCPT
SECT CONSULT ECO/TAC LEGIT ADMIN NAT/LISM ALL/VALS DIPLOM
...SOC OBS TREND STERTYP CMN/WLTH LEAGUE/NAT UK
PARLIAMENT 20. PAGE 45 B0916

B45
PASTUHOV V.D.,A GUIDE TO THE PRACTICE OF INT/ORG
INTERNATIONAL CONFERENCES. WOR+45 PLAN LEGIT DELIB/GP
ORD/FREE...MGT OBS RECORD VAL/FREE ILO LEAGUE/NAT
20. PAGE 81 B1640

B47
BARNARD C.,THE FUNCTIONS OF THE EXECUTIVE. USA+45 EXEC
ELITES INTELL LEGIT ATTIT DRIVE PERSON SKILL...PSY EX/STRUC
SOC METH/CNCPT SOC/EXP GEN/METH VAL/FREE 20. PAGE 9 ROUTINE
B0187

B48
BONAPARTE M.,MYTHS OF WAR. GERMANY WOR+45 WOR-45 ROUTINE
CULTURE SOCIETY NAT/G FORCES LEGIT ATTIT ALL/VALS MYTH
...CONCPT HIST/WRIT TIME/SEQ 20 JEWS. PAGE 13 B0271 WAR

B48
HULL C.,THE MEMOIRS OF CORDELL HULL (VOLUME ONE). BIOG
USA-45 WOR-45 CONSTN FAM LOC/G NAT/G PROVS DELIB/GP DIPLOM
FORCES LEGIS TOP/EX BAL/PWR LEGIT ADMIN EXEC WAR
ATTIT ORD/FREE PWR...MAJORIT SELF/OBS TIME/SEQ
TREND NAZI 20. PAGE 52 B1062

B49
BUSH V.,MODERN ARMS AND FREE MEN. WOR-45 SOCIETY TEC/DEV
NAT/G ECO/TAC DOMIN LEGIT EXEC COERCE DETER ATTIT FORCES
DRIVE ORD/FREE PWR...CONCPT MYTH COLD/WAR 20 NUC/PWR
COLD/WAR. PAGE 18 B0361 WAR

B50
HARTLAND P.C.,BALANCE OF INTERREGIONAL PAYMENTS OF ECO/DEV
NEW ENGLAND. USA+45 TEC/DEV ECO/TAC LEGIT ROUTINE FINAN
BAL/PAY PROFIT 20 NEW/ENGLND FED/RESERV. PAGE 47 REGION
B0962 PLAN

B50
LASSWELL H.D.,NATIONAL SECURITY AND INDIVIDUAL FACE/GP
FREEDOM. USA+45 R+D NAT/G VOL/ASSN CONSULT DELIB/GP ROUTINE
LEGIT ADMIN KNOWL ORD/FREE PWR...PLURIST TOT/POP BAL/PWR
COLD/WAR 20. PAGE 63 B1268

B51
LEITES N.,THE OPERATIONAL CODE OF THE POLITBURO. DELIB/GP
COM USSR CREATE PLAN DOMIN LEGIT COERCE ALL/VALS ADMIN
...SOC CONCPT MYTH TREND CON/ANAL GEN/LAWS 20 SOCISM
LENIN/VI STALIN/J. PAGE 64 B1284

B51
SMITH L.,AMERICAN DEMOCRACY AND MILITARY POWER. FORCES
USA+45 USA-45 CONSTN STRATA NAT/G LEGIS ACT/RES STRUCT
LEGIT ADMIN EXEC GOV/REL ALL/VALS...CONCPT WAR
HIST/WRIT CONGRESS 20. PAGE 98 B1982

L51
MANGONE G.,"THE IDEA AND PRACTICE OF WORLD INT/ORG
GOVERNMENT." FUT WOR+45 WOR-45 ECO/DEV LEGIS CREATE SOCIETY
LEGIT ROUTINE ATTIT MORAL PWR WEALTH...CONCPT INT/LAW
GEN/LAWS 20. PAGE 69 B1388

B52
EGLE W.P.,ECONOMIC STABILIZATION. USA+45 SOCIETY NAT/G
FINAN MARKET PLAN ECO/TAC DOMIN EDU/PROP LEGIT EXEC ECO/DEV
WEALTH...CONCPT METH/CNCPT TREND HYPO/EXP GEN/METH CAP/ISM
TOT/POP VAL/FREE 20. PAGE 32 B0656

B53
MEYER P.,THE JEWS IN THE SOVIET SATELLITES. COM
CZECHOSLVK POLAND SOCIETY STRATA NAT/G BAL/PWR SECT
ECO/TAC EDU/PROP LEGIT ADMIN COERCE ATTIT DISPL TOTALISM
PERCEPT HEALTH PWR RESPECT WEALTH...METH/CNCPT JEWS USSR
VAL/FREE NAZI 20. PAGE 73 B1474

B54
COMBS C.H.,DECISION PROCESSES. INTELL SOCIETY MATH
DELIB/GP CREATE TEC/DEV DOMIN LEGIT EXEC CHOOSE DECISION
DRIVE RIGID/FLEX KNOWL PWR...PHIL/SCI SOC
METH/CNCPT CONT/OBS REC/INT PERS/TEST SAMP/SIZ BIOG
SOC/EXP WORK. PAGE 22 B0455

B54
MANGONE G.,A SHORT HISTORY OF INTERNATIONAL INT/ORG
ORGANIZATION. MOD/EUR USA+45 USA-45 WOR+45 WOR-45 INT/LAW
LAW LEGIS CREATE LEGIT ROUTINE RIGID/FLEX PWR
...JURID CONCPT OBS TIME/SEQ STERTYP GEN/LAWS UN
TOT/POP VAL/FREE 18/20. PAGE 69 B1389

B54
MILLARD E.L.,FREEDOM IN A FEDERAL WORLD. FUT WOR+45 INT/ORG
VOL/ASSN TOP/EX LEGIT ROUTINE FEDERAL PEACE ATTIT CREATE
DISPL ORD/FREE PWR...MAJORIT INT/LAW JURID TREND ADJUD
COLD/WAR 20. PAGE 73 B1479 BAL/PWR

L54
FURNISS E.S.,"WEAKNESSES IN FRENCH FOREIGN POLICY- NAT/G
MAKING." EUR+WWI LEGIS LEGIT EXEC ATTIT RIGID/FLEX STRUCT
ORD/FREE...SOC CONCPT METH/CNCPT OBS 20. PAGE 38 DIPLOM
B0766 FRANCE

L54
ROSTOW W.W.,"ASIAN LEADERSHIP AND FREE-WORLD ATTIT
ALLIANCE." ASIA COM USA+45 CULTURE ELITES INTELL LEGIT
NAT/G TEC/DEV ECO/TAC EDU/PROP COLONIAL PARL/PROC DIPLOM
ROUTINE COERCE DRIVE ORD/FREE MARXISM...PSY CONCPT.
PAGE 90 B1829

S54
WOLFERS A.,"COLLECTIVE SECURITY AND THE WAR IN ACT/RES
KOREA." ASIA KOREA USA+45 INT/ORG DIPLOM ROUTINE LEGIT
...GEN/LAWS UN COLD/WAR 20. PAGE 117 B2370

B55
APTER D.E.,THE GOLD COAST IN TRANSITION. FUT CONSTN AFR
CULTURE SOCIETY ECO/UNDEV FAM KIN LOC/G NAT/G SOVEREIGN
POL/PAR LEGIS TOP/EX EDU/PROP LEGIT ADMIN ATTIT
PERSON PWR...CONCPT STAT INT CENSUS TOT/POP
VAL/FREE. PAGE 6 B0120

B55
CHOWDHURI R.N.,INTERNATIONAL MANDATES AND DELIB/GP
TRUSTEESHIP SYSTEMS. WOR+45 STRUCT ECO/UNDEV PLAN
INT/ORG LEGIS DOMIN EDU/PROP LEGIT ADJUD EXEC PWR SOVEREIGN
...CONCPT TIME/SEQ UN 20. PAGE 21 B0427

B56
ABELS J.,THE TRUMAN SCANDALS. USA+45 USA-45 POL/PAR CRIME
TAX LEGIT CT/SYS CHOOSE PRIVIL MORAL WEALTH 20 ADMIN
TRUMAN/HS PRESIDENT CONGRESS. PAGE 3 B0052 CHIEF
TRIBUTE

B56
SOHN L.B.,BASIC DOCUMENTS OF THE UNITED NATIONS. DELIB/GP
WOR+45 LAW INT/ORG LEGIT EXEC ROUTINE CHOOSE PWR CONSTN
...JURID CONCPT GEN/LAWS ANTHOL UN TOT/POP OAS FAO
ILO 20. PAGE 99 B1993

B56
WEBER M.,STAATSSOZIOLOGIE. STRUCT LEGIT ADMIN SOC
PARL/PROC SUPEGO CONSERVE JURID. PAGE 114 B2305 NAT/G
POL/PAR
LEAD

L56
PARSONS T.,"SUGGESTIONS FOR A SOCIOLOGICAL APPROACH SOC
TO THE THEORY OF ORGANIZATIONS - I" (BMR)" FINAN CONCPT
EX/STRUC LEGIT ALL/VALS...POLICY DECISION 20. ADMIN
PAGE 81 B1637 STRUCT

S56
KHAMA T.,"POLITICAL CHANGE IN AFRICAN SOCIETY." AFR
CONSTN SOCIETY LOC/G NAT/G POL/PAR EX/STRUC LEGIS ELITES
LEGIT ADMIN CHOOSE REPRESENT NAT/LISM MORAL
ORD/FREE PWR...CONCPT OBS TREND GEN/METH CMN/WLTH
17/20. PAGE 59 B1201

B57
BEAL J.R.,JOHN FOSTER DULLES, A BIOGRAPHY. USA+45 BIOG
USSR WOR+45 CONSTN INT/ORG NAT/G EX/STRUC LEGIT DIPLOM
ADMIN NUC/PWR DISPL PERSON ORD/FREE PWR SKILL
...POLICY PSY OBS RECORD COLD/WAR UN 20 DULLES/JF.
PAGE 10 B0200

B57
DJILAS M.,THE NEW CLASS: AN ANALYSIS OF THE COM
COMMUNIST SYSTEM. STRATA CAP/ISM ECO/TAC DOMIN POL/PAR
EDU/PROP LEGIT EXEC COERCE ATTIT PWR MARXISM USSR
...MARXIST MGT CONCPT TIME/SEQ GEN/LAWS 20. PAGE 29 YUGOSLAVIA
B0600

B57
HUNTINGTON S.P.,THE SOLDIER AND THE STATE: THE ACT/RES
THEORY AND POLITICS OF CIVIL-MILITARY RELATIONS. FORCES
USA+45 USA-45 NAT/G PROF/ORG CONSULT DOMIN LEGIT
ROUTINE ATTIT PWR...CONCPT TIME/SEQ COLD/WAR 20.
PAGE 53 B1065

B57
LOEWENSTEIN K.,POLITICAL POWER AND THE GOVERNMENTAL PWR
PROCESS. WOR+45 WOR-45 CONSTN NAT/G POL/PAR CONCPT
EX/STRUC LEGIS TOP/EX DOMIN EDU/PROP LEGIT ADMIN
REGION CHOOSE ATTIT...JURID STERTYP GEN/LAWS 20.
PAGE 66 B1336

B57
MURRAY J.N.,THE UNITED NATIONS TRUSTEESHIP SYSTEM. INT/ORG
AFR WOR+45 CONSTN CONSULT LEGIS EDU/PROP LEGIT EXEC DELIB/GP
ROUTINE...INT TIME/SEQ SOMALI UN 20. PAGE 77 B1547

B57
SHARMA S.R.,SOME ASPECTS OF THE INDIAN EXEC
ADMINISTRATIVE SYSTEM. INDIA WOR+45 TEC/DEV BUDGET DECISION
LEGIT ROUTINE ATTIT. PAGE 96 B1937 ADMIN
INGP/REL

L57
HAAS E.B.,"REGIONAL INTEGRATION AND NATIONAL INT/ORG
POLICY." WOR+45 VOL/ASSN DELIB/GP EX/STRUC ECO/TAC ORD/FREE
DOMIN EDU/PROP LEGIT COERCE ATTIT PERCEPT KNOWL REGION
...TIME/SEQ COLD/WAR 20 UN. PAGE 45 B0908

BROWNE C.G.,THE CONCEPT OF LEADERSHIP. UNIV FACE/GP EXEC
DOMIN EDU/PROP LEGIT LEAD DRIVE PERSON PWR...MGT
SOC OBS SELF/OBS CONT/OBS INT PERS/TEST STERTYP
GEN/LAWS. PAGE 16 B0328
EXEC
CONCPT
B58

HENKIN L.,ARMS CONTROL AND INSPECTION IN AMERICAN
LAW. LAW CONSTN INT/ORG LOC/G MUNIC NAT/G PROVS
EDU/PROP LEGIT EXEC NUC/PWR KNOWL ORD/FREE...OBS
TOT/POP CONGRESS 20. PAGE 49 B0990
USA+45
JURID
ARMS/CONT
B58

SPITZ D.,DEMOCRACY AND THE CHALLANGE OF POWER. FUT
USA+45 USA-45 LAW SOCIETY STRUCT LOC/G POL/PAR
PROVS DELIB/GP EX/STRUC LEGIS TOP/EX ACT/RES CREATE
DOMIN EDU/PROP LEGIT ADJUD ADMIN ATTIT DRIVE MORAL
ORD/FREE TOT/POP. PAGE 99 B2010
NAT/G
PWR
B58

HAVILAND H.F.,"FOREIGN AID AND THE POLICY PROCESS:
1957." USA FACE/GP POL/PAR VOL/ASSN CHIEF
DELIB/GP ACT/RES LEGIT EXEC GOV/REL ATTIT DRIVE PWR
...POLICY TESTS CONGRESS 20. PAGE 48 B0971
LEGIS
PLAN
FOR/AID
L58

BLAISDELL D.C.,"PRESSURE GROUPS, FOREIGN POLICIES,
AND INTERNATIONAL POLITICS." USA+45 WOR+45 INT/ORG
PLAN DOMIN EDU/PROP LEGIT ADMIN ROUTINE CHOOSE
...DECISION MGT METH/CNCPT CON/ANAL 20. PAGE 12
B0249
PROF/ORG
PWR
S58

DAHL R.A.,"A CRITIQUE OF THE RULING ELITE MODEL."
USA+45 LOC/G MUNIC NAT/G POL/PAR PROVS DOMIN LEGIT
ADMIN...METH/CNCPT HYPO/EXP. PAGE 25 B0520
CONCPT
STERTYP
ELITES
S58

DAVENPORT J.,"ARMS AND THE WELFARE STATE." INTELL
STRUCT FORCES CREATE ECO/TAC FOR/AID DOMIN LEGIT
ADMIN WAR ORD/FREE PWR...POLICY SOC CONCPT MYTH OBS
TREND COLD/WAR TOT/POP 20. PAGE 26 B0533
USA+45
NAT/G
USSR
S58

CHINA INSTITUTE OF AMERICA.,CHINA AND THE UNITED
NATIONS. CHINA/COM FUT STRUCT EDU/PROP LEGIT ADMIN
ATTIT KNOWL ORD/FREE PWR...OBS RECORD STAND/INT
TIME/SEQ UN LEAGUE/NAT UNESCO 20. PAGE 21 B0425
ASIA
INT/ORG
B59

GOODRICH L.,THE UNITED NATIONS. WOR+45 CONSTN
STRUCT ACT/RES LEGIT COERCE KNOWL ORD/FREE PWR
...GEN/LAWS UN 20. PAGE 41 B0825
INT/ORG
ROUTINE
B59

GORDENKER L.,THE UNITED NATIONS AND THE PEACEFUL
UNIFICATION OF KOREA. ASIA LAW LOC/G CONSULT
ACT/RES DIPLOM DOMIN LEGIT ADJUD ADMIN ORD/FREE
SOVEREIGN...INT GEN/METH UN COLD/WAR 20. PAGE 41
B0829
DELIB/GP
KOREA
INT/ORG
B59

SCHURZ W.L.,AMERICAN FOREIGN AFFAIRS: A GUIDE TO
INTERNATIONAL AFFAIRS. USA+45 WOR+45 WOR-45 NAT/G
FORCES LEGIS TOP/EX PLAN EDU/PROP LEGIT ADMIN
ROUTINE ATTIT ORD/FREE PWR...SOC CONCPT STAT
SAMP/SIZ CHARTS STERTYP 20. PAGE 95 B1910
INT/ORG
SOCIETY
DIPLOM
B59

SPIRO H.J.,GOVERNMENT BY CONSTITUTIONS: THE
POLITICAL SYSTEMS OF DEMOCRACY. CANADA EUR+WWI FUT
USA+45 WOR+45 WOR-45 LEGIS TOP/EX LEGIT ADMIN
CT/SYS ORD/FREE PWR...TREND TOT/POP VAL/FREE 20.
PAGE 99 B2008
NAT/G
CONSTN
B59

HARVEY M.F.,"THE PALESTINE REFUGEE PROBLEM:
ELEMENTS OF A SOLUTION." ISLAM LAW INT/ORG DELIB/GP
TOP/EX ECO/TAC ROUTINE DRIVE HEALTH LOVE ORD/FREE
PWR WEALTH...MAJORIT FAO 20. PAGE 48 B0964
ACT/RES
LEGIT
PEACE
ISRAEL
S59

HOFFMANN S.,"IMPLEMENTATION OF INTERNATIONAL
INSTRUMENTS ON HUMAN RIGHTS." WOR+45 VOL/ASSN
DELIB/GP JUDGE EDU/PROP LEGIT ROUTINE PEACE
COLD/WAR 20. PAGE 51 B1029
INT/ORG
MORAL
S59

SOHN L.B.,"THE DEFINITION OF AGGRESSION." FUT LAW
FORCES LEGIT ADJUD ROUTINE COERCE ORD/FREE PWR
...MAJORIT JURID QUANT COLD/WAR 20. PAGE 99 B1995
INT/ORG
CT/SYS
DETER
SOVEREIGN
S59

STOESSINGER J.G.,"THE INTERNATIONAL ATOMIC ENERGY
AGENCY: THE FIRST PHASE." FUT WOR+45 NAT/G VOL/ASSN
DELIB/GP BAL/PWR LEGIT ADMIN ROUTINE PWR...OBS
CON/ANAL GEN/LAWS VAL/FREE 20 IAEA. PAGE 101 B2040
INT/ORG
ECO/DEV
FOR/AID
NUC/PWR
S59

SUTTON F.X.,"REPRESENTATION AND THE NATURE OF
POLITICAL SYSTEMS." UNIV WOR-45 CULTURE SOCIETY
STRATA INT/ORG FORCES JUDGE DOMIN LEGIT EXEC REGION
REPRESENT ATTIT ORD/FREE RESPECT...SOC HIST/WRIT
TIME/SEQ. PAGE 102 B2057
NAT/G
CONCPT
S59

LENCZOWSKI G.,OIL AND STATE IN THE MIDDLE EAST. FUT
IRAN LAW ECO/UNDEV EXTR/IND NAT/G TOP/EX PLAN
TEC/DEV ECO/TAC LEGIT ADMIN COERCE ATTIT ALL/VALS
PWR...CHARTS 20. PAGE 64 B1288
ISLAM
INDUS
NAT/LISM
B60

LINDSAY K.,EUROPEAN ASSEMBLIES: THE EXPERIMENTAL
VOL/ASSN

PERIOD 1949-1959. EUR+WWI ECO/DEV NAT/G POL/PAR
LEGIS TOP/EX ACT/RES PLAN ECO/TAC DOMIN LEGIT
ROUTINE ATTIT DRIVE ORD/FREE PWR SKILL...SOC CONCPT
TREND CHARTS GEN/LAWS VAL/FREE. PAGE 65 B1315
INT/ORG
REGION
B60

MUNRO L.,UNITED NATIONS, HOPE FOR A DIVIDED WORLD.
FUT WOR+45 CONSTN DELIB/GP CREATE TEC/DEV DIPLOM
EDU/PROP LEGIT PEACE ATTIT HEALTH ORD/FREE PWR
...CONCPT TREND UN VAL/FREE 20. PAGE 76 B1540
INT/ORG
ROUTINE
S60

HUNTINGTON S.P.,"STRATEGIC PLANNING AND THE
POLITICAL PROCESS." USA+45 NAT/G DELIB/GP LEGIS
ACT/RES ECO/TAC LEGIT ROUTINE CHOOSE RIGID/FLEX PWR
...POLICY MAJORIT MGT 20. PAGE 53 B1066
EXEC
FORCES
NUC/PWR
WAR
S60

SCHACHTER O.,"THE ENFORCEMENT OF INTERNATIONAL
JUDICIAL AND ARBITRAL DECISIONS." WOR+45 NAT/G
ECO/TAC DOMIN LEGIT ROUTINE COERCE ATTIT DRIVE
ALL/VALS PWR...METH/CNCPT TREND TOT/POP 20 UN.
PAGE 93 B1878
INT/ORG
ADJUD
INT/LAW
B61

HAMILTON A.,THE FEDERALIST. USA-45 NAT/G VOL/ASSN
LEGIS TOP/EX EDU/PROP LEGIT CHOOSE ATTIT RIGID/FLEX
ORD/FREE PWR...MAJORIT JURID CONCPT ANTHOL. PAGE 46
B0931
EX/STRUC
CONSTN
B61

MACMAHON A.W.,DELEGATION AND AUTONOMY. INDIA STRUCT
LEGIS BARGAIN BUDGET ECO/TAC LEGIT EXEC REPRESENT
GOV/REL CENTRAL DEMAND EFFICIENCY PRODUC. PAGE 68
B1373
ADMIN
PLAN
FEDERAL
B61

STONE J.,QUEST FOR SURVIVAL. WOR+45 NAT/G VOL/ASSN
LEGIT ADMIN ARMS/CONT COERCE DISPL ORD/FREE PWR
...POLICY INT/LAW JURID COLD/WAR 20. PAGE 101 B2047
INT/ORG
ADJUD
SOVEREIGN
B61

STRAUSS E.,THE RULING SERVANTS. FRANCE UK USSR
WOR+45 WOR-45 NAT/G CONSULT DELIB/GP EX/STRUC
TOP/EX DOMIN EDU/PROP LEGIT ROUTINE...MGT TIME/SEQ
STERTYP 20. PAGE 101 B2051
ADMIN
PWR
ELITES
S61

BARTLEY H.J.,"COMMAND EXPERIENCE." USA+45 EX/STRUC
FORCES LEGIT ROUTINE SKILL...POLICY OBS HYPO/EXP
GEN/LAWS 20. PAGE 9 B0191
CONCPT
TREND
S61

EVAN W.M.,"A LABORATORY EXPERIMENT ON BUREAUCRATIC
AUTHORITY" WORKER CONTROL EXEC PRODUC ATTIT PERSON
...PSY SOC CHARTS SIMUL 20 WEBER/MAX. PAGE 34 B0687
ADMIN
LEGIT
LAB/EXP
EFFICIENCY
S61

HALPERIN M.H.,"THE GAITHER COMMITTEE AND THE POLICY
PROCESS." USA+45 NAT/G TOP/EX ACT/RES LEGIT ADMIN
BAL/PAY PERCEPT...CONCPT TOT/POP 20. PAGE 46 B0928
PLAN
POLICY
NUC/PWR
DELIB/GP
S61

LIEBENOW J.G.,"LEGITIMACY OF ALIEN RELATIONSHIP:
THE NYATURU OF TANGANYIKA" (BMR)" AFR UK ADMIN LEAD
CHOOSE 20 NYATURU TANGANYIKA. PAGE 65 B1312
COLONIAL
DOMIN
LEGIT
PWR
S61

MILLER E.,"LEGAL ASPECTS OF UN ACTION IN THE
CONGO." AFR CULTURE ADMIN PEACE DRIVE RIGID/FLEX
ORD/FREE...WELF/ST JURID OBS UN CONGO 20. PAGE 73
B1480
INT/ORG
LEGIT
S61

SCHILLING W.R.,"THE H-BOMB: HOW TO DECIDE WITHOUT
ACTUALLY CHOOSING." FUT USA+45 INTELL CONSULT ADMIN
CT/SYS MORAL...JURID OBS 20 TRUMAN/HS. PAGE 93
B1888
PERSON
LEGIT
NUC/PWR
S61

BINDER L.,IRAN: POLITICAL DEVELOPMENT IN A CHANGING
SOCIETY. IRAN OP/RES REV GP/REL CENTRAL RATIONAL
PWR...PHIL/SCI NAT/COMP GEN/LAWS 20. PAGE 12 B0239
LEGIT
NAT/G
ADMIN
STRUCT
B62

HADWEN J.G.,HOW UNITED NATIONS DECISIONS ARE MADE.
WOR+45 LAW EDU/PROP LEGIT ADMIN PWR...DECISION
SELF/OBS GEN/LAWS UN 20. PAGE 45 B0912
INT/ORG
ROUTINE
B62

LAWSON R.,INTERNATIONAL REGIONAL ORGANIZATIONS.
WOR+45 NAT/G VOL/ASSN CONSULT LEGIS EDU/PROP LEGIT
ADMIN EXEC ROUTINE HEALTH PWR WEALTH...JURID EEC
COLD/WAR 20 UN. PAGE 63 B1277
INT/ORG
DELIB/GP
REGION
B62

MODELSKI G.,A THEORY OF FOREIGN POLICY. WOR+45
WOR-45 NAT/G DELIB/GP EX/STRUC TOP/EX EDU/PROP
LEGIT ROUTINE...POLICY CONCPT TOT/POP COLD/WAR 20.
PAGE 74 B1494
PLAN
PWR
DIPLOM
B62

NICHOLAS H.G.,THE UNITED NATIONS AS A POLITICAL
INSTITUTION. WOR+45 CONSTN EX/STRUC ACT/RES LEGIT
PERCEPT KNOWL PWR...CONCPT TIME/SEQ CON/ANAL
ORG/CHARTS UN 20. PAGE 78 B1580
INT/ORG
ROUTINE
B62

SCHILLING W.R.,STRATEGY, POLITICS, AND DEFENSE
BUDGETS. USA+45 R+D NAT/G CONSULT DELIB/GP FORCES
LEGIS ACT/RES PLAN BAL/PWR LEGIT EXEC NUC/PWR
ROUTINE
POLICY

RIGID/FLEX PWR...TREND COLD/WAR CONGRESS 20
EISNHWR/DD. PAGE 93 B1890
                                                          B62
THIERRY S.S.,LE VATICAN SECRET. CHRIST-17C EUR+WWI   ADMIN
MOD/EUR VATICAN NAT/G SECT DELIB/GP DOMIN LEGIT   EX/STRUC
SOVEREIGN. PAGE 104 B2096   CATHISM
                                                          DECISION
                                                          L62
BAILEY S.D.,"THE TROIKA AND THE FUTURE OF THE UN."   FUT
CONSTN CREATE LEGIT EXEC CHOOSE ORD/FREE PWR   INT/ORG
...CONCPT NEW/IDEA UN COLD/WAR 20. PAGE 8 B0163   USSR
                                                          L62
MANGIN G.,"L'ORGANIZATION JUDICIAIRE DES ETATS   AFR
D'AFRIQUE ET DE MADAGASCAR." ISLAM WOR+45 STRATA   LEGIS
STRUCT ECO/UNDEV NAT/G LEGIT EXEC...JURID TIME/SEQ   COLONIAL
TOT/POP 20 SUPREME/CT. PAGE 69 B1387   MADAGASCAR
                                                          S62
FESLER J.W.,"FRENCH FIELD ADMINISTRATION: THE   EX/STRUC
BEGINNINGS." CHRIST-17C CULTURE SOCIETY STRATA   FRANCE
NAT/G ECO/TAC DOMIN EDU/PROP LEGIT ADJUD COERCE
ATTIT ALL/VALS...TIME/SEQ CON/ANAL GEN/METH
VAL/FREE 13/15. PAGE 35 B0714
                                                          S62
HUDSON G.F.,"SOVIET FEARS OF THE WEST." COM USA+45   ATTIT
SOCIETY DELIB/GP EX/STRUC TOP/EX ACT/RES CREATE   MYTH
DOMIN EDU/PROP LEGIT ADMIN ROUTINE DRIVE PERSON   GERMANY
RIGID/FLEX PWR...RECORD TIME/SEQ TOT/POP 20   USSR
STALIN/J. PAGE 52 B1057
                                                          S62
MARTIN L.W.,"POLITICAL SETTLEMENTS AND ARMS   CONCPT
CONTROL." COM EUR+WWI GERMANY USA+45 PROVS FORCES   ARMS/CONT
TOP/EX ACT/RES CREATE DOMIN LEGIT ROUTINE COERCE
ATTIT RIGID/FLEX ORD/FREE PWR...METH/CNCPT RECORD
GEN/LAWS 20. PAGE 70 B1410
                                                          S62
MURACCIOLE L.,"LES CONSTITUTIONS DES ETATS   NAT/G
AFRICAINS D'EXPRESSION FRANCAISE: LA CONSTITUTION   CONSTN
DU 16 AVRIL 1962 DE LA REPUBLIQUE DU" AFR CHAD
CHIEF LEGIS LEGIT COLONIAL EXEC ROUTINE ORD/FREE
SOVEREIGN...SOC CONCPT 20. PAGE 76 B1541
                                                          S62
MURACCIOLE L.,"LES MODIFICATIONS DE LA CONSTITUTION NAT/G
MALGACHE." AFR WOR+45 ECO/UNDEV LEGIT EXEC ALL/VALS   STRUCT
...JURID 20. PAGE 76 B1542   SOVEREIGN
                                                          MADAGASCAR
                                                          S62
PIQUEMAL M.,"LES PROBLEMES DES UNIONS D'ETATS EN   AFR
AFRIQUE NOIRE." FRANCE SOCIETY INT/ORG NAT/G   ECO/UNDEV
DELIB/GP PLAN LEGIT ADMIN COLONIAL ROUTINE ATTIT   REGION
ORD/FREE PWR...GEOG METH/CNCPT 20. PAGE 83 B1678
                                                          S62
SPRINGER H.W.,"FEDERATION IN THE CARIBBEAN: AN   VOL/ASSN
ATTEMPT THAT FAILED." L/A+17C ECO/UNDEV INT/ORG   NAT/G
POL/PAR PROVS LEGIS CREATE PLAN LEGIT ADMIN FEDERAL   REGION
ATTIT DRIVE PERSON ORD/FREE PWR...POLICY GEOG PSY
CONCPT OBS CARIBBEAN CMN/WLTH 20. PAGE 100 B2013
                                                          B63
BOWETT D.W.,THE LAW OF INTERNATIONAL INSTITUTIONS.   INT/ORG
WOR+45 WOR-45 CONSTN DELIB/GP EX/STRUC JUDGE   ADJUD
EDU/PROP LEGIT CT/SYS EXEC ROUTINE RIGID/FLEX   DIPLOM
ORD/FREE PWR...JURID CONCPT ORG/CHARTS GEN/METH
LEAGUE/NAT OAS OEEC 20 UN. PAGE 14 B0286
                                                          B63
DEBRAY P.,LE PORTUGAL ENTRE DEUX REVOLUTIONS.   NAT/G
EUR+WWI PORTUGAL CONSTN LEGIT ADMIN ATTIT ALL/VALS   DELIB/GP
...DECISION CONCPT 20 SALAZAR/A. PAGE 28 B0567   TOP/EX
                                                          B63
FISHER S.N.,THE MILITARY IN THE MIDDLE EAST: EX/STRUC
PROBLEMS IN SOCIETY AND GOVERNMENT. ISLAM USA+45   FORCES
NAT/G DOMIN LEGIT COERCE ORD/FREE PWR...TIME/SEQ
VAL/FREE 20. PAGE 36 B0725
                                                          B63
KOGAN N.,THE POLITICS OF ITALIAN FOREIGN POLICY.   NAT/G
EUR+WWI LEGIS DOMIN LEGIT EXEC PWR RESPECT SKILL   ROUTINE
...POLICY DECISION HUM SOC METH/CNCPT OBS INT   DIPLOM
CHARTS 20. PAGE 61 B1227   ITALY
                                                          B63
LANGROD G.,THE INTERNATIONAL CIVIL SERVICE: ITS   INT/ORG
ORIGINS, ITS NATURE, ITS EVALUATION. FUT WOR+45   ADMIN
WOR-45 DELIB/GP ACT/RES DOMIN LEGIT ATTIT
RIGID/FLEX SUPEGO ALL/VALS...MGT CONCPT STAT
TIME/SEQ ILO LEAGUE/NAT VAL/FREE 20 UN. PAGE 62
B1259
                                                          B63
LEWIS J.W.,LEADERSHIP IN COMMUNIST CHINA. ASIA   POL/PAR
INTELL ECO/UNDEV LOC/G MUNIC NAT/G PROVS ECO/TAC   DOMIN
EDU/PROP LEGIT ADMIN COERCE ATTIT ORD/FREE PWR   ELITES
...INT TIME/SEQ CHARTS TOT/POP VAL/FREE. PAGE 65
B1304
                                                          B63
MAYNE R.,THE COMMUNITY OF EUROPE. UK CONSTN NAT/G   EUR+WWI
CONSULT DELIB/GP CREATE PLAN ECO/TAC LEGIT ADMIN   INT/ORG
ROUTINE ORD/FREE PWR WEALTH...CONCPT TIME/SEQ EEC   REGION
EURATOM 20. PAGE 71 B1436
                                                          B63
STEVENSON A.E.,LOOKING OUTWARD: YEARS OF CRISIS AT   INT/ORG

THE UNITED NATIONS. COM CUBA USA+45 WOR+45 SOCIETY   CONCPT
NAT/G EX/STRUC ACT/RES LEGIT COLONIAL ATTIT PERSON   ARMS/CONT
SUPEGO ALL/VALS...POLICY HUM UN COLD/WAR CONGO 20.
PAGE 100 B2034
                                                          B63
SWERDLOW I.,DEVELOPMENT ADMINISTRATION: CONCEPTS   ECO/UNDEV
AND PROBLEMS. WOR+45 CULTURE SOCIETY STRATA   ADMIN
DELIB/GP EX/STRUC ACT/RES PLAN ECO/TAC DOMIN LEGIT
ATTIT RIGID/FLEX SUPEGO HEALTH PWR...MGT CONCPT
ANTHOL VAL/FREE. PAGE 102 B2062
                                                          B63
THOMETZ C.E.,THE DECISION-MAKERS: THE POWER   ELITES
STRUCTURE OF DALLAS. USA+45 CULTURE EX/STRUC DOMIN   MUNIC
LEGIT GP/REL ATTIT OBJECTIVE...INT CHARTS GP/COMP.   PWR
PAGE 104 B2101   DECISION
                                                          L63
EMERSON R.,"POLITICAL MODERNIZATION." WOR+45   POL/PAR
CULTURE ECO/UNDEV NAT/G FORCES ECO/TAC DOMIN   ADMIN
EDU/PROP LEGIT COERCE ALL/VALS...CONCPT TIME/SEQ
VAL/FREE 20. PAGE 33 B0672
                                                          L63
FREUND G.,"ADENAUER AND THE FUTURE OF GERMANY."   NAT/G
EUR+WWI FUT GERMANY/W FORCES LEGIT ADMIN ROUTINE   BIOG
ATTIT DRIVE PERSON PWR...POLICY TIME/SEQ TREND   DIPLOM
VAL/FREE 20 ADENAUER/K. PAGE 37 B0753   GERMANY
                                                          L63
SPITZ A.A.,"DEVELOPMENT ADMINISTRATION: AN   ADMIN
ANNOTATED BIBLIOGRAPHY." WOR+45 CULTURE SOCIETY   ECO/UNDEV
STRATA DELIB/GP EX/STRUC TOP/EX ACT/RES ECO/TAC
DOMIN EDU/PROP LEGIT COERCE ATTIT ALL/VALS...MGT
VAL/FREE. PAGE 99 B2009
                                                          S63
ANTHON C.G.,"THE END OF THE ADENAUER ERA." EUR+WWI   NAT/G
GERMANY/W CONSTN EX/STRUC CREATE DIPLOM LEGIT ATTIT   TOP/EX
PERSON ALL/VALS...RECORD 20 ADENAUER/K. PAGE 6   BAL/PWR
B0113   GERMANY
                                                          S63
BACHRACH P.,"DECISIONS AND NONDECISIONS: AN   PWR
ANALYTICAL FRAMEWORK." UNIV SOCIETY CREATE LEGIT   HYPO/EXP
ADMIN EXEC COERCE...DECISION PSY CONCPT CHARTS.
PAGE 8 B0156
                                                          S63
BRZEZINSKI Z.K.,"CINCINNATUS AND THE APPARATCHIK."   POL/PAR
COM USA+45 USA-45 ELITES LOC/G NAT/G PROVS CONSULT   USSR
LEGIS DOMIN LEGIT EXEC ROUTINE CHOOSE DRIVE PWR
SKILL...CONCPT CHARTS VAL/FREE COLD/WAR 20. PAGE 16
B0334
                                                          S63
HARRIS R.L.,"A COMPARATIVE ANALYSIS OF THE   DELIB/GP
ADMINISTRATIVE SYSTEMS OF CANADA AND CEYLON."   EX/STRUC
S/ASIA CULTURE SOCIETY STRATA TOP/EX ACT/RES DOMIN   CANADA
EDU/PROP LEGIT COERCE ATTIT SUPEGO ALL/VALS...MGT   CEYLON
CHARTS GEN/LAWS VAL/FREE 20. PAGE 47 B0955
                                                          S63
MANGONE G.,"THE UNITED NATIONS AND UNITED STATES   INT/ORG
FOREIGN POLICY." USA+45 WOR+45 ECO/UNDEV NAT/G   ECO/TAC
DIPLOM LEGIT ROUTINE ATTIT DRIVE...TIME/SEQ UN   FOR/AID
COLD/WAR 20. PAGE 69 B1390
                                                          S63
MODELSKI G.,"STUDY OF ALLIANCES." WOR+45 WOR-45   VOL/ASSN
INT/ORG NAT/G FORCES LEGIT ADMIN CHOOSE ALL/VALS   CON/ANAL
PWR SKILL...INT/LAW CONCPT GEN/LAWS 20 TREATY.   DIPLOM
PAGE 74 B1495
                                                          S63
MORGENTHAU H.J.,"THE POLITICAL CONDITIONS FOR AN   INT/ORG
INTERNATIONAL POLICE FORCE." FUT WOR+45 CREATE   FORCES
LEGIT ADMIN PEACE ORD/FREE 20. PAGE 75 B1524   ARMS/CONT
                                                          DETER
                                                          S63
SCHMITT H.A.,"THE EUROPEAN COMMUNITIES." EUR+WWI   VOL/ASSN
FRANCE DELIB/GP EX/STRUC TOP/EX CREATE TEC/DEV   ECO/DEV
ECO/TAC LEGIT REGION COERCE DRIVE ALL/VALS
...METH/CNCPT EEC 20. PAGE 94 B1897
                                                          B64
GUTTSMAN W.L.,THE BRITISH POLITICAL ELITE. EUR+WWI   NAT/G
MOD/EUR STRATA FAM LABOR POL/PAR SCHOOL VOL/ASSN   SOC
DELIB/GP LEGIS LEGIT EXEC CHOOSE ATTIT ALL/VALS   UK
...STAT BIOG TIME/SEQ CHARTS VAL/FREE. PAGE 45   ELITES
B0905
                                                          B64
MERILLAT H.C.L.,LEGAL ADVISERS AND FOREIGN AFFAIRS. CONSULT
WOR+45 WOR-45 ELITES INTELL NAT/G LEGIT ADMIN   EX/STRUC
PERCEPT ALL/VALS...MGT NEW/IDEA RECORD 20. PAGE 73   DIPLOM
B1469
                                                          B64
NEUSTADT R.,PRESIDENTIAL POWER. USA+45 CONSTN NAT/G   TOP/EX
CHIEF LEGIS CREATE EDU/PROP LEGIT ADMIN EXEC COERCE   SKILL
ATTIT PERSON RIGID/FLEX PWR CONGRESS 20 PRESIDENT
TRUMAN/HS EISNHWR/DD. PAGE 78 B1575
                                                          B64
PIPES R.,THE FORMATION OF THE SOVIET UNION. EUR+WWI COM
MOD/EUR STRUCT ECO/UNDEV NAT/G LEGIS DOMIN LEGIT   USSR
CT/SYS EXEC COERCE ALL/VALS...POLICY RELATIV   RUSSIA
HIST/WRIT TIME/SEQ TOT/POP 19/20. PAGE 83 B1677
                                                          B64
PLISCHKE E.,SYSTEMS OF INTEGRATING THE   INT/ORG

INTERNATIONAL COMMUNITY. WOR+45 NAT/G VOL/ASSN
ECO/TAC LEGIT PWR WEALTH...TIME/SEQ ANTHOL UN
TOT/POP 20. PAGE 83 B1684
    EX/STRUC REGION

POTTER D.C.,GOVERNMENT IN RURAL INDIA. INDIA LEGIT
INGP/REL EFFICIENCY ATTIT 20. PAGE 84 B1695
    B64 LOC/G ADMIN TAX PROB/SOLV

SINGER M.R.,THE EMERGING ELITE: A STUDY OF
POLITICAL LEADERSHIP IN CEYLON. S/ASIA ECO/UNDEV
AGRI KIN NAT/G SECT EX/STRUC LEGIT ATTIT PWR
RESPECT...SOC STAT CHARTS 20. PAGE 97 B1967
    B64 TOP/EX STRATA NAT/LISM CEYLON

UN PUB. INFORM. ORGAN.,EVERY MAN'S UNITED NATIONS.
UNIV WOR+45 CONSTN CULTURE SOCIETY ECO/DEV
ECO/UNDEV NAT/G ACT/RES PLAN ECO/TAC INT/TRADE
EDU/PROP LEGIT PEACE ATTIT ALL/VALS...POLICY HUM
INT/LAW CONCPT CHARTS UN TOT/POP 20. PAGE 106 B2150
    B64 INT/ORG ROUTINE

WAINHOUSE D.W.,REMNANTS OF EMPIRE: THE UNITED
NATIONS AND THE END OF COLONIALISM. FUT PORTUGAL
WOR+45 NAT/G CONSULT DOMIN LEGIT ADMIN ROUTINE
ATTIT ORD/FREE...POLICY JURID RECORD INT TIME/SEQ
UN CMN/WLTH 20. PAGE 113 B2275
    B64 INT/ORG TREND COLONIAL

MACKINTOSH J.P.,"NIGERIA'S EXTERNAL AFFAIRS." UK
CULTURE ECO/UNDEV NAT/G VOL/ASSN EDU/PROP LEGIT
ADMIN ATTIT ORD/FREE PWR 20. PAGE 68 B1365
    L64 AFR DIPLOM NIGERIA

MILLIS W.,"THE DEMILITARIZED WORLD." COM USA+45
USSR WOR+45 CONSTN NAT/G EX/STRUC PLAN LEGIT ATTIT
DRIVE...CONCPT TIME/SEQ STERTYP TOT/POP COLD/WAR
20. PAGE 74 B1486
    L64 FUT INT/ORG BAL/PWR PEACE

ROTBERG R.,"THE FEDERATION MOVEMENT IN BRITISH EAST
AND CENTRAL AFRICA." AFR RHODESIA UGANDA ECO/UNDEV
NAT/G POL/PAR FORCES DOMIN LEGIT ADMIN COERCE ATTIT
...CONCPT TREND 20 TANGANYIKA. PAGE 91 B1831
    L64 VOL/ASSN PWR REGION

SYMONDS R.,"REFLECTIONS IN LOCALISATION." AFR
S/ASIA UK STRATA INT/ORG NAT/G SCHOOL EDU/PROP
LEGIT KNOWL ORD/FREE PWR RESPECT CMN/WLTH 20.
PAGE 102 B2064
    L64 ADMIN MGT COLONIAL

WORLD PEACE FOUNDATION,"INTERNATIONAL
ORGANIZATIONS: SUMMARY OF ACTIVITIES." INDIA
PAKISTAN TURKEY WOR+45 CONSTN CONSULT EX/STRUC
ECO/TAC EDU/PROP LEGIT ORD/FREE...JURID SOC UN 20
CYPRESS. PAGE 118 B2375
    L64 INT/ORG ROUTINE

CLIGNET R.,"POTENTIAL ELITES IN GHANA AND THE IVORY
COAST: A PRELIMINARY SURVEY." AFR CULTURE ELITES
STRATA KIN NAT/G SECT DOMIN EXEC ORD/FREE RESPECT
SKILL...POLICY RELATIV GP/COMP NAT/COMP 20. PAGE 21
B0438
    S64 PWR LEGIT IVORY/CST GHANA

JOHNSON K.F.,"CAUSAL FACTORS IN LATIN AMERICAN
POLITICAL INSTABILITY." CULTURE NAT/G VOL/ASSN
EX/STRUC FORCES EDU/PROP LEGIT ADMIN COERCE REV
ATTIT KNOWL PWR...STYLE RECORD CHARTS WORK 20.
PAGE 57 B1144
    S64 L/A+17C PERCEPT ELITES

KHAN M.Z.,"THE PRESIDENT OF THE GENERAL ASSEMBLY."
WOR+45 CONSTN DELIB/GP EDU/PROP LEGIT ROUTINE PWR
RESPECT SKILL...DECISION SOC BIOG TREND UN 20.
PAGE 59 B1202
    S64 INT/ORG TOP/EX

LOW D.A.,"LION RAMPANT." EUR+WWI MOD/EUR S/ASIA
ECO/UNDEV NAT/G FORCES TEC/DEV ECO/TAC LEGIT ADMIN
COLONIAL COERCE ORD/FREE RESPECT 19/20. PAGE 67
B1344
    S64 AFR DOMIN DIPLOM UK

PARSONS T.,"EVOLUTIONARY UNIVERSALS IN SOCIETY."
UNIV SOCIETY STRATA MARKET EDU/PROP LEGIT ADJUD
ADMIN ALL/VALS...JURID OBS GEN/LAWS VAL/FREE 20.
PAGE 81 B1638
    S64 SOC CONCPT

FRIEDMAN L.,SOUTHERN JUSTICE. USA+45 PUB/INST LEGIT
ADMIN CT/SYS DISCRIM...DECISION ANTHOL 20 NEGRO
SOUTH/US CIV/RIGHTS. PAGE 37 B0758
    B65 ADJUD LAW CONSTN RACE/REL

PHELPS-FETHERS I.,SOVIET INTERNATIONAL FRONT
ORGANIZATIONS* A CONCISE HANDBOOK. DIPLOM DOMIN
LEGIT ADMIN EXEC GP/REL PEACE MARXISM...TIME/SEQ
GP/COMP. PAGE 83 B1668
    B65 USSR EDU/PROP ASIA COM

VIORST M.,HOSTILE ALLIES: FDR AND DE GAULLE.
EUR+WWI USA-45 ELITES NAT/G VOL/ASSN FORCES LEGIS
PLAN LEGIT ADMIN COERCE PERSON...BIOG TIME/SEQ 20
ROOSEVLT/F DEGAULLE/C. PAGE 112 B2263
    B65 TOP/EX PWR WAR FRANCE

VONGLAHN G.,LAW AMONG NATIONS: AN INTRODUCTION TO
PUBLIC INTERNATIONAL LAW. UNIV WOR+45 LAW INT/ORG
NAT/G LEGIT EXEC RIGID/FLEX...CONCPT TIME/SEQ
    B65 CONSTN JURID INT/LAW

GEN/LAWS UN TOT/POP 20. PAGE 112 B2267

HOOK S.,"SECOND THOUGHTS ON BERKELEY" USA+45 ELITES
INTELL LEGIT ADMIN COERCE REPRESENT GP/REL INGP/REL
TOTALISM AGE/Y MARXISM 20 BERKELEY FREE/SPEE
STUDNT/PWR. PAGE 51 B1040
    L65 ACADEM ORD/FREE POLICY CREATE

RUBIN A.P.,"UNITED STATES CONTEMPORARY PRACTICE
RELATING TO INTERNATIONAL LAW." USA+45 WOR+45
CONSTN INT/ORG NAT/G DELIB/GP EX/STRUC DIPLOM DOMIN
CT/SYS ROUTINE ORD/FREE...CONCPT COLD/WAR 20.
PAGE 91 B1848
    L65 LAW LEGIT INT/LAW

CHARLESWORTH J.C.,"ALLOCATION OF RESPONSIBILITIES
AND RESOURCES AMONG THE THREE LEVELS OF
GOVERNMENT." USA+45 USA-45 ECO/DEV MUNIC PLAN LEGIT
...PLURIST MGT. PAGE 20 B0415
    S65 PROVS NAT/G LG/CO WEALTH

RUBINSTEIN A.Z.,"YUGOSLAVIA'S OPENING SOCIETY." COM
USSR INTELL NAT/G LEGIS TOP/EX LEGIT CT/SYS
RIGID/FLEX ALL/VALS SOCISM...HUM TIME/SEQ TREND 20.
PAGE 92 B1851
    S65 CONSTN EX/STRUC YUGOSLAVIA

WILLNER A.R.,THE NEOTRADITIONAL ACCOMMODATION TO
POLITICAL INDEPENDENCE* THE CASE OF INDONESIA *
RESEARCH MONOGRAPH NO. 26. CULTURE ECO/UNDEV CREATE
PROB/SOLV FOR/AID LEGIT COLONIAL EFFICIENCY
NAT/LISM ALL/VALS SOC. PAGE 117 B2355
    B66 INDONESIA CONSERVE ELITES ADMIN

BLUMBERG A.S.,CRIMINAL JUSTICE. USA+45 CLIENT LAW
LOC/G FORCES JUDGE ACT/RES LEGIT ADMIN RATIONAL
MYTH. PAGE 13 B0259
    B67 JURID CT/SYS PROF/ORG CRIME

NIEDERHOFFER A.,BEHIND THE SHIELD: THE POLICE IN
URBAN SOCIETY. USA+45 LEGIT ADJUD ROUTINE COERCE
CRIME ADJUST...INT CHARTS 20 NEWYORK/C. PAGE 78
B1582
    B67 FORCES PERSON SOCIETY ATTIT

SCHLOSSBERG S.I.,ORGANIZING AND THE LAW. USA+45
WORKER PLAN LEGIT REPRESENT GP/REL...JURID MGT 20
NLRB. PAGE 94 B1893
    B67 LABOR CONSULT BARGAIN PRIVIL

GOULD W.B.,"THE STATUS OF UNAUTHORIZED AND
'WILDCAT' STRIKES UNDER THE NATIONAL LABOR
RELATIONS ACT." USA+45 ACT/RES BARGAIN ECO/TAC
LEGIT ADJUD ADMIN GP/REL MGT. PAGE 42 B0842
    L67 ECO/DEV INDUS LABOR POLICY

BEASLEY W.G.,"POLITICS AND THE SAMURAI CLASS
STRUCTURE IN SATSUMA, 18581868." STRATA FORCES
DOMIN LEGIT ADMIN LEAD 19 CHINJAP. PAGE 10 B0202
    S67 ELITES STRUCT ATTIT PRIVIL

BURKE E.M.,"THE SEARCH FOR AUTHORITY IN PLANNING."
MUNIC NEIGH CREATE PROB/SOLV LEGIT ADMIN CONTROL
EFFICIENCY PWR...METH/COMP SIMUL 20. PAGE 17 B0352
    S67 DECISION PLAN LOC/G METH

HALL B.,"THE PAINTER'S UNION: A PARTIAL VICTORY."
USA+45 PROB/SOLV LEGIT ADMIN REPRESENT 20. PAGE 45
B0922
    S67 LABOR CHIEF CHOOSE CRIME

LEIBNITZ/G....GOTTFRIED WILHELM VON LEIBNITZ

LEISERSON A. B1283

LEISURE....UNOBLIGATED TIME EXPENDITURES

CULLINGWORTH J.B.,TOWN AND COUNTRY PLANNING IN
ENGLAND AND WALES. UK LAW SOCIETY CONSULT ACT/RES
ADMIN ROUTINE LEISURE INGP/REL ADJUST PWR...GEOG 20
OPEN/SPACE URBAN/RNWL. PAGE 25 B0512
    B64 MUNIC PLAN NAT/G PROB/SOLV

PINNICK A.W.,COUNTRY PLANNERS IN ACTION. UK FINAN
SERV/IND NAT/G CONSULT DELIB/GP PRICE CONTROL
ROUTINE LEISURE AGE/C...GEOG 20 URBAN/RNWL. PAGE 83
B1674
    B64 MUNIC PLAN INDUS ATTIT

LAMBIRI I.,SOCIAL CHANGE IN A GREEK COUNTRY TOWN.
GREECE FAM PROB/SOLV ROUTINE TASK LEISURE INGP/REL
CONSEN ORD/FREE...SOC INT QU CHARTS 20. PAGE 62
B1252
    B65 INDUS WORKER CULTURE NEIGH

NJ DIVISION STATE-REGION PLAN,UTILIZATION OF NEW
JERSEY'S DELAWARE RIVER WATERFRONT (PAMPHLET). FUT
ADMIN REGION LEISURE GOV/REL DEMAND WEALTH...CHARTS
20 NEW/JERSEY. PAGE 78 B1586
    N65 UTIL PLAN ECO/TAC PROVS

MONEYPENNY P.,"UNIVERSITY PURPOSE, DISCIPLINE, AND
DUE PROCESS." USA+45 EDU/PROP ADJUD LEISURE
ORD/FREE. PAGE 74 B1500
    S67 ACADEM AGE/Y CONTROL ADMIN

LEITES N. B1076,B1284

LEMARCHAND R. B1285

LEMAY G.H. B1286

LEMBERG E. B1287

LENCZOWSKI G. B1288

LEND/LEASE....LEND-LEASE PROGRAM(S)

LENDVAI P. B1289

LENG S.C. B1290

LENGYEL P. B1291

LENIN V.I. B1292

LENIN/VI....VLADIMIR ILYICH LENIN

B48
TOWSTER J.,POLITICAL POWER IN THE USSR: 1917-1947. EX/STRUC
USSR CONSTN CULTURE ELITES CREATE PLAN COERCE NAT/G
CENTRAL ATTIT RIGID/FLEX ORD/FREE...BIBLIOG MARXISM
SOC/INTEG 20 LENIN/VI STALIN/J. PAGE 105 B2124 PWR

B51
LEITES N.,THE OPERATIONAL CODE OF THE POLITBURO. DELIB/GP
COM USSR CREATE PLAN DOMIN LEGIT COERCE ALL/VALS ADMIN
...SOC CONCPT MYTH TREND CON/ANAL GEN/LAWS 20 SOCISM
LENIN/VI STALIN/J. PAGE 64 B1284

S55
KAUTSKY J.H.,"THE NEW STRATEGY OF INTERNATIONAL COM
COMMUNISM." ASIA CHINA/COM FUT WOR+45 WOR-45 ADMIN POL/PAR
ROUTINE PERSON MARXISM SOCISM...TREND IDEA/COMP 20 TOTALISM
LENIN/VI MAO. PAGE 59 B1184 USSR

B67
BRZEZINSKI Z.K.,THE SOVIET BLOC: UNITY AND CONFLICT NAT/G
(2ND ED., REV., ENLARGED). COM POLAND USSR INTELL DIPLOM
CHIEF EX/STRUC CONTROL EXEC GOV/REL PWR MARXISM
...TREND IDEA/COMP 20 LENIN/VI MARX/KARL STALIN/J.
PAGE 16 B0336

LEONARD A.R. B0257

LEONARD T.J. B1293

LEPAWSKY A. B1294

LERNER A.P. B1295,B1296

LERNER D. B1270,B1297,B1687

LESAGE/J....J. LESAGE

LESSLER R.S. B2308

LESTER R.A. B1298,B1299

LEVCIK B. B1300

LEVELLERS....LEVELLERS PARTY

LEVIN J. B1189

LEVIN M.R. B1301

LEVINSON D.J. B1027

LEVY H.P. B1302

LEVY L.W. B1809,B1810

LEWIN E. B1303

LEWIS J.W. B1304

LEWIS P.H. B1305

LEWIS P.R. B1306

LEWIS V.B. B0786

LEWIS W.A. B1307

LEWIS/A....ARTHUR LEWIS

LEWIS/JL....JOHN L. LEWIS

B38
SALTER J.T.,THE AMERICAN POLITICIAN. USA-45 LABOR BIOG
POL/PAR EDU/PROP ADMIN CHOOSE ATTIT DRIVE PERSON LEAD
PWR...POLICY ANTHOL 20 THOMAS/N LEWIS/JL LAGUARD/F PROVS
GOVERNOR MAYOR. PAGE 92 B1865 LOC/G

LEWY G. B1308

LEYDER J. B1309

LEYS C.T. B1310

LFNA....LEAGUE OF FREE NATIONS ASSOCIATION

LG/CO....LARGE COMPANY

N
PRINCETON U INDUSTRIAL REL SEC,SELECTED REFERENCES BIBLIOG/A
OF THE INDUSTRIAL RELATIONS SECTION OF PRINCETON, INDUS
NEW JERSEY. LG/CO NAT/G LEGIS WORKER PLAN PROB/SOLV LABOR
PAY ADMIN ROUTINE TASK GP/REL...PSY 20. PAGE 84 MGT
B1708

N
VENKATESAN S.L.,BIBLIOGRAPHY ON PUBLIC ENTERPRISES BIBLIOG/A
IN INDIA. INDIA S/ASIA FINAN LG/CO LOC/G PLAN ADMIN
BUDGET SOCISM...MGT 20. PAGE 112 B2258 ECO/UNDEV
INDUS

WORKER
PERSONNEL ADMINISTRATION: THE JOURNAL OF THE MGT
SOCIETY FOR PERSONNEL ADMINISTRATION. USA+45 INDUS ADMIN
LG/CO SML/CO...BIBLIOG/A 20. PAGE 2 B0028 EX/STRUC

N
PERSONNEL. USA+45 LAW LABOR LG/CO WORKER CREATE BIBLIOG/A
GOV/REL PERS/REL ATTIT WEALTH. PAGE 2 B0030 ADMIN
MGT
GP/REL

N
FINANCIAL INDEX. CANADA UK USA+45 ECO/DEV LG/CO BIBLIOG
ADMIN 20. PAGE 2 B0032 INDUS
FINAN
PRESS

B19
DUNN A.,SCIENTIFIC SELLING AND ADVERTISING. CLIENT LG/CO
ADMIN DEMAND EFFICIENCY 20. PAGE 31 B0632 PERCEPT
PERS/REL
TASK

N19
BUREAU OF NAT'L AFFAIRS INC.,A CURRENT LOOK AT: DISCRIM
(1) THE NEGRO AND TITLE VII, (2) SEX AND TITLE VII SEX
(PAMPHLET). LAW LG/CO SML/CO RACE/REL...POLICY SOC WORKER
STAT DEEP/QU TREND CON/ANAL CHARTS 20 NEGRO MGT
CIV/RIGHTS. PAGE 17 B0350

B38
BALDWIN R.N.,CIVIL LIBERTIES AND INDUSTRIAL LABOR
CONFLICT. USA+45 STRATA WORKER INGP/REL...MGT 20 LG/CO
ACLU CIVIL/LIB. PAGE 9 B0175 INDUS
GP/REL

B40
BURT F.A.,AMERICAN ADVERTISING AGENCIES. BARGAIN LG/CO
BUDGET LICENSE WRITING PRICE PERS/REL COST DEMAND COM/IND
...ORG/CHARTS BIBLIOG 20. PAGE 18 B0358 ADMIN
EFFICIENCY

S43
GOLDEN C.S.,"NEW PATTERNS OF DEMOCRACY." NEIGH LABOR
DELIB/GP EDU/PROP EXEC PARTIC...MGT METH/CNCPT OBS REPRESENT
TREND. PAGE 40 B0815 LG/CO
GP/REL

B45
BAKER H.,PROBLEMS OF REEMPLOYMENT AND RETRAINING OF BIBLIOG/A
MANPOWER DURING THE TRANSITION FROM WAR TO PEACE. ADJUST
USA+45 INDUS LABOR LG/CO NAT/G PLAN ADMIN PEACE WAR
...POLICY MGT 20. PAGE 8 B0167 PROB/SOLV

B45
BENJAMIN H.C.,EMPLOYMENT TESTS IN INDUSTRY AND BIBLIOG/A
BUSINESS. LG/CO WORKER ROUTINE...MGT PSY SOC METH
CLASSIF PROBABIL STAT APT/TEST KNO/TEST PERS/TEST TESTS
20. PAGE 10 B0211 INDUS

B46
DAVIES E.,NATIONAL ENTERPRISE: THE DEVELOPMENT OF ADMIN
THE PUBLIC CORPORATION. UK LG/CO EX/STRUC WORKER NAT/G
PROB/SOLV COST ATTIT SOCISM 20. PAGE 26 B0536 CONTROL
INDUS

B47
BAERWALD F.,FUNDAMENTALS OF LABOR ECONOMICS. LAW ECO/DEV
INDUS LABOR LG/CO CONTROL GP/REL INCOME TOTALSM WORKER
...MGT CHARTS GEN/LAWS BIBLIOG 20. PAGE 8 B0158 MARKET

B47
WHITEHEAD T.N.,LEADERSHIP IN A FREE SOCIETY; A INDUS
STUDY IN HUMAN RELATIONS BASED ON AN ANALYSIS OF LEAD
PRESENT-DAY INDUSTRIAL CIVILIZATION. WOR-45 STRUCT ORD/FREE
R+D LABOR LG/CO SML/CO WORKER PLAN PROB/SOLV SOCIETY
TEC/DEV DRIVE...MGT 20. PAGE 116 B2341

B49
GLOVER J.D.,THE ADMINISTRATOR. ELITES LG/CO ADMIN
EX/STRUC ACT/RES CONTROL GP/REL INGP/REL PERS/REL MGT
AUTHORIT...POLICY CONCPT HIST/WRIT. PAGE 40 B0811 ATTIT
PROF/ORG

B49
LEPAWSKY A.,ADMINISTRATION. FINAN INDUS LG/CO ADMIN
SML/CO INGP/REL PERS/REL COST EFFICIENCY OPTIMAL MGT
SKILL 20. PAGE 64 B1294 WORKER

EX/STRUC
B49
WRIGHT J.H.,PUBLIC RELATIONS IN MANAGEMENT. USA+45   MGT
USA-45 ECO/DEV LG/CO SML/CO CONSULT EXEC TASK   PLAN
PROFIT ATTIT ROLE 20. PAGE 118 B2382   EDU/PROP
                                                       PARTIC
S50
DALTON M.,"CONFLICTS BETWEEN STAFF AND LINE   MGT
MANAGERIAL OFFICERS" (BMR)" USA+45 USA-45 ELITES   ATTIT
LG/CO WORKER PROB/SOLV ADMIN EXEC EFFICIENCY PRODUC   GP/REL
...GP/COMP 20. PAGE 26 B0526   INDUS
S50
TANNENBAUM R.,"PARTICIPATION BY SUBORDINATES IN THE   PARTIC
MANAGERIAL DECISIONMAKING PROCESS" (BMR)" WOR+45   DECISION
INDUS LG/CO WORKER INGP/REL...CONCPT GEN/LAWS 20.   MGT
PAGE 103 B2074   LG/CO
C50
SIMON H.A.,"PUBLIC ADMINISTRATION." LG/CO SML/CO   MGT
PLAN DOMIN LEAD GP/REL DRIVE PERCEPT ALL/VALS   ADMIN
...POLICY BIBLIOG/A 20. PAGE 97 B1957   DECISION
EX/STRUC
B51
DIMOCK M.E.,FREE ENTERPRISE AND THE ADMINISTRATIVE   CAP/ISM
STATE. FINAN LG/CO BARGAIN BUDGET DOMIN CONTROL   ADMIN
INGP/REL EFFICIENCY 20. PAGE 29 B0595   MGT
MARKET
B51
NIELANDER W.A.,PUBLIC RELATIONS. USA+45 COM/IND   PERS/REL
LOC/G NAT/G VOL/ASSN EX/STRUC DIPLOM EDU/PROP PRESS   GP/REL
TV...METH/CNCPT T 20. PAGE 78 B1583   LG/CO
ROUTINE
B52
DONHAM W.B.,ADMINISTRATION AND BLIND SPOTS. LG/CO   ADMIN
EX/STRUC BARGAIN ADJUD ROUTINE ROLE SUPEGO 20.   TOP/EX
PAGE 30 B0605   DECISION
POLICY
B52
MILLER M.,THE JUDGES AND THE JUDGED. USA+45 LG/CO   COM/IND
ACT/RES TV ROUTINE SANCTION NAT/LISM ATTIT ORD/FREE   DISCRIM
...POLICY ACLU. PAGE 73 B1481   EDU/PROP
MARXISM
S53
GABLE R.W.,"NAM: INFLUENTIAL LOBBY OR KISS OF   LOBBY
DEATH?" (BMR)" USA+45 LAW INSPECT EDU/PROP ADMIN   LEGIS
CONTROL INGP/REL EFFICIENCY PWR 20 CONGRESS NAM   INDUS
TAFT/HART. PAGE 38 B0769   LG/CO
B54
LOCKLIN D.P.,ECONOMICS OF TRANSPORTATION (4TH ED.).   ECO/DEV
USA+45 USA-45 SEA AIR LAW FINAN LG/CO EX/STRUC   DIST/IND
ADMIN CONTROL...STAT CHARTS 19/20 RAILROAD   ECO/TAC
PUB/TRANS. PAGE 66 B1335   TEC/DEV
B55
HOROWITZ M.,INCENTIVE WAGE SYSTEMS. INDUS LG/CO   BIBLIOG/A
WORKER CONTROL GP/REL...MGT PSY 20. PAGE 51 B1044   PAY
PLAN
TASK
S55
WEISS R.S.,"A METHOD FOR THE ANALYSIS OF THE   PROF/ORG
STRUCTURE OF COMPLEX ORGANIZATIONS." WOR+45 INDUS   SOC/EXP
LG/CO NAT/G EXEC ROUTINE ORD/FREE PWR SKILL...MGT
PSY SOC NEW/IDEA STAT INT REC/INT STAND/INT CHARTS
WORK. PAGE 115 B2316
B56
BLAU P.M.,BUREAUCRACY IN MODERN SOCIETY. STRUCT   SOC
INDUS LABOR LG/CO LOC/G NAT/G FORCES EDU/PROP   EX/STRUC
ROUTINE ORD/FREE 20 BUREAUCRCY. PAGE 12 B0252   ADMIN
EFFICIENCY
B56
WHYTE W.H. JR.,THE ORGANIZATION MAN. CULTURE FINAN   ADMIN
VOL/ASSN DOMIN EDU/PROP EXEC DISPL HABITAT ROLE   LG/CO
...PERS/TEST STERTYP. PAGE 116 B2343   PERSON
CONSEN
B58
CHEEK G.,ECONOMIC AND SOCIAL IMPLICATIONS OF   BIBLIOG/A
AUTOMATION: A BIBLIOGRAPHIC REVIEW (PAMPHLET).   SOCIETY
USA+45 LG/CO WORKER CREATE PLAN CONTROL ROUTINE   INDUS
PERS/REL EFFICIENCY PRODUC...METH/COMP 20. PAGE 20   AUTOMAT
B0416
B58
REDFIELD C.E.,COMMUNICATION IN MANAGEMENT. DELIB/GP   COM/IND
EX/STRUC WRITING LEAD PERS/REL...PSY INT METH 20.   MGT
PAGE 87 B1750   LG/CO
ADMIN
L58
CYERT R.M.,"THE ROLE OF EXPECTATIONS IN BUSINESS   LG/CO
DECISION-MAKING." PROB/SOLV PRICE RIGID/FLEX.   DECISION
PAGE 25 B0516   ROUTINE
EXEC
S58
ARGYRIS C.,"SOME PROBLEMS IN CONCEPTUALIZING   FINAN
ORGANIZATIONAL CLIMATE: A CASE STUDY OF A BANK"   CONCPT
(BMR)" USA+45 EX/STRUC ADMIN PERS/REL ADJUST PERSON   LG/CO
...POLICY HYPO/EXP SIMUL 20. PAGE 6 B0129   INGP/REL
S58
HELMER O.,"THE PROSPECTS OF A UNIFIED THEORY OF   SIMUL
ORGANIZATIONS" UNIV ACT/RES ADMIN...CONCPT HYPO/EXP   LG/CO

METH. PAGE 49 B0989   METH/CNCPT
GAME
S58
MANSFIELD E.,"A STUDY OF DECISION-MAKING WITHIN THE   OP/RES
FIRM." LG/CO WORKER INGP/REL COST EFFICIENCY PRODUC   PROB/SOLV
...CHARTS 20. PAGE 69 B1395   AUTOMAT
ROUTINE
B59
FAYERWEATHER J.,THE EXECUTIVE OVERSEAS: INT/TRADE
ADMINISTRATIVE ATTITUDES AND RELATIONSHIPS IN A   TOP/EX
FOREIGN CULTURE. USA+45 WOR+45 CULTURE LG/CO SML/CO   NAT/COMP
ATTIT...MGT PERS/COMP 20 MEXIC/AMER. PAGE 35 B0709   PERS/REL
B59
HANSON A.H.,THE STRUCTURE AND CONTROL OF STATE   NAT/G
ENTERPRISES IN TURKEY. TURKEY LAW ADMIN GOV/REL   LG/CO
EFFICIENCY...CHARTS 20. PAGE 46 B0939   OWN
CONTROL
S59
SIMPSON R.L.,"VERTICAL AND HORIZONTAL COMMUNICATION   PERS/REL
IN FORMAL ORGANIZATION" USA+45 LG/CO EX/STRUC DOMIN   AUTOMAT
CONTROL TASK INGP/REL TIME 20. PAGE 97 B1963   INDUS
WORKER
S59
UDY S.H. JR.,"'BUREAUCRACY' AND 'RATIONALITY' IN   GEN/LAWS
WEBER'S ORGANIZATION THEORY: AN EMPIRICAL STUDY"   METH/CNCPT
(BMR)" UNIV STRUCT INDUS LG/CO SML/CO VOL/ASSN   ADMIN
...SOC SIMUL 20 WEBER/MAX BUREAUCRCY. PAGE 106   RATIONAL
B2144
B60
ARGYRIS C.,UNDERSTANDING ORGANIZATIONAL BEHAVIOR.   LG/CO
OP/RES FEEDBACK...MGT PSY METH/CNCPT OBS INT SIMUL   PERSON
20. PAGE 6 B0130   ADMIN
ROUTINE
B60
BOULDING K.E.,LINEAR PROGRAMMING AND THE THEORY OF   LG/CO
THE FIRM. ACT/RES PLAN...MGT MATH. PAGE 14 B0283   NEW/IDEA
COMPUTER
B60
BRISTOL L.H. JR.,DEVELOPING THE CORPORATE IMAGE.   LG/CO
USA+45 SOCIETY ECO/DEV COM/IND SCHOOL EDU/PROP   ATTIT
PRESS TV...AUD/VIS ANTHOL. PAGE 15 B0312   MGT
ECO/TAC
B60
GILMORE D.R.,DEVELOPING THE "LITTLE" ECONOMIES.   ECO/TAC
USA+45 FINAN LG/CO PROF/ORG VOL/ASSN CREATE ADMIN.   LOC/G
PAGE 40 B0801   PROVS
PLAN
B60
INDIAN INST OF PUBLIC ADMIN.STATE UNDERTAKINGS: GOV/REL
REPORT OF A CONFERENCE, DECEMBER 19-20, 1959   ADMIN
(PAMPHLET). INDIA LG/CO DELIB/GP CONFER PARL/PROC   NAT/G
EFFICIENCY OWN...MGT 20. PAGE 53 B1081   LEGIS
S60
SMIGEL E.O.,"THE IMPACT OF RECRUITMENT ON THE   LG/CO
ORGANIZATION OF THE LARGE LAW FIRM" (BMR)" USA+45   ADMIN
STRUCT CONSULT PLAN GP/REL EFFICIENCY JURID.   LAW
PAGE 98 B1979   WORKER
S60
THOMPSON J.D.,"ORGANIZATIONAL MANAGEMENT OF   PROB/SOLV
CONFLICT" (BMR)" WOR+45 STRUCT LABOR LG/CO WORKER   PERS/REL
TEC/DEV INGP/REL ATTIT GP/COMP. PAGE 104 B2103   ADMIN
MGT
C60
SCHRAMM W.,"MASS COMMUNICATIONS: A BOOK OF READINGS   COM/IND
(2ND ED.)" LG/CO PRESS ADMIN CONTROL ROUTINE ATTIT   EDU/PROP
ROLE SUPEGO...CHARTS ANTHOL BIBLIOG 20. PAGE 94   CROWD
B1902   MAJORIT
B61
AGARWAL R.C.,STATE ENTERPRISE IN INDIA. FUT INDIA   ECO/UNDEV
UK FINAN INDUS ADMIN CONTROL OWN...POLICY CHARTS   SOCISM
BIBLIOG 20 RAILROAD. PAGE 3 B0064   GOV/REL
LG/CO
B61
AMERICAN MANAGEMENT ASSN.SUPERIOR-SUBORDINATE   MGT
COMMUNICATION IN MANAGEMENT. STRATA FINAN INDUS   ACT/RES
SML/CO WORKER CONTROL EXEC ATTIT 20. PAGE 4 B0086   PERS/REL
LG/CO
B61
DUBIN R.,HUMAN RELATIONS IN ADMINISTRATION. USA+45   PERS/REL
INDUS LABOR LG/CO EX/STRUC GP/REL DRIVE PWR   MGT
...DECISION SOC CHARTS ANTHOL 20. PAGE 31 B0623   ADMIN
EXEC
B61
FRIEDMANN W.G.,JOINT INTERNATIONAL BUSINESS   ECO/UNDEV
VENTURES. ASIA ISLAM L/A+17C ECO/DEV DIST/IND FINAN   INT/TRADE
PROC/MFG FACE/GP LG/CO NAT/G VOL/ASSN CONSULT
EX/STRUC PLAN ADMIN ROUTINE WEALTH...OLD/LIB WORK
20. PAGE 37 B0760
B61
GORDON R.A.,BUSINESS LEADERSHIP IN THE LARGE   LG/CO
CORPORATION. USA+45 SOCIETY EX/STRUC ADMIN CONTROL   LEAD
ROUTINE GP/REL PWR...MGT 20. PAGE 41 B0831   DECISION
LOBBY
B61
THAYER L.O.,ADMINISTRATIVE COMMUNICATION. DELIB/GP   GP/REL
ADMIN ROUTINE PERS/REL 20. PAGE 104 B2093   PSY

LG/CO
MGT

B62

CAIRNCROSS A.K.,FACTORS IN ECONOMIC DEVELOPMENT. MARKET
WOR+45 ECO/UNDEV INDUS R+D LG/CO NAT/G EX/STRUC ECO/DEV
PLAN TEC/DEV ECO/TAC ATTIT HEALTH KNOWL PWR WEALTH
...TIME/SEQ GEN/LAWS TOT/POP VAL/FREE 20. PAGE 18
B0363

B62

CHANDLER A.D.,STRATEGY AND STRUCTURE: CHAPTERS IN LG/CO
THE HISTORY OF THE INDUSTRIAL ENTERPRISE. USA+45 PLAN
USA-45 ECO/DEV EX/STRUC ECO/TAC EXEC...DECISION 20. ADMIN
PAGE 20 B0403 FINAN

B62

DIMOCK M.E.,THE NEW AMERICAN POLITICAL ECONOMY: A FEDERAL
SYNTHESIS OF POLITICS AND ECONOMICS. USA+45 FINAN ECO/TAC
LG/CO PLAN ADMIN REGION GP/REL CENTRAL MORAL 20. NAT/G
PAGE 29 B0598 PARTIC

B62

GRANICK D.,THE EUROPEAN EXECUTIVE. BELGIUM FRANCE MGT
GERMANY/W UK INDUS LABOR LG/CO SML/CO EX/STRUC PLAN ECO/DEV
TEC/DEV CAP/ISM COST DEMAND...POLICY CHARTS 20. ECO/TAC
PAGE 42 B0852 EXEC

B62

KUHN T.E.,PUBLIC ENTERPRISES, PROJECT PLANNING AND ECO/DEV
ECONOMIC DEVELOPMENT (PAMPHLET). ECO/UNDEV FINAN ECO/TAC
PLAN ADMIN EFFICIENCY OWN...MGT STAT CHARTS ANTHOL LG/CO
20. PAGE 61 B1240 NAT/G

B62

MEANS G.C.,THE CORPORATE REVOLUTION IN AMERICA: LG/CO
ECONOMIC REALITY VS. ECONOMIC THEORY. USA+45 USA-45 MARKET
INDUS WORKER PLAN CAP/ISM ADMIN...IDEA/COMP 20. CONTROL
PAGE 72 B1459 PRICE

B62

PRAKASH O.M.,THE THEORY AND WORKING OF STATE LG/CO
CORPORATIONS: WITH SPECIAL REFERENCE TO INDIA. ECO/UNDEV
INDIA UK USA+45 TOP/EX PRICE ADMIN EFFICIENCY...MGT GOV/REL
METH/COMP 20 TVA. PAGE 84 B1698 SOCISM

B62

PRESTHUS R.,THE ORGANIZATIONAL SOCIETY. USA+45 LG/CO
STRUCT ECO/DEV ADMIN ATTIT ALL/VALS...PSY SOC 20. WORKER
PAGE 84 B1703 PERS/REL
DRIVE

S62

BERNTHAL W.F.,"VALUE PERSPECTIVES IN MANAGEMENT MGT
DECISIONS." LG/CO OP/RES SUPEGO MORAL. PAGE 11 PROB/SOLV
B0229 DECISION

S62

READ W.H.,"UPWARD COMMUNICATION IN INDUSTRIAL ADMIN
HIERARCHIES." LG/CO TOP/EX PROB/SOLV DOMIN EXEC INGP/REL
PERS/REL ATTIT DRIVE PERCEPT...CORREL STAT CHARTS PSY
20. PAGE 86 B1747 MGT

B63

GANGULY D.S.,PUBLIC CORPORATIONS IN A NATIONAL ECO/UNDEV
ECONOMY. INDIA WOR+45 FINAN INDUS TOP/EX PRICE LG/CO
EFFICIENCY...MGT STAT CHARTS BIBLIOG 20. PAGE 38 SOCISM
B0779 GOV/REL

B63

HARGROVE M.M.,BUSINESS POLICY CASES-WITH BEHAVIORAL SOC/EXP
SCIENCE IMPLICATIONS. LG/CO SML/CO EX/STRUC TOP/EX INDUS
PLAN PROB/SOLV CONFER ADMIN CONTROL ROUTINE DECISION
EFFICIENCY. PAGE 47 B0946 MGT

B63

HOUGHTELING J.L. JR.,THE LEGAL ENVIRONMENT OF LAW
BUSINESS. LG/CO NAT/G CONSULT AGREE CONTROL MGT
...DICTIONARY T 20. PAGE 52 B1047 ADJUD
JURID

B63

KORNHAUSER W.,SCIENTISTS IN INDUSTRY: CONFLICT AND CREATE
ACCOMMODATION. USA+45 R+D LG/CO NAT/G TEC/DEV INDUS
CONTROL ADJUST ATTIT...MGT STAT INT BIBLIOG 20. PROF/ORG
PAGE 61 B1229 GP/REL

B63

PATRA A.C.,THE ADMINISTRATION OF JUSTICE UNDER THE ADMIN
EAST INDIA COMPANY IN BENGAL, BIHAR AND ORISSA. JURID
INDIA UK LG/CO CAP/ISM INT/TRADE ADJUD COLONIAL CONCPT
CONTROL CT/SYS...POLICY 20. PAGE 81 B1641

B63

RAUDSEPP E.,MANAGING CREATIVE SCIENTISTS AND MGT
ENGINEERS. USA+45 ECO/DEV LG/CO GP/REL PERS/REL CREATE
PRODUC. PAGE 86 B1742 R+D
ECO/TAC

B63

SINGH M.M.,MUNICIPAL GOVERNMENT IN THE CALCUTTA LOC/G
METROPOLITAN DISTRICT A PRELIMINARY SURVEY. FINAN HEALTH
LG/CO DELIB/GP BUDGET TAX ADMIN GP/REL 20 CALCUTTA. MUNIC
PAGE 97 B1969 JURID

B63

THORELLI H.B.,INTOP: INTERNATIONAL OPERATIONS GAME
SIMULATION: PLAYER'S MANUAL. BRAZIL FINAN OP/RES INT/TRADE
ADMIN GP/REL INGP/REL PRODUC PERCEPT...DECISION MGT EDU/PROP
EEC. PAGE 104 B2108 LG/CO

B63

US SENATE COMM ON JUDICIARY,ADMINISTERED PRICES. LG/CO
USA+45 RATION ADJUD CONTROL LOBBY...POLICY 20 PRICE
SENATE MONOPOLY. PAGE 110 B2229 ADMIN

DECISION

B64

CHANDLER A.D. JR.,GIANT ENTERPRISE: FORD, GENERAL LG/CO
MOTORS, AND THE AUTOMOBILE INDUSTRY; SOURCES AND DIST/IND
READINGS. USA+45 USA-45 FINAN MARKET CREATE ADMIN LABOR
...TIME/SEQ ANTHOL 20 AUTOMOBILE. PAGE 20 B0404 MGT

B64

FLORENCE P.S.,ECONOMICS AND SOCIOLOGY OF INDUSTRY; INDUS
A REALISTIC ANALYSIS OF DEVELOPMENT. ECO/UNDEV SOC
LG/CO NAT/G PLAN...GEOG MGT BIBLIOG 20. PAGE 36 ADMIN
B0729

B64

GROSS B.M.,THE MANAGING OF ORGANIZATIONS (VOL. I). ECO/TAC
USA+45 ECO/DEV LG/CO CAP/ISM EFFICIENCY ROLE...MGT ADMIN
20. PAGE 44 B0886 INDUS
POLICY

B64

MARRIS R.,THE ECONOMIC THEORY OF "MANAGERIAL" CAP/ISM
CAPITALISM. USA+45 ECO/DEV LG/CO ECO/TAC DEMAND MGT
...CHARTS BIBLIOG 20. PAGE 69 B1402 CONTROL
OP/RES

B64

MCNULTY J.E.,SOME ECONOMIC ASPECTS OF BUSINESS ADMIN
ORGANIZATION. ECO/DEV UTIL...MGT CHARTS BIBLIOG LG/CO
METH 20. PAGE 72 B1458 GEN/LAWS

B64

ORTH C.D.,ADMINISTERING RESEARCH AND DEVELOPMENT. MGT
FINAN PLAN PROB/SOLV ADMIN ROUTINE...METH/CNCPT R+D
STAT CHARTS METH 20. PAGE 80 B1616 LG/CO
INDUS

B64

SAYLES L.R.,MANAGERIAL BEHAVIOR: ADMINISTRATION IN CONCPT
COMPLEX ORGANIZATIONS. INDUS LG/CO PROB/SOLV ADMIN
CONTROL EXEC INGP/REL PERS/REL SKILL...MGT OBS TOP/EX
PREDICT GEN/LAWS 20. PAGE 93 B1874 EX/STRUC

B65

GOLEMBIEWSKI R.T.,MEN, MANAGEMENT, AND MORALITY; LG/CO
TOWARD A NEW ORGANIZATIONAL ETHIC. CONSTN EX/STRUC MGT
CREATE ADMIN CONTROL INGP/REL PERSON SUPEGO MORAL PROB/SOLV
PWR...GOV/COMP METH/COMP 20 BUREAUCRCY. PAGE 40
B0819

B65

GT BRIT ADMIN STAFF COLLEGE,THE ACCOUNTABILITY OF LG/CO
PUBLIC CORPORATIONS (REV. ED.). UK ECO/DEV FINAN NAT/G
DELIB/GP EX/STRUC BUDGET CAP/ISM CONFER PRICE ADMIN
PARL/PROC 20. PAGE 44 B0899 CONTROL

B65

HODGSON R.C.,THE EXECUTIVE ROLE CONSTELLATION: AN LG/CO
ANALYSIS OF PERSONALITY AND ROLE RELATIONS IN ADMIN
MANAGEMENT. USA+45 PUB/INST EXEC PERS/REL PERSON TOP/EX
...PSY PERS/COMP HYPO/EXP 20. PAGE 51 B1027 ROLE

B65

PRESTHUS R.,BEHAVIORAL APPROACHES TO PUBLIC GEN/METH
ADMINISTRATION. UK STRATA LG/CO PUB/INST VOL/ASSN DECISION
EX/STRUC TOP/EX EFFICIENCY HEALTH. PAGE 84 B1704 ADMIN
R+D

B65

STARR M.K.,EXECUTIVE READINGS IN MANAGEMENT MGT
SCIENCE. TOP/EX WORKER EDU/PROP ADMIN...DECISION EX/STRUC
GEN/LAWS ANTHOL METH T 20. PAGE 100 B2023 PLAN
LG/CO

B65

STEINER G.A.,THE CREATIVE ORGANIZATION. ELITES CREATE
LG/CO PLAN PROB/SOLV TEC/DEV INSPECT CAP/ISM MGT
CONTROL EXEC PERSON...METH/COMP HYPO/EXP 20. ADMIN
PAGE 100 B2029 SOC

S65

CHARLESWORTH J.C.,"ALLOCATION OF RESPONSIBILITIES PROVS
AND RESOURCES AMONG THE THREE LEVELS OF NAT/G
GOVERNMENT." USA+45 USA-45 ECO/DEV MUNIC PLAN LEGIT LG/CO
...PLURIST MGT. PAGE 20 B0415 WEALTH

B66

BIRKHEAD G.S.,ADMINISTRATIVE PROBLEMS IN PAKISTAN. ADMIN
PAKISTAN AGRI FINAN INDUS LG/CO ECO/TAC CONTROL PWR NAT/G
...CHARTS ANTHOL 20. PAGE 12 B0241 ORD/FREE
ECO/UNDEV

B66

COOK P.W. JR.,PROBLEMS OF CORPORATE POWER. WOR+45 ADMIN
FINAN INDUS BARGAIN GP/REL...MGT ANTHOL. PAGE 23 LG/CO
B0471 PWR
ECO/TAC

B66

FENN DH J.R.,BUSINESS DECISION MAKING AND DECISION
GOVERNMENT POLICY. SERV/IND LEGIS LICENSE ADMIN PLAN
CONTROL GP/REL INGP/REL 20 CASEBOOK. PAGE 35 B0711 NAT/G
LG/CO

B66

RAPHAEL J.S.,GOVERNMENTAL REGULATION OF BUSINESS. LG/CO
USA+45 LAW CONSTN TAX ADJUD ADMIN EFFICIENCY PWR GOV/REL
20. PAGE 86 B1736 CONTROL
ECO/DEV

B66

REDFORD E.S.,THE ROLE OF GOVERNMENT IN THE AMERICAN NAT/G
ECONOMY. USA+45 USA-45 FINAN INDUS LG/CO PROB/SOLV ECO/DEV
ADMIN INGP/REL INCOME PRODUC 18/20. PAGE 87 B1759 CAP/ISM
ECO/TAC

SZLADITS C.,A BIBLIOGRAPHY ON FOREIGN AND
COMPARATIVE LAW (SUPPLEMENT 1964). FINAN FAM LABOR
LG/CO LEGIS JUDGE ADMIN CRIME...CRIMLGY 20.
PAGE 102 B2066
B66 BIBLIOG/A CT/SYS INT/LAW

SNOWISS L.M.,"CONGRESSIONAL RECRUITMENT AND
REPRESENTATION." USA+45 LG/CO MUNIC POL/PAR ADMIN
REGION CONGRESS CHICAGO. PAGE 98 B1990
S66 LEGIS REPRESENT CHOOSE LOC/G

SHERMAN H.,"IT ALL DEPENDS." USA+45 FINAN MARKET
PLAN PROB/SOLV EXEC PARTIC INGP/REL SUPEGO
...DECISION BIBLIOG 20. PAGE 96 B1944
C66 LG/CO MGT ADMIN POLICY

ANGEL D.D.,ROMNEY. LABOR LG/CO NAT/G EXEC WAR
RACE/REL PERSON ORD/FREE...MGT WORSHIP 20
ROMNEY/GEO CIV/RIGHTS MORMON GOVERNOR. PAGE 5 B0108
B67 BIOG CHIEF PROVS POLICY

BUDER S.,PULLMAN: AN EXPERIMENT IN INDUSTRIAL ORDER
AND COMMUNITY PLANNING, 1880-1930. USA-45 SOCIETY
LABOR LG/CO CREATE PROB/SOLV CONTROL GP/REL
EFFICIENCY ATTIT...MGT BIBLIOG 19/20 PULLMAN.
PAGE 17 B0337
B67 DIST/IND INDUS MUNIC PLAN

GABRIEL P.P.,THE INTERNATIONAL TRANSFER OF
CORPORATE SKILLS: MANAGEMENT CONTRACTS IN LESS
DEVELOPED COUNTRIES. CLIENT INDUS LG/CO PLAN
PROB/SOLV CAP/ISM ECO/TAC FOR/AID INT/TRADE RENT
ADMIN SKILL 20. PAGE 38 B0771
B67 ECO/UNDEV AGREE MGT CONSULT

NARVER J.C.,CONGLOMERATE MERGERS AND MARKET
COMPETITION. USA+45 LAW STRUCT ADMIN LEAD RISK COST
PROFIT WEALTH...POLICY CHARTS BIBLIOG. PAGE 77
B1555
B67 DEMAND LG/CO MARKET MGT

UNIVERSAL REFERENCE SYSTEM,ADMINISTRATIVE
MANAGEMENT: PUBLIC AND PRIVATE BUREAUCRACY (VOLUME
IV). WOR+45 WOR-45 ECO/DEV LG/CO LOC/G PUB/INST
VOL/ASSN GOV/REL...COMPUT/IR GEN/METH. PAGE 107
B2164
B67 BIBLIOG/A MGT ADMIN NAT/G

ZELERMYER W.,BUSINESS LAW: NEW PERSPECTIVES IN
BUSINESS ECONOMICS. USA+45 LAW INDUS DELIB/GP
...JURID MGT ANTHOL BIBLIOG 20 NLRB. PAGE 119 B2400
B67 LABOR CAP/ISM LG/CO

TRAVERS H. JR.,"AN EXAMINATION OF THE CAB'S MERGER
POLICY." USA+45 USA-45 LAW NAT/G LEGIS PLAN ADMIN
...DECISION 20 CONGRESS. PAGE 105 B2125
L67 ADJUD LG/CO POLICY DIST/IND

ALPANDER G.G.,"ENTREPRENEURS AND PRIVATE ENTERPRISE
IN TURKEY." TURKEY INDUS PROC/MFG EDU/PROP ATTIT
DRIVE WEALTH...GEOG MGT SOC STAT TREND CHARTS 20.
PAGE 4 B0080
S67 ECO/UNDEV LG/CO NAT/G POLICY

HILL F.G.,"VEBLEN, BERLE AND THE MODERN
CORPORATION." FINAN ECO/TAC CONTROL OWN...MGT 20.
PAGE 50 B1010
S67 LG/CO ROLE INDUS ECO/DEV

LERNER A.P.,"EMPLOYMENT THEORY AND EMPLOYMENT
POLICY." ECO/DEV INDUS LABOR LG/CO BUDGET ADMIN
DEMAND PROFIT WEALTH LAISSEZ METH/COMP. PAGE 64
B1296
S67 CAP/ISM WORKER CONCPT

MORTON J.A.,"A SYSTEMS APPROACH TO THE INNOVATION
PROCESS: ITS USE IN THE BELL SYSTEM." USA+45 INTELL
INDUS LG/CO CONSULT WORKER COMPUTER AUTOMAT DEMAND
...MGT CHARTS 20. PAGE 76 B1531
S67 TEC/DEV GEN/METH R+D COM/IND

ROSE A.M.,"CONFIDENCE AND THE CORPORATION." LG/CO
CONTROL CRIME INCOME PROFIT 20. PAGE 90 B1818
S67 INDUS EX/STRUC VOL/ASSN RESPECT

GRAM H.A.,"BUSINESS ETHICS AND THE CORPORATION."
LG/CO SECT PROB/SOLV CONTROL EXEC GP/REL INGP/REL
PERS/REL ROLE MORAL PWR...DECISION 20. PAGE 42
B0850
S68 POLICY ADMIN MGT

LI C.M. B1311

LIB/INTRNT....LIBERAL INTERNATIONAL

LIB/PARTY....LIBERAL PARTY (ALL NATIONS)

FYFE H.,THE BRITISH LIBERAL PARTY. UK SECT ADMIN
LEAD CHOOSE GP/REL PWR SOCISM...MAJORIT TIME/SEQ
19/20 LIB/PARTY CONSRV/PAR. PAGE 38 B0768
B28 POL/PAR NAT/G REPRESENT POPULISM

LIBERALISM....SEE NEW/LIB, WELF/ST, OLD/LIB, LAISSEZ

LIBERIA....SEE ALSO AFR

LIBERTY....SEE ORD/FREE

LIBRARY....SEE OLD/STOR

LIBYA....SEE ALSO ISLAM

LICENSE....LEGAL PERMIT

BURT F.A.,AMERICAN ADVERTISING AGENCIES. BARGAIN
BUDGET LICENSE WRITING PRICE PERS/REL COST DEMAND
...ORG/CHARTS BIBLIOG 20. PAGE 18 B0358
B40 LG/CO COM/IND ADMIN EFFICIENCY

PALMER A.M.,ADMINISTRATION OF MEDICAL AND
PHARMACEUTICAL PATENTS (PAMPHLET). USA+45 PROF/ORG
ADMIN PHIL/SCI. PAGE 80 B1626
B55 HEAL ACADEM LAW LICENSE

BURRUS B.R.,ADMINSTRATIVE LAW AND LOCAL GOVERNMENT.
USA+45 PROVS LEGIS LICENSE ADJUD ORD/FREE 20.
PAGE 17 B0356
B63 EX/STRUC LOC/G JURID CONSTN

SZLADITS C.,BIBLIOGRAPHY ON FOREIGN AND COMPARATIVE
LAW: BOOKS AND ARTICLES IN ENGLISH (SUPPLEMENT
1962). FINAN INDUS JUDGE LICENSE ADMIN CT/SYS
PARL/PROC OWN...INT/LAW CLASSIF METH/COMP NAT/COMP
20. PAGE 102 B2065
B64 BIBLIOG/A JURID ADJUD LAW

FENN DH J.R.,BUSINESS DECISION MAKING AND
GOVERNMENT POLICY. SERV/IND LEGIS LICENSE ADMIN
CONTROL GP/REL INGP/REL 20 CASEBOOK. PAGE 35 B0711
B66 DECISION PLAN NAT/G LG/CO

LIEBENOW J.G. B1312

LIECHTENST....LIECHTENSTEIN; SEE ALSO APPROPRIATE
    TIME/SPACE/CULTURE INDEX

LIGHTFT/PM....PHIL M. LIGHTFOOT

LIKERT/R....RENSIS LIKERT

LIN/PIAO....LIN PIAO

LINCOLN/A....PRESIDENT ABRAHAM LINCOLN

LINDAHL/E....ERIK LINDAHL

LINDBERG L. B1313

LINDFORS G.V. B1314

LINDSAY K. B1315

LINDVEIT E.N. B1316

LINEBERRY R.L. B1317

LING....LINGUISTICS, LANGUAGE

CUMULATIVE BOOK INDEX. WOR+45 WOR-45 ADMIN PERSON
ALL/VALS ALL/IDEOS...HUM PHIL/SCI SOC LING 19/20.
PAGE 1 B0012
N INDEX NAT/G DIPLOM

NATHAN M.,THE SOUTH AFRICAN COMMONWEALTH:
CONSTITUTION, PROBLEMS, SOCIAL CONDITIONS.
SOUTH/AFR UK CULTURE INDUS EX/STRUC LEGIS BUDGET
EDU/PROP ADMIN CT/SYS GP/REL RACE/REL...LING 19/20
CMN/WLTH. PAGE 77 B1559
B19 CONSTN NAT/G POL/PAR SOCIETY

PERREN G.E.,LANGUAGE AND COMMUNICATION IN THE
COMMONWEALTH (PAMPHLET). FUT UK LAW ECO/DEV PRESS
TV WRITING ADJUD ADMIN COLONIAL CONTROL 20
CMN/WLTH. PAGE 82 B1660
N19 EDU/PROP LING GOV/REL COM/IND

BOUDET P.,BIBLIOGRAPHIE DE L'INDOCHINE FRANCAISE.
S/ASIA VIETNAM SECT...GEOG LING 20. PAGE 14 B0282
B29 BIBLIOG ADMIN COLONIAL DIPLOM

DE CENIVAL P.,BIBLIOGRAPHIE MAROCAINE: 1923-1933.
FRANCE MOROCCO SECT ADMIN LEAD GP/REL ATTIT...LING
20. PAGE 27 B0551
B34 BIBLIOG/A ISLAM NAT/G COLONIAL

LEVY H.P.,A STUDY IN PUBLIC RELATIONS: CASE HISTORY
OF THE RELATIONS MAINTAINED BETWEEN A DEPT OF
PUBLIC ASSISTANCE AND PEOPLE. USA-45 NAT/G PRESS
ADMIN LOBBY GP/REL DISCRIM...SOC/WK LING AUD/VIS 20
PENNSYLVAN. PAGE 64 B1302
B43 ATTIT RECEIVE WEALTH SERV/IND

B54

BENTLEY A.F.,INQUIRY INTO INQUIRIES: ESSAYS IN   EPIST
SOCIAL THEORY. UNIV LEGIS ADJUD ADMIN LOBBY   SOC
...PHIL/SCI PSY NEW/IDEA LING METH 20. PAGE 11   CONCPT
B0220

B57

CENTRAL ASIAN RESEARCH CENTRE,BIBLIOGRAPHY OF   BIBLIOG/A
RECENT SOVIET SOURCE MATERIAL ON SOVIET CENTRAL   COM
ASIA AND THE BORDERLANDS. AFGHANISTN INDIA PAKISTAN   CULTURE
UAR USSR ECO/UNDEV AGRI EXTR/IND INDUS ACADEM ADMIN   NAT/G
...HEAL HUM LING CON/ANAL 20. PAGE 19 B0399

B58

MASON J.B.,THAILAND BIBLIOGRAPHY. S/ASIA THAILAND   BIBLIOG/A
CULTURE EDU/PROP ADMIN...GEOG SOC LING 20. PAGE 70   ECO/UNDEV
B1423   DIPLOM
NAT/G

B58

ORTIZ R.P.,ANNUARIO BIBLIOGRAFICO COLOMBIANO,   BIBLIOG
1951-1956. LAW RECEIVE EDU/PROP ADMIN...LING STAT   SOC
20 COLOMB. PAGE 80 B1617

B58

UNIVERSITY OF LONDON,THE FAR EAST AND SOUTH-EAST   BIBLIOG
ASIA: A CUMULATED LIST OF PERIODICAL ARTICLES, MAY   SOC
1956-APRIL 1957. ASIA S/ASIA LAW ADMIN...LING 20.
PAGE 107 B2168

B63

CHOJNACKI S.,REGISTER ON CURRENT RESEARCH ON   BIBLIOG
ETHIOPIA AND THE HORN OF AFRICA. ETHIOPIA LAW   ACT/RES
CULTURE AGRI SECT EDU/PROP ADMIN...GEOG HEAL LING   INTELL
20. PAGE 21 B0426   ACADEM

B65

ANTHONY R.N.,PLANNING AND CONTROL SYSTEMS. UNIV   CONTROL
OP/RES...DECISION MGT LING. PAGE 6 B0114   PLAN
METH
HYPO/EXP

B65

BERNDT R.M.,ABORIGINAL MAN IN AUSTRALIA. LAW DOMIN   SOC
ADMIN COLONIAL MARRIAGE HABITAT ORD/FREE...LING   CULTURE
CHARTS ANTHOL BIBLIOG WORSHIP 20 AUSTRAL ABORIGINES   SOCIETY
MUSIC ELKIN/AP. PAGE 11 B0225   S.TRUCT

L65

MATTHEWS D.G.,"A CURRENT BIBLIOGRAPHY ON ETHIOPIAN   BIBLIOG/A
AFFAIRS: A SELECT BIBLIOGRAPHY FROM 1950-1964."   ADMIN
ETHIOPIA LAW CULTURE ECO/UNDEV INDUS LABOR SECT   POL/PAR
FORCES DIPLOM CIVMIL/REL RACE/REL...LING STAT 20.   NAT/G
PAGE 71 B1428

B66

BRAIBANTI R.,RESEARCH ON THE BUREAUCRACY OF   HABITAT
PAKISTAN. PAKISTAN LAW CULTURE INTELL ACADEM LOC/G   NAT/G
SECT PRESS CT/SYS...LING CHARTS 20 BUREAUCRCY.   ADMIN
PAGE 15 B0299   CONSTN

B66

GHOSH P.K.,THE CONSTITUTION OF INDIA: HOW IT HAS   CONSTN
BEEN FRAMED. INDIA LOC/G DELIB/GP EX/STRUC   NAT/G
PROB/SOLV BUDGET INT/TRADE CT/SYS CHOOSE...LING 20.   LEGIS
PAGE 39 B0795   FEDERAL

B66

WALL E.H.,THE COURT OF JUSTICE IN THE EUROPEAN   CT/SYS
COMMUNITIES: JURISDICTION AND PROCEDURE. EUR+WWI   INT/ORG
DIPLOM ADJUD ADMIN ROUTINE TASK...CONCPT LING 20.   LAW
PAGE 113 B2281   OP/RES

S66

AFRICAN BIBLIOGRAPHIC CENTER,"A CURRENT VIEW OF   BIBLIOG/A
AFRICANA: A SELECT AND ANNOTATED BIBLIOGRAPHICAL   NAT/G
PUBLISHING GUIDE, 1965-1966." AFR CULTURE INDUS   TEC/DEV
LABOR SECT FOR/AID ADMIN COLONIAL REV RACE/REL   POL/PAR
SOCISM...LING 20. PAGE 3 B0063

S66

MATTHEWS D.G.,"ETHIOPIAN OUTLINE: A BIBLIOGRAPHIC   BIBLIOG
RESEARCH GUIDE." ETHIOPIA LAW STRUCT ECO/UNDEV AGRI   NAT/G
LABOR SECT CHIEF DELIB/GP EX/STRUC ADMIN...LING   DIPLOM
ORG/CHARTS 20. PAGE 71 B1429   POL/PAR

B67

SCHUMACHER B.G.,COMPUTER DYNAMICS IN PUBLIC   COMPUTER
ADMINISTRATION. USA+45 CREATE PLAN TEC/DEV...MGT   COMPUT/IR
LING CON/ANAL BIBLIOG/A 20. PAGE 94 B1907   ADMIN
AUTOMAT

L67

TAMBIAH S.J.,"THE POLITICS OF LANGUAGE IN INDIA AND   POL/PAR
CEYLON." CEYLON INDIA NAT/G DOMIN ADMIN...SOC 20.   LING
PAGE 102 B2070   NAT/LISM
REGION

LINGUISTICS....SEE LING

LINK/AS....ARTHUR S. LINK

LIPPMANN W. B1318

LIPPMANN/W....WALTER LIPPMANN

LIPSET S.M. B1319,B1320,B1321,B1322

LISKA G. B1323

LITCHFIELD E.H. B1324

LITERACY....ABILITY TO READ AND WRITE

B02

MOREL E.D.,AFFAIRS OF WEST AFRICA. UK FINAN INDUS   COLONIAL
FAM KIN SECT CHIEF WORKER DIPLOM RACE/REL LITERACY   ADMIN
HEALTH...CHARTS 18/20 AFRICA/W NEGRO. PAGE 75 B1521   AFR

B61

KEE R.,REFUGEE WORLD. AUSTRIA EUR+WWI GERMANY NEIGH   NAT/G
EX/STRUC WORKER PROB/SOLV ECO/TAC RENT EDU/PROP   GIVE
INGP/REL COST LITERACY HABITAT 20 MIGRATION.   WEALTH
PAGE 59 B1186   STRANGE

B66

FISK E.K.,NEW GUINEA ON THE THRESHOLD; ASPECTS OF   ECO/UNDEV
SOCIAL, POLITICAL, AND ECONOMIC DEVELOPMENT. AGRI   SOCIETY
NAT/G INT/TRADE ADMIN ADJUST LITERACY ROLE...CHARTS
ANTHOL 20 NEW/GUINEA. PAGE 36 B0726

B82

MACDONALD D.,AFRICANA; OR, THE HEART OF HEATHEN   SECT
AFRICA. VOL. II: MISSION LIFE. SOCIETY STRATA KIN   AFR
CREATE EDU/PROP ADMIN COERCE LITERACY HEALTH...MYTH   CULTURE
WORSHIP 19 LIVNGSTN/D MISSION NEGRO. PAGE 67 B1355   ORD/FREE

B98

THOMPSON H.C.,RHODESIA AND ITS GOVERNMENT. AFR   COLONIAL
RHODESIA ECO/UNDEV INDUS KIN WORKER INT/TRADE   ADMIN
DISCRIM LITERACY ORD/FREE 19. PAGE 104 B2102   POLICY
ELITES

LITERARY ANALYSIS....SEE HUM

LITHUANIA....SEE ALSO USSR

B63

KLESMENT J.,LEGAL SOURCES AND BIBLIOGRAPHY OF THE   BIBLIOG/A
BALTIC STATES (ESTONIA, LATVIA, LITHUANIA). COM   JURID
ESTONIA LATVIA LITHUANIA LAW FINAN ADJUD CT/SYS   CONSTN
REGION CENTRAL MARXISM 19/20. PAGE 60 B1218   ADMIN

LITTERER J.A. B1325

LITTLE I.M.D. B1326

LITTLE HOOVER COMM B1327

LITTLEFIELD N. B1328

LIU K.C. B1329

LIU/SHAO....LIU SHAO-CHI

LIVERNASH E.R. B1330

LIVINGSTON J.C. B1331

LIVNGSTN/D....DAVID LIVINGSTON

B82

MACDONALD D.,AFRICANA; OR, THE HEART OF HEATHEN   SECT
AFRICA. VOL. II: MISSION LIFE. SOCIETY STRATA KIN   AFR
CREATE EDU/PROP ADMIN COERCE LITERACY HEALTH...MYTH   CULTURE
WORSHIP 19 LIVNGSTN/D MISSION NEGRO. PAGE 67 B1355   ORD/FREE

LIVY....LIVY

LLOYD K. B1332

LLOYD/HD....HENRY D. LLOYD

LLOYD-GEO/D....DAVID LLOYD GEORGE

LOANS....SEE RENT+GIVE+FOR/AID+FINAN

LOBBY....PRESSURE GROUP

N19

FIRMALINO T.,THE DISTRICT SCHOOL SUPERVISOR VS.   RIGID/FLEX
TEACHERS AND PARENTS: A PHILIPPINE CASE STUDY   SCHOOL
(PAMPHLET) (BMR). PHILIPPINE LOC/G PLAN EDU/PROP   ADMIN
LOBBY REGION PERS/REL 20. PAGE 36 B0722   CREATE

N19

MARSH J.F. JR.,THE FBI RETIREMENT BILL (PAMPHLET).   ADMIN
USA+45 EX/STRUC WORKER PLAN PROB/SOLV BUDGET LEAD   NAT/G
LOBBY PARL/PROC PERS/REL RIGID/FLEX...POLICY 20 FBI   SENIOR
PRESIDENT BUR/BUDGET. PAGE 70 B1405   GOV/REL

B28

HARDMAN J.B.,AMERICAN LABOR DYNAMICS. WORKER   LABOR
ECO/TAC DOMIN ADJUD LEAD LOBBY PWR...POLICY MGT.   INGP/REL
PAGE 47 B0944   ATTIT
GP/REL

B35

HOLECOMBE A.N.,GOVERNMENT IN A PLANNED DEMOCRACY.   ADMIN
USA+45 EX/STRUC 20. PAGE 51 B1035   REPRESENT
LOBBY
PLURISM

B37

BROOKS R.R.,WHEN LABOR ORGANIZES. FINAN EDU/PROP   LABOR
ADMIN LOBBY PARTIC REPRESENT WEALTH TREND. PAGE 16   GP/REL
B0318   POLICY

B0318   POLICY
                                                                 B41
GELLHORN W.,FEDERAL ADMINISTRATIVE PROCEEDINGS.   EX/STRUC
USA+45 CLIENT FACE/GP NAT/G LOBBY REPRESENT PWR 20. LAW
PAGE 39 B0788   ADJUD
                                                     POLICY
                                                                 B42
LEISERSON A.,ADMINISTRATIVE REGULATION: A STUDY IN   LOBBY
REPRESENTATION OF INTERESTS. NAT/G EX/STRUC   ADMIN
PROB/SOLV BARGAIN CONFER ROUTINE REPRESENT PERS/REL GP/REL
UTIL PWR POLICY. PAGE 63 B1283   GOV/REL
                                                                 S42
HUZAR E.,"LEGISLATIVE CONTROL OVER ADMINISTRATION: ADMIN
CONGRESS AND WPA" USA+45 FINAN DELIB/GP LOBBY   EX/STRUC
GOV/REL EFFICIENCY ATTIT...POLICY CONGRESS. PAGE 53 CONTROL
B1069   LEGIS
                                                                 B43
LEVY H.P.,A STUDY IN PUBLIC RELATIONS: CASE HISTORY ATTIT
OF THE RELATIONS MAINTAINED BETWEEN A DEPT OF   RECEIVE
PUBLIC ASSISTANCE AND PEOPLE. USA+45 NAT/G PRESS   WEALTH
ADMIN LOBBY GP/REL DISCRIM...SOC/WK LING AUD/VIS 20 SERV/IND
PENNSYLVAN. PAGE 64 B1302
                                                                 B45
APPLEBY P.H.,BIG DEMOCRACY. USA+45 LOBBY REPRESENT   ADMIN
PWR...MGT 20. PAGE 6 B0115   NAT/G
                                                     POLICY
                                                                 B46
CORRY J.A.,DEMOCRATIC GOVERNMENT AND POLITICS.   NAT/G
WOR-45 EX/STRUC LOBBY TOTALISM...MAJORIT CONCPT   CONSTN
METH/COMP NAT/COMP 20. PAGE 24 B0479   POL/PAR
                                                     JURID
                                                                 B47
KEFAUVER E.,A TWENTIETH-CENTURY CONGRESS. POL/PAR   LEGIS
EX/STRUC SENIOR ADMIN CONTROL EXEC LOBBY CHOOSE   DELIB/GP
EFFICIENCY PWR. PAGE 59 B1189   ROUTINE
                                                     TOP/EX
                                                                 B47
MILLETT J.D.,THE PROCESS AND ORGANIZATION OF   ADMIN
GOVERNMENT PLANNING. USA+45 DELIB/GP ACT/RES LEAD   NAT/G
LOBBY TASK...POLICY GEOG TIME 20 RESOURCE/N.   PLAN
PAGE 73 B1482   CONSULT
                                                                 C48
WALKER H.,"THE LEGISLATIVE PROCESS: LAWMAKING IN   PARL/PROC
THE UNITED STATES." NAT/G POL/PAR PROVS EX/STRUC   LEGIS
OP/RES PROB/SOLV CT/SYS LOBBY GOV/REL...CHARTS   LAW
BIBLIOG T 18/20 CONGRESS. PAGE 113 B2279   CONSTN
                                                                 B49
APPLEBY P.H.,POLICY AND ADMINISTRATION. USA+45   REPRESENT
NAT/G LOBBY PWR 20. PAGE 6 B0116   EXEC
                                                     ADMIN
                                                     CLIENT
                                                                 B49
STEIN H.,THE FOREIGN SERVICE ACT OF 1946. USA+45   DIPLOM
ELITES EX/STRUC PLAN PROB/SOLV LOBBY GOV/REL   LAW
PERS/REL RIGID/FLEX...POLICY IDEA/COMP 20 CONGRESS   NAT/G
BUR/BUDGET. PAGE 100 B2027   ADMIN
                                                                 B51
HARDMAN J.B.,THE HOUSE OF LABOR. LAW R+D NEIGH   LABOR
EDU/PROP LEAD ROUTINE REPRESENT GP/REL...POLICY   LOBBY
STAT. PAGE 47 B0945   ADMIN
                                                     PRESS
                                                                 B51
MAASS A.,MUDDY WATERS: THE ARMY ENGINEERS AND THE   FORCES
NATIONS RIVERS. USA-45 PROF/ORG CONSULT LEGIS ADMIN GP/REL
EXEC ROLE PWR...SOC PRESIDENT 20. PAGE 67 B1353   LOBBY
                                                     CONSTRUC
                                                                 S51
STEWART D.D.,"THE PLACE OF VOLUNTEER PARTICIPATION   ADMIN
IN BUREAUCRATIC ORGANIZATION." NAT/G DELIB/GP   PARTIC
OP/RES DOMIN LOBBY WAR ATTIT ROLE PWR. PAGE 101   VOL/ASSN
B2035   FORCES
                                                                 B52
APPLEBY P.H.,MORALITY AND ADMINISTRATION IN   REPRESENT
DEMOCRATIC GOVERNMENT. USA+45 CLIENT NAT/G EXEC   LOBBY
EFFICIENCY 20. PAGE 6 B0117   ADMIN
                                                     EX/STRUC
                                                                 B52
CORSON J.J.,EXECUTIVES FOR THE FEDERAL SERVICE.   LOBBY
USA+45 CHIEF...MGT 20. PAGE 24 B0480   ADMIN
                                                     EX/STRUC
                                                     PERS/REL
                                                                 B52
REDFORD E.S.,ADMINISTRATION OF NATIONAL ECONOMIC   ADMIN
CONTROL. ECO/DEV DELIB/GP ADJUD CONTROL EQUILIB 20. ROUTINE
PAGE 87 B1753   GOV/REL
                                                     LOBBY
                                                                 B52
SCHATTSCHNEIDER E.E.,A GUIDE TO THE STUDY OF PUBLIC ACT/RES
AFFAIRS. LAW LOC/G NAT/G LEGIS BUDGET PRESS ADMIN   INTELL
LOBBY...JURID CHARTS 20. PAGE 93 B1882   ACADEM
                                                     METH/COMP
                                                                 S52
EDELMAN M.,"GOVERNMENTAL ORGANIZATION AND PUBLIC   ADMIN
POLICY." DELIB/GP ADJUD DECISION. PAGE 32 B0652   PLURIST
                                                     LOBBY
                                                     EX/STRUC

                                                                 C52
LASSWELL H.D.,"THE COMPARATIVE STUDY OF ELITES: AN   ELITES
INTRODUCTION AND BIBLIOGRAPHY." STRATA·POL/PAR   LEAD
EDU/PROP ADMIN LOBBY COERCE ATTIT PERSON PWR   CONCPT
...BIBLIOG 20. PAGE 63 B1270   DOMIN
                                                                 B53
GROSS B.M.,THE LEGISLATIVE STRUGGLE: A STUDY IN   LEGIS
SOCIAL COMBAT. STRUCT LOC/G POL/PAR JUDGE EDU/PROP   DECISION
DEBATE ETIQUET ADMIN LOBBY CHOOSE GOV/REL INGP/REL   PERSON
HEREDITY ALL/VALS...SOC PRESIDENT. PAGE 44 B0885   LEAD
                                                                 B53
SECKLER-HUDSON C.,BIBLIOGRAPHY ON PUBLIC   BIBLIOG/A
ADMINISTRATION (4TH ED.). USA+45 LAW POL/PAR   ADMIN
DELIB/GP BUDGET ADJUD LOBBY GOV/REL GP/REL ATTIT   NAT/G
...JURID 20. PAGE 95 B1923   MGT
                                                                 S53
GABLE R.W.,"NAM: INFLUENTIAL LOBBY OR KISS OF   LOBBY
DEATH?" (BMR)" USA+45 LAW INSPECT EDU/PROP ADMIN   LEGIS
CONTROL INGP/REL EFFICIENCY PWR 20 CONGRESS NAM   INDUS
TAFT/HART. PAGE 38 B0769   LG/CO
                                                                 B54
BENTLEY A.F.,INQUIRY INTO INQUIRIES: ESSAYS IN   EPIST
SOCIAL THEORY. UNIV LEGIS ADJUD ADMIN LOBBY   SOC
...PHIL/SCI PSY NEW/IDEA LING METH 20. PAGE 11   CONCPT
B0220
                                                                 B54
TOMPKINS D.C.,STATE GOVERNMENT AND ADMINISTRATION: BIBLIOG/A
A BIBLIOGRAPHY. USA+45 USA+45 CONSTN LEGIS JUDGE   LOC/G
BUDGET CT/SYS LOBBY...CHARTS 20. PAGE 105 B2116   PROVS
                                                     ADMIN
                                                                 S54
APPLEBY P.H.,"BUREAUCRACY AND THE FUTURE." USA+45   EX/STRUC
NAT/G CONTROL EXEC...MAJORIT 20. PAGE 6 B0119   LOBBY
                                                     REPRESENT
                                                     ADMIN
                                                                 S54
CHILDS R.S.,"CITIZEN ORGANIZATION FOR CONTROL OF   CHOOSE
GOVERNMENT." USA+45 POL/PAR CONTROL LOBBY...MAJORIT REPRESENT
20. PAGE 21 B0424   ADMIN
                                                     EX/STRUC
                                                                 S54
LANE E.,"INTEREST GROUPS AND BUREAUCRACY." NAT/G   EX/STRUC
ADMIN GP/REL INGP/REL 20. PAGE 62 B1256   LOBBY
                                                     REPRESENT
                                                     PWR
                                                                 S54
STONE E.O.,"ADMINISTRATIVE INTEGRATION." USA+45   REPRESENT
NAT/G ADMIN CONTROL CENTRAL 20. PAGE 101 B2046   EFFICIENCY
                                                     LOBBY
                                                     EX/STRUC
                                                                 C54
ZELLER B.,"AMERICAN STATE LEGISLATURES: REPORT ON   REPRESENT
THE COMMITTEE ON AMERICAN LEGISLATURES." CONSTN   LEGIS
POL/PAR EX/STRUC CONFER ADMIN CONTROL EXEC LOBBY   PROVS
ROUTINE GOV/REL...POLICY BIBLIOG 20. PAGE 119 B2401 APPORT
                                                                 B56
BARBASH J.,THE PRACTICE OF UNIONISM. ECO/TAC LEAD   LABOR
LOBBY GP/REL INGP/REL DRIVE MARXISM BIBLIOG. PAGE 9 REPRESENT
B0182   CONTROL
                                                     ADMIN
                                                                 B56
REDFORD E.S.,PUBLIC ADMINISTRATION AND POLICY   EX/STRUC
FORMATION: STUDIES IN OIL, GAS, BANKING, RIVER   PROB/SOLV
DEVELOPMENT AND CORPORATE INVESTIGATIONS. USA+45   CONTROL
CLIENT NAT/G ADMIN LOBBY REPRESENT GOV/REL INGP/REL EXEC
20. PAGE 87 B1754
                                                                 S56
CLEVELAND H.,"THE EXECUTIVE AND THE PUBLIC   LOBBY
INTEREST." USA+45 DOMIN ADMIN PWR...POLICY 20.   REPRESENT
PAGE 21 B0437   CHIEF
                                                     EXEC
                                                                 B57
BABCOCK R.S.,STATE & LOCAL GOVERNMENT AND POLITICS. PROVS
USA+45 CONSTN POL/PAR EX/STRUC LEGIS BUDGET LOBBY   LOC/G
CHOOSE SUFF...CHARTS BIBLIOG T 20. PAGE 8 B0154   GOV/REL
                                                                 B57
SCARROW H.A.,THE HIGHER PUBLIC SERVICE OF THE   ADMIN
COMMONWEALTH OF AUSTRALIA. LAW SENIOR LOBBY ROLE 20 NAT/G
AUSTRAL CIVIL/SERV COMMONWLTH. PAGE 93 B1877   EX/STRUC
                                                     GOV/COMP
                                                                 B58
BERNSTEIN M.H.,THE JOB OF THE FEDERAL EXECUTIVE.   NAT/G
POL/PAR CHIEF LEGIS ADMIN EXEC LOBBY CHOOSE GOV/REL TOP/EX
ORD/FREE PWR...MGT TREND. PAGE 11 B0228   PERS/COMP
                                                                 B58
STEWART J.D.,BRITISH PRESSURE GROUPS: THEIR ROLE IN LOBBY
RELATION TO THE HOUSE OF COMMONS. UK CONSULT   LEGIS
DELIB/GP ADMIN ROUTINE CHOOSE REPRESENT ATTIT ROLE   PLAN
20 HOUSE/CMNS PARLIAMENT. PAGE 101 B2038   PARL/PROC
                                                                 B58
VAN RIPER P.P.,HISTORY OF THE UNITED STATES CIVIL   ADMIN
SERVICE. USA+45 USA+45 LABOR LOC/G DELIB/GP LEGIS   WORKER
PROB/SOLV LOBBY GOV/REL GP/REL INCOME...POLICY   NAT/G
18/20 PRESIDENT CIVIL/SERV. PAGE 111 B2251
                                                                 S58
ALMOND G.A.,"COMPARATIVE STUDY OF INTEREST GROUPS." LOBBY

USA+45 EX/STRUC PWR 20. PAGE 4 B0079
REPRESENT ADMIN VOL/ASSN

S58
DIAMANT A.,"A CASE STUDY OF ADMINISTRATIVE AUTONOMY: CONTROLS AND TENSIONS IN FRENCH ADMINISTRATION." FRANCE ADJUD LOBBY DEMAND EFFICIENCY 20. PAGE 29 B0585
ADMIN CONTROL LEGIS EXEC

S58
FREEMAN J.L.,"THE BUREAUCRACY IN PRESSURE POLITICS." USA+45 NAT/G CHIEF ADMIN EXEC 20. PAGE 37 B0752
CONTROL EX/STRUC REPRESENT LOBBY

S58
KEISER N.F.,"PUBLIC RESPONSIBILITY AND FEDERAL ADVISORY GROUPS: A CASE STUDY." NAT/G ADMIN CONTROL LOBBY...POLICY 20. PAGE 59 B1190
REPRESENT ELITES GP/REL EX/STRUC

S58
SALETAN E.N.,"ADMINISTRATIVE TRUSTIFICATION." NAT/G EX/STRUC ADMIN 20. PAGE 92 B1862
LOBBY PWR CONTROL REPRESENT

C58
REDFORD E.S.,"THE NEVER-ENDING SEARCH FOR THE PUBLIC INTEREST" IN E. REDFORD, IDEALS AND PRACTICE IN PUBLIC ADMINISTRATION (BMR)" USA+45 USA-45 SOCIETY PARTIC GP/REL ATTIT PLURISM...DECISION SOC 20. PAGE 87 B1755
LOBBY POLICY ADMIN MAJORIT

B59
DUVERGER M.,LA CINQUIEME REPUBLIQUE. FRANCE WOR+45 POL/PAR CHIEF EX/STRUC LOBBY. PAGE 31 B0636
NAT/G CONSTN GOV/REL PARL/PROC

B59
MOOS M.,THE CAMPUS AND THE STATE. LAW FINAN DELIB/GP LEGIS EXEC LOBBY GP/REL PWR...POLICY BIBLIOG. PAGE 75 B1517
EDU/PROP ACADEM PROVS CONTROL

B59
REDFORD E.S.,NATIONAL REGULATORY COMMISSIONS: NEED FOR A NEW LOOK (PAMPHLET). USA+45 CLIENT PROB/SOLV ADJUD LOBBY EFFICIENCY...POLICY 20. PAGE 87 B1757
REPRESENT CONTROL EXEC NAT/G

S59
JEWELL M.R.,"THE SENATE REPUBLICAN POLICY COMMITTEE AND FOREIGN POLICY." PLAN ADMIN CONTROL LEAD LOBBY EFFICIENCY PRESIDENT 20 REPUBLICAN. PAGE 56 B1139
POL/PAR NAT/G DELIB/GP POLICY

C59
DAHL R.A.,"SOCIAL SCIENCE RESEARCH ON BUSINESS: PRODUCT AND POTENTIAL" INDUS MARKET OP/RES CAP/ISM ADMIN LOBBY DRIVE...PSY CONCPT BIBLIOG/A 20. PAGE 26 B0521
MGT EFFICIENCY PROB/SOLV EX/STRUC

B60
BELL J.,THE SPLENDID MISERY: THE STORY OF THE PRESIDENCY AND POWER POLITICS AT CLOSE RANGE. USA+45 USA-45 PRESS ADMIN LEAD LOBBY GP/REL PERS/REL PERSON PRESIDENT. PAGE 10 B0208
EXEC TOP/EX LEGIS

B60
FOSS P.,POLITICS AND GRASS: THE ADMINISTRATION OF GRAZING ON THE PUBLIC DOMAIN. USA+45 LEGIS TOP/EX EXEC...DECISION 20. PAGE 37 B0743
REPRESENT ADMIN LOBBY EX/STRUC

B60
HAYNES G.H.,THE SENATE OF THE UNITED STATES: ITS HISTORY AND PRACTICE. CONSTN EX/STRUC TOP/EX CONFER DEBATE LEAD LOBBY PARL/PROC CHOOSE PWR SENATE CONGRESS. PAGE 48 B0977
LEGIS DELIB/GP

B60
HODGETTS J.E.,CANADIAN PUBLIC ADMINISTRATION. CANADA CONTROL LOBBY EFFICIENCY 20. PAGE 50 B1024
REPRESENT ADMIN EX/STRUC ADJUD

S60
TAYLOR M.G.,"THE ROLE OF THE MEDICAL PROFESSION IN THE FORMULATION AND EXECUTION OF PUBLIC POLICY" (BMR)" CANADA NAT/G CONSULT ADMIN REPRESENT GP/REL ROLE SOVEREIGN...DECISION 20 CMA. PAGE 103 B2088
PROF/ORG HEALTH LOBBY POLICY

B61
GORDON R.A.,BUSINESS LEADERSHIP IN THE LARGE CORPORATION. USA+45 SOCIETY EX/STRUC ADMIN CONTROL ROUTINE GP/REL PWR...MGT 20. PAGE 41 B0831
LG/CO LEAD DECISION LOBBY

B61
GRIFFITH E.S.,CONGRESS: ITS CONTEMPORARY ROLE. CONSTN POL/PAR CHIEF PLAN BUDGET DIPLOM CONFER ADMIN LOBBY...DECISION CONGRESS. PAGE 43 B0878
PARL/PROC EX/STRUC TOP/EX LEGIS

S61
ABLARD C.D.,"EX PARTE CONTACTS WITH FEDERAL ADMINISTRATIVE AGENCIES." USA+45 CLIENT NAT/G DELIB/GP ADMIN PWR 20. PAGE 3 B0055
EXEC ADJUD LOBBY REPRESENT

S61
EHRMANN H.W.,"FRENCH BUREAUCRACY AND ORGANIZED INTERESTS" (BMR)" FRANCE NAT/G DELIB/GP ROUTINE ...INT 20 BUREAUCRCY CIVIL/SERV. PAGE 32 B0657
ADMIN DECISION PLURISM LOBBY

B62
CARPER E.T.,ILLINOIS GOES TO CONGRESS FOR ARMY LAND. USA+45 LAW EXTR/IND PROVS REGION CIVMIL/REL GOV/REL FEDERAL ATTIT 20 ILLINOIS SENATE CONGRESS DIRKSEN/E DOUGLAS/P. PAGE 19 B0385
ADMIN LOBBY GEOG LEGIS

B62
LOWI T.J.,LEGISLATIVE POLITICS U.S.A. LAW LEGIS DIPLOM EXEC LOBBY CHOOSE SUFF FEDERAL PWR 19/20 CONGRESS. PAGE 67 B1345
PARL/PROC REPRESENT POLICY ROUTINE

B62
REICH C.A.,BUREAUCRACY AND THE FORESTS (PAMPHLET). USA+45 LOBBY...POLICY MGT 20. PAGE 87 B1762
ADMIN CONTROL EX/STRUC REPRESENT

B62
SCHULMAN S.,TOWARD JUDICIAL REFORM IN PENNSYLVANIA; A STUDY IN COURT REORGANIZATION. USA+45 CONSTN JUDGE PLAN ADMIN LOBBY SANCTION PRIVIL PWR...JURID 20 PENNSYLVAN. PAGE 94 B1905
CT/SYS ACT/RES PROB/SOLV

L62
BORCHARDT K.,"CONGRESSIONAL USE OF ADMINISTRATIVE ORGANIZATION AND PROCEDURE FOR POLICY-MAKING PURPOSES." USA+45 NAT/G EXEC LOBBY. PAGE 14 B0278
ADMIN LEGIS REPRESENT CONTROL

L62
CAVERS D.F.,"ADMINISTRATIVE DECISION-MAKING IN NUCLEAR FACILITIES LICENSING." USA+45 CLIENT ADMIN EXEC 20 AEC. PAGE 19 B0395
REPRESENT LOBBY PWR CONTROL

L62
ERDMANN H.H.,"ADMINISTRATIVE LAW AND FARM ECONOMICS." USA+45 LOC/G NAT/G PLAN PROB/SOLV LOBBY ...DECISION ANTHOL 20. PAGE 33 B0680
AGRI ADMIN ADJUD POLICY

C62
DE GRAZIA A.,"POLITICAL BEHAVIOR (REV. ED.)" STRATA POL/PAR LEAD LOBBY ROUTINE WAR CHOOSE REPRESENT CONSEN ATTIT ORD/FREE BIBLIOG. PAGE 27 B0555
PHIL/SCI OP/RES CONCPT

C62
TRUMAN D.B.,"THE GOVERNMENTAL PROCESS: POLITICAL INTERESTS AND PUBLIC OPINION." POL/PAR ADJUD ADMIN EXEC LEAD ROUTINE CHOOSE REPRESENT GOV/REL RIGID/FLEX...POLICY BIBLIOG/A 20. PAGE 105 B2131
LOBBY EDU/PROP GP/REL LEGIS

B63
CROUCH W.W.,SOUTHERN CALIFORNIA METROPOLIS: A STUDY IN DEVELOPMENT OF GOVERNMENT FOR A METROPOLITAN AREA. USA+45 USA-45 PROB/SOLV ADMIN LOBBY PARTIC CENTRAL ORD/FREE PWR...BIBLIOG 20 PROGRSV/M. PAGE 25 B0510
LOC/G MUNIC LEGIS DECISION

B63
HATHAWAY D.A.,GOVERNMENT AND AGRICULTURE: PUBLIC POLICY IN A DEMOCRATIC SOCIETY. USA+45 LEGIS ADMIN EXEC LOBBY REPRESENT PWR 20. PAGE 48 B0967
AGRI GOV/REL PROB/SOLV EX/STRUC

B63
HIGA M.,POLITICS AND PARTIES IN POSTWAR OKINAWA. USA+45 VOL/ASSN LEGIS CONTROL LOBBY CHOOSE NAT/LISM PWR SOVEREIGN MARXISM SOCISM 20 OKINAWA CHINJAP. PAGE 50 B1008
GOV/REL POL/PAR ADMIN FORCES

B63
ROYAL INSTITUTE PUBLIC ADMIN,BRITISH PUBLIC ADMINISTRATION. UK LAW FINAN INDUS LOC/G POL/PAR LEGIS LOBBY PARL/PROC CHOOSE JURID. PAGE 91 B1845
BIBLIOG ADMIN MGT NAT/G

B63
US SENATE COMM ON JUDICIARY,ADMINISTERED PRICES. USA+45 RATION ADJUD CONTROL LOBBY...POLICY 20 SENATE MONOPOLY. PAGE 110 B2229
LG/CO PRICE ADMIN DECISION

B64
BANTON M.,THE POLICEMAN IN THE COMMUNITY. UK USA+45 STRUCT PROF/ORG WORKER LOBBY ROUTINE COERCE CROWD GP/REL ADJUST DISCRIM PERCEPT 20. PAGE 9 B0181
FORCES ADMIN ROLE RACE/REL

B64
BENNETT H.A.,THE COMMISSION AND THE COMMON LAW: A STUDY IN ADMINISTRATIVE ADJUDICATION. LAW ADMIN CT/SYS LOBBY SANCTION GOV/REL 20 COMMON/LAW. PAGE 10 B0212
ADJUD DELIB/GP DIST/IND POLICY

B64
BOYER W.W.,BUREAUCRACY ON TRIAL: POLICY MAKING BY GOVERNMENT AGENCIES. USA+45 NAT/G REPRESENT 20. PAGE 14 B0294
ADMIN LOBBY EXEC EX/STRUC

B64
CATER D.,POWER IN WASHINGTON: A CRITICAL LOOK AT TODAY'S STRUGGLE TO GOVERN IN THE NATION'S CAPITAL. USA+45 NAT/G LEGIS ADMIN EXEC LOBBY PLURISM 20. PAGE 19 B0392
REPRESENT GOV/REL INGP/REL EX/STRUC

B64
COTTER C.P.,POLITICS WITHOUT POWER: THE NATIONAL PARTY COMMITTEES. USA+45 FINAN NAT/G LOBBY ROUTINE
CHOOSE POL/PAR

GP/REL ATTIT ROLE SUPEGO PWR 20. PAGE 24 B0491   REPRESENT DELIB/GP
B64

EATON H.,PRESIDENTIAL TIMBER: A HISTORY OF NOMINATING CONVENTIONS, 1868-1960. USA+45 USA-45 POL/PAR EX/STRUC DEBATE LOBBY ATTIT PERSON ALL/VALS ...MYTH 19/20 PRESIDENT. PAGE 32 B0646   DELIB/GP CHOOSE CHIEF NAT/G
B64

FISK W.M.,ADMINISTRATIVE PROCEDURE IN A REGULATORY AGENCY: THE CAB AND THE NEW YORK-CHICAGO CASE (PAMPHLET). USA+45 DIST/IND ADMIN CONTROL LOBBY GP/REL ROLE ORD/FREE NEWYORK/C CHICAGO CAB. PAGE 36 B0727   SERV/IND ECO/DEV AIR JURID
B64

KEEFE W.J.,THE AMERICAN LEGISLATIVE PROCESS: CONGRESS AND THE STATES. USA+45 LAW POL/PAR DELIB/GP DEBATE ADMIN LOBBY REPRESENT CONGRESS PRESIDENT. PAGE 59 B1187   LEGIS DECISION PWR PROVS
B64

LOWI T.J.,AT THE PLEASURE OF THE MAYOR. EX/STRUC PROB/SOLV BAL/PWR ADMIN PARTIC CHOOSE GP/REL ...CONT/OBS NET/THEORY CHARTS 20 NEWYORK/C MAYOR. PAGE 67 B1346   LOBBY LOC/G PWR MUNIC
B64

TURNER H.A.,THE GOVERNMENT AND POLITICS OF CALIFORNIA (2ND ED.). LAW FINAN MUNIC POL/PAR SCHOOL EX/STRUC LEGIS LOBBY CHOOSE...CHARTS T 20 CALIFORNIA. PAGE 106 B2138   PROVS ADMIN LOC/G CONSTN
S64

EAKIN T.C.,"LEGISLATIVE POLITICS -- I AND II THE WESTERN STATES, 19581964) (SUPPLEMENT)" USA+45 POL/PAR SCHOOL CONTROL LOBBY CHOOSE AGE. PAGE 32 B0641   PROVS LEGIS ROUTINE STRUCT
C64

SCOTT R.E.,"MEXICAN GOVERNMENT IN TRANSITION (REV ED)" CULTURE STRUCT POL/PAR CHIEF ADMIN LOBBY REV CHOOSE GP/REL DRIVE...BIBLIOG METH 20 MEXIC/AMER. PAGE 95 B1920   NAT/G L/A+17C ROUTINE CONSTN
B65

AIYAR S.P.,STUDIES IN INDIAN DEMOCRACY. INDIA STRATA ECO/UNDEV LABOR POL/PAR LEGIS DIPLOM LOBBY REGION CHOOSE ATTIT SOCISM...ANTHOL 20. PAGE 3 B0067   ORD/FREE REPRESENT ADMIN NAT/G
B65

BANFIELD E.C.,BIG CITY POLITICS. USA+45 CONSTN POL/PAR ADMIN LOBBY CHOOSE SUFF INGP/REL PWR...GEOG 20. PAGE 9 B0179   METH/COMP MUNIC STRUCT
B65

HADWIGER D.F.,PRESSURES AND PROTEST. NAT/G LEGIS PLAN LEAD PARTIC ROUTINE ATTIT POLICY. PAGE 45 B0913   AGRI GP/REL LOBBY CHOOSE
B65

REDFORD D.R.,POLITICS AND GOVERNMENT IN THE UNITED STATES. USA+45 USA-45 LOC/G PROVS FORCES DIPLOM CT/SYS LOBBY...JURID SUPREME/CT PRESIDENT. PAGE 87 B1751   NAT/G POL/PAR EX/STRUC LEGIS
S65

ANDERSON T.J.,"PRESSURE GROUPS AND INTERGOVERNMENTAL RELATIONS." USA+45 NAT/G ROLE 20. PAGE 5 B0097   ADMIN EX/STRUC LOBBY GOV/REL
S65

LONG T.G.,"THE ADMINISTRATIVE PROCESS: AGONIZING REAPPRAISAL IN THE FTC." NAT/G REPRESENT 20 FTC. PAGE 66 B1339   ADJUD LOBBY ADMIN EX/STRUC
B66

FINNISH POLITICAL SCIENCE ASSN,SCANDINAVIAN POLITICAL STUDIES (VOL. I). FINLAND DIPLOM ADMIN LOBBY PARL/PROC...CHARTS BIBLIOG 20 SCANDINAV. PAGE 36 B0721   ATTIT POL/PAR ACT/RES CHOOSE
B66

LIVINGSTON J.C.,THE CONSENT OF THE GOVERNED. USA+45 EX/STRUC BAL/PWR DOMIN CENTRAL PERSON PWR...POLICY CONCPT OBS IDEA/COMP 20 CONGRESS. PAGE 66 B1331   NAT/G LOBBY MAJORIT PARTIC
B66

NIEBURG H.L.,IN THE NAME OF SCIENCE. USA+45 EX/STRUC LEGIS TEC/DEV BUDGET PAY AUTOMAT LOBBY PWR ...OBS 20. PAGE 78 B1581   NAT/G INDUS TECHRACY
B66

RICHARD J.B.,GOVERNMENT AND POLITICS OF WYOMING. USA+45 POL/PAR EX/STRUC LEGIS CT/SYS LOBBY APPORT CHOOSE REPRESENT 20 WYOMING GOVERNOR. PAGE 88 B1773   PROVS LOC/G ADMIN
B66

SCHMIDT K.M.,AMERICAN STATE AND LOCAL GOVERNMENT IN ACTION. USA+45 CONSTN LOC/G POL/PAR CHIEF LEGIS PROB/SOLV ADJUD LOBBY GOV/REL...DECISION ANTHOL 20 GOVERNOR MAYOR URBAN/RNWL. PAGE 94 B1896   PROVS ADMIN MUNIC PLAN
B66

SEASHOLES B.,VOTING, INTEREST GROUPS, AND PARTIES. USA+45 FINAN LOC/G NAT/G ADMIN LEAD GP/REL INGP/REL ROLE...CHARTS ANTHOL 20. PAGE 95 B1922   CHOOSE POL/PAR LOBBY PARTIC

JACOB H.,"DIMENSIONS OF STATE POLITICS HEARD A. ED. STATE LEGIWLATURES IN AMERICAN POLITICS." CULTURE STRATA POL/PAR BUDGET TAX LOBBY ROUTINE GOV/REL ...TRADIT DECISION GEOG. PAGE 55 B1112   C66 PROVS LEGIS ROLE REPRESENT

TACHERON D.G.,"THE JOB OF THE CONGRESSMAN: AN INTRODUCTION TO SERVICES IN THE US HOUSE OF REPRESENTATIVES." DELIB/GP EX/STRUC PRESS SENIOR CT/SYS LOBBY CHOOSE GOV/REL...BIBLIOG 20 CONGRESS HOUSE/REP SENATE. PAGE 102 B2068   C66 LEGIS PARL/PROC ADMIN POL/PAR

FINCHER F.,THE GOVERNMENT OF THE UNITED STATES. USA+45 USA-45 POL/PAR CHIEF CT/SYS LOBBY GP/REL INGP/REL...CONCPT CHARTS BIBLIOG T 18/20 PRESIDENT CONGRESS SUPREME/CT. PAGE 35 B0719   B67 NAT/G EX/STRUC LEGIS OP/RES

SCHAEFER W.V.,THE SUSPECT AND SOCIETY: CRIMINAL PROCEDURE AND CONVERGING CONSTITUTIONAL DOCTRINES. USA+45 TEC/DEV LOBBY ROUTINE SANCTION...INT 20. PAGE 93 B1879   B67 CRIME FORCES CONSTN JURID

TOMA P.A.,THE POLITICS OF FOOD FOR PEACE: EXECUTIVE-LEGISLATIVE INTERACTION. USA+45 ECO/UNDEV POL/PAR DEBATE EXEC LOBBY CHOOSE PEACE...DECISION CHARTS. PAGE 104 B2113   B67 FOR/AID POLICY LEGIS AGRI

US SENATE COMM ON FOREIGN REL,HUMAN RIGHTS CONVENTIONS. USA+45 LABOR VOL/ASSN DELIB/GP DOMIN ADJUD REPRESENT...INT/LAW MGT CONGRESS. PAGE 110 B2225   B67 LEGIS ORD/FREE WORKER LOBBY

ANDERSON M.,"THE FRENCH PARLIAMENT." EUR+WWI FRANCE MOD/EUR CONSTN POL/PAR CHIEF LEGIS LOBBY ATTIT ROLE PWR 19/20. PAGE 5 B0095   S67 PARL/PROC LEAD GOV/COMP EX/STRUC

HOFMANN W.,"THE PUBLIC INTEREST PRESSURE GROUP: THE CASE OF THE DEUTSCHE STADTETAG." GERMANY GERMANY/W CONSTN STRUCT NAT/G CENTRAL FEDERAL PWR...TIME/SEQ 20. PAGE 51 B1030   S67 LOC/G VOL/ASSN LOBBY ADMIN

JOHNSON L.B.,"BULLETS DO NOT DISCRIMINATE-LANDLORDS DO." PROB/SOLV EXEC LOBBY DEMAND...REALPOL SOC 20. PAGE 57 B1145   S67 NAT/G DISCRIM POLICY

LASLETT J.H.M.,"SOCIALISM AND THE AMERICAN LABOR MOVEMENT* SOME NEW REFLECTIONS." USA-45 VOL/ASSN LOBBY PARTIC CENTRAL ALL/VALS SOCISM...GP/COMP 20. PAGE 63 B1265   S67 LABOR ROUTINE ATTIT GP/REL

SPACKMAN A.,"THE SENATE OF TRINIDAD AND TOBAGO." L/A+17C TRINIDAD WEST/IND NAT/G POL/PAR DELIB/GP OP/RES PROB/SOLV EDU/PROP EXEC LOBBY ROUTINE REPRESENT GP/REL 20. PAGE 99 B2002   S67 ELITES EFFICIENCY LEGIS DECISION

TIVEY L.,"THE POLITICAL CONSEQUENCES OF ECONOMIC PLANNING." UK CONSTN INDUS ACT/RES ADMIN CONTROL LOBBY REPRESENT EFFICIENCY SUPEGO SOVEREIGN ...DECISION 20. PAGE 104 B2112   S67 PLAN POLICY NAT/G

GUZZARDI W. JR.,"THE SECOND BATTLE OF BRITAIN." UK STRATA LABOR WORKER CREATE PROB/SOLV EDU/PROP ADMIN LEAD LOBBY...MGT SOC 20 GOLD/STAND. PAGE 45 B0907   S68 FINAN ECO/TAC ECO/DEV STRUCT

LOBBYING....SEE LOBBY

LOC/G....LOCAL GOVERNMENT

AUSTRALIAN NATIONAL RES COUN,AUSTRALIAN SOCIAL SCIENCE ABSTRACTS. NEW/ZEALND CULTURE SOCIETY LOC/G CT/SYS PARL/PROC...HEAL JURID PSY SOC 20 AUSTRAL. PAGE 7 B0149   N BIBLIOG/A POLICY NAT/G ADMIN

VENKATESAN S.L.,BIBLIOGRAPHY ON PUBLIC ENTERPRISES IN INDIA. INDIA S/ASIA FINAN LG/CO LOC/G PLAN BUDGET SOCISM...MGT 20. PAGE 112 B2258   N BIBLIOG/A ADMIN ECO/UNDEV INDUS

JOURNAL OF POLITICS. USA+45 USA-45 CONSTN POL/PAR EX/STRUC LEGIS PROB/SOLV DIPLOM CT/SYS CHOOSE RACE/REL 20. PAGE 1 B0005   N BIBLIOG/A NAT/G LAW LOC/G

BULLETIN OF THE PUBLIC AFFAIRS INFORMATION SERVICE. WOR+45 WOR-45 ECO/UNDEV FINAN LABOR LOC/G PROVS TEC/DEV DIPLOM EDU/PROP SOC. PAGE 1 B0010   N BIBLIOG NAT/G ECO/DEV ADMIN

LOCAL GOVERNMENT SERVICE....SOC BIBLIOG/A 20. PAGE 1 B0016   N LOC/G ADMIN MUNIC GOV/REL

SUBJECT GUIDE TO BOOKS IN PRINT: AN INDEX TO THE
PUBLISHERS' TRADE LIST ANNUAL. UNIV LAW LOC/G
DIPLOM WRITING ADMIN LEAD PERSON...MGT SOC. PAGE 1
B0023
N
BIBLIOG
ECO/DEV
POL/PAR
NAT/G

CARLETON UNIVERSITY LIBRARY,SELECTED LIST OF
CURRENT MATERIALS ON CANADIAN PUBLIC
ADMINISTRATION. CANADA LEGIS WORKER PLAN BUDGET 20.
PAGE 19 B0379
N
BIBLIOG
ADMIN
LOC/G
MUNIC

DEUTSCHE BUCHEREI,JAHRESVERZEICHNIS DES DEUTSCHEN
SCHRIFTUMS. AUSTRIA EUR+WWI GERMANY SWITZERLND LAW
LOC/G DIPLOM ADMIN...MGT SOC 19/20. PAGE 29 B0580
N
BIBLIOG
WRITING
NAT/G

FAUNT J.R.,A CHECKLIST OF SOUTH CAROLINA STATE
PUBLICATIONS. USA+45 CONSTN LEGIS ADMIN ATTIT 20.
PAGE 35 B0708
N
BIBLIOG
PROVS
LOC/G
GOV/REL

PUBLISHERS' CIRCULAR LIMITED,THE ENGLISH CATALOGUE
OF BOOKS. UK WOR+45 WOR-45 LAW CULTURE LOC/G NAT/G
ADMIN LEAD...MGT 19/20. PAGE 85 B1718
N
BIBLIOG
ALL/VALS
ALL/IDEOS
SOCIETY

STATE OF ILLINOIS,PUBLICATIONS OF THE STATE OF
ILLINOIS. USA+45 FINAN POL/PAR ADMIN LEAD 20
ILLINOIS. PAGE 100 B2024
N
BIBLIOG
PROVS
LOC/G
GOV/REL

US LIBRARY OF CONGRESS,CATALOG OF THE PUBLIC
DOCUMENTS OF THE UNITED STATES, 1893-1940. USA-45
LAW ECO/DEV AGRI PLAN PROB/SOLV ADMIN LEAD GOV/REL
ATTIT 19/20. PAGE 109 B2200
N
BIBLIOG
NAT/G
POLICY
LOC/G

US SUPERINTENDENT OF DOCUMENTS,EDUCATION (PRICE
LIST 31). USA+45 LAW FINAN LOC/G NAT/G DEBATE ADMIN
LEAD RACE/REL FEDERAL HEALTH POLICY. PAGE 111 B2238
N
BIBLIOG/A
EDU/PROP
ACADEM
SCHOOL

US SUPERINTENDENT OF DOCUMENTS,INTERSTATE COMMERCE
(PRICE LIST 59). USA+45 LAW LOC/G NAT/G LEGIS
TARIFFS TAX ADMIN CONTROL HEALTH DECISION. PAGE 111
B2239
N
BIBLIOG/A
DIST/IND
GOV/REL
PROVS

GOODNOW F.J.,THE PRINCIPLES OF THE ADMINISTRATIVE
LAW OF THE UNITED STATES. USA-45 LAW STRUCT
EX/STRUC LEGIS BAL/PWR CONTROL GOV/REL PWR...JURID
19/20 CIVIL/SERV. PAGE 41 B0822
B05
ADMIN
NAT/G
PROVS
LOC/G

MEYER H.H.B.,SELECT LIST OF REFERENCES ON
COMMISSION GOVERNMENT FOR CITIES (PAMPHLET). USA-45
EX/STRUC ADMIN 20. PAGE 73 B1473
B13
BIBLIOG
LOC/G
MUNIC
DELIB/GP

SAWYER R.A.,A LIST OF WORKS ON COUNTY GOVERNMENT.
LAW FINAN MUNIC TOP/EX ROUTINE CRIME...CLASSIF
RECORD 19/20. PAGE 93 B1871
B15
BIBLIOG/A
LOC/G
GOV/REL
ADMIN

LOS ANGELES BD CIV SERV COMNRS,ANNUAL REPORT: LOS
ANGELES CALIFORNIA: 1919-1936. USA-45 LAW GOV/REL
PRODUC...STAT 20. PAGE 66 B1340
B19
DELIB/GP
ADMIN
LOC/G
MUNIC

ANDERSON W.,THE UNITS OF GOVERNMENT IN THE UNITED
STATES (PAMPHLET). USA-45 NAT/G PROVS EFFICIENCY
...CHARTS 20. PAGE 5 B0098
N19
LOC/G
CENSUS
ADMIN
GOV/REL

FAHRNKOPF N.,STATE AND LOCAL GOVERNMENT IN ILLINOIS
(PAMPHLET). CONSTN ADMIN PARTIC CHOOSE REPRESENT
GOV/REL...JURID MGT 20 ILLINOIS. PAGE 34 B0696
N19
BIBLIOG
LOC/G
LEGIS
CT/SYS

FIRMALINO T.,THE DISTRICT SCHOOL SUPERVISOR VS.
TEACHERS AND PARENTS: A PHILIPPINE CASE STUDY
(PAMPHLET) (BMR). PHILIPPINE LOC/G PLAN EDU/PROP
LOBBY REGION PERS/REL 20. PAGE 36 B0722
N19
RIGID/FLEX
SCHOOL
ADMIN
CREATE

GINZBERG E.,MANPOWER FOR GOVERNMENT (PAMPHLET).
USA+45 FORCES PLAN PROB/SOLV PAY EDU/PROP ADMIN
GP/REL COST...MGT PREDICT TREND 20 CIVIL/SERV.
PAGE 40 B0803
N19
WORKER
CONSULT
NAT/G
LOC/G

GRIFFITH W.,THE PUBLIC SERVICE (PAMPHLET). UK LAW
LOC/G NAT/G PARTIC CHOOSE DRIVE ROLE SKILL...CHARTS
20 CIVIL/SERV. PAGE 44 B0880
N19
ADMIN
EFFICIENCY
EDU/PROP
GOV/REL

RIDLEY C.E.,MEASURING MUNICIPAL ACTIVITIES
(PAMPHLET). FINAN SERV/IND FORCES RECEIVE INGP/REL
HABITAT...POLICY SOC/WK 20. PAGE 88 B1779
N19
MGT
HEALTH
WEALTH
LOC/G

VERNON R.,THE MYTH AND REALITY OF OUR URBAN
N19
PLAN

PROBLEMS (PAMPHLET). USA+45 SOCIETY LOC/G ADMIN
COST 20 PRINCETN/U INTERVENT URBAN/RNWL. PAGE 112
B2261
MUNIC
HABITAT
PROB/SOLV
N19

WALL N.L.,MUNICIPAL REPORTING TO THE PUBLIC
(PAMPHLET). LOC/G PLAN WRITING ADMIN REPRESENT
EFFICIENCY...AUD/VIS CHARTS 20. PAGE 113 B2282
METH
MUNIC
GP/REL
COM/IND
C20

BLACHLY F.F.,"THE GOVERNMENT AND ADMINISTRATION OF
GERMANY." GERMANY CONSTN LOC/G PROVS DELIB/GP
EX/STRUC FORCES LEGIS TOP/EX CT/SYS...BIBLIOG/A
19/20. PAGE 12 B0246
NAT/G
GOV/REL
ADMIN
PHIL/SCI
B23

FRANK T.,A HISTORY OF ROME. MEDIT-7 INTELL SOCIETY
LOC/G NAT/G POL/PAR FORCES LEGIS DOMIN LEGIT
ALL/VALS...POLICY CONCPT TIME/SEQ GEN/LAWS ROM/EMP
ROM/EMP. PAGE 37 B0749
EXEC
STRUCT
ELITES
B24

KENT F.R.,THE GREAT GAME OF POLITICS. USA-45 LOC/G
NAT/G POL/PAR EX/STRUC PROB/SOLV BUDGET CHOOSE
GOV/REL 20. PAGE 59 B1194
ADMIN
OP/RES
STRUCT
B25

MATHEWS J.M.,AMERICAN STATE GOVERNMENT. USA-45
LOC/G CHIEF EX/STRUC LEGIS ADJUD CONTROL CT/SYS
ROUTINE GOV/REL PWR 20 GOVERNOR. PAGE 71 B1426
PROVS
ADMIN
FEDERAL
CONSTN
B28

BUELL R.,THE NATIVE PROBLEM IN AFRICA. KIN LABOR
LOC/G ECO/TAC ROUTINE ORD/FREE...REC/INT KNO/TEST
CENSUS TREND CHARTS SOC/EXP STERTYP 20. PAGE 17
B0339
AFR
CULTURE
B30

FAIRLIE J.A.,COUNTY GOVERNMENT AND ADMINISTRATION.
UK USA-45 NAT/G SCHOOL FORCES BUDGET TAX CT/SYS
CHOOSE...JURID BIBLIOG 11/20. PAGE 35 B0701
ADMIN
GOV/REL
LOC/G
MUNIC
B30

ZINK H.,CITY BOSSES IN THE UNITED STATES: A STUDY
OF TWENTY MUNICIPAL BOSSES. USA-45 INDUS MUNIC
NEIGH POL/PAR ADMIN CRIME INGP/REL PERS/REL PWR
...PERS/COMP 20 BOSSISM. PAGE 119 B2403
LOC/G
DOMIN
BIOG
LEAD
B33

BROMAGE A.W.,AMERICAN COUNTY GOVERNMENT. USA-45
NAT/G LEAD GOV/REL CENTRAL PWR...MGT BIBLIOG 18/20.
PAGE 15 B0314
LOC/G
CREATE
ADMIN
MUNIC
B33

GREER S.,A BIBLIOGRAPHY OF PUBLIC ADMINISTRATION.
WOR-45 CONSTN LOC/G MUNIC EX/STRUC LEGIS...CONCPT
20. PAGE 43 B0869
BIBLIOG/A
ADMIN
MGT
NAT/G
B34

RIDLEY C.E.,THE CITY-MANAGER PROFESSION. CHIEF PLAN
ADMIN CONTROL ROUTINE CHOOSE...TECHNIC CHARTS
GOV/COMP BIBLIOG 20. PAGE 88 B1780
MUNIC
EX/STRUC
LOC/G
EXEC
B35

GORER G.,AFRICA DANCES: A BOOK ABOUT WEST AFRICAN
NEGROES. STRUCT LOC/G SECT FORCES TAX ADMIN
COLONIAL...ART/METH MYTH WORSHIP 20 NEGRO AFRICA/W
CHRISTIAN RITUAL. PAGE 41 B0835
AFR
ATTIT
CULTURE
SOCIETY
B35

GREER S.,BIBLIOGRAPHY ON CIVIL SERVICE AND
PERSONNEL ADMINISTRATION. USA-45 LOC/G PROVS WORKER
PRICE SENIOR DRIVE...MGT 20. PAGE 43 B0870
BIBLIOG/A
ADMIN
NAT/G
ROUTINE
B37

GOSNELL H.F.,MACHINE POLITICS: CHICAGO MODEL.
COM/IND FACE/GP LOC/G EX/STRUC LEAD ROUTINE
SANCTION REPRESENT GOV/REL PWR...POLICY MATH OBS
INT CHARTS. PAGE 41 B0840
POL/PAR
MUNIC
ADMIN
CHOOSE
B37

HODGSON J.G.,THE OFFICIAL PUBLICATIONS OF AMERICAN
COUNTIES: A UNION LIST. SCHOOL BUDGET...HEAL MGT
SOC/WK 19/20. PAGE 51 B1026
BIBLIOG
LOC/G
PUB/INST
B38

MACDONALD G.E.,CHECK LIST OF LEGISLATIVE JOURNALS
OF THE STATES OF THE UNITED STATES OF AMERICA.
USA-45 ADMIN GOV/REL ATTIT...POLICY 18/20. PAGE 67
B1356
BIBLIOG
PROVS
LEGIS
LOC/G
B38

SALTER J.T.,THE AMERICAN POLITICIAN. USA-45 LABOR
POL/PAR EDU/PROP ADMIN CHOOSE ATTIT DRIVE PERSON
PWR...POLICY ANTHOL 20 THOMAS/N LEWIS/JL LAGUARD/F
GOVERNOR MAYOR. PAGE 92 B1865
BIOG
LEAD
PROVS
LOC/G
B39

ANDERSON W.,LOCAL GOVERNMENT IN EUROPE. FRANCE
GERMANY ITALY UK USSR MUNIC PROVS ADMIN GOV/REL
CENTRAL SOVEREIGN 20. PAGE 5 B0099
GOV/COMP
NAT/COMP
LOC/G
CONSTN
B39

BAKER G.,THE COUNTY AGENT. USA-45 LOC/G NAT/G
PROB/SOLV ADMIN...POLICY 20 ROOSEVLT/F NEW/DEAL
COUNTY/AGT. PAGE 8 B0166
AGRI
CONSULT
GOV/REL
EDU/PROP

MCHENRY D.E.,HIS MAJESTY'S OPPOSITION: STRUCTURE AND PROBLEMS OF THE BRITISH LABOUR PARTY 1931-1938. UK FINAN LABOR LOC/G DELIB/GP LEGIS EDU/PROP LEAD PARTIC CHOOSE GP/REL SOCISM...TREND 20 LABOR/PAR. PAGE 72 B1450
POL/PAR MGT NAT/G POLICY
B40

PATTERSON C.P.,STATE AND LOCAL GOVERNMENT IN TEXAS (3RD ED.). USA-45 EX/STRUC LEGIS CT/SYS CHOOSE 20 TEXAS. PAGE 81 B1642
CONSTN PROVS GOV/REL LOC/G
B40

COUNTY GOVERNMENT IN THE UNITED STATES: A LIST OF RECENT REFERENCES (PAMPHLET). USA-45 LAW PUB/INST PLAN BUDGET CT/SYS CENTRAL 20. PAGE 49 B0988
BIBLIOG/A LOC/G ADMIN MUNIC
N40

BROWN A.D.,LIST OF REFERENCES ON THE CIVIL SERVICE AND PERSONNEL ADMINISTRATION IN THE UNITED STATES (2ND MIMEOGRAPHED SUPPLEMENT). USA-45 LOC/G POL/PAR PROVS FEDERAL...TESTS 20. PAGE 16 B0319
BIBLIOG ADMIN MGT NAT/G
B42

JONES V.,METROPOLITAN GOVERNMENT. HABITAT ALL/VALS ...MGT SOC CHARTS. PAGE 57 B1151
LOC/G MUNIC ADMIN TECHRACY
B42

CARLO A.M.,ENSAYO DE UNA BIBLIOGRAFIA DE BIBLIOGRAFIAS MEXICANAS. ECO/UNDEV LOC/G ADMIN LEAD 20 MEXIC/AMER. PAGE 19 B0381
BIBLIOG L/A+17C NAT/G DIPLOM
B43

PUBLIC ADMINISTRATION SERVICE,YOUR BUSINESS OF GOVERNMENT: A CATALOG OF PUBLICATIONS IN THE FIELD OF PUBLIC ADMINISTRATION (PAMPHLET). FINAN R+D LOC/G ACT/RES OP/RES PLAN 20. PAGE 85 B1715
BIBLIOG ADMIN NAT/G MUNIC
B44

CONOVER H.F.,THE GOVERNMENTS OF THE MAJOR FOREIGN POWERS: A BIBLIOGRAPHY. FRANCE GERMANY ITALY UK USSR CONSTN LOC/G POL/PAR EX/STRUC FORCES ADMIN CT/SYS CIVMIL/REL TOTALISM...POLICY 19/20. PAGE 23 B0464
BIBLIOG NAT/G DIPLOM
B45

ROGERS W.C.,INTERNATIONAL ADMINISTRATION: A BIBLIOGRAPHY (PUBLICATION NO 92; A PAMPHLET). WOR-45 INT/ORG LOC/G NAT/G CENTRAL 20. PAGE 90 B1814
BIBLIOG/A ADMIN MGT DIPLOM
B45

FISHER M.J.,"PARTIES AND POLITICS IN THE LOCAL COMMUNITY." USA-45 NAT/G SCHOOL ADMIN PARTIC REPRESENT KNOWL...BIBLIOG 20. PAGE 36 B0724
CHOOSE LOC/G POL/PAR ROUTINE
C45

CONOVER H.F.,NON-SELF-GOVERNING AREAS. BELGIUM FRANCE ITALY UK WOR+45 CULTURE ECO/UNDEV INT/ORG LOC/G NAT/G ECO/TAC INT/TRADE ADMIN HEALTH...SOC UN. PAGE 23 B0465
BIBLIOG/A COLONIAL DIPLOM
B47

FLYNN E.J.,YOU'RE THE BOSS. USA-45 ELITES TOP/EX DOMIN CONTROL EXEC LEAD REPRESENT 19/20 NEWYORK/C ROOSEVLT/F FLYNN/BOSS BOSSISM. PAGE 36 B0732
LOC/G MUNIC BIOG POL/PAR
B47

HIRSHBERG H.S.,SUBJECT GUIDE TO UNITED STATES GOVERNMENT PUBLICATIONS. USA+45 USA-45 LAW ADMIN ...SOC 20. PAGE 50 B1017
BIBLIOG NAT/G DIPLOM LOC/G
B47

PUBLIC ADMINISTRATION SERVICE,CURRENT RESEARCH PROJECTS IN PUBLIC ADMINISTRATION (PAMPHLET). LAW CONSTN COM/IND LABOR LOC/G MUNIC PROVS ACT/RES DIPLOM RECEIVE EDU/PROP WAR 20. PAGE 85 B1716
BIBLIOG R+D MGT ADMIN
B48

HULL C.,THE MEMOIRS OF CORDELL HULL (VOLUME ONE). USA-45 WOR-45 CONSTN FAM LOC/G NAT/G PROVS DELIB/GP FORCES LEGIS TOP/EX BAL/PWR LEGIT ADMIN EXEC WAR ATTIT ORD/FREE PWR...MAJORIT SELF/OBS TIME/SEQ TREND NAZI 20. PAGE 52 B1062
BIOG DIPLOM
B48

PUBLIC ADMINISTRATION SERVICE,SOURCE MATERIALS IN PUBLIC ADMINISTRATION (PAS BIBLIOGRAPHY (PAS PUBLICATION NO. 102). USA+45 LAW FINAN LOC/G MUNIC NAT/G PLAN RECEIVE EDU/PROP CT/SYS CHOOSE HEALTH 20. PAGE 85 B1717
BIBLIOG/A GOV/REL MGT ADMIN
B48

STOKES W.S.,BIBLIOGRAPHY OF STANDARD AND CLASSICAL WORKS IN THE FIELDS OF AMERICAN POLITICAL SCIENCE. USA+45 USA-45 POL/PAR PROVS FORCES DIPLOM ADMIN CT/SYS APPORT 20 CONGRESS PRESIDENT. PAGE 101 B2043
BIBLIOG NAT/G LOC/G CONSTN
C48

BOLLENS J.C.,"THE PROBLEM OF GOVERNMENT IN THE SAN FRANCISCO BAY REGION." INDUS PROVS ADMIN GOV/REL ...SOC CHARTS BIBLIOG 20. PAGE 13 B0270
USA+45 MUNIC LOC/G PROB/SOLV
N48

YATES M.,ADMINISTRATIVE REORGANIZATION OF STATE
BIBLIOG

GOVERNMENTS: A BIBLIOGRAPHY (PAMPHLET). USA+45 USA-45 CONSTN OP/RES PLAN CONFER...POLICY 20. PAGE 118 B2390
LOC/G ADMIN PROVS
B49

SHISTER J.,ECONOMICS OF THE LABOR MARKET. LOC/G NAT/G WORKER TEC/DEV BARGAIN PAY PRICE EXEC GP/REL INCOME...MGT T 20. PAGE 96 B1949
MARKET LABOR INDUS
S49

STEINMETZ H.,"THE PROBLEMS OF THE LANDRAT: A STUDY OF COUNTY GOVERNMENT IN THE US ZONE OF GERMANY." GERMANY/W USA+45 INDUS PLAN DIPLOM EDU/PROP CONTROL WAR GOV/REL FEDERAL WEALTH PLURISM...GOV/COMP 20 LANDRAT. PAGE 100 B2031
LOC/G COLONIAL MGT TOP/EX
B50

GRAVES W.B.,PUBLIC ADMINISTRATION: A COMPREHENSIVE BIBLIOGRAPHY ON PUBLIC ADMINISTRATION IN THE UNITED STATES (PAMPHLET). USA+45 USA-45 LOC/G NAT/G LEGIS ADJUD INGP/REL...MGT 20. PAGE 42 B0858
BIBLIOG FINAN CONTROL ADMIN
B50

GREAT BRITAIN TREASURY,PUBLIC ADMINISTRATION: A BIBLIOGRAPHY FOR ORGANISATION AND METHODS (PAMPHLET). UK LOC/G NAT/G CONSULT EX/STRUC CONFER ROUTINE TASK EFFICIENCY...MGT 20. PAGE 43 B0862
BIBLIOG PLAN CONTROL ADMIN
B50

LITTLE HOOVER COMM,HOW TO ACHIEVE GREATER EFFICIENCY AND ECONOMY IN MINNESOTA'S GOVERNMENT (PAMPHLET). PLAN BUDGET ADMIN CHOOSE EFFICIENCY ALL/VALS 20 MINNESOTA. PAGE 66 B1327
TOP/EX LOC/G GOV/REL PROVS
B50

WARD R.E.,A GUIDE TO JAPANESE REFERENCE AND RESEARCH MATERIALS IN THE FIELD OF POLITICAL SCIENCE. LAW CONSTN LOC/G PRESS ADMIN...SOC CON/ANAL METH 19/20 CHINJAP. PAGE 113 B2289
BIBLIOG/A ASIA NAT/G
B50

MORLAN R.L.,"INTERGOVERNMENTAL RELATIONS IN EDUCATION." USA+45 FINAN LOC/G MUNIC NAT/G FORCES PROB/SOLV RECEIVE ADMIN RACE/REL COST...BIBLIOG INDIAN/AM. PAGE 76 B1526
SCHOOL GOV/REL ACADEM POLICY
C50

STEWART F.M.,"A HALF CENTURY OF MUNICIPAL REFORM." USA+45 CONSTN FINAN SCHOOL EX/STRUC PLAN PROB/SOLV EDU/PROP ADMIN CHOOSE GOV/REL BIBLIOG. PAGE 101 B2036
LOC/G VOL/ASSN MUNIC POLICY
C50

WAGER P.W.,"COUNTY GOVERNMENT ACROSS THE NATION." USA+45 CONSTN COM/IND FINAN SCHOOL DOMIN CT/SYS LEAD GOV/REL...STAT BIBLIOG 20. PAGE 112 B2272
LOC/G PROVS ADMIN ROUTINE
B51

ANDERSON W.,STATE AND LOCAL GOVERNMENT IN THE UNITED STATES. USA+45 CONSTN POL/PAR EX/STRUC LEGIS BUDGET TAX ADJUD CT/SYS CHOOSE...CHARTS T 20. PAGE 5 B0100
LOC/G MUNIC PROVS GOV/REL
B51

ANDERSON W.,GOVERNMENT IN THE FIFTY STATES. LAW CONSTN FINAN POL/PAR LEGIS EDU/PROP ADJUD ADMIN CT/SYS CHOOSE...CHARTS 20. PAGE 5 B0101
LOC/G PROVS GOV/REL
B51

CHRISTENSEN A.N.,THE EVOLUTION OF LATIN AMERICAN GOVERNMENT: A BOOK OF READINGS. ECO/UNDEV INDUS LOC/G POL/PAR EX/STRUC LEGIS FOR/AID CT/SYS ...SOC/WK 20 SOUTH/AMER. PAGE 21 B0428
NAT/G CONSTN DIPLOM L/A+17C
B51

NIELANDER W.A.,PUBLIC RELATIONS. USA+45 COM/IND LOC/G NAT/G VOL/ASSN EX/STRUC DIPLOM EDU/PROP PRESS TV...METH/CNCPT T 20. PAGE 78 B1583
PERS/REL GP/REL LG/CO ROUTINE
B52

DE GRAZIA A.,POLITICAL ORGANIZATION. CONSTN LOC/G MUNIC NAT/G CHIEF LEGIS TOP/EX ADJUD CT/SYS PERS/REL...INT/LAW MYTH UN. PAGE 27 B0553
FEDERAL LAW ADMIN
B52

LEGISLATIVE REFERENCE SERVICE,PROBLEMS OF LEGISLATIVE APPORTIONMENT ON BOTH FEDERAL AND STATE LEVELS: SELECTED REFERENCES (PAMPHLET). USA+45 LOC/G NAT/G LEGIS WRITING ADMIN APPORT 20 CONGRESS. PAGE 63 B1282
BIBLIOG REPRESENT CHOOSE PROVS
B52

SCHATTSCHNEIDER E.E.,A GUIDE TO THE STUDY OF PUBLIC AFFAIRS. LAW LOC/G NAT/G LEGIS BUDGET PRESS ADMIN LOBBY...JURID CHARTS 20. PAGE 93 B1882
ACT/RES INTELL ACADEM METH/COMP
S52

SNIDER C.F.,"AMERICAN COUNTY GOVERNMENT: A MID-CENTURY REVIEW" (BMR)" USA+45 USA-45 PROVS DELIB/GP EX/STRUC BUDGET TAX PWR 20. PAGE 98 B1988
LOC/G ADMIN GOV/REL REGION
C52

LANCASTER L.W.,"GOVERNMENT IN RURAL AMERICA." USA+45 ECO/DEV AGRI SCHOOL FORCES LEGIS JUDGE BUDGET TAX CT/SYS...CHARTS BIBLIOG. PAGE 62 B1253
GOV/REL LOC/G MUNIC ADMIN
B53

A BIBLIOGRAPHY AND SUBJECT INDEX OF PUBLICATIONS OF FLORIDA STATE AGENCIES. USA+45 LOC/G LEAD ATTIT 20 FLORIDA. PAGE 2 B0036
BIBLIOG PROVS GOV/REL

APPLEBY P.H.,PUBLIC ADMINISTRATION IN INDIA: REPORT OF A SURVEY. INDIA LOC/G OP/RES ATTIT ORD/FREE 20. PAGE 6 B0118
ADMIN B53
ADMIN NAT/G EX/STRUC GOV/REL

GROSS B.M.,THE LEGISLATIVE STRUGGLE: A STUDY IN SOCIAL COMBAT. STRUCT LOC/G POL/PAR JUDGE EDU/PROP DEBATE ETIQUET ADMIN LOBBY CHOOSE GOV/REL INGP/REL HEREDITY ALL/VALS...SOC PRESIDENT. PAGE 44 B0885
B53
LEGIS DECISION PERSON LEAD

STOUT H.M.,BRITISH GOVERNMENT. UK FINAN LOC/G POL/PAR DELIB/GP DIPLOM ADMIN COLONIAL CHOOSE ORD/FREE...JURID BIBLIOG 20 COMMONWLTH. PAGE 101 B2049
B53
NAT/G PARL/PROC CONSTN NEW/LIB

TOMPKINS D.C.,CIVIL DEFENSE IN THE STATES: A BIBLIOGRAPHY (DEFENSE BIBLIOGRAPHIES NO. 3; PAMPHLET). USA+45 LABOR LOC/G NAT/G PROVS LEGIS. PAGE 105 B2115
B53
BIBLIOG WAR ORD/FREE ADMIN

CHICAGO JOINT REFERENCE LIB,FEDERAL-STATE-LOCAL RELATIONS; A SELECTED BIBLIOGRAPHY. USA+45 AGRI LABOR LOC/G MUNIC EX/STRUC ADMIN REGION HEALTH CON/ANAL. PAGE 21 B0419
B54
BIBLIOG FEDERAL GOV/REL

SCHWARTZ B.,FRENCH ADMINISTRATIVE LAW AND THE COMMON-LAW WORLD. FRANCE CULTURE LOC/G NAT/G PROVS DELIB/GP EX/STRUC LEGIS PROB/SOLV CT/SYS EXEC GOV/REL...IDEA/COMP ENGLSH/LAW. PAGE 95 B1912
B54
JURID LAW METH/COMP ADJUD

TOMPKINS D.C.,STATE GOVERNMENT AND ADMINISTRATION: A BIBLIOGRAPHY. USA+45 USA-45 CONSTN LEGIS JUDGE BUDGET CT/SYS LOBBY...CHARTS 20. PAGE 105 B2116
B54
BIBLIOG/A LOC/G PROVS ADMIN

CALDWELL L.K.,"THE GOVERNMENT AND ADMINISTRATION OF NEW YORK." LOC/G MUNIC POL/PAR SCHOOL CHIEF LEGIS PLAN TAX CT/SYS...MGT SOC/WK BIBLIOG 20 NEWYORK/C. PAGE 18 B0366
C54
PROVS ADMIN CONSTN EX/STRUC

ROBSON W.A.,"GREAT CITIES OF THE WORLD: THEIR GOVERNMENT, POLITICS, AND PLANNING." LOC/G CONSTN FINAN EX/STRUC ADMIN EXEC CHOOSE GOV/REL...STAT TREND ANTHOL BIBLIOG 20. PAGE 89 B1806
C54
LOC/G MUNIC PLAN PROB/SOLV

APTER D.E.,THE GOLD COAST IN TRANSITION. FUT CONSTN CULTURE SOCIETY ECO/UNDEV FAM KIN LOC/G NAT/G POL/PAR LEGIS TOP/EX EDU/PROP LEGIT ADMIN ATTIT PERSON PWR...CONCPT STAT INT CENSUS TOT/POP VAL/FREE. PAGE 6 B0120
B55
AFR SOVEREIGN

CHAPMAN B.,THE PREFECTS AND PROVINCIAL FRANCE. FRANCE DELIB/GP WORKER ROLE PWR 19/20 PREFECT. PAGE 20 B0408
B55
ADMIN PROVS EX/STRUC LOC/G

GUAITA A.,BIBLIOGRAFIA ESPANOLA DE DERECHO ADMINISTRATIVO (PAMPHLET). SPAIN LOC/G MUNIC NAT/G PROVS JUDGE BAL/PWR GOV/REL OWN...JURID 18/19. PAGE 44 B0900
B55
BIBLIOG ADMIN CONSTN PWR

BLAU P.M.,BUREAUCRACY IN MODERN SOCIETY. STRUCT INDUS LABOR LG/CO LOC/G NAT/G FORCES EDU/PROP ROUTINE ORD/FREE 20 BUREAUCRCY. PAGE 12 B0252
B56
SOC EX/STRUC ADMIN EFFICIENCY

POWELL N.J.,PERSONNEL ADMINISTRATION IN GOVERNMENT. COM/IND POL/PAR LEGIS PAY CT/SYS ROUTINE GP/REL PERS/REL...POLICY METH 20 CIVIL/SERV. PAGE 84 B1697
B56
ADMIN WORKER LOC/G NAT/G

WASSERMAN P.,INFORMATION FOR ADMINISTRATORS: A GUIDE TO PUBLICATIONS AND SERVICES FOR MANAGEMENT IN BUSINESS AND GOVERNMENT. R+D LOC/G NAT/G PROF/ORG VOL/ASSN PRESS...PSY SOC STAT 20. PAGE 114 B2299
B56
BIBLIOG MGT KNOWL EDU/PROP

WILSON P.,GOVERNMENT AND POLITICS OF INDIA AND PAKISTAN: 1885-1955; A BIBLIOGRAPHY OF WORKS IN WESTERN LANGUAGES. INDIA PAKISTAN CONSTN LOC/G POL/PAR FORCES DIPLOM ADMIN WAR CHOOSE...BIOG CON/ANAL 19/20. PAGE 117 B2361
B56
BIBLIOG COLONIAL NAT/G S/ASIA

HEADY F.,"THE MICHIGAN DEPARTMENT OF ADMINISTRATION; A CASE STUDY IN THE POLITICS OF ADMINISTRATION" (BMR)" USA+45 POL/PAR PROVS CHIEF LEGIS GP/REL ATTIT 20 MICHIGAN. PAGE 48 B0980
S56
ADMIN DELIB/GP LOC/G

KHAMA T.,"POLITICAL CHANGE IN AFRICAN SOCIETY." CONSTN SOCIETY LOC/G NAT/G POL/PAR EX/STRUC LEGIS LEGIT ADMIN CHOOSE REPRESENT NAT/LISM MORAL ORD/FREE PWR...CONCPT OBS TREND GEN/METH CMN/WLTH 17/20. PAGE 59 B1201
S56
AFR ELITES

MARGOLIS J.,"ON MUNICIPAL LAND POLICY FOR FISCAL GAINS." USA+45 MUNIC PLAN TAX COST EFFICIENCY HABITAT KNOWL...MGT 20. PAGE 69 B1398
S56
BUDGET POLICY GEOG LOC/G

BABCOCK R.S.,STATE & LOCAL GOVERNMENT AND POLITICS. USA+45 CONSTN POL/PAR EX/STRUC LEGIS BUDGET LOBBY CHOOSE SUFF...CHARTS BIBLIOG T 20. PAGE 8 B0154
B57
PROVS LOC/G GOV/REL

CHICAGO U LAW SCHOOL,CONFERENCE ON JUDICIAL ADMINISTRATION. LOC/G MUNIC NAT/G PROVS...ANTHOL 20. PAGE 21 B0421
B57
CT/SYS ADJUD ADMIN GOV/REL

DE GRAZIA A.,GRASS ROOTS PRIVATE WELFARE. LOC/G SCHOOL ACT/RES EDU/PROP ROUTINE CROWD GP/REL DISCRIM HAPPINESS ILLEGIT AGE HABITAT. PAGE 27 B0554
B57
NEW/LIB HEALTH MUNIC VOL/ASSN

KNEIER C.M.,CITY GOVERNMENT IN THE UNITED STATES (3RD ED.). USA-45 FINAN NAT/G POL/PAR LEGIS EDU/PROP LEAD APPORT REPRESENT ATTIT...MGT 20 CITY/MGT. PAGE 60 B1219
B57
MUNIC LOC/G ADMIN GOV/REL

MEYER P.,ADMINISTRATIVE ORGANIZATION: A COMPARATIVE STUDY OF THE ORGANIZATION OF PUBLIC ADMINISTRATION. DENMARK FRANCE NORWAY SWEDEN UK USA+45 ELITES LOC/G CONSULT LEGIS ADJUD CONTROL LEAD PWR SKILL DECISION. PAGE 73 B1475
B57
ADMIN METH/COMP NAT/G CENTRAL

GULICK L.,"METROPOLITAN ORGANIZATION." LEGIS EXEC PARTIC CHOOSE REPRESENT GOV/REL...MAJORIT DECISION. PAGE 45 B0904
S57
REGION LOC/G MUNIC

HAILEY,"TOMORROW IN AFRICA." CONSTN SOCIETY LOC/G NAT/G DOMIN ADJUD ADMIN GP/REL DISCRIM NAT/LISM ATTIT MORAL ORD/FREE...PSY SOC CONCPT OBS RECORD TREND GEN/LAWS CMN/WLTH 20. PAGE 45 B0917
S57
AFR PERSON ELITES RACE/REL

ROBSON W.A.,"TWO-LEVEL GOVERNMENT FOR METROPOLITAN AREAS." MUNIC EX/STRUC LEGIS PARTIC REPRESENT MAJORITY. PAGE 89 B1807
S57
REGION LOC/G PLAN GOV/REL

CARTER G.M.,TRANSITION IN AFRICA; STUDIES IN POLITICAL ADAPTATION. AFR CENTRL/AFR GHANA NIGERIA CONSTN LOC/G POL/PAR ADMIN GP/REL FEDERAL...MAJORIT BIBLIOG 20. PAGE 19 B0389
B58
NAT/COMP PWR CONTROL NAT/G

COLEMAN J.S.,NIGERIA: BACKGROUND TO NATIONALISM. AFR SOCIETY ECO/DEV KIN LOC/G POL/PAR TEC/DEV DOMIN ADMIN DRIVE PWR RESPECT...TRADIT SOC INT SAMP TIME/SEQ 20. PAGE 22 B0452
B58
NAT/G NAT/LISM NIGERIA

COWAN L.G.,LOCAL GOVERNMENT IN WEST AFRICA. AFR FRANCE UK CULTURE KIN POL/PAR CHIEF LEGIS CREATE ADMIN PARTIC GOV/REL GP/REL...METH/COMP 20. PAGE 24 B0498
B58
LOC/G COLONIAL SOVEREIGN REPRESENT

DAVIS K.C.,ADMINISTRATIVE LAW; CASES, TEXT, PROBLEMS. LAW LOC/G NAT/G TOP/EX PAY CONTROL GOV/REL INGP/REL FEDERAL 20 SUPREME/CT. PAGE 27 B0541
B58
ADJUD JURID CT/SYS ADMIN

HENKIN L.,ARMS CONTROL AND INSPECTION IN AMERICAN LAW. LAW CONSTN INT/ORG LOC/G MUNIC NAT/G PROVS EDU/PROP LEGIT EXEC NUC/PWR KNOWL ORD/FREE...OBS TOT/POP CONGRESS 20. PAGE 49 B0990
B58
USA+45 JURID ARMS/CONT

INDIAN INST OF PUBLIC ADMIN,IMPROVING CITY GOVERNMENT. INDIA ECO/UNDEV PLAN BUDGET PARTIC GP/REL 20. PAGE 53 B1080
B58
LOC/G MUNIC PROB/SOLV ADMIN

NEAL F.W.,TITOISM IN ACTION. COM YUGOSLAVIA AGRI LOC/G DIPLOM TOTALISM...BIBLIOG 20 TITO/MARSH. PAGE 77 B1564
B58
MARXISM POL/PAR CHIEF ADMIN

SHAW S.J.,THE FINANCIAL AND ADMINISTRATIVE ORGANIZATION AND DEVELOPMENT OF OTTOMAN EGYPT 1517-1798. UAR LOC/G FORCES BUDGET INT/TRADE TAX EATING INCOME WEALTH...CHARTS BIBLIOG 16/18 OTTOMAN NAPOLEON/B. PAGE 96 B1940
B58
FINAN ADMIN GOV/REL CULTURE

SHERWOOD F.P.,SUPERVISORY METHODS IN MUNICIPAL ADMINISTRATION. USA+45 MUNIC WORKER EDU/PROP PARTIC INGP/REL PERS/REL 20 CITY/MGT. PAGE 96 B1945
B58
EX/STRUC LEAD ADMIN LOC/G

SPITZ D.,DEMOCRACY AND THE CHALLANGE OF POWER. FUT USA+45 USA-45 LAW SOCIETY STRUCT LOC/G POL/PAR PROVS DELIB/GP EX/STRUC LEGIS TOP/EX ACT/RES CREATE DOMIN EDU/PROP LEGIT ADJUD ADMIN ATTIT DRIVE MORAL ORD/FREE TOT/POP. PAGE 99 B2010
B58
NAT/G PWR

SWEENEY S.B.,EDUCATION FOR ADMINISTRATIVE CAREERS   B58
IN GOVERNMENT SERVICE. USA+45 ACADEM CONSULT CREATE   EDU/PROP
PLAN CONFER SKILL...TREND IDEA/COMP METH 20   ADMIN
CIVIL/SERV. PAGE 102 B2059   NAT/G
                                                       LOC/G
                                                        B58
VAN RIPER P.P.,HISTORY OF THE UNITED STATES CIVIL   ADMIN
SERVICE. USA+45 USA-45 LABOR LOC/G DELIB/GP LEGIS   WORKER
PROB/SOLV LOBBY GOV/REL GP/REL INCOME...POLICY   NAT/G
18/20 PRESIDENT CIVIL/SERV. PAGE 111 B2251
                                                        L58
JONAS F.H.,"BIBLIOGRAPHY ON WESTERN POLITICS."   BIBLIOG/A
USA+45 USA-45 ELITES MUNIC POL/PAR LEGIS ADJUD   LOC/G
ADMIN 20. PAGE 57 B1148   NAT/G
                                                       LAW
                                                        S58
DAHL R.A.,"A CRITIQUE OF THE RULING ELITE MODEL."   CONCPT
USA+45 LOC/G MUNIC NAT/G POL/PAR PROVS DOMIN LEGIT   STERTYP
ADMIN...METH/CNCPT HYPO/EXP. PAGE 25 B0520   ELITES

MAIR L.P.,"REPRESENTATIVE LOCAL GOVERNMENT AS A   AFR
PROBLEM IN SOCIAL CHANGE." ECO/UNDEV KIN LOC/G   PWR
NAT/G SCHOOL JUDGE ADMIN ROUTINE REPRESENT   ELITES
RIGID/FLEX RESPECT...CONCPT STERTYP CMN/WLTH 20.
PAGE 68 B1383
                                                        B59
BRUNTON R.L.,MANAGEMENT PRACTICES FOR SMALLER   ADMIN
CITIES. USA+45 MUNIC CONSULT PLAN BUDGET PERS/REL   LOC/G
20 CITY/MGT. PAGE 16 B0331   MGT
                                                       TOP/EX
                                                        B59
COUNCIL OF STATE GOVERNMENTS,STATE GOVERNMENT: AN   BIBLIOG/A
ANNOTATED BIBLIOGRAPHY (PAMPHLET). USA+45 LAW AGRI   PROVS
INDUS WORKER PLAN TAX ADJUST AGE/Y ORD/FREE...HEAL   LOC/G
MGT 20. PAGE 24 B0494   ADMIN
                                                        B59
DESMITH S.A.,JUDICIAL REVIEW OF ADMINISTRATIVE   ADJUD
ACTION. UK LOC/G CONSULT DELIB/GP ADMIN PWR   NAT/G
...DECISION JURID 20 ENGLSH/LAW. PAGE 28 B0576   PROB/SOLV
                                                       CT/SYS
                                                        B59
ELAZAR D.J.,INTERGOVERNMENTAL RELATIONS IN   FEDERAL
NINETEENTH CENTURY AMERICAN FEDERALISM (DOCTORAL   ADMIN
THESIS). USA-45 FINAN LOC/G NAT/G GP/REL 18/19.   PROVS
PAGE 33 B0662   GOV/REL
                                                        B59
GORDENKER L.,THE UNITED NATIONS AND THE PEACEFUL   DELIB/GP
UNIFICATION OF KOREA. ASIA LAW LOC/G CONSULT   KOREA
ACT/RES DIPLOM DOMIN LEGIT ADJUD ADMIN ORD/FREE   INT/ORG
SOVEREIGN...INT GEN/METH UN COLD/WAR 20. PAGE 41
B0829
                                                        B59
IPSEN H.P.,HAMBURGISCHES STAATS- UND   ADMIN
VERWALTUNGSRECHT. CONSTN LOC/G FORCES BUDGET CT/SYS   PROVS
...JURID 20 HAMBURG. PAGE 54 B1103   LEGIS
                                                       FINAN
                                                        B59
MAASS A.,AREA AND POWER: A THEORY OF LOCAL   LOC/G
GOVERNMENT. MUNIC PROVS EX/STRUC LEGIS CT/SYS   FEDERAL
CHOOSE PWR 20. PAGE 67 B1354   BAL/PWR
                                                       GOV/REL
                                                        B59
PARK R.L.,LEADERSHIP AND POLITICAL INSTITUTIONS IN   NAT/G
INDIA. S/ASIA CULTURE ECO/UNDEV KIN LOC/G MUNIC PROVS   EXEC
LEGIS PLAN ADMIN LEAD ORD/FREE WEALTH...GEOG SOC   INDIA
BIOG TOT/POP VAL/FREE 20. PAGE 81 B1633
                                                        B59
SAYER W.S.,AN AGENDA FOR RESEARCH IN PUBLIC   WORKER
PERSONNEL ADMINISTRATION. FUT USA+45 ACADEM LABOR   ADMIN
LOC/G NAT/G POL/PAR DELIB/GP MGT. PAGE 93 B1872   ACT/RES
                                                       CONSULT
                                                        B59
YALE UNIV BUR OF HIGHWAY TRAF,URBAN TRANSPORTATION   ADMIN
ADMINISTRATION. FUT USA+45 CONSTRUC ACT/RES BUDGET   DIST/IND
...CENSUS 20 PUB/TRANS. PAGE 118 B2388   LOC/G
                                                       PLAN
                                                        S59
PADELFORD N.J.,"REGIONAL COOPERATION IN THE SOUTH   INT/ORG
PACIFIC: THE SOUTH PACIFIC COMMISSION." FUT   ADMIN
NEW/ZEALND UK WOR+45 CULTURE ECO/UNDEV LOC/G
VOL/ASSN...OBS CON/ANAL UNESCO VAL/FREE AUSTRAL 20.
PAGE 80 B1622
                                                        B60
ADRIAN C.R.,STATE AND LOCAL GOVERNMENTS: A STUDY IN   LOC/G
THE POLITICAL PROCESS. USA+45 LAW FINAN MUNIC   PROVS
POL/PAR LEGIS ADJUD EXEC CHOOSE REPRESENT. PAGE 3   GOV/REL
B0060   ATTIT
                                                        B60
ALBI F.,TRATADO DE LOS MODOS DE GESTION DE LAS   LOC/G
CORPORACIONES LOCALES. SPAIN FINAN NAT/G BUDGET   LAW
CONTROL EXEC ROUTINE GOV/REL ORD/FREE SOVEREIGN   ADMIN
...MGT 20. PAGE 3 B0068   MUNIC
                                                        B60
ARGAL R.,MUNICIPAL GOVERNMENT IN INDIA. INDIA   LOC/G
BUDGET TAX ADMIN EXEC 19/20. PAGE 6 B0126   MUNIC
                                                       DELIB/GP

                                                       CONTROL
                                                        B60
AYEARST M.,THE BRITISH WEST INDIES: THE SEARCH FOR   CONSTN
SELF-GOVERNMENT. FUT WEST/IND LOC/G POL/PAR   COLONIAL
EX/STRUC LEGIS CHOOSE FEDERAL...NAT/COMP BIBLIOG   REPRESENT
17/20. PAGE 7 B0152   NAT/G
                                                        B60
FRYE R.J.,GOVERNMENT AND LABOR: THE ALABAMA   ADMIN
PROGRAM. USA+45 INDUS R+D LABOR WORKER BUDGET   LEGIS
EFFICIENCY AGE/Y HEALTH...CHARTS 20 ALABAMA.   LOC/G
PAGE 38 B0761   PROVS
                                                        B60
GILMORE D.R.,DEVELOPING THE "LITTLE" ECONOMIES.   ECO/TAC
USA+45 FINAN LG/CO PROF/ORG VOL/ASSN CREATE ADMIN.   LOC/G
PAGE 40 B0801   PROVS
                                                       PLAN
                                                        B60
HEAP D.,AN OUTLINE OF PLANNING LAW (3RD ED.). UK   MUNIC
LAW PROB/SOLV ADMIN CONTROL 20. PAGE 49 B0983   PLAN
                                                       JURID
                                                       LOC/G
                                                        B60
JONES V.,METROPOLITAN COMMUNITIES: A BIBLIOGRAPHY   BIBLIOG
WITH SPECIAL EMPHASIS UPON GOVERNMENT AND POLITICS,   LOC/G
1955-1957. STRUCT ECO/DEV FINAN FORCES PLAN   MUNIC
PROB/SOLV RECEIVE EDU/PROP CT/SYS...GEOG HEAL 20.   ADMIN
PAGE 57 B1152
                                                        B60
MARSHALL A.H.,FINANCIAL ADMINISTRATION IN LOCAL   FINAN
GOVERNMENT. UK DELIB/GP CONFER COST INCOME PERSON   LOC/G
...JURID 20. PAGE 70 B1408   BUDGET
                                                       ADMIN
                                                        B60
MATTOD P.K.,A STUDY OF LOCAL SELF GOVERNMENT IN   MUNIC
URBAN INDIA. INDIA FINAN DELIB/GP LEGIS BUDGET TAX   CONSTN
SOVEREIGN...MGT GP/COMP 20. PAGE 71 B1432   LOC/G
                                                       ADMIN
                                                        B60
PAGE T.,THE PUBLIC PERSONNEL AGENCY AND THE CHIEF   WORKER
EXECUTIVE (REPORT NO. 601). USA+45 LOC/G NAT/G   EXEC
GP/REL PERS/REL...ANTHOL 20. PAGE 80 B1624   ADMIN
                                                       MGT
                                                        B60
PENNSYLVANIA ECONOMY LEAGUE,URBAN RENEWAL IMPACT   PLAN
STUDY: ADMINISTRATIVE-LEGAL-FISCAL. USA+45 FINAN   BUDGET
LOC/G NEIGH ADMIN EFFICIENCY...CENSUS CHARTS 20   MUNIC
PENNSYLVAN. PAGE 82 B1652   ADJUD
                                                        B60
PFIFFNER J.M.,PUBLIC ADMINISTRATION. USA+45 FINAN   ADMIN
WORKER PLAN PROB/SOLV ADJUD CONTROL EXEC...T 20.   NAT/G
PAGE 82 B1666   LOC/G
                                                       MGT
                                                        B60
PHILLIPS J.C.,MUNICIPAL GOVERNMENT AND   MUNIC
ADMINISTRATION IN AMERICA. USA+45 LAW CONSTN FINAN   GOV/REL
FORCES PLAN RECEIVE OWN ORD/FREE 20 CIVIL/LIB.   LOC/G
PAGE 83 B1669   ADMIN
                                                        B60
POOLEY B.J.,THE EVOLUTION OF BRITISH PLANNING   PLAN
LEGISLATION. UK ECO/DEV LOC/G CONSULT DELIB/GP   MUNIC
ADMIN 20 URBAN/RNWL. PAGE 84 B1691   LEGIS
                                                       PROB/SOLV
                                                        B60
SMITH M.G.,GOVERNMENT IN ZAZZAU 1800-1950. NIGERIA   REGION
UK CULTURE SOCIETY LOC/G ADMIN COLONIAL   CONSTN
...METH/CNCPT NEW/IDEA METH 19/20. PAGE 98 B1983   KIN
                                                       ECO/UNDEV
                                                        L60
GRODZINS M.,"AMERICAN POLITICAL PARTIES AND THE   POL/PAR
AMERICAN SYSTEM" (BMR)" USA+45 LOC/G NAT/G LEGIS   FEDERAL
BAL/PWR ADMIN ROLE PWR...DECISION 20. PAGE 44 B0883   CENTRAL
                                                       GOV/REL
                                                        S60
BANFIELD E.C.,"THE POLITICAL IMPLICATIONS OF   TASK
METROPOLITAN GROWTH" (BMR)" UK USA+45 LOC/G   MUNIC
PROB/SOLV ADMIN GP/REL...METH/COMP NAT/COMP 20.   GOV/COMP
PAGE 9 B0176   CENSUS
                                                        S60
EMERSON R.,"THE EROSION OF DEMOCRACY." AFR FUT LAW   S/ASIA
CULTURE INTELL SOCIETY ECO/UNDEV FAM LOC/G NAT/G   POL/PAR
FORCES PLAN TEC/DEV ECO/TAC ADMIN CT/SYS ATTIT
ORD/FREE PWR...SOCIALIST SOC CONCPT STAND/INT
TIME/SEQ WORK 20. PAGE 33 B0671
                                                        S60
HERZ J.H.,"EAST GERMANY: PROGRESS AND PROSPECTS."   POL/PAR
COM AGRI FINAN INDUS LOC/G NAT/G FORCES PLAN   STRUCT
TEC/DEV DOMIN ADMIN COERCE DRIVE PERCEPT RIGID/FLEX   GERMANY
MORAL ORD/FREE PWR...MARXIST PSY SOC RECORD STERTYP
WORK. PAGE 49 B0997
                                                        S60
MARSHALL G.,"POLICE RESPONSIBILITY." UK LOC/G ADJUD   CONTROL
ADMIN EXEC 20. PAGE 70 B1409   REPRESENT
                                                       LAW
                                                       FORCES
                                                        S60
RAPHAELI N.,"SELECTED ARTICLES AND DOCUMENTS ON   BIBLIOG

COMPARATIVE PUBLIC ADMINISTRATION." USA+45 FINAN
LOC/G TOP/EX TEC/DEV EXEC GP/REL INGP/REL...GP/COMP
GOV/COMP METH/COMP. PAGE 86 B1738
    MGT
    ADMIN
    EX/STRUC
          S60

REISELBACH L.N.,"THE BASIS OF ISOLATIONIST
BEHAVIOR." USA+45 USA-45 CULTURE ECO/DEV LOC/G
NAT/G ADMIN ROUTINE CHOOSE BIO/SOC DRIVE RIGID/FLEX
...CENSUS SAMP TREND CHARTS TOT/POP 20. PAGE 87
B1765
    ATTIT
    DIPLOM
    ECO/TAC
          B61

AVERY M.W.,GOVERNMENT OF WASHINGTON STATE. USA+45
MUNIC DELIB/GP EX/STRUC LEGIS GIVE CT/SYS PARTIC
REGION EFFICIENCY 20 WASHINGT/G GOVERNOR. PAGE 7
B0151
    PROVS
    LOC/G
    ADMIN
    GOV/REL
          B61

BEASLEY K.E.,STATE SUPERVISION OF MUNICIPAL DEBT IN
KANSAS – A CASE STUDY. USA+45 USA-45 FINAN PROVS
BUDGET TAX ADJUD ADMIN CONTROL SUPEGO. PAGE 10
B0201
    MUNIC
    LOC/G
    LEGIS
    JURID
          B61

BURDETTE F.L.,POLITICAL SCIENCE: A SELECTED
BIBLIOGRAPHY OF BOOKS IN PRINT, WITH ANNOTATIONS
(PAMPHLET). LAW LOC/G NAT/G POL/PAR PROVS DIPLOM
EDU/PROP ADMIN CHOOSE ATTIT 20. PAGE 17 B0347
    BIBLIOG/A
    GOV/COMP
    CONCPT
    ROUTINE
          B61

DARRAH E.L.,FIFTY STATE GOVERNMENTS: A COMPILATION
OF EXECUTIVE ORGANIZATION CHARTS. USA+45 LOC/G
DELIB/GP LEGIS ADJUD LEAD PWR 20 GOVERNOR. PAGE 26
B0530
    EX/STRUC
    ADMIN
    ORG/CHARTS
    PROVS
          B61

DRAGNICH A.N.,MAJOR EUROPEAN GOVERNMENTS. FRANCE
GERMANY/W UK USSR LOC/G EX/STRUC CT/SYS PARL/PROC
ATTIT MARXISM...JURID MGT NAT/COMP 19/20. PAGE 30
B0615
    NAT/G
    LEGIS
    CONSTN
    POL/PAR
          B61

DRURY J.W.,THE GOVERNMENT OF KANSAS. USA+45 AGRI
INDUS CHIEF LEGIS WORKER PLAN BUDGET GIVE CT/SYS
GOV/REL...T 20 KANSAS GOVERNOR CITY/MGT. PAGE 31
B0621
    PROVS
    CONSTN
    ADMIN
    LOC/G
          B61

GARCIA E.,LA ADMINISTRACION ESPANOLA. SPAIN GOV/REL
...CONCPT METH/COMP 20. PAGE 39 B0780
    ADMIN
    NAT/G
    LOC/G
    DECISION
          B61

HICKS U.K.,DEVELOPMENT FROM BELOW. UK INDUS ADMIN
COLONIAL ROUTINE GOV/REL...POLICY METH/CNCPT CHARTS
19/20 CMN/WLTH. PAGE 50 B1006
    ECO/UNDEV
    LOC/G
    GOV/COMP
    METH/COMP
          B61

INTL UNION LOCAL AUTHORITIES,LOCAL GOVERNMENT IN
THE USA. USA+45 PUB/INST DELIB/GP CONFER AUTOMAT
GP/REL POPULISM...ANTHOL 20 CITY/MGT. PAGE 54 B1101
    LOC/G
    MUNIC
    ADMIN
    GOV/REL
          B61

LEE R.R.,ENGINEERING-ECONOMIC PLANNING
MISCELLANEOUS SUBJECTS: A SELECTED BIBLIOGRAPHY
(MIMEOGRAPHED). FINAN LOC/G MUNIC NEIGH ADMIN
CONTROL INGP/REL HABITAT...GEOG MGT SOC/WK 20
RESOURCE/N. PAGE 63 B1280
    BIBLIOG/A
    PLAN
    REGION
          B61

MACRIDIS R.C.,COMPARATIVE POLITICS: NOTES AND
READINGS. WOR+45 LOC/G MUNIC NAT/G PROVS VOL/ASSN
EDU/PROP ADMIN ATTIT PERSON ORD/FREE...SOC CONCPT
OBS RECORD TREND 20. PAGE 68 B1376
    POL/PAR
    CHOOSE
          B61

NARAIN J.P.,SWARAJ FOR THE PEOPLE. INDIA CONSTN
LOC/G MUNIC POL/PAR CHOOSE REPRESENT EFFICIENCY
ATTIT PWR SOVEREIGN 20. PAGE 77 B1553
    NAT/G
    ORD/FREE
    EDU/PROP
    EX/STRUC
          B61

PUGET H.,ESSAI DE BIBLIOGRAPHIE DES PRINCIPAUX
OUVRAGES DE DROIT PUBLIC.. QUI ONT PARU HORS DE
FRANCE DE 1945 A 1958. EUR+WWI USA+45 CONSTN LOC/G
...METH 20. PAGE 85 B1719
    BIBLIOG
    MGT
    ADMIN
    LAW
          B61

ROMANO F.,CIVIL SERVICE AND PUBLIC EMPLOYEE LAW IN
NEW JERSEY. CONSTN MUNIC WORKER GIVE PAY CHOOSE
UTIL 20. PAGE 90 B1816
    ADMIN
    PROVS
    ADJUD
    LOC/G
          B61

WEST F.J.,POLITICAL ADVANCEMENT IN THE SOUTH
PACIFIC. CONSTN CULTURE POL/PAR LEGIS DOMIN ADMIN
CHOOSE SOVEREIGN VAL/FREE 20 FIJI TAHITI SAMOA.
PAGE 115 B2325
    S/ASIA
    LOC/G
    COLONIAL
          L61

GERWIG R.,"PUBLIC AUTHORITIES IN THE UNITED
STATES." LAW CONSTN PROVS TAX ADMIN FEDERAL.
PAGE 39 B0793
    LOC/G
    MUNIC
    GOV/REL
    PWR
          S61

DYKMAN J.W.,"REVIEW ARTICLE* PLANNING AND DECISION
THEORY." ELITES LOC/G MUNIC CONSULT ADMIN...POLICY
MGT. PAGE 31 B0640
    DECISION
    PLAN
    RATIONAL
          C61

MOODIE G.C.,"THE GOVERNMENT OF GREAT BRITAIN." UK
    NAT/G

LAW STRUCT LOC/G POL/PAR DIPLOM RECEIVE ADMIN
COLONIAL CHOOSE...BIBLIOG 20 PARLIAMENT. PAGE 75
B1508
    SOCIETY
    PARL/PROC
    GOV/COMP
          B62

ARCO EDITORIAL BOARD,PUBLIC MANAGEMENT AND
ADMINISTRATION. PLAN BUDGET WRITING CONTROL ROUTINE
...TESTS CHARTS METH T 20. PAGE 6 B0125
    MGT
    ADMIN
    NAT/G
    LOC/G
          B62

CARTER G.M.,THE GOVERNMENT OF THE SOVIET UNION.
USSR CULTURE LOC/G DIPLOM ECO/TAC ADJUD CT/SYS LEAD
WEALTH...CHARTS T 20 COM/PARTY. PAGE 19 B0390
    NAT/G
    MARXISM
    POL/PAR
    EX/STRUC
          B62

COSTA RICA UNIVERSIDAD BIBL,LISTA DE TESIS DE GRADO
DE LA UNIVERSIDAD DE COSTA RICA. COSTA/RICA LAW
LOC/G ADMIN LEAD...SOC 20. PAGE 24 B0487
    BIBLIOG/A
    NAT/G
    DIPLOM
    ECO/UNDEV
          B62

FARBER W.O.,GOVERNMENT OF SOUTH DAKOTA. USA+45
DIST/IND POL/PAR CHIEF EX/STRUC LEGIS ECO/TAC GIVE
EDU/PROP CT/SYS PARTIC...T 20 SOUTH/DAK GOVERNOR.
PAGE 35 B0704
    PROVS
    LOC/G
    ADMIN
    CONSTN
          B62

GOVERNORS CONF STATE PLANNING,STATE PLANNING: A
POLICY STATEMENT (PAMPHLET). USA+45 LOC/G NAT/G
DELIB/GP LEGIS EXEC 20 GOVERNOR. PAGE 42 B0847
    GOV/REL
    PLAN
    ADMIN
    PROVS
          B62

GROVE J.W.,GOVERNMENT AND INDUSTRY IN BRITAIN. UK
FINAN LOC/G CONSULT DELIB/GP INT/TRADE ADMIN
CONTROL...BIBLIOG 20. PAGE 44 B0894
    ECO/TAC
    INDUS
    NAT/G
    GP/REL
          B62

HSUEH S.-S.,GOVERNMENT AND ADMINISTRATION OF HONG
KONG. CHIEF DELIB/GP LEGIS CT/SYS REPRESENT GOV/REL
20 HONG/KONG CITY/MGT CIVIL/SERV GOVERNOR. PAGE 52
B1055
    ADMIN
    LOC/G
    COLONIAL
    EX/STRUC
          B62

INAYATULLAH,BUREAUCRACY AND DEVELOPMENT IN
PAKISTAN. PAKISTAN ECO/UNDEV EDU/PROP CONFER
...ANTHOL DICTIONARY 20 BUREAUCRCY. PAGE 53 B1078
    EX/STRUC
    ADMIN
    NAT/G
    LOC/G
          B62

INST TRAINING MUNICIPAL ADMIN,MUNICIPAL FINANCE
ADMINISTRATION (6TH ED.). USA+45 ELITES ECO/DEV
LEGIS PLAN BUDGET TAX GP/REL BAL/PAY COST...POLICY
20 CITY/MGT. PAGE 54 B1089
    MUNIC
    ADMIN
    FINAN
    LOC/G
          B62

INSTITUTE JUDICIAL ADMIN,JUDGES: THEIR TEMPORARY
APPOINTMENT, ASSIGNMENT AND TRANSFER: SURVEY OF FED
AND STATE CONSTN'S STATUTES, ROLES OF CT. USA+45
CONSTN PROVS CT/SYS GOV/REL PWR JURID. PAGE 54
B1090
    NAT/G
    LOC/G
    JUDGE
    ADMIN
          B62

KARNJAHAPRAKORN C.,MUNICIPAL GOVERNMENT IN THAILAND
AS AN INSTITUTION AND PROCESS OF SELF-GOVERNMENT.
THAILAND CULTURE FINAN EX/STRUC LEGIS PLAN CONTROL
GOV/REL EFFICIENCY ATTIT...POLICY 20. PAGE 58 B1176
    LOC/G
    MUNIC
    ORD/FREE
    ADMIN
          B62

LITTLEFIELD N.,METROPOLITAN AREA PROBLEMS AND
MUNICIPAL HOME RULE. USA+45 PROVS ADMIN CONTROL
GP/REL PWR. PAGE 66 B1328
    LOC/G
    SOVEREIGN
    JURID
    LEGIS
          B62

MARTIN R.C.,GOVERNMENT AND THE SUBURBAN SCHOOL.
USA+45 FINAN EDU/PROP ADMIN HABITAT...TREND GP/COMP
20. PAGE 70 B1414
    SCHOOL
    LOC/G
    EX/STRUC
    ISOLAT
          B62

MUKERJI S.N.,ADMINISTRATION OF EDUCATION IN INDIA.
ACADEM LOC/G PROVS ROUTINE...POLICY STAT CHARTS 20.
PAGE 76 B1536
    SCHOOL
    ADMIN
    NAT/G
    EDU/PROP
          B62

MUNICIPAL MANPOWER COMMISSION,GOVERNMENTAL MANPOWER
FOR TOMORROW'S CITIES: A REPORT. USA+45 DELIB/GP
EX/STRUC PROB/SOLV TEC/DEV EDU/PROP ADMIN LEAD
HABITAT. PAGE 76 B1539
    LOC/G
    MUNIC
    LABOR
    GOV/REL
          B62

PHILLIPS O.H.,CONSTITUTIONAL AND ADMINISTRATIVE LAW
(3RD ED.). UK INT/ORG LOC/G CHIEF EX/STRUC LEGIS
BAL/PWR ADJUD COLONIAL CT/SYS PWR...CHARTS 20.
PAGE 83 B1670
    JURID
    ADMIN
    CONSTN
    NAT/G
          B62

PRESS C.,STATE MANUALS, BLUE BOOKS AND ELECTION
RESULTS. LAW LOC/G MUNIC LEGIS WRITING FEDERAL
SOVEREIGN...DECISION STAT CHARTS 20. PAGE 84 B1700
    BIBLIOG
    PROVS
    ADMIN
    CHOOSE
          B62

STAHL O.G.,PUBLIC PERSONNEL ADMINISTRATION. LOC/G
TOP/EX CREATE PLAN ROUTINE...TECHNIC MGT T.
PAGE 100 B2017
    ADMIN
    WORKER
    EX/STRUC
    NAT/G
          B62

US ADVISORY COMN INTERGOV REL,STATE CONSTITUTIONAL
    LOC/G

AND STATUTORY RESTRICTIONS UPON THE STRUCTURAL, FUNCTIONAL, AND PERSONAL POWERS OF LOCAL GOV'T. EX/STRUC ACT/RES DOMIN GOV/REL PWR...POLICY DECISION 17/20. PAGE 108 B2172 — CONSTN PROVS LAW

B62
WANGSNESS P.H.,THE POWER OF THE CITY MANAGER. USA+45 EX/STRUC BAL/PWR BUDGET TAX ADMIN REPRESENT CENTRAL EFFICIENCY DRIVE ROLE...POLICY 20 CITY/MGT. PAGE 113 B2286 — PWR TOP/EX MUNIC LOC/G

ERDMANN H.H.,"ADMINISTRATIVE LAW AND FARM ECONOMICS." USA+45 LOC/G NAT/G PLAN PROB/SOLV LOBBY ...DECISION ANTHOL 20. PAGE 33 B0680 — AGRI ADMIN ADJUD POLICY

L62
WATERSTON A.,"PLANNING IN MOROCCO, ORGANIZATION AND IMPLEMENTATION. BALTIMORE: HOPKINS ECON. DEVELOP. INT. BANK FOR." ISLAM ECO/DEV AGRI DIST/IND INDUS PROC/MFG SERV/IND LOC/G EX/STRUC ECO/TAC PWR WEALTH TOT/POP VAL/FREE 20. PAGE 114 B2302 — NAT/G PLAN MOROCCO

N62
UNIVERSITY PITT INST LOC GOVT,THE COUNCIL-MANAGER FORM OF GOVERNMENT IN PENNSYLVANIA (PAMPHLET). PROVS EX/STRUC REPRESENT GOV/REL EFFICIENCY ...CHARTS SIMUL 20 PENNSYLVAN CITY/MGT. PAGE 107 B2169 — LOC/G TOP/EX MUNIC PWR

B63
ADRIAN C.R.,GOVERNING OVER FIFTY STATES AND THEIR COMMUNITIES. USA+45 CONSTN FINAN MUNIC NAT/G POL/PAR EX/STRUC LEGIS ADMIN CONTROL CT/SYS ...CHARTS 20. PAGE 3 B0061 — PROVS LOC/G GOV/REL GOV/COMP

B63
BANFIELD E.C.,CITY POLITICS. CULTURE LABOR LOC/G POL/PAR LEGIS EXEC LEAD CHOOSE...DECISION NEGRO. PAGE 9 B0178 — MUNIC RIGID/FLEX ATTIT

B63
BASS M.E.,SELECTIVE BIBLIOGRAPHY ON MUNICIPAL GOVERNMENT FROM THE FILES OF THE MUNICIPAL TECHNICAL ADVISORY SERVICE. USA+45 FINAN SERV/IND PLAN 20. PAGE 9 B0194 — BIBLIOG LOC/G ADMIN MUNIC

B63
BOCK E.A., STATE AND LOCAL GOVERNMENT: A CASE BOOK. USA+45 MUNIC PROVS CONSULT GP/REL ATTIT...MGT 20 CASEBOOK GOVERNOR MAYOR. PAGE 12 B0254 — LOC/G ADMIN PROB/SOLV CHIEF

B63
BLONDEL J.,VOTERS, PARTIES, AND LEADERS. UK ELITES LOC/G NAT/G PROVS ACT/RES DOMIN REPRESENT GP/REL INGP/REL...SOC BIBLIOG 20. PAGE 12 B0255 — POL/PAR STRATA LEGIS ADMIN

B63
BOCK E.A.,STATE AND LOCAL GOVERNMENT: A CASE BOOK. USA+45 FINAN CHIEF PROB/SOLV TAX ATTIT...POLICY 20 CASEBOOK. PAGE 13 B0263 — PROVS LOC/G ADMIN GOV/REL

B63
BURRUS B.R.,ADMINSTRATIVE LAW AND LOCAL GOVERNMENT. USA+45 PROVS LEGIS LICENSE ADJUD ORD/FREE 20. PAGE 17 B0356 — EX/STRUC LOC/G JURID CONSTN

B63
CROUCH W.W.,SOUTHERN CALIFORNIA METROPOLIS: A STUDY IN DEVELOPMENT OF GOVERNMENT FOR A METROPOLITAN AREA. USA+45 USA-45 PROB/SOLV ADMIN LOBBY PARTIC CENTRAL ORD/FREE PWR...BIBLIOG 20 PROGRSV/M. PAGE 25 B0510 — LOC/G MUNIC LEGIS DECISION

B63
FORTES A.B.,HISTORIA ADMINISTRATIVA, JUDICIARIA E ECLESIASTICA DO RIO GRANDE DO SUL. BRAZIL L/A+17C LOC/G SECT COLONIAL CT/SYS ORD/FREE CATHISM 16/20. PAGE 37 B0742 — PROVS ADMIN JURID

B63
GARNER J.F.,ADMINISTRATIVE LAW. UK LAW LOC/G NAT/G EX/STRUC LEGIS JUDGE BAL/PWR BUDGET ADJUD CONTROL CT/SYS...BIBLIOG 20. PAGE 39 B0783 — ADMIN JURID PWR GOV/REL

B63
GOURNAY B.,PUBLIC ADMINISTRATION. FRANCE LAW CONSTN AGRI FINAN LABOR SCHOOL EX/STRUC CHOOSE...MGT METH/COMP 20. PAGE 42 B0846 — BIBLIOG/A ADMIN NAT/G LOC/G

B63
GRANT D.R.,STATE AND LOCAL GOVERNMENT IN AMERICA. USA+45 FINAN LOC/G MUNIC EX/STRUC FORCES EDU/PROP ADMIN CHOOSE FEDERAL ATTIT...JURID 20. PAGE 42 B0853 — PROVS POL/PAR LEGIS CONSTN

B63
HEARLE E.F.R.,A DATA PROCESSING SYSTEM FOR STATE AND LOCAL GOVERNMENTS. PLAN TEC/DEV AUTOMAT ROUTINE ...MGT METH/CNCPT CLASSIF 20. PAGE 49 B0984 — LOC/G PROVS COMPUTER COMPUT/IR

B63
HERMAN H.,NEW YORK STATE AND THE METROPOLITAN PROBLEM. USA+45 ECO/DEV PUB/INST SCHOOL LEGIS PLAN TAX EXEC PARL/PROC PARTIC...HEAL 20 NEW/YORK. PAGE 49 B0992 — GOV/REL PROVS LOC/G POLICY

B63
JACOB H.,GERMAN ADMINISTRATION SINCE BISMARCK: CENTRAL AUTHORITY VERSUS LOCAL AUTONOMY. GERMANY GERMANY/W LAW POL/PAR CONTROL CENTRAL TOTALISM FASCISM...MAJORIT DECISION STAT CHARTS GOV/COMP 19/20 BISMARCK/O HITLER/A WEIMAR/REP. PAGE 55 B1111 — ADMIN NAT/G LOC/G POLICY

B63
KAMMERER G.M.,THE URBAN POLITICAL COMMUNITY: PROFILES IN TOWN POLITICS. ELITES LOC/G LEAD ...DECISION GP/COMP. PAGE 57 B1162 — EXEC MUNIC PWR GOV/COMP

B63
LEWIS J.W.,LEADERSHIP IN COMMUNIST CHINA. ASIA INTELL ECO/UNDEV LOC/G MUNIC NAT/G PROVS ECO/TAC EDU/PROP LEGIT ADMIN COERCE ATTIT ORD/FREE PWR ...INT TIME/SEQ CHARTS TOT/POP VAL/FREE. PAGE 65 B1304 — POL/PAR DOMIN ELITES

B63
LOCKARD D.,THE POLITICS OF STATE AND LOCAL GOVERNMENT. USA+45 CONSTN EX/STRUC LEGIS CT/SYS FEDERAL...CHARTS BIBLIOG 20. PAGE 66 B1334 — LOC/G PROVS OP/RES ADMIN

B63
MAHESHWARI B.,STUDIES IN PANCHAYATI RAJ. INDIA POL/PAR EX/STRUC BUDGET EXEC REPRESENT CENTRAL EFFICIENCY...DECISION 20. PAGE 68 B1378 — FEDERAL LOC/G GOV/REL LEAD

B63
MONTER W.,THE GOVERNMENT OF GENEVA, 1536-1605 (DOCTORAL THESIS). SWITZERLND DIPLOM LEAD ORD/FREE SOVEREIGN 16/17 CALVIN/J ROME. PAGE 74 B1504 — SECT FINAN LOC/G ADMIN

B63
PALOTAI O.C.,PUBLICATIONS OF THE INSTITUTE OF GOVERNMENT, 1930-1962. LAW PROVS SCHOOL WORKER ACT/RES OP/RES CT/SYS GOV/REL...CRIMLGY SOC/WK. PAGE 81 B1629 — BIBLIOG/A ADMIN LOC/G FINAN

B63
PLISCHKE E.,GOVERNMENT AND POLITICS OF CONTEMPORARY BERLIN. GERMANY LAW CONSTN POL/PAR LEGIS WAR CHOOSE REPRESENT GOV/REL...CHARTS BIBLIOG 20 BERLIN. PAGE 83 B1683 — MUNIC LOC/G POLICY ADMIN

B63
ROBINSON K.,ESSAYS IN IMPERIAL GOVERNMENT. CAMEROON NIGERIA UK CONSTN LOC/G LEGIS ADMIN GOV/REL PWR ...POLICY ANTHOL BIBLIOG 17/20 PURHAM/M. PAGE 89 B1803 — COLONIAL AFR DOMIN

B63
ROYAL INSTITUTE PUBLIC ADMIN,BRITISH PUBLIC ADMINISTRATION. UK LAW FINAN INDUS LOC/G POL/PAR LEGIS LOBBY PARL/PROC CHOOSE JURID. PAGE 91 B1845 — BIBLIOG ADMIN MGT NAT/G

B63
SINGH M.M.,MUNICIPAL GOVERNMENT IN THE CALCUTTA METROPOLITAN DISTRICT A PRELIMINARY SURVEY. FINAN LG/CO DELIB/GP BUDGET TAX ADMIN GP/REL 20 CALCUTTA. PAGE 97 B1969 — LOC/G HEALTH MUNIC JURID

S63
BRZEZINSKI Z.K.,"CINCINNATUS AND THE APPARATCHIK." COM USA+45 USA-45 ELITES LOC/G NAT/G PROVS CONSULT LEGIS DOMIN LEGIT EXEC ROUTINE CHOOSE DRIVE PWR SKILL...CONCPT CHARTS VAL/FREE COLD/WAR 20. PAGE 16 B0334 — POL/PAR USSR

S63
GITTELL M.,"METROPOLITAN MAYOR: DEAD END." LOC/G PARTIC REGION ATTIT PWR GP/COMP. PAGE 40 B0804 — MUNIC LEAD EXEC

S63
JENNINGS M.K.,"PUBLIC ADMINISTRATORS AND COMMUNITY DECISION-MAKING." ELITES LOC/G LEAD...GP/COMP GOV/COMP. PAGE 56 B1134 — ADMIN MUNIC DECISION PWR

C63
CARLISLE D.,"PARTY LOYALTY: THE ELECTION PROCESS IN SOUTH CAROLINA." USA+45 LOC/G ADMIN ATTIT...TREND CHARTS BIBLIOG 17/20. PAGE 19 B0380 — CHOOSE POL/PAR PROVS SUFF

N63
GREAT BRITAIN DEPT TECH COOP,PUBLIC ADMINISTRATION: A SELECT BIBLIOGRAPHY (PAMPHLET). WOR+45 AGRI FINAN INDUS EX/STRUC OP/RES ECO/TAC...MGT METH/COMP NAT/COMP. PAGE 43 B0861 — BIBLIOG/A ADMIN NAT/G LOC/G

N63
INTERNATIONAL CITY MGRS ASSN,POST-ENTRY TRAINING IN THE LOCAL PUBLIC SERVICE (PAMPHLET). SCHOOL PLAN PROB/SOLV TEC/DEV ADMIN EFFICIENCY SKILL...POLICY AUD/VIS CHARTS BIBLIOG 20 CITY/MGT. PAGE 54 B1096 — LOC/G WORKER EDU/PROP METH/COMP

B64
ALDERFER H.O.,LOCAL GOVERNMENT IN DEVELOPING COUNTRIES. ASIA COM L/A+17C S/ASIA AGRI LOC/G MUNIC PROVS DOMIN CHOOSE PWR...POLICY MGT CONCPT 20. PAGE 3 B0070 — ADMIN ROUTINE

B64
BOUVIER-AJAM M.,MANUEL TECHNIQUE ET PRATIQUE DU MAIRE ET DES ELUS ET AGENTS COMMUNAUX. FRANCE LOC/G BUDGET CHOOSE GP/REL SUPEGO...JURID BIBLIOG 20 — MUNIC ADMIN CHIEF

MAYOR COMMUNES. PAGE 14 B0284
NEIGH

B64
BROMAGE A.W.,MANAGER PLAN ABANDONMENTS: WHY A FEW
HAVE DROPPED COUNCILMANAGER GOVERNMENT. USA+45
CREATE PARTIC CHOOSE...MGT CENSUS CHARTS 20.
PAGE 15 B0315
MUNIC
PLAN
CONSULT
LOC/G

B64
CONNECTICUT U INST PUBLIC SERV,SUMMARY OF CHARTER
PROVISIONS IN CONNECTICUT LOCAL GOVERNMENT
(PAMPHLET). USA+45 DELIB/GP LEGIS TOP/EX CHOOSE
REPRESENT 20 CONNECTICT CITY/MGT MAYOR. PAGE 23
B0462
CONSTN
MUNIC
LOC/G
EX/STRUC

B64
GOLDWIN R.A.,POLITICAL PARTIES, USA. USA+45 USA-45
LOC/G ADMIN LEAD EFFICIENCY ATTIT PWR...POLICY STAT
ANTHOL 18/20 CONGRESS. PAGE 40 B0818
POL/PAR
PARTIC
NAT/G
CONSTN

B64
GOODMAN W.,THE TWO-PARTY SYSTEM IN THE UNITED
STATES. USA+45 USA-45 STRATA LOC/G CHIEF EDU/PROP
ADMIN COST PWR POPULISM...PLURIST 18/20 PRESIDENT.
PAGE 41 B0821
POL/PAR
REPRESENT
CHOOSE
NAT/G

B64
GREBLER L.,URBAN RENEWAL IN EUROPEAN COUNTRIES: ITS
EMERGENCE AND POTENTIALS. EUR+WWI UK ECO/DEV LOC/G
NEIGH CREATE ADMIN ATTIT...TREND NAT/COMP 20
URBAN/RNWL. PAGE 43 B0863
MUNIC
PLAN
CONSTRUC
NAT/G

B64
HARMON R.B.,BIBLIOGRAPHY OF BIBLIOGRAPHIES IN
POLITICAL SCIENCE (MIMEOGRAPHED PAPER: LIMITED
EDITION). WOR+45 WOR-45 INT/ORG POL/PAR GOV/REL
ALL/IDEOS...INT/LAW JURID MGT 19/20. PAGE 47 B0949
BIBLIOG
NAT/G
DIPLOM
LOC/G

B64
INDIAN COMM PREVENTION CORRUPT,REPORT, 1964. INDIA
NAT/G GOV/REL ATTIT ORD/FREE...CRIMLGY METH 20.
PAGE 53 B1079
CRIME
ADMIN
LEGIS
LOC/G

B64
JACKSON W.V.,LIBRARY GUIDE FOR BRAZILIAN STUDIES.
BRAZIL USA+45 STRUCT DIPLOM ADMIN...SOC 20. PAGE 55
B1110
BIBLIOG
L/A+17C
NAT/G
LOC/G

B64
LOWI T.J.,AT THE PLEASURE OF THE MAYOR. EX/STRUC
PROB/SOLV BAL/PWR ADMIN PARTIC CHOOSE GP/REL
...CONT/OBS NET/THEORY CHARTS 20 NEWYORK/C MAYOR.
PAGE 67 B1346
LOBBY
LOC/G
PWR
MUNIC

B64
MAHAR J.M.,INDIA: A CRITICAL BIBLIOGRAPHY. INDIA
PAKISTAN CULTURE ECO/UNDEV LOC/G POL/PAR SECT
PROB/SOLV DIPLOM ADMIN COLONIAL PARL/PROC ATTIT 20.
PAGE 68 B1377
BIBLIOG/A
S/ASIA
NAT/G
LEAD

B64
NATIONAL BOOK LEAGUE,THE COMMONWEALTH IN BOOKS: AN
ANNOTATED LIST. CANADA UK LOC/G SECT ADMIN...SOC
BIOG 20 CMN/WLTH. PAGE 77 B1561
BIBLIOG/A
JURID
NAT/G

B64
NUQUIST A.E.,TOWN GOVERNMENT IN VERMONT. USA+45
FINAN TOP/EX PROB/SOLV BUDGET TAX REPRESENT SUFF
EFFICIENCY...OBS INT 20 VERMONT. PAGE 79 B1595
LOC/G
MUNIC
POPULISM
ADMIN

B64
PIERCE T.M.,FEDERAL, STATE, AND LOCAL GOVERNMENT IN
EDUCATION. FINAN LOC/G PROVS LEGIS PLAN EDU/PROP
ADMIN CONTROL CENTRAL COST KNOWL 20. PAGE 83 B1673
NAT/G
POLICY
SCHOOL
GOV/REL

B64
POTTER D.C.,GOVERNMENT IN RURAL INDIA. INDIA LEGIT
INGP/REL EFFICIENCY ATTIT 20. PAGE 84 B1695
LOC/G
ADMIN
TAX
PROB/SOLV

B64
PRESS C.,A BIBLIOGRAPHIC INTRODUCTION TO AMERICAN
STATE GOVERNMENT AND POLITICS (PAMPHLET). USA+45
USA-45 EX/STRUC ADJUD INGP/REL FEDERAL ORD/FREE 20.
PAGE 84 B1701
BIBLIOG
LEGIS
LOC/G
POL/PAR

B64
RICHARDSON I.L.,BIBLIOGRAFIA BRASILEIRA DE
ADMINISTRACAO PUBLICA E ASSUNTOS CORRELATOS. BRAZIL
CONSTN FINAN LOC/G NAT/G POL/PAR PLAN DIPLOM
RECEIVE ATTIT...METH 20. PAGE 88 B1776
BIBLIOG
MGT
ADMIN
LAW

B64
SHERIDAN R.G.,URBAN JUSTICE. USA+45 PROVS CREATE
ADMIN CT/SYS ORD/FREE 20 TENNESSEE. PAGE 96 B1943
LOC/G
JURID
ADJUD
MUNIC

B64
THE BRITISH COUNCIL,PUBLIC ADMINISTRATION: A SELECT
LIST OF BOOKS AND PERIODICALS. LAW CONSTN FINAN
POL/PAR SCHOOL CHOOSE...HEAL MGT METH/COMP 19/20
CMN/WLTH. PAGE 104 B2094
BIBLIOG
ADMIN
LOC/G
INDUS

B64
TURNER H.A.,THE GOVERNMENT AND POLITICS OF
CALIFORNIA (2ND ED.). LAW FINAN MUNIC POL/PAR
SCHOOL EX/STRUC LEGIS LOBBY CHOOSE...CHARTS T 20
CALIFORNIA. PAGE 106 B2138
PROVS
ADMIN
LOC/G
CONSTN

B64
VALEN H.,POLITICAL PARTIES IN NORWAY. NORWAY ACADEM
PARTIC ROUTINE INGP/REL KNOWL...QU 20. PAGE 111
B2249
LOC/G
POL/PAR
PERSON

B64
WEIDENBAUM M.L.,CONGRESS AND THE FEDERAL BUDGET:
FEDERAL BUDGETING AND THE RESPONSIBLE USE OF POWER.
LOC/G PLAN TAX CONGRESS. PAGE 114 B2309
LEGIS
EX/STRUC
BUDGET
ADMIN

B64
WRAITH R.,CORRUPTION IN DEVELOPING COUNTRIES.
NIGERIA UK LAW ELITES STRATA INDUS LOC/G NAT/G SECT
FORCES EDU/PROP ADMIN PWR WEALTH 18/20. PAGE 118
B2377
ECO/UNDEV
CRIME
SANCTION
ATTIT

L64
GILBERT C.E.,"NATIONAL POLITICAL ALIGNMENTS AND THE
POLITICS OF LARGE CITIES." ELITES LOC/G NAT/G LEGIS
EXEC LEAD PLURISM GOV/COMP. PAGE 39 B0800
MUNIC
CHOOSE
POL/PAR
PWR

S64
HADY T.F.,"CONGRESSIONAL TOWNSHIPS AS INCORPORATED
MUNICIPALITIES." NEIGH ADMIN REPRESENT ATTIT GEOG.
PAGE 45 B0914
MUNIC
REGION
LOC/G
GOV/COMP

S64
KAMMERER G.M.,"ROLE DIVERSITY OF CITY MANAGERS."
LOC/G ADMIN LEAD PERCEPT PWR GP/COMP. PAGE 57 B1163
MUNIC
EXEC
ATTIT
ROLE

S64
NEEDHAM T.,"SCIENCE AND SOCIETY IN EAST AND WEST."
INTELL STRATA R+D LOC/G NAT/G PROVS CONSULT ACT/RES
CREATE PLAN TEC/DEV EDU/PROP ADMIN ATTIT ALL/VALS
...POLICY RELATIV MGT CONCPT NEW/IDEA TIME/SEQ WORK
WORK. PAGE 77 B1565
ASIA
STRUCT

N64
US SENATE COMM GOVT OPERATIONS,METROPOLITAN
AMERICA: A SELECTED BIBLIOGRAPHY (PAMPHLET). USA+45
DIST/IND FINAN LOC/G EDU/PROP ADMIN HEALTH 20.
PAGE 110 B2214
BIBLIOG/A
MUNIC
GOV/REL
DECISION

B65
BUECHNER J.C.,DIFFERENCES IN ROLE PERCEPTIONS IN
COLORADO COUNCIL-MANAGER CITIES. USA+45 ADMIN
ROUTINE GP/REL CONSEN PERCEPT PERSON ROLE
...DECISION MGT STAT INT QU CHARTS 20 COLORADO
CITY/MGT. PAGE 17 B0338
MUNIC
CONSULT
LOC/G
IDEA/COMP

B65
COHN H.J.,THE GOVERNMENT OF THE RHINE PALATINATE IN
THE FIFTEENTH CENTURY. GERMANY FINAN LOC/G DELIB/GP
LEGIS CT/SYS CHOOSE CATHISM 14/15 PALATINATE.
PAGE 22 B0449
PROVS
JURID
GP/REL
ADMIN

B65
EAST J.P.,COUNCIL-MANAGER GOVERNMENT: THE POLITICAL
THOUGHT OF ITS FOUNDER, RICHARD S. CHILDS. USA+45
CREATE ADMIN CHOOSE...BIOG GEN/LAWS BIBLIOG 20
CHILDS/RS CITY/MGT. PAGE 32 B0642
SIMUL
LOC/G
MUNIC
EX/STRUC

B65
FISCHER F.C.,THE GOVERNMENT OF MICHIGAN. USA+45
NAT/G PUB/INST EX/STRUC LEGIS BUDGET GIVE EDU/PROP
CT/SYS CHOOSE GOV/REL...T MICHIGAN. PAGE 36 B0723
PROVS
LOC/G
ADMIN
CONSTN

B65
GREER S.,URBAN RENEWAL AND AMERICAN CITIES: THE
DILEMMA OF DEMOCRATIC INTERVENTION. USA+45 R+D
LOC/G VOL/ASSN ACT/RES BUDGET ADMIN GOV/REL...SOC
INT SAMP 20 BOSTON CHICAGO MIAMI URBAN/RNWL.
PAGE 43 B0871
MUNIC
PROB/SOLV
PLAN
NAT/G

B65
HARMON R.B.,POLITICAL SCIENCE: A BIBLIOGRAPHICAL
GUIDE TO THE LITERATURE. WOR+45 WOR-45 R+D INT/ORG
LOC/G NAT/G DIPLOM ADMIN...CONCPT METH. PAGE 47
B0950
BIBLIOG
POL/PAR
LAW
GOV/COMP

B65
MOORE C.H.,TUNISIA SINCE INDEPENDENCE. ELITES LOC/G
POL/PAR ADMIN COLONIAL CONTROL EXEC GOV/REL
TOTALISM MARXISM...INT 20 TUNIS. PAGE 75 B1513
NAT/G
EX/STRUC
SOCISM

B65
PARRISH W.E.,MISSOURI UNDER RADICAL RULE 1865-1870.
USA-45 SOCIETY INDUS LOC/G POL/PAR WORKER EDU/PROP
SUFF INGP/REL ATTIT...BIBLIOG 19 NEGRO MISSOURI.
PAGE 81 B1635
PROVS
ADMIN
RACE/REL
ORD/FREE

B65
PUSTAY J.S.,COUNTER-INSURGENCY WARFARE. COM USA+45
LOC/G NAT/G ACT/RES EDU/PROP ADMIN COERCE ATTIT
...CONCPT MARX/KARL 20. PAGE 85 B1722
FORCES
PWR
GUERRILLA

B65
REDFORD D.R.,POLITICS AND GOVERNMENT IN THE UNITED
STATES. USA+45 USA-45 LOC/G PROVS FORCES DIPLOM
CT/SYS LOBBY...JURID SUPREME/CT PRESIDENT. PAGE 87
B1751
NAT/G
POL/PAR
EX/STRUC
LEGIS

B65
RUBIN H.,PENSIONS AND EMPLOYEE MOBILITY IN THE
PUBLIC SERVICE. USA+45 WORKER PERSON ORD/FREE...SOC
QU. PAGE 91 B1849
ADMIN
NAT/G
LOC/G
SENIOR

SCHAPIRO L.,THE GOVERNMENT AND POLITICS OF THE
SOVIET UNION. USSR WOR+45 WOR-45 ADMIN PARTIC REV
CHOOSE REPRESENT PWR...POLICY IDEA/COMP 20. PAGE 93
B1880
MARXISM
GOV/REL
NAT/G
LOC/G
B65

SHARMA S.A.,PARLIAMENTARY GOVERNMENT IN INDIA.
INDIA FINAN LOC/G PROVS DELIB/GP PLAN ADMIN CT/SYS
FEDERAL...JURID 20. PAGE 96 B1936
NAT/G
CONSTN
PARL/PROC
LEGIS
B65

SNIDER C.F.,AMERICAN STATE AND LOCAL GOVERNMENT.
USA+45 FINAN CHIEF EX/STRUC TAX ADMIN CONTROL SUFF
INGP/REL PWR 20. PAGE 98 B1989
GOV/REL
MUNIC
PROVS
LOC/G
B65

STEINER K.,LOCAL GOVERNMENT IN JAPAN. CONSTN
CULTURE NAT/G ADMIN CHOOSE...SOC STAT 20 CHINJAP.
PAGE 100 B2030
LOC/G
SOCIETY
JURID
ORD/FREE
B65

WITHERELL J.W.,MADAGASCAR AND ADJACENT ISLANDS; A
GUIDE TO OFFICIAL PUBLICATIONS (PAMPHLET). FRANCE
MADAGASCAR S/ASIA UK LAW OP/RES PLAN DIPLOM
...POLICY CON/ANAL 19/20. PAGE 117 B2368
BIBLIOG
COLONIAL
LOC/G
ADMIN
S65

RAPHAELI N.,"SELECTED ARTICLES AND DOCUMENTS ON
COMPARATIVE PUBLIC ADMINISTRATION." USA+45 FINAN
LOC/G WORKER TEC/DEV CONTROL LEAD...SOC/WK GOV/COMP
METH/COMP. PAGE 86 B1739
BIBLIOG
ADMIN
NAT/G
MGT
N65

MOTE M.E.,SOVIET LOCAL AND REPUBLIC ELECTIONS. COM
USSR NAT/G PLAN PARTIC GOV/REL TOTALISM PWR
...CHARTS 20. PAGE 76 B1534
CHOOSE
ADMIN
CONTROL
LOC/G
B66

ADAMS J.C.,THE GOVERNMENT OF REPUBLICAN ITALY (2ND
ED.). ITALY LOC/G POL/PAR DELIB/GP LEGIS WORKER
ADMIN CT/SYS FASCISM...CHARTS BIBLIOG 20
PARLIAMENT. PAGE 3 B0057
NAT/G
CHOOSE
EX/STRUC
CONSTN
B66

ASHRAF A.,THE CITY GOVERNMENT OF CALCUTTA: A STUDY
OF INERTIA. INDIA ELITES INDUS NAT/G EX/STRUC
ACT/RES PLAN PROB/SOLV LEAD HABITAT...BIBLIOG 20
CALCUTTA. PAGE 7 B0141
LOC/G
MUNIC
ADMIN
ECO/UNDEV
B66

BHALERAO C.N.,PUBLIC SERVICE COMMISSIONS OF INDIA:
A STUDY. INDIA SERV/IND EX/STRUC ROUTINE CHOOSE
GOV/REL INGP/REL...KNO/TEST EXHIBIT 20. PAGE 11
B0233
NAT/G
OP/RES
LOC/G
ADMIN
B66

BRAIBANTI R.,RESEARCH ON THE BUREAUCRACY OF
PAKISTAN. PAKISTAN LAW CULTURE INTELL ACADEM LOC/G
SECT PRESS CT/SYS...LING CHARTS 20 BUREAUCRCY.
PAGE 15 B0299
HABITAT
NAT/G
ADMIN
CONSTN
B66

CARALEY D.,PARTY POLITICS AND NATIONAL ELECTIONS.
USA+45 STRATA LOC/G PROVS EX/STRUC BARGAIN ADMIN
SANCTION GP/REL ATTIT 20 DEMOCRAT REPUBLICAN.
PAGE 18 B0375
POL/PAR
CHOOSE
REPRESENT
NAT/G
B66

DUNCOMBE H.S.,COUNTY GOVERNMENT IN AMERICA. USA+45
FINAN MUNIC ADMIN ROUTINE GOV/REL...GOV/COMP 20.
PAGE 31 B0631
LOC/G
PROVS
CT/SYS
TOP/EX
B66

EPSTEIN F.T.,THE AMERICAN BIBLIOGRAPHY OF RUSSIAN
AND EAST EUROPEAN STUDIES FOR 1964. USSR LOC/G
NAT/G POL/PAR FORCES ADMIN ARMS/CONT...JURID CONCPT
20 UN. PAGE 33 B0678
BIBLIOG
COM
MARXISM
DIPLOM
B66

FINK M.,A SELECTIVE BIBLIOGRAPHY ON STATE
CONSTITUTIONAL REVISION (PAMPHLET). USA+45 FINAN
EX/STRUC LEGIS EDU/PROP ADMIN CT/SYS APPORT CHOOSE
GOV/REL 20. PAGE 35 B0720
BIBLIOG
PROVS
LOC/G
CONSTN
B66

GHOSH P.K.,THE CONSTITUTION OF INDIA: HOW IT HAS
BEEN FRAMED. INDIA LOC/G DELIB/GP EX/STRUC
PROB/SOLV BUDGET INT/TRADE CT/SYS CHOOSE...LING 20.
PAGE 39 B0795
CONSTN
NAT/G
LEGIS
FEDERAL
B66

GREENE L.E.,GOVERNMENT IN TENNESSEE (2ND ED.).
USA+45 DIST/IND INDUS POL/PAR EX/STRUC LEGIS PLAN
BUDGET GIVE CT/SYS...MGT T 20 TENNESSEE. PAGE 43
B0866
PROVS
LOC/G
CONSTN
ADMIN
B66

GROSS C.,A BIBLIOGRAPHY OF BRITISH MUNICIPAL
HISTORY (2ND ED.). UK LOC/G ADMIN 11/19. PAGE 44
B0888
BIBLIOG/A
MUNIC
CONSTN
B66

HARMON R.B.,SOURCES AND PROBLEMS OF BIBLIOGRAPHY IN
POLITICAL SCIENCE (PAMPHLET). INT/ORG LOC/G MUNIC
POL/PAR ADMIN GOV/REL ALL/IDEOS...JURID MGT CONCPT
19/20. PAGE 47 B0951
BIBLIOG
DIPLOM
INT/LAW
NAT/G
B66

HESSLER I.O.,29 WAYS TO GOVERN A CITY. EX/STRUC
MUNIC

TOP/EX PROB/SOLV PARTIC CHOOSE REPRESENT EFFICIENCY
...CHARTS 20 CITY/MGT MAYOR. PAGE 49 B0998
GOV/COMP
LOC/G
ADMIN
B66

MURDOCK J.C.,RESEARCH AND REGIONS. AGRI FINAN INDUS
LOC/G MUNIC NAT/G PROB/SOLV TEC/DEV ADMIN REGION
20. PAGE 76 B1545
BIBLIOG
ECO/DEV
COMPUT/IR
R+D
B66

NEUMANN R.G.,THE GOVERNMENT OF THE GERMAN FEDERAL
REPUBLIC. EUR+WWI GERMANY/W LOC/G EX/STRUC LEGIS
CT/SYS INGP/REL PWR...BIBLIOG 20 ADENAUER/K.
PAGE 78 B1573
NAT/G
POL/PAR
DIPLOM
CONSTN
B66

NYC TEMPORARY COMM CITY FINAN,MUNICIPAL COLLECTIVE
BARGAINING (NO. 8). USA+45 PLAN PROB/SOLV BARGAIN
BUDGET TAX EDU/PROP GOV/REL COST...MGT 20
NEWYORK/C. PAGE 79 B1596
MUNIC
FINAN
ADMIN
LOC/G
B66

RICHARD J.B.,GOVERNMENT AND POLITICS OF WYOMING.
USA+45 POL/PAR EX/STRUC LEGIS CT/SYS LOBBY APPORT
CHOOSE REPRESENT 20 WYOMING GOVERNOR. PAGE 88 B1773
PROVS
LOC/G
ADMIN
B66

ROSS R.M.,STATE AND LOCAL GOVERNMENT AND
ADMINISTRATION. USA+45 CONSTN POL/PAR EX/STRUC
LEGIS BUDGET EDU/PROP CONTROL CT/SYS CHOOSE GOV/REL
T. PAGE 90 B1827
LOC/G
PROVS
MUNIC
ADMIN
B66

SCHLESSINGER P.J.,ELEMENTS OF CALIFORNIA GOVERNMENT
(2ND ED.). USA+45 LAW ADJUD ADMIN CONTROL CT/SYS
EFFICIENCY...BIBLIOG T CALIFORNIA. PAGE 94 B1891
LOC/G
PROVS
GOV/REL
LEGIS
B66

SCHMIDT K.M.,AMERICAN STATE AND LOCAL GOVERNMENT IN
ACTION. USA+45 CONSTN LOC/G POL/PAR CHIEF LEGIS
PROB/SOLV ADJUD LOBBY GOV/REL...DECISION ANTHOL 20
GOVERNOR MAYOR URBAN/RNWL. PAGE 94 B1896
PROVS
ADMIN
MUNIC
PLAN
B66

SCHURMANN F.,IDEOLOGY AND ORGANIZATION IN COMMUNIST
CHINA. CHINA/COM LOC/G MUNIC POL/PAR ECO/TAC
CONTROL ATTIT...MGT STERTYP 20 COM/PARTY. PAGE 94
B1909
MARXISM
STRUCT
ADMIN
NAT/G
B66

SEASHOLES B.,VOTING, INTEREST GROUPS, AND PARTIES.
USA+45 FINAN LOC/G NAT/G ADMIN LEAD GP/REL INGP/REL
ROLE...CHARTS ANTHOL 20. PAGE 95 B1922
CHOOSE
POL/PAR
LOBBY
PARTIC
B66

WARREN R.O.,GOVERNMENT IN METROPOLITAN REGIONS: A
REAPPRAISAL OF FRACTIONATED POLITICAL ORGANIZATION.
USA+45 ACT/RES PROB/SOLV REGION...CHARTS METH/COMP
BIBLIOG CITY/MGT. PAGE 114 B2296
LOC/G
MUNIC
EX/STRUC
PLAN
B66

CRAIN R.L.,"STRUCTURE AND VALUES IN LOCAL POLITICAL
SYSTEMS: THE CASE OF FLUORIDATION DECISIONS."
EX/STRUC LEGIS LEAD PARTIC REPRESENT PWR...DECISION
GOV/COMP. PAGE 25 B0501
MUNIC
EDU/PROP
LOC/G
ATTIT
L66

SEYLER W.C.,"DOCTORAL DISSERTATIONS IN POLITICAL
SCIENCE IN UNIVERSITIES OF THE UNITED STATES AND
CANADA." INT/ORG LOC/G ADMIN...INT/LAW MGT
GOV/COMP. PAGE 96 B1930
BIBLIOG
LAW
NAT/G
L66

"FURTHER READING." INDIA LOC/G NAT/G PLAN ADMIN
WEALTH...GEOG SOC CONCPT CENSUS 20. PAGE 2 B0045
BIBLIOG
ECO/UNDEV
TEC/DEV
PROVS
S66

BURDETTE F.L.,"SELECTED ARTICLES AND DOCUMENTS ON
AMERICAN GOVERNMENT AND POLITICS." LAW LOC/G MUNIC
NAT/G POL/PAR PROVS LEGIS BAL/PWR ADMIN EXEC
REPRESENT MGT. PAGE 17 B0348
BIBLIOG
USA+45
JURID
CONSTN
S66

POLSBY N.W.,"BOOKS IN THE FIELD: POLITICAL
SCIENCE." LAW CONSTN LOC/G NAT/G LEGIS ADJUD PWR 20
SUPREME/CT. PAGE 83 B1686
BIBLIOG/A
ATTIT
ADMIN
JURID
S66

SNOWISS L.M.,"CONGRESSIONAL RECRUITMENT AND
REPRESENTATION." USA+45 LG/CO MUNIC POL/PAR ADMIN
REGION CONGRESS CHICAGO. PAGE 98 B1990
LEGIS
REPRESENT
CHOOSE
LOC/G
N66

AMERICAN SOCIETY PUBLIC ADMIN,PUBLIC ADMINISTRATION
AND THE WAR ON POVERTY (PAMPHLET). USA+45 SOCIETY
ECO/DEV FINAN LOC/G LEGIS CREATE EDU/PROP CONFER
GOV/REL GP/REL ROLE 20 POVRTY/WAR. PAGE 4 B0089
WEALTH
NAT/G
PLAN
ADMIN
N66

BACHELDER G.L.,THE LITERATURE OF FEDERALISM: A
SELECTED BIBLIOGRAPHY (REV ED) (A PAMPHLET). USA+45
USA-45 WOR+45 WOR-45 LAW CONSTN PROVS ADMIN CT/SYS
GOV/REL ROLE...CONCPT 19/20. PAGE 8 B0155
BIBLIOG
FEDERAL
NAT/G
LOC/G
B67

BLUMBERG A.S.,CRIMINAL JUSTICE. USA+45 CLIENT LAW
LOC/G FORCES JUDGE ACT/RES LEGIT ADMIN RATIONAL
MYTH. PAGE 13 B0259
JURID
CT/SYS
PROF/ORG

BULPITT J.G.,PARTY POLITICS IN ENGLISH LOCAL GOVERNMENT. UK CONSTN ACT/RES TAX CONTROL CHOOSE REPRESENT GOV/REL KNOWL 20. PAGE 17 B0344
CRIME
B67
POL/PAR
LOC/G
ELITES
EX/STRUC

BUREAU GOVERNMENT RES AND SERV,COUNTY GOVERNMENT REORGANIZATION - A SELECTED ANNOTATED BIBLIOGRAPHY (PAPER). USA+45 USA-45 LAW CONSTN MUNIC PROVS EX/STRUC CREATE PLAN PROB/SOLV REPRESENT GOV/REL 20. PAGE 17 B0349
B67
BIBLIOG/A
APPORT
LOC/G
ADMIN

COHEN R.,COMPARATIVE POLITICAL SYSTEMS: STUDIES IN THE POLITICS OF PRE-INDUSTRIAL SOCIETIES. WOR+45 WOR-45 CULTURE FAM KIN LOC/G NEIGH LEAD ADMIN MARRIAGE...BIBLIOG 20. PAGE 22 B0447
B67
ECO/UNDEV
STRUCT
SOCIETY
GP/COMP

FESLER J.W.,THE FIFTY STATES AND THEIR LOCAL GOVERNMENTS. FUT USA+45 POL/PAR LEGIS PROB/SOLV ADMIN CT/SYS CHOOSE GOV/REL FEDERAL...POLICY CHARTS 20 SUPREME/CT. PAGE 35 B0715
B67
PROVS
LOC/G

IANNACCONE L.,POLITICS IN EDUCATION. USA+45 LOC/G PROF/ORG BAL/PWR ADMIN...CHARTS SIMUL. PAGE 53 B1072
B67
EDU/PROP
GEN/LAWS
PROVS

KAPLAN H.,URBAN POLITICAL SYSTEMS: A FUNCTIONAL ANALYSIS OF METRO TORONTO. CANADA STRUCT NEIGH PLAN ADMIN...POLICY METH 20 TORONTO. PAGE 58 B1166
B67
GEN/LAWS
MUNIC
LOC/G
FEDERAL

KATZ J.,PSYCHOANALYSIS, PSYCHIATRY, AND LAW. USA+45 LOC/G NAT/G PUB/INST PROB/SOLV ADMIN HEALTH ...CRIMLGY CONCPT SAMP/SIZ IDEA/COMP. PAGE 58 B1180
B67
LAW
PSY
CT/SYS
ADJUD

KRISLOV S.,THE NEGRO IN FEDERAL EMPLOYMENT. LAW STRATA LOC/G CREATE PROB/SOLV INSPECT GOV/REL DISCRIM ROLE...DECISION INT TREND 20 NEGRO WWI CIVIL/SERV. PAGE 61 B1238
B67
WORKER
NAT/G
ADMIN
RACE/REL

LENG S.C.,JUSTICE IN COMMUNIST CHINA: A SURVEY OF THE JUDICIAL SYSTEM OF THE CHINESE PEOPLE'S REPUBLIC. CHINA/COM LAW CONSTN LOC/G NAT/G PROF/ORG CONSULT FORCES ADMIN CRIME ORD/FREE...BIBLIOG 20 MAO. PAGE 64 B1290
B67
CT/SYS
ADJUD
JURID
MARXISM

MILNE R.S.,GOVERNMENT AND POLITICS IN MALAYSIA. INDONESIA MALAYSIA LOC/G EX/STRUC FORCES DIPLOM GP/REL 20 SINGAPORE. PAGE 74 B1489
B67
NAT/G
LEGIS
ADMIN

PRINCE C.E.,NEW JERSEY'S JEFFERSONIAN REPUBLICANS; THE GENESIS OF AN EARLY PARTY MACHINE (1789-1817). USA+45 LOC/G EDU/PROP PRESS CONTROL CHOOSE...CHARTS 18/19 NEW/JERSEY REPUBLICAN. PAGE 84 B1707
B67
POL/PAR
CONSTN
ADMIN
PROVS

UNIVERSAL REFERENCE SYSTEM,ADMINISTRATIVE MANAGEMENT: PUBLIC AND PRIVATE BUREAUCRACY (VOLUME IV). WOR+45 WOR-45 ECO/DEV LG/CO LOC/G PUB/INST VOL/ASSN GOV/REL...COMPUT/IR GEN/METH. PAGE 107 B2164
B67
BIBLIOG/A
MGT
ADMIN
NAT/G

US DEPARTMENT OF THE ARMY,CIVILIAN IN PEACE, SOLDIER IN WAR: A BIBLIOGRAPHIC SURVEY OF THE ARMY AND AIR NATIONAL GUARD (PAMPHLET, NOS. 130-2). USA+45 USA-45 LOC/G NAT/G PROVS LEGIS PLAN ADMIN ATTIT ORD/FREE...POLICY 19/20 B2185
B67
BIBLIOG/A
FORCES
ROLE
DIPLOM

"A PROPOS DES INCITATIONS FINANCIERES AUX GROUPEMENTS DES COMMUNES: ESSAI D'INTERPRETATION." FRANCE NAT/G LEGIS ADMIN GOV/REL CENTRAL 20. PAGE 2 B0046
L67
LOC/G
ECO/TAC
APPORT
ADJUD

BURKE E.M.,"THE SEARCH FOR AUTHORITY IN PLANNING." MUNIC NEIGH CREATE PROB/SOLV LEGIT ADMIN CONTROL EFFICIENCY PWR...METH/COMP SIMUL 20. PAGE 17 B0352
S67
DECISION
PLAN
LOC/G
METH

DRYDEN S.,"LOCAL GOVERNMENT IN TANZANIA PART II" TANZANIA LAW NAT/G POL/PAR CONTROL PARTIC REPRESENT ...DECISION 20. PAGE 31 B0622
S67
LOC/G
GOV/REL
ADMIN
STRUCT

HOFMANN W.,"THE PUBLIC INTEREST PRESSURE GROUP: THE CASE OF THE DEUTSCHE STADTETAG." GERMANY GERMANY/W CONSTN STRUCT NAT/G CENTRAL FEDERAL PWR...TIME/SEQ 20. PAGE 51 B1030
S67
LOC/G
VOL/ASSN
LOBBY
ADMIN

HUMPHREY H.,"A MORE PERFECT UNION." USA+45 LOC/G NAT/G ACT/RES BUDGET RECEIVE CENTRAL CONGRESS. PAGE 52 B1063
S67
GOV/REL
FEDERAL
ADMIN
PROB/SOLV

LINEBERRY R.L.,"REFORMISM AND PUBLIC POLICIES IN AMERICAN CITIES." USA+45 POL/PAR EX/STRUC LEGIS
S67
DECISION
POLICY

BUDGET TAX GP/REL...STAT CHARTS. PAGE 65 B1317
MUNIC
LOC/G
S67

LLOYD K.,"URBAN RACE RIOTS V EFFECTIVE ANTI-DISCRIMINATION AGENCIES* AN END OR A BEGINNING?" USA+45 STRATA ACT/RES ADMIN ADJUST ORD/FREE RESPECT ...PLURIST DECISION SOC SOC/WK. PAGE 66 B1332
GP/REL
DISCRIM
LOC/G
CROWD
S67

PAYNE W.A.,"LOCAL GOVERNMENT STUDY COMMISSIONS: ORGANIZATION FOR ACTION." USA+45 LEGIS PWR...CHARTS 20. PAGE 81 B1646
LOC/G
DELIB/GP
PROB/SOLV
ADMIN
S67

ROWAT D.C.,"RECENT DEVELOPMENTS IN OMBUDSMANSHIP* A REVIEW ARTICLE." UK USA+45 STRUCT CONSULT INSPECT TASK EFFICIENCY...NEW/IDEA 20. PAGE 91 B1841
CANADA
ADMIN
LOC/G
NAT/G
S67

SUBRAMANIAM V.,"REPRESENTATIVE BUREAUCRACY: A REASSESSMENT." USA+45 ELITES LOC/G NAT/G ADMIN GOV/REL PRIVIL DRIVE ROLE...POLICY CENSUS 20 CIVIL/SERV BUREAUCRCY. PAGE 101 B2053
STRATA
GP/REL
MGT
GOV/COMP
S67

ZASLOW M.,"RECENT CONSTITUTIONAL DEVELOPMENTS IN CANADA'S NORTHERN TERRITORIES." CANADA LOC/G DELIB/GP EX/STRUC LEGIS ADMIN ORD/FREE...TREND 20. PAGE 119 B2398
GOV/REL
REGION
CONSTN
FEDERAL
B82

POOLE W.F.,INDEX TO PERIODICAL LITERATURE. LOC/G NAT/G DIPLOM ADMIN...HUM PHIL/SCI SOC 19. PAGE 84 B1690
BIBLIOG
USA-45
ALL/VALS
SOCIETY
B87

KINNEAR J.B.,PRINCIPLES OF CIVIL GOVERNMENT. MOD/EUR USA-45 CONSTN LOC/G EX/STRUC ADMIN PARL/PROC RACE/REL...CONCPT 18/19. PAGE 60 B1210
POL/PAR
NAT/G
GOV/COMP
REPRESENT

DRUCKER P.F.,"'MANAGEMENT SCIENCE' AND THE MANAGER." PLAN ROUTINE RIGID/FLEX...METH/CNCPT LOG HYPO/EXP. PAGE 30 B0620
S55
MGT
STRUCT
DECISION
RATIONAL
B57

HEATH S.,CITADEL, MARKET, AND ALTAR; EMERGING SOCIETY. SOCIETY ADMIN OPTIMAL OWN RATIONAL ORD/FREE...SOC LOG PREDICT GEN/LAWS DICTIONARY 20. PAGE 49 B0985
NEW/IDEA
STRUCT
UTOPIA
CREATE

HOWARD L.V.,TULANE STUDIES IN POLITICAL SCIENCE: CIVIL SERVICE DEVELOPMENT IN LOUISIANA VOLUME 3. LAW POL/PAR LEGIS CT/SYS ADJUST ORD/FREE...STAT CHARTS 19/20 LOUISIANA CIVIL/SERV. PAGE 52 B1050
B56
ADMIN
GOV/REL
PROVS
POLICY
B66

O'NEILL C.E.,CHURCH AND STATE IN FRENCH COLONIAL
COLONIAL

LOUISIANA: POLICY AND POLITICS TO 1732. PROVS   NAT/G
VOL/ASSN DELIB/GP ADJUD ADMIN GP/REL ATTIT DRIVE   SECT
...POLICY BIBLIOG 17/18 LOUISIANA CHURCH/STA.   PWR
PAGE 79 B1601

LOUISVILLE....LOUISVILLE, KENTUCKY

LOUVERT/T....L'OUVERTURE TOUSSANT

LOVE....AFFECTION, FRIENDSHIP, SEX RELATIONS

                                                                  B54
ALLPORT G.W.,THE NATURE OF PREJUDICE. USA+45 WOR+45   CULTURE
STRATA FACE/GP KIN NEIGH SECT ADMIN GP/REL DISCRIM   PERSON
ATTIT DRIVE LOVE RESPECT...PSY SOC MYTH QU/SEMANT   RACE/REL
20. PAGE 4 B0078
                                                                  B56
MANNONI D.O.,PROSPERO AND CALIBAN: THE PSYCHOLOGY   CULTURE
OF COLONIZATION. AFR EUR+WWI FAM KIN MUNIC SECT   COLONIAL
DOMIN ADMIN ATTIT DRIVE LOVE PWR RESPECT...PSY SOC
CONCPT MYTH OBS DEEP/INT BIOG GEN/METH MALAGASY 20.
PAGE 69 B1394
                                                                  S59
HARVEY M.F.,"THE PALESTINE REFUGEE PROBLEM: ACT/RES
ELEMENTS OF A SOLUTION." ISLAM LAW INT/ORG DELIB/GP   LEGIT
TOP/EX ECO/TAC ROUTINE DRIVE HEALTH LOVE ORD/FREE   PEACE
PWR WEALTH...MAJORIT FAO 20. PAGE 48 B0964   ISRAEL

LOVEDAY A. B1342

LOVEJOY D.S. B1343

LOVESTN/J....JAY LOVESTONE

LOW D.A. B1344

LOW J.O. B2293

LOWI T.J. B1345,B1346

LOWITH

LOYALTY....SEE SUPEGO

LUA....LUA, OR LAWA: VILLAGE PEOPLES OF NORTHERN THAILAND

LUANDA....LUANDA, ANGOLA

                                                                  B65
BOXER C.R.,PORTUGUESE SOCIETY IN THE TROPICS - THE   MUNIC
MUNICIPAL COUNCILS OF GAO, MACAO, BAHIA, AND   ADMIN
LUANDA, 1510-1800. EUR+WWI MOD/EUR PORTUGAL CONSTN   COLONIAL
EX/STRUC DOMIN CONTROL ROUTINE REPRESENT PRIVIL   DELIB/GP
...BIBLIOG/A 16/19 GENACCOUNT MACAO BAHIA LUANDA.
PAGE 14 B0290

LUBBOCK/TX....LUBBOCK, TEXAS

LUCE R. B1347

LUDWIG/BAV....LUDWIG THE BAVARIAN

LUMBERING....SEE EXTR/IND

LUTHER/M....MARTIN LUTHER

LUTZ V. B1348

LUVALE....LUVALE TRIBE, CENTRAL AFRICA

LUXEMBOURG....SEE ALSO APPROPRIATE TIME/SPACE/CULTURE INDEX

LUZON....LUZON, PHILIPPINES

LYNCH J. B1349

LYNCH M.C. B0696

LYONS G.M. B1350,B1351
                        —————— M ——————
M)%(*ROBINSON R.D. B1352

MAASS A. B1353,B1354

MACAO....MACAO

                                                                  B65
BOXER C.R.,PORTUGUESE SOCIETY IN THE TROPICS - THE   MUNIC
MUNICIPAL COUNCILS OF GAO, MACAO, BAHIA, AND   ADMIN
LUANDA, 1510-1800. EUR+WWI MOD/EUR PORTUGAL CONSTN   COLONIAL
EX/STRUC DOMIN CONTROL ROUTINE REPRESENT PRIVIL   DELIB/GP
...BIBLIOG/A 16/19 GENACCOUNT MACAO BAHIA LUANDA.
PAGE 14 B0290

MACAPAGL/D....DIOSDADO MACAPAGAL

MACARTHR/D....DOUGLAS MACARTHUR

MACDONALD D. B1355

MACDONALD G.E. B1356

MACDONALD G.J.F. B1357

MACDONALD R.W. B1358

MACFARQUHAR R. B1359

MACHIAVELLI N. B1360

MACHIAVELL....NICCOLO MACHIAVELLI

MACHIAVELLISM....SEE REALPOL, MACHIAVELL

MACIVER R.M. B1362

MACK R.T. B1363

MACKINTOSH J.M. B1364

MACKINTOSH J.P. B1365

MACLEISH/A....ARCHIBALD MACLEISH

MACMAHON A.W. B1366,B1367,B1368,B1369,B1370,B1371,B1372,B1373

MACMILLN/H....HAROLD MACMILLAN, PRIME MINISTER

MACNEIL N. B1374

MACPHERSON C. B1375

MACRIDIS R.C. B1376

MADAGASCAR....SEE ALSO AFR

                                                                  N
CONOVER H.F.,MADAGASCAR: A SELECTED LIST OF   BIBLIOG/A
REFERENCES. MADAGASCAR STRUCT ECO/UNDEV NAT/G ADMIN   SOCIETY
...SOC 19/20. PAGE 23 B0463   CULTURE
                                                       COLONIAL
                                                                  L62
MANGIN G.,"L'ORGANIZATION JUDICIAIRE DES ETATS   AFR
D'AFRIQUE ET DE MADAGASCAR." ISLAM WOR+45 STRATA   LEGIS
STRUCT ECO/UNDEV NAT/G LEGIT EXEC...JURID TIME/SEQ   COLONIAL
TOT/POP 20 SUPREME/CT. PAGE 69 B1387   MADAGASCAR
                                                                  S62
MURACCIOLE L.,"LES MODIFICATIONS DE LA CONSTITUTION   NAT/G
MALGACHE." AFR WOR+45 ECO/UNDEV LEGIT EXEC ALL/VALS   STRUCT
...JURID 20. PAGE 76 B1542   SOVEREIGN
                                                       MADAGASCAR
                                                                  B65
WITHERELL J.W.,MADAGASCAR AND ADJACENT ISLANDS; A   BIBLIOG
GUIDE TO OFFICIAL PUBLICATIONS (PAMPHLET). FRANCE   COLONIAL
MADAGASCAR S/ASIA UK LAW OP/RES PLAN DIPLOM   LOC/G
...POLICY CON/ANAL 19/20. PAGE 117 B2368   ADMIN

MADDEN F. B1803

MADERO/F....FRANCISCO MADERO

MADISON J. B0931

MADISON/J....PRESIDENT JAMES MADISON

MADOW W.G. B0577

MAFIA....MAFIA

MAGHREB....SEE ALSO ISLAM

MAGNA/CART....MAGNA CARTA

MAGON/F....FLORES MAGON

MAHAR J.M. B1377

MAHESHWARI B. B1378

MAIER N.R.F. B0529,B1379

MAILICK S. B1380

MAIMONIDES....MAIMONIDES

MAINE....MAINE

MAINZER L.C. B1381,B1382

MAIR L.P. B1383

MAITLAND/F....FREDERIC WILLIAM MAITLAND

MAJORIT....MAJORITARIAN

POOLE D.C.,THE CONDUCT OF FOREIGN RELATIONS UNDER
MODERN DEMOCRATIC CONDITIONS. EUR+WWI USA-45
INT/ORG PLAN LEGIT ADMIN KNOWL PWR...MAJORIT
OBS/ENVIR HIST/WRIT GEN/LAWS 20. PAGE 84 B1689
B24
NAT/G
EDU/PROP
DIPLOM

FYFE H.,THE BRITISH LIBERAL PARTY. UK SECT ADMIN
LEAD CHOOSE GP/REL PWR SOCISM...MAJORIT TIME/SEQ
19/20 LIB/PARTY CONSRV/PAR. PAGE 38 B0768
B28
POL/PAR
NAT/G
REPRESENT
POPULISM

STOKE H.W.,"EXECUTIVE LEADERSHIP AND THE GROWTH OF
PROPAGANDA." USA-45 NAT/G EX/STRUC LEGIS TOP/EX
PARL/PROC REPRESENT ORD/FREE PWR...MAJORIT 20.
PAGE 101 B2042
S41
EXEC
LEAD
EDU/PROP
ADMIN

BUSH V.,SCIENCE, THE ENDLESS FRONTIER. FUT USA-45
INTELL STRATA ACT/RES CREATE PLAN EDU/PROP ADMIN
NUC/PWR PEACE ATTIT HEALTH KNOWL...MAJORIT HEAL MGT
PHIL/SCI CONCPT OBS TREND 20. PAGE 18 B0360
B45
R+D
NAT/G

CORRY J.A.,DEMOCRATIC GOVERNMENT AND POLITICS.
WOR-45 EX/STRUC LOBBY TOTALISM...MAJORIT CONCPT
METH/COMP NAT/COMP 20. PAGE 24 B0479
B46
NAT/G
CONSTN
POL/PAR
JURID

HULL C.,THE MEMOIRS OF CORDELL HULL (VOLUME ONE).
USA-45 WOR-45 CONSTN FAM LOC/G NAT/G PROVS DELIB/GP
FORCES LEGIS TOP/EX BAL/PWR LEGIT ADMIN EXEC WAR
ATTIT ORD/FREE PWR...MAJORIT SELF/OBS TIME/SEQ
TREND NAZI 20. PAGE 52 B1062
B48
BIOG
DIPLOM

RIDDICK F.M.,THE UNITED STATES CONGRESS
ORGANIZATION AND PROCEDURE. POL/PAR DELIB/GP
PROB/SOLV DEBATE CONTROL EXEC LEAD INGP/REL PWR
...MAJORIT DECISION CONGRESS PRESIDENT. PAGE 88
B1777
B49
LEGIS
PARL/PROC
CHIEF
EX/STRUC

HOLCOMBE A.,"OUR MORE PERFECT UNION." USA+45 USA-45
POL/PAR JUDGE CT/SYS EQUILIB FEDERAL PWR...MAJORIT
TREND BIBLIOG 18/20 CONGRESS PRESIDENT. PAGE 51
B1031
C50
CONSTN
NAT/G
ADMIN
PLAN

SWISHER C.B.,THE THEORY AND PRACTICE OF AMERICAN
NATIONAL GOVERNMENT. CULTURE LEGIS DIPLOM ADJUD
ADMIN WAR PEACE ORD/FREE...MAJORIT 17/20. PAGE 102
B2063
B51
CONSTN
NAT/G
GOV/REL
GEN/LAWS

SHILS E.A.,"THE LEGISLATOR AND HIS ENVIRONMENT."
EX/STRUC DOMIN CONFER EFFICIENCY PWR MAJORIT.
PAGE 96 B1947
S51
LEGIS
TOP/EX
ADMIN
DELIB/GP

LIPSET S.M.,"DEMOCRACY IN PRIVATE GOVERNMENT; (A
CASE STUDY OF THE INTERNATIONAL TYPOGRAPHICAL
UNION)" (BMR)" POL/PAR CONTROL LEAD INGP/REL PWR
...MAJORIT DECISION PREDICT 20. PAGE 65 B1319
S52
LABOR
ADMIN
ELITES
REPRESENT

SAYLES L.R.,THE LOCAL UNION. CONSTN CULTURE
DELIB/GP PARTIC CHOOSE GP/REL INGP/REL ATTIT ROLE
...MAJORIT DECISION MGT. PAGE 93 B1873
B53
LABOR
LEAD
ADJUD
ROUTINE

LAPIERRE R.T.,A THEORY OF SOCIAL CONTROL. STRUCT
ADMIN ROUTINE SANCTION ANOMIE AUTHORIT DRIVE PERSON
PWR...MAJORIT CONCPT CLASSIF. PAGE 62 B1260
B54
CONTROL
VOL/ASSN
CULTURE

MILLARD E.L.,FREEDOM IN A FEDERAL WORLD. FUT WOR+45
VOL/ASSN TOP/EX LEGIT ROUTINE FEDERAL PEACE ATTIT
DISPL ORD/FREE PWR...MAJORIT INT/LAW JURID TREND
COLD/WAR 20. PAGE 73 B1479
B54
INT/ORG
CREATE
ADJUD
BAL/PWR

APPLEBY P.H.,"BUREAUCRACY AND THE FUTURE." USA+45
NAT/G CONTROL EXEC...MAJORIT 20. PAGE 6 B0119
S54
EX/STRUC
LOBBY
REPRESENT
ADMIN

CHILDS R.S.,"CITIZEN ORGANIZATION FOR CONTROL OF
GOVERNMENT." USA+45 POL/PAR CONTROL LOBBY...MAJORIT
20. PAGE 21 B0424
S54
CHOOSE
REPRESENT
ADMIN
EX/STRUC

NEUMANN S.,"MODERN POLITICAL PARTIES: APPROACHES TO
COMPARATIVE POLITIC. FRANCE UK EX/STRUC DOMIN ADMIN
LEAD REPRESENT TOTALISM ATTIT...POLICY TREND
METH/COMP ANTHOL BIBLIOG/A 20 CMN/WLTH. PAGE 78
B1574
C56
POL/PAR
GOV/COMP
ELITES
MAJORIT

JENNINGS I.,PARLIAMENT. UK FINAN INDUS POL/PAR
DELIB/GP EX/STRUC PLAN CONTROL...MAJORIT JURID
PARLIAMENT. PAGE 56 B1133
B57
PARL/PROC
TOP/EX
MGT
LEGIS

GULICK L.,"METROPOLITAN ORGANIZATION." LEGIS EXEC
S57
REGION

PARTIC CHOOSE REPRESENT GOV/REL...MAJORIT DECISION. LOC/G
PAGE 45 B0904
MUNIC

TANG P.S.H.,"COMMUNIST CHINA TODAY: DOMESTIC AND
FOREIGN POLICIES." CHINA/COM COM S/ASIA USSR STRATA
FORCES DIPLOM EDU/PROP COERCE GOV/REL...POLICY
MAJORIT BIBLIOG 20. PAGE 102 B2071
C57
POL/PAR
LEAD
ADMIN
CONSTN

CARTER G.M.,TRANSITION IN AFRICA; STUDIES IN
POLITICAL ADAPTATION. AFR CENTRL/AFR GHANA NIGERIA
CONSTN LOC/G POL/PAR ADMIN GP/REL FEDERAL...MAJORIT
BIBLIOG 20. PAGE 19 B0389
B58
NAT/COMP
PWR
CONTROL
NAT/G

LESTER R.A.,AS UNIONS MATURE. POL/PAR BARGAIN LEAD
PARTIC GP/REL CENTRAL...MAJORIT TIME/SEQ METH/COMP.
PAGE 64 B1299
B58
LABOR
INDUS
POLICY
MGT

REDFORD E.S.,"THE NEVER-ENDING SEARCH FOR THE
PUBLIC INTEREST" IN E. REDFORD, IDEALS AND PRACTICE
IN PUBLIC ADMINISTRATION (BMR)" USA+45 USA-45
SOCIETY PARTIC GP/REL ATTIT PLURISM...DECISION SOC
20. PAGE 87 B1755
C58
LOBBY
POLICY
ADMIN
MAJORIT

HARVEY M.F.,"THE PALESTINE REFUGEE PROBLEM:
ELEMENTS OF A SOLUTION." ISLAM LAW INT/ORG DELIB/GP
TOP/EX ECO/TAC ROUTINE DRIVE HEALTH LOVE ORD/FREE
PWR WEALTH...MAJORIT FAO 20. PAGE 48 B0964
S59
ACT/RES
LEGIT
PEACE
ISRAEL

SOHN L.B.,"THE DEFINITION OF AGGRESSION." FUT LAW
FORCES LEGIS LEGIT ADJUD ROUTINE COERCE ORD/FREE PWR
...MAJORIT JURID QUANT COLD/WAR 20. PAGE 99 B1995
S59
INT/ORG
CT/SYS
DETER
SOVEREIGN

HUNTINGTON S.P.,"STRATEGIC PLANNING AND THE
POLITICAL PROCESS." USA+45 NAT/G DELIB/GP LEGIS
ACT/RES ECO/TAC LEGIT ROUTINE CHOOSE RIGID/FLEX PWR
...POLICY MAJORIT MGT 20. PAGE 53 B1066
S60
EXEC
FORCES
NUC/PWR
WAR

ROURKE F.E.,"ADMINISTRATIVE SECRECY: A
CONGRESSIONAL DILEMMA." DELIB/GP CT/SYS ATTIT
...MAJORIT DECISION JURID. PAGE 91 B1837
S60
LEGIS
EXEC
ORD/FREE
POLICY

SCHRAMM W.,"MASS COMMUNICATIONS: A BOOK OF READINGS
(2ND ED.)" LG/CO PRESS ADMIN CONTROL ROUTINE ATTIT
ROLE SUPEGO...CHARTS ANTHOL BIBLIOG 20. PAGE 94
B1902
C60
COM/IND
EDU/PROP
CROWD
MAJORIT

HAMILTON A.,THE FEDERALIST. USA-45 NAT/G VOL/ASSN
LEGIS TOP/EX EDU/PROP LEGIT CHOOSE ATTIT RIGID/FLEX
ORD/FREE PWR...MAJORIT JURID CONCPT ANTHOL. PAGE 46
B0931
B61
EX/STRUC
CONSTN

ROWAT D.C.,BASIC ISSUES IN PUBLIC ADMINISTRATION.
STRUCT EX/STRUC PWR CONSERVE...MAJORIT DECISION MGT
T 20 BUREAUCRCY. PAGE 91 B1839
B61
NAT/G
ADJUD
ADMIN

JEWELL M.E.,SENATORIAL POLITICS AND FOREIGN POLICY.
NAT/G POL/PAR CHIEF DELIB/GP TOP/EX FOR/AID
EDU/PROP ROUTINE ATTIT PWR SKILL...MAJORIT
METH/CNCPT TIME/SEQ CONGRESS 20 PRESIDENT. PAGE 56
B1138
B62
USA+45
LEGIS
DIPLOM

JACOB H.,GERMAN ADMINISTRATION SINCE BISMARCK:
CENTRAL AUTHORITY VERSUS LOCAL AUTONOMY. GERMANY
GERMANY/W LAW POL/PAR CONTROL CENTRAL TOTALISM
FASCISM...MAJORIT DECISION STAT CHARTS GOV/COMP
19/20 BISMARCK/O HITLER/A WEIMAR/REP. PAGE 55 B1111
B63
ADMIN
NAT/G
LOC/G
POLICY

MEYNAUD J.,PLANIFICATION ET POLITIQUE. FRANCE ITALY
FINAN LABOR DELIB/GP LEGIS ADMIN EFFICIENCY
...MAJORIT DECISION 20. PAGE 73 B1477
B63
PLAN
ECO/TAC
PROB/SOLV

LIPSET S.M.,THE BERKELEY STUDENT REVOLT: FACTS AND
INTERPRETATIONS. USA+45 INTELL VOL/ASSN CONSULT
EDU/PROP PRESS DEBATE ADMIN REV HAPPINESS
RIGID/FLEX MAJORIT. PAGE 65 B1322
B65
CROWD
ACADEM
ATTIT
GP/REL

NATIONAL BOOK CENTRE PAKISTAN,BOOKS ON PAKISTAN: A
BIBLIOGRAPHY. PAKISTAN CULTURE DIPLOM ADMIN ATTIT
...MAJORIT SOC CONCPT 20. PAGE 77 B1560
B65
BIBLIOG
CONSTN
S/ASIA
NAT/G

NORDEN A.,WAR AND NAZI CRIMINALS IN WEST GERMANY:
STATE, ECONOMY, ADMINISTRATION, ARMY, JUSTICE,
SCIENCE. GERMANY GERMANY/W MOD/EUR ECO/DEV ACADEM
EX/STRUC FORCES DOMIN ADMIN CT/SYS...POLICY MAJORIT
PACIFIST 20. PAGE 78 B1587
B65
FASCIST
WAR
NAT/G
TOP/EX

STANLEY D.T.,CHANGING ADMINISTRATIONS. USA+45
POL/PAR DELIB/GP TOP/EX BUDGET GOV/REL GP/REL
PERS/REL PWR...MAJORIT DECISION MGT 20 PRESIDENT
SUCCESSION DEPT/STATE DEPT/DEFEN DEPT/HEW. PAGE 100
B2021
B65
NAT/G
CHIEF
ADMIN
EX/STRUC

ANDERSON S.V.,CANADIAN OMBUDSMAN PROPOSALS. CANADA LEGIS DEBATE PARL/PROC...MAJORIT JURID TIME/SEQ IDEA/COMP 20 OMBUDSMAN PARLIAMENT. PAGE 5 B0096
B66
NAT/G
CREATE
ADMIN
POL/PAR

HIDAYATULLAH M.,DEMOCRACY IN INDIA AND THE JUDICIAL PROCESS. INDIA EX/STRUC LEGIS LEAD GOV/REL ATTIT ORD/FREE...MAJORIT CONCPT 20 NEHRU/J. PAGE 50 B1007
B66
NAT/G
CT/SYS
CONSTN
JURID

LIVINGSTON J.C.,THE CONSENT OF THE GOVERNED. USA+45 EX/STRUC BAL/PWR DOMIN CENTRAL PERSON PWR...POLICY CONCPT OBS IDEA/COMP 20 CONGRESS. PAGE 66 B1331
NAT/G
LOBBY
MAJORIT
PARTIC

IDENBURG P.J.,"POLITICAL STRUCTURAL DEVELOPMENT IN TROPICAL AFRICA." UK ECO/UNDEV KIN POL/PAR CHIEF EX/STRUC CREATE COLONIAL CONTROL REPRESENT RACE/REL ...MAJORIT TREND 20. PAGE 53 B1074
S67
AFR
CONSTN
NAT/G
GOV/COMP

MAJORITY....BEHAVIOR OF MAJOR PARTS OF A GROUP; SEE ALSO CONSEN, MAJORIT

WILSON W.,CONGRESSIONAL GOVERNMENT. USA-45 NAT/G ADMIN EXEC PARL/PROC GP/REL MAJORITY ATTIT 19 SENATE HOUSE/REP. PAGE 117 B2364
B56
LEGIS
CHIEF
CONSTN
PWR

ROBSON W.A.,"TWO-LEVEL GOVERNMENT FOR METROPOLITAN AREAS." MUNIC EX/STRUC LEGIS PARTIC REPRESENT MAJORITY. PAGE 89 B1807
S57
REGION
LOC/G
PLAN
GOV/REL

HAIRE M.,MODERN ORGANIZATION THEORY. LABOR ROUTINE MAJORITY...CONCPT MODAL OBS CONT/OBS. PAGE 45 B0919
B61
PERS/REL
GP/REL
MGT
DECISION

MAJUMDAR B.B. B1384

MALAGASY

MANNONI D.O.,PROSPERO AND CALIBAN: THE PSYCHOLOGY OF COLONIZATION. AFR EUR+WWI FAM KIN MUNIC SECT DOMIN ADMIN ATTIT DRIVE LOVE PWR RESPECT...PSY SOC CONCPT MYTH OBS DEEP/INT BIOG GEN/METH MALAGASY 20. PAGE 69 B1394
B56
CULTURE
COLONIAL

MALAWI....SEE ALSO AFR

RHODESIA-NYASA NATL ARCHIVES.A SELECT BIBLIOGRAPHY OF RECENT PUBLICATIONS CONCERNING THE FEDERATION OF RHODESIA AND NYASALAND (PAMPHLET). MALAWI RHODESIA LAW CULTURE STRUCT ECO/UNDEV LEGIS...GEOG 20. PAGE 88 B1770
N60
BIBLIOG
ADMIN
ORD/FREE
NAT/G

MALAYA....MALAYA

MALAYSIA....SEE ALSO S/ASIA

MCKIE R.,MALAYSIA IN FOCUS. INDONESIA WOR+45 ECO/UNDEV FINAN NAT/G POL/PAR SECT FORCES PLAN ADMIN COLONIAL COERCE DRIVE ALL/VALS...POLICY RECORD CENSUS TIME/SEQ CMN/WLTH 20. PAGE 72 B1453
B63
S/ASIA
NAT/LISM
MALAYSIA

TILMAN R.O.,BUREAUCRATIC TRANSITION IN MALAYA. MALAYSIA S/ASIA UK NAT/G EX/STRUC DIPLOM...CHARTS BIBLIOG 20. PAGE 104 B2110
B64
ADMIN
COLONIAL
SOVEREIGN
EFFICIENCY

PURCELL V.,THE MEMOIRS OF A MALAYAN OFFICIAL. MALAYSIA UK ECO/UNDEV INDUS LABOR EDU/PROP COLONIAL CT/SYS WAR NAT/LISM TOTALISM ORD/FREE SOVEREIGN 20 UN CIVIL/SERV. PAGE 85 B1721
B65
BIOG
ADMIN
JURID
FORCES

MILNE R.S.,GOVERNMENT AND POLITICS IN MALAYSIA. INDONESIA MALAYSIA LOC/G EX/STRUC FORCES DIPLOM GP/REL 20 SINGAPORE. PAGE 74 B1489
B67
NAT/G
LEGIS
ADMIN

ROFF W.R.,THE ORIGINS OF MALAY NATIONALISM. MALAYSIA INTELL NAT/G ADMIN COLONIAL...BIBLIOG DICTIONARY 20 CMN/WLTH. PAGE 90 B1813
B67
NAT/LISM
ELITES
VOL/ASSN
SOCIETY

MALCOLM/X....MALCOLM X

MALDIVE....MALDIVE ISLAND; SEE ALSO S/ASIA, COMMONWLTH

MALE/SEX....MALE SEX

MALI....SEE ALSO AFR

FOLTZ W.J.,FROM FRENCH WEST AFRICA TO THE MALI FEDERATION. AFR FRANCE MALI ADMIN CONTROL FEDERAL ...DECISION 20. PAGE 36 B0734
B65
EXEC
TOP/EX
ELITES
LEAD

SNYDER F.G.,ONE-PARTY GOVERNMENT IN MALI: TRANSITION TOWARD CONTROL. MALI STRATA STRUCT SOC. PAGE 99 B1991
B65
ECO/UNDEV
POL/PAR
EX/STRUC
ADMIN

MALINOWSKI W.R. B1385

MALOF P. B0728

MALTA....SEE ALSO APPROPRIATE TIME/SPACE/CULTURE INDEX

MALTHUS....THOMAS ROBERT MALTHUS

MANAGEMENT....SEE MGT, EX/STRUC, ADMIN

MANAGEMENT BY OBJECTIVES....SEE MGT/OBJECT

MANCHESTER....MANCHESTER, ENGLAND

MANCHU/DYN....MANCHU DYNASTY

MANGIN G. B1386,B1387

MANGONE G. B1388,B1389,B1390

MANGONE G.J. B1391

MANITOBA....MANITOBA, CANADA

MANNE H.G. B1392

MANNERS....SEE ETIQUET

MANNHEIM K. B1393

MANNHEIM/K....KARL MANNHEIM

MANNONI D.O. B1394

MANPOWER....SEE LABOR

MANSFIELD E. B1395,B1396

MANTECON J. B0381

MANTON/M....MART MANTON

MANUFACTURING INDUSTRY....SEE PROC/MFG

MAO....MAO TSE-TUNG

KAUTSKY J.H.,"THE NEW STRATEGY OF INTERNATIONAL COMMUNISM." ASIA CHINA/COM FUT WOR+45 WOR-45 ADMIN ROUTINE PERSON MARXISM SOCISM...TREND IDEA/COMP 20 LENIN/VI MAO. PAGE 59 B1184
S55
COM
POL/PAR
TOTALISM
USSR

MACFARQUHAR R.,CHINA UNDER MAO: POLITICS TAKES COMMAND. CHINA/COM COM AGRI INDUS CHIEF FORCES DIPLOM INT/TRADE EDU/PROP TASK REV ADJUST...ANTHOL 20 MAO. PAGE 67 B1359
B66
ECO/UNDEV
TEC/DEV
ECO/TAC
ADMIN

LENG S.C.,JUSTICE IN COMMUNIST CHINA: A SURVEY OF THE JUDICIAL SYSTEM OF THE CHINESE PEOPLE'S REPUBLIC. CHINA/COM LAW CONSTN LOC/G NAT/G PROF/ORG CONSULT FORCES ADMIN CRIME ORD/FREE...BIBLIOG 20 MAO. PAGE 64 B1290
B67
CT/SYS
ADJUD
JURID
MARXISM

MAPS....MAPS AND ATLASES; SEE ALSO CHARTS

MARAJO....MARAJO, A BRAZILIAN ISLAND

MARANHAO....MARANHAO, BRAZIL

MARCANT/V....VITO MARCANTONIO

MARCH J.G. B0516,B0517,B0518,B1397

MARCUSE H. B1233

MARCUSE/H....HERBERT MARCUSE

MARGOLIS J. B1398

MARITAIN/J....JACQUES MARITAIN

KARIEL H.S.,IN SEARCH OF AUTHORITY: TWENTIETH-CENTURY POLITICAL THOUGHT. WOR+45 WOR-45 NAT/G EX/STRUC TOTALISM DRIVE PWR...MGT PHIL/SCI GEN/LAWS ORD/FREE
B64
CONSTN
CONCPT

19/20 NIETZSCH/F FREUD/S WEBER/MAX NIEBUHR/R   IDEA/COMP
MARITAIN/J. PAGE 58 B1173

MARITIME....MARITIME PROVINCES

MARKET RESEARCH....SEE MARKET

MARKET....MARKETING SYSTEM

INTERNATIONAL BIBLIOGRAPHY OF ECONOMICS. WOR+45   N
FINAN MARKET ADMIN DEMAND INCOME PRODUC...POLICY   BIBLIOG
IDEA/COMP METH. PAGE 1 B0003   ECO/DEV
                                                    ECO/UNDEV
                                                    INT/TRADE
                                                    N
THE MANAGEMENT REVIEW. FINAN EX/STRUC PROFIT   LABOR
BIBLIOG/A. PAGE 1 B0017   MGT
                                                    ADMIN
                                                    MARKET
                                                    N
MARKETING INFORMATION GUIDE. USA+45 ECO/DEV FINAN   BIBLIOG/A
ADMIN GP/REL. PAGE 1 B0018   DIST/IND
                                                    MARKET
                                                    ECO/TAC
                                                    N
ECONOMIC LIBRARY SELECTIONS. AGRI INDUS MARKET   BIBLIOG/A
ADMIN...STAT NAT/COMP 20. PAGE 2 B0026   WRITING
                                                    FINAN
                                                    N
BUSINESS LITERATURE. WOR+45 MARKET ADMIN MGT.   BIBLIOG/A
PAGE 2 B0031   INDUS
                                                    FINAN
                                                    POLICY
                                                    N19
KRIESBERG M..CANCELLATION OF THE RATION STAMPS   RATION
(PAMPHLET). USA+45 USA-45 MARKET PROB/SOLV PRICE   DECISION
GOV/REL RIGID/FLEX 20 OPA. PAGE 61 B1235   ADMIN
                                                    NAT/G
                                                    B28
CALKINS E.E..BUSINESS THE CIVILIZER. INDUS MARKET   LAISSEZ
WORKER TAX PAY ROUTINE COST DEMAND MORAL 19/20.   POLICY
PAGE 18 B0367   WEALTH
                                                    PROFIT
                                                    B37
PARSONS T..THE STRUCTURE OF SOCIAL ACTION. UNIV   CULTURE
INTELL SOCIETY INDUS MARKET ECO/TAC ROUTINE CHOOSE ATTIT
ALL/VALS...CONCPT OBS BIOG TREND GEN/LAWS 20.   CAP/ISM
PAGE 81 B1636
                                                    B38
DAY C..A HISTORY OF COMMERCE. CHRIST-17C EUR+WWI   MARKET
ISLAM MEDIT-7 MOD/EUR USA-45 ECO/DEV FINAN NAT/G   INT/TRADE
ECO/TAC EXEC ROUTINE PWR WEALTH HIST/WRIT. PAGE 27
B0546
                                                    B38
LANGE O..ON THE ECONOMIC THEORY OF SOCIALISM. UNIV MARKET
ECO/DEV FINAN INDUS INT/ORG PUB/INST ROUTINE ATTIT ECO/TAC
ALL/VALS...SOC CONCPT STAT TREND 20. PAGE 62 B1258 INT/TRADE
                                                    SOCISM
                                                    B40
GAUS J.M..PUBLIC ADMINISTRATION AND THE UNITED   ADMIN
STATES DEPARTMENT OF AGRICULTURE. USA+45 STRUCT   AGRI
DIST/IND FINAN MARKET EX/STRUC PROB/SOLV GIVE   DELIB/GP
PRODUC...POLICY GEOG CHARTS 20 DEPT/AGRI. PAGE 39   OP/RES
B0786
                                                    L44
HAILEY.."THE FUTURE OF COLONIAL PEOPLES." WOR-45   PLAN
CONSTN CULTURE ECO/UNDEV AGRI MARKET INT/ORG NAT/G CONCPT
SECT CONSULT ECO/TAC LEGIT ADMIN NAT/LISM ALL/VALS DIPLOM
...SOC OBS TREND STERTYP CMN/WLTH LEAGUE/NAT   UK
PARLIAMENT 20. PAGE 45 B0916
                                                    B47
BAERWALD F..FUNDAMENTALS OF LABOR ECONOMICS. LAW   ECO/DEV
INDUS LABOR LG/CO CONTROL GP/REL INCOME TOTALISM   WORKER
...MGT CHARTS GEN/LAWS BIBLIOG 20. PAGE 8 B0158   MARKET
                                                    B48
HOOVER E.M..THE LOCATION OF ECONOMIC ACTIVITY.   HABITAT
WOR+45 MARKET MUNIC WORKER PROB/SOLV INT/TRADE   INDUS
ADMIN COST...POLICY CHARTS T 20. PAGE 51 B1041   ECO/TAC
                                                    GEOG
                                                    B49
SHISTER J..ECONOMICS OF THE LABOR MARKET. LOC/G   MARKET
NAT/G WORKER TEC/DEV BARGAIN PAY PRICE EXEC GP/REL LABOR
INCOME...MGT T 20. PAGE 96 B1949   INDUS
                                                    B51
DIMOCK M.E..FREE ENTERPRISE AND THE ADMINISTRATIVE CAP/ISM
STATE. FINAN LG/CO BARGAIN BUDGET DOMIN CONTROL   ADMIN
INGP/REL EFFICIENCY 20. PAGE 29 B0595   MGT
                                                    MARKET
                                                    B52
EGLE W.P..ECONOMIC STABILIZATION. USA+45 SOCIETY   NAT/G
FINAN MARKET PLAN ECO/TAC DOMIN EDU/PROP LEGIT EXEC ECO/DEV
WEALTH...CONCPT METH/CNCPT TREND HYPO/EXP GEN/METH CAP/ISM
TOT/POP VAL/FREE 20. PAGE 32 B0656
                                                    B53
MILLIKAN M.F..INCOME STABILIZATION FOR A DEVELOPING ANTHOL
DEMOCRACY. USA+45 ECO/DEV LABOR BUDGET ECO/TAC TAX MARKET

ADMIN ADJUST PRODUC WEALTH...POLICY TREND 20.   EQUILIB
PAGE 73 B1484   EFFICIENCY
                                                    B53
ROBINSON E.A.G..THE STRUCTURE OF COMPETITIVE   INDUS
INDUSTRY. UK ECO/DEV DIST/IND MARKET TEC/DEV DIPLOM PRODUC
EDU/PROP ADMIN EFFICIENCY WEALTH...MGT 19/20.   WORKER
PAGE 89 B1798   OPTIMAL
                                                    B54
MOSK S.A..INDUSTRIAL REVOLUTION IN MEXICO. MARKET   INDUS
LABOR CREATE CAP/ISM ADMIN ATTIT SOCISM...POLICY 20 TEC/DEV
MEXIC/AMER. PAGE 76 B1533   ECO/UNDEV
                                                    NAT/G
                                                    B56
ALEXANDER R.S..INDUSTRIAL MARKETING. USA+45 ECO/DEV INDUS
DIST/IND FINAN NAT/G ACT/RES CAP/ISM PRICE CONTROL MARKET
...POLICY MGT 20. PAGE 4 B0072   ECO/TAC
                                                    PLAN
                                                    B58
ATOMIC INDUSTRIAL FORUM.MANAGEMENT AND ATOMIC   NUC/PWR
ENERGY. WOR+45 SEA LAW MARKET NAT/G TEC/DEV INSPECT INDUS
INT/TRADE CONFER PEACE HEALTH...ANTHOL 20. PAGE 7   MGT
B0145   ECO/TAC
                                                    B59
WASSERMAN P..MEASUREMENT AND ANALYSIS OF   BIBLIOG/A
ORGANIZATIONAL PERFORMANCE. FINAN MARKET EX/STRUC   ECO/TAC
TEC/DEV EDU/PROP CONTROL ROUTINE TASK...MGT 20.   OP/RES
PAGE 114 B2300   EFFICIENCY
                                                    B59
WELTON H..THE THIRD WORLD WAR; TRADE AND INDUSTRY, INT/TRADE
THE NEW BATTLEGROUND. WOR+45 ECO/DEV INDUS MARKET   PLAN
TASK...MGT IDEA/COMP COLD/WAR. PAGE 115 B2321   DIPLOM
                                                    S59
ZAUBERMAN A.."SOVIET BLOC ECONOMIC INTEGRATION."   MARKET
COM CULTURE INTELL ECO/DEV INDUS TOP/EX ACT/RES   INT/ORG
PLAN ECO/TAC INT/TRADE ROUTINE CHOOSE ATTIT   USSR
...TIME/SEQ 20. PAGE 119 B2399   TOTALISM
                                                    C59
DAHL R.A.."SOCIAL SCIENCE RESEARCH ON BUSINESS: MGT
PRODUCT AND POTENTIAL" INDUS MARKET OP/RES CAP/ISM EFFICIENCY
ADMIN LOBBY DRIVE...PSY CONCPT BIBLIOG/A 20.   PROB/SOLV
PAGE 26 B0521   EX/STRUC
                                                    B60
CAMPBELL R.W..SOVIET ECONOMIC POWER. COM USA+45   ECO/DEV
DIST/IND MARKET TOP/EX ACT/RES CAP/ISM ECO/TAC   PLAN
DOMIN EDU/PROP ADMIN ROUTINE DRIVE...MATH TIME/SEQ SOCISM
CHARTS WORK 20. PAGE 18 B0371   USSR
                                                    B60
HOVING W..THE DISTRIBUTION REVOLUTION. WOR+45   DIST/IND
ECO/DEV FINAN SERV/IND PRESS PRICE INCOME PRODUC   MARKET
...MGT 20. PAGE 52 B1049   ECO/TAC
                                                    TASK
                                                    B60
MOORE W.E..LABOR COMMITMENT AND SOCIAL CHANGE IN   LABOR
DEVELOPING AREAS. SOCIETY STRATA ECO/UNDEV MARKET   ORD/FREE
VOL/ASSN WORKER AUTHORIT SKILL...MGT NAT/COMP   ATTIT
SOC/INTEG 20. PAGE 75 B1514   INDUS
                                                    L60
STEIN E.."LEGAL REMEDIES OF ENTERPRISES IN THE   MARKET
EUROPEAN ECONOMIC COMMUNITY." EUR+WWI FUT ECO/DEV   ADJUD
INDUS PLAN ECO/TAC ADMIN PWR...MGT MATH STAT TREND
CON/ANAL EEC 20. PAGE 100 B2026
                                                    S60
GARNICK D.H.."ON THE ECONOMIC FEASIBILITY OF A   MARKET
MIDDLE EASTERN COMMON MARKET." AFR ISLAM CULTURE   INT/TRADE
INDUS NAT/G PLAN TEC/DEV ECO/TAC ADMIN ATTIT DRIVE
RIGID/FLEX...PLURIST STAT TREND GEN/LAWS 20.
PAGE 39 B0784
                                                    B61
BRADY R.A..ORGANIZATION, AUTOMATION, AND SOCIETY.   TEC/DEV
USA+45 AGRI COM/IND DIST/IND MARKET CREATE   INDUS
...DECISION MGT 20. PAGE 14 B0296   AUTOMAT
                                                    ADMIN
                                                    B61
HALL M..DISTRIBUTION IN GREAT BRITAIN AND NORTH   DIST/IND
AMERICA. CANADA UK USA+45 ECO/DEV INDUS MARKET   PRODUC
EFFICIENCY PROFIT...MGT CHARTS 20. PAGE 46 B0924   ECO/TAC
                                                    CAP/ISM
                                                    B61
MARX K..THE COMMUNIST MANIFESTO. IN (MENDEL A.   COM
ESSENTIAL WORKS OF MARXISM, NEW YORK: BANTAM. FUT   NEW/IDEA
MOD/EUR CULTURE ECO/DEV ECO/UNDEV AGRI FINAN INDUS CAP/ISM
MARKET PROC/MFG LABOR MUNIC POL/PAR CONSULT FORCES REV
CREATE PLAN ADMIN ATTIT DRIVE RIGID/FLEX ORD/FREE
PWR RESPECT MARX/KARL WORK. PAGE 70 B1421
                                                    B61
WILLSON F.M.G..ADMINISTRATORS IN ACTION. UK MARKET ADMIN
TEC/DEV PARL/PROC 20. PAGE 117 B2358   NAT/G
                                                    CONSTN
                                                    S61
LANFALUSSY A.."EUROPE'S PROGRESS: DUE TO COMMON   INT/ORG
MARKET." EUR+WWI ECO/DEV DELIB/GP PLAN ECO/TAC   MARKET
ROUTINE WEALTH...GEOG TREND EEC 20. PAGE 62 B1257
                                                    S61
VINER J.."ECONOMIC FOREIGN POLICY ON THE NEW   TOP/EX
FRONTIER." USA+45 ECO/UNDEV AGRI FINAN INDUS MARKET ECO/TAC
INT/ORG NAT/G FOR/AID INT/TRADE ADMIN ATTIT PWR 20 BAL/PAY

KENNEDY/JF. PAGE 112 B2262   TARIFFS

B62
BECKMAN T.N.,MARKETING (7TH ED.). USA+45 SOCIETY   MARKET
ECO/DEV NAT/G PRICE EFFICIENCY INCOME ATTIT WEALTH   ECO/TAC
...MGT BIBLIOG 20. PAGE 10 B0205   DIST/IND
                                                    POLICY
B62
CAIRNCROSS A.K.,FACTORS IN ECONOMIC DEVELOPMENT.   MARKET
WOR+45 ECO/UNDEV INDUS R+D LG/CO NAT/G EX/STRUC   ECO/DEV
PLAN TEC/DEV ECO/TAC ATTIT HEALTH KNOWL PWR WEALTH
...TIME/SEQ GEN/LAWS TOT/POP VAL/FREE 20. PAGE 18
B0363
B62
MEANS G.C.,THE CORPORATE REVOLUTION IN AMERICA: LG/CO
ECONOMIC REALITY VS. ECONOMIC THEORY. USA+45 USA-45 MARKET
INDUS WORKER PLAN CAP/ISM ADMIN...IDEA/COMP 20.   CONTROL
PAGE 72 B1459   PRICE
B62
NATIONAL BUREAU ECONOMIC RES,THE RATE AND DIRECTION DECISION
OF INVENTIVE ACTIVITY: ECONOMIC AND SOCIAL FACTORS. PROB/SOLV
STRUCT INDUS MARKET R+D CREATE OP/RES TEC/DEV   MGT
EFFICIENCY PRODUC RATIONAL UTIL...WELF/ST PHIL/SCI
METH/CNCPT TIME. PAGE 77 B1562
B62
SAMPSON A.,ANATOMY OF BRITAIN. UK LAW COM/IND FINAN ELITES
INDUS MARKET MUNIC POL/PAR EX/STRUC TOP/EX DIPLOM   PWR
LEAD REPRESENT PERSON PARLIAMENT WORSHIP. PAGE 92   STRUCT
B1866   FORCES
B63
BONINI C.P.,SIMULATION OF INFORMATION AND DECISION   INDUS
SYSTEMS IN THE FIRM. MARKET BUDGET DOMIN EDU/PROP   SIMUL
ADMIN COST ATTIT HABITAT PERCEPT PWR...CONCPT   DECISION
PROBABIL QUANT PREDICT HYPO/EXP BIBLIOG. PAGE 13   MGT
B0273
B63
HEYEL C.,THE ENCYCLOPEDIA OF MANAGEMENT. WOR+45   MGT
MARKET TOP/EX TEC/DEV AUTOMAT LEAD ADJUST...STAT   INDUS
CHARTS GAME ANTHOL BIBLIOG. PAGE 49 B1002   ADMIN
                                                    FINAN
B63
LINDBERG L.,POLITICAL DYNAMICS OF EUROPEAN ECONOMIC MARKET
INTEGRATION. EUR+WWI ECO/DEV INT/ORG VOL/ASSN   ECO/TAC
DELIB/GP ADMIN WEALTH...DECISION EEC 20. PAGE 65
B1313
B63
SCHOECK H.,THE NEW ARGUMENT IN ECONOMICS. UK USA+45 WELF/ST
INDUS MARKET LABOR NAT/G ECO/TAC ADMIN ROUTINE   FOR/AID
BAL/PAY PWR...POLICY BOLIV. PAGE 94 B1899   ECO/DEV
                                                    ALL/IDEOS
B63
SELF P.,THE STATE AND THE FARMER. UK ECO/DEV MARKET AGRI
WORKER PRICE CONTROL GP/REL...WELF/ST 20 DEPT/AGRI. NAT/G
PAGE 95 B1926   ADMIN
                                                    VOL/ASSN
S63
BARZANSKI S.,"REGIONAL UNDERDEVELOPMENT IN THE   ECO/UNDEV
EUROPEAN ECONOMIC COMMUNITY." EUR+WWI ELITES   PLAN
DIST/IND MARKET VOL/ASSN CONSULT EX/STRUC ECO/TAC
RIGID/FLEX WEALTH EEC OEEC 20. PAGE 9 B0192
B64
CHANDLER A.D. JR.,GIANT ENTERPRISE: FORD, GENERAL   LG/CO
MOTORS, AND THE AUTOMOBILE INDUSTRY; SOURCES AND   DIST/IND
READINGS. USA+45 USA-45 FINAN MARKET CREATE ADMIN   LABOR
...TIME/SEQ ANTHOL 20 AUTOMOBILE. PAGE 20 B0404   MGT
B64
COX R.,THEORY IN MARKETING. FUT USA+45 SOCIETY   MARKET
ECO/DEV PROB/SOLV PRICE RISK PRODUC ATTIT...ANTHOL   ECO/TAC
20. PAGE 24 B0499   PHIL/SCI
                                                    MGT
B64
GARFIELD PJ   LOVEJOY WF,PUBLIC UTILITY   T
ECONOMICS. DIST/IND FINAN MARKET MUNIC ADMIN COST   ECO/TAC
DEMAND...TECHNIC JURID 20 MONOPOLY. PAGE 39 B0782   OWN
                                                    SERV/IND
B64
LI C.M.,INDUSTRIAL DEVELOPMENT IN COMMUNIST CHINA.   ASIA
CHINA/COM ECO/DEV ECO/UNDEV AGRI FINAN INDUS MARKET TEC/DEV
LABOR NAT/G ECO/TAC INT/TRADE EXEC ALL/VALS
...POLICY RELATIV TREND WORK TOT/POP VAL/FREE 20.
PAGE 65 B1311
B64
WELLISZ S.,THE ECONOMICS OF THE SOVIET BLOC. COM   EFFICIENCY
USSR INDUS WORKER PLAN BUDGET INT/TRADE TAX PRICE   ADMIN
PRODUC WEALTH MARXISM...METH/COMP 20. PAGE 115   MARKET
B2319
B64
WILLIAMSON O.E.,THE ECONOMICS OF DISCRETIONARY   EFFICIENCY
BEHAVIOR: MANAGERIAL OBJECTIVES IN A THEORY OF THE   MGT
FIRM. MARKET BUDGET CAP/ISM PRODUC DRIVE PERSON   ECO/TAC
...STAT CHARTS BIBLIOG METH 20. PAGE 117 B2354   CHOOSE
L64
HAAS E.B.,"ECONOMICS AND DIFFERENTIAL PATTERNS OF   L/A+17C
POLITICAL INTEGRATION: PROJECTIONS ABOUT UNITY IN   INT/ORG
LATIN AMERICA." SOCIETY NAT/G DELIB/GP ACT/RES   MARKET
CREATE PLAN ECO/TAC REGION ROUTINE ATTIT DRIVE PWR
WEALTH...CONCPT TREND CHARTS LAFTA 20. PAGE 45

B0910
S64
HUELIN D.,"ECONOMIC INTEGRATION IN LATIN AMERICAN: MARKET
PROGRESS AND PROBLEMS." L/A+17C ECO/DEV AGRI   ECO/UNDEV
DIST/IND FINAN INDUS NAT/G VOL/ASSN CONSULT   INT/TRADE
DELIB/GP EX/STRUC ACT/RES PLAN TEC/DEV ECO/TAC
ROUTINE BAL/PAY WEALTH WORK 20. PAGE 52 B1058
S64
PARSONS T.,"EVOLUTIONARY UNIVERSALS IN SOCIETY."   SOC
UNIV SOCIETY STRATA MARKET EDU/PROP LEGIT ADJUD   CONCPT
ADMIN ALL/VALS...JURID OBS GEN/LAWS VAL/FREE 20.
PAGE 81 B1638
S64
RIGBY T.H.,"TRADITIONAL, MARKET, AND ORGANIZATIONAL MARKET
SOCIETIES AND THE USSR." COM ECO/DEV NAT/G POL/PAR   ADMIN
ECO/TAC DOMIN ORD/FREE PWR WEALTH...TIME/SEQ   USSR
GEN/LAWS VAL/FREE 20 STALIN/J. PAGE 88 B1784
B65
ALDERSON W.,DYNAMIC MARKETING BEHAVIOR. USA+45   MGT
FINAN CREATE TEC/DEV EDU/PROP PRICE COST 20. PAGE 3 MARKET
B0071   ATTIT
                                                    CAP/ISM
B65
DOWD L.P.,PRINCIPLES OF WORLD BUSINESS. SERV/IND   INT/TRADE
NAT/G DIPLOM ECO/TAC TARIFFS...INT/LAW JURID 20.   MGT
PAGE 30 B0614   FINAN
                                                    MARKET
B65
INT. BANK RECONSTR. DEVELOP.,ECONOMIC DEVELOPMENT   INDUS
OF KUWAIT. ISLAM KUWAIT AGRI FINAN MARKET EX/STRUC   NAT/G
TEC/DEV ECO/TAC ADMIN WEALTH...OBS CON/ANAL CHARTS
20. PAGE 54 B1092
B65
KELLEY E.J.,MARKETING: STRATEGY AND FUNCTIONS.   MARKET
ECO/DEV INDUS PLAN PRICE CONTROL ROUTINE...MGT   DIST/IND
BIBLIOG 20. PAGE 59 B1191   POLICY
                                                    ECO/TAC
B65
LATHAM E.,THE GROUP BASIS OF POLITICS: A STUDY IN   LEGIS
BASING-POINT LEGISLATION. INDUS MARKET POL/PAR   GP/COMP
DELIB/GP EX/STRUC DEBATE ADJUD...CHARTS PRESIDENT.   GP/REL
PAGE 63 B1274
L65
WILLIAMS S.,"NEGOTIATING INVESTMENT IN EMERGING   FINAN
COUNTRIES." USA+45 WOR+45 INDUS MARKET NAT/G TOP/EX ECO/UNDEV
TEC/DEV CAP/ISM ECO/TAC ADMIN SKILL WEALTH...POLICY
RELATIV MGT WORK 20. PAGE 117 B2353
B66
BOYD H.W.,MARKETING MANAGEMENT: CASES FROM EMERGING MGT
COUNTRIES. BRAZIL GHANA ISRAEL WOR+45 ADMIN   ECO/UNDEV
PERS/REL ATTIT HABITAT WEALTH...ANTHOL 20 ARGEN   PROB/SOLV
CASEBOOK. PAGE 14 B0292   MARKET
B66
GRETHER E.T.,MARKETING AND PUBLIC POLICY. USA+45   MARKET
ECO/DEV DIST/IND NAT/G PLAN CAP/ISM PRICE CONTROL   PROB/SOLV
...GEOG MGT 20. PAGE 43 B0874   ECO/TAC
                                                    POLICY
B66
KAESTNER K.,GESAMTWIRTSCHAFTLICHE PLANUNG IN EINER   ECO/TAC
GEMISCHTEN WIRTSCHAFTSORDNUNG   PLAN
(WIRTSCHAFTSPOLITISCHE STUDIEN 5). GERMANY/W WOR+45 POLICY
WOR-45 INDUS MARKET NAT/G ACT/RES GP/REL INGP/REL   PREDICT
PRODUC...ECOMETRIC MGT BIBLIOG 20. PAGE 57 B1159
B66
LINDFORS G.V.,INTERCOLLEGIATE BIBLIOGRAPHY; CASES   BIBLIOG/A
IN BUSINESS ADMINISTRATION (VOL. X). FINAN MARKET   ADMIN
LABOR CONSULT PLAN GP/REL PRODUC 20. PAGE 65 B1314   MGT
                                                    OP/RES
B66
SPINELLI A.,THE EUROCRATS; CONFLICT AND CRISIS IN   INT/ORG
THE EUROPEAN COMMUNITY (TRANS. BY C. GROVE HAINES). INGP/REL
EUR+WWI MARKET POL/PAR ECO/TAC PARL/PROC EEC OEEC   CONSTN
ECSC EURATOM. PAGE 99 B2007   ADMIN
S66
HANSON A.H.,"PLANNING AND THE POLITICIANS* SOME   PLAN
REFLECTIONS ON ECONOMIC PLANNING IN WESTERN   ECO/DEV
EUROPE." MARKET NAT/G TEC/DEV CONSEN ROLE   EUR+WWI
...METH/COMP NAT/COMP. PAGE 46 B0942   ADMIN
S66
MARKSHAK J.,"ECONOMIC PLANNING AND THE COST OF   ECO/UNDEV
THINKING." COM MARKET EX/STRUC...DECISION GEN/LAWS. ECO/TAC
PAGE 69 B1400   PLAN
                                                    ECO/DEV
C66
SHERMAN H.,"IT ALL DEPENDS." USA+45 FINAN MARKET   LG/CO
PLAN PROB/SOLV EXEC PARTIC INGP/REL SUPEGO   MGT
...DECISION BIBLIOG 20. PAGE 96 B1944   ADMIN
                                                    POLICY
B67
BRAYMAN H.,CORPORATE MANAGEMENT IN A WORLD OF   MGT
POLITICS. USA+45 ELITES MARKET CREATE BARGAIN   ECO/DEV
DIPLOM INT/TRADE ATTIT SKILL 20. PAGE 15 B0302   CAP/ISM
                                                    INDUS
B67
ROBINSON R.D., INTERNATIONAL MANAGEMENT. USA&45   INT/TRADE
FINAN R+D PLAN PRODUC...DECISION T. PAGE 67 B1352   MGT

INT/LAW
MARKET

B67
NARVER J.C.,CONGLOMERATE MERGERS AND MARKET
COMPETITION. USA+45 LAW STRUCT ADMIN LEAD RISK COST
PROFIT WEALTH...POLICY CHARTS BIBLIOG. PAGE 77
B1555
DEMAND
LG/CO
MARKET
MGT

B67
NORTHRUP H.R.,RESTRICTIVE LABOR PRACTICES IN THE
SUPERMARKET INDUSTRY. USA+45 INDUS WORKER TEC/DEV
BARGAIN PAY CONTROL GP/REL COST...STAT CHARTS NLRB.
PAGE 79 B1592
DIST/IND
MARKET
LABOR
MGT

S67
BRIMMER A.F.,"INITIATIVE AND INNOVATION IN CENTRAL
BANKING." USA+45 ECO/DEV MARKET ECO/TAC TAX CONTROL
DEMAND...MGT CHARTS FED/RESERV. PAGE 15 B0309
FINAN
CREATE
NAT/G
POLICY

S67
DIXON O.F.,"A SOCIAL SYSTEMS APPROACH TO
MARKETING." ECO/DEV ECO/TAC CONTROL EFFICIENCY
...DECISION 20. PAGE 29 B0599
MARKET
SOCIETY
GP/REL
MGT

S67
GOLIGHTLY H.O.,"THE AIRLINES: A CASE STUDY IN
MANAGEMENT INNOVATION." USA+45 AIR FINAN INDUS
TOP/EX CREATE PLAN PROB/SOLV ADMIN EXEC PROFIT
...DECISION 20. PAGE 40 B0820
DIST/IND
MARKET
MGT
TEC/DEV

MARKETING SYSTEM....SEE MARKET

MARKMANN C.L. B1399

MARKSHAK J. B1400

MARRIAGE....WEDLOCK; SEE ALSO LOVE

B65
BERNDT R.M.,ABORIGINAL MAN IN AUSTRALIA. LAW DOMIN
ADMIN COLONIAL MARRIAGE HABITAT ORD/FREE...LING
CHARTS ANTHOL BIBLIOG WORSHIP 20 AUSTRAL ABORIGINES
MUSIC ELKIN/AP. PAGE 11 B0225
SOC
CULTURE
SOCIETY
STRUCT

B67
COHEN R.,COMPARATIVE POLITICAL SYSTEMS: STUDIES IN
THE POLITICS OF PRE-INDUSTRIAL SOCIETIES. WOR+45
WOR-45 CULTURE FAM KIN LOC/G NEIGH ADMIN LEAD
MARRIAGE...BIBLIOG 20. PAGE 22 B0447
ECO/UNDEV
STRUCT
SOCIETY
GP/COMP

MARRIS P. B1401

MARRIS R. B1402

MARS D. B1403

MARSH D.C. B1404

MARSH J.F. B1405

MARSH R.M. B1406,B1407

MARSHALL A.H. B1408

MARSHALL G. B1409

MARSHALL/A....ALFRED MARSHALL

MARSHALL/J....JOHN MARSHALL

MARSHL/PLN....MARSHALL PLAN

MARTI/JOSE....JOSE MARTI

MARTIN E.D. B0194

MARTIN L.W. B1410,B1411

MARTIN N.H. B2294

MARTIN R. B1412

MARTIN R.C. B1413,B1414

MARTIN W.O. B1415

MARVICK D. B1416

MARX C.M. B1417

MARX F.M. B1418,B1419,B1420

MARX K. B1421

MARX/KARL....KARL MARX

B61
MARX K.,THE COMMUNIST MANIFESTO. IN (MENDEL A.,
ESSENTIAL WORKS OF MARXISM, NEW YORK: BANTAM. FUT
COM
NEW/IDEA

MOD/EUR CULTURE ECO/DEV ECO/UNDEV AGRI FINAN INDUS
MARKET PROC/MFG LABOR MUNIC POL/PAR CONSULT FORCES
CREATE PLAN ADMIN ATTIT DRIVE RIGID/FLEX ORD/FREE
PWR RESPECT MARX/KARL WORK. PAGE 70 B1421
CAP/ISM
REV

B63
TUCKER R.C.,THE SOVIET POLITICAL MIND. WOR+45
ELITES INT/ORG NAT/G POL/PAR PLAN DIPLOM ECO/TAC
DOMIN ADMIN NUC/PWR REV DRIVE PERSON SUPEGO PWR
WEALTH...POLICY MGT PSY CONCPT OBS BIOG TREND
COLD/WAR MARX/KARL 20. PAGE 106 B2134
COM
TOP/EX
USSR

B65
PUSTAY J.S.,COUNTER-INSURGENCY WARFARE. COM USA+45
LOC/G NAT/G ACT/RES EDU/PROP ADMIN COERCE ATTIT
...CONCPT MARX/KARL 20. PAGE 85 B1722
FORCES
PWR
GUERRILLA

B67
BRZEZINSKI Z.K.,THE SOVIET BLOC: UNITY AND CONFLICT
(2ND ED., REV., ENLARGED). COM POLAND USSR INTELL
CHIEF EX/STRUC CONTROL EXEC GOV/REL PWR MARXISM
...TREND IDEA/COMP 20 LENIN/VI MARX/KARL STALIN/J.
PAGE 16 B0336
NAT/G
DIPLOM

MARXISM....MARXISM, COMMUNISM; SEE ALSO MARXIST

N
MONPIED E.,BIBLIOGRAPHIE FEDERALISTE: ARTICLES ET
DOCUMENTS PUBLIES DANS LES PERIODIQUES PARUS EN
FRANCE NOV. 1945-OCT. 1950. EUR+WWI WOR+45 ADMIN
REGION ATTIT MARXISM PACIFISM 20 EEC. PAGE 74 B1501
BIBLIOG/A
FEDERAL
CENTRAL
INT/ORG

N
SOVIET-EAST EUROPEAN RES SERV,SOVIET SOCIETY. USSR
LABOR POL/PAR PRESS MARXISM...MARXIST 20. PAGE 99
B2001
BIBLIOG/A
EDU/PROP
ADMIN
SOC

N
KYRIAK T.E.,EAST EUROPE: BIBLIOGRAPHY--INDEX TO US
JPRS RESEARCH TRANSLATIONS. ALBANIA BULGARIA COM
CZECHOSLVK HUNGARY POLAND ROMANIA AGRI EXTR/IND
FINAN SERV/IND INT/TRADE WEAPON...GEOG MGT SOC 20.
PAGE 62 B1247
BIBLIOG/A
PRESS
MARXISM
INDUS

B38
HARPER S.N.,THE GOVERNMENT OF THE SOVIET UNION. COM
USSR LAW CONSTN ECO/DEV PLAN TEC/DEV DIPLOM
INT/TRADE ADMIN REV NAT/LISM...POLICY 20. PAGE 47
B0952
MARXISM
NAT/G
LEAD
POL/PAR

B44
BIENSTOCK G.,MANAGEMENT IN RUSSIAN INDUSTRY AND
AGRICULTURE. USSR CONSULT WORKER LEAD COST PROFIT
ATTIT DRIVE PWR...MGT METH/COMP DICTIONARY 20.
PAGE 12 B0236
ADMIN
MARXISM
SML/CO
AGRI

B48
TOWSTER J.,POLITICAL POWER IN THE USSR: 1917-1947.
USSR CONSTN CULTURE ELITES CREATE PLAN COERCE
CENTRAL ATTIT RIGID/FLEX ORD/FREE...BIBLIOG
SOC/INTEG 20 LENIN/VI STALIN/J. PAGE 105 B2124
EX/STRUC
NAT/G
MARXISM
PWR

S50
NEUMANN F.L.,"APPROACHES TO THE STUDY OF POLITICAL
POWER." POL/PAR TOP/EX ADMIN LEAD ATTIT ORD/FREE
CONSERVE LAISSEZ MARXISM...PSY SOC. PAGE 78 B1572
PWR
IDEA/COMP
CONCPT

B51
BERTON P.A.,MANCHURIA: AN ANNOTATED BIBLIOGRAPHY.
ASIA DIST/IND ADMIN...SOC 20. PAGE 11 B0231
BIBLIOG/A
MARXISM
ECO/UNDEV
COLONIAL

S51
SCHRAMM W.,"COMMUNICATION IN THE SOVIETIZED STATE,
AS DEMONSTRATED IN KOREA." ASIA COM KOREA COM/IND
FACE/GP POL/PAR SCHOOL FORCES ADMIN PWR MARXISM
...SOC CONCPT MYTH INT BIOG TOT/POP 20. PAGE 94
B1901
ATTIT
EDU/PROP
TOTALISM

C51
MOORE B.,"SOVIET POLITICS - THE DILEMMA OF POWER:
THE ROLE OF IDEAS IN SOCIAL CHANGE." USSR PROB/SOLV
DIPLOM EDU/PROP ADMIN LEAD ROUTINE REV...POLICY
DECISION BIBLIOG 20. PAGE 75 B1512
ATTIT
PWR
CONCPT
MARXISM

B52
MILLER M.,THE JUDGES AND THE JUDGED. USA+45 LG/CO
ACT/RES TV ROUTINE SANCTION NAT/LISM ATTIT ORD/FREE
...POLICY ACLU. PAGE 73 B1481
COM/IND
DISCRIM
EDU/PROP
MARXISM

B52
SELZNICK P.,THE ORGANIZATIONAL WEAPON: A STUDY OF
BOLSHEVIK STRATEGY AND TACTICS. USSR SOCIETY STRATA
LABOR DOMIN EDU/PROP PARTIC REV ATTIT PWR...POLICY
MGT CONCPT 20 BOLSHEVISM. PAGE 95 B1929
MARXISM
POL/PAR
LEAD
TOTALISM

B52
US DEPARTMENT OF STATE,RESEARCH ON EASTERN EUROPE
(EXCLUDING USSR). EUR+WWI LAW ECO/DEV NAT/G
PROB/SOLV DIPLOM ADMIN LEAD MARXISM...TREND 19/20.
PAGE 108 B2182
BIBLIOG
R+D
ACT/RES
COM

L54
ROSTOW W.W.,"ASIAN LEADERSHIP AND FREE-WORLD
ALLIANCE." ASIA COM USA+45 CULTURE ELITES INTELL
NAT/G TEC/DEV ECO/TAC EDU/PROP COLONIAL PARL/PROC
ROUTINE COERCE DRIVE ORD/FREE MARXISM...PSY CONCPT.
PAGE 90 B1829
ATTIT
LEGIT
DIPLOM

L55
ROSTOW W.W.,"RUSSIA AND CHINA UNDER COMMUNISM." COM
CHINA/COM USSR INTELL STRUCT INT/ORG NAT/G POL/PAR ASIA
TOP/EX ACT/RES PLAN ADMIN ATTIT ALL/VALS MARXISM
...CONCPT OBS TIME/SEQ TREND GOV/COMP VAL/FREE 20.
PAGE 91 B1830

S55
KAUTSKY J.H.,"THE NEW STRATEGY OF INTERNATIONAL COM
COMMUNISM." ASIA CHINA/COM FUT WOR+45 WOR-45 ADMIN POL/PAR
ROUTINE PERSON MARXISM SOCISM...TREND IDEA/COMP 20 TOTALISM
LENIN/VI MAO. PAGE 59 B1184 USSR

B56
BARBASH J.,THE PRACTICE OF UNIONISM. ECO/TAC LEAD LABOR
LOBBY GP/REL INGP/REL DRIVE MARXISM BIBLIOG. PAGE 9 REPRESENT
B0182 CONTROL
ADMIN

C56
FALL B.B.,"THE VIET-MINH REGIME." VIETNAM LAW NAT/G
ECO/UNDEV POL/PAR FORCES DOMIN WAR ATTIT MARXISM ADMIN
...BIOG PREDICT BIBLIOG/A 20. PAGE 35 B0703 EX/STRUC
LEAD

B57
DJILAS M.,THE NEW CLASS: AN ANALYSIS OF THE COM
COMMUNIST SYSTEM. STRATA CAP/ISM ECO/TAC DOMIN POL/PAR
EDU/PROP LEGIT EXEC COERCE ATTIT PWR MARXISM USSR
...MARXIST MGT CONCPT TIME/SEQ GEN/LAWS 20. PAGE 29 YUGOSLAVIA
B0600

B58
LAQUER W.Z.,THE MIDDLE EAST IN TRANSITION. COM USSR ISLAM
ECO/UNDEV NAT/G VOL/ASSN EDU/PROP EXEC ATTIT DRIVE TREND
PWR MARXISM COLD/WAR TOT/POP 20. PAGE 62 B1261 NAT/LISM

B58
NEAL F.W.,TITOISM IN ACTION. COM YUGOSLAVIA AGRI MARXISM
LOC/G DIPLOM TOTALISM...BIBLIOG 20 TITO/MARSH. POL/PAR
PAGE 77 B1564 CHIEF
ADMIN

B58
SCOTT D.J.R.,RUSSIAN POLITICAL INSTITUTIONS. RUSSIA NAT/G
USSR CONSTN AGRI DELIB/GP PLAN EDU/PROP CONTROL POL/PAR
CHOOSE EFFICIENCY ATTIT MARXISM...BIBLIOG/A 13/20. ADMIN
PAGE 95 B1919 DECISION

B59
EPSTEIN F.T.,EAST GERMANY: A SELECTED BIBLIOGRAPHY BIBLIOG/A
(PAMPHLET). COM GERMANY/E LAW AGRI FINAN INDUS INTELL
LABOR POL/PAR EDU/PROP ADMIN AGE/Y 20. PAGE 33 MARXISM
B0677 NAT/G

B60
WORLEY P.,ASIA TODAY (REV. ED.) (PAMPHLET). COM BIBLIOG/A
ECO/UNDEV AGRI FINAN INDUS POL/PAR FOR/AID ADMIN ASIA
MARXISM 20. PAGE 118 B2376 DIPLOM
NAT/G

B61
ARMSTRONG J.A.,AN ESSAY ON SOURCES FOR THE STUDY OF BIBLIOG/A
THE COMMUNIST PARTY OF THE SOVIET UNION, 1934-1960 COM
(EXTERNAL RESEARCH PAPER 137). USSR EX/STRUC ADMIN POL/PAR
LEAD REV 20. PAGE 7 B0134 MARXISM

B61
DRAGNICH A.N.,MAJOR EUROPEAN GOVERNMENTS. FRANCE NAT/G
GERMANY/W UK USSR LOC/G EX/STRUC CT/SYS PARL/PROC LEGIS
ATTIT MARXISM...JURID MGT NAT/COMP 19/20. PAGE 30 CONSTN
B0615 POL/PAR

B61
HOUN F.W.,TO CHANGE A NATION: PROPAGANDA AND DOMIN
INDOCTRINATION IN COMMUNIST CHINA. CHINA/COM COM EDU/PROP
ACT/RES PLAN PRESS ADMIN FEEDBACK CENTRAL TOTALISM
EFFICIENCY ATTIT...PSY SOC 20. PAGE 52 B1048 MARXISM

B61
LENIN V.I.,WHAT IS TO BE DONE? (1902). RUSSIA LABOR EDU/PROP
NAT/G POL/PAR WORKER CAP/ISM ECO/TAC ADMIN PARTIC PRESS
...MARXIST IDEA/COMP GEN/LAWS 19/20. PAGE 64 B1292 MARXISM
METH/COMP

B61
MOLLAU G.,INTERNATIONAL COMMUNISM AND WORLD COM
REVOLUTION: HISTORY AND METHODS. RUSSIA USSR REV
INT/ORG NAT/G POL/PAR VOL/ASSN FORCES BAL/PWR
DIPLOM EXEC REGION WAR ATTIT PWR MARXISM...CONCPT
TIME/SEQ COLD/WAR 19/20. PAGE 74 B1498

B61
NOVE A.,THE SOVIET ECONOMY. USSR ECO/DEV FINAN PLAN
NAT/G ECO/TAC PRICE ADMIN EFFICIENCY MARXISM PRODUC
...TREND BIBLIOG 20. PAGE 79 B1594 POLICY

S61
TOMASIC D.,"POLITICAL LEADERSHIP IN CONTEMPORARY SOCIETY
POLAND." COM EUR+WWI GERMANY NAT/G POL/PAR SECT ROUTINE
DELIB/GP PLAN ECO/TAC DOMIN EDU/PROP PWR MARXISM USSR
...MARXIST GEOG MGT CONCPT TIME/SEQ STERTYP 20. POLAND
PAGE 105 B2114

B62
CARTER G.M.,THE GOVERNMENT OF THE SOVIET UNION. NAT/G
USSR CULTURE LOC/G DIPLOM ECO/TAC ADJUD CT/SYS LEAD MARXISM
WEALTH...CHARTS T 20 COM/PARTY. PAGE 19 B0390 POL/PAR
EX/STRUC

B62
INTERNATIONAL LABOR OFFICE,WORKERS' MANAGEMENT IN WORKER
YUGOSLAVIA. COM YUGOSLAVIA LABOR DELIB/GP EX/STRUC CONTROL
PROB/SOLV ADMIN PWR MARXISM...CHARTS ORG/CHARTS MGT

BIBLIOG 20. PAGE 54 B1098 INDUS

S62
IOVTCHOUK M.T.,"ON SOME THEORETICAL PRINCIPLES AND COM
METHODS OF SOCIOLOGICAL INVESTIGATIONS (IN ECO/DEV
RUSSIAN)." FUT USA+45 STRATA R+D NAT/G POL/PAR CAP/ISM
TOP/EX ACT/RES PLAN ECO/TAC EDU/PROP ROUTINE ATTIT USSR
RIGID/FLEX MARXISM SOCISM...MARXIST METH/CNCPT OBS
TREND NAT/COMP GEN/LAWS 20. PAGE 54 B1102

B63
COM INTERNAT DES MOUVEMENTS,REPERTOIRE BIBLIOG/A
INTERNATIONAL DES SOURCES POUR L'ETUDE DES MARXISM
MOUVEMENTS SOCIAUX AUX XIXE ET XXE SIECLES (VOL. POL/PAR
III). MOD/EUR ADMIN...SOC 19. PAGE 22 B0454 LABOR

B63
HIGA M.,POLITICS AND PARTIES IN POSTWAR OKINAWA. GOV/REL
USA+45 VOL/ASSN LEGIS CONTROL LOBBY CHOOSE NAT/LISM POL/PAR
PWR SOVEREIGN MARXISM SOCISM 20 OKINAWA CHINJAP. ADMIN
PAGE 50 B1008 FORCES

B63
KLESMENT J.,LEGAL SOURCES AND BIBLIOGRAPHY OF THE BIBLIOG/A
BALTIC STATES (ESTONIA, LATVIA, LITHUANIA). COM JURID
ESTONIA LATVIA LITHUANIA LAW FINAN ADJUD CT/SYS CONSTN
REGION CENTRAL MARXISM 19/20. PAGE 60 B1218 ADMIN

B63
TUCKER R.C.,THE SOVIET POLITICAL MIND. COM INTELL STRUCT
NAT/G TOP/EX EDU/PROP ADMIN COERCE TOTALISM ATTIT RIGID/FLEX
PWR MARXISM...PSY MYTH HYPO/EXP 20. PAGE 106 B2135 ELITES
USSR

B64
ELDREDGE H.W.,THE SECOND AMERICAN REVOLUTION. ELITES
EDU/PROP NAT/LISM RATIONAL TOTALISM FASCISM MARXISM ORD/FREE
SOCISM. PAGE 33 B0664 ADMIN
PLAN

B64
FAINSOD M.,HOW RUSSIA IS RULED (REV. ED.). RUSSIA NAT/G
USSR AGRI PROC/MFG LABOR POL/PAR EX/STRUC CONTROL REV
PWR...POLICY BIBLIOG 19/20 KHRUSH/N COM/PARTY. MARXISM
PAGE 34 B0700

B64
GRZYBOWSKI K.,THE SOCIALIST COMMONWEALTH OF INT/LAW
NATIONS: ORGANIZATIONS AND INSTITUTIONS. FORCES COM
DIPLOM INT/TRADE ADJUD ADMIN LEAD WAR MARXISM REGION
SOCISM...BIBLIOG 20 COMECON WARSAW/P. PAGE 44 B0898 INT/ORG

B64
POPPINO R.E.,INTERNATIONAL COMMUNISM IN LATIN MARXISM
AMERICA: A HISTORY OF THE MOVEMENT 1917-1963. POL/PAR
CHINA/COM USSR INTELL STRATA LABOR WORKER ADMIN REV L/A+17C
ATTIT...POLICY 20 COLD/WAR. PAGE 84 B1692

B64
STOICOIU V.,LEGAL SOURCES AND BIBLIOGRAPHY OF BIBLIOG/A
ROMANIA. COM ROMANIA LAW FINAN POL/PAR LEGIS JUDGE JURID
ADJUD CT/SYS PARL/PROC MARXISM 20. PAGE 101 B2041 CONSTN
ADMIN

B64
WELLISZ S.,THE ECONOMICS OF THE SOVIET BLOC. COM EFFICIENCY
USSR INDUS WORKER PLAN BUDGET INT/TRADE TAX PRICE ADMIN
PRODUC WEALTH MARXISM...METH/COMP 20. PAGE 115 MARKET
B2319

S64
HORECKY P.L.,"LIBRARY OF CONGRESS PUBLICATIONS IN BIBLIOG/A
AID OF USSR AND EAST EUROPEAN RESEARCH." BULGARIA COM
CZECHOSLVK POLAND USSR YUGOSLAVIA NAT/G POL/PAR MARXISM
DIPLOM ADMIN GOV/REL...CLASSIF 20. PAGE 51 B1042

B65
CHEN T.H.,THE CHINESE COMMUNIST REGIME: A MARXISM
DOCUMENTARY STUDY (2 VOLS.). CHINA/COM LAW CONSTN POL/PAR
ELITES ECO/UNDEV LEGIS ECO/TAC ADMIN CONTROL PWR NAT/G
...SOC 20. PAGE 20 B0417

B65
KOUSOULAS D.G.,REVOLUTION AND DEFEAT: THE STORY OF REV
THE GREEK COMMUNIST PARTY. GREECE INT/ORG EX/STRUC MARXISM
DIPLOM FOR/AID EDU/PROP PARL/PROC ADJUST ATTIT 20 POL/PAR
COM/PARTY. PAGE 61 B1230 ORD/FREE

B65
MEYERHOFF A.E.,THE STRATEGY OF PERSUASION. USA+45 EDU/PROP
COM/IND CONSULT FOR/AID CONTROL COERCE COST ATTIT EFFICIENCY
PERCEPT MARXISM 20 COLD/WAR. PAGE 73 B1476 OP/RES
ADMIN

B65
MOORE C.H.,TUNISIA SINCE INDEPENDENCE. ELITES LOC/G NAT/G
POL/PAR ADMIN COLONIAL EXEC GOV/REL EX/STRUC
TOTALISM MARXISM...INT 20 TUNIS. PAGE 75 B1513 SOCISM

B65
MORGENTHAU H.,MORGENTHAU DIARY (CHINA) (2 VOLS.). DIPLOM
ASIA USA+45 USA-45 LAW DELIB/GP EX/STRUC PLAN ADMIN
FOR/AID INT/TRADE CONFER WAR MARXISM 20 CHINJAP.
PAGE 75 B1523

B65
ORG FOR ECO COOP AND DEVEL,THE MEDITERRANEAN EDU/PROP
REGIONAL PROJECT: YUGOSLAVIA; EDUCATION AND ACADEM
DEVELOPMENT. YUGOSLAVIA SOCIETY FINAN PROF/ORG PLAN SCHOOL
ADMIN COST DEMAND MARXISM...STAT TREND CHARTS METH ECO/UNDEV
20 OECD. PAGE 80 B1615

B65
PHELPS-FETHERS I.,SOVIET INTERNATIONAL FRONT USSR
ORGANIZATIONS: A CONCISE HANDBOOK. DIPLOM DOMIN EDU/PROP

LEGIT ADMIN EXEC GP/REL PEACE MARXISM...TIME/SEQ
GP/COMP. PAGE 83 B1668
ASIA
COM

B65

SCHAPIRO L.,THE GOVERNMENT AND POLITICS OF THE
SOVIET UNION. USSR WOR+45 WOR-45 ADMIN PARTIC REV
CHOOSE REPRESENT PWR...POLICY IDEA/COMP 20. PAGE 93
B1880
MARXISM
GOV/REL
NAT/G
LOC/G

L65

HOOK S.,"SECOND THOUGHTS ON BERKELEY" USA+45 ELITES
INTELL LEGIT ADMIN COERCE REPRESENT GP/REL INGP/REL
TOTALISM AGE/Y MARXISM 20 BERKELEY FREE/SPEE
STUDNT/PWR. PAGE 51 B1040
ACADEM
ORD/FREE
POLICY
CREATE

B66

BARBER W.F.,INTERNAL SECURITY AND MILITARY POWER*
COUNTERINSURGENCY AND CIVIC ACTION IN LATIN
AMERICA. ECO/UNDEV CREATE ADMIN REV ATTIT
RIGID/FLEX MARXISM...INT BIBLIOG OAS. PAGE 9 B0183
L/A+17C
FORCES
ORD/FREE
TASK

B66

EPSTEIN F.T.,THE AMERICAN BIBLIOGRAPHY OF RUSSIAN
AND EAST EUROPEAN STUDIES FOR 1964. USSR LOC/G
NAT/G POL/PAR FORCES ADMIN ARMS/CONT...JURID CONCPT
20 UN. PAGE 33 B0678
BIBLIOG
COM
MARXISM
DIPLOM

B66

KURAKOV I.G.,SCIENCE, TECHNOLOGY AND COMMUNISM:
SOME QUESTIONS OF DEVELOPMENT (TRANS. BY CARIN
DEDIJER). USSR INDUS PLAN PROB/SOLV COST PRODUC
...MGT MATH CHARTS METH 20. PAGE 61 B1243
CREATE
TEC/DEV
MARXISM
ECO/TAC

B66

SCHURMANN F.,IDEOLOGY AND ORGANIZATION IN COMMUNIST
CHINA. CHINA/COM LOC/G MUNIC POL/PAR ECO/TAC
CONTROL ATTIT...MGT STERTYP 20 COM/PARTY. PAGE 94
B1909
MARXISM
STRUCT
ADMIN
NAT/G

B66

US DEPARTMENT OF THE ARMY,COMMUNIST CHINA: A
STRATEGIC SURVEY: A BIBLIOGRAPHY (PAMPHLET NO.
20-67). CHINA/COM COM INDIA USSR NAT/G POL/PAR
EX/STRUC FORCES NUC/PWR REV ATTIT...POLICY GEOG
CHARTS. PAGE 108 B2184
BIBLIOG/A
MARXISM
S/ASIA
DIPLOM

C66

TARLING N.,"A CONCISE HISTORY OF SOUTHEAST ASIA."
BURMA CAMBODIA LAOS S/ASIA THAILAND VIETNAM
ECO/UNDEV POL/PAR FORCES ADMIN REV WAR CIVMIL/REL
ORD/FREE MARXISM SOCISM 13/20. PAGE 103 B2080
COLONIAL
DOMIN
INT/TRADE
NAT/LISM

B67

BRZEZINSKI Z.K.,IDEOLOGY AND POWER IN SOVIET
POLITICS. USSR NAT/G POL/PAR PWR...GEN/LAWS 19/20.
PAGE 16 B0335
DIPLOM
EX/STRUC
MARXISM

B67

BRZEZINSKI Z.K.,THE SOVIET BLOC: UNITY AND CONFLICT
(2ND ED., REV., ENLARGED). COM POLAND USSR INTELL
CHIEF EX/STRUC CONTROL EXEC GOV/REL PWR MARXISM
...TREND IDEA/COMP 20 LENIN/VI MARX/KARL STALIN/J.
PAGE 16 B0336
NAT/G
DIPLOM

B67

EVANS R.H.,COEXISTENCE: COMMUNISM AND ITS PRACTICE
IN BOLOGNA, 1945-1965. ITALY CAP/ISM ADMIN CHOOSE
PEACE ORD/FREE...SOC STAT DEEP/INT SAMP CHARTS
BIBLIOG 20. PAGE 34 B0690
MARXISM
CULTURE
MUNIC
POL/PAR

B67

FARNSWORTH B.,WILLIAM C. BULLITT AND THE SOVIET
UNION. USA-45 USSR NAT/G CHIEF CONSULT DELIB/GP
EX/STRUC WAR REPRESENT MARXISM 20 WILSON/W
ROOSEVLT/F STALIN/J BULLITT/WC. PAGE 35 B0705
DIPLOM
BIOG
POLICY

B67

GROSSMAN G.,ECONOMIC SYSTEMS. USA+45 USA-45 USSR
YUGOSLAVIA WORKER CAP/ISM PRICE GP/REL EQUILIB
WEALTH MARXISM SOCISM...MGT METH/COMP 19/20.
PAGE 44 B0892
ECO/DEV
PLAN
TEC/DEV
DEMAND

B67

GRUBER H.,INTERNATIONAL COMMUNISM IN THE ERA OF
LENIN. COM ADMIN REV GP/REL 20. PAGE 44 B0895
MARXISM
HIST/WRIT
POL/PAR

B67

JHANGIANI M.A.,JANA SANGH AND SWATANTRA: A PROFILE
OF THE RIGHTIST PARTIES IN INDIA. INDIA ADMIN
CHOOSE MARXISM SOCISM...INT CHARTS BIBLIOG 20.
PAGE 56 B1140
POL/PAR
LAISSEZ
NAT/LISM
ATTIT

B67

LENG S.C.,JUSTICE IN COMMUNIST CHINA: A SURVEY OF
THE JUDICIAL SYSTEM OF THE CHINESE PEOPLE'S
REPUBLIC. CHINA/COM LAW CONSTN LOC/G NAT/G PROF/ORG
CONSULT FORCES ADMIN CRIME ORD/FREE...BIBLIOG 20
MAO. PAGE 64 B1290
CT/SYS
ADJUD
JURID
MARXISM

B67

MACKINTOSH J.M.,JUGGERNAUT. USSR NAT/G POL/PAR
ADMIN LEAD CIVMIL/REL COST TOTALISM PWR MARXISM
...GOV/COMP 20. PAGE 68 B1364
WAR
FORCES
COM
PROF/ORG

B67

SABLE M.H.,A GUIDE TO LATIN AMERICAN STUDIES (2
VOLS). CONSTN FINAN INT/ORG LABOR MUNIC POL/PAR
FORCES CAP/ISM FOR/AID ADMIN MARXISM SOCISM OAS.
PAGE 92 B1861
BIBLIOG/A
L/A+17C
DIPLOM
NAT/LISM

B67

TANSKY L.,US AND USSR AID TO DEVELOPING COUNTRIES.
INDIA TURKEY UAR USA+45 USSR FINAN PLAN TEC/DEV
FOR/AID
ECO/UNDEV

ADMIN WEALTH...TREND METH/COMP 20. PAGE 103 B2076
MARXISM
CAP/ISM

S67

BASTID M.,"ORIGINES ET DEVELOPMENT DE LA REVOLUTION
CULTURELLE." CHINA/COM DOMIN ADMIN CONTROL LEAD
COERCE CROWD ATTIT DRIVE MARXISM...POLICY 20.
PAGE 10 B0195
REV
CULTURE
ACADEM
WORKER

S67

BAUM R.D.,"IDEOLOGY REDIVIVUS." CHINA/COM NAT/G
EDU/PROP ADMIN 20. PAGE 10 B0197
REV
MARXISM
CREATE
TEC/DEV

S67

BREGMAN A.,"WHITHER RUSSIA?" COM RUSSIA INTELL
POL/PAR DIPLOM PARTIC NAT/LISM TOTALISM ATTIT
ORD/FREE 20. PAGE 15 B0304
MARXISM
ELITES
ADMIN
CREATE

S67

GRUNDY K.W.,"THE POLITICAL USES OF IMAGINATION."
GHANA ELITES SOCIETY NAT/G DOMIN EDU/PROP COLONIAL
REGION REPRESENT GP/REL CENTRAL PWR MARXISM 20.
PAGE 44 B0897
NAT/LISM
EX/STRUC
AFR
LEAD

S67

HSUEH C.T.,"THE CULTURAL REVOLUTION AND LEADERSHIP
CRISIS IN COMMUNIST CHINA." CHINA/COM POL/PAR
EX/STRUC FORCES EDU/PROP ATTIT PWR...POLICY 20.
PAGE 52 B1054
LEAD
REV
CULTURE
MARXISM

S67

LENDVAI P.,"HUNGARY* CHANGE VS. IMMOBILISM."
HUNGARY LABOR NAT/G PLAN DEBATE ADMIN ROUTINE
CENTRAL EFFICIENCY MARXISM PLURISM...PREDICT 20.
PAGE 64 B1289
ECO/DEV
MGT
CHOOSE

S67

LEVCIK B.,"WAGES AND EMPLOYMENT PROBLEMS IN THE NEW
SYSTEM OF PLANNED MANAGEMENT IN CZECHOSLOVAKIA."
CZECHOSLVK EUR+WWI NAT/G OP/RES PLAN ADMIN ROUTINE
INGP/REL CENTRAL EFFICIENCY PRODUC DECISION.
PAGE 64 B1300
MARXISM
WORKER
MGT
PAY

S67

LIU K.C.,"DISINTEGRATION OF THE OLD ORDER." ASIA
SOCIETY PROB/SOLV ADMIN REGION TOTALISM ORD/FREE
MARXISM 19/20. PAGE 66 B1329
ADJUST
NAT/LISM

S67

WALLER D.J.,"CHINA: RED OR EXPERT." CHINA/COM
INTELL DOMIN REV ATTIT MARXISM 20. PAGE 113 B2283
CONTROL
FORCES
ADMIN
POL/PAR

MARXIST....MARXIST

N

SOVIET-EAST EUROPEAN RES SERV,SOVIET SOCIETY. USSR
LABOR POL/PAR PRESS MARXISM...MARXIST 20. PAGE 99
B2001
BIBLIOG/A
EDU/PROP
ADMIN
SOC

B46

BIBLIOGRAFIIA DISSERTATSII: DOKTORSKIE DISSERTATSII
ZA 19411944 (2 VOLS.). COM USSR LAW POL/PAR DIPLOM
ADMIN LEAD...PHIL/SCI SOC 20. PAGE 2 B0035
BIBLIOG
ACADEM
KNOWL
MARXIST

B57

DJILAS M.,THE NEW CLASS: AN ANALYSIS OF THE
COMMUNIST SYSTEM. STRATA CAP/ISM ECO/TAC DOMIN
EDU/PROP LEGIT EXEC COERCE ATTIT PWR MARXISM
...MARXIST MGT CONCPT TIME/SEQ GEN/LAWS 20. PAGE 29
B0600
COM
POL/PAR
USSR
YUGOSLAVIA

S60

HERZ J.H.,"EAST GERMANY: PROGRESS AND PROSPECTS."
COM AGRI FINAN INDUS LOC/G NAT/G FORCES PLAN
TEC/DEV DOMIN ADMIN COERCE DRIVE PERCEPT RIGID/FLEX
MORAL ORD/FREE PWR...MARXIST PSY SOC RECORD STERTYP
WORK. PAGE 49 B0997
POL/PAR
STRUCT
GERMANY

B61

LENIN V.I.,WHAT IS TO BE DONE? (1902). RUSSIA LABOR
NAT/G POL/PAR WORKER CAP/ISM ECO/TAC ADMIN PARTIC
...MARXIST IDEA/COMP GEN/LAWS 19/20. PAGE 64 B1292
EDU/PROP
PRESS
MARXISM
METH/COMP

S61

TOMASIC D.,"POLITICAL LEADERSHIP IN CONTEMPORARY
POLAND." COM EUR+WWI GERMANY NAT/G POL/PAR SECT
DELIB/GP PLAN ECO/TAC DOMIN EDU/PROP PWR MARXISM
...MARXIST MGT CONCPT TIME/SEQ STERTYP 20.
PAGE 105 B2114
SOCIETY
ROUTINE
USSR
POLAND

S62

IOVTCHOUK M.T.,"ON SOME THEORETICAL PRINCIPLES AND
METHODS OF SOCIOLOGICAL INVESTIGATIONS (IN
RUSSIAN)." FUT USA+45 STRATA R+D NAT/G POL/PAR
TOP/EX ACT/RES PLAN ECO/TAC EDU/PROP ROUTINE ATTIT
RIGID/FLEX MARXISM SOCISM...MARXIST METH/CNCPT OBS
TREND NAT/COMP GEN/LAWS 20. PAGE 54 B1102
COM
ECO/DEV
CAP/ISM
USSR

S66

JACOBS P.,"RE-RADICALIZING THE DE-RADICALIZED."
USA+45 SOCIETY STRUCT FINAN PLAN PROB/SOLV CAP/ISM
WEALTH CONSERVE NEW/LIB 20. PAGE 55 B1114
NAT/G
POLICY
MARXIST
ADMIN

MARYLAND....MARYLAND

MASLAND J.W. B1422

MASON J.B. B1423

MASON R.J. B0984

MASON W.S. B1460

MASS MEDIA....SEE EDU/PROP, COM/IND

MASSACHU....MASSACHUSETTS

ABBOT F.C.,THE CAMBRIDGE CITY MANAGER (PAMPHLET). PROB/SOLV ADMIN PERS/REL RIGID/FLEX PWR...MGT 20 MASSACHU CITY/MGT. PAGE 2 B0050 — MUNIC EX/STRUC TOP/EX GP/REL — N19

MASSARIK F. B2074

MASSART L. B1424

MASTERS N.A. B1425

MASUMI J. B1876

MATH....MATHEMATICS

GOSNELL H.F.,MACHINE POLITICS: CHICAGO MODEL. COM/IND FACE/GP LOC/G EX/STRUC LEAD ROUTINE SANCTION REPRESENT GOV/REL PWR...POLICY MATH OBS INT CHARTS. PAGE 41 B0840 — POL/PAR MUNIC ADMIN CHOOSE — B37

COMBS C.H.,DECISION PROCESSES. INTELL SOCIETY DELIB/GP CREATE TEC/DEV DOMIN LEGIT EXEC CHOOSE DRIVE RIGID/FLEX KNOWL PWR...PHIL/SCI SOC METH/CNCPT CONT/OBS REC/INT PERS/TEST SAMP/SIZ BIOG SOC/EXP WORK. PAGE 22 B0455 — MATH DECISION — B54

DUVERGER M.,POLITICAL PARTIES: THEIR ORGANIZATION AND ACTIVITY IN THE MODERN STATE. EUR+WWI MOD/EUR USA+45 USA-45 EDU/PROP ADMIN ROUTINE ATTIT DRIVE ORD/FREE PWR...SOC CONCPT MATH STAT TIME/SEQ TOT/POP 19/20. PAGE 31 B0635 — POL/PAR EX/STRUC ELITES — B54

CRONBACK L.J.,PSYCHOLOGICAL TESTS AND PERSONNEL DECISIONS. OP/RES PROB/SOLV CHOOSE PERSON...PSY STAT TESTS 20. PAGE 25 B0508 — MATH DECISION WORKER MGT — B57

SIMON H.A.,MODELS OF MAN, SOCIAL AND RATIONAL: MATHEMATICAL ESSAYS ON RATIONAL HUMAN BEHAVIOR IN A SOCIAL SETTING. UNIV LAW SOCIETY FACE/GP VOL/ASSN CONSULT EX/STRUC LEGIS CREATE ADMIN ROUTINE ATTIT DRIVE PWR...SOC CONCPT METH/CNCPT QUANT STAT TOT/POP VAL/FREE 20. PAGE 97 B1959 — MATH SIMUL — B57

OPERATIONS RESEARCH SOCIETY,A COMPREHENSIVE BIBLIOGRAPHY ON OPERATIONS RESEARCH; THROUGH 1956 WITH SUPPLEMENT FOR 1957. COM/IND DIST/IND INDUS ADMIN...DECISION MATH STAT METH 20. PAGE 80 B1612 — BIBLIOG/A COMPUT/IR OP/RES MGT — B58

CYERT R.M.,"MODELS IN A BEHAVIORAL THEORY OF THE FIRM." ROUTINE...DECISION MGT METH/CNCPT MATH. PAGE 25 B0517 — SIMUL GAME PREDICT INDUS — S59

ARROW K.J.,MATHEMATICAL METHODS IN THE SOCIAL SCIENCES, 1959. TEC/DEV CHOOSE UTIL PERCEPT ...KNO/TEST GAME SIMUL ANTHOL. PAGE 7 B0137 — MATH PSY MGT — B60

BOULDING K.E.,LINEAR PROGRAMMING AND THE THEORY OF THE FIRM. ACT/RES PLAN...MGT MATH. PAGE 14 B0283 — LG/CO NEW/IDEA COMPUTER — B60

CAMPBELL R.W.,SOVIET ECONOMIC POWER. COM USA+45 DIST/IND MARKET TOP/EX ACT/RES CAP/ISM ECO/TAC DOMIN EDU/PROP ADMIN ROUTINE DRIVE...MATH TIME/SEQ CHARTS WORK 20. PAGE 18 B0371 — ECO/DEV PLAN SOCISM USSR — B60

LERNER A.P.,THE ECONOMICS OF CONTROL. USA+45 ECO/UNDEV INT/ORG ACT/RES PLAN CAP/ISM INT/TRADE ATTIT WEALTH...SOC MATH STAT GEN/LAWS INDEX 20. PAGE 64 B1295 — ECO/DEV ROUTINE ECO/TAC SOCISM — B60

STEIN E.,"LEGAL REMEDIES OF ENTERPRISES IN THE EUROPEAN ECONOMIC COMMUNITY." EUR+WWI FUT ECO/DEV INDUS PLAN ECO/TAC ADMIN PWR...MGT MATH STAT TREND CON/ANAL EEC 20. PAGE 100 B2026 — MARKET ADJUD — L60

FRANKEL S.H.,"ECONOMIC ASPECTS OF POLITICAL INDEPENDENCE IN AFRICA." AFR FUT SOCIETY ECO/UNDEV COM/IND FINAN LEGIS PLAN TEC/DEV CAP/ISM ECO/TAC — NAT/G FOR/AID — S60

INT/TRADE ADMIN ATTIT DRIVE RIGID/FLEX PWR WEALTH ...MGT NEW/IDEA MATH TIME/SEQ VAL/FREE 20. PAGE 37 B0751

SCHATZ S.P.,"THE INFLENCE OF PLANNING ON DEVELOPMENT: THE NIGERIAN EXPERIENCE." AFR FUT FINAN INDUS NAT/G EX/STRUC ECO/TAC ADMIN ATTIT PERCEPT ORD/FREE PWR...MATH TREND CON/ANAL SIMUL VAL/FREE 20. PAGE 93 B1883 — ECO/UNDEV PLAN NIGERIA — S60

TANNENBAUM A.S.,"CONTROL AND EFFECTIVENESS IN A VOLUNTARY ORGANIZATION." USA+45 ADMIN...CORREL MATH REGRESS STAT TESTS SAMP/SIZ CHARTS SOC/EXP INDEX 20 LEAGUE/WV. PAGE 102 B2072 — EFFICIENCY VOL/ASSN CONTROL INGP/REL — S61

DUCKWORTH W.E.,A GUIDE TO OPERATIONAL RESEARCH. INDUS PLAN PROB/SOLV EXEC EFFICIENCY PRODUC KNOWL ...MGT MATH STAT SIMUL METH 20 MONTECARLO. PAGE 31 B0624 — OP/RES GAME DECISION ADMIN — B62

BURSK E.C.,NEW DECISION-MAKING TOOLS FOR MANAGERS. COMPUTER PLAN PROB/SOLV ROUTINE COST. PAGE 18 B0357 — DECISION MGT MATH RIGID/FLEX — B63

COOMBS C.H.,A THEORY OF DATA....MGT PHIL/SCI SOC CLASSIF MATH PROBABIL STAT QU. PAGE 23 B0472 — CON/ANAL GEN/METH TESTS PSY — B64

VEINOTT A.F. JR.,MATHEMATICAL STUDIES IN MANAGEMENT SCIENCE. UNIV INDUS COMPUTER ADMIN...DECISION NET/THEORY SIMUL 20. PAGE 112 B2257 — MATH MGT PLAN PRODUC — B65

FABRYCKY W.J.,OPERATIONS ECONOMY INDUSTRIAL APPLICATIONS OF OPERATIONS RESEARCH. INDUS PLAN ECO/TAC PRODUC...MATH PROBABIL STAT CHARTS 20. PAGE 34 B0695 — OP/RES MGT SIMUL DECISION — B66

KURAKOV I.G.,SCIENCE, TECHNOLOGY AND COMMUNISM; SOME QUESTIONS OF DEVELOPMENT (TRANS. BY CARIN DEDIJER). USSR INDUS PLAN PROB/SOLV COST PRODUC ...MGT MATH CHARTS METH 20. PAGE 61 B1243 — CREATE TEC/DEV MARXISM ECO/TAC — B66

OHLIN G.,AID AND INDEBTEDNESS. AUSTRIA FINAN INT/ORG PLAN DIPLOM GIVE...POLICY MATH CHARTS 20. PAGE 79 B1604 — FOR/AID ECO/UNDEV ADMIN WEALTH — B66

WESTON J.F.,THE SCOPE AND METHODOLOGY OF FINANCE. PLAN TEC/DEV CONTROL EFFICIENCY INCOME UTIL...MGT CONCPT MATH STAT TREND METH 20. PAGE 115 B2327 — FINAN ECO/DEV POLICY PRICE — B66

MATHEMATICS....SEE MATH, ALSO LOGIC, MATHEMATICS, AND LANGUAGE INDEX, P. XIV

MATHEWS J.M. B1426

MATRAS J. B1427

MATTEI/E....ENRICO MATTEI

MATTHEWS D.G. B1428,B1429,B1430

MATTHEWS D.R. B1431

MATTOD P.K. B1432

MAU/MAU....MAU MAU

MAUD....MILITARY APPLICATIONS OF URANIUM DETONATION (MAUD) (U.K. - WWII)

MAURITANIA....SEE ALSO AFR

MAURRAS/C....CHARLES MAURRAS

MAYDA J. B1433

MAYER C.S. B1434

MAYNE A. B1435

MAYNE R. B1436

MAYNTZ R. B1437

MAYO E. B1438

MAYO/ELTON....ELTON MAYO

MAYOR....MAYOR; SEE ALSO MUNIC, CHIEF

SALTER J.T.,THE AMERICAN POLITICIAN. USA-45 LABOR **B38**
POL/PAR EDU/PROP ADMIN CHOOSE ATTIT DRIVE PERSON BIOG
PWR...POLICY ANTHOL 20 THOMAS/N LEWIS/JL LAGUARD/F LEAD
GOVERNOR MAYOR. PAGE 92 B1865 PROVS
LOC/G

BOCK E.A., STATE AND LOCAL GOVERNMENT: A CASE BOOK. **B63**
USA+45 MUNIC PROVS CONSULT GP/REL ATTIT...MGT 20 LOC/G
CASEBOOK GOVERNOR MAYOR. PAGE 12 B0254 ADMIN
PROB/SOLV
CHIEF

BOUVIER-AJAM M.,MANUEL TECHNIQUE ET PRATIQUE DU **B64**
MAIRE ET DES ELUS ET AGENTS COMMUNAUX. FRANCE LOC/G MUNIC
BUDGET CHOOSE GP/REL SUPEGO...JURID BIBLIOG 20 ADMIN
MAYOR COMMUNES. PAGE 14 B0284 CHIEF
NEIGH

CONNECTICUT U INST PUBLIC SERV,SUMMARY OF CHARTER **B64**
PROVISIONS IN CONNECTICUT LOCAL GOVERNMENT CONSTN
(PAMPHLET). USA+45 DELIB/GP LEGIS TOP/EX CHOOSE MUNIC
REPRESENT 20 CONNECTICT CITY/MGT MAYOR. PAGE 23 LOC/G
B0462 EX/STRUC

FONTENEAU J.,LE CONSEIL MUNICIPAL: LE MAIRE-LES **B64**
ADJOINTS. FRANCE FINAN DELIB/GP EX/STRUC BUDGET TAX MUNIC
TASK COST INCOME ROLE SUPEGO 20 MAYOR. PAGE 36 NEIGH
B0735 ADMIN
TOP/EX

LOWI T.J.,AT THE PLEASURE OF THE MAYOR. EX/STRUC **B64**
PROB/SOLV BAL/PWR ADMIN PARTIC CHOOSE GP/REL LOBBY
...CONT/OBS NET/THEORY CHARTS 20 NEWYORK/C MAYOR. LOC/G
PAGE 67 B1346 PWR
MUNIC

HESSLER I.O.,29 WAYS TO GOVERN A CITY. EX/STRUC **B66**
TOP/EX PROB/SOLV PARTIC CHOOSE REPRESENT EFFICIENCY MUNIC
...CHARTS 20 CITY/MGT MAYOR. PAGE 49 B0998 GOV/COMP
LOC/G
ADMIN

SCHMIDT K.M.,AMERICAN STATE AND LOCAL GOVERNMENT IN **B66**
ACTION. USA+45 CONSTN LOC/G POL/PAR CHIEF LEGIS PROVS
PROB/SOLV ADJUD LOBBY GOV/REL...DECISION ANTHOL 20 ADMIN
GOVERNOR MAYOR URBAN/RNWL. PAGE 94 B1896 MUNIC
PLAN

MAZZINI J. B1439

MBEMBE....MBEMBE TRIBE

MCALISTER S.B. B1642

MCANAW R.L. B2379

MCAUSLAN J.P.W. B1440

MCCAMY J. B1441

MCCAMY J.L. B1442

MCCARTHY/E....EUGENE MCCARTHY

MCCARTHY/J....JOSEPH MCCARTHY

MCCLEERY R. B1443

MCCLELLAND C.A. B1444

MCCLELLN/J....JOHN MCCLELLAN

MCCLOSKEY J.F. B1445

MCCONNELL G. B1446

MCCORMICK E.M. B0968

MCDIARMID J. B1447

MCDONOUGH A.M. B1448

MCELHINEY P.T. B0706

MCGEORGE H. B0558

MCGREGOR D. B1449

MCHENRY D.E. B1450,B1451

MCKENZIE J.L. B1452

MCKERSIE R.B. B2285

MCKIE R. B1453

MCKINLEY/W....PRESIDENT WILLIAM MCKINLEY

MCKISACK M. B1454

MCLEAN J.M. B1455

MCLUHAN/M....MARSHALL MCLUHAN

MCMAHON....MCMAHON LINE

MCNAMARA R.L. B1456

MCNAMARA/R....ROBERT MCNAMARA

TANZER L.,THE KENNEDY CIRCLE. INTELL CONSULT **B61**
DELIB/GP TOP/EX CONTROL EXEC INGP/REL PERS/REL PWR EX/STRUC
...BIOG IDEA/COMP ANTHOL 20 KENNEDY/JF PRESIDENT NAT/G
DEMOCRAT MCNAMARA/R RUSK/D. PAGE 103 B2077 CHIEF

US SENATE COMM GOVT OPERATIONS,ADMINISTRATION OF **B62**
NATIONAL SECURITY. USA+45 CHIEF PLAN PROB/SOLV ORD/FREE
TEC/DEV DIPLOM ATTIT...POLICY DECISION 20 ADMIN
KENNEDY/JF RUSK/D MCNAMARA/R BUNDY/M HERTER/C. NAT/G
PAGE 110 B2212 CONTROL

RAYMOND J.,POWER AT THE PENTAGON (1ST ED.). ELITES **B64**
NAT/G PLAN EDU/PROP ARMS/CONT DETER WAR WEAPON PWR
...TIME/SEQ 20 PENTAGON MCNAMARA/R. PAGE 86 B1746 CIVMIL/REL
EX/STRUC
FORCES

BALDWIN H.,"SLOW-DOWN IN THE PENTAGON." USA+45 **S65**
CREATE PLAN GOV/REL CENTRAL COST EFFICIENCY PWR RECORD
...MGT MCNAMARA/R. PAGE 9 B0174 R+D
WEAPON
ADMIN

AUSLAND J.C.,"CRISIS MANAGEMENT* BERLIN, CYPRUS, **S66**
LAOS." CYPRUS LAOS FORCES CREATE PLAN EDU/PROP TASK OP/RES
CENTRAL PERSON RIGID/FLEX...DECISION MGT 20 BERLIN DIPLOM
KENNEDY/JF MCNAMARA/R RUSK. PAGE 7 B0148 RISK
ADMIN

ZUCKERT E.M.,"THE SERVICE SECRETARY* HAS HE A **S66**
USEFUL ROLE?" USA+45 TOP/EX PLAN ADMIN EXEC DETER OBS
NUC/PWR WEAPON...MGT RECORD MCNAMARA/R. PAGE 119 OP/RES
B2407 DIPLOM
FORCES

MCNAMEE B.J. B1457

MCNULTY J.E. B1458

MDTA....MANPOWER DEVELOPMENT AND TRAINING ACT (1962)

CHERNICK J.,THE SELECTION OF TRAINEES UNDER MDTA. **B62**
USA+45 NAT/G LEGIS PERSON...CENSUS 20 CIVIL/SERV EDU/PROP
MDTA. PAGE 20 B0418 WORKER
ADMIN
DELIB/GP

MEAD/GH....GEORGE HERBERT MEAD

MEAD/MARG....MARGARET MEAD

RUITENBEER H.M.,THE DILEMMA OF ORGANIZATIONAL **B63**
SOCIETY. CULTURE ECO/DEV MUNIC SECT TEC/DEV PERSON
EDU/PROP NAT/LISM ORD/FREE...NAT/COMP 20 RIESMAN/D ROLE
WHYTE/WF MERTON/R MEAD/MARG JASPERS/K. PAGE 92 ADMIN
B1855 WORKER

MEADVIL/PA....MEADVILLE, PA.

MEADVILLE, PA.....SEE MEADVIL/PA

MEANS G.C. B1459

MEDALIA N.Z. B1460

MEDIATION....SEE CONFER, CONSULT

MEDICAL CARE....SEE HEALTH

MEDITERRANEAN AND NEAR EAST, TO ISLAMIC PERIOD....SEE
MEDIT-7

MEDIT-7....MEDITERRANEAN AND NEAR EAST TO THE ISLAMIC
PERIOD (7TH CENTURY); SEE ALSO APPROPRIATE NATIONS

FRANK T.,A HISTORY OF ROME. MEDIT-7 INTELL SOCIETY **B23**
LOC/G NAT/G POL/PAR FORCES LEGIS DOMIN LEGIT EXEC
ALL/VALS...POLICY CONCPT TIME/SEQ GEN/LAWS ROM/EMP STRUCT
ROM/EMP. PAGE 37 B0749 ELITES

DAY C.,A HISTORY OF COMMERCE. CHRIST-17C EUR+WWI **B38**
ISLAM MEDIT-7 MOD/EUR USA-45 ECO/DEV FINAN NAT/G MARKET
ECO/TAC EXEC ROUTINE PWR WEALTH HIST/WRIT. PAGE 27 INT/TRADE
B0546

PLATO,THE REPUBLIC. MEDIT-7 UNIV SOCIETY STRUCT **B45**
EX/STRUC FORCES UTOPIA ATTIT PERCEPT HEALTH KNOWL PERSON
ORD/FREE PWR...HUM CONCPT STERTYP TOT/POP. PAGE 83 PHIL/SCI
B1681

MEEHAN E.J. B1461

MEEK C.K. B1462

MEIJI....MEIJI: THE REIGN OF EMPEROR MUTSUHITO OF JAPAN
   (1868-1912)

MEISEL J.H. B1463

MELANESIA....MELANESIA

MELINAT C.H. B1017

MELMAN S. B1464,B1465

MELTZER B.D. B1466

MENHENNET D. B1467

MENON/KRSH....KRISHNA MENON

MENSHEVIK....MENSHEVIKS

MENTAL DISORDERS....SEE HEALTH

MENTAL HEALTH....SEE HEALTH, PSY

MENTAL INSTITUTION....SEE PUB/INST

MENZEL J.M. B1468

MENZIES/RG....ROBERT G. MENZIES

MERCANTILISM....SEE ECO

MERCANTLST....MERCANTILIST ECONOMIC THEORY

MERCIER/E....ERNEST MERCIER

MEREDITH/J....JAMES MEREDITH

MERGERS....SEE INDUS, EX/STRUC, FINAN

MERILLAT H.C.L. B1469

MERON T. B1470

MERRIAM C.E. B1471,B1472

MERTHYR....MERTHYR, WALES

MERTON/R....ROBERT MERTON

B63
RUITENBEER H.M.,THE DILEMMA OF ORGANIZATIONAL   PERSON
SOCIETY. CULTURE ECO/DEV MUNIC SECT TEC/DEV   ROLE
EDU/PROP NAT/LISM ORD/FREE...NAT/COMP 20 RIESMAN/D   ADMIN
WHYTE/WF MERTON/R MEAD/MARG JASPERS/K. PAGE 92   WORKER
B1855

MESOPOTAM....MESOPOTAMIA

METH....HEAVILY EMPHASIZED METHODOLOGY OR TECHNIQUE OF STUDY

N
AMERICAN POLITICAL SCIENCE REVIEW. USA+45 USA-45   BIBLIOG/A
WOR+45 WOR-45 INT/ORG ADMIN...INT/LAW PHIL/SCI   DIPLOM
CONCPT METH 20 UN. PAGE 1 B0001   NAT/G
                                                      GOV/COMP
                                                      N
INTERNATIONAL BIBLIOGRAPHY OF ECONOMICS. WOR+45   BIBLIOG
FINAN MARKET ADMIN DEMAND INCOME PRODUC...POLICY   ECO/DEV
IDEA/COMP METH. PAGE 1 B0003   ECO/UNDEV
                                                      INT/TRADE
                                                      N19
WALL N.L.,MUNICIPAL REPORTING TO THE PUBLIC   METH
(PAMPHLET). LOC/G PLAN WRITING ADMIN REPRESENT   MUNIC
EFFICIENCY...AUD/VIS CHARTS 20. PAGE 113 B2282   GP/REL
                                                      COM/IND
                                                      N19
WRIGHT D.S.,AMERICAN STATE ADMINISTRATORS   QU
(PAMPHLET). USA+45 ATTIT PERSON...SAMP/SIZ CHARTS   TOP/EX
SOC/EXP METH 20. PAGE 118 B2379   ADMIN
                                                      PROVS
                                                      B24
BAGEHOT W.,THE ENGLISH CONSTITUTION AND OTHER   NAT/G
POLITICAL ESSAYS. UK DELIB/GP BAL/PWR ADMIN CONTROL   STRUCT
EXEC ROUTINE CONSERVE...METH PARLIAMENT 19/20.   CONCPT
PAGE 8 B0160
                                                      B31
BORCHARD E.H.,GUIDE TO THE LAW AND LEGAL LITERATURE   BIBLIOG/A
OF FRANCE. FRANCE FINAN INDUS LABOR SECT LEGIS   LAW
ADMIN COLONIAL CRIME OWN...INT/LAW 20. PAGE 14   CONSTN
B0277   METH

B40
PFIFFNER J.M.,RESEARCH METHODS IN PUBLIC   ADMIN
ADMINISTRATION. USA-45 R+D...MGT STAT INT QU T 20.   OP/RES
PAGE 82 B1665   METH
                                                      TEC/DEV
                                                      S43
SELZNICK P.,"AN APPROACH TO A THEORY OF   ROUTINE
BUREAUCRACY." INDUS WORKER CONTROL LEAD EFFICIENCY   ADMIN
OPTIMAL...SOC METH 20 BARNARD/C BUREAUCRCY   MGT
WEBER/MAX FRIEDRCH/C MICHELS/R. PAGE 95 B1928   EX/STRUC
                                                      B45
BENJAMIN H.C.,EMPLOYMENT TESTS IN INDUSTRY AND   BIBLIOG/A
BUSINESS. LG/CO WORKER ROUTINE...MGT PSY SOC   METH
CLASSIF PROBABIL STAT APT/TEST KNO/TEST PERS/TEST   TESTS
20. PAGE 10 B0211   INDUS
                                                      B50
WARD R.E.,A GUIDE TO JAPANESE REFERENCE AND   BIBLIOG/A
RESEARCH MATERIALS IN THE FIELD OF POLITICAL   ASIA
SCIENCE. LAW CONSTN LOC/G PRESS ADMIN...SOC   NAT/G
CON/ANAL METH 19/20 CHINJAP. PAGE 113 B2289
                                                      S51
LERNER D.,"THE POLICY SCIENCES: RECENT DEVELOPMENTS CONSULT
IN SCOPE AND METHODS." R+D SERV/IND CREATE DIPLOM   SOC
ROUTINE PWR...METH/CNCPT TREND GEN/LAWS METH 20.
PAGE 64 B1297
                                                      B53
ARGYRIS C.,EXECUTIVE LEADERSHIP: AN APPRAISAL OF A   MGT
MANAGER IN ACTION. TOP/EX ADMIN LEAD ADJUST ATTIT   EX/STRUC
...METH 20. PAGE 6 B0127   WORKER
                                                      PERS/REL
                                                      B54
BENTLEY A.F.,INQUIRY INTO INQUIRIES: ESSAYS IN   EPIST
SOCIAL THEORY. UNIV LEGIS ADJUD ADMIN LOBBY   SOC
...PHIL/SCI PSY NEW/IDEA LING METH 20. PAGE 11   CONCPT
B0220
                                                      B55
BAILEY S.K.,RESEARCH FRONTIERS IN POLITICS AND   R+D
GOVERNMENT. CONSTN LEGIS ADMIN REV CHOOSE...CONCPT   METH
IDEA/COMP GAME ANTHOL 20. PAGE 8 B0164   NAT/G
                                                      S55
TERRIEN F.W.,"THE EFFECT OF CHANGING SIZE UPON THE   SOC
INTERNAL STRUCTURE OF ORGANIZATIONS" (BMR)" WOR+45   ADMIN
WOR-45 CHARTS. PAGE 103 B2091   GP/REL
                                                      METH
                                                      B56
ECOLE NAT'L D'ADMINISTRATION,RECRUITMENT AND   ADMIN
TRAINING FOR THE HIGHER CIVIL SERVICE IN FRANCE.   MGT
FRANCE EX/STRUC PLAN EDU/PROP CONTROL ROUTINE TASK   EXEC
COST...METH 20 CIVIL/SERV. PAGE 32 B0650   ACADEM
                                                      B56
HICKMAN C.A.,INDIVIDUALS, GROUPS, AND ECONOMIC   MGT
BEHAVIOR. WORKER PAY CONTROL EXEC GP/REL INGP/REL   ADMIN
PERSON ROLE...PSY SOC PERS/COMP METH 20. PAGE 50   ECO/TAC
B1005   PLAN
                                                      B56
POWELL N.J.,PERSONNEL ADMINISTRATION IN GOVERNMENT.   ADMIN
COM/IND POL/PAR LEGIS PAY CT/SYS ROUTINE GP/REL   WORKER
PERS/REL...POLICY METH 20 CIVIL/SERV. PAGE 84 B1697   LOC/G
                                                      NAT/G
                                                      S57
ARGYRIS C.,"THE INDIVIDUAL AND ORGANIZATION: SOME   PERSON
PROBLEMS OF MUTUAL ADJUSTMENT" (BMR)" USA+45   METH
PROB/SOLV ADMIN CONTROL 20. PAGE 6 B0128   INGP/REL
                                                      TASK
                                                      S57
FESLER J.W.,"ADMINISTRATIVE LITERATURE AND THE   ADMIN
SECOND HOOVER COMMISSION REPORTS" (BMR)" USA+45   NAT/G
EX/STRUC LEGIS WRITING...DECISION METH 20. PAGE 35   OP/RES
B0713   DELIB/GP
                                                      B58
DEVLIN P.,THE CRIMINAL PROSECUTION IN ENGLAND. UK   CRIME
NAT/G ADMIN ROUTINE EFFICIENCY...JURID SOC 20.   LAW
PAGE 29 B0583   METH
                                                      CT/SYS
                                                      B58
OPERATIONS RESEARCH SOCIETY,A COMPREHENSIVE   BIBLIOG/A
BIBLIOGRAPHY ON OPERATIONS RESEARCH: THROUGH 1956   COMPUT/IR
WITH SUPPLEMENT FOR 1957. COM/IND DIST/IND INDUS   OP/RES
ADMIN...DECISION MATH STAT METH 20. PAGE 80 B1612   MGT
                                                      B58
REDFIELD C.E.,COMMUNICATION IN MANAGEMENT. DELIB/GP COM/IND
EX/STRUC WRITING LEAD PERS/REL...PSY INT METH 20.   MGT
PAGE 87 B1750   LG/CO
                                                      ADMIN
                                                      B58
SWEENEY S.B.,EDUCATION FOR ADMINISTRATIVE CAREERS   EDU/PROP
IN GOVERNMENT SERVICE. USA+45 ACADEM CONSULT CREATE   ADMIN
PLAN CONFER SKILL...TREND IDEA/COMP METH 20   NAT/G
CIVIL/SERV. PAGE 102 B2059   LOC/G
                                                      S58
HELMER O.,"THE PROSPECTS OF A UNIFIED THEORY OF   SIMUL
ORGANIZATIONS" UNIV ACT/RES ADMIN...CONCPT HYPO/EXP   LG/CO
METH. PAGE 49 B0989   METH/CNCPT
                                                      GAME
                                                      B59
SURRENCY E.C.,A GUIDE TO LEGAL RESEARCH. USA+45   NAT/G

ACADEM LEGIS ACT/RES ADMIN...DECISION METH/COMP
BIBLIOG METH. PAGE 102 B2055
PROVS
ADJUD
JURID
L59

"A BIBLIOGRAPHICAL ESSAY ON DECISION MAKING."
WOR+45 WOR-45 STRUCT OP/RES GP/REL...CONCPT
IDEA/COMP METH 20. PAGE 2 B0038
BIBLIOG/A
DECISION
ADMIN
LEAD
B60

KERSELL J.E.,PARLIAMENTARY SUPERVISION OF DELEGATED
LEGISLATION. UK EFFICIENCY PWR...POLICY CHARTS
BIBLIOG METH 20 PARLIAMENT. PAGE 59 B1198
LEGIS
CONTROL
NAT/G
EX/STRUC
B60

SMITH M.G.,GOVERNMENT IN ZAZZAU 1800-1950. NIGERIA
UK CULTURE SOCIETY LOC/G ADMIN COLONIAL
...METH/CNCPT NEW/IDEA METH 19/20. PAGE 98 B1983
REGION
CONSTN
KIN
ECO/UNDEV
S60

RIESELBACH Z.N.,"QUANTITATIVE TECHNIQUES FOR
STUDYING VOTING BEHAVIOR IN THE UNITED NATIONS
GENERAL ASSEMBLY." FUT S/ASIA USA+45 INT/ORG
BAL/PWR DIPLOM ECO/TAC FOR/AID ADMIN PWR...POLICY
METH/CNCPT METH UN 20. PAGE 88 B1783
QUANT
CHOOSE

FREYRE G.,THE PORTUGUESE AND THE TROPICS. L/A+17C
PORTUGAL SOCIETY PERF/ART ADMIN TASK GP/REL
...ART/METH CONCPT SOC/INTEG 20. PAGE 37 B0754
COLONIAL
METH
PLAN
CULTURE
B61

LASSWELL H.D.,PSYCOPATHOLOGY AND POLITICS. WOR-45
CULTURE SOCIETY FACE/GP NAT/G CONSULT CREATE
EDU/PROP EXEC ROUTINE DISPL DRIVE PERSON PWR
RESPECT...PSY CONCPT METH/CNCPT METH. PAGE 63 B1272
ATTIT
GEN/METH
B61

PUGET H.,ESSAI DE BIBLIOGRAPHIE DES PRINCIPAUX
OUVRAGES DE DROIT PUBLIC... QUI ONT PARU HORS DE
FRANCE DE 1945 A 1958. EUR+WWI USA+45 CONSTN LOC/G
...METH 20. PAGE 85 B1719
BIBLIOG
MGT
ADMIN
LAW
B61

SHARP W.R.,FIELD ADMINISTRATION IN THE UNITED
NATION SYSTEM: THE CONDUCT OF INTERNATIONAL
ECONOMIC AND SOCIAL PROGRAMS. FUT WOR+45 CONSTN
SOCIETY ECO/UNDEV R+D DELIB/GP ACT/RES PLAN TEC/DEV
EDU/PROP EXEC ROUTINE HEALTH WEALTH...HUM CONCPT
CHARTS METH ILO UNESCO VAL/FREE UN 20. PAGE 96
B1939
INT/ORG
CONSULT

VERBA S.,"SMALL GROUPS AND POLITICAL BEHAVIOR: A
STUDY OF LEADERSHIP" DOMIN PARTIC ROUTINE GP/REL
ATTIT DRIVE ALL/VALS...CONCPT IDEA/COMP LAB/EXP
BIBLIOG METH. PAGE 112 B2259
LEAD
ELITES
FACE/GP
C61

ARCO EDITORIAL BOARD,PUBLIC MANAGEMENT AND
ADMINISTRATION. PLAN BUDGET WRITING CONTROL ROUTINE
...TESTS CHARTS METH T 20. PAGE 6 B0125
MGT
ADMIN
NAT/G
LOC/G
B62

BROWN B.E.,NEW DIRECTIONS IN COMPARATIVE POLITICS.
AUSTRIA FRANCE GERMANY UK WOR+45 EX/STRUC LEGIS
ORD/FREE 20. PAGE 16 B0320
NAT/COMP
METH
POL/PAR
FORCES
B62

DUCKWORTH W.E.,A GUIDE TO OPERATIONAL RESEARCH.
INDUS PLAN PROB/SOLV EXEC EFFICIENCY PRODUC KNOWL
...MGT MATH STAT SIMUL METH 20 MONTECARLO. PAGE 31
B0624
OP/RES
GAME
DECISION
ADMIN
B62

HITCHNER D.G.,MODERN GOVERNMENT: A SURVEY OF
POLITICAL SCIENCE. WOR+45 INT/ORG LEGIS ADMIN
CT/SYS EXEC CHOOSE TOTALISM POPULISM...INT/LAW
PHIL/SCI METH 20. PAGE 50 B1019
CONCPT
NAT/G
STRUCT
B62

MARS D.,SUGGESTED LIBRARY IN PUBLIC ADMINISTRATION.
FINAN DELIB/GP EX/STRUC WORKER COMPUTER ADJUD
...DECISION PSY SOC METH/COMP 20. PAGE 69 B1403
BIBLIOG
ADMIN
METH
MGT
B62

SNYDER R.C.,FOREIGN POLICY DECISION-MAKING. FUT
KOREA WOR+45 R+D CREATE ADMIN ROUTINE PWR
...DECISION PSY SOC CONCPT METH/CNCPT CON/ANAL
CHARTS GEN/METH METH 20. PAGE 99 B1992
TEC/DEV
HYPO/EXP
DIPLOM
B62

TAYLOR J.K.L.,ATTITUDES AND METHODS OF
COMMUNICATION AND CONSULTATION BETWEEN EMPLOYERS
AND WORKERS AT INDIVIDUAL FIRM LEVEL. WOR+45 STRUCT
INDUS LABOR CONFER TASK GP/REL EFFICIENCY...MGT
BIBLIOG METH 20 OECD. PAGE 103 B2087
WORKER
ADMIN
ATTIT
EDU/PROP
B63

INDIAN INSTITUTE PUBLIC ADMIN,CASES IN INDIAN
ADMINISTRATION. INDIA AGRI NAT/G PROB/SOLV TEC/DEV
ECO/TAC ADMIN...ANTHOL METH 20. PAGE 53 B1083
DECISION
PLAN
MGT
ECO/UNDEV
B63

INTL INST ADMIN SCIENCES,EDUCATION IN PUBLIC
ADMINISTRATION: A SYMPOSIUM ON TEACHING METHODS AND
EDU/PROP
METH

MATERIALS. WOR+45 SCHOOL CONSULT CREATE CONFER
SKILL...OBS TREND IDEA/COMP METH/COMP 20. PAGE 54
B1100
ADMIN
ACADEM
B64

INDIAN COMM PREVENTION CORRUPT,REPORT, 1964. INDIA
NAT/G GOV/REL ATTIT ORD/FREE...CRIMLGY METH 20.
PAGE 53 B1079
CRIME
ADMIN
LEGIS
LOC/G
B64

MAYER C.S.,INTERVIEWING COSTS IN SURVEY RESEARCH.
USA+45 PLAN COST...MGT REC/INT SAMP METH/COMP
HYPO/EXP METH 20. PAGE 71 B1434
SIMUL
INT
R+D
EFFICIENCY
B64

MCNULTY J.E.,SOME ECONOMIC ASPECTS OF BUSINESS
ORGANIZATION. ECO/DEV UTIL...MGT CHARTS BIBLIOG
METH 20. PAGE 72 B1458
ADMIN
LG/CO
GEN/LAWS
B64

ORTH C.D.,ADMINISTERING RESEARCH AND DEVELOPMENT.
MGT FINAN PLAN PROB/SOLV ADMIN ROUTINE...METH/CNCPT
STAT CHARTS METH 20. PAGE 80 B1616
MGT
R+D
LG/CO
INDUS
B64

RICHARDSON I.L.,BIBLIOGRAFIA BRASILEIRA DE
ADMINISTRACAO PUBLICA E ASSUNTOS CORRELATOS. BRAZIL
CONSTN FINAN LOC/G NAT/G POL/PAR PLAN DIPLOM
RECEIVE ATTIT...METH 20. PAGE 88 B1776
BIBLIOG
MGT
ADMIN
LAW
B64

WILLIAMSON O.E.,THE ECONOMICS OF DISCRETIONARY
BEHAVIOR: MANAGERIAL OBJECTIVES IN A THEORY OF THE
FIRM. MARKET BUDGET CAP/ISM PRODUC DRIVE PERSON
...STAT CHARTS BIBLIOG METH 20. PAGE 117 B2354
EFFICIENCY
MGT
ECO/TAC
CHOOSE
C64

SCOTT R.E.,"MEXICAN GOVERNMENT IN TRANSITION (REV
ED)" CULTURE STRUCT POL/PAR CHIEF ADMIN LOBBY REV
CHOOSE GP/REL DRIVE...BIBLIOG METH 20 MEXIC/AMER.
PAGE 95 B1920
NAT/G
L/A+17C
ROUTINE
CONSTN
B65

ANTHONY R.N.,PLANNING AND CONTROL SYSTEMS. UNIV
OP/RES...DECISION MGT LING. PAGE 6 B0114
CONTROL
PLAN
METH
HYPO/EXP
B65

HARMON R.B.,POLITICAL SCIENCE: A BIBLIOGRAPHICAL
GUIDE TO THE LITERATURE. WOR+45 WOR-45 R+D INT/ORG
LOC/G NAT/G DIPLOM ADMIN...CONCPT METH. PAGE 47
B0950
BIBLIOG
POL/PAR
LAW
GOV/COMP
B65

ORG FOR ECO COOP AND DEVEL,THE MEDITERRANEAN
REGIONAL PROJECT: YUGOSLAVIA; EDUCATION AND
DEVELOPMENT. YUGOSLAVIA SOCIETY FINAN PROF/ORG PLAN
ADMIN COST DEMAND MARXISM...STAT TREND CHARTS METH
20 OECD. PAGE 80 B1615
EDU/PROP
ACADEM
SCHOOL
ECO/UNDEV
B65

STARR M.K.,EXECUTIVE READINGS IN MANAGEMENT
SCIENCE. TOP/EX WORKER EDU/PROP ADMIN...DECISION
GEN/LAWS ANTHOL METH T 20. PAGE 100 B2023
MGT
EX/STRUC
PLAN
LG/CO
B65

DAHLBERG J.S.,THE NEW YORK BUREAU OF MUNICIPAL
RESEARCH: PIONEER IN GOVERNMENT ADMINISTRATION.
CONSTN R+D BUDGET EDU/PROP PARTIC REPRESENT
EFFICIENCY ORD/FREE...BIBLIOG METH 20 NEW/YORK
NIPA. PAGE 26 B0522
PROVS
MUNIC
DELIB/GP
ADMIN
B66

KURAKOV I.G.,SCIENCE, TECHNOLOGY AND COMMUNISM;
SOME QUESTIONS OF DEVELOPMENT (TRANS. BY CARIN
DEDIJER). USSR INDUS PLAN PROB/SOLV COST PRODUC
...MGT MATH CHARTS METH 20. PAGE 61 B1243
CREATE
TEC/DEV
MARXISM
ECO/TAC
B66

WESTON J.F.,THE SCOPE AND METHODOLOGY OF FINANCE.
PLAN TEC/DEV CONTROL EFFICIENCY INCOME UTIL...MGT
CONCPT MATH STAT TREND METH 20. PAGE 115 B2327
FINAN
ECO/DEV
POLICY
PRICE
B67

DE BLIJ H.J.,SYSTEMATIC POLITICAL GEOGRAPHY. WOR+45
STRUCT INT/ORG NAT/G EDU/PROP ADMIN COLONIAL
ROUTINE ORD/FREE PWR...IDEA/COMP T 20. PAGE 27
B0550
GEOG
CONCPT
METH
B67

KAPLAN H.,URBAN POLITICAL SYSTEMS: A FUNCTIONAL
ANALYSIS OF METRO TORONTO. CANADA STRUCT NEIGH PLAN
ADMIN...POLICY METH 20 TORONTO. PAGE 58 B1166
GEN/LAWS
MUNIC
LOC/G
FEDERAL
S67

BURKE E.M.,"THE SEARCH FOR AUTHORITY IN PLANNING."
MUNIC NEIGH CREATE PROB/SOLV LEGIT ADMIN CONTROL
EFFICIENCY PWR...METH/COMP SIMUL 20. PAGE 17 B0352
DECISION
PLAN
LOC/G
METH
S67

MCNAMARA R.L.,"THE NEED FOR INNOVATIVENESS IN
DEVELOPING SOCIETIES." L/A+17C EDU/PROP ADMIN LEAD
WEALTH...POLICY PSY SOC METH 20 COLOMB. PAGE 72
B1456
PROB/SOLV
PLAN
ECO/UNDEV
NEW/IDEA
S67

MURRAY R.,"SECOND THOUGHTS ON GHANA." AFR GHANA
COLONIAL

NAT/G POL/PAR ADMIN REV GP/REL CENTRAL...SOCIALIST CONCPT METH 20. PAGE 77 B1548 — CONTROL REGION SOCISM

METH/CNCPT....METHODOLOGICAL CONCEPTS

METH/COMP....COMPARISON OF METHODS

N

WEIGLEY R.F.,HISTORY OF THE UNITED STATES ARMY. USA+45 USA-45 SOCIETY NAT/G LEAD WAR GP/REL PWR ...SOC METH/COMP COLD/WAR. PAGE 115 B2312 — FORCES ADMIN ROLE CIVMIL/REL

N

CATHERINE R.,LA REVUE ADMINISTRATIVE. FRANCE LAW NAT/G LEGIS...JURID BIBLIOG/A 20. PAGE 19 B0393 — ADMIN MGT FINAN METH/COMP

N19

ARNOW K.,SELF-INSURANCE IN THE TREASURY (PAMPHLET). USA+45 LAW RIGID/FLEX...POLICY METH/COMP 20 DEPT/TREAS. PAGE 7 B0135 — ADMIN PLAN EFFICIENCY NAT/G

N19

FOLSOM M.B.,BETTER MANAGEMENT OF THE PUBLIC'S BUSINESS (PAMPHLET). USA+45 DELIB/GP PAY CONFER CONTROL REGION GP/REL...METH/COMP ANTHOL 20. PAGE 36 B0733 — ADMIN NAT/G MGT PROB/SOLV

N19

GORWALA A.D.,THE ADMINISTRATIVE JUNGLE (PAMPHLET). INDIA NAT/G LEGIS ECO/TAC CONTROL GOV/REL ...METH/COMP 20. PAGE 41 B0838 — ADMIN POLICY PLAN ECO/UNDEV

N19

LA PALOMBARA J.G.,ALTERNATIVE STRATEGIES FOR DEVELOPING ADMINISTRATIVE CAPABILITIES IN EMERGING NATIONS (PAMPHLET). POL/PAR EX/STRUC PROB/SOLV PLURISM...POLICY METH/COMP. PAGE 62 B1248 — ECO/UNDEV MGT EXEC ADMIN

B33

ENSOR R.C.K.,COURTS AND JUDGES IN FRANCE, GERMANY, AND ENGLAND. FRANCE GERMANY UK LAW PROB/SOLV ADMIN ROUTINE CRIME ROLE...METH/COMP 20 CIVIL/LAW. PAGE 33 B0676 — CT/SYS EX/STRUC ADJUD NAT/COMP

B37

GULICK L.,PAPERS ON THE SCIENCE OF ADMINISTRATION. INDUS PROB/SOLV TEC/DEV COST EFFICIENCY PRODUC HABITAT...PHIL/SCI METH/COMP 20. PAGE 45 B0903 — OP/RES CONTROL ADMIN MGT

B41

COHEN E.W.,THE GROWTH OF THE BRITISH CIVIL SERVICE 1780-1939. UK NAT/G SENIOR ROUTINE GOV/REL...MGT METH/COMP BIBLIOG 18/20. PAGE 22 B0442 — OP/RES TIME/SEQ CENTRAL ADMIN

B44

BIENSTOCK G.,MANAGEMENT IN RUSSIAN INDUSTRY AND AGRICULTURE. USSR CONSULT WORKER LEAD COST PROFIT ATTIT DRIVE PWR...MGT METH/COMP DICTIONARY 20. PAGE 12 B0236 — ADMIN MARXISM SML/CO AGRI

B46

CORRY J.A.,DEMOCRATIC GOVERNMENT AND POLITICS. WOR-45 EX/STRUC LOBBY TOTALISM...MAJORIT CONCPT METH/COMP NAT/COMP 20. PAGE 24 B0479 — NAT/G CONSTN POL/PAR JURID

B48

SLESSER H.,THE ADMINISTRATION OF THE LAW. UK CONSTN EX/STRUC OP/RES PROB/SOLV CRIME ROLE...DECISION METH/COMP 20 CIVIL/LAW ENGLSH/LAW CIVIL/LAW. PAGE 98 B1977 — LAW CT/SYS ADJUD

B49

MCLEAN J.M.,THE PUBLIC SERVICE AND UNIVERSITY EDUCATION. UK USA-45 DELIB/GP EX/STRUC TOP/EX ADMIN ...GOV/COMP METH/COMP NAT/COMP ANTHOL 20. PAGE 72 B1455 — ACADEM NAT/G EXEC EDU/PROP

B50

COMMONS J.R.,THE ECONOMICS OF COLLECTIVE ACTION. USA-45 AGRI INDUS LABOR NAT/G LEGIS ADMIN EFFICIENCY...MGT METH/COMP BIBLIOG 20. PAGE 22 B0458 — ECO/DEV CAP/ISM ACT/RES CONCPT

B52

SCHATTSCHNEIDER E.E.,A GUIDE TO THE STUDY OF PUBLIC AFFAIRS. LAW LOC/G NAT/G LEGIS BUDGET PRESS ADMIN LOBBY...JURID CHARTS 20. PAGE 93 B1882 — ACT/RES INTELL ACADEM METH/COMP

B53

CALDWELL L.K.,RESEARCH METHODS IN PUBLIC ADMINISTRATION; AN OUTLINE OF TOPICS AND READINGS (PAMPHLET). LAW ACT/RES COMPUTER KNOWL...SOC STAT GEN/METH 20. PAGE 18 B0365 — BIBLIOG/A METH/COMP ADMIN OP/RES

N53

US PRES CONF ADMIN PROCEDURE,REPORT (PAMPHLET). USA+45 CONFER ADJUD...METH/COMP 20 PRESIDENT. PAGE 109 B2209 — NAT/G DELIB/GP ADJUST ADMIN

B54

MCCLOSKEY J.F.,OPERATIONS RESEARCH FOR MANAGEMENT. STRUCT COMPUTER ADMIN ROUTINE...PHIL/SCI CONCPT — OP/RES MGT

METH/CNCPT TREND ANTHOL BIBLIOG 20. PAGE 72 B1445 — METH/COMP TEC/DEV

B54

SCHWARTZ B.,FRENCH ADMINISTRATIVE LAW AND THE COMMON-LAW WORLD. FRANCE CULTURE LOC/G NAT/G PROVS DELIB/GP EX/STRUC LEGIS PROB/SOLV CT/SYS EXEC GOV/REL...IDEA/COMP ENGLSH/LAW. PAGE 95 B1912 — JURID LAW METH/COMP ADJUD

B55

BERNAYS E.L.,THE ENGINEERING OF CONSENT. VOL/ASSN OP/RES ROUTINE INGP/REL ATTIT RESPECT...POLICY METH/CNCPT METH/COMP 20. PAGE 11 B0224 — GP/REL PLAN ACT/RES ADJUST

C56

NEUMANN S.,"MODERN POLITICAL PARTIES: APPROACHES TO COMPARATIVE POLITIC. FRANCE UK EX/STRUC DOMIN ADMIN LEAD REPRESENT TOTALISM ATTIT...POLICY TREND METH/COMP ANTHOL BIBLIOG/A 20 CMN/WLTH. PAGE 78 B1574 — POL/PAR GOV/COMP ELITES MAJORIT

B57

MEYER P.,ADMINISTRATIVE ORGANIZATION: A COMPARATIVE STUDY OF THE ORGANIZATION OF PUBLIC ADMINISTRATION. DENMARK FRANCE NORWAY SWEDEN UK USA+45 ELITES LOC/G CONSULT LEGIS ADJUD CONTROL LEAD PWR SKILL DECISION. PAGE 73 B1475 — ADMIN METH/COMP NAT/G CENTRAL

B57

UDY S.H. JR.,THE ORGANIZATION OF PRODUCTION IN NONINDUSTRIAL CULTURE. VOL/ASSN DELIB/GP TEC/DEV ...CHARTS BIBLIOG. PAGE 106 B2143 — METH/COMP ECO/UNDEV PRODUC ADMIN

B57

WEIDLUND J.,COMPARATIVE PUBLIC ADMINISTRATION. EX/STRUC METH/COMP. PAGE 114 B2310 — ADMIN NAT/G GOV/COMP BIBLIOG/A

S57

HONEY J.C.,"RESEARCH IN PUBLIC ADMINISTRATION: A FURTHER NOTE." EX/STRUC 20. PAGE 51 B1038 — ADMIN EXEC METH/COMP METH/CNCPT

B58

CHEEK G.,ECONOMIC AND SOCIAL IMPLICATIONS OF AUTOMATION: A BIBLIOGRAPHIC REVIEW (PAMPHLET). USA+45 LG/CO WORKER CREATE PLAN CONTROL ROUTINE PERS/REL EFFICIENCY PRODUC...METH/COMP 20. PAGE 20 B0416 — BIBLIOG/A SOCIETY INDUS AUTOMAT

B58

COWAN L.G.,LOCAL GOVERNMENT IN WEST AFRICA. AFR FRANCE UK CULTURE KIN POL/PAR CHIEF LEGIS CREATE ADMIN PARTIC GOV/REL GP/REL...METH/COMP 20. PAGE 24 B0498 — LOC/G COLONIAL SOVEREIGN REPRESENT

B58

LAW COMMISSION OF INDIA,REFORM OF JUDICIAL ADMINISTRATION. INDIA TOP/EX ADMIN DISCRIM EFFICIENCY...METH/COMP 20. PAGE 63 B1276 — CT/SYS ADJUD GOV/REL CONTROL

B58

LESTER R.A.,AS UNIONS MATURE. POL/PAR BARGAIN LEAD PARTIC GP/REL CENTRAL...MAJORIT TIME/SEQ METH/COMP. PAGE 64 B1299 — LABOR INDUS POLICY MGT

B58

REDFORD E.S.,IDEAL AND PRACTICE IN PUBLIC ADMINISTRATION. CONSTN ELITES NAT/G CONSULT DELIB/GP LEAD UTOPIA ATTIT POPULISM...DECISION METH/COMP 20. PAGE 87 B1756 — POLICY EX/STRUC PLAN ADMIN

B59

SURRENCY E.C.,A GUIDE TO LEGAL RESEARCH. USA+45 ACADEM LEGIS ACT/RES ADMIN...DECISION METH/COMP BIBLIOG METH. PAGE 102 B2055 — NAT/G PROVS ADJUD JURID

B60

ECKHOFF T.,RATIONALITY AND RESPONSIBILITY IN ADMINISTRATIVE AND JUDICIAL DECISION-MAKING. ELITES LEAD INGP/REL ATTIT PWR...MGT METH/COMP GAME 20. PAGE 32 B0649 — ADMIN PROB/SOLV DECISION METH/CNCPT

B60

MEYRIAT J.,LA SCIENCE POLITIQUE EN FRANCE, 1945-1958; BIBLIOGRAPHIES FRANCAISES DE SCIENCES SOCIALES (VOL. I). EUR+WWI FRANCE POL/PAR DIPLOM ADMIN CHOOSE ATTIT...IDEA/COMP METH/COMP NAT/COMP 20. PAGE 73 B1478 — BIBLIOG/A NAT/G CONCPT PHIL/SCI

B60

PENTONY D.E.,UNITED STATES FOREIGN AID. INDIA LAOS USA+45 ECO/UNDEV INT/TRADE ADMIN PEACE ATTIT ...POLICY METH/COMP ANTHOL 20. PAGE 82 B1653 — FOR/AID DIPLOM ECO/TAC

B60

ROBINSON E.A.G.,ECONOMIC CONSEQUENCES OF THE SIZE OF NATIONS. AGRI INDUS DELIB/GP FOR/AID ADMIN EFFICIENCY...METH/COMP 20. PAGE 89 B1799 — CONCPT INT/ORG NAT/COMP

S60

BANFIELD E.C.,"THE POLITICAL IMPLICATIONS OF METROPOLITAN GROWTH" (BMR)" UK USA+45 LOC/G PROB/SOLV ADMIN GP/REL...METH/COMP NAT/COMP 20. PAGE 9 B0176 — TASK MUNIC GOV/COMP CENSUS

S60

FRIEDMAN L.,"DECISION MAKING IN COMPETITIVE — DECISION

SITUATIONS" OP/RES...MGT PROBABIL METH/COMP SIMUL 20. PAGE 37 B0757 — UTIL OPTIMAL GAME

S60
RAPHAELI N.,"SELECTED ARTICLES AND DOCUMENTS ON COMPARATIVE PUBLIC ADMINISTRATION." USA+45 FINAN LOC/G TOP/EX TEC/DEV EXEC. GP/REL INGP/REL...GP/COMP GOV/COMP METH/COMP. PAGE 86 B1738 — BIBLIOG MGT ADMIN EX/STRUC

B61
BAINS J.S.,STUDIES IN POLITICAL SCIENCE. INDIA WOR+45 WOR-45 CONSTN BAL/PWR ADJUD ADMIN PARL/PROC SOVEREIGN...SOC METH/COMP ANTHOL 17/20 UN. PAGE 8 B0165 — DIPLOM INT/LAW NAT/G

B61
CARNEY D.E.,GOVERNMENT AND ECONOMY IN BRITISH WEST AFRICA. GAMBIA GHANA NIGERIA SIER/LEONE DOMIN ADMIN GOV/REL SOVEREIGN WEALTH LAISSEZ...BIBLIOG 20 CMN/WLTH. PAGE 19 B0384 — METH/COMP COLONIAL ECO/TAC ECO/UNDEV

B61
CONFREY E.A.,ADMINISTRATION OF COMMUNITY HEALTH SERVICES. USA+45 R+D PUB/INST DELIB/GP PLAN BUDGET ROUTINE AGE/C HEALTH...MGT SOC/WK METH/COMP 20. PAGE 23 B0461 — HEAL ADMIN MUNIC BIO/SOC

B61
GARCIA E.,LA ADMINISTRACION ESPANOLA. SPAIN GOV/REL ...CONCPT METH/COMP 20. PAGE 39 B0780 — ADMIN NAT/G LOC/G DECISION

B61
HART H.C.,ADMINISTRATIVE ASPECTS OF RIVER VALLEY DEVELOPMENT. INDIA USA+45 INDUS CONTROL EFFICIENCY OPTIMAL PRODUC 20 TVA. PAGE 47 B0957 — ADMIN PLAN METH/COMP AGRI

B61
HICKS U.K.,DEVELOPMENT FROM BELOW. UK INDUS ADMIN COLONIAL ROUTINE GOV/REL...POLICY METH/CNCPT CHARTS 19/20 CMN/WLTH. PAGE 50 B1006 — ECO/UNDEV LOC/G GOV/COMP METH/COMP

B61
LENIN V.I.,WHAT IS TO BE DONE? (1902). RUSSIA LABOR NAT/G POL/PAR WORKER CAP/ISM ECO/TAC ADMIN PARTIC ...MARXIST IDEA/COMP GEN/LAWS 19/20. PAGE 64 B1292 — EDU/PROP PRESS MARXISM METH/COMP

B62
GALENSON W.,LABOR IN DEVELOPING COUNTRIES. BRAZIL INDONESIA ISRAEL PAKISTAN TURKEY AGRI INDUS WORKER PAY PRICE GP/REL WEALTH...MGT CHARTS METH/COMP NAT/COMP 20. PAGE 38 B0775 — LABOR ECO/UNDEV BARGAIN POL/PAR

B62
HATTERY L.H.,INFORMATION RETRIEVAL MANAGEMENT. CLIENT INDUS TOP/EX COMPUTER OP/RES TEC/DEV ROUTINE COST EFFICIENCY RIGID/FLEX...METH/COMP ANTHOL 20. PAGE 48 B0968 — R+D COMPUT/IR MGT CREATE

B62
MARS D.,SUGGESTED LIBRARY IN PUBLIC ADMINISTRATION. FINAN DELIB/GP EX/STRUC WORKER COMPUTER ADJUD ...DECISION PSY SOC METH/COMP 20. PAGE 69 B1403 — BIBLIOG ADMIN METH MGT

B62
PRAKASH O.M.,THE THEORY AND WORKING OF STATE CORPORATIONS: WITH SPECIAL REFERENCE TO INDIA. INDIA UK USA+45 TOP/EX PRICE ADMIN EFFICIENCY...MGT METH/COMP 20 TVA. PAGE 84 B1698 — LG/CO ECO/UNDEV GOV/REL SOCISM

B62
SRIVASTAVA G.L.,COLLECTIVE BARGAINING AND LABOR-MANAGEMENT RELATIONS IN INDIA. INDIA UK USA+45 INDUS LEGIS WORKER ADJUD EFFICIENCY PRODUC ...METH/COMP 20. PAGE 100 B2014 — LABOR MGT BARGAIN GP/REL

B62
US ADMINISTRATIVE CONFERENCE,FINAL REPORT OF THE ADMINISTRATIVE CONFERENCE OF THE US; SUGGESTIONS FOR IMPROVING PROCESSES - ADMIN. AGENCIES. USA+45 INGP/REL EFFICIENCY RATIONAL ORD/FREE...GP/COMP METH/COMP 20. PAGE 107 B2170 — ADMIN NAT/G DELIB/GP GOV/REL

B62
WENDT P.F.,HOUSING POLICY - THE SEARCH FOR SOLUTIONS. GERMANY/W SWEDEN UK USA+45 OP/RES HABITAT WEALTH...SOC/WK CHARTS 20. PAGE 115 B2322 — PLAN ADMIN METH/COMP NAT/G

B63
COUNCIL STATE GOVERNMENTS,HANDBOOK FOR LEGISLATIVE COMMITTEES. USA+45 LAW DELIB/GP EX/STRUC TOP/EX CHOOSE PWR...METH/COMP 20. PAGE 24 B0496 — LEGIS PARL/PROC PROVS ADJUD

B63
DUE J.F.,STATE SALES TAX ADMINISTRATION. OP/RES BUDGET PAY ADMIN EXEC ROUTINE COST EFFICIENCY PROFIT...CHARTS METH/COMP 20. PAGE 31 B0626 — PROVS TAX STAT GOV/COMP

B63
FRIED R.C.,THE ITALIAN PREFECTS. ITALY STRATA ECO/DEV NAT/LISM ALL/IDEOS...TREND CHARTS METH/COMP BIBLIOG 17/20 PREFECT. PAGE 37 B0755 — ADMIN NAT/G EFFICIENCY

B63
GOURNAY B.,PUBLIC ADMINISTRATION. FRANCE LAW CONSTN AGRI FINAN LABOR SCHOOL EX/STRUC CHOOSE...MGT — BIBLIOG/A ADMIN

METH/COMP 20. PAGE 42 B0846 — NAT/G LOC/G

B63
HONORD S.,PUBLIC RELATIONS IN ADMINISTRATION. WOR+45 NAT/G...SOC/WK BIBLIOG 20. PAGE 51 B1039 — PRESS DIPLOM MGT METH/COMP

B63
INTL INST ADMIN SCIENCES,EDUCATION IN PUBLIC ADMINISTRATION: A SYMPOSIUM ON TEACHING METHODS AND MATERIALS. WOR+45 SCHOOL CONSULT CREATE CONFER SKILL...OBS TREND IDEA/COMP METH/COMP 20. PAGE 54 B1100 — EDU/PROP METH ADMIN ACADEM

B63
LEONARD T.J.,THE FEDERAL SYSTEM OF INDIA. INDIA MUNIC NAT/G PROVS ADMIN SOVEREIGN...IDEA/COMP 20. PAGE 64 B1293 — FEDERAL MGT NAT/COMP METH/COMP

B63
SHANKS M.,THE LESSONS OF PUBLIC ENTERPRISE. UK LEGIS WORKER ECO/TAC ADMIN PARL/PROC GOV/REL ATTIT ...POLICY MGT METH/COMP NAT/COMP ANTHOL 20 PARLIAMENT. PAGE 96 B1931 — SOCISM OWN NAT/G INDUS

B63
WADE H.W.R.,TOWARDS ADMINISTRATIVE JUSTICE. UK USA+45 CONSTN CONSULT PROB/SOLV CT/SYS PARL/PROC ...POLICY JURID METH/COMP 20 ENGLSH/LAW. PAGE 112 B2270 — ADJUD IDEA/COMP ADMIN

S63
REES A.,"THE EFFECTS OF UNIONS ON RESOURCE ALLOCATION." USA+45 WORKER PRICE CONTROL GP/REL ...MGT METH/COMP 20. PAGE 87 B1761 — LABOR BARGAIN RATION INCOME

N63
GREAT BRITAIN DEPT TECH COOP,PUBLIC ADMINISTRATION: A SELECT BIBLIOGRAPHY (PAMPHLET). WOR+45 AGRI FINAN INDUS EX/STRUC OP/RES ECO/TAC...MGT METH/COMP NAT/COMP. PAGE 43 B0861 — BIBLIOG/A ADMIN NAT/G LOC/G

N63
INTERNATIONAL CITY MGRS ASSN,POST-ENTRY TRAINING IN THE LOCAL PUBLIC SERVICE (PAMPHLET). SCHOOL PLAN PROB/SOLV TEC/DEV ADMIN EFFICIENCY SKILL...EDU/PROP AUD/VIS CHARTS BIBLIOG 20 CITY/MGT. PAGE 54 B1096 — LOC/G WORKER EDU/PROP METH/COMP

B64
HODGETTS J.E.,ADMINISTERING THE ATOM FOR PEACE. OP/RES TEC/DEV ADMIN...IDEA/COMP METH/COMP 20. PAGE 50 B1025 — PROB/SOLV NUC/PWR PEACE MGT

B64
KILPATRICKFP,SOURCE BOOK OF OCCUPATIONAL VALUES AND THE IMAGE OF THE FEDERAL SERVICE. USA+45 EX/STRUC ...POLICY MGT INT METH/COMP 20. PAGE 60 B1205 — NAT/G ATTIT ADMIN WORKER

B64
KILPATRICKFP,THE IMAGE OF THE FEDERAL SERVICE. USA+45 EX/STRUC...POLICY MGT INT METH/COMP 20. PAGE 60 B1206 — NAT/G ATTIT ADMIN WORKER

B64
MAYER C.S.,INTERVIEWING COSTS IN SURVEY RESEARCH. USA+45 PLAN COST...MGT REC/INT SAMP METH/COMP HYPO/EXP METH 20. PAGE 71 B1434 — SIMUL INT R+D EFFICIENCY

B64
OECD SEMINAR REGIONAL DEV,REGIONAL DEVELOPMENT IN ISRAEL. ISRAEL STRUCT ECO/UNDEV NAT/G REGION...GEOG 20. PAGE 79 B1603 — ADMIN PROVS PLAN METH/COMP

B64
REDLICH F.,THE GERMAN MILITARY ENTERPRISER AND HIS WORK FORCE. CHRIST-17C GERMANY ELITES SOCIETY FINAN ECO/TAC CIVMIL/REL GP/REL INGP/REL...HIST/WRIT METH/COMP 14/17. PAGE 87 B1760 — EX/STRUC FORCES PROFIT WORKER

B64
STANLEY D.T.,THE HIGHER CIVIL SERVICE: AN EVALUATION OF FEDERAL PERSONNEL PRACTICES. USA+45 CREATE EXEC ROUTINE CENTRAL...MGT SAMP IDEA/COMP METH/COMP 20 CIVIL/SERV. PAGE 100 B2020 — NAT/G ADMIN CONTROL EFFICIENCY

B64
SZLADITS C.,BIBLIOGRAPHY ON FOREIGN AND COMPARATIVE LAW: BOOKS AND ARTICLES IN ENGLISH (SUPPLEMENT 1962). FINAN INDUS JUDGE LICENSE ADMIN CT/SYS PARL/PROC OWN...INT/LAW CLASSIF METH/COMP NAT/COMP 20. PAGE 102 B2065 — BIBLIOG/A JURID ADJUD LAW

B64
THE BRITISH COUNCIL,PUBLIC ADMINISTRATION: A SELECT LIST OF BOOKS AND PERIODICALS. LAW CONSTN FINAN POL/PAR SCHOOL CHOOSE...HEAL MGT METH/COMP 19/20 CMN/WLTH. PAGE 104 B2094 — BIBLIOG ADMIN LOC/G INDUS

B64
TULLY A.,WHERE DID YOUR MONEY GO. USA+45 USSR ECO/UNDEV ADMIN EFFICIENCY WEALTH...METH/COMP 20. PAGE 106 B2136 — FOR/AID DIPLOM CONTROL

B64
WELLISZ S.,THE ECONOMICS OF THE SOVIET BLOC. COM USSR INDUS WORKER PLAN BUDGET INT/TRADE TAX PRICE — EFFICIENCY ADMIN

PRODUC WEALTH MARXISM...METH/COMP 20. PAGE 115 MARKET
B2319
                                                    S64
LIPSET S.M.."SOCIOLOGY AND POLITICAL SCIENCE: A   BIBLIOG/A
BIBLIOGRAPHICAL NOTE." WOR+45 ELITES LEGIS ADJUD   SOC
ADMIN ATTIT IDEA/COMP. PAGE 65 B1321   METH/COMP
                                                    S64
NEWLYN W.T.."MONETARY SYSTEMS AND INTEGRATION" AFR ECO/UNDEV
BUDGET ADMIN FEDERAL PRODUC PROFIT UTIL...CHARTS 20 REGION
AFRICA/E. PAGE 78 B1578   METH/COMP
                                                    FINAN
                                                    S64
STONE P.A.."DECISION TECHNIQUES FOR TOWN   OP/RES
DEVELOPMENT." PLAN COST PROFIT...DECISION MGT   MUNIC
CON/ANAL CHARTS METH/COMP BIBLIOG 20. PAGE 101   ADMIN
B2048   PROB/SOLV
                                                    B65
BANFIELD E.C.,BIG CITY POLITICS. USA+45 CONSTN   METH/COMP
POL/PAR ADMIN LOBBY CHOOSE SUFF INGP/REL PWR...GEOG MUNIC
20. PAGE 9 B0179   STRUCT
                                                    B65
CAVERS D.F.,THE CHOICE-OF-LAW PROCESS. PROB/SOLV   JURID
ADJUD CT/SYS CHOOSE RATIONAL...IDEA/COMP 16/20   DECISION
TREATY. PAGE 19 B0396   METH/COMP
                                                    ADMIN
                                                    B65
CRAMER J.F.,CONTEMPORARY EDUCATION: A COMPARATIVE   EDU/PROP
STUDY OF NATIONAL SYSTEMS (2ND ED.). CHINA/COM   NAT/COMP
EUR+WWI INDIA USA+45 FINAN PROB/SOLV ADMIN CONTROL SCHOOL
ATTIT...IDEA/COMP METH/COMP 20 CHINJAP. PAGE 25   ACADEM
B0502
                                                    B65
DYER F.C.,BUREAUCRACY VS CREATIVITY. UNIV CONTROL   ADMIN
LEAD INGP/REL EFFICIENCY MGT. PAGE 31 B0639   DECISION
                                                    METH/COMP
                                                    CREATE
                                                    B65
GOLEMBIEWSKI R.T.,MEN, MANAGEMENT, AND MORALITY;   LG/CO
TOWARD A NEW ORGANIZATIONAL ETHIC. CONSTN EX/STRUC MGT
CREATE ADMIN CONTROL INGP/REL PERSON SUPEGO MORAL   PROB/SOLV
PWR...GOV/COMP METH/COMP 20 BUREAUCRCY. PAGE 40
B0819
                                                    B65
HAINES R.M.,THE ADMINISTRATION OF THE DIOCESE OF   ADMIN
WORCESTER IN THE FIRST HALF OF THE FOURTEENTH   EX/STRUC
CENTURY. UK CATHISM...METH/COMP 13/15. PAGE 45   SECT
B0918   DELIB/GP
                                                    B65
HUGHES J.M.,EDUCATION IN AMERICA (2ND ED.). USA+45 EDU/PROP
USA-45 GP/REL INGP/REL AGE/C AGE/Y ROLE...IDEA/COMP SCHOOL
BIBLIOG T 20. PAGE 52 B1059   ADMIN
                                                    METH/COMP
                                                    B65
ROWAT D.C.,THE OMBUDSMAN: CITIZEN'S DEFENDER.   INSPECT
DENMARK FINLAND NEW/ZEALND NORWAY SWEDEN CONSULT   CONSTN
PROB/SOLV FEEDBACK PARTIC GP/REL...SOC CONCPT   NAT/G
NEW/IDEA METH/COMP ANTHOL BIBLIOG 20. PAGE 91 B1840 ADMIN
                                                    B65
STEINER G.A.,THE CREATIVE ORGANIZATION. ELITES   CREATE
LG/CO PLAN PROB/SOLV TEC/DEV INSPECT CAP/ISM   MGT
CONTROL EXEC PERSON...METH/COMP HYPO/EXP 20.   ADMIN
PAGE 100 B2029   SOC
                                                    S65
ALEXANDER T.."SYNECTICS: INVENTING BY THE MADNESS   PROB/SOLV
METHOD." DELIB/GP TOP/EX ACT/RES TEC/DEV EXEC TASK OP/RES
KNOWL...MGT METH/COMP 20. PAGE 4 B0073   CREATE
                                                    CONSULT
                                                    S65
RAPHAELI N.."SELECTED ARTICLES AND DOCUMENTS ON   BIBLIOG
COMPARATIVE PUBLIC ADMINISTRATION." USA+45 FINAN   ADMIN
LOC/G WORKER TEC/DEV CONTROL LEAD...SOC/WK GOV/COMP NAT/G
METH/COMP. PAGE 86 B1739   MGT
                                                    B66
ANDREWS K.R.,THE EFFECTIVENESS OF UNIVERSITY   ECO/DEV
MANAGEMENT DEVELOPMENT PROGRAMS. FUT USA+45 ECO/TAC ACADEM
ADMIN...MGT QU METH/COMP 20. PAGE 5 B0103   TOP/EX
                                                    ATTIT
                                                    B66
FABAR R.,THE VISION AND THE NEED: LATE VICTORIAN   COLONIAL
IMPERIALIST AIMS. MOD/EUR UK WOR-45 CULTURE NAT/G   CONCPT
DIPLOM...TIME/SEQ METH/COMP 19 KIPLING/R   ADMIN
COMMONWLTH. PAGE 34 B0693   ATTIT
                                                    B66
HALPIN A.W.,THEORY AND RESEARCH IN ADMINISTRATION. GEN/LAWS
ACT/RES LEAD...MGT IDEA/COMP METH/COMP. PAGE 46   EDU/PROP
B0929   ADMIN
                                                    PHIL/SCI
                                                    B66
MONTGOMERY J.D.,APPROACHES TO DEVELOPMENT: ECO/UNDEV
POLITICS, ADMINISTRATION AND CHANGE. USA+45 AGRI   ADMIN
FOR/AID ORD/FREE...CONCPT IDEA/COMP METH/COMP   POLICY
ANTHOL. PAGE 75 B1507   ECO/TAC
                                                    B66
OWEN G.,INDUSTRY IN THE UNITED STATES. UK USA+45   METH/COMP
NAT/G WEALTH...DECISION NAT/COMP 20. PAGE 80 B1620 INDUS
                                                    MGT

                                                    PROB/SOLV
                                                    B66
SILBERMAN B.S.,MODERN JAPANESE LEADERSHIP;   LEAD
TRANSITION AND CHANGE. NAT/G POL/PAR CHIEF ADMIN   CULTURE
REPRESENT GP/REL ADJUST RIGID/FLEX...SOC METH/COMP ELITES
ANTHOL 19/20 CHINJAP CHRISTIAN. PAGE 97 B1952   MUNIC
                                                    B66
WARREN R.O.,GOVERNMENT IN METROPOLITAN REGIONS: A   LOC/G
REAPPRAISAL OF FRACTIONATED POLITICAL ORGANIZATION. MUNIC
USA+45 ACT/RES PROB/SOLV REGION...CHARTS METH/COMP EX/STRUC
BIBLIOG CITY/MGT. PAGE 114 B2296   PLAN
                                                    S66
HANSON A.H.,"PLANNING AND THE POLITICIANS* SOME   PLAN
REFLECTIONS ON ECONOMIC PLANNING IN WESTERN   ECO/DEV
EUROPE." MARKET NAT/G TEC/DEV CONSEN ROLE   EUR+WWI
...METH/COMP NAT/COMP. PAGE 46 B0942   ADMIN
                                                    B67
BROWN L.N.,FRENCH ADMINISTRATIVE LAW. FRANCE UK   EX/STRUC
CONSTN NAT/G LEGIS DOMIN CONTROL EXEC PARL/PROC PWR LAW
...JURID METH/COMP GEN/METH. PAGE 16 B0324   IDEA/COMP
                                                    CT/SYS
                                                    B67
GIFFORD P.,BRITAIN AND GERMANY IN AFRICA. AFR   COLONIAL
GERMANY UK ECO/UNDEV LEAD WAR NAT/LISM ATTIT   ADMIN
...POLICY HIST/WRIT METH/COMP ANTHOL BIBLIOG 19/20 DIPLOM
WWI. PAGE 39 B0797   NAT/COMP
                                                    B67
GROSSMAN G.,ECONOMIC SYSTEMS. USA+45 USA-45 USSR   ECO/DEV
YUGOSLAVIA WORKER CAP/ISM PRICE GP/REL EQUILIB   PLAN
WEALTH MARXISM SOCISM...MGT METH/COMP 19/20.   TEC/DEV
PAGE 44 B0892   DEMAND
                                                    B67
HIRSCHMAN A.O.,DEVELOPMENT PROJECTS OBSERVED. INDUS ECO/UNDEV
INT/ORG CONSULT EX/STRUC CREATE OP/RES ECO/TAC   R+D
DEMAND...POLICY MGT METH/COMP 20 WORLD/BANK.   FINAN
PAGE 50 B1016   PLAN
                                                    B67
MARRIS P.,DILEMMAS OF SOCIAL REFORM: POVERTY AND   STRUCT
COMMUNITY ACTION IN THE UNITED STATES. USA+45 NAT/G MUNIC
OP/RES ADMIN PARTIC EFFICIENCY WEALTH...SOC   PROB/SOLV
METH/COMP T 20 REFORMERS. PAGE 69 B1401   COST
                                                    B67
TANSKY L.,US AND USSR AID TO DEVELOPING COUNTRIES. FOR/AID
INDIA TURKEY UAR USA+45 USSR FINAN PLAN TEC/DEV   ECO/UNDEV
ADMIN WEALTH...TREND METH/COMP 20. PAGE 103 B2076   MARXISM
                                                    CAP/ISM
                                                    B67
WATERS M.,THE UNITED NATIONS* INTERNATIONAL   CONSTN
ORGANIZATION AND ADMINISTRATION. WOR+45 EX/STRUC   INT/ORG
FORCES DIPLOM LEAD REGION ARMS/CONT REPRESENT   ADMIN
INGP/REL ROLE...METH/COMP ANTHOL 20 UN LEAGUE/NAT. ADJUD
PAGE 114 B2301
                                                    S67
BURKE E.M.."THE SEARCH FOR AUTHORITY IN PLANNING." DECISION
MUNIC NEIGH CREATE PROB/SOLV LEGIT ADMIN CONTROL   PLAN
EFFICIENCY PWR...METH/COMP SIMUL 20. PAGE 17 B0352 LOC/G
                                                    METH
                                                    S67
DOERN G.B.."THE ROYAL COMMISSIONS IN THE GENERAL   R+D
POLICY PROCESS AND IN FEDERAL-PROVINCIAL   EX/STRUC
RELATIONS." CANADA CONSTN ACADEM PROVS CONSULT   GOV/REL
DELIB/GP LEGIS ACT/RES PROB/SOLV CONFER CONTROL   NAT/G
EFFICIENCY...METH/COMP 20 SENATE ROYAL/COMM.
PAGE 30 B0603
                                                    S67
DROR Y.."POLICY ANALYSTS." USA+45 COMPUTER OP/RES   NAT/G
ECO/TAC ADMIN ROUTINE...ECOMETRIC METH/COMP SIMUL   POLICY
20. PAGE 30 B0618   PLAN
                                                    DECISION
                                                    S67
GORHAM W.."NOTES OF A PRACTITIONER." USA+45 BUDGET DECISION
ADMIN COST...CON/ANAL METH/COMP 20 JOHNSON/LB.   NAT/G
PAGE 41 B0836   DELIB/GP
                                                    EFFICIENCY
                                                    S67
GRINYER P.H.."THE SYSTEMATIC EVALUATION OF METHODS OP/RES
OF WAGE PAYMENT." UK INDUS WORKER ADMIN EFFICIENCY COST
...MGT METH/COMP 20. PAGE 44 B0882   PAY
                                                    PRODUC
                                                    S67
LERNER A.P.."EMPLOYMENT THEORY AND EMPLOYMENT   CAP/ISM
POLICY." ECO/DEV INDUS LABOR LG/CO BUDGET ADMIN   WORKER
DEMAND PROFIT WEALTH LAISSEZ METH/COMP. PAGE 64   CONCPT
B1296
                                                    S67
RAUM O.."THE MODERN LEADERSHIP GROUP AMONG THE   RACE/REL
SOUTH AFRICAN XHOSA." SOUTH/AFR SOCIETY SECT   KIN
EX/STRUC REPRESENT GP/REL INGP/REL PERSON   LEAD
...METH/COMP 17/20 XHOSA NEGRO. PAGE 86 B1743   CULTURE
                                                    S67
ROSENZWEIG J.E.."MANAGERS AND MANAGEMENT SCIENTISTS EFFICIENCY
(TWO CULTURES)" INDUS CREATE TEC/DEV OPTIMAL   MGT
...NEW/IDEA 20. PAGE 90 B1823   INTELL
                                                    METH/COMP
                                                    S67
ZOETEWEIJ B.."INCOME POLICIES ABROAD: AN INTERIM   METH/COMP

REPORT." NAT/G PROB/SOLV BARGAIN BUDGET PRICE RISK **INCOME**
CENTRAL EFFICIENCY EQUILIB...MGT NAT/COMP 20. **POLICY**
PAGE 119 B2405 **LABOR**

METHOD, COMPARATIVE....SEE IDEA/COMP, METH/COMP

METHODOLOGY....SEE METH, PHIL/SCI, METHODOLOGICAL INDEXES,
PP. XIII-XIV

METRO/COUN....METROPOLITAN COUNCIL

METROPOLITAN....SEE MUNIC

METROPOLITAN COUNCIL....SEE METRO/COUN

METTRNCH/K....PRINCE K. VON METTERNICH

MEXIC/AMER....MEXICAN-AMERICANS; SEE ALSO SPAN/AMER

B43
CARLO A.M.,ENSAYO DE UNA BIBLIOGRAFIA DE **BIBLIOG**
BIBLIOGRAFIAS MEXICANAS. ECO/UNDEV LOC/G ADMIN LEAD **L/A+17C**
20 MEXIC/AMER. PAGE 19 B0381 **NAT/G**
DIPLOM

B54
MOSK S.A.,INDUSTRIAL REVOLUTION IN MEXICO. MARKET **INDUS**
LABOR CREATE CAP/ISM ADMIN ATTIT SOCISM...POLICY 20 **TEC/DEV**
MEXIC/AMER. PAGE 76 B1533 **ECO/UNDEV**
NAT/G

B59
FAYERWEATHER J.,THE EXECUTIVE OVERSEAS: **INT/TRADE**
ADMINISTRATIVE ATTITUDES AND RELATIONSHIPS IN A **TOP/EX**
FOREIGN CULTURE. USA+45 WOR+45 CULTURE LG/CO SML/CO **NAT/COMP**
ATTIT...MGT PERS/COMP 20 MEXIC/AMER. PAGE 35 B0709 **PERS/REL**

S61
NEEDLER M.C.,"THE POLITICAL DEVELOPMENT OF MEXICO." **L/A+17C**
STRUCT NAT/G ADMIN RIGID/FLEX...TIME/SEQ TREND **POL/PAR**
MEXIC/AMER TOT/POP VAL/FREE 19/20. PAGE 77 B1566

C64
SCOTT R.E.,"MEXICAN GOVERNMENT IN TRANSITION (REV **NAT/G**
ED)" CULTURE STRUCT POL/PAR CHIEF ADMIN LOBBY REV **L/A+17C**
CHOOSE GP/REL DRIVE...BIBLIOG METH 20 MEXIC/AMER. **ROUTINE**
PAGE 95 B1920 **CONSTN**

S67
FABREGA J.,"ANTECEDENTES EXTRANJEROS EN LA **CONSTN**
CONSTITUCION PANAMENA." CUBA L/A+17C PANAMA URUGUAY **JURID**
EX/STRUC LEGIS DIPLOM ORD/FREE 19/20 COLOMB **NAT/G**
MEXIC/AMER. PAGE 34 B0694 **PARL/PROC**

MEXICO....SEE ALSO L/A+17C

MEYER H.H.B. B1473

MEYER P. B1474,B1475

MEYERHOFF A.E. B1476

MEYNAUD J. B1477

MEYRIAT J. B0634,B1478

MGT....MANAGEMENT

MGT/OBJECT....MANAGEMENT BY OBJECTIVES

MIAMI

B65
GREER S.,URBAN RENEWAL AND AMERICAN CITIES: THE **MUNIC**
DILEMMA OF DEMOCRATIC INTERVENTION. USA+45 R+D **PROB/SOLV**
LOC/G VOL/ASSN ACT/RES BUDGET ADMIN GOV/REL...SOC **PLAN**
INT SAMP 20 BOSTON CHICAGO MIAMI URBAN/RNWL. **NAT/G**
PAGE 43 B0871

MICH/STA/U....MICHIGAN STATE UNIVERSITY

MICH/U....UNIVERSITY OF MICHIGAN

MICHELS/R

S43
SELZNICK P.,"AN APPROACH TO A THEORY OF **ROUTINE**
BUREAUCRACY." INDUS WORKER CONTROL LEAD EFFICIENCY **ADMIN**
OPTIMAL...SOC METH 20 BARNARD/C BUREAUCRCY **MGT**
WEBER/MAX FRIEDRCH/C MICHELS/R. PAGE 95 B1928 **EX/STRUC**

MICHIGAN STATE UNIVERSITY....SEE MICH/STA/U

MICHIGAN....MICHIGAN

S56
HEADY F.,"THE MICHIGAN DEPARTMENT OF **ADMIN**
ADMINISTRATION; A CASE STUDY IN THE POLITICS OF **DELIB/GP**
ADMINISTRATION" (BMR)" USA+45 POL/PAR PROVS CHIEF **LOC/G**
LEGIS GP/REL ATTIT 20 MICHIGAN. PAGE 48 B0980

B65
FISCHER F.C.,THE GOVERNMENT OF MICHIGAN. USA+45 **PROVS**
NAT/G PUB/INST EX/STRUC LEGIS BUDGET GIVE EDU/PROP **LOC/G**
CT/SYS CHOOSE GOV/REL...T MICHIGAN. PAGE 36 B0723 **ADMIN**
CONSTN

S67
BERRODIN E.F.,"AT THE BARGAINING TABLE." LABOR **PROVS**
DIPLOM ECO/TAC ADMIN...MGT 20 MICHIGAN. PAGE 11 **WORKER**
B0230 **LAW**
BARGAIN

MICRONESIA....MICRONESIA

MID/EAST....MIDDLE EAST

S67
TATU M.,"URSS: LES FLOTTEMENTS DE LA DIRECTION **POLICY**
COLLEGIALE." UAR USSR CHIEF LEAD INGP/REL **NAT/G**
EFFICIENCY...DECISION TREND 20 MID/EAST. PAGE 103 **EX/STRUC**
B2082 **DIPLOM**

MIDDLETON J. B0447

MIDDLETOWN....MIDDLETOWN: LOCATION OF LYND STUDY

MIDWEST/US....MIDWESTERN UNITED STATES

MIGRATION....MIGRATION; IMMIGRATION AND EMIGRATION; SEE
ALSO HABITAT, GEOG

B48
DAY P.,CRISIS IN SOUTH AFRICA. SOUTH/AFR UK KIN **RACE/REL**
MUNIC ECO/TAC RECEIVE 20 SMUTS/JAN MIGRATION. **COLONIAL**
PAGE 27 B0548 **ADMIN**
EXTR/IND

B59
LEMBERG E.,DIE VERTRIEBENEN IN WESTDEUTSCHLAND (3 **GP/REL**
VOLS.). GERMANY/W CULTURE STRUCT AGRI PROVS ADMIN **INGP/REL**
...JURID 20 MIGRATION. PAGE 64 B1287 **SOCIETY**

B61
KEE R.,REFUGEE WORLD. AUSTRIA EUR+WWI GERMANY NEIGH **NAT/G**
EX/STRUC WORKER PROB/SOLV ECO/TAC RENT EDU/PROP **GIVE**
INGP/REL COST LITERACY HABITAT 20 MIGRATION. **WEALTH**
PAGE 59 B1186 **STRANGE**

B63
BADI J.,THE GOVERNMENT OF THE STATE OF ISRAEL: A **NAT/G**
CRITICAL ACCOUNT OF ITS PARLIAMENT, EXECUTIVE, AND **CONSTN**
JUDICIARY. ISRAEL ECO/DEV CHIEF DELIB/GP LEGIS **EX/STRUC**
DIPLOM CT/SYS INGP/REL PEACE ORD/FREE...BIBLIOG 20 **POL/PAR**
PARLIAMENT ARABS MIGRATION. PAGE 8 B0157

MIL/ACAD....MILITARY ACADEMY

MILITARY....SEE FORCES

MILITARY APPLICATIONS OF URANIUM DETONATION....SEE MAUD

MILL/JAMES....JAMES MILL

MILL/JS....JOHN STUART MILL

MILLARD E.L. B1479

MILLER E. B1480

MILLER M. B1481

MILLER R.W. B1583

MILLETT J.D. B1367,B1482,B1483

MILLIKAN M.F. B1484

MILLIS H.A. B1485

MILLIS W. B1486

MILLS C.W. B1487

MILLS D.L. B2091

MILLS/CW....C. WRIGHT MILLS

MILLSAP K.F. B1827

MILNE R.S. B1488,B1489

MILNER/A....ALFRED MILNER

MILTON/J....MILTON, JOHN

MINING....SEE EXTR/IND

MINISTERE DE L'EDUC NATIONALE B1490

MINNESOTA....MINNESOTA

B50
LITTLE HOOVER COMM.,HOW TO ACHIEVE GREATER
EFFICIENCY AND ECONOMY IN MINNESOTA'S GOVERNMENT
(PAMPHLET). PLAN BUDGET ADMIN CHOOSE EFFICIENCY
ALL/VALS 20 MINNESOTA. PAGE 66 B1327
TOP/EX
LOC/G
GOV/REL
PROVS

MINORITY....SEE RACE/REL

MINTZ M. B1491

MISCEGEN....MISCEGENATION

MISSION....MISSIONARIES

B50
WELCH S.R.,PORTUGUESE RULE AND SPANISH CROWN IN
SOUTH AFRICA 1581-1640. PORTUGAL SOUTH/AFR SPAIN
SOCIETY KIN NEIGH SECT INT/TRADE ADMIN 16/17
MISSION. PAGE 115 B2317
DIPLOM
COLONIAL
WAR
PEACE

B63
GALBRAITH J.S.,RELUCTANT EMPIRE: BRITISH POLICY OF
THE SOUTH AFRICAN FRONTIER, 1834-1854. AFR
SOUTH/AFR UK GP/REL RACE/REL DISCRIM...CHARTS
BIBLIOG 19 MISSION. PAGE 38 B0774
COLONIAL
ADMIN
POLICY
SECT

B82
MACDONALD D.,AFRICANA; OR, THE HEART OF HEATHEN
AFRICA, VOL. II: MISSION LIFE. SOCIETY STRATA KIN
CREATE EDU/PROP ADMIN COERCE LITERACY HEALTH...MYTH
WORSHIP 19 LIVNGSTN/D MISSION NEGRO. PAGE 67 B1355
SECT
AFR
CULTURE
ORD/FREE

MISSISSIPP....MISSISSIPPI

MISSOURI RIVER BASIN PLAN....SEE MO/BASIN

MISSOURI....MISSOURI

S58
DERGE D.R.,"METROPOLITAN AND OUTSTATE ALIGNMENTS IN
ILLINOIS AND MISSOURI LEGISLATIVE DELEGATIONS"
(BMR)" USA+45 ADMIN PARTIC GOV/REL...MYTH CHARTS 20
ILLINOIS MISSOURI. PAGE 28 B0575
LEGIS
MUNIC
PROVS
POL/PAR

S59
DWYER R.J.,"THE ADMINISTRATIVE ROLE IN
DESEGREGATION." USA+45 LAW PROB/SOLV LEAD RACE/REL
ISOLAT STRANGE ROLE...POLICY SOC/INTEG MISSOURI
NEGRO CIV/RIGHTS. PAGE 31 B0638
ADMIN
SCHOOL
DISCRIM
ATTIT

B65
PARRISH W.E.,MISSOURI UNDER RADICAL RULE 1865-1870.
USA+45 SOCIETY INDUS LOC/G POL/PAR WORKER EDU/PROP
SUFF INGP/REL ATTIT...BIBLIOG 19 NEGRO MISSOURI.
PAGE 81 B1635
PROVS
ADMIN
RACE/REL
ORD/FREE

MITCHELL W.C. B1492

MNR....MOVIMIENTO NACIONALISTA REVOLUCIONARIO (BOLIVIA)

MO/BASIN....MISSOURI RIVER BASIN PLAN

MOB....SEE CROWD

MOBUTU/J....JOSEPH MOBUTU

MOCHE....MOCHE, PERU

MOD/EUR....MODERN EUROPE (1700-1918); SEE ALSO APPROPRIATE
NATIONS

B03
GRIFFIN A.P.C.,LIST OF BOOKS ON THE CABINETS OF
ENGLAND AND AMERICA (PAMPHLET). MOD/EUR UK USA+45
CONSTN NAT/G CONSULT EX/STRUC 19/20. PAGE 43 B0875
BIBLIOG/A
GOV/COMP
ADMIN
DELIB/GP

B20
HALDANE R.B.,BEFORE THE WAR. MOD/EUR SOCIETY
INT/ORG NAT/G DELIB/GP PLAN DOMIN EDU/PROP LEGIT
ADMIN COERCE ATTIT DRIVE MORAL ORD/FREE PWR...SOC
CONCPT SELF/OBS RECORD BIOG TIME/SEQ. PAGE 45 B0921
POLICY
DIPLOM
UK

B26
MOON P.T.,IMPERIALISM AND WORLD POLITICS. AFR ASIA
ISLAM MOD/EUR S/ASIA USA+45 SOCIETY NAT/G EX/STRUC
BAL/PWR DOMIN COLONIAL NAT/LISM ATTIT DRIVE PWR
...GEOG SOC 20. PAGE 75 B1510
WEALTH
TIME/SEQ
CAP/ISM
DIPLOM

B28
SOROKIN P.,CONTEMPORARY SOCIOLOGICAL THEORIES.
MOD/EUR UNIV SOCIETY R+D SCHOOL ECO/TAC EDU/PROP
ROUTINE ATTIT DRIVE...PSY CONCPT TIME/SEQ TREND
GEN/LAWS 20. PAGE 99 B1997
CULTURE
SOC
WAR

B38
DAY C.,A HISTORY OF COMMERCE. CHRIST-17C EUR+WWI
ISLAM MEDIT-7 MOD/EUR USA+45 ECO/DEV FINAN NAT/G
ECO/TAC EXEC ROUTINE PWR WEALTH HIST/WRIT. PAGE 27
B0546
MARKET
INT/TRADE

B38
PETTEE G.S.,THE PROCESS OF REVOLUTION. COM FRANCE
ITALY MOD/EUR RUSSIA SPAIN WOR-45 ELITES INTELL
SOCIETY STRATA STRUC INT/ORG NAT/G POL/PAR ACT/RES
COERCE
CONCPT
REV

PLAN EDU/PROP LEGIT EXEC...SOC MYTH TIME/SEQ
TOT/POP 18/20. PAGE 82 B1664

B39
HITLER A.,MEIN KAMPF. EUR+WWI FUT MOD/EUR STRUCT
INT/ORG LABOR NAT/G POL/PAR FORCES CREATE PLAN
BAL/PWR DIPLOM ECO/TAC DOMIN EDU/PROP ADMIN COERCE
ATTIT...SOCIALIST BIOG TREND NAZI. PAGE 50 B1020
PWR
NEW/IDEA
WAR

B41
YOUNG G.,FEDERALISM AND FREEDOM. EUR+WWI MOD/EUR
RUSSIA USA-45 WOR-45 SOCIETY STRUCT ECO/DEV INT/ORG
EXEC FEDERAL ATTIT PERSON ALL/VALS...OLD/LIB CONCPT
OBS TREND LEAGUE/NAT TOT/POP. PAGE 119 B2392
NAT/G
WAR

B42
SINGTON D.,THE GOEBBELS EXPERIMENT. GERMANY MOD/EUR
NAT/G EX/STRUC FORCES CONTROL ROUTINE WAR TOTALISM
PWR...ART/METH HUM 20 NAZI GOEBBELS/J. PAGE 97
B1970
FASCISM
EDU/PROP
ATTIT
COM/IND

S44
GRIFFITH E.S.,"THE CHANGING PATTERN OF PUBLIC
POLICY FORMATION." MOD/EUR WOR+45 FINAN CHIEF
CONFER ADMIN LEAD CONSERVE SOCISM TECHRACY...SOC
CHARTS CONGRESS. PAGE 43 B0877
LAW
POLICY
TEC/DEV

B46
CLOUGH S.B.,ECONOMIC HISTORY OF EUROPE. CHRIST-17C
EUR+WWI MOD/EUR WOR-45 SOCIETY EXEC ATTIT WEALTH
...CONCPT GEN/LAWS WORK TOT/POP VAL/FREE 7/20.
PAGE 22 B0440
ECO/TAC
CAP/ISM

B46
GRIFFIN G.G.,A GUIDE TO MANUSCRIPTS RELATING TO
AMERICAN HISTORY IN BRITISH DEPOSITORIES. CANADA
IRELAND MOD/EUR UK USA-45 LAW DIPLOM ADMIN COLONIAL
WAR NAT/LISM SOVEREIGN...GEOG INT/LAW 15/19
CMN/WLTH. PAGE 43 B0876
BIBLIOG/A
ALL/VALS
NAT/G

B49
DENNING A.,FREEDOM UNDER THE LAW. MOD/EUR UK LAW
SOCIETY CHIEF EX/STRUC LEGIS ADJUD CT/SYS PERS/REL
PERSON 17/20 ENGLSH/LAW. PAGE 28 B0573
ORD/FREE
JURID
NAT/G

B52
HIMMELFARB G.,LORD ACTON: A STUDY IN CONSCIENCE AND
POLITICS. MOD/EUR NAT/G POL/PAR SECT LEGIS TOP/EX
EDU/PROP ADMIN NAT/LISM ATTIT PERSON SUPEGO MORAL
ORD/FREE...CONCPT PARLIAMENT 19 ACTON/LORD. PAGE 50
B1014
PWR
BIOG

C53
DORWART R.A.,"THE ADMINISTRATIVE REFORMS OF
FREDRICK WILLIAM I OF PRUSSIA. GERMANY MOD/EUR
CHIEF CONTROL PWR...BIBLIOG 16/18. PAGE 30 B0608
ADMIN
NAT/G
CENTRAL
GOV/REL

B54
DUVERGER M.,POLITICAL PARTIES: THEIR ORGANIZATION
AND ACTIVITY IN THE MODERN STATE. EUR+WWI MOD/EUR
USA+45 EDU/PROP ADMIN ROUTINE ATTIT DRIVE
ORD/FREE PWR...SOC CONCPT MATH STAT TIME/SEQ
TOT/POP 19/20. PAGE 31 B0635
POL/PAR
EX/STRUC
ELITES

B54
MANGONE G.,A SHORT HISTORY OF INTERNATIONAL
ORGANIZATION. MOD/EUR USA+45 USA-45 WOR+45 WOR-45
LAW LEGIS CREATE LEGIT ROUTINE RIGID/FLEX PWR
...JURID CONCPT OBS TIME/SEQ STERTYP GEN/LAWS UN
TOT/POP VAL/FREE 18/20. PAGE 69 B1389
INT/ORG
INT/LAW

B55
GULICK C.A.,HISTORY AND THEORIES OF WORKING-CLASS
MOVEMENTS: A SELECT BIBLIOGRAPHY. EUR+WWI MOD/EUR
UK USA+45 INT/ORG. PAGE 44 B0902
BIBLIOG
WORKER
LABOR
ADMIN

B55
MAZZINI J.,THE DUTIES OF MAN. MOD/EUR LAW SOCIETY
FAM NAT/G POL/PAR SECT VOL/ASSN EX/STRUC ACT/RES
CREATE REV PEACE ATTIT ALL/VALS...GEN/LAWS WORK 19.
PAGE 71 B1439
SUPEGO
CONCPT
NAT/LISM

B57
MORSTEIN-MARX F.,THE ADMINISTRATIVE STATE: AN
INTRODUCTION TO BUREAUCRACY. EUR+WWI FUT MOD/EUR
USA+45 USA-45 NAT/G CONSULT ADMIN ROUTINE TOTALISM
DRIVE SKILL...TREND 19/20. PAGE 76 B1530
EXEC
MGT
CAP/ISM
ELITES

B58
TAYLOR H.,THE STATESMAN. MOD/EUR FACE/GP FAM NAT/G
POL/PAR DELIB/GP LEGIS ATTIT PERSON PWR...POLICY
CONCPT OBS GEN/LAWS. PAGE 103 B2086
EXEC
STRUCT

B59
CHAPMAN B.,THE PROFESSION OF GOVERNMENT: THE PUBLIC
SERVICE IN EUROPE. MOD/EUR LABOR CT/SYS...T 20
CIVIL/SERV. PAGE 20 B0409
ADMIN
CONTROL
ROUTINE
EX/STRUC

B60
LIPSET S.M.,POLITICAL MAN. AFR COM EUR+WWI L/A+17C
MOD/EUR S/ASIA USA+45 USA-45 STRUCT ECO/DEV
ECO/UNDEV POL/PAR SECT ADMIN WEALTH...CONCPT WORK
TOT/POP 20. PAGE 65 B1320
PWR
SOC

B61
BISHOP D.G.,THE ADMINISTRATION OF BRITISH FOREIGN
RELATIONS. EUR+WWI MOD/EUR INT/ORG NAT/G POL/PAR
DELIB/GP LEGIS TOP/EX ECO/TAC DOMIN EDU/PROP ADMIN
COERCE 20. PAGE 12 B0243
ROUTINE
PWR
DIPLOM
UK

B61
MARX K.,THE COMMUNIST MANIFESTO. IN (MENDEL A.
COM

ESSENTIAL WORKS OF MARXISM, NEW YORK: BANTAM. FUT   NEW/IDEA
MOD/EUR CULTURE ECO/DEV ECO/UNDEV AGRI FINAN INDUS   CAP/ISM
MARKET PROC/MFG LABOR MUNIC POL/PAR CONSULT FORCES   REV
CREATE PLAN ADMIN ATTIT DRIVE RIGID/FLEX ORD/FREE
PWR RESPECT MARX/KARL WORK. PAGE 70 B1421
                                                    B61
MONAS S.,THE THIRD SECTION: POLICE AND SOCIETY IN   ORD/FREE
RUSSIA UNDER NICHOLAS I. MOD/EUR RUSSIA ELITES   COM
STRUCT NAT/G EX/STRUC ADMIN CONTROL PWR CONSERVE   FORCES
...DECISION 19 NICHOLAS/I. PAGE 74 B1499   COERCE
                                                    B62
THIERRY S.S.,LE VATICAN SECRET. CHRIST-17C EUR+WWI   ADMIN
MOD/EUR VATICAN NAT/G SECT DELIB/GP DOMIN LEGIT   EX/STRUC
SOVEREIGN. PAGE 104 B2096   CATHISM
                                                    DECISION
                                                    B63
BOISSIER P.,HISTORIE DU COMITE INTERNATIONAL DE LA   INT/ORG
CROIX ROUGE. MOD/EUR WOR-45 CONSULT FORCES PLAN   HEALTH
DIPLOM EDU/PROP ADMIN MORAL ORD/FREE...SOC CONCPT   ARMS/CONT
RECORD TIME/SEQ GEN/LAWS TOT/POP VAL/FREE 19/20.   WAR
PAGE 13 B0267
                                                    B63
COM INTERNAT DES MOUVEMENTS,REPERTOIRE   BIBLIOG/A
INTERNATIONAL DES SOURCES POUR L'ETUDE DES   MARXISM
MOUVEMENTS SOCIAUX AUX XIXE ET XXE SIECLES (VOL.   POL/PAR
III). MOD/EUR ADMIN...SOC 19. PAGE 22 B0454   LABOR
                                                    B63
NORTH R.C.,CONTENT ANALYSIS: A HANDBOOK WITH   METH/CNCPT
APPLICATIONS FOR THE STUDY OF INTERNATIONAL CRISIS. COMPUT/IR
ASIA COM EUR+WWI MOD/EUR INT/ORG TEC/DEV DOMIN   USSR
EDU/PROP ROUTINE COERCE PERCEPT RIGID/FLEX ALL/VALS
...QUANT TESTS CON/ANAL SIMUL GEN/LAWS VAL/FREE.
PAGE 79 B1591
                                                    B63
OLSON M. JR.,THE ECONOMICS OF WARTIME SHORTAGE.   WAR
FRANCE GERMANY MOD/EUR UK AGRI PROB/SOLV ADMIN   ADJUST
DEMAND WEALTH...POLICY OLD/LIB 17/20. PAGE 80 B1608 ECO/TAC
                                                    NAT/COMP
                                                    B64
GUTTSMAN W.L.,THE BRITISH POLITICAL ELITE. EUR+WWI   NAT/G
MOD/EUR STRATA FAM LABOR POL/PAR SCHOOL VOL/ASSN   SOC
DELIB/GP LEGIS LEGIT EXEC CHOOSE ATTIT ALL/VALS   UK
...STAT BIOG TIME/SEQ CHARTS VAL/FREE. PAGE 45   ELITES
B0905
                                                    B64
PIPES R.,THE FORMATION OF THE SOVIET UNION. EUR+WWI COM
MOD/EUR STRUCT ECO/UNDEV NAT/G LEGIS DOMIN LEGIT   USSR
CT/SYS EXEC COERCE ALL/VALS...POLICY RELATIV   RUSSIA
HIST/WRIT TIME/SEQ TOT/POP 19/20. PAGE 83 B1677
                                                    S64
GROSS J.A.,"WHITEHALL AND THE COMMONWEALTH."   EX/STRUC
EUR+WWI MOD/EUR INT/ORG NAT/G CONSULT DELIB/GP   ATTIT
LEGIS DOMIN ADMIN COLONIAL ROUTINE PWR CMN/WLTH   TREND
19/20. PAGE 44 B0890
                                                    S64
LOW D.A.,"LION RAMPANT." EUR+WWI MOD/EUR S/ASIA   AFR
ECO/UNDEV NAT/G FORCES TEC/DEV ECO/TAC LEGIT ADMIN   DOMIN
COLONIAL COERCE ORD/FREE RESPECT 19/20. PAGE 67   DIPLOM
B1344   UK
                                                    B65
BOXER C.R.,PORTUGUESE SOCIETY IN THE TROPICS - THE   MUNIC
MUNICIPAL COUNCILS OF GAO, MACAO, BAHIA, AND   ADMIN
LUANDA, 1510-1800. EUR+WWI MOD/EUR PORTUGAL CONSTN   COLONIAL
EX/STRUC DOMIN CONTROL ROUTINE REPRESENT PRIVIL   DELIB/GP
...BIBLIOG/A 16/19 GENACCOUNT MACAO BAHIA LUANDA.
PAGE 14 B0290
                                                    B65
NORDEN A.,WAR AND NAZI CRIMINALS IN WEST GERMANY: FASCIST
STATE, ECONOMY, ADMINISTRATION, ARMY, JUSTICE,   WAR
SCIENCE. GERMANY GERMANY/W MOD/EUR ECO/DEV ACADEM   NAT/G
EX/STRUC FORCES DOMIN ADMIN CT/SYS...POLICY MAJORIT TOP/EX
PACIFIST 20. PAGE 78 B1587
                                                    S65
HOLSTI O.R.,"THE 1914 CASE." MOD/EUR COMPUTER   CON/ANAL
DIPLOM EDU/PROP EXEC...DECISION PSY PROBABIL STAT   PERCEPT
COMPUT/IR SOC/EXP TIME. PAGE 51 B1036   WAR
                                                    B66
FABAR R.,THE VISION AND THE NEED: LATE VICTORIAN   COLONIAL
IMPERIALIST AIMS. MOD/EUR UK WOR-45 CULTURE NAT/G   CONCPT
DIPLOM...TIME/SEQ METH/CMP 19 KIPLING/R   ADMIN
COMMONWLTH. PAGE 34 B0693   ATTIT
                                                    B66
MARTIN L.W.,DIPLOMACY IN MODERN EUROPEAN HISTORY.   DIPLOM
EUR+WWI MOD/EUR INT/ORG NAT/G EX/STRUC ROUTINE WAR   POLICY
PEACE TOTALISM PWR 15/20 COLD/WAR EUROPE/W. PAGE 70
B1411
                                                    B67
RALSTON D.B.,THE ARMY OF THE REPUBLIC; THE PLACE OF FORCES
THE MILITARY IN THE POLITICAL EVOLUTION OF FRANCE   NAT/G
1871-1914. FRANCE MOD/EUR EX/STRUC LEGIS TOP/EX   CIVMIL/REL
DIPLOM ADMIN WAR GP/REL ROLE...BIBLIOG 19/20.   POLICY
PAGE 86 B1730
                                                    S67
ANDERSON M.,"THE FRENCH PARLIAMENT." EUR+WWI FRANCE PARL/PROC
MOD/EUR CONSTN POL/PAR CHIEF LEGIS LOBBY ATTIT ROLE LEAD
PWR 19/20. PAGE 5 B0095   GOV/COMP

                                                    EX/STRUC
                                                    B87
KINNEAR J.B.,PRINCIPLES OF CIVIL GOVERNMENT.   POL/PAR
MOD/EUR USA-45 CONSTN LOC/G EX/STRUC ADMIN   NAT/G
PARL/PROC RACE/REL...CONCPT 18/19. PAGE 60 B1210   GOV/COMP
                                                    REPRESENT

MODAL....MODAL TYPES, FASHIONS

                                                    B61
HAIRE M.,MODERN ORGANIZATION THEORY. LABOR ROUTINE   PERS/REL
MAJORITY...CONCPT MODAL OBS CONT/OBS. PAGE 45 B0919 GP/REL
                                                    MGT
                                                    DECISION

MODELS....SEE SIMUL, MATH, ALSO MODELS INDEX, P. XIV

MODELSKI G. B1493,B1494,B1495

MODERNIZATION....SEE MODERNIZE

MODERNIZE....MODERNIZATION

MODZELEWSKI B1244

MOEN N.W. B1496

MOLEY R. B1497

MOLLAU G. B1498

MONACO....SEE ALSO APPROPRIATE TIME/SPACE/CULTURE INDEX

MONARCH....SEE CHIEF, KING

MONARCHY....SEE CONSERVE, CHIEF, KING

MONAS S. B1499

MONETARY POLICY....SEE FINAN, PLAN

MONEY....SEE FINAN, ECO

                                                    B42
WRIGHT D.M.,THE CREATION OF PURCHASING POWER.   FINAN
USA-45 NAT/G PRICE ADMIN WAR INCOME PRODUC...POLICY ECO/TAC
CONCPT IDEA/COMP BIBLIOG 20 MONEY. PAGE 118 B2378   ECO/DEV
                                                    CREATE
                                                    B62
BRIEFS H.W.,PRICING POWER AND "ADMINISTRATIVE"   ECO/DEV
INFLATION (PAMPHLET). USA+45 PROC/MFG CONTROL   PRICE
EFFICIENCY MONEY GOLD/STAND. PAGE 15 B0306   POLICY
                                                    EXEC

MONEYPENNY P. B1500

MONGOLIA....MONGOLIA; SEE ALSO USSR

                                                    L62
ABERLE D.F.,"CHAHAR AND DAGOR MONGOL BUREAUCRATIC   EX/STRUC
ADMINISTRATION: 19621945." ASIA MUNIC TOP/EX PWR   STRATA
...MGT OBS INT MONGOL 20. PAGE 3 B0053

MONOPOLY....MONOPOLIES, OLIGOPOLIES, AND ANTI-TRUST ACTIONS

                                                    N19
BURRUS B.R.,INVESTIGATION AND DISCOVERY IN STATE   NAT/G
ANTITRUST (PAMPHLET). USA+45 USA-45 LEGIS ECO/TAC   PROVS
ADMIN CONTROL CT/SYS CRIME GOV/REL PWR...JURID   LAW
CHARTS 19/20 FTC MONOPOLY. PAGE 17 B0355   INSPECT
                                                    B63
US SENATE COMM ON JUDICIARY,ADMINISTERED PRICES.   LG/CO
USA+45 RATION ADJUD CONTROL LOBBY...POLICY 20   PRICE
SENATE MONOPOLY. PAGE 110 B2229   ADMIN
                                                    DECISION
                                                    B64
GARFIELD PJ   LOVEJOY WF,PUBLIC UTILITY   T
ECONOMICS. DIST/IND FINAN MARKET MUNIC ADMIN COST   ECO/TAC
DEMAND...TECHNIC JURID 20 MONOPOLY. PAGE 39 B0782   OWN
                                                    SERV/IND
                                                    B64
WERNETTE J.P.,GOVERNMENT AND BUSINESS. LABOR   NAT/G
CAP/ISM ECO/TAC INT/TRADE TAX ADMIN AUTOMAT NUC/PWR FINAN
CIVMIL/REL DEMAND...MGT 20 MONOPOLY. PAGE 115 B2323 ECO/DEV
                                                    CONTROL

MONPIED E. B1501,B1502

MONROE/DOC....MONROE DOCTRINE

MONROE/J....PRESIDENT JAMES MONROE

MONTANA....MONTANA

MONTECARLO....MONTE CARLO - OPERATIONAL RESEARCH
   DECISION-MAKING MODEL

DUCKWORTH W.E.,A GUIDE TO OPERATIONAL RESEARCH. B62
INDUS PLAN PROB/SOLV EXEC EFFICIENCY PRODUC KNOWL OP/RES
...MGT MATH STAT SIMUL METH 20 MONTECARLO. PAGE 31 GAME
B0624 DECISION
ADMIN

MONTEIRO J.B. B1503

MONTER W. B1504

MONTESQ....MONTESQUIEU, CHARLES LOUIS DE SECONDAT

MONTGOMERY H. B1505

MONTGOMERY J.D. B1506,B1507

MONTGOMERY R.E. B1485

MONTGOMERY....MONTGOMERY, ALABAMA

MOODIE G.C. B1508

MOOMAW I.W. B1509

MOON P.T. B1510

MOOR E.J. B1511

MOORE B. B1512

MOORE C.H. B1513

MOORE W.E. B1514,B1515,B1516

MOOS M. B1517

MORA J.A. B1518

MORAL....RECTITUDE, MORALITY, GOODNESS (ALSO IMMORALITY)

HALDANE R.B.,BEFORE THE WAR. MOD/EUR SOCIETY B20
INT/ORG NAT/G DELIB/GP PLAN DOMIN EDU/PROP LEGIT POLICY
ADMIN COERCE ATTIT DRIVE MORAL ORD/FREE PWR...SOC DIPLOM
CONCPT SELF/OBS RECORD BIOG TIME/SEQ. PAGE 45 B0921 UK

CALKINS E.E.,BUSINESS THE CIVILIZER. INDUS MARKET B28
WORKER TAX PAY ROUTINE COST DEMAND MORAL 19/20. LAISSEZ
PAGE 18 B0367 POLICY
WEALTH
PROFIT

BUELL R.,INTERNATIONAL RELATIONS. WOR+45 WOR-45 B29
CONSTN STRATA FORCES TOP/EX ADMIN ATTIT DRIVE INT/ORG
SUPEGO MORAL ORD/FREE PWR SOVEREIGN...JURID SOC BAL/PWR
CONCPT 20. PAGE 17 B0340 DIPLOM

HYNEMAN C.S.,BUREAUCRACY IN A DEMOCRACY. CHIEF B50
LEGIS ADMIN CONTROL LEAD ROUTINE PERS/REL COST NAT/G
EFFICIENCY UTIL ATTIT AUTHORIT PERSON MORAL. CENTRAL
PAGE 53 B1071 EX/STRUC
MYTH

MANGONE G.,"THE IDEA AND PRACTICE OF WORLD L51
GOVERNMENT." FUT WOR+45 WOR-45 ECO/DEV LEGIS CREATE INT/ORG
LEGIT ROUTINE ATTIT MORAL PWR WEALTH...CONCPT SOCIETY
GEN/LAWS 20. PAGE 69 B1388 INT/LAW

HIMMELFARB G.,LORD ACTON: A STUDY IN CONSCIENCE AND B52
POLITICS. MOD/EUR NAT/G POL/PAR SECT LEGIS TOP/EX PWR
EDU/PROP ADMIN NAT/LISM ATTIT PERSON SUPEGO MORAL BIOG
ORD/FREE...CONCPT PARLIAMENT 19 ACTON/LORD. PAGE 50
B1014

BEISEL A.R.,CONTROL OVER ILLEGAL ENFORCEMENT OF THE B55
CRIMINAL LAW: ROLE OF THE SUPREME COURT. CONSTN ORD/FREE
ROUTINE MORAL PWR...SOC 20 SUPREME/CT. PAGE 10 LAW
B0207 CRIME

ABELS J.,THE TRUMAN SCANDALS. USA+45 USA-45 POL/PAR B56
TAX LEGIT CT/SYS CHOOSE PRIVIL MORAL WEALTH 20 CRIME
TRUMAN/HS PRESIDENT CONGRESS. PAGE 3 B0052 ADMIN
CHIEF
TRIBUTE

KHAMA T.,"POLITICAL CHANGE IN AFRICAN SOCIETY." S56
CONSTN SOCIETY LOC/G NAT/G POL/PAR EX/STRUC LEGIS AFR
LEGIT ADMIN CHOOSE REPRESENT NAT/LISM MORAL ELITES
ORD/FREE PWR...CONCPT OBS TREND GEN/METH CMN/WLTH
17/20. PAGE 59 B1201

KIETH-LUCAS A.,DECISIONS ABOUT PEOPLE IN NEED, A B57
STUDY OF ADMINISTRATIVE RESPONSIVENESS IN PUBLIC ADMIN
ASSISTANCE. USA+45 GIVE RECEIVE INGP/REL PERS/REL RIGID/FLEX
MORAL RESPECT WEALTH...SOC OBS BIBLIOG 20. PAGE 60 SOC/WK
B1204 DECISION

HAILEY,"TOMORROW IN AFRICA." CONSTN SOCIETY LOC/G S57
NAT/G DOMIN ADJUD ADMIN GP/REL DISCRIM NAT/LISM AFR
ATTIT MORAL ORD/FREE...PSY SOC CONCPT OBS RECORD PERSON
TREND GEN/LAWS CMN/WLTH 20. PAGE 45 B0917 ELITES
RACE/REL

SPITZ D.,DEMOCRACY AND THE CHALLANGE OF POWER. FUT B58
USA+45 USA-45 LAW SOCIETY STRUCT LOC/G POL/PAR NAT/G
PROVS DELIB/GP EX/STRUC LEGIS TOP/EX ACT/RES CREATE PWR
DOMIN EDU/PROP LEGIT ADJUD ADMIN ATTIT DRIVE MORAL
ORD/FREE TOT/POP. PAGE 99 B2010

WHITE L.D.,THE REPUBLICAN ERA: 1869-1901, A STUDY B58
IN ADMINISTRATIVE HISTORY. USA-45 FINAN PLAN MGT
NEUTRAL CRIME GP/REL MORAL LAISSEZ PRESIDENT PWR
REFORMERS 19 CONGRESS CIVIL/SERV. PAGE 116 B2340 DELIB/GP
ADMIN

GRABER D.,CRISIS DIPLOMACY. L/A+17C USA+45 USA-45 B59
NAT/G TOP/EX ECO/TAC COERCE ATTIT ORD/FREE...CONCPT ROUTINE
MYTH TIME/SEQ COLD/WAR 20. PAGE 42 B0848 MORAL
DIPLOM

HOFFMANN S.,"IMPLEMENTATION OF INTERNATIONAL S59
INSTRUMENTS ON HUMAN RIGHTS." WOR+45 VOL/ASSN INT/ORG
DELIB/GP JUDGE EDU/PROP LEGIT ROUTINE PEACE MORAL
COLD/WAR 20. PAGE 51 B1029

ROEPKE W.,A HUMANE ECONOMY: THE SOCIAL FRAMEWORK OF B60
THE FREE MARKET. FUT USSR WOR+45 CULTURE SOCIETY DRIVE
ECO/DEV PLAN ECO/TAC ADMIN ATTIT PERSON RIGID/FLEX EDU/PROP
SUPEGO MORAL WEALTH SOCISM...POLICY OLD/LIB CONCPT CAP/ISM
TREND GEN/LAWS 20. PAGE 90 B1811

HERZ J.H.,"EAST GERMANY: PROGRESS AND PROSPECTS." S60
COM AGRI FINAN INDUS LOC/G NAT/G FORCES PLAN POL/PAR
TEC/DEV DOMIN ADMIN COERCE DRIVE PERCEPT RIGID/FLEX STRUCT
MORAL ORD/FREE PWR...MARXIST PSY SOC RECORD STERTYP GERMANY
WORK. PAGE 49 B0997

THOMPSON K.W.,"MORAL PURPOSE IN FOREIGN POLICY: S60
REALITIES AND ILLUSIONS." WOR+45 WOR-45 LAW CULTURE MORAL
SOCIETY INT/ORG PLAN ADJUD ADMIN COERCE RIGID/FLEX JURID
SUPEGO KNOWL ORD/FREE PWR...SOC TREND SOC/EXP DIPLOM
TOT/POP 20. PAGE 104 B2104

CATHERINE R.,LE FONCTIONNAIRE FRANCAIS. FRANCE B61
NAT/G INGP/REL ATTIT MORAL ORD/FREE...T CIVIL/SERV. ADMIN
PAGE 19 B0394 GP/REL
LEAD
SUPEGO

NOVE A.,"THE SOVIET MODEL AND UNDERDEVELOPED S61
COUNTRIES." COM FUT USSR WOR+45 CULTURE ECO/DEV ECO/UNDEV
POL/PAR FOR/AID EDU/PROP ADMIN MORAL WEALTH PLAN
...POLICY RECORD HIST/WRIT 20. PAGE 79 B1593

SCHILLING W.R.,"THE H-BOMB: HOW TO DECIDE WITHOUT S61
ACTUALLY CHOOSING." FUT USA+45 INTELL CONSULT ADMIN PERSON
CT/SYS MORAL...JURID OBS 20 TRUMAN/HS. PAGE 93 LEGIT
B1888 NUC/PWR

DIMOCK M.E.,THE NEW AMERICAN POLITICAL ECONOMY: A B62
SYNTHESIS OF POLITICS AND ECONOMICS. USA+45 FINAN FEDERAL
LG/CO PLAN ADMIN REGION GP/REL CENTRAL MORAL 20. ECO/TAC
PAGE 29 B0598 NAT/G
PARTIC

SIMON Y.R.,A GENERAL THEORY OF AUTHORITY. DOMIN B62
ADMIN RATIONAL UTOPIA KNOWL MORAL PWR SOVEREIGN PERS/REL
...HUM CONCPT NEW/IDEA 20. PAGE 97 B1962 PERSON
SOCIETY
ORD/FREE

BERNTHAL W.F.,"VALUE PERSPECTIVES IN MANAGEMENT S62
DECISIONS." LG/CO OP/RES SUPEGO MORAL. PAGE 11 MGT
B0229 PROB/SOLV
DECISION

BRAIBANTI R.,"REFLECTIONS ON BUREAUCRATIC S62
CORRPUTION." LAW REPRESENT 20. PAGE 15 B0298 CONTROL
MORAL
ADMIN
GOV/COMP

MAINZER L.C.,"INJUSTICE AND BUREAUCRACY." ELITES S62
STRATA STRUCT EX/STRUC SENIOR CONTROL EXEC LEAD MORAL
ROUTINE INGP/REL ORD/FREE...CONCPT 20 BUREAUCRCY. MGT
PAGE 68 B1381 ADMIN

BOISSIER P.,HISTORIE DU COMITE INTERNATIONAL DE LA B63
CROIX ROUGE. MOD/EUR WOR-45 CONSULT FORCES PLAN INT/ORG
DIPLOM EDU/PROP ADMIN MORAL ORD/FREE...SOC CONCPT HEALTH
RECORD TIME/SEQ GEN/LAWS TOT/POP VAL/FREE 19/20. ARMS/CONT
PAGE 13 B0267 WAR

HEUSSLER R.,YESTERDAY'S RULERS: THE MAKING OF THE B63
BRITISH COLONIAL SERVICE. AFR EUR+WWI UK STRATA EX/STRUC
SECT DELIB/GP DOMIN EDU/PROP ATTIT PERCEPT MORAL
PERSON SUPEGO KNOWL ORD/FREE PWR...MGT SOC OBS INT ELITES
TIME/SEQ 20 CMN/WLTH. PAGE 49 B1000

SCHWELB E.,"OPERATION OF THE EUROPEAN CONVENTION ON INT/ORG S64

HUMAN RIGHTS." EUR+WWI LAW SOCIETY CREATE EDU/PROP   MORAL
ADJUD ADMIN PEACE ATTIT ORD/FREE PWR...POLICY
INT/LAW CONCPT OBS GEN/LAWS UN VAL/FREE ILO 20
ECHR. PAGE 95 B1916
                                                            B65
CONRAD J.P.,CRIME AND ITS CORRECTION: AN   CRIME
INTERNATIONAL SURVEY OF ATTITUDES AND PRACTICES.   PUB/INST
EUR+WWI NETHERLAND USA+45 USSR ATTIT MORAL 20   POLICY
SCANDINAV. PAGE 23 B0467   ADMIN
                                                            B65
GOLEMBIEWSKI R.T.,MEN, MANAGEMENT, AND MORALITY;   LG/CO
TOWARD A NEW ORGANIZATIONAL ETHIC. CONSTN EX/STRUC   MGT
CREATE ADMIN CONTROL INGP/REL PERSON SUPEGO MORAL   PROB/SOLV
PWR...GOV/COMP METH/COMP 20 BUREAUCRCY. PAGE 40
B0819
                                                            B66
PERROW C.,ORGANIZATION FOR TREATMENT: A COMPARATIVE AGE/Y
STUDY OF INSTITUTIONS FOR DELINQUENTS. LAW   PSY
PROB/SOLV ADMIN CRIME PERSON MORAL...SOC/WK OBS   PUB/INST
DEEP/QU CHARTS SOC/EXP SOC/INTEG 20. PAGE 82 B1661
                                                            B66
THOENES P.,THE ELITE IN THE WELFARE STATE ,TRANS.   ADMIN
BY J BINGHAM; ED. BY. STRATA NAT/G GP/REL HAPPINESS ELITES
INCOME OPTIMAL MORAL PWR WEALTH...POLICY CONCPT.   MGT
PAGE 104 B2097   WELF/ST
                                                            B66
VON HOFFMAN N.,THE MULTIVERSITY; A PERSONAL REPORT   EDU/PROP
ON WHAT HAPPENS TO TODAY'S STUDENTS AT AMERICAN   ACADEM
UNIVERSITIES. USA+45 SOCIETY ROUTINE ANOMIE ROLE   ATTIT
MORAL ORD/FREE SKILL...INT 20. PAGE 112 B2266   STRANGE
                                                            S67
MAINZER L.C.,"HONOR IN THE BUREAUCRATIC LIFE."   ADMIN
REPRESENT EFFICIENCY 20. PAGE 68 B1382   MORAL
                                                     EX/STRUC
                                                     EXEC
                                                            S68
GRAM H.A.,"BUSINESS ETHICS AND THE CORPORATION."   POLICY
LG/CO SECT PROB/SOLV CONTROL EXEC GP/REL INGP/REL   ADMIN
PERS/REL ROLE MORAL PWR...DECISION 20. PAGE 42   MGT
B0850

MORALES C.J. B1519

MORALITY....SEE MORAL, CULTURE, ALL/VALS, LAW/ETHIC

MORE S.S. B1520

MORE/THOM....SIR THOMAS MORE

MOREL E.D. B1521

MORGAN G.G. B1522

MORGAN J. B0188

MORGENTH/H.... HANS MORGENTHAU

MORGENTHAU H.J. B1523,B1524

MORISON E.E. B1525

MORL/MINTO....MORLEY-MINTO - ERA OF BRITISH RULE IN INDIA
(1905-1910)

MORLAN R.L. B1526

MORLEY/J....JOHN MORLEY

                                                            B64
DAS M.N.,INDIA UNDER MORLEY AND MINTO. INDIA UK   GOV/REL
ECO/UNDEV MUNIC PROVS EX/STRUC LEGIS DIPLOM CONTROL COLONIAL
REV 20 MORLEY/J. PAGE 26 B0531   POLICY
                                                     ADMIN

MORMON....MORMON PEOPLE AND MORMON FAITH

                                                            B67
ANGEL D.D.,ROMNEY. LABOR LG/CO NAT/G EXEC WAR   BIOG
RACE/REL PERSON ORD/FREE...MGT WORSHIP 20   CHIEF
ROMNEY/GEO CIV/RIGHTS MORMON GOVERNOR. PAGE 5 B0108 PROVS
                                                     POLICY

MOROCCO....SEE ALSO ISLAM

                                                            B34
DE CENIVAL P.,BIBLIOGRAPHIE MAROCAINE: 1923-1933.   BIBLIOG/A
FRANCE MOROCCO SECT ADMIN LEAD GP/REL ATTIT...LING   ISLAM
20. PAGE 27 B0551   NAT/G
                                                     COLONIAL
                                                            B61
LAHAYE R.,LES ENTREPRISES PUBLIQUES AU MAROC.   NAT/G
FRANCE MOROCCO LAW DIST/IND EXTR/IND FINAN CONSULT   INDUS
PLAN TEC/DEV ADMIN AGREE CONTROL OWN...POLICY 20.   ECO/UNDEV
PAGE 62 B1250   ECO/TAC

                                                            L62
WATERSTON A.,"PLANNING IN MOROCCO, ORGANIZATION AND NAT/G
IMPLEMENTATION. BALTIMORE: HOPKINS ECON. DEVELOP.   PLAN
INT. BANK FOR." ISLAM ECO/DEV AGRI DIST/IND INDUS   MOROCCO
PROC/MFG SERV/IND LOC/G EX/STRUC ECO/TAC PWR WEALTH
TOT/POP VAL/FREE 20. PAGE 114 B2302
                                                            B63
ROBERT J.,LA MONARCHIE MAROCAINE. MOROCCO LABOR   CHIEF
MUNIC POL/PAR EX/STRUC ORD/FREE PWR...JURID TREND T CONSERVE
20. PAGE 89 B1793   ADMIN
                                                     CONSTN
                                                            L63
ROBERT J.,"LES ELECTIONS LEGISLATIVES DU 17 MAI   CHOOSE
1963 ET L'EVOLUTION POLITIQUE INTERNE DU MAROC."   MOROCCO
ISLAM WOR+45 NAT/G POL/PAR EXEC ALL/VALS 20.
PAGE 89 B1792
                                                            S65
ASHFORD D.E.,"BUREAUCRATS AND CITIZENS." MOROCCO   GOV/COMP
PAKISTAN PARTIC 20 TUNIS. PAGE 7 B0140   ADMIN
                                                     EX/STRUC
                                                     ROLE
                                                            S65
THOMAS F.C. JR.,"THE PEACE CORPS IN MOROCCO."   MOROCCO
CULTURE MUNIC PROVS CREATE ROUTINE TASK ADJUST   FRANCE
STRANGE...OBS PEACE/CORP. PAGE 104 B2099   FOR/AID
                                                     EDU/PROP

MORRIS B.S. B1527

MORRIS H.C. B1528

MORRIS W.T. B1529

MORRIS/CW....C.W. MORRIS

MORRIS/G....G. MORRIS

MORROW/DW....DWIGHT W. MORROW

MORSTEIN-MARX F. B1530

MORTON J.A. B1531

MORTON L. B1351,B1532

MOSCA/G....GAETANO MOSCA

MOSCOW....MOSCOW, U.S.S.R.

MOSHER F.C. B1872

MOSK S.A. B1533

MOSSI....MOSSI TRIBE

MOTE M.E. B1534

MOTIVATION....SEE DRIVE

MOUTON J.S. B0250

MOVIES....SEE FILM

MOVIMIENTO NACIONALISTA REVOLUCIONARIO (BOLIVIA)....SEE
MNR

MOWER A.G. B1535

MOYNI/RPRT....MOYNIHAN REPORT

MOYNIHAN REPORT....SEE MOYNI/RPRT

MOZAMBIQUE LIBERATION FRONT....SEE FRELIMO

MOZAMBIQUE....MOZAMBIQUE

MUCKRAKER....MUCKRAKERS

MUGWUMP....MUGWUMP

MUKERJI S.N. B1536

MULATTO....MULATTO

MULLEY F.W. B1537

MULTIVAR....MULTIVARIATE ANALYSIS

MULTIVARIATE ANALYSIS....SEE MULTIVAR

MUNGER E.S. B1538

MUNIC....CITIES, TOWNS, VILLAGES

                                                            N
THE AMERICAN CITY. INDUS PROF/ORG PLAN GOV/REL   BIBLIOG/A

...MGT 20. PAGE 1 B0007   ADMIN
                                                 TEC/DEV
                                                 MUNIC
                                                 N

LOCAL GOVERNMENT SERVICE....SOC BIBLIOG/A 20.   LOC/G
PAGE 1 B0016   ADMIN
                                                 MUNIC
                                                 GOV/REL
                                                 N

CARLETON UNIVERSITY LIBRARY,SELECTED LIST OF   BIBLIOG
CURRENT MATERIALS ON CANADIAN PUBLIC   ADMIN
ADMINISTRATION. CANADA LEGIS WORKER PLAN BUDGET 20. LOC/G
PAGE 19 B0379   MUNIC
                                                 B05

RIORDAN W.L.,PLUNKITT OF TAMMANY HALL. USA-45   POL/PAR
SOCIETY PROB/SOLV EXEC LEAD TASK CHOOSE ALL/VALS MUNIC
...RECORD ANTHOL 20 REFORMERS TAMMANY NEWYORK/C CHIEF
PLUNKITT/G. PAGE 88 B1789   ATTIT
                                                 B13

MEYER H.H.B.,SELECT LIST OF REFERENCES ON   BIBLIOG
COMMISSION GOVERNMENT FOR CITIES (PAMPHLET). USA-45 LOC/G
EX/STRUC ADMIN 20. PAGE 73 B1473   MUNIC
                                                 DELIB/GP
                                                 B15

SAWYER R.A.,A LIST OF WORKS ON COUNTY GOVERNMENT. BIBLIOG/A
LAW FINAN MUNIC TOP/EX ROUTINE CRIME...CLASSIF   LOC/G
RECORD 19/20. PAGE 93 B1871   GOV/REL
                                                 ADMIN
                                                 B19

LOS ANGELES BD CIV SERV COMNRS,ANNUAL REPORT: LOS DELIB/GP
ANGELES CALIFORNIA: 1919-1936. USA-45 LAW GOV/REL ADMIN
PRODUC...STAT 20. PAGE 66 B1340   LOC/G
                                                 MUNIC
                                                 N19

ABBOT F.C.,THE CAMBRIDGE CITY MANAGER (PAMPHLET). MUNIC
PROB/SOLV ADMIN PERS/REL RIGID/FLEX PWR...MGT 20 EX/STRUC
MASSACHU CITY/MGT. PAGE 2 B0050   TOP/EX
                                                 GP/REL
                                                 N19

VERNON R.,THE MYTH AND REALITY OF OUR URBAN   PLAN
PROBLEMS (PAMPHLET). USA+45 SOCIETY LOC/G ADMIN MUNIC
COST 20 PRINCETN/U INTERVENT URBAN/RNWL. PAGE 112 HABITAT
B2261   PROB/SOLV
                                                 N19

WALL N.L.,MUNICIPAL REPORTING TO THE PUBLIC   METH
(PAMPHLET). LOC/G PLAN WRITING ADMIN REPRESENT   MUNIC
EFFICIENCY...AUD/VIS CHARTS 20. PAGE 113 B2282   GP/REL
                                                 COM/IND
                                                 B29

MERRIAM C.E.,CHICAGO: A MORE INTIMATE VIEW OF URBAN STRUCT
POLITICS. USA-45 CONSTN POL/PAR LEGIS ADMIN CRIME GP/REL
INGP/REL 18/20 CHICAGO. PAGE 73 B1472   MUNIC
                                                 B30

FAIRLIE J.A.,COUNTY GOVERNMENT AND ADMINISTRATION. ADMIN
UK USA-45 NAT/G SCHOOL FORCES BUDGET TAX CT/SYS GOV/REL
CHOOSE...JURID BIBLIOG 11/20. PAGE 35 B0701   LOC/G
                                                 MUNIC
                                                 B30

ZINK H.,CITY BOSSES IN THE UNITED STATES: A STUDY LOC/G
OF TWENTY MUNICIPAL BOSSES. USA-45 INDUS MUNIC   DOMIN
NEIGH POL/PAR ADMIN CRIME INGP/REL PERS/REL PWR BIOG
...PERS/COMP 20 BOSSISM. PAGE 119 B2403   LEAD
                                                 B32

MCKISACK M.,THE PARLIAMENTARY REPRESENTATION OF THE NAT/G
ENGLISH BOROUGHS DURING THE MIDDLE AGES. UK CONSTN MUNIC
CULTURE ELITES EX/STRUC TAX PAY ADJUD PARL/PROC LEGIS
APPORT FEDERAL...POLICY 13/15 PARLIAMENT. PAGE 72 CHOOSE
B1454   B33

BROMAGE A.W.,AMERICAN COUNTY GOVERNMENT. USA-45 LOC/G
NAT/G LEAD GOV/REL CENTRAL PWR...MGT BIBLIOG 18/20. CREATE
PAGE 15 B0314   ADMIN
                                                 MUNIC
                                                 B33

GREER S.,A BIBLIOGRAPHY OF PUBLIC ADMINISTRATION. BIBLIOG/A
WOR-45 CONSTN LOC/G MUNIC EX/STRUC LEGIS...CONCPT ADMIN
20. PAGE 43 B0869   MGT
                                                 NAT/G
                                                 B34

RIDLEY C.E.,THE CITY-MANAGER PROFESSION. CHIEF PLAN MUNIC
ADMIN CONTROL ROUTINE CHOOSE...TECHNIC CHARTS   EX/STRUC
GOV/COMP BIBLIOG 20. PAGE 88 B1780   LOC/G
                                                 EXEC
                                                 B36

US LIBRARY OF CONGRESS,CLASSIFIED GUIDE TO MATERIAL BIBLIOG
IN THE LIBRARY OF CONGRESS COVERING URBAN COMMUNITY CLASSIF
DEVELOPMENT. USA+45 CREATE PROB/SOLV ADMIN 20.   MUNIC
PAGE 109 B2202   PLAN
                                                 B37

GOSNELL H.F.,MACHINE POLITICS: CHICAGO MODEL.   POL/PAR
COM/IND FACE/GP LOC/G EX/STRUC LEAD ROUTINE   MUNIC
SANCTION REPRESENT GOV/REL PWR...POLICY MATH OBS ADMIN
INT CHARTS. PAGE 41 B0840   CHOOSE
                                                 B39

ANDERSON W.,LOCAL GOVERNMENT IN EUROPE. FRANCE   GOV/COMP
GERMANY ITALY UK USSR MUNIC PROVS ADMIN GOV/REL NAT/COMP

CENTRAL SOVEREIGN 20. PAGE 5 B0099   LOC/G
                                                 CONSTN
                                                 N40

COUNTY GOVERNMENT IN THE UNITED STATES: A LIST OF BIBLIOG/A
RECENT REFERENCES (PAMPHLET). USA-45 LAW PUB/INST LOC/G
PLAN BUDGET CT/SYS CENTRAL 20. PAGE 49 B0988   ADMIN
                                                 MUNIC
                                                 B42

JONES V.,METROPOLITAN GOVERNMENT. HABITAT ALL/VALS LOC/G
...MGT SOC CHARTS. PAGE 57 B1151   MUNIC
                                                 ADMIN
                                                 TECHRACY
                                                 B44

PUBLIC ADMINISTRATION SERVICE,YOUR BUSINESS OF   BIBLIOG
GOVERNMENT: A CATALOG OF PUBLICATIONS IN THE FIELD ADMIN
OF PUBLIC ADMINISTRATION (PAMPHLET). FINAN R+D   NAT/G
LOC/G ACT/RES OP/RES PLAN 20. PAGE 85 B1715   MUNIC
                                                 B47

FLYNN E.J.,YOU'RE THE BOSS. USA-45 ELITES TOP/EX LOC/G
DOMIN CONTROL EXEC LEAD REPRESENT 19/20 NEWYORK/C MUNIC
ROOSEVLT/F FLYNN/BOSS BOSSISM. PAGE 36 B0732   BIOG
                                                 POL/PAR
                                                 B47

PUBLIC ADMINISTRATION SERVICE,CURRENT RESEARCH   BIBLIOG
PROJECTS IN PUBLIC ADMINISTRATION (PAMPHLET). LAW R+D
CONSTN COM/IND LABOR LOC/G MUNIC PROVS ACT/RES   MGT
DIPLOM RECEIVE EDU/PROP WAR 20. PAGE 85 B1716   ADMIN
                                                 B47

TAPPAN P.W.,DELINQUENT GIRLS IN COURT. USA-45 MUNIC CT/SYS
EX/STRUC FORCES ADMIN EXEC ADJUST SEX RESPECT   AGE/Y
...JURID SOC/WK 20 NEWYORK/C FEMALE/SEX. PAGE 103 CRIME
B2078   ADJUD
                                                 B48

DAY P.,CRISIS IN SOUTH AFRICA. SOUTH/AFR UK KIN RACE/REL
MUNIC ECO/TAC RECEIVE 20 SMUTS/JAN MIGRATION.   COLONIAL
PAGE 27 B0548   ADMIN
                                                 EXTR/IND
                                                 B48

HOOVER E.M.,THE LOCATION OF ECONOMIC ACTIVITY.   HABITAT
WOR+45 MARKET MUNIC WORKER PROB/SOLV INT/TRADE   INDUS
ADMIN COST...POLICY CHARTS T 20. PAGE 51 B1041   ECO/TAC
                                                 GEOG
                                                 B48

PUBLIC ADMINISTRATION SERVICE,SOURCE MATERIALS IN BIBLIOG/A
PUBLIC ADMINISTRATION: A SELECTED BIBLIOGRAPHY (PAS GOV/REL
PUBLICATION NO. 102). USA+45 LAW FINAN LOC/G MUNIC MGT
NAT/G PLAN RECEIVE EDU/PROP CT/SYS CHOOSE HEALTH ADMIN
20. PAGE 85 B1717   C48

BOLLENS J.C.,"THE PROBLEM OF GOVERNMENT IN THE SAN USA+45
FRANCISCO BAY REGION." INDUS PROVS ADMIN GOV/REL MUNIC
...SOC CHARTS BIBLIOG 20. PAGE 13 B0270   LOC/G
                                                 PROB/SOLV
                                                 B49

HEADLAM-MORLEY,BIBLIOGRAPHY IN POLITICS FOR THE BIBLIOG
HONOUR SCHOOL OF PHILOSOPHY, POLITICS AND ECONOMICS NAT/G
(PAMPHLET). UK CONSTN LABOR MUNIC DIPLOM ADMIN   PHIL/SCI
19/20. PAGE 48 B0979   GOV/REL
                                                 B50

BROWN E.S.,MANUAL OF GOVERNMENT PUBLICATIONS.   BIBLIOG/A
WOR+45 WOR-45 CONSTN INT/ORG MUNIC PROVS DIPLOM NAT/G
ADMIN 20. PAGE 16 B0322   LAW
                                                 B50

DEES J.W. JR.,URBAN SOCIOLOGY AND THE EMERGING   PLAN
ATOMIC MEGALOPOLIS, PART I. USA+45 TEC/DEV ADMIN NEIGH
NUC/PWR HABITAT...SOC AUD/VIS CHARTS GEN/LAWS 20 MUNIC
WATER. PAGE 28 B0568   PROB/SOLV
                                                 B50

JENKINS W.S.,A GUIDE TO THE MICROFILM COLLECTION OF BIBLIOG
EARLY STATE RECORDS. USA+45 CONSTN MUNIC LEGIS   PROVS
PRESS ADMIN CT/SYS 18/20. PAGE 56 B1130   AUD/VIS
                                                 C50

MORLAN R.L.,"INTERGOVERNMENTAL RELATIONS IN   SCHOOL
EDUCATION." USA+45 FINAN LOC/G MUNIC NAT/G FORCES GOV/REL
PROB/SOLV RECEIVE ADMIN RACE/REL COST...BIBLIOG ACADEM
INDIAN/AM. PAGE 76 B1526   POLICY
                                                 C50

STEWART F.M.,"A HALF CENTURY OF MUNICIPAL REFORM." LOC/G
USA+45 CONSTN FINAN SCHOOL EX/STRUC PLAN PROB/SOLV VOL/ASSN
EDU/PROP ADMIN CHOOSE GOV/REL BIBLIOG. PAGE 101 MUNIC
B2036   POLICY
                                                 B51

ANDERSON W.,STATE AND LOCAL GOVERNMENT IN THE   LOC/G
UNITED STATES. USA+45 CONSTN POL/PAR EX/STRUC LEGIS MUNIC
BUDGET TAX ADJUD CT/SYS CHOOSE...CHARTS T 20.   PROVS
PAGE 5 B0100   GOV/REL
                                                 B52

DE GRAZIA A.,POLITICAL ORGANIZATION. CONSTN LOC/G FEDERAL
MUNIC NAT/G CHIEF LEGIS TOP/EX ADJUD CT/SYS   LAW
PERS/REL...INT/LAW MYTH UN. PAGE 27 B0553   ADMIN
                                                 C52

LANCASTER L.W.,"GOVERNMENT IN RURAL AMERICA."   GOV/REL
USA+45 ECO/DEV AGRI SCHOOL FORCES LEGIS JUDGE   LOC/G
BUDGET TAX CT/SYS...CHARTS BIBLIOG. PAGE 62 B1253 MUNIC
                                                 ADMIN

B53
MAJUMDAR B.B.,PROBLEMS OF PUBLIC ADMINISTRATION IN   ECO/UNDEV
INDIA. INDIA INDUS PLAN BUDGET ADJUD CENTRAL DEMAND   GOV/REL
WEALTH...WELF/ST ANTHOL 20 CIVIL/SERV. PAGE 68   ADMIN
B1384   MUNIC

B53
STENE E.O.,ABANDONMENTS OF THE MANAGER PLAN. LEGIS   MUNIC
LEAD GP/REL PWR DECISION. PAGE 100 B2032   EX/STRUC
                                                       REPRESENT
                                                       ADMIN

B54
BIESANZ J.,MODERN SOCIETY: AN INTRODUCTION TO   SOCIETY
SOCIAL SCIENCE. COM CONSTN STRUCT FAM MUNIC NAT/G   PROB/SOLV
SECT EX/STRUC LEGIS GP/REL PERSON...SOC 20. PAGE 12   CULTURE
B0237

B54
CHICAGO JOINT REFERENCE LIB,FEDERAL-STATE-LOCAL   BIBLIOG
RELATIONS; A SELECTED BIBLIOGRAPHY. USA+45 AGRI   FEDERAL
LABOR LOC/G MUNIC EX/STRUC ADMIN REGION HEALTH   GOV/REL
CON/ANAL. PAGE 21 B0419

B54
WILENSKY H.L.,SYLLABUS OF INDUSTRIAL RELATIONS: A   BIBLIOG
GUIDE TO READING AND RESEARCH. USA+45 MUNIC ADMIN   INDUS
INGP/REL...POLICY MGT PHIL/SCI 20. PAGE 117 B2351   LABOR
                                                       WORKER

C54
CALDWELL L.K.,"THE GOVERNMENT AND ADMINISTRATION OF   PROVS
NEW YORK." LOC/G MUNIC POL/PAR SCHOOL CHIEF LEGIS   ADMIN
PLAN TAX CT/SYS...MGT SOC/WK BIBLIOG 20 NEWYORK/C.   CONSTN
PAGE 18 B0366   EX/STRUC

C54
ROBSON W.A.,"GREAT CITIES OF THE WORLD: THEIR   LOC/G
GOVERNMENT, POLITICS, AND PLANNING." CONSTN FINAN   MUNIC
EX/STRUC ADMIN EXEC CHOOSE GOV/REL...STAT TREND   PLAN
ANTHOL BIBLIOG 20. PAGE 89 B1806   PROB/SOLV

B55
GUAITA A.,BIBLIOGRAFIA ESPANOLA DE DERECHO   BIBLIOG
ADMINISTRATIVO (PAMPHLET). SPAIN LOC/G MUNIC NAT/G   ADMIN
PROVS JUDGE BAL/PWR GOV/REL OWN...JURID 18/19.   CONSTN
PAGE 44 B0900   PWR

B55
UN ECONOMIC AND SOCIAL COUNCIL,BIBLIOGRAPHY OF   BIBLIOG/A
PUBLICATIONS OF THE UN AND SPECIALIZED AGENCIES IN   SOC/WK
THE SOCIAL WELFARE FIELD, 1946-1952. WOR+45 FAM   ADMIN
INT/ORG MUNIC ACT/RES PLAN PROB/SOLV EDU/PROP AGE/C   WEALTH
AGE/Y HABITAT...HEAL UN. PAGE 106 B2148

B56
BROWNE D.G.,THE RISE OF SCOTLAND YARD: A HISTORY OF   CRIMLGY
THE METROPOLITAN POLICE. UK MUNIC CHIEF ADMIN CRIME   LEGIS
GP/REL 19/20. PAGE 16 B0329   CONTROL
                                                       FORCES

B56
MANNONI D.O.,PROSPERO AND CALIBAN: THE PSYCHOLOGY   CULTURE
OF COLONIZATION. AFR EUR+WWI FAM KIN MUNIC SECT   COLONIAL
DOMIN ADMIN ATTIT DRIVE LOVE PWR RESPECT...PSY SOC
CONCPT MYTH OBS DEEP/INT BIOG GEN/METH MALAGASY 20.
PAGE 69 B1394

S56
MARGOLIS J.,"ON MUNICIPAL LAND POLICY FOR FISCAL   BUDGET
GAINS." USA+45 MUNIC PLAN TAX COST EFFICIENCY   POLICY
HABITAT KNOWL...MGT 20. PAGE 69 B1398   GEOG
                                                       LOC/G

B57
CHICAGO U LAW SCHOOL,CONFERENCE ON JUDICIAL   CT/SYS
ADMINISTRATION. LOC/G MUNIC NAT/G PROVS...ANTHOL   ADJUD
20. PAGE 21 B0421   ADMIN
                                                       GOV/REL

B57
DE GRAZIA A.,GRASS ROOTS PRIVATE WELFARE. LOC/G   NEW/LIB
SCHOOL ACT/RES EDU/PROP ROUTINE CROWD GP/REL   HEALTH
DISCRIM HAPPINESS ILLEGIT AGE HABITAT. PAGE 27   MUNIC
B0554   VOL/ASSN

B57
KNEIER C.M.,CITY GOVERNMENT IN THE UNITED STATES   MUNIC
(3RD ED.). USA-45 FINAN NAT/G POL/PAR LEGIS   LOC/G
EDU/PROP LEAD APPORT REPRESENT ATTIT...MGT 20   ADMIN
CITY/MGT. PAGE 60 B1219   GOV/REL

S57
GULICK L.,"METROPOLITAN ORGANIZATION." LEGIS EXEC   REGION
PARTIC CHOOSE REPRESENT GOV/REL...MAJORIT DECISION.   LOC/G
PAGE 45 B0904   MUNIC

S57
ROBSON W.A.,"TWO-LEVEL GOVERNMENT FOR METROPOLITAN   REGION
AREAS." MUNIC EX/STRUC LEGIS PARTIC REPRESENT   LOC/G
MAJORITY. PAGE 89 B1807   PLAN
                                                       GOV/REL

B58
HENKIN L.,ARMS CONTROL AND INSPECTION IN AMERICAN   USA+45
LAW. LAW CONSTN INT/ORG LOC/G MUNIC NAT/G PROVS   JURID
EDU/PROP LEGIT EXEC NUC/PWR KNOWL ORD/FREE...OBS   ARMS/CONT
TOT/POP CONGRESS 20. PAGE 49 B0990

B58
INDIAN INST OF PUBLIC ADMIN,IMPROVING CITY   LOC/G
GOVERNMENT. INDIA ECO/UNDEV PLAN BUDGET PARTIC   MUNIC
GP/REL 20. PAGE 53 B1080   PROB/SOLV
                                                       ADMIN

B58
SHERWOOD F.P.,SUPERVISORY METHODS IN MUNICIPAL   EX/STRUC
ADMINISTRATION. USA+45 MUNIC WORKER EDU/PROP PARTIC   LEAD
INGP/REL PERS/REL 20 CITY/MGT. PAGE 96 B1945   ADMIN
                                                       LOC/G

B58
WILENSKY H.L.,INDUSTRIAL SOCIETY AND SOCIAL   INDUS
WELFARE: IMPACT OF INDUSTRIALIZATION ON SUPPLY AND   ECO/DEV
ORGANIZATION OF SOC WELF SERVICES. ELITES SOCIETY   RECEIVE
STRATA SERV/IND FAM MUNIC PUB/INST CONSULT WORKER   PROF/ORG
ADMIN AUTOMAT ANOMIE 20. PAGE 117 B2352

L58
JONAS F.H.,"BIBLIOGRAPHY ON WESTERN POLITICS."   BIBLIOG/A
USA+45 USA-45 ELITES MUNIC POL/PAR LEGIS ADJUD   LOC/G
ADMIN 20. PAGE 57 B1148   NAT/G
                                                       LAW

S58
DAHL R.A.,"A CRITIQUE OF THE RULING ELITE MODEL."   CONCPT
USA+45 LOC/G MUNIC NAT/G POL/PAR PROVS DOMIN LEGIT   STERTYP
ADMIN...METH/CNCPT HYPO/EXP. PAGE 25 B0520   ELITES

S58
DERGE D.R.,"METROPOLITAN AND OUTSTATE ALIGNMENTS IN   LEGIS
ILLINOIS AND MISSOURI LEGISLATIVE DELEGATIONS"   MUNIC
(BMR)" USA+45 ADMIN PARTIC GOV/REL...MYTH CHARTS 20   PROVS
ILLINOIS MISSOURI. PAGE 28 B0575   POL/PAR

B59
BRUNTON R.L.,MANAGEMENT PRACTICES FOR SMALLER   ADMIN
CITIES. USA+45 MUNIC CONSULT PLAN BUDGET PERS/REL   LOC/G
20 CITY/MGT. PAGE 16 B0331   MGT
                                                       TOP/EX

B59
MAASS A.,AREA AND POWER: A THEORY OF LOCAL   LOC/G
GOVERNMENT. MUNIC PROVS EX/STRUC LEGIS CT/SYS   FEDERAL
CHOOSE PWR 20. PAGE 67 B1354   BAL/PWR
                                                       GOV/REL

B59
MAYNTZ R.,PARTEIGRUPPEN IN DER GROSSSTADT. GERMANY   MUNIC
STRATA STRUCT DOMIN CHOOSE 20. PAGE 71 B1437   MGT
                                                       POL/PAR
                                                       ATTIT

B59
PARK R.L.,LEADERSHIP AND POLITICAL INSTITUTIONS IN   NAT/G
INDIA. S/ASIA CULTURE ECO/UNDEV LOC/G MUNIC PROVS   EXEC
LEGIS PLAN ADMIN LEAD ORD/FREE WEALTH...GEOG SOC   INDIA
BIOG TOT/POP VAL/FREE 20. PAGE 81 B1633

B59
YANG C.K.,A CHINESE VILLAGE IN EARLY COMMUNIST   ASIA
TRANSITION. ECO/UNDEV AGRI FAM KIN MUNIC FORCES   ROUTINE
PLAN ECO/TAC DOMIN EDU/PROP ATTIT DRIVE PWR RESPECT   SOCISM
...SOC CONCPT METH/CNCPT OBS RECORD CON/ANAL CHARTS
WORK 20. PAGE 118 B2389

B60
ADRIAN C.R.,STATE AND LOCAL GOVERNMENTS: A STUDY IN   LOC/G
THE POLITICAL PROCESS. USA+45 LAW FINAN MUNIC   PROVS
POL/PAR LEGIS ADJUD EXEC CHOOSE REPRESENT. PAGE 3   GOV/REL
B0060   ATTIT

B60
ALBI F.,TRATADO DE LOS MODOS DE GESTION DE LAS   LOC/G
CORPORACIONES LOCALES. SPAIN FINAN NAT/G BUDGET   LAW
CONTROL EXEC ROUTINE GOV/REL ORD/FREE SOVEREIGN   ADMIN
...MGT 20. PAGE 3 B0068   MUNIC

B60
ARGAL R.,MUNICIPAL GOVERNMENT IN INDIA. INDIA   LOC/G
BUDGET TAX ADMIN EXEC 19/20. PAGE 6 B0126   MUNIC
                                                       DELIB/GP
                                                       CONTROL

B60
HEAP D.,AN OUTLINE OF PLANNING LAW (3RD ED.). UK   MUNIC
LAW PROB/SOLV ADMIN CONTROL 20. PAGE 49 B0983   PLAN
                                                       JURID
                                                       LOC/G

B60
JONES V.,METROPOLITAN COMMUNITIES: A BIBLIOGRAPHY   BIBLIOG
WITH SPECIAL EMPHASIS UPON GOVERNMENT AND POLITICS,   LOC/G
1955-1957. STRUCT ECO/DEV FINAN FORCES PLAN   MUNIC
PROB/SOLV RECEIVE EDU/PROP CT/SYS...GEOG HEAL 20.   ADMIN
PAGE 57 B1152

B60
MATTOD P.K.,A STUDY OF LOCAL SELF GOVERNMENT IN   MUNIC
URBAN INDIA. INDIA FINAN DELIB/GP LEGIS BUDGET TAX   CONSTN
SOVEREIGN...MGT GP/COMP 20. PAGE 71 B1432   LOC/G
                                                       ADMIN

B60
PENNSYLVANIA ECONOMY LEAGUE,URBAN RENEWAL IMPACT   PLAN
STUDY: ADMINISTRATIVE-LEGAL-FISCAL. USA+45 FINAN   BUDGET
LOC/G NEIGH ADMIN EFFICIENCY...CENSUS CHARTS 20   MUNIC
PENNSYLVAN. PAGE 82 B1652   ADJUD

B60
PHILLIPS J.C.,MUNICIPAL GOVERNMENT AND   MUNIC
ADMINISTRATION IN AMERICA. USA+45 LAW CONSTN FINAN   GOV/REL
FORCES PLAN RECEIVE OWN ORD/FREE 20 CIVIL/LIB.   LOC/G
PAGE 83 B1669   ADMIN

B60
POOLEY B.J.,THE EVOLUTION OF BRITISH PLANNING   PLAN
LEGISLATION. UK ECO/DEV LOC/G CONSULT DELIB/GP   MUNIC
ADMIN 20 URBAN/RNWL. PAGE 84 B1691   LEGIS

PROB/SOLV
B60

SAYRE W.S.,GOVERNING NEW YORK CITY; POLITICS IN THE MUNIC
METROPOLIS. POL/PAR CHIEF DELIB/GP LEGIS PLAN ADMIN
CT/SYS LEAD PARTIC CHOOSE...DECISION CHARTS BIBLIOG PROB/SOLV
20 NEWYORK/C BUREAUCRCY. PAGE 93 B1875

B60

WALDO D.,THE RESEARCH FUNCTION OF UNIVERSITY ADMIN
BUREAUS AND INSTITUTES FOR GOVERNMENTAL-RELATED R+D
RESEARCH. FINAN ACADEM NAT/G INGP/REL ROLE...POLICY MUNIC
CLASSIF GOV/COMP. PAGE 113 B2276

B60

WALTER B.,COMMUNICATIONS AND INFLUENCE: DEXISION MUNIC
MAKING IN A MUNICIPAL ADMINISTRATIVE HIERARCHY DECISION
(PH.D. DISS., UNPUBL.). LEAD CHOOSE PWR METH/CNCPT. ADMIN
PAGE 113 B2284 STRUCT

S60

BANFIELD E.C.,"THE POLITICAL IMPLICATIONS OF TASK
METROPOLITAN GROWTH" (BMR) UK USA+45 LOC/G MUNIC
PROB/SOLV ADMIN GP/REL...METH/COMP NAT/COMP 20. GOV/COMP
PAGE 9 B0176 CENSUS

B61

AVERY M.W.,GOVERNMENT OF WASHINGTON STATE. USA+45 PROVS
MUNIC DELIB/GP EX/STRUC LEGIS GIVE CT/SYS PARTIC LOC/G
REGION EFFICIENCY 20 WASHINGT/G GOVERNOR. PAGE 7 ADMIN
B0151 GOV/REL

B61

BANFIELD E.C.,URBAN GOVERNMENT; A READER IN MUNIC
POLITICS AND ADMINISTRATION. ELITES LABOR POL/PAR GEN/METH
EXEC CHOOSE REPRESENT GP/REL PWR PLURISM...PSY SOC. DECISION
PAGE 9 B0177

B61

BEASLEY K.E.,STATE SUPERVISION OF MUNICIPAL DEBT IN MUNIC
KANSAS - A CASE STUDY. USA+45 USA-45 FINAN PROVS LOC/G
BUDGET TAX ADJUD ADMIN CONTROL SUPEGO. PAGE 10 LEGIS
B0201 JURID

B61

CONFREY E.A.,ADMINISTRATION OF COMMUNITY HEALTH HEAL
SERVICES. USA+45 R+D PUB/INST DELIB/GP PLAN BUDGET ADMIN
ROUTINE AGE/C HEALTH...MGT SOC/WK METH/COMP 20. MUNIC
PAGE 23 B0461 BIO/SOC

B61

INTL UNION LOCAL AUTHORITIES,LOCAL GOVERNMENT IN LOC/G
THE USA. USA+45 PUB/INST DELIB/GP CONFER AUTOMAT MUNIC
GP/REL POPULISM...ANTHOL 20 CITY/MGT. PAGE 54 B1101 ADMIN
GOV/REL

B61

JACOBS J.,THE DEATH AND LIFE OF GREAT AMERICAN MUNIC
CITIES. USA+45 SOCIETY DIST/IND CREATE PROB/SOLV PLAN
ADMIN...GEOG SOC CENSUS 20 URBAN/RNWL. PAGE 55 ADJUST
B1113 HABITAT

B61

JANOWITZ M.,COMMUNITY POLITICAL SYSTEMS. USA+45 MUNIC
SOCIETY INDUS VOL/ASSN TEC/DEV ADMIN LEAD CHOOSE STRUCT
...SOC SOC/WK 20. PAGE 56 B1123 POL/PAR

B61

LEE R.R.,ENGINEERING-ECONOMIC PLANNING BIBLIOG/A
MISCELLANEOUS SUBJECTS: A SELECTED BIBLIOGRAPHY PLAN
(MIMEOGRAPHED). FINAN LOC/G MUNIC NEIGH ADMIN REGION
CONTROL INGP/REL HABITAT...GEOG MGT SOC/WK 20
RESOURCE/N. PAGE 63 B1280

B61

MACRIDIS R.C.,COMPARATIVE POLITICS: NOTES AND POL/PAR
READINGS. WOR+45 LOC/G MUNIC NAT/G PROVS VOL/ASSN CHOOSE
EDU/PROP ADMIN ATTIT PERSON ORD/FREE...SOC CONCPT
OBS RECORD TREND 20. PAGE 68 B1376

B61

MARX K.,THE COMMUNIST MANIFESTO. IN (MENDEL A. COM
ESSENTIAL WORKS OF MARXISM, NEW YORK: BANTAM. FUT NEW/IDEA
MOD/EUR CULTURE ECO/DEV ECO/UNDEV AGRI FINAN INDUS CAP/ISM
MARKET PROC/MFG LABOR MUNIC POL/PAR CONSULT FORCES REV
CREATE PLAN ADMIN ATTIT DRIVE RIGID/FLEX ORD/FREE
PWR RESPECT MARX/KARL WORK. PAGE 70 B1421

B61

NARAIN J.P.,SWARAJ FOR THE PEOPLE. INDIA CONSTN NAT/G
LOC/G MUNIC POL/PAR CHOOSE REPRESENT EFFICIENCY ORD/FREE
ATTIT PWR SOVEREIGN 20. PAGE 77 B1553 EDU/PROP
EX/STRUC

B61

ROMANO F.,CIVIL SERVICE AND PUBLIC EMPLOYEE LAW IN ADMIN
NEW JERSEY. CONSTN MUNIC WORKER GIVE PAY CHOOSE PROVS
UTIL 20. PAGE 90 B1816 ADJUD
LOC/G

L61

GERWIG R.,"PUBLIC AUTHORITIES IN THE UNITED LOC/G
STATES." LAW CONSTN PROVS TAX ADMIN FEDERAL. MUNIC
PAGE 39 B0793 GOV/REL
PWR

S61

BENNIS W.G.,"REVISIONIST THEORY OF LEADERSHIP" LEAD
MUNIC ACT/RES TEC/DEV...SIMUL 20. PAGE 11 B0215 ADMIN
PERS/REL
HYPO/EXP

S61

DYKMAN J.W.,"REVIEW ARTICLE* PLANNING AND DECISION DECISION
THEORY." ELITES LOC/G MUNIC CONSULT ADMIN...POLICY PLAN

MGT. PAGE 31 B0640 RATIONAL
S61

SHERBENOU E.L.,"CLASS, PARTICIPATION, AND THE REPRESENT
COUNCIL-MANAGER PLAN." ELITES STRUCT LEAD GP/REL MUNIC
ATTIT PWR DECISION. PAGE 96 B1942 EXEC

B62

INST TRAINING MUNICIPAL ADMIN,MUNICIPAL FINANCE MUNIC
ADMINISTRATION (6TH ED.). USA+45 ELITES ECO/DEV ADMIN
LEGIS PLAN BUDGET TAX GP/REL BAL/PAY COST...POLICY FINAN
20 CITY/MGT. PAGE 54 B1089 LOC/G

B62

KAMMERER G.M.,CITY MANAGERS IN POLITICS: AN MUNIC
ANALYSIS OF MANAGER TENURE AND TERMINATION. POL/PAR LEAD
LEGIS PARTIC CHOOSE PWR...DECISION GEOG METH/CNCPT. EXEC
PAGE 57 B1161

B62

KARNJAHAPRAKORN C.,MUNICIPAL GOVERNMENT IN THAILAND LOC/G
AS AN INSTITUTION AND PROCESS OF SELF-GOVERNMENT. MUNIC
THAILAND CULTURE FINAN EX/STRUC LEGIS PLAN CONTROL ORD/FREE
GOV/REL EFFICIENCY ATTIT...POLICY 20. PAGE 58 B1176 ADMIN

B62

MUNICIPAL MANPOWER COMMISSION,GOVERNMENTAL MANPOWER LOC/G
FOR TOMORROW'S CITIES: A REPORT. USA+45 DELIB/GP MUNIC
EX/STRUC PROB/SOLV TEC/DEV EDU/PROP ADMIN LEAD LABOR
HABITAT. PAGE 76 B1539 GOV/REL

B62

PRESS C.,STATE MANUALS, BLUE BOOKS AND ELECTION BIBLIOG
RESULTS. LAW LOC/G MUNIC LEGIS WRITING FEDERAL PROVS
SOVEREIGN...DECISION STAT CHARTS 20. PAGE 84 B1700 ADMIN
CHOOSE

B62

SAMPSON A.,ANATOMY OF BRITAIN. UK LAW COM/IND FINAN ELITES
INDUS MARKET MUNIC POL/PAR EX/STRUC TOP/EX DIPLOM PWR
LEAD REPRESENT PERSON PARLIAMENT WORSHIP. PAGE 92 STRUCT
B1866 FORCES

B62

WANGSNESS P.H.,THE POWER OF THE CITY MANAGER. PWR
USA+45 EX/STRUC BAL/PWR BUDGET TAX ADMIN REPRESENT TOP/EX
CENTRAL EFFICIENCY DRIVE ROLE...POLICY 20 CITY/MGT. MUNIC
PAGE 113 B2286 LOC/G

L62

ABERLE D.F.,"CHAHAR AND DAGOR MONGOL BUREAUCRATIC EX/STRUC
ADMINISTRATION: 19621945." ASIA MUNIC TOP/EX PWR STRATA
...MGT OBS INT MONGOL 20. PAGE 3 B0053

S62

BOOTH D.A.,"POWER STRUCTURE AND COMMUNITY CHANGE: A MUNIC
REPLICATION STUDY OF COMMUNITY A." STRATA LABOR ELITES
LEAD PARTIC REPRESENT...DECISION MGT TIME. PAGE 14 PWR
B0275

S62

DAKIN R.E.,"VARIATIONS IN POWER STRUCTURES AND MUNIC
ORGANIZING EFFICIENCY: A COMPARATIVE STUDY OF FOUR STRUCT
AREAS." STRATA EDU/PROP ADMIN LEAD GP/REL GOV/COMP. PWR
PAGE 26 B0524

S62

GEORGE P.,"MATERIAUX ET REFLEXIONS POUR UNE ECO/UNDEV
POLITIQUE URBAINE RATIONNELLE DANS LES PAYS EN PLAN
COURS DE DEVELOPPEMENT." FUT INTELL SOCIETY
SERV/IND MUNIC ACT/RES WEALTH...MGT 20. PAGE 39
B0790

S62

LOCKARD D.,"THE CITY MANAGER, ADMINISTRATIVE THEORY MUNIC
AND POLITICAL POWER." LEGIS ADMIN REPRESENT GP/REL EXEC
PWR. PAGE 66 B1333 LEAD
DECISION

N62

UNIVERSITY PITT INST LOC GOVT,THE COUNCIL-MANAGER LOC/G
FORM OF GOVERNMENT IN PENNSYLVANIA (PAMPHLET). TOP/EX
PROVS EX/STRUC REPRESENT GOV/REL EFFICIENCY MUNIC
...CHARTS SIMUL 20 PENNSYLVAN CITY/MGT. PAGE 107 PWR
B2169

N62

US ADVISORY COMN INTERGOV REL,ALTERNATIVE MUNIC
APPROACHES TO GOVERNMENTAL REORGANIZATION IN REGION
METROPOLITAN AREAS (PAMPHLET). EX/STRUC LEGIS EXEC PLAN
LEAD PWR...DECISION GEN/METH. PAGE 107 B2171 GOV/REL

B63

ADRIAN C.R.,GOVERNING OVER FIFTY STATES AND THEIR PROVS
COMMUNITIES. USA+45 CONSTN FINAN MUNIC NAT/G LOC/G
POL/PAR EX/STRUC LEGIS ADMIN CONTROL CT/SYS GOV/REL
...CHARTS 20. PAGE 3 B0061 GOV/COMP

B63

BANFIELD E.C.,CITY POLITICS. CULTURE LABOR LOC/G MUNIC
POL/PAR LEGIS EXEC LEAD CHOOSE...DECISION NEGRO. RIGID/FLEX
PAGE 9 B0178 ATTIT

B63

BASS M.E.,SELECTIVE BIBLIOGRAPHY ON MUNICIPAL BIBLIOG
GOVERNMENT FROM THE FILES OF THE MUNICIPAL LOC/G
TECHNICAL ADVISORY SERVICE. USA+45 FINAN SERV/IND ADMIN
PLAN 20. PAGE 9 B0194 MUNIC

B63

BOCK E.A., STATE AND LOCAL GOVERNMENT: A CASE BOOK. LOC/G
USA+45 MUNIC PROVS CONSULT GP/REL ATTIT...MGT 20 ADMIN
CASEBOOK GOVERNOR MAYOR. PAGE 12 B0254 PROB/SOLV
CHIEF

B63

CROUCH W.W.,SOUTHERN CALIFORNIA METROPOLIS: A STUDY LOC/G
IN DEVELOPMENT OF GOVERNMENT FOR A METROPOLITAN   MUNIC
AREA. USA+45 USA-45 PROB/SOLV ADMIN LOBBY PARTIC   LEGIS
CENTRAL ORD/FREE PWR...BIBLIOG 20 PROGRSV/M.   DECISION
PAGE 25 B0510

B63

GRANT D.R.,STATE AND LOCAL GOVERNMENT IN AMERICA.   PROVS
USA+45 FINAN LOC/G MUNIC EX/STRUC FORCES EDU/PROP   POL/PAR
ADMIN CHOOSE FEDERAL ATTIT...JURID 20. PAGE 42   LEGIS
B0853   CONSTN

B63

KAMMERER G.M.,THE URBAN POLITICAL COMMUNITY: EXEC
PROFILES IN TOWN POLITICS. ELITES LOC/G LEAD   MUNIC
...DECISION GP/COMP. PAGE 57 B1162   PWR
                                                       GOV/COMP

B63

LEONARD T.J.,THE FEDERAL SYSTEM OF INDIA. INDIA   FEDERAL
MUNIC NAT/G PROVS ADMIN SOVEREIGN...IDEA/COMP 20.   MGT
PAGE 64 B1293   NAT/COMP
                                                       METH/COMP

B63

LEWIS J.W.,LEADERSHIP IN COMMUNIST CHINA. ASIA   POL/PAR
INTELL ECO/UNDEV LOC/G MUNIC NAT/G PROVS ECO/TAC   DOMIN
EDU/PROP LEGIT ADMIN COERCE ATTIT ORD/FREE PWR   ELITES
...INT TIME/SEQ CHARTS TOT/POP VAL/FREE. PAGE 65
B1304

B63

MOORE W.E.,MAN, TIME, AND SOCIETY. UNIV STRUCT FAM   CONCPT
MUNIC VOL/ASSN ADMIN...SOC NEW/IDEA TIME/SEQ TREND   SOCIETY
TIME 20. PAGE 75 B1515   CONTROL

B63

NASA,CONFERENCE ON SPACE, SCIENCE, AND URBAN LIFE.   MUNIC
USA+45 SOCIETY INDUS ACADEM ACT/RES ECO/TAC ADMIN   SPACE
20. PAGE 77 B1556   TEC/DEV
                                                       PROB/SOLV

B63

PLISCHKE E.,GOVERNMENT AND POLITICS OF CONTEMPORARY   MUNIC
BERLIN. GERMANY LAW CONSTN POL/PAR LEGIS WAR CHOOSE   LOC/G
REPRESENT GOV/REL...CHARTS BIBLIOG 20 BERLIN.   POLICY
PAGE 83 B1683   ADMIN

B63

ROBERT J.,LA MONARCHIE MAROCAINE. MOROCCO LABOR   CHIEF
MUNIC POL/PAR EX/STRUC ORD/FREE PWR...JURID TREND T   CONSERVE
20. PAGE 89 B1793   ADMIN
                                                       CONSTN

B63

RUITENBEER H.M.,THE DILEMMA OF ORGANIZATIONAL   PERSON
SOCIETY. CULTURE ECO/DEV MUNIC SECT TEC/DEV   ROLE
EDU/PROP NAT/LISM ORD/FREE...NAT/COMP 20 RIESMAN/D   ADMIN
WHYTE/WF MERTON/R MEAD/MARG JASPERS/K. PAGE 92   WORKER
B1855

B63

SINGH M.M.,MUNICIPAL GOVERNMENT IN THE CALCUTTA   LOC/G
METROPOLITAN DISTRICT A PRELIMINARY SURVEY. FINAN   HEALTH
LG/CO DELIB/GP BUDGET TAX ADMIN GP/REL 20 CALCUTTA.   MUNIC
PAGE 97 B1969   JURID

B63

THOMETZ C.E.,THE DECISION-MAKERS: THE POWER   ELITES
STRUCTURE OF DALLAS. USA+45 CULTURE EX/STRUC DOMIN   MUNIC
LEGIT GP/REL ATTIT OBJECTIVE...INT CHARTS GP/COMP.   PWR
PAGE 104 B2101   DECISION

S63

GITTELL M.,"METROPOLITAN MAYOR: DEAD END." LOC/G   MUNIC
PARTIC REGION ATTIT PWR GP/COMP. PAGE 40 B0804   LEAD
                                                       EXEC

S63

JENNINGS M.K.,"PUBLIC ADMINISTRATORS AND COMMUNITY   ADMIN
DECISION-MAKING." ELITES LOC/G LEAD...GP/COMP   MUNIC
GOV/COMP. PAGE 56 B1134   DECISION
                                                       PWR

S63

WINGFIELD C.J.,"POWER STRUCTURE AND DECISION-MAKING   MUNIC
IN CITY PLANNING." EDU/PROP ADMIN LEAD PARTIC   PLAN
GP/REL ATTIT. PAGE 117 B2365   DECISION
                                                       PWR

B64

ALDERFER H.O.,LOCAL GOVERNMENT IN DEVELOPING   ADMIN
COUNTRIES. ASIA COM L/A+17C S/ASIA AGRI LOC/G MUNIC   ROUTINE
PROVS DOMIN CHOOSE PWR...POLICY MGT CONCPT 20.
PAGE 3 B0070

B64

BOUVIER-AJAM M.,MANUEL TECHNIQUE ET PRATIQUE DU   MUNIC
MAIRE ET DES ELUS ET AGENTS COMMUNAUX. FRANCE LOC/G   ADMIN
BUDGET CHOOSE GP/REL SUPEGO...JURID BIBLIOG 20   CHIEF
MAYOR COMMUNES. PAGE 14 B0284   NEIGH

B64

BROMAGE A.W.,MANAGER PLAN ABANDONMENTS: WHY A FEW   MUNIC
HAVE DROPPED COUNCILMANAGER GOVERNMENT. USA+45   PLAN
CREATE PARTIC CHOOSE...MGT CENSUS CHARTS 20.   CONSULT
PAGE 15 B0315   LOC/G

B64

CONNECTICUT U INST PUBLIC SERV,SUMMARY OF CHARTER   CONSTN
PROVISIONS IN CONNECTICUT LOCAL GOVERNMENT   MUNIC
(PAMPHLET). USA+45 DELIB/GP LEGIS TOP/EX CHOOSE   LOC/G
REPRESENT 20 CONNECTICT CITY/MGT MAYOR. PAGE 23   EX/STRUC

B0462

B64

CULLINGWORTH J.B.,TOWN AND COUNTRY PLANNING IN   MUNIC
ENGLAND AND WALES. UK LAW SOCIETY CONSULT ACT/RES   PLAN
ADMIN ROUTINE LEISURE INGP/REL ADJUST PWR...GEOG 20   NAT/G
OPEN/SPACE URBAN/RNWL. PAGE 25 B0512   PROB/SOLV

B64

DAS M.N.,INDIA UNDER MORLEY AND MINTO. INDIA UK   GOV/REL
ECO/UNDEV MUNIC PROVS EX/STRUC LEGIS DIPLOM CONTROL   COLONIAL
REV 20 MORLEY/J. PAGE 26 B0531   POLICY
                                                       ADMIN

B64

FONTENEAU J.,LE CONSEIL MUNICIPAL: LE MAIRE-LES   MUNIC
ADJOINTS. FRANCE FINAN DELIB/GP EX/STRUC BUDGET TAX   NEIGH
TASK COST INCOME ROLE SUPEGO 20 MAYOR. PAGE 36   ADMIN
B0735   TOP/EX

B64

GARFIELD PJ   LOVEJOY WF.PUBLIC UTILITY   T
ECONOMICS. DIST/IND FINAN MARKET MUNIC ADMIN COST   ECO/TAC
DEMAND...TECHNIC JURID 20 MONOPOLY. PAGE 39 B0782   OWN
                                                       SERV/IND

B64

GRAVIER J.F.,AMENAGEMENT DU TERRITOIRE ET L'AVENIR   PLAN
DES REGIONS FRANCAISES. FRANCE ECO/DEV AGRI INDUS   MUNIC
CREATE...GEOG CHARTS 20. PAGE 42 B0859   NEIGH
                                                       ADMIN

B64

GREBLER L.,URBAN RENEWAL IN EUROPEAN COUNTRIES: ITS   MUNIC
EMERGENCE AND POTENTIALS. EUR+WWI UK ECO/DEV LOC/G   PLAN
NEIGH CREATE ADMIN ATTIT...TREND NAT/COMP 20   CONSTRUC
URBAN/RNWL. PAGE 43 B0863   NAT/G

B64

HAMILTON B.L.S.,PROBLEMS OF ADMINISTRATION IN AN   ADMIN
EMERGENT NATION: CASE STUDY OF JAMAICA. JAMAICA UK   ECO/UNDEV
WOR+45 MUNIC COLONIAL HABITAT...CHARTS BIBLIOG 20   GOV/REL
CIVIL/SERV. PAGE 46 B0932   NAT/G

B64

INST D'ETUDE POL L'U GRENOBLE,ADMINISTRATION   ADMIN
TRADITIONELLE ET PLANIFICATION REGIONALE. FRANCE   MUNIC
LAW POL/PAR PROB/SOLV ADJUST RIGID/FLEX...CHARTS   PLAN
ANTHOL BIBLIOG T 20 REFORMERS. PAGE 54 B1087   CREATE

B64

KIESER P.J.,THE COST OF ADMINISTRATION, SUPERVISION   AFR
AND SERVICES IN URBAN BANTU TOWNSHIPS. SOUTH/AFR   MGT
SERV/IND MUNIC PROVS ADMIN COST...OBS QU CHARTS 20   FINAN
BANTU. PAGE 60 B1203

B64

LOWI T.J.,AT THE PLEASURE OF THE MAYOR. EX/STRUC   LOBBY
PROB/SOLV BAL/PWR ADMIN PARTIC CHOOSE GP/REL   LOC/G
...CONT/OBS NET/THEORY CHARTS 20 NEWYORK/C MAYOR.   PWR
PAGE 67 B1346   MUNIC

B64

NUQUIST A.E.,TOWN GOVERNMENT IN VERMONT. USA+45   LOC/G
FINAN TOP/EX PROB/SOLV BUDGET TAX REPRESENT SUFF   MUNIC
EFFICIENCY...OBS INT 20 VERMONT. PAGE 79 B1595   POPULISM
                                                       ADMIN

B64

PINNICK A.W.,COUNTRY PLANNERS IN ACTION. UK FINAN   MUNIC
SERV/IND NAT/G CONSULT DELIB/GP PRICE CONTROL   PLAN
ROUTINE LEISURE AGE/C...GEOG 20 URBAN/RNWL. PAGE 83   INDUS
B1674   ATTIT

B64

SHERIDAN R.G.,URBAN JUSTICE. USA+45 PROVS CREATE   LOC/G
ADMIN CT/SYS ORD/FREE 20 TENNESSEE. PAGE 96 B1943   JURID
                                                       ADJUD
                                                       MUNIC

B64

TURNER H.A.,THE GOVERNMENT AND POLITICS OF   PROVS
CALIFORNIA (2ND ED.). LAW FINAN MUNIC POL/PAR   ADMIN
SCHOOL EX/STRUC LEGIS LOBBY CHOOSE...CHARTS T 20   LOC/G
CALIFORNIA. PAGE 106 B2138   CONSTN

B64

WILDAVSKY A.,LEADERSHIP IN A SMALL TOWN. USA+45   LEAD
STRUCT PROB/SOLV EXEC PARTIC RACE/REL PWR PLURISM   MUNIC
...SOC 20 NEGRO WATER CIV/RIGHTS OBERLIN CITY/MGT.   ELITES
PAGE 116 B2348

L64

GILBERT C.E.,"NATIONAL POLITICAL ALIGNMENTS AND THE   MUNIC
POLITICS OF LARGE CITIES." ELITES LOC/G NAT/G LEGIS   CHOOSE
EXEC LEAD PLURISM GOV/COMP. PAGE 39 B0800   POL/PAR
                                                       PWR

S64

CASE H.L.,"GORDON R. CLAPP: THE ROLE OF FAITH,   ADMIN
PURPOSES AND PEOPLE IN ADMINISTRATION." INDUS MUNIC   BIOG
PROVS...POLICY 20. PAGE 19 B0391   EX/STRUC
                                                       DECISION

S64

HADY T.F.,"CONGRESSIONAL TOWNSHIPS AS INCORPORATED   MUNIC
MUNICIPALITIES." NEIGH ADMIN REPRESENT ATTIT GEOG.   REGION
PAGE 45 B0914   LOC/G
                                                       GOV/COMP

S64

KAMMERER G.M.,"ROLE DIVERSITY OF CITY MANAGERS."   MUNIC
LOC/G ADMIN LEAD PERCEPT PWR GP/COMP. PAGE 57 B1163   EXEC
                                                       ATTIT
                                                       ROLE

KAMMERER G.M.,"URBAN LEADERSHIP DURING CHANGE."
LEAD PARTIC REPRESENT GP/REL PLURISM...DECISION
GP/COMP. PAGE 58 B1164
MUNIC
PWR
ELITES
EXEC
S64

SALISBURY R.H.,"URBAN POLITICS: THE NEW CONVERGENCE
OF POWER." STRATA POL/PAR EX/STRUC PARTIC GP/REL
DECISION. PAGE 92 B1863
MUNIC
PWR
LEAD
S64

STONE P.A.,"DECISION TECHNIQUES FOR TOWN
DEVELOPMENT." PLAN COST PROFIT...DECISION MGT
CON/ANAL CHARTS METH/COMP BIBLIOG 20. PAGE 101
B2048
OP/RES
MUNIC
ADMIN
PROB/SOLV
S64

US SENATE COMM GOVT OPERATIONS,METROPOLITAN
AMERICA: A SELECTED BIBLIOGRAPHY (PAMPHLET). USA+45
DIST/IND FINAN LOC/G EDU/PROP ADMIN HEALTH 20.
PAGE 110 B2214
BIBLIOG/A
GOV/REL
DECISION
N64

ARTHUR D LITTLE INC,SAN FRANCISCO COMMUNITY RENEWAL
PROGRAM. USA+45 FINAN PROVS ADMIN INCOME...CHARTS
20 CALIFORNIA SAN/FRAN URBAN/RNWL. PAGE 7 B0138
HABITAT
MUNIC
PLAN
PROB/SOLV
B65

BANFIELD E.C.,BIG CITY POLITICS. USA+45 CONSTN
POL/PAR ADMIN LOBBY CHOOSE SUFF INGP/REL PWR...GEOG
20. PAGE 9 B0179
METH/COMP
MUNIC
STRUCT
B65

BOXER C.R.,PORTUGUESE SOCIETY IN THE TROPICS - THE
MUNICIPAL COUNCILS OF GOA, MACAO, BAHIA, AND
LUANDA, 1510-1800. EUR+WWI MOD/EUR PORTUGAL CONSTN
EX/STRUC DOMIN CONTROL ROUTINE REPRESENT PRIVIL
...BIBLIOG 16/19 GENACCOUNT MACAO BAHIA LUANDA.
PAGE 14 B0290
MUNIC
ADMIN
COLONIAL
DELIB/GP
B65

BUECHNER J.C.,DIFFERENCES IN ROLE PERCEPTIONS IN
COLORADO COUNCIL-MANAGER CITIES. USA+45 ADMIN
ROUTINE GP/REL CONSEN PERCEPT PERSON ROLE
...DECISION MGT STAT INT QU CHARTS 20 COLORADO
CITY/MGT. PAGE 17 B0338
MUNIC
CONSULT
LOC/G
IDEA/COMP
B65

DUGGAR G.S.,RENEWAL OF TOWN AND VILLAGE I: A WORLD-
WIDE SURVEY OF LOCAL GOVERNMENT EXPERIENCE. WOR+45
CONSTRUC INDUS CREATE BUDGET REGION GOV/REL...QU
NAT/COMP 20 URBAN/RNWL. PAGE 31 B0628
MUNIC
NEIGH
PLAN
ADMIN
B65

EAST J.P.,COUNCIL-MANAGER GOVERNMENT: THE POLITICAL
THOUGHT OF ITS FOUNDER, RICHARD S. CHILDS. USA+45
CREATE ADMIN CHOOSE...BIOG GEN/LAWS BIBLIOG 20
CHILDS/RS CITY/MGT. PAGE 32 B0642
SIMUL
LOC/G
MUNIC
EX/STRUC
B65

EVERETT R.O.,URBAN PROBLEMS AND PROSPECTS. USA+45
CREATE TEC/DEV EDU/PROP ADJUD ADMIN GOV/REL ATTIT
...ANTHOL 20 URBAN/RNWL. PAGE 34 B0691
MUNIC
PLAN
PROB/SOLV
NEIGH
B65

FRYE R.J.,HOUSING AND URBAN RENEWAL IN ALABAMA.
USA+45 NEIGH LEGIS BUDGET ADJUD ADMIN PARTIC...MGT
20 ALABAMA URBAN/RNWL. PAGE 38 B0762
MUNIC
PROB/SOLV
PLAN
GOV/REL
B65

GOODSELL C.T.,ADMINISTRATION OF A REVOLUTION.
PUERT/RICO ECO/UNDEV FINAN MUNIC POL/PAR PROVS
LEGIS PLAN BUDGET RECEIVE ADMIN COLONIAL LEAD 20
ROOSEVLT/F. PAGE 41 B0827
EXEC
SOC
B65

GREER S.,URBAN RENEWAL AND AMERICAN CITIES: THE
DILEMMA OF DEMOCRATIC INTERVENTION. USA+45 R+D
LOC/G VOL/ASSN ACT/RES BUDGET ADMIN GOV/REL...SOC
INT SAMP 20 BOSTON CHICAGO MIAMI URBAN/RNWL.
PAGE 43 B0871
MUNIC
PROB/SOLV
PLAN
NAT/G
B65

HOWE R.,THE STORY OF SCOTLAND YARD: A HISTORY OF
THE CID FROM THE EARLIEST TIMES TO THE PRESENT DAY.
UK MUNIC EDU/PROP 6/20 SCOT/YARD. PAGE 52 B1051
CRIMLGY
CRIME
FORCES
ADMIN
B65

INTERNATIONAL CITY MGRS ASSN,COUNCIL-MANAGER
GOVERNMENT, 1940-64: AN ANNOTATED BIBLIOGRAPHY.
USA+45 ADMIN GOV/REL ROLE...MGT 20. PAGE 54 B1097
BIBLIOG/A
MUNIC
CONSULT
PLAN
B65

KWEDER J.B.,THE ROLES OF THE MANAGER, MAYOR, AND
COUNCILMEN IN POLICYMAKING. LEGIS PERS/REL ATTIT
ROLE PWR GP/COMP. PAGE 62 B1246
MUNIC
EXEC
LEAD
DECISION
B65

PERLOFF H.S.,URBAN RESEARCH AND EDUCATION IN THE
NEW YORK METROPOLITAN REGION (VOL. II). FUT USA+45
NEIGH PROF/ORG ACT/RES PROB/SOLV EDU/PROP ADMIN
...STAT BIBLIOG 20 NEWYORK/C. PAGE 82 B1659
MUNIC
PLAN
ACADEM
GP/REL
B65

SNIDER C.F.,AMERICAN STATE AND LOCAL GOVERNMENT.
USA+45 FINAN CHIEF EX/STRUC TAX ADMIN CONTROL SUFF
INGP/REL PWR 20. PAGE 98 B1989
GOV/REL
MUNIC
PROVS

LOC/G
S65

CHARLESWORTH J.C.,"ALLOCATION OF RESPONSIBILITIES
AND RESOURCES AMONG THE THREE LEVELS OF
GOVERNMENT." USA+45 USA-45 ECO/DEV MUNIC PLAN LEGIT
...PLURIST MGT. PAGE 20 B0415
PROVS
NAT/G
LG/CO
WEALTH
S65

THOMAS F.C. JR.,"THE PEACE CORPS IN MOROCCO."
CULTURE MUNIC PROVS CREATE ROUTINE TASK ADJUST
STRANGE...OBS PEACE/CORP. PAGE 104 B2099
MOROCCO
FRANCE
FOR/AID
EDU/PROP
B66

ANDERSON D.L.,MUNICIPAL PUBLIC RELATIONS (1ST ED.).
USA+45 SOCIETY CONSULT FORCES PRESS ADMIN...CHARTS
BIBLIOG/A 20. PAGE 4 B0092
MUNIC
INGP/REL
EDU/PROP
ATTIT
B66

ASHRAF A.,THE CITY GOVERNMENT OF CALCUTTA: A STUDY
OF INERTIA. INDIA ELITES INDUS NAT/G EX/STRUC
ACT/RES PLAN PROB/SOLV LEAD HABITAT...BIBLIOG 20
CALCUTTA. PAGE 7 B0141
LOC/G
MUNIC
ADMIN
ECO/UNDEV
B66

DAHLBERG J.S.,THE NEW YORK BUREAU OF MUNICIPAL
RESEARCH: PIONEER IN GOVERNMENT ADMINISTRATION.
CONSTN R+D BUDGET EDU/PROP PARTIC REPRESENT
EFFICIENCY ORD/FREE...BIBLIOG METH 20 NEW/YORK
NIPA. PAGE 26 B0522
PROVS
MUNIC
DELIB/GP
ADMIN
B66

DUNCOMBE H.S.,COUNTY GOVERNMENT IN AMERICA. USA+45
FINAN MUNIC ADMIN ROUTINE GOV/REL...GOV/COMP 20.
PAGE 31 B0631
LOC/G
PROVS
CT/SYS
TOP/EX
B66

GROSS C.,A BIBLIOGRAPHY OF BRITISH MUNICIPAL
HISTORY (2ND ED.). UK LOC/G ADMIN 11/19. PAGE 44
B0888
BIBLIOG/A
MUNIC
CONSTN
B66

HARMON R.B.,SOURCES AND PROBLEMS OF BIBLIOGRAPHY IN
POLITICAL SCIENCE (PAMPHLET). INT/ORG LOC/G MUNIC
POL/PAR ADMIN GOV/REL ALL/IDEOS...JURID MGT CONCPT
19/20. PAGE 47 B0951
BIBLIOG
DIPLOM
INT/LAW
NAT/G
B66

HESSLER I.O.,29 WAYS TO GOVERN A CITY. EX/STRUC
TOP/EX PROB/SOLV PARTIC CHOOSE REPRESENT EFFICIENCY
...CHARTS 20 CITY/MGT MAYOR. PAGE 49 B0998
MUNIC
GOV/COMP
LOC/G
ADMIN
B66

MURDOCK J.C.,RESEARCH AND REGIONS. AGRI FINAN INDUS
LOC/G MUNIC NAT/G PROB/SOLV TEC/DEV ADMIN REGION
20. PAGE 76 B1545
BIBLIOG
ECO/DEV
COMPUT/IR
R+D
B66

NYC TEMPORARY COMM CITY FINAN,MUNICIPAL COLLECTIVE
BARGAINING (NO. 8). USA+45 PLAN PROB/SOLV BARGAIN
BUDGET TAX EDU/PROP GOV/REL COST...MGT 20
NEWYORK/C. PAGE 79 B1596
MUNIC
FINAN
ADMIN
LOC/G
B66

ROSS R.M.,STATE AND LOCAL GOVERNMENT AND
ADMINISTRATION. USA+45 CONSTN POL/PAR EX/STRUC
LEGIS BUDGET EDU/PROP CONTROL CT/SYS CHOOSE GOV/REL
T. PAGE 90 B1827
LOC/G
PROVS
MUNIC
ADMIN
B66

SCHMIDT K.M.,AMERICAN STATE AND LOCAL GOVERNMENT IN
ACTION. USA+45 CONSTN LOC/G POL/PAR CHIEF LEGIS
PROB/SOLV ADJUD LOBBY GOV/REL...DECISION ANTHOL 20
GOVERNOR MAYOR URBAN/RNWL. PAGE 94 B1896
PROVS
ADMIN
MUNIC
PLAN
B66

SCHURMANN F.,IDEOLOGY AND ORGANIZATION IN COMMUNIST
CHINA. CHINA/COM LOC/G MUNIC POL/PAR ECO/TAC
CONTROL ATTIT...MGT STERTYP 20 COM/PARTY. PAGE 94
B1909
MARXISM
STRUCT
ADMIN
NAT/G
B66

SILBERMAN B.S.,MODERN JAPANESE LEADERSHIP;
TRANSITION AND CHANGE. NAT/G POL/PAR CHIEF ADMIN
REPRESENT GP/REL ADJUST RIGID/FLEX...SOC METH/COMP
ANTHOL 19/20 CHINJAP CHRISTIAN. PAGE 97 B1952
LEAD
CULTURE
ELITES
MUNIC
B66

WARREN R.O.,GOVERNMENT IN METROPOLITAN REGIONS: A
REAPPRAISAL OF FRACTIONATED POLITICAL ORGANIZATION.
USA+45 ACT/RES PROB/SOLV REGION...CHARTS METH/COMP
BIBLIOG CITY/MGT. PAGE 114 B2296
LOC/G
MUNIC
EX/STRUC
PLAN
B66

WYLIE C.M.,RESEARCH IN PUBLIC HEALTH
ADMINISTRATION: SELECTED RECENT ABSTRACTS IV
(PAMPHLET). USA+45 MUNIC PUB/INST ACT/RES CREATE
OP/RES TEC/DEV GP/REL ROLE...MGT PHIL/SCI STAT.
PAGE 118 B2387
BIBLIOG/A
R+D
HEAL
ADMIN
L66

CRAIN R.L.,"STRUCTURE AND VALUES IN LOCAL POLITICAL
SYSTEMS: THE CASE OF FLUORIDATION DECISIONS."
EX/STRUC LEGIS LEAD PARTIC REPRESENT PWR...DECISION
GOV/COMP. PAGE 25 B0501
MUNIC
EDU/PROP
LOC/G
ATTIT
S66

BURDETTE F.L.,"SELECTED ARTICLES AND DOCUMENTS ON
AMERICAN GOVERNMENT AND POLITICS." LAW LOC/G MUNIC
NAT/G POL/PAR PROVS LEGIS BAL/PWR ADMIN EXEC
BIBLIOG
USA+45
JURID

REPRESENT MGT. PAGE 17 B0348   CONSTN

S66
SNOWISS L.M.,"CONGRESSIONAL RECRUITMENT AND   LEGIS
REPRESENTATION." USA+45 LG/CO MUNIC POL/PAR ADMIN   REPRESENT
REGION CONGRESS CHICAGO. PAGE 98 B1990   CHOOSE
                                                     LOC/G

S66
WOLFINGER R.E.,"POLITICAL ETHOS AND THE STRUCTURE   MUNIC
OF CITY GOVERNMENT." POL/PAR EX/STRUC REPRESENT   ATTIT
GP/REL PERS/REL RIGID/FLEX PWR. PAGE 118 B2371   STRATA
                                                     GOV/COMP

B67
BUDER S.,PULLMAN: AN EXPERIMENT IN INDUSTRIAL ORDER DIST/IND
AND COMMUNITY PLANNING, 1880-1930. USA-45 SOCIETY   INDUS
LABOR LG/CO CREATE PROB/SOLV CONTROL GP/REL   MUNIC
EFFICIENCY ATTIT...MGT BIBLIOG 19/20 PULLMAN.   PLAN
PAGE 17 B0337

B67
BUREAU GOVERNMENT RES AND SERV,COUNTY GOVERNMENT   BIBLIOG/A
REORGANIZATION - A SELECTED ANNOTATED BIBLIOGRAPHY   APPORT
(PAPER). USA+45 USA-45 LAW CONSTN MUNIC PROVS   LOC/G
EX/STRUC CREATE PLAN PROB/SOLV REPRESENT GOV/REL   ADMIN
20. PAGE 17 B0349

B67
EVANS R.H.,COEXISTENCE: COMMUNISM AND ITS PRACTICE   MARXISM
IN BOLOGNA, 1945-1965. ITALY CAP/ISM ADMIN CHOOSE   CULTURE
PEACE ORD/FREE...SOC STAT DEEP/INT SAMP CHARTS   MUNIC
BIBLIOG 20. PAGE 34 B0690   POL/PAR

B67
GITTELL M.,PARTICIPANTS AND PARTICIPATION: A STUDY   SCHOOL
OF SCHOOL POLICY IN NEW YORK. USA+45 MUNIC EX/STRUC DECISION
BUDGET PAY ATTIT...POLICY 20 NEWYORK/C. PAGE 40   PARTIC
B0806   ADMIN

B67
GREENE L.S.,AMERICAN GOVERNMENT POLICIES AND   POLICY
FUNCTIONS. USA+45 LAW AGRI DIST/IND LABOR MUNIC   NAT/G
BUDGET DIPLOM EDU/PROP ORD/FREE...BIBLIOG T 20.   ADMIN
PAGE 43 B0867   DECISION

B67
EDUCATION, INTERACTION, AND SOCIAL CHANGE. STRATA   EDU/PROP
MUNIC SCHOOL ADMIN RIGID/FLEX ROLE 20. PAGE 49   ADJUST
B0991   SOC
                                                     ACT/RES

B67
KAPLAN H.,URBAN POLITICAL SYSTEMS: A FUNCTIONAL   GEN/LAWS
ANALYSIS OF METRO TORONTO. CANADA STRUCT NEIGH PLAN MUNIC
ADMIN...POLICY METH 20 TORONTO. PAGE 58 B1166   LOC/G
                                                     FEDERAL

B67
MARRIS P.,DILEMMAS OF SOCIAL REFORM: POVERTY AND   STRUCT
COMMUNITY ACTION IN THE UNITED STATES. USA+45 NAT/G MUNIC
OP/RES ADMIN PARTIC EFFICIENCY WEALTH...SOC   PROB/SOLV
METH/COMP T 20 REFORMERS. PAGE 69 B1401   COST

B67
ROTHENBERG J.,ECONOMIC EVALUATION OF URBAN RENEWAL: PLAN
CONCEPTUAL FOUNDATION OF BENEFIT-COST ANALYSIS.   MUNIC
USA+45 ECO/DEV NEIGH TEC/DEV ADMIN GEN/LAWS.   PROB/SOLV
PAGE 91 B1834   COST

B67
SABLE M.H.,A GUIDE TO LATIN AMERICAN STUDIES (2   BIBLIOG/A
VOLS). CONSTN FINAN INT/ORG LABOR MUNIC POL/PAR   L/A+17C
FORCES CAP/ISM FOR/AID ADMIN MARXISM SOCISM OAS.   DIPLOM
PAGE 92 B1861   NAT/LISM

B67
US DEPARTMENT HEALTH EDUC WELF,NEW PROGRAMS IN   ADMIN
HEALTH, EDUCATION, WELFARE, HOUSING AND URBAN   HEALTH
DEVELOPMENT FOR PERSONS AND FAMILIES -LOW, MOD,   SCHOOL
INCOME. USA+45 MUNIC NAT/G EDU/PROP GOV/REL   HABITAT
INGP/REL ORD/FREE 20 DEPT/HEW DEPT/HUD. PAGE 108
B2180

B67
WESTON P.B.,THE ADMINISTRATION OF JUSTICE. USA+45   CRIME
CONSTN MUNIC NAT/G PROVS EX/STRUC JUDGE ADMIN   CT/SYS
CONTROL SANCTION ORD/FREE...CHARTS 20. PAGE 115   JURID
B2328   ADJUD

L67
CARMICHAEL D.M.,"FORTY YEARS OF WATER POLLUTION   HEALTH
CONTROL IN WISCONSIN: A CASE STUDY." LAW EXTR/IND   CONTROL
INDUS MUNIC DELIB/GP PLAN PROB/SOLV SANCTION   ADMIN
...CENSUS CHARTS 20 WISCONSIN. PAGE 19 B0382   ADJUD

S67
BURKE E.M.,"THE SEARCH FOR AUTHORITY IN PLANNING."   DECISION
MUNIC NEIGH CREATE PROB/SOLV LEGIT ADMIN CONTROL   PLAN
EFFICIENCY PWR...METH/COMP SIMUL 20. PAGE 17 B0352   LOC/G
                                                     METH

S67
DONNELL J.C.,"PACIFICATION REASSESSED." VIETNAM/S   ADMIN
NAT/LISM DRIVE SUPEGO ORD/FREE...SOC/WK 20. PAGE 30 GP/REL
B0606   EFFICIENCY
                                                     MUNIC

S67
EDWARDS H.T.,"POWER STRUCTURE AND ITS COMMUNICATION ELITES
IN SAN JOSE, COSTA RICA." COSTA/RICA L/A+17C STRATA INGP/REL
FACE/GP POL/PAR EX/STRUC PROB/SOLV ADMIN LEAD   MUNIC
GP/REL PWR...STAT INT 20. PAGE 32 B0655   DOMIN

S67
FERGUSON H.,"3-CITY CONSOLIDATION." USA+45 CONSTN   MUNIC
INDUS BARGAIN BUDGET CONFER ADMIN INGP/REL COST   CHOOSE
UTIL. PAGE 35 B0712   CREATE
                                                     PROB/SOLV

S67
FRYKENBURG R.E.,"STUDIES OF LAND CONTROL IN INDIAN   ECO/UNDEV
HISTORY: REVIEW ARTICLE." INDIA UK STRATA AGRI   CONTROL
MUNIC OP/RES COLONIAL REGION EFFICIENCY OWN HABITAT ADMIN
...CONCPT 16/20. PAGE 38 B0763

S67
GITTELL M.,"PROFESSIONALISM AND PUBLIC   DECISION
PARTICIPATION IN EDUCATIONAL POLICY MAKING." STRUCT PLAN
ADMIN GP/REL ATTIT PWR 20. PAGE 40 B0805   EDU/PROP
                                                     MUNIC

S67
GOBER J.L.,"FEDERALISM AT WORK." USA+45 NAT/G   MUNIC
CONSULT ACT/RES PLAN CONFER ADMIN LEAD PARTIC   TEC/DEV
FEDERAL ATTIT. PAGE 40 B0813   R+D
                                                     GOV/REL

S67
HUGON P.,"BLOCAGES ET DESEQUILIBRES DE LA   ECO/UNDEV
CROISSANCE ECONOMIQUE EN AFRIQUE NOIRE." AFR KIN   COLONIAL
MUNIC CREATE PLAN INT/TRADE REGION ADJUST CENTRAL   STRUCT
EQUILIB NAT/LISM ORD/FREE 20. PAGE 52 B1060   ADMIN

S67
LEVIN M.R.,"PLANNERS AND METROPOLITAN PLANNING."   PLAN
FUT USA+45 SOCIETY NAT/G PROVS PROB/SOLV LEAD   MUNIC
PARTIC GOV/REL RACE/REL HABITAT ROLE. PAGE 64 B1301 R+D
                                                     ADMIN

S67
LINEBERRY R.L.,"REFORMISM AND PUBLIC POLICIES IN   DECISION
AMERICAN CITIES." USA+45 POL/PAR EX/STRUC LEGIS   POLICY
BUDGET TAX GP/REL...STAT CHARTS. PAGE 65 B1317   MUNIC
                                                     LOC/G

N67
NATIONAL COMN COMMUNITY HEALTH,ACTION - PLANNING   PLAN
FOR COMMUNITY HEALTH SERVICES (PAMPHLET). USA+45   MUNIC
PROF/ORG DELIB/GP BUDGET ROUTINE GP/REL ATTIT   HEALTH
...HEAL SOC SOC/WK CHARTS TIME 20. PAGE 77 B1563   ADJUST

MUNICH....MUNICH, GERMANY

MUNICIPAL MANPOWER COMMISSION B1539

MUNICIPALITIES....SEE MUNIC

MUNRO L. B1540

MURACCIOLE L. B1541,B1542

MURCHISON C. B1543

MURDER....MURDER, ASSASSINATION; SEE ALSO CRIME

B65
FEERICK J.D.,FROM FAILING HANDS: THE STUDY OF   EX/STRUC
PRESIDENTIAL SUCCESSION. CONSTN NAT/G PROB/SOLV   CHIEF
LEAD PARL/PROC MURDER CHOOSE...NEW/IDEA BIBLIOG 20   LAW
KENNEDY/JF JOHNSON/LB PRESIDENT PRE/US/AM   LEGIS
VICE/PRES. PAGE 35 B0710

MURDESHWAR A.K. B1544

MURDOCK J.C. B1545

MURNGIN....MURNGIN, AN AUSTRALIAN TRIBE

MURRAY D. B1546

MURRAY J.N. B1547

MURRAY R. B1548

MURRAY/JC....JOHN COURTNEY MURRAY

MUSCAT....MUSCAT AND OMAN; SEE ALSO ISLAM

MUSHKIN S.J. B1549

MUSHRUSH G.J. B0702

MUSIC....MUSIC AND SONGS

B65
BERNDT R.M.,ABORIGINAL MAN IN AUSTRALIA. LAW DOMIN   SOC
ADMIN COLONIAL MARRIAGE HABITAT ORD/FREE...LING   CULTURE
CHARTS ANTHOL BIBLIOG WORSHIP 20 AUSTRAL ABORIGINES SOCIETY
MUSIC ELKIN/AP. PAGE 11 B0225   STRUCT

MUSLIM....MUSLIM PEOPLE AND RELIGION

MUSLIM/LG....MUSLIM LEAGUE

MUSOLF L.D. B1550

MUSSO AMBROSI L.A. B1551

MUSSOLIN/B....BENITO MUSSOLINI

FIELD G.L.,THE SYNDICAL AND CORPORATIVE INSTITUTIONS OF ITALIAN FASCISM. ITALY CONSTN STRATA LABOR EX/STRUC TOP/EX ADJUD ADMIN LEAD TOTALISM AUTHORIT...MGT 20 MUSSOLIN/B. PAGE 35 B0716 — B38 FASCISM INDUS NAT/G WORKER

MUSTE A.J. B0991

MYRDAL/G....GUNNAR MYRDAL

MYSTIC....MYSTICAL

MYSTICISM....SEE MYSTISM

MYSTISM....MYSTICISM

MYTH....FICTION

ANGELL N.,THE PUBLIC MIND. USA-45 SOCIETY EDU/PROP ROUTINE SUPEGO KNOWL...POLICY CONCPT MYTH OBS/ENVIR EUR+WW1 TOT/POP 20. PAGE 5 B0109 — B27 PERCEPT ATTIT DIPLOM NAT/LISM

GORER G.,AFRICA DANCES: A BOOK ABOUT WEST AFRICAN NEGROES. STRUCT LOC/G SECT FORCES TAX ADMIN COLONIAL...ART/METH MYTH WORSHIP 20 NEGRO AFRICA/W CHRISTIAN RITUAL. PAGE 41 B0835 — B35 AFR ATTIT CULTURE SOCIETY

PETTEE G.S.,THE PROCESS OF REVOLUTION. COM FRANCE ITALY MOD/EUR RUSSIA SPAIN WOR-45 ELITES INTELL SOCIETY STRATA STRUCT INT/ORG NAT/G POL/PAR ACT/RES PLAN EDU/PROP LEGIT EXEC...SOC MYTH TIME/SEQ TOT/POP 18/20. PAGE 82 B1664 — B38 COERCE CONCPT REV

BONAPARTE M.,MYTHS OF WAR. GERMANY WOR+45 WOR-45 CULTURE SOCIETY NAT/G FORCES LEGIT ATTIT ALL/VALS ...CONCPT HIST/WRIT TIME/SEQ 20 JEWS. PAGE 13 B0271 — B48 ROUTINE MYTH WAR

BUSH V.,MODERN ARMS AND FREE MEN. WOR+45 SOCIETY NAT/G ECO/TAC DOMIN LEGIT EXEC COERCE DETER ATTIT DRIVE ORD/FREE...CONCPT MYTH COLD/WAR 20 COLD/WAR. PAGE 18 B0361 — B49 TEC/DEV FORCES NUC/PWR WAR

HYNEMAN C.S.,BUREAUCRACY IN A DEMOCRACY. CHIEF LEGIS ADMIN CONTROL LEAD ROUTINE PERS/REL COST EFFICIENCY UTIL ATTIT AUTHORIT PERSON MORAL. PAGE 53 B1071 — B50 NAT/G CENTRAL EX/STRUC MYTH

LEITES N.,THE OPERATIONAL CODE OF THE POLITBURO. COM USSR CREATE PLAN DOMIN LEGIT COERCE ALL/VALS ...SOC CONCPT MYTH TREND CON/ANAL GEN/LAWS 20 LENIN/VI STALIN/J. PAGE 64 B1284 — B51 DELIB/GP ADMIN SOCISM

SCHRAMM W.,"COMMUNICATION IN THE SOVIETIZED STATE, AS DEMONSTRATED IN KOREA." ASIA COM KOREA COM/IND FACE/GP POL/PAR SCHOOL FORCES ADMIN PWR MARXISM ...SOC CONCPT MYTH INT BIOG TOT/POP 20. PAGE 94 B1901 — S51 ATTIT EDU/PROP TOTALISM

BRINTON C.,THE ANATOMY OF REVOLUTION. FRANCE UK USA-45 USSR WOR-45 ELITES INTELL ECO/DEV NAT/G EX/STRUC FORCES COERCE DRIVE ORD/FREE PWR SOVEREIGN ...MYTH HIST/WRIT GEN/LAWS. PAGE 15 B0311 — B52 SOCIETY CONCPT REV

DE GRAZIA A.,POLITICAL ORGANIZATION. CONSTN LOC/G MUNIC NAT/G CHIEF LEGIS TOP/EX ADJUD CT/SYS PERS/REL...INT/LAW MYTH UN. PAGE 27 B0553 — B52 FEDERAL LAW ADMIN

ALLPORT G.W.,THE NATURE OF PREJUDICE. USA+45 WOR+45 STRATA FACE/GP KIN NEIGH SECT ADMIN GP/REL DISCRIM ATTIT DRIVE LOVE RESPECT...PSY SOC MYTH QU/SEMANT 20. PAGE 4 B0078 — B54 CULTURE PERSON RACE/REL

MANNONI D.O.,PROSPERO AND CALIBAN: THE PSYCHOLOGY OF COLONIZATION. AFR EUR+WWI FAM KIN MUNIC SECT DOMIN ADMIN ATTIT DRIVE LOVE PWR RESPECT...PSY SOC CONCPT MYTH OBS DEEP/INT BIOG GEN/METH MALAGASY 20. PAGE 69 B1394 — B56 CULTURE COLONIAL

BAUER R.A.,"BRAINWASHING: PSYCHOLOGY OR DEMONOLOGY." ASIA CHINA/COM COM POL/PAR ECO/TAC ADMIN COERCE ATTIT DRIVE ORD/FREE...CONCPT MYTH 20. PAGE 10 B0196 — S57 EDU/PROP PSY TOTALISM

DAVENPORT J.,"ARMS AND THE WELFARE STATE." INTELL STRUCT FORCES CREATE ECO/TAC FOR/AID DOMIN LEGIT ADMIN WAR ORD/FREE PWR...POLICY SOC CONCPT MYTH OBS TREND COLD/WAR TOT/POP 20. PAGE 26 B0533 — S58 USA+45 NAT/G USSR

DERGE D.R.,"METROPOLITAN AND OUTSTATE ALIGNMENTS IN LEGIS — S58

ILLINOIS AND MISSOURI LEGISLATIVE DELEGATIONS" (BMR)" USA+45 ADMIN PARTIC GOV/REL...MYTH CHARTS 20 ILLINOIS MISSOURI. PAGE 28 B0575 — MUNIC PROVS POL/PAR

GRABER D.,CRISIS DIPLOMACY. L/A+17C USA+45 USA-45 NAT/G TOP/EX ECO/TAC COERCE ATTIT ORD/FREE...CONCPT MYTH TIME/SEQ COLD/WAR 20. PAGE 42 B0848 — B59 ROUTINE MORAL DIPLOM

DRAPER T.,AMERICAN COMMUNISM AND SOVIET RUSSIA. EUR+WWI USA+45 USSR INTELL AGRI COM/IND FINAN INDUS LABOR PROF/ORG VOL/ASSN PLAN TEC/DEV DOMIN EDU/PROP ADMIN COERCE REV PERSON PWR...POLICY CONCPT MYTH 19/20. PAGE 30 B0617 — B60 COM POL/PAR

NORTH R.C.,"DIE DISKREPANZ ZWISCHEN REALITAT UND WUNSCHBILD ALS INNENPOLITISCHER FAKTOR." ASIA CHINA/COM COM FUT ECO/UNDEV NAT/G PLAN DOMIN ADMIN COERCE PERCEPT...SOC MYTH GEN/METH WORK TOT/POP 20. PAGE 79 B1589 — S60 SOCIETY ECO/TAC

KOESTLER A.,THE LOTUS AND THE ROBOT. ASIA INDIA S/ASIA SOCIETY STRATA ECO/DEV AGRI INDUS FAM CREATE DOMIN EDU/PROP ADMIN COERCE ATTIT DRIVE SUPEGO ORD/FREE PWR RESPECT WEALTH...MYTH OBS 20 CHINJAP. PAGE 61 B1226 — B61 SECT ECO/UNDEV

CARLETON W.G.,"AMERICAN FOREIGN POLICY: MYTHS AND REALITIES." FUT USA+45 WOR+45 ECO/UNDEV INT/ORG EX/STRUC ARMS/CONT NUC/PWR WAR ATTIT...POLICY CONCPT CONT/OBS GEN/METH COLD/WAR TOT/POP 20. PAGE 19 B0378 — S61 PLAN MYTH DIPLOM

LIPPMANN W.,PREFACE TO POLITICS. LABOR CHIEF CONTROL LEAD...MYTH IDEA/COMP 19/20 ROOSEVLT/T TAMMANY WILSON/H SANTAYAN/G BERGSON/H. PAGE 65 B1318 — B62 PARTIC ATTIT ADMIN

HUDSON G.F.,"SOVIET FEARS OF THE WEST." COM USA+45 SOCIETY DELIB/GP EX/STRUC TOP/EX ACT/RES CREATE DOMIN EDU/PROP LEGIT ADMIN ROUTINE DRIVE PERSON RIGID/FLEX PWR...RECORD TIME/SEQ TOT/POP 20 STALIN/J. PAGE 52 B1057 — S62 ATTIT MYTH GERMANY USSR

TSOU T.,AMERICA'S FAILURE IN CHINA, 1941-1950. USA+45 USA-45 NAT/G ACT/RES PLAN DOMIN EDU/PROP ADMIN ROUTINE ATTIT PERSON ORD/FREE...DECISION CONCPT MYTH TIME/SEQ TREND STERTYP 20. PAGE 105 B2132 — B63 ASIA PERCEPT DIPLOM

TUCKER R.C.,THE SOVIET POLITICAL MIND. COM INTELL NAT/G TOP/EX EDU/PROP ADMIN COERCE TOTALISM ATTIT PWR MARXISM...PSY MYTH HYPO/EXP 20. PAGE 106 B2135 — B63 STRUCT RIGID/FLEX ELITES USSR

EATON H.,PRESIDENTIAL TIMBER: A HISTORY OF NOMINATING CONVENTIONS, 1868-1960. USA+45 USA-45 POL/PAR EX/STRUC DEBATE LOBBY ATTIT PERSON ALL/VALS ...MYTH 19/20 PRESIDENT. PAGE 32 B0646 — B64 DELIB/GP CHOOSE CHIEF NAT/G

DE GRAZIA A.,REPUBLIC IN CRISIS: CONGRESS AGAINST THE EXECUTIVE FORCE. USA+45 USA-45 SOCIETY POL/PAR CHIEF DOMIN ROLE ORD/FREE PWR...CONCPT MYTH BIBLIOG 20 CONGRESS. PAGE 27 B0556 — B65 LEGIS EXEC GOV/REL CONTROL

BLUMBERG A.S.,CRIMINAL JUSTICE. USA+45 CLIENT LAW LOC/G FORCES JUDGE ACT/RES LEGIT ADMIN RATIONAL MYTH. PAGE 13 B0259 — B67 JURID CT/SYS PROF/ORG CRIME

MACDONALD D.,AFRICANA; OR, THE HEART OF HEATHEN AFRICA. VOL. II: MISSION LIFE. SOCIETY STRATA KIN CREATE EDU/PROP ADMIN COERCE LITERACY HEALTH...MYTH WORSHIP 19 LIVNGSTN/D MISSION NEGRO. PAGE 67 B1355 — B82 SECT AFR CULTURE ORD/FREE

N

NAACP....NATIONAL ASSOCIATION FOR THE ADVANCEMENT OF COLORED PEOPLE

NABALOI....NABALOI TRIBE, PHILIPPINES

NADLER E.B. B1552

NAFTA....NORTH ATLANTIC FREE TRADE AREA

NAM....NATIONAL ASSOCIATION OF MANUFACTURERS

GABLE R.W.,"NAM: INFLUENTIAL LOBBY OR KISS OF DEATH?" (BMR)" USA+45 LAW INSPECT EDU/PROP ADMIN CONTROL INGP/REL EFFICIENCY PWR 20 CONGRESS NAM TAFT/HART. PAGE 38 B0769 — S53 LOBBY LEGIS INDUS LG/CO

NAM/TIEN....NAM TIEN

NAPOLEON/B....NAPOLEON BONAPARTE

B58
SHAW S.J.,.THE FINANCIAL AND ADMINISTRATIVE ORGANIZATION AND DEVELOPMENT OF OTTOMAN EGYPT 1517-1798. UAR LOC/G FORCES BUDGET INT/TRADE TAX EATING INCOME WEALTH...CHARTS BIBLIOG 16/18 OTTOMAN NAPOLEON/B. PAGE 96 B1940
FINAN
ADMIN
GOV/REL
CULTURE

NARAIN J.P. B1553

NARASIMHAN V.K. B1554

NARAYAN/J....JAYPRAKASH NARAYAN

NARCO/ACT....UNIFORM NARCOTIC DRUG ACT

NARVER J.C. B1555

NASA B1556

NASA....NATIONAL AERONAUTIC AND SPACE ADMINISTRATION

B63
DEAN A.L.,.FEDERAL AGENCY APPROACHES TO FIELD MANAGEMENT (PAMPHLET). R+D DELIB/GP EX/STRUC PROB/SOLV GOV/REL...CLASSIF BIBLIOG 20 FAA NASA DEPT/HEW POSTAL/SYS IRS. PAGE 28 B0563
ADMIN
MGT
NAT/G
OP/RES

B63
KAST F.E.,.SCIENCE, TECHNOLOGY, AND MANAGEMENT. SPACE USA+45 FORCES CONFER DETER NUC/PWR...PHIL/SCI CHARTS ANTHOL BIBLIOG 20 NASA. PAGE 58 B1179
MGT
PLAN
TEC/DEV
PROB/SOLV

B66
ROSHOLT R.L.,.AN ADMINISTRATIVE HISTORY OF NASA, 1958-1963. SPACE USA+45 FINAN LEAD...MGT CHARTS BIBLIOG 20 NASA. PAGE 90 B1824
ADMIN
EX/STRUC
ADJUST
DELIB/GP

S67
MACDONALD G.J.F.,."SCIENCE AND SPACE POLICY* HOW DOES IT GET PLANNED?" R+D CREATE TEC/DEV BUDGET ADMIN ROUTINE...DECISION NASA. PAGE 67 B1357
SPACE
PLAN
MGT
EX/STRUC

N67
US SUPERINTENDENT OF DOCUMENTS,SPACE: MISSILES, THE MOON, NASA, AND SATELLITES (PRICE LIST 79A). USA+45 COM/IND R+D NAT/G DIPLOM EDU/PROP ADMIN CONTROL HEALTH...POLICY SIMUL NASA CONGRESS. PAGE 111 B2244
BIBLIOG/A
SPACE
TEC/DEV
PEACE

N67
US SENATE COMM AERO SPACE SCI,.AERONAUTICAL RESEARCH AND DEVELOPMENT POLICY; HEARINGS, COMM ON AERONAUTICAL AND SPACE SCIENCES...1967 (PAMPHLET). R+D PROB/SOLV EXEC GOV/REL 20 DEPT/DEFEN FAA NASA CONGRESS. PAGE 109 B2210
DIST/IND
SPACE
NAT/G
PLAN

NASH B.D. B1557

NASH M. B1558

NASHVILLE....NASHVILLE, TENNESSEE

NASSER/G....GAMAL ABDUL NASSER

S66
PALMER M.,."THE UNITED ARAB REPUBLIC* AN ASSESSMENT OF ITS FAILURE." ELITES ECO/UNDEV POL/PAR FORCES ECO/TAC RUMOR ADMIN EXEC EFFICIENCY ATTIT SOCISM ...INT NASSER/G. PAGE 81 B1628
UAR
SYRIA
REGION
FEDERAL

NAT/COMP....COMPARISON OF NATIONS

N
ECONOMIC LIBRARY SELECTIONS. AGRI INDUS MARKET ADMIN...STAT NAT/COMP 20. PAGE 2 B0026
BIBLIOG/A
WRITING
FINAN

N
NEUE POLITISCHE LITERATUR; BERICHTE UBER DAS INTERNATIONALE SCHRIFTTUM ZUR POLITIK. WOR+45 LAW CONSTN POL/PAR ADMIN LEAD GOV/REL...POLICY IDEA/COMP. PAGE 2 B0027
BIBLIOG/A
DIPLOM
NAT/G
NAT/COMP

B18
WILSON W.,.THE STATE: ELEMENTS OF HISTORICAL AND PRACTICAL POLITICS. FRANCE GERMANY ITALY UK USSR CONSTN EX/STRUC LEGIS CT/SYS WAR PWR...POLICY GOV/COMP 20. PAGE 117 B2363
NAT/G
JURID
CONCPT
NAT/COMP

B33
ENSOR R.C.K.,.COURTS AND JUDGES IN FRANCE, GERMANY, AND ENGLAND. FRANCE GERMANY UK LAW PROB/SOLV ADMIN ROUTINE CRIME ROLE...METH/COMP 20 CIVIL/LAW. PAGE 33 B0676
CT/SYS
EX/STRUC
ADJUD
NAT/COMP

B39
ANDERSON W.,.LOCAL GOVERNMENT IN EUROPE. FRANCE GERMANY ITALY UK USSR MUNIC PROVS ADMIN GOV/REL CENTRAL SOVEREIGN 20. PAGE 5 B0099
GOV/COMP
NAT/COMP
LOC/G
CONSTN

B46
CORRY J.A.,.DEMOCRATIC GOVERNMENT AND POLITICS. WOR-45 EX/STRUC LOBBY TOTALISM...MAJORIT CONCPT
NAT/G
CONSTN

METH/COMP NAT/COMP 20. PAGE 24 B0479
POL/PAR
JURID

B49
MCLEAN J.M.,.THE PUBLIC SERVICE AND UNIVERSITY EDUCATION. UK USA-45 DELIB/GP EX/STRUC TOP/EX ADMIN ...GOV/COMP METH/COMP NAT/COMP ANTHOL 20. PAGE 72 B1455
ACADEM
NAT/G
EXEC
EDU/PROP

B58
CARTER G.M.,.TRANSITION IN AFRICA; STUDIES IN POLITICAL ADAPTATION. AFR CENTRL/AFR GHANA NIGERIA CONSTN LOC/G POL/PAR ADMIN GP/REL FEDERAL...MAJORIT BIBLIOG 20. PAGE 19 B0389
NAT/COMP
PWR
CONTROL
NAT/G

B58
KINTNER W.R.,.ORGANIZING FOR CONFLICT: A PROPOSAL. USSR STRUCT NAT/G LEGIS ADMIN EXEC PEACE ORD/FREE PWR...CONCPT OBS TREND NAT/COMP VAL/FREE COLD/WAR 20. PAGE 60 B1211
USA+45
PLAN
DIPLOM

B58
SHARMA M.P.,.PUBLIC ADMINISTRATION IN THEORY AND PRACTICE. INDIA UK USA+45 USA-45 EX/STRUC ADJUD ...POLICY CONCPT NAT/COMP 20. PAGE 96 B1935
MGT
ADMIN
DELIB/GP
JURID

B59
FAYERWEATHER J.,.THE EXECUTIVE OVERSEAS: ADMINISTRATIVE ATTITUDES AND RELATIONSHIPS IN A FOREIGN CULTURE. USA+45 WOR+45 CULTURE LG/CO SML/CO ATTIT...MGT PERS/COMP 20 MEXIC/AMER. PAGE 35 B0709
INT/TRADE
TOP/EX
NAT/COMP
PERS/REL

B60
AYEARST M.,.THE BRITISH WEST INDIES: THE SEARCH FOR SELF-GOVERNMENT. FUT WEST/IND LOC/G POL/PAR EX/STRUC LEGIS CHOOSE FEDERAL...NAT/COMP BIBLIOG 17/20. PAGE 7 B0152
CONSTN
COLONIAL
REPRESENT
NAT/G

B60
KERR C.,.INDUSTRIALISM AND INDUSTRIAL MAN. CULTURE SOCIETY ECO/UNDEV NAT/G ADMIN PRODUC WEALTH ...PREDICT TREND NAT/COMP 19/20. PAGE 59 B1197
WORKER
MGT
ECO/DEV
INDUS

B60
MEYRIAT J.,.LA SCIENCE POLITIQUE EN FRANCE, 1945-1958; BIBLIOGRAPHIES FRANCAISES DE SCIENCES SOCIALES (VOL. I). EUR+WWI FRANCE POL/PAR DIPLOM ADMIN CHOOSE ATTIT...IDEA/COMP METH/COMP NAT/COMP 20. PAGE 73 B1478
BIBLIOG/A
NAT/G
CONCPT
PHIL/SCI

B60
MOORE W.E.,.LABOR COMMITMENT AND SOCIAL CHANGE IN DEVELOPING AREAS. SOCIETY STRATA ECO/UNDEV MARKET VOL/ASSN WORKER AUTHORIT SKILL...MGT NAT/COMP SOC/INTEG 20. PAGE 75 B1514
LABOR
ORD/FREE
ATTIT
INDUS

B60
PINTO F.B.M.,.ENRIQUECIMENTO ILICITO NO EXERCICIO DE CARGOS PUBLICOS. BRAZIL L/A+17C USA+45 ELITES TRIBUTE CONTROL INGP/REL ORD/FREE PWR...NAT/COMP 20. PAGE 83 B1675
ADMIN
NAT/G
CRIME
LAW

B60
ROBINSON E.A.G.,.ECONOMIC CONSEQUENCES OF THE SIZE OF NATIONS. AGRI INDUS DELIB/GP FOR/AID ADMIN EFFICIENCY...METH/COMP 20. PAGE 89 B1799
CONCPT
INT/ORG
NAT/COMP

S60
BANFIELD E.C.,."THE POLITICAL IMPLICATIONS OF METROPOLITAN GROWTH" (BMR)" UK USA+45 LOC/G PROB/SOLV ADMIN GP/REL...METH/COMP NAT/COMP 20. PAGE 9 B0176
TASK
MUNIC
GOV/COMP
CENSUS

B61
DRAGNICH A.N.,.MAJOR EUROPEAN GOVERNMENTS. FRANCE GERMANY/W UK USSR LOC/G EX/STRUC CT/SYS PARL/PROC ATTIT MARXISM...JURID MGT NAT/COMP 19/20. PAGE 30 B0615
NAT/G
LEGIS
CONSTN
POL/PAR

B62
ANDREWS W.G.,.EUROPEAN POLITICAL INSTITUTIONS. FRANCE GERMANY UK USSR TOP/EX LEAD PARL/PROC CHOOSE 20. PAGE 5 B0104
NAT/COMP
POL/PAR
EX/STRUC
LEGIS

B62
BINDER L.,.IRAN: POLITICAL DEVELOPMENT IN A CHANGING SOCIETY. IRAN OP/RES REV GP/REL CENTRAL RATIONAL PWR...PHIL/SCI NAT/COMP GEN/LAWS 20. PAGE 12 B0239
LEGIT
NAT/G
ADMIN
STRUCT

B62
BROWN B.E.,.NEW DIRECTIONS IN COMPARATIVE POLITICS. AUSTRIA FRANCE GERMANY UK WOR+45 EX/STRUC LEGIS ORD/FREE 20. PAGE 16 B0320
NAT/COMP
METH
POL/PAR
FORCES

B62
FRIEDMANN W.,.METHODS AND POLICIES OF PRINCIPAL DONOR COUNTRIES IN PUBLIC INTERNATIONAL DEVELOPMENT FINANCING: PRELIMINARY APPRAISAL. FRANCE GERMANY/W UK USA+45 USSR WOR+45 FINAN TEC/DEV CAP/ISM DIPLOM ECO/TAC ATTIT 20 EEC. PAGE 37 B0759
INT/ORG
FOR/AID
NAT/COMP
ADMIN

B62
GALENSON W.,.LABOR IN DEVELOPING COUNTRIES. BRAZIL INDONESIA ISRAEL PAKISTAN TURKEY AGRI INDUS WORKER PAY PRICE GP/REL WEALTH...MGT CHARTS METH/COMP NAT/COMP 20. PAGE 38 B0775
LABOR
ECO/UNDEV
BARGAIN
POL/PAR

S62
IOVTCHOUK M.T.,."ON SOME THEORETICAL PRINCIPLES AND METHODS OF SOCIOLOGICAL INVESTIGATIONS (IN
COM
ECO/DEV

RUSSIAN)." FUT USA+45 STRATA R+D NAT/G POL/PAR CAP/ISM
TOP/EX ACT/RES PLAN ECO/TAC EDU/PROP ROUTINE ATTIT USSR
RIGID/FLEX MARXISM SOCISM...MARXIST METH/CNCPT OBS
TREND NAT/COMP GEN/LAWS 20. PAGE 54 B1102
B63

BROGAN D.W.,POLITICAL PATTERNS IN TODAY'S WORLD. NAT/COMP
FRANCE USA+45 USSR WOR+45 CONSTN STRUCT PLAN DIPLOM NEW/LIB
ADMIN LEAD ROLE SUPEGO...PHIL/SCI 20. PAGE 15 B0313 COM
TOTALISM
B63

KULZ H.R.,STAATSBURGER UND STAATSGEWALT (2 VOLS.). ADMIN
GERMANY SWITZERLND UK USSR CONSTN DELIB/GP TARIFFS ADJUD
TAX...JURID 20. PAGE 61 B1242 CT/SYS
NAT/COMP
B63

LEONARD T.J.,THE FEDERAL SYSTEM OF INDIA. INDIA FEDERAL
MUNIC NAT/G PROVS ADMIN SOVEREIGN...IDEA/COMP 20. MGT
PAGE 64 B1293 NAT/COMP
METH/COMP
B63

OLSON M. JR.,THE ECONOMICS OF WARTIME SHORTAGE. WAR
FRANCE GERMANY MOD/EUR UK AGRI PROB/SOLV ADMIN ADJUST
DEMAND WEALTH...POLICY OLD/LIB 17/20. PAGE 80 B1608 ECO/TAC
NAT/COMP
B63

RUITENBEER H.M.,THE DILEMMA OF ORGANIZATIONAL PERSON
SOCIETY. CULTURE ECO/DEV MUNIC SECT TEC/DEV ROLE
EDU/PROP NAT/LISM ORD/FREE...NAT/COMP 20 RIESMAN/D ADMIN
WHYTE/WF MERTON/R MEAD/MARG JASPERS/K. PAGE 92 WORKER
B1855
B63

SHANKS M.,THE LESSONS OF PUBLIC ENTERPRISE. UK SOCISM
LEGIS WORKER ECO/TAC ADMIN PARL/PROC GOV/REL ATTIT OWN
...POLICY MGT METH/COMP NAT/COMP ANTHOL 20 NAT/G
PARLIAMENT. PAGE 96 B1931 INDUS
B63

UN SECRETARY GENERAL,PLANNING FOR ECONOMIC PLAN
DEVELOPMENT. ECO/UNDEV FINAN BUDGET INT/TRADE ECO/TAC
TARIFFS TAX ADMIN 20 UN. PAGE 106 B2151 MGT
NAT/COMP
L63

BOLGAR V.,"THE PUBLIC INTEREST: A JURISPRUDENTIAL CONCPT
AND COMPARATIVE OVERVIEW OF SYMPOSIUM ON ORD/FREE
FUNDAMENTAL CONCEPTS OF PUBLIC LAW" COM FRANCE CONTROL
GERMANY SWITZERLND LAW ADJUD ADMIN AGREE LAISSEZ NAT/COMP
...JURID GEN/LAWS 20 EUROPE/E. PAGE 13 B0268
N63

GREAT BRITAIN DEPT TECH COOP,PUBLIC ADMINISTRATION: BIBLIOG/A
A SELECT BIBLIOGRAPHY (PAMPHLET). WOR+45 AGRI FINAN ADMIN
INDUS EX/STRUC OP/RES ECO/TAC...MGT METH/COMP NAT/G
NAT/COMP. PAGE 43 B0861 LOC/G
B64

AVASTHI A.,ASPECTS OF ADMINISTRATION. INDIA UK MGT
USA+45 FINAN ACADEM DELIB/GP LEGIS RECEIVE ADMIN
PARL/PROC PRIVIL...NAT/COMP 20. PAGE 7 B0150 SOC/WK
ORD/FREE
B64

GESELLSCHAFT RECHTSVERGLEICH,BIBLIOGRAPHIE DES BIBLIOG/A
DEUTSCHEN RECHTS (BIBLIOGRAPHY OF GERMAN LAW, JURID
TRANS. BY COURTLAND PETERSON). GERMANY FINAN INDUS CONSTN
LABOR SECT FORCES CT/SYS PARL/PROC CRIME...INT/LAW ADMIN
SOC NAT/COMP 20. PAGE 39 B0794
B64

GREBLER L.,URBAN RENEWAL IN EUROPEAN COUNTRIES: ITS MUNIC
EMERGENCE AND POTENTIALS. EUR+WWI UK ECO/DEV LOC/G PLAN
NEIGH CREATE ADMIN ATTIT...TREND NAT/COMP 20 CONSTRUC
URBAN/RNWL. PAGE 43 B0863 NAT/G
B64

HALLER W.,DER SCHWEDISCHE JUSTITIEOMBUDSMAN. JURID
DENMARK FINLAND NORWAY SWEDEN LEGIS ADJUD CONTROL PARL/PROC
PERSON ORD/FREE...NAT/COMP 20 OMBUDSMAN. PAGE 46 ADMIN
B0926 CHIEF
B64

RUSSET B.M.,WORLD HANDBOOK OF POLITICAL AND SOCIAL DIPLOM
INDICATORS. WOR+45 COM/IND ADMIN WEALTH...GEOG 20. STAT
PAGE 92 B1858 NAT/G
NAT/COMP
B64

SZLADITS C.,BIBLIOGRAPHY ON FOREIGN AND COMPARATIVE BIBLIOG/A
LAW: BOOKS AND ARTICLES IN ENGLISH (SUPPLEMENT JURID
1962). FINAN INDUS JUDGE LICENSE ADMIN CT/SYS ADJUD
PARL/PROC OWN...INT/LAW CLASSIF METH/COMP NAT/COMP LAW
20. PAGE 102 B2065
B64

WHEARE K.C.,FEDERAL GOVERNMENT (4TH ED.). WOR+45 FEDERAL
WOR-45 POL/PAR LEGIS BAL/PWR CT/SYS...POLICY JURID CONSTN
CONCPT GOV/COMP 17/20. PAGE 116 B2331 EX/STRUC
NAT/COMP
S64

CLIGNET R.,"POTENTIAL ELITES IN GHANA AND THE IVORY PWR
COAST: A PRELIMINARY SURVEY." AFR CULTURE ELITES LEGIT
STRATA KIN NAT/G SECT DOMIN EXEC ORD/FREE RESPECT IVORY/CST
SKILL...POLICY RELATIV GP/COMP NAT/COMP 20. PAGE 21 GHANA
B0438
S64

NASH M.,"SOCIAL PREREQUISITES TO ECONOMIC GROWTH IN ECO/DEV

LATIN AMERICA AND SOUTHEAST ASIA." L/A+17C S/ASIA PERCEPT
CULTURE SOCIETY ECO/UNDEV AGRI INDUS NAT/G PLAN
TEC/DEV EDU/PROP ROUTINE ALL/VALS...POLICY RELATIV
SOC NAT/COMP WORK TOT/POP 20. PAGE 77 B1558
B65

CRAMER J.F.,CONTEMPORARY EDUCATION: A COMPARATIVE EDU/PROP
STUDY OF NATIONAL SYSTEMS (2ND ED.). CHINA/COM NAT/COMP
EUR+WWI INDIA USA+45 FINAN PROB/SOLV ADMIN CONTROL SCHOOL
ATTIT...IDEA/COMP METH/COMP 20 CHINJAP. PAGE 25 ACADEM
B0502
B65

DUGGAR G.S.,RENEWAL OF TOWN AND VILLAGE I: A WORLD- MUNIC
WIDE SURVEY OF LOCAL GOVERNMENT EXPERIENCE. WOR+45 NEIGH
CONSTRUC INDUS CREATE BUDGET REGION GOV/REL...QU PLAN
NAT/COMP 20 URBAN/RNWL. PAGE 31 B0628 ADMIN
B65

GOPAL S.,BRITISH POLICY IN INDIA 1858-1905. INDIA COLONIAL
UK ELITES CHIEF DELIB/GP ECO/TAC GP/REL DISCRIM ADMIN
ATTIT...IDEA/COMP NAT/COMP PERS/COMP BIBLIOG/A POL/PAR
19/20. PAGE 41 B0828 ECO/UNDEV
B66

HEADY F.,PUBLIC ADMINISTRATION: A COMPARATIVE ADMIN
PERSPECTIVE. ECO/DEV ECO/UNDEV...GOV/COMP 20 NAT/COMP
BUREAUCRCY. PAGE 48 B0982 NAT/G
CIVMIL/REL
B66

OWEN G.,INDUSTRY IN THE UNITED STATES. UK USA+45 METH/COMP
NAT/G WEALTH...DECISION NAT/COMP 20. PAGE 80 B1620 INDUS
MGT
PROB/SOLV
B66

US SENATE COMM ON FOREIGN REL,HEARINGS ON S 2859 FOR/AID
AND S 2861. USA+45 WOR+45 FORCES BUDGET CAP/ISM DIPLOM
ADMIN DETER WEAPON TOTALISM...NAT/COMP 20 UN ORD/FREE
CONGRESS. PAGE 110 B2221 ECO/UNDEV
S66

HANSON A.H.,"PLANNING AND THE POLITICIANS* SOME PLAN
REFLECTIONS ON ECONOMIC PLANNING IN WESTERN ECO/DEV
EUROPE." MARKET NAT/G TEC/DEV CONSEN ROLE EUR+WWI
...METH/COMP NAT/COMP. PAGE 46 B0942 ADMIN
B67

ANDERSON C.W.,POLITICS AND ECONOMIC CHANGE IN LATIN ECO/UNDEV
AMERICA. L/A+17C INDUS NAT/G OP/RES ADMIN DEMAND PROB/SOLV
...POLICY STAT CHARTS NAT/COMP 20. PAGE 4 B0091 PLAN
ECO/TAC
B67

GELLHORN W.,OMBUDSMEN AND OTHERS: CITIZENS' NAT/COMP
PROTECTORS IN NINE COUNTRIES. WOR+45 LAW CONSTN REPRESENT
LEGIS INSPECT ADJUD ADMIN CONTROL CT/SYS CHOOSE INGP/REL
PERS/REL...STAT CHARTS 20. PAGE 39 B0789 PROB/SOLV
B67

GIFFORD P.,BRITAIN AND GERMANY IN AFRICA. AFR COLONIAL
GERMANY UK ECO/UNDEV LEAD WAR NAT/LISM ATTIT ADMIN
...POLICY HIST/WRIT METH/COMP ANTHOL BIBLIOG 19/20 DIPLOM
WWI. PAGE 39 B0797 NAT/COMP
B67

OVERSEAS DEVELOPMENT INSTIT,EFFECTIVE AID. WOR+45 FOR/AID
INT/ORG TEC/DEV DIPLOM INT/TRADE ADMIN. PAGE 80 ECO/UNDEV
B1619 ECO/TAC
NAT/COMP
S67

CARIAS B.,"EL CONTROL DE LAS EMPRESAS PUBLICAS POR WORKER
GRUPOS DE INTERESES DE LA COMUNIDAD." FRANCE UK REPRESENT
VENEZUELA INDUS NAT/G CONTROL OWN PWR...DECISION MGT
NAT/COMP 20. PAGE 18 B0377 SOCISM
S67

ZOETEWEIJ B.,"INCOME POLICIES ABROAD: AN INTERIM METH/COMP
REPORT." NAT/G PROB/SOLV BARGAIN BUDGET PRICE RISK INCOME
CENTRAL EFFICIENCY EQUILIB...MGT NAT/COMP 20. POLICY
PAGE 119 B2405 LABOR

NAT/FARMER....NATIONAL FARMERS' ASSOCIATION

NAT/G....NATIONAL GOVERNMENT

NAT/LISM....NATIONALISM
N19

JACKSON R.G.A.,THE CASE FOR AN INTERNATIONAL FOR/AID
DEVELOPMENT AUTHORITY (PAMPHLET). WOR+45 ECO/DEV INT/ORG
DIPLOM GIVE CONTROL GP/REL EFFICIENCY NAT/LISM ECO/UNDEV
SOVEREIGN 20. PAGE 55 B1108 ADMIN
B26

MOON P.T.,IMPERIALISM AND WORLD POLITICS. AFR ASIA WEALTH
ISLAM MOD/EUR S/ASIA USA-45 SOCIETY NAT/G EX/STRUC TIME/SEQ
BAL/PWR DOMIN COLONIAL NAT/LISM ATTIT DRIVE PWR CAP/ISM
...GEOG SOC 20. PAGE 75 B1510 DIPLOM
B27

ANGELL N.,THE PUBLIC MIND. USA-45 SOCIETY EDU/PROP PERCEPT
ROUTINE SUPEGO KNOWL...POLICY CONCPT MYTH OBS/ENVIR ATTIT
EUR+WW1 TOT/POP 20. PAGE 5 B0109 DIPLOM
NAT/LISM
B38

HARPER S.N.,THE GOVERNMENT OF THE SOVIET UNION. COM MARXISM
USSR LAW CONSTN ECO/DEV PLAN TEC/DEV DIPLOM NAT/G
INT/TRADE ADMIN REV NAT/LISM...POLICY 20. PAGE 47 LEAD

B0952   POL/PAR
                                                        B39
ZIMMERN A.,MODERN POLITICAL DOCTRINE. WOR-45   NAT/G
CULTURE SOCIETY ECO/UNDEV DELIB/GP EX/STRUC CREATE ECO/TAC
DOMIN COERCE NAT/LISM ATTIT RIGID/FLEX ORD/FREE PWR BAL/PWR
WEALTH...POLICY CONCPT OBS TIME/SEQ TREND TOT/POP   INT/TRADE
LEAGUE/NAT 20. PAGE 119 B2402
                                                        B42
BINGHAM A.M.,THE TECHNIQUES OF DEMOCRACY. USA-45   POPULISM
CONSTN STRUCT POL/PAR LEGIS PLAN PARTIC CHOOSE   ORD/FREE
REPRESENT NAT/LISM TOTALISM...MGT 20. PAGE 12 B0240 ADMIN
                                                   NAT/G
                                                        L44
HAILEY,"THE FUTURE OF COLONIAL PEOPLES." WOR-45   PLAN
CONSTN CULTURE ECO/UNDEV AGRI MARKET INT/ORG NAT/G CONCPT
SECT CONSULT ECO/TAC LEGIT ADMIN NAT/LISM ALL/VALS DIPLOM
...SOC OBS TREND STERTYP CMN/WLTH LEAGUE/NAT   UK
PARLIAMENT 20. PAGE 45 B0916
                                                        B46
GRIFFIN G.G.,A GUIDE TO MANUSCRIPTS RELATING TO   BIBLIOG/A
AMERICAN HISTORY IN BRITISH DEPOSITORIES. CANADA   ALL/VALS
IRELAND MOD/EUR UK USA-45 LAW DIPLOM ADMIN COLONIAL NAT/G
WAR NAT/LISM SOVEREIGN...GEOG INT/LAW 15/19
CMN/WLTH. PAGE 43 B0876
                                                        S50
EPSTEIN L.D.,"POLITICAL STERILIZATION OF CIVIL   ADMIN
SERVANTS: THE UNITED STATES AND GREAT BRITAIN." UK LEGIS
USA-45 USA-45 STRUCT TOP/EX OP/RES PARTIC CHOOSE   DECISION
NAT/LISM 20 CONGRESS CIVIL/SERV. PAGE 33 B0679   POL/PAR
                                                        B52
HIMMELFARB G.,LORD ACTON: A STUDY IN CONSCIENCE AND PWR
POLITICS. MOD/EUR NAT/G POL/PAR SECT LEGIS TOP/EX   BIOG
EDU/PROP ADMIN NAT/LISM ATTIT PERSON SUPEGO MORAL
ORD/FREE...CONCPT PARLIAMENT 19 ACTON/LORD. PAGE 50
B1014
                                                        B52
MILLER M.,THE JUDGES AND THE JUDGED. USA+45 LG/CO COM/IND
ACT/RES TV ROUTINE SANCTION NAT/LISM ATTIT ORD/FREE DISCRIM
...POLICY ACLU. PAGE 73 B1481   EDU/PROP
                                                   MARXISM
                                                        C54
LANDAU J.M.,"PARLIAMENTS AND PARTIES IN EGYPT." UAR ISLAM
NAT/G SECT CONSULT LEGIS TOP/EX PROB/SOLV ADMIN   NAT/LISM
COLONIAL...GEN/LAWS BIBLIOG 19/20. PAGE 62 B1254   PARL/PROC
                                                   POL/PAR
                                                        B55
MAZZINI J.,THE DUTIES OF MAN. MOD/EUR LAW SOCIETY SUPEGO
FAM NAT/G POL/PAR SECT VOL/ASSN EX/STRUC ACT/RES   CONCPT
CREATE REV PEACE ATTIT ALL/VALS...GEN/LAWS WORK 19. NAT/LISM
PAGE 71 B1439
                                                        S56
KHAMA T.,"POLITICAL CHANGE IN AFRICAN SOCIETY."   AFR
CONSTN SOCIETY LOC/G NAT/G POL/PAR EX/STRUC LEGIS   ELITES
LEGIT ADMIN CHOOSE REPRESENT NAT/LISM MORAL
ORD/FREE PWR...CONCPT OBS TREND GEN/METH CMN/WLTH
17/20. PAGE 59 B1201
                                                        S57
HAILEY,"TOMORROW IN AFRICA." CONSTN SOCIETY LOC/G AFR
NAT/G DOMIN ADJUD ADMIN GP/REL DISCRIM NAT/LISM   PERSON
ATTIT MORAL ORD/FREE...PSY SOC CONCPT OBS RECORD   ELITES
TREND GEN/LAWS CMN/WLTH 20. PAGE 45 B0917   RACE/REL
                                                        B58
COLEMAN J.S.,NIGERIA: BACKGROUND TO NATIONALISM.   NAT/G
AFR SOCIETY ECO/DEV KIN LOC/G POL/PAR TEC/DEV DOMIN NAT/LISM
ADMIN DRIVE PWR RESPECT...TRADIT SOC INT SAMP   NIGERIA
TIME/SEQ 20. PAGE 22 B0452
                                                        B58
LAQUER W.Z.,THE MIDDLE EAST IN TRANSITION. COM USSR ISLAM
ECO/UNDEV NAT/G VOL/ASSN EDU/PROP EXEC ATTIT DRIVE TREND
PWR MARXISM COLD/WAR TOT/POP 20. PAGE 62 B1261   NAT/LISM
                                                        S59
BAILEY S.D.,"THE FUTURE COMPOSITION OF THE   INT/ORG
TRUSTEESHIP COUNCIL." FUT WOR+45 CONSTN VOL/ASSN   NAT/LISM
ADMIN ATTIT PWR...OBS TREND CON/ANAL VAL/FREE UN   SOVEREIGN
20. PAGE 8 B0161
                                                        B60
HAUSER O.,PREUSSISCHE STAATSRASON UND NATIONALER   NAT/LISM
GEDANKE. PRUSSIA SOCIETY PRESS ADMIN...CONCPT   NAT/G
19/20. PAGE 48 B0969   ATTIT
                                                   PROVS
                                                        B60
LENCZOWSKI G.,OIL AND STATE IN THE MIDDLE EAST. FUT ISLAM
IRAN LAW ECO/UNDEV EXTR/IND NAT/G TOP/EX PLAN   INDUS
TEC/DEV ECO/TAC LEGIT ADMIN COERCE ATTIT ALL/VALS   NAT/LISM
PWR...CHARTS 20. PAGE 64 B1288
                                                        B60
PIERCE R.A.,RUSSIAN CENTRAL ASIA, 1867-1917. ASIA COLONIAL
RUSSIA CULTURE AGRI INDUS EDU/PROP REV NAT/LISM   DOMIN
...CHARTS BIBLIOG 19/20 BOLSHEVISM INTERVENT.   ADMIN
PAGE 83 B1672   ECO/UNDEV
                                                        S60
APTER D.E.,"THE ROLE OF TRADITIONALISM IN THE   CONSERVE
POLITICAL MODERNIZATION OF GHANA AND UGANDA" (BMR)" ADMIN
AFR GHANA UGANDA CULTURE NAT/G POL/PAR NAT/LISM   GOV/COMP
...CON/ANAL 20. PAGE 6 B0121   PROB/SOLV

                                                        S60
BOGARDUS E.S.,"THE SOCIOLOGY OF A STRUCTURED   INT/ORG
PEACE." FUT SOCIETY CREATE DIPLOM EDU/PROP ADJUD   SOC
ROUTINE ATTIT RIGID/FLEX KNOWL ORD/FREE RESPECT   NAT/LISM
...POLICY INT/LAW JURID NEW/IDEA SELF/OBS TOT/POP   PEACE
20 UN. PAGE 13 B0264
                                                        S60
SCHWARTZ B.,"THE INTELLIGENTSIA IN COMMUNIST CHINA: INTELL
A TENTATIVE COMPARISON." ASIA CHINA/COM COM RUSSIA RIGID/FLEX
ELITES SOCIETY STRATA POL/PAR VOL/ASSN CREATE ADMIN REV
COERCE NAT/LISM TOTALISM...POLICY TREND 20. PAGE 95
B1914
                                                        B62
INGHAM K.,A HISTORY OF EAST AFRICA. NAT/G DIPLOM   AFR
ADMIN WAR NAT/LISM...SOC BIOG BIBLIOG. PAGE 54   CONSTN
B1085   COLONIAL
                                                        B62
SCALAPINO R.A.,PARTIES AND POLITICS IN CONTEMPORARY POL/PAR
JAPAN. EX/STRUC DIPLOM CHOOSE NAT/LISM ATTIT   PARL/PROC
...POLICY 20 CHINJAP. PAGE 93 B1876   ELITES
                                                   DECISION
                                                        B63
CROZIER B.,THE MORNING AFTER; A STUDY OF   SOVEREIGN
INDEPENDENCE. WOR+45 EX/STRUC PLAN BAL/PWR COLONIAL NAT/LISM
GP/REL 20 COLD/WAR. PAGE 25 B0511   NAT/G
                                                   DIPLOM
                                                        B63
ELIAS T.O.,THE NIGERIAN LEGAL SYSTEM. NIGERIA LAW CT/SYS
FAM KIN SECT ADMIN NAT/LISM...JURID 18/20   ADJUD
ENGLSH/LAW COMMON/LAW. PAGE 33 B0665   COLONIAL
                                                   PROF/ORG
                                                        B63
FRIED R.C.,THE ITALIAN PREFECTS. ITALY STRATA   ADMIN
ECO/DEV NAT/LISM ALL/IDEOS...TREND CHARTS METH/COMP NAT/G
BIBLIOG 17/20 PREFECT. PAGE 37 B0755   EFFICIENCY
                                                        B63
HIGA M.,POLITICS AND PARTIES IN POSTWAR OKINAWA.   GOV/REL
USA+45 VOL/ASSN LEGIS CONTROL LOBBY CHOOSE NAT/LISM POL/PAR
PWR SOVEREIGN MARXISM SOCISM 20 OKINAWA CHINJAP.   ADMIN
PAGE 50 B1008   FORCES
                                                        B63
MCKIE R.,MALAYSIA IN FOCUS. INDONESIA WOR+45   S/ASIA
ECO/UNDEV FINAN NAT/G POL/PAR SECT FORCES PLAN   NAT/LISM
ADMIN COLONIAL COERCE DRIVE ALL/VALS...POLICY   MALAYSIA
RECORD CENSUS TIME/SEQ CMN/WLTH 20. PAGE 72 B1453
                                                        B63
RUITENBEER H.M.,THE DILEMMA OF ORGANIZATIONAL   PERSON
SOCIETY. CULTURE ECO/DEV MUNIC SECT TEC/DEV   ROLE
EDU/PROP NAT/LISM ORD/FREE...NAT/COMP 20 RIESMAN/D ADMIN
WHYTE/WF MERTON/R MEAD/MARG JASPERS/K. PAGE 92   WORKER
B1855
                                                        B63
SINGH H.L.,PROBLEMS AND POLICIES OF THE BRITISH IN COLONIAL
INDIA. 1885-1898. INDIA UK NAT/G FORCES LEGIS   PWR
PROB/SOLV CONTROL RACE/REL ADJUST DISCRIM NAT/LISM POLICY
RIGID/FLEX...MGT 19 CIVIL/SERV. PAGE 97 B1968   ADMIN
                                                        S63
RUSTOW D.A.,"THE MILITARY IN MIDDLE EASTERN SOCIETY FORCES
AND POLITICS." FUT ISLAM CONSTN SOCIETY FACE/GP   ELITES
NAT/G POL/PAR PROF/ORG CONSULT DOMIN ADMIN EXEC
REGION COERCE NAT/LISM ATTIT DRIVE PERSON ORD/FREE
PWR...POLICY CONCPT OBS STERTYP 20. PAGE 92 B1860
                                                        C63
BLUM J.M.,"THE NATIONAL EXPERIENCE." USA+45 USA-45 ADMIN
ECO/DEV DIPLOM WAR NAT/LISM...POLICY CHARTS BIBLIOG NAT/G
T 16/20 CONGRESS PRESIDENT COLD/WAR. PAGE 13 B0258 LEGIS
                                                   CHIEF
                                                        B64
ELDREDGE H.W.,THE SECOND AMERICAN REVOLUTION.   ELITES
EDU/PROP NAT/LISM RATIONAL TOTALISM FASCISM MARXISM ORD/FREE
SOCISM. PAGE 33 B0664   ADMIN
                                                   PLAN
                                                        B64
HANNA W.J.,INDEPENDENT BLACK AFRICA: THE POLITICS AFR
OF FREEDOM. ELITES INDUS KIN CHIEF COLONIAL CHOOSE ECO/UNDEV
GOV/REL RACE/REL NAT/LISM ATTIT PERSON 20 NEGRO.   ADMIN
PAGE 46 B0938   PROB/SOLV
                                                        B64
SINGER M.R.,THE EMERGING ELITE: A STUDY OF   TOP/EX
POLITICAL LEADERSHIP IN CEYLON. S/ASIA ECO/UNDEV   STRATA
AGRI KIN NAT/G SECT EX/STRUC LEGIT ATTIT PWR   NAT/LISM
RESPECT...SOC STAT CHARTS 20. PAGE 97 B1967   CEYLON
                                                        L64
RIPLEY R.B.,"INTERAGENCY COMMITTEES AND   EXEC
INCREMENTALISM: THE CASE OF AID TO INDIA." INDIA   MGT
USA+45 INTELL NAT/G DELIB/GP ACT/RES DIPLOM ROUTINE FOR/AID
NAT/LISM ATTIT PWR...SOC CONCPT NEW/IDEA TIME/SEQ
CON/ANAL VAL/FREE 20. PAGE 89 B1790
                                                        B65
INST INTL DES CIVILISATION DIF,THE CONSTITUTIONS   CONSTN
AND ADMINISTRATIVE INSTITUTIONS OF THE NEW STATES. ADMIN
AFR ISLAM S/ASIA NAT/G POL/PAR DELIB/GP EX/STRUC   ADJUD
CONFER EFFICIENCY NAT/LISM...JURID SOC 20. PAGE 54 ECO/UNDEV
B1088
                                                        B65
MATRAS J.,SOCIAL CHANGE IN ISRAEL. ISRAEL STRATA   SECT

FAM ACT/RES EDU/PROP ADMIN CHOOSE...STAT CENSUS 19/20 JEWS. PAGE 71 B1427
NAT/LISM GEOG STRUCT

B65
PURCELL V.,THE MEMOIRS OF A MALAYAN OFFICIAL. MALAYSIA UK ECO/UNDEV INDUS LABOR EDU/PROP COLONIAL CT/SYS WAR NAT/LISM TOTALISM ORD/FREE SOVEREIGN 20 UN CIVIL/SERV. PAGE 85 B1721
BIOG ADMIN JURID FORCES

B65
ROTBERG R.I.,A POLITICAL HISTORY OF TROPICAL AFRICA. EX/STRUC DIPLOM INT/TRADE DOMIN ADMIN RACE/REL NAT/LISM PWR SOVEREIGN...GEOG TIME/SEQ BIBLIOG 1/20. PAGE 91 B1832
AFR CULTURE COLONIAL

B65
YOUNG C.,POLITICS IN THE CONGO* DECOLONIZATION AND INDEPENDENCE. ELITES STRATA FORCES ADMIN REV RACE/REL FEDERAL SOVEREIGN...OBS INT CHARTS CONGO/LEOP. PAGE 118 B2391
BELGIUM COLONIAL NAT/LISM

B66
WILLNER A.R.,THE NEOTRADITIONAL ACCOMMODATION TO POLITICAL INDEPENDENCE* THE CASE OF INDONESIA * RESEARCH MONOGRAPH NO. 26. CULTURE ECO/UNDEV CREATE PROB/SOLV FOR/AID LEGIT COLONIAL EFFICIENCY NAT/LISM ALL/VALS SOC. PAGE 117 B2355
INDONESIA CONSERVE ELITES ADMIN

C66
TARLING N.,"A CONCISE HISTORY OF SOUTHEAST ASIA." BURMA CAMBODIA LAOS S/ASIA THAILAND VIETNAM ECO/UNDEV POL/PAR FORCES ADMIN REV WAR CIVMIL/REL ORD/FREE MARXISM SOCISM 13/20. PAGE 103 B2080
COLONIAL DOMIN INT/TRADE NAT/LISM

B67
GIFFORD P.,BRITAIN AND GERMANY IN AFRICA. AFR GERMANY UK ECO/UNDEV LEAD WAR NAT/LISM ATTIT ...POLICY HIST/WRIT METH/COMP ANTHOL BIBLIOG 19/20 WWI. PAGE 39 B0797
COLONIAL ADMIN DIPLOM NAT/COMP

B67
JHANGIANI M.A.,JANA SANGH AND SWATANTRA: A PROFILE OF THE RIGHTIST PARTIES IN INDIA. INDIA ADMIN CHOOSE MARXISM SOCISM...INT CHARTS BIBLIOG 20. PAGE 56 B1140
POL/PAR LAISSEZ NAT/LISM ATTIT

B67
NIVEN R.,NIGERIA. NIGERIA CONSTN INDUS EX/STRUC COLONIAL REV NAT/LISM...CHARTS 19/20. PAGE 78 B1584
NAT/G REGION CHOOSE GP/REL

B67
RAVKIN A.,THE NEW STATES OF AFRICA (HEADLINE SERIES, NO. 183((PAMPHLET). CULTURE STRUCT INDUS COLONIAL NAT/LISM...SOC 20. PAGE 86 B1744
AFR ECO/UNDEV SOCIETY ADMIN

B67
ROFF W.R.,THE ORIGINS OF MALAY NATIONALISM. MALAYSIA INTELL NAT/G ADMIN COLONIAL...BIBLIOG DICTIONARY 20 CMN/WLTH. PAGE 90 B1813
NAT/LISM ELITES VOL/ASSN SOCIETY

B67
SABLE M.H.,A GUIDE TO LATIN AMERICAN STUDIES (2 VOLS). CONSTN FINAN INT/ORG LABOR MUNIC POL/PAR FORCES CAP/ISM FOR/AID ADMIN MARXISM SOCISM OAS. PAGE 92 B1861
BIBLIOG/A L/A+17C DIPLOM NAT/LISM

B67
SCHEINMAN L.,EURATOM* NUCLEAR INTEGRATION IN EUROPE. EX/STRUC LEAD 20 EURATOM. PAGE 93 B1885
INT/ORG NAT/LISM NUC/PWR DIPLOM

L67
TAMBIAH S.J.,"THE POLITICS OF LANGUAGE IN INDIA AND CEYLON." CEYLON INDIA NAT/G DOMIN ADMIN...SOC 20. PAGE 102 B2070
POL/PAR LING NAT/LISM REGION

S67
BREGMAN A.,"WHITHER RUSSIA?" COM RUSSIA INTELL POL/PAR DIPLOM PARTIC NAT/LISM TOTALISM ATTIT ORD/FREE 20. PAGE 15 B0304
MARXISM ELITES ADMIN CREATE

S67
DONNELL J.C.,"PACIFICATION REASSESSED." VIETNAM/S NAT/LISM DRIVE SUPEGO ORD/FREE...SOC/WK 20. PAGE 30 B0606
ADMIN GP/REL EFFICIENCY MUNIC

S67
GRUNDY K.W.,"THE POLITICAL USES OF IMAGINATION." GHANA ELITES SOCIETY NAT/G DOMIN EDU/PROP COLONIAL REGION REPRESENT GP/REL CENTRAL PWR MARXISM 20. PAGE 44 B0897
NAT/LISM EX/STRUC AFR LEAD

S67
HUGON P.,"BLOCAGES ET DESEQUILIBRES DE LA CROISSANCE ECONOMIQUE EN AFRIQUE NOIRE." AFR KIN MUNIC CREATE PLAN INT/TRADE REGION ADJUST CENTRAL EQUILIB NAT/LISM ORD/FREE 20. PAGE 52 B1060
ECO/UNDEV COLONIAL STRUCT ADMIN

S67
LIU K.C.,"DISINTEGRATION OF THE OLD ORDER." ASIA SOCIETY PROB/SOLV ADMIN REGION TOTALISM ORD/FREE MARXISM 19/20. PAGE 66 B1329
ADJUST NAT/LISM

S67
NEUCHTERLEIN D.E.,"THAILAND* ANOTHER VIETNAM?" THAILAND ECO/UNDEV DIPLOM ADMIN REGION CENTRAL
WAR GUERRILLA

NAT/LISM...POLICY 20. PAGE 78 B1571
S/ASIA NAT/G

NAT/SAFETY....NATIONAL SAFETY COUNCIL

NAT/SERV....COMPULSORY NATIONAL SERVICE

NAT/UNITY....NATIONAL UNITY COMMITTEE (TURKEY)

NATAL

B67
KONCZACKI Z.A.,PUBLIC FINANCE AND ECONOMIC DEVELOPMENT OF NATAL 1893-1910. TAX ADMIN COLONIAL ...STAT CHARTS BIBLIOG 19/20 NATAL. PAGE 61 B1228
ECO/TAC FINAN NAT/G ECO/UNDEV

NATHAN M. B1559

NATIONAL AERONAUTIC AND SPACE ADMINISTRATION....SEE NASA

NATIONAL ASSOCIATION FOR THE ADVANCEMENT OF COLORED PEOPLE....SEE NAACP

NATIONAL ASSOCIATION OF MANUFACTURERS....SEE NAM

NATIONAL BELLAS HESS....SEE BELLAS/HES

NATIONAL COUNCIL OF CHURCHES....SEE NCC

NATIONAL DEBT....SEE DEBT

NATIONAL DIRECTORY (IRELAND)....SEE DIRECT/NAT

NATIONAL EDUCATION ASSOCIATION....SEE NEA

NATIONAL FARMERS' ASSOCIATION....SEE NAT/FARMER

NATIONAL GUARD....SEE NATL/GUARD

NATIONAL INSTITUTE OF HEALTH....SEE NIH

NATIONAL INSTITUTE OF PUBLIC ADMINISTRATION....SEE NIPA

NATIONAL LABOR RELATIONS BOARD....SEE NLRB

NATIONAL LIBERATION COUNCIL IN GHANA....SEE NLC

NATIONAL LIBERATION FRONT (OF SOUTH VIETNAM)....SEE NLF

NATIONAL RECOVERY ADMINISTRATION....SEE NRA

NATIONAL SAFETY COUNCIL....SEE NAT/SAFETY

NATIONAL SCIENCE FOUNDATION....SEE NSF

NATIONAL SECURITY COUNCIL....SEE NSC

NATIONAL SECURITY....SEE ORD/FREE

NATIONAL SOCIAL SCIENCE FOUNDATION....SEE NSSF

NATIONAL UNITY COMMITTEE....SEE NUC

NATIONAL WEALTH....SEE NAT/G+WEALTH

NATIONAL BOOK CENTRE PAKISTAN B1560

NATIONAL BOOK LEAGUE B1561

NATIONAL BUREAU ECONOMIC RES B1562

NATIONAL COMN COMMUNITY HEALTH B1563

NATIONALISM....SEE NAT/LISM

NATIONALIST CHINA....SEE TAIWAN

NATIONALIZATION....SEE SOCISM

NATL/GUARD....NATIONAL GUARD
NATL ADVANCED-TECH MGT CONF B1179
NATO....NORTH ATLANTIC TREATY ORGANIZATION; SEE ALSO VOL/ASSN, INT/ORG, FORCES, DETER

B61
KERTESZ S.D.,AMERICAN DIPLOMACY IN A NEW ERA. COM S/ASIA UK USA+45 FORCES PROB/SOLV BAL/PWR ECO/TAC ADMIN COLONIAL WAR PEACE ORD/FREE 20 NATO CONGRESS UN COLD/WAR. PAGE 59 B1199
ANTHOL DIPLOM TREND

S61
HAAS E.B.,"INTERNATIONAL INTEGRATION: THE EUROPEAN AND THE UNIVERSAL PROCESS." EUR+WWI FUT WOR+45 NAT/G EX/STRUC ATTIT DRIVE ORD/FREE PWR...CONCPT GEN/LAWS OEEC 20 NATO COUNCL/EUR. PAGE 45 B0909
INT/ORG TREND REGION

MULLEY F.W.,THE POLITICS OF WESTERN DEFENSE.   INT/ORG
EUR+WWI USA-45 WOR+45 VOL/ASSN EX/STRUC FORCES   DELIB/GP
COERCE DETER PEACE ATTIT ORD/FREE PWR...RECORD   NUC/PWR
TIME/SEQ CHARTS COLD/WAR 20 NATO. PAGE 76 B1537
                                                          B62

BOWIE R.,"STRATEGY AND THE ATLANTIC ALLIANCE."   FORCES
EUR+WWI VOL/ASSN BAL/PWR COERCE NUC/PWR ATTIT   ROUTINE
ORD/FREE PWR...DECISION GEN/LAWS NATO COLD/WAR 20.
PAGE 14 B0287
                                                          S63

STANLEY T.W.,"DECENTRALIZING NUCLEAR CONTROL IN   INT/ORG
NATO." EUR+WWI USA+45 ELITES FORCES ACT/RES ATTIT   EX/STRUC
ORD/FREE PWR...NEW/IDEA HYPO/EXP TOT/POP 20 NATO.   NUC/PWR
PAGE 100 B2022
                                                          S63

COTTRELL A.J.,THE POLITICS OF THE ATLANTIC   VOL/ASSN
ALLIANCE. EUR+WWI USA+45 INT/ORG NAT/G DELIB/GP   FORCES
EX/STRUC BAL/PWR DIPLOM REGION DETER ATTIT ORD/FREE
...CONCPT RECORD GEN/LAWS GEN/METH NATO. PAGE 24
B0493
                                                          B64

BROWN S.,"AN ALTERNATIVE TO THE GRAND DESIGN."   VOL/ASSN
EUR+WWI FUT USA+45 INT/ORG NAT/G EX/STRUC FORCES   CONCPT
CREATE BAL/PWR DOMIN RIGID/FLEX ORD/FREE   DIPLOM
...NEW/IDEA RECORD EEC NATO 20. PAGE 16 B0327
                                                          S65

BEAUFRE A.,NATO AND EUROPE. WOR+45 PLAN CONFER EXEC   INT/ORG
NUC/PWR ATTIT...POLICY 20 NATO EUROPE. PAGE 10   DETER
B0203   DIPLOM
                                                      ADMIN
                                                          B66

SPICER K.,A SAMARITAN STATE? AFR CANADA INDIA   DIPLOM
PAKISTAN UK USA+45 FINAN INDUS PRODUC...CHARTS 20   FOR/AID
NATO. PAGE 99 B2006   ECO/DEV
                                                      ADMIN
                                                          B66

NATURL/LAW....NATURAL LAW

NAVAHO....NAVAHO INDIANS

NAVAL/RES....OFFICE OF NAVAL RESEARCH

NAVY....NAVY (ALL NATIONS)

NAZI....NAZI MOVEMENT (ALL NATIONS); SEE ALSO GERMANY,
   NAT/LISM, FASCIST

RAPPARD W.E.,THE CRISIS OF DEMOCRACY. EUR+WWI UNIV   NAT/G
WOR-45 CULTURE SOCIETY ECO/DEV INT/ORG POL/PAR   CONCPT
ACT/RES EDU/PROP EXEC CHOOSE ATTIT ALL/VALS...SOC
OBS HIST/WRIT TIME/SEQ LEAGUE/NAT NAZI TOT/POP 20.
PAGE 86 B1741
                                                          B38

HITLER A.,MEIN KAMPF. EUR+WWI FUT MOD/EUR STRUCT   PWR
INT/ORG LABOR NAT/G POL/PAR FORCES CREATE PLAN   NEW/IDEA
BAL/PWR DIPLOM ECO/TAC DOMIN EDU/PROP ADMIN COERCE   WAR
ATTIT...SOCIALIST BIOG TREND NAZI. PAGE 50 B1020
                                                          B39

NEUBURGER O.,OFFICIAL PUBLICATIONS OF PRESENT-DAY   BIBLIOG/A
GERMANY: GOVERNMENT, CORPORATE ORGANIZATIONS, AND   FASCISM
NATIONAL SOCIALIST PARTY. GERMANY CONSTN COM/IND   NAT/G
POL/PAR EDU/PROP PRESS 20 NAZI. PAGE 78 B1570   ADMIN
                                                          B42

SINGTON D.,THE GOEBBELS EXPERIMENT. GERMANY MOD/EUR   FASCISM
NAT/G EX/STRUC FORCES CONTROL ROUTINE WAR TOTALISM   EDU/PROP
PWR...ART/METH HUM 20 NAZI GOEBBELS/J. PAGE 97   ATTIT
B1970   COM/IND
                                                          B42

LASSWELL H.D.,THE ANALYSIS OF POLITICAL BEHAVIOUR: R+D
AN EMPIRICAL APPROACH. WOR+45 CULTURE NAT/G FORCES   ACT/RES
EDU/PROP ADMIN ATTIT PERCEPT KNOWL...PHIL/SCI PSY   ELITES
SOC NEW/IDEA OBS INT GEN/METH NAZI 20. PAGE 63
B1267
                                                          B47

HULL C.,THE MEMOIRS OF CORDELL HULL (VOLUME ONE).   BIOG
USA-45 WOR-45 CONSTN FAM LOC/G PROVS DELIB/GP   DIPLOM
FORCES LEGIS TOP/EX BAL/PWR LEGIT ADMIN EXEC WAR
ATTIT ORD/FREE PWR...MAJORIT SELF/OBS TIME/SEQ
TREND NAZI 20. PAGE 52 B1062
                                                          B48

MEYER P.,THE JEWS IN THE SOVIET SATELLITES.   COM
CZECHOSLVK POLAND SOCIETY STRATA NAT/G BAL/PWR   SECT
ECO/TAC EDU/PROP LEGIT ADMIN COERCE ATTIT DISPL   TOTALISM
PERCEPT HEALTH PWR RESPECT WEALTH...METH/CNCPT JEWS   USSR
VAL/FREE NAZI 20. PAGE 73 B1474
                                                          B53

NCC....NATIONAL COUNCIL OF CHURCHES

NE/WIN....NE WIN

NEA....NATIONAL EDUCATION ASSOCIATION

NEAL F.W. B1564

NEAR EAST....SEE MEDIT-7, ISLAM

NEBRASKA....NEBRASKA

ZABEL O.H.,GOD AND CAESAR IN NEBRASKA: A STUDY OF   SECT
LEGAL RELATIONSHIP OF CHURCH AND STATE, 1854-1954.   PROVS
TAX GIVE ADMIN CONTROL GP/REL ROLE...GP/COMP 19/20   LAW
NEBRASKA. PAGE 119 B2396   EDU/PROP
                                                          B55

NEEDHAM T. B1565

NEEDLER M.C. B1566

NEESSE G. B2306

NEG/INCOME....NEGATIVE INCOME TAX

NEGATIVE INCOME TAX....SEE NEG/INCOME

NEGRITO....NEGRITO TRIBE, PHILIPPINES

NEGRO....NEGRO; SEE ALSO BLACK/PWR

MOREL E.D.,AFFAIRS OF WEST AFRICA. UK FINAN INDUS   COLONIAL
FAM KIN SECT CHIEF WORKER DIPLOM RACE/REL LITERACY   ADMIN
HEALTH...CHARTS 18/20 AFRICA/W NEGRO. PAGE 75 B1521   AFR
                                                          B02

BUREAU OF NAT'L AFFAIRS INC.,A CURRENT LOOK AT: DISCRIM
(1) THE NEGRO AND TITLE VII; (2) SEX AND TITLE VII   SEX
(PAMPHLET). LAW LG/CO SML/CO RACE/REL...POLICY SOC   WORKER
STAT DEEP/QU TREND CON/ANAL CHARTS 20 NEGRO   MGT
CIV/RIGHTS. PAGE 17 B0350
                                                          N19

GORER G.,AFRICA DANCES: A BOOK ABOUT WEST AFRICAN   AFR
NEGROES. STRUCT LOC/G SECT FORCES TAX ADMIN   ATTIT
COLONIAL...ART/METH MYTH WORSHIP 20 NEGRO AFRICA/W   CULTURE
CHRISTIAN RITUAL. PAGE 41 B0835   SOCIETY
                                                          B35

KESSELMAN L.C.,THE SOCIAL POLITICS OF THE FEPC.   POLICY
INDUS WORKER EDU/PROP GP/REL RACE/REL 20 NEGRO JEWS   NAT/G
FEPC. PAGE 59 B1200   ADMIN
                                                      DISCRIM
                                                          B48

DWYER R.J.,"THE ADMINISTRATIVE ROLE IN   ADMIN
DESEGREGATION." USA+45 LAW PROB/SOLV LEAD RACE/REL   SCHOOL
ISOLAT STRANGE ROLE...POLICY SOC/INTEG MISSOURI   DISCRIM
NEGRO CIV/RIGHTS. PAGE 31 B0638   ATTIT
                                                          S59

LEYDER J.,BIBLIOGRAPHIE DE L'ENSEIGNEMENT SUPERIEUR   BIBLIOG/A
ET DE LA RECHERCHE SCIENTIFIQUE EN AFRIQUE   ACT/RES
INTERTROPICALE (2 VOLS.). AFR CULTURE ECO/UNDEV   ACADEM
AGRI PLAN EDU/PROP ADMIN COLONIAL...GEOG SOC/INTEG   R+D
20 NEGRO. PAGE 65 B1309
                                                          B60

BANFIELD E.C.,CITY POLITICS. CULTURE LABOR LOC/G   MUNIC
POL/PAR LEGIS EXEC LEAD CHOOSE...DECISION NEGRO.   RIGID/FLEX
PAGE 9 B0178   ATTIT
                                                          B63

HANNA W.J.,INDEPENDENT BLACK AFRICA: THE POLITICS   AFR
OF FREEDOM. ELITES INDUS KIN CHIEF COLONIAL CHOOSE   ECO/UNDEV
GOV/REL RACE/REL NAT/LISM ATTIT PERSON 20 NEGRO.   ADMIN
PAGE 46 B0938   PROB/SOLV
                                                          B64

WILDAVSKY A.,LEADERSHIP IN A SMALL TOWN. USA+45   LEAD
STRUCT PROB/SOLV EXEC PARTIC RACE/REL PWR PLURISM   MUNIC
...SOC 20 NEGRO WATER CIV/RIGHTS OBERLIN CITY/MGT.   ELITES
PAGE 116 B2348
                                                          B64

NORGREN P.H.,"TOWARD FAIR EMPLOYMENT." USA+45 LAW   RACE/REL
STRATA LABOR NAT/G FORCES ACT/RES ADMIN ATTIT   DISCRIM
...POLICY BIBLIOG 20 NEGRO. PAGE 79 B1588   WORKER
                                                      MGT
                                                          C64

FRIEDMAN L.,SOUTHERN JUSTICE. USA+45 PUB/INST LEGIT   ADJUD
ADMIN CT/SYS DISCRIM...DECISION ANTHOL 20 NEGRO   LAW
SOUTH/US CIV/RIGHTS. PAGE 37 B0758   CONSTN
                                                      RACE/REL
                                                          B65

PARRISH W.E.,MISSOURI UNDER RADICAL RULE 1865-1870.   PROVS
USA-45 SOCIETY INDUS LOC/G POL/PAR WORKER EDU/PROP   ADMIN
SUFF INGP/REL ATTIT...BIBLIOG 19 NEGRO MISSOURI.   RACE/REL
PAGE 81 B1635   ORD/FREE
                                                          B65

JACOBSON J.,"COALITIONISM: FROM PROTEST TO   RACE/REL
POLITICKING" USA+45 ELITES NAT/G POL/PAR PROB/SOLV   LABOR
ADMIN LEAD DISCRIM ORD/FREE PWR CONSERVE 20 NEGRO   SOCIALIST
AFL/CIO CIV/RIGHTS BLACK/PWR. PAGE 55 B1116   VOL/ASSN
                                                          S66

KRISLOV S.,THE NEGRO IN FEDERAL EMPLOYMENT. LAW   WORKER
STRATA LOC/G CREATE PROB/SOLV INSPECT GOV/REL   NAT/G
DISCRIM ROLE...DECISION INT TREND 20 NEGRO WWI   ADMIN
CIVIL/SERV. PAGE 61 B1238   RACE/REL
                                                          B67

LANDES W.M.,"THE EFFECT OF STATE FAIR EMPLOYMENT   DISCRIM
                                                          S67

LAWS ON THE ECONOMIC POSITION OF NONWHITES." USA+45 LAW PROVS SECT LEGIS ADMIN GP/REL RACE/REL...JURID CONCPT CHARTS HYPO/EXP NEGRO. PAGE 62 B1255

LAW
WORKER

S67

O'DELL J.H.,"THE JULY REBELLIONS AND THE 'MILITARY STATE'." USA+45 VIETNAM STRATA CHIEF WORKER COLONIAL EXEC CROWD CIVMIL/REL RACE/REL TOTALISM ...WELF/ST PACIFIST 20 NEGRO JOHNSON/LB PRESIDENT CIV/RIGHTS. PAGE 79 B1599

PWR
NAT/G
COERCE
FORCES

S67

RAUM O.,"THE MODERN LEADERSHIP GROUP AMONG THE SOUTH AFRICAN XHOSA." SOUTH/AFR SOCIETY SECT EX/STRUC REPRESENT GP/REL INGP/REL PERSON ...METH/COMP 17/20 XHOSA NEGRO. PAGE 86 B1743

RACE/REL
KIN
LEAD
CULTURE

B82

MACDONALD D.,AFRICANA; OR, THE HEART OF HEATHEN AFRICA, VOL. II: MISSION LIFE. SOCIETY STRATA KIN CREATE EDU/PROP ADMIN COERCE LITERACY HEALTH...MYTH WORSHIP 19 LIVNGSTN/D MISSION NEGRO. PAGE 67 B1355

SECT
AFR
CULTURE
ORD/FREE

NEHRU/J....JAWAHARLAL NEHRU

B66

HIDAYATULLAH M.,DEMOCRACY IN INDIA AND THE JUDICIAL PROCESS. INDIA EX/STRUC LEGIS LEAD GOV/REL ATTIT ORD/FREE...MAJORIT CONCPT 20 NEHRU/J. PAGE 50 B1007

NAT/G
CT/SYS
CONSTN
JURID

B66

ZINKIN T.,CHALLENGES IN INDIA. INDIA PAKISTAN LAW AGRI FINAN INDUS TOP/EX TEC/DEV CONTROL ROUTINE ORD/FREE PWR 20 NEHRU/J SHASTRI/LB CIVIL/SERV. PAGE 119 B2404

NAT/G
ECO/TAC
POLICY
ADMIN

S67

SPEAR P.,"NEHRU." INDIA NAT/G POL/PAR ECO/TAC ADJUD GOV/REL CENTRAL RIGID/FLEX 20 NEHRU/J. PAGE 99 B2003

CHIEF
ATTIT
ADMIN
CREATE

NEHRU/PM....PANDIT MOTILAL NEHRU

NEIBURG H.L. B1567

NEIGH....NEIGHBORHOOD

B30

ZINK H.,CITY BOSSES IN THE UNITED STATES: A STUDY OF TWENTY MUNICIPAL BOSSES. USA-45 INDUS MUNIC NEIGH POL/PAR ADMIN CRIME INGP/REL PERS/REL PWR ...PERS/COMP 20 BOSSISM. PAGE 119 B2403

LOC/G
DOMIN
BIOG
LEAD

S43

GOLDEN C.S.,"NEW PATTERNS OF DEMOCRACY." NEIGH DELIB/GP EDU/PROP EXEC PARTIC...MGT METH/CNCPT OBS TREND. PAGE 40 B0815

LABOR
REPRESENT
LG/CO
GP/REL

B50

DEES J.W. JR.,URBAN SOCIOLOGY AND THE EMERGING ATOMIC MEGALOPOLIS, PART I. USA+45 TEC/DEV ADMIN NUC/PWR HABITAT...SOC AUD/VIS CHARTS GEN/LAWS 20 WATER. PAGE 28 B0568

PLAN
NEIGH
MUNIC
PROB/SOLV

B50

WELCH S.R.,PORTUGUESE RULE AND SPANISH CROWN IN SOUTH AFRICA 1581-1640. PORTUGAL SOUTH/AFR SPAIN SOCIETY KIN NEIGH SECT INT/TRADE ADMIN 16/17 MISSION. PAGE 115 B2317

DIPLOM
COLONIAL
WAR
PEACE

B51

HARDMAN J.B.,THE HOUSE OF LABOR. LAW R+D NEIGH EDU/PROP LEAD ROUTINE REPRESENT GP/REL...POLICY STAT. PAGE 47 B0945

LABOR
LOBBY
ADMIN
PRESS

B53

WAGLEY C.,AMAZON TOWN: A STUDY OF MAN IN THE TROPICS. BRAZIL L/A+17C STRATA STRUCT ECO/UNDEV AGRI EX/STRUC RACE/REL DISCRIM HABITAT WEALTH...OBS SOC/EXP 20. PAGE 113 B2273

SOC
NEIGH
CULTURE
INGP/REL

B54

ALLPORT G.W.,THE NATURE OF PREJUDICE. USA+45 WOR+45 STRATA FACE/GP KIN NEIGH SECT ADMIN GP/REL DISCRIM ATTIT DRIVE LOVE RESPECT...PSY SOC MYTH QU/SEMANT 20. PAGE 4 B0078

CULTURE
PERSON
RACE/REL

B57

SCHNEIDER E.V.,INDUSTRIAL SOCIOLOGY: THE SOCIAL RELATIONS OF INDUSTRY AND COMMUNITY. STRATA INDUS NAT/G NEIGH CREATE ADMIN PARTIC GP/REL RACE/REL ROLE PWR...POLICY BIBLIOG. PAGE 94 B1898

LABOR
MGT
INGP/REL
STRUCT

B60

PENNSYLVANIA ECONOMY LEAGUE.URBAN RENEWAL IMPACT STUDY: ADMINISTRATIVE-LEGAL-FISCAL. USA+45 FINAN LOC/G NEIGH ADMIN EFFICIENCY...CENSUS CHARTS 20 PENNSYLVAN. PAGE 82 B1652

PLAN
BUDGET
MUNIC
ADJUD

B61

BULLIS H.A.,MANIFESTO FOR AMERICANS. USA+45 AGRI LABOR NAT/G NEIGH FOR/AID INT/TRADE TAX EDU/PROP CHOOSE...POLICY MGT 20 UN UNESCO. PAGE 17 B0342

ECO/TAC
SOCIETY
INDUS
CAP/ISM

B61

KEE R.,REFUGEE WORLD. AUSTRIA EUR+WWI GERMANY NEIGH NAT/G

EX/STRUC WORKER PROB/SOLV ECO/TAC RENT EDU/PROP INGP/REL COST LITERACY HABITAT 20 MIGRATION. PAGE 59 B1186

GIVE
WEALTH
STRANGE

B61

LEE R.R.,ENGINEERING-ECONOMIC PLANNING MISCELLANEOUS SUBJECTS: A SELECTED BIBLIOGRAPHY (MIMEOGRAPHED). FINAN LOC/G MUNIC NEIGH ADMIN CONTROL INGP/REL HABITAT...GEOG MGT SOC/WK 20 RESOURCE/N. PAGE 63 B1280

BIBLIOG/A
PLAN
REGION

B61

TRECKER H.B.,NEW UNDERSTANDING OF ADMINISTRATION. NEIGH DELIB/GP CONTROL LEAD GP/REL INGP/REL ...POLICY DECISION BIBLIOG. PAGE 105 B2126

VOL/ASSN
PROF/ORG
ADMIN
PARTIC

B63

JOHNS R.,CONFRONTING ORGANIZATIONAL CHANGE. NEIGH DELIB/GP CREATE OP/RES ADMIN GP/REL DRIVE...WELF/ST SOC RECORD BIBLIOG. PAGE 56 B1142

SOC/WK
WEALTH
LEAD
VOL/ASSN

B64

BOUVIER-AJAM M.,MANUEL TECHNIQUE ET PRATIQUE DU MAIRE ET DES ELUS ET AGENTS COMMUNAUX. FRANCE LOC/G BUDGET CHOOSE GP/REL SUPEGO...JURID BIBLIOG 20 MAYOR COMMUNES. PAGE 14 B0284

MUNIC
ADMIN
CHIEF
NEIGH

B64

FONTENEAU J.,LE CONSEIL MUNICIPAL: LE MAIRE-LES ADJOINTS. FRANCE FINAN DELIB/GP EX/STRUC BUDGET TAX TASK COST INCOME ROLE SUPEGO 20 MAYOR. PAGE 36 B0735

MUNIC
NEIGH
ADMIN
TOP/EX

B64

GRAVIER J.F.,AMENAGEMENT DU TERRITOIRE ET L'AVENIR DES REGIONS FRANCAISES. FRANCE ECO/DEV AGRI INDUS CREATE...GEOG CHARTS 20. PAGE 42 B0859

PLAN
MUNIC
NEIGH
ADMIN

B64

GREBLER L.,URBAN RENEWAL IN EUROPEAN COUNTRIES: ITS EMERGENCE AND POTENTIALS. EUR+WWI UK ECO/DEV LOC/G NEIGH CREATE ADMIN ATTIT...TREND NAT/COMP 20 URBAN/RNWL. PAGE 43 B0863

MUNIC
PLAN
CONSTRUC
NAT/G

S64

HADY T.F.,"CONGRESSIONAL TOWNSHIPS AS INCORPORATED MUNICIPALITIES." NEIGH ADMIN REPRESENT ATTIT GEOG. PAGE 45 B0914

MUNIC
REGION
LOC/G
GOV/COMP

S64

MURRAY D.,"CHINESE EDUCATION IN SOUTH-EAST ASIA." SOCIETY NEIGH EDU/PROP ROUTINE PERSON KNOWL ...OBS/ENVIR STERTYP. PAGE 76 B1546

S/ASIA
SCHOOL
REGION
ASIA

B65

DUGGAR G.S.,RENEWAL OF TOWN AND VILLAGE I: A WORLD-WIDE SURVEY OF LOCAL GOVERNMENT EXPERIENCE. WOR+45 CONSTRUC INDUS CREATE BUDGET REGION GOV/REL...QU NAT/COMP 20 URBAN/RNWL. PAGE 31 B0628

MUNIC
NEIGH
PLAN
ADMIN

B65

EVERETT R.O.,URBAN PROBLEMS AND PROSPECTS. USA+45 CREATE TEC/DEV EDU/PROP ADJUD ADMIN GOV/REL ATTIT ...ANTHOL 20 URBAN/RNWL. PAGE 34 B0691

MUNIC
PLAN
PROB/SOLV
NEIGH

B65

FRYE R.J.,HOUSING AND URBAN RENEWAL IN ALABAMA. USA+45 NEIGH LEGIS BUDGET ADJUD ADMIN PARTIC...MGT 20 ALABAMA URBAN/RNWL. PAGE 38 B0762

MUNIC
PROB/SOLV
PLAN
GOV/REL

B65

LAMBIRI I.,SOCIAL CHANGE IN A GREEK COUNTRY TOWN. GREECE FAM PROB/SOLV ROUTINE TASK LEISURE INGP/REL CONSEN ORD/FREE...SOC INT QU CHARTS 20. PAGE 62 B1252

INDUS
WORKER
CULTURE
NEIGH

B65

PERLOFF H.S.,URBAN RESEARCH AND EDUCATION IN THE NEW YORK METROPOLITAN REGION (VOL. II). FUT USA+45 NEIGH PROF/ORG ACT/RES PROB/SOLV EDU/PROP ADMIN ...STAT BIBLIOG 20 NEWYORK/C. PAGE 82 B1659

MUNIC
PLAN
ACADEM
GP/REL

B67

COHEN R.,COMPARATIVE POLITICAL SYSTEMS: STUDIES IN THE POLITICS OF PRE-INDUSTRIAL SOCIETIES. WOR+45 WOR-45 CULTURE FAM KIN LOC/G NEIGH ADMIN LEAD MARRIAGE...BIBLIOG 20. PAGE 22 B0447

ECO/UNDEV
STRUCT
SOCIETY
GP/COMP

B67

KAPLAN H.,URBAN POLITICAL SYSTEMS: A FUNCTIONAL ANALYSIS OF METRO TORONTO. CANADA STRUCT NEIGH PLAN ADMIN...POLICY METH 20 TORONTO. PAGE 58 B1166

GEN/LAWS
MUNIC
LOC/G
FEDERAL

B67

ROTHENBERG J.,ECONOMIC EVALUATION OF URBAN RENEWAL: CONCEPTUAL FOUNDATION OF BENEFIT-COST ANALYSIS. USA+45 ECO/DEV NEIGH TEC/DEV ADMIN GEN/LAWS. PAGE 91 B1834

PLAN
MUNIC
PROB/SOLV
COST

B67

WEINBERG M.,SCHOOL INTEGRATION: A COMPREHENSIVE CLASSIFIED BIBLIOGRAPHY OF 3,100 REFERENCES. USA+45 LAW NAT/G NEIGH SECT PLAN ROUTINE AGE/C WEALTH SOC/INTEG INDIAN/AM. PAGE 115 B2314

BIBLIOG
SCHOOL
DISCRIM
RACE/REL

S67

BURKE E.M.,"THE SEARCH FOR AUTHORITY IN PLANNING." DECISION

MUNIC NEIGH CREATE PROB/SOLV LEGIT ADMIN CONTROL
EFFICIENCY PWR...METH/COMP SIMUL 20. PAGE 17 B0352
   PLAN
   LOC/G
   METH

S67
DODSON D.W.,"NEW FORCES OPERATING IN EDUCATIONAL
DECISION-MAKING." USA+45 NEIGH EDU/PROP ADMIN
SUPEGO DECISION. PAGE 30 B0602
   PROB/SOLV
   SCHOOL
   PERS/REL
   PWR

S67
FOX R.G.,"FAMILY, CASTE, AND COMMERCE IN A NORTH
INDIAN MARKET TOWN." INDIA STRATA AGRI FACE/GP FAM
NEIGH OP/RES BARGAIN ADMIN ROUTINE WEALTH...SOC
CHARTS 20. PAGE 37 B0747
   CULTURE
   GP/REL
   ECO/UNDEV
   DIST/IND

NELSON D.H. B1568

NELSON R.H. B1569

NEOLITHIC....NEOLITHIC PERIOD

NEPAL....SEE ALSO S/ASIA

B66
DEBENKO E.,RESEARCH SOURCES FOR SOUTH ASIAN STUDIES
IN ECONOMIC DEVELOPMENT: A SELECT BIBLIOGRAPHY OF
SERIAL PUBLICATIONS. CEYLON INDIA NEPAL PAKISTAN
PROB/SOLV ADMIN...POLICY 20. PAGE 28 B0566
   BIBLIOG
   ECO/UNDEV
   S/ASIA
   PLAN

NET/THEORY....NETWORK THEORY

B64
LOWI T.J.,AT THE PLEASURE OF THE MAYOR. EX/STRUC
PROB/SOLV BAL/PWR ADMIN PARTIC CHOOSE GP/REL
...CONT/OBS NET/THEORY CHARTS 20 NEWYORK/C MAYOR.
PAGE 67 B1346
   LOBBY
   LOC/G
   PWR
   MUNIC

B65
SINGER J.D.,HUMAN BEHAVIOR AND INTERNATINAL
POLITICS* CONTRIBUTIONS FROM THE SOCIAL-
PSYCHOLOGICAL SCIENCES. ACT/RES PLAN EDU/PROP ADMIN
KNOWL...DECISION PSY SOC NET/THEORY HYPO/EXP
LAB/EXP SOC/EXP GEN/METH ANTHOL BIBLIOG. PAGE 97
B1965
   DIPLOM
   PHIL/SCI
   QUANT
   SIMUL

B65
VEINOTT A.F. JR.,MATHEMATICAL STUDIES IN MANAGEMENT
SCIENCE. UNIV INDUS COMPUTER ADMIN...DECISION
NET/THEORY SIMUL 20. PAGE 112 B2257
   MATH
   MGT
   PLAN
   PRODUC

B66
YOUNG S.,MANAGEMENT: A SYSTEMS ANALYSIS. DELIB/GP
EX/STRUC ECO/TAC CONTROL EFFICIENCY...NET/THEORY
20. PAGE 119 B2394
   PROB/SOLV
   MGT
   DECISION
   SIMUL

B67
VOOS H.,ORGANIZATIONAL COMMUNICATION: A
BIBLIOGRAPHY. WOR+45 STRATA R+D PROB/SOLV FEEDBACK
COERCE...MGT PSY NET/THEORY HYPO/EXP. PAGE 112
B2268
   BIBLIOG/A
   COM/IND
   VOL/ASSN

NETH/IND....NETHERLAND EAST INDIES (PRE-INDONESIA)

NETHERLAND....NETHERLANDS; SEE ALSO APPROPRIATE TIME/SPACE/
CULTURE INDEX

B31
DEKAT A.D.A.,COLONIAL POLICY. S/ASIA CULTURE
EX/STRUC ECO/TAC DOMIN ADMIN COLONIAL ROUTINE
SOVEREIGN WEALTH...POLICY MGT RECORD KNO/TEST SAMP.
PAGE 28 B0570
   DRIVE
   PWR
   INDONESIA
   NETHERLAND

B65
CONRAD J.P.,CRIME AND ITS CORRECTION: AN
INTERNATIONAL SURVEY OF ATTITUDES AND PRACTICES.
EUR+WWI NETHERLAND USA+45 USSR ATTIT MORAL 20
SCANDINAV. PAGE 23 B0467
   CRIME
   PUB/INST
   POLICY
   ADMIN

B65
EDELMAN M.,THE POLITICS OF WAGE-PRICE DECISIONS.
GERMANY ITALY NETHERLAND UK INDUS LABOR POL/PAR
PROB/SOLV BARGAIN PRICE ROUTINE BAL/PAY COST DEMAND
20. PAGE 32 B0654
   GOV/COMP
   CONTROL
   ECO/TAC
   PLAN

B65
HICKMAN B.G.,QUANTITATIVE PLANNING OF ECONOMIC
POLICY. FRANCE NETHERLAND OP/RES PRICE ROUTINE UTIL
...POLICY DECISION ECOMETRIC METH/CNCPT STAT STYLE
CHINJAP. PAGE 50 B1004
   PROB/SOLV
   PLAN
   QUANT

NETWORK THEORY....SEE NET/THEORY

NEUBURGER O. B1570

NEUCHTERLEIN D.E. B1571

NEUMANN F.L. B1572

NEUMANN R.G. B1573

NEUMANN S. B1574

NEUSTADT R. B1575

NEUTRAL....POLITICAL NONALIGNMENT, LEGAL NEUTRALITY

L49
MARX C.M.,"ADMINISTRATIVE ETHICS AND THE RULE OF
LAW." USA+45 ELITES ACT/RES DOMIN NEUTRAL ROUTINE
INGP/REL ORD/FREE...JURID IDEA/COMP. PAGE 70 B1417
   ADMIN
   LAW

S56
KAUFMAN H.,"EMERGING CONFLICTS IN THE DOCTRINES OF
PUBLIC ADMINISTRATION" (BMR)" USA+45 USA-45 NAT/G
EX/STRUC LEGIS CONTROL NEUTRAL ATTIT PWR...TREND
20. PAGE 58 B1181
   ADMIN
   ORD/FREE
   REPRESENT
   LEAD

B58
WHITE L.D.,THE REPUBLICAN ERA: 1869-1901, A STUDY
IN ADMINISTRATIVE HISTORY. USA-45 FINAN PLAN
NEUTRAL CRIME GP/REL MORAL LAISSEZ PRESIDENT
REFORMERS 19 CONGRESS CIVIL/SERV. PAGE 116 B2340
   MGT
   PWR
   DELIB/GP
   ADMIN

B61
HARRISON S.,INDIA AND THE UNITED STATES. FUT S/ASIA
USA+45 WOR+45 INTELL ECO/DEV ECO/UNDEV AGRI INDUS
INT/ORG NAT/G CONSULT EX/STRUC TOP/EX PLAN ECO/TAC
NEUTRAL ALL/VALS...MGT TOT/POP 20. PAGE 47 B0956
   DELIB/GP
   ACT/RES
   FOR/AID
   INDIA

S63
HAVILAND H.F.,"BUILDING A POLITICAL COMMUNITY."
EUR+WWI FUT UK USA+45 ECO/DEV ECO/UNDEV INT/ORG
NAT/G DELIB/GP BAL/PWR ECO/TAC NEUTRAL ROUTINE
ATTIT PWR WEALTH...CONCPT COLD/WAR TOT/POP 20.
PAGE 48 B0972
   VOL/ASSN
   DIPLOM

B65
MACDONALD R.W.,THE LEAGUE OF ARAB STATES: A STUDY
IN THE DYNAMICS OF REGIONAL ORGANIZATION. ISRAEL
UAR USSR FINAN INT/ORG DELIB/GP ECO/TAC AGREE
NEUTRAL ORD/FREE PWR...DECISION BIBLIOG 20 TREATY
UN. PAGE 67 B1358
   ISLAM
   REGION
   DIPLOM
   ADMIN

NEVADA....NEVADA

NEVINS A. B1576

NEW ECONOMICS....SEE NEW/ECONOM

NEW LIBERALISM....SEE NEW/LIB

NEW STATES....SEE ECO/UNDEV+GEOGRAPHIC AREA+COLONIAL+
NAT/LISM
NEW YORK CITY....SEE NEWYORK/C
NEW YORK TIMES....SEE NEWY/TIMES

NEW ZEALAND COMM OF ST SERVICE B1577

NEW/BRUNS....NEW BRUNSWICK, CANADA

NEW/DEAL....NEW DEAL OF F.D.R.'S ADMINISTRATION

B39
BAKER G.,THE COUNTY AGENT. USA-45 LOC/G NAT/G
PROB/SOLV ADMIN...POLICY 20 ROOSEVLT/F NEW/DEAL
COUNTY/AGT. PAGE 8 B0166
   AGRI
   CONSULT
   GOV/REL
   EDU/PROP

B63
KARL B.D.,EXECUTIVE REORGANIZATION AND REFORM IN
THE NEW DEAL. ECO/DEV INDUS DELIB/GP EX/STRUC PLAN
BUDGET ADMIN EFFICIENCY PWR POPULISM...POLICY 20
PRESIDENT ROOSEVLT/F WILSON/W NEW/DEAL. PAGE 58
B1174
   BIOG
   EXEC
   CREATE
   CONTROL

NEW/DELHI....NEW DELHI (UNCTAD MEETING OF DEVELOPED AND
UNDERDEVELOPED NATIONS IN 1968)

NEW/ECO/MN....NEW ECONOMIC MECHANISM OF HUNGARY

NEW/ECONOM....NEW ECONOMICS

NEW/ENGLND....NEW ENGLAND

B50
HARTLAND P.C.,BALANCE OF INTERREGIONAL PAYMENTS OF
NEW ENGLAND. USA+45 TEC/DEV ECO/TAC LEGIT ROUTINE
BAL/PAY PROFIT 20 NEW/ENGLND FED/RESERV. PAGE 47
B0962
   ECO/DEV
   FINAN
   REGION
   PLAN

NEW/FRONTR....NEW FRONTIER OF J.F.KENNEDY

B61
MARKMANN C.L.,JOHN F. KENNEDY: A SENSE OF PURPOSE.
USA+45 INTELL FAM CONSULT DELIB/GP LEGIS PERSON
SKILL 20 KENNEDY/JF EISNHWR/DD ROOSEVLT/F
NEW/FRONTR PRESIDENT. PAGE 69 B1399
   CHIEF
   TOP/EX
   ADMIN
   BIOG

NEW/GUINEA....NEW GUINEA

B66
FISK E.K.,NEW GUINEA ON THE THRESHOLD; ASPECTS OF
SOCIAL, POLITICAL, AND ECONOMIC DEVELOPMENT. AGRI
NAT/G INT/TRADE ADMIN ADJUST LITERACY ROLE...CHARTS
   ECO/UNDEV
   SOCIETY

ANTHOL 20 NEW/GUINEA. PAGE 36 B0726

NEW/HAMPSH....NEW HAMPSHIRE

NEW/HEBRID....NEW HEBRIDES

NEW/IDEA....NEW CONCEPT

NEW/JERSEY....NEW JERSEY

S52
RICH B.M.,"ADMINISTRATION REORGANIZATION IN NEW | ADMIN
JERSEY" (BMR)" USA+45 DELIB/GP EX/STRUC WORKER | CONSTN
OP/RES BUDGET 20 NEW/JERSEY. PAGE 88 B1772 | PROB/SOLV
| PROVS
B62
NJ DEPARTMENT CIVIL SERV,THE CIVIL SERVICE RULES OF | ADMIN
THE STATE OF NEW JERSEY. USA+45 USA-45 PAY...JURID | PROVS
ANTHOL 20 CIVIL/SERV NEW/JERSEY. PAGE 78 B1585 | ROUTINE
| WORKER
B64
SCHERMER G.,MEETING SOCIAL NEEDS IN THE PENJERDEL | PLAN
REGION. SOCIETY FINAN ACT/RES EDU/PROP ADMIN | REGION
GOV/REL...SOC/WK 45 20 PENNSYLVAN DELAWARE | HEALTH
NEW/JERSEY. PAGE 93 B1887 | WEALTH
N65
NJ DIVISION STATE-REGION PLAN,UTILIZATION OF NEW | UTIL
JERSEY'S DELAWARE RIVER WATERFRONT (PAMPHLET). FUT | PLAN
ADMIN REGION LEISURE GOV/REL DEMAND WEALTH...CHARTS | ECO/TAC
20 NEW/JERSEY. PAGE 78 B1586 | PROVS
B67
PRINCE C.E.,NEW JERSEY'S JEFFERSONIAN REPUBLICANS; | POL/PAR
THE GENESIS OF AN EARLY PARTY MACHINE (1789-1817). | CONSTN
USA-45 LOC/G EDU/PROP PRESS CONTROL CHOOSE...CHARTS | ADMIN
18/19 NEW/JERSEY REPUBLICAN. PAGE 84 B1707 | PROVS

NEW/LEFT....THE NEW LEFT

NEW/LIB....NEW LIBERALISM

B34
WILCOX J.K.,GUIDE TO THE OFFICIAL PUBLICATIONS OF | BIBLIOG
THE NEW DEAL ADMINISTRATION (2 VOLS.). USA-45 CHIEF | NAT/G
LEGIS ADMIN...POLICY 20 CONGRESS ROOSEVLT/F. | NEW/LIB
PAGE 116 B2345 | RECEIVE
B52
SWENSON R.J.,FEDERAL ADMINISTRATIVE LAW: A STUDY OF | JURID
THE GROWTH, NATURE, AND CONTROL OF ADMINISTRATIVE | CONSTN
ACTION. USA-45 JUDGE ADMIN GOV/REL EFFICIENCY | LEGIS
PRIVIL ATTIT NEW/LIB SUPREME/CT. PAGE 102 B2061 | ADJUD
B53
STOUT H.M.,BRITISH GOVERNMENT. UK FINAN LOC/G | NAT/G
POL/PAR DELIB/GP DIPLOM ADMIN COLONIAL CHOOSE | PARL/PROC
ORD/FREE...JURID BIBLIOG 20 COMMONWLTH. PAGE 101 | CONSTN
B2049 | NEW/LIB
B56
DUNNILL F.,THE CIVIL SERVICE. UK LAW PLAN ADMIN | PERSON
EFFICIENCY DRIVE NEW/LIB...STAT CHARTS 20 | WORKER
PARLIAMENT CIVIL/SERV. PAGE 31 B0633 | STRATA
| SOC/WK
B57
DE GRAZIA A.,GRASS ROOTS PRIVATE WELFARE. LOC/G | NEW/LIB
SCHOOL ACT/RES EDU/PROP ROUTINE CROWD GP/REL | HEALTH
DISCRIM HAPPINESS ILLEGIT AGE HABITAT. PAGE 27 | MUNIC
B0554 | VOL/ASSN
B61
NARASIMHAN V.K.,THE PRESS, THE PUBLIC AND THE | NAT/G
ADMINISTRATION (PAMPHLET). INDIA COM/IND CONTROL | ADMIN
REPRESENT GOV/REL EFFICIENCY...ANTHOL 20. PAGE 77 | PRESS
B1554 | NEW/LIB
B62
MORE S.S.,REMODELLING OF DEMOCRACY FOR AFRO-ASIAN | ORD/FREE
NATIONS. AFR INDIA S/ASIA SOUTH/AFR CONSTN EX/STRUC | ECO/UNDEV
COLONIAL CHOOSE TOTALISM SOVEREIGN NEW/LIB SOCISM | ADMIN
...SOC/WK 20. PAGE 75 B1520 | LEGIS
B63
BROGAN D.W.,POLITICAL PATTERNS IN TODAY'S WORLD. | NAT/COMP
FRANCE USA+45 USSR WOR+45 CONSTN STRUCT PLAN DIPLOM | NEW/LIB
ADMIN LEAD ROLE SUPEGO...PHIL/SCI 20. PAGE 15 B0313 | COM
| TOTALISM
B64
MARSH D.C.,THE FUTURE OF THE WELFARE STATE. UK | NEW/LIB
CONSTN NAT/G POL/PAR...POLICY WELF/ST 20. PAGE 69 | ADMIN
B1404 | CONCPT
| INSPECT
B65
MUSOLF L.D.,PROMOTING THE GENERAL WELFARE: | ECO/TAC
GOVERNMENT AND THE ECONOMY. USA+45 ECO/DEV CAP/ISM | NAT/G
DEMAND OPTIMAL 20. PAGE 77 B1550 | EX/STRUC
| NEW/LIB
B65
PENNICK JL J.R.,THE POLITICS OF AMERICAN SCIENCE, | POLICY
1939 TO THE PRESENT. USA+45 USA-45 INTELL TEC/DEV | ADMIN
DIPLOM NEW/LIB...ANTHOL 20 COLD/WAR. PAGE 82 B1651 | PHIL/SCI
| NAT/G

B65
VAID K.N.,STATE AND LABOR IN INDIA. INDIA INDUS | LAW
WORKER PAY PRICE ADJUD CONTROL PARL/PROC GP/REL | LABOR
ORD/FREE 20. PAGE 111 B2248 | MGT
| NEW/LIB
S65
HAMILTON R.F.,"SKILL LEVEL AND POLITICS." USA+45 | SKILL
CULTURE STRATA STRUCT LABOR CONSERVE NEW/LIB. | ADMIN
PAGE 46 B0933
B66
WASHINGTON S.H.,BIBLIOGRAPHY: LABOR-MANAGEMENT | BIBLIOG
RELATIONS ACT, 1947 AS AMENDED BY LABOR-MANAGEMENT | LAW
REPORTING AND DISCLOSURE ACT, 1959. USA+45 CONSTN | LABOR
INDUS DELIB/GP LEGIS WORKER BARGAIN ECO/TAC ADJUD | MGT
GP/REL NEW/LIB...JURID CONGRESS. PAGE 114 B2298
S66
JACOBS P.,"RE-RADICALIZING THE DE-RADICALIZED." | NAT/G
USA+45 SOCIETY STRUCT FINAN PLAN PROB/SOLV CAP/ISM | POLICY
WEALTH CONSERVE NEW/LIB 20. PAGE 55 B1114 | MARXIST
| ADMIN

NEW/MEXICO....NEW MEXICO

NEW/YORK....NEW YORK STATE

S30
CRAWFORD F.G.,"THE EXECUTIVE BUDGET DECISION IN NEW | LEAD
YORK." LEGIS EXEC PWR NEW/YORK. PAGE 25 B0504 | BUDGET
| PROVS
| PROB/SOLV
B63
HERMAN H.,NEW YORK STATE AND THE METROPOLITAN | GOV/REL
PROBLEM. USA+45 ECO/DEV PUB/INST SCHOOL LEGIS PLAN | PROVS
TAX EXEC PARL/PROC PARTIC...HEAL 20 NEW/YORK. | LOC/G
PAGE 49 B0992 | POLICY
B66
DAHLBERG J.S.,THE NEW YORK BUREAU OF MUNICIPAL | PROVS
RESEARCH: PIONEER IN GOVERNMENT ADMINISTRATION. | MUNIC
CONSTN R+D BUDGET EDU/PROP PARTIC REPRESENT | DELIB/GP
EFFICIENCY ORD/FREE...BIBLIOG METH 20 NEW/YORK | ADMIN
NIPA. PAGE 26 B0522
B67
HEWITT W.H.,ADMINISTRATION OF CRIMINAL JUSTICE IN | CRIME
NEW YORK. LAW PROB/SOLV ADJUD ADMIN...CRIMLGY | ROLE
CHARTS T 20 NEW/YORK. PAGE 49 B1001 | CT/SYS
| FORCES
L67
GAINES J.E.,"THE YOUTH COURT CONCEPT AND ITS | CT/SYS
IMPLEMENTATION IN TOMPKINS COUNTY, NEW YORK." | AGE/Y
USA+45 LAW CONSTN JUDGE WORKER ADJUD ADMIN CHOOSE | INGP/REL
PERSON...JURID NEW/YORK. PAGE 38 B0772 | CRIME

NEW/ZEALND....NEW ZEALAND; SEE ALSO S/ASIA, COMMONWLTH

N
AUSTRALIAN NATIONAL RES COUN,AUSTRALIAN SOCIAL | BIBLIOG/A
SCIENCE ABSTRACTS. NEW/ZEALND CULTURE SOCIETY LOC/G | POLICY
CT/SYS PARL/PROC...HEAL JURID PSY SOC 20 AUSTRAL. | NAT/G
PAGE 7 B0149 | ADMIN
B21
BRYCE J.,MODERN DEMOCRACIES. FUT NEW/ZEALND USA+45 | NAT/G
LAW CONSTN POL/PAR PROVS VOL/ASSN EX/STRUC LEGIS | TREND
LEGIT CT/SYS EXEC KNOWL CONGRESS AUSTRAL 20. |
PAGE 16 B0332
S59
PADELFORD N.J.,"REGIONAL COOPERATION IN THE SOUTH | INT/ORG
PACIFIC: THE SOUTH PACIFIC COMMISSION." FUT | ADMIN
NEW/ZEALND UK WOR+45 CULTURE ECO/UNDEV LOC/G |
VOL/ASSN...OBS CON/ANAL UNESCO VAL/FREE AUSTRAL 20. |
PAGE 80 B1622
B62
NEW ZEALAND COMM OF ST SERVICE,THE STATE SERVICES | ADMIN
IN NEW ZEALAND. NEW/ZEALND CONSULT EX/STRUC ACT/RES | WORKER
...BIBLIOG 20. PAGE 78 B1577 | TEC/DEV
| NAT/G
B65
ROWAT D.C.,THE OMBUDSMAN: CITIZEN'S DEFENDER. | INSPECT
DENMARK FINLAND NEW/ZEALND NORWAY SWEDEN CONSULT | CONSTN
PROB/SOLV FEEDBACK PARTIC GP/REL...SOC CONCPT | NAT/G
NEW/IDEA METH/COMP ANTHOL BIBLIOG 20. PAGE 91 B1840 | ADMIN
S67
ANDERSON L.G.,"ADMINISTERING A GOVERNMENT SOCIAL | ADMIN
SERVICE" NEW/ZEALND EX/STRUC TASK ROLE 20. PAGE 5 | NAT/G
B0094 | DELIB/GP
| SOC/WK

NEWARK/NJ....NEWARK, N.J.

NEWFNDLND....NEWFOUNDLAND, CANADA

NEWLYN W.T. B1578

NEWMAN F.C. B1579

NEWY/TIMES....NEW YORK TIMES

NEWYORK/C....NEW YORK CITY

B05
RIORDAN W.L.,PLUNKITT OF TAMMANY HALL. USA-45   POL/PAR
SOCIETY PROB/SOLV EXEC LEAD TASK CHOOSE ALL/VALS   MUNIC
...RECORD ANTHOL 20 REFORMERS TAMMANY NEWYORK/C   CHIEF
PLUNKITT/G. PAGE 88 B1789   ATTIT

B47
FLYNN E.J.,YOU'RE THE BOSS. USA-45 ELITES TOP/EX   LOC/G
DOMIN CONTROL EXEC LEAD REPRESENT 19/20 NEWYORK/C   MUNIC
ROOSEVLT/F FLYNN/BOSS BOSSISM. PAGE 36 B0732   BIOG
                                                      POL/PAR
B47
TAPPAN P.W.,DELINQUENT GIRLS IN COURT. USA-45 MUNIC   CT/SYS
EX/STRUC FORCES ADMIN EXEC ADJUST SEX RESPECT   AGE/Y
...JURID SOC/WK 20 NEWYORK/C FEMALE/SEX. PAGE 103   CRIME
B2078   ADJUD

C54
CALDWELL L.K.,"THE GOVERNMENT AND ADMINISTRATION OF   PROVS
NEW YORK." LOC/G MUNIC POL/PAR SCHOOL CHIEF LEGIS   ADMIN
PLAN TAX CT/SYS...MGT SOC/WK BIBLIOG 20 NEWYORK/C.   CONSTN
PAGE 18 B0366   EX/STRUC

B60
SAYRE W.S.,GOVERNING NEW YORK CITY; POLITICS IN THE   MUNIC
METROPOLIS. POL/PAR CHIEF DELIB/GP LEGIS PLAN   ADMIN
CT/SYS LEAD PARTIC CHOOSE...DECISION CHARTS BIBLIOG   PROB/SOLV
20 NEWYORK/C BUREAUCRCY. PAGE 93 B1875

B64
FISK W.M.,ADMINISTRATIVE PROCEDURE IN A REGULATORY   SERV/IND
AGENCY: THE CAB AND THE NEW YORK-CHICAGO CASE   ECO/DEV
(PAMPHLET). USA+45 DIST/IND ADMIN CONTROL LOBBY   AIR
GP/REL ROLE ORD/FREE NEWYORK/C CHICAGO CAB. PAGE 36   JURID
B0727

B64
LOWI T.J.,AT THE PLEASURE OF THE MAYOR. EX/STRUC   LOBBY
PROB/SOLV BAL/PWR ADMIN PARTIC CHOOSE GP/REL   LOC/G
...CONT/OBS NET/THEORY CHARTS 20 NEWYORK/C MAYOR.   PWR
PAGE 67 B1346   MUNIC

B65
PERLOFF H.S.,URBAN RESEARCH AND EDUCATION IN THE   MUNIC
NEW YORK METROPOLITAN REGION (VOL. II). FUT USA+45   PLAN
NEIGH PROF/ORG ACT/RES PROB/SOLV EDU/PROP ADMIN   ACADEM
...STAT BIBLIOG 20 NEWYORK/C. PAGE 82 B1659   GP/REL

B65
REISS A.J. JR.,SCHOOLS IN A CHANGING SOCIETY.   SCHOOL
CULTURE PROB/SOLV INSPECT DOMIN CONFER INGP/REL   EX/STRUC
RACE/REL AGE/C AGE/Y ALL/VALS...ANTHOL SOC/INTEG 20   ADJUST
NEWYORK/C. PAGE 87 B1766   ADMIN

B66
NYC TEMPORARY COMM CITY FINAN.MUNICIPAL COLLECTIVE   MUNIC
BARGAINING (NO. 8). USA+45 PLAN PROB/SOLV BARGAIN   FINAN
BUDGET TAX EDU/PROP GOV/REL COST...MGT 20   ADMIN
NEWYORK/C. PAGE 79 B1596   LOC/G

B67
GITTELL M.,PARTICIPANTS AND PARTICIPATION: A STUDY   SCHOOL
OF SCHOOL POLICY IN NEW YORK. USA+45 MUNIC EX/STRUC   DECISION
BUDGET PAY ATTIT...POLICY 20 NEWYORK/C. PAGE 40   PARTIC
B0806   ADMIN

B67
NIEDERHOFFER A.,BEHIND THE SHIELD; THE POLICE IN   FORCES
URBAN SOCIETY. USA+45 LEGIT ADJUD ROUTINE COERCE   PERSON
CRIME ADJUST...INT CHARTS 20 NEWYORK/C. PAGE 78   SOCIETY
B1582   ATTIT

NICARAGUA....NICARAGUA; SEE ALSO L/A+17C

B47
DE NOIA J.,GUIDE TO OFFICIAL PUBLICATIONS OF THE   BIBLIOG/A
OTHER AMERICAN REPUBLICS: NICARAGUA (VOL. XIV).   EDU/PROP
NICARAGUA LAW LEGIS ADMIN CT/SYS...JURID 19/20.   NAT/G
PAGE 27 B0559   CONSTN

NICHOLAS H.G. B1580

NICHOLAS/I....CZAR NICHOLAS I

B61
MONAS S.,THE THIRD SECTION: POLICE AND SOCIETY IN   ORD/FREE
RUSSIA UNDER NICHOLAS I. MOD/EUR RUSSIA ELITES   COM
STRUCT NAT/G EX/STRUC ADMIN CONTROL PWR CONSERVE   FORCES
...DECISION 19 NICHOLAS/I. PAGE 74 B1499   COERCE

NICOLSON/A....SIR ARTHUR NICOLSON

NIEBUHR/R....REINHOLD NIEBUHR

B64
KARIEL H.S.,IN SEARCH OF AUTHORITY: TWENTIETH-   CONSTN
CENTURY POLITICAL THOUGHT. WOR+45 WOR-45 NAT/G   CONCPT
EX/STRUC TOTALISM DRIVE PWR...MGT PHIL/SCI GEN/LAWS   ORD/FREE
19/20 NIETZSCH/F FREUD/S WEBER/MAX NIEBUHR/R   IDEA/COMP
MARITAIN/J. PAGE 58 B1173

NIEBURG H.L. B1581

NIEBURG/HL....H.L. NIEBURG

NIEDERHOFFER A. B1582

NIELANDER W.A. B1583

NIETZSCH/F....FRIEDRICH NIETZSCHE

B64
KARIEL H.S.,IN SEARCH OF AUTHORITY: TWENTIETH-   CONSTN
CENTURY POLITICAL THOUGHT. WOR+45 WOR-45 NAT/G   CONCPT
EX/STRUC TOTALISM DRIVE PWR...MGT PHIL/SCI GEN/LAWS   ORD/FREE
19/20 NIETZSCH/F FREUD/S WEBER/MAX NIEBUHR/R   IDEA/COMP
MARITAIN/J. PAGE 58 B1173

NIGERIA....SEE ALSO AFR.

NC0
STOLPER W.,"SOCIAL FACTORS IN ECONOMIC PLANNING,   ECO/UNDEV
WITH SPECIAL REFERENCE TO NIGERIA" AFR NIGER   PLAN
CULTURE FAM SECT RECEIVE ETIQUET ADMIN DEMAND 20.   ADJUST
PAGE 101 B2045   RISK

B58
CARTER G.M.,TRANSITION IN AFRICA; STUDIES IN   NAT/COMP
POLITICAL ADAPTATION. AFR CENTRL/AFR GHANA NIGERIA   PWR
CONSTN LOC/G POL/PAR ADMIN GP/REL FEDERAL...MAJORIT   CONTROL
BIBLIOG 20. PAGE 19 B0389

B58
COLEMAN J.S.,NIGERIA: BACKGROUND TO NATIONALISM.   NAT/LISM
AFR SOCIETY KIN LOC/G POL/PAR TEC/DEV DOMIN ADMIN   NIGERIA
DRIVE PWR RESPECT...TRADIT SOC INT SAMP TIME/SEQ
20. PAGE 22 B0452

B59
CONOVER H.F.,NIGERIAN OFFICIAL PUBLICATIONS,   BIBLIOG
1869-1959: A GUIDE. NIGER CONSTN FINAN ACADEM   CON/ANAL
SCHOOL FORCES PRESS ADMIN COLONIAL...HIST/WRIT
19/20. PAGE 23 B0466

B60
SMITH M.G.,GOVERNMENT IN ZAZZAU 1800-1950. NIGERIA   REGION
UK CULTURE SOCIETY LOC/G ADMIN COLONIAL   CONSTN
...METH/CNCPT NEW/IDEA METH 19/20. PAGE 98 B1983   KIN
                                                      ECO/UNDEV
S60
SCHATZ S.P.,"THE INFLENCE OF PLANNING ON   ECO/UNDEV
DEVELOPMENT: THE NIGERIAN EXPERIENCE." AFR FUT   PLAN
FINAN INDUS EX/STRUC ECO/TAC ADMIN ATTIT PERCEPT   NIGERIA
ORD/FREE PWR...MATH TREND CON/ANAL SIMUL VAL/FREE
20. PAGE 93 B1883

B61
CARNEY D.E.,GOVERNMENT AND ECONOMY IN BRITISH WEST   METH/COMP
AFRICA. GAMBIA GHANA NIGERIA SIER/LEONE DOMIN ADMIN   COLONIAL
GOV/REL SOVEREIGN WEALTH LAISSEZ...BIBLIOG 20   ECO/TAC
CMN/WLTH. PAGE 19 B0384   ECO/UNDEV

B63
ELIAS T.O.,THE NIGERIAN LEGAL SYSTEM. NIGERIA LAW   CT/SYS
FAM KIN SECT ADMIN NAT/LISM...JURID 18/20   ADJUD
ENGLSH/LAW COMMON/LAW. PAGE 33 B0665   COLONIAL
                                                      PROF/ORG
B63
PREST A.R.,PUBLIC FINANCE IN UNDERDEVELOPED   FINAN
COUNTRIES. UK WOR-45 SOCIETY INT/ORG LEGIS ACT/RES   ECO/UNDEV
PLAN ECO/TAC ADMIN ROUTINE...CHARTS 20. PAGE 84   NIGERIA
B1702

B63
ROBINSON K.,ESSAYS IN IMPERIAL GOVERNMENT. CAMEROON   COLONIAL
NIGERIA UK CONSTN LOC/G LEGIS ADMIN GOV/REL PWR   AFR
...POLICY ANTHOL BIBLIOG 17/20 PURHAM/M. PAGE 89   DOMIN
B1803

B64
THE SPECIAL COMMONWEALTH AFRICAN ASSISTANCE PLAN.   ECO/UNDEV
AFR CANADA INDIA NIGERIA UK FINAN SCHOOL...CHARTS   TREND
20 COMMONWLTH. PAGE 2 B0041   FOR/AID
                                                      ADMIN
B64
BROWN C.V.,GOVERNMENT AND BANKING IN WESTERN   ADMIN
NIGERIA. AFR NIGERIA GOV/REL GP/REL...POLICY 20.   ECO/UNDEV
PAGE 16 B0321   FINAN

B64
WRAITH R.,CORRUPTION IN DEVELOPING COUNTRIES.   ECO/UNDEV
NIGERIA UK LAW ELITES STRATA INDUS LOC/G SECT   CRIME
FORCES EDU/PROP ADMIN PWR WEALTH 18/20. PAGE 118   SANCTION
B2377   ATTIT

L64
MACKINTOSH J.P.,"NIGERIA'S EXTERNAL AFFAIRS." UK   AFR
CULTURE ECO/UNDEV VOL/ASSN EDU/PROP LEGIT ADMIN   DIPLOM
ATTIT ORD/FREE PWR 20. PAGE 68 B1365   NIGERIA

B66
US LIBRARY OF CONGRESS,NIGERIA: A GUIDE TO OFFICIAL   BIBLIOG
PUBLICATIONS. CAMEROON NIGERIA UK DIPLOM...POLICY   ADMIN
19/20 UN LEAGUE/NAT. PAGE 109 B2207   COLONIAL

MATTHEWS D.G.,"PRELUDE-COUP D'ETAT-MILITARY GOVERNMENT: A BIBLIOGRAPHICAL AND RESEARCH GUIDE TO NIGERIAN POL AND GOVT, JAN. 1965-66." AFR NIGER LAW CONSTN POL/PAR LEGIS CIVMIL/REL GOV/REL...STAT 20. PAGE 71 B1430
S66
BIBLIOG
ADMIN
CHOOSE

NIVEN R.,NIGERIA. NIGERIA CONSTN INDUS EX/STRUC COLONIAL REV NAT/LISM...CHARTS 19/20. PAGE 78 B1584
B67
REGION
CHOOSE
GP/REL

NIH....NATIONAL INSTITUTE OF HEALTH

NIPA....NATIONAL INSTITUTE OF PUBLIC ADMINISTRATION

DAHLBERG J.S.,THE NEW YORK BUREAU OF MUNICIPAL RESEARCH: PIONEER IN GOVERNMENT ADMINISTRATION. CONSTN R+D BUDGET EDU/PROP PARTIC REPRESENT EFFICIENCY ORD/FREE...BIBLIOG METH 20 NEW/YORK NIPA. PAGE 26 B0522
B66
PROVS
MUNIC
DELIB/GP
ADMIN

NISEI....NISEI: JAPANESE AMERICANS

NIVEN R. B1584

NIXON H.C. B0853

NIXON/RM....PRESIDENT RICHARD M. NIXON

BENSON E.T.,CROSS FIRE: THE EIGHT YEARS WITH EISENHOWER. USA+45 DIPLOM LEAD ATTIT PERSON CONSERVE...TRADIT BIOG 20 EISNHWR/DD PRESIDENT TAFT/RA DULLES/JF NIXON/RM. PAGE 11 B0218
B62
ADMIN
POLICY
DELIB/GP
TOP/EX

NJ DEPARTMENT CIVIL SERV B1585

NJ DIVISION STATE-REGION PLAN B1586

NKRUMAH/K....KWAME NKRUMAH

NLC....NATIONAL LIBERATION COUNCIL IN GHANA

NLF....NATIONAL LIBERATION FRONT OF SOUTH VIETNAM

NLRB....NATIONAL LABOR RELATIONS BOARD

BUREAU OF NATIONAL AFFAIRS,LABOR RELATIONS REFERENCE MANUAL VOL 1, 1935-1937. BARGAIN DEBATE ROUTINE INGP/REL 20 NLRB. PAGE 17 B0351
B37
LABOR
ADMIN
ADJUD
NAT/G

US HOUSE COMM EDUC AND LABOR,ADMINISTRATION OF THE NATIONAL LABOR RELATIONS ACT. USA+45 DELIB/GP WORKER PROB/SOLV BARGAIN PAY CONTROL 20 NLRB CONGRESS. PAGE 108 B2188
B65
ADMIN
LABOR
GP/REL
INDUS

NORTHRUP H.R.,RESTRICTIVE LABOR PRACTICES IN THE SUPERMARKET INDUSTRY. USA+45 INDUS WORKER TEC/DEV BARGAIN PAY CONTROL GP/REL COST...STAT CHARTS NLRB. PAGE 79 B1592
B67
DIST/IND
MARKET
LABOR
MGT

SCHLOSSBERG S.I.,ORGANIZING AND THE LAW. USA+45 WORKER PLAN LEGIT REPRESENT GP/REL...JURID MGT 20 NLRB. PAGE 94 B1893
B67
LABOR
CONSULT
BARGAIN
PRIVIL

ZELERMYER W.,BUSINESS LAW: NEW PERSPECTIVES IN BUSINESS ECONOMICS. USA+45 LAW INDUS DELIB/GP ...JURID MGT ANTHOL BIBLIOG 20 NLRB. PAGE 119 B2400
B67
LABOR
CAP/ISM
LG/CO

NOBILITY....SEE ELITES

NOLTING O.F. B1780

NOMAD/MAX....MAX NOMAD

NOMADISM....SEE GEOG

NONALIGNED NATIONS....SEE THIRD/WRLD

NON-WHITE....SEE RACE/REL

NONVIOLENT....NONVIOLENCE (CONCEPT)

NORDEN A. B1587

NORGREN P.H. B1588

NORMS....SEE AVERAGE, ALSO APPROPRIATE VALUES AND DIMENSIONS OF GROUPS, STAT, LOG, ETC.

NORTH R.C. B1589,B1590,B1591

NORTH AFRICA....SEE AFRICA/N, ISLAM

NORTH ATLANTIC FREE TRADE AREA....SEE NAFTA

NORTH ATLANTIC TREATY ORGANIZATION....SEE NATO

NORTH KOREA....SEE KOREA/N

NORTH VIETNAM....SEE VIETNAM/N

NORTH/AMER....NORTH AMERICA, EXCLUSIVE OF CENTRAL AMERICA

NORTH/CAR....NORTH CAROLINA

NORTH/DAK....NORTH DAKOTA

NORTH/US....NORTHERN UNITED STATES

NORTHERN RHODESIA....SEE ZAMBIA

NORTHRUP H.R. B1592

NORTHW/TER....NORTHWEST TERRITORIES, CANADA

NORTHWEST TERRITORIES, CANADA....SEE NORTHW/TER

NORTHWST/U....NORTHWESTERN UNIVERSITY

NORWAY....SEE ALSO APPROPRIATE TIME/SPACE/CULTURE INDEX

MEYER P.,ADMINISTRATIVE ORGANIZATION: A COMPARATIVE STUDY OF THE ORGANIZATION OF PUBLIC ADMINISTRATION. DENMARK FRANCE NORWAY SWEDEN UK USA+45 ELITES LOC/G CONSULT LEGIS ADJUD CONTROL LEAD PWR SKILL DECISION. PAGE 73 B1475
B57
ADMIN
METH/COMP
NAT/G
CENTRAL

ANDREN N.,GOVERNMENT AND POLITICS IN THE NORDIC COUNTRIES: DENMARK, FINLAND, ICELAND, NORWAY, SWEDEN. DENMARK FINLAND ICELAND NORWAY SWEDEN POL/PAR CHIEF LEGIS ADMIN REGION REPRESENT ATTIT CONSERVE...CHARTS BIBLIOG/A 20. PAGE 5 B0102
B64
CONSTN
NAT/G
CULTURE
GOV/COMP

HALLER W.,DER SCHWEDISCHE JUSTITIEOMBUDSMAN. DENMARK FINLAND NORWAY SWEDEN LEGIS ADJUD CONTROL PERSON ORD/FREE...NAT/COMP 20 OMBUDSMAN. PAGE 46 B0926
B64
JURID
PARL/PROC
ADMIN
CHIEF

VALEN H.,POLITICAL PARTIES IN NORWAY. NORWAY ACADEM PARTIC ROUTINE INGP/REL KNOWL...QU 20. PAGE 111 B2249
B64
LOC/G
POL/PAR
PERSON

ROWAT D.C.,THE OMBUDSMAN: CITIZEN'S DEFENDER. DENMARK FINLAND NEW/ZEALND NORWAY SWEDEN CONSULT PROB/SOLV FEEDBACK PARTIC GP/REL...SOC CONCPT NEW/IDEA METH/COMP ANTHOL BIBLIOG 20. PAGE 91 B1840
B65
INSPECT
CONSTN
NAT/G
ADMIN

NOVA/SCOT....NOVA SCOTIA, CANADA

NOVE A. B1593,B1594

NOVOTNY/A....A. NOVOTNY

NRA....NATIONAL RECOVERY ADMINISTRATION

CHARLES S.,MINISTER OF RELIEF: HARRY HOPKINS AND THE DEPRESSION. EX/STRUC PROB/SOLV RATION PARL/PROC PERS/REL ALL/VALS 20 HOPKINS/H NRA. PAGE 20 B0414
B63
ADMIN
ECO/TAC
PLAN
BIOG

NSC....NATIONAL SECURITY COUNCIL

CUTLER R.,"THE DEVELOPMENT OF THE NATIONAL SECURITY COUNCIL." USA+45 INTELL CONSULT EX/STRUC DIPLOM LEAD 20 TRUMAN/HS EISNHWR/DD NSC. PAGE 25 B0514
S56
ORD/FREE
DELIB/GP
PROB/SOLV
NAT/G

NSF....NATIONAL SCIENCE FOUNDATION

NSSF....NATIONAL SOCIAL SCIENCE FOUNDATION

NUC....NATIONAL UNITY COMMITTEE (TURKEY)

NUC/PWR....NUCLEAR POWER, INCLUDING NUCLEAR WEAPONS

BUSH V.,SCIENCE, THE ENDLESS FRONTIER. FUT USA-45 INTELL STRATA ACT/RES CREATE PLAN EDU/PROP ADMIN NUC/PWR PEACE ATTIT HEALTH KNOWL...MAJORIT HEAL MGT PHIL/SCI CONCPT OBS TREND 20. PAGE 18 B0360
B45
R+D
NAT/G

BUSH V.,MODERN ARMS AND FREE MEN. WOR-45 SOCIETY NAT/G ECO/TAC DOMIN LEGIT EXEC COERCE DETER ATTIT DRIVE ORD/FREE PWR...CONCPT MYTH COLD/WAR 20
B49
TEC/DEV
FORCES
NUC/PWR

COLD/WAR. PAGE 18 B0361   WAR

B50
DEES J.W. JR.,URBAN SOCIOLOGY AND THE EMERGING   PLAN
ATOMIC MEGALOPOLIS. PART I. USA+45 TEC/DEV ADMIN   NEIGH
NUC/PWR HABITAT...SOC AUD/VIS CHARTS GEN/LAWS 20   MUNIC
WATER. PAGE 28 B0568   PROB/SOLV

B56
KAUFMANN W.W.,MILITARY POLICY AND NATIONAL   FORCES
SECURITY. USA+45 ELITES INTELL NAT/G TOP/EX PLAN   CREATE
BAL/PWR DIPLOM ROUTINE COERCE NUC/PWR ATTIT
ORD/FREE PWR 20 COLD/WAR. PAGE 58 B1182

B56
KOENIG L.W.,THE TRUMAN ADMINISTRATION: ITS   ADMIN
PRINCIPLES AND PRACTICE. USA+45 POL/PAR CHIEF LEGIS   POLICY
DIPLOM DEATH NUC/PWR WAR CIVMIL/REL PEACE   EX/STRUC
...DECISION 20 TRUMAN/HS PRESIDENT TREATY. PAGE 61   GOV/REL
B1224

B57
BEAL J.R.,JOHN FOSTER DULLES, A BIOGRAPHY. USA+45   BIOG
USSR WOR+45 CONSTN INT/ORG NAT/G EX/STRUC LEGIT   DIPLOM
ADMIN NUC/PWR DISPL PERSON ORD/FREE PWR SKILL
...POLICY PSY OBS RECORD COLD/WAR UN 20 DULLES/JF.
PAGE 10 B0200

B58
ATOMIC INDUSTRIAL FORUM,MANAGEMENT AND ATOMIC   NUC/PWR
ENERGY. WOR+45 SEA LAW MARKET NAT/G TEC/DEV INSPECT   INDUS
INT/TRADE CONFER PEACE HEALTH...ANTHOL 20. PAGE 7   MGT
B0145   ECO/TAC

B58
CONSERVATIVE POLITICAL CENTRE,A WORLD SECURITY   ORD/FREE
AUTHORITY? WOR+45 CONSTN ELITES FINAN DELIB/GP PLAN   CONSERVE
PROB/SOLV ADMIN CONTROL NUC/PWR GP/REL...IDEA/COMP   FORCES
20. PAGE 23 B0468   ARMS/CONT

B58
HENKIN L.,ARMS CONTROL AND INSPECTION IN AMERICAN   USA+45
LAW. LAW CONSTN INT/ORG LOC/G MUNIC NAT/G PROVS   JURID
EDU/PROP LEGIT EXEC NUC/PWR KNOWL ORD/FREE...OBS   ARMS/CONT
TOT/POP CONGRESS 20. PAGE 49 B0990

B59
MAYDA J.,ATOMIC ENERGY AND LAW. ECO/UNDEV FINAN   NUC/PWR
TEC/DEV FOR/AID EFFICIENCY PRODUC WEALTH...POLICY   L/A+17C
TECHNIC 20. PAGE 71 B1433   LAW
                                                      ADMIN

B59
U OF MICHIGAN LAW SCHOOL,ATOMS AND THE LAW. USA+45   NUC/PWR
PROVS WORKER PROB/SOLV DIPLOM ADMIN GOV/REL ANTHOL.   NAT/G
PAGE 106 B2142   CONTROL
                                                      LAW

S59
JANOWITZ M.,"CHANGING PATTERNS OF ORGANIZATIONAL   FORCES
AUTHORITY: THE MILITARY ESTABLISHMENT" (BMR)"   AUTHORIT
USA+45 ELITES STRUCT EX/STRUC PLAN DOMIN AUTOMAT   ADMIN
NUC/PWR WEAPON 20. PAGE 55 B1122   TEC/DEV

S59
STOESSINGER J.G.,"THE INTERNATIONAL ATOMIC ENERGY   INT/ORG
AGENCY: THE FIRST PHASE." FUT WOR+45 NAT/G VOL/ASSN   ECO/DEV
DELIB/GP BAL/PWR LEGIT ADMIN ROUTINE PWR...OBS   FOR/AID
CON/ANAL GEN/LAWS VAL/FREE 20 IAEA. PAGE 101 B2040   NUC/PWR

S60
HUNTINGTON S.P.,"STRATEGIC PLANNING AND THE   EXEC
POLITICAL PROCESS." USA+45 NAT/G DELIB/GP LEGIS   ACT/RES
ACT/RES ECO/TAC LEGIT ROUTINE CHOOSE RIGID/FLEX PWR   NUC/PWR
...POLICY MAJORIT MGT 20. PAGE 53 B1066   WAR

S60
HUTCHINSON C.E.,"AN INSTITUTE FOR NATIONAL SECURITY   POLICY
AFFAIRS." USA+45 R+D NAT/G CONSULT TOP/EX ACT/RES   METH/CNCPT
CREATE PLAN TEC/DEV EDU/PROP ROUTINE NUC/PWR ATTIT   ELITES
ORD/FREE PWR...DECISION MGT PHIL/SCI CONCPT RECORD   DIPLOM
GEN/LAWS GEN/METH 20. PAGE 53 B1068

B61
HAYTER W.,THE DIPLOMACY OF THE GREAT POWERS. FRANCE   DIPLOM
UK USSR WOR+45 EX/STRUC TOP/EX NUC/PWR PEACE...OBS   POLICY
20. PAGE 48 B0978   NAT/G

S61
CARLETON W.G.,"AMERICAN FOREIGN POLICY: MYTHS AND   PLAN
REALITIES." FUT USA+45 WOR+45 ECO/UNDEV INT/ORG   MYTH
EX/STRUC ARMS/CONT NUC/PWR WAR ATTIT...POLICY   DIPLOM
CONCPT CONT/OBS GEN/METH COLD/WAR TOT/POP 20.
PAGE 19 B0378

S61
HALPERIN M.H.,"THE GAITHER COMMITTEE AND THE POLICY   PLAN
PROCESS." USA+45 NAT/G TOP/EX ACT/RES LEGIT ADMIN   POLICY
BAL/PAY PERCEPT...CONCPT TOT/POP 20. PAGE 46 B0928   NUC/PWR
                                                      DELIB/GP

S61
LEWY G.,"SUPERIOR ORDERS, NUCLEAR WARFARE AND THE   DETER
DICTATES OF CONSCIENCE: THE DILEMMA OF MILITARY   INT/ORG
OBEDIENCE IN THE ATOMIC." FUT UNIV WOR+45 INTELL   LAW
SOCIETY FORCES TOP/EX ACT/RES ADMIN ROUTINE NUC/PWR   INT/LAW
PERCEPT RIGID/FLEX ALL/VALS...POLICY CONCPT 20.
PAGE 65 B1308

S61
SCHILLING W.R.,"THE H-BOMB: HOW TO DECIDE WITHOUT   PERSON
ACTUALLY CHOOSING." FUT USA+45 INTELL CONSULT ADMIN   LEGIT
CT/SYS MORAL...JURID OBS 20 TRUMAN/HS. PAGE 93   NUC/PWR
B1888

S61
TAUBENFELD H.J.,"OUTER SPACE--PAST POLITICS AND   PLAN
FUTURE POLICY." FUT USA+45 USA-45 WOR+45 AIR INTELL   SPACE
STRUCT ECO/DEV NAT/G TOP/EX ACT/RES ADMIN ROUTINE   INT/ORG
NUC/PWR ATTIT DRIVE...CONCPT TIME/SEQ TREND TOT/POP
20. PAGE 103 B2083

B62
KENNEDY J.F.,TO TURN THE TIDE. SPACE AGRI INT/ORG   DIPLOM
FORCES TEC/DEV ADMIN NUC/PWR PEACE WEALTH...ANTHOL   CHIEF
20 KENNEDY/JF CIV/RIGHTS. PAGE 59 B1193   POLICY
                                                      NAT/G

B62
MULLEY F.W.,THE POLITICS OF WESTERN DEFENSE.   INT/ORG
EUR+WWI USA-45 WOR+45 VOL/ASSN EX/STRUC FORCES   DELIB/GP
COERCE DETER PEACE ATTIT ORD/FREE PWR...RECORD   NUC/PWR
TIME/SEQ CHARTS COLD/WAR 20 NATO. PAGE 76 B1537

B62
SCHILLING W.R.,STRATEGY, POLITICS, AND DEFENSE   ROUTINE
BUDGETS. USA+45 R+D NAT/G CONSULT DELIB/GP FORCES   POLICY
LEGIS ACT/RES PLAN BAL/PWR LEGIT EXEC NUC/PWR
RIGID/FLEX PWR...TREND COLD/WAR CONGRESS 20
EISNHWR/DD. PAGE 93 B1890

L62
NEIBURG H.L.,"THE EISENHOWER AEC AND CONGRESS: A   CHIEF
STUDY IN EXECUTIVE-LEGISLATIVE RELATIONS." USA+45   LEGIS
NAT/G POL/PAR DELIB/GP EX/STRUC TOP/EX ADMIN EXEC   GOV/REL
LEAD ROUTINE PWR...POLICY COLD/WAR CONGRESS   NUC/PWR
PRESIDENT AEC. PAGE 77 B1567

S62
ALBONETTI A.,"IL SECONDO PROGRAMMA QUINQUENNALE   R+D
1963-67 ED IL BILANCIO RICERCHE ED INVESTIMENTI PER   PLAN
IL 1963 DELL'ERATOM." EUR+WWI FUT ITALY WOR+45   NUC/PWR
ECO/DEV SERV/IND NAT/G TEC/DEV ECO/TAC ATTIT
SKILL WEALTH...MGT TIME/SEQ OEEC 20. PAGE 3 B0069

S62
SCHILLING W.R.,"SCIENTISTS, FOREIGN POLICY AND   NAT/G
POLITICS." WOR+45 WOR-45 INTELL INT/ORG CONSULT   TEC/DEV
TOP/EX ACT/RES PLAN ADMIN KNOWL...CONCPT OBS TREND   DIPLOM
LEAGUE/NAT 20. PAGE 93 B1889   NUC/PWR

B63
GREEN H.P.,GOVERNMENT OF THE ATOM. USA+45 LEGIS   GOV/REL
PROB/SOLV ADMIN CONTROL PWR...POLICY DECISION 20   EX/STRUC
PRESIDENT CONGRESS. PAGE 43 B0864   NUC/PWR
                                                      DELIB/GP

B63
KAST F.E.,SCIENCE, TECHNOLOGY, AND MANAGEMENT.   MGT
SPACE USA+45 FORCES CONFER DETER NUC/PWR...PHIL/SCI   PLAN
CHARTS ANTHOL BIBLIOG 20 NASA. PAGE 58 B1179   TEC/DEV
                                                      PROB/SOLV

B63
ROETTER C.,THE DIPLOMATIC ART. USSR INT/ORG NAT/G   DIPLOM
DELIB/GP ROUTINE NUC/PWR PEACE...POLICY 20. PAGE 90   ELITES
B1812   TOP/EX

B63
TUCKER R.C.,THE SOVIET POLITICAL MIND. WOR+45   COM
ELITES INT/ORG NAT/G POL/PAR PLAN DIPLOM ECO/TAC   TOP/EX
DOMIN ADMIN NUC/PWR REV DRIVE PERSON SUPEGO PWR   USSR
WEALTH...POLICY MGT PSY CONCPT OBS BIOG TREND
COLD/WAR MARX/KARL 20. PAGE 106 B2134

S63
BOWIE R.,"STRATEGY AND THE ATLANTIC ALLIANCE."   FORCES
EUR+WWI VOL/ASSN BAL/PWR COERCE NUC/PWR ATTIT   ROUTINE
ORD/FREE PWR...DECISION GEN/LAWS NATO COLD/WAR 20.
PAGE 14 B0287

S63
STANLEY T.W.,"DECENTRALIZING NUCLEAR CONTROL IN   INT/ORG
NATO." EUR+WWI USA+45 ELITES FORCES ACT/RES ATTIT   EX/STRUC
ORD/FREE PWR...NEW/IDEA HYPO/EXP TOT/POP 20 NATO.   NUC/PWR
PAGE 100 B2022

B64
HODGETTS J.E.,ADMINISTERING THE ATOM FOR PEACE.   PROB/SOLV
OP/RES TEC/DEV ADMIN...IDEA/COMP METH/COMP 20.   NUC/PWR
PAGE 50 B1025   PEACE
                                                      MGT

B64
WERNETTE J.P.,GOVERNMENT AND BUSINESS. LABOR   NAT/G
CAP/ISM ECO/TAC INT/TRADE TAX ADMIN AUTOMAT NUC/PWR   FINAN
CIVMIL/REL DEMAND...MGT 20 MONOPOLY. PAGE 115 B2323   ECO/DEV
                                                      CONTROL

B65
GOTLIEB A.,DISARMAMENT AND INTERNATIONAL LAW* A   INT/LAW
STUDY OF THE ROLE OF LAW IN THE DISARMAMENT   INT/ORG
PROCESS. USA+45 USSR PROB/SOLV CONFER ADMIN ROUTINE   ARMS/CONT
NUC/PWR ORD/FREE SOVEREIGN UN TREATY. PAGE 42 B0841   IDEA/COMP

B66
BEAUFRE A.,NATO AND EUROPE. WOR+45 PLAN CONFER EXEC INT/ORG
NUC/PWR ATTIT...POLICY 20 NATO EUROPE. PAGE 10   DETER
B0203   DIPLOM
                                                      ADMIN

B66
US DEPARTMENT OF THE ARMY,COMMUNIST CHINA: A   BIBLIOG/A
STRATEGIC SURVEY: A BIBLIOGRAPHY (PAMPHLET NO.   MARXISM
20-67). CHINA/COM COM INDIA USSR NAT/G POL/PAR   S/ASIA
EX/STRUC FORCES NUC/PWR REV ATTIT...POLICY GEOG   DIPLOM
CHARTS. PAGE 108 B2184

YOUNG W.,EXISTING MECHANISMS OF ARMS CONTROL. PROC/MFG OP/RES DIPLOM TASK CENTRAL...MGT TREATY. PAGE 119 B2395
ARMS/CONT
ADMIN
NUC/PWR
ROUTINE

ZUCKERT E.M.,"THE SERVICE SECRETARY* HAS HE A USEFUL ROLE?" USA+45 TOP/EX PLAN ADMIN EXEC DETER NUC/PWR WEAPON...MGT RECORD MCNAMARA/R. PAGE 119 B2407
S66
OBS
OP/RES
DIPLOM
FORCES

AMERICAN FRIENDS SERVICE COMM.IN PLACE OF WAR. NAT/G ACT/RES DIPLOM ADMIN NUC/PWR EFFICIENCY ...POLICY 20. PAGE 4 B0085
B67
PEACE
PACIFISM
WAR
DETER

ENKE S.,DEFENSE MANAGEMENT. USA+45 R+D FORCES WORKER PLAN ECO/TAC ADMIN NUC/PWR BAL/PAY UTIL WEALTH...MGT DEPT/DEFEN. PAGE 33 B0675
B67
DECISION
DELIB/GP
EFFICIENCY
BUDGET

SCHEINMAN L.,EURATOM* NUCLEAR INTEGRATION IN EUROPE. EX/STRUC LEAD 20 EURATOM. PAGE 93 B1885
B67
INT/ORG
NAT/LISM
NUC/PWR
DIPLOM

UNIVERSAL REFERENCE SYSTEM,PUBLIC POLICY AND THE MANAGEMENT OF SCIENCE (VOLUME IX). FUT SPACE WOR+45 LAW NAT/G TEC/DEV CONTROL NUC/PWR GOV/REL ...COMPUT/IR GEN/METH. PAGE 107 B2165
B67
BIBLIOG/A
POLICY
MGT
PHIL/SCI

PASLEY R.S.,"ORGANIZATIONAL CONFLICTS OF INTEREST IN GOVERNMENT CONTRACTS." ELITES R+D ROUTINE NUC/PWR DEMAND EFFICIENCY 20. PAGE 81 B1639
L67
NAT/G
ECO/TAC
RATION
CONTROL

LALL B.G.,"GAPS IN THE ABM DEBATE." NAT/G DIPLOM DETER CIVMIL/REL 20. PAGE 62 B1251
S67
NUC/PWR
ARMS/CONT
EX/STRUC
FORCES

NUCLEAR POWER....SEE NUC/PWR

NUCLEAR WAR....SEE NUC/PWR+COERCE, WAR

NUMERICAL INDICES....SEE INDEX

NUQUIST A.E. B1595

NUREMBERG....NUREMBERG WAR TRIALS; SEE ALSO WAR/TRIAL

NYASALAND....SEE MALAWI

NYATURU....NYATURU, A TRIBE OF TANGANYIKA

LIEBENOW J.G.,"LEGITIMACY OF ALIEN RELATIONSHIP: THE NYATURU OF TANGANYIKA" (BMR)" AFR UK ADMIN LEAD CHOOSE 20 NYATURU TANGANYIKA. PAGE 65 B1312
S61
COLONIAL
DOMIN
LEGIT
PWR

NYC....NEW YORK CITY

NYC TEMPORARY COMM CITY FINAN B1596

NYE J.S. B1597,B1598

O'DELL J.H. B1599

O'HEARN P.J.T. B1600

O'LEARY M.K. B0535

O'NEILL C.E. B1601

OAS....ORGANIZATION OF AMERICAN STATES; SEE ALSO INT/ORG, VOL/ASSN

KISER M.,"ORGANIZATION OF AMERICAN STATES." L/A+17C USA+45 ECO/UNDEV INT/ORG NAT/G PLAN TEC/DEV DIPLOM ECO/TAC INT/TRADE EDU/PROP ADMIN ALL/VALS...POLICY MGT RECORD ORG/CHARTS OAS 20. PAGE 60 B1215
L55
VOL/ASSN
ECO/DEV
REGION

SOHN L.B.,BASIC DOCUMENTS OF THE UNITED NATIONS. WOR+45 LAW INT/ORG LEGIT EXEC ROUTINE CHOOSE PWR ...JURID CONCPT GEN/LAWS ANTHOL UN TOT/POP OAS FAO ILO 20. PAGE 99 B1993
B56
DELIB/GP
CONSTN

PAN AMERICAN UNION,REPERTORIO DE PUBLICACIONES PERIODICAS ACTUALES LATINO-AMERICANAS. CULTURE ECO/UNDEV ADMIN LEAD GOV/REL 20 OAS. PAGE 81 B1630
B58
BIBLIOG
L/A+17C
NAT/G
DIPLOM

"THE EMERGING COMMON MARKETS IN LATIN AMERICA." FUT L/A+17C STRATA DIST/IND INDUS LABOR NAT/G LEGIS
S60
FINAN
ECO/UNDEV

ECO/TAC ADMIN RIGID/FLEX HEALTH...NEW/IDEA TIME/SEQ INT/TRADE OAS 20. PAGE 2 B0039

MORA J.A.,"THE ORGANIZATION OF AMERICAN STATES." USA+45 LAW ECO/UNDEV VOL/ASSN DELIB/GP PLAN BAL/PWR EDU/PROP ADMIN DRIVE RIGID/FLEX ORD/FREE WEALTH ...TIME/SEQ GEN/LAWS OAS 20. PAGE 75 B1518
S60
L/A+17C
INT/ORG
REGION

ANGLIN D.,"UNITED STATES OPPOSITION TO CANADIAN MEMBERSHIP IN THE PAN AMERICAN UNION: A CANADIAN VIEW." L/A+17C UK USA+45 VOL/ASSN DELIB/GP EX/STRUC PLAN DIPLOM DOMIN REGION ATTIT RIGID/FLEX PWR ...RELATIV CONCPT CMN/WLTH OAS 20. PAGE 5 B0112
S61
INT/ORG
CANADA

MALINOWSKI W.R.,"CENTRALIZATION AND DE-CENTRALIZATION IN THE UNITED NATIONS' ECONOMIC AND SOCIAL ACTIVITIES." WOR+45 CONSTN ECO/UNDEV INT/ORG VOL/ASSN DELIB/GP ECO/TAC EDU/PROP ADMIN RIGID/FLEX ...OBS CHARTS UNESCO UN EEC OAS OEEC 20. PAGE 69 B1385
L62
CREATE
GEN/LAWS

BOWETT D.W.,THE LAW OF INTERNATIONAL INSTITUTIONS. WOR+45 WOR-45 CONSTN DELIB/GP EX/STRUC JUDGE EDU/PROP LEGIT CT/SYS EXEC ROUTINE RIGID/FLEX ORD/FREE PWR...JURID CONCPT ORG/CHARTS GEN/METH LEAGUE/NAT OAS OEEC 20 UN. PAGE 14 B0286
B63
INT/ORG
ADJUD
DIPLOM

BARBER W.F.,INTERNAL SECURITY AND MILITARY POWER* COUNTERINSURGENCY AND CIVIC ACTION IN LATIN AMERICA. ECO/UNDEV CREATE ADMIN REV ATTIT RIGID/FLEX MARXISM...INT BIBLIOG OAS. PAGE 9 B0183
B66
L/A+17C
FORCES
ORD/FREE
TASK

SABLE M.H.,A GUIDE TO LATIN AMERICAN STUDIES (2 VOLS). CONSTN FINAN INT/ORG LABOR MUNIC POL/PAR FORCES CAP/ISM FOR/AID ADMIN MARXISM SOCISM OAS. PAGE 92 B1861
B67
BIBLIOG/A
L/A+17C
DIPLOM
NAT/LISM

TURNER F.C. JR.,"EXPERIMENT IN INTER-AMERICAN PEACE-KEEPING." DOMIN/REP ADMIN ROUTINE REV ORD/FREE OAS 20. PAGE 106 B2137
S67
FORCES
ADJUD
PEACE

OATMAN M.E. B0246

OAU....ORGANIZATION FOR AFRICAN UNITY

OBERLIN....OBERLIN, OHIO

WILDAVSKY A.,LEADERSHIP IN A SMALL TOWN. USA+45 STRUCT PROB/SOLV EXEC PARTIC RACE/REL PWR PLURISM ...SOC 20 NEGRO WATER CIV/RIGHTS OBERLIN CITY/MGT. PAGE 116 B2348
B64
LEAD
MUNIC
ELITES

OBESITY....SEE HEALTH, EATING

OBJECTIVE....OBJECTIVE, OBJECTIVITY

MARX F.M.,"POLICY FORMULATION AND THE ADMINISTRATIVE PROCESS" ROUTINE ADJUST EFFICIENCY OPTIMAL PRIVIL DRIVE PERSON OBJECTIVE...DECISION OBS GEN/METH. PAGE 70 B1418
S39
ADMIN
LEAD
INGP/REL
MGT

THOMETZ C.E.,THE DECISION-MAKERS: THE POWER STRUCTURE OF DALLAS. USA+45 CULTURE EX/STRUC DOMIN LEGIT GP/REL ATTIT OBJECTIVE...INT CHARTS GP/COMP. PAGE 104 B2101
B63
ELITES
MUNIC
PWR
DECISION

WOLL P.,AMERICAN BUREAUCRACY. USA+45 USA-45 CONSTN NAT/G ADJUD PWR OBJECTIVE...MGT GP/COMP. PAGE 118 B2372
B63
LEGIS
EX/STRUC
ADMIN
GP/REL

OBLIGATION....SEE SUPEGO

OBS....OBSERVATION; SEE ALSO DIRECT OBSERVATION METHOD INDEX, P. XIV

SUTHERLAND G.,CONSTITUTIONAL POWER AND WORLD AFFAIRS. CONSTN STRUCT INT/ORG NAT/G CHIEF LEGIS ACT/RES PLAN GOV/REL ALL/VALS...OBS TIME/SEQ CONGRESS VAL/FREE 20 PRESIDENT. PAGE 102 B2056
B19
USA-45
EXEC
DIPLOM

STOWELL E.C.,INTERVENTION IN INTERNATIONAL LAW. UNIV LAW SOCIETY INT/ORG ACT/RES PLAN LEGIT ROUTINE WAR...JURID OBS GEN/LAWS 20. PAGE 101 B2050
B21
BAL/PWR
SOVEREIGN

MERRIAM C.E.,A HISTORY OF POLITICAL THEORIES - RECENT TIMES. USA-45 WOR-45 CULTURE SOCIETY ECO/DEV R+D EDU/PROP ROUTINE CHOOSE ATTIT PERSON ALL/VALS ...POLICY SOC CONCPT METH/CNCPT OBS HIST/WRIT TIME/SEQ TREND. PAGE 73 B1471
B24
UNIV
INTELL

HALL W.P.,EMPIRE TO COMMONWEALTH. FUT WOR-45 CONSTN
B28
VOL/ASSN

ECO/DEV ECO/UNDEV INT/ORG PROVS PLAN DIPLOM
EDU/PROP ADMIN COLONIAL PEACE PERSON ALL/VALS
...POLICY GEOG SOC OBS RECORD TREND CMN/WLTH
PARLIAMENT 19/20. PAGE 46 B0925
NAT/G
UK

B29
ROBERTS S.H.,HISTORY OF FRENCH COLONIAL POLICY. AFR
ASIA L/A+17C S/ASIA CULTURE ECO/DEV ECO/UNDEV FINAN
NAT/G PLAN ECO/TAC DOMIN ROUTINE SOVEREIGN...OBS
HIST/WRIT TREND CHARTS VAL/FREE 19/20. PAGE 89
B1796
INT/ORG
ACT/RES
FRANCE
COLONIAL

B30
MURCHISON C.,PSYCHOLOGIES OF 1930. UNIV USA-45
CULTURE INTELL SOCIETY STRATA FAM ROUTINE BIO/SOC
DRIVE RIGID/FLEX SUPEGO...NEW/IDEA OBS SELF/OBS
CONT/OBS 20. PAGE 76 B1543
CREATE
PERSON

B37
GOSNELL H.F.,MACHINE POLITICS: CHICAGO MODEL.
COM/IND FACE/GP LOC/G EX/STRUC LEAD ROUTINE
SANCTION REPRESENT GOV/REL PWR...POLICY MATH OBS
INT CHARTS. PAGE 41 B0840
POL/PAR
MUNIC
ADMIN
CHOOSE

B37
PARSONS T.,THE STRUCTURE OF SOCIAL ACTION. UNIV
INTELL SOCIETY INDUS MARKET ECO/TAC ROUTINE CHOOSE
ALL/VALS...CONCPT OBS BIOG TREND GEN/LAWS 20.
PAGE 81 B1636
CULTURE
ATTIT
CAP/ISM

B38
RAPPARD W.E.,THE CRISIS OF DEMOCRACY. EUR+WWI UNIV
WOR-45 CULTURE SOCIETY ECO/DEV INT/ORG POL/PAR
ACT/RES EDU/PROP EXEC CHOOSE ATTIT ALL/VALS...SOC
OBS HIST/WRIT TIME/SEQ LEAGUE/NAT NAZI TOT/POP 20.
PAGE 86 B1741
NAT/G
CONCPT

B39
ZIMMERN A.,MODERN POLITICAL DOCTRINE. WOR-45
CULTURE SOCIETY ECO/UNDEV DELIB/GP EX/STRUC CREATE
DOMIN COERCE NAT/LISM ATTIT RIGID/FLEX ORD/FREE PWR
WEALTH...POLICY CONCPT OBS TIME/SEQ TREND TOT/POP
LEAGUE/NAT 20. PAGE 119 B2402
NAT/G
ECO/TAC
BAL/PWR
INT/TRADE

S39
MARX F.M.,"POLICY FORMULATION AND THE
ADMINISTRATIVE PROCESS" ROUTINE ADJUST EFFICIENCY
OPTIMAL PRIVIL DRIVE PERSON OBJECTIVE...DECISION
OBS GEN/METH. PAGE 70 B1418
ADMIN
LEAD
INGP/REL
MGT

B41
YOUNG G.,FEDERALISM AND FREEDOM. EUR+WWI MOD/EUR
RUSSIA USA-45 WOR-45 SOCIETY STRUCT ECO/DEV INT/ORG
EXEC FEDERAL ATTIT PERSON ALL/VALS...OLD/LIB CONCPT
OBS TREND LEAGUE/NAT TOT/POP. PAGE 119 B2392
NAT/G
WAR

S43
GOLDEN C.S.,"NEW PATTERNS OF DEMOCRACY." NEIGH
DELIB/GP EDU/PROP EXEC PARTIC...MGT METH/CNCPT OBS
TREND. PAGE 40 B0815
LABOR
REPRESENT
LG/CO
GP/REL

B44
DAVIS H.E.,PIONEERS IN WORLD ORDER. WOR-45 CONSTN
ECO/TAC DOMIN EDU/PROP LEGIT ADJUD ADMIN ARMS/CONT
CHOOSE KNOWL ORD/FREE...POLICY JURID SOC STAT OBS
CENSUS TIME/SEQ ANTHOL LEAGUE/NAT 20. PAGE 26 B0537
INT/ORG
ROUTINE

L44
HAILEY,"THE FUTURE OF COLONIAL PEOPLES." WOR-45
CONSTN CULTURE ECO/UNDEV AGRI MARKET INT/ORG NAT/G
SECT CONSULT ECO/TAC LEGIT ADMIN NAT/LISM ALL/VALS
...SOC OBS TREND STERTYP CMN/WLTH LEAGUE/NAT
PARLIAMENT 20. PAGE 45 B0916
PLAN
CONCPT
DIPLOM
UK

B45
BUSH V.,SCIENCE, THE ENDLESS FRONTIER. FUT USA-45
INTELL STRATA ACT/RES CREATE PLAN EDU/PROP ADMIN
NUC/PWR PEACE ATTIT HEALTH KNOWL...MAJORIT HEAL MGT
PHIL/SCI CONCPT OBS TREND 20. PAGE 18 B0360
R+D
NAT/G

B45
PASTUHOV V.D.,A GUIDE TO THE PRACTICE OF
INTERNATIONAL CONFERENCES. WOR+45 PLAN LEGIT
ORD/FREE...MGT OBS RECORD VAL/FREE ILO LEAGUE/NAT
20. PAGE 81 B1640
INT/ORG
DELIB/GP

B47
CROCKER W.R.,ON GOVERNING COLONIES: BEING AN
OUTLINE OF THE REAL ISSUES AND A COMPARISON OF THE
BRITISH, FRENCH, AND BELGIAN... AFR BELGIUM FRANCE
UK CULTURE SOVEREIGN...OBS 20. PAGE 25 B0505
COLONIAL
POLICY
GOV/COMP
ADMIN

B47
LASSWELL H.D.,THE ANALYSIS OF POLITICAL BEHAVIOUR:
AN EMPIRICAL APPROACH. WOR+45 CULTURE NAT/G FORCES
EDU/PROP ADMIN ATTIT PERCEPT KNOWL...PHIL/SCI PSY
SOC NEW/IDEA OBS INT GEN/METH NAZI 20. PAGE 63
B1267
R+D
ACT/RES
ELITES

B49
KENT S.,STRATEGIC INTELLIGENCE FOR AMERICAN WORLD
POLICY. FUT USA+45 NAT/G ATTIT PERCEPT ORD/FREE
...OBS 20. PAGE 59 B1195
ACT/RES
EX/STRUC
DIPLOM

B51
LASSWELL H.D.,THE POLITICAL WRITINGS OF HAROLD D
LASSWELL. UNIV DOMIN EXEC LEAD RATIONAL ATTIT DRIVE
ROLE ALL/VALS...OBS BIOG 20. PAGE 63 B1269
PERSON
PSY
INGP/REL
CONCPT

S51
COHEN M.B.,"PERSONALITY AS A FACTOR IN
ADMINISTRATIVE DECISIONS." ADJUD PERS/REL ANOMIE
PERSON
ADMIN

SUPEGO...OBS SELF/OBS INT. PAGE 22 B0446
PROB/SOLV
PSY

C51
HOMANS G.C.,"THE WESTERN ELECTRIC RESEARCHES" IN S.
HOSLETT, ED.: HUMAN FACTORS IN MANAGEMENT (BMR)"
ACT/RES GP/REL HAPPINESS PRODUC DRIVE...MGT OBS 20.
PAGE 51 B1037
OP/RES
EFFICIENCY
SOC/EXP
WORKER

B52
DAY E.E.,EDUCATION FOR FREEDOM AND RESPONSIBILITY.
FUT USA+45 CULTURE CONSULT EDU/PROP ATTIT SKILL
...MGT CONCPT OBS GEN/LAWS COLD/WAR 20. PAGE 27
B0547
SCHOOL
KNOWL

B52
ULAM A.B.,TITOISM AND THE COMINFORM. USSR WOR+45
STRUCT INT/ORG NAT/G ACT/RES PLAN EXEC ATTIT DRIVE
ALL/VALS...CONCPT OBS VAL/FREE 20 COMINTERN
TITO/MARSH. PAGE 106 B2145
COM
POL/PAR
TOTALISM
YUGOSLAVIA

B53
WAGLEY C.,AMAZON TOWN: A STUDY OF MAN IN THE
TROPICS. BRAZIL L/A+17C STRATA STRUCT ECO/UNDEV
AGRI EX/STRUC RACE/REL DISCRIM HABITAT WEALTH...OBS
SOC/EXP 20. PAGE 113 B2273
SOC
NEIGH
CULTURE
INGP/REL

B54
MANGONE G.,A SHORT HISTORY OF INTERNATIONAL
ORGANIZATION. MOD/EUR USA-45 WOR+45 WOR-45
LAW LEGIS CREATE LEGIT ROUTINE RIGID/FLEX PWR
...JURID CONCPT OBS TIME/SEQ STERTYP GEN/LAWS UN
TOT/POP VAL/FREE 18/20. PAGE 69 B1389
INT/ORG
INT/LAW

L54
FURNISS E.S.,"WEAKNESSES IN FRENCH FOREIGN POLICY-
MAKING." EUR+WWI LEGIS LEGIT EXEC ATTIT RIGID/FLEX
ORD/FREE...SOC CONCPT METH/CNCPT OBS 20. PAGE 38
B0766
NAT/G
STRUCT
DIPLOM
FRANCE

L55
ROSTOW W.W.,"RUSSIA AND CHINA UNDER COMMUNISM."
CHINA/COM USSR INTELL STRUCT INT/ORG NAT/G POL/PAR
TOP/EX ACT/RES PLAN ADMIN ATTIT ALL/VALS MARXISM
...CONCPT OBS TIME/SEQ TREND GOV/COMP VAL/FREE 20.
PAGE 91 B1830
COM
ASIA

S55
ANGELL R.,"GOVERNMENTS AND PEOPLES AS A FOCI FOR
PEACE-ORIENTED RESEARCH." WOR+45 CULTURE SOCIETY
FACE/GP ACT/RES CREATE PLAN DIPLOM EDU/PROP ROUTINE
ATTIT PERCEPT SKILL...POLICY CONCPT OBS TREND
GEN/METH 20. PAGE 5 B0110
FUT
SOC
PEACE

S55
CHAPIN F.S.,"FORMALIZATION OBSERVED IN TEN
VOLUNTARY ORGANIZATIONS: CONCEPTS, MORPHOLOGY,
PROCESS." STRUCT INGP/REL PERS/REL...METH/CNCPT
CLASSIF OBS RECORD. PAGE 20 B0407
VOL/ASSN
ROUTINE
CONTROL
OP/RES

S55
TORRE M.,"PSYCHIATRIC OBSERVATIONS OF INTERNATIONAL
CONFERENCES." WOR+45 INT/ORG PROF/ORG VOL/ASSN
CONSULT EDU/PROP ROUTINE ATTIT DRIVE KNOWL...PSY
METH/CNCPT OBS/ENVIR STERTYP 20. PAGE 105 B2119
DELIB/GP
OBS
DIPLOM

B56
MANNONI D.O.,PROSPERO AND CALIBAN: THE PSYCHOLOGY
OF COLONIZATION. AFR EUR+WWI FAM KIN MUNIC SECT
DOMIN ADMIN ATTIT DRIVE LOVE PWR RESPECT...PSY SOC
CONCPT MYTH OBS DEEP/INT BIOG GEN/METH MALAGASY 20.
PAGE 69 B1394
CULTURE
COLONIAL

S56
KHAMA T.,"POLITICAL CHANGE IN AFRICAN SOCIETY."
CONSTN SOCIETY LOC/G NAT/G POL/PAR EX/STRUC LEGIS
LEGIT ADMIN CHOOSE REPRESENT NAT/LISM MORAL
ORD/FREE PWR...CONCPT OBS TREND GEN/METH CMN/WLTH
17/20. PAGE 59 B1201
AFR
ELITES

B57
BEAL J.R.,JOHN FOSTER DULLES, A BIOGRAPHY. USA+45
USSR WOR+45 CONSTN INT/ORG NAT/G EX/STRUC LEGIT
ADMIN NUC/PWR DISPL PERSON ORD/FREE PWR SKILL
...POLICY PSY OBS RECORD COLD/WAR UN 20 DULLES/JF.
PAGE 10 B0200
BIOG
DIPLOM

B57
KIETH-LUCAS A.,DECISIONS ABOUT PEOPLE IN NEED, A
STUDY OF ADMINISTRATIVE RESPONSIVENESS IN PUBLIC
ASSISTANCE. USA+45 GIVE RECEIVE INGP/REL PERS/REL
MORAL RESPECT WEALTH...SOC OBS BIBLIOG 20. PAGE 60
B1204
ADMIN
RIGID/FLEX
SOC/WK
DECISION

S57
HAILEY,"TOMORROW IN AFRICA." CONSTN SOCIETY LOC/G
NAT/G DOMIN ADJUD ADMIN GP/REL DISCRIM NAT/LISM
ATTIT MORAL ORD/FREE...PSY SOC CONCPT OBS RECORD
TREND GEN/LAWS CMN/WLTH 20. PAGE 45 B0917
AFR
PERSON
ELITES
RACE/REL

B58
BROWNE C.G.,THE CONCEPT OF LEADERSHIP. UNIV FACE/GP
DOMIN EDU/PROP LEGIT LEAD DRIVE PERSON PWR...MGT
SOC OBS SELF/OBS CONT/OBS INT PERS/TEST STERTYP
GEN/LAWS. PAGE 16 B0328
EXEC
CONCPT

B58
HENKIN L.,ARMS CONTROL AND INSPECTION IN AMERICAN
LAW. LAW CONSTN INT/ORG LOC/G MUNIC NAT/G PROVS
EDU/PROP LEGIT EXEC NUC/PWR KNOWL ORD/FREE...OBS
TOT/POP CONGRESS 20. PAGE 49 B0990
USA+45
JURID
ARMS/CONT

B58
KINTNER W.R.,ORGANIZING FOR CONFLICT: A PROPOSAL.
USA+45

USSR STRUCT NAT/G LEGIS ADMIN EXEC PEACE ORD/FREE PWR...CONCPT OBS TREND NAT/COMP VAL/FREE COLD/WAR 20. PAGE 60 B1211 — PLAN DIPLOM
B58

TAYLOR H..THE STATESMAN. MOD/EUR FACE/GP FAM NAT/G POL/PAR DELIB/GP LEGIS ATTIT PERSON PWR...POLICY CONCPT OBS GEN/LAWS. PAGE 103 B2086 — EXEC STRUCT
S58

DAVENPORT J.."ARMS AND THE WELFARE STATE." INTELL STRUCT FORCES CREATE ECO/TAC FOR/AID DOMIN LEGIT ADMIN WAR ORD/FREE PWR...POLICY SOC CONCPT MYTH OBS TREND COLD/WAR TOT/POP 20. PAGE 26 B0533 — USA+45 NAT/G USSR
B59

BOWLES C..THE COMING POLITICAL BREAKTHROUGH. USA+45 ECO/DEV EX/STRUC ATTIT...CONCPT OBS 20. PAGE 14 B0288 — DIPLOM CHOOSE PREDICT POL/PAR
B59

CHINA INSTITUTE OF AMERICA..CHINA AND THE UNITED NATIONS. CHINA/COM FUT STRUCT EDU/PROP LEGIT ADMIN ATTIT KNOWL ORD/FREE PWR...OBS RECORD STAND/INT TIME/SEQ UN LEAGUE/NAT UNESCO 20. PAGE 21 B0425 — ASIA INT/ORG
B59

ELLIOTT O..MEN AT THE TOP. USA+45 CULTURE EX/STRUC PRESS GOV/REL ATTIT ALL/VALS...OBS INT QU 20. PAGE 33 B0668 — TOP/EX PERSON LEAD POLICY
B59

YANG C.K..A CHINESE VILLAGE IN EARLY COMMUNIST TRANSITION. ECO/UNDEV AGRI FAM KIN MUNIC FORCES PLAN ECO/TAC DOMIN EDU/PROP ATTIT DRIVE PWR RESPECT ...SOC CONCPT METH/CNCPT OBS RECORD CON/ANAL CHARTS WORK 20. PAGE 118 B2389 — ASIA ROUTINE SOCISM
S59

BAILEY S.D.."THE FUTURE COMPOSITION OF THE TRUSTEESHIP COUNCIL." FUT WOR+45 CONSTN VOL/ASSN ADMIN ATTIT PWR...OBS TREND CON/ANAL VAL/FREE UN 20. PAGE 8 B0161 — INT/ORG NAT/LISM SOVEREIGN
S59

CHAPMAN B.."THE FRENCH CONSEIL D'ETAT." FRANCE NAT/G CONSULT OP/RES PROB/SOLV PWR...OBS 20. PAGE 20 B0410 — ADMIN LAW CT/SYS LEGIS
S59

LENGYEL P.."SOME TRENDS IN THE INTERNATIONAL CIVIL SERVICE." FUT WOR+45 INT/ORG CONSULT ATTIT...MGT OBS TREND CON/ANAL LEAGUE/NAT UNESCO 20. PAGE 64 B1291 — ADMIN EXEC
S59

PADELFORD N.J.."REGIONAL COOPERATION IN THE SOUTH PACIFIC: THE SOUTH PACIFIC COMMISSION." FUT NEW/ZEALND UK WOR+45 CULTURE ECO/UNDEV LOC/G VOL/ASSN...OBS CON/ANAL UNESCO VAL/FREE AUSTRAL 20. PAGE 80 B1622 — INT/ORG ADMIN
S59

STOESSINGER J.G.."THE INTERNATIONAL ATOMIC ENERGY AGENCY: THE FIRST PHASE." FUT WOR+45 NAT/G VOL/ASSN DELIB/GP BAL/PWR LEGIT ADMIN ROUTINE PWR...OBS CON/ANAL GEN/LAWS VAL/FREE 20 IAEA. PAGE 101 B2040 — INT/ORG ECO/DEV FOR/AID NUC/PWR
B60

ARGYRIS C..UNDERSTANDING ORGANIZATIONAL BEHAVIOR. OP/RES FEEDBACK...MGT PSY METH/CNCPT OBS INT SIMUL 20. PAGE 6 B0130 — LG/CO PERSON ADMIN ROUTINE
B60

BASS B.M..LEADERSHIP, PSYCHOLOGY, AND ORGANIZATIONAL BEHAVIOR. DOMIN CHOOSE DRIVE PERSON PWR RESPECT SKILL...SOC METH/CNCPT OBS. PAGE 9 B0193 — UNIV FACE/GP DELIB/GP ROUTINE
B60

MEEHAN E.J..THE BRITISH LEFT WING AND FOREIGN POLICY: A STUDY OF THE INFLUENCE OF IDEOLOGY. FUT UK UNIV WOR+45 INTELL TOP/EX PLAN ADMIN ROUTINE DRIVE...OBS TIME/SEQ GEN/LAWS PARLIAMENT 20. PAGE 72 B1461 — ACT/RES ATTIT DIPLOM
L60

MACPHERSON C.."TECHNICAL CHANGE AND POLITICAL DECISION." WOR+45 NAT/G CREATE CAP/ISM DIPLOM ROUTINE RIGID/FLEX...CONCPT OBS GEN/METH 20. PAGE 68 B1375 — TEC/DEV ADMIN
B61

BARNES W..THE FOREIGN SERVICE OF THE UNITED STATES. USA+45 USA-45 CONSTN INT/ORG POL/PAR CONSULT DELIB/GP LEGIS DOMIN EDU/PROP EXEC ATTIT RIGID/FLEX ORD/FREE PWR...POLICY CONCPT STAT OBS RECORD BIOG TIME/SEQ TREND. PAGE 9 B0188 — NAT/G MGT DIPLOM
B61

HAIRE M..MODERN ORGANIZATION THEORY. LABOR ROUTINE MAJORITY...CONCPT MODAL OBS CONT/OBS. PAGE 45 B0919 — PERS/REL GP/REL MGT DECISION
B61

HASAN H.S..PAKISTAN AND THE UN. ISLAM WOR+45 ECO/DEV ECO/UNDEV NAT/G TOP/EX ECO/TAC FOR/AID EDU/PROP ADMIN DRIVE PERCEPT...OBS TIME/SEQ UN 20. PAGE 48 B0965 — INT/ORG ATTIT PAKISTAN
B61

HAYTER W.,THE DIPLOMACY OF THE GREAT POWERS. FRANCE UK USSR WOR+45 EX/STRUC TOP/EX NUC/PWR PEACE...OBS 20. PAGE 48 B0978 — DIPLOM POLICY NAT/G
B61

KOESTLER A..THE LOTUS AND THE ROBOT. ASIA INDIA S/ASIA SOCIETY STRATA ECO/DEV AGRI INDUS FAM CREATE DOMIN EDU/PROP ADMIN COERCE ATTIT DRIVE SUPEGO ORD/FREE PWR RESPECT WEALTH...MYTH OBS 20 CHINJAP. PAGE 61 B1226 — SECT ECO/UNDEV
B61

MACRIDIS R.C..COMPARATIVE POLITICS: NOTES AND READINGS. WOR+45 LOC/G MUNIC NAT/G PROVS VOL/ASSN EDU/PROP ADMIN ATTIT PERSON ORD/FREE...SOC CONCPT OBS RECORD TREND 20. PAGE 68 B1376 — POL/PAR CHOOSE
B61

MARVICK D..POLITICAL DECISION-MAKERS. INTELL STRATA NAT/G POL/PAR EX/STRUC LEGIS DOMIN EDU/PROP ATTIT PERSON PWR...PSY STAT OBS CONT/OBS STAND/INT UNPLAN/INT TIME/SEQ CHARTS STERTYP VAL/FREE. PAGE 70 B1416 — TOP/EX BIOG ELITES
B61

TANNENBAUM R..LEADERSHIP AND ORGANIZATION. STRUCT ADMIN INGP/REL ATTIT PERCEPT...DECISION METH/CNCPT OBS CHARTS BIBLIOG. PAGE 103 B2075 — LEAD MGT RESPECT ROLE
S61

BARTLEY H.J.."COMMAND EXPERIENCE." USA+45 EX/STRUC FORCES LEGIT ROUTINE SKILL...POLICY OBS HYPO/EXP GEN/LAWS 20. PAGE 9 B0191 — CONCPT TREND
S61

JACKSON E.."CONSTITUTIONAL DEVELOPMENTS OF THE UNITED NATIONS: THE GROWTH OF ITS EXECUTIVE CAPACITY." FUT WOR+45 CONSTN STRUCT ACT/RES PLAN ALL/VALS...NEW/IDEA OBS COLD/WAR UN 20. PAGE 55 B1106 — INT/ORG EXEC
S61

MILLER E.."LEGAL ASPECTS OF UN ACTION IN THE CONGO." AFR CULTURE ADMIN PEACE DRIVE RIGID/FLEX ORD/FREE...WELF/ST JURID OBS UN CONGO 20. PAGE 73 B1480 — INT/ORG LEGIT
S61

RUDOLPH S.."CONSENSUS AND CONFLICT IN INDIAN POLITICS." S/ASIA WOR+45 NAT/G DELIB/GP DIPLOM EDU/PROP ADMIN CONSEN PERSON ALL/VALS...OBS TREND TOT/POP VAL/FREE 20. PAGE 92 B1854 — POL/PAR PERCEPT INDIA
S61

SCHILLING W.R.."THE H-BOMB: HOW TO DECIDE WITHOUT ACTUALLY CHOOSING." FUT USA+45 INTELL CONSULT ADMIN CT/SYS MORAL...JURID OBS 20 TRUMAN/HS. PAGE 93 B1888 — PERSON LEGIT NUC/PWR
B62

ARGYRIS C..INTERPERSONAL COMPETENCE AND ORGANIZATIONAL EFFECTIVENESS. CREATE PLAN PROB/SOLV EDU/PROP INGP/REL PERS/REL PRODUC...OBS INT SIMUL 20. PAGE 6 B0131 — EX/STRUC ADMIN CONSULT EFFICIENCY
L62

ABERLE D.F.."CHAHAR AND DAGOR MONGOL BUREAUCRATIC ADMINISTRATION: 19621945." ASIA MUNIC TOP/EX PWR ...MGT OBS INT MONGOL 20. PAGE 3 B0053 — EX/STRUC STRATA
L62

MALINOWSKI W.R.."CENTRALIZATION AND DE-CENTRALIZATION IN THE UNITED NATIONS' ECONOMIC AND SOCIAL ACTIVITIES." WOR+45 CONSTN ECO/UNDEV INT/ORG VOL/ASSN DELIB/GP ECO/TAC EDU/PROP ADMIN RIGID/FLEX ...OBS CHARTS UNESCO UN EEC OAS OEEC 20. PAGE 69 B1385 — CREATE GEN/LAWS
S62

BUENO M.."ASPECTOS SOCIOLOGICOS DE LA EDUCACION." FUT UNIV INTELL R+D SERV/IND SCHOOL CONSULT EX/STRUC ACT/RES PLAN...METH/CNCPT OBS 20. PAGE 17 B0341 — SOCIETY EDU/PROP PERSON
S62

IOVTCHOUK M.T.."ON SOME THEORETICAL PRINCIPLES AND METHODS OF SOCIOLOGICAL INVESTIGATIONS (IN RUSSIAN)." FUT USA+45 STRATA R+D NAT/G POL/PAR TOP/EX ACT/RES PLAN ECO/TAC EDU/PROP ROUTINE ATTIT RIGID/FLEX MARXISM SOCISM...MARXIST METH/CNCPT OBS TREND NAT/COMP GEN/LAWS 20. PAGE 54 B1102 — COM ECO/DEV CAP/ISM USSR
S62

JACOBSON H.K.."THE UNITED NATIONS AND COLONIALISM: A TENTATIVE APPRAISAL." AFR FUT S/ASIA USA+45 USSR WOR+45 NAT/G DELIB/GP PLAN DIPLOM ECO/TAC DOMIN ADMIN ROUTINE COERCE ATTIT RIGID/FLEX ORD/FREE PWR ...OBS STERTYP UN 20. PAGE 55 B1115 — INT/ORG CONCPT COLONIAL
S62

SCHILLING W.R.."SCIENTISTS, FOREIGN POLICY AND POLITICS." WOR+45 WOR-45 INTELL INT/ORG CONSULT TOP/EX ACT/RES PLAN ADMIN KNOWL...CONCPT OBS TREND LEAGUE/NAT 20. PAGE 93 B1889 — NAT/G TEC/DEV DIPLOM NUC/PWR
S62

SPRINGER H.W.."FEDERATION IN THE CARIBBEAN: AN ATTEMPT THAT FAILED." L/A+17C ECO/UNDEV INT/ORG POL/PAR PROVS LEGIS CREATE PLAN LEGIT ADMIN FEDERAL ATTIT DRIVE PERSON ORD/FREE PWR...POLICY GEOG PSY CONCPT OBS CARIBBEAN CMN/WLTH 20. PAGE 100 B2013 — VOL/ASSN NAT/G REGION

HEUSSLER R.,YESTERDAY'S RULERS: THE MAKING OF THE | B63
BRITISH COLONIAL SERVICE. AFR EUR+WWI UK STRATA | EX/STRUC
SECT DELIB/GP PLAN DOMIN EDU/PROP ATTIT PERCEPT | MORAL
PERSON SUPEGO KNOWL ORD/FREE PWR...MGT SOC OBS INT | ELITES
TIME/SEQ 20 CMN/WLTH. PAGE 49 B1000

INTL INST ADMIN SCIENCES,EDUCATION IN PUBLIC | B63
ADMINISTRATION: A SYMPOSIUM ON TEACHING METHODS AND | EDU/PROP
MATERIALS. WOR+45 SCHOOL CONSULT CREATE CONFER | METH
SKILL...OBS TREND IDEA/COMP METH/COMP 20. PAGE 54 | ADMIN
B1100 | ACADEM

KOGAN N.,THE POLITICS OF ITALIAN FOREIGN POLICY. | B63
EUR+WWI LEGIS DOMIN LEGIT EXEC PWR RESPECT SKILL | NAT/G
...POLICY DECISION HUM SOC METH/CNCPT OBS INT | ROUTINE
CHARTS 20. PAGE 61 B1227 | DIPLOM
 | ITALY

MACNEIL N.,FORGE OF DEMOCRACY: THE HOUSE OF | B63
REPRESENTATIVES. POL/PAR EX/STRUC TOP/EX DEBATE | LEGIS
LEAD PARL/PROC CHOOSE GOV/REL PWR...OBS HOUSE/REP. | DELIB/GP
PAGE 68 B1374

TUCKER R.C.,THE SOVIET POLITICAL MIND. WOR+45 | B63
ELITES INT/ORG NAT/G POL/PAR PLAN DIPLOM ECO/TAC | COM
DOMIN ADMIN NUC/PWR REV DRIVE PERSON SUPEGO PWR | TOP/EX
WEALTH...POLICY MGT PSY CONCPT OBS BIOG TREND | USSR
COLD/WAR MARX/KARL 20. PAGE 106 B2134

DUCROS B.,"MOBILISATION DES RESSOURCES PRODUCTIVES | S63
ET DEVELOPPEMENT." FUT INTELL SOCIETY COM/IND | ECO/UNDEV
DIST/IND EXTR/IND FINAN INDUS ROUTINE WEALTH | TEC/DEV
...METH/CNCPT OBS 20. PAGE 31 B0625

NYE J.S. JR.,"EAST AFRICAN ECONOMIC INTEGRATION." | S63
AFR UGANDA PROVS DELIB/GP PLAN ECO/TAC INT/TRADE | ECO/UNDEV
ADMIN ROUTINE ORD/FREE PWR WEALTH...OBS TIME/SEQ | INT/ORG
VAL/FREE 20. PAGE 79 B1597

RUSTOW D.A.,"THE MILITARY IN MIDDLE EASTERN SOCIETY | S63
AND POLITICS." FUT ISLAM CONSTN SOCIETY FACE/GP | FORCES
NAT/G POL/PAR PROF/ORG CONSULT DOMIN ADMIN EXEC | ELITES
REGION COERCE NAT/LISM ATTIT DRIVE PERSON ORD/FREE
PWR...POLICY CONCPT OBS STERTYP 20. PAGE 92 B1860

ADAMS V.,THE PEACE CORPS IN ACTION. USA+45 VOL/ASSN | B64
EX/STRUC GOV/REL PERCEPT ORD/FREE...OBS 20 | DIPLOM
KENNEDY/JF PEACE/CORP. PAGE 3 B0058 | FOR/AID
 | PERSON
 | DRIVE

JACKSON H.M.,THE SECRETARY OF STATE AND THE | B64
AMBASSADOR* JACKSON SUBCOMMITTEE PAPERS ON THE | GOV/REL
CONDUCT OF AMERICAN FOREIGN POLICY. USA+45 NAT/G | DIPLOM
FORCES ACT/RES OP/RES EDU/PROP CENTRAL EFFICIENCY | ADMIN
ORD/FREE...OBS RECORD ANTHOL CONGRESS PRESIDENT. | EX/STRUC
PAGE 55 B1107

KIESER P.J.,THE COST OF ADMINISTRATION, SUPERVISION | B64
AND SERVICES IN URBAN BANTU TOWNSHIPS. SOUTH/AFR | AFR
SERV/IND MUNIC PROVS ADMIN COST...OBS QU CHARTS 20 | MGT
BANTU. PAGE 60 B1203 | FINAN

NUQUIST A.E.,TOWN GOVERNMENT IN VERMONT. USA+45 | B64
FINAN TOP/EX PROB/SOLV BUDGET TAX REPRESENT SUFF | LOC/G
EFFICIENCY...OBS INT 20 VERMONT. PAGE 79 B1595 | MUNIC
 | POPULISM
 | ADMIN

SAYLES L.R.,MANAGERIAL BEHAVIOR: ADMINISTRATION IN | B64
COMPLEX ORGANIZATIONS. INDUS LG/CO PROB/SOLV | CONCPT
CONTROL EXEC INGP/REL PERS/REL SKILL...MGT OBS | ADMIN
PREDICT GEN/LAWS 20. PAGE 93 B1874 | TOP/EX
 | EX/STRUC

GALTUNE J.,"BALANCE OF POWER AND THE PROBLEM OF | S64
PERCEPTION. A LOGICAL ANALYSIS." WOR+45 CONSTN | PWR
SOCIETY NAT/G DELIB/GP EX/STRUC LEGIS DOMIN ADMIN | PSY
COERCE DRIVE ORD/FREE...POLICY CONCPT OBS TREND | ARMS/CONT
GEN/LAWS. PAGE 38 B0778 | WAR

PARSONS T.,"EVOLUTIONARY UNIVERSALS IN SOCIETY." | S64
UNIV SOCIETY STRATA MARKET EDU/PROP LEGIT ADJUD | SOC
ADMIN ALL/VALS...JURID OBS GEN/LAWS VAL/FREE 20. | CONCPT
PAGE 81 B1638

SCHWELB E.,"OPERATION OF THE EUROPEAN CONVENTION ON | S64
HUMAN RIGHTS." EUR+WWI LAW SOCIETY CREATE EDU/PROP | INT/ORG
ADJUD ADMIN PEACE ATTIT ORD/FREE PWR...POLICY | MORAL
INT/LAW CONCPT OBS GEN/LAWS UN VAL/FREE ILO 20
ECHR. PAGE 95 B1916

ECCLES H.E.,MILITARY CONCEPTS AND PHILOSOPHY. | B65
USA+45 STRUCT EXEC ROUTINE COERCE WAR CIVMIL/REL | PLAN
COST...OBS GEN/LAWS COLD/WAR. PAGE 32 B0648 | DRIVE
 | LEAD
 | FORCES

INT. BANK RECONSTR. DEVELOP.,ECONOMIC DEVELOPMENT | B65
OF KUWAIT. ISLAM KUWAIT AGRI FINAN MARKET EX/STRUC | INDUS
 | NAT/G
TEC/DEV ECO/TAC ADMIN WEALTH...OBS CON/ANAL CHARTS
20. PAGE 54 B1092

YOUNG C.,POLITICS IN THE CONGO* DECOLONIZATION AND | B65
INDEPENDENCE. ELITES STRATA FORCES ADMIN REV | BELGIUM
RACE/REL FEDERAL SOVEREIGN...OBS INT CHARTS | COLONIAL
CONGO/LEOP. PAGE 118 B2391 | NAT/LISM

THOMAS F.C. JR.,"THE PEACE CORPS IN MOROCCO." | S65
CULTURE MUNIC PROVS CREATE ROUTINE TASK ADJUST | MOROCCO
STRANGE...OBS PEACE/CORP. PAGE 104 B2099 | FRANCE
 | FOR/AID
 | EDU/PROP

DICKSON W.J.,COUNSELING IN AN ORGANIZATION: A | B66
SEQUEL TO THE HAWTHORNE RESEARCHES. CLIENT VOL/ASSN | INDUS
ACT/RES PROB/SOLV AUTOMAT ROUTINE PERS/REL | WORKER
HAPPINESS ANOMIE ROLE...OBS CHARTS 20 AT+T. PAGE 29 | PSY
B0588 | MGT

LIVINGSTON J.C.,THE CONSENT OF THE GOVERNED. USA+45 | B66
EX/STRUC BAL/PWR DOMIN CENTRAL PERSON PWR...POLICY | NAT/G
CONCPT OBS IDEA/COMP 20 CONGRESS. PAGE 66 B1331 | LOBBY
 | MAJORIT
 | PARTIC

NIEBURG H.L.,IN THE NAME OF SCIENCE. USA+45 | B66
EX/STRUC LEGIS TEC/DEV BUDGET PAY AUTOMAT LOBBY PWR | NAT/G
...OBS 20. PAGE 78 B1581 | INDUS
 | TECHRACY

PERROW C.,ORGANIZATION FOR TREATMENT: A COMPARATIVE | B66
STUDY OF INSTITUTIONS FOR DELINQUENTS. AGE/Y | PSY
PROB/SOLV ADMIN CRIME PERSON MORAL...SOC/WK OBS | PUB/INST
DEEP/QU CHARTS SOC/INTEG 20. PAGE 82 B1661

RUBENSTEIN R.,THE SHARING OF POWER IN A PSYCHIATRIC | B66
HOSPITAL. CLIENT PROF/ORG PUB/INST INGP/REL ATTIT | ADMIN
PWR...DECISION OBS RECORD. PAGE 91 B1847 | PARTIC
 | HEALTH
 | CONCPT

ZUCKERT E.M.,"THE SERVICE SECRETARY* HAS HE A | S66
USEFUL ROLE?" USA+45 TOP/EX PLAN ADMIN EXEC DETER | OBS
NUC/PWR WEAPON...MGT RECORD MCNAMARA/R. PAGE 119 | OP/RES
B2407 | DIPLOM
 | FORCES

ROBINSON D.W.,PROMISING PRACTICES IN CIVIC | B67
EDUCATION. FUT USA+45 CONTROL PARTIC GOV/REL...OBS | EDU/PROP
AUD/VIS 20. PAGE 89 B1797 | NAT/G
 | ADJUST
 | ADMIN

ZONDAG C.H.,THE BOLIVIAN ECONOMY 1952-65. L/A+17C | B67
TEC/DEV FOR/AID ADMIN...OBS TREND CHARTS BIBLIOG 20 | ECO/UNDEV
BOLIV. PAGE 119 B2406 | INDUS
 | PRODUC

BURACK E.H.,"INDUSTRIAL MANAGEMENT IN ADVANCED | S67
PRODUCTION SYSTEMS: SOME THEORETICAL CONCEPTS AND | ADMIN
PRELIMINARY FINDINGS." INDUS CREATE PLAN PRODUC | MGT
ROLE...OBS STAND/INT DEEP/QU HYPO/EXP ORG/CHARTS | TEC/DEV
20. PAGE 17 B0346 | EX/STRUC

SCOTT W.R.,"ORGANIZATIONAL EVALUATION AND | S67
AUTHORITY." CONTROL SANCTION PERS/REL ATTIT DRIVE | EXEC
...SOC CONCPT OBS CHARTS IDEA/COMP 20. PAGE 95 | WORKER
B1921 | INSPECT
 | EX/STRUC

OBS/ENVIR....SOCIAL MILIEU OF AND RESISTANCES TO OBSERVATIONS

POOLE D.C.,THE CONDUCT OF FOREIGN RELATIONS UNDER | B24
MODERN DEMOCRATIC CONDITIONS. EUR+WWI USA-45 | NAT/G
INT/ORG PLAN LEGIT ADMIN KNOWL PWR...MAJORIT | EDU/PROP
OBS/ENVIR HIST/WRIT GEN/LAWS 20. PAGE 84 B1689 | DIPLOM

ANGELL N.,THE PUBLIC MIND. USA-45 SOCIETY EDU/PROP | B27
ROUTINE SUPEGO KNOWL...POLICY CONCPT MYTH OBS/ENVIR | PERCEPT
EUR+WW1 TOT/POP 20. PAGE 5 B0109 | ATTIT
 | DIPLOM
 | NAT/LISM

TORRE M.,"PSYCHIATRIC OBSERVATIONS OF INTERNATIONAL | S55
CONFERENCES." WOR+45 INT/ORG PROF/ORG VOL/ASSN | DELIB/GP
CONSULT EDU/PROP ROUTINE ATTIT DRIVE KNOWL...PSY | OBS
METH/CNCPT OBS/ENVIR STERTYP 20. PAGE 105 B2119 | DIPLOM

MURRAY D.,"CHINESE EDUCATION IN SOUTH-EAST ASIA." | S64
SOCIETY NEIGH EDU/PROP ROUTINE PERSON KNOWL | S/ASIA
...OBS/ENVIR STERTYP. PAGE 76 B1546 | SCHOOL
 | REGION
 | ASIA

OBSCENITY....OBSCENITY

OBSERVATION....SEE DIRECT-OBSERVATION METHOD INDEX, P. XIV

OBSOLESCENCE, PLANNED....SEE OBSOLESCNC

OBSOLESCNC....OBSOLESCENCE, PLANNED

OCAM....SEE UAM

OCCUPATION....SEE WORKER

OCEANIA....OCEANIA: AUSTRALIA, NEW ZEALAND, MALAYSIA,
    MELANESIA, MICRONESIA, AND POLYNESIA

OCKERT R.A. B0902

ODEGARD/P....PETER ODEGARD

ODINGA/O....OGINGA ODINGA

OECD B1602

OECD....ORGANIZATION FOR ECONOMIC COOPERATION AND
    DEVELOPMENT

		B62
TAYLOR J.K.L.,ATTITUDES AND METHODS OF COMMUNICATION AND CONSULTATION BETWEEN EMPLOYERS AND WORKERS AT INDIVIDUAL FIRM LEVEL. WOR+45 STRUCT INDUS LABOR CONFER TASK GP/REL EFFICIENCY...MGT BIBLIOG METH 20 OECD. PAGE 103 B2087	WORKER ADMIN ATTIT EDU/PROP	
		B65
OECD,MEDITERRANEAN REGIONAL PROJECT: TURKEY; EDUCATION AND DEVELOPMENT. FUT TURKEY SOCIETY STRATA FINAN NAT/G PROF/ORG PLAN PROB/SOLV ADMIN COST...STAT CHARTS 20 OECD. PAGE 79 B1602	EDU/PROP ACADEM SCHOOL ECO/UNDEV	
		B65
ORG FOR ECO COOP AND DEVEL,THE MEDITERRANEAN REGIONAL PROJECT: AN EXPERIMENT IN PLANNING BY SIX COUNTRIES. FUT GREECE SPAIN TURKEY YUGOSLAVIA SOCIETY FINAN NAT/G PROF/ORG EDU/PROP ADMIN REGION COST...POLICY STAT CHARTS 20 OECD. PAGE 80 B1614	PLAN ECO/UNDEV ACADEM SCHOOL	
		B65
ORG FOR ECO COOP AND DEVEL,THE MEDITERRANEAN REGIONAL PROJECT: YUGOSLAVIA: EDUCATION AND DEVELOPMENT. YUGOSLAVIA SOCIETY FINAN PROF/ORG PLAN ADMIN COST DEMAND MARXISM...STAT TREND CHARTS METH 20 OECD. PAGE 80 B1615	EDU/PROP ACADEM SCHOOL ECO/UNDEV	

OECD SEMINAR REGIONAL DEV B1603

OEEC....ORGANIZATION FOR EUROPEAN ECONOMIC COOPERATION;
    SEE ALSO VOL/ASSN, INT/ORG

		S58
ELKIN A.B.,"OEEC-ITS STRUCTURE AND POWERS." EUR+WWI CONSTN INDUS INT/ORG NAT/G VOL/ASSN DELIB/GP ACT/RES PLAN ORD/FREE WEALTH...CHARTS ORG/CHARTS OEEC 20. PAGE 33 B0666	ECO/DEV EX/STRUC	
		S61
HAAS E.B.,"INTERNATIONAL INTEGRATION: THE EUROPEAN AND THE UNIVERSAL PROCESS." EUR+WWI FUT WOR+45 NAT/G EX/STRUC ATTIT DRIVE ORD/FREE PWR...CONCPT GEN/LAWS OEEC 20 NATO COUNCL/EUR. PAGE 45 B0909	INT/ORG TREND REGION	
		L62
MALINOWSKI W.R.,"CENTRALIZATION AND DE-CENTRALIZATION IN THE UNITED NATIONS' ECONOMIC AND SOCIAL ACTIVITIES." WOR+45 CONSTN ECO/UNDEV INT/ORG VOL/ASSN DELIB/GP ECO/TAC EDU/PROP ADMIN RIGID/FLEX ...OBS CHARTS UNESCO UN EEC OAS OEEC 20. PAGE 69 B1385	CREATE GEN/LAWS	
		S62
ALBONETTI A.,"IL SECONDO PROGRAMMA QUINQUENNALE 1963-67 ED IL BILANCIO RICERCHE ED INVESTIMENTI PER IL 1963 DELL'ERATOM." EUR+WWI FUT ITALY WOR+45 ECO/DEV SERV/IND INT/ORG TEC/DEV ECO/TAC ATTIT SKILL WEALTH...MGT TIME/SEQ OEEC 20. PAGE 3 B0069	R+D PLAN NUC/PWR	
		B63
BOWETT D.W.,THE LAW OF INTERNATIONAL INSTITUTIONS. WOR+45 WOR-45 CONSTN DELIB/GP EX/STRUC JUDGE EDU/PROP LEGIT CT/SYS EXEC ROUTINE RIGID/FLEX ORD/FREE PWR...JURID CONCPT CHARTS GEN/METH LEAGUE/NAT OAS OEEC 20 UN. PAGE 14 B0286	INT/ORG ADJUD DIPLOM	
		S63
BARZANSKI S.,"REGIONAL UNDERDEVELOPMENT IN THE EUROPEAN ECONOMIC COMMUNITY." EUR+WWI ELITES DIST/IND MARKET VOL/ASSN CONSULT EX/STRUC ECO/TAC RIGID/FLEX WEALTH EEC OEEC 20. PAGE 9 B0192	ECO/UNDEV PLAN	
		B66
SPINELLI A.,THE EUROCRATS; CONFLICT AND CRISIS IN THE EUROPEAN COMMUNITY (TRANS. BY C. GROVE HAINES). EUR+WWI MARKET POL/PAR ECO/TAC PARL/PROC EEC OEEC ECSC EURATOM. PAGE 99 B2007	INT/ORG INGP/REL CONSTN ADMIN	

OEO....OFFICE OF ECONOMIC OPPORTUNITY

OEP....OFFICE OF EMERGENCY PLANNING

OFFICE OF ECONOMIC OPPORTUNITY....SEE OEO

OFFICE OF EMERGENCY PLANNING....SEE OEP

OFFICE OF PRICE ADMINISTRATION....SEE OPA

OFFICE OF WAR INFORMATION....SEE OWI

OGDEN G. B1367

OGUL M.S. B1187

OHIO....OHIO

OHLIN G. B1604

OHLIN/HECK....OHLIN-HECKSCHER THEORY OF COMMODITY TRADE

OKELLO/J....JOHN OKELLO

OKINAWA....OKINAWA

		B63
HIGA M.,POLITICS AND PARTIES IN POSTWAR OKINAWA. USA+45 VOL/ASSN LEGIS CONTROL LOBBY CHOOSE NAT/LISM PWR SOVEREIGN MARXISM SOCISM 20 OKINAWA CHINJAP. PAGE 50 B1008	GOV/REL POL/PAR ADMIN FORCES	

OKLAHOMA....OKLAHOMA

OLAS....ORGANIZATION FOR LATIN AMERICAN SOLIDARITY

OLD LIBERAL....SEE OLD/LIB

OLD/LIB....OLD LIBERAL

		B41
YOUNG G.,FEDERALISM AND FREEDOM. EUR+WWI MOD/EUR RUSSIA USA-45 WOR-45 SOCIETY STRUCT ECO/DEV INT/ORG EXEC FEDERAL ATTIT PERSON ALL/VALS...OLD/LIB CONCPT OBS TREND LEAGUE/NAT TOT/POP. PAGE 119 B2392	NAT/G WAR	
		B60
ROEPKE W.,A HUMANE ECONOMY: THE SOCIAL FRAMEWORK OF THE FREE MARKET. FUT USSR WOR+45 CULTURE SOCIETY ECO/DEV PLAN ECO/TAC ADMIN ATTIT PERSON RIGID/FLEX SUPEGO MORAL WEALTH SOCISM...POLICY OLD/LIB CONCPT TREND GEN/LAWS 20. PAGE 90 B1811	DRIVE EDU/PROP CAP/ISM	
		B61
FRIEDMANN W.G.,JOINT INTERNATIONAL BUSINESS VENTURES. ASIA ISLAM L/A+17C ECO/DEV DIST/IND FINAN PROC/MFG FACE/GP LG/CO NAT/G VOL/ASSN CONSULT EX/STRUC PLAN ADMIN ROUTINE WEALTH...OLD/LIB WORK 20. PAGE 37 B0760	ECO/UNDEV INT/TRADE	
		B63
OLSON M. JR.,THE ECONOMICS OF WARTIME SHORTAGE. FRANCE GERMANY MOD/EUR UK AGRI PROB/SOLV ADMIN DEMAND WEALTH...POLICY OLD/LIB 17/20. PAGE 80 B1608	WAR ADJUST ECO/TAC NAT/COMP	

OLD/STOR....CONVENTIONAL INFORMATION-STORAGE SYSTEMS

OLIGARCHY....SEE ELITES

OLIGOPOLY....SEE MONOPOLY

OLIN/MTHSN....OLIN MATHIESON

OLIVARES....OLIVARES, HEAD OF SPAIN DURING CATALAN REV.,
    1640

OLIVE B.A. B1605

OLLE-LAPRUNE J. B1606

OLLERENSHAW K. B1607

OLSON M. B1608,B1609

OMBUDSMAN....OMBUDSMAN; DOMESTIC GRIEVANCE ORGAN

		B64
HALLER W.,DER SCHWEDISCHE JUSTITIEOMBUDSMAN. DENMARK FINLAND NORWAY SWEDEN LEGIS ADJUD CONTROL PERSON ORD/FREE...NAT/COMP 20 OMBUDSMAN. PAGE 46 B0926	JURID PARL/PROC ADMIN CHIEF	
		B66
AARON T.J.,THE CONTROL OF POLICE DISCRETION: THE DANISH EXPERIENCE. DENMARK LAW CREATE ADMIN INGP/REL SUPEGO PWR 20 OMBUDSMAN. PAGE 2 B0049	CONTROL FORCES REPRESENT PROB/SOLV	
		B66
ANDERSON S.V.,CANADIAN OMBUDSMAN PROPOSALS. CANADA LEGIS DEBATE PARL/PROC...MAJORIT JURID TIME/SEQ IDEA/COMP 20 OMBUDSMAN PARLIAMENT. PAGE 5 B0096	NAT/G CREATE ADMIN POL/PAR	
		B66
MONTEIRO J.B.,CORRUPTION: CONTROL OF MALADMINISTRATION. EUR+WWI INDIA USA+45 USSR NAT/G DELIB/GP ADMIN...GP/COMP 20 OMBUDSMAN. PAGE 74 B1503	CONTROL CRIME PROB/SOLV	

ONTARIO....ONTARIO, CANADA

ONYEMELUKWE C.C. B1610

OP/RES....OPERATIONS RESEARCH; SEE ALSO CREATE

N
WORLD PEACE FOUNDATION,DOCUMENTS OF INTERNATIONAL   BIBLIOG
ORGANIZATIONS: A SELECTED BIBLIOGRAPHY. WOR+45   DIPLOM
WOR-45 AGRI FINAN ACT/RES OP/RES INT/TRADE ADMIN   INT/ORG
...CON/ANAL 20 UN UNESCO LEAGUE/NAT. PAGE 118 B2374 REGION

B24
KENT F.R.,THE GREAT GAME OF POLITICS. USA+45 LOC/G   ADMIN
NAT/G POL/PAR EX/STRUC PROB/SOLV BUDGET CHOOSE   OP/RES
GOV/REL 20. PAGE 59 B1194   STRUCT

B27
WILLOUGHBY W.F.,PRINCIPLES OF PUBLIC ADMINISTRATION NAT/G
WITH SPECIAL REFERENCE TO THE NATIONAL AND STATE   EX/STRUC
GOVERNMENTS OF THE UNITED STATES. FINAN PROVS CHIEF OP/RES
CONSULT LEGIS CREATE BUDGET EXEC ROUTINE GOV/REL   ADMIN
CENTRAL...MGT 20 BUR/BUDGET CONGRESS PRESIDENT.
PAGE 117 B2356

B37
GULICK L.,PAPERS ON THE SCIENCE OF ADMINISTRATION. OP/RES
INDUS PROB/SOLV TEC/DEV COST EFFICIENCY PRODUC   CONTROL
HABITAT...PHIL/SCI METH/COMP 20. PAGE 45 B0903   ADMIN
  MGT

B39
JENNINGS W.I.,PARLIAMENT. UK POL/PAR OP/RES BUDGET PARL/PROC
LEAD CHOOSE GP/REL...MGT 20 PARLIAMENT HOUSE/LORD   LEGIS
HOUSE/CMNS. PAGE 56 B1135   CONSTN
  NAT/G

B40
GAUS J.M.,PUBLIC ADMINISTRATION AND THE UNITED   ADMIN
STATES DEPARTMENT OF AGRICULTURE. USA-45 STRUCT   AGRI
DIST/IND FINAN MARKET EX/STRUC PROB/SOLV GIVE   DELIB/GP
PRODUC...POLICY GEOG CHARTS 20 DEPT/AGRI. PAGE 39 OP/RES
B0786

B40
PFIFFNER J.M.,RESEARCH METHODS IN PUBLIC   ADMIN
ADMINISTRATION. USA-45 R+D...MGT STAT INT QU T 20. OP/RES
PAGE 82 B1665   METH
  TEC/DEV

B41
COHEN E.W.,THE GROWTH OF THE BRITISH CIVIL SERVICE OP/RES
1780-1939. UK NAT/G SENIOR ROUTINE GOV/REL...MGT   TIME/SEQ
METH/COMP BIBLIOG 18/20. PAGE 22 B0442   CENTRAL
  ADMIN

B41
THE TAX FOUNDATION,STUDIES IN ECONOMY AND   BIBLIOG
EFFICIENCY IN GOVERNMENT. FINAN R+D OP/RES BUDGET ADMIN
TAX 20. PAGE 104 B2095   EFFICIENCY
  NAT/G

B44
PUBLIC ADMINISTRATION SERVICE,YOUR BUSINESS OF   BIBLIOG
GOVERNMENT: A CATALOG OF PUBLICATIONS IN THE FIELD ADMIN
OF PUBLIC ADMINISTRATION (PAMPHLET). FINAN R+D   NAT/G
LOC/G ACT/RES OP/RES PLAN 20. PAGE 85 B1715   MUNIC

B47
SIMON H.A.,ADMINISTRATIVE BEHAVIOR: A STUDY OF   DECISION
DECISION-MAKING PROCESSES IN ADMINISTRATIVE   NEW/IDEA
ORGANIZATION. STRUCT COM/IND OP/RES PROB/SOLV   ADMIN
EFFICIENCY EQUILIB UTIL...PHIL/SCI PSY STYLE.   RATIONAL
PAGE 97 B1956

B48
SLESSER H.,THE ADMINISTRATION OF THE LAW. UK CONSTN LAW
EX/STRUC OP/RES PROB/SOLV CRIME ROLE...DECISION   CT/SYS
METH/COMP 20 CIVIL/LAW ENGLSH/LAW CIVIL/LAW.   ADJUD
PAGE 98 B1977

S48
COCH L.,"OVERCOMING RESISTANCE TO CHANGE" (BMR)"   WORKER
USA+45 CONSULT ADMIN ROUTINE GP/REL EFFICIENCY   OP/RES
PRODUC PERCEPT SKILL...CHARTS SOC/EXP 20. PAGE 22 PROC/MFG
B0441   RIGID/FLEX

S48
KNICKERBOCKER I.,"LEADERSHIP: A CONCEPTION AND SOME LEAD
IMPLICATIONS." INDUS OP/RES REPRESENT INGP/REL   CONCPT
DRIVE...MGT CLASSIF. PAGE 60 B1220   PERSON
  ROLE

C48
WALKER H.,"THE LEGISLATIVE PROCESS: LAWMAKING IN   PARL/PROC
THE UNITED STATES." NAT/G POL/PAR PROVS EX/STRUC   LEGIS
OP/RES PROB/SOLV CT/SYS LOBBY GOV/REL...CHARTS   LAW
BIBLIOG T 18/20 CONGRESS. PAGE 113 B2279   CONSTN

N48
YATES M.,ADMINISTRATIVE REORGANIZATION OF STATE   BIBLIOG
GOVERNMENTS: A BIBLIOGRAPHY (PAMPHLET). USA+45   LOC/G
USA-45 CONSTN OP/RES PLAN CONFER...POLICY 20.   ADMIN
PAGE 118 B2390   PROVS

B49
DE GRAZIA A.,HUMAN RELATIONS IN PUBLIC   BIBLIOG/A
ADMINISTRATION. INDUS ACT/RES CREATE PLAN PROB/SOLV ADMIN
TEC/DEV INGP/REL PERS/REL DRIVE...POLICY SOC 20.   PHIL/SCI
PAGE 27 B0552   OP/RES

S50
EPSTEIN L.D.,"POLITICAL STERILIZATION OF CIVIL   ADMIN
SERVANTS: THE UNITED STATES AND GREAT BRITAIN." UK LEGIS
USA+45 USA-45 STRUCT TOP/EX OP/RES PARTIC CHOOSE   DECISION
NAT/LISM 20 CONGRESS CIVIL/SERV. PAGE 33 B0679   POL/PAR

S51
STEWART D.D.,"THE PLACE OF VOLUNTEER PARTICIPATION ADMIN
IN BUREAUCRATIC ORGANIZATION." NAT/G DELIB/GP   PARTIC
OP/RES DOMIN LOBBY WAR ATTIT ROLE PWR. PAGE 101   VOL/ASSN
B2035   FORCES

C51
HOMANS G.C.,"THE WESTERN ELECTRIC RESEARCHES" IN S. OP/RES
HOSLETT, ED., HUMAN FACTORS IN MANAGEMENT (BMR)"   EFFICIENCY
ACT/RES GP/REL HAPPINESS PRODUC DRIVE...MGT OBS 20. SOC/EXP
PAGE 51 B1037   WORKER

S52
RICH B.M.,"ADMINISTRATION REORGANIZATION IN NEW   ADMIN
JERSEY" (BMR)" USA+45 DELIB/GP EX/STRUC WORKER   CONSTN
OP/RES BUDGET 20 NEW/JERSEY. PAGE 88 B1772   PROB/SOLV
  PROVS

B53
APPLEBY P.H.,PUBLIC ADMINISTRATION IN INDIA: REPORT ADMIN
OF A SURVEY. INDIA LOC/G OP/RES ATTIT ORD/FREE 20. NAT/G
PAGE 6 B0118   EX/STRUC
  GOV/REL

B53
CALDWELL L.K.,RESEARCH METHODS IN PUBLIC   BIBLIOG/A
ADMINISTRATION; AN OUTLINE OF TOPICS AND READINGS METH/COMP
(PAMPHLET). LAW ACT/RES COMPUTER KNOWL...SOC STAT ADMIN
GEN/METH 20. PAGE 18 B0365   OP/RES

B53
DIMOCK M.E.,PUBLIC ADMINISTRATION. USA+45 FINAN   ADMIN
WORKER BUDGET CONTROL CHOOSE...T 20. PAGE 29 B0596 STRUCT
  OP/RES
  POLICY

B54
GOULDNER A.W.,PATTERNS OF INDUSTRIAL BUREAUCRACY.   ADMIN
DOMIN ATTIT DRIVE...BIBLIOG 20 BUREAUCRCY. PAGE 42 INDUS
B0844   OP/RES
  WORKER

B54
MCCLOSKEY J.F.,OPERATIONS RESEARCH FOR MANAGEMENT. OP/RES
STRUCT COMPUTER ADMIN ROUTINE...PHIL/SCI CONCPT   MGT
METH/CNCPT TREND ANTHOL BIBLIOG 20. PAGE 72 B1445 METH/COMP
  TEC/DEV

C54
GOULDNER A.W.,"PATTERNS OF INDUSTRIAL BUREAUCRACY." ADMIN
GP/REL CONSEN ATTIT DRIVE...BIBLIOG 20. PAGE 42   INDUS
B0843   OP/RES
  WORKER

B55
BERNAYS E.L.,THE ENGINEERING OF CONSENT.   VOL/ASSN
OP/RES ROUTINE INGP/REL ATTIT RESPECT...POLICY   GP/REL
METH/CNCPT METH/COMP 20. PAGE 11 B0224   PLAN
  ACT/RES
  ADJUST

S55
CHAPIN F.S.,"FORMALIZATION OBSERVED IN TEN   VOL/ASSN
VOLUNTARY ORGANIZATIONS: CONCEPTS, MORPHOLOGY,   ROUTINE
PROCESS." STRUCT INGP/REL PERS/REL...METH/CNCPT   CONTROL
CLASSIF OBS RECORD. PAGE 20 B0407   OP/RES

L56
LITCHFIELD E.H.,"NOTES ON A GENERAL THEORY OF   ADMIN
ADMINISTRATION." USA+45 OP/RES PROB/SOLV EFFICIENCY ROUTINE
IDEA/COMP. PAGE 66 B1324   MGT

B57
CRONBACK L.J.,PSYCHOLOGICAL TESTS AND PERSONNEL   MATH
DECISIONS. OP/RES PROB/SOLV CHOOSE PERSON...PSY   DECISION
STAT TESTS 20. PAGE 25 B0508   WORKER
  MGT

B57
INDUSTRIAL RELATIONS RES ASSN,RESEARCH IN   INDUS
INDUSTRIAL HUMAN RELATIONS. INTELL ACT/RES OP/RES MGT
ADMIN 20. PAGE 54 B1084   LABOR
  GP/REL

S57
FESLER J.W.,"ADMINISTRATIVE LITERATURE AND THE   ADMIN
SECOND HOOVER COMMISSION REPORTS" (BMR)" USA+45   NAT/G
EX/STRUC LEGIS WRITING...DECISION METH 20. PAGE 35 OP/RES
B0713   DELIB/GP

S57
RAPAPORT R.N.,"'DEMOCRATIZATION' AND AUTHORITY IN A PUB/INST
THERAPEUTIC COMMUNITY." OP/RES ADMIN PARTIC CENTRAL HEALTH
ATTIT...POLICY DECISION. PAGE 86 B1735   DOMIN
  CLIENT

N57
MACMAHON A.W.,ADMINISTRATION AND FOREIGN POLICY   DIPLOM
(PAMPHLET). USA+45 CHIEF OP/RES ADMIN 20. PAGE 68 EX/STRUC
B1372   DECISION
  CONFER

B58
BRIGHT J.R.,AUTOMATION AND MANAGEMENT. INDUS LABOR AUTOMAT
WORKER OP/RES TEC/DEV INSPECT 20. PAGE 15 B0307   COMPUTER
  PLAN
  MGT

B58
MARCH J.G.,ORGANIZATIONS. USA+45 CREATE OP/RES PLAN MGT
PROB/SOLV PARTIC ROUTINE RATIONAL ATTIT PERCEPT   PERSON
...DECISION BIBLIOG. PAGE 69 B1397   DRIVE
  CONCPT

B58
MELMAN S.,DECISION-MAKING AND PRODUCTIVITY. INDUS LABOR

EX/STRUC WORKER OP/RES PROB/SOLV TEC/DEV ADMIN
ROUTINE RIGID/FLEX GP/COMP. PAGE 73 B1464
PRODUC
DECISION
MGT
B58

OPERATIONS RESEARCH SOCIETY,A COMPREHENSIVE
BIBLIOGRAPHY ON OPERATIONS RESEARCH; THROUGH 1956
WITH SUPPLEMENT FOR 1957. COM/IND DIST/IND INDUS
ADMIN...DECISION MATH STAT METH 20. PAGE 80 B1612
BIBLIOG/A
COMPUT/IR
OP/RES
MGT
L58

EISENSTADT S.N.,"BUREAUCRACY AND
BUREAUCRATIZATION." WOR+45 ECO/DEV INDUS R+D PLAN
GOV/REL...WELF/ST TREND BIBLIOG/A 20. PAGE 32 B0659
ADMIN
OP/RES
MGT
PHIL/SCI
S58

DEAN B.V.,"APPLICATION OF OPERATIONS RESEARCH TO
MANAGERIAL DECISION MAKING" STRATA ACT/RES
PROB/SOLV ROLE...SOC PREDICT SIMUL 20. PAGE 28
B0565
DECISION
OP/RES
MGT
METH/CNCPT
S58

MANSFIELD E.,"A STUDY OF DECISION-MAKING WITHIN THE
FIRM." LG/CO WORKER INGP/REL COST EFFICIENCY PRODUC
...CHARTS 20. PAGE 69 B1395
OP/RES
PROB/SOLV
AUTOMAT
ROUTINE
B59

BONNETT C.E.,LABOR-MANAGEMENT RELATIONS. USA+45
OP/RES PROB/SOLV EDU/PROP...AUD/VIS CHARTS 20.
PAGE 13 B0274
MGT
LABOR
INDUS
GP/REL
B59

JENNINGS W.I.,CABINET GOVERNMENT (3RD ED.). UK
POL/PAR CHIEF BUDGET ADMIN CHOOSE GP/REL 20.
PAGE 56 B1137
DELIB/GP
NAT/G
CONSTN
OP/RES
B59

WASSERMAN P.,MEASUREMENT AND ANALYSIS OF
ORGANIZATIONAL PERFORMANCE. FINAN MARKET EX/STRUC
TEC/DEV EDU/PROP CONTROL ROUTINE TASK...MGT 20.
PAGE 114 B2300
BIBLIOG/A
ECO/TAC
OP/RES
EFFICIENCY
L59

"A BIBLIOGRAPHICAL ESSAY ON DECISION MAKING."
WOR+45 WOR-45 STRUCT OP/RES GP/REL...CONCPT
IDEA/COMP METH 20. PAGE 2 B0038
BIBLIOG/A
DECISION
ADMIN
LEAD
L59

RHODE W.E.,"COMMITTEE CLEARANCE OF ADMINISTRATIVE
DECISIONS." DELIB/GP LEGIS BUDGET DOMIN CIVMIL/REL
20 CONGRESS. PAGE 87 B1768
DECISION
ADMIN
OP/RES
NAT/G
S59

CALKINS R.D.,"THE DECISION PROCESS IN
ADMINISTRATION." EX/STRUC PROB/SOLV ROUTINE MGT.
PAGE 18 B0368
ADMIN
OP/RES
DECISION
CON/ANAL
S59

CHAPMAN B.,"THE FRENCH CONSEIL D'ETAT." FRANCE
NAT/G CONSULT OP/RES PROB/SOLV PWR...OBS 20.
PAGE 20 B0410
ADMIN
LAW
CT/SYS
LEGIS
C59

DAHL R.A.,"SOCIAL SCIENCE RESEARCH ON BUSINESS:
PRODUCT AND POTENTIAL" INDUS MARKET OP/RES CAP/ISM
ADMIN LOBBY DRIVE...PSY CONCPT BIBLIOG/A 20.
PAGE 26 B0521
MGT
EFFICIENCY
PROB/SOLV
EX/STRUC
B60

ARGYRIS C.,UNDERSTANDING ORGANIZATIONAL BEHAVIOR.
OP/RES FEEDBACK...MGT PSY METH/CNCPT OBS INT SIMUL
20. PAGE 6 B0130
LG/CO
PERSON
ADMIN
ROUTINE
B60

MORRIS W.T.,ENGINEERING ECONOMY. AUTOMAT RISK
RATIONAL...PROBABIL STAT CHARTS GAME SIMUL BIBLIOG
T 20. PAGE 76 B1529
OP/RES
DECISION
MGT
PROB/SOLV
B60

US DEPARTMENT OF THE ARMY,SELECT BIBLIOGRAPHY ON
ADMINISTRATIVE ORGANIZATION(PAMPHLET). USA+45 INDUS
NAT/G EX/STRUC OP/RES CIVMIL/REL EFFICIENCY
ORD/FREE. PAGE 108 B2183
BIBLIOG/A
ADMIN
CONCPT
FORCES
S60

FRIEDMAN L.,"DECISION MAKING IN COMPETITIVE
SITUATIONS" OP/RES...MGT PROBABIL METH/COMP SIMUL
20. PAGE 37 B0757
DECISION
UTIL
OPTIMAL
GAME
B61

CHAPPLE E.D.,THE MEASURE OF MANAGEMENT. USA+45
WORKER ADMIN GP/REL EFFICIENCY...DECISION
ORG/CHARTS SIMUL 20. PAGE 20 B0412
MGT
OP/RES
PLAN
METH/CNCPT
B61

ETZIONI A.,COMPLEX ORGANIZATIONS: A SOCIOLOGICAL
READER. CLIENT CULTURE STRATA CREATE OP/RES ADMIN
...POLICY METH/CNCPT BUREAUCRCY. PAGE 34 B0683
VOL/ASSN
STRUCT
CLASSIF
PROF/ORG
C61

ETZIONI A.,"A COMPARATIVE ANALYSIS OF COMPLEX
ORGANIZATIONS: ON POWER, INVOLVEMENT AND THEIR
CON/ANAL
SOC

CORRELATES." ELITES CREATE OP/RES ROUTINE INGP/REL
PERS/REL CONSEN ATTIT DRIVE PWR...CONCPT BIBLIOG.
PAGE 34 B0684
LEAD
CONTROL
B62

BINDER L.,IRAN: POLITICAL DEVELOPMENT IN A CHANGING
SOCIETY. IRAN OP/RES REV GP/REL CENTRAL RATIONAL
PWR...PHIL/SCI NAT/COMP GEN/LAWS 20. PAGE 12 B0239
LEGIT
NAT/G
ADMIN
STRUCT
B62

BOWEN W.G.,THE FEDERAL GOVERNMENT AND PRINCETON
UNIVERSITY. USA+45 FINAN ACT/RES PROB/SOLV ADMIN
CONTROL COST...POLICY 20 PRINCETN/U. PAGE 14 B0285
NAT/G
ACADEM
GP/REL
OP/RES
B62

DUCKWORTH W.E.,A GUIDE TO OPERATIONAL RESEARCH.
INDUS PLAN PROB/SOLV EXEC EFFICIENCY PRODUC KNOWL
...MGT MATH STAT SIMUL METH 20 MONTECARLO. PAGE 31
B0624
OP/RES
GAME
DECISION
ADMIN
B62

FRIEDLANDER W.A.,INDIVIDUALISM AND SOCIAL WELFARE.
FRANCE ACADEM OP/RES ADMIN AGE/Y AGE/A ORD/FREE 20.
PAGE 37 B0756
GIVE
SOC/WK
SOC/EXP
FINAN
B62

HATTERY L.H.,INFORMATION RETRIEVAL MANAGEMENT.
CLIENT INDUS TOP/EX COMPUTER OP/RES TEC/DEV ROUTINE
COST EFFICIENCY RIGID/FLEX...METH/COMP ANTHOL 20.
PAGE 48 B0968
R+D
COMPUT/IR
MGT
CREATE
B62

NATIONAL BUREAU ECONOMIC RES,THE RATE AND DIRECTION
OF INVENTIVE ACTIVITY: ECONOMIC AND SOCIAL FACTORS.
STRUCT INDUS MARKET R+D CREATE OP/RES TEC/DEV
EFFICIENCY PRODUC RATIONAL UTIL...WELF/ST PHIL/SCI
METH/CNCPT TIME. PAGE 77 B1562
DECISION
PROB/SOLV
MGT
B62

WENDT P.F.,HOUSING POLICY - THE SEARCH FOR
SOLUTIONS. GERMANY/W SWEDEN UK USA+45 OP/RES
HABITAT WEALTH...SOC/WK CHARTS 20. PAGE 115 B2322
PLAN
ADMIN
METH/COMP
NAT/G
S62

BERNTHAL W.F.,"VALUE PERSPECTIVES IN MANAGEMENT
DECISIONS." LG/CO OP/RES SUPEGO MORAL. PAGE 11
B0229
MGT
PROB/SOLV
DECISION
C62

DE GRAZIA A.,"POLITICAL BEHAVIOR (REV. ED.)" STRATA
POL/PAR LEAD LOBBY ROUTINE WAR CHOOSE REPRESENT
CONSEN ATTIT ORD/FREE BIBLIOG. PAGE 27 B0555
PHIL/SCI
OP/RES
CONCPT
B63

ACKOFF R.L.,A MANAGER'S GUIDE TO OPERATIONS
RESEARCH. STRUCT INDUS PROB/SOLV ROUTINE 20. PAGE 3
B0056
OP/RES
MGT
GP/REL
ADMIN
B63

DEAN A.L.,FEDERAL AGENCY APPROACHES TO FIELD
MANAGEMENT (PAMPHLET). R+D DELIB/GP EX/STRUC
PROB/SOLV GOV/REL...CLASSIF BIBLIOG 20 FAA NASA
DEPT/HEW POSTAL/SYS IRS. PAGE 28 B0563
ADMIN
MGT
NAT/G
OP/RES
B63

DUE J.F.,STATE SALES TAX ADMINISTRATION. OP/RES
BUDGET PAY ADMIN EXEC ROUTINE COST EFFICIENCY
PROFIT...CHARTS METH/COMP 20. PAGE 31 B0626
PROVS
TAX
STAT
GOV/COMP
B63

ECOLE NATIONALE D'ADMIN,BIBLIOGRAPHIE SELECTIVE
D'OUVRAGES DE LANGUE FRANCAISE TRAITANT DES
PROBLEMES GOUVERNEMENTAUX ET ADMINISTRATIFS. NAT/G
FORCES ACT/RES OP/RES PLAN PROB/SOLV BUDGET ADJUD
COLONIAL LEAD 20. PAGE 32 B0651
BIBLIOG
AFR
ADMIN
EX/STRUC
B63

JOHNS R.,CONFRONTING ORGANIZATIONAL CHANGE. NEIGH
DELIB/GP CREATE OP/RES ADMIN GP/REL DRIVE...WELF/ST
SOC RECORD BIBLIOG. PAGE 56 B1142
SOC/WK
WEALTH
LEAD
VOL/ASSN
B63

LOCKARD D.,THE POLITICS OF STATE AND LOCAL
GOVERNMENT. USA+45 CONSTN EX/STRUC LEGIS CT/SYS
FEDERAL...CHARTS BIBLIOG 20. PAGE 66 B1334
LOC/G
PROVS
OP/RES
ADMIN
B63

MCDONOUGH A.M.,INFORMATION ECONOMICS AND MANAGEMENT
SYSTEMS. ECO/DEV OP/RES AUTOMAT EFFICIENCY 20.
PAGE 72 B1448
COMPUT/IR
MGT
CONCPT
COMPUTER
B63

PALOTAI O.C.,PUBLICATIONS OF THE INSTITUTE OF
GOVERNMENT, 1930-1962. LAW PROVS SCHOOL WORKER
ACT/RES OP/RES CT/SYS GOV/REL...CRIMLGY SOC/WK.
PAGE 81 B1629
BIBLIOG/A
ADMIN
LOC/G
FINAN
B63

THORELLI H.B.,INTOP: INTERNATIONAL OPERATIONS
SIMULATION: PLAYER'S MANUAL. BRAZIL FINAN OP/RES
ADMIN GP/REL INGP/REL PRODUC PERCEPT...DECISION MGT
EEC. PAGE 104 B2108
GAME
INT/TRADE
EDU/PROP
LG/CO
B63

US SENATE COMM GOVT OPERATIONS,ADMINISTRATION OF
NATIONAL SECURITY (9 PARTS). ADMIN...INT REC/INT
DELIB/GP
NAT/G

CHARTS 20 SENATE CONGRESS. PAGE 110 B2213
OP/RES
ORD/FREE

N63
GREAT BRITAIN DEPT TECH COOP,PUBLIC ADMINISTRATION: BIBLIOG/A
A SELECT BIBLIOGRAPHY (PAMPHLET). WOR+45 AGRI FINAN ADMIN
INDUS EX/STRUC OP/RES ECO/TAC...MGT METH/COMP NAT/G
NAT/COMP. PAGE 43 B0861 LOC/G

B64
BLAKE R.R.,MANAGING INTERGROUP CONFLICT IN CREATE
INDUSTRY. INDUS DELIB/GP EX/STRUC GP/REL PERS/REL PROB/SOLV
GAME. PAGE 12 B0250 OP/RES
ADJUD

B64
HAMBRIDGE G.,DYNAMICS OF DEVELOPMENT. AGRI FINAN ECO/UNDEV
INDUS LABOR INT/TRADE EDU/PROP ADMIN LEAD OWN ECO/TAC
HEALTH...ANTHOL BIBLIOG 20. PAGE 46 B0930 OP/RES
ACT/RES

B64
HODGETTS J.E.,ADMINISTERING THE ATOM FOR PEACE. PROB/SOLV
OP/RES TEC/DEV ADMIN...IDEA/COMP METH/COMP 20. NUC/PWR
PAGE 50 B1025 PEACE
MGT

B64
JACKSON H.M.,THE SECRETARY OF STATE AND THE GOV/REL
AMBASSADOR* JACKSON SUBCOMMITTEE PAPERS ON THE DIPLOM
CONDUCT OF AMERICAN FOREIGN POLICY. USA+45 NAT/G ADMIN
FORCES ACT/RES OP/RES EDU/PROP CENTRAL EFFICIENCY EX/STRUC
ORD/FREE...OBS RECORD ANTHOL CONGRESS PRESIDENT.
PAGE 55 B1107

B64
KAHNG T.J.,LAW, POLITICS, AND THE SECURITY COUNCIL* DELIB/GP
AN INQUIRY INTO THE HANDLING OF LEGAL QUESTIONS. ADJUD
LAW CONSTN NAT/G ACT/RES OP/RES CT/SYS TASK PWR ROUTINE
...INT/LAW BIBLIOG UN. PAGE 57 B1160

B64
MARRIS R.,THE ECONOMIC THEORY OF "MANAGERIAL" CAP/ISM
CAPITALISM. USA+45 ECO/DEV LG/CO ECO/TAC DEMAND MGT
...CHARTS BIBLIOG 20. PAGE 69 B1402 CONTROL
OP/RES

B64
PARET P.,FRENCH REVOLUTIONARY WARFARE FROM FRANCE
INDOCHINA TO ALGERIA* THE ANALYSIS OF A POLITICAL GUERRILLA
AND MILITARY DOCTRINE. ALGERIA VIETNAM FORCES GEN/LAWS
OP/RES TEC/DEV ROUTINE REV ATTIT...PSY BIBLIOG.
PAGE 81 B1632

B64
RIDDLE D.H.,THE TRUMAN COMMITTEE: A STUDY IN LEGIS
CONGRESSIONAL RESPONSIBILITY. INDUS FORCES OP/RES DELIB/GP
DOMIN ADMIN LEAD PARL/PROC WAR PRODUC SUPEGO CONFER
...BIBLIOG CONGRESS. PAGE 88 B1778

B64
WILSON L.,THE ACADEMIC MAN. STRUCT FINAN PROF/ORG ACADEM
OP/RES ADMIN AUTHORIT ROLE RESPECT...SOC STAT. INGP/REL
PAGE 117 B2360 STRATA
DELIB/GP

S64
STONE P.A.,"DECISION TECHNIQUES FOR TOWN OP/RES
DEVELOPMENT." PLAN COST PROFIT...DECISION MGT MUNIC
CON/ANAL CHARTS METH/COMP BIBLIOG 20. PAGE 101 ADMIN
B2048 PROB/SOLV

B65
ANTHONY R.N.,PLANNING AND CONTROL SYSTEMS. UNIV CONTROL
OP/RES...DECISION MGT LING. PAGE 6 B0114 PLAN
METH
HYPO/EXP

B65
BARISH N.N.,MANAGEMENT SCIENCES IN THE EMERGING ECO/UNDEV
COUNTRIES. AFR CHINA/COM WOR+45 FINAN INDUS PLAN OP/RES
PRODUC HABITAT...ANTHOL 20. PAGE 9 B0184 MGT
TEC/DEV

B65
BARNETT V.M. JR.,THE REPRESENTATION OF THE UNITED USA+45
STATES ABROAD* REVISED EDITION. ECO/UNDEV ACADEM DIPLOM
INT/ORG FORCES ACT/RES CREATE OP/RES FOR/AID REGION ADMIN
CENTRAL...CLASSIF ANTHOL. PAGE 9 B0189

B65
BOGUSLAW R.,THE NEW UTOPIANS. OP/RES ADMIN CONTROL UTOPIA
PWR...IDEA/COMP SIMUL 20. PAGE 13 B0265 AUTOMAT
COMPUTER
PLAN

B65
ELDER R.E.,OVERSEAS REPRESENTATION AND SERVICES FOR OP/RES
FEDERAL DOMESTIC AGENCIES. USA+45 NAT/G ACT/RES DIPLOM
FOR/AID EDU/PROP SENIOR ROUTINE TASK ADJUST...MGT GOV/REL
ORG/CHARTS. PAGE 33 B0663 ADMIN

B65
HARR J.E.,THE DEVELOPMENT OF CAREERS IN THE FOREIGN OP/RES
SERVICE. CREATE SENIOR EXEC FEEDBACK GOV/REL MGT
EFFICIENCY ATTIT RESPECT ORG/CHARTS. PAGE 47 B0953 ADMIN
DIPLOM

B65
HICKMAN B.G.,QUANTITATIVE PLANNING OF ECONOMIC PROB/SOLV
POLICY. FRANCE NETHERLAND OP/RES PRICE ROUTINE UTIL PLAN
...POLICY DECISION ECOMETRIC METH/CNCPT STAT STYLE QUANT
CHINJAP. PAGE 50 B1004

B65
JONES A.G.,THE EVOLUTION OF PERSONNEL SYSTEMS FOR DIPLOM
US FOREIGN AFFAIRS* A HISTORY OF REFORM EFFORTS. ADMIN
USA+45 USA-45 ACADEM OP/RES GOV/REL...MGT CONGRESS. ACT/RES
PAGE 57 B1149 EFFICIENCY

B65
MEYERHOFF A.E.,THE STRATEGY OF PERSUASION. USA+45 EDU/PROP
COM/IND CONSULT FOR/AID CONTROL COERCE COST ATTIT EFFICIENCY
PERCEPT MARXISM 20 COLD/WAR. PAGE 73 B1476 OP/RES
ADMIN

B65
WITHERELL J.W.,MADAGASCAR AND ADJACENT ISLANDS; A BIBLIOG
GUIDE TO OFFICIAL PUBLICATIONS (PAMPHLET). FRANCE COLONIAL
MADAGASCAR S/ASIA UK LAW OP/RES PLAN DIPLOM LOC/G
...POLICY CON/ANAL 19/20. PAGE 117 B2368 ADMIN

S65
ALEXANDER T.,"SYNECTICS: INVENTING BY THE MADNESS PROB/SOLV
METHOD." DELIB/GP TOP/EX ACT/RES TEC/DEV EXEC TASK OP/RES
KNOWL...MGT METH/COMP 20. PAGE 4 B0073 CREATE
CONSULT

S65
HAMMOND P.Y.,"FOREIGN POLICY-MAKING AND DIPLOM
ADMINISTRATIVE POLITICS." CREATE ADMIN COST STRUCT
...DECISION CONCPT GAME CONGRESS PRESIDENT. PAGE 46 IDEA/COMP
B0935 OP/RES

B66
BHALERAO C.N.,PUBLIC SERVICE COMMISSIONS OF INDIA: NAT/G
A STUDY. INDIA SERV/IND EX/STRUC ROUTINE CHOOSE OP/RES
GOV/REL INGP/REL...KNO/TEST EXHIBIT 20. PAGE 11 LOC/G
B0233 ADMIN

B66
CLEGG R.K.,THE ADMINISTRATOR IN PUBLIC WELFARE. ADMIN
USA+45 STRUCT NAT/G PROVS PROB/SOLV BUDGET ECO/TAC GIVE
GP/REL ROLE...SOC/WK 20 PUBLIC/REL. PAGE 21 B0434 GOV/REL
OP/RES

B66
DAVIS R.G.,PLANNING HUMAN RESOURCE DEVELOPMENT, PLAN
EDUCATIONAL MODELS AND SCHEMATA. WORKER OP/RES EFFICIENCY
ECO/TAC EDU/PROP CONTROL COST PRODUC...GEOG STAT SIMUL
CHARTS 20. PAGE 27 B0544 ROUTINE

B66
FABRYCKY W.J.,OPERATIONS ECONOMY INDUSTRIAL OP/RES
APPLICATIONS OF OPERATIONS RESEARCH. INDUS PLAN MGT
ECO/TAC PRODUC...MATH PROBABIL STAT CHARTS 20. SIMUL
PAGE 34 B0695 DECISION

B66
LINDFORS G.V.,INTERCOLLEGIATE BIBLIOGRAPHY; CASES BIBLIOG/A
IN BUSINESS ADMINISTRATION (VOL. X). FINAN MARKET ADMIN
LABOR CONSULT PLAN GP/REL PRODUC 20. PAGE 65 B1314 MGT
OP/RES

B66
MANSFIELD E.,MANAGERIAL ECONOMICS AND OPERATIONS ECO/TAC
RESEARCH; A NONMATHEMATICAL INTRODUCTION. USA+45 OP/RES
ELITES ECO/DEV CONSULT EX/STRUC PROB/SOLV ROUTINE MGT
EFFICIENCY OPTIMAL...GAME T 20. PAGE 69 B1396 COMPUTER

B66
WALL E.H.,THE COURT OF JUSTICE IN THE EUROPEAN CT/SYS
COMMUNITIES: JURISDICTION AND PROCEDURE. EUR+WWI INT/ORG
DIPLOM ADJUD ADMIN ROUTINE TASK...CONCPT LING 20. LAW
PAGE 113 B2281 OP/RES

B66
WYLIE C.M.,RESEARCH IN PUBLIC HEALTH BIBLIOG/A
ADMINISTRATION; SELECTED RECENT ABSTRACTS IV R+D
(PAMPHLET). USA+45 MUNIC PUB/INST ACT/RES CREATE HEAL
OP/RES TEC/DEV GP/REL ROLE...MGT PHIL/SCI STAT. ADMIN
PAGE 118 B2387

B66
YOUNG W.,EXISTING MECHANISMS OF ARMS CONTROL. ARMS/CONT
PROC/MFG OP/RES DIPLOM TASK CENTRAL...MGT TREATY. ADMIN
PAGE 119 B2395 NUC/PWR
ROUTINE

S66
AUSLAND J.C.,"CRISIS MANAGEMENT* BERLIN, CYPRUS, OP/RES
LAOS." CYPRUS LAOS FORCES CREATE PLAN EDU/PROP TASK DIPLOM
CENTRAL PERSON RIGID/FLEX...DECISION MGT 20 BERLIN RISK
KENNEDY/JF MCNAMARA/R RUSK. PAGE 7 B0148 ADMIN

S66
DIEBOLD J.,"COMPUTERS, PROGRAM MANAGEMENT AND COMPUTER
FOREIGN AFFAIRS." USA+45 INDUS OP/RES TEC/DEV...MGT DIPLOM
GP/COMP GEN/LAWS. PAGE 29 B0590 ROUTINE
ACT/RES

S66
ZUCKERT E.M.,"THE SERVICE SECRETARY* HAS HE A OBS
USEFUL ROLE?" USA+45 TOP/EX PLAN ADMIN EXEC DETER OP/RES
NUC/PWR WEAPON...MGT RECORD MCNAMARA/R. PAGE 119 DIPLOM
B2407 FORCES

B67
ANDERSON C.W.,POLITICS AND ECONOMIC CHANGE IN LATIN ECO/UNDEV
AMERICA. L/A+17C INDUS NAT/G OP/RES ADMIN DEMAND PROB/SOLV
...POLICY STAT CHARTS NAT/COMP 20. PAGE 4 B0091 PLAN
ECO/TAC

B67
FINCHER F.,THE GOVERNMENT OF THE UNITED STATES. NAT/G
USA+45 USA-45 POL/PAR CHIEF CT/SYS LOBBY GP/REL EX/STRUC
INGP/REL...CONCPT CHARTS BIBLIOG T 18/20 PRESIDENT LEGIS
CONGRESS SUPREME/CT. PAGE 35 B0719 OP/RES

HIRSCHMAN A.O.,DEVELOPMENT PROJECTS OBSERVED. INDUS
INT/ORG CONSULT EX/STRUC CREATE OP/RES ECO/TAC
DEMAND...POLICY MGT METH/COMP 20 WORLD/BANK.
PAGE 50 B1016
 B67
 ECO/UNDEV
 R+D
 FINAN
 PLAN

MARRIS P.,DILEMMAS OF SOCIAL REFORM: POVERTY AND
COMMUNITY ACTION IN THE UNITED STATES. USA+45 NAT/G
OP/RES ADMIN PARTIC EFFICIENCY WEALTH...SOC
METH/COMP T 20 REFORMERS. PAGE 69 B1401
 B67
 STRUCT
 MUNIC
 PROB/SOLV
 COST

US HOUSE COMM SCI ASTRONAUT,GOVERNMENT, SCIENCE,
AND INTERNATIONAL POLICY. R+D OP/RES PLAN 20.
PAGE 109 B2198
 B67
 ADMIN
 PHIL/SCI
 ACT/RES
 DIPLOM

BERLINER J.S.,"RUSSIA'S BUREAUCRATS - WHY THEY'RE
REACTIONARY." USSR NAT/G OP/RES PROB/SOLV TEC/DEV
CONTROL SANCTION EFFICIENCY DRIVE PERSON...TECHNIC
SOC 20. PAGE 11 B0223
 S67
 CREATE
 ADMIN
 INDUS
 PRODUC

DROR Y.,"POLICY ANALYSTS." USA+45 COMPUTER OP/RES
ECO/TAC ADMIN ROUTINE...ECOMETRIC METH/COMP SIMUL
20. PAGE 30 B0618
 S67
 NAT/G
 POLICY
 PLAN
 DECISION

DUGGAR J.W.,"THE DEVELOPMENT OF MONEY SUPPLY IN
ETHIOPIA." ETHIOPIA ISLAM CONSULT OP/RES BUDGET
CONTROL ROUTINE EFFICIENCY EQUILIB WEALTH...MGT 20.
PAGE 31 B0629
 S67
 ECO/UNDEV
 FINAN
 BAL/PAY
 ECOMETRIC

FOX R.G.,"FAMILY, CASTE, AND COMMERCE IN A NORTH
INDIAN MARKET TOWN." INDIA STRATA AGRI FACE/GP FAM
NEIGH OP/RES BARGAIN ADMIN ROUTINE WEALTH...SOC
CHARTS 20. PAGE 37 B0747
 S67
 CULTURE
 GP/REL
 ECO/UNDEV
 DIST/IND

FRYKENBURG R.E.,"STUDIES OF LAND CONTROL IN INDIAN
HISTORY: REVIEW ARTICLE." INDIA UK STRATA AGRI
MUNIC OP/RES COLONIAL REGION EFFICIENCY OWN HABITAT
...CONCPT 16/20. PAGE 38 B0763
 S67
 ECO/UNDEV
 CONTROL
 ADMIN

GRINYER P.H.,"THE SYSTEMATIC EVALUATION OF METHODS
OF WAGE PAYMENT." UK INDUS WORKER ADMIN EFFICIENCY
...MGT METH/COMP 20. PAGE 44 B0882
 S67
 OP/RES
 COST
 PAY
 PRODUC

HAIRE M.,"MANAGING MANAGEMENT MANPOWER." EX/STRUC
OP/RES PAY EDU/PROP COST EFFICIENCY...PREDICT SIMUL
20. PAGE 45 B0920
 S67
 MGT
 EXEC
 LEAD
 INDUS

LEVCIK B.,"WAGES AND EMPLOYMENT PROBLEMS IN THE NEW
SYSTEM OF PLANNED MANAGEMENT IN CZECHOSLOVAKIA."
CZECHOSLVK EUR+WWI NAT/G OP/RES PLAN ADMIN ROUTINE
INGP/REL CENTRAL EFFICIENCY PRODUC DECISION.
PAGE 64 B1300
 S67
 MARXISM
 WORKER
 MGT
 PAY

MOOR E.J.,"THE INTERNATIONAL IMPACT OF AUTOMATION."
WOR+45 ACT/RES COMPUTER CREATE PLAN CAP/ISM ROUTINE
EFFICIENCY PREDICT. PAGE 75 B1511
 S67
 TEC/DEV
 OP/RES
 AUTOMAT
 INDUS

OLIVE B.A.,"THE ADMINISTRATION OF HIGHER EDUCATION:
A BIBLIOGRAPHICAL SURVEY." USA+45 ATTIT. PAGE 79
B1605
 S67
 ACADEM
 ADMIN
 OP/RES

SKOLNICK J.H.,"SOCIAL CONTROL IN THE ADVERSARY
SYSTEM." USA+45 CONSULT OP/RES ADMIN CONTROL.
PAGE 98 B1975
 S67
 PROB/SOLV
 PERS/REL
 ADJUD
 CT/SYS

SPACKMAN A.,"THE SENATE OF TRINIDAD AND TOBAGO."
L/A+17C TRINIDAD WEST/IND NAT/G POL/PAR DELIB/GP
OP/RES PROB/SOLV EDU/PROP EXEC LOBBY ROUTINE
REPRESENT GP/REL 20. PAGE 99 B2002
 S67
 ELITES
 EFFICIENCY
 LEGIS
 DECISION

VERGIN R.C.,"COMPUTER INDUCED ORGANIZATION
CHANGES." FUT USA+45 R+D CREATE OP/RES TEC/DEV
ADJUST CENTRAL...MGT INT CON/ANAL COMPUT/IR.
PAGE 112 B2260
 S67
 COMPUTER
 DECISION
 AUTOMAT
 EX/STRUC

US SENATE COMM ON FOREIGN REL,ARMS SALES AND
FOREIGN POLICY (PAMPHLET). FINAN FOR/AID CONTROL
20. PAGE 110 B2222
 N67
 ARMS/CONT
 ADMIN
 OP/RES
 DIPLOM

OPA....OFFICE OF PRICE ADMINISTRATION

KRIESBERG M.,CANCELLATION OF THE RATION STAMPS
(PAMPHLET). USA+45 USA-45 MARKET PROB/SOLV PRICE
GOV/REL RIGID/FLEX 20 OPA. PAGE 61 B1235
 N19
 RATION
 DECISION
 ADMIN
 NAT/G

REDFORD E.S.,FIELD ADMINISTRATION OF WARTIME
RATIONING. USA-45 CONSTN ELITES DIST/IND WORKER
 B47
 ADMIN
 NAT/G

CONTROL WAR GOV/REL ADJUST RIGID/FLEX 20 OPA.
PAGE 87 B1752
 PROB/SOLV
 RATION

OPEN/SPACE....OPEN SPACE - TOWN AND COUNTRY PLANNING

CULLINGWORTH J.B.,TOWN AND COUNTRY PLANNING IN
ENGLAND AND WALES. UK LAW SOCIETY CONSULT ACT/RES
ADMIN ROUTINE LEISURE INGP/REL ADJUST PWR...GEOG 20
OPEN/SPACE URBAN/RNWL. PAGE 25 B0512
 B64
 MUNIC
 PLAN
 NAT/G
 PROB/SOLV

OPERATIONAL RESEARCH AND RELATED MANAGEMENT SCIENCE....
 SEE OR/MS

OPERATIONS AND POLICY RESEARCH B1611

OPERATIONS RESEARCH SOCIETY B1612

OPERATIONS RESEARCH....SEE OP/RES

OPINION TESTS AND POLLS....SEE KNO/TEST

OPINIONS....SEE ATTIT

OPOTOWSKY S. B1613

OPTIMAL....OPTIMALITY

MARX F.M.,"POLICY FORMULATION AND THE
ADMINISTRATIVE PROCESS" ROUTINE ADJUST EFFICIENCY
OPTIMAL PRIVIL DRIVE PERSON OBJECTIVE...DECISION
OBS GEN/METH. PAGE 70 B1418
 S39
 ADMIN
 LEAD
 INGP/REL
 MGT

SELZNICK P.,"AN APPROACH TO A THEORY OF
BUREAUCRACY." INDUS WORKER CONTROL LEAD EFFICIENCY
OPTIMAL...SOC METH 20 BARNARD/C BUREAUCRCY
WEBER/MAX FRIEDRCH/C MICHELS/R. PAGE 95 B1928
 S43
 ROUTINE
 ADMIN
 MGT
 EX/STRUC

LEPAWSKY A.,ADMINISTRATION. FINAN INDUS LG/CO
SML/CO INGP/REL PERS/REL COST EFFICIENCY OPTIMAL
SKILL 20. PAGE 64 B1294
 B49
 ADMIN
 MGT
 WORKER
 EX/STRUC

ROBINSON E.A.G.,THE STRUCTURE OF COMPETITIVE
INDUSTRY. UK ECO/DEV DIST/IND MARKET TEC/DEV DIPLOM
EDU/PROP ADMIN EFFICIENCY WEALTH...MGT 19/20.
PAGE 89 B1798
 B53
 INDUS
 PRODUC
 WORKER
 OPTIMAL

RILEY V.,INTERINDUSTRY ECONOMIC STUDIES. USA+45
COMPUTER ADMIN OPTIMAL PRODUC...MGT CLASSIF STAT.
PAGE 88 B1788
 B55
 BIBLIOG
 ECO/DEV
 PLAN
 STRUCT

HEATH S.,CITADEL, MARKET, AND ALTAR; EMERGING
SOCIETY. SOCIETY ADMIN OPTIMAL OWN RATIONAL
ORD/FREE...SOC LOG PREDICT GEN/LAWS DICTIONARY 20.
PAGE 49 B0985
 B57
 NEW/IDEA
 STRUCT
 UTOPIA
 CREATE

GLOVER J.D.,A CASE STUDY OF HIGH LEVEL
ADMINISTRATION IN A LARGE ORGANIZATION. EX/STRUC
EXEC LEAD ROUTINE INGP/REL OPTIMAL ATTIT PERSON
...POLICY DECISION INT QU. PAGE 40 B0812
 B60
 ADMIN
 TOP/EX
 FORCES
 NAT/G

FRIEDMAN L.,"DECISION MAKING IN COMPETITIVE
SITUATIONS" OP/RES...MGT PROBABIL METH/COMP SIMUL
20. PAGE 37 B0757
 S60
 DECISION
 UTIL
 OPTIMAL
 GAME

HART H.C.,ADMINISTRATIVE ASPECTS OF RIVER VALLEY
DEVELOPMENT. INDIA USA+45 INDUS CONTROL EFFICIENCY
OPTIMAL PRODUC 20 TVA. PAGE 47 B0957
 B61
 ADMIN
 PLAN
 METH/COMP
 AGRI

MUSOLF L.D.,PROMOTING THE GENERAL WELFARE:
GOVERNMENT AND THE ECONOMY. USA+45 ECO/DEV CAP/ISM
DEMAND OPTIMAL 20. PAGE 77 B1550
 B65
 ECO/TAC
 NAT/G
 EX/STRUC
 NEW/LIB

GRENIEWSKI H.,"INTENTION AND PERFORMANCE: A PRIMER
OF CYBERNETICS OF PLANNING." EFFICIENCY OPTIMAL
KNOWL SKILL...DECISION MGT EQUILIB. PAGE 43 B0873
 S65
 SIMUL
 GAME
 GEN/METH
 PLAN

MANSFIELD E.,MANAGERIAL ECONOMICS AND OPERATIONS
RESEARCH; A NONMATHEMATICAL INTRODUCTION. USA+45
ELITES ECO/DEV CONSULT EX/STRUC PROB/SOLV ROUTINE
EFFICIENCY OPTIMAL...GAME T 20. PAGE 69 B1396
 B66
 ECO/TAC
 OP/RES
 MGT
 COMPUTER

THOENES P.,THE ELITE IN THE WELFARE STATE ,TRANS.
BY J BINGHAM; ED. BY. STRATA NAT/G GP/REL HAPPINESS
INCOME OPTIMAL MORAL PWR WEALTH...POLICY CONCPT.
PAGE 104 B2097
 B66
 ADMIN
 ELITES
 MGT
 WELF/ST

ROSENZWEIG J.E.,"MANAGERS AND MANAGEMENT SCIENTISTS
(TWO CULTURES)" INDUS CREATE TEC/DEV OPTIMAL
 S67
 EFFICIENCY
 MGT

...NEW/IDEA 20. PAGE 90 B1823 — INTELL METH/COMP

S67
WRIGHT F.K.,"INVESTMENT CRITERIA AND THE COST OF CAPITAL." FINAN PLAN BUDGET OPTIMAL PRODUC...POLICY DECISION 20. PAGE 118 B2380 — COST PROFIT INDUS MGT

N67
US CONGRESS JT COMM ECO GOVT,BACKGROUND MATERIAL ON ECONOMY IN GOVERNMENT 1967 (PAMPHLET). WOR+45 ECO/DEV BARGAIN PRICE DEMAND OPTIMAL...STAT DEPT/DEFEN. PAGE 108 B2178 — BUDGET COST MGT NAT/G

S68
PEARSON A.W.,"RESOURCE ALLOCATION." PLAN PROB/SOLV BUDGET ADMIN CONTROL CHOOSE EFFICIENCY...DECISION MGT 20. PAGE 82 B1649 — PROFIT OPTIMAL COST INDUS

OR/MS....OPERATIONAL RESEARCH AND RELATED MANAGEMENT SCIENCE

ORANGE FREE STATE....SEE ORANGE/STA

ORANGE/STA....ORANGE FREE STATE

ORD/FREE....SECURITY, ORDER, RESTRAINT, LIBERTY, FREEDOM

B00
SANDERSON E.,AFRICA IN THE NINETEENTH CENTURY. FRANCE UK EXTR/IND FORCES LEGIS ADMIN WAR DISCRIM ORD/FREE...GEOG GP/COMP SOC/INTEG 19. PAGE 92 B1867 — COLONIAL AFR DIPLOM

B05
MACHIAVELLI N.,THE ART OF WAR. CHRIST-17C TOP/EX DRIVE ORD/FREE PWR SKILL...MGT CHARTS. PAGE 67 B1360 — NAT/G FORCES WAR ITALY

B20
HALDANE R.B.,BEFORE THE WAR. MOD/EUR SOCIETY INT/ORG NAT/G DELIB/GP PLAN DOMIN EDU/PROP LEGIT ADMIN COERCE ATTIT DRIVE MORAL ORD/FREE PWR...SOC CONCPT SELF/OBS RECORD BIOG TIME/SEQ. PAGE 45 B0921 — POLICY DIPLOM UK

B27
DICKINSON J.,ADMINISTRATIVE JUSTICE AND THE SUPREMACY OF LAW IN THE UNITED STATES. USA-45 LAW INDUS DOMIN EDU/PROP CONTROL EXEC GP/REL ORD/FREE ...POLICY JURID 19/20. PAGE 29 B0586 — CT/SYS ADJUD ADMIN NAT/G

B28
BUELL R.,THE NATIVE PROBLEM IN AFRICA. KIN LABOR LOC/G ECO/TAC ROUTINE ORD/FREE...REC/INT KNO/TEST CENSUS TREND CHARTS SOC/EXP STERTYP 20. PAGE 17 B0339 — AFR CULTURE

B29
BUELL R.,INTERNATIONAL RELATIONS. WOR+45 WOR-45 CONSTN STRATA FORCES TOP/EX ADMIN ATTIT DRIVE SUPEGO MORAL ORD/FREE PWR SOVEREIGN...JURID SOC CONCPT 20. PAGE 17 B0340 — INT/ORG BAL/PWR DIPLOM

B36
GAUS J.M.,THE FRONTIERS OF PUBLIC ADMINISTRATION. EFFICIENCY PERCEPT RIGID/FLEX ORD/FREE 20. PAGE 39 B0785 — ROUTINE GOV/REL ELITES PROB/SOLV

B39
ZIMMERN A.,MODERN POLITICAL DOCTRINE. WOR-45 CULTURE SOCIETY ECO/UNDEV DELIB/GP EX/STRUC CREATE DOMIN COERCE NAT/LISM ATTIT RIGID/FLEX ORD/FREE PWR WEALTH...POLICY CONCPT OBS TIME/SEQ TREND TOT/POP LEAGUE/NAT 20. PAGE 119 B2402 — NAT/G ECO/TAC BAL/PWR INT/TRADE

B40
HART J.,AN INTRODUCTION TO ADMINISTRATIVE LAW, WITH SELECTED CASES. USA-45 CONSTN SOCIETY NAT/G EX/STRUC ADJUD CT/SYS LEAD CRIME ORD/FREE ...DECISION JURID 20 CASEBOOK. PAGE 47 B0958 — LAW ADMIN LEGIS PWR

S41
STOKE H.W.,"EXECUTIVE LEADERSHIP AND THE GROWTH OF PROPAGANDA." USA-45 NAT/G EX/STRUC LEGIS TOP/EX PARL/PROC REPRESENT ORD/FREE PWR...MAJORIT 20. PAGE 101 B2042 — EXEC LEAD EDU/PROP ADMIN

B42
BINGHAM A.M.,THE TECHNIQUES OF DEMOCRACY. USA-45 CONSTN STRUCT POL/PAR LEGIS PLAN PARTIC CHOOSE REPRESENT NAT/LISM TOTALISM...MGT 20. PAGE 12 B0240 — POPULISM ORD/FREE ADMIN NAT/G

B43
CLARKE M.P.,PARLIAMENTARY PRIVILEGE IN THE AMERICAN COLONIES. PROVS DOMIN ADMIN REPRESENT GOV/REL ORD/FREE...BIBLIOG/A 17/18. PAGE 21 B0433 — LEGIS PWR COLONIAL PARL/PROC

B44
DAVIS H.E.,PIONEERS IN WORLD ORDER. WOR-45 CONSTN ECO/TAC DOMIN EDU/PROP LEGIT ADJUD ADMIN ARMS/CONT CHOOSE KNOWL ORD/FREE...POLICY JURID SOC STAT OBS CENSUS TIME/SEQ ANTHOL LEAGUE/NAT 20. PAGE 26 B0537 — INT/ORG ROUTINE

B45
PASTUHOV V.D.,A GUIDE TO THE PRACTICE OF INTERNATIONAL CONFERENCES. WOR+45 PLAN LEGIT ORD/FREE...MGT OBS RECORD VAL/FREE ILO LEAGUE/NAT — INT/ORG DELIB/GP

20. PAGE 81 B1640

B45
PLATO,THE REPUBLIC. MEDIT-7 UNIV SOCIETY STRUCT EX/STRUC FORCES UTOPIA ATTIT PERCEPT HEALTH KNOWL ORD/FREE PWR...HUM CONCPT STERTYP TOT/POP. PAGE 83 B1681 — PERSON PHIL/SCI

B45
RANSHOFFEN-WERTHEIMER EF,THE INTERNATIONAL SECRETARIAT: A GREAT EXPERIMENT IN INTERNATIONAL ADMINISTRATION. EUR+WWI FUT CONSTN FACE/GP CONSULT DELIB/GP ACT/RES ADMIN ROUTINE PEACE ORD/FREE...MGT RECORD ORG/CHARTS LEAGUE/NAT WORK 20. PAGE 86 B1731 — INT/ORG EXEC

B47
WHITEHEAD T.N.,LEADERSHIP IN A FREE SOCIETY: A STUDY IN HUMAN RELATIONS BASED ON AN ANALYSIS OF PRESENT-DAY INDUSTRIAL CIVILIZATION. WOR-45 STRUCT R+D LABOR LG/CO SML/CO WORKER PLAN PROB/SOLV TEC/DEV DRIVE...MGT 20. PAGE 116 B2341 — INDUS LEAD ORD/FREE SOCIETY

B48
HULL C.,THE MEMOIRS OF CORDELL HULL (VOLUME ONE). USA-45 WOR-45 CONSTN FAM LOC/G NAT/G PROVS DELIB/GP FORCES LEGIS TOP/EX BAL/PWR LEGIT ADMIN EXEC WAR ATTIT ORD/FREE PWR...MAJORIT SELF/OBS TIME/SEQ TREND NAZI 20. PAGE 52 B1062 — BIOG DIPLOM

B48
ROSSITER C.L.,CONSTITUTIONAL DICTATORSHIP: CRISIS GOVERNMENT IN THE MODERN DEMOCRACIES. FRANCE GERMANY UK USA-45 WOR-45 EX/STRUC BAL/PWR CONTROL COERCE WAR CENTRAL ORD/FREE...DECISION 19/20. PAGE 90 B1828 — NAT/G AUTHORIT CONSTN TOTALISM

B48
TOWSTER J.,POLITICAL POWER IN THE USSR: 1917-1947. USSR CONSTN CULTURE ELITES CREATE PLAN COERCE CENTRAL ATTIT RIGID/FLEX ORD/FREE...BIBLIOG SOC/INTEG 20 LENIN/VI STALIN/J. PAGE 105 B2124 — EX/STRUC NAT/G MARXISM PWR

B49
ASPINALL A.,POLITICS AND THE PRESS 1780-1850. UK LAW ELITES FINAN PROF/ORG LEGIS ADMIN ATTIT ...POLICY 18/19. PAGE 7 B0142 — PRESS CONTROL POL/PAR ORD/FREE

B49
BUSH V.,MODERN ARMS AND FREE MEN. WOR-45 SOCIETY NAT/G ECO/TAC DOMIN LEGIT EXEC COERCE DETER ATTIT DRIVE ORD/FREE PWR...CONCPT MYTH COLD/WAR 20 COLD/WAR. PAGE 18 B0361 — TEC/DEV FORCES NUC/PWR WAR

B49
DENNING A.,FREEDOM UNDER THE LAW. MOD/EUR UK LAW SOCIETY CHIEF EX/STRUC LEGIS ADJUD CT/SYS PERS/REL PERSON 17/20 ENGLSH/LAW. PAGE 28 B0573 — ORD/FREE JURID NAT/G

B49
KENT S.,STRATEGIC INTELLIGENCE FOR AMERICAN WORLD POLICY. FUT USA+45 NAT/G ATTIT PERCEPT ORD/FREE ...OBS 20. PAGE 59 B1195 — ACT/RES EX/STRUC DIPLOM

B49
WALINE M.,LE CONTROLE JURIDICTIONNEL DE L'ADMINISTRATION. BELGIUM FRANCE UAR JUDGE BAL/PWR ADJUD CONTROL CT/SYS...GP/COMP 20. PAGE 113 B2277 — JURID ADMIN PWR ORD/FREE

L49
MARX C.M.,"ADMINISTRATIVE ETHICS AND THE RULE OF LAW." USA+45 ELITES ACT/RES DOMIN NEUTRAL ROUTINE INGP/REL ORD/FREE...JURID IDEA/COMP. PAGE 70 B1417 — ADMIN LAW

B50
LASSWELL H.D.,NATIONAL SECURITY AND INDIVIDUAL FREEDOM. USA+45 R+D NAT/G VOL/ASSN CONSULT DELIB/GP LEGIT ADMIN KNOWL ORD/FREE PWR...PLURIST TOT/POP COLD/WAR 20. PAGE 63 B1268 — FACE/GP ROUTINE BAL/PWR

S50
NEUMANN F.L.,"APPROACHES TO THE STUDY OF POLITICAL POWER." POL/PAR TOP/EX ADMIN LEAD ATTIT ORD/FREE CONSERVE LAISSEZ MARXISM...PSY SOC. PAGE 78 B1572 — PWR IDEA/COMP CONCPT

B51
DAVIS K.C.,ADMINISTRATIVE LAW. USA+45 USA-45 NAT/G PROB/SOLV BAL/PWR CONTROL ORD/FREE...POLICY 20 SUPREME/CT. PAGE 26 B0539 — ADMIN JURID EX/STRUC ADJUD

B51
PETERSON F.,SURVEY OF LABOR ECONOMICS (REV. ED.). STRATA ECO/DEV LABOR INSPECT BARGAIN PAY PRICE EXEC ROUTINE GP/REL ALL/VALS ORD/FREE 20 AFL/CIO DEPT/LABOR. PAGE 82 B1662 — WORKER DEMAND IDEA/COMP T

B51
SWISHER C.B.,THE THEORY AND PRACTICE OF AMERICAN NATIONAL GOVERNMENT. CULTURE LEGIS DIPLOM ADJUD ADMIN WAR PEACE ORD/FREE...MAJORIT 17/20. PAGE 102 B2063 — CONSTN NAT/G GOV/REL GEN/LAWS

B52
BRINTON C.,THE ANATOMY OF REVOLUTION. FRANCE UK USA-45 USSR WOR-45 ELITES INTELL ECO/DEV NAT/G EX/STRUC FORCES COERCE DRIVE ORD/FREE PWR SOVEREIGN ...MYTH HIST/WRIT GEN/LAWS. PAGE 15 B0311 — SOCIETY CONCPT REV

B52
HIMMELFARB G.,LORD ACTON: A STUDY IN CONSCIENCE AND POLITICS. MOD/EUR NAT/G POL/PAR SECT LEGIS TOP/EX EDU/PROP ADMIN NAT/LISM ATTIT PERSON SUPEGO MORAL ORD/FREE...CONCPT PARLIAMENT 19 ACTON/LORD. PAGE 50 — PWR BIOG

B1014

MILLER M.,THE JUDGES AND THE JUDGED. USA+45 LG/CO   COM/IND
ACT/RES TV ROUTINE SANCTION NAT/LISM ATTIT ORD/FREE DISCRIM
...POLICY ACLU. PAGE 73 B1481   EDU/PROP
                                                     MARXISM

                                                      B53
APPLEBY P.H.,PUBLIC ADMINISTRATION IN INDIA: REPORT ADMIN
OF A SURVEY. INDIA LOC/G OP/RES ATTIT ORD/FREE 20.   NAT/G
PAGE 6 B0118   EX/STRUC
                                                     GOV/REL

                                                      B53
STOUT H.M.,BRITISH GOVERNMENT. UK FINAN LOC/G   NAT/G
POL/PAR DELIB/GP DIPLOM ADMIN COLONIAL CHOOSE   PARL/PROC
ORD/FREE...JURID BIBLIOG 20 COMMONWLTH. PAGE 101   CONSTN
B2049   NEW/LIB

                                                      B53
TOMPKINS D.C.,CIVIL DEFENSE IN THE STATES: A   BIBLIOG
BIBLIOGRAPHY (DEFENSE BIBLIOGRAPHIES NO. 3;   WAR
PAMPHLET). USA+45 LABOR LOC/G NAT/G PROVS LEGIS.   ORD/FREE
PAGE 105 B2115   ADMIN

                                                      S53
PERKINS J.A.,"ADMINISTRATION OF THE NATIONAL   CONTROL
SECURITY PROGRAM." USA+45 EX/STRUC FORCES ADMIN   GP/REL
CIVMIL/REL ORD/FREE 20. PAGE 82 B1657   REPRESENT
                                                     PROB/SOLV

                                                      B54
DUVERGÉR M.,POLITICAL PARTIES: THEIR ORGANIZATION   POL/PAR
AND ACTIVITY IN THE MODERN STATE. EUR+WWI MOD/EUR   EX/STRUC
USA+45 USA-45 EDU/PROP ADMIN ROUTINE ATTIT DRIVE   ELITES
ORD/FREE PWR...SOC CONCPT MATH STAT TIME/SEQ
TOT/POP 19/20. PAGE 31 B0635

                                                      B54
HOBBS E.H.,BEHIND THE PRESIDENT - A STUDY OF   EX/STRUC
EXECUTIVE OFFICE AGENCIES. USA+45 NAT/G PLAN BUDGET DELIB/GP
ECO/TAC EXEC ORD/FREE 20 BUR/BUDGET. PAGE 50 B1022   CONFER
                                                     CONSULT

                                                      B54
MILLARD E.L.,FREEDOM IN A FEDERAL WORLD. FUT WOR+45 INT/ORG
VOL/ASSN TOP/EX LEGIT ROUTINE FEDERAL PEACE ATTIT   CREATE
DISPL ORD/FREE PWR...MAJORIT INT/LAW JURID TREND   ADJUD
COLD/WAR 20. PAGE 73 B1479   BAL/PWR

                                                      L54
FURNISS E.S.,"WEAKNESSES IN FRENCH FOREIGN POLICY-   NAT/G
MAKING." EUR+WWI LEGIS LEGIT EXEC ATTIT RIGID/FLEX   STRUCT
ORD/FREE...SOC CONCPT METH/CNCPT OBS 20. PAGE 38   DIPLOM
B0766   FRANCE

                                                      L54
ROSTOW W.W.,"ASIAN LEADERSHIP AND FREE-WORLD   ATTIT
ALLIANCE." ASIA COM USA+45 CULTURE ELITES INTELL   LEGIT
NAT/G TEC/DEV ECO/TAC EDU/PROP COLONIAL PARL/PROC   DIPLOM
ROUTINE COERCE DRIVE ORD/FREE MARXISM...PSY CONCPT.
PAGE 90 B1829

                                                      B55
BEISEL A.R.,CONTROL OVER ILLEGAL ENFORCEMENT OF THE ORD/FREE
CRIMINAL LAW: ROLE OF THE SUPREME COURT. CONSTN   LAW
ROUTINE MORAL PWR...SOC 20 SUPREME/CT. PAGE 10   CRIME
B0207

                                                      B55
DE ARAGAO J.G.,LA JURIDICTION ADMINISTRATIVE AU   EX/STRUC
BRESIL. BRAZIL ADJUD COLONIAL CT/SYS REV FEDERAL   ADMIN
ORD/FREE...BIBLIOG 19/20. PAGE 27 B0549   NAT/G

                                                      B55
UN HEADQUARTERS LIBRARY,BIBLIOGRAPHIE DE LA CHARTE   BIBLIOG/A
DES NATIONS UNIES. CHINA/COM KOREA WOR+45 VOL/ASSN   INT/ORG
CONFER ADMIN COERCE PEACE ATTIT ORD/FREE SOVEREIGN   DIPLOM
...INT/LAW 20 UNESCO UN. PAGE 106 B2149

                                                      S55
WEISS R.S.,"A METHOD FOR THE ANALYSIS OF THE   PROF/ORG
STRUCTURE OF COMPLEX ORGANIZATIONS." WOR+45 INDUS   SOC/EXP
LG/CO NAT/G EXEC ROUTINE ORD/FREE PWR SKILL...MGT
PSY SOC NEW/IDEA STAT INT REC/INT STAND/INT CHARTS
WORK. PAGE 115 B2316

                                                      B56
BLAU P.M.,BUREAUCRACY IN MODERN SOCIETY. STRUCT   SOC
INDUS LABOR LG/CO NAT/G FORCES EDU/PROP   EX/STRUC
ROUTINE ORD/FREE 20 BUREAUCRCY. PAGE 12 B0252   ADMIN
                                                     EFFICIENCY

                                                      B56
HOWARD L.V.,TULANE STUDIES IN POLITICAL SCIENCE: ADMIN
CIVIL SERVICE DEVELOPMENT IN LOUISIANA VOLUME 3.   GOV/REL
LAW POL/PAR LEGIS CT/SYS ADJUST ORD/FREE...STAT   PROVS
CHARTS 19/20 LOUISIANA CIVIL/SERV. PAGE 52 B1050   POLICY

                                                      B56
KAUFMANN W.W.,MILITARY POLICY AND NATIONAL   FORCES
SECURITY. USA+45 ELITES INTELL NAT/G TOP/EX PLAN   CREATE
BAL/PWR DIPLOM ROUTINE COERCE NUC/PWR ATTIT
ORD/FREE PWR 20 COLD/WAR. PAGE 58 B1182

                                                      B56
SOHN L.B.,CASES ON UNITED NATIONS LAW. STRUCT   INT/ORG
DELIB/GP WAR PEACE ORD/FREE...DECISION ANTHOL 20   INT/LAW
UN. PAGE 99 B1994   ADMIN
                                                     ADJUD

                                                      B56
WIGGINS J.R.,FREEDOM OR SECRECY. USA+45 USA-45   ORD/FREE
DELIB/GP EX/STRUC FORCES ADJUD SANCTION KNOWL PWR   PRESS

...AUD/VIS CONGRESS 20. PAGE 116 B2344   NAT/G
                                                     CONTROL

                                                      S56
CUTLER R.,"THE DEVELOPMENT OF THE NATIONAL SECURITY ORD/FREE
COUNCIL." USA+45 INTELL CONSULT EX/STRUC DIPLOM   DELIB/GP
LEAD 20 TRUMAN/HS EISNHWR/DD NSC. PAGE 25 B0514   PROB/SOLV
                                                     NAT/G

                                                      S56
KAUFMAN H.,"EMERGING CONFLICTS IN THE DOCTRINES OF   ADMIN
PUBLIC ADMINISTRATION" (BMR) USA+45 USA-45 NAT/G   ORD/FREE
EX/STRUC LEGIS CONTROL NEUTRAL ATTIT PWR...TREND   REPRESENT
20. PAGE 58 B1181   LEAD

                                                      S56
KHAMA T.,"POLITICAL CHANGE IN AFRICAN SOCIETY."   AFR
CONSTN SOCIETY LOC/G NAT/G POL/PAR EX/STRUC LEGIS   ELITES
LEGIT ADMIN CHOOSE REPRESENT NAT/LISM MORAL
ORD/FREE PWR...CONCPT OBS TREND GEN/METH CMN/WLTH
17/20. PAGE 59 B1201

                                                      B57
BEAL J.R.,JOHN FOSTER DULLES, A BIOGRAPHY. USA+45   BIOG
USSR WOR+45 CONSTN INT/ORG NAT/G EX/STRUC LEGIT   DIPLOM
ADMIN NUC/PWR DISPL PERSON ORD/FREE PWR SKILL
...POLICY PSY OBS RECORD COLD/WAR UN 20 DULLES/JF.
PAGE 10 B0200

                                                      B57
HEATH S.,CITADEL, MARKET, AND ALTAR: EMERGING   NEW/IDEA
SOCIETY. SOCIETY ADMIN OPTIMAL OWN RATIONAL   STRUCT
ORD/FREE...SOC LOG PREDICT GEN/LAWS DICTIONARY 20.   UTOPIA
PAGE 49 B0985   CREATE

                                                      B57
PYE L.W.,THE POLICY IMPLICATIONS OF SOCIAL CHANGE   SOCIETY
IN NON-WESTERN SOCIETIES. ASIA USA+45 CULTURE   ORD/FREE
STRUCT NAT/G ECO/TAC ADMIN ROLE...POLICY SOC.   ECO/UNDEV
PAGE 85 B1723   DIPLOM

                                                      B57
SCHLOCHAUER H.J.,OFFENTLICHES RECHT. GERMANY/W   CONSTN
FINAN EX/STRUC LEGIS DIPLOM FEDERAL ORD/FREE   JURID
...INT/LAW 20. PAGE 94 B1892   ADMIN
                                                     CT/SYS

                                                      L57
HAAS E.B.,"REGIONAL INTEGRATION AND NATIONAL   INT/ORG
POLICY." WOR+45 VOL/ASSN DELIB/GP EX/STRUC ECO/TAC   ORD/FREE
DOMIN EDU/PROP LEGIT COERCE ATTIT PERCEPT KNOWL   REGION
...TIME/SEQ COLD/WAR 20 UN. PAGE 45 B0908

                                                      S57
BAUER R.A.,"BRAINWASHING: PSYCHOLOGY OR   EDU/PROP
DEMONOLOGY." ASIA CHINA/COM COM POL/PAR ECO/TAC   PSY
ADMIN COERCE ATTIT DRIVE ORD/FREE...CONCPT MYTH 20. TOTALISM
PAGE 10 B0196

                                                      S57
HAILEY,"TOMORROW IN AFRICA." CONSTN SOCIETY LOC/G   AFR
NAT/G DOMIN ADJUD ADMIN GP/REL DISCRIM NAT/LISM   PERSON
ATTIT MORAL ORD/FREE...PSY SOC CONCPT OBS RECORD   ELITES
TREND GEN/LAWS CMN/WLTH 20. PAGE 45 B0917   RACE/REL

                                                      B58
BERNSTEIN M.H.,THE JOB OF THE FEDERAL EXECUTIVE.   NAT/G
POL/PAR CHIEF LEGIS ADMIN EXEC LOBBY CHOOSE GOV/REL TOP/EX
ORD/FREE PWR...MGT TREND. PAGE 11 B0228   PERS/COMP

                                                      B58
CONSERVATIVE POLITICAL CENTRE,A WORLD SECURITY   ORD/FREE
AUTHORITY? WOR+45 CONSTN ELITES FINAN DELIB/GP PLAN CONSERVE
PROB/SOLV ADMIN CONTROL NUC/PWR GP/REL...IDEA/COMP   FORCES
20. PAGE 23 B0468   ARMS/CONT

                                                      B58
HENKIN L.,ARMS CONTROL AND INSPECTION IN AMERICAN   USA+45
LAW. LAW CONSTN INT/ORG LOC/G MUNIC NAT/G PROVS   JURID
EDU/PROP LEGIT EXEC NUC/PWR KNOWL ORD/FREE...OBS   ARMS/CONT
TOT/POP CONGRESS 20. PAGE 49 B0990

                                                      B58
KINTNER W.R.,ORGANIZING FOR CONFLICT: A PROPOSAL.   USA+45
USSR STRUCT NAT/G LEGIS ADMIN EXEC PEACE ORD/FREE   PLAN
PWR...CONCPT OBS TREND NAT/COMP VAL/FREE COLD/WAR   DIPLOM
20. PAGE 60 B1211

                                                      B58
SPITZ D.,DEMOCRACY AND THE CHALLENGE OF POWER. FUT   NAT/G
USA+45 USA-45 LAW SOCIETY STRUCT LOC/G POL/PAR   PWR
PROVS DELIB/GP EX/STRUC LEGIS TOP/EX ACT/RES CREATE
DOMIN EDU/PROP LEGIT ADJUD ADMIN ATTIT DRIVE MORAL
ORD/FREE TOT/POP. PAGE 99 B2010

                                                      B58
US HOUSE COMM GOVT OPERATIONS,HEARINGS BEFORE A   FOR/AID
SUBCOMMITTEE OF THE COMMITTEE ON GOVERNMENT   DIPLOM
OPERATIONS. CAMBODIA PHILIPPINE USA+45 CONSTRUC   ORD/FREE
TEC/DEV ADMIN CONTROL WEAPON EFFICIENCY HOUSE/REP.   ECO/UNDEV
PAGE 108 B2189

                                                      S58
DAVENPORT J.,"ARMS AND THE WELFARE STATE." INTELL   USA+45
STRUCT FORCES CREATE ECO/TAC FOR/AID DOMIN LEGIT   NAT/G
ADMIN WAR ORD/FREE PWR...POLICY SOC CONCPT MYTH OBS USSR
TREND COLD/WAR TOT/POP 20. PAGE 26 B0533

                                                      S58
ELKIN A.B.,"OEEC-ITS STRUCTURE AND POWERS." EUR+WWI ECO/DEV
CONSTN INDUS INT/ORG NAT/G VOL/ASSN DELIB/GP   EX/STRUC
ACT/RES PLAN ORD/FREE WEALTH...CHARTS ORG/CHARTS
OEEC 20. PAGE 33 B0666

S58
MITCHELL W.C.,"OCCUPATIONAL ROLE STRAINS: THE   ANOMIE
AMERICAN ELECTIVE PUBLIC OFFICIAL." CONTROL   DRIVE
RIGID/FLEX SUPEGO HEALTH ORD/FREE...SOC INT QU.   ROUTINE
PAGE 74 B1492   PERSON

S58
STAAR R.F.,"ELECTIONS IN COMMUNIST POLAND." EUR+WWI   COM
SOCIETY INT/ORG NAT/G POL/PAR LEGIS ACT/RES ECO/TAC   CHOOSE
EDU/PROP ADJUD ADMIN ROUTINE COERCE TOTALISM ATTIT   POLAND
ORD/FREE PWR 20. PAGE 100 B2015

B59
CHINA INSTITUTE OF AMERICA,,CHINA AND THE UNITED   ASIA
NATIONS. CHINA/COM FUT STRUCT EDU/PROP ADMIN   INT/ORG
ATTIT KNOWL ORD/FREE PWR...OBS RECORD STAND/INT
TIME/SEQ UN LEAGUE/NAT UNESCO 20. PAGE 21 B0425

B59
COUNCIL OF STATE GOVERNMENTS,STATE GOVERNMENT: AN   BIBLIOG/A
ANNOTATED BIBLIOGRAPHY (PAMPHLET). USA+45 LAW AGRI   PROVS
INDUS WORKER PLAN TAX ADJUST AGE/Y ORD/FREE...HEAL   LOC/G
MGT 20. PAGE 24 B0494   ADMIN

B59
DAVIS K.C.,ADMINISTRATIVE LAW TEXT. USA+45 NAT/G   ADJUD
DELIB/GP EX/STRUC CONTROL ORD/FREE...T 20   ADMIN
SUPREME/CT. PAGE 27 B0542   JURID
  CT/SYS

B59
DIEBOLD W. JR.,THE SCHUMAN PLAN: A STUDY IN   INT/ORG
ECONOMIC COOPERATION, 1950-1959. EUR+WWI FRANCE   REGION
GERMANY USA+45 EXTR/IND CONSULT DELIB/GP PLAN
DIPLOM ECO/TAC INT/TRADE ROUTINE ORD/FREE WEALTH
...METH/CNCPT STAT CONT/OBS INT TIME/SEQ ECSC 20.
PAGE 29 B0591

B59
ELLIOTT S.D.,IMPROVING OUR COURTS. LAW EX/STRUC   CT/SYS
PLAN PROB/SOLV ADJUD ADMIN TASK CRIME EFFICIENCY   JURID
ORD/FREE 20. PAGE 33 B0669   GOV/REL
  NAT/G

B59
GOODRICH L.,THE UNITED NATIONS. WOR+45 CONSTN   INT/ORG
STRUCT ACT/RES LEGIT COERCE KNOWL ORD/FREE PWR   ROUTINE
...GEN/LAWS UN 20. PAGE 41 B0825

B59
GORDENKER L.,THE UNITED NATIONS AND THE PEACEFUL   DELIB/GP
UNIFICATION OF KOREA. ASIA LAW LOC/G CONSULT   KOREA
ACT/RES DIPLOM DOMIN LEGIT ADJUD ADMIN ORD/FREE   INT/ORG
SOVEREIGN...INT GEN/METH UN COLD/WAR 20. PAGE 41
B0829

B59
GRABER D.,CRISIS DIPLOMACY. L/A+17C USA+45 USA-45   ROUTINE
NAT/G TOP/EX ECO/TAC COERCE ATTIT ORD/FREE...CONCPT   MORAL
MYTH TIME/SEQ COLD/WAR 20. PAGE 42 B0848   DIPLOM

B59
GREENEWALT C.H.,THE UNCOMMON MAN. UNIV ECO/DEV   TASK
ADMIN PERS/REL PERSON SUPEGO WEALTH 20. PAGE 43   ORD/FREE
B0868   DRIVE
  EFFICIENCY

B59
JANOWITZ M.,SOCIOLOGY AND THE MILITARY   FORCES
ESTABLISHMENT. USA+45 WOR+45 CULTURE SOCIETY   SOC
PROF/ORG CONSULT EX/STRUC PLAN TEC/DEV DIPLOM DOMIN
COERCE DRIVE RIGID/FLEX ORD/FREE PWR SKILL COLD/WAR
20. PAGE 55 B1121

B59
LOEWENSTEIN K.,VERFASSUNGSRECHT UND   CONSTN
VERFASSUNGSPRAXIS DER VEREINIGTEN STAATEN. USA+45   POL/PAR
USA-45 COLONIAL CT/SYS GP/REL RACE/REL ORD/FREE   EX/STRUC
...JURID 18/20 SUPREME/CT CONGRESS PRESIDENT   NAT/G
BILL/RIGHT CIVIL/LIB. PAGE 66 B1337

B59
PARK R.L.,LEADERSHIP AND POLITICAL INSTITUTIONS IN   NAT/G
INDIA. S/ASIA CULTURE ECO/UNDEV LOC/G MUNIC PROVS   EXEC
LEGIS PLAN ADMIN LEAD ORD/FREE WEALTH...GEOG SOC   INDIA
BIOG TOT/POP VAL/FREE 20. PAGE 81 B1633

B59
SCHURZ W.L.,AMERICAN FOREIGN AFFAIRS: A GUIDE TO   INT/ORG
INTERNATIONAL AFFAIRS. USA+45 WOR+45 WOR-45 NAT/G   SOCIETY
FORCES LEGIS TOP/EX PLAN EDU/PROP LEGIT ADMIN   DIPLOM
ROUTINE ATTIT ORD/FREE PWR...SOC CONCPT STAT
SAMP/SIZ CHARTS STERTYP 20. PAGE 95 B1910

B59
SINHA H.N.,OUTLINES OF POLITICAL SCIENCE. NAT/G   JURID
POL/PAR EX/STRUC LEGIS CT/SYS CHOOSE REPRESENT 20.   CONCPT
PAGE 98 B1971   ORD/FREE
  SOVEREIGN

B59
SISSON C.H.,THE SPIRIT OF BRITISH ADMINISTRATION   GOV/COMP
AND SOME EUROPEAN COMPARISONS. FRANCE GERMANY/W   ADMIN
SWEDEN UK LAW EX/STRUC INGP/REL EFFICIENCY ORD/FREE   ELITES
...DECISION 20. PAGE 98 B1972   ATTIT

B59
SPIRO H.J.,GOVERNMENT BY CONSTITUTIONS: THE   NAT/G
POLITICAL SYSTEMS OF DEMOCRACY. CANADA EUR+WWI FUT   CONSTN
USA+45 WOR+45 WOR-45 LEGIS TOP/EX LEGIT ADMIN
CT/SYS ORD/FREE PWR...TREND TOT/POP VAL/FREE 20.
PAGE 99 B2008

B59
US PRES COMM STUDY MIL ASSIST,COMPOSITE REPORT.   FOR/AID
USA+45 ECO/UNDEV PLAN BUDGET DIPLOM EFFICIENCY   FORCES
...POLICY MGT 20. PAGE 109 B2208   WEAPON
  ORD/FREE

S59
HARVEY M.F.,"THE PALESTINE REFUGEE PROBLEM: ACT/RES
ELEMENTS OF A SOLUTION." ISLAM LAW INT/ORG DELIB/GP   LEGIT
TOP/EX ECO/TAC ROUTINE DRIVE HEALTH LOVE ORD/FREE   PEACE
PWR WEALTH...MAJORIT FAO 20. PAGE 48 B0964   ISRAEL

S59
SOHN L.B.,"THE DEFINITION OF AGGRESSION." FUT LAW   INT/ORG
FORCES LEGIT ADJUD ROUTINE COERCE ORD/FREE PWR   CT/SYS
...MAJORIT JURID QUANT COLD/WAR 20. PAGE 99 B1995   DETER
  SOVEREIGN

S59
SUTTON F.X.,"REPRESENTATION AND THE NATURE OF   NAT/G
POLITICAL SYSTEMS." UNIV WOR-45 CULTURE SOCIETY   CONCPT
STRATA INT/ORG FORCES JUDGE DOMIN LEGIT EXEC REGION
REPRESENT ATTIT ORD/FREE RESPECT...SOC HIST/WRIT
TIME/SEQ. PAGE 102 B2057

B60
JUNZ A.J., PRESENT TRENDS IN AMERICAN NATIONAL   POL/PAR
GOVERNMENT. LEGIS DIPLOM ADMIN CT/SYS ORD/FREE   CHOOSE
...CONCPT ANTHOL 20 CONGRESS PRESIDENT SUPREME/CT.   CONSTN
PAGE 2 B0048   NAT/G

B60
ALBI F.,TRATADO DE LOS MODOS DE GESTION DE LAS   LOC/G
CORPORACIONES LOCALES. SPAIN FINAN NAT/G BUDGET   LAW
CONTROL EXEC ROUTINE GOV/REL ORD/FREE SOVEREIGN   ADMIN
...MGT 20. PAGE 3 B0068   MUNIC

B60
CORSON J.J.,GOVERNANCE OF COLLEGES AND   ADMIN
UNIVERSITIES. STRUCT FINAN DELIB/GP DOMIN EDU/PROP   EXEC
LEAD CHOOSE GP/REL CENTRAL COST PRIVIL SUPEGO   ACADEM
ORD/FREE PWR...DECISION BIBLIOG. PAGE 24 B0481   HABITAT

B60
EASTON S.C.,THE TWILIGHT OF EUROPEAN COLONIALISM.   FINAN
AFR S/ASIA CONSTN SOCIETY STRUCT ECO/UNDEV INDUS   ADMIN
NAT/G FORCES ECO/TAC COLONIAL CT/SYS ATTIT KNOWL
ORD/FREE PWR...SOCIALIST TIME/SEQ TREND CON/ANAL
20. PAGE 32 B0645

B60
GRUNDLICH T.,DIE TECHNIK DER DIKTATUR. ADMIN   COERCE
TOTALISM ATTIT PWR...MGT CONCPT ARISTOTLE. PAGE 44   DOMIN
B0896   ORD/FREE
  WAR

B60
HAYEK F.A.,THE CONSTITUTION OF LIBERTY. UNIV LAW   ORD/FREE
CONSTN WORKER TAX EDU/PROP ADMIN CT/SYS COERCE   CHOOSE
DISCRIM...IDEA/COMP 20. PAGE 48 B0974   NAT/G
  CONCPT

B60
KINGSTON-MCCLOUG E.,DEFENSE; POLICY AND STRATEGY.   FORCES
UK SEA AIR TEC/DEV DIPLOM ADMIN LEAD WAR ORD/FREE   PLAN
...CHARTS 20. PAGE 60 B1209   POLICY
  DECISION

B60
LINDSAY K.,EUROPEAN ASSEMBLIES: THE EXPERIMENTAL   VOL/ASSN
PERIOD 1949-1959. EUR+WWI ECO/DEV NAT/G POL/PAR   INT/ORG
LEGIS TOP/EX ACT/RES PLAN ECO/TAC DOMIN LEGIT   REGION
ROUTINE ATTIT DRIVE ORD/FREE PWR SKILL...SOC CONCPT
TREND CHARTS GEN/LAWS VAL/FREE. PAGE 65 B1315

B60
MOORE W.E.,LABOR COMMITMENT AND SOCIAL CHANGE IN   LABOR
DEVELOPING AREAS. SOCIETY STRATA ECO/UNDEV MARKET   ORD/FREE
VOL/ASSN WORKER AUTHORIT SKILL...MGT NAT/COMP   ATTIT
SOC/INTEG 20. PAGE 75 B1514   INDUS

B60
MUNRO L.,UNITED NATIONS, HOPE FOR A DIVIDED WORLD.   INT/ORG
FUT WOR+45 CONSTN DELIB/GP CREATE TEC/DEV DIPLOM   ROUTINE
EDU/PROP LEGIT PEACE ATTIT HEALTH ORD/FREE PWR
...CONCPT TREND UN VAL/FREE 20. PAGE 76 B1540

B60
PHILLIPS J.C.,MUNICIPAL GOVERNMENT AND   MUNIC
ADMINISTRATION IN AMERICA. USA+45 LAW CONSTN FINAN   GOV/REL
FORCES PLAN RECEIVE OWN ORD/FREE 20 CIVIL/LIB.   LOC/G
PAGE 83 B1669   ADMIN

B60
PINTO F.B.M.,ENRIQUECIMENTO ILICITO NO EXERCICIO DE   ADMIN
CARGOS PUBLICOS. BRAZIL L/A+17C USA+45 ELITES   NAT/G
TRIBUTE CONTROL INGP/REL ORD/FREE PWR...NAT/COMP   CRIME
20. PAGE 83 B1675   LAW

B60
US DEPARTMENT OF THE ARMY,SELECT BIBLIOGRAPHY ON   BIBLIOG/A
ADMINISTRATIVE ORGANIZATION(PAMPHLET). USA+45 INDUS   ADMIN
NAT/G EX/STRUC OP/RES CIVMIL/REL EFFICIENCY   CONCPT
ORD/FREE. PAGE 108 B2183   FORCES

B60
WEBSTER J.A.,A GENERAL STUDY OF THE DEPARTMENT OF   ORD/FREE
DEFENSE INTERNAL SECURITY PROGRAM. USA+45 WORKER   PLAN
TEC/DEV ADJUD CONTROL CT/SYS EXEC GOV/REL COST   ADMIN
...POLICY DECISION MGT 20 DEPT/DEFEN SUPREME/CT.   NAT/G
PAGE 114 B2307

L60
DEAN A.W.,"SECOND GENEVA CONFERENCE OF THE LAW OF   INT/ORG

THE SEA: THE FIGHT FOR FREEDOM OF THE SEAS." FUT
USA+45 USSR WOR+45 WOR-45 SEA CONSTN STRUCT PLAN
INT/TRADE ADJUD ADMIN ORD/FREE...DECISION RECORD
TREND GEN/LAWS 20 TREATY. PAGE 28 B0564
JURID
INT/LAW

S60
BOGARDUS E.S.,"THE SOCIOLOGY OF A STRUCTURED
PEACE." FUT SOCIETY CREATE DIPLOM EDU/PROP ADJUD
ROUTINE ATTIT RIGID/FLEX KNOWL ORD/FREE RESPECT
...POLICY INT/LAW JURID NEW/IDEA SELF/OBS TOT/POP
20 UN. PAGE 13 B0264
INT/ORG
SOC
NAT/LISM
PEACE

S60
EMERSON R.,"THE EROSION OF DEMOCRACY." AFR FUT LAW
CULTURE INTELL SOCIETY ECO/UNDEV FAM LOC/G NAT/G
FORCES PLAN TEC/DEV ECO/TAC ADMIN CT/SYS ATTIT
ORD/FREE PWR...SOCIALIST SOC CONCPT STAND/INT
TIME/SEQ WORK 20. PAGE 33 B0671
S/ASIA
POL/PAR

S60
HERZ J.H.,"EAST GERMANY: PROGRESS AND PROSPECTS."
COM AGRI FINAN INDUS LOC/G NAT/G FORCES PLAN
TEC/DEV DOMIN ADMIN COERCE DRIVE PERCEPT RIGID/FLEX
MORAL ORD/FREE PWR...MARXIST PSY SOC RECORD STERTYP
WORK. PAGE 49 B0997
POL/PAR
STRUCT
GERMANY

S60
HUTCHINSON C.E.,"AN INSTITUTE FOR NATIONAL SECURITY
AFFAIRS." USA+45 R+D NAT/G CONSULT TOP/EX ACT/RES
CREATE PLAN TEC/DEV EDU/PROP ROUTINE NUC/PWR ATTIT
ORD/FREE PWR...DECISION MGT PHIL/SCI CONCPT RECORD
GEN/LAWS GEN/METH 20. PAGE 53 B1068
POLICY
METH/CNCPT
ELITES
DIPLOM

S60
MORA J.A.,"THE ORGANIZATION OF AMERICAN STATES."
USA+45 LAW ECO/UNDEV VOL/ASSN DELIB/GP PLAN BAL/PWR
EDU/PROP ADMIN DRIVE RIGID/FLEX ORD/FREE WEALTH
...TIME/SEQ GEN/LAWS OAS 20. PAGE 75 B1518
L/A+17C
INT/ORG
REGION

S60
ROURKE F.E.,"ADMINISTRATIVE SECRECY: A
CONGRESSIONAL DILEMMA." DELIB/GP CT/SYS ATTIT
...MAJORIT DECISION JURID. PAGE 91 B1837
LEGIS
EXEC
ORD/FREE
POLICY

S60
SCHATZ S.P.,"THE INFLENCE OF PLANNING ON
DEVELOPMENT: THE NIGERIAN EXPERIENCE." AFR FUT
FINAN INDUS NAT/G EX/STRUC ECO/TAC ADMIN ATTIT
PERCEPT ORD/FREE PWR...MATH TREND CON/ANAL SIMUL
VAL/FREE 20. PAGE 93 B1883
ECO/UNDEV
PLAN
NIGERIA

S60
THOMPSON K.W.,"MORAL PURPOSE IN FOREIGN POLICY:
REALITIES AND ILLUSIONS." WOR+45 WOR-45 LAW CULTURE
SOCIETY INT/ORG PLAN ADJUD ADMIN COERCE RIGID/FLEX
SUPEGO KNOWL ORD/FREE PWR...SOC TREND SOC/EXP
TOT/POP 20. PAGE 104 B2104
MORAL
JURID
DIPLOM

N60
RHODESIA-NYASA NATL ARCHIVES,A SELECT BIBLIOGRAPHY
OF RECENT PUBLICATIONS CONCERNING THE FEDERATION OF
RHODESIA AND NYASALAND (PAMPHLET). MALAWI RHODESIA
LAW CULTURE STRUCT ECO/UNDEV LEGIS...GEOG 20.
PAGE 88 B1770
BIBLIOG
ADMIN
ORD/FREE
NAT/G

B61
BARNES W.,THE FOREIGN SERVICE OF THE UNITED STATES.
USA+45 USA-45 CONSTN INT/ORG POL/PAR CONSULT
DELIB/GP LEGIS DOMIN EDU/PROP EXEC ATTIT RIGID/FLEX
ORD/FREE PWR...POLICY CONCPT STAT OBS RECORD BIOG
TIME/SEQ TREND. PAGE 9 B0188
NAT/G
MGT
DIPLOM

B61
CATHERINE R.,LE FONCTIONNAIRE FRANCAIS. FRANCE
NAT/G INGP/REL ATTIT MORAL ORD/FREE...T CIVIL/SERV.
PAGE 19 B0394
ADMIN
GP/REL
LEAD
SUPEGO

B61
HAMILTON A.,THE FEDERALIST. USA-45 NAT/G VOL/ASSN
LEGIS TOP/EX EDU/PROP LEGIT CHOOSE ATTIT RIGID/FLEX
ORD/FREE PWR...MAJORIT JURID CONCPT ANTHOL. PAGE 46
B0931
EX/STRUC
CONSTN

B61
KERTESZ S.D.,AMERICAN DIPLOMACY IN A NEW ERA. COM
S/ASIA UK USA+45 FORCES PROB/SOLV BAL/PWR ECO/TAC
ADMIN COLONIAL WAR PEACE ORD/FREE 20 NATO CONGRESS
UN COLD/WAR. PAGE 59 B1199
ANTHOL
DIPLOM
TREND

B61
KOESTLER A.,THE LOTUS AND THE ROBOT. ASIA INDIA
S/ASIA SOCIETY STRATA ECO/DEV AGRI INDUS FAM CREATE
DOMIN EDU/PROP ADMIN COERCE ATTIT DRIVE SUPEGO
ORD/FREE PWR RESPECT WEALTH...MYTH OBS 20 CHINJAP.
PAGE 61 B1226
SECT
ECO/UNDEV

B61
MACRIDIS R.C.,COMPARATIVE POLITICS: NOTES AND
READINGS. WOR+45 LOC/G MUNIC NAT/G PROVS VOL/ASSN
EDU/PROP ADMIN ATTIT PERSON ORD/FREE...SOC CONCPT
OBS RECORD TREND 20. PAGE 68 B1376
POL/PAR
CHOOSE

B61
MARX K.,THE COMMUNIST MANIFESTO. IN (MENDEL A.
ESSENTIAL WORKS OF MARXISM, NEW YORK: BANTAM. FUT
MOD/EUR CULTURE ECO/DEV ECO/UNDEV AGRI FINAN INDUS
MARKET PROC/MFG LABOR MUNIC POL/PAR CONSULT FORCES
CREATE PLAN ADMIN ATTIT DRIVE RIGID/FLEX ORD/FREE
PWR RESPECT MARX/KARL WORK. PAGE 70 B1421
COM
NEW/IDEA
CAP/ISM
REV

B61
MONAS S.,THE THIRD SECTION: POLICE AND SOCIETY IN
RUSSIA UNDER NICHOLAS I. MOD/EUR RUSSIA ELITES
STRUCT NAT/G EX/STRUC ADMIN CONTROL PWR CONSERVE
...DECISION 19 NICHOLAS/I. PAGE 74 B1499
ORD/FREE
COM
FORCES
COERCE

B61
NARAIN J.P.,SWARAJ FOR THE PEOPLE. INDIA CONSTN
LOC/G MUNIC POL/PAR CHOOSE REPRESENT EFFICIENCY
ATTIT PWR SOVEREIGN 20. PAGE 77 B1553
NAT/G
ORD/FREE
EDU/PROP
EX/STRUC

B61
RAO K.V.,PARLIAMENTARY DEMOCRACY OF INDIA. INDIA
EX/STRUC TOP/EX COLONIAL CT/SYS PARL/PROC ORD/FREE
...POLICY CONCPT TREND 20 PARLIAMENT. PAGE 86 B1733
CONSTN
ADJUD
NAT/G
FEDERAL

B61
STONE J.,QUEST FOR SURVIVAL. WOR+45 NAT/G VOL/ASSN
LEGIT ADMIN ARMS/CONT COERCE DISPL ORD/FREE PWR
...POLICY INT/LAW JURID COLD/WAR 20. PAGE 101 B2047
INT/ORG
ADJUD
SOVEREIGN

S61
HAAS E.B.,"INTERNATIONAL INTEGRATION: THE EUROPEAN
AND THE UNIVERSAL PROCESS." EUR+WWI FUT WOR+45
NAT/G EX/STRUC ATTIT DRIVE ORD/FREE PWR...CONCPT
GEN/LAWS OEEC 20 NATO COUNCL/EUR. PAGE 45 B0909
INT/ORG
TREND
REGION

S61
MILLER E.,"LEGAL ASPECTS OF UN ACTION IN THE
CONGO." AFR CULTURE ADMIN PEACE DRIVE RIGID/FLEX
ORD/FREE...WELF/ST JURID OBS UN CONGO 20. PAGE 73
B1480
INT/ORG
LEGIT

B62
BOCK E.A.,CASE STUDIES IN AMERICAN GOVERNMENT.
USA+45 ECO/DEV CHIEF EDU/PROP CT/SYS RACE/REL
ORD/FREE...JURID MGT PHIL/SCI PRESIDENT CASEBOOK.
PAGE 13 B0262
POLICY
LEGIS
IDEA/COMP
NAT/G

B62
BROWN B.E.,NEW DIRECTIONS IN COMPARATIVE POLITICS.
AUSTRIA FRANCE GERMANY UK WOR+45 EX/STRUC LEGIS
ORD/FREE 20. PAGE 16 B0320
NAT/COMP
METH
POL/PAR
FORCES

B62
FOSS P.O.,REORGANIZATION AND REASSIGNMENT IN THE
CALIFORNIA HIGHWAY PATROL (PAMPHLET). USA+45 STRUCT
WORKER EDU/PROP CONTROL COERCE INGP/REL ORD/FREE
PWR...DECISION 20 CALIFORNIA. PAGE 37 B0744
FORCES
ADMIN
PROVS
PLAN

B62
FRIEDLANDER W.A.,INDIVIDUALISM AND SOCIAL WELFARE.
FRANCE ACADEM OP/RES ADMIN AGE/Y AGE/A ORD/FREE 20.
PAGE 37 B0756
GIVE
SOC/WK
SOC/EXP
FINAN

B62
HARARI M.,GOVERNMENT AND POLITICS OF THE MIDDLE
EAST. ISLAM USA+45 NAT/G SECT CHIEF ADMIN ORD/FREE
20. PAGE 47 B0943
DIPLOM
ECO/UNDEV
TEC/DEV
POLICY

B62
INTERNAT CONGRESS OF JURISTS,EXECUTIVE ACTION AND
THE RULE OF RULE: REPORTION PROCEEDINGS OF INT'T
CONGRESS OF JURISTS,--RIO DE JANEIRO, BRAZIL. WOR+45
ACADEM CONSULT JUDGE EDU/PROP ADJUD CT/SYS INGP/REL
PERSON DEPT/DEFEN. PAGE 54 B1094
JURID
EXEC
ORD/FREE
CONTROL

B62
KARNJAHAPRAKORN C.,MUNICIPAL GOVERNMENT IN THAILAND
AS AN INSTITUTION AND PROCESS OF SELF-GOVERNMENT.
THAILAND CULTURE FINAN EX/STRUC LEGIS PLAN CONTROL
GOV/REL EFFICIENCY ATTIT...POLICY 20. PAGE 58 B1176
LOC/G
MUNIC
ORD/FREE
ADMIN

B62
MORE S.S.,REMODELLING OF DEMOCRACY FOR AFRO-ASIAN
NATIONS. AFR INDIA S/ASIA SOUTH/AFR CONSTN EX/STRUC
COLONIAL CHOOSE TOTALISM SOVEREIGN NEW/LIB SOCISM
...SOC/WK 20. PAGE 75 B1520
ORD/FREE
ECO/UNDEV
ADMIN
LEGIS

B62
MULLEY F.W.,THE POLITICS OF WESTERN DEFENSE.
EUR+WWI USA+45 WOR+45 VOL/ASSN EX/STRUC FORCES
COERCE DETER PEACE ATTIT ORD/FREE PWR...RECORD
TIME/SEQ CHARTS COLD/WAR 20 NATO. PAGE 76 B1537
INT/ORG
DELIB/GP
NUC/PWR

B62
SIMON Y.R.,A GENERAL THEORY OF AUTHORITY. DOMIN
ADMIN RATIONAL UTOPIA KNOWL MORAL PWR SOVEREIGN
...HUM CONCPT NEW/IDEA 20. PAGE 97 B1962
PERS/REL
PERSON
SOCIETY
ORD/FREE

B62
TAYLOR D.,THE BRITISH IN AFRICA. UK CULTURE
ECO/UNDEV INDUS DIPLOM INT/TRADE ADMIN WAR RACE/REL
ORD/FREE SOVEREIGN...POLICY BIBLIOG 15/20 CMN/WLTH.
PAGE 103 B2084
AFR
COLONIAL
DOMIN

B62
US ADMINISTRATIVE CONFERENCE,FINAL REPORT OF THE
ADMINISTRATIVE CONFERENCE OF THE US; SUGGESTIONS
FOR IMPROVING PROCESSES - ADMIN. AGENCIES. USA+45
INGP/REL EFFICIENCY RATIONAL ORD/FREE...GP/COMP
METH/COMP 20. PAGE 107 B2170
ADMIN
NAT/G
DELIB/GP
GOV/REL

B62
US SENATE COMM GOVT OPERATIONS,ADMINISTRATION OF
NATIONAL SECURITY. USA+45 CHIEF PLAN PROB/SOLV
TEC/DEV DIPLOM ATTIT...POLICY DECISION 20
KENNEDY/JF RUSK/D MCNAMARA/R BUNDY/M HERTER/C.
ORD/FREE
ADMIN
NAT/G
CONTROL

PAGE 110 B2212

B62

US SENATE COMM ON JUDICIARY,STATE DEPARTMENT   CONTROL
SECURITY. USA+45 CHIEF TEC/DEV DOMIN ADMIN EXEC   WORKER
ATTIT ORD/FREE...POLICY CONGRESS DEPT/STATE   NAT/G
PRESIDENT KENNEDY/JF KENNEDY/JF SENATE 20. PAGE 110 GOV/REL
B2228

L62

BAILEY S.D.,"THE TROIKA AND THE FUTURE OF THE UN."   FUT
CONSTN CREATE LEGIT EXEC CHOOSE ORD/FREE PWR   INT/ORG
...CONCPT NEW/IDEA UN COLD/WAR 20. PAGE 8 B0163   USSR

S62

JACOBSON H.K.,"THE UNITED NATIONS AND COLONIALISM: INT/ORG
A TENTATIVE APPRAISAL." AFR FUT S/ASIA USA+45 USSR   CONCPT
WOR+45 NAT/G DELIB/GP PLAN DIPLOM ECO/TAC DOMIN   COLONIAL
ADMIN ROUTINE COERCE ATTIT RIGID/FLEX ORD/FREE PWR
...OBS STERTYP UN 20. PAGE 55 B1115

S62

MAINZER L.C.,"INJUSTICE AND BUREAUCRACY." ELITES   MORAL
STRATA STRUCT EX/STRUC SENIOR CONTROL EXEC LEAD   MGT
ROUTINE INGP/REL ORD/FREE...CONCPT 20 BUREAUCRCY.   ADMIN
PAGE 68 B1381

S62

MARTIN L.W.,"POLITICAL SETTLEMENTS AND ARMS   CONCPT
CONTROL." COM EUR+WWI GERMANY USA+45 PROVS FORCES   ARMS/CONT
TOP/EX ACT/RES CREATE DOMIN LEGIT ROUTINE COERCE
ATTIT RIGID/FLEX ORD/FREE PWR...METH/CNCPT RECORD
GEN/LAWS 20. PAGE 70 B1410

S62

MCCLELLAND C.A.,"DECISIONAL OPPORTUNITY AND   ACT/RES
POLITICAL CONTROVERSY." USA+45 NAT/G POL/PAR FORCES PERCEPT
TOP/EX DOMIN ADMIN PEACE DRIVE ORD/FREE PWR   DIPLOM
...DECISION SIMUL 20. PAGE 72 B1444

S62

MURACCIOLE L.,"LES CONSTITUTIONS DES ETATS   NAT/G
AFRICAINS D'EXPRESSION FRANCAISE: LA CONSTITUTION   CONSTN
DU 16 AVRIL 1962 DE LA REPUBLIQUE DU" AFR CHAD
CHIEF LEGIS LEGIT COLONIAL EXEC ROUTINE ORD/FREE
SOVEREIGN...SOC CONCPT 20. PAGE 76 B1541

S62

PIQUEMAL M.,"LES PROBLEMES DES UNIONS D'ETATS EN   AFR
AFRIQUE NOIRE." FRANCE SOCIETY INT/ORG NAT/G   ECO/UNDEV
DELIB/GP PLAN LEGIT ADMIN COLONIAL ROUTINE ATTIT   REGION
ORD/FREE PWR...GEOG METH/CNCPT 20. PAGE 83 B1678

S62

SPRINGER H.W.,"FEDERATION IN THE CARIBBEAN: AN   VOL/ASSN
ATTEMPT THAT FAILED." L/A+17C ECO/UNDEV INT/ORG   NAT/G
POL/PAR PROVS LEGIS CREATE PLAN LEGIT ADMIN FEDERAL REGION
ATTIT DRIVE PERSON ORD/FREE PWR...POLICY GEOG PSY
CONCPT OBS CARIBBEAN CMN/WLTH 20. PAGE 100 B2013

C62

DE GRAZIA A.,"POLITICAL BEHAVIOR (REV. ED.)" STRATA PHIL/SCI
POL/PAR LEAD LOBBY ROUTINE WAR CHOOSE REPRESENT   OP/RES
CONSEN ATTIT ORD/FREE BIBLIOG. PAGE 27 B0555   CONCPT

B63

BADI J.,THE GOVERNMENT OF THE STATE OF ISRAEL: A   NAT/G
CRITICAL ACCOUNT OF ITS PARLIAMENT, EXECUTIVE, AND   CONSTN
JUDICIARY. ISRAEL ECO/DEV CHIEF DELIB/GP LEGIS   EX/STRUC
DIPLOM CT/SYS INGP/REL PEACE ORD/FREE...BIBLIOG 20   POL/PAR
PARLIAMENT ARABS MIGRATION. PAGE 8 B0157

B63

BOISSIER P.,HISTORIE DU COMITE INTERNATIONAL DE LA   INT/ORG
CROIX ROUGE. MOD/EUR WOR-45 CONSULT FORCES PLAN   HEALTH
DIPLOM EDU/PROP ADMIN MORAL ORD/FREE...SOC CONCPT   ARMS/CONT
RECORD TIME/SEQ GEN/LAWS TOT/POP VAL/FREE 19/20.   WAR
PAGE 13 B0267

B63

BOWETT D.W.,THE LAW OF INTERNATIONAL INSTITUTIONS.   INT/ORG
WOR+45 WOR-45 CONSTN DELIB/GP EX/STRUC JUDGE   ADJUD
EDU/PROP LEGIT CT/SYS EXEC ROUTINE RIGID/FLEX   DIPLOM
ORD/FREE PWR...JURID CONCPT ORG/CHARTS GEN/METH
LEAGUE/NAT OAS OEEC 20 UN. PAGE 14 B0286

B63

BURRUS B.R.,ADMINSTRATIVE LAW AND LOCAL GOVERNMENT. EX/STRUC
USA+45 PROVS LEGIS LICENSE ADJUD ORD/FREE 20.   LOC/G
PAGE 17 B0356   JURID
                                                     CONSTN

B63

CONF ON FUTURE OF COMMONWEALTH,THE FUTURE OF THE   DIPLOM
COMMONWEALTH. UK ECO/UNDEV AGRI EDU/PROP ADMIN   RACE/REL
SOC/INTEG 20 COMMONWLTH. PAGE 23 B0460   ORD/FREE
                                                     TEC/DEV

B63

CROUCH W.W.,SOUTHERN CALIFORNIA METROPOLIS: A STUDY LOC/G
IN DEVELOPMENT OF GOVERNMENT FOR A METROPOLITAN   MUNIC
AREA. USA+45 USA-45 PROB/SOLV ADMIN LOBBY PARTIC   LEGIS
CENTRAL ORD/FREE PWR...BIBLIOG 20 PROGRSV/M.   DECISION
PAGE 25 B0510

B63

DE VRIES E.,SOCIAL ASPECTS OF ECONOMIC DEVELOPMENT   L/A+17C
IN LATIN AMERICA. CULTURE SOCIETY STRATA FINAN   ECO/UNDEV
INDUS INT/ORG DELIB/GP ACT/RES ECO/TAC EDU/PROP
ADMIN ATTIT SUPEGO HEALTH KNOWL ORD/FREE...SOC STAT
TREND ANTHOL TOT/POP VAL/FREE. PAGE 28 B0562

B63

FISHER S.N.,THE MILITARY IN THE MIDDLE EAST: EX/STRUC

PROBLEMS IN SOCIETY AND GOVERNMENT. ISLAM USA+45   FORCES
NAT/G DOMIN LEGIT COERCE ORD/FREE PWR...TIME/SEQ
VAL/FREE 20. PAGE 36 B0725

B63

FORTES A.B.,HISTORIA ADMINISTRATIVA, JUDICIARIA E   PROVS
ECLESIASTICA DO RIO GRANDE DO SUL. BRAZIL L/A+17C   ADMIN
LOC/G SECT COLONIAL CT/SYS ORD/FREE CATHISM 16/20.   JURID
PAGE 37 B0742

B63

HEUSSLER R.,YESTERDAY'S RULERS: THE MAKING OF THE   EX/STRUC
BRITISH COLONIAL SERVICE. AFR EUR+WWI UK STRATA   MORAL
SECT DELIB/GP PLAN DOMIN EDU/PROP ATTIT PERCEPT   ELITES
PERSON SUPEGO KNOWL ORD/FREE PWR...MGT SOC OBS INT
TIME/SEQ 20 CMN/WLTH. PAGE 49 B1000

B63

LEWIS J.W.,LEADERSHIP IN COMMUNIST CHINA. ASIA   POL/PAR
INTELL ECO/UNDEV LOC/G MUNIC NAT/G PROVS ECO/TAC   DOMIN
EDU/PROP LEGIT ADMIN COERCE ATTIT ORD/FREE PWR   ELITES
...INT TIME/SEQ CHARTS TOT/POP VAL/FREE. PAGE 65
B1304

B63

MAYNE R.,THE COMMUNITY OF EUROPE. UK CONSTN NAT/G   EUR+WWI
CONSULT DELIB/GP CREATE PLAN ECO/TAC LEGIT ADMIN   INT/ORG
ROUTINE ORD/FREE PWR WEALTH...CONCPT TIME/SEQ EEC   REGION
EURATOM 20. PAGE 71 B1436

B63

MONTER W.,THE GOVERNMENT OF GENEVA, 1536-1605   SECT
(DOCTORAL THESIS). SWITZERLND DIPLOM LEAD ORD/FREE   FINAN
SOVEREIGN 16/17 CALVIN/J ROME. PAGE 74 B1504   LOC/G
                                                     ADMIN

B63

ROBERT J.,LA MONARCHIE MAROCAINE. MOROCCO LABOR   CHIEF
MUNIC POL/PAR EX/STRUC ORD/FREE PWR...JURID TREND T CONSERVE
20. PAGE 89 B1793   ADMIN
                                                     CONSTN

B63

RUITENBEER H.M.,THE DILEMMA OF ORGANIZATIONAL   PERSON
SOCIETY. CULTURE ECO/DEV MUNIC SECT TEC/DEV   ROLE
EDU/PROP NAT/LISM ORD/FREE...NAT/COMP 20 RIESMAN/D   ADMIN
WHYTE/WF MERTON/R MEAD/MARG JASPERS/K. PAGE 92   WORKER
B1855

B63

TSOU T.,AMERICA'S FAILURE IN CHINA, 1941-1950.   ASIA
USA+45 USA-45 NAT/G ACT/RES PLAN DOMIN EDU/PROP   PERCEPT
ADMIN ROUTINE ATTIT PERSON ORD/FREE...DECISION   DIPLOM
CONCPT MYTH TIME/SEQ TREND STERTYP 20. PAGE 105
B2132

B63

US CONGRESS: SENATE,HEARINGS OF THE COMMITTEE ON   LEGIS
THE JUDICIARY. USA+45 CONSTN NAT/G ADMIN GOV/REL 20 LAW
CONGRESS. PAGE 108 B2179   ORD/FREE
                                                     DELIB/GP

B63

US SENATE COMM GOVT OPERATIONS,ADMINISTRATION OF   DELIB/GP
NATIONAL SECURITY (9 PARTS). ADMIN...INT REC/INT   NAT/G
CHARTS 20 SENATE CONGRESS. PAGE 110 B2213   OP/RES
                                                     ORD/FREE

B63

VAN SLYCK P.,PEACE: THE CONTROL OF NATIONAL POWER.   ARMS/CONT
CUBA WOR+45 FINAN NAT/G FORCES PROB/SOLV TEC/DEV   PEACE
BAL/PWR ADMIN CONTROL ORD/FREE...POLICY INT/LAW UN   INT/ORG
COLD/WAR TREATY. PAGE 112 B2253   DIPLOM

L63

BOLGAR V.,"THE PUBLIC INTEREST: A JURISPRUDENTIAL   CONCPT
AND COMPARATIVE OVERVIEW OF SYMPOSIUM ON   ORD/FREE
FUNDAMENTAL CONCEPTS OF PUBLIC LAW" COM FRANCE   CONTROL
GERMANY SWITZERLND LAW ADJUD ADMIN AGREE LAISSEZ   NAT/COMP
...JURID GEN/LAWS 20 EUROPE/E. PAGE 13 B0268

L63

LIVERNASH E.R.,"THE RELATION OF POWER TO THE   LABOR
STRUCTURE AND PROCESS OF COLLECTIVE BARGAINING."   GP/REL
ADJUD ORD/FREE...POLICY MGT CLASSIF GP/COMP.   PWR
PAGE 66 B1330   ECO/TAC

S63

BECHHOEFER B.G.,"UNITED NATIONS PROCEDURES IN CASE   INT/ORG
OF VIOLATIONS OF DISARMAMENT AGREEMENTS." COM   DELIB/GP
USA+45 USSR LAW CONSTN NAT/G EX/STRUC FORCES LEGIS
BAL/PWR EDU/PROP CT/SYS ARMS/CONT ORD/FREE PWR
...POLICY STERTYP UN VAL/FREE 20. PAGE 10 B0204

S63

BOWIE R.,"STRATEGY AND THE ATLANTIC ALLIANCE."   FORCES
EUR+WWI VOL/ASSN BAL/PWR COERCE NUC/PWR ATTIT   ROUTINE
ORD/FREE PWR...DECISION GEN/LAWS NATO COLD/WAR 20.
PAGE 14 B0287

S63

JOELSON M.R.,"THE DISMISSAL OF CIVIL SERVANTS IN   USA+45
THE INTERESTS OF NATIONAL SECURITY." EUR+WWI LAW   NAT/G
DELIB/GP ROUTINE ORD/FREE...MGT VAL/FREE 20.   UK
PAGE 56 B1141   FRANCE

S63

MORGENTHAU H.J.,"THE POLITICAL CONDITIONS FOR AN   INT/ORG
INTERNATIONAL POLICE FORCE." FUT WOR+45 CREATE   FORCES
LEGIT ADMIN PEACE ORD/FREE 20. PAGE 75 B1524   ARMS/CONT
                                                     DETER

S63

NYE J.S. JR.,"EAST AFRICAN ECONOMIC INTEGRATION."   ECO/UNDEV

AFR UGANDA PROVS DELIB/GP PLAN ECO/TAC INT/TRADE   INT/ORG
ADMIN ROUTINE ORD/FREE PWR WEALTH...OBS TIME/SEQ
VAL/FREE 20. PAGE 79 B1597
                                                            S63
RUSTOW D.A.,"THE MILITARY IN MIDDLE EASTERN SOCIETY   FORCES
AND POLITICS." FUT ISLAM CONSTN SOCIETY FACE/GP   ELITES
NAT/G POL/PAR PROF/ORG CONSULT DOMIN ADMIN EXEC
REGION COERCE NAT/LISM ATTIT DRIVE PERSON ORD/FREE
PWR...POLICY CONCPT OBS STERTYP 20. PAGE 92 B1860
                                                            S63
STANLEY T.W.,"DECENTRALIZING NUCLEAR CONTROL IN   INT/ORG
NATO." EUR+WWI USA+45 ELITES FORCES ACT/RES ATTIT   EX/STRUC
ORD/FREE PWR...NEW/IDEA HYPO/EXP TOT/POP 20 NATO.   NUC/PWR
PAGE 100 B2022
                                                            B64
ADAMS V.,THE PEACE CORPS IN ACTION. USA+45 VOL/ASSN   DIPLOM
EX/STRUC GOV/REL PERCEPT ORD/FREE...OBS 20   FOR/AID
KENNEDY/JF PEACE/CORP. PAGE 3 B0058   PERSON
                                                      DRIVE
                                                            B64
AVASTHI A.,ASPECTS OF ADMINISTRATION. INDIA UK   MGT
USA+45 FINAN ACADEM DELIB/GP LEGIS RECEIVE   ADMIN
PARL/PROC PRIVIL...NAT/COMP 20. PAGE 7 B0150   SOC/WK
                                                      ORD/FREE
                                                            B64
BLACKSTOCK P.W.,THE STRATEGY OF SUBVERSION. USA+45   ORD/FREE
FORCES EDU/PROP ADMIN COERCE GOV/REL...DECISION MGT   DIPLOM
20 DEPT/DEFEN CIA DEPT/STATE. PAGE 12 B0247   CONTROL
                                                            B64
BOTTOMORE T.B.,ELITES AND SOCIETY. INTELL STRATA   ELITES
ECO/DEV ECO/UNDEV ADMIN GP/REL ORD/FREE...CONCPT   IDEA/COMP
BIBLIOG 20. PAGE 14 B0281   SOCIETY
                                                      SOC
                                                            B64
COTTRELL A.J.,THE POLITICS OF THE ATLANTIC   VOL/ASSN
ALLIANCE. EUR+WWI USA+45 INT/ORG NAT/G DELIB/GP   FORCES
EX/STRUC BAL/PWR DIPLOM REGION DETER ATTIT ORD/FREE
...CONCPT RECORD GEN/LAWS GEN/METH NATO 20. PAGE 24
B0493
                                                            B64
ELDREDGE H.W.,THE SECOND AMERICAN REVOLUTION.   ELITES
EDU/PROP NAT/LISM RATIONAL TOTALSM FASCISM MARXISM   ORD/FREE
SOCISM. PAGE 33 B0664   ADMIN
                                                      PLAN
                                                            B64
FISK W.M.,ADMINISTRATIVE PROCEDURE IN A REGULATORY   SERV/IND
AGENCY: THE CAB AND THE NEW YORK-CHICAGO CASE   ECO/DEV
(PAMPHLET). USA+45 DIST/IND ADMIN CONTROL LOBBY   AIR
GP/REL ROLE ORD/FREE NEWYORK/C CHICAGO CAB. PAGE 36   JURID
B0727
                                                            B64
HALLER W.,DER SCHWEDISCHE JUSTITIEOMBUDSMAN.   JURID
DENMARK FINLAND NORWAY SWEDEN LEGIS ADJUD CONTROL   PARL/PROC
PERSON ORD/FREE...NAT/COMP 20 OMBUDSMAN. PAGE 46   ADMIN
B0926   CHIEF
                                                            B64
INDIAN COMM PREVENTION CORRUPT,REPORT, 1964. INDIA   CRIME
NAT/G GOV/REL ATTIT ORD/FREE...CRIMLGY METH 20.   ADMIN
PAGE 53 B1079   LEGIS
                                                      LOC/G
                                                            B64
JACKSON H.M.,THE SECRETARY OF STATE AND THE   GOV/REL
AMBASSADOR* JACKSON SUBCOMMITTEE PAPERS ON THE   DIPLOM
CONDUCT OF AMERICAN FOREIGN POLICY. USA+45 NAT/G   ADMIN
FORCES ACT/RES OP/RES EDU/PROP CENTRAL EFFICIENCY   EX/STRUC
ORD/FREE...OBS RECORD ANTHOL CONGRESS PRESIDENT.
PAGE 55 B1107
                                                            B64
JACKSON R.M.,THE MACHINERY OF JUSTICE IN ENGLAND.   CT/SYS
UK EDU/PROP CONTROL COST ORD/FREE...MGT 20   ADJUD
ENGLSH/LAW. PAGE 55 B1109   JUDGE
                                                      JURID
                                                            B64
KARIEL H.S.,IN SEARCH OF AUTHORITY: TWENTIETH-   CONSTN
CENTURY POLITICAL THOUGHT. WOR+45 WOR-45 NAT/G   CONCPT
EX/STRUC TOTALSM DRIVE PWR...MGT PHIL/SCI GEN/LAWS   ORD/FREE
19/20 NIETZSCH/F FREUD/S WEBER/MAX NIEBUHR/R   IDEA/COMP
MARITAIN/J. PAGE 58 B1173
                                                            B64
PRESS C.,A BIBLIOGRAPHIC INTRODUCTION TO AMERICAN   BIBLIOG
STATE GOVERNMENT AND POLITICS (PAMPHLET). USA+45   LEGIS
USA-45 EX/STRUC ADJUD INGP/REL FEDERAL ORD/FREE 20.   LOC/G
PAGE 84 B1701   POL/PAR
                                                            B64
RIKER W.H.,FEDERALISM. WOR+45 WOR-45 CONSTN CHIEF   FEDERAL
LEGIS ADMIN COLONIAL CONTROL CT/SYS PWR...BIBLIOG/A   NAT/G
18/20. PAGE 88 B1787   ORD/FREE
                                                      CENTRAL
                                                            B64
RUSSELL R.B.,UNITED NATIONS EXPERIENCE WITH   FORCES
MILITARY FORCES: POLITICAL AND LEGAL ASPECTS. AFR   DIPLOM
KOREA WOR+45 LEGIS PROB/SOLV ADMIN CONTROL   SANCTION
EFFICIENCY PEACE...POLICY INT/LAW BIBLIOG UN.   ORD/FREE
PAGE 92 B1857
                                                            B64
SHERIDAN R.G.,URBAN JUSTICE. USA+45 PROVS CREATE   LOC/G

ADMIN CT/SYS ORD/FREE 20 TENNESSEE. PAGE 96 B1943   JURID
                                                      ADJUD
                                                      MUNIC
                                                            B64
TOMPKINS D.C.,PROBATION SINCE WORLD WAR II. USA+45   BIBLIOG
FORCES ADMIN ROUTINE PERS/REL AGE...CRIMLGY HEAL   PUB/INST
20. PAGE 105 B2118   ORD/FREE
                                                      CRIME
                                                            B64
US SENATE COMM GOVT OPERATIONS,ADMINISTRATION OF   ADMIN
NATIONAL SECURITY. USA+45 CHIEF TOP/EX PLAN DIPLOM   FORCES
CONTROL PEACE...POLICY DECISION 20 PRESIDENT   ORD/FREE
CONGRESS. PAGE 110 B2216   NAT/G
                                                            B64
WAINHOUSE D.W.,REMNANTS OF EMPIRE: THE UNITED   INT/ORG
NATIONS AND THE END OF COLONIALISM. FUT PORTUGAL   TREND
WOR+45 NAT/G CONSULT DOMIN LEGIT ADMIN ROUTINE   COLONIAL
ATTIT ORD/FREE...POLICY JURID RECORD INT TIME/SEQ
UN CMN/WLTH 20. PAGE 113 B2275
                                                            B64
WHEELER-BENNETT J.W.,THE NEMESIS OF POWER (2ND   FORCES
ED.). EUR+WWI GERMANY TOP/EX TEC/DEV ADMIN WAR   NAT/G
PERS/REL RIGID/FLEX ROLE ORD/FREE PWR FASCISM 20   GP/REL
HITLER/A. PAGE 116 B2332   STRUCT
                                                            L64
MACKINTOSH J.P.,"NIGERIA'S EXTERNAL AFFAIRS." UK   AFR
CULTURE ECO/UNDEV NAT/G VOL/ASSN EDU/PROP LEGIT   DIPLOM
ADMIN ATTIT ORD/FREE PWR 20. PAGE 68 B1365   NIGERIA
                                                            L64
SYMONDS R.,"REFLECTIONS IN LOCALISATION." AFR   ADMIN
S/ASIA UK STRATA INT/ORG NAT/G SCHOOL EDU/PROP   MGT
LEGIT KNOWL ORD/FREE PWR RESPECT CMN/WLTH 20.   COLONIAL
PAGE 102 B2064
                                                            L64
WORLD PEACE FOUNDATION,"INTERNATIONAL   INT/ORG
ORGANIZATIONS: SUMMARY OF ACTIVITIES." INDIA   ROUTINE
PAKISTAN TURKEY WOR+45 CONSTN CONSULT EX/STRUC
ECO/TAC EDU/PROP LEGIT ORD/FREE...JURID SOC UN 20
CYPRESS. PAGE 118 B2375
                                                            S64
CLIGNET R.,"POTENTIAL ELITES IN GHANA AND THE IVORY   PWR
COAST: A PRELIMINARY SURVEY." AFR CULTURE ELITES   LEGIT
STRATA KIN NAT/G SECT DOMIN EXEC ORD/FREE RESPECT   IVORY/CST
SKILL...POLICY RELATIV GP/COMP NAT/COMP 20. PAGE 21   GHANA
B0438
                                                            S64
GALTUNE J.,"BALANCE OF POWER AND THE PROBLEM OF   PWR
PERCEPTION, A LOGICAL ANALYSIS." WOR+45 CONSTN   PSY
SOCIETY NAT/G DELIB/GP EX/STRUC LEGIS DOMIN ADMIN   ARMS/CONT
COERCE DRIVE ORD/FREE...POLICY CONCPT OBS TREND   WAR
GEN/LAWS. PAGE 38 B0778
                                                            S64
HOSCH L.G.,"PUBLIC ADMINISTRATION ON THE   INT/ORG
INTERNATIONAL FRONTIER." WOR+45 R+D NAT/G EDU/PROP   MGT
EXEC KNOWL ORD/FREE VAL/FREE 20 UN. PAGE 52 B1046
                                                            S64
KASSOF A.,"THE ADMINISTERED SOCIETY: SOCIETY
TOTALITARIANISM WITHOUT TERROR." COM USSR STRATA   DOMIN
AGRI INDUS NAT/G PERF/ART SCHOOL TOP/EX EDU/PROP   TOTALSM
ADMIN ORD/FREE PWR...POLICY SOC TIME/SEQ GEN/LAWS
VAL/FREE 20. PAGE 58 B1178
                                                            S64
LOW D.A.,"LION RAMPANT." EUR+WWI MOD/EUR S/ASIA   AFR
ECO/UNDEV NAT/G FORCES TEC/DEV ECO/TAC LEGIT ADMIN   DOMIN
COLONIAL COERCE ORD/FREE RESPECT 19/20. PAGE 67   DIPLOM
B1344   UK
                                                            S64
RIGBY T.H.,"TRADITIONAL, MARKET, AND ORGANIZATIONAL   MARKET
SOCIETIES AND THE USSR." COM ECO/DEV NAT/G POL/PAR   ADMIN
ECO/TAC DOMIN ORD/FREE PWR WEALTH...TIME/SEQ   USSR
GEN/LAWS VAL/FREE 20 STALIN/J. PAGE 88 B1784
                                                            S64
SCHWELB E.,"OPERATION OF THE EUROPEAN CONVENTION ON   INT/ORG
HUMAN RIGHTS." EUR+WWI LAW SOCIETY CREATE EDU/PROP   MORAL
ADJUD ADMIN PEACE ATTIT ORD/FREE PWR...POLICY
INT/LAW CONCPT OBS GEN/LAWS UN VAL/FREE ILO 20
ECHR. PAGE 95 B1916
                                                            S64
THOMPSON V.A.,"ADMINISTRATIVE OBJECTIVES FOR   ECO/UNDEV
DEVELOPMENT ADMINISTRATION." WOR+45 CREATE PLAN   MGT
DOMIN EDU/PROP EXEC ROUTINE ATTIT ORD/FREE PWR
...POLICY GEN/LAWS VAL/FREE. PAGE 104 B2107
                                                            B65
AIYAR S.P.,STUDIES IN INDIAN DEMOCRACY. INDIA   ORD/FREE
STRATA ECO/UNDEV LABOR POL/PAR LEGIS DIPLOM LOBBY   REPRESENT
REGION CHOOSE ATTIT SOCISM...ANTHOL 20. PAGE 3   ADMIN
B0067   NAT/G
                                                            B65
BERNDT R.M.,ABORIGINAL MAN IN AUSTRALIA. LAW DOMIN   SOC
ADMIN COLONIAL MARRIAGE HABITAT ORD/FREE...LING   CULTURE
CHARTS ANTHOL BIBLIOG WORSHIP 20 AUSTRAL ABORIGINES   SOCIETY
MUSIC ELKIN/AP. PAGE 11 B0225   STRUCT
                                                            B65
BOCK E.,GOVERNMENT REGULATION OF BUSINESS. USA+45   MGT
LAW EX/STRUC LEGIS EXEC ORD/FREE PWR...ANTHOL   ADMIN
CONGRESS. PAGE 13 B0261   NAT/G

DE GRAZIA A.,REPUBLIC IN CRISIS: CONGRESS AGAINST THE EXECUTIVE FORCE. USA+45 USA-45 SOCIETY POL/PAR CHIEF DOMIN ROLE ORD/FREE PWR...CONCPT MYTH BIBLIOG 20 CONGRESS. PAGE 27 B0556
CONTROL
B65
LEGIS
EXEC
GOV/REL
CONTROL
B65

GOTLIEB A.,DISARMAMENT AND INTERNATIONAL LAW* A STUDY OF THE ROLE OF LAW IN THE DISARMAMENT PROCESS. USA+45 USSR PROB/SOLV CONFER ADMIN ROUTINE NUC/PWR ORD/FREE SOVEREIGN UN TREATY. PAGE 42 B0841
INT/LAW
INT/ORG
ARMS/CONT
IDEA/COMP
B65

KOUSOULAS D.G.,REVOLUTION AND DEFEAT; THE STORY OF THE GREEK COMMUNIST PARTY. GREECE INT/ORG EX/STRUC DIPLOM FOR/AID EDU/PROP PARL/PROC ADJUST ATTIT 20 COM/PARTY. PAGE 61 B1230
REV
MARXISM
POL/PAR
ORD/FREE
B65

KRIESBERG M.,PUBLIC ADMINISTRATION IN DEVELOPING COUNTRIES: PROCEEDINGS OF AN INTERNATIONAL CONFERENCE HELD IN BOGOTA, COLUMBIA,1963. FUT EDU/PROP ORD/FREE...MGT 20 CIVIL/SERV. PAGE 61 B1237
NAT/G
ECO/UNDEV
SOCIETY
ADMIN
B65

LAMBIRI I.,SOCIAL CHANGE IN A GREEK COUNTRY TOWN. GREECE FAM PROB/SOLV ROUTINE TASK LEISURE INGP/REL CONSEN ORD/FREE...SOC INT QU CHARTS 20. PAGE 62 B1252
INDUS
WORKER
CULTURE
NEIGH
B65

LEMAY G.H.,BRITISH SUPREMACY IN SOUTH AFRICA 1899-1907. SOUTH/AFR UK ADMIN CONTROL LEAD GP/REL ORD/FREE 19/20. PAGE 64 B1286
WAR
COLONIAL
DOMIN
POLICY
B65

LUTZ V.,FRENCH PLANNING. FRANCE TEC/DEV RIGID/FLEX ORD/FREE 20. PAGE 67 B1348
PLAN
ADMIN
FUT
B65

MACDONALD R.W.,THE LEAGUE OF ARAB STATES: A STUDY IN THE DYNAMICS OF REGIONAL ORGANIZATION. ISRAEL UAR USSR FINAN INT/ORG DELIB/GP ECO/TAC AGREE NEUTRAL ORD/FREE PWR...DECISION BIBLIOG 20 TREATY UN. PAGE 67 B1358
ISLAM
REGION
DIPLOM
ADMIN
B65

MOORE W.E.,THE IMPACT OF INDUSTRY. CULTURE STRUCT ORD/FREE...TREND 20. PAGE 75 B1516
INDUS
MGT
TEC/DEV
ECO/UNDEV
B65

OLSON M. JR.,DROIT PUBLIC. FRANCE NAT/G LEGIS SUFF GP/REL PRIVIL...TREND 18/20. PAGE 80 B1609
CONSTN
FINAN
ADMIN
ORD/FREE
B65

PARRISH W.E.,MISSOURI UNDER RADICAL RULE 1865-1870. USA-45 SOCIETY INDUS LOC/G POL/PAR WORKER EDU/PROP SUFF INGP/REL ATTIT...BIBLIOG 19 NEGRO MISSOURI. PAGE 81 B1635
PROVS
USA-45
RACE/REL
ORD/FREE
B65

PURCELL V.,THE MEMOIRS OF A MALAYAN OFFICIAL. MALAYSIA UK ECO/UNDEV INDUS LABOR EDU/PROP COLONIAL CT/SYS WAR NAT/LISM TOTALISM ORD/FREE SOVEREIGN 20 UN CIVIL/SERV. PAGE 85 B1721
BIOG
ADMIN
JURID
FORCES
B65

RUBIN H.,PENSIONS AND EMPLOYEE MOBILITY IN THE PUBLIC SERVICE. USA+45 WORKER PERSON ORD/FREE...SOC QU. PAGE 91 B1849
ADMIN
NAT/G
LOC/G
SENIOR
B65

RUBINSTEIN A.Z.,THE CHALLENGE OF POLITICS: IDEAS AND ISSUES (2ND ED.). UNIV ELITES SOCIETY EX/STRUC BAL/PWR PARL/PROC AUTHORIT...DECISION ANTHOL 20. PAGE 92 B1852
NAT/G
DIPLOM
GP/REL
ORD/FREE
B65

STEINER K.,LOCAL GOVERNMENT IN JAPAN. CONSTN CULTURE NAT/G ADMIN CHOOSE...SOC STAT 20 CHINJAP. PAGE 100 B2030
LOC/G
SOCIETY
JURID
ORD/FREE
B65

US SENATE COMM GOVT OPERATIONS,ADMINISTRATION OF NATIONAL SECURITY. USA+45 DELIB/GP ADMIN ROLE ...POLICY CHARTS SENATE. PAGE 110 B2218
NAT/G
ORD/FREE
DIPLOM
PROB/SOLV
B65

VAID K.N.,STATE AND LABOR IN INDIA. INDIA INDUS WORKER PAY PRICE ADJUD CONTROL PARL/PROC GP/REL ORD/FREE 20. PAGE 111 B2248
LAW
LABOR
MGT
NEW/LIB
L65

HOOK S.,"SECOND THOUGHTS ON BERKELEY" USA+45 ELITES INTELL LEGIT ADMIN COERCE REPRESENT GP/REL INGP/REL TOTALISM AGE/Y MARXISM 20 BERKELEY FREE/SPEE STUDNT/PWR. PAGE 51 B1040
ACADEM
ORD/FREE
POLICY
CREATE
L65

RUBIN A.P.,"UNITED STATES CONTEMPORARY PRACTICE RELATING TO INTERNATIONAL LAW." USA+45 WOR+45 CONSTN INT/ORG NAT/G DELIB/GP EX/STRUC DIPLOM DOMIN
LAW
LEGIT
INT/LAW

CT/SYS ROUTINE ORD/FREE...CONCPT COLD/WAR 20. PAGE 91 B1848
S65

BROWN S.,"AN ALTERNATIVE TO THE GRAND DESIGN." EUR+WWI FUT USA+45 INT/ORG NAT/G EX/STRUC FORCES CREATE BAL/PWR DOMIN RIGID/FLEX ORD/FREE PWR ...NEW/IDEA RECORD EEC NATO 20. PAGE 16 B0327
VOL/ASSN
CONCPT
DIPLOM
S65

QUADE Q.L.,"THE TRUMAN ADMINISTRATION AND THE SEPARATION OF POWERS: THE CASE OF THE MARSHALL PLAN." SOCIETY INT/ORG NAT/G CONSULT DELIB/GP LEGIS PLAN ECO/TAC ROUTINE DRIVE PERCEPT RIGID/FLEX ORD/FREE PWR WEALTH...DECISION GEOG NEW/IDEA TREND 20 TRUMAN/HS. PAGE 85 B1726
USA+45
ECO/UNDEV
DIPLOM
S65

ALI S.,PLANNING, DEVELOPMENT AND CHANGE: AN ANNOTATED BIBLIOGRAPHY ON DEVELOPMENTAL ADMINISTRATION. PAKISTAN SOCIETY ORD/FREE 20. PAGE 4 B0077
BIBLIOG/A
ADMIN
ECO/UNDEV
PLAN
B66

BARBER W.F.,INTERNAL SECURITY AND MILITARY POWER* COUNTERINSURGENCY AND CIVIC ACTION IN LATIN AMERICA. ECO/UNDEV CREATE ADMIN REV ATTIT RIGID/FLEX MARXISM...INT BIBLIOG OAS. PAGE 9 B0183
L/A+17C
FORCES
ORD/FREE
TASK
B66

BIRKHEAD G.S.,ADMINISTRATIVE PROBLEMS IN PAKISTAN. PAKISTAN AGRI FINAN INDUS LG/CO ECO/TAC CONTROL PWR ...CHARTS ANTHOL 20. PAGE 12 B0241
ADMIN
NAT/G
ORD/FREE
ECO/UNDEV
B66

DAHLBERG J.S.,THE NEW YORK BUREAU OF MUNICIPAL RESEARCH: PIONEER IN GOVERNMENT ADMINISTRATION. CONSTN R+D BUDGET EDU/PROP PARTIC REPRESENT EFFICIENCY ORD/FREE...BIBLIOG METH 20 NEW/YORK NIPA. PAGE 26 B0522
PROVS
MUNIC
DELIB/GP
ADMIN
B66

HIDAYATULLAH M.,DEMOCRACY IN INDIA AND THE JUDICIAL PROCESS. INDIA EX/STRUC LEGIS LEAD GOV/REL ATTIT ORD/FREE...MAJORIT CONCPT 20 NEHRU/J. PAGE 50 B1007
NAT/G
CT/SYS
CONSTN
JURID
B66

JOHNSON N.,PARLIAMENT AND ADMINISTRATION: THE ESTIMATES COMMITTEE 1945-65. FUT UK NAT/G EX/STRUC PLAN BUDGET ORD/FREE...T 20 PARLIAMENT HOUSE/CMNS. PAGE 57 B1147
LEGIS
ADMIN
FINAN
DELIB/GP
B66

KAUNDA K.,ZAMBIA: INDEPENDENCE AND BEYOND: THE SPEECHES OF KENNETH KAUNDA. AFR FUT ZAMBIA SOCIETY ECO/UNDEV NAT/G PROB/SOLV ECO/TAC ADMIN RACE/REL SOVEREIGN 20. PAGE 59 B1183
ORD/FREE
COLONIAL
CONSTN
LEAD
B66

MCKENZIE J.L.,AUTHORITY IN THE CHURCH. STRUCT LEAD INGP/REL PERS/REL CENTRAL ANOMIE ATTIT ORD/FREE RESPECT CATH. PAGE 72 B1452
SECT
AUTHORIT
PWR
ADMIN
B66

MONTGOMERY J.D.,APPROACHES TO DEVELOPMENT: POLITICS, ADMINISTRATION AND CHANGE. USA+45 AGRI FOR/AID ORD/FREE...CONCPT IDEA/COMP METH/COMP ANTHOL. PAGE 75 B1507
ECO/UNDEV
ADMIN
POLICY
ECO/TAC
B66

PERKINS J.A.,THE UNIVERSITY IN TRANSITION. USA+45 SOCIETY FINAN INDUS NAT/G EX/STRUC ADMIN INGP/REL COST EFFICIENCY ATTIT 20. PAGE 82 B1658
ACADEM
ORD/FREE
CREATE
ROLE
B66

US SENATE COMM ON FOREIGN REL,HEARINGS ON S 2859 AND S 2861. USA+45 WOR+45 FORCES BUDGET CAP/ISM ADMIN DETER WEAPON TOTALISM...NAT/COMP 20 UN CONGRESS. PAGE 110 B2221
FOR/AID
DIPLOM
ORD/FREE
ECO/UNDEV
B66

VON HOFFMAN N.,THE MULTIVERSITY; A PERSONAL REPORT ON WHAT HAPPENS TO TODAY'S STUDENTS AT AMERICAN UNIVERSITIES. USA+45 SOCIETY ROUTINE ANOMIE ROLE MORAL ORD/FREE SKILL...INT 20. PAGE 112 B2266
EDU/PROP
ACADEM
ATTIT
STRANGE
B66

WILSON G.,CASES AND MATERIALS ON CONSTITUTIONAL AND ADMINISTRATIVE LAW. UK LAW NAT/G EX/STRUC LEGIS BAL/PWR BUDGET DIPLOM ADJUD CONTROL CT/SYS GOV/REL ORD/FREE 20 PARLIAMENT ENGLSH/LAW. PAGE 117 B2359
JURID
ADMIN
CONSTN
PWR
B66

ZINKIN T.,CHALLENGES IN INDIA. INDIA PAKISTAN LAW AGRI FINAN INDUS TOP/EX TEC/DEV CONTROL ROUTINE ORD/FREE PWR 20 NEHRU/J SHASTRI/LB CIVIL/SERV. PAGE 119 B2404
NAT/G
ECO/TAC
POLICY
ADMIN
S66

JACOBSON J.,"COALITIONISM: FROM PROTEST TO POLITICKING" USA+45 ELITES NAT/G POL/PAR PROB/SOLV ADMIN LEAD DISCRIM ORD/FREE PWR CONSERVE 20 NEGRO AFL/CIO CIV/RIGHTS BLACK/PWR. PAGE 55 B1116
RACE/REL
LABOR
SOCIALIST
VOL/ASSN
C66

TARLING N.,"A CONCISE HISTORY OF SOUTHEAST ASIA." BURMA CAMBODIA LAOS S/ASIA THAILAND VIETNAM ECO/UNDEV POL/PAR FORCES ADMIN REV WAR CIVMIL/REL ORD/FREE MARXISM SOCISM 13/20. PAGE 103 B2080
COLONIAL
DOMIN
INT/TRADE
NAT/LISM

ANGEL D.D.,ROMNEY. LABOR LG/CO NAT/G EXEC WAR
RACE/REL PERSON ORD/FREE...MGT WORSHIP 20
ROMNEY/GEO CIV/RIGHTS MORMON GOVERNOR. PAGE 5 B0108
BIOG
CHIEF
PROVS
POLICY
B67

DE BLIJ H.J.,SYSTEMATIC POLITICAL GEOGRAPHY. WOR+45
STRUCT INT/ORG NAT/G EDU/PROP ADMIN COLONIAL
ROUTINE ORD/FREE PWR...IDEA/COMP T 20. PAGE 27
B0550
GEOG
CONCPT
METH
B67

EVANS R.H.,COEXISTENCE: COMMUNISM AND ITS PRACTICE
IN BOLOGNA, 1945-1965. ITALY CAP/ISM ADMIN CHOOSE
PEACE NAT/G ORD/FREE...SOC STAT DEEP/INT SAMP CHARTS
BIBLIOG 20. PAGE 34 B0690
MARXISM
CULTURE
MUNIC
POL/PAR
B67

GREENE L.S.,AMERICAN GOVERNMENT POLICIES AND
FUNCTIONS. USA+45 LAW AGRI DIST/IND LABOR MUNIC
BUDGET DIPLOM EDU/PROP ORD/FREE...BIBLIOG T 20.
PAGE 43 B0867
POLICY
NAT/G
ADMIN
DECISION
B67

LENG S.C.,JUSTICE IN COMMUNIST CHINA: A SURVEY OF
THE JUDICIAL SYSTEM OF THE CHINESE PEOPLE'S
REPUBLIC. CHINA/COM LAW CONSTN LOC/G NAT/G PROF/ORG
CONSULT FORCES ADMIN CRIME ORD/FREE...BIBLIOG 20
MAO. PAGE 64 B1290
CT/SYS
ADJUD
JURID
MARXISM
B67

PAULSEN F.R.,AMERICAN EDUCATION: CHALLENGES AND
IMAGES. FUT USA+45 ADMIN AGE/C AGE/Y SUPEGO HEALTH
...ANTHOL 20. PAGE 81 B1644
EDU/PROP
SCHOOL
ORD/FREE
GOV/REL
B67

PLANO J.C.,FORGING WORLD ORDER: THE POLITICS OF
INTERNATIONAL ORGANIZATION. PROB/SOLV DIPLOM
CONTROL CENTRAL RATIONAL ORD/FREE...INT/LAW CHARTS
BIBLIOG 20 UN LEAGUE/NAT. PAGE 83 B1679
INT/ORG
ADMIN
JURID
B67

US DEPARTMENT HEALTH EDUC WELF,NEW PROGRAMS IN
HEALTH, EDUCATION, WELFARE, HOUSING AND URBAN
DEVELOPMENT FOR PERSONS AND FAMILIES -LOW, MOD,
INCOME. USA+45 MUNIC NAT/G EDU/PROP GOV/REL
INGP/REL ORD/FREE 20 DEPT/HEW DEPT/HUD. PAGE 108
B2180
ADMIN
HEALTH
SCHOOL
HABITAT
B67

US DEPARTMENT OF THE ARMY,CIVILIAN IN PEACE,
SOLDIER IN WAR: A BIBLIOGRAPHIC SURVEY OF THE ARMY
AND AIR NATIONAL GUARD (PAMPHLET, NOS. 130-2).
USA+45 USA-45 LOC/G NAT/G PROVS LEGIS PLAN ADMIN
ATTIT ORD/FREE...POLICY 19/20. PAGE 108 B2185
BIBLIOG/A
FORCES
ROLE
DIPLOM
B67

US SENATE COMM ON FOREIGN REL,HUMAN RIGHTS
CONVENTIONS. USA+45 LABOR VOL/ASSN DELIB/GP DOMIN
ADJUD REPRESENT...INT/LAW MGT CONGRESS. PAGE 110
B2225
LEGIS
ORD/FREE
WORKER
LOBBY
B67

WESTON P.B.,THE ADMINISTRATION OF JUSTICE. USA+45
CONSTN MUNIC NAT/G PROVS EX/STRUC JUDGE ADMIN
CONTROL SANCTION ORD/FREE...CHARTS 20. PAGE 115
B2328
CRIME
CT/SYS
JURID
ADJUD
L67

"RESTRICTIVE SOVEREIGN IMMUNITY, THE STATE
DEPARTMENT, AND THE COURTS." USA+45 USA-45 EX/STRUC
DIPLOM ADJUD CONTROL GOV/REL 19/20 DEPT/STATE
SUPREME/CT. PAGE 2 B0047
SOVEREIGN
ORD/FREE
PRIVIL
CT/SYS
L67

ROBERTS J.C.,"CIVIL RESTRAINT, MENTAL ILLNESS, AND
THE RIGHT TO TREATMENT." PROB/SOLV ADMIN PERSON
HEAL. PAGE 89 B1795
HEALTH
ORD/FREE
COERCE
LAW
S67

BRADLEY A.W.,"CONSTITUTION-MAKING IN UGANDA."
UGANDA LAW CHIEF DELIB/GP LEGIS ADMIN EXEC
PARL/PROC RACE/REL ORD/FREE...GOV/COMP 20. PAGE 14
B0295
NAT/G
CREATE
CONSTN
FEDERAL
S67

BREGMAN A.,"WHITHER RUSSIA?" COM RUSSIA INTELL
POL/PAR DIPLOM PARTIC NAT/LISM TOTALISM ATTIT
ORD/FREE 20. PAGE 15 B0304
MARXISM
ELITES
ADMIN
CREATE
S67

CHAMBERLAIN N.W.,"STRIKES IN CONTEMPORARY CONTEXT."
LAW INDUS NAT/G CHIEF CONFER COST ATTIT ORD/FREE
...POLICY MGT 20. PAGE 20 B0400
LABOR
BARGAIN
EFFICIENCY
PROB/SOLV
S67

DONNELL J.C.,"PACIFICATION REASSESSED." VIETNAM/S
NAT/LISM DRIVE SUPEGO ORD/FREE...SOC/WK 20. PAGE 30
B0606
ADMIN
GP/REL
EFFICIENCY
MUNIC
S67

DRAPER A.P.,"UNIONS AND THE WAR IN VIETNAM." USA+45
CONFER ADMIN LEAD WAR ORD/FREE PACIFIST 20. PAGE 30
B0616
LABOR
PACIFISM
ATTIT
ELITES
S67

FABREGA J.,"ANTECEDENTES EXTRANJEROS EN LA
CONSTN

CONSTITUCION PANAMENA." CUBA L/A+17C PANAMA URUGUAY
EX/STRUC LEGIS DIPLOM ORD/FREE 19/20 COLOMB
MEXIC/AMER. PAGE 34 B0694
JURID
NAT/G
PARL/PROC
S67

GORMAN W.,"ELLUL - A PROPHETIC VOICE." WOR+45
ELITES SOCIETY ACT/RES PLAN BAL/PWR DOMIN CONTROL
PARTIC TOTALISM PWR 20. PAGE 41 B0837
CREATE
ORD/FREE
EX/STRUC
UTOPIA
S67

HALL B.,"THE COALITION AGAINST DISHWASHERS." USA+45
POL/PAR PROB/SOLV BARGAIN LEAD CHOOSE REPRESENT
GP/REL ORD/FREE PWR...POLICY 20. PAGE 46 B0923
LABOR
ADMIN
DOMIN
WORKER
S67

HUGON P.,"BLOCAGES ET DESEQUILIBRES DE LA
CROISSANCE ECONOMIQUE EN AFRIQUE NOIRE." AFR KIN
MUNIC CREATE PLAN INT/TRADE REGION ADJUST CENTRAL
EQUILIB NAT/LISM ORD/FREE 20. PAGE 52 B1060
ECO/UNDEV
COLONIAL
STRUCT
ADMIN
S67

LIU K.C.,"DISINTEGRATION OF THE OLD ORDER." ASIA
SOCIETY PROB/SOLV ADMIN REGION TOTALISM ORD/FREE
MARXISM 19/20. PAGE 66 B1329
ADJUST
NAT/LISM
S67

LLOYD K.,"URBAN RACE RIOTS V EFFECTIVE ANTI-
DISCRIMINATION AGENCIES* AN END OR A BEGINNING?"
USA+45 STRATA ACT/RES ADMIN ADJUST ORD/FREE RESPECT
...PLURIST DECISION SOC SOC/WK. PAGE 66 B1332
GP/REL
DISCRIM
LOC/G
CROWD
S67

MONEYPENNY P.,"UNIVERSITY PURPOSE, DISCIPLINE, AND
DUE PROCESS." USA+45 EDU/PROP ADJUD LEISURE
ORD/FREE. PAGE 74 B1500
ACADEM
AGE/Y
CONTROL
ADMIN
S67

SMITH W.H.T.,"THE IMPLICATIONS OF THE AMERICAN BAR
ASSOCIATION ADVISORY COMMITTEE RECOMMENDATIONS FOR
POLICE ADMINISTRATION." ADMIN...JURID 20 ABA.
PAGE 98 B1986
EDU/PROP
CONTROL
GP/REL
ORD/FREE
S67

TURNER F.C. JR.,"EXPERIMENT IN INTER-AMERICAN
PEACE-KEEPING." DOMIN/REP ADMIN ROUTINE REV
ORD/FREE OAS 20. PAGE 106 B2137
FORCES
ADJUD
PEACE
S67

ZASLOW M.,"RECENT CONSTITUTIONAL DEVELOPMENTS IN
CANADA'S NORTHERN TERRITORIES." CANADA LOC/G
DELIB/GP EX/STRUC LEGIS ADMIN ORD/FREE...TREND 20.
PAGE 119 B2398
GOV/REL
REGION
CONSTN
FEDERAL
B82

MACDONALD D.,AFRICANA; OR, THE HEART OF HEATHEN
AFRICA, VOL. II: MISSION LIFE. SOCIETY STRATA KIN
CREATE EDU/PROP ADMIN COERCE LITERACY HEALTH...MYTH
WORSHIP 19 LIVNGSTN/D MISSION NEGRO. PAGE 67 B1355
SECT
AFR
CULTURE
ORD/FREE
L86

GOODNOW F.J.,"AN EXECUTIVE AND THE COURTS: JUDICIAL
REMEDIES AGAINST ADMINISTRATIVE ACTION" FRANCE UK
USA-45 WOR-45 LAW CONSTN SANCTION ORD/FREE 19.
PAGE 41 B0823
CT/SYS
GOV/REL
ADMIN
ADJUD
B98

THOMPSON H.C.,RHODESIA AND ITS GOVERNMENT. AFR
RHODESIA ECO/UNDEV INDUS KIN WORKER INT/TRADE
DISCRIM LITERACY ORD/FREE 19. PAGE 104 B2102
COLONIAL
ADMIN
POLICY
ELITES

ORDER....SEE ORD/FREE

OREGON....OREGON

ORG FOR ECO COOP AND DEVEL B1614,B1615

ORG/CHARTS....ORGANIZATIONAL CHARTS, BLUEPRINTS

ORGANIZATION FOR AFRICAN UNITY....SEE OAU

ORGANIZATION FOR ECONOMIC COOPERATION AND DEVELOPMENT....
     SEE OECD

ORGANIZATION FOR EUROPEAN ECONOMIC COOPERATION....SEE OEEC

ORGANIZATION FOR LATIN AMERICAN SOLIDARITY....SEE OLAS

ORGANIZATION OF AFRICAN STATES.... SEE AFR/STATES

ORGANIZATION OF AMERICAN STATES....SEE OAS

ORGANIZATION, INTERNATIONAL....SEE INT/ORG

ORGANIZATION, LABOR....SEE LABOR

ORGANIZATION, POLITICAL....SEE POL/PAR

ORGANIZATION, PROFESSIONAL....SEE PROF/ORG

ORGANIZATION, VOLUNTARY....SEE VOL/ASSN

ORGANIZATIONAL BEHAVIOR, NONEXECUTIVE....SEE ADMIN

ORGANIZATIONAL CHARTS....SEE ORG/CHARTS

ORTH C.D. B1052,B1616

ORTHO/GK....GREEK ORTHODOX CHURCH

ORTHO/RUSS....RUSSIAN ORTHODOX CATHOLIC

ORTHODOX EASTERN CHURCH....SEE ORTHO/GK

ORTIZ R.P. B1617

ORWELL/G....GEORGE ORWELL

OSHOGBO....OSHOGBO, WEST AFRICA

OSSIPOV G. B1102

OSTGAARD E. B1618

OTTOMAN....OTTOMAN EMPIRE

                                          L56

EISENTADT S.N.,"POLITICAL STRUGGLE IN BUREAUCRATIC ADMIN
SOCIETIES" ASIA CULTURE ADJUD SANCTION PWR CHIEF
BUREAUCRCY OTTOMAN BYZANTINE. PAGE 33 B0661 CONTROL
ROUTINE
B58

SHAW S.J.,THE FINANCIAL AND ADMINISTRATIVE FINAN
ORGANIZATION AND DEVELOPMENT OF OTTOMAN EGYPT ADMIN
1517-1798. UAR LOC/G FORCES BUDGET INT/TRADE TAX GOV/REL
EATING INCOME WEALTH...CHARTS BIBLIOG 16/18 OTTOMAN CULTURE
NAPOLEON/B. PAGE 96 B1940

OUTER SPACE....SEE SPACE

OUTER/MONG....OUTER MONGOLIA

OVERSEAS DEVELOPMENT INSTITUTE....SEE OVRSEA/DEV

OVERSEAS DEVELOPMENT INSTIT B1619

OVIMBUNDU....OVIMBUNDU PEOPLES OF ANGOLA

OVRSEA/DEV....OVERSEAS DEVELOPMENT INSTITUTE

                                          B66

HAYER T.,FRENCH AID. AFR FRANCE AGRI FINAN BUDGET TEC/DEV
ADMIN WAR PRODUC...CHARTS 18/20 THIRD/WRLD COLONIAL
OVRSEA/DEV. PAGE 48 B0975 FOR/AID
ECO/UNDEV

OWEN G. B1620

OWEN/RBT....ROBERT OWEN

OWI....OFFICE OF WAR INFORMATION

OWN....OWNERSHIP, OWNER

                                          N

US SUPERINTENDENT OF DOCUMENTS,TARIFF AND TAXATION BIBLIOG/A
(PRICE LIST 37). USA+45 LAW INT/TRADE ADJUD ADMIN TAX
CT/SYS INCOME OWN...DECISION GATT. PAGE 111 B2242 TARIFFS
NAT/G
B31

BORCHARD E.H.,GUIDE TO THE LAW AND LEGAL LITERATURE BIBLIOG/A
OF FRANCE. FRANCE FINAN INDUS LABOR SECT LEGIS LAW
ADMIN COLONIAL CRIME OWN...INT/LAW 20. PAGE 14 CONSTN
B0277 METH
B55

GUAITA A.,BIBLIOGRAFIA ESPANOLA DE DERECHO BIBLIOG
ADMINISTRATIVO (PAMPHLET). SPAIN LOC/G MUNIC NAT/G ADMIN
PROVS JUDGE BAL/PWR GOV/REL OWN...JURID 18/19. CONSTN
PAGE 44 B0900 PWR
B57

HEATH S.,CITADEL, MARKET, AND ALTAR; EMERGING NEW/IDEA
SOCIETY. SOCIETY ADMIN OPTIMAL OWN RATIONAL STRUCT
ORD/FREE...SOC LOG PREDICT GEN/LAWS DICTIONARY 20. UTOPIA
PAGE 49 B0985 CREATE
B57

MURDESHWAR A.K.,ADMINISTRATIVE PROBLEMS RELATING TO NAT/G
NATIONALISATION: WITH SPECIAL REFERENCE TO INDIAN OWN
STATE ENTERPRISES. CZECHOSLVK FRANCE INDIA UK INDUS
USA+45 LEGIS WORKER PROB/SOLV BUDGET PRICE CONTROL ADMIN
...MGT GEN/LAWS 20 PARLIAMENT. PAGE 76 B1544
B59

GINSBURG M.,LAW AND OPINION IN ENGLAND. UK CULTURE JURID
KIN LABOR LEGIS EDU/PROP ADMIN CT/SYS CRIME OWN POLICY
HEALTH...ANTHOL 20 ENGLSH/LAW. PAGE 40 B0802 ECO/TAC
B59

HANSON A.H.,THE STRUCTURE AND CONTROL OF STATE NAT/G
ENTERPRISES IN TURKEY. TURKEY LAW ADMIN GOV/REL LG/CO
EFFICIENCY...CHARTS 20. PAGE 46 B0939 OWN
CONTROL
B60

BHAMBHRI C.P.,PARLIAMENTARY CONTROL OVER STATE NAT/G
ENTERPRISE IN INDIA. INDIA DELIB/GP ADMIN CONTROL OWN

INGP/REL EFFICIENCY 20 PARLIAMENT. PAGE 11 B0235 INDUS
PARL/PROC
B60

INDIAN INST OF PUBLIC ADMIN,STATE UNDERTAKINGS: GOV/REL
REPORT OF A CONFERENCE, DECEMBER 19-20, 1959 ADMIN
(PAMPHLET). INDIA LG/CO DELIB/GP CONFER PARL/PROC NAT/G
EFFICIENCY OWN...MGT 20. PAGE 53 B1081 LEGIS
B60

PHILLIPS J.C.,MUNICIPAL GOVERNMENT AND MUNIC
ADMINISTRATION IN AMERICA. USA+45 LAW CONSTN FINAN GOV/REL
FORCES PLAN RECEIVE OWN ORD/FREE 20 CIVIL/LIB. LOC/G
PAGE 83 B1669 ADMIN
B61

AGARWAL R.C.,STATE ENTERPRISE IN INDIA. FUT INDIA ECO/UNDEV
UK FINAN INDUS ADMIN CONTROL OWN...POLICY CHARTS SOCISM
BIBLIOG 20 RAILROAD. PAGE 3 B0064 GOV/REL
LG/CO
B61

LAHAYE R.,LES ENTREPRISES PUBLIQUES AU MAROC. NAT/G
FRANCE MOROCCO LAW DIST/IND EXTR/IND FINAN CONSULT INDUS
PLAN TEC/DEV ADMIN AGREE CONTROL OWN...POLICY 20. ECO/UNDEV
PAGE 62 B1250 ECO/TAC
B61

SHARMA T.R.,THE WORKING OF STATE ENTERPRISES IN NAT/G
INDIA. INDIA DELIB/GP LEGIS WORKER BUDGET PRICE INDUS
CONTROL GP/REL OWN ATTIT...MGT CHARTS 20. PAGE 96 ADMIN
B1938 SOCISM
B62

KUHN T.E.,PUBLIC ENTERPRISES, PROJECT PLANNING AND ECO/DEV
ECONOMIC DEVELOPMENT (PAMPHLET). ECO/UNDEV FINAN ECO/TAC
PLAN ADMIN EFFICIENCY OWN...MGT STAT CHARTS ANTHOL LG/CO
20. PAGE 61 B1240 NAT/G
B63

HANSON A.H.,NATIONALIZATION: A BOOK OF READINGS. NAT/G
WOR+45 FINAN DELIB/GP LEGIS WORKER BUDGET ADMIN OWN
GP/REL EFFICIENCY SOCISM...MGT ANTHOL. PAGE 46 INDUS
B0941 CONTROL
B63

SHANKS M.,THE LESSONS OF PUBLIC ENTERPRISE. UK SOCISM
LEGIS WORKER ECO/TAC ADMIN PARL/PROC GOV/REL ATTIT OWN
...POLICY MGT METH/COMP NAT/COMP ANTHOL 20 NAT/G
PARLIAMENT. PAGE 96 B1931 INDUS
B63

SPRING D.,THE ENGLISH LANDED ESTATE IN THE STRATA
NINETEENTH CENTURY: ITS ADMINISTRATION. UK ELITES PERS/REL
STRUCT AGRI NAT/G GP/REL OWN PWR WEALTH...BIBLIOG MGT
19 HOUSE/LORD. PAGE 99 B2012
B64

GARFIELD PJ   LOVEJOY WF,PUBLIC UTILITY T
ECONOMICS. DIST/IND FINAN MARKET MUNIC ADMIN COST ECO/TAC
DEMAND...TECHNIC JURID 20 MONOPOLY. PAGE 39 B0782 OWN
SERV/IND
B64

HAMBRIDGE G.,DYNAMICS OF DEVELOPMENT. AGRI FINAN ECO/UNDEV
INDUS LABOR INT/TRADE EDU/PROP ADMIN LEAD OWN ECO/TAC
HEALTH...ANTHOL BIBLIOG 20. PAGE 46 B0930 OP/RES
ACT/RES
B64

SZLADITS C.,BIBLIOGRAPHY ON FOREIGN AND COMPARATIVE BIBLIOG/A
LAW: BOOKS AND ARTICLES IN ENGLISH (SUPPLEMENT JURID
1962). FINAN INDUS JUDGE LICENSE ADMIN CT/SYS ADJUD
PARL/PROC OWN...INT/LAW CLASSIF METH/COMP NAT/COMP LAW
20. PAGE 102 B2065
B65

WARD R.,BACKGROUND MATERIAL ON ECONOMIC IMPACT OF ECO/DEV
FEDERAL PROCUREMENT - 1965: FOR JOINT ECONOMIC NAT/G
COMMITTEE US CONGRESS. FINAN ROUTINE WEAPON OWN
CIVMIL/REL EFFICIENCY...STAT CHARTS 20 CONGRESS. GOV/REL
PAGE 113 B2288
B67

JAIN R.K.,MANAGEMENT OF STATE ENTERPRISES. INDIA NAT/G
SOCIETY FINAN WORKER BUDGET ADMIN CONTROL OWN 20. SOCISM
PAGE 55 B1118 INDUS
MGT
S67

CARIAS B.,"EL CONTROL DE LAS EMPRESAS PUBLICAS POR WORKER
GRUPOS DE INTERESES DE LA COMUNIDAD." FRANCE UK REPRESENT
VENEZUELA INDUS NAT/G CONTROL OWN PWR...DECISION MGT
NAT/COMP 20. PAGE 18 B0377 SOCISM
S67

FRYKENBURG R.E.,"STUDIES OF LAND CONTROL IN INDIAN ECO/UNDEV
HISTORY: REVIEW ARTICLE." INDIA UK STRATA AGRI CONTROL
MUNIC OP/RES COLONIAL REGION EFFICIENCY OWN HABITAT ADMIN
...CONCPT 16/20. PAGE 38 B0763
S67

HILL F.G.,"VEBLEN, BERLE AND THE MODERN LG/CO
CORPORATION." FINAN ECO/TAC CONTROL OWN...MGT 20. ROLE
PAGE 50 B1010 INDUS
ECO/DEV
S67

JENCKS C.E.,"SOCIAL STATUS OF COAL MINERS IN EXTR/IND
BRITAIN SINCE NATIONALIZATION." UK STRATA STRUCT WORKER
LABOR RECEIVE GP/REL INCOME OWN ATTIT HABITAT...MGT CONTROL
T 20. PAGE 56 B1128 NAT/G
S67

KURON J.,"AN OPEN LETTER TO THE PARTY." CONSTN ELITES

WORKER BUDGET EDU/PROP ADMIN REPRESENT SUFF OWN
...SOCIALIST 20. PAGE 62 B1244
STRUCT
POL/PAR
ECO/TAC

OXFORD/GRP....OXFORD GROUP

P

PACIFIC/IS....PACIFIC ISLANDS: US TRUST TERRITORY OF THE
PACIFIC ISLANDS - CAROLINE ISLANDS, MARSHALL ISLANDS,
AND MARIANA ISLANDS

PACIFISM....SEE ALSO ARMS/CONT, PEACE

N
MONPIED E.,BIBLIOGRAPHIE FEDERALISTE: ARTICLES ET
DOCUMENTS PUBLIES DANS LES PERIODIQUES PARUS EN
FRANCE NOV. 1945-OCT. 1950. EUR+WWI WOR+45 ADMIN
REGION ATTIT MARXISM PACIFISM 20 EEC. PAGE 74 B1501
BIBLIOG/A
FEDERAL
CENTRAL
INT/ORG
B50

MONPIED E.,BIBLIOGRAPHIE FEDERALISTE: OUVRAGES
CHOISIS (VOL. I. MIMEOGRAPHED PAPER). EUR+WWI
DIPLOM ADMIN REGION ATTIT PACIFISM SOCISM...INT/LAW
19/20. PAGE 74 B1502
BIBLIOG/A
FEDERAL
CENTRAL
INT/ORG
B67

AMERICAN FRIENDS SERVICE COMM.IN PLACE OF WAR.
NAT/G ACT/RES DIPLOM ADMIN NUC/PWR EFFICIENCY
...POLICY 20. PAGE 4 B0085
PEACE
PACIFISM
WAR
DETER
S67

DRAPER A.P.,"UNIONS AND THE WAR IN VIETNAM." USA+45
CONFER ADMIN LEAD WAR ORD/FREE PACIFIST 20. PAGE 30
B0616
LABOR
PACIFISM
ATTIT
ELITES

PACIFIST....PACIFIST; SEE ALSO PEACE

B65
NORDEN A.,WAR AND NAZI CRIMINALS IN WEST GERMANY:
STATE, ECONOMY, ADMINISTRATION, ARMY, JUSTICE,
SCIENCE. GERMANY GERMANY/W MOD/EUR ECO/DEV ACADEM
EX/STRUC FORCES DOMIN ADMIN CT/SYS...POLICY MAJORIT
PACIFIST 20. PAGE 78 B1587
FASCIST
WAR
NAT/G
TOP/EX
S67

DRAPER A.P.,"UNIONS AND THE WAR IN VIETNAM." USA+45
CONFER ADMIN LEAD WAR ORD/FREE PACIFIST 20. PAGE 30
B0616
LABOR
PACIFISM
ATTIT
ELITES
S67

O'DELL J.H.,"THE JULY REBELLIONS AND THE 'MILITARY
STATE'." USA+45 VIETNAM STRATA CHIEF WORKER
COLONIAL EXEC CROWD CIVMIL/REL RACE/REL TOTALISM
...WELF/ST PACIFIST 20 NEGRO JOHNSON/LB PRESIDENT
CIV/RIGHTS. PAGE 79 B1599
PWR
NAT/G
COERCE
FORCES

PACKARD V. B1621

PADELFORD N.J. B1622

PADOVER S.K. B1623

PAGE T. B1624,B1625

PAIN....SEE HEALTH

PAKISTAN....SEE ALSO S/ASIA

B56
JENNINGS W.I.,THE APPROACH TO SELF-GOVERNMENT.
CEYLON INDIA PAKISTAN S/ASIA UK SOCIETY POL/PAR
DELIB/GP LEGIS ECO/TAC EDU/PROP ADMIN EXEC CHOOSE
ATTIT ALL/VALS...JURID CONCPT GEN/METH TOT/POP 20.
PAGE 56 B1136
NAT/G
CONSTN
COLONIAL
B56

WILSON P.,GOVERNMENT AND POLITICS OF INDIA AND
PAKISTAN: 1885-1955; A BIBLIOGRAPHY OF WORKS IN
WESTERN LANGUAGES. INDIA PAKISTAN CONSTN LOC/G
POL/PAR FORCES DIPLOM ADMIN WAR CHOOSE...BIOG
CON/ANAL 19/20. PAGE 117 B2361
BIBLIOG
COLONIAL
NAT/G
S/ASIA
B57

CENTRAL ASIAN RESEARCH CENTRE,BIBLIOGRAPHY OF
RECENT SOVIET SOURCE MATERIAL ON SOVIET CENTRAL
ASIA AND THE BORDERLANDS. AFGHANISTN INDIA PAKISTAN
UAR USSR ECO/UNDEV AGRI EXTR/IND INDUS ACADEM ADMIN
...HEAL HUM LING CON/ANAL 20. PAGE 19 B0399
BIBLIOG/A
COM
CULTURE
NAT/G
B61

HASAN H.S.,PAKISTAN AND THE UN. ISLAM WOR+45
ECO/DEV ECO/UNDEV NAT/G TOP/EX ECO/TAC FOR/AID
EDU/PROP ADMIN DRIVE PERCEPT...OBS TIME/SEQ UN 20.
PAGE 48 B0965
INT/ORG
ATTIT
PAKISTAN
B62

GALENSON W.,LABOR IN DEVELOPING COUNTRIES. BRAZIL
INDONESIA ISRAEL PAKISTAN TURKEY AGRI INDUS WORKER
PAY PRICE GP/REL WEALTH...MGT CHARTS METH/COMP
NAT/COMP 20. PAGE 38 B0775
LABOR
ECO/UNDEV
BARGAIN
POL/PAR
B62

INAYATULLAH,BUREAUCRACY AND DEVELOPMENT IN
PAKISTAN. PAKISTAN ECO/UNDEV EDU/PROP CONFER
EX/STRUC
ADMIN

...ANTHOL DICTIONARY 20 BUREAUCRCY. PAGE 53 B1078
NAT/G
LOC/G
B63

WEINER M.,POLITICAL CHANGE IN SOUTH ASIA. CEYLON
INDIA PAKISTAN S/ASIA CULTURE ELITES ECO/UNDEV
EX/STRUC ADMIN CONTROL CHOOSE CONSERVE...GOV/COMP
ANTHOL 20. PAGE 115 B2315
NAT/G
CONSTN
TEC/DEV
B64

AHMAD M.,THE CIVIL SERVANT IN PAKISTAN. PAKISTAN
ECO/UNDEV COLONIAL INGP/REL...SOC CHARTS BIBLIOG 20
CIVIL/SERV. PAGE 3 B0065
WELF/ST
ADMIN
ATTIT
STRATA
B64

GOODNOW H.F.,THE CIVIL SERVICE OF PAKISTAN:
BUREAUCRACY IN A NEW NATION. INDIA PAKISTAN S/ASIA
ECO/UNDEV PROVS CHIEF PARTIC CHOOSE EFFICIENCY PWR
...BIBLIOG 20. PAGE 41 B0824
ADMIN
GOV/REL
LAW
NAT/G
B64

MAHAR J.M.,INDIA: A CRITICAL BIBLIOGRAPHY. INDIA
PAKISTAN CULTURE ECO/UNDEV LOC/G POL/PAR SECT
PROB/SOLV DIPLOM ADMIN COLONIAL PARL/PROC ATTIT 20.
PAGE 68 B1377
BIBLIOG/A
S/ASIA
NAT/G
LEAD
L64

WORLD PEACE FOUNDATION,"INTERNATIONAL
ORGANIZATIONS: SUMMARY OF ACTIVITIES." INDIA
PAKISTAN TURKEY WOR+45 CONSTN CONSULT EX/STRUC
ECO/TAC EDU/PROP LEGIT ORD/FREE...JURID SOC UN 20
CYPRESS. PAGE 118 B2375
INT/ORG
ROUTINE
B65

NATIONAL BOOK CENTRE PAKISTAN,BOOKS ON PAKISTAN: A
BIBLIOGRAPHY. PAKISTAN CULTURE DIPLOM ADMIN ATTIT
...MAJORIT SOC CONCPT 20. PAGE 77 B1560
BIBLIOG
CONSTN
S/ASIA
NAT/G
S65

ASHFORD D.E.,"BUREAUCRATS AND CITIZENS." MOROCCO
PAKISTAN PARTIC 20 TUNIS. PAGE 7 B0140
GOV/COMP
ADMIN
EX/STRUC
ROLE
B66

ALI S.,PLANNING, DEVELOPMENT AND CHANGE: AN
ANNOTATED BIBLIOGRAPHY ON DEVELOPMENTAL
ADMINISTRATION. PAKISTAN SOCIETY ORD/FREE 20.
PAGE 4 B0077
BIBLIOG/A
ADMIN
ECO/UNDEV
PLAN
B66

BIRKHEAD G.S.,ADMINISTRATIVE PROBLEMS IN PAKISTAN.
PAKISTAN AGRI FINAN INDUS LG/CO ECO/TAC CONTROL PWR
...CHARTS ANTHOL 20. PAGE 12 B0241
ADMIN
NAT/G
ORD/FREE
ECO/UNDEV
B66

BRAIBANTI R.,RESEARCH ON THE BUREAUCRACY OF
PAKISTAN. PAKISTAN LAW CULTURE INTELL ACADEM LOC/G
SECT PRESS CT/SYS...LING CHARTS 20 BUREAUCRCY.
PAGE 15 B0299
HABITAT
NAT/G
ADMIN
CONSTN
B66

DEBENKO E.,RESEARCH SOURCES FOR SOUTH ASIAN STUDIES
IN ECONOMIC DEVELOPMENT: A SELECT BIBLIOGRAPHY OF
SERIAL PUBLICATIONS. CEYLON INDIA NEPAL PAKISTAN
PROB/SOLV ADMIN...POLICY 20. PAGE 28 B0566
BIBLIOG
ECO/UNDEV
S/ASIA
PLAN
B66

SPICER K.,A SAMARITAN STATE? AFR CANADA INDIA
PAKISTAN UK USA+45 FINAN INDUS PRODUC...CHARTS 20
NATO. PAGE 99 B2006
DIPLOM
FOR/AID
ECO/DEV
ADMIN
B66

ZINKIN T.,CHALLENGES IN INDIA. INDIA PAKISTAN LAW
AGRI FINAN INDUS TOP/EX TEC/DEV CONTROL ROUTINE
ORD/FREE PWR 20 NEHRU/J SHASTRI/LB CIVIL/SERV.
PAGE 119 B2404
NAT/G
ECO/TAC
POLICY
ADMIN

PAKISTAN/E.....EAST PAKISTAN

PALATINATE

B65
COHN H.J.,THE GOVERNMENT OF THE RHINE PALATINATE IN
THE FIFTEENTH CENTURY. GERMANY FINAN LOC/G DELIB/GP
LEGIS CT/SYS CHOOSE CATHISM 14/15 PALATINATE.
PAGE 22 B0449
PROVS
JURID
GP/REL
ADMIN

PALESTINE....PALESTINE (PRE-1948 ISRAEL); SEE ALSO ISRAEL

PALMER A.M. B1626

PALMER J. B1467

PALMER J.M. B1627

PALMER M. B1628

PALOTAI O.C. B1629

PAN AFRICAN FREEDOM MOVEMENT....SEE PANAF/FREE

PAN AMERICAN UNION B1630

PANAF/FREE....PAN AFRICAN FREEDOM MOVEMENT

PANAFR/ISM....PAN-AFRICANISM

PANAMA CANAL ZONE....SEE CANAL/ZONE

PANAMA....PANAMA

N
US SUPERINTENDENT OF DOCUMENTS,TRANSPORTATION: HIGHWAYS, ROADS, AND POSTAL SERVICE (PRICE LIST 25). PANAMA USA+45 LAW FORCES DIPLOM ADMIN GOV/REL HEALTH MGT. PAGE 111 B2243
BIBLIOG/A
DIST/IND
SERV/IND
NAT/G

B47
DE NOIA J.,GUIDE TO OFFICIAL PUBLICATIONS OF THE OTHER AMERICAN REPUBLICS: PANAMA (VOL. XV). PANAMA LAW LEGIS EDU/PROP CT/SYS 20. PAGE 27 B0560
BIBLIOG/A
CONSTN
ADMIN
NAT/G

S67
FABREGA J.,"ANTECEDENTES EXTRANJEROS EN LA CONSTITUCION PANAMENA." CUBA L/A+17C PANAMA URUGUAY EX/STRUC LEGIS DIPLOM ORD/FREE 19/20 COLOMB MEXIC/AMER. PAGE 34 B0694
CONSTN
JURID
NAT/G
PARL/PROC

PAN-AFRICANISM....SEE PANAFR/ISM

PANJAB, PANJABI PEOPLE....SEE PUNJAB

PANJABI K.L. B1631

PANKHURST R. B0426

PAPUA....PAPUA

PARAGUAY....SEE ALSO L/A+17C

S67
LEWIS P.H.,"LEADERSHIP AND CONFLICT WITHIN FEBRERISTA PARTY OF PARAGUAY." L/A+17C PARAGUAY EX/STRUC DOMIN SENIOR CONTROL INGP/REL CENTRAL FEDERAL ATTIT 20. PAGE 65 B1305
POL/PAR
ELITES
LEAD

PARANTAPE H.K. B2258

PARET P. B1632

PARETO/V....VILFREDO PARETO

PARIS....PARIS, FRANCE

PARISH H.C. B1423

PARITY....SEE ECO

PARK R.L. B1633

PARK/R....ROBERT PARK

PARKER/H....HENRY PARKER

PARKFOREST....PARK FOREST, ILLINOIS

PARKINSON C.N. B1634

PARL/PROC....PARLIAMENTARY PROCESSES; SEE ALSO LEGIS

N
AUSTRALIAN NATIONAL RES COUN,AUSTRALIAN SOCIAL SCIENCE ABSTRACTS. NEW/ZEALND CULTURE SOCIETY LOC/G CT/SYS PARL/PROC...HEAL JURID PSY SOC 20 AUSTRAL. PAGE 7 B0149
BIBLIOG/A
POLICY
NAT/G
ADMIN

B08
WILSON W.,CONSTITUTIONAL GOVERNMENT IN THE UNITED STATES. USA+45 LAW POL/PAR PROVS CHIEF LEGIS BAL/PWR ADJUD EXEC FEDERAL PWR 18/20 SUPREME/CT HOUSE/REP SENATE. PAGE 117 B2362
NAT/G
GOV/REL
CONSTN
PARL/PROC

B17
HARLOW R.V.,THE HISTORY OF LEGISLATIVE METHODS IN THE PERIOD BEFORE 1825. USA-45 EX/STRUC ADMIN COLONIAL LEAD PARL/PROC ROUTINE...GP/COMP GOV/COMP HOUSE/REP. PAGE 47 B0948
LEGIS
DELIB/GP
PROVS
POL/PAR

N19
ADMINISTRATIVE STAFF COLLEGE,THE ACCOUNTABILITY OF GOVERNMENT DEPARTMENTS (PAMPHLET) (REV. ED.). UK CONSTN FINAN NAT/G CONSULT ADMIN INGP/REL CONSEN PRIVIL 20 PARLIAMENT. PAGE 3 B0059
PARL/PROC
ELITES
SANCTION
PROB/SOLV

N19
MARSH J.F. JR.,THE FBI RETIREMENT BILL (PAMPHLET). USA+45 EX/STRUC WORKER PLAN PROB/SOLV BUDGET LEAD LOBBY PARL/PROC PERS/REL RIGID/FLEX...POLICY 20 FBI PRESIDENT BUR/BUDGET. PAGE 70 B1405
ADMIN
NAT/G
SENIOR
GOV/REL

N19
TREVELYAN G.M.,THE TWO-PARTY SYSTEM IN ENGLISH POLITICAL HISTORY (PAMPHLET). UK CHIEF LEGIS COLONIAL EXEC REV CHOOSE 17/19. PAGE 105 B2128
PARL/PROC
POL/PAR
NAT/G
PWR

B32
MCKISACK M.,THE PARLIAMENTARY REPRESENTATION OF THE
NAT/G

ENGLISH BOROUGHS DURING THE MIDDLE AGES. UK CONSTN CULTURE ELITES EX/STRUC TAX PAY ADJUD PARL/PROC APPORT FEDERAL...POLICY 13/15 PARLIAMENT. PAGE 72 B1454
MUNIC
LEGIS
CHOOSE

L34
GOSNELL H.F.,"BRITISH ROYAL COMMISSIONS OF INQUIRY" UK CONSTN LEGIS PRESS ADMIN PARL/PROC...DECISION 20 PARLIAMENT. PAGE 41 B0839
DELIB/GP
INSPECT
POLICY
NAT/G

B39
JENNINGS W.I.,PARLIAMENT. UK POL/PAR OP/RES BUDGET LEAD CHOOSE GP/REL...MGT 20 PARLIAMENT HOUSE/LORD HOUSE/CMNS. PAGE 56 B1135
PARL/PROC
LEGIS
CONSTN
NAT/G

S40
PERKINS J.A.,"CONGRESSIONAL INVESTIGATIONS OF MATTERS OF INTERNATIONAL IMPORT." DELIB/GP DIPLOM ADMIN CONTROL 20 CONGRESS. PAGE 82 B1656
POL/PAR
DECISION
PARL/PROC
GOV/REL

S41
STOKE H.W.,"EXECUTIVE LEADERSHIP AND THE GROWTH OF PROPAGANDA." USA-45 NAT/G EX/STRUC LEGIS TOP/EX PARL/PROC REPRESENT ORD/FREE PWR...MAJORIT 20. PAGE 101 B2042
EXEC
LEAD
EDU/PROP
ADMIN

B43
CLARKE M.P.,PARLIAMENTARY PRIVILEGE IN THE AMERICAN COLONIES. PROVS DOMIN ADMIN REPRESENT GOV/REL ORD/FREE...BIBLIOG/A 17/18. PAGE 21 B0433
LEGIS
PWR
COLONIAL
PARL/PROC

S43
PRICE D.K.,"THE PARLIAMENTARY AND PRESIDENTIAL SYSTEMS" (BMR)" USA+45 NAT/G EX/STRUC PARL/PROC GOV/REL PWR 20 PRESIDENT CONGRESS PARLIAMENT. PAGE 84 B1706
LEGIS
REPRESENT
ADMIN
GOV/COMP

B48
BISHOP H.M.,BASIC ISSUES OF AMERICAN DEMOCRACY. USA+45 USA-45 POL/PAR EX/STRUC LEGIS ADJUD FEDERAL ...BIBLIOG 18/20. PAGE 12 B0244
NAT/G
PARL/PROC
CONSTN

C48
WALKER H.,"THE LEGISLATIVE PROCESS: LAWMAKING IN THE UNITED STATES." NAT/G POL/PAR PROVS EX/STRUC OP/RES PROB/SOLV CT/SYS LOBBY GOV/REL...CHARTS BIBLIOG T 18/20 CONGRESS. PAGE 113 B2279
PARL/PROC
LEGIS
LAW
CONSTN

B49
RIDDICK F.M.,THE UNITED STATES CONGRESS ORGANIZATION AND PROCEDURE. POL/PAR DELIB/GP PROB/SOLV DEBATE CONTROL EXEC LEAD INGP/REL PWR ...MAJORIT DECISION CONGRESS PRESIDENT. PAGE 88 B1777
LEGIS
PARL/PROC
CHIEF
EX/STRUC

B50
WADE E.C.S.,CONSTITUTIONAL LAW: AN OUTLINE OF THE LAW AND PRACTICE OF THE CONSTITUTION. UK LEGIS DOMIN ADMIN GP/REL 16/20 CMN/WLTH PARLIAMENT ENGLSH/LAW. PAGE 112 B2269
CONSTN
NAT/G
PARL/PROC
LAW

S50
HUMPHREY H.H.,"THE SENATE ON TRIAL." USA+45 POL/PAR DEBATE REPRESENT EFFICIENCY ATTIT RIGID/FLEX ...TRADIT SENATE. PAGE 52 B1064
PARL/PROC
ROUTINE
PWR
LEGIS

S51
MARX F.M.,"SIGNIFICANCE FOR THE ADMINISTRATIVE PROCESS." POL/PAR LEAD PARL/PROC GOV/REL EFFICIENCY SUPEGO...POLICY CONGRESS. PAGE 70 B1420
LEGIS
ADMIN
CHIEF

B53
STOUT H.M.,BRITISH GOVERNMENT. UK FINAN LOC/G POL/PAR DELIB/GP DIPLOM ADMIN COLONIAL CHOOSE ORD/FREE...JURID BIBLIOG 20 COMMONWLTH. PAGE 101 B2049
NAT/G
PARL/PROC
CONSTN
NEW/LIB

B54
JENNINGS I.,THE QUEEN'S GOVERNMENT. UK POL/PAR DELIB/GP ADJUD ADMIN CT/SYS PARL/PROC REPRESENT CONSERVE 13/20 PARLIAMENT. PAGE 56 B1132
NAT/G
CONSTN
LEGIS
CHIEF

L54
ROSTOW W.W.,"ASIAN LEADERSHIP AND FREE-WORLD ALLIANCE." ASIA COM USA+45 CULTURE ELITES INTELL NAT/G TEC/DEV ECO/TAC EDU/PROP COLONIAL PARL/PROC ROUTINE COERCE DRIVE ORD/FREE MARXISM...PSY CONCPT. PAGE 90 B1829
ATTIT
LEGIT
DIPLOM

C54
LANDAU J.M.,"PARLIAMENTS AND PARTIES IN EGYPT." UAR NAT/G SECT CONSULT LEGIS TOP/EX PROB/SOLV ADMIN COLONIAL...GEN/LAWS BIBLIOG 19/20. PAGE 62 B1254
ISLAM
NAT/LISM
PARL/PROC
POL/PAR

B55
GALLOWAY G.B.,CONGRESS AND PARLIAMENT: THEIR ORGANIZATION AND OPERATION IN THE US AND THE UK: PLANNING PAMPHLET NO. 93. POL/PAR EX/STRUC DEBATE CONTROL LEAD ROUTINE EFFICIENCY PWR...POLICY CONGRESS PARLIAMENT. PAGE 38 B0777
DELIB/GP
LEGIS
PARL/PROC
GOV/COMP

B56
WAUGH E.W.,SECOND CONSUL. USA+45 USA-45 CONSTN POL/PAR PROB/SOLV PARL/PROC CHOOSE PERS/REL ATTIT ...BIBLIOG 18/20 VICE/PRES. PAGE 114 B2304
NAT/G
EX/STRUC
PWR
CHIEF

B56

WEBER M.,STAATSSOZIOLOGIE. STRUCT LEGIT ADMIN
PARL/PROC SUPEGO CONSERVE JURID. PAGE 114 B2305
SOC
NAT/G
POL/PAR
LEAD

B56

WILSON W.,CONGRESSIONAL GOVERNMENT. USA-45 NAT/G
ADMIN EXEC PARL/PROC GP/REL MAJORITY ATTIT 19
SENATE HOUSE/REP. PAGE 117 B2364
LEGIS
CHIEF
CONSTN
PWR

B57

JENNINGS I.,PARLIAMENT. UK FINAN INDUS POL/PAR
DELIB/GP EX/STRUC PLAN CONTROL...MAJORIT JURID
PARLIAMENT. PAGE 56 B1133
PARL/PROC
TOP/EX
MGT
LEGIS

S57

COTTER C.P.,"ADMINISTRATIVE ACCOUNTABILITY;
REPORTING TO CONGRESS." USA+45 CONSULT DELIB/GP
PARL/PROC PARTIC GOV/REL ATTIT PWR DECISION.
PAGE 24 B0490
LEGIS
EX/STRUC
REPRESENT
CONTROL

S57

HARRIS J.P.,"LEGISLATIVE CONTROL OF ADMINISTRATION:
SOME COMPARISONS OF AMERICAN AND EUROPEAN
PRACTICES." DEBATE PARL/PROC ROUTINE GOV/REL
EFFICIENCY SUPEGO DECISION. PAGE 47 B0954
LEGIS
CONTROL
EX/STRUC
REPRESENT

B58

JAPAN MINISTRY OF JUSTICE,CRIMINAL JUSTICE IN
JAPAN. LAW PROF/ORG PUB/INST FORCES CONTROL CT/SYS
PARL/PROC 20 CHINJAP. PAGE 56 B1125
CONSTN
CRIME
JURID
ADMIN

B58

MOEN N.W.,THE GOVERNMENT OF SCOTLAND 1603 - 1625.
UK JUDGE ADMIN GP/REL PWR 17 SCOTLAND COMMON/LAW.
PAGE 74 B1496
CHIEF
JURID
CONTROL
PARL/PROC

B58

STEWART J.D.,BRITISH PRESSURE GROUPS: THEIR ROLE IN
RELATION TO THE HOUSE OF COMMONS. UK CONSULT
DELIB/GP ADMIN ROUTINE CHOOSE REPRESENT ATTIT ROLE
20 HOUSE/CMNS PARLIAMENT. PAGE 101 B2038
LOBBY
LEGIS
PLAN
PARL/PROC

B58

US SENATE COMM POST OFFICE,TO PROVIDE AN EFFECTIVE
SYSTEM OF PERSONNEL ADMINISTRATION. USA+45 NAT/G
EX/STRUC PARL/PROC GOV/REL...JURID 20 SENATE
CIVIL/SERV. PAGE 111 B2234
INT
LEGIS
CONFER
ADMIN

C58

GOLAY J.F.,"THE FOUNDING OF THE FEDERAL REPUBLIC OF
GERMANY." GERMANY/W CONSTN EX/STRUC DIPLOM ADMIN
CHOOSE...DECISION BIBLIOG 20. PAGE 40 B0814
FEDERAL
NAT/G
PARL/PROC
POL/PAR

C58

WILDING N.,"AN ENCYCLOPEDIA OF PARLIAMENT." UK LAW
CONSTN CHIEF PROB/SOLV DIPLOM DEBATE WAR INGP/REL
PRIVIL...BIBLIOG DICTIONARY 13/20 CMN/WLTH
PARLIAMENT. PAGE 116 B2350
PARL/PROC
POL/PAR
NAT/G
ADMIN

B59

DUVERGER M.,LA CINQUIEME REPUBLIQUE. FRANCE WOR+45
POL/PAR CHIEF EX/STRUC LOBBY. PAGE 31 B0636
NAT/G
CONSTN
GOV/REL
PARL/PROC

S59

ROBINSON J.A.,"THE ROLE OF THE RULES COMMITTEE IN
ARRANGING THE PROGRAM OF THE UNITED STATES HOUSE OF
REPRESENTATIVES." USA+45 DEBATE CONTROL AUTHORIT
HOUSE/REP. PAGE 89 B1801
PARL/PROC
DELIB/GP
ROUTINE
LEGIS

B60

BHAMBHRI C.P.,PARLIAMENTARY CONTROL OVER STATE
ENTERPRISE IN INDIA. INDIA DELIB/GP ADMIN CONTROL
INGP/REL EFFICIENCY 20 PARLIAMENT. PAGE 11 B0235
NAT/G
OWN
INDUS
PARL/PROC

B60

HAYNES G.H.,THE SENATE OF THE UNITED STATES: ITS
HISTORY AND PRACTICE. CONSTN EX/STRUC TOP/EX CONFER
DEBATE LEAD LOBBY PARL/PROC CHOOSE PWR SENATE
CONGRESS. PAGE 48 B0977
LEGIS
DELIB/GP

B60

INDIAN INST OF PUBLIC ADMIN,STATE UNDERTAKINGS:
REPORT OF A CONFERENCE, DECEMBER 19-20, 1959
(PAMPHLET). INDIA LG/CO DELIB/GP CONFER PARL/PROC
EFFICIENCY OWN...MGT 20. PAGE 53 B1081
GOV/REL
ADMIN
NAT/G
LEGIS

B60

US LIBRARY OF CONGRESS,INDEX TO LATIN AMERICAN
LEGISLATION: 1950-1960 (2 VOLS.). NAT/G DELIB/GP
ADMIN PARL/PROC 20. PAGE 109 B2205
BIBLIOG/A
LEGIS
L/A+17C
JURID

B60

US SENATE COMM ON JUDICIARY,FEDERAL ADMINISTRATIVE
PROCEDURE. USA+45 CONSTN NAT/G PROB/SOLV CONFER
GOV/REL...JURID INT 20 SENATE. PAGE 110 B2226
PARL/PROC
LEGIS
ADMIN
LAW

B60

US SENATE COMM ON JUDICIARY,ADMINISTRATIVE
PROCEDURE LEGISLATION. USA+45 CONSTN NAT/G
PROB/SOLV CONFER ROUTINE GOV/REL...INT 20 SENATE.
PAGE 110 B2227
PARL/PROC
LEGIS
ADMIN
JURID

B61

BAINS J.S.,STUDIES IN POLITICAL SCIENCE. INDIA
WOR+45 WOR-45 CONSTN BAL/PWR ADJUD ADMIN PARL/PROC
SOVEREIGN...SOC METH/COMP ANTHOL 17/20 UN. PAGE 8
B0165
DIPLOM
INT/LAW
NAT/G

B61

DRAGNICH A.N.,MAJOR EUROPEAN GOVERNMENTS. FRANCE
GERMANY/W UK USSR LOC/G EX/STRUC PARL/PROC
ATTIT MARXISM...JURID MGT NAT/COMP 19/20. PAGE 30
B0615
NAT/G
LEGIS
CONSTN
POL/PAR

B61

GRIFFITH E.S.,CONGRESS: ITS CONTEMPORARY ROLE.
CONSTN POL/PAR CHIEF PLAN BUDGET DIPLOM CONFER
ADMIN LOBBY...DECISION CONGRESS. PAGE 43 B0878
PARL/PROC
EX/STRUC
TOP/EX
LEGIS

B61

MUNGER E.S.,AFRICAN FIELD REPORTS 1952-1961.
SOUTH/AFR SOCIETY ECO/UNDEV NAT/G POL/PAR COLONIAL
EXEC PARL/PROC GUERRILLA RACE/REL ALL/IDEOS...SOC
AUD/VIS 20. PAGE 76 B1538
AFR
DISCRIM
RECORD

B61

RAO K.V.,PARLIAMENTARY DEMOCRACY OF INDIA. INDIA
EX/STRUC TOP/EX COLONIAL CT/SYS PARL/PROC ORD/FREE
...POLICY CONCPT TREND 20 PARLIAMENT. PAGE 86 B1733
CONSTN
ADJUD
NAT/G
FEDERAL

B61

WILLSON F.M.G.,ADMINISTRATORS IN ACTION. UK MARKET
TEC/DEV PARL/PROC 20. PAGE 117 B2358
ADMIN
NAT/G
CONSTN

C61

MOODIE G.C.,"THE GOVERNMENT OF GREAT BRITAIN." UK
LAW STRUCT LOC/G POL/PAR DIPLOM RECEIVE ADMIN
COLONIAL CHOOSE...BIBLIOG 20 PARLIAMENT. PAGE 75
B1508
NAT/G
SOCIETY
PARL/PROC
GOV/COMP

B62

ANDREWS W.G.,EUROPEAN POLITICAL INSTITUTIONS.
FRANCE GERMANY UK USSR TOP/EX LEAD PARL/PROC CHOOSE
20. PAGE 5 B0104
NAT/COMP
POL/PAR
EX/STRUC
LEGIS

B62

LOWI T.J.,LEGISLATIVE POLITICS U.S.A. LAW LEGIS
DIPLOM EXEC LOBBY CHOOSE SUFF FEDERAL PWR 19/20
CONGRESS. PAGE 67 B1345
PARL/PROC
REPRESENT
POLICY
ROUTINE

B62

SCALAPINO R.A.,PARTIES AND POLITICS IN CONTEMPORARY
JAPAN. EX/STRUC DIPLOM CHOOSE NAT/LISM ATTIT
...POLICY 20 CHINJAP. PAGE 93 B1876
POL/PAR
PARL/PROC
ELITES
DECISION

B63

CHARLES S.,MINISTER OF RELIEF: HARRY HOPKINS AND
THE DEPRESSION. EX/STRUC PROB/SOLV RATION PARL/PROC
PERS/REL ALL/VALS 20 HOPKINS/H NRA. PAGE 20 B0414
ADMIN
ECO/TAC
PLAN
BIOG

B63

COUNCIL STATE GOVERNMENTS,HANDBOOK FOR LEGISLATIVE
COMMITTEES. USA+45 LAW DELIB/GP EX/STRUC TOP/EX
CHOOSE PWR...METH/COMP 20. PAGE 24 B0496
LEGIS
PARL/PROC
PROVS
ADJUD

B63

HERMAN H.,NEW YORK STATE AND THE METROPOLITAN
PROBLEM. USA+45 ECO/DEV PUB/INST SCHOOL LEGIS PLAN
TAX EXEC PARL/PROC PARTIC...HEAL 20 NEW/YORK.
PAGE 49 B0992
GOV/REL
PROVS
LOC/G
POLICY

B63

MACNEIL N.,FORGE OF DEMOCRACY: THE HOUSE OF
REPRESENTATIVES. POL/PAR EX/STRUC TOP/EX DEBATE
LEAD PARL/PROC CHOOSE GOV/REL PWR...OBS HOUSE/REP.
PAGE 68 B1374
LEGIS
DELIB/GP

B63

RICHARDSON H.G.,THE ADMINISTRATION OF IRELAND
1172-1377. IRELAND CONSTN EX/STRUC LEGIS JUDGE
CT/SYS PARL/PROC...CHARTS BIBLIOG 12/14. PAGE 88
B1775
ADMIN
NAT/G
PWR

B63

ROYAL INSTITUTE PUBLIC ADMIN,BRITISH PUBLIC
ADMINISTRATION. UK LAW FINAN INDUS LOC/G POL/PAR
LEGIS LOBBY PARL/PROC CHOOSE JURID. PAGE 91 B1845
BIBLIOG
ADMIN
MGT
NAT/G

B63

SHANKS M.,THE LESSONS OF PUBLIC ENTERPRISE. UK
LEGIS WORKER ECO/TAC ADMIN PARL/PROC GOV/REL ATTIT
...POLICY MGT METH/COMP NAT/COMP ANTHOL 20
PARLIAMENT. PAGE 96 B1931
SOCISM
OWN
NAT/G
INDUS

B63

SMITH R.M.,STATE GOVERNMENT IN TRANSITION. USA+45
POL/PAR LEGIS PARL/PROC GOV/REL 20 PENNSYLVAN
GOVERNOR. PAGE 98 B1984
PROVS
POLICY
EX/STRUC
PLAN

B63

US SENATE COMM ON JUDICIARY,ADMINISTRATIVE
CONFERENCE OF THE UNITED STATES. USA+45 CONSTN
NAT/G PROB/SOLV CONFER GOV/REL...INT 20 SENATE.
PAGE 110 B2230
PARL/PROC
JURID
ADMIN
LEGIS

B63

WADE H.W.R.,TOWARDS ADMINISTRATIVE JUSTICE. UK
ADJUD

USA+45 CONSTN CONSULT PROB/SOLV CT/SYS PARL/PROC   IDEA/COMP
...POLICY JURID METH/COMP 20 ENGLSH/LAW. PAGE 112   ADMIN
B2270

B64
AVASTHI A.,ASPECTS OF ADMINISTRATION. INDIA UK   MGT
USA+45 FINAN ACADEM DELIB/GP LEGIS RECEIVE   ADMIN
PARL/PROC PRIVIL...NAT/COMP 20. PAGE 7 B0150   SOC/WK
ORD/FREE

B64
FORBES A.H.,CURRENT RESEARCH IN BRITISH STUDIES. UK   BIBLIOG
CONSTN CULTURE POL/PAR SECT DIPLOM ADMIN...JURID   PERSON
BIOG WORSHIP 20. PAGE 36 B0736   NAT/G
PARL/PROC

B64
GESELLSCHAFT RECHTSVERGLEICH,BIBLIOGRAPHIE DES   BIBLIOG/A
DEUTSCHEN RECHTS (BIBLIOGRAPHY OF GERMAN LAW,   JURID
TRANS. BY COURTLAND PETERSON). GERMANY FINAN INDUS   CONSTN
LABOR SECT FORCES CT/SYS PARL/PROC CRIME...INT/LAW   ADMIN
SOC NAT/COMP 20. PAGE 39 B0794

B64
GJUPANOVIC H.,LEGAL SOURCES AND BIBLIOGRAPHY OF   BIBLIOG/A
YUGOSLAVIA. COM YUGOSLAVIA LAW LEGIS DIPLOM ADMIN   JURID
PARL/PROC REGION CRIME CENTRAL 20. PAGE 40 B0807   CONSTN
ADJUD

B64
HALLER W.,DER SCHWEDISCHE JUSTITIEOMBUDSMAN.   JURID
DENMARK FINLAND NORWAY SWEDEN LEGIS ADJUD CONTROL   PARL/PROC
PERSON ORD/FREE...NAT/COMP 20 OMBUDSMAN. PAGE 46   ADMIN
B0926   CHIEF

B64
KAACK H.,DIE PARTEIEN IN DER   POL/PAR
VERFASSUNGSWIRKLICHKEIT DER BUNDESREPUBLIK.   PROVS
GERMANY/W ADMIN PARL/PROC CHOOSE...JURID 20.   NAT/G
PAGE 57 B1157

B64
MAHAR J.M.,INDIA: A CRITICAL BIBLIOGRAPHY. INDIA   BIBLIOG/A
PAKISTAN CULTURE ECO/UNDEV LOC/G POL/PAR SECT   S/ASIA
PROB/SOLV DIPLOM ADMIN COLONIAL PARL/PROC ATTIT 20.   NAT/G
PAGE 68 B1377   LEAD

B64
O'HEARN P.J.T.,PEACE, ORDER AND GOOD GOVERNMENT; A   NAT/G
NEW CONSTITUTION FOR CANADA. CANADA EX/STRUC LEGIS   CONSTN
CT/SYS PARL/PROC...BIBLIOG 20. PAGE 79 B1600   LAW
CREATE

B64
RIDDLE D.H.,THE TRUMAN COMMITTEE: A STUDY IN   LEGIS
CONGRESSIONAL RESPONSIBILITY. INDUS FORCES OP/RES   DELIB/GP
DOMIN ADMIN LEAD PARL/PROC WAR PRODUC SUPEGO   CONFER
...BIBLIOG CONGRESS. PAGE 88 B1778

B64
STOICOIU V.,LEGAL SOURCES AND BIBLIOGRAPHY OF   BIBLIOG/A
ROMANIA. COM ROMANIA LAW FINAN POL/PAR LEGIS JUDGE   JURID
ADJUD CT/SYS PARL/PROC MARXISM 20. PAGE 101 B2041   CONSTN
ADMIN

B64
SZLADITS C.,BIBLIOGRAPHY ON FOREIGN AND COMPARATIVE   BIBLIOG/A
LAW: BOOKS AND ARTICLES IN ENGLISH (SUPPLEMENT   JURID
1962). FINAN INDUS JUDGE LICENSE ADMIN CT/SYS   ADJUD
PARL/PROC OWN...INT/LAW CLASSIF METH/COMP NAT/COMP   LAW
20. PAGE 102 B2065

B64
US SENATE COMM ON JUDICIARY,ADMINISTRATIVE   PARL/PROC
PROCEDURE ACT. USA+45 CONSTN NAT/G PROB/SOLV CONFER   LEGIS
GOV/REL PWR...INT 20 SENATE. PAGE 110 B2231   JURID
ADMIN

S64
REDFORD E.S.,"THE PROTECTION OF THE PUBLIC INTEREST   ADMIN
WITH SPECIAL REFERENCE TO ADMINISTRATIVE   VOL/ASSN
REGULATION." POL/PAR LEGIS PRESS PARL/PROC. PAGE 87   EX/STRUC
B1758   GP/REL

B65
FEERICK J.D.,FROM FAILING HANDS: THE STUDY OF   EX/STRUC
PRESIDENTIAL SUCCESSION. CONSTN NAT/G PROB/SOLV   CHIEF
LEAD PARL/PROC MURDER CHOOSE...NEW/IDEA BIBLIOG 20   LAW
KENNEDY/JF JOHNSON/LB PRESIDENT PRE/US/AM   LEGIS
VICE/PRES. PAGE 35 B0710

B65
GT BRIT ADMIN STAFF COLLEGE,THE ACCOUNTABILITY OF   LG/CO
PUBLIC CORPORATIONS (REV. ED.). UK ECO/DEV FINAN   NAT/G
DELIB/GP EX/STRUC BUDGET CAP/ISM CONFER PRICE   ADMIN
PARL/PROC 20. PAGE 44 B0899   CONTROL

B65
KOUSOULAS D.G.,REVOLUTION AND DEFEAT; THE STORY OF   REV
THE GREEK COMMUNIST PARTY. GREECE INT/ORG EX/STRUC   MARXISM
DIPLOM FOR/AID EDU/PROP PARL/PROC ADJUST ATTIT 20   POL/PAR
COM/PARTY. PAGE 61 B1230   ORD/FREE

B65
PYLEE M.V.,CONSTITUTIONAL GOVERNMENT IN INDIA (2ND   CONSTN
REV. ED.). INDIA POL/PAR EX/STRUC DIPLOM COLONIAL   NAT/G
CT/SYS PARL/PROC PRIVIL...JURID 16/20. PAGE 85   PROVS
B1725   FEDERAL

B65
RUBINSTEIN A.Z.,THE CHALLENGE OF POLITICS: IDEAS   NAT/G
AND ISSUES (2ND ED.). UNIV ELITES SOCIETY EX/STRUC   DIPLOM
BAL/PWR PARL/PROC AUTHORIT...DECISION ANTHOL 20.   GP/REL
PAGE 92 B1852   ORD/FREE

B65
SHARMA S.A.,PARLIAMENTARY GOVERNMENT IN INDIA.   NAT/G
INDIA FINAN LOC/G PROVS DELIB/GP PLAN ADMIN CT/SYS   CONSTN
FEDERAL...JURID 20. PAGE 96 B1936   PARL/PROC
LEGIS

B65
VAID K.N.,STATE AND LABOR IN INDIA. INDIA INDUS   LAW
WORKER PAY PRICE ADJUD CONTROL PARL/PROC GP/REL   LABOR
ORD/FREE 20. PAGE 111 B2248   MGT
NEW/LIB

B66
ANDERSON S.V.,CANADIAN OMBUDSMAN PROPOSALS. CANADA   NAT/G
LEGIS DEBATE PARL/PROC...MAJORIT JURID TIME/SEQ   CREATE
IDEA/COMP 20 OMBUDSMAN PARLIAMENT. PAGE 5 B0096   ADMIN
POL/PAR

B66
BURNS A.C.,PARLIAMENT AS AN EXPORT. WOR+45 CONSTN   PARL/PROC
BARGAIN DEBATE ROUTINE GOV/REL EFFICIENCY...ANTHOL   POL/PAR
COMMONWLTH PARLIAMENT. PAGE 17 B0353   CT/SYS
CHIEF

B66
CHAPMAN B.,THE PROFESSION OF GOVERNMENT: THE PUBLIC   BIBLIOG
SERVICE IN EUROPE. CONSTN NAT/G POL/PAR EX/STRUC   ADMIN
LEGIS TOP/EX PROB/SOLV DEBATE EXEC PARL/PROC PARTIC   EUR+WWI
20. PAGE 20 B0411   GOV/COMP

B66
DAVIDSON R.H.,CONGRESS IN CRISIS: POLITICS AND   LEGIS
CONGRESSIONAL REFORM. USA+45 SOCIETY POL/PAR   PARL/PROC
CONTROL LEAD ROUTINE GOV/REL ATTIT PWR...POLICY 20   PROB/SOLV
CONGRESS. PAGE 26 B0535   NAT/G

B66
DILLEY M.R.,BRITISH POLICY IN KENYA COLONY (2ND   COLONIAL
ED.). AFR INDIA UK LABOR BUDGET TAX ADMIN PARL/PROC   REPRESENT
GP/REL...BIBLIOG 20 PARLIAMENT. PAGE 29 B0594   SOVEREIGN

B66
FINNISH POLITICAL SCIENCE ASSN,SCANDINAVIAN   ATTIT
POLITICAL STUDIES (VOL. I). FINLAND DIPLOM ADMIN   POL/PAR
LOBBY PARL/PROC...CHARTS BIBLIOG 20 SCANDINAV.   ACT/RES
PAGE 36 B0721   CHOOSE

B66
INTERPARLIAMENTARY UNION,PARLIAMENTS: COMPARATIVE   PARL/PROC
STUDY ON STRUCTURE AND FUNCTIONING OF   LEGIS
REPRESENTATIVE INSTITUTIONS IN FIFTY-FIVE   GOV/COMP
COUNTRIES. WOR+45 POL/PAR DELIB/GP BUDGET ADMIN   EX/STRUC
CONTROL CHOOSE. PAGE 54 B1099

B66
SPINELLI A.,THE EUROCRATS; CONFLICT AND CRISIS IN   INT/ORG
THE EUROPEAN COMMUNITY (TRANS. BY C. GROVE HAINES).   INGP/REL
EUR+WWI MARKET POL/PAR ECO/TAC PARL/PROC EEC OEEC   CONSTN
ECSC EURATOM. PAGE 99 B2007   ADMIN

C66
TACHERON D.G.,"THE JOB OF THE CONGRESSMAN: AN   LEGIS
INTRODUCTION TO SERVICES IN THE US HOUSE OF   PARL/PROC
REPRESENTATIVES." DELIB/GP EX/STRUC PRESS SENIOR   ADMIN
CT/SYS LOBBY CHOOSE GOV/REL...BIBLIOG 20 CONGRESS   POL/PAR
HOUSE/REP SENATE. PAGE 102 B2068

B67
BROWN L.N.,FRENCH ADMINISTRATIVE LAW. FRANCE UK   EX/STRUC
CONSTN NAT/G LEGIS DOMIN CONTROL EXEC PARL/PROC PWR   LAW
...JURID METH/COMP GEN/METH. PAGE 16 B0324   IDEA/COMP
CT/SYS

B67
MENHENNET D.,PARLIAMENT IN PERSPECTIVE. UK ROUTINE   LEGIS
REPRESENT ROLE PWR 20 PARLIAMENT. PAGE 73 B1467   PARL/PROC
CONCPT
POPULISM

S67
ANDERSON M.,"THE FRENCH PARLIAMENT." EUR+WWI FRANCE   PARL/PROC
MOD/EUR CONSTN POL/PAR CHIEF LEGIS LOBBY ATTIT ROLE   LEAD
PWR 19/20. PAGE 5 B0095   GOV/COMP
EX/STRUC

S67
BRADLEY A.W.,"CONSTITUTION-MAKING IN UGANDA."   NAT/G
UGANDA LAW CHIEF DELIB/GP LEGIS ADMIN EXEC   CREATE
PARL/PROC RACE/REL ORD/FREE...GOV/COMP 20. PAGE 14   CONSTN
B0295   FEDERAL

S67
FABREGA J.,"ANTECEDENTES EXTRANJEROS EN LA   CONSTN
CONSTITUCION PANAMENA." CUBA L/A+17C PANAMA URUGUAY   JURID
EX/STRUC LEGIS DIPLOM ORD/FREE 19/20 COLOMB   NAT/G
MEXIC/AMER. PAGE 34 B0694   PARL/PROC

B87
KINNEAR J.B.,PRINCIPLES OF CIVIL GOVERNMENT.   POL/PAR
MOD/EUR USA-45 CONSTN LOC/G EX/STRUC ADMIN   NAT/G
PARL/PROC RACE/REL...CONCPT 18/19. PAGE 60 B1210   GOV/COMP
REPRESENT

PARLIAMENTARY PROCESSES....SEE PARL/PROC

PARLIAMENT....PARLIAMENT (ALL NATIONS); SEE ALSO LEGIS

N19
ADMINISTRATIVE STAFF COLLEGE,THE ACCOUNTABILITY OF   PARL/PROC
GOVERNMENT DEPARTMENTS (PAMPHLET) (REV. ED.). UK   ELITES
CONSTN FINAN NAT/G CONSULT ADMIN INGP/REL CONSEN   SANCTION
PRIVIL 20 PARLIAMENT. PAGE 3 B0059   PROB/SOLV

N19

HIGGINS R.,THE ADMINISTRATION OF UNITED KINGDOM
FOREIGN POLICY THROUGH THE UNITED NATIONS
(PAMPHLET). UK NAT/G ADMIN GOV/REL...CHARTS 20 UN
PARLIAMENT. PAGE 50 B1009

DIPLOM
POLICY
INT/ORG

B24

BAGEHOT W.,THE ENGLISH CONSTITUTION AND OTHER
POLITICAL ESSAYS. UK DELIB/GP BAL/PWR ADMIN CONTROL
EXEC ROUTINE CONSERVE...METH PARLIAMENT 19/20.
PAGE 8 B0160

NAT/G
STRUCT
CONCPT

B24

HOLDSWORTH W.S.,A HISTORY OF ENGLISH LAW; THE
COMMON LAW AND ITS RIVALS (VOL. V). UK SEA EX/STRUC
WRITING ADMIN...INT/LAW JURID CONCPT IDEA/COMP
WORSHIP 16/17 PARLIAMENT ENGLSH/LAW COMMON/LAW.
PAGE 51 B1033

LAW
LEGIS
ADJUD
CT/SYS

B24

HOLDSWORTH W.S.,A HISTORY OF ENGLISH LAW; THE
COMMON LAW AND ITS RIVALS (VOL. VI). UK STRATA
EX/STRUC ADJUD ADMIN CONTROL CT/SYS...JURID CONCPT
GEN/LAWS 17 COMMONWLTH PARLIAMENT ENGLSH/LAW
COMMON/LAW. PAGE 51 B1034

LAW
CONSTN
LEGIS
CHIEF

B28

HALL W.P.,EMPIRE TO COMMONWEALTH. FUT WOR-45 CONSTN
ECO/DEV ECO/UNDEV INT/ORG PROVS PLAN DIPLOM
EDU/PROP ADMIN COLONIAL PEACE PERSON ALL/VALS
...POLICY GEOG SOC OBS RECORD TREND CMN/WLTH
PARLIAMENT 19/20. PAGE 46 B0925

VOL/ASSN
NAT/G
UK

B32

MCKISACK M.,THE PARLIAMENTARY REPRESENTATION OF THE
ENGLISH BOROUGHS DURING THE MIDDLE AGES. UK CONSTN
CULTURE ELITES EX/STRUC TAX PAY ADJUD PARL/PROC
APPORT FEDERAL...POLICY 13/15 PARLIAMENT. PAGE 72
B1454

NAT/G
MUNIC
LEGIS
CHOOSE

L34

GOSNELL H.F.,"BRITISH ROYAL COMMISSIONS OF INQUIRY"
UK CONSTN LEGIS PRESS ADMIN PARL/PROC...DECISION 20
PARLIAMENT. PAGE 41 B0839

DELIB/GP
INSPECT
POLICY
NAT/G

B39

JENNINGS W.I.,PARLIAMENT. UK POL/PAR OP/RES BUDGET
LEAD CHOOSE GP/REL...MGT 20 PARLIAMENT HOUSE/LORD
HOUSE/CMNS. PAGE 56 B1135

PARL/PROC
LEGIS
CONSTN
NAT/G

S43

PRICE D.K.,"THE PARLIAMENTARY AND PRESIDENTIAL
SYSTEMS" (BMR)" USA-45 NAT/G EX/STRUC PARL/PROC
GOV/REL PWR 20 PRESIDENT CONGRESS PARLIAMENT.
PAGE 84 B1706

LEGIS
REPRESENT
ADMIN
GOV/COMP

L44

HAILEY,"THE FUTURE OF COLONIAL PEOPLES." WOR-45
CONSTN CULTURE ECO/UNDEV AGRI MARKET INT/ORG NAT/G
SECT CONSULT ECO/TAC LEGIT ADMIN NAT/LISM ALL/VALS
...SOC OBS TREND STFRTYP CMN/WLTH LEAGUE/NAT
PARLIAMENT 20. PAGE 45 B0916

PLAN
CONCPT
DIPLOM
UK

B50

WADE E.C.S.,CONSTITUTIONAL LAW; AN OUTLINE OF THE
LAW AND PRACTICE OF THE CONSTITUTION. UK LEGIS
DOMIN ADMIN GP/REL 16/20 CMN/WLTH PARLIAMENT
ENGLSH/LAW. PAGE 112 B2269

CONSTN
NAT/G
PARL/PROC
LAW

B52

HIMMELFARB G.,LORD ACTON: A STUDY IN CONSCIENCE AND
POLITICS. MOD/EUR NAT/G POL/PAR SECT LEGIS TOP/EX
EDU/PROP ADMIN NAT/LISM ATTIT PERSON SUPEGO MORAL
ORD/FREE...CONCPT PARLIAMENT 19 ACTON/LORD. PAGE 50
B1014

PWR
BIOG

C53

BULNER-THOMAS I.,"THE PARTY SYSTEM IN GREAT
BRITAIN." UK CONSTN SECT PRESS CONFER GP/REL ATTIT
...POLICY TREND BIBLIOG 19/20 PARLIAMENT. PAGE 17
B0343

NAT/G
POL/PAR
ADMIN
ROUTINE

B54

JENNINGS I.,THE QUEEN'S GOVERNMENT. UK POL/PAR
DELIB/GP ADJUD ADMIN CT/SYS PARL/PROC REPRESENT
CONSERVE 13/20 PARLIAMENT. PAGE 56 B1132

NAT/G
CONSTN
LEGIS
CHIEF

B55

CRAIG J.,BIBLIOGRAPHY OF PUBLIC ADMINISTRATION IN
AUSTRALIA. CONSTN FINAN EX/STRUC LEGIS PLAN DIPLOM
RECEIVE ADJUD ROUTINE...HEAL 19/20 AUSTRAL
PARLIAMENT. PAGE 24 B0500

BIBLIOG
GOV/REL
ADMIN
NAT/G

B55

GALLOWAY G.B.,CONGRESS AND PARLIAMENT: THEIR
ORGANIZATION AND OPERATION IN THE US AND THE UK:
PLANNING PAMPHLET NO. 93. POL/PAR EX/STRUC DEBATE
CONTROL LEAD ROUTINE EFFICIENCY PWR...POLICY
CONGRESS PARLIAMENT. PAGE 38 B0777

DELIB/GP
LEGIS
PARL/PROC
GOV/COMP

B56

CARTER B.E.,THE OFFICE OF THE PRIME MINISTER. UK
ADMIN REPRESENT PARLIAMENT 20. PAGE 19 B0388

GOV/REL
CHIEF
EX/STRUC
LEAD

B56

DUNNILL F.,THE CIVIL SERVICE. UK LAW PLAN ADMIN
EFFICIENCY DRIVE NEW/LIB...STAT CHARTS 20
PARLIAMENT CIVIL/SERV. PAGE 31 B0633

PERSON
WORKER
STRATA

SOC/WK

B57

JENNINGS I.,PARLIAMENT. UK FINAN INDUS POL/PAR
DELIB/GP EX/STRUC PLAN CONTROL...MAJORIT JURID
PARLIAMENT. PAGE 56 B1133

PARL/PROC
TOP/EX
MGT
LEGIS

B57

MURDESHWAR A.K.,ADMINISTRATIVE PROBLEMS RELATING TO
NATIONALISATION: WITH SPECIAL REFERENCE TO INDIAN
STATE ENTERPRISES. CZECHOSLVK FRANCE INDIA UK
USA+45 LEGIS WORKER PROB/SOLV BUDGET PRICE CONTROL
...MGT GEN/LAWS 20 PARLIAMENT. PAGE 76 B1544

NAT/G
OWN
INDUS
ADMIN

B58

STEWART J.D.,BRITISH PRESSURE GROUPS: THEIR ROLE IN
RELATION TO THE HOUSE OF COMMONS. UK CONSULT
DELIB/GP ADMIN ROUTINE CHOOSE REPRESENT ATTIT ROLE
20 HOUSE/CMNS PARLIAMENT. PAGE 101 B2038

LOBBY
LEGIS
PLAN
PARL/PROC

C58

WILDING N.,"AN ENCYCLOPEDIA OF PARLIAMENT." UK LAW
CONSTN CHIEF PROB/SOLV DIPLOM DEBATE WAR INGP/REL
PRIVIL...BIBLIOG DICTIONARY 13/20 CMN/WLTH
PARLIAMENT. PAGE 116 B2350

PARL/PROC
POL/PAR
NAT/G
ADMIN

B60

BHAMBHRI C.P.,PARLIAMENTARY CONTROL OVER STATE
ENTERPRISE IN INDIA. INDIA DELIB/GP ADMIN CONTROL
INGP/REL EFFICIENCY 20 PARLIAMENT. PAGE 11 B0235

NAT/G
OWN
INDUS
PARL/PROC

B60

KERSELL J.E.,PARLIAMENTARY SUPERVISION OF DELEGATED
LEGISLATION. UK EFFICIENCY PWR...POLICY CHARTS
BIBLIOG METH 20 PARLIAMENT. PAGE 59 B1198

LEGIS
CONTROL
NAT/G
EX/STRUC

B60

MEEHAN E.J.,THE BRITISH LEFT WING AND FOREIGN
POLICY: A STUDY OF THE INFLUENCE OF IDEOLOGY. FUT
UK UNIV WOR+45 INTELL TOP/EX PLAN ADMIN ROUTINE
DRIVE...OBS TIME/SEQ GEN/LAWS PARLIAMENT 20.
PAGE 72 B1461

ACT/RES
ATTIT
DIPLOM

B61

RAO K.V.,PARLIAMENTARY DEMOCRACY OF INDIA. INDIA
EX/STRUC TOP/EX COLONIAL CT/SYS PARL/PROC ORD/FREE
...POLICY CONCPT TREND 20 PARLIAMENT. PAGE 86 B1733

CONSTN
ADJUD
NAT/G
FEDERAL

S61

JOHNSON N.,"PARLIAMENTARY QUESTIONS AND THE CONDUCT
OF ADMINISTRATION." UK REPRESENT PARLIAMENT 20.
PAGE 57 B1146

CONTROL
EXEC
EX/STRUC

C61

MOODIE G.C.,"THE GOVERNMENT OF GREAT BRITAIN." UK
LAW STRUCT LOC/G POL/PAR DIPLOM RECEIVE ADMIN
COLONIAL CHOOSE...BIBLIOG 20 PARLIAMENT. PAGE 75
B1508

NAT/G
SOCIETY
PARL/PROC
GOV/COMP

B62

HANSON A.H.,MANAGERIAL PROBLEMS IN PUBLIC
ENTERPRISE. INDIA DELIB/GP GP/REL INGP/REL
EFFICIENCY 20 PARLIAMENT. PAGE 46 B0940

MGT
NAT/G
INDUS
PROB/SOLV

B62

SAMPSON A.,ANATOMY OF BRITAIN. UK LAW COM/IND FINAN
INDUS MARKET MUNIC POL/PAR EX/STRUC TOP/EX DIPLOM
LEAD REPRESENT PERSON PARLIAMENT WORSHIP. PAGE 92
B1866

ELITES
PWR
STRUCT
FORCES

B63

BADI J.,THE GOVERNMENT OF THE STATE OF ISRAEL: A
CRITICAL ACCOUNT OF ITS PARLIAMENT, EXECUTIVE, AND
JUDICIARY. ISRAEL ECO/DEV CHIEF DELIB/GP LEGIS
DIPLOM CT/SYS INGP/REL PEACE ORD/FREE...BIBLIOG 20
PARLIAMENT ARABS MIGRATION. PAGE 8 B0157

NAT/G
CONSTN
EX/STRUC
POL/PAR

B63

SHANKS M.,THE LESSONS OF PUBLIC ENTERPRISE. UK
LEGIS WORKER ECO/TAC ADMIN PARL/PROC GOV/REL ATTIT
...POLICY MGT METH/COMP NAT/COMP ANTHOL 20
PARLIAMENT. PAGE 96 B1931

SOCISM
OWN
NAT/G
INDUS

B66

ADAMS J.C.,THE GOVERNMENT OF REPUBLICAN ITALY (2ND
ED.). ITALY LOC/G POL/PAR DELIB/GP LEGIS WORKER
ADMIN CT/SYS FASCISM...CHARTS BIBLIOG 20
PARLIAMENT. PAGE 3 B0057

NAT/G
CHOOSE
EX/STRUC
CONSTN

B66

ANDERSON S.V.,CANADIAN OMBUDSMAN PROPOSALS. CANADA
LEGIS DEBATE PARL/PROC...MAJORIT JURID TIME/SEQ
IDEA/COMP 20 OMBUDSMAN PARLIAMENT. PAGE 5 B0096

NAT/G
CREATE
ADMIN
POL/PAR

B66

BURNS A.C.,PARLIAMENT AS AN EXPORT. WOR+45 CONSTN
BARGAIN DEBATE ROUTINE GOV/REL EFFICIENCY...ANTHOL
COMMONWLTH PARLIAMENT. PAGE 17 B0353

PARL/PROC
POL/PAR
CT/SYS
CHIEF

B66

DILLEY M.R.,BRITISH POLICY IN KENYA COLONY (2ND
ED.). AFR INDIA UK LABOR BUDGET TAX ADMIN PARL/PROC
GP/REL...BIBLIOG 20 PARLIAMENT. PAGE 29 B0594

COLONIAL
REPRESENT
SOVEREIGN

B66

JOHNSON N.,PARLIAMENT AND ADMINISTRATION: THE
ESTIMATES COMMITTEE 1945-65. FUT UK NAT/G EX/STRUC
PLAN BUDGET ORD/FREE...T 20 PARLIAMENT HOUSE/CMNS.

LEGIS
ADMIN
FINAN

PAGE 57 B1147 — DELIB/GP
B66

WILSON G.,CASES AND MATERIALS ON CONSTITUTIONAL AND JURID
ADMINISTRATIVE LAW. UK LAW NAT/G EX/STRUC LEGIS — ADMIN
BAL/PWR BUDGET DIPLOM ADJUD CONTROL CT/SYS GOV/REL — CONSTN
ORD/FREE 20 PARLIAMENT ENGLSH/LAW. PAGE 117 B2359 — PWR
B67

MENHENNET D.,PARLIAMENT IN PERSPECTIVE. UK ROUTINE — LEGIS
REPRESENT ROLE PWR 20 PARLIAMENT. PAGE 73 B1467 — PARL/PROC
CONCPT
POPULISM
B86

BOLINSBROKE H ST J.,A DISSERTATION UPON PARTIES — CONSERVE
(1729). UK LEGIS CHOOSE GOV/REL SOVEREIGN...TRADIT — POL/PAR
18 PARLIAMENT. PAGE 13 B0269 — CHIEF
EX/STRUC

PARNELL/CS....CHARLES STEWART PARNELL

PAROLE....SEE PUB/INST, ROUTINE, CRIME

PARRISH W.E. B1635

PARSONS T. B1636,B1637,B1638

PARSONS/T....TALCOTT PARSONS

PARTH/SASS....PARTHO-SASSANIAN EMPIRE

PARTHEMOS G.S. B0867

PARTIC....PARTICIPATION; CIVIC ACTIVITY AND NONACTIVITY

CIVIL SERVICE JOURNAL. PARTIC INGP/REL PERS/REL — ADMIN
...MGT BIBLIOG/A 20. PAGE 1 B0011 — NAT/G
SERV/IND
WORKER
N19

FAHRNKOPF N.,STATE AND LOCAL GOVERNMENT IN ILLINOIS BIBLIOG
(PAMPHLET). CONSTN ADMIN PARTIC CHOOSE REPRESENT — LOC/G
GOV/REL...JURID MGT 20 ILLINOIS. PAGE 34 B0696 — LEGIS
CT/SYS
N19

GRIFFITH W.,THE PUBLIC SERVICE (PAMPHLET). UK LAW — ADMIN
LOC/G NAT/G PARTIC CHOOSE DRIVE ROLE SKILL...CHARTS — EFFICIENCY
20 CIVIL/SERV. PAGE 44 B0880 — EDU/PROP
GOV/REL
B36

HERRING E.P.,PUBLIC ADMINISTRATION AND THE PUBLIC — GP/REL
INTEREST. LABOR NAT/G PARTIC EFFICIENCY 20. PAGE 49 — DECISION
B0995 — PROB/SOLV
ADMIN
B37

BROOKS R.R.,WHEN LABOR ORGANIZES. FINAN EDU/PROP — LABOR
ADMIN LOBBY PARTIC REPRESENT WEALTH TREND. PAGE 16 — GP/REL
B0318 — POLICY
B39

MCCAMY J.L.,GOVERNMENT PUBLICITY: ITS PRACTICE IN — EDU/PROP
FEDERAL ADMINISTRATION. USA-45 COM/IND ADMIN — NAT/G
CONTROL EXEC PARTIC INGP/REL...SOC 20. PAGE 71 — PLAN
B1442 — ATTIT
B40

MCHENRY D.E.,HIS MAJESTY'S OPPOSITION: STRUCTURE — POL/PAR
AND PROBLEMS OF THE BRITISH LABOUR PARTY 1931-1938. — MGT
UK FINAN LABOR LOC/G DELIB/GP LEGIS EDU/PROP LEAD — NAT/G
PARTIC CHOOSE GP/REL SOCISM...TREND 20 LABOR/PAR. — POLICY
PAGE 72 B1450
B42

BINGHAM A.M.,THE TECHNIQUES OF DEMOCRACY. USA-45 — POPULISM
CONSTN STRUCT POL/PAR LEGIS PLAN PARTIC CHOOSE — ORD/FREE
REPRESENT NAT/LISM TOTALISM...MGT 20. PAGE 12 B0240 — ADMIN
NAT/G
S43

GOLDEN C.S.,"NEW PATTERNS OF DEMOCRACY." NEIGH — LABOR
DELIB/GP EDU/PROP EXEC PARTIC...MGT METH/CNCPT OBS — REPRESENT
TREND. PAGE 40 B0815 — LG/CO
GP/REL
S45

TRUMAN D.B.,"PUBLIC OPINION RESEARCH AS A TOOL OF — REPRESENT
PUBLIC ADMINISTRATION" ADMIN PARTIC ROLE...DECISION — METH/CNCPT
20. PAGE 105 B2130 — ATTIT
EX/STRUC
C45

FISHER M.J.,"PARTIES AND POLITICS IN THE LOCAL — CHOOSE
COMMUNITY." USA-45 NAT/G SCHOOL ADMIN PARTIC — LOC/G
REPRESENT KNOWL...BIBLIOG 20. PAGE 36 B0724 — POL/PAR
ROUTINE
S46

CAMPBELL A.,"THE USES OF INTERVIEW SURVEYS IN — INT
FEDERAL ADMINSTRATION" PROB/SOLV EXEC PARTIC — ADMIN
DECISION. PAGE 18 B0369 — EX/STRUC
REPRESENT
B49

WRIGHT J.H.,PUBLIC RELATIONS IN MANAGEMENT. USA+45 — MGT
USA-45 ECO/DEV LG/CO SML/CO CONSULT EXEC TASK — PLAN

PROFIT ATTIT ROLE 20. PAGE 118 B2382 — EDU/PROP
PARTIC
B50

AMERICAN POLITICAL SCI ASSN,TOWARD A MORE — POL/PAR
RESPONSIBLE TWO-PARTY SYSTEM. USA+45 CONSTN — TASK
VOL/ASSN LEGIS LEAD CHOOSE...POLICY MGT 20. PAGE 4 — PARTIC
B0087 — ACT/RES
S50

EPSTEIN L.D.,"POLITICAL STERILIZATION OF CIVIL — ADMIN
SERVANTS: THE UNITED STATES AND GREAT BRITAIN." UK — LEGIS
USA+45 USA-45 STRUCT TOP/EX OP/RES PARTIC CHOOSE — DECISION
NAT/LISM 20 CONGRESS CIVIL/SERV. PAGE 33 B0679 — POL/PAR
S50

TANNENBAUM R.,"PARTICIPATION BY SUBORDINATES IN THE PARTIC
MANAGERIAL DECISIONMAKING PROCESS" (BMR)" WOR+45 — DECISION
INDUS SML/CO WORKER INGP/REL...CONCPT GEN/LAWS 20. — MGT
PAGE 103 B2074 — LG/CO
S51

STEWART D.D.,"THE PLACE OF VOLUNTEER PARTICIPATION — ADMIN
IN BUREAUCRATIC ORGANIZATION." NAT/G DELIB/GP — PARTIC
OP/RES DOMIN LOBBY WAR ATTIT ROLE PWR. PAGE 101 — VOL/ASSN
B2035 — FORCES
S52

GOLDSTEIN J.,THE GOVERNMENT OF BRITISH TRADE — LABOR
UNIONS. UK ECO/DEV EX/STRUC INGP/REL...BIBLIOG 20. — PARTIC
PAGE 40 B0817
B52

SELZNICK P.,THE ORGANIZATIONAL WEAPON: A STUDY OF — MARXISM
BOLSHEVIK STRATEGY AND TACTICS. USSR SOCIETY STRATA POL/PAR
LABOR DOMIN EDU/PROP PARTIC REV ATTIT PWR...POLICY — LEAD
MGT CONCPT 20 BOLSHEVISM. PAGE 95 B1929 — TOTALISM
B53

SAYLES L.R.,THE LOCAL UNION. CONSTN CULTURE — LABOR
DELIB/GP PARTIC CHOOSE GP/REL INGP/REL ATTIT ROLE — LEAD
...MAJORIT DECISION MGT. PAGE 93 B1873 — ADJUD
ROUTINE
S53

DRUCKER P.F.,"THE EMPLOYEE SOCIETY." STRUCT BAL/PWR LABOR
PARTIC REPRESENT PWR...DECISION CONCPT. PAGE 30 — MGT
B0619 — WORKER
CULTURE
S55

MARTIN R.C.,"ADMINISTRATIVE LEADERSHIP IN — TOP/EX
GOVERNMENT." NAT/G PARTIC ROUTINE INGP/REL...MGT — ADMIN
20. PAGE 70 B1413 — EXEC
REPRESENT
B56

CONAWAY O.B.,DEMOCRACY IN FEDERAL ADMINISTRATION — ADMIN
(PAMPHLET). USA+45 LEGIS PARTIC ATTIT...TREND — SERV/IND
ANTHOL 20. PAGE 23 B0459 — NAT/G
GP/REL
B56

GLADDEN E.N.,CIVIL SERVICE OR BUREAUCRACY? UK LAW — ADMIN
STRATA LABOR TOP/EX PLAN SENIOR AUTOMAT CONTROL — GOV/REL
PARTIC CHOOSE HAPPINESS...CHARTS 19/20 CIVIL/SERV — EFFICIENCY
BUREAUCRCY. PAGE 40 B0808 — PROVS
B57

SCHNEIDER E.V.,INDUSTRIAL SOCIOLOGY: THE SOCIAL — LABOR
RELATIONS OF INDUSTRY AND COMMUNITY. STRATA INDUS — MGT
NAT/G NEIGH CREATE ADMIN PARTIC GP/REL RACE/REL — INGP/REL
ROLE PWR...POLICY BIBLIOG. PAGE 94 B1898 — STRUCT
S57

COTTER C.P.,"ADMINISTRATIVE ACCOUNTABILITY; — LEGIS
REPORTING TO CONGRESS." USA+45 CONSULT DELIB/GP — EX/STRUC
PARL/PROC PARTIC GOV/REL ATTIT PWR DECISION. — REPRESENT
PAGE 24 B0490 — CONTROL
S57

GULICK L.,"METROPOLITAN ORGANIZATION." LEGIS EXEC — REGION
PARTIC CHOOSE REPRESENT GOV/REL...MAJORIT DECISION. LOC/G
PAGE 45 B0904 — MUNIC
S57

RAPAPORT R.N.,"'DEMOCRATIZATION' AND AUTHORITY IN A PUB/INST
THERAPEUTIC COMMUNITY." OP/RES ADMIN PARTIC CENTRAL HEALTH
ATTIT...POLICY DECISION. PAGE 86 B1735 — DOMIN
CLIENT
S57

ROBSON W.A.,"TWO-LEVEL GOVERNMENT FOR METROPOLITAN — REGION
AREAS." MUNIC EX/STRUC LEGIS PARTIC REPRESENT — LOC/G
MAJORITY. PAGE 89 B1807 — PLAN
GOV/REL
B58

COWAN L.G.,LOCAL GOVERNMENT IN WEST AFRICA. AFR — LOC/G
FRANCE UK CULTURE KIN POL/PAR CHIEF LEGIS CREATE — COLONIAL
ADMIN PARTIC GOV/REL GP/REL...METH/COMP 20. PAGE 24 SOVEREIGN
B0498 — REPRESENT
B58

INDIAN INST OF PUBLIC ADMIN,IMPROVING CITY — LOC/G
GOVERNMENT. INDIA ECO/UNDEV PLAN BUDGET PARTIC — MUNIC
GP/REL 20. PAGE 53 B1080 — PROB/SOLV
ADMIN
B58

LESTER R.A.,AS UNIONS MATURE. POL/PAR BARGAIN LEAD — LABOR
PARTIC GP/REL CENTRAL...MAJORIT TIME/SEQ METH/COMP. INDUS
PAGE 64 B1299 — POLICY
MGT

B58
MARCH J.G.,ORGANIZATIONS. USA+45 CREATE OP/RES PLAN MGT
PROB/SOLV PARTIC ROUTINE RATIONAL ATTIT PERCEPT PERSON
...DECISION BIBLIOG. PAGE 69 B1397 DRIVE
CONCPT

B58
SHERWOOD F.P.,SUPERVISORY METHODS IN MUNICIPAL EX/STRUC
ADMINISTRATION. USA+45 MUNIC WORKER EDU/PROP PARTIC LEAD
INGP/REL PERS/REL 20 CITY/MGT. PAGE 96 B1945 ADMIN
LOC/G

S58
DERGE D.R.,"METROPOLITAN AND OUTSTATE ALIGNMENTS IN LEGIS
ILLINOIS AND MISSOURI LEGISLATIVE DELEGATIONS" MUNIC
(BMR)" USA+45 ADMIN PARTIC GOV/REL...MYTH CHARTS 20 PROVS
ILLINOIS MISSOURI. PAGE 28 B0575 POL/PAR

C58
REDFORD E.S.,"THE NEVER-ENDING SEARCH FOR THE LOBBY
PUBLIC INTEREST" IN E. REDFORD, IDEALS AND PRACTICE POLICY
IN PUBLIC ADMINISTRATION (BMR)" USA+45 USA-45 ADMIN
SOCIETY PARTIC GP/REL ATTIT PLURISM...DECISION SOC MAJORIT
20. PAGE 87 B1755

S59
GABLE R.W.,"CULTURE AND ADMINISTRATION IN IRAN." ADMIN
IRAN EXEC PARTIC REPRESENT PWR. PAGE 38 B0770 CULTURE
EX/STRUC
INGP/REL

B60
BERNSTEIN I.,THE LEAN YEARS. SOCIETY STRATA PARTIC WORKER
GP/REL ATTIT...SOC 20 DEPRESSION. PAGE 11 B0227 LABOR
WEALTH
MGT

B60
SAYRE W.S.,GOVERNING NEW YORK CITY: POLITICS IN THE MUNIC
METROPOLIS. POL/PAR CHIEF DELIB/GP LEGIS PLAN ADMIN
CT/SYS LEAD PARTIC CHOOSE...DECISION CHARTS BIBLIOG PROB/SOLV
20 NEWYORK/C BUREAUCRCY. PAGE 93 B1875

B61
AVERY M.W.,GOVERNMENT OF WASHINGTON STATE. USA+45 PROVS
MUNIC DELIB/GP EX/STRUC LEGIS GIVE CT/SYS PARTIC LOC/G
REGION EFFICIENCY 20 WASHINGT/G GOVERNOR. PAGE 7 ADMIN
B0151 GOV/REL

B61
LENIN V.I.,WHAT IS TO BE DONE? (1902). RUSSIA LABOR EDU/PROP
NAT/G POL/PAR WORKER CAP/ISM ECO/TAC ADMIN PARTIC PRESS
...MARXIST IDEA/COMP GEN/LAWS 19/20. PAGE 64 B1292 MARXISM
METH/COMP

B61
TRECKER H.B.,NEW UNDERSTANDING OF ADMINISTRATION. VOL/ASSN
NEIGH DELIB/GP CONTROL LEAD GP/REL INGP/REL PROF/ORG
...POLICY DECISION BIBLIOG. PAGE 105 B2126 ADMIN
PARTIC

S61
LYONS G.M.,"THE NEW CIVIL-MILITARY RELATIONS." CIVMIL/REL
USA+45 NAT/G EX/STRUC TOP/EX PROB/SOLV ADMIN EXEC PWR
PARTIC 20. PAGE 67 B1350 REPRESENT

C61
VERBA S.,"SMALL GROUPS AND POLITICAL BEHAVIOR: A LEAD
STUDY OF LEADERSHIP" DOMIN PARTIC ROUTINE GP/REL ELITES
ATTIT DRIVE ALL/VALS...CONCPT IDEA/COMP LAB/EXP FACE/GP
BIBLIOG METH. PAGE 112 B2259

B62
DIMOCK M.E.,THE NEW AMERICAN POLITICAL ECONOMY: A FEDERAL
SYNTHESIS OF POLITICS AND ECONOMICS. USA+45 FINAN ECO/TAC
LG/CO PLAN ADMIN REGION GP/REL CENTRAL MORAL 20. NAT/G
PAGE 29 B0598 PARTIC

B62
DODDS H.W.,THE ACADEMIC PRESIDENT "EDUCATOR OR ACADEM
CARETAKER? FINAN DELIB/GP EDU/PROP PARTIC ATTIT ADMIN
ROLE PWR...POLICY RECORD INT. PAGE 30 B0601 LEAD
CONTROL

B62
FARBER W.O.,GOVERNMENT OF SOUTH DAKOTA. USA+45 PROVS
DIST/IND POL/PAR CHIEF EX/STRUC LEGIS ECO/TAC GIVE LOC/G
EDU/PROP CT/SYS PARTIC...T 20 SOUTH/DAK GOVERNOR. ADMIN
PAGE 35 B0704 CONSTN

B62
KAMMERER G.M.,CITY MANAGERS IN POLITICS: AN MUNIC
ANALYSIS OF MANAGER TENURE AND TERMINATION. POL/PAR LEAD
LEGIS PARTIC CHOOSE PWR...DECISION GEOG METH/CNCPT. EXEC
PAGE 57 B1161

B62
LIPPMANN W.,PREFACE TO POLITICS. LABOR CHIEF PARTIC
CONTROL LEAD...MYTH IDEA/COMP 19/20 ROOSEVLT/T ATTIT
TAMMANY WILSON/H SANTAYAN/G BERGSON/H. PAGE 65 ADMIN
B1318

B62
LYNCH J.,ADMINISTRATION COLONIAL ESPANOLA COLONIAL
1782-1810. SPAIN PROVS TOP/EX PARTIC 18/19 ARGEN. CONTROL
PAGE 67 B1349 ADJUD
ADMIN

S62
BOOTH D.A.,"POWER STRUCTURE AND COMMUNITY CHANGE: A MUNIC
REPLICATION STUDY OF COMMUNITY A." STRATA LABOR ELITES
LEAD PARTIC REPRESENT...DECISION MGT TIME. PAGE 14 PWR
B0275

S62
TANNENBAUM A.S.,"CONTROL IN ORGANIZATIONS: ADMIN
INDIVIDUAL ADJUSTMENT AND ORGANIZATIONAL MGT
PERFORMANCE." DOMIN PARTIC REPRESENT INGP/REL STRUCT
PRODUC ATTIT DRIVE PWR...PSY CORREL. PAGE 102 B2073 CONTROL

B63
BERNE E.,THE STRUCTURE AND DYNAMICS OF INGP/REL
ORGANIZATIONS AND GROUPS. CLIENT PARTIC DRIVE AUTHORIT
HEALTH...MGT PSY ORG/CHARTS. PAGE 11 B0226 ROUTINE
CLASSIF

B63
CROUCH W.W.,SOUTHERN CALIFORNIA METROPOLIS: A STUDY LOC/G
IN DEVELOPMENT OF GOVERNMENT FOR A METROPOLITAN MUNIC
AREA. USA+45 USA-45 PROB/SOLV ADMIN LOBBY PARTIC LEGIS
CENTRAL ORD/FREE PWR...BIBLIOG 20 PROGRSV/M. DECISION
PAGE 25 B0510

B63
HAYMAN D.,POLITICAL ACTIVITY RESTRICTION: AN CONTROL
ANALYSIS WITH RECOMMENDATIONS (PAMPHLET). USA+45 ADMIN
EXEC PARTIC ROLE PWR 20. PAGE 48 B0976 INGP/REL
REPRESENT

B63
HERMAN H.,NEW YORK STATE AND THE METROPOLITAN GOV/REL
PROBLEM. USA+45 ECO/DEV PUB/INST SCHOOL LEGIS PLAN PROVS
TAX EXEC PARL/PROC PARTIC...HEAL 20 NEW/YORK. LOC/G
PAGE 49 B0992 POLICY

S63
GITTELL M.,"METROPOLITAN MAYOR: DEAD END." LOC/G MUNIC
PARTIC REGION ATTIT PWR GP/COMP. PAGE 40 B0804 LEAD
EXEC

S63
WINGFIELD C.J.,"POWER STRUCTURE AND DECISION-MAKING MUNIC
IN CITY PLANNING." EDU/PROP ADMIN LEAD PARTIC PLAN
GP/REL ATTIT. PAGE 117 B2365 DECISION
PWR

B64
ARGYRIS C.,INTEGRATING THE INDIVIDUAL AND THE ADMIN
ORGANIZATION. WORKER PROB/SOLV LEAD SANCTION PERS/REL
REPRESENT ADJUST EFFICIENCY DRIVE PERSON...PSY VOL/ASSN
METH/CNCPT ORG/CHARTS. PAGE 6 B0132 PARTIC

B64
BROMAGE A.W.,MANAGER PLAN ABANDONMENTS: WHY A FEW MUNIC
HAVE DROPPED COUNCILMANAGER GOVERNMENT. USA+45 PLAN
CREATE PARTIC CHOOSE...MGT CENSUS CHARTS 20. CONSULT
PAGE 15 B0315 LOC/G

B64
GOLDWIN R.A.,POLITICAL PARTIES. USA. USA+45 USA-45 POL/PAR
LOC/G ADMIN LEAD EFFICIENCY ATTIT PWR...POLICY STAT PARTIC
ANTHOL 18/20 CONGRESS. PAGE 40 B0818 NAT/G
CONSTN

B64
GOODNOW H.F.,THE CIVIL SERVICE OF PAKISTAN: ADMIN
BUREAUCRACY IN A NEW NATION. INDIA PAKISTAN S/ASIA GOV/REL
ECO/UNDEV PROVS CHIEF PARTIC CHOOSE EFFICIENCY PWR LAW
...BIBLIOG 20. PAGE 41 B0824 NAT/G

B64
LOWI T.J.,AT THE PLEASURE OF THE MAYOR. EX/STRUC LOBBY
PROB/SOLV BAL/PWR ADMIN PARTIC CHOOSE GP/REL LOC/G
...CONT/OBS NET/THEORY CHARTS 20 NEWYORK/C MAYOR. PWR
PAGE 67 B1346 MUNIC

B64
RAPHAEL M.,PENSIONS AND PUBLIC SERVANTS. UK PLAN ADMIN
EDU/PROP PARTIC GOV/REL HEALTH...POLICY CHARTS SENIOR
17/20 CIVIL/SERV. PAGE 86 B1737 PAY
AGE/O

B64
RIDLEY F.,PUBLIC ADMINISTRATION IN FRANCE. FRANCE ADMIN
UK EX/STRUC CONTROL PARTIC EFFICIENCY 20. PAGE 88 REPRESENT
B1781 GOV/COMP
PWR

B64
ROBSON W.A.,THE GOVERNORS AND THE GOVERNED. USA+45 EX/STRUC
PROB/SOLV DOMIN ADMIN CONTROL CHOOSE...POLICY ATTIT
PRESIDENT. PAGE 89 B1808 PARTIC
LEAD

B64
VALEN H.,POLITICAL PARTIES IN NORWAY. NORWAY ACADEM LOC/G
PARTIC ROUTINE INGP/REL KNOWL...QU 20. PAGE 111 POL/PAR
B2249 PERSON

B64
WILDAVSKY A.,LEADERSHIP IN A SMALL TOWN. USA+45 LEAD
STRUCT PROB/SOLV EXEC PARTIC RACE/REL PWR PLURISM MUNIC
...SOC 20 NEGRO WATER CIV/RIGHTS OBERLIN CITY/MGT. ELITES
PAGE 116 B2348

S64
KAMMERER G.M.,"URBAN LEADERSHIP DURING CHANGE." MUNIC
LEAD PARTIC REPRESENT GP/REL PLURISM...DECISION PWR
GP/COMP. PAGE 58 B1164 ELITES
EXEC

S64
SALISBURY R.H.,"URBAN POLITICS: THE NEW CONVERGENCE MUNIC
OF POWER." STRATA POL/PAR EX/STRUC PARTIC GP/REL PWR
DECISION. PAGE 92 B1863 LEAD

B65
FRYE R.J.,HOUSING AND URBAN RENEWAL IN ALABAMA. MUNIC
USA+45 NEIGH LEGIS BUDGET ADJUD ADMIN PARTIC...MGT PROB/SOLV

20 ALABAMA URBAN/RNWL. PAGE 38 B0762
PLAN
GOV/REL

B65

GOULDNER A.W.,STUDIES IN LEADERSHIP. LABOR EDU/PROP
CONTROL PARTIC...CONCPT CLASSIF. PAGE 42 B0845
LEAD
ADMIN
AUTHORIT

B65

HADWIGER D.F.,PRESSURES AND PROTEST. NAT/G LEGIS
PLAN LEAD PARTIC ROUTINE ATTIT POLICY. PAGE 45
B0913
AGRI
GP/REL
LOBBY
CHOOSE

B65

MASTERS N.A.,COMMITTEE ASSIGNMENTS IN THE HOUSE OF
REPRESENTATIVES (BMR). USA+45 ELITES POL/PAR
EX/STRUC PARTIC REPRESENT GP/REL PERS/REL ATTIT PWR
...STAT CHARTS 20 HOUSE/REP. PAGE 71 B1425
LEAD
LEGIS
CHOOSE
DELIB/GP

B65

ROWAT D.C.,THE OMBUDSMAN: CITIZEN'S DEFENDER.
DENMARK FINLAND NEW/ZEALND NORWAY SWEDEN CONSULT
PROB/SOLV FEEDBACK PARTIC GP/REL...SOC CONCPT
NEW/IDEA METH/COMP ANTHOL BIBLIOG 20. PAGE 91 B1840
INSPECT
CONSTN
NAT/G
ADMIN

B65

SCHAPIRO L.,THE GOVERNMENT AND POLITICS OF THE
SOVIET UNION. USSR WOR+45 WOR-45 ADMIN PARTIC REV
CHOOSE REPRESENT PWR...POLICY IDEA/COMP 20. PAGE 93
B1880
MARXISM
GOV/REL
NAT/G
LOC/G

B65

WARD W.E.,GOVERNMENT IN WEST AFRICA. WOR+45 POL/PAR
EX/STRUC PLAN PARTIC GP/REL SOVEREIGN 20 AFRICA/W.
PAGE 114 B2291
GOV/COMP
CONSTN
COLONIAL
ECO/UNDEV

S65

ASHFORD D.E.,"BUREAUCRATS AND CITIZENS." MOROCCO
PAKISTAN PARTIC 20 TUNIS. PAGE 7 B0140
GOV/COMP
ADMIN
EX/STRUC
ROLE

N65

MOTE M.E.,SOVIET LOCAL AND REPUBLIC ELECTIONS. COM
USSR NAT/G PLAN PARTIC GOV/REL TOTALISM PWR
...CHARTS 20. PAGE 76 B1534
CHOOSE
ADMIN
CONTROL
LOC/G

B66

CHAPMAN B.,THE PROFESSION OF GOVERNMENT: THE PUBLIC
SERVICE IN EUROPE. CONSTN NAT/G POL/PAR EX/STRUC
LEGIS TOP/EX PROB/SOLV DEBATE EXEC PARL/PROC PARTIC
20. PAGE 20 B0411
BIBLIOG
ADMIN
EUR+WWI
GOV/COMP

B66

CORNWELL E.E. JR.,THE AMERICAN PRESIDENCY: VITAL
CENTER. USA+45 USA-45 POL/PAR LEGIS PROB/SOLV
CONTROL PARTIC GOV/REL 18/20 PRESIDENT. PAGE 23
B0478
CHIEF
EX/STRUC
NAT/G
ADMIN

B66

DAHLBERG J.S.,THE NEW YORK BUREAU OF MUNICIPAL
RESEARCH: PIONEER IN GOVERNMENT ADMINISTRATION.
CONSTN R+D BUDGET EDU/PROP PARTIC REPRESENT
EFFICIENCY ORD/FREE...BIBLIOG METH 20 NEW/YORK
NIPA. PAGE 26 B0522
PROVS
MUNIC
DELIB/GP
ADMIN

B66

HESSLER I.O.,29 WAYS TO GOVERN A CITY. EX/STRUC
TOP/EX PROB/SOLV PARTIC CHOOSE REPRESENT EFFICIENCY
...CHARTS 20 CITY/MGT MAYOR. PAGE 49 B0998
MUNIC
GOV/COMP
LOC/G
ADMIN

B66

LIVINGSTON J.C.,THE CONSENT OF THE GOVERNED. USA+45
EX/STRUC BAL/PWR DOMIN CENTRAL PERSON PWR...POLICY
CONCPT OBS IDEA/COMP 20 CONGRESS. PAGE 66 B1331
NAT/G
LOBBY
MAJORIT
PARTIC

B66

RUBENSTEIN R.,THE SHARING OF POWER IN A PSYCHIATRIC
HOSPITAL. CLIENT PROF/ORG PUB/INST INGP/REL ATTIT
PWR...DECISION OBS RECORD. PAGE 91 B1847
ADMIN
PARTIC
HEALTH
CONCPT

B66

SEASHOLES B.,VOTING, INTEREST GROUPS, AND PARTIES.
USA+45 FINAN LOC/G NAT/G ADMIN LEAD GP/REL INGP/REL
ROLE...CHARTS ANTHOL 20. PAGE 95 B1922
CHOOSE
POL/PAR
LOBBY
PARTIC

B66

STREET D.,ORGANIZATION FOR TREATMENT. CLIENT PROVS
PUB/INST PLAN CONTROL PARTIC REPRESENT ATTIT PWR
...POLICY BIBLIOG. PAGE 101 B2052
GP/COMP
AGE/Y
ADMIN
VOL/ASSN

B66

TOTTEN G.O.,THE SOCIAL DEMOCRATIC MOVEMENT IN
PREWAR JAPAN. ASIA CHIEF EX/STRUC LEGIS DOMIN LEAD
ROUTINE WAR 20 CHINJAP. PAGE 105 B2122
POL/PAR
SOCISM
PARTIC
STRATA

L66

CRAIN R.L.,"STRUCTURE AND VALUES IN LOCAL POLITICAL
SYSTEMS: THE CASE OF FLUORIDATION DECISIONS."
EX/STRUC LEGIS LEAD PARTIC REPRESENT PWR...DECISION
GOV/COMP. PAGE 25 B0501
MUNIC
EDU/PROP
LOC/G
ATTIT

C66

SHERMAN H.,"IT ALL DEPENDS." USA+45 FINAN MARKET
PLAN PROB/SOLV EXEC PARTIC INGP/REL SUPEGO
...DECISION BIBLIOG 20. PAGE 96 B1944
LG/CO
MGT
ADMIN

POLICY

B67

GITTELL M.,PARTICIPANTS AND PARTICIPATION: A STUDY
OF SCHOOL POLICY IN NEW YORK. USA+45 MUNIC EX/STRUC
BUDGET PAY ATTIT...POLICY 20 NEWYORK/C. PAGE 40
B0806
SCHOOL
DECISION
PARTIC
ADMIN

B67

MARRIS P.,DILEMMAS OF SOCIAL REFORM: POVERTY AND
COMMUNITY ACTION IN THE UNITED STATES. USA+45 NAT/G
OP/RES ADMIN PARTIC EFFICIENCY WEALTH...SOC
METH/COMP T 20 REFORMERS. PAGE 69 B1401
STRUCT
MUNIC
PROB/SOLV
COST

B67

ROBINSON D.W.,PROMISING PRACTICES IN CIVIC
EDUCATION. FUT USA+45 CONTROL PARTIC GOV/REL...OBS
AUD/VIS 20. PAGE 89 B1797
EDU/PROP
NAT/G
ADJUST
ADMIN

S67

BREGMAN A.,"WHITHER RUSSIA?" COM RUSSIA INTELL
POL/PAR DIPLOM PARTIC NAT/LISM TOTALISM ATTIT
ORD/FREE 20. PAGE 15 B0304
MARXISM
ELITES
ADMIN
CREATE

S67

DRYDEN S.,"LOCAL GOVERNMENT IN TANZANIA PART II"
TANZANIA LAW NAT/G POL/PAR CONTROL PARTIC REPRESENT
...DECISION 20. PAGE 31 B0622
LOC/G
GOV/REL
ADMIN
STRUCT

S67

GOBER J.L.,"FEDERALISM AT WORK." USA+45 NAT/G
CONSULT ACT/RES PLAN CONFER ADMIN LEAD PARTIC
FEDERAL ATTIT. PAGE 40 B0813
MUNIC
TEC/DEV
R+D
GOV/REL

S67

GORMAN W.,"ELLUL - A PROPHETIC VOICE." WOR+45
ELITES SOCIETY ACT/RES PLAN BAL/PWR DOMIN CONTROL
PARTIC TOTALISM PWR 20. PAGE 41 B0837
CREATE
ORD/FREE
EX/STRUC
UTOPIA

S67

LASLETT J.H.M.,"SOCIALISM AND THE AMERICAN LABOR
MOVEMENT* SOME NEW REFLECTIONS." USA-45 VOL/ASSN
LOBBY PARTIC CENTRAL ALL/VALS SOCISM...GP/COMP 20.
PAGE 63 B1265
LABOR
ROUTINE
ATTIT
GP/REL

S67

LEVIN M.R.,"PLANNERS AND METROPOLITAN PLANNING."
FUT USA+45 SOCIETY NAT/G PROVS PROB/SOLV LEAD
PARTIC GOV/REL RACE/REL HABITAT ROLE. PAGE 64 B1301
PLAN
MUNIC
R+D
ADMIN

N19

DOTSON A.,PRODUCTION PLANNING IN THE PATENT OFFICE
(PAMPHLET). USA+45 DIST/IND PROB/SOLV PRODUC...MGT
PHIL/SCI 20 BUR/BUDGET PATENT/OFF. PAGE 30 B0610
EFFICIENCY
PLAN
NAT/G
ADMIN

N

PRINCETON U INDUSTRIAL REL SEC,SELECTED REFERENCES
OF THE INDUSTRIAL RELATIONS SECTION OF PRINCETON,
NEW JERSEY. LG/CO NAT/G LEGIS WORKER PLAN PROB/SOLV
PAY ADMIN ROUTINE TASK GP/REL...PSY 20. PAGE 84
B1708
BIBLIOG/A
INDUS
LABOR
MGT

N19

FIKS M.,PUBLIC ADMINISTRATION IN ISRAEL (PAMPHLET).
ISRAEL SCHOOL EX/STRUC BUDGET PAY INGP/REL
...DECISION 20 CIVIL/SERV. PAGE 35 B0718
EDU/PROP
NAT/G
ADMIN
WORKER

N19
FOLSOM M.B.,BETTER MANAGEMENT OF THE PUBLIC'S
BUSINESS (PAMPHLET). USA+45 DELIB/GP PAY CONFER
CONTROL REGION GP/REL...METH/COMP ANTHOL 20.
PAGE 36 B0733

ADMIN
NAT/G
MGT
PROB/SOLV

N19
GINZBERG E.,MANPOWER FOR GOVERNMENT (PAMPHLET).
USA+45 FORCES PLAN PROB/SOLV PAY EDU/PROP ADMIN
GP/REL COST...MGT PREDICT TREND 20 CIVIL/SERV.
PAGE 40 B0803

WORKER
CONSULT
NAT/G
LOC/G

B28
CALKINS E.E.,BUSINESS THE CIVILIZER. INDUS MARKET
WORKER TAX PAY ROUTINE COST DEMAND MORAL 19/20.
PAGE 18 B0367

LAISSEZ
POLICY
WEALTH
PROFIT

B32
MCKISACK M.,THE PARLIAMENTARY REPRESENTATION OF THE
ENGLISH BOROUGHS DURING THE MIDDLE AGES. UK CONSTN
CULTURE ELITES EX/STRUC TAX PAY ADJUD PARL/PROC
APPORT FEDERAL...POLICY 13/15 PARLIAMENT. PAGE 72
B1454

NAT/G
MUNIC
LEGIS
CHOOSE

B41
LESTER R.A.,ECONOMICS OF LABOR. UK USA-45 TEC/DEV
BARGAIN PAY INGP/REL INCOME...MGT 19/20. PAGE 64
B1298

LABOR
ECO/DEV
INDUS
WORKER

B41
SLICHTER S.H.,UNION POLICIES AND INDUSTRIAL
MANAGEMENT. USA-45 INDUS TEC/DEV PAY GP/REL
INGP/REL COST EFFICIENCY PRODUC...POLICY 20.
PAGE 98 B1978

BARGAIN
LABOR
MGT
WORKER

B49
SHISTER J.,ECONOMICS OF THE LABOR MARKET. LOC/G
NAT/G WORKER TEC/DEV BARGAIN PAY PRICE EXEC GP/REL
INCOME...MGT T 20. PAGE 96 B1949

MARKET
LABOR
INDUS

B51
PETERSON F.,SURVEY OF LABOR ECONOMICS (REV. ED.).
STRATA ECO/DEV LABOR INSPECT BARGAIN PAY PRICE EXEC
ROUTINE GP/REL ALL/VALS ORD/FREE 20 AFL/CIO
DEPT/LABOR. PAGE 82 B1662

WORKER
DEMAND
IDEA/COMP
T

B54
GOLDNER A.W.,WILDCAT STRIKE. LABOR TEC/DEV PAY
ADMIN LEAD PERS/REL ATTIT RIGID/FLEX PWR...MGT
CONCPT. PAGE 40 B0816

INDUS
WORKER
GP/REL
SOC

B55
HOROWITZ M.,INCENTIVE WAGE SYSTEMS. INDUS LG/CO
WORKER CONTROL GP/REL...MGT PSY 20. PAGE 51 B1044

BIBLIOG/A
PAY
PLAN
TASK

B56
HICKMAN C.A.,INDIVIDUALS, GROUPS, AND ECONOMIC
BEHAVIOR. WORKER PAY CONTROL EXEC GP/REL INGP/REL
PERSON ROLE...PSY SOC PERS/COMP METH 20. PAGE 50
B1005

MGT
ADMIN
ECO/TAC
PLAN

B56
POWELL N.J.,PERSONNEL ADMINISTRATION IN GOVERNMENT.
COM/IND POL/PAR LEGIS PAY CT/SYS ROUTINE GP/REL
PERS/REL...POLICY METH 20 CIVIL/SERV. PAGE 84 B1697

ADMIN
WORKER
LOC/G
NAT/G

B58
DAVIS K.C.,ADMINISTRATIVE LAW; CASES, TEXT,
PROBLEMS. LAW LOC/G NAT/G TOP/EX PAY CONTROL
GOV/REL INGP/REL FEDERAL 20 SUPREME/CT. PAGE 27
B0541

ADJUD
JURID
CT/SYS
ADMIN

B59
CHRISTENSON R.M.,THE BRANNAN PLAN: FARM POLITICS
AND POLICY. USA+45 ECO/DEV CONSULT PLAN PAY GOV/REL
...POLICY 20. PAGE 21 B0429

AGRI
NAT/G
ADMIN
ECO/TAC

B59
COUNCIL OF STATE GOVERNORS,AMERICAN LEGISLATURES:
STRUCTURE AND PROCEDURES. SUMMARY AND TABULATIONS
OF A 1959 SURVEY. PUERT/RICO USA+45 PAY ADJUD ADMIN
APPORT...IDEA/COMP 20 GUAM VIRGIN/ISL. PAGE 24
B0495

LEGIS
CHARTS
PROVS
REPRESENT

B59
ROSOLIO D.,TEN YEARS OF THE CIVIL SERVICE IN ISRAEL
(1948-1958) (PAMPHLET). ISRAEL NAT/G RECEIVE 20.
PAGE 90 B1825

ADMIN
WORKER
GOV/REL
PAY

B59
THARAMATHAJ C.,A STUDY OF THE COMPOSITION OF THE
THAI CIVIL SERVICE (PAPER). THAILAND PAY ROLE
...CHARTS 20 CIVIL/SERV FEMALE/SEX. PAGE 103 B2092

ADMIN
EX/STRUC
STRATA
INGP/REL

B60
LINDVEIT E.N.,SCIENTISTS IN GOVERNMENT. USA+45 PAY
EDU/PROP ADMIN DRIVE HABITAT ROLE...TECHNIC BIBLIOG
20. PAGE 65 B1316

TEC/DEV
ECO/TAC
PHIL/SCI
GOV/REL

B61
AYLMER G.,THE KING'S SERVANTS. UK ELITES CHIEF PAY
CT/SYS WEALTH 17 CROMWELL/O CHARLES/I. PAGE 7 B0153

ADMIN
ROUTINE
EX/STRUC
NAT/G

B61
QURESHI S.,INCENTIVES IN AMERICAN EMPLOYMENT
(THESIS, UNIVERSITY OF PENNSYLVANIA). DELIB/GP
TOP/EX BUDGET ROUTINE SANCTION COST TECHRACY MGT.
PAGE 85 B1727

SERV/IND
ADMIN
PAY
EX/STRUC

B61
ROMANO F.,CIVIL SERVICE AND PUBLIC EMPLOYEE LAW IN
NEW JERSEY. CONSTN MUNIC WORKER GIVE PAY CHOOSE
UTIL 20. PAGE 90 B1816

ADMIN
PROVS
ADJUD
LOC/G

B61
ROSE D.L.,THE VIETNAMESE CIVIL SERVICE. VIETNAM
CONSULT DELIB/GP GIVE PAY EDU/PROP COLONIAL GOV/REL
UTIL...CHARTS 20. PAGE 90 B1819

ADMIN
EFFICIENCY
STAT
NAT/G

B62
GALENSON W.,LABOR IN DEVELOPING COUNTRIES. BRAZIL
INDONESIA ISRAEL PAKISTAN TURKEY AGRI INDUS WORKER
PAY PRICE GP/REL WEALTH...MGT CHARTS METH/COMP
NAT/COMP 20. PAGE 38 B0775

LABOR
ECO/UNDEV
BARGAIN
POL/PAR

B62
NJ DEPARTMENT CIVIL SERV,THE CIVIL SERVICE RULES OF
THE STATE OF NEW JERSEY. USA+45 USA-45 PAY...JURID
ANTHOL 20 CIVIL/SERV NEW/JERSEY. PAGE 78 B1585

ADMIN
PROVS
ROUTINE
WORKER

L62
BELSHAW D.G.R.,"PUBLIC INVESTMENT IN AGRICULTURE
AND ECONOMIC DEVELOPMENT OF UGANDA" UGANDA AGRI
INDUS R+D ECO/TAC RATION TAX PAY COLONIAL 20
WORLD/BANK. PAGE 10 B0209

ECO/UNDEV
PLAN
ADMIN
CENTRAL

B63
DUE J.F.,STATE SALES TAX ADMINISTRATION. OP/RES
BUDGET PAY ADMIN EXEC ROUTINE COST EFFICIENCY
PROFIT...CHARTS METH/COMP 20. PAGE 31 B0626

PROVS
TAX
STAT
GOV/COMP

B63
US HOUSE COM ON ED AND LABOR,ADMINISTRATION OF
AGING. USA+45 R+D EX/STRUC PLAN BUDGET PAY EDU/PROP
ROUTINE COST CONGRESS. PAGE 108 B2187

AGE/O
ADMIN
DELIB/GP
GIVE

S63
MEDALIA N.Z.,"POSITION AND PROSPECTS OF
SOCIOLOGISTS IN FEDERAL EMPLOYMENT." USA+45 CONSULT
PAY SENIOR ADMIN GOV/REL...TREND CHARTS 20
CIVIL/SERV. PAGE 72 B1460

NAT/G
WORKER
SOC
SKILL

B64
COMMITTEE ECONOMIC DEVELOPMENT,IMPROVING EXECUTIVE
MANAGEMENT IN THE FEDERAL GOVERNMENT. USA+45 CHIEF
DELIB/GP WORKER PLAN PAY SENIOR ADMIN EFFICIENCY 20
PRESIDENT. PAGE 22 B0457

EXEC
MGT
TOP/EX
NAT/G

B64
RAPHAEL M.,PENSIONS AND PUBLIC SERVANTS. UK PLAN
EDU/PROP PARTIC GOV/REL HEALTH...POLICY CHARTS
17/20 CIVIL/SERV. PAGE 86 B1737

ADMIN
SENIOR
PAY
AGE/O

B65
RHODES G.,PUBLIC SECTOR PENSIONS. UK FINAN LEGIS
BUDGET TAX PAY INCOME...CHARTS 20 CIVIL/SERV.
PAGE 88 B1769

ADMIN
RECEIVE
AGE/O
WORKER

B65
US HOUSE COMM EDUC AND LABOR,ADMINISTRATION OF THE
NATIONAL LABOR RELATIONS ACT. USA+45 DELIB/GP
WORKER PROB/SOLV BARGAIN PAY CONTROL 20 NLRB
CONGRESS. PAGE 108 B2188

ADMIN
LABOR
GP/REL
INDUS

B65
VAID K.N.,STATE AND LABOR IN INDIA. INDIA INDUS
WORKER PAY PRICE ADJUD CONTROL PARL/PROC GP/REL
ORD/FREE 20. PAGE 111 B2248

LAW
LABOR
MGT
NEW/LIB

B66
NIEBURG H.L.,IN THE NAME OF SCIENCE. USA+45
EX/STRUC LEGIS TEC/DEV BUDGET PAY AUTOMAT LOBBY PWR
...OBS 20. PAGE 78 B1581

NAT/G
INDUS
TECHRACY

B66
US SENATE COMM GOVT OPERATIONS,INTERGOVERNMENTAL
PERSONNEL ACT OF 1966. USA+45 NAT/G CONSULT
DELIB/GP WORKER TEC/DEV PAY AUTOMAT UTIL 20
CONGRESS. PAGE 110 B2219

ADMIN
LEGIS
EFFICIENCY
EDU/PROP

B67
GITTELL M.,PARTICIPANTS AND PARTICIPATION: A STUDY
OF SCHOOL POLICY IN NEW YORK. USA+45 MUNIC EX/STRUC
BUDGET PAY ATTIT...POLICY 20 NEWYORK/C. PAGE 40
B0806

SCHOOL
DECISION
PARTIC
ADMIN

B67
NORTHRUP H.R.,RESTRICTIVE LABOR PRACTICES IN THE
SUPERMARKET INDUSTRY. USA+45 INDUS WORKER TEC/DEV
BARGAIN PAY CONTROL GP/REL COST...STAT CHARTS NLRB.
PAGE 79 B1592

DIST/IND
MARKET
LABOR
MGT

S67
GRINYER P.H.,"THE SYSTEMATIC EVALUATION OF METHODS
OF WAGE PAYMENT." UK INDUS WORKER ADMIN EFFICIENCY
...MGT METH/COMP 20. PAGE 44 B0882

OP/RES
COST
PAY
PRODUC

S67
HAIRE M.,"MANAGING MANAGEMENT MANPOWER." EX/STRUC

MGT

OP/RES PAY EDU/PROP COST EFFICIENCY...PREDICT SIMUL EXEC LEAD INDUS
20. PAGE 45 B0920

S67
LEVCIK B.,"WAGES AND EMPLOYMENT PROBLEMS IN THE NEW MARXISM
SYSTEM OF PLANNED MANAGEMENT IN CZECHOSLOVAKIA." WORKER
CZECHOSLVK EUR+WWI NAT/G OP/RES PLAN ADMIN ROUTINE MGT
INGP/REL CENTRAL EFFICIENCY PRODUC DECISION. PAY
PAGE 64 B1300

S67
MERON T.,"THE UN'S 'COMMON SYSTEM' OF SALARY, ADMIN
ALLOWANCE, AND BENEFITS: CRITICAL APPR'SAL OF COORD EX/STRUC
IN PERSONNEL MATTERS." VOL/ASSN PAY EFFICIENCY INT/ORG
...CHARTS 20 UN. PAGE 73 B1470 BUDGET

PAYNE E.M. B1457

PAYNE J.L. B1645

PAYNE W.A. B1646

PEABODY R.L. B1647,B1648

PEACE CORPS....SEE PEACE/CORP

PEACE OF WESTPHALIA....SEE WESTPHALIA

PEACE....SEE ALSO ORD/FREE

N
UNITED NATIONS,UNITED NATIONS PUBLICATIONS. WOR+45 BIBLIOG
ECO/UNDEV AGRI FINAN FORCES ADMIN LEAD WAR PEACE INT/ORG
...POLICY INT/LAW 20 UN. PAGE 107 B2160 DIPLOM

B18
US LIBRARY OF CONGRESS,LIST OF REFERENCES ON A BIBLIOG
LEAGUE OF NATIONS. DIPLOM WAR PEACE 20 LEAGUE/NAT. INT/ORG
PAGE 109 B2201 ADMIN
EX/STRUC

B28
HALL W.P.,EMPIRE TO COMMONWEALTH. FUT WOR-45 CONSTN VOL/ASSN
ECO/DEV ECO/UNDEV INT/ORG PROVS PLAN DIPLOM NAT/G
EDU/PROP ADMIN COLONIAL PEACE PERSON ALL/VALS UK
...POLICY GEOG SOC OBS RECORD TREND CMN/WLTH
PARLIAMENT 19/20. PAGE 46 B0925

L44
CORWIN E.S.,"THE CONSTITUTION AND WORLD INT/ORG
ORGANIZATION." FUT USA+45 USA-45 NAT/G EX/STRUC CONSTN
LEGIS PEACE KNOWL...CON/ANAL UN 20. PAGE 24 B0484 SOVEREIGN

B45
BAKER H.,PROBLEMS OF REEMPLOYMENT AND RETRAINING OF BIBLIOG/A
MANPOWER DURING THE TRANSITION FROM WAR TO PEACE. ADJUST
USA+45 INDUS LABOR LG/CO NAT/G PLAN ADMIN PEACE WAR
...POLICY MGT 20. PAGE 8 B0167 PROB/SOLV

B45
BUSH V.,SCIENCE, THE ENDLESS FRONTIER. FUT USA-45 R+D
INTELL STRATA ACT/RES CREATE PLAN EDU/PROP ADMIN NAT/G
NUC/PWR PEACE ATTIT HEALTH KNOWL...MAJORIT HEAL MGT
PHIL/SCI CONCPT OBS TREND 20. PAGE 18 B0360

B45
RANSHOFFEN-WERTHEIMER EF,THE INTERNATIONAL INT/ORG
SECRETARIAT: A GREAT EXPERIMENT IN INTERNATIONAL EXEC
ADMINISTRATION. EUR+WWI FUT CONSTN FACE/GP CONSULT
DELIB/GP ACT/RES ADMIN ROUTINE PEACE ORD/FREE...MGT
RECORD ORG/CHARTS LEAGUE/NAT WORK 20. PAGE 86 B1731

B50
WELCH S.R.,PORTUGUESE RULE AND SPANISH CROWN IN DIPLOM
SOUTH AFRICA 1581-1640. PORTUGAL SOUTH/AFR SPAIN COLONIAL
SOCIETY KIN NEIGH SECT INT/TRADE ADMIN 16/17 WAR
MISSION. PAGE 115 B2317 PEACE

L50
US SENATE COMM. GOVT. OPER.,"REVISION OF THE UN INT/ORG
CHARTER." FUT USA+45 WOR+45 CONSTN ECO/DEV LEGIS
ECO/UNDEV NAT/G DELIB/GP ACT/RES CREATE PLAN EXEC PEACE
ROUTINE CHOOSE ALL/VALS...POLICY CONCPT CONGRESS UN
TOT/POP 20 COLD/WAR. PAGE 111 B2235

B51
SWISHER C.B.,THE THEORY AND PRACTICE OF AMERICAN CONSTN
NATIONAL GOVERNMENT. CULTURE LEGIS DIPLOM ADJUD NAT/G
ADMIN WAR PEACE ORD/FREE...MAJORIT 17/20. PAGE 102 GOV/REL
B2063 GEN/LAWS

B52
ELLIOTT W.,UNITED STATES FOREIGN POLICY, ITS LEGIS
ORGANIZATION AND CONTROL. USA+45 USA-45 CONSTN EX/STRUC
NAT/G FORCES TOP/EX PEACE...TIME/SEQ CONGRESS DIPLOM
LEAGUE/NAT 20. PAGE 33 B0670

B52
VANDENBOSCH A.,THE UN: BACKGROUND, ORGANIZATION, DELIB/GP
FUNCTIONS, ACTIVITIES. WOR+45 LAW CONSTN STRUCT TIME/SEQ
INT/ORG CONSULT BAL/PWR EDU/PROP EXEC ALL/VALS PEACE
...POLICY CONCPT UN 20. PAGE 112 B2254

S52
SCHWEBEL S.M.,"THE SECRETARY-GENERAL OF THE UN." INT/ORG
FUT INTELL CONSULT DELIB/GP ADMIN PEACE ATTIT TOP/EX
...JURID MGT CONCPT TREND UN CONGRESS 20. PAGE 95
B1915

S53
CORY R.H. JR.,"FORGING A PUBLIC INFORMATION POLICY INT/ORG
FOR THE UNITED NATIONS." FUT WOR+45 SOCIETY ADMIN EDU/PROP
PEACE ATTIT PERSON SKILL...CONCPT 20 UN. PAGE 24 BAL/PWR
B0486

S54
MILLARD E.L.,FREEDOM IN A FEDERAL WORLD. FUT WOR+45 INT/ORG
VOL/ASSN TOP/EX LEGIT ROUTINE FEDERAL PEACE ATTIT CREATE
DISPL ORD/FREE PWR...MAJORIT INT/LAW JURID TREND ADJUD
COLD/WAR 20. PAGE 73 B1479 BAL/PWR

B55
MAZZINI J.,THE DUTIES OF MAN. MOD/EUR LAW SOCIETY SUPEGO
FAM NAT/G POL/PAR SECT VOL/ASSN EX/STRUC ACT/RES CONCPT
CREATE REV PEACE ATTIT ALL/VALS...GEN/LAWS WORK 19. NAT/LISM
PAGE 71 B1439

B55
UN HEADQUARTERS LIBRARY,BIBLIOGRAPHIE DE LA CHARTE BIBLIOG/A
DES NATIONS UNIES. CHINA/COM KOREA WOR+45 VOL/ASSN INT/ORG
CONFER ADMIN COERCE PEACE ATTIT ORD/FREE SOVEREIGN DIPLOM
...INT/LAW 20 UNESCO UN. PAGE 106 B2149

S55
ANGELL R.,"GOVERNMENTS AND PEOPLES AS A FOCI FOR FUT
PEACE-ORIENTED RESEARCH." WOR+45 CULTURE SOCIETY SOC
FACE/GP ACT/RES CREATE PLAN DIPLOM EDU/PROP ROUTINE PEACE
ATTIT PERCEPT SKILL...POLICY CONCPT OBS TREND
GEN/METH 20. PAGE 5 B0110

S55
WRIGHT Q.,"THE PEACEFUL ADJUSTMENT OF INTERNATIONAL R+D
RELATIONS: PROBLEMS AND RESEARCH APPROACHES." UNIV METH/CNCPT
INTELL EDU/PROP ADJUD ROUTINE KNOWL SKILL...INT/LAW PEACE
JURID PHIL/SCI CLASSIF 20. PAGE 118 B2385

B56
KIRK G.,THE CHANGING ENVIRONMENT OF INTERNATIONAL FUT
RELATIONS. ASIA S/ASIA USA+45 WOR+45 ECO/UNDEV EXEC
INT/ORG NAT/G FOR/AID EDU/PROP PEACE KNOWL DIPLOM
...PLURIST COLD/WAR TOT/POP 20. PAGE 60 B1214

B56
KOENIG L.W.,THE TRUMAN ADMINISTRATION: ITS ADMIN
PRINCIPLES AND PRACTICE. USA+45 POL/PAR CHIEF LEGIS POLICY
DIPLOM DEATH NUC/PWR WAR CIVMIL/REL PEACE EX/STRUC
...DECISION 20 TRUMAN/HS PRESIDENT TREATY. PAGE 61 GOV/REL
B1224

B56
SOHN L.B.,CASES ON UNITED NATIONS LAW. STRUCT INT/ORG
DELIB/GP WAR PEACE ORD/FREE...DECISION ANTHOL 20 INT/LAW
UN. PAGE 99 B1994 ADMIN
ADJUD

B58
ATOMIC INDUSTRIAL FORUM,MANAGEMENT AND ATOMIC NUC/PWR
ENERGY. WOR+45 SEA LAW MARKET NAT/G TEC/DEV INSPECT INDUS
INT/TRADE CONFER PEACE HEALTH...ANTHOL 20. PAGE 7 MGT
B0145 ECO/TAC

B58
ISLAM R.,INTERNATIONAL ECONOMIC COOPERATION AND THE INT/ORG
UNITED NATIONS. FINAN PLAN EXEC TASK WAR PEACE DIPLOM
...SOC METH/CNCPT 20 UN LEAGUE/NAT. PAGE 55 B1105 ADMIN

B58
KINTNER W.R.,ORGANIZING FOR CONFLICT: A PROPOSAL. USA+45
USSR STRUCT NAT/G LEGIS ADMIN EXEC PEACE ORD/FREE PLAN
PWR...CONCPT OBS TREND NAT/COMP VAL/FREE COLD/WAR DIPLOM
20. PAGE 60 B1211

B58
MILLS C.W.,THE CAUSES OF WORLD WAR THREE. FUT CONSULT
USA+45 INTELL NAT/G DOMIN EDU/PROP ADMIN WAR ATTIT PWR
SOC. PAGE 74 B1487 ELITES
PEACE

S59
HARVEY M.F.,"THE PALESTINE REFUGEE PROBLEM: ACT/RES
ELEMENTS OF A SOLUTION." ISLAM LAW INT/ORG DELIB/GP LEGIT
TOP/EX ECO/TAC ROUTINE DRIVE HEALTH LOVE ORD/FREE PEACE
PWR WEALTH...MAJORIT FAO 20. PAGE 48 B0964 ISRAEL

S59
HOFFMANN S.,"IMPLEMENTATION OF INTERNATIONAL INT/ORG
INSTRUMENTS ON HUMAN RIGHTS." WOR+45 VOL/ASSN MORAL
DELIB/GP JUDGE EDU/PROP LEGIT ROUTINE PEACE
COLD/WAR 20. PAGE 51 B1029

S59
LASSWELL H.D.,"UNIVERSALITY IN PERSPECTIVE." FUT INT/ORG
UNIV SOCIETY CONSULT TOP/EX PLAN EDU/PROP ADJUD JURID
ROUTINE ARMS/CONT COERCE PEACE ATTIT PERSON TOTALISM
ALL/VALS. PAGE 63 B1271

B60
MORISON E.E.,TURMOIL AND TRADITION: A STUDY OF THE BIOG
LIFE AND TIMES OF HENRY L. STIMSON. ASIA USA+45 USA-45 NAT/G
POL/PAR CHIEF DELIB/GP FORCES BAL/PWR DIPLOM EX/STRUC
ARMS/CONT WAR PEACE 19/20 STIMSON/HL ROOSEVLT/F
TAFT/WH HOOVER/H REPUBLICAN. PAGE 75 B1525

B60
MUNRO L.,UNITED NATIONS, HOPE FOR A DIVIDED WORLD. INT/ORG
FUT WOR+45 CONSTN DELIB/GP CREATE TEC/DEV DIPLOM ROUTINE
EDU/PROP LEGIT PEACE ATTIT HEALTH ORD/FREE PWR
...CONCPT TREND UN VAL/FREE 20. PAGE 76 B1540

B60
PENTONY D.E.,UNITED STATES FOREIGN AID. INDIA LAOS FOR/AID
USA+45 ECO/UNDEV INT/TRADE ADMIN PEACE ATTIT DIPLOM
...POLICY METH/COMP ANTHOL 20. PAGE 82 B1653 ECO/TAC

SOUTH AFRICAN CONGRESS OF DEM.FACE THE FUTURE.
SOUTH/AFR ELITES LEGIS ADMIN REGION COERCE PEACE
ATTIT 20. PAGE 99 B1999
RACE/REL
DISCRIM
CONSTN
NAT/G
B60

BOGARDUS E.S.,"THE SOCIOLOGY OF A STRUCTURED
PEACE." FUT SOCIETY CREATE DIPLOM EDU/PROP ADJUD
ROUTINE ATTIT RIGID/FLEX KNOWL ORD/FREE RESPECT
...POLICY INT/LAW JURID NEW/IDEA SELF/OBS TOT/POP
20 UN. PAGE 13 B0264
S60
INT/ORG
SOC
NAT/LISM
PEACE

NELSON R.H.,"LEGISLATIVE PARTICIPATION IN THE
TREATY AND AGREEMENT MAKING PROCESS." CONSTN
POL/PAR PLAN EXEC PWR FAO UN CONGRESS. PAGE 78
B1569
S60
LEGIS
PEACE
DECISION
DIPLOM

HAYTER W.,THE DIPLOMACY OF THE GREAT POWERS. FRANCE
UK USSR WOR+45 EX/STRUC TOP/EX NUC/PWR PEACE...OBS
20. PAGE 48 B0978
B61
DIPLOM
POLICY
NAT/G

KERTESZ S.D.,AMERICAN DIPLOMACY IN A NEW ERA. COM
S/ASIA UK USA+45 FORCES PROB/SOLV BAL/PWR ECO/TAC
ADMIN COLONIAL WAR PEACE ORD/FREE 20 NATO CONGRESS
UN COLD/WAR. PAGE 59 B1199
B61
ANTHOL
DIPLOM
TREND

JUVILER P.H.,"INTERPARLIAMENTARY CONTACTS IN SOVIET
FOREIGN POLICY." COM FUT WOR+45 WOR-45 SOCIETY
CONSULT ACT/RES DIPLOM ADMIN PEACE ATTIT RIGID/FLEX
WEALTH...WELF/ST SOC TOT/POP CONGRESS 19/20.
PAGE 57 B1156
S61
INT/ORG
DELIB/GP
USSR

MILLER E.,"LEGAL ASPECTS OF UN ACTION IN THE
CONGO." AFR CULTURE ADMIN PEACE DRIVE RIGID/FLEX
ORD/FREE...WELF/ST JURID OBS UN CONGO 20. PAGE 73
B1480
S61
INT/ORG
LEGIT

PADOVER S.K.,"PSYCHOLOGICAL WARFARE AND FOREIGN
POLICY." FUT UNIV USA+45 INTELL SOCIETY CREATE
EDU/PROP ADMIN WAR PEACE PERCEPT...POLICY
METH/CNCPT TESTS TIME/SEQ 20. PAGE 80 B1623
S61
ROUTINE
DIPLOM

BAILEY S.D.,THE SECRETARIAT OF THE UNITED NATIONS.
FUT WOR+45 DELIB/GP PLAN BAL/PWR DOMIN EDU/PROP
ADMIN PEACE ATTIT PWR...DECISION CONCPT TREND
CON/ANAL CHARTS UN VAL/FREE COLD/WAR 20. PAGE 8
B0162
B62
INT/ORG
EXEC
DIPLOM

BRIMMER B.,A GUIDE TO THE USE OF UNITED NATIONS
DOCUMENTS. WOR+45 ECO/UNDEV AGRI EX/STRUC FORCES
PROB/SOLV ADMIN WAR PEACE WEALTH...POLICY UN.
PAGE 15 B0310
B62
BIBLIOG/A
INT/ORG
DIPLOM

EVANS M.S.,THE FRINGE ON TOP. USSR EX/STRUC FORCES
DIPLOM ECO/TAC PEACE CONSERVE SOCISM...TREND 20
KENNEDY/JF. PAGE 34 B0689
B62
NAT/G
PWR
CENTRAL
POLICY

KENNEDY J.F.,TO TURN THE TIDE. SPACE AGRI INT/ORG
FORCES TEC/DEV ADMIN NUC/PWR PEACE WEALTH...ANTHOL
20 KENNEDY/JF CIV/RIGHTS. PAGE 59 B1193
B62
DIPLOM
CHIEF
POLICY
NAT/G

MULLEY F.W.,THE POLITICS OF WESTERN DEFENSE.
EUR+WWI USA-45 WOR+45 VOL/ASSN EX/STRUC FORCES
COERCE DETER PEACE ATTIT ORD/FREE PWR...RECORD
TIME/SEQ CHARTS COLD/WAR 20 NATO. PAGE 76 B1537
B62
INT/ORG
DELIB/GP
NUC/PWR

MCCLELLAND C.A.,"DECISIONAL OPPORTUNITY AND
POLITICAL CONTROVERSY." USA+45 NAT/G POL/PAR FORCES
TOP/EX DOMIN ADMIN PEACE DRIVE ORD/FREE PWR
...DECISION SIMUL 20. PAGE 72 B1444
S62
ACT/RES
PERCEPT
DIPLOM

BADI J.,THE GOVERNMENT OF THE STATE OF ISRAEL: A
CRITICAL ACCOUNT OF ITS PARLIAMENT, EXECUTIVE, AND
JUDICIARY. ISRAEL ECO/DEV CHIEF DELIB/GP LEGIS
DIPLOM CT/SYS INGP/REL PEACE ORD/FREE...BIBLIOG 20
PARLIAMENT ARABS MIGRATION. PAGE 8 B0157
B63
NAT/G
CONSTN
EX/STRUC
POL/PAR

ROETTER C.,THE DIPLOMATIC ART. USSR INT/ORG NAT/G
DELIB/GP ROUTINE NUC/PWR PEACE...POLICY 20. PAGE 90
B1812
B63
DIPLOM
ELITES
TOP/EX

VAN SLYCK P.,PEACE: THE CONTROL OF NATIONAL POWER.
CUBA WOR+45 FINAN NAT/G FORCES PROB/SOLV TEC/DEV
BAL/PWR ADMIN CONTROL ORD/FREE...POLICY INT/LAW UN
COLD/WAR TREATY. PAGE 112 B2253
B63
ARMS/CONT
PEACE
INT/ORG
DIPLOM

MORGENTHAU H.J.,"THE POLITICAL CONDITIONS FOR AN
INTERNATIONAL POLICE FORCE." FUT WOR+45 CREATE
LEGIT ADMIN PEACE ORD/FREE 20. PAGE 75 B1524
S63
INT/ORG
FORCES
ARMS/CONT
DETER

HODGETTS J.E.,ADMINISTERING THE ATOM FOR PEACE.
OP/RES TEC/DEV ADMIN...IDEA/COMP METH/COMP 20.
PAGE 50 B1025
B64
PROB/SOLV
NUC/PWR
PEACE

RUSSELL R.B.,UNITED NATIONS EXPERIENCE WITH
MILITARY FORCES: POLITICAL AND LEGAL ASPECTS. AFR
KOREA WOR+45 LEGIS PROB/SOLV ADMIN CONTROL
EFFICIENCY PEACE...POLICY INT/LAW BIBLIOG UN.
PAGE 92 B1857
MGT
B64
FORCES
DIPLOM
SANCTION
ORD/FREE

SARROS P.P.,CONGRESS AND THE NEW DIPLOMACY: THE
FORMULATION OF MUTUAL SECURITY POLICY: 1953-60
(THESIS). USA+45 CHIEF EX/STRUC REGION ROUTINE
CHOOSE GOV/REL PEACE ROLE...POLICY 20 PRESIDENT
CONGRESS. PAGE 92 B1869
B64
DIPLOM
POL/PAR
NAT/G

SULLIVAN G.,THE STORY OF THE PEACE CORPS. USA+45
WOR+45 INTELL FACE/GP NAT/G SCHOOL VOL/ASSN CONSULT
EX/STRUC PLAN EDU/PROP ADMIN ATTIT DRIVE ALL/VALS
...POLICY HEAL SOC CONCPT INT QU BIOG TREND SOC/EXP
WORK. PAGE 102 B2054
B64
INT/ORG
ECO/UNDEV
FOR/AID
PEACE

UN PUB. INFORM. ORGAN.,EVERY MAN'S UNITED NATIONS.
UNIV WOR+45 CONSTN CULTURE SOCIETY ECO/DEV
ECO/UNDEV NAT/G ACT/RES PLAN ECO/TAC INT/TRADE
EDU/PROP LEGIT PEACE ATTIT ALL/VALS...POLICY HUM
INT/LAW CONCPT CHARTS UN TOT/POP 20. PAGE 106 B2150
B64
INT/ORG
ROUTINE

US SENATE COMM GOVT OPERATIONS,ADMINISTRATION OF
NATIONAL SECURITY. USA+45 CHIEF TOP/EX PLAN DIPLOM
CONTROL PEACE...POLICY DECISION 20 PRESIDENT
CONGRESS. PAGE 110 B2216
B64
ADMIN
FORCES
ORD/FREE
NAT/G

MILLIS W.,"THE DEMILITARIZED WORLD." COM USA+45
USSR WOR+45 CONSTN NAT/G EX/STRUC PLAN LEGIT ATTIT
DRIVE...CONCPT TIME/SEQ STERTYP TOT/POP COLD/WAR
20. PAGE 74 B1486
L64
FUT
INT/ORG
BAL/PWR
PEACE

SCHWELB E.,"OPERATION OF THE EUROPEAN CONVENTION ON
HUMAN RIGHTS." EUR+WWI LAW SOCIETY CREATE EDU/PROP
ADJUD ADMIN PEACE ATTIT ORD/FREE PWR...POLICY
INT/LAW CONCPT OBS GEN/LAWS UN VAL/FREE ILO 20
ECHR. PAGE 95 B1916
S64
INT/ORG
MORAL

FORGAC A.A.,NEW DIPLOMACY AND THE UNITED NATIONS.
FRANCE GERMANY UK USSR INT/ORG DELIB/GP EX/STRUC
PEACE...INT/LAW CONCPT UN. PAGE 36 B0740
B65
DIPLOM
ETIQUET
NAT/G

PHELPS-FETHERS I.,SOVIET INTERNATIONAL FRONT
ORGANIZATIONS* A CONCISE HANDBOOK. DIPLOM DOMIN
LEGIT ADMIN EXEC GP/REL PEACE MARXISM...TIME/SEQ
GP/COMP. PAGE 83 B1668
B65
USSR
EDU/PROP
ASIA
COM

MARTIN L.W.,DIPLOMACY IN MODERN EUROPEAN HISTORY.
EUR+WWI MOD/EUR INT/ORG NAT/G EX/STRUC ROUTINE WAR
PEACE TOTALISM PWR 15/20 COLD/WAR EUROPE/W. PAGE 70
B1411
B66
DIPLOM
POLICY

US HOUSE COMM GOVT OPERATIONS,AN INVESTIGATION OF
THE US ECONOMIC AND MILITARY ASSISTANCE PROGRAMS IN
VIETNAM. USA+45 VIETNAM/S SOCIETY CONSTRUC FINAN
FORCES BUDGET INT/TRADE PEACE HEALTH...MGT
HOUSE/REP AID. PAGE 108 B2191
B66
FOR/AID
ECO/UNDEV
WAR
INSPECT

AMERICAN FRIENDS SERVICE COMM,IN PLACE OF WAR.
NAT/G ACT/RES DIPLOM ADMIN NUC/PWR EFFICIENCY
...POLICY 20. PAGE 4 B0085
B67
PEACE
PACIFISM
WAR
DETER

EVANS R.H.,COEXISTENCE: COMMUNISM AND ITS PRACTICE
IN BOLOGNA, 1945-1965. ITALY CAP/ISM ADMIN CHOOSE
PEACE ORD/FREE...SOC STAT DEEP/INT SAMP CHARTS
BIBLIOG 20. PAGE 36 B0690
B67
MARXISM
CULTURE
MUNIC
POL/PAR

TOMA P.A.,THE POLITICS OF FOOD FOR PEACE:
EXECUTIVE-LEGISLATIVE INTERACTION. USA+45 ECO/UNDEV
POL/PAR DEBATE EXEC LOBBY CHOOSE PEACE...DECISION
CHARTS. PAGE 104 B2113
B67
FOR/AID
POLICY
LEGIS
AGRI

COHEN M.,"THE DEMISE OF UNEF." CONSTN DIPLOM ADMIN
AGREE LEAD COERCE 20 UNEF U/THANT HAMMARSK/D.
PAGE 22 B0445
L67
INT/ORG
FORCES
PEACE
POLICY

SATHYAMURTHY T.V.,"TWENTY YEARS OF UNESCO: AN
INTERPRETATION." SOCIETY PROB/SOLV LEAD PEACE
UNESCO. PAGE 92 B1870
S67
ADMIN
CONSTN
INT/ORG
TIME/SEQ

TACKABERRY R.B.,"ORGANIZING AND TRAINING PEACE-
KEEPING FORCES* THE CANADIAN VIEW." CANADA PLAN
DIPLOM CONFER ADJUD ADMIN CIVMIL/REL 20 UN.
PAGE 102 B2069
S67
PEACE
FORCES
INT/ORG
CONSULT

TOURNELLE G.,"DIPLOMATIE D' HIER ET D'AUJOURD'
HUI." CONFER ADMIN ROUTINE PEACE. PAGE 105 B2123
S67
DIPLOM
ROLE
INT/ORG

S67
TURNER F.C. JR.,"EXPERIMENT IN INTER-AMERICAN   FORCES
PEACE-KEEPING." DOMIN/REP ADMIN ROUTINE REV   ADJUD
ORD/FREE OAS 20. PAGE 106 B2137   PEACE

N67
US SUPERINTENDENT OF DOCUMENTS,SPACE: MISSILES, THE   BIBLIOG/A
MOON, NASA, AND SATELLITES (PRICE LIST 79A). USA+45   SPACE
COM/IND R+D NAT/G DIPLOM EDU/PROP TEC/DEV   TEC/DEV
HEALTH...POLICY SIMUL NASA CONGRESS. PAGE 111 B2244   PEACE

N67
US SENATE COMM ON FOREIGN REL,THE UNITED NATIONS AT   INT/ORG
TWENTY-ONE (PAMPHLET). WOR+45 BUDGET ADMIN SENATE   DIPLOM
UN. PAGE 110 B2223   PEACE

N67
US SENATE COMM ON FOREIGN REL,THE UNITED NATIONS   INT/ORG
PEACEKEEPING DILEMMA (PAMPHLET). ISLAM WOR+45   DIPLOM
PROB/SOLV BUDGET ADMIN SENATE UN. PAGE 110 B2224   PEACE

PEACE/CORP....PEACE CORPS

B64
ADAMS V.,THE PEACE CORPS IN ACTION. USA+45 VOL/ASSN   DIPLOM
EX/STRUC GOV/REL PERCEPT ORD/FREE...OBS 20   FOR/AID
KENNEDY/JF PEACE/CORP. PAGE 3 B0058   PERSON
                                                      DRIVE

S65
THOMAS F.C. JR.,"THE PEACE CORPS IN MOROCCO."   MOROCCO
CULTURE MUNIC PROVS CREATE ROUTINE TASK ADJUST   FRANCE
STRANGE...OBS PEACE/CORP. PAGE 104 B2099   FOR/AID
                                                      EDU/PROP

PEACEFUL COEXISTENCE....SEE PEACE+COLD/WAR

PEALY R.H. B0980

PEARSON A.W. B1649

PEARSON/L....LESTER PEARSON

N64
CANADA NATL JT COUN PUB SERV,THE CANADA NATIONAL   GP/REL
JOINT COUNCIL OF THE PUBLIC SERVICE 1944-1964   NAT/G
(PAMPHLET). CANADA EX/STRUC PERS/REL DRIVE...MGT 20   LABOR
PEARSON/L. PAGE 18 B0373   EFFICIENCY

PEASLEE A.J. B1650

PEASNT/WAR....PEASANT WAR (1525)

PENICK J.L. JR. B1651

PENN/WM....WILLIAM PENN

PENNIMAN C. B0101

PENNSYLVANIA ECONOMY LEAGUE B1652

PENNSYLVAN....PENNSYLVANIA

B43
LEVY H.P.,A STUDY IN PUBLIC RELATIONS: CASE HISTORY   ATTIT
OF THE RELATIONS MAINTAINED BETWEEN A DEPT OF   RECEIVE
PUBLIC ASSISTANCE AND PEOPLE. USA-45 NAT/G PRESS   WEALTH
ADMIN LOBBY GP/REL DISCRIM...SOC/WK LING AUD/VIS 20   SERV/IND
PENNSYLVAN. PAGE 64 B1302

B60
PENNSYLVANIA ECONOMY LEAGUE,URBAN RENEWAL IMPACT   PLAN
STUDY: ADMINISTRATIVE-LEGAL-FISCAL. USA+45 FINAN   BUDGET
LOC/G NEIGH ADMIN EFFICIENCY...CENSUS CHARTS 20   MUNIC
PENNSYLVAN. PAGE 82 B1652   ADJUD

B62
SCHULMAN S.,TOWARD JUDICIAL REFORM IN PENNSYLVANIA;   CT/SYS
A STUDY IN COURT REORGANIZATION. USA+45 CONSTN   ACT/RES
JUDGE PLAN ADMIN LOBBY SANCTION PRIVIL PWR...JURID   PROB/SOLV
20 PENNSYLVAN. PAGE 94 B1905

N62
UNIVERSITY PITT INST LOC GOVT,THE COUNCIL-MANAGER   LOC/G
FORM OF GOVERNMENT IN PENNSYLVANIA (PAMPHLET).   TOP/EX
PROVS EX/STRUC REPRESENT GOV/REL EFFICIENCY   MUNIC
...CHARTS SIMUL 20 PENNSYLVAN CITY/MGT. PAGE 107   PWR
B2169

B63
SMITH R.M.,STATE GOVERNMENT IN TRANSITION. USA+45   PROVS
POL/PAR LEGIS PARL/PROC GOV/REL 20 PENNSYLVAN   POLICY
GOVERNOR. PAGE 98 B1984   EX/STRUC
                                                      PLAN

B64
SCHERMER G.,MEETING SOCIAL NEEDS IN THE PENJERDEL   PLAN
REGION. SOCIETY FINAN ACT/RES EDU/PROP ADMIN   REGION
GOV/REL...SOC/WK 45 20 PENNSYLVAN DELAWARE   HEALTH
NEW/JERSEY. PAGE 93 B1887   WEALTH

PENOLOGY....SEE CRIME

PENTAGON....PENTAGON

PAGE 640

B64
RAYMOND J.,POWER AT THE PENTAGON (1ST ED.). ELITES   PWR
NAT/G PLAN EDU/PROP ARMS/CONT DETER WAR WEAPON   CIVMIL/REL
...TIME/SEQ 20 PENTAGON MCNAMARA/R. PAGE 86 B1746   EX/STRUC
                                                      FORCES

PENTONY D.E. B1653

PEOPLE'S REPUBLIC OF CHINA....SEE CHINA/COM

PERCEPT....PERCEPTION AND COGNITION

B19
DUNN A.,SCIENTIFIC SELLING AND ADVERTISING. CLIENT   LG/CO
ADMIN DEMAND EFFICIENCY 20. PAGE 31 B0632   PERCEPT
                                                      PERS/REL
                                                      TASK

B27
ANGELL N.,THE PUBLIC MIND. USA-45 SOCIETY EDU/PROP   PERCEPT
ROUTINE SUPEGO KNOWL...POLICY CONCPT MYTH OBS/ENVIR   ATTIT
EUR+WW1 TOT/POP 20. PAGE 5 B0109   DIPLOM
                                                      NAT/LISM

B36
GAUS J.M.,THE FRONTIERS OF PUBLIC ADMINISTRATION.   ROUTINE
EFFICIENCY PERCEPT RIGID/FLEX ORD/FREE 20. PAGE 39   GOV/REL
B0785   ELITES
                                                      PROB/SOLV

S41
ABEL T.,"THE ELEMENT OF DECISION IN THE PATTERN OF   TEC/DEV
WAR." EUR+WWI FUT NAT/G TOP/EX DIPLOM ROUTINE   FORCES
COERCE DISPL PERCEPT PWR...SOC METH/CNCPT HIST/WRIT   WAR
TREND GEN/LAWS 20. PAGE 2 B0051

B45
PLATO,THE REPUBLIC. MEDIT-7 UNIV SOCIETY STRUCT   PERSON
EX/STRUC FORCES UTOPIA ATTIT PERCEPT HEALTH KNOWL   PHIL/SCI
ORD/FREE PWR...HUM CONCPT STERTYP TOT/POP. PAGE 83
B1681

B47
LASSWELL H.D.,THE ANALYSIS OF POLITICAL BEHAVIOUR: R+D
AN EMPIRICAL APPROACH. WOR+45 CULTURE NAT/G FORCES   ACT/RES
EDU/PROP ADMIN ATTIT PERCEPT KNOWL...PHIL/SCI PSY   ELITES
SOC NEW/IDEA OBS INT GEN/METH NAZI 20. PAGE 63
B1267

S48
COCH L.,"OVERCOMING RESISTANCE TO CHANGE" (BMR)"   WORKER
USA+45 CONSULT ADMIN ROUTINE GP/REL EFFICIENCY   OP/RES
PRODUC PERCEPT SKILL...CHARTS SOC/EXP 20. PAGE 22   PROC/MFG
B0441   RIGID/FLEX

B49
KENT S.,STRATEGIC INTELLIGENCE FOR AMERICAN WORLD   ACT/RES
POLICY. FUT USA+45 NAT/G ATTIT PERCEPT ORD/FREE   EX/STRUC
...OBS 20. PAGE 59 B1195   DIPLOM

C50
SIMON H.A.,"PUBLIC ADMINISTRATION." LG/CO SML/CO   MGT
PLAN DOMIN LEAD GP/REL DRIVE PERCEPT ALL/VALS   ADMIN
...POLICY BIBLIOG/A 20. PAGE 97 B1957   DECISION
                                                      EX/STRUC

S51
INKELES A.,"UNDERSTANDING A FOREIGN SOCIETY: A   SOC
SOCIOLOGIST'S VIEW." SOCIETY ROUTINE KNOWL...PSY   METH/CNCPT
CONCPT GEN/METH 20. PAGE 54 B1086   PERCEPT
                                                      ATTIT

B52
MAIER N.R.F.,PRINCIPLES OF HUMAN RELATIONS. WOR+45   INDUS
WOR-45 CULTURE SOCIETY ROUTINE ATTIT DRIVE PERCEPT
PERSON RIGID/FLEX SUPEGO PWR...PSY CONT/OBS RECORD
TOT/POP VAL/FREE 20. PAGE 68 B1379

S52
TAYLOR D.W.,"TWENTY QUESTIONS: EFFICIENCY IN   PROB/SOLV
PROBLEM SOLVING AS A FUNCTION OF SIZE OF GROUP"   EFFICIENCY
WOR+45 CONFER ROUTINE INGP/REL...PSY GP/COMP 20.   SKILL
PAGE 103 B2085   PERCEPT

B53
MEYER P.,THE JEWS IN THE SOVIET SATELLITES.   COM
CZECHOSLVK POLAND SOCIETY STRATA NAT/G BAL/PWR   SECT
ECO/TAC EDU/PROP LEGIT ADMIN COERCE ATTIT DISPL   TOTALISM
PERCEPT HEALTH PWR RESPECT WEALTH...METH/CNCPT JEWS   USSR
VAL/FREE NAZI 20. PAGE 73 B1474

B54
CONWAY O.B. JR.,LEGISLATIVE-EXECUTIVE RELATIONS IN   BAL/PWR
THE GOVERNMENT OF THE UNITED STATES (PAMPHLET).   FEDERAL
BUDGET ATTIT PERCEPT...DECISION 20. PAGE 23 B0470   GOV/REL
                                                      EX/STRUC

S55
ANGELL R.,"GOVERNMENTS AND PEOPLES AS A FOCI FOR   FUT
PEACE-ORIENTED RESEARCH." WOR+45 CULTURE SOCIETY   SOC
FACE/GP ACT/RES CREATE PLAN DIPLOM EDU/PROP ROUTINE   PEACE
ATTIT PERCEPT SKILL...POLICY CONCPT OBS TREND
GEN/METH 20. PAGE 5 B0110

B57
HOLCOMBE A.N.,STRENGTHENING THE UNITED NATIONS.   INT/ORG
USA+45 ACT/RES CREATE PLAN EDU/PROP ATTIT PERCEPT   ROUTINE
PWR...METH/CNCPT CONT/OBS RECORD UN COLD/WAR 20.
PAGE 51 B1032

L57
HAAS E.B.,"REGIONAL INTEGRATION AND NATIONAL   INT/ORG

POLICY." WOR+45 VOL/ASSN DELIB/GP EX/STRUC ECO/TAC   ORD/FREE
DOMIN EDU/PROP LEGIT COERCE ATTIT PERCEPT KNOWL   REGION
...TIME/SEQ COLD/WAR 20 UN. PAGE 45 B0908
                                                                          B58
MARCH J.G.,ORGANIZATIONS. USA+45 CREATE OP/RES PLAN   MGT
PROB/SOLV PARTIC ROUTINE RATIONAL ATTIT PERCEPT   PERSON
...DECISION BIBLIOG. PAGE 69 B1397   DRIVE
                                                          CONCPT
                                                                          B60
ARROW K.J.,MATHEMATICAL METHODS IN THE SOCIAL   MATH
SCIENCES, 1959. TEC/DEV CHOOSE UTIL PERCEPT   PSY
...KNO/TEST GAME SIMUL ANTHOL. PAGE 7 B0137   MGT
                                                                          S60
HERZ J.H.,"EAST GERMANY: PROGRESS AND PROSPECTS."   POL/PAR
COM AGRI FINAN INDUS LOC/G NAT/G FORCES PLAN   STRUCT
TEC/DEV DOMIN ADMIN COERCE DRIVE PERCEPT RIGID/FLEX   GERMANY
MORAL ORD/FREE PWR...MARXIST PSY SOC RECORD STERTYP
WORK. PAGE 49 B0997
                                                                          S60
NORTH R.C.,"DIE DISKREPANZ ZWISCHEN REALITAT UND   SOCIETY
WUNSCHBILD ALS INNENPOLITISCHER FAKTOR." ASIA   ECO/TAC
CHINA/COM COM FUT ECO/UNDEV NAT/G PLAN DOMIN ADMIN
COERCE PERCEPT...SOC MYTH GEN/METH WORK TOT/POP 20.
PAGE 79 B1589
                                                                          S60
SCHATZ S.P.,"THE INFLENCE OF PLANNING ON   ECO/UNDEV
DEVELOPMENT: THE NIGERIAN EXPERIENCE." AFR FUT   PLAN
FINAN INDUS NAT/G EX/STRUC ECO/TAC ADMIN ATTIT   NIGERIA
PERCEPT ORD/FREE PWR...MATH TREND CON/ANAL SIMUL
VAL/FREE 20. PAGE 93 B1883
                                                                          B61
BENOIT E.,EUROPE AT SIXES AND SEVENS: THE COMMON   FINAN
MARKET, THE FREE TRADE ASSOCIATION AND THE UNITED   ECO/DEV
STATES. EUR+WWI FUT USA+45 INDUS CONSULT DELIB/GP   VOL/ASSN
EX/STRUC TOP/EX ACT/RES ECO/TAC EDU/PROP ROUTINE
CHOOSE PERCEPT WEALTH...MGT TREND EEC TOT/POP 20
EFTA. PAGE 11 B0217
                                                                          B61
HASAN H.S.,PAKISTAN AND THE UN. ISLAM WOR+45   INT/ORG
ECO/DEV ECO/UNDEV NAT/G TOP/EX ECO/TAC FOR/AID   ATTIT
EDU/PROP ADMIN DRIVE PERCEPT...OBS TIME/SEQ UN 20.   PAKISTAN
PAGE 48 B0965
                                                                          B61
TANNENBAUM R.,LEADERSHIP AND ORGANIZATION. STRUCT   LEAD
ADMIN INGP/REL ATTIT PERCEPT...DECISION METH/CNCPT   MGT
OBS CHARTS BIBLIOG. PAGE 103 B2075   RESPECT
                                                          ROLE
                                                                          S61
GORDON L.,"ECONOMIC REGIONALISM RECONSIDERED." FUT   ECO/DEV
USA+45 WOR+45 INDUS NAT/G TEC/DEV DIPLOM ROUTINE   ATTIT
PERCEPT WEALTH...WELF/ST METH/CNCPT WORK 20.   CAP/ISM
PAGE 41 B0830   REGION
                                                                          S61
HALPERIN M.H.,"THE GAITHER COMMITTEE AND THE POLICY   PLAN
PROCESS." USA+45 NAT/G TOP/EX ACT/RES LEGIT ADMIN   POLICY
BAL/PAY PERCEPT...CONCPT TOT/POP 20. PAGE 46 B0928   NUC/PWR
                                                          DELIB/GP
                                                                          S61
LEWY G.,"SUPERIOR ORDERS, NUCLEAR WARFARE AND THE   DETER
DICTATES OF CONSCIENCE: THE DILEMMA OF MILITARY   INT/ORG
OBEDIENCE IN THE ATOMIC." FUT UNIV WOR+45 INTELL   LAW
SOCIETY FORCES TOP/EX ACT/RES ADMIN ROUTINE NUC/PWR   INT/LAW
PERCEPT RIGID/FLEX ALL/VALS...POLICY CONCPT 20.
PAGE 65 B1308
                                                                          S61
PADOVER S.K.,"PSYCHOLOGICAL WARFARE AND FOREIGN   ROUTINE
POLICY." FUT UNIV USA+45 INTELL SOCIETY CREATE   DIPLOM
EDU/PROP ADMIN WAR PEACE PERCEPT...POLICY
METH/CNCPT TESTS TIME/SEQ 20. PAGE 80 B1623
                                                                          S61
RUDOLPH S.,"CONSENSUS AND CONFLICT IN INDIAN   POL/PAR
POLITICS." S/ASIA WOR+45 NAT/G DELIB/GP DIPLOM   PERCEPT
EDU/PROP ADMIN CONSEN PERSON ALL/VALS...OBS TREND   INDIA
TOT/POP VAL/FREE 20. PAGE 92 B1854
                                                                          B62
NICHOLAS H.G.,THE UNITED NATIONS AS A POLITICAL   INT/ORG
INSTITUTION. WOR+45 CONSTN EX/STRUC ACT/RES LEGIT   ROUTINE
PERCEPT KNOWL PWR...CONCPT TIME/SEQ CON/ANAL
ORG/CHARTS UN 20. PAGE 78 B1580
                                                                          S62
BRZEZINSKI Z.K.,"DEVIATION CONTROL: A STUDY IN THE   RIGID/FLEX
DYNAMICS OF DOCTRINAL CONFLICT." WOR+45 WOR-45   ATTIT
VOL/ASSN CREATE BAL/PWR DOMIN EXEC DRIVE PERCEPT
PWR...METH/CNCPT TIME/SEQ TREND 20. PAGE 16 B0333
                                                                          S62
IKLE F.C.,"POLITICAL NEGOTIATION AS A PROCESS OF   ROUTINE
MODIFYING UTILITIES." WOR+45 FACE/GP LABOR NAT/G   DECISION
FORCES ACT/RES EDU/PROP DETER PERCEPT ALL/VALS   DIPLOM
...PSY NEW/IDEA HYPO/EXP GEN/METH 20. PAGE 53 B1076
                                                                          S62
LARSON R.L.,"HOW TO DEFINE ADMINISTRATIVE   UNIV
PROBLEMS." ROUTINE PERCEPT KNOWL SKILL...MGT   FACE/GP
METH/CNCPT CHARTS TOT/POP. PAGE 63 B1263   INDUS
                                                          EXEC
                                                                          S62
MANGIN G.,"LES ACCORDS DE COOPERATION EN MATIERE DE   INT/ORG

JUSTICE ENTRE LA FRANCE ET LES ETATS AFRICAINS ET   LAW
MALGACHE." AFR ISLAM WOR+45 STRUCT ECO/UNDEV NAT/G   FRANCE
DELIB/GP PERCEPT ALL/VALS...JURID MGT TIME/SEQ 20.
PAGE 69 B1386
                                                                          S62
MCCLELLAND C.A.,"DECISIONAL OPPORTUNITY AND   ACT/RES
POLITICAL CONTROVERSY." USA+45 NAT/G POL/PAR FORCES   PERCEPT
TOP/EX DOMIN ADMIN PEACE DRIVE ORD/FREE PWR   DIPLOM
...DECISION SIMUL 20. PAGE 72 B1444
                                                                          S62
NORTH R.C.,"DECISION MAKING IN CRISIS: AN   INT/ORG
INTRODUCTION." WOR+45 WOR-45 NAT/G CONSULT DELIB/GP   ROUTINE
TEC/DEV PERCEPT KNOWL...POLICY DECISION PSY   DIPLOM
METH/CNCPT CONT/OBS TREND VAL/FREE 20. PAGE 79
B1590
                                                                          S62
READ W.H.,"UPWARD COMMUNICATION IN INDUSTRIAL   ADMIN
HIERARCHIES." LG/CO TOP/EX PROB/SOLV DOMIN EXEC   INGP/REL
PERS/REL ATTIT DRIVE PERCEPT...CORREL STAT CHARTS   PSY
20. PAGE 86 B1747   MGT
                                                                          B63
BONINI C.P.,SIMULATION OF INFORMATION AND DECISION   INDUS
SYSTEMS IN THE FIRM. MARKET BUDGET DOMIN EDU/PROP   SIMUL
ADMIN COST ATTIT HABITAT PERCEPT PWR...CONCPT   DECISION
PROBABIL QUANT PREDICT HYPO/EXP BIBLIOG. PAGE 13   MGT
B0273
                                                                          B63
COSTELLO T.W.,PSYCHOLOGY IN ADMINISTRATION: A   PSY
RESEARCH ORIENTATION. CREATE PROB/SOLV PERS/REL   MGT
ADJUST ANOMIE ATTIT DRIVE PERCEPT ROLE...DECISION   EXEC
BIBLIOG T 20. PAGE 24 B0488   ADMIN
                                                                          B63
DE GUZMAN R.P.,PATTERNS IN DECISION-MAKING: CASE   ADMIN
STUDIES IN PHILIPPINE PUBLIC ADMINISTRATION.   DECISION
PHILIPPINE LAW CHIEF PROB/SOLV INGP/REL DRIVE   POLICY
PERCEPT ROLE...ANTHOL T 20. PAGE 27 B0557   GOV/REL
                                                                          B63
HEUSSLER R.,YESTERDAY'S RULERS: THE MAKING OF THE   EX/STRUC
BRITISH COLONIAL SERVICE. AFR EUR+WWI UK STRATA   MORAL
SECT DELIB/GP PLAN DOMIN EDU/PROP ATTIT PERCEPT   ELITES
PERSON SUPEGO KNOWL ORD/FREE PWR...MGT SOC OBS INT
TIME/SEQ 20 CMN/WLTH. PAGE 49 B1000
                                                                          B63
NORTH R.C.,CONTENT ANALYSIS: A HANDBOOK WITH   METH/CNCPT
APPLICATIONS FOR THE STUDY OF INTERNATIONAL CRISIS.   COMPUT/IR
ASIA COM EUR+WWI MOD/EUR INT/ORG TEC/DEV DOMIN   USSR
EDU/PROP ROUTINE COERCE PERCEPT RIGID/FLEX ALL/VALS
...QUANT TESTS CON/ANAL SIMUL GEN/LAWS VAL/FREE.
PAGE 79 B1591
                                                                          B63
THORELLI H.B.,INTOP: INTERNATIONAL OPERATIONS   GAME
SIMULATION: PLAYER'S MANUAL. BRAZIL FINAN OP/RES   INT/TRADE
ADMIN GP/REL INGP/REL PRODUC PERCEPT...DECISION MGT   EDU/PROP
EEC. PAGE 104 B2108   LG/CO
                                                                          B63
TSOU T.,AMERICA'S FAILURE IN CHINA, 1941-1950.   ASIA
USA+45 USA-45 NAT/G ACT/RES PLAN DOMIN EDU/PROP   PERCEPT
ADMIN ROUTINE ATTIT PERSON ORD/FREE...DECISION   DIPLOM
CONCPT MYTH TIME/SEQ TREND STERTYP 20. PAGE 105
B2132
                                                                          S63
ARASTEH R.,"THE ROLE OF INTELLECTUALS IN   INTELL
ADMINISTRATIVE DEVELOPMENT AND SOCIAL CHANGE IN   ADMIN
MODERN IRAN." ISLAM CULTURE NAT/G CONSULT ACT/RES   IRAN
EDU/PROP EXEC ATTIT BIO/SOC PERCEPT SUPEGO ALL/VALS
...POLICY MGT PSY SOC CONCPT 20. PAGE 6 B0123
                                                                          S63
ROUGEMONT D.,"LES NOUVELLES CHANCES DE L'EUROPE."   ECO/UNDEV
EUR+WWI FUT ECO/DEV INT/ORG NAT/G ACT/RES PLAN   PERCEPT
TEC/DEV EDU/PROP ADMIN COLONIAL FEDERAL ATTIT PWR
SKILL...TREND 20. PAGE 91 B1835
                                                                          S63
WAGRET M.,"L'ASCENSION POLITIQUE DE L'U.D.D.I.A.   EX/STRUC
(CONGO) ET SA PRISE DU POUVOIR (1956-1959)." AFR   CHOOSE
WOR+45 NAT/G POL/PAR CONSULT DELIB/GP LEGIS PERCEPT   FRANCE
ALL/VALS SOVEREIGN...TIME/SEQ CONGO. PAGE 113 B2274
                                                                          B64
ADAMS V.,THE PEACE CORPS IN ACTION. USA+45 VOL/ASSN   DIPLOM
EX/STRUC GOV/REL PERCEPT ORD/FREE...OBS 20   FOR/AID
KENNEDY/JF PEACE/CORP. PAGE 3 B0058   PERSON
                                                          DRIVE
                                                                          B64
APTER D.E.,IDEOLOGY AND DISCONTENT. FUT WOR+45   ACT/RES
CONSTN CULTURE INTELL SOCIETY STRUCT INT/ORG NAT/G   ATTIT
DELIB/GP LEGIS CREATE PLAN TEC/DEV EDU/PROP EXEC
PERCEPT PERSON RIGID/FLEX ALL/VALS...POLICY
TOT/POP. PAGE 6 B0122
                                                                          B64
BANTON M.,THE POLICEMAN IN THE COMMUNITY. UK USA+45   FORCES
STRUCT PROF/ORG WORKER LOBBY ROUTINE COERCE CROWD   ADMIN
GP/REL ADJUST DISCRIM PERCEPT 20. PAGE 9 B0181   ROLE
                                                          RACE/REL
                                                                          B64
MERILLAT H.C.L.,LEGAL ADVISERS AND FOREIGN AFFAIRS.   CONSULT
WOR+45 WOR-45 ELITES INTELL NAT/G LEGIT ADMIN   EX/STRUC
PERCEPT ALL/VALS...MGT NEW/IDEA RECORD 20. PAGE 73   DIPLOM

B1469

JOHNSON K.F.,"CAUSAL FACTORS IN LATIN AMERICAN
POLITICAL INSTABILITY." CULTURE NAT/G VOL/ASSN
EX/STRUC FORCES EDU/PROP LEGIT ADMIN COERCE REV
ATTIT KNOWL PWR...STYLE RECORD CHARTS WORK 20.
PAGE 57 B1144
S64 L/A+17C PERCEPT ELITES

KAMMERER G.M.,"ROLE DIVERSITY OF CITY MANAGERS."
LOC/G ADMIN LEAD PERCEPT PWR GP/COMP. PAGE 57 B1163
S64 MUNIC EXEC ATTIT ROLE

KENNAN G.F.,"POLYCENTRISM AND WESTERN POLICY." ASIA
CHINA/COM COM FUT USA+45 USSR NAT/G ACT/RES DOMIN
EDU/PROP EXEC COERCE DISPL PERCEPT...POLICY
COLD/WAR 20. PAGE 59 B1192
S64 RIGID/FLEX ATTIT DIPLOM

NASH M.,"SOCIAL PREREQUISITES TO ECONOMIC GROWTH IN
LATIN AMERICA AND SOUTHEAST ASIA." L/A+17C S/ASIA
CULTURE SOCIETY ECO/UNDEV AGRI INDUS NAT/G PLAN
TEC/DEV EDU/PROP ROUTINE ALL/VALS...POLICY RELATIV
SOC NAT/COMP WORK TOT/POP 20. PAGE 77 B1558
S64 ECO/DEV PERCEPT

BUECHNER J.C.,DIFFERENCES IN ROLE PERCEPTIONS IN
COLORADO COUNCIL-MANAGER CITIES. USA+45 ADMIN
ROUTINE GP/REL CONSEN PERCEPT PERSON ROLE
...DECISION MGT STAT INT QU CHARTS 20 COLORADO
CITY/MGT. PAGE 17 B0338
B65 MUNIC CONSULT LOC/G IDEA/COMP

MEYERHOFF A.E.,THE STRATEGY OF PERSUASION. USA+45
COM/IND CONSULT FOR/AID CONTROL COERCE COST ATTIT
PERCEPT MARXISM 20 COLD/WAR. PAGE 73 B1476
B65 EDU/PROP EFFICIENCY OP/RES ADMIN

HOLSTI O.R.,"THE 1914 CASE." MOD/EUR COMPUTER
DIPLOM EDU/PROP EXEC...DECISION PSY PROBABIL STAT
COMPUT/IR SOC/EXP TIME. PAGE 51 B1036
S65 CON/ANAL PERCEPT WAR

OSTGAARD E.,"FACTORS INFLUENCING THE FLOW OF NEWS."
COM/IND BUDGET DIPLOM EXEC GP/REL COST ATTIT SAMP.
PAGE 80 B1618
S65 EDU/PROP PERCEPT RECORD

POLK W.R.,"PROBLEMS OF GOVERNMENT UTILIZATION OF
SCHOLARLY RESEARCH IN INTERNATIONAL AFFAIRS." FINAN
NAT/G EDU/PROP CONTROL TASK GP/REL ATTIT PERCEPT
KNOWL...POLICY TIME. PAGE 83 B1685
S65 ACT/RES ACADEM PLAN ADMIN

QUADE Q.L.,"THE TRUMAN ADMINISTRATION AND THE
SEPARATION OF POWERS: THE CASE OF THE MARSHALL
PLAN." SOCIETY INT/ORG NAT/G CONSULT DELIB/GP LEGIS
PLAN ECO/TAC ROUTINE DRIVE PERCEPT RIGID/FLEX
ORD/FREE PWR WEALTH...DECISION GEOG NEW/IDEA TREND
20 TRUMAN/HS. PAGE 85 B1726
S65 USA+45 ECO/UNDEV DIPLOM

SCHMIDT F.,PUBLIC RELATIONS IN HEALTH AND WELFARE.
USA+45 ACADEM RECEIVE PRESS FEEDBACK GOV/REL
PERS/REL DEMAND EFFICIENCY ATTIT PERCEPT WEALTH 20
PUBLIC/REL. PAGE 94 B1895
B66 PROF/ORG EDU/PROP ADMIN HEALTH

SKOLNIKOFF E.B.,"MAKING FOREIGN POLICY" PROB/SOLV
EFFICIENCY PERCEPT PWR...MGT METH/CNCPT CLASSIF 20.
PAGE 98 B1976
S67 TEC/DEV CONTROL USA+45 NAT/G

PERCEPTION....SEE PERCEPT

PERCY/CHAS....CHARLES PERCY

PERF/ART....PERFORMING ARTS

FREYRE G.,THE PORTUGUESE AND THE TROPICS. L/A+17C
PORTUGAL SOCIETY PERF/ART ADMIN TASK GP/REL
...ART/METH CONCPT SOC/INTEG 20. PAGE 37 B0754
B61 COLONIAL METH PLAN CULTURE

KASSOF A.,"THE ADMINISTERED SOCIETY:
TOTALITARIANISM WITHOUT TERROR." COM USSR STRATA
AGRI INDUS NAT/G PERF/ART SCHOOL TOP/EX EDU/PROP
ADMIN ORD/FREE PWR...POLICY SOC TIME/SEQ GEN/LAWS
VAL/FREE 20. PAGE 58 B1178
S64 SOCIETY DOMIN TOTALISM

PERFORMING ARTS....SEE PERF/ART; ALSO ART/METH

PERHAM M. B1654,B1655

PERKINS J.A. B1656,B1657,B1658

PERLOFF H.S. B1659

PERON/JUAN....JUAN PERON

PERREN G.E. B1660

PERROW C. B1661,B2052

PERS/COMP....COMPARISON OF PERSONS

ZINK H.,CITY BOSSES IN THE UNITED STATES: A STUDY
OF TWENTY MUNICIPAL BOSSES. USA-45 INDUS MUNIC
NEIGH POL/PAR ADMIN CRIME INGP/REL PERS/REL PWR
...PERS/COMP 20 BOSSISM. PAGE 119 B2403
B30 LOC/G DOMIN BIOG LEAD

HICKMAN C.A.,INDIVIDUALS, GROUPS, AND ECONOMIC
BEHAVIOR. WORKER PAY CONTROL EXEC GP/REL INGP/REL
PERSON ROLE...PSY SOC PERS/COMP METH 20. PAGE 50
B1005
B56 MGT ADMIN ECO/TAC PLAN

BERNSTEIN M.H.,THE JOB OF THE FEDERAL EXECUTIVE.
NAT/G POL/PAR CHIEF LEGIS ADMIN EXEC LOBBY CHOOSE GOV/REL
ORD/FREE PWR...MGT TREND. PAGE 11 B0228
B58 NAT/G TOP/EX PERS/COMP

FAYERWEATHER J.,THE EXECUTIVE OVERSEAS:
ADMINISTRATIVE ATTITUDES AND RELATIONSHIPS IN A
FOREIGN CULTURE. USA+45 WOR+45 CULTURE LG/CO SML/CO
ATTIT...MGT PERS/COMP 20 MEXIC/AMER. PAGE 35 B0709
B59 INT/TRADE TOP/EX NAT/COMP PERS/REL

BENNIS W.G.,"A NEW ROLE FOR THE BEHAVIORAL
SCIENCES: EFFECTING ORGANIZATIONAL CHANGE." ACT/RES
...MGT GP/COMP PERS/COMP SOC/EXP ORG/CHARTS.
PAGE 11 B0216
L63 METH/CNCPT CREATE STRUCT SOC

GOPAL S.,BRITISH POLICY IN INDIA 1858-1905. INDIA
UK ELITES CHIEF DELIB/GP ECO/TAC GP/REL DISCRIM
ATTIT...IDEA/COMP NAT/COMP PERS/COMP BIBLIOG/A
19/20. PAGE 41 B0828
B65 COLONIAL ADMIN POL/PAR ECO/UNDEV

HODGSON R.C.,THE EXECUTIVE ROLE CONSTELLATION: AN
ANALYSIS OF PERSONALITY AND ROLE RELATIONS IN
MANAGEMENT. USA+45 PUB/INST EXEC PERS/REL PERSON
...PSY PERS/COMP HYPO/EXP 20. PAGE 51 B1027
B65 LG/CO ADMIN TOP/EX ROLE

LYONS G.M.,SCHOOLS FOR STRATEGY* EDUCATION AND
RESEARCH IN NATIONAL SECURITY AFFAIRS. USA+45 FINAN
NAT/G VOL/ASSN FORCES TEC/DEV ADMIN WAR...GP/COMP
IDEA/COMP PERS/COMP COLD/WAR. PAGE 67 B1351
B65 ACADEM ACT/RES INTELL

DANELSKI D.J.,"CONFLICT AND ITS RESOLUTION IN THE
SUPREME COURT." PROB/SOLV LEAD ROUTINE PERSON...PSY
PERS/COMP BIBLIOG 20. PAGE 26 B0527
S67 ROLE JURID JUDGE INGP/REL

PERS/REL....RELATIONS BETWEEN PERSONS AND INTERPERSONAL
        COMMUNICATION

CIVIL SERVICE JOURNAL. PARTIC INGP/REL PERS/REL
...MGT BIBLIOG/A 20. PAGE 1 B0011
N ADMIN NAT/G SERV/IND WORKER

PERSONNEL. USA+45 LAW LABOR LG/CO WORKER CREATE
GOV/REL PERS/REL ATTIT WEALTH. PAGE 2 B0030
N BIBLIOG/A ADMIN MGT GP/REL

DUNN A.,SCIENTIFIC SELLING AND ADVERTISING. CLIENT
ADMIN DEMAND EFFICIENCY 20. PAGE 31 B0632
B19 LG/CO PERCEPT PERS/REL TASK

ABBOT F.C.,THE CAMBRIDGE CITY MANAGER (PAMPHLET).
PROB/SOLV ADMIN PERS/REL RIGID/FLEX PWR...MGT 20
MASSACHU CITY/MGT. PAGE 2 B0050
N19 MUNIC EX/STRUC TOP/EX GP/REL

FIRMALINO T.,THE DISTRICT SCHOOL SUPERVISOR VS.
TEACHERS AND PARENTS: A PHILIPPINE CASE STUDY
(PAMPHLET) (BMR). PHILIPPINE LOC/G PLAN EDU/PROP
LOBBY REGION PERS/REL 20. PAGE 36 B0722
N19 RIGID/FLEX SCHOOL ADMIN CREATE

MARSH J.F. JR.,THE FBI RETIREMENT BILL (PAMPHLET).
USA+45 EX/STRUC WORKER PLAN PROB/SOLV BUDGET LEAD
LOBBY PARL/PROC PERS/REL RIGID/FLEX...POLICY 20 FBI
PRESIDENT BUR/BUDGET. PAGE 70 B1405
N19 ADMIN NAT/G SENIOR GOV/REL

ZINK H.,CITY BOSSES IN THE UNITED STATES: A STUDY
OF TWENTY MUNICIPAL BOSSES. USA-45 INDUS MUNIC
NEIGH POL/PAR ADMIN CRIME INGP/REL PERS/REL PWR
...PERS/COMP 20 BOSSISM. PAGE 119 B2403
B30 LOC/G DOMIN BIOG LEAD

BURT F.A.,AMERICAN ADVERTISING AGENCIES. BARGAIN
BUDGET LICENSE WRITING PRICE PERS/REL COST DEMAND
...ORG/CHARTS BIBLIOG 20. PAGE 18 B0358
B40 LG/CO COM/IND ADMIN EFFICIENCY

LEISERSON A.,ADMINISTRATIVE REGULATION: A STUDY IN
REPRESENTATION OF INTERESTS. NAT/G EX/STRUC
PROB/SOLV BARGAIN CONFER ROUTINE REPRESENT PERS/REL
UTIL PWR POLICY. PAGE 63 B1283
B42 LOBBY ADMIN GP/REL GOV/REL

B45
MAYO E.,THE SOCIAL PROBLEMS OF AN INDUSTRIAL CIVILIZATION. USA+45 SOCIETY LABOR CROWD PERS/REL LAISSEZ. PAGE 71 B1438
INDUS GP/REL MGT WORKER

B48
HART J.,THE AMERICAN PRESIDENCY IN ACTION 1789: A STUDY IN CONSTITUTIONAL HISTORY. USA-45 POL/PAR DELIB/GP FORCES LEGIS ADJUD ADMIN LEAD GP/REL PERS/REL 18 PRESIDENT CONGRESS. PAGE 47 B0959
NAT/G CONSTN CHIEF EX/STRUC

B48
WHITE L.D.,THE FEDERALISTS: A STUDY IN ADMINISTRATIVE HISTORY. STRUCT DELIB/GP LEGIS BUDGET ROUTINE GOV/REL GP/REL PERS/REL PWR...BIOG 18/19 PRESIDENT CONGRESS WASHINGT/G JEFFERSN/T HAMILTON/A. PAGE 116 B2337
ADMIN NAT/G POLICY PROB/SOLV

B49
DE GRAZIA A.,HUMAN RELATIONS IN PUBLIC ADMINISTRATION. INDUS ACT/RES CREATE PLAN PROB/SOLV TEC/DEV INGP/REL PERS/REL DRIVE...POLICY SOC 20. PAGE 27 B0552
BIBLIOG/A ADMIN PHIL/SCI OP/RES

B49
DENNING A.,FREEDOM UNDER THE LAW. MOD/EUR UK LAW SOCIETY CHIEF EX/STRUC LEGIS ADJUD CT/SYS PERS/REL PERSON 17/20 ENGLSH/LAW. PAGE 28 B0573
ORD/FREE JURID NAT/G

B49
GLOVER J.D.,THE ADMINISTRATOR. ELITES LG/CO EX/STRUC ACT/RES CONTROL GP/REL INGP/REL PERS/REL AUTHORIT...POLICY CONCPT HIST/WRIT. PAGE 40 B0811
ADMIN MGT ATTIT PROF/ORG

B49
LEPAWSKY A.,ADMINISTRATION. FINAN INDUS LG/CO SML/CO INGP/REL PERS/REL COST EFFICIENCY OPTIMAL SKILL 20. PAGE 64 B1294
ADMIN MGT WORKER EX/STRUC

B49
STEIN H.,THE FOREIGN SERVICE ACT OF 1946. USA+45 ELITES EX/STRUC PLAN PROB/SOLV LOBBY GOV/REL PERS/REL RIGID/FLEX...POLICY IDEA/COMP 20 CONGRESS BUR/BUDGET. PAGE 100 B2027
DIPLOM LAW NAT/G ADMIN

S49
REISSMAN L.,"A STUDY OF ROLE CONCEPTIONS IN BUREAUCRACY" (BMR)" PERS/REL ROLE...SOC CONCPT NEW/IDEA IDEA/COMP SOC/EXP 20 BUREAUCRCY. PAGE 87 B1767
ADMIN METH/CNCPT GEN/LAWS PROB/SOLV

B50
BAKKE E.W.,BONDS OF ORGANIZATION (2ND ED.). USA+45 COM/IND FINAN ADMIN LEAD PERS/REL...INT SOC/INTEG 20. PAGE 8 B0169
ECO/DEV MGT LABOR GP/REL

B50
HYNEMAN C.S.,BUREAUCRACY IN A DEMOCRACY. CHIEF LEGIS ADMIN CONTROL LEAD ROUTINE PERS/REL COST EFFICIENCY UTIL ATTIT AUTHORIT PERSON MORAL. PAGE 53 B1071
NAT/G CENTRAL EX/STRUC MYTH

B51
NIELANDER W.A.,PUBLIC RELATIONS. USA+45 COM/IND LOC/G NAT/G VOL/ASSN EX/STRUC DIPLOM EDU/PROP PRESS TV...METH/CNCPT T 20. PAGE 78 B1583
PERS/REL GP/REL LG/CO ROUTINE

S51
COHEN M.B.,"PERSONALITY AS A FACTOR IN ADMINISTRATIVE DECISIONS." ADJUD PERS/REL ANOMIE SUPEGO...OBS SELF/OBS INT. PAGE 22 B0446
PERSON ADMIN PROB/SOLV PSY

B52
CORSON J.J.,EXECUTIVES FOR THE FEDERAL SERVICE. USA+45 CHIEF...MGT 20. PAGE 24 B0480
LOBBY ADMIN EX/STRUC PERS/REL

B52
DE GRAZIA A.,POLITICAL ORGANIZATION. CONSTN LOC/G MUNIC NAT/G CHIEF LEGIS TOP/EX ADJUD CT/SYS PERS/REL...INT/LAW MYTH UN. PAGE 27 B0553
FEDERAL LAW ADMIN

B53
ARGYRIS C.,EXECUTIVE LEADERSHIP: AN APPRAISAL OF A MANAGER IN ACTION. TOP/EX ADMIN LEAD ADJUST ATTIT ...METH 20. PAGE 6 B0127
MGT EX/STRUC WORKER PERS/REL

B54
GOLDNER A.W.,WILDCAT STRIKE. LABOR TEC/DEV PAY ADMIN LEAD PERS/REL ATTIT RIGID/FLEX PWR...MGT CONCPT. PAGE 40 B0816
INDUS WORKER GP/REL SOC

B55
BLAU P.M.,THE DYNAMICS OF BUREAUCRACY: A STUDY OF INTERPERSONAL RELATIONS IN TWO GOVERNMENT AGENCIES. USA+45 EX/STRUC REPRESENT INGP/REL PERS/REL. PAGE 12 B0251
CLIENT ADMIN EXEC ROUTINE

S55
CHAPIN F.S.,"FORMALIZATION OBSERVED IN TEN VOLUNTARY ORGANIZATIONS: CONCEPTS, MORPHOLOGY, PROCESS." STRUCT INGP/REL PERS/REL...METH/CNCPT CLASSIF OBS RECORD. PAGE 20 B0407
VOL/ASSN ROUTINE CONTROL OP/RES

S55
CROCKETT W.H.,"EMERGENT LEADERSHIP IN SMALL DECISION MAKING GROUPS." ACT/RES ROUTINE PERS/REL ATTIT...STAT CONT/OBS SOC/EXP SIMUL. PAGE 25 B0507
DELIB/GP ADMIN PSY DECISION

B56
POWELL N.J.,PERSONNEL ADMINISTRATION IN GOVERNMENT. COM/IND POL/PAR LEGIS PAY CT/SYS ROUTINE GP/REL PERS/REL...POLICY METH 20 CIVIL/SERV. PAGE 84 B1697
ADMIN WORKER LOC/G NAT/G

B56
WAUGH E.W.,SECOND CONSUL. USA+45 USA-45 CONSTN POL/PAR PROB/SOLV PARL/PROC CHOOSE PERS/REL ATTIT ...BIBLIOG 18/20 VICE/PRES. PAGE 114 B2304
NAT/G EX/STRUC PWR CHIEF

B57
KIETH-LUCAS A.,DECISIONS ABOUT PEOPLE IN NEED, A STUDY OF ADMINISTRATIVE RESPONSIVENESS IN PUBLIC ASSISTANCE. USA+45 GIVE RECEIVE INGP/REL PERS/REL MORAL RESPECT WEALTH...SOC OBS BIBLIOG 20. PAGE 60 B1204
ADMIN RIGID/FLEX SOC/WK DECISION

S57
BAUMGARTEL H.,"LEADERSHIP STYLE AS A VARIABLE IN RESEARCH ADMINISTRATION." USA+45 ADMIN REPRESENT PERS/REL 20. PAGE 10 B0198
LEAD EXEC MGT INGP/REL

B58
CHEEK G.,ECONOMIC AND SOCIAL IMPLICATIONS OF AUTOMATION: A BIBLIOGRAPHIC REVIEW (PAMPHLET). USA+45 LG/CO WORKER CREATE PLAN CONTROL ROUTINE PERS/REL EFFICIENCY PRODUC...METH/COMP 20. PAGE 20 B0416
BIBLIOG/A SOCIETY INDUS AUTOMAT

B58
DWARKADAS R.,ROLE OF HIGHER CIVIL SERVICE IN INDIA. INDIA ECO/UNDEV LEGIS PROB/SOLV GP/REL PERS/REL ...POLICY WELF/ST DECISION ORG/CHARTS BIBLIOG 20 CIVIL/SERV INTRVN/ECO. PAGE 31 B0637
ADMIN NAT/G ROLE PLAN

B58
REDFIELD C.E.,COMMUNICATION IN MANAGEMENT. DELIB/GP EX/STRUC WRITING LEAD PERS/REL...PSY INT METH 20. PAGE 87 B1750
COM/IND MGT LG/CO ADMIN

B58
SHERWOOD F.P.,SUPERVISORY METHODS IN MUNICIPAL ADMINISTRATION. USA+45 MUNIC WORKER EDU/PROP PARTIC INGP/REL PERS/REL 20 CITY/MGT. PAGE 96 B1945
EX/STRUC LEAD ADMIN LOC/G

S58
ARGYRIS C.,"SOME PROBLEMS IN CONCEPTUALIZING ORGANIZATIONAL CLIMATE: A CASE STUDY OF A BANK" (BMR)" USA+45 EX/STRUC ADMIN PERS/REL ADJUST PERSON ...POLICY HYPO/EXP SIMUL 20. PAGE 6 B0129
FINAN CONCPT LG/CO INGP/REL

B59
BRUNTON R.L.,MANAGEMENT PRACTICES FOR SMALLER CITIES. USA+45 MUNIC CONSULT PLAN BUDGET PERS/REL 20 CITY/MGT. PAGE 16 B0331
ADMIN LOC/G MGT TOP/EX

B59
FAYERWEATHER J.,THE EXECUTIVE OVERSEAS: ADMINISTRATIVE ATTITUDES AND RELATIONSHIPS IN A FOREIGN CULTURE. USA+45 WOR+45 CULTURE LG/CO SML/CO ATTIT...MGT PERS/COMP 20 MEXIC/AMER. PAGE 35 B0709
INT/TRADE TOP/EX NAT/COMP PERS/REL

B59
GREENEWALT C.H.,THE UNCOMMON MAN. UNIV ECO/DEV ADMIN PERS/REL PERSON SUPEGO WEALTH 20. PAGE 43 B0868
TASK ORD/FREE DRIVE EFFICIENCY

B59
WARNER W.L.,INDUSTRIAL MAN. USA+45 USA-45 ELITES INDUS LABOR TOP/EX WORKER ADMIN INGP/REL PERS/REL ...CHARTS ANTHOL 20. PAGE 114 B2294
EXEC LEAD PERSON MGT

L59
BENNIS W.G.,"LEADERSHIP THEORY AND ADMINISTRATIVE BEHAVIOR: THE PROBLEM OF AUTHORITY." ROUTINE...MGT HYPO/EXP. PAGE 10 B0214
LEAD ADMIN DOMIN PERS/REL

S59
SIMPSON R.L.,"VERTICAL AND HORIZONTAL COMMUNICATION IN FORMAL ORGANIZATION" USA+45 LG/CO EX/STRUC DOMIN CONTROL TASK INGP/REL TIME 20. PAGE 97 B1963
PERS/REL AUTOMAT INDUS WORKER

B60
BELL J.,THE SPLENDID MISERY: THE STORY OF THE PRESIDENCY AND POWER POLITICS AT CLOSE RANGE. USA+45 USA-45 PRESS ADMIN LEAD LOBBY GP/REL PERS/REL PERSON PRESIDENT. PAGE 10 B0208
EXEC TOP/EX LEGIS

B60
PAGE T.,THE PUBLIC PERSONNEL AGENCY AND THE CHIEF EXECUTIVE (REPORT NO. 601). USA+45 LOC/G NAT/G GP/REL PERS/REL...ANTHOL 20. PAGE 80 B1624
WORKER EXEC ADMIN MGT

S60
BAVELAS A.,"LEADERSHIP: MAN AND FUNCTION." WORKER CREATE PLAN CONTROL PERS/REL PERSON PWR...MGT 20. PAGE 10 B0199
LEAD ADMIN ROUTINE ROLE

S60

THOMPSON J.D.,"ORGANIZATIONAL MANAGEMENT OF   PROB/SOLV
CONFLICT" (BMR)" WOR+45 STRUCT LABOR LG/CO WORKER PERS/REL
TEC/DEV INGP/REL ATTIT GP/COMP. PAGE 104 B2103   ADMIN
                                                   MGT

C60

MCCLEERY R.,"COMMUNICATION PATTERNS AS BASES OF   PERS/REL
SYSTEMS OF AUTHORITY AND POWER" IN THEORETICAL   PUB/INST
STUDIES IN SOCIAL ORGAN. OF PRISON-BMR. USA+45   PWR
SOCIETY STRUCT EDU/PROP ADMIN CONTROL COERCE CRIME DOMIN
GP/REL AUTHORIT...SOC 20. PAGE 71 B1443

B61

AMERICAN MANAGEMENT ASSN.SUPERIOR-SUBORDINATE   MGT
COMMUNICATION IN MANAGEMENT. STRATA FINAN INDUS   ACT/RES
SML/CO WORKER CONTROL EXEC ATTIT 20. PAGE 4 B0086 PERS/REL
                                                   LG/CO

B61

DUBIN R.,HUMAN RELATIONS IN ADMINISTRATION. USA+45 PERS/REL
INDUS LABOR LG/CO EX/STRUC GP/REL DRIVE PWR   MGT
...DECISION SOC CHARTS ANTHOL 20. PAGE 31 B0623   ADMIN
                                                   EXEC

B61

HAIRE M.,MODERN ORGANIZATION THEORY. LABOR ROUTINE PERS/REL
MAJORITY...CONCPT MODAL OBS CONT/OBS. PAGE 45 B0919 GP/REL
                                                   MGT
                                                   DECISION

B61

KRUPP S.,PATTERN IN ORGANIZATIONAL ANALYSIS: A   MGT
CRITICAL EXAMINATION. INGP/REL PERS/REL RATIONAL   CONTROL
ATTIT AUTHORIT DRIVE PWR...DECISION PHIL/SCI SOC   CONCPT
IDEA/COMP. PAGE 61 B1239   METH/CNCPT

B61

PETRULLO L.,LEADERSHIP AND INTERPERSONAL BEHAVIOR. PERSON
FACE/GP FAM PROF/ORG EX/STRUC FORCES DOMIN WAR   ATTIT
GP/REL PERS/REL EFFICIENCY PRODUC PWR...MGT PSY.   LEAD
PAGE 82 B1663   HABITAT

B61

TANZER L.,THE KENNEDY CIRCLE. INTELL CONSULT   EX/STRUC
DELIB/GP TOP/EX CONTROL EXEC INGP/REL PERS/REL PWR NAT/G
...BIOG IDEA/COMP ANTHOL 20 KENNEDY/JF PRESIDENT   CHIEF
DEMOCRAT MCNAMARA/R RUSK/D. PAGE 103 B2077

B61

THAYER L.O.,ADMINISTRATIVE COMMUNICATION. DELIB/GP GP/REL
ADMIN ROUTINE PERS/REL 20. PAGE 104 B2093   PSY
                                                   LG/CO
                                                   MGT

L61

THOMPSON V.A.,"HIERARACHY, SPECIALIZATION, AND   PERS/REL
ORGANIZATIONAL CONFLICT" (BMR)" WOR+45 STRATA   PROB/SOLV
STRUCT WORKER TEC/DEV GP/REL INGP/REL ATTIT   ADMIN
AUTHORIT 20 BUREAUCRCY. PAGE 104 B2106   EX/STRUC

S61

BENNIS W.G.,"REVISIONIST THEORY OF LEADERSHIP"   LEAD
MUNIC ACT/RES TEC/DEV...SIMUL 20. PAGE 11 B0215   ADMIN
                                                   PERS/REL
                                                   HYPO/EXP

C61

ETZIONI A.,"A COMPARATIVE ANALYSIS OF COMPLEX   CON/ANAL
ORGANIZATIONS: ON POWER, INVOLVEMENT AND THEIR   SOC
CORRELATES." ELITES CREATE OP/RES ROUTINE INGP/REL LEAD
PERS/REL CONSEN ATTIT DRIVE PWR...CONCPT BIBLIOG. CONTROL
PAGE 34 B0684

B62

ARGYRIS C.,INTERPERSONAL COMPETENCE AND   EX/STRUC
ORGANIZATIONAL EFFECTIVENESS. CREATE PLAN PROB/SOLV ADMIN
EDU/PROP INGP/REL PERS/REL PRODUC...OBS INT SIMUL CONSULT
20. PAGE 6 B0131   EFFICIENCY

B62

GRAY R.K.,EIGHTEEN ACRES UNDER GLASS. ELITES   CHIEF
CONSULT EX/STRUC DIPLOM PRESS CONFER WAR PERS/REL ADMIN
PERSON 20 EISNHWR/DD TRUMAN/HS CABINET. PAGE 43   TOP/EX
B0860   NAT/G

B62

PACKARD V.,THE PYRAMID CLIMBERS. USA+45 ELITES   INDUS
SOCIETY CREATE PROB/SOLV EFFICIENCY ATTIT...MGT 20. TOP/EX
PAGE 80 B1621   PERS/REL
                                                   DRIVE

B62

PRESTHUS R.,THE ORGANIZATIONAL SOCIETY. USA+45   LG/CO
STRUCT ECO/DEV ADMIN ATTIT ALL/VALS...PSY SOC 20. WORKER
PAGE 84 B1703   PERS/REL
                                                   DRIVE

B62

SIMON Y.R.,A GENERAL THEORY OF AUTHORITY. DOMIN   PERS/REL
ADMIN RATIONAL UTOPIA KNOWL MORAL PWR SOVEREIGN   PERSON
...HUM CONCPT NEW/IDEA 20. PAGE 97 B1962   SOCIETY
                                                   ORD/FREE

S62

READ W.H.,"UPWARD COMMUNICATION IN INDUSTRIAL   ADMIN
HIERARCHIES." LG/CO TOP/EX PROB/SOLV DOMIN EXEC   INGP/REL
PERS/REL ATTIT DRIVE PERCEPT...CORREL STAT CHARTS PSY
20. PAGE 86 B1747   MGT

B63

CHARLES S.,MINISTER OF RELIEF: HARRY HOPKINS AND   ADMIN
THE DEPRESSION. EX/STRUC PROB/SOLV RATION PARL/PROC ECO/TAC
PERS/REL ALL/VALS 20 HOPKINS/H NRA. PAGE 20 B0414 PLAN

BIOG

B63

COSTELLO T.W.,PSYCHOLOGY IN ADMINISTRATION: A   PSY
RESEARCH ORIENTATION. CREATE PROB/SOLV PERS/REL   MGT
ADJUST ANOMIE ATTIT DRIVE PERCEPT ROLE...DECISION EXEC
BIBLIOG T 20. PAGE 24 B0488   ADMIN

B63

HOWER R.M.,MANAGERS AND SCIENTISTS. EX/STRUC CREATE R+D
ADMIN REPRESENT ATTIT DRIVE ROLE PWR SKILL...SOC   MGT
INT. PAGE 52 B1052   PERS/REL
                                                   INGP/REL

B63

RAUDSEPP E.,MANAGING CREATIVE SCIENTISTS AND   MGT
ENGINEERS. USA+45 ECO/DEV LG/CO GP/REL PERS/REL   CREATE
PRODUC. PAGE 86 B1742   R+D
                                                   ECO/TAC

B63

SPRING D.,THE ENGLISH LANDED ESTATE IN THE   STRATA
NINETEENTH CENTURY: ITS ADMINISTRATION. UK ELITES PERS/REL
STRUCT AGRI NAT/G GP/REL OWN PWR WEALTH...BIBLIOG   MGT
19 HOUSE/LORD. PAGE 99 B2012

S63

BAKER R.J.,"DISCUSSION AND DECISION-MAKING IN THE EXEC
CIVIL SERVICE." UK CONTROL REPRESENT INGP/REL   EX/STRUC
PERS/REL EFFICIENCY 20. PAGE 8 B0168   PROB/SOLV
                                                   ADMIN

S63

HILLS R.J.,"THE REPRESENTATIVE FUNCTION: NEGLECTED LEAD
DIMENSION OF LEADERSHIP BEHAVIOR" USA+45 CLIENT   ADMIN
STRUCT SCHOOL PERS/REL...STAT QU SAMP LAB/EXP 20. EXEC
PAGE 50 B1012   ACT/RES

B64

ARGYRIS C.,INTEGRATING THE INDIVIDUAL AND THE   ADMIN
ORGANIZATION. WORKER PROB/SOLV LEAD SANCTION   PERS/REL
REPRESENT ADJUST EFFICIENCY DRIVE PERSON...PSY   VOL/ASSN
METH/CNCPT ORG/CHARTS. PAGE 6 B0132   PARTIC

B64

BLAKE R.R.,MANAGING INTERGROUP CONFLICT IN   CREATE
INDUSTRY. INDUS DELIB/GP EX/STRUC GP/REL PERS/REL PROB/SOLV
GAME. PAGE 12 B0250   OP/RES
                                                   ADJUD

B64

ETZIONI A.,MODERN ORGANIZATIONS. CLIENT STRUCT   MGT
DOMIN CONTROL LEAD PERS/REL AUTHORIT...CLASSIF   ADMIN
BUREAUCRCY. PAGE 34 B0685   PLAN
                                                   CULTURE

B64

GORE W.J.,ADMINISTRATIVE DECISION-MAKING* A   DECISION
HEURISTIC MODEL. EX/STRUC ADMIN LEAD ROUTINE   MGT
PERS/REL...METH/CNCPT ORG/CHARTS. PAGE 41 B0834   SIMUL
                                                   GEN/METH

B64

RIES J.C.,THE MANAGEMENT OF DEFENSE: ORGANIZATION FORCES
AND CONTROL OF THE US ARMED SERVICES. PROF/ORG   ACT/RES
DELIB/GP EX/STRUC LEGIS GOV/REL PERS/REL CENTRAL   DECISION
RATIONAL PWR...POLICY TREND GOV/COMP BIBLIOG.   CONTROL
PAGE 88 B1782

B64

SAYLES L.R.,MANAGERIAL BEHAVIOR: ADMINISTRATION IN CONCPT
COMPLEX ORGANIZATIONS. INDUS LG/CO PROB/SOLV   ADMIN
CONTROL EXEC INGP/REL PERS/REL SKILL...MGT OBS   TOP/EX
PREDICT GEN/LAWS 20. PAGE 93 B1874   EX/STRUC

B64

TOMPKINS D.C.,PROBATION SINCE WORLD WAR II. USA+45 BIBLIOG
FORCES ADMIN ROUTINE PERS/REL AGE...CRIMLGY HEAL   PUB/INST
20. PAGE 105 B2118   ORD/FREE
                                                   CRIME

B64

WHEELER-BENNETT J.W.,THE NEMESIS OF POWER (2ND   FORCES
ED.). EUR+WWI GERMANY TOP/EX TEC/DEV ADMIN WAR   NAT/G
PERS/REL RIGID/FLEX ROLE ORD/FREE PWR FASCISM 20   GP/REL
HITLER/A. PAGE 116 B2332   STRUCT

N64

CANADA NATL JT COUN PUB SERV.THE CANADA NATIONAL   GP/REL
JOINT COUNCIL OF THE PUBLIC SERVICE 1944-1964   NAT/G
(PAMPHLET). CANADA EX/STRUC PERS/REL DRIVE...MGT 20 LABOR
PEARSON/L. PAGE 18 B0373   EFFICIENCY

B65

DAVISON W.P.,INTERNATIONAL POLITICAL COMMUNICATION. EDU/PROP
COM USA+45 WOR+45 CULTURE ECO/UNDEV NAT/G PROB/SOLV DIPLOM
PRESS TV ADMIN 20 FILM. PAGE 27 B0545   PERS/REL
                                                   COM/IND

B65

HAIGHT D.E.,THE PRESIDENT: ROLES AND POWERS. USA+45 CHIEF
USA-45 POL/PAR PLAN DIPLOM CHOOSE PERS/REL PWR   LEGIS
18/20 PRESIDENT CONGRESS. PAGE 45 B0915   TOP/EX
                                                   EX/STRUC

B65

HODGSON R.C.,THE EXECUTIVE ROLE CONSTELLATION: AN LG/CO
ANALYSIS OF PERSONALITY AND ROLE RELATIONS IN   ADMIN
MANAGEMENT. USA+45 PUB/INST EXEC PERS/REL PERSON   TOP/EX
...PSY PERS/COMP HYPO/EXP 20. PAGE 51 B1027   ROLE

B65

KWEDER J.B.,THE ROLES OF THE MANAGER, MAYOR, AND   MUNIC
COUNCILMEN IN POLICYMAKING. LEGIS PERS/REL ATTIT   EXEC
ROLE PWR GP/COMP. PAGE 62 B1246   LEAD

DECISION
B65

MASTERS N.A.,COMMITTEE ASSIGNMENTS IN THE HOUSE OF   LEAD
REPRESENTATIVES (BMR). USA+45 ELITES POL/PAR   LEGIS
EX/STRUC PARTIC REPRESENT GP/REL PERS/REL ATTIT PWR   CHOOSE
...STAT CHARTS 20 HOUSE/REP. PAGE 71 B1425   DELIB/GP
B65

STANLEY D.T.,CHANGING ADMINISTRATIONS. USA+45   NAT/G
POL/PAR DELIB/GP TOP/EX BUDGET GOV/REL GP/REL   CHIEF
PERS/REL PWR...MAJORIT DECISION MGT 20 PRESIDENT   ADMIN
SUCCESSION DEPT/STATE DEPT/DEFEN DEPT/HEW. PAGE 100   EX/STRUC
B2021
B66

BOYD H.W.,MARKETING MANAGEMENT: CASES FROM EMERGING   MGT
COUNTRIES. BRAZIL GHANA ISRAEL WOR+45 ADMIN   ECO/UNDEV
PERS/REL ATTIT HABITAT WEALTH...ANTHOL 20 ARGEN   PROB/SOLV
CASEBOOK. PAGE 14 B0292   MARKET
B66

DICKSON W.J.,COUNSELING IN AN ORGANIZATION: A   INDUS
SEQUEL TO THE HAWTHORNE RESEARCHES. CLIENT VOL/ASSN   WORKER
ACT/RES PROB/SOLV AUTOMAT ROUTINE PERS/REL   PSY
HAPPINESS ANOMIE ROLE...OBS CHARTS 20 AT+T. PAGE 29   MGT
B0588
B66

MCKENZIE J.L.,AUTHORITY IN THE CHURCH. STRUCT LEAD   SECT
INGP/REL PERS/REL CENTRAL ANOMIE ATTIT ORD/FREE   AUTHORIT
RESPECT CATH. PAGE 72 B1452   PWR
ADMIN
B66

RAEFF M.,ORIGINS OF THE RUSSIAN INTELLIGENTSIA: THE   INTELL
EIGHTEENTH-CENTURY NOBILITY. RUSSIA FAM NAT/G   ELITES
EDU/PROP ADMIN PERS/REL ATTIT...HUM BIOG 18.   STRATA
PAGE 85 B1728   CONSERVE
B66

SCHMIDT F.,PUBLIC RELATIONS IN HEALTH AND WELFARE.   PROF/ORG
USA+45 ACADEM RECEIVE PRESS FEEDBACK GOV/REL   EDU/PROP
PERS/REL DEMAND EFFICIENCY ATTIT PERCEPT WEALTH 20   ADMIN
PUBLIC/REL. PAGE 94 B1895   HEALTH
B66

SIMON R.,PERSPECTIVES IN PUBLIC RELATIONS. USA+45   GP/REL
INDUS ACT/RES PLAN ADMIN ATTIT MGT. PAGE 97 B1961   PERS/REL
COM/IND
SOCIETY
S66

WOLFINGER R.E.,"POLITICAL ETHOS AND THE STRUCTURE   MUNIC
OF CITY GOVERNMENT." POL/PAR EX/STRUC REPRESENT   ATTIT
GP/REL PERS/REL RIGID/FLEX PWR. PAGE 118 B2371   STRATA
GOV/COMP
B67

CECIL L.,ALBERT BALLIN: BUSINESS AND POLITICS IN   DIPLOM
IMPERIAL GERMANY 1888-1918. GERMANY UK INT/TRADE   CONSTN
LEAD WAR PERS/REL ADJUST PWR WEALTH...MGT BIBLIOG   ECO/DEV
19/20. PAGE 19 B0397   TOP/EX
B67

GELLHORN W.,OMBUDSMEN AND OTHERS: CITIZENS'   NAT/COMP
PROTECTORS IN NINE COUNTRIES. WOR+45 LAW CONSTN   REPRESENT
LEGIS INSPECT ADJUD ADMIN CONTROL CT/SYS CHOOSE   INGP/REL
PERS/REL...STAT CHARTS 20. PAGE 39 B0789   PROB/SOLV
S67

CROCKETT D.G.,"THE MP AND HIS CONSTITUENTS." UK   EXEC
POL/PAR...DECISION 20. PAGE 25 B0506   NAT/G
PERS/REL
REPRESENT
S67

DODSON D.W.,"NEW FORCES OPERATING IN EDUCATIONAL   PROB/SOLV
DECISION-MAKING." USA+45 NEIGH EDU/PROP ADMIN   SCHOOL
SUPEGO DECISION. PAGE 30 B0602   PERS/REL
PWR
S67

LA PORTE T.,"DIFFUSION AND DISCONTINUITY IN   INTELL
SCIENCE, TECHNOLOGY AND PUBLIC AFFAIRS: RESULTS OF   ADMIN
A SEARCH IN THE FIELD." USA+45 ACT/RES TEC/DEV   ACADEM
PERS/REL ATTIT PHIL/SCI. PAGE 62 B1249   GP/REL
S67

ROSENBERG B.,"ETHNIC LIBERALISM AND EMPLOYMENT   RACE/REL
DISCRIMINATION IN THE NORTH." USA+45 TOP/EX   ATTIT
PROB/SOLV ADMIN REGION PERS/REL DISCRIM...INT   WORKER
IDEA/COMP. PAGE 90 B1820   EXEC
S67

SCOTT W.R.,"ORGANIZATIONAL EVALUATION AND   EXEC
AUTHORITY." CONTROL SANCTION PERS/REL ATTIT DRIVE   WORKER
...SOC CONCPT OBS CHARTS IDEA/COMP 20. PAGE 95   INSPECT
B1921   EX/STRUC
S67

SKOLNICK J.H.,"SOCIAL CONTROL IN THE ADVERSARY   PROB/SOLV
SYSTEM." USA+45 CONSULT OP/RES ADMIN CONTROL.   PERS/REL
PAGE 98 B1975   ADJUD
CT/SYS
S68

GRAM H.A.,"BUSINESS ETHICS AND THE CORPORATION."   POLICY
LG/CO SECT PROB/SOLV CONTROL EXEC GP/REL INGP/REL   ADMIN
PERS/REL ROLE MORAL PWR...DECISION 20. PAGE 42   MGT
B0850

PERS/TEST....PERSONALITY TESTS

B45
BENJAMIN H.C.,EMPLOYMENT TESTS IN INDUSTRY AND   BIBLIOG/A
BUSINESS. LG/CO WORKER ROUTINE...MGT PSY SOC   METH
CLASSIF PROBABIL STAT APT/TEST KNO/TEST PERS/TEST   TESTS
20. PAGE 10 B0211   INDUS
B51

GUETZKOW H.,GROUPS, LEADERSHIP, AND MEN. FACE/GP   ATTIT
SECT EDU/PROP EXEC PERSON RESPECT...PERS/TEST   SOC
GEN/METH 20. PAGE 44 B0901   ELITES
B54

COMBS C.H.,DECISION PROCESSES. INTELL SOCIETY   MATH
DELIB/GP CREATE TEC/DEV DOMIN LEGIT EXEC CHOOSE   DECISION
DRIVE RIGID/FLEX KNOWL PWR...PHIL/SCI SOC
METH/CNCPT CONT/OBS REC/INT PERS/TEST SAMP/SIZ BIOG
SOC/EXP WORK. PAGE 22 B0455
B56

WHYTE W.H. JR.,THE ORGANIZATION MAN. CULTURE FINAN   ADMIN
VOL/ASSN DOMIN EDU/PROP EXEC DISPL HABITAT ROLE   LG/CO
...PERS/TEST STERTYP. PAGE 116 B2343   PERSON
CONSEN
B58

BROWNE C.G.,THE CONCEPT OF LEADERSHIP. UNIV FACE/GP   EXEC
DOMIN EDU/PROP LEGIT LEAD DRIVE PERSON PWR...MGT   CONCPT
SOC OBS SELF/OBS CONT/OBS INT PERS/TEST STERTYP
GEN/LAWS. PAGE 16 B0328
B62

CHICAGO U CTR PROG GOVT ADMIN,EDUCATION FOR   EDU/PROP
INNOVATIVE BEHAVIOR IN EXECUTIVES. UNIV ELITES   CREATE
ADMIN EFFICIENCY DRIVE PERSON...MGT APT/TEST   EXEC
PERS/TEST CHARTS LAB/EXP BIBLIOG 20. PAGE 21 B0420   STAT

PERSIA....PERSIA: ANCIENT IRAN

PERSON....PERSONALITY AND HUMAN NATURE

N
BIBLIO. CATALOGUE DES OUVRAGES PARUS EN LANGUE   BIBLIOG
FRANCAISE DANS LE MONDE ENTIER. FRANCE WOR+45 ADMIN   NAT/G
LEAD PERSON...SOC 20. PAGE 1 B0008   DIPLOM
ECO/DEV
N

CUMULATIVE BOOK INDEX. WOR+45 WOR-45 ADMIN PERSON   INDEX
ALL/VALS ALL/IDEOS...HUM PHIL/SCI SOC LING 19/20.   NAT/G
PAGE 1 B0012   DIPLOM
N

DEUTSCHE BIBLIOGRAPHIE. HALBJAHRESVERZEICHNIS.   BIBLIOG
WOR+45 LAW ADMIN PERSON. PAGE 1 B0013   NAT/G
DIPLOM
N

PUBLISHERS' TRADE LIST ANNUAL. LAW POL/PAR ADMIN   BIBLIOG
PERSON ALL/IDEOS...HUM SOC 19/20. PAGE 1 B0020   NAT/G
DIPLOM
POLICY
N

READERS GUIDE TO PERIODICAL LITERATURE. WOR+45   BIBLIOG
WOR-45 LAW ADMIN ATTIT PERSON...HUM PSY SOC 20.   WRITING
PAGE 1 B0021   DIPLOM
NAT/G
N

SUBJECT GUIDE TO BOOKS IN PRINT: AN INDEX TO THE   BIBLIOG
PUBLISHERS' TRADE LIST ANNUAL. UNIV LAW LOC/G   ECO/DEV
DIPLOM WRITING ADMIN LEAD PERSON...MGT SOC. PAGE 1   POL/PAR
B0023   NAT/G
N

SUBJECT GUIDE TO BOOKS IN PRINT: AN INDEX TO THE   BIBLIOG
PUBLISHERS' TRADE LIST ANNUAL. WOR+45 WOR-45 LAW   NAT/G
CULTURE ADMIN LEAD PERSON...HUM MGT SOC. PAGE 2   DIPLOM
B0029
N

DEUTSCHE BUCHEREI,JAHRESVERZEICHNIS DER DEUTSCHEN   BIBLIOG
HOCHSCHULSCHRIFTEN. EUR+WWI GERMANY LAW ADMIN   WRITING
PERSON...MGT SOC 19/20. PAGE 28 B0579   ACADEM
INTELL
N

DEUTSCHE BUCHEREI,DEUTSCHES BUCHERVERZEICHNIS.   BIBLIOG
GERMANY LAW CULTURE POL/PAR ADMIN LEAD ATTIT PERSON   NAT/G
...SOC 20. PAGE 29 B0581   DIPLOM
ECO/DEV
N19

BOHLKE R.H.,BUREAUCRATS AND INTELLECTUALS: A   PERSON
CRITIQUE OF C. WRIGHT MILLS (PAMPHLET). ADMIN   SOC
SOCISM. PAGE 13 B0266   ELITES
ACADEM
N19

WRIGHT D.S.,AMERICAN STATE ADMINISTRATORS   QU
(PAMPHLET). USA+45 ATTIT PERSON...SAMP/SIZ CHARTS   TOP/EX
SOC/EXP METH 20. PAGE 118 B2379   ADMIN
PROVS
B24

MERRIAM C.E.,A HISTORY OF POLITICAL THEORIES -   UNIV
RECENT TIMES. USA-45 WOR-45 CULTURE SOCIETY ECO/DEV   INTELL
R+D EDU/PROP ROUTINE CHOOSE ATTIT PERSON ALL/VALS
...POLICY SOC CONCPT METH/CNCPT OBS HIST/WRIT
TIME/SEQ TREND. PAGE 73 B1471
B28

HALL W.P.,EMPIRE TO COMMONWEALTH. FUT WOR-45 CONSTN VOL/ASSN

ECO/DEV ECO/UNDEV INT/ORG PROVS PLAN DIPLOM   NAT/G
EDU/PROP ADMIN COLONIAL PEACE PERSON ALL/VALS   UK
...POLICY GEOG SOC OBS RECORD TREND CMN/WLTH
PARLIAMENT 19/20. PAGE 46 B0925

B30
MURCHISON C.,PSYCHOLOGIES OF 1930. UNIV USA-45   CREATE
CULTURE INTELL SOCIETY STRATA FAM ROUTINE BIO/SOC   PERSON
DRIVE RIGID/FLEX SUPEGO...NEW/IDEA OBS SELF/OBS
CONT/OBS 20. PAGE 76 B1543

B38
SALTER J.T.,THE AMERICAN POLITICIAN. USA-45 LABOR   BIOG
POL/PAR EDU/PROP ADMIN CHOOSE ATTIT DRIVE PERSON   LEAD
PWR...POLICY ANTHOL 20 THOMAS/N LEWIS/JL LAGUARD/F   PROVS
GOVERNOR MAYOR. PAGE 92 B1865   LOC/G

S39
MARX F.M.,"POLICY FORMULATION AND THE   ADMIN
ADMINISTRATIVE PROCESS" ROUTINE ADJUST EFFICIENCY   LEAD
OPTIMAL PRIVIL DRIVE PERSON OBJECTIVE...DECISION   INGP/REL
OBS GEN/METH. PAGE 70 B1418   MGT

B41
YOUNG G.,FEDERALISM AND FREEDOM. EUR+WWI MOD/EUR   NAT/G
RUSSIA USA-45 WOR-45 SOCIETY STRUCT ECO/DEV INT/ORG WAR
EXEC FEDERAL ATTIT PERSON ALL/VALS...OLD/LIB CONCPT
OBS TREND LEAGUE/NAT TOT/POP. PAGE 119 B2392

B42
US STATE DEPT.,PEACE AND WAR: UNITED STATES FOREIGN DIPLOM
POLICY, 1931-41. CULTURE FORCES ROUTINE CHOOSE   USA-45
ATTIT DRIVE PERSON 20. PAGE 111 B2237   PLAN

B45
PLATO,THE REPUBLIC. MEDIT-7 UNIV SOCIETY STRUCT   PERSON
EX/STRUC FORCES UTOPIA ATTIT PERCEPT HEALTH KNOWL   PHIL/SCI
ORD/FREE PWR...HUM CONCPT STERTYP TOT/POP. PAGE 83
B1681

B47
BARNARD C.,THE FUNCTIONS OF THE EXECUTIVE. USA+45   EXEC
ELITES INTELL LEGIT ATTIT DRIVE PERSON SKILL...PSY   EX/STRUC
SOC METH/CNCPT SOC/EXP GEN/METH VAL/FREE 20. PAGE 9 ROUTINE
B0187

S47
TURNER R.H.,"THE NAVY DISBURSING OFFICER AS A   FORCES
BUREAUCRAT" (BMR)" USA-45 LAW STRATA DIST/IND WAR   ADMIN
PWR...SOC 20 BUREAUCRCY. PAGE 106 B2140   PERSON
                                                     ROLE

B48
SHERWOOD R.E.,ROOSEVELT AND HOPKINS. UK USA+45 USSR TOP/EX
NAT/G EX/STRUC FORCES ADMIN ROUTINE PERSON PWR   BIOG
...TIME/SEQ 20 ROOSEVLT/F HOPKINS/H. PAGE 96 B1946   DIPLOM
                                                     WAR

S48
KNICKERBOCKER I.,"LEADERSHIP: A CONCEPTION AND SOME LEAD
IMPLICATIONS." INDUS OP/RES REPRESENT INGP/REL   CONCPT
DRIVE...MGT CLASSIF. PAGE 60 B1220   PERSON
                                                     ROLE

B49
DENNING A.,FREEDOM UNDER THE LAW. MOD/EUR UK LAW   ORD/FREE
SOCIETY CHIEF EX/STRUC LEGIS ADJUD CT/SYS PERS/REL   JURID
PERSON 17/20 ENGLSH/LAW. PAGE 28 B0573   NAT/G

B50
HYNEMAN C.S.,BUREAUCRACY IN A DEMOCRACY. CHIEF   NAT/G
LEGIS ADMIN CONTROL LEAD ROUTINE PERS/REL COST   CENTRAL
EFFICIENCY UTIL ATTIT AUTHORIT PERSON MORAL.   EX/STRUC
PAGE 53 B1071   MYTH

B51
GUETZKOW H.,GROUPS, LEADERSHIP, AND MEN. FACE/GP   ATTIT
SECT EDU/PROP EXEC PERSON RESPECT...PERS/TEST   SOC
GEN/METH 20. PAGE 44 B0901   ELITES

B51
LASSWELL H.D.,THE POLITICAL WRITINGS OF HAROLD D   PERSON
LASSWELL. UNIV DOMIN EXEC LEAD RATIONAL ATTIT DRIVE PSY
ROLE ALL/VALS...OBS BIOG 20. PAGE 63 B1269   INGP/REL
                                                     CONCPT

S51
COHEN M.B.,"PERSONALITY AS A FACTOR IN   PERSON
ADMINISTRATIVE DECISIONS." ADJUD PERS/REL ANOMIE   ADMIN
SUPEGO...OBS SELF/OBS INT. PAGE 22 B0446   PROB/SOLV
                                                     PSY

B52
HIMMELFARB G.,LORD ACTON: A STUDY IN CONSCIENCE AND PWR
POLITICS. MOD/EUR NAT/G POL/PAR SECT LEGIS TOP/EX   BIOG
EDU/PROP ADMIN NAT/LISM ATTIT PERSON SUPEGO MORAL
ORD/FREE...CONCPT PARLIAMENT 19 ACTON/LORD. PAGE 50
B1014

B52
MAIER N.R.F.,PRINCIPLES OF HUMAN RELATIONS. WOR+45   INDUS
WOR-45 CULTURE SOCIETY ROUTINE ATTIT DRIVE PERCEPT
PERSON RIGID/FLEX SUPEGO PWR...PSY CONT/OBS RECORD
TOT/POP VAL/FREE 20. PAGE 68 B1379

B52
POOL I.,SYMBOLS OF DEMOCRACY. WOR+45 WOR-45 POL/PAR INTELL
FORCES ADMIN PERSON PWR...CONCPT 20. PAGE 83 B1687   SOCIETY
                                                     USSR

S52
JOSEPHSON E.,"IRRATIONAL LEADERSHIP IN FORMAL   ADMIN
ORGANIZATIONS." EX/STRUC PLAN LEAD GP/REL INGP/REL   RATIONAL
EFFICIENCY AUTHORIT DRIVE PSY. PAGE 57 B1154   CONCPT
                                                     PERSON

C52
LASSWELL H.D.,"THE COMPARATIVE STUDY OF ELITES: AN   ELITES
INTRODUCTION AND BIBLIOGRAPHY." STRATA POL/PAR   LEAD
EDU/PROP ADMIN LOBBY COERCE ATTIT PERSON PWR   CONCPT
...BIBLIOG 20. PAGE 63 B1270   DOMIN

B53
GROSS B.M.,THE LEGISLATIVE STRUGGLE: A STUDY IN   LEGIS
SOCIAL COMBAT. STRUCT LOC/G POL/PAR JUDGE EDU/PROP   DECISION
DEBATE ETIQUET ADMIN LOBBY CHOOSE GOV/REL INGP/REL   PERSON
HEREDITY ALL/VALS...SOC PRESIDENT. PAGE 44 B0885   LEAD

S53
CORY R.H. JR.,"FORGING A PUBLIC INFORMATION POLICY   INT/ORG
FOR THE UNITED NATIONS." FUT WOR+45 SOCIETY   ADMIN
PEACE ATTIT PERSON SKILL...CONCPT 20 UN. PAGE 24   EDU/PROP
B0486   BAL/PWR

B54
ALLPORT G.W.,THE NATURE OF PREJUDICE. USA+45 WOR+45 CULTURE
STRATA FACE/GP KIN NEIGH SECT ADMIN GP/REL DISCRIM   PERSON
ATTIT DRIVE LOVE RESPECT...PSY SOC MYTH QU/SEMANT   RACE/REL
20. PAGE 4 B0078

B54
BIESANZ J.,MODERN SOCIETY: AN INTRODUCTION TO   SOCIETY
SOCIAL SCIENCE. COM CONSTN STRUCT FAM MUNIC NAT/G   PROB/SOLV
SECT EX/STRUC LEGIS GP/REL PERSON...SOC 20. PAGE 12 CULTURE
B0237

B54
LAPIERRE R.T.,A THEORY OF SOCIAL CONTROL. STRUCT   CONTROL
ADMIN ROUTINE SANCTION ANOMIE AUTHORIT DRIVE PERSON VOL/ASSN
PWR...MAJORIT CONCPT CLASSIF. PAGE 62 B1260   CULTURE

B54
MATTHEWS D.R.,THE SOCIAL BACKGROUND OF POLITICAL   DECISION
DECISION-MAKERS. CULTURE SOCIETY STRATA FAM   BIOG
EX/STRUC LEAD ATTIT BIO/SOC DRIVE PERSON ALL/VALS   SOC
HIST/WRIT. PAGE 71 B1431

B55
APTER D.E.,THE GOLD COAST IN TRANSITION. FUT CONSTN AFR
CULTURE SOCIETY ECO/UNDEV FAM KIN LOC/G NAT/G   SOVEREIGN
POL/PAR LEGIS TOP/EX EDU/PROP LEGIT ADMIN ATTIT
PERSON PWR...CONCPT STAT INT CENSUS TOT/POP
VAL/FREE. PAGE 6 B0120

S55
BUNZEL J.H.,"THE GENERAL IDEOLOGY OF AMERICAN SMALL ALL/IDEOS
BUSINESS" (BMR)" USA+45 USA-45 AGRI GP/REL INGP/REL ATTIT
PERSON...MGT IDEA/COMP 18/20. PAGE 17 B0345   SML/CO
                                                     INDUS

S55
KAUTSKY J.H.,"THE NEW STRATEGY OF INTERNATIONAL   COM
COMMUNISM." ASIA CHINA/COM FUT WOR+45 WOR-45 ADMIN   POL/PAR
ROUTINE PERSON MARXISM SOCISM...TREND IDEA/COMP 20   TOTALISM
LENIN/VI MAO. PAGE 59 B1184   USSR

B56
DUNNILL F.,THE CIVIL SERVICE. UK LAW PLAN ADMIN   PERSON
EFFICIENCY DRIVE NEW/LIB...STAT CHARTS 20   WORKER
PARLIAMENT CIVIL/SERV. PAGE 31 B0633   STRATA
                                                     SOC/WK

B56
HICKMAN C.A.,INDIVIDUALS, GROUPS, AND ECONOMIC   MGT
BEHAVIOR. WORKER PAY CONTROL EXEC GP/REL INGP/REL   ADMIN
PERSON ROLE...PSY SOC PERS/COMP METH 20. PAGE 50   ECO/TAC
B1005   PLAN

B56
WHYTE W.H. JR.,THE ORGANIZATION MAN. CULTURE FINAN   ADMIN
VOL/ASSN DOMIN EDU/PROP EXEC DISPL HABITAT ROLE   LG/CO
...PERS/TEST STERTYP. PAGE 116 B2343   PERSON
                                                     CONSEN

B57
BEAL J.R.,JOHN FOSTER DULLES, A BIOGRAPHY. USA+45   BIOG
USSR WOR+45 CONSTN INT/ORG NAT/G EX/STRUC LEGIT   DIPLOM
ADMIN NUC/PWR DISPL PERSON ORD/FREE PWR SKILL
...POLICY PSY OBS RECORD COLD/WAR UN 20 DULLES/JF.
PAGE 10 B0200

B57
COOPER F.E.,THE LAWYER AND ADMINISTRATIVE AGENCIES. CONSULT
USA+45 CLIENT LAW PROB/SOLV CT/SYS PERSON ROLE.   ADMIN
PAGE 23 B0473   ADJUD
                                                     DELIB/GP

B57
CRONBACK L.J.,PSYCHOLOGICAL TESTS AND PERSONNEL   MATH
DECISIONS. OP/RES PROB/SOLV CHOOSE PERSON...PSY   DECISION
STAT TESTS 20. PAGE 25 B0508   WORKER
                                                     MGT

B57
KAPLAN M.A.,SYSTEM AND PROCESS OF INTERNATIONAL   INT/ORG
POLITICS. FUT WOR+45 WOR-45 SOCIETY PLAN BAL/PWR   DIPLOM
ADMIN ATTIT PERSON RIGID/FLEX PWR SOVEREIGN
...DECISION TREND VAL/FREE. PAGE 58 B1168

B57
PARKINSON C.N.,PARKINSON'S LAW. UNIV EX/STRUC PLAN   ADMIN
ATTIT PERSON TIME. PAGE 81 B1634   EXEC
                                                     FINAN
                                                     ECOMETRIC

S57
ARGYRIS C.,"THE INDIVIDUAL AND ORGANIZATION: SOME   PERSON
PROBLEMS OF MUTUAL ADJUSTMENT" (BMR)" USA+45   METH
PROB/SOLV ADMIN CONTROL 20. PAGE 6 B0128   INGP/REL
                                                     TASK

S57

HAILEY,"TOMORROW IN AFRICA." CONSTN SOCIETY LOC/G AFR
NAT/G DOMIN ADJUD ADMIN GP/REL DISCRIM NAT/LISM PERSON
ATTIT MORAL ORD/FREE...PSY SOC CONCPT OBS RECORD ELITES
TREND GEN/LAWS CMN/WLTH 20. PAGE 45 B0917 RACE/REL

B58

BROWNE C.G.,THE CONCEPT OF LEADERSHIP. UNIV FACE/GP EXEC
DOMIN EDU/PROP LEGIT LEAD DRIVE PERSON PWR...MGT CONCPT
SOC OBS SELF/OBS CONT/OBS INT PERS/TEST STERTYP
GEN/LAWS. PAGE 16 B0328

B58

CLEMENTS R.V.,MANAGERS - A STUDY OF THEIR CAREERS MGT
IN INDUSTRY. STRATA INDUS TASK PERSON SKILL 20. ELITES
PAGE 21 B0435 EDU/PROP
TOP/EX

B58

MARCH J.G.,ORGANIZATIONS. USA+45 CREATE OP/RES PLAN MGT
PROB/SOLV PARTIC ROUTINE RATIONAL ATTIT PERCEPT PERSON
...DECISION BIBLIOG. PAGE 69 B1397 DRIVE
CONCPT

B58

SKINNER G.W.,LEADERSHIP AND POWER IN THE CHINESE SOC
COMMUNITY OF THAILAND. ASIA S/ASIA STRATA FACE/GP ELITES
KIN PROF/ORG VOL/ASSN EX/STRUC DOMIN PERSON RESPECT THAILAND
...METH/CNCPT STAT INT QU BIOG CHARTS 20. PAGE 98
B1974

B58

TAYLOR H.,THE STATESMAN. MOD/EUR FACE/GP FAM NAT/G EXEC
POL/PAR DELIB/GP LEGIS ATTIT PERSON PWR...POLICY STRUCT
CONCPT OBS GEN/LAWS. PAGE 103 B2086

S58

ARGYRIS C.,"SOME PROBLEMS IN CONCEPTUALIZING FINAN
ORGANIZATIONAL CLIMATE: A CASE STUDY OF A BANK" CONCPT
(BMR)" USA+45 EX/STRUC ADMIN PERS/REL ADJUST PERSON LG/CO
...POLICY HYPO/EXP SIMUL 20. PAGE 6 B0129 INGP/REL

S58

MITCHELL W.C.,"OCCUPATIONAL ROLE STRAINS: THE ANOMIE
AMERICAN ELECTIVE PUBLIC OFFICIAL." CONTROL DRIVE
RIGID/FLEX SUPEGO HEALTH ORD/FREE...SOC INT QU. ROUTINE
PAGE 74 B1492 PERSON

B59

ELLIOTT O.,MEN AT THE TOP. USA+45 CULTURE EX/STRUC TOP/EX
PRESS GOV/REL ATTIT ALL/VALS...OBS INT QU 20. PERSON
PAGE 33 B0668 LEAD
POLICY

B59

GREENEWALT C.H.,THE UNCOMMON MAN. UNIV ECO/DEV TASK
ADMIN PERS/REL PERSON SUPEGO WEALTH 20. PAGE 43 ORD/FREE
B0868 DRIVE
EFFICIENCY

B59

WARNER W.L.,INDUSTRIAL MAN. USA+45 USA-45 ELITES EXEC
INDUS LABOR TOP/EX WORKER ADMIN INGP/REL PERS/REL LEAD
...CHARTS ANTHOL 20. PAGE 114 B2294 PERSON
MGT

S59

LASSWELL H.D.,"UNIVERSALITY IN PERSPECTIVE." FUT INT/ORG
UNIV SOCIETY CONSULT TOP/EX PLAN EDU/PROP ADJUD JURID
ROUTINE ARMS/CONT COERCE PEACE ATTIT PERSON TOTALISM
ALL/VALS. PAGE 63 B1271

B60

ARGYRIS C.,UNDERSTANDING ORGANIZATIONAL BEHAVIOR. LG/CO
OP/RES FEEDBACK...MGT PSY METH/CNCPT OBS INT SIMUL PERSON
20. PAGE 6 B0130 ADMIN
ROUTINE

B60

BASS B.M.,LEADERSHIP, PSYCHOLOGY, AND UNIV
ORGANIZATIONAL BEHAVIOR. DOMIN CHOOSE DRIVE PERSON FACE/GP
PWR RESPECT SKILL...SOC METH/CNCPT OBS. PAGE 9 DELIB/GP
B0193 ROUTINE

B60

BELL J.,THE SPLENDID MISERY: THE STORY OF THE EXEC
PRESIDENCY AND POWER POLITICS AT CLOSE RANGE. TOP/EX
USA+45 USA-45 PRESS ADMIN LEAD LOBBY GP/REL LEGIS
PERS/REL PERSON PRESIDENT. PAGE 10 B0208

B60

DRAPER T.,AMERICAN COMMUNISM AND SOVIET RUSSIA. COM
EUR+WWI USA+45 USSR INTELL AGRI COM/IND FINAN INDUS POL/PAR
LABOR PROF/ORG VOL/ASSN PLAN TEC/DEV DOMIN EDU/PROP
ADMIN COERCE REV PERSON PWR...POLICY CONCPT MYTH
19/20. PAGE 30 B0617

B60

GLOVER J.D.,A CASE STUDY OF HIGH LEVEL ADMIN
ADMINISTRATION IN A LARGE ORGANIZATION. EX/STRUC TOP/EX
EXEC LEAD ROUTINE INGP/REL OPTIMAL ATTIT PERSON FORCES
...POLICY DECISION INT QU. PAGE 40 B0812 NAT/G

B60

MARSHALL A.H.,FINANCIAL ADMINISTRATION IN LOCAL FINAN
GOVERNMENT. UK DELIB/GP CONFER COST INCOME PERSON LOC/G
...JURID 20. PAGE 70 B1408 BUDGET
ADMIN

B60

ROEPKE W.,A HUMANE ECONOMY: THE SOCIAL FRAMEWORK OF DRIVE
THE FREE MARKET. FUT USSR WOR+45 CULTURE SOCIETY EDU/PROP
ECO/DEV PLAN ECO/TAC ADMIN ATTIT PERSON RIGID/FLEX CAP/ISM
SUPEGO MORAL WEALTH SOCISM...POLICY OLD/LIB CONCPT

TREND GEN/LAWS 20. PAGE 90 B1811

B60

US SENATE COMM. GOVT. OPER.,ORGANIZING FOR NATIONAL CONSULT
SECURITY. USA+45 USA-45 INTELL STRUCT SML/CO EXEC
ACT/RES ADMIN ATTIT PERSON PWR SKILL...DECISION 20.
PAGE 111 B2236

S60

BAVELAS A.,"LEADERSHIP: MAN AND FUNCTION." WORKER LEAD
CREATE PLAN CONTROL PERS/REL PERSON PWR...MGT 20. ADMIN
PAGE 10 B0199 ROUTINE
ROLE

B61

BIRNBACH B.,NEO-FREUDIAN SOCIAL PHILOSOPHY. TEC/DEV SOCIETY
INGP/REL ADJUST HAPPINESS SUPEGO HEALTH...CONCPT PSY
GEN/LAWS BIBLIOG 20. PAGE 12 B0242 PERSON
ADMIN

B61

LASSWELL H.D.,PSYCOPATHOLOGY AND POLITICS. WOR-45 ATTIT
CULTURE SOCIETY FACE/GP NAT/G CONSULT CREATE GEN/METH
EDU/PROP EXEC ROUTINE DISPL DRIVE PERSON PWR
RESPECT...PSY CONCPT METH/CNCPT METH. PAGE 63 B1272

B61

MACRIDIS R.C.,COMPARATIVE POLITICS: NOTES AND POL/PAR
READINGS. WOR+45 LOC/G MUNIC NAT/G PROVS VOL/ASSN CHOOSE
EDU/PROP ADMIN ATTIT PERSON ORD/FREE...SOC CONCPT
OBS RECORD TREND 20. PAGE 68 B1376

B61

MARKMANN C.L.,JOHN F. KENNEDY: A SENSE OF PURPOSE. CHIEF
USA+45 INTELL FAM CONSULT DELIB/GP LEGIS PERSON TOP/EX
SKILL 20 KENNEDY/JF EISNHWR/DD ROOSEVLT/F ADMIN
NEW/FRONTR PRESIDENT. PAGE 69 B1399 BIOG

B61

MARVICK D.,POLITICAL DECISION-MAKERS. INTELL STRATA TOP/EX
NAT/G POL/PAR EX/STRUC LEGIS DOMIN EDU/PROP ATTIT BIOG
PERSON PWR...PSY STAT OBS CONT/OBS STAND/INT ELITES
UNPLAN/INT TIME/SEQ CHARTS STERTYP VAL/FREE.
PAGE 70 B1416

B61

OPOTOWSKY S.,THE KENNEDY GOVERNMENT. NAT/G CONSULT ADMIN
EX/STRUC LEAD PERSON...POLICY 20 KENNEDY/JF BIOG
CONGRESS CABINET. PAGE 80 B1613 ELITES
TOP/EX

B61

PETRULLO L.,LEADERSHIP AND INTERPERSONAL BEHAVIOR. PERSON
FACE/GP FAM PROF/ORG EX/STRUC FORCES DOMIN WAR ATTIT
GP/REL PERS/REL EFFICIENCY PRODUC PWR...MGT PSY. LEAD
PAGE 82 B1663 HABITAT

S61

DEUTSCH K.W.,"A NOTE ON THE APPEARANCE OF WISDOM IN ADMIN
LARGE BUREAUCRATIC ORGANIZATIONS." ROUTINE PERSON PROBABIL
KNOWL SKILL...DECISION STAT. PAGE 28 B0577 PROB/SOLV
SIMUL

S61

EVAN W.M.,"A LABORATORY EXPERIMENT ON BUREAUCRATIC ADMIN
AUTHORITY" WORKER CONTROL EXEC PRODUC ATTIT PERSON LEGIT
...PSY SOC CHARTS SIMUL 20 WEBER/MAX. PAGE 34 B0687 LAB/EXP
EFFICIENCY

S61

RUDOLPH S.,"CONSENSUS AND CONFLICT IN INDIAN POL/PAR
POLITICS." S/ASIA WOR+45 NAT/G DELIB/GP DIPLOM PERCEPT
EDU/PROP ADMIN CONSEN PERSON ALL/VALS...OBS TREND INDIA
TOT/POP VAL/FREE 20. PAGE 92 B1854

S61

SCHILLING W.R.,"THE H-BOMB: HOW TO DECIDE WITHOUT PERSON
ACTUALLY CHOOSING." FUT USA+45 INTELL CONSULT ADMIN LEGIT
CT/SYS MORAL...JURID OBS 20 TRUMAN/HS. PAGE 93 NUC/PWR
B1888

B62

BENSON E.T.,CROSS FIRE: THE EIGHT YEARS WITH ADMIN
EISENHOWER. USA+45 DIPLOM LEAD ATTIT PERSON POLICY
CONSERVE...TRADIT BIOG 20 EISNHWR/DD PRESIDENT DELIB/GP
TAFT/RA DULLES/JF NIXON/RM. PAGE 11 B0218 TOP/EX

B62

CHERNICK J.,THE SELECTION OF TRAINEES UNDER MDTA. EDU/PROP
USA+45 NAT/G LEGIS PERSON...CENSUS 20 CIVIL/SERV WORKER
MDTA. PAGE 20 B0418 ADMIN
DELIB/GP

B62

CHICAGO U CTR PROG GOVT ADMIN,EDUCATION FOR EDU/PROP
INNOVATIVE BEHAVIOR IN EXECUTIVES. UNIV ELITES CREATE
ADMIN EFFICIENCY DRIVE PERSON...MGT APT/TEST EXEC
PERS/TEST CHARTS LAB/EXP BIBLIOG 20. PAGE 21 B0420 STAT

B62

GRAY R.K.,EIGHTEEN ACRES UNDER GLASS. ELITES CHIEF
CONSULT EX/STRUC DIPLOM PRESS CONFER WAR PERS/REL ADMIN
PERSON 20 EISNHWR/DD TRUMAN/HS CABINET. PAGE 43 TOP/EX
B0860 NAT/G

B62

INTERNAT CONGRESS OF JURISTS,EXECUTIVE ACTION AND JURID
THE RULE OF RULE: REPORTION PROCEEDINGS OF INT'T EXEC
CONGRESS OF JURISTS,-RIO DE JANEIRO, BRAZIL. WOR+45 ORD/FREE
ACADEM CONSULT JUDGE EDU/PROP ADJUD CT/SYS INGP/REL CONTROL
PERSON DEPT/DEFEN. PAGE 54 B1094

B62

OLLE-LAPRUNE J.,LA STABILITE DES MINISTRES SOUS LA LEGIS
TROISIEME REPUBLIQUE, 1879-1940. FRANCE CONSTN NAT/G

POL/PAR LEAD WAR INGP/REL RIGID/FLEX PWR...POLICY ADMIN
CHARTS 19/20. PAGE 79 B1606 PERSON

B62
SAMPSON A..ANATOMY OF BRITAIN. UK LAW COM/IND FINAN ELITES
INDUS MARKET MUNIC POL/PAR EX/STRUC TOP/EX DIPLOM PWR
LEAD REPRESENT PERSON PARLIAMENT WORSHIP. PAGE 92 STRUCT
B1866 FORCES

B62
SIMON Y.R..A GENERAL THEORY OF AUTHORITY. DOMIN PERS/REL
ADMIN RATIONAL UTOPIA KNOWL MORAL PWR SOVEREIGN PERSON
...HUM CONCPT NEW/IDEA 20. PAGE 97 B1962 SOCIETY
ORD/FREE

S62
BUENO M.."ASPECTOS SOCIOLOGICOS DE LA EDUCACION." SOCIETY
FUT UNIV INTELL R+D SERV/IND SCHOOL CONSULT EDU/PROP
EX/STRUC ACT/RES PLAN...METH/CNCPT OBS 20. PAGE 17 PERSON
B0341

S62
HUDSON G.F.."SOVIET FEARS OF THE WEST." COM USA+45 ATTIT
SOCIETY DELIB/GP EX/STRUC TOP/EX ACT/RES CREATE MYTH
DOMIN EDU/PROP LEGIT ADMIN ROUTINE DRIVE PERSON GERMANY
RIGID/FLEX PWR...RECORD TIME/SEQ TOT/POP 20 USSR
STALIN/J. PAGE 52 B1057

S62
SPRINGER H.W.."FEDERATION IN THE CARIBBEAN: AN VOL/ASSN
ATTEMPT THAT FAILED." L/A+17C ECO/UNDEV INT/ORG NAT/G
POL/PAR PROVS LEGIS CREATE PLAN LEGIT ADMIN FEDERAL REGION
ATTIT DRIVE PERSON ORD/FREE PWR...POLICY GEOG PSY
CONCPT OBS CARIBBEAN CMN/WLTH 20. PAGE 100 B2013

B63
BRAIBANTI R.J.D..ADMINISTRATION AND ECONOMIC ECO/UNDEV
DEVELOPMENT IN INDIA. INDIA S/ASIA SOCIETY STRATA ADMIN
ECO/TAC PERSON WEALTH...MGT GEN/LAWS TOT/POP
VAL/FREE 20. PAGE 15 B0300

B63
CLARK J.S..THE SENATE ESTABLISHMENT. USA+45 NAT/G LEGIS
POL/PAR ADMIN CHOOSE PERSON SENATE. PAGE 21 B0431 ROUTINE
LEAD
SENIOR

B63
HEUSSLER R..YESTERDAY'S RULERS: THE MAKING OF THE EX/STRUC
BRITISH COLONIAL SERVICE. AFR EUR+WWI UK STRATA MORAL
SECT DELIB/GP PLAN DOMIN EDU/PROP ATTIT PERCEPT ELITES
PERSON KNOWL ORD/FREE PWR...MGT SOC OBS INT
TIME/SEQ 20 CMN/WLTH. PAGE 49 B1000

B63
RUITENBEER H.M..THE DILEMMA OF ORGANIZATIONAL PERSON
SOCIETY. CULTURE ECO/DEV MUNIC SECT TEC/DEV ROLE
EDU/PROP NAT/LISM ORD/FREE...NAT/COMP 20 RIESMAN/D ADMIN
WHYTE/WF MERTON/R MEAD/MARG JASPERS/K. PAGE 92 WORKER
B1855

B63
SIDEY H..JOHN F. KENNEDY, PRESIDENT. USA+45 INTELL BIOG
FAM CONSULT DELIB/GP LEGIS ADMIN LEAD 20 KENNEDY/JF TOP/EX
PRESIDENT. PAGE 97 B1951 SKILL
PERSON

B63
STEVENSON A.E..LOOKING OUTWARD: YEARS OF CRISIS AT INT/ORG
THE UNITED NATIONS. COM CUBA USA+45 WOR+45 SOCIETY CONCPT
NAT/G EX/STRUC ACT/RES LEGIT COLONIAL ATTIT PERSON ARMS/CONT
SUPEGO ALL/VALS...POLICY HUM UN COLD/WAR CONGO 20.
PAGE 100 B2034

B63
TSOU T..AMERICA'S FAILURE IN CHINA, 1941-1950. ASIA
USA+45 USA-45 NAT/G ACT/RES PLAN DOMIN EDU/PROP PERCEPT
ADMIN ROUTINE ATTIT PERSON ORD/FREE...DECISION DIPLOM
CONCPT MYTH TIME/SEQ TREND STERTYP 20. PAGE 105
B2132

B63
TUCKER R.C..THE SOVIET POLITICAL MIND. WOR+45 COM
ELITES INT/ORG NAT/G POL/PAR PLAN DIPLOM ECO/TAC TOP/EX
DOMIN ADMIN NUC/PWR REV DRIVE PERSON SUPEGO PWR USSR
WEALTH...POLICY MGT PSY CONCPT OBS BIOG TREND
COLD/WAR MARX/KARL 20. PAGE 106 B2134

L63
FREUND G.."ADENAUER AND THE FUTURE OF GERMANY." NAT/G
EUR+WWI FUT GERMANY/W FORCES LEGIT ADMIN ROUTINE BIOG
ATTIT DRIVE PERSON PWR...POLICY TIME/SEQ TREND DIPLOM
VAL/FREE 20 ADENAUER/K. PAGE 37 B0753 GERMANY

S63
ANTHON C.G.."THE END OF THE ADENAUER ERA." EUR+WWI NAT/G
GERMANY/W CONSTN EX/STRUC CREATE DIPLOM LEGIT ATTIT TOP/EX
PERSON ALL/VALS...RECORD 20 ADENAUER/K. PAGE 6 BAL/PWR
B0113 GERMANY

S63
RUSTOW D.A.."THE MILITARY IN MIDDLE EASTERN SOCIETY FORCES
AND POLITICS." FUT ISLAM CONSTN SOCIETY FACE/GP ELITES
NAT/G POL/PAR PROF/ORG CONSULT DOMIN ADMIN EXEC
REGION COERCE NAT/LISM ATTIT DRIVE PERSON ORD/FREE
PWR...POLICY CONCPT OBS STERTYP 20. PAGE 92 B1860

S63
USEEM J.."MEN IN THE MIDDLE OF THE THIRD CULTURE: ADMIN
THE ROLES OF AMERICAN AND NON-WESTERN PEOPLE IN SOCIETY
CROSS-CULTURAL ADMINIS-." FUT WOR+45 DELIB/GP PERSON
EX/STRUC LEGIS ATTIT ALL/VALS...MGT INT TIME/SEQ
GEN/LAWS VAL/FREE. PAGE 111 B2247

B64
ADAMS V..THE PEACE CORPS IN ACTION. USA+45 VOL/ASSN DIPLOM
EX/STRUC GOV/REL PERCEPT ORD/FREE...OBS 20 FOR/AID
KENNEDY/JF PEACE/CORP. PAGE 3 B0058 PERSON
DRIVE

B64
APTER D.E..IDEOLOGY AND DISCONTENT. FUT WOR+45 ACT/RES
CONSTN CULTURE INTELL SOCIETY STRUCT INT/ORG NAT/G ATTIT
DELIB/GP LEGIS CREATE PLAN TEC/DEV EDU/PROP EXEC
PERCEPT PERSON RIGID/FLEX ALL/VALS...POLICY
TOT/POP. PAGE 6 B0122

B64
ARGYRIS C..INTEGRATING THE INDIVIDUAL AND THE ADMIN
ORGANIZATION. WORKER PROB/SOLV LEAD SANCTION PERS/REL
REPRESENT ADJUST EFFICIENCY DRIVE PERSON...PSY VOL/ASSN
METH/CNCPT ORG/CHARTS. PAGE 6 B0132 PARTIC

B64
BRIGHT J.R..RESEARCH, DEVELOPMENT AND TECHNOLOGICAL TEC/DEV
INNOVATION. CULTURE R+D CREATE PLAN PROB/SOLV NEW/IDEA
AUTOMAT RISK PERSON...DECISION CONCPT PREDICT INDUS
BIBLIOG. PAGE 15 B0308 MGT

B64
EATON H..PRESIDENTIAL TIMBER: A HISTORY OF DELIB/GP
NOMINATING CONVENTIONS, 1868-1960. USA+45 USA-45 CHOOSE
POL/PAR EX/STRUC POL/PAR DEBATE LOBBY ATTIT PERSON ALL/VALS CHIEF
...MYTH 19/20 PRESIDENT. PAGE 32 B0646 NAT/G

B64
EWING D.W..THE MANAGERIAL MIND. SOCIETY STRUCT MGT
INDUS PERSON KNOWL 20. PAGE 34 B0692 ATTIT
CREATE
EFFICIENCY

B64
FORBES A.H..CURRENT RESEARCH IN BRITISH STUDIES. UK BIBLIOG
CONSTN CULTURE POL/PAR SECT DIPLOM ADMIN...JURID PERSON
BIOG WORSHIP 20. PAGE 36 B0736 NAT/G
PARL/PROC

B64
HALLER W..DER SCHWEDISCHE JUSTITIEOMBUDSMAN. JURID
DENMARK FINLAND NORWAY SWEDEN LEGIS ADJUD CONTROL PARL/PROC
PERSON ORD/FREE...NAT/COMP 20 OMBUDSMAN. PAGE 46 ADMIN
B0926 CHIEF

B64
HANNA W.J..INDEPENDENT BLACK AFRICA: THE POLITICS AFR
OF FREEDOM. ELITES INDUS KIN CHIEF COLONIAL CHOOSE ECO/UNDEV
GOV/REL RACE/REL NAT/LISM ATTIT PERSON 20 NEGRO. ADMIN
PAGE 46 B0938 PROB/SOLV

B64
NEUSTADT R..PRESIDENTIAL POWER. USA+45 CONSTN NAT/G TOP/EX
CHIEF LEGIS CREATE EDU/PROP LEGIT ADMIN EXEC COERCE SKILL
ATTIT PERSON RIGID/FLEX PWR CONGRESS 20 PRESIDENT
TRUMAN/HS EISNHWR/DD. PAGE 78 B1575

B64
VALEN H..POLITICAL PARTIES IN NORWAY. NORWAY ACADEM LOC/G
PARTIC ROUTINE INGP/REL KNOWL...QU 20. PAGE 111 POL/PAR
B2249 PERSON

B64
WILLIAMSON O.E..THE ECONOMICS OF DISCRETIONARY EFFICIENCY
BEHAVIOR: MANAGERIAL OBJECTIVES IN A THEORY OF THE MGT
FIRM. MARKET BUDGET CAP/ISM PRODUC DRIVE PERSON ECO/TAC
...STAT CHARTS BIBLIOG METH 20. PAGE 117 B2354 CHOOSE

S64
MURRAY D.."CHINESE EDUCATION IN SOUTH-EAST ASIA." S/ASIA
SOCIETY NEIGH EDU/PROP ROUTINE PERSON KNOWL SCHOOL
...OBS/ENVIR STERTYP. PAGE 76 B1546 REGION
ASIA

B65
BUECHNER J.C..DIFFERENCES IN ROLE PERCEPTIONS IN MUNIC
COLORADO COUNCIL-MANAGER CITIES. USA+45 ADMIN CONSULT
ROUTINE GP/REL CONSEN PERCEPT PERSON ROLE LOC/G
...DECISION MGT STAT INT QU CHARTS 20 COLORADO IDEA/COMP
CITY/MGT. PAGE 17 B0338

B65
GOLEMBIEWSKI R.T..MEN, MANAGEMENT, AND MORALITY: LG/CO
TOWARD A NEW ORGANIZATIONAL ETHIC. CONSTN EX/STRUC MGT
CREATE ADMIN CONTROL INGP/REL PERSON SUPEGO MORAL PROB/SOLV
PWR...GOV/COMP METH/COMP 20 BUREAUCRCY. PAGE 40
B0819

B65
HODGSON R.C..THE EXECUTIVE ROLE CONSTELLATION: AN LG/CO
ANALYSIS OF PERSONALITY AND ROLE RELATIONS IN ADMIN
MANAGEMENT. USA+45 PUB/INST EXEC PERS/REL PERSON TOP/EX
...PSY PERS/COMP HYPO/EXP 20. PAGE 51 B1027 ROLE

B65
RUBIN H..PENSIONS AND EMPLOYEE MOBILITY IN THE ADMIN
PUBLIC SERVICE. USA+45 WORKER PERSON ORD/FREE...SOC NAT/G
QU. PAGE 91 B1849 LOC/G
SENIOR

B65
STEINER G.A..THE CREATIVE ORGANIZATION. ELITES CREATE
LG/CO PLAN PROB/SOLV TEC/DEV INSPECT CAP/ISM MGT
CONTROL EXEC PERSON...METH/COMP HYPO/EXP 20. ADMIN
PAGE 100 B2029 SOC

B65
VIORST M..HOSTILE ALLIES: FDR AND DE GAULLE. TOP/EX
EUR+WWI USA-45 ELITES NAT/G VOL/ASSN FORCES LEGIS PWR
PLAN LEGIT ADMIN COERCE PERSON...BIOG TIME/SEQ 20 WAR

ROOSEVLT/F DEGAULLE/C. PAGE 112 B2263   FRANCE
B66

BROWN R.E.,JUDGMENT IN ADMINISTRATION. DRIVE PERSON ADMIN
KNOWL...DECISION 20. PAGE 16 B0326   EXEC
    SKILL
    PROB/SOLV
B66

LIVINGSTON J.C.,THE CONSENT OF THE GOVERNED. USA+45 NAT/G
EX/STRUC BAL/PWR DOMIN CENTRAL PERSON PWR...POLICY LOBBY
CONCPT OBS IDEA/COMP 20 CONGRESS. PAGE 66 B1331   MAJORIT
    PARTIC
B66

PERROW C.,ORGANIZATION FOR TREATMENT: A COMPARATIVE AGE/Y
STUDY OF INSTITUTIONS FOR DELINQUENTS. LAW   PSY
PROB/SOLV ADMIN CRIME PERSON MORAL...SOC/WK OBS   PUB/INST
DEEP/QU CHARTS SOC/EXP SOC/INTEG 20. PAGE 82 B1661
B66

ZALEZNIK A.,HUMAN DILEMMAS OF LEADERSHIP. ELITES   LEAD
INDUS EX/STRUC INGP/REL ATTIT...PSY 20. PAGE 119   PERSON
B2397   EXEC
    MGT
S66

AUSLAND J.C.,"CRISIS MANAGEMENT* BERLIN, CYPRUS,   OP/RES
LAOS." CYPRUS LAOS FORCES CREATE PLAN EDU/PROP TASK DIPLOM
CENTRAL PERSON RIGID/FLEX...DECISION MGT 20 BERLIN RISK
KENNEDY/JF MCNAMARA/R RUSK. PAGE 7 B0148   ADMIN
B67

ANGEL D.D.,ROMNEY. LABOR LG/CO NAT/G EXEC WAR   BIOG
RACE/REL PERSON ORD/FREE...MGT WORSHIP 20   CHIEF
ROMNEY/GEO CIV/RIGHTS MORMON GOVERNOR. PAGE 5 B0108 PROVS
    POLICY
B67

NIEDERHOFFER A.,BEHIND THE SHIELD; THE POLICE IN   FORCES
URBAN SOCIETY. USA+45 LEGIT ADJUD ROUTINE COERCE   PERSON
CRIME ADJUST...INT CHARTS 20 NEWYORK/C. PAGE 78   SOCIETY
B1582   ATTIT
L67

GAINES J.E.,"THE YOUTH COURT CONCEPT AND ITS   CT/SYS
IMPLEMENTATION IN TOMPKINS COUNTY, NEW YORK."   AGE/Y
USA+45 LAW CONSTN JUDGE WORKER ADJUD ADMIN CHOOSE INGP/REL
PERSON...JURID NEW/YORK. PAGE 38 B0772   CRIME
L67

ROBERTS J.C.,"CIVIL RESTRAINT, MENTAL ILLNESS, AND HEALTH
THE RIGHT TO TREATMENT." PROB/SOLV ADMIN PERSON   ORD/FREE
HEAL. PAGE 89 B1795   COERCE
    LAW
S67

BERLINER J.S.,"RUSSIA'S BUREAUCRATS - WHY THEY'RE   CREATE
REACTIONARY." USSR NAT/G OP/RES PROB/SOLV TEC/DEV ADMIN
CONTROL SANCTION EFFICIENCY DRIVE PERSON...TECHNIC INDUS
SOC 20. PAGE 11 B0223   PRODUC
S67

DANELSKI D.J.,"CONFLICT AND ITS RESOLUTION IN THE   ROLE
SUPREME COURT." PROB/SOLV LEAD ROUTINE PERSON...PSY JURID
PERS/COMP BIBLIOG 20. PAGE 26 B0527   JUDGE
    INGP/REL
S67

RAUM O.,"THE MODERN LEADERSHIP GROUP AMONG THE   RACE/REL
SOUTH AFRICAN XHOSA." SOUTH/AFR SOCIETY SECT   KIN
EX/STRUC REPRESENT GP/REL INGP/REL PERSON   LEAD
...METH/COMP 17/20 XHOSA NEGRO. PAGE 86 B1743   CULTURE

PERSONAL RELATIONS....SEE PERS/REL

PERSONALITY....SEE PERSON, ALSO PERSONALITY INDEX, P. XIII

PERSONALITY TESTS....SEE PERS/TEST

PERSUASION....SEE LOBBY, EDU/PROP

PERU....SEE ALSO L/A+17C

N19

OPERATIONS AND POLICY RESEARCH,PERU ELECTION   CHOOSE
MEMORANDA (PAMPHLET). L/A+17C PERU POL/PAR LEGIS   CONSTN
EXEC APPORT REPRESENT 20. PAGE 80 B1611   SUFF
    NAT/G
B48

DE NOIA J.,GUIDE TO OFFICIAL PUBLICATIONS OF OTHER BIBLIOG/A
AMERICAN REPUBLICS: PERU (VOL. XVII). PERU LAW   CONSTN
LEGIS ADMIN CT/SYS...JURID 19/20. PAGE 28 B0561   NAT/G
    EDU/PROP
B65

PAYNE J.L.,LABOR AND POLITICS IN PERU; THE SYSTEM   LABOR
OF POLITICAL BARGAINING. PERU CONSTN VOL/ASSN   POL/PAR
EX/STRUC LEAD PWR...CHARTS 20. PAGE 81 B1645   BARGAIN
    GP/REL

PETAIN/HP....H.P. PETAIN

PETERS....PETERS V. NEW YORK

PETERSON F. B1662

PETRULLO L. B1663

PETTEE G.S. B1664

PFIFFNER J.M. B1665,B1666,B1667

PHELPS-FETHERS I. B1668

PHIL/SCI....SCIENTIFIC METHOD AND PHILOSOPHY OF SCIENCE

B

DEUTSCHE BIBLIOTH FRANKF A M,DEUTSCHE   BIBLIOG
BIBLIOGRAPHIE. EUR+WWI GERMANY ECO/DEV FORCES   LAW
DIPLOM LEAD...POLICY PHIL/SCI SOC 20. PAGE 28 B0578 ADMIN
    NAT/G
N

AMERICAN POLITICAL SCIENCE REVIEW. USA+45 USA-45   BIBLIOG/A
WOR+45 WOR-45 INT/ORG ADMIN...INT/LAW PHIL/SCI   DIPLOM
CONCPT METH 20 UN. PAGE 1 B0001   NAT/G
    GOV/COMP
N

REVIEW OF POLITICS. WOR+45 WOR-45 CONSTN LEGIS   BIBLIOG/A
PROB/SOLV ADMIN LEAD ALL/IDEOS...PHIL/SCI 20.   DIPLOM
PAGE 1 B0006   INT/ORG
    NAT/G
N

CUMULATIVE BOOK INDEX. WOR+45 WOR-45 ADMIN PERSON INDEX
ALL/VALS ALL/IDEOS...HUM PHIL/SCI SOC LING 19/20. NAT/G
PAGE 1 B0012   DIPLOM
N

THE JAPAN SCIENCE REVIEW: LAW AND POLITICS: LIST OF BIBLIOG
BOOKS AND ARTICLES ON LAW AND POLITICS. CONSTN AGRI LAW
INDUS LABOR DIPLOM TAX ADMIN CRIME...INT/LAW SOC 20 S/ASIA
CHINJAP. PAGE 1 B0025   PHIL/SCI
N19

DOTSON A.,PRODUCTION PLANNING IN THE PATENT OFFICE EFFICIENCY
(PAMPHLET). USA+45 DIST/IND PROB/SOLV PRODUC...MGT PLAN
PHIL/SCI 20 BUR/BUDGET PATENT/OFF. PAGE 30 B0610   NAT/G
    ADMIN
C20

BLACHLY F.F.,"THE GOVERNMENT AND ADMINISTRATION OF NAT/G
GERMANY." GERMANY CONSTN LOC/G PROVS DELIB/GP   GOV/REL
EX/STRUC FORCES LEGIS TOP/EX CT/SYS...BIBLIOG/A   ADMIN
19/20. PAGE 12 B0246   PHIL/SCI
B26

INTERNATIONAL BIBLIOGRAPHY OF POLITICAL SCIENCE.   BIBLIOG
WOR+45 NAT/G POL/PAR EX/STRUC LEGIS CT/SYS LEAD   DIPLOM
CHOOSE GOV/REL ATTIT...PHIL/SCI 20. PAGE 2 B0034   CONCPT
    ADMIN
B37

GULICK L.,PAPERS ON THE SCIENCE OF ADMINISTRATION. OP/RES
INDUS PROB/SOLV TEC/DEV COST EFFICIENCY PRODUC   CONTROL
HABITAT...PHIL/SCI METH/COMP 20. PAGE 45 B0903   ADMIN
    MGT
B45

BUSH V.,SCIENCE, THE ENDLESS FRONTIER. FUT USA-45   R+D
INTELL STRATA ACT/RES CREATE PLAN EDU/PROP ADMIN   NAT/G
NUC/PWR PEACE ATTIT HEALTH KNOWL...MAJORIT HEAL MGT
PHIL/SCI CONCPT OBS TREND 20. PAGE 18 B0360
B45

PLATO,THE REPUBLIC. MEDIT-7 UNIV SOCIETY STRUCT   PERSON
EX/STRUC FORCES UTOPIA ATTIT PERCEPT HEALTH KNOWL PHIL/SCI
ORD/FREE PWR...HUM CONCPT STERTYP TOT/POP. PAGE 83
B1681
B46

BIBLIOGRAFIIA DISSERTATSII: DOKTORSKIE DISSERTATSII BIBLIOG
ZA 19411944 (2 VOLS.). COM USSR LAW POL/PAR DIPLOM ACADEM
ADMIN LEAD...PHIL/SCI SOC 20. PAGE 2 B0035   KNOWL
    MARXIST
B47

LASSWELL H.D.,THE ANALYSIS OF POLITICAL BEHAVIOUR: R+D
AN EMPIRICAL APPROACH. WOR+45 CULTURE NAT/G FORCES ACT/RES
EDU/PROP ADMIN ATTIT PERCEPT KNOWL...PHIL/SCI PSY ELITES
SOC NEW/IDEA OBS INT GEN/METH NAZI 20. PAGE 63
B1267
B47

SIMON H.A.,ADMINISTRATIVE BEHAVIOR: A STUDY OF   DECISION
DECISION-MAKING PROCESSES IN ADMINISTRATIVE   NEW/IDEA
ORGANIZATION. STRUCT COM/IND OP/RES PROB/SOLV   ADMIN
EFFICIENCY EQUILIB UTIL...PHIL/SCI PSY STYLE.   RATIONAL
PAGE 97 B1956
B49

DE GRAZIA A.,HUMAN RELATIONS IN PUBLIC   BIBLIOG/A
ADMINISTRATION. INDUS ACT/RES CREATE PLAN PROB/SOLV ADMIN
TEC/DEV INGP/REL PERS/REL DRIVE...POLICY SOC 20.   PHIL/SCI
PAGE 27 B0552   OP/RES
B49

HEADLAM-MORLEY,BIBLIOGRAPHY IN POLITICS FOR THE   BIBLIOG
HONOUR SCHOOL OF PHILOSOPHY, POLITICS AND ECONOMICS NAT/G
(PAMPHLET). UK CONSTN LABOR MUNIC DIPLOM ADMIN   PHIL/SCI
19/20. PAGE 48 B0979   GOV/REL
B54

BENTLEY A.F.,INQUIRY INTO INQUIRIES: ESSAYS IN   EPIST
SOCIAL THEORY. UNIV LEGIS ADJUD ADMIN LOBBY   SOC
...PHIL/SCI PSY NEW/IDEA LING METH 20. PAGE 11   CONCPT
B0220
B54

COMBS C.H.,DECISION PROCESSES. INTELL SOCIETY   MATH

DELIB/GP CREATE TEC/DEV DOMIN LEGIT EXEC CHOOSE DRIVE RIGID/FLEX KNOWL PWR...PHIL/SCI SOC METH/CNCPT CONT/OBS REC/INT PERS/TEST SAMP/SIZ BIOG SOC/EXP WORK. PAGE 22 B0455 — DECISION

B54

MCCLOSKEY J.F.,OPERATIONS RESEARCH FOR MANAGEMENT. STRUCT COMPUTER ADMIN ROUTINE...PHIL/SCI CONCPT METH/CNCPT TREND ANTHOL BIBLIOG 20. PAGE 72 B1445 — OP/RES MGT METH/COMP TEC/DEV

B54

WILENSKY H.L.,SYLLABUS OF INDUSTRIAL RELATIONS: A GUIDE TO READING AND RESEARCH. USA+45 MUNIC ADMIN INGP/REL...POLICY MGT PHIL/SCI 20. PAGE 117 B2351 — BIBLIOG INDUS LABOR WORKER

B55

JAPAN MOMBUSHO DAIGAKU GAKIYUT,BIBLIOGRAPHY OF THE STUDIES ON LAW AND POLITICS (PAMPHLET). CONSTN INDUS LABOR DIPLOM TAX ADMIN...CRIMLGY INT/LAW 20 CHINJAP. PAGE 56 B1126 — BIBLIOG LAW PHIL/SCI

B55

PALMER A.M.,ADMINISTRATION OF MEDICAL AND PHARMACEUTICAL PATENTS (PAMPHLET). USA+45 PROF/ORG ADMIN PHIL/SCI. PAGE 80 B1626 — HEAL ACADEM LAW LICENSE

B55

STEPHENS O.,FACTS TO A CANDID WORLD. USA+45 WOR+45 COM/IND EX/STRUC PRESS ROUTINE EFFICIENCY ATTIT ...PSY 20. PAGE 100 B2033 — EDU/PROP PHIL/SCI NAT/G DIPLOM

S55

WRIGHT Q.,"THE PEACEFUL ADJUSTMENT OF INTERNATIONAL RELATIONS: PROBLEMS AND RESEARCH APPROACHES." UNIV INTELL EDU/PROP ADJUD ROUTINE KNOWL SKILL...INT/LAW JURID PHIL/SCI CLASSIF 20. PAGE 118 B2385 — R+D METH/CNCPT PEACE

C55

BONER H.A.,"HUNGRY GENERATIONS." UK WOR+45 WOR-45 STRATA INDUS FAM LABOR CAP/ISM...MGT BIBLIOG 19/20. PAGE 13 B0272 — ECO/DEV PHIL/SCI CONCPT WEALTH

L58

EISENSTADT S.N.,"BUREAUCRACY AND BUREAUCRATIZATION." WOR+45 ECO/DEV INDUS R+D PLAN GOV/REL...WELF/ST TREND BIBLIOG/A 20. PAGE 32 B0659 — ADMIN OP/RES MGT PHIL/SCI

B60

LINDVEIT E.N.,SCIENTISTS IN GOVERNMENT. USA+45 PAY EDU/PROP ADMIN DRIVE HABITAT ROLE...TECHNIC BIBLIOG 20. PAGE 65 B1316 — TEC/DEV ECO/TAC PHIL/SCI GOV/REL

B60

MEYRIAT J.,LA SCIENCE POLITIQUE EN FRANCE, 1945-1958; BIBLIOGRAPHIES FRANCAISES DE SCIENCES SOCIALES (VOL. I). EUR+WWI FRANCE POL/PAR DIPLOM ADMIN CHOOSE ATTIT...IDEA/COMP METH/COMP NAT/COMP 20. PAGE 73 B1478 — BIBLIOG/A NAT/G CONCPT PHIL/SCI

S60

HUTCHINSON C.E.,"AN INSTITUTE FOR NATIONAL SECURITY AFFAIRS." USA+45 R+D CONSULT TOP/EX ACT/RES CREATE PLAN TEC/DEV EDU/PROP ROUTINE NUC/PWR ATTIT ORD/FREE PWR...DECISION MGT PHIL/SCI CONCPT RECORD GEN/LAWS GEN/METH 20. PAGE 53 B1068 — POLICY METH/CNCPT ELITES DIPLOM

B61

KRUPP S.,PATTERN IN ORGANIZATIONAL ANALYSIS: A CRITICAL EXAMINATION. INGP/REL PERS/REL RATIONAL ATTIT AUTHORIT DRIVE PWR...DECISION PHIL/SCI SOC IDEA/COMP. PAGE 61 B1239 — MGT CONTROL CONCPT METH/CNCPT

B61

WARD R.E.,JAPANESE POLITICAL SCIENCE: A GUIDE TO JAPANESE REFERENCE AND RESEARCH MATERIALS (2ND ED.). LAW CONSTN STRATA NAT/G POL/PAR DELIB/GP LEGIS ADMIN CHOOSE GP/REL...INT/LAW 19/20 CHINJAP. PAGE 113 B2290 — BIBLIOG/A PHIL/SCI

B62

BINDER L.,IRAN: POLITICAL DEVELOPMENT IN A CHANGING SOCIETY. IRAN OP/RES REV GP/REL CENTRAL RATIONAL PWR...PHIL/SCI NAT/COMP GEN/LAWS 20. PAGE 12 B0239 — LEGIT NAT/G ADMIN STRUCT

B62

BOCK E.A.,CASE STUDIES IN AMERICAN GOVERNMENT. USA+45 ECO/DEV CHIEF EDU/PROP CT/SYS RACE/REL ORD/FREE...JURID MGT PHIL/SCI PRESIDENT CASEBOOK. PAGE 13 B0262 — POLICY LEGIS IDEA/COMP NAT/G

B62

HITCHNER D.G.,MODERN GOVERNMENT: A SURVEY OF POLITICAL SCIENCE. WOR+45 INT/ORG LEGIS ADMIN CT/SYS EXEC CHOOSE TOTALISM POPULISM...INT/LAW PHIL/SCI METH 20. PAGE 50 B1019 — CONCPT NAT/G STRUCT

B62

NATIONAL BUREAU ECONOMIC RES,THE RATE AND DIRECTION OF INVENTIVE ACTIVITY: ECONOMIC AND SOCIAL FACTORS. STRUCT INDUS MARKET R+D CREATE OP/RES TEC/DEV EFFICIENCY PRODUC RATIONAL UTIL...WELF/ST PHIL/SCI METH/CNCPT TIME. PAGE 77 B1562 — DECISION PROB/SOLV MGT

C62

DE GRAZIA A.,"POLITICAL BEHAVIOR (REV. ED.)" STRATA POL/PAR LEAD LOBBY ROUTINE WAR CHOOSE REPRESENT — PHIL/SCI OP/RES

CONSEN ATTIT ORD/FREE BIBLIOG. PAGE 27 B0555 — CONCPT

B63

BROGAN D.W.,POLITICAL PATTERNS IN TODAY'S WORLD. FRANCE USA+45 USSR WOR+45 CONSTN STRUCT PLAN DIPLOM ADMIN LEAD ROLE SUPEGO...PHIL/SCI 20. PAGE 15 B0313 — NAT/COMP NEW/LIB COM TOTALISM

B63

KAST F.E.,SCIENCE, TECHNOLOGY, AND MANAGEMENT. SPACE USA+45 FORCES CONFER DETER NUC/PWR...PHIL/SCI CHARTS ANTHOL BIBLIOG 20 NASA. PAGE 58 B1179 — MGT PLAN TEC/DEV PROB/SOLV

B64

COOMBS C.H.,A THEORY OF DATA....MGT PHIL/SCI SOC CLASSIF MATH PROBABIL STAT QU. PAGE 23 B0472 — CON/ANAL GEN/METH TESTS PSY

B64

COX R.,THEORY IN MARKETING. FUT USA+45 SOCIETY ECO/DEV PROB/SOLV PRICE RISK PRODUC ATTIT...ANTHOL 20. PAGE 24 B0499 — MARKET ECO/TAC PHIL/SCI MGT

B64

KARIEL H.S.,IN SEARCH OF AUTHORITY: TWENTIETH-CENTURY POLITICAL THOUGHT. WOR+45 WOR-45 NAT/G EX/STRUC TOTALISM DRIVE PWR...MGT PHIL/SCI GEN/LAWS 19/20 NIETZSCH/F FREUD/S WEBER/MAX NIEBUHR/R MARITAIN/J. PAGE 58 B1173 — CONSTN CONCPT ORD/FREE IDEA/COMP

B65

PENNICK JL J.R.,THE POLITICS OF AMERICAN SCIENCE, 1939 TO THE PRESENT. USA+45 USA-45 INTELL TEC/DEV DIPLOM NEW/LIB...ANTHOL 20 COLD/WAR. PAGE 82 B1651 — POLICY ADMIN PHIL/SCI NAT/G

B65

SINGER J.D.,HUMAN BEHAVIOR AND INTERNATINAL POLITICS* CONTRIBUTIONS FROM THE SOCIAL-PSYCHOLOGICAL SCIENCES. ACT/RES PLAN EDU/PROP ADMIN KNOWL...DECISION PSY SOC NET/THEORY HYPO/EXP LAB/EXP SOC/EXP GEN/METH ANTHOL BIBLIOG. PAGE 97 B1965 — DIPLOM PHIL/SCI QUANT SIMUL

B65

UNIVERSAL REFERENCE SYSTEM,INTERNATIONAL AFFAIRS: VOLUME I IN THE POLITICAL SCIENCE, GOVERNMENT, AND PUBLIC POLICY SERIES....DECISION ECOMETRIC GEOG INT/LAW JURID MGT PHIL/SCI PSY SOC. PAGE 107 B2163 — BIBLIOG/A GEN/METH COMPUT/IR DIPLOM

S65

SILVERT K.H.,"AMERICAN ACADEMIC ETHICS AND SOCIAL RESEARCH ABROAD* THE LESSON OF PROJECT CAMELOT." CHILE L/A+17C USA+45 FINAN ADMIN...PHIL/SCI SOC GEN/LAWS CAMELOT. PAGE 97 B1953 — ACADEM NAT/G ACT/RES POLICY

B66

HALPIN A.W.,THEORY AND RESEARCH IN ADMINISTRATION. ACT/RES LEAD...MGT IDEA/COMP METH/COMP. PAGE 46 B0929 — GEN/LAWS EDU/PROP ADMIN PHIL/SCI

B66

US BUREAU OF THE BUDGET,THE ADMINISTRATION OF GOVERNMENT SUPPORTED RESEARCH AT UNIVERSITIES (PAMPHLET). USA+45 CONSULT TOP/EX ADMIN INCOME WEALTH...MGT PHIL/SCI INT. PAGE 108 B2174 — ACT/RES NAT/G ACADEM GP/REL

B66

WYLIE C.M.,RESEARCH IN PUBLIC HEALTH ADMINISTRATION; SELECTED RECENT ABSTRACTS IV (PAMPHLET). USA+45 MUNIC PUB/INST ACT/RES CREATE OP/RES TEC/DEV GP/REL ROLE...MGT PHIL/SCI STAT. PAGE 118 B2387 — BIBLIOG/A R+D HEAL ADMIN

B67

UNIVERSAL REFERENCE SYSTEM,PUBLIC POLICY AND THE MANAGEMENT OF SCIENCE (VOLUME IX). FUT SPACE WOR+45 LAW NAT/G TEC/DEV CONTROL NUC/PWR GOV/REL ...COMPUT/IR GEN/METH. PAGE 107 B2165 — BIBLIOG/A POLICY MGT PHIL/SCI

B67

US HOUSE COMM SCI ASTRONAUT,GOVERNMENT, SCIENCE, AND INTERNATIONAL POLICY. R+D OP/RES PLAN 20. PAGE 109 B2198 — ADMIN PHIL/SCI ACT/RES DIPLOM

S67

LA PORTE T.,"DIFFUSION AND DISCONTINUITY IN SCIENCE, TECHNOLOGY AND PUBLIC AFFAIRS: RESULTS OF A SEARCH IN THE FIELD." USA+45 ACT/RES TEC/DEV PERS/REL ATTIT PHIL/SCI. PAGE 62 B1249 — INTELL ADMIN ACADEM GP/REL

B82

POOLE W.F.,INDEX TO PERIODICAL LITERATURE. LOC/G NAT/G DIPLOM ADMIN...HUM PHIL/SCI SOC 19. PAGE 84 B1690 — BIBLIOG USA-45 ALL/VALS SOCIETY

PHILADELPH....PHILADELPHIA, PENNSYLVANIA

PHILANTHROPY....SEE GIVE+WEALTH

PHILIP/J....JOHN PHILIP

PHILIPPINE....PHILIPPINESL SEE ALSO S/ASIA

PHILIPPINES....SEE PHILIPPINE; S/ASIA

B21

STOWELL E.C.,INTERVENTION IN INTERNATIONAL LAW.   BAL/PWR
UNIV LAW SOCIETY INT/ORG ACT/RES PLAN LEGIT ROUTINE.   SOVEREIGN
WAR...JURID OBS GEN/LAWS 20. PAGE 101 B2050

L23

DOUGLAS P.H.,"OCCUPATIONAL V PROPORTIONAL   REPRESENT
REPRESENTATION." INDUS NAT/G PLAN ROUTINE SUFF   PROF/ORG
CONSEN DRIVE...CONCPT CLASSIF. PAGE 30 B0612   DOMIN
                                                        INGP/REL

B24

POOLE D.C.,THE CONDUCT OF FOREIGN RELATIONS UNDER   NAT/G
MODERN DEMOCRATIC CONDITIONS. EUR+WWI USA-45   EDU/PROP
INT/ORG PLAN LEGIT ADMIN KNOWL PWR...MAJORIT   DIPLOM
OBS/ENVIR HIST/WRIT GEN/LAWS 20. PAGE 84 B1689

C27

HSIAO K.C.,"POLITICAL PLURALISM." LAW CONSTN   STRUCT
POL/PAR LEGIS PLAN ADMIN CENTRAL SOVEREIGN   GEN/LAWS
...INT/LAW BIBLIOG 19/20. PAGE 52 B1053   PLURISM

B28

HALL W.P.,EMPIRE TO COMMONWEALTH. FUT WOR-45 CONSTN   VOL/ASSN
ECO/DEV ECO/UNDEV INT/ORG PROVS PLAN DIPLOM   NAT/G
EDU/PROP ADMIN COLONIAL PEACE PERSON ALL/VALS   UK
...POLICY GEOG SOC OBS RECORD TREND CMN/WLTH
PARLIAMENT 19/20. PAGE 46 B0925

B29

ROBERTS S.H.,HISTORY OF FRENCH COLONIAL POLICY. AFR   INT/ORG
ASIA L/A+17C S/ASIA CULTURE ECO/DEV ECO/UNDEV FINAN   ACT/RES
NAT/G PLAN ECO/TAC DOMIN ROUTINE SOVEREIGN...OBS   FRANCE
HIST/WRIT TREND CHARTS VAL/FREE 19/20. PAGE 89   COLONIAL
B1796

B32

WRIGHT Q.,GOLD AND MONETARY STABILIZATION. FUT   FINAN
USA-45 WOR-45 INTELL ECO/DEV INT/ORG NAT/G CONSULT   POLICY
PLAN ECO/TAC ADMIN ATTIT WEALTH...CONCPT TREND 20.
PAGE 118 B2383

B34

RIDLEY C.E.,THE CITY-MANAGER PROFESSION. CHIEF PLAN   MUNIC
ADMIN CONTROL ROUTINE CHOOSE...TECHNIC CHARTS   EX/STRUC
GOV/COMP BIBLIOG 20. PAGE 88 B1780   LOC/G
                                                        EXEC

B36

ROBINSON H.,DEVELOPMENT OF THE BRITISH EMPIRE.   NAT/G
WOR-45 CULTURE SOCIETY STRUCT ECO/DEV ECO/UNDEV   HIST/WRIT
INT/ORG VOL/ASSN FORCES CREATE PLAN DOMIN EDU/PROP   UK
ADMIN COLONIAL PWR WEALTH...POLICY GEOG CHARTS
CMN/WLTH 16/20. PAGE 89 B1800

B36

US LIBRARY OF CONGRESS,CLASSIFIED GUIDE TO MATERIAL   BIBLIOG
IN THE LIBRARY OF CONGRESS COVERING URBAN COMMUNITY   CLASSIF
DEVELOPMENT. USA+45 CREATE PROB/SOLV ADMIN 20.   MUNIC
PAGE 109 B2202   PLAN

B37

GALLOWAY G.B.,AMERICAN PAMPHLET LITERATURE OF   BIBLIOG/A
PUBLIC AFFAIRS (PAMPHLET). USA-45 ECO/DEV LABOR   PLAN
ADMIN...MGT 20. PAGE 38 B0776   DIPLOM
                                                        NAT/G

B37

ROBBINS L.,ECONOMIC PLANNING AND INTERNATIONAL   INT/ORG
ORDER. WOR-45 SOCIETY FINAN INDUS NAT/G ECO/TAC   PLAN
ROUTINE WEALTH...SOC TIME/SEQ GEN/METH WORK 20   INT/TRADE
KEYNES/JM. PAGE 89 B1791

B37

ROYAL INST. INT. AFF.,THE COLONIAL PROBLEM. WOR-45   INT/ORG
LAW ECO/DEV ECO/UNDEV NAT/G PLAN ECO/TAC EDU/PROP   ACT/RES
ADMIN ATTIT ALL/VALS...CONCPT 20. PAGE 91 B1844   SOVEREIGN
                                                        COLONIAL

B38

HARPER S.N.,THE GOVERNMENT OF THE SOVIET UNION. COM   MARXISM
USSR LAW CONSTN ECO/DEV PLAN TEC/DEV DIPLOM   NAT/G
INT/TRADE ADMIN REV NAT/LISM...POLICY 20. PAGE 47   LEAD
B0952   POL/PAR

B38

PETTEE G.S.,THE PROCESS OF REVOLUTION. COM FRANCE   COERCE
ITALY MOD/EUR RUSSIA SPAIN WOR-45 ELITES INTELL   CONCPT
SOCIETY STRATA STRUCT INT/ORG NAT/G POL/PAR ACT/RES   REV
PLAN EDU/PROP LEGIT EXEC...SOC MYTH TIME/SEQ
TOT/POP 18/20. PAGE 82 B1664

B39

HITLER A.,MEIN KAMPF. EUR+WWI FUT MOD/EUR STRUCT   PWR
INT/ORG LABOR NAT/G POL/PAR FORCES CREATE PLAN   NEW/IDEA
BAL/PWR DIPLOM ECO/TAC DOMIN EDU/PROP ADMIN COERCE   WAR
ATTIT...SOCIALIST BIOG TREND NAZI. PAGE 50 B1020

B39

MCCAMY J.L.,GOVERNMENT PUBLICITY: ITS PRACTICE IN   EDU/PROP
FEDERAL ADMINISTRATION. USA-45 COM/IND. ADMIN   NAT/G
CONTROL EXEC PARTIC INGP/REL...SOC 20. PAGE 71   PLAN
B1442   ATTIT

N40

COUNTY GOVERNMENT IN THE UNITED STATES: A LIST OF   BIBLIOG/A
RECENT REFERENCES (PAMPHLET). USA-45 LAW PUB/INST   LOC/G
PLAN BUDGET CT/SYS CENTRAL 20. PAGE 49 B0988   ADMIN
                                                        MUNIC

B42

BINGHAM A.M.,THE TECHNIQUES OF DEMOCRACY. USA-45   POPULISM
CONSTN STRUCT POL/PAR LEGIS PLAN PARTIC CHOOSE   ORD/FREE
REPRESENT NAT/LISM TOTALISM...MGT 20. PAGE 12 B0240   ADMIN

NAT/G

B42

US STATE DEPT.,PEACE AND WAR: UNITED STATES FOREIGN   DIPLOM
POLICY, 1931-41. CULTURE FORCES ROUTINE CHOOSE   USA-45
ATTIT DRIVE PERSON 20. PAGE 111 B2237   PLAN

B44

DAHL D.,SICKNESS BENEFITS AND GROUP PURCHASE OF   BIBLIOG/A
MEDICAL CARE FOR INDUSTRIAL EMPLOYEES. FAM LABOR   INDUS
NAT/G PLAN...POLICY MGT SOC STAT 20. PAGE 25 B0519   WORKER
                                                        HEAL

B44

PUBLIC ADMINISTRATION SERVICE,YOUR BUSINESS OF   BIBLIOG
GOVERNMENT: A CATALOG OF PUBLICATIONS IN THE FIELD   ADMIN
OF PUBLIC ADMINISTRATION (PAMPHLET). FINAN R+D   NAT/G
LOC/G ACT/RES OP/RES PLAN 20. PAGE 85 B1715   MUNIC

B44

WRIGHT H.R.,SOCIAL SERVICE IN WARTIME. FINAN NAT/G   GIVE
VOL/ASSN PLAN GP/REL ROLE. PAGE 118 B2381   WAR
                                                        SOC/WK
                                                        ADMIN

L44

HAILEY,"THE FUTURE OF COLONIAL PEOPLES." WOR-45   PLAN
CONSTN CULTURE ECO/UNDEV AGRI MARKET INT/ORG NAT/G   CONCPT
SECT CONSULT ECO/TAC LEGIT ADMIN NAT/LISM ALL/VALS   DIPLOM
...SOC OBS TREND STERTYP CMN/WLTH LEAGUE/NAT   UK
PARLIAMENT 20. PAGE 45 B0916

B45

BAKER H.,PROBLEMS OF REEMPLOYMENT AND RETRAINING OF   BIBLIOG/A
MANPOWER DURING THE TRANSITION FROM WAR TO PEACE.   ADJUST
USA+45 INDUS LABOR LG/CO NAT/G PLAN ADMIN PEACE   WAR
...POLICY MGT 20. PAGE 8 B0167   PROB/SOLV

B45

BUSH V.,SCIENCE, THE ENDLESS FRONTIER. FUT USA-45   R+D
INTELL STRATA ACT/RES CREATE PLAN EDU/PROP ADMIN   NAT/G
NUC/PWR PEACE ATTIT HEALTH KNOWL...MAJORIT HEAL MGT
PHIL/SCI CONCPT OBS TREND 20. PAGE 18 B0360

B45

CLAPP G.R.,NEW HORIZONS IN PUBLIC ADMINISTRATION: A   ADMIN
SYMPOSIUM. USA-45 LEGIS PLAN DIPLOM REGION   EX/STRUC
EFFICIENCY 20. PAGE 21 B0430   MGT
                                                        NAT/G

B45

PASTUHOV V.D.,A GUIDE TO THE PRACTICE OF   INT/ORG
INTERNATIONAL CONFERENCES. WOR+45 PLAN LEGIT   DELIB/GP
ORD/FREE...MGT OBS RECORD VAL/FREE ILO LEAGUE/NAT
20. PAGE 81 B1640

S45

WHITE L.D.,"CONGRESSIONAL CONTROL OF THE PUBLIC   LEGIS
SERVICE." USA-45 NAT/G CONSULT DELIB/GP PLAN SENIOR   EXEC
CONGRESS. PAGE 116 B2335   POLICY
                                                        CONTROL

B47

MILLETT J.D.,THE PROCESS AND ORGANIZATION OF   ADMIN
GOVERNMENT PLANNING. USA+45 DELIB/GP ACT/RES LEAD   NAT/G
LOBBY TASK...POLICY GEOG TIME 20 RESOURCE/N.   PLAN
PAGE 73 B1482   CONSULT

B47

WHITEHEAD T.N.,LEADERSHIP IN A FREE SOCIETY; A   INDUS
STUDY IN HUMAN RELATIONS BASED ON AN ANALYSIS OF   LEAD
PRESENT-DAY INDUSTRIAL CIVILIZATION. WOR-45 STRUCT   ORD/FREE
R+D LABOR LG/CO SML/CO WORKER PLAN PROB/SOLV   SOCIETY
TEC/DEV DRIVE...MGT 20. PAGE 116 B2341

B48

PUBLIC ADMINISTRATION SERVICE,SOURCE MATERIALS IN   BIBLIOG/A
PUBLIC ADMINISTRATION: A SELECTED BIBLIOGRAPHY (PAS   GOV/REL
PUBLICATION NO. 102). USA+45 LAW FINAN LOC/G MUNIC   MGT
NAT/G PLAN RECEIVE EDU/PROP CT/SYS CHOOSE HEALTH   ADMIN
20. PAGE 85 B1717

B48

ROSENFARB J.,FREEDOM AND THE ADMINISTRATIVE STATE.   ECO/DEV
NAT/G ROUTINE EFFICIENCY PRODUC RATIONAL UTIL   INDUS
...TECHNIC WELF/ST MGT 20 BUREAUCRCY. PAGE 90 B1821   PLAN
                                                        WEALTH

B48

TOWSTER J.,POLITICAL POWER IN THE USSR: 1917-1947.   EX/STRUC
USSR CONSTN CULTURE ELITES CREATE PLAN COERCE   NAT/G
CENTRAL ATTIT RIGID/FLEX ORD/FREE...BIBLIOG   MARXISM
SOC/INTEG 20 LENIN/VI STALIN/J. PAGE 105 B2124   PWR

B48

WHITE L.D.,INTRODUCTION OT THE STUDY OF PUBLIC   ADMIN
ADMINISTRATION. STRUCT PLAN PROB/SOLV EXEC ROUTINE   MGT
GOV/REL EFFICIENCY PWR CHARTS. PAGE 116 B2336   EX/STRUC
                                                        NAT/G

N48

YATES M.,ADMINISTRATIVE REORGANIZATION OF STATE   BIBLIOG
GOVERNMENTS: A BIBLIOGRAPHY (PAMPHLET). USA+45   LOC/G
USA-45 CONSTN OP/RES PLAN CONFER...POLICY 20.   ADMIN
PAGE 118 B2390   PROVS

B49

DE GRAZIA A.,HUMAN RELATIONS IN PUBLIC   BIBLIOG/A
ADMINISTRATION. INDUS ACT/RES CREATE PLAN PROB/SOLV   ADMIN
TEC/DEV INGP/REL PERS/REL DRIVE...POLICY SOC 20.   PHIL/SCI
PAGE 27 B0552   OP/RES

B49

ROSENHAUPT H.W.,HOW TO WAGE PEACE. USA+45 SOCIETY   INTELL
STRATA STRUCT R+D INT/ORG POL/PAR LEGIS ACT/RES   CONCPT

CREATE PLAN EDU/PROP ADMIN EXEC ATTIT ALL/VALS   DIPLOM
...TIME/SEQ TREND COLD/WAR 20. PAGE 90 B1822
                                                            B49
SINGER K.,THE IDEA OF CONFLICT. UNIV INTELL INT/ORG ACT/RES
NAT/G PLAN ROUTINE ATTIT DRIVE ALL/VALS...POLICY   SOC
CONCPT TIME/SEQ. PAGE 97 B1966
                                                            B49
STEIN H.,THE FOREIGN SERVICE ACT OF 1946. USA+45   DIPLOM
ELITES EX/STRUC PLAN PROB/SOLV LOBBY GOV/REL   LAW
PERS/REL RIGID/FLEX...POLICY IDEA/COMP 20 CONGRESS NAT/G
BUR/BUDGET. PAGE 100 B2027   ADMIN
                                                            B49
WRIGHT J.H.,PUBLIC RELATIONS IN MANAGEMENT. USA+45 MGT
USA-45 ECO/DEV LG/CO SML/CO CONSULT EXEC TASK   PLAN
PROFIT ATTIT ROLE 20. PAGE 118 B2382   EDU/PROP
                                                   PARTIC
                                                            S49
STEINMETZ H.,"THE PROBLEMS OF THE LANDRAT: A STUDY LOC/G
OF COUNTY GOVERNMENT IN THE US ZONE OF GERMANY."   COLONIAL
GERMANY/W USA+45 INDUS PLAN DIPLOM EDU/PROP CONTROL MGT
WAR GOV/REL FEDERAL WEALTH PLURISM...GOV/COMP 20   TOP/EX
LANDRAT. PAGE 100 B2031
                                                            B50
DEES J.W. JR.,URBAN SOCIOLOGY AND THE EMERGING   PLAN
ATOMIC MEGALOPOLIS, PART I. USA+45 TEC/DEV ADMIN   NEIGH
NUC/PWR HABITAT...SOC AUD/VIS CHARTS GEN/LAWS 20   MUNIC
WATER. PAGE 28 B0568   PROB/SOLV
                                                            B50
GREAT BRITAIN TREASURY,PUBLIC ADMINISTRATION: A   BIBLIOG
BIBLIOGRAPHY FOR ORGANISATION AND METHODS   PLAN
(PAMPHLET). LOC/G NAT/G CONSULT EX/STRUC CONFER   CONTROL
ROUTINE TASK EFFICIENCY...MGT 20. PAGE 43 B0862   ADMIN
                                                            B50
HARTLAND P.C.,BALANCE OF INTERREGIONAL PAYMENTS OF ECO/DEV
NEW ENGLAND. USA+45 TEC/DEV ECO/TAC LEGIT ROUTINE   FINAN
BAL/PAY PROFIT 20 NEW/ENGLND FED/RESERV. PAGE 47   REGION
B0962   PLAN
                                                            B50
KOENIG L.W.,THE SALE OF THE TANKERS. USA+45 SEA   NAT/G
DIST/IND POL/PAR DIPLOM ADMIN CIVMIL/REL ATTIT   POLICY
...DECISION 20 PRESIDENT DEPT/STATE. PAGE 60 B1223 PLAN
                                                   GOV/REL
                                                            B50
LITTLE HOOVER COMM,HOW TO ACHIEVE GREATER   TOP/EX
EFFICIENCY AND ECONOMY IN MINNESOTA'S GOVERNMENT   LOC/G
(PAMPHLET). PLAN BUDGET ADMIN CHOOSE EFFICIENCY   GOV/REL
ALL/VALS 20 MINNESOTA. PAGE 66 B1327   PROVS
                                                            B50
MANNHEIM K.,FREEDOM, POWER, AND DEMOCRATIC   TEC/DEV
PLANNING. FUT USSR WOR+45 ELITES INTELL SOCIETY   PLAN
NAT/G EDU/PROP ROUTINE ATTIT DRIVE SUPEGO SKILL   CAP/ISM
...POLICY PSY CONCPT TREND GEN/LAWS 20. PAGE 69   UK
B1393
                                                            B50
MCCAMY J.,THE ADMINISTRATION OF AMERICAN FOREIGN   EXEC
AFFAIRS. USA+45 SOCIETY INT/ORG NAT/G ACT/RES PLAN STRUCT
INT/TRADE EDU/PROP ADJUD ALL/VALS...METH/CNCPT   DIPLOM
TIME/SEQ CONGRESS 20. PAGE 71 B1441
                                                            L50
US SENATE COMM. GOVT. OPER.,"REVISION OF THE UN   INT/ORG
CHARTER." FUT USA+45 WOR+45 CONSTN ECO/DEV   LEGIS
ECO/UNDEV NAT/G DELIB/GP ACT/RES CREATE PLAN EXEC   PEACE
ROUTINE CHOOSE ALL/VALS...POLICY CONCPT CONGRESS UN
TOT/POP 20 COLD/WAR. PAGE 111 B2235
                                                            C50
HOLCOMBE A.,"OUR MORE PERFECT UNION." USA+45 USA-45 CONSTN
POL/PAR JUDGE CT/SYS EQUILIB FEDERAL PWR...MAJORIT NAT/G
TREND BIBLIOG 18/20 CONGRESS PRESIDENT. PAGE 51   ADMIN
B1031   PLAN
                                                            C50
SIMON H.A.,"PUBLIC ADMINISTRATION." LG/CO SML/CO   MGT
PLAN DOMIN LEAD GP/REL DRIVE PERCEPT ALL/VALS   ADMIN
...POLICY BIBLIOG/A 20. PAGE 97 B1957   DECISION
                                                   EX/STRUC
                                                            C50
STEWART F.M.,"A HALF CENTURY OF MUNICIPAL REFORM." LOC/G
USA+45 CONSTN FINAN SCHOOL EX/STRUC PLAN PROB/SOLV VOL/ASSN
EDU/PROP ADMIN CHOOSE GOV/REL BIBLIOG. PAGE 101   MUNIC
B2036   POLICY
                                                            B51
LEITES N.,THE OPERATIONAL CODE OF THE POLITBURO.   DELIB/GP
COM USSR PLAN CREATE PLAN DOMIN LEGIT COERCE ALL/VALS ADMIN
...SOC CONCPT MYTH TREND CON/ANAL GEN/LAWS 20   SOCISM
LENIN/VI STALIN/J. PAGE 64 B1284
                                                            B52
EGLE W.P.,ECONOMIC STABILIZATION. USA+45 SOCIETY   NAT/G
FINAN MARKET PLAN ECO/TAC DOMIN EDU/PROP LEGIT EXEC ECO/DEV
WEALTH...CONCPT METH/CNCPT TREND HYPO/EXP GEN/METH CAP/ISM
TOT/POP VAL/FREE 20. PAGE 32 B0656
                                                            B52
JANSE R.S.,SOVIET TRANSPORTATION AND   BIBLIOG/A
COMMUNICATIONS: A BIBLIOGRAPHY. COM USSR PLAN   COM/IND
...DICTIONARY 20. PAGE 56 B1124   LEGIS
                                                   ADMIN
                                                            B52
ULAM A.B.,TITOISM AND THE COMINFORM. USSR WOR+45   COM

STRUCT INT/ORG NAT/G ACT/RES PLAN EXEC ATTIT DRIVE POL/PAR
ALL/VALS...CONCPT OBS VAL/FREE 20 COMINTERN   TOTALISM
TITO/MARSH. PAGE 106 B2145   YUGOSLAVIA
                                                            S52
JOSEPHSON E.,"IRRATIONAL LEADERSHIP IN FORMAL   ADMIN
ORGANIZATIONS." EX/STRUC PLAN LEAD GP/REL INGP/REL RATIONAL
EFFICIENCY AUTHORIT DRIVE PSY. PAGE 57 B1154   CONCPT
                                                   PERSON
                                                            B53
LARSEN K.,NATIONAL BIBLIOGRAPHIC SERVICES: THEIR   BIBLIOG/A
CREATION AND OPERATION. WOR+45 COM/IND CREATE PLAN INT/ORG
DIPLOM PRESS ADMIN ROUTINE...MGT UNESCO. PAGE 62   WRITING
B1262
                                                            B53
MAJUMDAR B.B.,PROBLEMS OF PUBLIC ADMINISTRATION IN ECO/UNDEV
INDIA. INDIA INDUS PLAN BUDGET ADJUD CENTRAL DEMAND GOV/REL
WEALTH...WELF/ST ANTHOL 20 CIVIL/SERV. PAGE 68   ADMIN
B1384   MUNIC
                                                            S53
BLOUGH R.,"THE ROLE OF THE ECONOMIST IN FEDERAL   DELIB/GP
POLICY MAKING." USA+45 ELITES INTELL ECO/DEV NAT/G ECO/TAC
CONSULT EX/STRUC ACT/RES PLAN INT/TRADE BAL/PAY
WEALTH...POLICY CONGRESS 20. PAGE 13 B0256
                                                            S53
MORRIS B.S.,"THE COMINFORM: A FIVE YEAR   VOL/ASSN
PERSPECTIVE." COM UNIV USSR WOR+45 ECO/DEV POL/PAR EDU/PROP
TOP/EX PLAN DOMIN ADMIN TOTALISM ATTIT ALL/VALS   DIPLOM
...CONCPT TIME/SEQ TREND CON/ANAL WORK VAL/FREE 20.
PAGE 76 B1527
                                                            B54
BINANI G.D.,INDIA AT A GLANCE (REV. ED.). INDIA   INDEX
COM/IND FINAN INDUS LABOR PROVS SCHOOL PLAN DIPLOM CON/ANAL
INT/TRADE ADMIN...JURID 20. PAGE 12 B0238   NAT/G
                                                   ECO/UNDEV
                                                            B54
HOBBS E.H.,BEHIND THE PRESIDENT - A STUDY OF   EX/STRUC
EXECUTIVE OFFICE AGENCIES. USA+45 NAT/G PLAN BUDGET DELIB/GP
ECO/TAC EXEC ORD/FREE 20 BUR/BUDGET. PAGE 50 B1022 CONFER
                                                   CONSULT
                                                            L54
ARCIENEGAS G.,"POST-WAR SOVIET FOREIGN POLICY: A   INTELL
WORLD PERSPECTIVE." COM USA+45 STRUCT NAT/G POL/PAR ACT/RES
TOP/EX PLAN ADMIN ALL/VALS...TREND COLD/WAR TOT/POP USSR
20. PAGE 6 B0124
                                                            C54
CALDWELL L.K.,"THE GOVERNMENT AND ADMINISTRATION OF PROVS
NEW YORK." LOC/G MUNIC POL/PAR SCHOOL CHIEF LEGIS   ADMIN
PLAN TAX CT/SYS...MGT SOC/WK BIBLIOG 20 NEWYORK/C. CONSTN
PAGE 18 B0366   EX/STRUC
                                                            C54
ROBSON W.A.,"GREAT CITIES OF THE WORLD: THEIR   LOC/G
GOVERNMENT, POLITICS, AND PLANNING." CONSTN FINAN   MUNIC
EX/STRUC ADMIN EXEC CHOOSE GOV/REL...STAT TREND   PLAN
ANTHOL BIBLIOG 20. PAGE 89 B1806   PROB/SOLV
                                                            B55
BERNAYS E.L.,THE ENGINEERING OF CONSENT. VOL/ASSN   GP/REL
OP/RES ROUTINE INGP/REL ATTIT RESPECT...POLICY   PLAN
METH/CNCPT METH/COMP 20. PAGE 11 B0224   ACT/RES
                                                   ADJUST
                                                            B55
CHOWDHURI R.N.,INTERNATIONAL MANDATES AND   DELIB/GP
TRUSTEESHIP SYSTEMS. WOR+45 STRUCT ECO/UNDEV   PLAN
INT/ORG LEGIS DOMIN EDU/PROP LEGIT ADJUD EXEC PWR   SOVEREIGN
...CONCPT TIME/SEQ UN 20. PAGE 21 B0427
                                                            B55
CRAIG J.,BIBLIOGRAPHY OF PUBLIC ADMINISTRATION IN   BIBLIOG
AUSTRALIA. CONSTN FINAN EX/STRUC LEGIS PLAN DIPLOM GOV/REL
RECEIVE ADJUD ROUTINE...HEAL 19/20 AUSTRAL   ADMIN
PARLIAMENT. PAGE 24 B0500   NAT/G
                                                            B55
HOROWITZ M.,INCENTIVE WAGE SYSTEMS. INDUS LG/CO   BIBLIOG/A
WORKER CONTROL GP/REL...MGT PSY 20. PAGE 51 B1044   PAY
                                                   PLAN
                                                   TASK
                                                            B55
RILEY V.,INTERINDUSTRY ECONOMIC STUDIES. USA+45   BIBLIOG
COMPUTER ADMIN OPTIMAL PRODUC...MGT CLASSIF STAT.   ECO/DEV
PAGE 88 B1788   PLAN
                                                   STRUCT
                                                            B55
RUSTOW D.A.,THE POLITICS OF COMPROMISE. SWEDEN   POL/PAR
LABOR EX/STRUC LEGIS PLAN REPRESENT SOCISM...SOC   NAT/G
19/20. PAGE 92 B1859   POLICY
                                                   ECO/TAC
                                                            B55
UN ECONOMIC AND SOCIAL COUNCIL,BIBLIOGRAPHY OF   BIBLIOG/A
PUBLICATIONS OF THE UN AND SPECIALIZED AGENCIES IN SOC/WK
THE SOCIAL WELFARE FIELD, 1946-1952. WOR+45 FAM   ADMIN
INT/ORG MUNIC ACT/RES PLAN PROB/SOLV EDU/PROP AGE/C WEALTH
AGE/Y HABITAT...HEAL UN. PAGE 106 B2148
                                                            L55
KISER M.,"ORGANIZATION OF AMERICAN STATES." L/A+17C VOL/ASSN
USA+45 ECO/UNDEV INT/ORG NAT/G PLAN TEC/DEV DIPLOM ECO/DEV
ECO/TAC INT/TRADE EDU/PROP ADMIN ALL/VALS...POLICY REGION
MGT RECORD ORG/CHARTS OAS 20. PAGE 60 B1215

L55

ROSTOW W.W.,"RUSSIA AND CHINA UNDER COMMUNISM."   COM
CHINA/COM USSR INTELL STRUCT INT/ORG NAT/G POL/PAR   ASIA
TOP/EX ACT/RES PLAN ADMIN ATTIT ALL/VALS MARXISM
...CONCPT OBS TIME/SEQ TREND GOV/COMP VAL/FREE 20.
PAGE 91 B1830

S55

ANGELL R.,"GOVERNMENTS AND PEOPLES AS A FOCI FOR   FUT
PEACE-ORIENTED RESEARCH." WOR+45 CULTURE SOCIETY   SOC
FACE/GP ACT/RES CREATE PLAN DIPLOM EDU/PROP ROUTINE PEACE
ATTIT PERCEPT SKILL...POLICY CONCPT OBS TREND
GEN/METH 20. PAGE 5 B0110

S55

DRUCKER P.F.,"'MANAGEMENT SCIENCE' AND THE   MGT
MANAGER." PLAN ROUTINE RIGID/FLEX...METH/CNCPT LOG   STRUCT
HYPO/EXP. PAGE 30 B0620   DECISION
  RATIONAL

C55

GRASSMUCK G.L.,"A MANUAL OF LEBANESE   ADMIN
ADMINISTRATION." LEBANON PLAN...CHARTS BIBLIOG/A   NAT/G
20. PAGE 42 B0854   ISLAM
  EX/STRUC

B56

ALEXANDER R.S.,INDUSTRIAL MARKETING. USA+45 ECO/DEV   INDUS
DIST/IND FINAN NAT/G ACT/RES CAP/ISM PRICE CONTROL   MARKET
...POLICY MGT 20. PAGE 4 B0072   ECO/TAC
  PLAN

B56

DUNNILL F.,THE CIVIL SERVICE. UK LAW PLAN ADMIN   PERSON
EFFICIENCY DRIVE NEW/LIB...STAT CHARTS 20   WORKER
PARLIAMENT CIVIL/SERV. PAGE 31 B0633   STRATA
  SOC/WK

B56

ECOLE NAT'L D'ADMINISTRATION,RECRUITMENT AND   ADMIN
TRAINING FOR THE HIGHER CIVIL SERVICE IN FRANCE.   MGT
FRANCE EX/STRUC PLAN EDU/PROP CONTROL ROUTINE TASK   EXEC
COST...METH 20 CIVIL/SERV. PAGE 32 B0650   ACADEM

B56

GARDNER R.N.,STERLING-DOLLAR DIPLOMACY. EUR+WWI   ECO/DEV
USA+45 INT/ORG NAT/G PLAN INT/TRADE EDU/PROP ADMIN   DIPLOM
KNOWL PWR WEALTH...POLICY SOC METH/CNCPT STAT
CHARTS SIMUL GEN/LAWS 20. PAGE 39 B0781

B56

GLADDEN E.N.,CIVIL SERVICE OR BUREAUCRACY? UK LAW   ADMIN
STRATA LABOR TOP/EX PLAN SENIOR AUTOMAT CONTROL   GOV/REL
PARTIC CHOOSE HAPPINESS...CHARTS 19/20 CIVIL/SERV   EFFICIENCY
BUREAUCRCY. PAGE 40 B0808   PROVS

B56

HICKMAN C.A.,INDIVIDUALS, GROUPS, AND ECONOMIC   MGT
BEHAVIOR. WORKER PAY CONTROL EXEC GP/REL INGP/REL   ADMIN
PERSON ROLE...PSY SOC PERS/COMP METH 20. PAGE 50   ECO/TAC
B1005   PLAN

B56

KAUFMANN W.W.,MILITARY POLICY AND NATIONAL   FORCES
SECURITY. USA+45 ELITES INTELL NAT/G TOP/EX PLAN   CREATE
BAL/PWR DIPLOM ROUTINE COERCE NUC/PWR ATTIT
ORD/FREE PWR 20 COLD/WAR. PAGE 58 B1182

S56

MARGOLIS J.,"ON MUNICIPAL LAND POLICY FOR FISCAL   BUDGET
GAINS." USA+45 MUNIC PLAN TAX COST EFFICIENCY   POLICY
HABITAT KNOWL...MGT 20. PAGE 69 B1398   GEOG
  LOC/G

B57

ASHER R.E.,THE UNITED NATIONS AND THE PROMOTION OF   INT/ORG
THE GENERAL WELFARE. WOR+45 WOR-45 ECO/UNDEV   CONSULT
EX/STRUC ACT/RES PLAN DIPLOM EDU/PROP ROUTINE HEALTH...HUM
CONCPT CHARTS UNESCO UN ILO 20. PAGE 7 B0139

B57

CHANDRA S.,PARTIES AND POLITICS AT THE MUGHAL   POL/PAR
COURT: 1707-1740. INDIA CULTURE EX/STRUC CREATE   ELITES
PLAN PWR...BIBLIOG/A 18. PAGE 20 B0405   NAT/G

B57

HOLCOMBE A.N.,STRENGTHENING THE UNITED NATIONS.   INT/ORG
USA+45 ACT/RES CREATE PLAN EDU/PROP ATTIT PERCEPT   ROUTINE
PWR...METH/CNCPT CONT/OBS RECORD UN COLD/WAR 20.
PAGE 51 B1032

B57

JENNINGS I.,PARLIAMENT. UK FINAN INDUS POL/PAR   PARL/PROC
DELIB/GP EX/STRUC PLAN CONTROL...MAJORIT JURID   TOP/EX
PARLIAMENT. PAGE 56 B1133   MGT
  LEGIS

B57

KAPLAN M.A.,SYSTEM AND PROCESS OF INTERNATIONAL   INT/ORG
POLITICS. FUT WOR+45 WOR-45 SOCIETY PLAN BAL/PWR   DIPLOM
ADMIN ATTIT PERSON RIGID/FLEX PWR SOVEREIGN
...DECISION TREND VAL/FREE. PAGE 58 B1168

B57

PARKINSON C.N.,PARKINSON'S LAW. UNIV EX/STRUC PLAN   ADMIN
ATTIT PERSON TIME. PAGE 81 B1634   EXEC
  FINAN
  ECOMETRIC

B57

US HOUSE COMM ON POST OFFICE,MANPOWER UTILIZATION   NAT/G
IN THE FEDERAL GOVERNMENT. USA+45 FORCES WORKER   ADMIN
CREATE PLAN EFFICIENCY UTIL 20 CONGRESS CIVIL/SERV   LABOR
POSTAL/SYS DEPT/DEFEN. PAGE 109 B2193   EX/STRUC

S57

ROBSON W.A.,"TWO-LEVEL GOVERNMENT FOR METROPOLITAN   REGION
AREAS." MUNIC EX/STRUC LEGIS PARTIC REPRESENT   LOC/G
MAJORITY. PAGE 89 B1807   PLAN
  GOV/REL

S57

ROURKE F.E.,"THE POLITICS OF ADMINISTRATIVE   POLICY
ORGANIZATION: A CASE HISTORY." USA+45 LABOR WORKER   ATTIT
PLAN ADMIN TASK EFFICIENCY 20 DEPT/LABOR CONGRESS.   MGT
PAGE 91 B1836   GP/COMP

S57

TAYLOR P.S.,"THE RELATION OF RESEARCH TO   DECISION
LEGISLATIVE AND ADMINISTRATIVE DECISIONS." ELITES   LEGIS
ACT/RES PLAN PROB/SOLV CONFER CHOOSE POLICY.   MGT
PAGE 103 B2089   PWR

B58

LIST OF PUBLICATIONS (PERIODICAL OR AD HOC) ISSUED   BIBLIOG
BY VARIOUS MINISTRIES OF THE GOVERNMENT OF INDIA   NAT/G
(3RD ED.). INDIA ECO/UNDEV PLAN...POLICY MGT 20.   ADMIN
PAGE 2 B0037

B58

AMERICAN SOCIETY PUBLIC ADMIN,STRENGTHENING   ADMIN
MANAGEMENT FOR DEMOCRATIC GOVERNMENT. USA+45 ACADEM   NAT/G
EX/STRUC WORKER PLAN BUDGET CONFER CT/SYS   EXEC
EFFICIENCY ANTHOL. PAGE 4 B0088   MGT

B58

BRIGHT J.R.,AUTOMATION AND MANAGEMENT. INDUS LABOR   AUTOMAT
WORKER OP/RES TEC/DEV INSPECT 20. PAGE 15 B0307   COMPUTER
  PLAN
  MGT

B58

CHEEK G.,ECONOMIC AND SOCIAL IMPLICATIONS OF   BIBLIOG/A
AUTOMATION: A BIBLIOGRAPHIC REVIEW (PAMPHLET).   SOCIETY
USA+45 LG/CO WORKER CREATE PLAN CONTROL ROUTINE   INDUS
PERS/REL EFFICIENCY PRODUC...METH/COMP 20. PAGE 20   AUTOMAT
B0416

B58

CONSERVATIVE POLITICAL CENTRE,A WORLD SECURITY   ORD/FREE
AUTHORITY? WOR+45 CONSTN ELITES FINAN DELIB/GP PLAN   CONSERVE
PROB/SOLV ADMIN CONTROL NUC/PWR GP/REL...IDEA/COMP   FORCES
20. PAGE 23 B0468   ARMS/CONT

B58

DWARKADAS R.,ROLE OF HIGHER CIVIL SERVICE IN INDIA.   ADMIN
INDIA ECO/UNDEV LEGIS PROB/SOLV GP/REL PERS/REL   NAT/G
...POLICY WELF/ST DECISION ORG/CHARTS BIBLIOG 20   ROLE
CIVIL/SERV INTRVN/ECO. PAGE 31 B0637   PLAN

B58

GROSSMAN J.,BIBLIOGRAPHY ON PUBLIC ADMINISTRATION   BIBLIOG
IN LATIN AMERICA. ECO/UNDEV FINAN PLAN BUDGET   L/A+17C
ECO/TAC TARIFFS TAX...STAT 20. PAGE 44 B0893   NAT/G
  ADMIN

B58

INDIAN INST OF PUBLIC ADMIN,IMPROVING CITY   LOC/G
GOVERNMENT. INDIA ECO/UNDEV PLAN BUDGET PARTIC   MUNIC
GP/REL 20. PAGE 53 B1080   PROB/SOLV
  ADMIN

B58

ISLAM R.,INTERNATIONAL ECONOMIC COOPERATION AND THE   INT/ORG
UNITED NATIONS. FINAN PLAN EXEC TASK WAR PEACE   DIPLOM
...SOC METH/CNCPT 20 UN LEAGUE/NAT. PAGE 55 B1105   ADMIN

B58

KINTNER W.R.,ORGANIZING FOR CONFLICT: A PROPOSAL.   USA+45
USSR STRUCT NAT/G LEGIS ADMIN EXEC PEACE ORD/FREE   PLAN
PWR...CONCPT OBS TREND NAT/COMP VAL/FREE COLD/WAR   DIPLOM
20. PAGE 60 B1211

B58

MARCH J.G.,ORGANIZATIONS. USA+45 CREATE OP/RES PLAN   MGT
PROB/SOLV PARTIC ROUTINE RATIONAL ATTIT PERCEPT   PERSON
...DECISION BIBLIOG. PAGE 69 B1397   DRIVE
  CONCPT

B58

REDFORD E.S.,IDEAL AND PRACTICE IN PUBLIC   POLICY
ADMINISTRATION. CONSTN ELITES NAT/G CONSULT   EX/STRUC
DELIB/GP LEAD UTOPIA ATTIT POPULISM...DECISION   PLAN
METH/COMP 20. PAGE 87 B1756   ADMIN

B58

SCOTT D.J.R.,RUSSIAN POLITICAL INSTITUTIONS. RUSSIA   NAT/G
USSR CONSTN AGRI DELIB/GP PLAN EDU/PROP CONTROL   POL/PAR
CHOOSE EFFICIENCY ATTIT MARXISM...BIBLIOG/A 13/20.   ADMIN
PAGE 95 B1919   DECISION

B58

STEWART J.D.,BRITISH PRESSURE GROUPS: THEIR ROLE IN   LOBBY
RELATION TO THE HOUSE OF COMMONS. UK CONSULT   LEGIS
DELIB/GP ADMIN ROUTINE CHOOSE REPRESENT ATTIT ROLE   PLAN
20 HOUSE/CMNS PARLIAMENT. PAGE 101 B2038   PARL/PROC

B58

SWEENEY S.B.,EDUCATION FOR ADMINISTRATIVE CAREERS   EDU/PROP
IN GOVERNMENT SERVICE. USA+45 ACADEM CONSULT CREATE   ADMIN
PLAN CONFER SKILL...TREND IDEA/COMP METH 20   NAT/G
CIVIL/SERV. PAGE 102 B2059   LOC/G

B58

WHITE L.D.,THE REPUBLICAN ERA: 1869-1901, A STUDY   MGT
IN ADMINISTRATIVE HISTORY. USA-45 FINAN PLAN   PWR
NEUTRAL CRIME GP/REL MORAL LAISSEZ PRESIDENT   DELIB/GP
REFORMERS 19 CONGRESS CIVIL/SERV. PAGE 116 B2340   ADMIN

L58

EISENSTADT S.N.,"BUREAUCRACY AND
BUREAUCRATIZATION." WOR+45 ECO/DEV INDUS R+D PLAN
GOV/REL...WELF/ST TREND BIBLIOG/A 20. PAGE 32 B0659

ADMIN
OP/RES
MGT
PHIL/SCI

L58

HAVILAND H.F.,"FOREIGN AID AND THE POLICY PROCESS:
1957." USA+45 FACE/GP POL/PAR VOL/ASSN CHIEF
DELIB/GP ACT/RES LEGIT EXEC GOV/REL ATTIT DRIVE PWR
...POLICY TESTS CONGRESS 20. PAGE 48 B0971

LEGIS
PLAN
FOR/AID

S58

BLAISDELL D.C.,"PRESSURE GROUPS, FOREIGN POLICIES,
AND INTERNATIONAL POLITICS." USA+45 WOR+45 INT/ORG
PLAN DOMIN EDU/PROP LEGIT ADMIN ROUTINE CHOOSE
...DECISION MGT METH/CNCPT CON/ANAL 20. PAGE 12
B0249

PROF/ORG
PWR

S58

ELKIN A.B.,"OEEC-ITS STRUCTURE AND POWERS." EUR+WWI
CONSTN INDUS INT/ORG NAT/G VOL/ASSN DELIB/GP
ACT/RES PLAN ORD/FREE WEALTH...CHARTS ORG/CHARTS
OEEC 20. PAGE 33 B0666

ECO/DEV
EX/STRUC

S58

JORDAN A.,"MILITARY ASSISTANCE AND NATIONAL
POLICY." ASIA FUT USA+45 WOR+45 ECO/DEV ECO/UNDEV
INT/ORG NAT/G PLAN ECO/TAC ROUTINE WEAPON ATTIT
RIGID/FLEX PWR...CONCPT TREND 20. PAGE 57 B1153

FORCES
POLICY
FOR/AID
DIPLOM

B59

BRUNTON R.L.,MANAGEMENT PRACTICES FOR SMALLER
CITIES. USA+45 MUNIC CONSULT PLAN BUDGET PERS/REL
20 CITY/MGT. PAGE 16 B0331

ADMIN
LOC/G
MGT
TOP/EX

B59

CHRISTENSON R.M.,THE BRANNAN PLAN: FARM POLITICS
AND POLICY. USA+45 ECO/DEV CONSULT PLAN PAY GOV/REL
...POLICY 20. PAGE 21 B0429

AGRI
NAT/G
ADMIN
ECO/TAC

B59

COUNCIL OF STATE GOVERNMENTS,STATE GOVERNMENT: AN
ANNOTATED BIBLIOGRAPHY (PAMPHLET). USA+45 LAW AGRI
INDUS WORKER PLAN TAX ADJUST AGE/Y ORD/FREE...HEAL
MGT 20. PAGE 24 B0494

BIBLIOG/A
PROVS
LOC/G
ADMIN

B59

DIEBOLD W. JR.,THE SCHUMAN PLAN: A STUDY IN
ECONOMIC COOPERATION, 1950-1959. EUR+WWI FRANCE
GERMANY USA+45 EXTR/IND CONSULT DELIB/GP PLAN
DIPLOM ECO/TAC INT/TRADE ROUTINE ORD/FREE WEALTH
...METH/CNCPT STAT CONT/OBS INT TIME/SEQ ECSC 20.
PAGE 29 B0591

INT/ORG
REGION

B59

ELLIOTT S.D.,IMPROVING OUR COURTS. LAW EX/STRUC
PLAN PROB/SOLV ADJUD ADMIN TASK CRIME EFFICIENCY
ORD/FREE 20. PAGE 33 B0669

CT/SYS
JURID
GOV/REL
NAT/G

B59

INDIAN INSTITUTE PUBLIC ADMIN,MORALE IN THE PUBLIC
SERVICES: REPORT OF A CONFERENCE JAN., 3-4, 1959.
INDIA S/ASIA ECO/UNDEV PROVS PLAN EDU/PROP CONFER
GOV/REL EFFICIENCY DRIVE ROLE 20 CIVIL/SERV.
PAGE 53 B1082

HAPPINESS
ADMIN
WORKER
INGP/REL

B59

JANOWITZ M.,SOCIOLOGY AND THE MILITARY
ESTABLISHMENT. USA+45 WOR+45 CULTURE SOCIETY
PROF/ORG CONSULT EX/STRUC PLAN TEC/DEV DIPLOM DOMIN
COERCE DRIVE RIGID/FLEX ORD/FREE PWR SKILL COLD/WAR
20. PAGE 55 B1121

FORCES
SOC

B59

PARK R.L.,LEADERSHIP AND POLITICAL INSTITUTIONS IN
INDIA. S/ASIA CULTURE ECO/UNDEV LOC/G MUNIC PROVS
LEGIS PLAN ADMIN LEAD ORD/FREE WEALTH...GEOG SOC
BIOG TOT/POP VAL/FREE 20. PAGE 81 B1633

NAT/G
EXEC
INDIA

B59

SCHURZ W.L.,AMERICAN FOREIGN AFFAIRS: A GUIDE TO
INTERNATIONAL AFFAIRS. USA+45 WOR+45 NAT/G
FORCES LEGIS TOP/EX PLAN EDU/PROP LEGIT ADMIN
ROUTINE ATTIT ORD/FREE PWR...SOC CONCPT STAT
SAMP/SIZ CHARTS STERTYP 20. PAGE 95 B1910

INT/ORG
SOCIETY
DIPLOM

B59

US HOUSE COMM GOVT OPERATIONS,UNITED STATES AID
OPERATIONS IN LAOS. LAOS USA+45 PLAN INSPECT
HOUSE/REP. PAGE 108 B2190

FOR/AID
ADMIN
FORCES
ECO/UNDEV

B59

US PRES COMM STUDY MIL ASSIST,COMPOSITE REPORT.
USA+45 ECO/UNDEV PLAN BUDGET DIPLOM EFFICIENCY
...POLICY MGT 20. PAGE 109 B2208

FOR/AID
FORCES
WEAPON
ORD/FREE

B59

WELTON H.,THE THIRD WORLD WAR; TRADE AND INDUSTRY,
THE NEW BATTLEGROUND. WOR+45 ECO/DEV INDUS MARKET
TASK...MGT IDEA/COMP COLD/WAR. PAGE 115 B2321

INT/TRADE
PLAN
DIPLOM

B59

YALE UNIV BUR OF HIGHWAY TRAF,URBAN TRANSPORTATION
ADMINISTRATION. FUT USA+45 CONSTRUC ACT/RES BUDGET
...CENSUS 20 PUB/TRANS. PAGE 118 B2388

ADMIN
DIST/IND
LOC/G
PLAN

B59

YANG C.K.,A CHINESE VILLAGE IN EARLY COMMUNIST
TRANSITION. ECO/UNDEV AGRI FAM KIN MUNIC FORCES
PLAN ECO/TAC DOMIN EDU/PROP ATTIT DRIVE PWR RESPECT
...SOC CONCPT METH/CNCPT OBS RECORD CON/ANAL CHARTS
WORK 20. PAGE 118 B2389

ASIA
ROUTINE
SOCISM

S59

JANOWITZ M.,"CHANGING PATTERNS OF ORGANIZATIONAL
AUTHORITY: THE MILITARY ESTABLISHMENT" (BMR)"
USA+45 ELITES STRUCT EX/STRUC PLAN DOMIN AUTOMAT
NUC/PWR WEAPON 20. PAGE 55 B1122

FORCES
AUTHORIT
ADMIN
TEC/DEV

S59

JEWELL M.R.,"THE SENATE REPUBLICAN POLICY COMMITTEE
AND FOREIGN POLICY." PLAN ADMIN CONTROL LEAD LOBBY
EFFICIENCY PRESIDENT 20 REPUBLICAN. PAGE 56 B1139

POL/PAR
NAT/G
DELIB/GP
POLICY

S59

LASSWELL H.D.,"UNIVERSALITY IN PERSPECTIVE." FUT
UNIV SOCIETY CONSULT TOP/EX PLAN EDU/PROP ADJUD
ROUTINE ARMS/CONT COERCE PEACE ATTIT PERSON
ALL/VALS. PAGE 63 B1271

INT/ORG
JURID
TOTALISM

S59

STINCHCOMBE A.L.,"BUREAUCRATIC AND CRAFT
ADMINISTRATION OF PRODUCTION: A COMPARATIVE STUDY"
(BMR)" USA+45 STRUCT EX/STRUC ECO/TAC GP/REL
...CLASSIF GP/COMP IDEA/COMP GEN/LAWS 20 WEBER/MAX.
PAGE 101 B2039

CONSTRUC
PROC/MFG
ADMIN
PLAN

S59

ZAUBERMAN A.,"SOVIET BLOC ECONOMIC INTEGRATION."
COM CULTURE INTELL ECO/DEV INDUS TOP/EX ACT/RES
PLAN ECO/TAC INT/TRADE ROUTINE CHOOSE ATTIT
...TIME/SEQ 20. PAGE 119 B2399

MARKET
INT/ORG
USSR
TOTALISM

B60

BOULDING K.E.,LINEAR PROGRAMMING AND THE THEORY OF
THE FIRM. ACT/RES PLAN...MGT MATH. PAGE 14 B0283

LG/CO
NEW/IDEA
COMPUTER

B60

CAMPBELL R.W.,SOVIET ECONOMIC POWER. COM USA+45
DIST/IND MARKET TOP/EX ACT/RES CAP/ISM ECO/TAC
DOMIN EDU/PROP ADMIN ROUTINE DRIVE...MATH TIME/SEQ
CHARTS WORK 20. PAGE 18 B0371

ECO/DEV
PLAN
SOCISM
USSR

B60

DRAPER T.,AMERICAN COMMUNISM AND SOVIET RUSSIA.
EUR+WWI USA+45 USSR INTELL AGRI COM/IND FINAN INDUS
LABOR PROF/ORG VOL/ASSN PLAN TEC/DEV DOMIN EDU/PROP
ADMIN COERCE REV PERSON PWR...POLICY CONCPT MYTH
19/20. PAGE 30 B0617

COM
POL/PAR

B60

GILMORE D.R.,DEVELOPING THE "LITTLE" ECONOMIES.
USA+45 FINAN LG/CO PROF/ORG VOL/ASSN CREATE ADMIN.
PAGE 40 B0801

ECO/TAC
LOC/G
PROVS
PLAN

B60

GRANICK D.,THE RED EXECUTIVE. COM USA+45 SOCIETY
ECO/DEV INDUS NAT/G POL/PAR EX/STRUC PLAN ECO/TAC
EDU/PROP ADMIN EXEC ATTIT DRIVE...GP/COMP 20.
PAGE 42 B0851

PWR
STRATA
USSR
ELITES

B60

HEAP D.,AN OUTLINE OF PLANNING LAW (3RD ED.). UK
LAW PROB/SOLV ADMIN CONTROL 20. PAGE 49 B0983

MUNIC
PLAN
JURID
LOC/G

B60

HYDE L.K.G.,THE US AND THE UN. WOR+45 STRUCT
ECO/DEV ECO/UNDEV NAT/G ACT/RES PLAN DIPLOM
EDU/PROP ADMIN ALL/VALS...CONCPT TIME/SEQ GEN/LAWS
UN VAL/FREE 20. PAGE 53 B1070

USA+45
INT/ORG
FOR/AID

B60

JONES V.,METROPOLITAN COMMUNITIES: A BIBLIOGRAPHY
WITH SPECIAL EMPHASIS UPON GOVERNMENT AND POLITICS,
1955-1957. STRUCT ECO/DEV FINAN FORCES PLAN
PROB/SOLV RECEIVE EDU/PROP CT/SYS...GEOG HEAL 20.
PAGE 57 B1152

BIBLIOG
LOC/G
MUNIC
ADMIN

B60

KINGSTON-MCCLOUG E.,DEFENSE; POLICY AND STRATEGY.
UK SEA AIR TEC/DEV DIPLOM ADMIN LEAD WAR ORD/FREE
...CHARTS 20. PAGE 60 B1209

FORCES
PLAN
POLICY
DECISION

B60

LENCZOWSKI G.,OIL AND STATE IN THE MIDDLE EAST. FUT
IRAN LAW ECO/UNDEV EXTR/IND NAT/G TOP/EX PLAN
TEC/DEV ECO/TAC LEGIT ADMIN COERCE ATTIT ALL/VALS
PWR...CHARTS 20. PAGE 64 B1288

ISLAM
INDUS
NAT/LISM

B60

LERNER A.P.,THE ECONOMICS OF CONTROL. USA+45
ECO/UNDEV INT/ORG ACT/RES PLAN CAP/ISM INT/TRADE
ATTIT WEALTH...SOC MATH STAT GEN/LAWS INDEX 20.
PAGE 64 B1295

ECO/DEV
ROUTINE
ECO/TAC
SOCISM

B60

LEYDER J.,BIBLIOGRAPHIE DE L'ENSEIGNEMENT SUPERIEUR
ET DE LA RECHERCHE SCIENTIFIQUE EN AFRIQUE
INTERTROPICALE (2 VOLS.). AFR CULTURE ECO/UNDEV
AGRI PLAN EDU/PROP ADMIN COLONIAL...GEOG SOC/INTEG
20 NEGRO. PAGE 65 B1309

BIBLIOG/A
ACT/RES
ACADEM
R+D

B60

LINDSAY K.,EUROPEAN ASSEMBLIES: THE EXPERIMENTAL

VOL/ASSN

PERIOD 1949-1959. EUR+WWI ECO/DEV NAT/G POL/PAR INT/ORG
LEGIS TOP/EX ACT/RES PLAN ECO/TAC DOMIN LEGIT REGION
ROUTINE ATTIT DRIVE ORD/FREE PWR SKILL...SOC CONCPT
TREND CHARTS GEN/LAWS VAL/FREE. PAGE 65 B1315

B60
MEEHAN E.J.,THE BRITISH LEFT WING AND FOREIGN ACT/RES
POLICY: A STUDY OF THE INFLUENCE OF IDEOLOGY. FUT ATTIT
UK UNIV WOR+45 INTELL TOP/EX PLAN ADMIN ROUTINE DIPLOM
DRIVE...OBS TIME/SEQ GEN/LAWS PARLIAMENT 20.
PAGE 72 B1461

B60
PENNSYLVANIA ECONOMY LEAGUE.URBAN RENEWAL IMPACT PLAN
STUDY: ADMINISTRATIVE-LEGAL-FISCAL. USA+45 FINAN BUDGET
LOC/G NEIGH ADMIN EFFICIENCY...CENSUS CHARTS 20 MUNIC
PENNSYLVAN. PAGE 82 B1652 ADJUD

B60
PFIFFNER J.M.,PUBLIC ADMINISTRATION. USA+45 FINAN ADMIN
WORKER PLAN PROB/SOLV ADJUD CONTROL EXEC...T 20. NAT/G
PAGE 82 B1666 LOC/G
MGT

B60
PHILLIPS J.C.,MUNICIPAL GOVERNMENT AND MUNIC
ADMINISTRATION IN AMERICA. USA+45 LAW CONSTN FINAN GOV/REL
FORCES PLAN RECEIVE OWN ORD/FREE 20 CIVIL/LIB. LOC/G
PAGE 83 B1669 ADMIN

B60
POOLEY B.J.,THE EVOLUTION OF BRITISH PLANNING PLAN
LEGISLATION. UK ECO/DEV LOC/G CONSULT DELIB/GP MUNIC
ADMIN 20 URBAN/RNWL. PAGE 84 B1691 LEGIS
PROB/SOLV

B60
RAO V.K.R.,INTERNATIONAL AID FOR ECONOMIC FOR/AID
DEVELOPMENT - POSSIBILITIES AND LIMITATIONS. FINAN DIPLOM
PLAN TEC/DEV ADMIN TASK EFFICIENCY...POLICY SOC INT/ORG
METH/CNCPT CHARTS 20 UN. PAGE 86 B1734 ECO/UNDEV

B60
ROEPKE W.,A HUMANE ECONOMY: THE SOCIAL FRAMEWORK OF DRIVE
THE FREE MARKET. FUT USSR WOR+45 CULTURE SOCIETY EDU/PROP
ECO/DEV PLAN ECO/TAC ADMIN ATTIT PERSON RIGID/FLEX CAP/ISM
SUPEGO MORAL WEALTH SOCISM...POLICY OLD/LIB CONCPT
TREND GEN/LAWS 20. PAGE 90 B1811

B60
SAYRE W.S.,GOVERNING NEW YORK CITY; POLITICS IN THE MUNIC
METROPOLIS. POL/PAR CHIEF DELIB/GP LEGIS PLAN ADMIN
CT/SYS LEAD PARTIC CHOOSE...DECISION CHARTS BIBLIOG PROB/SOLV
20 NEWYORK/C BUREAUCRCY. PAGE 93 B1875

B60
SCHUBERT G.,THE PUBLIC INTEREST. USA+45 CONSULT POLICY
PLAN PROB/SOLV ADJUD ADMIN GP/REL PWR ALL/IDEOS 20. DELIB/GP
PAGE 94 B1903 REPRESENT
POL/PAR

B60
STANFORD RESEARCH INSTITUTE.AFRICAN DEVELOPMENT: A FOR/AID
TEST FOR INTERNATIONAL COOPERATION. AFR USA+45 ECO/UNDEV
WOR+45 FINAN INT/ORG PLAN PROB/SOLV ECO/TAC ATTIT
INT/TRADE ADMIN...CHARTS 20. PAGE 100 B2018 DIPLOM

B60
WEBSTER J.A.,A GENERAL STUDY OF THE DEPARTMENT OF ORD/FREE
DEFENSE INTERNAL SECURITY PROGRAM. USA+45 WORKER PLAN
TEC/DEV ADJUD CONTROL CT/SYS EXEC GOV/REL COST ADMIN
...POLICY DECISION MGT 20 DEPT/DEFEN SUPREME/CT. NAT/G
PAGE 114 B2307

L60
BRENNAN D.G.,"SETTING AND GOALS OF ARMS CONTROL." FORCES
FUT USA+45 USSR WOR+45 INTELL INT/ORG NAT/G COERCE
VOL/ASSN CONSULT PLAN DIPLOM ECO/TAC ADMIN KNOWL ARMS/CONT
PWR...POLICY CONCPT TREND COLD/WAR 20. PAGE 15 DETER
B0305

L60
DEAN A.W.,"SECOND GENEVA CONFERENCE OF THE LAW OF INT/ORG
THE SEA: THE FIGHT FOR FREEDOM OF THE SEAS." FUT JURID
USA+45 USSR WOR+45 WOR-45 SEA CONSTN STRUCT PLAN INT/LAW
INT/TRADE ADJUD ADMIN ORD/FREE...DECISION RECORD
TREND GEN/LAWS 20 TREATY. PAGE 28 B0564

L60
STEIN E.,"LEGAL REMEDIES OF ENTERPRISES IN THE MARKET
EUROPEAN ECONOMIC COMMUNITY." EUR+WWI FUT ECO/DEV ADJUD
INDUS PLAN ECO/TAC ADMIN PWR...MGT MATH STAT TREND
CON/ANAL EEC 20. PAGE 100 B2026

S60
BAVELAS A.,"LEADERSHIP: MAN AND FUNCTION." WORKER LEAD
CREATE PLAN CONTROL PERS/REL PERSON PWR...MGT 20. ADMIN
PAGE 10 B0199 ROUTINE
ROLE

S60
EMERSON R.,"THE EROSION OF DEMOCRACY." AFR FUT LAW S/ASIA
CULTURE INTELL SOCIETY ECO/UNDEV FAM LOC/G NAT/G POL/PAR
FORCES PLAN TEC/DEV ECO/TAC ADMIN CT/SYS ATTIT
ORD/FREE PWR...SOCIALIST SOC CONCPT STAND/INT
TIME/SEQ WORK 20. PAGE 33 B0671

S60
FRANKEL S.H.,"ECONOMIC ASPECTS OF POLITICAL NAT/G
INDEPENDENCE IN AFRICA." AFR FUT SOCIETY ECO/UNDEV FOR/AID
COM/IND FINAN LEGIS PLAN TEC/DEV CAP/ISM ECO/TAC
INT/TRADE ADMIN ATTIT DRIVE RIGID/FLEX PWR WEALTH
...MGT NEW/IDEA MATH TIME/SEQ VAL/FREE 20. PAGE 37

B0751

S60
GARNICK D.H.,"ON THE ECONOMIC FEASIBILITY OF A MARKET
MIDDLE EASTERN COMMON MARKET." AFR ISLAM CULTURE INT/TRADE
INDUS NAT/G PLAN TEC/DEV ECO/TAC ADMIN ATTIT DRIVE
RIGID/FLEX...PLURIST STAT TREND GEN/LAWS 20.
PAGE 39 B0784

S60
GROSSMAN G.,"SOVIET GROWTH: ROUTINE, INERTIA, AND POL/PAR
PRESSURE." COM STRATA NAT/G DELIB/GP PLAN TEC/DEV ECO/DEV
ECO/TAC EDU/PROP ADMIN ROUTINE DRIVE WEALTH USSR
COLD/WAR 20. PAGE 44 B0891

S60
HALPERIN M.H.,"IS THE SENATE'S FOREIGN RELATIONS PLAN
RESEARCH WORTHWHILE." COM FUT USA+45 USSR ACT/RES DIPLOM
BAL/PWR EDU/PROP ADMIN ALL/VALS CONGRESS VAL/FREE
20 COLD/WAR. PAGE 46 B0927

S60
HERRERA F.,"THE INTER-AMERICAN DEVELOPMENT BANK." L/A+17C
USA+45 ECO/UNDEV INT/ORG CONSULT DELIB/GP PLAN FOR/AID
ECO/TAC INT/TRADE ROUTINE WEALTH...STAT 20. PAGE 49 REGION
B0994

S60
HERZ J.H.,"EAST GERMANY: PROGRESS AND PROSPECTS." POL/PAR
COM AGRI FINAN INDUS LOC/G NAT/G FORCES PLAN STRUCT
TEC/DEV DOMIN ADMIN COERCE DRIVE PERCEPT RIGID/FLEX GERMANY
MORAL ORD/FREE PWR...MARXIST PSY SOC RECORD STERTYP
WORK. PAGE 49 B0997

S60
HUTCHINSON C.E.,"AN INSTITUTE FOR NATIONAL SECURITY POLICY
AFFAIRS." USA+45 R+D NAT/G CONSULT TOP/EX ACT/RES METH/CNCPT
CREATE PLAN TEC/DEV EDU/PROP ROUTINE NUC/PWR ATTIT ELITES
ORD/FREE PWR...DECISION MGT PHIL/SCI CONCPT RECORD DIPLOM
GEN/LAWS GEN/METH 20. PAGE 53 B1068

S60
MODELSKI G.,"AUSTRALIA AND SEATO." S/ASIA USA+45 INT/ORG
CULTURE ECO/DEV NAT/G PLAN DIPLOM ADMIN ACT/RES
ROUTINE ATTIT SKILL...MGT TIME/SEQ AUSTRAL 20
SEATO. PAGE 74 B1493

S60
MORA J.A.,"THE ORGANIZATION OF AMERICAN STATES." L/A+17C
USA+45 LAW ECO/UNDEV VOL/ASSN DELIB/GP PLAN BAL/PWR INT/ORG
EDU/PROP ADMIN DRIVE RIGID/FLEX ORD/FREE WEALTH REGION
...TIME/SEQ GEN/LAWS OAS 20. PAGE 75 B1518

S60
NELSON R.H.,"LEGISLATIVE PARTICIPATION IN THE LEGIS
TREATY AND AGREEMENT MAKING PROCESS." CONSTN PEACE
POL/PAR PLAN EXEC PWR FAO UN CONGRESS. PAGE 78 DECISION
B1569 DIPLOM

S60
NORTH R.C.,"DIE DISKREPANZ ZWISCHEN REALITAT UND SOCIETY
WUNSCHBILD ALS INNENPOLITISCHER FAKTOR." ASIA ECO/TAC
CHINA/COM COM FUT ECO/UNDEV NAT/G PLAN DOMIN ADMIN
COERCE PERCEPT...SOC MYTH GEN/METH WORK TOT/POP 20.
PAGE 79 B1589

S60
SCHATZ S.P.,"THE INFLENCE OF PLANNING ON ECO/UNDEV
DEVELOPMENT: THE NIGERIAN EXPERIENCE." AFR FUT PLAN
FINAN INDUS NAT/G EX/STRUC ECO/TAC ADMIN ATTIT NIGERIA
PERCEPT ORD/FREE PWR...MATH TREND CON/ANAL SIMUL
VAL/FREE 20. PAGE 93 B1883

S60
SMIGEL E.O.,"THE IMPACT OF RECRUITMENT ON THE LG/CO
ORGANIZATION OF THE LARGE LAW FIRM" (BMR)" USA+45 ADMIN
STRUCT CONSULT PLAN GP/REL EFFICIENCY JURID. LAW
PAGE 98 B1979 WORKER

S60
THOMPSON K.W.,"MORAL PURPOSE IN FOREIGN POLICY: MORAL
REALITIES AND ILLUSIONS." WOR+45 WOR-45 LAW CULTURE JURID
SOCIETY INT/ORG PLAN ADJUD ADMIN COERCE RIGID/FLEX DIPLOM
SUPEGO KNOWL ORD/FREE PWR...SOC TREND SOC/EXP
TOT/POP 20. PAGE 104 B2104

B61
CHAPPLE E.D.,THE MEASURE OF MANAGEMENT. USA+45 MGT
WORKER ADMIN GP/REL EFFICIENCY...DECISION OP/RES
ORG/CHARTS SIMUL 20. PAGE 20 B0412 PLAN
METH/CNCPT

B61
CONFREY E.A.,ADMINISTRATION OF COMMUNITY HEALTH HEAL
SERVICES. USA+45 R+D PUB/INST DELIB/GP PLAN BUDGET ADMIN
ROUTINE AGE/C HEALTH...MGT SOC/WK METH/COMP 20. MUNIC
PAGE 23 B0461 BIO/SOC

B61
DRURY J.W.,THE GOVERNMENT OF KANSAS. USA+45 AGRI PROVS
INDUS CHIEF LEGIS WORKER PLAN BUDGET GIVE CT/SYS CONSTN
GOV/REL...T 20 KANSAS GOVERNOR CITY/MGT. PAGE 31 ADMIN
B0621 LOC/G

B61
FREYRE G.,THE PORTUGUESE AND THE TROPICS. L/A+17C COLONIAL
PORTUGAL SOCIETY PERF/ART ADMIN TASK GP/REL METH
...ART/METH CONCPT SOC/INTEG 20. PAGE 37 B0754 PLAN
CULTURE

B61
FRIEDMANN W.G.,JOINT INTERNATIONAL BUSINESS ECO/UNDEV
VENTURES. ASIA ISLAM L/A+17C ECO/DEV DIST/IND FINAN INT/TRADE
PROC/MFG FACE/GP LG/CO NAT/G VOL/ASSN CONSULT

EX/STRUC PLAN ADMIN ROUTINE WEALTH...OLD/LIB WORK
20. PAGE 37 B0760

B61
GORDON W.J.J.,SYNECTICS; THE DEVELOPMENT OF
CREATIVE CAPACITY. USA+45 PLAN TEC/DEV KNOWL WEALTH
...DECISION MGT 20. PAGE 41 B0832
CREATE
PROB/SOLV
ACT/RES
TOP/EX

B61
GRIFFITH E.S.,CONGRESS: ITS CONTEMPORARY ROLE.
CONSTN POL/PAR CHIEF PLAN BUDGET DIPLOM CONFER
ADMIN LOBBY...DECISION CONGRESS. PAGE 43 B0878
PARL/PROC
EX/STRUC
TOP/EX
LEGIS

B61
HARRISON S.,INDIA AND THE UNITED STATES. FUT S/ASIA
USA+45 WOR+45 INTELL ECO/DEV ECO/UNDEV AGRI INDUS
INT/ORG NAT/G CONSULT EX/STRUC TOP/EX PLAN ECO/TAC
NEUTRAL ALL/VALS...MGT TOT/POP 20. PAGE 47 B0956
DELIB/GP
ACT/RES
FOR/AID
INDIA

B61
HART H.C.,ADMINISTRATIVE ASPECTS OF RIVER VALLEY
DEVELOPMENT. INDIA USA+45 INDUS CONTROL EFFICIENCY
OPTIMAL PRODUC 20 TVA. PAGE 47 B0957
ADMIN
PLAN
METH/COMP
AGRI

B61
HORVATH B.,THE CHARACTERISTICS OF YUGOSLAV ECONOMIC
DEVELOPMENT. COM ECO/UNDEV AGRI INDUS PLAN CAP/ISM
ECO/TAC ROUTINE WEALTH...SOCIALIST STAT CHARTS
STERTYP WORK 20. PAGE 52 B1045
ACT/RES
YUGOSLAVIA

B61
HOUN F.W.,TO CHANGE A NATION; PROPAGANDA AND
INDOCTRINATION IN COMMUNIST CHINA. CHINA/COM COM
ACT/RES PLAN PRESS ADMIN FEEDBACK CENTRAL
EFFICIENCY ATTIT...PSY SOC 20. PAGE 52 B1048
DOMIN
EDU/PROP
TOTALISM
MARXISM

B61
JACOBS J.,THE DEATH AND LIFE OF GREAT AMERICAN
CITIES. USA+45 SOCIETY DIST/IND CREATE PROB/SOLV
ADMIN...GEOG SOC CENSUS 20 URBAN/RNWL. PAGE 55
B1113
MUNIC
PLAN
ADJUST
HABITAT

B61
LAHAYE R.,LES ENTREPRISES PUBLIQUES AU MAROC.
FRANCE MOROCCO LAW DIST/IND EXTR/IND FINAN CONSULT
PLAN TEC/DEV ADMIN AGREE CONTROL OWN...POLICY 20.
PAGE 62 B1250
NAT/G
INDUS
ECO/UNDEV
ECO/TAC

B61
LEE R.R.,ENGINEERING-ECONOMIC PLANNING
MISCELLANEOUS SUBJECTS: A SELECTED BIBLIOGRAPHY
(MIMEOGRAPHED). FINAN LOC/G MUNIC NEIGH ADMIN
CONTROL INGP/REL HABITAT...GEOG MGT SOC/WK 20
RESOURCE/N. PAGE 63 B1280
BIBLIOG/A
PLAN
REGION

B61
MACMAHON A.W.,DELEGATION AND AUTONOMY. INDIA STRUCT
LEGIS BARGAIN BUDGET ECO/TAC LEGIT EXEC REPRESENT
GOV/REL CENTRAL DEMAND EFFICIENCY PRODUC. PAGE 68
B1373
ADMIN
PLAN
FEDERAL

B61
MARX K.,THE COMMUNIST MANIFESTO. IN (MENDEL A.
ESSENTIAL WORKS OF MARXISM. NEW YORK: BANTAM. FUT
MOD/EUR CULTURE ECO/DEV ECO/UNDEV AGRI FINAN INDUS
MARKET PROC/MFG LABOR MUNIC POL/PAR CONSULT FORCES
CREATE PLAN ADMIN ATTIT DRIVE RIGID/FLEX ORD/FREE
PWR RESPECT MARX/KARL WORK. PAGE 70 B1421
COM
NEW/IDEA
CAP/ISM
REV

B61
MAYNE A.,DESIGNING AND ADMINISTERING A REGIONAL
ECONOMIC DEVELOPMENT PLAN WITH SPECIFIC REFERENCE
TO PUERTO RICO (PAMPHLET). PUERT/RICO SOCIETY NAT/G
DELIB/GP REGION...DECISION 20. PAGE 71 B1435
ECO/UNDEV
PLAN
CREATE
ADMIN

B61
NOVE A.,THE SOVIET ECONOMY. USSR ECO/DEV FINAN
NAT/G ECO/TAC PRICE ADMIN EFFICIENCY MARXISM
...TREND BIBLIOG 20. PAGE 79 B1594
PLAN
PRODUC
POLICY

B61
SHARP W.R.,FIELD ADMINISTRATION IN THE UNITED
NATION SYSTEM: THE CONDUCT OF INTERNATIONAL
ECONOMIC AND SOCIAL PROGRAMS. FUT WOR+45 CONSTN
SOCIETY ECO/UNDEV R+D DELIB/GP ACT/RES PLAN TEC/DEV
EDU/PROP EXEC ROUTINE HEALTH WEALTH...HUM CONCPT
CHARTS METH ILO UNESCO VAL/FREE UN 20. PAGE 96
B1939
INT/ORG
CONSULT

B61
SINGER J.D.,FINANCING INTERNATIONAL ORGANIZATION:
THE UNITED NATIONS BUDGET PROCESS. WOR+45 FINAN
ACT/RES CREATE PLAN BUDGET ECO/TAC ADMIN ROUTINE
ATTIT KNOWL...DECISION METH/CNCPT TIME/SEQ UN 20.
PAGE 97 B1964
INT/ORG
MGT

S61
ALGER C.F.,"NON-RESOLUTION CONSEQUENCES OF THE
UNITED NATIONS AND THEIR EFFECT ON INTERNATIONAL
CONFLICT." WOR+45 CONSTN ECO/DEV NAT/G CONSULT
DELIB/GP TOP/EX ACT/RES PLAN DIPLOM EDU/PROP
ROUTINE ATTIT ALL/VALS...INT/LAW TOT/POP UN 20.
PAGE 4 B0075
INT/ORG
DRIVE
BAL/PWR

S61
ANGLIN D.,"UNITED STATES OPPOSITION TO CANADIAN
MEMBERSHIP IN THE PAN AMERICAN UNION: A CANADIAN
VIEW." L/A+17C UK USA+45 VOL/ASSN DELIB/GP EX/STRUC
PLAN DIPLOM DOMIN REGION ATTIT RIGID/FLEX PWR
...RELATIV CONCPT STERTYP CMN/WLTH OAS 20. PAGE 5
INT/ORG
CANADA

B0112

S61
CARLETON W.G.,"AMERICAN FOREIGN POLICY: MYTHS AND
REALITIES." FUT USA+45 WOR+45 ECO/UNDEV INT/ORG
EX/STRUC ARMS/CONT NUC/PWR WAR ATTIT...POLICY
CONCPT CONT/OBS GEN/METH COLD/WAR TOT/POP 20.
PAGE 19 B0378
PLAN
MYTH
DIPLOM

S61
DYKMAN J.W.,"REVIEW ARTICLE* PLANNING AND DECISION
THEORY." ELITES LOC/G MUNIC CONSULT ADMIN...POLICY
MGT. PAGE 31 B0640
DECISION
PLAN
RATIONAL

S61
HALPERIN M.H.,"THE GAITHER COMMITTEE AND THE POLICY
PROCESS." USA+45 NAT/G TOP/EX ACT/RES LEGIT ADMIN
BAL/PAY PERCEPT...CONCPT TOT/POP 20. PAGE 46 B0928
PLAN
POLICY
NUC/PWR
DELIB/GP

S61
JACKSON E.,"CONSTITUTIONAL DEVELOPMENTS OF THE
UNITED NATIONS: THE GROWTH OF ITS EXECUTIVE
CAPACITY." FUT WOR+45 CONSTN STRUCT ACT/RES PLAN
ALL/VALS...NEW/IDEA OBS COLD/WAR UN 20. PAGE 55
B1106
INT/ORG
EXEC

S61
LANFALUSSY A.,"EUROPE'S PROGRESS: DUE TO COMMON
MARKET." EUR+WWI ECO/DEV DELIB/GP PLAN ECO/TAC
ROUTINE WEALTH...GEOG TREND EEC 20. PAGE 62 B1257
INT/ORG
MARKET

S61
NOVE A.,"THE SOVIET MODEL AND UNDERDEVELOPED
COUNTRIES." COM FUT USSR WOR+45 CULTURE ECO/DEV
POL/PAR FOR/AID EDU/PROP ADMIN MORAL WEALTH
...POLICY RECORD HIST/WRIT 20. PAGE 79 B1593
ECO/UNDEV
PLAN

S61
TAUBENFELD H.J.,"OUTER SPACE--PAST POLITICS AND
FUTURE POLICY." FUT USA+45 USA-45 WOR+45 AIR INTELL
STRUCT ECO/DEV NAT/G TOP/EX ACT/RES ADMIN ROUTINE
NUC/PWR ATTIT DRIVE...CONCPT TIME/SEQ TREND TOT/POP
20. PAGE 103 B2083
PLAN
SPACE
INT/ORG

S61
TOMASIC D.,"POLITICAL LEADERSHIP IN CONTEMPORARY
POLAND." COM EUR+WWI GERMANY NAT/G POL/PAR SECT
DELIB/GP PLAN ECO/TAC DOMIN EDU/PROP PWR MARXISM
...MARXIST GEOG MGT CONCPT TIME/SEQ STERTYP 20.
PAGE 105 B2114
SOCIETY
ROUTINE
USSR
POLAND

B62
ARCO EDITORIAL BOARD,PUBLIC MANAGEMENT AND
ADMINISTRATION. PLAN BUDGET WRITING CONTROL ROUTINE
...TESTS CHARTS METH T 20. PAGE 6 B0125
MGT
ADMIN
NAT/G
LOC/G

B62
ARGYRIS C.,INTERPERSONAL COMPETENCE AND
ORGANIZATIONAL EFFECTIVENESS. CREATE PLAN PROB/SOLV
EDU/PROP INGP/REL PERS/REL PRODUC...OBS INT SIMUL
20. PAGE 6 B0131
EX/STRUC
ADMIN
CONSULT
EFFICIENCY

B62
BAILEY S.D.,THE SECRETARIAT OF THE UNITED NATIONS.
FUT WOR+45 DELIB/GP PLAN BAL/PWR DOMIN EDU/PROP
ADMIN PEACE ATTIT PWR...DECISION CONCPT TREND
CON/ANAL CHARTS UN VAL/FREE COLD/WAR 20. PAGE 8
B0162
INT/ORG
EXEC
DIPLOM

B62
CAIRNCROSS A.K.,FACTORS IN ECONOMIC DEVELOPMENT.
WOR+45 ECO/UNDEV INDUS R+D LG/CO NAT/G EX/STRUC
PLAN TEC/DEV ECO/TAC ATTIT HEALTH KNOWL PWR WEALTH
...TIME/SEQ GEN/LAWS TOT/POP VAL/FREE 20. PAGE 18
B0363
MARKET
ECO/DEV

B62
CHANDLER A.D.,STRATEGY AND STRUCTURE: CHAPTERS IN
THE HISTORY OF THE INDUSTRIAL ENTERPRISE. USA+45
USA-45 ECO/DEV EX/STRUC ECO/TAC EXEC...DECISION 20.
PAGE 20 B0403
LG/CO
PLAN
ADMIN
FINAN

B62
DIMOCK M.E.,THE NEW AMERICAN POLITICAL ECONOMY: A
SYNTHESIS OF POLITICS AND ECONOMICS. USA+45 FINAN
LG/CO PLAN ADMIN REGION GP/REL CENTRAL MORAL 20.
PAGE 29 B0598
FEDERAL
ECO/TAC
NAT/G
PARTIC

B62
DUCKWORTH W.E.,A GUIDE TO OPERATIONAL RESEARCH.
INDUS PLAN PROB/SOLV EXEC EFFICIENCY PRODUC KNOWL
...MGT MATH STAT SIMUL METH 20 MONTECARLO. PAGE 31
B0624
OP/RES
GAME
DECISION
ADMIN

B62
FOSS P.O.,REORGANIZATION AND REASSIGNMENT IN THE
CALIFORNIA HIGHWAY PATROL (PAMPHLET). USA+45 STRUCT
WORKER EDU/PROP CONTROL COERCE INGP/REL ORD/FREE
PWR...DECISION 20 CALIFORNIA. PAGE 37 B0744
FORCES
ADMIN
PROVS
PLAN

B62
GOVERNORS CONF STATE PLANNING,STATE PLANNING: A
POLICY STATEMENT (PAMPHLET). USA+45 LOC/G NAT/G
DELIB/GP LEGIS EXEC 20 GOVERNOR. PAGE 42 B0847
GOV/REL
PLAN
ADMIN
PROVS

B62
GRANICK D.,THE EUROPEAN EXECUTIVE. BELGIUM FRANCE
GERMANY/W UK INDUS LABOR LG/CO EX/STRUC PLAN
TEC/DEV CAP/ISM COST DEMAND...POLICY CHARTS 20.
PAGE 42 B0852
MGT
ECO/DEV
ECO/TAC
EXEC

B62
INST TRAINING MUNICIPAL ADMIN,MUNICIPAL FINANCE   MUNIC
ADMINISTRATION (6TH ED.). USA+45 ELITES ECO/DEV   ADMIN
LEGIS PLAN BUDGET TAX GP/REL BAL/PAY COST...POLICY   FINAN
20 CITY/MGT. PAGE 54 B1089   LOC/G
                                                          B62
KARNJAHAPRAKORN C.,MUNICIPAL GOVERNMENT IN THAILAND LOC/G
AS AN INSTITUTION AND PROCESS OF SELF-GOVERNMENT.   MUNIC
THAILAND CULTURE FINAN EX/STRUC LEGIS PLAN CONTROL   ORD/FREE
GOV/REL EFFICIENCY ATTIT...POLICY 20. PAGE 58 B1176 ADMIN
                                                          B62
KUHN T.E.,PUBLIC ENTERPRISES, PROJECT PLANNING AND   ECO/DEV
ECONOMIC DEVELOPMENT (PAMPHLET). ECO/UNDEV FINAN   ECO/TAC
PLAN ADMIN EFFICIENCY OWN...MGT STAT CHARTS ANTHOL   LG/CO
20. PAGE 61 B1240   NAT/G
                                                          B62
MEANS G.C.,THE CORPORATE REVOLUTION IN AMERICA: LG/CO
ECONOMIC REALITY VS. ECONOMIC THEORY. USA+45 USA-45 MARKET
INDUS WORKER PLAN CAP/ISM ADMIN...IDEA/COMP 20.   CONTROL
PAGE 72 B1459   PRICE
                                                          B62
MODELSKI G.,A THEORY OF FOREIGN POLICY. WOR+45   PLAN
WOR-45 NAT/G DELIB/GP EX/STRUC TOP/EX EDU/PROP   PWR
LEGIT ROUTINE...POLICY CONCPT TOT/POP COLD/WAR 20.   DIPLOM
PAGE 74 B1494
                                                          B62
MORTON L.,STRATEGY AND COMMAND: THE FIRST TWO   WAR
YEARS. USA-45 NAT/G CONTROL EXEC LEAD WEAPON   FORCES
CIVMIL/REL PWR...POLICY AUD/VIS CHARTS 20 CHINJAP.   PLAN
PAGE 76 B1532   DIPLOM
                                                          B62
ROBINSON M.,THE COMING OF AGE OF THE LANGLEY PORTER PUB/INST
CLINIC (PAMPHLET). USA+45 PROF/ORG PROVS PLAN...MGT ADMIN
PSY 20 CALIFORNIA LANGLEY. PAGE 89 B1804   EFFICIENCY
                                                         HEAL
                                                          B62
SCHILLING W.R.,STRATEGY, POLITICS, AND DEFENSE   ROUTINE
BUDGETS. USA+45 R+D NAT/G CONSULT DELIB/GP FORCES   POLICY
LEGIS ACT/RES PLAN BAL/PWR LEGIT EXEC NUC/PWR
RIGID/FLEX PWR...TREND COLD/WAR CONGRESS 20
EISNHWR/DD. PAGE 93 B1890
                                                          B62
SCHULMAN S.,TOWARD JUDICIAL REFORM IN PENNSYLVANIA: CT/SYS
A STUDY IN COURT REORGANIZATION. USA+45 CONSTN   ACT/RES
JUDGE PLAN ADMIN LOBBY SANCTION PRIVIL PWR...JURID PROB/SOLV
20 PENNSYLVAN. PAGE 94 B1905
                                                          B62
STAHL O.G.,PUBLIC PERSONNEL ADMINISTRATION. LOC/G   ADMIN
TOP/EX CREATE PLAN ROUTINE...TECHNIC MGT T.   WORKER
PAGE 100 B2017   EX/STRUC
                                                         NAT/G
                                                          B62
UNECA LIBRARY,NEW ACQUISITIONS IN THE UNECA   BIBLIOG
LIBRARY. LAW NAT/G PLAN PROB/SOLV TEC/DEV ADMIN   AFR
REGION...GEOG SOC 20 UN. PAGE 106 B2152   ECO/UNDEV
                                                         INT/ORG
                                                          B62
US SENATE COMM GOVT OPERATIONS,ADMINISTRATION OF   ORD/FREE
NATIONAL SECURITY. USA+45 CHIEF PLAN PROB/SOLV   ADMIN
TEC/DEV DIPLOM ATTIT...POLICY DECISION 20   NAT/G
KENNEDY/JF RUSK/D MCNAMARA/R BUNDY/M HERTER/C.   CONTROL
PAGE 110 B2212
                                                          B62
WEDDING N.,ADVERTISING MANAGEMENT. USA+45 ECO/DEV   ECO/TAC
BUDGET CAP/ISM PRODUC PROFIT ATTIT...DECISION MGT   COM/IND
PSY 20. PAGE 114 B2308   PLAN
                                                         EDU/PROP
                                                          B62
WENDT P.F.,HOUSING POLICY - THE SEARCH FOR   PLAN
SOLUTIONS. GERMANY/W SWEDEN UK USA+45 OP/RES   ADMIN
HABITAT WEALTH...SOC/WK CHARTS 20. PAGE 115 B2322 METH/COMP
                                                         NAT/G
                                                          L62
BELSHAW D.G.R.,"PUBLIC INVESTMENT IN AGRICULTURE   ECO/UNDEV
AND ECONOMIC DEVELOPMENT OF UGANDA" UGANDA AGRI   PLAN
INDUS R+D ECO/TAC RATION TAX PAY COLONIAL 20   ADMIN
WORLD/BANK. PAGE 10 B0209   CENTRAL
                                                          L62
ERDMANN H.H.,"ADMINISTRATIVE LAW AND FARM   AGRI
ECONOMICS." USA+45 LOC/G NAT/G PLAN PROB/SOLV LOBBY ADMIN
...DECISION ANTHOL 20. PAGE 33 B0680   ADJUD
                                                         POLICY
                                                          L62
GALBRAITH J.K.,"ECONOMIC DEVELOPMENT IN   ECO/UNDEV
PERSPECTIVE." CAP/ISM ECO/TAC ROUTINE ATTIT WEALTH PLAN
...TREND CHARTS SOC/EXP WORK 20. PAGE 38 B0773
                                                          L62
HOFFHERR R.,"LE PROBLEME DE L'ENCADREMENT DANS LES   AFR
JEUNES ETATS DE LANGUE FRANCAISE EN AFRIQUE   STRUCT
CENTRALE ET A MADAGASCAR." FUT ECO/UNDEV CONSULT FRANCE
PLAN ECO/TAC COLONIAL ATTIT...MGT TIME/SEQ VAL/FREE
20. PAGE 51 B1028
                                                          L62
WATERSTON A.,"PLANNING IN MOROCCO, ORGANIZATION AND NAT/G
IMPLEMENTATION. BALTIMORE: HOPKINS ECON. DEVELOP.   PLAN
INT. BANK FOR." ISLAM ECO/DEV AGRI DIST/IND INDUS   MOROCCO

PROC/MFG SERV/IND LOC/G EX/STRUC ECO/TAC PWR WEALTH
TOT/POP VAL/FREE 20. PAGE 114 B2302
                                                          S62
ALBONETTI A.,"IL SECONDO PROGRAMMA QUINQUENNALE   R+D
1963-67 ED IL BILANCIO RICERCHE ED INVESTIMENTI PER PLAN
IL 1963 DELL'ERATOM." EUR+WWI FUT ITALY WOR+45   NUC/PWR
ECO/DEV SERV/IND INT/ORG TEC/DEV ECO/TAC ATTIT
SKILL WEALTH...MGT TIME/SEQ OEEC 20. PAGE 3 B0069
                                                          S62
BUENO M.,"ASPECTOS SOCIOLOGICOS DE LA EDUCACION."   SOCIETY
FUT UNIV INTELL R+D SERV/IND SCHOOL CONSULT   EDU/PROP
EX/STRUC ACT/RES PLAN...METH/CNCPT OBS 20. PAGE 17 PERSON
B0341
                                                          S62
GEORGE P.,"MATERIAUX ET REFLEXIONS POUR UNE   ECO/UNDEV
POLITIQUE URBAINE RATIONNELLE DANS LES PAYS EN   PLAN
COURS DE DEVELOPPEMENT." FUT INTELL SOCIETY
SERV/IND MUNIC ACT/RES WEALTH...MGT 20. PAGE 39
B0790
                                                          S62
IOVTCHOUK M.T.,"ON SOME THEORETICAL PRINCIPLES AND   COM
METHODS OF SOCIOLOGICAL INVESTIGATIONS (IN   ECO/DEV
RUSSIAN)." FUT USA+45 STRATA R+D NAT/G POL/PAR   CAP/ISM
TOP/EX ACT/RES PLAN ECO/TAC EDU/PROP ROUTINE ATTIT USSR
RIGID/FLEX MARXISM SOCISM...MARXIST METH/CNCPT OBS
TREND NAT/COMP GEN/LAWS 20. PAGE 54 B1102
                                                          S62
JACOBSON H.K.,"THE UNITED NATIONS AND COLONIALISM: INT/ORG
A TENTATIVE APPRAISAL." AFR FUT S/ASIA USA+45 USSR CONCPT
WOR+45 NAT/G DELIB/GP PLAN DIPLOM ECO/TAC DOMIN   COLONIAL
ADMIN ROUTINE COERCE ATTIT RIGID/FLEX ORD/FREE PWR
...OBS STERTYP UN 20. PAGE 55 B1115
                                                          S62
JOHNSON H.,"CANADA IN A CHANGING WORLD." EUR+WWI   ECO/DEV
USA+45 NAT/G CAP/ISM ECO/TAC ADMIN ATTIT WEALTH   PLAN
...TREND TOT/POP 20 EEC. PAGE 57 B1143   CANADA
                                                          S62
PIQUEMAL M.,"LES PROBLEMES DES UNIONS D'ETATS EN   AFR
AFRIQUE NOIRE." FRANCE SOCIETY INT/ORG NAT/G   ECO/UNDEV
DELIB/GP PLAN LEGIT ADMIN COLONIAL ROUTINE ATTIT   REGION
ORD/FREE PWR...GEOG METH/CNCPT 20. PAGE 83 B1678
                                                          S62
SCHILLING W.R.,"SCIENTISTS, FOREIGN POLICY AND   NAT/G
POLITICS." WOR+45 WOR-45 INTELL INT/ORG CONSULT   TEC/DEV
TOP/EX ACT/RES PLAN ADMIN KNOWL...CONCPT OBS TREND DIPLOM
LEAGUE/NAT 20. PAGE 93 B1889   NUC/PWR
                                                          S62
SPRINGER H.W.,"FEDERATION IN THE CARIBBEAN: AN   VOL/ASSN
ATTEMPT THAT FAILED." L/A+17C ECO/UNDEV INT/ORG   NAT/G
POL/PAR PROVS LEGIS CREATE PLAN LEGIT ADMIN FEDERAL REGION
ATTIT DRIVE PERSON ORD/FREE PWR...POLICY GEOG PSY
CONCPT OBS CARIBBEAN CMN/WLTH 20. PAGE 100 B2013
                                                          N62
US ADVISORY COMN INTERGOV REL,ALTERNATIVE   MUNIC
APPROACHES TO GOVERNMENTAL REORGANIZATION IN   REGION
METROPOLITAN AREAS (PAMPHLET). EX/STRUC LEGIS EXEC PLAN
LEAD PWR...DECISION GEN/METH. PAGE 107 B2171   GOV/REL
                                                          B63
BASS M.E.,SELECTIVE BIBLIOGRAPHY ON MUNICIPAL   BIBLIOG
GOVERNMENT FROM THE FILES OF THE MUNICIPAL   LOC/G
TECHNICAL ADVISORY SERVICE. USA+45 FINAN SERV/IND ADMIN
PLAN 20. PAGE 9 B0194   MUNIC
                                                          B63
BOISSIER P.,HISTORIE DU COMITE INTERNATIONAL DE LA INT/ORG
CROIX ROUGE. MOD/EUR WOR-45 CONSULT FORCES PLAN   HEALTH
DIPLOM EDU/PROP ADMIN MORAL ORD/FREE...SOC CONCPT ARMS/CONT
RECORD TIME/SEQ GEN/LAWS TOT/POP VAL/FREE 19/20. WAR
PAGE 13 B0267
                                                          B63
BROGAN D.W.,POLITICAL PATTERNS IN TODAY'S WORLD.   NAT/COMP
FRANCE USA+45 USSR WOR+45 CONSTN STRUCT PLAN DIPLOM NEW/LIB
ADMIN LEAD ROLE SUPEGO...PHIL/SCI 20. PAGE 15 B0313 COM
                                                         TOTALISM
                                                          B63
BURSK E.C.,NEW DECISION-MAKING TOOLS FOR MANAGERS. DECISION
COMPUTER PLAN PROB/SOLV ROUTINE COST. PAGE 18 B0357 MGT
                                                         MATH
                                                         RIGID/FLEX
                                                          B63
CHARLES S.,MINISTER OF RELIEF: HARRY HOPKINS AND   ADMIN
THE DEPRESSION. EX/STRUC PROB/SOLV RATION PARL/PROC ECO/TAC
PERS/REL ALL/VALS 20 HOPKINS/H NRA. PAGE 20 B0414 PLAN
                                                         BIOG
                                                          B63
CROZIER B.,THE MORNING AFTER; A STUDY OF   SOVEREIGN
INDEPENDENCE. WOR+45 EX/STRUC PLAN BAL/PWR COLONIAL NAT/LISM
GP/REL 20 COLD/WAR. PAGE 25 B0511   NAT/G
                                                         DIPLOM
                                                          B63
DALAND R.T.,PERSPECTIVES OF BRAZILIAN PUBLIC   ADMIN
ADMINISTRATION (VOL. I). BRAZIL LAW ECO/UNDEV   NAT/G
SCHOOL CHIEF TEC/DEV CONFER CONTROL GP/REL ATTIT PLAN
ROLE PWR...ANTHOL 20. PAGE 26 B0525   GOV/REL
                                                          B63
ECOLE NATIONALE D'ADMIN,BIBLIOGRAPHIE SELECTIVE   BIBLIOG
D'OUVRAGES DE LANGUE FRANCAISE TRAITANT DES   AFR

PROBLEMES GOUVERNEMENTAUX ET ADMINISTRATIFS. NAT/G
FORCES ACT/RES OP/RES PLAN PROB/SOLV BUDGET ADJUD
COLONIAL LEAD 20. PAGE 32 B0651
ADMIN
EX/STRUC

B63

HARGROVE M.M.,BUSINESS POLICY CASES-WITH BEHAVIORAL
SCIENCE IMPLICATIONS. LG/CO SML/CO EX/STRUC TOP/EX
PLAN PROB/SOLV CONFER ADMIN CONTROL ROUTINE
EFFICIENCY. PAGE 47 B0946
SOC/EXP
INDUS
DECISION
MGT

B63

HAUSMAN W.H.,MANAGING ECONOMIC DEVELOPMENT IN
AFRICA. AFR USA+45 LAW FINAN WORKER TEC/DEV WEALTH
...ANTHOL 20. PAGE 48 B0970
ECO/UNDEV
PLAN
FOR/AID
MGT

B63

HEARLE E.F.R.,A DATA PROCESSING SYSTEM FOR STATE
AND LOCAL GOVERNMENTS. PLAN TEC/DEV AUTOMAT ROUTINE
...MGT METH/CNCPT CLASSIF 20. PAGE 49 B0984
LOC/G
PROVS
COMPUTER
COMPUT/IR

B63

HERMAN H.,NEW YORK STATE AND THE METROPOLITAN
PROBLEM. USA+45 ECO/DEV PUB/INST SCHOOL LEGIS PLAN
TAX EXEC PARL/PROC PARTIC...HEAL 20 NEW/YORK.
PAGE 49 B0992
GOV/REL
PROVS
LOC/G
POLICY

B63

HEUSSLER R.,YESTERDAY'S RULERS: THE MAKING OF THE
BRITISH COLONIAL SERVICE. AFR EUR+WWI UK STRATA
SECT DELIB/GP PLAN DOMIN EDU/PROP ATTIT PERCEPT
PERSON SUPEGO KNOWL ORD/FREE PWR...MGT SOC OBS INT
TIME/SEQ 20 CMN/WLTH. PAGE 49 B1000
EX/STRUC
MORAL
ELITES

B63

INDIAN INSTITUTE PUBLIC ADMIN.,CASES IN INDIAN
ADMINISTRATION. INDIA AGRI NAT/G PROB/SOLV TEC/DEV
ECO/TAC ADMIN...ANTHOL METH 20. PAGE 53 B1083
DECISION
PLAN
MGT
ECO/UNDEV

B63

KARL B.D.,EXECUTIVE REORGANIZATION AND REFORM IN
THE NEW DEAL. ECO/DEV INDUS DELIB/GP EX/STRUC PLAN
BUDGET ADMIN EFFICIENCY PWR POPULISM...POLICY 20
PRESIDENT ROOSEVLT/F WILSON/W NEW/DEAL. PAGE 58
B1174
BIOG
EXEC
CREATE
CONTROL

B63

KAST F.E.,SCIENCE, TECHNOLOGY, AND MANAGEMENT.
SPACE USA+45 FORCES CONFER DETER NUC/PWR...PHIL/SCI
CHARTS ANTHOL BIBLIOG 20 NASA. PAGE 58 B1179
MGT
PLAN
TEC/DEV
PROB/SOLV

B63

LITTERER J.A.,ORGANIZATIONS: STRUCTURE AND
BEHAVIOR. PLAN DOMIN CONTROL LEAD ROUTINE SANCTION
INGP/REL EFFICIENCY PRODUC DRIVE RIGID/FLEX PWR.
PAGE 66 B1325
ADMIN
CREATE
MGT
ADJUST

B63

MAYNE R.,THE COMMUNITY OF EUROPE. UK CONSTN NAT/G
CONSULT DELIB/GP CREATE PLAN ECO/TAC LEGIT ADMIN
ROUTINE ORD/FREE PWR WEALTH...CONCPT TIME/SEQ EEC
EURATOM 20. PAGE 71 B1436
EUR+WWI
INT/ORG
REGION

B63

MCKIE R.,MALAYSIA IN FOCUS. INDONESIA WOR+45
ECO/UNDEV FINAN NAT/G POL/PAR SECT FORCES PLAN
ADMIN COLONIAL COERCE DRIVE ALL/VALS...POLICY
RECORD CENSUS TIME/SEQ CMN/WLTH 20. PAGE 72 B1453
S/ASIA
NAT/LISM
MALAYSIA

B63

MEYNAUD J.,PLANIFICATION ET POLITIQUE. FRANCE ITALY
FINAN LABOR DELIB/GP LEGIS ADMIN EFFICIENCY
...MAJORIT DECISION 20. PAGE 73 B1477
PLAN
ECO/TAC
PROB/SOLV

B63

PREST A.R.,PUBLIC FINANCE IN UNDERDEVELOPED
COUNTRIES. UK WOR+45 WOR-45 SOCIETY INT/ORG NAT/G
LEGIS ACT/RES PLAN ECO/TAC ADMIN ROUTINE...CHARTS
20. PAGE 84 B1702
FINAN
ECO/UNDEV
NIGERIA

B63

SCHRADER R.,SCIENCE AND POLICY. WOR+45 ECO/DEV
ECO/UNDEV R+D FORCES PLAN DIPLOM GOV/REL TECHRACY
BIBLIOG. PAGE 94 B1900
TEC/DEV
NAT/G
POLICY
ADMIN

B63

SMITH R.M.,STATE GOVERNMENT IN TRANSITION. USA+45
POL/PAR LEGIS PARL/PROC GOV/REL 20 PENNSYLVAN
GOVERNOR. PAGE 98 B1984
PROVS
POLICY
EX/STRUC
PLAN

B63

STEIN H.,AMERICAN CIVIL-MILITARY DECISION. USA+45
USA-45 EX/STRUC FORCES LEGIS TOP/EX PLAN DIPLOM
FOR/AID ATTIT 20 CONGRESS. PAGE 100 B2028
CIVMIL/REL
DECISION
WAR
BUDGET

B63

SWEENEY S.B.,ACHIEVING EXCELLENCE IN PUBLIC
SERVICE. FUT USA+45 NAT/G ACT/RES GOV/REL...POLICY
ANTHOL 20 CIVIL/SERV. PAGE 102 B2060
ADMIN
WORKER
TASK
PLAN

B63

SWERDLOW I.,DEVELOPMENT ADMINISTRATION: CONCEPTS
AND PROBLEMS. WOR+45 CULTURE SOCIETY STRATA
DELIB/GP EX/STRUC ACT/RES PLAN ECO/TAC DOMIN LEGIT
ATTIT RIGID/FLEX SUPEGO HEALTH PWR...MGT CONCPT
ANTHOL VAL/FREE. PAGE 102 B2062
ECO/UNDEV
ADMIN

TSOU T.,AMERICA'S FAILURE IN CHINA, 1941-1950.
USA+45 USA-45 NAT/G ACT/RES PLAN DOMIN EDU/PROP
ADMIN ROUTINE ATTIT PERSON ORD/FREE...DECISION
CONCPT MYTH TIME/SEQ TREND STERTYP 20. PAGE 105
B2132
ASIA
PERCEPT
DIPLOM

B63

TUCKER R.C.,THE SOVIET POLITICAL MIND. WOR+45
ELITES INT/ORG NAT/G POL/PAR PLAN DIPLOM ECO/TAC
DOMIN ADMIN NUC/PWR REV DRIVE PERSON SUPEGO PWR
WEALTH...POLICY MGT PSY CONCPT OBS BIOG TREND
COLD/WAR MARX/KARL 20. PAGE 106 B2134
COM
TOP/EX
USSR

B63

UN SECRETARY GENERAL,PLANNING FOR ECONOMIC
DEVELOPMENT. ECO/UNDEV FINAN BUDGET INT/TRADE
TARIFFS TAX ADMIN 20 UN. PAGE 106 B2151
PLAN
ECO/TAC
MGT
NAT/COMP

B63

US HOUSE COM ON ED AND LABOR,ADMINISTRATION OF
AGING. USA+45 R+D EX/STRUC PLAN BUDGET PAY EDU/PROP
ROUTINE COST CONGRESS. PAGE 108 B2187
AGE/O
ADMIN
DELIB/GP
GIVE

B63

WALKER A.A.,OFFICIAL PUBLICATIONS OF SIERRA LEONE
AND GAMBIA. GAMBIA SIER/LEONE UK LAW CONSTN LEGIS
PLAN BUDGET DIPLOM...SOC SAMP CON/ANAL 20. PAGE 113
B2278
BIBLIOG
NAT/G
COLONIAL
ADMIN

S63

BARZANSKI S.,"REGIONAL UNDERDEVELOPMENT IN THE
EUROPEAN ECONOMIC COMMUNITY." EUR+WWI ELITES
DIST/IND MARKET VOL/ASSN CONSULT EX/STRUC ECO/TAC
RIGID/FLEX WEALTH EEC OEEC 20. PAGE 9 B0192
ECO/UNDEV
PLAN

S63

CLEMHOUT S.,"PRODUCTION FUNCTION ANALYSIS APPLIED
TO THE LEONTIEF SCARCE-FACTOR PARADOX OF
INTERNATIONAL TRADE." EUR+WWI USA+45 DIST/IND NAT/G
PLAN TEC/DEV DIPLOM PWR WEALTH...MGT METH/CNCPT
CONT/OBS CON/ANAL CHARTS SIMUL GEN/LAWS 20. PAGE 21
B0436
ECO/DEV
ECO/TAC

S63

MASSART L.,"L'ORGANISATION DE LA RECHERCHE
SCIENTIFIQUE EN EUROPE." EUR+WWI WOR+45 ACT/RES
PLAN TEC/DEV EDU/PROP EXEC KNOWL...METH/CNCPT EEC
20. PAGE 70 B1424
R+D
CREATE

S63

NADLER E.B.,"SOME ECONOMIC DISADVANTAGES OF THE
ARMS RACE." USA+45 INDUS R+D FORCES PLAN TEC/DEV
ECO/TAC FOR/AID EDU/PROP PWR WEALTH...TREND
COLD/WAR 20. PAGE 77 B1552
ECO/DEV
MGT
BAL/PAY

S63

NYE J.S. JR.,"EAST AFRICAN ECONOMIC INTEGRATION."
AFR UGANDA PROVS DELIB/GP PLAN ECO/TAC INT/TRADE
ADMIN ROUTINE ORD/FREE PWR WEALTH...OBS TIME/SEQ
VAL/FREE 20. PAGE 79 B1597
ECO/UNDEV
INT/ORG

S63

ROUGEMONT D.,"LES NOUVELLES CHANCES DE L'EUROPE."
EUR+WWI FUT ECO/DEV INT/ORG NAT/G ACT/RES PLAN
TEC/DEV EDU/PROP ADMIN COLONIAL FEDERAL ATTIT PWR
SKILL...TREND 20. PAGE 91 B1835
ECO/UNDEV
PERCEPT

S63

SCHURMANN F.,"ECONOMIC POLICY AND POLITICAL POWER
IN COMMUNIST CHINA." ASIA CHINA/COM USSR SOCIETY
ECO/UNDEV AGRI INDUS CREATE ADMIN ROUTINE ATTIT
DRIVE RIGID/FLEX PWR WEALTH...HIST/WRIT TREND
CHARTS WORK 20. PAGE 94 B1908
PLAN
ECO/TAC

S63

WINGFIELD C.J.,"POWER STRUCTURE AND DECISION-MAKING
IN CITY PLANNING." EDU/PROP ADMIN LEAD PARTIC
GP/REL ATTIT. PAGE 117 B2365
MUNIC
PLAN
DECISION
PWR

N63

INTERNATIONAL CITY MGRS ASSN,POST-ENTRY TRAINING IN
THE LOCAL PUBLIC SERVICE (PAMPHLET). SCHOOL PLAN
PROB/SOLV TEC/DEV ADMIN EFFICIENCY SKILL...POLICY
AUD/VIS CHARTS BIBLIOG 20 CITY/MGT. PAGE 54 B1096
LOC/G
WORKER
EDU/PROP
METH/COMP

B64

RECENT PUBLICATIONS ON GOVERNMENTAL PROBLEMS. FINAN
INDUS ACADEM PLAN PROB/SOLV EDU/PROP ADJUD ADMIN
BIO/SOC...MGT SOC. PAGE 2 B0040
BIBLIOG
AUTOMAT
LEGIS
JURID

B64

APTER D.E.,IDEOLOGY AND DISCONTENT. FUT WOR+45
CONSTN CULTURE INTELL SOCIETY STRUCT INT/ORG NAT/G
DELIB/GP ACT/RES CREATE PLAN TEC/DEV EDU/PROP EXEC
PERCEPT PERSON RIGID/FLEX ALL/VALS...POLICY
TOT/POP. PAGE 6 B0122
ACT/RES
ATTIT

B64

BRIGHT J.R.,RESEARCH, DEVELOPMENT AND TECHNOLOGICAL
INNOVATION. CULTURE R+D CREATE PLAN PROB/SOLV
AUTOMAT RISK PERSON...DECISION CONCPT PREDICT
BIBLIOG. PAGE 15 B0308
TEC/DEV
NEW/IDEA
INDUS
MGT

B64

BROMAGE A.W.,MANAGER PLAN ABANDONMENTS: WHY A FEW
HAVE DROPPED COUNCILMANAGER GOVERNMENT. USA+45
CREATE PARTIC CHOOSE...MGT CENSUS CHARTS 20.
PAGE 15 B0315
MUNIC
PLAN
CONSULT
LOC/G

B64
COMMITTEE ECONOMIC DEVELOPMENT,IMPROVING EXECUTIVE EXEC
MANAGEMENT IN THE FEDERAL GOVERNMENT. USA+45 CHIEF MGT
DELIB/GP WORKER PLAN PAY SENIOR ADMIN EFFICIENCY 20 TOP/EX
PRESIDENT. PAGE 22 B0457 NAT/G

B64
CULLINGWORTH J.B.,TOWN AND COUNTRY PLANNING IN MUNIC
ENGLAND AND WALES. UK LAW SOCIETY CONSULT ACT/RES PLAN
ADMIN ROUTINE LEISURE INGP/REL ADJUST PWR...GEOG 20 NAT/G
OPEN/SPACE URBAN/RNWL. PAGE 25 B0512 PROB/SOLV

B64
ELDREDGE H.W.,THE SECOND AMERICAN REVOLUTION. ELITES
EDU/PROP NAT/LISM RATIONAL TOTALISM FASCISM MARXISM ORD/FREE
SOCISM. PAGE 33 B0664 ADMIN
PLAN

B64
ETZIONI A.,MODERN ORGANIZATIONS. CLIENT STRUCT MGT
DOMIN CONTROL LEAD PERS/REL AUTHORIT...CLASSIF ADMIN
BUREAUCRCY. PAGE 34 B0685 PLAN
CULTURE

B64
FALK L.A.,ADMINISTRATIVE ASPECTS OF GROUP PRACTICE. BIBLIOG/A
USA+45 FINAN PROF/ORG PLAN MGT. PAGE 35 B0702 HEAL
ADMIN
SERV/IND

B64
FLORENCE P.S.,ECONOMICS AND SOCIOLOGY OF INDUSTRY; INDUS
A REALISTIC ANALYSIS OF DEVELOPMENT. ECO/UNDEV SOC
LG/CO NAT/G PLAN...GEOG MGT BIBLIOG 20. PAGE 36 ADMIN
B0729

B64
GRAVIER J.F.,AMENAGEMENT DU TERRITOIRE ET L'AVENIR PLAN
DES REGIONS FRANCAISES. FRANCE ECO/DEV AGRI INDUS MUNIC
CREATE...GEOG CHARTS 20. PAGE 42 B0859 NEIGH
ADMIN

B64
GREBLER L.,URBAN RENEWAL IN EUROPEAN COUNTRIES: ITS MUNIC
EMERGENCE AND POTENTIALS. EUR+WWI UK ECO/DEV LOC/G PLAN
NEIGH CREATE ADMIN ATTIT...TREND NAT/COMP 20 CONSTRUC
URBAN/RNWL. PAGE 43 B0863 NAT/G

B64
HERSKOVITS M.J.,ECONOMIC TRANSITION IN AFRICA. FUT AFR
INT/ORG NAT/G WORKER PROB/SOLV TEC/DEV INT/TRADE ECO/UNDEV
EQUILIB INCOME...ANTHOL 20. PAGE 49 B0996 PLAN
ADMIN

B64
INST D'ETUDE POL L'U GRENOBLE,ADMINISTRATION ADMIN
TRADITIONELLE ET PLANIFICATION REGIONALE. FRANCE MUNIC
LAW POL/PAR PROB/SOLV ADJUST RIGID/FLEX...CHARTS PLAN
ANTHOL BIBLIOG T 20 REFORMERS. PAGE 54 B1087 CREATE

B64
KAPP E.,THE MERGER OF THE EXECUTIVES OF THE CENTRAL
EUROPEAN COMMUNITIES. LAW CONSTN STRUCT ACT/RES EX/STRUC
PLAN PROB/SOLV ADMIN REGION TASK...INT/LAW MGT ECSC
EEC. PAGE 58 B1170

B64
MAYER C.S.,INTERVIEWING COSTS IN SURVEY RESEARCH. SIMUL
USA+45 PLAN COST...MGT REC/INT SAMP METH/COMP INT
HYPO/EXP METH 20. PAGE 71 B1434 R+D
EFFICIENCY

B64
OECD SEMINAR REGIONAL DEV,REGIONAL DEVELOPMENT IN ADMIN
ISRAEL. ISRAEL STRUCT ECO/UNDEV NAT/G REGION...GEOG PROVS
20. PAGE 79 B1603 PLAN
METH/COMP

B64
ORTH C.D.,ADMINISTERING RESEARCH AND DEVELOPMENT. MGT
FINAN PLAN PROB/SOLV ADMIN ROUTINE...METH/CNCPT R+D
STAT CHARTS METH 20. PAGE 80 B1616 LG/CO
INDUS

B64
PEABODY R.L.,ORGANIZATIONAL AUTHORITY. SCHOOL ADMIN
WORKER PLAN SENIOR GOV/REL UTIL DRIVE PWR...PSY EFFICIENCY
CHARTS BIBLIOG 20. PAGE 82 B1648 TASK
GP/REL

B64
PIERCE T.M.,FEDERAL, STATE, AND LOCAL GOVERNMENT IN NAT/G
EDUCATION. FINAN LOC/G PROVS LEGIS PLAN EDU/PROP POLICY
ADMIN CONTROL CENTRAL COST KNOWL 20. PAGE 83 B1673 SCHOOL
GOV/REL

B64
PINNICK A.W.,COUNTRY PLANNERS IN ACTION. UK FINAN MUNIC
SERV/IND NAT/G CONSULT DELIB/GP PRICE CONTROL PLAN
ROUTINE LEISURE AGE/C...GEOG 20 URBAN/RNWL. PAGE 83 INDUS
B1674 ATTIT

B64
RAPHAEL M.,PENSIONS AND PUBLIC SERVANTS. UK PLAN ADMIN
EDU/PROP PARTIC GOV/REL HEALTH...POLICY CHARTS SENIOR
17/20 CIVIL/SERV. PAGE 86 B1737 PAY
AGE/O

B64
RAYMOND J.,POWER AT THE PENTAGON (1ST ED.). ELITES PWR
NAT/G PLAN EDU/PROP ARMS/CONT DETER WAR WEAPON CIVMIL/REL
...TIME/SEQ 20 PENTAGON MCNAMARA/R. PAGE 86 B1746 EX/STRUC
FORCES

B64
RICHARDSON I.L.,BIBLIOGRAFIA BRASILEIRA DE BIBLIOG
ADMINISTRACAO PUBLICA E ASSUNTOS CORRELATOS. BRAZIL MGT
CONSTN FINAN LOC/G NAT/G POL/PAR PLAN DIPLOM ADMIN
RECEIVE ATTIT...METH 20. PAGE 88 B1776 LAW

B64
RIGGS F.W.,ADMINISTRATION IN DEVELOPING COUNTRIES. ECO/UNDEV
FUT WOR+45 STRUCT AGRI INDUS NAT/G PLAN TEC/DEV ADMIN
ECO/TAC EDU/PROP RIGID/FLEX KNOWL WEALTH...POLICY
MGT CONCPT METH/CNCPT TREND 20. PAGE 88 B1785

B64
RIGGS R.E.,THE MOVEMENT FOR ADMINISTRATIVE ADMIN
REORGANIZATION IN ARIZONA. USA+45 LAW POL/PAR PROVS
DELIB/GP LEGIS PROB/SOLV CONTROL RIGID/FLEX PWR CREATE
...ORG/CHARTS 20 ARIZONA DEMOCRAT REPUBLICAN. PLAN
PAGE 88 B1786

B64
SCHERMER G.,MEETING SOCIAL NEEDS IN THE PENJERDEL PLAN
REGION. SOCIETY FINAN ACT/RES EDU/PROP ADMIN REGION
GOV/REL...SOC/WK 45 20 PENNSYLVAN DELAWARE HEALTH
NEW/JERSEY. PAGE 93 B1887 WEALTH

B64
SULLIVAN G.,THE STORY OF THE PEACE CORPS. USA+45 INT/ORG
WOR+45 INTELL FACE/GP NAT/G SCHOOL VOL/ASSN CONSULT ECO/UNDEV
EX/STRUC PLAN EDU/PROP ADMIN ATTIT DRIVE ALL/VALS FOR/AID
...POLICY HEAL SOC CONCPT INT QU BIOG TREND SOC/EXP PEACE
WORK. PAGE 102 B2054

B64
TINBERGEN J.,CENTRAL PLANNING. COM INTELL ECO/DEV PLAN
ECO/UNDEV FINAN INT/ORG PROB/SOLV ECO/TAC CONTROL INDUS
EXEC ROUTINE DECISION. PAGE 104 B2111 MGT
CENTRAL

B64
UN PUB. INFORM. ORGAN.,EVERY MAN'S UNITED NATIONS. INT/ORG
UNIV WOR+45 CONSTN CULTURE SOCIETY ECO/DEV ROUTINE
ECO/UNDEV NAT/G ACT/RES PLAN ECO/TAC INT/TRADE
EDU/PROP LEGIT PEACE ATTIT ALL/VALS...POLICY HUM
INT/LAW CONCPT CHARTS UN TOT/POP 20. PAGE 106 B2150

B64
US SENATE COMM GOVT OPERATIONS,THE SECRETARY OF DIPLOM
STATE AND THE AMBASSADOR. USA+45 CHIEF CONSULT DELIB/GP
EX/STRUC FORCES PLAN ADMIN EXEC INGP/REL ROLE NAT/G
...ANTHOL 20 PRESIDENT DEPT/STATE. PAGE 110 B2215

B64
US SENATE COMM GOVT OPERATIONS,ADMINISTRATION OF ADMIN
NATIONAL SECURITY. USA+45 CHIEF TOP/EX PLAN DIPLOM FORCES
CONTROL PEACE...POLICY DECISION 20 PRESIDENT ORD/FREE
CONGRESS. PAGE 110 B2216 NAT/G

B64
WEIDENBAUM M.L.,CONGRESS AND THE FEDERAL BUDGET: LEGIS
FEDERAL BUDGETING AND THE RESPONSIBLE USE OF POWER. EX/STRUC
LOC/G PLAN TAX CONGRESS. PAGE 114 B2309 BUDGET
ADMIN

B64
WELLISZ S.,THE ECONOMICS OF THE SOVIET BLOC. COM EFFICIENCY
USSR INDUS WORKER PLAN BUDGET INT/TRADE TAX PRICE ADMIN
PRODUC WEALTH MARXISM...METH/COMP 20. PAGE 115 MARKET
B2319

L64
HAAS E.B.,"ECONOMICS AND DIFFERENTIAL PATTERNS OF L/A+17C
POLITICAL INTEGRATION: PROJECTIONS ABOUT UNITY IN INT/ORG
LATIN AMERICA." SOCIETY NAT/G DELIB/GP ACT/RES MARKET
CREATE PLAN ECO/TAC REGION ROUTINE ATTIT DRIVE PWR
WEALTH...CONCPT TREND CHARTS LAFTA 20. PAGE 45
B0910

L64
MILLIS W.,"THE DEMILITARIZED WORLD." COM USA+45 FUT
USSR WOR+45 CONSTN NAT/G EX/STRUC PLAN LEGIT ATTIT INT/ORG
DRIVE...CONCPT TIME/SEQ STERTYP TOT/POP COLD/WAR BAL/PWR
20. PAGE 74 B1486 PEACE

S64
FLORINSKY M.T.,"TRENDS IN THE SOVIET ECONOMY." COM ECO/DEV
USA+45 USSR INDUS LABOR NAT/G PLAN TEC/DEV ECO/TAC AGRI
ALL/VALS SOCISM...MGT METH/CNCPT STYLE CON/ANAL
GEN/METH WORK 20. PAGE 36 B0731

S64
HUELIN D.,"ECONOMIC INTEGRATION IN LATIN AMERICAN: MARKET
PROGRESS AND PROBLEMS." L/A+17C ECO/DEV AGRI ECO/UNDEV
DIST/IND FINAN INDUS NAT/G VOL/ASSN CONSULT INT/TRADE
DELIB/GP EX/STRUC ACT/RES PLAN TEC/DEV ECO/TAC
ROUTINE BAL/PAY WEALTH WORK 20. PAGE 52 B1058

S64
NASH M.,"SOCIAL PREREQUISITES TO ECONOMIC GROWTH IN ECO/DEV
LATIN AMERICA AND SOUTHEAST ASIA." L/A+17C S/ASIA PERCEPT
CULTURE SOCIETY ECO/UNDEV AGRI INDUS NAT/G PLAN
TEC/DEV EDU/PROP ROUTINE ALL/VALS...POLICY RELATIV
SOC NAT/COMP WORK TOT/POP 20. PAGE 77 B1558

S64
NEEDHAM T.,"SCIENCE AND SOCIETY IN EAST AND WEST." ASIA
INTELL STRATA R+D LOC/G NAT/G PROVS CONSULT ACT/RES STRUCT
CREATE PLAN TEC/DEV EDU/PROP ADMIN ATTIT ALL/VALS
...POLICY RELATIV MGT CONCPT NEW/IDEA TIME/SEQ WORK
WORK. PAGE 77 B1565

S64
STONE P.A.,"DECISION TECHNIQUES FOR TOWN OP/RES
DEVELOPMENT." PLAN COST PROFIT...DECISION MGT MUNIC

CON/ANAL CHARTS METH/COMP BIBLIOG 20. PAGE 101
B2048
ADMIN
PROB/SOLV
S64

THOMPSON V.A.,"ADMINISTRATIVE OBJECTIVES FOR
DEVELOPMENT ADMINISTRATION." WOR+45 CREATE PLAN
DOMIN EDU/PROP EXEC ROUTINE ATTIT ORD/FREE PWR
...POLICY GEN/LAWS VAL/FREE. PAGE 104 B2107
ECO/UNDEV
MGT
N64

US BOARD GOVERNORS FEDL RESRV,SELECTED BIBLIOGRAPHY
ON MONETARY POLICY AND MANAGEMENT OF THE PUBLIC
DEBT 1947-1960 AND 1961-1963 SUPPLEMENT (PAMPH.).
USA+45 PLAN...POLICY MGT 20. PAGE 108 B2173
BIBLIOG
FINAN
NAT/G
B65

AMERICAN ECONOMIC ASSOCIATION,INDEX OF ECONOMIC
JOURNALS 1886-1965 (7 VOLS.). UK USA+45 USA-45 AGRI
FINAN PLAN ECO/TAC INT/TRADE ADMIN...STAT CENSUS
19/20. PAGE 4 B0083
BIBLIOG
WRITING
INDUS
B65

ANTHONY R.N.,PLANNING AND CONTROL SYSTEMS. UNIV
OP/RES...DECISION MGT LING. PAGE 6 B0114
CONTROL
PLAN
METH
HYPO/EXP
B65

ARTHUR D LITTLE INC,SAN FRANCISCO COMMUNITY RENEWAL
PROGRAM. USA+45 FINAN PROVS ADMIN INCOME...CHARTS
20 CALIFORNIA SAN/FRAN URBAN/RNWL. PAGE 7 B0138
HABITAT
MUNIC
PLAN
PROB/SOLV
B65

BARISH N.N.,MANAGEMENT SCIENCES IN THE EMERGING
COUNTRIES. AFR CHINA/COM WOR+45 FINAN INDUS PLAN
PRODUC HABITAT...ANTHOL 20. PAGE 9 B0184
ECO/UNDEV
OP/RES
MGT
TEC/DEV
B65

BOGUSLAW R.,THE NEW UTOPIANS. OP/RES ADMIN CONTROL
PWR...IDEA/COMP SIMUL 20. PAGE 13 B0265
UTOPIA
AUTOMAT
COMPUTER
PLAN
B65

CAMPBELL G.A.,THE CIVIL SERVICE IN BRITAIN (2ND
ED.). UK DELIB/GP FORCES WORKER CREATE PLAN
...POLICY AUD/VIS 19/20 CIVIL/SERV. PAGE 18 B0370
ADMIN
LEGIS
NAT/G
FINAN
B65

COOPER F.E.,STATE ADMINISTRATIVE LAW (2 VOLS.). LAW
LEGIS PLAN TAX ADJUD CT/SYS FEDERAL PWR...CONCPT
20. PAGE 23 B0474
JURID
CONSTN
ADMIN
PROVS
B65

COPELAND M.A.,OUR FREE ENTERPRISE ECONOMY. USA+45
INDUS LABOR ADMIN CONTROL GP/REL MGT. PAGE 23 B0476
CAP/ISM
PLAN
FINAN
ECO/DEV
B65

DUGGAR G.S.,RENEWAL OF TOWN AND VILLAGE I: A WORLD-
WIDE SURVEY OF LOCAL GOVERNMENT EXPERIENCE. WOR+45
CONSTRUC INDUS CREATE BUDGET REGION GOV/REL...QU
NAT/COMP 20 URBAN/RNWL. PAGE 31 B0628
MUNIC
NEIGH
PLAN
ADMIN
B65

ECCLES H.E.,MILITARY CONCEPTS AND PHILOSOPHY.
USA+45 STRUCT EXEC ROUTINE COERCE WAR CIVMIL/REL
COST...OBS GEN/LAWS COLD/WAR. PAGE 32 B0648
PLAN
DRIVE
LEAD
FORCES
B65

EDELMAN M.,THE POLITICS OF WAGE-PRICE DECISIONS.
GERMANY ITALY NETHERLAND UK INDUS LABOR POL/PAR
PROB/SOLV BARGAIN PRICE ROUTINE BAL/PAY COST DEMAND
20. PAGE 32 B0654
GOV/COMP
CONTROL
ECO/TAC
PLAN
B65

EVERETT R.O.,URBAN PROBLEMS AND PROSPECTS. USA+45
CREATE TEC/DEV EDU/PROP ADJUD ADMIN GOV/REL ATTIT
...ANTHOL 20 URBAN/RNWL. PAGE 34 B0691
MUNIC
PLAN
PROB/SOLV
NEIGH
B65

FRYE R.J.,HOUSING AND URBAN RENEWAL IN ALABAMA.
USA+45 NEIGH LEGIS BUDGET ADJUD ADMIN PARTIC...MGT
20 ALABAMA URBAN/RNWL. PAGE 38 B0762
MUNIC
PROB/SOLV
PLAN
GOV/REL
B65

GOODSELL C.T.,ADMINISTRATION OF A REVOLUTION.
PUERT/RICO ECO/UNDEV FINAN MUNIC POL/PAR PROVS
LEGIS PLAN BUDGET RECEIVE ADMIN COLONIAL LEAD 20
ROOSEVLT/F. PAGE 41 B0827
EXEC
SOC
B65

GREER S.,URBAN RENEWAL AND AMERICAN CITIES: THE
DILEMMA OF DEMOCRATIC INTERVENTION. USA+45 R+D
LOC/G VOL/ASSN ACT/RES BUDGET ADMIN GOV/REL...SOC
INT SAMP 20 BOSTON CHICAGO MIAMI URBAN/RNWL.
PAGE 43 B0871
MUNIC
PROB/SOLV
PLAN
NAT/G
B65

HADWIGER D.F.,PRESSURES AND PROTEST. NAT/G LEGIS
PLAN LEAD PARTIC ROUTINE ATTIT POLICY. PAGE 45
B0913
AGRI
GP/REL
LOBBY
CHOOSE
B65

HAIGHT D.E.,THE PRESIDENT; ROLES AND POWERS. USA+45
USA-45 POL/PAR PLAN DIPLOM CHOOSE PERS/REL PWR
CHIEF
LEGIS

18/20 PRESIDENT CONGRESS. PAGE 45 B0915
TOP/EX
EX/STRUC
B65

HICKMAN B.G.,QUANTITATIVE PLANNING OF ECONOMIC
POLICY. FRANCE NETHERLAND OP/RES PRICE ROUTINE UTIL
...POLICY DECISION ECOMETRIC METH/CNCPT STAT STYLE
CHINJAP. PAGE 50 B1004
PROB/SOLV
PLAN
QUANT
B65

INTERNATIONAL CITY MGRS ASSN,COUNCIL-MANAGER
GOVERNMENT, 1940-64: AN ANNOTATED BIBLIOGRAPHY.
USA+45 ADMIN GOV/REL ROLE...MGT 20. PAGE 54 B1097
BIBLIOG/A
MUNIC
CONSULT
PLAN
B65

KASER M.,COMECON* INTEGRATION PROBLEMS OF THE
PLANNED ECONOMIES. INT/ORG TEC/DEV INT/TRADE PRICE
ADMIN ADJUST CENTRAL...STAT TIME/SEQ ORG/CHARTS
COMECON. PAGE 58 B1177
PLAN
ECO/DEV
COM
REGION
B65

KELLEY E.J.,MARKETING: STRATEGY AND FUNCTIONS.
ECO/DEV INDUS PLAN PRICE CONTROL ROUTINE...MGT
BIBLIOG 20. PAGE 59 B1191
MARKET
DIST/IND
POLICY
ECO/TAC
B65

LEYS C.T.,FEDERATION IN EAST AFRICA. LAW AGRI
DIST/IND FINAN INT/ORG LABOR INT/TRADE CONFER ADMIN
CONTROL GP/REL...ANTHOL 20 AFRICA/E. PAGE 65 B1310
FEDERAL
REGION
ECO/UNDEV
PLAN
B65

LUTZ V.,FRENCH PLANNING. FRANCE TEC/DEV RIGID/FLEX
ORD/FREE 20. PAGE 67 B1348
PLAN
ADMIN
FUT
B65

MORGENTHAU H.,MORGENTHAU DIARY (CHINA) (2 VOLS.).
ASIA USA+45 USA-45 LAW DELIB/GP EX/STRUC PLAN
FOR/AID INT/TRADE CONFER WAR MARXISM 20 CHINJAP.
PAGE 75 B1523
DIPLOM
ADMIN
B65

MUSHKIN S.J.,STATE PROGRAMMING. USA+45 PLAN BUDGET
TAX ADMIN REGION GOV/REL...BIBLIOG 20. PAGE 77
B1549
PROVS
POLICY
CREATE
ECO/DEV
B65

OECD,MEDITERRANEAN REGIONAL PROJECT: TURKEY;
EDUCATION AND DEVELOPMENT. FUT TURKEY SOCIETY
STRATA FINAN NAT/G PROF/ORG PLAN PROB/SOLV ADMIN
COST...STAT CHARTS 20 OECD. PAGE 79 B1602
EDU/PROP
ACADEM
SCHOOL
ECO/UNDEV
B65

ORG FOR ECO COOP AND DEVEL,THE MEDITERRANEAN
REGIONAL PROJECT: AN EXPERIMENT IN PLANNING BY SIX
COUNTRIES. FUT GREECE SPAIN TURKEY YUGOSLAVIA
SOCIETY FINAN NAT/G PROF/ORG EDU/PROP ADMIN REGION
COST...POLICY STAT CHARTS 20 OECD. PAGE 80 B1614
PLAN
ECO/UNDEV
ACADEM
SCHOOL
B65

ORG FOR ECO COOP AND DEVEL,THE MEDITERRANEAN
REGIONAL PROJECT: YUGOSLAVIA; EDUCATION AND
DEVELOPMENT. YUGOSLAVIA SOCIETY FINAN PROF/ORG PLAN
ADMIN COST DEMAND MARXISM...STAT TREND CHARTS METH
20 OECD. PAGE 80 B1615
EDU/PROP
ACADEM
SCHOOL
ECO/UNDEV
B65

PERLOFF H.S.,URBAN RESEARCH AND EDUCATION IN THE
NEW YORK METROPOLITAN REGION (VOL. II). FUT USA+45
NEIGH PROF/ORG ACT/RES PROB/SOLV EDU/PROP ADMIN
...STAT BIBLIOG 20 NEWYORK/C. PAGE 82 B1659
MUNIC
PLAN
ACADEM
GP/REL
B65

ROWE J.Z.,THE PUBLIC-PRIVATE CHARACTER OF UNITED
STATES CENTRAL BANKING. USA+45 NAT/G EX/STRUC
...BIBLIOG 20 FED/RESERV. PAGE 91 B1842
FINAN
PLAN
FEDERAL
LAW
B65

SHARMA S.A.,PARLIAMENTARY GOVERNMENT IN INDIA.
INDIA FINAN LOC/G PROVS DELIB/GP PLAN ADMIN CT/SYS
FEDERAL...JURID 20. PAGE 96 B1936
NAT/G
CONSTN
PARL/PROC
LEGIS
B65

SINGER J.D.,HUMAN BEHAVIOR AND INTERNATINAL
POLITICS* CONTRIBUTIONS FROM THE SOCIAL-
PSYCHOLOGICAL SCIENCES. ACT/RES PLAN EDU/PROP ADMIN
KNOWL...DECISION PSY SOC NET/THEORY HYPO/EXP
LAB/EXP SOC/EXP GEN/METH ANTHOL BIBLIOG. PAGE 97
B1965
DIPLOM
PHIL/SCI
QUANT
SIMUL
B65

STARR M.K.,EXECUTIVE READINGS IN MANAGEMENT
SCIENCE. TOP/EX WORKER EDU/PROP ADMIN...DECISION
GEN/LAWS ANTHOL METH T 20. PAGE 100 B2023
MGT
EX/STRUC
PLAN
LG/CO
B65

STEINER G.A.,THE CREATIVE ORGANIZATION. ELITES
LG/CO PLAN PROB/SOLV TEC/DEV INSPECT CAP/ISM
CONTROL EXEC PERSON...METH/COMP HYPO/EXP 20.
PAGE 100 B2029
CREATE
MGT
ADMIN
SOC
B65

VEINOTT A.F. JR.,MATHEMATICAL STUDIES IN MANAGEMENT
SCIENCE. UNIV INDUS COMPUTER ADMIN...DECISION
NET/THEORY SIMUL 20. PAGE 112 B2257
MATH
MGT
PLAN
PRODUC

B65
VIORST M.,HOSTILE ALLIES: FDR AND DE GAULLE. EUR+WWI USA-45 ELITES NAT/G VOL/ASSN FORCES LEGIS PLAN LEGIT ADMIN COERCE PERSON...BIOG TIME/SEQ 20 ROOSEVLT/F DEGAULLE/C. PAGE 112 B2263
TOP/EX
PWR
WAR
FRANCE

B65
WARD W.E.,GOVERNMENT IN WEST AFRICA. WOR+45 POL/PAR EX/STRUC PLAN PARTIC GP/REL SOVEREIGN 20 AFRICA/W. PAGE 114 B2291
GOV/COMP
CONSTN
COLONIAL
ECO/UNDEV

B65
WATERSTON A.,DEVELOPMENT PLANNING* LESSONS OF EXPERIENCE. ECO/TAC CENTRAL...MGT QUANT BIBLIOG. PAGE 114 B2303
ECO/UNDEV
CREATE
PLAN
ADMIN

B65
WHITE J.,GERMAN AID. GERMANY/W FINAN PLAN TEC/DEV INT/TRADE ADMIN ATTIT...POLICY 20. PAGE 116 B2334
FOR/AID
ECO/UNDEV
DIPLOM
ECO/TAC

B65
WITHERELL J.W.,MADAGASCAR AND ADJACENT ISLANDS; A GUIDE TO OFFICIAL PUBLICATIONS (PAMPHLET). FRANCE MADAGASCAR S/ASIA UK LAW OP/RES PLAN DIPLOM ...POLICY CON/ANAL 19/20. PAGE 117 B2368
BIBLIOG
COLONIAL
LOC/G
ADMIN

S65
BALDWIN H.,"SLOW-DOWN IN THE PENTAGON." USA+45 CREATE PLAN GOV/REL CENTRAL COST EFFICIENCY PWR ...MGT MCNAMARA/R. PAGE 9 B0174
RECORD
R+D
WEAPON
ADMIN

S65
CHARLESWORTH J.C.,"ALLOCATION OF RESPONSIBILITIES AND RESOURCES AMONG THE THREE LEVELS OF GOVERNMENT." USA+45 USA-45 ECO/DEV MUNIC PLAN LEGIT ...PLURIST MGT. PAGE 20 B0415
PROVS
NAT/G
LG/CO
WEALTH

S65
GRENIEWSKI H.,"INTENTION AND PERFORMANCE: A PRIMER OF CYBERNETICS OF PLANNING." EFFICIENCY OPTIMAL KNOWL SKILL...DECISION MGT EQULIB. PAGE 43 B0873
SIMUL
GAME
GEN/METH
PLAN

S65
POLK W.R.,"PROBLEMS OF GOVERNMENT UTILIZATION OF SCHOLARLY RESEARCH IN INTERNATIONAL AFFAIRS." FINAN NAT/G EDU/PROP CONTROL TASK GP/REL ATTIT PERCEPT KNOWL...POLICY TIME. PAGE 83 B1685
ACT/RES
ACADEM
PLAN
ADMIN

S65
POSVAR W.W.,"NATIONAL SECURITY POLICY* THE REALM OF OBSCURITY." CREATE PLAN PROB/SOLV ADMIN LEAD GP/REL CONSERVE...DECISION GEOG. PAGE 84 B1694
DIPLOM
USA+45
RECORD

S65
QUADE Q.L.,"THE TRUMAN ADMINISTRATION AND THE SEPARATION OF POWERS: THE CASE OF THE MARSHALL PLAN." SOCIETY INT/ORG NAT/G CONSULT DELIB/GP LEGIS PLAN ECO/TAC ROUTINE DRIVE PERCEPT RIGID/FLEX ORD/FREE PWR WEALTH...DECISION GEOG NEW/IDEA TREND 20 TRUMAN/HS. PAGE 85 B1726
USA+45
ECO/UNDEV
DIPLOM

S65
TABORSKY E.,"CHANGE IN CZECHOSLOVAKIA." COM USSR ELITES INTELL AGRI INDUS NAT/G DELIB/GP EX/STRUC ECO/TAC TOTALISM ATTIT RIGID/FLEX SOCISM...MGT CONCPT TREND 20. PAGE 102 B2067
ECO/DEV
PLAN
CZECHOSLVK

N65
MOTE M.E.,SOVIET LOCAL AND REPUBLIC ELECTIONS. COM USSR NAT/G PLAN PARTIC GOV/REL TOTALISM PWR ...CHARTS 20. PAGE 76 B1534
CHOOSE
ADMIN
CONTROL
LOC/G

N65
NJ DIVISION STATE-REGION PLAN,UTILIZATION OF NEW JERSEY'S DELAWARE RIVER WATERFRONT (PAMPHLET). FUT ADMIN REGION LEISURE GOV/REL DEMAND WEALTH...CHARTS 20 NEW/JERSEY. PAGE 78 B1586
UTIL
PLAN
ECO/TAC
PROVS

B66
ALEXANDER Y.,INTERNATIONAL TECHNICAL ASSISTANCE EXPERTS* A CASE STUDY OF THE U.N. EXPERIENCE. ECO/UNDEV CONSULT EX/STRUC CREATE PLAN DIPLOM FOR/AID TASK EFFICIENCY...ORG/CHARTS UN. PAGE 4 B0074
ECO/TAC
INT/ORG
ADMIN
MGT

B66
ALI S.,PLANNING, DEVELOPMENT AND CHANGE: AN ANNOTATED BIBLIOGRAPHY ON DEVELOPMENTAL ADMINISTRATION. PAKISTAN SOCIETY ORD/FREE 20. PAGE 4 B0077
BIBLIOG/A
ADMIN
ECO/UNDEV
PLAN

B66
ASHRAF A.,THE CITY GOVERNMENT OF CALCUTTA: A STUDY OF INERTIA. INDIA ELITES INDUS NAT/G EX/STRUC ACT/RES PLAN PROB/SOLV LEAD HABITAT...BIBLIOG 20 CALCUTTA. PAGE 7 B0141
LOC/G
MUNIC
ADMIN
ECO/UNDEV

B66
BEAUFRE A.,NATO AND EUROPE. WOR+45 PLAN CONFER EXEC NUC/PWR ATTIT...POLICY 20 NATO EUROPE. PAGE 10 B0203
INT/ORG
DETER
DIPLOM
ADMIN

B66
DAVIS R.G.,PLANNING HUMAN RESOURCE DEVELOPMENT, EDUCATIONAL MODELS AND SCHEMATA. WORKER OP/RES ECO/TAC EDU/PROP CONTROL COST PRODUC...GEOG STAT CHARTS 20. PAGE 27 B0544
PLAN
EFFICIENCY
SIMUL
ROUTINE

B66
DEBENKO E.,RESEARCH SOURCES FOR SOUTH ASIAN STUDIES IN ECONOMIC DEVELOPMENT: A SELECT BIBLIOGRAPHY OF SERIAL PUBLICATIONS. CEYLON INDIA NEPAL PAKISTAN PROB/SOLV ADMIN...POLICY 20. PAGE 28 B0566
BIBLIOG
ECO/UNDEV
S/ASIA
PLAN

B66
FABRYCKY W.J.,OPERATIONS ECONOMY INDUSTRIAL APPLICATIONS OF OPERATIONS RESEARCH. INDUS PLAN ECO/TAC PRODUC...MATH PROBABIL STAT CHARTS 20. PAGE 34 B0695
OP/RES
MGT
SIMUL
DECISION

B66
FENN DH J.R.,BUSINESS DECISION MAKING AND GOVERNMENT POLICY. SERV/IND LEGIS LICENSE ADMIN CONTROL GP/REL INGP/REL 20 CASEBOOK. PAGE 35 B0711
DECISION
PLAN
NAT/G
LG/CO

B66
FOX K.A.,THE THEORY OF QUANTITATIVE ECONOMIC POLICY WITH APPLICATIONS TO ECONOMIC GROWTH AND STABILIZATION. ECO/DEV AGRI NAT/G PLAN ADMIN RISK ...DECISION IDEA/COMP SIMUL T. PAGE 37 B0746
ECO/TAC
ECOMETRIC
EQUILIB
GEN/LAWS

B66
GLAZER M.,THE FEDERAL GOVERNMENT AND THE UNIVERSITY. CHILE PROB/SOLV DIPLOM GIVE ADMIN WAR ...POLICY SOC 20. PAGE 40 B0810
BIBLIOG/A
NAT/G
PLAN
ACADEM

B66
GREENE L.E.,GOVERNMENT IN TENNESSEE (2ND ED.). USA+45 DIST/IND INDUS POL/PAR EX/STRUC LEGIS PLAN BUDGET GIVE CT/SYS...MGT T 20 TENNESSEE. PAGE 43 B0866
PROVS
LOC/G
CONSTN
ADMIN

B66
GRETHER E.T.,MARKETING AND PUBLIC POLICY. USA+45 ECO/DEV DIST/IND NAT/G PLAN CAP/ISM PRICE CONTROL ...GEOG MGT 20. PAGE 43 B0874
MARKET
PROB/SOLV
ECO/TAC
POLICY

B66
GROSS H.,MAKE OR BUY. USA+45 FINAN INDUS CREATE PRICE PRODUC 20. PAGE 44 B0889
ECO/TAC
PLAN
MGT
COST

B66
HASTINGS P.G.,THE MANAGEMENT OF BUSINESS FINANCE. ECO/DEV PLAN BUDGET CONTROL COST...DECISION CHARTS BIBLIOG T 20. PAGE 48 B0966
FINAN
MGT
INDUS
ECO/TAC

B66
JOHNSON N.,PARLIAMENT AND ADMINISTRATION: THE ESTIMATES COMMITTEE 1945-65. FUT UK NAT/G EX/STRUC PLAN BUDGET ORD/FREE...T 20 PARLIAMENT HOUSE/CMNS. PAGE 57 B1147
LEGIS
ADMIN
FINAN
DELIB/GP

B66
KAESTNER K.,GESAMTWIRTSCHAFTLICHE PLANUNG IN EINER GEMISCHTEN WIRTSCHAFTSORDNUNG (WIRTSCHAFTSPOLITISCHE STUDIEN 5). GERMANY/W WOR+45 WOR-45 INDUS MARKET NAT/G ACT/RES GP/REL INGP/REL PRODUC...ECOMETRIC MGT BIBLIOG 20. PAGE 57 B1159
ECO/TAC
PLAN
POLICY
PREDICT

B66
KIRDAR U.,THE STRUCTURE OF UNITED NATIONS ECONOMIC AID TO UNDERDEVELOPED COUNTRIES. AGRI FINAN INDUS NAT/G EX/STRUC PLAN GIVE TASK...POLICY 20 UN. PAGE 60 B1213
INT/ORG
FOR/AID
ECO/UNDEV
ADMIN

B66
KURAKOV I.G.,SCIENCE, TECHNOLOGY AND COMMUNISM; SOME QUESTIONS OF DEVELOPMENT (TRANS. BY CARIN DEDIJER). USSR INDUS PLAN PROB/SOLV COST PRODUC ...MGT MATH CHARTS METH 20. PAGE 61 B1243
CREATE
TEC/DEV
MARXISM
ECO/TAC

B66
LEWIS W.A.,DEVELOPMENT PLANNING; THE ESSENTIALS OF ECONOMIC POLICY. USA+45 FINAN INDUS NAT/G WORKER FOR/AID INT/TRADE ADMIN ROUTINE WEALTH...CONCPT STAT. PAGE 65 B1307
PLAN
ECO/DEV
POLICY
CREATE

B66
LINDFORS G.V.,INTERCOLLEGIATE BIBLIOGRAPHY; CASES IN BUSINESS ADMINISTRATION (VOL. X). FINAN MARKET LABOR CONSULT PLAN GP/REL PRODUC 20. PAGE 65 B1314
BIBLIOG/A
ADMIN
MGT
OP/RES

B66
MOOMAW I.W.,THE CHALLENGE OF HUNGER. USA+45 PLAN ADMIN EATING 20. PAGE 75 B1509
FOR/AID
DIPLOM
ECO/UNDEV
ECO/TAC

B66
NYC TEMPORARY COMM CITY FINAN,MUNICIPAL COLLECTIVE BARGAINING (NO. 8). USA+45 PLAN PROB/SOLV BARGAIN BUDGET TAX EDU/PROP GOV/REL COST...MGT 20 NEWYORK/C. PAGE 79 B1596
MUNIC
FINAN
ADMIN
LOC/G

B66
OHLIN G.,AID AND INDEBTEDNESS. AUSTRIA FINAN INT/ORG PLAN DIPLOM GIVE...POLICY MATH CHARTS 20. PAGE 79 B1604
FOR/AID
ECO/UNDEV
ADMIN
WEALTH

B66
ONYEMELUKWE C.C.,PROBLEMS OF INDUSTRIAL PLANNING AND MANAGEMENT IN NIGERIA. AFR FINAN LABOR DELIB/GP TEC/DEV ADJUST...MGT TREND BIBLIOG. PAGE 80 B1610
ECO/UNDEV
ECO/TAC
INDUS

SAPIN B.M.,THE MAKING OF UNITED STATES FOREIGN
POLICY. USA+45 INT/ORG DELIB/GP FORCES PLAN ECO/TAC
CIVMIL/REL PRESIDENT. PAGE 92 B1868
> B66
> PLAN
> DIPLOM
> EX/STRUC
> DECISION
> NAT/G

SCHMIDT K.M.,AMERICAN STATE AND LOCAL GOVERNMENT IN
ACTION. USA+45 CONSTN LOC/G POL/PAR CHIEF LEGIS
PROB/SOLV ADJUD LOBBY GOV/REL...DECISION ANTHOL 20
GOVERNOR MAYOR URBAN/RNWL. PAGE 94 B1896
> B66
> PROVS
> ADMIN
> MUNIC
> PLAN

SIMON R.,PERSPECTIVES IN PUBLIC RELATIONS. USA+45
INDUS ACT/RES PLAN ADMIN ATTIT MGT. PAGE 97 B1961
> B66
> GP/REL
> PERS/REL
> COM/IND
> SOCIETY

SMITH H.E.,READINGS IN ECONOMIC DEVELOPMENT AND
ADMINISTRATION IN TANZANIA. TANZANIA FINAN INDUS
LABOR NAT/G PLAN PROB/SOLV INT/TRADE COLONIAL
REGION...ANTHOL BIBLIOG 20 AFRICA/E. PAGE 98 B1981
> B66
> TEC/DEV
> ADMIN
> GOV/REL

STREET D.,ORGANIZATION FOR TREATMENT. CLIENT PROVS
PUB/INST PLAN CONTROL PARTIC REPRESENT ATTIT PWR
...POLICY BIBLIOG. PAGE 101 B2052
> B66
> GP/COMP
> AGE/Y
> ADMIN
> VOL/ASSN

UN ECAFE,ADMINISTRATIVE ASPECTS OF FAMILY PLANNING
PROGRAMMES (PAMPHLET). ASIA THAILAND WOR+45
VOL/ASSN PROB/SOLV BUDGET FOR/AID EDU/PROP CONFER
CONTROL GOV/REL TIME 20 UN BIRTH/CON. PAGE 106
B2147
> B66
> PLAN
> CENSUS
> FAM
> ADMIN

WARBURG J.P.,THE UNITED STATES IN THE POSTWAR
WORLD. USA+45 ECO/TAC...POLICY 20 COLD/WAR.
PAGE 113 B2287
> B66
> FOR/AID
> DIPLOM
> PLAN
> ADMIN

WARREN R.O.,GOVERNMENT IN METROPOLITAN REGIONS: A
REAPPRAISAL OF FRACTIONATED POLITICAL ORGANIZATION.
USA+45 ACT/RES PROB/SOLV REGION...CHARTS METH/COMP
BIBLIOG CITY/MGT. PAGE 114 B2296
> B66
> LOC/G
> MUNIC
> EX/STRUC
> PLAN

WESTON J.F.,THE SCOPE AND METHODOLOGY OF FINANCE.
PLAN TEC/DEV CONTROL EFFICIENCY INCOME UTIL...MGT
CONCPT MATH STAT TREND METH 20. PAGE 115 B2327
> B66
> FINAN
> ECO/DEV
> POLICY
> PRICE

AMERICAN ECONOMIC REVIEW,"SIXTY-THIRD LIST OF
DOCTORAL DISSERTATIONS IN POLITICAL ECONOMY IN
AMERICAN UNIVERSITIES AND COLLEGES." ECO/DEV AGRI
FINAN LABOR WORKER PLAN BUDGET INT/TRADE ADMIN
DEMAND...MGT STAT 20. PAGE 4 B0084
> L66
> BIBLIOG/A
> CONCPT
> ACADEM

"FURTHER READING." INDIA LOC/G NAT/G PLAN ADMIN
WEALTH...GEOG SOC CONCPT CENSUS 20. PAGE 2 B0045
> S66
> BIBLIOG
> ECO/UNDEV
> TEC/DEV
> PROVS

AUSLAND J.C.,"CRISIS MANAGEMENT* BERLIN, CYPRUS,
LAOS." CYPRUS LAOS FORCES CREATE PLAN EDU/PROP TASK
CENTRAL PERSON RIGID/FLEX...DECISION MGT 20 BERLIN
KENNEDY/JF MCNAMARA/R RUSK. PAGE 7 B0148
> S66
> OP/RES
> DIPLOM
> RISK
> ADMIN

HANSON A.H.,"PLANNING AND THE POLITICIANS* SOME
REFLECTIONS ON ECONOMIC PLANNING IN WESTERN
EUROPE." MARKET NAT/G TEC/DEV CONSEN ROLE
...METH/COMP NAT/COMP. PAGE 46 B0942
> S66
> PLAN
> ECO/DEV
> EUR+WWI
> ADMIN

JACOBS P.,"RE-RADICALIZING THE DE-RADICALIZED."
USA+45 SOCIETY STRUCT FINAN PLAN PROB/SOLV CAP/ISM
WEALTH CONSERVE NEW/LIB 20. PAGE 55 B1114
> S66
> NAT/G
> POLICY
> MARXIST
> ADMIN

MARKSHAK J.,"ECONOMIC PLANNING AND THE COST OF
THINKING." COM MARKET EX/STRUC...DECISION GEN/LAWS.
PAGE 69 B1400
> S66
> ECO/UNDEV
> ECO/TAC
> PLAN
> ECO/DEV

ZUCKERT E.M.,"THE SERVICE SECRETARY* HAS HE A
USEFUL ROLE?" USA+45 TOP/EX PLAN ADMIN EXEC DETER
NUC/PWR WEAPON...MGT RECORD MCNAMARA/R. PAGE 119
B2407
> S66
> OBS
> OP/RES
> DIPLOM
> FORCES

SHERMAN H.,"IT ALL DEPENDS." USA+45 FINAN MARKET
PLAN PROB/SOLV EXEC PARTIC INGP/REL SUPEGO
...DECISION BIBLIOG 20. PAGE 96 B1944
> C66
> LG/CO
> MGT
> ADMIN
> POLICY

AMERICAN SOCIETY PUBLIC ADMIN,PUBLIC ADMINISTRATION
AND THE WAR ON POVERTY (PAMPHLET). USA+45 SOCIETY
ECO/DEV FINAN LOC/G LEGIS CREATE EDU/PROP CONFER
GOV/REL GP/REL ROLE 20 POVRTY/WAR. PAGE 4 B0089
> N66
> WEALTH
> NAT/G
> PLAN
> ADMIN

ANDERSON C.W.,POLITICS AND ECONOMIC CHANGE IN LATIN
AMERICA. L/A+17C INDUS NAT/G OP/RES ADMIN DEMAND
> B67
> ECO/UNDEV
> PROB/SOLV

...POLICY STAT CHARTS NAT/COMP 20. PAGE 4 B0091
> PLAN
> ECO/TAC

BALDWIN G.B.,PLANNING AND DEVELOPMENT IN IRAN. IRAN
AGRI INDUS CONSULT WORKER EDU/PROP BAL/PAY...CHARTS
20. PAGE 8 B0173
> B67
> PLAN
> ECO/UNDEV
> ADMIN
> PROB/SOLV

BUDER S.,PULLMAN: AN EXPERIMENT IN INDUSTRIAL ORDER
AND COMMUNITY PLANNING, 1880-1930. USA-45 SOCIETY
LABOR LG/CO CREATE PROB/SOLV CONTROL GP/REL
EFFICIENCY ATTIT...MGT BIBLIOG 19/20 PULLMAN.
PAGE 17 B0337
> B67
> DIST/IND
> INDUS
> MUNIC
> PLAN

BUREAU GOVERNMENT RES AND SERV,COUNTY GOVERNMENT
REORGANIZATION - A SELECTED ANNOTATED BIBLIOGRAPHY
(PAPER). USA+45 USA-45 LAW CONSTN MUNIC PROVS
EX/STRUC CREATE PLAN PROB/SOLV REPRESENT GOV/REL
20. PAGE 17 B0349
> B67
> BIBLIOG/A
> APPORT
> LOC/G
> ADMIN

ENKE S.,DEFENSE MANAGEMENT. USA+45 R+D FORCES
WORKER PLAN ECO/TAC ADMIN NUC/PWR BAL/PAY UTIL
WEALTH...MGT DEPT/DEFEN. PAGE 33 B0675
> B67
> DECISION
> DELIB/GP
> EFFICIENCY
> BUDGET

GABRIEL P.P.,THE INTERNATIONAL TRANSFER OF
CORPORATE SKILLS: MANAGEMENT CONTRACTS IN LESS
DEVELOPED COUNTRIES. CLIENT INDUS LG/CO PLAN
PROB/SOLV CAP/ISM ECO/TAC FOR/AID INT/TRADE RENT
ADMIN SKILL 20. PAGE 38 B0771
> B67
> ECO/UNDEV
> AGREE
> MGT
> CONSULT

GROSSMAN G.,ECONOMIC SYSTEMS. USA+45 USA-45 USSR
YUGOSLAVIA WORKER CAP/ISM PRICE GP/REL EQUILIB
WEALTH MARXISM SOCISM...MGT METH/COMP 19/20.
PAGE 44 B0892
> B67
> ECO/DEV
> PLAN
> TEC/DEV
> DEMAND

HIRSCHMAN A.O.,DEVELOPMENT PROJECTS OBSERVED. INDUS
INT/ORG CONSULT EX/STRUC CREATE OP/RES ECO/TAC
DEMAND...POLICY MGT METH/COMP 20 WORLD/BANK.
PAGE 50 B1016
> B67
> ECO/UNDEV
> R+D
> FINAN
> PLAN

ILLINOIS COMMISSION,IMPROVING THE STATE
LEGISLATURE. USA+45 LAW CONSTN NAT/G PROB/SOLV
EDU/PROP ADMIN TASK CHOOSE INGP/REL EFFICIENCY
ILLINOIS. PAGE 53 B1077
> B67
> PROVS
> LEGIS
> REPRESENT
> PLAN

JAKUBAUSKAS E.B.,HUMAN RESOURCES DEVELOPMENT.
USA+45 AGRI INDUS SERV/IND ACT/RES PLAN ADMIN
RACE/REL DISCRIM...TREND GEN/LAWS. PAGE 55 B1119
> B67
> PROB/SOLV
> ECO/TAC
> EDU/PROP
> WORKER

KAPLAN H.,URBAN POLITICAL SYSTEMS: A FUNCTIONAL
ANALYSIS OF METRO TORONTO. CANADA STRUCT NEIGH PLAN
ADMIN...POLICY METH 20 TORONTO. PAGE 58 B1166
> B67
> GEN/LAWS
> MUNIC
> LOC/G
> FEDERAL

LEACH R.H.,GOVERNING THE AMERICAN NATION. FUT
USA+45 USA-45 CONSTN POL/PAR PLAN ADJUD EXEC CONSEN
CONGRESS PRESIDENT. PAGE 63 B1278
> B67
> NAT/G
> LEGIS
> PWR

ROBINSON R.D., INTERNATIONAL MANAGEMENT USA+45
FINAN R+D PLAN PRODUC...DECISION T. PAGE 67 B1352
> B67
> INT/TRADE
> MGT
> INT/LAW
> MARKET

MINTZ M.,BY PRESCRIPTION ONLY. USA+45 NAT/G
EX/STRUC PLAN TEC/DEV EXEC EFFICIENCY HEALTH...MGT
SOC/WK 20. PAGE 74 B1491
> B67
> BIO/SOC
> PROC/MFG
> CONTROL
> POLICY

POSNER M.V.,ITALIAN PUBLIC ENTERPRISE. ITALY
ECO/DEV FINAN INDUS CREATE FCO/TAC ADMIN CONTROL
EFFICIENCY PRODUC...TREND CHARTS 20. PAGE 84 B1693
> B67
> NAT/G
> PLAN
> CAP/ISM
> SOCISM

ROTHENBERG J.,ECONOMIC EVALUATION OF URBAN RENEWAL:
CONCEPTUAL FOUNDATION OF BENEFIT-COST ANALYSIS.
USA+45 ECO/DEV NEIGH TEC/DEV ADMIN GEN/LAWS.
PAGE 91 B1834
> B67
> PLAN
> MUNIC
> PROB/SOLV
> COST

SCHLOSSBERG S.I.,ORGANIZING AND THE LAW. USA+45
WORKER PLAN LEGIT REPRESENT GP/REL...JURID MGT 20
NLRB. PAGE 94 B1893
> B67
> LABOR
> CONSULT
> BARGAIN
> PRIVIL

SCHUMACHER B.G.,COMPUTER DYNAMICS IN PUBLIC
ADMINISTRATION. USA+45 CREATE PLAN TEC/DEV...MGT
LING CON/ANAL BIBLIOG/A 20. PAGE 94 B1907
> B67
> COMPUTER
> COMPUT/IR
> ADMIN
> AUTOMAT

TANSKY L.,US AND USSR AID TO DEVELOPING COUNTRIES.
INDIA TURKEY UAR USA+45 USSR FINAN PLAN TEC/DEV
ADMIN WEALTH...TREND METH/COMP 20. PAGE 103 B2076
> B67
> FOR/AID
> ECO/UNDEV
> MARXISM
> CAP/ISM

US DEPARTMENT OF THE ARMY,CIVILIAN IN PEACE,
> B67
> BIBLIOG/A

SOLDIER IN WAR: A BIBLIOGRAPHIC SURVEY OF THE ARMY FORCES
AND AIR NATIONAL GUARD (PAMPHLET, NOS. 130-2). ROLE
USA+45 USA-45 LOC/G NAT/G PROVS LEGIS PLAN ADMIN DIPLOM
ATTIT ORD/FREE...POLICY 19/20. PAGE 108 B2185
B67

US HOUSE COMM SCI ASTRONAUT,GOVERNMENT, SCIENCE, ADMIN
AND INTERNATIONAL POLICY. R+D OP/RES PLAN 20. PHIL/SCI
PAGE 109 B2198 ACT/RES
DIPLOM
B67

WEINBERG M.,SCHOOL INTEGRATION: A COMPREHENSIVE BIBLIOG
CLASSIFIED BIBLIOGRAPHY OF 3,100 REFERENCES. USA+45 SCHOOL
LAW NAT/G NEIGH SECT PLAN ROUTINE AGE/C WEALTH DISCRIM
SOC/INTEG INDIAN/AM. PAGE 115 B2314 RACE/REL
L67

CARMICHAEL D.M.,"FORTY YEARS OF WATER POLLUTION HEALTH
CONTROL IN WISCONSIN: A CASE STUDY." LAW EXTR/IND CONTROL
INDUS MUNIC DELIB/GP PLAN PROB/SOLV SANCTION ADMIN
...CENSUS CHARTS 20 WISCONSIN. PAGE 19 B0382 ADJUD
L67

TRAVERS H. JR.,"AN EXAMINATION OF THE CAB'S MERGER ADJUD
POLICY." USA+45 USA-45 LAW NAT/G LEGIS PLAN ADMIN LG/CO
...DECISION 20 CONGRESS. PAGE 105 B2125 POLICY
DIST/IND
S67

ATKIN J.M.,"THE FEDERAL GOVERNMENT, BIG BUSINESS, SCHOOL
AND COLLEGES OF EDUCATION." PROF/ORG CONSULT CREATE ACADEM
PLAN PROB/SOLV ADMIN EFFICIENCY. PAGE 7 B0144 NAT/G
INDUS
S67

BURACK E.H.,"INDUSTRIAL MANAGEMENT IN ADVANCED ADMIN
PRODUCTION SYSTEMS: SOME THEORETICAL CONCEPTS AND MGT
PRELIMINARY FINDINGS." INDUS CREATE PLAN PRODUC TEC/DEV
ROLE...OBS STAND/INT DEEP/QU HYPO/EXP ORG/CHARTS EX/STRUC
20. PAGE 17 B0346
S67

BURKE E.M.,"THE SEARCH FOR AUTHORITY IN PLANNING." DECISION
MUNIC NEIGH CREATE PROB/SOLV LEGIT ADMIN CONTROL PLAN
EFFICIENCY PWR...METH/COMP SIMUL 20. PAGE 17 B0352 LOC/G
METH
S67

CONWAY J.E.,"MAKING RESEARCH EFFECTIVE IN ACT/RES
LEGISLATION." LAW R+D CONSULT EX/STRUC PLAN CONFER POLICY
ADMIN LEAD ROUTINE TASK INGP/REL DECISION. PAGE 23 LEGIS
B0469 PROB/SOLV
S67

DROR Y.,"POLICY ANALYSTS." USA+45 COMPUTER OP/RES NAT/G
ECO/TAC ADMIN ROUTINE...ECOMETRIC METH/COMP SIMUL POLICY
20. PAGE 30 B0618 PLAN
DECISION
S67

GITTELL M.,"PROFESSIONALISM AND PUBLIC DECISION
PARTICIPATION IN EDUCATIONAL POLICY MAKING." STRUCT PLAN
ADMIN GP/REL ATTIT PWR 20. PAGE 40 B0805 EDU/PROP
MUNIC
S67

GOBER J.L.,"FEDERALISM AT WORK." USA+45 NAT/G MUNIC
CONSULT ACT/RES PLAN CONFER ADMIN LEAD PARTIC TEC/DEV
FEDERAL ATTIT. PAGE 40 B0813 R+D
GOV/REL
S67

GOLIGHTLY H.O.,"THE AIRLINES: A CASE STUDY IN DIST/IND
MANAGEMENT INNOVATION." USA+45 AIR FINAN INDUS MARKET
TOP/EX CREATE PLAN PROB/SOLV ADMIN EXEC PROFIT MGT
...DECISION 20. PAGE 40 B0820 TEC/DEV
S67

GORMAN W.,"ELLUL - A PROPHETIC VOICE." WOR+45 CREATE
ELITES SOCIETY ACT/RES PLAN BAL/PWR DOMIN CONTROL ORD/FREE
PARTIC TOTALISM PWR 20. PAGE 41 B0837 EX/STRUC
UTOPIA
S67

HUGON P.,"BLOCAGES ET DESEQUILIBRES DE LA ECO/UNDEV
CROISSANCE ECONOMIQUE EN AFRIQUE NOIRE." AFR KIN COLONIAL
MUNIC CREATE PLAN INT/TRADE REGION ADJUST CENTRAL STRUCT
EQUILIB NAT/LISM ORD/FREE 20. PAGE 52 B1060 ADMIN
S67

JONES G.S.,"STRATEGIC PLANNING." USA+45 EX/STRUC PLAN
FORCES DETER WAR 20 PRESIDENT. PAGE 57 B1150 DECISION
DELIB/GP
POLICY
S67

KAYSEN C.,"DATA BANKS AND DOSSIERS." FUT USA+45 CENTRAL
COM/IND NAT/G PLAN PROB/SOLV TEC/DEV BUDGET ADMIN EFFICIENCY
ROUTINE. PAGE 59 B1185 CENSUS
ACT/RES
S67

LEES J.P.,"LEGISLATIVE REVIEW AND BUREAUCRATIC SUPEGO
RESPONSIBILITY." USA+45 FINAN NAT/G DELIB/GP PLAN BUDGET
PROB/SOLV CONFER CONTROL GP/REL DEMAND...DECISION LEGIS
20 CONGRESS PRESIDENT HOUSE/REP BUREAUCRCY. PAGE 63 EXEC
B1281
S67

LENDVAI P.,"HUNGARY* CHANGE VS. IMMOBILISM." ECO/DEV
HUNGARY LABOR NAT/G PLAN DEBATE ADMIN ROUTINE MGT
CENTRAL EFFICIENCY MARXISM PLURISM...PREDICT 20. CHOOSE
PAGE 64 B1289

LEVCIK B.,"WAGES AND EMPLOYMENT PROBLEMS IN THE NEW MARXISM
SYSTEM OF PLANNED MANAGEMENT IN CZECHOSLOVAKIA." WORKER
CZECHOSLVK EUR+WWI NAT/G OP/RES PLAN ADMIN ROUTINE MGT
INGP/REL CENTRAL EFFICIENCY PRODUC DECISION. PAY
PAGE 64 B1300
S67

LEVIN M.R.,"PLANNERS AND METROPOLITAN PLANNING." PLAN
FUT USA+45 SOCIETY NAT/G PROVS PROB/SOLV LEAD MUNIC
PARTIC GOV/REL RACE/REL HABITAT ROLE. PAGE 64 B1301 R+D
ADMIN
S67

MACDONALD G.J.F.,"SCIENCE AND SPACE POLICY* HOW SPACE
DOES IT GET PLANNED?" R+D CREATE TEC/DEV BUDGET PLAN
ADMIN ROUTINE...DECISION NASA. PAGE 67 B1357 MGT
EX/STRUC
S67

MCNAMARA R.L.,"THE NEED FOR INNOVATIVENESS IN PROB/SOLV
DEVELOPING SOCIETIES." L/A+17C EDU/PROP ADMIN LEAD PLAN
WEALTH...POLICY PSY SOC METH 20 COLOMB. PAGE 72 ECO/UNDEV
B1456 NEW/IDEA
S67

MOOR E.J.,"THE INTERNATIONAL IMPACT OF AUTOMATION." TEC/DEV
WOR+45 ACT/RES COMPUTER CREATE PLAN CAP/ISM ROUTINE OP/RES
EFFICIENCY PREDICT. PAGE 75 B1511 AUTOMAT
INDUS
S67

PRATT R.C.,"THE ADMINISTRATION OF ECONOMIC PLANNING NAT/G
IN A NEWLY INDEPEND ENT STATE* THE TANZANIAN DELIB/GP
EXPERIENCE 1963-1966." AFR TANZANIA ECO/UNDEV PLAN PLAN
CONTROL ROUTINE TASK EFFICIENCY 20. PAGE 84 B1699 ADMIN
TEC/DEV
S67

ROBERTS E.B.,"THE PROBLEM OF AGING ORGANIZATIONS." INDUS
INTELL PROB/SOLV ADMIN EXEC FEEDBACK EFFICIENCY R+D
PRODUC...GEN/LAWS 20. PAGE 89 B1794 MGT
PLAN
S67

TACKABERRY R.B.,"ORGANIZING AND TRAINING PEACE- PEACE
KEEPING FORCES* THE CANADIAN VIEW." CANADA PLAN FORCES
DIPLOM CONFER ADJUD ADMIN CIVMIL/REL 20 UN. INT/ORG
PAGE 102 B2069 CONSULT
S67

TIVEY L.,"THE POLITICAL CONSEQUENCES OF ECONOMIC PLAN
PLANNING." UK CONSTN INDUS ACT/RES ADMIN CONTROL POLICY
LOBBY REPRESENT EFFICIENCY SUPEGO SOVEREIGN NAT/G
...DECISION 20. PAGE 104 B2112
S67

WRIGHT F.K.,"INVESTMENT CRITERIA AND THE COST OF COST
CAPITAL." FINAN PLAN BUDGET OPTIMAL PRODUC...POLICY PROFIT
DECISION 20. PAGE 118 B2380 INDUS
MGT
N67

NATIONAL COMN COMMUNITY HEALTH,ACTION - PLANNING PLAN
FOR COMMUNITY HEALTH SERVICES (PAMPHLET). USA+45 MUNIC
PROF/ORG DELIB/GP BUDGET ROUTINE GP/REL ATTIT HEALTH
...HEAL SOC SOC/WK CHARTS TIME 20. PAGE 77 B1563 ADJUST
N67

PRINCETON U INDUSTRIAL REL SEC,OUTSTANDING BOOKS ON BIBLIOG/A
INDUSTRIAL RELATIONS, 1966 (PAMPHLET NO. 134). INDUS
WOR+45 LABOR WORKER PLAN PRICE CONTROL INCOME...MGT GP/REL
20. PAGE 85 B1711 POLICY
N67

US SENATE COMM AERO SPACE SCI,AERONAUTICAL RESEARCH DIST/IND
AND DEVELOPMENT POLICY; HEARINGS, COMM ON SPACE
AERONAUTICAL AND SPACE SCIENCES...1967 (PAMPHLET). NAT/G
R+D PROB/SOLV EXEC GOV/REL 20 DEPT/DEFEN FAA NASA PLAN
CONGRESS. PAGE 109 B2210
S68

PEARSON A.W.,"RESOURCE ALLOCATION." PLAN PROB/SOLV PROFIT
BUDGET ADMIN CONTROL CHOOSE EFFICIENCY...DECISION OPTIMAL
MGT 20. PAGE 82 B1649 COST
INDUS

PLAN/UNIT....PLANNED UNIT DEVELOPMENT

PLANO J.C. B1679

PLANTEY A. B1680

PLATO B1681

PLATO....PLATO

PLEKHNV/GV....G.V. PLEKHANOV

PLISCHKE E. B1683,B1684

PLUNKITT/G....G.W. PLUNKITT, TAMMANY BOSS

B05
RIORDAN W.L.,PLUNKITT OF TAMMANY HALL. USA-45 POL/PAR
SOCIETY PROB/SOLV EXEC LEAD TASK CHOOSE ALL/VALS MUNIC
...RECORD ANTHOL 20 REFORMERS TAMMANY NEWYORK/C CHIEF
PLUNKITT/G. PAGE 88 B1789 ATTIT

PLURALISM....SEE PLURISM, PLURIST

PLURISM....PLURALISM, SOCIO-POLITICAL ORDER OF AUTONOMOUS
        GROUPS

N19
LA PALOMBARA J.G.,ALTERNATIVE STRATEGIES FOR | ECO/UNDEV
DEVELOPING ADMINISTRATIVE CAPABILITIES IN EMERGING | MGT
NATIONS (PAMPHLET). POL/PAR EX/STRUC PROB/SOLV | EXEC
PLURISM...POLICY METH/COMP. PAGE 62 B1248 | ADMIN

C27
HSIAO K.C.,"POLITICAL PLURALISM." LAW CONSTN | STRUCT
POL/PAR LEGIS PLAN ADMIN CENTRAL SOVEREIGN | GEN/LAWS
...INT/LAW BIBLIOG 19/20. PAGE 52 B1053 | PLURISM

B35
HOLECOMBE A.N.,GOVERNMENT IN A PLANNED DEMOCRACY. | ADMIN
USA+45 NAT/G EX/STRUC 20. PAGE 51 B1035 | REPRESENT
| LOBBY
| PLURISM

S49
STEINMETZ H.,"THE PROBLEMS OF THE LANDRAT: A STUDY | LOC/G
OF COUNTY GOVERNMENT IN THE US ZONE OF GERMANY." | COLONIAL
GERMANY/W USA+45 INDUS PLAN DIPLOM EDU/PROP CONTROL | MGT
WAR GOV/REL FEDERAL WEALTH PLURISM...GOV/COMP 20 | TOP/EX
LANDRAT. PAGE 100 B2031

C58
REDFORD E.S.,"THE NEVER-ENDING SEARCH FOR THE | LOBBY
PUBLIC INTEREST" IN E. REDFORD, IDEALS AND PRACTICE | POLICY
IN PUBLIC ADMINISTRATION (BMR)" USA+45 USA-45 | ADMIN
SOCIETY PARTIC GP/REL ATTIT PLURISM...DECISION SOC | MAJORIT
20. PAGE 87 B1755

B59
DAHRENDORF R.,CLASS AND CLASS CONFLICT IN | VOL/ASSN
INDUSTRIAL SOCIETY. LABOR NAT/G COERCE ROLE PLURISM | STRUCT
...POLICY MGT CONCPT CLASSIF. PAGE 26 B0523 | SOC
| GP/REL

S59
SEIDMAN H.,"THE GOVERNMENT CORPORATION IN THE | CONTROL
UNITED STATES." USA+45 LEGIS ADMIN PLURISM 20. | GOV/REL
PAGE 95 B1925 | EX/STRUC
| EXEC

B61
BANFIELD E.C.,URBAN GOVERNMENT; A READER IN | MUNIC
POLITICS AND ADMINISTRATION. ELITES LABOR POL/PAR | GEN/METH
EXEC CHOOSE REPRESENT GP/REL PWR PLURISM...PSY SOC. | DECISION
PAGE 9 B0177

S61
EHRMANN H.W.,"FRENCH BUREAUCRACY AND ORGANIZED | ADMIN
INTERESTS" (BMR)" FRANCE NAT/G DELIB/GP ROUTINE | DECISION
...INT 20 BUREAUCRCY CIVIL/SERV. PAGE 32 B0657 | PLURISM
| LOBBY

B64
CATER D.,POWER IN WASHINGTON: A CRITICAL LOOK AT | REPRESENT
TODAY'S STRUGGLE TO GOVERN IN THE NATION'S CAPITAL. | GOV/REL
USA+45 NAT/G LEGIS ADMIN EXEC LOBBY PLURISM 20. | INGP/REL
PAGE 19 B0392 | EX/STRUC

B64
WILDAVSKY A.,LEADERSHIP IN A SMALL TOWN. USA+45 | LEAD
STRUCT PROB/SOLV EXEC PARTIC RACE/REL PWR PLURISM | MUNIC
...SOC 20 NEGRO WATER CIV/RIGHTS OBERLIN CITY/MGT. | ELITES
PAGE 116 B2348

L64
GILBERT C.E.,"NATIONAL POLITICAL ALIGNMENTS AND THE | MUNIC
POLITICS OF LARGE CITIES." ELITES LOC/G NAT/G LEGIS | CHOOSE
EXEC LEAD PLURISM GOV/COMP. PAGE 39 B0800 | POL/PAR
| PWR

S64
KAMMERER G.M.,"URBAN LEADERSHIP DURING CHANGE." | MUNIC
LEAD PARTIC REPRESENT GP/REL PLURISM...DECISION | PWR
GP/COMP. PAGE 58 B1164 | ELITES
| EXEC

B65
KOENIG C.W.,OFFICIAL MAKERS OF PUBLIC POLICY: | CHIEF
CONGRESS AND THE PRESIDENT. USA+45 USA-45 NAT/G | LEGIS
EX/STRUC PROB/SOLV PWR. PAGE 60 B1222 | GOV/REL
| PLURISM

S67
LENDVAI P.,"HUNGARY* CHANGE VS. IMMOBILISM." | ECO/DEV
HUNGARY LABOR NAT/G PLAN DEBATE ADMIN ROUTINE | MGT
CENTRAL EFFICIENCY MARXISM PLURISM...PREDICT 20. | CHOOSE
PAGE 64 B1289

S67
WEIL G.L.,"THE MERGER OF THE INSTITUTIONS OF THE | ECO/TAC
EUROPEAN COMMUNITIES" EUR+WWI ECO/DEV INT/TRADE | INT/ORG
CONSEN PLURISM...DECISION MGT 20 EEC EURATOM ECSC | CENTRAL
TREATY. PAGE 115 B2313 | INT/LAW

PLURIST....PLURALIST

B50
LASSWELL H.D.,NATIONAL SECURITY AND INDIVIDUAL | FACE/GP
FREEDOM. USA+45 R+D NAT/G VOL/ASSN CONSULT DELIB/GP | ROUTINE
LEGIT ADMIN KNOWL ORD/FREE PWR...PLURIST TOT/POP | BAL/PWR
COLD/WAR 20. PAGE 63 B1268

S52
EDELMAN M.,"GOVERNMENTAL ORGANIZATION AND PUBLIC | ADMIN
POLICY." DELIB/GP ADJUD DECISION. PAGE 32 B0652 | PLURIST
| LOBBY

EX/STRUC
B56
KIRK G.,THE CHANGING ENVIRONMENT OF INTERNATIONAL | FUT
RELATIONS. ASIA S/ASIA USA+45 WOR+45 ECO/UNDEV | EXEC
INT/ORG NAT/G FOR/AID EDU/PROP PEACE KNOWL | DIPLOM
...PLURIST COLD/WAR TOT/POP 20. PAGE 60 B1214

S59
KISSINGER H.A.,"THE POLICYMAKER AND THE | INTELL
INTELLECTUAL." USA+45 CONSULT DELIB/GP ACT/RES | CREATE
ADMIN ATTIT DRIVE RIGID/FLEX KNOWL PWR...POLICY
PLURIST MGT METH/CNCPT GEN/LAWS GEN/METH 20.
PAGE 60 B1216

S60
GARNICK D.H.,"ON THE ECONOMIC FEASIBILITY OF A | MARKET
MIDDLE EASTERN COMMON MARKET." AFR ISLAM CULTURE | INT/TRADE
INDUS NAT/G PLAN TEC/DEV ECO/TAC ADMIN ATTIT DRIVE
RIGID/FLEX...PLURIST STAT TREND GEN/LAWS 20.
PAGE 39 B0784

S61
KUIC V.,"THEORY AND PRACTICE OF THE AMERICAN | EXEC
PRESIDENCY." USA+45 USA-45 NAT/G ADMIN REPRESENT | EX/STRUC
...PLURIST 20 PRESIDENT. PAGE 61 B1241 | PWR
| CHIEF

B64
GOODMAN W.,THE TWO-PARTY SYSTEM IN THE UNITED | POL/PAR
STATES. USA+45 USA-45 STRATA LOC/G CHIEF EDU/PROP | REPRESENT
ADMIN COST PWR POPULISM...PLURIST 18/20 PRESIDENT. | CHOOSE
PAGE 41 B0821 | NAT/G

S65
CHARLESWORTH J.C.,"ALLOCATION OF RESPONSIBILITIES | PROVS
AND RESOURCES AMONG THE THREE LEVELS OF | NAT/G
GOVERNMENT." USA+45 USA-45 ECO/DEV MUNIC PLAN LEGIT | LG/CO
...PLURIST MGT. PAGE 20 B0415 | WEALTH

S67
LLOYD K.,"URBAN RACE RIOTS V EFFECTIVE ANTI- | GP/REL
DISCRIMINATION AGENCIES* AN END OR A BEGINNING?" | DISCRIM
USA+45 STRATA ACT/RES ADMIN ADJUST ORD/FREE RESPECT | LOC/G
...PLURIST DECISION SOC SOC/WK. PAGE 66 B1332 | CROWD

POL....POLITICAL AND POWER PROCESS

POL/PAR....POLITICAL PARTIES

N
SOVIET-EAST EUROPEAN RES SERV,SOVIET SOCIETY. USSR | BIBLIOG/A
LABOR POL/PAR PRESS MARXISM...MARXIST 20. PAGE 99 | EDU/PROP
B2001 | ADMIN
| SOC

N
JOURNAL OF POLITICS. USA+45 USA-45 CONSTN POL/PAR | BIBLIOG/A
EX/STRUC LEGIS PROB/SOLV DIPLOM CT/SYS CHOOSE | NAT/G
RACE/REL 20. PAGE 1 B0005 | LAW
| LOC/G

N
HANDBOOK OF LATIN AMERICAN STUDIES. LAW CULTURE | BIBLIOG/A
ECO/UNDEV POL/PAR ADMIN LEAD...SOC 20. PAGE 1 B0014 | L/A+17C
| NAT/G
| DIPLOM

N
PUBLISHERS' TRADE LIST ANNUAL. LAW POL/PAR ADMIN | BIBLIOG
PERSON ALL/IDEOS...HUM SOC 19/20. PAGE 1 B0020 | NAT/G
| DIPLOM
| POLICY

N
SUBJECT GUIDE TO BOOKS IN PRINT: AN INDEX TO THE | BIBLIOG
PUBLISHERS' TRADE LIST ANNUAL. UNIV LAW LOC/G | ECO/DEV
DIPLOM WRITING ADMIN LEAD PERSON...MGT SOC. PAGE 1 | POL/PAR
B0023 | NAT/G

N
NEUE POLITISCHE LITERATUR; BERICHTE UBER DAS | BIBLIOG/A
INTERNATIONALE SCHRIFTTUM ZUR POLITIK. WOR+45 LAW | DIPLOM
CONSTN POL/PAR ADMIN LEAD GOV/REL...POLICY | NAT/G
IDEA/COMP. PAGE 2 B0027 | NAT/COMP

N
DEUTSCHE BUCHEREI,DEUTSCHES BUCHERVERZEICHNIS. | BIBLIOG
GERMANY LAW CULTURE POL/PAR ADMIN LEAD ATTIT PERSON | NAT/G
...SOC 20. PAGE 29 B0581 | DIPLOM
| ECO/DEV

N
STATE OF ILLINOIS,PUBLICATIONS OF THE STATE OF | BIBLIOG
ILLINOIS. USA+45 FINAN POL/PAR ADMIN LEAD 20 | PROVS
ILLINOIS. PAGE 100 B2024 | LOC/G
| GOV/REL

N
VIRGINIA STATE LIBRARY,CHECK-LIST OF VIRGINIA STATE | BIBLIOG/A
PUBLICATIONS. USA+45 USA-45 ECO/DEV POL/PAR LEGIS | PROVS
ADJUD LEAD 18/20. PAGE 112 B2265 | ADMIN
| GOV/REL

B05
RIORDAN W.L.,PLUNKITT OF TAMMANY HALL. USA-45 | POL/PAR
SOCIETY PROB/SOLV EXEC LEAD TASK CHOOSE ALL/VALS | MUNIC
...RECORD ANTHOL 20 REFORMERS TAMMANY NEWYORK/C | CHIEF
PLUNKITT/G. PAGE 88 B1789 | ATTIT

B08
WILSON W.,CONSTITUTIONAL GOVERNMENT IN THE UNITED | NAT/G
STATES. USA-45 LAW POL/PAR PROVS CHIEF LEGIS | GOV/REL

BAL/PWR ADJUD EXEC FEDERAL PWR 18/20 SUPREME/CT HOUSE/REP SENATE. PAGE 117 B2362 — CONSTN PARL/PROC

B17
HARLOW R.V.,THE HISTORY OF LEGISLATIVE METHODS IN THE PERIOD BEFORE 1825. USA-45 EX/STRUC ADMIN COLONIAL LEAD PARL/PROC ROUTINE...GP/COMP GOV/COMP HOUSE/REP. PAGE 47 B0948 — LEGIS DELIB/GP PROVS POL/PAR

B19
NATHAN M.,THE SOUTH AFRICAN COMMONWEALTH: CONSTITUTION, PROBLEMS, SOCIAL CONDITIONS. SOUTH/AFR UK CULTURE INDUS EX/STRUC LEGIS BUDGET EDU/PROP ADMIN CT/SYS GP/REL RACE/REL...LING 19/20 CMN/WLTH. PAGE 77 B1559 — CONSTN NAT/G POL/PAR SOCIETY

N19
LA PALOMBARA J.G.,ALTERNATIVE STRATEGIES FOR DEVELOPING ADMINISTRATIVE CAPABILITIES IN EMERGING NATIONS (PAMPHLET). POL/PAR EX/STRUC PROB/SOLV PLURISM...POLICY METH/COMP. PAGE 62 B1248 — ECO/UNDEV MGT EXEC ADMIN

N19
OPERATIONS AND POLICY RESEARCH,PERU ELECTION MEMORANDA (PAMPHLET). L/A+17C PERU POL/PAR LEGIS EXEC APPORT REPRESENT 20. PAGE 80 B1611 — CHOOSE CONSTN SUFF NAT/G

N19
TREVELYAN G.M.,THE TWO-PARTY SYSTEM IN ENGLISH POLITICAL HISTORY (PAMPHLET). UK CHIEF LEGIS COLONIAL EXEC REV CHOOSE 17/19. PAGE 105 B2128 — PARL/PROC POL/PAR NAT/G PWR

B21
BRYCE J.,MODERN DEMOCRACIES. FUT NEW/ZEALND USA-45 LAW CONSTN POL/PAR PROVS VOL/ASSN EX/STRUC LEGIS LEGIT CT/SYS EXEC KNOWL CONGRESS AUSTRAL 20. PAGE 16 B0332 — NAT/G TREND

B23
FRANK T.,A HISTORY OF ROME. MEDIT-7 INTELL SOCIETY LOC/G NAT/G POL/PAR FORCES LEGIS DOMIN LEGIT ALL/VALS...POLICY CONCPT TIME/SEQ GEN/LAWS ROM/EMP ROM/EMP. PAGE 37 B0749 — EXEC STRUCT ELITES

B24
KENT F.R.,THE GREAT GAME OF POLITICS. USA-45 LOC/G NAT/G POL/PAR EX/STRUC PROB/SOLV BUDGET CHOOSE GOV/REL 20. PAGE 59 B1194 — ADMIN OP/RES STRUCT

B26
INTERNATIONAL BIBLIOGRAPHY OF POLITICAL SCIENCE. WOR+45 NAT/G POL/PAR EX/STRUC LEGIS CT/SYS LEAD CHOOSE GOV/REL ATTIT...PHIL/SCI 20. PAGE 2 B0034 — BIBLIOG DIPLOM CONCPT ADMIN

C27
HSIAO K.C.,"POLITICAL PLURALISM." LAW CONSTN POL/PAR LEGIS PLAN ADMIN CENTRAL SOVEREIGN ...INT/LAW BIBLIOG 19/20. PAGE 52 B1053 — STRUCT GEN/LAWS PLURISM

B28
FYFE H.,THE BRITISH LIBERAL PARTY. UK SECT ADMIN LEAD CHOOSE GP/REL PWR SOCISM...MAJORIT TIME/SEQ 19/20 LIB/PARTY CONSRV/PAR. PAGE 38 B0768 — POL/PAR NAT/G REPRESENT POPULISM

B29
MERRIAM C.E.,CHICAGO: A MORE INTIMATE VIEW OF URBAN POLITICS. USA-45 CONSTN POL/PAR LEGIS ADMIN CRIME INGP/REL 18/20 CHICAGO. PAGE 73 B1472 — STRUCT GP/REL MUNIC

B29
MOLEY R.,POLITICS AND CRIMINAL PROSECUTION. USA-45 POL/PAR EX/STRUC LEGIT CONTROL LEAD ROUTINE CHOOSE INGP/REL...JURID CHARTS 20. PAGE 74 B1497 — PWR CT/SYS CRIME ADJUD

B30
ZINK H.,CITY BOSSES IN THE UNITED STATES: A STUDY OF TWENTY MUNICIPAL BOSSES. USA-45 INDUS MUNIC NEIGH POL/PAR ADMIN CRIME INGP/REL PERS/REL PWR ...PERS/COMP 20 BOSSISM. PAGE 119 B2403 — LOC/G DOMIN BIOG LEAD

B37
CLOKIE H.M.,ROYAL COMMISSIONS OF INQUIRY; THE SIGNIFICANCE OF INVESTIGATIONS IN BRITISH POLITICS. UK POL/PAR CONFER ROUTINE...POLICY DECISION TIME/SEQ 16/20. PAGE 22 B0439 — NAT/G DELIB/GP INSPECT

B37
GOSNELL H.F.,MACHINE POLITICS: CHICAGO MODEL. COM/IND FACE/GP LOC/G EX/STRUC LEAD ROUTINE SANCTION REPRESENT GOV/REL PWR...POLICY MATH OBS INT CHARTS. PAGE 41 B0840 — POL/PAR MUNIC ADMIN CHOOSE

B38
HARPER S.N.,THE GOVERNMENT OF THE SOVIET UNION. COM USSR LAW CONSTN ECO/DEV PLAN TEC/DEV DIPLOM INT/TRADE ADMIN REV NAT/LISM...POLICY 20. PAGE 47 B0952 — MARXISM NAT/G LEAD POL/PAR

B38
PETTEE G.S.,THE PROCESS OF REVOLUTION. COM FRANCE ITALY MOD/EUR RUSSIA SPAIN WOR-45 ELITES INTELL SOCIETY STRATA STRUCT INT/ORG NAT/G POL/PAR ACT/RES PLAN EDU/PROP LEGIT EXEC...SOC MYTH TIME/SEQ TOT/POP 18/20. PAGE 82 B1664 — COERCE CONCPT REV

B38
RAPPARD W.E.,THE CRISIS OF DEMOCRACY. EUR+WWI UNIV WOR-45 CULTURE SOCIETY ECO/DEV INT/ORG POL/PAR ACT/RES EDU/PROP EXEC CHOOSE ATTIT ALL/VALS...SOC OBS HIST/WRIT TIME/SEQ LEAGUE/NAT NAZI TOT/POP 20. — NAT/G CONCPT

PAGE 86 B1741

B38
SALTER J.T.,THE AMERICAN POLITICIAN. USA-45 LABOR POL/PAR EDU/PROP ADMIN CHOOSE ATTIT DRIVE PERSON PWR...POLICY ANTHOL 20 THOMAS/N LEWIS/JL LAGUARD/F GOVERNOR MAYOR. PAGE 92 B1865 — BIOG LEAD PROVS LOC/G

B39
HITLER A.,MEIN KAMPF. EUR+WWI FUT MOD/EUR STRUCT INT/ORG LABOR NAT/G POL/PAR FORCES CREATE PLAN BAL/PWR DIPLOM ECO/TAC DOMIN EDU/PROP ADMIN COERCE ATTIT...SOCIALIST BIOG TREND NAZI. PAGE 50 B1020 — PWR NEW/IDEA WAR

B39
JENNINGS W.I.,PARLIAMENT. UK POL/PAR OP/RES BUDGET LEAD CHOOSE GP/REL...MGT 20 PARLIAMENT HOUSE/LORD HOUSE/CMNS. PAGE 56 B1135 — PARL/PROC LEGIS CONSTN NAT/G

C39
REISCHAUER R.,"JAPAN'S GOVERNMENT--POLITICS." CONSTN STRATA POL/PAR FORCES LEGIS DIPLOM ADMIN EXEC CENTRAL...POLICY BIBLIOG 20 CHINJAP. PAGE 87 B1764 — NAT/G S/ASIA CONCPT ROUTINE

B40
MCHENRY D.E.,HIS MAJESTY'S OPPOSITION: STRUCTURE AND PROBLEMS OF THE BRITISH LABOUR PARTY 1931-1938. UK FINAN LABOR LOC/G DELIB/GP LEGIS EDU/PROP LEAD PARTIC CHOOSE GP/REL SOCISM...TREND 20 LABOR/PAR. PAGE 72 B1450 — POL/PAR MGT NAT/G POLICY

S40
FAHS C.B.,"POLITICAL GROUPS IN THE JAPANESE HOUSE OF PEERS." ELITES NAT/G ADMIN GP/REL...TREND CHINJAP. PAGE 34 B0697 — ROUTINE POL/PAR LEGIS

S40
GERTH H.,"THE NAZI PARTY: ITS LEADERSHIP AND COMPOSITION" (BMR)" GERMANY ELITES STRATA STRUCT EX/STRUC FORCES ECO/TAC CT/SYS CHOOSE TOTALISM AGE/Y AUTHORIT PWR 20. PAGE 39 B0792 — POL/PAR DOMIN LEAD ADMIN

S40
PERKINS J.A.,"CONGRESSIONAL INVESTIGATIONS OF MATTERS OF INTERNATIONAL IMPORT." DELIB/GP DIPLOM ADMIN CONTROL 20 CONGRESS. PAGE 82 B1656 — POL/PAR DECISION PARL/PROC GOV/REL

B42
BINGHAM A.M.,THE TECHNIQUES OF DEMOCRACY. USA-45 CONSTN STRUCT POL/PAR LEGIS PLAN PARTIC CHOOSE REPRESENT NAT/LISM TOTALISM...MGT 20. PAGE 12 B0240 — POPULISM ORD/FREE ADMIN NAT/G

B42
BROWN A.D.,LIST OF REFERENCES ON THE CIVIL SERVICE AND PERSONNEL ADMINISTRATION IN THE UNITED STATES (2ND MIMEOGRAPHED SUPPLEMENT). USA-45 LOC/G POL/PAR PROVS FEDERAL...TESTS 20. PAGE 16 B0319 — BIBLIOG ADMIN MGT NAT/G

B42
NEUBURGER O.,OFFICIAL PUBLICATIONS OF PRESENT-DAY GERMANY: GOVERNMENT, CORPORATE ORGANIZATIONS, AND NATIONAL SOCIALIST PARTY. GERMANY CONSTN COM/IND POL/PAR EDU/PROP PRESS 20 NAZI. PAGE 78 B1570 — BIBLIOG/A FASCISM NAT/G ADMIN

B45
CONOVER H.F.,THE GOVERNMENTS OF THE MAJOR FOREIGN POWERS: A BIBLIOGRAPHY. FRANCE GERMANY ITALY UK USSR CONSTN LOC/G POL/PAR EX/STRUC FORCES ADMIN CT/SYS CIVMIL/REL TOTALISM...POLICY 19/20. PAGE 23 B0464 — BIBLIOG NAT/G DIPLOM

C45
FISHER M.J.,"PARTIES AND POLITICS IN THE LOCAL COMMUNITY." USA-45 NAT/G SCHOOL ADMIN PARTIC REPRESENT KNOWL...BIBLIOG 20. PAGE 36 B0724 — CHOOSE LOC/G POL/PAR ROUTINE

B46
BIBLIOGRAFIIA DISSERTATSII: DOKTORSKIE DISSERTATSII ZA 19411944 (2 VOLS). COM USSR LAW POL/PAR DIPLOM ADMIN LEAD...PHIL/SCI SOC 20. PAGE 2 B0035 — BIBLIOG ACADEM KNOWL MARXIST

B46
CORRY J.A.,DEMOCRATIC GOVERNMENT AND POLITICS. WOR-45 EX/STRUC LOBBY TOTALISM...MAJORIT CONCPT METH/COMP NAT/COMP 20. PAGE 24 B0479 — NAT/G CONSTN POL/PAR JURID

B47
BORGESE G.,COMMON CAUSE. LAW CONSTN SOCIETY STRATA ECO/DEV INT/ORG POL/PAR FORCES LEGIS TOP/EX CAP/ISM DIPLOM ADMIN EXEC ATTIT PWR 20. PAGE 14 B0279 — WOR+45 NAT/G SOVEREIGN REGION

B47
FLYNN E.J.,YOU'RE THE BOSS. USA-45 ELITES TOP/EX DOMIN CONTROL EXEC LEAD REPRESENT 19/20 NEWYORK/C ROOSEVLT/F FLYNN/BOSS BOSSISM. PAGE 36 B0732 — LOC/G MUNIC BIOG POL/PAR

B47
KEFAUVER E.,A TWENTIETH-CENTURY CONGRESS. POL/PAR EX/STRUC SENIOR ADMIN CONTROL EXEC LOBBY CHOOSE EFFICIENCY PWR. PAGE 59 B1189 — LEGIS DELIB/GP ROUTINE TOP/EX

B47
PATTERSON C.P.,PRESIDENTIAL GOVERNMENT IN THE UNITED STATES - THE UNWRITTEN CONSTITUTION. USA+45 DELIB/GP EX/STRUC ADJUD ADMIN EXEC...DECISION — CHIEF NAT/G CONSTN

PRESIDENT. PAGE 81 B1643   POL/PAR

B48

BISHOP H.M.,BASIC ISSUES OF AMERICAN DEMOCRACY.   NAT/G
USA+45 USA-45 POL/PAR EX/STRUC LEGIS ADJUD FEDERAL PARL/PROC
...BIBLIOG 18/20. PAGE 12 B0244   CONSTN

B48

HART J.,THE AMERICAN PRESIDENCY IN ACTION 1789: A   NAT/G
STUDY IN CONSTITUTIONAL HISTORY. USA+45 POL/PAR   CONSTN
DELIB/GP FORCES LEGIS ADJUD ADMIN LEAD GP/REL   CHIEF
PERS/REL 18 PRESIDENT CONGRESS. PAGE 47 B0959   EX/STRUC

B48

STOKES W.S.,BIBLIOGRAPHY OF STANDARD AND CLASSICAL BIBLIOG
WORKS IN THE FIELDS OF AMERICAN POLITICAL SCIENCE. NAT/G
USA+45 USA-45 POL/PAR PROVS FORCES DIPLOM ADMIN   LOC/G
CT/SYS APPORT 20 CONGRESS PRESIDENT. PAGE 101 B2043 CONSTN

C48

WALKER H.,"THE LEGISLATIVE PROCESS; LAWMAKING IN   PARL/PROC
THE UNITED STATES." NAT/G POL/PAR PROVS EX/STRUC   LEGIS
OP/RES PROB/SOLV CT/SYS LOBBY GOV/REL...CHARTS   LAW
BIBLIOG T 18/20 CONGRESS. PAGE 113 B2279   CONSTN

B49

ASPINALL A.,POLITICS AND THE PRESS 1780-1850. UK   PRESS
LAW ELITES FINAN PROF/ORG LEGIS ADMIN ATTIT   CONTROL
...POLICY 18/19. PAGE 7 B0142   POL/PAR
                                                    ORD/FREE

B49

RIDDICK F.M.,THE UNITED STATES CONGRESS   LEGIS
ORGANIZATION AND PROCEDURE. POL/PAR DELIB/GP   PARL/PROC
PROB/SOLV DEBATE CONTROL EXEC LEAD INGP/REL PWR   CHIEF
...MAJORIT DECISION CONGRESS PRESIDENT. PAGE 88   EX/STRUC
B1777

B49

ROSENHAUPT H.W.,HOW TO WAGE PEACE. USA+45 SOCIETY   INTELL
STRATA STRUCT R+D INT/ORG POL/PAR LEGIS ACT/RES   CONCPT
CREATE PLAN EDU/PROP ADMIN EXEC ATTIT ALL/VALS   DIPLOM
...TIME/SEQ TREND COLD/WAR 20. PAGE 90 B1822

B50

AMERICAN POLITICAL SCI ASSN,TOWARD A MORE   POL/PAR
RESPONSIBLE TWO-PARTY SYSTEM. USA+45 CONSTN   TASK
VOL/ASSN LEGIS LEAD CHOOSE...POLICY MGT 20. PAGE 4 PARTIC
B0087   ACT/RES

B50

KOENIG L.W.,THE SALE OF THE TANKERS. USA+45 SEA   NAT/G
DIST/IND POL/PAR DIPLOM ADMIN CIVMIL/REL ATTIT   POLICY
...DECISION 20 PRESIDENT DEPT/STATE. PAGE 60 B1223 PLAN
                                                    GOV/REL

B50

MCHENRY D.E.,THE THIRD FORCE IN CANADA: THE   POL/PAR
COOPERATIVE COMMONWEALTH FEDERATION, 1932-1948.   ADMIN
CANADA EX/STRUC LEGIS REPRESENT 20 LABOR/PAR.   CHOOSE
PAGE 72 B1451   POLICY

B50

MONTGOMERY H.,CRACKER PARTIES. CULTURE EX/STRUC   POL/PAR
LEAD PWR POPULISM...TIME/SEQ 19 GEORGIA CALHOUN/JC PROVS
COBB/HOWLL JACKSON/A. PAGE 74 B1505   ELITES
                                                    BIOG

S50

EPSTEIN L.D.,"POLITICAL STERILIZATION OF CIVIL   ADMIN
SERVANTS: THE UNITED STATES AND GREAT BRITAIN." UK LEGIS
USA+45 USA-45 STRUCT TOP/EX OP/RES PARTIC CHOOSE   DECISION
NAT/LISM 20 CONGRESS CIVIL/SERV. PAGE 33 B0679   POL/PAR

S50

HUMPHREY H.H.,"THE SENATE ON TRIAL." USA+45 POL/PAR PARL/PROC
DEBATE REPRESENT EFFICIENCY ATTIT RIGID/FLEX   ROUTINE
...TRADIT SENATE. PAGE 52 B1064   PWR
                                                    LEGIS

S50

NEUMANN F.L.,"APPROACHES TO THE STUDY OF POLITICAL PWR
POWER." POL/PAR TOP/EX ADMIN LEAD ATTIT ORD/FREE   IDEA/COMP
CONSERVE LAISSEZ MARXISM...PSY SOC. PAGE 78 B1572   CONCPT

C50

HOLCOMBE A.,"OUR MORE PERFECT UNION." USA+45 USA-45 CONSTN
POL/PAR JUDGE CT/SYS EQUILIB FEDERAL PWR...MAJORIT NAT/G
TREND BIBLIOG 18/20 CONGRESS PRESIDENT. PAGE 51   ADMIN
B1031   PLAN

C50

STOKES W.S.,"HONDURAS: AN AREA STUDY IN   CONSTN
GOVERNMENT." HONDURAS NAT/G POL/PAR COLONIAL CT/SYS LAW
ROUTINE CHOOSE REPRESENT...GEOG RECORD BIBLIOG   L/A+17C
19/20. PAGE 101 B2044   ADMIN

B51

ANDERSON W.,STATE AND LOCAL GOVERNMENT IN THE   LOC/G
UNITED STATES. USA+45 CONSTN POL/PAR EX/STRUC LEGIS MUNIC
BUDGET TAX ADJUD CT/SYS CHOOSE...CHARTS T 20.   PROVS
PAGE 5 B0100   GOV/REL

B51

ANDERSON W.,GOVERNMENT IN THE FIFTY STATES. LAW   LOC/G
CONSTN FINAN POL/PAR LEGIS EDU/PROP ADJUD ADMIN   PROVS
CT/SYS CHOOSE...CHARTS 20. PAGE 5 B0101   GOV/REL

B51

CHRISTENSEN A.N.,THE EVOLUTION OF LATIN AMERICAN   NAT/G
GOVERNMENT: A BOOK OF READINGS. ECO/UNDEV INDUS   CONSTN
LOC/G POL/PAR EX/STRUC LEGIS FOR/AID CT/SYS   DIPLOM
...SOC/WK 20 SOUTH/AMER. PAGE 21 B0428   L/A+17C

B51

US LIBRARY OF CONGRESS,EAST EUROPEAN ACCESSIONS   BIBLIOG/A

LIST (VOL. I). POL/PAR DIPLOM ADMIN LEAD 20.   COM
PAGE 109 B2204   SOCIETY
                                                    NAT/G

B51

WHITE L.D.,THE JEFFERSONIANS: A STUDY IN   ADMIN
ADMINISTRATIVE HISTORY 18011829. USA+45 DELIB/GP   NAT/G
LEGIS TOP/EX PROB/SOLV BUDGET ECO/TAC GP/REL   POLICY
FEDERAL...BIOG IDEA/COMP 19 PRESIDENT CONGRESS   POL/PAR
JEFFERSN/T. PAGE 116 B2338

S51

MARX F.M.,"SIGNIFICANCE FOR THE ADMINISTRATIVE   LEGIS
PROCESS." POL/PAR LEAD PARL/PROC GOV/REL EFFICIENCY ADMIN
SUPEGO...POLICY CONGRESS. PAGE 70 B1420   CHIEF

S51

SCHRAMM W.,"COMMUNICATION IN THE SOVIETIZED STATE, ATTIT
AS DEMONSTRATED IN KOREA." ASIA COM KOREA COM/IND   EDU/PROP
FACE/GP POL/PAR SCHOOL FORCES ADMIN PWR MARXISM   TOTALISM
...SOC CONCPT MYTH INT BIOG TOT/POP 20. PAGE 94
B1901

B52

HIMMELFARB G.,LORD ACTON: A STUDY IN CONSCIENCE AND PWR
POLITICS. MOD/EUR NAT/G POL/PAR SECT LEGIS TOP/EX   BIOG
EDU/PROP ADMIN NAT/LISM ATTIT PERSON SUPEGO MORAL
ORD/FREE...CONCPT PARLIAMENT 19 ACTON/LORD. PAGE 50
B1014

B52

POOL I.,SYMBOLS OF DEMOCRACY. WOR+45 WOR-45 POL/PAR INTELL
FORCES ADMIN PERSON PWR...CONCPT 20. PAGE 83 B1687 SOCIETY
                                                    USSR

B52

SELZNICK P.,THE ORGANIZATIONAL WEAPON: A STUDY OF   MARXISM
BOLSHEVIK STRATEGY AND TACTICS. USSR SOCIETY STRATA POL/PAR
LABOR DOMIN EDU/PROP PARTIC REV ATTIT PWR...POLICY LEAD
MGT CONCPT 20 BOLSHEVISM. PAGE 95 B1929   TOTALISM

B52

ULAM A.B.,TITOISM AND THE COMINFORM. USSR WOR+45   COM
STRUCT INT/ORG NAT/G ACT/RES PLAN EXEC ATTIT DRIVE POL/PAR
ALL/VALS...CONCPT OBS VAL/FREE 20 COMINTERN   TOTALISM
TITO/MARSH. PAGE 106 B2145   YUGOSLAVIA

S52

LIPSET S.M.,"DEMOCRACY IN PRIVATE GOVERNMENT; (A   LABOR
CASE STUDY OF THE INTERNATIONAL TYPOGRAPHICAL   ADMIN
UNION)" (BMR)" POL/PAR CONTROL LEAD INGP/REL PWR   ELITES
...MAJORIT DECISION PREDICT 20. PAGE 65 B1319   REPRESENT

C52

LASSWELL H.D.,"THE COMPARATIVE STUDY OF ELITES: AN ELITES
INTRODUCTION AND BIBLIOGRAPHY." STRATA POL/PAR   LEAD
EDU/PROP ADMIN LOBBY COERCE ATTIT PERSON PWR   CONCPT
...BIBLIOG 20. PAGE 63 B1270   DOMIN

B53

GROSS B.M.,THE LEGISLATIVE STRUGGLE: A STUDY IN   LEGIS
SOCIAL COMBAT. STRUCT LOC/G POL/PAR JUDGE EDU/PROP DECISION
DEBATE ETIQUET ADMIN LOBBY CHOOSE GOV/REL INGP/REL PERSON
HEREDITY ALL/VALS...SOC PRESIDENT. PAGE 44 B0885   LEAD

B53

SECKLER-HUDSON C.,BIBLIOGRAPHY ON PUBLIC   BIBLIOG/A
ADMINISTRATION (4TH ED.). USA+45 LAW POL/PAR   ADMIN
DELIB/GP BUDGET ADJUD LOBBY GOV/REL GP/REL ATTIT   NAT/G
...JURID 20. PAGE 95 B1923   MGT

B53

STOUT H.M.,BRITISH GOVERNMENT. UK FINAN LOC/G   NAT/G
POL/PAR DELIB/GP DIPLOM ADMIN COLONIAL CHOOSE   PARL/PROC
ORD/FREE...JURID BIBLIOG 20 COMMONWLTH. PAGE 101   CONSTN
B2049   NEW/LIB

S53

MORRIS B.S.,"THE COMINFORM: A FIVE YEAR   VOL/ASSN
PERSPECTIVE." COM UNIV USSR WOR+45 ECO/DEV POL/PAR EDU/PROP
TOP/EX PLAN DOMIN ADMIN TOTALISM ATTIT ALL/VALS   DIPLOM
...CONCPT TIME/SEQ TREND CON/ANAL WORK VAL/FREE 20.
PAGE 76 B1527

C53

BULNER-THOMAS I.,"THE PARTY SYSTEM IN GREAT   NAT/G
BRITAIN." UK CONSTN SECT PRESS CONFER GP/REL ATTIT POL/PAR
...POLICY TREND BIBLIOG 19/20 PARLIAMENT. PAGE 17   ADMIN
B0343   ROUTINE

B54

DUVERGER M.,POLITICAL PARTIES: THEIR ORGANIZATION   POL/PAR
AND ACTIVITY IN THE MODERN STATE. EUR+WWI MOD/EUR   EX/STRUC
USA+45 USA-45 EDU/PROP ADMIN ROUTINE ATTIT DRIVE   ELITES
ORD/FREE PWR...SOC CONCPT MATH STAT TIME/SEQ
TOT/POP 19/20. PAGE 31 B0635

B54

JENNINGS I.,THE QUEEN'S GOVERNMENT. UK POL/PAR   NAT/G
DELIB/GP ADJUD ADMIN CT/SYS PARL/PROC REPRESENT   CONSTN
CONSERVE 13/20 PARLIAMENT. PAGE 56 B1132   LEGIS
                                                    CHIEF

B54

WHITE L.D.,THE JACKSONIANS: A STUDY IN   NAT/G
ADMINISTRATIVE HISTORY 1829-1861. USA+45 CONSTN   ADMIN
POL/PAR CHIEF DELIB/GP LEGIS CREATE PROB/SOLV   POLICY
ECO/TAC LEAD REGION GP/REL 19 PRESIDENT CONGRESS
JACKSON/A. PAGE 116 B2339

L54

ARCIENEGAS G.,"POST-WAR SOVIET FOREIGN POLICY: A   INTELL
WORLD PERSPECTIVE." COM USA+45 STRUCT NAT/G POL/PAR ACT/RES
TOP/EX PLAN ADMIN ALL/VALS...TREND COLD/WAR TOT/POP USSR

20. PAGE 6 B0124

S54
CHILDS R.S.,"CITIZEN ORGANIZATION FOR CONTROL OF GOVERNMENT." USA+45 POL/PAR CONTROL LOBBY...MAJORIT 20. PAGE 21 B0424
CHOOSE REPRESENT ADMIN EX/STRUC

C54
CALDWELL L.K.,"THE GOVERNMENT AND ADMINISTRATION OF NEW YORK." LOC/G MUNIC POL/PAR SCHOOL CHIEF LEGIS PLAN TAX CT/SYS...MGT SOC/WK BIBLIOG 20 NEWYORK/C. PAGE 18 B0366
PROVS ADMIN CONSTN EX/STRUC

C54
LANDAU J.M.,"PARLIAMENTS AND PARTIES IN EGYPT." UAR NAT/G SECT CONSULT LEGIS TOP/EX PROB/SOLV ADMIN COLONIAL...GEN/LAWS BIBLIOG 19/20. PAGE 62 B1254
ISLAM NAT/LISM PARL/PROC POL/PAR

C54
ZELLER B.,"AMERICAN STATE LEGISLATURES: REPORT ON THE COMMITTEE ON AMERICAN LEGISLATURES." CONSTN POL/PAR EX/STRUC CONFER ADMIN CONTROL EXEC LOBBY ROUTINE GOV/REL...POLICY BIBLIOG 20. PAGE 119 B2401
REPRESENT LEGIS PROVS APPORT

B55
APTER D.E.,THE GOLD COAST IN TRANSITION. FUT CONSTN CULTURE SOCIETY ECO/UNDEV FAM KIN LOC/G NAT/G POL/PAR LEGIS TOP/EX EDU/PROP LEGIT ADMIN ATTIT PERSON PWR...CONCPT STAT INT CENSUS TOT/POP VAL/FREE. PAGE 6 B0120
AFR SOVEREIGN

B55
GALLOWAY G.B.,CONGRESS AND PARLIAMENT: THEIR ORGANIZATION AND OPERATION IN THE US AND THE UK: PLANNING PAMPHLET NO. 93. POL/PAR EX/STRUC DEBATE CONTROL LEAD ROUTINE EFFICIENCY PWR...POLICY CONGRESS PARLIAMENT. PAGE 38 B0777
DELIB/GP LEGIS PARL/PROC GOV/COMP

B55
MAZZINI J.,THE DUTIES OF MAN. MOD/EUR LAW SOCIETY FAM NAT/G POL/PAR SECT VOL/ASSN EX/STRUC ACT/RES CREATE REV PEACE ATTIT ALL/VALS...GEN/LAWS WORK 19. PAGE 71 B1439
SUPEGO CONCPT NAT/LISM

B55
RUSTOW D.A.,THE POLITICS OF COMPROMISE. SWEDEN LABOR EX/STRUC LEGIS PLAN REPRESENT SOCISM...SOC 19/20. PAGE 92 B1859
POL/PAR NAT/G POLICY ECO/TAC

L55
ROSTOW W.W.,"RUSSIA AND CHINA UNDER COMMUNISM." CHINA/COM USSR INTELL STRUCT INT/ORG NAT/G POL/PAR TOP/EX ACT/RES PLAN ADMIN ATTIT ALL/VALS MARXISM ...CONCPT OBS TIME/SEQ TREND GOV/COMP VAL/FREE 20. PAGE 91 B1830
COM ASIA

S55
KAUTSKY J.H.,"THE NEW STRATEGY OF INTERNATIONAL COMMUNISM." ASIA CHINA/COM FUT WOR+45 WOR-45 ADMIN ROUTINE PERSON MARXISM SOCISM...TREND IDEA/COMP 20 LENIN/VI MAO. PAGE 59 B1184
COM POL/PAR TOTALISM USSR

B56
ABELS J.,THE TRUMAN SCANDALS. USA+45 USA-45 POL/PAR TAX LEGIT CT/SYS CHOOSE PRIVIL MORAL WEALTH 20 TRUMAN/HS PRESIDENT CONGRESS. PAGE 3 B0052
CRIME ADMIN CHIEF TRIBUTE

B56
DEGRAS J.,THE COMMUNIST INTERNATIONAL, 1919-1943: DOCUMENTS (3 VOLS.). EX/STRUC...ANTHOL BIBLIOG 20. PAGE 28 B0569
COM DIPLOM POLICY POL/PAR

B56
HOWARD L.V.,TULANE STUDIES IN POLITICAL SCIENCE: CIVIL SERVICE DEVELOPMENT IN LOUISIANA VOLUME 3. LAW POL/PAR LEGIS CT/SYS ADJUST ORD/FREE...STAT CHARTS 19/20 LOUISIANA CIVIL/SERV. PAGE 52 B1050
ADMIN GOV/REL PROVS POLICY

B56
JENNINGS W.I.,THE APPROACH TO SELF-GOVERNMENT. CEYLON INDIA PAKISTAN S/ASIA UK SOCIETY POL/PAR DELIB/GP LEGIS ECO/TAC EDU/PROP ADMIN EXEC CHOOSE ATTIT ALL/VALS...JURID CONCPT GEN/METH TOT/POP 20. PAGE 56 B1136
NAT/G CONSTN COLONIAL

B56
KOENIG L.W.,THE TRUMAN ADMINISTRATION: ITS PRINCIPLES AND PRACTICE. USA+45 POL/PAR CHIEF LEGIS DIPLOM DEATH NUC/PWR WAR CIVMIL/REL PEACE ...DECISION 20 TRUMAN/HS PRESIDENT TREATY. PAGE 61 B1224
ADMIN POLICY EX/STRUC GOV/REL

B56
POWELL N.J.,PERSONNEL ADMINISTRATION IN GOVERNMENT. COM/IND POL/PAR LEGIS PAY CT/SYS ROUTINE GP/REL PERS/REL...POLICY METH 20 CIVIL/SERV. PAGE 84 B1697
ADMIN WORKER LOC/G NAT/G

B56
RANSONE C.B.,THE OFFICE OF GOVERNOR IN THE UNITED STATES. USA+45 ADMIN...MGT INT CHARTS 20 GOVERNOR. PAGE 86 B1732
PROVS TOP/EX POL/PAR EX/STRUC

B56
WAUGH E.W.,SECOND CONSUL. USA+45 USA-45 CONSTN POL/PAR PROB/SOLV PARL/PROC CHOOSE PERS/REL ATTIT ...BIBLIOG 18/20 VICE/PRES. PAGE 114 B2304
NAT/G EX/STRUC PWR CHIEF

B56
WEBER M.,STAATSSOZIOLOGIE. STRUCT LEGIT ADMIN PARL/PROC SUPEGO CONSERVE JURID. PAGE 114 B2305
SOC NAT/G POL/PAR LEAD

B56
WILSON P.,GOVERNMENT AND POLITICS OF INDIA AND PAKISTAN: 1885-1955; A BIBLIOGRAPHY OF WORKS IN WESTERN LANGUAGES. INDIA PAKISTAN CONSTN LOC/G POL/PAR FORCES DIPLOM ADMIN WAR CHOOSE...BIOG CON/ANAL 19/20. PAGE 117 B2361
BIBLIOG COLONIAL NAT/G S/ASIA

B56
WU E.,LEADERS OF TWENTIETH-CENTURY CHINA; AN ANNOTATED BIBLIOGRAPHY OF SELECTED CHINESE BIOGRAPHICAL WORKS IN HOOVER LIBRARY. ASIA INDUS POL/PAR DIPLOM ADMIN REV WAR...HUM MGT 20. PAGE 118 B2386
BIBLIOG/A BIOG INTELL CHIEF

L56
MACMAHON A.W.,"WOODROW WILSON AS LEGISLATIVE LEADER AND ADMINISTRATOR." CONSTN POL/PAR ADMIN...POLICY HIST/WRIT WILSON/W PRESIDENT. PAGE 68 B1371
LEGIS CHIEF LEAD BIOG

S56
HEADY F.,"THE MICHIGAN DEPARTMENT OF ADMINISTRATION; A CASE STUDY IN THE POLITICS OF ADMINISTRATION" (BMR)" USA+45 POL/PAR PROVS CHIEF LEGIS GP/REL ATTIT 20 MICHIGAN. PAGE 48 B0980
ADMIN DELIB/GP LOC/G

S56
KHAMA T.,"POLITICAL CHANGE IN AFRICAN SOCIETY." CONSTN SOCIETY LOC/G NAT/G POL/PAR EX/STRUC LEGIS LEGIT ADMIN CHOOSE REPRESENT NAT/LISM MORAL ORD/FREE PWR...CONCPT OBS TREND GEN/METH CMN/WLTH 17/20. PAGE 59 B1201
AFR ELITES

C56
FALL B.B.,"THE VIET-MINH REGIME." VIETNAM LAW ECO/UNDEV POL/PAR FORCES DOMIN WAR ATTIT MARXISM ...BIOG PREDICT BIBLIOG/A 20. PAGE 35 B0703
NAT/G ADMIN EX/STRUC LEAD

C56
NEUMANN S.,"MODERN POLITICAL PARTIES: APPROACHES TO COMPARATIVE POLITIC. FRANCE UK EX/STRUC DOMIN ADMIN LEAD REPRESENT TOTALISM ATTIT...POLICY TREND METH/COMP ANTHOL BIBLIOG/A 20 CMN/WLTH. PAGE 78 B1574
POL/PAR GOV/COMP ELITES MAJORIT

B57
BABCOCK R.S.,STATE & LOCAL GOVERNMENT AND POLITICS. USA+45 CONSTN POL/PAR EX/STRUC LEGIS BUDGET LOBBY CHOOSE SUFF...CHARTS BIBLIOG T 20. PAGE 8 B0154
PROVS LOC/G GOV/REL

B57
CHANDRA S.,PARTIES AND POLITICS AT THE MUGHAL COURT: 1707-1740. INDIA CULTURE EX/STRUC CREATE PLAN PWR...BIBLIOG/A 18. PAGE 20 B0405
POL/PAR ELITES NAT/G

B57
DJILAS M.,THE NEW CLASS: AN ANALYSIS OF THE COMMUNIST SYSTEM. STRATA CAP/ISM ECO/TAC DOMIN EDU/PROP LEGIT EXEC COERCE ATTIT PWR MARXISM ...MARXIST MGT CONCPT TIME/SEQ GEN/LAWS 20. PAGE 29 B0600
COM POL/PAR USSR YUGOSLAVIA

B57
IKE N.,JAPANESE POLITICS. INTELL STRUCT AGRI INDUS FAM KIN LABOR PRESS CHOOSE ATTIT...DECISION BIBLIOG 19/20 CHINJAP. PAGE 53 B1075
NAT/G ADMIN POL/PAR CULTURE

B57
JENNINGS I.,PARLIAMENT. UK FINAN INDUS POL/PAR DELIB/GP EX/STRUC PLAN CONTROL...MAJORIT JURID PARLIAMENT. PAGE 56 B1133
PARL/PROC TOP/EX MGT LEGIS

B57
KNEIER C.M.,CITY GOVERNMENT IN THE UNITED STATES (3RD ED.). USA-45 FINAN NAT/G POL/PAR LEGIS EDU/PROP LEAD APPORT REPRESENT ATTIT...MGT 20 CITY/MGT. PAGE 60 B1219
MUNIC LOC/G ADMIN GOV/REL

B57
LOEWENSTEIN K.,POLITICAL POWER AND THE GOVERNMENTAL PROCESS. WOR+45 WOR-45 CONSTN NAT/G POL/PAR EX/STRUC LEGIS TOP/EX DOMIN EDU/PROP LEGIT ADMIN REGION CHOOSE ATTIT...JURID STERTYP GEN/LAWS 20. PAGE 66 B1336
PWR CONCPT

S57
BAUER R.A.,"BRAINWASHING: PSYCHOLOGY OR DEMONOLOGY." ASIA CHINA/COM COM POL/PAR ECO/TAC ADMIN COERCE ATTIT DRIVE ORD/FREE...CONCPT MYTH 20 PAGE 10 B0196
EDU/PROP PSY TOTALISM

S57
HUITT R.K.,"THE MORSE COMMITTEE ASSIGNMENT CONTROVERSY: A STUDY IN SENATE NORMS." USA+45 USA-45 POL/PAR SENIOR ROLE SUPEGO SENATE. PAGE 52 B1061
LEGIS ETIQUET PWR ROUTINE

C57
TANG P.S.H.,"COMMUNIST CHINA TODAY: DOMESTIC AND FOREIGN POLICIES." CHINA/COM COM S/ASIA USSR STRATA FORCES DIPLOM EDU/PROP COERCE GOV/REL...POLICY MAJORIT BIBLIOG 20. PAGE 102 B2071
POL/PAR LEAD ADMIN CONSTN

B58
BERNSTEIN M.H.,THE JOB OF THE FEDERAL EXECUTIVE.
NAT/G

POL/PAR CHIEF LEGIS ADMIN EXEC LOBBY CHOOSE GOV/REL TOP/EX
ORD/FREE PWR...MGT TREND. PAGE 11 B0228   PERS/COMP
                                                       B58
CARTER G.M..TRANSITION IN AFRICA; STUDIES IN   NAT/COMP
POLITICAL ADAPTATION. AFR CENTRL/AFR GHANA NIGERIA   PWR
CONSTN LOC/G POL/PAR ADMIN GP/REL FEDERAL...MAJORIT   CONTROL
BIBLIOG 20. PAGE 19 B0389   NAT/G
                                                       B58
COLEMAN J.S..NIGERIA: BACKGROUND TO NATIONALISM.   NAT/G
AFR SOCIETY ECO/DEV KIN LOC/G POL/PAR TEC/DEV DOMIN   NAT/LISM
ADMIN DRIVE PWR RESPECT...TRADIT SOC INT SAMP   NIGERIA
TIME/SEQ 20. PAGE 22 B0452   B58
COWAN L.G..LOCAL GOVERNMENT IN WEST AFRICA. AFR   LOC/G
FRANCE UK CULTURE KIN POL/PAR CHIEF LEGIS CREATE   COLONIAL
ADMIN PARTIC GOV/REL GP/REL...METH/COMP 20. PAGE 24   SOVEREIGN
B0498   REPRESENT
                                                       B58
KAPLAN H.E..THE LAW OF CIVIL SERVICE. USA+45 LAW   ADJUD
POL/PAR CT/SYS CRIME GOV/REL...POLICY JURID 20.   NAT/G
PAGE 58 B1167   ADMIN
                                                       CONSTN
                                                       B58
LESTER R.A..AS UNIONS MATURE. POL/PAR BARGAIN LEAD   LABOR
PARTIC GP/REL CENTRAL...MAJORIT TIME/SEQ METH/COMP.   INDUS
PAGE 64 B1299   POLICY
                                                       MGT
                                                       B58
NEAL F.W..TITOISM IN ACTION. COM YUGOSLAVIA AGRI   MARXISM
LOC/G DIPLOM TOTALISM...BIBLIOG 20 TITO/MARSH.   POL/PAR
PAGE 77 B1564   CHIEF
                                                       ADMIN
                                                       B58
SCOTT D.J.R..RUSSIAN POLITICAL INSTITUTIONS. RUSSIA   NAT/G
USSR CONSTN AGRI DELIB/GP PLAN EDU/PROP CONTROL   POL/PAR
CHOOSE EFFICIENCY ATTIT MARXISM...BIBLIOG/A 13/20.   ADMIN
PAGE 95 B1919   DECISION
                                                       B58
SPITZ D..DEMOCRACY AND THE CHALLANGE OF POWER. FUT   NAT/G
USA+45 USA-45 LAW SOCIETY STRUCT LOC/G POL/PAR   PWR
PROVS DELIB/GP EX/STRUC LEGIS TOP/EX ACT/RES CREATE
DOMIN EDU/PROP LEGIT ADJUD ADMIN ATTIT DRIVE MORAL
ORD/FREE TOT/POP. PAGE 99 B2010
                                                       B58
TAYLOR H..THE STATESMAN. MOD/EUR FACE/GP FAM NAT/G   EXEC
POL/PAR DELIB/GP LEGIS ATTIT PERSON PWR...POLICY   STRUCT
CONCPT OBS GEN/LAWS. PAGE 103 B2086
                                                       L58
HAVILAND H.F.."FOREIGN AID AND THE POLICY PROCESS: LEGIS
1957." USA+45 FACE/GP POL/PAR VOL/ASSN CHIEF   PLAN
DELIB/GP ACT/RES LEGIT EXEC GOV/REL ATTIT DRIVE PWR   FOR/AID
...POLICY TESTS CONGRESS 20. PAGE 48 B0971
                                                       L58
JONAS F.H.."BIBLIOGRAPHY ON WESTERN POLITICS."   BIBLIOG/A
USA+45 USA-45 ELITES MUNIC POL/PAR LEGIS ADJUD   LOC/G
ADMIN 20. PAGE 57 B1148   NAT/G
                                                       LAW
                                                       S58
DAHL R.A.."A CRITIQUE OF THE RULING ELITE MODEL."   CONCPT
USA+45 LOC/G MUNIC NAT/G POL/PAR PROVS DOMIN LEGIT   STERTYP
ADMIN...METH/CNCPT HYPO/EXP. PAGE 25 B0520   ELITES
                                                       S58
DERGE D.R.."METROPOLITAN AND OUTSTATE ALIGNMENTS IN   LEGIS
ILLINOIS AND MISSOURI LEGISLATIVE DELEGATIONS"   MUNIC
(BMR)" USA+45 ADMIN PARTIC GOV/REL...MYTH CHARTS 20   PROVS
ILLINOIS MISSOURI. PAGE 28 B0575   POL/PAR
                                                       S58
STAAR R.F.."ELECTIONS IN COMMUNIST POLAND." EUR+WWI   COM
SOCIETY IND/ORG NAT/G POL/PAR LEGIS ACT/RES ECO/TAC   CHOOSE
EDU/PROP ADJUD ADMIN ROUTINE COERCE TOTALISM ATTIT   POLAND
ORD/FREE PWR 20. PAGE 100 B2015
                                                       C58
GOLAY J.F.."THE FOUNDING OF THE FEDERAL REPUBLIC OF   FEDERAL
GERMANY." GERMANY/W CONSTN EX/STRUC DIPLOM ADMIN   NAT/G
CHOOSE...DECISION BIBLIOG 20. PAGE 40 B0814   PARL/PROC
                                                       POL/PAR
                                                       C58
WILDING N.."AN ENCYCLOPEDIA OF PARLIAMENT." UK LAW   PARL/PROC
CONSTN CHIEF PROB/SOLV DIPLOM DEBATE WAR INGP/REL   POL/PAR
PRIVIL...BIBLIOG DICTIONARY 13/20 CMN/WLTH   NAT/G
PARLIAMENT. PAGE 116 B2350   ADMIN
                                                       B59
BOWLES C..THE COMING POLITICAL BREAKTHROUGH. USA+45   DIPLOM
ECO/DEV EX/STRUC ATTIT...CONCPT OBS 20. PAGE 14   CHOOSE
B0288   PREDICT
                                                       POL/PAR
                                                       B59
DUVERGER M..LA CINQUIEME REPUBLIQUE. FRANCE WOR+45   NAT/G
POL/PAR CHIEF EX/STRUC LOBBY. PAGE 31 B0636   CONSTN
                                                       GOV/REL
                                                       PARL/PROC
                                                       B59
EPSTEIN F.T..EAST GERMANY: A SELECTED BIBLIOGRAPHY   BIBLIOG/A
(PAMPHLET). COM GERMANY/E LAW AGRI FINAN INDUS   INTELL
LABOR POL/PAR EDU/PROP ADMIN AGE/Y 20. PAGE 33   MARXISM
B0677   NAT/G

                                                       B59
JENNINGS W.I..CABINET GOVERNMENT (3RD ED.). UK   DELIB/GP
POL/PAR CHIEF BUDGET ADMIN CHOOSE GP/REL 20.   NAT/G
PAGE 56 B1137   CONSTN
                                                       OP/RES
                                                       B59
LOEWENSTEIN K..VERFASSUNGSRECHT UND   CONSTN
VERFASSUNGSPRAXIS DER VEREINIGTEN STAATEN. USA+45   POL/PAR
USA-45 COLONIAL CT/SYS GP/REL RACE/REL ORD/FREE   EX/STRUC
...JURID 18/20 SUPREME/CT CONGRESS PRESIDENT   NAT/G
BILL/RIGHT CIVIL/LIB. PAGE 66 B1337
                                                       B59
MAYNTZ R..PARTEIGRUPPEN IN DER GROSSSTADT. GERMANY   MUNIC
STRATA STRUCT DOMIN CHOOSE 20. PAGE 71 B1437   MGT
                                                       POL/PAR
                                                       ATTIT
                                                       B59
SAYER W.S..AN AGENDA FOR RESEARCH IN PUBLIC   WORKER
PERSONNEL ADMINISTRATION. FUT USA+45 ACADEM LABOR   ADMIN
LOC/G NAT/G POL/PAR DELIB/GP MGT. PAGE 93 B1872   ACT/RES
                                                       CONSULT
                                                       B59
SINHA H.N..OUTLINES OF POLITICAL SCIENCE. NAT/G   JURID
POL/PAR EX/STRUC LEGIS CT/SYS CHOOSE REPRESENT 20.   CONCPT
PAGE 98 B1971   ORD/FREE
                                                       SOVEREIGN
                                                       S59
JEWELL M.R.."THE SENATE REPUBLICAN POLICY COMMITTEE   POL/PAR
AND FOREIGN POLICY." PLAN ADMIN CONTROL LEAD LOBBY   NAT/G
EFFICIENCY PRESIDENT 20 REPUBLICAN. PAGE 56 B1139   DELIB/GP
                                                       POLICY
                                                       B60
JUNZ A.J., PRESENT TRENDS IN AMERICAN NATIONAL   POL/PAR
GOVERNMENT. LEGIS DIPLOM ADMIN CT/SYS ORD/FREE   CHOOSE
...CONCPT ANTHOL 20 CONGRESS PRESIDENT SUPREME/CT.   CONSTN
PAGE 2 B0048   NAT/G
                                                       B60
ADRIAN C.R..STATE AND LOCAL GOVERNMENTS: A STUDY IN   LOC/G
THE POLITICAL PROCESS. USA+45 LAW FINAN MUNIC   PROVS
POL/PAR LEGIS ADJUD EXEC CHOOSE REPRESENT. PAGE 3   GOV/REL
B0060   ATTIT
                                                       B60
AYEARST M..THE BRITISH WEST INDIES: THE SEARCH FOR   CONSTN
SELF-GOVERNMENT. FUT WEST/IND LOC/G POL/PAR   COLONIAL
EX/STRUC LEGIS CHOOSE FEDERAL...NAT/COMP BIBLIOG   REPRESENT
17/20. PAGE 7 B0152   NAT/G
                                                       B60
DRAPER T..AMERICAN COMMUNISM AND SOVIET RUSSIA.   COM
EUR+WWI USA+45 USSR INTELL AGRI COM/IND FINAN INDUS   POL/PAR
LABOR PROF/ORG VOL/ASSN PLAN TEC/DEV DOMIN EDU/PROP
ADMIN COERCE REV PERSON PWR...POLICY CONCPT MYTH
19/20. PAGE 30 B0617
                                                       B60
GRANICK D..THE RED EXECUTIVE. COM USA+45 SOCIETY   PWR
ECO/DEV INDUS NAT/G POL/PAR EX/STRUC PLAN ECO/TAC   STRATA
EDU/PROP ADMIN EXEC ATTIT DRIVE...GP/COMP 20.   USSR
PAGE 42 B0851   ELITES
                                                       B60
LINDSAY K..EUROPEAN ASSEMBLIES: THE EXPERIMENTAL   VOL/ASSN
PERIOD 1949-1959. EUR+WWI ECO/DEV NAT/G POL/PAR   INT/ORG
LEGIS TOP/EX ACT/RES PLAN ECO/TAC DOMIN LEGIT   REGION
ROUTINE ATTIT DRIVE ORD/FREE PWR SKILL...SOC CONCPT
TREND CHARTS GEN/LAWS VAL/FREE. PAGE 65 B1315
                                                       B60
LIPSET S.M..POLITICAL MAN. AFR COM EUR+WWI L/A+17C   PWR
MOD/EUR S/ASIA USA+45 STRUCT ECO/DEV   SOC
ECO/UNDEV POL/PAR SECT ADMIN WEALTH...CONCPT WORK
TOT/POP 20. PAGE 65 B1320
                                                       B60
MEYRIAT J..LA SCIENCE POLITIQUE EN FRANCE,   BIBLIOG/A
1945-1958; BIBLIOGRAPHIES FRANCAISES DE SCIENCES   NAT/G
SOCIALES (VOL. I). EUR+WWI FRANCE POL/PAR DIPLOM   CONCPT
ADMIN CHOOSE ATTIT...IDEA/COMP METH/COMP NAT/COMP   PHIL/SCI
20. PAGE 73 B1478
                                                       B60
MORISON E.E..TURMOIL AND TRADITION: A STUDY OF THE   BIOG
LIFE AND TIMES OF HENRY L. STIMSON. USA+45 USA-45   NAT/G
POL/PAR CHIEF DELIB/GP FORCES BAL/PWR DIPLOM   EX/STRUC
ARMS/CONT WAR PEACE 19/20 STIMSON/HL ROOSEVLT/F
TAFT/WH HOOVER/H REPUBLICAN. PAGE 75 B1525
                                                       B60
ROY N.C..THE CIVIL SERVICE IN INDIA. INDIA POL/PAR   ADMIN
ECO/TAC INCOME...JURID MGT 20 CIVIL/SERV. PAGE 91   NAT/G
B1843   DELIB/GP
                                                       CONFER
                                                       B60
SAYRE W.S..GOVERNING NEW YORK CITY; POLITICS IN THE   MUNIC
METROPOLIS. POL/PAR CHIEF DELIB/GP LEGIS PLAN   ADMIN
CT/SYS LEAD PARTIC CHOOSE...DECISION CHARTS BIBLIOG   PROB/SOLV
20 NEWYORK/C BUREAUCRCY. PAGE 93 B1875
                                                       B60
SCHUBERT G..THE PUBLIC INTEREST. USA+45 CONSULT   POLICY
PLAN PROB/SOLV ADJUD ADMIN GP/REL PWR ALL/IDEOS 20.   DELIB/GP
PAGE 94 B1903   REPRESENT
                                                       POL/PAR

B60
WORLEY P.,ASIA TODAY (REV. ED.) (PAMPHLET). COM
ECO/UNDEV AGRI FINAN INDUS POL/PAR FOR/AID ADMIN
MARXISM 20. PAGE 118 B2376
BIBLIOG/A
ASIA
DIPLOM
NAT/G

L60
GRODZINS M.,"AMERICAN POLITICAL PARTIES AND THE
AMERICAN SYSTEM" (BMR)" USA+45 LOC/G NAT/G LEGIS
BAL/PWR ADMIN ROLE PWR...DECISION 20. PAGE 44 B0883
POL/PAR
FEDERAL
CENTRAL
GOV/REL

S60
APTER D.E.,"THE ROLE OF TRADITIONALISM IN THE
POLITICAL MODERNIZATION OF GHANA AND UGANDA" (BMR)"
AFR GHANA UGANDA CULTURE NAT/G POL/PAR NAT/LISM
...CON/ANAL 20. PAGE 6 B0121
CONSERVE
ADMIN
GOV/COMP
PROB/SOLV

S60
EMERSON R.,"THE EROSION OF DEMOCRACY." AFR FUT LAW
CULTURE INTELL SOCIETY ECO/UNDEV FAM LOC/G NAT/G
FORCES PLAN TEC/DEV ECO/TAC ADMIN CT/SYS ATTIT
ORD/FREE PWR...SOCIALIST SOC CONCPT STAND/INT
TIME/SEQ WORK 20. PAGE 33 B0671
S/ASIA
POL/PAR

S60
GROSSMAN G.,"SOVIET GROWTH: ROUTINE, INERTIA, AND
PRESSURE." COM STRATA NAT/G DELIB/GP PLAN TEC/DEV
ECO/TAC EDU/PROP ADMIN ROUTINE DRIVE WEALTH
COLD/WAR 20. PAGE 44 B0891
POL/PAR
ECO/DEV
USSR

S60
HERZ J.H.,"EAST GERMANY: PROGRESS AND PROSPECTS."
COM AGRI FINAN INDUS LOC/G NAT/G FORCES PLAN
TEC/DEV DOMIN ADMIN COERCE DRIVE PERCEPT RIGID/FLEX
MORAL ORD/FREE PWR...MARXIST PSY SOC RECORD STERTYP
WORK. PAGE 49 B0997
POL/PAR
STRUCT
GERMANY

S60
NELSON R.H.,"LEGISLATIVE PARTICIPATION IN THE
TREATY AND AGREEMENT MAKING PROCESS." CONSTN
POL/PAR PLAN EXEC PWR FAO UN CONGRESS. PAGE 78
B1569
LEGIS
PEACE
DECISION
DIPLOM

S60
SCHWARTZ B.,"THE INTELLIGENTSIA IN COMMUNIST CHINA:
A TENTATIVE COMPARISON." ASIA CHINA/COM COM RUSSIA
ELITES SOCIETY STRATA POL/PAR VOL/ASSN CREATE ADMIN
COERCE NAT/LISM TOTALISM...POLICY TREND 20. PAGE 95
B1914
INTELL
RIGID/FLEX
REV

C60
SCHAPIRO L.B.,"THE COMMUNIST PARTY OF THE SOVIET
UNION." USSR INTELL CHIEF EX/STRUC FORCES DOMIN
ADMIN LEAD WAR ATTIT SOVEREIGN...POLICY BIBLIOG 20.
PAGE 93 B1881
POL/PAR
COM
REV

B61
ARMSTRONG J.A.,AN ESSAY ON SOURCES FOR THE STUDY OF
THE COMMUNIST PARTY OF THE SOVIET UNION, 1934-1960
(EXTERNAL RESEARCH PAPER 137). USSR EX/STRUC ADMIN
LEAD REV 20. PAGE 7 B0134
BIBLIOG/A
COM
POL/PAR
MARXISM

B61
BANFIELD E.C.,URBAN GOVERNMENT; A READER IN
POLITICS AND ADMINISTRATION. ELITES LABOR POL/PAR
EXEC CHOOSE REPRESENT GP/REL PWR PLURISM...PSY SOC.
PAGE 9 B0177
MUNIC
GEN/METH
DECISION

B61
BARNES W.,THE FOREIGN SERVICE OF THE UNITED STATES.
USA+45 USA-45 CONSTN INT/ORG POL/PAR CONSULT
DELIB/GP LEGIS DOMIN EDU/PROP EXEC ATTIT RIGID/FLEX
ORD/FREE PWR...POLICY CONCPT STAT OBS RECORD BIOG
TIME/SEQ TREND. PAGE 9 B0188
NAT/G
MGT
DIPLOM

B61
BISHOP D.G.,THE ADMINISTRATION OF BRITISH FOREIGN
RELATIONS. EUR+WWI MOD/EUR INT/ORG NAT/G POL/PAR
DELIB/GP LEGIS TOP/EX ECO/TAC DOMIN EDU/PROP ADMIN
COERCE 20. PAGE 12 B0243
ROUTINE
PWR
DIPLOM
UK

B61
BURDETTE F.L.,POLITICAL SCIENCE: A SELECTED
BIBLIOGRAPHY OF BOOKS IN PRINT, WITH ANNOTATIONS
(PAMPHLET). LAW LOC/G NAT/G POL/PAR PROVS DIPLOM
EDU/PROP ADMIN CHOOSE ATTIT 20. PAGE 17 B0347
BIBLIOG/A
GOV/COMP
CONCPT
ROUTINE

B61
DRAGNICH A.N.,MAJOR EUROPEAN GOVERNMENTS. FRANCE
GERMANY/W UK USSR LOC/G EX/STRUC CT/SYS PARL/PROC
ATTIT MARXISM...JURID MGT NAT/COMP 19/20. PAGE 30
B0615
NAT/G
LEGIS
CONSTN
POL/PAR

B61
GRIFFITH E.S.,CONGRESS: ITS CONTEMPORARY ROLE.
CONSTN POL/PAR CHIEF PLAN BUDGET DIPLOM CONFER
ADMIN LOBBY...DECISION CONGRESS. PAGE 43 B0878
PARL/PROC
EX/STRUC
TOP/EX
LEGIS

B61
JANOWITZ M.,COMMUNITY POLITICAL SYSTEMS. USA+45
SOCIETY INDUS VOL/ASSN TEC/DEV ADMIN LEAD CHOOSE
...SOC SOC/WK 20. PAGE 56 B1123
MUNIC
STRUCT
POL/PAR

B61
LENIN V.I.,WHAT IS TO BE DONE? (1902). RUSSIA LABOR
NAT/G POL/PAR WORKER CAP/ISM ECO/TAC ADMIN PARTIC
...MARXIST IDEA/COMP GEN/LAWS 19/20. PAGE 64 B1292
EDU/PROP
PRESS
MARXISM
METH/COMP

B61
MACRIDIS R.C.,COMPARATIVE POLITICS: NOTES AND
READINGS. WOR+45 LOC/G MUNIC NAT/G PROVS VOL/ASSN
POL/PAR
CHOOSE

EDU/PROP ADMIN ATTIT PERSON ORD/FREE...SOC CONCPT
OBS RECORD TREND 20. PAGE 68 B1376

B61
MARVICK D.,POLITICAL DECISION-MAKERS. INTELL STRATA
NAT/G POL/PAR EX/STRUC LEGIS DOMIN EDU/PROP ATTIT
PERSON PWR...PSY STAT OBS CONT/OBS STAND/INT
UNPLAN/INT TIME/SEQ CHARTS STERTYP VAL/FREE.
PAGE 70 B1416
TOP/EX
BIOG
ELITES

B61
MARX K.,THE COMMUNIST MANIFESTO. IN (MENDEL A.
ESSENTIAL WORKS OF MARXISM. NEW YORK: BANTAM. FUT
MOD/EUR CULTURE ECO/DEV ECO/UNDEV AGRI FINAN INDUS
MARKET PROC/MFG LABOR MUNIC POL/PAR CONSULT FORCES
CREATE PLAN ADMIN ATTIT DRIVE RIGID/FLEX ORD/FREE
PWR RESPECT MARX/KARL WORK. PAGE 70 B1421
COM
NEW/IDEA
CAP/ISM
REV

B61
MOLLAU G.,INTERNATIONAL COMMUNISM AND WORLD
REVOLUTION: HISTORY AND METHODS. RUSSIA USSR
INT/ORG NAT/G POL/PAR VOL/ASSN FORCES BAL/PWR
DIPLOM EXEC REGION WAR ATTIT PWR MARXISM...CONCPT
TIME/SEQ COLD/WAR 19/20. PAGE 74 B1498
COM
REV

B61
MUNGER E.S.,AFRICAN FIELD REPORTS 1952-1961.
SOUTH/AFR SOCIETY ECO/UNDEV NAT/G POL/PAR COLONIAL
EXEC PARL/PROC GUERRILLA RACE/REL ALL/IDEOS...SOC
AUD/VIS 20. PAGE 76 B1538
AFR
DISCRIM
RECORD

B61
NARAIN J.P.,SWARAJ FOR THE PEOPLE. INDIA CONSTN
LOC/G MUNIC POL/PAR CHOOSE REPRESENT EFFICIENCY
ATTIT PWR SOVEREIGN 20. PAGE 77 B1553
NAT/G
ORD/FREE
EDU/PROP
EX/STRUC

B61
PAGE T.,STATE PERSONNEL REORGANIZATION IN ILLINOIS.
USA+45 POL/PAR CHIEF TEC/DEV LEAD ADJUST 20.
PAGE 80 B1625
ADMIN
PROVS
WORKER
DELIB/GP

B61
WARD R.E.,JAPANESE POLITICAL SCIENCE: A GUIDE TO
JAPANESE REFERENCE AND RESEARCH MATERIALS (2ND
ED.). LAW CONSTN STRATA NAT/G POL/PAR DELIB/GP
LEGIS ADMIN CHOOSE GP/REL...INT/LAW 19/20 CHINJAP.
PAGE 113 B2290
BIBLIOG/A
PHIL/SCI

B61
WEST F.J.,POLITICAL ADVANCEMENT IN THE SOUTH
PACIFIC. CONSTN CULTURE POL/PAR LEGIS DOMIN ADMIN
CHOOSE SOVEREIGN VAL/FREE 20 FIJI TAHITI SAMOA.
PAGE 115 B2325
S/ASIA
LOC/G
COLONIAL

S61
NEEDLER M.C.,"THE POLITICAL DEVELOPMENT OF MEXICO."
STRUCT NAT/G ADMIN RIGID/FLEX...TIME/SEQ TREND
MEXIC/AMER TOT/POP VAL/FREE 19/20. PAGE 77 B1566
L/A+17C
POL/PAR

S61
NOVE A.,"THE SOVIET MODEL AND UNDERDEVELOPED
COUNTRIES." COM FUT USSR WOR+45 CULTURE ECO/DEV
POL/PAR FOR/AID EDU/PROP ADMIN MORAL WEALTH
...POLICY RECORD HIST/WRIT 20. PAGE 79 B1593
ECO/UNDEV
PLAN

S61
ROBINSON J.A.,"PROCESS SATISFACTION AND POLICY
APPROVAL IN STATE DEPARTMENT - CONGRESSIONAL
RELATIONS." ELITES CHIEF LEGIS CONFER DEBATE ADMIN
FEEDBACK ROLE...CHARTS 20 CONGRESS PRESIDENT
DEPT/STATE. PAGE 89 B1802
GOV/REL
EX/STRUC
POL/PAR
DECISION

S61
RUDOLPH S.,"CONSENSUS AND CONFLICT IN INDIAN
POLITICS." S/ASIA WOR+45 NAT/G DELIB/GP DIPLOM
EDU/PROP ADMIN CONSEN PERSON ALL/VALS...OBS TREND
TOT/POP VAL/FREE 20. PAGE 92 B1854
POL/PAR
PERCEPT
INDIA

S61
TOMASIC D.,"POLITICAL LEADERSHIP IN CONTEMPORARY
POLAND." COM EUR+WWI GERMANY NAT/G POL/PAR SECT
DELIB/GP PLAN ECO/TAC DOMIN EDU/PROP PWR MARXISM
...MARXIST GEOG MGT CONCPT TIME/SEQ STERTYP 20.
PAGE 105 B2114
SOCIETY
ROUTINE
USSR
POLAND

C61
MOODIE G.C.,"THE GOVERNMENT OF GREAT BRITAIN." UK
LAW STRUCT LOC/G POL/PAR DIPLOM RECEIVE ADMIN
COLONIAL CHOOSE...BIBLIOG 20 PARLIAMENT. PAGE 75
B1508
NAT/G
SOCIETY
PARL/PROC
GOV/COMP

B62
ANDREWS W.G.,EUROPEAN POLITICAL INSTITUTIONS.
FRANCE GERMANY UK USSR TOP/EX LEAD PARL/PROC CHOOSE
20. PAGE 5 B0104
NAT/COMP
POL/PAR
EX/STRUC
LEGIS

B62
ANDREWS W.G.,FRENCH POLITICS AND ALGERIA: THE
PROCESS OF POLICY FORMATION 1954-1962. ALGERIA
FRANCE CONSTN ELITES POL/PAR CHIEF DELIB/GP LEGIS
DIPLOM PRESS CHOOSE 20. PAGE 5 B0105
GOV/COMP
EXEC
COLONIAL

B62
BROWN B.E.,NEW DIRECTIONS IN COMPARATIVE POLITICS.
AUSTRIA FRANCE GERMANY UK WOR+45 EX/STRUC LEGIS
ORD/FREE 20. PAGE 16 B0320
NAT/COMP
METH
POL/PAR
FORCES

B62
CARTER G.M.,THE GOVERNMENT OF THE SOVIET UNION.
USSR CULTURE LOC/G DIPLOM ECO/TAC ADJUD CT/SYS LEAD
NAT/G
MARXISM

WEALTH...CHARTS T 20 COM/PARTY. PAGE 19 B0390 POL/PAR
EX/STRUC
B62

FARBER W.O.,GOVERNMENT OF SOUTH DAKOTA. USA+45 PROVS
DIST/IND POL/PAR CHIEF EX/STRUC LEGIS ECO/TAC GIVE LOC/G
EDU/PROP CT/SYS PARTIC...T 20 SOUTH/DAK GOVERNOR. ADMIN
PAGE 35 B0704 CONSTN
B62

GALENSON W.,LABOR IN DEVELOPING COUNTRIES. BRAZIL LABOR
INDONESIA ISRAEL PAKISTAN TURKEY AGRI INDUS WORKER ECO/UNDEV
PAY PRICE GP/REL WEALTH...MGT CHARTS METH/COMP BARGAIN
NAT/COMP. PAGE 38 B0775 POL/PAR
B62

JEWELL M.E.,SENATORIAL POLITICS AND FOREIGN POLICY. USA+45
NAT/G POL/PAR CHIEF DELIB/GP TOP/EX FOR/AID LEGIS
EDU/PROP ROUTINE ATTIT PWR SKILL...MAJORIT DIPLOM
METH/CNCPT TIME/SEQ CONGRESS 20 PRESIDENT. PAGE 56
B1138
B62

KAMMERER G.M.,CITY MANAGERS IN POLITICS: AN MUNIC
ANALYSIS OF MANAGER TENURE AND TERMINATION. POL/PAR LEAD
LEGIS PARTIC CHOOSE PWR...DECISION GEOG METH/CNCPT. EXEC
PAGE 57 B1161
B62

OLLE-LAPRUNE J.,LA STABILITE DES MINISTRES SOUS LA LEGIS
TROISIEME REPUBLIQUE, 1879-1940. FRANCE CONSTN NAT/G
POL/PAR LEAD WAR INGP/REL RIGID/FLEX PWR...POLICY ADMIN
CHARTS 19/20. PAGE 79 B1606 PERSON
B62

SAMPSON A.,ANATOMY OF BRITAIN. UK LAW COM/IND FINAN ELITES
INDUS MARKET MUNIC POL/PAR EX/STRUC TOP/EX DIPLOM PWR
LEAD REPRESENT PERSON PARLIAMENT WORSHIP. PAGE 92 STRUCT
B1866 FORCES
B62

SCALAPINO R.A.,PARTIES AND POLITICS IN CONTEMPORARY POL/PAR
JAPAN. EX/STRUC DIPLOM CHOOSE NAT/LISM ATTIT PARL/PROC
...POLICY 20 CHINJAP. PAGE 93 B1876 ELITES
DECISION
L62

NEIBURG H.L.,"THE EISENHOWER AEC AND CONGRESS: A CHIEF
STUDY IN EXECUTIVE-LEGISLATIVE RELATIONS." USA+45 LEGIS
NAT/G POL/PAR DELIB/GP EX/STRUC TOP/EX ADMIN EXEC GOV/REL
LEAD ROUTINE PWR...POLICY COLD/WAR CONGRESS NUC/PWR
PRESIDENT AEC. PAGE 77 B1567
S62

IOVTCHOUK M.T.,"ON SOME THEORETICAL PRINCIPLES AND COM
METHODS OF SOCIOLOGICAL INVESTIGATIONS (IN ECO/DEV
RUSSIAN)." FUT USA+45 STRATA R+D NAT/G POL/PAR CAP/ISM
TOP/EX ACT/RES PLAN ECO/TAC EDU/PROP ROUTINE ATTIT USSR
RIGID/FLEX MARXISM SOCISM...MARXIST METH/CNCPT OBS
TREND NAT/COMP GEN/LAWS 20. PAGE 54 B1102
S62

MCCLELLAND C.A.,"DECISIONAL OPPORTUNITY AND ACT/RES
POLITICAL CONTROVERSY." USA+45 NAT/G POL/PAR FORCES PERCEPT
TOP/EX DOMIN ADMIN PEACE DRIVE ORD/FREE PWR DIPLOM
...DECISION SIMUL 20. PAGE 72 B1444
S62

SPRINGER H.W.,"FEDERATION IN THE CARIBBEAN: AN VOL/ASSN
ATTEMPT THAT FAILED." L/A+17C ECO/UNDEV INT/ORG NAT/G
POL/PAR PROVS LEGIS CREATE PLAN LEGIT ADMIN FEDERAL REGION
ATTIT DRIVE PERSON ORD/FREE PWR...POLICY GEOG PSY
CONCPT OBS CARIBBEAN CMN/WLTH 20. PAGE 100 B2013
S62

TRUMAN D.,"THE DOMESTIC POLITICS OF FOREIGN AID." ROUTINE
USA+45 WOR+45 NAT/G POL/PAR LEGIS DIPLOM ECO/TAC FOR/AID
EDU/PROP ADMIN CHOOSE ATTIT PWR CONGRESS 20
CONGRESS. PAGE 105 B2129
C62

DE GRAZIA A.,"POLITICAL BEHAVIOR (REV. ED.)" STRATA PHIL/SCI
POL/PAR LEAD LOBBY ROUTINE WAR CHOOSE REPRESENT OP/RES
CONSEN ATTIT ORD/FREE BIBLIOG. PAGE 27 B0555 CONCPT
C62

TRUMAN D.B.,"THE GOVERNMENTAL PROCESS: POLITICAL LOBBY
INTERESTS AND PUBLIC OPINION." POL/PAR ADJUD ADMIN EDU/PROP
EXEC LEAD ROUTINE CHOOSE REPRESENT GOV/REL GP/REL
RIGID/FLEX...POLICY BIBLIOG/A 20. PAGE 105 B2131 LEGIS
B63

ADRIAN C.R.,GOVERNING OVER FIFTY STATES AND THEIR PROVS
COMMUNITIES. USA+45 CONSTN FINAN MUNIC NAT/G LOC/G
POL/PAR EX/STRUC LEGIS ADMIN CONTROL CT/SYS GOV/REL
...CHARTS 20. PAGE 3 B0061 GOV/COMP
B63

BADI J.,THE GOVERNMENT OF THE STATE OF ISRAEL: A NAT/G
CRITICAL ACCOUNT OF ITS PARLIAMENT, EXECUTIVE, AND CONSTN
JUDICIARY. ISRAEL ECO/DEV CHIEF DELIB/GP LEGIS EX/STRUC
DIPLOM CT/SYS INGP/REL PEACE ORD/FREE...BIBLIOG 20 POL/PAR
PARLIAMENT ARABS MIGRATION. PAGE 8 B0157
B63

BANFIELD E.C.,CITY POLITICS. CULTURE LABOR LOC/G MUNIC
POL/PAR LEGIS EXEC LEAD CHOOSE...DECISION NEGRO. RIGID/FLEX
PAGE 9 B0178 ATTIT
B63

BLONDEL J.,VOTERS, PARTIES, AND LEADERS. UK ELITES POL/PAR
LOC/G NAT/G PROVS ACT/RES DOMIN REPRESENT GP/REL STRATA
INGP/REL...SOC BIBLIOG 20. PAGE 12 B0255 LEGIS
ADMIN

B63
CLARK J.S.,THE SENATE ESTABLISHMENT. USA+45 NAT/G LEGIS
POL/PAR ADMIN CHOOSE PERSON SENATE. PAGE 21 B0431 ROUTINE
LEAD
SENIOR
B63

COM INTERNAT DES MOUVEMENTS,REPERTOIRE BIBLIOG/A
INTERNATIONAL DES SOURCES POUR L'ETUDE DES MARXISM
MOUVEMENTS SOCIAUX AUX XIXE ET XXE SIECLES (VOL. POL/PAR
III). MOD/EUR ADMIN...SOC 19. PAGE 22 B0454 LABOR
B63

GRANT D.R.,STATE AND LOCAL GOVERNMENT IN AMERICA. PROVS
USA+45 FINAN LOC/G MUNIC EX/STRUC FORCES EDU/PROP POL/PAR
ADMIN CHOOSE FEDERAL ATTIT...JURID 20. PAGE 42 LEGIS
B0853 CONSTN
B63

HERNDON J.,A SELECTED BIBLIOGRAPHY OF MATERIALS IN BIBLIOG
STATE GOVERNMENT AND POLITICS (PAMPHLET). USA+45 GOV/COMP
POL/PAR LEGIS ADMIN CHOOSE MGT. PAGE 49 B0993 PROVS
DECISION
B63

HIGA M.,POLITICS AND PARTIES IN POSTWAR OKINAWA. GOV/REL
USA+45 VOL/ASSN LEGIS CONTROL LOBBY CHOOSE NAT/LISM POL/PAR
PWR SOVEREIGN MARXISM SOCISM 20 OKINAWA CHINJAP. ADMIN
PAGE 50 B1008 FORCES
B63

JACOB H.,GERMAN ADMINISTRATION SINCE BISMARCK: ADMIN
CENTRAL AUTHORITY VERSUS LOCAL AUTONOMY. GERMANY NAT/G
GERMANY/W LAW POL/PAR CONTROL CENTRAL TOTALISM LOC/G
FASCISM...MAJORIT DECISION STAT CHARTS GOV/COMP POLICY
19/20 BISMARCK/O HITLER/A WEIMAR/REP. PAGE 55 B1111
B63

LEWIS J.W.,LEADERSHIP IN COMMUNIST CHINA. ASIA POL/PAR
INTELL ECO/UNDEV LOC/G MUNIC NAT/G PROVS ECO/TAC DOMIN
EDU/PROP LEGIT ADMIN COERCE ATTIT ORD/FREE PWR ELITES
...INT TIME/SEQ CHARTS TOT/POP VAL/FREE. PAGE 65
B1304
B63

MACNEIL N.,FORGE OF DEMOCRACY: THE HOUSE OF LEGIS
REPRESENTATIVES. POL/PAR EX/STRUC TOP/EX DEBATE DELIB/GP
LEAD PARL/PROC CHOOSE GOV/REL PWR...OBS HOUSE/REP.
PAGE 68 B1374
B63

MAHESHWARI B.,STUDIES IN PANCHAYATI RAJ. INDIA FEDERAL
POL/PAR EX/STRUC BUDGET EXEC REPRESENT CENTRAL LOC/G
EFFICIENCY...DECISION 20. PAGE 68 B1378 GOV/REL
LEAD
B63

MCKIE R.,MALAYSIA IN FOCUS. INDONESIA WOR+45 S/ASIA
ECO/UNDEV FINAN NAT/G POL/PAR SECT FORCES PLAN NAT/LISM
ADMIN COLONIAL COERCE DRIVE ALL/VALS...POLICY MALAYSIA
RECORD CENSUS TIME/SEQ CMN/WLTH 20. PAGE 72 B1453
B63

PLISCHKE E.,GOVERNMENT AND POLITICS OF CONTEMPORARY MUNIC
BERLIN. GERMANY LAW CONSTN POL/PAR LEGIS WAR CHOOSE LOC/G
REPRESENT GOV/REL...CHARTS BIBLIOG 20 BERLIN. POLICY
PAGE 83 B1683 ADMIN
B63

RICHARDS P.G.,PATRONAGE IN BRITISH GOVERNMENT. EX/STRUC
ELITES DELIB/GP TOP/EX PROB/SOLV CONTROL CT/SYS REPRESENT
EXEC PWR. PAGE 88 B1774 POL/PAR
ADMIN
B63

ROBERT J.,LA MONARCHIE MAROCAINE. MOROCCO LABOR CHIEF
MUNIC POL/PAR EX/STRUC ORD/FREE PWR...JURID TREND T CONSERVE
20. PAGE 89 B1793 ADMIN
CONSTN
B63

ROYAL INSTITUTE PUBLIC ADMIN,BRITISH PUBLIC BIBLIOG
ADMINISTRATION. UK LAW FINAN INDUS LOC/G POL/PAR ADMIN
LEGIS LOBBY PARL/PROC CHOOSE JURID. PAGE 91 B1845 MGT
NAT/G
B63

SMITH R.M.,STATE GOVERNMENT IN TRANSITION. USA+45 PROVS
POL/PAR LEGIS PARL/PROC GOV/REL 20 PENNSYLVAN POLICY
GOVERNOR. PAGE 98 B1984 EX/STRUC
PLAN
B63

TUCKER R.C.,THE SOVIET POLITICAL MIND. WOR+45 COM
ELITES INT/ORG NAT/G POL/PAR PLAN DIPLOM ECO/TAC TOP/EX
DOMIN ADMIN NUC/PWR REV DRIVE PERSON SUPEGO PWR USSR
WEALTH...POLICY MGT PSY CONCPT OBS BIOG TREND
COLD/WAR MARX/KARL 20. PAGE 106 B2134
L63

EMERSON R.,"POLITICAL MODERNIZATION." WOR+45 POL/PAR
CULTURE ECO/UNDEV NAT/G FORCES ECO/TAC DOMIN ADMIN
EDU/PROP LEGIT COERCE ALL/VALS...CONCPT TIME/SEQ
VAL/FREE 20. PAGE 33 B0672
L63

ROBERT J.,"LES ELECTIONS LEGISLATIVES DU 17 MAI CHOOSE
1963 ET L'EVOLUTION POLITIQUE INTERNE DU MAROC." MOROCCO
ISLAM WOR+45 NAT/G POL/PAR EXEC ALL/VALS 20.
PAGE 89 B1792
S63

BRZEZINSKI Z.K.,"CINCINNATUS AND THE APPARATCHIK." POL/PAR
COM USA+45 USA-45 ELITES LOC/G NAT/G PROVS CONSULT USSR

LEGIS DOMIN LEGIT EXEC ROUTINE CHOOSE DRIVE PWR
SKILL...CONCPT CHARTS VAL/FREE COLD/WAR 20. PAGE 16
B0334

S63
DELLIN L.A.D.,"BULGARIA UNDER SOVIET LEADERSHIP." AGRI
BULGARIA COM USA+45 USSR ECO/DEV INDUS POL/PAR NAT/G
EX/STRUC TOP/EX COERCE ATTIT RIGID/FLEX...POLICY TOTALISM
TIME/SEQ 20. PAGE 28 B0572

S63
RUSTOW D.A.,"THE MILITARY IN MIDDLE EASTERN SOCIETY FORCES
AND POLITICS." FUT ISLAM CONSTN SOCIETY FACE/GP ELITES
NAT/G POL/PAR PROF/ORG CONSULT DOMIN ADMIN EXEC
REGION COERCE NAT/LISM ATTIT DRIVE PERSON ORD/FREE
PWR...POLICY CONCPT OBS STERTYP 20. PAGE 92 B1860

S63
WAGRET M.,"L'ASCENSION POLITIQUE DE L'U.D.D.I.A. EX/STRUC
(CONGO) ET SA PRISE DU POUVOIR (1956-1959)." AFR CHOOSE
WOR+45 NAT/G POL/PAR CONSULT DELIB/GP LEGIS PERCEPT FRANCE
ALL/VALS SOVEREIGN...TIME/SEQ CONGO. PAGE 113 B2274

C63
CARLISLE D.,"PARTY LOYALTY; THE ELECTION PROCESS IN CHOOSE
SOUTH CAROLINA." USA+45 LOC/G ADMIN ATTIT...TREND POL/PAR
CHARTS BIBLIOG 17/20. PAGE 19 B0380 PROVS
SUFF

B64
ANDREN N.,GOVERNMENT AND POLITICS IN THE NORDIC CONSTN
COUNTRIES: DENMARK, FINLAND, ICELAND, NORWAY, NAT/G
SWEDEN. DENMARK FINLAND ICELAND NORWAY SWEDEN CULTURE
POL/PAR CHIEF LEGIS ADMIN REGION REPRESENT ATTIT GOV/COMP
CONSERVE...CHARTS BIBLIOG/A 20. PAGE 5 B0102

B64
CLARK J.S.,CONGRESS: THE SAPLESS BRANCH. DELIB/GP LEGIS
SENIOR ATTIT CONGRESS. PAGE 21 B0432 ROUTINE
ADMIN
POL/PAR

B64
COTTER C.P.,POLITICS WITHOUT POWER: THE NATIONAL CHOOSE
PARTY COMMITTEES. USA+45 FINAN NAT/G LOBBY ROUTINE POL/PAR
GP/REL ATTIT ROLE SUPEGO PWR 20. PAGE 24 B0491 REPRESENT
DELIB/GP

B64
EATON H.,PRESIDENTIAL TIMBER: A HISTORY OF DELIB/GP
NOMINATING CONVENTIONS, 1868-1960. USA+45 USA-45 CHOOSE
POL/PAR EX/STRUC DEBATE LOBBY ATTIT PERSON ALL/VALS CHIEF
...MYTH 19/20 PRESIDENT. PAGE 32 B0646 NAT/G

B64
FAINSOD M.,HOW RUSSIA IS RULED (REV. ED.). RUSSIA NAT/G
USSR AGRI PROC/MFG LABOR POL/PAR EX/STRUC CONTROL REV
PWR...POLICY BIBLIOG 19/20 KHRUSH/N COM/PARTY. MARXISM
PAGE 34 B0700

B64
FORBES A.H.,CURRENT RESEARCH IN BRITISH STUDIES. UK BIBLIOG
CONSTN CULTURE POL/PAR SECT DIPLOM ADMIN...JURID PERSON
BIOG WORSHIP 20. PAGE 36 B0736 NAT/G
PARL/PROC

B64
GOLDWIN R.A.,POLITICAL PARTIES. USA. USA+45 USA-45 POL/PAR
LOC/G ADMIN LEAD EFFICIENCY ATTIT PWR...POLICY STAT PARTIC
ANTHOL 18/20 CONGRESS. PAGE 40 B0818 NAT/G
CONSTN

B64
GOODMAN W.,THE TWO-PARTY SYSTEM IN THE UNITED POL/PAR
STATES. USA+45 USA-45 STRATA LOC/G CHIEF EDU/PROP REPRESENT
ADMIN COST PWR POPULISM...PLURIST 18/20 PRESIDENT. CHOOSE
PAGE 41 B0821 NAT/G

B64
GUTTSMAN W.L.,THE BRITISH POLITICAL ELITE. EUR+WWI NAT/G
MOD/EUR STRATA FAM LABOR POL/PAR SCHOOL VOL/ASSN SOC
DELIB/GP LEGIS LEGIT EXEC CHOOSE ATTIT ALL/VALS UK
...STAT BIOG TIME/SEQ CHARTS VAL/FREE. PAGE 45 ELITES
B0905

B64
HARMON R.B.,BIBLIOGRAPHY OF BIBLIOGRAPHIES IN BIBLIOG
POLITICAL SCIENCE (MIMEOGRAPHED PAPER: LIMITED NAT/G
EDITION). WOR+45 WOR-45 INT/ORG POL/PAR GOV/REL DIPLOM
ALL/IDEOS...INT/LAW JURID MGT 19/20. PAGE 47 B0949 LOC/G

B64
INST D'ETUDE POL L'U GRENOBLE,ADMINISTRATION ADMIN
TRADITIONELLE ET PLANIFICATION REGIONALE. FRANCE MUNIC
LAW POL/PAR PROB/SOLV ADJUST RIGID/FLEX...CHARTS PLAN
ANTHOL BIBLIOG T 20 REFORMERS. PAGE 54 B1087 CREATE

B64
KAACK H.,DIE PARTEIEN IN DER POL/PAR
VERFASSUNGSWIRKLICHKEIT DER BUNDESREPUBLIK. PROVS
GERMANY/W ADMIN PARL/PROC CHOOSE...JURID 20. NAT/G
PAGE 57 B1157

B64
KEEFE W.J.,THE AMERICAN LEGISLATIVE PROCESS: LEGIS
CONGRESS AND THE STATES. USA+45 LAW POL/PAR DECISION
DELIB/GP DEBATE ADMIN LOBBY REPRESENT CONGRESS PWR
PRESIDENT. PAGE 59 B1187 PROVS

B64
MAHAR J.M.,INDIA: A CRITICAL BIBLIOGRAPHY. INDIA BIBLIOG/A
PAKISTAN CULTURE ECO/UNDEV LOC/G POL/PAR SECT S/ASIA
PROB/SOLV DIPLOM ADMIN COLONIAL PARL/PROC ATTIT 20. NAT/G
PAGE 68 B1377 LEAD

B64
MARSH D.C.,THE FUTURE OF THE WELFARE STATE. UK NEW/LIB
CONSTN NAT/G POL/PAR...POLICY WELF/ST 20. PAGE 69 ADMIN
B1404 CONCPT
INSPECT

B64
POPPINO R.E.,INTERNATIONAL COMMUNISM IN LATIN MARXISM
AMERICA: A HISTORY OF THE MOVEMENT 1917-1963. POL/PAR
CHINA/COM USSR INTELL STRATA LABOR WORKER ADMIN REV L/A+17C
ATTIT...POLICY 20 COLD/WAR. PAGE 84 B1692

B64
PRESS C.,A BIBLIOGRAPHIC INTRODUCTION TO AMERICAN BIBLIOG
STATE GOVERNMENT AND POLITICS (PAMPHLET). USA+45 LEGIS
USA-45 EX/STRUC ADJUD INGP/REL FEDERAL ORD/FREE 20. LOC/G
PAGE 84 B1701 POL/PAR

B64
RICHARDSON I.L.,BIBLIOGRAFIA BRASILEIRA DE BIBLIOG
ADMINISTRACAO PUBLICA E ASSUNTOS CORRELATOS. BRAZIL MGT
CONSTN FINAN LOC/G NAT/G POL/PAR PLAN DIPLOM ADMIN
RECEIVE ATTIT...METH 20. PAGE 88 B1776 LAW

B64
RIGGS R.E.,THE MOVEMENT FOR ADMINISTRATIVE ADMIN
REORGANIZATION IN ARIZONA. USA+45 LAW POL/PAR PROVS
DELIB/GP LEGIS PROB/SOLV CONTROL RIGID/FLEX PWR CREATE
...ORG/CHARTS 20 ARIZONA DEMOCRAT REPUBLICAN. PLAN
PAGE 88 B1786

B64
SARROS P.P.,CONGRESS AND THE NEW DIPLOMACY: THE DIPLOM
FORMULATION OF MUTUAL SECURITY POLICY: 1953-60 POL/PAR
(THESIS). USA+45 CHIEF EX/STRUC REGION ROUTINE NAT/G
CHOOSE GOV/REL PEACE ROLE...POLICY 20 PRESIDENT
CONGRESS. PAGE 92 B1869

B64
STOICOIU V.,LEGAL SOURCES AND BIBLIOGRAPHY OF BIBLIOG/A
ROMANIA. COM ROMANIA LAW FINAN POL/PAR LEGIS JUDGE JURID
ADJUD CT/SYS PARL/PROC MARXISM 20. PAGE 101 B2041 CONSTN
ADMIN

B64
THE BRITISH COUNCIL,PUBLIC ADMINISTRATION: A SELECT BIBLIOG
LIST OF BOOKS AND PERIODICALS. LAW CONSTN FINAN ADMIN
POL/PAR SCHOOL CHOOSE...HEAL MGT METH/COMP 19/20 LOC/G
CMN/WLTH. PAGE 104 B2094 INDUS

B64
TURNER H.A.,THE GOVERNMENT AND POLITICS OF PROVS
CALIFORNIA (2ND ED.). LAW FINAN MUNIC POL/PAR ADMIN
SCHOOL EX/STRUC LEGIS LOBBY CHOOSE...CHARTS T 20 LOC/G
CALIFORNIA. PAGE 106 B2138 CONSTN

B64
VALEN H.,POLITICAL PARTIES IN NORWAY. NORWAY ACADEM LOC/G
PARTIC ROUTINE INGP/REL KNOWL...QU 20. PAGE 111 POL/PAR
B2249 PERSON

B64
WHEARE K.C.,FEDERAL GOVERNMENT (4TH ED.). WOR+45 FEDERAL
WOR-45 POL/PAR LEGIS BAL/PWR CT/SYS...POLICY JURID CONSTN
CONCPT GOV/COMP 17/20. PAGE 116 B2331 EX/STRUC
NAT/COMP

L64
GILBERT C.E.,"NATIONAL POLITICAL ALIGNMENTS AND THE MUNIC
POLITICS OF LARGE CITIES." ELITES LOC/G NAT/G LEGIS CHOOSE
EXEC LEAD PLURISM GOV/COMP. PAGE 39 B0800 POL/PAR
PWR

L64
ROTBERG R.,"THE FEDERATION MOVEMENT IN BRITISH EAST VOL/ASSN
AND CENTRAL AFRICA." AFR RHODESIA UGANDA ECO/UNDEV PWR
NAT/G POL/PAR FORCES DOMIN LEGIT ADMIN COERCE ATTIT REGION
...CONCPT TREND 20 TANGANYIKA. PAGE 91 B1831

S64
EAKIN T.C.,"LEGISLATIVE POLITICS -- I AND II THE PROVS
WESTERN STATES, 19581964" (SUPPLEMENT)" USA+45 LEGIS
POL/PAR SCHOOL CONTROL LOBBY CHOOSE AGE. PAGE 32 ROUTINE
B0641 STRUCT

S64
HORECKY P.L.,"LIBRARY OF CONGRESS PUBLICATIONS IN BIBLIOG/A
AID OF USSR AND EAST EUROPEAN RESEARCH." BULGARIA COM
CZECHOSLVK POLAND USSR YUGOSLAVIA NAT/G POL/PAR MARXISM
DIPLOM ADMIN GOV/REL...CLASSIF 20. PAGE 51 B1042

S64
REDFORD E.S.,"THE PROTECTION OF THE PUBLIC INTEREST ADMIN
WITH SPECIAL REFERENCE TO ADMINISTRATIVE VOL/ASSN
REGULATION." POL/PAR LEGIS PRESS PARL/PROC. PAGE 87 EX/STRUC
B1758 GP/REL

S64
RIGBY T.H.,"TRADITIONAL, MARKET, AND ORGANIZATIONAL MARKET
SOCIETIES AND THE USSR." COM ECO/DEV NAT/G POL/PAR ADMIN
ECO/TAC DOMIN ORD/FREE PWR WEALTH...TIME/SEQ USSR
GEN/LAWS VAL/FREE 20 STALIN/J. PAGE 88 B1784

S64
SALISBURY R.H.,"URBAN POLITICS: THE NEW CONVERGENCE MUNIC
OF POWER." STRATA POL/PAR EX/STRUC PARTIC GP/REL PWR
DECISION. PAGE 92 B1863 LEAD

S64
SWEARER H.R.,"AFTER KHRUSHCHEV: WHAT NEXT." COM FUT EX/STRUC
USSR CONSTN ELITES NAT/G POL/PAR CHIEF DELIB/GP PWR
LEGIS DOMIN LEAD...RECORD TREND STERTYP GEN/METH
20. PAGE 102 B2058

SCOTT R.E.,"MEXICAN GOVERNMENT IN TRANSITION (REV ED)" CULTURE STRUCT POL/PAR CHIEF ADMIN LOBBY REV CHOOSE GP/REL DRIVE...BIBLIOG METH 20 MEXIC/AMER. PAGE 95 B1920
C64
NAT/G
L/A+17C
ROUTINE
CONSTN

AIYAR S.P.,STUDIES IN INDIAN DEMOCRACY. INDIA STRATA ECO/UNDEV LABOR POL/PAR LEGIS DIPLOM LOBBY REGION CHOOSE ATTIT SOCISM...ANTHOL 20. PAGE 3 B0067
B65
ORD/FREE
REPRESENT
ADMIN
NAT/G

AMERICAN ASSEMBLY COLUMBIA U.THE FEDERAL GOVERNMENT SERVICE. USA+45 POL/PAR EX/STRUC EXEC 20. PAGE 4 B0082
B65
ADMIN
MGT
NAT/G
INGP/REL

BANFIELD E.C.,BIG CITY POLITICS. USA+45 CONSTN POL/PAR ADMIN LOBBY CHOOSE SUFF INGP/REL PWR...GEOG 20. PAGE 9 B0179
B65
METH/COMP
MUNIC
STRUCT

CHANDA A.,FEDERALISM IN INDIA. INDIA UK ELITES FINAN NAT/G POL/PAR EX/STRUC LEGIS DIPLOM TAX GOV/REL POPULISM...POLICY 20. PAGE 20 B0402
B65
CONSTN
CENTRAL
FEDERAL

CHEN T.H.,THE CHINESE COMMUNIST REGIME: A DOCUMENTARY STUDY (2 VOLS.). CHINA/COM LAW CONSTN ELITES ECO/UNDEV LEGIS ECO/TAC ADMIN CONTROL PWR ...SOC 20. PAGE 20 B0417
B65
MARXISM
POL/PAR
NAT/G

DE GRAZIA A.,REPUBLIC IN CRISIS: CONGRESS AGAINST THE EXECUTIVE FORCE. USA+45 USA-45 SOCIETY POL/PAR CHIEF DOMIN ROLE ORD/FREE PWR...CONCPT MYTH BIBLIOG 20 CONGRESS. PAGE 27 B0556
B65
LEGIS
EXEC
GOV/REL
CONTROL

EDELMAN M.,THE POLITICS OF WAGE-PRICE DECISIONS. GERMANY ITALY NETHERLAND UK INDUS LABOR POL/PAR PROB/SOLV BARGAIN PRICE ROUTINE BAL/PAY COST DEMAND 20. PAGE 32 B0654
B65
GOV/COMP
CONTROL
ECO/TAC
PLAN

GOODSELL C.T.,ADMINISTRATION OF A REVOLUTION. PUERT/RICO ECO/UNDEV FINAN MUNIC POL/PAR PROVS LEGIS PLAN BUDGET RECEIVE ADMIN COLONIAL LEAD 20 ROOSEVLT/F. PAGE 41 B0827
B65
EXEC
SOC

GOPAL S.,BRITISH POLICY IN INDIA 1858-1905. INDIA UK ELITES CHIEF DELIB/GP ECO/TAC GP/REL DISCRIM ATTIT...IDEA/COMP NAT/COMP PERS/COMP BIBLIOG/A 19/20. PAGE 41 B0828
B65
COLONIAL
ADMIN
POL/PAR
ECO/UNDEV

GREGG J.L.,POLITICAL PARTIES AND PARTY SYSTEMS IN GUATEMALA, 1944-1963. GUATEMALA L/A+17C EX/STRUC FORCES CREATE CONTROL REV CHOOSE PWR...TREND IDEA/COMP 20. PAGE 43 B0872
B65
LEAD
POL/PAR
NAT/G
CHIEF

HAIGHT D.E.,THE PRESIDENT; ROLES AND POWERS. USA+45 USA-45 POL/PAR PLAN DIPLOM CHOOSE PERS/REL PWR 18/20 PRESIDENT CONGRESS. PAGE 45 B0915
B65
CHIEF
LEGIS
TOP/EX
EX/STRUC

HARMON R.B.,POLITICAL SCIENCE: A BIBLIOGRAPHICAL GUIDE TO THE LITERATURE. WOR+45 WOR-45 R+D INT/ORG LOC/G NAT/G DIPLOM ADMIN...CONCPT METH. PAGE 47 B0950
B65
BIBLIOG
POL/PAR
LAW
GOV/COMP

INST INTL DES CIVILISATION DIF,THE CONSTITUTIONS AND ADMINISTRATIVE INSTITUTIONS OF THE NEW STATES. AFR ISLAM S/ASIA NAT/G POL/PAR DELIB/GP EX/STRUC CONFER EFFICIENCY NAT/LISM...JURID SOC 20. PAGE 54 B1088
B65
CONSTN
ADMIN
ADJUD
ECO/UNDEV

KOUSOULAS D.G.,REVOLUTION AND DEFEAT; THE STORY OF THE GREEK COMMUNIST PARTY. GREECE INT/ORG EX/STRUC DIPLOM FOR/AID EDU/PROP PARL/PROC ADJUST ATTIT 20 COM/PARTY. PAGE 61 B1230
B65
REV
MARXISM
POL/PAR
ORD/FREE

LATHAM E.,THE GROUP BASIS OF POLITICS: A STUDY IN BASING-POINT LEGISLATION. INDUS MARKET POL/PAR DELIB/GP EX/STRUC DEBATE ADJUD...CHARTS PRESIDENT. PAGE 63 B1274
B65
LEGIS
GP/COMP
GP/REL

MASTERS N.A.,COMMITTEE ASSIGNMENTS IN THE HOUSE OF REPRESENTATIVES (BMR). USA+45 ELITES POL/PAR EX/STRUC PARTIC REPRESENT GP/REL PERS/REL ATTIT PWR ...STAT CHARTS 20 HOUSE/REP. PAGE 71 B1425
B65
LEAD
LEGIS
CHOOSE
DELIB/GP

MOORE C.H.,TUNISIA SINCE INDEPENDENCE. ELITES LOC/G POL/PAR ADMIN COLONIAL CONTROL EXEC GOV/REL TOTALISM MARXISM...INT 20 TUNIS. PAGE 75 B1513
B65
NAT/G
EX/STRUC
SOCISM

PARRISH W.E.,MISSOURI UNDER RADICAL RULE 1865-1870. USA-45 SOCIETY INDUS LOC/G POL/PAR WORKER EDU/PROP SUFF INGP/REL ATTIT...BIBLIOG 19 NEGRO MISSOURI. PAGE 81 B1635
B65
PROVS
ADMIN
RACE/REL
ORD/FREE

PAYNE J.L.,LABOR AND POLITICS IN PERU; THE SYSTEM OF POLITICAL BARGAINING. PERU CONSTN VOL/ASSN
LABOR
POL/PAR

EX/STRUC LEAD PWR...CHARTS 20. PAGE 81 B1645
BARGAIN
GP/REL
B65

PYLEE M.V.,CONSTITUTIONAL GOVERNMENT IN INDIA (2ND REV. ED.). INDIA POL/PAR EX/STRUC DIPLOM COLONIAL CT/SYS PARL/PROC PRIVIL...JURID 16/20. PAGE 85 B1725
CONSTN
NAT/G
PROVS
FEDERAL

SNYDER F.G.,ONE-PARTY GOVERNMENT IN MALI: TRANSITION TOWARD CONTROL. MALI STRATA STRUCT SOC. PAGE 99 B1991
B65
ECO/UNDEV
POL/PAR
EX/STRUC
ADMIN

STANLEY D.T.,CHANGING ADMINISTRATIONS. USA+45 POL/PAR DELIB/GP TOP/EX BUDGET GOV/REL GP/REL PERS/REL PWR...MAJORIT DECISION MGT 20 PRESIDENT SUCCESSION DEPT/STATE DEPT/DEFEN DEPT/HEW. PAGE 100 B2021
B65
NAT/G
CHIEF
ADMIN
EX/STRUC

WARD W.E.,GOVERNMENT IN WEST AFRICA. WOR+45 POL/PAR EX/STRUC PLAN PARTIC GP/REL SOVEREIGN 20 AFRICA/W. PAGE 114 B2291
B65
GOV/COMP
CONSTN
COLONIAL
ECO/UNDEV

WILDER B.E.,BIBLIOGRAPHY OF THE OFFICIAL PUBLICATIONS OF KANSAS, 1854-1958. USA+45 USA-45 ECO/DEV POL/PAR EX/STRUC LEGIS ADJUD ATTIT 19/20. PAGE 116 B2349
B65
BIBLIOG
PROVS
GOV/REL
ADMIN

MATTHEWS D.G.,"A CURRENT BIBLIOGRAPHY ON ETHIOPIAN AFFAIRS: A SELECT BIBLIOGRAPHY FROM 1950-1964." ETHIOPIA LAW CULTURE ECO/UNDEV INDUS LABOR SECT FORCES DIPLOM CIVMIL/REL RACE/REL...LING STAT 20. PAGE 71 B1428
L65
BIBLIOG/A
ADMIN
POL/PAR
NAT/G

ADAMS J.C.,THE GOVERNMENT OF REPUBLICAN ITALY (2ND ED.). ITALY LOC/G POL/PAR DELIB/GP LEGIS WORKER ADMIN CT/SYS FASCISM...CHARTS BIBLIOG 20 PARLIAMENT. PAGE 3 B0057
B66
NAT/G
CHOOSE
EX/STRUC
CONSTN

ANDERSON S.V.,CANADIAN OMBUDSMAN PROPOSALS. CANADA LEGIS DEBATE PARL/PROC...MAJORIT JURID TIME/SEQ IDEA/COMP 20 OMBUDSMAN PARLIAMENT. PAGE 5 B0096
B66
NAT/G
CREATE
ADMIN
POL/PAR

BURNS A.C.,PARLIAMENT AS AN EXPORT. WOR+45 CONSTN BARGAIN DEBATE ROUTINE GOV/REL EFFICIENCY...ANTHOL COMMONWLTH PARLIAMENT. PAGE 17 B0353
B66
PARL/PROC
POL/PAR
CT/SYS
CHIEF

CARALEY D.,PARTY POLITICS AND NATIONAL ELECTIONS. USA+45 STRATA LOC/G PROVS EX/STRUC BARGAIN ADMIN SANCTION GP/REL ATTIT 20 DEMOCRAT REPUBLICAN. PAGE 18 B0375
B66
POL/PAR
CHOOSE
REPRESENT
NAT/G

CHAPMAN B.,THE PROFESSION OF GOVERNMENT: THE PUBLIC SERVICE IN EUROPE. CONSTN NAT/G POL/PAR EX/STRUC LEGIS TOP/EX PROB/SOLV DEBATE EXEC PARL/PROC PARTIC 20. PAGE 20 B0411
B66
BIBLIOG
ADMIN
EUR+WWI
GOV/COMP

CORNWELL E.E. JR.,THE AMERICAN PRESIDENCY: VITAL CENTER. USA+45 USA-45 POL/PAR LEGIS PROB/SOLV CONTROL PARTIC GOV/REL 18/20 PRESIDENT. PAGE 23 B0478
B66
CHIEF
EX/STRUC
NAT/G
ADMIN

DAVIDSON R.H.,CONGRESS IN CRISIS: POLITICS AND CONGRESSIONAL REFORM. USA+45 SOCIETY POL/PAR CONTROL LEAD ROUTINE GOV/REL ATTIT PWR...POLICY 20 CONGRESS. PAGE 26 B0535
B66
LEGIS
PARL/PROC
PROB/SOLV
NAT/G

EPSTEIN F.T.,THE AMERICAN BIBLIOGRAPHY OF RUSSIAN AND EAST EUROPEAN STUDIES FOR 1964. USSR LOC/G NAT/G POL/PAR FORCES ADMIN ARMS/CONT...JURID CONCPT 20 UN. PAGE 33 B0678
B66
BIBLIOG
COM
MARXISM
DIPLOM

FINNISH POLITICAL SCIENCE ASSN,SCANDINAVIAN POLITICAL STUDIES (VOL. I). FINLAND DIPLOM ADMIN LOBBY PARL/PROC...CHARTS BIBLIOG 20 SCANDINAV. PAGE 36 B0721
B66
ATTIT
POL/PAR
ACT/RES
CHOOSE

GREENE L.E.,GOVERNMENT IN TENNESSEE (2ND ED.). USA+45 DIST/IND INDUS POL/PAR EX/STRUC LEGIS PLAN BUDGET GIVE CT/SYS...MGT T 20 TENNESSEE. PAGE 43 B0866
B66
PROVS
LOC/G
CONSTN
ADMIN

HARMON R.B.,SOURCES AND PROBLEMS OF BIBLIOGRAPHY IN POLITICAL SCIENCE (PAMPHLET). INT/ORG LOC/G MUNIC POL/PAR ADMIN GOV/REL ALL/IDEOS...JURID MGT CONCPT 19/20. PAGE 47 B0951
B66
BIBLIOG
DIPLOM
INT/LAW
NAT/G

INTERPARLIAMENTARY UNION,PARLIAMENTS: COMPARATIVE
PARL/PROC
B66

STUDY ON STRUCTURE AND FUNCTIONING OF
REPRESENTATIVE INSTITUTIONS IN FIFTY-FIVE
COUNTRIES. WOR+45 POL/PAR DELIB/GP BUDGET ADMIN
CONTROL CHOOSE. PAGE 54 B1099
LEGIS
GOV/COMP
EX/STRUC

B66
NEUMANN R.G.,THE GOVERNMENT OF THE GERMAN FEDERAL
REPUBLIC. EUR+WWI GERMANY/W LOC/G EX/STRUC LEGIS
CT/SYS INGP/REL PWR...BIBLIOG 20 ADENAUER/K.
PAGE 78 B1573
NAT/G
POL/PAR
DIPLOM
CONSTN

B66
RICHARD J.B.,GOVERNMENT AND POLITICS OF WYOMING.
USA+45 POL/PAR EX/STRUC LEGIS CT/SYS LOBBY APPORT
CHOOSE REPRESENT 20 WYOMING GOVERNOR. PAGE 88 B1773
PROVS
LOC/G
ADMIN

B66
ROSS R.M.,STATE AND LOCAL GOVERNMENT AND
ADMINISTRATION. USA+45 CONSTN POL/PAR EX/STRUC
LEGIS BUDGET EDU/PROP CONTROL CT/SYS CHOOSE GOV/REL
T. PAGE 90 B1827
LOC/G
PROVS
MUNIC
ADMIN

B66
SCHMIDT K.M.,AMERICAN STATE AND LOCAL GOVERNMENT IN
ACTION. USA+45 CONSTN LOC/G POL/PAR CHIEF LEGIS
PROB/SOLV ADJUD LOBBY GOV/REL...DECISION ANTHOL 20
GOVERNOR MAYOR URBAN/RNWL. PAGE 94 B1896
PROVS
ADMIN
MUNIC
PLAN

B66
SCHURMANN F.,IDEOLOGY AND ORGANIZATION IN COMMUNIST
CHINA. CHINA/COM LOC/G MUNIC POL/PAR ECO/TAC
CONTROL ATTIT...MGT STERTYP 20 COM/PARTY. PAGE 94
B1909
MARXISM
STRUCT
ADMIN
NAT/G

B66
SEASHOLES B.,VOTING, INTEREST GROUPS, AND PARTIES.
USA+45 FINAN LOC/G NAT/G ADMIN LEAD GP/REL INGP/REL
ROLE...CHARTS ANTHOL 20. PAGE 95 B1922
CHOOSE
POL/PAR
LOBBY
PARTIC

B66
SILBERMAN B.S.,MODERN JAPANESE LEADERSHIP;
TRANSITION AND CHANGE. NAT/G POL/PAR CHIEF ADMIN
REPRESENT GP/REL ADJUST RIGID/FLEX...SOC METH/COMP
ANTHOL 19/20 CHINJAP CHRISTIAN. PAGE 97 B1952
LEAD
CULTURE
ELITES
MUNIC

B66
SPINELLI A.,THE EUROCRATS; CONFLICT AND CRISIS IN
THE EUROPEAN COMMUNITY (TRANS. BY C. GROVE HAINES).
EUR+WWI MARKET POL/PAR ECO/TAC PARL/PROC EEC OEEC
ECSC EURATOM. PAGE 99 B2007
INT/ORG
INGP/REL
CONSTN
ADMIN

B66
TOTTEN G.O.,THE SOCIAL DEMOCRATIC MOVEMENT IN
PREWAR JAPAN. ASIA CHIEF EX/STRUC LEGIS DOMIN LEAD
ROUTINE WAR 20 CHINJAP. PAGE 105 B2122
POL/PAR
SOCISM
PARTIC
STRATA

B66
US DEPARTMENT OF THE ARMY,COMMUNIST CHINA: A
STRATEGIC SURVEY: A BIBLIOGRAPHY (PAMPHLET NO.
20-67). CHINA/COM COM INDIA USSR NAT/G POL/PAR
EX/STRUC FORCES NUC/PWR REV ATTIT...POLICY GEOG
CHARTS. PAGE 108 B2184
BIBLIOG/A
MARXISM
S/ASIA
DIPLOM

L66
MCAUSLAN J.P.W.,"CONSTITUTIONAL INNOVATION AND
POLITICAL STABILITY IN TANZANIA: A PRELIMINARY
ASSESSMENT." AFR TANZANIA ELITES CHIEF EX/STRUC
RIGID/FLEX PWR 20 PRESIDENT BUREAUCRCY. PAGE 71
B1440
CONSTN
NAT/G
EXEC
POL/PAR

S66
AFRICAN BIBLIOGRAPHIC CENTER,"A CURRENT VIEW OF
AFRICANA: A SELECT AND ANNOTATED BIBLIOGRAPHICAL
PUBLISHING GUIDE, 1965-1966." AFR CULTURE INDUS
LABOR SECT FOR/AID ADMIN COLONIAL REV RACE/REL
SOCISM...LING 20. PAGE 3 B0063
BIBLIOG/A
NAT/G
TEC/DEV
POL/PAR

S66
BURDETTE F.L.,"SELECTED ARTICLES AND DOCUMENTS ON
AMERICAN GOVERNMENT AND POLITICS." LAW LOC/G MUNIC
NAT/G POL/PAR PROVS LEGIS BAL/PWR ADMIN EXEC
REPRESENT MGT. PAGE 17 B0343
BIBLIOG
USA+45
JURID
CONSTN

S66
JACOBSON J.,"COALITIONISM: FROM PROTEST TO
POLITICKING" USA+45 ELITES NAT/G POL/PAR PROB/SOLV
ADMIN LEAD DISCRIM ORD/FREE PWR CONSERVE 20 NEGRO
AFL/CIO CIV/RIGHTS BLACK/PWR. PAGE 55 B1116
RACE/REL
LABOR
SOCIALIST
VOL/ASSN

S66
MATTHEWS D.G.,"ETHIOPIAN OUTLINE: A BIBLIOGRAPHIC
RESEARCH GUIDE." ETHIOPIA LAW STRUCT ECO/UNDEV AGRI
LABOR SECT CHIEF DELIB/GP EX/STRUC ADMIN...LING
ORG/CHARTS 20. PAGE 71 B1429
BIBLIOG
NAT/G
DIPLOM
POL/PAR

S66
MATTHEWS D.G.,"PRELUDE-COUP D'ETAT-MILITARY
GOVERNMENT: A BIBLIOGRAPHICAL AND RESEARCH GUIDE TO
NIGERIAN POL AND GOVT, JAN, 1965-66." AFR NIGER LAW
CONSTN POL/PAR LEGIS CIVMIL/REL GOV/REL...STAT 20.
PAGE 71 B1430
BIBLIOG
NAT/G
ADMIN
CHOOSE

S66
PALMER M.,"THE UNITED ARAB REPUBLIC* AN ASSESSMENT
OF ITS FAILURE." ELITES ECO/UNDEV POL/PAR FORCES
ECO/TAC RUMOR ADMIN EXEC EFFICIENCY ATTIT SOCISM
...INT NASSER/G. PAGE 81 B1628
UAR
SYRIA
REGION
FEDERAL

S66
SNOWISS L.M.,"CONGRESSIONAL RECRUITMENT AND
REPRESENTATION." USA+45 LG/CO MUNIC POL/PAR ADMIN
REGION CONGRESS CHICAGO. PAGE 98 B1990
LEGIS
REPRESENT
CHOOSE

LOC/G
S66
WOLFINGER R.E.,"POLITICAL ETHOS AND THE STRUCTURE
OF CITY GOVERNMENT." POL/PAR EX/STRUC REPRESENT
GP/REL PERS/REL RIGID/FLEX PWR. PAGE 118 B2371
MUNIC
ATTIT
STRATA
GOV/COMP

C66
JACOB H.,"DIMENSIONS OF STATE POLITICS HEARD A. ED.
STATE LEGIWLATURES IN AMERICAN POLITICS." CULTURE
STRATA POL/PAR BUDGET TAX LOBBY ROUTINE GOV/REL
...TRADIT DECISION GEOG. PAGE 55 B1112
PROVS
LEGIS
ROLE
REPRESENT

C66
TACHERON D.G.,"THE JOB OF THE CONGRESSMAN: AN
INTRODUCTION TO SERVICES IN THE US HOUSE OF
REPRESENTATIVES." DELIB/GP EX/STRUC PRESS SENIOR
CT/SYS LOBBY CHOOSE GOV/REL...BIBLIOG 20 CONGRESS
HOUSE/REP SENATE. PAGE 102 B2068
LEGIS
PARL/PROC
ADMIN
POL/PAR

C66
TARLING N.,"A CONCISE HISTORY OF SOUTHEAST ASIA."
BURMA CAMBODIA LAOS S/ASIA THAILAND VIETNAM
ECO/UNDEV POL/PAR FORCES ADMIN REV WAR CIVMIL/REL
ORD/FREE MARXISM SOCISM 13/20. PAGE 103 B2080
COLONIAL
DOMIN
INT/TRADE
NAT/LISM

B67
BRZEZINSKI Z.K.,IDEOLOGY AND POWER IN SOVIET
POLITICS. USSR NAT/G POL/PAR PWR...GEN/LAWS 19/20.
PAGE 16 B0335
DIPLOM
EX/STRUC
MARXISM

B67
BULPITT J.G.,PARTY POLITICS IN ENGLISH LOCAL
GOVERNMENT. UK CONSTN ACT/RES TAX CONTROL CHOOSE
REPRESENT GOV/REL KNOWL 20. PAGE 17 B0344
POL/PAR
LOC/G
ELITES
EX/STRUC

B67
CROTTY W.J.,APPROACHES TO THE STUDY OF PARTY
ORGANIZATION. USA+45 SOCIETY GP/REL...ANTHOL 20.
PAGE 25 B0509
POL/PAR
STRUCT
GEN/LAWS
ADMIN

B67
DOSSICK J.J.,DOCTORAL RESEARCH ON PUERTO RICO AND
PUERTO RICANS. PUERT/RICO USA+45 USA-45 ADMIN 20.
PAGE 30 B0609
BIBLIOG
CONSTN
POL/PAR
DIPLOM

B67
EVANS R.H.,COEXISTENCE: COMMUNISM AND ITS PRACTICE
IN BOLOGNA, 1945-1965. ITALY CAP/ISM ADMIN CHOOSE
PEACE ORD/FREE...SOC STAT DEEP/INT SAMP CHARTS
BIBLIOG 20. PAGE 34 B0690
MARXISM
CULTURE
MUNIC
POL/PAR

B67
FESLER J.W.,THE FIFTY STATES AND THEIR LOCAL
GOVERNMENTS. FUT USA+45 POL/PAR LEGIS PROB/SOLV
ADMIN CT/SYS CHOOSE GOV/REL FEDERAL...POLICY CHARTS
20 SUPREME/CT. PAGE 35 B0715
PROVS
LOC/G

B67
FINCHER F.,THE GOVERNMENT OF THE UNITED STATES.
USA+45 USA-45 POL/PAR CHIEF CT/SYS LOBBY GP/REL
INGP/REL...CONCPT CHARTS BIBLIOG T 18/20 PRESIDENT
CONGRESS SUPREME/CT. PAGE 35 B0719
NAT/G
EX/STRUC
LEGIS
OP/RES

B67
GRUBER H.,INTERNATIONAL COMMUNISM IN THE ERA OF
LENIN. COM ADMIN REV GP/REL 20. PAGE 44 B0895
MARXISM
HIST/WRIT
POL/PAR

B67
JHANGIANI M.A.,JANA SANGH AND SWATANTRA: A PROFILE
OF THE RIGHTIST PARTIES IN INDIA. INDIA ADMIN
CHOOSE MARXISM SOCISM...INT CHARTS BIBLIOG 20.
PAGE 56 B1140
POL/PAR
LAISSEZ
NAT/LISM
ATTIT

B67
LEACH R.H.,GOVERNING THE AMERICAN NATION. FUT
USA+45 USA-45 CONSTN POL/PAR PLAN ADJUD EXEC CONSEN
CONGRESS PRESIDENT. PAGE 63 B1278
NAT/G
LEGIS
PWR

B67
MACKINTOSH J.M.,JUGGERNAUT. USSR NAT/G POL/PAR
ADMIN LEAD CIVMIL/REL COST TOTALISM PWR MARXISM
...GOV/COMP 20. PAGE 68 B1364
WAR
FORCES
COM
PROF/ORG

B67
PRINCE C.E.,NEW JERSEY'S JEFFERSONIAN REPUBLICANS;
THE GENESIS OF AN EARLY PARTY MACHINE (1789-1817).
USA-45 LOC/G EDU/PROP PRESS CONTROL CHOOSE...CHARTS
18/19 NEW/JERSEY REPUBLICAN. PAGE 84 B1707
POL/PAR
CONSTN
ADMIN
PROVS

B67
PYE L.W.,SOUTHEAST ASIA'S POLITICAL SYSTEMS. ASIA
S/ASIA STRUCT ECO/UNDEV EX/STRUC CAP/ISM DIPLOM
ALL/IDEOS...TREND CHARTS. PAGE 85 B1724
NAT/G
POL/PAR
GOV/COMP

B67
SABLE M.H.,A GUIDE TO LATIN AMERICAN STUDIES (2
VOLS). CONSTN FINAN INT/ORG LABOR MUNIC POL/PAR
FORCES CAP/ISM FOR/AID ADMIN MARXISM SOCISM OAS.
PAGE 92 B1861
BIBLIOG/A
L/A+17C
DIPLOM
NAT/LISM

B67
TOMA P.A.,THE POLITICS OF FOOD FOR PEACE;
EXECUTIVE-LEGISLATIVE INTERACTION. USA+45 ECO/UNDEV
POL/PAR DEBATE EXEC LOBBY CHOOSE PEACE...DECISION
CHARTS. PAGE 104 B2113
FOR/AID
POLICY
LEGIS
AGRI

B67
WARREN S.,THE AMERICAN PRESIDENT. POL/PAR FORCES
LEGIS DIPLOM ECO/TAC ADMIN EXEC PWR...ANTHOL 18/20
CHIEF
LEAD

ROOSEVLT/F KENNEDY/JF JOHNSON/LB TRUMAN/HS
WILSON/W. PAGE 114 B2297

NAT/G
CONSTN

L67

TAMBIAH S.J.,"THE POLITICS OF LANGUAGE IN INDIA AND
CEYLON." CEYLON INDIA NAT/G DOMIN ADMIN...SOC 20.
PAGE 102 B2070

POL/PAR
LING
NAT/LISM
REGION

S67

ANDERSON M.,"THE FRENCH PARLIAMENT." EUR+WWI FRANCE
MOD/EUR CONSTN POL/PAR CHIEF LEGIS LOBBY ATTIT ROLE
PWR 19/20. PAGE 5 B0095

PARL/PROC
LEAD
GOV/COMP
EX/STRUC

S67

BREGMAN A.,"WHITHER RUSSIA?" COM RUSSIA INTELL
POL/PAR DIPLOM PARTIC NAT/LISM TOTALISM ATTIT
ORD/FREE 20. PAGE 15 B0304

MARXISM
ELITES
ADMIN
CREATE

S67

CROCKETT D.G.,"THE MP AND HIS CONSTITUENTS." UK
POL/PAR...DECISION 20. PAGE 25 B0506

EXEC
NAT/G
PERS/REL
REPRESENT

S67

DRYDEN S.,"LOCAL GOVERNMENT IN TANZANIA PART II"
TANZANIA LAW NAT/G POL/PAR CONTROL PARTIC REPRESENT
...DECISION 20. PAGE 31 B0622

LOC/G
GOV/REL
ADMIN
STRUCT

S67

EDWARDS H.T.,"POWER STRUCTURE AND ITS COMMUNICATION
IN SAN JOSE, COSTA RICA." COSTA/RICA L/A+17C STRATA
FACE/GP POL/PAR EX/STRUC PROB/SOLV ADMIN LEAD
GP/REL PWR...STAT INT 20. PAGE 32 B0655

ELITES
INGP/REL
MUNIC
DOMIN

S67

HALL B.,"THE COALITION AGAINST DISHWASHERS." USA+45
POL/PAR PROB/SOLV BARGAIN LEAD CHOOSE REPRESENT
GP/REL ORD/FREE PWR...POLICY 20. PAGE 46 B0923

LABOR
ADMIN
DOMIN
WORKER

S67

HSUEH C.T.,"THE CULTURAL REVOLUTION AND LEADERSHIP
CRISIS IN COMMUNIST CHINA." CHINA/COM POL/PAR
EX/STRUC FORCES EDU/PROP ATTIT PWR...POLICY 20.
PAGE 52 B1054

LEAD
REV
CULTURE
MARXISM

S67

IDENBURG P.J.,"POLITICAL STRUCTURAL DEVELOPMENT IN
TROPICAL AFRICA." UK ECO/UNDEV KIN POL/PAR CHIEF
EX/STRUC CREATE COLONIAL CONTROL REPRESENT RACE/REL
...MAJORIT TREND 20. PAGE 53 B1074

AFR
CONSTN
NAT/G
GOV/COMP

S67

KURON J.,"AN OPEN LETTER TO THE PARTY." CONSTN
WORKER BUDGET EDU/PROP ADMIN REPRESENT SUFF OWN
...SOCIALIST 20. PAGE 62 B1244

ELITES
STRUCT
POL/PAR
ECO/TAC

S67

LEWIS P.H.,"LEADERSHIP AND CONFLICT WITHIN
FEBRERISTA PARTY OF PARAGUAY." L/A+17C PARAGUAY
EX/STRUC DOMIN SENIOR CONTROL INGP/REL CENTRAL
FEDERAL ATTIT 20. PAGE 65 B1305

POL/PAR
ELITES
LEAD

S67

LINEBERRY R.L.,"REFORMISM AND PUBLIC POLICIES IN
AMERICAN CITIES." USA+45 POL/PAR EX/STRUC LEGIS
BUDGET TAX GP/REL...STAT CHARTS. PAGE 65 B1317

DECISION
POLICY
MUNIC
LOC/G

S67

MURRAY R.,"SECOND THOUGHTS ON GHANA." AFR GHANA
NAT/G POL/PAR ADMIN REV GP/REL CENTRAL...SOCIALIST
CONCPT METH 20. PAGE 77 B1548

COLONIAL
CONTROL
REGION
SOCISM

S67

SPACKMAN A.,"THE SENATE OF TRINIDAD AND TOBAGO."
L/A+17C TRINIDAD WEST/IND NAT/G POL/PAR DELIB/GP
OP/RES PROB/SOLV EDU/PROP EXEC LOBBY ROUTINE
REPRESENT GP/REL 20. PAGE 99 B2002

ELITES
EFFICIENCY
LEGIS
DECISION

S67

SPEAR P.,"NEHRU." INDIA NAT/G POL/PAR ECO/TAC ADJUD
GOV/REL CENTRAL RIGID/FLEX 20 NEHRU/J. PAGE 99
B2003

CHIEF
ATTIT
ADMIN
CREATE

S67

WALLER D.J.,"CHINA: RED OR EXPERT." CHINA/COM
INTELL DOMIN REV ATTIT MARXISM 20. PAGE 113 B2283

CONTROL
FORCES
ADMIN
POL/PAR

B86

BOLINSBROKE H ST J.,A DISSERTATION UPON PARTIES
(1729). UK LEGIS CHOOSE GOV/REL SOVEREIGN...TRADIT
18 PARLIAMENT. PAGE 13 B0269

CONSERVE
POL/PAR
CHIEF
EX/STRUC

B87

KINNEAR J.B.,PRINCIPLES OF CIVIL GOVERNMENT.
MOD/EUR USA-45 CONSTN LOC/G EX/STRUC ADMIN
PARL/PROC RACE/REL...CONCPT 18/19. PAGE 60 B1210

POL/PAR
NAT/G
GOV/COMP
REPRESENT

POLAND O.F. B0530

POLAND....SEE ALSO COM

N

KYRIAK T.E.,EAST EUROPE: BIBLIOGRAPHY--INDEX TO US
JPRS RESEARCH TRANSLATIONS. ALBANIA BULGARIA COM
CZECHOSLVK HUNGARY POLAND ROMANIA AGRI EXTR/IND
FINAN SERV/IND INT/TRADE WEAPON...GEOG MGT SOC 20.
PAGE 62 B1247

BIBLIOG/A
PRESS
MARXISM
INDUS

B53

MEYER P.,THE JEWS IN THE SOVIET SATELLITES.
CZECHOSLVK POLAND SOCIETY STRATA NAT/G BAL/PWR
ECO/TAC EDU/PROP LEGIT ADMIN COERCE ATTIT DISPL
PERCEPT HEALTH PWR RESPECT WEALTH...METH/CNCPT JEWS
VAL/FREE NAZI 20. PAGE 73 B1474

COM
SECT
TOTALISM
USSR

B55

POOL I.,SATELLITE GENERALS: A STUDY OF MILITARY
ELITES IN THE SOVIET SPHERE. ASIA CHINA/COM COM
CZECHOSLVK FUT HUNGARY POLAND ROMANIA USSR ELITES
STRATA ADMIN ATTIT PWR SKILL...METH/CNCPT BIOG 20.
PAGE 84 B1688

FORCES
CHOOSE

S58

STAAR R.F.,"ELECTIONS IN COMMUNIST POLAND." EUR+WWI
SOCIETY INT/ORG NAT/G POL/PAR LEGIS ACT/RES ECO/TAC
EDU/PROP ADJUD ADMIN ROUTINE COERCE TOTALISM ATTIT
ORD/FREE PWR 20. PAGE 100 B2015

COM
CHOOSE
POLAND

S61

TOMASIC D.,"POLITICAL LEADERSHIP IN CONTEMPORARY
POLAND." COM EUR+WWI GERMANY NAT/G POL/PAR SECT
DELIB/GP PLAN ECO/TAC DOMIN EDU/PROP PWR MARXISM
...MARXIST GEOG MGT CONCPT TIME/SEQ STERTYP 20.
PAGE 105 B2114

SOCIETY
ROUTINE
USSR
POLAND

S64

HORECKY P.L.,"LIBRARY OF CONGRESS PUBLICATIONS IN
AID OF USSR AND EAST EUROPEAN RESEARCH." BULGARIA
CZECHOSLVK POLAND USSR YUGOSLAVIA NAT/G POL/PAR
DIPLOM ADMIN GOV/REL...CLASSIF 20. PAGE 51 B1042

BIBLIOG/A
COM
MARXISM

B67

BRZEZINSKI Z.K.,THE SOVIET BLOC: UNITY AND CONFLICT
(2ND ED., REV., ENLARGED). COM POLAND USSR INTELL
CHIEF EX/STRUC CONTROL EXEC GOV/REL PWR MARXISM
...TREND IDEA/COMP 20 LENIN/VI MARX/KARL STALIN/J.
PAGE 16 B0336

NAT/G
DIPLOM

POLICE....SEE FORCES

POLICY....ETHICS OF PUBLIC POLICIES

POLIT/ACTN....POLITICAL ACTION COMMITTEE

POLITBURO....POLITBURO (U.S.S.R.)

POLITICAL BEHAVIOR....SEE POL

POLITICAL FINANCING....SEE POL+FINAN

POLITICAL MACHINE....SEE POL+ADMIN

POLITICAL MOVEMENT....SEE IDEOLOGICAL TOPIC INDEX

POLITICAL ORGANIZATION....SEE POL/PAR

POLITICAL PROCESS....SEE LEGIS, POL

POLITICAL SCIENCE....SEE POL

POLITICAL SYSTEMS....SEE IDEOLOGICAL TOPIC INDEX

POLITICAL SYSTEMS THEORY....SEE GEN/LAWS+NET/THEORY+POL

POLITICAL THEORY....SEE IDEOLOGICAL TOPIC INDEX

POLITICS....SEE POL

POLK W.R. B1685

POLK/JAMES....PRESIDENT JAMES POLK

POLLACK/N....NORMAN POLLACK

POLLOCK R. B0534

POLLUTION....AIR OR WATER POLLUTION

POLSBY N.W. B1647,B1686

POLYNESIA....POLYNESIA

POOL I. B1687,B1688

POOLE D.C. B1689

POOLE W.F. B1690

POOLEY B.J. B1691

POONA....POONA, INDIA

POPE....POPE

POPPER/K....KARL POPPER

POPPINO R.E. B1692

POPULATION....SEE GEOG, CENSUS

POPULISM....MAJORITARIANISM

FYFE H.,THE BRITISH LIBERAL PARTY. UK SECT ADMIN LEAD CHOOSE GP/REL PWR SOCISM...MAJORIT TIME/SEQ 19/20 LIB/PARTY CONSRV/PAR. PAGE 38 B0768 — POL/PAR NAT/G REPRESENT POPULISM — B28

REICH N.,LABOR RELATIONS IN REPUBLICAN GERMANY. GERMANY CONSTN ECO/DEV INDUS NAT/G ADMIN CONTROL GP/REL FASCISM POPULISM 20 WEIMAR/REP. PAGE 87 B1763 — WORKER MGT LABOR BARGAIN — B38

BINGHAM A.M.,THE TECHNIQUES OF DEMOCRACY. USA-45 CONSTN STRUCT POL/PAR LEGIS PLAN PARTIC CHOOSE REPRESENT NAT/LISM TOTALISM...MGT 20. PAGE 12 B0240 — POPULISM ORD/FREE ADMIN NAT/G — B42

MONTGOMERY H.,CRACKER PARTIES. CULTURE EX/STRUC LEAD PWR POPULISM...TIME/SEQ 19 GEORGIA CALHOUN/JC COBB/HOWLL JACKSON/A. PAGE 74 B1505 — POL/PAR PROVS ELITES BIOG — B50

WHEARE K.C.,GOVERNMENT BY COMMITTEE; AN ESSAY ON THE BRITISH CONSTITUTION. UK NAT/G LEGIS INSPECT CONFER ADJUD ADMIN CONTROL TASK EFFICIENCY ROLE POPULISM 20. PAGE 115 B2329 — DELIB/GP CONSTN LEAD GP/COMP — B55

REDFORD E.S.,IDEAL AND PRACTICE IN PUBLIC ADMINISTRATION. CONSTN ELITES NAT/G CONSULT DELIB/GP LEAD UTOPIA ATTIT POPULISM...DECISION METH/COMP 20. PAGE 87 B1756 — POLICY EX/STRUC PLAN ADMIN — B58

BHAMBHRI C.P.,SUBSTANCE OF HINDU POLITY. INDIA S/ASIA LAW EX/STRUC JUDGE TAX COERCE GP/REL POPULISM 20 HINDU. PAGE 11 B0234 — GOV/REL WRITING SECT PROVS — B59

INTL UNION LOCAL AUTHORITIES,LOCAL GOVERNMENT IN THE USA. USA+45 PUB/INST DELIB/GP CONFER AUTOMAT GP/REL POPULISM...ANTHOL 20 CITY/MGT. PAGE 54 B1101 — LOC/G MUNIC ADMIN GOV/REL — B61

HITCHNER D.G.,MODERN GOVERNMENT: A SURVEY OF POLITICAL SCIENCE. WOR+45 INT/ORG LEGIS ADMIN CT/SYS EXEC CHOOSE TOTALISM POPULISM...INT/LAW PHIL/SCI METH 20. PAGE 50 B1019 — CONCPT NAT/G STRUCT — B62

KARL B.D.,EXECUTIVE REORGANIZATION AND REFORM IN THE NEW DEAL. ECO/DEV INDUS DELIB/GP EX/STRUC PLAN BUDGET ADMIN EFFICIENCY PWR POPULISM...POLICY 20 PRESIDENT ROOSEVLT/F WILSON/W NEW/DEAL. PAGE 58 B1174 — BIOG EXEC CREATE CONTROL — B63

GOODMAN W.,THE TWO-PARTY SYSTEM IN THE UNITED STATES. USA+45 USA-45 STRATA LOC/G CHIEF EDU/PROP ADMIN COST PWR POPULISM...PLURIST 18/20 PRESIDENT. PAGE 41 B0821 — POL/PAR REPRESENT CHOOSE NAT/G — B64

NUQUIST A.E.,TOWN GOVERNMENT IN VERMONT. USA+45 FINAN TOP/EX PROB/SOLV BUDGET TAX REPRESENT SUFF EFFICIENCY...OBS INT 20 VERMONT. PAGE 79 B1595 — LOC/G MUNIC POPULISM ADMIN — B64

CHANDA A.,FEDERALISM IN INDIA. INDIA UK ELITES FINAN NAT/G POL/PAR EX/STRUC LEGIS DIPLOM TAX GOV/REL POPULISM...POLICY 20. PAGE 20 B0402 — CONSTN CENTRAL FEDERAL — B65

MENHENNET D.,PARLIAMENT IN PERSPECTIVE. UK ROUTINE REPRESENT ROLE PWR 20 PARLIAMENT. PAGE 73 B1467 — LEGIS PARL/PROC CONCPT POPULISM — B67

PORTUGAL....SEE ALSO APPROPRIATE TIME/SPACE/CULTURE INDEX

FIGANIERE J.C.,BIBLIOTHECA HISTORICA PORTUGUEZA. BRAZIL PORTUGAL SECT ADMIN. PAGE 35 B0717 — BIBLIOG NAT/G DIPLOM COLONIAL — B50

WELCH S.R.,PORTUGUESE RULE AND SPANISH CROWN IN SOUTH AFRICA 1581-1640. PORTUGAL SOUTH/AFR SPAIN SOCIETY KIN NEIGH SECT INT/TRADE ADMIN 16/17 MISSION. PAGE 115 B2317 — DIPLOM COLONIAL WAR PEACE — B50

FREYRE G.,THE PORTUGUESE AND THE TROPICS. L/A+17C PORTUGAL SOCIETY PERF/ART ADMIN TASK GP/REL ...ART/METH CONCPT SOC/INTEG 20. PAGE 37 B0754 — COLONIAL METH PLAN CULTURE — B61

DEBRAY P.,LE PORTUGAL ENTRE DEUX REVOLUTIONS. EUR+WWI PORTUGAL CONSTN LEGIT ADMIN ATTIT ALL/VALS ...DECISION CONCPT 20 SALAZAR/A. PAGE 28 B0567 — NAT/G DELIB/GP TOP/EX — B63

WAINHOUSE D.W.,REMNANTS OF EMPIRE: THE UNITED NATIONS AND THE END OF COLONIALISM. FUT PORTUGAL WOR+45 NAT/G CONSULT DOMIN LEGIT ADMIN ROUTINE ATTIT ORD/FREE...POLICY JURID RECORD INT TIME/SEQ UN CMN/WLTH 20. PAGE 113 B2275 — INT/ORG TREND COLONIAL — B64

BOXER C.R.,PORTUGUESE SOCIETY IN THE TROPICS - THE MUNICIPAL COUNCILS OF GAO, MACAO, BAHIA, AND LUANDA, 1510-1800. EUR+WWI MOD/EUR PORTUGAL CONSTN EX/STRUC DOMIN CONTROL ROUTINE REPRESENT PRIVIL ...BIBLIOG/A 16/19 GENACCOUNT MACAO BAHIA LUANDA. PAGE 14 B0290 — MUNIC ADMIN COLONIAL DELIB/GP — B65

HISPANIC SOCIETY OF AMERICA,CATALOGUE (10 VOLS.). PORTUGAL PRE/AMER SPAIN NAT/G ADMIN...POLICY SOC 15/20. PAGE 50 B1018 — BIBLIOG L/A+17C COLONIAL DIPLOM — B65

POSITIVISM....SEE GEN/METH

POSNER M.V. B1693

POSTAL/SYS....POSTAL SYSTEMS

THE GOVERNMENT OF SOUTH AFRICA (VOL. II). SOUTH/AFR STRATA EXTR/IND EX/STRUC TOP/EX BUDGET ADJUD ADMIN CT/SYS PRODUC...CORREL CENSUS 19 RAILROAD CIVIL/SERV POSTAL/SYS. PAGE 2 B0033 — CONSTN FINAN LEGIS NAT/G — B08

US HOUSE COMM ON POST OFFICE,MANPOWER UTILIZATION IN THE FEDERAL GOVERNMENT. USA+45 FORCES WORKER CREATE PLAN EFFICIENCY UTIL 20 CONGRESS CIVIL/SERV POSTAL/SYS DEPT/DEFEN. PAGE 109 B2193 — NAT/G ADMIN LABOR EX/STRUC — B57

US HOUSE COMM ON POST OFFICE,TO PROVIDE AN EFFECTIVE SYSTEM OF PERSONNEL ADMINISTRATION. USA+45 DELIB/GP CONTROL EFFICIENCY 20 CONGRESS PRESIDENT CIVIL/SERV POSTAL/SYS. PAGE 109 B2194 — ADMIN NAT/G EX/STRUC LAW — B58

US SENATE COMM ON POST OFFICE,TO PROVIDE FOR AN EFFECTIVE SYSTEM OF PERSONNEL ADMINISTRATION. EFFICIENCY...MGT 20 CONGRESS CIVIL/SERV POSTAL/SYS YARBROGH/R. PAGE 111 B2233 — ADMIN NAT/G EX/STRUC LAW — B59

DEAN A.L.,FEDERAL AGENCY APPROACHES TO FIELD MANAGEMENT (PAMPHLET). R+D DELIB/GP EX/STRUC PROB/SOLV GOV/REL...CLASSIF BIBLIOG 20 FAA NASA DEPT/HEW POSTAL/SYS IRS. PAGE 28 B0563 — ADMIN MGT NAT/G OP/RES — B63

POSTOFFICE....POST OFFICE DEPARTMENT

POSVAR W.W. B1694

POTSDAM....POTSDAM

POTTER D.C. B1695

POUND R. B1696

POUND/ROS....ROSCOE POUND

POVERTY....SEE WEALTH, INCOME

POVRTY/WAR....WAR ON POVERTY; SEE ALSO GREAT/SOC, JOHNSN/LB

AMERICAN SOCIETY PUBLIC ADMIN,PUBLIC ADMINISTRATION AND THE WAR ON POVERTY (PAMPHLET). USA+45 SOCIETY ECO/DEV FINAN LOC/G LEGIS CREATE EDU/PROP CONFER GOV/REL GP/REL ROLE 20 POVRTY/WAR. PAGE 4 B0089 — WEALTH NAT/G PLAN ADMIN — N66

POWELL N.J. B1697

POWELL/AC....ADAM CLAYTON POWELL

POWER....SEE PWR

PPBS....PLANNING-PROGRAMMING-BUDGETING SYSTEM

PRAGMATICS....SEE LOG

PRAKASH O.M. B1698

PRATT R.C. B1699

PRE/AMER....PRE-EUROPEAN AMERICAS

DOHERTY D.K.,PRELIMINARY BIBLIOGRAPHY OF COLONIZATION AND SETTLEMENT IN LATIN AMERICA AND — BIBLIOG COLONIAL — N

ANGLO-AMERICA. L/A+17C PRE/AMER USA-45 ECO/UNDEV   ADMIN
NAT/G 15/20. PAGE 30 B0604   DIPLOM

                               B65

HISPANIC SOCIETY OF AMERICA,CATALOGUE (10 VOLS.).   BIBLIOG
PORTUGAL PRE/AMER SPAIN NAT/G ADMIN...POLICY SOC   L/A+17C
15/20. PAGE 50 B1018   COLONIAL
                                  DIPLOM

PRE/US/AM....PRE-1776 UNITED STATES (THE COLONIES)

                               B41

PALMER J.M.,AMERICA IN ARMS: THE EXPERIENCE OF THE   FORCES
UNITED STATES WITH MILITARY ORGANIZATION. FUT   NAT/G
USA-45 LEAD REV PWR 18/20 WASHINGT/G KNOX/HENRY   ADMIN
PRE/US/AM. PAGE 81 B1627   WAR

                               B65

FEERICK J.D.,FROM FAILING HANDS: THE STUDY OF   EX/STRUC
PRESIDENTIAL SUCCESSION. CONSTN NAT/G PROB/SOLV   CHIEF
LEAD PARL/PROC MURDER CHOOSE...NEW/IDEA BIBLIOG 20   LAW
KENNEDY/JF JOHNSON/LB PRESIDENT PRE/US/AM   LEGIS
VICE/PRES. PAGE 35 B0710

PREDICT....PREDICTION OF FUTURE EVENTS, SEE ALSO FUT

                               N19

GINZBERG E.,MANPOWER FOR GOVERNMENT (PAMPHLET).   WORKER
USA+45 FORCES PLAN PROB/SOLV PAY EDU/PROP ADMIN   CONSULT
GP/REL COST...MGT PREDICT TREND 20 CIVIL/SERV.   NAT/G
PAGE 40 B0803   LOC/G

                               B49

BURNS J.M.,CONGRESS ON TRIAL: THE LEGISLATIVE   LEGIS
PROCESS AND THE ADMINISTRATIVE STATE. USA+45 NAT/G   EXEC
ADMIN ROUTINE REPRESENT...PREDICT TREND. PAGE 17   GP/REL
B0354   PWR

                               S52

LIPSET S.M.,"DEMOCRACY IN PRIVATE GOVERNMENT; (A   LABOR
CASE STUDY OF THE INTERNATIONAL TYPOGRAPHICAL   ADMIN
UNION)" (BMR)" POL/PAR CONTROL LEAD INGP/REL PWR   ELITES
...MAJORIT DECISION PREDICT 20. PAGE 65 B1319   REPRESENT

                               C56

FALL B.B.,"THE VIET-MINH REGIME." VIETNAM LAW   NAT/G
ECO/UNDEV POL/PAR FORCES DOMIN WAR ATTIT MARXISM   ADMIN
...BIOG PREDICT BIBLIOG/A 20. PAGE 35 B0703   EX/STRUC
                                  LEAD

                               B57

HEATH S.,CITADEL, MARKET, AND ALTAR; EMERGING   NEW/IDEA
SOCIETY. SOCIETY ADMIN OPTIMAL OWN RATIONAL   STRUCT
ORD/FREE...SOC LOG PREDICT GEN/LAWS DICTIONARY 20.   UTOPIA
PAGE 49 B0985   CREATE

                               S58

DEAN B.V.,"APPLICATION OF OPERATIONS RESEARCH TO   DECISION
MANAGERIAL DECISION MAKING" STRATA ACT/RES   OP/RES
PROB/SOLV ROLE...SOC PREDICT SIMUL 20. PAGE 28   MGT
B0565   METH/CNCPT

                               B59

BOWLES C.,THE COMING POLITICAL BREAKTHROUGH. USA+45   DIPLOM
ECO/DEV EX/STRUC ATTIT...CONCPT OBS 20. PAGE 14   CHOOSE
B0288   PREDICT
                                  POL/PAR

                               S59

CYERT R.M.,"MODELS IN A BEHAVIORAL THEORY OF THE   SIMUL
FIRM." ROUTINE...DECISION MGT METH/CNCPT MATH.   GAME
PAGE 25 B0517   PREDICT
                                  INDUS

                               B60

KERR C.,INDUSTRIALISM AND INDUSTRIAL MAN. CULTURE   WORKER
SOCIETY ECO/UNDEV NAT/G ADMIN PRODUC WEALTH   MGT
...PREDICT TREND NAT/COMP 19/20. PAGE 59 B1197   ECO/DEV
                                  INDUS

                               B63

BONINI C.P.,SIMULATION OF INFORMATION AND DECISION   INDUS
SYSTEMS IN THE FIRM. MARKET BUDGET DOMIN EDU/PROP   SIMUL
ADMIN COST ATTIT HABITAT PERCEPT PWR...CONCPT   DECISION
PROBABIL QUANT PREDICT HYPO/EXP BIBLIOG. PAGE 13   MGT
B0273

                               B64

BRIGHT J.R.,RESEARCH, DEVELOPMENT AND TECHNOLOGICAL   TEC/DEV
INNOVATION. CULTURE R+D CREATE PLAN PROB/SOLV   NEW/IDEA
AUTOMAT RISK PERSON...DECISION CONCPT PREDICT   INDUS
BIBLIOG. PAGE 15 B0308   MGT

                               B64

SAYLES L.R.,MANAGERIAL BEHAVIOR: ADMINISTRATION IN   CONCPT
COMPLEX ORGANIZATIONS. INDUS LG/CO PROB/SOLV   ADMIN
CONTROL EXEC INGP/REL PERS/REL SKILL...MGT OBS   TOP/EX
PREDICT GEN/LAWS 20. PAGE 93 B1874   EX/STRUC

                               B66

AMER ENTERPRISE INST PUB POL,CONGRESS: THE FIRST   EFFICIENCY
BRANCH OF GOVERNMENT. EX/STRUC FEEDBACK REPRESENT   LEGIS
INGP/REL PWR...DECISION METH/CNCPT PREDICT. PAGE 4   DELIB/GP
B0081   CONTROL

                               B66

KAESTNER K.,GESAMTWIRTSCHAFTLICHE PLANUNG IN EINER   ECO/TAC
GEMISCHTEN WIRTSCHAFTSORDNUNG   PLAN
(WIRTSCHAFTSPOLITISCHE STUDIEN 5). GERMANY/W WOR+45   POLICY
WOR-45 INDUS MARKET NAT/G ACT/RES GP/REL INGP/REL   PREDICT
PRODUC...ECOMETRIC MGT BIBLIOG 20. PAGE 57 B1159

                               S67

BRADY R.H.,"COMPUTERS IN TOP-LEVEL DECISION MAKING"   COMPUTER
FUT WOR+45 CONTROL...PREDICT CHARTS. PAGE 15 B0297   MGT
                                  DECISION
                                  TEC/DEV

                               S67

HAIRE M.,"MANAGING MANAGEMENT MANPOWER." EX/STRUC   MGT
OP/RES PAY EDU/PROP COST EFFICIENCY...PREDICT SIMUL   EXEC
20. PAGE 45 B0920   LEAD
                                  INDUS

                               S67

LENDVAI P.,"HUNGARY* CHANGE VS. IMMOBILISM."   ECO/DEV
HUNGARY LABOR NAT/G PLAN DEBATE ADMIN ROUTINE   MGT
CENTRAL EFFICIENCY MARXISM PLURISM...PREDICT 20.   CHOOSE
PAGE 64 B1289

                               S67

MOOR E.J.,"THE INTERNATIONAL IMPACT OF AUTOMATION."   TEC/DEV
WOR+45 ACT/RES COMPUTER CREATE PLAN CAP/ISM ROUTINE   OP/RES
EFFICIENCY PREDICT. PAGE 75 B1511   AUTOMAT
                                  INDUS

PREDICTION....SEE PREDICT, FUT

PREFECT....PREFECTS AND PREFECTORALISM

                               B55

CHAPMAN B.,THE PREFECTS AND PROVINCIAL FRANCE.   ADMIN
FRANCE DELIB/GP WORKER ROLE PWR 19/20 PREFECT.   PROVS
PAGE 20 B0408   EX/STRUC
                                  LOC/G

                               B63

FRIED R.C.,THE ITALIAN PREFECTS. ITALY STRATA   ADMIN
ECO/DEV NAT/LISM ALL/IDEOS...TREND CHARTS METH/COMP   NAT/G
BIBLIOG 17/20 PREFECT. PAGE 37 B0755   EFFICIENCY

PREHIST....PREHISTORIC SOCIETY, PRIOR TO 3000 B.C.

PREHISTORIC SOCIETY....SEE PREHIST

PREJUDICE....SEE DISCRIM

PRESIDENT....PRESIDENCY (ALL NATIONS); SEE ALSO CHIEF

                               N

US SUPERINTENDENT OF DOCUMENTS,POLITICAL SCIENCE: BIBLIOG/A
GOVERNMENT, CRIME, DISTRICT OF COLUMBIA (PRICE LIST   NAT/G
54). USA+45 LAW CONSTN EX/STRUC WORKER ADJUD ADMIN   CRIME
CT/SYS CHOOSE INGP/REL RACE/REL CONGRESS PRESIDENT.
PAGE 111 B2241

                               B17

CORWIN E.S.,THE PRESIDENT'S CONTROL OF FOREIGN   TOP/EX
RELATIONS. FUT USA-45 CONSTN STRATA NAT/G CHIEF   PWR
EX/STRUC LEGIS KNOWL RESPECT...JURID CONCPT TREND   DIPLOM
CONGRESS VAL/FREE 20 PRESIDENT. PAGE 24 B0483
                               B19

SUTHERLAND G.,CONSTITUTIONAL POWER AND WORLD   USA-45
AFFAIRS. CONSTN STRUCT INT/ORG NAT/G CHIEF LEGIS   EXEC
ACT/RES PLAN GOV/REL ALL/VALS...OBS TIME/SEQ   DIPLOM
CONGRESS VAL/FREE 20 PRESIDENT. PAGE 102 B2056
                               N19

MARSH J.F. JR.,THE FBI RETIREMENT BILL (PAMPHLET).   ADMIN
USA+45 EX/STRUC WORKER PLAN PROB/SOLV BUDGET LEAD   NAT/G
LOBBY PARL/PROC PERS/REL RIGID/FLEX...POLICY 20 FBI   SENIOR
PRESIDENT BUR/BUDGET. PAGE 70 B1405   GOV/REL
                               B27

WILLOUGHBY W.F.,PRINCIPLES OF PUBLIC ADMINISTRATION   NAT/G
WITH SPECIAL REFERENCE TO THE NATIONAL AND STATE   EX/STRUC
GOVERNMENTS OF THE UNITED STATES. FINAN PROVS CHIEF   OP/RES
CONSULT LEGIS CREATE BUDGET EXEC ROUTINE GOV/REL   ADMIN
CENTRAL...MGT 20 BUR/BUDGET CONGRESS PRESIDENT.
PAGE 117 B2356
                               S43

PRICE D.K.,"THE PARLIAMENTARY AND PRESIDENTIAL   LEGIS
SYSTEMS" (BMR)" USA-45 NAT/G EX/STRUC PARL/PROC   REPRESENT
GOV/REL PWR 20 PRESIDENT CONGRESS PARLIAMENT.   ADMIN
PAGE 84 B1706   GOV/COMP
                               B47

MARX F.M.,THE PRESIDENT AND HIS STAFF SERVICES   CONSTN
PUBLIC ADMINISTRATION SERVICES NUMBER 98   CHIEF
(PAMPHLET). FINAN ADMIN CT/SYS REPRESENT PWR 20   NAT/G
PRESIDENT. PAGE 70 B1419   EX/STRUC
                               B47

PATTERSON C.P.,PRESIDENTIAL GOVERNMENT IN THE   CHIEF
UNITED STATES - THE UNWRITTEN CONSTITUTION. USA+45   NAT/G
DELIB/GP EX/STRUC ADJUD ADMIN EXEC...DECISION   CONSTN
PRESIDENT. PAGE 81 B1643   POL/PAR
                               B48

HART J.,THE AMERICAN PRESIDENCY IN ACTION 1789: A   NAT/G
STUDY IN CONSTITUTIONAL HISTORY. USA-45 POL/PAR   CONSTN
DELIB/GP FORCES LEGIS ADJUD ADMIN LEAD GP/REL   CHIEF
PERS/REL 18 PRESIDENT CONGRESS. PAGE 47 B0959   EX/STRUC
                               B48

STOKES W.S.,BIBLIOGRAPHY OF STANDARD AND CLASSICAL   BIBLIOG
WORKS IN THE FIELDS OF AMERICAN POLITICAL SCIENCE.   NAT/G
USA+45 USA-45 POL/PAR PROVS FORCES DIPLOM ADMIN   LOC/G
CT/SYS APPORT 20 CONGRESS PRESIDENT. PAGE 101 B2043   CONSTN

WHITE L.D.,THE FEDERALISTS: A STUDY IN
ADMINISTRATIVE HISTORY. STRUCT DELIB/GP LEGIS
BUDGET ROUTINE GOV/REL GP/REL PERS/REL PWR...BIOG
18/19 PRESIDENT CONGRESS WASHINGT/G JEFFERSN/T
HAMILTON/A. PAGE 116 B2337
ADMIN
NAT/G
POLICY
PROB/SOLV
B48

GRAVES W.B.,BASIC INFORMATION ON THE REORGANIZATION
OF THE EXECUTIVE BRANCH: 1912-1948. USA-45 BUDGET
ADMIN CONTROL GP/REL EFFICIENCY...MGT CHARTS
ORG/CHARTS 20 PRESIDENT. PAGE 42 B0857
BIBLIOG/A
EX/STRUC
NAT/G
CHIEF
B49

RIDDICK F.M.,THE UNITED STATES CONGRESS
ORGANIZATION AND PROCEDURE. POL/PAR DELIB/GP
PROB/SOLV DEBATE CONTROL EXEC LEAD INGP/REL PWR
...MAJORIT DECISION CONGRESS PRESIDENT. PAGE 88
B1777
LEGIS
PARL/PROC
CHIEF
EX/STRUC
B49

CORWIN E.S.,"THE PRESIDENCY IN PERSPECTIVE." USA+45
USA-45 NAT/G LEAD 20 PRESIDENT. PAGE 24 B0485
CHIEF
PWR
REPRESENT
EXEC
S49

KOENIG L.W.,THE SALE OF THE TANKERS. USA+45 SEA
DIST/IND POL/PAR DIPLOM ADMIN CIVMIL/REL ATTIT
...DECISION 20 PRESIDENT DEPT/STATE. PAGE 60 B1223
NAT/G
POLICY
PLAN
GOV/REL
B50

HOLCOMBE A.,"OUR MORE PERFECT UNION." USA+45 USA-45
POL/PAR JUDGE CT/SYS EQUILIB FEDERAL PWR...MAJORIT
TREND BIBLIOG 18/20 CONGRESS PRESIDENT. PAGE 51
B1031
CONSTN
NAT/G
ADMIN
PLAN
C50

MAASS A.,MUDDY WATERS: THE ARMY ENGINEERS AND THE
NATIONS RIVERS. USA-45 PROF/ORG CONSULT LEGIS ADMIN
EXEC ROLE PWR...SOC PRESIDENT 20. PAGE 67 B1353
FORCES
GP/REL
LOBBY
CONSTRUC
B51

WHITE L.D.,THE JEFFERSONIANS: A STUDY IN
ADMINISTRATIVE HISTORY 18011829. USA-45 DELIB/GP
LEGIS TOP/EX PROB/SOLV BUDGET ECO/TAC GP/REL
FEDERAL...BIOG IDEA/COMP 19 PRESIDENT CONGRESS
JEFFERSN/T. PAGE 116 B2338
ADMIN
NAT/G
POLICY
POL/PAR
B51

NASH B.D.,STAFFING THE PRESIDENCY: PLANNING
PAMPHLET NO. 80 (PAMPHLET). NAT/G CHIEF CONSULT
DELIB/GP CONFER ADMIN 20 PRESIDENT. PAGE 77 B1557
EX/STRUC
EXEC
TOP/EX
ROLE
B52

SOMERS H.M.,"THE PRESIDENT AS ADMINISTRATOR."
USA+45 NAT/G ADMIN REPRESENT GOV/REL 20 PRESIDENT.
PAGE 99 B1996
CONTROL
EFFICIENCY
EX/STRUC
EXEC
S52

GROSS B.M.,THE LEGISLATIVE STRUGGLE: A STUDY IN
SOCIAL COMBAT. STRUCT LOC/G POL/PAR JUDGE EDU/PROP
DEBATE ETIQUET ADMIN LOBBY CHOOSE GOV/REL INGP/REL
HEREDITY ALL/VALS...SOC PRESIDENT. PAGE 44 B0885
LEGIS
DECISION
PERSON
LEAD
B53

US PRES CONF ADMIN PROCEDURE,REPORT (PAMPHLET).
USA+45 CONFER ADJUD...METH/COMP 20 PRESIDENT.
PAGE 109 B2209
NAT/G
DELIB/GP
ADJUST
ADMIN
N53

WHITE L.D.,THE JACKSONIANS: A STUDY IN
ADMINISTRATIVE HISTORY 1829-1861. USA-45 CONSTN
POL/PAR CHIEF DELIB/GP LEGIS CREATE PROB/SOLV
ECO/TAC LEAD REGION GP/REL 19 PRESIDENT CONGRESS
JACKSON/A. PAGE 116 B2339
NAT/G
ADMIN
POLICY
B54

SMITHIES A.,THE BUDGETARY PROCESS IN THE UNITED
STATES. ECO/DEV AGRI EX/STRUC FORCES LEGIS
PROB/SOLV TAX ROUTINE EFFICIENCY...MGT CONGRESS
PRESIDENT. PAGE 98 B1987
NAT/G
ADMIN
BUDGET
GOV/REL
B55

ABELS J.,THE TRUMAN SCANDALS. USA+45 USA-45 POL/PAR
TAX LEGIT CT/SYS CHOOSE PRIVIL MORAL WEALTH 20
TRUMAN/HS PRESIDENT CONGRESS. PAGE 3 B0052
CRIME
ADMIN
CHIEF
TRIBUTE
B56

KOENIG L.W.,THE TRUMAN ADMINISTRATION: ITS
PRINCIPLES AND PRACTICE. USA+45 POL/PAR CHIEF LEGIS
DIPLOM DEATH NUC/PWR WAR CIVMIL/REL PEACE
...DECISION 20 TRUMAN/HS PRESIDENT TREATY. PAGE 61
B1224
ADMIN
POLICY
EX/STRUC
GOV/REL
B56

MACMAHON A.W.,"WOODROW WILSON AS LEGISLATIVE LEADER
AND ADMINISTRATOR." CONSTN POL/PAR ADMIN...POLICY
HIST/WRIT WILSON/W PRESIDENT. PAGE 68 B1371
LEGIS
CHIEF
LEAD
BIOG
L56

US HOUSE COMM ON POST OFFICE,TO PROVIDE AN
EFFECTIVE SYSTEM OF PERSONNEL ADMINISTRATION.
USA+45 DELIB/GP CONTROL EFFICIENCY 20 CONGRESS
PRESIDENT CIVIL/SERV POSTAL/SYS. PAGE 109 B2194
ADMIN
NAT/G
EX/STRUC
LAW
B58

VAN RIPER P.P.,HISTORY OF THE UNITED STATES CIVIL
SERVICE. USA+45 USA-45 LABOR LOC/G DELIB/GP LEGIS
PROB/SOLV LOBBY GOV/REL GP/REL INCOME...POLICY
18/20 PRESIDENT CIVIL/SERV. PAGE 111 B2251
ADMIN
WORKER
NAT/G
B58

WHITE L.D.,THE REPUBLICAN ERA: 1869-1901, A STUDY
IN ADMINISTRATIVE HISTORY. USA-45 FINAN PLAN
NEUTRAL CRIME GP/REL MORAL LAISSEZ PRESIDENT
REFORMERS 19 CONGRESS CIVIL/SERV. PAGE 116 B2340
MGT
PWR
DELIB/GP
ADMIN
B58

LOEWENSTEIN K.,VERFASSUNGSRECHT UND
VERFASSUNGSPRAXIS DER VEREINIGTEN STAATEN. USA+45
USA-45 COLONIAL CT/SYS GP/REL RACE/REL ORD/FREE
...JURID 18/20 SUPREME/CT CONGRESS PRESIDENT
BILL/RIGHT CIVIL/LIB. PAGE 66 B1337
CONSTN
POL/PAR
EX/STRUC
NAT/G
B59

JEWELL M.R.,"THE SENATE REPUBLICAN POLICY COMMITTEE
AND FOREIGN POLICY." PLAN ADMIN CONTROL LEAD LOBBY
EFFICIENCY PRESIDENT 20 REPUBLICAN. PAGE 56 B1139
POL/PAR
NAT/G
DELIB/GP
POLICY
S59

JUNZ A.J., PRESENT TRENDS IN AMERICAN NATIONAL
GOVERNMENT. LEGIS DIPLOM ADMIN CT/SYS ORD/FREE
...CONCPT ANTHOL 20 CONGRESS PRESIDENT SUPREME/CT.
PAGE 2 B0048
POL/PAR
CHOOSE
CONSTN
NAT/G
B60

BELL J.,THE SPLENDID MISERY: THE STORY OF THE
PRESIDENCY AND POWER POLITICS AT CLOSE RANGE.
USA+45 USA-45 PRESS ADMIN LEAD LOBBY GP/REL
PERS/REL PERSON PRESIDENT. PAGE 10 B0208
EXEC
TOP/EX
LEGIS
B60

MARKMANN C.L.,JOHN F. KENNEDY: A SENSE OF PURPOSE.
USA+45 INTELL FAM CONSULT DELIB/GP LEGIS PERSON
SKILL 20 KENNEDY/JF EISNHWR/DD ROOSEVLT/F
NEW/FRONTR PRESIDENT. PAGE 69 B1399
CHIEF
TOP/EX
ADMIN
BIOG
B61

TANZER L.,THE KENNEDY CIRCLE. INTELL CONSULT
DELIB/GP TOP/EX CONTROL EXEC INGP/REL PERS/REL PWR
...BIOG IDEA/COMP ANTHOL 20 KENNEDY/JF PRESIDENT
DEMOCRAT MCNAMARA/R RUSK/D. PAGE 103 B2077
EX/STRUC
NAT/G
CHIEF
B61

TOMPKINS D.C.,CONFLICT OF INTEREST IN THE FEDERAL
GOVERNMENT: A BIBLIOGRAPHY. USA+45 EX/STRUC LEGIS
ADJUD ADMIN CRIME CONGRESS PRESIDENT. PAGE 105
B2117
BIBLIOG
ROLE
NAT/G
LAW
B61

KUIC V.,"THEORY AND PRACTICE OF THE AMERICAN
PRESIDENCY." USA+45 USA-45 NAT/G ADMIN REPRESENT
...PLURIST 20 PRESIDENT. PAGE 61 B1241
EXEC
EX/STRUC
PWR
CHIEF
S61

ROBINSON J.A.,"PROCESS SATISFACTION AND POLICY
APPROVAL IN STATE DEPARTMENT - CONGRESSIONAL
RELATIONS." ELITES CHIEF LEGIS CONFER DEBATE ADMIN
FEEDBACK ROLE...CHARTS 20 CONGRESS PRESIDENT
DEPT/STATE. PAGE 89 B1802
GOV/REL
EX/STRUC
POL/PAR
DECISION
S61

BENSON E.T.,CROSS FIRE: THE EIGHT YEARS WITH
EISENHOWER. USA+45 DIPLOM LEAD ATTIT PERSON
CONSERVE...TRADIT BIOG 20 EISNHWR/DD PRESIDENT
TAFT/RA DULLES/JF NIXON/RM. PAGE 11 B0218
ADMIN
POLICY
DELIB/GP
TOP/EX
B62

BOCK E.A.,CASE STUDIES IN AMERICAN GOVERNMENT.
USA+45 ECO/DEV CHIEF EDU/PROP CT/SYS RACE/REL
ORD/FREE...JURID MGT PHIL/SCI PRESIDENT CASEBOOK.
PAGE 13 B0262
POLICY
LEGIS
IDEA/COMP
NAT/G
B62

JEWELL M.E.,SENATORIAL POLITICS AND FOREIGN POLICY.
NAT/G POL/PAR CHIEF DELIB/GP TOP/EX FOR/AID
EDU/PROP ROUTINE ATTIT PWR SKILL...MAJORIT
METH/CNCPT TIME/SEQ CONGRESS 20 PRESIDENT. PAGE 56
B1138
USA+45
LEGIS
DIPLOM
B62

US SENATE COMM ON JUDICIARY,STATE DEPARTMENT
SECURITY. USA+45 CHIEF TEC/DEV DOMIN ADMIN EXEC
ATTIT ORD/FREE...POLICY CONGRESS DEPT/STATE
PRESIDENT KENNEDY/JF KENNEDY/JF SENATE 20. PAGE 110
B2228
CONTROL
WORKER
NAT/G
GOV/REL
B62

NEIBURG H.L.,"THE EISENHOWER AEC AND CONGRESS: A
STUDY IN EXECUTIVE-LEGISLATIVE RELATIONS." USA+45
NAT/G POL/PAR DELIB/GP EX/STRUC TOP/EX ADMIN EXEC
LEAD ROUTINE PWR...POLICY COLD/WAR CONGRESS
PRESIDENT AEC. PAGE 77 B1567
CHIEF
LEGIS
GOV/REL
NUC/PWR
L62

GREEN H.P.,GOVERNMENT OF THE ATOM. USA+45 LEGIS
PROB/SOLV ADMIN CONTROL PWR...POLICY DECISION 20
PRESIDENT CONGRESS. PAGE 43 B0864
GOV/REL
EX/STRUC
NUC/PWR
DELIB/GP
B63

KARL B.D.,EXECUTIVE REORGANIZATION AND REFORM IN
THE NEW DEAL. ECO/DEV INDUS DELIB/GP EX/STRUC PLAN
BUDGET ADMIN EFFICIENCY PWR POPULISM...POLICY 20
PRESIDENT ROOSEVLT/F WILSON/W NEW/DEAL. PAGE 58
B1174
BIOG
EXEC
CREATE
CONTROL
B63

B63

SIDEY H.,JOHN F. KENNEDY, PRESIDENT. USA+45 INTELL   BIOG
FAM CONSULT DELIB/GP LEGIS ADMIN LEAD 20 KENNEDY/JF   TOP/EX
PRESIDENT. PAGE 97 B1951   SKILL
                                                     PERSON
                                                       B63
WARNER W.L.,THE AMERICAN FEDERAL EXECUTIVE. USA+45   ELITES
USA-45 CONSULT EX/STRUC GP/REL DRIVE ALL/VALS...PSY   NAT/G
DEEP/QU CHARTS 19/20 PRESIDENT. PAGE 114 B2295   TOP/EX
                                                     ADMIN
                                                       C63
BLUM J.M.,"THE NATIONAL EXPERIENCE." USA+45 USA-45   ADMIN
ECO/DEV DIPLOM WAR NAT/LISM...POLICY CHARTS BIBLIOG   NAT/G
T 16/20 CONGRESS PRESIDENT COLD/WAR. PAGE 13 B0258   LEGIS
                                                     CHIEF
                                                       B64
COMMITTEE ECONOMIC DEVELOPMENT,IMPROVING EXECUTIVE   EXEC
MANAGEMENT IN THE FEDERAL GOVERNMENT. USA+45 CHIEF   MGT
DELIB/GP WORKER PLAN PAY SENIOR ADMIN EFFICIENCY 20   TOP/EX
PRESIDENT. PAGE 22 B0457   NAT/G
                                                       B64
EATON H.,PRESIDENTIAL TIMBER: A HISTORY OF   DELIB/GP
NOMINATING CONVENTIONS, 1868-1960. USA+45 USA-45   CHOOSE
POL/PAR EX/STRUC DEBATE LOBBY ATTIT PERSON ALL/VALS CHIEF
...MYTH 19/20 PRESIDENT. PAGE 32 B0646   NAT/G
                                                       B64
GOODMAN W.,THE TWO-PARTY SYSTEM IN THE UNITED   POL/PAR
STATES. USA+45 USA-45 STRATA LOC/G CHIEF EDU/PROP   REPRESENT
ADMIN COST PWR POPULISM...PLURIST 18/20 PRESIDENT.   CHOOSE
PAGE 41 B0821   NAT/G
                                                       B64
JACKSON H.M.,THE SECRETARY OF STATE AND THE   GOV/REL
AMBASSADOR* JACKSON SUBCOMMITTEE PAPERS ON THE   DIPLOM
CONDUCT OF AMERICAN FOREIGN POLICY. USA+45 NAT/G   ADMIN
FORCES ACT/RES OP/RES EDU/PROP CENTRAL EFFICIENCY   EX/STRUC
ORD/FREE...OBS RECORD ANTHOL CONGRESS PRESIDENT.
PAGE 55 B1107
                                                       B64
KEEFE W.J.,THE AMERICAN LEGISLATIVE PROCESS: LEGIS
CONGRESS AND THE STATES. USA+45 LAW POL/PAR   DECISION
DELIB/GP DEBATE ADMIN LOBBY REPRESENT CONGRESS   PWR
PRESIDENT. PAGE 59 B1187   PROVS
                                                       B64
NEUSTADT R.,PRESIDENTIAL POWER. USA+45 CONSTN NAT/G TOP/EX
CHIEF LEGIS CREATE EDU/PROP LEGIT ADMIN EXEC COERCE SKILL
ATTIT PERSON RIGID/FLEX PWR CONGRESS 20 PRESIDENT
TRUMAN/HS EISNHWR/DD. PAGE 78 B1575
                                                       B64
ROBSON W.A.,THE GOVERNORS AND THE GOVERNED. USA+45   EX/STRUC
PROB/SOLV DOMIN ADMIN CONTROL CHOOSE...POLICY   ATTIT
PRESIDENT. PAGE 89 B1808   PARTIC
                                                     LEAD
                                                       B64
ROCHE J.P.,THE PRESIDENCY. USA+45 USA-45 CONSTN   EX/STRUC
NAT/G CHIEF BAL/PWR DIPLOM GP/REL 18/20 PRESIDENT.   PWR
PAGE 90 B1810
                                                       B64
SARROS P.P.,CONGRESS AND THE NEW DIPLOMACY: THE   DIPLOM
FORMULATION OF MUTUAL SECURITY POLICY: 1953-60   POL/PAR
(THESIS). USA+45 CHIEF EX/STRUC REGION ROUTINE   NAT/G
CHOOSE GOV/REL PEACE ROLE...POLICY 20 PRESIDENT
CONGRESS. PAGE 92 B1869
                                                       B64
US SENATE COMM GOVT OPERATIONS,THE SECRETARY OF   DIPLOM
STATE AND THE AMBASSADOR. USA+45 CHIEF CONSULT   DELIB/GP
EX/STRUC FORCES PLAN ADMIN EXEC INGP/REL ROLE   NAT/G
...ANTHOL 20 PRESIDENT DEPT/STATE. PAGE 110 B2215
                                                       B64
US SENATE COMM GOVT OPERATIONS,ADMINISTRATION OF   ADMIN
NATIONAL SECURITY. USA+45 CHIEF TOP/EX PLAN DIPLOM   FORCES
CONTROL PEACE...POLICY DECISION 20 PRESIDENT   ORD/FREE
CONGRESS. PAGE 110 B2216   NAT/G
                                                       B65
FEERICK J.D.,FROM FAILING HANDS: THE STUDY OF   EX/STRUC
PRESIDENTIAL SUCCESSION. CONSTN NAT/G PROB/SOLV   CHIEF
LEAD PARL/PROC MURDER CHOOSE...NEW/IDEA BIBLIOG 20   LAW
KENNEDY/JF JOHNSON/LB PRESIDENT PRE/US/AM   LEGIS
VICE/PRES. PAGE 35 B0710
                                                       B65
HAIGHT D.E.,THE PRESIDENT: ROLES AND POWERS. USA+45 CHIEF
USA-45 POL/PAR PLAN DIPLOM CHOOSE PERS/REL PWR   LEGIS
18/20 PRESIDENT CONGRESS. PAGE 45 B0915   TOP/EX
                                                     EX/STRUC
                                                       B65
KOENIG L.W.,OFFICIAL MAKERS OF PUBLIC POLICY: POLICY
CONGRESS AND THE PRESIDENT. USA+45 USA-45 EX/STRUC   LEGIS
ADMIN CONTROL GOV/REL PWR 18/20 CONGRESS PRESIDENT. CHIEF
PAGE 61 B1225   NAT/G
                                                       B65
LATHAM E.,THE GROUP BASIS OF POLITICS: A STUDY IN   LEGIS
BASING-POINT LEGISLATION. INDUS MARKET POL/PAR   GP/COMP
DELIB/GP EX/STRUC DEBATE ADJUD...CHARTS PRESIDENT.   GP/REL
PAGE 63 B1274
                                                       B65
REDFORD D.R.,POLITICS AND GOVERNMENT IN THE UNITED   NAT/G
STATES. USA+45 USA-45 LOC/G PROVS FORCES DIPLOM   POL/PAR

CT/SYS LOBBY...JURID SUPREME/CT PRESIDENT. PAGE 87   EX/STRUC
B1751   LEGIS
                                                       B65
STANLEY D.T.,CHANGING ADMINISTRATIONS. USA+45   NAT/G
POL/PAR DELIB/GP TOP/EX BUDGET GOV/REL GP/REL   CHIEF
PERS/REL PWR...MAJORIT DECISION MGT 20 PRESIDENT   ADMIN
SUCCESSION DEPT/STATE DEPT/DEFEN DEPT/HEW. PAGE 100 EX/STRUC
B2021
                                                       S65
HAMMOND P.Y.,"FOREIGN POLICY-MAKING AND   DIPLOM
ADMINISTRATIVE POLITICS." CREATE ADMIN COST   STRUCT
...DECISION CONCPT GAME CONGRESS PRESIDENT. PAGE 46 IDEA/COMP
B0935   OP/RES
                                                       B66
CORNWELL E.E. JR.,THE AMERICAN PRESIDENCY: VITAL   CHIEF
CENTER. USA+45 USA-45 POL/PAR LEGIS PROB/SOLV   EX/STRUC
CONTROL PARTIC GOV/REL 18/20 PRESIDENT. PAGE 23   NAT/G
B0478   ADMIN
                                                       B66
SAPIN B.M.,THE MAKING OF UNITED STATES FOREIGN   DIPLOM
POLICY. USA+45 INT/ORG DELIB/GP FORCES PLAN ECO/TAC EX/STRUC
CIVMIL/REL PRESIDENT. PAGE 92 B1868   DECISION
                                                     NAT/G
                                                       L66
MCAUSLAN J.P.W.,"CONSTITUTIONAL INNOVATION AND   CONSTN
POLITICAL STABILITY IN TANZANIA: A PRELIMINARY   NAT/G
ASSESSMENT." AFR TANZANIA ELITES CHIEF EX/STRUC   EXEC
RIGID/FLEX PWR 20 PRESIDENT BUREAUCRCY. PAGE 71   POL/PAR
B1440
                                                       B67
FINCHER F.,THE GOVERNMENT OF THE UNITED STATES.   NAT/G
USA+45 USA-45 POL/PAR CHIEF CT/SYS LOBBY GP/REL   EX/STRUC
INGP/REL...CONCPT CHARTS BIBLIOG T 18/20 PRESIDENT   LEGIS
CONGRESS SUPREME/CT. PAGE 35 B0719   OP/RES
                                                       B67
LEACH R.H.,GOVERNING THE AMERICAN NATION. FUT   NAT/G
USA+45 USA-45 CONSTN POL/PAR PLAN ADJUD EXEC CONSEN LEGIS
CONGRESS PRESIDENT. PAGE 63 B1278   PWR
                                                       S67
JONES G.S.,"STRATEGIC PLANNING." USA+45 EX/STRUC   PLAN
FORCES DETER WAR 20 PRESIDENT. PAGE 57 B1150   DECISION
                                                     DELIB/GP
                                                     POLICY
                                                       S67
LEES J.P.,"LEGISLATIVE REVIEW AND BUREAUCRATIC   SUPEGO
RESPONSIBILITY." USA+45 FINAN NAT/G DELIB/GP PLAN   BUDGET
PROB/SOLV CONFER CONTROL GP/REL DEMAND...DECISION   LEGIS
20 CONGRESS PRESIDENT HOUSE/REP BUREAUCRCY. PAGE 63 EXEC
B1281
                                                       S67
O'DELL J.H.,"THE JULY REBELLIONS AND THE 'MILITARY PWR
STATE'." USA+45 VIETNAM STRATA CHIEF WORKER   NAT/G
COLONIAL EXEC CROWD CIVMIL/REL RACE/REL TOTALISM   COERCE
...WELF/ST PACIFIST 20 NEGRO JOHNSON/LB PRESIDENT   FORCES
CIV/RIGHTS. PAGE 79 B1599

PRESS C. B0993,B1700,B1701

PRESS....PRESS, OPERATIONS OF ALL PRINTED MEDIA, EXCEPT
     FILM AND TV (Q.V.), JOURNALISM; SEE ALSO COM/IND

                                                       N
SOVIET-EAST EUROPEAN RES SERV,SOVIET SOCIETY. USSR BIBLIOG/A
LABOR POL/PAR PRESS MARXISM...MARXIST 20. PAGE 99   EDU/PROP
B2001   ADMIN
                                                     SOC
                                                       N
CONGRESSIONAL MONITOR. CONSULT DELIB/GP PROB/SOLV   BIBLIOG
PRESS DEBATE ROUTINE...POLICY CONGRESS. PAGE 1   LEGIS
B0002   REPRESENT
                                                     USA+45
                                                       N
FINANCIAL INDEX. CANADA UK USA+45 ECO/DEV LG/CO   BIBLIOG
ADMIN 20. PAGE 2 B0032   INDUS
                                                     FINAN
                                                     PRESS
                                                       N
KYRIAK T.E.,EAST EUROPE: BIBLIOGRAPHY--INDEX TO US BIBLIOG/A
JPRS RESEARCH TRANSLATIONS. ALBANIA BULGARIA COM   PRESS
CZECHOSLVK HUNGARY POLAND ROMANIA AGRI EXTR/IND   MARXISM
FINAN SERV/IND INT/TRADE WEAPON...GEOG MGT SOC 20. INDUS
PAGE 62 B1247
                                                       N
UNIVERSITY MICROFILMS INC,DISSERTATION ABSTRACTS: BIBLIOG/A
ABSTRACTS OF DISSERTATIONS AND MONOGRAPHS IN   ACADEM
MICROFILM. CANADA DIPLOM ADMIN...INDEX 20. PAGE 107 PRESS
B2166   WRITING
                                                       N19
PERREN G.E.,LANGUAGE AND COMMUNICATION IN THE   EDU/PROP
COMMONWEALTH (PAMPHLET). FUT UK LAW ECO/DEV PRESS   LING
TV WRITING ADJUD ADMIN COLONIAL CONTROL 20   GOV/REL
CMN/WLTH. PAGE 82 B1660   COM/IND
                                                       L34
GOSNELL H.F.,"BRITISH ROYAL COMMISSIONS OF INQUIRY" DELIB/GP
UK CONSTN LEGIS PRESS ADMIN PARL/PROC...DECISION 20 INSPECT
PARLIAMENT. PAGE 41 B0839   POLICY

B42

NEUBURGER O.,OFFICIAL PUBLICATIONS OF PRESENT-DAY GERMANY: GOVERNMENT, CORPORATE ORGANIZATIONS, AND NATIONAL SOCIALIST PARTY. GERMANY CONSTN COM/IND POL/PAR EDU/PROP PRESS 20 NAZI. PAGE 78 B1570 — NAT/G BIBLIOG/A FASCISM NAT/G ADMIN

B43

LEVY H.P.,A STUDY IN PUBLIC RELATIONS: CASE HISTORY OF THE RELATIONS MAINTAINED BETWEEN A DEPT OF PUBLIC ASSISTANCE AND PEOPLE. USA-45 NAT/G PRESS ADMIN LOBBY GP/REL DISCRIM...SOC/WK LING AUD/VIS 20 PENNSYLVAN. PAGE 64 B1302 — ATTIT RECEIVE WEALTH SERV/IND

B49

ASPINALL A.,POLITICS AND THE PRESS 1780-1850. UK LAW ELITES FINAN PROF/ORG LEGIS ADMIN ATTIT ...POLICY 18/19. PAGE 7 B0142 — PRESS CONTROL POL/PAR ORD/FREE

B49

BOYD A.M.,UNITED STATES GOVERNMENT PUBLICATIONS (3RD ED.). USA+45 EX/STRUC LEGIS ADMIN...JURID CHARTS 20. PAGE 14 B0291 — BIBLIOG/A PRESS NAT/G EDU/PROP

B50

JENKINS W.S.,A GUIDE TO THE MICROFILM COLLECTION OF EARLY STATE RECORDS. USA+45 CONSTN MUNIC LEGIS PRESS ADMIN CT/SYS 18/20. PAGE 56 B1130 — BIBLIOG PROVS AUD/VIS

B50

WARD R.E.,A GUIDE TO JAPANESE REFERENCE AND RESEARCH MATERIALS IN THE FIELD OF POLITICAL SCIENCE. LAW CONSTN LOC/G PRESS ADMIN...SOC CON/ANAL METH 19/20 CHINJAP. PAGE 113 B2289 — BIBLIOG/A ASIA NAT/G

B51

HARDMAN J.B.,THE HOUSE OF LABOR. LAW R+D NEIGH EDU/PROP LEAD ROUTINE REPRESENT GP/REL...POLICY STAT. PAGE 47 B0945 — LABOR LOBBY ADMIN PRESS

B51

NIELANDER W.A.,PUBLIC RELATIONS. USA+45 COM/IND LOC/G NAT/G VOL/ASSN EX/STRUC DIPLOM EDU/PROP PRESS TV...METH/CNCPT T 20. PAGE 78 B1583 — PERS/REL GP/REL LG/CO ROUTINE

B52

SCHATTSCHNEIDER E.E.,A GUIDE TO THE STUDY OF PUBLIC AFFAIRS. LAW LOC/G NAT/G LEGIS BUDGET PRESS ADMIN LOBBY...JURID CHARTS 20. PAGE 93 B1882 — ACT/RES INTELL ACADEM METH/COMP

B53

LARSEN K.,NATIONAL BIBLIOGRAPHIC SERVICES: THEIR CREATION AND OPERATION. WOR+45 COM/IND CREATE PLAN DIPLOM PRESS ADMIN ROUTINE...MGT UNESCO. PAGE 62 B1262 — BIBLIOG/A INT/ORG WRITING

C53

BULNER-THOMAS I.,"THE PARTY SYSTEM IN GREAT BRITAIN." UK CONSTN SECT PRESS CONFER GP/REL ATTIT ...POLICY TREND BIBLIOG 19/20 PARLIAMENT. PAGE 17 B0343 — NAT/G POL/PAR ADMIN ROUTINE

B55

STEPHENS O.,FACTS TO A CANDID WORLD. USA+45 WOR+45 COM/IND EX/STRUC PRESS ROUTINE EFFICIENCY ATTIT ...PSY 20. PAGE 100 B2033 — EDU/PROP PHIL/SCI NAT/G DIPLOM

B56

WASSERMAN P.,INFORMATION FOR ADMINISTRATORS: A GUIDE TO PUBLICATIONS AND SERVICES FOR MANAGEMENT IN BUSINESS AND GOVERNMENT. R+D LOC/G NAT/G PROF/ORG VOL/ASSN PRESS...PSY SOC STAT 20. PAGE 114 B2299 — BIBLIOG MGT KNOWL EDU/PROP

B56

WIGGINS J.R.,FREEDOM OR SECRECY. USA+45 USA-45 DELIB/GP EX/STRUC FORCES ADJUD SANCTION KNOWL PWR ...AUD/VIS CONGRESS 20. PAGE 116 B2344 — ORD/FREE PRESS NAT/G CONTROL

B57

IKE N.,JAPANESE POLITICS. INTELL STRUCT AGRI INDUS FAM KIN LABOR PRESS CHOOSE ATTIT...DECISION BIBLIOG 19/20 CHINJAP. PAGE 53 B1075 — NAT/G ADMIN POL/PAR CULTURE

B59

CONOVER H.F.,NIGERIAN OFFICIAL PUBLICATIONS, 1869-1959: A GUIDE. NIGER CONSTN FINAN ACADEM SCHOOL FORCES PRESS ADMIN COLONIAL...HIST/WRIT 19/20. PAGE 23 B0466 — BIBLIOG NAT/G CON/ANAL

B59

ELLIOTT O.,MEN AT THE TOP. USA+45 CULTURE EX/STRUC PRESS GOV/REL ATTIT ALL/VALS...OBS INT QU 20. PAGE 33 B0668 — TOP/EX PERSON LEAD POLICY

B60

ANDRIOT J.L.,GUIDE TO POPULAR GOVERNMENT PUBLICATIONS. USA+45 CONSTN ADMIN 20. PAGE 5 B0106 — BIBLIOG/A PRESS NAT/G

B60

BELL J.,THE SPLENDID MISERY: THE STORY OF THE PRESIDENCY AND POWER POLITICS AT CLOSE RANGE. USA+45 USA-45 PRESS ADMIN LEAD LOBBY GP/REL PERS/REL PERSON PRESIDENT. PAGE 10 B0208 — EXEC TOP/EX LEGIS

B60

BRISTOL L.H. JR.,DEVELOPING THE CORPORATE IMAGE. USA+45 SOCIETY ECO/DEV COM/IND SCHOOL EDU/PROP PRESS TV...AUD/VIS ANTHOL. PAGE 15 B0312 — LG/CO ATTIT MGT ECO/TAC

B60

HAUSER O.,PREUSSISCHE STAATSRASON UND NATIONALER GEDANKE. PRUSSIA SOCIETY PRESS ADMIN...CONCPT 19/20. PAGE 48 B0969 — NAT/LISM NAT/G ATTIT PROVS

B60

HOVING W.,THE DISTRIBUTION REVOLUTION. WOR+45 ECO/DEV FINAN SERV/IND PRESS PRICE INCOME PRODUC ...MGT 20. PAGE 52 B1049 — DIST/IND MARKET ECO/TAC TASK

C60

SCHRAMM W.,"MASS COMMUNICATIONS: A BOOK OF READINGS (2ND ED.)" LG/CO PRESS ADMIN CONTROL ROUTINE ATTIT ROLE SUPEGO...CHARTS ANTHOL BIBLIOG 20. PAGE 94 B1902 — COM/IND EDU/PROP CROWD MAJORIT

B61

HOUN F.W.,TO CHANGE A NATION: PROPAGANDA AND INDOCTRINATION IN COMMUNIST CHINA. CHINA/COM COM ACT/RES PLAN PRESS ADMIN FEEDBACK CENTRAL EFFICIENCY ATTIT...PSY SOC 20. PAGE 52 B1048 — DOMIN EDU/PROP TOTALISM MARXISM

B61

LENIN V.I.,WHAT IS TO BE DONE? (1902). RUSSIA LABOR NAT/G POL/PAR WORKER CAP/ISM ECO/TAC ADMIN PARTIC ...MARXIST IDEA/COMP GEN/LAWS 19/20. PAGE 64 B1292 — EDU/PROP PRESS MARXISM METH/COMP

B61

NARASIMHAN V.K.,THE PRESS, THE PUBLIC AND THE ADMINISTRATION (PAMPHLET). INDIA COM/IND CONTROL REPRESENT GOV/REL EFFICIENCY...ANTHOL 20. PAGE 77 B1554 — NAT/G ADMIN PRESS NEW/LIB

B62

ANDREWS W.G.,FRENCH POLITICS AND ALGERIA: THE PROCESS OF POLICY FORMATION 1954-1962. ALGERIA FRANCE CONSTN ELITES POL/PAR CHIEF DELIB/GP LEGIS DIPLOM PRESS CHOOSE 20. PAGE 5 B0105 — GOV/COMP EXEC COLONIAL

B62

GRAY R.K.,EIGHTEEN ACRES UNDER GLASS. ELITES CONSULT EX/STRUC DIPLOM PRESS CONFER WAR PERS/REL PERSON 20 EISNHWR/DD TRUMAN/HS CABINET. PAGE 43 B0860 — CHIEF ADMIN TOP/EX NAT/G

B63

HONORD S.,PUBLIC RELATIONS IN ADMINISTRATION. WOR+45 NAT/G...SOC/WK BIBLIOG 20. PAGE 51 B1039 — PRESS DIPLOM MGT METH/COMP

B64

MUSSO AMBROSI L.A.,BIBLIOGRAFIA DE BIBLIOGRAFIAS URUGUAYAS. URUGUAY DIPLOM ADMIN ATTIT...SOC 20. PAGE 77 B1551 — BIBLIOG NAT/G L/A+17C PRESS

S64

REDFORD E.S.,"THE PROTECTION OF THE PUBLIC INTEREST WITH SPECIAL REFERENCE TO ADMINISTRATIVE REGULATION." POL/PAR LEGIS PRESS PARL/PROC. PAGE 87 B1758 — ADMIN VOL/ASSN EX/STRUC GP/REL

B65

CUTLIP S.M.,A PUBLIC RELATIONS BIBLIOGRAPHY. INDUS LABOR NAT/G PROF/ORG SCHOOL DIPLOM PRESS TV GOV/REL GP/REL...PSY SOC/WK 20. PAGE 25 B0515 — BIBLIOG/A MGT COM/IND ADMIN

B65

DAVISON W.P.,INTERNATIONAL POLITICAL COMMUNICATION. COM USA+45 WOR+45 CULTURE ECO/UNDEV NAT/G PROB/SOLV PRESS TV ADMIN 20 FILM. PAGE 27 B0545 — EDU/PROP DIPLOM PERS/REL COM/IND

B65

LIPSET S.M.,THE BERKELEY STUDENT REVOLT: FACTS AND INTERPRETATIONS. USA+45 INTELL VOL/ASSN CONSULT EDU/PROP PRESS DEBATE ADMIN REV HAPPINESS RIGID/FLEX MAJORIT. PAGE 65 B1322 — CROWD ACADEM ATTIT GP/REL

B65

ROMASCO A.U.,THE POVERTY OF ABUNDANCE: HOOVER, THE NATION, THE DEPRESSION. USA-45 AGRI LEGIS WORKER GIVE PRESS LEAD 20 HOOVER/H. PAGE 90 B1817 — ECO/TAC ADMIN NAT/G FINAN

B66

ANDERSON D.L.,MUNICIPAL PUBLIC RELATIONS (1ST ED.). USA+45 SOCIETY CONSULT FORCES PRESS ADMIN...CHARTS BIBLIOG/A 20. PAGE 4 B0092 — MUNIC INGP/REL EDU/PROP ATTIT

B66

BRAIBANTI R.,RESEARCH ON THE BUREAUCRACY OF PAKISTAN. PAKISTAN LAW CULTURE INTELL ACADEM LOC/G SECT PRESS CT/SYS...LING CHARTS 20 BUREAUCRCY. PAGE 15 B0299 — HABITAT NAT/G ADMIN CONSTN

B66

SCHMIDT F.,PUBLIC RELATIONS IN HEALTH AND WELFARE. USA+45 ACADEM RECEIVE PRESS FEEDBACK GOV/REL PERS/REL DEMAND EFFICIENCY ATTIT PERCEPT WEALTH 20 PUBLIC/REL. PAGE 94 B1895 — PROF/ORG EDU/PROP ADMIN HEALTH

B65
KELLEY E.J.,MARKETING: STRATEGY AND FUNCTIONS.   MARKET
ECO/DEV INDUS PLAN PRICE CONTROL ROUTINE...MGT   DIST/IND
BIBLIOG 20. PAGE 59 B1191   POLICY
                                                              ECO/TAC
                                                                 B65
VAID K.N.,STATE AND LABOR IN INDIA. INDIA INDUS   LAW
WORKER PAY PRICE ADJUD CONTROL PARL/PROC GP/REL   LABOR
ORD/FREE 20. PAGE 111 B2248   MGT
                                                             NEW/LIB
                                                                 B66
GRETHER E.T.,MARKETING AND PUBLIC POLICY. USA+45   MARKET
ECO/DEV DIST/IND NAT/G PLAN CAP/ISM PRICE CONTROL   PROB/SOLV
...GEOG MGT 20. PAGE 43 B0874   ECO/TAC
                                                              POLICY
                                                                 B66
GROSS H.,MAKE OR BUY. USA+45 FINAN INDUS CREATE   ECO/TAC
PRICE PRODUC 20. PAGE 44 B0889   PLAN
                                                               MGT
                                                               COST
                                                                 B66
WESTON J.F.,THE SCOPE AND METHODOLOGY OF FINANCE.   FINAN
PLAN TEC/DEV CONTROL EFFICIENCY INCOME UTIL...MGT   ECO/DEV
CONCPT MATH STAT TREND METH 20. PAGE 115 B2327   POLICY
                                                              PRICE
                                                                 B67
GROSSMAN G.,ECONOMIC SYSTEMS. USA+45 USA-45 USSR   ECO/DEV
YUGOSLAVIA WORKER CAP/ISM PRICE GP/REL EQUILIB   PLAN
WEALTH MARXISM SOCISM...MGT METH/COMP 19/20.   TEC/DEV
PAGE 44 B0892   DEMAND
                                                                 S67
ZOETEWEIJ B.,"INCOME POLICIES ABROAD: AN INTERIM   METH/COMP
REPORT." NAT/G PROB/SOLV BARGAIN BUDGET PRICE RISK   INCOME
CENTRAL EFFICIENCY EQUILIB...MGT NAT/COMP 20.   POLICY
PAGE 119 B2405   LABOR
                                                                 N67
PRINCETON U INDUSTRIAL REL SEC,OUTSTANDING BOOKS ON   BIBLIOG/A
INDUSTRIAL RELATIONS, 1966 (PAMPHLET NO. 134).   INDUS
WOR+45 LABOR WORKER PLAN PRICE CONTROL INCOME...MGT   GP/REL
20. PAGE 85 B1711   POLICY
                                                                 N67
US CONGRESS JT COMM ECO GOVT,BACKGROUND MATERIAL ON   BUDGET
ECONOMY IN GOVERNMENT 1967 (PAMPHLET). WOR+45   COST
ECO/DEV BARGAIN PRICE DEMAND OPTIMAL...STAT   MGT
DEPT/DEFEN. PAGE 108 B2178   NAT/G

PRICING....SEE PRICE, ECO, ACT/RES

PRIMARIES....ELECTORAL PRIMARIES

PRIME/MIN....PRIME MINISTER

PRINCE C.E. B1707

PRINCETN/U....PRINCETON UNIVERSITY

                                                                 N19
VERNON R.,THE MYTH AND REALITY OF OUR URBAN   PLAN
PROBLEMS (PAMPHLET). USA+45 SOCIETY LOC/G ADMIN   MUNIC
COST 20 PRINCETN/U INTERVENT URBAN/RNWL. PAGE 112   HABITAT
B2261   PROB/SOLV
                                                                 B62
BOWEN W.G.,THE FEDERAL GOVERNMENT AND PRINCETON   NAT/G
UNIVERSITY. USA+45 FINAN ACT/RES PROB/SOLV ADMIN   ACADEM
CONTROL COST...POLICY 20 PRINCETN/U. PAGE 14 B0285   GP/REL
                                                            OP/RES

PRINCETON U INDUSTRIAL REL SEC B1708,B1709,B1710,B1711

PRINCETON UNIVERSITY B1712

PRISON....PRISONS; SEE ALSO PUB/INST

PRIVACY....PRIVACY AND ITS INVASION

PRIVIL....PRIVILEGED, AS CONDITION

                                                                 N19
ADMINISTRATIVE STAFF COLLEGE,THE ACCOUNTABILITY OF   PARL/PROC
GOVERNMENT DEPARTMENTS (PAMPHLET) (REV. ED.). UK   ELITES
CONSTN FINAN NAT/G CONSULT ADMIN INGP/REL CONSEN   SANCTION
PRIVIL 20 PARLIAMENT. PAGE 3 B0059   PROB/SOLV
                                                                 S39
MARX F.M.,"POLICY FORMULATION AND THE   ADMIN
ADMINISTRATIVE PROCESS" ROUTINE ADJUST EFFICIENCY   LEAD
OPTIMAL PRIVIL DRIVE PERSON OBJECTIVE...DECISION   INGP/REL
OBS GEN/METH. PAGE 70 B1418   MGT
                                                                 B52
SWENSON R.J.,FEDERAL ADMINISTRATIVE LAW: A STUDY OF   JURID
THE GROWTH, NATURE, AND CONTROL OF ADMINISTRATIVE   CONSTN
ACTION. USA-45 JUDGE ADMIN GOV/REL EFFICIENCY   LEGIS
PRIVIL ATTIT NEW/LIB SUPREME/CT. PAGE 102 B2061   ADJUD
                                                                 B56
ABELS J.,THE TRUMAN SCANDALS. USA+45 USA-45 POL/PAR   CRIME
TAX LEGIT CT/SYS CHOOSE PRIVIL MORAL WEALTH 20   ADMIN
TRUMAN/HS PRESIDENT CONGRESS. PAGE 3 B0052   CHIEF

                                                              TRIBUTE
                                                                 C58
WILDING N.,"AN ENCYCLOPEDIA OF PARLIAMENT." UK LAW   PARL/PROC
CONSTN CHIEF PROB/SOLV DIPLOM DEBATE WAR INGP/REL   POL/PAR
PRIVIL...BIBLIOG DICTIONARY 13/20 CMN/WLTH   NAT/G
PARLIAMENT. PAGE 116 B2350   ADMIN
                                                                 B60
CORSON J.J.,GOVERNANCE OF COLLEGES AND   ADMIN
UNIVERSITIES. STRUCT FINAN DELIB/GP DOMIN EDU/PROP   EXEC
LEAD CHOOSE GP/REL CENTRAL COST PRIVIL SUPEGO   ACADEM
ORD/FREE PWR...DECISION BIBLIOG. PAGE 24 B0481   HABITAT
                                                                 B62
SCHULMAN S.,TOWARD JUDICIAL REFORM IN PENNSYLVANIA;   CT/SYS
A STUDY IN COURT REORGANIZATION. USA+45 CONSTN   ACT/RES
JUDGE PLAN ADMIN LOBBY SANCTION PRIVIL PWR...JURID   PROB/SOLV
20 PENNSYLVAN. PAGE 94 B1905
                                                                 B64
AVASTHI A.,ASPECTS OF ADMINISTRATION. INDIA UK   MGT
USA+45 FINAN ACADEM DELIB/GP LEGIS RECEIVE   ADMIN
PARL/PROC PRIVIL...NAT/COMP 20. PAGE 7 B0150   SOC/WK
                                                            ORD/FREE
                                                                 B65
BOXER C.R.,PORTUGUESE SOCIETY IN THE TROPICS - THE   MUNIC
MUNICIPAL COUNCILS OF GAO, MACAO, BAHIA, AND   ADMIN
LUANDA, 1510-1800. EUR+WWI MOD/EUR PORTUGAL CONSTN   COLONIAL
EX/STRUC DOMIN CONTROL ROUTINE REPRESENT PRIVIL   DELIB/GP
...BIBLIOG/A 16/19 GENACCOUNT MACAO BAHIA LUANDA.
PAGE 14 B0290
                                                                 B65
OLSON M. JR.,DROIT PUBLIC. FRANCE NAT/G LEGIS SUFF   CONSTN
GP/REL PRIVIL...TREND 18/20. PAGE 80 B1609   FINAN
                                                            ADMIN
                                                            ORD/FREE
                                                                 B65
PYLEE M.V.,CONSTITUTIONAL GOVERNMENT IN INDIA (2ND   CONSTN
REV.). INDIA POL/PAR EX/STRUC DIPLOM COLONIAL   NAT/G
CT/SYS PARL/PROC PRIVIL...JURID 16/20. PAGE 85   PROVS
B1725   FEDERAL
                                                                 B66
LEE L.T.,VIENNA CONVENTION ON CONSULAR RELATIONS.   AGREE
WOR+45 LAW INT/ORG CONFER GP/REL PRIVIL...INT/LAW   DIPLOM
20 TREATY VIENNA/CNV. PAGE 63 B1279   ADMIN
                                                                 B67
SCHLOSSBERG S.I.,ORGANIZING AND THE LAW. USA+45   LABOR
WORKER PLAN LEGIT REPRESENT GP/REL...JURID MGT 20   CONSULT
NLRB. PAGE 94 B1893   BARGAIN
                                                           PRIVIL
                                                                 L67
"RESTRICTIVE SOVEREIGN IMMUNITY, THE STATE   SOVEREIGN
DEPARTMENT, AND THE COURTS." USA+45 USA-45 EX/STRUC   ORD/FREE
DIPLOM ADJUD CONTROL GOV/REL 19/20 DEPT/STATE   PRIVIL
SUPREME/CT. PAGE 2 B0047   CT/SYS
                                                                 S67
BEASLEY W.G.,"POLITICS AND THE SAMURAI CLASS   ELITES
STRUCTURE IN SATSUMA, 18581868." STRATA FORCES   STRUCT
DOMIN LEGIT ADMIN LEAD 19 CHINJAP. PAGE 10 B0202   ATTIT
                                                          PRIVIL
                                                                 S67
SUBRAMANIAM V.,"REPRESENTATIVE BUREAUCRACY: A   STRATA
REASSESSMENT." USA+45 ELITES LOC/G NAT/G ADMIN   GP/REL
GOV/REL PRIVIL DRIVE ROLE...POLICY CENSUS 20   MGT
CIVIL/SERV BUREAUCRCY. PAGE 101 B2053   GOV/COMP

PRIVILEGE....SEE PRIVIL

PROB/SOLV....PROBLEM SOLVING

                                                                 N
PRINCETON U INDUSTRIAL REL SEC,SELECTED REFERENCES   BIBLIOG/A
OF THE INDUSTRIAL RELATIONS SECTION OF PRINCETON,   INDUS
NEW JERSEY. LG/CO NAT/G LEGIS WORKER PLAN PROB/SOLV   LABOR
PAY ADMIN ROUTINE TASK GP/REL...PSY 20. PAGE 84   MGT
B1708
                                                                 N
CONGRESSIONAL MONITOR. CONSULT DELIB/GP PROB/SOLV   BIBLIOG
PRESS DEBATE ROUTINE...POLICY CONGRESS. PAGE 1   LEGIS
B0002   REPRESENT
                                                          USA+45
                                                                 N
INTERNATIONAL REVIEW OF ADMINISTRATIVE SCIENCES.   BIBLIOG/A
WOR+45 WOR-45 STRATA ECO/DEV ECO/UNDEV CREATE PLAN   ADMIN
PROB/SOLV DIPLOM CONTROL REPRESENT...MGT 20. PAGE 1   INT/ORG
B0004   NAT/G
                                                                 N
JOURNAL OF POLITICS. USA+45 USA-45 CONSTN POL/PAR   BIBLIOG/A
EX/STRUC LEGIS PROB/SOLV DIPLOM CT/SYS CHOOSE   NAT/G
RACE/REL 20. PAGE 1 B0005   LAW
                                                          LOC/G
                                                                 N
REVIEW OF POLITICS. WOR+45 WOR-45 CONSTN LEGIS   BIBLIOG/A
PROB/SOLV ADMIN LEAD ALL/IDEOS...PHIL/SCI 20.   DIPLOM
PAGE 1 B0006   INT/ORG
                                                          NAT/G
                                                                 N
PUBLIC ADMINISTRATION ABSTRACTS AND INDEX OF   BIBLIOG/A
ARTICLES. WOR+45 PLAN PROB/SOLV...POLICY 20. PAGE 1 ADMIN

B0019   ECO/UNDEV
                                                         NAT/G
                                                         N
UNESCO,INTERNATIONAL BIBLIOGRAPHY OF POLITICAL   BIBLIOG
SCIENCE (VOLUMES 1-8). WOR+45 LAW NAT/G EX/STRUC   CONCPT
LEGIS PROB/SOLV DIPLOM ADMIN GOV/REL 20 UNESCO.   IDEA/COMP
PAGE 107 B2153

                                                         N
US LIBRARY OF CONGRESS,CATALOG OF THE PUBLIC   BIBLIOG
DOCUMENTS OF THE UNITED STATES, 1893-1940. USA-45   NAT/G
LAW ECO/DEV AGRI PLAN PROB/SOLV ADMIN LEAD GOV/REL   POLICY
ATTIT 19/20. PAGE 109 B2200   LOC/G
                                                         B05
RIORDAN W.L.,PLUNKITT OF TAMMANY HALL. USA-45   POL/PAR
SOCIETY PROB/SOLV EXEC LEAD TASK CHOOSE ALL/VALS   MUNIC
...RECORD ANTHOL 20 REFORMERS TAMMANY NEWYORK/C   CHIEF
PLUNKITT/G. PAGE 88 B1789   ATTIT
                                                         N19
ABBOT F.C.,THE CAMBRIDGE CITY MANAGER (PAMPHLET).   MUNIC
PROB/SOLV ADMIN PERS/REL RIGID/FLEX PWR...MGT 20   EX/STRUC
MASSACHU CITY/MGT. PAGE 2 B0050   TOP/EX
                                                         GP/REL
                                                         N19
ABERNATHY B.R.,SOME PERSISTING QUESTIONS CONCERNING   PROVS
THE CONSTITUTIONAL STATE EXECUTIVE (PAMPHLET).   EX/STRUC
CONSTN TOP/EX TEC/DEV GOV/REL EFFICIENCY TIME 20   PROB/SOLV
GOVERNOR. PAGE 3 B0054   PWR
                                                         N19
ADMINISTRATIVE STAFF COLLEGE,THE ACCOUNTABILITY OF   PARL/PROC
GOVERNMENT DEPARTMENTS (PAMPHLET) (REV. ED.). UK   ELITES
CONSTN FINAN NAT/G CONSULT ADMIN INGP/REL CONSEN   SANCTION
PRIVIL 20 PARLIAMENT. PAGE 3 B0059   PROB/SOLV
                                                         N19
ANDERSON J.,THE ORGANIZATION OF ECONOMIC STUDIES IN   ECO/TAC
RELATION TO THE PROBLEMS OF GOVERNMENT (PAMPHLET).   ACT/RES
UK FINAN INDUS DELIB/GP PLAN PROB/SOLV ADMIN 20.   NAT/G
PAGE 5 B0093   CENTRAL
                                                         N19
DOTSON A.,PRODUCTION PLANNING IN THE PATENT OFFICE   EFFICIENCY
(PAMPHLET). USA+45 DIST/IND PROB/SOLV PRODUC...MGT   PLAN
PHIL/SCI 20 BUR/BUDGET PATENT/OFF. PAGE 30 B0610   NAT/G
                                                         ADMIN
                                                         N19
EAST KENTUCKY REGIONAL PLAN,PROGRAM 60: A DECADE OF   REGION
ACTION FOR PROGRESS IN EASTERN KENTUCKY (PAMPHLET).   ADMIN
USA+45 AGRI CONSTRUC INDUS CONSULT ACT/RES   PLAN
PROB/SOLV EDU/PROP GOV/REL HEALTH KENTUCKY. PAGE 32   ECO/UNDEV
B0643
                                                         N19
EAST KENTUCKY REGIONAL PLAN,PROGRAM 60 REPORT: REGION
ACTION FOR PORGRESS IN EASTERN KENTUCKY (PAMPHLET).   PLAN
USA+45 CONSTRUC INDUS ACT/RES PROB/SOLV EDU/PROP   ECO/UNDEV
ADMIN GOV/REL KENTUCKY. PAGE 32 B0644   CONSULT
                                                         N19
FOLSOM M.B.,BETTER MANAGEMENT OF THE PUBLIC'S   ADMIN
BUSINESS (PAMPHLET). USA+45 DELIB/GP PAY CONFER   NAT/G
CONTROL REGION GP/REL...METH/COMP ANTHOL 20.   MGT
PAGE 36 B0733   PROB/SOLV
                                                         N19
GINZBERG E.,MANPOWER FOR GOVERNMENT (PAMPHLET).   WORKER
USA+45 FORCES PLAN PROB/SOLV PAY EDU/PROP ADMIN   CONSULT
GP/REL COST...MGT PREDICT TREND 20 CIVIL/SERV.   NAT/G
PAGE 40 B0803   LOC/G
                                                         N19
KRIESBERG M.,CANCELLATION OF THE RATION STAMPS   RATION
(PAMPHLET). USA+45 USA-45 MARKET PROB/SOLV PRICE   DECISION
GOV/REL RIGID/FLEX 20 OPA. PAGE 61 B1235   ADMIN
                                                         NAT/G
                                                         N19
LA PALOMBARA J.G.,ALTERNATIVE STRATEGIES FOR   ECO/UNDEV
DEVELOPING ADMINISTRATIVE CAPABILITIES IN EMERGING   MGT
NATIONS (PAMPHLET). POL/PAR EX/STRUC PROB/SOLV   EXEC
PLURISM...POLICY METH/COMP. PAGE 62 B1248   ADMIN
                                                         N19
MARSH J.F. JR.,THE FBI RETIREMENT BILL (PAMPHLET).   ADMIN
USA+45 EX/STRUC WORKER PLAN PROB/SOLV BUDGET LEAD   NAT/G
LOBBY PARL/PROC PERS/REL RIGID/FLEX...POLICY 20 FBI   SENIOR
PRESIDENT BUR/BUDGET. PAGE 70 B1405   GOV/REL
                                                         N19
SOUTH AFRICA COMMISSION ON FUT,INTERIM AND FINAL   CONSTN
REPORTS ON FUTURE FORM OF GOVERNMENT IN THE SOUTH-   REPRESENT
WEST AFRICAN PROTECTORATE (PAMPHLET). SOUTH/AFR   ADMIN
NAT/G FORCES CONFER COLONIAL CONTROL 20 AFRICA/SW.   PROB/SOLV
PAGE 99 B1998
                                                         N19
VERNON R.,THE MYTH AND REALITY OF OUR URBAN   PLAN
PROBLEMS (PAMPHLET). USA+45 SOCIETY LOC/G ADMIN   MUNIC
COST 20 PRINCETN/U INTERVENT URBAN/RNWL. PAGE 112   HABITAT
B2261   PROB/SOLV
                                                         B24
KENT F.R.,THE GREAT GAME OF POLITICS. USA-45 LOC/G   ADMIN
NAT/G POL/PAR EX/STRUC PROB/SOLV BUDGET CHOOSE   OP/RES
GOV/REL 20. PAGE 59 B1194   STRUCT
                                                         S30
CRAWFORD F.G.,"THE EXECUTIVE BUDGET DECISION IN NEW   LEAD
YORK." LEGIS EXEC PWR NEW/YORK. PAGE 25 B0504   BUDGET

                                                         PROVS
                                                         PROB/SOLV
                                                         B33
ENSOR R.C.K.,COURTS AND JUDGES IN FRANCE, GERMANY,   CT/SYS
AND ENGLAND. FRANCE GERMANY UK LAW PROB/SOLV ADMIN   EX/STRUC
ROUTINE CRIME ROLE...METH/COMP 20 CIVIL/LAW.   ADJUD
PAGE 33 B0676   NAT/COMP
                                                         B36
GAUS J.M.,THE FRONTIERS OF PUBLIC ADMINISTRATION.   ROUTINE
EFFICIENCY PERCEPT RIGID/FLEX ORD/FREE 20. PAGE 39   GOV/REL
B0785   ELITES
                                                         PROB/SOLV
                                                         B36
HERRING E.P.,PUBLIC ADMINISTRATION AND THE PUBLIC   GP/REL
INTEREST. LABOR NAT/G PARTIC EFFICIENCY 20. PAGE 49   DECISION
B0995   PROB/SOLV
                                                         ADMIN
                                                         B36
US LIBRARY OF CONGRESS,CLASSIFIED GUIDE TO MATERIAL   BIBLIOG
IN THE LIBRARY OF CONGRESS COVERING URBAN COMMUNITY   CLASSIF
DEVELOPMENT. USA+45 CREATE PROB/SOLV ADMIN 20.   MUNIC
PAGE 109 B2202   PLAN
                                                         B37
GULICK L.,PAPERS ON THE SCIENCE OF ADMINISTRATION.   OP/RES
INDUS PROB/SOLV TEC/DEV COST EFFICIENCY PRODUC   CONTROL
HABITAT...PHIL/SCI METH/COMP 20. PAGE 45 B0903   ADMIN
                                                         MGT
                                                         B39
BAKER G.,THE COUNTY AGENT. USA-45 LOC/G NAT/G   AGRI
PROB/SOLV ADMIN...POLICY 20 ROOSEVLT/F NEW/DEAL   CONSULT
COUNTY/AGT. PAGE 8 B0166   GOV/REL
                                                         EDU/PROP
                                                         B40
GAUS J.M.,PUBLIC ADMINISTRATION AND THE UNITED   ADMIN
STATES DEPARTMENT OF AGRICULTURE. USA-45 STRUCT   AGRI
DIST/IND FINAN MARKET EX/STRUC PROB/SOLV GIVE   DELIB/GP
PRODUC...POLICY GEOG CHARTS 20 DEPT/AGRI. PAGE 39   OP/RES
B0786
                                                         B42
LEISERSON A.,ADMINISTRATIVE REGULATION: A STUDY IN   LOBBY
REPRESENTATION OF INTERESTS. NAT/G EX/STRUC   ADMIN
PROB/SOLV BARGAIN CONFER ROUTINE REPRESENT PERS/REL   GP/REL
UTIL PWR POLICY. PAGE 63 B1283   GOV/REL
                                                         B45
BAKER H.,PROBLEMS OF REEMPLOYMENT AND RETRAINING OF   BIBLIOG/A
MANPOWER DURING THE TRANSITION FROM WAR TO PEACE.   ADJUST
USA+45 INDUS LABOR LG/CO NAT/G PLAN ADMIN PEACE   WAR
...POLICY MGT 20. PAGE 8 B0167   PROB/SOLV
                                                         B45
BRECHT A.,FEDERALISM AND REGIONALISM IN GERMANY;   FEDERAL
THE DIVISION OF PRUSSIA. GERMANY PRUSSIA WOR-45   REGION
CREATE ADMIN WAR TOTALISM PWR...CHARTS 20 HITLER/A.   PROB/SOLV
PAGE 15 B0303   CONSTN
                                                         B46
DAVIES E.,NATIONAL ENTERPRISE: THE DEVELOPMENT OF   ADMIN
THE PUBLIC CORPORATION. UK LG/CO EX/STRUC WORKER   NAT/G
PROB/SOLV COST ATTIT SOCISM 20. PAGE 26 B0536   CONTROL
                                                         INDUS
                                                         L46
FORRESTAL J.,"THE NAVY: A STUDY IN ADMINISTRATION."   FORCES
ELITES FACE/GP EX/STRUC PROB/SOLV REPRESENT   INGP/REL
EFFICIENCY PRODUC. PAGE 37 B0741   ROUTINE
                                                         EXEC
                                                         S46
CAMPBELL A.,"THE USES OF INTERVIEW SURVEYS IN   INT
FEDERAL ADMNISTRATION" PROB/SOLV EXEC PARTIC   ADMIN
DECISION. PAGE 18 B0369   EX/STRUC
                                                         REPRESENT
                                                         B47
REDFORD E.S.,FIELD ADMINISTRATION OF WARTIME   ADMIN
RATIONING. USA-45 CONSTN ELITES DIST/IND WORKER   NAT/G
CONTROL WAR GOV/REL ADJUST RIGID/FLEX 20 OPA.   PROB/SOLV
PAGE 87 B1752   RATION
                                                         B47
SIMON H.A.,ADMINISTRATIVE BEHAVIOR: A STUDY OF   DECISION
DECISION-MAKING PROCESSES IN ADMINISTRATIVE   NEW/IDEA
ORGANIZATION. STRUCT COM/IND OP/RES PROB/SOLV   ADMIN
EFFICIENCY EQUILIB UTIL...PHIL/SCI PSY STYLE.   RATIONAL
PAGE 97 B1956
                                                         B47
WHITEHEAD T.N.,LEADERSHIP IN A FREE SOCIETY; A   INDUS
STUDY IN HUMAN RELATIONS BASED ON AN ANALYSIS OF   LEAD
PRESENT-DAY INDUSTRIAL CIVILIZATION. WOR-45 STRUCT   ORD/FREE
R+D LABOR LG/CO SML/CO WORKER PLAN PROB/SOLV   SOCIETY
TEC/DEV DRIVE...MGT 20. PAGE 116 B2341
                                                         B48
HOOVER E.M.,THE LOCATION OF ECONOMIC ACTIVITY.   HABITAT
WOR+45 MARKET MUNIC WORKER PROB/SOLV INT/TRADE   INDUS
ADMIN COST...POLICY CHARTS T 20. PAGE 51 B1041   ECO/TAC
                                                         GEOG
                                                         B48
SLESSER H.,THE ADMINISTRATION OF THE LAW. UK CONSTN   LAW
EX/STRUC OP/RES PROB/SOLV CRIME ROLE...DECISION   CT/SYS
METH/COMP 20 CIVIL/LAW ENGLSH/LAW CIVIL/LAW.   ADJUD
PAGE 98 B1977

B48

WHITE L.D.,INTRODUCTION OT THE STUDY OF PUBLIC   ADMIN
ADMINISTRATION. STRUCT PLAN PROB/SOLV EXEC ROUTINE   MGT
GOV/REL EFFICIENCY PWR CHARTS. PAGE 116 B2336   EX/STRUC
                                                        NAT/G
                                                              B48
WHITE L.D.,THE FEDERALISTS: A STUDY IN   ADMIN
ADMINISTRATIVE HISTORY. STRUCT DELIB/GP LEGIS   NAT/G
BUDGET ROUTINE GOV/REL GP/REL PERS/REL PWR...BIOG   POLICY
18/19 PRESIDENT CONGRESS WASHINGT/G JEFFERSN/T   PROB/SOLV
HAMILTON/A. PAGE 116 B2337
                                                              C48
BOLLENS J.C.,"THE PROBLEM OF GOVERNMENT IN THE SAN   USA+45
FRANCISCO BAY REGION." INDUS PROVS ADMIN GOV/REL   MUNIC
...SOC CHARTS BIBLIOG 20. PAGE 13 B0270   LOC/G
                                                        PROB/SOLV
                                                              C48
WALKER H.,"THE LEGISLATIVE PROCESS: LAWMAKING IN   PARL/PROC
THE UNITED STATES." NAT/G POL/PAR PROVS EX/STRUC   LEGIS
OP/RES PROB/SOLV CT/SYS LOBBY GOV/REL...CHARTS   LAW
BIBLIOG T 18/20 CONGRESS. PAGE 113 B2279   CONSTN
                                                              B49
DE GRAZIA A.,HUMAN RELATIONS IN PUBLIC   BIBLIOG/A
ADMINISTRATION. INDUS ACT/RES CREATE PLAN PROB/SOLV   ADMIN
TEC/DEV INGP/REL PERS/REL DRIVE...POLICY SOC 20.   PHIL/SCI
PAGE 27 B0552   OP/RES
                                                              B49
RIDDICK F.M.,THE UNITED STATES CONGRESS   LEGIS
ORGANIZATION AND PROCEDURE. POL/PAR DELIB/GP   PARL/PROC
PROB/SOLV DEBATE CONTROL EXEC LEAD INGP/REL PWR   CHIEF
...MAJORIT DECISION CONGRESS PRESIDENT. PAGE 88   EX/STRUC
B1777
                                                              B49
STEIN H.,THE FOREIGN SERVICE ACT OF 1946. USA+45   DIPLOM
ELITES EX/STRUC PLAN PROB/SOLV LOBBY GOV/REL   LAW
PERS/REL RIGID/FLEX...POLICY IDEA/COMP 20 CONGRESS   NAT/G
BUR/BUDGET. PAGE 100 B2027   ADMIN
                                                              S49
REISSMAN L.,"A STUDY OF ROLE CONCEPTIONS IN   ADMIN
BUREAUCRACY" (BMR)" PERS/REL ROLE...SOC CONCPT   METH/CNCPT
NEW/IDEA IDEA/COMP SOC/EXP 20 BUREAUCRCY. PAGE 87   GEN/LAWS
B1767   PROB/SOLV
                                                              B50
DEES J.W. JR.,URBAN SOCIOLOGY AND THE EMERGING   PLAN
ATOMIC MEGALOPOLIS, PART I. USA+45 TEC/DEV ADMIN   NEIGH
NUC/PWR HABITAT...SOC AUD/VIS CHARTS GEN/LAWS 20   MUNIC
WATER. PAGE 28 B0568   PROB/SOLV
                                                              S50
DALTON M.,"CONFLICTS BETWEEN STAFF AND LINE   MGT
MANAGERIAL OFFICERS" (BMR). USA+45 USA-45 ELITES   ATTIT
LG/CO WORKER PROB/SOLV ADMIN EXEC EFFICIENCY PRODUC   GP/REL
...GP/COMP 20. PAGE 26 B0526   INDUS
                                                              C50
MORLAN R.L.,"INTERGOVERNMENTAL RELATIONS IN   SCHOOL
EDUCATION." USA+45 FINAN LOC/G MUNIC NAT/G FORCES   GOV/REL
PROB/SOLV RECEIVE ADMIN RACE/REL COST...BIBLIOG   ACADEM
INDIAN/AM. PAGE 76 B1526   POLICY
                                                              C50
STEWART F.M.,"A HALF CENTURY OF MUNICIPAL REFORM."   LOC/G
USA+45 CONSTN FINAN SCHOOL EX/STRUC PLAN PROB/SOLV   VOL/ASSN
EDU/PROP ADMIN CHOOSE GOV/REL BIBLIOG. PAGE 101   MUNIC
B2036   POLICY
                                                              B51
DAVIS K.C.,ADMINISTRATIVE LAW. USA+45 USA-45 NAT/G   ADMIN
PROB/SOLV BAL/PWR CONTROL ORD/FREE...POLICY 20   JURID
SUPREME/CT. PAGE 26 B0539   EX/STRUC
                                                        ADJUD
                                                              B51
WHITE L.D.,THE JEFFERSONIANS: A STUDY IN   ADMIN
ADMINISTRATIVE HISTORY 18011829. USA-45 DELIB/GP   NAT/G
LEGIS TOP/EX PROB/SOLV BUDGET ECO/TAC GP/REL   POLICY
FEDERAL...BIOG IDEA/COMP 19 PRESIDENT CONGRESS   POL/PAR
JEFFERSN/T. PAGE 116 B2338
                                                              S51
COHEN M.B.,"PERSONALITY AS A FACTOR IN   PERSON
ADMINISTRATIVE DECISIONS." ADJUD PERS/REL ANOMIE   ADMIN
SUPEGO...OBS SELF/OBS INT. PAGE 22 B0446   PROB/SOLV
                                                        PSY
                                                              C51
MOORE B.,"SOVIET POLITICS - THE DILEMMA OF POWER: ATTIT
THE ROLE OF IDEAS IN SOCIAL CHANGE." USSR PROB/SOLV   PWR
DIPLOM EDU/PROP ADMIN LEAD ROUTINE REV...POLICY   CONCPT
DECISION BIBLIOG 20. PAGE 75 B1512   MARXISM
                                                              B52
US DEPARTMENT OF STATE,RESEARCH ON EASTERN EUROPE   BIBLIOG
(EXCLUDING USSR). EUR+WWI LAW ECO/DEV NAT/G   R+D
PROB/SOLV DIPLOM ADMIN LEAD MARXISM...TREND 19/20.   ACT/RES
PAGE 108 B2182   COM
                                                              S52
MASLAND J.W.,"THE NATIONAL WAR COLLEGE AND THE   CIVMIL/REL
ADMINISTRATION OF FOREIGN AFFAIRS." USA+45 NAT/G   EX/STRUC
FORCES EXEC 20. PAGE 70 B1422   REPRESENT
                                                        PROB/SOLV
                                                              S52
RICH B.M.,"ADMINISTRATION REORGANIZATION IN NEW   ADMIN
JERSEY" (BMR)" USA+45 DELIB/GP EX/STRUC WORKER   CONSTN

OP/RES BUDGET 20 NEW/JERSEY. PAGE 88 B1772   PROB/SOLV
                                                        PROVS
                                                              S52
TAYLOR D.W.,"TWENTY QUESTIONS: EFFICIENCY IN   PROB/SOLV
PROBLEM SOLVING AS A FUNCTION OF SIZE OF GROUP"   EFFICIENCY
WOR+45 CONFER ROUTINE INGP/REL...PSY GP/COMP 20.   SKILL
PAGE 103 B2085   PERCEPT
                                                              B53
THOMAS S.B.,GOVERNMENT AND ADMINISTRATION IN   PWR
COMMUNIST CHINA (MONOGRAPH). CHINA/COM PROB/SOLV   EX/STRUC
EDU/PROP 20. PAGE 104 B2100   REPRESENT
                                                        ELITES
                                                              S53
PERKINS J.A.,"ADMINISTRATION OF THE NATIONAL   CONTROL
SECURITY PROGRAM." USA+45 EX/STRUC FORCES ADMIN   GP/REL
CIVMIL/REL ORD/FREE 20. PAGE 82 B1657   REPRESENT
                                                        PROB/SOLV
                                                              B54
BIESANZ J.,MODERN SOCIETY: AN INTRODUCTION TO   SOCIETY
SOCIAL SCIENCE. COM CONSTN STRUCT FAM MUNIC NAT/G   PROB/SOLV
SECT EX/STRUC LEGIS GP/REL PERSON...SOC 20. PAGE 12   CULTURE
B0237
                                                              B54
SCHWARTZ B.,FRENCH ADMINISTRATIVE LAW AND THE   JURID
COMMON-LAW WORLD. FRANCE CULTURE LOC/G NAT/G PROVS   LAW
DELIB/GP EX/STRUC LEGIS PROB/SOLV CT/SYS EXEC   METH/COMP
GOV/REL...IDEA/COMP ENGLSH/LAW. PAGE 95 B1912   ADJUD
                                                              B54
WHITE L.D.,THE JACKSONIANS: A STUDY IN   NAT/G
ADMINISTRATIVE HISTORY 1829-1861. USA-45 CONSTN   ADMIN
POL/PAR CHIEF DELIB/GP LEGIS CREATE PROB/SOLV   POLICY
ECO/TAC LEAD REGION GP/REL 19 PRESIDENT CONGRESS
JACKSON/A. PAGE 116 B2339
                                                              S54
LONG N.E.,"PUBLIC POLICY AND ADMINISTRATION: THE   PROB/SOLV
GOALS OF RATIONALITY AND RESPONSIBILITY." EX/STRUC   EXEC
ADMIN LEAD 20. PAGE 66 B1338   REPRESENT
                                                              C54
LANDAU J.M.,"PARLIAMENTS AND PARTIES IN EGYPT." UAR   ISLAM
NAT/G SECT CONSULT LEGIS TOP/EX PROB/SOLV ADMIN   NAT/LISM
COLONIAL...GEN/LAWS BIBLIOG 19/20. PAGE 62 B1254   PARL/PROC
                                                        POL/PAR
                                                              C54
ROBSON W.A.,"GREAT CITIES OF THE WORLD: THEIR   LOC/G
GOVERNMENT, POLITICS, AND PLANNING." CONSTN FINAN   MUNIC
EX/STRUC ADMIN EXEC CHOOSE GOV/REL...STAT TREND   PLAN
ANTHOL BIBLIOG 20. PAGE 89 B1806   PROB/SOLV
                                                              B55
CUSHMAN R.E.,LEADING CONSTITUTIONAL DECISIONS.   CONSTN
USA+45 USA-45 NAT/G EX/STRUC LEGIS JUDGE TAX   PROB/SOLV
FEDERAL...DECISION 20 SUPREME/CT CASEBOOK. PAGE 25   JURID
B0513   CT/SYS
                                                              B55
SMITHIES A.,THE BUDGETARY PROCESS IN THE UNITED   NAT/G
STATES. ECO/DEV AGRI EX/STRUC FORCES LEGIS   ADMIN
PROB/SOLV TAX ROUTINE EFFICIENCY...MGT CONGRESS   BUDGET
PRESIDENT. PAGE 98 B1987   GOV/REL
                                                              B55
UN ECONOMIC AND SOCIAL COUNCIL,BIBLIOGRAPHY OF   BIBLIOG/A
PUBLICATIONS OF THE UN AND SPECIALIZED AGENCIES IN   SOC/WK
THE SOCIAL WELFARE FIELD, 1946-1952. WOR+45 FAM   ADMIN
INT/ORG MUNIC ACT/RES PLAN PROB/SOLV EDU/PROP AGE/C   WEALTH
AGE/Y HABITAT...HEAL UN. PAGE 106 B2148
                                                              B56
REDFORD E.S.,PUBLIC ADMINISTRATION AND POLICY   EX/STRUC
FORMATION: STUDIES IN OIL, GAS, BANKING, RIVER   PROB/SOLV
DEVELOPMENT AND CORPORATE INVESTIGATIONS. USA+45   CONTROL
CLIENT NAT/G ADMIN LOBBY REPRESENT GOV/REL INGP/REL   EXEC
20. PAGE 87 B1754
                                                              B56
WAUGH E.W.,SECOND CONSUL. USA+45 USA-45 CONSTN   NAT/G
POL/PAR PROB/SOLV PARL/PROC CHOOSE PERS/REL ATTIT   EX/STRUC
...BIBLIOG 18/20 VICE/PRES. PAGE 114 B2304   PWR
                                                        CHIEF
                                                              L56
LITCHFIELD E.H.,"NOTES ON A GENERAL THEORY OF   ADMIN
ADMINISTRATION." USA+45 OP/RES PROB/SOLV EFFICIENCY   ROUTINE
IDEA/COMP. PAGE 66 B1324   MGT
                                                              S56
CUTLER R.,"THE DEVELOPMENT OF THE NATIONAL SECURITY   ORD/FREE
COUNCIL." USA+45 INTELL CONSULT EX/STRUC DIPLOM   DELIB/GP
LEAD 20 TRUMAN/HS EISNHWR/DD NSC. PAGE 25 B0514   PROB/SOLV
                                                        NAT/G
                                                              S56
GORE W.J.,"ADMINISTRATIVE DECISION-MAKING IN   DECISION
FEDERAL FIELD OFFICES." USA+45 PROVS PWR CONT/OBS.   PROB/SOLV
PAGE 41 B0833   FEDERAL
                                                        ADMIN
                                                              C56
AUMANN F.R.,"THE ISTRUMENTALITIES OF JUSTICE: THEIR   JURID
FORMS, FUNCTIONS, AND LIMITATIONS." WOR+45 WOR-45   ADMIN
JUDGE PROB/SOLV ROUTINE ATTIT...BIBLIOG 20. PAGE 7   CT/SYS
B0147   ADJUD
                                                              B57
COOPER F.E.,THE LAWYER AND ADMINISTRATIVE AGENCIES.   CONSULT
USA+45 CLIENT LAW PROB/SOLV CT/SYS PERSON ROLE.   ADMIN

PAGE 23 B0473

ADJUD
DELIB/GP
B57

CRONBACK L.J.,PSYCHOLOGICAL TESTS AND PERSONNEL
DECISIONS. OP/RES PROB/SOLV CHOOSE PERSON...PSY
STAT TESTS 20. PAGE 25 B0508

MATH
DECISION
WORKER
MGT
B57

HINDERLING A.,DIE REFORMATORISCHE
VERWALTUNGSGERICHTSBARKEIT. GERMANY/W PROB/SOLV
ADJUD SUPEGO PWR...CONCPT 20. PAGE 50 B1015

ADMIN
CT/SYS
JURID
CONTROL
B57

MURDESHWAR A.K.,ADMINISTRATIVE PROBLEMS RELATING TO
NATIONALISATION: WITH SPECIAL REFERENCE TO INDIAN
STATE ENTERPRISES. CZECHOSLVK FRANCE INDIA UK
USA+45 LEGIS WORKER PROB/SOLV BUDGET PRICE CONTROL
...MGT GEN/LAWS 20 PARLIAMENT. PAGE 76 B1544

NAT/G
OWN
INDUS
ADMIN
B57

SELZNICK,LEADERSHIP IN ADMINISTRATION: A
SOCIOLOGICAL INTERPRETATION. CREATE PROB/SOLV EXEC
ROUTINE EFFICIENCY RATIONAL KNOWL...POLICY PSY.
PAGE 95 B1927

LEAD
ADMIN
DECISION
NAT/G
S57

ARGYRIS C.,"THE INDIVIDUAL AND ORGANIZATION: SOME
PROBLEMS OF MUTUAL ADJUSTMENT" (BMR)" USA+45
PROB/SOLV ADMIN CONTROL 20. PAGE 6 B0128

PERSON
METH
INGP/REL
TASK
S57

DANIELSON L.E.,"SUPERVISORY PROBLEMS IN DECISION
MAKING." WORKER ADMIN ROUTINE TASK MGT. PAGE 26
B0529

PROB/SOLV
DECISION
CONTROL
GP/REL
S57

JANOWITZ M.,"THE BUREAUCRAT AND THE PUBLIC: A STUDY
OF INFORMATIONAL PERSPECTIVES." USA+45 PROB/SOLV
ATTIT 20. PAGE 55 B1120

REPRESENT
ADMIN
EX/STRUC
CLIENT
S57

SCHUBERT G.A.,"'THE PUBLIC INTEREST' IN
ADMINISTRATIVE DECISION-MAKING: THEOREM, THEOSOPHY
OR THEORY" USA+45 EX/STRUC PROB/SOLV...METH/CNCPT
STAT. PAGE 94 B1904

ADMIN
DECISION
POLICY
EXEC
S57

TAYLOR P.S.,"THE RELATION OF RESEARCH TO
LEGISLATIVE AND ADMINISTRATIVE DECISIONS." ELITES
ACT/RES PLAN PROB/SOLV CONFER CHOOSE POLICY.
PAGE 103 B2089

DECISION
LEGIS
MGT
PWR
B58

CONSERVATIVE POLITICAL CENTRE,A WORLD SECURITY
AUTHORITY? WOR+45 CONSTN ELITES FINAN DELIB/GP PLAN
PROB/SOLV ADMIN CONTROL NUC/PWR GP/REL...IDEA/COMP
20. PAGE 23 B0468

ORD/FREE
CONSERVE
FORCES
ARMS/CONT
B58

DAVIS K.C.,ADMINISTRATIVE LAW TREATISE (VOLS. I AND
IV). NAT/G JUDGE PROB/SOLV ADJUD GP/REL 20
SUPREME/CT. PAGE 26 B0540

ADMIN
JURID
CT/SYS
EX/STRUC
B58

DWARKADAS R.,ROLE OF HIGHER CIVIL SERVICE IN INDIA.
INDIA ECO/UNDEV LEGIS PROB/SOLV GP/REL PERS/REL
...POLICY WELF/ST DECISION ORG/CHARTS BIBLIOG 20
CIVIL/SERV INTRVN/ECO. PAGE 31 B0637

ADMIN
NAT/G
ROLE
PLAN
B58

INDIAN INST OF PUBLIC ADMIN,IMPROVING CITY
GOVERNMENT. INDIA ECO/UNDEV PLAN BUDGET PARTIC
GP/REL 20. PAGE 53 B1080

LOC/G
MUNIC
PROB/SOLV
ADMIN
B58

MARCH J.G.,ORGANIZATIONS. USA+45 CREATE OP/RES PLAN
PROB/SOLV PARTIC ROUTINE RATIONAL ATTIT PERCEPT
...DECISION BIBLIOG. PAGE 69 B1397

MGT
PERSON
DRIVE
CONCPT
B58

MELMAN S.,DECISION-MAKING AND PRODUCTIVITY. INDUS
EX/STRUC WORKER OP/RES PROB/SOLV TEC/DEV ADMIN
ROUTINE RIGID/FLEX GP/COMP. PAGE 73 B1464

LABOR
PRODUC
DECISION
MGT
B58

VAN RIPER P.P.,HISTORY OF THE UNITED STATES CIVIL
SERVICE. USA+45 USA-45 LABOR LOC/G DELIB/GP LEGIS
PROB/SOLV LOBBY GOV/REL GP/REL INCOME...POLICY
18/20 PRESIDENT CIVIL/SERV. PAGE 111 B2251

ADMIN
WORKER
NAT/G
B58

WARNER A.W.,CONCEPTS AND CASES IN ECONOMIC
ANALYSIS. PROB/SOLV BARGAIN CONTROL INCOME PRODUC
...ECOMETRIC MGT CONCPT CLASSIF CHARTS 20
KEYNES/JM. PAGE 114 B2292

ECO/TAC
DEMAND
EQUILIB
COST
L58

CYERT R.M.,"THE ROLE OF EXPECTATIONS IN BUSINESS
DECISION-MAKING." PROB/SOLV PRICE RIGID/FLEX.
PAGE 25 B0516

LG/CO
DECISION
ROUTINE
EXEC
S58

DEAN B.V.,"APPLICATION OF OPERATIONS RESEARCH TO
MANAGERIAL DECISION MAKING" STRATA ACT/RES

DECISION
OP/RES

PROB/SOLV ROLE...SOC PREDICT SIMUL 20. PAGE 28
B0565

MGT
METH/CNCPT
S58

MANSFIELD E.,"A STUDY OF DECISION-MAKING WITHIN THE
FIRM." LG/CO WORKER INGP/REL COST EFFICIENCY PRODUC
...CHARTS 20. PAGE 69 B1395

OP/RES
PROB/SOLV
AUTOMAT
ROUTINE
C58

WILDING N.,"AN ENCYCLOPEDIA OF PARLIAMENT." UK LAW
CONSTN CHIEF PROB/SOLV DIPLOM DEBATE WAR INGP/REL
PRIVIL...BIBLIOG DICTIONARY 13/20 CMN/WLTH
PARLIAMENT. PAGE 116 B2350

PARL/PROC
POL/PAR
NAT/G
ADMIN
B59

BONNETT C.E.,LABOR-MANAGEMENT RELATIONS. USA+45
OP/RES PROB/SOLV EDU/PROP...AUD/VIS CHARTS 20.
PAGE 13 B0274

MGT
LABOR
INDUS
GP/REL
B59

DESMITH S.A.,JUDICIAL REVIEW OF ADMINISTRATIVE
ACTION. UK LOC/G CONSULT DELIB/GP ADMIN PWR
...DECISION JURID 20 ENGLSH/LAW. PAGE 28 B0576

ADJUD
NAT/G
PROB/SOLV
CT/SYS
B59

DIMOCK M.E.,ADMINISTRATIVE VITALITY: THE CONFLICT
WITH BUREAUCRACY. PROB/SOLV EXEC 20. PAGE 29 B0597

REPRESENT
ADMIN
EX/STRUC
ROUTINE
B59

ELLIOTT S.D.,IMPROVING OUR COURTS. LAW EX/STRUC
PLAN PROB/SOLV ADJUD ADMIN TASK CRIME EFFICIENCY
ORD/FREE 20. PAGE 33 B0669

CT/SYS
JURID
GOV/REL
NAT/G
B59

MONTGOMERY J.D.,CASES IN VIETNAMESE ADMINISTRATION.
VIETNAM/S EX/STRUC 20. PAGE 75 B1506

ADMIN
DECISION
PROB/SOLV
LEAD
B59

REDFORD E.S.,NATIONAL REGULATORY COMMISSIONS: NEED
FOR A NEW LOOK (PAMPHLET). USA+45 CLIENT PROB/SOLV
ADJUD LOBBY EFFICIENCY...POLICY 20. PAGE 87 B1757

REPRESENT
CONTROL
EXEC
NAT/G
B59

U OF MICHIGAN LAW SCHOOL,ATOMS AND THE LAW. USA+45
PROVS WORKER PROB/SOLV DIPLOM ADMIN GOV/REL ANTHOL.
PAGE 106 B2142

NUC/PWR
NAT/G
CONTROL
LAW
S59

CALKINS R.D.,"THE DECISION PROCESS IN
ADMINISTRATION." EX/STRUC PROB/SOLV ROUTINE MGT.
PAGE 18 B0368

ADMIN
OP/RES
DECISION
CON/ANAL
S59

CHAPMAN B.,"THE FRENCH CONSEIL D'ETAT." FRANCE
NAT/G CONSULT OP/RES PROB/SOLV PWR...OBS 20.
PAGE 20 B0410

ADMIN
LAW
CT/SYS
LEGIS
S59

DWYER R.J.,"THE ADMINISTRATIVE ROLE IN
DESEGREGATION." USA+45 LAW PROB/SOLV LEAD RACE/REL
ISOLAT STRANGE ROLE...POLICY SOC/INTEG MISSOURI
NEGRO CIV/RIGHTS. PAGE 31 B0638

ADMIN
SCHOOL
DISCRIM
ATTIT
S59

HILSMAN R.,"THE FOREIGN-POLICY CONSENSUS: AN
INTERIM RESEARCH REPORT." USA+45 INT/ORG LEGIS
TEC/DEV EXEC WAR CONSEN KNOWL...DECISION COLD/WAR.
PAGE 50 B1013

PROB/SOLV
NAT/G
DELIB/GP
DIPLOM
C59

DAHL R.A.,"SOCIAL SCIENCE RESEARCH ON BUSINESS:
PRODUCT AND POTENTIAL" INDUS MARKET OP/RES CAP/ISM
ADMIN LOBBY DRIVE...PSY CONCPT BIBLIOG/A 20.
PAGE 26 B0521

MGT
EFFICIENCY
PROB/SOLV
EX/STRUC
B60

DAVIS K.C.,ADMINISTRATIVE LAW AND GOVERNMENT.
USA+45 EX/STRUC PROB/SOLV ADJUD GP/REL PWR...POLICY
20 SUPREME/CT. PAGE 27 B0543

ADMIN
JURID
CT/SYS
NAT/G
B60

ECKHOFF T.,RATIONALITY AND RESPONSIBILITY IN
ADMINISTRATIVE AND JUDICIAL DECISION-MAKING. ELITES
LEAD INGP/REL ATTIT PWR...MGT METH/COMP GAME 20.
PAGE 32 B0649

ADMIN
PROB/SOLV
DECISION
METH/CNCPT
B60

GRAHAM G.A.,AMERICA'S CAPACITY TO GOVERN: SOME
PRELIMINARY THOUGHTS FOR PROSPECTIVE
ADMINISTRATORS. USA+45 SOCIETY DELIB/GP TOP/EX
CREATE PROB/SOLV RATIONAL 20. PAGE 42 B0849

MGT
LEAD
CHOOSE
ADMIN
B60

HEAP D.,AN OUTLINE OF PLANNING LAW (3RD ED.). UK
LAW PROB/SOLV ADMIN CONTROL 20. PAGE 49 B0983

MUNIC
PLAN
JURID
LOC/G
B60

JONES V.,METROPOLITAN COMMUNITIES: A BIBLIOGRAPHY
WITH SPECIAL EMPHASIS UPON GOVERNMENT AND POLITICS,
1955-1957. STRUCT ECO/DEV FINAN FORCES PLAN

BIBLIOG
LOC/G
MUNIC

PROB/SOLV RECEIVE EDU/PROP CT/SYS...GEOG HEAL 20. PAGE 57 B1152 — ADMIN

B60
MORRIS W.T.,ENGINEERING ECONOMY. AUTOMAT RISK RATIONAL...PROBABIL STAT CHARTS GAME SIMUL BIBLIOG T 20. PAGE 76 B1529 — OP/RES DECISION MGT PROB/SOLV

B60
PFIFFNER J.M.,PUBLIC ADMINISTRATION. USA+45 FINAN WORKER PLAN PROB/SOLV ADJUD CONTROL EXEC...T 20. PAGE 82 B1666 — ADMIN NAT/G LOC/G MGT

B60
POOLEY B.J.,THE EVOLUTION OF BRITISH PLANNING LEGISLATION. UK ECO/DEV LOC/G CONSULT DELIB/GP ADMIN 20 URBAN/RNWL. PAGE 84 B1691 — PLAN MUNIC LEGIS PROB/SOLV

B60
SAYRE W.S.,GOVERNING NEW YORK CITY; POLITICS IN THE METROPOLIS. POL/PAR CHIEF DELIB/GP LEGIS PLAN CT/SYS LEAD PARTIC CHOOSE...DECISION CHARTS BIBLIOG 20 NEWYORK/C BUREAUCRCY. PAGE 93 B1875 — MUNIC ADMIN PROB/SOLV

B60
SCHUBERT G.,THE PUBLIC INTEREST. USA+45 CONSULT PLAN PROB/SOLV ADJUD ADMIN GP/REL PWR ALL/IDEOS 20. PAGE 94 B1903 — POLICY DELIB/GP REPRESENT POL/PAR

B60
STANFORD RESEARCH INSTITUTE,AFRICAN DEVELOPMENT: A TEST FOR INTERNATIONAL COOPERATION. AFR USA+45 WOR+45 FINAN INT/ORG PLAN PROB/SOLV ECO/TAC INT/TRADE ADMIN...CHARTS 20. PAGE 100 B2018 — FOR/AID ECO/UNDEV ATTIT DIPLOM

B60
US SENATE COMM ON JUDICIARY,FEDERAL ADMINISTRATIVE PROCEDURE. USA+45 CONSTN NAT/G PROB/SOLV CONFER GOV/REL...JURID INT 20 SENATE. PAGE 110 B2226 — PARL/PROC LEGIS ADMIN LAW

B60
US SENATE COMM ON JUDICIARY,ADMINISTRATIVE PROCEDURE LEGISLATION. USA+45 CONSTN NAT/G PROB/SOLV CONFER ROUTINE GOV/REL...INT 20 SENATE. PAGE 110 B2227 — PARL/PROC LEGIS ADMIN JURID

S60
APTER D.E.,"THE ROLE OF TRADITIONALISM IN THE POLITICAL MODERNIZATION OF GHANA AND UGANDA" (BMR)" AFR GHANA UGANDA CULTURE NAT/G POL/PAR NAT/LISM ...CON/ANAL 20. PAGE 6 B0121 — CONSERVE ADMIN GOV/COMP PROB/SOLV

S60
BANFIELD E.C.,"THE POLITICAL IMPLICATIONS OF METROPOLITAN GROWTH" (BMR)" UK USA+45 LOC/G PROB/SOLV ADMIN GP/REL...METH/COMP NAT/COMP 20. PAGE 9 B0176 — TASK MUNIC GOV/COMP CENSUS

S60
THOMPSON J.D.,"ORGANIZATIONAL MANAGEMENT OF CONFLICT" (BMR)" WOR+45 STRUCT LABOR LG/CO WORKER TEC/DEV INGP/REL ATTIT GP/COMP. PAGE 104 B2103 — PROB/SOLV PERS/REL ADMIN MGT

B61
PROCEEDINGS OF THE CONFERENCE ON BUSINESS GAMES AS TEACHING DEVICES. PROB/SOLV ECO/TAC CONFER ADMIN TASK...MGT ANTHOL 20. PAGE 29 B0593 — GAME DECISION EDU/PROP EFFICIENCY

B61
GORDON W.J.J.,SYNECTICS; THE DEVELOPMENT OF CREATIVE CAPACITY. USA+45 PLAN TEC/DEV KNOWL WEALTH ...DECISION MGT 20. PAGE 41 B0832 — CREATE PROB/SOLV ACT/RES TOP/EX

B61
JACOBS J.,THE DEATH AND LIFE OF GREAT AMERICAN CITIES. USA+45 SOCIETY DIST/IND CREATE PROB/SOLV ADMIN...GEOG SOC CENSUS 20 URBAN/RNWL. PAGE 55 B1113 — MUNIC PLAN ADJUST HABITAT

B61
KEE R.,REFUGEE WORLD. AUSTRIA EUR+WWI GERMANY NEIGH EX/STRUC WORKER PROB/SOLV ECO/TAC RENT EDU/PROP INGP/REL COST LITERACY HABITAT 20 MIGRATION. PAGE 59 B1186 — NAT/G GIVE WEALTH STRANGE

B61
KERTESZ S.D.,AMERICAN DIPLOMACY IN A NEW ERA. COM S/ASIA UK USA+45 FORCES PROB/SOLV BAL/PWR ECO/TAC ADMIN COLONIAL WAR PEACE ORD/FREE 20 NATO CONGRESS UN COLD/WAR. PAGE 59 B1199 — ANTHOL DIPLOM TREND

B61
SHAPP W.R.,FIELD ADMINISTRATION IN THE UNITED NATIONS SYSTEM. FINAN PROB/SOLV INSPECT DIPLOM EXEC REGION ROUTINE EFFICIENCY ROLE...INT CHARTS 20 UN. PAGE 96 B1933 — INT/ORG ADMIN GP/REL FOR/AID

L61
THOMPSON V.A.,"HIERARACHY, SPECIALIZATION, AND ORGANIZATIONAL CONFLICT" (BMR)" WOR+45 STRATA STRUCT WORKER TEC/DEV GP/REL INGP/REL ATTIT AUTHORIT 20 BUREAUCRCY. PAGE 104 B2106 — PERS/REL PROB/SOLV ADMIN EX/STRUC

S61
CYERT R.M.,"TWO EXPERIMENTS ON BIAS AND CONFLICT IN ORGANIZATIONAL ESTIMATION." WORKER PROB/SOLV EFFICIENCY...MGT PSY STAT CHARTS. PAGE 25 B0518 — LAB/EXP ROUTINE ADMIN DECISION

S61
DEUTSCH K.W.,"A NOTE ON THE APPEARANCE OF WISDOM IN LARGE BUREAUCRATIC ORGANIZATIONS." ROUTINE PERSON KNOWL SKILL...DECISION STAT. PAGE 28 B0577 — ADMIN PROBABIL PROB/SOLV SIMUL

S61
LYONS G.M.,"THE NEW CIVIL-MILITARY RELATIONS." USA+45 NAT/G EX/STRUC TOP/EX PROB/SOLV ADMIN EXEC PARTIC 20. PAGE 67 B1350 — CIVMIL/REL PWR REPRESENT

B62
ARGYRIS C.,INTERPERSONAL COMPETENCE AND ORGANIZATIONAL EFFECTIVENESS. CREATE PLAN PROB/SOLV EDU/PROP INGP/REL PERS/REL PRODUC...OBS INT SIMUL 20. PAGE 6 B0131 — EX/STRUC ADMIN CONSULT EFFICIENCY

B62
BOWEN W.G.,THE FEDERAL GOVERNMENT AND PRINCETON UNIVERSITY. USA+45 FINAN ACT/RES PROB/SOLV ADMIN CONTROL COST...POLICY 20 PRINCETN/U. PAGE 14 B0285 — NAT/G ACADEM GP/REL OP/RES

B62
BRIMMER B.,A GUIDE TO THE USE OF UNITED NATIONS DOCUMENTS. WOR+45 ECO/UNDEV AGRI EX/STRUC FORCES PROB/SOLV ADMIN WAR PEACE WEALTH...POLICY UN. PAGE 15 B0310 — BIBLIOG/A INT/ORG DIPLOM

B62
DUCKWORTH W.E.,A GUIDE TO OPERATIONAL RESEARCH. INDUS PLAN PROB/SOLV EXEC EFFICIENCY PRODUC KNOWL ...MGT MATH STAT SIMUL METH 20 MONTECARLO. PAGE 31 B0624 — OP/RES GAME DECISION ADMIN

B62
ESCUELA SUPERIOR DE ADMIN PUBL,INFORME DEL SEMINARIO SOBRE SERVICIO CIVIL O CARRERA ADMINISTRATIVA. L/A+17C ELITES STRATA CONFER CONTROL GOV/REL INGP/REL SUPEGO 20 CENTRAL/AM CIVIL/SERV. PAGE 33 B0681 — ADMIN NAT/G PROB/SOLV ATTIT

B62
HANSON A.H.,MANAGERIAL PROBLEMS IN PUBLIC ENTERPRISE. INDIA DELIB/GP GP/REL INGP/REL EFFICIENCY 20 PARLIAMENT. PAGE 46 B0940 — MGT NAT/G INDUS PROB/SOLV

B62
INTERNATIONAL LABOR OFFICE,WORKERS' MANAGEMENT IN YUGOSLAVIA. COM YUGOSLAVIA LABOR DELIB/GP EX/STRUC PROB/SOLV ADMIN PWR MARXISM...CHARTS ORG/CHARTS BIBLIOG 20. PAGE 54 B1098 — WORKER CONTROL MGT INDUS

B62
MAILICK S.,CONCEPTS AND ISSUES IN ADMINISTRATIVE BEHAVIOR. EX/STRUC TOP/EX ROUTINE INGP/REL EFFICIENCY. PAGE 68 B1380 — DECISION MGT EXEC PROB/SOLV

B62
MUNICIPAL MANPOWER COMMISSION,GOVERNMENTAL MANPOWER FOR TOMORROW'S CITIES: A REPORT. USA+45 DELIB/GP EX/STRUC PROB/SOLV TEC/DEV EDU/PROP ADMIN LEAD HABITAT. PAGE 76 B1539 — LOC/G MUNIC LABOR GOV/REL

B62
NATIONAL BUREAU ECONOMIC RES,THE RATE AND DIRECTION OF INVENTIVE ACTIVITY: ECONOMIC AND SOCIAL FACTORS. STRUCT INDUS MARKET R+D CREATE OP/RES TEC/DEV EFFICIENCY PRODUC RATIONAL UTIL...WELF/ST PHIL/SCI METH/CNCPT TIME. PAGE 77 B1562 — DECISION PROB/SOLV MGT

B62
PACKARD V.,THE PYRAMID CLIMBERS. USA+45 ELITES SOCIETY CREATE PROB/SOLV EFFICIENCY ATTIT...MGT 20. PAGE 80 B1621 — INDUS TOP/EX PERS/REL DRIVE

B62
SCHULMAN S.,TOWARD JUDICIAL REFORM IN PENNSYLVANIA; A STUDY IN COURT REORGANIZATION. USA+45 CONSTN JUDGE PLAN ADMIN LOBBY SANCTION PRIVIL PWR...JURID 20 PENNSYLVAN. PAGE 94 B1905 — CT/SYS ACT/RES PROB/SOLV

B62
UNECA LIBRARY,NEW ACQUISITIONS IN THE UNECA LIBRARY. LAW NAT/G PLAN PROB/SOLV TEC/DEV ADMIN REGION...GEOG SOC 20 UN. PAGE 106 B2152 — BIBLIOG AFR ECO/UNDEV INT/ORG

B62
US SENATE COMM GOVT OPERATIONS,ADMINISTRATION OF NATIONAL SECURITY. USA+45 CHIEF PLAN PROB/SOLV TEC/DEV DIPLOM ATTIT...POLICY DECISION 20 KENNEDY/JF RUSK/D MCNAMARA/R BUNDY/M HERTER/C. PAGE 110 B2212 — ORD/FREE ADMIN NAT/G CONTROL

L62
ERDMANN H.H.,"ADMINISTRATIVE LAW AND FARM ECONOMICS." USA+45 LOC/G NAT/G PLAN PROB/SOLV LOBBY ...DECISION ANTHOL 20. PAGE 33 B0680 — AGRI ADMIN ADJUD POLICY

S62
BERNTHAL W.F.,"VALUE PERSPECTIVES IN MANAGEMENT DECISIONS." LG/CO OP/RES SUPEGO MORAL. PAGE 11 B0229 — MGT PROB/SOLV DECISION

S62
READ W.H.,"UPWARD COMMUNICATION IN INDUSTRIAL HIERARCHIES." LG/CO TOP/EX PROB/SOLV DOMIN EXEC PERS/REL ATTIT DRIVE PERCEPT...CORREL STAT CHARTS — ADMIN INGP/REL PSY

20. PAGE 86 B1747 — MGT

ACKOFF R.L.,A MANAGER'S GUIDE TO OPERATIONS
RESEARCH. STRUCT INDUS PROB/SOLV ROUTINE 20. PAGE 3
B0056 — OP/RES MGT GP/REL ADMIN

BOCK E.A., STATE AND LOCAL GOVERNMENT: A CASE BOOK.
USA+45 MUNIC PROVS CONSULT GP/REL ATTIT...MGT 20
CASEBOOK GOVERNOR MAYOR. PAGE 12 B0254 — LOC/G ADMIN PROB/SOLV CHIEF

BOCK E.A.,STATE AND LOCAL GOVERNMENT: A CASE BOOK.
USA+45 FINAN CHIEF PROB/SOLV TAX ATTIT...POLICY 20
CASEBOOK. PAGE 13 B0263 — PROVS LOC/G ADMIN GOV/REL

BURSK E.C.,NEW DECISION-MAKING TOOLS FOR MANAGERS.
COMPUTER PLAN PROB/SOLV ROUTINE COST. PAGE 18 B0357 — DECISION MGT MATH RIGID/FLEX

CHARLES S.,MINISTER OF RELIEF: HARRY HOPKINS AND
THE DEPRESSION. EX/STRUC PROB/SOLV RATION PARL/PROC
PERS/REL ALL/VALS 20 HOPKINS/H NRA. PAGE 20 B0414 — ADMIN ECO/TAC PLAN BIOG

CORSON J.J.,PUBLIC ADMINISTRATION IN MODERN
SOCIETY. INDUS FORCES CONTROL CENTRAL EFFICIENCY
20. PAGE 24 B0482 — MGT NAT/G PROB/SOLV INGP/REL

COSTELLO T.W.,PSYCHOLOGY IN ADMINISTRATION: A
RESEARCH ORIENTATION. CREATE PROB/SOLV PERS/REL
ADJUST ANOMIE ATTIT DRIVE PERCEPT ROLE...DECISION
BIBLIOG T 20. PAGE 24 B0488 — PSY MGT EXEC ADMIN

CROUCH W.W.,SOUTHERN CALIFORNIA METROPOLIS: A STUDY
IN DEVELOPMENT OF GOVERNMENT FOR A METROPOLITAN
AREA. USA+45 USA-45 PROB/SOLV ADMIN LOBBY PARTIC
CENTRAL ORD/FREE PWR...BIBLIOG 20 PROGRSV/M.
PAGE 25 B0510 — LOC/G MUNIC LEGIS DECISION

DE GUZMAN R.P.,PATTERNS IN DECISION-MAKING: CASE
STUDIES IN PHILIPPINE PUBLIC ADMINISTRATION.
PHILIPPINE LAW CHIEF PROB/SOLV INGP/REL DRIVE
PERCEPT ROLE...ANTHOL T 20. PAGE 27 B0557 — ADMIN DECISION POLICY GOV/REL

DEAN A.L.,FEDERAL AGENCY APPROACHES TO FIELD
MANAGEMENT (PAMPHLET). R+D DELIB/GP EX/STRUC
PROB/SOLV GOV/REL...CLASSIF BIBLIOG 20 FAA NASA
DEPT/HEW POSTAL/SYS IRS. PAGE 28 B0563 — ADMIN MGT NAT/G OP/RES

ECOLE NATIONALE D'ADMIN,BIBLIOGRAPHIE SELECTIVE
D'OUVRAGES DE LANGUE FRANCAISE TRAITANT DES
PROBLEMES GOUVERNEMENTAUX ET ADMINISTRATIFS. NAT/G
FORCES ACT/RES OP/RES PLAN PROB/SOLV BUDGET ADJUD
COLONIAL LEAD 20. PAGE 32 B0651 — BIBLIOG AFR ADMIN EX/STRUC

GREEN H.P.,GOVERNMENT OF THE ATOM. USA+45 LEGIS
PROB/SOLV ADMIN CONTROL PWR...POLICY DECISION 20
PRESIDENT CONGRESS. PAGE 43 B0864 — GOV/REL EX/STRUC NUC/PWR DELIB/GP

HARGROVE M.M.,BUSINESS POLICY CASES-WITH BEHAVIORAL
SCIENCE IMPLICATIONS. LG/CO SML/CO EX/STRUC TOP/EX
PLAN PROB/SOLV CONFER ADMIN CONTROL ROUTINE
EFFICIENCY. PAGE 47 B0946 — SOC/EXP INDUS DECISION MGT

HATHAWAY D.A.,GOVERNMENT AND AGRICULTURE: PUBLIC
POLICY IN A DEMOCRATIC SOCIETY. USA+45 LEGIS ADMIN
EXEC LOBBY REPRESENT PWR 20. PAGE 48 B0967 — AGRI GOV/REL PROB/SOLV EX/STRUC

INDIAN INSTITUTE PUBLIC ADMIN,CASES IN INDIAN
ADMINISTRATION. INDIA AGRI NAT/G PROB/SOLV TEC/DEV
ECO/TAC ADMIN...ANTHOL METH 20. PAGE 53 B1083 — DECISION PLAN MGT ECO/UNDEV

KAST F.E.,SCIENCE, TECHNOLOGY, AND MANAGEMENT.
SPACE USA+45 FORCES CONFER DETER NUC/PWR...PHIL/SCI
CHARTS ANTHOL BIBLIOG 20 NASA. PAGE 58 B1179 — MGT PLAN TEC/DEV PROB/SOLV

MEYNAUD J.,PLANIFICATION ET POLITIQUE. FRANCE ITALY
FINAN LABOR DELIB/GP LEGIS ADMIN EFFICIENCY
...MAJORIT DECISION 20. PAGE 73 B1477 — PLAN ECO/TAC PROB/SOLV

NASA,CONFERENCE ON SPACE, SCIENCE, AND URBAN LIFE.
USA+45 SOCIETY INDUS ACADEM ACT/RES ECO/TAC ADMIN
20. PAGE 77 B1556 — MUNIC SPACE TEC/DEV PROB/SOLV

OLSON M. JR.,THE ECONOMICS OF WARTIME SHORTAGE.
FRANCE GERMANY MOD/EUR UK AGRI PROB/SOLV ADMIN
DEMAND WEALTH...POLICY OLD/LIB 17/20. PAGE 80 B1608 — WAR ADJUST ECO/TAC

NAT/COMP

PLANTEY A.,TRAITE PRATIQUE DE LA FONCTION PUBLIQUE
(2ND ED., 2 VOLS.). FRANCE FINAN EX/STRUC PROB/SOLV
GP/REL ATTIT...SOC 20 CIVIL/SERV. PAGE 83 B1680 — ADMIN SUPEGO JURID

RICHARDS P.G.,PATRONAGE IN BRITISH GOVERNMENT.
ELITES DELIB/GP TOP/EX PROB/SOLV CONTROL CT/SYS
EXEC PWR. PAGE 88 B1774 — EX/STRUC REPRESENT POL/PAR ADMIN

SINGH H.L.,PROBLEMS AND POLICIES OF THE BRITISH IN
INDIA, 1885-1898. INDIA UK NAT/G FORCES LEGIS
PROB/SOLV CONTROL RACE/REL ADJUST DISCRIM NAT/LISM
RIGID/FLEX...MGT 19 CIVIL/SERV. PAGE 97 B1968 — COLONIAL PWR POLICY ADMIN

US SENATE COMM ON JUDICIARY,ADMINISTRATIVE
CONFERENCE OF THE UNITED STATES. USA+45 CONSTN
NAT/G PROB/SOLV CONFER GOV/REL...INT 20 SENATE.
PAGE 110 B2230 — PARL/PROC JURID ADMIN LEGIS

VAN SLYCK P.,PEACE: THE CONTROL OF NATIONAL POWER.
CUBA WOR+45 FINAN NAT/G FORCES PROB/SOLV TEC/DEV
BAL/PWR ADMIN CONTROL ORD/FREE...POLICY INT/LAW UN
COLD/WAR TREATY. PAGE 112 B2253 — ARMS/CONT PEACE INT/ORG DIPLOM

WADE H.W.R.,TOWARDS ADMINISTRATIVE JUSTICE. UK
USA+45 CONSTN CONSULT PROB/SOLV CT/SYS PARL/PROC
...POLICY JURID METH/COMP 20 ENGLSH/LAW. PAGE 112
B2270 — ADJUD IDEA/COMP ADMIN

BAKER R.J.,"DISCUSSION AND DECISION-MAKING IN THE
CIVIL SERVICE." UK CONTROL REPRESENT INGP/REL
PERS/REL EFFICIENCY 20. PAGE 8 B0168 — EXEC EX/STRUC PROB/SOLV ADMIN

PIPER D.C.,"THE ROLE OF INTER-GOVERNMENTAL
MACHINERY IN CANADIANAMERICAN RELATIONS." CANADA
USA+45 PROB/SOLV REPRESENT 20. PAGE 83 B1676 — GOV/REL ADMIN EX/STRUC CONFER

INTERNATIONAL CITY MGRS ASSN,POST-ENTRY TRAINING IN
THE LOCAL PUBLIC SERVICE (PAMPHLET). SCHOOL PLAN
PROB/SOLV TEC/DEV ADMIN EFFICIENCY SKILL...POLICY
AUD/VIS CHARTS BIBLIOG 20 CITY/MGT. PAGE 54 B1096 — LOC/G WORKER EDU/PROP METH/COMP

RECENT PUBLICATIONS ON GOVERNMENTAL PROBLEMS. FINAN
INDUS ACADEM PLAN PROB/SOLV EDU/PROP ADJUD ADMIN
BIO/SOC...MGT SOC. PAGE 2 B0040 — BIBLIOG AUTOMAT LEGIS JURID

ARGYRIS C.,INTEGRATING THE INDIVIDUAL AND THE
ORGANIZATION. WORKER PROB/SOLV LEAD SANCTION
REPRESENT ADJUST EFFICIENCY DRIVE PERSON...PSY
METH/CNCPT ORG/CHARTS. PAGE 6 B0132 — ADMIN PERS/REL VOL/ASSN PARTIC

BLAKE R.R.,MANAGING INTERGROUP CONFLICT IN
INDUSTRY. INDUS DELIB/GP EX/STRUC GP/REL PERS/REL
GAME. PAGE 12 B0250 — CREATE PROB/SOLV OP/RES ADJUD

BRIGHT J.R.,RESEARCH, DEVELOPMENT AND TECHNOLOGICAL
INNOVATION. CULTURE R+D CREATE PLAN PROB/SOLV
AUTOMAT RISK PERSON...DECISION CONCPT PREDICT
BIBLIOG. PAGE 15 B0308 — TEC/DEV NEW/IDEA INDUS MGT

COLLINS B.E.,A SOCIAL PSYCHOLOGY OF GROUP PROCESSES
FOR DECISION-MAKING. PROB/SOLV ROUTINE...SOC CHARTS
HYPO/EXP. PAGE 22 B0453 — FACE/GP DECISION NAT/G INDUS

COX R.,THEORY IN MARKETING. FUT USA+45 SOCIETY
ECO/DEV PROB/SOLV PRICE RISK PRODUC ATTIT...ANTHOL
20. PAGE 24 B0499 — MARKET ECO/TAC PHIL/SCI MGT

CULLINGWORTH J.B.,TOWN AND COUNTRY PLANNING IN
ENGLAND AND WALES. UK LAW SOCIETY CONSULT ACT/RES
ADMIN ROUTINE LEISURE INGP/REL ADJUST PWR...GEOG 20
OPEN/SPACE URBAN/RNWL. PAGE 25 B0512 — MUNIC PLAN NAT/G PROB/SOLV

HANNA W.J.,INDEPENDENT BLACK AFRICA: THE POLITICS
OF FREEDOM. ELITES INDUS KIN CHIEF COLONIAL CHOOSE
GOV/REL RACE/REL NAT/LISM ATTIT PERSON 20 NEGRO.
PAGE 46 B0938 — AFR ECO/UNDEV ADMIN PROB/SOLV

HERSKOVITS M.J.,ECONOMIC TRANSITION IN AFRICA. FUT
INT/ORG NAT/G WORKER PROB/SOLV TEC/DEV INT/TRADE
EQUILIB INCOME...ANTHOL 20. PAGE 49 B0996 — AFR ECO/UNDEV PLAN ADMIN

HODGETTS J.E.,ADMINISTERING THE ATOM FOR PEACE.
OP/RES TEC/DEV ADMIN...IDEA/COMP METH/COMP 20.
PAGE 50 B1025 — PROB/SOLV NUC/PWR PEACE MGT

B63
B63
B63
B63
B63
B63
B63
B63
B63
B63
B63
B63
B63
B63
B63
B63
B63
B63
S63
S63
N63
B64
B64
B64
B64
B64
B64
B64
B64

B64

INST D'ETUDE POL L'U GRENOBLE.ADMINISTRATION
TRADITIONELLE ET PLANIFICATION REGIONALE. FRANCE
LAW POL/PAR PROB/SOLV ADJUST RIGID/FLEX...CHARTS
ANTHOL BIBLIOG T 20 REFORMERS. PAGE 54 B1087
    ADMIN MUNIC PLAN CREATE

B64

KAPP E..THE MERGER OF THE EXECUTIVES OF THE
EUROPEAN COMMUNITIES. LAW CONSTN STRUCT ACT/RES
PLAN PROB/SOLV ADMIN REGION TASK...INT/LAW MGT ECSC
EEC. PAGE 58 B1170
    CENTRAL EX/STRUC

B64

KIMBROUGH R.B..POLITICAL POWER AND EDUCATIONAL
DECISION-MAKING. USA+45 FINAN ADMIN LEAD GP/REL
ATTIT PWR PROG/TEAC. PAGE 60 B1207
    EDU/PROP PROB/SOLV DECISION SCHOOL

B64

LOWI T.J..AT THE PLEASURE OF THE MAYOR. EX/STRUC
PROB/SOLV BAL/PWR ADMIN PARTIC CHOOSE GP/REL
...CONT/OBS NET/THEORY CHARTS 20 NEWYORK/C MAYOR.
PAGE 67 B1346
    LOBBY LOC/G PWR MUNIC

B64

MAHAR J.M..INDIA: A CRITICAL BIBLIOGRAPHY. INDIA
PAKISTAN CULTURE ECO/UNDEV LOC/G POL/PAR SECT
PROB/SOLV DIPLOM ADMIN COLONIAL PARL/PROC ATTIT 20.
PAGE 68 B1377
    BIBLIOG/A S/ASIA NAT/G LEAD

B64

NUQUIST A.E..TOWN GOVERNMENT IN VERMONT. USA+45
FINAN TOP/EX PROB/SOLV BUDGET TAX REPRESENT SUFF
EFFICIENCY...OBS INT 20 VERMONT. PAGE 79 B1595
    LOC/G MUNIC POPULISM ADMIN

B64

ORTH C.D..ADMINISTERING RESEARCH AND DEVELOPMENT.
FINAN PLAN PROB/SOLV ADMIN ROUTINE...METH/CNCPT
STAT CHARTS METH 20. PAGE 80 B1616
    MGT R+D LG/CO INDUS

B64

POTTER D.C..GOVERNMENT IN RURAL INDIA. INDIA LEGIT
INGP/REL EFFICIENCY ATTIT 20. PAGE 84 B1695
    LOC/G ADMIN TAX PROB/SOLV

B64

RIGGS R.E..THE MOVEMENT FOR ADMINISTRATIVE
REORGANIZATION IN ARIZONA. USA+45 LAW POL/PAR
DELIB/GP LEGIS PROB/SOLV CONTROL RIGID/FLEX PWR
...ORG/CHARTS 20 ARIZONA DEMOCRAT REPUBLICAN.
PAGE 88 B1786
    ADMIN PROVS CREATE PLAN

B64

ROBSON W.A..THE GOVERNORS AND THE GOVERNED. USA+45
PROB/SOLV DOMIN ADMIN CONTROL CHOOSE...POLICY
PRESIDENT. PAGE 89 B1808
    EX/STRUC ATTIT PARTIC LEAD

B64

RUSSELL R.B..UNITED NATIONS EXPERIENCE WITH
MILITARY FORCES: POLITICAL AND LEGAL ASPECTS. AFR
KOREA WOR+45 LEGIS PROB/SOLV ADMIN CONTROL
EFFICIENCY PEACE...POLICY INT/LAW BIBLIOG UN.
PAGE 92 B1857
    FORCES DIPLOM SANCTION ORD/FREE

B64

SAYLES L.R..MANAGERIAL BEHAVIOR: ADMINISTRATION IN
COMPLEX ORGANIZATIONS. INDUS LG/CO PROB/SOLV
CONTROL EXEC INGP/REL PERS/REL SKILL...MGT OBS
PREDICT GEN/LAWS 20. PAGE 93 B1874
    CONCPT ADMIN TOP/EX EX/STRUC

B64

TINBERGEN J..CENTRAL PLANNING. COM INTELL ECO/DEV
ECO/UNDEV FINAN INT/ORG PROB/SOLV ECO/TAC CONTROL
EXEC ROUTINE DECISION. PAGE 104 B2111
    PLAN INDUS MGT CENTRAL

B64

US SENATE COMM ON JUDICIARY.ADMINISTRATIVE
PROCEDURE ACT. USA+45 CONSTN NAT/G PROB/SOLV CONFER
GOV/REL PWR...INT 20 SENATE. PAGE 110 B2231
    PARL/PROC LEGIS JURID ADMIN

B64

WILDAVSKY A..LEADERSHIP IN A SMALL TOWN. USA+45
STRUCT PROB/SOLV EXEC PARTIC RACE/REL PWR PLURISM
...SOC 20 NEGRO WATER CIV/RIGHTS OBERLIN CITY/MGT.
PAGE 116 B2348
    LEAD MUNIC ELITES

L64

PRUITT D.G.."PROBLEM SOLVING IN THE DEPARTMENT OF
STATE." USA+45 NAT/G CONSULT PROB/SOLV EXEC PWR
...DECISION INT ORG/CHARTS 20. PAGE 85 B1713
    ROUTINE MGT DIPLOM

S64

RUSK D.."THE MAKING OF FOREIGN POLICY" USA+45 CHIEF
DELIB/GP WORKER PROB/SOLV ADMIN ATTIT PWR
...DECISION 20 DEPT/STATE RUSK/D GOLDMAN/E. PAGE 92
B1856
    DIPLOM INT POLICY

S64

STONE P.A.."DECISION TECHNIQUES FOR TOWN
DEVELOPMENT." PLAN COST PROFIT...DECISION MGT
CON/ANAL CHARTS METH/COMP BIBLIOG 20. PAGE 101
B2048
    OP/RES MUNIC ADMIN PROB/SOLV

B65

ARTHUR D LITTLE INC.SAN FRANCISCO COMMUNITY RENEWAL
PROGRAM. USA+45 FINAN PROVS ADMIN INCOME...CHARTS
20 CALIFORNIA SAN/FRAN URBAN/RNWL. PAGE 7 B0138
    HABITAT MUNIC PLAN PROB/SOLV

B65

CAVERS D.F..THE CHOICE-OF-LAW PROCESS. PROB/SOLV
ADJUD CT/SYS CHOOSE RATIONAL...IDEA/COMP 16/20
TREATY. PAGE 19 B0396
    JURID DECISION METH/COMP ADMIN

B65

CRAMER J.F..CONTEMPORARY EDUCATION: A COMPARATIVE
STUDY OF NATIONAL SYSTEMS (2ND ED.). CHINA/COM
EUR+WWI INDIA USA+45 FINAN PROB/SOLV ADMIN CONTROL
ATTIT...IDEA/COMP METH/COMP 20 CHINJAP. PAGE 25
B0502
    EDU/PROP NAT/COMP SCHOOL ACADEM

B65

DAVISON W.P..INTERNATIONAL POLITICAL COMMUNICATION.
COM USA+45 WOR+45 CULTURE ECO/UNDEV NAT/G PROB/SOLV
PRESS TV ADMIN 20 FILM. PAGE 27 B0545
    EDU/PROP DIPLOM PERS/REL COM/IND

B65

EDELMAN M..THE POLITICS OF WAGE-PRICE DECISIONS.
GERMANY ITALY NETHERLAND UK INDUS LABOR POL/PAR
PROB/SOLV BARGAIN PRICE ROUTINE BAL/PAY COST DEMAND
20. PAGE 32 B0654
    GOV/COMP CONTROL ECO/TAC PLAN

B65

EVERETT R.O..URBAN PROBLEMS AND PROSPECTS. USA+45
CREATE TEC/DEV EDU/PROP ADJUD ADMIN GOV/REL ATTIT
...ANTHOL 20 URBAN/RNWL. PAGE 34 B0691
    MUNIC PLAN PROB/SOLV NEIGH

B65

FEERICK J.D..FROM FAILING HANDS: THE STUDY OF
PRESIDENTIAL SUCCESSION. CONSTN NAT/G PROB/SOLV
LEAD PARL/PROC MURDER CHOOSE...NEW/IDEA BIBLIOG 20
KENNEDY/JF JOHNSON/LB PRESIDENT PRE/US/AM
VICE/PRES. PAGE 35 B0710
    EX/STRUC CHIEF LAW LEGIS

B65

FRYE R.J..HOUSING AND URBAN RENEWAL IN ALABAMA.
USA+45 NEIGH LEGIS BUDGET ADJUD ADMIN PARTIC...MGT
20 ALABAMA URBAN/RNWL. PAGE 38 B0762
    MUNIC PROB/SOLV PLAN GOV/REL

B65

GOLEMBIEWSKI R.T..MEN, MANAGEMENT, AND MORALITY:
TOWARD A NEW ORGANIZATIONAL ETHIC. CONSTN EX/STRUC
CREATE ADMIN CONTROL INGP/REL PERSON SUPEGO MORAL
PWR...GOV/COMP METH/COMP 20 BUREAUCRCY. PAGE 40
B0819
    LG/CO MGT PROB/SOLV

B65

GOTLIEB A..DISARMAMENT AND INTERNATIONAL LAW* A
STUDY OF THE ROLE OF LAW IN THE DISARMAMENT
PROCESS. USA+45 USSR PROB/SOLV CONFER ADMIN ROUTINE
NUC/PWR ORD/FREE SOVEREIGN UN TREATY. PAGE 42 B0841
    INT/LAW INT/ORG ARMS/CONT IDEA/COMP

B65

GREER S..URBAN RENEWAL AND AMERICAN CITIES: THE
DILEMMA OF DEMOCRATIC INTERVENTION. USA+45 R+D
LOC/G VOL/ASSN ACT/RES BUDGET ADMIN GOV/REL...SOC
INT SAMP 20 BOSTON CHICAGO MIAMI URBAN/RNWL.
PAGE 43 B0871
    MUNIC PROB/SOLV PLAN NAT/G

B65

HICKMAN B.G..QUANTITATIVE PLANNING OF ECONOMIC
POLICY. FRANCE NETHERLAND OP/RES PRICE ROUTINE UTIL
...POLICY DECISION ECOMETRIC METH/CNCPT STAT STYLE
CHINJAP. PAGE 50 B1004
    PROB/SOLV PLAN QUANT

B65

KOENIG C.W..OFFICIAL MAKERS OF PUBLIC POLICY:
CONGRESS AND THE PRESIDENT. USA+45 USA-45 NAT/G
EX/STRUC PROB/SOLV PWR. PAGE 60 B1222
    CHIEF LEGIS GOV/REL PLURISM

B65

LAMBIRI I..SOCIAL CHANGE IN A GREEK COUNTRY TOWN.
GREECE FAM PROB/SOLV ROUTINE TASK LEISURE INGP/REL
CONSEN ORD/FREE...SOC INT QU CHARTS 20. PAGE 62
B1252
    INDUS WORKER CULTURE NEIGH

B65

OECD.MEDITERRANEAN REGIONAL PROJECT: TURKEY;
EDUCATION AND DEVELOPMENT. FUT TURKEY SOCIETY
STRATA FINAN NAT/G PROF/ORG PLAN PROB/SOLV ADMIN
COST...STAT CHARTS 20 OECD. PAGE 79 B1602
    EDU/PROP ACADEM SCHOOL ECO/UNDEV

B65

PERLOFF H.S..URBAN RESEARCH AND EDUCATION IN THE
NEW YORK METROPOLITAN REGION (VOL. II). FUT USA+45
NEIGH PROF/ORG ACT/RES PROB/SOLV EDU/PROP ADMIN
...STAT BIBLIOG 20 NEWYORK/C. PAGE 82 B1659
    MUNIC PLAN ACADEM GP/REL

B65

REISS A.J. JR..SCHOOLS IN A CHANGING SOCIETY.
CULTURE PROB/SOLV INSPECT DOMIN CONFER INGP/REL
RACE/REL AGE/C AGE/Y ALL/VALS...ANTHOL SOC/INTEG 20
NEWYORK/C. PAGE 87 B1766
    SCHOOL EX/STRUC ADJUST ADMIN

B65

ROSS P..THE GOVERNMENT AS A SOURCE OF UNION POWER.
USA+45 LAW ECO/DEV PROB/SOLV ECO/TAC LEAD GP/REL
...MGT 20. PAGE 90 B1826
    LABOR BARGAIN POLICY NAT/G

B65

ROWAT D.C..THE OMBUDSMAN: CITIZEN'S DEFENDER.
DENMARK FINLAND NEW/ZEALND NORWAY SWEDEN CONSULT
PROB/SOLV FEEDBACK PARTIC GP/REL...SOC CONCPT
NEW/IDEA METH/COMP ANTHOL BIBLIOG 20. PAGE 91 B1840
    INSPECT CONSTN NAT/G ADMIN

B65

STEINER G.A..THE CREATIVE ORGANIZATION. ELITES
    CREATE

LG/CO PLAN PROB/SOLV TEC/DEV INSPECT CAP/ISM
CONTROL EXEC PERSON...METH/COMP HYPO/EXP 20.
PAGE 100 B2029
MGT
ADMIN
SOC
B65

US HOUSE COMM EDUC AND LABOR,ADMINISTRATION OF THE
NATIONAL LABOR RELATIONS ACT. USA+45 DELIB/GP
WORKER PROB/SOLV BARGAIN PAY CONTROL 20 NLRB
CONGRESS. PAGE 108 B2188
ADMIN
LABOR
GP/REL
INDUS
B65

US SENATE COMM GOVT OPERATIONS,ADMINISTRATION OF
NATIONAL SECURITY. USA+45 DELIB/GP ADMIN ROLE
...POLICY CHARTS SENATE. PAGE 110 B2218
NAT/G
ORD/FREE
DIPLOM
PROB/SOLV
B65

WALTON R.E.,A BEHAVIORAL THEORY OF LABOR
NEGOTIATIONS: AN ANALYSIS OF A SOCIAL INTERACTION
SYSTEM. USA+45 FINAN PROB/SOLV ECO/TAC GP/REL
INGP/REL...DECISION BIBLIOG. PAGE 113 B2285
SOC
LABOR
BARGAIN
ADMIN
L65

SHARKANSKY I.,"FOUR AGENCIES AND AN APPROPRIATIONS
SUBCOMMITTEE: A COMPARATIVE STUDY OF BUDGET
STRATEGIES." USA+45 EX/STRUC TOP/EX PROB/SOLV
CONTROL ROUTINE CONGRESS. PAGE 96 B1934
ADMIN
EDU/PROP
NAT/G
LEGIS
S65

ALEXANDER T.,"SYNECTICS: INVENTING BY THE MADNESS
METHOD." DELIB/GP TOP/EX ACT/RES TEC/DEV EXEC TASK
KNOWL...MGT METH/COMP 20. PAGE 4 B0073
PROB/SOLV
OP/RES
CREATE
CONSULT
S65

POSVAR W.W.,"NATIONAL SECURITY POLICY* THE REALM OF
OBSCURITY." CREATE PLAN PROB/SOLV ADMIN LEAD GP/REL
CONSERVE...DECISION GEOG. PAGE 84 B1694
DIPLOM
USA+45
RECORD
B66

AARON T.J.,THE CONTROL OF POLICE DISCRETION: THE
DANISH EXPERIENCE. DENMARK LAW CREATE ADMIN
INGP/REL SUPEGO PWR 20 OMBUDSMAN. PAGE 2 B0049
CONTROL
FORCES
REPRESENT
PROB/SOLV
B66

ASHRAF A.,THE CITY GOVERNMENT OF CALCUTTA: A STUDY
OF INERTIA. INDIA ELITES INDUS NAT/G EX/STRUC
ACT/RES PLAN PROB/SOLV LEAD HABITAT...BIBLIOG 20
CALCUTTA. PAGE 7 B0141
LOC/G
MUNIC
ADMIN
ECO/UNDEV
B66

BOYD H.W.,MARKETING MANAGEMENT: CASES FROM EMERGING
COUNTRIES. BRAZIL GHANA ISRAEL WOR+45 ADMIN
PERS/REL ATTIT HABITAT WEALTH...ANTHOL 20 ARGEN
CASEBOOK. PAGE 14 B0292
MGT
ECO/UNDEV
PROB/SOLV
MARKET
B66

BROWN R.E.,JUDGMENT IN ADMINISTRATION. DRIVE PERSON
KNOWL...DECISION 20. PAGE 16 B0326
ADMIN
EXEC
SKILL
PROB/SOLV
B66

CHAPMAN B.,THE PROFESSION OF GOVERNMENT: THE PUBLIC
SERVICE IN EUROPE. CONSTN NAT/G POL/PAR EX/STRUC
LEGIS TOP/EX PROB/SOLV DEBATE EXEC PARL/PROC PARTIC
20. PAGE 20 B0411
BIBLIOG
ADMIN
EUR+WWI
GOV/COMP
B66

CLEGG R.K.,THE ADMINISTRATOR IN PUBLIC WELFARE.
USA+45 STRUCT NAT/G PROVS PROB/SOLV BUDGET ECO/TAC
GP/REL ROLE...SOC/WK 20 PUBLIC/REL. PAGE 21 B0434
ADMIN
GIVE
GOV/REL
OP/RES
B66

CORNWELL E.E. JR.,THE AMERICAN PRESIDENCY: VITAL
CENTER. USA+45 USA-45 POL/PAR LEGIS PROB/SOLV
CONTROL PARTIC GOV/REL 18/20 PRESIDENT. PAGE 23
B0478
CHIEF
EX/STRUC
NAT/G
ADMIN
B66

DAVIDSON R.H.,CONGRESS IN CRISIS: POLITICS AND
CONGRESSIONAL REFORM. USA+45 SOCIETY POL/PAR
CONTROL LEAD ROUTINE GOV/REL ATTIT PWR...POLICY 20
CONGRESS. PAGE 26 B0535
LEGIS
PARL/PROC
PROB/SOLV
NAT/G
B66

DEBENKO E.,RESEARCH SOURCES FOR SOUTH ASIAN STUDIES
IN ECONOMIC DEVELOPMENT: A SELECT BIBLIOGRAPHY OF
SERIAL PUBLICATIONS. CEYLON INDIA NEPAL PAKISTAN
PROB/SOLV ADMIN...POLICY 20. PAGE 28 B0566
BIBLIOG
ECO/UNDEV
S/ASIA
PLAN
B66

DICKSON W.J.,COUNSELING IN AN ORGANIZATION: A
SEQUEL TO THE HAWTHORNE RESEARCHES. CLIENT VOL/ASSN
ACT/RES PROB/SOLV AUTOMAT ROUTINE PERS/REL
HAPPINESS ANOMIE ROLE...OBS CHARTS 20 AT+T. PAGE 29
B0588
INDUS
WORKER
PSY
MGT
B66

GERBERDING W.P.,UNITED STATES FOREIGN POLICY:
PERSPECTIVES AND ANALYSIS. USA+45 LEGIS EXEC LEAD
REPRESENT PWR 20. PAGE 39 B0791
PROB/SOLV
CHIEF
EX/STRUC
CONTROL
B66

GHOSH P.K.,THE CONSTITUTION OF INDIA: HOW IT HAS
BEEN FRAMED. INDIA LOC/G DELIB/GP EX/STRUC
PROB/SOLV BUDGET INT/TRADE CT/SYS CHOOSE...LING 20.
PAGE 39 B0795
CONSTN
NAT/G
LEGIS
FEDERAL
B66

GLAZER M.,THE FEDERAL GOVERNMENT AND THE
UNIVERSITY. CHILE PROB/SOLV DIPLOM GIVE ADMIN WAR
BIBLIOG/A
NAT/G

...POLICY SOC 20. PAGE 40 B0810
PLAN
ACADEM
B66

GRETHER E.T.,MARKETING AND PUBLIC POLICY. USA+45
ECO/DEV DIST/IND NAT/G PLAN CAP/ISM PRICE CONTROL
...GEOG MGT 20. PAGE 43 B0874
MARKET
PROB/SOLV
ECO/TAC
POLICY
B66

HESSLER I.O.,29 WAYS TO GOVERN A CITY. EX/STRUC
TOP/EX PROB/SOLV PARTIC CHOOSE REPRESENT EFFICIENCY
...CHARTS 20 CITY/MGT MAYOR. PAGE 49 B0998
MUNIC
GOV/COMP
LOC/G
ADMIN
B66

KAUNDA K.,ZAMBIA: INDEPENDENCE AND BEYOND: THE
SPEECHES OF KENNETH KAUNDA. AFR FUT ZAMBIA SOCIETY
ECO/UNDEV NAT/G PROB/SOLV ECO/TAC ADMIN RACE/REL
SOVEREIGN 20. PAGE 59 B1183
ORD/FREE
COLONIAL
CONSTN
LEAD
B66

KURAKOV I.G.,SCIENCE, TECHNOLOGY AND COMMUNISM;
SOME QUESTIONS OF DEVELOPMENT (TRANS. BY CARIN
DEDIJER). USSR INDUS PLAN PROB/SOLV COST PRODUC
...MGT MATH CHARTS METH 20. PAGE 61 B1243
CREATE
TEC/DEV
MARXISM
ECO/TAC
B66

MANSFIELD E.,MANAGERIAL ECONOMICS AND OPERATIONS
RESEARCH; A NONMATHEMATICAL INTRODUCTION. USA+45
ELITES ECO/DEV CONSULT EX/STRUC PROB/SOLV ROUTINE
EFFICIENCY OPTIMAL...GAME T 20. PAGE 69 B1396
ECO/TAC
OP/RES
MGT
COMPUTER
B66

MONTEIRO J.B.,CORRUPTION: CONTROL OF
MALADMINISTRATION. EUR+WWI INDIA USA+45 USSR NAT/G
DELIB/GP ADMIN...GP/COMP 20 OMBUDSMAN. PAGE 74
B1503
CONTROL
CRIME
PROB/SOLV
B66

MURDOCK J.C.,RESEARCH AND REGIONS. AGRI FINAN INDUS
LOC/G MUNIC NAT/G PROB/SOLV TEC/DEV ADMIN REGION
20. PAGE 76 B1545
BIBLIOG
ECO/DEV
COMPUT/IR
R+D
B66

NYC TEMPORARY COMM CITY FINAN,MUNICIPAL COLLECTIVE
BARGAINING (NO. 8). USA+45 PLAN PROB/SOLV BARGAIN
BUDGET TAX EDU/PROP GOV/REL COST...MGT 20
NEWYORK/C. PAGE 79 B1596
MUNIC
FINAN
ADMIN
LOC/G
B66

OWEN G.,INDUSTRY IN THE UNITED STATES. UK USA+45
NAT/G WEALTH...DECISION NAT/COMP 20. PAGE 80 B1620
METH/COMP
INDUS
MGT
PROB/SOLV
B66

PERROW C.,ORGANIZATION FOR TREATMENT: A COMPARATIVE
STUDY OF INSTITUTIONS FOR DELINQUENTS. LAW
PROB/SOLV ADMIN CRIME PERSON MORAL...SOC/WK OBS
DEEP/QU CHARTS SOC/EXP SOC/INTEG 20. PAGE 82 B1661
AGE/Y
PSY
PUB/INST
B66

REDFORD E.S.,THE ROLE OF GOVERNMENT IN THE AMERICAN
ECONOMY. USA+45 USA-45 FINAN INDUS LG/CO PROB/SOLV
ADMIN INGP/REL INCOME PRODUC 18/20. PAGE 87 B1759
NAT/G
ECO/DEV
CAP/ISM
ECO/TAC
B66

SCHMIDT K.M.,AMERICAN STATE AND LOCAL GOVERNMENT IN
ACTION. USA+45 CONSTN LOC/G POL/PAR CHIEF LEGIS
PROB/SOLV ADJUD LOBBY GOV/REL...DECISION ANTHOL 20
GOVERNOR MAYOR URBAN/RNWL. PAGE 94 B1896
PROVS
ADMIN
MUNIC
PLAN
B66

SMITH H.E.,READINGS IN ECONOMIC DEVELOPMENT AND
ADMINISTRATION IN TANZANIA. TANZANIA FINAN INDUS
LABOR NAT/G PLAN PROB/SOLV INT/TRADE COLONIAL
REGION...ANTHOL BIBLIOG 20 AFRICA/E. PAGE 98 B1981
TEC/DEV
ADMIN
GOV/REL
B66

UN ECAFE,ADMINISTRATIVE ASPECTS OF FAMILY PLANNING
PROGRAMMES (PAMPHLET). ASIA THAILAND WOR+45
VOL/ASSN PROB/SOLV BUDGET FOR/AID EDU/PROP CONFER
CONTROL GOV/REL TIME 20 UN BIRTH/CON. PAGE 106
B2147
PLAN
CENSUS
FAM
ADMIN
B66

WADIA M.,THE NATURE AND SCOPE OF MANAGEMENT.
DELIB/GP EX/STRUC CREATE AUTOMAT CONTROL EFFICIENCY
...ANTHOL 20. PAGE 112 B2271
MGT
PROB/SOLV
IDEA/COMP
ECO/TAC
B66

WARREN R.O.,GOVERNMENT IN METROPOLITAN REGIONS: A
REAPPRAISAL OF FRACTIONATED POLITICAL ORGANIZATION.
USA+45 ACT/RES PROB/SOLV REGION...CHARTS METH/COMP
BIBLIOG CITY/MGT. PAGE 114 B2296
LOC/G
MUNIC
EX/STRUC
PLAN
B66

WILLNER A.R.,THE NEOTRADITIONAL ACCOMMODATION TO
POLITICAL INDEPENDENCE* THE CASE OF INDONESIA *
RESEARCH MONOGRAPH NO. 26. CULTURE ECO/UNDEV CREATE
PROB/SOLV FOR/AID LEGIT COLONIAL EFFICIENCY
NAT/LISM ALL/VALS SOC. PAGE 117 B2355
INDONESIA
CONSERVE
ELITES
ADMIN
B66

YOUNG S.,MANAGEMENT: A SYSTEMS ANALYSIS. DELIB/GP
EX/STRUC ECO/TAC CONTROL EFFICIENCY...NET/THEORY
20. PAGE 119 B2394
PROB/SOLV
MGT
DECISION
SIMUL
S66

JACOBS P.,"RE-RADICALIZING THE DE-RADICALIZED."
NAT/G

USA+45 SOCIETY STRUCT FINAN PLAN PROB/SOLV CAP/ISM POLICY
WEALTH CONSERVE NEW/LIB 20. PAGE 55 B1114   MARXIST
                                                 ADMIN
                                                          S66
JACOBSON J.,"COALITIONISM: FROM PROTEST TO   RACE/REL
POLITICKING" USA+45 ELITES NAT/G POL/PAR PROB/SOLV LABOR
ADMIN LEAD DISCRIM ORD/FREE PWR CONSERVE 20 NEGRO   SOCIALIST
AFL/CIO CIV/RIGHTS BLACK/PWR. PAGE 55 B1116   VOL/ASSN
                                                          C66
SHERMAN H.,"IT ALL DEPENDS." USA+45 FINAN MARKET   LG/CO
PLAN PROB/SOLV EXEC PARTIC INGP/REL SUPEGO   MGT
...DECISION BIBLIOG 20. PAGE 96 B1944   ADMIN
                                                    POLICY
                                                          B67
ANDERSON C.W.,POLITICS AND ECONOMIC CHANGE IN LATIN ECO/UNDEV
AMERICA. L/A+17C INDUS NAT/G OP/RES ADMIN DEMAND   PROB/SOLV
...POLICY STAT CHARTS NAT/COMP 20. PAGE 4 B0091   PLAN
                                                    ECO/TAC
                                                          B67
BALDWIN G.B.,PLANNING AND DEVELOPMENT IN IRAN. IRAN PLAN
AGRI INDUS CONSULT WORKER EDU/PROP BAL/PAY...CHARTS ECO/UNDEV
20. PAGE 8 B0173   ADMIN
                                                    PROB/SOLV
                                                          B67
BUDER S.,PULLMAN: AN EXPERIMENT IN INDUSTRIAL ORDER DIST/IND
AND COMMUNITY PLANNING, 1880-1930. USA-45 SOCIETY   INDUS
LABOR LG/CO CREATE PROB/SOLV CONTROL GP/REL   MUNIC
EFFICIENCY ATTIT...MGT BIBLIOG 19/20 PULLMAN.   PLAN
PAGE 17 B0337
                                                          B67
BUREAU GOVERNMENT RES AND SERV,COUNTY GOVERNMENT   BIBLIOG/A
REORGANIZATION - A SELECTED ANNOTATED BIBLIOGRAPHY APPORT
(PAPER). USA+45 USA-45 LAW CONSTN MUNIC PROVS   LOC/G
EX/STRUC CREATE PLAN PROB/SOLV REPRESENT GOV/REL   ADMIN
20. PAGE 17 B0349
                                                          B67
FESLER J.W.,THE FIFTY STATES AND THEIR LOCAL   PROVS
GOVERNMENTS. FUT USA+45 POL/PAR LEGIS PROB/SOLV   LOC/G
ADMIN CT/SYS CHOOSE GOV/REL FEDERAL...POLICY CHARTS
20 SUPREME/CT. PAGE 35 B0715
                                                          B67
GABRIEL P.P.,THE INTERNATIONAL TRANSFER OF   ECO/UNDEV
CORPORATE SKILLS: MANAGEMENT CONTRACTS IN LESS   AGREE
DEVELOPED COUNTRIES. CLIENT INDUS LG/CO PLAN   MGT
PROB/SOLV CAP/ISM ECO/TAC FOR/AID INT/TRADE RENT   CONSULT
ADMIN SKILL 20. PAGE 38 B0771
                                                          B67
GELLHORN W.,OMBUDSMEN AND OTHERS: CITIZENS'   NAT/COMP
PROTECTORS IN NINE COUNTRIES. WOR+45 LAW CONSTN   REPRESENT
LEGIS INSPECT ADJUD ADMIN CONTROL CT/SYS CHOOSE   INGP/REL
PERS/REL...STAT CHARTS 20. PAGE 39 B0789   PROB/SOLV
                                                          B67
HEWITT W.H.,ADMINISTRATION OF CRIMINAL JUSTICE IN   CRIME
NEW YORK. LAW PROB/SOLV ADJUD ADMIN...CRIMLGY   ROLE
CHARTS T 20 NEW/YORK. PAGE 49 B1001   CT/SYS
                                                    FORCES
                                                          B67
ILLINOIS COMMISSION,IMPROVING THE STATE   PROVS
LEGISLATURE. USA+45 LAW CONSTN NAT/G PROB/SOLV   LEGIS
EDU/PROP ADMIN TASK CHOOSE INGP/REL EFFICIENCY   REPRESENT
ILLINOIS. PAGE 53 B1077   PLAN
                                                          B67
JAKUBAUSKAS E.B.,HUMAN RESOURCES DEVELOPMENT.   PROB/SOLV
USA+45 AGRI INDUS SERV/IND ACT/RES PLAN ADMIN   ECO/TAC
RACE/REL DISCRIM...TREND GEN/LAWS. PAGE 55 B1119   EDU/PROP
                                                    WORKER
                                                          B67
KATZ J.,PSYCHOANALYSIS, PSYCHIATRY, AND LAW. USA+45 LAW
LOC/G NAT/G PUB/INST PROB/SOLV ADMIN HEALTH   PSY
...CRIMLGY CONCPT SAMP/SIZ IDEA/COMP. PAGE 58 B1180 CT/SYS
                                                    ADJUD
                                                          B67
KRISLOV S.,THE NEGRO IN FEDERAL EMPLOYMENT. LAW   WORKER
STRATA LOC/G CREATE PROB/SOLV INSPECT GOV/REL   NAT/G
DISCRIM ROLE...DECISION INT TREND 20 NEGRO WWI   ADMIN
CIVIL/SERV. PAGE 61 B1238   RACE/REL
                                                          B67
MARRIS P.,DILEMMAS OF SOCIAL REFORM: POVERTY AND   STRUCT
COMMUNITY ACTION IN THE UNITED STATES. USA+45 NAT/G MUNIC
OP/RES ADMIN PARTIC EFFICIENCY WEALTH...SOC   PROB/SOLV
METH/COMP T 20 REFORMERS. PAGE 69 B1401   COST
                                                          B67
PLANO J.C.,FORGING WORLD ORDER: THE POLITICS OF   INT/ORG
INTERNATIONAL ORGANIZATION. PROB/SOLV DIPLOM   ADMIN
CONTROL CENTRAL RATIONAL ORD/FREE...INT/LAW CHARTS JURID
BIBLIOG 20 UN LEAGUE/NAT. PAGE 83 B1679
                                                          B67
ROTHENBERG J.,ECONOMIC EVALUATION OF URBAN RENEWAL: PLAN
CONCEPTUAL FOUNDATION OF BENEFIT-COST ANALYSIS.   MUNIC
USA+45 ECO/DEV NEIGH TEC/DEV ADMIN GEN/LAWS.   PROB/SOLV
PAGE 91 B1834   COST
                                                          B67
SKIDMORE T.E.,POLITICS IN BRAZIL 1930-1964. BRAZIL CONSTN
L/A+17C INDUS NAT/G PROB/SOLV ATTIT 20. PAGE 98   ECO/TAC
B1973   ADMIN

                                                          B67
US DEPARTMENT OF JUSTICE,ANNUAL REPORT OF THE   ADMIN
OFFICE OF ADMINISTRATIVE PROCEDURE. USA+45   NAT/G
PROB/SOLV EDU/PROP EXEC INGP/REL EFFICIENCY KNOWL   ROUTINE
...POLICY STAT 20. PAGE 108 B2181   GOV/REL
                                                          B67
VOOS H.,ORGANIZATIONAL COMMUNICATION: A   BIBLIOG/A
BIBLIOGRAPHY. WOR+45 STRATA R+D PROB/SOLV FEEDBACK INDUS
COERCE...MGT PSY NET/THEORY HYPO/EXP. PAGE 112   COM/IND
B2268   VOL/ASSN
                                                          L67
CAHIERS P.,"LE RECOURS EN CONSTATATION DE   INT/ORG
MANQUEMENTS DES ETATS MEMBRES DEVANT LA COUR DES   CONSTN
COMMUNAUTES EUROPEENNES." LAW PROB/SOLV DIPLOM   ROUTINE
ADMIN CT/SYS SANCTION ATTIT...POLICY DECISION JURID ADJUD
ECSC EEC. PAGE 18 B0362
                                                          L67
CARMICHAEL D.M.,"FORTY YEARS OF WATER POLLUTION   HEALTH
CONTROL IN WISCONSIN: A CASE STUDY." LAW EXTR/IND   CONTROL
INDUS MUNIC DELIB/GP PLAN PROB/SOLV SANCTION   ADMIN
...CENSUS CHARTS 20 WISCONSIN. PAGE 19 B0382   ADJUD
                                                          L67
ROBERTS J.C.,"CIVIL RESTRAINT, MENTAL ILLNESS, AND HEALTH
THE RIGHT TO TREATMENT." PROB/SOLV ADMIN PERSON   ORD/FREE
HEAL. PAGE 89 B1795   COERCE
                                                    LAW
                                                          S67
ATKIN J.M.,"THE FEDERAL GOVERNMENT, BIG BUSINESS,   SCHOOL
AND COLLEGES OF EDUCATION." PROF/ORG CONSULT CREATE ACADEM
PLAN PROB/SOLV ADMIN EFFICIENCY. PAGE 7 B0144   NAT/G
                                                    INDUS
                                                          S67
BERLINER J.S.,"RUSSIA'S BUREAUCRATS - WHY THEY'RE   CREATE
REACTIONARY." USSR NAT/G OP/RES PROB/SOLV TEC/DEV   ADMIN
CONTROL SANCTION EFFICIENCY DRIVE PERSON...TECHNIC INDUS
SOC 20. PAGE 11 B0223   PRODUC
                                                          S67
BURKE E.M.,"THE SEARCH FOR AUTHORITY IN PLANNING." DECISION
MUNIC NEIGH CREATE PROB/SOLV LEGIT ADMIN CONTROL   PLAN
EFFICIENCY PWR...METH/COMP SIMUL 20. PAGE 17 B0352 LOC/G
                                                    METH
                                                          S67
CHAMBERLAIN N.W.,"STRIKES IN CONTEMPORARY CONTEXT." LABOR
LAW INDUS NAT/G CHIEF CONFER COST ATTIT ORD/FREE   BARGAIN
...POLICY MGT 20. PAGE 20 B0400   EFFICIENCY
                                                    PROB/SOLV
                                                          S67
CONWAY J.E.,"MAKING RESEARCH EFFECTIVE IN   ACT/RES
LEGISLATION." LAW R+D CONSULT EX/STRUC PLAN CONFER POLICY
ADMIN LEAD ROUTINE TASK INGP/REL DECISION. PAGE 23 LEGIS
B0469   PROB/SOLV
                                                          S67
DANELSKI D.J.,"CONFLICT AND ITS RESOLUTION IN THE   ROLE
SUPREME COURT." PROB/SOLV LEAD ROUTINE PERSON...PSY JURID
PERS/COMP BIBLIOG 20. PAGE 26 B0527   JUDGE
                                                    INGP/REL
                                                          S67
DODSON D.W.,"NEW FORCES OPERATING IN EDUCATIONAL   PROB/SOLV
DECISION-MAKING." USA+45 NEIGH EDU/PROP ADMIN   SCHOOL
SUPEGO DECISION. PAGE 30 B0602   PERS/REL
                                                    PWR
                                                          S67
DOERN G.B.,"THE ROYAL COMMISSIONS IN THE GENERAL   R+D
POLICY PROCESS AND IN FEDERAL-PROVINCIAL   EX/STRUC
RELATIONS." CANADA CONSTN ACADEM PROVS CONSULT   GOV/REL
DELIB/GP LEGIS ACT/RES PROB/SOLV CONFER CONTROL   NAT/G
EFFICIENCY...METH/COMP 20 SENATE ROYAL/COMM.
PAGE 30 B0603
                                                          S67
EDWARDS H.T.,"POWER STRUCTURE AND ITS COMMUNICATION ELITES
IN SAN JOSE, COSTA RICA." COSTA/RICA L/A+17C STRATA INGP/REL
FACE/GP POL/PAR EX/STRUC PROB/SOLV ADMIN LEAD   MUNIC
GP/REL PWR...STAT INT 20. PAGE 32 B0655   DOMIN
                                                          S67
FERGUSON H.,"3-CITY CONSOLIDATION." USA+45 CONSTN   MUNIC
INDUS BARGAIN BUDGET CONFER ADMIN INGP/REL COST   CHOOSE
UTIL. PAGE 35 B0712   CREATE
                                                    PROB/SOLV
                                                          S67
GOLIGHTLY H.O.,"THE AIRLINES: A CASE STUDY IN   DIST/IND
MANAGEMENT INNOVATION." USA+45 AIR FINAN INDUS   MARKET
TOP/EX CREATE PLAN PROB/SOLV ADMIN EXEC PROFIT   MGT
...DECISION 20. PAGE 40 B0820   TEC/DEV
                                                          S67
HALL B.,"THE PAINTER'S UNION: A PARTIAL VICTORY."   LABOR
USA+45 PROB/SOLV LEGIT ADMIN REPRESENT 20. PAGE 45 CHIEF
B0922   CHOOSE
                                                    CRIME
                                                          S67
HALL B.,"THE COALITION AGAINST DISHWASHERS." USA+45 LABOR
POL/PAR PROB/SOLV BARGAIN LEAD CHOOSE REPRESENT   ADMIN
GP/REL ORD/FREE PWR...POLICY 20. PAGE 46 B0923   DOMIN
                                                    WORKER
                                                          S67
HUMPHREY H.,"A MORE PERFECT UNION." USA+45 LOC/G   GOV/REL
NAT/G ACT/RES BUDGET RECEIVE CENTRAL CONGRESS.   FEDERAL

PAGE 52 B1063 — ADMIN PROB/SOLV

S67

JOHNSON L.B.,"BULLETS DO NOT DISCRIMINATE-LANDLORDS DO." PROB/SOLV EXEC LOBBY DEMAND...REALPOL SOC 20. PAGE 57 B1145 — NAT/G DISCRIM POLICY

S67

KAYSEN C.,"DATA BANKS AND DOSSIERS." FUT USA+45 COM/IND NAT/G PLAN PROB/SOLV TEC/DEV BUDGET ADMIN ROUTINE. PAGE 59 B1185 — CENTRAL EFFICIENCY CENSUS ACT/RES

S67

LEES J.P.,"LEGISLATIVE REVIEW AND BUREAUCRATIC RESPONSIBILITY." USA+45 FINAN NAT/G DELIB/GP PLAN PROB/SOLV CONFER CONTROL GP/REL DEMAND...DECISION 20 CONGRESS PRESIDENT HOUSE/REP BUREAUCRCY. PAGE 63 B1281 — SUPEGO BUDGET LEGIS EXEC

S67

LEVIN M.R.,"PLANNERS AND METROPOLITAN PLANNING." FUT USA+45 SOCIETY NAT/G PROVS PROB/SOLV LEAD PARTIC GOV/REL RACE/REL HABITAT ROLE. PAGE 64 B1301 — PLAN MUNIC R+D ADMIN

S67

LIU K.C.,"DISINTEGRATION OF THE OLD ORDER." ASIA SOCIETY PROB/SOLV ADMIN REGION TOTALSM ORD/FREE MARXISM 19/20. PAGE 66 B1329 — ADJUST NAT/LISM

S67

MCNAMARA R.L.,"THE NEED FOR INNOVATIVENESS IN DEVELOPING SOCIETIES." L/A+17C EDU/PROP ADMIN LEAD WEALTH...POLICY PSY SOC METH 20 COLOMB. PAGE 72 B1456 — PROB/SOLV PLAN ECO/UNDEV NEW/IDEA

S67

MELTZER B.D.,"RUMINATIONS ABOUT IDEOLOGY, LAW, AND LABOR ARBITRATION." USA+45 ECO/DEV PROB/SOLV CONFER MGT. PAGE 73 B1466 — JURID ADJUD LABOR CONSULT

S67

PAYNE W.A.,"LOCAL GOVERNMENT STUDY COMMISSIONS: ORGANIZATION FOR ACTION." USA+45 LEGIS PWR...CHARTS 20. PAGE 81 B1646 — LOC/G DELIB/GP PROB/SOLV ADMIN

S67

ROBERTS E.B.,"THE PROBLEM OF AGING ORGANIZATIONS." INTELL PROB/SOLV ADMIN EXEC FEEDBACK EFFICIENCY PRODUC...GEN/LAWS 20. PAGE 89 B1794 — INDUS R+D MGT PLAN

S67

ROSENBERG B.,"ETHNIC LIBERALISM AND EMPLOYMENT DISCRIMINATION IN THE NORTH." USA+45 TOP/EX PROB/SOLV ADMIN REGION PERS/REL DISCRIM...INT IDEA/COMP. PAGE 90 B1820 — RACE/REL ATTIT WORKER EXEC

S67

SATHYAMURTHY T.V.,"TWENTY YEARS OF UNESCO: AN INTERPRETATION." SOCIETY PROB/SOLV LEAD PEACE UNESCO. PAGE 92 B1870 — ADMIN CONSTN INT/ORG TIME/SEQ

S67

SKOLNICK J.H.,"SOCIAL CONTROL IN THE ADVERSARY SYSTEM." USA+45 CONSULT OP/RES ADMIN CONTROL. PAGE 98 B1975 — PROB/SOLV PERS/REL ADJUD CT/SYS

S67

SKOLNIKOFF E.B.,"MAKING FOREIGN POLICY" PROB/SOLV EFFICIENCY PERCEPT PWR...MGT METH/CNCPT CLASSIF 20. PAGE 98 B1976 — TEC/DEV CONTROL USA+45 NAT/G

S67

SPACKMAN A.,"THE SENATE OF TRINIDAD AND TOBAGO." L/A+17C TRINIDAD WEST/IND NAT/G POL/PAR DELIB/GP OP/RES PROB/SOLV EDU/PROP EXEC LOBBY ROUTINE REPRESENT GP/REL 20. PAGE 99 B2002 — ELITES EFFICIENCY LEGIS DECISION

S67

WINTHROP H.,"THE MEANING OF DECENTRALIZATION FOR TWENTIETH-CENTURY MAN." FUT WOR+45 SOCIETY TEC/DEV. PAGE 117 B2366 — ADMIN STRUCT CENTRAL PROB/SOLV

S67

ZOETEWEIJ B.,"INCOME POLICIES ABROAD: AN INTERIM REPORT." NAT/G PROB/SOLV BARGAIN BUDGET PRICE RISK CENTRAL EFFICIENCY EQUILIB...MGT NAT/COMP 20. PAGE 119 B2405 — METH/COMP INCOME POLICY LABOR

N67

US SENATE COMM AERO SPACE SCI,AERONAUTICAL RESEARCH AND DEVELOPMENT POLICY; HEARINGS, COMM ON AERONAUTICAL AND SPACE SCIENCES...1967 (PAMPHLET). R+D PROB/SOLV EXEC GOV/REL 20 DEPT/DEFEN FAA NASA CONGRESS. PAGE 109 B2210 — DIST/IND SPACE NAT/G PLAN

N67

US SENATE COMM ON FOREIGN REL,THE UNITED NATIONS PEACEKEEPING DILEMMA (PAMPHLET). ISLAM WOR+45 PROB/SOLV BUDGET ADMIN SENATE UN. PAGE 110 B2224 — INT/ORG DIPLOM PEACE

S68

GRAM H.A.,"BUSINESS ETHICS AND THE CORPORATION." LG/CO SECT PROB/SOLV CONTROL EXEC GP/REL INGP/REL PERS/REL ROLE MORAL PWR...DECISION 20. PAGE 42 B0850 — POLICY ADMIN MGT

S68

GUZZARDI W. JR.,"THE SECOND BATTLE OF BRITAIN." UK STRATA LABOR WORKER CREATE PROB/SOLV EDU/PROP ADMIN LEAD LOBBY...MGT SOC 20 GOLD/STAND. PAGE 45 B0907 — FINAN ECO/TAC ECO/DEV STRUCT

S68

PEARSON A.W.,"RESOURCE ALLOCATION." PLAN PROB/SOLV BUDGET ADMIN CONTROL CHOOSE EFFICIENCY...DECISION MGT 20. PAGE 82 B1649 — PROFIT OPTIMAL COST INDUS

PROBABIL....PROBABILITY; SEE ALSO GAMBLE

B45

BENJAMIN H.C.,EMPLOYMENT TESTS IN INDUSTRY AND BUSINESS. LG/CO WORKER ROUTINE...MGT PSY SOC CLASSIF PROBABIL STAT APT/TEST KNO/TEST PERS/TEST 20. PAGE 10 B0211 — BIBLIOG/A METH TESTS INDUS

B60

MORRIS W.T.,ENGINEERING ECONOMY. AUTOMAT RISK RATIONAL...PROBABIL STAT CHARTS GAME SIMUL BIBLIOG T 20. PAGE 76 B1529 — OP/RES DECISION MGT PROB/SOLV

S60

FRIEDMAN L.,"DECISION MAKING IN COMPETITIVE SITUATIONS" OP/RES...MGT PROBABIL METH/COMP SIMUL 20. PAGE 37 B0757 — DECISION UTIL OPTIMAL GAME

S61

DEUTSCH K.W.,"A NOTE ON THE APPEARANCE OF WISDOM IN LARGE BUREAUCRATIC ORGANIZATIONS." ROUTINE PERSON KNOWL SKILL...DECISION STAT. PAGE 28 B0577 — ADMIN PROBABIL PROB/SOLV SIMUL

B63

BONINI C.P.,SIMULATION OF INFORMATION AND DECISION SYSTEMS IN THE FIRM. MARKET BUDGET DOMIN EDU/PROP ADMIN COST ATTIT HABITAT PERCEPT PWR...CONCPT PROBABIL QUANT PREDICT HYPO/EXP BIBLIOG. PAGE 13 B0273 — INDUS SIMUL DECISION MGT

B64

COOMBS C.H.,A THEORY OF DATA....MGT PHIL/SCI SOC CLASSIF MATH PROBABIL STAT QU. PAGE 23 B0472 — CON/ANAL GEN/METH TESTS PSY

S65

HOLSTI O.R.,"THE 1914 CASE." MOD/EUR COMPUTER DIPLOM EDU/PROP EXEC...DECISION PSY PROBABIL STAT COMPUT/IR SOC/EXP TIME. PAGE 51 B1036 — CON/ANAL PERCEPT WAR

B66

FABRYCKY W.J.,OPERATIONS ECONOMY INDUSTRIAL APPLICATIONS OF OPERATIONS RESEARCH. INDUS PLAN ECO/TAC PRODUC...MATH PROBABIL STAT CHARTS 20. PAGE 34 B0695 — OP/RES MGT SIMUL DECISION

PROBABILITY....SEE PROBABIL

PROBLEM SOLVING....SEE PROB/SOLV

PROC/MFG....PROCESSING OR MANUFACTURING INDUSTRIES

B47

WARNER W.L.,THE SOCIAL SYSTEM OF THE MODERN FACTORY; THE STRIKE: AN ANALYSIS. USA+45 STRATA WORKER ECO/TAC GP/REL INGP/REL...MGT SOC CHARTS 20 YANKEE/C. PAGE 114 B2293 — ROLE STRUCT LABOR PROC/MFG

S48

COCH L.,"OVERCOMING RESISTANCE TO CHANGE" (BMR)" USA+45 CONSULT ADMIN ROUTINE GP/REL EFFICIENCY PRODUC PERCEPT SKILL...CHARTS SOC/EXP 20. PAGE 22 B0441 — WORKER OP/RES PROC/MFG RIGID/FLEX

S59

STINCHCOMBE A.L.,"BUREAUCRATIC AND CRAFT ADMINISTRATION OF PRODUCTION: A COMPARATIVE STUDY" (BMR)" USA+45 STRUCT EX/STRUC ECO/TAC GP/REL ...CLASSIF GP/COMP IDEA/COMP GEN/LAWS 20 WEBER/MAX. PAGE 101 B2039 — CONSTRUC PROC/MFG ADMIN PLAN

B61

FRIEDMANN W.G.,JOINT INTERNATIONAL BUSINESS VENTURES. ASIA ISLAM L/A+17C ECO/DEV DIST/IND FINAN PROC/MFG FACE/GP LG/CO NAT/G VOL/ASSN CONSULT EX/STRUC PLAN ADMIN ROUTINE WEALTH...OLD/LIB WORK 20. PAGE 37 B0760 — ECO/UNDEV INT/TRADE

B61

MARX K.,THE COMMUNIST MANIFESTO. IN (MENDEL A. ESSENTIAL WORKS OF MARXISM, NEW YORK: BANTAM. FUT MOD/EUR CULTURE ECO/DEV ECO/UNDEV AGRI FINAN INDUS MARKET PROC/MFG LABOR MUNIC POL/PAR CONSULT FORCES CREATE PLAN ADMIN ATTIT DRIVE RIGID/FLEX ORD/FREE PWR RESPECT MARX/KARL WORK. PAGE 70 B1421 — COM NEW/IDEA CAP/ISM REV

B62

BRIEFS H.W.,PRICING POWER AND "ADMINISTRATIVE" INFLATION (PAMPHLET). USA+45 PROC/MFG CONTROL EFFICIENCY MONEY GOLD/STAND. PAGE 15 B0306 — ECO/DEV PRICE POLICY EXEC

L62

WATERSTON A.,"PLANNING IN MOROCCO, ORGANIZATION AND — NAT/G

IMPLEMENTATION. BALTIMORE: HOPKINS ECON. DEVELOP.   PLAN
INT. BANK FOR." ISLAM ECO/DEV AGRI DIST/IND INDUS   MOROCCO
PROC/MFG SERV/IND LOC/G EX/STRUC ECO/TAC PWR WEALTH
TOT/POP VAL/FREE 20. PAGE 114 B2302

                               B64
FAINSOD M.,HOW RUSSIA IS RULED (REV. ED.). RUSSIA   NAT/G
USSR AGRI PROC/MFG LABOR POL/PAR EX/STRUC CONTROL   REV
PWR...POLICY BIBLIOG 19/20 KHRUSH/N COM/PARTY.   MARXISM
PAGE 34 B0700

                               B66
YOUNG W.,EXISTING MECHANISMS OF ARMS CONTROL.   ARMS/CONT
PROC/MFG OP/RES DIPLOM TASK CENTRAL...MGT TREATY.   ADMIN
PAGE 119 B2395   NUC/PWR
                                                     ROUTINE
                               B67
MINTZ M.,BY PRESCRIPTION ONLY. USA+45 NAT/G   BIO/SOC
EX/STRUC PLAN TEC/DEV EXEC EFFICIENCY HEALTH...MGT   PROC/MFG
SOC/WK 20. PAGE 74 B1491   CONTROL
                                                     POLICY
                               S67
ALPANDER G.G.,"ENTREPRENEURS AND PRIVATE ENTERPRISE   ECO/UNDEV
IN TURKEY." TURKEY INDUS PROC/MFG EDU/PROP ATTIT   LG/CO
DRIVE WEALTH...GEOG MGT SOC STAT TREND CHARTS 20.   NAT/G
PAGE 4 B0080   POLICY

PROCEDURAL SYSTEMS....SEE ROUTINE, ALSO PROCESSES AND
    PRACTICES INDEX

PROCESSING OR MANUFACTURING INDUSTRY....SEE PROC/MFG

PRODUC....PRODUCTIVITY; SEE ALSO PLAN

                               N
INTERNATIONAL BIBLIOGRAPHY OF ECONOMICS. WOR+45   BIBLIOG
FINAN MARKET ADMIN DEMAND INCOME PRODUC...POLICY   ECO/DEV
IDEA/COMP METH. PAGE 1 B0003   ECO/UNDEV
                                                     INT/TRADE
                               N
US SUPERINTENDENT OF DOCUMENTS,LABOR (PRICE LIST   BIBLIOG/A
33). USA+45 LAW AGRI CONSTRUC INDUS NAT/G BARGAIN   WORKER
PRICE ADMIN AUTOMAT PRODUC MGT. PAGE 111 B2240   LABOR
                                                     LEGIS
                               B08
THE GOVERNMENT OF SOUTH AFRICA (VOL. II). SOUTH/AFR   CONSTN
STRATA EXTR/IND EX/STRUC TOP/EX BUDGET ADJUD ADMIN   FINAN
CT/SYS PRODUC...CORREL CENSUS 19 RAILROAD   LEGIS
CIVIL/SERV POSTAL/SYS. PAGE 2 B0033   NAT/G
                                                     B19
LOS ANGELES BD CIV SERV COMNRS,ANNUAL REPORT: LOS   DELIB/GP
ANGELES CALIFORNIA: 1919-1936. USA-45 LAW GOV/REL   ADMIN
PRODUC...STAT 20. PAGE 66 B1340   LOC/G
                                                     MUNIC
                               N19
DOTSON A.,PRODUCTION PLANNING IN THE PATENT OFFICE   EFFICIENCY
(PAMPHLET). USA+45 DIST/IND PROB/SOLV PRODUC...MGT   PLAN
PHIL/SCI 20 BUR/BUDGET PATENT/OFF. PAGE 30 B0610   NAT/G
                                                     ADMIN
                               B37
GULICK L.,PAPERS ON THE SCIENCE OF ADMINISTRATION.   OP/RES
INDUS PROB/SOLV TEC/DEV COST EFFICIENCY PRODUC   CONTROL
HABITAT...PHIL/SCI METH/COMP 20. PAGE 45 B0903   ADMIN
                                                     MGT
                               B40
GAUS J.M.,PUBLIC ADMINISTRATION AND THE UNITED   ADMIN
STATES DEPARTMENT OF AGRICULTURE. USA-45 STRUCT   AGRI
DIST/IND FINAN MARKET EX/STRUC PROB/SOLV GIVE   DELIB/GP
PRODUC...POLICY GEOG CHARTS 20 DEPT/AGRI. PAGE 39   OP/RES
B0786
                                                     B41
SLICHTER S.H.,UNION POLICIES AND INDUSTRIAL   BARGAIN
MANAGEMENT. USA-45 INDUS TEC/DEV PAY GP/REL   LABOR
INGP/REL COST EFFICIENCY PRODUC...POLICY 20.   MGT
PAGE 98 B1978   WORKER
                                                     B42
WRIGHT D.M.,THE CREATION OF PURCHASING POWER.   FINAN
USA-45 NAT/G PRICE ADMIN WAR INCOME PRODUC...POLICY   ECO/TAC
CONCPT IDEA/COMP BIBLIOG 20 MONEY. PAGE 118 B2378   ECO/DEV
                                                     CREATE
                               B46
WILCOX J.K.,OFFICIAL DEFENSE PUBLICATIONS,   BIBLIOG/A
1941-1945 (NINE VOLS.). USA-45 AGRI INDUS R+D LABOR   WAR
FORCES TEC/DEV EFFICIENCY PRODUC SKILL WEALTH 20.   CIVMIL/REL
PAGE 116 B2347   ADMIN
                                                     L46
FORRESTAL J.,"THE NAVY: A STUDY IN ADMINISTRATION."   FORCES
ELITES FACE/GP EX/STRUC PROB/SOLV REPRESENT   INGP/REL
EFFICIENCY PRODUC. PAGE 37 B0741   ROUTINE
                                                     EXEC
                               B48
ROSENFARB J.,FREEDOM AND THE ADMINISTRATIVE STATE.   ECO/DEV
NAT/G ROUTINE EFFICIENCY PRODUC RATIONAL UTIL   INDUS
...TECHNIC WELF/ST MGT 20 BUREAUCRCY. PAGE 90 B1821   PLAN
                                                     WEALTH
                               S48
COCH L.,"OVERCOMING RESISTANCE TO CHANGE" (BMR)"   WORKER
USA+45 CONSULT ADMIN ROUTINE GP/REL EFFICIENCY   OP/RES

PRODUC PERCEPT SKILL...CHARTS SOC/EXP 20. PAGE 22   PROC/MFG
B0441   RIGID/FLEX
                                                     S50
DALTON M.,"CONFLICTS BETWEEN STAFF AND LINE   MGT
MANAGERIAL OFFICERS" (BMR). USA+45 USA-45 ELITES   ATTIT
LG/CO WORKER PROB/SOLV ADMIN EXEC EFFICIENCY PRODUC   GP/REL
...GP/COMP 20. PAGE 26 B0526   INDUS
                                                     C51
HOMANS G.C.,"THE WESTERN ELECTRIC RESEARCHES" IN S.   OP/RES
HOSLETT, ED., HUMAN FACTORS IN MANAGEMENT (BMR)"   EFFICIENCY
ACT/RES GP/REL HAPPINESS PRODUC DRIVE...MGT OBS 20.   SOC/EXP
PAGE 51 B1037   WORKER
                                                     B53
MILLIKAN M.F.,INCOME STABILIZATION FOR A DEVELOPING   ANTHOL
DEMOCRACY. USA+45 ECO/DEV LABOR BUDGET ECO/TAC TAX   MARKET
ADMIN ADJUST PRODUC WEALTH...POLICY TREND 20.   EQUILIB
PAGE 73 B1484   EFFICIENCY
                                                     B53
ROBINSON E.A.G.,THE STRUCTURE OF COMPETITIVE   INDUS
INDUSTRY. UK ECO/DEV DIST/IND MARKET TEC/DEV DIPLOM   PRODUC
EDU/PROP ADMIN EFFICIENCY WEALTH...MGT 19/20.   WORKER
PAGE 89 B1798   OPTIMAL
                                                     B55
RILEY V.,INTERINDUSTRY ECONOMIC STUDIES. USA+45   BIBLIOG
COMPUTER ADMIN OPTIMAL PRODUC...MGT CLASSIF STAT.   ECO/DEV
PAGE 88 B1788   PLAN
                                                     STRUCT
                               B57
UDY S.H. JR.,THE ORGANIZATION OF PRODUCTION IN   METH/COMP
NONINDUSTRIAL CULTURE. VOL/ASSN DELIB/GP TEC/DEV   ECO/UNDEV
...CHARTS BIBLIOG. PAGE 106 B2143   PRODUC
                                                     ADMIN
                               B58
CHEEK G.,ECONOMIC AND SOCIAL IMPLICATIONS OF   BIBLIOG/A
AUTOMATION: A BIBLIOGRAPHIC REVIEW (PAMPHLET).   SOCIETY
USA+45 LG/CO WORKER CREATE PLAN CONTROL ROUTINE   INDUS
PERS/REL EFFICIENCY PRODUC...METH/COMP 20. PAGE 20   AUTOMAT
B0416
                                                     B58
MELMAN S.,DECISION-MAKING AND PRODUCTIVITY. INDUS   LABOR
EX/STRUC WORKER OP/RES PROB/SOLV TEC/DEV ADMIN   PRODUC
ROUTINE RIGID/FLEX GP/COMP. PAGE 73 B1464   DECISION
                                                     MGT
                               B58
WARNER A.W.,CONCEPTS AND CASES IN ECONOMIC   ECO/TAC
ANALYSIS. PROB/SOLV BARGAIN CONTROL INCOME PRODUC   DEMAND
...ECOMETRIC MGT CONCPT CLASSIF CHARTS 20   EQUILIB
KEYNES/JM. PAGE 114 B2292   COST
                                                     S58
MANSFIELD E.,"A STUDY OF DECISION-MAKING WITHIN THE   OP/RES
FIRM." LG/CO WORKER INGP/REL COST EFFICIENCY PRODUC   PROB/SOLV
...CHARTS 20. PAGE 69 B1395   AUTOMAT
                                                     ROUTINE
                               B59
MAYDA J.,ATOMIC ENERGY AND LAW. ECO/UNDEV FINAN   NUC/PWR
TEC/DEV FOR/AID EFFICIENCY PRODUC WEALTH...POLICY   L/A+17C
TECHNIC 20. PAGE 71 B1433   LAW
                                                     ADMIN
                               B60
HOVING W.,THE DISTRIBUTION REVOLUTION. WOR+45   DIST/IND
ECO/DEV FINAN SERV/IND PRESS PRICE INCOME PRODUC   MARKET
...MGT 20. PAGE 52 B1049   ECO/TAC
                                                     TASK
                               B60
KERR C.,INDUSTRIALISM AND INDUSTRIAL MAN. CULTURE   WORKER
SOCIETY ECO/UNDEV NAT/G ADMIN PRODUC WEALTH   MGT
...PREDICT TREND NAT/COMP 19/20. PAGE 59 B1197   ECO/DEV
                                                     INDUS
                               B61
HALL M.,DISTRIBUTION IN GREAT BRITAIN AND NORTH   DIST/IND
AMERICA. CANADA UK USA+45 ECO/DEV INDUS MARKET   PRODUC
EFFICIENCY PROFIT...MGT CHARTS 20. PAGE 46 B0924   ECO/TAC
                                                     CAP/ISM
                               B61
HART H.C.,ADMINISTRATIVE ASPECTS OF RIVER VALLEY   ADMIN
DEVELOPMENT. INDIA USA+45 INDUS CONTROL EFFICIENCY   PLAN
OPTIMAL PRODUC 20 TVA. PAGE 47 B0957   METH/COMP
                                                     AGRI
                               B61
MACMAHON A.W.,DELEGATION AND AUTONOMY. INDIA STRUCT   ADMIN
LEGIS BARGAIN BUDGET ECO/TAC LEGIT EXEC REPRESENT   PLAN
GOV/REL CENTRAL DEMAND EFFICIENCY PRODUC. PAGE 68   FEDERAL
B1373
                                                     B61
NOVE A.,THE SOVIET ECONOMY. USSR ECO/DEV FINAN   PLAN
NAT/G ECO/TAC PRICE ADMIN EFFICIENCY MARXISM   PRODUC
...TREND BIBLIOG 20. PAGE 79 B1594   POLICY
                                                     B61
PETRULLO L.,LEADERSHIP AND INTERPERSONAL BEHAVIOR.   PERSON
FACE/GP FAM PROF/ORG EX/STRUC FORCES DOMIN WAR   ATTIT
GP/REL PERS/REL EFFICIENCY PRODUC PWR...MGT PSY.   LEAD
PAGE 82 B1663   HABITAT
                                                     S61
EVAN W.M.,"A LABORATORY EXPERIMENT ON BUREAUCRATIC   ADMIN
AUTHORITY" WORKER CONTROL EXEC PRODUC ATTIT PERSON   LEGIT
...PSY SOC CHARTS SIMUL 20 WEBER/MAX. PAGE 34 B0687   LAB/EXP

ARGYRIS C.,INTERPERSONAL COMPETENCE AND
ORGANIZATIONAL EFFECTIVENESS. CREATE PLAN PROB/SOLV
EDU/PROP INGP/REL PERS/REL PRODUC...OBS INT SIMUL
20. PAGE 6 B0131

EFFICIENCY
B62
EX/STRUC
ADMIN
CONSULT

DUCKWORTH W.E.,A GUIDE TO OPERATIONAL RESEARCH.
INDUS PLAN PROB/SOLV EXEC EFFICIENCY PRODUC KNOWL
...MGT MATH STAT SIMUL METH 20 MONTECARLO. PAGE 31
B0624

EFFICIENCY
B62
OP/RES
GAME
DECISION
ADMIN

NATIONAL BUREAU ECONOMIC RES,THE RATE AND DIRECTION
OF INVENTIVE ACTIVITY: ECONOMIC AND SOCIAL FACTORS.
STRUCT INDUS MARKET R+D CREATE OP/RES TEC/DEV
EFFICIENCY PRODUC RATIONAL UTIL...WELF/ST PHIL/SCI
METH/CNCPT TIME. PAGE 77 B1562

B62
DECISION
PROB/SOLV
MGT

SRIVASTAVA G.L.,COLLECTIVE BARGAINING AND LABOR-
MANAGEMENT RELATIONS IN INDIA. INDIA UK USA+45
INDUS LEGIS WORKER ADJUD EFFICIENCY PRODUC
...METH/COMP 20. PAGE 100 B2014

B62
LABOR
MGT
BARGAIN
GP/REL

WEDDING N.,ADVERTISING MANAGEMENT. USA+45 ECO/DEV
BUDGET CAP/ISM PRODUC PROFIT ATTIT...DECISION MGT
PSY 20. PAGE 114 B2308

B62
ECO/TAC
COM/IND
PLAN
EDU/PROP

TANNENBAUM A.S.,"CONTROL IN ORGANIZATIONS:
INDIVIDUAL ADJUSTMENT AND ORGANIZATIONAL
PERFORMANCE." DOMIN PARTIC REPRESENT INGP/REL
PRODUC ATTIT DRIVE PWR...PSY CORREL. PAGE 102 B2073

S62
ADMIN
MGT
STRUCT
CONTROL

LITTERER J.A.,ORGANIZATIONS: STRUCTURE AND
BEHAVIOR. PLAN DOMIN CONTROL LEAD ROUTINE SANCTION
INGP/REL EFFICIENCY PRODUC DRIVE RIGID/FLEX PWR.
PAGE 66 B1325

B63
ADMIN
CREATE
MGT
ADJUST

RAUDSEPP E.,MANAGING CREATIVE SCIENTISTS AND
ENGINEERS. USA+45 ECO/DEV LG/CO GP/REL PERS/REL
PRODUC. PAGE 86 B1742

B63
MGT
CREATE
R+D
ECO/TAC

THORELLI H.B.,INTOP: INTERNATIONAL OPERATIONS
SIMULATION: PLAYER'S MANUAL. BRAZIL FINAN OP/RES
ADMIN GP/REL INGP/REL PRODUC PERCEPT...DECISION MGT
EEC. PAGE 104 B2108

B63
GAME
INT/TRADE
EDU/PROP
LG/CO

COX R.,THEORY IN MARKETING. FUT USA+45 SOCIETY
ECO/DEV PROB/SOLV PRICE RISK PRODUC ATTIT...ANTHOL
20. PAGE 24 B0499

B64
MARKET
ECO/TAC
PHIL/SCI
MGT

RIDDLE D.H.,THE TRUMAN COMMITTEE: A STUDY IN
CONGRESSIONAL RESPONSIBILITY. INDUS FORCES OP/RES
DOMIN ADMIN LEAD PARL/PROC WAR PRODUC SUPEGO
...BIBLIOG CONGRESS. PAGE 88 B1778

B64
LEGIS
DELIB/GP
CONFER

WELLISZ S.,THE ECONOMICS OF THE SOVIET BLOC. COM
USSR INDUS WORKER PLAN BUDGET INT/TRADE TAX PRICE
PRODUC WEALTH MARXISM...METH/COMP 20. PAGE 115
B2319

B64
EFFICIENCY
ADMIN
MARKET

WILLIAMSON O.E.,THE ECONOMICS OF DISCRETIONARY
BEHAVIOR: MANAGERIAL OBJECTIVES IN A THEORY OF THE
FIRM. MARKET BUDGET CAP/ISM PRODUC DRIVE PERSON
...STAT CHARTS BIBLIOG METH 20. PAGE 117 B2354

B64
EFFICIENCY
MGT
ECO/TAC
CHOOSE

NEWLYN W.T.,"MONETARY SYSTEMS AND INTEGRATION" AFR
BUDGET ADMIN FEDERAL PRODUC PROFIT UTIL...CHARTS 20
AFRICA/E. PAGE 78 B1578

S64
ECO/UNDEV
REGION
METH/COMP
FINAN

BARISH N.N.,MANAGEMENT SCIENCES IN THE EMERGING
COUNTRIES. AFR CHINA/COM WOR+45 FINAN INDUS PLAN
PRODUC HABITAT...ANTHOL 20. PAGE 9 B0184

B65
ECO/UNDEV
OP/RES
MGT
TEC/DEV

VEINOTT A.F. JR.,MATHEMATICAL STUDIES IN MANAGEMENT
SCIENCE. UNIV INDUS COMPUTER ADMIN...DECISION
NET/THEORY SIMUL 20. PAGE 112 B2257

B65
MATH
MGT
PLAN
PRODUC

DAVIS R.G.,PLANNING HUMAN RESOURCE DEVELOPMENT.
EDUCATIONAL MODELS AND SCHEMATA. WORKER OP/RES
ECO/TAC EDU/PROP CONTROL COST PRODUC...GEOG STAT
CHARTS 20. PAGE 27 B0544

B66
PLAN
EFFICIENCY
SIMUL
ROUTINE

FABRYCKY W.J.,OPERATIONS ECONOMY INDUSTRIAL
APPLICATIONS OF OPERATIONS RESEARCH. INDUS PLAN
ECO/TAC PRODUC...MATH PROBABIL STAT CHARTS 20.
PAGE 34 B0695

B66
OP/RES
MGT
SIMUL
DECISION

GROSS H.,MAKE OR BUY. USA+45 FINAN INDUS CREATE
PRICE PRODUC 20. PAGE 44 B0889

ECO/TAC
PLAN
MGT

COST
B66

HAYER T.,FRENCH AID. AFR FRANCE AGRI FINAN BUDGET
ADMIN WAR PRODUC...CHARTS 18/20 THIRD/WRLD
OVRSEA/DEV. PAGE 48 B0975

TEC/DEV
COLONIAL
FOR/AID
ECO/UNDEV
B66

KAESTNER K.,GESAMTWIRTSCHAFTLICHE PLANUNG IN EINER
GEMISCHTEN WIRTSCHAFTSORDNUNG
(WIRTSCHAFTSPOLITISCHE STUDIEN 5). GERMANY/W WOR+45
WOR-45 INDUS MARKET NAT/G ACT/RES GP/REL INGP/REL
PRODUC...ECOMETRIC MGT BIBLIOG 20. PAGE 57 B1159

ECO/TAC
PLAN
POLICY
PREDICT

B66

KURAKOV I.G.,SCIENCE, TECHNOLOGY AND COMMUNISM;
SOME QUESTIONS OF DEVELOPMENT (TRANS. BY CARIN
DEDIJER). USSR INDUS PLAN PROB/SOLV COST PRODUC
...MGT MATH CHARTS METH 20. PAGE 61 B1243

CREATE
TEC/DEV
MARXISM
ECO/TAC
B66

LINDFORS G.V.,INTERCOLLEGIATE BIBLIOGRAPHY; CASES
IN BUSINESS ADMINISTRATION (VOL. X). FINAN MARKET
LABOR CONSULT PLAN GP/REL PRODUC 20. PAGE 65 B1314

BIBLIOG/A
ADMIN
MGT
OP/RES
B66

REDFORD E.S.,THE ROLE OF GOVERNMENT IN THE AMERICAN
ECONOMY. USA+45 USA-45 FINAN INDUS LG/CO PROB/SOLV
ADMIN INGP/REL INCOME PRODUC 18/20. PAGE 87 B1759

NAT/G
ECO/DEV
CAP/ISM
ECO/TAC
B66

SPICER K.,A SAMARITAN STATE? AFR CANADA INDIA
PAKISTAN UK USA+45 FINAN INDUS PRODUC...CHARTS 20
NATO. PAGE 99 B2006

DIPLOM
FOR/AID
ECO/DEV
ADMIN
B67

ROBINSON R.D., INTERNATIONAL MANAGEMENT USA+45
FINAN R+D PLAN PRODUC...DECISION T. PAGE 67 B1352

INT/TRADE
MGT
INT/LAW
MARKET
B67

POSNER M.V.,ITALIAN PUBLIC ENTERPRISE. ITALY
ECO/DEV FINAN INDUS CREATE ECO/TAC ADMIN CONTROL
EFFICIENCY PRODUC...TREND CHARTS 20. PAGE 84 B1693

NAT/G
PLAN
CAP/ISM
SOCISM
B67

ZONDAG C.H.,THE BOLIVIAN ECONOMY 1952-65. L/A+17C
TEC/DEV FOR/AID ADMIN...OBS TREND CHARTS BIBLIOG 20
BOLIV. PAGE 119 B2406

ECO/UNDEV
INDUS
PRODUC
S67

BERLINER J.S.,"RUSSIA'S BUREAUCRATS - WHY THEY'RE
REACTIONARY." USSR NAT/G OP/RES PROB/SOLV TEC/DEV
CONTROL SANCTION EFFICIENCY DRIVE PERSON...TECHNIC
SOC 20. PAGE 11 B0223

CREATE
ADMIN
INDUS
PRODUC
S67

BURACK E.H.,"INDUSTRIAL MANAGEMENT IN ADVANCED
PRODUCTION SYSTEMS: SOME THEORETICAL CONCEPTS AND
PRELIMINARY FINDINGS." INDUS CREATE PLAN PRODUC
ROLE...OBS STAND/INT DEEP/QU HYPO/EXP ORG/CHARTS
20. PAGE 17 B0346

ADMIN
MGT
TEC/DEV
EX/STRUC
S67

GRINYER P.H.,"THE SYSTEMATIC EVALUATION OF METHODS
OF WAGE PAYMENT." UK INDUS WORKER ADMIN EFFICIENCY
...MGT METH/COMP 20. PAGE 44 B0882

OP/RES
COST
PAY
PRODUC
S67

LEVCIK B.,"WAGES AND EMPLOYMENT PROBLEMS IN THE NEW
SYSTEM OF PLANNED MANAGEMENT IN CZECHOSLOVAKIA."
CZECHOSLVK EUR+WWI NAT/G OP/RES PLAN ADMIN ROUTINE
INGP/REL CENTRAL EFFICIENCY PRODUC DECISION.
PAGE 64 B1300

MARXISM
WORKER
MGT
PAY

S67

ROBERTS E.B.,"THE PROBLEM OF AGING ORGANIZATIONS."
INTELL PROB/SOLV ADMIN EXEC FEEDBACK EFFICIENCY
PRODUC...GEN/LAWS 20. PAGE 89 B1794

INDUS
R+D
MGT
PLAN
S67

WRIGHT F.K.,"INVESTMENT CRITERIA AND THE COST OF
CAPITAL." FINAN PLAN BUDGET OPTIMAL PRODUC...POLICY
DECISION 20. PAGE 118 B2380

COST
PROFIT
INDUS
MGT

PRODUCTIVITY....SEE PRODUC

PROF/ORG....PROFESSIONAL ORGANIZATIONS

N

THE AMERICAN CITY. INDUS PROF/ORG PLAN GOV/REL
...MGT 20. PAGE 1 B0007

BIBLIOG/A
ADMIN
TEC/DEV
MUNIC
L23

DOUGLAS P.H.,"OCCUPATIONAL V PROPORTIONAL
REPRESENTATION." INDUS NAT/G PLAN ROUTINE SUFF
CONSEN DRIVE...CONCPT CLASSIF. PAGE 30 B0612

REPRESENT
PROF/ORG
DOMIN
INGP/REL
B49

ASPINALL A.,POLITICS AND THE PRESS 1780-1850. UK
LAW ELITES FINAN PROF/ORG LEGIS ADMIN ATTIT

PRESS
CONTROL

...POLICY 18/19. PAGE 7 B0142 — POL/PAR ORD/FREE

B49
GLOVER J.D.,THE ADMINISTRATOR. ELITES LG/CO EX/STRUC ACT/RES CONTROL GP/REL INGP/REL PERS/REL AUTHORIT...POLICY CONCPT HIST/WRIT. PAGE 40 B0811 — ADMIN MGT ATTIT PROF/ORG

B51
MAASS A.,MUDDY WATERS: THE ARMY ENGINEERS AND THE NATIONS RIVERS. USA-45 PROF/ORG CONSULT LEGIS ADMIN EXEC ROLE PWR...SOC PRESIDENT 20. PAGE 67 B1353 — FORCES GP/REL LOBBY CONSTRUC

B55
PALMER A.M.,ADMINISTRATION OF MEDICAL AND PHARMACEUTICAL PATENTS (PAMPHLET). USA+45 PROF/ORG ADMIN PHIL/SCI. PAGE 80 B1626 — HEAL ACADEM LAW LICENSE

S55
TORRE M.,"PSYCHIATRIC OBSERVATIONS OF INTERNATIONAL CONFERENCES." WOR+45 INT/ORG PROF/ORG VOL/ASSN CONSULT EDU/PROP ROUTINE ATTIT DRIVE KNOWL...PSY METH/CNCPT OBS/ENVIR STERTYP 20. PAGE 105 B2119 — DELIB/GP OBS DIPLOM

S55
WEISS R.S.,"A METHOD FOR THE ANALYSIS OF THE STRUCTURE OF COMPLEX ORGANIZATIONS." WOR+45 INDUS LG/CO NAT/G EXEC ROUTINE ORD/FREE PWR SKILL...MGT PSY SOC NEW/IDEA STAT INT REC/INT STAND/INT CHARTS WORK. PAGE 115 B2316 — PROF/ORG SOC/EXP

B56
WASSERMAN P.,INFORMATION FOR ADMINISTRATORS: A GUIDE TO PUBLICATIONS AND SERVICES FOR MANAGEMENT IN BUSINESS AND GOVERNMENT. R+D LOC/G NAT/G PROF/ORG VOL/ASSN PRESS...PSY SOC STAT 20. PAGE 114 B2299 — BIBLIOG MGT KNOWL EDU/PROP

B57
HUNTINGTON S.P.,THE SOLDIER AND THE STATE: THE THEORY AND POLITICS OF CIVIL-MILITARY RELATIONS. USA+45 USA-45 NAT/G PROF/ORG CONSULT DOMIN LEGIT ROUTINE ATTIT PWR...CONCPT TIME/SEQ COLD/WAR 20. PAGE 53 B1065 — ACT/RES FORCES

B58
JAPAN MINISTRY OF JUSTICE,CRIMINAL JUSTICE IN JAPAN. LAW PROF/ORG PUB/INST FORCES CONTROL CT/SYS PARL/PROC 20 CHINJAP. PAGE 56 B1125 — CONSTN CRIME JURID ADMIN

B58
SKINNER G.W.,LEADERSHIP AND POWER IN THE CHINESE COMMUNITY OF THAILAND. ASIA S/ASIA STRATA FACE/GP KIN PROF/ORG VOL/ASSN EX/STRUC DOMIN PERSON RESPECT ...METH/CNCPT STAT INT QU BIOG CHARTS 20. PAGE 98 B1974 — SOC ELITES THAILAND

B58
WILENSKY H.L.,INDUSTRIAL SOCIETY AND SOCIAL WELFARE: IMPACT OF INDUSTRIALIZATION ON SUPPLY AND ORGANIZATION OF SOC WELF SERVICES. ELITES SOCIETY STRATA SERV/IND FAM MUNIC PUB/INST CONSULT WORKER ADMIN AUTOMAT ANOMIE 20. PAGE 117 B2352 — INDUS ECO/DEV RECEIVE PROF/ORG

S58
BLAISDELL D.C.,"PRESSURE GROUPS, FOREIGN POLICIES, AND INTERNATIONAL POLITICS." USA+45 WOR+45 INT/ORG PLAN DOMIN EDU/PROP LEGIT ADMIN ROUTINE CHOOSE ...DECISION MGT METH/CNCPT CON/ANAL 20. PAGE 12 B0249 — PROF/ORG PWR

B59
JANOWITZ M.,SOCIOLOGY AND THE MILITARY ESTABLISHMENT. USA+45 WOR+45 CULTURE SOCIETY PROF/ORG CONSULT EX/STRUC PLAN TEC/DEV DIPLOM DOMIN COERCE DRIVE RIGID/FLEX ORD/FREE PWR SKILL COLD/WAR 20. PAGE 55 B1121 — FORCES SOC

B60
DRAPER T.,AMERICAN COMMUNISM AND SOVIET RUSSIA. EUR+WWI USA+45 USSR INTELL AGRI COM/IND FINAN INDUS LABOR PROF/ORG VOL/ASSN PLAN TEC/DEV DOMIN EDU/PROP ADMIN COERCE REV PERSON PWR...POLICY CONCPT MYTH 19/20. PAGE 30 B0617 — COM POL/PAR

B60
GILMORE D.R.,DEVELOPING THE "LITTLE" ECONOMIES. USA+45 FINAN LG/CO PROF/ORG VOL/ASSN CREATE ADMIN. PAGE 40 B0801 — ECO/TAC LOC/G PROVS PLAN

S60
TAYLOR M.G.,"THE ROLE OF THE MEDICAL PROFESSION IN THE FORMULATION AND EXECUTION OF PUBLIC POLICY" (BMR)" CANADA NAT/G CONSULT ADMIN REPRESENT GP/REL ROLE SOVEREIGN...DECISION 20 CMA. PAGE 103 B2088 — PROF/ORG HEALTH LOBBY POLICY

B61
ETZIONI A.,COMPLEX ORGANIZATIONS: A SOCIOLOGICAL READER. CLIENT CULTURE STRATA CREATE OP/RES ADMIN ...POLICY METH/CNCPT BUREAUCRCY. PAGE 34 B0683 — VOL/ASSN STRUCT CLASSIF PROF/ORG

B61
LOSCHELDER W.,AUSBILDUNG UND AUSLESE DER BEAMTEN. GERMANY/W ELITES NAT/G ADMIN GP/REL ATTIT...JURID 20 CIVIL/SERV. PAGE 67 B1341 — PROF/ORG EDU/PROP EX/STRUC CHOOSE

B61
MARSH R.M.,THE MANDARINS: THE CIRCULATION OF ELITES IN CHINA, 1600-1900. ASIA STRUCT PROF/ORG...SOC CHARTS BIBLIOG DICTIONARY 17/20. PAGE 70 B1406 — ELITES ADMIN FAM STRATA

B61
PETRULLO L.,LEADERSHIP AND INTERPERSONAL BEHAVIOR. FACE/GP FAM PROF/ORG EX/STRUC FORCES DOMIN WAR GP/REL PERS/REL EFFICIENCY PRODUC PWR...MGT PSY. PAGE 82 B1663 — PERSON ATTIT LEAD HABITAT

B61
TRECKER H.B.,NEW UNDERSTANDING OF ADMINISTRATION. NEIGH DELIB/GP CONTROL LEAD GP/REL INGP/REL ...POLICY DECISION BIBLIOG. PAGE 105 B2126 — VOL/ASSN PROF/ORG ADMIN PARTIC

B62
ROBINSON M.,THE COMING OF AGE OF THE LANGLEY PORTER CLINIC (PAMPHLET). USA+45 PROF/ORG PROVS PLAN...MGT PSY 20 CALIFORNIA LANGLEY. PAGE 89 B1804 — PUB/INST ADMIN EFFICIENCY HEAL

B63
ELIAS T.O.,THE NIGERIAN LEGAL SYSTEM. NIGERIA LAW FAM KIN SECT ADMIN NAT/LISM...JURID 18/20 ENGLSH/LAW COMMON/LAW. PAGE 33 B0665 — CT/SYS ADJUD COLONIAL PROF/ORG

B63
KORNHAUSER W.,SCIENTISTS IN INDUSTRY: CONFLICT AND ACCOMMODATION. USA+45 R+D LG/CO NAT/G TEC/DEV CONTROL ADJUST ATTIT...MGT STAT INT BIBLIOG 20. PAGE 61 B1229 — CREATE INDUS PROF/ORG GP/REL

S63
COUTY P.,"L'ASSISTANCE POUR LE DEVELOPPEMENT: POINT DE VUE SCANDINAVES." EUR+WWI FINLAND FUT SWEDEN WOR+45 ECO/DEV ECO/UNDEV COM/IND LABOR NAT/G PROF/ORG ACT/RES SKILL WEALTH TOT/POP 20. PAGE 24 B0497 — FINAN ROUTINE FOR/AID

S63
RUSTOW D.A.,"THE MILITARY IN MIDDLE EASTERN SOCIETY AND POLITICS." FUT ISLAM CONSTN SOCIETY FACE/GP NAT/G POL/PAR PROF/ORG CONSULT DOMIN ADMIN EXEC REGION COERCE NAT/LISM ATTIT DRIVE PERSON ORD/FREE PWR...POLICY CONCPT OBS STERTYP 20. PAGE 92 B1860 — FORCES ELITES

B64
BANTON M.,THE POLICEMAN IN THE COMMUNITY. UK USA+45 STRUCT PROF/ORG WORKER LOBBY ROUTINE COERCE CROWD GP/REL ADJUST DISCRIM PERCEPT 20. PAGE 9 B0181 — FORCES ADMIN ROLE RACE/REL

B64
FALK L.A.,ADMINISTRATIVE ASPECTS OF GROUP PRACTICE. USA+45 FINAN PROF/ORG PLAN MGT. PAGE 35 B0702 — BIBLIOG/A HEAL ADMIN SERV/IND

B64
RIES J.C.,THE MANAGEMENT OF DEFENSE: ORGANIZATION AND CONTROL OF THE US ARMED SERVICES. PROF/ORG DELIB/GP EX/STRUC LEGIS GOV/REL PERS/REL CENTRAL RATIONAL PWR...POLICY TREND GOV/COMP BIBLIOG. PAGE 88 B1782 — FORCES ACT/RES DECISION CONTROL

B64
WILSON L.,THE ACADEMIC MAN. STRUCT FINAN PROF/ORG OP/RES ADMIN AUTHORIT ROLE RESPECT...SOC STAT. PAGE 117 B2360 — ACADEM INGP/REL STRATA DELIB/GP

B65
CUTLIP S.M.,A PUBLIC RELATIONS BIBLIOGRAPHY. INDUS LABOR NAT/G PROF/ORG SCHOOL DIPLOM PRESS TV GOV/REL GP/REL...PSY SOC/WK 20. PAGE 25 B0515 — BIBLIOG/A MGT COM/IND ADMIN

B65
OECD,MEDITERRANEAN REGIONAL PROJECT: TURKEY; EDUCATION AND DEVELOPMENT. FUT TURKEY SOCIETY STRATA FINAN NAT/G PROF/ORG PLAN PROB/SOLV ADMIN COST...STAT CHARTS 20 OECD. PAGE 79 B1602 — EDU/PROP ACADEM SCHOOL ECO/UNDEV

B65
ORG FOR ECO COOP AND DEVEL,THE MEDITERRANEAN REGIONAL PROJECT: AN EXPERIMENT IN PLANNING BY SIX COUNTRIES. FUT GREECE SPAIN TURKEY YUGOSLAVIA SOCIETY FINAN NAT/G PROF/ORG EDU/PROP ADMIN REGION COST...POLICY STAT CHARTS 20 OECD. PAGE 80 B1614 — PLAN ECO/UNDEV ACADEM SCHOOL

B65
ORG FOR ECO COOP AND DEVEL,THE MEDITERRANEAN REGIONAL PROJECT: YUGOSLAVIA; EDUCATION AND DEVELOPMENT. YUGOSLAVIA SOCIETY FINAN PROF/ORG PLAN ADMIN COST DEMAND MARXISM...STAT TREND CHARTS METH 20 OECD. PAGE 80 B1615 — EDU/PROP ACADEM SCHOOL ECO/UNDEV

B65
PERLOFF H.S.,URBAN RESEARCH AND EDUCATION IN THE NEW YORK METROPOLITAN REGION (VOL. II). FUT USA+45 NEIGH PROF/ORG ACT/RES PROB/SOLV EDU/PROP ADMIN ...STAT BIBLIOG 20 NEWYORK/C. PAGE 82 B1659 — MUNIC PLAN ACADEM GP/REL

B65
UNESCO,INTERNATIONAL ORGANIZATIONS IN THE SOCIAL SCIENCES(REV. ED.). LAW ADMIN ATTIT...CRIMLGY GEOG INT/LAW PSY SOC STAT 20 UNESCO. PAGE 107 B2157 — INT/ORG R+D PROF/ORG ACT/RES

B66
RUBENSTEIN R.,,THE SHARING OF POWER IN A PSYCHIATRIC | ADMIN
HOSPITAL. CLIENT PROF/ORG PUB/INST INGP/REL ATTIT | PARTIC
PWR...DECISION OBS RECORD. PAGE 91 B1847 | HEALTH
| CONCPT

B66
SCHMIDT F.,PUBLIC RELATIONS IN HEALTH AND WELFARE. | PROF/ORG
USA+45 ACADEM RECEIVE PRESS FEEDBACK GOV/REL | EDU/PROP
PERS/REL DEMAND EFFICIENCY ATTIT PERCEPT WEALTH 20 | ADMIN
PUBLIC/REL. PAGE 94 B1895 | HEALTH

B67
BLUMBERG A.S.,CRIMINAL JUSTICE. USA+45 CLIENT LAW | JURID
LOC/G FORCES JUDGE ACT/RES LEGIT ADMIN RATIONAL | CT/SYS
MYTH. PAGE 13 B0259 | PROF/ORG
| CRIME

B67
IANNACCONE L.,POLITICS IN EDUCATION. USA+45 LOC/G | EDU/PROP
PROF/ORG BAL/PWR ADMIN...CHARTS SIMUL. PAGE 53 | GEN/LAWS
B1072 | PROVS

B67
LENG S.C.,JUSTICE IN COMMUNIST CHINA: A SURVEY OF | CT/SYS
THE JUDICIAL SYSTEM OF THE CHINESE PEOPLE'S | ADJUD
REPUBLIC. CHINA/COM LAW CONSTN LOC/G NAT/G PROF/ORG | JURID
CONSULT FORCES ADMIN CRIME ORD/FREE...BIBLIOG 20 | MARXISM
MAO. PAGE 64 B1290

B67
MACKINTOSH J.M.,JUGGERNAUT. USSR NAT/G POL/PAR | WAR
ADMIN LEAD CIVMIL/REL COST TOTALISM PWR MARXISM | FORCES
...GOV/COMP 20. PAGE 68 B1364 | COM
| PROF/ORG

S67
ATKIN J.M.,"THE FEDERAL GOVERNMENT, BIG BUSINESS, | SCHOOL
AND COLLEGES OF EDUCATION." PROF/ORG CONSULT CREATE | ACADEM
PLAN PROB/SOLV ADMIN EFFICIENCY. PAGE 7 B0144 | NAT/G
| INDUS

S67
RUBIN R.I.,"THE LEGISLATIVE-EXECUTIVE RELATIONS OF | LEGIS
THE UNITED STATES INFORMATION AGENCY." USA+45 | EX/STRUC
EDU/PROP TASK INGP/REL EFFICIENCY ISOLAT ATTIT ROLE | GP/REL
USIA CONGRESS. PAGE 91 B1850 | PROF/ORG

N67
NATIONAL COMN COMMUNITY HEALTH,ACTION - PLANNING | PLAN
FOR COMMUNITY HEALTH SERVICES (PAMPHLET). USA+45 | MUNIC
PROF/ORG DELIB/GP BUDGET ROUTINE GP/REL ATTIT | HEALTH
...HEAL SOC SOC/WK CHARTS TIME 20. PAGE 77 B1563 | ADJUST

PROFESSIONAL ORGANIZATION....SEE PROF/ORG

PROFIT....SEE ALSO ECO

N
THE MANAGEMENT REVIEW. FINAN EX/STRUC PROFIT | LABOR
BIBLIOG/A. PAGE 1 B0017 | MGT
| ADMIN
| MARKET

B28
CALKINS E.E.,BUSINESS THE CIVILIZER. INDUS MARKET | LAISSEZ
WORKER TAX PAY ROUTINE COST DEMAND MORAL 19/20. | POLICY
PAGE 18 B0367 | WEALTH
| PROFIT

B44
BIENSTOCK G.,MANAGEMENT IN RUSSIAN INDUSTRY AND | ADMIN
AGRICULTURE. USSR CONSULT WORKER LEAD COST PROFIT | MARXISM
ATTIT DRIVE PWR...MGT METH/COMP DICTIONARY 20. | SML/CO
PAGE 12 B0236 | AGRI

B49
WRIGHT J.H.,PUBLIC RELATIONS IN MANAGEMENT. USA+45 | MGT
USA-45 ECO/DEV LG/CO SML/CO CONSULT EXEC TASK | PLAN
PROFIT ATTIT ROLE 20. PAGE 118 B2382 | EDU/PROP
| PARTIC

B50
HARTLAND P.C.,BALANCE OF INTERREGIONAL PAYMENTS OF | ECO/DEV
NEW ENGLAND. USA+45 TEC/DEV ECO/TAC LEGIT ROUTINE | FINAN
BAL/PAY PROFIT 20 NEW/ENGLND FED/RESERV. PAGE 47 | REGION
B0962 | PLAN

B61
HALL M.,DISTRIBUTION IN GREAT BRITAIN AND NORTH | DIST/IND
AMERICA. CANADA UK USA+45 ECO/DEV INDUS MARKET | PRODUC
EFFICIENCY PROFIT...MGT CHARTS 20. PAGE 46 B0924 | ECO/TAC
| CAP/ISM

B62
WEDDING N.,ADVERTISING MANAGEMENT. USA+45 ECO/DEV | ECO/TAC
BUDGET CAP/ISM PRODUC PROFIT ATTIT...DECISION MGT | COM/IND
PSY 20. PAGE 114 B2308 | PLAN
| EDU/PROP

B63
DUE J.F.,STATE SALES TAX ADMINISTRATION. OP/RES | PROVS
BUDGET PAY ADMIN EXEC ROUTINE COST EFFICIENCY | TAX
PROFIT...CHARTS METH/COMP 20. PAGE 31 B0626 | STAT
| GOV/COMP

B64
REDLICH F.,THE GERMAN MILITARY ENTERPRISER AND HIS | EX/STRUC
WORK FORCE. CHRIST-17C GERMANY ELITES SOCIETY FINAN | FORCES
ECO/TAC CIVMIL/REL GP/REL INGP/REL...HIST/WRIT | PROFIT
METH/COMP 14/17. PAGE 87 B1760 | WORKER

S64
NEWLYN W.T.,"MONETARY SYSTEMS AND INTEGRATION" AFR | ECO/UNDEV
BUDGET ADMIN FEDERAL PRODUC PROFIT UTIL...CHARTS 20 | REGION
AFRICA/E. PAGE 78 B1578 | METH/COMP
| FINAN

S64
STONE P.A.,"DECISION TECHNIQUES FOR TOWN | OP/RES
DEVELOPMENT." PLAN COST PROFIT...DECISION MGT | MUNIC
CON/ANAL CHARTS METH/COMP BIBLIOG 20. PAGE 101 | ADMIN
B2048 | PROB/SOLV

B65
TYBOUT R.A.,ECONOMICS OF RESEARCH AND DEVELOPMENT. | R+D
ECO/DEV ECO/UNDEV INDUS PROFIT DECISION. PAGE 106 | FORCES
B2141 | ADMIN
| DIPLOM

B67
NARVER J.C.,CONGLOMERATE MERGERS AND MARKET | DEMAND
COMPETITION. USA+45 LAW STRUCT ADMIN LEAD RISK COST | LG/CO
PROFIT WEALTH...POLICY CHARTS BIBLIOG. PAGE 77 | MARKET
B1555 | MGT

S67
GOLIGHTLY H.O.,"THE AIRLINES: A CASE STUDY IN | DIST/IND
MANAGEMENT INNOVATION." USA+45 AIR FINAN INDUS | MARKET
TOP/EX CREATE PLAN PROB/SOLV ADMIN EXEC PROFIT | MGT
...DECISION 20. PAGE 40 B0820 | TEC/DEV

S67
LERNER A.P.,"EMPLOYMENT THEORY AND EMPLOYMENT | CAP/ISM
POLICY." ECO/DEV INDUS LABOR LG/CO BUDGET ADMIN | WORKER
DEMAND PROFIT WEALTH LAISSEZ METH/COMP. PAGE 64 | CONCPT
B1296

S67
ROSE A.M.,"CONFIDENCE AND THE CORPORATION." LG/CO | INDUS
CONTROL CRIME INCOME PROFIT 20. PAGE 90 B1818 | EX/STRUC
| VOL/ASSN
| RESPECT

S67
WRIGHT F.K.,"INVESTMENT CRITERIA AND THE COST OF | COST
CAPITAL." FINAN PLAN BUDGET OPTIMAL PRODUC...POLICY | PROFIT
DECISION 20. PAGE 118 B2380 | INDUS
| MGT

S68
PEARSON A.W.,"RESOURCE ALLOCATION." PLAN PROB/SOLV | PROFIT
BUDGET ADMIN CONTROL CHOOSE EFFICIENCY...DECISION | OPTIMAL
MGT 20. PAGE 82 B1649 | COST
| INDUS

PROFUMO/J....JOHN PROFUMO, THE PROFUMO AFFAIR

PROG/TEAC....PROGRAMMED INSTRUCTION

B64
KIMBROUGH R.B.,POLITICAL POWER AND EDUCATIONAL | EDU/PROP
DECISION-MAKING. USA+45 FINAN ADMIN LEAD GP/REL | PROB/SOLV
ATTIT PWR PROG/TEAC. PAGE 60 B1207 | DECISION
| SCHOOL

B66
BALDWIN D.A.,FOREIGN AID AND AMERICAN FOREIGN | FOR/AID
POLICY; A DOCUMENTARY ANALYSIS. USA+45 ECO/UNDEV | DIPLOM
ADMIN...ECOMETRIC STAT STYLE CHARTS PROG/TEAC | IDEA/COMP
GEN/LAWS ANTHOL. PAGE 8 B0172

PROGRAMMED INSTRUCTION....SEE PROG/TEAC

PROGRAMMING....SEE COMPUTER

PROGRSV/M....PROGRESSIVE MOVEMENT (ALL NATIONS)

B63
CROUCH W.W.,SOUTHERN CALIFORNIA METROPOLIS: A STUDY | LOC/G
IN DEVELOPMENT OF GOVERNMENT FOR A METROPOLITAN | MUNIC
AREA. USA+45 USA-45 PROB/SOLV ADMIN LOBBY PARTIC | LEGIS
CENTRAL ORD/FREE PWR...BIBLIOG 20 PROGRSV/M. | DECISION
PAGE 25 B0510

PROJ/TEST....PROJECTIVE TESTS

PROJECTION....SEE DISPL

PROPAGANDA....SEE EDU/PROP

PROPERTY TAX....SEE PROPERTY/TX

PROPERTY/TX....PROPERTY TAX

PROSTITUTN....SEE ALSO SEX + CRIME

PROTECTIONISM....SEE PROTECTNSM

PROTECTNSM....PROTECTIONISM

PROTEST....SEE COERCE

PROTESTANT....PROTESTANTS, PROTESTANTISM

PROUDHON/P....PIERRE JOSEPH PROUDHON

PROVS....STATE AND PROVINCES

BULLETIN OF THE PUBLIC AFFAIRS INFORMATION SERVICE. BIBLIOG
WOR+45 WOR-45 ECO/UNDEV FINAN LABOR LOC/G PROVS NAT/G
TEC/DEV DIPLOM EDU/PROP SOC. PAGE 1 B0010 ECO/DEV
   N ADMIN

FAUNT J.R.,A CHECKLIST OF SOUTH CAROLINA STATE BIBLIOG
PUBLICATIONS. USA+45 CONSTN LEGIS ADMIN ATTIT 20. PROVS
PAGE 35 B0708 LOC/G
   N GOV/REL

KENTUCKY STATE ARCHIVES,CHECKLIST OF KENTUCKY STATE BIBLIOG/A
PUBLICATIONS AND STATE DIRECTORY. USA+45 LAW ACADEM PROVS
EX/STRUC LEGIS EDU/PROP LEAD...JURID 20. PAGE 59 PUB/INST
B1196 ADMIN
   N

MARTIN W.O. JR.,STATE OF LOUISIANA OFFICIAL BIBLIOG
PUBLICATIONS. USA+45 USA-45 LEGIS ADMIN LEAD 19/20. PROVS
PAGE 70 B1415 GOV/REL
   N

STATE OF ILLINOIS,PUBLICATIONS OF THE STATE OF BIBLIOG
ILLINOIS. USA+45 FINAN POL/PAR ADMIN LEAD 20 PROVS
ILLINOIS. PAGE 100 B2024 LOC/G
   N GOV/REL

US SUPERINTENDENT OF DOCUMENTS,INTERSTATE COMMERCE BIBLIOG/A
(PRICE LIST 59). USA+45 LAW LOC/G NAT/G LEGIS DIST/IND
TARIFFS TAX ADMIN CONTROL HEALTH DECISION. PAGE 111 GOV/REL
B2239 PROVS
   N

VIRGINIA STATE LIBRARY,CHECK-LIST OF VIRGINIA STATE BIBLIOG/A
PUBLICATIONS. USA+45 USA-45 ECO/DEV POL/PAR LEGIS PROVS
ADJUD LEAD 18/20. PAGE 112 B2265 ADMIN
   N GOV/REL

GOODNOW F.J.,THE PRINCIPLES OF THE ADMINISTRATIVE ADMIN
LAW OF THE UNITED STATES. USA-45 LAW STRUCT NAT/G
EX/STRUC LEGIS BAL/PWR CONTROL GOV/REL PWR...JURID PROVS
19/20 CIVIL/SERV. PAGE 41 B0822 LOC/G
   B05

HAASE A.R.,INDEX OF ECONOMIC MATERIAL IN DOCUMENTS BIBLIOG
OF STATES OF THE UNITED STATES (13 VOLS.). USA-45 ECO/DEV
NAT/G GOV/REL...POLICY 18/20. PAGE 45 B0911 PROVS
   B07 ADMIN

WILSON W.,CONSTITUTIONAL GOVERNMENT IN THE UNITED NAT/G
STATES. USA-45 LAW POL/PAR PROVS CHIEF LEGIS GOV/REL
BAL/PWR ADJUD EXEC FEDERAL PWR 18/20 SUPREME/CT CONSTN
HOUSE/REP SENATE. PAGE 117 B2362 PARL/PROC
   B08

HARLOW R.V.,THE HISTORY OF LEGISLATIVE METHODS IN LEGIS
THE PERIOD BEFORE 1825. USA-45 EX/STRUC ADMIN DELIB/GP
COLONIAL LEAD PARL/PROC ROUTINE...GP/COMP GOV/COMP PROVS
HOUSE/REP. PAGE 47 B0948 POL/PAR
   B17

ABERNATHY B.R.,SOME PERSISTING QUESTIONS CONCERNING PROVS
THE CONSTITUTIONAL STATE EXECUTIVE (PAMPHLET). EX/STRUC
CONSTN TOP/EX TEC/DEV GOV/REL EFFICIENCY TIME 20 PROB/SOLV
GOVERNOR. PAGE 3 B0054 PWR
   N19

ANDERSON W.,THE UNITS OF GOVERNMENT IN THE UNITED LOC/G
STATES (PAMPHLET). USA-45 NAT/G PROVS EFFICIENCY CENSUS
...CHARTS 20. PAGE 5 B0098 ADMIN
   N19 GOV/REL

BURRUS B.R.,INVESTIGATION AND DISCOVERY IN STATE NAT/G
ANTITRUST (PAMPHLET). USA+45 USA-45 LEGIS ECO/TAC PROVS
ADMIN CONTROL CT/SYS CRIME GOV/REL PWR...JURID LAW
CHARTS 19/20 FTC MONOPOLY. PAGE 17 B0355 INSPECT
   N19

WRIGHT D.S.,AMERICAN STATE ADMINISTRATORS QU
(PAMPHLET). USA+45 ATTIT PERSON...SAMP/SIZ CHARTS TOP/EX
SOC/EXP METH 20. PAGE 118 B2379 ADMIN
   PROVS

BLACHLY F.F.,"THE GOVERNMENT AND ADMINISTRATION OF NAT/G
GERMANY." GERMANY CONSTN LOC/G PROVS DELIB/GP GOV/REL
EX/STRUC FORCES LEGIS TOP/EX CT/SYS...BIBLIOG/A ADMIN
19/20. PAGE 12 B0246 PHIL/SCI
   B21

BRYCE J.,MODERN DEMOCRACIES. FUT NEW/ZEALND USA-45 NAT/G
LAW CONSTN POL/PAR PROVS VOL/ASSN EX/STRUC LEGIS TREND
LEGIT CT/SYS EXEC KNOWL CONGRESS AUSTRAL 20.
PAGE 16 B0332
   B25

MATHEWS J.M.,AMERICAN STATE GOVERNMENT. USA-45 PROVS
LOC/G CHIEF EX/STRUC LEGIS ADJUD CONTROL CT/SYS ADMIN
ROUTINE GOV/REL PWR 20 GOVERNOR. PAGE 71 B1426 FEDERAL
   CONSTN

   B27

WILLOUGHBY W.F.,PRINCIPLES OF PUBLIC ADMINISTRATION NAT/G
WITH SPECIAL REFERENCE TO THE NATIONAL AND STATE EX/STRUC
GOVERNMENTS OF THE UNITED STATES. FINAN PROVS CHIEF OP/RES
CONSULT LEGIS CREATE BUDGET EXEC ROUTINE GOV/REL ADMIN

CENTRAL...MGT 20 BUR/BUDGET CONGRESS PRESIDENT.
PAGE 117 B2356
   B28

HALL W.P.,EMPIRE TO COMMONWEALTH. FUT WOR-45 CONSTN VOL/ASSN
ECO/DEV ECO/UNDEV INT/ORG PROVS PLAN DIPLOM NAT/G
EDU/PROP ADMIN COLONIAL PEACE PERSON ALL/VALS UK
...POLICY GEOG SOC OBS RECORD TREND CMN/WLTH
PARLIAMENT 19/20. PAGE 46 B0925
   S30

CRAWFORD F.G.,"THE EXECUTIVE BUDGET DECISION IN NEW LEAD
YORK." LEGIS EXEC PWR NEW/YORK. PAGE 25 B0504 BUDGET
   PROVS
   PROB/SOLV
   B35

GREER S.,BIBLIOGRAPHY ON CIVIL SERVICE AND BIBLIOG/A
PERSONNEL ADMINISTRATION. USA-45 LOC/G PROVS WORKER ADMIN
PRICE SENIOR DRIVE...MGT 20. PAGE 43 B0870 NAT/G
   ROUTINE
   B36

GRAVES W.B.,AMERICAN STATE GOVERNMENT. CONSTN FINAN NAT/G
EX/STRUC FORCES LEGIS BUDGET TAX CT/SYS REPRESENT PROVS
GOV/REL...BIBLIOG/A 19/20. PAGE 42 B0855 ADMIN
   FEDERAL
   B38

MACDONALD G.E.,CHECK LIST OF LEGISLATIVE JOURNALS BIBLIOG
OF THE STATES OF THE UNITED STATES OF AMERICA. PROVS
USA-45 ADMIN GOV/REL ATTIT...POLICY 18/20. PAGE 67 LEGIS
B1356 LOC/G
   B38

SALTER J.T.,THE AMERICAN POLITICIAN. USA-45 LABOR BIOG
POL/PAR EDU/PROP ADMIN CHOOSE ATTIT DRIVE PERSON LEAD
PWR...POLICY ANTHOL 20 THOMAS/N LEWIS/JL LAGUARD/F PROVS
GOVERNOR MAYOR. PAGE 92 B1865 LOC/G
   B39

ANDERSON W.,LOCAL GOVERNMENT IN EUROPE. FRANCE GOV/COMP
GERMANY ITALY UK USSR MUNIC PROVS ADMIN GOV/REL NAT/COMP
CENTRAL SOVEREIGN 20. PAGE 5 B0099 LOC/G
   CONSTN
   B40

PATTERSON C.P.,STATE AND LOCAL GOVERNMENT IN TEXAS CONSTN
(3RD ED.). USA-45 EX/STRUC LEGIS CT/SYS CHOOSE 20 PROVS
TEXAS. PAGE 81 B1642 GOV/REL
   LOC/G
   B40

WILCOX J.K.,MANUAL ON THE USE OF STATE BIBLIOG/A
PUBLICATIONS. USA-45 FINAN LEGIS TAX GOV/REL PROVS
...CHARTS 20. PAGE 116 B2346 ADMIN
   LAW
   B42

BROWN A.D.,LIST OF REFERENCES ON THE CIVIL SERVICE BIBLIOG
AND PERSONNEL ADMINISTRATION IN THE UNITED STATES ADMIN
(2ND MIMEOGRAPHED SUPPLEMENT). USA-45 LOC/G POL/PAR MGT
PROVS FEDERAL...TESTS 20. PAGE 16 B0319 NAT/G
   B43

CLARKE M.P.,PARLIAMENTARY PRIVILEGE IN THE AMERICAN LEGIS
COLONIES. PROVS DOMIN ADMIN REPRESENT GOV/REL PWR
ORD/FREE...BIBLIOG/A 17/18. PAGE 21 B0433 COLONIAL
   PARL/PROC
   B47

JENKINS W.S.,COLLECTED PUBLIC DOCUMENTS OF THE BIBLIOG
STATES: A CHECK LIST. USA-45 ECO/DEV NAT/G ADMIN PROVS
GOV/REL 20. PAGE 56 B1129 LEGIS
   TOP/EX
   B47

PUBLIC ADMINISTRATION SERVICE,CURRENT RESEARCH BIBLIOG
PROJECTS IN PUBLIC ADMINISTRATION (PAMPHLET). LAW R+D
CONSTN COM/IND LABOR LOC/G MUNIC PROVS ACT/RES MGT
DIPLOM RECEIVE EDU/PROP WAR 20. PAGE 85 B1716 ADMIN

CALDWELL L.K.,"STRENGTHENING STATE LEGISLATURES" PROVS
FUT DELIB/GP WEALTH REFORMERS. PAGE 18 B0364 LEGIS
   ROUTINE
   BUDGET
   B48

HULL C.,THE MEMOIRS OF CORDELL HULL (VOLUME ONE). BIOG
USA-45 WOR-45 CONSTN FAM LOC/G NAT/G PROVS DELIB/GP DIPLOM
FORCES LEGIS TOP/EX BAL/PWR LEGIT ADMIN EXEC WAR
ATTIT ORD/FREE PWR...MAJORIT SELF/OBS TIME/SEQ
TREND NAZI 20. PAGE 52 B1062
   B48

STOKES W.S.,BIBLIOGRAPHY OF STANDARD AND CLASSICAL BIBLIOG
WORKS IN THE FIELDS OF AMERICAN POLITICAL SCIENCE. NAT/G
USA+45 USA-45 POL/PAR PROVS FORCES DIPLOM ADMIN LOC/G
CT/SYS APPORT 20 CONGRESS PRESIDENT. PAGE 101 B2043 CONSTN
   C48

BOLLENS J.C.,"THE PROBLEM OF GOVERNMENT IN THE SAN USA+45
FRANCISCO BAY REGION." INDUS PROVS ADMIN GOV/REL MUNIC
...SOC CHARTS BIBLIOG 20. PAGE 13 B0270 LOC/G
   PROB/SOLV
   C48

WALKER H.,"THE LEGISLATIVE PROCESS; LAWMAKING IN PARL/PROC
THE UNITED STATES." NAT/G POL/PAR PROVS EX/STRUC LEGIS
OP/RES PROB/SOLV CT/SYS LOBBY GOV/REL...CHARTS LAW
BIBLIOG T 18/20 CONGRESS. PAGE 113 B2279 CONSTN
   N48

YATES M.,ADMINISTRATIVE REORGANIZATION OF STATE BIBLIOG

GOVERNMENTS: A BIBLIOGRAPHY (PAMPHLET). USA+45 LOC/G
USA-45 CONSTN OP/RES PLAN CONFER...POLICY 20. ADMIN
PAGE 118 B2390 PROVS
B50

BROWN E.S.,MANUAL OF GOVERNMENT PUBLICATIONS. BIBLIOG/A
WOR+45 WOR-45 CONSTN INT/ORG MUNIC PROVS DIPLOM NAT/G
ADMIN 20. PAGE 16 B0322 LAW
B50

JENKINS W.S.,A GUIDE TO THE MICROFILM COLLECTION OF BIBLIOG
EARLY STATE RECORDS. USA+45 CONSTN MUNIC LEGIS PROVS
PRESS ADMIN CT/SYS 18/20. PAGE 56 B1130 AUD/VIS
B50

LITTLE HOOVER COMM,HOW TO ACHIEVE GREATER TOP/EX
EFFICIENCY AND ECONOMY IN MINNESOTA'S GOVERNMENT LOC/G
(PAMPHLET). PLAN BUDGET ADMIN CHOOSE EFFICIENCY GOV/REL
ALL/VALS 20 MINNESOTA. PAGE 66 B1327 PROVS
B50

MONTGOMERY H.,CRACKER PARTIES. CULTURE EX/STRUC POL/PAR
LEAD PWR POPULISM...TIME/SEQ 19 GEORGIA CALHOUN/JC PROVS
COBB/HOWLL JACKSON/A. PAGE 74 B1505 ELITES
BIOG
C50

WAGER P.W.,"COUNTY GOVERNMENT ACROSS THE NATION." LOC/G
USA+45 CONSTN COM/IND FINAN SCHOOL DOMIN CT/SYS PROVS
LEAD GOV/REL...STAT BIBLIOG 20. PAGE 112 B2272 ADMIN
ROUTINE
B51

ANDERSON W.,STATE AND LOCAL GOVERNMENT IN THE LOC/G
UNITED STATES. USA+45 CONSTN POL/PAR EX/STRUC LEGIS MUNIC
BUDGET TAX ADJUD CT/SYS CHOOSE...CHARTS T 20. PROVS
PAGE 5 B0100 GOV/REL
B51

ANDERSON W.,GOVERNMENT IN THE FIFTY STATES. LAW LOC/G
CONSTN FINAN POL/PAR LEGIS EDU/PROP ADJUD ADMIN PROVS
CT/SYS CHOOSE...CHARTS 20. PAGE 5 B0101 GOV/REL
B52

LEGISLATIVE REFERENCE SERVICE,PROBLEMS OF BIBLIOG
LEGISLATIVE APPORTIONMENT ON BOTH FEDERAL AND STATE REPRESENT
LEVELS: SELECTED REFERENCES (PAMPHLET). USA+45 CHOOSE
USA-45 LOC/G NAT/G LEGIS WRITING ADMIN APPORT 20 PROVS
CONGRESS. PAGE 63 B1282
S52

RICH B.M.,"ADMINISTRATION REORGANIZATION IN NEW ADMIN
JERSEY" (BMR)" USA+45 DELIB/GP EX/STRUC WORKER CONSTN
OP/RES BUDGET 20 NEW/JERSEY. PAGE 88 B1772 PROB/SOLV
PROVS
S52

SNIDER C.F.,"AMERICAN COUNTY GOVERNMENT: A MID- LOC/G
CENTURY REVIEW" (BMR)" USA+45 USA-45 PROVS DELIB/GP ADMIN
EX/STRUC BUDGET TAX PWR 20. PAGE 98 B1988 GOV/REL
REGION
B53

A BIBLIOGRAPHY AND SUBJECT INDEX OF PUBLICATIONS OF BIBLIOG
FLORIDA STATE AGENCIES. USA+45 LOC/G LEAD ATTIT 20 PROVS
FLORIDA. PAGE 2 B0036 GOV/REL
ADMIN
B53

TOMPKINS D.C.,CIVIL DEFENSE IN THE STATES: A BIBLIOG
BIBLIOGRAPHY (DEFENSE BIBLIOGRAPHIES NO. 3; WAR
PAMPHLET). USA+45 LABOR LOC/G NAT/G PROVS LEGIS. ORD/FREE
PAGE 105 B2115 ADMIN
S53

BOSWORTH K.A.,"THE POLITICS OF MANAGEMENT PWR
IMPROVEMENT IN THE STATES" USA+45 POLICY. PAGE 14 PROVS
B0280 LEGIS
EXEC
B54

BINANI G.D.,INDIA AT A GLANCE (REV. ED.). INDIA INDEX
COM/IND FINAN INDUS LABOR PROVS SCHOOL PLAN DIPLOM CON/ANAL
INT/TRADE ADMIN...JURID 20. PAGE 12 B0238 NAT/G
ECO/UNDEV
B54

PUBLIC ADMIN CLEARING HOUSE,PUBLIC ADMINISTRATIONS INDEX
ORGANIZATIONS: A DIRECTORY, 1954. USA+45 R+D PROVS VOL/ASSN
ACT/RES...MGT 20. PAGE 85 B1714 NAT/G
ADMIN
B54

SCHWARTZ B.,FRENCH ADMINISTRATIVE LAW AND THE JURID
COMMON-LAW WORLD. FRANCE CULTURE LOC/G NAT/G PROVS LAW
DELIB/GP EX/STRUC LEGIS PROB/SOLV CT/SYS EXEC METH/COMP
GOV/REL...IDEA/COMP ENGLSH/LAW. PAGE 95 B1912 ADJUD
B54

SHELTON W.L.,CHECKLIST OF NEW MEXICO PUBLICATIONS, BIBLIOG
1850-1953. USA+45 USA-45 LEGIS ADMIN LEAD 19/20. PROVS
PAGE 96 B1941 GOV/REL
B54

THORNTON M.L.,OFFICIAL PUBLICATIONS OF THE COLONY BIBLIOG
AND STATE OF NORTH CAROLINA, 1749-1939. USA+45 ADMIN
USA-45 LEGIS LEAD GOV/REL ATTIT 18/20. PAGE 104 PROVS
B2109 ACADEM
B54

TOMPKINS D.C.,STATE GOVERNMENT AND ADMINISTRATION: BIBLIOG/A
A BIBLIOGRAPHY. USA+45 USA-45 CONSTN LEGIS JUDGE LOC/G
BUDGET CT/SYS LOBBY...CHARTS 20. PAGE 105 B2116 PROVS
ADMIN

C54

CALDWELL L.K.,"THE GOVERNMENT AND ADMINISTRATION OF PROVS
NEW YORK." LOC/G MUNIC POL/PAR SCHOOL CHIEF LEGIS ADMIN
PLAN TAX CT/SYS...MGT SOC/WK BIBLIOG 20 NEWYORK/C. CONSTN
PAGE 18 B0366 EX/STRUC
C54

ZELLER B.,"AMERICAN STATE LEGISLATURES: REPORT ON REPRESENT
THE COMMITTEE ON AMERICAN LEGISLATURES." CONSTN LEGIS
POL/PAR EX/STRUC CONFER ADMIN CONTROL EXEC LOBBY PROVS
ROUTINE GOV/REL...POLICY BIBLIOG 20. PAGE 119 B2401 APPORT
B55

CHAPMAN B.,THE PREFECTS AND PROVINCIAL FRANCE. ADMIN
FRANCE DELIB/GP WORKER ROLE PWR 19/20 PREFECT. PROVS
PAGE 20 B0408 EX/STRUC
LOC/G
B55

GUAITA A.,BIBLIOGRAFIA ESPANOLA DE DERECHO BIBLIOG
ADMINISTRATIVO (PAMPHLET). SPAIN LOC/G MUNIC NAT/G ADMIN
PROVS JUDGE BAL/PWR GOV/REL OWN...JURID 18/19. CONSTN
PAGE 44 B0900 PWR
B55

PULLEN W.R.,A CHECK LIST OF LEGISLATIVE JOURNALS BIBLIOG
ISSUED SINCE 1937 BY THE STATES OF THE UNITED PROVS
STATES OF AMERICA (PAMPHLET). USA+45 USA-45 LAW EDU/PROP
WRITING ADJUD ADMIN...JURID 20. PAGE 85 B1720 LEGIS
B55

ZABEL O.H.,GOD AND CAESAR IN NEBRASKA: A STUDY OF SECT
LEGAL RELATIONSHIP OF CHURCH AND STATE, 1854-1954. PROVS
TAX GIVE ADMIN CONTROL GP/REL ROLE...GP/COMP 19/20 LAW
NEBRASKA. PAGE 119 B2396 EDU/PROP
B56

GLADDEN E.N.,CIVIL SERVICE OR BUREAUCRACY? UK LAW ADMIN
STRATA LABOR TOP/EX PLAN SENIOR AUTOMAT CONTROL GOV/REL
PARTIC CHOOSE HAPPINESS...CHARTS 19/20 CIVIL/SERV EFFICIENCY
BUREAUCRCY. PAGE 40 B0808 PROVS
B56

HOWARD L.V.,TULANE STUDIES IN POLITICAL SCIENCE: ADMIN
CIVIL SERVICE DEVELOPMENT IN LOUISIANA VOLUME 3. GOV/REL
LAW POL/PAR LEGIS CT/SYS ADJUST ORD/FREE...STAT PROVS
CHARTS 19/20 LOUISIANA CIVIL/SERV. PAGE 52 B1050 POLICY
B56

RANSONE C.B.,THE OFFICE OF GOVERNOR IN THE UNITED PROVS
STATES. USA+45 ADMIN...MGT INT CHARTS 20 GOVERNOR. TOP/EX
PAGE 86 B1732 POL/PAR
EX/STRUC
S56

GORE W.J.,"ADMINISTRATIVE DECISION-MAKING IN DECISION
FEDERAL FIELD OFFICES." USA+45 PROVS PWR CONT/OBS. PROB/SOLV
PAGE 41 B0833 FEDERAL
ADMIN
S56

HEADY F.,"THE MICHIGAN DEPARTMENT OF ADMIN
ADMINISTRATION: A CASE STUDY IN THE POLITICS OF DELIB/GP
ADMINISTRATION" (BMR)" USA+45 POL/PAR PROVS CHIEF LOC/G
LEGIS GP/REL ATTIT 20 MICHIGAN. PAGE 48 B0980
B57

BABCOCK R.S.,STATE & LOCAL GOVERNMENT AND POLITICS. PROVS
USA+45 CONSTN POL/PAR EX/STRUC LEGIS BUDGET LOBBY LOC/G
CHOOSE SUFF...CHARTS T 20. PAGE 8 B0154 GOV/REL
B57

CHICAGO U LAW SCHOOL,CONFERENCE ON JUDICIAL CT/SYS
ADMINISTRATION. LOC/G MUNIC NAT/G PROVS...ANTHOL ADJUD
20. PAGE 21 B0421 ADMIN
GOV/REL
B58

HENKIN L.,ARMS CONTROL AND INSPECTION IN AMERICAN USA+45
LAW. LAW CONSTN INT/ORG LOC/G MUNIC NAT/G PROVS JURID
EDU/PROP LEGIT EXEC NUC/PWR KNOWL ORD/FREE...OBS ARMS/CONT
TOT/POP CONGRESS 20. PAGE 49 B0990
B58

SPITZ D.,DEMOCRACY AND THE CHALLANGE OF POWER. FUT NAT/G
USA+45 USA-45 LAW CONSTN INT/ORG LOC/G POL/PAR PWR
PROVS DELIB/GP EX/STRUC LEGIS TOP/EX ACT/RES CREATE
DOMIN EDU/PROP LEGIT ADJUD ADMIN ATTIT DRIVE MORAL
ORD/FREE TOT/POP. PAGE 99 B2010
S58

DAHL R.A.,"A CRITIQUE OF THE RULING ELITE MODEL." CONCPT
USA+45 LOC/G MUNIC NAT/G POL/PAR PROVS DOMIN LEGIT STERTYP
ADMIN...METH/CNCPT HYPO/EXP. PAGE 25 B0520 ELITES
S58

DERGE D.R.,"METROPOLITAN AND OUTSTATE ALIGNMENTS IN LEGIS
ILLINOIS AND MISSOURI LEGISLATIVE DELEGATIONS" MUNIC
(BMR)" USA+45 ADMIN PARTIC GOV/REL...MYTH CHARTS 20 PROVS
ILLINOIS MISSOURI. PAGE 28 B0575 POL/PAR
B59

BHAMBHRI C.P.,SUBSTANCE OF HINDU POLITY. INDIA GOV/REL
S/ASIA LAW EX/STRUC JUDGE TAX COERCE GP/REL WRITING
POPULISM 20 HINDU. PAGE 11 B0234 SECT
PROVS
B59

COUNCIL OF STATE GOVERNMENTS,STATE GOVERNMENT: AN BIBLIOG/A
ANNOTATED BIBLIOGRAPHY (PAMPHLET). USA+45 LAW AGRI PROVS
INDUS WORKER PLAN TAX ADJUST AGE/Y ORD/FREE...HEAL LOC/G
MGT 20. PAGE 24 B0494 ADMIN
B59

COUNCIL OF STATE GOVERNORS,AMERICAN LEGISLATURES: LEGIS

STRUCTURE AND PROCEDURES. SUMMARY AND TABULATIONS OF A 1959 SURVEY. PUERT/RICO USA+45 PAY ADJUD ADMIN APPORT...IDEA/COMP 20 GUAM VIRGIN/ISL. PAGE 24 B0495
CHARTS PROVS REPRESENT
B59

ELAZAR D.J.,INTERGOVERNMENTAL RELATIONS IN NINETEENTH CENTURY AMERICAN FEDERALISM (DOCTORAL THESIS). USA-45 FINAN LOC/G NAT/G GP/REL 18/19. PAGE 33 B0662
FEDERAL ADMIN PROVS GOV/REL
B59

INDIAN INSTITUTE PUBLIC ADMIN,MORALE IN THE PUBLIC SERVICES: REPORT OF A CONFERENCE JAN., 3-4, 1959. INDIA S/ASIA ECO/UNDEV PROVS PLAN EDU/PROP CONFER GOV/REL EFFICIENCY DRIVE ROLE 20 CIVIL/SERV. PAGE 53 B1082
HAPPINESS ADMIN WORKER INGP/REL
B59

IPSEN H.P.,HAMBURGISCHES STAATS- UND VERWALTUNGSRECHT. CONSTN LOC/G FORCES BUDGET CT/SYS ...JURID 20 HAMBURG. PAGE 54 B1103
ADMIN PROVS LEGIS FINAN
B59

LEMBERG E.,DIE VERTRIEBENEN IN WESTDEUTSCHLAND (3 VOLS.). GERMANY/W CULTURE STRUCT AGRI PROVS ADMIN ...JURID 20 MIGRATION. PAGE 64 B1287
GP/REL INGP/REL SOCIETY
B59

MAASS A.,AREA AND POWER: A THEORY OF LOCAL GOVERNMENT. MUNIC PROVS EX/STRUC LEGIS CT/SYS CHOOSE PWR 20. PAGE 67 B1354
LOC/G FEDERAL BAL/PWR GOV/REL
B59

MOOS M.,THE CAMPUS AND THE STATE. LAW FINAN DELIB/GP LEGIS EXEC LOBBY GP/REL PWR...POLICY BIBLIOG. PAGE 75 B1517
EDU/PROP ACADEM PROVS CONTROL
B59

PARK R.L.,LEADERSHIP AND POLITICAL INSTITUTIONS IN INDIA. S/ASIA CULTURE ECO/UNDEV LOC/G MUNIC PROVS LEGIS PLAN ADMIN LEAD ORD/FREE WEALTH...GEOG SOC BIOG TOT/POP VAL/FREE 20. PAGE 81 B1633
NAT/G EXEC INDIA
B59

SURRENCY E.C.,A GUIDE TO LEGAL RESEARCH. USA+45 ACADEM LEGIS ACT/RES ADMIN...DECISION METH/COMP BIBLIOG METH. PAGE 102 B2055
NAT/G PROVS ADJUD JURID
B59

U OF MICHIGAN LAW SCHOOL,ATOMS AND THE LAW. USA+45 PROVS WORKER PROB/SOLV DIPLOM ADMIN GOV/REL ANTHOL. PAGE 106 B2142
NUC/PWR NAT/G CONTROL LAW
B60

ADRIAN C.R.,STATE AND LOCAL GOVERNMENTS: A STUDY IN THE POLITICAL PROCESS. USA+45 LAW FINAN MUNIC POL/PAR LEGIS ADJUD EXEC CHOOSE REPRESENT. PAGE 3 B0060
LOC/G PROVS GOV/REL ATTIT
B60

FRYE R.J.,GOVERNMENT AND LABOR: THE ALABAMA PROGRAM. USA+45 INDUS R+D LABOR WORKER BUDGET EFFICIENCY AGE/Y HEALTH...CHARTS 20 ALABAMA. PAGE 38 B0761
ADMIN LEGIS LOC/G PROVS
B60

GILMORE D.R.,DEVELOPING THE "LITTLE" ECONOMIES. USA+45 FINAN LG/CO PROF/ORG VOL/ASSN CREATE ADMIN. PAGE 40 B0801
ECO/TAC LOC/G PROVS PLAN
B60

HAUSER O.,PREUSSISCHE STAATSRASON UND NATIONALER GEDANKE. PRUSSIA SOCIETY PRESS ADMIN...CONCPT 19/20. PAGE 48 B0969
NAT/LISM NAT/G ATTIT PROVS
B60

WEIDNER E.W.,INTERGOVERNMENTAL RELATIONS AS SEEN BY PUBLIC OFFICIALS. USA+45 PROVS EX/STRUC EXEC FEDERAL...QU 20. PAGE 115 B2311
ATTIT GP/REL GOV/REL ADMIN
B60

AVERY M.W.,GOVERNMENT OF WASHINGTON STATE. USA+45 MUNIC DELIB/GP EX/STRUC LEGIS GIVE CT/SYS PARTIC REGION EFFICIENCY 20 WASHINGT/G GOVERNOR. PAGE 7 B0151
PROVS LOC/G ADMIN GOV/REL
B61

BEASLEY K.E.,STATE SUPERVISION OF MUNICIPAL DEBT IN KANSAS - A CASE STUDY. USA+45 USA-45 FINAN PROVS BUDGET TAX ADJUD ADMIN CONTROL SUPEGO. PAGE 10 B0201
MUNIC LOC/G LEGIS JURID
B61

BURDETTE F.L.,POLITICAL SCIENCE: A SELECTED BIBLIOGRAPHY OF BOOKS IN PRINT, WITH ANNOTATIONS (PAMPHLET). LAW LOC/G NAT/G POL/PAR PROVS DIPLOM EDU/PROP ADMIN CHOOSE ATTIT 20. PAGE 17 B0347
BIBLIOG/A GOV/COMP CONCPT ROUTINE
B61

DARRAH E.L.,FIFTY STATE GOVERNMENTS: A COMPILATION OF EXECUTIVE ORGANIZATION CHARTS. USA+45 LOC/G DELIB/GP LEGIS ADJUD LEAD PWR 20 GOVERNOR. PAGE 26 B0530
EX/STRUC ADMIN ORG/CHARTS PROVS
B61

DRURY J.W.,THE GOVERNMENT OF KANSAS. USA+45 AGRI
PROVS

INDUS CHIEF LEGIS WORKER PLAN BUDGET GIVE CT/SYS GOV/REL...T 20 KANSAS GOVERNOR CITY/MGT. PAGE 31 B0621
CONSTN ADMIN LOC/G
B61

MACRIDIS R.C.,COMPARATIVE POLITICS: NOTES AND READINGS. WOR+45 LOC/G MUNIC NAT/G PROVS VOL/ASSN EDU/PROP ADMIN ATTIT PERSON ORD/FREE...SOC CONCPT OBS RECORD TREND 20. PAGE 68 B1376
POL/PAR CHOOSE
B61

PAGE T.,STATE PERSONNEL REORGANIZATION IN ILLINOIS. USA+45 POL/PAR CHIEF TEC/DEV LEAD ADJUST 20. PAGE 80 B1625
ADMIN PROVS WORKER DELIB/GP
B61

ROMANO F.,CIVIL SERVICE AND PUBLIC EMPLOYEE LAW IN NEW JERSEY. CONSTN MUNIC WORKER GIVE PAY CHOOSE UTIL 20. PAGE 90 B1816
ADMIN PROVS ADJUD LOC/G
L61

GERWIG R.,"PUBLIC AUTHORITIES IN THE UNITED STATES." LAW CONSTN PROVS TAX ADMIN FEDERAL. PAGE 39 B0793
LOC/G MUNIC GOV/REL PWR
L61

MCNAMEE B.J.,"CONFLICT OF INTEREST: STATE GOVERNMENT EMPLOYEES." USA+45 PROVS 20. PAGE 72 B1457
LAW REPRESENT ADMIN CONTROL
B62

CARPER E.T.,ILLINOIS GOES TO CONGRESS FOR ARMY LAND. USA+45 LAW EXTR/IND PROVS REGION CIVMIL/REL GOV/REL FEDERAL ATTIT 20 ILLINOIS SENATE CONGRESS DIRKSEN/E DOUGLAS/P. PAGE 19 B0385
ADMIN LOBBY GEOG LEGIS
B62

EATON J.W.,STONE WALLS NOT A PRISON MAKE: THE ANATOMY OF PLANNED ADMINISTRATIVE CHANGE. USA+45 PROVS EDU/PROP 20. PAGE 32 B0647
CRIMLGY ADMIN EXEC POLICY
B62

FARBER W.O.,GOVERNMENT OF SOUTH DAKOTA. USA+45 DIST/IND POL/PAR CHIEF EX/STRUC LEGIS ECO/TAC GIVE EDU/PROP CT/SYS PARTIC...T 20 SOUTH/DAK GOVERNOR. PAGE 35 B0704
PROVS LOC/G ADMIN CONSTN
B62

FOSS P.O.,REORGANIZATION AND REASSIGNMENT IN THE CALIFORNIA HIGHWAY PATROL (PAMPHLET). USA+45 STRUCT WORKER EDU/PROP CONTROL COERCE INGP/REL ORD/FREE PWR...DECISION 20 CALIFORNIA. PAGE 37 B0744
FORCES ADMIN PROVS PLAN
B62

GOVERNORS CONF STATE PLANNING,STATE PLANNING: A POLICY STATEMENT (PAMPHLET). USA+45 LOC/G NAT/G DELIB/GP LEGIS EXEC 20 GOVERNOR. PAGE 42 B0847
GOV/REL PLAN ADMIN PROVS
B62

INSTITUTE JUDICIAL ADMIN,JUDGES: THEIR TEMPORARY APPOINTMENT, ASSIGNMENT AND TRANSFER: SURVEY OF FED AND STATE CONSTN'S STATUTES, ROLES OF CT. USA+45 CONSTN PROVS CT/SYS GOV/REL PWR JURID. PAGE 54 B1090
NAT/G LOC/G JUDGE ADMIN
B62

LITTLEFIELD N.,METROPOLITAN AREA PROBLEMS AND MUNICIPAL HOME RULE. USA+45 PROVS ADMIN CONTROL GP/REL PWR. PAGE 66 B1328
LOC/G SOVEREIGN JURID LEGIS
B62

LYNCH J.,ADMINISTRATION COLONIAL ESPANOLA 1782-1810. SPAIN PROVS TOP/EX PARTIC 18/19 ARGEN. PAGE 67 B1349
COLONIAL CONTROL ADJUD ADMIN
B62

MUKERJI S.N.,ADMINISTRATION OF EDUCATION IN INDIA. ACADEM LOC/G PROVS ROUTINE...POLICY STAT CHARTS 20. PAGE 76 B1536
SCHOOL ADMIN NAT/G EDU/PROP
B62

NEVINS A.,THE STATE UNIVERSITIES AND DEMOCRACY. AGRI FINAN SCHOOL ADMIN EXEC EFFICIENCY ATTIT. PAGE 78 B1576
ACADEM PROVS EDU/PROP POLICY
B62

NJ DEPARTMENT CIVIL SERV,THE CIVIL SERVICE RULES OF THE STATE OF NEW JERSEY. USA+45 USA-45 PAY...JURID ANTHOL 20 CIVIL/SERV NEW/JERSEY. PAGE 78 B1585
ADMIN PROVS ROUTINE WORKER
B62

PRESS C.,STATE MANUALS, BLUE BOOKS AND ELECTION RESULTS. LAW LOC/G MUNIC LEGIS WRITING FEDERAL SOVEREIGN...DECISION STAT CHARTS 20. PAGE 84 B1700
BIBLIOG PROVS ADMIN CHOOSE
B62

ROBINSON M.,THE COMING OF AGE OF THE LANGLEY PORTER CLINIC (PAMPHLET). USA+45 PROF/ORG PROVS PLAN...MGT PSY 20 CALIFORNIA LANGLEY. PAGE 89 B1804
PUB/INST ADMIN EFFICIENCY HEAL
B62

US ADVISORY COMN INTERGOV REL,STATE CONSTITUTIONAL
LOC/G

AND STATUTORY RESTRICTIONS UPON THE STRUCTURAL,
FUNCTIONAL, AND PERSONAL POWERS OF LOCAL GOV'T.
EX/STRUC ACT/RES DOMIN GOV/REL PWR...POLICY
DECISION 17/20. PAGE 108 B2172
CONSTN PROVS LAW
S62

MARTIN L.W.,"POLITICAL SETTLEMENTS AND ARMS
CONTROL." COM EUR+WWI GERMANY USA+45 PROVS FORCES
TOP/EX ACT/RES CREATE DOMIN LEGIT ROUTINE COERCE
ATTIT RIGID/FLEX ORD/FREE PWR...METH/CNCPT RECORD
GEN/LAWS 20. PAGE 70 B1410
CONCPT ARMS/CONT
S62

SPRINGER H.W.,"FEDERATION IN THE CARIBBEAN: AN
ATTEMPT THAT FAILED." L/A+17C ECO/UNDEV INT/ORG
POL/PAR PROVS LEGIS CREATE PLAN LEGIT ADMIN FEDERAL
ATTIT DRIVE PERSON ORD/FREE PWR...POLICY GEOG PSY
CONCPT OBS CARIBBEAN CMN/WLTH 20. PAGE 100 B2013
VOL/ASSN NAT/G REGION
N62

UNIVERSITY PITT INST LOC GOVT,THE COUNCIL-MANAGER
FORM OF GOVERNMENT IN PENNSYLVANIA (PAMPHLET).
PROVS EX/STRUC REPRESENT GOV/REL EFFICIENCY
...CHARTS SIMUL 20 PENNSYLVAN CITY/MGT. PAGE 107
B2169
LOC/G TOP/EX MUNIC PWR
B63

ADRIAN C.R.,GOVERNING OVER FIFTY STATES AND THEIR
COMMUNITIES. USA+45 CONSTN FINAN MUNIC NAT/G
POL/PAR EX/STRUC LEGIS ADMIN CONTROL CT/SYS
...CHARTS 20. PAGE 3 B0061
PROVS LOC/G GOV/REL GOV/COMP
B63

BOCK E.A., STATE AND LOCAL GOVERNMENT: A CASE BOOK.
USA+45 MUNIC PROVS CONSULT GP/REL ATTIT...MGT 20
CASEBOOK GOVERNOR MAYOR. PAGE 12 B0254
LOC/G ADMIN PROB/SOLV CHIEF
B63

BLONDEL J.,VOTERS, PARTIES, AND LEADERS. UK ELITES
LOC/G NAT/G PROVS ACT/RES DOMIN REPRESENT GP/REL
INGP/REL...SOC BIBLIOG 20. PAGE 12 B0255
POL/PAR STRATA LEGIS ADMIN
B63

BOCK E.A.,STATE AND LOCAL GOVERNMENT: A CASE BOOK.
USA+45 FINAN CHIEF PROB/SOLV TAX ATTIT...POLICY 20
CASEBOOK. PAGE 13 B0263
PROVS LOC/G ADMIN GOV/REL
B63

BURRUS B.R.,ADMINSTRATIVE LAW AND LOCAL GOVERNMENT.
USA+45 PROVS LEGIS LICENSE ADJUD ORD/FREE 20.
PAGE 17 B0356
EX/STRUC LOC/G JURID CONSTN
B63

COUNCIL STATE GOVERNMENTS,HANDBOOK FOR LEGISLATIVE
COMMITTEES. USA+45 LAW DELIB/GP EX/STRUC TOP/EX
CHOOSE PWR...METH/COMP 20. PAGE 24 B0496
LEGIS PARL/PROC PROVS ADJUD
B63

DUE J.F.,STATE SALES TAX ADMINISTRATION. OP/RES
BUDGET PAY ADMIN EXEC ROUTINE COST EFFICIENCY
PROFIT...CHARTS METH/COMP 20. PAGE 31 B0626
PROVS TAX STAT GOV/COMP
B63

FORTES A.B.,HISTORIA ADMINISTRATIVA, JUDICIARIA E
ECLESIASTICA DO RIO GRANDE DO SUL. BRAZIL L/A+17C
LOC/G SECT COLONIAL CT/SYS ORD/FREE CATHISM 16/20.
PAGE 37 B0742
PROVS ADMIN JURID
B63

GRANT D.R.,STATE AND LOCAL GOVERNMENT IN AMERICA.
USA+45 FINAN LOC/G MUNIC EX/STRUC FORCES EDU/PROP
ADMIN CHOOSE FEDERAL ATTIT...JURID 20. PAGE 42
B0853
PROVS POL/PAR LEGIS CONSTN
B63

HEARLE E.F.R.,A DATA PROCESSING SYSTEM FOR STATE
AND LOCAL GOVERNMENTS. PLAN TEC/DEV AUTOMAT ROUTINE
...MGT METH/CNCPT CLASSIF 20. PAGE 49 B0984
LOC/G PROVS COMPUTER COMPUT/IR
B63

HERMAN H.,NEW YORK STATE AND THE METROPOLITAN
PROBLEM. USA+45 ECO/DEV PUB/INST SCHOOL LEGIS PLAN
TAX EXEC PARL/PROC PARTIC...HEAL 20 NEW/YORK.
PAGE 49 B0992
GOV/REL PROVS LOC/G POLICY
B63

HERNDON J.,A SELECTED BIBLIOGRAPHY OF MATERIALS IN
STATE GOVERNMENT AND POLITICS (PAMPHLET). USA+45
POL/PAR LEGIS ADMIN CHOOSE MGT. PAGE 49 B0993
BIBLIOG GOV/COMP PROVS DECISION
B63

LEONARD T.J.,THE FEDERAL SYSTEM OF INDIA. INDIA
MUNIC NAT/G PROVS ADMIN SOVEREIGN...IDEA/COMP 20.
PAGE 64 B1293
FEDERAL MGT NAT/COMP METH/COMP
B63

LEWIS J.W.,LEADERSHIP IN COMMUNIST CHINA. ASIA
INTELL ECO/UNDEV LOC/G MUNIC NAT/G PROVS ECO/TAC
EDU/PROP LEGIT ADMIN COERCE ATTIT ORD/FREE PWR
...INT TIME/SEQ CHARTS TOT/POP VAL/FREE. PAGE 65
B1304
POL/PAR DOMIN ELITES
B63

LOCKARD D.,THE POLITICS OF STATE AND LOCAL
GOVERNMENT. USA+45 CONSTN EX/STRUC LEGIS CT/SYS
LOC/G PROVS

FEDERAL...CHARTS BIBLIOG 20. PAGE 66 B1334
OP/RES ADMIN
B63

PALOTAI O.C.,PUBLICATIONS OF THE INSTITUTE OF
GOVERNMENT, 1930-1962. LAW PROVS SCHOOL WORKER
ACT/RES OP/RES CT/SYS GOV/REL...CRIMLGY SOC/WK.
PAGE 81 B1629
BIBLIOG/A ADMIN LOC/G FINAN
B63

SMITH R.M.,STATE GOVERNMENT IN TRANSITION. USA+45
POL/PAR LEGIS PARL/PROC GOV/REL 20 PENNSYLVAN
GOVERNOR. PAGE 98 B1984
PROVS POLICY EX/STRUC PLAN
S63

BRZEZINSKI Z.K.,"CINCINNATUS AND THE APPARATCHIK."
COM USA+45 USA-45 ELITES LOC/G NAT/G PROVS CONSULT
LEGIS DOMIN LEGIT EXEC ROUTINE CHOOSE DRIVE PWR
SKILL...CONCPT CHARTS VAL/FREE COLD/WAR 20. PAGE 16
B0334
POL/PAR USSR
S63

NYE J.S. JR.,"EAST AFRICAN ECONOMIC INTEGRATION."
AFR UGANDA PROVS DELIB/GP PLAN ECO/TAC INT/TRADE
ADMIN ROUTINE ORD/FREE PWR WEALTH...OBS TIME/SEQ
VAL/FREE 20. PAGE 79 B1597
ECO/UNDEV INT/ORG
C63

CARLISLE D.,"PARTY LOYALTY; THE ELECTION PROCESS IN
SOUTH CAROLINA." USA+45 LOC/G ADMIN ATTIT...TREND
CHARTS BIBLIOG 17/20. PAGE 19 B0380
CHOOSE POL/PAR PROVS SUFF
B64

ALDERFER H.O.,LOCAL GOVERNMENT IN DEVELOPING
COUNTRIES. ASIA COM L/A+17C S/ASIA AGRI LOC/G MUNIC
PROVS DOMIN CHOOSE PWR...POLICY MGT CONCPT 20.
PAGE 3 B0070
ADMIN ROUTINE
B64

DAS M.N.,INDIA UNDER MORLEY AND MINTO. INDIA UK
ECO/UNDEV MUNIC PROVS EX/STRUC LEGIS DIPLOM CONTROL
REV 20 MORLEY/J. PAGE 26 B0531
GOV/REL COLONIAL POLICY ADMIN
B64

DIEBOLD J.,BEYOND AUTOMATION: MANAGERIAL PROBLEMS
OF AN EXPLODING TECHNOLOGY. SOCIETY ECO/DEV CREATE
ECO/TAC AUTOMAT SKILL...TECHNIC MGT WORK. PAGE 29
B0589
FUT INDUS PROVS NAT/G
B64

GOODNOW H.F.,THE CIVIL SERVICE OF PAKISTAN:
BUREAUCRACY IN A NEW NATION. INDIA PAKISTAN S/ASIA
ECO/UNDEV PROVS CHIEF PARTIC CHOOSE EFFICIENCY PWR
...BIBLIOG 20. PAGE 41 B0824
ADMIN GOV/REL LAW NAT/G
B64

KAACK H.,DIE PARTEIEN IN DER
VERFASSUNGSWIRKLICHKEIT DER BUNDESREPUBLIK.
GERMANY/W ADMIN PARL/PROC CHOOSE...JURID 20.
PAGE 57 B1157
POL/PAR PROVS NAT/G
B64

KEEFE W.J.,THE AMERICAN LEGISLATIVE PROCESS:
CONGRESS AND THE STATES. USA+45 LAW POL/PAR
DELIB/GP DEBATE ADMIN LOBBY REPRESENT CONGRESS
PRESIDENT. PAGE 59 B1187
LEGIS DECISION PWR PROVS
B64

KIESER P.J.,THE COST OF ADMINISTRATION, SUPERVISION
AND SERVICES IN URBAN BANTU TOWNSHIPS. SOUTH/AFR
SERV/IND MUNIC PROVS ADMIN COST...OBS QU CHARTS 20
BANTU. PAGE 60 B1203
AFR MGT FINAN
B64

OECD SEMINAR REGIONAL DEV,REGIONAL DEVELOPMENT IN
ISRAEL. ISRAEL STRUCT ECO/UNDEV NAT/G REGION...GEOG
20. PAGE 79 B1603
ADMIN PROVS PLAN METH/COMP
B64

PIERCE T.M.,FEDERAL, STATE, AND LOCAL GOVERNMENT IN
EDUCATION. FINAN LOC/G PROVS LEGIS PLAN EDU/PROP
ADMIN CONTROL CENTRAL COST KNOWL 20. PAGE 83 B1673
NAT/G POLICY SCHOOL GOV/REL
B64

RIGGS R.E.,THE MOVEMENT FOR ADMINISTRATIVE
REORGANIZATION IN ARIZONA. USA+45 LAW POL/PAR
DELIB/GP LEGIS PROB/SOLV CONTROL RIGID/FLEX PWR
...ORG/CHARTS 20 ARIZONA DEMOCRAT REPUBLICAN.
PAGE 88 B1786
ADMIN PROVS CREATE PLAN
B64

SHERIDAN R.G.,URBAN JUSTICE. USA+45 PROVS CREATE
ADMIN CT/SYS ORD/FREE 20 TENNESSEE. PAGE 96 B1943
LOC/G JURID ADJUD MUNIC
B64

TURNER H.A.,THE GOVERNMENT AND POLITICS OF
CALIFORNIA (2ND ED.). LAW FINAN MUNIC POL/PAR
SCHOOL EX/STRUC LEGIS LOBBY CHOOSE...CHARTS T 20
CALIFORNIA. PAGE 106 B2138
PROVS ADMIN LOC/G CONSTN
S64

CASE H.L.,"GORDON R. CLAPP: THE ROLE OF FAITH,
PURPOSES AND PEOPLE IN ADMINISTRATION." INDUS MUNIC
PROVS...POLICY 20. PAGE 19 B0391
ADMIN BIOG EX/STRUC DECISION
S64

EAKIN T.C.,"LEGISLATIVE POLITICS -- I AND II THE
PROVS

WESTERN STATES, 19581964" (SUPPLEMENT)" USA+45   LEGIS
POL/PAR SCHOOL CONTROL LOBBY CHOOSE AGE. PAGE 32   ROUTINE
B0641   STRUCT
                                      S64

NEEDHAM T.,"SCIENCE AND SOCIETY IN EAST AND WEST."   ASIA
INTELL STRATA R+D LOC/G NAT/G PROVS CONSULT ACT/RES   STRUCT
CREATE PLAN TEC/DEV EDU/PROP ADMIN ATTIT ALL/VALS
...POLICY RELATIV MGT CONCPT NEW/IDEA TIME/SEQ WORK
WORK. PAGE 77 B1565
                                       B65

ARTHUR D LITTLE INC,SAN FRANCISCO COMMUNITY RENEWAL   HABITAT
PROGRAM. USA+45 FINAN PROVS ADMIN INCOME...CHARTS   MUNIC
20 CALIFORNIA SAN/FRAN URBAN/RNWL. PAGE 7 B0138   PLAN
                                      PROB/SOLV
                                      B65

COHN H.J.,THE GOVERNMENT OF THE RHINE PALATINATE IN   PROVS
THE FIFTEENTH CENTURY. GERMANY FINAN LOC/G DELIB/GP   JURID
LEGIS CT/SYS CHOOSE CATHISM 14/15 PALATINATE.   GP/REL
PAGE 22 B0449   ADMIN
                                      B65

COOPER F.E.,STATE ADMINISTRATIVE LAW (2 VOLS.). LAW   JURID
LEGIS PLAN TAX ADJUD CT/SYS FEDERAL PWR...CONCPT   CONSTN
20. PAGE 23 B0474   ADMIN
                                      PROVS
                                      B65

FISCHER F.C.,THE GOVERNMENT OF MICHIGAN. USA+45   PROVS
NAT/G PUB/INST EX/STRUC LEGIS BUDGET GIVE EDU/PROP   LOC/G
CT/SYS CHOOSE GOV/REL...T MICHIGAN. PAGE 36 B0723   ADMIN
                                      CONSTN
                                      B65

GOODSELL C.T.,ADMINISTRATION OF A REVOLUTION.   EXEC
PUERT/RICO ECO/UNDEV FINAN MUNIC POL/PAR PROVS   SOC
LEGIS PLAN BUDGET RECEIVE ADMIN COLONIAL LEAD 20
ROOSEVLT/F. PAGE 41 B0827
                                       B65

KAAS L.,DIE GEISTLICHE GERICHTSBARKEIT DER   JURID
KATHOLISCHEN KIRCHE IN PREUSSEN (2 VOLS.). PRUSSIA   CATHISM
CONSTN NAT/G PROVS SECT ADJUD ADMIN ATTIT 16/20.   GP/REL
PAGE 57 B1158   CT/SYS
                                      B65

MUSHKIN S.J.,STATE PROGRAMMING. USA+45 PLAN BUDGET   PROVS
TAX ADMIN REGION GOV/REL...BIBLIOG 20. PAGE 77   POLICY
B1549   CREATE
                                      ECO/DEV
                                      B65

PARRISH W.E.,MISSOURI UNDER RADICAL RULE 1865-1870.   PROVS
USA-45 SOCIETY INDUS LOC/G POL/PAR WORKER EDU/PROP   ADMIN
SUFF INGP/REL ATTIT...BIBLIOG 19 NEGRO MISSOURI.   RACE/REL
PAGE 81 B1635   ORD/FREE
                                      B65

PYLEE M.V.,CONSTITUTIONAL GOVERNMENT IN INDIA (2ND   CONSTN
REV. ED.). INDIA POL/PAR EX/STRUC DIPLOM COLONIAL   NAT/G
CT/SYS PARL/PROC PRIVIL...JURID 16/20. PAGE 85   PROVS
B1725   FEDERAL
                                      B65

REDFORD D.R.,POLITICS AND GOVERNMENT IN THE UNITED   NAT/G
STATES. USA+45 USA-45 LOC/G PROVS FORCES DIPLOM   POL/PAR
CT/SYS LOBBY...JURID SUPREME/CT PRESIDENT. PAGE 87   EX/STRUC
B1751   LEGIS
                                      B65

SHARMA S.A.,PARLIAMENTARY GOVERNMENT IN INDIA.   NAT/G
INDIA FINAN LOC/G PROVS DELIB/GP PLAN ADMIN CT/SYS   CONSTN
FEDERAL...JURID 20. PAGE 96 B1936   PARL/PROC
                                      LEGIS
                                      B65

SNIDER C.F.,AMERICAN STATE AND LOCAL GOVERNMENT.   GOV/REL
USA+45 FINAN CHIEF EX/STRUC TAX ADMIN CONTROL SUFF   MUNIC
INGP/REL PWR 20. PAGE 98 B1989   PROVS
                                      LOC/G
                                      B65

WILDER B.E.,BIBLIOGRAPHY OF THE OFFICIAL   BIBLIOG
PUBLICATIONS OF KANSAS, 1854-1958. USA+45 USA-45   PROVS
ECO/DEV POL/PAR EX/STRUC LEGIS ADJUD ATTIT 19/20.   GOV/REL
PAGE 116 B2349   ADMIN
                                      S65

CHARLESWORTH J.C.,"ALLOCATION OF RESPONSIBILITIES   PROVS
AND RESOURCES AMONG THE THREE LEVELS OF   NAT/G
GOVERNMENT." USA+45 USA-45 ECO/DEV MUNIC PLAN LEGIT   LG/CO
...PLURIST 20 B0415   WEALTH
                                      S65

THOMAS F.C. JR.,"THE PEACE CORPS IN MOROCCO."   MOROCCO
CULTURE MUNIC PROVS CREATE ROUTINE TASK ADJUST   FRANCE
STRANGE...OBS PEACE/CORP. PAGE 104 B2099   FOR/AID
                                      EDU/PROP
                                      N65

NJ DIVISION STATE-REGION PLAN,UTILIZATION OF NEW   UTIL
JERSEY'S DELAWARE RIVER WATERFRONT (PAMPHLET). FUT   PLAN
ADMIN REGION LEISURE GOV/REL DEMAND WEALTH...CHARTS   ECO/TAC
20 NEW/JERSEY. PAGE 78 B1586   PROVS
                                      B66

CARALEY D.,PARTY POLITICS AND NATIONAL ELECTIONS.   POL/PAR
USA+45 STRATA LOC/G PROVS EX/STRUC BARGAIN ADMIN   CHOOSE
SANCTION GP/REL ATTIT 20 DEMOCRAT REPUBLICAN.   REPRESENT
PAGE 18 B0375   NAT/G
                                      B66

CLEGG R.K.,THE ADMINISTRATOR IN PUBLIC WELFARE.   ADMIN

USA+45 STRUCT NAT/G PROVS PROB/SOLV BUDGET ECO/TAC   GIVE
GP/REL ROLE...SOC/WK 20 PUBLIC/REL. PAGE 21 B0434   GOV/REL
                                      OP/RES
                                      B66

DAHLBERG J.S.,THE NEW YORK BUREAU OF MUNICIPAL   PROVS
RESEARCH: PIONEER IN GOVERNMENT ADMINISTRATION.   MUNIC
CONSTN R+D BUDGET EDU/PROP PARTIC REPRESENT   DELIB/GP
EFFICIENCY ORD/FREE...BIBLIOG METH 20 NEW/YORK   ADMIN
NIPA. PAGE 26 B0522
                                      B66

DUNCOMBE H.S.,COUNTY GOVERNMENT IN AMERICA. USA+45   LOC/G
FINAN MUNIC ADMIN ROUTINE GOV/REL...GOV/COMP 20.   PROVS
PAGE 31 B0631   CT/SYS
                                      TOP/EX
                                      B66

FINK M.,A SELECTIVE BIBLIOGRAPHY ON STATE   BIBLIOG
CONSTITUTIONAL REVISION (PAMPHLET). USA+45 FINAN   PROVS
EX/STRUC LEGIS EDU/PROP ADMIN CT/SYS APPORT CHOOSE   LOC/G
GOV/REL 20. PAGE 35 B0720   CONSTN
                                      B66

GREENE L.E.,GOVERNMENT IN TENNESSEE (2ND ED.).   PROVS
USA+45 DIST/IND INDUS POL/PAR EX/STRUC LEGIS PLAN   LOC/G
BUDGET GIVE CT/SYS...MGT T 20 TENNESSEE. PAGE 43   CONSTN
B0866   ADMIN
                                      B66

O'NEILL C.E.,CHURCH AND STATE IN FRENCH COLONIAL   COLONIAL
LOUISIANA: POLICY AND POLITICS TO 1732. PROVS   NAT/G
VOL/ASSN DELIB/GP ADJUD ADMIN GP/REL ATTIT DRIVE   SECT
...POLICY BIBLIOG 17/18 LOUISIANA CHURCH/STA.   PWR
PAGE 79 B1601
                                      B66

RICHARD J.B.,GOVERNMENT AND POLITICS OF WYOMING.   PROVS
USA+45 POL/PAR EX/STRUC LEGIS CT/SYS LOBBY APPORT   LOC/G
CHOOSE REPRESENT 20 WYOMING GOVERNOR. PAGE 88 B1773   ADMIN
                                      B66

ROSS R.M.,STATE AND LOCAL GOVERNMENT AND   LOC/G
ADMINISTRATION. USA+45 CONSTN POL/PAR EX/STRUC   PROVS
LEGIS BUDGET EDU/PROP CONTROL CT/SYS CHOOSE GOV/REL   MUNIC
T. PAGE 90 B1827   ADMIN
                                      B66

SCHLESSINGER P.J.,ELEMENTS OF CALIFORNIA GOVERNMENT   LOC/G
(2ND ED.). USA+45 LAW ADJUD ADMIN CONTROL CT/SYS   PROVS
EFFICIENCY...BIBLIOG T CALIFORNIA. PAGE 94 B1891   GOV/REL
                                      LEGIS
                                      B66

SCHMIDT K.M.,AMERICAN STATE AND LOCAL GOVERNMENT IN   PROVS
ACTION. USA+45 CONSTN LOC/G POL/PAR CHIEF LEGIS   ADMIN
PROB/SOLV ADJUD LOBBY GOV/REL...DECISION ANTHOL 20   MUNIC
GOVERNOR MAYOR URBAN/RNWL. PAGE 94 B1896   PLAN
                                      B66

STREET D.,ORGANIZATION FOR TREATMENT. CLIENT PROVS   GP/COMP
PUB/INST PLAN CONTROL PARTIC REPRESENT ATTIT PWR   AGE/Y
...POLICY BIBLIOG. PAGE 101 B2052   ADMIN
                                      VOL/ASSN
                                      S66

"FURTHER READING." INDIA LOC/G NAT/G PLAN ADMIN   BIBLIOG
WEALTH...GEOG SOC CONCPT CENSUS 20. PAGE 2 B0045   ECO/UNDEV
                                      TEC/DEV
                                      PROVS
                                      S66

BURDETTE F.L.,"SELECTED ARTICLES AND DOCUMENTS ON   BIBLIOG
AMERICAN GOVERNMENT AND POLITICS." LAW LOC/G MUNIC   USA+45
NAT/G POL/PAR PROVS LEGIS BAL/PWR ADMIN EXEC   JURID
REPRESENT MGT. PAGE 17 B0348   CONSTN
                                      C66

JACOB H.,"DIMENSIONS OF STATE POLITICS HEARD A. ED.   PROVS
STATE LEGIWLATURES IN AMERICAN POLITICS." CULTURE   LEGIS
STRATA POL/PAR BUDGET TAX LOBBY ROUTINE GOV/REL   ROLE
...TRADIT DECISION GEOG. PAGE 55 B1112   REPRESENT
                                      N66

BACHELDER G.L.,THE LITERATURE OF FEDERALISM: A   BIBLIOG
SELECTED BIBLIOGRAPHY (REV ED) (A PAMPHLET). USA+45   FEDERAL
USA-45 WOR+45 WOR-45 LAW CONSTN PROVS ADMIN CT/SYS   NAT/G
GOV/REL ROLE...CONCPT 19/20. PAGE 8 B0155   LOC/G
                                      B67

ANGEL D.D.,ROMNEY. LABOR LG/CO NAT/G EXEC WAR   BIOG
RACE/REL PERSON ORD/FREE...MGT WORSHIP 20   CHIEF
ROMNEY/GEO CIV/RIGHTS MORMON GOVERNOR. PAGE 5 B0108   PROVS
                                      POLICY
                                      B67

BUREAU GOVERNMENT RES AND SERV,COUNTY GOVERNMENT   BIBLIOG/A
REORGANIZATION - A SELECTED ANNOTATED BIBLIOGRAPHY   APPORT
(PAPER). USA+45 USA-45 LAW CONSTN MUNIC PROVS   LOC/G
EX/STRUC CREATE PLAN PROB/SOLV REPRESENT GOV/REL   ADMIN
20. PAGE 17 B0349
                                      B67

FESLER J.W.,THE FIFTY STATES AND THEIR LOCAL   PROVS
GOVERNMENTS. FUT USA+45 POL/PAR LEGIS PROB/SOLV   LOC/G
ADMIN CT/SYS CHOOSE GOV/REL FEDERAL...POLICY CHARTS
20 SUPREME/CT. PAGE 35 B0715
                                      B67

IANNACCONE L.,POLITICS IN EDUCATION. USA+45 LOC/G   EDU/PROP
PROF/ORG BAL/PWR ADMIN...CHARTS SIMUL. PAGE 53   GEN/LAWS
B1072   PROVS
                                      B67

ILLINOIS COMMISSION,IMPROVING THE STATE   PROVS

LEGISLATURE. USA+45 LAW CONSTN NAT/G PROB/SOLV   LEGIS
EDU/PROP ADMIN TASK CHOOSE INGP/REL EFFICIENCY   REPRESENT
ILLINOIS. PAGE 53 B1077   PLAN
                                                       B67
PRINCE C.E.,NEW JERSEY'S JEFFERSONIAN REPUBLICANS;   POL/PAR
THE GENESIS OF AN EARLY PARTY MACHINE (1789-1817).   CONSTN
USA-45 LOC/G EDU/PROP PRESS CONTROL CHOOSE...CHARTS   ADMIN
18/19 NEW/JERSEY REPUBLICAN. PAGE 84 B1707   PROVS
                                                       B67
US DEPARTMENT OF THE ARMY,CIVILIAN IN PEACE,   BIBLIOG/A
SOLDIER IN WAR: A BIBLIOGRAPHIC SURVEY OF THE ARMY   FORCES
AND AIR NATIONAL GUARD (PAMPHLET NOS. 130-2).   ROLE
USA+45 USA-45 LOC/G NAT/G PROVS LEGIS PLAN ADMIN   DIPLOM
ATTIT ORD/FREE...POLICY 19/20. PAGE 108 B2185
                                                       B67
WESTON P.B.,THE ADMINISTRATION OF JUSTICE. USA+45   CRIME
CONSTN MUNIC NAT/G PROVS EX/STRUC JUDGE ADMIN   CT/SYS
CONTROL SANCTION ORD/FREE...CHARTS 20. PAGE 115   JURID
B2328   ADJUD
                                                       S67
BERRODIN E.F.,"AT THE BARGAINING TABLE." LABOR   PROVS
DIPLOM ECO/TAC ADMIN...MGT 20 MICHIGAN. PAGE 11   WORKER
B0230   LAW
                                                       BARGAIN
                                                       S67
DOERN G.B.,"THE ROYAL COMMISSIONS IN THE GENERAL   R+D
POLICY PROCESS AND IN FEDERAL-PROVINCIAL   EX/STRUC
RELATIONS." CANADA CONSTN ACADEM PROVS CONSULT   GOV/REL
DELIB/GP LEGIS ACT/RES PROB/SOLV CONFER CONTROL   NAT/G
EFFICIENCY...METH/COMP 20 SENATE ROYAL/COMM.
PAGE 30 B0603
                                                       S67
LANDES W.M.,"THE EFFECT OF STATE FAIR EMPLOYMENT   DISCRIM
LAWS ON THE ECONOMIC POSITION OF NONWHITES." USA+45   LAW
PROVS SECT LEGIS ADMIN GP/REL RACE/REL...JURID   WORKER
CONCPT CHARTS HYPO/EXP NEGRO. PAGE 62 B1255
                                                       S67
LEVIN M.R.,"PLANNERS AND METROPOLITAN PLANNING."   PLAN
FUT USA+45 SOCIETY NAT/G PROVS PROB/SOLV LEAD   MUNIC
PARTIC GOV/REL RACE/REL HABITAT ROLE. PAGE 64 B1301   R+D
                                                       ADMIN
                                                       S67
RAI H.,"DISTRICT MAGISTRATE AND POLICE   STRUCT
SUPERINTENDENT IN INDIA: THE CONTROVERSY OF DUAL   CONTROL
CONTROL" INDIA LAW PROVS ADMIN PWR 19/20. PAGE 86   ROLE
B1729   FORCES

PRUITT D.G. B1713

PRUITT/DG....DEAN G. PRUITT

PRUSSIA.....PRUSSIA

                                                       B45
BRECHT A.,FEDERALISM AND REGIONALISM IN GERMANY;   FEDERAL
THE DIVISION OF PRUSSIA. GERMANY PRUSSIA WOR-45   REGION
CREATE ADMIN WAR TOTALISM PWR...CHARTS 20 HITLER/A.   PROB/SOLV
PAGE 15 B0303   CONSTN
                                                       B60
HAUSER O.,PREUSSISCHE STAATSRASON UND NATIONALER   NAT/LISM
GEDANKE. PRUSSIA SOCIETY PRESS ADMIN...CONCPT   NAT/G
19/20. PAGE 48 B0969   ATTIT
                                                       PROVS
                                                       B65
KAAS L.,DIE GEISTLICHE GERICHTSBARKEIT DER   JURID
KATHOLISCHEN KIRCHE IN PREUSSEN (2 VOLS.). PRUSSIA   CATHISM
CONSTN NAT/G PROVS SECT ADJUD ADMIN ATTIT 16/20.   GP/REL
PAGE 57 B1158   CT/SYS

PSY....PSYCHOLOGY

                                                       N
AUSTRALIAN NATIONAL RES COUN,AUSTRALIAN SOCIAL   BIBLIOG/A
SCIENCE ABSTRACTS. NEW/ZEALND CULTURE SOCIETY LOC/G   POLICY
CT/SYS PARL/PROC...HEAL JURID PSY SOC 20 AUSTRAL.   NAT/G
PAGE 7 B0149   ADMIN
                                                       N
PRINCETON U INDUSTRIAL REL SEC,SELECTED REFERENCES   BIBLIOG/A
OF THE INDUSTRIAL RELATIONS SECTION OF PRINCETON,   INDUS
NEW JERSEY. LG/CO NAT/G LEGIS WORKER PLAN PROB/SOLV   LABOR
PAY ADMIN ROUTINE TASK GP/REL...PSY 20. PAGE 84   MGT
B1708
                                                       N
READERS GUIDE TO PERIODICAL LITERATURE. WOR+45   BIBLIOG
WOR-45 LAW ADMIN ATTIT PERSON...HUM PSY SOC 20.   WRITING
PAGE 1 B0021   DIPLOM
                                                       NAT/G
                                                       B28
SOROKIN P.,CONTEMPORARY SOCIOLOGICAL THEORIES.   CULTURE
MOD/EUR UNIV SOCIETY R+D SCHOOL ECO/TAC EDU/PROP   SOC
ROUTINE ATTIT DRIVE...PSY CONCPT TIME/SEQ TREND   WAR
GEN/LAWS 20. PAGE 99 B1997
                                                       B45
BENJAMIN H.C.,EMPLOYMENT TESTS IN INDUSTRY AND   BIBLIOG/A
BUSINESS. LG/CO WORKER ROUTINE...MGT PSY SOC   METH
CLASSIF PROBABIL STAT APT/TEST KNO/TEST PERS/TEST   TESTS

20. PAGE 10 B0211   INDUS
                                                       B47
BARNARD C.,THE FUNCTIONS OF THE EXECUTIVE. USA+45   EXEC
ELITES INTELL LEGIT ATTIT DRIVE PERSON SKILL...PSY   EX/STRUC
SOC METH/CNCPT SOC/EXP GEN/METH VAL/FREE 20. PAGE 9   ROUTINE
B0187
                                                       B47
LASSWELL H.D.,THE ANALYSIS OF POLITICAL BEHAVIOUR: R+D
AN EMPIRICAL APPROACH. WOR+45 CULTURE NAT/G FORCES   ACT/RES
EDU/PROP ADMIN ATTIT PERCEPT KNOWL...PHIL/SCI PSY   ELITES
SOC NEW/IDEA OBS INT GEN/METH NAZI 20. PAGE 63
B1267
                                                       B47
SIMON H.A.,ADMINISTRATIVE BEHAVIOR: A STUDY OF   DECISION
DECISION-MAKING PROCESSES IN ADMINISTRATIVE   NEW/IDEA
ORGANIZATION. STRUCT COM/IND OP/RES PROB/SOLV   ADMIN
EFFICIENCY EQUILIB UTIL...PHIL/SCI PSY STYLE.   RATIONAL
PAGE 97 B1956
                                                       B49
FORD FOUNDATION,REPORT OF THE STUDY FOR THE FORD   WEALTH
FOUNDATION ON POLICY AND PROGRAM. SOCIETY R+D   GEN/LAWS
ACT/RES CAP/ISM FOR/AID EDU/PROP ADMIN KNOWL
...POLICY PSY SOC 20. PAGE 36 B0739
                                                       B50
MANNHEIM K.,FREEDOM, POWER, AND DEMOCRATIC   TEC/DEV
PLANNING. FUT USSR WOR+45 ELITES INTELL SOCIETY   PLAN
NAT/G EDU/PROP ROUTINE ATTIT DRIVE SUPEGO SKILL   CAP/ISM
...POLICY PSY CONCPT TREND GEN/LAWS 20. PAGE 69   UK
B1393
                                                       S50
NEUMANN F.L.,"APPROACHES TO THE STUDY OF POLITICAL   PWR
POWER." POL/PAR TOP/EX ADMIN LEAD ATTIT ORD/FREE   IDEA/COMP
CONSERVE LAISSEZ MARXISM...PSY SOC. PAGE 78 B1572   CONCPT
                                                       B51
LASSWELL H.D.,THE POLITICAL WRITINGS OF HAROLD D   PERSON
LASSWELL. UNIV DOMIN EXEC LEAD RATIONAL ATTIT DRIVE   PSY
ROLE ALL/VALS...OBS BIOG 20. PAGE 63 B1269   INGP/REL
                                                       CONCPT
                                                       S51
COHEN M.B.,"PERSONALITY AS A FACTOR IN   PERSON
ADMINISTRATIVE DECISIONS." ADJUD PERS/REL ANOMIE   ADMIN
SUPEGO...OBS SELF/OBS INT. PAGE 22 B0446   PROB/SOLV
                                                       PSY
                                                       S51
INKELES A.,"UNDERSTANDING A FOREIGN SOCIETY: A   SOC
SOCIOLOGIST'S VIEW." SOCIETY ROUTINE KNOWL...PSY   METH/CNCPT
CONCPT GEN/METH 20. PAGE 54 B1086   PERCEPT
                                                       ATTIT
                                                       B52
MAIER N.R.F.,PRINCIPLES OF HUMAN RELATIONS. WOR+45   INDUS
WOR-45 CULTURE SOCIETY ROUTINE ATTIT DRIVE PERCEPT
PERSON RIGID/FLEX SUPEGO PWR...PSY CONT/OBS RECORD
TOT/POP VAL/FREE 20. PAGE 68 B1379
                                                       B52
UNESCO,THESES DE SCIENCES SOCIALES: CATALOGUE   BIBLIOG
ANALYTIQUE INTERNATIONAL DE THESES INEDITES DE   ACADEM
DOCTORAT, 1940-1950. INT/ORG DIPLOM EDU/PROP...GEOG   WRITING
INT/LAW MGT PSY SOC 20. PAGE 107 B2155
                                                       S52
JOSEPHSON E.,"IRRATIONAL LEADERSHIP IN FORMAL   ADMIN
ORGANIZATIONS." EX/STRUC PLAN LEAD GP/REL INGP/REL   RATIONAL
EFFICIENCY AUTHORIT DRIVE PSY. PAGE 57 B1154   CONCPT
                                                       PERSON
                                                       S52
TAYLOR D.W.,"TWENTY QUESTIONS: EFFICIENCY IN   PROB/SOLV
PROBLEM SOLVING AS A FUNCTION OF SIZE OF GROUP"   EFFICIENCY
WOR+45 CONFER ROUTINE INGP/REL...PSY GP/COMP 20.   SKILL
PAGE 103 B2085   PERCEPT
                                                       B54
ALLPORT G.W.,THE NATURE OF PREJUDICE. USA+45 WOR+45   CULTURE
STRATA FACE/GP KIN NEIGH SECT ADMIN GP/REL DISCRIM   PERSON
ATTIT DRIVE LOVE RESPECT...PSY SOC MYTH QU/SEMANT   RACE/REL
20. PAGE 4 B0078
                                                       B54
BENTLEY A.F.,INQUIRY INTO INQUIRIES: ESSAYS IN   EPIST
SOCIAL THEORY. UNIV LEGIS ADJUD ADMIN LOBBY   SOC
...PHIL/SCI PSY NEW/IDEA LING METH 20. PAGE 11   CONCPT
B0220
                                                       L54
ROSTOW W.W.,"ASIAN LEADERSHIP AND FREE-WORLD   ATTIT
ALLIANCE." ASIA COM USA+45 CULTURE ELITES INTELL   LEGIT
NAT/G TEC/DEV ECO/TAC EDU/PROP COLONIAL PARL/PROC   DIPLOM
ROUTINE COERCE DRIVE ORD/FREE MARXISM...PSY CONCPT.
PAGE 90 B1829
                                                       B55
HOROWITZ M.,INCENTIVE WAGE SYSTEMS. INDUS LG/CO   BIBLIOG/A
WORKER CONTROL GP/REL...MGT PSY 20. PAGE 51 B1044   PAY
                                                       PLAN
                                                       TASK
                                                       B55
STEPHENS O.,FACTS TO A CANDID WORLD. USA+45 WOR+45   EDU/PROP
COM/IND EX/STRUC PRESS ROUTINE EFFICIENCY ATTIT   PHIL/SCI
...PSY 20. PAGE 100 B2033   NAT/G
                                                       DIPLOM
                                                       S55
CROCKETT W.H.,"EMERGENT LEADERSHIP IN SMALL   DELIB/GP

DECISION MAKING GROUPS." ACT/RES ROUTINE PERS/REL ADMIN
ATTIT...STAT CONT/OBS SOC/EXP SIMUL. PAGE 25 B0507 PSY
DECISION
S55

TORRE M.,"PSYCHIATRIC OBSERVATIONS OF INTERNATIONAL DELIB/GP
CONFERENCES." WOR+45 INT/ORG PROF/ORG VOL/ASSN OBS
CONSULT EDU/PROP ROUTINE ATTIT DRIVE KNOWL...PSY DIPLOM
METH/CNCPT OBS/ENVIR STERTYP 20. PAGE 105 B2119
S55

WEISS R.S.,"A METHOD FOR THE ANALYSIS OF THE PROF/ORG
STRUCTURE OF COMPLEX ORGANIZATIONS." WOR+45 INDUS SOC/EXP
LG/CO NAT/G EXEC ROUTINE ORD/FREE PWR SKILL...MGT
PSY SOC NEW/IDEA STAT INT REC/INT STAND/INT CHARTS
WORK. PAGE 115 B2316
B56

HICKMAN C.A.,INDIVIDUALS, GROUPS, AND ECONOMIC MGT
BEHAVIOR. WORKER PAY CONTROL EXEC GP/REL INGP/REL ADMIN
PERSON ROLE...PSY SOC PERS/COMP METH 20. PAGE 50 ECO/TAC
B1005 PLAN
B56

MANNONI D.O.,PROSPERO AND CALIBAN: THE PSYCHOLOGY CULTURE
OF COLONIZATION. AFR EUR+WWI FAM KIN MUNIC SECT COLONIAL
DOMIN ADMIN ATTIT DRIVE LOVE PWR RESPECT...PSY SOC
CONCPT MYTH OBS DEEP/INT BIOG GEN/METH MALAGASY 20.
PAGE 69 B1394
B56

WASSERMAN P.,INFORMATION FOR ADMINISTRATORS: A BIBLIOG
GUIDE TO PUBLICATIONS AND SERVICES FOR MANAGEMENT MGT
IN BUSINESS AND GOVERNMENT. R+D LOC/G NAT/G KNOWL
PROF/ORG VOL/ASSN PRESS...PSY SOC STAT 20. PAGE 114 EDU/PROP
B2299
B57

BEAL J.R.,JOHN FOSTER DULLES, A BIOGRAPHY. USA+45 BIOG
USSR WOR+45 CONSTN INT/ORG NAT/G EX/STRUC LEGIT DIPLOM
ADMIN NUC/PWR DISPL PERSON ORD/FREE PWR SKILL
...POLICY PSY OBS RECORD COLD/WAR UN 20 DULLES/JF.
PAGE 10 B0200
B57

CRONBACK L.J.,PSYCHOLOGICAL TESTS AND PERSONNEL MATH
DECISIONS. OP/RES PROB/SOLV CHOOSE PERSON...PSY DECISION
STAT TESTS 20. PAGE 25 B0508 WORKER
MGT
B57

SELZNICK,LEADERSHIP IN ADMINISTRATION: A LEAD
SOCIOLOGICAL INTERPRETATION. CREATE PROB/SOLV EXEC ADMIN
ROUTINE EFFICIENCY RATIONAL KNOWL...POLICY PSY. DECISION
PAGE 95 B1927 NAT/G
S57

BAUER R.A.,"BRAINWASHING: PSYCHOLOGY OR EDU/PROP
DEMONOLOGY." ASIA CHINA/COM COM POL/PAR ECO/TAC PSY
ADMIN COERCE ATTIT DRIVE ORD/FREE...CONCPT MYTH 20. TOTALISM
PAGE 10 B0196
S57

HAILEY,"TOMORROW IN AFRICA." CONSTN SOCIETY LOC/G AFR
NAT/G DOMIN ADJUD ADMIN GP/REL DISCRIM NAT/LISM PERSON
ATTIT MORAL ORD/FREE...PSY SOC CONCPT OBS RECORD ELITES
TREND GEN/LAWS CMN/WLTH 20. PAGE 45 B0917 RACE/REL
B58

REDFIELD C.E.,COMMUNICATION IN MANAGEMENT. DELIB/GP COM/IND
EX/STRUC WRITING LEAD PERS/REL...PSY INT METH 20. MGT
PAGE 87 B1750 LG/CO
ADMIN
C59

DAHL R.A.,"SOCIAL SCIENCE RESEARCH ON BUSINESS: MGT
PRODUCT AND POTENTIAL" INDUS MARKET OP/RES CAP/ISM EFFICIENCY
ADMIN LOBBY DRIVE...PSY CONCPT BIBLIOG/A 20. PROB/SOLV
PAGE 26 B0521 EX/STRUC
B60

ARGYRIS C.,UNDERSTANDING ORGANIZATIONAL BEHAVIOR. LG/CO
OP/RES FEEDBACK...MGT PSY METH/CNCPT OBS INT SIMUL PERSON
20. PAGE 6 B0130 ADMIN
ROUTINE
B60

ARROW K.J.,MATHEMATICAL METHODS IN THE SOCIAL MATH
SCIENCES, 1959. TEC/DEV CHOOSE UTIL PERCEPT PSY
...KNO/TEST GAME SIMUL ANTHOL. PAGE 7 B0137 MGT
S60

HERZ J.H.,"EAST GERMANY: PROGRESS AND PROSPECTS." POL/PAR
COM AGRI FINAN INDUS LOC/G NAT/G FORCES PLAN STRUCT
TEC/DEV DOMIN ADMIN COERCE DRIVE PERCEPT RIGID/FLEX GERMANY
MORAL ORD/FREE PWR...MARXIST PSY SOC RECORD STERTYP
WORK. PAGE 49 B0997
B61

BANFIELD E.C.,URBAN GOVERNMENT; A READER IN MUNIC
POLITICS AND ADMINISTRATION. ELITES LABOR POL/PAR GEN/METH
EXEC CHOOSE REPRESENT GP/REL PWR PLURISM...PSY SOC. DECISION
PAGE 9 B0177
B61

BIRNBACH B.,NEO-FREUDIAN SOCIAL PHILOSOPHY. TEC/DEV SOCIETY
INGP/REL ADJUST HAPPINESS SUPEGO HEALTH...CONCPT PSY
GEN/LAWS BIBLIOG 20. PAGE 12 B0242 PERSON
ADMIN
B61

HOUN F.W.,TO CHANGE A NATION; PROPAGANDA AND DOMIN
INDOCTRINATION IN COMMUNIST CHINA. CHINA/COM COM EDU/PROP
ACT/RES PLAN PRESS ADMIN FEEDBACK CENTRAL TOTALISM

EFFICIENCY ATTIT...PSY SOC 20. PAGE 52 B1048 MARXISM
B61

LASSWELL H.D.,PSYCOPATHOLOGY AND POLITICS. WOR-45 ATTIT
CULTURE SOCIETY FACE/GP NAT/G CONSULT CREATE GEN/METH
EDU/PROP EXEC ROUTINE DISPL DRIVE PERSON PWR
RESPECT...PSY CONCPT METH/CNCPT METH. PAGE 63 B1272
B61

MARVICK D.,POLITICAL DECISION-MAKERS. INTELL STRATA TOP/EX
NAT/G POL/PAR EX/STRUC LEGIS DOMIN EDU/PROP ATTIT BIOG
PERSON PWR...PSY STAT OBS CONT/OBS STAND/INT ELITES
UNPLAN/INT TIME/SEQ CHARTS STERTYP VAL/FREE.
PAGE 70 B1416
B61

PETRULLO L.,LEADERSHIP AND INTERPERSONAL BEHAVIOR. PERSON
FACE/GP FAM PROF/ORG EX/STRUC FORCES DOMIN WAR ATTIT
GP/REL PERS/REL EFFICIENCY PRODUC PWR...MGT PSY. LEAD
PAGE 82 B1663 HABITAT
B61

THAYER L.O.,ADMINISTRATIVE COMMUNICATION. DELIB/GP GP/REL
ADMIN ROUTINE PERS/REL 20. PAGE 104 B2093 PSY
LG/CO
MGT
B61

WALKER N.,MORALE IN THE CIVIL SERVICE. UK EXEC LEAD ATTIT
INGP/REL EFFICIENCY HAPPINESS 20. PAGE 113 B2280 WORKER
ADMIN
PSY
S61

BROWN M.,"THE DEMISE OF STATE DEPARTMENT PUBLIC EDU/PROP
OPINION POLLS: A STUDY IN LEGISLATIVE OVERSIGHT." NAT/G
PWR...POLICY PSY SAMP. PAGE 16 B0325 LEGIS
ADMIN
S61

CYERT R.M.,"TWO EXPERIMENTS ON BIAS AND CONFLICT IN LAB/EXP
ORGANIZATIONAL ESTIMATION." WORKER PROB/SOLV ROUTINE
EFFICIENCY...MGT PSY STAT CHARTS. PAGE 25 B0518 ADMIN
DECISION
S61

EVAN W.M.,"A LABORATORY EXPERIMENT ON BUREAUCRATIC ADMIN
AUTHORITY" WORKER CONTROL EXEC PRODUC ATTIT PERSON LEGIT
...PSY SOC CHARTS SIMUL 20 WEBER/MAX. PAGE 34 B0687 LAB/EXP
EFFICIENCY
B62

MARS D.,SUGGESTED LIBRARY IN PUBLIC ADMINISTRATION. BIBLIOG
FINAN DELIB/GP EX/STRUC WORKER COMPUTER ADJUD ADMIN
...DECISION PSY SOC METH/COMP 20. PAGE 69 B1403 METH
MGT
B62

PRESTHUS R.,THE ORGANIZATIONAL SOCIETY. USA+45 LG/CO
STRUCT ECO/DEV ADMIN ATTIT ALL/VALS...PSY SOC 20. WORKER
PAGE 84 B1703 PERS/REL
DRIVE
B62

ROBINSON M.,THE COMING OF AGE OF THE LANGLEY PORTER PUB/INST
CLINIC (PAMPHLET). USA+45 PROF/ORG PROVS PLAN...MGT ADMIN
PSY 20 CALIFORNIA LANGLEY. PAGE 89 B1804 EFFICIENCY
HEAL
B62

SNYDER R.C.,FOREIGN POLICY DECISION-MAKING. FUT TEC/DEV
KOREA WOR+45 R+D CREATE ADMIN ROUTINE PWR HYPO/EXP
...DECISION PSY SOC CONCPT METH/CNCPT CON/ANAL DIPLOM
CHARTS GEN/METH METH 20. PAGE 99 B1992
B62

WEDDING N.,ADVERTISING MANAGEMENT. USA+45 ECO/DEV ECO/TAC
BUDGET CAP/ISM PRODUC PROFIT ATTIT...DECISION MGT COM/IND
PSY 20. PAGE 114 B2308 PLAN
EDU/PROP
S62

IKLE F.C.,"POLITICAL NEGOTIATION AS A PROCESS OF ROUTINE
MODIFYING UTILITIES." WOR+45 FACE/GP LABOR NAT/G DECISION
FORCES ACT/RES EDU/PROP DETER PERCEPT ALL/VALS DIPLOM
...PSY NEW/IDEA HYPO/EXP GEN/METH 20. PAGE 53 B1076
S62

NORTH R.C.,"DECISION MAKING IN CRISIS: AN INT/ORG
INTRODUCTION." WOR+45 WOR-45 NAT/G CONSULT DELIB/GP ROUTINE
TEC/DEV PERCEPT KNOWL...POLICY DECISION PSY DIPLOM
METH/CNCPT CONT/OBS TREND VAL/FREE 20. PAGE 79
B1590
S62

READ W.H.,"UPWARD COMMUNICATION IN INDUSTRIAL ADMIN
HIERARCHIES." LG/CO TOP/EX PROB/SOLV DOMIN EXEC INGP/REL
PERS/REL ATTIT DRIVE PERCEPT...CORREL STAT CHARTS PSY
20. PAGE 86 B1747 MGT
S62

SPRINGER H.W.,"FEDERATION IN THE CARIBBEAN: AN VOL/ASSN
ATTEMPT THAT FAILED." L/A+17C ECO/UNDEV INT/ORG NAT/G
POL/PAR PROVS LEGIS CREATE PLAN LEGIT ADMIN FEDERAL REGION
ATTIT DRIVE PERSON ORD/FREE PWR...POLICY GEOG PSY
CONCPT OBS CARIBBEAN CMN/WLTH 20. PAGE 100 B2013
S62

TANNENBAUM A.S.,"CONTROL IN ORGANIZATIONS: ADMIN
INDIVIDUAL ADJUSTMENT AND ORGANIZATIONAL MGT
PERFORMANCE." DOMIN PARTIC REPRESENT INGP/REL STRUCT
PRODUC ATTIT DRIVE PWR...PSY CORREL. PAGE 102 B2073 CONTROL
B63

BERNE E.,THE STRUCTURE AND DYNAMICS OF INGP/REL

ORGANIZATIONS AND GROUPS. CLIENT PARTIC DRIVE HEALTH...MGT PSY ORG/CHARTS. PAGE 11 B0226

AUTHORIT
ROUTINE
CLASSIF
B63

COSTELLO T.W.,PSYCHOLOGY IN ADMINISTRATION: A RESEARCH ORIENTATION. CREATE PROB/SOLV PERS/REL ADJUST ANOMIE ATTIT DRIVE PERCEPT ROLE...DECISION BIBLIOG T 20. PAGE 24 B0488

PSY
MGT
EXEC
ADMIN
B63

TUCKER R.C.,THE SOVIET POLITICAL MIND. WOR+45 ELITES INT/ORG NAT/G POL/PAR PLAN DIPLOM ECO/TAC DOMIN ADMIN NUC/PWR REV DRIVE PERSON SUPEGO PWR WEALTH...POLICY MGT PSY CONCPT OBS BIOG TREND COLD/WAR MARX/KARL 20. PAGE 106 B2134

COM
TOP/EX
USSR
B63

TUCKER R.C.,THE SOVIET POLITICAL MIND. COM INTELL NAT/G TOP/EX EDU/PROP ADMIN COERCE TOTALISM ATTIT PWR MARXISM...PSY MYTH HYPO/EXP 20. PAGE 106 B2135

STRUCT
RIGID/FLEX
ELITES
USSR
B63

WARNER W.L.,THE AMERICAN FEDERAL EXECUTIVE. USA+45 USA-45 CONSULT EX/STRUC GP/REL DRIVE ALL/VALS...PSY DEEP/QU CHARTS 19/20 PRESIDENT. PAGE 114 B2295

ELITES
NAT/G
TOP/EX
ADMIN
S63

ARASTEH R.,"THE ROLE OF INTELLECTUALS IN ADMINISTRATIVE DEVELOPMENT AND SOCIAL CHANGE IN MODERN IRAN." ISLAM CULTURE NAT/G CONSULT ACT/RES EDU/PROP EXEC ATTIT BIO/SOC PERCEPT SUPEGO ALL/VALS ...POLICY MGT PSY SOC CONCPT 20. PAGE 6 B0123

INTELL
ADMIN
IRAN

S63

BACHRACH P.,"DECISIONS AND NONDECISIONS: AN ANALYTICAL FRAMEWORK." UNIV SOCIETY CREATE LEGIT ADMIN EXEC COERCE...DECISION PSY CONCPT CHARTS. PAGE 8 B0156

PWR
HYPO/EXP

B64

ARGYRIS C.,INTEGRATING THE INDIVIDUAL AND THE ORGANIZATION. WORKER PROB/SOLV LEAD SANCTION REPRESENT ADJUST EFFICIENCY DRIVE PERSON...PSY METH/CNCPT ORG/CHARTS. PAGE 6 B0132

ADMIN
PERS/REL
VOL/ASSN
PARTIC
B64

COOMBS C.H.,A THEORY OF DATA....MGT PHIL/SCI SOC CLASSIF MATH PROBABIL STAT QU. PAGE 23 B0472

CON/ANAL
GEN/METH
TESTS
PSY
B64

PARET P.,FRENCH REVOLUTIONARY WARFARE FROM INDOCHINA TO ALGERIA* THE ANALYSIS OF A POLITICAL AND MILITARY DOCTRINE. ALGERIA VIETNAM FORCES OP/RES TEC/DEV ROUTINE REV ATTIT...PSY BIBLIOG. PAGE 81 B1632

FRANCE
GUERRILLA
GEN/LAWS

B64

PEABODY R.L.,ORGANIZATIONAL AUTHORITY. SCHOOL WORKER PLAN SENIOR GOV/REL UTIL DRIVE PWR...PSY CHARTS BIBLIOG 20. PAGE 82 B1648

ADMIN
EFFICIENCY
TASK
GP/REL
S64

GALTUNE J.,"BALANCE OF POWER AND THE PROBLEM OF PERCEPTION, A LOGICAL ANALYSIS." WOR+45 CONSTN SOCIETY NAT/G DELIB/GP EX/STRUC LEGIS DOMIN ADMIN COERCE DRIVE ORD/FREE...POLICY CONCPT OBS TREND GEN/LAWS. PAGE 38 B0778

PWR
PSY
ARMS/CONT
WAR

B65

CUTLIP S.M.,A PUBLIC RELATIONS BIBLIOGRAPHY. INDUS LABOR NAT/G PROF/ORG SCHOOL DIPLOM PRESS TV GOV/REL GP/REL...PSY SOC/WK 20. PAGE 25 B0515

BIBLIOG/A
MGT
COM/IND
ADMIN
B65

HODGSON R.C.,THE EXECUTIVE ROLE CONSTELLATION: AN ANALYSIS OF PERSONALITY AND ROLE RELATIONS IN MANAGEMENT. USA+45 PUB/INST EXEC PERS/REL PERSON ...PSY PERS/COMP HYPO/EXP 20. PAGE 51 B1027

LG/CO
ADMIN
TOP/EX
ROLE
B65

SINGER J.D.,HUMAN BEHAVIOR AND INTERNATIONAL POLITICS* CONTRIBUTIONS FROM THE SOCIAL-PSYCHOLOGICAL SCIENCES. ACT/RES PLAN EDU/PROP ADMIN KNOWL...DECISION PSY SOC NET/THEORY HYPO/EXP LAB/EXP SOC/EXP GEN/METH ANTHOL BIBLIOG. PAGE 97 B1965

DIPLOM
PHIL/SCI
QUANT
SIMUL

B65

UNESCO,INTERNATIONAL ORGANIZATIONS IN THE SOCIAL SCIENCES(REV. ED.). LAW ADMIN ATTIT...CRIMLGY GEOG INT/LAW PSY SOC STAT 20 UNESCO. PAGE 107 B2157

INT/ORG
R+D
PROF/ORG
ACT/RES
B65

UNIVERSAL REFERENCE SYSTEM,INTERNATIONAL AFFAIRS: VOLUME I IN THE POLITICAL SCIENCE, GOVERNMENT, AND PUBLIC POLICY SERIES....DECISION ECOMETRIC GEOG INT/LAW JURID MGT PHIL/SCI PSY SOC. PAGE 107 B2163

BIBLIOG/A
GEN/METH
COMPUT/IR
DIPLOM
L65

HAMMOND A.,"COMPREHENSIVE VERSUS INCREMENTAL BUDGETING IN THE DEPARTMENT OF AGRICULTURE" USA+45 GP/REL ATTIT...PSY INT 20 DEPT/AGRI. PAGE 46 B0934

TOP/EX
EX/STRUC
AGRI
BUDGET
S65

HOLSTI O.R.,"THE 1914 CASE." MOD/EUR COMPUTER

CON/ANAL

DIPLOM EDU/PROP EXEC...DECISION PSY PROBABIL STAT COMPUT/IR SOC/EXP TIME. PAGE 51 B1036

PERCEPT
WAR
B66

DICKSON W.J.,COUNSELING IN AN ORGANIZATION: A SEQUEL TO THE HAWTHORNE RESEARCHES. CLIENT VOL/ASSN ACT/RES PROB/SOLV AUTOMAT ROUTINE PERS/REL HAPPINESS ANOMIE ROLE...OBS CHARTS 20 AT+T. PAGE 29 B0588

INDUS
WORKER
PSY
MGT

B66

PERROW C.,ORGANIZATION FOR TREATMENT: A COMPARATIVE STUDY OF INSTITUTIONS FOR DELINQUENTS. LAW PROB/SOLV ADMIN CRIME PERSON MORAL...SOC/WK OBS DEEP/QU CHARTS SOC/EXP SOC/INTEG 20. PAGE 82 B1661

AGE/Y
PSY
PUB/INST

B66

ZALEZNIK A.,HUMAN DILEMMAS OF LEADERSHIP. ELITES INDUS EX/STRUC INGP/REL ATTIT...PSY 20. PAGE 119 B2397

LEAD
PERSON
EXEC
MGT
B67

KATZ J.,PSYCHOANALYSIS, PSYCHIATRY, AND LAW. USA+45 LOC/G NAT/G PUB/INST PROB/SOLV ADMIN HEALTH ...CRIMLGY CONCPT SAMP/SIZ IDEA/COMP. PAGE 58 B1180

LAW
PSY
CT/SYS
ADJUD
B67

VOOS H.,ORGANIZATIONAL COMMUNICATION: A BIBLIOGRAPHY. WOR+45 STRATA R+D PROB/SOLV FEEDBACK COERCE...MGT PSY NET/THEORY HYPO/EXP. PAGE 112 B2268

BIBLIOG/A
INDUS
COM/IND
VOL/ASSN
S67

DANELSKI D.J.,"CONFLICT AND ITS RESOLUTION IN THE SUPREME COURT." PROB/SOLV LEAD ROUTINE PERSON...PSY PERS/COMP BIBLIOG 20. PAGE 26 B0527

ROLE
JURID
JUDGE
INGP/REL
S67

MCNAMARA R.L.,"THE NEED FOR INNOVATIVENESS IN DEVELOPING SOCIETIES." L/A+17C EDU/PROP ADMIN LEAD WEALTH...POLICY PSY SOC METH 20 COLOMB. PAGE 72 B1456

PROB/SOLV
PLAN
ECO/UNDEV
NEW/IDEA

PSY/WAR....PSYCHOLOGICAL WARFARE: SEE ALSO PSY + EDU/PROP + WAR

PSYCHIATRY....SEE PSY

PSYCHOANALYSIS....SEE BIOG, PSY

PSYCHO-DRAMA....SEE SELF/OBS

PSYCHOLOGICAL WARFARE....SEE PSY+EDU/PROP+WAR

PSYCHOLOGY....SEE PSY

PUB/INST....MENTAL, CORRECTIONAL, AND OTHER HABITATIONAL INSTITUTIONS

N

KENTUCKY STATE ARCHIVES,CHECKLIST OF KENTUCKY STATE PUBLICATIONS AND STATE DIRECTORY. USA+45 LAW ACADEM EX/STRUC LEGIS EDU/PROP LEAD...JURID 20. PAGE 59 B1196

BIBLIOG/A
PROVS
PUB/INST
ADMIN
B37

HODGSON J.G.,THE OFFICIAL PUBLICATIONS OF AMERICAN COUNTIES: A UNION LIST. SCHOOL BUDGET...HEAL MGT SOC/WK 19/20. PAGE 51 B1026

BIBLIOG
LOC/G
PUB/INST
B37

UNION OF SOUTH AFRICA,REPORT CONCERNING ADMINISTRATION OF SOUTH WEST AFRICA (6 VOLS.). SOUTH/AFR INDUS PUB/INST FORCES LEGIS BUDGET DIPLOM EDU/PROP ADJUD CT/SYS...GEOG CHARTS 20 AFRICA/SW LEAGUE/NAT. PAGE 107 B2158

NAT/G
ADMIN
COLONIAL
CONSTN

B38

LANGE O.,ON THE ECONOMIC THEORY OF SOCIALISM. UNIV ECO/DEV FINAN INDUS INT/ORG PUB/INST ROUTINE ATTIT ALL/VALS...SOC CONCPT STAT TREND 20. PAGE 62 B1258

MARKET
ECO/TAC
INT/TRADE
SOCISM
N40

COUNTY GOVERNMENT IN THE UNITED STATES: A LIST OF RECENT REFERENCES (PAMPHLET). USA-45 LAW PUB/INST PLAN BUDGET CT/SYS CENTRAL 20. PAGE 49 B0988

BIBLIOG/A
LOC/G
ADMIN
MUNIC
S57

RAPAPORT R.N.,"'DEMOCRATIZATION' AND AUTHORITY IN A THERAPEUTIC COMMUNITY." OP/RES ADMIN PARTIC CENTRAL ATTIT...POLICY DECISION. PAGE 86 B1735

PUB/INST
HEALTH
DOMIN
CLIENT
B58

JAPAN MINISTRY OF JUSTICE,CRIMINAL JUSTICE IN JAPAN. LAW PROF/ORG PUB/INST FORCES CONTROL CT/SYS PARL/PROC 20 CHINJAP. PAGE 56 B1125

CONSTN
CRIME
JURID
ADMIN
B58

WILENSKY H.L.,INDUSTRIAL SOCIETY AND SOCIAL WELFARE: IMPACT OF INDUSTRIALIZATION ON SUPPLY AND ORGANIZATION OF SOC WELF SERVICES. ELITES SOCIETY STRATA SERV/IND FAM MUNIC PUB/INST CONSULT WORKER ADMIN AUTOMAT ANOMIE 20. PAGE 117 B2352

INDUS
ECO/DEV
RECEIVE
PROF/ORG

C60

MCCLEERY R.,"COMMUNICATION PATTERNS AS BASES OF   PERS/REL
SYSTEMS OF AUTHORITY AND POWER" IN THEORETICAL   PUB/INST
STUDIES IN SOCIAL ORGAN. OF PRISON-BMR. USA+45   PWR
SOCIETY STRUCT EDU/PROP ADMIN CONTROL COERCE CRIME   DOMIN
GP/REL AUTHORIT...SOC 20. PAGE 71 B1443

B61

CONFREY E.A.,ADMINISTRATION OF COMMUNITY HEALTH   HEAL
SERVICES. USA+45 R+D PUB/INST DELIB/GP PLAN BUDGET   ADMIN
ROUTINE AGE/C HEALTH...MGT SOC/WK METH/COMP 20.   MUNIC
PAGE 23 B0461   BIO/SOC

B61

INTL UNION LOCAL AUTHORITIES,LOCAL GOVERNMENT IN   LOC/G
THE USA. USA+45 PUB/INST DELIB/GP CONFER AUTOMAT   MUNIC
GP/REL POPULISM...ANTHOL 20 CITY/MGT. PAGE 54 B1101   ADMIN
                                                        GOV/REL

B62

ROBINSON M.,THE COMING OF AGE OF THE LANGLEY PORTER   PUB/INST
CLINIC (PAMPHLET). USA+45 PROF/ORG PROVS PLAN...MGT   ADMIN
PSY 20 CALIFORNIA LANGLEY. PAGE 89 B1804   EFFICIENCY
                                                        HEAL

B62

RUDOLPH F.,THE AMERICAN COLLEGE AND UNIVERSITY.   ACADEM
CLIENT FINAN PUB/INST DELIB/GP EDU/PROP CONTROL   INGP/REL
EXEC CONSEN ATTIT POLICY. PAGE 92 B1853   PWR
                                                        ADMIN

B63

HERMAN H.,NEW YORK STATE AND THE METROPOLITAN   GOV/REL
PROBLEM. USA+45 ECO/DEV PUB/INST SCHOOL LEGIS PLAN   PROVS
TAX EXEC PARL/PROC PARTIC...HEAL 20 NEW/YORK.   LOC/G
PAGE 49 B0992   POLICY

B64

TOMPKINS D.C.,PROBATION SINCE WORLD WAR II. USA+45   BIBLIOG
FORCES ADMIN ROUTINE PERS/REL AGE...CRIMLGY HEAL   PUB/INST
20. PAGE 105 B2118   ORD/FREE
                                                        CRIME

B65

CONRAD J.P.,CRIME AND ITS CORRECTION: AN   CRIME
INTERNATIONAL SURVEY OF ATTITUDES AND PRACTICES.   PUB/INST
EUR+WWI NETHERLAND USA+45 USSR ATTIT MORAL 20   POLICY
SCANDINAV. PAGE 23 B0467   ADMIN

B65

FISCHER F.C.,THE GOVERNMENT OF MICHIGAN. USA+45   PROVS
NAT/G PUB/INST EX/STRUC LEGIS BUDGET GIVE EDU/PROP   LOC/G
CT/SYS CHOOSE GOV/REL...T MICHIGAN. PAGE 36 B0723   ADMIN
                                                        CONSTN

B65

FRIEDMAN L.,SOUTHERN JUSTICE. USA+45 PUB/INST LEGIT   ADJUD
ADMIN CT/SYS DISCRIM...DECISION ANTHOL 20 NEGRO   LAW
SOUTH/US CIV/RIGHTS. PAGE 37 B0758   CONSTN
                                                        RACE/REL

B65

HODGSON R.C.,THE EXECUTIVE ROLE CONSTELLATION: AN   LG/CO
ANALYSIS OF PERSONALITY AND ROLE RELATIONS IN   ADMIN
MANAGEMENT. USA+45 PUB/INST EXEC PERS/REL PERSON   TOP/EX
...PSY PERS/COMP HYPO/EXP 20. PAGE 51 B1027   ROLE

B65

PRESTHUS R.,BEHAVIORAL APPROACHES TO PUBLIC   GEN/METH
ADMINISTRATION. UK STRATA LG/CO PUB/INST VOL/ASSN   DECISION
EX/STRUC TOP/EX EFFICIENCY HEALTH. PAGE 84 B1704   ADMIN
                                                        R+D

B66

PERROW C.,ORGANIZATION FOR TREATMENT: A COMPARATIVE   AGE/Y
STUDY OF INSTITUTIONS FOR DELINQUENTS. LAW   PSY
PROB/SOLV ADMIN CRIME PERSON MORAL...SOC/WK OBS   PUB/INST
DEEP/QU CHARTS SOC/EXP SOC/INTEG 20. PAGE 82 B1661

B66

RUBENSTEIN R.,THE SHARING OF POWER IN A PSYCHIATRIC   ADMIN
HOSPITAL. CLIENT PROF/ORG PUB/INST INGP/REL ATTIT   PARTIC
PWR...DECISION OBS RECORD. PAGE 91 B1847   HEALTH
                                                        CONCPT

B66

STREET D.,ORGANIZATION FOR TREATMENT. CLIENT PROVS   GP/COMP
PUB/INST PLAN CONTROL PARTIC REPRESENT ATTIT PWR   AGE/Y
...POLICY BIBLIOG. PAGE 101 B2052   ADMIN
                                                        VOL/ASSN

B66

WYLIE C.M.,RESEARCH IN PUBLIC HEALTH   BIBLIOG/A
ADMINISTRATION; SELECTED RECENT ABSTRACTS IV   R+D
(PAMPHLET). USA+45 MUNIC PUB/INST ACT/RES CREATE   HEAL
OP/RES TEC/DEV GP/REL ROLE...MGT PHIL/SCI STAT.   ADMIN
PAGE 118 B2387

B67

KATZ J.,PSYCHOANALYSIS, PSYCHIATRY, AND LAW. USA+45   LAW
LOC/G NAT/G PUB/INST PROB/SOLV ADMIN HEALTH   PSY
...CRIMLGY CONCPT SAMP/SIZ IDEA/COMP. PAGE 58 B1180   CT/SYS
                                                        ADJUD

B67

UNIVERSAL REFERENCE SYSTEM,ADMINISTRATIVE   BIBLIOG/A
MANAGEMENT: PUBLIC AND PRIVATE BUREAUCRACY (VOLUME   MGT
IV). WOR+45 WOR-45 ECO/DEV LG/CO LOC/G PUB/INST   ADMIN
VOL/ASSN GOV/REL...COMPUT/IR GEN/METH. PAGE 107   NAT/G
B2164

PUB/TRANS....PUBLIC TRANSPORTATION

B54

LOCKLIN D.P.,ECONOMICS OF TRANSPORTATION (4TH ED.).   ECO/DEV
USA+45 USA-45 SEA AIR LAW FINAN LG/CO EX/STRUC   DIST/IND
ADMIN CONTROL...STAT CHARTS 19/20 RAILROAD   ECO/TAC
PUB/TRANS. PAGE 66 B1335   TEC/DEV

B59

YALE UNIV BUR OF HIGHWAY TRAF,URBAN TRANSPORTATION   ADMIN
ADMINISTRATION. FUT USA+45 CONSTRUC ACT/RES BUDGET   DIST/IND
...CENSUS 20 PUB/TRANS. PAGE 118 B2388   LOC/G
                                                        PLAN

PUBL/WORKS....PUBLIC WORKS

PUBLIC ADMINISTRATION....SEE ADMIN, NAT/G

PUBLIC HEALTH SERVICE....SEE PHS

PUBLIC OPINION....SEE ATTIT

PUBLIC POLICY....SEE NAT/G+PLAN

PUBLIC RELATIONS....SEE NAT/G+RELATIONS INDEX

PUBLIC WORKS....SEE PUBL/WORKS

PUBLIC ADMIN CLEARING HOUSE B1714

PUBLIC ADMINISTRATION SERVICE B1715,B1716,B1717

PUBLIC/EDU....PUBLIC EDUCATION ASSOCIATION

PUBLIC/REL....PUBLIC RELATIONS; SEE ALSO NAT/G + RELATIONS
    INDEX

B66

CLEGG R.K.,THE ADMINISTRATOR IN PUBLIC WELFARE.   ADMIN
USA+45 STRUCT NAT/G PROVS PROB/SOLV BUDGET ECO/TAC   GIVE
GP/REL ROLE...SOC/WK 20 PUBLIC/REL. PAGE 21 B0434   GOV/REL
                                                        OP/RES

B66

SCHMIDT F.,PUBLIC RELATIONS IN HEALTH AND WELFARE.   PROF/ORG
USA+45 ACADEM RECEIVE PRESS FEEDBACK GOV/REL   EDU/PROP
PERS/REL DEMAND EFFICIENCY ATTIT PERCEPT WEALTH 20   ADMIN
PUBLIC/REL. PAGE 94 B1895   HEALTH

PUBLIC/USE....PUBLIC USE

PUBLISHERS' CIRCULAR LIMITED B1718

PUEBLO....PUEBLO INCIDENT; SEE ALSO KOREA/N

PUERT/RICN....PUERTO RICAN

PUERT/RICO....PUERTO RICO; SEE ALSO L/A+17C

B59

COUNCIL OF STATE GOVERNORS,AMERICAN LEGISLATURES: LEGIS
STRUCTURE AND PROCEDURES. SUMMARY AND TABULATIONS   CHARTS
OF A 1959 SURVEY. PUERT/RICO USA+45 PAY ADJUD ADMIN   PROVS
APPORT...IDEA/COMP 20 GUAM VIRGIN/ISL. PAGE 24   REPRESENT
B0495

B61

MAYNE A.,DESIGNING AND ADMINISTERING A REGIONAL   ECO/UNDEV
ECONOMIC DEVELOPMENT PLAN WITH SPECIFIC REFERENCE   PLAN
TO PUERTO RICO (PAMPHLET). PUERT/RICO SOCIETY NAT/G   CREATE
DELIB/GP REGION...DECISION 20. PAGE 71 B1435   ADMIN

B65

GOODSELL C.T.,ADMINISTRATION OF A REVOLUTION.   EXEC
PUERT/RICO ECO/UNDEV FINAN MUNIC POL/PAR PROVS   SOC
LEGIS PLAN BUDGET RECEIVE ADMIN COLONIAL LEAD 20
ROOSEVLT/F. PAGE 41 B0827

B67

DOSSICK J.J.,DOCTORAL RESEARCH ON PUERTO RICO AND   BIBLIOG
PUERTO RICANS. PUERT/RICO USA+45 USA-45 ADMIN 20.   CONSTN
PAGE 30 B0609   POL/PAR
                                                        DIPLOM

PUERTO RICANS....SEE PUERT/RICN

PUGET H. B1719

PULLEN W.R. B1720

PULLMAN....PULLMAN, ILLINOIS

B67

BUDER S.,PULLMAN: AN EXPERIMENT IN INDUSTRIAL ORDER   DIST/IND
AND COMMUNITY PLANNING, 1880-1930. USA-45 SOCIETY   INDUS
LABOR LG/CO CREATE PROB/SOLV CONTROL GP/REL   MUNIC
EFFICIENCY ATTIT...MGT BIBLIOG 19/20 PULLMAN.   PLAN
PAGE 17 B0337

PUNISHMENT....SEE ADJUD, LAW, LEGIT, SANCTION

PUNJAB....THE PUNJAB AND ITS PEOPLES

PUNTA DEL ESTE....SEE PUNTA/ESTE

PUNTA/ESTE....PUNTA DEL ESTE

PURCELL V. B1721

PURGE....PURGES

PURHAM/M....MARGERY PURHAM

B63
ROBINSON K.,ESSAYS IN IMPERIAL GOVERNMENT. CAMEROON COLONIAL
NIGERIA UK CONSTN LOC/G LEGIS ADMIN GOV/REL PWR
...POLICY ANTHOL BIBLIOG 17/20 PURHAM/M. PAGE 89 AFR
B1803 DOMIN

PURITAN....PURITANS

PURSELL CW J.R. B1651

PUSTAY J.S. B1722

PWR....POWER, PARTICIPATION IN DECISION-MAKING

N
WEIGLEY R.F.,HISTORY OF THE UNITED STATES ARMY. FORCES
USA+45 USA-45 SOCIETY NAT/G LEAD WAR GP/REL PWR ADMIN
...SOC METH/COMP COLD/WAR. PAGE 115 B2312 ROLE
CIVMIL/REL
B05
GOODNOW F.J.,THE PRINCIPLES OF THE ADMINISTRATIVE ADMIN
LAW OF THE UNITED STATES. USA-45 LAW STRUCT NAT/G
EX/STRUC LEGIS BAL/PWR CONTROL GOV/REL PWR...JURID PROVS
19/20 CIVIL/SERV. PAGE 41 B0822 LOC/G
B05
MACHIAVELLI N.,THE ART OF WAR. CHRIST-17C TOP/EX NAT/G
DRIVE ORD/FREE PWR SKILL...MGT CHARTS. PAGE 67 FORCES
B1360 WAR
ITALY
B08
WILSON W.,CONSTITUTIONAL GOVERNMENT IN THE UNITED NAT/G
STATES. USA-45 LAW POL/PAR PROVS CHIEF LEGIS GOV/REL
BAL/PWR ADJUD EXEC FEDERAL PWR 18/20 SUPREME/CT CONSTN
HOUSE/REP SENATE. PAGE 117 B2362 PARL/PROC
B16
TREITSCHKE H.,POLITICS. UNIV SOCIETY STRATA NAT/G EXEC
EX/STRUC LEGIS DOMIN EDU/PROP ATTIT PWR RESPECT ELITES
...CONCPT TIME/SEQ GEN/LAWS TOT/POP 20. PAGE 105 GERMANY
B2127
B17
CORWIN E.S.,THE PRESIDENT'S CONTROL OF FOREIGN TOP/EX
RELATIONS. FUT USA-45 CONSTN STRATA NAT/G CHIEF PWR
EX/STRUC LEGIS KNOWL RESPECT...JURID CONCPT TREND DIPLOM
CONGRESS VAL/FREE 20 PRESIDENT. PAGE 24 B0483
B18
WILSON W.,THE STATE: ELEMENTS OF HISTORICAL AND NAT/G
PRACTICAL POLITICS. FRANCE GERMANY ITALY UK USSR JURID
CONSTN EX/STRUC LEGIS CT/SYS WAR PWR...POLICY CONCPT
GOV/COMP 20. PAGE 117 B2363 NAT/COMP
N19
ABBOT F.C.,THE CAMBRIDGE CITY MANAGER (PAMPHLET). MUNIC
PROB/SOLV ADMIN PERS/REL RIGID/FLEX PWR...MGT 20 EX/STRUC
MASSACHU CITY/MGT. PAGE 2 B0050 TOP/EX
GP/REL
N19
ABERNATHY B.R.,SOME PERSISTING QUESTIONS CONCERNING PROVS
THE CONSTITUTIONAL STATE EXECUTIVE (PAMPHLET). EX/STRUC
CONSTN TOP/EX TEC/DEV GOV/REL EFFICIENCY TIME 20 PROB/SOLV
GOVERNOR. PAGE 3 B0054 PWR
N19
BURRUS B.R.,INVESTIGATION AND DISCOVERY IN STATE NAT/G
ANTITRUST (PAMPHLET). USA+45 USA-45 LEGIS ECO/TAC PROVS
ADMIN CONTROL CT/SYS CRIME GOV/REL PWR...JURID LAW
CHARTS 19/20 FTC MONOPOLY. PAGE 17 B0355 INSPECT
N19
TREVELYAN G.M.,THE TWO-PARTY SYSTEM IN ENGLISH PARL/PROC
POLITICAL HISTORY (PAMPHLET). UK CHIEF LEGIS POL/PAR
COLONIAL EXEC REV CHOOSE 17/19. PAGE 105 B2128 NAT/G
PWR
B20
HALDANE R.B.,BEFORE THE WAR. MOD/EUR SOCIETY POLICY
INT/ORG NAT/G DELIB/GP PLAN DOMIN EDU/PROP LEGIT DIPLOM
ADMIN COERCE ATTIT DRIVE MORAL ORD/FREE PWR...SOC UK
CONCPT SELF/OBS RECORD BIOG TIME/SEQ. PAGE 45 B0921
B24
POOLE D.C.,THE CONDUCT OF FOREIGN RELATIONS UNDER NAT/G
MODERN DEMOCRATIC CONDITIONS. EUR+WWI USA-45 EDU/PROP
INT/ORG PLAN LEGIT ADMIN KNOWL PWR...MAJORIT DIPLOM
OBS/ENVIR HIST/WRIT GEN/LAWS 20. PAGE 84 B1689
B25
MATHEWS J.M.,AMERICAN STATE GOVERNMENT. USA-45 PROVS
LOC/G CHIEF EX/STRUC LEGIS ADJUD CONTROL CT/SYS ADMIN
ROUTINE GOV/REL PWR 20 GOVERNOR. PAGE 71 B1426 FEDERAL
CONSTN
B26
MOON P.T.,IMPERIALISM AND WORLD POLITICS. AFR ASIA WEALTH

ISLAM MOD/EUR S/ASIA USA-45 SOCIETY NAT/G EX/STRUC TIME/SEQ
BAL/PWR DOMIN COLONIAL NAT/LISM ATTIT DRIVE PWR CAP/ISM
...GEOG SOC 20. PAGE 75 B1510 DIPLOM
B28
FYFE H.,THE BRITISH LIBERAL PARTY. UK SECT ADMIN POL/PAR
LEAD CHOOSE GP/REL PWR SOCISM...MAJORIT TIME/SEQ NAT/G
19/20 LIB/PARTY CONSRV/PAR. PAGE 38 B0768 REPRESENT
POPULISM
B28
HARDMAN J.B.,AMERICAN LABOR DYNAMICS. WORKER LABOR
ECO/TAC DOMIN ADJUD LEAD LOBBY PWR...POLICY MGT. INGP/REL
PAGE 47 B0944 ATTIT
GP/REL
B29
BUELL R.,INTERNATIONAL RELATIONS. WOR+45 WOR-45 INT/ORG
CONSTN STRATA FORCES TOP/EX ADMIN ATTIT DRIVE BAL/PWR
SUPEGO MORAL ORD/FREE PWR SOVEREIGN...JURID SOC DIPLOM
CONCPT 20. PAGE 17 B0340
B29
MOLEY R.,POLITICS AND CRIMINAL PROSECUTION. USA-45 PWR
POL/PAR EX/STRUC LEGIT CONTROL LEAD ROUTINE CHOOSE CT/SYS
INGP/REL...JURID CHARTS 20. PAGE 74 B1497 CRIME
ADJUD
B30
ZINK H.,CITY BOSSES IN THE UNITED STATES: A STUDY LOC/G
OF TWENTY MUNICIPAL BOSSES. USA-45 INDUS MUNIC DOMIN
NEIGH POL/PAR ADMIN CRIME INGP/REL PERS/REL PWR BIOG
...PERS/COMP 20 BOSSISM. PAGE 119 B2403 LEAD
S30
CRAWFORD F.G.,"THE EXECUTIVE BUDGET DECISION IN NEW LEAD
YORK." LEGIS EXEC PWR NEW/YORK. PAGE 25 B0504 BUDGET
PROVS
PROB/SOLV
B31
DEKAT A.D.A.,COLONIAL POLICY. S/ASIA CULTURE DRIVE
EX/STRUC ECO/TAC DOMIN ADMIN COLONIAL ROUTINE PWR
SOVEREIGN WEALTH...POLICY MGT RECORD KNO/TEST SAMP. INDONESIA
PAGE 28 B0570 NETHERLAND
B33
BROMAGE A.W.,AMERICAN COUNTY GOVERNMENT. USA-45 LOC/G
NAT/G LEAD GOV/REL CENTRAL PWR...MGT BIBLIOG 18/20. CREATE
PAGE 15 B0314 ADMIN
MUNIC
B36
ROBINSON H.,DEVELOPMENT OF THE BRITISH EMPIRE. NAT/G
WOR-45 CULTURE SOCIETY STRUCT ECO/DEV ECO/UNDEV HIST/WRIT
INT/ORG VOL/ASSN FORCES CREATE PLAN DOMIN EDU/PROP UK
ADMIN COLONIAL PWR WEALTH...POLICY GEOG CHARTS
CMN/WLTH 16/20. PAGE 89 B1800
B37
GOSNELL H.F.,MACHINE POLITICS: CHICAGO MODEL. POL/PAR
COM/IND FACE/GP LOC/G EX/STRUC LEAD ROUTINE MUNIC
SANCTION REPRESENT GOV/REL PWR...POLICY MATH OBS ADMIN
INT CHARTS. PAGE 41 B0840 CHOOSE
B38
DAY C.,A HISTORY OF COMMERCE. CHRIST-17C EUR+WWI MARKET
ISLAM MEDIT-7 MOD/EUR USA-45 ECO/DEV FINAN NAT/G INT/TRADE
ECO/TAC EXEC ROUTINE PWR WEALTH HIST/WRIT. PAGE 27
B0546
B38
SALTER J.T.,THE AMERICAN POLITICIAN. USA-45 LABOR BIOG
POL/PAR EDU/PROP ADMIN CHOOSE ATTIT DRIVE PERSON LEAD
PWR...POLICY ANTHOL 20 THOMAS/N LEWIS/JL LAGUARD/F PROVS
GOVERNOR MAYOR. PAGE 92 B1865 LOC/G
B39
HITLER A.,MEIN KAMPF. EUR+WWI FUT MOD/EUR STRUCT PWR
INT/ORG LABOR NAT/G POL/PAR FORCES CREATE PLAN NEW/IDEA
BAL/PWR DIPLOM ECO/TAC DOMIN EDU/PROP ADMIN COERCE WAR
ATTIT...SOCIALIST BIOG TREND NAZI. PAGE 50 B1020
B39
ZIMMERN A.,MODERN POLITICAL DOCTRINE. WOR-45 NAT/G
CULTURE SOCIETY ECO/UNDEV DELIB/GP EX/STRUC CREATE ECO/TAC
DOMIN COERCE NAT/LISM ATTIT RIGID/FLEX ORD/FREE PWR BAL/PWR
WEALTH...POLICY CONCPT OBS TIME/SEQ TREND TOT/POP INT/TRADE
LEAGUE/NAT 20. PAGE 119 B2402
B40
HART J.,AN INTRODUCTION TO ADMINISTRATIVE LAW, WITH LAW
SELECTED CASES. USA-45 CONSTN SOCIETY NAT/G ADMIN
EX/STRUC ADJUD CT/SYS LEAD CRIME ORD/FREE LEGIS
...DECISION JURID 20 CASEBOOK. PAGE 47 B0958 PWR
S40
GERTH H.,"THE NAZI PARTY: ITS LEADERSHIP AND POL/PAR
COMPOSITION" (BMR)" GERMANY ELITES STRATA STRUCT DOMIN
EX/STRUC FORCES ECO/TAC CT/SYS CHOOSE TOTALISM LEAD
AGE/Y AUTHORIT PWR 20. PAGE 39 B0792 ADMIN
B41
BURTON M.E.,THE ASSEMBLY OF THE LEAGUE OF NATIONS. DELIB/GP
WOR-45 CONSTN SOCIETY STRUCT INT/ORG NAT/G CREATE EX/STRUC
ATTIT RIGID/FLEX PWR...POLICY TIME/SEQ LEAGUE/NAT DIPLOM
20. PAGE 18 B0359
B41
GELLHORN W.,FEDERAL ADMINISTRATIVE PROCEEDINGS. EX/STRUC
USA+45 CLIENT FACE/GP NAT/G LOBBY REPRESENT PWR 20. LAW
PAGE 39 B0788 ADJUD
POLICY

GOVERNMENT." FUT WOR+45 WOR-45 ECO/DEV LEGIS CREATE SOCIETY
LEGIT ROUTINE ATTIT MORAL PWR WEALTH...CONCPT INT/LAW
GEN/LAWS 20. PAGE 69 B1388

S51
LERNER D.,"THE POLICY SCIENCES: RECENT DEVELOPMENTS CONSULT
IN SCOPE AND METHODS." R+D SERV/IND CREATE DIPLOM SOC
ROUTINE PWR...METH/CNCPT TREND GEN/LAWS METH 20.
PAGE 64 B1297

S51
SCHRAMM W.,"COMMUNICATION IN THE SOVIETIZED STATE, ATTIT
AS DEMONSTRATED IN KOREA." ASIA COM KOREA COM/IND EDU/PROP
FACE/GP POL/PAR SCHOOL FORCES ADMIN PWR MARXISM TOTALISM
...SOC CONCPT MYTH INT BIOG TOT/POP 20. PAGE 94
B1901

S51
SHILS E.A.,"THE LEGISLATOR AND HIS ENVIRONMENT." LEGIS
EX/STRUC DOMIN CONFER EFFICIENCY PWR MAJORIT. TOP/EX
PAGE 96 B1947 ADMIN
DELIB/GP

S51
STEWART D.D.,"THE PLACE OF VOLUNTEER PARTICIPATION ADMIN
IN BUREAUCRATIC ORGANIZATION." NAT/G DELIB/GP PARTIC
OP/RES DOMIN LOBBY WAR ATTIT ROLE PWR. PAGE 101 VOL/ASSN
B2035 FORCES

C51
MOORE B.,"SOVIET POLITICS - THE DILEMMA OF POWER: ATTIT
THE ROLE OF IDEAS IN SOCIAL CHANGE." USSR PROB/SOLV PWR
DIPLOM EDU/PROP ADMIN LEAD ROUTINE REV...POLICY CONCPT
DECISION BIBLIOG 20. PAGE 75 B1512 MARXISM

B52
BRINTON C.,THE ANATOMY OF REVOLUTION. FRANCE UK SOCIETY
USA-45 USSR WOR-45 ELITES INTELL ECO/DEV NAT/G CONCPT
EX/STRUC FORCES COERCE DRIVE ORD/FREE PWR SOVEREIGN REV
...MYTH HIST/WRIT GEN/LAWS. PAGE 15 B0311

B52
HIMMELFARB G.,LORD ACTON: A STUDY IN CONSCIENCE AND PWR
POLITICS. MOD/EUR NAT/G POL/PAR SECT LEGIS TOP/EX BIOG
EDU/PROP ADMIN NAT/LISM ATTIT PERSON SUPEGO MORAL
ORD/FREE...CONCPT PARLIAMENT 19 ACTON/LORD. PAGE 50
B1014

B52
MAIER N.R.F.,PRINCIPLES OF HUMAN RELATIONS. WOR+45 INDUS
WOR-45 CULTURE SOCIETY ROUTINE ATTIT DRIVE PERCEPT
PERSON RIGID/FLEX SUPEGO PWR...PSY CONT/OBS RECORD
TOT/POP VAL/FREE 20. PAGE 68 B1379

B52
POOL I.,SYMBOLS OF DEMOCRACY. WOR+45 WOR-45 POL/PAR INTELL
FORCES ADMIN PERSON PWR...CONCPT 20. PAGE 83 B1687 SOCIETY
USSR

B52
SELZNICK P.,THE ORGANIZATIONAL WEAPON: A STUDY OF MARXISM
BOLSHEVIK STRATEGY AND TACTICS. USSR SOCIETY STRATA POL/PAR
LABOR DOMIN EDU/PROP PARTIC REV ATTIT PWR...POLICY LEAD
MGT CONCPT 20 BOLSHEVISM. PAGE 95 B1929 TOTALISM

S52
BRUEGEL J.W.,"DIE INTERNAZIONALE VOL/ASSN
GEWERKSCHAFTSBEWEGUNG." COM EUR+WWI USA+45 WOR+45 LABOR
DELIB/GP EX/STRUC ECO/TAC EDU/PROP ATTIT PWR TOTALISM
RESPECT SKILL WEALTH WORK 20. PAGE 16 B0330

S52
LIPSET S.M.,"DEMOCRACY IN PRIVATE GOVERNMENT; (A LABOR
CASE STUDY OF THE INTERNATIONAL TYPOGRAPHICAL ADMIN
UNION)" (BMR)" POL/PAR CONTROL LEAD INGP/REL PWR ELITES
...MAJORIT DECISION PREDICT 20. PAGE 65 B1319 REPRESENT

S52
SNIDER C.F.,"AMERICAN COUNTY GOVERNMENT: A MID- LOC/G
CENTURY REVIEW" (BMR)" USA+45 USA-45 PROVS DELIB/GP ADMIN
EX/STRUC BUDGET TAX PWR 20. PAGE 98 B1988 GOV/REL
REGION

C52
LASSWELL H.D.,"THE COMPARATIVE STUDY OF ELITES: AN ELITES
INTRODUCTION AND BIBLIOGRAPHY." STRATA POL/PAR LEAD
EDU/PROP ADMIN LOBBY COERCE ATTIT PERSON PWR CONCPT
...BIBLIOG 20. PAGE 63 B1270 DOMIN

B53
MACMAHON A.W.,ADMINISTRATION IN FOREIGN AFFAIRS. USA+45
NAT/G CONSULT DELIB/GP LEGIS ACT/RES CREATE ADMIN ROUTINE
EXEC RIGID/FLEX PWR...METH/CNCPT TIME/SEQ TOT/POP FOR/AID
VAL/FREE 20. PAGE 68 B1369 DIPLOM

B53
MEYER P.,THE JEWS IN THE SOVIET SATELLITES. COM
CZECHOSLVK POLAND SOCIETY STRATA NAT/G BAL/PWR SECT
ECO/TAC EDU/PROP LEGIT ADMIN COERCE ATTIT DISPL TOTALISM
PERCEPT HEALTH PWR RESPECT WEALTH...METH/CNCPT JEWS USSR
VAL/FREE NAZI 20. PAGE 73 B1474

B53
STENE E.O.,ABANDONMENTS OF THE MANAGER PLAN. LEGIS MUNIC
LEAD GP/REL PWR DECISION. PAGE 100 B2032 EX/STRUC
REPRESENT
ADMIN

B53
THOMAS S.B.,GOVERNMENT AND ADMINISTRATION IN PWR
COMMUNIST CHINA (MONOGRAPH). CHINA/COM PROB/SOLV EX/STRUC
EDU/PROP 20. PAGE 104 B2100 REPRESENT
ELITES

L53
NEWMAN F.C.,"CONGRESS AND THE FAITHFUL EXECUTION OF REPRESENT
LAWS - SHOULD LEGISLATORS SUPERVISE CONTROL
ADMINISTRATORS." USA+45 NAT/G EX/STRUC EXEC PWR ADMIN
POLICY. PAGE 78 B1579 LEGIS

S53
BOSWORTH K.A.,"THE POLITICS OF MANAGEMENT PWR
IMPROVEMENT IN THE STATES" USA+45 POLICY. PAGE 14 PROVS
B0280 LEGIS
EXEC

S53
DRUCKER P.F.,"THE EMPLOYEE SOCIETY." STRUCT BAL/PWR LABOR
PARTIC REPRESENT PWR...DECISION CONCPT. PAGE 30 MGT
B0619 WORKER
CULTURE

S53
GABLE R.W.,"NAM: INFLUENTIAL LOBBY OR KISS OF LOBBY
DEATH?" (BMR)" USA+45 LAW INSPECT EDU/PROP ADMIN LEGIS
CONTROL INGP/REL EFFICIENCY PWR 20 CONGRESS NAM INDUS
TAFT/HART. PAGE 38 B0769 LG/CO

C53
DORWART R.A.,"THE ADMINISTRATIVE REFORMS OF ADMIN
FREDRICK WILLIAM I OF PRUSSIA. GERMANY MOD/EUR NAT/G
CHIEF CONTROL PWR...BIBLIOG 16/18. PAGE 30 B0608 CENTRAL
GOV/REL

B54
COMBS C.H.,DECISION PROCESSES. INTELL SOCIETY MATH
DELIB/GP CREATE TEC/DEV DOMIN LEGIT EXEC CHOOSE DECISION
DRIVE RIGID/FLEX KNOWL PWR...PHIL/SCI SOC
METH/CNCPT CONT/OBS REC/INT PERS/TEST SAMP/SIZ BIOG
SOC/EXP WORK. PAGE 22 B0455

B54
DUVERGER M.,POLITICAL PARTIES: THEIR ORGANIZATION POL/PAR
AND ACTIVITY IN THE MODERN STATE. EUR+WWI MOD/EUR EX/STRUC
USA+45 USA-45 EDU/PROP ADMIN ROUTINE ATTIT DRIVE ELITES
ORD/FREE PWR...SOC CONCPT MATH STAT TIME/SEQ
TOT/POP 19/20. PAGE 31 B0635

B54
GOLDNER A.W.,WILDCAT STRIKE. LABOR TEC/DEV PAY INDUS
ADMIN LEAD PERS/REL ATTIT RIGID/FLEX PWR...MGT WORKER
CONCPT. PAGE 40 B0816 GP/REL
SOC

B54
LAPIERRE R.T.,A THEORY OF SOCIAL CONTROL. STRUCT CONTROL
ADMIN ROUTINE SANCTION ANOMIE AUTHORIT DRIVE PERSON VOL/ASSN
PWR...MAJORIT CONCPT CLASSIF. PAGE 62 B1260 CULTURE

B54
MANGONE G.,A SHORT HISTORY OF INTERNATIONAL INT/ORG
ORGANIZATION. MOD/EUR USA+45 USA-45 WOR+45 WOR-45 INT/LAW
LAW LEGIS CREATE LEGIT ROUTINE RIGID/FLEX PWR
...JURID CONCPT OBS TIME/SEQ STERTYP GEN/LAWS UN
TOT/POP VAL/FREE 18/20. PAGE 69 B1389

B54
MILLARD E.L.,FREEDOM IN A FEDERAL WORLD. FUT WOR+45 INT/ORG
VOL/ASSN TOP/EX LEGIT ROUTINE FEDERAL PEACE ATTIT CREATE
DISPL ORD/FREE PWR...MAJORIT INT/LAW JURID TREND ADJUD
COLD/WAR 20. PAGE 73 B1479 BAL/PWR

S54
COOPER L.,"ADMINISTRATIVE JUSTICE." UK ADMIN LAW
REPRESENT PWR...POLICY 20. PAGE 23 B0475 ADJUD
CONTROL
EX/STRUC

S54
LANE E.,"INTEREST GROUPS AND BUREAUCRACY." NAT/G EX/STRUC
ADMIN GP/REL INGP/REL 20. PAGE 62 B1256 LOBBY
REPRESENT
PWR

B55
APTER D.E.,THE GOLD COAST IN TRANSITION. FUT CONSTN AFR
CULTURE SOCIETY ECO/UNDEV FAM KIN LOC/G NAT/G SOVEREIGN
POL/PAR LEGIS TOP/EX EDU/PROP LEGIT ADMIN ATTIT
PERSON PWR...CONCPT STAT INT CENSUS TOT/POP
VAL/FREE. PAGE 6 B0120

B55
BEISEL A.R.,CONTROL OVER ILLEGAL ENFORCEMENT OF THE ORD/FREE
CRIMINAL LAW: ROLE OF THE SUPREME COURT. CONSTN LAW
ROUTINE MORAL PWR...SOC 20 SUPREME/CT. PAGE 10 CRIME
B0207

B55
CHAPMAN B.,THE PREFECTS AND PROVINCIAL FRANCE. ADMIN
FRANCE DELIB/GP WORKER ROLE PWR 19/20 PREFECT. PROVS
PAGE 20 B0408 EX/STRUC
LOC/G

B55
CHOWDHURI R.N.,INTERNATIONAL MANDATES AND DELIB/GP
TRUSTEESHIP SYSTEMS. WOR+45 STRUCT ECO/UNDEV PLAN
INT/ORG LEGIS DOMIN EDU/PROP LEGIT ADJUD EXEC PWR SOVEREIGN
...CONCPT TIME/SEQ UN 20. PAGE 21 B0427

B55
GALLOWAY G.B.,CONGRESS AND PARLIAMENT: THEIR DELIB/GP
ORGANIZATION AND OPERATION IN THE US AND THE UK: LEGIS
PLANNING PAMPHLET NO. 93. POL/PAR EX/STRUC DEBATE PARL/PROC
CONTROL LEAD ROUTINE EFFICIENCY PWR...POLICY GOV/COMP
CONGRESS PARLIAMENT. PAGE 38 B0777

B55
GUAITA A.,BIBLIOGRAFIA ESPANOLA DE DERECHO BIBLIOG

ADMINISTRATIVO (PAMPHLET). SPAIN LOC/G MUNIC NAT/G
PROVS JUDGE BAL/PWR GOV/REL OWN...JURID 18/19.
PAGE 44 B0900
ADMIN
CONSTN
PWR
B55

POOL I.,SATELLITE GENERALS: A STUDY OF MILITARY
ELITES IN THE SOVIET SPHERE. ASIA CHINA/COM COM
CZECHOSLVK FUT HUNGARY POLAND ROMANIA USSR ELITES
STRATA ADMIN ATTIT PWR SKILL...METH/CNCPT BIOG 20.
PAGE 84 B1688
FORCES
CHOOSE
S55

WEISS R.S.,"A METHOD FOR THE ANALYSIS OF THE
STRUCTURE OF COMPLEX ORGANIZATIONS." WOR+45 INDUS
LG/CO NAT/G EXEC ROUTINE ORD/FREE PWR SKILL...MGT
PSY SOC NEW/IDEA STAT INT REC/INT STAND/INT CHARTS
WORK. PAGE 115 B2316
PROF/ORG
SOC/EXP

GARDNER R.N.,STERLING-DOLLAR DIPLOMACY. EUR+WWI
USA+45 INT/ORG NAT/G PLAN INT/TRADE EDU/PROP ADMIN
KNOWL PWR WEALTH...POLICY SOC METH/CNCPT STAT
CHARTS SIMUL GEN/LAWS 20. PAGE 39 B0781
ECO/DEV
DIPLOM
B56

KAUFMANN W.W.,MILITARY POLICY AND NATIONAL
SECURITY. USA+45 ELITES INTELL NAT/G TOP/EX PLAN
BAL/PWR DIPLOM ROUTINE COERCE NUC/PWR ATTIT
ORD/FREE PWR 20 COLD/WAR. PAGE 58 B1182
FORCES
CREATE
B56

MANNONI D.O.,PROSPERO AND CALIBAN: THE PSYCHOLOGY
OF COLONIZATION. AFR EUR+WWI FAM KIN MUNIC SECT
DOMIN ADMIN ATTIT DRIVE LOVE PWR RESPECT...PSY SOC
CONCPT MYTH OBS DEEP/INT BIOG GEN/METH MALAGASY 20.
PAGE 69 B1394
CULTURE
COLONIAL
B56

SOHN L.B.,BASIC DOCUMENTS OF THE UNITED NATIONS.
WOR+45 LAW INT/ORG LEGIT EXEC ROUTINE CHOOSE PWR
...JURID CONCPT GEN/LAWS ANTHOL UN TOT/POP OAS FAO
ILO 20. PAGE 99 B1993
DELIB/GP
CONSTN
B56

US HOUSE RULES COMM,HEARINGS BEFORE A SPECIAL
SUBCOMMITTEE: ESTABLISHMENT OF A STANDING COMMITTEE
ON ADMINISTRATIVE PROCEDURE, PRACTICE. USA+45 LAW
EX/STRUC ADJUD CONTROL EXEC GOV/REL EFFICIENCY PWR
...POLICY INT 20 CONGRESS. PAGE 109 B2199
ADMIN
DOMIN
DELIB/GP
NAT/G
B56

WAUGH E.W.,SECOND CONSUL. USA+45 USA-45 CONSTN
POL/PAR PROB/SOLV PARL/PROC CHOOSE PERS/REL ATTIT
...BIBLIOG 18/20 VICE/PRES. PAGE 114 B2304
NAT/G
EX/STRUC
PWR
CHIEF
B56

WIGGINS J.R.,FREEDOM OR SECRECY. USA+45 USA-45
DELIB/GP EX/STRUC FORCES ADJUD SANCTION KNOWL PWR
...AUD/VIS CONGRESS 20. PAGE 116 B2344
ORD/FREE
PRESS
NAT/G
CONTROL
B56

WILSON W.,CONGRESSIONAL GOVERNMENT. USA-45 NAT/G
ADMIN EXEC PARL/PROC GP/REL MAJORITY ATTIT 19
SENATE HOUSE/REP. PAGE 117 B2364
LEGIS
CHIEF
CONSTN
PWR
L56

EISENTADT S.N.,"POLITICAL STRUGGLE IN BUREAUCRATIC
SOCIETIES" ASIA CULTURE ADJUD SANCTION PWR
BUREAUCRCY OTTOMAN BYZANTINE. PAGE 33 B0661
ADMIN
CHIEF
CONTROL
ROUTINE
S56

CLEVELAND H.,"THE EXECUTIVE AND THE PUBLIC
INTEREST." USA+45 DOMIN ADMIN PWR...POLICY 20.
PAGE 21 B0437
LOBBY
REPRESENT
CHIEF
EXEC
S56

COTTER C.P.,"ADMINISTRATIVE ACCOUNTABILITY TO
CONGRESS: THE CONCURRENT RESOLUTION." USA+45 NAT/G
EXEC REPRESENT PWR 20. PAGE 24 B0489
CONTROL
GOV/REL
LEGIS
EX/STRUC
S56

GORE W.J.,"ADMINISTRATIVE DECISION-MAKING IN
FEDERAL FIELD OFFICES." USA+45 PROVS PWR CONT/OBS.
PAGE 41 B0833
DECISION
PROB/SOLV
FEDERAL
ADMIN
S56

KAUFMAN H.,"EMERGING CONFLICTS IN THE DOCTRINES OF
PUBLIC ADMINISTRATION" (BMR)" USA+45 USA-45 NAT/G
EX/STRUC LEGIS CONTROL NEUTRAL ATTIT PWR...TREND
20. PAGE 58 B1181
ADMIN
ORD/FREE
REPRESENT
LEAD
S56

KHAMA T.,"POLITICAL CHANGE IN AFRICAN SOCIETY."
CONSTN SOCIETY LOC/G NAT/G POL/PAR EX/STRUC LEGIS
LEGIT ADMIN CHOOSE REPRESENT NAT/LISM MORAL
ORD/FREE PWR...CONCPT OBS TREND GEN/METH CMN/WLTH
17/20. PAGE 59 B1201
AFR
ELITES
S56

MILNE R.S.,"CONTROL OF GOVERNMENT CORPORATIONS IN
THE UNITED STATES." USA+45 NAT/G CHIEF LEGIS BUDGET
20 GENACCOUNT. PAGE 74 B1488
CONTROL
EX/STRUC
GOV/REL
PWR
B57

BEAL J.R.,JOHN FOSTER DULLES, A BIOGRAPHY. USA+45
USSR WOR+45 CONSTN INT/ORG NAT/G EX/STRUC LEGIT
BIOG
DIPLOM

ADMIN NUC/PWR DISPL PERSON ORD/FREE PWR SKILL
...POLICY PSY OBS RECORD COLD/WAR UN 20 DULLES/JF.
PAGE 10 B0200
B57

CHANDRA S.,PARTIES AND POLITICS AT THE MUGHAL
COURT: 1707-1740. INDIA CULTURE EX/STRUC CREATE
PLAN PWR...BIBLIOG/A 18. PAGE 20 B0405
POL/PAR
ELITES
NAT/G
B57

DJILAS M.,THE NEW CLASS: AN ANALYSIS OF THE
COMMUNIST SYSTEM. STRATA CAP/ISM ECO/TAC DOMIN
EDU/PROP LEGIT EXEC COERCE ATTIT PWR MARXISM
...MARXIST MGT CONCPT TIME/SEQ GEN/LAWS 20. PAGE 29
B0600
COM
POL/PAR
USSR
YUGOSLAVIA
B57

HINDERLING A.,DIE REFORMATORISCHE
VERWALTUNGSGERICHTSBARKEIT. GERMANY/W PROB/SOLV
ADJUD SUPEGO PWR...CONCPT 20. PAGE 50 B1015
ADMIN
CT/SYS
JURID
CONTROL
B57

HOLCOMBE A.N.,STRENGTHENING THE UNITED NATIONS.
USA+45 ACT/RES CREATE PLAN EDU/PROP ATTIT PERCEPT
PWR...METH/CNCPT CONT/OBS RECORD UN COLD/WAR 20.
PAGE 51 B1032
INT/ORG
ROUTINE
B57

HUNTINGTON S.P.,THE SOLDIER AND THE STATE: THE
THEORY AND POLITICS OF CIVIL-MILITARY RELATIONS.
USA+45 USA-45 NAT/G PROF/ORG CONSULT DOMIN LEGIT
ROUTINE ATTIT PWR...CONCPT TIME/SEQ COLD/WAR 20.
PAGE 53 B1065
ACT/RES
FORCES
B57

KAPLAN M.A.,SYSTEM AND PROCESS OF INTERNATIONAL
POLITICS. FUT WOR+45 WOR-45 SOCIETY PLAN BAL/PWR
ADMIN ATTIT PERSON RIGID/FLEX PWR SOVEREIGN
...DECISION TREND VAL/FREE. PAGE 58 B1168
INT/ORG
DIPLOM
B57

LOEWENSTEIN K.,POLITICAL POWER AND THE GOVERNMENTAL
PROCESS. WOR+45 WOR-45 CONSTN NAT/G POL/PAR
EX/STRUC LEGIS TOP/EX DOMIN EDU/PROP LEGIT ADMIN
REGION CHOOSE ATTIT...JURID STERTYP GEN/LAWS 20.
PAGE 66 B1336
PWR
CONCPT
B57

MEYER P.,ADMINISTRATIVE ORGANIZATION: A COMPARATIVE
STUDY OF THE ORGANIZATION OF PUBLIC ADMINISTRATION.
DENMARK FRANCE NORWAY SWEDEN UK USA+45 ELITES LOC/G
CONSULT LEGIS ADJUD CONTROL LEAD PWR SKILL
DECISION. PAGE 73 B1475
ADMIN
METH/COMP
NAT/G
CENTRAL
B57

SCHNEIDER E.V.,INDUSTRIAL SOCIOLOGY: THE SOCIAL
RELATIONS OF INDUSTRY AND COMMUNITY. STRATA INDUS
NAT/G NEIGH CREATE ADMIN PARTIC GP/REL RACE/REL
ROLE PWR...POLICY BIBLIOG. PAGE 94 B1898
LABOR
MGT
INGP/REL
STRUCT
B57

SIMON H.A.,MODELS OF MAN, SOCIAL AND RATIONAL:
MATHEMATICAL ESSAYS ON RATIONAL HUMAN BEHAVIOR IN A
SOCIAL SETTING. UNIV LAW SOCIETY FACE/GP VOL/ASSN
CONSULT EX/STRUC LEGIS CREATE ADMIN ROUTINE ATTIT
DRIVE PWR...SOC CONCPT METH/CNCPT QUANT STAT
TOT/POP VAL/FREE 20. PAGE 97 B1959
MATH
SIMUL
L57

DOTSON A.,"FUNDAMENTAL APPROACHES TO
RESPONSIBILITY." USA+45 NAT/G PWR 20. PAGE 30 B0611
ADMIN
REPRESENT
EXEC
CONTROL
S57

COTTER C.P.,"ADMINISTRATIVE ACCOUNTABILITY:
REPORTING TO CONGRESS." USA+45 CONSULT DELIB/GP
PARL/PROC PARTIC GOV/REL ATTIT PWR DECISION.
PAGE 24 B0490
LEGIS
EX/STRUC
REPRESENT
CONTROL
S57

HUITT R.K.,"THE MORSE COMMITTEE ASSIGNMENT
CONTROVERSY: A STUDY IN SENATE NORMS." USA+45
USA-45 POL/PAR SENIOR ROLE SUPEGO SENATE. PAGE 52
B1061
LEGIS
ETIQUET
PWR
ROUTINE
S57

TAYLOR P.S.,"THE RELATION OF RESEARCH TO
LEGISLATIVE AND ADMINISTRATIVE DECISIONS." ELITES
ACT/RES PLAN PROB/SOLV CONFER CHOOSE POLICY.
PAGE 103 B2089
DECISION
LEGIS
MGT
PWR
B58

BERNSTEIN M.H.,THE JOB OF THE FEDERAL EXECUTIVE.
POL/PAR CHIEF LEGIS ADMIN EXEC LOBBY CHOOSE GOV/REL
ORD/FREE PWR...MGT TREND. PAGE 11 B0228
NAT/G
TOP/EX
PERS/COMP
B58

BROWNE C.G.,THE CONCEPT OF LEADERSHIP. UNIV FACE/GP
DOMIN EDU/PROP LEGIT LEAD DRIVE PERSON PWR...MGT
SOC OBS SELF/OBS CONT/OBS INT PERS/TEST STERTYP
GEN/LAWS. PAGE 16 B0328
EXEC
CONCPT
B58

CARTER G.M.,TRANSITION IN AFRICA; STUDIES IN
POLITICAL ADAPTATION. AFR CENTRL/AFR GHANA NIGERIA
CONSTN LOC/G POL/PAR ADMIN GP/REL FEDERAL...MAJORIT
BIBLIOG 20. PAGE 19 B0389
NAT/COMP
PWR
CONTROL
NAT/G
B58

COLEMAN J.S.,NIGERIA: BACKGROUND TO NATIONALISM.
AFR SOCIETY ECO/DEV KIN LOC/G POL/PAR TEC/DEV DOMIN
ADMIN DRIVE PWR RESPECT...TRADIT SOC INT SAMP
NAT/G
NAT/LISM
NIGERIA

B58

KINTNER W.R.,ORGANIZING FOR CONFLICT: A PROPOSAL.
USSR STRUCT NAT/G LEGIS ADMIN EXEC PEACE ORD/FREE
PWR...CONCPT OBS TREND NAT/COMP VAL/FREE COLD/WAR
20. PAGE 60 B1211
USA+45
PLAN
DIPLOM

B58

LAQUER W.Z.,THE MIDDLE EAST IN TRANSITION. COM USSR
ECO/UNDEV NAT/G VOL/ASSN EDU/PROP EXEC ATTIT DRIVE
PWR MARXISM COLD/WAR TOT/POP 20. PAGE 62 B1261
ISLAM
TREND
NAT/LISM

B58

MILLS C.W.,THE CAUSES OF WORLD WAR THREE. FUT
USA+45 INTELL NAT/G DOMIN EDU/PROP ADMIN WAR ATTIT
SOC. PAGE 74 B1487
CONSULT
PWR
ELITES
PEACE

B58

MOEN N.W.,THE GOVERNMENT OF SCOTLAND 1603 - 1625.
UK JUDGE ADMIN GP/REL PWR 17 SCOTLAND COMMON/LAW.
PAGE 74 B1496
CHIEF
JURID
CONTROL
PARL/PROC

B58

SPITZ D.,DEMOCRACY AND THE CHALLANGE OF POWER. FUT
USA+45 USA-45 LAW SOCIETY STRUCT LOC/G POL/PAR
PROVS DELIB/GP EX/STRUC LEGIS TOP/EX ACT/RES CREATE
DOMIN EDU/PROP LEGIT ADJUD ADMIN ATTIT DRIVE MORAL
ORD/FREE TOT/POP. PAGE 99 B2010
NAT/G
PWR

B58

TAYLOR H.,THE STATESMAN. MOD/EUR FACE/GP FAM NAT/G
POL/PAR DELIB/GP LEGIS ATTIT PERSON PWR...POLICY
CONCPT OBS GEN/LAWS. PAGE 103 B2086
EXEC
STRUCT

B58

WHITE L.D.,THE REPUBLICAN ERA: 1869-1901. A STUDY
IN ADMINISTRATIVE HISTORY. USA-45 FINAN PLAN
NEUTRAL CRIME GP/REL MORAL LAISSEZ PRESIDENT
REFORMERS 19 CONGRESS CIVIL/SERV. PAGE 116 B2340
MGT
PWR
DELIB/GP
ADMIN

L58

HAVILAND H.F.,"FOREIGN AID AND THE POLICY PROCESS:
1957." USA+45 FACE/GP POL/PAR VOL/ASSN CHIEF
DELIB/GP ACT/RES LEGIT EXEC GOV/REL ATTIT DRIVE PWR
...POLICY TESTS CONGRESS 20. PAGE 48 B0971
LEGIS
PLAN
FOR/AID

S58

ALMOND G.A.,"COMPARATIVE STUDY OF INTEREST GROUPS."
USA+45 EX/STRUC PWR 20. PAGE 4 B0079
LOBBY
REPRESENT
ADMIN
VOL/ASSN

S58

BLAISDELL D.C.,"PRESSURE GROUPS, FOREIGN POLICIES,
AND INTERNATIONAL POLITICS." USA+45 WOR+45 INT/ORG
PLAN DOMIN EDU/PROP LEGIT ADMIN ROUTINE CHOOSE
...DECISION MGT METH/CNCPT CON/ANAL 20. PAGE 12
B0249
PROF/ORG
PWR

S58

DAVENPORT J.,"ARMS AND THE WELFARE STATE." INTELL
STRUCT FORCES CREATE ECO/TAC FOR/AID DOMIN LEGIT
ADMIN WAR ORD/FREE PWR...POLICY SOC CONCPT MYTH OBS
TREND COLD/WAR TOT/POP 20. PAGE 26 B0533
USA+45
NAT/G
USSR

S58

EISENSTADT S.N.,"INTERNAL CONTRADICTIONS IN
BUREAUCRATIC POLITICS." ADMIN EXEC CENTRAL. PAGE 32
B0658
ELITES
LEAD
PWR
EX/STRUC

S58

JORDAN A.,"MILITARY ASSISTANCE AND NATIONAL
POLICY." ASIA FUT USA+45 WOR+45 ECO/DEV ECO/UNDEV
INT/ORG NAT/G PLAN ECO/TAC ROUTINE WEAPON ATTIT
RIGID/FLEX PWR...CONCPT TREND 20. PAGE 57 B1153
FORCES
POLICY
FOR/AID
DIPLOM

S58

MAIR L.P.,"REPRESENTATIVE LOCAL GOVERNMENT AS A
PROBLEM IN SOCIAL CHANGE." AFR ECO/UNDEV KIN LOC/G
NAT/G SCHOOL JUDGE ADMIN ROUTINE REPRESENT
RIGID/FLEX RESPECT...CONCPT STERTYP CMN/WLTH 20.
PAGE 68 B1383
AFR
PWR
ELITES

S58

SALETAN E.N.,"ADMINISTRATIVE TRUSTIFICATION." NAT/G
EX/STRUC ADMIN 20. PAGE 92 B1862
LOBBY
PWR
CONTROL
REPRESENT

S58

STAAR R.F.,"ELECTIONS IN COMMUNIST POLAND." EUR+WWI
SOCIETY INT/ORG NAT/G POL/PAR LEGIS ACT/RES ECO/TAC
EDU/PROP ADJUD ADMIN ROUTINE COERCE TOTALISM ATTIT
ORD/FREE PWR 20. PAGE 100 B2015
COM
CHOOSE
POLAND

B59

CHINA INSTITUTE OF AMERICA,,CHINA AND THE UNITED
NATIONS. CHINA/COM FUT STRUCT EDU/PROP LEGIT ADMIN
ATTIT KNOWL ORD/FREE PWR...OBS RECORD STAND/INT
TIME/SEQ UN LEAGUE/NAT UNESCO 20. PAGE 21 B0425
ASIA
INT/ORG

B59

DESMITH S.A.,JUDICIAL REVIEW OF ADMINISTRATIVE
ACTION. UK LOC/G CONSULT DELIB/GP ADMIN PWR
...DECISION JURID 20 ENGLSH/LAW. PAGE 28 B0576
ADJUD
NAT/G
PROB/SOLV
CT/SYS

B59

GOODRICH L.,THE UNITED NATIONS. WOR+45 CONSTN
STRUCT ACT/RES LEGIT COERCE KNOWL ORD/FREE PWR
...GEN/LAWS UN 20. PAGE 41 B0825
INT/ORG
ROUTINE

B59

JANOWITZ M.,SOCIOLOGY AND THE MILITARY
ESTABLISHMENT. USA+45 WOR+45 CULTURE SOCIETY
PROF/ORG CONSULT EX/STRUC PLAN TEC/DEV DIPLOM DOMIN
COERCE DRIVE RIGID/FLEX ORD/FREE PWR SKILL COLD/WAR
20. PAGE 55 B1121
FORCES
SOC

B59

MAASS A.,AREA AND POWER: A THEORY OF LOCAL
GOVERNMENT. MUNIC PROVS EX/STRUC LEGIS CT/SYS
CHOOSE PWR 20. PAGE 67 B1354
LOC/G
FEDERAL
BAL/PWR
GOV/REL

B59

MILLETT J.D.,GOVERNMENT AND PUBLIC ADMINISTRATION:
THE QUEST FOR RESPONSIBLE PERFORMANCE. USA+45 NAT/G
DELIB/GP LEGIS CT/SYS EXEC...DECISION MGT. PAGE 73
B1483
ADMIN
PWR
CONSTN
ROLE

B59

MOOS M.,THE CAMPUS AND THE STATE. LAW FINAN
DELIB/GP LEGIS EXEC LOBBY GP/REL PWR...POLICY
BIBLIOG. PAGE 75 B1517
EDU/PROP
ACADEM
PROVS
CONTROL

B59

SCHURZ W.L.,AMERICAN FOREIGN AFFAIRS: A GUIDE TO
INTERNATIONAL AFFAIRS. USA+45 WOR+45 WOR-45 NAT/G
FORCES LEGIS TOP/EX PLAN EDU/PROP LEGIT ADMIN
ROUTINE ATTIT ORD/FREE PWR...SOC CONCPT STAT
SAMP/SIZ CHARTS STERTYP 20. PAGE 95 B1910
INT/ORG
SOCIETY
DIPLOM

B59

SPIRO H.J.,GOVERNMENT BY CONSTITUTIONS: THE
POLITICAL SYSTEMS OF DEMOCRACY. CANADA EUR+WWI FUT
USA+45 WOR+45 WOR-45 LEGIS TOP/EX LEGIT ADMIN
CT/SYS ORD/FREE PWR...TREND TOT/POP VAL/FREE 20.
PAGE 99 B2008
NAT/G
CONSTN

B59

YANG C.K.,A CHINESE VILLAGE IN EARLY COMMUNIST
TRANSITION. ECO/UNDEV AGRI FAM KIN MUNIC FORCES
PLAN ECO/TAC DOMIN EDU/PROP ATTIT DRIVE PWR RESPECT
...SOC CONCPT METH/CNCPT OBS RECORD CON/ANAL CHARTS
WORK 20. PAGE 118 B2389
ASIA
ROUTINE
SOCISM

S59

BAILEY S.D.,"THE FUTURE COMPOSITION OF THE
TRUSTEESHIP COUNCIL." FUT WOR+45 CONSTN VOL/ASSN
ADMIN ATTIT PWR...OBS TREND CON/ANAL VAL/FREE UN
20. PAGE 8 B0161
INT/ORG
NAT/LISM
SOVEREIGN

S59

CHAPMAN B.,"THE FRENCH CONSEIL D'ETAT." FRANCE
NAT/G CONSULT OP/RES PROB/SOLV PWR...OBS 20.
PAGE 20 B0410
ADMIN
LAW
CT/SYS
LEGIS

S59

GABLE R.W.,"CULTURE AND ADMINISTRATION IN IRAN."
IRAN EXEC PARTIC REPRESENT PWR. PAGE 38 B0770
ADMIN
CULTURE
EX/STRUC
INGP/REL

S59

HARVEY M.F.,"THE PALESTINE REFUGEE PROBLEM:
ELEMENTS OF A SOLUTION." ISLAM LAW INT/ORG DELIB/GP
TOP/EX ECO/TAC ROUTINE DRIVE HEALTH LOVE ORD/FREE
PWR WEALTH...MAJORIT FAO 20. PAGE 48 B0964
ACT/RES
LEGIT
PEACE
ISRAEL

S59

KISSINGER H.A.,"THE POLICYMAKER AND THE
INTELLECTUAL." USA+45 CONSULT DELIB/GP ACT/RES
ADMIN ATTIT DRIVE RIGID/FLEX KNOWL PWR...POLICY
PLURIST MGT METH/CNCPT GEN/LAWS GEN/METH 20.
PAGE 60 B1216
INTELL
CREATE

S59

SOHN L.B.,"THE DEFINITION OF AGGRESSION." FUT LAW
FORCES LEGIT ADJUD ROUTINE COERCE ORD/FREE PWR
...MAJORIT JURID QUANT COLD/WAR 20. PAGE 99 B1995
INT/ORG
CT/SYS
DETER
SOVEREIGN

S59

STOESSINGER J.G.,"THE INTERNATIONAL ATOMIC ENERGY
AGENCY: THE FIRST PHASE." FUT WOR+45 NAT/G VOL/ASSN
DELIB/GP BAL/PWR LEGIT ADMIN ROUTINE PWR...OBS
CON/ANAL GEN/LAWS VAL/FREE 20 IAEA. PAGE 101 B2040
INT/ORG
ECO/DEV
FOR/AID
NUC/PWR

B60

BASS B.M.,LEADERSHIP, PSYCHOLOGY, AND
ORGANIZATIONAL BEHAVIOR. DOMIN CHOOSE DRIVE PERSON
PWR RESPECT SKILL...SOC METH/CNCPT OBS. PAGE 9
B0193
UNIV
FACE/GP
DELIB/GP
ROUTINE

B60

CORSON J.J.,GOVERNANCE OF COLLEGES AND
UNIVERSITIES. STRUCT FINAN DELIB/GP DOMIN EDU/PROP
LEAD CHOOSE GP/REL CENTRAL COST PRIVIL SUPEGO
ORD/FREE PWR...DECISION BIBLIOG. PAGE 24 B0481
ADMIN
EXEC
ACADEM
HABITAT

B60

DAVIS K.C.,ADMINISTRATIVE LAW AND GOVERNMENT.
USA+45 EX/STRUC PROB/SOLV ADJUD GP/REL PWR...POLICY
20 SUPREME/CT. PAGE 27 B0543
ADMIN
JURID
CT/SYS
NAT/G

B60

DRAPER T.,AMERICAN COMMUNISM AND SOVIET RUSSIA.
EUR+WWI USA+45 USSR INTELL AGRI COM/IND FINAN INDUS
LABOR PROF/ORG VOL/ASSN PLAN TEC/DEV DOMIN EDU/PROP
ADMIN COERCE REV PERSON PWR...POLICY CONCPT MYTH
19/20. PAGE 30 B0617
COM
POL/PAR

EASTON S.C.,THE TWILIGHT OF EUROPEAN COLONIALISM. AFR S/ASIA CONSTN SOCIETY STRUCT ECO/UNDEV INDUS NAT/G FORCES ECO/TAC COLONIAL CT/SYS ATTIT KNOWL ORD/FREE PWR...SOCIALIST TIME/SEQ TREND CON/ANAL 20. PAGE 32 B0645
B60
FINAN
ADMIN

ECKHOFF T.,RATIONALITY AND RESPONSIBILITY IN ADMINISTRATIVE AND JUDICIAL DECISION-MAKING. ELITES LEAD INGP/REL ATTIT PWR...MGT METH/COMP GAME 20. PAGE 32 B0649
B60
ADMIN
PROB/SOLV
DECISION
METH/CNCPT

FURNISS E.S.,FRANCE, TROUBLED ALLY. EUR+WWI FUT CULTURE SOCIETY BAL/PWR ADMIN ATTIT DRIVE PWR ...TREND TOT/POP 20 DEGAULLE/C. PAGE 38 B0767
B60
NAT/G
FRANCE

GRANICK D.,THE RED EXECUTIVE. COM USA+45 SOCIETY ECO/DEV INDUS NAT/G POL/PAR EX/STRUC PLAN ECO/TAC EDU/PROP ADMIN EXEC ATTIT DRIVE...GP/COMP 20. PAGE 42 B0851
B60
PWR
STRATA
USSR
ELITES

GRUNDLICH T.,DIE TECHNIK DER DIKTATUR. ADMIN TOTALISM ATTIT PWR...MGT CONCPT ARISTOTLE. PAGE 44 B0896
B60
COERCE
DOMIN
ORD/FREE
WAR

HAYNES G.H.,THE SENATE OF THE UNITED STATES: ITS HISTORY AND PRACTICE. CONSTN EX/STRUC TOP/EX CONFER DEBATE LEAD LOBBY PARL/PROC CHOOSE PWR SENATE CONGRESS. PAGE 48 B0977
B60
LEGIS
DELIB/GP

KERSELL J.E.,PARLIAMENTARY SUPERVISION OF DELEGATED LEGISLATION. UK EFFICIENCY PWR...POLICY CHARTS BIBLIOG METH 20 PARLIAMENT. PAGE 59 B1198
B60
LEGIS
CONTROL
NAT/G
EX/STRUC

LENCZOWSKI G.,OIL AND STATE IN THE MIDDLE EAST. FUT IRAN LAW ECO/UNDEV EXTR/IND NAT/G TOP/EX PLAN TEC/DEV ECO/TAC LEGIT ADMIN COERCE ATTIT ALL/VALS PWR...CHARTS 20. PAGE 64 B1288
B60
ISLAM
INDUS
NAT/LISM

LINDSAY K.,EUROPEAN ASSEMBLIES: THE EXPERIMENTAL PERIOD 1949-1959. EUR+WWI ECO/DEV NAT/G POL/PAR LEGIS TOP/EX ACT/RES PLAN ECO/TAC DOMIN LEGIT ROUTINE ATTIT DRIVE ORD/FREE PWR SKILL...SOC CONCPT TREND CHARTS GEN/LAWS VAL/FREE. PAGE 65 B1315
B60
VOL/ASSN
INT/ORG
REGION

LIPSET S.M.,POLITICAL MAN. AFR COM EUR+WWI L/A+17C MOD/EUR S/ASIA USA+45 STRUCT ECO/DEV ECO/UNDEV POL/PAR SECT ADMIN WEALTH...CONCPT WORK TOT/POP 20. PAGE 65 B1320
B60
PWR
SOC

LISKA G.,THE NEW STATECRAFT. WOR+45 WOR-45 LEGIS DIPLOM ADMIN ATTIT PWR WEALTH...HIST/WRIT TREND COLD/WAR 20. PAGE 66 B1323
B60
ECO/TAC
CONCPT
FOR/AID

MUNRO L.,UNITED NATIONS, HOPE FOR A DIVIDED WORLD. FUT WOR+45 CONSTN DELIB/GP CREATE TEC/DEV DIPLOM EDU/PROP LEGIT PEACE ATTIT HEALTH ORD/FREE PWR ...CONCPT TREND UN VAL/FREE 20. PAGE 76 B1540
B60
INT/ORG
ROUTINE

PINTO F.B.M.,ENRIQUECIMENTO ILICITO NO EXERCICIO DE CARGOS PUBLICOS. BRAZIL L/A+17C USA+45 ELITES TRIBUTE CONTROL INGP/REL ORD/FREE PWR...NAT/COMP 20. PAGE 83 B1675
B60
ADMIN
NAT/G
CRIME
LAW

SCHUBERT G.,THE PUBLIC INTEREST. USA+45 CONSULT PLAN PROB/SOLV ADJUD ADMIN GP/REL PWR ALL/IDEOS 20. PAGE 94 B1903
B60
POLICY
DELIB/GP
REPRESENT
POL/PAR

US SENATE COMM. GOVT. OPER.,ORGANIZING FOR NATIONAL SECURITY. USA+45 USA-45 INTELL STRUCT SML/CO ACT/RES ADMIN ATTIT PERSON PWR SKILL...DECISION 20. PAGE 111 B2236
B60
CONSULT
EXEC

WALTER B.,COMMUNICATIONS AND INFLUENCE: DEXISION MAKING IN A MUNICIPAL ADMINISTRATIVE HIERARCHY (PH.D. DISS., UNPUBL.). LEAD CHOOSE PWR METH/CNCPT. PAGE 113 B2284
B60
MUNIC
DECISION
ADMIN
STRUCT

BRENNAN D.G.,"SETTING AND GOALS OF ARMS CONTROL." FUT USA+45 USSR WOR+45 INTELL INT/ORG NAT/G VOL/ASSN CONSULT PLAN DIPLOM ECO/TAC ADMIN KNOWL PWR...POLICY CONCPT TREND COLD/WAR 20. PAGE 15 B0305
L60
FORCES
COERCE
ARMS/CONT
DETER

GRODZINS M.,"AMERICAN POLITICAL PARTIES AND THE AMERICAN SYSTEM" (BMR)" USA+45 LOC/G NAT/G LEGIS BAL/PWR ADMIN ROLE PWR...DECISION 20. PAGE 44 B0883
L60
POL/PAR
FEDERAL
CENTRAL
GOV/REL

STEIN E.,"LEGAL REMEDIES OF ENTERPRISES IN THE EUROPEAN ECONOMIC COMMUNITY." EUR+WWI FUT ECO/DEV INDUS PLAN ECO/TAC ADMIN PWR...MGT MATH STAT TREND CON/ANAL EEC 20. PAGE 100 B2026
L60
MARKET
ADJUD

BAVELAS A.,"LEADERSHIP: MAN AND FUNCTION." WORKER CREATE PLAN CONTROL PERS/REL PERSON PWR...MGT 20. PAGE 10 B0199
S60
LEAD
ADMIN
ROUTINE
ROLE

EMERSON R.,"THE EROSION OF DEMOCRACY." AFR FUT LAW CULTURE INTELL SOCIETY ECO/UNDEV FAM LOC/G NAT/G FORCES PLAN TEC/DEV ECO/TAC ADMIN CT/SYS ATTIT ORD/FREE PWR...SOCIALIST SOC CONCPT STAND/INT TIME/SEQ WORK 20. PAGE 33 B0671
S60
S/ASIA
POL/PAR

FRANKEL S.H.,"ECONOMIC ASPECTS OF POLITICAL INDEPENDENCE IN AFRICA." AFR FUT SOCIETY ECO/UNDEV COM/IND FINAN LEGIS PLAN TEC/DEV CAP/ISM ECO/TAC INT/TRADE ADMIN ATTIT DRIVE RIGID/FLEX PWR WEALTH ...MGT NEW/IDEA MATH TIME/SEQ VAL/FREE 20. PAGE 37 B0751
S60
NAT/G
FOR/AID

HERZ J.H.,"EAST GERMANY: PROGRESS AND PROSPECTS." COM AGRI FINAN INDUS LOC/G NAT/G FORCES PLAN TEC/DEV DOMIN ADMIN COERCE DRIVE PERCEPT RIGID/FLEX MORAL ORD/FREE PWR...MARXIST PSY SOC RECORD STERTYP WORK. PAGE 49 B0997
S60
POL/PAR
STRUCT
GERMANY

HUNTINGTON S.P.,"STRATEGIC PLANNING AND THE POLITICAL PROCESS." USA+45 NAT/G DELIB/GP LEGIS ACT/RES ECO/TAC LEGIT ROUTINE CHOOSE RIGID/FLEX PWR ...POLICY MAJORIT MGT 20. PAGE 53 B1066
S60
EXEC
FORCES
NUC/PWR
WAR

HUTCHINSON C.E.,"AN INSTITUTE FOR NATIONAL SECURITY AFFAIRS." USA+45 R+D NAT/G CONSULT TOP/EX ACT/RES CREATE PLAN TEC/DEV EDU/PROP ROUTINE NUC/PWR ATTIT ORD/FREE PWR...DECISION MGT PHIL/SCI CONCPT RECORD GEN/LAWS GEN/METH 20. PAGE 53 B1068
S60
POLICY
METH/CNCPT
ELITES
DIPLOM

NELSON R.H.,"LEGISLATIVE PARTICIPATION IN THE TREATY AND AGREEMENT MAKING PROCESS." CONSTN POL/PAR PLAN EXEC PWR FAO UN CONGRESS. PAGE 78 B1569
S60
LEGIS
PEACE
DECISION
DIPLOM

RIESELBACH Z.N.,"QUANTITATIVE TECHNIQUES FOR STUDYING VOTING BEHAVIOR IN THE UNITED NATIONS GENERAL ASSEMBLY." S/ASIA USA+45 INT/ORG BAL/PWR DIPLOM ECO/TAC FOR/AID ADMIN PWR...POLICY METH/CNCPT METH UN 20. PAGE 88 B1783
S60
QUANT
CHOOSE

SCHACHTER O.,"THE ENFORCEMENT OF INTERNATIONAL JUDICIAL AND ARBITRAL DECISIONS." WOR+45 NAT/G ECO/TAC DOMIN LEGIT ROUTINE COERCE ATTIT DRIVE ALL/VALS PWR...METH/CNCPT TREND TOT/POP 20 UN. PAGE 93 B1878
S60
INT/ORG
ADJUD
INT/LAW

SCHATZ S.P.,"THE INFLENCE OF PLANNING ON DEVELOPMENT: THE NIGERIAN EXPERIENCE." AFR FUT FINAN INDUS NAT/G EX/STRUC ECO/TAC ADMIN ATTIT PERCEPT ORD/FREE PWR...MATH TREND CON/ANAL SIMUL VAL/FREE 20. PAGE 93 B1883
S60
ECO/UNDEV
PLAN
NIGERIA

SCHER S.,"CONGRESSIONAL COMMITTEE MEMBERS AND INDEPENDENT AGENCY OVERSEERS: A CASE STUDY." DELIB/GP EX/STRUC JUDGE TOP/EX DOMIN ADMIN CONTROL PWR...SOC/EXP HOUSE/REP CONGRESS. PAGE 93 B1886
S60
LEGIS
GOV/REL
LABOR
ADJUD

THOMPSON K.W.,"MORAL PURPOSE IN FOREIGN POLICY: REALITIES AND ILLUSIONS." WOR+45 WOR-45 LAW CULTURE SOCIETY INT/ORG PLAN ADJUD ADMIN COERCE RIGID/FLEX SUPEGO KNOWL ORD/FREE PWR...SOC TREND SOC/EXP TOT/POP 20. PAGE 104 B2104
S60
MORAL
JURID
DIPLOM

MCCLEERY R.,"COMMUNICATION PATTERNS AS BASES OF SYSTEMS OF AUTHORITY AND POWER" IN THEORETICAL STUDIES IN SOCIAL ORGAN. OF PRISON-BMR. USA+45 SOCIETY STRUCT EDU/PROP ADMIN CONTROL COERCE CRIME GP/REL AUTHORIT...SOC 20. PAGE 71 B1443
C60
PERS/REL
PUB/INST
PWR
DOMIN

BANFIELD E.C.,URBAN GOVERNMENT; A READER IN POLITICS AND ADMINISTRATION. ELITES LABOR POL/PAR EXEC CHOOSE REPRESENT GP/REL PWR PLURISM...PSY SOC. PAGE 9 B0177
B61
MUNIC
GEN/METH
DECISION

BARNES W.,THE FOREIGN SERVICE OF THE UNITED STATES. USA+45 USA-45 CONSTN INT/ORG POL/PAR CONSULT DELIB/GP LEGIS DOMIN EDU/PROP EXEC ATTIT RIGID/FLEX ORD/FREE PWR...POLICY CONCPT STAT OBS RECORD BIOG TIME/SEQ TREND. PAGE 9 B0188
B61
NAT/G
MGT
DIPLOM

BARRASH J.,LABOR'S GRASS ROOTS; A STUDY OF THE LOCAL UNION. STRATA BARGAIN LEAD REPRESENT DEMAND ATTIT PWR. PAGE 9 B0190
B61
LABOR
USA+45
INGP/REL
EXEC

BISHOP D.G.,THE ADMINISTRATION OF BRITISH FOREIGN RELATIONS. EUR+WWI MOD/EUR INT/ORG NAT/G POL/PAR DELIB/GP LEGIS TOP/EX ECO/TAC DOMIN EDU/PROP ADMIN COERCE 20. PAGE 12 B0243
B61
ROUTINE
PWR
DIPLOM
UK

B61
DARRAH E.L.,FIFTY STATE GOVERNMENTS: A COMPILATION OF EXECUTIVE ORGANIZATION CHARTS. USA+45 LOC/G DELIB/GP LEGIS ADJUD LEAD PWR 20 GOVERNOR. PAGE 26 B0530
EX/STRUC ADMIN ORG/CHARTS PROVS

B61
DUBIN R.,HUMAN RELATIONS IN ADMINISTRATION. USA+45 INDUS LABOR LG/CO EX/STRUC GP/REL DRIVE PWR ...DECISION SOC CHARTS ANTHOL 20. PAGE 31 B0623
PERS/REL MGT ADMIN EXEC

B61
GORDON R.A.,BUSINESS LEADERSHIP IN THE LARGE CORPORATION. USA+45 SOCIETY EX/STRUC ADMIN CONTROL ROUTINE GP/REL PWR...MGT 20. PAGE 41 B0831
LG/CO LEAD DECISION LOBBY

B61
HAMILTON A.,THE FEDERALIST. USA-45 NAT/G VOL/ASSN LEGIS TOP/EX EDU/PROP LEGIT CHOOSE ATTIT RIGID/FLEX ORD/FREE PWR...MAJORIT JURID CONCPT ANTHOL. PAGE 46 B0931
EX/STRUC CONSTN

B61
KOESTLER A.,THE LOTUS AND THE ROBOT. ASIA INDIA S/ASIA SOCIETY STRATA ECO/DEV AGRI INDUS FAM CREATE DOMIN EDU/PROP ADMIN COERCE ATTIT DRIVE SUPEGO ORD/FREE PWR RESPECT WEALTH...MYTH OBS 20 CHINJAP. PAGE 61 B1226
SECT ECO/UNDEV

B61
KRUPP S.,PATTERN IN ORGANIZATIONAL ANALYSIS: A CRITICAL EXAMINATION. INGP/REL PERS/REL RATIONAL ATTIT AUTHORIT DRIVE PWR...DECISION PHIL/SCI SOC IDEA/COMP. PAGE 61 B1239
MGT CONTROL CONCPT METH/CNCPT

B61
LASSWELL H.D.,PSYCOPATHOLOGY AND POLITICS. WOR-45 CULTURE SOCIETY FACE/GP NAT/G CONSULT CREATE EDU/PROP EXEC ROUTINE DISPL DRIVE PERSON PWR RESPECT...PSY CONCPT METH/CNCPT METH. PAGE 63 B1272
ATTIT GEN/METH

B61
MARVICK D.,POLITICAL DECISION-MAKERS. INTELL STRATA NAT/G POL/PAR EX/STRUC LEGIS DOMIN EDU/PROP ATTIT PERSON PWR...PSY STAT OBS CONT/OBS STAND/INT UNPLAN/INT TIME/SEQ CHARTS STERTYP VAL/FREE. PAGE 70 B1416
TOP/EX BIOG ELITES

B61
MARX K.,THE COMMUNIST MANIFESTO. IN (MENDEL A., ESSENTIAL WORKS OF MARXISM, NEW YORK: BANTAM. FUT MOD/EUR CULTURE ECO/DEV ECO/UNDEV AGRI FINAN INDUS MARKET PROC/MFG LABOR MUNIC POL/PAR CONSULT FORCES CREATE PLAN ADMIN ATTIT DRIVE RIGID/FLEX ORD/FREE PWR RESPECT MARX/KARL WORK. PAGE 70 B1421
COM NEW/IDEA CAP/ISM REV

B61
MOLLAU G.,INTERNATIONAL COMMUNISM AND WORLD REVOLUTION: HISTORY AND METHODS. RUSSIA USSR INT/ORG NAT/G POL/PAR VOL/ASSN FORCES BAL/PWR DIPLOM EXEC REGION WAR ATTIT PWR MARXISM...CONCPT TIME/SEQ COLD/WAR 19/20. PAGE 74 B1498
COM REV

B61
MONAS S.,THE THIRD SECTION: POLICE AND SOCIETY IN RUSSIA UNDER NICHOLAS I. MOD/EUR RUSSIA ELITES STRUCT NAT/G EX/STRUC ADMIN CONTROL PWR CONSERVE ...DECISION 19 NICHOLAS/I. PAGE 74 B1499
ORD/FREE COM FORCES COERCE

B61
NARAIN J.P.,SWARAJ FOR THE PEOPLE. INDIA CONSTN LOC/G MUNIC POL/PAR CHOOSE REPRESENT EFFICIENCY ATTIT PWR SOVEREIGN 20. PAGE 77 B1553
NAT/G ORD/FREE EDU/PROP EX/STRUC

B61
PETRULLO L.,LEADERSHIP AND INTERPERSONAL BEHAVIOR. FACE/GP FAM PROF/ORG EX/STRUC FORCES DOMIN WAR GP/REL PERS/REL EFFICIENCY PRODUC PWR...MGT PSY. PAGE 82 B1663
PERSON ATTIT LEAD HABITAT

B61
ROWAT D.C.,BASIC ISSUES IN PUBLIC ADMINISTRATION. STRUCT EX/STRUC PWR CONSERVE...MAJORIT DECISION MGT T 20 BUREAUCRCY. PAGE 91 B1839
NAT/G ADJUD ADMIN

B61
STONE J.,QUEST FOR SURVIVAL. WOR+45 NAT/G VOL/ASSN LEGIT ADMIN ARMS/CONT COERCE DISPL ORD/FREE PWR ...POLICY INT/LAW JURID COLD/WAR 20. PAGE 101 B2047
INT/ORG ADJUD SOVEREIGN

B61
STRAUSS E.,THE RULING SERVANTS. FRANCE UK USSR WOR+45 WOR-45 NAT/G CONSULT DELIB/GP EX/STRUC TOP/EX DOMIN EDU/PROP LEGIT ROUTINE...MGT TIME/SEQ STERTYP 20. PAGE 101 B2051
ADMIN PWR ELITES

B61
TANZER L.,THE KENNEDY CIRCLE. INTELL CONSULT DELIB/GP TOP/EX CONTROL EXEC INGP/REL PERS/REL PWR ...BIOG IDEA/COMP ANTHOL 20 KENNEDY/JF PRESIDENT DEMOCRAT MCNAMARA/R RUSK/D. PAGE 103 B2077
EX/STRUC NAT/G CHIEF

L61
GERWIG R.,"PUBLIC AUTHORITIES IN THE UNITED STATES." LAW CONSTN PROVS TAX ADMIN FEDERAL. PAGE 39 B0793
LOC/G MUNIC GOV/REL PWR

L61
KRAMER R.,"EXECUTIVE PRIVILEGE - A STUDY OF THE PERIOD 1953-1960." NAT/G CHIEF EX/STRUC LEGIS PWR.
REPRESENT LEAD

PAGE 61 B1233
EXEC GOV/REL

S61
ABLARD C.D.,"EX PARTE CONTACTS WITH FEDERAL ADMINISTRATIVE AGENCIES." USA+45 CLIENT NAT/G DELIB/GP ADMIN PWR 20. PAGE 3 B0055
EXEC ADJUD LOBBY REPRESENT

S61
ANGLIN D.,"UNITED STATES OPPOSITION TO CANADIAN MEMBERSHIP IN THE PAN AMERICAN UNION: A CANADIAN VIEW." L/A+17C UK USA+45 VOL/ASSN DELIB/GP EX/STRUC PLAN DIPLOM DOMIN REGION ATTIT RIGID/FLEX PWR ...RELATIV CONCPT STERTYP CMN/WLTH OAS 20. PAGE 5 B0112
INT/ORG CANADA

S61
BROWN M.,"THE DEMISE OF STATE DEPARTMENT PUBLIC OPINION POLLS: A STUDY IN LEGISLATIVE OVERSIGHT." PWR...POLICY PSY SAMP. PAGE 16 B0325
EDU/PROP NAT/G LEGIS ADMIN

S61
HAAS E.B.,"INTERNATIONAL INTEGRATION: THE EUROPEAN AND THE UNIVERSAL PROCESS." EUR+WWI FUT WOR+45 NAT/G EX/STRUC ATTIT DRIVE ORD/FREE PWR...CONCPT GEN/LAWS OEEC 20 NATO COUNCL/EUR. PAGE 45 B0909
INT/ORG TREND REGION

S61
KUIC V.,"THEORY AND PRACTICE OF THE AMERICAN PRESIDENCY." USA+45 USA-45 NAT/G ADMIN REPRESENT ...PLURIST 20 PRESIDENT. PAGE 61 B1241
EXEC EX/STRUC PWR CHIEF

S61
LIEBENOW J.G.,"LEGITIMACY OF ALIEN RELATIONSHIP: THE NYATURU OF TANGANYIKA" (BMR)" AFR UK ADMIN LEAD CHOOSE 20 NYATURU TANGANYIKA. PAGE 65 B1312
COLONIAL DOMIN LEGIT PWR

S61
LYONS G.M.,"THE NEW CIVIL-MILITARY RELATIONS." USA+45 NAT/G EX/STRUC TOP/EX PROB/SOLV ADMIN EXEC PARTIC 20. PAGE 67 B1350
CIVMIL/REL PWR REPRESENT

S61
REAGAN M.O.,"THE POLITICAL STRUCTURE OF THE FEDERAL RESERVE SYSTEM." USA+45 FINAN NAT/G ADMIN 20. PAGE 87 B1748
PWR EX/STRUC EXEC LEAD

S61
SHERBENOU E.L.,"CLASS, PARTICIPATION, AND THE COUNCIL-MANAGER PLAN." ELITES STRUCT LEAD GP/REL ATTIT PWR DECISION. PAGE 96 B1942
REPRESENT MUNIC EXEC

S61
TOMASIC D.,"POLITICAL LEADERSHIP IN CONTEMPORARY POLAND." COM EUR+WWI GERMANY NAT/G POL/PAR SECT DELIB/GP PLAN ECO/TAC DOMIN EDU/PROP PWR MARXISM ...MARXIST GEOG MGT CONCPT TIME/SEQ STERTYP 20. PAGE 105 B2114
SOCIETY ROUTINE USSR POLAND

S61
VINER J.,"ECONOMIC FOREIGN POLICY ON THE NEW FRONTIER." USA+45 ECO/UNDEV AGRI FINAN INDUS MARKET INT/ORG NAT/G FOR/AID INT/TRADE ADMIN ATTIT PWR 20 KENNEDY/JF. PAGE 112 B2262
TOP/EX ECO/TAC BAL/PAY TARIFFS

C61
ETZIONI A.,"A COMPARATIVE ANALYSIS OF COMPLEX ORGANIZATIONS: ON POWER, INVOLVEMENT AND THEIR CORRELATES." ELITES CREATE OP/RES ROUTINE INGP/REL PERS/REL CONSEN ATTIT DRIVE PWR...CONCPT BIBLIOG. PAGE 34 B0684
CON/ANAL SOC LEAD CONTROL

B62
BAILEY S.D.,THE SECRETARIAT OF THE UNITED NATIONS. FUT WOR+45 DELIB/GP PLAN BAL/PWR DOMIN EDU/PROP ADMIN PEACE ATTIT PWR...DECISION CONCPT TREND CON/ANAL CHARTS UN VAL/FREE COLD/WAR 20. PAGE 8 B0162
INT/ORG EXEC DIPLOM

B62
BINDER L.,IRAN: POLITICAL DEVELOPMENT IN A CHANGING SOCIETY. IRAN OP/RES REV GP/REL CENTRAL RATIONAL PWR...PHIL/SCI NAT/COMP GEN/LAWS 20. PAGE 12 B0239
LEGIT NAT/G ADMIN STRUCT

B62
CAIRNCROSS A.K.,FACTORS IN ECONOMIC DEVELOPMENT. WOR+45 ECO/UNDEV INDUS R+D LG/CO NAT/G EX/STRUC PLAN TEC/DEV ECO/TAC ATTIT HEALTH KNOWL PWR WEALTH ...TIME/SEQ GEN/LAWS TOT/POP VAL/FREE 20. PAGE 18 B0363
MARKET ECO/DEV

B62
DODDS H.W.,THE ACADEMIC PRESIDENT "EDUCATOR OR CARETAKER? FINAN DELIB/GP EDU/PROP PARTIC ATTIT ROLE PWR...POLICY RECORD INT. PAGE 30 B0601
ACADEM ADMIN LEAD CONTROL

B62
EVANS M.S.,THE FRINGE ON TOP. USSR EX/STRUC FORCES DIPLOM ECO/TAC PEACE CONSERVE SOCISM...TREND 20 KENNEDY/JF. PAGE 34 B0689
NAT/G PWR CENTRAL POLICY

B62
FOSS P.O.,REORGANIZATION AND REASSIGNMENT IN THE CALIFORNIA HIGHWAY PATROL (PAMPHLET). USA+45 STRUCT WORKER EDU/PROP CONTROL COERCE INGP/REL ORD/FREE PWR...DECISION 20 CALIFORNIA. PAGE 37 B0744
FORCES ADMIN PROVS PLAN

HADWEN J.G.,HOW UNITED NATIONS DECISIONS ARE MADE. INT/ORG
WOR+45 LAW EDU/PROP LEGIT ADMIN PWR...DECISION ROUTINE
SELF/OBS GEN/LAWS UN 20. PAGE 45 B0912 B62

INSTITUTE JUDICIAL ADMIN.JUDGES: THEIR TEMPORARY NAT/G
APPOINTMENT, ASSIGNMENT AND TRANSFER: SURVEY OF FED LOC/G
AND STATE CONSTN'S STATUTES, ROLES OF CT. USA+45 JUDGE
CONSTN PROVS CT/SYS GOV/REL PWR JURID. PAGE 54 ADMIN
B1090 B62

INTERNATIONAL LABOR OFFICE,WORKERS' MANAGEMENT IN WORKER
YUGOSLAVIA. COM YUGOSLAVIA LABOR DELIB/GP EX/STRUC CONTROL
PROB/SOLV ADMIN PWR MARXISM...CHARTS ORG/CHARTS MGT
BIBLIOG 20. PAGE 54 B1098 INDUS B62

JEWELL M.E.,SENATORIAL POLITICS AND FOREIGN POLICY. USA+45
NAT/G POL/PAR CHIEF DELIB/GP TOP/EX FOR/AID LEGIS
EDU/PROP ROUTINE ATTIT PWR SKILL...MAJORIT DIPLOM
METH/CNCPT TIME/SEQ CONGRESS 20 PRESIDENT. PAGE 56
B1138 B62

KAMMERER G.M.,CITY MANAGERS IN POLITICS: AN MUNIC
ANALYSIS OF MANAGER TENURE AND TERMINATION. POL/PAR LEAD
LEGIS PARTIC CHOOSE PWR...DECISION GEOG METH/CNCPT. EXEC
PAGE 57 B1161 B62

LAWSON R.,INTERNATIONAL REGIONAL ORGANIZATIONS. INT/ORG
WOR+45 NAT/G VOL/ASSN CONSULT LEGIS EDU/PROP LEGIT DELIB/GP
ADMIN EXEC ROUTINE HEALTH PWR WEALTH...JURID EEC REGION
COLD/WAR 20 UN. PAGE 63 B1277 B62

LITTLEFIELD N.,METROPOLITAN AREA PROBLEMS AND LOC/G
MUNICIPAL HOME RULE. USA+45 PROVS ADMIN CONTROL SOVEREIGN
GP/REL PWR. PAGE 66 B1328 JURID
LEGIS B62

LOWI T.J.,LEGISLATIVE POLITICS U.S.A. LAW LEGIS PARL/PROC
DIPLOM EXEC LOBBY CHOOSE SUFF FEDERAL PWR 19/20 REPRESENT
CONGRESS. PAGE 67 B1345 POLICY
ROUTINE B62

MODELSKI G.,A THEORY OF FOREIGN POLICY. WOR+45 PLAN
WOR-45 NAT/G DELIB/GP EX/STRUC TOP/EX EDU/PROP PWR
LEGIT ROUTINE...POLICY CONCPT TOT/POP COLD/WAR 20. DIPLOM
PAGE 74 B1494 B62

MORTON L.,STRATEGY AND COMMAND: THE FIRST TWO WAR
YEARS. USA-45 NAT/G CONTROL EXEC LEAD WEAPON FORCES
CIVMIL/REL PWR...POLICY AUD/VIS CHARTS 20 CHINJAP. PLAN
PAGE 76 B1532 DIPLOM B62

MULLEY F.W.,THE POLITICS OF WESTERN DEFENSE. INT/ORG
EUR+WWI USA-45 WOR+45 VOL/ASSN EX/STRUC FORCES DELIB/GP
COERCE DETER PEACE ATTIT ORD/FREE PWR...RECORD NUC/PWR
TIME/SEQ CHARTS COLD/WAR 20 NATO. PAGE 76 B1537 B62

NICHOLAS H.G.,THE UNITED NATIONS AS A POLITICAL INT/ORG
INSTITUTION. WOR+45 CONSTN EX/STRUC ACT/RES LEGIT ROUTINE
PERCEPT KNOWL PWR...CONCPT TIME/SEQ CON/ANAL
ORG/CHARTS UN 20. PAGE 78 B1580 B62

OLLE-LAPRUNE J.,LA STABILITE DES MINISTRES SOUS LA LEGIS
TROISIEME REPUBLIQUE, 1879-1940. FRANCE CONSTN NAT/G
POL/PAR LEAD WAR INGP/REL RIGID/FLEX PWR...POLICY ADMIN
CHARTS 19/20. PAGE 79 B1606 PERSON B62

PHILLIPS O.H.,CONSTITUTIONAL AND ADMINISTRATIVE LAW JURID
(3RD ED.). UK INT/ORG LOC/G CHIEF EX/STRUC LEGIS ADMIN
BAL/PWR ADJUD COLONIAL CT/SYS PWR...CHARTS 20. CONSTN
PAGE 83 B1670 NAT/G B62

RUDOLPH F.,THE AMERICAN COLLEGE AND UNIVERSITY. ACADEM
CLIENT FINAN PUB/INST DELIB/GP EDU/PROP CONTROL INGP/REL
EXEC CONSEN ATTIT POLICY. PAGE 92 B1853 PWR
ADMIN B62

SAMPSON A.,ANATOMY OF BRITAIN. UK LAW COM/IND FINAN ELITES
INDUS MARKET MUNIC POL/PAR EX/STRUC TOP/EX DIPLOM PWR
LEAD REPRESENT PERSON PARLIAMENT WORSHIP. PAGE 92 STRUCT
B1866 FORCES B62

SCHILLING W.R.,STRATEGY, POLITICS, AND DEFENSE ROUTINE
BUDGETS. USA+45 R+D NAT/G CONSULT DELIB/GP FORCES POLICY
LEGIS ACT/RES PLAN BAL/PWR LEGIT EXEC NUC/PWR
RIGID/FLEX PWR...TREND COLD/WAR CONGRESS 20
EISNHWR/DD. PAGE 93 B1890 B62

SCHULMAN S.,TOWARD JUDICIAL REFORM IN PENNSYLVANIA; CT/SYS
A STUDY IN COURT REORGANIZATION. USA+45 CONSTN ACT/RES
JUDGE PLAN ADMIN LOBBY SANCTION PRIVIL PWR...JURID PROB/SOLV
20 PENNSYLVAN. PAGE 94 B1905 B62

SIMON Y.R.,A GENERAL THEORY OF AUTHORITY. DOMIN PERS/REL
ADMIN RATIONAL UTOPIA KNOWL MORAL PWR SOVEREIGN PERSON
...HUM CONCPT NEW/IDEA 20. PAGE 97 B1962 SOCIETY

SNYDER R.C.,FOREIGN POLICY DECISION-MAKING. FUT ORD/FREE
KOREA WOR+45 R+D CREATE ADMIN ROUTINE PWR B62
...DECISION PSY SOC CONCPT METH/CNCPT CON/ANAL TEC/DEV
CHARTS GEN/METH METH 20. PAGE 99 B1992 HYPO/EXP
DIPLOM

US ADVISORY COMN INTERGOV REL,STATE CONSTITUTIONAL LOC/G B62
AND STATUTORY RESTRICTIONS UPON THE STRUCTURAL, CONSTN
FUNCTIONAL, AND PERSONAL POWERS OF LOCAL GOV'T. PROVS
EX/STRUC ACT/RES DOMIN GOV/REL PWR...POLICY LAW
DECISION 17/20. PAGE 108 B2172

WANGSNESS P.H.,THE POWER OF THE CITY MANAGER. PWR B62
USA+45 EX/STRUC BAL/PWR BUDGET TAX ADMIN REPRESENT TOP/EX
CENTRAL EFFICIENCY DRIVE ROLE...POLICY 20 CITY/MGT. MUNIC
PAGE 113 B2286 LOC/G

ABERLE D.F.,"CHAHAR AND DAGOR MONGOL BUREAUCRATIC EX/STRUC L62
ADMINISTRATION: 19621945." ASIA MUNIC TOP/EX PWR STRATA
...MGT OBS INT MONGOL 20. PAGE 3 B0053

BAILEY S.D.,"THE TROIKA AND THE FUTURE OF THE UN." FUT L62
CONSTN CREATE LEGIT EXEC CHOOSE ORD/FREE PWR INT/ORG
...CONCPT NEW/IDEA UN COLD/WAR 20. PAGE 8 B0163 USSR

CAVERS D.F.,"ADMINISTRATIVE DECISION-MAKING IN REPRESENT L62
NUCLEAR FACILITIES LICENSING." USA+45 CLIENT ADMIN LOBBY
EXEC 20 AEC. PAGE 19 B0395 PWR
CONTROL

NEIBURG H.L.,"THE EISENHOWER AEC AND CONGRESS: A CHIEF L62
STUDY IN EXECUTIVE-LEGISLATIVE RELATIONS." USA+45 LEGIS
NAT/G POL/PAR DELIB/GP EX/STRUC TOP/EX ADMIN EXEC GOV/REL
LEAD ROUTINE PWR...POLICY COLD/WAR CONGRESS NUC/PWR
PRESIDENT AEC. PAGE 77 B1567

WATERSTON A.,"PLANNING IN MOROCCO, ORGANIZATION AND NAT/G L62
IMPLEMENTATION. BALTIMORE: HOPKINS ECON. DEVELOP. PLAN
INT. BANK FOR." ISLAM ECO/DEV AGRI DIST/IND INDUS MOROCCO
PROC/MFG SERV/IND LOC/G EX/STRUC ECO/TAC PWR WEALTH
TOT/POP VAL/FREE 20. PAGE 114 B2302

BOOTH D.A.,"POWER STRUCTURE AND COMMUNITY CHANGE: A MUNIC S62
REPLICATION STUDY OF COMMUNITY A." STRATA LABOR ELITES
LEAD PARTIC REPRESENT...DECISION MGT TIME. PAGE 14 PWR
B0275

BRZEZINSKI Z.K.,"DEVIATION CONTROL: A STUDY IN THE RIGID/FLEX S62
DYNAMICS OF DOCTRINAL CONFLICT." WOR+45 WOR-45 ATTIT
VOL/ASSN CREATE BAL/PWR DOMIN EXEC DRIVE PERCEPT
PWR...METH/CNCPT TIME/SEQ TREND 20. PAGE 16 B0333

DAKIN R.E.,"VARIATIONS IN POWER STRUCTURES AND MUNIC S62
ORGANIZING EFFICIENCY: A COMPARATIVE STUDY OF FOUR STRUCT
AREAS." STRATA EDU/PROP ADMIN LEAD GP/REL GOV/COMP. PWR
PAGE 26 B0524

GUYOT J.F.,"GOVERNMENT BUREAUCRATS ARE DIFFERENT." ATTIT S62
USA+45 REPRESENT PWR 20. PAGE 45 B0906 DRIVE
TOP/EX
ADMIN

HUDSON G.F.,"SOVIET FEARS OF THE WEST." COM USA+45 ATTIT S62
SOCIETY DELIB/GP EX/STRUC TOP/EX ACT/RES CREATE MYTH
DOMIN EDU/PROP LEGIT ADMIN ROUTINE DRIVE PERSON GERMANY
RIGID/FLEX PWR...RECORD TIME/SEQ TOT/POP 20 USSR
STALIN/J. PAGE 52 B1057

JACOBSON H.K.,"THE UNITED NATIONS AND COLONIALISM: INT/ORG S62
A TENTATIVE APPRAISAL." AFR FUT S/ASIA USA+45 USSR CONCPT
WOR+45 NAT/G DELIB/GP PLAN DIPLOM ECO/TAC DOMIN COLONIAL
ADMIN ROUTINE COERCE ATTIT RIGID/FLEX ORD/FREE PWR
...OBS STERTYP UN 20. PAGE 55 B1115

LOCKARD D.,"THE CITY MANAGER, ADMINISTRATIVE THEORY MUNIC S62
AND POLITICAL POWER." LEGIS ADMIN REPRESENT GP/REL EXEC
PWR. PAGE 66 B1333 LEAD
DECISION

MARTIN L.W.,"POLITICAL SETTLEMENTS AND ARMS CONCPT S62
CONTROL." COM EUR+WWI GERMANY USA+45 PROVS FORCES ARMS/CONT
TOP/EX ACT/RES CREATE DOMIN LEGIT ROUTINE COERCE
ATTIT RIGID/FLEX ORD/FREE PWR...METH/CNCPT RECORD
GEN/LAWS 20. PAGE 70 B1410

MCCLELLAND C.A.,"DECISIONAL OPPORTUNITY AND ACT/RES S62
POLITICAL CONTROVERSY." USA+45 NAT/G POL/PAR FORCES PERCEPT
TOP/EX DOMIN ADMIN PEACE DRIVE ORD/FREE PWR DIPLOM
...DECISION SIMUL 20. PAGE 72 B1444

PIQUEMAL M.,"LES PROBLEMES DES UNIONS D'ETATS EN AFR S62
AFRIQUE NOIRE." FRANCE SOCIETY INT/ORG NAT/G ECO/UNDEV
DELIB/GP PLAN LEGIT ADMIN COLONIAL ROUTINE ATTIT REGION
ORD/FREE PWR...GEOG METH/CNCPT 20. PAGE 83 B1678

S62

SPRINGER H.W.,"FEDERATION IN THE CARIBBEAN: AN
ATTEMPT THAT FAILED." L/A+17C ECO/UNDEV INT/ORG
POL/PAR PROVS LEGIS CREATE PLAN LEGIT ADMIN FEDERAL
ATTIT DRIVE PERSON ORD/FREE PWR...POLICY GEOG PSY
CONCPT OBS CARIBBEAN CMN/WLTH 20. PAGE 100 B2013

VOL/ASSN
NAT/G
INT/ORG
REGION

S62

TANNENBAUM A.S.,"CONTROL IN ORGANIZATIONS:
INDIVIDUAL ADJUSTMENT AND ORGANIZATIONAL
PERFORMANCE." DOMIN PARTIC REPRESENT INGP/REL
PRODUC ATTIT DRIVE PWR...PSY CORREL. PAGE 102 B2073

ADMIN
MGT
STRUCT
CONTROL

S62

TRUMAN D.,"THE DOMESTIC POLITICS OF FOREIGN AID."
USA+45 WOR+45 NAT/G POL/PAR LEGIS DIPLOM ECO/TAC
EDU/PROP ADMIN CHOOSE ATTIT PWR CONGRESS 20
CONGRESS. PAGE 105 B2129

ROUTINE
FOR/AID

N62

UNIVERSITY PITT INST LOC GOVT,THE COUNCIL-MANAGER
FORM OF GOVERNMENT IN PENNSYLVANIA (PAMPHLET).
PROVS EX/STRUC REPRESENT GOV/REL EFFICIENCY
...CHARTS SIMUL 20 PENNSYLVAN CITY/MGT. PAGE 107
B2169

LOC/G
TOP/EX
MUNIC
PWR

N62

US ADVISORY COMN INTERGOV REL,ALTERNATIVE
APPROACHES TO GOVERNMENTAL REORGANIZATION IN
METROPOLITAN AREAS (PAMPHLET). EX/STRUC LEGIS EXEC
LEAD PWR...DECISION GEN/METH. PAGE 107 B2171

MUNIC
REGION
PLAN
GOV/REL

B63

BONINI C.P.,SIMULATION OF INFORMATION AND DECISION
SYSTEMS IN THE FIRM. MARKET BUDGET DOMIN ECO/PROP
ADMIN COST ATTIT HABITAT PERCEPT PWR...CONCPT
PROBABIL QUANT PREDICT HYPO/EXP BIBLIOG. PAGE 13
B0273

INDUS
SIMUL
DECISION
MGT

B63

BOWETT D.W.,THE LAW OF INTERNATIONAL INSTITUTIONS.
WOR+45 WOR-45 CONSTN DELIB/GP EX/STRUC JUDGE
EDU/PROP LEGIT CT/SYS EXEC ROUTINE RIGID/FLEX
ORD/FREE PWR...JURID CONCPT ORG/CHARTS GEN/METH
LEAGUE/NAT OAS OEEC 20 UN. PAGE 14 B0286

INT/ORG
ADJUD
DIPLOM

B63

CORLEY R.N.,THE LEGAL ENVIRONMENT OF BUSINESS.
CONSTN LEGIS TAX ADMIN CT/SYS DISCRIM ATTIT PWR
...TREND 18/20. PAGE 23 B0477

NAT/G
INDUS
JURID
DECISION

B63

COUNCIL STATE GOVERNMENTS,HANDBOOK FOR LEGISLATIVE
COMMITTEES. USA+45 LAW DELIB/GP EX/STRUC TOP/EX
CHOOSE PWR...METH/COMP 20. PAGE 24 B0496

LEGIS
PARL/PROC
PROVS
ADJUD

B63

CROUCH W.W.,SOUTHERN CALIFORNIA METROPOLIS: A STUDY
IN DEVELOPMENT OF GOVERNMENT FOR A METROPOLITAN
AREA. USA+45 USA-45 PROB/SOLV ADMIN LOBBY PARTIC
CENTRAL ORD/FREE PWR...BIBLIOG 20 PROGRSV/M.
PAGE 25 B0510

LOC/G
MUNIC
LEGIS
DECISION

B63

DALAND R.T.,PERSPECTIVES OF BRAZILIAN PUBLIC
ADMINISTRATION (VOL. I). BRAZIL LAW ECO/UNDEV
SCHOOL CHIEF TEC/DEV CONFER CONTROL GP/REL ATTIT
ROLE PWR...ANTHOL 20. PAGE 26 B0525

ADMIN
NAT/G
PLAN
GOV/REL

B63

FISHER S.N.,THE MILITARY IN THE MIDDLE EAST:
PROBLEMS IN SOCIETY AND GOVERNMENT. ISLAM USA+45
NAT/G DOMIN LEGIT COERCE ORD/FREE PWR...TIME/SEQ
VAL/FREE 20. PAGE 36 B0725

EX/STRUC
FORCES

B63

GARNER U.F.,ADMINISTRATIVE LAW. UK LAW LOC/G NAT/G
EX/STRUC LEGIS JUDGE BAL/PWR BUDGET ADJUD CONTROL
CT/SYS...BIBLIOG 20. PAGE 39 B0783

ADMIN
JURID
PWR
GOV/REL

B63

GREEN H.P.,GOVERNMENT OF THE ATOM. USA+45 LEGIS
PROB/SOLV ADMIN CONTROL PWR...POLICY DECISION 20
PRESIDENT CONGRESS. PAGE 43 B0864

GOV/REL
EX/STRUC
NUC/PWR
DELIB/GP

B63

GRIFFITH J.A.G.,PRINCIPLES OF ADMINISTRATIVE LAW
(3RD ED.). UK CONSTN EX/STRUC LEGIS ADJUD CONTROL
CT/SYS PWR...CHARTS 20. PAGE 43 B0879

JURID
ADMIN
NAT/G
BAL/PWR

B63

HATHAWAY D.A.,GOVERNMENT AND AGRICULTURE: PUBLIC
POLICY IN A DEMOCRATIC SOCIETY. USA+45 LEGIS ADMIN
EXEC LOBBY REPRESENT PWR 20. PAGE 48 B0967

AGRI
GOV/REL
PROB/SOLV
EX/STRUC

B63

HAYMAN D.,POLITICAL ACTIVITY RESTRICTION; AN
ANALYSIS WITH RECOMMENDATIONS (PAMPHLET). USA+45
EXEC PARTIC ROLE PWR 20. PAGE 48 B0976

CONTROL
ADMIN
INGP/REL
REPRESENT

B63

HEUSSLER R.,YESTERDAY'S RULERS: THE MAKING OF THE
BRITISH COLONIAL SERVICE. AFR EUR+WWI UK STRATA
SECT DELIB/GP PLAN DOMIN EDU/PROP ATTIT PERCEPT
PERSON SUPEGO KNOWL ORD/FREE PWR...MGT SOC OBS INT
TIME/SEQ 20 CMN/WLTH. PAGE 49 B1000

EX/STRUC
MORAL
ELITES

B63

HIGA M.,POLITICS AND PARTIES IN POSTWAR OKINAWA.
USA+45 VOL/ASSN LEGIS CONTROL LOBBY CHOOSE NAT/LISM
PWR SOVEREIGN MARXISM SOCISM 20 OKINAWA CHINJAP.
PAGE 50 B1008

GOV/REL
POL/PAR
ADMIN
FORCES

B63

HOWER R.M.,MANAGERS AND SCIENTISTS. EX/STRUC CREATE
ADMIN REPRESENT ATTIT DRIVE ROLE PWR SKILL...SOC
INT. PAGE 52 B1052

R+D
MGT
PERS/REL
INGP/REL

B63

KAMMERER G.M.,THE URBAN POLITICAL COMMUNITY:
PROFILES IN TOWN POLITICS. ELITES LOC/G LEAD
...DECISION GP/COMP. PAGE 57 B1162

EXEC
MUNIC
PWR
GOV/COMP

B63

KARL B.D.,EXECUTIVE REORGANIZATION AND REFORM IN
THE NEW DEAL. ECO/DEV INDUS DELIB/GP EX/STRUC PLAN
BUDGET ADMIN EFFICIENCY PWR POPULISM...POLICY 20
PRESIDENT ROOSEVLT/F WILSON/W NEW/DEAL. PAGE 58
B1174

BIOG
EXEC
CREATE
CONTROL

B63

KOGAN N.,THE POLITICS OF ITALIAN FOREIGN POLICY.
EUR+WWI LEGIS DOMIN EXEC LEGIT PWR RESPECT SKILL
...POLICY DECISION HUM SOC METH/CNCPT OBS INT
CHARTS 20. PAGE 61 B1227

NAT/G
ROUTINE
DIPLOM
ITALY

B63

LEWIS J.W.,LEADERSHIP IN COMMUNIST CHINA. ASIA
INTELL ECO/UNDEV LOC/G MUNIC NAT/G PROVS ECO/TAC
EDU/PROP LEGIT ADMIN COERCE ATTIT ORD/FREE PWR
...INT TIME/SEQ CHARTS TOT/POP VAL/FREE. PAGE 65
B1304

POL/PAR
DOMIN
ELITES

B63

LITTERER J.A.,ORGANIZATIONS: STRUCTURE AND
BEHAVIOR. PLAN DOMIN CONTROL LEAD ROUTINE SANCTION
INGP/REL EFFICIENCY PRODUC DRIVE RIGID/FLEX PWR.
PAGE 66 B1325

ADMIN
CREATE
MGT
ADJUST

B63

MACNEIL N.,FORGE OF DEMOCRACY: THE HOUSE OF
REPRESENTATIVES. POL/PAR EX/STRUC TOP/EX DEBATE
LEAD PARL/PROC CHOOSE GOV/REL PWR...OBS HOUSE/REP.
PAGE 68 B1374

LEGIS
DELIB/GP

B63

MAYNE R.,THE COMMUNITY OF EUROPE. UK CONSTN NAT/G
CONSULT DELIB/GP CREATE PLAN ECO/TAC LEGIT ADMIN
ROUTINE ORD/FREE PWR WEALTH...CONCPT TIME/SEQ EEC
EURATOM 20. PAGE 71 B1436

EUR+WWI
INT/ORG
REGION

B63

PEABODY R.L.,NEW PERSPECTIVES ON THE HOUSE OF
REPRESENTATIVES. AGRI FINAN SCHOOL FORCES CONFER
LEAD CHOOSE REPRESENT FEDERAL...POLICY DECISION
HOUSE/REP. PAGE 82 B1647

NEW/IDEA
LEGIS
PWR
ADMIN

B63

RICHARDS P.G.,PATRONAGE IN BRITISH GOVERNMENT.
ELITES DELIB/GP TOP/EX PROB/SOLV CONTROL CT/SYS
EXEC PWR. PAGE 88 B1774

EX/STRUC
REPRESENT
POL/PAR
ADMIN

B63

RICHARDSON H.G.,THE ADMINISTRATION OF IRELAND
1172-1377. IRELAND CONSTN EX/STRUC LEGIS JUDGE
CT/SYS PARL/PROC...CHARTS BIBLIOG 12/14. PAGE 88
B1775

ADMIN
NAT/G
PWR

B63

ROBERT J.,LA MONARCHIE MAROCAINE. MOROCCO LABOR
MUNIC POL/PAR EX/STRUC ORD/FREE PWR...JURID TREND T
20. PAGE 89 B1793

CHIEF
CONSERVE
ADMIN
CONSTN

B63

ROBINSON K.,ESSAYS IN IMPERIAL GOVERNMENT. CAMEROON
NIGERIA UK CONSTN LOC/G LEGIS ADMIN GOV/REL PWR
...POLICY ANTHOL BIBLIOG 17/20 PURHAM/M. PAGE 89
B1803

COLONIAL
AFR
DOMIN

B63

SCHOECK H.,THE NEW ARGUMENT IN ECONOMICS. UK USA+45
INDUS MARKET LABOR NAT/G ECO/TAC ADMIN ROUTINE
BAL/PAY PWR...POLICY BOLIV. PAGE 94 B1899

WELF/ST
FOR/AID
ECO/DEV
ALL/IDEOS

B63

SINGH H.L.,PROBLEMS AND POLICIES OF THE BRITISH IN
INDIA, 1885-1898. INDIA UK NAT/G FORCES LEGIS
PROB/SOLV CONTROL RACE/REL ADJUST DISCRIM NAT/LISM
RIGID/FLEX...MGT 19 CIVIL/SERV. PAGE 97 B1968

COLONIAL
PWR
POLICY
ADMIN

B63

SPRING D.,THE ENGLISH LANDED ESTATE IN THE
NINETEENTH CENTURY: ITS ADMINISTRATION. UK ELITES
STRUCT AGRI NAT/G GP/REL OWN PWR WEALTH...BIBLIOG
19 HOUSE/LORD. PAGE 99 B2012

STRATA
PERS/REL
MGT

B63

SWERDLOW I.,DEVELOPMENT ADMINISTRATION: CONCEPTS
AND PROBLEMS. WOR+45 CULTURE SOCIETY STRATA
DELIB/GP EX/STRUC ACT/RES PLAN ECO/TAC DOMIN LEGIT
ATTIT RIGID/FLEX SUPEGO HEALTH PWR...MGT CONCPT
ANTHOL VAL/FREE. PAGE 102 B2062

ECO/UNDEV
ADMIN

B63

THOMETZ C.E.,THE DECISION-MAKERS: THE POWER
STRUCTURE OF DALLAS. USA+45 CULTURE EX/STRUC DOMIN

ELITES
MUNIC

LEGIT GP/REL ATTIT OBJECTIVE...INT CHARTS GP/COMP. PAGE 104 B2101
PWR
DECISION
B63

TUCKER R.C.,THE SOVIET POLITICAL MIND. WOR+45 ELITES INT/ORG NAT/G POL/PAR PLAN DIPLOM ECO/TAC DOMIN ADMIN NUC/PWR REV DRIVE PERSON SUPEGO PWR WEALTH...POLICY MGT PSY CONCPT OBS BIOG TREND COLD/WAR MARX/KARL 20. PAGE 106 B2134
COM
TOP/EX
USSR
B63

TUCKER R.C.,THE SOVIET POLITICAL MIND. COM INTELL NAT/G TOP/EX EDU/PROP ADMIN COERCE TOTALISM ATTIT PWR MARXISM...PSY MYTH HYPO/EXP 20. PAGE 106 B2135
STRUCT
RIGID/FLEX
ELITES
USSR
B63

WOLL P.,AMERICAN BUREAUCRACY. USA+45 USA-45 CONSTN NAT/G ADJUD PWR OBJECTIVE...MGT GP/COMP. PAGE 118 B2372
LEGIS
EX/STRUC
ADMIN
GP/REL
L63

FREUND G.,"ADENAUER AND THE FUTURE OF GERMANY." EUR+WWI FUT GERMANY/W FORCES LEGIT ADMIN ROUTINE ATTIT DRIVE PERSON PWR...POLICY TIME/SEQ TREND VAL/FREE 20 ADENAUER/K. PAGE 37 B0753
NAT/G
BIOG
DIPLOM
GERMANY
L63

LIVERNASH E.R.,"THE RELATION OF POWER TO THE STRUCTURE AND PROCESS OF COLLECTIVE BARGAINING." ADJUD ORD/FREE...POLICY MGT CLASSIF GP/COMP. PAGE 66 B1330
LABOR
GP/REL
PWR
ECO/TAC
S63

BACHRACH P.,"DECISIONS AND NONDECISIONS: AN ANALYTICAL FRAMEWORK." UNIV SOCIETY CREATE LEGIT ADMIN EXEC COERCE...DECISION PSY CONCPT CHARTS. PAGE 8 B0156
PWR
HYPO/EXP

S63

BANFIELD J.,"FEDERATION IN EAST-AFRICA." AFR UGANDA ELITES INT/ORG NAT/G VOL/ASSN LEGIS ECO/TAC FEDERAL ATTIT SOVEREIGN TOT/POP 20 TANGANYIKA. PAGE 9 B0180
EX/STRUC
PWR
REGION
S63

BECHHOEFER B.G.,"UNITED NATIONS PROCEDURES IN CASE OF VIOLATIONS OF DISARMAMENT AGREEMENTS." COM USA+45 USSR LAW CONSTN NAT/G EX/STRUC FORCES LEGIS BAL/PWR EDU/PROP CT/SYS ARMS/CONT ORD/FREE PWR ...POLICY STERTYP UN VAL/FREE 20. PAGE 10 B0204
INT/ORG
DELIB/GP

S63

BOWIE R.,"STRATEGY AND THE ATLANTIC ALLIANCE." EUR+WWI VOL/ASSN BAL/PWR COERCE NUC/PWR ATTIT ORD/FREE PWR...DECISION GEN/LAWS NATO COLD/WAR 20. PAGE 14 B0287
FORCES
ROUTINE

S63

BRZEZINSKI Z.K.,"CINCINNATUS AND THE APPARATCHIK." COM USA+45 USA-45 ELITES LOC/G NAT/G PROVS CONSULT LEGIS DOMIN LEGIT EXEC ROUTINE CHOOSE DRIVE PWR SKILL...CONCPT CHARTS VAL/FREE COLD/WAR 20. PAGE 16 B0334
POL/PAR
USSR

S63

CLEMHOUT S.,"PRODUCTION FUNCTION ANALYSIS APPLIED TO THE LEONTIEF SCARCE-FACTOR PARADOX OF INTERNATIONAL TRADE." EUR+WWI USA+45 USA-45 DIST/IND NAT/G PLAN TEC/DEV DIPLOM PWR WEALTH...MGT METH/CNCPT CONT/OBS CON/ANAL CHARTS SIMUL GEN/LAWS 20. PAGE 21 B0436
ECO/DEV
ECO/TAC

S63

EVANS L.H.,"SOME MANAGEMENT PROBLEMS OF UNESCO." WOR+45 EX/STRUC LEGIS PWR UNESCO VAL/FREE 20. PAGE 34 B0688
INT/ORG
MGT

S63

GITTELL M.,"METROPOLITAN MAYOR: DEAD END." LOC/G PARTIC REGION ATTIT PWR GP/COMP. PAGE 40 B0804
MUNIC
LEAD
EXEC
S63

HAVILAND H.F.,"BUILDING A POLITICAL COMMUNITY." EUR+WWI FUT UK USA+45 ECO/DEV ECO/UNDEV INT/ORG NAT/G DELIB/GP BAL/PWR ECO/TAC NEUTRAL ROUTINE ATTIT PWR WEALTH...CONCPT COLD/WAR TOT/POP 20. PAGE 48 B0972
VOL/ASSN
DIPLOM

S63

JENNINGS M.K.,"PUBLIC ADMINISTRATORS AND COMMUNITY DECISION-MAKING." ELITES LOC/G LEAD...GP/COMP GOV/COMP. PAGE 56 B1134
ADMIN
MUNIC
DECISION
PWR
S63

MODELSKI G.,"STUDY OF ALLIANCES." WOR+45 WOR-45 INT/ORG NAT/G FORCES LEGIT ADMIN CHOOSE ALL/VALS PWR SKILL...INT/LAW CONCPT GEN/LAWS 20 TREATY. PAGE 74 B1495
VOL/ASSN
CON/ANAL
DIPLOM

S63

NADLER E.B.,"SOME ECONOMIC DISADVANTAGES OF THE ARMS RACE." USA+45 INDUS R+D FORCES PLAN TEC/DEV ECO/TAC FOR/AID EDU/PROP PWR WEALTH...TREND COLD/WAR 20. PAGE 77 B1552
ECO/DEV
MGT
BAL/PAY

S63

NYE J.S. JR.,"EAST AFRICAN ECONOMIC INTEGRATION." AFR UGANDA PROVS DELIB/GP PLAN ECO/TAC INT/TRADE ADMIN ROUTINE ORD/FREE PWR WEALTH...OBS TIME/SEQ VAL/FREE 20. PAGE 79 B1597
ECO/UNDEV
INT/ORG

S63

ROUGEMONT D.,"LES NOUVELLES CHANCES DE L'EUROPE." EUR+WWI FUT ECO/DEV INT/ORG NAT/G ACT/RES PLAN TEC/DEV EDU/PROP ADMIN COLONIAL FEDERAL ATTIT PWR SKILL...TREND 20. PAGE 91 B1835
ECO/UNDEV
PERCEPT

S63

RUSTOW D.A.,"THE MILITARY IN MIDDLE EASTERN SOCIETY AND POLITICS." FUT ISLAM CONSTN SOCIETY FACE/GP NAT/G POL/PAR PROF/ORG CONSULT DOMIN ADMIN EXEC REGION COERCE NAT/LISM ATTIT DRIVE PERSON ORD/FREE PWR...POLICY CONCPT OBS STERTYP 20. PAGE 92 B1860
FORCES
ELITES

S63

SCHURMANN F.,"ECONOMIC POLICY AND POLITICAL POWER IN COMMUNIST CHINA." ASIA CHINA/COM USSR SOCIETY ECO/UNDEV AGRI INDUS CREATE ADMIN ROUTINE ATTIT DRIVE RIGID/FLEX PWR WEALTH...HIST/WRIT TREND CHARTS WORK 20. PAGE 94 B1908
PLAN
ECO/TAC

S63

SHIMKIN D.B.,"STRUCTURE OF SOVIET POWER." COM FUT USA+45 USSR WOR+45 NAT/G FORCES ECO/TAC DOMIN EXEC COERCE CHOOSE ATTIT WEALTH...TIME/SEQ COLD/WAR TOT/POP VAL/FREE 20. PAGE 96 B1948
PWR

S63

STANLEY T.W.,"DECENTRALIZING NUCLEAR CONTROL IN NATO." EUR+WWI USA+45 ELITES FORCES ACT/RES ATTIT ORD/FREE PWR...NEW/IDEA HYPO/EXP TOT/POP 20 NATO. PAGE 100 B2022
INT/ORG
EX/STRUC
NUC/PWR

S63

WINGFIELD C.J.,"POWER STRUCTURE AND DECISION-MAKING IN CITY PLANNING." EDU/PROP ADMIN LEAD PARTIC GP/REL ATTIT. PAGE 117 B2365
MUNIC
PLAN
DECISION
PWR
B64

ALDERFER H.O.,LOCAL GOVERNMENT IN DEVELOPING COUNTRIES. ASIA COM L/A+17C S/ASIA AGRI LOC/G MUNIC PROVS DOMIN CHOOSE PWR...POLICY MGT CONCPT 20. PAGE 3 B0070
ADMIN
ROUTINE

B64

COTTER C.P.,POLITICS WITHOUT POWER: THE NATIONAL PARTY COMMITTEES. USA+45 FINAN NAT/G LOBBY ROUTINE GP/REL ATTIT ROLE SUPEGO PWR 20. PAGE 24 B0491
CHOOSE
POL/PAR
REPRESENT
DELIB/GP
B64

CULLINGWORTH J.B.,TOWN AND COUNTRY PLANNING IN ENGLAND AND WALES. UK LAW SOCIETY CONSULT ACT/RES ADMIN ROUTINE LEISURE INGP/REL ADJUST PWR...GEOG 20 OPEN/SPACE URBAN/RNWL. PAGE 25 B0512
MUNIC
PLAN
NAT/G
PROB/SOLV
B64

DUROSELLE J.B.,POLITIQUES NATIONALES ENVERS LES JEUNES ETATS. FRANCE ISRAEL ITALY UK USA+45 USSR YUGOSLAVIA ECO/DEV FINAN ECO/TAC INT/TRADE ADMIN PWR 20. PAGE 31 B0634
DIPLOM
ECO/UNDEV
COLONIAL
DOMIN
B64

EDELMAN M.,THE SYMBOLIC USES OF POWER. USA+45 EX/STRUC CONTROL GP/REL INGP/REL...MGT T. PAGE 32 B0653
CLIENT
PWR
EXEC
ELITES
B64

FAINSOD M.,HOW RUSSIA IS RULED (REV. ED.). RUSSIA USSR AGRI PROC/MFG LABOR POL/PAR EX/STRUC CONTROL PWR...POLICY BIBLIOG 19/20 KHRUSH/N COM/PARTY. PAGE 34 B0700
NAT/G
REV
MARXISM
B64

GOLDWIN R.A.,POLITICAL PARTIES, USA. USA+45 USA-45 LOC/G ADMIN LEAD EFFICIENCY ATTIT PWR...POLICY STAT ANTHOL 18/20 CONGRESS. PAGE 40 B0818
POL/PAR
PARTIC
NAT/G
CONSTN
B64

GOODMAN W.,THE TWO-PARTY SYSTEM IN THE UNITED STATES. USA+45 USA-45 STRATA LOC/G CHIEF EDU/PROP ADMIN COST PWR POPULISM...PLURIST 18/20 PRESIDENT. PAGE 41 B0821
POL/PAR
REPRESENT
CHOOSE
NAT/G
B64

GOODNOW H.F.,THE CIVIL SERVICE OF PAKISTAN: BUREAUCRACY IN A NEW NATION. INDIA PAKISTAN S/ASIA ECO/UNDEV PROVS CHIEF PARTIC CHOOSE EFFICIENCY PWR ...BIBLIOG 20. PAGE 41 B0824
ADMIN
GOV/REL
LAW
NAT/G
B64

KAHNG T.J.,LAW, POLITICS, AND THE SECURITY COUNCIL* AN INQUIRY INTO THE HANDLING OF LEGAL QUESTIONS. LAW CONSTN NAT/G ACT/RES OP/RES CT/SYS TASK PWR ...INT/LAW BIBLIOG UN. PAGE 57 B1160
DELIB/GP
ADJUD
ROUTINE

B64

KARIEL H.S.,IN SEARCH OF AUTHORITY: TWENTIETH-CENTURY POLITICAL THOUGHT. WOR+45 WOR-45 NAT/G EX/STRUC TOTALISM DRIVE PWR...MGT PHIL/SCI GEN/LAWS 19/20 NIETZSCH/F FREUD/S WEBER/MAX NIEBUHR/R MARITAIN/J. PAGE 58 B1173
CONSTN
CONCPT
ORD/FREE
IDEA/COMP
B64

KEEFE W.J.,THE AMERICAN LEGISLATIVE PROCESS: CONGRESS AND THE STATES. USA+45 LAW POL/PAR DELIB/GP DEBATE ADMIN LOBBY REPRESENT CONGRESS PRESIDENT. PAGE 59 B1187
LEGIS
DECISION
PWR
PROVS
B64

KIMBROUGH R.B.,POLITICAL POWER AND EDUCATIONAL DECISION-MAKING. USA+45 FINAN ADMIN LEAD GP/REL
EDU/PROP
PROB/SOLV

ATTIT PWR PROG/TEAC. PAGE 60 B1207 — DECISION SCHOOL

B64

LOWI T.J.,AT THE PLEASURE OF THE MAYOR. EX/STRUC PROB/SOLV BAL/PWR ADMIN PARTIC CHOOSE GP/REL ...CONT/OBS NET/THEORY CHARTS 20 NEWYORK/C MAYOR. PAGE 67 B1346 — LOBBY LOC/G PWR MUNIC

B64

NEUSTADT R.,PRESIDENTIAL POWER. USA+45 CONSTN NAT/G CHIEF LEGIS CREATE EDU/PROP LEGIT ADMIN EXEC COERCE ATTIT PERSON RIGID/FLEX PWR CONGRESS 20 PRESIDENT TRUMAN/HS EISNHWR/DD. PAGE 78 B1575 — TOP/EX SKILL

B64

PEABODY R.L.,ORGANIZATIONAL AUTHORITY. SCHOOL WORKER PLAN SENIOR GOV/REL UTIL DRIVE PWR...PSY CHARTS BIBLIOG 20. PAGE 82 B1648 — ADMIN EFFICIENCY TASK GP/REL

B64

PLISCHKE E.,SYSTEMS OF INTEGRATING THE INTERNATIONAL COMMUNITY. WOR+45 NAT/G VOL/ASSN ECO/TAC LEGIT PWR WEALTH...TIME/SEQ ANTHOL UN TOT/POP 20. PAGE 83 B1684 — INT/ORG EX/STRUC REGION

B64

RAYMOND J.,POWER AT THE PENTAGON (1ST ED.). ELITES NAT/G PLAN EDU/PROP ARMS/CONT DETER WAR WEAPON ...TIME/SEQ 20 PENTAGON MCNAMARA/R. PAGE 86 B1746 — PWR CIVMIL/REL EX/STRUC FORCES

B64

RIDLEY F.,PUBLIC ADMINISTRATION IN FRANCE. FRANCE UK EX/STRUC CONTROL PARTIC EFFICIENCY 20. PAGE 88 B1781 — ADMIN REPRESENT GOV/COMP PWR

B64

RIES J.C.,THE MANAGEMENT OF DEFENSE: ORGANIZATION AND CONTROL OF THE US ARMED SERVICES. PROF/ORG DELIB/GP EX/STRUC LEGIS GOV/REL PERS/REL CENTRAL RATIONAL PWR...POLICY TREND GOV/COMP BIBLIOG. PAGE 88 B1782 — FORCES ACT/RES DECISION CONTROL

B64

RIGGS R.E.,THE MOVEMENT FOR ADMINISTRATIVE REORGANIZATION IN ARIZONA. USA+45 LAW POL/PAR DELIB/GP LEGIS PROB/SOLV CONTROL RIGID/FLEX PWR ...ORG/CHARTS 20 ARIZONA DEMOCRAT REPUBLICAN. PAGE 88 B1786 — ADMIN PROVS CREATE PLAN

B64

RIKER W.H.,FEDERALISM. WOR+45 WOR-45 CONSTN CHIEF LEGIS ADMIN COLONIAL CONTROL CT/SYS PWR...BIBLIOG/A 18/20. PAGE 88 B1787 — FEDERAL NAT/G ORD/FREE CENTRAL

B64

ROCHE J.P.,THE CONGRESS. EX/STRUC BAL/PWR DIPLOM DEBATE ADJUD LEAD PWR. PAGE 89 B1809 — INGP/REL LEGIS DELIB/GP SENIOR

B64

ROCHE J.P.,THE PRESIDENCY. USA+45 USA-45 CONSTN NAT/G CHIEF BAL/PWR DIPLOM GP/REL 18/20 PRESIDENT. PAGE 90 B1810 — EX/STRUC PWR

B64

SINGER M.R.,THE EMERGING ELITE: A STUDY OF POLITICAL LEADERSHIP IN CEYLON. S/ASIA ECO/UNDEV AGRI KIN NAT/G SECT EX/STRUC LEGIT ATTIT PWR RESPECT...SOC STAT CHARTS 20. PAGE 97 B1967 — TOP/EX STRATA NAT/LISM CEYLON

B64

US SENATE COMM ON JUDICIARY,ADMINISTRATIVE PROCEDURE ACT. USA+45 CONSTN NAT/G PROB/SOLV CONFER GOV/REL PWR...INT 20 SENATE. PAGE 110 B2231 — PARL/PROC LEGIS JURID ADMIN

B64

WHEELER-BENNETT J.W.,THE NEMESIS OF POWER (2ND ED.). EUR+WWI GERMANY TOP/EX TEC/DEV ADMIN WAR PERS/REL RIGID/FLEX ROLE ORD/FREE PWR FASCISM 20 HITLER/A. PAGE 116 B2332 — FORCES NAT/G GP/REL STRUCT

B64

WILDAVSKY A.,LEADERSHIP IN A SMALL TOWN. USA+45 STRUCT PROB/SOLV EXEC PARTIC RACE/REL PWR PLURISM ...SOC 20 NEGRO WATER CIV/RIGHTS OBERLIN CITY/MGT. PAGE 116 B2348 — LEAD MUNIC ELITES

B64

WRAITH R.,CORRUPTION IN DEVELOPING COUNTRIES. NIGERIA UK LAW ELITES STRATA INDUS LOC/G NAT/G SECT FORCES EDU/PROP ADMIN PWR WEALTH 18/20. PAGE 118 B2377 — ECO/UNDEV CRIME SANCTION ATTIT

L64

FOX G.H.,"PERCEPTIONS OF THE VIETNAMESE PUBLIC ADMINISTRATION SYSTEM" VIETNAM ELITES CONTROL EXEC LEAD PWR...INT 20. PAGE 37 B0745 — ADMIN EX/STRUC INGP/REL ROLE

L64

GILBERT C.E.,"NATIONAL POLITICAL ALIGNMENTS AND THE POLITICS OF LARGE CITIES." ELITES LOC/G NAT/G LEGIS EXEC LEAD PLURISM GOV/COMP. PAGE 39 B0800 — MUNIC CHOOSE POL/PAR PWR

L64

HAAS E.B.,"ECONOMICS AND DIFFERENTIAL PATTERNS OF POLITICAL INTEGRATION: PROJECTIONS ABOUT UNITY IN — L/A+17C INT/ORG

LATIN AMERICA." SOCIETY NAT/G DELIB/GP ACT/RES CREATE PLAN ECO/TAC REGION ROUTINE ATTIT DRIVE PWR WEALTH...CONCPT TREND CHARTS LAFTA 20. PAGE 45 B0910 — MARKET

L64

MACKINTOSH J.P.,"NIGERIA'S EXTERNAL AFFAIRS." UK CULTURE ECO/UNDEV NAT/G VOL/ASSN EDU/PROP LEGIT ADMIN ATTIT ORD/FREE PWR 20. PAGE 68 B1365 — AFR DIPLOM NIGERIA

L64

PRUITT D.G.,"PROBLEM SOLVING IN THE DEPARTMENT OF STATE." USA+45 NAT/G CONSULT PROB/SOLV EXEC PWR ...DECISION INT ORG/CHARTS 20. PAGE 85 B1713 — ROUTINE MGT DIPLOM

L64

RIPLEY R.B.,"INTERAGENCY COMMITTEES AND INCREMENTALISM: THE CASE OF AID TO INDIA." INDIA USA+45 INTELL NAT/G DELIB/GP ACT/RES DIPLOM ROUTINE NAT/LISM ATTIT PWR...SOC CONCPT NEW/IDEA TIME/SEQ CON/ANAL VAL/FREE 20. PAGE 89 B1790 — EXEC MGT FOR/AID

L64

ROTBERG R.,"THE FEDERATION MOVEMENT IN BRITISH EAST AND CENTRAL AFRICA." AFR RHODESIA UGANDA ECO/UNDEV NAT/G POL/PAR FORCES DOMIN LEGIT ADMIN COERCE ATTIT ...CONCPT TREND 20 TANGANYIKA. PAGE 91 B1831 — VOL/ASSN PWR REGION

L64

SYMONDS R.,"REFLECTIONS IN LOCALISATION." AFR S/ASIA UK STRATA INT/ORG NAT/G SCHOOL EDU/PROP LEGIT KNOWL ORD/FREE PWR RESPECT CMN/WLTH 20. PAGE 102 B2064 — ADMIN MGT COLONIAL

S64

CLIGNET R.,"POTENTIAL ELITES IN GHANA AND THE IVORY COAST: A PRELIMINARY SURVEY." AFR CULTURE ELITES STRATA KIN NAT/G SECT DOMIN EXEC ORD/FREE RESPECT SKILL...POLICY RELATIV GP/COMP NAT/COMP 20. PAGE 21 B0438 — PWR LEGIT IVORY/CST GHANA

S64

GALTUNE J.,"BALANCE OF POWER AND THE PROBLEM OF PERCEPTION. A LOGICAL ANALYSIS." WOR+45 CONSTN SOCIETY NAT/G DELIB/GP EX/STRUC LEGIS DOMIN ADMIN COERCE DRIVE ORD/FREE...POLICY CONCPT OBS TREND GEN/LAWS. PAGE 38 B0778 — PWR PSY ARMS/CONT WAR

S64

GROSS J.A.,"WHITEHALL AND THE COMMONWEALTH." EUR+WWI MOD/EUR INT/ORG NAT/G CONSULT DELIB/GP LEGIS DOMIN ADMIN COLONIAL ROUTINE PWR CMN/WLTH 19/20. PAGE 44 B0890 — EX/STRUC ATTIT TREND

S64

JOHNSON K.F.,"CAUSAL FACTORS IN LATIN AMERICAN POLITICAL INSTABILITY." CULTURE NAT/G VOL/ASSN EX/STRUC FORCES EDU/PROP LEGIT ADMIN COERCE REV ATTIT KNOWL PWR...STYLE RECORD CHARTS WORK 20. PAGE 57 B1144 — L/A+17C PERCEPT ELITES

S64

KAMMERER G.M.,"ROLE DIVERSITY OF CITY MANAGERS." LOC/G ADMIN LEAD PERCEPT PWR GP/COMP. PAGE 57 B1163 — MUNIC EXEC ATTIT ROLE

S64

KAMMERER G.M.,"URBAN LEADERSHIP DURING CHANGE." LEAD PARTIC REPRESENT GP/REL PLURISM...DECISION GP/COMP. PAGE 58 B1164 — MUNIC PWR ELITES EXEC

S64

KASSOF A.,"THE ADMINISTERED SOCIETY: TOTALITARIANISM WITHOUT TERROR." COM USSR STRATA AGRI INDUS NAT/G PERF/ART SCHOOL TOP/EX EDU/PROP ADMIN ORD/FREE PWR...POLICY SOC TIME/SEQ GEN/LAWS VAL/FREE 20. PAGE 58 B1178 — SOCIETY DOMIN TOTALISM

S64

KHAN M.Z.,"THE PRESIDENT OF THE GENERAL ASSEMBLY." WOR+45 CONSTN DELIB/GP EDU/PROP LEGIT ROUTINE PWR RESPECT SKILL...DECISION SOC BIOG TREND UN 20. PAGE 59 B1202 — INT/ORG TOP/EX

S64

MOWER A.G.,"THE OFFICIAL PRESSURE GROUP OF THE COUNCIL OF EUROPE'S CONSULATIVE ASSEMBLY." EUR+WWI SOCIETY STRUCT FINAN CONSULT ECO/TAC ADMIN ROUTINE ATTIT PWR WEALTH...STAT CHARTS 20 COUNCL/EUR. PAGE 76 B1535 — INT/ORG EDU/PROP

S64

RIGBY T.H.,"TRADITIONAL, MARKET, AND ORGANIZATIONAL SOCIETIES AND THE USSR." COM ECO/DEV NAT/G POL/PAR ECO/TAC DOMIN ORD/FREE PWR WEALTH...TIME/SEQ GEN/LAWS VAL/FREE 20 STALIN/J. PAGE 88 B1784 — MARKET ADMIN USSR

S64

ROGOW A.A.,"CONGRESSIONAL GOVERNMENT: LEGISLATIVE POWER V. DOMESTIC PROCESSES." USA+45 CHIEF DELIB/GP ADMIN GOV/REL CONGRESS. PAGE 90 B1815 — PWR DIPLOM LEGIS POLICY

S64

RUSK D.,"THE MAKING OF FOREIGN POLICY" USA+45 CHIEF DELIB/GP WORKER PROB/SOLV ADMIN ATTIT PWR ...DECISION 20 DEPT/STATE RUSK/D GOLDMAN/E. PAGE 92 B1856 — DIPLOM INT POLICY

S64

SALISBURY R.H.,"URBAN POLITICS: THE NEW CONVERGENCE OF POWER." STRATA POL/PAR EX/STRUC PARTIC GP/REL — MUNIC PWR

DECISION. PAGE 92 B1863   LEAD
S64

SCHWELB E.,"OPERATION OF THE EUROPEAN CONVENTION ON   INT/ORG
HUMAN RIGHTS." EUR+WWI LAW SOCIETY CREATE EDU/PROP   MORAL
ADJUD ADMIN PEACE ATTIT ORD/FREE PWR...POLICY
INT/LAW CONCPT OBS GEN/LAWS UN VAL/FREE ILO 20
ECHR. PAGE 95 B1916
S64

SWEARER H.R.,"AFTER KHRUSHCHEV: WHAT NEXT." COM FUT   EX/STRUC
USSR CONSTN ELITES NAT/G POL/PAR CHIEF DELIB/GP   PWR
LEGIS DOMIN LEAD...RECORD TREND STERTYP GEN/METH
20. PAGE 102 B2058
S64

THOMPSON V.A.,"ADMINISTRATIVE OBJECTIVES FOR   ECO/UNDEV
DEVELOPMENT ADMINISTRATION." WOR+45 CREATE PLAN   MGT
DOMIN EDU/PROP EXEC ADMIN ATTIT ORD/FREE PWR
...POLICY GEN/LAWS VAL/FREE. PAGE 104 B2107
B65

BANFIELD E.C.,BIG CITY POLITICS. USA+45 CONSTN   METH/COMP
POL/PAR ADMIN LOBBY CHOOSE SUFF INGP/REL PWR...GEOG   MUNIC
20. PAGE 9 B0179   STRUCT
B65

BOCK E.,GOVERNMENT REGULATION OF BUSINESS. USA+45   MGT
LAW EX/STRUC LEGIS EXEC ORD/FREE PWR...ANTHOL   ADMIN
CONGRESS. PAGE 13 B0261   NAT/G
  CONTROL
B65

BOGUSLAW R.,THE NEW UTOPIANS. OP/RES ADMIN CONTROL   UTOPIA
PWR...IDEA/COMP SIMUL 20. PAGE 13 B0265   AUTOMAT
  COMPUTER
  PLAN
B65

CHEN T.H.,THE CHINESE COMMUNIST REGIME: A   MARXISM
DOCUMENTARY STUDY (2 VOLS.). CHINA/COM LAW CONSTN   POL/PAR
ELITES ECO/UNDEV LEGIS ECO/TAC ADMIN CONTROL PWR   NAT/G
...SOC 20. PAGE 20 B0417
B65

COOPER F.E.,STATE ADMINISTRATIVE LAW (2 VOLS.). LAW   JURID
LEGIS PLAN TAX ADJUD CT/SYS FEDERAL PWR...CONCPT   CONSTN
20. PAGE 23 B0474   ADMIN
  PROVS
B65

DE GRAZIA A.,REPUBLIC IN CRISIS: CONGRESS AGAINST   LEGIS
THE EXECUTIVE FORCE. USA+45 USA-45 SOCIETY POL/PAR   EXEC
CHIEF DOMIN ROLE ORD/FREE PWR...CONCPT MYTH BIBLIOG   GOV/REL
20 CONGRESS. PAGE 27 B0556   CONTROL
B65

GOLEMBIEWSKI R.T.,MEN, MANAGEMENT, AND MORALITY;   LG/CO
TOWARD A NEW ORGANIZATIONAL ETHIC. CONSTN EX/STRUC   MGT
CREATE ADMIN CONTROL INGP/REL PERSON SUPEGO MORAL   PROB/SOLV
PWR...GOV/COMP METH/COMP 20 BUREAUCRCY. PAGE 40
B0819
B65

GREGG J.L.,POLITICAL PARTIES AND PARTY SYSTEMS IN   LEAD
GUATEMALA, 1944-1963. GUATEMALA L/A+17C EX/STRUC   POL/PAR
FORCES CREATE CONTROL REV CHOOSE PWR...TREND   NAT/G
IDEA/COMP 20. PAGE 43 B0872   CHIEF
B65

HAIGHT D.E.,THE PRESIDENT; ROLES AND POWERS. USA+45   CHIEF
USA-45 POL/PAR PLAN DIPLOM CHOOSE PERS/REL PWR   LEGIS
18/20 PRESIDENT CONGRESS. PAGE 45 B0915   TOP/EX
  EX/STRUC
B65

KOENIG C.W.,OFFICIAL MAKERS OF PUBLIC POLICY: CHIEF
CONGRESS AND THE PRESIDENT. USA+45 USA-45 NAT/G   LEGIS
EX/STRUC PROB/SOLV PWR. PAGE 60 B1222   GOV/REL
  PLURISM
B65

KOENIG L.W.,OFFICIAL MAKERS OF PUBLIC POLICY: POLICY
CONGRESS AND THE PRESIDENT. USA+45 USA-45 EX/STRUC   LEGIS
ADMIN CONTROL GOV/REL PWR 18/20 CONGRESS PRESIDENT.   CHIEF
PAGE 61 B1225   NAT/G
B65

KWEDER J.B.,THE ROLES OF THE MANAGER, MAYOR, AND   MUNIC
COUNCILMEN IN POLICYMAKING. LEGIS PERS/REL ATTIT   EXEC
ROLE PWR GP/COMP. PAGE 62 B1246   LEAD
  DECISION
B65

MACDONALD R.W.,THE LEAGUE OF ARAB STATES: A STUDY   ISLAM
IN THE DYNAMICS OF REGIONAL ORGANIZATION. ISRAEL   REGION
UAR USSR FINAN INT/ORG DELIB/GP ECO/TAC AGREE   DIPLOM
NEUTRAL ORD/FREE PWR...DECISION BIBLIOG 20 TREATY   ADMIN
UN. PAGE 67 B1358
B65

MASTERS N.A.,COMMITTEE ASSIGNMENTS IN THE HOUSE OF   LEAD
REPRESENTATIVES (BMR). USA+45 ELITES POL/PAR   LEGIS
EX/STRUC PARTIC REPRESENT GP/REL PERS/REL ATTIT PWR   CHOOSE
...STAT CHARTS 20 HOUSE/REP. PAGE 71 B1425   DELIB/GP
B65

MEISEL J.H.,PARETO & MOSCA. ITALY STRUCT ADMIN   PWR
...SOC CON/ANAL ANTHOL BIBLIOG 19/20. PAGE 72 B1463   ELITES
  CONTROL
  LAISSEZ
B65

PAYNE J.L.,LABOR AND POLITICS IN PERU; THE SYSTEM   LABOR
OF POLITICAL BARGAINING. PERU CONSTN VOL/ASSN   POL/PAR

EX/STRUC LEAD PWR...CHARTS 20. PAGE 81 B1645   BARGAIN
  GP/REL
B65

PUSTAY J.S.,COUNTER-INSURGENCY WARFARE. COM USA+45   FORCES
LOC/G NAT/G ACT/RES EDU/PROP ADMIN COERCE ATTIT   PWR
...CONCPT MARX/KARL 20. PAGE 85 B1722   GUERRILLA
B65

ROTBERG R.I.,A POLITICAL HISTORY OF TROPICAL   AFR
AFRICA. EX/STRUC DIPLOM INT/TRADE DOMIN ADMIN   CULTURE
RACE/REL NAT/LISM PWR SOVEREIGN...GEOG TIME/SEQ   COLONIAL
BIBLIOG 1/20. PAGE 91 B1832
B65

ROURKE F.E.,BUREAUCRATIC POWER IN NATIONAL   EX/STRUC
POLITICS. ADMIN CONTROL EXEC GOV/REL INGP/REL 20.   EFFICIENCY
PAGE 91 B1838   REPRESENT
  PWR
B65

SCHAPIRO L.,THE GOVERNMENT AND POLITICS OF THE   MARXISM
SOVIET UNION. USSR WOR+45 WOR-45 ADMIN PARTIC REV   GOV/REL
CHOOSE REPRESENT PWR...POLICY IDEA/COMP 20. PAGE 93   NAT/G
B1880   LOC/G
B65

SNIDER C.F.,AMERICAN STATE AND LOCAL GOVERNMENT.   GOV/REL
USA+45 FINAN CHIEF EX/STRUC TAX ADMIN CONTROL SUFF   MUNIC
INGP/REL PWR 20. PAGE 98 B1989   PROVS
  LOC/G
B65

STANLEY D.T.,CHANGING ADMINISTRATIONS. USA+45   NAT/G
POL/PAR DELIB/GP TOP/EX BUDGET GOV/REL GP/REL   CHIEF
PERS/REL PWR...MAJORIT DECISION MGT 20 PRESIDENT   ADMIN
SUCCESSION DEPT/STATE DEPT/DEFEN DEPT/HEW. PAGE 100   EX/STRUC
B2021
B65

VIORST M.,HOSTILE ALLIES: FDR AND DE GAULLE.   TOP/EX
EUR+WWI USA-45 ELITES NAT/G VOL/ASSN FORCES LEGIS   PWR
PLAN LEGIT ADMIN COERCE PERSON...BIOG TIME/SEQ 20   WAR
ROOSEVLT/F DEGAULLE/C. PAGE 112 B2263   FRANCE
L65

LASSWELL H.D.,"THE POLICY SCIENCES OF DEVELOPMENT."   PWR
CULTURE SOCIETY EX/STRUC CREATE ADMIN ATTIT KNOWL   METH/CNCPT
...SOC CONCPT SIMUL GEN/METH. PAGE 63 B1273   DIPLOM
S65

AMLUND C.A.,"EXECUTIVE-LEGISLATIVE IMBALANCE: LEGIS
TRUMAN TO KENNEDY." USA+45 NAT/G GOV/REL PWR.   EXEC
PAGE 4 B0090   DECISION
S65

BALDWIN H.,"SLOW-DOWN IN THE PENTAGON." USA+45   RECORD
CREATE PLAN GOV/REL CENTRAL COST EFFICIENCY PWR   R+D
...MGT MCNAMARA/R. PAGE 9 B0174   WEAPON
  ADMIN
S65

BROWN S.,"AN ALTERNATIVE TO THE GRAND DESIGN."   VOL/ASSN
EUR+WWI FUT USA+45 INT/ORG NAT/G EX/STRUC FORCES   CONCPT
CREATE BAL/PWR DOMIN RIGID/FLEX ORD/FREE PWR   DIPLOM
...NEW/IDEA RECORD EEC NATO 20. PAGE 16 B0327
S65

QUADE Q.L.,"THE TRUMAN ADMINISTRATION AND THE   USA+45
SEPARATION OF POWERS: THE CASE OF THE MARSHALL   ECO/UNDEV
PLAN." SOCIETY INT/ORG NAT/G CONSULT DELIB/GP LEGIS   DIPLOM
PLAN ECO/TAC ROUTINE DRIVE PERCEPT RIGID/FLEX
ORD/FREE PWR WEALTH...DECISION GEOG NEW/IDEA TREND
20 TRUMAN/HS. PAGE 85 B1726
C65

HUNTINGTON S.P.,"CONGRESSIONAL RESPONSES TO THE   FUT
TWENTIETH CENTURY IN D. TRUMAN, ED. THE CONGRESS   LEAD
AND AMERICA'S FUTURE." USA+45 USA-45 DIPLOM SENIOR   NAT/G
ADMIN EXEC PWR...SOC 20 CONGRESS. PAGE 53 B1067   LEGIS
N65

MOTE M.E.,SOVIET LOCAL AND REPUBLIC ELECTIONS. COM   CHOOSE
USSR NAT/G PLAN PARTIC GOV/REL TOTALISM PWR   ADMIN
...CHARTS 20. PAGE 76 B1534   CONTROL
  LOC/G
B66

AARON T.J.,THE CONTROL OF POLICE DISCRETION: THE   CONTROL
DANISH EXPERIENCE. DENMARK LAW CREATE ADMIN   FORCES
INGP/REL SUPEGO PWR 20 OMBUDSMAN. PAGE 2 B0049   REPRESENT
  PROB/SOLV
B66

AMER ENTERPRISE INST PUB POL,CONGRESS: THE FIRST   EFFICIENCY
BRANCH OF GOVERNMENT. EX/STRUC FEEDBACK REPRESENT   LEGIS
INGP/REL PWR...DECISION METH/CNCPT PREDICT. PAGE 4   DELIB/GP
B0081   CONTROL
B66

BIRKHEAD G.S.,ADMINISTRATIVE PROBLEMS IN PAKISTAN.   ADMIN
PAKISTAN AGRI FINAN INDUS LG/CO ECO/TAC CONTROL PWR   NAT/G
...CHARTS ANTHOL 20. PAGE 12 B0241   ORD/FREE
  ECO/UNDEV
B66

COOK P.W. JR.,PROBLEMS OF CORPORATE POWER. WOR+45   ADMIN
FINAN INDUS BARGAIN GP/REL...MGT ANTHOL. PAGE 23   LG/CO
B0471   PWR
  ECO/TAC
B66

DAVIDSON R.H.,CONGRESS IN CRISIS: POLITICS AND   LEGIS
CONGRESSIONAL REFORM. USA+45 SOCIETY POL/PAR   PARL/PROC
CONTROL LEAD ROUTINE GOV/REL ATTIT PWR...POLICY 20   PROB/SOLV

CONGRESS. PAGE 26 B0535   NAT/G

B66
GERBERDING W.P.,UNITED STATES FOREIGN POLICY: PROB/SOLV
PERSPECTIVES AND ANALYSIS. USA+45 LEGIS EXEC LEAD   CHIEF
REPRESENT PWR 20. PAGE 39 B0791   EX/STRUC
                                         CONTROL
B66
LIVINGSTON J.C.,THE CONSENT OF THE GOVERNED. USA+45 NAT/G
EX/STRUC BAL/PWR DOMIN CENTRAL PERSON PWR...POLICY   LOBBY
CONCPT OBS IDEA/COMP 20 CONGRESS. PAGE 66 B1331   MAJORIT
                                         PARTIC
B66
MARTIN L.W.,DIPLOMACY IN MODERN EUROPEAN HISTORY.   DIPLOM
EUR+WWI MOD/EUR INT/ORG NAT/G EX/STRUC ROUTINE WAR   POLICY
PEACE TOTALISM PWR 15/20 COLD/WAR EUROPE/W. PAGE 70
B1411
B66
MCKENZIE J.L.,AUTHORITY IN THE CHURCH. STRUCT LEAD   SECT
INGP/REL PERS/REL CENTRAL ANOMIE ATTIT ORD/FREE   AUTHORIT
RESPECT CATH. PAGE 72 B1452   PWR
                                         ADMIN
B66
NEUMANN R.G.,THE GOVERNMENT OF THE GERMAN FEDERAL   NAT/G
REPUBLIC. EUR+WWI GERMANY/W LOC/G EX/STRUC LEGIS   POL/PAR
CT/SYS INGP/REL PWR...BIBLIOG 20 ADENAUER/K.   DIPLOM
PAGE 78 B1573   CONSTN
B66
NIEBURG H.L.,IN THE NAME OF SCIENCE. USA+45   NAT/G
EX/STRUC LEGIS TEC/DEV BUDGET PAY AUTOMAT LOBBY PWR INDUS
...OBS 20. PAGE 78 B1581   TECHRACY
B66
O'NEILL C.E.,CHURCH AND STATE IN FRENCH COLONIAL   COLONIAL
LOUISIANA: POLICY AND POLITICS TO 1732. PROVS   NAT/G
VOL/ASSN DELIB/GP ADJUD ADMIN GP/REL ATTIT DRIVE   SECT
...POLICY BIBLIOG 17/18 LOUISIANA CHURCH/STA.   PWR
PAGE 79 B1601
B66
RAPHAEL J.S.,GOVERNMENTAL REGULATION OF BUSINESS.   LG/CO
USA+45 LAW CONSTN TAX ADJUD ADMIN EFFICIENCY PWR   GOV/REL
20. PAGE 86 B1736   CONTROL
                                         ECO/DEV
B66
RUBENSTEIN R.,THE SHARING OF POWER IN A PSYCHIATRIC ADMIN
HOSPITAL. CLIENT PROF/ORG PUB/INST INGP/REL ATTIT   PARTIC
PWR...DECISION OBS RECORD. PAGE 91 B1847   HEALTH
                                         CONCPT
B66
STREET D.,ORGANIZATION FOR TREATMENT. CLIENT PROVS   GP/COMP
PUB/INST PLAN CONTROL PARTIC REPRESENT ATTIT PWR   AGE/Y
...POLICY BIBLIOG. PAGE 101 B2052   ADMIN
                                         VOL/ASSN
B66
THOENES P.,THE ELITE IN THE WELFARE STATE ,TRANS.   ADMIN
BY J BINGHAM; ED. BY. STRATA NAT/G GP/REL HAPPINESS ELITES
INCOME OPTIMAL MORAL PWR WEALTH...POLICY CONCPT.   MGT
PAGE 104 B2097   WELF/ST
B66
WILSON G.,CASES AND MATERIALS ON CONSTITUTIONAL AND JURID
ADMINISTRATIVE LAW. UK LAW NAT/G EX/STRUC LEGIS   ADMIN
BAL/PWR BUDGET DIPLOM ADJUD CONTROL CT/SYS GOV/REL   CONSTN
ORD/FREE 20 PARLIAMENT ENGLSH/LAW. PAGE 117 B2359   PWR
B66
ZINKIN T.,CHALLENGES IN INDIA. INDIA PAKISTAN LAW   NAT/G
AGRI FINAN INDUS TOP/EX TEC/DEV CONTROL ROUTINE   ECO/TAC
ORD/FREE PWR 20 NEHRU/J SHASTRI/LB CIVIL/SERV.   POLICY
PAGE 119 B2404   ADMIN
L66
CRAIN R.L.,"STRUCTURE AND VALUES IN LOCAL POLITICAL MUNIC
SYSTEMS: THE CASE OF FLUORIDATION DECISIONS."   EDU/PROP
EX/STRUC LEGIS LEAD PARTIC REPRESENT PWR...DECISION LOC/G
GOV/COMP. PAGE 25 B0501   ATTIT
L66
LEMARCHAND R.,"SOCIAL CHANGE AND POLITICAL   NAT/G
MODERNISATION IN BURUNDI." AFR BURUNDI STRATA CHIEF STRUCT
EX/STRUC RIGID/FLEX PWR...SOC 20. PAGE 64 B1285   ELITES
                                         CONSERVE
L66
MCAUSLAN J.P.W.,"CONSTITUTIONAL INNOVATION AND   CONSTN
POLITICAL STABILITY IN TANZANIA: A PRELIMINARY   NAT/G
ASSESSMENT." AFR TANZANIA ELITES CHIEF EX/STRUC   EXEC
RIGID/FLEX PWR 20 PRESIDENT BUREAUCRCY. PAGE 71   POL/PAR
B1440
S66
JACOBSON J.,"COALITIONISM: FROM PROTEST TO   RACE/REL
POLITICKING" USA+45 ELITES NAT/G POL/PAR PROB/SOLV   LABOR
ADMIN LEAD DISCRIM ORD/FREE PWR CONSERVE 20 NEGRO   SOCIALIST
AFL/CIO CIV/RIGHTS BLACK/PWR. PAGE 55 B1116   VOL/ASSN
S66
POLSBY N.W.,"BOOKS IN THE FIELD: POLITICAL   BIBLIOG/A
SCIENCE." LAW CONSTN LOC/G NAT/G LEGIS ADJUD PWR 20 ATTIT
SUPREME/CT. PAGE 83 B1686   ADMIN
                                         JURID
S66
WOLFINGER R.E.,"POLITICAL ETHOS AND THE STRUCTURE   MUNIC
OF CITY GOVERNMENT." POL/PAR EX/STRUC REPRESENT   ATTIT
GP/REL PERS/REL RIGID/FLEX PWR. PAGE 118 B2371   STRATA

                                         GOV/COMP
N66
PRINCETON U INDUSTRIAL REL SEC,OUTSTANDING BOOKS ON BIBLIOG/A
INDUSTRIAL RELATIONS, 1965 (PAMPHLET NO. 128).   INDUS
WOR+45 LABOR BARGAIN GOV/REL RACE/REL HEALTH PWR   GP/REL
...MGT 20. PAGE 85 B1709   POLICY
B67
BROWN L.N.,FRENCH ADMINISTRATIVE LAW. FRANCE UK   EX/STRUC
CONSTN NAT/G LEGIS DOMIN CONTROL EXEC PARL/PROC PWR LAW
...JURID METH/COMP GEN/METH. PAGE 16 B0324   IDEA/COMP
                                         CT/SYS
B67
BRZEZINSKI Z.K.,IDEOLOGY AND POWER IN SOVIET   DIPLOM
POLITICS. USSR NAT/G POL/PAR PWR...GEN/LAWS 19/20.   EX/STRUC
PAGE 16 B0335   MARXISM
B67
BRZEZINSKI Z.K.,THE SOVIET BLOC: UNITY AND CONFLICT   NAT/G
(2ND ED., REV., ENLARGED). COM POLAND USSR INTELL   DIPLOM
CHIEF EX/STRUC CONTROL EXEC GOV/REL PWR MARXISM
...TREND IDEA/COMP 20 LENIN/VI MARX/KARL STALIN/J.
PAGE 16 B0336
B67
CECIL L.,ALBERT BALLIN: BUSINESS AND POLITICS IN   DIPLOM
IMPERIAL GERMANY 1888-1918. GERMANY UK INT/TRADE   CONSTN
LEAD WAR PERS/REL ADJUST PWR WEALTH...MGT BIBLIOG   ECO/DEV
19/20. PAGE 19 B0397   TOP/EX
B67
DE BLIJ H.J.,SYSTEMATIC POLITICAL GEOGRAPHY. WOR+45 GEOG
STRUCT INT/ORG NAT/G EDU/PROP ADMIN COLONIAL   CONCPT
ROUTINE ORD/FREE PWR...IDEA/COMP T 20. PAGE 27   METH
B0550
B67
LEACH R.H.,GOVERNING THE AMERICAN NATION. FUT   NAT/G
USA+45 USA-45 CONSTN POL/PAR PLAN ADJUD EXEC CONSEN LEGIS
CONGRESS PRESIDENT. PAGE 63 B1278   PWR
B67
MACKINTOSH J.M.,JUGGERNAUT. USSR NAT/G POL/PAR   WAR
ADMIN LEAD CIVMIL/REL COST TOTALISM PWR MARXISM   FORCES
...GOV/COMP 20. PAGE 68 B1364   COM
                                         PROF/ORG
B67
MCCONNELL G.,THE MODERN PRESIDENCY. USA+45 CONSTN   NAT/G
TOP/EX DOMIN EXEC CHOOSE PWR...MGT 20. PAGE 72   CHIEF
B1446   EX/STRUC
B67
MENHENNET D.,PARLIAMENT IN PERSPECTIVE. UK ROUTINE   LEGIS
REPRESENT ROLE PWR 20 PARLIAMENT. PAGE 73 B1467   PARL/PROC
                                         CONCPT
                                         POPULISM
B67
RAWLINSON J.L.,CHINA'S STRUGGLE FOR NAVAL   SEA
DEVELOPMENT 1839-1895. ASIA DIPLOM ADMIN WAR   FORCES
...BIBLIOG DICTIONARY 19 CHINJAP. PAGE 86 B1745   PWR
B67
WARREN S.,THE AMERICAN PRESIDENT. POL/PAR FORCES   CHIEF
LEGIS DIPLOM ECO/TAC ADMIN EXEC PWR...ANTHOL 18/20   LEAD
ROOSEVLT/F KENNEDY/JF JOHNSON/LB TRUMAN/HS   NAT/G
WILSON/W. PAGE 114 B2297   CONSTN
B67
WESSON R.G.,THE IMPERIAL ORDER. WOR-45 STRUCT SECT   PWR
DOMIN ADMIN COLONIAL LEAD CONSERVE...CONCPT BIBLIOG CHIEF
20. PAGE 115 B2324   CONTROL
                                         SOCIETY
S67
ANDERSON M.,"THE FRENCH PARLIAMENT." EUR+WWI FRANCE PARL/PROC
MOD/EUR CONSTN POL/PAR CHIEF LEGIS LOBBY ATTIT ROLE LEAD
PWR 19/20. PAGE 5 B0095   GOV/COMP
                                         EX/STRUC
S67
BURKE E.M.,"THE SEARCH FOR AUTHORITY IN PLANNING."   DECISION
MUNIC NEIGH CREATE PROB/SOLV LEGIT ADMIN CONTROL   PLAN
EFFICIENCY PWR...METH/COMP SIMUL 20. PAGE 17 B0352   LOC/G
                                         METH
S67
CARIAS B.,"EL CONTROL DE LAS EMPRESAS PUBLICAS POR   WORKER
GRUPOS DE INTERESES DE LA COMUNIDAD." FRANCE UK   REPRESENT
VENEZUELA INDUS NAT/G CONTROL OWN PWR...DECISION   MGT
NAT/COMP 20. PAGE 18 B0377   SOCISM
S67
DODSON D.W.,"NEW FORCES OPERATING IN EDUCATIONAL   PROB/SOLV
DECISION-MAKING." USA+45 NEIGH EDU/PROP ADMIN   SCHOOL
SUPEGO DECISION. PAGE 30 B0602   PERS/REL
                                         PWR
S67
EDWARDS H.T.,"POWER STRUCTURE AND ITS COMMUNICATION ELITES
IN SAN JOSE, COSTA RICA." COSTA/RICA L/A+17C STRATA INGP/REL
FACE/GP POL/PAR EX/STRUC PROB/SOLV ADMIN LEAD   MUNIC
GP/REL PWR...STAT INT 20. PAGE 32 B0655   DOMIN
S67
GITTELL M.,"PROFESSIONALISM AND PUBLIC   DECISION
PARTICIPATION IN EDUCATIONAL POLICY MAKING." STRUCT PLAN
ADMIN GP/REL ATTIT PWR 20. PAGE 40 B0805   EDU/PROP
                                         MUNIC
S67
GORMAN W.,"ELLUL - A PROPHETIC VOICE." WOR+45   CREATE
ELITES SOCIETY ACT/RES PLAN BAL/PWR DOMIN CONTROL   ORD/FREE

PARTIC TOTALISM PWR 20. PAGE 41 B0837 | EX/STRUC UTOPIA

S67
GRUNDY K.W.,"THE POLITICAL USES OF IMAGINATION." GHANA ELITES SOCIETY NAT/G DOMIN EDU/PROP COLONIAL REGION REPRESENT GP/REL CENTRAL PWR MARXISM 20. PAGE 44 B0897 | NAT/LISM EX/STRUC AFR LEAD

S67
HALL B.,"THE COALITION AGAINST DISHWASHERS." USA+45 POL/PAR PROB/SOLV BARGAIN LEAD CHOOSE REPRESENT GP/REL ORD/FREE PWR...POLICY 20. PAGE 46 B0923 | LABOR ADMIN DOMIN WORKER

S67
HOFMANN W.,"THE PUBLIC INTEREST PRESSURE GROUP: THE CASE OF THE DEUTSCHE STADTETAG." GERMANY GERMANY/W CONSTN STRUCT NAT/G CENTRAL FEDERAL PWR...TIME/SEQ 20. PAGE 51 B1030 | LOC/G VOL/ASSN LOBBY ADMIN

S67
HSUEH C.T.,"THE CULTURAL REVOLUTION AND LEADERSHIP CRISIS IN COMMUNIST CHINA." CHINA/COM POL/PAR EX/STRUC FORCES EDU/PROP ATTIT PWR...POLICY 20. PAGE 52 B1054 | LEAD REV CULTURE MARXISM

S67
O'DELL J.H.,"THE JULY REBELLIONS AND THE 'MILITARY STATE'." USA+45 VIETNAM STRATA CHIEF WORKER COLONIAL EXEC CROWD CIVMIL/REL RACE/REL TOTALISM ...WELF/ST PACIFIST 20 NEGRO JOHNSON/LB PRESIDENT CIV/RIGHTS. PAGE 79 B1599 | PWR NAT/G COERCE FORCES

S67
PAYNE W.A.,"LOCAL GOVERNMENT STUDY COMMISSIONS: ORGANIZATION FOR ACTION." USA+45 LEGIS PWR...CHARTS 20. PAGE 81 B1646 | LOC/G DELIB/GP PROB/SOLV ADMIN

S67
RAI H.,"DISTRICT MAGISTRATE AND POLICE SUPERINTENDENT IN INDIA: THE CONTROVERSY OF DUAL CONTROL" INDIA LAW PROVS ADMIN PWR 19/20. PAGE 86 B1729 | STRUCT CONTROL ROLE FORCES

S67
SHOEMAKER R.L.,"JAPANESE ARMY AND THE WEST." ASIA ELITES EX/STRUC DIPLOM DOMIN EDU/PROP COERCE ATTIT AUTHORIT PWR 1/20 CHINJAP. PAGE 96 B1950 | FORCES TEC/DEV WAR TOTALISM

S67
SKOLNIKOFF E.B.,"MAKING FOREIGN POLICY" PROB/SOLV EFFICIENCY PERCEPT PWR...MGT METH/CNCPT CLASSIF 20. PAGE 98 B1976 | TEC/DEV CONTROL USA+45 NAT/G

S68
GRAM H.A.,"BUSINESS ETHICS AND THE CORPORATION." LG/CO SECT PROB/SOLV CONTROL EXEC GP/REL INGP/REL PERS/REL ROLE MORAL PWR...DECISION 20. PAGE 42 B0850 | POLICY ADMIN MGT

PYE L.W. B1723,B1724

PYLEE M.V. B1725

Q

QU....QUESTIONNAIRES; SEE ALSO QUESTIONNAIRES INDEX, P. XIV

N19
WRIGHT D.S.,AMERICAN STATE ADMINISTRATORS (PAMPHLET). USA+45 ATTIT PERSON...SAMP/SIZ CHARTS SOC/EXP METH 20. PAGE 118 B2379 | QU TOP/EX ADMIN PROVS

B40
PFIFFNER J.M.,RESEARCH METHODS IN PUBLIC ADMINISTRATION. USA-45 R+D...MGT STAT INT QU T 20. PAGE 82 B1665 | ADMIN OP/RES METH TEC/DEV

S45
KRIESBERG M.,"WHAT CONGRESSMEN AND ADMINISTRATORS THINK OF THE POLLS." USA-45 CONTROL PWR...INT QU. PAGE 61 B1236 | LEGIS ATTIT EDU/PROP ADMIN

B56
FRANCIS R.G.,SERVICE AND PROCEDURE IN BUREAUCRACY. EXEC LEAD ROUTINE...QU 20. PAGE 37 B0748 | CLIENT ADMIN INGP/REL REPRESENT

B57
BERGER M.,BUREAUCRACY AND SOCIETY IN MODERN EGYPT; A STUDY OF THE HIGHER CIVIL SERVICE. UAR REPRESENT ...QU 20. PAGE 11 B0221 | ATTIT EXEC ADMIN ROUTINE

B57
FULLER C.D.,TRAINING OF SPECIALISTS IN INTERNATIONAL RELATIONS. FUT USA+45 USA-45 INTELL INT/ORG...MGT METH/CNCPT INT QU GEN/METH 20. PAGE 38 B0765 | KNOWL DIPLOM

B58
SKINNER G.W.,LEADERSHIP AND POWER IN THE CHINESE COMMUNITY OF THAILAND. ASIA S/ASIA STRATA FACE/GP KIN PROF/ORG VOL/ASSN EX/STRUC DOMIN PERSON RESPECT ...METH/CNCPT STAT INT QU BIOG CHARTS 20. PAGE 98 B1974 | SOC ELITES THAILAND

S58
MITCHELL W.C.,"OCCUPATIONAL ROLE STRAINS: THE AMERICAN ELECTIVE PUBLIC OFFICIAL." CONTROL RIGID/FLEX SUPEGO HEALTH ORD/FREE...SOC INT QU. PAGE 74 B1492 | ANOMIE DRIVE ROUTINE PERSON

B59
ELLIOTT O.,MEN AT THE TOP. USA+45 CULTURE EX/STRUC PRESS GOV/REL ATTIT ALL/VALS...OBS INT QU 20. PAGE 33 B0668 | TOP/EX PERSON LEAD POLICY

B60
GLOVER J.D.,A CASE STUDY OF HIGH LEVEL ADMINISTRATION IN A LARGE ORGANIZATION. EX/STRUC EXEC LEAD ROUTINE INGP/REL OPTIMAL ATTIT PERSON ...POLICY DECISION INT QU. PAGE 40 B0812 | ADMIN TOP/EX FORCES NAT/G

B60
WEIDNER E.W.,INTERGOVERNMENTAL RELATIONS AS SEEN BY PUBLIC OFFICIALS. USA+45 PROVS EX/STRUC EXEC FEDERAL...QU 20. PAGE 115 B2311 | ATTIT GP/REL GOV/REL ADMIN

S63
HILLS R.J.,"THE REPRESENTATIVE FUNCTION: NEGLECTED DIMENSION OF LEADERSHIP BEHAVIOR" USA+45 CLIENT STRUCT SCHOOL PERS/REL...STAT QU SAMP LAB/EXP 20. PAGE 50 B1012 | LEAD ADMIN EXEC ACT/RES

B64
COOMBS C.H.,A THEORY OF DATA....MGT PHIL/SCI SOC CLASSIF MATH PROBABIL STAT QU. PAGE 23 B0472 | CON/ANAL GEN/METH TESTS PSY

B64
KIESER P.J.,THE COST OF ADMINISTRATION, SUPERVISION AND SERVICES IN URBAN BANTU TOWNSHIPS. SOUTH/AFR SERV/IND MUNIC PROVS ADMIN COST...OBS QU CHARTS 20 BANTU. PAGE 60 B1203 | AFR MGT FINAN

B64
SULLIVAN G.,THE STORY OF THE PEACE CORPS. USA+45 WOR+45 INTELL FACE/GP NAT/G SCHOOL VOL/ASSN CONSULT EX/STRUC PLAN EDU/PROP ADMIN ATTIT DRIVE ALL/VALS ...POLICY HEAL SOC CONCPT INT QU BIOG TREND SOC/EXP WORK. PAGE 102 B2054 | INT/ORG ECO/UNDEV FOR/AID PEACE

B64
VALEN H.,POLITICAL PARTIES IN NORWAY. NORWAY ACADEM PARTIC ROUTINE INGP/REL KNOWL...QU 20. PAGE 111 B2249 | LOC/G POL/PAR PERSON

B65
BUECHNER J.C.,DIFFERENCES IN ROLE PERCEPTIONS IN COLORADO COUNCIL-MANAGER CITIES. USA+45 ADMIN ROUTINE GP/REL CONSEN PERCEPT PERSON ROLE ...DECISION MGT STAT INT QU CHARTS 20 COLORADO CITY/MGT. PAGE 17 B0338 | MUNIC CONSULT LOC/G IDEA/COMP

B65
DUGGAR G.S.,RENEWAL OF TOWN AND VILLAGE I: A WORLD-WIDE SURVEY OF LOCAL GOVERNMENT EXPERIENCE. WOR+45 CONSTRUC INDUS CREATE BUDGET REGION GOV/REL...QU NAT/COMP 20 URBAN/RNWL. PAGE 31 B0628 | MUNIC NEIGH PLAN ADMIN

B65
LAMBIRI I.,SOCIAL CHANGE IN A GREEK COUNTRY TOWN. GREECE FAM PROB/SOLV ROUTINE TASK LEISURE INGP/REL CONSEN ORD/FREE...SOC INT QU CHARTS 20. PAGE 62 B1252 | INDUS WORKER CULTURE NEIGH

B65
RUBIN H.,PENSIONS AND EMPLOYEE MOBILITY IN THE PUBLIC SERVICE. USA+45 WORKER PERSON ORD/FREE...SOC QU. PAGE 91 B1849 | ADMIN NAT/G LOC/G SENIOR

B66
ANDREWS K.R.,THE EFFECTIVENESS OF UNIVERSITY MANAGEMENT DEVELOPMENT PROGRAMS. FUT USA+45 ECO/TAC ADMIN...MGT QU METH/COMP 20. PAGE 5 B0103 | ECO/DEV ACADEM TOP/EX ATTIT

QU/SEMANT....SEMANTIC AND SOCIAL PROBLEMS OF QUESTIONNAIRES

B54
ALLPORT G.W.,THE NATURE OF PREJUDICE. USA+45 WOR+45 STRATA FACE/GP KIN NEIGH SECT ADMIN GP/REL DISCRIM ATTIT DRIVE LOVE RESPECT...PSY SOC MYTH QU/SEMANT 20. PAGE 4 B0078 | CULTURE PERSON RACE/REL

QUADE Q.L. B1726

QUAKER....QUAKER

QUANT....QUANTIFICATION

B57
SIMON H.A.,MODELS OF MAN, SOCIAL AND RATIONAL: MATHEMATICAL ESSAYS ON RATIONAL HUMAN BEHAVIOR IN A SOCIAL SETTING. UNIV LAW SOCIETY FACE/GP VOL/ASSN CONSULT EX/STRUC LEGIS CREATE ADMIN ROUTINE ATTIT DRIVE PWR...SOC CONCPT METH/CNCPT QUANT STAT TOT/POP VAL/FREE 20. PAGE 97 B1959 | MATH SIMUL

S59
SOHN L.B.,"THE DEFINITION OF AGGRESSION." FUT LAW FORCES LEGIT ADJUD ROUTINE COERCE ORD/FREE PWR | INT/ORG CT/SYS

...MAJORIT JURID QUANT COLD/WAR 20. PAGE 99 B1995 — DETER SOVEREIGN

S60

RIESELBACH Z.N.,"QUANTITATIVE TECHNIQUES FOR STUDYING VOTING BEHAVIOR IN THE UNITED NATIONS GENERAL ASSEMBLY." FUT S/ASIA USA+45 INT/ORG BAL/PWR DIPLOM ECO/TAC FOR/AID ADMIN PWR...POLICY METH/CNCPT METH UN 20. PAGE 88 B1783 — QUANT CHOOSE

B63

BONINI C.P.,SIMULATION OF INFORMATION AND DECISION SYSTEMS IN THE FIRM. MARKET BUDGET DOMIN EDU/PROP ADMIN COST ATTIT HABITAT PERCEPT PWR...CONCPT PROBABIL QUANT PREDICT HYPO/EXP BIBLIOG. PAGE 13 B0273 — INDUS SIMUL DECISION MGT

B63

NORTH R.C.,CONTENT ANALYSIS: A HANDBOOK WITH APPLICATIONS FOR THE STUDY OF INTERNATIONAL CRISIS. ASIA COM EUR+WWI MOD/EUR INT/ORG TEC/DEV DOMIN EDU/PROP ROUTINE COERCE PERCEPT RIGID/FLEX ALL/VALS ...QUANT TESTS CON/ANAL SIMUL GEN/LAWS VAL/FREE. PAGE 79 B1591 — METH/CNCPT COMPUT/IR USSR

B65

HICKMAN B.G.,QUANTITATIVE PLANNING OF ECONOMIC POLICY. FRANCE NETHERLAND OP/RES PRICE ROUTINE UTIL ...POLICY DECISION ECOMETRIC METH/CNCPT STAT STYLE CHINJAP. PAGE 50 B1004 — PROB/SOLV PLAN QUANT

B65

SINGER J.D.,HUMAN BEHAVIOR AND INTERNATIONAL POLITICS* CONTRIBUTIONS FROM THE SOCIAL-PSYCHOLOGICAL SCIENCES. ACT/RES PLAN EDU/PROP ADMIN KNOWL...DECISION PSY SOC NET/THEORY HYPO/EXP LAB/EXP SOC/EXP GEN/METH ANTHOL BIBLIOG. PAGE 97 B1965 — DIPLOM PHIL/SCI QUANT SIMUL

B65

WATERSTON A.,DEVELOPMENT PLANNING* LESSONS OF EXPERIENCE. ECO/TAC CENTRAL...MGT QUANT BIBLIOG. PAGE 114 B2303 — ECO/UNDEV CREATE PLAN ADMIN

QUANTIFICATION....SEE QUANT

QUANTITATIVE CONTENT ANALYSIS....SEE CON/ANAL

QUEBEC....QUEBEC, CANADA

QUESTIONNAIRES....SEE QU

QURESHI S. B1727

R

R+D....RESEARCH AND DEVELOPMENT GROUP

B24

MERRIAM C.E.,A HISTORY OF POLITICAL THEORIES - RECENT TIMES. USA-45 WOR-45 CULTURE SOCIETY ECO/DEV R+D EDU/PROP ROUTINE CHOOSE ATTIT PERSON ALL/VALS ...POLICY SOC CONCPT METH/CNCPT OBS HIST/WRIT TIME/SEQ TREND. PAGE 73 B1471 — UNIV INTELL

B28

SOROKIN P.,CONTEMPORARY SOCIOLOGICAL THEORIES. MOD/EUR UNIV SOCIETY R+D SCHOOL ECO/TAC EDU/PROP ROUTINE ATTIT DRIVE...PSY CONCPT TIME/SEQ TREND GEN/LAWS 20. PAGE 99 B1997 — CULTURE SOC WAR

B40

PFIFFNER J.M.,RESEARCH METHODS IN PUBLIC ADMINISTRATION. USA-45 R+D...MGT STAT INT QU T 20. PAGE 82 B1665 — ADMIN OP/RES METH TEC/DEV

B41

THE TAX FOUNDATION,STUDIES IN ECONOMY AND EFFICIENCY IN GOVERNMENT. FINAN R+D OP/RES BUDGET TAX 20. PAGE 104 B2095 — BIBLIOG ADMIN EFFICIENCY NAT/G

B44

PUBLIC ADMINISTRATION SERVICE,YOUR BUSINESS OF GOVERNMENT: A CATALOG OF PUBLICATIONS IN THE FIELD OF PUBLIC ADMINISTRATION (PAMPHLET). FINAN R+D LOC/G ACT/RES OP/RES PLAN 20. PAGE 85 B1715 — BIBLIOG ADMIN NAT/G MUNIC

B45

BUSH V.,SCIENCE, THE ENDLESS FRONTIER. FUT USA-45 INTELL STRATA ACT/RES CREATE PLAN EDU/PROP ADMIN NUC/PWR PEACE ATTIT HEALTH KNOWL...MAJORIT HEAL MGT PHIL/SCI CONCPT OBS TREND 20. PAGE 18 B0360 — R+D NAT/G

B46

WILCOX J.K.,OFFICIAL DEFENSE PUBLICATIONS. 1941-1945 (NINE VOLS.). USA-45 AGRI INDUS R+D LABOR FORCES TEC/DEV EFFICIENCY PRODUC SKILL WEALTH 20. PAGE 116 B2347 — BIBLIOG/A WAR CIVMIL/REL ADMIN

B47

LASSWELL H.D.,THE ANALYSIS OF POLITICAL BEHAVIOUR: AN EMPIRICAL APPROACH. WOR+45 CULTURE NAT/G FORCES EDU/PROP ADMIN ATTIT PERCEPT KNOWL...PHIL/SCI PSY SOC NEW/IDEA OBS INT GEN/METH NAZI 20. PAGE 63 B1267 — R+D ACT/RES ELITES

B47

PUBLIC ADMINISTRATION SERVICE,CURRENT RESEARCH PROJECTS IN PUBLIC ADMINISTRATION (PAMPHLET). LAW — BIBLIOG R+D

CONSTN COM/IND LABOR LOC/G MUNIC PROVS ACT/RES DIPLOM RECEIVE EDU/PROP WAR 20. PAGE 85 B1716 — MGT ADMIN

B47

WHITEHEAD T.N.,LEADERSHIP IN A FREE SOCIETY; A STUDY IN HUMAN RELATIONS BASED ON AN ANALYSIS OF PRESENT-DAY INDUSTRIAL CIVILIZATION. WOR-45 STRUCT R+D LABOR LG/CO SML/CO WORKER PLAN PROB/SOLV TEC/DEV DRIVE...MGT 20. PAGE 116 B2341 — INDUS LEAD ORD/FREE SOCIETY

B48

STEWART I.,ORGANIZING SCIENTIFIC RESEARCH FOR WAR: ADMINISTRATIVE HISTORY OF OFFICE OF SCIENTIFIC RESEARCH AND DEVELOPMENT. USA-45 INTELL R+D LABOR WORKER CREATE BUDGET WEAPON CIVMIL/REL GP/REL EFFICIENCY...POLICY 20. PAGE 101 B2037 — DELIB/GP ADMIN WAR TEC/DEV

B49

FORD FOUNDATION,REPORT OF THE STUDY FOR THE FORD FOUNDATION ON POLICY AND PROGRAM. SOCIETY R+D ACT/RES CAP/ISM FOR/AID EDU/PROP ADMIN KNOWL ...POLICY PSY SOC 20. PAGE 36 B0739 — WEALTH GEN/LAWS

B49

ROSENHAUPT H.W.,HOW TO WAGE PEACE. USA+45 SOCIETY STRATA STRUCT R+D INT/ORG POL/PAR LEGIS ACT/RES CREATE PLAN EDU/PROP ADMIN EXEC ATTIT ALL/VALS ...TIME/SEQ TREND COLD/WAR 20. PAGE 90 B1822 — INTELL CONCPT DIPLOM

B50

LASSWELL H.D.,NATIONAL SECURITY AND INDIVIDUAL FREEDOM. USA+45 R+D NAT/G VOL/ASSN CONSULT DELIB/GP LEGIT ADMIN KNOWL ORD/FREE PWR...PLURIST TOT/POP COLD/WAR 20. PAGE 63 B1268 — FACE/GP ROUTINE BAL/PWR

B51

HARDMAN J.B.,THE HOUSE OF LABOR. LAW R+D NEIGH EDU/PROP LEAD ROUTINE REPRESENT GP/REL...POLICY STAT. PAGE 47 B0945 — LABOR LOBBY ADMIN PRESS

S51

LERNER D.,"THE POLICY SCIENCES: RECENT DEVELOPMENTS IN SCOPE AND METHODS." R+D SERV/IND CREATE DIPLOM ROUTINE PWR...METH/CNCPT TREND GEN/LAWS METH 20. PAGE 64 B1297 — CONSULT SOC

B52

US DEPARTMENT OF STATE,RESEARCH ON EASTERN EUROPE (EXCLUDING USSR). EUR+WWI LAW ECO/DEV NAT/G PROB/SOLV DIPLOM ADMIN LEAD MARXISM...TREND 19/20. PAGE 108 B2182 — BIBLIOG R+D ACT/RES COM

B54

PUBLIC ADMIN CLEARING HOUSE,PUBLIC ADMINISTRATIONS ORGANIZATIONS: A DIRECTORY, 1954. USA+45 R+D PROVS ACT/RES...MGT 20. PAGE 85 B1714 — INDEX VOL/ASSN NAT/G ADMIN

B55

BAILEY S.K.,RESEARCH FRONTIERS IN POLITICS AND GOVERNMENT. CONSTN LEGIS ADMIN REV CHOOSE...CONCPT IDEA/COMP GAME ANTHOL 20. PAGE 8 B0164 — R+D METH NAT/G

S55

WRIGHT Q.,"THE PEACEFUL ADJUSTMENT OF INTERNATIONAL RELATIONS: PROBLEMS AND RESEARCH APPROACHES." UNIV INTELL EDU/PROP ADJUD ROUTINE KNOWL SKILL...INT/LAW JURID PHIL/SCI CLASSIF 20. PAGE 118 B2385 — R+D METH/CNCPT PEACE

B56

UNITED NATIONS,BIBLIOGRAPHY ON INDUSTRIALIZATION IN UNDER-DEVELOPED COUNTRIES. WOR+45 R+D INT/ORG NAT/G FOR/AID ADMIN LEAD 20 UN. PAGE 107 B2161 — BIBLIOG ECO/UNDEV INDUS TEC/DEV

B56

WASSERMAN P.,INFORMATION FOR ADMINISTRATORS: A GUIDE TO PUBLICATIONS AND SERVICES FOR MANAGEMENT IN BUSINESS AND GOVERNMENT. R+D LOC/G NAT/G PROF/ORG VOL/ASSN PRESS...PSY SOC STAT 20. PAGE 114 B2299 — BIBLIOG MGT KNOWL EDU/PROP

L58

EISENSTADT S.N.,"BUREAUCRACY AND BUREAUCRATIZATION." WOR+45 ECO/DEV INDUS R+D PLAN GOV/REL...WELF/ST TREND BIBLIOG/A 20. PAGE 32 B0659 — ADMIN OP/RES MGT PHIL/SCI

B60

FRYE R.J.,GOVERNMENT AND LABOR: THE ALABAMA PROGRAM. USA+45 INDUS R+D LABOR WORKER BUDGET EFFICIENCY AGE/Y HEALTH...CHARTS 20 ALABAMA. PAGE 38 B0761 — ADMIN LEGIS LOC/G PROVS

B60

LEYDER J.,BIBLIOGRAPHIE DE L'ENSEIGNEMENT SUPERIEUR ET DE LA RECHERCHE SCIENTIFIQUE EN AFRIQUE INTERTROPICALE (2 VOLS.). AFR CULTURE ECO/UNDEV AGRI PLAN EDU/PROP ADMIN COLONIAL...GEOG SOC/INTEG 20 NEGRO. PAGE 65 B1309 — BIBLIOG/A ACT/RES ACADEM R+D

B60

WALDO D.,THE RESEARCH FUNCTION OF UNIVERSITY BUREAUS AND INSTITUTES FOR GOVERNMENTAL-RELATED RESEARCH. FINAN ACADEM NAT/G INGP/REL ROLE...POLICY CLASSIF GOV/COMP. PAGE 113 B2276 — ADMIN R+D MUNIC

S60

BOYER W.W.,"POLICY MAKING BY GOVERNMENT AGENCIES." USA+45 WOR+45 R+D DELIB/GP TOP/EX EDU/PROP ROUTINE ATTIT BIO/SOC DRIVE...CONCPT TREND TOT/POP 20. PAGE 14 B0293 — NAT/G DIPLOM

HUTCHINSON C.E.,"AN INSTITUTE FOR NATIONAL SECURITY POLICY
AFFAIRS." USA+45 R+D NAT/G CONSULT TOP/EX ACT/RES   METH/CNCPT
CREATE PLAN TEC/DEV EDU/PROP ROUTINE NUC/PWR ATTIT   ELITES
ORD/FREE PWR...DECISION MGT PHIL/SCI CONCPT RECORD   DIPLOM
GEN/LAWS GEN/METH 20. PAGE 53 B1068
                                                    S60

CONFREY E.A.,ADMINISTRATION OF COMMUNITY HEALTH   HEAL
SERVICES. USA+45 R+D PUB/INST DELIB/GP PLAN BUDGET ADMIN
ROUTINE AGE/C HEALTH...MGT SOC/WK METH/COMP 20.   MUNIC
PAGE 23 B0461   BIO/SOC
                                                    B61

SHARP W.R.,FIELD ADMINISTRATION IN THE UNITED   INT/ORG
NATION SYSTEM: THE CONDUCT OF INTERNATIONAL   CONSULT
ECONOMIC AND SOCIAL PROGRAMS. FUT WOR+45 CONSTN
SOCIETY ECO/UNDEV R+D DELIB/GP ACT/RES PLAN TEC/DEV
EDU/PROP EXEC ROUTINE HEALTH WEALTH...HUM CONCPT
CHARTS METH ILO UNESCO VAL/FREE UN 20. PAGE 96
B1939
                                                    B62

CAIRNCROSS A.K.,FACTORS IN ECONOMIC DEVELOPMENT.   MARKET
WOR+45 ECO/UNDEV INDUS R+D LG/CO NAT/G EX/STRUC   ECO/DEV
PLAN TEC/DEV ECO/TAC ATTIT HEALTH KNOWL PWR WEALTH
...TIME/SEQ GEN/LAWS TOT/POP VAL/FREE 20. PAGE 18
B0363
                                                    B62

HATTERY L.H.,INFORMATION RETRIEVAL MANAGEMENT.   R+D
CLIENT INDUS TOP/EX COMPUTER OP/RES TEC/DEV ROUTINE COMPUT/IR
COST EFFICIENCY RIGID/FLEX...METH/COMP ANTHOL 20.   MGT
PAGE 48 B0968   CREATE
                                                    B62

NATIONAL BUREAU ECONOMIC RES,THE RATE AND DIRECTION DECISION
OF INVENTIVE ACTIVITY: ECONOMIC AND SOCIAL FACTORS. PROB/SOLV
STRUCT INDUS MARKET R+D CREATE OP/RES TEC/DEV   MGT
EFFICIENCY PRODUC RATIONAL UTIL...WELF/ST PHIL/SCI
METH/CNCPT TIME. PAGE 77 B1562
                                                    B62

SCHILLING W.R.,STRATEGY, POLITICS, AND DEFENSE   ROUTINE
BUDGETS. USA+45 R+D NAT/G CONSULT DELIB/GP FORCES   POLICY
LEGIS ACT/RES PLAN BAL/PWR LEGIT EXEC NUC/PWR
RIGID/FLEX PWR...TREND COLD/WAR CONGRESS 20
EISNHWR/DD. PAGE 93 B1890
                                                    B62

SNYDER R.C.,FOREIGN POLICY DECISION-MAKING. FUT   TEC/DEV
KOREA WOR+45 R+D CREATE ADMIN ROUTINE PWR   HYPO/EXP
...DECISION PSY SOC CONCPT METH/CNCPT CON/ANAL   DIPLOM
CHARTS GEN/METH METH 20. PAGE 99 B1992
                                                    L62

BELSHAW D.G.R.,"PUBLIC INVESTMENT IN AGRICULTURE   ECO/UNDEV
AND ECONOMIC DEVELOPMENT OF UGANDA" UGANDA AGRI   PLAN
INDUS R+D ECO/TAC RATION TAX PAY COLONIAL 20   ADMIN
WORLD/BANK. PAGE 10 B0209   CENTRAL
                                                    S62

ALBONETTI A.,"IL SECONDO PROGRAMMA QUINQUENNALE   R+D
1963-67 ED IL BILANCIO RICERCHE ED INVESTIMENTI PER PLAN
IL 1963 DELL'ERATOM." EUR+WWI FUT ITALY WOR+45   NUC/PWR
ECO/DEV SERV/IND INT/ORG TEC/DEV ECO/TAC ATTIT
SKILL WEALTH...MGT TIME/SEQ OEEC 20. PAGE 3 B0069
                                                    S62

BUENO M.,"ASPECTOS SOCIOLOGICOS DE LA EDUCACION."   SOCIETY
FUT UNIV INTELL R+D SERV/IND SCHOOL CONSULT   EDU/PROP
EX/STRUC ACT/RES PLAN...METH/CNCPT OBS 20. PAGE 17 PERSON
B0341
                                                    S62

IOVTCHOUK M.T.,"ON SOME THEORETICAL PRINCIPLES AND COM
METHODS OF SOCIOLOGICAL INVESTIGATIONS (IN   ECO/DEV
RUSSIAN)." FUT USA+45 STRATA R+D NAT/G POL/PAR   CAP/ISM
TOP/EX ACT/RES PLAN ECO/TAC EDU/PROP ROUTINE ATTIT USSR
RIGID/FLEX MARXISM SOCISM...MARXIST METH/CNCPT OBS
TREND NAT/COMP GEN/LAWS 20. PAGE 54 B1102
                                                    B63

DEAN A.L.,FEDERAL AGENCY APPROACHES TO FIELD   ADMIN
MANAGEMENT (PAMPHLET). R+D DELIB/GP EX/STRUC   MGT
PROB/SOLV GOV/REL...CLASSIF BIBLIOG 20 FAA NASA   NAT/G
DEPT/HEW POSTAL/SYS IRS. PAGE 28 B0563   OP/RES
                                                    B63

HOWER R.M.,MANAGERS AND SCIENTISTS. EX/STRUC CREATE R+D
ADMIN REPRESENT ATTIT DRIVE ROLE PWR SKILL...SOC   MGT
INT. PAGE 52 B1052   PERS/REL
                                                    INGP/REL
                                                    B63

KORNHAUSER W.,SCIENTISTS IN INDUSTRY: CONFLICT AND CREATE
ACCOMMODATION. USA+45 R+D LG/CO NAT/G TEC/DEV   INDUS
CONTROL ADJUST ATTIT...MGT STAT INT BIBLIOG 20.   PROF/ORG
PAGE 61 B1229   GP/REL
                                                    B63

RAUDSEPP E.,MANAGING CREATIVE SCIENTISTS AND   MGT
ENGINEERS. USA+45 ECO/DEV LG/CO GP/REL PERS/REL   CREATE
PRODUC. PAGE 86 B1742   R+D
                                                    ECO/TAC
                                                    B63

SCHRADER R.,SCIENCE AND POLICY. WOR+45 ECO/DEV   TEC/DEV
ECO/UNDEV R+D FORCES PLAN DIPLOM GOV/REL TECHRACY   NAT/G
BIBLIOG. PAGE 94 B1900   POLICY
                                                    ADMIN

US HOUSE COM ON ED AND LABOR,ADMINISTRATION OF   AGE/O
AGING. USA+45 R+D EX/STRUC PLAN BUDGET PAY EDU/PROP ADMIN
ROUTINE COST CONGRESS. PAGE 108 B2187   DELIB/GP
                                                    GIVE
                                                    L63

BEGUIN H.,"ASPECTS GEOGRAPHIQUE DE LA   ECO/UNDEV
POLARISATION." FUT WOR+45 SOCIETY STRUCT ECO/DEV   GEOG
R+D BAL/PWR ADMIN ATTIT RIGID/FLEX HEALTH WEALTH   DIPLOM
...CHARTS 20. PAGE 10 B0206
                                                    S63

MASSART L.,"L'ORGANISATION DE LA RECHERCHE   R+D
SCIENTIFIQUE EN EUROPE." EUR+WWI WOR+45 ACT/RES   CREATE
PLAN TEC/DEV EDU/PROP EXEC KNOWL...METH/CNCPT EEC
20. PAGE 70 B1424
                                                    S63

NADLER E.B.,"SOME ECONOMIC DISADVANTAGES OF THE   ECO/DEV
ARMS RACE." USA+45 INDUS R+D FORCES PLAN TEC/DEV   MGT
ECO/TAC FOR/AID EDU/PROP PWR WEALTH...TREND   BAL/PAY
COLD/WAR 20. PAGE 77 B1552
                                                    B64

BRIGHT J.R.,RESEARCH, DEVELOPMENT AND TECHNOLOGICAL TEC/DEV
INNOVATION. CULTURE R+D CREATE PLAN PROB/SOLV   NEW/IDEA
AUTOMAT RISK PERSON...DECISION CONCPT PREDICT   INDUS
BIBLIOG. PAGE 15 B0308   MGT
                                                    B64

MAYER C.S.,INTERVIEWING COSTS IN SURVEY RESEARCH.   SIMUL
USA+45 PLAN COST...MGT REC/INT SAMP METH/COMP   INT
HYPO/EXP METH 20. PAGE 71 B1434   R+D
                                                    EFFICIENCY
                                                    B64

ORTH C.D.,ADMINISTERING RESEARCH AND DEVELOPMENT.   MGT
FINAN PLAN PROB/SOLV ADMIN ROUTINE...METH/CNCPT   R+D
STAT CHARTS METH 20. PAGE 80 B1616   LG/CO
                                                    INDUS
                                                    B64

HOSCH L.G.,"PUBLIC ADMINISTRATION ON THE   INT/ORG
INTERNATIONAL FRONTIER." WOR+45 R+D NAT/G EDU/PROP MGT
EXEC KNOWL ORD/FREE VAL/FREE 20 UN. PAGE 52 B1046
                                                    S64

KAPLAN N.,"RESEARCH ADMINISTRATION AND THE   R+D
ADMINISTRATOR: USSR AND US." COM USA+45 INTELL   ADMIN
EX/STRUC KNOWL...MGT 20. PAGE 58 B1169   USSR
                                                    S64

NEEDHAM T.,"SCIENCE AND SOCIETY IN EAST AND WEST." ASIA
INTELL STRATA R+D LOC/G NAT/G PROVS CONSULT ACT/RES STRUCT
CREATE PLAN TEC/DEV EDU/PROP ADMIN ATTIT ALL/VALS
...POLICY RELATIV MGT CONCPT NEW/IDEA TIME/SEQ WORK
WORK. PAGE 77 B1565
                                                    B65

GREER S.,URBAN RENEWAL AND AMERICAN CITIES: THE   MUNIC
DILEMMA OF DEMOCRATIC INTERVENTION. USA+45 R+D   PROB/SOLV
LOC/G VOL/ASSN ACT/RES BUDGET ADMIN GOV/REL...SOC   PLAN
INT SAMP 20 BOSTON CHICAGO MIAMI URBAN/RNWL.   NAT/G
PAGE 43 B0871
                                                    B65

HARMON R.B.,POLITICAL SCIENCE: A BIBLIOGRAPHICAL   BIBLIOG
GUIDE TO THE LITERATURE. WOR+45 WOR-45 R+D INT/ORG POL/PAR
LOC/G NAT/G DIPLOM ADMIN...CONCPT METH. PAGE 47   LAW
B0950   GOV/COMP
                                                    B65

PRESTHUS R.,BEHAVIORAL APPROACHES TO PUBLIC   GEN/METH
ADMINISTRATION. UK STRATA LG/CO PUB/INST VOL/ASSN   DECISION
EX/STRUC TOP/EX EFFICIENCY HEALTH. PAGE 84 B1704   ADMIN
                                                    R+D
                                                    B65

TYBOUT R.A.,ECONOMICS OF RESEARCH AND DEVELOPMENT. R+D
ECO/DEV ECO/UNDEV INDUS PROFIT DECISION. PAGE 106   FORCES
B2141   ADMIN
                                                    DIPLOM
                                                    B65

UNESCO,INTERNATIONAL ORGANIZATIONS IN THE SOCIAL   INT/ORG
SCIENCES(REV. ED.). LAW ADMIN ATTIT...CRIMLGY GEOG R+D
INT/LAW PSY SOC STAT 20 UNESCO. PAGE 107 B2157   PROF/ORG
                                                    ACT/RES
                                                    S65

BALDWIN H.,"SLOW-DOWN IN THE PENTAGON." USA+45   RECORD
CREATE PLAN GOV/REL CENTRAL COST EFFICIENCY PWR   R+D
...MGT MCNAMARA/R. PAGE 9 B0174   WEAPON
                                                    ADMIN
                                                    B66

DAHLBERG J.S.,THE NEW YORK BUREAU OF MUNICIPAL   PROVS
RESEARCH: PIONEER IN GOVERNMENT ADMINISTRATION.   MUNIC
CONSTN R+D BUDGET EDU/PROP PARTIC REPRESENT   DELIB/GP
EFFICIENCY ORD/FREE...BIBLIOG METH 20 NEW/YORK   ADMIN
NIPA. PAGE 26 B0522
                                                    B66

MURDOCK J.C.,RESEARCH AND REGIONS. AGRI FINAN INDUS BIBLIOG
LOC/G MUNIC NAT/G PROB/SOLV TEC/DEV ADMIN REGION   ECO/DEV
20. PAGE 76 B1545   COMPUT/IR
                                                    R+D
                                                    B66

WYLIE C.M.,RESEARCH IN PUBLIC HEALTH   BIBLIOG/A
ADMINISTRATION; SELECTED RECENT ABSTRACTS IV   R+D
(PAMPHLET). USA+45 MUNIC PUB/INST ACT/RES CREATE   HEAL
OP/RES TEC/DEV GP/REL ROLE...MGT PHIL/SCI STAT.   ADMIN

PAGE 118 B2387

B67
ENKE S.,DEFENSE MANAGEMENT. USA+45 R+D FORCES WORKER PLAN ECO/TAC ADMIN NUC/PWR BAL/PAY UTIL WEALTH...MGT DEPT/DEFEN. PAGE 33 B0675
DECISION DELIB/GP EFFICIENCY BUDGET

B67
HIRSCHMAN A.O.,DEVELOPMENT PROJECTS OBSERVED. INDUS INT/ORG CONSULT EX/STRUC CREATE OP/RES ECO/TAC DEMAND...POLICY MGT METH/COMP 20 WORLD/BANK. PAGE 50 B1016
ECO/UNDEV R+D FINAN PLAN

B67
ROBINSON R.D., INTERNATIONAL MANAGEMENT USA+45 FINAN R+D PLAN PRODUC...DECISION T. PAGE 67 B1352
INT/TRADE MGT INT/LAW MARKET

B67
US HOUSE COMM SCI ASTRONAUT,GOVERNMENT, SCIENCE, AND INTERNATIONAL POLICY. R+D OP/RES PLAN 20. PAGE 109 B2198
ADMIN PHIL/SCI ACT/RES DIPLOM

B67
VOOS H.,ORGANIZATIONAL COMMUNICATION: A BIBLIOGRAPHY. WOR+45 STRATA R+D PROB/SOLV FEEDBACK COERCE...MGT PSY NET/THEORY HYPO/EXP. PAGE 112 B2268
BIBLIOG/A INDUS COM/IND VOL/ASSN

L67
PASLEY R.S.,"ORGANIZATIONAL CONFLICTS OF INTEREST IN GOVERNMENT CONTRACTS." ELITES R+D ROUTINE NUC/PWR DEMAND EFFICIENCY 20. PAGE 81 B1639
NAT/G ECO/TAC RATION CONTROL

S67
CONWAY J.E.,"MAKING RESEARCH EFFECTIVE IN LEGISLATION." LAW R+D CONSULT EX/STRUC PLAN CONFER ADMIN LEAD ROUTINE TASK INGP/REL DECISION. PAGE 23 B0469
ACT/RES POLICY LEGIS PROB/SOLV

S67
DOERN G.B.,"THE ROYAL COMMISSIONS IN THE GENERAL POLICY PROCESS AND IN FEDERAL-PROVINCIAL RELATIONS." CANADA CONSTN ACADEM PROVS CONSULT DELIB/GP LEGIS ACT/RES PROB/SOLV CONFER CONTROL EFFICIENCY...METH/COMP 20 SENATE ROYAL/COMM. PAGE 30 B0603
R+D EX/STRUC GOV/REL NAT/G

S67
GOBER J.L.,"FEDERALISM AT WORK." USA+45 NAT/G CONSULT ACT/RES PLAN CONFER ADMIN LEAD PARTIC FEDERAL ATTIT. PAGE 40 B0813
MUNIC TEC/DEV R+D GOV/REL

S67
LEVIN M.R.,"PLANNERS AND METROPOLITAN PLANNING." FUT USA+45 SOCIETY NAT/G PROVS PROB/SOLV LEAD PARTIC GOV/REL RACE/REL HABITAT ROLE. PAGE 64 B1301
PLAN MUNIC R+D ADMIN

S67
MACDONALD G.J.F.,"SCIENCE AND SPACE POLICY* HOW DOES IT GET PLANNED?" R+D CREATE TEC/DEV BUDGET ADMIN ROUTINE...DECISION NASA. PAGE 67 B1357
SPACE PLAN MGT EX/STRUC

S67
MORTON J.A.,"A SYSTEMS APPROACH TO THE INNOVATION PROCESS: ITS USE IN THE BELL SYSTEM." USA+45 INTELL INDUS LG/CO CONSULT WORKER COMPUTER AUTOMAT DEMAND ...MGT CHARTS 20. PAGE 76 B1531
TEC/DEV GEN/METH R+D COM/IND

S67
ROBERTS E.B.,"THE PROBLEM OF AGING ORGANIZATIONS." INTELL PROB/SOLV ADMIN EXEC FEEDBACK EFFICIENCY PRODUC...GEN/LAWS 20. PAGE 89 B1794
INDUS R+D MGT PLAN

S67
VERGIN R.C.,"COMPUTER INDUCED ORGANIZATION CHANGES." FUT USA+45 R+D CREATE OP/RES TEC/DEV ADJUST CENTRAL...MGT INT CON/ANAL COMPUT/IR. PAGE 112 B2260
COMPUTER DECISION AUTOMAT EX/STRUC

N67
US SUPERINTENDENT OF DOCUMENTS,SPACE: MISSILES, THE MOON, NASA, AND SATELLITES (PRICE LIST 79A). USA+45 COM/IND R+D NAT/G DIPLOM EDU/PROP ADMIN CONTROL HEALTH...POLICY SIMUL NASA CONGRESS. PAGE 111 B2244
BIBLIOG/A SPACE TEC/DEV PEACE

N67
US SENATE COMM AERO SPACE SCI,AERONAUTICAL RESEARCH AND DEVELOPMENT POLICY; HEARINGS, COMM ON AERONAUTICAL AND SPACE SCIENCES...1967 (PAMPHLET). R+D PROB/SOLV EXEC GOV/REL 20 DEPT/DEFEN FAA NASA CONGRESS. PAGE 109 B2210
DIST/IND SPACE NAT/G PLAN

RACE....SEE RACE/REL, KIN

RACE/REL....RACE RELATIONS; SEE ALSO DISCRIM, ISOLAT, KIN

N
JOURNAL OF POLITICS. USA+45 USA-45 CONSTN POL/PAR EX/STRUC LEGIS PROB/SOLV DIPLOM CT/SYS CHOOSE RACE/REL 20. PAGE 1 B0005
BIBLIOG/A NAT/G LAW LOC/G

N
US SUPERINTENDENT OF DOCUMENTS,EDUCATION (PRICE LIST 31). USA+45 LAW FINAN LOC/G NAT/G DEBATE ADMIN LEAD RACE/REL FEDERAL HEALTH POLICY. PAGE 111 B2238
BIBLIOG/A EDU/PROP ACADEM SCHOOL

N
US SUPERINTENDENT OF DOCUMENTS,POLITICAL SCIENCE: GOVERNMENT, CRIME, DISTRICT OF COLUMBIA (PRICE LIST 54). USA+45 LAW CONSTN EX/STRUC WORKER ADJUD ADMIN CT/SYS CHOOSE INGP/REL RACE/REL CONGRESS PRESIDENT. PAGE 111 B2241
BIBLIOG/A NAT/G CRIME

B02
MOREL E.D.,AFFAIRS OF WEST AFRICA. UK FINAN INDUS FAM KIN SECT CHIEF WORKER DIPLOM RACE/REL LITERACY HEALTH...CHARTS 18/20 AFRICA/W NEGRO. PAGE 75 B1521
COLONIAL ADMIN AFR

B19
NATHAN M.,THE SOUTH AFRICAN COMMONWEALTH: CONSTITUTION, PROBLEMS, SOCIAL CONDITIONS. SOUTH/AFR UK CULTURE INDUS EX/STRUC LEGIS BUDGET EDU/PROP ADMIN CT/SYS GP/REL RACE/REL...LING 19/20 CMN/WLTH. PAGE 77 B1559
CONSTN NAT/G POL/PAR SOCIETY

N19
BUREAU OF NAT'L AFFAIRS INC.,A CURRENT LOOK AT: (1) THE NEGRO AND TITLE VII, (2) SEX AND TITLE VII (PAMPHLET). LAW LG/CO SML/CO RACE/REL...POLICY SOC STAT DEEP/QU TREND CON/ANAL CHARTS 20 NEGRO CIV/RIGHTS. PAGE 17 B0350
DISCRIM SEX WORKER MGT

B48
DAY P.,CRISIS IN SOUTH AFRICA. SOUTH/AFR UK KIN MUNIC ECO/TAC RECEIVE 20 SMUTS/JAN MIGRATION. PAGE 27 B0548
RACE/REL COLONIAL ADMIN EXTR/IND

B48
KESSELMAN L.C.,THE SOCIAL POLITICS OF THE FEPC. INDUS WORKER EDU/PROP GP/REL RACE/REL 20 NEGRO JEWS FEPC. PAGE 59 B1200
POLICY NAT/G ADMIN DISCRIM

C50
MORLAN R.L.,"INTERGOVERNMENTAL RELATIONS IN EDUCATION." USA+45 FINAN LOC/G MUNIC NAT/G FORCES PROB/SOLV RECEIVE ADMIN RACE/REL COST...BIBLIOG INDIAN/AM. PAGE 76 B1526
SCHOOL GOV/REL ACADEM POLICY

B53
WAGLEY C.,AMAZON TOWN: A STUDY OF MAN IN THE TROPICS. BRAZIL L/A+17C STRATA STRUCT ECO/UNDEV AGRI EX/STRUC RACE/REL DISCRIM HABITAT WEALTH...OBS SOC/EXP 20. PAGE 113 B2273
SOC NEIGH CULTURE INGP/REL

B54
ALLPORT G.W.,THE NATURE OF PREJUDICE. USA+45 WOR+45 STRATA FACE/GP KIN NEIGH SECT ADMIN GP/REL DISCRIM ATTIT DRIVE LOVE RESPECT...PSY SOC MYTH QU/SEMANT 20. PAGE 4 B0078
CULTURE PERSON RACE/REL

B56
IRIKURA J.K.,SOUTHEAST ASIA: SELECTED ANNOTATED BIBLIOGRAPHY OF JAPANESE PUBLICATIONS. CULTURE ADMIN RACE/REL 20 CHINJAP. PAGE 55 B1104
BIBLIOG/A S/ASIA DIPLOM

B57
SCHNEIDER E.V.,INDUSTRIAL SOCIOLOGY: THE SOCIAL RELATIONS OF INDUSTRY AND COMMUNITY. STRATA INDUS NAT/G NEIGH CREATE ADMIN PARTIC GP/REL RACE/REL ROLE PWR...POLICY BIBLIOG. PAGE 94 B1898
LABOR MGT INGP/REL STRUCT

S57
HAILEY,"TOMORROW IN AFRICA." CONSTN SOCIETY LOC/G NAT/G DOMIN ADJUD ADMIN GP/REL DISCRIM NAT/LISM ATTIT MORAL ORD/FREE...PSY SOC CONCPT OBS RECORD TREND GEN/LAWS CMN/WLTH 20. PAGE 45 B0917
AFR PERSON ELITES RACE/REL

B59
LOEWENSTEIN K.,VERFASSUNGSRECHT UND VERFASSUNGSPRAXIS DER VEREINIGTEN STAATEN. USA+45 USA-45 COLONIAL CT/SYS GP/REL RACE/REL ORD/FREE ...JURID 18/20 SUPREME/CT CONGRESS PRESIDENT BILL/RIGHT CIVIL/LIB. PAGE 66 B1337
CONSTN POL/PAR EX/STRUC NAT/G

S59
DWYER R.J.,"THE ADMINISTRATIVE ROLE IN DESEGREGATION." USA+45 LAW PROB/SOLV LEAD RACE/REL ISOLAT STRANGE ROLE...POLICY SOC/INTEG MISSOURI NEGRO CIV/RIGHTS. PAGE 31 B0638
ADMIN SCHOOL DISCRIM ATTIT

B60
ASPREMONT-LYNDEN H.,RAPPORT SUR L'ADMINISTRATION BELGE DU RUANDA-URUNDI PENDANT L'ANNEE 1959. BELGIUM RWANDA AGRI INDUS DIPLOM ECO/TAC INT/TRADE DOMIN ADMIN RACE/REL...GEOG CENSUS 20 UN. PAGE 7 B0143
AFR COLONIAL ECO/UNDEV INT/ORG

B60
SOUTH AFRICAN CONGRESS OF DEM,FACE THE FUTURE. SOUTH/AFR ELITES LEGIS ADMIN REGION COERCE PEACE ATTIT 20. PAGE 99 B1999
RACE/REL DISCRIM CONSTN NAT/G

C60
FITZSIMMONS T.,"USSR: ITS PEOPLE, ITS SOCIETY, ITS CULTURE." USSR FAM SECT DIPLOM EDU/PROP ADMIN RACE/REL ATTIT...POLICY CHARTS BIBLIOG 20. PAGE 36 B0728
CULTURE STRUCT SOCIETY COM

C60
SMITH T.E.,"ELECTIONS IN DEVELOPING COUNTRIES: A STUDY OF ELECTORAL PROCEDURES USED IN TOPICAL AFRICA, SOUTH-EAST ASIA..." AFR S/ASIA UK ROUTINE GOV/REL RACE/REL...GOV/COMP BIBLIOG 20. PAGE 98
ECO/UNDEV CHOOSE REPRESENT ADMIN

B1985

B61

MUNGER E.S.,AFRICAN FIELD REPORTS 1952-1961.   AFR
SOUTH/AFR SOCIETY ECO/UNDEV NAT/G POL/PAR COLONIAL   DISCRIM
EXEC PARL/PROC GUERRILLA RACE/REL ALL/IDEOS...SOC   RECORD
AUD/VIS 20. PAGE 76 B1538

B62

BOCK E.A.,CASE STUDIES IN AMERICAN GOVERNMENT.   POLICY
USA+45 ECO/DEV CHIEF EDU/PROP CT/SYS RACE/REL   LEGIS
ORD/FREE...JURID MGT PHIL/SCI PRESIDENT CASEBOOK.   IDEA/COMP
PAGE 13 B0262   NAT/G

B62

SHAPIRO D.,A SELECT BIBLIOGRAPHY OF WORKS IN   BIBLIOG
ENGLISH ON RUSSIAN HISTORY, 1801-1917. COM USSR   DIPLOM
STRATA FORCES EDU/PROP ADMIN REV RACE/REL ATTIT   COLONIAL
19/20. PAGE 96 B1932

B62

TAYLOR D.,THE BRITISH IN AFRICA. UK CULTURE   AFR
ECO/UNDEV INDUS DIPLOM INT/TRADE ADMIN WAR RACE/REL   COLONIAL
ORD/FREE SOVEREIGN...POLICY BIBLIOG 15/20 CMN/WLTH.   DOMIN
PAGE 103 B2084

B63

CONF ON FUTURE OF COMMONWEALTH,THE FUTURE OF THE   DIPLOM
COMMONWEALTH. UK ECO/UNDEV AGRI EDU/PROP ADMIN   RACE/REL
SOC/INTEG 20 COMMONWLTH. PAGE 23 B0460   ORD/FREE
                                                      TEC/DEV

B63

GALBRAITH J.S.,RELUCTANT EMPIRE: BRITISH POLICY OF   COLONIAL
THE SOUTH AFRICAN FRONTIER, 1834-1854. AFR   ADMIN
SOUTH/AFR UK GP/REL RACE/REL DISCRIM...CHARTS   POLICY
BIBLIOG 19 MISSION. PAGE 38 B0774   SECT

B63

SINGH H.L.,PROBLEMS AND POLICIES OF THE BRITISH IN   COLONIAL
INDIA, 1885-1898. INDIA UK NAT/G FORCES LEGIS   PWR
PROB/SOLV CONTROL RACE/REL ADJUST DISCRIM NAT/LISM   POLICY
RIGID/FLEX...MGT 19 CIVIL/SERV. PAGE 97 B1968   ADMIN

B64

BANTON M.,THE POLICEMAN IN THE COMMUNITY. UK USA+45   FORCES
STRUCT PROF/ORG WORKER LOBBY ROUTINE COERCE CROWD   ADMIN
GP/REL ADJUST DISCRIM PERCEPT 20. PAGE 9 B0181   ROLE
                                                      RACE/REL

B64

HANNA W.J.,INDEPENDENT BLACK AFRICA: THE POLITICS   AFR
OF FREEDOM. ELITES INDUS KIN CHIEF COLONIAL CHOOSE   ECO/UNDEV
GOV/REL RACE/REL NAT/LISM ATTIT PERSON 20 NEGRO.   ADMIN
PAGE 46 B0938   PROB/SOLV

B64

WILDAVSKY A.,LEADERSHIP IN A SMALL TOWN. USA+45   LEAD
STRUCT PROB/SOLV EXEC PARTIC RACE/REL PWR PLURISM   MUNIC
...SOC 20 NEGRO WATER CIV/RIGHTS OBERLIN CITY/MGT.   ELITES
PAGE 116 B2348

C64

NORGREN P.H.,"TOWARD FAIR EMPLOYMENT." USA+45 LAW   RACE/REL
STRATA LABOR NAT/G FORCES ACT/RES ADMIN ATTIT   DISCRIM
...POLICY BIBLIOG 20 NEGRO. PAGE 79 B1588   WORKER
                                                      MGT

B65

FRIEDMAN L.,SOUTHERN JUSTICE. USA+45 PUB/INST LEGIT   ADJUD
ADMIN CT/SYS DISCRIM...DECISION ANTHOL 20 NEGRO   LAW
SOUTH/US CIV/RIGHTS. PAGE 37 B0758   CONSTN
                                                      RACE/REL

B65

PANJABI K.L.,THE CIVIL SERVANT IN INDIA. INDIA UK   ADMIN
NAT/G CONSULT EX/STRUC REGION GP/REL RACE/REL 20.   WORKER
PAGE 81 B1631   BIOG
                                                      COLONIAL

B65

PARRISH W.E.,MISSOURI UNDER RADICAL RULE 1865-1870.   PROVS
USA-45 SOCIETY INDUS LOC/G POL/PAR WORKER EDU/PROP   ADMIN
SUFF INGP/REL ATTIT...BIBLIOG 19 NEGRO MISSOURI.   RACE/REL
PAGE 81 B1635   ORD/FREE

B65

REISS A.J. JR.,SCHOOLS IN A CHANGING SOCIETY.   SCHOOL
CULTURE PROB/SOLV INSPECT DOMIN CONFER INGP/REL   EX/STRUC
RACE/REL AGE/C AGE/Y ALL/VALS...ANTHOL SOC/INTEG 20   ADJUST
NEWYORK/C. PAGE 87 B1766   ADMIN

B65

ROTBERG R.I.,A POLITICAL HISTORY OF TROPICAL   AFR
AFRICA. EX/STRUC DIPLOM INT/TRADE DOMIN ADMIN   CULTURE
RACE/REL NAT/LISM PWR SOVEREIGN...GEOG TIME/SEQ   COLONIAL
BIBLIOG 1/20. PAGE 91 B1832

B65

YOUNG C.,POLITICS IN THE CONGO* DECOLONIZATION AND   BELGIUM
INDEPENDENCE. ELITES STRATA FORCES ADMIN REV   COLONIAL
RACE/REL FEDERAL SOVEREIGN...OBS INT CHARTS   NAT/LISM
CONGO/LEOP. PAGE 118 B2391

L65

MATTHEWS D.G.,"A CURRENT BIBLIOGRAPHY ON ETHIOPIAN   BIBLIOG/A
AFFAIRS: A SELECT BIBLIOGRAPHY FROM 1950-1964."   ADMIN
ETHIOPIA LAW CULTURE ECO/UNDEV INDUS LABOR SECT   POL/PAR
FORCES DIPLOM CIVMIL/REL RACE/REL...LING STAT 20.   NAT/G
PAGE 71 B1428

B66

DAVIS J.A.,SOUTHERN AFRICA IN TRANSITION. SOUTH/AFR   AFR
USA+45 FINAN NAT/G DELIB/GP EDU/PROP ADMIN COLONIAL   ADJUST
REGION RACE/REL ATTIT SOVEREIGN...ANTHOL 20   CONSTN

RESOURCE/N. PAGE 26 B0538

B66

KAUNDA K.,ZAMBIA: INDEPENDENCE AND BEYOND: THE   ORD/FREE
SPEECHES OF KENNETH KAUNDA. AFR FUT ZAMBIA SOCIETY   COLONIAL
ECO/UNDEV NAT/G PROB/SOLV ECO/TAC ADMIN RACE/REL   CONSTN
SOVEREIGN 20. PAGE 59 B1183   LEAD

S66

AFRICAN BIBLIOGRAPHIC CENTER,"A CURRENT VIEW OF   BIBLIOG/A
AFRICANA: A SELECT AND ANNOTATED BIBLIOGRAPHICAL   NAT/G
PUBLISHING GUIDE, 1965-1966." AFR CULTURE INDUS   TEC/DEV
LABOR SECT FOR/AID ADMIN COLONIAL REV RACE/REL   POL/PAR
SOCISM...LING 20. PAGE 3 B0063

S66

JACOBSON J.,"COALITIONISM: FROM PROTEST TO   RACE/REL
POLITICKING" USA+45 ELITES NAT/G POL/PAR PROB/SOLV   LABOR
ADMIN LEAD DISCRIM ORD/FREE PWR CONSERVE 20 NEGRO   SOCIALIST
AFL/CIO CIV/RIGHTS BLACK/PWR. PAGE 55 B1116   VOL/ASSN

N66

PRINCETON U INDUSTRIAL REL SEC,OUTSTANDING BOOKS ON   BIBLIOG/A
INDUSTRIAL RELATIONS, 1965 (PAMPHLET NO. 128).   INDUS
WOR+45 LABOR BARGAIN GOV/REL RACE/REL HEALTH PWR   GP/REL
...MGT 20. PAGE 85 B1709   POLICY

B67

ANGEL D.D.,ROMNEY. LABOR LG/CO NAT/G EXEC WAR   BIOG
RACE/REL PERSON ORD/FREE...MGT WORSHIP 20   CHIEF
ROMNEY/GEO CIV/RIGHTS MORMON GOVERNOR. PAGE 5 B0108   PROVS
                                                      POLICY

B67

JAKUBAUSKAS E.B.,HUMAN RESOURCES DEVELOPMENT.   PROB/SOLV
USA+45 AGRI INDUS SERV/IND ACT/RES PLAN ADMIN   ECO/TAC
RACE/REL DISCRIM...TREND GEN/LAWS. PAGE 55 B1119   EDU/PROP
                                                      WORKER

B67

KRISLOV S.,THE NEGRO IN FEDERAL EMPLOYMENT. LAW   WORKER
STRATA LOC/G CREATE PROB/SOLV INSPECT GOV/REL   NAT/G
DISCRIM ROLE...DECISION INT TREND 20 NEGRO WWI   ADMIN
CIVIL/SERV. PAGE 61 B1238   RACE/REL

B67

WEINBERG M.,SCHOOL INTEGRATION: A COMPREHENSIVE   BIBLIOG
CLASSIFIED BIBLIOGRAPHY OF 3,100 REFERENCES. USA+45   SCHOOL
LAW NAT/G NEIGH SECT PLAN ROUTINE AGE/C WEALTH   DISCRIM
SOC/INTEG INDIAN/AM. PAGE 115 B2314   RACE/REL

S67

BRADLEY A.W.,"CONSTITUTION-MAKING IN UGANDA."   NAT/G
UGANDA LAW CHIEF DELIB/GP LEGIS ADMIN EXEC   CREATE
PARL/PROC RACE/REL ORD/FREE...GOV/COMP 20. PAGE 14   CONSTN
B0295   FEDERAL

S67

IDENBURG P.J.,"POLITICAL STRUCTURAL DEVELOPMENT IN   AFR
TROPICAL AFRICA." UK ECO/UNDEV KIN POL/PAR CHIEF   CONSTN
EX/STRUC CREATE COLONIAL CONTROL REPRESENT RACE/REL   NAT/G
...MAJORIT TREND 20. PAGE 53 B1074   GOV/COMP

S67

LANDES W.M.,"THE EFFECT OF STATE FAIR EMPLOYMENT   DISCRIM
LAWS ON THE ECONOMIC POSITION OF NONWHITES." USA+45   LAW
PROVS SECT LEGIS ADMIN GP/REL RACE/REL...JURID   WORKER
CONCPT CHARTS HYPO/EXP NEGRO. PAGE 62 B1255

S67

LEVIN M.R.,"PLANNERS AND METROPOLITAN PLANNING."   PLAN
FUT USA+45 SOCIETY NAT/G PROVS PROB/SOLV LEAD   MUNIC
PARTIC GOV/REL RACE/REL HABITAT ROLE. PAGE 64 B1301   R+D
                                                      ADMIN

S67

O'DELL J.H.,"THE JULY REBELLIONS AND THE 'MILITARY   PWR
STATE'." USA+45 VIETNAM STRATA CHIEF WORKER   NAT/G
COLONIAL EXEC CROWD CIVMIL/REL RACE/REL TOTALISM   COERCE
...WELF/ST PACIFIST 20 NEGRO JOHNSON/LB PRESIDENT   FORCES
CIV/RIGHTS. PAGE 79 B1599

S67

RAUM O.,"THE MODERN LEADERSHIP GROUP AMONG THE   RACE/REL
SOUTH AFRICAN XHOSA." SOUTH/AFR SOCIETY SECT   KIN
EX/STRUC REPRESENT GP/REL INGP/REL PERSON   LEAD
...METH/COMP 17/20 XHOSA NEGRO. PAGE 86 B1743   CULTURE

S67

ROSENBERG B.,"ETHNIC LIBERALISM AND EMPLOYMENT   RACE/REL
DISCRIMINATION IN THE NORTH." USA+45 TOP/EX   ATTIT
PROB/SOLV ADMIN REGION PERS/REL DISCRIM...INT   WORKER
IDEA/COMP. PAGE 90 B1820   EXEC

S67

ROTBERG R.I.,"COLONIALISM AND AFTER: THE POLITICAL   BIBLIOG/A
LITERATURE OF CENTRAL AFRICA - A BIBLIOGRAPHIC   COLONIAL
ESSAY." AFR CHIEF EX/STRUC REV INGP/REL RACE/REL   DIPLOM
SOVEREIGN 20. PAGE 91 B1833   NAT/G

B87

KINNEAR J.B.,PRINCIPLES OF CIVIL GOVERNMENT.   POL/PAR
MOD/EUR USA-45 CONSTN LOC/G EX/STRUC ADMIN   NAT/G
PARL/PROC RACE/REL...CONCPT 18/19. PAGE 60 B1210   GOV/COMP
                                                      REPRESENT

RAEFF M. B1728

RAF....ROYAL AIR FORCE

RAHMAN/TA....TUNKU ABDUL RAHMAN

RAI H. B1729

RAILROAD....RAILROADS AND RAILWAY SYSTEMS

B08

THE GOVERNMENT OF SOUTH AFRICA (VOL. II). SOUTH/AFR CONSTN
STRATA EXTR/IND EX/STRUC TOP/EX BUDGET ADJUD ADMIN FINAN
CT/SYS PRODUC...CORREL CENSUS 19 RAILROAD LEGIS
CIVIL/SERV POSTAL/SYS. PAGE 2 B0033 NAT/G

B54

LOCKLIN D.P.,ECONOMICS OF TRANSPORTATION (4TH ED.). ECO/DEV
USA+45 SEA AIR LAW FINAN LG/CO EX/STRUC DIST/IND
ADMIN CONTROL...STAT CHARTS 19/20 RAILROAD ECO/TAC
PUB/TRANS. PAGE 66 B1335 TEC/DEV

B61

AGARWAL R.C.,STATE ENTERPRISE IN INDIA. FUT INDIA ECO/UNDEV
UK FINAN INDUS ADMIN CONTROL OWN...POLICY CHARTS SOCISM
BIBLIOG 20 RAILROAD. PAGE 3 B0064 GOV/REL
LG/CO

RAJARATAM/S....S. RAJARATAM

RAJASTHAN....RAJASTHAN

RALSTON D.B. B1730

RAMA RAO T.V. B0238

RANDALL C.B. B0175

RANDOMNESS....SEE PROB/SOLV

RANKE/L....LEOPOLD VON RANKE

RANKING SYSTEMS....SEE SENIOR

RANKOVIC/A....ALEXANDER RANKOVIC, YUGOSLAVIA0S FORMER VICE
     PRESIDENT

RANSHOFFEN-WERTHEIMER EF B1731

RANSONE C.B. B1732

RAO K.V. B1733

RAO V.K.R. B1734

RAPAPORT R.N. B1735

RAPAPORT R.S. B1735

RAPHAEL J.S. B1736

RAPHAEL M. B1737

RAPHAELI N. B1738,B1739

RAPP W.F. B1740

RAPPARD W.E. B1741

RATION....RATIONING

N19

KRIESBERG M.,CANCELLATION OF THE RATION STAMPS RATION
(PAMPHLET). USA+45 USA-45 MARKET PROB/SOLV PRICE DECISION
GOV/REL RIGID/FLEX 20 OPA. PAGE 61 B1235 ADMIN
NAT/G

B47

REDFORD E.S.,FIELD ADMINISTRATION OF WARTIME ADMIN
RATIONING. USA-45 CONSTN ELITES DIST/IND WORKER NAT/G
CONTROL WAR GOV/REL ADJUST RIGID/FLEX 20 OPA. PROB/SOLV
PAGE 87 B1752 RATION

L62

BELSHAW D.G.R.,"PUBLIC INVESTMENT IN AGRICULTURE ECO/UNDEV
AND ECONOMIC DEVELOPMENT OF UGANDA" UGANDA AGRI PLAN
INDUS R+D ECO/TAC RATION TAX PAY COLONIAL 20 ADMIN
WORLD/BANK. PAGE 10 B0209 CENTRAL

B63

CHARLES S.,MINISTER OF RELIEF: HARRY HOPKINS AND ADMIN
THE DEPRESSION. EX/STRUC PROB/SOLV RATION PARL/PROC ECO/TAC
PERS/REL ALL/VALS 20 HOPKINS/H NRA. PAGE 20 B0414 PLAN
BIOG

B63

US SENATE COMM ON JUDICIARY,ADMINISTERED PRICES. LG/CO
USA+45 RATION ADJUD CONTROL LOBBY...POLICY 20 PRICE
SENATE MONOPOLY. PAGE 110 B2229 ADMIN
DECISION

S63

REES A.,"THE EFFECTS OF UNIONS ON RESOURCE LABOR
ALLOCATION." USA+45 WORKER PRICE CONTROL GP/REL BARGAIN
...MGT METH/COMP 20. PAGE 87 B1761 RATION
INCOME

L67

PASLEY R.S.,"ORGANIZATIONAL CONFLICTS OF INTEREST NAT/G
IN GOVERNMENT CONTRACTS." ELITES R+D ROUTINE ECO/TAC
NUC/PWR DEMAND EFFICIENCY 20. PAGE 81 B1639 RATION
CONTROL

RATIONAL....RATIONALITY

B47

SIMON H.A.,ADMINISTRATIVE BEHAVIOR: A STUDY OF DECISION
DECISION-MAKING PROCESSES IN ADMINISTRATIVE NEW/IDEA
ORGANIZATION. STRUCT COM/IND OP/RES PROB/SOLV ADMIN
EFFICIENCY EQUILIB UTIL...PHIL/SCI PSY STYLE. RATIONAL
PAGE 97 B1956

B48

ROSENFARB J.,FREEDOM AND THE ADMINISTRATIVE STATE. ECO/DEV
NAT/G ROUTINE EFFICIENCY PRODUC RATIONAL UTIL INDUS
...TECHNIC WELF/ST MGT 20 BUREAUCRCY. PAGE 90 B1821 PLAN
WEALTH

B51

LASSWELL H.D.,THE POLITICAL WRITINGS OF HAROLD D PERSON
LASSWELL. UNIV DOMIN EXEC LEAD RATIONAL ATTIT DRIVE PSY
ROLE ALL/VALS...OBS BIOG 20. PAGE 63 B1269 INGP/REL
CONCPT

S52

JOSEPHSON E.,"IRRATIONAL LEADERSHIP IN FORMAL ADMIN
ORGANIZATIONS." EX/STRUC PLAN LEAD GP/REL INGP/REL RATIONAL
EFFICIENCY AUTHORIT DRIVE PSY. PAGE 57 B1154 CONCPT
PERSON

S55

DRUCKER P.F.,"'MANAGEMENT SCIENCE' AND THE MGT
MANAGER." PLAN ROUTINE RIGID/FLEX...METH/CNCPT LOG STRUCT
HYPO/EXP. PAGE 30 B0620 DECISION
RATIONAL

B57

HEATH S.,CITADEL, MARKET, AND ALTAR; EMERGING NEW/IDEA
SOCIETY. SOCIETY ADMIN OPTIMAL OWN RATIONAL STRUCT
ORD/FREE...SOC LOG PREDICT GEN/LAWS DICTIONARY 20. UTOPIA
PAGE 49 B0985 CREATE

B57

SELZNICK,LEADERSHIP IN ADMINISTRATION: A LEAD
SOCIOLOGICAL INTERPRETATION. CREATE PROB/SOLV EXEC ADMIN
ROUTINE EFFICIENCY RATIONAL KNOWL...POLICY PSY. DECISION
PAGE 95 B1927 NAT/G

B58

MARCH J.G.,ORGANIZATIONS. USA+45 CREATE OP/RES PLAN MGT
PROB/SOLV PARTIC ROUTINE RATIONAL ATTIT PERCEPT PERSON
...DECISION BIBLIOG. PAGE 69 B1397 DRIVE
CONCPT

S59

UDY S.H. JR.,"'BUREAUCRACY' AND 'RATIONALITY' IN GEN/LAWS
WEBER'S ORGANIZATION THEORY: AN EMPIRICAL STUDY" METH/CNCPT
(BMR)" UNIV STRUCT INDUS LG/CO SML/CO VOL/ASSN ADMIN
...SOC SIMUL 20 WEBER/MAX BUREAUCRCY. PAGE 106 RATIONAL
B2144

B60

GRAHAM G.A.,AMERICA'S CAPACITY TO GOVERN: SOME MGT
PRELIMINARY THOUGHTS FOR PROSPECTIVE LEAD
ADMINISTRATORS. USA+45 SOCIETY DELIB/GP TOP/EX CHOOSE
CREATE PROB/SOLV RATIONAL 20. PAGE 42 B0849 ADMIN

B60

MORRIS W.T.,ENGINEERING ECONOMY. AUTOMAT RISK OP/RES
RATIONAL...PROBABIL STAT CHARTS GAME SIMUL BIBLIOG DECISION
T 20. PAGE 76 B1529 MGT
PROB/SOLV

S60

PFIFFNER J.M.,"ADMINISTRATIVE RATIONALITY" (BMR)" ADMIN
UNIV CONTROL...POLICY IDEA/COMP SIMUL. PAGE 83 DECISION
B1667 RATIONAL

B61

KRUPP S.,PATTERN IN ORGANIZATIONAL ANALYSIS: A MGT
CRITICAL EXAMINATION. INGP/REL PERS/REL RATIONAL CONTROL
ATTIT AUTHORIT DRIVE PWR...DECISION PHIL/SCI SOC CONCPT
IDEA/COMP. PAGE 61 B1239 METH/CNCPT

S61

DYKMAN J.W.,"REVIEW ARTICLE* PLANNING AND DECISION DECISION
THEORY." ELITES LOC/G MUNIC CONSULT ADMIN...POLICY PLAN
MGT. PAGE 31 B0640 RATIONAL

B62

BINDER L.,IRAN: POLITICAL DEVELOPMENT IN A CHANGING LEGIT
SOCIETY. IRAN OP/RES REV GP/REL CENTRAL RATIONAL NAT/G
PWR...PHIL/SCI NAT/COMP GEN/LAWS 20. PAGE 12 B0239 ADMIN
STRUCT

B62

NATIONAL BUREAU ECONOMIC RES,THE RATE AND DIRECTION DECISION
OF INVENTIVE ACTIVITY: ECONOMIC AND SOCIAL FACTORS. PROB/SOLV
STRUCT INDUS MARKET R+D CREATE OP/RES TEC/DEV MGT
EFFICIENCY PRODUC RATIONAL UTIL...WELF/ST PHIL/SCI
METH/CNCPT TIME. PAGE 77 B1562

B62

SIMON Y.R.,A GENERAL THEORY OF AUTHORITY. DOMIN PERS/REL
ADMIN RATIONAL UTOPIA KNOWL MORAL PWR SOVEREIGN PERSON
...HUM CONCPT NEW/IDEA 20. PAGE 97 B1962 SOCIETY
ORD/FREE

B62

US ADMINISTRATIVE CONFERENCE,FINAL REPORT OF THE ADMIN
ADMINISTRATIVE CONFERENCE OF THE US; SUGGESTIONS NAT/G
FOR IMPROVING PROCESSES - ADMIN. AGENCIES. USA+45 DELIB/GP
INGP/REL EFFICIENCY RATIONAL ORD/FREE...GP/COMP GOV/REL
METH/COMP 20. PAGE 107 B2170

B64

ELDREDGE H.W.,THE SECOND AMERICAN REVOLUTION. ELITES

EDU/PROP NAT/LISM RATIONAL TOTALISM FASCISM MARXISM ORD/FREE
SOCISM. PAGE 33 B0664   ADMIN
                                                     PLAN
                                                               B64
RIES J.C.,THE MANAGEMENT OF DEFENSE: ORGANIZATION   FORCES
AND CONTROL OF THE US ARMED SERVICES. PROF/ORG   ACT/RES
DELIB/GP EX/STRUC LEGIS GOV/REL PERS/REL CENTRAL   DECISION
RATIONAL PWR...POLICY TREND GOV/COMP BIBLIOG.   CONTROL
PAGE 88 B1782
                                                               B65
CAVERS D.F.,THE CHOICE-OF-LAW PROCESS. PROB/SOLV   JURID
ADJUD CT/SYS CHOOSE RATIONAL...IDEA/COMP 16/20   DECISION
TREATY. PAGE 19 B0396   METH/COMP
                                                     ADMIN
                                                               B67
BLUMBERG A.S.,CRIMINAL JUSTICE. USA+45 CLIENT LAW   JURID
LOC/G FORCES JUDGE ACT/RES LEGIT ADMIN RATIONAL   CT/SYS
MYTH. PAGE 13 B0259   PROF/ORG
                                                     CRIME
                                                               B67
PLANO J.C.,FORGING WORLD ORDER: THE POLITICS OF   INT/ORG
INTERNATIONAL ORGANIZATION. PROB/SOLV DIPLOM   ADMIN
CONTROL CENTRAL RATIONAL ORD/FREE...INT/LAW CHARTS   JURID
BIBLIOG 20 UN LEAGUE/NAT. PAGE 83 B1679

RAUDSEPP E. B1742

RAUM O. B1743

RAVKIN A. B1744

RAWLINSON J.L. B1745

RAYMOND J. B1746

READ W.H. B1747

REAGAN M.O. B1748

REAGAN/RON....RONALD REAGAN

REALPOL....REALPOLITIK, PRACTICAL POLITICS

                                                               S67
JOHNSON L.B.,"BULLETS DO NOT DISCRIMINATE-LANDLORDS NAT/G
DO." PROB/SOLV EXEC LOBBY DEMAND...REALPOL SOC 20.   DISCRIM
PAGE 57 B1145   POLICY

REALPOLITIK....SEE REALPOL

REC/INT....RECORDING OF INTERVIEWS

                                                               B28
BUELL R.,THE NATIVE PROBLEM IN AFRICA. KIN LABOR   AFR
LOC/G ECO/TAC ROUTINE ORD/FREE...REC/INT KNO/TEST   CULTURE
CENSUS TREND CHARTS SOC/EXP STERTYP 20. PAGE 17
B0339
                                                               B54
COMBS C.H.,DECISION PROCESSES. INTELL SOCIETY   MATH
DELIB/GP CREATE TEC/DEV DOMIN LEGIT EXEC CHOOSE   DECISION
DRIVE RIGID/FLEX KNOWL PWR...PHIL/SCI SOC
METH/CNCPT CONT/OBS REC/INT PERS/TEST SAMP/SIZ BIOG
SOC/EXP WORK. PAGE 22 B0455
                                                               S55
WEISS R.S.,"A METHOD FOR THE ANALYSIS OF THE   PROF/ORG
STRUCTURE OF COMPLEX ORGANIZATIONS." WOR+45 INDUS   SOC/EXP
LG/CO NAT/G EXEC ROUTINE ORD/FREE PWR SKILL...MGT
PSY SOC NEW/IDEA STAT INT REC/INT STAND/INT CHARTS
WORK. PAGE 115 B2316
                                                               B63
US SENATE COMM GOVT OPERATIONS,ADMINISTRATION OF   DELIB/GP
NATIONAL SECURITY (9 PARTS). ADMIN...INT REC/INT   NAT/G
CHARTS 20 SENATE CONGRESS. PAGE 110 B2213   OP/RES
                                                     ORD/FREE
                                                               B64
MAYER C.S.,INTERVIEWING COSTS IN SURVEY RESEARCH.   SIMUL
USA+45 PLAN COST...MGT REC/INT SAMP METH/COMP   INT
HYPO/EXP METH 20. PAGE 71 B1434   R+D
                                                     EFFICIENCY

RECALL....RECALL PROCEDURE

RECEIVE....RECEIVING (IN WELFARE SENSE)

                                                               NCO
STOLPER W.,"SOCIAL FACTORS IN ECONOMIC PLANNING,   ECO/UNDEV
WITH SPECIAL REFERENCE TO NIGERIA" AFR NIGER   PLAN
CULTURE FAM SECT RECEIVE ETIQUET ADMIN DEMAND 20.   ADJUST
PAGE 101 B2045   RISK
                                                               N19
RIDLEY C.E.,MEASURING MUNICIPAL ACTIVITIES   MGT
(PAMPHLET). FINAN SERV/IND FORCES RECEIVE INGP/REL   HEALTH
HABITAT...POLICY SOC/WK 20. PAGE 88 B1779   WEALTH
                                                     LOC/G
                                                               B34
WILCOX J.K.,GUIDE TO THE OFFICIAL PUBLICATIONS OF   BIBLIOG

THE NEW DEAL ADMINISTRATION (2 VOLS.). USA-45 CHIEF NAT/G
LEGIS ADMIN...POLICY 20 CONGRESS ROOSEVLT/F.   NEW/LIB
PAGE 116 B2345   RECEIVE
                                                               B43
LEVY H.P.,A STUDY IN PUBLIC RELATIONS: CASE HISTORY ATTIT
OF THE RELATIONS MAINTAINED BETWEEN A DEPT OF   RECEIVE
PUBLIC ASSISTANCE AND PEOPLE. USA-45 NAT/G PRESS   WEALTH
ADMIN LOBBY GP/REL DISCRIM...SOC/WK LING AUD/VIS 20 SERV/IND
PENNSYLVAN. PAGE 64 B1302
                                                               B47
PUBLIC ADMINISTRATION SERVICE,CURRENT RESEARCH   BIBLIOG
PROJECTS IN PUBLIC ADMINISTRATION (PAMPHLET). LAW   R+D
CONSTN COM/IND LABOR LOC/G MUNIC PROVS ACT/RES   MGT
DIPLOM RECEIVE EDU/PROP WAR 20. PAGE 85 B1716   ADMIN
                                                               B48
DAY P.,CRISIS IN SOUTH AFRICA. SOUTH/AFR UK KIN   RACE/REL
MUNIC ECO/TAC RECEIVE 20 SMUTS/JAN MIGRATION.   COLONIAL
PAGE 27 B0548   ADMIN
                                                     EXTR/IND
                                                               B48
PUBLIC ADMINISTRATION SERVICE,SOURCE MATERIALS IN   BIBLIOG/A
PUBLIC ADMINISTRATION: A SELECTED BIBLIOGRAPHY (PAS GOV/REL
PUBLICATION NO. 102). USA+45 LAW FINAN LOC/G MUNIC   MGT
NAT/G PLAN RECEIVE EDU/PROP CT/SYS CHOOSE HEALTH   ADMIN
20. PAGE 85 B1717
                                                               C50
MORLAN R.L.,"INTERGOVERNMENTAL RELATIONS IN   SCHOOL
EDUCATION." USA+45 FINAN LOC/G MUNIC NAT/G FORCES   GOV/REL
PROB/SOLV RECEIVE ADMIN RACE/REL COST...BIBLIOG   ACADEM
INDIAN/AM. PAGE 76 B1526   POLICY
                                                               B55
CRAIG J.,BIBLIOGRAPHY OF PUBLIC ADMINISTRATION IN   BIBLIOG
AUSTRALIA. CONSTN FINAN EX/STRUC LEGIS PLAN DIPLOM   GOV/REL
RECEIVE ADJUD ROUTINE...HEAL 19/20 AUSTRAL   ADMIN
PARLIAMENT. PAGE 24 B0500   NAT/G
                                                               B57
KIETH-LUCAS A.,DECISIONS ABOUT PEOPLE IN NEED, A   ADMIN
STUDY OF ADMINISTRATIVE RESPONSIVENESS IN PUBLIC   RIGID/FLEX
ASSISTANCE. USA+45 GIVE RECEIVE INGP/REL PERS/REL   SOC/WK
MORAL RESPECT WEALTH...SOC OBS BIBLIOG 20. PAGE 60   DECISION
B1204
                                                               B58
ORTIZ R.P.,ANNUARIO BIBLIOGRAFICO COLOMBIANO,   BIBLIOG
1951-1956. LAW RECEIVE EDU/PROP ADMIN...LING STAT   SOC
20 COLOMB. PAGE 80 B1617
                                                               B58
WILENSKY H.L.,INDUSTRIAL SOCIETY AND SOCIAL   INDUS
WELFARE: IMPACT OF INDUSTRIALIZATION ON SUPPLY AND   ECO/DEV
ORGANIZATION OF SOC WELF SERVICES. ELITES SOCIETY   RECEIVE
STRATA SERV/IND FAM MUNIC PUB/INST CONSULT WORKER   PROF/ORG
ADMIN AUTOMAT ANOMIE 20. PAGE 117 B2352
                                                               B59
ROSOLIO D.,TEN YEARS OF THE CIVIL SERVICE IN ISRAEL ADMIN
(1948-1958) (PAMPHLET). ISRAEL NAT/G RECEIVE 20.   WORKER
PAGE 90 B1825   GOV/REL
                                                     PAY
                                                               B60
JONES V.,METROPOLITAN COMMUNITIES: A BIBLIOGRAPHY   BIBLIOG
WITH SPECIAL EMPHASIS UPON GOVERNMENT AND POLITICS, LOC/G
1955-1957. STRUCT ECO/DEV FINAN FORCES PLAN   MUNIC
PROB/SOLV RECEIVE EDU/PROP CT/SYS...GEOG HEAL 20.   ADMIN
PAGE 57 B1152
                                                               B60
PHILLIPS J.C.,MUNICIPAL GOVERNMENT AND   MUNIC
ADMINISTRATION IN AMERICA. USA+45 LAW CONSTN FINAN   GOV/REL
FORCES PLAN RECEIVE OWN ORD/FREE 20 CIVIL/LIB.   LOC/G
PAGE 83 B1669   ADMIN
                                                               C61
MOODIE G.C.,"THE GOVERNMENT OF GREAT BRITAIN." UK   NAT/G
LAW STRUCT LOC/G POL/PAR DIPLOM RECEIVE ADMIN   SOCIETY
COLONIAL CHOOSE...BIBLIOG 20 PARLIAMENT. PAGE 75   PARL/PROC
B1508   GOV/COMP
                                                               B64
AVASTHI A.,ASPECTS OF ADMINISTRATION. INDIA UK   MGT
USA+45 FINAN ACADEM DELIB/GP LEGIS RECEIVE   ADMIN
PARL/PROC PRIVIL...NAT/COMP 20. PAGE 7 B0150   SOC/WK
                                                     ORD/FREE
                                                               B64
RICHARDSON I.L.,BIBLIOGRAFIA BRASILEIRA DE   BIBLIOG
ADMINISTRACAO PUBLICA E ASSUNTOS CORRELATOS. BRAZIL MGT
CONSTN FINAN LOC/G NAT/G POL/PAR PLAN DIPLOM   ADMIN
RECEIVE ATTIT...METH 20. PAGE 88 B1776   LAW
                                                               B65
GOODSELL C.T.,ADMINISTRATION OF A REVOLUTION.   EXEC
PUERT/RICO ECO/UNDEV FINAN MUNIC POL/PAR PROVS   SOC
LEGIS PLAN BUDGET RECEIVE ADMIN COLONIAL LEAD 20
ROOSEVLT/F. PAGE 41 B0827
                                                               B65
RHODES G.,PUBLIC SECTOR PENSIONS. UK FINAN LEGIS   ADMIN
BUDGET TAX PAY INCOME...CHARTS 20 CIVIL/SERV.   RECEIVE
PAGE 88 B1769   AGE/O
                                                     WORKER
                                                               B66
SCHMIDT F.,PUBLIC RELATIONS IN HEALTH AND WELFARE.   PROF/ORG
USA+45 ACADEM RECEIVE PRESS FEEDBACK GOV/REL   EDU/PROP
PERS/REL DEMAND EFFICIENCY ATTIT PERCEPT WEALTH 20   ADMIN

PUBLIC/REL. PAGE 94 B1895   HEALTH

HUMPHREY H.,"A MORE PERFECT UNION." USA+45 LOC/G   GOV/REL
NAT/G ACT/RES BUDGET RECEIVE CENTRAL CONGRESS.   FEDERAL
PAGE 52 B1063   ADMIN
  PROB/SOLV
  S67

JENCKS C.E.,"SOCIAL STATUS OF COAL MINERS IN   EXTR/IND
BRITAIN SINCE NATIONALIZATION." UK STRATA STRUCT   WORKER
LABOR RECEIVE GP/REL INCOME OWN ATTIT HABITAT...MGT   CONTROL
T 20. PAGE 56 B1128   NAT/G

RECIFE....RECIFE, BRAZIL

RECIPROCITY....SEE SANCTION

RECK D. B1749

RECONSTRUCTION PERIOD....SEE CIVIL/WAR

RECORD....RECORDING OF DIRECT OBSERVATIONS

  B05

RIORDAN W.L.,PLUNKITT OF TAMMANY HALL. USA-45   POL/PAR
SOCIETY PROB/SOLV EXEC LEAD TASK CHOOSE ALL/VALS   MUNIC
...RECORD ANTHOL 20 REFORMERS TAMMANY NEWYORK/C   CHIEF
PLUNKITT/G. PAGE 88 B1789   ATTIT
  B15

SAWYER R.A.,A LIST OF WORKS ON COUNTY GOVERNMENT.   BIBLIOG/A
LAW FINAN MUNIC TOP/EX ROUTINE CRIME...CLASSIF   LOC/G
RECORD 19/20. PAGE 93 B1871   GOV/REL
  ADMIN
  B20

HALDANE R.B.,BEFORE THE WAR. MOD/EUR SOCIETY   POLICY
INT/ORG NAT/G DELIB/GP PLAN DOMIN EDU/PROP LEGIT   DIPLOM
ADMIN COERCE ATTIT DRIVE MORAL ORD/FREE PWR...SOC   UK
CONCPT SELF/OBS RECORD BIOG TIME/SEQ. PAGE 45 B0921
  B28

HALL W.P.,EMPIRE TO COMMONWEALTH. FUT WOR-45 CONSTN   VOL/ASSN
ECO/DEV ECO/UNDEV INT/ORG PROVS PLAN DIPLOM   NAT/G
EDU/PROP ADMIN COLONIAL PEACE PERSON ALL/VALS   UK
...POLICY GEOG SOC RECORD TREND CMN/WLTH
PARLIAMENT 19/20. PAGE 46 B0925
  B31

DEKAT A.D.A.,COLONIAL POLICY. S/ASIA CULTURE   DRIVE
EX/STRUC ECO/TAC DOMIN ADMIN COLONIAL ROUTINE   PWR
SOVEREIGN WEALTH...POLICY MGT RECORD KNO/TEST SAMP.   INDONESIA
PAGE 28 B0570   NETHERLAND
  B45

PASTUHOV V.D.,A GUIDE TO THE PRACTICE OF   INT/ORG
INTERNATIONAL CONFERENCES. WOR+45 PLAN LEGIT   DELIB/GP
ORD/FREE...MGT OBS RECORD VAL/FREE ILO LEAGUE/NAT
20. PAGE 81 B1640
  B45

RANSHOFFEN-WERTHEIMER EF,THE INTERNATIONAL   INT/ORG
SECRETARIAT: A GREAT EXPERIMENT IN INTERNATIONAL   EXEC
ADMINISTRATION. EUR+WWI FUT CONSTN FACE/GP CONSULT
DELIB/GP ACT/RES ADMIN ROUTINE PEACE ORD/FREE...MGT
RECORD ORG/CHARTS LEAGUE/NAT WORK 20. PAGE 86 B1731
  C50

STOKES W.S.,"HONDURAS: AN AREA STUDY IN   CONSTN
GOVERNMENT. HONDURAS NAT/G POL/PAR COLONIAL CT/SYS   LAW
ROUTINE CHOOSE REPRESENT...GEOG RECORD BIBLIOG   L/A+17C
19/20. PAGE 101 B2044   ADMIN
  B52

MAIER N.R.F.,PRINCIPLES OF HUMAN RELATIONS. WOR+45   INDUS
WOR-45 CULTURE SOCIETY ROUTINE ATTIT DRIVE PERCEPT
PERSON RIGID/FLEX SUPEGO PWR...PSY CONT/OBS RECORD
TOT/POP VAL/FREE 20. PAGE 68 B1379
  B55

MACMAHON A.W.,FEDERALISM: MATURE AND EMERGENT.   STRUCT
EUR+WWI FUT WOR+45 WOR-45 INT/ORG NAT/G REPRESENT   CONCPT
FEDERAL...POLICY MGT RECORD TREND GEN/LAWS 20.
PAGE 68 B1370
  L55

KISER M.,"ORGANIZATION OF AMERICAN STATES." L/A+17C   VOL/ASSN
USA+45 ECO/UNDEV INT/ORG NAT/G PLAN TEC/DEV DIPLOM   ECO/DEV
ECO/TAC INT/TRADE EDU/PROP ADMIN ALL/VALS...POLICY   REGION
MGT RECORD ORG/CHARTS OAS 20. PAGE 60 B1215
  S55

CHAPIN F.S.,"FORMALIZATION OBSERVED IN TEN   VOL/ASSN
VOLUNTARY ORGANIZATIONS: CONCEPTS, MORPHOLOGY,   ROUTINE
PROCESS." STRUCT INGP/REL PERS/REL...METH/CNCPT   CONTROL
CLASSIF OBS RECORD. PAGE 20 B0407   OP/RES
  B57

BEAL J.R.,JOHN FOSTER DULLES, A BIOGRAPHY. USA+45   BIOG
USSR WOR+45 CONSTN INT/ORG NAT/G EX/STRUC LEGIT   DIPLOM
ADMIN NUC/PWR DISPL PERSON ORD/FREE PWR SKILL
...POLICY PSY OBS RECORD COLD/WAR UN 20 DULLES/JF.
PAGE 10 B0200
  B57

HOLCOMBE A.N.,STRENGTHENING THE UNITED NATIONS.   INT/ORG
USA+45 ACT/RES CREATE PLAN EDU/PROP ATTIT PERCEPT   ROUTINE
PWR...METH/CNCPT CONT/OBS RECORD UN COLD/WAR 20.
PAGE 51 B1032

  S57

HAILEY,"TOMORROW IN AFRICA." CONSTN SOCIETY LOC/G   AFR
NAT/G DOMIN ADJUD ADMIN GP/REL DISCRIM NAT/LISM   PERSON
ATTIT MORAL ORD/FREE...PSY SOC CONCPT OBS RECORD   ELITES
TREND GEN/LAWS CMN/WLTH 20. PAGE 45 B0917   RACE/REL
  B58

WESTIN A.F.,THE ANATOMY OF A CONSTITUTIONAL LAW   CT/SYS
CASE. USA+45 LAW LEGIS ADMIN EXEC...DECISION MGT   INDUS
SOC RECORD 20 SUPREME/CT. PAGE 115 B2326   ADJUD
  CONSTN
  B59

CHINA INSTITUTE OF AMERICA,,CHINA AND THE UNITED   ASIA
NATIONS. CHINA/COM FUT STRUCT EDU/PROP LEGIT ADMIN   INT/ORG
ATTIT KNOWL ORD/FREE PWR...OBS RECORD STAND/INT
TIME/SEQ UN LEAGUE/NAT UNESCO 20. PAGE 21 B0425
  B59

YANG C.K.,A CHINESE VILLAGE IN EARLY COMMUNIST   ASIA
TRANSITION. ECO/UNDEV AGRI FAM KIN MUNIC FORCES   ROUTINE
PLAN ECO/TAC DOMIN EDU/PROP ATTIT DRIVE PWR RESPECT   SOCISM
...SOC CONCPT METH/CNCPT OBS RECORD CON/ANAL CHARTS
WORK 20. PAGE 118 B2389
  L60

DEAN A.W.,"SECOND GENEVA CONFERENCE OF THE LAW OF   INT/ORG
THE SEA: THE FIGHT FOR FREEDOM OF THE SEAS." FUT   JURID
USA+45 USSR WOR+45 WOR-45 SEA CONSTN STRUCT PLAN   INT/LAW
INT/TRADE ADJUD ADMIN ORD/FREE...DECISION RECORD
TREND GEN/LAWS 20 TREATY. PAGE 28 B0564
  S60

HERZ J.H.,"EAST GERMANY: PROGRESS AND PROSPECTS."   POL/PAR
COM AGRI FINAN INDUS LOC/G NAT/G FORCES PLAN   STRUCT
TEC/DEV DOMIN ADMIN COERCE DRIVE PERCEPT RIGID/FLEX   GERMANY
MORAL ORD/FREE PWR...MARXIST PSY SOC RECORD STERTYP
WORK. PAGE 49 B0997
  S60

HUTCHINSON C.E.,"AN INSTITUTE FOR NATIONAL SECURITY   POLICY
AFFAIRS." USA+45 R+D NAT/G CONSULT TOP/EX ACT/RES   METH/CNCPT
CREATE PLAN TEC/DEV EDU/PROP ROUTINE NUC/PWR ATTIT   ELITES
ORD/FREE PWR...DECISION MGT PHIL/SCI CONCPT RECORD   DIPLOM
GEN/LAWS GEN/METH 20. PAGE 53 B1068
  B61

BARNES W.,THE FOREIGN SERVICE OF THE UNITED STATES.   NAT/G
USA+45 USA-45 CONSTN INT/ORG POL/PAR CONSULT   MGT
DELIB/GP LEGIS DOMIN EDU/PROP EXEC ATTIT RIGID/FLEX   DIPLOM
ORD/FREE PWR...POLICY CONCPT STAT OBS RECORD BIOG
TIME/SEQ TREND. PAGE 9 B0188
  B61

MACRIDIS R.C.,COMPARATIVE POLITICS: NOTES AND   POL/PAR
READINGS. WOR+45 LOC/G MUNIC NAT/G PROVS VOL/ASSN   CHOOSE
EDU/PROP ADMIN ATTIT PERSON ORD/FREE...SOC CONCPT
OBS RECORD TREND 20. PAGE 68 B1376
  B61

MUNGER E.S.,AFRICAN FIELD REPORTS 1952-1961.   AFR
SOUTH/AFR SOCIETY ECO/UNDEV NAT/G POL/PAR COLONIAL   DISCRIM
EXEC PARL/PROC GUERRILLA RACE/REL ALL/IDEOS...SOC   RECORD
AUD/VIS 20. PAGE 76 B1538
  S61

NOVE A.,"THE SOVIET MODEL AND UNDERDEVELOPED   ECO/UNDEV
COUNTRIES." COM FUT USSR WOR+45 CULTURE ECO/DEV   PLAN
POL/PAR FOR/AID EDU/PROP ADMIN MORAL WEALTH
...POLICY RECORD HIST/WRIT 20. PAGE 79 B1593
  B62

DODDS H.W.,THE ACADEMIC PRESIDENT "EDUCATOR OR   ACADEM
CARETAKER? FINAN DELIB/GP EDU/PROP PARTIC ATTIT   ADMIN
ROLE PWR...POLICY RECORD INT. PAGE 30 B0601   LEAD
  CONTROL
  B62

MULLEY F.W.,THE POLITICS OF WESTERN DEFENSE.   INT/ORG
EUR+WWI USA-45 WOR+45 VOL/ASSN EX/STRUC FORCES   DELIB/GP
COERCE DETER PEACE ATTIT ORD/FREE PWR...RECORD   NUC/PWR
TIME/SEQ CHARTS COLD/WAR 20 NATO. PAGE 76 B1537
  S62

HUDSON G.F.,"SOVIET FEARS OF THE WEST." COM USA+45   ATTIT
SOCIETY DELIB/GP EX/STRUC TOP/EX ACT/RES CREATE   MYTH
DOMIN EDU/PROP LEGIT ADMIN ROUTINE DRIVE PERSON   GERMANY
RIGID/FLEX PWR...RECORD TIME/SEQ TOT/POP 20   USSR
STALIN/J. PAGE 52 B1057
  S62

MARTIN L.W.,"POLITICAL SETTLEMENTS AND ARMS   CONCPT
CONTROL." COM EUR+WWI GERMANY USA+45 PROVS FORCES   ARMS/CONT
TOP/EX ACT/RES CREATE DOMIN LEGIT ROUTINE COERCE
ATTIT RIGID/FLEX ORD/FREE PWR...METH/CNCPT RECORD
GEN/LAWS 20. PAGE 70 B1410
  B63

BOISSIER P.,HISTORIE DU COMITE INTERNATIONAL DE LA   INT/ORG
CROIX ROUGE. MOD/EUR WOR-45 CONSULT FORCES PLAN   HEALTH
DIPLOM EDU/PROP ADMIN MORAL ORD/FREE...SOC CONCPT   ARMS/CONT
RECORD TIME/SEQ GEN/LAWS TOT/POP VAL/FREE 19/20.   WAR
PAGE 13 B0267
  B63

JOHNS R.,CONFRONTING ORGANIZATIONAL CHANGE. NEIGH   SOC/WK
DELIB/GP CREATE OP/RES ADMIN GP/REL DRIVE...WELF/ST   WEALTH
SOC RECORD BIBLIOG. PAGE 56 B1142   LEAD
  VOL/ASSN
  B63

MCKIE R.,MALAYSIA IN FOCUS. INDONESIA WOR+45   S/ASIA
ECO/UNDEV FINAN NAT/G POL/PAR SECT FORCES PLAN   NAT/LISM

ADMIN COLONIAL COERCE DRIVE ALL/VALS...POLICY   MALAYSIA
RECORD CENSUS TIME/SEQ CMN/WLTH 20. PAGE 72 B1453
                                                                S63
ANTHON C.G.,"THE END OF THE ADENAUER ERA." EUR+WWI   NAT/G
GERMANY/W CONSTN EX/STRUC CREATE DIPLOM LEGIT ATTIT   TOP/EX
PERSON ALL/VALS...RECORD 20 ADENAUER/K. PAGE 6   BAL/PWR
B0113   GERMANY
                                                                B64
COTTRELL A.J.,THE POLITICS OF THE ATLANTIC   VOL/ASSN
ALLIANCE. EUR+WWI USA+45 INT/ORG NAT/G DELIB/GP   FORCES
EX/STRUC BAL/PWR DIPLOM REGION DETER ATTIT ORD/FREE
...CONCPT RECORD GEN/LAWS GEN/METH NATO 20. PAGE 24
B0493
                                                                B64
JACKSON H.M.,THE SECRETARY OF STATE AND THE   GOV/REL
AMBASSADOR* JACKSON SUBCOMMITTEE PAPERS ON THE   DIPLOM
CONDUCT OF AMERICAN FOREIGN POLICY. USA+45 NAT/G   ADMIN
FORCES ACT/RES OP/RES EDU/PROP CENTRAL EFFICIENCY   EX/STRUC
ORD/FREE...OBS RECORD ANTHOL CONGRESS PRESIDENT.
PAGE 55 B1107
                                                                B64
MERILLAT H.C.L.,LEGAL ADVISERS AND FOREIGN AFFAIRS.   CONSULT
WOR+45 WOR-45 ELITES INTELL NAT/G LEGIT ADMIN   EX/STRUC
PERCEPT ALL/VALS...MGT NEW/IDEA RECORD 20. PAGE 73   DIPLOM
B1469
                                                                B64
WAINHOUSE D.W.,REMNANTS OF EMPIRE: THE UNITED   INT/ORG
NATIONS AND THE END OF COLONIALISM. FUT PORTUGAL   TREND
WOR+45 NAT/G CONSULT DOMIN LEGIT ADMIN ROUTINE   COLONIAL
ATTIT ORD/FREE...POLICY JURID RECORD INT TIME/SEQ
UN CMN/WLTH 20. PAGE 113 B2275
                                                                S64
CARNEGIE ENDOWMENT INT. PEACE,"ADMINISTRATION AND   INT/ORG
BUDGET (ISSUES BEFORE THE NINETEENTH GENERAL   ADMIN
ASSEMBLY)." WOR+45 FINAN BUDGET ECO/TAC ROUTINE
COST...STAT RECORD UN. PAGE 19 B0383
                                                                S64
JOHNSON K.F.,"CAUSAL FACTORS IN LATIN AMERICAN   L/A+17C
POLITICAL INSTABILITY." CULTURE NAT/G VOL/ASSN   PERCEPT
EX/STRUC FORCES EDU/PROP LEGIT ADMIN COERCE REV   ELITES
ATTIT KNOWL PWR...STYLE RECORD CHARTS WORK 20.
PAGE 57 B1144
                                                                S64
SWEARER H.R.,"AFTER KHRUSHCHEV: WHAT NEXT." COM FUT   EX/STRUC
USSR CONSTN ELITES NAT/G POL/PAR CHIEF DELIB/GP   PWR
LEGIS DOMIN LEAD...RECORD TREND STERTYP GEN/METH
20. PAGE 102 B2058
                                                                S65
BALDWIN H.,"SLOW-DOWN IN THE PENTAGON." USA+45   RECORD
CREATE PLAN GOV/REL CENTRAL COST EFFICIENCY PWR   R+D
...MGT MCNAMARA/R. PAGE 9 B0174   WEAPON
                                                           ADMIN
                                                                S65
BROWN S.,"AN ALTERNATIVE TO THE GRAND DESIGN."   VOL/ASSN
EUR+WWI FUT USA+45 INT/ORG NAT/G EX/STRUC FORCES   CONCPT
CREATE BAL/PWR DOMIN RIGID/FLEX ORD/FREE PWR   DIPLOM
...NEW/IDEA RECORD EEC NATO 20. PAGE 16 B0327
                                                                S65
OSTGAARD E.,"FACTORS INFLUENCING THE FLOW OF NEWS."   EDU/PROP
COM/IND BUDGET DIPLOM EXEC GP/REL COST ATTIT SAMP.   PERCEPT
PAGE 80 B1618   RECORD
                                                                S65
POSVAR W.W.,"NATIONAL SECURITY POLICY* THE REALM OF   DIPLOM
OBSCURITY." CREATE PLAN PROB/SOLV ADMIN LEAD GP/REL   USA+45
CONSERVE...DECISION GEOG. PAGE 84 B1694   RECORD
                                                                B66
RUBENSTEIN R.,THE SHARING OF POWER IN A PSYCHIATRIC   ADMIN
HOSPITAL. CLIENT PROF/ORG PUB/INST INGP/REL ATTIT   PARTIC
PWR...DECISION OBS RECORD. PAGE 91 B1847   HEALTH
                                                           CONCPT
                                                                S66
ZUCKERT E.M.,"THE SERVICE SECRETARY* HAS HE A   OBS
USEFUL ROLE?" USA+45 TOP/EX PLAN ADMIN EXEC DETER   OP/RES
NUC/PWR WEAPON...MGT RECORD MCNAMARA/R. PAGE 119   DIPLOM
B2407   FORCES

RECORDING OF INTERVIEWS....SEE REC/INT

RECORDS....SEE OLD/STOR

RECTITUDE....SEE MORAL

RED/CROSS
                                                                B59
JOYCE J.A.,RED CROSS INTERNATIONAL AND THE STRATEGY   VOL/ASSN
OF PEACE. WOR+45 WOR-45 EX/STRUC SUPEGO ALL/VALS   HEALTH
...CONCPT GEN/LAWS TOT/POP 19/20 RED/CROSS. PAGE 57
B1155

RED/GUARD....RED GUARD

REDFIELD C.E. B1750

REDFIELD/R....ROBERT REDFIELD

REDFORD D.R. B1751

REDFORD E.S. B1752,B1753,B1754,B1755,B1756,B1757,B1758,B1759

REDLICH F. B1760

REED/STAN....JUSTICE STANLEY REED

REES A. B1761

REFERENDUM....REFERENDUM; SEE ALSO PARTIC

REFORMERS....REFORMERS
                                                                B05
RIORDAN W.L.,PLUNKITT OF TAMMANY HALL. USA-45   POL/PAR
SOCIETY PROB/SOLV EXEC LEAD TASK CHOOSE ALL/VALS   MUNIC
...RECORD ANTHOL 20 REFORMERS TAMMANY NEWYORK/C   CHIEF
PLUNKITT/G. PAGE 88 B1789   ATTIT
                                                                B43
YOUNG R.,THIS IS CONGRESS. FUT SENIOR ADMIN GP/REL   LEGIS
PWR...DECISION REFORMERS CONGRESS. PAGE 119 B2393   DELIB/GP
                                                          CHIEF
                                                          ROUTINE
                                                                S44
KEFAUVER E.,"THE NEED FOR BETTER EXECUTIVE-   LEGIS
LEGISLATIVE TEAMWORK IN THE NATIONAL GOVERNMENT."   EXEC
USA-45 CONSTN NAT/G ROUTINE...TRADIT CONGRESS   CONFER
REFORMERS. PAGE 59 B1188   LEAD
                                                                S47
CALDWELL L.K.,"STRENGTHENING STATE LEGISLATURES"   PROVS
FUT DELIB/GP WEALTH REFORMERS. PAGE 18 B0364   LEGIS
                                                          ROUTINE
                                                          BUDGET
                                                                B58
WHITE L.D.,THE REPUBLICAN ERA: 1869-1901, A STUDY   MGT
IN ADMINISTRATIVE HISTORY. USA-45 FINAN PLAN   PWR
NEUTRAL CRIME GP/REL MORAL LAISSEZ PRESIDENT   DELIB/GP
REFORMERS 19 CONGRESS CIVIL/SERV. PAGE 116 B2340   ADMIN
                                                                B64
INST D'ETUDE POL L'U GRENOBLE,ADMINISTRATION   ADMIN
TRADITIONELLE ET PLANIFICATION REGIONALE. FRANCE   MUNIC
LAW POL/PAR PROB/SOLV ADJUST RIGID/FLEX...CHARTS   PLAN
ANTHOL BIBLIOG T 20 REFORMERS. PAGE 54 B1087   CREATE
                                                                B67
MARRIS P.,DILEMMAS OF SOCIAL REFORM: POVERTY AND   STRUCT
COMMUNITY ACTION IN THE UNITED STATES. USA+45 NAT/G   MUNIC
OP/RES ADMIN PARTIC EFFICIENCY WEALTH...SOC   PROB/SOLV
METH/COMP T 20 REFORMERS. PAGE 69 B1401   COST

REGION....REGIONALISM
                                                                N
MONPIED E.,BIBLIOGRAPHIE FEDERALISTE: ARTICLES ET   BIBLIOG/A
DOCUMENTS PUBLIES DANS LES PERIODIQUES PARUS EN   FEDERAL
FRANCE NOV. 1945-OCT. 1950. EUR+WWI WOR+45 ADMIN   CENTRAL
REGION ATTIT MARXISM PACIFISM 20 EEC. PAGE 74 B1501   INT/ORG
                                                                N
WORLD PEACE FOUNDATION,DOCUMENTS OF INTERNATIONAL   BIBLIOG
ORGANIZATIONS: A SELECTED BIBLIOGRAPHY. WOR+45   DIPLOM
WOR-45 AGRI FINAN ACT/RES OP/RES INT/TRADE ADMIN   INT/ORG
...CON/ANAL 20 UN UNESCO LEAGUE/NAT. PAGE 118 B2374   REGION
                                                                N19
EAST KENTUCKY REGIONAL PLAN,PROGRAM 60: A DECADE OF   REGION
ACTION FOR PROGRESS IN EASTERN KENTUCKY (PAMPHLET).   ADMIN
USA+45 AGRI CONSTRUC INDUS CONSULT ACT/RES   PLAN
PROB/SOLV EDU/PROP GOV/REL HEALTH KENTUCKY. PAGE 32   ECO/UNDEV
B0643
                                                                N19
EAST KENTUCKY REGIONAL PLAN,PROGRAM 60 REPORT: REGION
ACTION FOR PORGRESS IN EASTERN KENTUCKY (PAMPHLET).   PLAN
USA+45 CONSTN CONSTRUC INDUS ACT/RES PROB/SOLV EDU/PROP   ECO/UNDEV
ADMIN GOV/REL KENTUCKY. PAGE 32 B0644   CONSULT
                                                                N19
FIRMALINO T.,THE DISTRICT SCHOOL SUPERVISOR VS.   RIGID/FLEX
TEACHERS AND PARENTS: A PHILIPPINE CASE STUDY   SCHOOL
(PAMPHLET) (BMR). PHILIPPINE LOC/G PLAN EDU/PROP   ADMIN
LOBBY REGION PERS/REL 20. PAGE 36 B0722   CREATE
                                                                N19
FOLSOM M.B.,BETTER MANAGEMENT OF THE PUBLIC'S   ADMIN
BUSINESS (PAMPHLET). USA+45 DELIB/GP PAY CONFER   NAT/G
CONTROL REGION GP/REL...METH/COMP ANTHOL 20.   MGT
PAGE 36 B0733   PROB/SOLV
                                                                B45
BRECHT A.,FEDERALISM AND REGIONALISM IN GERMANY;   FEDERAL
THE DIVISION OF PRUSSIA. GERMANY PRUSSIA WOR-45   REGION
CREATE ADMIN WAR TOTALISM PWR...CHARTS 20 HITLER/A.   PROB/SOLV
PAGE 15 B0303   CONSTN
                                                                B45
CLAPP G.R.,NEW HORIZONS IN PUBLIC ADMINISTRATION: A   ADMIN
SYMPOSIUM. USA-45 LEGIS PLAN DIPLOM REGION   EX/STRUC
EFFICIENCY 20. PAGE 21 B0430   MGT
                                                        NAT/G
                                                                B47
BORGESE G.,COMMON CAUSE. LAW CONSTN SOCIETY STRATA   WOR+45
ECO/DEV INT/ORG POL/PAR FORCES LEGIS TOP/EX CAP/ISM   NAT/G

DIPLOM ADMIN EXEC ATTIT PWR 20. PAGE 14 B0279   SOVEREIGN
                                                       REGION

                                                          B50
HARTLAND P.C.,BALANCE OF INTERREGIONAL PAYMENTS OF   ECO/DEV
NEW ENGLAND. USA+45 TEC/DEV ECO/TAC LEGIT ROUTINE   FINAN
BAL/PAY PROFIT 20 NEW/ENGLND FED/RESERV. PAGE 47   REGION
B0962   PLAN

                                                          B50
MONPIED E.,BIBLIOGRAPHIE FEDERALISTE: OUVRAGES   BIBLIOG/A
CHOISIS (VOL. I, MIMEOGRAPHED PAPER). EUR+WWI   FEDERAL
DIPLOM ADMIN REGION ATTIT PACIFISM SOCISM...INT/LAW   CENTRAL
19/20. PAGE 74 B1502   INT/ORG

                                                          S52
SNIDER C.F.,"AMERICAN COUNTY GOVERNMENT: A MID-   LOC/G
CENTURY REVIEW" (BMR)" USA+45 USA-45 PROVS DELIB/GP   ADMIN
EX/STRUC BUDGET TAX PWR 20. PAGE 98 B1988   GOV/REL
                                                       REGION

                                                          B54
CHICAGO JOINT REFERENCE LIB,FEDERAL-STATE-LOCAL   BIBLIOG
RELATIONS; A SELECTED BIBLIOGRAPHY. USA+45 AGRI   FEDERAL
LABOR LOC/G MUNIC EX/STRUC ADMIN REGION HEALTH   GOV/REL
CON/ANAL. PAGE 21 B0419

                                                          B54
WHITE L.D.,THE JACKSONIANS: A STUDY IN   NAT/G
ADMINISTRATIVE HISTORY 1829-1861. USA-45 CONSTN   ADMIN
POL/PAR CHIEF DELIB/GP LEGIS CREATE PROB/SOLV   POLICY
ECO/TAC LEAD REGION GP/REL 19 PRESIDENT CONGRESS
JACKSON/A. PAGE 116 B2339

                                                          L55
KISER M.,"ORGANIZATION OF AMERICAN STATES." L/A+17C   VOL/ASSN
USA+45 ECO/UNDEV INT/ORG NAT/G PLAN TEC/DEV DIPLOM   ECO/DEV
ECO/TAC INT/TRADE EDU/PROP ADMIN ALL/VALS...POLICY   REGION
MGT RECORD ORG/CHARTS OAS 20. PAGE 60 B1215

                                                          B57
LOEWENSTEIN K.,POLITICAL POWER AND THE GOVERNMENTAL   PWR
PROCESS. WOR+45 WOR-45 CONSTN NAT/G POL/PAR   CONCPT
EX/STRUC LEGIS TOP/EX DOMIN EDU/PROP LEGIT ADMIN
REGION CHOOSE ATTIT...JURID STERTYP GEN/LAWS 20.
PAGE 66 B1336

                                                          L57
HAAS E.B.,"REGIONAL INTEGRATION AND NATIONAL   INT/ORG
POLICY." WOR+45 VOL/ASSN DELIB/GP EX/STRUC ECO/TAC   ORD/FREE
DOMIN EDU/PROP LEGIT COERCE ATTIT PERCEPT KNOWL   REGION
...TIME/SEQ COLD/WAR 20 UN. PAGE 45 B0908

                                                          S57
GULICK L.,"METROPOLITAN ORGANIZATION." LEGIS EXEC   REGION
PARTIC CHOOSE REPRESENT GOV/REL...MAJORIT DECISION.   LOC/G
PAGE 45 B0904   MUNIC

                                                          S57
ROBSON W.A.,"TWO-LEVEL GOVERNMENT FOR METROPOLITAN   REGION
AREAS." MUNIC EX/STRUC LEGIS PARTIC REPRESENT   LOC/G
MAJORITY. PAGE 89 B1807   PLAN
                                                       GOV/REL

                                                          B59
DIEBOLD W. JR.,THE SCHUMAN PLAN: A STUDY IN   INT/ORG
ECONOMIC COOPERATION, 1950-1959. EUR+WWI FRANCE   REGION
GERMANY USA+45 EXTR/IND CONSULT DELIB/GP PLAN
DIPLOM ECO/TAC INT/TRADE ROUTINE ORD/FREE WEALTH
...METH/CNCPT STAT CONT/OBS INT TIME/SEQ ECSC 20.
PAGE 29 B0591

                                                          S59
SUTTON F.X.,"REPRESENTATION AND THE NATURE OF   NAT/G
POLITICAL SYSTEMS." UNIV WOR-45 CULTURE SOCIETY   CONCPT
STRATA INT/ORG FORCES JUDGE DOMIN LEGIT EXEC REGION
REPRESENT ATTIT ORD/FREE RESPECT...SOC HIST/WRIT
TIME/SEQ. PAGE 102 B2057

                                                          B60
LINDSAY K.,EUROPEAN ASSEMBLIES: THE EXPERIMENTAL   VOL/ASSN
PERIOD 1949-1959. EUR+WWI ECO/DEV NAT/G POL/PAR   INT/ORG
LEGIS TOP/EX ACT/RES PLAN EXEC ROUTINE DOMIN LEGIT   REGION
ROUTINE ATTIT DRIVE ORD/FREE PWR SKILL...SOC CONCPT
TREND CHARTS GEN/LAWS VAL/FREE. PAGE 65 B1315

                                                          B60
SMITH M.G.,GOVERNMENT IN ZAZZAU 1800-1950. NIGERIA   REGION
UK CULTURE SOCIETY LOC/G ADMIN COLONIAL   CONSTN
...METH/CNCPT NEW/IDEA METH 19/20. PAGE 98 B1983   KIN
                                                       ECO/UNDEV

                                                          B60
SOUTH AFRICAN CONGRESS OF DEM,FACE THE FUTURE.   RACE/REL
SOUTH/AFR ELITES LEGIS ADMIN REGION COERCE PEACE   DISCRIM
ATTIT 20. PAGE 99 B1999   CONSTN
                                                       NAT/G

                                                          S60
HERRERA F.,"THE INTER-AMERICAN DEVELOPMENT BANK."   L/A+17C
USA+45 ECO/UNDEV INT/ORG CONSULT DELIB/GP PLAN   FINAN
ECO/TAC INT/TRADE ROUTINE WEALTH...STAT 20. PAGE 49   FOR/AID
B0994   REGION

                                                          S60
MORA J.A.,"THE ORGANIZATION OF AMERICAN STATES."   L/A+17C
USA+45 LAW ECO/UNDEV VOL/ASSN DELIB/GP PLAN BAL/PWR   INT/ORG
EDU/PROP ADMIN DRIVE RIGID/FLEX ORD/FREE WEALTH   REGION
...TIME/SEQ GEN/LAWS OAS 20. PAGE 75 B1518

                                                          S60
MORALES C.J.,"TRADE AND ECONOMIC INTEGRATION IN   FINAN
LATIN AMERICA." FUT L/A+17C LAW STRATA ECO/UNDEV   INT/TRADE
DIST/IND INDUS LABOR NAT/G LEGIS ECO/TAC ADMIN   REGION

RIGID/FLEX WEALTH...CONCPT NEW/IDEA CONT/OBS
TIME/SEQ WORK 20. PAGE 75 B1519

                                                          B61
AVERY M.W.,GOVERNMENT OF WASHINGTON STATE. USA+45   PROVS
MUNIC DELIB/GP EX/STRUC LEGIS GIVE CT/SYS PARTIC   LOC/G
REGION EFFICIENCY 20 WASHINGT/G GOVERNOR. PAGE 7   ADMIN
B0151   GOV/REL

                                                          B61
LEE R.R.,ENGINEERING-ECONOMIC PLANNING   BIBLIOG/A
MISCELLANEOUS SUBJECTS: A SELECTED BIBLIOGRAPHY   PLAN
(MIMEOGRAPHED). FINAN LOC/G MUNIC NEIGH ADMIN   REGION
CONTROL INGP/REL HABITAT...GEOG MGT SOC/WK 20
RESOURCE/N. PAGE 63 B1280

                                                          B61
MAYNE A.,DESIGNING AND ADMINISTERING A REGIONAL   ECO/UNDEV
ECONOMIC DEVELOPMENT PLAN WITH SPECIFIC REFERENCE   PLAN
TO PUERTO RICO (PAMPHLET). PUERT/RICO SOCIETY NAT/G   CREATE
DELIB/GP REGION...DECISION 20. PAGE 71 B1435   ADMIN

                                                          B61
MOLLAU G.,INTERNATIONAL COMMUNISM AND WORLD   COM
REVOLUTION: HISTORY AND METHODS. RUSSIA USSR   REV
INT/ORG NAT/G POL/PAR VOL/ASSN FORCES BAL/PWR
DIPLOM EXEC REGION WAR ATTIT PWR MARXISM...CONCPT
TIME/SEQ COLD/WAR 19/20. PAGE 74 B1498

                                                          B61
SHAPP W.R.,FIELD ADMINISTRATION IN THE UNITED   INT/ORG
NATIONS SYSTEM. FINAN PROB/SOLV INSPECT DIPLOM EXEC   ADMIN
REGION ROUTINE EFFICIENCY ROLE...INT CHARTS 20. UN.   GP/REL
PAGE 96 B1933   FOR/AID

                                                          S61
ANGLIN D.,"UNITED STATES OPPOSITION TO CANADIAN   INT/ORG
MEMBERSHIP IN THE PAN AMERICAN UNION: A CANADIAN   CANADA
VIEW." L/A+17C UK USA+45 VOL/ASSN DELIB/GP EX/STRUC
PLAN DIPLOM DOMIN REGION ATTIT RIGID/FLEX PWR
...RELATIV CONCPT STERTYP CMN/WLTH OAS 20. PAGE 5
B0112

                                                          S61
GORDON L.,"ECONOMIC REGIONALISM RECONSIDERED." FUT   ECO/DEV
USA+45 WOR+45 INDUS NAT/G TEC/DEV DIPLOM ROUTINE   ATTIT
PERCEPT WEALTH...WELF/ST METH/CNCPT WORK 20.   CAP/ISM
PAGE 41 B0830   REGION

                                                          S61
HAAS E.B.,"INTERNATIONAL INTEGRATION: THE EUROPEAN   INT/ORG
AND THE UNIVERSAL PROCESS." EUR+WWI FUT WOR+45   TREND
NAT/G EX/STRUC ATTIT DRIVE ORD/FREE PWR...CONCPT   REGION
GEN/LAWS OEEC 20 NATO COUNCL/EUR. PAGE 45 B0909

                                                          B62
CARPER E.T.,ILLINOIS GOES TO CONGRESS FOR ARMY   ADMIN
LAND. USA+45 LAW EXTR/IND PROVS REGION CIVMIL/REL   LOBBY
GOV/REL FEDERAL ATTIT 20 ILLINOIS SENATE CONGRESS   GEOG
DIRKSEN/E DOUGLAS/P. PAGE 19 B0385   LEGIS

                                                          B62
DIMOCK M.E.,THE NEW AMERICAN POLITICAL ECONOMY: A   FEDERAL
SYNTHESIS OF POLITICS AND ECONOMICS. USA+45 FINAN   ECO/TAC
LG/CO PLAN ADMIN REGION GP/REL CENTRAL MORAL 20.   NAT/G
PAGE 29 B0598   PARTIC

                                                          B62
LAWSON R.,INTERNATIONAL REGIONAL ORGANIZATIONS.   INT/ORG
WOR+45 NAT/G VOL/ASSN CONSULT LEGIS EDU/PROP LEGIT   DELIB/GP
ADMIN EXEC ROUTINE HEALTH PWR WEALTH...JURID EEC   REGION
COLD/WAR 20 UN. PAGE 63 B1277

                                                          B62
UNECA LIBRARY,NEW ACQUISITIONS IN THE UNECA   BIBLIOG
LIBRARY. LAW NAT/G PLAN PROB/SOLV TEC/DEV ADMIN   AFR
REGION...GEOG SOC 20 UN. PAGE 106 B2152   ECO/UNDEV
                                                       INT/ORG

                                                          S62
PIQUEMAL M.,"LES PROBLEMES DES UNIONS D'ETATS EN   AFR
AFRIQUE NOIRE." FRANCE SOCIETY INT/ORG NAT/G   ECO/UNDEV
DELIB/GP PLAN LEGIT ADMIN COLONIAL ROUTINE ATTIT   REGION
ORD/FREE PWR...GEOG METH/CNCPT 20. PAGE 83 B1678

                                                          S62
SPRINGER H.W.,"FEDERATION IN THE CARIBBEAN: AN   VOL/ASSN
ATTEMPT THAT FAILED." L/A+17C ECO/UNDEV INT/ORG   NAT/G
POL/PAR PROVS LEGIS CREATE PLAN LEGIT ADMIN FEDERAL   REGION
ATTIT DRIVE PERSON ORD/FREE PWR...POLICY GEOG PSY
CONCPT OBS CARIBBEAN CMN/WLTH 20. PAGE 100 B2013

                                                          N62
US ADVISORY COMN INTERGOV REL,ALTERNATIVE   MUNIC
APPROACHES TO GOVERNMENTAL REORGANIZATION IN   REGION
METROPOLITAN AREAS (PAMPHLET). EX/STRUC LEGIS EXEC   PLAN
LEAD PWR...DECISION GEN/METH. PAGE 107 B2171   GOV/REL

                                                          B63
KLESMENT J.,LEGAL SOURCES AND BIBLIOGRAPHY OF THE   BIBLIOG/A
BALTIC STATES (ESTONIA, LATVIA, LITHUANIA). COM   JURID
ESTONIA LATVIA LITHUANIA LAW FINAN ADJUD CT/SYS   CONSTN
REGION CENTRAL MARXISM 19/20. PAGE 60 B1218   ADMIN

                                                          B63
MAYNE R.,THE COMMUNITY OF EUROPE. UK CONSTN NAT/G   EUR+WWI
CONSULT DELIB/GP CREATE PLAN ECO/TAC LEGIT ADMIN   INT/ORG
ROUTINE ORD/FREE PWR WEALTH...CONCPT TIME/SEQ EEC   REGION
EURATOM 20. PAGE 71 B1436

                                                          S63
BANFIELD J.,"FEDERATION IN EAST-AFRICA." AFR UGANDA   EX/STRUC
ELITES INT/ORG NAT/G VOL/ASSN LEGIS ECO/TAC FEDERAL   PWR
ATTIT SOVEREIGN TOT/POP 20 TANGANYIKA. PAGE 9 B0180   REGION

GITTELL M.,"METROPOLITAN MAYOR: DEAD END." LOC/G   MUNIC
PARTIC REGION ATTIT PWR GP/COMP. PAGE 40 B0804   LEAD
                                                    EXEC
                                              S63

RUSTOW D.A.,"THE MILITARY IN MIDDLE EASTERN SOCIETY FORCES
AND POLITICS." FUT ISLAM CONSTN SOCIETY FACE/GP   ELITES
NAT/G POL/PAR PROF/ORG CONSULT DOMIN ADMIN EXEC
REGION COERCE NAT/LISM ATTIT DRIVE PERSON ORD/FREE
PWR...POLICY CONCPT OBS STERTYP 20. PAGE 92 B1860
                                              S63

SCHMITT H.A.,"THE EUROPEAN COMMUNITIES." EUR+WWI   VOL/ASSN
FRANCE DELIB/GP EX/STRUC TOP/EX CREATE TEC/DEV   ECO/DEV
ECO/TAC LEGIT REGION COERCE DRIVE ALL/VALS
...METH/CNCPT EEC 20. PAGE 94 B1897
                                              B64

ANDREN N.,GOVERNMENT AND POLITICS IN THE NORDIC   CONSTN
COUNTRIES: DENMARK, FINLAND, ICELAND, NORWAY,   NAT/G
SWEDEN. DENMARK FINLAND ICELAND NORWAY SWEDEN   CULTURE
POL/PAR CHIEF LEGIS ADMIN REGION REPRESENT ATTIT   GOV/COMP
CONSERVE...CHARTS BIBLIOG/A 20. PAGE 5 B0102
                                              B64

COTTRELL A.J.,THE POLITICS OF THE ATLANTIC   VOL/ASSN
ALLIANCE. EUR+WWI USA+45 INT/ORG NAT/G DELIB/GP   FORCES
EX/STRUC BAL/PWR DIPLOM REGION DETER ATTIT ORD/FREE
...CONCPT RECORD GEN/LAWS GEN/METH NATO 20. PAGE 24
B0493
                                              B64

GJUPANOVIC H.,LEGAL SOURCES AND BIBLIOGRAPHY OF   BIBLIOG/A
YUGOSLAVIA. COM YUGOSLAVIA LAW LEGIS DIPLOM ADMIN   JURID
PARL/PROC REGION CRIME CENTRAL 20. PAGE 40 B0807   CONSTN
                                                    ADJUD
                                              B64

GRZYBOWSKI K.,THE SOCIALIST COMMONWEALTH OF   INT/LAW
NATIONS: ORGANIZATIONS AND INSTITUTIONS. FORCES   COM
DIPLOM INT/TRADE ADJUD ADMIN LEAD WAR MARXISM   REGION
SOCISM...BIBLIOG 20 COMECON WARSAW/P. PAGE 44 B0898 INT/ORG
                                              B64

KAPP E.,THE MERGER OF THE EXECUTIVES OF THE   CENTRAL
EUROPEAN COMMUNITIES. LAW CONSTN STRUCT ACT/RES   EX/STRUC
PLAN PROB/SOLV ADMIN REGION TASK...INT/LAW MGT ECSC
EEC. PAGE 58 B1170
                                              B64

OECD SEMINAR REGIONAL DEV,REGIONAL DEVELOPMENT IN   ADMIN
ISRAEL. ISRAEL STRUCT ECO/UNDEV NAT/G REGION...GEOG PROVS
20. PAGE 79 B1603   PLAN
                                                    METH/COMP
                                              B64

PLISCHKE E.,SYSTEMS OF INTEGRATING THE   INT/ORG
INTERNATIONAL COMMUNITY. WOR+45 NAT/G VOL/ASSN   EX/STRUC
ECO/TAC LEGIT PWR WEALTH...TIME/SEQ ANTHOL UN   REGION
TOT/POP 20. PAGE 83 B1684
                                              B64

SARROS P.P.,CONGRESS AND THE NEW DIPLOMACY: THE   DIPLOM
FORMULATION OF MUTUAL SECURITY POLICY: 1953-60   POL/PAR
(THESIS). USA+45 CHIEF EX/STRUC REGION ROUTINE   NAT/G
CHOOSE GOV/REL PEACE ROLE...POLICY 20 PRESIDENT
CONGRESS. PAGE 92 B1869
                                              B64

SCHERMER G.,MEETING SOCIAL NEEDS IN THE PENJERDEL   PLAN
REGION. SOCIETY FINAN ACT/RES EDU/PROP ADMIN   REGION
GOV/REL...SOC/WK 45 20 PENNSYLVAN DELAWARE   HEALTH
NEW/JERSEY. PAGE 93 B1887   WEALTH
                                              L64

HAAS E.B.,"ECONOMICS AND DIFFERENTIAL PATTERNS OF   L/A+17C
POLITICAL INTEGRATION: PROJECTIONS ABOUT UNITY IN   INT/ORG
LATIN AMERICA." SOCIETY NAT/G DELIB/GP ACT/RES   MARKET
CREATE PLAN ECO/TAC REGION ROUTINE ATTIT DRIVE PWR
WEALTH...CONCPT TREND CHARTS LAFTA 20. PAGE 45
B0910
                                              L64

ROTBERG R.,"THE FEDERATION MOVEMENT IN BRITISH EAST VOL/ASSN
AND CENTRAL AFRICA." AFR RHODESIA UGANDA ECO/UNDEV PWR
NAT/G POL/PAR FORCES DOMIN LEGIT ADMIN COERCE ATTIT REGION
...CONCPT TREND 20 TANGANYIKA. PAGE 91 B1831
                                              S64

HADY T.F.,"CONGRESSIONAL TOWNSHIPS AS INCORPORATED MUNIC
MUNICIPALITIES." NEIGH ADMIN REPRESENT ATTIT GEOG. REGION
PAGE 45 B0914   LOC/G
                                                    GOV/COMP
                                              S64

MURRAY D.,"CHINESE EDUCATION IN SOUTH-EAST ASIA."   S/ASIA
SOCIETY NEIGH EDU/PROP ROUTINE PERSON KNOWL   SCHOOL
...OBS/ENVIR STERTYP. PAGE 76 B1546   REGION
                                                    ASIA
                                              S64

NEWLYN W.T.,"MONETARY SYSTEMS AND INTEGRATION" AFR ECO/UNDEV
BUDGET ADMIN FEDERAL PRODUC PROFIT UTIL...CHARTS 20 REGION
AFRICA/E. PAGE 78 B1578   METH/COMP
                                                    FINAN
                                              B65

AIYAR S.P.,STUDIES IN INDIAN DEMOCRACY. INDIA   ORD/FREE
STRATA ECO/UNDEV LABOR POL/PAR LEGIS DIPLOM LOBBY   REPRESENT
REGION CHOOSE ATTIT SOCISM...ANTHOL 20. PAGE 3   ADMIN
B0067   NAT/G

BARNETT V.M. JR.,THE REPRESENTATION OF THE UNITED   USA+45
STATES ABROAD* REVISED EDITION. ECO/UNDEV ACADEM   DIPLOM
INT/ORG FORCES ACT/RES CREATE OP/RES FOR/AID REGION ADMIN
CENTRAL...CLASSIF ANTHOL. PAGE 9 B0189
                                              B65

DUGGAR G.S.,RENEWAL OF TOWN AND VILLAGE I: A WORLD- MUNIC
WIDE SURVEY OF LOCAL GOVERNMENT EXPERIENCE. WOR+45 NEIGH
CONSTRUC INDUS CREATE BUDGET REGION GOV/REL...QU   PLAN
NAT/COMP 20 URBAN/RNWL. PAGE 31 B0628   ADMIN
                                              B65

ETZIONI A.,POLITICAL UNIFICATION* A COMPARATIVE   INT/ORG
STUDY OF LEADERS AND FORCES. EUR+WWI ISLAM L/A+17C FORCES
WOR+45 ELITES STRATA EXEC WEALTH...TIME/SEQ TREND   ECO/TAC
SOC/EXP. PAGE 34 B0686   REGION
                                              B65

KASER M.,COMECON* INTEGRATION PROBLEMS OF THE   PLAN
PLANNED ECONOMIES. INT/ORG TEC/DEV INT/TRADE PRICE ECO/DEV
ADMIN ADJUST CENTRAL...STAT TIME/SEQ ORG/CHARTS   COM
COMECON. PAGE 58 B1177   REGION
                                              B65

LEYS C.T.,FEDERATION IN EAST AFRICA. LAW AGRI   FEDERAL
DIST/IND FINAN INT/ORG LABOR INT/TRADE CONFER ADMIN REGION
CONTROL GP/REL...ANTHOL 20 AFRICA/E. PAGE 65 B1310 ECO/UNDEV
                                                    PLAN
                                              B65

MACDONALD R.W.,THE LEAGUE OF ARAB STATES: A STUDY   ISLAM
IN THE DYNAMICS OF REGIONAL ORGANIZATION. ISRAEL   REGION
UAR USSR FINAN INT/ORG DELIB/GP ECO/TAC AGREE   DIPLOM
NEUTRAL ORD/FREE PWR...DECISION BIBLIOG 20 TREATY   ADMIN
UN. PAGE 67 B1358
                                              B65

MUSHKIN S.J.,STATE PROGRAMMING. USA+45 PLAN BUDGET PROVS
TAX ADMIN REGION GOV/REL...BIBLIOG 20. PAGE 77   POLICY
B1549   CREATE
                                                    ECO/DEV
                                              B65

ORG FOR ECO COOP AND DEVEL,THE MEDITERRANEAN   PLAN
REGIONAL PROJECT: AN EXPERIMENT IN PLANNING BY SIX ECO/UNDEV
COUNTRIES. FUT GREECE SPAIN TURKEY YUGOSLAVIA   ACADEM
SOCIETY FINAN NAT/G PROF/ORG EDU/PROP ADMIN REGION SCHOOL
COST...POLICY STAT CHARTS 20 OECD. PAGE 80 B1614
                                              B65

PANJABI K.L.,THE CIVIL SERVANT IN INDIA. INDIA UK   ADMIN
NAT/G CONSULT EX/STRUC REGION GP/REL RACE/REL 20.   WORKER
PAGE 81 B1631   BIOG
                                                    COLONIAL
                                              B65

SPEECKAERT G.P.,SELECT BIBLIOGRAPHY ON   BIBLIOG
INTERNATIONAL ORGANIZATION, 1885-1964. WOR+45   INT/ORG
WOR-45 EX/STRUC DIPLOM ADMIN REGION 19/20 UN.   GEN/LAWS
PAGE 99 B2004   STRATA
                                              N65

NJ DIVISION STATE-REGION PLAN,UTILIZATION OF NEW   UTIL
JERSEY'S DELAWARE RIVER WATERFRONT (PAMPHLET). FUT PLAN
ADMIN REGION LEISURE GOV/REL DEMAND WEALTH...CHARTS ECO/TAC
20 NEW/JERSEY. PAGE 78 B1586   PROVS
                                              B66

DAVIS J.A.,SOUTHERN AFRICA IN TRANSITION. SOUTH/AFR AFR
USA+45 FINAN NAT/G DELIB/GP EDU/PROP ADMIN COLONIAL ADJUST
REGION RACE/REL ATTIT SOVEREIGN...ANTHOL 20   CONSTN
RESOURCE/N. PAGE 26 B0538
                                              B66

MANGONE G.J.,UN ADMINISTRATION OF ECONOMIC AND   ADMIN
AOCIAL PROGRAMS. CONSULT BUDGET INT/TRADE REGION 20 MGT
UN. PAGE 69 B1391   ECO/TAC
                                                    DELIB/GP
                                              B66

MURDOCK J.C.,RESEARCH AND REGIONS. AGRI FINAN INDUS BIBLIOG
LOC/G MUNIC NAT/G PROB/SOLV TEC/DEV ADMIN REGION   ECO/DEV
20. PAGE 76 B1545   COMPUT/IR
                                                    R+D
                                              B66

SMITH H.E.,READINGS IN ECONOMIC DEVELOPMENT AND   TEC/DEV
ADMINISTRATION IN TANZANIA. TANZANIA FINAN INDUS   ADMIN
LABOR NAT/G PLAN PROB/SOLV INT/TRADE COLONIAL   GOV/REL
REGION...ANTHOL BIBLIOG 20 AFRICA/E. PAGE 98 B1981
                                              B66

WARREN R.O.,GOVERNMENT IN METROPOLITAN REGIONS: A   LOC/G
REAPPRAISAL OF FRACTIONATED POLITICAL ORGANIZATION. MUNIC
USA+45 ACT/RES PROB/SOLV REGION...CHARTS METH/COMP EX/STRUC
BIBLIOG CITY/MGT. PAGE 114 B2296   PLAN
                                              S66

PALMER M.,"THE UNITED ARAB REPUBLIC* AN ASSESSMENT UAR
OF ITS FAILURE." ELITES ECO/UNDEV POL/PAR FORCES   SYRIA
ECO/TAC RUMOR ADMIN EXEC EFFICIENCY ATTIT SOCISM   REGION
...INT NASSER/G. PAGE 81 B1628   FEDERAL
                                              S66

SNOWISS L.M.,"CONGRESSIONAL RECRUITMENT AND   LEGIS
REPRESENTATION." USA+45 LG/CO MUNIC POL/PAR ADMIN   REPRESENT
REGION CONGRESS CHICAGO. PAGE 98 B1990   CHOOSE
                                                    LOC/G
                                              B67

NIVEN R.,NIGERIA. NIGERIA CONSTN INDUS EX/STRUC   NAT/G
COLONIAL REV NAT/LISM...CHARTS 19/20. PAGE 78 B1584 REGION
                                                    CHOOSE

WATERS M.,THE UNITED NATIONS* INTERNATIONAL ORGANIZATION AND ADMINISTRATION. WOR+45 EX/STRUC FORCES DIPLOM LEAD REGION ARMS/CONT REPRESENT INGP/REL ROLE...METH/COMP ANTHOL 20 UN LEAGUE/NAT. PAGE 114 B2301
GP/REL B67 CONSTN INT/ORG ADMIN ADJUD

TAMBIAH S.J.,"THE POLITICS OF LANGUAGE IN INDIA AND CEYLON." CEYLON INDIA NAT/G DOMIN ADMIN...SOC 20. PAGE 102 B2070
L67 POL/PAR LING NAT/LISM REGION

FRYKENBURG R.E.,"STUDIES OF LAND CONTROL IN INDIAN HISTORY: REVIEW ARTICLE." INDIA UK STRATA AGRI MUNIC OP/RES COLONIAL REGION EFFICIENCY OWN HABITAT ...CONCPT 16/20. PAGE 38 B0763
S67 ECO/UNDEV CONTROL ADMIN

GRUNDY K.W.,"THE POLITICAL USES OF IMAGINATION." GHANA ELITES SOCIETY NAT/G DOMIN EDU/PROP COLONIAL REGION REPRESENT GP/REL CENTRAL PWR MARXISM 20. PAGE 44 B0897
S67 NAT/LISM EX/STRUC AFR LEAD

HUGON P.,"BLOCAGES ET DESEQUILIBRES DE LA CROISSANCE ECONOMIQUE EN AFRIQUE NOIRE." AFR KIN MUNIC CREATE PLAN INT/TRADE REGION ADJUST CENTRAL EQUILIB NAT/LISM ORD/FREE 20. PAGE 52 B1060
S67 ECO/UNDEV COLONIAL STRUCT ADMIN

LIU K.C.,"DISINTEGRATION OF THE OLD ORDER." ASIA SOCIETY PROB/SOLV ADMIN REGION TOTALISM ORD/FREE MARXISM 19/20. PAGE 66 B1329
S67 ADJUST NAT/LISM

MURRAY R.,"SECOND THOUGHTS ON GHANA." AFR GHANA NAT/G POL/PAR ADMIN REV GP/REL CENTRAL...SOCIALIST CONCPT METH 20. PAGE 77 B1548
S67 COLONIAL CONTROL REGION SOCISM

NEUCHTERLEIN D.E.,"THAILAND* ANOTHER VIETNAM?" THAILAND ECO/UNDEV DIPLOM ADMIN REGION CENTRAL NAT/LISM...POLICY 20. PAGE 78 B1571
S67 WAR GUERRILLA S/ASIA NAT/G

ROSENBERG B.,"ETHNIC LIBERALISM AND EMPLOYMENT DISCRIMINATION IN THE NORTH." USA+45 TOP/EX PROB/SOLV ADMIN REGION PERS/REL DISCRIM...INT IDEA/COMP. PAGE 90 B1820
S67 RACE/REL ATTIT WORKER EXEC

ZASLOW M.,"RECENT CONSTITUTIONAL DEVELOPMENTS IN CANADA'S NORTHERN TERRITORIES." CANADA LOC/G DELIB/GP EX/STRUC LEGIS ADMIN ORD/FREE...TREND 20. PAGE 119 B2398
S67 GOV/REL REGION CONSTN FEDERAL

REGRESS....REGRESSION ANALYSIS; SEE ALSO CON/ANAL

TANNENBAUM A.S.,"CONTROL AND EFFECTIVENESS IN A VOLUNTARY ORGANIZATION." USA+45 ADMIN...CORREL MATH REGRESS STAT TESTS SAMP/SIZ CHARTS SOC/EXP INDEX 20 LEAGUE/WV. PAGE 102 B2072
S61 EFFICIENCY VOL/ASSN CONTROL INGP/REL

REGRESSION ANALYSIS....SEE REGRESS

REHABILITATION....SEE REHABILITN

REHABILITN....REHABILITATION

REICH C.A. B1762

REICH N. B1763

REIN M. B1401

REISCHAUER R. B1764

REISELBACH L.N. B1765

REISS A.J. B1766

REISSMAN L. B1767

RELATIONS AMONG GROUPS....SEE GP/REL

RELATISM....RELATIVISM

RELATIV....RELATIVITY

ANGLIN D.,"UNITED STATES OPPOSITION TO CANADIAN MEMBERSHIP IN THE PAN AMERICAN UNION: A CANADIAN VIEW." L/A+17C UK USA+45 VOL/ASSN DELIB/GP EX/STRUC PLAN DIPLOM DOMIN REGION ATTIT RIGID/FLEX PWR ...RELATIV CONCPT STERTYP CMN/WLTH OAS 20. PAGE 5 B0112
S61 INT/ORG CANADA

LI C.M.,INDUSTRIAL DEVELOPMENT IN COMMUNIST CHINA. ASIA CHINA/COM ECO/DEV ECO/UNDEV AGRI FINAN INDUS MARKET TEC/DEV
B64

LABOR NAT/G ECO/TAC INT/TRADE EXEC ALL/VALS ...POLICY RELATIV TREND WORK TOT/POP VAL/FREE 20. PAGE 65 B1311

PIPES R.,THE FORMATION OF THE SOVIET UNION. EUR+WWI MOD/EUR STRUCT ECO/UNDEV NAT/G LEGIS DOMIN LEGIT CT/SYS EXEC COERCE ALL/VALS...POLICY RELATIV HIST/WRIT TIME/SEQ TOT/POP 19/20. PAGE 83 B1677
B64 COM USSR RUSSIA

CLIGNET R.,"POTENTIAL ELITES IN GHANA AND THE IVORY COAST: A PRELIMINARY SURVEY." AFR CULTURE ELITES STRATA KIN NAT/G SECT DOMIN EXEC ORD/FREE RESPECT SKILL...POLICY RELATIV GP/COMP NAT/COMP 20. PAGE 21 B0438
S64 PWR LEGIT IVORY/CST GHANA

NASH M.,"SOCIAL PREREQUISITES TO ECONOMIC GROWTH IN LATIN AMERICA AND SOUTHEAST ASIA." L/A+17C S/ASIA CULTURE SOCIETY ECO/UNDEV AGRI INDUS NAT/G PLAN TEC/DEV EDU/PROP ROUTINE ALL/VALS...POLICY RELATIV SOC NAT/COMP WORK TOT/POP 20. PAGE 77 B1558
S64 ECO/DEV PERCEPT

NEEDHAM T.,"SCIENCE AND SOCIETY IN EAST AND WEST." ASIA INTELL STRATA R+D LOC/G NAT/G PROVS CONSULT ACT/RES CREATE PLAN TEC/DEV EDU/PROP ADMIN ATTIT ALL/VALS ...POLICY RELATIV MGT CONCPT NEW/IDEA TIME/SEQ WORK WORK. PAGE 77 B1565
S64 ASIA STRUCT

WILLIAMS S.,"NEGOTIATING INVESTMENT IN EMERGING COUNTRIES." USA+45 WOR+45 INDUS MARKET NAT/G TOP/EX TEC/DEV CAP/ISM ECO/TAC ADMIN SKILL WEALTH...POLICY RELATIV MGT WORK 20. PAGE 117 B2353
L65 FINAN ECO/UNDEV

RELATIVISM....SEE RELATISM, RELATIV

RELATIVITY....SEE RELATIV

RELIABILITY....SEE METH/CNCPT

RELIGION....SEE SECT, WORSHIP

RELIGIOUS GROUP....SEE SECT

RENAISSAN....RENAISSANCE

RENT....RENTING

KEE R.,REFUGEE WORLD. AUSTRIA EUR+WWI GERMANY NEIGH EX/STRUC WORKER PROB/SOLV ECO/TAC RENT EDU/PROP INGP/REL COST LITERACY HABITAT 20 MIGRATION. PAGE 59 B1186
B61 NAT/G GIVE WEALTH STRANGE

BALDWIN D.A.,"CONGRESSIONAL INITIATIVE IN FOREIGN POLICY." NAT/G BARGAIN DIPLOM FOR/AID RENT GIVE ...DECISION CONGRESS. PAGE 8 B0171
S66 EXEC TOP/EX GOV/REL

GABRIEL P.P.,THE INTERNATIONAL TRANSFER OF CORPORATE SKILLS: MANAGEMENT CONTRACTS IN LESS DEVELOPED COUNTRIES. CLIENT INDUS LG/CO PLAN PROB/SOLV CAP/ISM ECO/TAC FOR/AID INT/TRADE RENT ADMIN SKILL 20. PAGE 38 B0771
B67 ECO/UNDEV AGREE MGT CONSULT

REP/CONVEN....REPUBLICAN (PARTY - U.S.) NATIONAL CONVENTION

REPAR....REPARATIONS; SEE ALSO INT/REL, SANCTION

REPARATIONS....SEE REPAR

REPRESENT....REPRESENTATION; SEE ALSO LEGIS

CONGRESSIONAL MONITOR. CONSULT DELIB/GP PROB/SOLV PRESS DEBATE ROUTINE...POLICY CONGRESS. PAGE 1 B0002
N BIBLIOG LEGIS REPRESENT USA+45

INTERNATIONAL REVIEW OF ADMINISTRATIVE SCIENCES. WOR+45 WOR-45 STRATA ECO/DEV ECO/UNDEV CREATE PLAN PROB/SOLV DIPLOM CONTROL REPRESENT...MGT 20. PAGE 1 B0004
N BIBLIOG/A ADMIN INT/ORG NAT/G

FAHRNKOPF N.,STATE AND LOCAL GOVERNMENT IN ILLINOIS (PAMPHLET). CONSTN ADMIN PARTIC CHOOSE REPRESENT GOV/REL...JURID MGT 20 ILLINOIS. PAGE 34 B0696
N19 BIBLIOG LOC/G LEGIS CT/SYS

OPERATIONS AND POLICY RESEARCH,PERU ELECTION MEMORANDA (PAMPHLET). L/A+17C PERU POL/PAR LEGIS EXEC APPORT REPRESENT 20. PAGE 80 B1611
N19 CHOOSE CONSTN SUFF NAT/G

SOUTH AFRICA COMMISSION ON FUT,INTERIM AND FINAL REPORTS ON FUTURE FORM OF GOVERNMENT IN THE SOUTH-WEST AFRICAN PROTECTORATE (PAMPHLET). SOUTH/AFR NAT/G FORCES CONFER COLONIAL CONTROL 20 AFRICA/SW. PAGE 99 B1998
N19 CONSTN REPRESENT ADMIN PROB/SOLV

SOMERS H.M.,"THE PRESIDENT AS ADMINISTRATOR."
USA+45 NAT/G ADMIN REPRESENT GOV/REL 20 PRESIDENT.
PAGE 99 B1996

PROB/SOLV
S52
CONTROL
EFFICIENCY
EX/STRUC
EXEC

STENE E.O.,ABANDONMENTS OF THE MANAGER PLAN. LEGIS
LEAD GP/REL PWR DECISION. PAGE 100 B2032

B53
MUNIC
EX/STRUC
REPRESENT
ADMIN

THOMAS S.B.,GOVERNMENT AND ADMINISTRATION IN
COMMUNIST CHINA (MONOGRAPH). CHINA/COM PROB/SOLV
EDU/PROP 20. PAGE 104 B2100

B53
PWR
EX/STRUC
REPRESENT
ELITES

NEWMAN F.C.,"CONGRESS AND THE FAITHFUL EXECUTION OF
LAWS - SHOULD LEGISLATORS SUPERVISE
ADMINISTRATORS." USA+45 NAT/G EX/STRUC EXEC PWR
POLICY. PAGE 78 B1579

L53
REPRESENT
CONTROL
ADMIN
LEGIS

DRUCKER P.F.,"THE EMPLOYEE SOCIETY." STRUCT BAL/PWR
PARTIC REPRESENT PWR...DECISION CONCPT. PAGE 30
B0619

S53
LABOR
MGT
WORKER
CULTURE

PERKINS J.A.,"ADMINISTRATION OF THE NATIONAL
SECURITY PROGRAM." USA+45 EX/STRUC FORCES ADMIN
CIVMIL/REL ORD/FREE 20. PAGE 82 B1657

S53
CONTROL
GP/REL
REPRESENT
PROB/SOLV

JENNINGS I.,THE QUEEN'S GOVERNMENT. UK POL/PAR
DELIB/GP ADJUD ADMIN CT/SYS PARL/PROC REPRESENT
CONSERVE 13/20 PARLIAMENT. PAGE 56 B1132

B54
NAT/G
CONSTN
LEGIS
CHIEF

US SENATE COMM ON FOREIGN REL,REVIEW OF THE UNITED
NATIONS CHARTER: A COLLECTION OF DOCUMENTS. LEGIS
DIPLOM ADMIN ARMS/CONT WAR REPRESENT SOVEREIGN
...INT/LAW 20 UN. PAGE 110 B2220

B54
BIBLIOG
CONSTN
INT/ORG
DEBATE

APPLEBY P.H.,"BUREAUCRACY AND THE FUTURE." USA+45
NAT/G CONTROL EXEC...MAJORIT 20. PAGE 6 B0119

S54
EX/STRUC
LOBBY
REPRESENT
ADMIN

CHILDS R.S.,"CITIZEN ORGANIZATION FOR CONTROL OF
GOVERNMENT." USA+45 POL/PAR CONTROL LOBBY...MAJORIT
20. PAGE 21 B0424

S54
CHOOSE
REPRESENT
ADMIN
EX/STRUC

COLE T.,"LESSONS FROM RECENT EUROPEAN EXPERIENCE."
EUR+WWI EX/STRUC 20. PAGE 22 B0450

S54
GOV/COMP
ADMIN
REPRESENT

COOPER L.,"ADMINISTRATIVE JUSTICE." UK ADMIN
REPRESENT PWR...POLICY 20. PAGE 23 B0475

S54
LAW
ADJUD
CONTROL
EX/STRUC

GILBERT C.E.,"LEGISLATIVE CONTROL OF THE
BUREAUCRACY." USA+45 NAT/G ADMIN EXEC 20. PAGE 39
B0798

S54
CONTROL
EX/STRUC
REPRESENT
GOV/REL

HART J.,"ADMINISTRATION AND THE COURTS." USA+45
NAT/G REPRESENT 20. PAGE 47 B0960

S54
ADMIN
GOV/REL
CT/SYS
FEDERAL

LANE E.,"INTEREST GROUPS AND BUREAUCRACY." NAT/G
ADMIN GP/REL INGP/REL 20. PAGE 62 B1256

S54
EX/STRUC
LOBBY
REPRESENT
PWR

LONG N.E.,"PUBLIC POLICY AND ADMINISTRATION: THE
GOALS OF RATIONALITY AND RESPONSIBILITY." EX/STRUC
ADMIN LEAD 20. PAGE 66 B1338

S54
PROB/SOLV
EXEC
REPRESENT

STONE E.O.,"ADMINISTRATIVE INTEGRATION." USA+45
NAT/G ADMIN CONTROL CENTRAL 20. PAGE 101 B2046

S54
REPRESENT
EFFICIENCY
LOBBY
EX/STRUC

ZELLER B.,"AMERICAN STATE LEGISLATURES: REPORT ON
THE COMMITTEE ON AMERICAN LEGISLATURES." CONSTN
POL/PAR EX/STRUC CONFER ADMIN CONTROL EXEC LOBBY
ROUTINE GOV/REL...POLICY BIBLIOG 20. PAGE 119 B2401

C54
REPRESENT
LEGIS
PROVS
APPORT

BLAU P.M.,THE DYNAMICS OF BUREAUCRACY: A STUDY OF
INTERPERSONAL RELATIONS IN TWO GOVERNMENT AGENCIES.
USA+45 EX/STRUC REPRESENT INGP/REL PERS/REL.
PAGE 12 B0251

B55
CLIENT
ADMIN
EXEC
ROUTINE

MACMAHON A.W.,FEDERALISM: MATURE AND EMERGENT.

B55
STRUCT

EUR+WWI FUT WOR+45 WOR-45 INT/ORG NAT/G REPRESENT
FEDERAL...POLICY MGT RECORD TREND GEN/LAWS 20.
PAGE 68 B1370

CONCPT

B55

RUSTOW D.A.,THE POLITICS OF COMPROMISE. SWEDEN
LABOR EX/STRUC LEGIS PLAN REPRESENT SOCISM...SOC
19/20. PAGE 92 B1859

POL/PAR
NAT/G
POLICY
ECO/TAC

S55

MARTIN R.C.,"ADMINISTRATIVE LEADERSHIP IN
GOVERNMENT." NAT/G PARTIC ROUTINE INGP/REL...MGT
20. PAGE 70 B1413

TOP/EX
ADMIN
EXEC
REPRESENT

S55

STAHL O.G.,"DEMOCRACY AND PUBLIC EMPLOYEE
MORALITY." USA+45 NAT/G EDU/PROP EXEC ROLE 20.
PAGE 100 B2016

REPRESENT
POLICY
ADMIN

B56

BARBASH J.,THE PRACTICE OF UNIONISM. ECO/TAC LEAD
LOBBY GP/REL INGP/REL DRIVE MARXISM BIBLIOG. PAGE 9
B0182

LABOR
REPRESENT
CONTROL
ADMIN

B56

CARTER B.E.,THE OFFICE OF THE PRIME MINISTER. UK
ADMIN REPRESENT PARLIAMENT 20. PAGE 19 B0388

GOV/REL
CHIEF
EX/STRUC
LEAD

B56

FRANCIS R.G.,SERVICE AND PROCEDURE IN BUREAUCRACY.
EXEC LEAD ROUTINE...QU 20. PAGE 37 B0748

CLIENT
ADMIN
INGP/REL
REPRESENT

B56

REDFORD E.S.,PUBLIC ADMINISTRATION AND POLICY
FORMATION: STUDIES IN OIL, GAS, BANKING, RIVER
DEVELOPMENT AND CORPORATE INVESTIGATIONS. USA+45
CLIENT NAT/G ADMIN LOBBY REPRESENT GOV/REL INGP/REL
20. PAGE 87 B1754

EX/STRUC
PROB/SOLV
CONTROL
EXEC

S56

CLEVELAND H.,"THE EXECUTIVE AND THE PUBLIC
INTEREST." USA+45 DOMIN ADMIN PWR...POLICY 20.
PAGE 21 B0437

LOBBY
REPRESENT
CHIEF
EXEC

S56

COTTER C.P.,"ADMINISTRATIVE ACCOUNTABILITY TO
CONGRESS: THE CONCURRENT RESOLUTION." USA+45 NAT/G
EXEC REPRESENT PWR 20. PAGE 24 B0489

CONTROL
GOV/REL
LEGIS
EX/STRUC

S56

EMMERICH H.,"COOPERATION AMONG ADMINISTRATIVE
AGENCIES." USA+45 NAT/G EX/STRUC ADMIN 20. PAGE 33
B0673

DELIB/GP
REPRESENT
GOV/REL
EXEC

S56

KAUFMAN H.,"EMERGING CONFLICTS IN THE DOCTRINES OF
PUBLIC ADMINISTRATION" (BMR)" USA+45 USA-45 NAT/G
EX/STRUC LEGIS CONTROL NEUTRAL ATTIT PWR...TREND
20. PAGE 58 B1181

ADMIN
ORD/FREE
REPRESENT
LEAD

S56

KHAMA T.,"POLITICAL CHANGE IN AFRICAN SOCIETY."
CONSTN SOCIETY LOC/G NAT/G POL/PAR EX/STRUC LEGIS
LEGIT ADMIN CHOOSE REPRESENT NAT/LISM MORAL
ORD/FREE PWR...CONCPT OBS TREND GEN/METH CMN/WLTH
17/20. PAGE 59 B1201

AFR
ELITES

S56

TSUJI K.,"THE CABINET, ADMINISTRATIVE ORGANIZATION,
AND THE BUREAUCRACY." EXEC 19/20 CHINJAP. PAGE 106
B2133

GOV/REL
EX/STRUC
ADMIN
REPRESENT

C56

NEUMANN S.,"MODERN POLITICAL PARTIES: APPROACHES TO
COMPARATIVE POLITIC. FRANCE UK EX/STRUC DOMIN ADMIN
LEAD REPRESENT TOTALISM ATTIT...POLICY TREND
METH/COMP ANTHOL BIBLIOG/A 20 CMN/WLTH. PAGE 78
B1574

POL/PAR
GOV/COMP
ELITES
MAJORIT

B57

BERGER M.,BUREAUCRACY AND SOCIETY IN MODERN EGYPT;
A STUDY OF THE HIGHER CIVIL SERVICE. UAR REPRESENT
...QU 20. PAGE 11 B0221

ATTIT
EXEC
ADMIN
ROUTINE

B57

KNEIER C.M.,CITY GOVERNMENT IN THE UNITED STATES
(3RD ED.). USA-45 FINAN NAT/G POL/PAR LEGIS
EDU/PROP LEAD APPORT REPRESENT ATTIT...MGT 20
CITY/MGT. PAGE 60 B1219

MUNIC
LOC/G
ADMIN
GOV/REL

L57

DOTSON A.,"FUNDAMENTAL APPROACHES TO
RESPONSIBILITY." USA+45 NAT/G PWR 20. PAGE 30 B0611

ADMIN
REPRESENT
EXEC
CONTROL

S57

BAUMGARTEL H.,"LEADERSHIP STYLE AS A VARIABLE IN
RESEARCH ADMINISTRATION." USA+45 ADMIN REPRESENT
PERS/REL 20. PAGE 10 B0198

LEAD
EXEC
MGT
INGP/REL

COTTER C.P.,"ADMINISTRATIVE ACCOUNTABILITY: REPORTING TO CONGRESS." USA+45 CONSULT DELIB/GP PARL/PROC PARTIC GOV/REL ATTIT PWR DECISION. PAGE 24 B0490
S57
LEGIS
EX/STRUC
REPRESENT
CONTROL

COTTER C.R.,"ADMINISTRATIVE RESPONSIBILITY: CONGRESSIONAL PRESCRIPTION OF INTERAGENCY RELATIONSHIPS." USA+45 NAT/G ADMIN 20. PAGE 24 B0492
S57
GOV/REL
LEGIS
REPRESENT
EX/STRUC

GULICK L.,"METROPOLITAN ORGANIZATION." LEGIS EXEC PARTIC CHOOSE REPRESENT GOV/REL...MAJORIT DECISION. PAGE 45 B0904
S57
REGION
LOC/G
MUNIC

HARRIS J.P.,"LEGISLATIVE CONTROL OF ADMINISTRATION: SOME COMPARISONS OF AMERICAN AND EUROPEAN PRACTICES." DEBATE PARL/PROC ROUTINE GOV/REL EFFICIENCY SUPEGO DECISION. PAGE 47 B0954
S57
LEGIS
CONTROL
EX/STRUC
REPRESENT

JANOWITZ M.,"THE BUREAUCRAT AND THE PUBLIC: A STUDY OF INFORMATIONAL PERSPECTIVES." USA+45 PROB/SOLV ATTIT 20. PAGE 55 B1120
S57
REPRESENT
ADMIN
EX/STRUC
CLIENT

ROBSON W.A.,"TWO-LEVEL GOVERNMENT FOR METROPOLITAN AREAS." MUNIC EX/STRUC LEGIS PARTIC REPRESENT MAJORITY. PAGE 89 B1807
S57
REGION
LOC/G
PLAN
GOV/REL

COWAN L.G.,LOCAL GOVERNMENT IN WEST AFRICA. AFR FRANCE UK CULTURE KIN POL/PAR CHIEF LEGIS CREATE ADMIN PARTIC GOV/REL GP/REL...METH/COMP 20. PAGE 24 B0498
B58
LOC/G
COLONIAL
SOVEREIGN
REPRESENT

LOVEJOY D.S.,RHODE ISLAND POLITICS AND THE AMERICAN REVOLUTION 1760-1776. UK USA-45 ELITES EX/STRUC TAX LEAD REPRESENT GOV/REL GP/REL ATTIT 18 RHODE/ISL. PAGE 67 B1343
B58
REV
COLONIAL
ECO/TAC
SOVEREIGN

STEWART J.D.,BRITISH PRESSURE GROUPS: THEIR ROLE IN RELATION TO THE HOUSE OF COMMONS. UK CONSULT DELIB/GP ADMIN ROUTINE CHOOSE REPRESENT ATTIT ROLE 20 HOUSE/CMNS PARLIAMENT. PAGE 101 B2038
B58
LOBBY
LEGIS
PLAN
PARL/PROC

VASEY W.,GOVERNMENT AND SOCIAL WELFARE: ROLES OF FEDERAL , STATE AND LOCAL GOVERNMENTS IN ADMINISTERING WELFARE SERVICES. USA+45 EDU/PROP 20. PAGE 112 B2255
B58
REPRESENT
ADMIN
EX/STRUC
SOC/WK

ALMOND G.A.,"COMPARATIVE STUDY OF INTEREST GROUPS." USA+45 EX/STRUC PWR 20. PAGE 4 B0079
S58
LOBBY
REPRESENT
ADMIN
VOL/ASSN

FREEMAN J.L.,"THE BUREAUCRACY IN PRESSURE POLITICS." USA+45 NAT/G CHIEF ADMIN EXEC 20. PAGE 37 B0752
S58
CONTROL
EX/STRUC
REPRESENT
LOBBY

KEISER N.F.,"PUBLIC RESPONSIBILITY AND FEDERAL ADVISORY GROUPS: A CASE STUDY." NAT/G ADMIN CONTROL LOBBY...POLICY 20. PAGE 59 B1190
S58
REPRESENT
ELITES
GP/REL
EX/STRUC

MAIR L.P.,"REPRESENTATIVE LOCAL GOVERNMENT AS A PROBLEM IN SOCIAL CHANGE." ECO/UNDEV KIN LOC/G NAT/G SCHOOL JUDGE ADMIN ROUTINE REPRESENT RIGID/FLEX RESPECT...CONCPT STERTYP CMN/WLTH 20. PAGE 68 B1383
S58
AFR
PWR
ELITES

SALETAN E.N.,"ADMINISTRATIVE TRUSTIFICATION." NAT/G EX/STRUC ADMIN 20. PAGE 92 B1862
S58
LOBBY
PWR
CONTROL
REPRESENT

COUNCIL OF STATE GOVERNORS,AMERICAN LEGISLATURES: STRUCTURE AND PROCEDURES. SUMMARY AND TABULATIONS OF A 1959 SURVEY. PUERT/RICO USA+45 PAY ADJUD ADMIN APPORT...IDEA/COMP 20 GUAM VIRGIN/ISL. PAGE 24 B0495
B59
LEGIS
CHARTS
PROVS
REPRESENT

DIMOCK M.E.,ADMINISTRATIVE VITALITY: THE CONFLICT WITH BUREAUCRACY. PROB/SOLV EXEC 20. PAGE 29 B0597
B59
REPRESENT
ADMIN
EX/STRUC
ROUTINE

REDFORD E.S.,NATIONAL REGULATORY COMMISSIONS: NEED FOR A NEW LOOK (PAMPHLET). USA+45 CLIENT PROB/SOLV ADJUD LOBBY EFFICIENCY...POLICY 20. PAGE 87 B1757
B59
REPRESENT
CONTROL
EXEC
NAT/G

SINHA H.N.,OUTLINES OF POLITICAL SCIENCE. NAT/G POL/PAR EX/STRUC LEGIS CT/SYS CHOOSE REPRESENT 20. PAGE 98 B1971
B59
JURID
CONCPT
ORD/FREE
SOVEREIGN

GILBERT C.E.,"THE FRAMEWORK OF ADMINISTRATIVE RESPONSIBILITY." USA+45 20. PAGE 39 B0799
L59
REPRESENT
EXEC
EX/STRUC
CONTROL

HECTOR L.J.,"GOVERNMENT BY ANONYMITY: WHO WRITES OUR REGULATORY OPINIONS?" USA+45 NAT/G TOP/EX CONTROL EXEC. PAGE 49 B0987
L59
ADJUD
REPRESENT
EX/STRUC
ADMIN

GABLE R.W.,"CULTURE AND ADMINISTRATION IN IRAN." IRAN EXEC PARTIC REPRESENT PWR. PAGE 38 B0770
S59
ADMIN
CULTURE
EX/STRUC
INGP/REL

SUTTON F.X.,"REPRESENTATION AND THE NATURE OF POLITICAL SYSTEMS." UNIV WOR-45 CULTURE SOCIETY STRATA INT/ORG FORCES JUDGE DOMIN LEGIT EXEC REGION REPRESENT ATTIT ORD/FREE RESPECT...SOC HIST/WRIT TIME/SEQ. PAGE 102 B2057
S59
NAT/G
CONCPT

ADRIAN C.R.,STATE AND LOCAL GOVERNMENTS: A STUDY IN THE POLITICAL PROCESS. USA+45 LAW FINAN MUNIC POL/PAR LEGIS ADJUD EXEC CHOOSE REPRESENT. PAGE 3 B0060
B60
LOC/G
PROVS
GOV/REL
ATTIT

AYEARST M.,THE BRITISH WEST INDIES: THE SEARCH FOR SELF-GOVERNMENT. FUT WEST/IND LOC/G POL/PAR EX/STRUC LEGIS CHOOSE FEDERAL...NAT/COMP BIBLIOG 17/20. PAGE 7 B0152
B60
CONSTN
COLONIAL
REPRESENT
NAT/G

FOSS P.,POLITICS AND GRASS: THE ADMINISTRATION OF GRAZING ON THE PUBLIC DOMAIN. USA+45 LEGIS TOP/EX EXEC...DECISION 20. PAGE 37 B0743
B60
REPRESENT
ADMIN
LOBBY
EX/STRUC

HODGETTS J.E.,CANADIAN PUBLIC ADMINISTRATION. CANADA CONTROL LOBBY EFFICIENCY 20. PAGE 50 B1024
B60
REPRESENT
ADMIN
EX/STRUC
ADJUD

SCHUBERT G.,THE PUBLIC INTEREST. USA+45 CONSULT PLAN PROB/SOLV ADJUD ADMIN GP/REL PWR ALL/IDEOS 20. PAGE 94 B1903
B60
POLICY
DELIB/GP
REPRESENT
POL/PAR

FUCHS R.F.,"FAIRNESS AND EFFECTIVENESS IN ADMINISTRATIVE AGENCY ORGANIZATION AND PROCEDURES." USA+45 ADJUD ADMIN REPRESENT. PAGE 38 B0764
L60
EFFICIENCY
EX/STRUC
EXEC
POLICY

MARSHALL G.,"POLICE RESPONSIBILITY." UK LOC/G ADJUD ADMIN EXEC 20. PAGE 70 B1409
S60
CONTROL
REPRESENT
LAW
FORCES

TAYLOR M.G.,"THE ROLE OF THE MEDICAL PROFESSION IN THE FORMULATION AND EXECUTION OF PUBLIC POLICY" (BMR)" CANADA NAT/G CONSULT ADMIN REPRESENT GP/REL ROLE SOVEREIGN...DECISION 20 CMA. PAGE 103 B2088
S60
PROF/ORG
HEALTH
LOBBY
POLICY

SMITH T.E.,"ELECTIONS IN DEVELOPING COUNTRIES: A STUDY OF ELECTORAL PROCEDURES USED IN TOPICAL AFRICA, SOUTH-EAST ASIA..." AFR S/ASIA UK ROUTINE GOV/REL RACE/REL...GOV/COMP BIBLIOG 20. PAGE 98 B1985
C60
ECO/UNDEV
CHOOSE
REPRESENT
ADMIN

BANFIELD E.C.,URBAN GOVERNMENT: A READER IN POLITICS AND ADMINISTRATION. ELITES LABOR POL/PAR EXEC CHOOSE REPRESENT GP/REL PWR PLURISM...PSY SOC. PAGE 9 B0177
B61
MUNIC
GEN/METH
DECISION

BARRASH J.,LABOR'S GRASS ROOTS: A STUDY OF THE LOCAL UNION. STRATA BARGAIN LEAD REPRESENT DEMAND ATTIT PWR. PAGE 9 B0190
B61
LABOR
USA+45
INGP/REL
EXEC

HART W.R.,COLLECTIVE BARGAINING IN THE FEDERAL CIVIL SERVICE. NAT/G EX/STRUC ADMIN EXEC 20. PAGE 47 B0961
B61
INGP/REL
MGT
REPRESENT
LABOR

MACMAHON A.W.,DELEGATION AND AUTONOMY. INDIA STRUCT LEGIS BARGAIN BUDGET ECO/TAC LEGIT EXEC REPRESENT GOV/REL CENTRAL DEMAND EFFICIENCY PRODUC. PAGE 68 B1373
B61
ADMIN
PLAN
FEDERAL

NARAIN J.P.,SWARAJ FOR THE PEOPLE. INDIA CONSTN LOC/G MUNIC POL/PAR CHOOSE REPRESENT EFFICIENCY ATTIT PWR SOVEREIGN 20. PAGE 77 B1553
B61
NAT/G
ORD/FREE
EDU/PROP
EX/STRUC

NARASIMHAN V.K.,THE PRESS, THE PUBLIC AND THE ADMINISTRATION (PAMPHLET). INDIA COM/IND CONTROL REPRESENT GOV/REL EFFICIENCY...ANTHOL 20. PAGE 77
B61
NAT/G
ADMIN
PRESS

B1554

NEW/LIB
B61

THOMPSON V.A.,MODERN ORGANIZATION. REPRESENT
EFFICIENCY. PAGE 104 B2105

ADMIN
EX/STRUC
EXEC
L61

KRAMER R.,"EXECUTIVE PRIVILEGE - A STUDY OF THE
PERIOD 1953-1960." NAT/G CHIEF EX/STRUC LEGIS PWR.
PAGE 61 B1233

REPRESENT
LEAD
EXEC
GOV/REL
L61

MCNAMEE B.J.,"CONFLICT OF INTEREST: STATE
GOVERNMENT EMPLOYEES." USA+45 PROVS 20. PAGE 72
B1457

LAW
REPRESENT
ADMIN
CONTROL
S61

ABLARD C.D.,"EX PARTE CONTACTS WITH FEDERAL
ADMINISTRATIVE AGENCIES." USA+45 CLIENT NAT/G
DELIB/GP ADMIN PWR 20. PAGE 3 B0055

EXEC
ADJUD
LOBBY
REPRESENT
S61

DEXTER L.A.,"HAS THE PUBLIC OFFICIAL ON OBLIGATION
TO RESTRICT HIS FRIENDSHIPS?" NAT/G EX/STRUC TOP/EX
20. PAGE 29 B0584

ADMIN
ATTIT
REPRESENT
POLICY
S61

JOHNSON N.,"PARLIAMENTARY QUESTIONS AND THE CONDUCT
OF ADMINISTRATION." UK REPRESENT PARLIAMENT 20.
PAGE 57 B1146

CONTROL
EXEC
EX/STRUC
S61

KUIC V.,"THEORY AND PRACTICE OF THE AMERICAN
PRESIDENCY." USA+45 USA-45 NAT/G ADMIN REPRESENT
...PLURIST 20 PRESIDENT. PAGE 61 B1241

EXEC
EX/STRUC
PWR
CHIEF
S61

LYONS G.M.,"THE NEW CIVIL-MILITARY RELATIONS."
USA+45 NAT/G EX/STRUC TOP/EX PROB/SOLV ADMIN EXEC
PARTIC 20. PAGE 67 B1350

CIVMIL/REL
PWR
REPRESENT
S61

SHERBENOU E.L.,"CLASS, PARTICIPATION, AND THE
COUNCIL-MANAGER PLAN." ELITES STRUCT LEAD GP/REL
ATTIT PWR DECISION. PAGE 96 B1942

REPRESENT
MUNIC
EXEC
B62

HSUEH S.-S.,GOVERNMENT AND ADMINISTRATION OF HONG
KONG. CHIEF DELIB/GP LEGIS CT/SYS REPRESENT GOV/REL
20 HONG/KONG CITY/MGT CIVIL/SERV GOVERNOR. PAGE 52
B1055

ADMIN
LOC/G
COLONIAL
EX/STRUC
B62

LOWI T.J.,LEGISLATIVE POLITICS U.S.A. LAW LEGIS
DIPLOM EXEC LOBBY CHOOSE SUFF FEDERAL PWR 19/20
CONGRESS. PAGE 67 B1345

PARL/PROC
REPRESENT
POLICY
ROUTINE
B62

REICH C.A.,BUREAUCRACY AND THE FORESTS (PAMPHLET).
USA+45 LOBBY...POLICY MGT 20. PAGE 87 B1762

ADMIN
CONTROL
EX/STRUC
REPRESENT
B62

SAMPSON A.,ANATOMY OF BRITAIN. UK LAW COM/IND FINAN
INDUS MARKET MUNIC POL/PAR EX/STRUC TOP/EX DIPLOM
LEAD REPRESENT PERSON PARLIAMENT WORSHIP. PAGE 92
B1866

ELITES
PWR
STRUCT
FORCES
B62

WANGSNESS P.H.,THE POWER OF THE CITY MANAGER.
USA+45 EX/STRUC BAL/PWR BUDGET TAX ADMIN REPRESENT
CENTRAL EFFICIENCY DRIVE ROLE...POLICY 20 CITY/MGT.
PAGE 113 B2286

PWR
TOP/EX
MUNIC
LOC/G
L62

BORCHARDT K.,"CONGRESSIONAL USE OF ADMINISTRATIVE
ORGANIZATION AND PROCEDURE FOR POLICY-MAKING
PURPOSES." USA+45 NAT/G EXEC LOBBY. PAGE 14 B0278

ADMIN
LEGIS
REPRESENT
CONTROL
L62

CAVERS D.F.,"ADMINISTRATIVE DECISION-MAKING IN
NUCLEAR FACILITIES LICENSING." USA+45 CLIENT ADMIN
EXEC 20 AEC. PAGE 19 B0395

REPRESENT
LOBBY
PWR
CONTROL
S62

BOOTH D.A.,"POWER STRUCTURE AND COMMUNITY CHANGE: A
REPLICATION STUDY OF COMMUNITY A." STRATA LABOR
LEAD PARTIC REPRESENT...DECISION MGT TIME. PAGE 14
B0275

MUNIC
ELITES
PWR
S62

BRAIBANTI R.,"REFLECTIONS ON BUREAUCRATIC
CORRPUTION." LAW REPRESENT 20. PAGE 15 B0298

CONTROL
MORAL
ADMIN
GOV/COMP
S62

GUYOT J.F.,"GOVERNMENT BUREAUCRATS ARE DIFFERENT."
USA+45 REPRESENT PWR 20. PAGE 45 B0906

ATTIT
DRIVE
TOP/EX
ADMIN
S62

LOCKARD D.,"THE CITY MANAGER, ADMINISTRATIVE THEORY
AND POLITICAL POWER." LEGIS ADMIN REPRESENT GP/REL
PWR. PAGE 66 B1333

MUNIC
EXEC
LEAD

DECISION
S62

OLLERENSHAW K.,"SHARING RESPONSIBLITY." UK DELIB/GP
EDU/PROP EFFICIENCY 20. PAGE 80 B1607

REPRESENT
GP/REL
ADMIN
EX/STRUC
S62

TANNENBAUM A.S.,"CONTROL IN ORGANIZATIONS:
INDIVIDUAL ADJUSTMENT AND ORGANIZATIONAL
PERFORMANCE." DOMIN PARTIC REPRESENT INGP/REL
PRODUC ATTIT DRIVE PWR...PSY CORREL. PAGE 102 B2073

ADMIN
MGT
STRUCT
CONTROL
C62

DE GRAZIA A.,"POLITICAL BEHAVIOR (REV. ED.)" STRATA
POL/PAR LEAD LOBBY ROUTINE WAR CHOOSE REPRESENT
CONSEN ATTIT ORD/FREE BIBLIOG. PAGE 27 B0555

PHIL/SCI
OP/RES
CONCPT
C62

TRUMAN D.B.,"THE GOVERNMENTAL PROCESS: POLITICAL
INTERESTS AND PUBLIC OPINION." POL/PAR ADJUD ADMIN
EXEC LEAD ROUTINE CHOOSE REPRESENT GOV/REL
RIGID/FLEX...POLICY BIBLIOG/A 20. PAGE 105 B2131

LOBBY
EDU/PROP
GP/REL
LEGIS
N62

UNIVERSITY PITT INST LOC GOVT,THE COUNCIL-MANAGER
FORM OF GOVERNMENT IN PENNSYLVANIA (PAMPHLET).
PROVS EX/STRUC REPRESENT GOV/REL EFFICIENCY
...CHARTS SIMUL 20 PENNSYLVAN CITY/MGT. PAGE 107
B2169

LOC/G
TOP/EX
MUNIC
PWR
B63

BLONDEL J.,VOTERS, PARTIES, AND LEADERS. UK ELITES
LOC/G NAT/G PROVS ACT/RES DOMIN REPRESENT GP/REL
INGP/REL...SOC BIBLIOG 20. PAGE 12 B0255

POL/PAR
STRATA
LEGIS
ADMIN
B63

BLUM H.L.,PUBLIC ADMINISTRATION - A PUBLIC HEALTH
VIEWPOINT. USA+45 NAT/G 20. PAGE 13 B0257

REPRESENT
EX/STRUC
EXEC
ADMIN
B63

DOUGLASS H.R.,MODERN ADMINISTRATION OF SECONDARY
SCHOOLS. CLIENT DELIB/GP WORKER REPRESENT INGP/REL
AUTHORIT...TREND BIBLIOG. PAGE 30 B0613

EDU/PROP
ADMIN
SCHOOL
MGT
B63

HATHAWAY D.A.,GOVERNMENT AND AGRICULTURE: PUBLIC
POLICY IN A DEMOCRATIC SOCIETY. USA+45 LEGIS ADMIN
EXEC LOBBY REPRESENT PWR 20. PAGE 48 B0967

AGRI
GOV/REL
PROB/SOLV
EX/STRUC
B63

HAYMAN D.,POLITICAL ACTIVITY RESTRICTION; AN
ANALYSIS WITH RECOMMENDATIONS (PAMPHLET). USA+45
EXEC PARTIC ROLE PWR 20. PAGE 48 B0976

CONTROL
ADMIN
INGP/REL
REPRESENT
B63

HOWER R.M.,MANAGERS AND SCIENTISTS. EX/STRUC CREATE
ADMIN REPRESENT ATTIT DRIVE ROLE PWR SKILL...SOC
INT. PAGE 52 B1052

R+D
MGT
PERS/REL
INGP/REL
B63

MAHESHWARI B.,STUDIES IN PANCHAYATI RAJ. INDIA
POL/PAR EX/STRUC BUDGET EXEC REPRESENT CENTRAL
EFFICIENCY...DECISION 20. PAGE 68 B1378

FEDERAL
LOC/G
GOV/REL
LEAD
B63

PEABODY R.L.,NEW PERSPECTIVES ON THE HOUSE OF
REPRESENTATIVES. AGRI FINAN SCHOOL FORCES CONFER
LEAD CHOOSE REPRESENT FEDERAL...POLICY DECISION
HOUSE/REP. PAGE 82 B1647

NEW/IDEA
LEGIS
PWR
ADMIN
B63

PLISCHKE E.,GOVERNMENT AND POLITICS OF CONTEMPORARY
BERLIN. GERMANY LAW CONSTN POL/PAR LEGIS WAR CHOOSE
REPRESENT GOV/REL...CHARTS BIBLIOG 20 BERLIN.
PAGE 83 B1683

MUNIC
LOC/G
POLICY
ADMIN
B63

RICHARDS P.G.,PATRONAGE IN BRITISH GOVERNMENT.
ELITES DELIB/GP TOP/EX PROB/SOLV CONTROL CT/SYS
EXEC PWR. PAGE 88 B1774

EX/STRUC
REPRESENT
POL/PAR
ADMIN
B63

WOLL P.,ADMINISTRATIVE LAW: THE INFORMAL PROCESS.
USA+45 NAT/G CONTROL EFFICIENCY 20. PAGE 118 B2373

ADMIN
ADJUD
REPRESENT
EX/STRUC
S63

BAKER R.J.,"DISCUSSION AND DECISION-MAKING IN THE
CIVIL SERVICE." UK CONTROL REPRESENT INGP/REL
PERS/REL EFFICIENCY 20. PAGE 8 B0168

EXEC
EX/STRUC
PROB/SOLV
ADMIN
S63

PIPER D.C.,"THE ROLE OF INTER-GOVERNMENTAL
MACHINERY IN CANADIANAMERICAN RELATIONS." CANADA
USA+45 PROB/SOLV REPRESENT 20. PAGE 83 B1676

GOV/REL
ADMIN
EX/STRUC
CONFER
B64

ANDREN N.,GOVERNMENT AND POLITICS IN THE NORDIC
COUNTRIES: DENMARK, FINLAND, ICELAND, NORWAY,
SWEDEN. DENMARK FINLAND ICELAND NORWAY SWEDEN
POL/PAR CHIEF LEGIS ADMIN REGION REPRESENT ATTIT

CONSTN
NAT/G
CULTURE
GOV/COMP

CONSERVE...CHARTS BIBLIOG/A 20. PAGE 5 B0102

B64
ARGYRIS C.,INTEGRATING THE INDIVIDUAL AND THE ADMIN
ORGANIZATION. WORKER PROB/SOLV LEAD SANCTION PERS/REL
REPRESENT ADJUST EFFICIENCY DRIVE PERSON...PSY VOL/ASSN
METH/CNCPT ORG/CHARTS. PAGE 6 B0132 PARTIC

B64
BOYER W.W.,BUREAUCRACY ON TRIAL: POLICY MAKING BY ADMIN
GOVERNMENT AGENCIES. USA+45 NAT/G REPRESENT 20. LOBBY
PAGE 14 B0294 EXEC
EX/STRUC

B64
CATER D.,POWER IN WASHINGTON: A CRITICAL LOOK AT REPRESENT
TODAY'S STRUGGLE TO GOVERN IN THE NATION'S CAPITAL. GOV/REL
USA+45 NAT/G LEGIS ADMIN EXEC LOBBY PLURISM 20. INGP/REL
PAGE 19 B0392 EX/STRUC

B64
CONNECTICUT U INST PUBLIC SERV.SUMMARY OF CHARTER CONSTN
PROVISIONS IN CONNECTICUT LOCAL GOVERNMENT MUNIC
(PAMPHLET). USA+45 DELIB/GP LEGIS TOP/EX CHOOSE LOC/G
REPRESENT 20 CONNECTICT CITY/MGT MAYOR. PAGE 23 EX/STRUC
B0462

B64
COTTER C.P.,POLITICS WITHOUT POWER: THE NATIONAL CHOOSE
PARTY COMMITTEES. USA+45 FINAN NAT/G LOBBY ROUTINE POL/PAR
GP/REL ATTIT ROLE SUPEGO PWR 20. PAGE 24 B0491 REPRESENT
DELIB/GP

B64
ENDACOTT G.B.,GOVERNMENT AND PEOPLE IN HONG KONG CONSTN
1841-1962: A CONSTITUTIONAL HISTORY. UK LEGIS ADJUD COLONIAL
REPRESENT ATTIT 19/20 HONG/KONG. PAGE 33 B0674 CONTROL
ADMIN

B64
GOODMAN W.,THE TWO-PARTY SYSTEM IN THE UNITED POL/PAR
STATES. USA+45 USA-45 STRATA LOC/G CHIEF EDU/PROP REPRESENT
ADMIN COST PWR POPULISM...PLURIST 18/20 PRESIDENT. CHOOSE
PAGE 41 B0821 NAT/G

B64
KEEFE W.J.,THE AMERICAN LEGISLATIVE PROCESS: LEGIS
CONGRESS AND THE STATES. USA+45 LAW POL/PAR DECISION
DELIB/GP DEBATE ADMIN LOBBY REPRESENT CONGRESS PWR
PRESIDENT. PAGE 59 B1187 PROVS

B64
NELSON D.H.,ADMINISTRATIVE AGENCIES OF THE USA: ADMIN
THEIR DECISIONS AND AUTHORITY. USA+45 NAT/G CONTROL EX/STRUC
CT/SYS REPRESENT...DECISION 20. PAGE 78 B1568 ADJUD
LAW

B64
NUQUIST A.E.,TOWN GOVERNMENT IN VERMONT. USA+45 LOC/G
FINAN TOP/EX PROB/SOLV BUDGET TAX REPRESENT SUFF MUNIC
EFFICIENCY...OBS INT 20 VERMONT. PAGE 79 B1595 POPULISM
ADMIN

B64
RIDLEY F.,PUBLIC ADMINISTRATION IN FRANCE. FRANCE ADMIN
UK EX/STRUC CONTROL PARTIC EFFICIENCY 20. PAGE 88 REPRESENT
B1781 GOV/COMP
PWR

S64
HADY T.F.,"CONGRESSIONAL TOWNSHIPS AS INCORPORATED MUNIC
MUNICIPALITIES." NEIGH ADMIN REPRESENT ATTIT GEOG. REGION
PAGE 45 B0914 LOC/G
GOV/COMP

S64
KAMMERER G.M.,"URBAN LEADERSHIP DURING CHANGE." MUNIC
LEAD PARTIC REPRESENT GP/REL PLURISM...DECISION PWR
GP/COMP. PAGE 58 B1164 ELITES
EXEC

B65
AIYAR S.P.,STUDIES IN INDIAN DEMOCRACY. INDIA ORD/FREE
STRATA ECO/UNDEV LABOR POL/PAR LEGIS DIPLOM LOBBY REPRESENT
REGION CHOOSE ATTIT SOCISM...ANTHOL 20. PAGE 3 ADMIN
B0067 NAT/G

B65
BOXER C.R.,PORTUGUESE SOCIETY IN THE TROPICS - THE MUNIC
MUNICIPAL COUNCILS OF GAO, MACAO, BAHIA, AND ADMIN
LUANDA, 1510-1800. EUR+WWI MOD/EUR PORTUGAL CONSTN COLONIAL
EX/STRUC DOMIN CONTROL ROUTINE REPRESENT PRIVIL DELIB/GP
...BIBLIOG/A 16/19 GENACCOUNT MACAO BAHIA LUANDA.
PAGE 14 B0290

B65
COHEN H.,THE DEMONICS OF BUREAUCRACY: PROBLEMS OF EXEC
CHANGE IN A GOVERNMENT AGENCY. USA+45 CLIENT EX/STRUC
ROUTINE REPRESENT 20. PAGE 22 B0443 INGP/REL
ADMIN

B65
MARTIN R.,PUBLIC ADMINISTRATION AND DEMOCRACY. EX/STRUC
ELITES NAT/G ADMIN EXEC ROUTINE INGP/REL. PAGE 70 DECISION
B1412 REPRESENT
GP/REL

B65
MASTERS N.A.,COMMITTEE ASSIGNMENTS IN THE HOUSE OF LEAD
REPRESENTATIVES (BMR). USA+45 ELITES POL/PAR LEGIS
EX/STRUC PARTIC REPRESENT GP/REL PERS/REL ATTIT PWR CHOOSE
...STAT CHARTS 20 HOUSE/REP. PAGE 71 B1425 DELIB/GP

B65
ROURKE F.E.,BUREAUCRATIC POWER IN NATIONAL EX/STRUC

POLITICS. ADMIN CONTROL EXEC GOV/REL INGP/REL 20. EFFICIENCY
PAGE 91 B1838 REPRESENT
PWR

B65
SCHAPIRO L.,THE GOVERNMENT AND POLITICS OF THE MARXISM
SOVIET UNION. USSR WOR+45 WOR-45 ADMIN PARTIC REV GOV/REL
CHOOSE REPRESENT PWR...POLICY IDEA/COMP 20. PAGE 93 NAT/G
B1880 LOC/G

L65
HOOK S.,"SECOND THOUGHTS ON BERKELEY" USA+45 ELITES ACADEM
INTELL LEGIT ADMIN COERCE REPRESENT GP/REL INGP/REL ORD/FREE
TOTALISM AGE/Y MARXISM 20 BERKELEY FREE/SPEE POLICY
STUDNT/PWR. PAGE 51 B1040 CREATE

S65
LONG T.G.,"THE ADMINISTRATIVE PROCESS: AGONIZING ADJUD
REAPPRAISAL IN THE FTC." NAT/G REPRESENT 20 FTC. LOBBY
PAGE 66 B1339 ADMIN
EX/STRUC

B66
AARON T.J.,THE CONTROL OF POLICE DISCRETION: THE CONTROL
DANISH EXPERIENCE. DENMARK LAW CREATE ADMIN FORCES
INGP/REL SUPEGO PWR 20 OMBUDSMAN. PAGE 2 B0049 REPRESENT
PROB/SOLV

B66
AMER ENTERPRISE INST PUB POL.CONGRESS: THE FIRST EFFICIENCY
BRANCH OF GOVERNMENT. EX/STRUC FEEDBACK REPRESENT LEGIS
INGP/REL PWR...DECISION METH/CNCPT PREDICT. PAGE 4 DELIB/GP
B0081 CONTROL

B66
BAKKE E.W.,MUTUAL SURVIVAL: THE GOAL OF UNION AND MGT
MANAGEMENT (2ND ED.). USA+45 ELITES ECO/DEV ECO/TAC LABOR
CONFER ADMIN REPRESENT GP/REL INGP/REL ATTIT BARGAIN
...GP/COMP 20. PAGE 8 B0170 INDUS

B66
CARALEY D.,PARTY POLITICS AND NATIONAL ELECTIONS. POL/PAR
USA+45 STRATA LOC/G PROVS EX/STRUC BARGAIN ADMIN CHOOSE
SANCTION GP/REL ATTIT 20 DEMOCRAT REPUBLICAN. REPRESENT
PAGE 18 B0375 NAT/G

B66
DAHLBERG J.S.,THE NEW YORK BUREAU OF MUNICIPAL PROVS
RESEARCH: PIONEER IN GOVERNMENT ADMINISTRATION. MUNIC
CONSTN R+D BUDGET EDU/PROP PARTIC REPRESENT DELIB/GP
EFFICIENCY ORD/FREE...BIBLIOG METH 20 NEW/YORK ADMIN
NIPA. PAGE 26 B0522

B66
DILLEY M.R.,BRITISH POLICY IN KENYA COLONY (2ND COLONIAL
ED.). AFR INDIA UK LABOR BUDGET TAX ADMIN PARL/PROC REPRESENT
GP/REL...BIBLIOG 20 PARLIAMENT. PAGE 29 B0594 SOVEREIGN

B66
GERBERDING W.P.,UNITED STATES FOREIGN POLICY: PROB/SOLV
PERSPECTIVES AND ANALYSIS. USA+45 LEGIS EXEC LEAD CHIEF
REPRESENT PWR 20. PAGE 39 B0791 EX/STRUC
CONTROL

B66
HESSLER I.O.,29 WAYS TO GOVERN A CITY. EX/STRUC MUNIC
TOP/EX PROB/SOLV PARTIC CHOOSE REPRESENT EFFICIENCY GOV/COMP
...CHARTS 20 CITY/MGT MAYOR. PAGE 49 B0998 LOC/G
ADMIN

B66
RICHARD J.B.,GOVERNMENT AND POLITICS OF WYOMING. PROVS
USA+45 POL/PAR EX/STRUC LEGIS CT/SYS LOBBY APPORT LOC/G
CHOOSE REPRESENT 20 WYOMING GOVERNOR. PAGE 88 B1773 ADMIN

B66
SILBERMAN B.S.,MODERN JAPANESE LEADERSHIP; LEAD
TRANSITION AND CHANGE. NAT/G POL/PAR CHIEF ADMIN CULTURE
REPRESENT GP/REL ADJUST RIGID/FLEX...SOC METH/COMP ELITES
ANTHOL 19/20 CHINJAP CHRISTIAN. PAGE 97 B1952 MUNIC

B66
STREET D.,ORGANIZATION FOR TREATMENT. CLIENT PROVS GP/COMP
PUB/INST PLAN CONTROL PARTIC REPRESENT ATTIT PWR AGE/Y
...POLICY BIBLIOG. PAGE 101 B2052 ADMIN
VOL/ASSN

L66
CRAIN R.L.,"STRUCTURE AND VALUES IN LOCAL POLITICAL MUNIC
SYSTEMS: THE CASE OF FLUORIDATION DECISIONS." EDU/PROP
EX/STRUC LEGIS LEAD PARTIC REPRESENT PWR...DECISION LOC/G
GOV/COMP. PAGE 25 B0501 ATTIT

S66
BURDETTE F.L.,"SELECTED ARTICLES AND DOCUMENTS ON BIBLIOG
AMERICAN GOVERNMENT AND POLITICS." LAW LOC/G MUNIC USA+45
NAT/G POL/PAR PROVS LEGIS BAL/PWR ADMIN EXEC JURID
REPRESENT MGT. PAGE 17 B0348 CONSTN

S66
SNOWISS L.M.,"CONGRESSIONAL RECRUITMENT AND LEGIS
REPRESENTATION." USA+45 LG/CO MUNIC POL/PAR ADMIN REPRESENT
REGION CONGRESS CHICAGO. PAGE 98 B1990 CHOOSE
LOC/G

S66
WOLFINGER R.E.,"POLITICAL ETHOS AND THE STRUCTURE MUNIC
OF CITY GOVERNMENT." POL/PAR EX/STRUC REPRESENT ATTIT
GP/REL PERS/REL RIGID/FLEX PWR. PAGE 118 B2371 STRATA
GOV/COMP

C66
JACOB H.,"DIMENSIONS OF STATE POLITICS HEARD A. ED. PROVS
STATE LEGIWLATURES IN AMERICAN POLITICS." CULTURE LEGIS
STRATA POL/PAR BUDGET TAX LOBBY ROUTINE GOV/REL ROLE

...TRADIT DECISION GEOG. PAGE 55 B1112   REPRESENT
                                                          B67
BULPITT J.G.,PARTY POLITICS IN ENGLISH LOCAL   POL/PAR
GOVERNMENT. UK CONSTN ACT/RES TAX CONTROL CHOOSE   LOC/G
REPRESENT GOV/REL KNOWL 20. PAGE 17 B0344   ELITES
                                                     EX/STRUC
                                                          B67
BUREAU GOVERNMENT RES AND SERV,COUNTY GOVERNMENT   BIBLIOG/A
REORGANIZATION - A SELECTED ANNOTATED BIBLIOGRAPHY   APPORT
(PAPER). USA+45 USA-45 LAW CONSTN MUNIC PROVS   LOC/G
EX/STRUC CREATE PLAN PROB/SOLV REPRESENT GOV/REL   ADMIN
20. PAGE 17 B0349
                                                          B67
FARNSWORTH B.,WILLIAM C. BULLITT AND THE SOVIET   DIPLOM
UNION. COM USA-45 USSR NAT/G CHIEF CONSULT DELIB/GP BIOG
EX/STRUC WAR REPRESENT MARXISM 20 WILSON/W   POLICY
ROOSEVLT/F STALIN/J BULLITT/WC. PAGE 35 B0705
                                                          B67
GELLHORN W.,OMBUDSMEN AND OTHERS: CITIZENS'   NAT/COMP
PROTECTORS IN NINE COUNTRIES. WOR+45 LAW CONSTN   REPRESENT
LEGIS INSPECT ADJUD ADMIN CONTROL CT/SYS CHOOSE   INGP/REL
PERS/REL...STAT CHARTS 20. PAGE 39 B0789   PROB/SOLV
                                                          B67
ILLINOIS COMMISSION,IMPROVING THE STATE   PROVS
LEGISLATURE. USA+45 LAW CONSTN NAT/G PROB/SOLV   LEGIS
EDU/PROP ADMIN TASK CHOOSE INGP/REL EFFICIENCY   REPRESENT
ILLINOIS. PAGE 53 B1077   PLAN
                                                          B67
MENHENNET D.,PARLIAMENT IN PERSPECTIVE. UK ROUTINE   LEGIS
REPRESENT ROLE PWR 20 PARLIAMENT. PAGE 73 B1467   PARL/PROC
                                                     CONCPT
                                                     POPULISM
                                                          B67
SCHLOSSBERG S.I.,ORGANIZING AND THE LAW. USA+45   LABOR
WORKER PLAN LEGIT REPRESENT GP/REL...JURID MGT 20   CONSULT
NLRB. PAGE 94 B1893   BARGAIN
                                                     PRIVIL
                                                          B67
US SENATE COMM ON FOREIGN REL,HUMAN RIGHTS   LEGIS
CONVENTIONS. USA+45 LABOR VOL/ASSN DELIB/GP DOMIN   ORD/FREE
ADJUD REPRESENT...INT/LAW MGT CONGRESS. PAGE 110   WORKER
B2225   LOBBY
                                                          B67
WATERS M.,THE UNITED NATIONS* INTERNATIONAL   CONSTN
ORGANIZATION AND ADMINISTRATION. WOR+45 EX/STRUC   INT/ORG
FORCES DIPLOM LEAD REGION ARMS/CONT REPRESENT   ADMIN
INGP/REL ROLE...METH/COMP ANTHOL 20 UN LEAGUE/NAT.   ADJUD
PAGE 114 B2301
                                                          S67
CARIAS B.,"EL CONTROL DE LAS EMPRESAS PUBLICAS POR   WORKER
GRUPOS DE INTERESES DE LA COMUNIDAD." FRANCE UK   REPRESENT
VENEZUELA INDUS NAT/G CONTROL OWN PWR...DECISION   MGT
NAT/COMP 20. PAGE 18 B0377   SOCISM
                                                          S67
CROCKETT D.G.,"THE MP AND HIS CONSTITUENTS." UK   EXEC
POL/PAR...DECISION 20. PAGE 25 B0506   NAT/G
                                                     PERS/REL
                                                     REPRESENT
                                                          S67
DRYDEN S.,"LOCAL GOVERNMENT IN TANZANIA PART II"   LOC/G
TANZANIA LAW NAT/G POL/PAR CONTROL PARTIC REPRESENT GOV/REL
...DECISION 20. PAGE 31 B0622   ADMIN
                                                     STRUCT
                                                          S67
GRUNDY K.W.,"THE POLITICAL USES OF IMAGINATION."   NAT/LISM
GHANA ELITES SOCIETY NAT/G DOMIN EDU/PROP COLONIAL   EX/STRUC
REGION REPRESENT GP/REL CENTRAL PWR MARXISM 20.   AFR
PAGE 44 B0897   LEAD
                                                          S67
HALL B.,"THE PAINTER'S UNION: A PARTIAL VICTORY."   LABOR
USA+45 PROB/SOLV LEGIT ADMIN REPRESENT 20. PAGE 45   CHIEF
B0922   CHOOSE
                                                     CRIME
                                                          S67
HALL B.,"THE COALITION AGAINST DISHWASHERS." USA+45 LABOR
POL/PAR PROB/SOLV BARGAIN LEAD CHOOSE REPRESENT   ADMIN
GP/REL ORD/FREE PWR...POLICY 20. PAGE 46 B0923   DOMIN
                                                     WORKER
                                                          S67
IDENBURG P.J.,"POLITICAL STRUCTURAL DEVELOPMENT IN   AFR
TROPICAL AFRICA." UK ECO/UNDEV KIN POL/PAR CHIEF   CONSTN
EX/STRUC CREATE COLONIAL CONTROL REPRESENT RACE/REL NAT/G
...MAJORIT TREND 20. PAGE 53 B1074   GOV/COMP
                                                          S67
KURON J.,"AN OPEN LETTER TO THE PARTY." CONSTN   ELITES
WORKER BUDGET EDU/PROP ADMIN REPRESENT SUFF OWN   STRUCT
...SOCIALIST 20. PAGE 62 B1244   POL/PAR
                                                     ECO/TAC
                                                          S67
MAINZER L.C.,"HONOR IN THE BUREAUCRATIC LIFE."   ADMIN
REPRESENT EFFICIENCY 20. PAGE 68 B1382   MORAL
                                                     EX/STRUC
                                                     EXEC
                                                          S67
RAUM O.,"THE MODERN LEADERSHIP GROUP AMONG THE   RACE/REL
SOUTH AFRICAN XHOSA." SOUTH/AFR SOCIETY SECT   KIN

EX/STRUC REPRESENT GP/REL INGP/REL PERSON   LEAD
...METH/COMP 17/20 XHOSA NEGRO. PAGE 86 B1743   CULTURE
                                                          S67
SPACKMAN A.,"THE SENATE OF TRINIDAD AND TOBAGO."   ELITES
L/A+17C TRINIDAD WEST/IND NAT/G POL/PAR DELIB/GP   EFFICIENCY
OP/RES PROB/SOLV EDU/PROP EXEC LOBBY ROUTINE   LEGIS
REPRESENT GP/REL 20. PAGE 99 B2002   DECISION
                                                          S67
TIVEY L.,"THE POLITICAL CONSEQUENCES OF ECONOMIC   PLAN
PLANNING." UK CONSTN INDUS ACT/RES ADMIN CONTROL   POLICY
LOBBY REPRESENT EFFICIENCY SUPEGO SOVEREIGN   NAT/G
...DECISION 20. PAGE 104 B2112
                                                          B87
KINNEAR J.B.,PRINCIPLES OF CIVIL GOVERNMENT.   POL/PAR
MOD/EUR USA-45 CONSTN LOC/G EX/STRUC ADMIN   NAT/G
PARL/PROC RACE/REL...CONCPT 18/19. PAGE 60 B1210   GOV/COMP
                                                     REPRESENT

REPUBLIC OF CHINA....SEE TAIWAN

REPUBLICAN....REPUBLICAN PARTY (ALL NATIONS)

                                                          S59
JEWELL M.R.,"THE SENATE REPUBLICAN POLICY COMMITTEE POL/PAR
AND FOREIGN POLICY." PLAN ADMIN CONTROL LEAD LOBBY   NAT/G
EFFICIENCY PRESIDENT 20 REPUBLICAN. PAGE 56 B1139   DELIB/GP
                                                     POLICY
                                                          B60
MORISON E.E.,TURMOIL AND TRADITION: A STUDY OF THE   BIOG
LIFE AND TIMES OF HENRY L. STIMSON. USA+45 USA-45   NAT/G
POL/PAR CHIEF DELIB/GP FORCES BAL/PWR DIPLOM   EX/STRUC
ARMS/CONT WAR PEACE 19/20 STIMSON/HL ROOSEVLT/F
TAFT/WH HOOVER/H REPUBLICAN. PAGE 75 B1525
                                                          B64
RIGGS R.E.,THE MOVEMENT FOR ADMINISTRATIVE   ADMIN
REORGANIZATION IN ARIZONA. USA+45 LAW POL/PAR   PROVS
DELIB/GP LEGIS PROB/SOLV CONTROL RIGID/FLEX PWR   CREATE
...ORG/CHARTS 20 ARIZONA DEMOCRAT REPUBLICAN.   PLAN
PAGE 88 B1786
                                                          B66
CARALEY D.,PARTY POLITICS AND NATIONAL ELECTIONS.   POL/PAR
USA+45 STRATA LOC/G PROVS EX/STRUC BARGAIN ADMIN   CHOOSE
SANCTION GP/REL ATTIT 20 DEMOCRAT REPUBLICAN.   REPRESENT
PAGE 18 B0375   NAT/G
                                                          B67
PRINCE C.E.,NEW JERSEY'S JEFFERSONIAN REPUBLICANS;   POL/PAR
THE GENESIS OF AN EARLY PARTY MACHINE (1789-1817).   CONSTN
USA-45 LOC/G EDU/PROP PRESS CONTROL CHOOSE...CHARTS ADMIN
18/19 NEW/JERSEY REPUBLICAN. PAGE 84 B1707   PROVS

RESEARCH....SEE ACT/RES, OP/RES, R+D, CREATE

RESEARCH AND DEVELOPMENT GROUP....SEE R+D

RESERVE SYSTEM, FEDERAL....SEE FED/RESERV

RESIST/INT....SOCIAL RESISTANCE TO INTERVIEWS

RESOURCE/N....NATURAL RESOURCES

                                                          B47
MILLETT J.D.,THE PROCESS AND ORGANIZATION OF   ADMIN
GOVERNMENT PLANNING. USA+45 DELIB/GP ACT/RES LEAD   NAT/G
LOBBY TASK...POLICY GEOG TIME 20 RESOURCE/N.   PLAN
PAGE 73 B1482   CONSULT
                                                          B61
LEE R.R.,ENGINEERING-ECONOMIC PLANNING   BIBLIOG/A
MISCELLANEOUS SUBJECTS: A SELECTED BIBLIOGRAPHY   PLAN
(MIMEOGRAPHED). FINAN LOC/G MUNIC NEIGH ADMIN   REGION
CONTROL INGP/REL HABITAT...GEOG MGT SOC/WK 20
RESOURCE/N. PAGE 63 B1280
                                                          B66
DAVIS J.A.,SOUTHERN AFRICA IN TRANSITION. SOUTH/AFR AFR
USA+45 FINAN NAT/G DELIB/GP EDU/PROP ADMIN COLONIAL ADJUST
REGION RACE/REL ATTIT SOVEREIGN...ANTHOL 20   CONSTN
RESOURCE/N. PAGE 26 B0538

RESPECT....RESPECT, SOCIAL CLASS, STRATIFICATION (CONTEMPT)

                                                          B16
TREITSCHKE H.,POLITICS. UNIV SOCIETY STRATA NAT/G   EXEC
EX/STRUC LEGIS DOMIN EDU/PROP ATTIT PWR RESPECT   ELITES
...CONCPT TIME/SEQ GEN/LAWS TOT/POP 20. PAGE 105   GERMANY
B2127
                                                          B17
CORWIN E.S.,THE PRESIDENT'S CONTROL OF FOREIGN   TOP/EX
RELATIONS. FUT USA-45 CONSTN STRATA NAT/G CHIEF   PWR
EX/STRUC LEGIS KNOWL RESPECT...JURID CONCPT TREND   DIPLOM
CONGRESS VAL/FREE 20 PRESIDENT. PAGE 24 B0483
                                                          S44
SIMON H.A.,"DECISION-MAKING AND ADMINISTRATIVE   DECISION
ORGANIZATION" (BMR)" WOR-45 CHOOSE INGP/REL   ADMIN
EFFICIENCY ATTIT RESPECT...MGT 20. PAGE 97 B1955   CONTROL
                                                     WORKER
                                                          B47
TAPPAN P.W.,DELINQUENT GIRLS IN COURT. USA-45 MUNIC CT/SYS

EX/STRUC FORCES ADMIN EXEC ADJUST SEX RESPECT ...JURID SOC/WK 20 NEWYORK/C FEMALE/SEX. PAGE 103 B2078
AGE/Y CRIME ADJUD

GUETZKOW H.,GROUPS, LEADERSHIP, AND MEN. FACE/GP SECT EDU/PROP EXEC PERSON RESPECT...PERS/TEST GEN/METH 20. PAGE 44 B0901
B51 ATTIT SOC ELITES

BRUEGEL J.W.,"DIE INTERNAZIONALE GEWERKSCHAFTSBEWEGUNG." COM EUR+WWI USA+45 WOR+45 DELIB/GP EX/STRUC ECO/TAC EDU/PROP ATTIT PWR RESPECT SKILL WEALTH WORK 20. PAGE 16 B0330
S52 VOL/ASSN LABOR TOTALISM

MEYER P.,THE JEWS IN THE SOVIET SATELLITES. CZECHOSLVK POLAND SOCIETY STRATA NAT/G BAL/PWR ECO/TAC EDU/PROP LEGIT ADMIN COERCE ATTIT DISPL PERCEPT HEALTH PWR RESPECT WEALTH...METH/CNCPT JEWS VAL/FREE NAZI 20. PAGE 73 B1474
B53 COM SECT TOTALISM USSR

ALLPORT G.W.,THE NATURE OF PREJUDICE. USA+45 WOR+45 STRATA FACE/GP KIN NEIGH SECT ADMIN GP/REL DISCRIM ATTIT DRIVE LOVE RESPECT...PSY SOC MYTH QU/SEMANT 20. PAGE 4 B0078
B54 CULTURE PERSON RACE/REL

BERNAYS E.L.,THE ENGINEERING OF CONSENT. VOL/ASSN OP/RES ROUTINE INGP/REL ATTIT RESPECT...POLICY METH/CNCPT METH/COMP 20. PAGE 11 B0224
B55 GP/REL PLAN ACT/RES ADJUST

MANNONI D.O.,PROSPERO AND CALIBAN: THE PSYCHOLOGY OF COLONIZATION. AFR EUR+WWI FAM KIN MUNIC SECT DOMIN ADMIN ATTIT DRIVE LOVE PWR RESPECT...PSY SOC CONCPT MYTH OBS DEEP/INT BIOG GEN/METH MALAGASY 20. PAGE 69 B1394
B56 CULTURE COLONIAL

KIETH-LUCAS A.,DECISIONS ABOUT PEOPLE IN NEED, A STUDY OF ADMINISTRATIVE RESPONSIVENESS IN PUBLIC ASSISTANCE. USA+45 GIVE RECEIVE INGP/REL PERS/REL MORAL RESPECT WEALTH...SOC OBS BIBLIOG 20. PAGE 60 B1204
B57 ADMIN RIGID/FLEX SOC/WK DECISION

COLEMAN J.S.,NIGERIA: BACKGROUND TO NATIONALISM. AFR SOCIETY ECO/DEV KIN LOC/G POL/PAR TEC/DEV DOMIN ADMIN DRIVE PWR RESPECT...TRADIT SOC INT SAMP TIME/SEQ 20. PAGE 22 B0452
B58 NAT/G NAT/LISM NIGERIA

SKINNER G.W.,LEADERSHIP AND POWER IN THE CHINESE COMMUNITY OF THAILAND. ASIA S/ASIA STRATA FACE/GP KIN PROF/ORG VOL/ASSN EX/STRUC DOMIN PERSON RESPECT ...METH/CNCPT STAT INT QU BIOG CHARTS 20. PAGE 98 B1974
B58 SOC ELITES THAILAND

MAIR L.P.,"REPRESENTATIVE LOCAL GOVERNMENT AS A PROBLEM IN SOCIAL CHANGE." ECO/UNDEV KIN LOC/G NAT/G SCHOOL JUDGE ADMIN ROUTINE REPRESENT RIGID/FLEX RESPECT...CONCPT STERTYP CMN/WLTH 20. PAGE 68 B1383
S58 AFR PWR ELITES

YANG C.K.,A CHINESE VILLAGE IN EARLY COMMUNIST TRANSITION. ECO/UNDEV AGRI FAM KIN MUNIC FORCES PLAN ECO/TAC DOMIN EDU/PROP ATTIT DRIVE PWR RESPECT ...SOC CONCPT METH/CNCPT OBS RECORD CON/ANAL CHARTS WORK 20. PAGE 118 B2389
B59 ASIA ROUTINE SOCISM

SUTTON F.X.,"REPRESENTATION AND THE NATURE OF POLITICAL SYSTEMS." UNIV WOR-45 CULTURE SOCIETY STRATA INT/ORG FORCES JUDGE DOMIN LEGIT EXEC REGION REPRESENT ATTIT ORD/FREE RESPECT...SOC HIST/WRIT TIME/SEQ. PAGE 102 B2057
S59 NAT/G CONCPT

BASS B.M.,LEADERSHIP, PSYCHOLOGY, AND ORGANIZATIONAL BEHAVIOR. DOMIN CHOOSE DRIVE PERSON PWR RESPECT SKILL...SOC METH/CNCPT OBS. PAGE 9 B0193
B60 UNIV FACE/GP DELIB/GP ROUTINE

BOGARDUS E.S.,"THE SOCIOLOGY OF A STRUCTURED PEACE." FUT SOCIETY CREATE DIPLOM EDU/PROP ADJUD ROUTINE ATTIT RIGID/FLEX KNOWL ORD/FREE RESPECT ...POLICY INT/LAW JURID NEW/IDEA SELF/OBS TOT/POP 20 UN. PAGE 13 B0264
S60 INT/ORG SOC NAT/LISM PEACE

KOESTLER A.,THE LOTUS AND THE ROBOT. ASIA INDIA S/ASIA SOCIETY STRATA ECO/DEV AGRI INDUS FAM CREATE DOMIN EDU/PROP ADMIN COERCE ATTIT DRIVE SUPEGO ORD/FREE PWR RESPECT WEALTH...MYTH OBS 20 CHINJAP. PAGE 61 B1226
B61 SECT ECO/UNDEV

LASSWELL H.D.,PSYCOPATHOLOGY AND POLITICS. WOR-45 CULTURE SOCIETY FACE/GP NAT/G CONSULT CREATE EDU/PROP EXEC ROUTINE DISPL DRIVE PERSON PWR RESPECT...PSY CONCPT METH/CNCPT METH. PAGE 63 B1272
B61 ATTIT GEN/METH

MARX K.,THE COMMUNIST MANIFESTO. IN (MENDEL A. ESSENTIAL WORKS OF MARXISM, NEW YORK: BANTAM. FUT MOD/EUR CULTURE ECO/DEV ECO/UNDEV AGRI FINAN INDUS MARKET PROC/MFG LABOR MUNIC POL/PAR CONSULT FORCES
B61 COM NEW/IDEA CAP/ISM REV

CREATE PLAN ADMIN ATTIT DRIVE RIGID/FLEX ORD/FREE PWR RESPECT MARX/KARL WORK. PAGE 70 B1421

TANNENBAUM R.,LEADERSHIP AND ORGANIZATION. STRUCT ADMIN INGP/REL ATTIT PERCEPT...DECISION METH/CNCPT OBS CHARTS BIBLIOG. PAGE 103 B2075
B61 LEAD MGT RESPECT ROLE

KOGAN N.,THE POLITICS OF ITALIAN FOREIGN POLICY. EUR+WWI LEGIS DOMIN LEGIT EXEC PWR RESPECT SKILL ...POLICY DECISION HUM SOC METH/CNCPT OBS INT CHARTS 20. PAGE 61 B1227
B63 NAT/G ROUTINE DIPLOM ITALY

SINGER M.R.,THE EMERGING ELITE: A STUDY OF POLITICAL LEADERSHIP IN CEYLON. S/ASIA ECO/UNDEV AGRI KIN NAT/G SECT EX/STRUC LEGIT ATTIT DRIVE RESPECT...SOC STAT CHARTS 20. PAGE 97 B1967
B64 TOP/EX STRATA NAT/LISM CEYLON

WILSON L.,THE ACADEMIC MAN. STRUCT FINAN PROF/ORG OP/RES ADMIN AUTHORIT ROLE RESPECT...SOC STAT. PAGE 117 B2360
B64 ACADEM INGP/REL STRATA DELIB/GP

SYMONDS R.,"REFLECTIONS IN LOCALISATION." AFR S/ASIA UK STRATA INT/ORG NAT/G SCHOOL EDU/PROP LEGIT KNOWL ORD/FREE PWR RESPECT CMN/WLTH 20. PAGE 102 B2064
L64 ADMIN MGT COLONIAL

CLIGNET R.,"POTENTIAL ELITES IN GHANA AND THE IVORY COAST: A PRELIMINARY SURVEY." AFR CULTURE ELITES STRATA KIN NAT/G SECT DOMIN EXEC ORD/FREE RESPECT SKILL...POLICY RELATIV GP/COMP NAT/COMP 20. PAGE 21 B0438
S64 PWR LEGIT IVORY/CST GHANA

KHAN M.Z.,"THE PRESIDENT OF THE GENERAL ASSEMBLY." WOR+45 CONSTN DELIB/GP EDU/PROP LEGIT ROUTINE PWR RESPECT SKILL...DECISION SOC BIOG TREND UN 20. PAGE 59 B1202
S64 INT/ORG TOP/EX

LOW D.A.,"LION RAMPANT." EUR+WWI MOD/EUR S/ASIA ECO/UNDEV NAT/G FORCES TEC/DEV ECO/TAC LEGIT ADMIN COLONIAL COERCE ORD/FREE RESPECT 19/20. PAGE 67 B1344
S64 AFR DOMIN DIPLOM UK

HARR J.E.,THE DEVELOPMENT OF CAREERS IN THE FOREIGN SERVICE. CREATE SENIOR EXEC FEEDBACK GOV/REL EFFICIENCY ATTIT RESPECT ORG/CHARTS. PAGE 47 B0953
B65 OP/RES MGT ADMIN DIPLOM

MCKENZIE J.L.,AUTHORITY IN THE CHURCH. STRUCT LEAD INGP/REL PERS/REL CENTRAL ANOMIE ATTIT ORD/FREE RESPECT CATH. PAGE 72 B1452
B66 SECT AUTHORIT PWR ADMIN

LLOYD K.,"URBAN RACE RIOTS V EFFECTIVE ANTI-DISCRIMINATION AGENCIES* AN END OR A BEGINNING?" USA+45 STRATA ACT/RES ADMIN ADJUST ORD/FREE RESPECT ...PLURIST DECISION SOC SOC/WK. PAGE 66 B1332
S67 GP/REL DISCRIM LOC/G CROWD

ROSE A.M.,"CONFIDENCE AND THE CORPORATION." LG/CO CONTROL CRIME INCOME PROFIT 20. PAGE 90 B1818
S67 INDUS EX/STRUC VOL/ASSN RESPECT

RESPONSIBILITY....SEE SUPEGO, RESPECT

RESPONSIVENESS....SEE RIGID/FLEX

RESTRAINT....SEE ORD/FREE

RETAILING....SEE MARKET

RETIREMENT....SEE SENIOR, ADMIN

REUTHER/W....WALTER REUTHER

REV....REVOLUTION; SEE ALSO WAR

TREVELYAN G.M.,THE TWO-PARTY SYSTEM IN ENGLISH POLITICAL HISTORY (PAMPHLET). UK CHIEF LEGIS COLONIAL EXEC REV CHOOSE 17/19. PAGE 105 B2128
N19 PARL/PROC POL/PAR NAT/G PWR

HARPER S.N.,THE GOVERNMENT OF THE SOVIET UNION. COM USSR LAW CONSTN ECO/DEV PLAN TEC/DEV DIPLOM INT/TRADE ADMIN REV NAT/LISM...POLICY 20. PAGE 47 B0952
B38 MARXISM NAT/G LEAD POL/PAR

PETTEE G.S.,THE PROCESS OF REVOLUTION. COM FRANCE ITALY MOD/EUR RUSSIA SPAIN WOR-45 ELITES INTELL SOCIETY STRATA STRUCT INT/ORG NAT/G POL/PAR ACT/RES PLAN EDU/PROP LEGIT EXEC...SOC MYTH TIME/SEQ TOT/POP 18/20. PAGE 82 B1664
B38 COERCE CONCPT REV

PALMER J.M.,AMERICA IN ARMS: THE EXPERIENCE OF THE
B41 FORCES

UNITED STATES WITH MILITARY ORGANIZATION. FUT
USA-45 LEAD REV PWR 18/20 WASHINGT/G KNOX/HENRY
PRE/US/AM. PAGE 81 B1627
  NAT/G ADMIN WAR

           B50
PERHAM M.,COLONIAL GOVERNMENT: ANNOTATED READING
LIST ON BRITISH COLONIAL GOVERNMENT. UK WOR+45
WOR-45 ECO/UNDEV INT/ORG LEGIS FOR/AID INT/TRADE
DOMIN ADMIN REV 20. PAGE 82 B1655
  BIBLIOG/A COLONIAL GOV/REL NAT/G

           C51
MOORE B.,"SOVIET POLITICS - THE DILEMMA OF POWER:
THE ROLE OF IDEAS IN SOCIAL CHANGE." USSR PROB/SOLV
DIPLOM EDU/PROP ADMIN LEAD ROUTINE REV...POLICY
DECISION BIBLIOG 20. PAGE 75 B1512
  ATTIT PWR CONCPT MARXISM

           B52
BRINTON C.,THE ANATOMY OF REVOLUTION. FRANCE UK
USA-45 USSR WOR+45 WOR-45 ELITES INTELL ECO/DEV NAT/G
EX/STRUC FORCES COERCE DRIVE ORD/FREE PWR SOVEREIGN
...MYTH HIST/WRIT GEN/LAWS. PAGE 15 B0311
  SOCIETY CONCPT REV

           B52
SELZNICK P.,THE ORGANIZATIONAL WEAPON: A STUDY OF
BOLSHEVIK STRATEGY AND TACTICS. USSR SOCIETY STRATA
LABOR DOMIN EDU/PROP PARTIC REV ATTIT PWR...POLICY
MGT CONCPT 20 BOLSHEVISM. PAGE 95 B1929
  MARXISM POL/PAR LEAD TOTALISM

           B55
BAILEY S.K.,RESEARCH FRONTIERS IN POLITICS AND
GOVERNMENT. CONSTN LEGIS ADMIN REV CHOOSE...CONCPT
IDEA/COMP GAME ANTHOL 20. PAGE 8 B0164
  R+D METH NAT/G

           B55
DE ARAGAO J.G.,LA JURIDICTION ADMINISTRATIVE AU
BRESIL. BRAZIL ADJUD COLONIAL CT/SYS REV FEDERAL
ORD/FREE...BIBLIOG 19/20. PAGE 27 B0549
  EX/STRUC ADMIN NAT/G

           B55
MAZZINI J.,THE DUTIES OF MAN. MOD/EUR LAW SOCIETY
FAM NAT/G POL/PAR SECT VOL/ASSN EX/STRUC ACT/RES
CREATE REV PEACE ATTIT ALL/VALS...GEN/LAWS WORK 19.
PAGE 71 B1439
  SUPEGO CONCPT NAT/LISM

           B56
WU E.,LEADERS OF TWENTIETH-CENTURY CHINA; AN
ANNOTATED BIBLIOGRAPHY OF SELECTED CHINESE
BIOGRAPHICAL WORKS IN HOOVER LIBRARY. ASIA INDUS
POL/PAR DIPLOM ADMIN REV WAR...HUM MGT 20. PAGE 118
B2386
  BIBLIOG/A BIOG INTELL CHIEF

           B58
LOVEJOY D.S.,RHODE ISLAND POLITICS AND THE AMERICAN
REVOLUTION 1760-1776. UK USA-45 ELITES EX/STRUC TAX
LEAD REPRESENT GOV/REL GP/REL ATTIT 18 RHODE/ISL.
PAGE 67 B1343
  REV COLONIAL ECO/TAC SOVEREIGN

           B60
DRAPER T.,AMERICAN COMMUNISM AND SOVIET RUSSIA.
EUR+WWI USA+45 USSR INTELL AGRI COM/IND FINAN INDUS
LABOR PROF/ORG VOL/ASSN PLAN TEC/DEV DOMIN EDU/PROP
ADMIN COERCE REV PERSON PWR...POLICY CONCPT MYTH
19/20. PAGE 30 B0617
  COM POL/PAR

           B60
PIERCE R.A.,RUSSIAN CENTRAL ASIA, 1867-1917. ASIA
RUSSIA CULTURE AGRI INDUS EDU/PROP REV NAT/LISM
...CHARTS BIBLIOG 19/20 BOLSHEVISM INTERVENT.
PAGE 83 B1672
  COLONIAL DOMIN ADMIN ECO/UNDEV

           S60
SCHWARTZ B.,"THE INTELLIGENTSIA IN COMMUNIST CHINA:
A TENTATIVE COMPARISON." ASIA CHINA/COM COM RUSSIA
ELITES SOCIETY STRATA POL/PAR VOL/ASSN CREATE ADMIN
COERCE NAT/LISM TOTALISM...POLICY TREND 20. PAGE 95
B1914
  INTELL RIGID/FLEX REV

           C60
SCHAPIRO L.B.,"THE COMMUNIST PARTY OF THE SOVIET
UNION." USSR INTELL CHIEF EX/STRUC FORCES DOMIN
ADMIN LEAD WAR ATTIT SOVEREIGN...POLICY BIBLIOG 20.
PAGE 93 B1881
  POL/PAR COM REV

           B61
ARMSTRONG J.A.,AN ESSAY ON SOURCES FOR THE STUDY OF
THE COMMUNIST PARTY OF THE SOVIET UNION, 1934-1960
(EXTERNAL RESEARCH PAPER 137). USSR EX/STRUC ADMIN
LEAD REV 20. PAGE 7 B0134
  BIBLIOG/A COM POL/PAR MARXISM

           B61
MARX K.,THE COMMUNIST MANIFESTO. IN (MENDEL A.
ESSENTIAL WORKS OF MARXISM. NEW YORK: BANTAM. FUT
MOD/EUR CULTURE ECO/DEV ECO/UNDEV AGRI FINAN INDUS
MARKET PROC/MFG LABOR MUNIC POL/PAR CONSULT FORCES
CREATE PLAN ADMIN ATTIT DRIVE RIGID/FLEX ORD/FREE
PWR RESPECT MARX/KARL WORK. PAGE 70 B1421
  COM NEW/IDEA CAP/ISM REV

           B61
MOLLAU G.,INTERNATIONAL COMMUNISM AND WORLD
REVOLUTION: HISTORY AND METHODS. RUSSIA USSR
INT/ORG NAT/G POL/PAR VOL/ASSN FORCES BAL/PWR
DIPLOM EXEC REGION WAR ATTIT PWR MARXISM...CONCPT
TIME/SEQ COLD/WAR 19/20. PAGE 74 B1498
  COM REV

           B62
BINDER L.,IRAN: POLITICAL DEVELOPMENT IN A CHANGING
SOCIETY. IRAN OP/RES REV GP/REL CENTRAL RATIONAL
PWR...PHIL/SCI NAT/COMP GEN/LAWS 20. PAGE 12 B0239
  LEGIT NAT/G ADMIN STRUCT

           B62
SHAPIRO D.,A SELECT BIBLIOGRAPHY OF WORKS IN
ENGLISH ON RUSSIAN HISTORY, 1801-1917. COM USSR
STRATA FORCES EDU/PROP ADMIN REV RACE/REL ATTIT
  BIBLIOG DIPLOM COLONIAL

19/20. PAGE 96 B1932

           B63
TUCKER R.C.,THE SOVIET POLITICAL MIND. WOR+45
ELITES INT/ORG NAT/G POL/PAR PLAN DIPLOM ECO/TAC
DOMIN ADMIN NUC/PWR REV DRIVE PERSON SUPEGO PWR
WEALTH...POLICY MGT PSY CONCPT OBS BIOG TREND
COLD/WAR MARX/KARL 20. PAGE 106 B2134
  COM TOP/EX USSR

           B64
DAS M.N.,INDIA UNDER MORLEY AND MINTO. INDIA UK
ECO/UNDEV MUNIC PROVS EX/STRUC LEGIS DIPLOM CONTROL
REV 20 MORLEY/J. PAGE 26 B0531
  GOV/REL COLONIAL POLICY ADMIN

           B64
FAINSOD M.,HOW RUSSIA IS RULED (REV. ED.). RUSSIA
USSR AGRI PROC/MFG LABOR POL/PAR EX/STRUC CONTROL
PWR...POLICY BIBLIOG 19/20 KHRUSH/N COM/PARTY.
PAGE 34 B0700
  NAT/G REV MARXISM

           B64
PARET P.,FRENCH REVOLUTIONARY WARFARE FROM
INDOCHINA TO ALGERIA: THE ANALYSIS OF A POLITICAL
AND MILITARY DOCTRINE. ALGERIA VIETNAM FORCES
OP/RES TEC/DEV ROUTINE REV ATTIT...PSY BIBLIOG.
PAGE 81 B1632
  FRANCE GUERRILLA GEN/LAWS

           B64
POPPINO R.E.,INTERNATIONAL COMMUNISM IN LATIN
AMERICA: A HISTORY OF THE MOVEMENT 1917-1963.
CHINA/COM USSR INTELL STRATA LABOR WORKER ADMIN REV
ATTIT...POLICY 20 COLD/WAR. PAGE 84 B1692
  MARXISM POL/PAR L/A+17C

           S64
JOHNSON K.F.,"CAUSAL FACTORS IN LATIN AMERICAN
POLITICAL INSTABILITY." CULTURE NAT/G VOL/ASSN
EX/STRUC FORCES EDU/PROP LEGIT ADMIN COERCE REV
ATTIT KNOWL PWR...STYLE RECORD CHARTS WORK 20.
PAGE 57 B1144
  L/A+17C PERCEPT ELITES

           C64
SCOTT R.E.,"MEXICAN GOVERNMENT IN TRANSITION (REV
ED)" CULTURE STRUCT POL/PAR CHIEF ADMIN LOBBY REV
CHOOSE GP/REL DRIVE...BIBLIOG METH 20 MEXIC/AMER.
PAGE 95 B1920
  NAT/G L/A+17C ROUTINE CONSTN

           B65
GREGG J.L.,POLITICAL PARTIES AND PARTY SYSTEMS IN
GUATEMALA, 1944-1963. GUATEMALA L/A+17C EX/STRUC
FORCES CREATE CONTROL REV CHOOSE PWR...TREND
IDEA/COMP 20. PAGE 43 B0872
  LEAD POL/PAR NAT/G CHIEF

           B65
KOUSOULAS D.G.,REVOLUTION AND DEFEAT; THE STORY OF
THE GREEK COMMUNIST PARTY. GREECE INT/ORG EX/STRUC
DIPLOM FOR/AID EDU/PROP PARL/PROC ADJUST ATTIT 20
COM/PARTY. PAGE 61 B1230
  REV MARXISM POL/PAR ORD/FREE

           B65
LIPSET S.M.,THE BERKELEY STUDENT REVOLT: FACTS AND
INTERPRETATIONS. USA+45 INTELL VOL/ASSN CONSULT
EDU/PROP PRESS DEBATE ADMIN REV HAPPINESS
RIGID/FLEX MAJORIT. PAGE 65 B1322
  CROWD ACADEM ATTIT GP/REL

           B65
SCHAPIRO L.,THE GOVERNMENT AND POLITICS OF THE
SOVIET UNION. USSR WOR+45 WOR-45 ADMIN PARTIC REV
CHOOSE REPRESENT PWR...POLICY IDEA/COMP 20. PAGE 93
B1880
  MARXISM GOV/REL NAT/G LOC/G

           B65
YOUNG C.,POLITICS IN THE CONGO: DECOLONIZATION AND
INDEPENDENCE. ELITES STRATA FORCES ADMIN REV
RACE/REL FEDERAL SOVEREIGN...OBS INT CHARTS
CONGO/LEOP. PAGE 118 B2391
  BELGIUM COLONIAL NAT/LISM

           B66
BARBER W.F.,INTERNAL SECURITY AND MILITARY POWER:
COUNTERINSURGENCY AND CIVIC ACTION IN LATIN
AMERICA. ECO/UNDEV CREATE ADMIN REV ATTIT
RIGID/FLEX MARXISM...INT BIBLIOG OAS. PAGE 9 B0183
  L/A+17C FORCES ORD/FREE TASK

           B66
MACFARQUHAR R.,CHINA UNDER MAO: POLITICS TAKES
COMMAND. CHINA/COM COM AGRI INDUS CHIEF FORCES
DIPLOM INT/TRADE EDU/PROP TASK REV ADJUST...ANTHOL
20 MAO. PAGE 67 B1359
  ECO/UNDEV TEC/DEV ECO/TAC ADMIN

           B66
US DEPARTMENT OF THE ARMY,COMMUNIST CHINA: A
STRATEGIC SURVEY: A BIBLIOGRAPHY (PAMPHLET NO.
20-67). CHINA/COM COM INDIA USSR NAT/G POL/PAR
EX/STRUC FORCES NUC/PWR REV ATTIT...POLICY GEOG
CHARTS. PAGE 108 B2184
  BIBLIOG/A MARXISM S/ASIA DIPLOM

           S66
AFRICAN BIBLIOGRAPHIC CENTER,"A CURRENT VIEW OF
AFRICANA: A SELECT AND ANNOTATED BIBLIOGRAPHICAL
PUBLISHING GUIDE, 1965-1966." AFR CULTURE INDUS
LABOR SECT FOR/AID ADMIN COLONIAL REV RACE/REL
SOCISM...LING 20. PAGE 3 B0063
  BIBLIOG/A NAT/G TEC/DEV POL/PAR

           C66
TARLING N.,"A CONCISE HISTORY OF SOUTHEAST ASIA."
BURMA CAMBODIA LAOS S/ASIA THAILAND VIETNAM
ECO/UNDEV POL/PAR FORCES ADMIN REV WAR CIVMIL/REL
ORD/FREE MARXISM SOCISM 13/20. PAGE 103 B2080
  COLONIAL DOMIN INT/TRADE NAT/LISM

           B67
GRUBER H.,INTERNATIONAL COMMUNISM IN THE ERA OF
LENIN. COM ADMIN REV GP/REL 20. PAGE 44 B0895
  MARXISM HIST/WRIT POL/PAR

NIVEN R.,NIGERIA. NIGERIA CONSTN INDUS EX/STRUC   NAT/G
COLONIAL REV NAT/LISM...CHARTS 19/20. PAGE 78 B1584   REGION
                                                        CHOOSE
                                                        GP/REL
                                                                S67
BASTID M.,"ORIGINES ET DEVELOPMENT DE LA REVOLUTION   REV
CULTURELLE." CHINA/COM DOMIN ADMIN CONTROL LEAD   CULTURE
COERCE CROWD ATTIT DRIVE MARXISM...POLICY 20.   ACADEM
PAGE 10 B0195   WORKER
                                                                S67
BAUM R.D.,"IDEOLOGY REDIVIVUS." CHINA/COM NAT/G   REV
EDU/PROP ADMIN 20. PAGE 10 B0197   MARXISM
                                                        CREATE
                                                        TEC/DEV
                                                                S67
HSUEH C.T.,"THE CULTURAL REVOLUTION AND LEADERSHIP   LEAD
CRISIS IN COMMUNIST CHINA." CHINA/COM POL/PAR   REV
EX/STRUC FORCES EDU/PROP ATTIT PWR...POLICY 20.   CULTURE
PAGE 52 B1054   MARXISM
                                                                S67
MURRAY R.,"SECOND THOUGHTS ON GHANA." AFR GHANA   COLONIAL
NAT/G POL/PAR ADMIN REV GP/REL CENTRAL...SOCIALIST   CONTROL
CONCPT METH 20. PAGE 77 B1548   REGION
                                                        SOCISM
                                                                S67
ROTBERG R.I.,"COLONIALISM AND AFTER: THE POLITICAL   BIBLIOG/A
LITERATURE OF CENTRAL AFRICA - A BIBLIOGRAPHIC   COLONIAL
ESSAY." AFR CHIEF EX/STRUC REV INGP/REL RACE/REL   DIPLOM
SOVEREIGN 20. PAGE 91 B1833   NAT/G
                                                                S67
TURNER F.C. JR.,"EXPERIMENT IN INTER-AMERICAN   FORCES
PEACE-KEEPING." DOMIN/REP ADMIN ROUTINE REV   ADJUD
ORD/FREE OAS 20. PAGE 106 B2137   PEACE
                                                                S67
WALLER D.J.,"CHINA: RED OR EXPERT." CHINA/COM   CONTROL
INTELL DOMIN REV ATTIT MARXISM 20. PAGE 113 B2283   FORCES
                                                        ADMIN
                                                        POL/PAR

REVOLUTION....SEE REV

REWARD....SEE SANCTION

RHENMAN E. B0444

RHODE W.E. B1768

RHODE/ISL....RHODE ISLAND
                                                                B58
LOVEJOY D.S.,RHODE ISLAND POLITICS AND THE AMERICAN   REV
REVOLUTION 1760-1776. UK USA-45 ELITES EX/STRUC TAX   COLONIAL
LEAD REPRESENT GOV/REL GP/REL ATTIT 18 RHODE/ISL.   ECO/TAC
PAGE 67 B1343   SOVEREIGN

RHODES G. B1769

RHODES/C....CECIL RHODES

RHODESIA....SEE ALSO AFR
                                                                N60
RHODESIA-NYASA NATL ARCHIVES,A SELECT BIBLIOGRAPHY   BIBLIOG
OF RECENT PUBLICATIONS CONCERNING THE FEDERATION OF   ADMIN
RHODESIA AND NYASALAND (PAMPHLET). MALAWI RHODESIA   ORD/FREE
LAW CULTURE STRUCT ECO/UNDEV LEGIS...GEOG 20.   NAT/G
PAGE 88 B1770
                                                                L64
ROTBERG R.,"THE FEDERATION MOVEMENT IN BRITISH EAST   VOL/ASSN
AND CENTRAL AFRICA." AFR RHODESIA UGANDA ECO/UNDEV   PWR
NAT/G POL/PAR FORCES DOMIN LEGIT ADMIN COERCE ATTIT   REGION
...CONCPT TREND 20 TANGANYIKA. PAGE 91 B1831
                                                                B98
THOMPSON H.C.,RHODESIA AND ITS GOVERNMENT. AFR   COLONIAL
RHODESIA ECO/UNDEV INDUS KIN WORKER INT/TRADE   ADMIN
DISCRIM LITERACY ORD/FREE 19. PAGE 104 B2102   POLICY
                                                        ELITES

RHODESIA-NYASA NATL ARCHIVES B1770

RICARDO/D....DAVID RICARDO

RICE R.R. B0641

RICH B.M. B1772

RICHARD J.B. B1773

RICHARD/H....HENRY RICHARD (WELSH POLITICIAN - 19TH CENTURY)

RICHARDS P.G. B1774

RICHARDSON H.F. B0148

RICHARDSON H.G. B1775

RICHARDSON I.L. B1776

RIDDICK F.M. B1777

RIDDLE D.H. B1778

RIDLEY C.E. B1779,B1780

RIDLEY F. B1781

RIES J.C. B1782

RIESELBACH L.N. B1783

RIESMAN/D....DAVID RIESMAN
                                                                B63
RUITENBEER H.M.,THE DILEMMA OF ORGANIZATIONAL   PERSON
SOCIETY. CULTURE ECO/DEV MUNIC SECT TEC/DEV   ROLE
EDU/PROP NAT/LISM ORD/FREE...NAT/COMP 20 RIESMAN/D   ADMIN
WHYTE/WF MERTON/R MEAD/MARG JASPERS/K. PAGE 92   WORKER
B1855

RIGBY T.H. B1784

RIGGS F.W. B1785

RIGGS R.E. B1679,B1786

RIGGS/FRED....FRED W. RIGGS

RIGHTS/MAN....RIGHTS OF MAN

RIGID/FLEX....DEGREE OF RESPONSIVENESS TO NEW IDEAS, METHODS,
    AND PEOPLE
                                                                N19
ABBOT F.C.,THE CAMBRIDGE CITY MANAGER (PAMPHLET).   MUNIC
PROB/SOLV ADMIN PERS/REL RIGID/FLEX PWR...MGT 20   EX/STRUC
MASSACHU CITY/MGT. PAGE 2 B0050   TOP/EX
                                                        GP/REL
                                                                N19
ARNOW K.,SELF-INSURANCE IN THE TREASURY (PAMPHLET).   ADMIN
USA+45 LAW RIGID/FLEX...POLICY METH/COMP 20   PLAN
DEPT/TREAS. PAGE 7 B0135   EFFICIENCY
                                                        NAT/G
                                                                N19
FIRMALINO T.,THE DISTRICT SCHOOL SUPERVISOR VS.   RIGID/FLEX
TEACHERS AND PARENTS: A PHILIPPINE CASE STUDY   SCHOOL
(PAMPHLET) (BMR). PHILIPPINE LOC/G PLAN EDU/PROP   ADMIN
LOBBY REGION PERS/REL 20. PAGE 36 B0722   CREATE
                                                                N19
KRIESBERG M.,CANCELLATION OF THE RATION STAMPS   RATION
(PAMPHLET). USA+45 USA-45 MARKET PROB/SOLV PRICE   DECISION
GOV/REL RIGID/FLEX 20 OPA. PAGE 61 B1235   ADMIN
                                                        NAT/G
                                                                N19
MARSH J.F. JR.,THE FBI RETIREMENT BILL (PAMPHLET).   ADMIN
USA+45 EX/STRUC WORKER PLAN PROB/SOLV BUDGET LEAD   NAT/G
LOBBY PARL/PROC PERS/REL RIGID/FLEX...POLICY 20 FBI   SENIOR
PRESIDENT BUR/BUDGET. PAGE 70 B1405   GOV/REL
                                                                B30
MURCHISON C.,PSYCHOLOGIES OF 1930. UNIV USA-45   CREATE
CULTURE INTELL SOCIETY STRATA FAM ROUTINE BIO/SOC   PERSON
DRIVE RIGID/FLEX SUPEGO...NEW/IDEA OBS SELF/OBS
CONT/OBS 20. PAGE 76 B1543   B36
GAUS J.M.,THE FRONTIERS OF PUBLIC ADMINISTRATION.   ROUTINE
EFFICIENCY PERCEPT RIGID/FLEX ORD/FREE 20. PAGE 39   GOV/REL
B0785   ELITES
                                                        PROB/SOLV
                                                                B39
ZIMMERN A.,MODERN POLITICAL DOCTRINE. WOR-45   NAT/G
CULTURE SOCIETY ECO/UNDEV DELIB/GP EX/STRUC CREATE   ECO/TAC
DOMIN COERCE NAT/LISM ATTIT RIGID/FLEX ORD/FREE PWR   BAL/PWR
WEALTH...POLICY CONCPT OBS TIME/SEQ TREND TOT/POP   INT/TRADE
LEAGUE/NAT 20. PAGE 119 B2402
                                                                B41
BURTON M.E.,THE ASSEMBLY OF THE LEAGUE OF NATIONS.   DELIB/GP
WOR-45 CONSTN SOCIETY STRUCT INT/ORG NAT/G CREATE   EX/STRUC
ATTIT RIGID/FLEX PWR...POLICY TIME/SEQ LEAGUE/NAT   DIPLOM
20. PAGE 18 B0359
                                                                B47
REDFORD E.S.,FIELD ADMINISTRATION OF WARTIME   ADMIN
RATIONING. USA-45 CONSTN ELITES DIST/IND WORKER   NAT/G
CONTROL WAR GOV/REL ADJUST RIGID/FLEX 20 OPA.   PROB/SOLV
PAGE 87 B1752   RATION
                                                                B48
TOWSTER J.,POLITICAL POWER IN THE USSR: 1917-1947.   EX/STRUC
USSR CONSTN CULTURE ELITES CREATE PLAN COERCE   NAT/G
CENTRAL ATTIT RIGID/FLEX ORD/FREE...BIBLIOG   MARXISM
SOC/INTEG 20 LENIN/VI STALIN/J. PAGE 105 B2124   PWR
                                                                S48
COCH L.,"OVERCOMING RESISTANCE TO CHANGE" (BMR)"   WORKER
USA+45 CONSULT ADMIN ROUTINE GP/REL EFFICIENCY   OP/RES
PRODUC PERCEPT SKILL...CHARTS SOC/EXP 20. PAGE 22   PROC/MFG

B0441   RIGID/FLEX
                                               B49
STEIN H..THE FOREIGN SERVICE ACT OF 1946. USA+45   DIPLOM
ELITES EX/STRUC PLAN PROB/SOLV LOBBY GOV/REL   LAW
PERS/REL RIGID/FLEX...POLICY IDEA/COMP 20 CONGRESS   NAT/G
BUR/BUDGET. PAGE 100 B2027   ADMIN
                                               S50
HUMPHREY H.H.."THE SENATE ON TRIAL." USA+45 POL/PAR PARL/PROC
DEBATE REPRESENT EFFICIENCY ATTIT RIGID/FLEX   ROUTINE
...TRADIT SENATE. PAGE 52 B1064   PWR
                                                    LEGIS
                                               B52
MAIER N.R.F..PRINCIPLES OF HUMAN RELATIONS. WOR+45 INDUS
WOR-45 CULTURE SOCIETY ROUTINE DRIVE PERCEPT
PERSON RIGID/FLEX SUPEGO PWR...PSY CONT/OBS RECORD
TOT/POP VAL/FREE 20. PAGE 68 B1379
                                               L52
WRIGHT Q.."CONGRESS AND THE TREATY-MAKING POWER."   ROUTINE
USA+45 WOR+45 CONSTN INTELL NAT/G CHIEF CONSULT   DIPLOM
EX/STRUC LEGIS TOP/EX CREATE GOV/REL DISPL DRIVE   INT/LAW
RIGID/FLEX...TREND TOT/POP CONGRESS CONGRESS 20   DELIB/GP
TREATY. PAGE 118 B2384
                                               B53
MACMAHON A.W..ADMINISTRATION IN FOREIGN AFFAIRS.   USA+45
NAT/G CONSULT DELIB/GP LEGIS ACT/RES CREATE ADMIN   ROUTINE
EXEC RIGID/FLEX PWR...METH/CNCPT TIME/SEQ TOT/POP   FOR/AID
VAL/FREE 20. PAGE 68 B1369   DIPLOM
                                               B54
COMBS C.H..DECISION PROCESSES. INTELL SOCIETY   MATH
DELIB/GP CREATE TEC/DEV DOMIN LEGIT EXEC CHOOSE   DECISION
DRIVE RIGID/FLEX KNOWL PWR...PHIL/SCI SOC
METH/CNCPT CONT/OBS REC/INT PERS/TEST SAMP/SIZ BIOG
SOC/EXP WORK. PAGE 22 B0455
                                               B54
GOLDNER A.W..WILDCAT STRIKE. LABOR TEC/DEV PAY   INDUS
ADMIN LEAD PERS/REL ATTIT RIGID/FLEX PWR...MGT   WORKER
CONCPT. PAGE 40 B0816   GP/REL
                                                    SOC
                                               B54
MANGONE G..A SHORT HISTORY OF INTERNATIONAL   INT/ORG
ORGANIZATION. MOD/EUR USA+45 USA-45 WOR+45 WOR-45   INT/LAW
LAW LEGIS CREATE LEGIT ROUTINE RIGID/FLEX PWR
...JURID CONCPT OBS TIME/SEQ STERTYP GEN/LAWS UN
TOT/POP VAL/FREE 18/20. PAGE 69 B1389
                                               L54
FURNISS E.S.."WEAKNESSES IN FRENCH FOREIGN POLICY- NAT/G
MAKING." EUR+WWI LEGIS LEGIT EXEC ATTIT RIGID/FLEX   STRUCT
ORD/FREE...SOC CONCPT METH/CNCPT OBS 20. PAGE 38   DIPLOM
B0766   FRANCE
                                               S55
DRUCKER P.F.."'MANAGEMENT SCIENCE' AND THE   MGT
MANAGER." PLAN ROUTINE RIGID/FLEX...METH/CNCPT LOG   STRUCT
HYPO/EXP. PAGE 30 B0620   DECISION
                                                    RATIONAL
                                               B57
KAPLAN M.A..SYSTEM AND PROCESS OF INTERNATIONAL   INT/ORG
POLITICS. FUT WOR+45 WOR-45 SOCIETY PLAN BAL/PWR   DIPLOM
ADMIN ATTIT PERSON RIGID/FLEX PWR SOVEREIGN
...DECISION TREND VAL/FREE. PAGE 58 B1168
                                               B57
KIETH-LUCAS A..DECISIONS ABOUT PEOPLE IN NEED, A   ADMIN
STUDY OF ADMINISTRATIVE RESPONSIVENESS IN PUBLIC   RIGID/FLEX
ASSISTANCE. USA+45 GIVE RECEIVE INGP/REL PERS/REL   SOC/WK
MORAL RESPECT WEALTH...SOC OBS BIBLIOG 20. PAGE 60   DECISION
B1204
                                               B58
MELMAN S..DECISION-MAKING AND PRODUCTIVITY. INDUS   LABOR
EX/STRUC WORKER OP/RES PROB/SOLV TEC/DEV ADMIN   PRODUC
ROUTINE RIGID/FLEX GP/COMP. PAGE 73 B1464   DECISION
                                                    MGT
                                               L58
CYERT R.M.."THE ROLE OF EXPECTATIONS IN BUSINESS   LG/CO
DECISION-MAKING." PROB/SOLV PRICE RIGID/FLEX.   DECISION
PAGE 25 B0516   ROUTINE
                                                    EXEC
                                               S58
JORDAN A.."MILITARY ASSISTANCE AND NATIONAL   FORCES
POLICY." ASIA FUT USA+45 WOR+45 ECO/DEV ECO/UNDEV   POLICY
INT/ORG NAT/G PLAN ECO/TAC ROUTINE WEAPON ATTIT   FOR/AID
RIGID/FLEX PWR...CONCPT TREND 20. PAGE 57 B1153   DIPLOM
                                               S58
MAIR L.P.."REPRESENTATIVE LOCAL GOVERNMENT AS A   AFR
PROBLEM IN SOCIAL CHANGE." ECO/UNDEV KIN LOC/G   PWR
NAT/G SCHOOL JUDGE ADMIN ROUTINE REPRESENT   ELITES
RIGID/FLEX PWR RESPECT...CONCPT STERTYP CMN/WLTH 20.
PAGE 68 B1383
                                               S58
MITCHELL W.C.."OCCUPATIONAL ROLE STRAINS: THE   ANOMIE
AMERICAN ELECTIVE PUBLIC OFFICIAL." CONTROL   DRIVE
RIGID/FLEX SUPEGO HEALTH ORD/FREE...SOC INT QU.   ROUTINE
PAGE 74 B1492   PERSON
                                               B59
JANOWITZ M..SOCIOLOGY AND THE MILITARY   FORCES
ESTABLISHMENT. USA+45 WOR+45 CULTURE SOCIETY   SOC
PROF/ORG CONSULT EX/STRUC PLAN TEC/DEV DIPLOM DOMIN
COERCE DRIVE RIGID/FLEX ORD/FREE PWR SKILL COLD/WAR

20. PAGE 55 B1121
                                               S59
KISSINGER H.A.."THE POLICYMAKER AND THE   INTELL
INTELLECTUAL." USA+45 CONSULT DELIB/GP ACT/RES   CREATE
ADMIN ATTIT DRIVE RIGID/FLEX KNOWL PWR...POLICY
PLURIST MGT METH/CNCPT GEN/LAWS GEN/METH 20.
PAGE 60 B1216
                                               B60
ROEPKE W..A HUMANE ECONOMY: THE SOCIAL FRAMEWORK OF DRIVE
THE FREE MARKET. FUT USSR WOR+45 CULTURE SOCIETY   EDU/PROP
ECO/DEV PLAN ECO/TAC ADMIN ATTIT PERSON RIGID/FLEX   CAP/ISM
SUPEGO MORAL WEALTH SOCISM...POLICY OLD/LIB CONCPT
TREND GEN/LAWS 20. PAGE 90 B1811
                                               L60
MACPHERSON C.."TECHNICAL CHANGE AND POLITICAL   TEC/DEV
DECISION." WOR+45 NAT/G CREATE CAP/ISM DIPLOM   ADMIN
ROUTINE RIGID/FLEX...CONCPT OBS GEN/METH 20.
PAGE 68 B1375
                                               S60
"THE EMERGING COMMON MARKETS IN LATIN AMERICA." FUT FINAN
L/A+17C STRATA DIST/IND INDUS LABOR NAT/G LEGIS   ECO/UNDEV
ECO/TAC ADMIN RIGID/FLEX HEALTH...NEW/IDEA TIME/SEQ INT/TRADE
OAS 20. PAGE 2 B0039
                                               S60
BOGARDUS E.S.."THE SOCIOLOGY OF A STRUCTURED   INT/ORG
PEACE." FUT SOCIETY CREATE DIPLOM EDU/PROP ADJUD   SOC
ROUTINE ATTIT RIGID/FLEX KNOWL ORD/FREE RESPECT   NAT/LISM
...POLICY INT/LAW JURID NEW/IDEA SELF/OBS TOT/POP   PEACE
20 UN. PAGE 13 B0264
                                               S60
FRANKEL S.H.."ECONOMIC ASPECTS OF POLITICAL   NAT/G
INDEPENDENCE IN AFRICA." AFR FUT SOCIETY ECO/UNDEV   FOR/AID
COM/IND FINAN LEGIS PLAN TEC/DEV CAP/ISM ECO/TAC
INT/TRADE ADMIN ATTIT DRIVE RIGID/FLEX PWR WEALTH
...MGT NEW/IDEA MATH TIME/SEQ VAL/FREE 20. PAGE 37
B0751
                                               S60
GARNICK D.H.."ON THE ECONOMIC FEASIBILITY OF A   MARKET
MIDDLE EASTERN COMMON MARKET." AFR ISLAM CULTURE   INT/TRADE
INDUS NAT/G PLAN TEC/DEV ECO/TAC ADMIN ATTIT DRIVE
RIGID/FLEX...PLURIST STAT TREND GEN/LAWS 20.
PAGE 39 B0784
                                               S60
HERZ J.H.."EAST GERMANY: PROGRESS AND PROSPECTS."   POL/PAR
COM AGRI FINAN INDUS LOC/G NAT/G FORCES PLAN   STRUCT
TEC/DEV DOMIN ADMIN COERCE DRIVE PERCEPT RIGID/FLEX GERMANY
MORAL ORD/FREE PWR...MARXIST PSY SOC RECORD STERTYP
WORK. PAGE 49 B0997
                                               S60
HUNTINGTON S.P.."STRATEGIC PLANNING AND THE   EXEC
POLITICAL PROCESS." USA+45 NAT/G DELIB/GP LEGIS   FORCES
ACT/RES ECO/TAC LEGIT ROUTINE CHOOSE RIGID/FLEX PWR NUC/PWR
...POLICY MAJORIT MGT 20. PAGE 53 B1066   WAR
                                               S60
MORA J.A.."THE ORGANIZATION OF AMERICAN STATES."   L/A+17C
USA+45 LAW ECO/UNDEV VOL/ASSN DELIB/GP PLAN BAL/PWR INT/ORG
EDU/PROP ADMIN DRIVE RIGID/FLEX ORD/FREE WEALTH   REGION
...TIME/SEQ GEN/LAWS OAS 20. PAGE 75 B1518
                                               S60
MORALES C.J.."TRADE AND ECONOMIC INTEGRATION IN   FINAN
LATIN AMERICA." FUT L/A+17C LAW STRATA ECO/UNDEV   INT/TRADE
DIST/IND INDUS LABOR NAT/G LEGIS ECO/TAC ADMIN   REGION
RIGID/FLEX WEALTH...CONCPT NEW/IDEA CONT/OBS
TIME/SEQ WORK 20. PAGE 75 B1519
                                               S60
REISELBACH L.N.."THE BASIS OF ISOLATIONIST   ATTIT
BEHAVIOR." USA+45 USA-45 CULTURE ECO/DEV LOC/G   DIPLOM
NAT/G ADMIN ROUTINE CHOOSE BIO/SOC DRIVE RIGID/FLEX ECO/TAC
...CENSUS SAMP TREND CHARTS TOT/POP 20. PAGE 87
B1765
                                               S60
SCHWARTZ B.."THE INTELLIGENTSIA IN COMMUNIST CHINA: INTELL
A TENTATIVE COMPARISON." ASIA CHINA/COM COM RUSSIA RIGID/FLEX
ELITES SOCIETY STRATA POL/PAR VOL/ASSN CREATE ADMIN REV
COERCE NAT/LISM TOTALISM...POLICY TREND 20. PAGE 95
B1914
                                               S60
THOMPSON K.W.."MORAL PURPOSE IN FOREIGN POLICY: MORAL
REALITIES AND ILLUSIONS." WOR+45 WOR-45 LAW CULTURE JURID
SOCIETY INT/ORG PLAN ADJUD ADMIN COERCE RIGID/FLEX   DIPLOM
SUPEGO KNOWL ORD/FREE PWR...SOC TREND SOC/EXP
TOT/POP 20. PAGE 104 B2104
                                               B61
BARNES W..THE FOREIGN SERVICE OF THE UNITED STATES. NAT/G
USA+45 USA-45 CONSTN INT/ORG POL/PAR CONSULT   MGT
DELIB/GP LEGIS DOMIN EDU/PROP EXEC ATTIT RIGID/FLEX DIPLOM
ORD/FREE PWR...POLICY CONCPT STAT OBS RECORD BIOG
TIME/SEQ TREND. PAGE 9 B0188
                                               B61
HAMILTON A..THE FEDERALIST. USA-45 NAT/G VOL/ASSN   EX/STRUC
LEGIS TOP/EX EDU/PROP LEGIT CHOOSE ATTIT RIGID/FLEX CONSTN
ORD/FREE PWR...MAJORIT JURID CONCPT ANTHOL. PAGE 46
B0931
                                               B61
MARX K..THE COMMUNIST MANIFESTO. IN (MENDEL A.   COM
ESSENTIAL WORKS OF MARXISM, NEW YORK: BANTAM. FUT   NEW/IDEA

MOD/EUR CULTURE ECO/DEV ECO/UNDEV AGRI FINAN INDUS CAP/ISM
MARKET PROC/MFG LABOR MUNIC POL/PAR CONSULT FORCES REV
CREATE PLAN ADMIN ATTIT DRIVE RIGID/FLEX ORD/FREE
PWR RESPECT MARX/KARL WORK. PAGE 70 B1421

S61
ANGLIN D.,"UNITED STATES OPPOSITION TO CANADIAN INT/ORG
MEMBERSHIP IN THE PAN AMERICAN UNION: A CANADIAN CANADA
VIEW." L/A+17C UK USA+45 VOL/ASSN DELIB/GP EX/STRUC
PLAN DIPLOM DOMIN REGION ATTIT RIGID/FLEX PWR
...RELATIV CONCPT STERTYP CMN/WLTH OAS 20. PAGE 5
B0112

S61
DEVINS J.H.,"THE INITIATIVE." COM USA+45 USA-45 FORCES
USSR SOCIETY NAT/G ACT/RES CREATE BAL/PWR ROUTINE CONCPT
COERCE DETER RIGID/FLEX SKILL...STERTYP COLD/WAR WAR
20. PAGE 29 B0582

S61
JUVILER P.H.,"INTERPARLIAMENTARY CONTACTS IN SOVIET INT/ORG
FOREIGN POLICY." COM FUT WOR+45 WOR-45 SOCIETY DELIB/GP
CONSULT ACT/RES DIPLOM ADMIN PEACE ATTIT RIGID/FLEX USSR
WEALTH...WELF/ST SOC TOT/POP CONGRESS 19/20.
PAGE 57 B1156

S61
LEWY G.,"SUPERIOR ORDERS, NUCLEAR WARFARE AND THE DETER
DICTATES OF CONSCIENCE: THE DILEMMA OF MILITARY INT/ORG
OBEDIENCE IN THE ATOMIC." FUT UNIV WOR+45 INTELL LAW
SOCIETY FORCES TOP/EX ACT/RES ADMIN ROUTINE NUC/PWR INT/LAW
PERCEPT RIGID/FLEX ALL/VALS...POLICY CONCPT 20.
PAGE 65 B1308

S61
MILLER E.,"LEGAL ASPECTS OF UN ACTION IN THE INT/ORG
CONGO." AFR CULTURE ADMIN PEACE DRIVE RIGID/FLEX LEGIT
ORD/FREE...WELF/ST JURID OBS UN CONGO 20. PAGE 73
B1480

S61
NEEDLER M.C.,"THE POLITICAL DEVELOPMENT OF MEXICO." L/A+17C
STRUCT NAT/G ADMIN RIGID/FLEX...TIME/SEQ TREND POL/PAR
MEXIC/AMER TOT/POP VAL/FREE 19/20. PAGE 77 B1566

B62
HATTERY L.H.,INFORMATION RETRIEVAL MANAGEMENT. R+D
CLIENT INDUS TOP/EX COMPUTER OP/RES TEC/DEV ROUTINE COMPUT/IR
COST EFFICIENCY RIGID/FLEX...METH/COMP ANTHOL 20. MGT
PAGE 48 B0968 CREATE

B62
OLLE-LAPRUNE J.,LA STABILITE DES MINISTRES SOUS LA LEGIS
TROISIEME REPUBLIQUE, 1879-1940. FRANCE CONSTN NAT/G
POL/PAR LEAD WAR INGP/REL RIGID/FLEX PWR...POLICY ADMIN
CHARTS 19/20. PAGE 79 B1606 PERSON

B62
SCHILLING W.R.,STRATEGY, POLITICS, AND DEFENSE ROUTINE
BUDGETS. USA+45 R+D NAT/G CONSULT DELIB/GP FORCES POLICY
LEGIS ACT/RES PLAN BAL/PWR LEGIT EXEC NUC/PWR
RIGID/FLEX PWR...TREND COLD/WAR CONGRESS 20
EISNHWR/DD. PAGE 93 B1890

L62
MALINOWSKI W.R.,"CENTRALIZATION AND DE- CREATE
CENTRALIZATION IN THE UNITED NATIONS' ECONOMIC AND GEN/LAWS
SOCIAL ACTIVITIES." WOR+45 CONSTN ECO/UNDEV INT/ORG
VOL/ASSN DELIB/GP ECO/TAC EDU/PROP ADMIN RIGID/FLEX
...OBS CHARTS UNESCO UN EEC OAS OEEC 20. PAGE 69
B1385

S62
BRZEZINSKI Z.K.,"DEVIATION CONTROL: A STUDY IN THE RIGID/FLEX
DYNAMICS OF DOCTRINAL CONFLICT." WOR+45 WOR-45 ATTIT
VOL/ASSN CREATE BAL/PWR DOMIN EXEC DRIVE PERCEPT
PWR...METH/CNCPT TIME/SEQ TREND 20. PAGE 16 B0333

S62
HUDSON G.F.,"SOVIET FEARS OF THE WEST." COM USA+45 ATTIT
SOCIETY DELIB/GP EX/STRUC TOP/EX ACT/RES CREATE MYTH
DOMIN EDU/PROP LEGIT ADMIN ROUTINE DRIVE PERSON GERMANY
RIGID/FLEX PWR...RECORD TIME/SEQ TOT/POP 20 USSR
STALIN/J. PAGE 52 B1057

S62
IOVTCHOUK M.T.,"ON SOME THEORETICAL PRINCIPLES AND COM
METHODS OF SOCIOLOGICAL INVESTIGATIONS (IN ECO/DEV
RUSSIAN)." FUT USA+45 STRATA R+D NAT/G POL/PAR CAP/ISM
TOP/EX ACT/RES PLAN ECO/TAC EDU/PROP ROUTINE ATTIT USSR
RIGID/FLEX MARXISM SOCISM...MARXIST METH/CNCPT OBS
TREND NAT/COMP GEN/LAWS 20. PAGE 54 B1102

S62
JACOBSON H.K.,"THE UNITED NATIONS AND COLONIALISM: INT/ORG
A TENTATIVE APPRAISAL." AFR FUT S/ASIA USA+45 USSR CONCPT
WOR+45 NAT/G DELIB/GP PLAN DIPLOM ECO/TAC DOMIN COLONIAL
ADMIN ROUTINE COERCE ATTIT RIGID/FLEX ORD/FREE PWR
...OBS STERTYP UN 20. PAGE 55 B1115

S62
MARTIN L.W.,"POLITICAL SETTLEMENTS AND ARMS CONCPT
CONTROL." COM EUR+WWI GERMANY USA+45 PROVS FORCES ARMS/CONT
TOP/EX ACT/RES CREATE DOMIN LEGIT ROUTINE COERCE
ATTIT RIGID/FLEX ORD/FREE PWR...METH/CNCPT RECORD
GEN/LAWS 20. PAGE 70 B1410

C62
TRUMAN D.B.,"THE GOVERNMENTAL PROCESS: POLITICAL LOBBY
INTERESTS AND PUBLIC OPINION." POL/PAR ADJUD ADMIN EDU/PROP
EXEC LEAD ROUTINE CHOOSE REPRESENT GOV/REL GP/REL
RIGID/FLEX...POLICY BIBLIOG/A 20. PAGE 105 B2131 LEGIS

B63
BANFIELD E.C.,CITY POLITICS. CULTURE LABOR LOC/G MUNIC
POL/PAR LEGIS EXEC LEAD CHOOSE...DECISION NEGRO. RIGID/FLEX
PAGE 9 B0178 ATTIT

B63
BOWETT D.W.,THE LAW OF INTERNATIONAL INSTITUTIONS. INT/ORG
WOR+45 WOR-45 CONSTN DELIB/GP EX/STRUC JUDGE ADJUD
EDU/PROP LEGIT CT/SYS EXEC ROUTINE RIGID/FLEX DIPLOM
ORD/FREE PWR...JURID CONCPT ORG/CHARTS GEN/METH
LEAGUE/NAT OAS OEEC 20 UN. PAGE 14 B0286

B63
BURSK E.C.,NEW DECISION-MAKING TOOLS FOR MANAGERS. DECISION
COMPUTER PLAN PROB/SOLV ROUTINE COST. PAGE 18 B0357 MGT
MATH
RIGID/FLEX

B63
LANGROD G.,THE INTERNATIONAL CIVIL SERVICE: ITS INT/ORG
ORIGINS, ITS NATURE, ITS EVALUATION. FUT WOR+45 ADMIN
WOR-45 DELIB/GP ACT/RES DOMIN LEGIT ATTIT
RIGID/FLEX SUPEGO ALL/VALS...MGT CONCPT STAT
TIME/SEQ ILO LEAGUE/NAT VAL/FREE 20 UN. PAGE 62
B1259

B63
LITTERER J.A.,ORGANIZATIONS: STRUCTURE AND ADMIN
BEHAVIOR. PLAN DOMIN CONTROL LEAD ROUTINE SANCTION CREATE
INGP/REL EFFICIENCY PRODUC DRIVE RIGID/FLEX PWR. MGT
PAGE 66 B1325 ADJUST

B63
NORTH R.C.,CONTENT ANALYSIS: A HANDBOOK WITH METH/CNCPT
APPLICATIONS FOR THE STUDY OF INTERNATIONAL CRISIS. COMPUT/IR
ASIA COM EUR+WWI MOD/EUR INT/ORG TEC/DEV DOMIN USSR
EDU/PROP ROUTINE COERCE PERCEPT RIGID/FLEX ALL/VALS
...QUANT TESTS CON/ANAL SIMUL GEN/LAWS VAL/FREE.
PAGE 91 B1591

B63
SINGH H.L.,PROBLEMS AND POLICIES OF THE BRITISH IN COLONIAL
INDIA, 1885-1898. INDIA UK NAT/G FORCES LEGIS PWR
PROB/SOLV CONTROL RACE/REL ADJUST DISCRIM NAT/LISM POLICY
RIGID/FLEX...MGT 19 CIVIL/SERV. PAGE 97 B1968 ADMIN

B63
SWERDLOW I.,DEVELOPMENT ADMINISTRATION: CONCEPTS ECO/UNDEV
AND PROBLEMS. WOR+45 CULTURE SOCIETY STRATA ADMIN
DELIB/GP EX/STRUC ACT/RES PLAN ECO/TAC DOMIN LEGIT
ATTIT RIGID/FLEX SUPEGO HEALTH PWR...MGT CONCPT
ANTHOL VAL/FREE. PAGE 102 B2062

B63
TUCKER R.C.,THE SOVIET POLITICAL MIND. COM INTELL STRUCT
NAT/G TOP/EX EDU/PROP ADMIN COERCE TOTALISM ATTIT RIGID/FLEX
PWR MARXISM...PSY MYTH HYPO/EXP 20. PAGE 106 B2135 ELITES
USSR

L63
BEGUIN H.,"ASPECTS GEOGRAPHIQUE DE LA ECO/UNDEV
POLARISATION." FUT WOR+45 SOCIETY STRUCT ECO/DEV GEOG
R+D BAL/PWR ADMIN ATTIT RIGID/FLEX HEALTH WEALTH DIPLOM
...CHARTS 20. PAGE 10 B0206

S63
BARZANSKI S.,"REGIONAL UNDERDEVELOPMENT IN THE ECO/UNDEV
EUROPEAN ECONOMIC COMMUNITY." EUR+WWI ELITES PLAN
DIST/IND MARKET VOL/ASSN CONSULT EX/STRUC ECO/TAC
RIGID/FLEX WEALTH EEC OEEC 20. PAGE 9 B0192

S63
DELLIN L.A.D.,"BULGARIA UNDER SOVIET LEADERSHIP." AGRI
BULGARIA COM USA+45 USSR ECO/DEV INDUS POL/PAR NAT/G
EX/STRUC TOP/EX COERCE ATTIT RIGID/FLEX...POLICY TOTALISM
TIME/SEQ 20. PAGE 28 B0572

S63
ETIENNE G.,"'LOIS OBJECTIVES' ET PROBLEMES DE TOTALISM
DEVELOPPEMENT DANS LE CONTEXTE CHINE-URSS." ASIA USSR
CHINA/COM COM FUT STRUCT INT/ORG VOL/ASSN TOP/EX
TEC/DEV ECO/TAC ATTIT RIGID/FLEX...GEOG MGT
TIME/SEQ TOT/POP 20. PAGE 34 B0682

S63
SCHURMANN F.,"ECONOMIC POLICY AND POLITICAL POWER PLAN
IN COMMUNIST CHINA." ASIA CHINA/COM USSR SOCIETY ECO/TAC
ECO/UNDEV AGRI INDUS CREATE ADMIN ROUTINE ATTIT
DRIVE RIGID/FLEX PWR WEALTH...HIST/WRIT TREND
CHARTS WORK 20. PAGE 94 B1908

B64
APTER D.E.,IDEOLOGY AND DISCONTENT. FUT WOR+45 ACT/RES
CONSTN CULTURE INTELL SOCIETY STRUCT INT/ORG NAT/G ATTIT
DELIB/GP LEGIS CREATE PLAN TEC/DEV EDU/PROP EXEC
PERCEPT PERSON RIGID/FLEX ALL/VALS...POLICY
TOT/POP. PAGE 6 B0122

B64
INST D'ETUDE POL L'U GRENOBLE,ADMINISTRATION ADMIN
TRADITIONELLE ET PLANIFICATION REGIONALE. FRANCE MUNIC
LAW POL/PAR PROB/SOLV ADJUST RIGID/FLEX...CHARTS PLAN
ANTHOL BIBLIOG T 20 REFORMERS. PAGE 54 B1087 CREATE

B64
NEUSTADT R.,PRESIDENTIAL POWER. USA+45 CONSTN NAT/G TOP/EX
CHIEF LEGIS CREATE EDU/PROP LEGIT ADMIN EXEC COERCE SKILL
ATTIT PERSON RIGID/FLEX PWR CONGRESS 20 PRESIDENT
TRUMAN/HS EISNHWR/DD. PAGE 78 B1575

B64
RIGGS F.W.,ADMINISTRATION IN DEVELOPING COUNTRIES. ECO/UNDEV
FUT WOR+45 STRUCT AGRI INDUS NAT/G PLAN TEC/DEV ADMIN

ROBINSON H. B1800

ROBINSON J.A. B1801,B1802

ROBINSON J.W. B0439

ROBINSON K. B1803

ROBINSON M. B1804

ROBINSON M.E. B1805
ROBINSON R.D. B1352
ROBINSON/H....HENRY ROBINSON

ROBSON P. B1310

ROBSON W.A. B1806,B1807,B1808

ROCHE J.P. B1809,B1810

RODBRTUS/C....CARL RODBERTUS

ROEPKE W. B1811

ROETHLISBERGER F.J. B0588

ROETTER C. B1812

ROFF W.R. B1813

ROGERS W.C. B1814

ROGGEVEEN V.J. B1280

ROGOW A.A. B1815

ROLE....ROLE, REFERENCE GROUP, CROSS-PRESSURES

WEIGLEY R.F.,HISTORY OF THE UNITED STATES ARMY. | FORCES | N
USA+45 USA-45 SOCIETY NAT/G LEAD WAR GP/REL PWR | ADMIN
...SOC METH/COMP COLD/WAR. PAGE 115 B2312 | ROLE
| CIVMIL/REL
| N19
GRIFFITH W.,THE PUBLIC SERVICE (PAMPHLET). UK LAW | ADMIN
LOC/G NAT/G PARTIC CHOOSE DRIVE ROLE SKILL...CHARTS | EFFICIENCY
20 CIVIL/SERV. PAGE 44 B0880 | EDU/PROP
| GOV/REL
| B33
ENSOR R.C.K.,COURTS AND JUDGES IN FRANCE, GERMANY, | CT/SYS
AND ENGLAND. FRANCE GERMANY UK LAW PROB/SOLV ADMIN | EX/STRUC
ROUTINE CRIME ROLE...METH/COMP 20 CIVIL/LAW. | ADJUD
PAGE 33 B0676 | NAT/COMP
| B44
BARKER E.,THE DEVELOPMENT OF PUBLIC SERVICES IN | GOV/COMP
WESTERN WUROPE: 1660-1930. FRANCE GERMANY UK SCHOOL | ADMIN
CONTROL REPRESENT ROLE...WELF/ST 17/20. PAGE 9 | EX/STRUC
B0185 |
| B44
WRIGHT H.R.,SOCIAL SERVICE IN WARTIME. FINAN NAT/G | GIVE
VOL/ASSN PLAN GP/REL ROLE. PAGE 118 B2381 | WAR
| SOC/WK
| ADMIN
| S45
TRUMAN D.B.,"PUBLIC OPINION RESEARCH AS A TOOL OF | REPRESENT
PUBLIC ADMINISTRATION" ADMIN PARTIC ROLE...DECISION | METH/CNCPT
20. PAGE 105 B2130 | ATTIT
| EX/STRUC
| B47
WARNER W.L.,THE SOCIAL SYSTEM OF THE MODERN | ROLE
FACTORY; THE STRIKE: AN ANALYSIS. USA-45 STRATA | STRUCT
WORKER ECO/TAC GP/REL INGP/REL...MGT SOC CHARTS 20 | LABOR
YANKEE/C. PAGE 114 B2293 | PROC/MFG
| S47
TURNER R.H.,"THE NAVY DISBURSING OFFICER AS A | FORCES
BUREAUCRAT" (BMR) USA-45 LAW STRATA DIST/IND WAR | ADMIN
PWR...SOC 20 BUREAUCRCY. PAGE 106 B2140 | PERSON
| ROLE
| B48
SLESSER H.,THE ADMINISTRATION OF THE LAW. UK CONSTN | LAW
EX/STRUC OP/RES PROB/SOLV CRIME ROLE...DECISION | CT/SYS
METH/COMP 20 CIVIL/LAW ENGLSH/LAW CIVIL/LAW. | ADJUD
PAGE 98 B1977 |
| S48
KNICKERBOCKER I.,"LEADERSHIP: A CONCEPTION AND SOME | LEAD
IMPLICATIONS." INDUS OP/RES REPRESENT INGP/REL | CONCPT
DRIVE...MGT CLASSIF. PAGE 60 B1220 | PERSON
| ROLE
| B49
WRIGHT J.H.,PUBLIC RELATIONS IN MANAGEMENT. USA+45 | MGT
USA-45 ECO/DEV LG/CO SML/CO CONSULT EXEC TASK | PLAN
PROFIT ATTIT ROLE 20. PAGE 118 B2382 | EDU/PROP
| PARTIC
| S49
REISSMAN L.,"A STUDY OF ROLE CONCEPTIONS IN | ADMIN
BUREAUCRACY" (BMR)" PERS/REL ROLE...SOC CONCPT | METH/CNCPT

NEW/IDEA IDEA/COMP SOC/EXP 20 BUREAUCRCY. PAGE 87 | GEN/LAWS
B1767 | PROB/SOLV
| N49
UN DEPARTMENT PUBLIC INF,SELECTED BIBLIOGRAPHY OF | BIBLIOG
THE SPECIALIZED AGENCIES RELATED TO THE UNITED | INT/ORG
NATIONS (PAMPHLET). USA+45 ROLE 20 UN. PAGE 106 | EX/STRUC
B2146 | ADMIN
| B51
LASSWELL H.D.,THE POLITICAL WRITINGS OF HAROLD D | PERSON
LASSWELL. UNIV DOMIN EXEC LEAD RATIONAL ATTIT DRIVE | PSY
ROLE ALL/VALS...OBS BIOG 20. PAGE 63 B1269 | INGP/REL
| CONCPT
| B51
MAASS A.,MUDDY WATERS: THE ARMY ENGINEERS AND THE | FORCES
NATIONS RIVERS. USA-45 PROF/ORG CONSULT LEGIS ADMIN | GP/REL
EXEC ROLE PWR...SOC PRESIDENT 20. PAGE 67 B1353 | LOBBY
| CONSTRUC
| S51
STEWART D.D.,"THE PLACE OF VOLUNTEER PARTICIPATION | ADMIN
IN BUREAUCRATIC ORGANIZATION." NAT/G DELIB/GP | PARTIC
OP/RES DOMIN LOBBY WAR ATTIT ROLE PWR. PAGE 101 | VOL/ASSN
B2035 | FORCES
| B52
DONHAM W.B.,ADMINISTRATION AND BLIND SPOTS. LG/CO | ADMIN
EX/STRUC BARGAIN ADJUD ROUTINE ROLE SUPEGO 20. | TOP/EX
PAGE 30 B0605 | DECISION
| POLICY
| B52
NASH B.D.,STAFFING THE PRESIDENCY: PLANNING | EX/STRUC
PAMPHLET NO. 80 (PAMPHLET). NAT/G CHIEF CONSULT | EXEC
DELIB/GP CONFER ADMIN 20 PRESIDENT. PAGE 77 B1557 | TOP/EX
| ROLE
| B53
SAYLES L.R.,THE LOCAL UNION. CONSTN CULTURE | LABOR
DELIB/GP PARTIC CHOOSE GP/REL INGP/REL ATTIT ROLE | LEAD
...MAJORIT DECISION MGT. PAGE 93 B1873 | ADJUD
| ROUTINE
| B55
CHAPMAN B.,THE PREFECTS AND PROVINCIAL FRANCE. | ADMIN
FRANCE DELIB/GP WORKER ROLE PWR 19/20 PREFECT. | PROVS
PAGE 20 B0408 | EX/STRUC
| LOC/G
| B55
WHEARE K.C.,GOVERNMENT BY COMMITTEE; AN ESSAY ON | DELIB/GP
THE BRITISH CONSTITUTION. UK NAT/G LEGIS INSPECT | CONSTN
CONFER ADJUD ADMIN CONTROL TASK EFFICIENCY ROLE | LEAD
POPULISM 20. PAGE 115 B2329 | GP/COMP
| B55
ZABEL O.H.,GOD AND CAESAR IN NEBRASKA: A STUDY OF | SECT
LEGAL RELATIONSHIP OF CHURCH AND STATE, 1854-1954. | PROVS
TAX GIVE ADMIN CONTROL GP/REL ROLE...GP/COMP 19/20 | LAW
NEBRASKA. PAGE 119 B2396 | EDU/PROP
| S55
STAHL O.G.,"DEMOCRACY AND PUBLIC EMPLOYEE | REPRESENT
MORALITY." USA+45 NAT/G EDU/PROP EXEC ROLE 20. | POLICY
PAGE 100 B2016 | ADMIN
| B56
HICKMAN C.A.,INDIVIDUALS, GROUPS, AND ECONOMIC | MGT
BEHAVIOR. WORKER PAY CONTROL EXEC GP/REL INGP/REL | ADMIN
PERSON ROLE...PSY SOC PERS/COMP METH 20. PAGE 50 | ECO/TAC
B1005 | PLAN
| B56
WHYTE W.H. JR.,THE ORGANIZATION MAN. CULTURE FINAN | ADMIN
VOL/ASSN DOMIN EDU/PROP EXEC DISPL HABITAT ROLE | LG/CO
...PERS/TEST STERTYP. PAGE 116 B2343 | PERSON
| CONSEN
| B57
COOPER F.E.,THE LAWYER AND ADMINISTRATIVE AGENCIES. | CONSULT
USA+45 CLIENT LAW PROB/SOLV CT/SYS PERSON ROLE. | ADMIN
PAGE 23 B0473 | ADJUD
| DELIB/GP
| B57
PYE L.W.,THE POLICY IMPLICATIONS OF SOCIAL CHANGE | SOCIETY
IN NON-WESTERN SOCIETIES. ASIA USA+45 CULTURE | ORD/FREE
STRUCT NAT/G ECO/TAC ADMIN ROLE...POLICY SOC. | ECO/UNDEV
PAGE 85 B1723 | DIPLOM
| B57
SCARROW H.A.,THE HIGHER PUBLIC SERVICE OF THE | ADMIN
COMMONWEALTH OF AUSTRALIA. LAW SENIOR LOBBY ROLE 20 | NAT/G
AUSTRAL CIVIL/SERV COMMONWLTH. PAGE 93 B1877 | EX/STRUC
| GOV/COMP
| B57
SCHNEIDER E.V.,INDUSTRIAL SOCIOLOGY: THE SOCIAL | LABOR
RELATIONS OF INDUSTRY AND COMMUNITY. STRATA INDUS | MGT
NAT/G NEIGH CREATE ADMIN PARTIC GP/REL RACE/REL | INGP/REL
ROLE PWR...POLICY BIBLIOG. PAGE 94 B1898 | STRUCT
| S57
HUITT R.K.,"THE MORSE COMMITTEE ASSIGNMENT | LEGIS
CONTROVERSY: A STUDY IN SENATE NORMS." USA+45 | ETIQUET
USA-45 POL/PAR SENIOR ROLE SUPEGO SENATE. PAGE 52 | PWR
B1061 | ROUTINE
| B58
DWARKADAS R.,ROLE OF HIGHER CIVIL SERVICE IN INDIA. | ADMIN
INDIA ECO/UNDEV LEGIS PROB/SOLV GP/REL PERS/REL | NAT/G
...POLICY WELF/ST DECISION ORG/CHARTS BIBLIOG 20 | ROLE
CIVIL/SERV INTRVN/ECO. PAGE 31 B0637 | PLAN

B58
STEWART J.D.,BRITISH PRESSURE GROUPS: THEIR ROLE IN LOBBY
RELATION TO THE HOUSE OF COMMONS. UK CONSULT LEGIS
DELIB/GP ADMIN ROUTINE CHOOSE REPRESENT ATTIT ROLE PLAN
20 HOUSE/CMNS PARLIAMENT. PAGE 101 B2038 PARL/PROC
S58
DEAN B.V.,"APPLICATION OF OPERATIONS RESEARCH TO DECISION
MANAGERIAL DECISION MAKING" STRATA ACT/RES OP/RES
PROB/SOLV ROLE...SOC PREDICT SIMUL 20. PAGE 28 MGT
B0565 METH/CNCPT
B59
DAHRENDORF R.,CLASS AND CLASS CONFLICT IN VOL/ASSN
INDUSTRIAL SOCIETY. LABOR NAT/G COERCE ROLE PLURISM STRUCT
...POLICY MGT CONCPT CLASSIF. PAGE 26 B0523 SOC
GP/REL
B59
INDIAN INSTITUTE PUBLIC ADMIN,MORALE IN THE PUBLIC HAPPINESS
SERVICES: REPORT OF A CONFERENCE JAN., 3-4, 1959. ADMIN
INDIA S/ASIA ECO/UNDEV PROVS PLAN EDU/PROP CONFER WORKER
GOV/REL EFFICIENCY DRIVE ROLE 20 CIVIL/SERV. INGP/REL
PAGE 53 B1082
B59
MILLETT J.D.,GOVERNMENT AND PUBLIC ADMINISTRATION: ADMIN
THE QUEST FOR RESPONSIBLE PERFORMANCE. USA+45 NAT/G PWR
DELIB/GP LEGIS CT/SYS EXEC...DECISION MGT. PAGE 73 CONSTN
B1483 ROLE
B59
THARAMATHAJ C.,A STUDY OF THE COMPOSITION OF THE ADMIN
THAI CIVIL SERVICE (PAPER). THAILAND PAY ROLE EX/STRUC
...CHARTS 20 CIVIL/SERV FEMALE/SEX. PAGE 103 B2092 STRATA
INGP/REL
S59
DWYER R.J.,"THE ADMINISTRATIVE ROLE IN ADMIN
DESEGREGATION." USA+45 LAW PROB/SOLV LEAD RACE/REL SCHOOL
ISOLAT STRANGE ROLE...POLICY SOC/INTEG MISSOURI DISCRIM
NEGRO CIV/RIGHTS. PAGE 31 B0638 ATTIT
B60
HANBURY H.G.,ENGLISH COURTS OF LAW. UK EX/STRUC JURID
LEGIS CRIME ROLE 12/20 COMMON/LAW ENGLSH/LAW. CT/SYS
PAGE 46 B0936 CONSTN
GOV/REL
B60
LINDVEIT E.N.,SCIENTISTS IN GOVERNMENT. USA+45 PAY TEC/DEV
EDU/PROP ADMIN DRIVE HABITAT ROLE...TECHNIC BIBLIOG ECO/TAC
20. PAGE 65 B1316 PHIL/SCI
GOV/REL
B60
WALDO D.,THE RESEARCH FUNCTION OF UNIVERSITY ADMIN
BUREAUS AND INSTITUTES FOR GOVERNMENTAL-RELATED R+D
RESEARCH. FINAN ACADEM NAT/G INGP/REL ROLE...POLICY MUNIC
CLASSIF GOV/COMP. PAGE 113 B2276
L60
GRODZINS M.,"AMERICAN POLITICAL PARTIES AND THE POL/PAR
AMERICAN SYSTEM" (BMR)" USA+45 LOC/G NAT/G LEGIS FEDERAL
BAL/PWR ADMIN ROLE PWR...DECISION 20. PAGE 44 B0883 CENTRAL
GOV/REL
S60
BAVELAS A.,"LEADERSHIP: MAN AND FUNCTION." WORKER LEAD
CREATE PLAN CONTROL PERS/REL PERSON PWR...MGT 20. ADMIN
PAGE 10 B0199 ROUTINE
ROLE
S60
TAYLOR M.G.,"THE ROLE OF THE MEDICAL PROFESSION IN PROF/ORG
THE FORMULATION AND EXECUTION OF PUBLIC POLICY" HEALTH
(BMR)" CANADA NAT/G CONSULT ADMIN REPRESENT GP/REL LOBBY
ROLE SOVEREIGN...DECISION 20 CMA. PAGE 103 B2088 POLICY
C60
SCHRAMM W.,"MASS COMMUNICATIONS: A BOOK OF READINGS COM/IND
(2ND ED.)" LG/CO PRESS ADMIN CONTROL ROUTINE ATTIT EDU/PROP
ROLE SUPEGO...CHARTS ANTHOL BIBLIOG 20. PAGE 94 CROWD
B1902 MAJORIT
B61
ROBINSON M.E.,EDUCATION FOR SOCIAL CHANGE: FOR/AID
ESTABLISHING INSTITUTES OF PUBLIC AND BUSINESS EDU/PROP
ADMINISTRATION ABROAD (PAMPHLET). WOR+45 SOCIETY MGT
ACADEM CONFER INGP/REL ROLE...SOC CHARTS BIBLIOG 20 ADJUST
ICA. PAGE 89 B1805
B61
SHAPP W.R.,FIELD ADMINISTRATION IN THE UNITED INT/ORG
NATIONS SYSTEM. FINAN PROB/SOLV INSPECT DIPLOM EXEC ADMIN
REGION ROUTINE EFFICIENCY ROLE...INT CHARTS 20 UN. GP/REL
PAGE 96 B1933 FOR/AID
B61
TANNENBAUM R.,LEADERSHIP AND ORGANIZATION. STRUCT LEAD
ADMIN INGP/REL ATTIT PERCEPT...DECISION METH/CNCPT MGT
OBS CHARTS BIBLIOG. PAGE 103 B2075 RESPECT
ROLE
B61
TOMPKINS D.C.,CONFLICT OF INTEREST IN THE FEDERAL BIBLIOG
GOVERNMENT: A BIBLIOGRAPHY. USA+45 EX/STRUC LEGIS ROLE
ADJUD ADMIN CRIME CONGRESS PRESIDENT. PAGE 105 NAT/G
B2117 LAW
S61
ROBINSON J.A.,"PROCESS SATISFACTION AND POLICY GOV/REL
APPROVAL IN STATE DEPARTMENT - CONGRESSIONAL EX/STRUC
RELATIONS." ELITES CHIEF LEGIS CONFER DEBATE ADMIN POL/PAR

FEEDBACK ROLE...CHARTS 20 CONGRESS PRESIDENT DECISION
DEPT/STATE. PAGE 89 B1802
B62
DODDS H.W.,THE ACADEMIC PRESIDENT "EDUCATOR OR ACADEM
CARETAKER? FINAN DELIB/GP EDU/PROP PARTIC ATTIT ADMIN
ROLE PWR...POLICY RECORD INT. PAGE 30 B0601 LEAD
CONTROL
B62
WANGSNESS P.H.,THE POWER OF THE CITY MANAGER. PWR
USA+45 EX/STRUC BAL/PWR BUDGET TAX ADMIN REPRESENT TOP/EX
CENTRAL EFFICIENCY DRIVE ROLE...POLICY 20 CITY/MGT. MUNIC
PAGE 113 B2286 LOC/G
B63
BROGAN D.W.,POLITICAL PATTERNS IN TODAY'S WORLD. NAT/COMP
FRANCE USA+45 USSR WOR+45 CONSTN STRUCT PLAN DIPLOM NEW/LIB
ADMIN LEAD ROLE SUPEGO...PHIL/SCI 20. PAGE 15 B0313 COM
TOTALISM
B63
COSTELLO T.W.,PSYCHOLOGY IN ADMINISTRATION: A PSY
RESEARCH ORIENTATION. CREATE PROB/SOLV PERS/REL MGT
ADJUST ANOMIE ATTIT DRIVE PERCEPT ROLE...DECISION EXEC
BIBLIOG T 20. PAGE 24 B0488 ADMIN
B63
DALAND R.T.,PERSPECTIVES OF BRAZILIAN PUBLIC ADMIN
ADMINISTRATION (VOL. I). BRAZIL LAW ECO/UNDEV NAT/G
SCHOOL CHIEF TEC/DEV CONFER CONTROL GP/REL ATTIT PLAN
ROLE PWR...ANTHOL 20. PAGE 26 B0525 GOV/REL
B63
DE GUZMAN R.P.,PATTERNS IN DECISION-MAKING: CASE ADMIN
STUDIES IN PHILIPPINE PUBLIC ADMINISTRATION. DECISION
PHILIPPINE LAW CHIEF PROB/SOLV INGP/REL DRIVE POLICY
PERCEPT ROLE...ANTHOL T 20. PAGE 27 B0557 GOV/REL
B63
HAYMAN D.,POLITICAL ACTIVITY RESTRICTION: AN CONTROL
ANALYSIS WITH RECOMMENDATIONS (PAMPHLET). USA+45 ADMIN
EXEC PARTIC ROLE PWR 20. PAGE 48 B0976 INGP/REL
REPRESENT
B63
HOWER R.M.,MANAGERS AND SCIENTISTS. EX/STRUC CREATE R+D
ADMIN REPRESENT ATTIT DRIVE ROLE PWR SKILL...SOC MGT
INT. PAGE 52 B1052 PERS/REL
INGP/REL
B63
MENZEL J.M.,THE CHINESE CIVIL SERVICE: CAREER OPEN ADMIN
TO TALENT? ASIA ROUTINE INGP/REL DISCRIM ATTIT ROLE NAT/G
KNOWL ANTHOL. PAGE 73 B1468 DECISION
ELITES
B63
RUITENBEER H.M.,THE DILEMMA OF ORGANIZATIONAL PERSON
SOCIETY. CULTURE ECO/DEV MUNIC SECT TEC/DEV ROLE
EDU/PROP NAT/LISM ORD/FREE...NAT/COMP 20 RIESMAN/D ADMIN
WHYTE/WF MERTON/R MEAD/MARG JASPERS/K. PAGE 92 WORKER
B1855
B64
BANTON M.,THE POLICEMAN IN THE COMMUNITY. UK USA+45 FORCES
STRUCT PROF/ORG WORKER LOBBY ROUTINE COERCE CROWD ADMIN
GP/REL ADJUST DISCRIM PERCEPT 20. PAGE 9 B0181 ROLE
RACE/REL
B64
COTTER C.P.,POLITICS WITHOUT POWER: THE NATIONAL CHOOSE
PARTY COMMITTEES. USA+45 FINAN NAT/G LOBBY ROUTINE POL/PAR
GP/REL ATTIT ROLE SUPEGO PWR 20. PAGE 24 B0491 REPRESENT
DELIB/GP
B64
FISK W.M.,ADMINISTRATIVE PROCEDURE IN A REGULATORY SERV/IND
AGENCY: THE CAB AND THE NEW YORK-CHICAGO CASE ECO/DEV
(PAMPHLET). USA+45 DIST/IND ADMIN CONTROL LOBBY AIR
GP/REL ROLE ORD/FREE NEWYORK/C CHICAGO CAB. PAGE 36 JURID
B0727
B64
FONTENEAU J.,LE CONSEIL MUNICIPAL: LE MAIRE-LES MUNIC
ADJOINTS. FRANCE FINAN DELIB/GP EX/STRUC BUDGET TAX NEIGH
TASK COST INCOME ROLE SUPEGO 20 MAYOR. PAGE 36 ADMIN
B0735 TOP/EX
B64
GROSS B.M.,THE MANAGING OF ORGANIZATIONS (VOL. I). ECO/TAC
USA+45 ECO/DEV LG/CO CAP/ISM EFFICIENCY ROLE...MGT ADMIN
20. PAGE 44 B0886 INDUS
POLICY
B64
SARROS P.P.,CONGRESS AND THE NEW DIPLOMACY: THE DIPLOM
FORMULATION OF MUTUAL SECURITY POLICY: 1953-60 POL/PAR
(THESIS). USA+45 CHIEF EX/STRUC REGION ROUTINE NAT/G
CHOOSE GOV/REL PEACE ROLE...POLICY 20 PRESIDENT
CONGRESS. PAGE 92 B1869
B64
US SENATE COMM GOVT OPERATIONS,THE SECRETARY OF DIPLOM
STATE AND THE AMBASSADOR. USA+45 CHIEF CONSULT DELIB/GP
EX/STRUC FORCES PLAN ADMIN EXEC INGP/REL ROLE NAT/G
...ANTHOL 20 PRESIDENT DEPT/STATE. PAGE 110 B2215
B64
WHEELER-BENNETT J.W.,THE NEMESIS OF POWER (2ND FORCES
ED.). EUR+WWI GERMANY TOP/EX TEC/DEV ADMIN WAR NAT/G
PERS/REL RIGID/FLEX ROLE ORD/FREE PWR FASCISM 20 GP/REL
HITLER/A. PAGE 116 B2332 STRUCT

WILSON L.,THE ACADEMIC MAN. STRUCT FINAN PROF/ORG OP/RES ADMIN AUTHORIT ROLE RESPECT...SOC STAT. PAGE 117 B2360
B64
ACADEM
INGP/REL
STRATA
DELIB/GP

FOX G.H.,"PERCEPTIONS OF THE VIETNAMESE PUBLIC ADMINISTRATION SYSTEM" VIETNAM ELITES CONTROL EXEC LEAD PWR...INT 20. PAGE 37 B0745
L64
ADMIN
EX/STRUC
INGP/REL
ROLE

KAMMERER G.M.,"ROLE DIVERSITY OF CITY MANAGERS." LOC/G ADMIN LEAD PERCEPT PWR GP/COMP. PAGE 57 B1163
S64
MUNIC.
EXEC
ATTIT
ROLE

BUECHNER J.C.,DIFFERENCES IN ROLE PERCEPTIONS IN COLORADO COUNCIL-MANAGER CITIES. USA+45 ADMIN ROUTINE GP/REL CONSEN PERCEPT PERSON ROLE ...DECISION MGT STAT INT QU CHARTS 20 COLORADO CITY/MGT. PAGE 17 B0338
B65
MUNIC
CONSULT
LOC/G
IDEA/COMP

DE GRAZIA A.,REPUBLIC IN CRISIS: CONGRESS AGAINST THE EXECUTIVE FORCE. USA+45 USA-45 SOCIETY POL/PAR CHIEF DOMIN ROLE ORD/FREE PWR...CONCPT MYTH BIBLIOG 20 CONGRESS. PAGE 27 B0556
B65
LEGIS
EXEC
GOV/REL
CONTROL

HODGSON R.C.,THE EXECUTIVE ROLE CONSTELLATION: AN ANALYSIS OF PERSONALITY AND ROLE RELATIONS IN MANAGEMENT. USA+45 PUB/INST EXEC PERS/REL PERSON ...PSY PERS/COMP HYPO/EXP 20. PAGE 51 B1027
B65
LG/CO
ADMIN
TOP/EX
ROLE

HUGHES J.M.,EDUCATION IN AMERICA (2ND ED.). USA+45 USA-45 GP/REL INGP/REL AGE/C AGE/Y ROLE...IDEA/COMP BIBLIOG T 20. PAGE 52 B1059
B65
EDU/PROP
SCHOOL
ADMIN
METH/COMP

INTERNATIONAL CITY MGRS ASSN,COUNCIL-MANAGER GOVERNMENT, 1940-64: AN ANNOTATED BIBLIOGRAPHY. USA+45 ADMIN GOV/REL ROLE...MGT 20. PAGE 54 B1097
B65
BIBLIOG/A
MUNIC
CONSULT
PLAN

KWEDER J.B.,THE ROLES OF THE MANAGER, MAYOR, AND COUNCILMEN IN POLICYMAKING. LEGIS PERS/REL ATTIT ROLE PWR GP/COMP. PAGE 62 B1246
B65
MUNIC
EXEC
LEAD
DECISION

US SENATE COMM GOVT OPERATIONS,ADMINISTRATION OF NATIONAL SECURITY. USA+45 DELIB/GP ADMIN ROLE ...POLICY CHARTS SENATE. PAGE 110 B2218
B65
NAT/G
ORD/FREE
DIPLOM
PROB/SOLV

ANDERSON T.J.,"PRESSURE GROUPS AND INTERGOVERNMENTAL RELATIONS." USA+45 NAT/G ROLE 20. PAGE 5 B0097
S65
ADMIN
EX/STRUC
LOBBY
GOV/REL

ASHFORD D.E.,"BUREAUCRATS AND CITIZENS." MOROCCO PAKISTAN PARTIC 20 TUNIS. PAGE 7 B0140
S65
GOV/COMP
ADMIN
EX/STRUC
ROLE

CLEGG R.K.,THE ADMINISTRATOR IN PUBLIC WELFARE. USA+45 STRUCT NAT/G PROVS PROB/SOLV BUDGET ECO/TAC GP/REL ROLE...SOC/WK 20 PUBLIC/REL. PAGE 21 B0434
B66
GIVE
GOV/REL
OP/RES

DICKSON W.J.,COUNSELING IN AN ORGANIZATION: A SEQUEL TO THE HAWTHORNE RESEARCHES. CLIENT VOL/ASSN ACT/RES PROB/SOLV AUTOMAT ROUTINE PERS/REL HAPPINESS ANOMIE ROLE...OBS CHARTS 20 AT+T. PAGE 29 B0588
B66
INDUS
WORKER
PSY
MGT

FISK E.K.,NEW GUINEA ON THE THRESHOLD; ASPECTS OF SOCIAL, POLITICAL, AND ECONOMIC DEVELOPMENT. AGRI NAT/G INT/TRADE ADMIN ADJUST LITERACY ROLE...CHARTS ANTHOL 20 NEW/GUINEA. PAGE 36 B0726
B66
ECO/UNDEV
SOCIETY

PERKINS J.A.,THE UNIVERSITY IN TRANSITION. USA+45 SOCIETY FINAN INDUS NAT/G EX/STRUC ADMIN INGP/REL COST EFFICIENCY ATTIT 20. PAGE 82.B1658
B66
ACADEM
ORD/FREE
CREATE
ROLE

SEASHOLES B.,VOTING, INTEREST GROUPS, AND PARTIES. USA+45 FINAN LOC/G NAT/G ADMIN LEAD GP/REL INGP/REL ROLE...CHARTS ANTHOL 20. PAGE 95 B1922
B66
CHOOSE
POL/PAR
LOBBY
PARTIC

VON HOFFMAN N.,THE MULTIVERSITY; A PERSONAL REPORT ON WHAT HAPPENS TO TODAY'S STUDENTS AT AMERICAN UNIVERSITIES. USA+45 SOCIETY ROUTINE ANOMIE ROLE MORAL ORD/FREE SKILL...INT 20. PAGE 112 B2266
B66
EDU/PROP
ACADEM
ATTIT
STRANGE

WYLIE C.M.,RESEARCH IN PUBLIC HEALTH ADMINISTRATION; SELECTED RECENT ABSTRACTS IV (PAMPHLET). USA+45 MUNIC PUB/INST ACT/RES CREATE
B66
BIBLIOG/A
R+D
HEAL

OP/RES TEC/DEV GP/REL ROLE...MGT PHIL/SCI STAT. PAGE 118 B2387
ADMIN

HANSON A.H.,"PLANNING AND THE POLITICIANS* SOME REFLECTIONS ON ECONOMIC PLANNING IN WESTERN EUROPE." MARKET NAT/G TEC/DEV CONSEN ROLE ...METH/COMP NAT/COMP. PAGE 46 B0942
S66
PLAN
ECO/DEV
EUR+WWI
ADMIN

JACOB H.,"DIMENSIONS OF STATE POLITICS HEARD A. ED. STATE LEGIWLATURES IN AMERICAN POLITICS." CULTURE STRATA POL/PAR BUDGET TAX LOBBY ROUTINE GOV/REL ...TRADIT DECISION GEOG. PAGE 55 B1112
C66
PROVS
LEGIS
ROLE
REPRESENT

AMERICAN SOCIETY PUBLIC ADMIN,PUBLIC ADMINISTRATION AND THE WAR ON POVERTY (PAMPHLET). USA+45 SOCIETY ECO/DEV FINAN LOC/G LEGIS CREATE EDU/PROP GOV/REL GP/REL ROLE 20 POVRTY/WAR. PAGE 4 B0089
N66
WEALTH
NAT/G
PLAN
ADMIN

BACHELDER G.L.,THE LITERATURE OF FEDERALISM: A SELECTED BIBLIOGRAPHY (REV ED) (A PAMPHLET). USA+45 USA-45 WOR+45 WOR-45 LAW CONSTN PROVS ADMIN CT/SYS GOV/REL ROLE...CONCPT 19/20. PAGE 8 B0155
N66
BIBLIOG
FEDERAL
NAT/G
LOC/G

EDUCATION, INTERACTION, AND SOCIAL CHANGE. STRATA MUNIC SCHOOL ADMIN RIGID/FLEX ROLE 20. PAGE 49 B0991
B67
EDU/PROP
ADJUST
SOC
ACT/RES

HEWITT W.H.,ADMINISTRATION OF CRIMINAL JUSTICE IN NEW YORK. LAW PROB/SOLV ADJUD ADMIN...CRIMLGY CHARTS T 20 NEW/YORK. PAGE 49 B1001
B67
CRIME
ROLE
CT/SYS
FORCES

KRISLOV S.,THE NEGRO IN FEDERAL EMPLOYMENT. LAW STRATA LOC/G CREATE PROB/SOLV INSPECT GOV/REL DISCRIM ROLE...DECISION INT TREND 20 NEGRO WWI CIVIL/SERV. PAGE 61 B1238
B67
WORKER
NAT/G
ADMIN
RACE/REL

MENHENNET D.,PARLIAMENT IN PERSPECTIVE. UK ROUTINE REPRESENT ROLE PWR 20 PARLIAMENT. PAGE 73 B1467
B67
LEGIS
PARL/PROC
CONCPT
POPULISM

RALSTON D.B.,THE ARMY OF THE REPUBLIC; THE PLACE OF THE MILITARY IN THE POLITICAL EVOLUTION OF FRANCE 1871-1914. FRANCE MOD/EUR EX/STRUC LEGIS TOP/EX DIPLOM ADMIN WAR GP/REL ROLE...BIBLIOG 19/20. PAGE 86 B1730
B67
FORCES
NAT/G
CIVMIL/REL
POLICY

US DEPARTMENT OF THE ARMY,CIVILIAN IN PEACE, SOLDIER IN WAR: A BIBLIOGRAPHIC SURVEY OF THE ARMY AND AIR NATIONAL GUARD (PAMPHLET, NOS. 130-2). USA+45 USA-45 LOC/G NAT/G PROVS LEGIS PLAN ADMIN ATTIT ORD/FREE...POLICY 19/20. PAGE 108 B2185
B67
BIBLIOG/A
FORCES
ROLE
DIPLOM

WATERS M.,THE UNITED NATIONS* INTERNATIONAL ORGANIZATION AND ADMINISTRATION. WOR+45 EX/STRUC FORCES DIPLOM LEAD REGION ARMS/CONT REPRESENT INGP/REL ROLE...METH/COMP ANTHOL 20 UN LEAGUE/NAT. PAGE 114 B2301
B67
CONSTN
INT/ORG
ADMIN
ADJUD

BESCOBY I.,"A COLONIAL ADMINISTRATION* AN ANALYSIS OF ADMINISTRATION IN BRITISH COLUMBIA 1869-1871." UK STRATA EX/STRUC LEGIS TASK GOV/REL EFFICIENCY ROLE...MGT CHARTS 19. PAGE 11 B0232
L67
ADMIN
CANADA
COLONIAL
LEAD

BLUMBERG A.S.,"THE PRACTICE OF LAW AS CONFIDENCE GAME; ORGANIZATIONAL COOPTATION OF A PROFESSION." USA+45 CLIENT SOCIETY CONSULT ROLE JURID. PAGE 13 B0260
L67
CT/SYS
ADJUD
GP/REL
ADMIN

ANDERSON L.G.,"ADMINISTERING A GOVERNMENT SOCIAL SERVICE" NEW/ZEALND EX/STRUC TASK ROLE 20. PAGE 5 B0094
S67
ADMIN
NAT/G
DELIB/GP
SOC/WK

ANDERSON M.,"THE FRENCH PARLIAMENT." EUR+WWI FRANCE MOD/EUR CONSTN POL/PAR CHIEF LEGIS LOBBY ATTIT ROLE PWR 19/20. PAGE 5 B0095
S67
PARL/PROC
LEAD
GOV/COMP
EX/STRUC

BURACK E.H.,"INDUSTRIAL MANAGEMENT IN ADVANCED PRODUCTION SYSTEMS: SOME THEORETICAL CONCEPTS AND PRELIMINARY FINDINGS." INDUS CREATE PLAN PRODUC ROLE...OBS STAND/INT DEEP/QU HYPO/EXP ORG/CHARTS 20. PAGE 17 B0346
S67
ADMIN
MGT
TEC/DEV
EX/STRUC

DANELSKI D.J.,"CONFLICT AND ITS RESOLUTION IN THE SUPREME COURT." PROB/SOLV LEAD ROUTINE PERSON...PSY PERS/COMP BIBLIOG 20. PAGE 26 B0527
S67
ROLE
JURID
JUDGE
INGP/REL

HILL F.G.,"VEBLEN, BERLE AND THE MODERN CORPORATION." FINAN ECO/TAC CONTROL OWN...MGT 20. PAGE 50 B1010
S67
LG/CO
ROLE
INDUS
ECO/DEV

HUDDLESTON J.,"TRADE UNIONS IN THE GERMAN FEDERAL   S67
REPUBLIC." EUR+WWI GERMANY/W UK LAW INDUS WORKER   LABOR
CREATE CENTRAL...MGT GP/COMP 20. PAGE 52 B1056   GP/REL
                                         SCHOOL
                                         ROLE

LEVIN M.R.,"PLANNERS AND METROPOLITAN PLANNING."   S67
FUT USA+45 SOCIETY NAT/G PROVS PROB/SOLV LEAD   PLAN
PARTIC GOV/REL RACE/REL HABITAT ROLE. PAGE 64 B1301   MUNIC
                                         R+D
                                         ADMIN

RAI H.,"DISTRICT MAGISTRATE AND POLICE   S67
SUPERINTENDENT IN INDIA: THE CONTROVERSY OF DUAL   STRUCT
CONTROL" INDIA LAW PROVS ADMIN PWR 19/20. PAGE 86   CONTROL
B1729   ROLE
                                         FORCES

RUBIN R.I.,"THE LEGISLATIVE-EXECUTIVE RELATIONS OF   S67
THE UNITED STATES INFORMATION AGENCY." USA+45   LEGIS
EDU/PROP TASK INGP/REL EFFICIENCY ISOLAT ATTIT ROLE   EX/STRUC
USIA CONGRESS. PAGE 91 B1850   GP/REL
                                         PROF/ORG

SUBRAMANIAM V.,"REPRESENTATIVE BUREAUCRACY: A   S67
REASSESSMENT." USA+45 ELITES LOC/G ADMIN GOV/REL   STRATA
PRIVIL DRIVE ROLE...POLICY CENSUS 20 CIVIL/SERV   GP/REL
BUREAUCRCY. PAGE 101 B2053   MGT
                                         GOV/COMP

TOURNELLE G.,"DIPLOMATIE D' HIER ET D'AUJOURD'   S67
HUI." CONFER ADMIN ROUTINE PEACE. PAGE 105 B2123   DIPLOM
                                         ROLE
                                         INT/ORG

GRAM H.A.,"BUSINESS ETHICS AND THE CORPORATION."   S68
LG/CO SECT PROB/SOLV CONTROL EXEC GP/REL INGP/REL   POLICY
PERS/REL ROLE MORAL PWR 20. PAGE 42 B0850   ADMIN
                                         MGT

ROLL E.   B0773

ROMAN CATHOLIC....SEE CATH, CATHISM

ROMAN/EMP....ROMAN EMPIRE

FRANK T.,A HISTORY OF ROME. MEDIT-7 INTELL SOCIETY   B23
LOC/G POL/PAR FORCES LEGIS DOMIN LEGIT ALL/VALS   EXEC
...POLICY CONCPT TIME/SEQ GEN/LAWS ROM/EMP ROM/EMP.   STRUCT
PAGE 37 B0749   ELITES

DIESNER H.J.,KIRCHE UND STAAT IM SPATROMISCHEN   B63
REICH. ROMAN/EMP EX/STRUC COLONIAL COERCE ATTIT   SECT
CATHISM 4/5 AFRICA/N CHURCH/STA. PAGE 29 B0592   GP/REL
                                         DOMIN
                                         JURID

ROMAN/LAW....ROMAN LAW

ROMAN/REP....ROMAN REPUBLIC

ROMANIA....SEE ALSO COM

KYRIAK T.E.,EAST EUROPE: BIBLIOGRAPHY--INDEX TO US   N
JPRS RESEARCH TRANSLATIONS. ALBANIA BULGARIA COM   BIBLIOG/A
CZECHOSLVK HUNGARY POLAND ROMANIA AGRI EXTR/IND   PRESS
FINAN SERV/IND INT/TRADE WEAPON...GEOG MGT SOC 20.   MARXISM
PAGE 62 B1247   INDUS

POOL I.,SATELLITE GENERALS: A STUDY OF MILITARY   B55
ELITES IN THE SOVIET SPHERE. ASIA CHINA/COM COM   FORCES
CZECHOSLVK FUT HUNGARY POLAND ROMANIA USSR ELITES   CHOOSE
STRATA ADMIN ATTIT PWR SKILL...METH/CNCPT BIOG 20.
PAGE 84 B1688

STOICOIU V.,LEGAL SOURCES AND BIBLIOGRAPHY OF   B64
ROMANIA. COM ROMANIA LAW FINAN POL/PAR LEGIS JUDGE   BIBLIOG/A
ADJUD CT/SYS PARL/PROC MARXISM 20. PAGE 101 B2041   JURID
                                         CONSTN
                                         ADMIN

ROMANO F. B1816

ROMASCO A.U. B1817

ROME....ROME

MONTER W.,THE GOVERNMENT OF GENEVA, 1536-1605   B63
(DOCTORAL THESIS). SWITZERLND DIPLOM LEAD ORD/FREE   SECT
SOVEREIGN 16/17 CALVIN/J ROME. PAGE 74 B1504   FINAN
                                         LOC/G
                                         ADMIN

ROME/ANC....ANCIENT ROME; SEE ALSO ROM/REP, ROM/EMP

ROMNEY/GEO....GEORGE ROMNEY

ANGEL D.D.,ROMNEY. LABOR LG/CO NAT/G EXEC WAR   B67
RACE/REL PERSON ORD/FREE...MGT WORSHIP 20   BIOG
ROMNEY/GEO CIV/RIGHTS MORMON GOVERNOR. PAGE 5 B0108   CHIEF
                                         PROVS
                                         POLICY

RONNING C.N. B0183

ROOSEVLT/F....PRESIDENT FRANKLIN D. ROOSEVELT

WILCOX J.K.,GUIDE TO THE OFFICIAL PUBLICATIONS OF   B34
THE NEW DEAL ADMINISTRATION (2 VOLS.). USA-45 CHIEF   BIBLIOG
LEGIS ADMIN...POLICY 20 CONGRESS ROOSEVLT/F.   NAT/G
PAGE 116 B2345   NEW/LIB
                                         RECEIVE

BAKER G.,THE COUNTY AGENT. USA-45 LOC/G NAT/G   B39
PROB/SOLV ADMIN...POLICY 20 ROOSEVLT/F NEW/DEAL   AGRI
COUNTY/AGT. PAGE 8 B0166   CONSULT
                                         GOV/REL
                                         EDU/PROP

FLYNN E.J.,YOU'RE THE BOSS. USA-45 ELITES TOP/EX   B47
DOMIN CONTROL EXEC LEAD REPRESENT 19/20 NEWYORK/C   LOC/G
ROOSEVLT/F FLYNN/BOSS BOSSISM. PAGE 36 B0732   MUNIC
                                         BIOG
                                         POL/PAR

SHERWOOD R.E.,ROOSEVELT AND HOPKINS. UK USA+45 USSR   B48
NAT/G EX/STRUC FORCES ADMIN ROUTINE PERSON PWR   TOP/EX
...TIME/SEQ 20 ROOSEVLT/F HOPKINS/H. PAGE 96 B1946   BIOG
                                         DIPLOM
                                         WAR

MORISON E.E.,TURMOIL AND TRADITION: A STUDY OF THE   B60
LIFE AND TIMES OF HENRY L. STIMSON. USA+45 USA-45   BIOG
POL/PAR CHIEF DELIB/GP FORCES BAL/PWR DIPLOM   NAT/G
ARMS/CONT WAR PEACE 19/20 STIMSON/HL ROOSEVLT/F   EX/STRUC
TAFT/WH HOOVER/H REPUBLICAN. PAGE 75 B1525

MARKMANN C.L.,JOHN F. KENNEDY: A SENSE OF PURPOSE.   B61
USA+45 INTELL FAM CONSULT DELIB/GP LEGIS PERSON   CHIEF
SKILL 20 KENNEDY/JF EISNHWR/DD ROOSEVLT/F   TOP/EX
NEW/FRONTR PRESIDENT. PAGE 69 B1399   ADMIN
                                         BIOG

KARL B.D.,EXECUTIVE REORGANIZATION AND REFORM IN   B63
THE NEW DEAL. ECO/DEV INDUS DELIB/GP EX/STRUC PLAN   BIOG
BUDGET ADMIN EFFICIENCY PWR POPULISM...POLICY 20   EXEC
PRESIDENT ROOSEVLT/F WILSON/W NEW/DEAL. PAGE 58   CREATE
B1174   CONTROL

GOODSELL C.T.,ADMINISTRATION OF A REVOLUTION.   B65
PUERT/RICO ECO/UNDEV FINAN MUNIC POL/PAR PROVS   EXEC
LEGIS PLAN BUDGET RECEIVE ADMIN COLONIAL LEAD 20   SOC
ROOSEVLT/F. PAGE 41 B0827

VIORST M.,HOSTILE ALLIES: FDR AND DE GAULLE.   B65
EUR+WWI USA-45 ELITES NAT/G VOL/ASSN FORCES LEGIS   TOP/EX
PLAN LEGIT ADMIN COERCE PERSON...BIOG TIME/SEQ 20   PWR
ROOSEVLT/F DEGAULLE/C. PAGE 112 B2263   WAR
                                         FRANCE

FARNSWORTH B.,WILLIAM C. BULLITT AND THE SOVIET   B67
UNION. COM USA-45 USSR NAT/G CHIEF CONSULT DELIB/GP   DIPLOM
EX/STRUC WAR REPRESENT MARXISM 20 WILSON/W   BIOG
ROOSEVLT/F STALIN/J BULLITT/WC. PAGE 35 B0705   POLICY

SALMOND J.A.,THE CIVILIAN CONSERVATION CORPS,   B67
1933-1942. USA-45 NAT/G CREATE EXEC EFFICIENCY   ADMIN
WEALTH...BIBLIOG 20 ROOSEVLT/F. PAGE 92 B1864   ECO/TAC
                                         TASK
                                         AGRI

WARREN S.,THE AMERICAN PRESIDENT. POL/PAR FORCES   B67
LEGIS DIPLOM ECO/TAC ADMIN EXEC PWR...ANTHOL 18/20   CHIEF
ROOSEVLT/F KENNEDY/JF JOHNSON/LB TRUMAN/HS   LEAD
WILSON/W. PAGE 114 B2297   NAT/G
                                         CONSTN

ROOSEVLT/T....PRESIDENT THEODORE ROOSEVELT

LIPPMANN W.,PREFACE TO POLITICS. LABOR CHIEF   B62
CONTROL LEAD...MYTH IDEA/COMP 19/20 ROOSEVLT/T   PARTIC
TAMMANY WILSON/H SANTAYAN/G BERGSON/H. PAGE 65   ATTIT
B1318   ADMIN

ROSE A.M. B1818

ROSE D.L. B1819

ROSENBERG B. B1820

ROSENFARB J. B1821

ROSENHAUPT H.W. B1822

ROSENTHAL A. B0864

N
PRINCETON U INDUSTRIAL REL SEC.SELECTED REFERENCES   BIBLIOG/A
OF THE INDUSTRIAL RELATIONS SECTION OF PRINCETON,   INDUS
NEW JERSEY. LG/CO NAT/G LEGIS WORKER PLAN PROB/SOLV LABOR
PAY ADMIN ROUTINE TASK GP/REL...PSY 20. PAGE 84   MGT
B1708

N
CONGRESSIONAL MONITOR. CONSULT DELIB/GP PROB/SOLV   BIBLIOG
PRESS DEBATE ROUTINE...POLICY CONGRESS. PAGE 1   LEGIS
B0002   REPRESENT
                                                     USA+45

N
REVUE FRANCAISE DE SCIENCE POLITIQUE. FRANCE UK   NAT/G
...BIBLIOG/A 20. PAGE 1 B0022   DIPLOM
                                                     CONCPT
                                                     ROUTINE

B00
MORRIS H.C.,THE HISTORY OF COLONIZATION. WOR+45   DOMIN
WOR-45 ECO/DEV ECO/UNDEV INT/ORG ACT/RES PLAN   SOVEREIGN
ECO/TAC LEGIT ROUTINE COERCE ATTIT DRIVE ALL/VALS   COLONIAL
...GEOG TREND 19. PAGE 76 B1528

B15
SAWYER R.A.,A LIST OF WORKS ON COUNTY GOVERNMENT.   BIBLIOG/A
LAW FINAN MUNIC TOP/EX ROUTINE CRIME...CLASSIF   LOC/G
RECORD 19/20. PAGE 93 B1871   GOV/REL
                                                     ADMIN

B17
HARLOW R.V.,THE HISTORY OF LEGISLATIVE METHODS IN   LEGIS
THE PERIOD BEFORE 1825. USA-45 EX/STRUC ADMIN   DELIB/GP
COLONIAL LEAD PARL/PROC ROUTINE...GP/COMP GOV/COMP   PROVS
HOUSE/REP. PAGE 47 B0948   POL/PAR

B21
STOWELL E.C.,INTERVENTION IN INTERNATIONAL LAW.   BAL/PWR
UNIV LAW SOCIETY INT/ORG ACT/RES PLAN LEGIT ROUTINE SOVEREIGN
WAR...JURID OBS GEN/LAWS 20. PAGE 101 B2050

L23
DOUGLAS P.H.,"OCCUPATIONAL V PROPORTIONAL   REPRESENT
REPRESENTATION." INDUS NAT/G PLAN ROUTINE SUFF   PROF/ORG
CONSEN DRIVE...CONCPT CLASSIF. PAGE 30 B0612   DOMIN
                                                     INGP/REL

B24
BAGEHOT W.,THE ENGLISH CONSTITUTION AND OTHER   NAT/G
POLITICAL ESSAYS. UK DELIB/GP BAL/PWR ADMIN CONTROL STRUCT
EXEC ROUTINE CONSERVE...METH PARLIAMENT 19/20.   CONCPT
PAGE 8 B0160

B24
MERRIAM C.E.,A HISTORY OF POLITICAL THEORIES -   UNIV
RECENT TIMES. USA-45 WOR-45 CULTURE SOCIETY ECO/DEV INTELL
R+D EDU/PROP ROUTINE CHOOSE ATTIT PERSON ALL/VALS
...POLICY SOC CONCPT METH/CNCPT OBS HIST/WRIT
TIME/SEQ TREND. PAGE 73 B1471

B25
MATHEWS J.M.,AMERICAN STATE GOVERNMENT. USA-45   PROVS
LOC/G CHIEF EX/STRUC LEGIS ADJUD CONTROL CT/SYS   ADMIN
ROUTINE GOV/REL PWR 20 GOVERNOR. PAGE 71 B1426   FEDERAL
                                                     CONSTN

B25
THOMAS F.,THE ENVIRONMENTAL BASIS OF SOCIETY.   SOCIETY
USA-45 WOR-45 STRATA ECO/DEV EXTR/IND CONSULT   GEOG
ECO/TAC ROUTINE ATTIT ALL/VALS...SOC TIME/SEQ.
PAGE 104 B2098

B27
ANGELL N.,THE PUBLIC MIND. USA-45 SOCIETY EDU/PROP   PERCEPT
ROUTINE SUPEGO KNOWL...POLICY CONCPT MYTH OBS/ENVIR ATTIT
EUR+WW1 TOT/POP 20. PAGE 5 B0109   DIPLOM
                                                     NAT/LISM

B27
WILLOUGHBY W.F.,PRINCIPLES OF PUBLIC ADMINISTRATION NAT/G
WITH SPECIAL REFERENCE TO THE NATIONAL AND STATE   EX/STRUC
GOVERNMENTS OF THE UNITED STATES. FINAN PROVS CHIEF OP/RES
CONSULT LEGIS CREATE BUDGET EXEC ROUTINE GOV/REL   ADMIN
CENTRAL...MGT 20 BUR/BUDGET CONGRESS PRESIDENT.
PAGE 117 B2356

B28
BUELL R.,THE NATIVE PROBLEM IN AFRICA. KIN LABOR   AFR
LOC/G ECO/TAC ROUTINE ORD/FREE...REC/INT KNO/TEST   CULTURE
CENSUS TREND CHARTS SOC/EXP STERTYP 20. PAGE 17
B0339

B28
CALKINS E.E.,BUSINESS THE CIVILIZER. INDUS MARKET   LAISSEZ
WORKER TAX PAY ROUTINE COST DEMAND MORAL 19/20.   POLICY
PAGE 18 B0367   WEALTH
                                                     PROFIT

B28
SOROKIN P.,CONTEMPORARY SOCIOLOGICAL THEORIES.   CULTURE
MOD/EUR EUR UNIV SOCIETY R+D SCHOOL ECO/TAC EDU/PROP SOC
ROUTINE ATTIT DRIVE...PSY CONCPT TIME/SEQ TREND   WAR
GEN/LAWS 20. PAGE 99 B1997

B29
MOLEY R.,POLITICS AND CRIMINAL PROSECUTION. USA-45   PWR
POL/PAR EX/STRUC LEGIT CONTROL LEAD ROUTINE CHOOSE   CT/SYS
INGP/REL...JURID CHARTS 20. PAGE 74 B1497   CRIME
                                                     ADJUD

B29
ROBERTS S.H.,HISTORY OF FRENCH COLONIAL POLICY. AFR INT/ORG
ASIA L/A+17C S/ASIA CULTURE ECO/DEV ECO/UNDEV FINAN ACT/RES
NAT/G PLAN ECO/TAC DOMIN ROUTINE SOVEREIGN...OBS   FRANCE
HIST/WRIT TREND CHARTS VAL/FREE 19/20. PAGE 89   COLONIAL
B1796

B30
MURCHISON C.,PSYCHOLOGIES OF 1930. UNIV USA-45   CREATE
CULTURE INTELL SOCIETY STRATA FAM ROUTINE BIO/SOC   PERSON
DRIVE RIGID/FLEX SUPEGO...NEW/IDEA OBS SELF/OBS
CONT/OBS 20. PAGE 76 B1543

B31
DEKAT A.D.A.,COLONIAL POLICY. S/ASIA CULTURE   DRIVE
EX/STRUC ECO/TAC DOMIN ADMIN COLONIAL ROUTINE   PWR
SOVEREIGN WEALTH...POLICY MGT RECORD KNO/TEST SAMP. INDONESIA
PAGE 28 B0570   NETHERLAND

B33
ENSOR R.C.K.,COURTS AND JUDGES IN FRANCE, GERMANY,   CT/SYS
AND ENGLAND. FRANCE GERMANY UK LAW PROB/SOLV ADMIN   EX/STRUC
ROUTINE CRIME ROLE...METH/COMP 20 CIVIL/LAW.   ADJUD
PAGE 33 B0676   NAT/COMP

B33
HETTINGER H.S.,A DECADE OF RADIO ADVERTISING.   EDU/PROP
USA-45 ECO/DEV CAP/ISM PRICE...CHARTS 20. PAGE 49   COM/IND
B0999   ECO/TAC
                                                     ROUTINE

B34
RIDLEY C.E.,THE CITY-MANAGER PROFESSION. CHIEF PLAN MUNIC
ADMIN CONTROL ROUTINE CHOOSE...TECHNIC CHARTS   EX/STRUC
GOV/COMP BIBLIOG 20. PAGE 88 B1780   LOC/G
                                                     EXEC

B35
GREER S.,BIBLIOGRAPHY ON CIVIL SERVICE AND   BIBLIOG/A
PERSONNEL ADMINISTRATION. USA-45 LOC/G PROVS WORKER ADMIN
PRICE SENIOR DRIVE...MGT 20. PAGE 43 B0870   NAT/G
                                                     ROUTINE

B36
GAUS J.M.,THE FRONTIERS OF PUBLIC ADMINISTRATION.   ROUTINE
EFFICIENCY PERCEPT RIGID/FLEX ORD/FREE 20. PAGE 39   GOV/REL
B0785   ELITES
                                                     PROB/SOLV

B37
BUREAU OF NATIONAL AFFAIRS,LABOR RELATIONS   LABOR
REFERENCE MANUAL VOL 1, 1935-1937. BARGAIN DEBATE   ADMIN
ROUTINE INGP/REL 20 NLRB. PAGE 17 B0351   ADJUD
                                                     NAT/G

B37
CLOKIE H.M.,ROYAL COMMISSIONS OF INQUIRY; THE   NAT/G
SIGNIFICANCE OF INVESTIGATIONS IN BRITISH POLITICS. DELIB/GP
UK POL/PAR CONFER ROUTINE...POLICY DECISION   INSPECT
TIME/SEQ 16/20. PAGE 22 B0439

B37
GOSNELL H.F.,MACHINE POLITICS: CHICAGO MODEL.   POL/PAR
COM/IND FACE/GP LOC/G EX/STRUC LEAD ROUTINE   MUNIC
SANCTION REPRESENT GOV/REL PWR...POLICY MATH OBS   ADMIN
INT CHARTS. PAGE 41 B0840   CHOOSE

B37
PARSONS T.,THE STRUCTURE OF SOCIAL ACTION. UNIV   CULTURE
INTELL SOCIETY INDUS MARKET ECO/TAC ROUTINE CHOOSE   ATTIT

ALL/VALS...CONCPT OBS BIOG TREND GEN/LAWS 20.
PAGE 81 B1636   CAP/ISM

                                                          B37
ROBBINS L.,ECONOMIC PLANNING AND INTERNATIONAL   INT/ORG
ORDER. WOR-45 SOCIETY FINAN INDUS NAT/G ECO/TAC   PLAN
ROUTINE WEALTH...SOC TIME/SEQ GEN/METH WORK 20   INT/TRADE
KEYNES/JM. PAGE 89 B1791

                                                          B38
DAY C.,A HISTORY OF COMMERCE. CHRIST-17C EUR+WWI   MARKET
ISLAM MEDIT-7 MOD/EUR USA-45 ECO/DEV FINAN NAT/G   INT/TRADE
ECO/TAC EXEC ROUTINE PWR WEALTH HIST/WRIT. PAGE 27
B0546

                                                          B38
LANGE O.,ON THE ECONOMIC THEORY OF SOCIALISM. UNIV   MARKET
ECO/DEV FINAN INDUS INT/ORG PUB/INST ROUTINE ATTIT   ECO/TAC
ALL/VALS...SOC CONCPT STAT TREND 20. PAGE 62 B1258   INT/TRADE
                                                       SOCISM
                                                          S39
MARX F.M.,"POLICY FORMULATION AND THE   ADMIN
ADMINISTRATIVE PROCESS" ROUTINE ADJUST EFFICIENCY   LEAD
OPTIMAL PRIVIL DRIVE PERSON OBJECTIVE...DECISION   INGP/REL
OBS GEN/METH. PAGE 70 B1418   MGT
                                                          C39
REISCHAUER R.,"JAPAN'S GOVERNMENT--POLITICS."   NAT/G
CONSTN STRATA POL/PAR FORCES LEGIS DIPLOM ADMIN   S/ASIA
EXEC CENTRAL...POLICY BIBLIOG 20 CHINJAP. PAGE 87   CONCPT
B1764   ROUTINE
                                                          S40
FAHS C.B.,"POLITICAL GROUPS IN THE JAPANESE HOUSE   ROUTINE
OF PEERS." ELITES NAT/G ADMIN GP/REL...TREND   POL/PAR
CHINJAP. PAGE 34 B0697   LEGIS
                                                          B41
COHEN E.W.,THE GROWTH OF THE BRITISH CIVIL SERVICE   OP/RES
1780-1939. UK NAT/G SENIOR ROUTINE GOV/REL...MGT   TIME/SEQ
METH/COMP BIBLIOG 18/20. PAGE 22 B0442   CENTRAL
                                                       ADMIN
                                                          S41
ABEL T.,"THE ELEMENT OF DECISION IN THE PATTERN OF   TEC/DEV
WAR." EUR+WWI NAT/G NAT/G TOP/EX DIPLOM ROUTINE   FORCES
COERCE DISPL PERCEPT PWR...SOC METH/CNCPT HIST/WRIT   WAR
TREND GEN/LAWS 20. PAGE 2 B0051
                                                          B42
DENNISON E.,THE SENATE FOREIGN RELATIONS COMMITTEE.   LEGIS
USA-45 NAT/G DELIB/GP ROUTINE CHOOSE PWR CONGRESS   ACT/RES
20. PAGE 28 B0574   DIPLOM
                                                          B42
HARLOW R.F.,PUBLIC RELATIONS IN WAR AND PEACE. FUT   WAR
USA-45 ECO/DEV ECO/TAC ROUTINE 20. PAGE 47 B0947   ATTIT
                                                       SOCIETY
                                                       INGP/REL
                                                          B42
LEISERSON A.,ADMINISTRATIVE REGULATION: A STUDY IN   LOBBY
REPRESENTATION OF INTERESTS. NAT/G EX/STRUC   GP/REL
PROB/SOLV BARGAIN CONFER ROUTINE REPRESENT PERS/REL   GOV/REL
UTIL PWR POLICY. PAGE 63 B1283
                                                          B42
SINGTON D.,THE GOEBBELS EXPERIMENT. GERMANY MOD/EUR   FASCISM
NAT/G EX/STRUC FORCES CONTROL ROUTINE WAR TOTALISM   EDU/PROP
PWR...ART/METH HUM 20 NAZI GOEBBELS/J. PAGE 97   ATTIT
B1970   COM/IND
                                                          B42
US STATE DEPT.,PEACE AND WAR: UNITED STATES FOREIGN   DIPLOM
POLICY, 1931-41. CULTURE FORCES ROUTINE CHOOSE   USA-45
ATTIT DRIVE PERSON 20. PAGE 111 B2237   PLAN
                                                          B43
YOUNG R.,THIS IS CONGRESS. FUT SENIOR ADMIN GP/REL   LEGIS
PWR...DECISION REFORMERS CONGRESS. PAGE 119 B2393   DELIB/GP
                                                       CHIEF
                                                       ROUTINE
                                                          L43
MACMAHON A.W.,"CONGRESSIONAL OVERSIGHT OF   LEGIS
ADMINISTRATION: THE POWER OF THE PURSE." USA-45   DELIB/GP
BUDGET ROUTINE GOV/REL PWR...POLICY CONGRESS.   ADMIN
PAGE 68 B1368   CONTROL
                                                          S43
SELZNICK P.,"AN APPROACH TO A THEORY OF   ROUTINE
BUREAUCRACY." INDUS WORKER CONTROL LEAD EFFICIENCY   ADMIN
OPTIMAL...SOC METH 20 BARNARD/C BUREAUCRCY   MGT
WEBER/MAX FRIEDRCH/C MICHELS/R. PAGE 95 B1928   EX/STRUC
                                                          B44
DAVIS H.E.,PIONEERS IN WORLD ORDER. WOR-45 CONSTN   INT/ORG
ECO/TAC DOMIN EDU/PROP LEGIT ADJUD ADMIN ARMS/CONT   ROUTINE
CHOOSE KNOWL ORD/FREE...POLICY JURID SOC STAT OBS
CENSUS TIME/SEQ ANTHOL LEAGUE/NAT 20. PAGE 26 B0537
                                                          S44
KEFAUVER E.,"THE NEED FOR BETTER EXECUTIVE-   LEGIS
LEGISLATIVE TEAMWORK IN THE NATIONAL GOVERNMENT."   EXEC
USA-45 CONSTN NAT/G ROUTINE...TRADIT CONGRESS   CONFER
REFORMERS. PAGE 59 B1188   LEAD
                                                          B45
BENJAMIN H.C.,EMPLOYMENT TESTS IN INDUSTRY AND   BIBLIOG/A
BUSINESS. LG/CO WORKER ROUTINE...MGT PSY SOC   METH
CLASSIF PROBABIL STAT APT/TEST KNO/TEST PERS/TEST   TESTS
20. PAGE 10 B0211   INDUS
                                                          B45
MILLIS H.A.,ORGANIZED LABOR (FIRST ED.). LAW STRUCT   LABOR

DELIB/GP WORKER ECO/TAC ADJUD CONTROL REPRESENT   POLICY
INGP/REL INCOME MGT. PAGE 74 B1485   ROUTINE
                                                       GP/REL
                                                          B45
RANSHOFFEN-WERTHEIMER EF.THE INTERNATIONAL   INT/ORG
SECRETARIAT: A GREAT EXPERIMENT IN INTERNATIONAL   EXEC
ADMINISTRATION. EUR+WWI FUT CONSTN FACE/GP CONSULT
DELIB/GP ACT/RES ADMIN ROUTINE PEACE ORD/FREE...MGT
RECORD ORG/CHARTS LEAGUE/NAT WORK 20. PAGE 86 B1731
                                                          C45
FISHER M.J.,"PARTIES AND POLITICS IN THE LOCAL   CHOOSE
COMMUNITY." USA-45 NAT/G SCHOOL ADMIN PARTIC   LOC/G
REPRESENT KNOWL...BIBLIOG 20. PAGE 36 B0724   POL/PAR
                                                       ROUTINE
                                                          L46
FORRESTAL J.,"THE NAVY: A STUDY IN ADMINISTRATION."   FORCES
ELITES FACE/GP EX/STRUC PROB/SOLV REPRESENT   INGP/REL
EFFICIENCY PRODUC. PAGE 37 B0741   ROUTINE
                                                       EXEC
                                                          B47
BARNARD C.,THE FUNCTIONS OF THE EXECUTIVE. USA+45   EXEC
ELITES INTELL LEGIT ATTIT DRIVE PERSON SKILL...PSY   EX/STRUC
SOC METH/CNCPT SOC/EXP GEN/METH VAL/FREE 20. PAGE 9   ROUTINE
B0187
                                                          B47
KEFAUVER E.,A TWENTIETH-CENTURY CONGRESS. POL/PAR   LEGIS
EX/STRUC SENIOR ADMIN CONTROL EXEC LOBBY CHOOSE   DELIB/GP
EFFICIENCY PWR. PAGE 59 B1189   ROUTINE
                                                       TOP/EX
                                                          S47
CALDWELL L.K.,"STRENGTHENING STATE LEGISLATURES"   PROVS
FUT DELIB/GP WEALTH REFORMERS. PAGE 18 B0364   LEGIS
                                                       ROUTINE
                                                       BUDGET
                                                          S47
GRAVES W.B.,"LEGISLATIVE REFERENCE SYSTEM FOR THE   LEGIS
CONGRESS OF THE UNITED STATES." ROUTINE...CLASSIF   STRUCT
TREND EXHIBIT CONGRESS. PAGE 42 B0856
                                                          B48
BONAPARTE M.,MYTHS OF WAR. GERMANY WOR+45 WOR-45   ROUTINE
CULTURE SOCIETY NAT/G FORCES LEGIT ATTIT ALL/VALS   MYTH
...CONCPT HIST/WRIT TIME/SEQ 20 JEWS. PAGE 13 B0271   WAR
                                                          B48
CHILDS J.R.,AMERICAN FOREIGN SERVICE. USA+45   DIPLOM
SOCIETY NAT/G ROUTINE GOV/REL 20 DEPT/STATE   ADMIN
CIVIL/SERV. PAGE 21 B0423   GP/REL
                                                          B48
ROSENFARB J.,FREEDOM AND THE ADMINISTRATIVE STATE.   ECO/DEV
NAT/G ROUTINE EFFICIENCY PRODUC RATIONAL UTIL   INDUS
...TECHNIC WELF/ST MGT 20 BUREAUCRCY. PAGE 90 B1821   PLAN
                                                       WEALTH
                                                          B48
SHERWOOD R.E.,ROOSEVELT AND HOPKINS. UK USA+45 USSR   TOP/EX
NAT/G EX/STRUC FORCES ADMIN ROUTINE PERSON PWR   BIOG
...TIME/SEQ 20 ROOSEVLT/F HOPKINS/H. PAGE 96 B1946   DIPLOM
                                                       WAR
                                                          B48
WHITE L.D.,INTRODUCTION OT THE STUDY OF PUBLIC   ADMIN
ADMINISTRATION. STRUCT PLAN PROB/SOLV EXEC ROUTINE   MGT
GOV/REL EFFICIENCY PWR CHARTS. PAGE 116 B2336   EX/STRUC
                                                       NAT/G
                                                          B48
WHITE L.D.,THE FEDERALISTS: A STUDY IN   ADMIN
ADMINISTRATIVE HISTORY. STRUCT DELIB/GP LEGIS   NAT/G
BUDGET ROUTINE GOV/REL GP/REL PERS/REL PWR...BIOG   POLICY
18/19 PRESIDENT CONGRESS WASHINGT/G JEFFERSN/T   PROB/SOLV
HAMILTON/A. PAGE 116 B2337
                                                          S48
COCH L.,"OVERCOMING RESISTANCE TO CHANGE" (BMR)"   WORKER
USA+45 CONSULT ADMIN ROUTINE GP/REL EFFICIENCY   OP/RES
PRODUC PERCEPT SKILL...CHARTS SOC/EXP 20. PAGE 22   PROC/MFG
B0441   RIGID/FLEX
                                                          B49
BURNS J.M.,CONGRESS ON TRIAL: THE LEGISLATIVE   LEGIS
PROCESS AND THE ADMINISTRATIVE STATE. USA+45 NAT/G   EXEC
ADMIN ROUTINE REPRESENT...PREDICT TREND. PAGE 17   GP/REL
B0354   PWR
                                                          B49
SINGER K.,THE IDEA OF CONFLICT. UNIV INTELL INT/ORG   ACT/RES
NAT/G PLAN ROUTINE ATTIT DRIVE ALL/VALS...POLICY   SOC
CONCPT TIME/SEQ. PAGE 97 B1966
                                                          L49
MARX C.M.,"ADMINISTRATIVE ETHICS AND THE RULE OF   ADMIN
LAW." USA+45 ELITES ACT/RES DOMIN NEUTRAL ROUTINE   LAW
INGP/REL ORD/FREE...JURID IDEA/COMP. PAGE 70 B1417
                                                          B50
GREAT BRITAIN TREASURY,PUBLIC ADMINISTRATION: A   BIBLIOG
BIBLIOGRAPHY FOR ORGANISATION AND METHODS   PLAN
(PAMPHLET). LOC/G NAT/G CONSULT EX/STRUC CONFER   CONTROL
ROUTINE TASK EFFICIENCY...MGT 20. PAGE 43 B0862   ADMIN
                                                          B50
HARTLAND P.C.,BALANCE OF INTERREGIONAL PAYMENTS OF   ECO/DEV
NEW ENGLAND. USA+45 TEC/DEV ECO/TAC LEGIT ROUTINE   FINAN
BAL/PAY PROFIT 20 NEW/ENGLND FED/RESERV. PAGE 47   REGION
B0962   PLAN

HYNEMAN C.S.,BUREAUCRACY IN A DEMOCRACY. CHIEF
LEGIS ADMIN CONTROL LEAD ROUTINE PERS/REL COST
EFFICIENCY UTIL ATTIT AUTHORIT PERSON MORAL.
PAGE 53 B1071
NAT/G CENTRAL EX/STRUC MYTH — B50

LASSWELL H.D.,NATIONAL SECURITY AND INDIVIDUAL
FREEDOM. USA+45 R+D NAT/G VOL/ASSN CONSULT DELIB/GP
LEGIT ADMIN KNOWL ORD/FREE PWR...PLURIST TOT/POP
COLD/WAR 20. PAGE 63 B1268
FACE/GP ROUTINE BAL/PWR — B50

MANNHEIM K.,FREEDOM, POWER, AND DEMOCRATIC
PLANNING. FUT USSR WOR+45 ELITES INTELL SOCIETY
NAT/G EDU/PROP ROUTINE ATTIT DRIVE SUPEGO SKILL
...POLICY PSY CONCPT TREND GEN/LAWS 20. PAGE 69
B1393
TEC/DEV PLAN CAP/ISM UK — B50

US SENATE COMM. GOVT. OPER.,"REVISION OF THE UN
CHARTER." FUT USA+45 WOR+45 CONSTN ECO/DEV
ECO/UNDEV NAT/G DELIB/GP ACT/RES CREATE PLAN EXEC
ROUTINE CHOOSE ALL/VALS...POLICY CONCPT CONGRESS UN
TOT/POP 20 COLD/WAR. PAGE 111 B2235
INT/ORG LEGIS PEACE — L50

HUMPHREY H.H.,"THE SENATE ON TRIAL." USA+45 POL/PAR
DEBATE REPRESENT EFFICIENCY ATTIT RIGID/FLEX
...TRADIT SENATE. PAGE 52 B1064
PARL/PROC ROUTINE PWR LEGIS — S50

STOKES W.S.,"HONDURAS: AN AREA STUDY IN
GOVERNMENT." HONDURAS NAT/G POL/PAR COLONIAL CT/SYS
ROUTINE CHOOSE REPRESENT...GEOG RECORD BIBLIOG
19/20. PAGE 101 B2044
CONSTN LAW L/A+17C ADMIN — C50

WAGER P.W.,"COUNTY GOVERNMENT ACROSS THE NATION."
USA+45 CONSTN COM/IND FINAN SCHOOL DOMIN CT/SYS
LEAD GOV/REL...STAT BIBLIOG 20. PAGE 112 B2272
LOC/G PROVS ADMIN ROUTINE — C50

HARDMAN J.B.,THE HOUSE OF LABOR. LAW R+D NEIGH
EDU/PROP LEAD ROUTINE REPRESENT GP/REL...POLICY
STAT. PAGE 47 B0945
LABOR LOBBY ADMIN PRESS — B51

NIELANDER W.A.,PUBLIC RELATIONS. USA+45 COM/IND
LOC/G NAT/G VOL/ASSN EX/STRUC DIPLOM EDU/PROP PRESS
TV...METH/CNCPT T 20. PAGE 78 B1583
PERS/REL GP/REL LG/CO ROUTINE — B51

PETERSON F.,SURVEY OF LABOR ECONOMICS (REV. ED.).
STRATA ECO/DEV LABOR INSPECT BARGAIN PAY PRICE EXEC
ROUTINE GP/REL ALL/VALS ORD/FREE 20 AFL/CIO
DEPT/LABOR. PAGE 82 B1662
WORKER DEMAND IDEA/COMP T — B51

MANGONE G.,"THE IDEA AND PRACTICE OF WORLD
GOVERNMENT." FUT WOR+45 WOR-45 ECO/DEV LEGIS CREATE
LEGIT ROUTINE ATTIT MORAL PWR WEALTH...CONCPT
GEN/LAWS 20. PAGE 69 B1388
INT/ORG SOCIETY INT/LAW — L51

INKELES A.,"UNDERSTANDING A FOREIGN SOCIETY: A
SOCIOLOGIST'S VIEW." SOCIETY ROUTINE KNOWL...PSY
CONCPT GEN/METH 20. PAGE 54 B1086
SOC METH/CNCPT PERCEPT ATTIT — S51

LERNER D.,"THE POLICY SCIENCES: RECENT DEVELOPMENTS
IN SCOPE AND METHODS." R+D SERV/IND CREATE DIPLOM
ROUTINE PWR...METH/CNCPT TREND GEN/LAWS METH 20.
PAGE 64 B1297
CONSULT SOC — S51

MOORE B.,"SOVIET POLITICS - THE DILEMMA OF POWER:
THE ROLE OF IDEAS IN SOCIAL CHANGE." USSR PROB/SOLV
DIPLOM EDU/PROP ADMIN LEAD ROUTINE REV...POLICY
DECISION BIBLIOG 20. PAGE 75 B1512
ATTIT PWR CONCPT MARXISM — C51

DONHAM W.B.,ADMINISTRATION AND BLIND SPOTS. LG/CO
EX/STRUC BARGAIN ADJUD ROUTINE ROLE SUPEGO 20.
PAGE 30 B0605
ADMIN TOP/EX DECISION POLICY — B52

MAIER N.R.F.,PRINCIPLES OF HUMAN RELATIONS. WOR+45
WOR-45 CULTURE SOCIETY ROUTINE ATTIT DRIVE PERCEPT
PERSON RIGID/FLEX SUPEGO PWR...PSY CONT/OBS RECORD
TOT/POP VAL/FREE 20. PAGE 68 B1379
INDUS — B52

MILLER M.,THE JUDGES AND THE JUDGED. USA+45 LG/CO
ACT/RES TV ROUTINE SANCTION NAT/LISM ATTIT ORD/FREE
...POLICY ACLU. PAGE 73 B1481
COM/IND DISCRIM EDU/PROP MARXISM — B52

REDFORD E.S.,ADMINISTRATION OF NATIONAL ECONOMIC
CONTROL. ECO/DEV DELIB/GP ADJUD CONTROL EQUILIB 20.
PAGE 87 B1753
ADMIN ROUTINE GOV/REL LOBBY — B52

WRIGHT Q.,"CONGRESS AND THE TREATY-MAKING POWER."
USA+45 WOR+45 CONSTN INTELL NAT/G CHIEF CONSULT
EX/STRUC LEGIS TOP/EX CREATE GOV/REL DISPL DRIVE
ROUTINE DIPLOM INT/LAW — L52

RIGID/FLEX...TREND TOT/POP CONGRESS CONGRESS 20
TREATY. PAGE 118 B2384
DELIB/GP — S52

TAYLOR D.W.,"TWENTY QUESTIONS: EFFICIENCY IN
PROBLEM SOLVING AS A FUNCTION OF SIZE OF GROUP"
WOR+45 CONFER ROUTINE INGP/REL...PSY GP/COMP 20.
PAGE 103 B2085
PROB/SOLV EFFICIENCY SKILL PERCEPT — S52

LARSEN K.,NATIONAL BIBLIOGRAPHIC SERVICES: THEIR
CREATION AND OPERATION. WOR+45 COM/IND CREATE PLAN
DIPLOM PRESS ADMIN ROUTINE...MGT UNESCO. PAGE 62
B1262
BIBLIOG/A INT/ORG WRITING — B53

MACMAHON A.W.,ADMINISTRATION IN FOREIGN AFFAIRS.
NAT/G CONSULT DELIB/GP LEGIS ACT/RES CREATE ADMIN
EXEC RIGID/FLEX PWR...METH/CNCPT TIME/SEQ TOT/POP
VAL/FREE 20. PAGE 68 B1369
USA+45 ROUTINE FOR/AID DIPLOM — B53

SAYLES L.R.,THE LOCAL UNION. CONSTN CULTURE
DELIB/GP PARTIC CHOOSE GP/REL INGP/REL ATTIT ROLE
...MAJORIT DECISION MGT. PAGE 93 B1873
LABOR LEAD ADJUD ROUTINE — B53

BULNER-THOMAS I.,"THE PARTY SYSTEM IN GREAT
BRITAIN." UK CONSTN SECT PRESS CONFER GP/REL ATTIT
...POLICY TREND BIBLIOG 19/20 PARLIAMENT. PAGE 17
B0343
NAT/G POL/PAR ADMIN ROUTINE — C53

DUVERGER M.,POLITICAL PARTIES: THEIR ORGANIZATION
AND ACTIVITY IN THE MODERN STATE. EUR+WWI MOD/EUR
USA+45 USA-45 EDU/PROP ADMIN ROUTINE ATTIT DRIVE
ORD/FREE PWR...SOC CONCPT MATH STAT TIME/SEQ
TOT/POP 19/20. PAGE 31 B0635
POL/PAR EX/STRUC ELITES — B54

LAPIERRE R.T.,A THEORY OF SOCIAL CONTROL. STRUCT
ADMIN ROUTINE SANCTION ANOMIE AUTHORIT DRIVE PERSON
PWR...MAJORIT CONCPT CLASSIF. PAGE 62 B1260
CONTROL VOL/ASSN CULTURE — B54

MANGONE G.,A SHORT HISTORY OF INTERNATIONAL
ORGANIZATION. MOD/EUR USA+45 USA-45 WOR+45 WOR-45
LAW LEGIS CREATE LEGIT ROUTINE RIGID/FLEX PWR
...JURID CONCPT OBS TIME/SEQ STERTYP GEN/LAWS UN
TOT/POP VAL/FREE 18/20. PAGE 69 B1389
INT/ORG INT/LAW — B54

MCCLOSKEY J.F.,OPERATIONS RESEARCH FOR MANAGEMENT.
STRUCT COMPUTER ADMIN ROUTINE...PHIL/SCI CONCPT
METH/CNCPT TREND ANTHOL BIBLIOG 20. PAGE 72 B1445
OP/RES MGT METH/COMP TEC/DEV — B54

MILLARD E.L.,FREEDOM IN A FEDERAL WORLD. FUT WOR+45
VOL/ASSN TOP/EX LEGIT ROUTINE FEDERAL PEACE ATTIT
DISPL ORD/FREE PWR...MAJORIT INT/LAW JURID TREND
COLD/WAR 20. PAGE 73 B1479
INT/ORG CREATE ADJUD BAL/PWR — B54

ROSTOW W.W.,"ASIAN LEADERSHIP AND FREE-WORLD
ALLIANCE." ASIA COM USA+45 CULTURE ELITES INTELL
NAT/G TEC/DEV ECO/TAC EDU/PROP COLONIAL PARL/PROC
ROUTINE COERCE DRIVE ORD/FREE MARXISM...PSY CONCPT.
PAGE 90 B1829
ATTIT LEGIT DIPLOM — L54

WOLFERS A.,"COLLECTIVE SECURITY AND THE WAR IN
KOREA." ASIA KOREA USA+45 INT/ORG DIPLOM ROUTINE
...GEN/LAWS UN COLD/WAR 20. PAGE 117 B2370
ACT/RES LEGIT — S54

ZELLER B.,"AMERICAN STATE LEGISLATURES: REPORT ON
THE COMMITTEE ON AMERICAN LEGISLATURES." CONSTN
POL/PAR EX/STRUC CONFER ADMIN CONTROL EXEC LOBBY
ROUTINE GOV/REL...POLICY BIBLIOG 20. PAGE 119 B2401
REPRESENT LEGIS PROVS APPORT — C54

BEISEL A.R.,CONTROL OVER ILLEGAL ENFORCEMENT OF THE
CRIMINAL LAW: ROLE OF THE SUPREME COURT. CONSTN
ROUTINE MORAL PWR...SOC 20 SUPREME/CT. PAGE 10
B0207
ORD/FREE LAW CRIME — B55

BERNAYS E.L.,THE ENGINEERING OF CONSENT. VOL/ASSN
OP/RES ROUTINE INGP/REL ATTIT RESPECT...POLICY
METH/CNCPT METH/COMP 20. PAGE 11 B0224
GP/REL PLAN ACT/RES ADJUST — B55

BLAU P.M.,THE DYNAMICS OF BUREAUCRACY: A STUDY OF
INTERPERSONAL RELATIONS IN TWO GOVERNMENT AGENCIES.
USA+45 EX/STRUC REPRESENT INGP/REL PERS/REL.
PAGE 12 B0251
CLIENT ADMIN EXEC ROUTINE — B55

BRAUN K.,LABOR DISPUTES AND THEIR SETTLEMENT.
ECO/TAC ROUTINE TASK GP/REL...DECISION GEN/LAWS.
PAGE 15 B0301
INDUS LABOR BARGAIN ADJUD — B55

CRAIG J.,BIBLIOGRAPHY OF PUBLIC ADMINISTRATION IN
AUSTRALIA. CONSTN FINAN EX/STRUC LEGIS PLAN DIPLOM
RECEIVE ADJUD ROUTINE...HEAL 19/20 AUSTRAL
PARLIAMENT. PAGE 24 B0500
BIBLIOG GOV/REL ADMIN NAT/G — B55

GALLOWAY G.B.,CONGRESS AND PARLIAMENT: THEIR
ORGANIZATION AND OPERATION IN THE US AND THE UK:
DELIB/GP LEGIS — B55

PLANNING PAMPHLET NO. 93. POL/PAR EX/STRUC DEBATE
CONTROL LEAD ROUTINE EFFICIENCY PWR...POLICY
CONGRESS PARLIAMENT. PAGE 38 B0777

PARL/PROC
GOV/COMP

B55

SMITHIES A.,THE BUDGETARY PROCESS IN THE UNITED
STATES. ECO/DEV AGRI EX/STRUC FORCES LEGIS
PROB/SOLV TAX ROUTINE EFFICIENCY...MGT CONGRESS
PRESIDENT. PAGE 98 B1987

NAT/G
ADMIN
BUDGET
GOV/REL

B55

STEPHENS O.,FACTS TO A CANDID WORLD. USA+45 WOR+45
COM/IND EX/STRUC PRESS ROUTINE EFFICIENCY ATTIT
...PSY 20. PAGE 100 B2033

EDU/PROP
PHIL/SCI
NAT/G
DIPLOM

S55

ANGELL R.,"GOVERNMENTS AND PEOPLES AS A FOCI FOR
PEACE-ORIENTED RESEARCH." WOR+45 CULTURE SOCIETY
FACE/GP ACT/RES CREATE PLAN DIPLOM EDU/PROP ROUTINE
ATTIT PERCEPT SKILL...POLICY CONCPT OBS TREND
GEN/METH 20. PAGE 5 B0110

FUT
SOC
PEACE

S55

CHAPIN F.S.,"FORMALIZATION OBSERVED IN TEN
VOLUNTARY ORGANIZATIONS: CONCEPTS, MORPHOLOGY,
PROCESS." STRUCT INGP/REL PERS/REL...METH/CNCPT
CLASSIF OBS RECORD. PAGE 20 B0407

VOL/ASSN
ROUTINE
CONTROL
OP/RES

S55

CROCKETT W.H.,"EMERGENT LEADERSHIP IN SMALL
DECISION MAKING GROUPS." ACT/RES ROUTINE PERS/REL
ATTIT...STAT CONT/OBS SOC/EXP SIMUL. PAGE 25 B0507

DELIB/GP
ADMIN
PSY
DECISION

S55

DRUCKER P.F.,"'MANAGEMENT SCIENCE' AND THE
MANAGER." PLAN ROUTINE RIGID/FLEX...METH/CNCPT LOG
HYPO/EXP. PAGE 30 B0620

MGT
STRUCT
DECISION
RATIONAL

S55

KAUTSKY J.H.,"THE NEW STRATEGY OF INTERNATIONAL
COMMUNISM." ASIA CHINA/COM FUT WOR+45 WOR-45 ADMIN
ROUTINE PERSON MARXISM SOCISM...TREND IDEA/COMP 20
LENIN/VI MAO. PAGE 59 B1184

COM
POL/PAR
TOTALISM
USSR

S55

MARTIN R.C.,"ADMINISTRATIVE LEADERSHIP IN
GOVERNMENT." NAT/G PARTIC ROUTINE INGP/REL...MGT
20. PAGE 70 B1413

TOP/EX
ADMIN
EXEC
REPRESENT

S55

TORRE M.,"PSYCHIATRIC OBSERVATIONS OF INTERNATIONAL
CONFERENCES." WOR+45 INT/ORG PROF/ORG VOL/ASSN
CONSULT EDU/PROP ROUTINE ATTIT DRIVE KNOWL...PSY
METH/CNCPT OBS/ENVIR STERTYP 20. PAGE 105 B2119

DELIB/GP
OBS
DIPLOM

S55

WEISS R.S.,"A METHOD FOR THE ANALYSIS OF THE
STRUCTURE OF COMPLEX ORGANIZATIONS." WOR+45 INDUS
LG/CO NAT/G EXEC ROUTINE ORD/FREE PWR SKILL...MGT
PSY SOC NEW/IDEA STAT INT REC/INT STAND/INT CHARTS
WORK. PAGE 115 B2316

PROF/ORG
SOC/EXP

S55

WRIGHT Q.,"THE PEACEFUL ADJUSTMENT OF INTERNATIONAL
RELATIONS: PROBLEMS AND RESEARCH APPROACHES." UNIV
INTELL EDU/PROP ADJUD ROUTINE KNOWL SKILL...INT/LAW
JURID PHIL/SCI CLASSIF 20. PAGE 118 B2385

R+D
METH/CNCPT
PEACE

B56

BLAU P.M.,BUREAUCRACY IN MODERN SOCIETY. STRUCT
INDUS LABOR LG/CO LOC/G NAT/G FORCES EDU/PROP
ROUTINE ORD/FREE 20 BUREAUCRCY. PAGE 12 B0252

SOC
EX/STRUC
ADMIN
EFFICIENCY

B56

ECOLE NAT'L D'ADMINISTRATION,RECRUITMENT AND
TRAINING FOR THE HIGHER CIVIL SERVICE IN FRANCE.
FRANCE EX/STRUC PLAN EDU/PROP CONTROL ROUTINE TASK
COST...METH 20 CIVIL/SERV. PAGE 32 B0650

ADMIN
MGT
EXEC
ACADEM

B56

FRANCIS R.G.,SERVICE AND PROCEDURE IN BUREAUCRACY.
EXEC LEAD ROUTINE...QU 20. PAGE 37 B0748

CLIENT
ADMIN
INGP/REL
REPRESENT

B56

KAUFMANN W.W.,MILITARY POLICY AND NATIONAL
SECURITY. USA+45 ELITES INTELL NAT/G TOP/EX PLAN
BAL/PWR DIPLOM ROUTINE COERCE NUC/PWR ATTIT
ORD/FREE PWR 20 COLD/WAR. PAGE 58 B1182

FORCES
CREATE

B56

LOVEDAY A.,REFLECTIONS ON INTERNATIONAL
ADMINISTRATION. WOR+45 WOR-45 DELIB/GP ACT/RES
ADMIN EXEC ROUTINE DRIVE...METH/CNCPT TIME/SEQ
CON/ANAL SIMUL TOT/POP 20. PAGE 67 B1342

INT/ORG
MGT

B56

POWELL N.J.,PERSONNEL ADMINISTRATION IN GOVERNMENT.
COM/IND POL/PAR LEGIS PAY CT/SYS ROUTINE GP/REL
PERS/REL...POLICY METH 20 CIVIL/SERV. PAGE 84 B1697

ADMIN
WORKER
LOC/G
NAT/G

B56

SOHN L.B.,BASIC DOCUMENTS OF THE UNITED NATIONS.
WOR+45 LAW INT/ORG LEGIT EXEC ROUTINE CHOOSE PWR
...JURID CONCPT GEN/LAWS ANTHOL UN TOT/POP OAS FAO
ILO 20. PAGE 99 B1993

DELIB/GP
CONSTN

EISENTADT S.N.,"POLITICAL STRUGGLE IN BUREAUCRATIC
SOCIETIES" ASIA CULTURE ADJUD SANCTION PWR
BUREAUCRCY OTTOMAN BYZANTINE. PAGE 33 B0661

L56

ADMIN
CHIEF
CONTROL
ROUTINE

L56

LITCHFIELD E.H.,"NOTES ON A GENERAL THEORY OF
ADMINISTRATION." USA+45 OP/RES PROB/SOLV EFFICIENCY
IDEA/COMP. PAGE 66 B1324

ADMIN
ROUTINE
MGT

C56

AUMANN F.R.,"THE ISTRUMENTALITIES OF JUSTICE: THEIR
FORMS, FUNCTIONS, AND LIMITATIONS." WOR+45 WOR-45
JUDGE PROB/SOLV ROUTINE ATTIT...BIBLIOG 20. PAGE 7
B0147

JURID
ADMIN
CT/SYS
ADJUD

B57

ASHER R.E.,THE UNITED NATIONS AND THE PROMOTION OF
THE GENERAL WELFARE. WOR+45 ECO/UNDEV
EX/STRUC ACT/RES PLAN EDU/PROP ROUTINE HEALTH...HUM
CONCPT CHARTS UNESCO UN ILO 20. PAGE 7 B0139

INT/ORG
CONSULT

B57

BERGER M.,BUREAUCRACY AND SOCIETY IN MODERN EGYPT;
A STUDY OF THE HIGHER CIVIL SERVICE. UAR REPRESENT
...QU 20. PAGE 11 B0221

ATTIT
EXEC
ADMIN
ROUTINE

B57

DE GRAZIA A.,GRASS ROOTS PRIVATE WELFARE. LOC/G
SCHOOL ACT/RES EDU/PROP ROUTINE CROWD GP/REL
DISCRIM HAPPINESS ILLEGIT AGE HABITAT. PAGE 27
B0554

NEW/LIB
HEALTH
MUNIC
VOL/ASSN

B57

HOLCOMBE A.N.,STRENGTHENING THE UNITED NATIONS.
USA+45 ACT/RES CREATE PLAN EDU/PROP ATTIT PERCEPT
PWR...METH/CNCPT CONT/OBS RECORD UN COLD/WAR 20.
PAGE 51 B1032

INT/ORG
ROUTINE

B57

HUNTINGTON S.P.,THE SOLDIER AND THE STATE: THE
THEORY AND POLITICS OF CIVIL-MILITARY RELATIONS.
USA+45 USA-45 NAT/G PROF/ORG CONSULT DOMIN LEGIT
ROUTINE ATTIT PWR...CONCPT TIME/SEQ COLD/WAR 20.
PAGE 53 B1065

ACT/RES
FORCES

B57

MORSTEIN-MARX F.,THE ADMINISTRATIVE STATE: AN
INTRODUCTION TO BUREAUCRACY. EUR+WWI FUT MOD/EUR
USA+45 USA-45 NAT/G CONSULT ADMIN ROUTINE TOTALISM
DRIVE SKILL...TREND 19/20. PAGE 76 B1530

EXEC
MGT
CAP/ISM
ELITES

B57

MURRAY J.N.,THE UNITED NATIONS TRUSTEESHIP SYSTEM.
AFR WOR+45 CONSTN CONSULT LEGIS EDU/PROP LEGIT EXEC
ROUTINE...INT TIME/SEQ SOMALI UN 20. PAGE 77 B1547

INT/ORG
DELIB/GP

B57

SELZNICK,LEADERSHIP IN ADMINISTRATION: A
SOCIOLOGICAL INTERPRETATION. CREATE PROB/SOLV EXEC
ROUTINE EFFICIENCY RATIONAL KNOWL...POLICY PSY.
PAGE 95 B1927

LEAD
ADMIN
DECISION
NAT/G

B57

SHARMA S.R.,SOME ASPECTS OF THE INDIAN
ADMINISTRATIVE SYSTEM. INDIA WOR+45 TEC/DEV BUDGET
LEGIT ROUTINE ATTIT. PAGE 96 B1937

EXEC
DECISION
ADMIN
INGP/REL

B57

SIMON H.A.,MODELS OF MAN, SOCIAL AND RATIONAL:
MATHEMATICAL ESSAYS ON RATIONAL HUMAN BEHAVIOR IN A
SOCIAL SETTING. UNIV LAW SOCIETY FACE/GP VOL/ASSN
CONSULT EX/STRUC LEGIS CREATE ADMIN ROUTINE ATTIT
DRIVE PWR...SOC CONCPT METH/CNCPT QUANT STAT
TOT/POP VAL/FREE 20. PAGE 97 B1959

MATH
SIMUL

S57

DANIELSON L.E.,"SUPERVISORY PROBLEMS IN DECISION
MAKING." WORKER ADMIN ROUTINE TASK MGT. PAGE 26
B0529

PROB/SOLV
DECISION
CONTROL
GP/REL

S57

HARRIS J.P.,"LEGISLATIVE CONTROL OF ADMINISTRATION:
SOME COMPARISONS OF AMERICAN AND EUROPEAN
PRACTICES." DEBATE PARL/PROC ROUTINE GOV/REL
EFFICIENCY SUPEGO DECISION. PAGE 47 B0954

LEGIS
CONTROL
EX/STRUC
REPRESENT

S57

HODGETTS J.E.,"THE CIVIL SERVICE AND POLICY
FORMATION." CANADA NAT/G EX/STRUC ROUTINE GOV/REL
20. PAGE 50 B1023

ADMIN
DECISION
EFFICIENCY
POLICY

S57

HUITT R.K.,"THE MORSE COMMITTEE ASSIGNMENT
CONTROVERSY: A STUDY IN SENATE NORMS." USA+45
USA-45 POL/PAR SENIOR ROLE SUPEGO SENATE. PAGE 52
B1061

LEGIS
ETIQUET
PWR
ROUTINE

B58

CHEEK G.,ECONOMIC AND SOCIAL IMPLICATIONS OF
AUTOMATION: A BIBLIOGRAPHIC REVIEW (PAMPHLET).
USA+45 LG/CO WORKER CREATE PLAN CONTROL ROUTINE
PERS/REL EFFICIENCY PRODUC...METH/COMP 20. PAGE 20
B0416

BIBLIOG/A
SOCIETY
INDUS
AUTOMAT

B58

DEVLIN P.,THE CRIMINAL PROSECUTION IN ENGLAND. UK
NAT/G ADMIN ROUTINE EFFICIENCY...JURID SOC 20.
PAGE 29 B0583

CRIME
LAW
METH

MARCH J.G.,ORGANIZATIONS. USA+45 CREATE OP/RES PLAN
PROB/SOLV PARTIC ROUTINE RATIONAL ATTIT PERCEPT
...DECISION BIBLIOG. PAGE 69 B1397
`CT/SYS` `B58` `MGT` `PERSON` `DRIVE` `CONCPT`

MELMAN S.,DECISION-MAKING AND PRODUCTIVITY. INDUS
EX/STRUC WORKER OP/RES PROB/SOLV TEC/DEV ADMIN
ROUTINE RIGID/FLEX GP/COMP. PAGE 73 B1464
`B58` `LABOR` `PRODUC` `DECISION` `MGT`

STEWART J.D.,BRITISH PRESSURE GROUPS: THEIR ROLE IN
RELATION TO THE HOUSE OF COMMONS. UK CONSULT
DELIB/GP ADMIN ROUTINE CHOOSE REPRESENT ATTIT ROLE
20 HOUSE/CMNS PARLIAMENT. PAGE 101 B2038
`B58` `LOBBY` `LEGIS` `PLAN` `PARL/PROC`

CYERT R.M.,"THE ROLE OF EXPECTATIONS IN BUSINESS
DECISION-MAKING." PROB/SOLV PRICE RIGID/FLEX.
PAGE 25 B0516
`L58` `LG/CO` `DECISION` `ROUTINE` `EXEC`

BLAISDELL D.C.,"PRESSURE GROUPS, FOREIGN POLICIES,
AND INTERNATIONAL POLITICS." USA+45 WOR+45 INT/ORG
PLAN DOMIN EDU/PROP LEGIT ADMIN ROUTINE CHOOSE
...DECISION MGT METH/CNCPT CON/ANAL 20. PAGE 12
B0249
`S58` `PROF/ORG` `PWR`

JORDAN A.,"MILITARY ASSISTANCE AND NATIONAL
POLICY." ASIA FUT USA+45 WOR+45 ECO/DEV ECO/UNDEV
INT/ORG NAT/G PLAN ECO/TAC ROUTINE WEAPON
RIGID/FLEX PWR...CONCPT TREND 20. PAGE 57 B1153
`S58` `FORCES` `POLICY` `FOR/AID` `DIPLOM`

MAIR L.P.,"REPRESENTATIVE LOCAL GOVERNMENT AS A
PROBLEM IN SOCIAL CHANGE." ECO/UNDEV KIN LOC/G
NAT/G SCHOOL JUDGE ADMIN ROUTINE REPRESENT
RIGID/FLEX RESPECT...CONCPT STERTYP CMN/WLTH 20.
PAGE 68 B1383
`S58` `AFR` `PWR` `ELITES`

MANSFIELD E.,"A STUDY OF DECISION-MAKING WITHIN THE
FIRM." LG/CO WORKER INGP/REL COST EFFICIENCY PRODUC
...CHARTS 20. PAGE 69 B1395
`S58` `OP/RES` `PROB/SOLV` `AUTOMAT` `ROUTINE`

MITCHELL W.C.,"OCCUPATIONAL ROLE STRAINS: THE
AMERICAN ELECTIVE PUBLIC OFFICIAL." CONTROL
RIGID/FLEX SUPEGO HEALTH ORD/FREE...SOC INT QU.
PAGE 74 B1492
`S58` `ANOMIE` `DRIVE` `ROUTINE` `PERSON`

STAAR R.F.,"ELECTIONS IN COMMUNIST POLAND." EUR+WWI
SOCIETY INT/ORG NAT/G POL/PAR LEGIS ACT/RES ECO/TAC
EDU/PROP ADJUD ADMIN ROUTINE COERCE TOTALISM ATTIT
ORD/FREE PWR 20. PAGE 100 B2015
`S58` `COM` `CHOOSE` `POLAND`

CHAPMAN B.,THE PROFESSION OF GOVERNMENT: THE PUBLIC
SERVICE IN EUROPE. MOD/EUR LABOR CT/SYS...T 20
CIVIL/SERV. PAGE 20 B0409
`B59` `ADMIN` `CONTROL` `ROUTINE` `EX/STRUC`

DIEBOLD W. JR.,THE SCHUMAN PLAN: A STUDY IN
ECONOMIC COOPERATION, 1950-1959. EUR+WWI FRANCE
GERMANY USA+45 EXTR/IND CONSULT DELIB/GP PLAN
DIPLOM ECO/TAC INT/TRADE ROUTINE ORD/FREE WEALTH
...METH/CNCPT STAT CONT/OBS INT TIME/SEQ ECSC 20.
PAGE 29 B0591
`B59` `INT/ORG` `REGION`

DIMOCK M.E.,ADMINISTRATIVE VITALITY: THE CONFLICT
WITH BUREAUCRACY. PROB/SOLV EXEC 20. PAGE 29 B0597
`B59` `REPRESENT` `ADMIN` `EX/STRUC` `ROUTINE`

GOODRICH L.,THE UNITED NATIONS. WOR+45 CONSTN
STRUCT ACT/RES LEGIT COERCE KNOWL ORD/FREE PWR
...GEN/LAWS UN 20. PAGE 41 B0825
`B59` `INT/ORG` `ROUTINE`

GRABER D.,CRISIS DIPLOMACY. L/A+17C USA+45 USA-45
NAT/G TOP/EX ECO/TAC COERCE ATTIT ORD/FREE...CONCPT
MYTH TIME/SEQ COLD/WAR 20. PAGE 42 B0848
`B59` `ROUTINE` `MORAL` `DIPLOM`

SCHURZ W.L.,AMERICAN FOREIGN AFFAIRS: A GUIDE TO
INTERNATIONAL AFFAIRS. USA+45 WOR+45 WOR-45 NAT/G
FORCES LEGIS TOP/EX PLAN EDU/PROP LEGIT ADMIN
ROUTINE ATTIT ORD/FREE PWR...SOC CONCPT STAT
SAMP/SIZ CHARTS STERTYP 20. PAGE 95 B1910
`B59` `INT/ORG` `SOCIETY` `DIPLOM`

WASSERMAN P.,MEASUREMENT AND ANALYSIS OF
ORGANIZATIONAL PERFORMANCE. FINAN MARKET EX/STRUC
TEC/DEV EDU/PROP CONTROL ROUTINE TASK...MGT 20.
PAGE 114 B2300
`B59` `BIBLIOG/A` `ECO/TAC` `OP/RES` `EFFICIENCY`

YANG C.K.,A CHINESE VILLAGE IN EARLY COMMUNIST
TRANSITION. ECO/UNDEV AGRI FAM KIN MUNIC FORCES
PLAN ECO/TAC DOMIN EDU/PROP ATTIT DRIVE PWR RESPECT
...SOC CONCPT METH/CNCPT OBS RECORD CON/ANAL CHARTS
WORK 20. PAGE 118 B2389
`B59` `ASIA` `ROUTINE` `SOCISM`

BENNIS W.G.,"LEADERSHIP THEORY AND ADMINISTRATIVE
BEHAVIOR: THE PROBLEM OF AUTHORITY." ROUTINE...MGT
HYPO/EXP. PAGE 10 B0214
`L59` `LEAD` `ADMIN` `DOMIN` `PERS/REL`

CALKINS R.D.,"THE DECISION PROCESS IN
ADMINISTRATION." EX/STRUC PROB/SOLV ROUTINE MGT.
PAGE 18 B0368
`S59` `ADMIN` `OP/RES` `DECISION` `CON/ANAL`

CYERT R.M.,"MODELS IN A BEHAVIORAL THEORY OF THE
FIRM." ROUTINE...DECISION MGT METH/CNCPT MATH.
PAGE 25 B0517
`S59` `SIMUL` `GAME` `PREDICT` `INDUS`

HARVEY M.F.,"THE PALESTINE REFUGEE PROBLEM:
ELEMENTS OF A SOLUTION." ISLAM LAW INT/ORG DELIB/GP
TOP/EX ECO/TAC ROUTINE DRIVE HEALTH LOVE ORD/FREE
PWR WEALTH...MAJORIT FAO 20. PAGE 48 B0964
`S59` `ACT/RES` `LEGIT` `PEACE` `ISRAEL`

HOFFMANN S.,"IMPLEMENTATION OF INTERNATIONAL
INSTRUMENTS ON HUMAN RIGHTS." WOR+45 VOL/ASSN
DELIB/GP JUDGE EDU/PROP LEGIT ROUTINE PEACE
COLD/WAR 20. PAGE 51 B1029
`S59` `INT/ORG` `MORAL`

LASSWELL H.D.,"UNIVERSALITY IN PERSPECTIVE." FUT
UNIV SOCIETY CONSULT TOP/EX PLAN EDU/PROP ADJUD
ROUTINE ARMS/CONT COERCE PEACE ATTIT PERSON
ALL/VALS. PAGE 63 B1271
`S59` `INT/ORG` `JURID` `TOTALISM`

ROBINSON J.A.,"THE ROLE OF THE RULES COMMITTEE IN
ARRANGING THE PROGRAM OF THE UNITED STATES HOUSE OF
REPRESENTATIVES." USA+45 DEBATE CONTROL AUTHORIT
HOUSE/REP. PAGE 89 B1801
`S59` `PARL/PROC` `DELIB/GP` `ROUTINE` `LEGIS`

SOHN L.B.,"THE DEFINITION OF AGGRESSION." FUT LAW
FORCES LEGIT ADJUD ROUTINE COERCE ORD/FREE PWR
...MAJORIT JURID QUANT COLD/WAR 20. PAGE 99 B1995
`S59` `INT/ORG` `CT/SYS` `DETER` `SOVEREIGN`

STOESSINGER J.G.,"THE INTERNATIONAL ATOMIC ENERGY
AGENCY: THE FIRST PHASE." FUT WOR+45 NAT/G VOL/ASSN
DELIB/GP BAL/PWR LEGIT ADMIN ROUTINE PWR...OBS
CON/ANAL GEN/LAWS VAL/FREE 20 IAEA. PAGE 101 B2040
`S59` `INT/ORG` `ECO/DEV` `FOR/AID` `NUC/PWR`

ZAUBERMAN A.,"SOVIET BLOC ECONOMIC INTEGRATION."
COM CULTURE INTELL ECO/DEV INDUS TOP/EX ACT/RES
PLAN ECO/TAC INT/TRADE ROUTINE CHOOSE ATTIT
...TIME/SEQ 20. PAGE 119 B2399
`S59` `MARKET` `INT/ORG` `USSR` `TOTALISM`

ALBI F.,TRATADO DE LOS MODOS DE GESTION DE LAS
CORPORACIONES LOCALES. SPAIN FINAN NAT/G BUDGET
CONTROL EXEC ROUTINE GOV/REL ORD/FREE SOVEREIGN
...MGT 20. PAGE 3 B0068
`B60` `LOC/G` `LAW` `ADMIN` `MUNIC`

ARGYRIS C.,UNDERSTANDING ORGANIZATIONAL BEHAVIOR.
OP/RES FEEDBACK...MGT PSY METH/CNCPT OBS INT SIMUL
20. PAGE 6 B0130
`B60` `LG/CO` `PERSON` `ADMIN` `ROUTINE`

BAERWALD F.,ECONOMIC SYSTEM ANALYSIS: CONCEPTS AND
PERSPECTIVES. USA+45 ECO/DEV NAT/G COMPUTER EQUILIB
INCOME ATTIT...DECISION CONCPT IDEA/COMP. PAGE 8
B0159
`B60` `ACT/RES` `ECO/TAC` `ROUTINE` `FINAN`

BASS B.M.,LEADERSHIP, PSYCHOLOGY, AND
ORGANIZATIONAL BEHAVIOR. DOMIN CHOOSE DRIVE PERSON
PWR RESPECT SKILL...SOC METH/CNCPT OBS. PAGE 9
B0193
`B60` `UNIV` `FACE/GP` `DELIB/GP` `ROUTINE`

CAMPBELL R.W.,SOVIET ECONOMIC POWER. COM USA+45
DIST/IND MARKET TOP/EX ACT/RES CAP/ISM ECO/TAC
DOMIN EDU/PROP ADMIN ROUTINE DRIVE...MATH TIME/SEQ
CHARTS WORK 20. PAGE 18 B0371
`B60` `ECO/DEV` `PLAN` `SOCISM` `USSR`

GLOVER J.D.,A CASE STUDY OF HIGH LEVEL
ADMINISTRATION IN A LARGE ORGANIZATION. EX/STRUC
EXEC LEAD ROUTINE INGP/REL OPTIMAL ATTIT PERSON
...POLICY DECISION INT QU. PAGE 40 B0812
`B60` `ADMIN` `TOP/EX` `FORCES` `NAT/G`

LERNER A.P.,THE ECONOMICS OF CONTROL. USA+45
ECO/UNDEV INT/ORG ACT/RES PLAN CAP/ISM INT/TRADE
ATTIT WEALTH...SOC MATH STAT GEN/LAWS INDEX 20.
PAGE 64 B1295
`B60` `ECO/DEV` `ROUTINE` `ECO/TAC` `SOCISM`

LINDSAY K.,EUROPEAN ASSEMBLIES: THE EXPERIMENTAL
PERIOD 1949-1959. EUR+WWI ECO/DEV NAT/G POL/PAR
LEGIS TOP/EX ACT/RES PLAN ECO/TAC DOMIN LEGIT
ROUTINE ATTIT DRIVE ORD/FREE PWR SKILL...SOC CONCPT
TREND CHARTS GEN/LAWS VAL/FREE. PAGE 65 B1315
`B60` `VOL/ASSN` `INT/ORG` `REGION`

MCGREGOR D.,THE HUMAN SIDE OF ENTERPRISE. USA+45
LEAD ROUTINE GP/REL INGP/REL...CONCPT GEN/LAWS 20.
PAGE 72 B1449
`B60` `MGT` `ATTIT` `SKILL` `EDU/PROP`

B60
MEEHAN E.J.,THE BRITISH LEFT WING AND FOREIGN
POLICY: A STUDY OF THE INFLUENCE OF IDEOLOGY. FUT
UK UNIV WOR+45 INTELL TOP/EX PLAN ADMIN ROUTINE
DRIVE...OBS TIME/SEQ GEN/LAWS PARLIAMENT 20.
PAGE 72 B1461
ACT/RES
ATTIT
DIPLOM

B60
MUNRO L.,UNITED NATIONS, HOPE FOR A DIVIDED WORLD.
FUT WOR+45 CONSTN DELIB/GP CREATE TEC/DEV DIPLOM
EDU/PROP LEGIT PEACE ATTIT HEALTH ORD/FREE PWR
...CONCPT TREND UN VAL/FREE 20. PAGE 76 B1540
INT/ORG
ROUTINE

B60
RUBENSTEIN A.H.,SOME THEORIES OF ORGANIZATION.
ROUTINE ATTIT...DECISION ECOMETRIC. PAGE 91 B1846
SOCIETY
ECO/DEV
INDUS
TOP/EX

B60
US SENATE COMM ON JUDICIARY,ADMINISTRATIVE
PROCEDURE LEGISLATION. USA+45 CONSTN NAT/G
PROB/SOLV CONFER ROUTINE GOV/REL...INT 20 SENATE.
PAGE 110 B2227
PARL/PROC
LEGIS
ADMIN
JURID

L60
MACPHERSON C.,"TECHNICAL CHANGE AND POLITICAL
DECISION." WOR+45 NAT/G CREATE CAP/ISM DIPLOM
ROUTINE RIGID/FLEX...CONCPT OBS GEN/METH 20.
PAGE 68 B1375
TEC/DEV
ADMIN

S60
BAVELAS A.,"LEADERSHIP: MAN AND FUNCTION." WORKER
CREATE PLAN CONTROL PERS/REL PERSON PWR...MGT 20.
PAGE 10 B0199
LEAD
ADMIN
ROUTINE
ROLE

S60
BOGARDUS E.S.,"THE SOCIOLOGY OF A STRUCTURED
PEACE." FUT SOCIETY CREATE DIPLOM EDU/PROP ADJUD
ROUTINE ATTIT RIGID/FLEX KNOWL ORD/FREE RESPECT
...POLICY INT/LAW JURID NEW/IDEA SELF/OBS TOT/POP
20 UN. PAGE 13 B0264
INT/ORG
SOC
NAT/LISM
PEACE

S60
BOYER W.W.,"POLICY MAKING BY GOVERNMENT AGENCIES."
USA+45 WOR+45 R+D DELIB/GP TOP/EX EDU/PROP ROUTINE
ATTIT BIO/SOC DRIVE...CONCPT TREND TOT/POP 20.
PAGE 14 B0293
NAT/G
DIPLOM

S60
GROSSMAN G.,"SOVIET GROWTH: ROUTINE, INERTIA, AND
PRESSURE." COM STRATA NAT/G DELIB/GP PLAN TEC/DEV
ECO/TAC EDU/PROP ADMIN ROUTINE DRIVE WEALTH
COLD/WAR 20. PAGE 44 B0891
POL/PAR
ECO/DEV
USSR

S60
HERRERA F.,"THE INTER-AMERICAN DEVELOPMENT BANK."
USA+45 ECO/UNDEV INT/ORG CONSULT DELIB/GP PLAN
ECO/TAC INT/TRADE ROUTINE WEALTH...STAT 20. PAGE 49
B0994
L/A+17C
FINAN
FOR/AID
REGION

S60
HUNTINGTON S.P.,"STRATEGIC PLANNING AND THE
POLITICAL PROCESS." USA+45 NAT/G DELIB/GP LEGIS
ACT/RES ECO/TAC LEGIT ROUTINE CHOOSE RIGID/FLEX PWR
...POLICY MAJORIT MGT 20. PAGE 53 B1066
EXEC
FORCES
NUC/PWR
WAR

S60
HUTCHINSON C.E.,"AN INSTITUTE FOR NATIONAL SECURITY
AFFAIRS." USA+45 R+D NAT/G CONSULT TOP/EX ACT/RES
CREATE PLAN TEC/DEV EDU/PROP ROUTINE NUC/PWR ATTIT
ORD/FREE PWR...DECISION MGT PHIL/SCI CONCPT RECORD
GEN/LAWS GEN/METH 20. PAGE 53 B1068
POLICY
METH/CNCPT
ELITES
DIPLOM

S60
MODELSKI G.,"AUSTRALIA AND SEATO." S/ASIA USA+45
CULTURE INTELL ECO/DEV NAT/G PLAN DIPLOM ADMIN
ROUTINE ATTIT SKILL...MGT TIME/SEQ AUSTRAL 20
SEATO. PAGE 74 B1493
INT/ORG
ACT/RES

S60
REISELBACH L.N.,"THE BASIS OF ISOLATIONIST
BEHAVIOR." USA+45 USA-45 CULTURE ECO/DEV LOC/G
NAT/G ADMIN ROUTINE CHOOSE BIO/SOC DRIVE RIGID/FLEX
...CENSUS SAMP TREND CHARTS TOT/POP 20. PAGE 87
B1765
ATTIT
DIPLOM
ECO/TAC

S60
SCHACHTER O.,"THE ENFORCEMENT OF INTERNATIONAL
JUDICIAL AND ARBITRAL DECISIONS." WOR+45 NAT/G
ECO/TAC DOMIN LEGIT ROUTINE COERCE ATTIT DRIVE
ALL/VALS PWR...METH/CNCPT TREND TOT/POP 20 UN.
PAGE 93 B1878
INT/ORG
ADJUD
INT/LAW

C60
SCHRAMM W.,"MASS COMMUNICATIONS: A BOOK OF READINGS
(2ND ED.)" LG/CO PRESS ADMIN CONTROL ROUTINE ATTIT
ROLE SUPEGO...CHARTS ANTHOL BIBLIOG 20. PAGE 94
B1902
COM/IND
EDU/PROP
CROWD
MAJORIT

C60
SMITH T.E.,"ELECTIONS IN DEVELOPING COUNTRIES: A
STUDY OF ELECTORAL PROCEDURES USED IN TOPICAL
AFRICA, SOUTH-EAST ASIA..." AFR S/ASIA UK ROUTINE
GOV/REL RACE/REL...GOV/COMP BIBLIOG 20. PAGE 98
B1985
ECO/UNDEV
CHOOSE
REPRESENT
ADMIN

B61
AYLMER G.,THE KING'S SERVANTS. UK ELITES CHIEF PAY
CT/SYS WEALTH 17 CROMWELL/O CHARLES/I. PAGE 7 B0153
ADMIN
ROUTINE
EX/STRUC
NAT/G

B61
BENOIT E.,EUROPE AT SIXES AND SEVENS: THE COMMON
MARKET, THE FREE TRADE ASSOCIATION AND THE UNITED
STATES. EUR+WWI FUT USA+45 INDUS CONSULT DELIB/GP
EX/STRUC TOP/EX ACT/RES ECO/TAC EDU/PROP ROUTINE
CHOOSE PERCEPT WEALTH...MGT TREND EEC TOT/POP 20
EFTA. PAGE 11 B0217
FINAN
ECO/DEV
VOL/ASSN

B61
BISHOP D.G.,THE ADMINISTRATION OF BRITISH FOREIGN
RELATIONS. EUR+WWI MOD/EUR INT/ORG NAT/G POL/PAR
DELIB/GP LEGIS TOP/EX ECO/TAC DOMIN EDU/PROP ADMIN
COERCE 20. PAGE 12 B0243
ROUTINE
PWR
DIPLOM
UK

B61
BURDETTE F.L.,POLITICAL SCIENCE: A SELECTED
BIBLIOGRAPHY OF BOOKS IN PRINT, WITH ANNOTATIONS
(PAMPHLET). LAW LOC/G NAT/G POL/PAR PROVS DIPLOM
EDU/PROP ADMIN CHOOSE ATTIT 20. PAGE 17 B0347
BIBLIOG/A
GOV/COMP
CONCPT
ROUTINE

B61
CONFREY E.A.,ADMINISTRATION OF COMMUNITY HEALTH
SERVICES. USA+45 R+D PUB/INST DELIB/GP PLAN BUDGET
ROUTINE AGE/C HEALTH...MGT SOC/WK METH/COMP 20.
PAGE 23 B0461
HEAL
ADMIN
MUNIC
BIO/SOC

B61
FRIEDMANN W.G.,JOINT INTERNATIONAL BUSINESS
VENTURES. ASIA ISLAM L/A+17C ECO/DEV DIST/IND FINAN
PROC/MFG FACE/GP LG/CO NAT/G VOL/ASSN CONSULT
EX/STRUC PLAN ADMIN ROUTINE WEALTH...OLD/LIB WORK
20. PAGE 37 B0760
ECO/UNDEV
INT/TRADE

B61
GORDON R.A.,BUSINESS LEADERSHIP IN THE LARGE
CORPORATION. USA+45 SOCIETY EX/STRUC ADMIN CONTROL
ROUTINE GP/REL PWR...MGT 20. PAGE 41 B0831
LG/CO
LEAD
DECISION
LOBBY

B61
HAIRE M.,MODERN ORGANIZATION THEORY. LABOR ROUTINE
MAJORITY...CONCPT MODAL OBS CONT/OBS. PAGE 45 B0919
PERS/REL
GP/REL
MGT
DECISION

B61
HICKS U.K.,DEVELOPMENT FROM BELOW. UK INDUS ADMIN
COLONIAL ROUTINE GOV/REL...POLICY METH/CNCPT CHARTS
19/20 CMN/WLTH. PAGE 50 B1006
ECO/UNDEV
LOC/G
GOV/COMP
METH/COMP

B61
HORVATH B.,THE CHARACTERISTICS OF YUGOSLAV ECONOMIC
DEVELOPMENT. COM ECO/UNDEV AGRI INDUS PLAN CAP/ISM
ECO/TAC ROUTINE WEALTH...SOCIALIST STAT CHARTS
STERTYP WORK 20. PAGE 52 B1045
ACT/RES
YUGOSLAVIA

B61
LASSWELL H.D.,PSYCOPATHOLOGY AND POLITICS. WOR-45
CULTURE SOCIETY FACE/GP NAT/G CONSULT CREATE
EDU/PROP EXEC ROUTINE DISPL DRIVE PERSON PWR
RESPECT...PSY CONCPT METH/CNCPT METH. PAGE 63 B1272
ATTIT
GEN/METH

B61
PEASLEE A.J.,INTERNATIONAL GOVERNMENT
ORGANIZATIONS, CONSTITUTIONAL DOCUMENTS. WOR+45
WOR-45 CONSTN VOL/ASSN DELIB/GP EX/STRUC ROUTINE
KNOWL TOT/POP 20. PAGE 82 B1650
INT/ORG
STRUCT

B61
QURESHI S.,INCENTIVES IN AMERICAN EMPLOYMENT
(THESIS, UNIVERSITY OF PENNSYLVANIA). DELIB/GP
TOP/EX BUDGET ROUTINE SANCTION COST TECHRACY MGT.
PAGE 85 B1727
SERV/IND
ADMIN
PAY
EX/STRUC

B61
SHAPP W.R.,FIELD ADMINISTRATION IN THE UNITED
NATIONS SYSTEM. FINAN PROB/SOLV INSPECT DIPLOM EXEC
REGION ROUTINE EFFICIENCY ROLE...INT CHARTS 20 UN.
PAGE 96 B1933
INT/ORG
ADMIN
GP/REL
FOR/AID

B61
SHARP W.R.,FIELD ADMINISTRATION IN THE UNITED
NATION SYSTEM: THE CONDUCT OF INTERNATIONAL
ECONOMIC AND SOCIAL PROGRAMS. FUT WOR+45 CONSTN
SOCIETY ECO/UNDEV R+D DELIB/GP ACT/RES PLAN TEC/DEV
EDU/PROP EXEC ROUTINE HEALTH WEALTH...HUM CONCPT
CHARTS METH ILO UNESCO VAL/FREE UN 20. PAGE 96
B1939
INT/ORG
CONSULT

B61
SINGER J.D.,FINANCING INTERNATIONAL ORGANIZATION:
THE UNITED NATIONS BUDGET PROCESS. WOR+45 FINAN
ACT/RES CREATE PLAN BUDGET ECO/TAC ADMIN ROUTINE
ATTIT KNOWL...DECISION METH/CNCPT TIME/SEQ UN 20.
PAGE 97 B1964
INT/ORG
MGT

B61
STRAUSS E.,THE RULING SERVANTS. FRANCE UK USSR
WOR+45 WOR-45 NAT/G CONSULT DELIB/GP EX/STRUC
TOP/EX DOMIN EDU/PROP LEGIT ROUTINE...MGT TIME/SEQ
STERTYP 20. PAGE 101 B2051
ADMIN
PWR
ELITES

B61
THAYER L.O.,ADMINISTRATIVE COMMUNICATION. DELIB/GP
ADMIN ROUTINE PERS/REL 20. PAGE 104 B2093
GP/REL
PSY
LG/CO
MGT

B61
WILLOUGHBY W.R.,THE ST LAWRENCE WATERWAY: A STUDY
IN POLITICS AND DIPLOMACY. USA+45 ECO/DEV COM/IND
INT/ORG CONSULT DELIB/GP ACT/RES TEC/DEV DIPLOM
LEGIS
INT/TRADE
CANADA

ECO/TAC ROUTINE...TIME/SEQ 20. PAGE 117 B2357   DIST/IND

S61

ALGER C.F.,"NON-RESOLUTION CONSEQUENCES OF THE   INT/ORG
UNITED NATIONS AND THEIR EFFECT ON INTERNATIONAL   DRIVE
CONFLICT." WOR+45 CONSTN ECO/DEV NAT/G CONSULT   BAL/PWR
DELIB/GP TOP/EX ACT/RES PLAN DIPLOM EDU/PROP
ROUTINE ATTIT ALL/VALS...INT/LAW TOT/POP UN 20.
PAGE 4 B0075

S61

BARTLEY H.J.,"COMMAND EXPERIENCE." USA+45 EX/STRUC   CONCPT
FORCES LEGIT ROUTINE SKILL...POLICY OBS HYPO/EXP   TREND
GEN/LAWS 20. PAGE 9 B0191

S61

CYERT R.M.,"TWO EXPERIMENTS ON BIAS AND CONFLICT IN   LAB/EXP
ORGANIZATIONAL ESTIMATION." WORKER PROB/SOLV   ROUTINE
EFFICIENCY...MGT PSY STAT CHARTS. PAGE 25 B0518   ADMIN
                                                       DECISION

S61

DEUTSCH K.W.,"A NOTE ON THE APPEARANCE OF WISDOM IN   ADMIN
LARGE BUREAUCRATIC ORGANIZATIONS." ROUTINE PERSON   PROBABIL
KNOWL SKILL...DECISION STAT. PAGE 28 B0577   PROB/SOLV
                                                       SIMUL

S61

DEVINS J.H.,"THE INITIATIVE." COM USA+45 USA-45   FORCES
USSR SOCIETY NAT/G ACT/RES CREATE BAL/PWR ROUTINE   CONCPT
COERCE DETER RIGID/FLEX SKILL...STERTYP COLD/WAR   WAR
20. PAGE 29 B0582

S61

EHRMANN H.W.,"FRENCH BUREAUCRACY AND ORGANIZED   ADMIN
INTERESTS" (BMR)" FRANCE NAT/G DELIB/GP ROUTINE   DECISION
...INT 20 BUREAUCRCY CIVIL/SERV. PAGE 32 B0657   PLURISM
                                                       LOBBY

S61

GORDON L.,"ECONOMIC REGIONALISM RECONSIDERED." FUT   ECO/DEV
USA+45 WOR+45 INDUS NAT/G TEC/DEV DIPLOM ROUTINE   ATTIT
PERCEPT WEALTH...WELF/ST METH/CNCPT WORK 20.   CAP/ISM
PAGE 41 B0830   REGION

S61

LANFALUSSY A.,"EUROPE'S PROGRESS: DUE TO COMMON   INT/ORG
MARKET." EUR+WWI ECO/DEV DELIB/GP PLAN ECO/TAC   MARKET
ROUTINE WEALTH...GEOG TREND EEC 20. PAGE 62 B1257

S61

LEWY G.,"SUPERIOR ORDERS, NUCLEAR WARFARE AND THE   DETER
DICTATES OF CONSCIENCE: THE DILEMMA OF MILITARY   INT/ORG
OBEDIENCE IN THE ATOMIC." FUT UNIV WOR+45 INTELL   LAW
SOCIETY FORCES TOP/EX ACT/RES ADMIN ROUTINE NUC/PWR   INT/LAW
PERCEPT RIGID/FLEX ALL/VALS...POLICY CONCPT 20.
PAGE 65 B1308

S61

PADOVER S.K.,"PSYCHOLOGICAL WARFARE AND FOREIGN   ROUTINE
POLICY." FUT UNIV USA+45 INTELL SOCIETY CREATE   DIPLOM
EDU/PROP ADMIN WAR PEACE PERCEPT...POLICY
METH/CNCPT TESTS TIME/SEQ 20. PAGE 80 B1623

S61

TAUBENFELD H.J.,"OUTER SPACE--PAST POLITICS AND   PLAN
FUTURE POLICY." FUT USA+45 USA-45 WOR+45 AIR INTELL   SPACE
STRUCT ECO/DEV NAT/G TOP/EX ACT/RES ADMIN ROUTINE   INT/ORG
NUC/PWR ATTIT DRIVE...CONCPT TIME/SEQ TREND TOT/POP
20. PAGE 103 B2083

S61

TOMASIC D.,"POLITICAL LEADERSHIP IN CONTEMPORARY   SOCIETY
POLAND." COM EUR+WWI GERMANY NAT/G POL/PAR SECT   ROUTINE
DELIB/GP PLAN ECO/TAC DOMIN EDU/PROP PWR MARXISM   USSR
...MARXIST GEOG MGT CONCPT TIME/SEQ STERTYP 20.   POLAND
PAGE 105 B2114

C61

ETZIONI A.,"A COMPARATIVE ANALYSIS OF COMPLEX   CON/ANAL
ORGANIZATIONS: ON POWER, INVOLVEMENT AND THEIR   SOC
CORRELATES." ELITES CREATE OP/RES ROUTINE INGP/REL   LEAD
PERS/REL CONSEN ATTIT DRIVE PWR...CONCPT BIBLIOG.   CONTROL
PAGE 34 B0684

C61

VERBA S.,"SMALL GROUPS AND POLITICAL BEHAVIOR: A   LEAD
STUDY OF LEADERSHIP" DOMIN PARTIC ROUTINE GP/REL   ELITES
ATTIT DRIVE ALL/VALS...CONCPT IDEA/COMP LAB/EXP   FACE/GP
BIBLIOG METH. PAGE 112 B2259

B62

ARCO EDITORIAL BOARD.PUBLIC MANAGEMENT AND   MGT
ADMINISTRATION. PLAN BUDGET WRITING CONTROL ROUTINE   ADMIN
...TESTS CHARTS METH T 20. PAGE 6 B0125   NAT/G
                                                       LOC/G

B62

HADWEN J.G.,HOW UNITED NATIONS DECISIONS ARE MADE.   INT/ORG
WOR+45 LAW EDU/PROP LEGIT ADMIN PWR...DECISION   ROUTINE
SELF/OBS GEN/LAWS UN 20. PAGE 45 B0912

B62

HATTERY L.H.,INFORMATION RETRIEVAL MANAGEMENT.   R+D
CLIENT INDUS TOP/EX COMPUTER OP/RES TEC/DEV ROUTINE   COMPUT/IR
COST EFFICIENCY RIGID/FLEX...METH/COMP ANTHOL 20.   MGT
PAGE 48 B0968   CREATE

B62

JEWELL M.E.,SENATORIAL POLITICS AND FOREIGN POLICY.   USA+45
NAT/G POL/PAR CHIEF DELIB/GP TOP/EX FOR/AID   LEGIS
EDU/PROP ROUTINE ATTIT PWR SKILL...MAJORIT   DIPLOM
METH/CNCPT TIME/SEQ CONGRESS 20 PRESIDENT. PAGE 56
B1138

B62

LAWSON R.,INTERNATIONAL REGIONAL ORGANIZATIONS.   INT/ORG
WOR+45 NAT/G VOL/ASSN CONSULT LEGIS EDU/PROP LEGIT   DELIB/GP
ADMIN EXEC ROUTINE HEALTH PWR WEALTH...JURID EEC   REGION
COLD/WAR 20 UN. PAGE 63 B1277

B62

LOWI T.J.,LEGISLATIVE POLITICS U.S.A. LAW LEGIS   PARL/PROC
DIPLOM EXEC LOBBY CHOOSE SUFF FEDERAL PWR 19/20   REPRESENT
CONGRESS. PAGE 67 B1345   POLICY
                                                       ROUTINE

B62

MAILICK S.,CONCEPTS AND ISSUES IN ADMINISTRATIVE   DECISION
BEHAVIOR. EX/STRUC TOP/EX ROUTINE INGP/REL   MGT
EFFICIENCY. PAGE 68 B1380   EXEC
                                                       PROB/SOLV

B62

MODELSKI G.,A THEORY OF FOREIGN POLICY. WOR+45   PLAN
WOR-45 NAT/G DELIB/GP EX/STRUC TOP/EX EDU/PROP   PWR
LEGIT ROUTINE...POLICY CONCPT TOT/POP COLD/WAR 20.   DIPLOM
PAGE 74 B1494

B62

MUKERJI S.N.,ADMINISTRATION OF EDUCATION IN INDIA.   SCHOOL
ACADEM LOC/G PROVS ROUTINE...POLICY STAT CHARTS 20.   ADMIN
PAGE 76 B1536   NAT/G
                                                       EDU/PROP

B62

NICHOLAS H.G.,THE UNITED NATIONS AS A POLITICAL   INT/ORG
INSTITUTION. WOR+45 CONSTN EX/STRUC ACT/RES LEGIT   ROUTINE
PERCEPT KNOWL PWR...CONCPT TIME/SEQ CON/ANAL
ORG/CHARTS UN 20. PAGE 78 B1580

B62

NJ DEPARTMENT CIVIL SERV.THE CIVIL SERVICE RULES OF   ADMIN
THE STATE OF NEW JERSEY. USA+45 USA-45 PAY...JURID   PROVS
ANTHOL 20 CIVIL/SERV NEW/JERSEY. PAGE 78 B1585   ROUTINE
                                                       WORKER

B62

SCHILLING W.R.,STRATEGY, POLITICS, AND DEFENSE   ROUTINE
BUDGETS. USA+45 R+D NAT/G DELIB/GP FORCES   POLICY
LEGIS ACT/RES PLAN BAL/PWR LEGIT EXEC NUC/PWR
RIGID/FLEX PWR...TREND COLD/WAR CONGRESS 20
EISNHWR/DD. PAGE 93 B1890

B62

SNYDER R.C.,FOREIGN POLICY DECISION-MAKING. FUT   TEC/DEV
KOREA WOR+45 R+D CREATE ADMIN ROUTINE PWR   HYPO/EXP
...DECISION PSY SOC CONCPT METH/CNCPT CON/ANAL   DIPLOM
CHARTS GEN/METH METH 20. PAGE 99 B1992

B62

STAHL O.G.,PUBLIC PERSONNEL ADMINISTRATION. LOC/G   ADMIN
TOP/EX CREATE PLAN ROUTINE...TECHNIC MGT T.   WORKER
PAGE 100 B2017   EX/STRUC
                                                       NAT/G

L62

GALBRAITH J.K.,"ECONOMIC DEVELOPMENT IN   ECO/UNDEV
PERSPECTIVE." CAP/ISM ECO/TAC ROUTINE ATTIT WEALTH   PLAN
...TREND CHARTS SOC/EXP WORK 20. PAGE 38 B0773

L62

NEIBURG H.L.,"THE EISENHOWER AEC AND CONGRESS: A   CHIEF
STUDY IN EXECUTIVE-LEGISLATIVE RELATIONS." USA+45   LEGIS
NAT/G POL/PAR DELIB/GP EX/STRUC TOP/EX ADMIN EXEC   GOV/REL
LEAD ROUTINE PWR...POLICY COLD/WAR CONGRESS   NUC/PWR
PRESIDENT AEC. PAGE 77 B1567

S62

DONNELLY D.,"THE POLITICS AND ADMINISTRATION OF   GOV/REL
PLANNING." UK ROUTINE FEDERAL 20. PAGE 30 B0607   EFFICIENCY
                                                       ADMIN
                                                       EX/STRUC

S62

GIDWANI K.A.,"LEADER BEHAVIOUR IN ELECTED AND NON-   LEAD
ELECTED GROUPS." DELIB/GP ROUTINE TASK HAPPINESS   INGP/REL
AUTHORIT...SOC STAT CHARTS SOC/EXP. PAGE 39 B0796   GP/COMP
                                                       CHOOSE

S62

HUDSON G.F.,"SOVIET FEARS OF THE WEST." COM USA+45   ATTIT
SOCIETY DELIB/GP EX/STRUC TOP/EX ACT/RES CREATE   MYTH
DOMIN EDU/PROP LEGIT ADMIN ROUTINE DRIVE PERSON   GERMANY
RIGID/FLEX PWR...RECORD TIME/SEQ TOT/POP 20   USSR
STALIN/J. PAGE 52 B1057

S62

IKLE F.C.,"POLITICAL NEGOTIATION AS A PROCESS OF   ROUTINE
MODIFYING UTILITIES." WOR+45 FACE/GP LABOR NAT/G   DECISION
FORCES ACT/RES EDU/PROP DETER PERCEPT ALL/VALS   DIPLOM
...PSY NEW/IDEA HYPO/EXP GEN/METH 20. PAGE 53 B1076

S62

IOVTCHOUK M.T.,"ON SOME THEORETICAL PRINCIPLES AND   COM
METHODS OF SOCIOLOGICAL INVESTIGATIONS (IN   ECO/DEV
RUSSIAN)." FUT USA+45 STRATA R+D NAT/G POL/PAR   CAP/ISM
TOP/EX ACT/RES PLAN ECO/TAC EDU/PROP ROUTINE ATTIT   USSR
RIGID/FLEX MARXISM SOCISM...MARXIST METH/CNCPT OBS
TREND NAT/COMP GEN/LAWS 20. PAGE 54 B1102

S62

JACOBSON H.K.,"THE UNITED NATIONS AND COLONIALISM: INT/ORG
A TENTATIVE APPRAISAL." AFR FUT S/ASIA USA+45 USSR   CONCPT
WOR+45 NAT/G DELIB/GP PLAN DIPLOM ECO/TAC DOMIN   COLONIAL
ADMIN ROUTINE COERCE ATTIT RIGID/FLEX ORD/FREE PWR
...OBS STERTYP UN 20. PAGE 55 B1115

LARSON R.L.,"HOW TO DEFINE ADMINISTRATIVE
PROBLEMS." ROUTINE PERCEPT KNOWL SKILL...MGT
METH/CNCPT CHARTS TOT/POP. PAGE 63 B1263
`S62` `UNIV` `FACE/GP` `INDUS` `EXEC`

MAINZER L.C.,"INJUSTICE AND BUREAUCRACY." ELITES
STRATA STRUCT EX/STRUC SENIOR CONTROL EXEC LEAD
ROUTINE INGP/REL ORD/FREE...CONCPT 20 BUREAUCRCY.
PAGE 68 B1381
`S62` `MORAL` `MGT` `ADMIN`

MARTIN L.W.,"POLITICAL SETTLEMENTS AND ARMS
CONTROL." COM EUR+WWI GERMANY USA+45 PROVS FORCES
TOP/EX ACT/RES CREATE DOMIN LEGIT ROUTINE COERCE
ATTIT RIGID/FLEX ORD/FREE PWR...METH/CNCPT RECORD
GEN/LAWS 20. PAGE 70 B1410
`S62` `CONCPT` `ARMS/CONT`

MURACCIOLE L.,"LES CONSTITUTIONS DES ETATS
AFRICAINS D'EXPRESSION FRANCAISE: LA CONSTITUTION
DU 16 AVRIL 1962 DE LA REPUBLIQUE DU" AFR CHAD
CHIEF LEGIS LEGIT COLONIAL EXEC ROUTINE ORD/FREE
SOVEREIGN...SOC CONCPT 20. PAGE 76 B1541
`S62` `NAT/G` `CONSTN`

NORTH R.C.,"DECISION MAKING IN CRISIS: AN
INTRODUCTION." WOR+45 WOR-45 NAT/G CONSULT DELIB/GP
TEC/DEV PERCEPT KNOWL...POLICY DECISION PSY
METH/CNCPT CONT/OBS TREND VAL/FREE 20. PAGE 79
B1590
`S62` `INT/ORG` `ROUTINE` `DIPLOM`

PIQUEMAL M.,"LES PROBLEMES DES UNIONS D'ETATS EN
AFRIQUE NOIRE." FRANCE SOCIETY INT/ORG NAT/G
DELIB/GP PLAN LEGIT ADMIN COLONIAL ROUTINE ATTIT
ORD/FREE PWR...GEOG METH/CNCPT 20. PAGE 83 B1678
`S62` `AFR` `ECO/UNDEV` `REGION`

TRUMAN D.,"THE DOMESTIC POLITICS OF FOREIGN AID."
USA+45 WOR+45 NAT/G POL/PAR LEGIS DIPLOM ECO/TAC
EDU/PROP ADMIN CHOOSE ATTIT PWR CONGRESS 20
CONGRESS. PAGE 105 B2129
`S62` `ROUTINE` `FOR/AID`

DE GRAZIA A.,"POLITICAL BEHAVIOR (REV. ED.)" STRATA
POL/PAR LEAD LOBBY ROUTINE WAR CHOOSE REPRESENT
CONSEN ATTIT ORD/FREE BIBLIOG. PAGE 27 B0555
`C62` `PHIL/SCI` `OP/RES` `CONCPT`

MORGAN G.G.,"SOVIET ADMINISTRATIVE LEGALITY: THE
ROLE OF THE ATTORNEY GENERAL'S OFFICE." COM USSR
CONTROL ROUTINE...CONCPT BIBLIOG 18/20. PAGE 75
B1522
`C62` `LAW` `CONSTN` `LEGIS` `ADMIN`

TRUMAN D.B.,"THE GOVERNMENTAL PROCESS: POLITICAL
INTERESTS AND PUBLIC OPINION." POL/PAR ADJUD ADMIN
EXEC LEAD ROUTINE CHOOSE REPRESENT GOV/REL
RIGID/FLEX...POLICY BIBLIOG/A 20. PAGE 105 B2131
`C62` `LOBBY` `EDU/PROP` `GP/REL` `LEGIS`

VAN DER SPRENKEL S.,"LEGAL INSTITUTIONS IN MANCHU
CHINA." ASIA STRUCT CT/SYS ROUTINE GOV/REL GP/REL
...CONCPT BIBLIOG 17/20. PAGE 111 B2250
`C62` `LAW` `JURID` `ADMIN` `ADJUD`

ACKOFF R.L.,A MANAGER'S GUIDE TO OPERATIONS
RESEARCH. STRUCT INDUS PROB/SOLV ROUTINE 20. PAGE 3
B0056
`B63` `OP/RES` `MGT` `GP/REL` `ADMIN`

BERNE E.,THE STRUCTURE AND DYNAMICS OF
ORGANIZATIONS AND GROUPS. CLIENT PARTIC DRIVE
HEALTH...MGT PSY ORG/CHARTS. PAGE 11 B0226
`B63` `INGP/REL` `AUTHORIT` `ROUTINE` `CLASSIF`

BOWETT D.W.,THE LAW OF INTERNATIONAL INSTITUTIONS.
WOR+45 WOR-45 CONSTN DELIB/GP EX/STRUC JUDGE
EDU/PROP LEGIT CT/SYS EXEC ROUTINE RIGID/FLEX
ORD/FREE PWR...JURID CONCPT ORG/CHARTS GEN/METH
LEAGUE/NAT OAS OEEC 20 UN. PAGE 14 B0286
`B63` `INT/ORG` `ADJUD` `DIPLOM`

BURSK E.C.,NEW DECISION-MAKING TOOLS FOR MANAGERS.
COMPUTER PLAN PROB/SOLV ROUTINE COST. PAGE 18 B0357
`B63` `DECISION` `MGT` `MATH` `RIGID/FLEX`

CLARK J.S.,THE SENATE ESTABLISHMENT. USA+45 NAT/G
POL/PAR ADMIN CHOOSE PERSON SENATE. PAGE 21 B0431
`B63` `LEGIS` `ROUTINE` `LEAD` `SENIOR`

DUE J.F.,STATE SALES TAX ADMINISTRATION. OP/RES
BUDGET PAY ADMIN EXEC ROUTINE COST EFFICIENCY
PROFIT...CHARTS METH/COMP 20. PAGE 31 B0626
`B63` `PROVS` `TAX` `STAT` `GOV/COMP`

HARGROVE M.M.,BUSINESS POLICY CASES-WITH BEHAVIORAL
SCIENCE IMPLICATIONS. LG/CO SML/CO EX/STRUC TOP/EX
PLAN PROB/SOLV CONFER ADMIN CONTROL ROUTINE
EFFICIENCY. PAGE 47 B0946
`B63` `SOC/EXP` `INDUS` `DECISION` `MGT`

HEARLE E.F.R.,A DATA PROCESSING SYSTEM FOR STATE
AND LOCAL GOVERNMENTS. PLAN TEC/DEV AUTOMAT ROUTINE
`B63` `LOC/G` `PROVS`

...MGT METH/CNCPT CLASSIF 20. PAGE 49 B0984
`COMPUTER` `COMPUT/IR`

KOGAN N.,THE POLITICS OF ITALIAN FOREIGN POLICY.
EUR+WWI LEGIS DOMIN LEGIT EXEC PWR RESPECT SKILL
...POLICY DECISION HUM SOC METH/CNCPT OBS INT
CHARTS 20. PAGE 61 B1227
`B63` `NAT/G` `ROUTINE` `DIPLOM` `ITALY`

LITTERER J.A.,ORGANIZATIONS: STRUCTURE AND
BEHAVIOR. PLAN DOMIN CONTROL LEAD ROUTINE SANCTION
INGP/REL EFFICIENCY PRODUC DRIVE RIGID/FLEX PWR.
PAGE 66 B1325
`B63` `ADMIN` `CREATE` `MGT` `ADJUST`

MAYNE R.,THE COMMUNITY OF EUROPE. UK CONSTN NAT/G
CONSULT DELIB/GP CREATE PLAN ECO/TAC LEGIT ADMIN
ROUTINE ORD/FREE PWR WEALTH...CONCPT TIME/SEQ EEC
EURATOM 20. PAGE 71 B1436
`B63` `EUR+WWI` `INT/ORG` `REGION`

MENZEL J.M.,THE CHINESE CIVIL SERVICE: CAREER OPEN
TO TALENT? ASIA ROUTINE INGP/REL DISCRIM ATTIT ROLE
KNOWL ANTHOL. PAGE 73 B1468
`B63` `ADMIN` `NAT/G` `DECISION` `ELITES`

NORTH R.C.,CONTENT ANALYSIS: A HANDBOOK WITH
APPLICATIONS FOR THE STUDY OF INTERNATIONAL CRISIS.
ASIA COM EUR+WWI MOD/EUR INT/ORG TEC/DEV DOMIN
EDU/PROP ROUTINE COERCE PERCEPT RIGID/FLEX ALL/VALS
...QUANT TESTS CON/ANAL SIMUL GEN/LAWS VAL/FREE.
PAGE 79 B1591
`B63` `METH/CNCPT` `COMPUT/IR` `USSR`

PREST A.R.,PUBLIC FINANCE IN UNDERDEVELOPED
COUNTRIES. UK WOR+45 WOR-45 SOCIETY INT/ORG NAT/G
LEGIS ACT/RES PLAN ECO/TAC ADMIN ROUTINE...CHARTS
20. PAGE 84 B1702
`B63` `FINAN` `ECO/UNDEV` `NIGERIA`

ROETTER C.,THE DIPLOMATIC ART. USSR INT/ORG NAT/G
DELIB/GP ROUTINE NUC/PWR PEACE...POLICY 20. PAGE 90
B1812
`B63` `DIPLOM` `ELITES` `TOP/EX`

SCHOECK H.,THE NEW ARGUMENT IN ECONOMICS. UK USA+45
INDUS MARKET LABOR NAT/G ECO/TAC ADMIN ROUTINE
BAL/PAY PWR...POLICY BOLIV. PAGE 94 B1899
`B63` `WELF/ST` `FOR/AID` `ECO/DEV` `ALL/IDEOS`

TSOU T.,AMERICA'S FAILURE IN CHINA, 1941-1950.
USA+45 USA-45 NAT/G ACT/RES PLAN DOMIN EDU/PROP
ADMIN ROUTINE ATTIT PERSON ORD/FREE...DECISION
CONCPT MYTH TIME/SEQ TREND STERTYP 20. PAGE 105
B2132
`B63` `ASIA` `PERCEPT` `DIPLOM`

US HOUSE COM ON ED AND LABOR,ADMINISTRATION OF
AGING. USA+45 R+D EX/STRUC PLAN BUDGET PAY EDU/PROP
ROUTINE COST CONGRESS. PAGE 108 B2187
`B63` `AGE/O` `ADMIN` `DELIB/GP` `GIVE`

FREUND G.,"ADENAUER AND THE FUTURE OF GERMANY."
EUR+WWI FUT GERMANY/W FORCES LEGIT ADMIN ROUTINE
ATTIT DRIVE PERSON PWR...POLICY TIME/SEQ TREND
VAL/FREE 20 ADENAUER/K. PAGE 37 B0753
`L63` `NAT/G` `BIOG` `DIPLOM` `GERMANY`

BOWIE R.,"STRATEGY AND THE ATLANTIC ALLIANCE."
EUR+WWI VOL/ASSN BAL/PWR COERCE NUC/PWR ATTIT
ORD/FREE PWR...DECISION GEN/LAWS NATO COLD/WAR 20.
PAGE 14 B0287
`S63` `FORCES` `ROUTINE`

BRZEZINSKI Z.K.,"CINCINNATUS AND THE APPARATCHIK."
COM USA+45 USA-45 ELITES LOC/G NAT/G PROVS CONSULT
LEGIS DOMIN LEGIT EXEC ROUTINE CHOOSE DRIVE PWR
SKILL...CONCPT CHARTS VAL/FREE COLD/WAR 20. PAGE 16
B0334
`S63` `POL/PAR` `USSR`

COUTY P.,"L'ASSISTANCE POUR LE DEVELOPPEMENT: POINT
DE VUE SCANDINAVES." EUR+WWI FINLAND FUT SWEDEN
WOR+45 ECO/DEV ECO/UNDEV COM/IND LABOR NAT/G
PROF/ORG ACT/RES SKILL WEALTH TOT/POP 20. PAGE 24
B0497
`S63` `FINAN` `ROUTINE` `FOR/AID`

DAVEE R.,"POUR UN FONDS DE DEVELOPPEMENT SOCIAL."
FUT WOR+45 INTELL SOCIETY ECO/DEV FINAN TEC/DEV
ROUTINE WEALTH...TREND TOT/POP VAL/FREE UN 20.
PAGE 26 B0532
`S63` `INT/ORG` `SOC` `FOR/AID`

DUCROS B.,"MOBILISATION DES RESSOURCES PRODUCTIVES
ET DEVELOPPEMENT." FUT INTELL SOCIETY COM/IND
DIST/IND EXTR/IND FINAN INDUS ROUTINE WEALTH
...METH/CNCPT OBS 20. PAGE 31 B0625
`S63` `ECO/UNDEV` `TEC/DEV`

HAVILAND H.F.,"BUILDING A POLITICAL COMMUNITY."
EUR+WWI FUT UK USA+45 ECO/DEV ECO/UNDEV INT/ORG
NAT/G DELIB/GP BAL/PWR ECO/TAC NEUTRAL ROUTINE
ATTIT PWR WEALTH...CONCPT COLD/WAR TOT/POP 20.
PAGE 48 B0972
`S63` `VOL/ASSN` `DIPLOM`

JOELSON M.R.,"THE DISMISSAL OF CIVIL SERVANTS IN
THE INTERESTS OF NATIONAL SECURITY." EUR+WWI LAW
DELIB/GP ROUTINE ORD/FREE...MGT VAL/FREE 20.
`S63` `USA+45` `NAT/G` `UK`

PAGE 56 B1141   FRANCE

S63

MANGONE G.,"THE UNITED NATIONS AND UNITED STATES INT/ORG
FOREIGN POLICY." USA+45 WOR+45 ECO/UNDEV NAT/G ECO/TAC
DIPLOM LEGIT ROUTINE ATTIT DRIVE...TIME/SEQ UN FOR/AID
COLD/WAR 20. PAGE 69 B1390

S63

NYE J.S. JR.,"EAST AFRICAN ECONOMIC INTEGRATION." ECO/UNDEV
AFR UGANDA PROVS DELIB/GP PLAN ECO/TAC INT/TRADE INT/ORG
ADMIN ROUTINE ORD/FREE PWR WEALTH...OBS TIME/SEQ
VAL/FREE 20. PAGE 79 B1597

S63

SCHURMANN F.,"ECONOMIC POLICY AND POLITICAL POWER PLAN
IN COMMUNIST CHINA." ASIA CHINA/COM USSR SOCIETY ECO/TAC
ECO/UNDEV AGRI INDUS CREATE ADMIN ROUTINE ATTIT
DRIVE RIGID/FLEX PWR WEALTH...HIST/WRIT TREND
CHARTS WORK 20. PAGE 94 B1908

B64

ALDERFER H.O.,LOCAL GOVERNMENT IN DEVELOPING ADMIN
COUNTRIES. ASIA COM L/A+17C S/ASIA AGRI LOC/G MUNIC ROUTINE
PROVS DOMIN CHOOSE PWR...POLICY MGT CONCPT 20.
PAGE 3 B0070

B64

BANTON M.,THE POLICEMAN IN THE COMMUNITY. UK USA+45 FORCES
STRUCT PROF/ORG WORKER LOBBY ROUTINE COERCE CROWD ADMIN
GP/REL ADJUST DISCRIM PERCEPT 20. PAGE 9 B0181 ROLE
              RACE/REL

B64

CLARK J.S.,CONGRESS: THE SAPLESS BRANCH. DELIB/GP LEGIS
SENIOR ATTIT CONGRESS. PAGE 21 B0432 ROUTINE
              ADMIN
              POL/PAR

B64

COLLINS B.E.,A SOCIAL PSYCHOLOGY OF GROUP PROCESSES FACE/GP
FOR DECISION-MAKING. PROB/SOLV ROUTINE...SOC CHARTS DECISION
HYPO/EXP. PAGE 22 B0453 NAT/G
              INDUS

B64

COTTER C.P.,POLITICS WITHOUT POWER: THE NATIONAL CHOOSE
PARTY COMMITTEES. USA+45 FINAN NAT/G LOBBY ROUTINE POL/PAR
GP/REL ATTIT ROLE SUPEGO PWR 20. PAGE 24 B0491 REPRESENT
              DELIB/GP

B64

CULLINGWORTH J.B.,TOWN AND COUNTRY PLANNING IN MUNIC
ENGLAND AND WALES. UK LAW SOCIETY CONSULT ACT/RES PLAN
ADMIN ROUTINE LEISURE INGP/REL ADJUST PWR...GEOG 20 NAT/G
OPEN/SPACE URBAN/RNWL. PAGE 25 B0512 PROB/SOLV

B64

GORE W.J.,ADMINISTRATIVE DECISION-MAKING* A DECISION
HEURISTIC MODEL. EX/STRUC ADMIN LEAD ROUTINE MGT
PERS/REL...METH/CNCPT ORG/CHARTS. PAGE 41 B0834 SIMUL
              GEN/METH

B64

KAHNG T.J.,LAW, POLITICS, AND THE SECURITY COUNCIL* DELIB/GP
AN INQUIRY INTO THE HANDLING OF LEGAL QUESTIONS. ADJUD
LAW CONSTN NAT/G ACT/RES OP/RES CT/SYS TASK PWR ROUTINE
...INT/LAW BIBLIOG UN. PAGE 57 B1160

B64

KARLEN D.,THE CITIZEN IN COURT. USA+45 LAW ADMIN CT/SYS
ROUTINE CRIME GP/REL...JURID 20. PAGE 58 B1175 ADJUD
              GOV/REL
              JUDGE

B64

ORTH C.D.,ADMINISTERING RESEARCH AND DEVELOPMENT. MGT
FINAN PLAN PROB/SOLV ADMIN ROUTINE...METH/CNCPT R+D
STAT CHARTS METH 20. PAGE 80 B1616 LG/CO
              INDUS

B64

PARET P.,FRENCH REVOLUTIONARY WARFARE FROM FRANCE
INDOCHINA TO ALGERIA* THE ANALYSIS OF A POLITICAL GUERRILLA
AND MILITARY DOCTRINE. ALGERIA VIETNAM FORCES GEN/LAWS
OP/RES TEC/DEV ROUTINE REV ATTIT...PSY BIBLIOG.
PAGE 81 B1632

B64

PINNICK A.W.,COUNTRY PLANNERS IN ACTION. UK FINAN MUNIC
SERV/IND NAT/G CONSULT DELIB/GP PRICE CONTROL PLAN
ROUTINE LEISURE AGE/C...GEOG 20 URBAN/RNWL. PAGE 83 INDUS
B1674   ATTIT

B64

SARROS P.P.,CONGRESS AND THE NEW DIPLOMACY: THE DIPLOM
FORMULATION OF MUTUAL SECURITY POLICY: 1953-60 POL/PAR
(THESIS). USA+45 CHIEF EX/STRUC REGION ROUTINE NAT/G
CHOOSE GOV/REL PEACE ROLE...POLICY 20 PRESIDENT
CONGRESS. PAGE 92 B1869

B64

STANLEY D.T.,THE HIGHER CIVIL SERVICE: AN NAT/G
EVALUATION OF FEDERAL PERSONNEL PRACTICES. USA+45 ADMIN
CREATE EXEC ROUTINE CENTRAL...MGT SAMP IDEA/COMP CONTROL
METH/COMP 20 CIVIL/SERV. PAGE 100 B2020 EFFICIENCY

B64

TINBERGEN J.,CENTRAL PLANNING. COM INTELL ECO/DEV PLAN
ECO/UNDEV FINAN INT/ORG PROB/SOLV ECO/TAC CONTROL INDUS
EXEC ROUTINE DECISION. PAGE 104 B2111 MGT
              CENTRAL

B64

TOMPKINS D.C.,PROBATION SINCE WORLD WAR II. USA+45 BIBLIOG

FORCES ADMIN ROUTINE PERS/REL AGE...CRIMLGY HEAL PUB/INST
20. PAGE 105 B2118 ORD/FREE
              CRIME

B64

UN PUB. INFORM. ORGAN.,EVERY MAN'S UNITED NATIONS. INT/ORG
UNIV WOR+45 CONSTN CULTURE SOCIETY ECO/DEV ROUTINE
ECO/UNDEV NAT/G ACT/RES PLAN ECO/TAC INT/TRADE
EDU/PROP LEGIT PEACE ATTIT ALL/VALS...POLICY HUM
INT/LAW CONCPT CHARTS UN TOT/POP 20. PAGE 106 B2150

B64

VALEN H.,POLITICAL PARTIES IN NORWAY. NORWAY ACADEM LOC/G
PARTIC ROUTINE INGP/REL KNOWL...QU 20. PAGE 111 POL/PAR
B2249   PERSON

B64

WAINHOUSE D.W.,REMNANTS OF EMPIRE: THE UNITED INT/ORG
NATIONS AND THE END OF COLONIALISM. FUT PORTUGAL TREND
WOR+45 NAT/G CONSULT DOMIN LEGIT ADMIN ROUTINE COLONIAL
ATTIT ORD/FREE...POLICY JURID RECORD INT TIME/SEQ
UN CMN/WLTH 20. PAGE 113 B2275

L64

HAAS E.B.,"ECONOMICS AND DIFFERENTIAL PATTERNS OF L/A+17C
POLITICAL INTEGRATION: PROJECTIONS ABOUT UNITY IN INT/ORG
LATIN AMERICA." SOCIETY NAT/G DELIB/GP ACT/RES MARKET
CREATE PLAN ECO/TAC REGION ROUTINE ATTIT DRIVE PWR
WEALTH...CONCPT TREND CHARTS LAFTA 20. PAGE 45
B0910

L64

PRUITT D.G.,"PROBLEM SOLVING IN THE DEPARTMENT OF ROUTINE
STATE." USA+45 NAT/G CONSULT PROB/SOLV EXEC PWR MGT
...DECISION INT ORG/CHARTS 20. PAGE 85 B1713 DIPLOM

L64

RIPLEY R.B.,"INTERAGENCY COMMITTEES AND EXEC
INCREMENTALISM: THE CASE OF AID TO INDIA." INDIA MGT
USA+45 INTELL NAT/G DELIB/GP ACT/RES DIPLOM ROUTINE FOR/AID
NAT/LISM ATTIT PWR...SOC CONCPT NEW/IDEA TIME/SEQ
CON/ANAL VAL/FREE 20. PAGE 89 B1790

L64

WORLD PEACE FOUNDATION,"INTERNATIONAL INT/ORG
ORGANIZATIONS: SUMMARY OF ACTIVITIES." INDIA ROUTINE
PAKISTAN TURKEY WOR+45 CONSTN CONSULT EX/STRUC
ECO/TAC EDU/PROP LEGIT ORD/FREE...JURID SOC UN 20
CYPRESS. PAGE 118 B2375

S64

CARNEGIE ENDOWMENT INT. PEACE,"ADMINISTRATION AND INT/ORG
BUDGET (ISSUES BEFORE THE NINETEENTH GENERAL ADMIN
ASSEMBLY)." WOR+45 FINAN BUDGET ECO/TAC ROUTINE
COST...STAT RECORD UN. PAGE 19 B0383

S64

EAKIN T.C.,"LEGISLATIVE POLITICS -- I AND II THE PROVS
WESTERN STATES, 19581964" (SUPPLEMENT)" USA+45 LEGIS
POL/PAR SCHOOL CONTROL LOBBY CHOOSE AGE. PAGE 32 ROUTINE
B0641   STRUCT

S64

GROSS J.A.,"WHITEHALL AND THE COMMONWEALTH." EX/STRUC
EUR+WWI MOD/EUR INT/ORG NAT/G CONSULT DELIB/GP ATTIT
LEGIS DOMIN ADMIN COLONIAL ROUTINE PWR CMN/WLTH TREND
19/20. PAGE 44 B0890

S64

HUELIN D.,"ECONOMIC INTEGRATION IN LATIN AMERICAN: MARKET
PROGRESS AND PROBLEMS." L/A+17C ECO/DEV AGRI ECO/UNDEV
DIST/IND FINAN INDUS NAT/G VOL/ASSN CONSULT INT/TRADE
DELIB/GP EX/STRUC ACT/RES PLAN TEC/DEV ECO/TAC
ROUTINE BAL/PAY WEALTH WORK 20. PAGE 52 B1058

S64

KHAN M.Z.,"THE PRESIDENT OF THE GENERAL ASSEMBLY." INT/ORG
WOR+45 CONSTN DELIB/GP EDU/PROP LEGIT ROUTINE PWR TOP/EX
RESPECT SKILL...DECISION SOC BIOG TREND UN 20.
PAGE 59 B1202

S64

MOWER A.G.,"THE OFFICIAL PRESSURE GROUP OF THE INT/ORG
COUNCIL OF EUROPE'S CONSULATIVE ASSEMBLY." EUR+WWI EDU/PROP
SOCIETY STRUCT FINAN CONSULT ECO/TAC ADMIN ROUTINE
ATTIT PWR WEALTH...STAT CHARTS 20 COUNCL/EUR.
PAGE 76 B1535

S64

MURRAY D.,"CHINESE EDUCATION IN SOUTH-EAST ASIA." S/ASIA
SOCIETY NEIGH EDU/PROP ROUTINE PERSON KNOWL SCHOOL
...OBS/ENVIR STERTYP. PAGE 76 B1546 REGION
              ASIA

S64

NASH M.,"SOCIAL PREREQUISITES TO ECONOMIC GROWTH IN ECO/DEV
LATIN AMERICA AND SOUTHEAST ASIA." L/A+17C S/ASIA PERCEPT
CULTURE SOCIETY ECO/UNDEV AGRI INDUS NAT/G PLAN
TEC/DEV EDU/PROP ROUTINE ALL/VALS...POLICY RELATIV
SOC NAT/COMP WORK TOT/POP 20. PAGE 77 B1558

S64

THOMPSON V.A.,"ADMINISTRATIVE OBJECTIVES FOR ECO/UNDEV
DEVELOPMENT ADMINISTRATION." WOR+45 CREATE PLAN MGT
DOMIN EDU/PROP EXEC ROUTINE ATTIT ORD/FREE PWR
...POLICY GEN/LAWS VAL/FREE. PAGE 104 B2107

C64

SCOTT R.E.,"MEXICAN GOVERNMENT IN TRANSITION (REV NAT/G
ED)" CULTURE STRUCT POL/PAR CHIEF ADMIN LOBBY REV L/A+17C
CHOOSE GP/REL DRIVE...BIBLIOG METH 20 MEXIC/AMER. ROUTINE
PAGE 95 B1920   CONSTN

B65
BOXER C.R.,PORTUGUESE SOCIETY IN THE TROPICS - THE   MUNIC
MUNICIPAL COUNCILS OF GAO, MACAO, BAHIA, AND   ADMIN
LUANDA, 1510-1800. EUR+WWI MOD/EUR PORTUGAL CONSTN   COLONIAL
EX/STRUC DOMIN CONTROL ROUTINE REPRESENT PRIVIL   DELIB/GP
...BIBLIOG/A 16/19 GENACCOUNT MACAO BAHIA LUANDA.
PAGE 14 B0290

B65
BUECHNER J.C.,DIFFERENCES IN ROLE PERCEPTIONS IN   MUNIC
COLORADO COUNCIL-MANAGER CITIES. USA+45 ADMIN   CONSULT
ROUTINE GP/REL CONSEN PERCEPT PERSON ROLE   LOC/G
...DECISION MGT STAT INT QU CHARTS 20 COLORADO   IDEA/COMP
CITY/MGT. PAGE 17 B0338

B65
COHEN H.,THE DEMONICS OF BUREAUCRACY: PROBLEMS OF   EXEC
CHANGE IN A GOVERNMENT AGENCY. USA+45 CLIENT   EX/STRUC
ROUTINE REPRESENT 20. PAGE 22 B0443   INGP/REL
                                                             ADMIN

B65
ECCLES H.E.,MILITARY CONCEPTS AND PHILOSOPHY.   PLAN
USA+45 STRUCT EXEC ROUTINE COERCE WAR CIVMIL/REL   DRIVE
COST...OBS GEN/LAWS COLD/WAR. PAGE 32 B0648   LEAD
                                                            FORCES

B65
EDELMAN M.,THE POLITICS OF WAGE-PRICE DECISIONS.   GOV/COMP
GERMANY ITALY NETHERLAND UK INDUS LABOR POL/PAR   CONTROL
PROB/SOLV BARGAIN PRICE ROUTINE BAL/PAY COST DEMAND   ECO/TAC
20. PAGE 32 B0654   PLAN

B65
ELDER R.E.,OVERSEAS REPRESENTATION AND SERVICES FOR   OP/RES
FEDERAL DOMESTIC AGENCIES. USA+45 NAT/G ACT/RES   DIPLOM
FOR/AID EDU/PROP SENIOR ROUTINE TASK ADJUST...MGT   GOV/REL
ORG/CHARTS. PAGE 33 B0663   ADMIN

B65
GOTLIEB A.,DISARMAMENT AND INTERNATIONAL LAW* A   INT/LAW
STUDY OF THE ROLE OF LAW IN THE DISARMAMENT   INT/ORG
PROCESS. USA+45 USSR PROB/SOLV CONFER ADMIN ROUTINE   ARMS/CONT
NUC/PWR ORD/FREE SOVEREIGN UN TREATY. PAGE 42 B0841   IDEA/COMP

B65
HADWIGER D.F.,PRESSURES AND PROTEST. NAT/G LEGIS   AGRI
PLAN LEAD PARTIC ROUTINE ATTIT POLICY. PAGE 45   GP/REL
B0913   LOBBY
                                                          CHOOSE

B65
HICKMAN B.G.,QUANTITATIVE PLANNING OF ECONOMIC   PROB/SOLV
POLICY. FRANCE NETHERLAND OP/RES PRICE ROUTINE UTIL   PLAN
...POLICY DECISION ECOMETRIC METH/CNCPT STAT STYLE   QUANT
CHINJAP. PAGE 50 B1004

B65
KELLEY E.J.,MARKETING: STRATEGY AND FUNCTIONS.   MARKET
ECO/DEV INDUS PLAN PRICE CONTROL ROUTINE...MGT   DIST/IND
BIBLIOG 20. PAGE 59 B1191   POLICY
                                                          ECO/TAC

B65
LAMBIRI I.,SOCIAL CHANGE IN A GREEK COUNTRY TOWN.   INDUS
GREECE FAM PROB/SOLV ROUTINE TASK LEISURE INGP/REL   WORKER
CONSEN ORD/FREE...SOC INT QU CHARTS 20. PAGE 62   CULTURE
B1252   NEIGH

B65
MARTIN R.,PUBLIC ADMINISTRATION AND DEMOCRACY.   EX/STRUC
ELITES NAT/G ADMIN EXEC ROUTINE INGP/REL. PAGE 70   DECISION
B1412   REPRESENT
                                                          GP/REL

B65
SCOTT A.M.,THE REVOLUTION IN STATECRAFT: INFORMAL   DIPLOM
PENETRATION. WOR+45 WOR-45 CULTURE INT/ORG FORCES   EDU/PROP
ECO/TAC ROUTINE...BIBLIOG 20. PAGE 95 B1918   FOR/AID

B65
US SENATE COMM GOVT OPERATIONS,ORGANIZATION OF   ADMIN
FEDERAL EXECUTIVE DEPARTMENTS AND AGENCIES: REPORT   EX/STRUC
OF MARCH 23, 1965. USA+45 FORCES LEGIS DIPLOM   GOV/REL
ROUTINE CIVMIL/REL EFFICIENCY FEDERAL...MGT STAT.   ORG/CHARTS
PAGE 110 B2217

B65
US SENATE COMM ON JUDICIARY,HEARINGS BEFORE   ROUTINE
SUBCOMMITTEE ON ADMINISTRATIVE PRACTICE AND   DELIB/GP
PROCEDURE ABOUT ADMINISTRATIVE PROCEDURE ACT 1965.   ADMIN
USA+45 LEGIS EDU/PROP ADJUD GOV/REL INGP/REL   NAT/G
EFFICIENCY...POLICY INT 20 CONGRESS. PAGE 110 B2232

B65
WARD R.,BACKGROUND MATERIAL ON ECONOMIC IMPACT OF   ECO/DEV
FEDERAL PROCUREMENT - 1965: FOR JOINT ECONOMIC   NAT/G
COMMITTEE US CONGRESS. FINAN ROUTINE WEAPON   OWN
CIVMIL/REL EFFICIENCY...STAT CHARTS 20 CONGRESS.   GOV/REL
PAGE 113 B2288

L65
RUBIN A.P.,"UNITED STATES CONTEMPORARY PRACTICE   LAW
RELATING TO INTERNATIONAL LAW." USA+45 WOR+45   LEGIT
CONSTN INT/ORG NAT/G DELIB/GP EX/STRUC DIPLOM DOMIN   INT/LAW
CT/SYS ROUTINE ORD/FREE...CONCPT COLD/WAR 20.
PAGE 91 B1848

L65
SHARKANSKY I.,"FOUR AGENCIES AND AN APPROPRIATIONS   ADMIN
SUBCOMMITTEE: A COMPARATIVE STUDY OF BDUGET   EDU/PROP
STRATEGIES." USA+45 EX/STRUC TOP/EX PROB/SOLV   NAT/G
CONTROL ROUTINE CONGRESS. PAGE 96 B1934   LEGIS

S65
QUADE Q.L.,"THE TRUMAN ADMINISTRATION AND THE   USA+45
SEPARATION OF POWERS: THE CASE OF THE MARSHALL   ECO/UNDEV
PLAN." SOCIETY INT/ORG NAT/G CONSULT DELIB/GP LEGIS DIPLOM
PLAN ECO/TAC ROUTINE DRIVE PERCEPT RIGID/FLEX
ORD/FREE PWR WEALTH...DECISION GEOG NEW/IDEA TREND
20 TRUMAN/HS. PAGE 85 B1726

S65
THOMAS F.C. JR.,"THE PEACE CORPS IN MOROCCO."   MOROCCO
CULTURE MUNIC PROVS CREATE ROUTINE TASK ADJUST   FRANCE
STRANGE...OBS PEACE/CORP. PAGE 104 B2099   FOR/AID
                                                         EDU/PROP

B66
BHALERAO C.N.,PUBLIC SERVICE COMMISSIONS OF INDIA: NAT/G
A STUDY. INDIA SERV/IND EX/STRUC ROUTINE CHOOSE   OP/RES
GOV/REL INGP/REL...KNO/TEST EXHIBIT 20. PAGE 11   LOC/G
B0233   ADMIN

B66
BURNS A.C.,PARLIAMENT AS AN EXPORT. WOR+45 CONSTN   PARL/PROC
BARGAIN DEBATE ROUTINE GOV/REL EFFICIENCY...ANTHOL   POL/PAR
COMMONWLTH PARLIAMENT. PAGE 17 B0353   CT/SYS
                                                         CHIEF

B66
DAVIDSON R.H.,CONGRESS IN CRISIS: POLITICS AND   LEGIS
CONGRESSIONAL REFORM. USA+45 SOCIETY POL/PAR   PARL/PROC
CONTROL LEAD ROUTINE GOV/REL ATTIT PWR...POLICY 20   PROB/SOLV
CONGRESS. PAGE 26 B0535   NAT/G

B66
DAVIS R.G.,PLANNING HUMAN RESOURCE DEVELOPMENT,   PLAN
EDUCATIONAL MODELS AND SCHEMATA. WORKER OP/RES   EFFICIENCY
ECO/TAC EDU/PROP CONTROL COST PRODUC...GEOG STAT   SIMUL
CHARTS 20. PAGE 27 B0544   ROUTINE

B66
DICKSON W.J.,COUNSELING IN AN ORGANIZATION: A   INDUS
SEQUEL TO THE HAWTHORNE RESEARCHES. CLIENT VOL/ASSN   WORKER
ACT/RES PROB/SOLV AUTOMAT ROUTINE PERS/REL   PSY
HAPPINESS ANOMIE ROLE...OBS CHARTS 20 AT+T. PAGE 29   MGT
B0588

B66
DUNCOMBE H.S.,COUNTY GOVERNMENT IN AMERICA. USA+45   LOC/G
FINAN MUNIC ADMIN ROUTINE GOV/REL...GOV/COMP 20.   PROVS
PAGE 31 B0631   CT/SYS
                                                       TOP/EX

B66
LEWIS W.A.,DEVELOPMENT PLANNING; THE ESSENTIALS OF   PLAN
ECONOMIC POLICY. USA+45 FINAN INDUS NAT/G WORKER   ECO/DEV
FOR/AID INT/TRADE ADMIN ROUTINE WEALTH...CONCPT   POLICY
STAT. PAGE 65 B1307   CREATE

B66
MANSFIELD E.,MANAGERIAL ECONOMICS AND OPERATIONS   ECO/TAC
RESEARCH; A NONMATHEMATICAL INTRODUCTION. USA+45   OP/RES
ELITES ECO/DEV CONSULT EX/STRUC PROB/SOLV ROUTINE   MGT
EFFICIENCY OPTIMAL...GAME T 20. PAGE 69 B1396   COMPUTER

B66
MARTIN L.W.,DIPLOMACY IN MODERN EUROPEAN HISTORY.   DIPLOM
EUR+WWI MOD/EUR INT/ORG NAT/G EX/STRUC ROUTINE WAR   POLICY
PEACE TOTALISM PWR 15/20 COLD/WAR EUROPE/W. PAGE 70
B1411

B66
TOTTEN G.O.,THE SOCIAL DEMOCRATIC MOVEMENT IN   POL/PAR
PREWAR JAPAN. ASIA CHIEF EX/STRUC LEGIS DOMIN LEAD   SOCISM
ROUTINE WAR 20 CHINJAP. PAGE 105 B2122   PARTIC
                                                     STRATA

B66
VON HOFFMAN N.,THE MULTIVERSITY; A PERSONAL REPORT   EDU/PROP
ON WHAT HAPPENS TO TODAY'S STUDENTS AT AMERICAN   ACADEM
UNIVERSITIES. USA+45 SOCIETY ROUTINE ANOMIE ROLE   ATTIT
MORAL ORD/FREE SKILL...INT 20. PAGE 112 B2266   STRANGE

B66
WALL E.H.,THE COURT OF JUSTICE IN THE EUROPEAN   CT/SYS
COMMUNITIES: JURISDICTION AND PROCEDURE. EUR+WWI   INT/ORG
DIPLOM ADJUD ADMIN ROUTINE TASK...CONCPT LING 20.   LAW
PAGE 113 B2281   OP/RES

B66
WHITNAH D.R.,SAFER SKYWAYS. DIST/IND DELIB/GP   ADMIN
FORCES TOP/EX WORKER TEC/DEV ROUTINE WAR CIVMIL/REL NAT/G
COST...TIME/SEQ 20 FAA CAB. PAGE 116 B2342   AIR
                                                     GOV/REL

B66
YOUNG W.,EXISTING MECHANISMS OF ARMS CONTROL.   ARMS/CONT
PROC/MFG OP/RES DIPLOM TASK CENTRAL...MGT TREATY.   ADMIN
PAGE 119 B2395   NUC/PWR
                                                     ROUTINE

B66
ZINKIN T.,CHALLENGES IN INDIA. INDIA PAKISTAN LAW   NAT/G
AGRI FINAN INDUS TOP/EX TEC/DEV CONTROL ROUTINE   ECO/TAC
ORD/FREE PWR 20 NEHRU/J SHASTRI/LB CIVIL/SERV.   POLICY
PAGE 119 B2404   ADMIN

S66
DIEBOLD J.,"COMPUTERS, PROGRAM MANAGEMENT AND   COMPUTER
FOREIGN AFFAIRS." USA+45 INDUS OP/RES TEC/DEV...MGT DIPLOM
GP/COMP GEN/LAWS. PAGE 29 B0590   ROUTINE
                                                     ACT/RES

C66
JACOB H.,"DIMENSIONS OF STATE POLITICS HEARD A. ED. PROVS
STATE LEGIWLATURES IN AMERICAN POLITICS." CULTURE   LEGIS

STRATA POL/PAR BUDGET TAX LOBBY ROUTINE GOV/REL   ROLE
...TRADIT DECISION GEOG. PAGE 55 B1112   REPRESENT
                  B67

DE BLIJ H.J.,SYSTEMATIC POLITICAL GEOGRAPHY. WOR+45 GEOG
STRUCT INT/ORG NAT/G EDU/PROP ADMIN COLONIAL   CONCPT
ROUTINE ORD/FREE PWR...IDEA/COMP T 20. PAGE 27   METH
B0550
                  B67

MENHENNET D.,PARLIAMENT IN PERSPECTIVE. UK ROUTINE LEGIS
REPRESENT ROLE PWR 20 PARLIAMENT. PAGE 73 B1467   PARL/PROC
                  CONCPT
                  POPULISM
                  B67

NIEDERHOFFER A.,BEHIND THE SHIELD; THE POLICE IN   FORCES
URBAN SOCIETY. USA+45 LEGIT ADJUD ROUTINE COERCE   PERSON
CRIME ADJUST...INT CHARTS 20 NEWYORK/C. PAGE 78   SOCIETY
B1582   ATTIT
                  B67

SCHAEFER W.V.,THE SUSPECT AND SOCIETY: CRIMINAL   CRIME
PROCEDURE AND CONVERGING CONSTITUTIONAL DOCTRINES.   FORCES
USA+45 TEC/DEV LOBBY ROUTINE SANCTION...INT 20.   CONSTN
PAGE 93 B1879   JURID
                  B67

US DEPARTMENT OF JUSTICE,ANNUAL REPORT OF THE   ADMIN
OFFICE OF ADMINISTRATIVE PROCEDURE. USA+45   NAT/G
PROB/SOLV EDU/PROP EXEC INGP/REL EFFICIENCY KNOWL   ROUTINE
...POLICY STAT 20. PAGE 108 B2181   GOV/REL
                  B67

WEINBERG M.,SCHOOL INTEGRATION: A COMPREHENSIVE   BIBLIOG
CLASSIFIED BIBLIOGRAPHY OF 3,100 REFERENCES. USA+45 SCHOOL
LAW NAT/G NEIGH SECT PLAN ROUTINE AGE/C WEALTH   DISCRIM
SOC/INTEG INDIAN/AM. PAGE 115 B2314   RACE/REL
                  L67

CAHIERS P.,"LE RECOURS EN CONSTATATION DE   INT/ORG
MANQUEMENTS DES ETATS MEMBRES DEVANT LA COUR DES   CONSTN
COMMUNAUTES EUROPEENNES." LAW PROB/SOLV DIPLOM   ROUTINE
ADMIN CT/SYS SANCTION ATTIT...POLICY DECISION JURID ADJUD
ECSC EEC. PAGE 18 B0362
                  L67

PASLEY R.S.,"ORGANIZATIONAL CONFLICTS OF INTEREST   NAT/G
IN GOVERNMENT CONTRACTS." ELITES R+D ROUTINE   ECO/TAC
NUC/PWR DEMAND EFFICIENCY 20. PAGE 81 B1639   RATION
                  CONTROL
                  S67

CONWAY J.E.,"MAKING RESEARCH EFFECTIVE IN   ACT/RES
LEGISLATION." LAW R+D CONSULT EX/STRUC PLAN CONFER POLICY
ADMIN LEAD ROUTINE TASK INGP/REL DECISION. PAGE 23 LEGIS
B0469   PROB/SOLV
                  S67

DANELSKI D.J.,"CONFLICT AND ITS RESOLUTION IN THE   ROLE
SUPREME COURT." PROB/SOLV LEAD ROUTINE PERSON...PSY JURID
PERS/COMP BIBLIOG 20. PAGE 26 B0527   JUDGE
                  INGP/REL
                  S67

DROR Y.,"POLICY ANALYSTS." USA+45 COMPUTER OP/RES   NAT/G
ECO/TAC ADMIN ROUTINE...ECOMETRIC METH/COMP SIMUL POLICY
20. PAGE 30 B0618   PLAN
                  DECISION
                  S67

DUGGAR J.W.,"THE DEVELOPMENT OF MONEY SUPPLY IN   ECO/UNDEV
ETHIOPIA." ETHIOPIA ISLAM CONSULT OP/RES BUDGET   FINAN
CONTROL ROUTINE EFFICIENCY EQUILIB WEALTH...MGT 20. BAL/PAY
PAGE 31 B0629   ECOMETRIC
                  S67

FOX R.G.,"FAMILY, CASTE, AND COMMERCE IN A NORTH   CULTURE
INDIAN MARKET TOWN." INDIA STRATA AGRI FACE/GP FAM GP/REL
NEIGH OP/RES BARGAIN ADMIN ROUTINE WEALTH...SOC   ECO/UNDEV
CHARTS 20. PAGE 37 B0747   DIST/IND
                  S67

KAYSEN C.,"DATA BANKS AND DOSSIERS." FUT USA+45   CENTRAL
COM/IND NAT/G PLAN PROB/SOLV TEC/DEV BUDGET ADMIN   EFFICIENCY
ROUTINE. PAGE 59 B1185   CENSUS
                  ACT/RES
                  S67

LASLETT J.H.M.,"SOCIALISM AND THE AMERICAN LABOR   LABOR
MOVEMENT* SOME NEW REFLECTIONS." USA-45 VOL/ASSN   ROUTINE
LOBBY PARTIC CENTRAL ALL/VALS SOCISM...GP/COMP 20.   ATTIT
PAGE 63 B1265   GP/REL
                  S67

LENDVAI P.,"HUNGARY* CHANGE VS. IMMOBILISM."   ECO/DEV
HUNGARY LABOR NAT/G PLAN DEBATE ADMIN ROUTINE   MGT
CENTRAL EFFICIENCY MARXISM PLURISM...PREDICT 20.   CHOOSE
PAGE 64 B1289
                  S67

LEVCIK B.,"WAGES AND EMPLOYMENT PROBLEMS IN THE NEW MARXISM
SYSTEM OF PLANNED MANAGEMENT IN CZECHOSLOVAKIA."   WORKER
CZECHOSLVK EUR+WWI NAT/G OP/RES PLAN ADMIN ROUTINE MGT
INGP/REL CENTRAL EFFICIENCY PRODUC DECISION.   PAY
PAGE 64 B1300
                  S67

MACDONALD G.J.F.,"SCIENCE AND SPACE POLICY* HOW   SPACE
DOES IT GET PLANNED?" R+D CREATE TEC/DEV BUDGET   PLAN
ADMIN ROUTINE...DECISION NASA. PAGE 67 B1357   MGT
                  EX/STRUC
                  S67

MOOR E.J.,"THE INTERNATIONAL IMPACT OF AUTOMATION." TEC/DEV

WOR+45 ACT/RES COMPUTER CREATE PLAN CAP/ISM ROUTINE OP/RES
EFFICIENCY PREDICT. PAGE 75 B1511   AUTOMAT
                  INDUS
                  S67

PRATT R.C.,"THE ADMINISTRATION OF ECONOMIC PLANNING NAT/G
IN A NEWLY INDEPEND ENT STATE* THE TANZANIAN   DELIB/GP
EXPERIENCE 1963-1966." AFR TANZANIA ECO/UNDEV PLAN ADMIN
CONTROL ROUTINE TASK EFFICIENCY 20. PAGE 84 B1699 TEC/DEV
                  S67

SPACKMAN A.,"THE SENATE OF TRINIDAD AND TOBAGO."   ELITES
L/A+17C TRINIDAD WEST/IND NAT/G POL/PAR DELIB/GP   EFFICIENCY
OP/RES PROB/SOLV EDU/PROP EXEC LOBBY ROUTINE   LEGIS
REPRESENT GP/REL 20. PAGE 99 B2002   DECISION
                  S67

TOURNELLE G.,"DIPLOMATIE D' HIER ET D'AUJOURD'   DIPLOM
HUI." CONFER ADMIN ROUTINE PEACE. PAGE 105 B2123   ROLE
                  INT/ORG
                  S67

TURNER F.C. JR.,"EXPERIMENT IN INTER-AMERICAN   FORCES
PEACE-KEEPING." DOMIN/REP ADMIN ROUTINE REV   ADJUD
ORD/FREE OAS 20. PAGE 106 B2137   PEACE
                  N67

NATIONAL COMN COMMUNITY HEALTH,ACTION - PLANNING   PLAN
FOR COMMUNITY HEALTH SERVICES (PAMPHLET). USA+45   MUNIC
PROF/ORG DELIB/GP BUDGET ROUTINE GP/REL ATTIT   HEALTH
...HEAL SOC SOC/WK CHARTS TIME 20. PAGE 77 B1563   ADJUST

ROWAT D.C. B1839,B1840,B1841

ROWE J.Z. B1842

ROY N.C. B1843

ROY/MN....M.N. ROY

ROYAL AIR FORCE....SEE RAF

ROYAL INST. INT. AFF. B1844

ROYAL INSTITUTE PUBLIC ADMIN B1845

ROYAL/COMM

                  S67
DOERN G.B.,"THE ROYAL COMMISSIONS IN THE GENERAL   R+D
POLICY PROCESS AND IN FEDERAL-PROVINCIAL   EX/STRUC
RELATIONS." CANADA CONSTN ACADEM PROVS CONSULT   GOV/REL
DELIB/GP LEGIS ACT/RES PROB/SOLV CONFER CONTROL   NAT/G
EFFICIENCY...METH/COMP 20 SENATE ROYAL/COMM.
PAGE 30 B0603

RUBENSTEIN A.H. B1846

RUBENSTEIN R. B1847

RUBIN A.P. B1848

RUBIN H. B1849

RUBIN R.I. B1850

RUBINSTEIN A.Z. B1851,B1852

RUDOLPH F. B1853

RUDOLPH S. B1854

RUEF/ABE....ABRAHAM RUEF

RUITENBEER H.M. B1855

RULES/COMM....RULES COMMITTEES OF CONGRESS

RUMOR....SEE ALSO PERS/REL

                  S66
PALMER M.,"THE UNITED ARAB REPUBLIC* AN ASSESSMENT UAR
OF ITS FAILURE." ELITES ECO/UNDEV POL/PAR FORCES   SYRIA
ECO/TAC RUMOR ADMIN EXEC EFFICIENCY ATTIT SOCISM   REGION
...INT NASSER/G. PAGE 81 B1628   FEDERAL

RURAL....RURAL AREAS, PEOPLE, ETC.

RUSK D. B1856

RUSK/D

                  B61
TANZER L.,THE KENNEDY CIRCLE. INTELL CONSULT   EX/STRUC
DELIB/GP TOP/EX CONTROL EXEC INGP/REL PERS/REL PWR CHIEF
...BIOG IDEA/COMP ANTHOL 20 KENNEDY/JF PRESIDENT
DEMOCRAT MCNAMARA/R RUSK/D. PAGE 103 B2077

B62
US SENATE COMM GOVT OPERATIONS.ADMINISTRATION OF
NATIONAL SECURITY. USA+45 CHIEF PLAN PROB/SOLV
TEC/DEV DIPLOM ATTIT...POLICY 20 KENNEDY/JF RUSK/D
MCNAMARA/R BUNDY/M HERTER/C. PAGE 110 B2212
ORD/FREE
ADMIN
CONTROL

S64
RUSK D.."THE MAKING OF FOREIGN POLICY" USA+45 CHIEF
DELIB/GP WORKER PROB/SOLV ADMIN ATTIT PWR 20
DEPT/STATE RUSK/D GOLDMAN/E. PAGE 92 B1856
DIPLOM
INT
POLICY

S66
AUSLAND J.C.."CRISIS MANAGEMENT* BERLIN, CYPRUS,
LAOS." CYPRUS LAOS FORCES CREATE PLAN EDU/PROP TASK
CENTRAL PERSON RIGID/FLEX...MGT 20 BERLIN
KENNEDY/JF MCNAMARA/R RUSK. PAGE 7 B0148
OP/RES
DIPLOM
RISK
ADMIN

RUSKIN/J....JOHN RUSKIN

RUSSELL R.B. B1857

RUSSELL/B....BERTRAND RUSSELL

RUSSETT B.M. B1858

RUSSIA....PRE-REVOLUTIONARY RUSSIA; SEE ALSO APPROPRIATE
    TIME/SPACE/CULTURE INDEX

B38
PETTEE G.S..THE PROCESS OF REVOLUTION. COM FRANCE
ITALY MOD/EUR RUSSIA SPAIN WOR-45 ELITES INTELL
SOCIETY STRATA STRUCT INT/ORG NAT/G POL/PAR ACT/RES
PLAN EDU/PROP LEGIT EXEC...SOC MYTH TIME/SEQ
TOT/POP 18/20. PAGE 82 B1664
COERCE
CONCPT
REV

B41
YOUNG G..FEDERALISM AND FREEDOM. EUR+WWI MOD/EUR
RUSSIA USA-45 WOR-45 SOCIETY STRUCT ECO/DEV INT/ORG
EXEC FEDERAL ATTIT PERSON ALL/VALS...OLD/LIB CONCPT
OBS TREND LEAGUE/NAT TOT/POP. PAGE 119 B2392
NAT/G
WAR

S50
WITTFOGEL K.A.."RUSSIA AND ASIA: PROBLEMS OF
CONTEMPORARY AREA STUDIES AND INTERNATIONAL
RELATIONS." ASIA COM USA+45 SOCIETY NAT/G DIPLOM
ECO/TAC FOR/AID EDU/PROP KNOWL...HIST/WRIT TOT/POP
20. PAGE 117 B2369
ECO/DEV
ADMIN
RUSSIA
USSR

B58
SCOTT D.J.R..RUSSIAN POLITICAL INSTITUTIONS. RUSSIA
USSR CONSTN AGRI DELIB/GP PLAN EDU/PROP CONTROL
CHOOSE EFFICIENCY ATTIT MARXISM...BIBLIOG/A 13/20.
PAGE 95 B1919
NAT/G
POL/PAR
ADMIN
DECISION

B60
PIERCE R.A..RUSSIAN CENTRAL ASIA, 1867-1917. ASIA
RUSSIA CULTURE AGRI INDUS EDU/PROP REV NAT/LISM
...CHARTS BIBLIOG 19/20 BOLSHEVISM INTERVENT.
PAGE 83 B1672
COLONIAL
DOMIN
ADMIN
ECO/UNDEV

S60
SCHWARTZ B.."THE INTELLIGENTSIA IN COMMUNIST CHINA:
A TENTATIVE COMPARISON." ASIA CHINA/COM COM RUSSIA
ELITES SOCIETY STRATA POL/PAR VOL/ASSN CREATE ADMIN
COERCE NAT/LISM TOTALISM...POLICY TREND 20. PAGE 95
B1914
INTELL
RIGID/FLEX
REV

B61
LENIN V.I..WHAT IS TO BE DONE? (1902). RUSSIA LABOR
NAT/G POL/PAR WORKER CAP/ISM ECO/TAC ADMIN PARTIC
...MARXIST IDEA/COMP GEN/LAWS 19/20. PAGE 64 B1292
EDU/PROP
PRESS
MARXISM
METH/COMP

B61
MOLLAU G..INTERNATIONAL COMMUNISM AND WORLD
REVOLUTION: HISTORY AND METHODS. RUSSIA USSR
INT/ORG NAT/G POL/PAR VOL/ASSN FORCES BAL/PWR
DIPLOM EXEC REGION WAR ATTIT PWR MARXISM...CONCPT
TIME/SEQ COLD/WAR 19/20. PAGE 74 B1498
COM
REV

B61
MONAS S..THE THIRD SECTION: POLICE AND SOCIETY IN
RUSSIA UNDER NICHOLAS I. MOD/EUR RUSSIA ELITES
STRUCT NAT/G EX/STRUC ADMIN CONTROL PWR CONSERVE
...DECISION 19 NICHOLAS/I. PAGE 74 B1499
ORD/FREE
COM
FORCES
COERCE

B64
FAINSOD M..HOW RUSSIA IS RULED (REV. ED.). RUSSIA
USSR AGRI PROC/MFG LABOR POL/PAR EX/STRUC CONTROL
PWR...POLICY BIBLIOG 19/20 KHRUSH/N COM/PARTY.
PAGE 34 B0700
NAT/G
REV
MARXISM

B64
PIPES R..THE FORMATION OF THE SOVIET UNION. EUR+WWI
MOD/EUR STRUCT ECO/UNDEV NAT/G LEGIS DOMIN LEGIT
CT/SYS EXEC COERCE ALL/VALS...POLICY RELATIV
HIST/WRIT TIME/SEQ TOT/POP 19/20. PAGE 83 B1677
COM
USSR
RUSSIA

B66
RAEFF M..ORIGINS OF THE RUSSIAN INTELLIGENTSIA: THE
EIGHTEENTH-CENTURY NOBILITY. RUSSIA FAM NAT/G
EDU/PROP ADMIN PERS/REL ATTIT...HUM BIOG 18.
PAGE 85 B1728
INTELL
ELITES
STRATA
CONSERVE

S67
BREGMAN A.."WHITHER RUSSIA?" COM RUSSIA INTELL
MARXISM

POL/PAR DIPLOM PARTIC NAT/LISM TOTALISM ATTIT
ORD/FREE 20. PAGE 15 B0304
ELITES
ADMIN
CREATE

RUSTOW D.A. B1859,B1860

RWANDA....SEE ALSO AFR

B60
ASPREMONT-LYNDEN H..RAPPORT SUR L'ADMINISTRATION
BELGE DU RUANDA-URUNDI PENDANT L'ANNEE 1959.
BELGIUM RWANDA AGRI INDUS DIPLOM ECO/TAC INT/TRADE
DOMIN ADMIN RACE/REL...GEOG CENSUS 20 UN. PAGE 7
B0143
AFR
COLONIAL
ECO/UNDEV
INT/ORG

RYUKYUS....RYUKYU ISLANDS

S

S/AFR....SOUTH AFRICA, SEE ALSO AFR

S/ASIA....SOUTHEAST ASIA; SEE ALSO APPROPRIATE NATIONS

N
VENKATESAN S.L..BIBLIOGRAPHY ON PUBLIC ENTERPRISES
IN INDIA. INDIA S/ASIA FINAN LG/CO LOC/G PLAN
BUDGET SOCISM...MGT 20. PAGE 112 B2258
BIBLIOG/A
ADMIN
ECO/UNDEV
INDUS

N
THE JAPAN SCIENCE REVIEW: LAW AND POLITICS: LIST OF
BOOKS AND ARTICLES ON LAW AND POLITICS. CONSTN AGRI
INDUS LABOR DIPLOM TAX ADMIN CRIME...INT/LAW SOC 20
CHINJAP. PAGE 1 B0025
BIBLIOG
LAW
S/ASIA
PHIL/SCI

B26
MOON P.T..IMPERIALISM AND WORLD POLITICS. AFR ASIA
ISLAM MOD/EUR S/ASIA USA+45 SOCIETY NAT/G EX/STRUC
BAL/PWR DOMIN COLONIAL NAT/LISM ATTIT DRIVE PWR
...GEOG SOC 20. PAGE 75 B1510
WEALTH
TIME/SEQ
CAP/ISM
DIPLOM

B29
BOUDET P..BIBLIOGRAPHIE DE L'INDOCHINE FRANCAISE.
S/ASIA VIETNAM SECT...GEOG LING 20. PAGE 14 B0282
BIBLIOG
ADMIN
COLONIAL
DIPLOM

B29
ROBERTS S.H..HISTORY OF FRENCH COLONIAL POLICY. AFR
ASIA L/A+17C S/ASIA CULTURE ECO/DEV ECO/UNDEV FINAN
NAT/G PLAN ECO/TAC DOMIN ROUTINE SOVEREIGN...OBS
HIST/WRIT TREND CHARTS VAL/FREE 19/20. PAGE 89
B1796
INT/ORG
ACT/RES
FRANCE
COLONIAL

B31
DEKAT A.D.A..COLONIAL POLICY. S/ASIA CULTURE
EX/STRUC ECO/TAC DOMIN ADMIN COLONIAL ROUTINE
SOVEREIGN WEALTH...POLICY MGT RECORD KNO/TEST SAMP.
PAGE 28 B0570
DRIVE
PWR
INDONESIA
NETHERLAND

C39
REISCHAUER R.."JAPAN'S GOVERNMENT--POLITICS."
CONSTN STRATA POL/PAR FORCES LEGIS DIPLOM ADMIN
EXEC CENTRAL...POLICY BIBLIOG 20 CHINJAP. PAGE 87
B1764
NAT/G
S/ASIA
CONCPT
ROUTINE

B56
IRIKURA J.K..SOUTHEAST ASIA: SELECTED ANNOTATED
BIBLIOGRAPHY OF JAPANESE PUBLICATIONS. CULTURE
ADMIN RACE/REL 20 CHINJAP. PAGE 55 B1104
BIBLIOG/A
S/ASIA
DIPLOM

B56
JENNINGS W.I..THE APPROACH TO SELF-GOVERNMENT.
CEYLON INDIA PAKISTAN S/ASIA UK SOCIETY POL/PAR
DELIB/GP LEGIS ECO/TAC EDU/PROP ADMIN EXEC CHOOSE
ATTIT ALL/VALS...JURID CONCPT GEN/METH TOT/POP 20.
PAGE 56 B1136
NAT/G
CONSTN
COLONIAL

B56
KIRK G..THE CHANGING ENVIRONMENT OF INTERNATIONAL
RELATIONS. ASIA S/ASIA USA+45 WOR+45 ECO/UNDEV
INT/ORG NAT/G FOR/AID EDU/PROP PEACE KNOWL
...PLURIST COLD/WAR TOT/POP 20. PAGE 60 B1214
FUT
EXEC
DIPLOM

B56
WILSON P..GOVERNMENT AND POLITICS OF INDIA AND
PAKISTAN: 1885-1955; A BIBLIOGRAPHY OF WORKS IN
WESTERN LANGUAGES. INDIA PAKISTAN CONSTN LOC/G
POL/PAR FORCES DIPLOM ADMIN WAR CHOOSE...BIOG
CON/ANAL 19/20. PAGE 117 B2361
BIBLIOG
COLONIAL
NAT/G
S/ASIA

B57
SOUTH PACIFIC COMMISSION.INDEX OF SOCIAL SCIENCE
RESEARCH THESES ON THE SOUTH PACIFIC. S/ASIA ACADEM
ADMIN COLONIAL...SOC 20. PAGE 99 B2000
BIBLIOG/A
ACT/RES
SECT
CULTURE

C57
TANG P.S.H.."COMMUNIST CHINA TODAY: DOMESTIC AND
FOREIGN POLICIES." CHINA/COM COM S/ASIA USSR STRATA
FORCES DIPLOM EDU/PROP COERCE GOV/REL...POLICY
MAJORIT BIBLIOG 20. PAGE 102 B2071
POL/PAR
LEAD
ADMIN
CONSTN

B58
MASON J.B..THAILAND BIBLIOGRAPHY. S/ASIA THAILAND
CULTURE EDU/PROP ADMIN...GEOG SOC LING 20. PAGE 70
B1423
BIBLIOG/A
ECO/UNDEV
DIPLOM
NAT/G

B58
SKINNER G.W..LEADERSHIP AND POWER IN THE CHINESE
COMMUNITY OF THAILAND. ASIA S/ASIA STRATA FACE/GP
SOC
ELITES

KIN PROF/ORG VOL/ASSN EX/STRUC DOMIN PERSON RESPECT THAILAND
...METH/CNCPT STAT INT QU BIOG CHARTS 20. PAGE 98
B1974

B58
UNIVERSITY OF LONDON,THE FAR EAST AND SOUTH-EAST   BIBLIOG
ASIA: A CUMULATED LIST OF PERIODICAL ARTICLES, MAY SOC
1956-APRIL 1957. ASIA S/ASIA LAW ADMIN...LING 20.
PAGE 107 B2168

B59
BHAMBHRI C.P.,SUBSTANCE OF HINDU POLITY. INDIA   GOV/REL
S/ASIA LAW EX/STRUC JUDGE TAX COERCE GP/REL   WRITING
POPULISM 20 HINDU. PAGE 11 B0234   SECT
                                                    PROVS
B59
INDIAN INSTITUTE PUBLIC ADMIN.MORALE IN THE PUBLIC HAPPINESS
SERVICES: REPORT OF A CONFERENCE JAN., 3-4, 1959.   ADMIN
INDIA S/ASIA ECO/UNDEV PROVS PLAN EDU/PROP CONFER   WORKER
GOV/REL EFFICIENCY DRIVE ROLE 20 CIVIL/SERV.   INGP/REL
PAGE 53 B1082

B59
PARK R.L.,LEADERSHIP AND POLITICAL INSTITUTIONS IN NAT/G
INDIA. S/ASIA CULTURE ECO/UNDEV LOC/G MUNIC PROVS   EXEC
LEGIS PLAN ADMIN LEAD ORD/FREE WEALTH...GEOG SOC   INDIA
BIOG TOT/POP VAL/FREE 20. PAGE 81 B1633

B60
EASTON S.C.,THE TWILIGHT OF EUROPEAN COLONIALISM.   FINAN
AFR S/ASIA CONSTN SOCIETY STRUCT ECO/UNDEV INDUS   ADMIN
NAT/G FORCES ECO/TAC COLONIAL CT/SYS ATTIT KNOWL
ORD/FREE PWR...SOCIALIST TIME/SEQ TREND CON/ANAL
20. PAGE 32 B0645

B60
LIPSET S.M.,POLITICAL MAN. AFR COM EUR+WWI L/A+17C PWR
MOD/EUR S/ASIA USA+45 USA-45 STRUCT ECO/DEV   SOC
ECO/UNDEV POL/PAR SECT ADMIN WEALTH...CONCPT WORK
TOT/POP 20. PAGE 65 B1320

S60
EMERSON R.,"THE EROSION OF DEMOCRACY." AFR FUT LAW S/ASIA
CULTURE INTELL SOCIETY ECO/UNDEV FAM LOC/G NAT/G   POL/PAR
FORCES PLAN TEC/DEV ECO/TAC ADMIN CT/SYS ATTIT
ORD/FREE PWR...SOCIALIST SOC CONCPT STAND/INT
TIME/SEQ WORK 20. PAGE 33 B0671

S60
MODELSKI G.,"AUSTRALIA AND SEATO." S/ASIA USA+45   INT/ORG
CULTURE INTELL ECO/DEV NAT/G PLAN DIPLOM ADMIN   ACT/RES
ROUTINE ATTIT SKILL...MGT TIME/SEQ AUSTRAL 20
SEATO. PAGE 74 B1493

S60
RIESELBACH Z.N.,"QUANTITATIVE TECHNIQUES FOR   QUANT
STUDYING VOTING BEHAVIOR IN THE UNITED NATIONS   CHOOSE
GENERAL ASSEMBLY." FUT S/ASIA USA+45 INT/ORG
BAL/PWR DIPLOM ECO/TAC FOR/AID ADMIN PWR...POLICY
METH/CNCPT METH UN 20. PAGE 88 B1783

C60
SMITH T.E.,"ELECTIONS IN DEVELOPING COUNTRIES: A   ECO/UNDEV
STUDY OF ELECTORAL PROCEDURES USED IN TOPICAL   CHOOSE
AFRICA, SOUTH-EAST ASIA..." AFR S/ASIA UK ROUTINE   REPRESENT
GOV/REL RACE/REL...GOV/COMP BIBLIOG 20. PAGE 98   ADMIN
B1985

B61
COHN B.S.,DEVELOPMENT AND IMPACT OF BRITISH   BIBLIOG/A
ADMINISTRATION IN INDIA: A BIBLIOGRAPHIC ESSAY.   COLONIAL
INDIA UK ECO/UNDEV NAT/G DOMIN...POLICY MGT SOC   S/ASIA
19/20. PAGE 22 B0448   ADMIN

B61
HARRISON S.,INDIA AND THE UNITED STATES. FUT S/ASIA DELIB/GP
USA+45 WOR+45 INTELL ECO/DEV ECO/UNDEV AGRI INDUS   ACT/RES
INT/ORG NAT/G CONSULT EX/STRUC TOP/EX PLAN ECO/TAC FOR/AID
NEUTRAL ALL/VALS...MGT TOT/POP 20. PAGE 47 B0956   INDIA

B61
KERTESZ S.D.,AMERICAN DIPLOMACY IN A NEW ERA. COM   ANTHOL
S/ASIA UK USA+45 FORCES PROB/SOLV BAL/PWR ECO/TAC   DIPLOM
ADMIN COLONIAL WAR PEACE ORD/FREE 20 NATO CONGRESS TREND
UN COLD/WAR. PAGE 59 B1199

B61
KOESTLER A.,THE LOTUS AND THE ROBOT. ASIA INDIA   SECT
S/ASIA SOCIETY STRATA ECO/DEV AGRI INDUS FAM CREATE ECO/UNDEV
DOMIN EDU/PROP ADMIN COERCE ATTIT DRIVE SUPEGO
ORD/FREE PWR RESPECT WEALTH...MYTH OBS 20 CHINJAP.
PAGE 61 B1226

B61
WEST F.J.,POLITICAL ADVANCEMENT IN THE SOUTH   S/ASIA
PACIFIC. CONSTN CULTURE POL/PAR LEGIS DOMIN ADMIN   LOC/G
CHOOSE SOVEREIGN VAL/FREE 20 FIJI TAHITI SAMOA.   COLONIAL
PAGE 115 B2325

S61
RUDOLPH S.,"CONSENSUS AND CONFLICT IN INDIAN   POL/PAR
POLITICS." S/ASIA WOR+45 NAT/G DELIB/GP DIPLOM   PERCEPT
EDU/PROP ADMIN CONSEN PERSON ALL/VALS...OBS TREND   INDIA
TOT/POP VAL/FREE 20. PAGE 92 B1854

B62
MORE S.S.,REMODELLING OF DEMOCRACY FOR AFRO-ASIAN   ORD/FREE
NATIONS. AFR INDIA S/ASIA SOUTH/AFR CONSTN EX/STRUC ECO/UNDEV
COLONIAL CHOOSE TOTALISM SOVEREIGN NEW/LIB SOCISM   ADMIN
...SOC/WK 20. PAGE 75 B1520   LEGIS

S62
JACOBSON H.K.,"THE UNITED NATIONS AND COLONIALISM: INT/ORG

A TENTATIVE APPRAISAL." AFR FUT S/ASIA USA+45 USSR CONCPT
WOR+45 NAT/G DELIB/GP PLAN DIPLOM ECO/TAC DOMIN   COLONIAL
ADMIN ROUTINE COERCE ATTIT RIGID/FLEX ORD/FREE PWR
...OBS STERTYP UN 20. PAGE 55 B1115

B63
BRAIBANTI R.J.D.,ADMINISTRATION AND ECONOMIC   ECO/UNDEV
DEVELOPMENT IN INDIA. INDIA S/ASIA SOCIETY STRATA   ADMIN
ECO/TAC PERSON WEALTH...MGT GEN/LAWS TOT/POP
VAL/FREE 20. PAGE 15 B0300

B63
KAPP W.K.,HINDU CULTURE: ECONOMIC DEVELOPMENT AND   SECT
ECONOMIC PLANNING IN INDIA. INDIA S/ASIA CULTURE   ECO/UNDEV
ECO/TAC EDU/PROP ADMIN ALL/VALS...POLICY MGT
TIME/SEQ VAL/FREE 20. PAGE 58 B1171

B63
MCKIE R.,MALAYSIA IN FOCUS. INDONESIA WOR+45   S/ASIA
ECO/UNDEV FINAN NAT/G POL/PAR SECT FORCES PLAN   NAT/LISM
ADMIN COLONIAL COERCE DRIVE ALL/VALS...POLICY   MALAYSIA
RECORD CENSUS TIME/SEQ CMN/WLTH 20. PAGE 72 B1453

B63
WEINER M.,POLITICAL CHANGE IN SOUTH ASIA. CEYLON   NAT/G
INDIA PAKISTAN S/ASIA CULTURE ELITES ECO/UNDEV   CONSTN
EX/STRUC ADMIN CONTROL CHOOSE CONSERVE...GOV/COMP   TEC/DEV
ANTHOL 20. PAGE 115 B2315

S63
HARRIS R.L.,"A COMPARATIVE ANALYSIS OF THE   DELIB/GP
ADMINISTRATIVE SYSTEMS OF CANADA AND CEYLON."   EX/STRUC
S/ASIA CULTURE SOCIETY STRATA TOP/EX ACT/RES DOMIN CANADA
EDU/PROP LEGIT COERCE ATTIT SUPEGO ALL/VALS...MGT   CEYLON
CHARTS GEN/LAWS VAL/FREE 20. PAGE 47 B0955

B64
ALDERFER H.O.,LOCAL GOVERNMENT IN DEVELOPING   ADMIN
COUNTRIES. ASIA COM L/A+17C S/ASIA AGRI LOC/G MUNIC ROUTINE
PROVS DOMIN CHOOSE PWR...POLICY MGT CONCPT 20.
PAGE 3 B0070

B64
GOODNOW H.F.,THE CIVIL SERVICE OF PAKISTAN: ADMIN
BUREAUCRACY IN A NEW NATION. INDIA PAKISTAN S/ASIA GOV/REL
ECO/UNDEV PROVS CHIEF PARTIC CHOOSE EFFICIENCY PWR LAW
...BIBLIOG 20. PAGE 41 B0824   NAT/G

B64
HICKEY G.C.,VILLAGE IN VIETNAM. USA+45 VIETNAM LAW CULTURE
AGRI FAM SECT ADMIN ATTIT...SOC CHARTS WORSHIP 20. SOCIETY
PAGE 49 B1003   STRUCT
                                                    S/ASIA
B64
MAHAR J.M.,INDIA: A CRITICAL BIBLIOGRAPHY. INDIA   BIBLIOG/A
PAKISTAN CULTURE ECO/UNDEV LOC/G POL/PAR SECT   S/ASIA
PROB/SOLV DIPLOM ADMIN COLONIAL PARL/PROC ATTIT 20. NAT/G
PAGE 68 B1377   LEAD

B64
SINGER M.R.,THE EMERGING ELITE: A STUDY OF   TOP/EX
POLITICAL LEADERSHIP IN CEYLON. S/ASIA ECO/UNDEV   STRATA
AGRI KIN NAT/G SECT EX/STRUC LEGIT ATTIT PWR   NAT/LISM
RESPECT...SOC STAT CHARTS 20. PAGE 97 B1967   CEYLON

B64
TILMAN R.O.,BUREAUCRATIC TRANSITION IN MALAYA.   ADMIN
MALAYSIA S/ASIA UK NAT/G EX/STRUC DIPLOM...CHARTS   COLONIAL
BIBLIOG 20. PAGE 104 B2110   SOVEREIGN
                                                    EFFICIENCY
L64
SYMONDS R.,"REFLECTIONS IN LOCALISATION." AFR   ADMIN
S/ASIA UK STRATA INT/ORG NAT/G SCHOOL EDU/PROP   MGT
LEGIT KNOWL ORD/FREE PWR RESPECT CMN/WLTH 20.   COLONIAL
PAGE 102 B2064

S64
LOW D.A.,"LION RAMPANT." EUR+WWI MOD/EUR S/ASIA   AFR
ECO/UNDEV NAT/G FORCES TEC/DEV ECO/TAC LEGIT ADMIN DOMIN
COLONIAL COERCE ORD/FREE RESPECT 19/20. PAGE 67   DIPLOM
B1344   UK

S64
MURRAY D.,"CHINESE EDUCATION IN SOUTH-EAST ASIA."   S/ASIA
SOCIETY NEIGH EDU/PROP ROUTINE PERSON KNOWL   SCHOOL
...OBS/ENVIR STERTYP. PAGE 76 B1546   REGION
                                                    ASIA
S64
NASH M.,"SOCIAL PREREQUISITES TO ECONOMIC GROWTH IN ECO/DEV
LATIN AMERICA AND SOUTHEAST ASIA." L/A+17C S/ASIA   PERCEPT
CULTURE SOCIETY ECO/UNDEV AGRI INDUS NAT/G PLAN
TEC/DEV EDU/PROP ROUTINE ALL/VALS...POLICY RELATIV
SOC NAT/COMP WORK TOT/POP 20. PAGE 77 B1558

B65
INST INTL DES CIVILISATION DIF,THE CONSTITUTIONS   CONSTN
AND ADMINISTRATIVE INSTITUTIONS OF THE NEW STATES. ADMIN
AFR ISLAM S/ASIA NAT/G POL/PAR DELIB/GP EX/STRUC   ADJUD
CONFER EFFICIENCY NAT/LISM...JURID SOC 20. PAGE 54 ECO/UNDEV
B1088

B65
NATIONAL BOOK CENTRE PAKISTAN,BOOKS ON PAKISTAN: A BIBLIOG
BIBLIOGRAPHY. PAKISTAN CULTURE DIPLOM ADMIN ATTIT   CONSTN
...MAJORIT SOC CONCPT 20. PAGE 77 B1560   S/ASIA
                                                    NAT/G
B65
WITHERELL J.W.,MADAGASCAR AND ADJACENT ISLANDS; A   BIBLIOG
GUIDE TO OFFICIAL PUBLICATIONS (PAMPHLET). FRANCE   COLONIAL
MADAGASCAR S/ASIA UK LAW OP/RES PLAN DIPLOM   LOC/G

...POLICY CON/ANAL 19/20. PAGE 117 B2368   ADMIN

B66
DEBENKO E.,RESEARCH SOURCES FOR SOUTH ASIAN STUDIES   BIBLIOG
IN ECONOMIC DEVELOPMENT: A SELECT BIBLIOGRAPHY OF   ECO/UNDEV
SERIAL PUBLICATIONS. CEYLON INDIA NEPAL PAKISTAN   S/ASIA
PROB/SOLV ADMIN...POLICY 20. PAGE 28 B0566   PLAN

B66
US DEPARTMENT OF THE ARMY,COMMUNIST CHINA: A   BIBLIOG/A
STRATEGIC SURVEY: A BIBLIOGRAPHY (PAMPHLET NO.   MARXISM
20-67). CHINA/COM COM INDIA USSR NAT/G POL/PAR   S/ASIA
EX/STRUC FORCES NUC/PWR REV ATTIT...POLICY GEOG   DIPLOM
CHARTS. PAGE 108 B2184

C66
TARLING N.,"A CONCISE HISTORY OF SOUTHEAST ASIA."   COLONIAL
BURMA CAMBODIA LAOS S/ASIA THAILAND VIETNAM   DOMIN
ECO/UNDEV POL/PAR FORCES CIVMIL/REL WAR CIVMIL/REL   INT/TRADE
ORD/FREE MARXISM SOCISM 13/20. PAGE 103 B2080   NAT/LISM

B67
PYE L.W.,SOUTHEAST ASIA'S POLITICAL SYSTEMS. ASIA   NAT/G
S/ASIA STRUCT ECO/UNDEV EX/STRUC CAP/ISM DIPLOM   POL/PAR
ALL/IDEOS...TREND CHARTS. PAGE 85 B1724   GOV/COMP

S67
NEUCHTERLEIN D.E.,"THAILAND* ANOTHER VIETNAM?"   WAR
THAILAND ECO/UNDEV DIPLOM ADMIN REGION CENTRAL   GUERRILLA
NAT/LISM...POLICY 20. PAGE 78 B1571   S/ASIA
                                                       NAT/G

S/EASTASIA.....SOUTHEAST ASIA: CAMBODIA, LAOS, NORTH AND
     SOUTH VIETNAM, AND THAILAND

SABAH....SABAH, MALAYSIA

SABBATINO....SABBATINO CASE

SABLE M.H. B1861

SABRAN B. B0567

SAINT AUGUSTINE....SEE AUGUSTINE

SAINT/PIER....JACQUES SAINT-PIERRE

SAINTSIMON....COMTE DE SAINT-SIMON

SALARY....SEE WORKER, WEALTH, ROUTINE

SALARY INFORMATION RETRIEVAL SYSTEM....SEE SIRS

SALAZAR/A....ANTONIO DE OLIVERA SALAZAR

B63
DEBRAY P.,LE PORTUGAL ENTRE DEUX REVOLUTIONS.   NAT/G
EUR+WWI PORTUGAL CONSTN LEGIT ADMIN ATTIT ALL/VALS   DELIB/GP
...DECISION CONCPT 20 SALAZAR/A. PAGE 28 B0567   TOP/EX

SALETAN E.N. B1862

SALIBI K. B0854

SALIENCE....SALIENCE

SALINGER/P....PIERRE SALINGER

SALISBURY R.H. B1863

SALMOND J.A. B1864

SALO....SALO REPUBLIC

SALOMA JS B2309

SALTER J.T. B1865

SAMBURU....SAMBURU TRIBE OF EAST AFRICA

SAMOA....SEE ALSO WEST/SAMOA

B61
WEST F.J.,POLITICAL ADVANCEMENT IN THE SOUTH   S/ASIA
PACIFIC. CONSTN CULTURE POL/PAR LEGIS DOMIN ADMIN   LOC/G
CHOOSE SOVEREIGN VAL/FREE 20 FIJI TAHITI SAMOA.   COLONIAL
PAGE 115 B2325

SAMP....SAMPLE SURVEY

B31
DEKAT A.D.A.,COLONIAL POLICY. S/ASIA CULTURE   DRIVE
EX/STRUC ECO/TAC DOMIN ADMIN COLONIAL ROUTINE   PWR
SOVEREIGN WEALTH...POLICY MGT RECORD KNO/TEST SAMP.   INDONESIA
PAGE 28 B0570   NETHERLAND

B58
COLEMAN J.S.,NIGERIA: BACKGROUND TO NATIONALISM.   NAT/G
AFR SOCIETY ECO/DEV KIN LOC/G POL/PAR TEC/DEV DOMIN   NAT/LISM
ADMIN DRIVE PWR RESPECT...TRADIT SOC INT SAMP   NIGERIA
TIME/SEQ 20. PAGE 22 B0452

S60
REISELBACH L.N.,"THE BASIS OF ISOLATIONIST   ATTIT
BEHAVIOR." USA+45 USA-45 CULTURE ECO/DEV LOC/G   DIPLOM
NAT/G ADMIN ROUTINE CHOOSE BIO/SOC DRIVE RIGID/FLEX   ECO/TAC
...CENSUS SAMP TREND CHARTS TOT/POP 20. PAGE 87
B1765

S61
BROWN M.,"THE DEMISE OF STATE DEPARTMENT PUBLIC   EDU/PROP
OPINION POLLS: A STUDY IN LEGISLATIVE OVERSIGHT."   NAT/G
PWR...POLICY PSY SAMP. PAGE 16 B0325   LEGIS
                                                      ADMIN

B63
WALKER A.A.,OFFICIAL PUBLICATIONS OF SIERRA LEONE   BIBLIOG
AND GAMBIA. GAMBIA SIER/LEONE UK LAW CONSTN LEGIS   NAT/G
PLAN BUDGET DIPLOM...SOC SAMP CON/ANAL 20. PAGE 113   COLONIAL
B2278   ADMIN

S63
HILLS R.J.,"THE REPRESENTATIVE FUNCTION: NEGLECTED   LEAD
DIMENSION OF LEADERSHIP BEHAVIOR" USA+45 CLIENT   ADMIN
STRUCT SCHOOL PERS/REL...STAT QU SAMP LAB/EXP 20.   EXEC
PAGE 50 B1012   ACT/RES

B64
MAYER C.S.,INTERVIEWING COSTS IN SURVEY RESEARCH.   SIMUL
USA+45 PLAN COST...MGT REC/INT SAMP METH/COMP   INT
HYPO/EXP METH 20. PAGE 71 B1434   R+D
                                                      EFFICIENCY

B64
STANLEY D.T.,THE HIGHER CIVIL SERVICE: AN   NAT/G
EVALUATION OF FEDERAL PERSONNEL PRACTICES. USA+45   ADMIN
CREATE EXEC ROUTINE CENTRAL...MGT SAMP IDEA/COMP   CONTROL
METH/COMP 20 CIVIL/SERV. PAGE 100 B2020   EFFICIENCY

B65
GREER S.,URBAN RENEWAL AND AMERICAN CITIES: THE   MUNIC
DILEMMA OF DEMOCRATIC INTERVENTION. USA+45 R+D   PROB/SOLV
LOC/G VOL/ASSN ACT/RES BUDGET ADMIN GOV/REL...SOC   PLAN
INT SAMP 20 BOSTON CHICAGO MIAMI URBAN/RNWL.   NAT/G
PAGE 43 B0871

S65
OSTGAARD E.,"FACTORS INFLUENCING THE FLOW OF NEWS."   EDU/PROP
COM/IND BUDGET DIPLOM EXEC GP/REL COST ATTIT SAMP.   PERCEPT
PAGE 80 B1618   RECORD

B67
EVANS R.H.,COEXISTENCE: COMMUNISM AND ITS PRACTICE   MARXISM
IN BOLOGNA, 1945-1965. ITALY CAP/ISM ADMIN CHOOSE   CULTURE
PEACE ORD/FREE...SOC STAT DEEP/INT SAMP CHARTS   MUNIC
BIBLIOG 20. PAGE 34 B0690   POL/PAR

SAMP/SIZ....SIZES AND TECHNIQUES OF SAMPLING

N19
WRIGHT D.S.,AMERICAN STATE ADMINISTRATORS   QU
(PAMPHLET). USA+45 ATTIT PERSON...SAMP/SIZ CHARTS   TOP/EX
SOC/EXP METH 20. PAGE 118 B2379   ADMIN
                                                      PROVS

B54
COMBS C.H.,DECISION PROCESSES. INTELL SOCIETY   MATH
DELIB/GP CREATE TEC/DEV DOMIN LEGIT EXEC CHOOSE   DECISION
DRIVE RIGID/FLEX KNOWL PWR...PHIL/SCI SOC
METH/CNCPT CONT/OBS REC/INT PERS/TEST SAMP/SIZ BIOG
SOC/EXP WORK. PAGE 22 B0455

B59
SCHURZ W.L.,AMERICAN FOREIGN AFFAIRS: A GUIDE TO   INT/ORG
INTERNATIONAL AFFAIRS. USA+45 WOR+45 WOR-45 NAT/G   SOCIETY
FORCES LEGIS TOP/EX PLAN EDU/PROP LEGIT ADMIN   DIPLOM
ROUTINE ATTIT ORD/FREE PWR...SOC CONCPT STAT
SAMP/SIZ CHARTS STERTYP 20. PAGE 95 B1910

S61
TANNENBAUM A.S.,"CONTROL AND EFFECTIVENESS IN A   EFFICIENCY
VOLUNTARY ORGANIZATION." USA+45 ADMIN...CORREL MATH   VOL/ASSN
REGRESS STAT TESTS SAMP/SIZ CHARTS SOC/EXP INDEX 20   CONTROL
LEAGUE/WV. PAGE 102 B2072   INGP/REL

B67
KATZ J.,PSYCHOANALYSIS, PSYCHIATRY, AND LAW. USA+45   LAW
LOC/G NAT/G PUB/INST PROB/SOLV ADMIN HEALTH   PSY
...CRIMLGY CONCPT SAMP/SIZ IDEA/COMP. PAGE 58 B1180   CT/SYS
                                                      ADJUD

SAMPLE....SEE SAMP

SAMPLE AND SAMPLING....SEE UNIVERSES AND SAMPLING INDEX,
  P. XIV

SAMPSON A. B1866

SAMUEL CLEMENS....SEE TWAIN/MARK

SAMUELSN/P....PAUL SAMUELSON

SAN/FRAN....SAN FRANCISCO

B65
ARTHUR D LITTLE INC,SAN FRANCISCO COMMUNITY RENEWAL   HABITAT
PROGRAM. USA+45 FINAN PROVS ADMIN INCOME...CHARTS   MUNIC
20 CALIFORNIA SAN/FRAN URBAN/RNWL. PAGE 7 B0138   PLAN
                                                      PROB/SOLV

SAN/MARINO....SAN MARINO

SAN/MARTIN....JOSE DE SAN MARTIN

SAN/QUENTN....SAN QUENTIN PRISON

SANCTION....SANCTION OF LAW AND SEMI-LEGAL PRIVATE
    ASSOCIATIONS AND SOCIAL GROUPS

	N19
ADMINISTRATIVE STAFF COLLEGE.THE ACCOUNTABILITY OF	PARL/PROC
GOVERNMENT DEPARTMENTS (PAMPHLET) (REV. ED.). UK	ELITES
CONSTN FINAN NAT/G CONSULT ADMIN INGP/REL CONSEN	SANCTION
PRIVIL 20 PARLIAMENT. PAGE 3 B0059	PROB/SOLV
	B37
GOSNELL H.F.,MACHINE POLITICS: CHICAGO MODEL.	POL/PAR
COM/IND FACE/GP LOC/G EX/STRUC LEAD ROUTINE	MUNIC
SANCTION REPRESENT GOV/REL PWR...POLICY MATH OBS	ADMIN
INT CHARTS. PAGE 41 B0840	CHOOSE
	B52
MILLER M.,THE JUDGES AND THE JUDGED. USA+45 LG/CO	COM/IND
ACT/RES TV ROUTINE SANCTION NAT/LISM ATTIT ORD/FREE	DISCRIM
...POLICY ACLU. PAGE 73 B1481	EDU/PROP
	MARXISM
	B54
LAPIERRE R.T.,A THEORY OF SOCIAL CONTROL. STRUCT	CONTROL
ADMIN ROUTINE SANCTION ANOMIE AUTHORIT DRIVE PERSON	VOL/ASSN
PWR...MAJORIT CONCPT CLASSIF. PAGE 62 B1260	CULTURE
	B56
WIGGINS J.R.,FREEDOM OR SECRECY. USA+45 USA-45	ORD/FREE
DELIB/GP EX/STRUC FORCES ADJUD SANCTION KNOWL PWR	PRESS
...AUD/VIS CONGRESS 20. PAGE 116 B2344	NAT/G
	CONTROL
	L56
EISENTADT S.N.,"POLITICAL STRUGGLE IN BUREAUCRATIC	ADMIN
SOCIETIES" ASIA CULTURE ADJUD SANCTION PWR	CHIEF
BUREAUCRCY OTTOMAN BYZANTINE. PAGE 33 B0661	CONTROL
	ROUTINE
	B61
QURESHI S.,INCENTIVES IN AMERICAN EMPLOYMENT	SERV/IND
(THESIS, UNIVERSITY OF PENNSYLVANIA). DELIB/GP	ADMIN
TOP/EX BUDGET ROUTINE SANCTION COST TECHRACY MGT.	PAY
PAGE 85 B1727	EX/STRUC
	B62
SCHULMAN S.,TOWARD JUDICIAL REFORM IN PENNSYLVANIA;	CT/SYS
A STUDY IN COURT REORGANIZATION. USA+45 CONSTN	ACT/RES
JUDGE PLAN ADMIN LOBBY SANCTION PRIVIL PWR...JURID	PROB/SOLV
20 PENNSYLVAN. PAGE 94 B1905	
	B63
LITTERER J.A.,ORGANIZATIONS: STRUCTURE AND	ADMIN
BEHAVIOR. PLAN DOMIN CONTROL LEAD ROUTINE SANCTION	CREATE
INGP/REL EFFICIENCY PRODUC DRIVE RIGID/FLEX PWR.	MGT
PAGE 66 B1325	ADJUST
	B64
ARGYRIS C.,INTEGRATING THE INDIVIDUAL AND THE	ADMIN
ORGANIZATION. WORKER PROB/SOLV LEAD SANCTION	PERS/REL
REPRESENT ADJUST EFFICIENCY DRIVE PERSON...PSY	VOL/ASSN
METH/CNCPT ORG/CHARTS. PAGE 6 B0132	PARTIC
	B64
BENNETT H.A.,THE COMMISSION AND THE COMMON LAW: A	ADJUD
STUDY IN ADMINISTRATIVE ADJUDICATION. LAW ADMIN	DELIB/GP
CT/SYS LOBBY SANCTION GOV/REL 20 COMMON/LAW.	DIST/IND
PAGE 10 B0212	POLICY
	B64
RUSSELL R.B.,UNITED NATIONS EXPERIENCE WITH	FORCES
MILITARY FORCES: POLITICAL AND LEGAL ASPECTS. AFR	DIPLOM
KOREA WOR+45 LEGIS PROB/SOLV ADMIN CONTROL	SANCTION
EFFICIENCY PEACE...POLICY INT/LAW BIBLIOG UN.	ORD/FREE
PAGE 92 B1857	
	B64
WRAITH R.,CORRUPTION IN DEVELOPING COUNTRIES.	ECO/UNDEV
NIGERIA UK LAW ELITES STRATA INDUS LOC/G NAT/G SECT	CRIME
FORCES EDU/PROP ADMIN PWR WEALTH 18/20. PAGE 118	SANCTION
B2377	ATTIT
	B66
CARALEY D.,PARTY POLITICS AND NATIONAL ELECTIONS.	POL/PAR
USA+45 STRATA LOC/G PROVS EX/STRUC BARGAIN ADMIN	CHOOSE
SANCTION GP/REL ATTIT 20 DEMOCRAT REPUBLICAN.	REPRESENT
PAGE 18 B0375	NAT/G
	B67
DUN J.L.,THE ESSENCE OF CHINESE CIVILIZATION. ASIA	CULTURE
FAM NAT/G TEC/DEV ADMIN SANCTION WAR HABITAT	SOCIETY
...ANTHOL WORSHIP. PAGE 31 B0630	
	B67
SCHAEFER W.V.,THE SUSPECT AND SOCIETY: CRIMINAL	CRIME
PROCEDURE AND CONVERGING CONSTITUTIONAL DOCTRINES.	FORCES
USA+45 TEC/DEV LOBBY ROUTINE SANCTION...INT 20.	CONSTN
PAGE 93 B1879	JURID
	B67
WESTON P.B.,THE ADMINISTRATION OF JUSTICE. USA+45	CRIME
CONSTN MUNIC NAT/G PROVS EX/STRUC JUDGE ADMIN	CT/SYS
CONTROL SANCTION ORD/FREE...CHARTS 20. PAGE 115	JURID
B2328	ADJUD
	L67
BERGER R.,"ADMINISTRATIVE ARBITRARINESS* A SEQUEL."	LAW
USA+45 CONSTN ADJUD CT/SYS SANCTION INGP/REL	LABOR

...POLICY JURID. PAGE 11 B0222	BARGAIN
	ADMIN
	L67
CAHIERS P.,"LE RECOURS EN CONSTATATION DE	INT/ORG
MANQUEMENTS DES ETATS MEMBRES DEVANT LA COUR DES	CONSTN
COMMUNAUTES EUROPEENNES." LAW PROB/SOLV DIPLOM	ROUTINE
ADMIN CT/SYS SANCTION ATTIT...POLICY DECISION JURID	ADJUD
ECSC EEC. PAGE 18 B0362	
	L67
CARMICHAEL D.M.,"FORTY YEARS OF WATER POLLUTION	HEALTH
CONTROL IN WISCONSIN: A CASE STUDY." LAW EXTR/IND	CONTROL
INDUS MUNIC DELIB/GP PLAN PROB/SOLV SANCTION	ADMIN
...CENSUS CHARTS 20 WISCONSIN. PAGE 19 B0382	ADJUD
	L67
JACOBY S.B.,"THE 89TH CONGRESS AND GOVERNMENT	LAW
LITIGATION." USA+45 ADMIN COST...JURID 20 CONGRESS.	NAT/G
PAGE 55 B1117	ADJUD
	SANCTION
	L67
MANNE H.G.,"OUR TWO CORPORATION SYSTEMS* LAW AND	INDUS
ECONOMICS." LAW CONTROL SANCTION GP/REL...JURID 20.	ELITES
PAGE 69 B1392	CAP/ISM
	ADMIN
	S67
BERLINER J.S.,"RUSSIA'S BUREAUCRATS - WHY THEY'RE	CREATE
REACTIONARY." USSR NAT/G OP/RES PROB/SOLV TEC/DEV	ADMIN
CONTROL SANCTION EFFICIENCY DRIVE PERSON...TECHNIC	INDUS
SOC 20. PAGE 11 B0223	PRODUC
	S67
SCOTT W.R.,"ORGANIZATIONAL EVALUATION AND	EXEC
AUTHORITY." CONTROL SANCTION PERS/REL ATTIT DRIVE	WORKER
...SOC CONCPT OBS CHARTS IDEA/COMP 20. PAGE 95	INSPECT
B1921	EX/STRUC
	L86
GOODNOW F.J.,"AN EXECUTIVE AND THE COURTS: JUDICIAL	CT/SYS
REMEDIES AGAINST ADMINISTRATIVE ACTION" FRANCE UK	GOV/REL
USA-45 WOR-45 LAW CONSTN SANCTION ORD/FREE 19.	ADMIN
PAGE 41 B0823	ADJUD

SANDERSON E. B1867

SANTAYAN/G....GEORGE SANTAYANA

	B62
LIPPMANN W.,PREFACE TO POLITICS. LABOR CHIEF	PARTIC
CONTROL LEAD...MYTH IDEA/COMP 19/20 ROOSEVLT/T	ATTIT
TAMMANY WILSON/H SANTAYAN/G BERGSON/H. PAGE 65	ADMIN
B1318	

SAO/PAULO....SAO PAULO, BRAZIL

SAPIN B. B1992

SAPIN B.M. B1868

SAPIR/EDW....EDWARD SAPIR

SARAWAK....SARAWAK, MALAYSIA

SARROS P.P. B1869

SARTRE/J....JEAN-PAUL SARTRE

SARVODAYA....SARVODAYA - GANDHIAN SOCIALIST POLITICAL IDEAL
    OF UNIVERSAL MATERIAL AND SPIRITUAL WELFARE; SEE ALSO
    GANDHI/M

SASKATCH....SASKATCHEWAN, CANADA

SASKATCHEWAN, CANADA...SEE SASKATCH

SATELLITE....SPACE SATELLITES

SATHYAMURTHY T.V. B1870

SATISFACTION....SEE HAPPINESS

SAUDI/ARAB....SAUDI ARABIA; SEE ALSO ISLAM

SAWYER R.A. B1871

SAX/JOSEPH....JOSEPH SAX

SAY/EMIL....EMIL SAY

SAYER W.S. B1872

SAYLES G.O. B1775

SAYLES L.R. B0412,B1873,B1874

SAYRE W.S. B1875

SBA....SMALL BUSINESS ADMINISTRATION

SCALAPINO R.A. B1876

SCALES....SEE TESTS AND SCALES INDEX, P. XIV

SCANDINAV....SCANDINAVIAN COUNTRIES

B65
CONRAD J.P.,CRIME AND ITS CORRECTION: AN
INTERNATIONAL SURVEY OF ATTITUDES AND PRACTICES.
EUR+WWI NETHERLAND USA+45 USSR ATTIT MORAL 20
SCANDINAV. PAGE 23 B0467
CRIME
PUB/INST
POLICY
ADMIN

B66
FINNISH POLITICAL SCIENCE ASSN,SCANDINAVIAN
POLITICAL STUDIES (VOL. I). FINLAND DIPLOM ADMIN
LOBBY PARL/PROC...CHARTS BIBLIOG 20 SCANDINAV.
PAGE 36 B0721
ATTIT
POL/PAR
ACT/RES
CHOOSE

SCANLON/H....HUGH SCANLON

SCARROW H.A. B1877

SCHACHTER O. B1878

SCHAEFER W.V. B1879

SCHAPIRO L. B1880, B1881

SCHATTSCHNEIDER E.E. B1882

SCHATZ S.P. B1883

SCHECHTER A.H. B1884

SCHEINMAN L. B1885

SCHER S. B1886

SCHERMER G. B1887

SCHEURER/K....AUGUSTE SCHEURER-KESTNER

SCHEURER-KESTNER, AUGUSTE....SEE SCHEURER/K

SCHILLING W.R. B1888,B1889,B1890

SCHINDLR/P....PAULINE SCHINDLER

SCHIZO....SCHIZOPHRENIA

SCHLESSINGER P.J. B1891

SCHLOCHAUER H.J. B1892

SCHLOSSBERG S.I. B1893

SCHMECKEBIER L. B1894

SCHMIDT F. B1895

SCHMIDT K.M. B1896

SCHMITT H.A. B1897

SCHMITTER P.C. B0910

SCHNEIDER E.V. B1898

SCHOECK H. B1899

SCHOLASTIC....SCHOLASTICISM (MEDIEVAL)

SCHOOL....SCHOOLS, EXCEPT UNIVERSITIES

N
US SUPERINTENDENT OF DOCUMENTS,EDUCATION (PRICE
LIST 31). USA+45 LAW FINAN LOC/G NAT/G DEBATE ADMIN
LEAD RACE/REL FEDERAL HEALTH POLICY. PAGE 111 B2238
BIBLIOG/A
EDU/PROP
ACADEM
SCHOOL

N19
FIKS M.,PUBLIC ADMINISTRATION IN ISRAEL (PAMPHLET).
ISRAEL SCHOOL EX/STRUC BUDGET PAY INGP/REL
...DECISION 20 CIVIL/SERV. PAGE 35 B0718
EDU/PROP
NAT/G
ADMIN
WORKER

N19
FIRMALINO T.,THE DISTRICT SCHOOL SUPERVISOR VS.
TEACHERS AND PARENTS: A PHILIPPINE CASE STUDY
(PAMPHLET) (BMR). PHILIPPINE LOC/G PLAN EDU/PROP
LOBBY REGION PERS/REL 20. PAGE 36 B0722
RIGID/FLEX
SCHOOL
ADMIN
CREATE

B28
SOROKIN P.,CONTEMPORARY SOCIOLOGICAL THEORIES.
MOD/EUR UNIV SOCIETY R+D SCHOOL ECO/TAC EDU/PROP
ROUTINE ATTIT DRIVE...PSY CONCPT TIME/SEQ TREND
GEN/LAWS 20. PAGE 99 B1997
CULTURE
SOC
WAR

B30
FAIRLIE J.A.,COUNTY GOVERNMENT AND ADMINISTRATION.
UK USA-45 NAT/G SCHOOL FORCES BUDGET TAX CT/SYS
ADMIN
GOV/REL

CHOOSE...JURID BIBLIOG 11/20. PAGE 35 B0701
LOC/G
MUNIC

B37
HODGSON J.G.,THE OFFICIAL PUBLICATIONS OF AMERICAN
COUNTIES: A UNION LIST. SCHOOL BUDGET...HEAL MGT
SOC/WK 19/20. PAGE 51 B1026
BIBLIOG
LOC/G
PUB/INST

B44
BARKER E.,THE DEVELOPMENT OF PUBLIC SERVICES IN
WESTERN WUROPE: 1660-1930. FRANCE GERMANY UK SCHOOL
CONTROL REPRESENT ROLE...WELF/ST 17/20. PAGE 9
B0185
GOV/COMP
ADMIN
EX/STRUC

C45
FISHER M.J.,"PARTIES AND POLITICS IN THE LOCAL
COMMUNITY." USA-45 NAT/G SCHOOL ADMIN PARTIC
REPRESENT KNOWL...BIBLIOG 20. PAGE 36 B0724
CHOOSE
LOC/G
POL/PAR
ROUTINE

C50
MORLAN R.L.,"INTERGOVERNMENTAL RELATIONS IN
EDUCATION." USA+45 FINAN LOC/G MUNIC NAT/G FORCES
PROB/SOLV RECEIVE ADMIN RACE/REL COST...BIBLIOG
INDIAN/AM. PAGE 76 B1526
SCHOOL
GOV/REL
ACADEM
POLICY

C50
STEWART F.M.,"A HALF CENTURY OF MUNICIPAL REFORM."
USA+45 CONSTN FINAN SCHOOL EX/STRUC PLAN PROB/SOLV
EDU/PROP ADMIN CHOOSE GOV/REL BIBLIOG. PAGE 101
B2036
LOC/G
VOL/ASSN
MUNIC
POLICY

C50
WAGER P.W.,"COUNTY GOVERNMENT ACROSS THE NATION."
USA+45 CONSTN COM/IND FINAN SCHOOL DOMIN CT/SYS
LEAD GOV/REL...STAT BIBLIOG 20. PAGE 112 B2272
LOC/G
PROVS
ADMIN
ROUTINE

S51
SCHRAMM W.,"COMMUNICATION IN THE SOVIETIZED STATE,
AS DEMONSTRATED IN KOREA." ASIA COM KOREA COM/IND
FACE/GP POL/PAR SCHOOL FORCES ADMIN PWR MARXISM
...SOC CONCPT MYTH INT BIOG TOT/POP 20. PAGE 94
B1901
ATTIT
EDU/PROP
TOTALISM

B52
DAY E.E.,EDUCATION FOR FREEDOM AND RESPONSIBILITY.
FUT USA+45 CULTURE CONSULT EDU/PROP ATTIT SKILL
...MGT CONCPT OBS GEN/LAWS COLD/WAR 20. PAGE 27
B0547
SCHOOL
KNOWL

C52
LANCASTER L.W.,"GOVERNMENT IN RURAL AMERICA."
USA+45 ECO/DEV AGRI SCHOOL FORCES LEGIS JUDGE
BUDGET TAX CT/SYS...CHARTS BIBLIOG. PAGE 62 B1253
GOV/REL
LOC/G
MUNIC
ADMIN

B54
BINANI G.D.,INDIA AT A GLANCE (REV. ED.). INDIA
COM/IND FINAN INDUS LABOR PROVS SCHOOL PLAN DIPLOM
INT/TRADE ADMIN...JURID 20. PAGE 12 B0238
INDEX
CON/ANAL
NAT/G
ECO/UNDEV

C54
CALDWELL L.K.,"THE GOVERNMENT AND ADMINISTRATION OF
NEW YORK." LOC/G MUNIC POL/PAR SCHOOL CHIEF LEGIS
PLAN TAX CT/SYS...MGT SOC/WK BIBLIOG 20 NEWYORK/C.
PAGE 18 B0366
PROVS
ADMIN
CONSTN
EX/STRUC

B57
DE GRAZIA A.,GRASS ROOTS PRIVATE WELFARE. LOC/G
SCHOOL ACT/RES EDU/PROP ROUTINE CROWD GP/REL
DISCRIM HAPPINESS ILLEGIT AGE HABITAT. PAGE 27
B0554
NEW/LIB
HEALTH
MUNIC
VOL/ASSN

S58
MAIR L.P.,"REPRESENTATIVE LOCAL GOVERNMENT AS A
PROBLEM IN SOCIAL CHANGE." ECO/UNDEV KIN LOC/G
NAT/G SCHOOL JUDGE ADMIN ROUTINE REPRESENT
RIGID/FLEX RESPECT...CONCPT STERTYP CMN/WLTH 20.
PAGE 68 B1383
AFR
PWR
ELITES

B59
CONOVER H.F.,NIGERIAN OFFICIAL PUBLICATIONS,
1869-1959: A GUIDE. NIGER CONSTN FINAN ACADEM
SCHOOL FORCES PRESS ADMIN COLONIAL...HIST/WRIT
19/20. PAGE 23 B0466
BIBLIOG
NAT/G
CON/ANAL

S59
DWYER R.J.,"THE ADMINISTRATIVE ROLE IN
DESEGREGATION." USA+45 LAW PROB/SOLV LEAD RACE/REL
ISOLAT STRANGE ROLE...POLICY SOC/INTEG MISSOURI
NEGRO CIV/RIGHTS. PAGE 31 B0638
ADMIN
SCHOOL
DISCRIM
ATTIT

B60
BRISTOL L.H. JR.,DEVELOPING THE CORPORATE IMAGE.
USA+45 SOCIETY ECO/DEV COM/IND SCHOOL EDU/PROP
PRESS TV...AUD/VIS ANTHOL. PAGE 15 B0312
LG/CO
ATTIT
MGT
ECO/TAC

B62
MARTIN R.C.,GOVERNMENT AND THE SUBURBAN SCHOOL.
USA+45 FINAN EDU/PROP ADMIN HABITAT...TREND GP/COMP
20. PAGE 70 B1414
SCHOOL
LOC/G
EX/STRUC
ISOLAT

B62
MUKERJI S.N.,ADMINISTRATION OF EDUCATION IN INDIA.
ACADEM LOC/G PROVS ROUTINE...POLICY STAT CHARTS 20.
PAGE 76 B1536
SCHOOL
ADMIN
NAT/G
EDU/PROP

B62
NEVINS A.,THE STATE UNIVERSITIES AND DEMOCRACY.
AGRI FINAN SCHOOL ADMIN EXEC EFFICIENCY ATTIT.
ACADEM
PROVS

PAGE 78 B1576

EDU/PROP
POLICY

S62

BUENO M.,"ASPECTOS SOCIOLOGICOS DE LA EDUCACION."
FUT UNIV INTELL R+D SERV/IND SCHOOL CONSULT
EX/STRUC ACT/RES PLAN...METH/CNCPT OBS 20. PAGE 17
B0341

SOCIETY
EDU/PROP
PERSON

B63

DALAND R.T.,PERSPECTIVES OF BRAZILIAN PUBLIC
ADMINISTRATION (VOL. I). BRAZIL LAW ECO/UNDEV
SCHOOL CHIEF TEC/DEV CONFER CONTROL GP/REL ATTIT
ROLE PWR...ANTHOL 20. PAGE 26 B0525

ADMIN
NAT/G
PLAN
GOV/REL

B63

DOUGLASS H.R.,MODERN ADMINISTRATION OF SECONDARY
SCHOOLS. CLIENT DELIB/GP WORKER REPRESENT INGP/REL
AUTHORIT...TREND BIBLIOG. PAGE 30 B0613

EDU/PROP
ADMIN
SCHOOL
MGT

B63

GOURNAY B.,PUBLIC ADMINISTRATION. FRANCE LAW CONSTN
AGRI FINAN LABOR SCHOOL EX/STRUC CHOOSE...MGT
METH/COMP 20. PAGE 42 B0846

BIBLIOG/A
ADMIN
NAT/G
LOC/G

B63

HERMAN H.,NEW YORK STATE AND THE METROPOLITAN
PROBLEM. USA+45 ECO/DEV PUB/INST SCHOOL LEGIS PLAN
TAX EXEC PARL/PROC PARTIC...HEAL 20 NEW/YORK.
PAGE 49 B0992

GOV/REL
PROVS
LOC/G
POLICY

B63

INTL INST ADMIN SCIENCES,EDUCATION IN PUBLIC
ADMINISTRATION: A SYMPOSIUM ON TEACHING METHODS AND
MATERIALS. WOR+45 SCHOOL CONSULT CREATE CONFER
SKILL...OBS TREND IDEA/COMP METH/COMP 20. PAGE 54
B1100

EDU/PROP
METH
ADMIN
ACADEM

B63

PALOTAI O.C.,PUBLICATIONS OF THE INSTITUTE OF
GOVERNMENT, 1930-1962. LAW PROVS SCHOOL WORKER
ACT/RES OP/RES CT/SYS GOV/REL...CRIMLGY SOC/WK.
PAGE 81 B1629

BIBLIOG/A
ADMIN
LOC/G
FINAN

B63

PEABODY R.L.,NEW PERSPECTIVES ON THE HOUSE OF
REPRESENTATIVES. AGRI FINAN SCHOOL FORCES CONFER
LEAD CHOOSE REPRESENT FEDERAL...POLICY DECISION
HOUSE/REP. PAGE 82 B1647

NEW/IDEA
LEGIS
PWR
ADMIN

S63

HILLS R.J.,"THE REPRESENTATIVE FUNCTION: NEGLECTED
DIMENSION OF LEADERSHIP BEHAVIOR" USA+45 CLIENT
STRUCT SCHOOL PERS/REL...STAT QU SAMP LAB/EXP 20.
PAGE 50 B1012

LEAD
ADMIN
EXEC
ACT/RES

N63

INTERNATIONAL CITY MGRS ASSN,POST-ENTRY TRAINING IN
THE LOCAL PUBLIC SERVICE (PAMPHLET). SCHOOL PLAN
PROB/SOLV TEC/DEV ADMIN EFFICIENCY SKILL...POLICY
AUD/VIS CHARTS BIBLIOG 20 CITY/MGT. PAGE 54 B1096

LOC/G
WORKER
EDU/PROP
METH/COMP

B64

THE SPECIAL COMMONWEALTH AFRICAN ASSISTANCE PLAN.
AFR CANADA INDIA NIGERIA UK FINAN SCHOOL...CHARTS
20 COMMONWLTH. PAGE 2 B0041

ECO/UNDEV
TREND
FOR/AID
ADMIN

B64

GUTTSMAN W.L.,THE BRITISH POLITICAL ELITE. EUR+WWI
MOD/EUR STRATA FAM LABOR POL/PAR SCHOOL VOL/ASSN
DELIB/GP LEGIS LEGIT EXEC CHOOSE ATTIT ALL/VALS
...STAT BIOG TIME/SEQ CHARTS VAL/FREE. PAGE 45
B0905

NAT/G
SOC
UK
ELITES

B64

KIMBROUGH R.B.,POLITICAL POWER AND EDUCATIONAL
DECISION-MAKING. USA+45 FINAN ADMIN LEAD GP/REL
ATTIT PWR PROG/TEAC. PAGE 60 B1207

EDU/PROP
PROB/SOLV
DECISION
SCHOOL

B64

PEABODY R.L.,ORGANIZATIONAL AUTHORITY. SCHOOL
WORKER PLAN SENIOR GOV/REL UTIL DRIVE PWR...PSY
CHARTS BIBLIOG 20. PAGE 82 B1648

ADMIN
EFFICIENCY
TASK
GP/REL

B64

PIERCE T.M.,FEDERAL, STATE, AND LOCAL GOVERNMENT IN
EDUCATION. FINAN LOC/G PROVS LEGIS PLAN EDU/PROP
ADMIN CONTROL CENTRAL COST KNOWL 20. PAGE 83 B1673

NAT/G
POLICY
SCHOOL
GOV/REL

B64

SULLIVAN G.,THE STORY OF THE PEACE CORPS. USA+45
WOR+45 INTELL FACE/GP NAT/G SCHOOL VOL/ASSN CONSULT
EX/STRUC PLAN EDU/PROP ADMIN ATTIT DRIVE ALL/VALS
...POLICY HEAL SOC CONCPT INT QU BIOG TREND SOC/EXP
WORK. PAGE 102 B2054

INT/ORG
ECO/UNDEV
FOR/AID
PEACE

B64

THE BRITISH COUNCIL,PUBLIC ADMINISTRATION: A SELECT
LIST OF BOOKS AND PERIODICALS. LAW CONSTN FINAN
POL/PAR SCHOOL CHOOSE...HEAL MGT METH/COMP 19/20
CMN/WLTH. PAGE 104 B2094

BIBLIOG
ADMIN
LOC/G
INDUS

B64

TURNER H.A.,THE GOVERNMENT AND POLITICS OF
CALIFORNIA (2ND ED.). LAW FINAN MUNIC POL/PAR
SCHOOL EX/STRUC LEGIS LOBBY CHOOSE...CHARTS T 20
CALIFORNIA. PAGE 106 B2138

PROVS
ADMIN
LOC/G
CONSTN

L64

SYMONDS R.,"REFLECTIONS IN LOCALISATION." AFR
S/ASIA UK STRATA INT/ORG NAT/G SCHOOL EDU/PROP
LEGIT KNOWL ORD/FREE PWR RESPECT CMN/WLTH 20.
PAGE 102 B2064

ADMIN
MGT
COLONIAL

S64

EAKIN T.C.,"LEGISLATIVE POLITICS -- I AND II THE
WESTERN STATES, 19581964" (SUPPLEMENT)" USA+45
POL/PAR SCHOOL CONTROL LOBBY CHOOSE AGE. PAGE 32
B0641

PROVS
LEGIS
ROUTINE
STRUCT

S64

KASSOF A.,"THE ADMINISTERED SOCIETY:
TOTALITARIANISM WITHOUT TERROR." COM USSR STRATA
AGRI INDUS NAT/G PERF/ART SCHOOL TOP/EX EDU/PROP
ADMIN ORD/FREE PWR...POLICY SOC TIME/SEQ GEN/LAWS
VAL/FREE 20. PAGE 58 B1178

SOCIETY
DOMIN
TOTALISM

S64

MURRAY D.,"CHINESE EDUCATION IN SOUTH-EAST ASIA."
SOCIETY NEIGH EDU/PROP ROUTINE PERSON KNOWL
...OBS/ENVIR STERTYP. PAGE 76 B1546

S/ASIA
SCHOOL
REGION
ASIA

B65

CRAMER J.F.,CONTEMPORARY EDUCATION: A COMPARATIVE
STUDY OF NATIONAL SYSTEMS (2ND ED.). CHINA/COM
EUR+WWI INDIA USA+45 FINAN PROB/SOLV ADMIN CONTROL
ATTIT...IDEA/COMP METH/COMP 20 CHINJAP. PAGE 25
B0502

EDU/PROP
NAT/COMP
SCHOOL
ACADEM

B65

CUTLIP S.M.,A PUBLIC RELATIONS BIBLIOGRAPHY. INDUS
LABOR NAT/G PROF/ORG SCHOOL DIPLOM PRESS TV GOV/REL
GP/REL...PSY SOC/WK 20. PAGE 25 B0515

BIBLIOG/A
MGT
COM/IND
ADMIN

B65

HUGHES J.M.,EDUCATION IN AMERICA (2ND ED.). USA+45
USA-45 GP/REL INGP/REL AGE/C AGE/Y ROLE...IDEA/COMP
BIBLIOG T 20. PAGE 52 B1059

EDU/PROP
SCHOOL
ADMIN
METH/COMP

B65

OECD,MEDITERRANEAN REGIONAL PROJECT: TURKEY;
EDUCATION AND DEVELOPMENT. FUT TURKEY SOCIETY
STRATA FINAN NAT/G PROF/ORG PLAN PROB/SOLV ADMIN
COST...STAT CHARTS 20 OECD. PAGE 79 B1602

EDU/PROP
ACADEM
SCHOOL
ECO/UNDEV

B65

ORG FOR ECO COOP AND DEVEL,THE MEDITERRANEAN
REGIONAL PROJECT: AN EXPERIMENT IN PLANNING BY SIX
COUNTRIES. FUT GREECE SPAIN TURKEY YUGOSLAVIA
SOCIETY FINAN NAT/G PROF/ORG EDU/PROP ADMIN REGION
COST...POLICY STAT CHARTS 20 OECD. PAGE 80 B1614

PLAN
ECO/UNDEV
ACADEM
SCHOOL

B65

ORG FOR ECO COOP AND DEVEL,THE MEDITERRANEAN
REGIONAL PROJECT: YUGOSLAVIA; EDUCATION AND
DEVELOPMENT. YUGOSLAVIA SOCIETY FINAN PROF/ORG PLAN
ADMIN COST DEMAND MARXISM...STAT TREND CHARTS METH
20 OECD. PAGE 80 B1615

EDU/PROP
ACADEM
SCHOOL
ECO/UNDEV

B65

REISS A.J. JR.,SCHOOLS IN A CHANGING SOCIETY.
CULTURE PROB/SOLV INSPECT DOMIN CONFER INGP/REL
RACE/REL AGE/C AGE/Y ALL/VALS...ANTHOL SOC/INTEG 20
NEWYORK/C. PAGE 87 B1766

SCHOOL
EX/STRUC
ADJUST
ADMIN

S65

"FURTHER READING." INDIA NAT/G ADMIN 20. PAGE 2
B0043

BIBLIOG
EDU/PROP
SCHOOL
ACADEM

B67

GITTELL M.,PARTICIPANTS AND PARTICIPATION: A STUDY
OF SCHOOL POLICY IN NEW YORK. USA+45 MUNIC EX/STRUC
BUDGET PAY ATTIT...POLICY 20 NEWYORK/C. PAGE 40
B0806

SCHOOL
DECISION
PARTIC
ADMIN

B67

EDUCATION, INTERACTION, AND SOCIAL CHANGE. STRATA
MUNIC SCHOOL ADMIN RIGID/FLEX ROLE 20. PAGE 49
B0991

EDU/PROP
ADJUST
SOC
ACT/RES

B67

PAULSEN F.R.,AMERICAN EDUCATION: CHALLENGES AND
IMAGES. FUT USA+45 ADMIN AGE/C AGE/Y SUPEGO HEALTH
...ANTHOL 20. PAGE 81 B1644

EDU/PROP
SCHOOL
ORD/FREE
GOV/REL

B67

US DEPARTMENT HEALTH EDUC WELF,NEW PROGRAMS IN
HEALTH, EDUCATION, WELFARE, HOUSING AND URBAN
DEVELOPMENT FOR PERSONS AND FAMILIES -LOW, MOD'
INCOME. USA+45 MUNIC NAT/G EDU/PROP GOV/REL
INGP/REL ORD/FREE 20 DEPT/HEW DEPT/HUD. PAGE 108
B2180

ADMIN
HEALTH
SCHOOL
HABITAT

B67

WEINBERG M.,SCHOOL INTEGRATION: A COMPREHENSIVE
CLASSIFIED BIBLIOGRAPHY OF 3,100 REFERENCES. USA+45
LAW NAT/G NEIGH SECT PLAN ROUTINE AGE/C WEALTH
SOC/INTEG INDIAN/AM. PAGE 115 B2314

BIBLIOG
SCHOOL
DISCRIM
RACE/REL

S67

ATKIN J.M.,"THE FEDERAL GOVERNMENT, BIG BUSINESS,
AND COLLEGES OF EDUCATION." PROF/ORG CONSULT CREATE
PLAN PROB/SOLV ADMIN EFFICIENCY. PAGE 7 B0144

SCHOOL
ACADEM
NAT/G
INDUS

DODSON D.W.,"NEW FORCES OPERATING IN EDUCATIONAL DECISION-MAKING." USA+45 NEIGH EDU/PROP ADMIN SUPEGO DECISION. PAGE 30 B0602
S67
PROB/SOLV
SCHOOL
PERS/REL
PWR

HUDDLESTON J.,"TRADE UNIONS IN THE GERMAN FEDERAL REPUBLIC." EUR+WWI GERMANY/W UK LAW INDUS WORKER CREATE CENTRAL...MGT GP/COMP 20. PAGE 52 B1056
S67
LABOR
GP/REL
SCHOOL
ROLE

SCHRADER R. B1900

SCHRAMM W. B1901,B1902

SCHUBERT G. B1903

SCHUBERT G.A. B1904

SCHULMAN S. B1905

SCHULTZ W.J. B1906

SCHUMACHER B.G. B1907

SCHUMCHR/K....KURT SCHUMACHER

SCHUMPTR/J....JOSEPH SCHUMPETER

SCHURMANN F. B1908,B1909

SCHURZ W.L. B1910

SCHWARTZ B. B1911,B1912,B1913,B1914

SCHWARZ S.M. B0236

SCHWEBEL S.M. B1915

SCHWELB E. B1916

SCHWERIN K. B1917

SCHWINN....ARNOLD, SCHWINN + COMPANY

SCI/ADVSRY....SCIENCE ADVISORY COMMISSION

SCIENCE....SEE PHIL/SCI, CREATE

SCIENCE ADVISORY COMMISSION....SEE SCI/ADVSRY

SCIENTIFIC METHOD....SEE PHIL/SCI

SCOT/YARD....SCOTLAND YARD - LONDON POLICE HEADQUARTERS AND DETECTIVE BUREAU

HOWE R.,THE STORY OF SCOTLAND YARD: A HISTORY OF THE CID FROM THE EARLIEST TIMES TO THE PRESENT DAY. UK MUNIC EDU/PROP 6/20 SCOT/YARD. PAGE 52 B1051
B65
CRIMLGY
CRIME
FORCES
ADMIN

SCOTLAND....SCOTLAND

MOEN N.W.,THE GOVERNMENT OF SCOTLAND 1603 - 1625. UK JUDGE ADMIN GP/REL PWR 17 SCOTLAND COMMON/LAW. PAGE 74 B1496
B58
CHIEF
JURID
CONTROL
PARL/PROC

SCOTT A.M. B1918

SCOTT D.J.R. B1919

SCOTT R.E. B1920

SCOTT W.R. B0253,B1921

SCREENING AND SELECTION....SEE CHOOSE, SAMP

SDR....SPECIAL DRAWING RIGHTS

SDS....STUDENTS FOR A DEMOCRATIC SOCIETY

SEA....LOCALE OF SUBJECT ACTIVITY IS AQUATIC

HOLDSWORTH W.S.,A HISTORY OF ENGLISH LAW: THE COMMON LAW AND ITS RIVALS (VOL. V). UK SEA EX/STRUC WRITING ADMIN...INT/LAW JURID CONCPT IDEA/COMP WORSHIP 16/17 PARLIAMENT ENGLSH/LAW COMMON/LAW. PAGE 51 B1033
B24
LAW
LEGIS
ADJUD
CT/SYS

KOENIG L.W.,THE SALE OF THE TANKERS. USA+45 SEA DIST/IND POL/PAR DIPLOM ADMIN CIVMIL/REL ATTIT ...DECISION 20 PRESIDENT DEPT/STATE. PAGE 60 B1223
B50
NAT/G
POLICY
PLAN

LOCKLIN D.P.,ECONOMICS OF TRANSPORTATION (4TH ED.). USA+45 USA-45 SEA AIR LAW FINAN LG/CO EX/STRUC ADMIN CONTROL...STAT CHARTS 19/20 RAILROAD PUB/TRANS. PAGE 66 B1335
GOV/REL
B54
ECO/DEV
DIST/IND
ECO/TAC
TEC/DEV

ATOMIC INDUSTRIAL FORUM,MANAGEMENT AND ATOMIC ENERGY. WOR+45 SEA LAW MARKET NAT/G TEC/DEV INSPECT INT/TRADE CONFER PEACE HEALTH...ANTHOL 20. PAGE 7 B0145
B58
NUC/PWR
INDUS
MGT
ECO/TAC

KINGSTON-MCCLOUG E.,DEFENSE: POLICY AND STRATEGY. UK SEA AIR TEC/DEV DIPLOM ADMIN LEAD WAR ORD/FREE ...CHARTS 20. PAGE 60 B1209
B60
FORCES
PLAN
POLICY
DECISION

DEAN A.W.,"SECOND GENEVA CONFERENCE OF THE LAW OF THE SEA: THE FIGHT FOR FREEDOM OF THE SEAS." FUT USA+45 USSR WOR+45 WOR-45 SEA CONSTN STRUCT PLAN INT/TRADE ADJUD ADMIN ORD/FREE...DECISION RECORD TREND GEN/LAWS 20 TREATY. PAGE 28 B0564
L60
INT/ORG
JURID
INT/LAW

RAWLINSON J.L.,CHINA'S STRUGGLE FOR NAVAL DEVELOPMENT 1839-1895. ASIA DIPLOM ADMIN WAR ...BIBLIOG DICTIONARY 19 CHINJAP. PAGE 86 B1745
B67
SEA
FORCES
PWR

SEARCH FOR EDUCATION, ELEVATION, AND KNOWLEDGE....SEE SEEK

SEASHOLES B. B1922

SEATO....SOUTH EAST ASIA TREATY ORGANIZATION; SEE ALSO INT/ORG, VOL/ASSN, FORCES, DETER

MODELSKI G.,"AUSTRALIA AND SEATO." S/ASIA USA+45 CULTURE INTELL ECO/DEV NAT/G PLAN DIPLOM ADMIN ROUTINE ATTIT SKILL...MGT TIME/SEQ AUSTRAL 20 SEATO. PAGE 74 B1493
S60
INT/ORG
ACT/RES

SEATTLE....SEATTLE, WASHINGTON

SEC/EXCHNG....SECURITY EXCHANGE COMMISSION

SEC/REFORM....SECOND REFORM ACT OF 1867 (U.K.)

SEC/STATE....U.S. SECRETARY OF STATE

SECKLER-HUDSON C. B1923

SECOND REFORM ACT OF 1867 (U.K.)....SEE SEC/REFORM

SECRETARY OF STATE (U.S.)....SEE SEC/STATE

SECT....CHURCH, SECT, RELIGIOUS GROUP

STOLPER W.,"SOCIAL FACTORS IN ECONOMIC PLANNING, WITH SPECIAL REFERENCE TO NIGERIA" AFR NIGER CULTURE FAM SECT RECEIVE ETIQUET ADMIN DEMAND 20. PAGE 101 B2045
NCO
ECO/UNDEV
PLAN
ADJUST
RISK

MOREL E.D.,AFFAIRS OF WEST AFRICA. UK FINAN INDUS FAM KIN SECT CHIEF WORKER DIPLOM RACE/REL LITERACY HEALTH...CHARTS 18/20 AFRICA/W NEGRO. PAGE 75 B1521
B02
COLONIAL
ADMIN
AFR

FYFE H.,THE BRITISH LIBERAL PARTY. UK SECT ADMIN LEAD CHOOSE GP/REL PWR SOCISM...MAJORIT TIME/SEQ 19/20 LIB/PARTY CONSRV/PAR. PAGE 38 B0768
B28
POL/PAR
NAT/G
REPRESENT
POPULISM

BOUDET P.,BIBLIOGRAPHIE DE L'INDOCHINE FRANCAISE. S/ASIA VIETNAM SECT...GEOG LING 20. PAGE 14 B0282
B29
BIBLIOG
ADMIN
COLONIAL
DIPLOM

BORCHARD E.H.,GUIDE TO THE LAW AND LEGAL LITERATURE OF FRANCE. FRANCE FINAN INDUS LABOR SECT LEGIS ADMIN COLONIAL CRIME OWN...INT/LAW 20. PAGE 14 B0277
B31
BIBLIOG/A
LAW
CONSTN
METH

DE CENIVAL P.,BIBLIOGRAPHIE MAROCAINE: 1923-1933. FRANCE MOROCCO SECT ADMIN LEAD GP/REL ATTIT...LING 20. PAGE 27 B0551
B34
BIBLIOG/A
ISLAM
NAT/G
COLONIAL

GORER G.,AFRICA DANCES: A BOOK ABOUT WEST AFRICAN NEGROES. STRUCT LOC/G SECT FORCES TAX ADMIN COLONIAL...ART/METH MYTH WORSHIP 20 NEGRO AFRICA/W CHRISTIAN RITUAL. PAGE 41 B0835
B35
AFR
ATTIT
CULTURE
SOCIETY

HAILEY,"THE FUTURE OF COLONIAL PEOPLES." WOR-45 CONSTN CULTURE ECO/UNDEV AGRI MARKET INT/ORG NAT/G SECT CONSULT ECO/TAC LEGIT ADMIN NAT/LISM ALL/VALS ...SOC OBS TREND STERTYP CMN/WLTH LEAGUE/NAT PARLIAMENT 20. PAGE 45 B0916
L44
PLAN
CONCPT
DIPLOM
UK

B50
FIGANIERE J.C.,BIBLIOTHECA HISTORICA PORTUGUEZA.   BIBLIOG
BRAZIL PORTUGAL SECT ADMIN. PAGE 35 B0717   NAT/G
                                                       DIPLOM
                                                       COLONIAL

B50
WELCH S.R.,PORTUGUESE RULE AND SPANISH CROWN IN   DIPLOM
SOUTH AFRICA 1581-1640. PORTUGAL SOUTH/AFR SPAIN   COLONIAL
SOCIETY KIN NEIGH SECT INT/TRADE ADMIN 16/17   WAR
MISSION. PAGE 115 B2317   PEACE

B51
GUETZKOW H.,GROUPS, LEADERSHIP, AND MEN. FACE/GP   ATTIT
SECT EDU/PROP EXEC PERSON RESPECT...PERS/TEST   SOC
GEN/METH 20. PAGE 44 B0901   ELITES

B52
HIMMELFARB G.,LORD ACTON: A STUDY IN CONSCIENCE AND   PWR
POLITICS. MOD/EUR NAT/G POL/PAR SECT LEGIS TOP/EX   BIOG
EDU/PROP ADMIN NAT/LISM ATTIT PERSON SUPEGO MORAL
ORD/FREE...CONCPT PARLIAMENT 19 ACTON/LORD. PAGE 50
B1014

B53
MEYER P.,THE JEWS IN THE SOVIET SATELLITES.   COM
CZECHOSLVK POLAND SOCIETY STRATA NAT/G BAL/PWR   SECT
ECO/TAC EDU/PROP LEGIT ADMIN COERCE ATTIT DISPL   TOTALISM
PERCEPT HEALTH PWR RESPECT...METH/CNCPT JEWS   USSR
VAL/FREE NAZI 20. PAGE 73 B1474

C53
BULNER-THOMAS I.,"THE PARTY SYSTEM IN GREAT   NAT/G
BRITAIN." UK CONSTN SECT PRESS CONFER GP/REL ATTIT   POL/PAR
...POLICY TREND BIBLIOG 19/20 PARLIAMENT. PAGE 17   ADMIN
B0343   ROUTINE

B54
ALLPORT G.W.,THE NATURE OF PREJUDICE. USA+45 WOR+45   CULTURE
STRATA FACE/GP KIN NEIGH SECT ADMIN GP/REL DISCRIM   PERSON
ATTIT DRIVE LOVE RESPECT...PSY SOC MYTH QU/SEMANT   RACE/REL
20. PAGE 4 B0078

B54
BIESANZ J.,MODERN SOCIETY: AN INTRODUCTION TO   SOCIETY
SOCIAL SCIENCE. COM CONSTN STRUCT FAM MUNIC NAT/G   PROB/SOLV
SECT EX/STRUC LEGIS GP/REL PERSON...SOC 20. PAGE 12   CULTURE
B0237

C54
LANDAU J.M.,"PARLIAMENTS AND PARTIES IN EGYPT." UAR   ISLAM
NAT/G SECT CONSULT LEGIS TOP/EX PROB/SOLV ADMIN   NAT/LISM
COLONIAL...GEN/LAWS BIBLIOG 19/20. PAGE 62 B1254   PARL/PROC
                                                       POL/PAR

B55
MAZZINI J.,THE DUTIES OF MAN. MOD/EUR LAW SOCIETY   SUPEGO
FAM NAT/G POL/PAR SECT VOL/ASSN EX/STRUC ACT/RES   CONCPT
CREATE REV PEACE ATTIT ALL/VALS...GEN/LAWS WORK 19.   NAT/LISM
PAGE 71 B1439

B55
ZABEL O.H.,GOD AND CAESAR IN NEBRASKA: A STUDY OF   SECT
LEGAL RELATIONSHIP OF CHURCH AND STATE, 1854-1954.   PROVS
TAX GIVE ADMIN CONTROL GP/REL ROLE...GP/COMP 19/20   LAW
NEBRASKA. PAGE 119 B2396   EDU/PROP

B56
MANNONI D.O.,PROSPERO AND CALIBAN: THE PSYCHOLOGY   CULTURE
OF COLONIZATION. AFR EUR+WWI FAM KIN MUNIC SECT   COLONIAL
DOMIN ADMIN ATTIT DRIVE LOVE PWR RESPECT...PSY SOC
CONCPT MYTH OBS DEEP/INT BIOG GEN/METH MALAGASY 20.
PAGE 69 B1394

B57
SOUTH PACIFIC COMMISSION,INDEX OF SOCIAL SCIENCE   BIBLIOG/A
RESEARCH THESES ON THE SOUTH PACIFIC. S/ASIA ACADEM   ACT/RES
ADMIN COLONIAL...SOC 20. PAGE 99 B2000   SECT
                                                       CULTURE

B59
BHAMBHRI C.P.,SUBSTANCE OF HINDU POLITY. INDIA   GOV/REL
S/ASIA LAW EX/STRUC JUDGE TAX COERCE GP/REL   WRITING
POPULISM 20 HINDU. PAGE 11 B0234   SECT
                                                       PROVS

B60
LIPSET S.M.,POLITICAL MAN. AFR COM EUR+WWI L/A+17C   PWR
MOD/EUR S/ASIA USA+45 USA-45 STRUCT ECO/DEV   SOC
ECO/UNDEV POL/PAR SECT ADMIN WEALTH...CONCPT WORK
TOT/POP 20. PAGE 65 B1320

C60
FITZSIMMONS T.,"USSR: ITS PEOPLE, ITS SOCIETY, ITS   CULTURE
CULTURE." USSR FAM SECT DIPLOM EDU/PROP ADMIN   STRUCT
RACE/REL ATTIT...POLICY CHARTS BIBLIOG 20. PAGE 36   SOCIETY
B0728   COM

B61
KOESTLER A.,THE LOTUS AND THE ROBOT. ASIA INDIA   SECT
S/ASIA SOCIETY STRATA ECO/DEV AGRI INDUS FAM CREATE   ECO/UNDEV
DOMIN EDU/PROP ADMIN COERCE ATTIT DRIVE SUPEGO
ORD/FREE PWR RESPECT WEALTH...MYTH OBS 20 CHINJAP.
PAGE 61 B1226

S61
TOMASIC D.,"POLITICAL LEADERSHIP IN CONTEMPORARY   SOCIETY
POLAND." COM EUR+WWI GERMANY NAT/G POL/PAR SECT   ROUTINE
DELIB/GP PLAN ECO/TAC DOMIN EDU/PROP PWR MARXISM   USSR
...MARXIST GEOG MGT CONCPT TIME/SEQ STERTYP 20.   POLAND
PAGE 105 B2114

B62
HARARI M.,GOVERNMENT AND POLITICS OF THE MIDDLE   DIPLOM

EAST. ISLAM USA+45 NAT/G SECT CHIEF ADMIN ORD/FREE   ECO/UNDEV
20. PAGE 47 B0943   TEC/DEV
                                                       POLICY

B62
THIERRY S.S.,LE VATICAN SECRET. CHRIST-17C EUR+WWI   ADMIN
MOD/EUR VATICAN NAT/G SECT DELIB/GP DOMIN LEGIT   EX/STRUC
SOVEREIGN. PAGE 104 B2096   CATHISM
                                                       DECISION

B62
US LIBRARY OF CONGRESS,A LIST OF AMERICAN DOCTORAL   BIBLIOG
DISSERTATIONS ON AFRICA. SOCIETY SECT DIPLOM   AFR
EDU/PROP ADMIN...GEOG 19/20. PAGE 109 B2206   ACADEM
                                                       CULTURE

B63
CHOJNACKI S.,REGISTER ON CURRENT RESEARCH ON   BIBLIOG
ETHIOPIA AND THE HORN OF AFRICA. ETHIOPIA LAW   ACT/RES
CULTURE AGRI SECT EDU/PROP ADMIN...GEOG HEAL LING   INTELL
20. PAGE 21 B0426   ACADEM

B63
DIESNER H.J.,KIRCHE UND STAAT IM SPATROMISCHEN   SECT
REICH. ROMAN/EMP EX/STRUC COLONIAL COERCE ATTIT   GP/REL
CATHISM 4/5 AFRICA/N CHURCH/STA. PAGE 29 B0592   DOMIN
                                                       JURID

B63
ELIAS T.O.,THE NIGERIAN LEGAL SYSTEM. NIGERIA LAW   CT/SYS
FAM KIN SECT ADMIN NAT/LISM...JURID 18/20   ADJUD
ENGLSH/LAW COMMON/LAW. PAGE 33 B0665   COLONIAL
                                                       PROF/ORG

B63
FORTES A.B.,HISTORIA ADMINISTRATIVA, JUDICIARIA E   PROVS
ECLESIASTICA DO RIO GRANDE DO SUL. BRAZIL L/A+17C   ADMIN
LOC/G SECT COLONIAL CT/SYS ORD/FREE CATHISM 16/20.   JURID
PAGE 37 B0742

B63
GALBRAITH J.S.,RELUCTANT EMPIRE: BRITISH POLICY OF   COLONIAL
THE SOUTH AFRICAN FRONTIER, 1834-1854. AFR   ADMIN
SOUTH/AFR UK GP/REL RACE/REL DISCRIM...CHARTS   POLICY
BIBLIOG 19 MISSION. PAGE 38 B0774   SECT

B63
HEUSSLER R.,YESTERDAY'S RULERS: THE MAKING OF THE   EX/STRUC
BRITISH COLONIAL SERVICE. AFR EUR+WWI UK STRATA   MORAL
SECT DELIB/GP PLAN DOMIN EDU/PROP ATTIT PERCEPT   ELITES
PERSON SUPEGO KNOWL ORD/FREE PWR...MGT SOC OBS INT
TIME/SEQ 20 CMN/WLTH. PAGE 49 B1000

B63
KAPP W.K.,HINDU CULTURE: ECONOMIC DEVELOPMENT AND   SECT
ECONOMIC PLANNING IN INDIA. INDIA S/ASIA CULTURE   ECO/UNDEV
ECO/TAC EDU/PROP ADMIN ALL/VALS...POLICY MGT
TIME/SEQ VAL/FREE 20. PAGE 58 B1171

B63
MCKIE R.,MALAYSIA IN FOCUS. INDONESIA WOR+45   S/ASIA
ECO/UNDEV FINAN NAT/G POL/PAR SECT FORCES PLAN   NAT/LISM
ADMIN COLONIAL COERCE DRIVE ALL/VALS...POLICY   MALAYSIA
RECORD CENSUS TIME/SEQ CMN/WLTH 20. PAGE 72 B1453

B63
MONTER W.,THE GOVERNMENT OF GENEVA, 1536-1605   SECT
(DOCTORAL THESIS). SWITZERLND DIPLOM LEAD ORD/FREE   FINAN
SOVEREIGN 16/17 CALVIN/J ROME. PAGE 74 B1504   LOC/G
                                                       ADMIN

B63
RUITENBEER H.M.,THE DILEMMA OF ORGANIZATIONAL   PERSON
SOCIETY. CULTURE ECO/DEV MUNIC SECT TEC/DEV   ROLE
EDU/PROP NAT/LISM ORD/FREE...NAT/COMP 20 RIESMAN/D   ADMIN
WHYTE/WF MERTON/R MEAD/MARG JASPERS/K. PAGE 92   WORKER
B1855

B64
FORBES A.H.,CURRENT RESEARCH IN BRITISH STUDIES. UK   BIBLIOG
CONSTN CULTURE POL/PAR SECT DIPLOM ADMIN...JURID   PERSON
BIOG WORSHIP 20. PAGE 36 B0736   NAT/G
                                                       PARL/PROC

B64
GESELLSCHAFT RECHTSVERGLEICH,BIBLIOGRAPHIE DES   BIBLIOG/A
DEUTSCHEN RECHTS (BIBLIOGRAPHY OF GERMAN LAW,   JURID
TRANS. BY COURTLAND PETERSON). GERMANY FINAN INDUS   CONSTN
LABOR SECT FORCES CT/SYS PARL/PROC CRIME...INT/LAW   ADMIN
SOC NAT/COMP 20. PAGE 39 B0794

B64
HICKEY G.C.,VILLAGE IN VIETNAM. USA+45 VIETNAM LAW   CULTURE
AGRI FAM SECT ADMIN ATTIT...SOC CHARTS WORSHIP 20.   SOCIETY
PAGE 49 B1003   STRUCT
                                                       S/ASIA

B64
MAHAR J.M.,INDIA: A CRITICAL BIBLIOGRAPHY. INDIA   BIBLIOG/A
PAKISTAN CULTURE ECO/UNDEV LOC/G POL/PAR SECT   S/ASIA
PROB/SOLV DIPLOM ADMIN COLONIAL PARL/PROC ATTIT 20.   NAT/G
PAGE 68 B1377   LEAD

B64
NATIONAL BOOK LEAGUE,THE COMMONWEALTH IN BOOKS: AN   BIBLIOG/A
ANNOTATED LIST. CANADA UK LOC/G SECT ADMIN...SOC   JURID
BIOG 20 CMN/WLTH. PAGE 77 B1561   NAT/G

B64
SINGER M.R.,THE EMERGING ELITE: A STUDY OF   TOP/EX
POLITICAL LEADERSHIP IN CEYLON. S/ASIA ECO/UNDEV   STRATA
AGRI KIN NAT/G SECT EX/STRUC LEGIT ATTIT PWR   NAT/LISM
RESPECT...SOC STAT CHARTS 20. PAGE 97 B1967   CEYLON

B64
WRAITH R.,CORRUPTION IN DEVELOPING COUNTRIES.   ECO/UNDEV
NIGERIA UK LAW ELITES STRATA INDUS LOC/G NAT/G SECT   CRIME
FORCES EDU/PROP ADMIN PWR WEALTH 18/20. PAGE 118   SANCTION
B2377   ATTIT

S64
CLIGNET R.,"POTENTIAL ELITES IN GHANA AND THE IVORY   PWR
COAST: A PRELIMINARY SURVEY." AFR CULTURE ELITES   LEGIT
STRATA KIN NAT/G SECT DOMIN EXEC ORD/FREE RESPECT   IVORY/CST
SKILL...POLICY RELATIV GP/COMP NAT/COMP 20. PAGE 21   GHANA
B0438

B65
HAINES R.M.,THE ADMINISTRATION OF THE DIOCESE OF   ADMIN
WORCESTER IN THE FIRST HALF OF THE FOURTEENTH   EX/STRUC
CENTURY. UK CATHISM...METH/COMP 13/15. PAGE 45   SECT
B0918   DELIB/GP

B65
KAAS L.,DIE GEISTLICHE GERICHTSBARKEIT DER   JURID
KATHOLISCHEN KIRCHE IN PREUSSEN (2 VOLS.). PRUSSIA   CATHISM
CONSTN NAT/G PROVS SECT ADJUD ADMIN ATTIT 16/20.   GP/REL
PAGE 57.B1158   CT/SYS

B65
MATRAS J.,SOCIAL CHANGE IN ISRAEL. ISRAEL STRATA   SECT
FAM ACT/RES EDU/PROP ADMIN CHOOSE...STAT CENSUS   NAT/LISM
19/20 JEWS. PAGE 71 B1427   GEOG
                                                             STRUCT

L65
MATTHEWS D.G.,"A CURRENT BIBLIOGRAPHY ON ETHIOPIAN   BIBLIOG/A
AFFAIRS: A SELECT BIBLIOGRAPHY FROM 1950-1964."   ADMIN
ETHIOPIA LAW CULTURE ECO/UNDEV INDUS LABOR SECT   POL/PAR
FORCES DIPLOM CIVMIL/REL RACE/REL...LING STAT 20.   NAT/G
PAGE 71 B1428

B66
BRAIBANTI R.,RESEARCH ON THE BUREAUCRACY OF   HABITAT
PAKISTAN. PAKISTAN LAW CULTURE INTELL ACADEM LOC/G   NAT/G
SECT PRESS CT/SYS...LING CHARTS 20 BUREAUCRCY.   ADMIN
PAGE 15 B0299   CONSTN

B66
MCKENZIE J.L.,AUTHORITY IN THE CHURCH. STRUCT LEAD   SECT
INGP/REL PERS/REL CENTRAL ANOMIE ATTIT ORD/FREE   AUTHORIT
RESPECT CATH. PAGE 72 B1452   PWR
                                                             ADMIN

B66
O'NEILL C.E.,CHURCH AND STATE IN FRENCH COLONIAL   COLONIAL
LOUISIANA: POLICY AND POLITICS TO 1732. PROVS   NAT/G
VOL/ASSN DELIB/GP ADJUD ADMIN GP/REL ATTIT DRIVE   SECT
...POLICY BIBLIOG 17/18 LOUISIANA CHURCH/STA.   PWR
PAGE 79 B1601

S66
AFRICAN BIBLIOGRAPHIC CENTER,"A CURRENT VIEW OF   BIBLIOG/A
AFRICANA: A SELECT AND ANNOTATED BIBLIOGRAPHICAL   NAT/G
PUBLISHING GUIDE, 1965-1966." AFR CULTURE INDUS   TEC/DEV
LABOR SECT FOR/AID ADMIN COLONIAL REV RACE/REL   POL/PAR
SOCISM...LING 20. PAGE 3 B0063

S66
MATTHEWS D.G.,"ETHIOPIAN OUTLINE: A BIBLIOGRAPHIC   BIBLIOG
RESEARCH GUIDE." ETHIOPIA LAW STRUCT ECO/UNDEV AGRI   NAT/G
LABOR SECT CHIEF DELIB/GP EX/STRUC ADMIN...LING   DIPLOM
ORG/CHARTS 20. PAGE 71 B1429   POL/PAR

B67
BENNETT J.W.,HUTTERIAN BRETHREN; THE AGRICULTURAL   SECT
ECONOMY AND SOCIAL ORGANIZATION OF A COMMUNAL   AGRI
PEOPLE. USA+45 SOCIETY FAM KIN TEC/DEV ADJUST...MGT   STRUCT
AUD/VIS GP/COMP 20. PAGE 10 B0213   GP/REL

B67
WEINBERG M.,SCHOOL INTEGRATION: A COMPREHENSIVE   BIBLIOG
CLASSIFIED BIBLIOGRAPHY OF 3,100 REFERENCES. USA+45   SCHOOL
LAW NAT/G NEIGH SECT PLAN ROUTINE AGE/C WEALTH   DISCRIM
SOC/INTEG INDIAN/AM. PAGE 115 B2314   RACE/REL

B67
WESSON R.G.,THE IMPERIAL ORDER. WOR-45 STRUCT SECT   PWR
DOMIN ADMIN COLONIAL LEAD CONSERVE...CONCPT BIBLIOG   CHIEF
20. PAGE 115 B2324   CONTROL
                                                             SOCIETY

S67
LANDES W.M.,"THE EFFECT OF STATE FAIR EMPLOYMENT   DISCRIM
LAWS ON THE ECONOMIC POSITION OF NONWHITES." USA+45   LAW
PROVS SECT LEGIS ADMIN GP/REL RACE/REL...JURID   WORKER
CONCPT CHARTS HYPO/EXP NEGRO. PAGE 62 B1255

S67
RAUM O.,"THE MODERN LEADERSHIP GROUP AMONG THE   RACE/REL
SOUTH AFRICAN XHOSA." SOUTH/AFR SOCIETY SECT   KIN
EX/STRUC REPRESENT GP/REL INGP/REL PERSON   LEAD
...METH/COMP 17/20 XHOSA NEGRO. PAGE 86 B1743   CULTURE

S68
GRAM H.A.,"BUSINESS ETHICS AND THE CORPORATION."   POLICY
LG/CO SECT PROB/SOLV CONTROL EXEC GP/REL INGP/REL   ADMIN
PERS/REL ROLE MORAL PWR...DECISION 20. PAGE 42   MGT
B0850

B82
MACDONALD D.,AFRICANA; OR, THE HEART OF HEATHEN   SECT
AFRICA, VOL. II: MISSION LIFE. SOCIETY STRATA KIN   AFR
CREATE EDU/PROP ADMIN COERCE LITERACY HEALTH...MYTH   CULTURE
WORSHIP 19 LIVNGSTN/D MISSION NEGRO. PAGE 67 B1355   ORD/FREE

B95
LATIMER E.W.,EUROPE IN AFRICA IN THE NINETEENTH   AFR

CENTURY. ECO/UNDEV KIN SECT DIPLOM DOMIN ADMIN   COLONIAL
DISCRIM 17/18. PAGE 63 B1275   WAR
                                                             FINAN

SECUR/COUN....UNITED NATIONS SECURITY COUNCIL

SECUR/PROG....SECURITY PROGRAM

SECURITIES....SEE FINAN

SECURITY....SEE ORD/FREE

SECURITY COUNCIL....SEE UN+DELIB/GP+PWR

SECURITY EXCHANGE COMMISSION....SEE SEC/EXCHNG

SECURITY PROGRAM....SEE SECUR/PROG

SEDITION....SEDITION

SEEK....SEARCH FOR EDUCATION, ELEVATION, AND KNOWLEDGE

SEGREGATION....SEE NEGRO, SOUTH/US, RACE/REL, SOC/INTEG,
   CIV/RIGHTS, DISCRIM, MISCEGEN, ISOLAT, SCHOOL,
   STRANGE, ANOMIE

SEGUNDO-SANCHEZ M. B1924

SEIDMAN H. B1925

SELASSIE/H....HAILE SELASSIE

SELBORNE/W....WILLIAM SELBORNE

SELEC/SERV....SELECTIVE SERVICE

SELF P. B1926

SELF/OBS....SELF/OBSERVATION

B20
HALDANE R.B.,BEFORE THE WAR. MOD/EUR SOCIETY   POLICY
INT/ORG NAT/G DELIB/GP PLAN DOMIN EDU/PROP LEGIT   DIPLOM
ADMIN COERCE ATTIT DRIVE MORAL ORD/FREE PWR...SOC   UK
CONCPT SELF/OBS RECORD BIOG TIME/SEQ. PAGE 45 B0921

B30
MURCHISON C.,PSYCHOLOGIES OF 1930. UNIV USA-45   CREATE
CULTURE INTELL SOCIETY STRATA FAM ROUTINE BIO/SOC   PERSON
DRIVE RIGID/FLEX SUPEGO...NEW/IDEA OBS SELF/OBS
CONT/OBS 20. PAGE 76 B1543

B48
HULL C.,THE MEMOIRS OF CORDELL HULL (VOLUME ONE).   BIOG
USA-45 WOR-45 CONSTN FAM LOC/G NAT/G PROVS DELIB/GP   DIPLOM
FORCES LEGIS TOP/EX BAL/PWR LEGIT ADMIN EXEC WAR
ATTIT ORD/FREE PWR...MAJORIT SELF/OBS TIME/SEQ
TREND NAZI 20. PAGE 52 B1062

S51
COHEN M.B.,"PERSONALITY AS A FACTOR IN   PERSON
ADMINISTRATIVE DECISIONS." ADJUD PERS/REL ANOMIE   ADMIN
SUPEGO...OBS SELF/OBS INT. PAGE 22 B0446   PROB/SOLV
                                                             PSY

B58
BROWNE C.G.,THE CONCEPT OF LEADERSHIP. UNIV FACE/GP   EXEC
DOMIN EDU/PROP LEGIT LEAD DRIVE PERSON PWR...MGT   CONCPT
SOC OBS SELF/OBS CONT/OBS INT PERS/TEST STERTYP
GEN/LAWS. PAGE 16 B0328

S60
BOGARDUS E.S.,"THE SOCIOLOGY OF A STRUCTURED   INT/ORG
PEACE." FUT SOCIETY CREATE DIPLOM ADJUD ROUTINE   SOC
ATTIT RIGID/FLEX KNOWL ORD/FREE RESPECT   NAT/LISM
...POLICY INT/LAW JURID NEW/IDEA SELF/OBS TOT/POP   PEACE
20 UN. PAGE 13 B0264

B62
HADWEN J.G.,HOW UNITED NATIONS DECISIONS ARE MADE.   INT/ORG
WOR+45 LAW EDU/PROP LEGIT ADMIN PWR...DECISION   ROUTINE
SELF/OBS GEN/LAWS UN 20. PAGE 45 B0912

SELZNICK B1927

SELZNICK P. B1928,B1929

SEMANTICS...SEE LOG

SEN/SPACE....UNITED STATES SENATE SPECIAL COMMITTEE ON
   SPACE ASTRONAUTICS

SENATE SPECIAL COMMITTEE ON SPACE ASTRONAUTICS....SEE
   SEN/SPACE

SENATE....SENATE (ALL NATIONS); SEE ALSO CONGRESS, LEGIS

B08
WILSON W.,CONSTITUTIONAL GOVERNMENT IN THE UNITED   NAT/G
STATES. USA-45 LAW POL/PAR PROVS CHIEF LEGIS   GOV/REL
BAL/PWR ADJUD EXEC FEDERAL PWR 18/20 SUPREME/CT   CONSTN
HOUSE/REP SENATE. PAGE 117 B2362   PARL/PROC

HUMPHREY H.H.,"THE SENATE ON TRIAL." USA+45 POL/PAR PARL/PROC DEBATE REPRESENT EFFICIENCY ATTIT RIGID/FLEX ...TRADIT SENATE. PAGE 52 B1064
S50
PARL/PROC
ROUTINE
PWR
LEGIS

WILSON W.,CONGRESSIONAL GOVERNMENT. USA-45 NAT/G ADMIN EXEC PARL/PROC GP/REL MAJORITY ATTIT 19 SENATE HOUSE/REP. PAGE 117 B2364
B56
LEGIS
CHIEF
CONSTN
PWR

HUITT R.K.,"THE MORSE COMMITTEE ASSIGNMENT CONTROVERSY: A STUDY IN SENATE NORMS." USA+45 USA-45 POL/PAR SENIOR ROLE SUPEGO SENATE. PAGE 52 B1061
S57
LEGIS
ETIQUET
PWR
ROUTINE

US SENATE COMM POST OFFICE,TO PROVIDE AN EFFECTIVE SYSTEM OF PERSONNEL ADMINISTRATION. USA+45 NAT/G EX/STRUC PARL/PROC GOV/REL...JURID 20 SENATE CIVIL/SERV. PAGE 111 B2234
B58
INT
LEGIS
CONFER
ADMIN

HAYNES G.H.,THE SENATE OF THE UNITED STATES: ITS HISTORY AND PRACTICE. CONSTN EX/STRUC TOP/EX CONFER DEBATE LEAD LOBBY PARL/PROC CHOOSE PWR SENATE CONGRESS. PAGE 48 B0977
B60
LEGIS
DELIB/GP

US SENATE COMM ON JUDICIARY,FEDERAL ADMINISTRATIVE PROCEDURE. USA+45 CONSTN NAT/G PROB/SOLV CONFER GOV/REL...JURID INT 20 SENATE. PAGE 110 B2226
B60
PARL/PROC
LEGIS
ADMIN
LAW

US SENATE COMM ON JUDICIARY,ADMINISTRATIVE PROCEDURE LEGISLATION. USA+45 CONSTN NAT/G PROB/SOLV CONFER ROUTINE GOV/REL...INT 20 SENATE. PAGE 110 B2227
B60
PARL/PROC
LEGIS
ADMIN
JURID

CARPER E.T.,ILLINOIS GOES TO CONGRESS FOR ARMY LAND. USA+45 LAW EXTR/IND PROVS REGION CIVMIL/REL GOV/REL FEDERAL ATTIT 20 ILLINOIS SENATE CONGRESS DIRKSEN/E DOUGLAS/P. PAGE 19 B0385
B62
ADMIN
LOBBY
GEOG
LEGIS

US SENATE COMM ON JUDICIARY,STATE DEPARTMENT SECURITY. USA+45 CHIEF TEC/DEV DOMIN ADMIN EXEC ATTIT ORD/FREE...POLICY CONGRESS DEPT/STATE PRESIDENT KENNEDY/JF KENNEDY/JF SENATE 20. PAGE 110 B2228
B62
CONTROL
WORKER
NAT/G
GOV/REL

CLARK J.S.,THE SENATE ESTABLISHMENT. USA+45 NAT/G POL/PAR ADMIN CHOOSE PERSON SENATE. PAGE 21 B0431
B63
LEGIS
ROUTINE
LEAD
SENIOR

US SENATE COMM GOVT OPERATIONS,ADMINISTRATION OF NATIONAL SECURITY (9 PARTS). ADMIN...INT REC/INT CHARTS 20 SENATE CONGRESS. PAGE 110 B2213
B63
DELIB/GP
NAT/G
OP/RES
ORD/FREE

US SENATE COMM ON JUDICIARY,ADMINISTERED PRICES. USA+45 RATION ADJUD CONTROL LOBBY...POLICY 20 SENATE MONOPOLY. PAGE 110 B2229
B63
LG/CO
PRICE
ADMIN
DECISION

US SENATE COMM ON JUDICIARY,ADMINISTRATIVE CONFERENCE OF THE UNITED STATES. USA+45 CONSTN NAT/G PROB/SOLV CONFER GOV/REL...INT 20 SENATE. PAGE 110 B2230
B63
PARL/PROC
JURID
ADMIN
LEGIS

US SENATE COMM ON JUDICIARY,ADMINISTRATIVE PROCEDURE ACT. USA+45 CONSTN NAT/G PROB/SOLV CONFER GOV/REL PWR...INT 20 SENATE. PAGE 110 B2231
B64
PARL/PROC
LEGIS
JURID
ADMIN

US SENATE COMM GOVT OPERATIONS,ADMINISTRATION OF NATIONAL SECURITY. USA+45 DELIB/GP ADMIN ROLE ...POLICY CHARTS SENATE. PAGE 110 B2218
B65
NAT/G
ORD/FREE
DIPLOM
PROB/SOLV

TACHERON D.G.,"THE JOB OF THE CONGRESSMAN: AN INTRODUCTION TO SERVICES IN THE US HOUSE OF REPRESENTATIVES." DELIB/GP EX/STRUC PRESS SENIOR CT/SYS LOBBY CHOOSE GOV/REL...BIBLIOG 20 CONGRESS HOUSE/REP SENATE. PAGE 102 B2068
C66
LEGIS
PARL/PROC
ADMIN
POL/PAR

DOERN G.B.,"THE ROYAL COMMISSIONS IN THE GENERAL POLICY PROCESS AND IN FEDERAL-PROVINCIAL RELATIONS." CANADA CONSTN ACADEM PROVS CONSULT DELIB/GP LEGIS ACT/RES PROB/SOLV CONFER CONTROL EFFICIENCY...METH/COMP 20 SENATE ROYAL/COMM. PAGE 30 B0603
S67
R+D
EX/STRUC
GOV/REL
NAT/G

US SENATE COMM ON FOREIGN REL,THE UNITED NATIONS AT TWENTY-ONE (PAMPHLET). WOR+45 BUDGET ADMIN SENATE UN. PAGE 110 B2223
N67
INT/ORG
DIPLOM
PEACE

US SENATE COMM ON FOREIGN REL,THE UNITED NATIONS PEACEKEEPING DILEMMA (PAMPHLET). ISLAM WOR+45
N67
INT/ORG
DIPLOM

PROB/SOLV BUDGET ADMIN SENATE UN. PAGE 110 B2224   PEACE

SENEGAL....SEE ALSO AFR

SENGUPTA J.K. B0746

SENIOR....SENIORITY; SEE ALSO ADMIN, ROUTINE

MARSH J.F. JR.,THE FBI RETIREMENT BILL (PAMPHLET). USA+45 EX/STRUC WORKER PLAN PROB/SOLV BUDGET LEAD LOBBY PARL/PROC PERS/REL RIGID/FLEX...POLICY 20 FBI PRESIDENT BUR/BUDGET. PAGE 70 B1405
N19
ADMIN
NAT/G
SENIOR
GOV/REL

GREER S.,BIBLIOGRAPHY ON CIVIL SERVICE AND PERSONNEL ADMINISTRATION. USA-45 LOC/G PROVS WORKER PRICE SENIOR DRIVE...MGT 20. PAGE 43 B0870
B35
BIBLIOG/A
ADMIN
NAT/G
ROUTINE

COHEN E.W.,THE GROWTH OF THE BRITISH CIVIL SERVICE 1780-1939. UK NAT/G SENIOR ROUTINE GOV/REL...MGT METH/COMP BIBLIOG 18/20. PAGE 22 B0442
B41
OP/RES
TIME/SEQ
CENTRAL
ADMIN

YOUNG R.,THIS IS CONGRESS. FUT SENIOR ADMIN GP/REL PWR...DECISION REFORMERS CONGRESS. PAGE 119 B2393
B43
LEGIS
DELIB/GP
CHIEF
ROUTINE

WHITE L.D.,"CONGRESSIONAL CONTROL OF THE PUBLIC SERVICE." USA-45 NAT/G CONSULT DELIB/GP PLAN SENIOR CONGRESS. PAGE 116 B2335
S45
LEGIS
EXEC
POLICY
CONTROL

KEFAUVER E.,A TWENTIETH-CENTURY CONGRESS. POL/PAR EX/STRUC SENIOR ADMIN CONTROL EXEC LOBBY CHOOSE EFFICIENCY PWR. PAGE 59 B1189
B47
LEGIS
DELIB/GP
ROUTINE
TOP/EX

GLADDEN E.N.,CIVIL SERVICE OR BUREAUCRACY? UK LAW STRATA LABOR TOP/EX PLAN SENIOR AUTOMAT CONTROL PARTIC CHOOSE HAPPINESS...CHARTS 19/20 CIVIL/SERV BUREAUCRCY. PAGE 40 B0808
B56
ADMIN
GOV/REL
EFFICIENCY
PROVS

SCARROW H.A.,THE HIGHER PUBLIC SERVICE OF THE COMMONWEALTH OF AUSTRALIA. LAW SENIOR LOBBY ROLE 20 AUSTRAL CIVIL/SERV COMMONWLTH. PAGE 93 B1877
B57
ADMIN
NAT/G
EX/STRUC
GOV/COMP

HUITT R.K.,"THE MORSE COMMITTEE ASSIGNMENT CONTROVERSY: A STUDY IN SENATE NORMS." USA+45 USA-45 POL/PAR SENIOR ROLE SUPEGO SENATE. PAGE 52 B1061
S57
LEGIS
ETIQUET
PWR
ROUTINE

MAINZER L.C.,"INJUSTICE AND BUREAUCRACY." ELITES STRATA STRUCT EX/STRUC SENIOR CONTROL EXEC LEAD ROUTINE INGP/REL ORD/FREE...CONCPT 20 BUREAUCRCY. PAGE 68 B1381
S62
MORAL
MGT
ADMIN

CLARK J.S.,THE SENATE ESTABLISHMENT. USA+45 NAT/G POL/PAR ADMIN CHOOSE PERSON SENATE. PAGE 21 B0431
B63
LEGIS
ROUTINE
LEAD
SENIOR

MEDALIA N.Z.,"POSITION AND PROSPECTS OF SOCIOLOGISTS IN FEDERAL EMPLOYMENT." USA+45 CONSULT PAY SENIOR ADMIN GOV/REL...TREND CHARTS 20 CIVIL/SERV. PAGE 72 B1460
S63
NAT/G
WORKER
SOC
SKILL

CLARK J.S.,CONGRESS: THE SAPLESS BRANCH. DELIB/GP SENIOR ATTIT CONGRESS. PAGE 21 B0432
B64
LEGIS
ROUTINE
ADMIN
POL/PAR

COMMITTEE ECONOMIC DEVELOPMENT,IMPROVING EXECUTIVE MANAGEMENT IN THE FEDERAL GOVERNMENT. USA+45 CHIEF DELIB/GP WORKER PLAN PAY SENIOR ADMIN EFFICIENCY 20 PRESIDENT. PAGE 22 B0457
B64
EXEC
MGT
TOP/EX
NAT/G

PEABODY R.L.,ORGANIZATIONAL AUTHORITY. SCHOOL WORKER PLAN SENIOR GOV/REL UTIL DRIVE PWR...PSY CHARTS BIBLIOG 20. PAGE 82 B1648
B64
ADMIN
EFFICIENCY
TASK
GP/REL

RAPHAEL M.,PENSIONS AND PUBLIC SERVANTS. UK PLAN EDU/PROP PARTIC GOV/REL HEALTH...POLICY CHARTS 17/20 CIVIL/SERV. PAGE 86 B1737
B64
ADMIN
SENIOR
PAY
AGE/O

ROCHE J.P.,THE CONGRESS. EX/STRUC BAL/PWR DIPLOM DEBATE ADJUD LEAD PWR. PAGE 89 B1809
B64
INGP/REL
LEGIS
DELIB/GP
SENIOR

ELDER R.E.,OVERSEAS REPRESENTATION AND SERVICES FOR FEDERAL DOMESTIC AGENCIES. USA+45 NAT/G ACT/RES
B65
OP/RES
DIPLOM

FOR/AID EDU/PROP SENIOR ROUTINE TASK ADJUST...MGT GOV/REL
ORG/CHARTS. PAGE 33 B0663 ADMIN
B65

HARR J.E.,THE DEVELOPMENT OF CAREERS IN THE FOREIGN OP/RES
SERVICE. CREATE SENIOR EXEC FEEDBACK GOV/REL MGT
EFFICIENCY ATTIT RESPECT ORG/CHARTS. PAGE 47 B0953 ADMIN
DIPLOM
B65

RUBIN H.,PENSIONS AND EMPLOYEE MOBILITY IN THE ADMIN
PUBLIC SERVICE. USA+45 WORKER PERSON ORD/FREE...SOC NAT/G
QU. PAGE 91 B1849 LOC/G
SENIOR
C65

HUNTINGTON S.P.,"CONGRESSIONAL RESPONSES TO THE FUT
TWENTIETH CENTURY IN D. TRUMAN, ED. THE CONGRESS LEAD
AND AMERICA'S FUTURE." USA+45 USA-45 DIPLOM SENIOR NAT/G
ADMIN EXEC PWR...SOC 20 CONGRESS. PAGE 53 B1067 LEGIS
C66

TACHERON D.G.,"THE JOB OF THE CONGRESSMAN: AN LEGIS
INTRODUCTION TO SERVICES IN THE US HOUSE OF PARL/PROC
REPRESENTATIVES." DELIB/GP EX/STRUC PRESS SENIOR ADMIN
CT/SYS LOBBY CHOOSE GOV/REL...BIBLIOG 20 CONGRESS POL/PAR
HOUSE/REP SENATE. PAGE 102 B2068
S67

LEWIS P.H.,"LEADERSHIP AND CONFLICT WITHIN POL/PAR
FEBRERISTA PARTY OF PARAGUAY." L/A+17C PARAGUAY ELITES
EX/STRUC DOMIN SENIOR CONTROL INGP/REL CENTRAL LEAD
FEDERAL ATTIT 20. PAGE 65 B1305

SEPARATION....SEE ISOLAT, DISCRIM, RACE/REL

SERBIA....SERBIA

SERENO R. B1266

SERV/IND....SERVICE INDUSTRY

CIVIL SERVICE JOURNAL. PARTIC INGP/REL PERS/REL ADMIN
...MGT BIBLIOG/A 20. PAGE 1 B0011 NAT/G
SERV/IND
WORKER
N

KYRIAK T.E.,EAST EUROPE: BIBLIOGRAPHY--INDEX TO US BIBLIOG/A
JPRS RESEARCH TRANSLATIONS. ALBANIA BULGARIA COM PRESS
CZECHOSLVK HUNGARY POLAND ROMANIA AGRI EXTR/IND MARXISM
FINAN SERV/IND INT/TRADE WEAPON...GEOG MGT SOC 20. INDUS
PAGE 62 B1247
N

US SUPERINTENDENT OF DOCUMENTS,TRANSPORTATION: BIBLIOG/A
HIGHWAYS, ROADS, AND POSTAL SERVICE (PRICE LIST DIST/IND
25). PANAMA USA+45 LAW FORCES DIPLOM ADMIN GOV/REL SERV/IND
HEALTH MGT. PAGE 111 B2243 NAT/G
N19

RIDLEY C.E.,MEASURING MUNICIPAL ACTIVITIES MGT
(PAMPHLET). FINAN SERV/IND FORCES RECEIVE INGP/REL HEALTH
HABITAT...POLICY SOC/WK 20. PAGE 88 B1779 WEALTH
LOC/G
B43

LEVY H.P.,A STUDY IN PUBLIC RELATIONS: CASE HISTORY ATTIT
OF THE RELATIONS MAINTAINED BETWEEN A DEPT OF RECEIVE
PUBLIC ASSISTANCE AND PEOPLE. USA+45 NAT/G PRESS WEALTH
ADMIN LOBBY GP/REL DISCRIM...SOC/WK LING AUD/VIS 20 SERV/IND
PENNSYLVAN. PAGE 64 B1302
S51

LERNER D.,"THE POLICY SCIENCES: RECENT DEVELOPMENTS CONSULT
IN SCOPE AND METHODS." R+D SERV/IND CREATE DIPLOM SOC
ROUTINE PWR...METH/CNCPT TREND GEN/LAWS METH 20.
PAGE 64 B1297
B56

CONAWAY O.B.,DEMOCRACY IN FEDERAL ADMINISTRATION ADMIN
(PAMPHLET). USA+45 LEGIS PARTIC ATTIT...TREND SERV/IND
ANTHOL 20. PAGE 23 B0459 NAT/G
GP/REL
B58

WILENSKY H.L.,INDUSTRIAL SOCIETY AND SOCIAL INDUS
WELFARE: IMPACT OF INDUSTRIALIZATION ON SUPPLY AND ECO/DEV
ORGANIZATION OF SOC WELF SERVICES. ELITES SOCIETY RECEIVE
STRATA SERV/IND FAM MUNIC PUB/INST CONSULT WORKER PROF/ORG
ADMIN AUTOMAT ANOMIE 20. PAGE 117 B2352
B60

HOVING W.,THE DISTRIBUTION REVOLUTION. WOR+45 DIST/IND
ECO/DEV FINAN SERV/IND PRESS PRICE INCOME PRODUC MARKET
...MGT 20. PAGE 52 B1049 ECO/TAC
TASK
B61

QURESHI S.,INCENTIVES IN AMERICAN EMPLOYMENT SERV/IND
(THESIS, UNIVERSITY OF PENNSYLVANIA). DELIB/GP ADMIN
TOP/EX BUDGET ROUTINE SANCTION COST TECHRACY MGT. PAY
PAGE 85 B1727 EX/STRUC
L62

WATERSTON A.,"PLANNING IN MOROCCO, ORGANIZATION AND NAT/G
IMPLEMENTATION. BALTIMORE: HOPKINS ECON. DEVELOP. PLAN
INT. BANK FOR." ISLAM ECO/DEV AGRI DIST/IND INDUS MOROCCO
PROC/MFG SERV/IND LOC/G EX/STRUC ECO/TAC PWR WEALTH
TOT/POP VAL/FREE 20. PAGE 114 B2302

ALBONETTI A.,"IL SECONDO PROGRAMMA QUINQUENNALE R+D
1963-67 ED IL BILANCIO RICERCHE ED INVESTIMENTI PER PLAN
IL 1963 DELL'ERATOM." EUR+WWI FUT ITALY WOR+45 NUC/PWR
ECO/DEV SERV/IND INT/ORG TEC/DEV ECO/TAC ATTIT
SKILL WEALTH...MGT TIME/SEQ OEEC 20. PAGE 3 B0069
S62

BUENO M.,"ASPECTOS SOCIOLOGICOS DE LA EDUCACION." SOCIETY
FUT UNIV INTELL R+D SERV/IND SCHOOL CONSULT EDU/PROP
EX/STRUC ACT/RES PLAN...METH/CNCPT OBS 20. PAGE 17 PERSON
B0341
S62

GEORGE P.,"MATERIAUX ET REFLEXIONS POUR UNE ECO/UNDEV
POLITIQUE URBAINE RATIONNELLE DANS LES PAYS EN PLAN
COURS DE DEVELOPPEMENT." FUT INTELL SOCIETY
SERV/IND MUNIC ACT/RES WEALTH...MGT 20. PAGE 39
B0790
B63

BASS M.E.,SELECTIVE BIBLIOGRAPHY ON MUNICIPAL BIBLIOG
GOVERNMENT FROM THE FILES OF THE MUNICIPAL LOC/G
TECHNICAL ADVISORY SERVICE. USA+45 FINAN SERV/IND ADMIN
PLAN 20. PAGE 9 B0194 MUNIC
B64

FALK L.A.,ADMINISTRATIVE ASPECTS OF GROUP PRACTICE. BIBLIOG/A
USA+45 FINAN PROF/ORG PLAN MGT. PAGE 35 B0702 HEAL
ADMIN
SERV/IND
B64

FISK W.M.,ADMINISTRATIVE PROCEDURE IN A REGULATORY SERV/IND
AGENCY: THE CAB AND THE NEW YORK-CHICAGO CASE ECO/DEV
(PAMPHLET). USA+45 DIST/IND ADMIN CONTROL LOBBY AIR
GP/REL ROLE ORD/FREE NEWYORK/C CHICAGO CAB. PAGE 36 JURID
B0727
B64

GARFIELD PJ   LOVEJOY WF,PUBLIC UTILITY T
ECONOMICS. DIST/IND FINAN MARKET MUNIC ADMIN COST ECO/TAC
DEMAND...TECHNIC JURID 20 MONOPOLY. PAGE 39 B0782 OWN
SERV/IND
B64

KIESER P.J.,THE COST OF ADMINISTRATION, SUPERVISION AFR
AND SERVICES IN URBAN BANTU TOWNSHIPS. SOUTH/AFR MGT
SERV/IND MUNIC PROVS ADMIN COST...OBS QU CHARTS 20 FINAN
BANTU. PAGE 60 B1203
B64

PINNICK A.W.,COUNTRY PLANNERS IN ACTION. UK FINAN MUNIC
SERV/IND NAT/G CONSULT DELIB/GP PRICE CONTROL PLAN
ROUTINE LEISURE AGE/C...GEOG 20 URBAN/RNWL. PAGE 83 INDUS
B1674 ATTIT
B65

DOWD L.P.,PRINCIPLES OF WORLD BUSINESS. SERV/IND INT/TRADE
NAT/G DIPLOM ECO/TAC TARIFFS...INT/LAW JURID 20. MGT
PAGE 30 B0614 FINAN
MARKET
B66

BHALERAO C.N.,PUBLIC SERVICE COMMISSIONS OF INDIA: NAT/G
A STUDY. INDIA SERV/IND EX/STRUC ROUTINE CHOOSE OP/RES
GOV/REL INGP/REL...KNO/TEST EXHIBIT 20. PAGE 11 LOC/G
B0233 ADMIN
B66

FENN DH J.R.,BUSINESS DECISION MAKING AND DECISION
GOVERNMENT POLICY. SERV/IND LEGIS LICENSE ADMIN PLAN
CONTROL GP/REL INGP/REL 20 CASEBOOK. PAGE 35 B0711 NAT/G
LG/CO
B67

JAKUBAUSKAS E.B.,HUMAN RESOURCES DEVELOPMENT. PROB/SOLV
USA+45 AGRI INDUS SERV/IND ACT/RES PLAN ADMIN ECO/TAC
RACE/REL DISCRIM...TREND GEN/LAWS. PAGE 55 B1119 EDU/PROP
WORKER

SERVAN/JJ....JEAN JACQUES SERVAN-SCHREIBER

SERVAN-SCHREIBER, JEAN-JACQUES....SEE SERVAN/JJ

SERVICE INDUSTRY....SEE SERV/IND

SET THEORY....SEE CLASSIF

SEVENTHDAY....SEVENTH DAY ADVENTISTS

SEX DIFFERENCES....SEE SEX

SEX....SEE ALSO BIO/SOC

BUREAU OF NAT'L AFFAIRS INC.,A CURRENT LOOK AT: DISCRIM
(1) THE NEGRO AND TITLE VII, (2) SEX AND TITLE VII SEX
(PAMPHLET). LAW LG/CO SML/CO RACE/REL...POLICY SOC WORKER
STAT DEEP/QU TREND CON/ANAL CHARTS 20 NEGRO MGT
CIV/RIGHTS. PAGE 17 B0350
B47

TAPPAN P.W.,DELINQUENT GIRLS IN COURT. USA-45 MUNIC CT/SYS
EX/STRUC FORCES ADMIN EXEC ADJUST SEX RESPECT AGE/Y
...JURID SOC/WK 20 NEWYORK/C FEMALE/SEX. PAGE 103 CRIME
B2078 ADJUD

SEXUAL BEHAVIOR....SEE SEX, PERSON

SEYLER W.C. B1930

SHACK W.A. B0426

SHANGHAI....SHANGHAI

SHANKS M. B1931

SHAPIRO D. B1932

SHAPIRO S.J. B0499

SHAPP W.R. B1933

SHARKANSKY I. B1934

SHARMA M.P. B1935

SHARMA S.A. B1936

SHARMA S.R. B1937

SHARMA T.R. B1938

SHARP W.R. B1939

SHASTRI/LB....LAL BAHADUR SHASTRI

B66
ZINKIN T.,CHALLENGES IN INDIA. INDIA PAKISTAN LAW   NAT/G
AGRI FINAN INDUS TOP/EX TEC/DEV CONTROL ROUTINE   ECO/TAC
ORD/FREE PWR 20 NEHRU/J SHASTRI/LB CIVIL/SERV.   POLICY
PAGE 119 B2404   ADMIN

SHAW P.C. B0155

SHAW S.J. B1940

SHELTON W.L. B1941

SHEPARD H.A. B0250

SHEPPARD/S....SAMUEL SHEPPARD

SHERBENOU E.L. B1942

SHERIDAN R.G. B1943

SHERMAN H. B1944

SHERMN/ACT....SHERMAN ANTI-TRUST ACT; SEE ALSO MONOPOLY

SHERWIN M. B1399

SHERWOOD F.P. B1945

SHERWOOD R.E. B1946

SHILS E.A. B1947

SHIMKIN D.B. B1948

SHISTER J. B1949

SHOEMAKER R.L. B1950

SHORT TAKE-OFF AND LANDING AIRCRAFT....SEE STOL

SHOUP/C....C. SHOUP

SHRIVER/S....SARGENT SHRIVER

SIBERIA....SIBERIA

SIBRON....SIBRON V. NEW YORK

SICILY....SICILY

SICKNESS....SEE HEALTH

SIDEY H. B1951

SIDGWICK/H....HENRY SIDGWICK

SIER/LEONE....SIERRA LEONE; SEE ALSO AFR

B61
CARNEY D.E.,GOVERNMENT AND ECONOMY IN BRITISH WEST   METH/COMP
AFRICA. GAMBIA GHANA NIGERIA SIER/LEONE DOMIN ADMIN   COLONIAL
GOV/REL SOVEREIGN WEALTH LAISSEZ...BIBLIOG 20   ECO/TAC
CMN/WLTH. PAGE 19 B0384   ECO/UNDEV
B63
WALKER A.A.,OFFICIAL PUBLICATIONS OF SIERRA LEONE   BIBLIOG
AND GAMBIA. GAMBIA SIER/LEONE UK LAW CONSTN LEGIS   NAT/G
PLAN BUDGET DIPLOM...SOC SAMP CON/ANAL 20. PAGE 113   COLONIAL
B2278   ADMIN

SIFFIN W.J. B1507

SIHANOUK....NORODOM SIHANOUK

SIKKIM....SEE ALSO S/ASIA

SILBERMAN B.S. B1952

SILVER....SILVER STANDARD AND POLICIES RELATING TO SILVER

SILVERT K.H. B1953

SIMMEL/G....GEORG SIMMEL

SIMOES DOS REIS A. B1954

SIMON H.A. B0164,B1397,B1779,B1955,B1956,B1957,B1959,B1960

SIMON R. B1961

SIMON Y.R. B1962

SIMPKINS E. B2377

SIMPSON R.L. B1963

SIMPSON....SIMPSON V. UNION OIL COMPANY

SIMUL....SCIENTIFIC MODELS

S55
CROCKETT W.H.,"EMERGENT LEADERSHIP IN SMALL   DELIB/GP
DECISION MAKING GROUPS." ACT/RES ROUTINE PERS/REL   ADMIN
ATTIT...STAT CONT/OBS SOC/EXP SIMUL. PAGE 25 B0507   PSY
                                                      DECISION
B56
GARDNER R.N.,STERLING-DOLLAR DIPLOMACY. EUR+WWI   ECO/DEV
USA+45 INT/ORG NAT/G PLAN INT/TRADE EDU/PROP ADMIN   DIPLOM
KNOWL PWR WEALTH...POLICY SOC METH/CNCPT STAT
CHARTS SIMUL GEN/LAWS 20. PAGE 39 B0781
B56
LOVEDAY A.,REFLECTIONS ON INTERNATIONAL   INT/ORG
ADMINISTRATION. WOR+45 WOR-45 DELIB/GP ACT/RES   MGT
ADMIN EXEC ROUTINE DRIVE...METH/CNCPT TIME/SEQ
CON/ANAL SIMUL TOT/POP 20. PAGE 67 B1342
B57
SIMON H.A.,MODELS OF MAN, SOCIAL AND RATIONAL: MATH
MATHEMATICAL ESSAYS ON RATIONAL HUMAN BEHAVIOR IN A   SIMUL
SOCIAL SETTING. UNIV LAW SOCIETY FACE/GP VOL/ASSN
CONSULT EX/STRUC LEGIS CREATE ADMIN ROUTINE ATTIT
DRIVE PWR...SOC CONCPT METH/CNCPT QUANT STAT
TOT/POP VAL/FREE 20. PAGE 97 B1959
S58
ARGYRIS C.,"SOME PROBLEMS IN CONCEPTUALIZING   FINAN
ORGANIZATIONAL CLIMATE: A CASE STUDY OF A BANK"   CONCPT
(BMR)" USA+45 EX/STRUC ADMIN PERS/REL ADJUST PERSON   LG/CO
...POLICY HYPO/EXP SIMUL 20. PAGE 6 B0129   INGP/REL
S58
DEAN B.V.,"APPLICATION OF OPERATIONS RESEARCH TO   DECISION
MANAGERIAL DECISION MAKING" STRATA ACT/RES   OP/RES
PROB/SOLV ROLE...SOC PREDICT SIMUL 20. PAGE 28   MGT
B0565   METH/CNCPT
S58
HELMER O.,"THE PROSPECTS OF A UNIFIED THEORY OF   SIMUL
ORGANIZATIONS" UNIV ACT/RES ADMIN...CONCPT HYPO/EXP   LG/CO
METH. PAGE 49 B0989   METH/CNCPT
                                                      GAME
S59
CYERT R.M.,"MODELS IN A BEHAVIORAL THEORY OF THE   SIMUL
FIRM." ROUTINE...DECISION MGT METH/CNCPT MATH.   GAME
PAGE 25 B0517   PREDICT
                                                      INDUS
S59
UDY S.H. JR.,"'BUREAUCRACY' AND 'RATIONALITY' IN   GEN/LAWS
WEBER'S ORGANIZATION THEORY: AN EMPIRICAL STUDY"   METH/CNCPT
(BMR)" UNIV STRUCT INDUS LG/CO SML/CO VOL/ASSN   ADMIN
...SOC SIMUL 20 WEBER/MAX BUREAUCRCY. PAGE 106   RATIONAL
B2144
B60
ARGYRIS C.,UNDERSTANDING ORGANIZATIONAL BEHAVIOR.   LG/CO
OP/RES FEEDBACK...MGT PSY METH/CNCPT OBS INT SIMUL   PERSON
20. PAGE 6 B0130   ADMIN
                                                      ROUTINE
B60
ARROW K.J.,MATHEMATICAL METHODS IN THE SOCIAL   MATH
SCIENCES, 1959. TEC/DEV CHOOSE UTIL PERCEPT   PSY
...KNO/TEST GAME SIMUL ANTHOL. PAGE 7 B0137   MGT
B60
MORRIS W.T.,ENGINEERING ECONOMY. AUTOMAT RISK   OP/RES
RATIONAL...PROBABIL STAT CHARTS GAME SIMUL BIBLIOG   DECISION
T 20. PAGE 76 B1529   MGT
                                                      PROB/SOLV
S60
FRIEDMAN L.,"DECISION MAKING IN COMPETITIVE   DECISION
SITUATIONS" OP/RES...MGT PROBABIL METH/COMP SIMUL   UTIL
20. PAGE 37 B0757   OPTIMAL

PFIFFNER J.M.,"ADMINISTRATIVE RATIONALITY" (BMR)"
UNIV CONTROL...POLICY IDEA/COMP SIMUL. PAGE 83
B1667

GAME
S60
ADMIN
DECISION
RATIONAL
S60

SCHATZ S.P.,"THE INFLENCE OF PLANNING ON
DEVELOPMENT: THE NIGERIAN EXPERIENCE." AFR FUT
FINAN INDUS NAT/G EX/STRUC ECO/TAC ADMIN ATTIT
PERCEPT ORD/FREE PWR...MATH TREND CON/ANAL SIMUL
VAL/FREE 20. PAGE 93 B1883

ECO/UNDEV
PLAN
NIGERIA

B61

CHAPPLE E.D.,"THE MEASURE OF MANAGEMENT. USA+45
WORKER ADMIN GP/REL EFFICIENCY...DECISION
ORG/CHARTS SIMUL 20. PAGE 20 B0412

MGT
OP/RES
PLAN
METH/CNCPT
S61

BENNIS W.G.,"REVISIONIST THEORY OF LEADERSHIP"
MUNIC ACT/RES TEC/DEV...SIMUL 20. PAGE 11 B0215

LEAD
ADMIN
PERS/REL
HYPO/EXP
S61

DEUTSCH K.W.,"A NOTE ON THE APPEARANCE OF WISDOM IN
LARGE BUREAUCRATIC ORGANIZATIONS." ROUTINE PERSON
KNOWL SKILL...DECISION STAT. PAGE 28 B0577

ADMIN
PROBABIL
PROB/SOLV
SIMUL
S61

EVAN W.M.,"A LABORATORY EXPERIMENT ON BUREAUCRATIC
AUTHORITY" WORKER CONTROL EXEC PRODUC ATTIT PERSON
...PSY SOC CHARTS SIMUL 20 WEBER/MAX. PAGE 34 B0687

ADMIN
LEGIT
LAB/EXP
EFFICIENCY
B62

ARGYRIS C.,INTERPERSONAL COMPETENCE AND
ORGANIZATIONAL EFFECTIVENESS. CREATE PLAN PROB/SOLV
EDU/PROP INGP/REL PERS/REL PRODUC...OBS INT SIMUL
20. PAGE 6 B0131

EX/STRUC
ADMIN
CONSULT
EFFICIENCY
B62

DUCKWORTH W.E.,A GUIDE TO OPERATIONAL RESEARCH.
INDUS PLAN PROB/SOLV EXEC EFFICIENCY PRODUC KNOWL
...MGT MATH STAT SIMUL METH 20 MONTECARLO. PAGE 31
B0624

OP/RES
GAME
DECISION
ADMIN
S62

MCCLELLAND C.A.,"DECISIONAL OPPORTUNITY AND
POLITICAL CONTROVERSY." USA+45 NAT/G POL/PAR FORCES
TOP/EX DOMIN ADMIN PEACE DRIVE ORD/FREE PWR
...DECISION SIMUL 20. PAGE 72 B1444

ACT/RES
PERCEPT
DIPLOM

N62

UNIVERSITY PITT INST LOC GOVT,THE COUNCIL-MANAGER
FORM OF GOVERNMENT IN PENNSYLVANIA (PAMPHLET).
PROVS EX/STRUC REPRESENT GOV/REL EFFICIENCY
...CHARTS SIMUL 20 PENNSYLVAN CITY/MGT. PAGE 107
B2169

LOC/G
TOP/EX
MUNIC
PWR

B63

BONINI C.P.,SIMULATION OF INFORMATION AND DECISION
SYSTEMS IN THE FIRM. MARKET BUDGET DOMIN EDU/PROP
ADMIN COST ATTIT HABITAT PERCEPT PWR...CONCPT
PROBABIL QUANT PREDICT HYPO/EXP BIBLIOG. PAGE 13
B0273

INDUS
SIMUL
DECISION
MGT

B63

NORTH R.C.,CONTENT ANALYSIS: A HANDBOOK WITH
APPLICATIONS FOR THE STUDY OF INTERNATIONAL CRISIS.
ASIA COM EUR+WWI MOD/EUR INT/ORG TEC/DEV DOMIN
EDU/PROP ROUTINE COERCE PERCEPT RIGID/FLEX ALL/VALS
...QUANT TESTS CON/ANAL SIMUL GEN/LAWS VAL/FREE.
PAGE 79 B1591

METH/CNCPT
COMPUT/IR
USSR

S63

CLEMHOUT S.,"PRODUCTION FUNCTION ANALYSIS APPLIED
TO THE LEONTIEF SCARCE-FACTOR PARADOX OF
INTERNATIONAL TRADE." EUR+WWI USA+45 DIST/IND NAT/G
PLAN TEC/DEV DIPLOM PWR WEALTH...MGT METH/CNCPT
CONT/OBS CON/ANAL CHARTS SIMUL GEN/LAWS 20. PAGE 21
B0436

ECO/DEV
ECO/TAC

B64

CAPLOW T.,PRINCIPLES OF ORGANIZATION. UNIV CULTURE
STRUCT CREATE INGP/REL UTOPIA...GEN/LAWS TIME.
PAGE 18 B0374

VOL/ASSN
CONCPT
SIMUL
EX/STRUC
B64

GORE W.J.,ADMINISTRATIVE DECISION-MAKING* A
HEURISTIC MODEL. EX/STRUC ADMIN LEAD ROUTINE
PERS/REL...METH/CNCPT ORG/CHARTS. PAGE 41 B0834

DECISION
MGT
SIMUL
GEN/METH
B64

MAYER C.S.,INTERVIEWING COSTS IN SURVEY RESEARCH.
USA+45 PLAN COST...MGT REC/INT SAMP METH/COMP
HYPO/EXP METH 20. PAGE 71 B1434

SIMUL
INT
R+D
EFFICIENCY
B65

BOGUSLAW R.,THE NEW UTOPIANS. OP/RES ADMIN CONTROL
PWR...IDEA/COMP SIMUL 20. PAGE 13 B0265

UTOPIA
AUTOMAT
COMPUTER
PLAN
B65

EAST J.P.,COUNCIL-MANAGER GOVERNMENT: THE POLITICAL
THOUGHT OF ITS FOUNDER, RICHARD S. CHILDS. USA+45
CREATE ADMIN CHOOSE...BIOG GEN/LAWS BIBLIOG 20

SIMUL
LOC/G
MUNIC

CHILDS/RS CITY/MGT. PAGE 32 B0642

EX/STRUC
B65

SINGER J.D.,HUMAN BEHAVIOR AND INTERNATINAL
POLITICS* CONTRIBUTIONS FROM THE SOCIAL-
PSYCHOLOGICAL SCIENCES. ACT/RES PLAN EDU/PROP ADMIN
KNOWL...DECISION PSY SOC NET/THEORY HYPO/EXP
LAB/EXP SOC/EXP GEN/METH ANTHOL BIBLIOG. PAGE 97
B1965

DIPLOM
PHIL/SCI
QUANT
SIMUL

B65

VEINOTT A.F. JR.,MATHEMATICAL STUDIES IN MANAGEMENT
SCIENCE. UNIV INDUS COMPUTER ADMIN...DECISION
NET/THEORY SIMUL 20. PAGE 112 B2257

MATH
MGT
PLAN
PRODUC
L65

LASSWELL H.D.,"THE POLICY SCIENCES OF DEVELOPMENT."
CULTURE SOCIETY EX/STRUC CREATE ADMIN ATTIT KNOWL
...SOC CONCPT SIMUL GEN/METH. PAGE 63 B1273

PWR
METH/CNCPT
DIPLOM
S65

GRENIEWSKI H.,"INTENTION AND PERFORMANCE: A PRIMER
OF CYBERNETICS OF PLANNING." EFFICIENCY OPTIMAL
KNOWL SKILL...DECISION MGT EQULIB. PAGE 43 B0873

SIMUL
GAME
GEN/METH
PLAN
B66

DAVIS R.G.,PLANNING HUMAN RESOURCE DEVELOPMENT,
EDUCATIONAL MODELS AND SCHEMATA. WORKER OP/RES
ECO/TAC EDU/PROP CONTROL COST PRODUC...GEOG STAT
CHARTS 20. PAGE 27 B0544

PLAN
EFFICIENCY
SIMUL
ROUTINE
B66

FABRYCKY W.J.,OPERATIONS ECONOMY INDUSTRIAL
APPLICATIONS OF OPERATIONS RESEARCH. INDUS PLAN
ECO/TAC PRODUC...MATH PROBABIL STAT CHARTS 20.
PAGE 34 B0695

OP/RES
MGT
SIMUL
DECISION
B66

FOX K.A.,THE THEORY OF QUANTITATIVE ECONOMIC POLICY
WITH APPLICATIONS TO ECONOMIC GROWTH AND
STABILIZATION. ECO/DEV AGRI NAT/G PLAN ADMIN RISK
...DECISION IDEA/COMP SIMUL T. PAGE 37 B0746

ECO/TAC
ECOMETRIC
EQUILIB
GEN/LAWS
B66

YOUNG S.,MANAGEMENT: A SYSTEMS ANALYSIS. DELIB/GP
EX/STRUC ECO/TAC CONTROL EFFICIENCY...NET/THEORY
20. PAGE 119 B2394

PROB/SOLV
MGT
DECISION
SIMUL
B67

IANNACCONE L.,POLITICS IN EDUCATION. USA+45 LOC/G
PROF/ORG BAL/PWR ADMIN...CHARTS SIMUL. PAGE 53
B1072

EDU/PROP
GEN/LAWS
PROVS
S67

BURKE E.M.,"THE SEARCH FOR AUTHORITY IN PLANNING."
MUNIC NEIGH CREATE PROB/SOLV LEGIT ADMIN CONTROL
EFFICIENCY PWR...METH/COMP SIMUL 20. PAGE 17 B0352

DECISION
PLAN
LOC/G
METH
S67

DROR Y.,"POLICY ANALYSTS." USA+45 COMPUTER OP/RES
ECO/TAC ADMIN ROUTINE...ECOMETRIC METH/COMP SIMUL
20. PAGE 30 B0618

NAT/G
POLICY
PLAN
DECISION
S67

HAIRE M.,"MANAGING MANAGEMENT MANPOWER." EX/STRUC
OP/RES PAY EDU/PROP COST EFFICIENCY...PREDICT SIMUL
20. PAGE 45 B0920

MGT
EXEC
LEAD
INDUS
N67

US SUPERINTENDENT OF DOCUMENTS,SPACE: MISSILES, THE
MOON, NASA, AND SATELLITES (PRICE LIST 79A). USA+45
COM/IND R+D NAT/G DIPLOM EDU/PROP ADMIN CONTROL
HEALTH...POLICY SIMUL NASA CONGRESS. PAGE 111 B2244

BIBLIOG/A
SPACE
TEC/DEV
PEACE

SIMULATION....SEE SIMUL, MODELS INDEX

SINAI....SINAI

SIND....SIND - REGION OF PAKISTAN

SINGAPORE....SINGAPORE; SEE ALSO MALAYSIA

B67

MILNE R.S.,GOVERNMENT AND POLITICS IN MALAYSIA.
INDONESIA MALAYSIA LOC/G EX/STRUC FORCES DIPLOM
GP/REL 20 SINGAPORE. PAGE 74 B1489

NAT/G
LEGIS
ADMIN

SINGER J.D. B1964,B1965

SINGER K. B1966

SINGER M.R. B1967

SINGH H.L. B1968

SINGH M.M. B1969

SINGTON D. B1970

SINHA H.N. B1971

SINO/SOV....SINO-SOVIET RELATIONSHIPS

SINO-SOVIET RELATIONS....SEE SINO/SOV

SINYAVSK/A....ANDREY SINYAVSKY

SIRS....SALARY INFORMATION RETRIEVAL SYSTEM

SISSON C.H. B1972

SKIDMORE T.E. B1973

SKILL....DEXTERITY

B05
MACHIAVELLI N.,THE ART OF WAR. CHRIST-17C TOP/EX | NAT/G
DRIVE ORD/FREE PWR SKILL...MGT CHARTS. PAGE 67 | FORCES
B1360 | WAR
| ITALY

N19
GRIFFITH W.,THE PUBLIC SERVICE (PAMPHLET). UK LAW | ADMIN
LOC/G NAT/G PARTIC CHOOSE DRIVE ROLE SKILL...CHARTS | EFFICIENCY
20 CIVIL/SERV. PAGE 44 B0880 | EDU/PROP
| GOV/REL

S37
LASSWELL H.D.,"GOVERNMENTAL AND PARTY LEADERS IN | ELITES
FASCIST ITALY." ITALY CRIME SKILL...BIOG CHARTS | FASCISM
GP/COMP 20. PAGE 63 B1266 | ADMIN

B46
WILCOX J.K.,OFFICIAL DEFENSE PUBLICATIONS, | BIBLIOG/A
1941-1945 (NINE VOLS.). USA-45 AGRI INDUS R+D LABOR | WAR
FORCES TEC/DEV EFFICIENCY PRODUC SKILL WEALTH 20. | CIVMIL/REL
PAGE 116 B2347 | ADMIN

B47
BARNARD C.,THE FUNCTIONS OF THE EXECUTIVE. USA+45 | EXEC
ELITES INTELL LEGIT ATTIT DRIVE PERSON SKILL...PSY | EX/STRUC
SOC METH/CNCPT SOC/EXP GEN/METH VAL/FREE 20. PAGE 9 | ROUTINE
B0187

S48
COCH L.,"OVERCOMING RESISTANCE TO CHANGE" (BMR)" | WORKER
USA+45 CONSULT ADMIN ROUTINE GP/REL EFFICIENCY | OP/RES
PRODUC PERCEPT SKILL...CHARTS SOC/EXP 20. PAGE 22 | PROC/MFG
B0441 | RIGID/FLEX

B49
LEPAWSKY A.,ADMINISTRATION. FINAN INDUS LG/CO | ADMIN
SML/CO INGP/REL PERS/REL COST EFFICIENCY OPTIMAL | MGT
SKILL 20. PAGE 64 B1294 | WORKER
| EX/STRUC

B50
MANNHEIM K.,FREEDOM, POWER, AND DEMOCRATIC | TEC/DEV
PLANNING. FUT USSR WOR+45 ELITES INTELL SOCIETY | PLAN
NAT/G EDU/PROP ROUTINE ATTIT DRIVE SUPEGO SKILL | CAP/ISM
...POLICY PSY CONCPT TREND GEN/LAWS 20. PAGE 69 | UK
B1393

B52
DAY E.E.,EDUCATION FOR FREEDOM AND RESPONSIBILITY. | SCHOOL
FUT USA+45 CULTURE CONSULT EDU/PROP ATTIT SKILL | KNOWL
...MGT CONCPT OBS GEN/LAWS COLD/WAR 20. PAGE 27
B0547

S52
BRUEGEL J.W.,"DIE INTERNAZIONALE | VOL/ASSN
GEWERKSCHAFTSBEWEGUNG." COM EUR+WWI USA+45 WOR+45 | LABOR
DELIB/GP EX/STRUC ECO/TAC EDU/PROP ATTIT PWR | TOTALISM
RESPECT SKILL WEALTH WORK 20. PAGE 16 B0330

S52
TAYLOR D.W.,"TWENTY QUESTIONS: EFFICIENCY IN | PROB/SOLV
PROBLEM SOLVING AS A FUNCTION OF SIZE OF GROUP" | EFFICIENCY
WOR+45 CONFER ROUTINE INGP/REL...PSY GP/COMP 20. | SKILL
PAGE 103 B2085 | PERCEPT

S53
CORY R.H. JR.,"FORGING A PUBLIC INFORMATION POLICY | INT/ORG
FOR THE UNITED NATIONS." FUT WOR+45 SOCIETY ADMIN | EDU/PROP
PEACE ATTIT PERSON SKILL...CONCPT 20 UN. PAGE 24 | BAL/PWR
B0486

B55
POOL I.,SATELLITE GENERALS: A STUDY OF MILITARY | FORCES
ELITES IN THE SOVIET SPHERE. ASIA CHINA/COM COM | CHOOSE
CZECHOSLVK FUT HUNGARY POLAND ROMANIA USSR ELITES
STRATA ADMIN ATTIT PWR SKILL...METH/CNCPT BIOG 20.
PAGE 84 B1688

S55
ANGELL R.,"GOVERNMENTS AND PEOPLES AS A FOCI FOR | FUT
PEACE-ORIENTED RESEARCH." WOR+45 CULTURE SOCIETY | SOC
FACE/GP ACT/RES CREATE PLAN DIPLOM EDU/PROP ROUTINE | PEACE
ATTIT PERCEPT SKILL...POLICY CONCPT OBS TREND
GEN/METH 20. PAGE 5 B0110

S55
WEISS R.S.,"A METHOD FOR THE ANALYSIS OF THE | PROF/ORG
STRUCTURE OF COMPLEX ORGANIZATIONS." WOR+45 INDUS | SOC/EXP
LG/CO NAT/G EXEC ROUTINE ORD/FREE PWR SKILL...MGT
PSY SOC NEW/IDEA STAT INT REC/INT STAND/INT CHARTS
WORK. PAGE 115 B2316

S55
WRIGHT Q.,"THE PEACEFUL ADJUSTMENT OF INTERNATIONAL | R+D
RELATIONS: PROBLEMS AND RESEARCH APPROACHES." UNIV | METH/CNCPT
INTELL EDU/PROP ADJUD ROUTINE KNOWL SKILL...INT/LAW | PEACE
JURID PHIL/SCI CLASSIF 20. PAGE 118 B2385

B57
BEAL J.R.,JOHN FOSTER DULLES, A BIOGRAPHY. USA+45 | BIOG
USSR WOR+45 CONSTN INT/ORG NAT/G EX/STRUC LEGIT | DIPLOM
ADMIN NUC/PWR DISPL PERSON ORD/FREE PWR SKILL
...POLICY PSY OBS RECORD COLD/WAR UN 20 DULLES/JF.
PAGE 10 B0200

B57
MEYER P.,ADMINISTRATIVE ORGANIZATION: A COMPARATIVE | ADMIN
STUDY OF THE ORGANIZATION OF PUBLIC ADMINISTRATION. | METH/COMP
DENMARK FRANCE NORWAY SWEDEN UK USA+45 ELITES LOC/G | NAT/G
CONSULT LEGIS ADJUD CONTROL LEAD PWR SKILL | CENTRAL
DECISION. PAGE 73 B1475

B57
MORSTEIN-MARX F.,THE ADMINISTRATIVE STATE: AN | EXEC
INTRODUCTION TO BUREAUCRACY. EUR+WWI FUT MOD/EUR | MGT
USA+45 USA-45 NAT/G CONSULT ADMIN ROUTINE TOTALISM | CAP/ISM
DRIVE SKILL...TREND 19/20. PAGE 76 B1530 | ELITES

B58
CLEMENTS R.V.,MANAGERS - A STUDY OF THEIR CAREERS | MGT
IN INDUSTRY. STRATA INDUS TASK PERSON SKILL 20. | ELITES
PAGE 21 B0435 | EDU/PROP
| TOP/EX

B58
SWEENEY S.B.,EDUCATION FOR ADMINISTRATIVE CAREERS | EDU/PROP
IN GOVERNMENT SERVICE. USA+45 ACADEM CONSULT CREATE | ADMIN
PLAN CONFER SKILL...TREND IDEA/COMP METH 20 | NAT/G
CIVIL/SERV. PAGE 102 B2059 | LOC/G

B58
US HOUSE COMM POST OFFICE,TRAINING OF FEDERAL | LEGIS
EMPLOYEES. USA+45 DIST/IND NAT/G EX/STRUC EDU/PROP | DELIB/GP
CONFER GOV/REL EFFICIENCY SKILL 20 CONGRESS | WORKER
CIVIL/SERV. PAGE 109 B2197 | ADMIN

B59
JANOWITZ M.,SOCIOLOGY AND THE MILITARY | FORCES
ESTABLISHMENT. USA+45 WOR+45 CULTURE SOCIETY | SOC
PROF/ORG CONSULT EX/STRUC PLAN TEC/DEV DIPLOM DOMIN
COERCE DRIVE RIGID/FLEX ORD/FREE PWR SKILL COLD/WAR
20. PAGE 55 B1121

B60
BASS B.M.,LEADERSHIP, PSYCHOLOGY, AND | UNIV
ORGANIZATIONAL BEHAVIOR. DOMIN CHOOSE DRIVE PERSON | FACE/GP
PWR RESPECT SKILL...SOC METH/CNCPT OBS. PAGE 9 | DELIB/GP
B0193 | ROUTINE

B60
LINDSAY K.,EUROPEAN ASSEMBLIES: THE EXPERIMENTAL | VOL/ASSN
PERIOD 1949-1959. EUR+WWI ECO/DEV NAT/G POL/PAR | INT/ORG
LEGIS TOP/EX ACT/RES PLAN ECO/TAC DOMIN LEGIT | REGION
ROUTINE ATTIT DRIVE ORD/FREE PWR SKILL...SOC CONCPT
TREND CHARTS GEN/LAWS VAL/FREE. PAGE 65 B1315

B60
MCGREGOR D.,THE HUMAN SIDE OF ENTERPRISE. USA+45 | MGT
LEAD ROUTINE GP/REL INGP/REL...CONCPT GEN/LAWS 20. | ATTIT
PAGE 72 B1449 | SKILL
| EDU/PROP

B60
MOORE W.E.,LABOR COMMITMENT AND SOCIAL CHANGE IN | LABOR
DEVELOPING AREAS. SOCIETY STRATA ECO/UNDEV MARKET | ORD/FREE
VOL/ASSN WORKER AUTHORIT SKILL...MGT NAT/COMP | ATTIT
SOC/INTEG 20. PAGE 75 B1514 | INDUS

B60
US SENATE COMM. GOVT. OPER.,ORGANIZING FOR NATIONAL | CONSULT
SECURITY. USA+45 USA-45 INTELL STRUCT SML/CO | EXEC
ACT/RES ADMIN ATTIT PERSON PWR SKILL...DECISION 20.
PAGE 111 B2236

S60
MODELSKI G.,"AUSTRALIA AND SEATO." S/ASIA USA+45 | INT/ORG
CULTURE INTELL ECO/DEV NAT/G PLAN DIPLOM ADMIN | ACT/RES
ROUTINE ATTIT SKILL...MGT TIME/SEQ AUSTRAL 20
SEATO. PAGE 74 B1493

B61
MARKMANN C.L.,JOHN F. KENNEDY: A SENSE OF PURPOSE. | CHIEF
USA+45 INTELL FAM CONSULT DELIB/GP LEGIS PERSON | TOP/EX
SKILL 20 KENNEDY/JF EISNHWR/DD ROOSEVLT/F | ADMIN
NEW/FRONTR PRESIDENT. PAGE 69 B1399 | BIOG

S61
BARTLEY H.J.,"COMMAND EXPERIENCE." USA+45 EX/STRUC | CONCPT
FORCES LEGIT ROUTINE SKILL...POLICY OBS HYPO/EXP | TREND
GEN/LAWS 20. PAGE 9 B0191

S61
DEUTSCH K.W.,"A NOTE ON THE APPEARANCE OF WISDOM IN | ADMIN
LARGE BUREAUCRATIC ORGANIZATIONS." ROUTINE PERSON | PROBABIL
KNOWL SKILL...DECISION STAT. PAGE 28 B0577 | PROB/SOLV
| SIMUL

S61
DEVINS J.H.,"THE INITIATIVE." COM USA+45 USA-45 | FORCES
USSR SOCIETY NAT/G ACT/RES CREATE BAL/PWR ROUTINE | CONCPT
COERCE DETER RIGID/FLEX SKILL...STERTYP COLD/WAR | WAR
20. PAGE 29 B0582

B62
JEWELL M.E.,SENATORIAL POLITICS AND FOREIGN POLICY. | USA+45
NAT/G POL/PAR CHIEF DELIB/GP TOP/EX FOR/AID | LEGIS
EDU/PROP ROUTINE ATTIT PWR SKILL...MAJORIT | DIPLOM
METH/CNCPT TIME/SEQ CONGRESS 20 PRESIDENT. PAGE 56
B1138

S62
ALBONETTI A.,"IL SECONDO PROGRAMMA QUINQUENNALE | R+D

1963-67 ED IL BILANCIO RICERCHE ED INVESTIMENTI PER PLAN
IL 1963 DELL'ERATOM." EUR+WWI FUT ITALY WOR+45   NUC/PWR
ECO/DEV SERV/IND INT/ORG TEC/DEV ECO/TAC ATTIT
SKILL WEALTH...MGT TIME/SEQ OEEC 20. PAGE 3 B0069
                                                            S62
LARSON R.L.,"HOW TO DEFINE ADMINISTRATIVE   UNIV
PROBLEMS." ROUTINE PERCEPT KNOWL SKILL...MGT   FACE/GP
METH/CNCPT CHARTS TOT/POP. PAGE 63 B1263   INDUS
                                                    EXEC
                                                            B63
HOWER R.M.,MANAGERS AND SCIENTISTS. EX/STRUC CREATE R+D
ADMIN REPRESENT ATTIT DRIVE ROLE PWR SKILL...SOC   MGT
INT. PAGE 52 B1052   PERS/REL
                                                    INGP/REL
                                                            B63
INTL INST ADMIN SCIENCES,EDUCATION IN PUBLIC   EDU/PROP
ADMINISTRATION: A SYMPOSIUM ON TEACHING METHODS AND METH
MATERIALS. WOR+45 SCHOOL CONSULT CREATE CONFER   ADMIN
SKILL...OBS TREND IDEA/COMP METH/COMP 20. PAGE 54   ACADEM
B1100
                                                            B63
KOGAN N.,THE POLITICS OF ITALIAN FOREIGN POLICY.   NAT/G
EUR+WWI LEGIS DOMIN LEGIT EXEC PWR RESPECT SKILL   ROUTINE
...POLICY DECISION HUM SOC METH/CNCPT OBS INT   DIPLOM
CHARTS 20. PAGE 61 B1227   ITALY
                                                            B63
SIDEY H.,JOHN F. KENNEDY, PRESIDENT. USA+45 INTELL BIOG
FAM CONSULT DELIB/GP LEGIS ADMIN LEAD 20 KENNEDY/JF TOP/EX
PRESIDENT. PAGE 97 B1951   SKILL
                                                    PERSON
                                                            B63
US SENATE COMM APPROPRIATIONS,PERSONNEL   ADMIN
ADMINISTRATION AND OPERATIONS OF AGENCY FOR   FOR/AID
INTERNATIONAL DEVELOPMENT: SPECIAL HEARING. FINAN   EFFICIENCY
LEAD COST UTIL SKILL...CHARTS 20 CONGRESS AID   DIPLOM
CIVIL/SERV. PAGE 109 B2211
                                                            S63
BRZEZINSKI Z.K.,"CINCINNATUS AND THE APPARATCHIK." POL/PAR
COM USA+45 USA-45 ELITES LOC/G NAT/G PROVS CONSULT USSR
LEGIS DOMIN LEGIT EXEC ROUTINE CHOOSE DRIVE PWR
SKILL...CONCPT CHARTS VAL/FREE COLD/WAR 20. PAGE 16
B0334
                                                            S63
COUTY P.,"L'ASSISTANCE POUR LE DEVELOPPEMENT: POINT FINAN
DE VUE SCANDINAVES." EUR+WWI FINLAND FUT SWEDEN   ROUTINE
WOR+45 ECO/DEV ECO/UNDEV COM/IND LABOR NAT/G   FOR/AID
PROF/ORG ACT/RES SKILL WEALTH TOT/POP 20. PAGE 24
B0497
                                                            S63
MEDALIA N.Z.,"POSITION AND PROSPECTS OF   NAT/G
SOCIOLOGISTS IN FEDERAL EMPLOYMENT." USA+45 CONSULT WORKER
PAY SENIOR ADMIN GOV/REL...TREND CHARTS 20   SOC
CIVIL/SERV. PAGE 72 B1460   SKILL
                                                            S63
MODELSKI G.,"STUDY OF ALLIANCES." WOR+45 WOR-45   VOL/ASSN
INT/ORG NAT/G FORCES LEGIT ADMIN CHOOSE ALL/VALS   CON/ANAL
PWR SKILL...INT/LAW CONCPT GEN/LAWS 20 TREATY.   DIPLOM
PAGE 74 B1495
                                                            S63
ROUGEMONT D.,"LES NOUVELLES CHANCES DE L'EUROPE."   ECO/UNDEV
EUR+WWI FUT ECO/DEV INT/ORG NAT/G ACT/RES PLAN   PERCEPT
TEC/DEV EDU/PROP ADMIN COLONIAL FEDERAL ATTIT PWR
SKILL...TREND 20. PAGE 91 B1835
                                                            N63
INTERNATIONAL CITY MGRS ASSN,POST-ENTRY TRAINING IN LOC/G
THE LOCAL PUBLIC SERVICE (PAMPHLET). SCHOOL PLAN   WORKER
PROB/SOLV TEC/DEV ADMIN EFFICIENCY SKILL...POLICY   EDU/PROP
AUD/VIS CHARTS BIBLIOG 20 CITY/MGT. PAGE 54 B1096   METH/COMP
                                                            B64
DIEBOLD J.,BEYOND AUTOMATION: MANAGERIAL PROBLEMS   FUT
OF AN EXPLODING TECHNOLOGY. SOCIETY ECO/DEV CREATE INDUS
ECO/TAC AUTOMAT SKILL...TECHNIC MGT WORK. PAGE 29   PROVS
B0589   NAT/G
                                                            B64
NEUSTADT R.,PRESIDENTIAL POWER. USA+45 CONSTN NAT/G TOP/EX
CHIEF LEGIS CREATE EDU/PROP LEGIT ADMIN EXEC COERCE SKILL
ATTIT PERSON RIGID/FLEX PWR CONGRESS 20 PRESIDENT
TRUMAN/HS EISNHWR/DD. PAGE 78 B1575
                                                            B64
SAYLES L.R.,MANAGERIAL BEHAVIOR: ADMINISTRATION IN CONCPT
COMPLEX ORGANIZATIONS. INDUS LG/CO PROB/SOLV   ADMIN
CONTROL EXEC INGP/REL PERS/REL SKILL...MGT OBS   TOP/EX
PREDICT GEN/LAWS 20. PAGE 93 B1874   EX/STRUC
                                                            S64
CLIGNET R.,"POTENTIAL ELITES IN GHANA AND THE IVORY PWR
COAST: A PRELIMINARY SURVEY." AFR CULTURE ELITES   LEGIT
STRATA KIN NAT/G SECT DOMIN EXEC ORD/FREE RESPECT   IVORY/CST
SKILL...POLICY RELATIV GP/COMP NAT/COMP 20. PAGE 21 GHANA
B0438
                                                            S64
KHAN M.Z.,"THE PRESIDENT OF THE GENERAL ASSEMBLY." INT/ORG
WOR+45 CONSTN DELIB/GP EDU/PROP LEGIT ROUTINE PWR   TOP/EX
RESPECT SKILL...DECISION SOC BIOG TREND UN 20.
PAGE 59 B1202
                                                            L65
WILLIAMS S.,"NEGOTIATING INVESTMENT IN EMERGING   FINAN

COUNTRIES." USA+45 WOR+45 INDUS MARKET NAT/G TOP/EX ECO/UNDEV
TEC/DEV CAP/ISM ECO/TAC ADMIN SKILL WEALTH...POLICY
RELATIV MGT WORK 20. PAGE 117 B2353
                                                            S65
GRENIEWSKI H.,"INTENTION AND PERFORMANCE: A PRIMER SIMUL
OF CYBERNETICS OF PLANNING." EFFICIENCY OPTIMAL   GAME
KNOWL SKILL...DECISION MGT EQULIB. PAGE 43 B0873   GEN/METH
                                                    PLAN
                                                            S65
HAMILTON R.F.,"SKILL LEVEL AND POLITICS." USA+45   SKILL
CULTURE STRATA STRUCT LABOR CONSERVE NEW/LIB.   ADMIN
PAGE 46 B0933
                                                            B66
BROWN R.E.,JUDGMENT IN ADMINISTRATION. DRIVE PERSON ADMIN
KNOWL...DECISION 20. PAGE 16 B0326   EXEC
                                                    SKILL
                                                    PROB/SOLV
                                                            B66
VON HOFFMAN N.,THE MULTIVERSITY; A PERSONAL REPORT EDU/PROP
ON WHAT HAPPENS TO TODAY'S STUDENTS AT AMERICAN   ACADEM
UNIVERSITIES. USA+45 SOCIETY ROUTINE ANOMIE ROLE   ATTIT
MORAL ORD/FREE SKILL...INT 20. PAGE 112 B2266   STRANGE
                                                            B67
BRAYMAN H.,CORPORATE MANAGEMENT IN A WORLD OF   MGT
POLITICS. USA+45 ELITES MARKET CREATE BARGAIN   ECO/DEV
DIPLOM INT/TRADE ATTIT SKILL 20. PAGE 15 B0302   CAP/ISM
                                                    INDUS
                                                            B67
GABRIEL P.P.,THE INTERNATIONAL TRANSFER OF   ECO/UNDEV
CORPORATE SKILLS: MANAGEMENT CONTRACTS IN LESS   AGREE
DEVELOPED COUNTRIES. CLIENT INDUS LG/CO PLAN   MGT
PROB/SOLV CAP/ISM ECO/TAC FOR/AID INT/TRADE RENT   CONSULT
ADMIN SKILL 20. PAGE 38 B0771

SKINNER G.W. B1974

SKOLNICK J.H. B1975

SKOLNIKOFF E.B. B1976

SKRABUT P.A. B0772

SKRIVANEK M.S. B0702

SLAV/MACED....SLAVO-MACEDONIANS

SLAVERY....SEE ORD/FREE, DOMIN

SLAVS....SLAVS - PERTAINING TO THE SLAVIC PEOPLE AND
    SLAVOPHILISM

SLEEP....SLEEPING AND FATIGUE

SLESSER H. B1977

SLICHTER S.H. B1978

SLUMS....SLUMS

SMALL BUSINESS ADMINISTRATION....SEE SBA

SMIGEL E.O. B1979

SMITH C. B1980

SMITH H.E. B1981

SMITH J.M. B0489,B0490,B0492

SMITH L. B1982

SMITH M.G. B1983

SMITH R.M. B1984

SMITH T.E. B1985

SMITH W.H.T. B1986

SMITH/ACT....SMITH ACT

SMITH/ADAM....ADAM SMITH

SMITH/ALF....ALFRED E. SMITH

SMITH/IAN....IAN SMITH

SMITH/JOS....JOSEPH SMITH

SMITH/LEVR....SMITH-LEVER ACT

SMITHBURG D.W. B1957

SMITHIES A. B1987

SML/CO....SMALL COMPANY

PERSONNEL ADMINISTRATION: THE JOURNAL OF THE
SOCIETY FOR PERSONNEL ADMINISTRATION. USA+45 INDUS
LG/CO SML/CO...BIBLIOG/A 20. PAGE 2 B0028
> N
> WORKER
> MGT
> ADMIN
> EX/STRUC

BUREAU OF NAT'L AFFAIRS INC.,A CURRENT LOOK AT:
(1) THE NEGRO AND TITLE VII, (2) SEX AND TITLE VII
(PAMPHLET). LAW LG/CO SML/CO RACE/REL...POLICY SOC
STAT DEEP/QU TREND CON/ANAL CHARTS 20 NEGRO
CIV/RIGHTS. PAGE 17 B0350
> N19
> DISCRIM
> SEX
> WORKER
> MGT

BIENSTOCK G.,MANAGEMENT IN RUSSIAN INDUSTRY AND
AGRICULTURE. USSR CONSULT WORKER LEAD COST PROFIT
ATTIT DRIVE PWR...MGT METH/COMP DICTIONARY 20.
PAGE 12 B0236
> B44
> ADMIN
> MARXISM
> SML/CO
> AGRI

WHITEHEAD T.N.,LEADERSHIP IN A FREE SOCIETY; A
STUDY IN HUMAN RELATIONS BASED ON AN ANALYSIS OF
PRESENT-DAY INDUSTRIAL CIVILIZATION. WOR-45 STRUCT
R+D LABOR LG/CO SML/CO WORKER PLAN PROB/SOLV
TEC/DEV DRIVE...MGT 20. PAGE 116 B2341
> B47
> INDUS
> LEAD
> ORD/FREE
> SOCIETY

LEPAWSKY A.,ADMINISTRATION. FINAN INDUS LG/CO
SML/CO INGP/REL PERS/REL COST EFFICIENCY OPTIMAL
SKILL 20. PAGE 64 B1294
> B49
> ADMIN
> MGT
> WORKER
> EX/STRUC

WRIGHT J.H.,PUBLIC RELATIONS IN MANAGEMENT. USA+45
USA-45 ECO/DEV LG/CO SML/CO CONSULT EXEC TASK
PROFIT ATTIT ROLE 20. PAGE 118 B2382
> B49
> MGT
> PLAN
> EDU/PROP
> PARTIC

TANNENBAUM R.,"PARTICIPATION BY SUBORDINATES IN THE
MANAGERIAL DECISIONMAKING PROCESS" (BMR)" WOR+45
INDUS SML/CO WORKER INGP/REL...CONCPT GEN/LAWS 20.
PAGE 103 B2074
> S50
> PARTIC
> DECISION
> MGT
> LG/CO

SIMON H.A.,"PUBLIC ADMINISTRATION." LG/CO SML/CO
PLAN DOMIN LEAD GP/REL DRIVE PERCEPT ALL/VALS
...POLICY BIBLIOG/A 20. PAGE 97 B1957
> C50
> MGT
> ADMIN
> DECISION
> EX/STRUC

BUNZEL J.H.,"THE GENERAL IDEOLOGY OF AMERICAN SMALL
BUSINESS"(BMR)" USA+45 USA-45 AGRI GP/REL INGP/REL
PERSON...MGT IDEA/COMP 18/20. PAGE 17 B0345
> S55
> ALL/IDEOS
> ATTIT
> SML/CO
> INDUS

FAYERWEATHER J.,THE EXECUTIVE OVERSEAS:
ADMINISTRATIVE ATTITUDES AND RELATIONSHIPS IN A
FOREIGN CULTURE. USA+45 WOR+45 CULTURE LG/CO SML/CO
ATTIT...MGT PERS/COMP 20 MEXIC/AMER. PAGE 35 B0709
> B59
> INT/TRADE
> TOP/EX
> NAT/COMP
> PERS/REL

UDY S.H. JR.,"'BUREAUCRACY' AND 'RATIONALITY' IN
WEBER'S ORGANIZATION THEORY: AN EMPIRICAL STUDY"
(BMR)" UNIV STRUCT INDUS LG/CO SML/CO VOL/ASSN
...SOC SIMUL 20 WEBER/MAX BUREAUCRCY. PAGE 106
B2144
> S59
> GEN/LAWS
> METH/CNCPT
> ADMIN
> RATIONAL

US SENATE COMM. GOVT. OPER.,ORGANIZING FOR NATIONAL
SECURITY. USA+45 USA-45 INTELL STRUCT SML/CO
ACT/RES ADMIN ATTIT PERSON PWR SKILL...DECISION 20.
PAGE 111 B2236
> B60
> CONSULT
> EXEC

AMERICAN MANAGEMENT ASSN,SUPERIOR-SUBORDINATE
COMMUNICATION IN MANAGEMENT. STRATA FINAN INDUS
SML/CO WORKER CONTROL EXEC ATTIT 20. PAGE 4 B0086
> B61
> MGT
> ACT/RES
> PERS/REL
> LG/CO

GRANICK D.,THE EUROPEAN EXECUTIVE. BELGIUM FRANCE
GERMANY/W UK INDUS LABOR LG/CO SML/CO EX/STRUC PLAN
TEC/DEV CAP/ISM COST DEMAND...POLICY CHARTS 20.
PAGE 42 B0852
> B62
> MGT
> ECO/DEV
> ECO/TAC
> EXEC

HARGROVE M.M.,BUSINESS POLICY CASES-WITH BEHAVIORAL
SCIENCE IMPLICATIONS. LG/CO SML/CO EX/STRUC TOP/EX
PLAN PROB/SOLV CONFER ADMIN CONTROL ROUTINE
EFFICIENCY. PAGE 47 B0946
> B63
> SOC/EXP
> INDUS
> DECISION
> MGT

SMUTS/JAN....JAN CHRISTIAN SMUTS

DAY P.,CRISIS IN SOUTH AFRICA. SOUTH/AFR UK KIN
MUNIC ECO/TAC RECEIVE 20 SMUTS/JAN MIGRATION.
PAGE 27 B0548
> B48
> RACE/REL
> COLONIAL
> ADMIN
> EXTR/IND

SNCC....STUDENT NONVIOLENT COORDINATING COMMITTEE; SEE ALSO
   STUDNT/PWR

SNIDER C.F. B1988,B1989

SNOWISS L.M. B1990

SNYDER F.G. B1991

SNYDER O.H. B1890

SNYDER R.C. B1992

SOC....SOCIOLOGY

AUSTRALIAN NATIONAL RES COUN,AUSTRALIAN SOCIAL
SCIENCE ABSTRACTS. NEW/ZEALND CULTURE SOCIETY LOC/G
CT/SYS PARL/PROC...HEAL JURID PSY SOC 20 AUSTRAL.
PAGE 7 B0149
> N
> BIBLIOG/A
> POLICY
> NAT/G
> ADMIN

CONOVER H.F.,MADAGASCAR: A SELECTED LIST OF
REFERENCES. MADAGASCAR STRUCT ECO/UNDEV NAT/G ADMIN
...SOC 19/20. PAGE 23 B0463
> N
> BIBLIOG/A
> SOCIETY
> CULTURE
> COLONIAL

SOVIET-EAST EUROPEAN RES SERV,SOVIET SOCIETY. USSR
LABOR POL/PAR PRESS MARXISM...MARXIST 20. PAGE 99
B2001
> N
> BIBLIOG/A
> EDU/PROP
> ADMIN
> SOC

WEIGLEY R.F.,HISTORY OF THE UNITED STATES ARMY.
USA+45 USA-45 SOCIETY NAT/G LEAD WAR GP/REL PWR
...SOC METH/COMP COLD/WAR. PAGE 115 B2312
> N
> FORCES
> ADMIN
> ROLE
> CIVMIL/REL

WELLS A.J.,THE BRITISH NATIONAL BIBLIOGRAPHY
CUMULATED SUBJECT CATALOGUE, 1951-1954. UK WOR+45
LAW ADMIN LEAD...HUM SOC 20. PAGE 115 B2320
> N
> BIBLIOG
> NAT/G

DEUTSCHE BIBLIOTH FRANKF A M,DEUTSCHE
BIBLIOGRAPHIE. EUR+WWI GERMANY ECO/DEV FORCES
DIPLOM LEAD...POLICY PHIL/SCI SOC 20. PAGE 28 B0578
> B
> BIBLIOG
> LAW
> ADMIN
> NAT/G

BIBLIO, CATALOGUE DES OUVRAGES PARUS EN LANGUE
FRANCAISE DANS LE MONDE ENTIER. FRANCE WOR+45 ADMIN
LEAD PERSON...SOC 20. PAGE 1 B0008
> N
> BIBLIOG
> NAT/G
> DIPLOM
> ECO/DEV

WHITAKER'S CUMULATIVE BOOKLIST. UK ADMIN...HUM SOC
20. PAGE 1 B0009
> N
> BIBLIOG/A
> WRITING
> CON/ANAL

BULLETIN OF THE PUBLIC AFFAIRS INFORMATION SERVICE.
WOR+45 WOR-45 ECO/UNDEV FINAN LABOR LOC/G PROVS
TEC/DEV DIPLOM EDU/PROP SOC. PAGE 1 B0010
> N
> BIBLIOG
> NAT/G
> ECO/DEV
> ADMIN

CUMULATIVE BOOK INDEX. WOR+45 WOR-45 ADMIN PERSON
ALL/VALS ALL/IDEOS...HUM PHIL/SCI SOC LING 19/20.
PAGE 1 B0012
> N
> INDEX
> NAT/G
> DIPLOM

HANDBOOK OF LATIN AMERICAN STUDIES. LAW CULTURE
ECO/UNDEV POL/PAR ADMIN LEAD...SOC 20. PAGE 1 B0014
> N
> BIBLIOG/A
> L/A+17C
> NAT/G
> DIPLOM

LOCAL GOVERNMENT SERVICE....SOC BIBLIOG/A 20.
PAGE 1 B0016
> N
> LOC/G
> ADMIN
> MUNIC
> GOV/REL

PUBLISHERS' TRADE LIST ANNUAL. LAW POL/PAR ADMIN
PERSON ALL/IDEOS...HUM SOC 19/20. PAGE 1 B0020
> N
> BIBLIOG
> NAT/G
> DIPLOM
> POLICY

READERS GUIDE TO PERIODICAL LITERATURE. WOR+45
WOR-45 LAW ADMIN ATTIT PERSON...HUM PSY SOC 20.
PAGE 1 B0021
> N
> BIBLIOG
> WRITING
> DIPLOM
> NAT/G

SUBJECT GUIDE TO BOOKS IN PRINT: AN INDEX TO THE
PUBLISHERS' TRADE LIST ANNUAL. UNIV LAW LOC/G
DIPLOM WRITING ADMIN LEAD PERSON...MGT SOC. PAGE 1
B0023
> N
> BIBLIOG
> ECO/DEV
> POL/PAR
> NAT/G

THE JAPAN SCIENCE REVIEW: LAW AND POLITICS: LIST OF
BOOKS AND ARTICLES ON LAW AND POLITICS. CONSTN AGRI
INDUS LABOR DIPLOM TAX ADMIN CRIME...INT/LAW SOC 20
CHINJAP. PAGE 1 B0025
> BIBLIOG
> LAW
> S/ASIA
> PHIL/SCI

SUBJECT GUIDE TO BOOKS IN PRINT; AN INDEX TO THE
PUBLISHERS' TRADE LIST ANNUAL. WOR+45 WOR-45 LAW
CULTURE ADMIN LEAD PERSON...HUM MGT SOC. PAGE 2
B0029
> N
> BIBLIOG
> NAT/G
> DIPLOM

DEUTSCHE BUCHEREI,JAHRESVERZEICHNIS DER DEUTSCHEN
HOCHSCHULSCHRIFTEN. EUR+WWI GERMANY LAW ADMIN
PERSON...MGT SOC 19/20. PAGE 28 B0579
> N
> BIBLIOG
> WRITING
> ACADEM
> INTELL

DEUTSCHE BUCHEREI,JAHRESVERZEICHNIS DES DEUTSCHEN
SCHRIFTUMS. AUSTRIA EUR+WWI GERMANY SWITZERLND LAW
> N
> BIBLIOG
> WRITING

LOC/G DIPLOM ADMIN...MGT SOC 19/20. PAGE 29 B0580   NAT/G

N

DEUTSCHE BUCHEREI,DEUTSCHES BUCHERVERZEICHNIS.   BIBLIOG
GERMANY LAW CULTURE POL/PAR ADMIN LEAD ATTIT PERSON NAT/G
...SOC 20. PAGE 29 B0581   DIPLOM
ECO/DEV

N

KYRIAK T.E.,EAST EUROPE: BIBLIOGRAPHY--INDEX TO US   BIBLIOG/A
JPRS RESEARCH TRANSLATIONS. ALBANIA BULGARIA COM   PRESS
CZECHOSLVK HUNGARY POLAND ROMANIA AGRI EXTR/IND   MARXISM
FINAN SERV/IND INT/TRADE WEAPON...GEOG MGT SOC 20.   INDUS
PAGE 62 B1247

N

MINISTERE DE L'EDUC NATIONALE,CATALOGUE DES THESES   BIBLIOG
DE DOCTORAT SOUTENNES DEVANT LES UNIVERSITAIRES   ACADEM
FRANCAISES. FRANCE LAW DIPLOM ADMIN...HUM SOC 20.   KNOWL
PAGE 74 B1490   NAT/G

N19

BOHLKE R.H.,BUREAUCRATS AND INTELLECTUALS: A   PERSON
CRITIQUE OF C. WRIGHT MILLS (PAMPHLET). ADMIN   SOC
SOCISM. PAGE 13 B0266   ELITES
ACADEM

N19

BUREAU OF NAT'L AFFAIRS INC.,A CURRENT LOOK AT: DISCRIM
(1) THE NEGRO AND TITLE VII, (2) SEX AND TITLE VII   SEX
(PAMPHLET). LAW LG/CO SML/CO RACE/REL...POLICY SOC   WORKER
STAT DEEP/QU TREND CON/ANAL CHARTS 20 NEGRO   MGT
CIV/RIGHTS. PAGE 17 B0350

B20

HALDANE R.B.,BEFORE THE WAR. MOD/EUR SOCIETY   POLICY
INT/ORG NAT/G DELIB/GP PLAN DOMIN EDU/PROP LEGIT   DIPLOM
ADMIN COERCE ATTIT DRIVE MORAL ORD/FREE PWR...SOC   UK
CONCPT SELF/OBS RECORD BIOG TIME/SEQ. PAGE 45 B0921

B24

MERRIAM C.E.,A HISTORY OF POLITICAL THEORIES -   UNIV
RECENT TIMES. USA-45 WOR-45 CULTURE SOCIETY ECO/DEV   INTELL
R+D EDU/PROP ROUTINE CHOOSE ATTIT PERSON ALL/VALS
...POLICY SOC CONCPT METH/CNCPT OBS HIST/WRIT
TIME/SEQ TREND. PAGE 73 B1471

B25

THOMAS F.,THE ENVIRONMENTAL BASIS OF SOCIETY.   SOCIETY
USA-45 WOR-45 STRATA ECO/DEV EXTR/IND CONSULT   GEOG
ECO/TAC ROUTINE ATTIT ALL/VALS...SOC TIME/SEQ.
PAGE 104 B2098

B26

MOON P.T.,IMPERIALISM AND WORLD POLITICS. AFR ASIA   WEALTH
ISLAM MOD/EUR S/ASIA USA-45 SOCIETY NAT/G EX/STRUC   TIME/SEQ
BAL/PWR DOMIN COLONIAL NAT/LISM ATTIT DRIVE PWR   CAP/ISM
...GEOG SOC 20. PAGE 75 B1510   DIPLOM

B28

HALL W.P.,EMPIRE TO COMMONWEALTH. FUT WOR-45 CONSTN   VOL/ASSN
ECO/DEV ECO/UNDEV INT/ORG PROVS PLAN DIPLOM   NAT/G
EDU/PROP ADMIN COLONIAL PEACE PERSON ALL/VALS   UK
...POLICY GEOG SOC OBS RECORD TREND CMN/WLTH
PARLIAMENT 19/20. PAGE 46 B0925

B28

SOROKIN P.,CONTEMPORARY SOCIOLOGICAL THEORIES.   CULTURE
MOD/EUR UNIV SOCIETY R+D SCHOOL ECO/TAC EDU/PROP   SOC
ROUTINE ATTIT DRIVE...PSY CONCPT TIME/SEQ TREND   WAR
GEN/LAWS 20. PAGE 99 B1997

B29

BUELL R.,INTERNATIONAL RELATIONS. WOR+45 WOR-45   INT/ORG
CONSTN STRATA FORCES TOP/EX ADMIN ATTIT DRIVE   BAL/PWR
SUPEGO MORAL ORD/FREE PWR SOVEREIGN...JURID SOC   DIPLOM
CONCPT 20. PAGE 17 B0340

B37

ROBBINS L.,ECONOMIC PLANNING AND INTERNATIONAL   INT/ORG
ORDER. WOR-45 SOCIETY FINAN INDUS NAT/G ECO/TAC   PLAN
ROUTINE WEALTH...SOC TIME/SEQ GEN/METH WORK 20   INT/TRADE
KEYNES/JM. PAGE 89 B1791

B38

LANGE O.,ON THE ECONOMIC THEORY OF SOCIALISM. UNIV   MARKET
ECO/DEV FINAN INDUS INT/ORG PUB/INST ROUTINE ATTIT   ECO/TAC
ALL/VALS...SOC CONCPT STAT TREND 20. PAGE 62 B1258   INT/TRADE
SOCISM

B38

PETTEE G.S.,THE PROCESS OF REVOLUTION. COM FRANCE   COERCE
ITALY MOD/EUR RUSSIA SPAIN WOR-45 ELITES INTELL   CONCPT
SOCIETY STRATA STRUCT INT/ORG NAT/G POL/PAR ACT/RES   REV
PLAN EDU/PROP LEGIT EXEC...SOC MYTH TIME/SEQ
TOT/POP 18/20. PAGE 82 B1664

B38

RAPPARD W.E.,THE CRISIS OF DEMOCRACY. EUR+WWI UNIV   NAT/G
WOR-45 CULTURE SOCIETY ECO/DEV INT/ORG POL/PAR   CONCPT
ACT/RES EDU/PROP EXEC CHOOSE ATTIT ALL/VALS...SOC
OBS HIST/WRIT TIME/SEQ LEAGUE/NAT NAZI TOT/POP 20.
PAGE 86 B1741

B39

MCCAMY J.L.,GOVERNMENT PUBLICITY: ITS PRACTICE IN   EDU/PROP
FEDERAL ADMINISTRATION. USA-45 COM/IND ADMIN   NAT/G
CONTROL EXEC PARTIC INGP/REL...SOC 20. PAGE 71   PLAN
B1442   ATTIT

S41

ABEL T.,"THE ELEMENT OF DECISION IN THE PATTERN OF   TEC/DEV
WAR." EUR+WWI FUT NAT/G TOP/EX DIPLOM ROUTINE   FORCES
COERCE DISPL PERCEPT PWR...SOC METH/CNCPT HIST/WRIT   WAR

TREND GEN/LAWS 20. PAGE 2 B0051

B42

JONES V.,METROPOLITAN GOVERNMENT. HABITAT ALL/VALS   LOC/G
...MGT SOC CHARTS. PAGE 57 B1151   MUNIC
ADMIN
TECHRACY

S43

SELZNICK P.,"AN APPROACH TO A THEORY OF   ROUTINE
BUREAUCRACY." INDUS WORKER CONTROL LEAD EFFICIENCY   ADMIN
OPTIMAL...SOC METH 20 BARNARD/C BUREAUCRCY   MGT
WEBER/MAX FRIEDRCH/C MICHELS/R. PAGE 95 B1928   EX/STRUC

B44

DAHL D.,SICKNESS BENEFITS AND GROUP PURCHASE OF   BIBLIOG/A
MEDICAL CARE FOR INDUSTRIAL EMPLOYEES. FAM LABOR   INDUS
NAT/G PLAN...POLICY MGT SOC STAT 20. PAGE 25 B0519   WORKER
HEAL

B44

DAVIS H.E.,PIONEERS IN WORLD ORDER. WOR-45 CONSTN   INT/ORG
ECO/TAC DOMIN EDU/PROP LEGIT ADJUD ADMIN ARMS/CONT   ROUTINE
CHOOSE KNOWL ORD/FREE...POLICY JURID SOC STAT OBS
CENSUS TIME/SEQ ANTHOL LEAGUE/NAT 20. PAGE 26 B0537

L44

HAILEY,"THE FUTURE OF COLONIAL PEOPLES." WOR-45   PLAN
CONSTN CULTURE ECO/UNDEV AGRI MARKET INT/ORG NAT/G   CONCPT
SECT CONSULT ECO/TAC LEGIT ADMIN NAT/LISM ALL/VALS   DIPLOM
...SOC OBS TREND STERTYP CMN/WLTH LEAGUE/NAT   UK
PARLIAMENT 20. PAGE 45 B0916

S44

GRIFFITH E.S.,"THE CHANGING PATTERN OF PUBLIC   LAW
POLICY FORMATION." MOD/EUR WOR+45 FINAN CHIEF   POLICY
CONFER ADMIN LEAD CONSERVE SOCISM TECHRACY...SOC   TEC/DEV
CHARTS CONGRESS. PAGE 43 B0877

B45

BENJAMIN H.C.,EMPLOYMENT TESTS IN INDUSTRY AND   BIBLIOG/A
BUSINESS. LG/CO WORKER ROUTINE...MGT PSY SOC   METH
CLASSIF PROBABIL STAT APT/TEST KNO/TEST PERS/TEST   TESTS
20. PAGE 10 B0211   INDUS

C45

MCDIARMID J.,"THE MOBILIZATION OF SOCIAL   INTELL
SCIENTISTS," IN L. WHITE'S CIVIL CIVIL SERVICE IN   WAR
WARTIME." USA-45 TEC/DEV CENTRAL...SOC 20   DELIB/GP
CIVIL/SERV. PAGE 72 B1447   ADMIN

B46

BIBLIOGRAFIIA DISSERTATSII: DOKTORSKIE DISSERTATSII   BIBLIOG
ZA 19411944 (2 VOLS.). COM USSR LAW POL/PAR DIPLOM   ACADEM
ADMIN LEAD...PHIL/SCI SOC 20. PAGE 2 B0035   KNOWL
MARXIST

B47

BARNARD C.,THE FUNCTIONS OF THE EXECUTIVE. USA+45   EXEC
ELITES INTELL LEGIT ATTIT DRIVE PERSON SKILL...PSY   EX/STRUC
SOC METH/CNCPT SOC/EXP GEN/METH VAL/FREE 20. PAGE 9   ROUTINE
B0187

B47

CONOVER H.F.,NON-SELF-GOVERNING AREAS. BELGIUM   BIBLIOG/A
FRANCE ITALY UK WOR+45 CULTURE ECO/UNDEV INT/ORG   COLONIAL
LOC/G NAT/G ECO/TAC INT/TRADE ADMIN HEALTH...SOC   DIPLOM
UN. PAGE 23 B0465

B47

HIRSHBERG H.S.,SUBJECT GUIDE TO UNITED STATES   BIBLIOG
GOVERNMENT PUBLICATIONS. USA+45 USA-45 LAW ADMIN   NAT/G
...SOC 20. PAGE 50 B1017   DIPLOM
LOC/G

B47

LASSWELL H.D.,THE ANALYSIS OF POLITICAL BEHAVIOUR: R+D
AN EMPIRICAL APPROACH. WOR+45 CULTURE NAT/G FORCES   ACT/RES
EDU/PROP ADMIN ATTIT PERCEPT KNOWL...PHIL/SCI PSY   ELITES
SOC NEW/IDEA OBS INT GEN/METH NAZI 20. PAGE 63
B1267

B47

WARNER W.L.,THE SOCIAL SYSTEM OF THE MODERN   ROLE
FACTORY; THE STRIKE: AN ANALYSIS. USA-45 STRATA   STRUCT
WORKER ECO/TAC GP/REL INGP/REL...MGT SOC CHARTS 20   LABOR
YANKEE/C. PAGE 114 B2293   PROC/MFG

S47

TURNER R.H.,"THE NAVY DISBURSING OFFICER AS A   FORCES
BUREAUCRAT" (BMR)" USA-45 LAW STRATA DIST/IND WAR   ADMIN
PWR...SOC 20 BUREAUCRCY. PAGE 106 B2140   PERSON
ROLE

B48

MEEK C.K.,COLONIAL LAW; A BIBLIOGRAPHY WITH SPECIAL   COLONIAL
REFERENCE TO NATIVE AFRICAN SYSTEMS OF LAW AND LAND   ADMIN
TENURE. AFR ECO/UNDEV AGRI CT/SYS...JURID SOC 20.   LAW
PAGE 72 B1462   CONSTN

C48

BOLLENS J.C.,"THE PROBLEM OF GOVERNMENT IN THE SAN   USA+45
FRANCISCO BAY REGION." INDUS PROVS ADMIN GOV/REL   MUNIC
...SOC CHARTS BIBLIOG 20. PAGE 13 B0270   LOC/G
PROB/SOLV

B49

BORBA DE MORAES R.,MANUAL BIBLIOGRAFICO DE ESTUDOS   BIBLIOG
BRASILEIROS. BRAZIL DIPLOM ADMIN LEAD...SOC 20.   L/A+17C
PAGE 14 B0276   NAT/G
ECO/UNDEV

B49

DE GRAZIA A.,HUMAN RELATIONS IN PUBLIC   BIBLIOG/A
ADMINISTRATION. INDUS ACT/RES CREATE PLAN PROB/SOLV   ADMIN

TEC/DEV INGP/REL PERS/REL DRIVE...POLICY SOC 20.
PAGE 27 B0552
PHIL/SCI
OP/RES

B49

FORD FOUNDATION,REPORT OF THE STUDY FOR THE FORD
FOUNDATION ON POLICY AND PROGRAM. SOCIETY R+D
ACT/RES CAP/ISM FOR/AID EDU/PROP ADMIN KNOWL
...POLICY PSY SOC 20. PAGE 36 B0739
WEALTH
GEN/LAWS

B49

SINGER K.,THE IDEA OF CONFLICT. UNIV INTELL INT/ORG
NAT/G PLAN ROUTINE ATTIT DRIVE ALL/VALS...POLICY
CONCPT TIME/SEQ. PAGE 97 B1966
ACT/RES
SOC

S49

REISSMAN L.,"A STUDY OF ROLE CONCEPTIONS IN
BUREAUCRACY" (BMR)" PERS/REL ROLE...SOC CONCPT
NEW/IDEA IDEA/COMP SOC/EXP 20 BUREAUCRCY. PAGE 87
B1767
ADMIN
METH/CNCPT
GEN/LAWS
PROB/SOLV

B50

DEES J.W. JR.,URBAN SOCIOLOGY AND THE EMERGING
ATOMIC MEGALOPOLIS, PART I. USA+45 TEC/DEV ADMIN
NUC/PWR HABITAT...SOC AUD/VIS CHARTS GEN/LAWS 20
WATER. PAGE 28 B0568
PLAN
NEIGH
MUNIC
PROB/SOLV

B50

WARD R.E.,A GUIDE TO JAPANESE REFERENCE AND
RESEARCH MATERIALS IN THE FIELD OF POLITICAL
SCIENCE. UNIV LAW CONSTN LOC/G PRESS ADMIN...SOC
CON/ANAL METH 19/20 CHINJAP. PAGE 113 B2289
BIBLIOG/A
ASIA
NAT/G

S50

NEUMANN F.L.,"APPROACHES TO THE STUDY OF POLITICAL
POWER." POL/PAR TOP/EX ADMIN LEAD ATTIT ORD/FREE
CONSERVE LAISSEZ MARXISM...PSY SOC. PAGE 78 B1572
PWR
IDEA/COMP
CONCPT

B51

BERTON P.A.,MANCHURIA: AN ANNOTATED BIBLIOGRAPHY.
ASIA DIST/IND ADMIN...SOC 20. PAGE 11 B0231
BIBLIOG/A
MARXISM
ECO/UNDEV
COLONIAL

B51

GUETZKOW H.,GROUPS, LEADERSHIP, AND MEN. FACE/GP
SECT EDU/PROP EXEC PERSON RESPECT...PERS/TEST
GEN/METH 20. PAGE 44 B0901
ATTIT
SOC
ELITES

B51

LEITES N.,THE OPERATIONAL CODE OF THE POLITBURO.
COM USSR CREATE PLAN LEGIT COERCE ALL/VALS
...SOC CONCPT MYTH TREND CON/ANAL GEN/LAWS 20
LENIN/VI STALIN/J. PAGE 64 B1284
DELIB/GP
ADMIN
SOCISM

B51

MAASS A.,MUDDY WATERS: THE ARMY ENGINEERS AND THE
NATIONS RIVERS. USA-45 PROF/ORG CONSULT LEGIS ADMIN
EXEC ROLE PWR...SOC PRESIDENT 20. PAGE 67 B1353
FORCES
GP/REL
LOBBY
CONSTRUC

S51

INKELES A.,"UNDERSTANDING A FOREIGN SOCIETY: A
SOCIOLOGIST'S VIEW." SOCIETY ROUTINE KNOWL...PSY
CONCPT GEN/METH 20. PAGE 54 B1086
SOC
METH/CNCPT
PERCEPT
ATTIT

S51

LERNER D.,"THE POLICY SCIENCES: RECENT DEVELOPMENTS
IN SCOPE AND METHODS." R+D SERV/IND CREATE DIPLOM
ROUTINE PWR...METH/CNCPT TREND GEN/LAWS METH 20.
PAGE 64 B1297
CONSULT
SOC

S51

SCHRAMM W.,"COMMUNICATION IN THE SOVIETIZED STATE,
AS DEMONSTRATED IN KOREA." ASIA COM KOREA COM/IND
FACE/GP POL/PAR SCHOOL FORCES ADMIN PWR MARXISM
...SOC CONCPT MYTH INT BIOG TOT/POP 20. PAGE 94
B1901
ATTIT
EDU/PROP
TOTALISM

B52

UNESCO,THESES DE SCIENCES SOCIALES: CATALOGUE
ANALYTIQUE INTERNATIONAL DE THESES INEDITES DE
DOCTORAT, 1940-1950. INT/ORG DIPLOM EDU/PROP...GEOG
INT/LAW MGT PSY SOC 20. PAGE 107 B2155
BIBLIOG
ACADEM
WRITING

B53

CALDWELL L.K.,RESEARCH METHODS IN PUBLIC
ADMINISTRATION; AN OUTLINE OF TOPICS AND READINGS
(PAMPHLET). LAW ACT/RES COMPUTER KNOWL...SOC STAT
GEN/METH 20. PAGE 18 B0365
BIBLIOG/A
METH/COMP
ADMIN
OP/RES

B53

GROSS B.M.,THE LEGISLATIVE STRUGGLE: A STUDY IN
SOCIAL COMBAT. STRUCT LOC/G POL/PAR JUDGE EDU/PROP
DEBATE ETIQUET ADMIN LOBBY CHOOSE GOV/REL INGP/REL
HEREDITY ALL/VALS...SOC PRESIDENT. PAGE 44 B0885
LEGIS
DECISION
PERSON
LEAD

B53

PIERCE R.A.,RUSSIAN CENTRAL ASIA, 1867-1917: A
SELECTED BIBLIOGRAPHY (PAMPHLET). USSR LAW CULTURE
NAT/G EDU/PROP WAR...GEOG SOC 19/20. PAGE 83 B1671
BIBLIOG
COLONIAL
ADMIN
COM

B53

WAGLEY C.,AMAZON TOWN: A STUDY OF MAN IN THE
TROPICS. BRAZIL L/A+17C STRATA STRUCT ECO/UNDEV
AGRI EX/STRUC RACE/REL DISCRIM HABITAT WEALTH...OBS
SOC/EXP 20. PAGE 113 B2273
SOC
NEIGH
CULTURE
INGP/REL

B54

ALLPORT G.W.,THE NATURE OF PREJUDICE. USA+45 WOR+45
STRATA FACE/GP KIN NEIGH SECT ADMIN GP/REL DISCRIM
ATTIT DRIVE LOVE RESPECT...PSY SOC MYTH QU/SEMANT
20. PAGE 4 B0078
CULTURE
PERSON
RACE/REL

B54

BENTLEY A.F.,INQUIRY INTO INQUIRIES: ESSAYS IN
SOCIAL THEORY. UNIV LEGIS ADJUD ADMIN LOBBY
...PHIL/SCI PSY NEW/IDEA LING METH 20. PAGE 11
B0220
EPIST
SOC
CONCPT

B54

BIESANZ J.,MODERN SOCIETY: AN INTRODUCTION TO
SOCIAL SCIENCE. COM CONSTN STRUCT FAM MUNIC NAT/G
SECT EX/STRUC LEGIS GP/REL PERSON...SOC 20. PAGE 12
B0237
SOCIETY
PROB/SOLV
CULTURE

B54

COMBS C.H.,DECISION PROCESSES. INTELL SOCIETY
DELIB/GP CREATE TEC/DEV DOMIN LEGIT EXEC CHOOSE
DRIVE RIGID/FLEX KNOWL PWR...PHIL/SCI
METH/CNCPT CONT/OBS REC/INT PERS/TEST SAMP/SIZ BIOG
SOC/EXP WORK. PAGE 22 B0455
MATH
DECISION

B54

DUVERGER M.,POLITICAL PARTIES: THEIR ORGANIZATION
AND ACTIVITY IN THE MODERN STATE. EUR+WWI MOD/EUR
USA+45 USA-45 EDU/PROP ADMIN ROUTINE ATTIT DRIVE
ORD/FREE PWR...SOC CONCPT MATH STAT TIME/SEQ
TOT/POP 19/20. PAGE 31 B0635
POL/PAR
EX/STRUC
ELITES

B54

GOLDNER A.W.,WILDCAT STRIKE. LABOR TEC/DEV PAY
ADMIN LEAD PERS/REL ATTIT RIGID/FLEX PWR...MGT
CONCPT. PAGE 40 B0816
INDUS
WORKER
GP/REL
SOC

B54

MATTHEWS D.R.,THE SOCIAL BACKGROUND OF POLITICAL
DECISION-MAKERS. CULTURE SOCIETY STRATA FAM
EX/STRUC LEAD ATTIT BIO/SOC DRIVE PERSON ALL/VALS
HIST/WRIT. PAGE 71 B1431
DECISION
BIOG
SOC

B54

TOTOK W.,HANDBUCH DER BIBLIOGRAPHISCHEN
NACHSCHLAGEWERKE. GERMANY LAW CULTURE ADMIN...SOC
20. PAGE 105 B2121
BIBLIOG/A
NAT/G
DIPLOM
POLICY

L54

FURNISS E.S.,"WEAKNESSES IN FRENCH FOREIGN POLICY-
MAKING." EUR+WWI LEGIS LEGIT EXEC ATTIT RIGID/FLEX
ORD/FREE...SOC CONCPT METH/CNCPT OBS 20. PAGE 38
B0766
NAT/G
STRUCT
DIPLOM
FRANCE

B55

BEISEL A.R.,CONTROL OVER ILLEGAL ENFORCEMENT OF THE
CRIMINAL LAW: ROLE OF THE SUPREME COURT. CONSTN
ROUTINE MORAL PWR...SOC 20 SUPREME/CT. PAGE 10
B0207
ORD/FREE
LAW
CRIME

B55

RUSTOW D.A.,THE POLITICS OF COMPROMISE. SWEDEN
LABOR EX/STRUC LEGIS PLAN REPRESENT SOCISM...SOC
19/20. PAGE 92 B1859
POL/PAR
NAT/G
POLICY
ECO/TAC

S55

ANGELL R.,"GOVERNMENTS AND PEOPLES AS A FOCI FOR
PEACE-ORIENTED RESEARCH." WOR+45 CULTURE SOCIETY
FACE/GP ACT/RES CREATE PLAN DIPLOM EDU/PROP ROUTINE
ATTIT PERCEPT SKILL...POLICY CONCPT OBS TREND
GEN/METH 20. PAGE 5 B0110
FUT
SOC
PEACE

S55

TERRIEN F.W.,"THE EFFECT OF CHANGING SIZE UPON THE
INTERNAL STRUCTURE OF ORGANIZATIONS" (BMR)" WOR+45
WOR-45 CHARTS. PAGE 103 B2091
SOC
ADMIN
GP/REL
METH

S55

WEISS R.S.,"A METHOD FOR THE ANALYSIS OF THE
STRUCTURE OF COMPLEX ORGANIZATIONS." WOR+45 INDUS
LG/CO NAT/G EXEC ROUTINE ORD/FREE PWR SKILL...MGT
PSY SOC NEW/IDEA STAT INT REC/INT STAND/INT CHARTS
WORK. PAGE 115 B2316
PROF/ORG
SOC/EXP

B56

BLAU P.M.,BUREAUCRACY IN MODERN SOCIETY. STRUCT
INDUS LABOR LG/CO LOC/G NAT/G FORCES EDU/PROP
ROUTINE ORD/FREE 20 BUREAUCRCY. PAGE 12 B0252
SOC
EX/STRUC
ADMIN
EFFICIENCY

B56

GARDNER R.N.,STERLING-DOLLAR DIPLOMACY. EUR+WWI
USA+45 INT/ORG NAT/G PLAN INT/TRADE EDU/PROP ADMIN
KNOWL PWR WEALTH...POLICY SOC METH/CNCPT STAT
CHARTS SIMUL GEN/LAWS 20. PAGE 39 B0781
ECO/DEV
DIPLOM

B56

HICKMAN C.A.,INDIVIDUALS, GROUPS, AND ECONOMIC
BEHAVIOR. WORKER PAY CONTROL EXEC GP/REL INGP/REL
PERSON ROLE...PSY SOC PERS/COMP METH 20. PAGE 50
B1005
MGT
ADMIN
ECO/TAC
PLAN

B56

INTERNATIONAL AFRICAN INST,SELECT ANNOTATED
BIBLIOGRAPHY OF TROPICAL AFRICA. NAT/G EDU/PROP
ADMIN HEALTH. PAGE 54 B1095
BIBLIOG/A
AFR
SOC
HABITAT

B56

MANNONI D.O.,PROSPERO AND CALIBAN: THE PSYCHOLOGY
OF COLONIZATION. AFR EUR+WWI FAM KIN MUNIC SECT
DOMIN ADMIN ATTIT DRIVE LOVE PWR RESPECT...PSY SOC
CONCPT MYTH OBS DEEP/INT BIOG GEN/METH MALAGASY 20.
PAGE 69 B1394
CULTURE
COLONIAL

B56

WASSERMAN P.,INFORMATION FOR ADMINISTRATORS: A
GUIDE TO PUBLICATIONS AND SERVICES FOR MANAGEMENT
IN BUSINESS AND GOVERNMENT. R+D LOC/G NAT/G
PROF/ORG VOL/ASSN PRESS...PSY SOC STAT 20. PAGE 114
B2299
BIBLIOG
MGT
KNOWL
EDU/PROP

B56

WEBER M.,STAATSSOZIOLOGIE. STRUCT LEGIT ADMIN
PARL/PROC SUPEGO CONSERVE JURID. PAGE 114 B2305
SOC
NAT/G
POL/PAR
LEAD

L56

PARSONS T.,"SUGGESTIONS FOR A SOCIOLOGICAL APPROACH
TO THE THEORY OF ORGANIZATIONS - I" (BMR)" FINAN
EX/STRUC LEGIT ALL/VALS...POLICY DECISION 20.
PAGE 81 B1637
SOC
CONCPT
ADMIN
STRUCT

B57

HEATH S.,CITADEL, MARKET, AND ALTAR; EMERGING
SOCIETY. SOCIETY ADMIN OPTIMAL OWN RATIONAL
ORD/FREE...SOC LOG PREDICT GEN/LAWS DICTIONARY 20.
PAGE 49 B0985
NEW/IDEA
STRUCT
UTOPIA
CREATE

B57

KIETH-LUCAS A.,DECISIONS ABOUT PEOPLE IN NEED, A
STUDY OF ADMINISTRATIVE RESPONSIVENESS IN PUBLIC
ASSISTANCE. USA+45 GIVE RECEIVE INGP/REL PERS/REL
MORAL RESPECT WEALTH...SOC OBS BIBLIOG 20. PAGE 60
B1204
ADMIN
RIGID/FLEX
SOC/WK
DECISION

B57

PYE L.W.,THE POLICY IMPLICATIONS OF SOCIAL CHANGE
IN NON-WESTERN SOCIETIES. ASIA USA+45 CULTURE
STRUCT NAT/G ECO/TAC ADMIN ROLE...POLICY SOC.
PAGE 85 B1723
SOCIETY
ORD/FREE
ECO/UNDEV
DIPLOM

B57

SIMON H.A.,MODELS OF MAN, SOCIAL AND RATIONAL:
MATHEMATICAL ESSAYS ON RATIONAL HUMAN BEHAVIOR IN A
SOCIAL SETTING. UNIV LAW SOCIETY FACE/GP VOL/ASSN
CONSULT EX/STRUC LEGIS CREATE ADMIN ROUTINE ATTIT
DRIVE PWR...SOC CONCPT METH/CNCPT QUANT STAT
TOT/POP VAL/FREE 20. PAGE 97 B1959
MATH
SIMUL

B57

SOUTH PACIFIC COMMISSION,INDEX OF SOCIAL SCIENCE
RESEARCH THESES ON THE SOUTH PACIFIC. S/ASIA ACADEM
ADMIN COLONIAL...SOC 20. PAGE 99 B2000
BIBLIOG/A
ACT/RES
SECT
CULTURE

S57

HAILEY,"TOMORROW IN AFRICA." CONSTN SOCIETY LOC/G
NAT/G DOMIN ADJUD ADMIN GP/REL DISCRIM NAT/LISM
ATTIT MORAL ORD/FREE...PSY SOC CONCPT OBS RECORD
TREND GEN/LAWS CMN/WLTH 20. PAGE 45 B0917
AFR
PERSON
ELITES
RACE/REL

B58

BROWNE C.G.,THE CONCEPT OF LEADERSHIP. UNIV FACE/GP
DOMIN EDU/PROP LEGIT LEAD DRIVE PERSON PWR...MGT
SOC OBS SELF/OBS CONT/OBS INT PERS/TEST STERTYP
GEN/LAWS. PAGE 16 B0328
EXEC
CONCPT

B58

COLEMAN J.S.,NIGERIA: BACKGROUND TO NATIONALISM.
AFR SOCIETY ECO/DEV KIN LOC/G POL/PAR TEC/DEV DOMIN
ADMIN DRIVE PWR RESPECT...TRADIT SOC INT SAMP
TIME/SEQ 20. PAGE 22 B0452
NAT/G
NAT/LISM
NIGERIA

B58

DEVLIN P.,THE CRIMINAL PROSECUTION IN ENGLAND. UK
NAT/G ADMIN ROUTINE EFFICIENCY...JURID SOC 20.
PAGE 29 B0583
CRIME
LAW
METH
CT/SYS

B58

ISLAM R.,INTERNATIONAL ECONOMIC COOPERATION AND THE
UNITED NATIONS. FINAN PLAN EXEC TASK WAR PEACE
...SOC METH/CNCPT 20 UN LEAGUE/NAT. PAGE 55 B1105
INT/ORG
DIPLOM
ADMIN

B58

MASON J.B.,THAILAND BIBLIOGRAPHY. S/ASIA THAILAND
CULTURE EDU/PROP ADMIN...GEOG SOC LING 20. PAGE 70
B1423
BIBLIOG/A
ECO/UNDEV
DIPLOM
NAT/G

B58

MILLS C.W.,THE CAUSES OF WORLD WAR THREE. FUT
USA+45 INTELL NAT/G DOMIN EDU/PROP ADMIN WAR ATTIT
SOC. PAGE 74 B1487
CONSULT
PWR
ELITES
PEACE

B58

ORTIZ R.P.,ANNUARIO BIBLIOGRAFICO COLOMBIANO,
1951-1956. LAW RECEIVE EDU/PROP ADMIN...LING STAT
20 COLOMB. PAGE 80 B1617
BIBLIOG
SOC

B58

SKINNER G.W.,LEADERSHIP AND POWER IN THE CHINESE
COMMUNITY OF THAILAND. ASIA S/ASIA STRATA FACE/GP
KIN PROF/ORG VOL/ASSN EX/STRUC DOMIN PERSON RESPECT
...METH/CNCPT STAT INT QU BIOG CHARTS 20. PAGE 98
B1974
SOC
ELITES
THAILAND

B58

UNESCO,UNESCO PUBLICATIONS: CHECK LIST (2ND REV.
ED.). WOR+45 DIPLOM FOR/AID WEALTH...POLICY SOC
UNESCO. PAGE 107 B2156
BIBLIOG
INT/ORG
ECO/UNDEV
ADMIN

B58

UNIVERSITY OF LONDON,THE FAR EAST AND SOUTH-EAST
ASIA: A CUMULATED LIST OF PERIODICAL ARTICLES, MAY
BIBLIOG
SOC

1956-APRIL 1957. ASIA S/ASIA LAW ADMIN...LING 20.
PAGE 107 B2168

B58

WESTIN A.F.,THE ANATOMY OF A CONSTITUTIONAL LAW
CASE. USA+45 LAW LEGIS ADMIN EXEC...DECISION MGT
SOC RECORD 20 SUPREME/CT. PAGE 115 B2326
CT/SYS
INDUS
ADJUD
CONSTN

S58

DAVENPORT J.,"ARMS AND THE WELFARE STATE." INTELL
STRUCT FORCES CREATE ECO/TAC FOR/AID DOMIN LEGIT
ADMIN WAR ORD/FREE PWR...POLICY SOC CONCPT MYTH OBS
TREND COLD/WAR TOT/POP 20. PAGE 26 B0533
USA+45
NAT/G
USSR

S58

DEAN B.V.,"APPLICATION OF OPERATIONS RESEARCH TO
MANAGERIAL DECISION MAKING" STRATA ACT/RES
PROB/SOLV ROLE...SOC PREDICT SIMUL 20. PAGE 28
B0565
DECISION
OP/RES
MGT
METH/CNCPT

S58

MITCHELL W.C.,"OCCUPATIONAL ROLE STRAINS: THE
AMERICAN ELECTIVE PUBLIC OFFICIAL." CONTROL
RIGID/FLEX SUPEGO HEALTH ORD/FREE...SOC INT QU.
PAGE 74 B1492
ANOMIE
DRIVE
ROUTINE
PERSON

C58

REDFORD E.S.,"THE NEVER-ENDING SEARCH FOR THE
PUBLIC INTEREST" IN E. REDFORD, IDEALS AND PRACTICE
IN PUBLIC ADMINISTRATION (BMR)" USA+45 USA-45
SOCIETY PARTIC GP/REL ATTIT PLURISM...DECISION SOC
20. PAGE 87 B1755
LOBBY
POLICY
ADMIN
MAJORIT

B59

DAHRENDORF R.,CLASS AND CLASS CONFLICT IN
INDUSTRIAL SOCIETY. LABOR NAT/G COERCE ROLE PLURISM
...POLICY MGT CONCPT CLASSIF. PAGE 26 B0523
VOL/ASSN
STRUCT
SOC
GP/REL

B59

INTERAMERICAN CULTURAL COUN,LISTA DE LIBROS
REPRESENTAVOS DE AMERICA. CULTURE DIPLOM ADMIN 20.
PAGE 54 B1093
BIBLIOG/A
NAT/G
L/A+17C
SOC

B59

JANOWITZ M.,SOCIOLOGY AND THE MILITARY
ESTABLISHMENT. USA+45 WOR+45 CULTURE SOCIETY
PROF/ORG CONSULT EX/STRUC PLAN TEC/DEV DIPLOM DOMIN
COERCE DRIVE RIGID/FLEX ORD/FREE PWR SKILL COLD/WAR
20. PAGE 55 B1121
FORCES
SOC

B59

PARK R.L.,LEADERSHIP AND POLITICAL INSTITUTIONS IN
INDIA. S/ASIA CULTURE ECO/UNDEV LOC/G MUNIC PROVS
LEGIS PLAN ADMIN LEAD ORD/FREE WEALTH...GEOG SOC
BIOG TOT/POP VAL/FREE 20. PAGE 81 B1633
NAT/G
EXEC
INDIA

B59

SCHURZ W.L.,AMERICAN FOREIGN AFFAIRS: A GUIDE TO
INTERNATIONAL AFFAIRS. USA+45 WOR+45 WOR-45 NAT/G
FORCES LEGIS TOP/EX PLAN EDU/PROP LEGIT ADMIN
ROUTINE ATTIT ORD/FREE PWR...SOC CONCPT STAT
SAMP/SIZ CHARTS STERTYP 20. PAGE 95 B1910
INT/ORG
SOCIETY
DIPLOM

B59

YANG C.K.,A CHINESE VILLAGE IN EARLY COMMUNIST
TRANSITION. ECO/UNDEV AGRI FAM KIN MUNIC FORCES
PLAN ECO/TAC DOMIN EDU/PROP ATTIT DRIVE PWR RESPECT
...SOC CONCPT METH/CNCPT OBS RECORD CON/ANAL CHARTS
WORK 20. PAGE 118 B2389
ASIA
ROUTINE
SOCISM

S59

SUTTON F.X.,"REPRESENTATION AND THE NATURE OF
POLITICAL SYSTEMS." UNIV WOR-45 CULTURE SOCIETY
STRATA INT/ORG FORCES JUDGE DOMIN LEGIT EXEC REGION
REPRESENT ATTIT ORD/FREE RESPECT...SOC HIST/WRIT
TIME/SEQ. PAGE 102 B2057
NAT/G
CONCPT

S59

UDY S.H. JR.,"'BUREAUCRACY' AND 'RATIONALITY' IN
WEBER'S ORGANIZATION THEORY: AN EMPIRICAL STUDY"
(BMR)" UNIV STRUCT INDUS LG/CO SML/CO VOL/ASSN
...SOC SIMUL 20 WEBER/MAX BUREAUCRCY. PAGE 106
B2144
GEN/LAWS
METH/CNCPT
ADMIN
RATIONAL

B60

ANGERS F.A.,ESSAI SUR LA CENTRALISATION: ANALYSE
DES PRINCIPES ET PERSPECTIVES CANADIENNES. CANADA
ECO/TAC CONTROL...SOC IDEA/COMP BIBLIOG 20. PAGE 5
B0111
CENTRAL
ADMIN

B60

BASS B.M.,LEADERSHIP, PSYCHOLOGY, AND
ORGANIZATIONAL BEHAVIOR. DOMIN CHOOSE DRIVE PERSON
PWR RESPECT SKILL...SOC METH/CNCPT OBS. PAGE 9
B0193
UNIV
FACE/GP
DELIB/GP
ROUTINE

B60

BERNSTEIN I.,THE LEAN YEARS. SOCIETY STRATA PARTIC
GP/REL ATTIT...SOC 20 DEPRESSION. PAGE 11 B0227
WORKER
LABOR
WEALTH
MGT

B60

FLORES R.H.,CATALOGO DE TESIS DOCTORALES DE LAS
FACULTADES DE LA UNIVERSIDAD DE EL SALVADOR.
EL/SALVADR LAW DIPLOM ADMIN LEAD GOV/REL...SOC
19/20. PAGE 36 B0730
BIBLIOG
ACADEM
L/A+17C
NAT/G

B60

LERNER A.P.,THE ECONOMICS OF CONTROL. USA+45
ECO/UNDEV INT/ORG ACT/RES PLAN CAP/ISM INT/TRADE
ECO/DEV
ROUTINE

ATTIT WEALTH...SOC MATH STAT GEN/LAWS INDEX 20.
PAGE 64 B1295
   ECO/TAC
   SOCISM
   B60

LEWIS P.R.,LITERATURE OF THE SOCIAL SCIENCES: AN
INTRODUCTORY SURVEY AND GUIDE. UK LAW INDUS DIPLOM
INT/TRADE ADMIN...MGT 19/20. PAGE 65 B1306
   BIBLIOG/A
   SOC
   B60

LINDSAY K.,EUROPEAN ASSEMBLIES: THE EXPERIMENTAL
PERIOD 1949-1959. EUR+WWI ECO/DEV NAT/G POL/PAR
LEGIS TOP/EX ACT/RES PLAN ECO/TAC DOMIN LEGIT
ROUTINE ATTIT DRIVE ORD/FREE PWR SKILL...SOC CONCPT
TREND CHARTS GEN/LAWS VAL/FREE. PAGE 65 B1315
   VOL/ASSN
   INT/ORG
   REGION
   B60

LIPSET S.M.,POLITICAL MAN. AFR COM EUR+WWI L/A+17C
MOD/EUR S/ASIA USA+45 STRUCT ECO/DEV
ECO/UNDEV POL/PAR SECT ADMIN WEALTH...CONCPT WORK
TOT/POP 20. PAGE 65 B1320
   PWR
   SOC
   B60

RAO V.K.R.,INTERNATIONAL AID FOR ECONOMIC
DEVELOPMENT - POSSIBILITIES AND LIMITATIONS. FINAN
PLAN TEC/DEV ADMIN TASK EFFICIENCY...POLICY SOC
METH/CNCPT CHARTS 20 UN. PAGE 86 B1734
   FOR/AID
   DIPLOM
   INT/ORG
   ECO/UNDEV
   S60

BOGARDUS E.S.,"THE SOCIOLOGY OF A STRUCTURED
PEACE." FUT SOCIETY CREATE DIPLOM EDU/PROP ADJUD
ROUTINE ATTIT RIGID/FLEX KNOWL ORD/FREE RESPECT
...POLICY INT/LAW JURID NEW/IDEA SELF/OBS TOT/POP
20 UN. PAGE 13 B0264
   INT/ORG
   SOC
   NAT/LISM
   PEACE
   S60

EMERSON R.,"THE EROSION OF DEMOCRACY." AFR FUT LAW
CULTURE INTELL SOCIETY ECO/UNDEV FAM LOC/G NAT/G
FORCES PLAN TEC/DEV ECO/TAC ADMIN CT/SYS ATTIT
ORD/FREE PWR...SOCIALIST SOC CONCPT STAND/INT
TIME/SEQ WORK 20. PAGE 33 B0671
   S/ASIA
   POL/PAR
   S60

HERZ J.H.,"EAST GERMANY: PROGRESS AND PROSPECTS."
COM AGRI FINAN INDUS LOC/G NAT/G FORCES PLAN
TEC/DEV ADMIN COERCE DRIVE PERCEPT RIGID/FLEX
MORAL ORD/FREE PWR...MARXIST PSY SOC RECORD STERTYP
WORK. PAGE 49 B0997
   POL/PAR
   STRUCT
   GERMANY
   S60

NORTH R.C.,"DIE DISKREPANZ ZWISCHEN REALITAT UND
WUNSCHBILD ALS INNENPOLITISCHER FAKTOR." ASIA
CHINA/COM COM FUT ECO/UNDEV NAT/G PLAN DOMIN ADMIN
COERCE PERCEPT...SOC MYTH GEN/METH WORK TOT/POP 20.
PAGE 79 B1589
   SOCIETY
   ECO/TAC
   S60

THOMPSON K.W.,"MORAL PURPOSE IN FOREIGN POLICY:
REALITIES AND ILLUSIONS." WOR+45 WOR-45 LAW CULTURE
SOCIETY INT/ORG PLAN ADJUD ADMIN COERCE RIGID/FLEX
SUPEGO KNOWL ORD/FREE PWR...SOC TREND SOC/EXP
TOT/POP 20. PAGE 104 B2104
   MORAL
   JURID
   DIPLOM
   C60

MCCLEERY R.,"COMMUNICATION PATTERNS AS BASES OF
SYSTEMS OF AUTHORITY AND POWER" IN THEORETICAL
STUDIES IN SOCIAL ORGAN. OF PRISON-BMR. USA+45
SOCIETY STRUCT EDU/PROP ADMIN CONTROL COERCE CRIME
GP/REL AUTHORIT...SOC. PAGE 71 B1443
   PERS/REL
   PUB/INST
   PWR
   DOMIN
   B61

BAINS J.S.,STUDIES IN POLITICAL SCIENCE. INDIA
WOR+45 WOR-45 CONSTN BAL/PWR ADJUD ADMIN PARL/PROC
SOVEREIGN...SOC METH/COMP ANTHOL 17/20 UN. PAGE 8
B0165
   DIPLOM
   INT/LAW
   NAT/G
   B61

BANFIELD E.C.,URBAN GOVERNMENT: A READER IN
POLITICS AND ADMINISTRATION. ELITES LABOR POL/PAR
EXEC CHOOSE REPRESENT GP/REL PWR PLURISM...PSY SOC.
PAGE 9 B0177
   MUNIC
   GEN/METH
   DECISION
   B61

COHN B.S.,DEVELOPMENT AND IMPACT OF BRITISH
ADMINISTRATION IN INDIA: A BIBLIOGRAPHIC ESSAY.
INDIA UK ECO/UNDEV NAT/G DOMIN...POLICY MGT SOC
19/20. PAGE 22 B0448
   BIBLIOG/A
   COLONIAL
   S/ASIA
   ADMIN
   B61

DUBIN R.,HUMAN RELATIONS IN ADMINISTRATION. USA+45
INDUS LABOR LG/CO EX/STRUC GP/REL DRIVE PWR
...DECISION SOC CHARTS ANTHOL 20. PAGE 31 B0623
   PERS/REL
   MGT
   ADMIN
   EXEC
   B61

HOUN F.W.,TO CHANGE A NATION: PROPAGANDA AND
INDOCTRINATION IN COMMUNIST CHINA. CHINA/COM COM
ACT/RES PLAN PRESS ADMIN FEEDBACK CENTRAL
EFFICIENCY ATTIT...PSY SOC 20. PAGE 52 B1048
   DOMIN
   EDU/PROP
   TOTALISM
   MARXISM
   B61

JACOBS J.,THE DEATH AND LIFE OF GREAT AMERICAN
CITIES. USA+45 SOCIETY DIST/IND CREATE PROB/SOLV
ADMIN...GEOG SOC CENSUS 20 URBAN/RNWL. PAGE 55
B1113
   MUNIC
   PLAN
   ADJUST
   HABITAT
   B61

JANOWITZ M.,COMMUNITY POLITICAL SYSTEMS. USA+45
SOCIETY INDUS VOL/ASSN TEC/DEV ADMIN LEAD CHOOSE
...SOC SOC/WK 20. PAGE 56 B1123
   MUNIC
   STRUCT
   POL/PAR
   B61

KRUPP S.,PATTERN IN ORGANIZATIONAL ANALYSIS: A
CRITICAL EXAMINATION. INGP/REL PERS/REL RATIONAL
ATTIT AUTHORIT DRIVE PWR...DECISION PHIL/SCI SOC
   MGT
   CONTROL
   CONCPT

IDEA/COMP. PAGE 61 B1239
   METH/CNCPT
   B61

MACRIDIS R.C.,COMPARATIVE POLITICS: NOTES AND
READINGS. WOR+45 LOC/G MUNIC NAT/G PROVS VOL/ASSN
EDU/PROP ADMIN ATTIT PERSON ORD/FREE...SOC CONCPT
OBS RECORD TREND 20. PAGE 68 B1376
   POL/PAR
   CHOOSE
   B61

MARSH R.M.,THE MANDARINS: THE CIRCULATION OF ELITES
IN CHINA. 1600-1900. ASIA STRUCT PROF/ORG...SOC
CHARTS BIBLIOG DICTIONARY 17/20. PAGE 70 B1406
   ELITES
   ADMIN
   FAM
   STRATA
   B61

MUNGER E.S.,AFRICAN FIELD REPORTS 1952-1961.
SOUTH/AFR SOCIETY ECO/UNDEV NAT/G POL/PAR COLONIAL
EXEC PARL/PROC GUERRILLA RACE/REL ALL/IDEOS...SOC
AUD/VIS 20. PAGE 76 B1538
   AFR
   DISCRIM
   RECORD
   B61

ROBINSON M.E.,EDUCATION FOR SOCIAL CHANGE:
ESTABLISHING INSTITUTES OF PUBLIC AND BUSINESS
ADMINISTRATION ABROAD (PAMPHLET). WOR+45 SOCIETY
ACADEM CONFER INGP/REL ROLE...SOC CHARTS BIBLIOG 20
ICA. PAGE 89 B1805
   FOR/AID
   EDU/PROP
   MGT
   ADJUST
   S61

EVAN W.M.,"A LABORATORY EXPERIMENT ON BUREAUCRATIC
AUTHORITY" WORKER CONTROL EXEC PRODUC ATTIT PERSON
...PSY SOC CHARTS SIMUL 20 WEBER/MAX. PAGE 34 B0687
   ADMIN
   LEGIT
   LAB/EXP
   EFFICIENCY
   S61

JUVILER P.H.,"INTERPARLIAMENTARY CONTACTS IN SOVIET
FOREIGN POLICY." COM FUT WOR+45 WOR-45 SOCIETY
CONSULT ACT/RES DIPLOM ADMIN PEACE ATTIT RIGID/FLEX
WEALTH...WELF/ST SOC TOT/POP CONGRESS 19/20.
PAGE 57 B1156
   INT/ORG
   DELIB/GP
   USSR
   S61

MARSH R.M.,"FORMAL ORGANIZATION AND PROMOTION IN A
PRE-INDUSTRIAL SOCIETY" (BMR)" ASIA FAM EX/STRUC
LEAD...SOC CHARTS 19 WEBER/MAX. PAGE 70 B1407
   ADMIN
   STRUCT
   ECO/UNDEV
   STRATA
   C61

ETZIONI A.,"A COMPARATIVE ANALYSIS OF COMPLEX
ORGANIZATIONS: ON POWER, INVOLVEMENT AND THEIR
CORRELATES." ELITES CREATE OP/RES ROUTINE INGP/REL
PERS/REL CONSEN ATTIT DRIVE PWR...CONCPT BIBLIOG.
PAGE 34 B0684
   CON/ANAL
   SOC
   LEAD
   CONTROL
   B62

COSTA RICA UNIVERSIDAD BIBL,LISTA DE TESIS DE GRADO
DE LA UNIVERSIDAD DE COSTA RICA. COSTA/RICA LAW
LOC/G ADMIN LEAD...SOC 20. PAGE 24 B0487
   BIBLIOG/A
   NAT/G
   DIPLOM
   ECO/UNDEV
   B62

INGHAM K.,A HISTORY OF EAST AFRICA. NAT/G DIPLOM
ADMIN WAR NAT/LISM...SOC BIOG BIBLIOG. PAGE 54
B1085
   AFR
   CONSTN
   COLONIAL
   B62

MARS D.,SUGGESTED LIBRARY IN PUBLIC ADMINISTRATION.
FINAN DELIB/GP EX/STRUC WORKER COMPUTER ADJUD
...DECISION PSY SOC METH/COMP 20. PAGE 69 B1403
   BIBLIOG
   ADMIN
   METH
   MGT
   B62

PRESTHUS R.,THE ORGANIZATIONAL SOCIETY. USA+45
STRUCT ECO/DEV ADMIN ATTIT ALL/VALS...PSY SOC 20.
PAGE 84 B1703
   LG/CO
   WORKER
   PERS/REL
   DRIVE
   B62

SNYDER R.C.,FOREIGN POLICY DECISION-MAKING. FUT
KOREA WOR+45 R+D CREATE ADMIN ROUTINE PWR
...DECISION PSY SOC CONCPT METH/CNCPT CON/ANAL
CHARTS GEN/METH METH 20. PAGE 99 B1992
   TEC/DEV
   HYPO/EXP
   DIPLOM
   B62

UNECA LIBRARY,NEW ACQUISITIONS IN THE UNECA
LIBRARY. LAW NAT/G PLAN PROB/SOLV TEC/DEV ADMIN
REGION...GEOG SOC 20 UN. PAGE 106 B2152
   BIBLIOG
   AFR
   ECO/UNDEV
   INT/ORG
   S62

ALGER C.F.,"THE EXTERNAL BUREAUCRACY IN UNITED
STATES FOREIGN AFFAIRS." USA+45 WOR+45 SOCIETY
COM/IND INT/ORG NAT/G CONSULT EX/STRUC ACT/RES
...MGT SOC CONCPT TREND 20. PAGE 4 B0076
   ADMIN
   ATTIT
   DIPLOM
   S62

DUFTY N.F.,"THE IMPLEMENTATION OF A DECISION."
STRATA ACT/RES...MGT CHARTS SOC/EXP ORG/CHARTS.
PAGE 31 B0627
   DECISION
   CREATE
   METH/CNCPT
   SOC
   S62

GIDWANI K.A.,"LEADER BEHAVIOUR IN ELECTED AND NON-
ELECTED GROUPS." DELIB/GP ROUTINE TASK HAPPINESS
AUTHORIT...SOC STAT CHARTS SOC/EXP. PAGE 39 B0796
   LEAD
   INGP/REL
   GP/COMP
   CHOOSE
   S62

MURACCIOLE L.,"LES CONSTITUTIONS DES ETATS
AFRICAINS D'EXPRESSION FRANCAISE: LA CONSTITUTION
DU 16 AVRIL 1962 DE LA REPUBLIQUE DU" AFR CHAD
CHIEF LEGIS LEGIT COLONIAL EXEC ROUTINE ORD/FREE
SOVEREIGN...SOC CONCPT 20. PAGE 76 B1541
   NAT/G
   CONSTN
   C62

BLAU P.M.,"FORMAL ORGANIZATIONS." WOR+45 SOCIETY
   ADMIN

STRUCT ECO/DEV GP/REL ATTIT...METH/CNCPT BIBLIOG   SOC
20. PAGE 12 B0253   GEN/METH
                                                    INGP/REL
                                                                    B63
BLONDEL J.,VOTERS, PARTIES, AND LEADERS. UK ELITES POL/PAR
LOC/G NAT/G PROVS ACT/RES DOMIN REPRESENT GP/REL   STRATA
INGP/REL...SOC BIBLIOG 20. PAGE 12 B0255   LEGIS
                                                    ADMIN
                                                                    B63
BOISSIER P.,HISTORIE DU COMITE INTERNATIONAL DE LA INT/ORG
CROIX ROUGE. MOD/EUR WOR-45 CONSULT FORCES PLAN   HEALTH
DIPLOM EDU/PROP ADMIN MORAL ORD/FREE...SOC CONCPT   ARMS/CONT
RECORD TIME/SEQ GEN/LAWS TOT/POP VAL/FREE 19/20.   WAR
PAGE 13 B0267
                                                                    B63
COM INTERNAT DES MOUVEMENTS,REPERTOIRE   BIBLIOG/A
INTERNATIONAL DES SOURCES POUR L'ETUDE DES   MARXISM
MOUVEMENTS SOCIAUX AUX XIXE ET XXE SIECLES (VOL.   POL/PAR
III). MOD/EUR ADMIN...SOC 19. PAGE 22 B0454   LABOR
                                                                    B63
COMISION DE HISTORIO,GUIA DE LOS DOCUMENTOS   BIBLIOG
MICROFOTOGRAFIADOS POR LA UNIDAD MOVIL DE LA   NAT/G
UNESCO. SOCIETY ECO/UNDEV INT/ORG ADMIN...SOC 20   L/A+17C
UNESCO. PAGE 22 B0456   DIPLOM
                                                                    B63
DE VRIES E.,SOCIAL ASPECTS OF ECONOMIC DEVELOPMENT L/A+17C
IN LATIN AMERICA. CULTURE SOCIETY STRATA FINAN   ECO/UNDEV
INDUS INT/ORG DELIB/GP ACT/RES ECO/TAC EDU/PROP
ADMIN ATTIT SUPEGO HEALTH KNOWL ORD/FREE...SOC STAT
TREND ANTHOL TOT/POP VAL/FREE. PAGE 28 B0562
                                                                    B63
HEUSSLER R.,YESTERDAY'S RULERS: THE MAKING OF THE   EX/STRUC
BRITISH COLONIAL SERVICE. AFR EUR+WWI UK STRATA   MORAL
SECT DELIB/GP PLAN DOMIN EDU/PROP ATTIT PERCEPT   ELITES
PERSON SUPEGO KNOWL ORD/FREE PWR...MGT SOC OBS INT
TIME/SEQ 20 CMN/WLTH. PAGE 49 B1000
                                                                    B63
HOWER R.M.,MANAGERS AND SCIENTISTS. EX/STRUC CREATE R+D
ADMIN REPRESENT ATTIT DRIVE ROLE PWR SKILL...SOC   MGT
INT. PAGE 52 B1052   PERS/REL
                                                    INGP/REL
                                                                    B63
JOHNS R.,CONFRONTING ORGANIZATIONAL CHANGE. NEIGH   SOC/WK
DELIB/GP CREATE OP/RES ADMIN GP/REL DRIVE...WELF/ST WEALTH
SOC RECORD BIBLIOG. PAGE 56 B1142   LEAD
                                                    VOL/ASSN
                                                                    B63
KOGAN N.,THE POLITICS OF ITALIAN FOREIGN POLICY.   NAT/G
EUR+WWI LEGIS DOMIN LEGIT EXEC PWR RESPECT SKILL   ROUTINE
...POLICY DECISION HUM SOC METH/CNCPT OBS INT   DIPLOM
CHARTS 20. PAGE 61 B1227   ITALY
                                                                    B63
MOORE W.E.,MAN, TIME, AND SOCIETY. UNIV STRUCT FAM CONCPT
MUNIC VOL/ASSN ADMIN...SOC NEW/IDEA TIME/SEQ TREND SOCIETY
TIME 20. PAGE 75 B1515   CONTROL
                                                                    B63
PLANTEY A.,TRAITE PRATIQUE DE LA FONCTION PUBLIQUE ADMIN
(2ND ED., 2 VOLS.). FRANCE FINAN EX/STRUC PROB/SOLV SUPEGO
GP/REL ATTIT...SOC 20 CIVIL/SERV. PAGE 83 B1680   JURID
                                                                    B63
WALKER A.A.,OFFICIAL PUBLICATIONS OF SIERRA LEONE   BIBLIOG
AND GAMBIA. GAMBIA SIER/LEONE UK LAW CONSTN LEGIS   NAT/G
PLAN BUDGET DIPLOM...SOC SAMP CON/ANAL 20. PAGE 113 COLONIAL
B2278   ADMIN
                                                                    L63
BENNIS W.G.,"A NEW ROLE FOR THE BEHAVIORAL   METH/CNCPT
SCIENCES: EFFECTING ORGANIZATIONAL CHANGE." ACT/RES CREATE
...MGT GP/COMP PERS/COMP SOC/EXP ORG/CHARTS.   STRUCT
PAGE 11 B0216   SOC
                                                                    S63
ARASTEH R.,"THE ROLE OF INTELLECTUALS IN   INTELL
ADMINISTRATIVE DEVELOPMENT AND SOCIAL CHANGE IN   ADMIN
MODERN IRAN." ISLAM CULTURE NAT/G CONSULT ACT/RES   IRAN
EDU/PROP EXEC ATTIT BIO/SOC PERCEPT SUPEGO ALL/VALS
...POLICY MGT PSY SOC CONCPT 20. PAGE 6 B0123
                                                                    S63
DAVEE R.,"POUR UN FONDS DE DEVELOPPEMENT SOCIAL."   INT/ORG
FUT WOR+45 INTELL SOCIETY ECO/DEV FINAN TEC/DEV   SOC
ROUTINE WEALTH...TREND TOT/POP VAL/FREE UN 20.   FOR/AID
PAGE 26 B0532
                                                                    S63
MEDALIA N.Z.,"POSITION AND PROSPECTS OF   NAT/G
SOCIOLOGISTS IN FEDERAL EMPLOYMENT." USA+45 CONSULT WORKER
PAY SENIOR ADMIN GOV/REL...TREND CHARTS 20   SOC
CIVIL/SERV. PAGE 72 B1460   SKILL
                                                                    B64
RECENT PUBLICATIONS ON GOVERNMENTAL PROBLEMS. FINAN BIBLIOG
INDUS ACADEM PLAN PROB/SOLV EDU/PROP ADJUD ADMIN   AUTOMAT
BIO/SOC...MGT SOC. PAGE 2 B0040   LEGIS
                                                    JURID
                                                                    B64
AHMAD M.,THE CIVIL SERVANT IN PAKISTAN. PAKISTAN   WELF/ST
ECO/UNDEV COLONIAL INGP/REL...SOC CHARTS BIBLIOG 20 ADMIN
CIVIL/SERV. PAGE 3 B0065   ATTIT
                                                    STRATA

                                                                    B64
BOTTOMORE T.B.,ELITES AND SOCIETY. INTELL STRATA   ELITES
ECO/DEV ECO/UNDEV ADMIN GP/REL ORD/FREE...CONCPT   IDEA/COMP
BIBLIOG 20. PAGE 14 B0281   SOCIETY
                                                    SOC
                                                                    B64
COLLINS B.E.,A SOCIAL PSYCHOLOGY OF GROUP PROCESSES FACE/GP
FOR DECISION-MAKING. PROB/SOLV ROUTINE...SOC CHARTS DECISION
HYPO/EXP. PAGE 22 B0453   NAT/G
                                                    INDUS
                                                                    B64
COOMBS C.H.,A THEORY OF DATA....MGT PHIL/SCI SOC   CON/ANAL
CLASSIF MATH PROBABIL STAT QU. PAGE 23 B0472   GEN/METH
                                                    TESTS
                                                    PSY
                                                                    B64
FLORENCE P.S.,ECONOMICS AND SOCIOLOGY OF INDUSTRY; INDUS
A REALISTIC ANALYSIS OF DEVELOPMENT. ECO/UNDEV   SOC
LG/CO NAT/G PLAN...GEOG MGT BIBLIOG 20. PAGE 36   ADMIN
B0729
                                                                    B64
GESELLSCHAFT RECHTSVERGLEICH,BIBLIOGRAPHIE DES   BIBLIOG/A
DEUTSCHEN RECHTS (BIBLIOGRAPHY OF GERMAN LAW,   JURID
TRANS. BY COURTLAND PETERSON). GERMANY FINAN INDUS CONSTN
LABOR SECT FORCES CT/SYS PARL/PROC CRIME...INT/LAW ADMIN
SOC NAT/COMP 20. PAGE 39 B0794
                                                                    B64
GUTTSMAN W.L.,THE BRITISH POLITICAL ELITE. EUR+WWI NAT/G
MOD/EUR STRATA FAM LABOR POL/PAR SCHOOL VOL/ASSN   SOC
DELIB/GP LEGIS LEGIT EXEC CHOOSE ATTIT ALL/VALS   UK
...STAT BIOG TIME/SEQ CHARTS VAL/FREE. PAGE 45   ELITES
B0905
                                                                    B64
HICKEY G.C.,VILLAGE IN VIETNAM. USA+45 VIETNAM LAW CULTURE
AGRI FAM SECT ADMIN ATTIT...SOC CHARTS WORSHIP 20. SOCIETY
PAGE 49 B1003   STRUCT
                                                    S/ASIA
                                                                    B64
IBERO-AMERICAN INSTITUTES,IBEROAMERICANA. STRUCT   BIBLIOG
ADMIN SOC. PAGE 53 B1073   L/A+17C
                                                    NAT/G
                                                    DIPLOM
                                                                    B64
JACKSON W.V.,LIBRARY GUIDE FOR BRAZILIAN STUDIES.   BIBLIOG
BRAZIL USA+45 STRUCT DIPLOM ADMIN...SOC 20. PAGE 55 L/A+17C
B1110   NAT/G
                                                    LOC/G
                                                                    B64
MUSSO AMBROSI L.A.,BIBLIOGRAFIA DE BIBLIOGRAFIAS   BIBLIOG
URUGUAYAS. URUGUAY DIPLOM ADMIN ATTIT...SOC 20.   NAT/G
PAGE 77 B1551   L/A+17C
                                                    PRESS
                                                                    B64
NATIONAL BOOK LEAGUE,THE COMMONWEALTH IN BOOKS: AN BIBLIOG/A
ANNOTATED LIST. CANADA UK LOC/G SECT ADMIN...SOC   JURID
BIOG 20 CMN/WLTH. PAGE 77 B1561   NAT/G
                                                                    B64
SINGER M.R.,THE EMERGING ELITE: A STUDY OF   TOP/EX
POLITICAL LEADERSHIP IN CEYLON. S/ASIA ECO/UNDEV   STRATA
AGRI KIN NAT/G SECT EX/STRUC LEGIT ATTIT PWR   NAT/LISM
RESPECT...SOC STAT CHARTS 20. PAGE 97 B1967   CEYLON
                                                                    B64
SULLIVAN G.,THE STORY OF THE PEACE CORPS. USA+45   INT/ORG
WOR+45 INTELL FACE/GP NAT/G SCHOOL VOL/ASSN CONSULT ECO/UNDEV
EX/STRUC PLAN EDU/PROP ADMIN ATTIT DRIVE ALL/VALS   FOR/AID
...POLICY HEAL SOC CONCPT INT QU BIOG TREND SOC/EXP PEACE
WORK. PAGE 102 B2054
                                                                    B64
TURNER M.C.,LIBROS EN VENTA EN HISPANOAMERICA Y   BIBLIOG
ESPANA. SPAIN LAW CONSTN CULTURE ADMIN LEAD...HUM   L/A+17C
SOC 20. PAGE 106 B2139   NAT/G
                                                    DIPLOM
                                                                    B64
WILDAVSKY A.,LEADERSHIP IN A SMALL TOWN. USA+45   LEAD
STRUCT PROB/SOLV EXEC PARTIC RACE/REL PWR PLURISM   MUNIC
...SOC 20 NEGRO WATER CIV/RIGHTS OBERLIN CITY/MGT. ELITES
PAGE 116 B2348
                                                                    B64
WILSON L.,THE ACADEMIC MAN. STRUCT FINAN PROF/ORG   ACADEM
OP/RES ADMIN AUTHORIT ROLE RESPECT...SOC STAT.   INGP/REL
PAGE 117 B2360   STRATA
                                                    DELIB/GP
                                                                    L64
RIPLEY R.B.,"INTERAGENCY COMMITTEES AND   EXEC
INCREMENTALISM: THE CASE OF AID TO INDIA." INDIA   MGT
USA+45 INTELL NAT/G DELIB/GP ACT/RES DIPLOM ROUTINE FOR/AID
NAT/LISM ATTIT PWR...SOC CONCPT NEW/IDEA TIME/SEQ
CON/ANAL VAL/FREE 20. PAGE 89 B1790
                                                                    L64
WORLD PEACE FOUNDATION,"INTERNATIONAL   INT/ORG
ORGANIZATIONS: SUMMARY OF ACTIVITIES." INDIA   ROUTINE
PAKISTAN TURKEY WOR+45 CONSTN CONSULT EX/STRUC
ECO/TAC EDU/PROP LEGIT ORD/FREE...JURID SOC UN 20
CYPRESS. PAGE 118 B2375
                                                                    S64
KASSOF A.,"THE ADMINISTERED SOCIETY: SOCIETY

TOTALITARIANISM WITHOUT TERROR." COM USSR STRATA   DOMIN
AGRI INDUS NAT/G PERF/ART SCHOOL TOP/EX EDU/PROP   TOTALISM
ADMIN ORD/FREE PWR...POLICY SOC TIME/SEQ GEN/LAWS
VAL/FREE 20. PAGE 58 B1178
                                                         S64
KHAN M.Z.,"THE PRESIDENT OF THE GENERAL ASSEMBLY."   INT/ORG
WOR+45 CONSTN DELIB/GP EDU/PROP LEGIT ROUTINE PWR   TOP/EX
RESPECT SKILL...DECISION SOC BIOG TREND UN 20.
PAGE 59 B1202
                                                         S64
LIPSET S.M.,"SOCIOLOGY AND POLITICAL SCIENCE: A   BIBLIOG/A
BIBLIOGRAPHICAL NOTE." WOR+45 ELITES LEGIS ADJUD   SOC
ADMIN ATTIT IDEA/COMP. PAGE 65 B1321   METH/COMP
                                                         S64
NASH M.,"SOCIAL PREREQUISITES TO ECONOMIC GROWTH IN   ECO/DEV
LATIN AMERICA AND SOUTHEAST ASIA." L/A+17C S/ASIA   PERCEPT
CULTURE SOCIETY ECO/UNDEV AGRI INDUS NAT/G PLAN
TEC/DEV EDU/PROP ROUTINE ALL/VALS...POLICY RELATIV
SOC NAT/COMP WORK TOT/POP 20. PAGE 77 B1558
                                                         S64
PARSONS T.,"EVOLUTIONARY UNIVERSALS IN SOCIETY."   SOC
UNIV SOCIETY STRATA MARKET EDU/PROP LEGIT ADJUD   CONCPT
ADMIN ALL/VALS...JURID OBS GEN/LAWS VAL/FREE 20.
PAGE 81 B1638
                                                         B65
BERNDT R.M.,ABORIGINAL MAN IN AUSTRALIA. LAW DOMIN   SOC
ADMIN COLONIAL MARRIAGE HABITAT ORD/FREE...LING   CULTURE
CHARTS ANTHOL BIBLIOG WORSHIP 20 AUSTRAL ABORIGINES   SOCIETY
MUSIC ELKIN/AP. PAGE 11 B0225   STRUCT
                                                         B65
CHEN T.H.,THE CHINESE COMMUNIST REGIME: A   MARXISM
DOCUMENTARY STUDY (2 VOLS.). CHINA/COM LAW CONSTN   POL/PAR
ELITES ECO/UNDEV LEGIS ECO/TAC ADMIN CONTROL PWR   NAT/G
...SOC 20. PAGE 20 B0417
                                                         B65
GOODSELL C.T.,ADMINISTRATION OF A REVOLUTION.   EXEC
PUERT/RICO ECO/UNDEV FINAN MUNIC POL/PAR PROVS   SOC
LEGIS PLAN BUDGET RECEIVE ADMIN COLONIAL LEAD 20
ROOSEVLT/F. PAGE 41 B0827
                                                         B65
GREER S.,URBAN RENEWAL AND AMERICAN CITIES: THE   MUNIC
DILEMMA OF DEMOCRATIC INTERVENTION. USA+45 R+D   PROB/SOLV
LOC/G VOL/ASSN ACT/RES BUDGET ADMIN GOV/REL...SOC   PLAN
INT SAMP 20 BOSTON CHICAGO MIAMI URBAN/RNWL.   NAT/G
PAGE 43 B0871
                                                         B65
HISPANIC SOCIETY OF AMERICA,CATALOGUE (10 VOLS.).   BIBLIOG
PORTUGAL PRE/AMER SPAIN NAT/G ADMIN...POLICY SOC   L/A+17C
15/20. PAGE 50 B1018   COLONIAL
                                                         DIPLOM
                                                         B65
INST INTL DES CIVILISATION DIF,THE CONSTITUTIONS   CONSTN
AND ADMINISTRATIVE INSTITUTIONS OF THE NEW STATES.   ADMIN
AFR ISLAM S/ASIA NAT/G POL/PAR DELIB/GP EX/STRUC   ADJUD
CONFER EFFICIENCY NAT/LISM...JURID SOC 20. PAGE 54   ECO/UNDEV
B1088
                                                         B65
LAMBIRI I.,SOCIAL CHANGE IN A GREEK COUNTRY TOWN.   INDUS
GREECE FAM PROB/SOLV ROUTINE TASK LEISURE INGP/REL   WORKER
CONSEN ORD/FREE...SOC INT QU CHARTS 20. PAGE 62   CULTURE
B1252   NEIGH
                                                         B65
MEISEL J.H.,PARETO & MOSCA. ITALY STRUCT ADMIN   PWR
...SOC CON/ANAL ANTHOL BIBLIOG 19/20. PAGE 72 B1463   ELITES
                                                         CONTROL
                                                         LAISSEZ
                                                         B65
NATIONAL BOOK CENTRE PAKISTAN,BOOKS ON PAKISTAN: A   BIBLIOG
BIBLIOGRAPHY. PAKISTAN CULTURE DIPLOM ADMIN ATTIT   CONSTN
...MAJORIT SOC CONCPT 20. PAGE 77 B1560   S/ASIA
                                                         NAT/G
                                                         B65
ROWAT D.C.,THE OMBUDSMAN: CITIZEN'S DEFENDER.   INSPECT
DENMARK FINLAND NEW/ZEALND NORWAY SWEDEN CONSULT   CONSTN
PROB/SOLV FEEDBACK PARTIC GP/REL...SOC CONCPT   NAT/G
NEW/IDEA METH/COMP ANTHOL BIBLIOG 20. PAGE 91 B1840   ADMIN
                                                         B65
RUBIN H.,PENSIONS AND EMPLOYEE MOBILITY IN THE   ADMIN
PUBLIC SERVICE. USA+45 WORKER PERSON ORD/FREE...SOC   NAT/G
QU. PAGE 91 B1849   LOC/G
                                                         SENIOR
                                                         B65
SINGER J.D.,HUMAN BEHAVIOR AND INTERNATIONAL   DIPLOM
POLITICS* CONTRIBUTIONS FROM THE SOCIAL-   PHIL/SCI
PSYCHOLOGICAL SCIENCES. ACT/RES PLAN EDU/PROP ADMIN   QUANT
KNOWL...DECISION PSY SOC NET/THEORY HYPO/EXP   SIMUL
LAB/EXP SOC/EXP GEN/METH ANTHOL BIBLIOG. PAGE 97
B1965
                                                         B65
SNYDER F.G.,ONE-PARTY GOVERNMENT IN MALI: ECO/UNDEV
TRANSITION TOWARD CONTROL. MALI STRATA STRUCT SOC.   POL/PAR
PAGE 99 B1991   EX/STRUC
                                                         ADMIN
                                                         B65
STEINER G.A.,THE CREATIVE ORGANIZATION. ELITES   CREATE
LG/CO PLAN PROB/SOLV TEC/DEV INSPECT CAP/ISM   MGT

CONTROL EXEC PERSON...METH/COMP HYPO/EXP 20.   ADMIN
PAGE 100 B2029   SOC
                                                         B65
STEINER K.,LOCAL GOVERNMENT IN JAPAN. CONSTN   LOC/G
CULTURE NAT/G ADMIN CHOOSE...SOC STAT 20 CHINJAP.   SOCIETY
PAGE 100 B2030   JURID
                                                         ORD/FREE
                                                         B65
UNESCO,INTERNATIONAL ORGANIZATIONS IN THE SOCIAL   INT/ORG
SCIENCES(REV. ED.). LAW ADMIN ATTIT...CRIMLGY GEOG   R+D
INT/LAW PSY SOC STAT 20 UNESCO. PAGE 107 B2157   PROF/ORG
                                                         ACT/RES
                                                         B65
UNIVERSAL REFERENCE SYSTEM,INTERNATIONAL AFFAIRS: BIBLIOG/A
VOLUME I IN THE POLITICAL SCIENCE, GOVERNMENT, AND   GEN/METH
PUBLIC POLICY SERIES....DECISION ECOMETRIC GEOG   COMPUT/IR
INT/LAW JURID MGT PHIL/SCI PSY SOC. PAGE 107 B2163   DIPLOM
                                                         B65
WALTON R.E.,A BEHAVIORAL THEORY OF LABOR   SOC
NEGOTIATIONS: AN ANALYSIS OF A SOCIAL INTERACTION   LABOR
SYSTEM. USA+45 FINAN PROB/SOLV ECO/TAC GP/REL   BARGAIN
INGP/REL...DECISION BIBLIOG. PAGE 113 B2285   ADMIN
                                                         L65
LASSWELL H.D.,"THE POLICY SCIENCES OF DEVELOPMENT."   PWR
CULTURE SOCIETY EX/STRUC CREATE ADMIN ATTIT KNOWL   METH/CNCPT
...SOC CONCPT SIMUL GEN/METH. PAGE 63 B1273   DIPLOM
                                                         S65
SILVERT K.H.,"AMERICAN ACADEMIC ETHICS AND SOCIAL   ACADEM
RESEARCH ABROAD* THE LESSON OF PROJECT CAMELOT."   NAT/G
CHILE L/A+17C USA+45 FINAN ADMIN...PHIL/SCI SOC   ACT/RES
GEN/LAWS CAMELOT. PAGE 97 B1953   POLICY
                                                         C65
HUNTINGTON S.P.,"CONGRESSIONAL RESPONSES TO THE   FUT
TWENTIETH CENTURY IN D. TRUMAN, ED. THE CONGRESS   LEAD
AND AMERICA'S FUTURE." USA+45 USA-45 DIPLOM SENIOR   NAT/G
ADMIN EXEC PWR...SOC 20 CONGRESS. PAGE 53 B1067   LEGIS
                                                         B66
GLAZER M.,THE FEDERAL GOVERNMENT AND THE   BIBLIOG/A
UNIVERSITY. CHILE PROB/SOLV DIPLOM GIVE ADMIN WAR   NAT/G
...POLICY SOC 20. PAGE 40 B0810   PLAN
                                                         ACADEM
                                                         B66
HANKE L.,HANDBOOK OF LATIN AMERICAN STUDIES.   BIBLIOG/A
ECO/UNDEV ADMIN LEAD...HUM SOC 20. PAGE 46 B0937   L/A+17C
                                                         INDEX
                                                         NAT/G
                                                         B66
SILBERMAN B.S.,MODERN JAPANESE LEADERSHIP: LEAD
TRANSITION AND CHANGE. NAT/G POL/PAR CHIEF ADMIN   CULTURE
REPRESENT GP/REL ADJUST RIGID/FLEX...SOC METH/COMP   ELITES
ANTHOL 19/20 CHINJAP CHRISTIAN. PAGE 97 B1952   MUNIC
                                                         B66
WILLNER A.R.,THE NEOTRADITIONAL ACCOMMODATION TO   INDONESIA
POLITICAL INDEPENDENCE* THE CASE OF INDONESIA *   CONSERVE
RESEARCH MONOGRAPH NO. 26. CULTURE ECO/UNDEV CREATE   ELITES
PROB/SOLV FOR/AID LEGIT COLONIAL EFFICIENCY   ADMIN
NAT/LISM ALL/VALS SOC. PAGE 117 B2355
                                                         L66
LEMARCHAND R.,"SOCIAL CHANGE AND POLITICAL   NAT/G
MODERNISATION IN BURUNDI." AFR BURUNDI STRATA CHIEF   STRUCT
EX/STRUC RIGID/FLEX PWR...SOC 20. PAGE 64 B1285   ELITES
                                                         CONSERVE
                                                         S66
"FURTHER READING." INDIA LOC/G NAT/G PLAN ADMIN   BIBLIOG
WEALTH...GEOG SOC CONCPT CENSUS 20. PAGE 2 B0045   ECO/UNDEV
                                                         TEC/DEV
                                                         PROVS
                                                         B67
DICKSON P.G.M.,THE FINANCIAL REVOLUTION IN ENGLAND.   ECO/DEV
UK NAT/G TEC/DEV ADMIN GOV/REL...SOC METH/CNCPT   FINAN
CHARTS GP/COMP BIBLIOG 17/18. PAGE 29 B0587   CAP/ISM
                                                         MGT
                                                         B67
EVANS R.H.,COEXISTENCE: COMMUNISM AND ITS PRACTICE   MARXISM
IN BOLOGNA, 1945-1965. ITALY CAP/ISM ADMIN CHOOSE   CULTURE
PEACE ORD/FREE...SOC STAT DEEP/INT SAMP CHARTS   MUNIC
BIBLIOG 20. PAGE 34 B0690   POL/PAR
                                                         B67
EDUCATION, INTERACTION, AND SOCIAL CHANGE. STRATA   EDU/PROP
MUNIC SCHOOL ADMIN RIGID/FLEX ROLE 20. PAGE 49   ADJUST
B0991   SOC
                                                         ACT/RES
                                                         B67
HOROWITZ I.L.,THE RISE AND FALL OF PROJECT CAMELOT: NAT/G
STUDIES IN THE RELATIONSHIP BETWEEN SOCIAL SCIENCE   ACADEM
AND PRACTICAL POLITICS. USA+45 WOR+45 CULTURE   ACT/RES
FORCES LEGIS EXEC CIVMIL/REL KNOWL...POLICY SOC   GP/REL
METH/CNCPT 20. PAGE 51 B1043
                                                         B67
MARRIS P.,DILEMMAS OF SOCIAL REFORM: POVERTY AND   STRUCT
COMMUNITY ACTION IN THE UNITED STATES. USA+45 NAT/G   MUNIC
OP/RES ADMIN PARTIC EFFICIENCY WEALTH...SOC   PROB/SOLV
METH/COMP T 20 REFORMERS. PAGE 69 B1401   COST
                                                         B67
RAVKIN A.,THE NEW STATES OF AFRICA (HEADLINE   AFR
SERIES, NO. 183((PAMPHLET). CULTURE STRUCT INDUS   ECO/UNDEV

COLONIAL NAT/LISM...SOC 20. PAGE 86 B1744 — SOCIETY ADMIN

L67

TAMBIAH S.J.,"THE POLITICS OF LANGUAGE IN INDIA AND CEYLON." CEYLON INDIA NAT/G DOMIN ADMIN...SOC 20. PAGE 102 B2070 — POL/PAR LING NAT/LISM REGION

S67

ALPANDER G.G.,"ENTREPRENEURS AND PRIVATE ENTERPRISE IN TURKEY." TURKEY INDUS PROC/MFG EDU/PROP ATTIT DRIVE WEALTH...GEOG MGT SOC STAT TREND CHARTS 20. PAGE 4 B0080 — ECO/UNDEV LG/CO NAT/G POLICY

S67

BERLINER J.S.,"RUSSIA'S BUREAUCRATS - WHY THEY'RE REACTIONARY." USSR NAT/G OP/RES PROB/SOLV TEC/DEV CONTROL SANCTION EFFICIENCY DRIVE PERSON...TECHNIC SOC 20. PAGE 11 B0223 — CREATE ADMIN INDUS PRODUC

S67

FOX R.G.,"FAMILY, CASTE, AND COMMERCE IN A NORTH INDIAN MARKET TOWN." INDIA STRATA AGRI FACE/GP FAM NEIGH OP/RES BARGAIN ADMIN ROUTINE WEALTH...SOC CHARTS 20. PAGE 37 B0747 — CULTURE GP/REL ECO/UNDEV DIST/IND

S67

JOHNSON L.B.,"BULLETS DO NOT DISCRIMINATE-LANDLORDS DO." PROB/SOLV EXEC LOBBY DEMAND...REALPOL SOC 20. PAGE 57 B1145 — NAT/G DISCRIM POLICY

S67

LLOYD K.,"URBAN RACE RIOTS V EFFECTIVE ANTI-DISCRIMINATION AGENCIES* AN END OR A BEGINNING?" USA+45 STRATA ACT/RES ADMIN ADJUST ORD/FREE RESPECT ...PLURIST DECISION SOC SOC/WK. PAGE 66 B1332 — GP/REL DISCRIM LOC/G CROWD

S67

MCNAMARA R.L.,"THE NEED FOR INNOVATIVENESS IN DEVELOPING SOCIETIES." L/A+17C EDU/PROP ADMIN LEAD WEALTH...POLICY PSY SOC METH 20 COLOMB. PAGE 72 B1456 — PROB/SOLV PLAN ECO/UNDEV NEW/IDEA

S67

SCOTT W.R.,"ORGANIZATIONAL EVALUATION AND AUTHORITY." CONTROL SANCTION PERS/REL ATTIT DRIVE ...SOC CONCPT OBS CHARTS IDEA/COMP 20. PAGE 95 B1921 — EXEC WORKER INSPECT EX/STRUC

N67

NATIONAL COMN COMMUNITY HEALTH,ACTION - PLANNING FOR COMMUNITY HEALTH SERVICES (PAMPHLET). USA+45 PROF/ORG DELIB/GP BUDGET ROUTINE GP/REL ATTIT ...HEAL SOC SOC/WK CHARTS TIME 20. PAGE 77 B1563 — PLAN MUNIC HEALTH ADJUST

S68

GUZZARDI W. JR.,"THE SECOND BATTLE OF BRITAIN." UK STRATA LABOR WORKER CREATE PROB/SOLV EDU/PROP ADMIN LEAD LOBBY...MGT SOC 20 GOLD/STAND. PAGE 45 B0907 — FINAN ECO/TAC ECO/DEV STRUCT

B82

POOLE W.F.,INDEX TO PERIODICAL LITERATURE. LOC/G NAT/G DIPLOM ADMIN...HUM PHIL/SCI SOC 19. PAGE 84 B1690 — BIBLIOG USA+45 ALL/VALS SOCIETY

SOC/DEMPAR....SOCIAL DEMOCRATIC PARTY (USE WITH SPECIFIC NATION)

SOC/EXP...."SOCIAL" EXPERIMENTATION UNDER UNCONTROLLED CONDITIONS

N19

WRIGHT D.S.,AMERICAN STATE ADMINISTRATORS (PAMPHLET). USA+45 ATTIT PERSON...SAMP/SIZ CHARTS SOC/EXP METH 20. PAGE 118 B2379 — QU TOP/EX ADMIN PROVS

B28

BUELL R.,THE NATIVE PROBLEM IN AFRICA. KIN LABOR LOC/G ECO/TAC ROUTINE ORD/FREE...REC/INT KNO/TEST CENSUS TREND CHARTS SOC/EXP STERTYP 20. PAGE 17 B0339 — AFR CULTURE

B47

BARNARD C.,THE FUNCTIONS OF THE EXECUTIVE. USA+45 ELITES INTELL LEGIT ATTIT DRIVE PERSON SKILL...PSY SOC METH/CNCPT SOC/EXP GEN/METH VAL/FREE 20. PAGE 9 B0187 — EXEC EX/STRUC ROUTINE

S48

COCH L.,"OVERCOMING RESISTANCE TO CHANGE" (BMR)" USA+45 CONSULT ADMIN ROUTINE GP/REL EFFICIENCY PRODUC PERCEPT SKILL...CHARTS SOC/EXP 20. PAGE 22 B0441 — WORKER OP/RES PROC/MFG RIGID/FLEX

S49

REISSMAN L.,"A STUDY OF ROLE CONCEPTIONS IN BUREAUCRACY" (BMR)" PERS/REL ROLE...SOC CONCPT NEW/IDEA IDEA/COMP SOC/EXP 20 BUREAUCRCY. PAGE 87 B1767 — ADMIN METH/CNCPT GEN/LAWS PROB/SOLV

C51

HOMANS G.C.,"THE WESTERN ELECTRIC RESEARCHES" IN S. HOSLETT, ED., HUMAN FACTORS IN MANAGEMENT (BMR)" ACT/RES GP/REL HAPPINESS PRODUC DRIVE...MGT OBS 20. PAGE 51 B1037 — OP/RES EFFICIENCY SOC/EXP WORKER

B53

WAGLEY C.,AMAZON TOWN: A STUDY OF MAN IN THE TROPICS. BRAZIL L/A+17C STRATA STRUCT ECO/UNDEV — SOC NEIGH

AGRI EX/STRUC RACE/REL DISCRIM HABITAT WEALTH...OBS SOC/EXP 20. PAGE 113 B2273 — CULTURE INGP/REL

B54

COMBS C.H.,DECISION PROCESSES. INTELL SOCIETY DELIB/GP CREATE TEC/DEV DOMIN LEGIT EXEC CHOOSE DRIVE RIGID/FLEX KNOWL PWR...PHIL/SCI SOC METH/CNCPT CONT/OBS REC/INT PERS/TEST SAMP/SIZ BIOG SOC/EXP WORK. PAGE 22 B0455 — MATH DECISION

S55

CROCKETT W.H.,"EMERGENT LEADERSHIP IN SMALL DECISION MAKING GROUPS." ACT/RES ROUTINE PERS/REL ATTIT...STAT CONT/OBS SOC/EXP SIMUL. PAGE 25 B0507 — DELIB/GP ADMIN PSY DECISION

S55

WEISS R.S.,"A METHOD FOR THE ANALYSIS OF THE STRUCTURE OF COMPLEX ORGANIZATIONS." WOR+45 INDUS LG/CO NAT/G EXEC ROUTINE ORD/FREE PWR SKILL...MGT PSY SOC NEW/IDEA STAT INT REC/INT STAND/INT CHARTS WORK. PAGE 115 B2316 — PROF/ORG SOC/EXP

S60

SCHER S.,"CONGRESSIONAL COMMITTEE MEMBERS AND INDEPENDENT AGENCY OVERSEERS: A CASE STUDY." DELIB/GP EX/STRUC JUDGE TOP/EX DOMIN ADMIN CONTROL PWR...SOC/EXP HOUSE/REP CONGRESS. PAGE 93 B1886 — LEGIS GOV/REL LABOR ADJUD

S60

THOMPSON K.W.,"MORAL PURPOSE IN FOREIGN POLICY: REALITIES AND ILLUSIONS." WOR+45 WOR-45 LAW CULTURE SOCIETY INT/ORG PLAN ADJUD ADMIN COERCE RIGID/FLEX SUPEGO KNOWL ORD/FREE PWR...SOC TREND SOC/EXP TOT/POP 20. PAGE 104 B2104 — MORAL JURID DIPLOM

S61

TANNENBAUM A.S.,"CONTROL AND EFFECTIVENESS IN A VOLUNTARY ORGANIZATION." USA+45 ADMIN...CORREL MATH REGRESS STAT TESTS SAMP/SIZ CHARTS SOC/EXP INDEX 20 LEAGUE/WV. PAGE 102 B2072 — EFFICIENCY VOL/ASSN CONTROL INGP/REL

B62

FRIEDLANDER W.A.,INDIVIDUALISM AND SOCIAL WELFARE. FRANCE ACADEM OP/RES ADMIN AGE/Y AGE/A ORD/FREE 20. PAGE 37 B0756 — GIVE SOC/WK SOC/EXP FINAN

L62

GALBRAITH J.K.,"ECONOMIC DEVELOPMENT IN PERSPECTIVE." CAP/ISM ECO/TAC ROUTINE ATTIT WEALTH ...TREND CHARTS SOC/EXP WORK 20. PAGE 38 B0773 — ECO/UNDEV PLAN

S62

DUFTY N.F.,"THE IMPLEMENTATION OF A DECISION." STRATA ACT/RES...MGT CHARTS SOC/EXP ORG/CHARTS. PAGE 31 B0627 — DECISION CREATE METH/CNCPT SOC

S62

GIDWANI K.A.,"LEADER BEHAVIOUR IN ELECTED AND NON-ELECTED GROUPS." DELIB/GP ROUTINE TASK HAPPINESS AUTHORIT...SOC STAT CHARTS SOC/EXP. PAGE 39 B0796 — LEAD INGP/REL GP/COMP CHOOSE

B63

HARGROVE M.M.,BUSINESS POLICY CASES-WITH BEHAVIORAL SCIENCE IMPLICATIONS. LG/CO SML/CO EX/STRUC TOP/EX PLAN PROB/SOLV CONFER ADMIN CONTROL ROUTINE EFFICIENCY. PAGE 47 B0946 — SOC/EXP INDUS DECISION MGT

L63

BENNIS W.G.,"A NEW ROLE FOR THE BEHAVIORAL SCIENCES: EFFECTING ORGANIZATIONAL CHANGE." ACT/RES ...MGT GP/COMP PERS/COMP SOC/EXP ORG/CHARTS. PAGE 11 B0216 — METH/CNCPT CREATE STRUCT SOC

B64

SULLIVAN G.,THE STORY OF THE PEACE CORPS. USA+45 WOR+45 INTELL FACE/GP NAT/G SCHOOL VOL/ASSN CONSULT EX/STRUC PLAN EDU/PROP ADMIN ATTIT DRIVE ALL/VALS ...POLICY HEAL SOC CONCPT INT QU BIOG TREND SOC/EXP WORK. PAGE 102 B2054 — INT/ORG ECO/UNDEV FOR/AID PEACE

B65

ETZIONI A.,POLITICAL UNIFICATION* A COMPARATIVE STUDY OF LEADERS AND FORCES. EUR+WWI ISLAM L/A+17C WOR+45 ELITES STRATA EXEC WEALTH...TIME/SEQ TREND SOC/EXP. PAGE 34 B0686 — INT/ORG FORCES ECO/TAC REGION

B65

SINGER J.D.,HUMAN BEHAVIOR AND INTERNATIONAL POLITICS* CONTRIBUTIONS FROM THE SOCIAL-PSYCHOLOGICAL SCIENCES. ACT/RES PLAN EDU/PROP ADMIN KNOWL...DECISION PSY SOC NET/THEORY HYPO/EXP LAB/EXP SOC/EXP GEN/METH ANTHOL BIBLIOG. PAGE 97 B1965 — DIPLOM PHIL/SCI QUANT SIMUL

S65

HOLSTI O.R.,"THE 1914 CASE." MOD/EUR COMPUTER DIPLOM EDU/PROP EXEC...DECISION PSY PROBABIL STAT COMPUT/IR SOC/EXP TIME. PAGE 51 B1036 — CON/ANAL PERCEPT WAR

B66

PERROW C.,ORGANIZATION FOR TREATMENT: A COMPARATIVE STUDY OF INSTITUTIONS FOR DELINQUENTS. LAW PROB/SOLV ADMIN CRIME PERSON MORAL...SOC/WK OBS DEEP/QU CHARTS SOC/EXP SOC/INTEG 20. PAGE 82 B1661 — AGE/Y PSY PUB/INST

SOC/INTEG....SOCIAL INTEGRATION; SEE ALSO CONSEN, RACE/REL

B00

SANDERSON E.,AFRICA IN THE NINETEENTH CENTURY. — COLONIAL

FRANCE UK EXTR/IND FORCES LEGIS ADMIN WAR DISCRIM AFR
ORD/FREE...GEOG GP/COMP SOC/INTEG 19. PAGE 92 B1867 DIPLOM

                                                           B48
TOWSTER J..POLITICAL POWER IN THE USSR: 1917-1947. EX/STRUC
USSR CONSTN CULTURE ELITES CREATE PLAN COERCE NAT/G
CENTRAL ATTIT RIGID/FLEX ORD/FREE...BIBLIOG MARXISM
SOC/INTEG 20 LENIN/VI STALIN/J. PAGE 105 B2124 PWR

                                                           B50
BAKKE E.W..BONDS OF ORGANIZATION (2ND ED.). USA+45 ECO/DEV
COM/IND FINAN ADMIN LEAD PERS/REL...INT SOC/INTEG MGT
20. PAGE 8 B0169 LABOR
                                                           GP/REL
                                                           S59
DWYER R.J.."THE ADMINISTRATIVE ROLE IN ADMIN
DESEGREGATION." USA+45 LAW PROB/SOLV LEAD RACE/REL SCHOOL
ISOLAT STRANGE ROLE...POLICY SOC/INTEG MISSOURI DISCRIM
NEGRO CIV/RIGHTS. PAGE 31 B0638 ATTIT

                                                           B60
LEYDER J..BIBLIOGRAPHIE DE L'ENSEIGNEMENT SUPERIEUR BIBLIOG/A
ET DE LA RECHERCHE SCIENTIFIQUE EN AFRIQUE ACT/RES
INTERTROPICALE (2 VOLS.). AFR CULTURE ECO/UNDEV ACADEM
AGRI PLAN EDU/PROP ADMIN COLONIAL...GEOG SOC/INTEG R+D
20 NEGRO. PAGE 65 B1309

                                                           B60
MOORE W.E..LABOR COMMITMENT AND SOCIAL CHANGE IN LABOR
DEVELOPING AREAS. SOCIETY STRATA ECO/UNDEV MARKET ORD/FREE
VOL/ASSN WORKER AUTHORIT SKILL...MGT NAT/COMP ATTIT
SOC/INTEG 20. PAGE 75 B1514 INDUS

                                                           B61
FREYRE G..THE PORTUGUESE AND THE TROPICS. L/A+17C COLONIAL
PORTUGAL SOCIETY PERF/ART ADMIN TASK GP/REL METH
...ART/METH CONCPT SOC/INTEG 20. PAGE 37 B0754 PLAN
                                                           CULTURE
                                                           B63
CONF ON FUTURE OF COMMONWEALTH.THE FUTURE OF THE DIPLOM
COMMONWEALTH. UK ECO/UNDEV AGRI EDU/PROP ADMIN RACE/REL
SOC/INTEG 20 COMMONWLTH. PAGE 23 B0460 ORD/FREE
                                                           TEC/DEV
                                                           B65
REISS A.J. JR..SCHOOLS IN A CHANGING SOCIETY. SCHOOL
CULTURE PROB/SOLV INSPECT DOMIN CONFER INGP/REL EX/STRUC
RACE/REL AGE/C AGE/Y ALL/VALS...ANTHOL SOC/INTEG 20 ADJUST
NEWYORK/C. PAGE 87 B1766 ADMIN

                                                           B66
PERROW C..ORGANIZATION FOR TREATMENT: A COMPARATIVE AGE/Y
STUDY OF INSTITUTIONS FOR DELINQUENTS. LAW PSY
PROB/SOLV ADMIN CRIME PERSON MORAL...SOC/WK OBS PUB/INST
DEEP/QU CHARTS SOC/EXP SOC/INTEG 20. PAGE 82 B1661

                                                           B67
WEINBERG M..SCHOOL INTEGRATION: A COMPREHENSIVE BIBLIOG
CLASSIFIED BIBLIOGRAPHY OF 3,100 REFERENCES. USA+45 SCHOOL
LAW NAT/G NEIGH SECT PLAN ROUTINE AGE/C WEALTH DISCRIM
SOC/INTEG INDIAN/AM. PAGE 115 B2314 RACE/REL

SOC/PAR....SOCIALIST PARTY (USE WITH SPECIFIC NATION)

SOC/REVPAR....SOCIALIST REVOLUTIONARY PARTY (USE WITH
     SPECIFIC NATION)

SOC/SECUR....SOCIAL SECURITY

SOC/WK....SOCIAL WORK, SOCIAL SERVICE ORGANIZATION

                                                           N19
RIDLEY C.E..MEASURING MUNICIPAL ACTIVITIES MGT
(PAMPHLET). FINAN SERV/IND FORCES RECEIVE INGP/REL HEALTH
HABITAT...POLICY SOC/WK 20. PAGE 88 B1779 WEALTH
                                                           LOC/G
                                                           B37
HODGSON J.G..THE OFFICIAL PUBLICATIONS OF AMERICAN BIBLIOG
COUNTIES: A UNION LIST. SCHOOL BUDGET...HEAL MGT LOC/G
SOC/WK 19/20. PAGE 51 B1026 PUB/INST
                                                           B43
LEVY H.P..A STUDY IN PUBLIC RELATIONS: CASE HISTORY ATTIT
OF THE RELATIONS MAINTAINED BETWEEN A DEPT OF RECEIVE
PUBLIC ASSISTANCE AND PEOPLE. USA-45 NAT/G PRESS WEALTH
ADMIN LOBBY GP/REL DISCRIM...SOC/WK LING AUD/VIS 20 SERV/IND
PENNSYLVAN. PAGE 64 B1302
                                                           B44
WRIGHT H.R..SOCIAL SERVICE IN WARTIME. FINAN NAT/G GIVE
VOL/ASSN PLAN GP/REL ROLE. PAGE 118 B2381 WAR
                                                           SOC/WK
                                                           ADMIN
                                                           B47
TAPPAN P.W..DELINQUENT GIRLS IN COURT. USA-45 MUNIC CT/SYS
EX/STRUC FORCES ADMIN EXEC ADJUST SEX RESPECT AGE/Y
...JURID SOC/WK 20 NEWYORK/C FEMALE/SEX. PAGE 103 CRIME
B2078 ADJUD
                                                           B51
CHRISTENSEN A.N..THE EVOLUTION OF LATIN AMERICAN NAT/G
GOVERNMENT: A BOOK OF READINGS. ECO/UNDEV INDUS CONSTN
LOC/G POL/PAR EX/STRUC LEGIS FOR/AID CT/SYS DIPLOM
...SOC/WK 20 SOUTH/AMER. PAGE 21 B0428 L/A+17C
                                                           C54
CALDWELL L.K.."THE GOVERNMENT AND ADMINISTRATION OF PROVS
NEW YORK." LOC/G MUNIC POL/PAR SCHOOL CHIEF LEGIS ADMIN

PLAN TAX CT/SYS...MGT SOC/WK BIBLIOG 20 NEWYORK/C. CONSTN
PAGE 18 B0366 EX/STRUC
                                                           B55
UN ECONOMIC AND SOCIAL COUNCIL.BIBLIOGRAPHY OF BIBLIOG/A
PUBLICATIONS OF THE UN AND SPECIALIZED AGENCIES IN SOC/WK
THE SOCIAL WELFARE FIELD, 1946-1952. WOR+45 FAM ADMIN
INT/ORG MUNIC ACT/RES PLAN PROB/SOLV EDU/PROP AGE/C WEALTH
AGE/Y HABITAT...HEAL UN. PAGE 106 B2148

                                                           B56
DUNNILL F..THE CIVIL SERVICE. UK LAW PLAN ADMIN PERSON
EFFICIENCY DRIVE NEW/LIB...STAT CHARTS 20 WORKER
PARLIAMENT CIVIL/SERV. PAGE 31 B0633 STRATA
                                                           SOC/WK
                                                           B57
KIETH-LUCAS A..DECISIONS ABOUT PEOPLE IN NEED, A ADMIN
STUDY OF ADMINISTRATIVE RESPONSIVENESS IN PUBLIC RIGID/FLEX
ASSISTANCE. USA+45 GIVE RECEIVE INGP/REL PERS/REL SOC/WK
MORAL RESPECT WEALTH...SOC OBS BIBLIOG 20. PAGE 60 DECISION
B1204
                                                           B58
VASEY W..GOVERNMENT AND SOCIAL WELFARE: ROLES OF REPRESENT
FEDERAL , STATE AND LOCAL GOVERNMENTS IN ADMIN
ADMINISTERING WELFARE SERVICES. USA+45 EDU/PROP 20. EX/STRUC
PAGE 112 B2255 SOC/WK
                                                           B61
CONFREY E.A..ADMINISTRATION OF COMMUNITY HEALTH HEAL
SERVICES. USA+45 R+D PUB/INST DELIB/GP PLAN BUDGET ADMIN
ROUTINE AGE/C HEALTH...MGT SOC/WK METH/COMP 20. MUNIC
PAGE 23 B0461 BIO/SOC
                                                           B61
JANOWITZ M..COMMUNITY POLITICAL SYSTEMS. USA+45 MUNIC
SOCIETY INDUS VOL/ASSN TEC/DEV ADMIN LEAD CHOOSE STRUCT
...SOC SOC/WK 20. PAGE 56 B1123 POL/PAR
                                                           B61
LEE R.R..ENGINEERING-ECONOMIC PLANNING BIBLIOG/A
MISCELLANEOUS SUBJECTS: A SELECTED BIBLIOGRAPHY PLAN
(MIMEOGRAPHED). FINAN LOC/G MUNIC NEIGH ADMIN REGION
CONTROL INGP/REL HABITAT...GEOG MGT SOC/WK 20
RESOURCE/N. PAGE 63 B1280
                                                           B62
FRIEDLANDER W.A..INDIVIDUALISM AND SOCIAL WELFARE. GIVE
FRANCE ACADEM OP/RES ADMIN AGE/Y AGE/A ORD/FREE 20. SOC/WK
PAGE 37 B0756 SOC/EXP
                                                           FINAN
                                                           B62
MORE S.S..REMODELLING OF DEMOCRACY FOR AFRO-ASIAN ORD/FREE
NATIONS. AFR INDIA S/ASIA SOUTH/AFR CONSTN EX/STRUC ECO/UNDEV
COLONIAL CHOOSE TOTALISM SOVEREIGN NEW/LIB SOCISM ADMIN
...SOC/WK 20. PAGE 75 B1520 LEGIS
                                                           B62
WENDT P.F..HOUSING POLICY - THE SEARCH FOR PLAN
SOLUTIONS. GERMANY/W SWEDEN UK USA+45 OP/RES ADMIN
HABITAT WEALTH...SOC/WK CHARTS 20. PAGE 115 B2322 METH/COMP
                                                           NAT/G
                                                           B63
HONORD S..PUBLIC RELATIONS IN ADMINISTRATION. PRESS
WOR+45 NAT/G...SOC/WK BIBLIOG 20. PAGE 51 B1039 DIPLOM
                                                           MGT
                                                           METH/COMP
                                                           B63
JOHNS R..CONFRONTING ORGANIZATIONAL CHANGE. NEIGH SOC/WK
DELIB/GP CREATE OP/RES ADMIN GP/REL DRIVE...WELF/ST WEALTH
SOC RECORD BIBLIOG. PAGE 56 B1142 LEAD
                                                           VOL/ASSN
                                                           B63
PALOTAI O.C..PUBLICATIONS OF THE INSTITUTE OF BIBLIOG/A
GOVERNMENT, 1930-1962. LAW PROVS SCHOOL WORKER ADMIN
ACT/RES OP/RES CT/SYS GOV/REL...CRIMLGY SOC/WK. LOC/G
PAGE 81 B1629 FINAN
                                                           B64
AVASTHI A..ASPECTS OF ADMINISTRATION. INDIA UK MGT
USA+45 FINAN ACADEM DELIB/GP LEGIS RECEIVE ADMIN
PARL/PROC PRIVIL...NAT/COMP 20. PAGE 7 B0150 SOC/WK
                                                           ORD/FREE
                                                           B64
SCHERMER G..MEETING SOCIAL NEEDS IN THE PENJERDEL PLAN
REGION. SOCIETY FINAN ACT/RES EDU/PROP ADMIN REGION
GOV/REL...SOC/WK 45 20 PENNSYLVAN DELAWARE HEALTH
NEW/JERSEY. PAGE 93 B1887 WEALTH
                                                           B65
CUTLIP S.M..A PUBLIC RELATIONS BIBLIOGRAPHY. INDUS BIBLIOG/A
LABOR NAT/G PROF/ORG SCHOOL DIPLOM PRESS TV GOV/REL MGT
GP/REL...PSY SOC/WK 20. PAGE 25 B0515 COM/IND
                                                           ADMIN
                                                           S65
RAPHAELI N.."SELECTED ARTICLES AND DOCUMENTS ON BIBLIOG
COMPARATIVE PUBLIC ADMINISTRATION." USA+45 FINAN ADMIN
LOC/G WORKER TEC/DEV CONTROL LEAD...SOC/WK GOV/COMP NAT/G
METH/COMP. PAGE 86 B1739 MGT
                                                           B66
CLEGG R.K..THE ADMINISTRATOR IN PUBLIC WELFARE. ADMIN
USA+45 STRUCT NAT/G PROVS PROB/SOLV BUDGET ECO/TAC GIVE
GP/REL ROLE...SOC/WK 20 PUBLIC/REL. PAGE 21 B0434 GOV/REL
                                                           OP/RES
                                                           B66
PERROW C..ORGANIZATION FOR TREATMENT: A COMPARATIVE AGE/Y

STUDY OF INSTITUTIONS FOR DELINQUENTS. LAW   PSY
PROB/SOLV ADMIN CRIME PERSON MORAL...SOC/WK OBS   PUB/INST
DEEP/QU CHARTS SOC/EXP SOC/INTEG 20. PAGE 82 B1661
                                           B67

MINTZ M.,BY PRESCRIPTION ONLY. USA+45 NAT/G   BIO/SOC
EX/STRUC PLAN TEC/DEV EXEC EFFICIENCY HEALTH...MGT   PROC/MFG
SOC/WK 20. PAGE 74 B1491   CONTROL
                                         POLICY
                                         S67

ANDERSON L.G.,"ADMINISTERING A GOVERNMENT SOCIAL   ADMIN
SERVICE" NEW/ZEALND EX/STRUC TASK ROLE 20. PAGE 5   NAT/G
B0094   DELIB/GP
                                         SOC/WK
                                         S67

DONNELL J.C.,"PACIFICATION REASSESSED." VIETNAM/S   ADMIN
NAT/LISM DRIVE SUPEGO ORD/FREE...SOC/WK 20. PAGE 30   GP/REL
B0606   EFFICIENCY
                                         MUNIC
                                         S67

LLOYD K.,"URBAN RACE RIOTS V EFFECTIVE ANTI-   GP/REL
DISCRIMINATION AGENCIES* AN END OR A BEGINNING?"   DISCRIM
USA+45 STRATA ACT/RES ADMIN ADJUST ORD/FREE RESPECT   LOC/G
...PLURIST DECISION SOC SOC/WK. PAGE 66 B1332   CROWD
                                         N67

NATIONAL COMN COMMUNITY HEALTH.ACTION - PLANNING   PLAN
FOR COMMUNITY HEALTH SERVICES (PAMPHLET). USA+45   MUNIC
PROF/ORG DELIB/GP BUDGET ROUTINE GP/REL ATTIT   HEALTH
...HEAL SOC SOC/WK CHARTS TIME 20. PAGE 77 B1563   ADJUST

SOCIAL ANALYSIS....SEE SOC

SOCIAL DEMOCRATIC PARTY (ALL NATIONS)....SEE SOC/DEMPAR

SOCIAL CLASS....SEE STRATA

SOCIAL INSTITUTIONS....SEE INSTITUTIONAL INDEX

SOCIAL MOBILITY....SEE STRATA

SOCIAL PSYCHOLOGY (GROUPS)....SEE SOC

SOCIAL PSYCHOLOGY (INDIVIDUALS)....SEE PSY

SOCIAL STRUCTURE....SEE STRUCT

SOCIAL WORK....SEE SOC/WK

SOCIAL REVOLUTIONARY PARTY (ALL NATIONS)....SEE SOC/REVPAR

SOCIAL STRUCTURE....SEE STRUCT, STRATA

SOCIALISM....SEE SOCISM, SOCIALIST

SOCIALIST....NON-COMMUNIST SOCIALIST; SEE ALSO SOCISM

                                         B39

HITLER A.,MEIN KAMPF. EUR+WWI FUT MOD/EUR STRUCT   PWR
INT/ORG LABOR NAT/G POL/PAR FORCES CREATE PLAN   NEW/IDEA
BAL/PWR DIPLOM ECO/TAC DOMIN EDU/PROP COERCE   WAR
ATTIT...SOCIALIST BIOG TREND NAZI. PAGE 50 B1020
                                         B60

EASTON S.C.,THE TWILIGHT OF EUROPEAN COLONIALISM.   FINAN
AFR S/ASIA CONSTN SOCIETY STRUCT ECO/UNDEV INDUS   ADMIN
NAT/G FORCES ECO/TAC COLONIAL CT/SYS ATTIT KNOWL
ORD/FREE PWR...SOCIALIST TIME/SEQ TREND CON/ANAL
20. PAGE 32 B0645
                                         S60

EMERSON R.,"THE EROSION OF DEMOCRACY." AFR FUT LAW   S/ASIA
CULTURE INTELL SOCIETY ECO/UNDEV FAM LOC/G NAT/G   POL/PAR
FORCES PLAN TEC/DEV ECO/TAC ADMIN CT/SYS ATTIT
ORD/FREE PWR...SOCIALIST SOC CONCPT STAND/INT
TIME/SEQ WORK 20. PAGE 33 B0671
                                         B61

HORVATH B.,THE CHARACTERISTICS OF YUGOSLAV ECONOMIC   ACT/RES
DEVELOPMENT. COM ECO/UNDEV AGRI INDUS PLAN CAP/ISM   YUGOSLAVIA
ECO/TAC ROUTINE WEALTH...SOCIALIST STAT CHARTS
STERTYP WORK 20. PAGE 52 B1045
                                         S66

JACOBSON J.,"COALITIONISM: FROM PROTEST TO   RACE/REL
POLITICKING" USA+45 ELITES NAT/G POL/PAR PROB/SOLV   LABOR
ADMIN LEAD DISCRIM ORD/FREE PWR CONSERVE 20 NEGRO   SOCIALIST
AFL/CIO CIV/RIGHTS BLACK/PWR. PAGE 55 B1116   VOL/ASSN
                                         S67

KURON J.,"AN OPEN LETTER TO THE PARTY." CONSTN   ELITES
WORKER BUDGET EDU/PROP ADMIN REPRESENT SUFF OWN   STRUCT
...SOCIALIST 20. PAGE 62 B1244   POL/PAR
                                         ECO/TAC
                                         S67

MURRAY R.,"SECOND THOUGHTS ON GHANA." AFR GHANA   COLONIAL
NAT/G POL/PAR ADMIN REV GP/REL CENTRAL...SOCIALIST   CONTROL
CONCPT METH 20. PAGE 77 B1548   REGION
                                         SOCISM

SOCIALIZATION....SEE ADJUST

SOCIETY....SOCIETY AS A WHOLE

SOCIOLOGY....SEE SOC

SOCIOLOGY OF KNOWLEDGE....SEE EPIST

SOCIOMETRY, AS THEORY....SEE GEN/METH

SOCISM....SOCIALISM; SEE ALSO SOCIALIST

                                         N

VENKATESAN S.L.,BIBLIOGRAPHY ON PUBLIC ENTERPRISES   BIBLIOG/A
IN INDIA. INDIA S/ASIA FINAN LG/CO LOC/G PLAN   ADMIN
BUDGET SOCISM...MGT 20. PAGE 112 B2258   ECO/UNDEV
                                         INDUS
                                         N19

BOHLKE R.H.,BUREAUCRATS AND INTELLECTUALS: A   PERSON
CRITIQUE OF C. WRIGHT MILLS (PAMPHLET). ADMIN   SOC
SOCISM. PAGE 13 B0266   ELITES
                                         ACADEM
                                         B28

FYFE H.,THE BRITISH LIBERAL PARTY. UK SECT ADMIN   POL/PAR
LEAD CHOOSE GP/REL PWR SOCISM...MAJORIT TIME/SEQ   NAT/G
19/20 LIB/PARTY CONSRV/PAR. PAGE 38 B0768   REPRESENT
                                         POPULISM
                                         B38

LANGE O.,ON THE ECONOMIC THEORY OF SOCIALISM. UNIV   MARKET
ECO/DEV FINAN INDUS INT/ORG PUB/INST ROUTINE ATTIT   ECO/TAC
ALL/VALS...SOC CONCPT STAT TREND 20. PAGE 62 B1258   INT/TRADE
                                         SOCISM
                                         B40

MCHENRY D.E.,HIS MAJESTY'S OPPOSITION: STRUCTURE   POL/PAR
AND PROBLEMS OF THE BRITISH LABOUR PARTY 1931-1938.   MGT
UK FINAN LABOR LOC/G DELIB/GP LEGIS EDU/PROP LEAD   NAT/G
PARTIC CHOOSE GP/REL SOCISM...TREND 20 LABOR/PAR.   POLICY
PAGE 72 B1450
                                         S44

GRIFFITH E.S.,"THE CHANGING PATTERN OF PUBLIC   LAW
POLICY FORMATION." MOD/EUR WOR+45 FINAN CHIEF   POLICY
CONFER ADMIN LEAD CONSERVE SOCISM TECHRACY...SOC   TEC/DEV
CHARTS CONGRESS. PAGE 43 B0877
                                         B46

DAVIES E.,NATIONAL ENTERPRISE: THE DEVELOPMENT OF   ADMIN
THE PUBLIC CORPORATION. UK LG/CO EX/STRUC WORKER   NAT/G
PROB/SOLV COST ATTIT SOCISM 20. PAGE 26 B0536   CONTROL
                                         INDUS
                                         B50

MONPIED E.,BIBLIOGRAPHIE FEDERALISTE: OUVRAGES   BIBLIOG/A
CHOISIS (VOL. I, MIMEOGRAPHED PAPER). EUR+WWI   FEDERAL
DIPLOM ADMIN REGION ATTIT PACIFISM SOCISM...INT/LAW   CENTRAL
19/20. PAGE 74 B1502   INT/ORG
                                         B51

LEITES N.,THE OPERATIONAL CODE OF THE POLITBURO.   DELIB/GP
COM USSR CREATE PLAN DOMIN LEGIT COERCE ALL/VALS   ADMIN
...SOC CONCPT MYTH TREND CON/ANAL GEN/LAWS 20   SOCISM
LENIN/VI STALIN/J. PAGE 64 B1284
                                         B54

MOSK S.A.,INDUSTRIAL REVOLUTION IN MEXICO. MARKET   INDUS
LABOR CREATE CAP/ISM ADMIN ATTIT SOCISM...POLICY 20   TEC/DEV
MEXIC/AMER. PAGE 76 B1533   ECO/UNDEV
                                         NAT/G
                                         B55

RUSTOW D.A.,THE POLITICS OF COMPROMISE. SWEDEN   POL/PAR
LABOR EX/STRUC LEGIS PLAN REPRESENT SOCISM...SOC   NAT/G
19/20. PAGE 92 B1859   POLICY
                                         ECO/TAC
                                         S55

KAUTSKY J.H.,"THE NEW STRATEGY OF INTERNATIONAL   COM
COMMUNISM." ASIA CHINA/COM FUT WOR+45 WOR-45 ADMIN   POL/PAR
ROUTINE PERSON MARXISM SOCISM...TREND IDEA/COMP 20   TOTALISM
LENIN/VI MAO. PAGE 59 B1184   USSR
                                         B59

YANG C.K.,A CHINESE VILLAGE IN EARLY COMMUNIST   ASIA
TRANSITION. ECO/UNDEV AGRI FAM KIN MUNIC FORCES   ROUTINE
PLAN ECO/TAC DOMIN EDU/PROP ATTIT DRIVE PWR RESPECT   SOCISM
...SOC CONCPT METH/CNCPT OBS RECORD CON/ANAL CHARTS
WORK 20. PAGE 118 B2389
                                         B60

CAMPBELL R.W.,SOVIET ECONOMIC POWER. COM USA+45   ECO/DEV
DIST/IND MARKET TOP/EX ACT/RES CAP/ISM ECO/TAC   PLAN
DOMIN EDU/PROP ADMIN ROUTINE DRIVE...MATH TIME/SEQ   SOCISM
CHARTS WORK 20. PAGE 18 B0371   USSR
                                         B60

LERNER A.P.,THE ECONOMICS OF CONTROL. USA+45   ECO/DEV
ECO/UNDEV INT/ORG ACT/RES PLAN CAP/ISM INT/TRADE   ROUTINE
ATTIT WEALTH...SOC MATH STAT GEN/LAWS INDEX 20.   ECO/TAC
PAGE 64 B1295   SOCISM
                                         B60

ROEPKE W.,A HUMANE ECONOMY: THE SOCIAL FRAMEWORK OF   DRIVE
THE FREE MARKET. FUT USSR WOR+45 CULTURE SOCIETY   EDU/PROP
ECO/DEV PLAN ECO/TAC ADMIN ATTIT PERSON RIGID/FLEX   CAP/ISM
SUPEGO MORAL WEALTH SOCISM...POLICY OLD/LIB CONCPT
TREND GEN/LAWS 20. PAGE 90 B1811
                                         B61

AGARWAL R.C.,STATE ENTERPRISE IN INDIA. FUT INDIA   ECO/UNDEV
UK FINAN INDUS ADMIN CONTROL OWN...POLICY CHARTS   SOCISM
BIBLIOG 20 RAILROAD. PAGE 3 B0064   GOV/REL
                                         LG/CO

SHARMA T.R.,THE WORKING OF STATE ENTERPRISES IN
INDIA. INDIA DELIB/GP LEGIS WORKER BUDGET PRICE
CONTROL GP/REL OWN ATTIT...MGT CHARTS 20. PAGE 96
B1938
     NAT/G INDUS ADMIN SOCISM
     B61

EVANS M.S.,THE FRINGE ON TOP. USSR EX/STRUC FORCES
DIPLOM ECO/TAC PEACE CONSERVE SOCISM...TREND 20
KENNEDY/JF. PAGE 34 B0689
     NAT/G PWR CENTRAL POLICY
     B62

MORE S.S.,REMODELLING OF DEMOCRACY FOR AFRO-ASIAN
NATIONS. AFR INDIA S/ASIA SOUTH/AFR CONSTN EX/STRUC
COLONIAL CHOOSE TOTALISM SOVEREIGN NEW/LIB SOCISM
...SOC/WK 20. PAGE 75 B1520
     ORD/FREE ECO/UNDEV ADMIN LEGIS
     B62

PRAKASH O.M.,THE THEORY AND WORKING OF STATE
CORPORATIONS: WITH SPECIAL REFERENCE TO INDIA.
INDIA UK USA+45 TOP/EX PRICE ADMIN EFFICIENCY...MGT
METH/COMP 20 TVA. PAGE 84 B1698
     LG/CO ECO/UNDEV GOV/REL SOCISM
     S62

IOVTCHOUK M.T.,"ON SOME THEORETICAL PRINCIPLES AND
METHODS OF SOCIOLOGICAL INVESTIGATIONS (IN
RUSSIAN)." FUT USA+45 STRATA R+D NAT/G POL/PAR
TOP/EX ACT/RES PLAN ECO/TAC EDU/PROP ROUTINE ATTIT
RIGID/FLEX MARXISM SOCISM...MARXIST METH/CNCPT OBS
TREND NAT/COMP GEN/LAWS 20. PAGE 54 B1102
     COM ECO/DEV CAP/ISM USSR

GANGULY D.S.,PUBLIC CORPORATIONS IN A NATIONAL
ECONOMY. INDIA WOR+45 FINAN INDUS TOP/EX PRICE
EFFICIENCY...MGT STAT CHARTS BIBLIOG 20. PAGE 38
B0779
     ECO/UNDEV LG/CO SOCISM GOV/REL
     B63

HANSON A.H.,NATIONALIZATION: A BOOK OF READINGS.
WOR+45 FINAN DELIB/GP LEGIS WORKER BUDGET ADMIN
GP/REL EFFICIENCY SOCISM...MGT ANTHOL. PAGE 46
B0941
     NAT/G OWN INDUS CONTROL
     B63

HIGA M.,POLITICS AND PARTIES IN POSTWAR OKINAWA.
USA+45 VOL/ASSN LEGIS CONTROL LOBBY CHOOSE NAT/LISM
PWR SOVEREIGN MARXISM SOCISM 20 OKINAWA CHINJAP.
PAGE 50 B1008
     GOV/REL POL/PAR ADMIN FORCES
     B63

SHANKS M.,THE LESSONS OF PUBLIC ENTERPRISE. UK
LEGIS WORKER ECO/TAC ADMIN PARL/PROC GOV/REL ATTIT
...POLICY MGT METH/COMP NAT/COMP ANTHOL 20
PARLIAMENT. PAGE 96 B1931
     SOCISM OWN NAT/G INDUS
     B64

ELDREDGE H.W.,THE SECOND AMERICAN REVOLUTION.
EDU/PROP NAT/LISM RATIONAL TOTALISM FASCISM MARXISM
SOCISM. PAGE 33 B0664
     ELITES ORD/FREE ADMIN PLAN
     B64

GRZYBOWSKI K.,THE SOCIALIST COMMONWEALTH OF
NATIONS: ORGANIZATIONS AND INSTITUTIONS. FORCES
DIPLOM INT/TRADE ADJUD ADMIN LEAD WAR MARXISM
SOCISM...BIBLIOG 20 COMECON WARSAW/P. PAGE 44 B0898
     INT/LAW COM REGION INT/ORG
     S64

FLORINSKY M.T.,"TRENDS IN THE SOVIET ECONOMY." COM
USA+45 USSR INDUS LABOR NAT/G PLAN TEC/DEV ECO/TAC
ALL/VALS SOCISM...MGT METH/CNCPT STYLE CON/ANAL
GEN/METH WORK 20. PAGE 36 B0731
     ECO/DEV AGRI

AIYAR S.P.,STUDIES IN INDIAN DEMOCRACY. INDIA
STRATA ECO/UNDEV LABOR POL/PAR LEGIS DIPLOM LOBBY
REGION CHOOSE ATTIT SOCISM...ANTHOL 20. PAGE 3
B0067
     ORD/FREE REPRESENT ADMIN NAT/G
     B65

MOORE C.H.,TUNISIA SINCE INDEPENDENCE. ELITES LOC/G
POL/PAR ADMIN COLONIAL CONTROL EXEC GOV/REL
TOTALISM MARXISM...INT 20 TUNIS. PAGE 75 B1513
     NAT/G EX/STRUC SOCISM
     B65

RUBINSTEIN A.Z.,"YUGOSLAVIA'S OPENING SOCIETY." COM
USSR INTELL NAT/G LEGIS TOP/EX LEGIT CT/SYS
RIGID/FLEX ALL/VALS SOCISM...HUM TIME/SEQ TREND 20.
PAGE 92 B1851
     CONSTN EX/STRUC YUGOSLAVIA
     S65

TABORSKY E.,"CHANGE IN CZECHOSLOVAKIA." COM USSR
ELITES INTELL AGRI INDUS NAT/G DELIB/GP EX/STRUC
ECO/TAC TOTALISM ATTIT RIGID/FLEX SOCISM...MGT
CONCPT TREND 20. PAGE 102 B2067
     ECO/DEV PLAN CZECHOSLVK
     S65

TOTTEN G.O.,THE SOCIAL DEMOCRATIC MOVEMENT IN
PREWAR JAPAN. ASIA CHIEF EX/STRUC LEGIS DOMIN LEAD
ROUTINE WAR 20 CHINJAP. PAGE 105 B2122
     POL/PAR SOCISM PARTIC STRATA
     B66

AFRICAN BIBLIOGRAPHIC CENTER,"A CURRENT VIEW OF
AFRICANA: A SELECT AND ANNOTATED BIBLIOGRAPHICAL
PUBLISHING GUIDE, 1965-1966." AFR CULTURE INDUS
LABOR SECT FOR/AID ADMIN COLONIAL REV RACE/REL
SOCISM...LING 20. PAGE 3 B0063
     BIBLIOG/A NAT/G TEC/DEV POL/PAR
     S66

PALMER M.,"THE UNITED ARAB REPUBLIC* AN ASSESSMENT
OF ITS FAILURE." ELITES ECO/UNDEV POL/PAR FORCES
ECO/TAC RUMOR ADMIN EXEC EFFICIENCY ATTIT SOCISM
     UAR SYRIA REGION

...INT NASSER/G. PAGE 81 B1628
     FEDERAL
     C66

TARLING N.,"A CONCISE HISTORY OF SOUTHEAST ASIA."
BURMA CAMBODIA LAOS S/ASIA THAILAND VIETNAM
ECO/UNDEV POL/PAR FORCES ADMIN REV WAR CIVMIL/REL
ORD/FREE MARXISM SOCISM 13/20. PAGE 103 B2080
     COLONIAL DOMIN INT/TRADE NAT/LISM
     B67

GROSSMAN G.,ECONOMIC SYSTEMS. USA+45 USA-45 USSR
YUGOSLAVIA WORKER CAP/ISM PRICE GP/REL EQUILIB
WEALTH MARXISM SOCISM...MGT METH/COMP 19/20.
PAGE 44 B0892
     ECO/DEV PLAN TEC/DEV DEMAND
     B67

JAIN R.K.,MANAGEMENT OF STATE ENTERPRISES. INDIA
SOCIETY FINAN WORKER BUDGET ADMIN CONTROL OWN 20.
PAGE 55 B1118
     NAT/G SOCISM INDUS MGT
     B67

JHANGIANI M.A.,JANA SANGH AND SWATANTRA: A PROFILE
OF THE RIGHTIST PARTIES IN INDIA. INDIA ADMIN
CHOOSE MARXISM SOCISM...INT CHARTS BIBLIOG 20.
PAGE 56 B1140
     POL/PAR LAISSEZ NAT/LISM ATTIT
     B67

POSNER M.V.,ITALIAN PUBLIC ENTERPRISE. ITALY
ECO/DEV FINAN INDUS CREATE ECO/TAC ADMIN CONTROL
EFFICIENCY PRODUC...TREND CHARTS 20. PAGE 84 B1693
     NAT/G PLAN CAP/ISM SOCISM
     B67

SABLE M.H.,A GUIDE TO LATIN AMERICAN STUDIES (2
VOLS). CONSTN FINAN INT/ORG LABOR MUNIC POL/PAR
FORCES CAP/ISM FOR/AID ADMIN MARXISM SOCISM OAS.
PAGE 92 B1861
     BIBLIOG/A L/A+17C DIPLOM NAT/LISM
     S67

CARIAS B.,"EL CONTROL DE LAS EMPRESAS PUBLICAS POR
GRUPOS DE INTERESES DE LA COMUNIDAD." FRANCE UK
VENEZUELA INDUS NAT/G CONTROL OWN PWR...DECISION
NAT/COMP 20. PAGE 18 B0377
     WORKER REPRESENT MGT SOCISM
     S67

LASLETT J.H.M.,"SOCIALISM AND THE AMERICAN LABOR
MOVEMENT* SOME NEW REFLECTIONS." USA-45 VOL/ASSN
LOBBY PARTIC CENTRAL ALL/VALS SOCISM...GP/COMP 20.
PAGE 63 B1265
     LABOR ROUTINE ATTIT GP/REL
     S67

MURRAY R.,"SECOND THOUGHTS ON GHANA." AFR GHANA
NAT/G POL/PAR ADMIN REV GP/REL CENTRAL...SOCIALIST
CONCPT METH 20. PAGE 77 B1548
     COLONIAL CONTROL REGION SOCISM

SOCRATES....SOCRATES

SOHN L.B. B1993,B1994,B1995

SOLOMONS....THE SOLOMON ISLANDS

SOMALI
     B57

     MURRAY J.N.,THE UNITED NATIONS TRUSTEESHIP SYSTEM. INT/ORG
     AFR WOR+45 CONSTN CONSULT LEGIS EDU/PROP LEGIT EXEC DELIB/GP
     ROUTINE...INT TIME/SEQ SOMALI UN 20. PAGE 77 B1547

SOMALIA....SOMALIA; SEE ALSO AFR

SOMERS H.M. B1996

SONGAI....SONGAI EMPIRES (AFRICA)

SOREL/G....GEORGES SOREL

SOROKIN P. B1997

SOUPHANGOU....PRINCE SOUPHANGOU-VONG (LEADER OF PATHET LAO)

SOUTH AFRICA....SEE SOUTH/AFR

SOUTH ARABIA....SEE ARABIA/SOU

SOUTH KOREA....SEE KOREA/S

SOUTH VIETNAM....SEE VIETNAM/S

SOUTH WEST AFRICA....SEE AFRICA/SW

SOUTH AFRICA COMMISSION ON FUT B1998

SOUTH AFRICAN CONGRESS OF DEM B1999

SOUTH PACIFIC COMMISSION B2000

SOUTH/AFR....UNION OF SOUTH AFRICA
     B08

     THE GOVERNMENT OF SOUTH AFRICA (VOL. II). SOUTH/AFR CONSTN
     STRATA EXTR/IND EX/STRUC TOP/EX BUDGET ADJUD ADMIN FINAN
     CT/SYS PRODUC...CORREL CENSUS 19 RAILROAD LEGIS
     CIVIL/SERV POSTAL/SYS. PAGE 2 B0033 NAT/G

B19
NATHAN M.,THE SOUTH AFRICAN COMMONWEALTH: CONSTN
CONSTITUTION, PROBLEMS, SOCIAL CONDITIONS. NAT/G
SOUTH/AFR UK CULTURE INDUS EX/STRUC LEGIS BUDGET POL/PAR
EDU/PROP ADMIN CT/SYS GP/REL RACE/REL...LING 19/20 SOCIETY
CMN/WLTH. PAGE 77 B1559

N19
SOUTH AFRICA COMMISSION ON FUT,INTERIM AND FINAL CONSTN
REPORTS ON FUTURE FORM OF GOVERNMENT IN THE SOUTH- REPRESENT
WEST AFRICAN PROTECTORATE (PAMPHLET). SOUTH/AFR ADMIN
NAT/G FORCES CONFER COLONIAL CONTROL 20 AFRICA/SW. PROB/SOLV
PAGE 99 B1998

B37
UNION OF SOUTH AFRICA,REPORT CONCERNING NAT/G
ADMINISTRATION OF SOUTH WEST AFRICA (6 VOLS.). ADMIN
SOUTH/AFR INDUS PUB/INST FORCES LEGIS BUDGET DIPLOM COLONIAL
EDU/PROP ADJUD CT/SYS...GEOG CHARTS 20 AFRICA/SW CONSTN
LEAGUE/NAT. PAGE 107 B2158

B48
DAY P.,CRISIS IN SOUTH AFRICA. SOUTH/AFR UK KIN RACE/REL
MUNIC ECO/TAC RECEIVE 20 SMUTS/JAN MIGRATION. COLONIAL
PAGE 27 B0548 ADMIN
EXTR/IND

B50
WELCH S.R.,PORTUGUESE RULE AND SPANISH CROWN IN DIPLOM
SOUTH AFRICA 1581-1640. PORTUGAL SOUTH/AFR SPAIN COLONIAL
SOCIETY KIN NEIGH SECT INT/TRADE ADMIN 16/17 WAR
MISSION. PAGE 115 B2317 PEACE

B60
SOUTH AFRICAN CONGRESS OF DEM,FACE THE FUTURE. RACE/REL
SOUTH/AFR ELITES LEGIS ADMIN REGION COERCE PEACE DISCRIM
ATTIT 20. PAGE 99 B1999 CONSTN
NAT/G

B61
MUNGER E.S.,AFRICAN FIELD REPORTS 1952-1961. AFR
SOUTH/AFR SOCIETY ECO/UNDEV NAT/G POL/PAR COLONIAL DISCRIM
EXEC PARL/PROC GUERRILLA RACE/REL ALL/IDEOS...SOC RECORD
AUD/VIS 20. PAGE 76 B1538

B62
MORE S.S.,REMODELLING OF DEMOCRACY FOR AFRO-ASIAN ORD/FREE
NATIONS. AFR INDIA S/ASIA SOUTH/AFR CONSTN EX/STRUC ECO/UNDEV
COLONIAL CHOOSE TOTALISM SOVEREIGN NEW/LIB SOCISM ADMIN
...SOC/WK 20. PAGE 75 B1520 LEGIS

B63
GALBRAITH J.S.,RELUCTANT EMPIRE: BRITISH POLICY OF COLONIAL
THE SOUTH AFRICAN FRONTIER, 1834-1854. AFR ADMIN
SOUTH/AFR UK GP/REL RACE/REL DISCRIM...CHARTS POLICY
BIBLIOG 19 MISSION. PAGE 38 B0774 SECT

B64
KIESER P.J.,THE COST OF ADMINISTRATION, SUPERVISION AFR
AND SERVICES IN URBAN BANTU TOWNSHIPS. SOUTH/AFR MGT
SERV/IND MUNIC PROVS ADMIN COST...OBS QU CHARTS 20 FINAN
BANTU. PAGE 60 B1203

B65
LEMAY G.H.,BRITISH SUPREMACY IN SOUTH AFRICA WAR
1899-1907. SOUTH/AFR UK ADMIN CONTROL LEAD GP/REL COLONIAL
ORD/FREE 19/20. PAGE 64 B1286 DOMIN
POLICY

B66
DAVIS J.A.,SOUTHERN AFRICA IN TRANSITION. SOUTH/AFR AFR
USA+45 FINAN NAT/G DELIB/GP EDU/PROP ADMIN COLONIAL ADJUST
REGION RACE/REL ATTIT SOVEREIGN...ANTHOL 20 CONSTN
RESOURCE/N. PAGE 26 B0538

S67
RAUM O.,"THE MODERN LEADERSHIP GROUP AMONG THE RACE/REL
SOUTH AFRICAN XHOSA." SOUTH/AFR SOCIETY SECT KIN
EX/STRUC REPRESENT GP/REL INGP/REL PERSON LEAD
...METH/COMP 17/20 XHOSA NEGRO. PAGE 86 B1743 CULTURE

SOUTH/AMER....SOUTH AMERICA

B51
CHRISTENSEN A.N.,THE EVOLUTION OF LATIN AMERICAN NAT/G
GOVERNMENT: A BOOK OF READINGS. ECO/UNDEV INDUS CONSTN
LOC/G POL/PAR EX/STRUC LEGIS FOR/AID CT/SYS DIPLOM
...SOC/WK 20 SOUTH/AMER. PAGE 21 B0428 L/A+17C

SOUTH/CAR....SOUTH CAROLINA

SOUTH/DAK....SOUTH DAKOTA

B62
FARBER W.O.,GOVERNMENT OF SOUTH DAKOTA. USA+45 PROVS
DIST/IND POL/PAR CHIEF EX/STRUC LEGIS ECO/TAC GIVE LOC/G
EDU/PROP CT/SYS PARTIC...T 20 SOUTH/DAK GOVERNOR. ADMIN
PAGE 35 B0704 CONSTN

SOUTH/US....SOUTH (UNITED STATES)

B65
FRIEDMAN L.,SOUTHERN JUSTICE. USA+45 PUB/INST LEGIT ADJUD
ADMIN CT/SYS DISCRIM...DECISION ANTHOL 20 NEGRO LAW
SOUTH/US CIV/RIGHTS. PAGE 37 B0758 CONSTN
RACE/REL

SOUTHEAST ASIA....SEE S/EASTASIA, S/ASIA

SOUTHEAST ASIA TREATY ORGANIZATION....SEE SEATO

SOUTHERN RHODESIA....SEE RHODESIA, COMMONWLTH

SOVEREIGN....SOVEREIGNTY

B00
MORRIS H.C.,THE HISTORY OF COLONIZATION. WOR+45 DOMIN
WOR-45 ECO/DEV ECO/UNDEV INT/ORG ACT/RES PLAN SOVEREIGN
ECO/TAC LEGIT ROUTINE COERCE ATTIT DRIVE ALL/VALS COLONIAL
...GEOG TREND 19. PAGE 76 B1528

N19
JACKSON R.G.A.,THE CASE FOR AN INTERNATIONAL FOR/AID
DEVELOPMENT AUTHORITY (PAMPHLET). WOR+45 ECO/DEV INT/ORG
DIPLOM GIVE CONTROL GP/REL EFFICIENCY NAT/LISM ECO/UNDEV
SOVEREIGN 20. PAGE 55 B1108 ADMIN

B21
STOWELL E.C.,INTERVENTION IN INTERNATIONAL LAW. BAL/PWR
UNIV LAW SOCIETY INT/ORG ACT/RES PLAN LEGIT ROUTINE SOVEREIGN
WAR...JURID OBS GEN/LAWS 20. PAGE 101 B2050

C27
HSIAO K.C.,"POLITICAL PLURALISM." LAW CONSTN STRUCT
POL/PAR LEGIS PLAN ADMIN CENTRAL SOVEREIGN GEN/LAWS
...INT/LAW BIBLIOG 19/20. PAGE 52 B1053 PLURISM

B29
BUELL R.,INTERNATIONAL RELATIONS. WOR+45 WOR-45 INT/ORG
CONSTN STRATA FORCES TOP/EX ADMIN ATTIT DRIVE BAL/PWR
SUPEGO MORAL ORD/FREE PWR SOVEREIGN...JURID SOC DIPLOM
CONCPT 20. PAGE 17 B0340

B29
ROBERTS S.H.,HISTORY OF FRENCH COLONIAL POLICY. AFR INT/ORG
ASIA L/A+17C S/ASIA CULTURE ECO/DEV ECO/UNDEV FINAN ACT/RES
NAT/G PLAN ECO/TAC DOMIN ROUTINE SOVEREIGN...OBS FRANCE
HIST/WRIT TREND CHARTS VAL/FREE 19/20. PAGE 89 COLONIAL
B1796

B31
DEKAT A.D.A.,COLONIAL POLICY. S/ASIA CULTURE DRIVE
EX/STRUC ECO/TAC DOMIN ADMIN COLONIAL ROUTINE PWR
SOVEREIGN WEALTH...POLICY MGT RECORD KNO/TEST SAMP. INDONESIA
PAGE 28 B0570 NETHERLAND

B37
ROYAL INST. INT. AFF.,THE COLONIAL PROBLEM. WOR-45 INT/ORG
LAW ECO/DEV ECO/UNDEV NAT/G PLAN ECO/TAC EDU/PROP ACT/RES
ADMIN ATTIT ALL/VALS...CONCPT 20. PAGE 91 B1844 SOVEREIGN
COLONIAL

B39
ANDERSON W.,LOCAL GOVERNMENT IN EUROPE. FRANCE GOV/COMP
GERMANY ITALY UK USSR MUNIC PROVS ADMIN GOV/REL NAT/COMP
CENTRAL SOVEREIGN 20. PAGE 5 B0099 LOC/G
CONSTN

C40
FAHS C.B.,"GOVERNMENT IN JAPAN." FINAN FORCES LEGIS ASIA
TOP/EX BUDGET INT/TRADE EDU/PROP SOVEREIGN DIPLOM
...CON/ANAL BIBLIOG/A 20 CHINJAP. PAGE 34 B0698 NAT/G
ADMIN

L44
CORWIN E.S.,"THE CONSTITUTION AND WORLD INT/ORG
ORGANIZATION." FUT USA+45 USA-45 NAT/G EX/STRUC CONSTN
LEGIS PEACE KNOWL...CON/ANAL UN 20. PAGE 24 B0484 SOVEREIGN

B46
GRIFFIN G.G.,A GUIDE TO MANUSCRIPTS RELATING TO BIBLIOG/A
AMERICAN HISTORY IN BRITISH DEPOSITORIES. CANADA ALL/VALS
IRELAND MOD/EUR UK USA-45 LAW DIPLOM ADMIN COLONIAL NAT/G
WAR NAT/LISM SOVEREIGN...GEOG INT/LAW 15/19
CMN/WLTH. PAGE 43 B0876

B47
BORGESE G.,COMMON CAUSE. LAW CONSTN SOCIETY STRATA WOR+45
ECO/DEV INT/ORG POL/PAR FORCES LEGIS TOP/EX CAP/ISM NAT/G
DIPLOM ADMIN EXEC ATTIT PWR 20. PAGE 14 B0279 SOVEREIGN
REGION

B47
CROCKER W.R.,ON GOVERNING COLONIES: BEING AN COLONIAL
OUTLINE OF THE REAL ISSUES AND A COMPARISON OF THE POLICY
BRITISH, FRENCH, AND BELGIAN... AFR BELGIUM FRANCE GOV/COMP
UK CULTURE SOVEREIGN...OBS 20. PAGE 25 B0505 ADMIN

B48
SPERO S.D.,GOVERNMENT AS EMPLOYER. USA+45 NAT/G SOVEREIGN
EX/STRUC ADMIN CONTROL EXEC 20. PAGE 99 B2005 INGP/REL
REPRESENT
CONFER

B52
BRINTON C.,THE ANATOMY OF REVOLUTION. FRANCE UK SOCIETY
USA-45 USSR WOR-45 ELITES INTELL ECO/DEV NAT/G CONCPT
EX/STRUC FORCES COERCE DRIVE ORD/FREE PWR SOVEREIGN REV
...MYTH HIST/WRIT GEN/LAWS. PAGE 15 B0311

B54
US SENATE COMM ON FOREIGN REL,REVIEW OF THE UNITED BIBLIOG
NATIONS CHARTER: A COLLECTION OF DOCUMENTS. LEGIS CONSTN
DIPLOM ADMIN ARMS/CONT WAR REPRESENT SOVEREIGN INT/ORG
...INT/LAW 20 UN. PAGE 110 B2220 DEBATE

B55
APTER D.E.,THE GOLD COAST IN TRANSITION. FUT CONSTN AFR
CULTURE SOCIETY ECO/UNDEV FAM KIN LOC/G NAT/G SOVEREIGN
POL/PAR LEGIS TOP/EX EDU/PROP LEGIT ADMIN ATTIT
PERSON PWR...CONCPT STAT INT CENSUS TOT/POP
VAL/FREE. PAGE 6 B0120

B55

CHOWDHURI R.N.,INTERNATIONAL MANDATES AND
TRUSTEESHIP SYSTEMS. WOR+45 STRUCT ECO/UNDEV
INT/ORG LEGIS DOMIN EDU/PROP LEGIT ADJUD EXEC PWR
...CONCPT TIME/SEQ UN 20. PAGE 21 B0427
DELIB/GP
PLAN
SOVEREIGN

B55

UN HEADQUARTERS LIBRARY,BIBLIOGRAPHIE DE LA CHARTE
DES NATIONS UNIES. CHINA/COM KOREA WOR+45 VOL/ASSN
CONFER ADMIN COERCE PEACE ATTIT ORD/FREE SOVEREIGN
...INT/LAW 20 UNESCO UN. PAGE 106 B2149
BIBLIOG/A
INT/ORG
DIPLOM

B57

KAPLAN M.A.,SYSTEM AND PROCESS OF INTERNATIONAL
POLITICS. FUT WOR+45 WOR-45 SOCIETY PLAN BAL/PWR
ADMIN ATTIT PERSON RIGID/FLEX PWR SOVEREIGN
...DECISION TREND VAL/FREE. PAGE 58 B1168
INT/ORG
DIPLOM

B58

COWAN L.G.,LOCAL GOVERNMENT IN WEST AFRICA. AFR
FRANCE UK CULTURE KIN POL/PAR CHIEF LEGIS CREATE
ADMIN PARTIC GOV/REL GP/REL...METH/COMP 20. PAGE 24
B0498
LOC/G
COLONIAL
SOVEREIGN
REPRESENT

B58

LOVEJOY D.S.,RHODE ISLAND POLITICS AND THE AMERICAN
REVOLUTION 1760-1776. UK USA-45 ELITES EX/STRUC TAX
LEAD REPRESENT GOV/REL GP/REL ATTIT 18 RHODE/ISL.
PAGE 67 B1343
REV
COLONIAL
ECO/TAC
SOVEREIGN

B59

GORDENKER L.,THE UNITED NATIONS AND THE PEACEFUL
UNIFICATION OF KOREA. ASIA LAW LOC/G CONSULT
ACT/RES DIPLOM DOMIN LEGIT ADJUD ADMIN ORD/FREE
SOVEREIGN...INT GEN/METH UN COLD/WAR 20. PAGE 41
B0829
DELIB/GP
KOREA
INT/ORG

B59

SINHA H.N.,OUTLINES OF POLITICAL SCIENCE. NAT/G
POL/PAR EX/STRUC LEGIS CT/SYS CHOOSE REPRESENT 20.
PAGE 98 B1971
JURID
CONCPT
ORD/FREE
SOVEREIGN

S59

BAILEY S.D.,"THE FUTURE COMPOSITION OF THE
TRUSTEESHIP COUNCIL." FUT WOR+45 CONSTN VOL/ASSN
ADMIN ATTIT PWR...OBS TREND CON/ANAL VAL/FREE UN
20. PAGE 8 B0161
INT/ORG
NAT/LISM
SOVEREIGN

S59

SOHN L.B.,"THE DEFINITION OF AGGRESSION." FUT LAW
FORCES LEGIT ADJUD ROUTINE COERCE ORD/FREE PWR
...MAJORIT JURID QUANT COLD/WAR 20. PAGE 99 B1995
INT/ORG
CT/SYS
DETER
SOVEREIGN

B60

ALBI F.,TRATADO DE LOS MODOS DE GESTION DE LAS
CORPORACIONES LOCALES. SPAIN FINAN NAT/G BUDGET
CONTROL EXEC ROUTINE GOV/REL ORD/FREE SOVEREIGN
...MGT 20. PAGE 3 B0068
LOC/G
LAW
ADMIN
MUNIC

B60

MATTOD P.K.,A STUDY OF LOCAL SELF GOVERNMENT IN
URBAN INDIA. INDIA FINAN DELIB/GP LEGIS BUDGET TAX
SOVEREIGN...MGT GP/COMP 20. PAGE 71 B1432
MUNIC
CONSTN
LOC/G
ADMIN

B60

WHEARE K.C.,THE CONSTITUTIONAL STRUCTURE OF THE
COMMONWEALTH. UK EX/STRUC DIPLOM DOMIN ADMIN
COLONIAL CONTROL LEAD INGP/REL SUPEGO 20 CMN/WLTH.
PAGE 115 B2330
CONSTN
INT/ORG
VOL/ASSN
SOVEREIGN

S60

TAYLOR M.G.,"THE ROLE OF THE MEDICAL PROFESSION IN
THE FORMULATION AND EXECUTION OF PUBLIC POLICY
(BMR)." CANADA NAT/G CONSULT ADMIN REPRESENT GP/REL
ROLE SOVEREIGN...DECISION 20 CMA. PAGE 103 B2088
PROF/ORG
HEALTH
LOBBY
POLICY

C60

SCHAPIRO L.B.,"THE COMMUNIST PARTY OF THE SOVIET
UNION." USSR INTELL CHIEF EX/STRUC FORCES DOMIN
ADMIN LEAD WAR ATTIT SOVEREIGN...POLICY BIBLIOG 20.
PAGE 93 B1881
POL/PAR
COM
REV

B61

BAINS J.S.,STUDIES IN POLITICAL SCIENCE. INDIA
WOR+45 WOR-45 CONSTN BAL/PWR ADJUD ADMIN PARL/PROC
SOVEREIGN...SOC METH/COMP ANTHOL 17/20 UN. PAGE 8
B0165
DIPLOM
INT/LAW
NAT/G

B61

CARNEY D.E.,GOVERNMENT AND ECONOMY IN BRITISH WEST
AFRICA. GAMBIA GHANA NIGERIA SIER/LEONE DOMIN ADMIN
GOV/REL SOVEREIGN WEALTH LAISSEZ...BIBLIOG 20
CMN/WLTH. PAGE 19 B0384
METH/COMP
COLONIAL
ECO/TAC
ECO/UNDEV

B61

NARAIN J.P.,SWARAJ FOR THE PEOPLE. INDIA CONSTN
LOC/G MUNIC POL/PAR CHOOSE REPRESENT EFFICIENCY
ATTIT PWR SOVEREIGN 20. PAGE 77 B1553
NAT/G
ORD/FREE
EDU/PROP
EX/STRUC

B61

STONE J.,QUEST FOR SURVIVAL. WOR+45 NAT/G VOL/ASSN
LEGIT ADMIN ARMS/CONT COERCE DISPL ORD/FREE PWR
...POLICY INT/LAW JURID COLD/WAR 20. PAGE 101 B2047
INT/ORG
ADJUD
SOVEREIGN

B61

WEST F.J.,POLITICAL ADVANCEMENT IN THE SOUTH
PACIFIC. CONSTN CULTURE POL/PAR LEGIS DOMIN ADMIN
CHOOSE SOVEREIGN VAL/FREE 20 FIJI TAHITI SAMOA.
PAGE 115 B2325
S/ASIA
LOC/G
COLONIAL

B62

LITTLEFIELD N.,METROPOLITAN AREA PROBLEMS AND
MUNICIPAL HOME RULE. USA+45 PROVS ADMIN CONTROL
GP/REL PWR. PAGE 66 B1328
LOC/G
SOVEREIGN
JURID
LEGIS

B62

MORE S.S.,REMODELLING OF DEMOCRACY FOR AFRO-ASIAN
NATIONS. AFR INDIA S/ASIA SOUTH/AFR CONSTN EX/STRUC
COLONIAL CHOOSE TOTALISM SOVEREIGN NEW/LIB SOCISM
...SOC/WK 20. PAGE 75 B1520
ORD/FREE
ECO/UNDEV
ADMIN
LEGIS

B62

PRESS C.,STATE MANUALS, BLUE BOOKS AND ELECTION
RESULTS. LAW LOC/G MUNIC LEGIS WRITING FEDERAL
SOVEREIGN...DECISION STAT CHARTS 20. PAGE 84 B1700
BIBLIOG
PROVS
ADMIN
CHOOSE

B62

SIMON Y.R.,A GENERAL THEORY OF AUTHORITY. DOMIN
ADMIN RATIONAL UTOPIA KNOWL MORAL PWR SOVEREIGN
...HUM CONCPT NEW/IDEA 20. PAGE 97 B1962
PERS/REL
PERSON
SOCIETY
ORD/FREE

B62

TAYLOR D.,THE BRITISH IN AFRICA. UK CULTURE
ECO/UNDEV INDUS DIPLOM INT/TRADE ADMIN WAR RACE/REL
ORD/FREE SOVEREIGN...POLICY BIBLIOG 15/20 CMN/WLTH.
PAGE 103 B2084
AFR
COLONIAL
DOMIN

B62

THIERRY S.S.,LE VATICAN SECRET. CHRIST-17C EUR+WWI
MOD/EUR VATICAN NAT/G SECT DELIB/GP DOMIN LEGIT
SOVEREIGN. PAGE 104 B2096
ADMIN
EX/STRUC
CATHISM
DECISION

S62

MURACCIOLE L.,"LES CONSTITUTIONS DES ETATS
AFRICAINS D'EXPRESSION FRANCAISE: LA CONSTITUTION
DU 16 AVRIL 1962 DE LA REPUBLIQUE DU" AFR CHAD
CHIEF LEGIS LEGIT COLONIAL EXEC ROUTINE ORD/FREE
SOVEREIGN...SOC CONCPT 20. PAGE 76 B1541
NAT/G
CONSTN

S62

MURACCIOLE L.,"LES MODIFICATIONS DE LA CONSTITUTION
MALGACHE." AFR WOR+45 ECO/UNDEV LEGIT EXEC ALL/VALS
...JURID 20. PAGE 76 B1542
NAT/G
STRUCT
SOVEREIGN
MADAGASCAR

B63

CROZIER B.,THE MORNING AFTER: A STUDY OF
INDEPENDENCE. WOR+45 EX/STRUC PLAN BAL/PWR COLONIAL
GP/REL 20 COLD/WAR. PAGE 25 B0511
SOVEREIGN
NAT/LISM
NAT/G
DIPLOM

B63

HIGA M.,POLITICS AND PARTIES IN POSTWAR OKINAWA.
USA+45 VOL/ASSN LEGIS CONTROL LOBBY CHOOSE NAT/LISM
PWR SOVEREIGN MARXISM SOCISM 20 OKINAWA CHINJAP.
PAGE 50 B1008
GOV/REL
POL/PAR
ADMIN
FORCES

B63

LEONARD T.J.,THE FEDERAL SYSTEM OF INDIA. INDIA
MUNIC NAT/G PROVS ADMIN SOVEREIGN...IDEA/COMP 20.
PAGE 64 B1293
FEDERAL
MGT
NAT/COMP
METH/COMP

B63

MONTER W.,THE GOVERNMENT OF GENEVA, 1536-1605
(DOCTORAL THESIS). SWITZERLND DIPLOM LEAD ORD/FREE
SOVEREIGN 16/17 CALVIN/J ROME. PAGE 74 B1504
SECT
FINAN
LOC/G
ADMIN

S63

BANFIELD J.,"FEDERATION IN EAST-AFRICA." AFR UGANDA
ELITES INT/ORG NAT/G VOL/ASSN LEGIS ECO/TAC FEDERAL
ATTIT SOVEREIGN TOT/POP 20 TANGANYIKA. PAGE 9 B0180
EX/STRUC
PWR
REGION

S63

WAGRET M.,"L'ASCENSION POLITIQUE DE L'U.D.D.I.A.
(CONGO) ET SA PRISE DU POUVOIR (1956-1959)." AFR
WOR+45 NAT/G POL/PAR CONSULT DELIB/GP LEGIS PERCEPT
ALL/VALS SOVEREIGN...TIME/SEQ CONGO. PAGE 113 B2274
EX/STRUC
CHOOSE
FRANCE

B64

SCHECHTER A.H.,INTERPRETATION OF AMBIGUOUS
DOCUMENTS BY INTERNATIONAL ADMINISTRATIVE
TRIBUNALS. WOR+45 EX/STRUC INT/TRADE CT/SYS
SOVEREIGN 20 UN ILO EURCT/JUST. PAGE 93 B1884
INT/LAW
DIPLOM
INT/ORG
ADJUD

B64

TILMAN R.O.,BUREAUCRATIC TRANSITION IN MALAYA.
MALAYSIA S/ASIA UK NAT/G EX/STRUC DIPLOM...CHARTS
BIBLIOG 20. PAGE 104 B2110
ADMIN
COLONIAL
SOVEREIGN
EFFICIENCY

B64

VECCHIO G.D.,L'ETAT ET LE DROIT. ITALY CONSTN
EX/STRUC LEGIS DIPLOM CT/SYS...JURID 20 UN.
PAGE 112 B2256
NAT/G
SOVEREIGN
CONCPT
INT/LAW

B65

ADU A.L.,THE CIVIL SERVICE IN NEW AFRICAN STATES.
AFR GHANA FINAN SOVEREIGN...POLICY 20 CIVIL/SERV
AFRICA/E AFRICA/W. PAGE 3 B0062
ECO/UNDEV
ADMIN
COLONIAL
NAT/G

B65

GOTLIEB A.,DISARMAMENT AND INTERNATIONAL LAW* A
STUDY OF THE ROLE OF LAW IN THE DISARMAMENT
PROCESS. USA+45 USSR PROB/SOLV CONFER ADMIN ROUTINE
NUC/PWR ORD/FREE SOVEREIGN UN TREATY. PAGE 42 B0841
INT/LAW
INT/ORG
ARMS/CONT
IDEA/COMP

PURCELL V..THE MEMOIRS OF A MALAYAN OFFICIAL.
MALAYSIA UK ECO/UNDEV INDUS LABOR EDU/PROP COLONIAL
CT/SYS WAR NAT/LISM TOTALISM ORD/FREE SOVEREIGN 20
UN CIVIL/SERV. PAGE 85 B1721
B65
BIOG
ADMIN
JURID
FORCES

ROTBERG R.I..A POLITICAL HISTORY OF TROPICAL
AFRICA. EX/STRUC DIPLOM INT/TRADE DOMIN ADMIN
RACE/REL NAT/LISM TOTALSM ORD/FREE SOVEREIGN...GEOG TIME/SEQ
BIBLIOG 1/20. PAGE 91 B1832
B65
AFR
CULTURE
COLONIAL

WARD W.E..GOVERNMENT IN WEST AFRICA. WOR+45 POL/PAR
EX/STRUC PLAN PARTIC GP/REL SOVEREIGN 20 AFRICA/W.
PAGE 114 B2291
B65
GOV/COMP
CONSTN
COLONIAL
ECO/UNDEV

YOUNG C..POLITICS IN THE CONGO* DECOLONIZATION AND
INDEPENDENCE. ELITES STRATA FORCES ADMIN REV
RACE/REL FEDERAL SOVEREIGN...OBS INT CHARTS
CONGO/LEOP. PAGE 118 B2391
B65
BELGIUM
COLONIAL
NAT/LISM

DAVIS J.A..SOUTHERN AFRICA IN TRANSITION. SOUTH/AFR
USA+45 FINAN NAT/G DELIB/GP EDU/PROP ADMIN COLONIAL
REGION RACE/REL ATTIT SOVEREIGN...ANTHOL 20
RESOURCE/N. PAGE 26 B0538
B66
AFR
ADJUST
CONSTN

DILLEY M.R..BRITISH POLICY IN KENYA COLONY (2ND
ED.). AFR INDIA UK LABOR BUDGET TAX ADMIN PARL/PROC
GP/REL...BIBLIOG 20 PARLIAMENT. PAGE 29 B0594
B66
COLONIAL
REPRESENT
SOVEREIGN

KAUNDA K..ZAMBIA: INDEPENDENCE AND BEYOND: THE
SPEECHES OF KENNETH KAUNDA. AFR FUT ZAMBIA SOCIETY
ECO/UNDEV NAT/G PROB/SOLV ECO/TAC ADMIN RACE/REL
SOVEREIGN 20. PAGE 59 B1183
B66
ORD/FREE
COLONIAL
CONSTN
LEAD

"RESTRICTIVE SOVEREIGN IMMUNITY, THE STATE
DEPARTMENT, AND THE COURTS." USA+45 USA-45 EX/STRUC
DIPLOM ADJUD CONTROL GOV/REL 19/20 DEPT/STATE
SUPREME/CT. PAGE 2 B0047
L67
SOVEREIGN
ORD/FREE
PRIVIL
CT/SYS

ROTBERG R.I.."COLONIALISM AND AFTER: THE POLITICAL
LITERATURE OF CENTRAL AFRICA - A BIBLIOGRAPHIC
ESSAY." AFR CHIEF EX/STRUC REV INGP/REL RACE/REL
SOVEREIGN 20. PAGE 91 B1833
S67
BIBLIOG/A
COLONIAL
DIPLOM
NAT/G

TIVEY L.."THE POLITICAL CONSEQUENCES OF ECONOMIC
PLANNING." UK CONSTN INDUS ACT/RES ADMIN CONTROL
LOBBY REPRESENT EFFICIENCY SUPEGO SOVEREIGN
...DECISION 20. PAGE 104 B2112
S67
PLAN
POLICY
NAT/G

BOLINSBROKE H ST J..A DISSERTATION UPON PARTIES
(1729). UK LEGIS CHOOSE GOV/REL SOVEREIGN...TRADIT
18 PARLIAMENT. PAGE 13 B0269
B86
CONSERVE
POL/PAR
CHIEF
EX/STRUC

SOVEREIGNTY....SEE SOVEREIGN

SOVIET UNION....SEE USSR

SOVIET-EAST EUROPEAN RES SERV B2001

SPACE....OUTER SPACE, SPACE LAW

TAUBENFELD H.J.."OUTER SPACE--PAST POLITICS AND
FUTURE POLICY." FUT USA+45 USA-45 WOR+45 AIR INTELL
STRUCT ECO/DEV NAT/G TOP/EX ACT/RES ADMIN ROUTINE
NUC/PWR ATTIT DRIVE...CONCPT TIME/SEQ TREND TOT/POP
20. PAGE 103 B2083
S61
PLAN
SPACE
INT/ORG

KENNEDY J.F..TO TURN THE TIDE. SPACE AGRI INT/ORG
FORCES TEC/DEV ADMIN NUC/PWR PEACE WEALTH...ANTHOL
20 KENNEDY/JF CIV/RIGHTS. PAGE 59 B1193
B62
DIPLOM
CHIEF
POLICY
NAT/G

KAST F.E..SCIENCE, TECHNOLOGY, AND MANAGEMENT.
SPACE USA+45 FORCES CONFER DETER NUC/PWR...PHIL/SCI
CHARTS ANTHOL BIBLIOG 20 NASA. PAGE 58 B1179
B63
MGT
PLAN
TEC/DEV
PROB/SOLV

NASA,CONFERENCE ON SPACE, SCIENCE, AND URBAN LIFE.
USA+45 SOCIETY INDUS ACADEM ACT/RES ECO/TAC ADMIN
20. PAGE 77 B1556
B63
MUNIC
SPACE
TEC/DEV
PROB/SOLV

MELMANS S..OUR DEPLETED SOCIETY. SPACE USA+45
ECO/DEV FORCES BUDGET ECO/TAC ADMIN WEAPON
EFFICIENCY 20 COLD/WAR. PAGE 73 B1465
B65
CIVMIL/REL
INDUS
EDU/PROP
CONTROL

ROSHOLT R.L..AN ADMINISTRATIVE HISTORY OF NASA,
1958-1963. SPACE USA+45 FINAN LEAD...MGT CHARTS
BIBLIOG 20 NASA. PAGE 90 B1824
B66
ADMIN
EX/STRUC
ADJUST
DELIB/GP

UNIVERSAL REFERENCE SYSTEM,PUBLIC POLICY AND THE
B67
BIBLIOG/A

MANAGEMENT OF SCIENCE (VOLUME IX). FUT SPACE WOR+45
LAW NAT/G TEC/DEV CONTROL NUC/PWR GOV/REL
...COMPUT/IR GEN/METH. PAGE 107 B2165
POLICY
MGT
PHIL/SCI

MACDONALD G.J.F.."SCIENCE AND SPACE POLICY* HOW
DOES IT GET PLANNED?" R+D CREATE TEC/DEV BUDGET
ADMIN ROUTINE...DECISION NASA. PAGE 67 B1357
S67
SPACE
PLAN
MGT
EX/STRUC

US SUPERINTENDENT OF DOCUMENTS,SPACE: MISSILES, THE
MOON, NASA, AND SATELLITES (PRICE LIST 79A). USA+45
COM/IND R+D NAT/G DIPLOM EDU/PROP ADMIN CONTROL
HEALTH...POLICY SIMUL NASA CONGRESS. PAGE 111 B2244
N67
BIBLIOG/A
SPACE
TEC/DEV
PEACE

US SENATE COMM AERO SPACE SCI,AERONAUTICAL RESEARCH
AND DEVELOPMENT POLICY; HEARINGS, COMM ON
AERONAUTICAL AND SPACE SCIENCES...1967 (PAMPHLET).
R+D PROB/SOLV EXEC GOV/REL 20 DEPT/DEFEN FAA NASA
CONGRESS. PAGE 109 B2210
N67
DIST/IND
SPACE
NAT/G
PLAN

SPACKMAN A. B2002

SPAIN....SPAIN

PETTEE G.S..THE PROCESS OF REVOLUTION. COM FRANCE
ITALY MOD/EUR RUSSIA SPAIN WOR-45 ELITES INTELL
SOCIETY STRATA STRUCT INT/ORG NAT/G POL/PAR ACT/RES
PLAN EDU/PROP LEGIT EXEC...SOC MYTH TIME/SEQ
TOT/POP 18/20. PAGE 82 B1664
B38
COERCE
CONCPT
REV

WELCH S.R..PORTUGUESE RULE AND SPANISH CROWN IN
SOUTH AFRICA 1581-1640. PORTUGAL SOUTH/AFR SPAIN
SOCIETY KIN NEIGH SECT INT/TRADE ADMIN 16/17
MISSION. PAGE 115 B2317
B50
DIPLOM
COLONIAL
WAR
PEACE

GUAITA A..BIBLIOGRAFIA ESPANOLA DE DERECHO
ADMINISTRATIVO (PAMPHLET). SPAIN LOC/G MUNIC NAT/G
PROVS JUDGE BAL/PWR GOV/REL OWN...JURID 18/19.
PAGE 44 B0900
B55
BIBLIOG
ADMIN
CONSTN
PWR

ALBI F..TRATADO DE LOS MODOS DE GESTION DE LAS
CORPORACIONES LOCALES. SPAIN FINAN NAT/G BUDGET
CONTROL EXEC ROUTINE GOV/REL ORD/FREE SOVEREIGN
...MGT 20. PAGE 3 B0068
B60
LOC/G
LAW
ADMIN
MUNIC

GARCIA E..LA ADMINISTRACION ESPANOLA. SPAIN GOV/REL
...CONCPT METH/COMP 20. PAGE 39 B0780
B61
ADMIN
NAT/G
LOC/G
DECISION

LYNCH J..ADMINISTRATION COLONIAL ESPANOLA
1782-1810. SPAIN PROVS TOP/EX PARTIC 18/19 ARGEN.
PAGE 67 B1349
B62
COLONIAL
CONTROL
ADJUD
ADMIN

TURNER M.C..LIBROS EN VENTA EN HISPANOAMERICA Y
ESPANA. SPAIN LAW CONSTN CULTURE ADMIN LEAD...HUM
SOC 20. PAGE 106 B2139
B64
BIBLIOG
L/A+17C
NAT/G
DIPLOM

HISPANIC SOCIETY OF AMERICA,CATALOGUE (10 VOLS.).
PORTUGAL PRE/AMER SPAIN NAT/G ADMIN...POLICY SOC
15/20. PAGE 50 B1018
B65
BIBLIOG
L/A+17C
COLONIAL
DIPLOM

ORG FOR ECO COOP AND DEVEL,THE MEDITERRANEAN
REGIONAL PROJECT: AN EXPERIMENT IN PLANNING BY SIX
COUNTRIES. FUT GREECE SPAIN TURKEY YUGOSLAVIA
SOCIETY FINAN NAT/G PROF/ORG EDU/PROP ADMIN REGION
COST...POLICY STAT CHARTS 20 OECD. PAGE 80 B1614
B65
PLAN
ECO/UNDEV
ACADEM
SCHOOL

SPAN/AMER....SPANISH-AMERICAN CULTURE

SPEAKER OF THE HOUSE....SEE CONGRESS, HOUSE/REP, LEGIS,
    PARLIAMENT

SPEAR P. B2003

SPEAR/BRWN....SPEARMAN BROWN PREDICTION FORMULA

SPECIAL DRAWING RIGHTS....SEE SDR

SPECIALIZATION....SEE TASK, SKILL

SPECULATION....SEE GAMBLE, RISK

SPEECKAERT G.P. B2004

SPENCER/H....HERBERT SPENCER

SPENGLER J.J. B0300

SPENGLER/O....OSWALD SPENGLER

SPERO S.D. B2005

SPICER K. B2006

SPINELLI A. B2007

SPINOZA/B....BARUCH (OR BENEDICT) SPINOZA

SPIRO H.J. B2008

SPITZ A.A. B2009

SPITZ D. B2010

SPIVEY W.A. B0283

SPOCK/B....BENJAMIN SPOCK

SPORTS....SPORTS AND ATHLETIC COMPETITIONS

SPRING D. B2012

SPRINGER H.W. B2013

SRAFFA/P....PIERO SRAFFA

SRINIVASAN R. B0067

SRIVASTAVA G.L. B2014

SST....SUPERSONIC TRANSPORT

ST/LOUIS....ST. LOUIS, MO.

ST/PAUL....SAINT PAUL, MINNESOTA

STAAR R.F. B2015

STAGES....SEE TIME/SEQ

STAHL O.G. B0976,B2016,B2017

STALIN/J....JOSEPH STALIN

B48
TOWSTER J.,POLITICAL POWER IN THE USSR: 1917-1947. EX/STRUC
USSR CONSTN CULTURE ELITES CREATE PLAN COERCE NAT/G
CENTRAL ATTIT RIGID/FLEX ORD/FREE...BIBLIOG MARXISM
SOC/INTEG 20 LENIN/VI STALIN/J. PAGE 105 B2124 PWR

B51
LEITES N.,THE OPERATIONAL CODE OF THE POLITBURO. DELIB/GP
COM USSR CREATE PLAN DOMIN LEGIT COERCE ALL/VALS ADMIN
...SOC CONCPT MYTH TREND CON/ANAL GEN/LAWS 20 SOCISM
LENIN/VI STALIN/J. PAGE 64 B1284

S62
HUDSON G.F.,"SOVIET FEARS OF THE WEST." COM USA+45 ATTIT
SOCIETY DELIB/GP EX/STRUC TOP/EX ACT/RES CREATE MYTH
DOMIN EDU/PROP LEGIT ADMIN ROUTINE DRIVE PERSON GERMANY
RIGID/FLEX PWR...RECORD TIME/SEQ TOT/POP 20 USSR
STALIN/J. PAGE 52 B1057

S64
RIGBY T.H.,"TRADITIONAL, MARKET, AND ORGANIZATIONAL MARKET
SOCIETIES AND THE USSR." COM ECO/DEV NAT/G POL/PAR ADMIN
ECO/TAC DOMIN ORD/FREE PWR WEALTH...TIME/SEQ USSR
GEN/LAWS VAL/FREE 20 STALIN/J. PAGE 88 B1784

B67
BRZEZINSKI Z.K.,THE SOVIET BLOC: UNITY AND CONFLICT NAT/G
(2ND ED., REV., ENLARGED). COM POLAND USSR INTELL DIPLOM
CHIEF EX/STRUC CONTROL EXEC GOV/REL PWR MARXISM
...TREND IDEA/COMP 20 LENIN/VI MARX/KARL STALIN/J.
PAGE 16 B0336

B67
FARNSWORTH B.,WILLIAM C. BULLITT AND THE SOVIET DIPLOM
UNION. COM USA+45 USSR NAT/G CHIEF CONSULT DELIB/GP BIOG
EX/STRUC WAR REPRESENT MARXISM 20 WILSON/W POLICY
ROOSEVLT/F STALIN/J BULLITT/WC. PAGE 35 B0705

STAMMLER/R....RUDOLF STAMMLER

STAND/INT....STANDARDIZED INTERVIEWS

S55
WEISS R.S.,"A METHOD FOR THE ANALYSIS OF THE PROF/ORG
STRUCTURE OF COMPLEX ORGANIZATIONS." WOR+45 INDUS SOC/EXP
LG/CO NAT/G EXEC ROUTINE ORD/FREE PWR SKILL...MGT
PSY SOC NEW/IDEA STAT INT REC/INT STAND/INT CHARTS
WORK. PAGE 115 B2316

B59
CHINA INSTITUTE OF AMERICA,,CHINA AND THE UNITED ASIA
NATIONS. CHINA/COM FUT STRUCT EDU/PROP LEGIT ADMIN INT/ORG
ATTIT KNOWL ORD/FREE PWR...OBS RECORD STAND/INT
TIME/SEQ UN LEAGUE/NAT UNESCO 20. PAGE 21 B0425

S60
EMERSON R.,"THE EROSION OF DEMOCRACY." AFR FUT LAW S/ASIA
CULTURE INTELL SOCIETY ECO/UNDEV FAM LOC/G NAT/G POL/PAR
FORCES PLAN TEC/DEV ECO/TAC ADMIN CT/SYS ATTIT
ORD/FREE PWR...SOCIALIST SOC CONCPT STAND/INT
TIME/SEQ WORK 20. PAGE 33 B0671

B61
MARVICK D.,,POLITICAL DECISION-MAKERS. INTELL STRATA TOP/EX
NAT/G POL/PAR EX/STRUC LEGIS DOMIN EDU/PROP ATTIT BIOG
PERSON PWR...PSY STAT OBS CONT/OBS STAND/INT ELITES
UNPLAN/INT TIME/SEQ CHARTS STERTYP VAL/FREE.
PAGE 70 B1416

S67
BURACK E.H.,"INDUSTRIAL MANAGEMENT IN ADVANCED ADMIN
PRODUCTION SYSTEMS: SOME THEORETICAL CONCEPTS AND MGT
PRELIMINARY FINDINGS." INDUS CREATE PLAN PRODUC TEC/DEV
ROLE...OBS STAND/INT DEEP/QU HYPO/EXP ORG/CHARTS EX/STRUC
20. PAGE 17 B0346

STANDARDIZED INTERVIEWS....SEE STAND/INT

STANFORD RESEARCH INSTITUTE B2018

STANFORD/U....STANFORD UNIVERSITY

STANKIEW/W.....W.J. STANKIEWICZ

STANKIEWICZ, W.J.....SEE STANKIEW/W

STANLEY D.T. B2019,B2020,B2021

STANLEY T.W. B2022

STAR/CARR....STAR-CARR, A PREHISTORIC SOCIETY

STARBUCK W.H. B0518

STARR M.K. B2023

STARRATT E.E. B0724

STAT....STATISTICS; SEE ALSO ACCT

N
ECONOMIC LIBRARY SELECTIONS. AGRI INDUS MARKET BIBLIOG/A
ADMIN...STAT NAT/COMP 20. PAGE 2 B0026 WRITING
FINAN

B19
LOS ANGELES BD CIV SERV COMNRS,ANNUAL REPORT: LOS DELIB/GP
ANGELES CALIFORNIA: 1919-1936. USA-45 LAW GOV/REL ADMIN
PRODUC...STAT 20. PAGE 66 B1340 LOC/G
MUNIC

N19
BUREAU OF NAT'L AFFAIRS INC.,A CURRENT LOOK AT: DISCRIM
(1) THE NEGRO AND TITLE VII, (2) SEX AND TITLE VII SEX
(PAMPHLET). LAW LG/CO SML/CO RACE/REL...POLICY SOC WORKER
STAT DEEP/QU TREND CON/ANAL CHARTS 20 NEGRO MGT
CIV/RIGHTS. PAGE 17 B0350

B33
DANGERFIELD R.,IN DEFENSE OF THE SENATE. USA-45 LEGIS
CONSTN NAT/G EX/STRUC TOP/EX ATTIT KNOWL DELIB/GP
...METH/CNCPT STAT TIME/SEQ TREND CON/ANAL CHARTS DIPLOM
CONGRESS 20 TREATY. PAGE 26 B0528

B38
LANGE O.,ON THE ECONOMIC THEORY OF SOCIALISM. UNIV MARKET
ECO/DEV FINAN INDUS INT/ORG PUB/INST ROUTINE ATTIT ECO/TAC
ALL/VALS...SOC CONCPT STAT TREND 20. PAGE 62 B1258 INT/TRADE
SOCISM

B40
PFIFFNER J.M.,RESEARCH METHODS IN PUBLIC ADMIN
ADMINISTRATION. USA-45 R+D...MGT STAT INT QU T 20. OP/RES
PAGE 82 B1665 METH
TEC/DEV

B44
DAHL D.,SICKNESS BENEFITS AND GROUP PURCHASE OF BIBLIOG/A
MEDICAL CARE FOR INDUSTRIAL EMPLOYEES. FAM LABOR INDUS
NAT/G PLAN...POLICY MGT SOC STAT 20. PAGE 25 B0519 WORKER
HEAL

B44
DAVIS H.E.,PIONEERS IN WORLD ORDER. WOR-45 CONSTN INT/ORG
ECO/TAC DOMIN EDU/PROP LEGIT ADJUD ADMIN ARMS/CONT ROUTINE
CHOOSE KNOWL ORD/FREE...POLICY JURID SOC STAT OBS
CENSUS TIME/SEQ ANTHOL LEAGUE/NAT 20. PAGE 26 B0537

B45
BENJAMIN H.C.,EMPLOYMENT TESTS IN INDUSTRY AND BIBLIOG/A
BUSINESS. LG/CO WORKER ROUTINE...MGT PSY SOC METH
CLASSIF PROBABIL STAT APT/TEST KNO/TEST PERS/TEST TESTS
20. PAGE 10 B0211 INDUS

C50
WAGER P.W.,"COUNTY GOVERNMENT ACROSS THE NATION." LOC/G
USA+45 CONSTN COM/IND FINAN SCHOOL DOMIN CT/SYS PROVS
LEAD GOV/REL...STAT BIBLIOG 20. PAGE 112 B2272 ADMIN
ROUTINE

B51
HARDMAN J.B.,THE HOUSE OF LABOR. LAW R+D NEIGH LABOR
EDU/PROP LEAD ROUTINE REPRESENT GP/REL...POLICY LOBBY
STAT. PAGE 47 B0945 ADMIN
PRESS

B51
US TARIFF COMMISSION,LIST OF PUBLICATIONS OF THE BIBLIOG
TARIFF COMMISSION (PAMPHLET). USA+45 USA-45 AGRI TARIFFS
EXTR/IND INDUS INT/TRADE...STAT 20. PAGE 111 B2245 NAT/G

ADMIN
B53

CALDWELL L.K.,RESEARCH METHODS IN PUBLIC   BIBLIOG/A
ADMINISTRATION: AN OUTLINE OF TOPICS AND READINGS   METH/COMP
(PAMPHLET). LAW ACT/RES COMPUTER KNOWL...SOC STAT   ADMIN
GEN/METH 20. PAGE 18 B0365   OP/RES

B53

MACK R.T.,RAISING THE WORLDS STANDARD OF LIVING.   WOR+45
IRAN INT/ORG VOL/ASSN EX/STRUC ECO/TAC WEALTH...MGT   FOR/AID
METH/CNCPT STAT CONT/OBS INT TOT/POP VAL/FREE 20   INT/TRADE
UN. PAGE 67 B1363

B54

DUVERGER M.,POLITICAL PARTIES: THEIR ORGANIZATION   POL/PAR
AND ACTIVITY IN THE MODERN STATE. EUR+WWI MOD/EUR   EX/STRUC
USA+45 USA-45 EDU/PROP ADMIN ROUTINE ATTIT DRIVE   ELITES
ORD/FREE PWR...SOC CONCPT MATH STAT TIME/SEQ
TOT/POP 19/20. PAGE 31 B0635

B54

LOCKLIN D.P.,ECONOMICS OF TRANSPORTATION (4TH ED.).   ECO/DEV
USA+45 USA-45 SEA AIR LAW FINAN LG/CO EX/STRUC   DIST/IND
ADMIN CONTROL...STAT CHARTS 19/20 RAILROAD   ECO/TAC
PUB/TRANS. PAGE 66 B1335   TEC/DEV

C54

ROBSON W.A.,"GREAT CITIES OF THE WORLD: THEIR   LOC/G
GOVERNMENT, POLITICS, AND PLANNING." CONSTN FINAN   MUNIC
EX/STRUC ADMIN EXEC CHOOSE GOV/REL...STAT TREND   PLAN
ANTHOL BIBLIOG 20. PAGE 89 B1806   PROB/SOLV

B55

APTER D.E.,THE GOLD COAST IN TRANSITION. FUT CONSTN   AFR
CULTURE SOCIETY ECO/UNDEV FAM KIN LOC/G NAT/G   SOVEREIGN
POL/PAR LEGIS TOP/EX EDU/PROP LEGIT ADMIN ATTIT
PERSON PWR...CONCPT STAT INT CENSUS TOT/POP
VAL/FREE. PAGE 6 B0120

B55

RILEY V.,INTERINDUSTRY ECONOMIC STUDIES. USA+45   BIBLIOG
COMPUTER ADMIN OPTIMAL PRODUC...MGT CLASSIF STAT.   ECO/DEV
PAGE 88 B1788   PLAN
STRUCT

S55

CROCKETT W.H.,"EMERGENT LEADERSHIP IN SMALL   DELIB/GP
DECISION MAKING GROUPS." ACT/RES ROUTINE PERS/REL   ADMIN
ATTIT...STAT CONT/OBS SOC/EXP SIMUL. PAGE 25 B0507   PSY
DECISION

S55

WEISS R.S.,"A METHOD FOR THE ANALYSIS OF THE   PROF/ORG
STRUCTURE OF COMPLEX ORGANIZATIONS." WOR+45 INDUS   SOC/EXP
LG/CO NAT/G EXEC ROUTINE ORD/FREE PWR SKILL...MGT
PSY SOC NEW/IDEA STAT INT REC/INT STAND/INT CHARTS
WORK. PAGE 115 B2316

B56

DUNNILL F.,THE CIVIL SERVICE. UK LAW PLAN ADMIN   PERSON
EFFICIENCY DRIVE NEW/LIB...STAT CHARTS 20   WORKER
PARLIAMENT CIVIL/SERV. PAGE 31 B0633   STRATA
SOC/WK

B56

GARDNER R.N.,STERLING-DOLLAR DIPLOMACY. EUR+WWI   ECO/DEV
USA+45 INT/ORG NAT/G PLAN INT/TRADE EDU/PROP ADMIN   DIPLOM
KNOWL PWR WEALTH...POLICY SOC METH/CNCPT STAT
CHARTS SIMUL GEN/LAWS 20. PAGE 39 B0781

B56

HOWARD L.V.,TULANE STUDIES IN POLITICAL SCIENCE: ADMIN
CIVIL SERVICE DEVELOPMENT IN LOUISIANA VOLUME 3.   GOV/REL
LAW POL/PAR LEGIS CT/SYS ADJUST ORD/FREE...STAT   PROVS
CHARTS 19/20 LOUISIANA CIVIL/SERV. PAGE 52 B1050   POLICY

B56

WASSERMAN P.,INFORMATION FOR ADMINISTRATORS: A   BIBLIOG
GUIDE TO PUBLICATIONS AND SERVICES FOR MANAGEMENT   MGT
IN BUSINESS AND GOVERNMENT. R+D LOC/G NAT/G   KNOWL
PROF/ORG VOL/ASSN PRESS...PSY SOC STAT 20. PAGE 114   EDU/PROP
B2299

B57

CRONBACK L.J.,PSYCHOLOGICAL TESTS AND PERSONNEL   MATH
DECISIONS. OP/RES PROB/SOLV CHOOSE PERSON...PSY   DECISION
STAT TESTS 20. PAGE 25 B0508   WORKER
MGT

B57

SIMON H.A.,MODELS OF MAN, SOCIAL AND RATIONAL: MATH
MATHEMATICAL ESSAYS ON RATIONAL HUMAN BEHAVIOR IN A   SIMUL
SOCIAL SETTING. UNIV LAW SOCIETY FACE/GP VOL/ASSN
CONSULT EX/STRUC LEGIS CREATE ADMIN ROUTINE ATTIT
DRIVE PWR...SOC CONCPT METH/CNCPT QUANT STAT
TOT/POP VAL/FREE 20. PAGE 97 B1959

S57

SCHUBERT G.A.,"'THE PUBLIC INTEREST' IN   ADMIN
ADMINISTRATIVE DECISION-MAKING: THEOREM, THEOSOPHY   DECISION
OR THEORY" USA+45 EX/STRUC PROB/SOLV...METH/CNCPT   POLICY
STAT. PAGE 94 B1904   EXEC

B58

GROSSMAN J.,BIBLIOGRAPHY ON PUBLIC ADMINISTRATION   BIBLIOG
IN LATIN AMERICA. ECO/UNDEV FINAN PLAN BUDGET   L/A+17C
ECO/TAC TARIFFS TAX...STAT 20. PAGE 44 B0893   NAT/G
ADMIN

B58

OPERATIONS RESEARCH SOCIETY,A COMPREHENSIVE   BIBLIOG/A
BIBLIOGRAPHY ON OPERATIONS RESEARCH: THROUGH 1956   COMPUT/IR
WITH SUPPLEMENT FOR 1957. COM/IND DIST/IND INDUS   OP/RES

ADMIN...DECISION MATH STAT METH 20. PAGE 80 B1612   MGT

B58

ORTIZ R.P.,ANNUARIO BIBLIOGRAFICO COLOMBIANO,   BIBLIOG
1951-1956. LAW RECEIVE EDU/PROP ADMIN...LING STAT   SOC
20 COLOMB. PAGE 80 B1617

B58

SKINNER G.W.,LEADERSHIP AND POWER IN THE CHINESE   SOC
COMMUNITY OF THAILAND. ASIA S/ASIA STRATA FACE/GP   ELITES
KIN PROF/ORG VOL/ASSN EX/STRUC DOMIN PERSON RESPECT   THAILAND
...METH/CNCPT STAT INT QU BIOG CHARTS 20. PAGE 98
B1974

B59

DIEBOLD W. JR.,THE SCHUMAN PLAN: A STUDY IN   INT/ORG
ECONOMIC COOPERATION, 1950-1959. EUR+WWI FRANCE   REGION
GERMANY USA+45 EXTR/IND CONSULT DELIB/GP PLAN
DIPLOM ECO/TAC INT/TRADE ROUTINE ORD/FREE WEALTH
...METH/CNCPT STAT CONT/OBS INT TIME/SEQ ECSC 20.
PAGE 29 B0591

B59

SCHURZ W.L.,AMERICAN FOREIGN AFFAIRS: A GUIDE TO   INT/ORG
INTERNATIONAL AFFAIRS. USA+45 WOR+45 WOR-45 NAT/G   SOCIETY
FORCES LEGIS TOP/EX PLAN EDU/PROP LEGIT ADMIN   DIPLOM
ROUTINE ATTIT ORD/FREE PWR...SOC CONCPT STAT
SAMP/SIZ CHARTS STERTYP 20. PAGE 95 B1910

B60

LERNER A.P.,THE ECONOMICS OF CONTROL. USA+45   ECO/DEV
ECO/UNDEV INT/ORG ACT/RES PLAN CAP/ISM INT/TRADE   ROUTINE
ATTIT WEALTH...SOC MATH STAT GEN/LAWS INDEX 20.   ECO/TAC
PAGE 64 B1295   SOCISM

B60

MORRIS W.T.,ENGINEERING ECONOMY. AUTOMAT RISK   OP/RES
RATIONAL...PROBABIL STAT CHARTS GAME SIMUL BIBLIOG   DECISION
T 20. PAGE 76 B1529   MGT
PROB/SOLV

L60

STEIN E.,"LEGAL REMEDIES OF ENTERPRISES IN THE   MARKET
EUROPEAN ECONOMIC COMMUNITY." EUR+WWI FUT ECO/DEV   ADJUD
INDUS PLAN ECO/TAC ADMIN PWR...MGT MATH STAT TREND
CON/ANAL EEC 20. PAGE 100 B2026

S60

GARNICK D.H.,"ON THE ECONOMIC FEASIBILITY OF A   MARKET
MIDDLE EASTERN COMMON MARKET." AFR ISLAM CULTURE   INT/TRADE
INDUS NAT/G PLAN TEC/DEV ECO/TAC ADMIN ATTIT DRIVE
RIGID/FLEX...PLURIST STAT TREND GEN/LAWS 20.
PAGE 39 B0784

S60

HERRERA F.,"THE INTER-AMERICAN DEVELOPMENT BANK."   L/A+17C
USA+45 ECO/UNDEV INT/ORG CONSULT DELIB/GP PLAN   FINAN
ECO/TAC INT/TRADE ROUTINE WEALTH...STAT 20. PAGE 49   FOR/AID
B0994   REGION

B61

BARNES W.,THE FOREIGN SERVICE OF THE UNITED STATES.   NAT/G
USA+45 USA-45 CONSTN INT/ORG POL/PAR CONSULT   MGT
DELIB/GP LEGIS DOMIN EDU/PROP EXEC ATTIT RIGID/FLEX   DIPLOM
ORD/FREE PWR...POLICY CONCPT STAT OBS RECORD BIOG
TIME/SEQ TREND. PAGE 9 B0188

B61

HORVATH B.,THE CHARACTERISTICS OF YUGOSLAV ECONOMIC   ACT/RES
DEVELOPMENT. COM ECO/UNDEV AGRI INDUS PLAN CAP/ISM   YUGOSLAVIA
ECO/TAC ROUTINE WEALTH...SOCIALIST STAT CHARTS
STERTYP WORK 20. PAGE 52 B1045

B61

MARVICK D.,POLITICAL DECISION-MAKERS. INTELL STRATA   TOP/EX
NAT/G POL/PAR EX/STRUC LEGIS DOMIN EDU/PROP ATTIT   BIOG
PERSON PWR...PSY STAT OBS CONT/OBS STAND/INT   ELITES
UNPLAN/INT TIME/SEQ CHARTS STERTYP VAL/FREE.
PAGE 70 B1416

B61

ROSE D.L.,THE VIETNAMESE CIVIL SERVICE. VIETNAM   ADMIN
CONSULT DELIB/GP GIVE PAY EDU/PROP COLONIAL GOV/REL   EFFICIENCY
UTIL...CHARTS 20. PAGE 90 B1819   STAT
NAT/G

S61

CYERT R.M.,"TWO EXPERIMENTS ON BIAS AND CONFLICT IN   LAB/EXP
ORGANIZATIONAL ESTIMATION." WORKER PROB/SOLV   ROUTINE
EFFICIENCY...MGT PSY STAT CHARTS. PAGE 25 B0518   ADMIN
DECISION

S61

DEUTSCH K.W.,"A NOTE ON THE APPEARANCE OF WISDOM IN   ADMIN
LARGE BUREAUCRATIC ORGANIZATIONS." ROUTINE PERSON   PROBABIL
KNOWL SKILL...DECISION STAT. PAGE 28 B0577   PROB/SOLV
SIMUL

S61

TANNENBAUM A.S.,"CONTROL AND EFFECTIVENESS IN A   EFFICIENCY
VOLUNTARY ORGANIZATION." USA+45 ADMIN...CORREL MATH   VOL/ASSN
REGRESS STAT TESTS SAMP/SIZ CHARTS SOC/EXP INDEX 20   CONTROL
LEAGUE/WV. PAGE 102 B2072   INGP/REL

B62

CHICAGO U CTR PROG GOVT ADMIN,EDUCATION FOR   EDU/PROP
INNOVATIVE BEHAVIOR IN EXECUTIVES. UNIV ELITES   CREATE
ADMIN EFFICIENCY DRIVE PERSON...MGT APT/TEST   EXEC
PERS/TEST CHARTS LAB/EXP BIBLIOG 20. PAGE 21 B0420   STAT

B62

DUCKWORTH W.E.,A GUIDE TO OPERATIONAL RESEARCH.   OP/RES
INDUS PLAN PROB/SOLV EXEC EFFICIENCY PRODUC KNOWL   GAME
...MGT MATH STAT SIMUL METH 20 MONTECARLO. PAGE 31   DECISION

B0624   ADMIN

B62

FORD A.G.,THE GOLD STANDARD 1880-1914: BRITAIN AND ARGENTINA. UK ECO/UNDEV INT/TRADE ADMIN GOV/REL DEMAND EFFICIENCY...STAT CHARTS 19/20 ARGEN GOLD/STAND. PAGE 36 B0737
FINAN
ECO/TAC
BUDGET
BAL/PAY

B62

KUHN T.E.,PUBLIC ENTERPRISES, PROJECT PLANNING AND ECONOMIC DEVELOPMENT (PAMPHLET). ECO/UNDEV FINAN PLAN ADMIN EFFICIENCY OWN...MGT STAT CHARTS ANTHOL 20. PAGE 61 B1240
ECO/DEV
ECO/TAC
LG/CO
NAT/G

B62

MUKERJI S.N.,ADMINISTRATION OF EDUCATION IN INDIA. ACADEM LOC/G PROVS ROUTINE...POLICY STAT CHARTS 20. PAGE 76 B1536
SCHOOL
ADMIN
NAT/G
EDU/PROP

B62

PRESS C.,STATE MANUALS, BLUE BOOKS AND ELECTION RESULTS. LAW LOC/G MUNIC LEGIS WRITING FEDERAL SOVEREIGN...DECISION STAT CHARTS 20. PAGE 84 B1700
BIBLIOG
PROVS
ADMIN
CHOOSE

L62

SCHWERIN K.,"LAW LIBRARIES AND FOREIGN LAW COLLECTION IN THE USA." USA+45 USA-45...INT/LAW STAT 20. PAGE 95 B1917
BIBLIOG
LAW
ACADEM
ADMIN

S62

GIDWANI K.A.,"LEADER BEHAVIOUR IN ELECTED AND NON-ELECTED GROUPS." DELIB/GP ROUTINE TASK HAPPINESS AUTHORIT...SOC STAT CHARTS SOC/EXP. PAGE 39 B0796
LEAD
INGP/REL
GP/COMP
CHOOSE

S62

READ W.H.,"UPWARD COMMUNICATION IN INDUSTRIAL HIERARCHIES." LG/CO TOP/EX PROB/SOLV DOMIN EXEC PERS/REL ATTIT DRIVE PERCEPT...CORREL STAT CHARTS 20. PAGE 86 B1747
ADMIN
INGP/REL
PSY
MGT

B63

DE VRIES E.,SOCIAL ASPECTS OF ECONOMIC DEVELOPMENT IN LATIN AMERICA. CULTURE SOCIETY STRATA FINAN INDUS INT/ORG DELIB/GP ACT/RES ECO/TAC EDU/PROP ADMIN ATTIT SUPEGO HEALTH KNOWL ORD/FREE...SOC STAT TREND ANTHOL TOT/POP VAL/FREE. PAGE 28 B0562
L/A+17C
ECO/UNDEV

B63

DUE J.F.,STATE SALES TAX ADMINISTRATION. OP/RES BUDGET PAY ADMIN EXEC ROUTINE COST EFFICIENCY PROFIT...CHARTS METH/COMP 20. PAGE 31 B0626
PROVS
TAX
STAT
GOV/COMP

B63

GANGULY D.S.,PUBLIC CORPORATIONS IN A NATIONAL ECONOMY. INDIA WOR+45 FINAN INDUS TOP/EX PRICE EFFICIENCY...MGT STAT CHARTS BIBLIOG 20. PAGE 38 B0779
ECO/UNDEV
LG/CO
SOCISM
GOV/REL

B63

HEYEL C.,THE ENCYCLOPEDIA OF MANAGEMENT. WOR+45 MARKET TOP/EX TEC/DEV AUTOMAT LEAD ADJUST...STAT CHARTS GAME ANTHOL BIBLIOG. PAGE 49 B1002
MGT
INDUS
ADMIN
FINAN

B63

JACOB H.,GERMAN ADMINISTRATION SINCE BISMARCK: CENTRAL AUTHORITY VERSUS LOCAL AUTONOMY. GERMANY GERMANY/W LAW POL/PAR CONTROL CENTRAL TOTALISM FASCISM...MAJORIT DECISION STAT CHARTS GOV/COMP 19/20 BISMARCK/O HITLER/A WEIMAR/REP. PAGE 55 B1111
ADMIN
NAT/G
LOC/G
POLICY

B63

KORNHAUSER W.,SCIENTISTS IN INDUSTRY: CONFLICT AND ACCOMMODATION. USA+45 R+D LG/CO NAT/G TEC/DEV CONTROL ADJUST ATTIT...MGT STAT INT BIBLIOG 20. PAGE 61 B1229
CREATE
INDUS
PROF/ORG
GP/REL

B63

LANGROD G.,THE INTERNATIONAL CIVIL SERVICE: ITS ORIGINS, ITS NATURE, ITS EVALUATION. FUT WOR+45 WOR-45 DELIB/GP ACT/RES DOMIN LEGIT ATTIT RIGID/FLEX SUPEGO ALL/VALS...MGT CONCPT STAT TIME/SEQ ILO LEAGUE/NAT VAL/FREE 20 UN. PAGE 62 B1259
INT/ORG
ADMIN

S63

HILLS R.J.,"THE REPRESENTATIVE FUNCTION: NEGLECTED DIMENSION OF LEADERSHIP BEHAVIOR" USA+45 CLIENT STRUCT SCHOOL PERS/REL...STAT QU SAMP LAB/EXP 20. PAGE 50 B1012
LEAD
ADMIN
EXEC
ACT/RES

B64

COOMBS C.H.,A THEORY OF DATA....MGT PHIL/SCI SOC CLASSIF MATH PROBABIL STAT QU. PAGE 23 B0472
CON/ANAL
GEN/METH
TESTS
PSY

B64

GOLDWIN R.A.,POLITICAL PARTIES, USA. USA+45 USA-45 LOC/G ADMIN LEAD EFFICIENCY ATTIT PWR...POLICY STAT ANTHOL 18/20 CONGRESS. PAGE 40 B0818
POL/PAR
PARTIC
NAT/G
CONSTN

B64

GUTTSMAN W.L.,THE BRITISH POLITICAL ELITE. EUR+WWI MOD/EUR STRATA FAM LABOR POL/PAR SCHOOL VOL/ASSN DELIB/GP LEGIS LEGIT EXEC CHOOSE ATTIT ALL/VALS ...STAT BIOG TIME/SEQ CHARTS VAL/FREE. PAGE 45 B0905
NAT/G
SOC
UK
ELITES

B64

ORTH C.D.,ADMINISTERING RESEARCH AND DEVELOPMENT. FINAN PLAN PROB/SOLV ADMIN ROUTINE...METH/CNCPT STAT CHARTS METH 20. PAGE 80 B1616
MGT
R+D
LG/CO
INDUS

B64

RUSSET B.M.,WORLD HANDBOOK OF POLITICAL AND SOCIAL INDICATORS. WOR+45 COM/IND ADMIN WEALTH...GEOG 20. PAGE 92 B1858
DIPLOM
STAT
NAT/G
NAT/COMP

B64

SINGER M.R.,THE EMERGING ELITE: A STUDY OF POLITICAL LEADERSHIP IN CEYLON. S/ASIA ECO/UNDEV AGRI KIN NAT/G SECT EX/STRUC LEGIT ATTIT PWR RESPECT...SOC STAT CHARTS 20. PAGE 97 B1967
TOP/EX
STRATA
NAT/LISM
CEYLON

B64

WILLIAMSON O.E.,THE ECONOMICS OF DISCRETIONARY BEHAVIOR: MANAGERIAL OBJECTIVES IN A THEORY OF THE FIRM. MARKET BUDGET CAP/ISM PRODUC DRIVE PERSON ...STAT CHARTS BIBLIOG METH 20. PAGE 117 B2354
EFFICIENCY
MGT
ECO/TAC
CHOOSE

B64

WILSON L.,THE ACADEMIC MAN. STRUCT FINAN PROF/ORG OP/RES ADMIN AUTHORIT ROLE RESPECT...SOC STAT. PAGE 117 B2360
ACADEM
INGP/REL
STRATA
DELIB/GP

S64

CARNEGIE ENDOWMENT INT. PEACE,"ADMINISTRATION AND BUDGET (ISSUES BEFORE THE NINETEENTH GENERAL ASSEMBLY)." WOR+45 FINAN BUDGET ECO/TAC ROUTINE COST...STAT RECORD UN. PAGE 19 B0383
INT/ORG
ADMIN

S64

MOWER A.G.,"THE OFFICIAL PRESSURE GROUP OF THE COUNCIL OF EUROPE'S CONSULATIVE ASSEMBLY." EUR+WWI SOCIETY STRUCT FINAN CONSULT ECO/TAC ADMIN ROUTINE ATTIT PWR WEALTH...STAT CHARTS 20 COUNCL/EUR. PAGE 76 B1535
INT/ORG
EDU/PROP

B65

AMERICAN ECONOMIC ASSOCIATION,INDEX OF ECONOMIC JOURNALS 1886-1965 (7 VOLS.). UK USA+45 USA-45 AGRI FINAN PLAN ECO/TAC INT/TRADE ADMIN...STAT CENSUS 19/20. PAGE 4 B0083
BIBLIOG
WRITING
INDUS

B65

BUECHNER J.C.,DIFFERENCES IN ROLE PERCEPTIONS IN COLORADO COUNCIL-MANAGER CITIES. USA+45 ADMIN ROUTINE GP/REL CONSEN PERCEPT PERSON ROLE ...DECISION MGT STAT INT QU CHARTS 20 COLORADO CITY/MGT. PAGE 17 B0338
MUNIC
CONSULT
LOC/G
IDEA/COMP

B65

HICKMAN B.G.,QUANTITATIVE PLANNING OF ECONOMIC POLICY. FRANCE NETHERLAND OP/RES PRICE ROUTINE UTIL ...POLICY DECISION ECOMETRIC METH/CNCPT STAT STYLE CHINJAP. PAGE 50 B1004
PROB/SOLV
PLAN
QUANT

B65

KASER M.,COMECON* INTEGRATION PROBLEMS OF THE PLANNED ECONOMIES. INT/ORG TEC/DEV INT/TRADE PRICE ADMIN ADJUST CENTRAL...STAT TIME/SEQ ORG/CHARTS COMECON. PAGE 58 B1177
PLAN
ECO/DEV
COM
REGION

B65

MASTERS N.A.,COMMITTEE ASSIGNMENTS IN THE HOUSE OF REPRESENTATIVES (BMR). USA+45 ELITES POL/PAR EX/STRUC PARTIC GP/REL PERS/REL ATTIT PWR ...STAT CHARTS 20 HOUSE/REP. PAGE 71 B1425
LEAD
LEGIS
CHOOSE
DELIB/GP

B65

MATRAS J.,SOCIAL CHANGE IN ISRAEL. ISRAEL STRATA FAM ACT/RES EDU/PROP ADMIN CHOOSE...STAT CENSUS 19/20 JEWS. PAGE 71 B1427
SECT
NAT/LISM
GEOG
STRUCT

B65

OECD,MEDITERRANEAN REGIONAL PROJECT: TURKEY; EDUCATION AND DEVELOPMENT. FUT TURKEY SOCIETY STRATA FINAN NAT/G PROF/ORG PLAN PROB/SOLV ADMIN COST...STAT CHARTS 20 OECD. PAGE 79 B1602
EDU/PROP
ACADEM
SCHOOL
ECO/UNDEV

B65

ORG FOR ECO COOP AND DEVEL,THE MEDITERRANEAN REGIONAL PROJECT: AN EXPERIMENT IN PLANNING BY SIX COUNTRIES. FUT GREECE SPAIN TURKEY YUGOSLAVIA SOCIETY FINAN NAT/G PROF/ORG EDU/PROP ADMIN REGION COST...POLICY STAT CHARTS 20 OECD. PAGE 80 B1614
PLAN
ECO/UNDEV
ACADEM
SCHOOL

B65

ORG FOR ECO COOP AND DEVEL,THE MEDITERRANEAN REGIONAL PROJECT: YUGOSLAVIA; EDUCATION AND DEVELOPMENT. YUGOSLAVIA SOCIETY FINAN PROF/ORG PLAN ADMIN COST DEMAND MARXISM...STAT TREND CHARTS METH 20 OECD. PAGE 80 B1615
EDU/PROP
ACADEM
SCHOOL
ECO/UNDEV

B65

PERLOFF H.S.,URBAN RESEARCH AND EDUCATION IN THE NEW YORK METROPOLITAN REGION (VOL. II). FUT USA+45 NEIGH PROF/ORG ACT/RES PROB/SOLV EDU/PROP ADMIN ...STAT BIBLIOG 20 NEWYORK/C. PAGE 82 B1659
MUNIC
PLAN
ACADEM
GP/REL

B65

STEINER K.,LOCAL GOVERNMENT IN JAPAN. CONSTN CULTURE NAT/G ADMIN CHOOSE...SOC STAT 20 CHINJAP. PAGE 100 B2030
LOC/G
SOCIETY
JURID
ORD/FREE

B65

UNESCO,INTERNATIONAL ORGANIZATIONS IN THE SOCIAL   INT/ORG

SCIENCES(REV. ED.). LAW ADMIN ATTIT...CRIMLGY GEOG   R+D
INT/LAW PSY SOC STAT 20 UNESCO. PAGE 107 B2157   PROF/ORG
    ACT/RES
    B65

US SENATE COMM GOVT OPERATIONS,ORGANIZATION OF   ADMIN
FEDERAL EXECUTIVE DEPARTMENTS AND AGENCIES: REPORT   EX/STRUC
OF MARCH 23, 1965. USA+45 FORCES LEGIS DIPLOM   GOV/REL
ROUTINE CIVMIL/REL EFFICIENCY FEDERAL...MGT STAT.   ORG/CHARTS
PAGE 110 B2217
    B65

WARD R.,BACKGROUND MATERIAL ON ECONOMIC IMPACT OF   ECO/DEV
FEDERAL PROCUREMENT - 1965: FOR JOINT ECONOMIC   NAT/G
COMMITTEE US CONGRESS. FINAN ROUTINE WEAPON   OWN
CIVMIL/REL EFFICIENCY...STAT CHARTS 20 CONGRESS.   GOV/REL
PAGE 113 B2288
    L65

MATTHEWS D.G.,"A CURRENT BIBLIOGRAPHY ON ETHIOPIAN   BIBLIOG/A
AFFAIRS: A SELECT BIBLIOGRAPHY FROM 1950-1964."   ADMIN
ETHIOPIA LAW CULTURE ECO/UNDEV INDUS LABOR SECT   POL/PAR
FORCES DIPLOM CIVMIL/REL RACE/REL...LING STAT 20.   NAT/G
PAGE 71 B1428
    S65

HOLSTI O.R.,"THE 1914 CASE." MOD/EUR COMPUTER   CON/ANAL
DIPLOM EDU/PROP EXEC...DECISION PSY PROBABIL STAT   PERCEPT
COMPUT/IR SOC/EXP TIME. PAGE 51 B1036   WAR
    B66

BALDWIN D.A.,FOREIGN AID AND AMERICAN FOREIGN   FOR/AID
POLICY; A DOCUMENTARY ANALYSIS. USA+45 ECO/UNDEV   DIPLOM
ADMIN...ECOMETRIC STAT STYLE CHARTS PROG/TEAC   IDEA/COMP
GEN/LAWS ANTHOL. PAGE 8 B0172
    B66

DAVIS R.G.,PLANNING HUMAN RESOURCE DEVELOPMENT,   PLAN
EDUCATIONAL MODELS AND SCHEMATA. WORKER OP/RES   EFFICIENCY
ECO/TAC EDU/PROP CONTROL COST PRODUC...GEOG STAT   SIMUL
CHARTS 20. PAGE 27 B0544   ROUTINE
    B66

FABRYCKY W.J.,OPERATIONS ECONOMY INDUSTRIAL   OP/RES
APPLICATIONS OF OPERATIONS RESEARCH. INDUS PLAN   MGT
ECO/TAC PRODUC...MATH PROBABIL STAT CHARTS 20.   SIMUL
PAGE 34 B0695   DECISION
    B66

LEWIS W.A.,DEVELOPMENT PLANNING; THE ESSENTIALS OF   PLAN
ECONOMIC POLICY. USA+45 FINAN INDUS NAT/G WORKER   ECO/DEV
FOR/AID INT/TRADE ADMIN ROUTINE WEALTH...CONCPT   POLICY
STAT. PAGE 65 B1307   CREATE
    B66

WESTON J.F.,THE SCOPE AND METHODOLOGY OF FINANCE.   FINAN
PLAN TEC/DEV CONTROL EFFICIENCY INCOME UTIL...MGT   ECO/DEV
CONCPT MATH STAT TREND METH 20. PAGE 115 B2327   POLICY
    PRICE
    B66

WYLIE C.M.,RESEARCH IN PUBLIC HEALTH   BIBLIOG/A
ADMINISTRATION; SELECTED RECENT ABSTRACTS IV   R+D
(PAMPHLET). USA+45 MUNIC PUB/INST ACT/RES CREATE   HEAL
OP/RES TEC/DEV GP/REL ROLE...MGT PHIL/SCI STAT.   ADMIN
PAGE 118 B2387
    L66

AMERICAN ECONOMIC REVIEW,"SIXTY-THIRD LIST OF   BIBLIOG/A
DOCTORAL DISSERTATIONS IN POLITICAL ECONOMY IN   CONCPT
AMERICAN UNIVERSITIES AND COLLEGES." ECO/DEV AGRI   ACADEM
FINAN LABOR WORKER PLAN BUDGET INT/TRADE ADMIN
DEMAND...MGT STAT 20. PAGE 4 B0084
    S66

MATTHEWS D.G.,"PRELUDE-COUP D'ETAT-MILITARY   BIBLIOG
GOVERNMENT: A BIBLIOGRAPHICAL AND RESEARCH GUIDE TO   NAT/G
NIGERIAN POL AND GOVT, JAN, 1965-66." AFR NIGER LAW   ADMIN
CONSTN POL/PAR LEGIS CIVMIL/REL GOV/REL...STAT 20.   CHOOSE
PAGE 71 B1430
    B67

ANDERSON C.W.,POLITICS AND ECONOMIC CHANGE IN LATIN   ECO/UNDEV
AMERICA. L/A+17C INDUS NAT/G OP/RES ADMIN DEMAND   PROB/SOLV
...POLICY STAT CHARTS NAT/COMP 20. PAGE 4 B0091   PLAN
    ECO/TAC
    B67

EVANS R.H.,COEXISTENCE: COMMUNISM AND ITS PRACTICE   MARXISM
IN BOLOGNA, 1945-1965. ITALY CAP/ISM ADMIN CHOOSE   CULTURE
PEACE ORD/FREE...SOC STAT DEEP/INT SAMP CHARTS   MUNIC
BIBLIOG 20. PAGE 34 B0690   POL/PAR
    B67

GELLHORN W.,OMBUDSMEN AND OTHERS: CITIZENS'   NAT/COMP
PROTECTORS IN NINE COUNTRIES. WOR+45 LAW CONSTN   REPRESENT
LEGIS INSPECT ADJUD ADMIN CONTROL CT/SYS CHOOSE   INGP/REL
PERS/REL...STAT CHARTS 20. PAGE 39 B0789   PROB/SOLV
    B67

KARDOUCHE G.K.,THE UAR IN DEVELOPMENT. UAR ECO/TAC   FINAN
INT/TRADE BAL/PAY...STAT CHARTS BIBLIOG 20. PAGE 58   MGT
B1172   CAP/ISM
    ECO/UNDEV
    B67

KONCZACKI Z.A.,PUBLIC FINANCE AND ECONOMIC   ECO/TAC
DEVELOPMENT OF NATAL 1893-1910. TAX ADMIN COLONIAL   FINAN
...STAT CHARTS BIBLIOG 19/20 NATAL. PAGE 61 B1228   NAT/G
    ECO/UNDEV
    B67

NORTHRUP H.R.,RESTRICTIVE LABOR PRACTICES IN THE   DIST/IND
SUPERMARKET INDUSTRY. USA+45 INDUS WORKER TEC/DEV   MARKET

BARGAIN PAY CONTROL GP/REL COST...STAT CHARTS NLRB.   LABOR
PAGE 79 B1592   MGT
    B67

US DEPARTMENT OF JUSTICE,ANNUAL REPORT OF THE   ADMIN
OFFICE OF ADMINISTRATIVE PROCEDURE. USA+45   NAT/G
PROB/SOLV EDU/PROP EXEC INGP/REL EFFICIENCY KNOWL   ROUTINE
...POLICY STAT 20. PAGE 108 B2181   GOV/REL
    S67

ALPANDER G.G.,"ENTREPRENEURS AND PRIVATE ENTERPRISE   ECO/UNDEV
IN TURKEY." TURKEY INDUS PROC/MFG EDU/PROP ATTIT   LG/CO
DRIVE WEALTH...GEOG MGT SOC STAT TREND CHARTS 20.   NAT/G
PAGE 4 B0080   POLICY
    S67

EDWARDS H.T.,"POWER STRUCTURE AND ITS COMMUNICATION   ELITES
IN SAN JOSE, COSTA RICA." COSTA/RICA L/A+17C STRATA   INGP/REL
FACE/GP POL/PAR EX/STRUC PROB/SOLV ADMIN LEAD   MUNIC
GP/REL PWR...STAT INT 20. PAGE 32 B0655   DOMIN
    S67

LINEBERRY R.L.,"REFORMISM AND PUBLIC POLICIES IN   DECISION
AMERICAN CITIES." USA+45 POL/PAR EX/STRUC LEGIS   POLICY
BUDGET TAX GP/REL...STAT CHARTS. PAGE 65 B1317   MUNIC
    LOC/G
    N67

US CONGRESS JT COMM ECO GOVT,BACKGROUND MATERIAL ON   BUDGET
ECONOMY IN GOVERNMENT 1967 (PAMPHLET). WOR+45   COST
ECO/DEV BARGAIN PRICE DEMAND OPTIMAL...STAT   MGT
DEPT/DEFEN. PAGE 108 B2178   NAT/G

STATE GOVERNMENT....SEE PROVS

STATE DEPARTMENT....SEE DEPT/STATE

STATIST REICHSAMTE B2025

STATISTICS....SEE STAT, ALSO LOGIC, MATHEMATICS, AND
    LANGUAGE INDEX, P. XIV

STEIN E. B2026

STEIN H. B2027,B2028

STEINER G.A. B2029

STEINER K. B2030

STEINMETZ H. B2031

STENE E.O. B2032

STEPHENS O. B2033

STEREOTYPE....SEE STERTYP

STERN/GANG....STERN GANG (PALESTINE)

STEROTYPE....SEE STERTYP

STERTYP....STEREOTYPE

    B28

BUELL R.,THE NATIVE PROBLEM IN AFRICA. KIN LABOR   AFR
LOC/G ECO/TAC ROUTINE ORD/FREE...REC/INT KNO/TEST   CULTURE
CENSUS TREND CHARTS SOC/EXP STERTYP 20. PAGE 17
B0339
    L44

HAILEY,"THE FUTURE OF COLONIAL PEOPLES." WOR-45   PLAN
CONSTN CULTURE ECO/UNDEV AGRI MARKET INT/ORG NAT/G   CONCPT
SECT CONSULT ECO/TAC LEGIT ADMIN NAT/LISM ALL/VALS   DIPLOM
...SOC OBS TREND STERTYP CMN/WLTH LEAGUE/NAT   UK
PARLIAMENT 20. PAGE 45 B0916
    B45

PLATO,THE REPUBLIC. MEDIT-7 UNIV SOCIETY STRUCT   PERSON
EX/STRUC FORCES UTOPIA ATTIT PERCEPT HEALTH KNOWL   PHIL/SCI
ORD/FREE PWR...HUM CONCPT STERTYP TOT/POP. PAGE 83
B1681
    B54

MANGONE G.,A SHORT HISTORY OF INTERNATIONAL   INT/ORG
ORGANIZATION. MOD/EUR USA+45 USA-45 WOR+45 WOR-45   INT/LAW
LAW LEGIS CREATE LEGIT ROUTINE RIGID/FLEX PWR
...JURID CONCPT OBS TIME/SEQ STERTYP GEN/LAWS UN
TOT/POP VAL/FREE 18/20. PAGE 69 B1389
    S55

TORRE M.,"PSYCHIATRIC OBSERVATIONS OF INTERNATIONAL   DELIB/GP
CONFERENCES." WOR+45 INT/ORG PROF/ORG VOL/ASSN   OBS
CONSULT EDU/PROP ROUTINE ATTIT DRIVE KNOWL...PSY   DIPLOM
METH/CNCPT OBS/ENVIR STERTYP 20. PAGE 105 B2119
    B56

WHYTE W.H. JR.,THE ORGANIZATION MAN. CULTURE FINAN   ADMIN
VOL/ASSN DOMIN EDU/PROP EXEC DISPL HABITAT ROLE   LG/CO
...PERS/TEST STERTYP. PAGE 116 B2343   PERSON
    CONSEN
    B57

LOEWENSTEIN K.,POLITICAL POWER AND THE GOVERNMENTAL   PWR
PROCESS. WOR+45 WOR-45 CONSTN NAT/G POL/PAR   CONCPT

EX/STRUC LEGIS TOP/EX DOMIN EDU/PROP LEGIT ADMIN
REGION CHOOSE ATTIT...JURID STERTYP GEN/LAWS 20.
PAGE 66 B1336

B58
BROWNE C.G.,THE CONCEPT OF LEADERSHIP. UNIV FACE/GP EXEC
DOMIN EDU/PROP LEGIT LEAD DRIVE PERSON PWR...MGT   CONCPT
SOC OBS SELF/OBS CONT/OBS INT PERS/TEST STERTYP
GEN/LAWS. PAGE 16 B0328

S58
DAHL R.A.,"A CRITIQUE OF THE RULING ELITE MODEL."   CONCPT
USA+45 LOC/G MUNIC NAT/G POL/PAR PROVS DOMIN LEGIT   STERTYP
ADMIN...METH/CNCPT HYPO/EXP. PAGE 25 B0520   ELITES

S58
MAIR L.P.,"REPRESENTATIVE LOCAL GOVERNMENT AS A   AFR
PROBLEM IN SOCIAL CHANGE." ECO/UNDEV KIN LOC/G   PWR
NAT/G SCHOOL JUDGE ADMIN ROUTINE REPRESENT   ELITES
RIGID/FLEX RESPECT...CONCPT STERTYP CMN/WLTH 20.
PAGE 68 B1383

B59
SCHURZ W.L.,AMERICAN FOREIGN AFFAIRS: A GUIDE TO   INT/ORG
INTERNATIONAL AFFAIRS. USA+45 WOR+45 WOR-45 NAT/G   SOCIETY
FORCES LEGIS TOP/EX PLAN EDU/PROP LEGIT ADMIN   DIPLOM
ROUTINE ATTIT ORD/FREE PWR...SOC CONCPT STAT
SAMP/SIZ CHARTS STERTYP 20. PAGE 95 B1910

S60
HERZ J.H.,"EAST GERMANY: PROGRESS AND PROSPECTS."   POL/PAR
COM AGRI FINAN INDUS LOC/G NAT/G FORCES PLAN   STRUCT
TEC/DEV DOMIN ADMIN COERCE DRIVE PERCEPT RIGID/FLEX GERMANY
MORAL ORD/FREE PWR...MARXIST PSY SOC RECORD STERTYP
WORK. PAGE 49 B0997

B61
HORVATH B.,THE CHARACTERISTICS OF YUGOSLAV ECONOMIC ACT/RES
DEVELOPMENT. COM ECO/UNDEV AGRI INDUS PLAN CAP/ISM   YUGOSLAVIA
ECO/TAC ROUTINE WEALTH...SOCIALIST STAT CHARTS
STERTYP WORK 20. PAGE 52 B1045

B61
MARVICK D.,POLITICAL DECISION-MAKERS. INTELL STRATA TOP/EX
NAT/G POL/PAR EX/STRUC LEGIS DOMIN EDU/PROP ATTIT   BIOG
PERSON PWR...PSY STAT OBS CONT/OBS STAND/INT   ELITES
UNPLAN/INT TIME/SEQ CHARTS STERTYP VAL/FREE.
PAGE 70 B1416

B61
STRAUSS E.,THE RULING SERVANTS. FRANCE UK USSR   ADMIN
WOR+45 WOR-45 NAT/G CONSULT DELIB/GP EX/STRUC   PWR
TOP/EX DOMIN EDU/PROP LEGIT ROUTINE...MGT TIME/SEQ   ELITES
STERTYP 20. PAGE 101 B2051

S61
ANGLIN D.,"UNITED STATES OPPOSITION TO CANADIAN   INT/ORG
MEMBERSHIP IN THE PAN AMERICAN UNION: A CANADIAN   CANADA
VIEW." L/A+17C UK USA+45 VOL/ASSN DELIB/GP EX/STRUC
PLAN DIPLOM DOMIN REGION ATTIT RIGID/FLEX PWR
...RELATIV CONCPT STERTYP CMN/WLTH OAS 20. PAGE 5
B0112

S61
DEVINS J.H.,"THE INITIATIVE." COM USA+45 USA-45   FORCES
USSR SOCIETY NAT/G ACT/RES CREATE BAL/PWR ROUTINE   CONCPT
COERCE DETER RIGID/FLEX SKILL...STERTYP COLD/WAR   WAR
20. PAGE 29 B0582

S61
TOMASIC D.,"POLITICAL LEADERSHIP IN CONTEMPORARY   SOCIETY
POLAND." COM EUR+WWI GERMANY NAT/G POL/PAR SECT   ROUTINE
DELIB/GP PLAN ECO/TAC DOMIN EDU/PROP PWR MARXISM   USSR
...MARXIST GEOG MGT CONCPT TIME/SEQ STERTYP 20.   POLAND
PAGE 105 B2114

S62
JACOBSON H.K.,"THE UNITED NATIONS AND COLONIALISM: INT/ORG
A TENTATIVE APPRAISAL." AFR FUT S/ASIA USA+45 USSR   CONCPT
WOR+45 NAT/G DELIB/GP PLAN DIPLOM ECO/TAC DOMIN   COLONIAL
ADMIN ROUTINE COERCE ATTIT RIGID/FLEX ORD/FREE PWR
...OBS STERTYP UN 20. PAGE 55 B1115

B63
TSOU T.,AMERICA'S FAILURE IN CHINA, 1941-1950.   ASIA
USA+45 USA-45 NAT/G ACT/RES PLAN DOMIN EDU/PROP   PERCEPT
ADMIN ROUTINE ATTIT PERSON ORD/FREE...DECISION   DIPLOM
CONCPT MYTH TIME/SEQ TREND STERTYP 20. PAGE 105
B2132

S63
BECHHOEFER B.G.,"UNITED NATIONS PROCEDURES IN CASE   INT/ORG
OF VIOLATIONS OF DISARMAMENT AGREEMENTS." COM   DELIB/GP
USA+45 USSR LAW CONSTN NAT/G EX/STRUC FORCES LEGIS
BAL/PWR EDU/PROP CT/SYS ARMS/CONT ORD/FREE PWR
...POLICY STERTYP UN VAL/FREE 20. PAGE 10 B0204

S63
RUSTOW D.A.,"THE MILITARY IN MIDDLE EASTERN SOCIETY FORCES
AND POLITICS." FUT ISLAM CONSTN SOCIETY FACE/GP   ELITES
NAT/G POL/PAR PROF/ORG CONSULT DOMIN ADMIN EXEC
REGION COERCE NAT/LISM ATTIT DRIVE PERSON ORD/FREE
PWR...POLICY CONCPT OBS STERTYP 20. PAGE 92 B1860

L64
MILLIS W.,"THE DEMILITARIZED WORLD." COM USA+45   FUT
USSR WOR+45 CONSTN NAT/G EX/STRUC PLAN LEGIT ATTIT   INT/ORG
DRIVE...CONCPT TIME/SEQ STERTYP TOT/POP COLD/WAR   BAL/PWR
20. PAGE 74 B1486   PEACE

S64
MURRAY D.,"CHINESE EDUCATION IN SOUTH-EAST ASIA."   S/ASIA
SOCIETY NEIGH EDU/PROP ROUTINE PERSON KNOWL   SCHOOL

...OBS/ENVIR STERTYP. PAGE 76 B1546   REGION
                                                     ASIA
S64
SWEARER H.R.,"AFTER KHRUSHCHEV: WHAT NEXT." COM FUT EX/STRUC
USSR CONSTN ELITES NAT/G POL/PAR CHIEF DELIB/GP   PWR
LEGIS DOMIN LEAD...RECORD TREND STERTYP GEN/METH
20. PAGE 102 B2058

B66
SCHURMANN F.,IDEOLOGY AND ORGANIZATION IN COMMUNIST MARXISM
CHINA. CHINA/COM LOC/G MUNIC POL/PAR ECO/TAC   STRUCT
CONTROL ATTIT...MGT STERTYP 20 COM/PARTY. PAGE 94   ADMIN
B1909   NAT/G

STEVENSN/A.....ADLAI STEVENSON

STEVENSON A.E. B2034

STEWARD/JH....JULIAN H. STEWARD

STEWART D.D. B2035

STEWART F.M. B2036

STEWART I. B2037

STEWART J.D. B2038

STIMSON/HL....HENRY L. STIMSON

B60
MORISON E.E.,TURMOIL AND TRADITION: A STUDY OF THE   BIOG
LIFE AND TIMES OF HENRY L. STIMSON. USA+45 USA-45   NAT/G
POL/PAR CHIEF DELIB/GP FORCES BAL/PWR DIPLOM   EX/STRUC
ARMS/CONT WAR PEACE 19/20 STIMSON/HL ROOSEVLT/F
TAFT/WH HOOVER/H REPUBLICAN. PAGE 75 B1525

STINCHCOMBE A.L. B2039

STOCHASTIC PROCESSES....SEE PROB/SOLV, MODELS INDEX

STOCKHOLM....STOCKHOLM

STOESSINGER J.G. B2040

STOICOIU V. B2041

STOKE H.W. B2042

STOKES W.S. B2043,B2044

STOKES/CB....CARL B. STOKES

STOL....SHORT TAKE-OFF AND LANDING AIRCRAFT

STOLPER W. B2045

STONE E.O. B2046

STONE J. B2047

STONE P.A. B2048

STONE R.C. B0748

STONE/HF....HARLAN FISKE STONE

STONE/IF....I.F. STONE

STORING H.J. B1926

STORING/HJ....H.J. STORING

STOUT H.M. B2049

STOWELL E.C. B2050

STRANGE....ESTRANGEMENT, ALIENATION, IMPERSONALITY

S59
DWYER R.J.,"THE ADMINISTRATIVE ROLE IN   ADMIN
DESEGREGATION." USA+45 LAW PROB/SOLV LEAD RACE/REL   SCHOOL
ISOLAT STRANGE ROLE...POLICY SOC/INTEG MISSOURI   DISCRIM
NEGRO CIV/RIGHTS. PAGE 31 B0638   ATTIT
B61
KEE R.,REFUGEE WORLD. AUSTRIA EUR+WWI GERMANY NEIGH NAT/G
EX/STRUC WORKER PROB/SOLV ECO/TAC RENT EDU/PROP   GIVE
INGP/REL COST LITERACY HABITAT 20 MIGRATION.   WEALTH
PAGE 59 B1186   STRANGE
S65
THOMAS F.C. JR.,"THE PEACE CORPS IN MOROCCO."   MOROCCO
CULTURE MUNIC PROVS CREATE ROUTINE TASK ADJUST   FRANCE
STRANGE...OBS PEACE/CORP. PAGE 104 B2099   FOR/AID
                                                     EDU/PROP
B66
VON HOFFMAN N.,THE MULTIVERSITY; A PERSONAL REPORT   EDU/PROP
ON WHAT HAPPENS TO TODAY'S STUDENTS AT AMERICAN   ACADEM

UNIVERSITIES. USA+45 SOCIETY ROUTINE ANOMIE ROLE   ATTIT
MORAL ORD/FREE SKILL...INT 20. PAGE 112 B2266   STRANGE

STRASBOURG....STRASBOURG PLAN

STRATA....SOCIAL STRATA, CLASS DIVISION

   N

INTERNATIONAL REVIEW OF ADMINISTRATIVE SCIENCES.   BIBLIOG/A
WOR+45 WOR-45 STRATA ECO/DEV ECO/UNDEV CREATE PLAN   ADMIN
PROB/SOLV DIPLOM CONTROL REPRESENT...MGT 20. PAGE 1   INT/ORG
B0004   NAT/G

   B08
THE GOVERNMENT OF SOUTH AFRICA (VOL. II). SOUTH/AFR   CONSTN
STRATA EXTR/IND EX/STRUC TOP/EX BUDGET ADJUD ADMIN   FINAN
CT/SYS PRODUC...CORREL CENSUS 19 RAILROAD   LEGIS
CIVIL/SERV POSTAL/SYS. PAGE 2 B0033   NAT/G

   B16
TREITSCHKE H.,POLITICS. UNIV SOCIETY STRATA NAT/G   EXEC
EX/STRUC LEGIS DOMIN EDU/PROP ATTIT PWR RESPECT   ELITES
...CONCPT TIME/SEQ GEN/LAWS TOT/POP 20. PAGE 105   GERMANY
B2127

   B17
CORWIN E.S.,THE PRESIDENT'S CONTROL OF FOREIGN   TOP/EX
RELATIONS. FUT USA-45 CONSTN STRATA NAT/G CHIEF   PWR
EX/STRUC LEGIS KNOWL RESPECT...JURID CONCPT TREND   DIPLOM
CONGRESS VAL/FREE 20 PRESIDENT. PAGE 24 B0483

   B24
HOLDSWORTH W.S.,A HISTORY OF ENGLISH LAW; THE   LAW
COMMON LAW AND ITS RIVALS (VOL. VI). UK STRATA   CONSTN
EX/STRUC ADJUD ADMIN CONTROL CT/SYS...JURID CONCPT   LEGIS
GEN/LAWS 17 COMMONWLTH PARLIAMENT ENGLSH/LAW   CHIEF
COMMON/LAW. PAGE 51 B1034

   B25
THOMAS F.,THE ENVIRONMENTAL BASIS OF SOCIETY.   SOCIETY
USA+45 WOR+45 STRATA ECO/DEV EXTR/IND CONSULT   GEOG
ECO/TAC ROUTINE ATTIT ALL/VALS...SOC TIME/SEQ.
PAGE 104 B2098

   B29
BUELL R.,INTERNATIONAL RELATIONS. WOR+45 WOR-45   INT/ORG
CONSTN STRATA FORCES TOP/EX ADMIN ATTIT DRIVE   BAL/PWR
SUPEGO MORAL ORD/FREE PWR SOVEREIGN...JURID SOC   DIPLOM
CONCPT 20. PAGE 17 B0340

   B30
MURCHISON C.,PSYCHOLOGIES OF 1930. UNIV USA-45   CREATE
CULTURE INTELL SOCIETY STRATA FAM ROUTINE BIO/SOC   PERSON
DRIVE RIGID/FLEX SUPEGO...NEW/IDEA OBS SELF/OBS
CONT/OBS 20. PAGE 76 B1543

   B38
BALDWIN R.N.,CIVIL LIBERTIES AND INDUSTRIAL   LABOR
CONFLICT. USA+45 STRATA WORKER INGP/REL...MGT 20   LG/CO
ACLU CIVIL/LIB. PAGE 9 B0175   INDUS
  GP/REL

   B38
FIELD G.L.,THE SYNDICAL AND CORPORATIVE   FASCISM
INSTITUTIONS OF ITALIAN FASCISM. ITALY CONSTN   INDUS
STRATA LABOR EX/STRUC TOP/EX ADJUD ADMIN LEAD   NAT/G
TOTALISM AUTHORIT...MGT 20 MUSSOLIN/B. PAGE 35   WORKER
B0716

   B38
PETTEE G.S.,THE PROCESS OF REVOLUTION. COM FRANCE   COERCE
ITALY MOD/EUR RUSSIA SPAIN WOR-45 ELITES INTELL   CONCPT
SOCIETY STRATA STRUCT INT/ORG NAT/G POL/PAR ACT/RES   REV
PLAN EDU/PROP LEGIT EXEC...SOC MYTH TIME/SEQ
TOT/POP 18/20. PAGE 82 B1664

   C39
REISCHAUER R.,"JAPAN'S GOVERNMENT--POLITICS."   NAT/G
CONSTN STRATA POL/PAR FORCES LEGIS DIPLOM ADMIN   S/ASIA
EXEC CENTRAL...POLICY BIBLIOG 20 CHINJAP. PAGE 87   CONCPT
B1764   ROUTINE

   S40
GERTH H.,"THE NAZI PARTY: ITS LEADERSHIP AND   POL/PAR
COMPOSITION" (BMR)" GERMANY ELITES STRATA STRUCT   DOMIN
EX/STRUC FORCES ECO/TAC CT/SYS CHOOSE TOTALISM   LEAD
AGE/Y AUTHORIT PWR 20. PAGE 39 B0792   ADMIN

   B45
BUSH V.,SCIENCE, THE ENDLESS FRONTIER. FUT USA+45   R+D
INTELL STRATA ACT/RES CREATE PLAN EDU/PROP ADMIN   NAT/G
NUC/PWR PEACE ATTIT HEALTH KNOWL...MAJORIT HEAL MGT
PHIL/SCI CONCPT OBS TREND 20. PAGE 18 B0360

   B47
BORGESE G.,COMMON CAUSE. LAW CONSTN SOCIETY STRATA   WOR+45
ECO/DEV INT/ORG POL/PAR FORCES LEGIS TOP/EX CAP/ISM   NAT/G
DIPLOM ADMIN EXEC ATTIT PWR 20. PAGE 14 B0279   SOVEREIGN
  REGION

   B47
WARNER W.L.,THE SOCIAL SYSTEM OF THE MODERN   ROLE
FACTORY; THE STRIKE: AN ANALYSIS. USA-45 STRATA   STRUCT
WORKER ECO/TAC GP/REL INGP/REL...MGT SOC CHARTS 20   LABOR
YANKEE/C. PAGE 114 B2293   PROC/MFG

   S47
TURNER R.H.,"THE NAVY DISBURSING OFFICER AS A   FORCES
BUREAUCRAT" (BMR)" USA-45 LAW STRATA DIST/IND WAR   ADMIN
PWR...SOC 20 BUREAUCRCY. PAGE 106 B2140   PERSON
  ROLE

   B49
ROSENHAUPT H.W.,HOW TO WAGE PEACE. USA+45 SOCIETY   INTELL
STRATA STRUCT R+D INT/ORG POL/PAR LEGIS ACT/RES   CONCPT
CREATE PLAN EDU/PROP ADMIN EXEC ATTIT ALL/VALS   DIPLOM
...TIME/SEQ TREND COLD/WAR 20. PAGE 90 B1822

   B51
PETERSON F.,SURVEY OF LABOR ECONOMICS (REV. ED.).   WORKER
STRATA ECO/DEV LABOR INSPECT BARGAIN PAY PRICE EXEC   DEMAND
ROUTINE GP/REL ALL/VALS ORD/FREE 20 AFL/CIO   IDEA/COMP
DEPT/LABOR. PAGE 82 B1662   T

   B51
SMITH L.,AMERICAN DEMOCRACY AND MILITARY POWER.   FORCES
USA+45 USA-45 CONSTN STRATA NAT/G LEGIS ACT/RES   STRUCT
LEGIT ADMIN EXEC GOV/REL ALL/VALS...CONCPT   WAR
HIST/WRIT CONGRESS 20. PAGE 98 B1982

   B52
SELZNICK P.,THE ORGANIZATIONAL WEAPON: A STUDY OF   MARXISM
BOLSHEVIK STRATEGY AND TACTICS. USSR SOCIETY STRATA   POL/PAR
LABOR DOMIN EDU/PROP PARTIC REV ATTIT PWR...POLICY   LEAD
MGT CONCPT 20 BOLSHEVISM. PAGE 95 B1929   TOTALISM

   C52
LASSWELL H.D.,"THE COMPARATIVE STUDY OF ELITES: AN   ELITES
INTRODUCTION AND BIBLIOGRAPHY." STRATA POL/PAR   LEAD
EDU/PROP ADMIN LOBBY COERCE ATTIT PERSON PWR   CONCPT
...BIBLIOG 20. PAGE 63 B1270   DOMIN

   B53
MEYER P.,THE JEWS IN THE SOVIET SATELLITES.   COM
CZECHOSLVK POLAND SOCIETY STRATA NAT/G BAL/PWR   SECT
ECO/TAC EDU/PROP LEGIT ADMIN COERCE ATTIT DISPL   TOTALISM
PERCEPT HEALTH PWR RESPECT WEALTH...METH/CNCPT JEWS   USSR
VAL/FREE NAZI 20. PAGE 73 B1474

   B53
WAGLEY C.,AMAZON TOWN: A STUDY OF MAN IN THE   SOC
TROPICS. BRAZIL L/A+17C STRATA STRUCT ECO/UNDEV   NEIGH
AGRI EX/STRUC RACE/REL DISCRIM HABITAT WEALTH...OBS   CULTURE
SOC/EXP 20. PAGE 113 B2273   INGP/REL

   B54
ALLPORT G.W.,THE NATURE OF PREJUDICE. USA+45 WOR+45   CULTURE
STRATA FACE/GP KIN NEIGH SECT ADMIN GP/REL DISCRIM   PERSON
ATTIT DRIVE LOVE RESPECT...PSY SOC MYTH QU/SEMANT   RACE/REL
20. PAGE 4 B0078

   B54
MATTHEWS D.R.,THE SOCIAL BACKGROUND OF POLITICAL   DECISION
DECISION-MAKERS. CULTURE SOCIETY STRATA FAM   BIOG
EX/STRUC LEAD ATTIT BIO/SOC DRIVE PERSON ALL/VALS   SOC
HIST/WRIT. PAGE 71 B1431

   B55
POOL I.,SATELLITE GENERALS: A STUDY OF MILITARY   FORCES
ELITES IN THE SOVIET SPHERE. ASIA CHINA/COM COM   CHOOSE
CZECHOSLVK FUT HUNGARY POLAND ROMANIA USSR ELITES
STRATA ADMIN ATTIT PWR SKILL...METH/CNCPT BIOG 20.
PAGE 84 B1688

   C55
BONER H.A.,"HUNGRY GENERATIONS." UK WOR+45 WOR-45   ECO/DEV
STRATA INDUS FAM LABOR CAP/ISM...MGT BIBLIOG 19/20.   PHIL/SCI
PAGE 13 B0272   CONCPT
  WEALTH

   B56
DUNNILL F.,THE CIVIL SERVICE. UK LAW PLAN ADMIN   PERSON
EFFICIENCY DRIVE NEW/LIB...STAT CHARTS 20   WORKER
PARLIAMENT CIVIL/SERV. PAGE 31 B0633   STRATA
  SOC/WK

   B56
GLADDEN E.N.,CIVIL SERVICE OR BUREAUCRACY? UK LAW   ADMIN
STRATA LABOR TOP/EX PLAN SENIOR AUTOMAT CONTROL   GOV/REL
PARTIC CHOOSE HAPPINESS...CHARTS 19/20 CIVIL/SERV   EFFICIENCY
BUREAUCRCY. PAGE 40 B0808   PROVS

   B57
DJILAS M.,THE NEW CLASS: AN ANALYSIS OF THE   COM
COMMUNIST SYSTEM. STRATA CAP/ISM ECO/TAC DOMIN   POL/PAR
EDU/PROP LEGIT EXEC COERCE ATTIT PWR MARXISM   USSR
...MARXIST MGT CONCPT TIME/SEQ GEN/LAWS 20. PAGE 29   YUGOSLAVIA
B0600

   B57
SCHNEIDER E.V.,INDUSTRIAL SOCIOLOGY: THE SOCIAL   LABOR
RELATIONS OF INDUSTRY AND COMMUNITY. STRATA INDUS   MGT
NAT/G NEIGH CREATE ADMIN PARTIC GP/REL RACE/REL   INGP/REL
ROLE PWR...POLICY BIBLIOG. PAGE 94 B1898   STRUCT

   C57
TANG P.S.H.,"COMMUNIST CHINA TODAY: DOMESTIC AND   POL/PAR
FOREIGN POLICIES." CHINA/COM COM S/ASIA USSR STRATA   LEAD
FORCES DIPLOM EDU/PROP COERCE GOV/REL...POLICY   ADMIN
MAJORIT BIBLIOG 20. PAGE 102 B2071   CONSTN

   B58
CLEMENTS R.V.,MANAGERS - A STUDY OF THEIR CAREERS   MGT
IN INDUSTRY. STRATA INDUS TASK PERSON SKILL 20.   ELITES
PAGE 21 B0435   EDU/PROP
  TOP/EX

   B58
SKINNER G.W.,LEADERSHIP AND POWER IN THE CHINESE   SOC
COMMUNITY OF THAILAND. ASIA S/ASIA STRATA FACE/GP   ELITES
KIN PROF/ORG VOL/ASSN EX/STRUC DOMIN PERSON RESPECT   THAILAND
...METH/CNCPT STAT INT QU BIOG CHARTS 20. PAGE 98
B1974

   B58
WILENSKY H.L.,INDUSTRIAL SOCIETY AND SOCIAL   INDUS

WELFARE: IMPACT OF INDUSTRIALIZATION ON SUPPLY AND ORGANIZATION OF SOC WELF WELF SERVICES. ELITES SOCIETY STRATA SERV/IND FAM MUNIC PUB/INST CONSULT WORKER ADMIN AUTOMAT ANOMIE 20. PAGE 117 B2352
ECO/DEV
RECEIVE
PROF/ORG

S58
DEAN B.V.,"APPLICATION OF OPERATIONS RESEARCH TO MANAGERIAL DECISION MAKING" STRATA ACT/RES PROB/SOLV ROLE...SOC PREDICT SIMUL 20. PAGE 28 B0565
DECISION
OP/RES
MGT
METH/CNCPT

B59
MAYNTZ R.,PARTEIGRUPPEN IN DER GROSSSTADT. GERMANY STRATA STRUCT DOMIN CHOOSE 20. PAGE 71 B1437
MUNIC
MGT
POL/PAR
ATTIT

B59
THARAMATHAJ C.,A STUDY OF THE COMPOSITION OF THE THAI CIVIL SERVICE (PAPER). THAILAND PAY ROLE ...CHARTS 20 CIVIL/SERV FEMALE/SEX. PAGE 103 B2092
ADMIN
EX/STRUC
STRATA
INGP/REL

S59
SUTTON F.X.,"REPRESENTATION AND THE NATURE OF POLITICAL SYSTEMS." UNIV WOR-45 CULTURE SOCIETY STRATA INT/ORG FORCES JUDGE DOMIN LEGIT EXEC REGION REPRESENT ATTIT ORD/FREE RESPECT...SOC HIST/WRIT TIME/SEQ. PAGE 102 B2057
NAT/G
CONCPT

B60
BERNSTEIN I.,THE LEAN YEARS. SOCIETY STRATA PARTIC GP/REL ATTIT...SOC 20 DEPRESSION. PAGE 11 B0227
WORKER
LABOR
WEALTH
MGT

B60
FRANKE W.,THE REFORM AND ABOLITION OF THE TRADITIONAL CHINESE EXAMINATION SYSTEM. ASIA STRUCT 19/20 CIVIL/SERV. PAGE 37 B0750
ADJUST
ADMIN
TESTS
STRATA

B60
GRANICK D.,THE RED EXECUTIVE. COM USA+45 SOCIETY ECO/DEV INDUS NAT/G POL/PAR EX/STRUC PLAN ECO/TAC EDU/PROP ADMIN EXEC ATTIT DRIVE...GP/COMP 20. PAGE 42 B0851
PWR
STRATA
USSR
ELITES

B60
MOORE W.E.,LABOR COMMITMENT AND SOCIAL CHANGE IN DEVELOPING AREAS. SOCIETY STRATA ECO/UNDEV MARKET VOL/ASSN WORKER AUTHORIT SKILL...MGT NAT/COMP SOC/INTEG 20. PAGE 75 B1514
LABOR
ORD/FREE
ATTIT
INDUS

S60
"THE EMERGING COMMON MARKETS IN LATIN AMERICA." FUT L/A+17C STRATA DIST/IND INDUS LABOR NAT/G LEGIS ECO/TAC ADMIN RIGID/FLEX HEALTH...NEW/IDEA TIME/SEQ OAS 20. PAGE 2 B0039
FINAN
ECO/UNDEV
INT/TRADE

S60
GROSSMAN G.,"SOVIET GROWTH: ROUTINE, INERTIA, AND PRESSURE." COM STRATA NAT/G DELIB/GP PLAN TEC/DEV ECO/TAC EDU/PROP ADMIN ROUTINE DRIVE WEALTH COLD/WAR 20. PAGE 44 B0891
POL/PAR
ECO/DEV
USSR

S60
MORALES C.J.,"TRADE AND ECONOMIC INTEGRATION IN LATIN AMERICA." FUT L/A+17C LAW STRATA ECO/UNDEV DIST/IND INDUS LABOR NAT/G LEGIS ECO/TAC ADMIN RIGID/FLEX WEALTH...CONCPT NEW/IDEA CONT/OBS TIME/SEQ WORK 20. PAGE 75 B1519
FINAN
INT/TRADE
REGION

S60
SCHWARTZ B.,"THE INTELLIGENTSIA IN COMMUNIST CHINA: A TENTATIVE COMPARISON." ASIA CHINA/COM COM RUSSIA ELITES SOCIETY STRATA POL/PAR VOL/ASSN CREATE ADMIN COERCE NAT/LISM TOTALISM...POLICY TREND 20. PAGE 95 B1914
INTELL
RIGID/FLEX
REV

B61
AMERICAN MANAGEMENT ASSN.SUPERIOR-SUBORDINATE COMMUNICATION IN MANAGEMENT. STRATA FINAN INDUS SML/CO WORKER CONTROL EXEC ATTIT 20. PAGE 4 B0086
MGT
ACT/RES
PERS/REL
LG/CO

B61
BARRASH J.,LABOR'S GRASS ROOTS; A STUDY OF THE LOCAL UNION. STRATA BARGAIN LEAD REPRESENT DEMAND ATTIT PWR. PAGE 9 B0190
LABOR
USA+45
INGP/REL
EXEC

B61
ETZIONI A.,COMPLEX ORGANIZATIONS: A SOCIOLOGICAL READER. CLIENT CULTURE STRATA CREATE OP/RES ADMIN ...POLICY METH/CNCPT BUREAUCRCY. PAGE 34 B0683
VOL/ASSN
STRUCT
CLASSIF
PROF/ORG

B61
KOESTLER A.,THE LOTUS AND THE ROBOT. ASIA INDIA S/ASIA SOCIETY STRATA ECO/DEV AGRI INDUS FAM CREATE DOMIN EDU/PROP ADMIN COERCE ATTIT DRIVE SUPEGO ORD/FREE PWR RESPECT WEALTH...MYTH OBS 20 CHINJAP. PAGE 61 B1226
SECT
ECO/UNDEV

B61
MARSH R.M.,THE MANDARINS: THE CIRCULATION OF ELITES IN CHINA, 1600-1900. ASIA STRUCT PROF/ORG...SOC CHARTS BIBLIOG DICTIONARY 17/20. PAGE 70 B1406
ELITES
ADMIN
FAM
STRATA

B61
MARVICK D.,POLITICAL DECISION-MAKERS. INTELL STRATA NAT/G POL/PAR EX/STRUC LEGIS DOMIN EDU/PROP ATTIT
TOP/EX
BIOG

PERSON PWR...PSY STAT OBS CONT/OBS STAND/INT UNPLAN/INT TIME/SEQ CHARTS STERTYP VAL/FREE. PAGE 70 B1416
ELITES

B61
WARD R.E.,JAPANESE POLITICAL SCIENCE: A GUIDE TO JAPANESE REFERENCE AND RESEARCH MATERIALS (2ND ED.). LAW CONSTN STRATA NAT/G POL/PAR DELIB/GP LEGIS ADMIN CHOOSE GP/REL...INT/LAW 19/20 CHINJAP. PAGE 113 B2290
BIBLIOG/A
PHIL/SCI

L61
THOMPSON V.A.,"HIERARACHY, SPECIALIZATION, AND ORGANIZATIONAL CONFLICT" (BMR)" WOR+45 STRATA STRUCT WORKER TEC/DEV GP/REL INGP/REL ATTIT AUTHORIT 20 BUREAUCRCY. PAGE 104 B2106
PERS/REL
PROB/SOLV
ADMIN
EX/STRUC

S61
MARSH R.M.,"FORMAL ORGANIZATION AND PROMOTION IN A PRE-INDUSTRIAL SOCIETY" (BMR)" ASIA FAM EX/STRUC LEAD...SOC CHARTS 19 WEBER/MAX. PAGE 70 B1407
ADMIN
STRUCT
ECO/UNDEV
STRATA

B62
ESCUELA SUPERIOR DE ADMIN PUBL.INFORME DEL SEMINARIO SOBRE SERVICIO CIVIL O CARRERA ADMINISTRATIVA. L/A+17C ELITES STRATA CONFER CONTROL GOV/REL INGP/REL SUPEGO 20 CENTRAL/AM CIVIL/SERV. PAGE 33 B0681
ADMIN
NAT/G
PROB/SOLV
ATTIT

B62
SHAPIRO D.,A SELECT BIBLIOGRAPHY OF WORKS IN ENGLISH ON RUSSIAN HISTORY, 1801-1917. COM USSR STRATA FORCES EDU/PROP ADMIN REV RACE/REL ATTIT 19/20. PAGE 96 B1932
BIBLIOG
DIPLOM
COLONIAL

L62
ABERLE D.F.,"CHAHAR AND DAGOR MONGOL BUREAUCRATIC ADMINISTRATION: 19621945." ASIA MUNIC TOP/EX PWR ...MGT OBS INT MONGOL 20. PAGE 3 B0053
EX/STRUC
STRATA

L62
MANGIN G.,"L'ORGANIZATION JUDICIAIRE DES ETATS D'AFRIQUE ET DE MADAGASCAR." ISLAM WOR+45 STRATA STRUCT ECO/UNDEV NAT/G LEGIT EXEC...JURID TIME/SEQ TOT/POP 20 SUPREME/CT. PAGE 69 B1387
AFR
LEGIS
COLONIAL
MADAGASCAR

S62
BOOTH D.A.,"POWER STRUCTURE AND COMMUNITY CHANGE: A REPLICATION STUDY OF COMMUNITY A." STRATA LABOR LEAD PARTIC REPRESENT...DECISION MGT TIME. PAGE 14 B0275
MUNIC
ELITES
PWR

S62
DAKIN R.E.,"VARIATIONS IN POWER STRUCTURES AND ORGANIZING EFFICIENCY: A COMPARATIVE STUDY OF FOUR AREAS." STRATA EDU/PROP ADMIN LEAD GP/REL GOV/COMP. PAGE 26 B0524
MUNIC
STRUCT
PWR

S62
DUFTY N.F.,"THE IMPLEMENTATION OF A DECISION." STRATA ACT/RES...MGT CHARTS SOC/EXP ORG/CHARTS. PAGE 31 B0627
DECISION
CREATE
METH/CNCPT
SOC

S62
FESLER J.W.,"FRENCH FIELD ADMINISTRATION: THE BEGINNINGS." CHRIST-17C CULTURE SOCIETY STRATA NAT/G ECO/TAC DOMIN EDU/PROP LEGIT ADJUD COERCE ATTIT ALL/VALS...TIME/SEQ CON/ANAL GEN/METH VAL/FREE 13/15. PAGE 35 B0714
EX/STRUC
FRANCE

S62
IOVTCHOUK M.T.,"ON SOME THEORETICAL PRINCIPLES AND METHODS OF SOCIOLOGICAL INVESTIGATIONS (IN RUSSIAN)." FUT WOR+45 STRATA R+D NAT/G POL/PAR TOP/EX ACT/RES PLAN ECO/TAC EDU/PROP ROUTINE ATTIT RIGID/FLEX MARXISM SOCISM...MARXIST METH/CNCPT OBS TREND NAT/COMP GEN/LAWS 20. PAGE 54 B1102
COM
ECO/DEV
CAP/ISM
USSR

S62
MAINZER L.C.,"INJUSTICE AND BUREAUCRACY." ELITES STRATA STRUCT EX/STRUC SENIOR CONTROL EXEC LEAD ROUTINE INGP/REL ORD/FREE...CONCPT 20 BUREAUCRCY. PAGE 68 B1381
MORAL
MGT
ADMIN

C62
DE GRAZIA A.,"POLITICAL BEHAVIOR (REV. ED.)" STRATA POL/PAR LEAD LOBBY ROUTINE WAR CHOOSE REPRESENT CONSEN ATTIT ORD/FREE BIBLIOG. PAGE 27 B0555
PHIL/SCI
OP/RES
CONCPT

B63
BLONDEL J.,VOTERS, PARTIES, AND LEADERS. UK ELITES LOC/G NAT/G PROVS ACT/RES DOMIN REPRESENT GP/REL INGP/REL...SOC BIBLIOG 20. PAGE 12 B0255
POL/PAR
STRATA
LEGIS
ADMIN

B63
BRAIBANTI R.J.D.,ADMINISTRATION AND ECONOMIC DEVELOPMENT IN INDIA. INDIA S/ASIA SOCIETY STRATA ECO/TAC PERSON WEALTH...MGT GEN/LAWS TOT/POP VAL/FREE 20. PAGE 15 B0300
ECO/UNDEV
ADMIN

B63
DE VRIES E.,SOCIAL ASPECTS OF ECONOMIC DEVELOPMENT IN LATIN AMERICA. CULTURE SOCIETY STRATA FINAN INDUS INT/ORG DELIB/GP ACT/RES ECO/TAC EDU/PROP ADMIN ATTIT SUPEGO HEALTH KNOWL ORD/FREE...SOC STAT TREND ANTHOL TOT/POP VAL/FREE. PAGE 28 B0562
L/A+17C
ECO/UNDEV

B63
FRIED R.C.,THE ITALIAN PREFECTS. ITALY STRATA ECO/DEV NAT/LISM ALL/IDEOS...TREND CHARTS METH/COMP BIBLIOG 17/20 PREFECT. PAGE 37 B0755
ADMIN
NAT/G
EFFICIENCY

HEUSSLER R.,YESTERDAY'S RULERS: THE MAKING OF THE BRITISH COLONIAL SERVICE. AFR EUR+WWI UK STRATA SECT DELIB/GP PLAN DOMIN EDU/PROP ATTIT PERCEPT PERSON SUPEGO KNOWL ORD/FREE PWR...MGT SOC OBS INT TIME/SEQ 20 CMN/WLTH. PAGE 49 B1000
B63 EX/STRUC MORAL ELITES

SPRING D.,THE ENGLISH LANDED ESTATE IN THE NINETEENTH CENTURY: ITS ADMINISTRATION. UK ELITES STRUCT AGRI NAT/G GP/REL OWN PWR WEALTH...BIBLIOG 19 HOUSE/LORD. PAGE 99 B2012
B63 STRATA PERS/REL MGT

SWERDLOW I.,DEVELOPMENT ADMINISTRATION: CONCEPTS AND PROBLEMS. WOR+45 CULTURE SOCIETY STRATA DELIB/GP EX/STRUC ACT/RES PLAN ECO/TAC DOMIN LEGIT ATTIT RIGID/FLEX SUPEGO HEALTH PWR...MGT CONCPT ANTHOL VAL/FREE. PAGE 102 B2062
B63 ECO/UNDEV ADMIN

SPITZ A.A.,"DEVELOPMENT ADMINISTRATION: AN ANNOTATED BIBLIOGRAPHY." WOR+45 CULTURE SOCIETY STRATA DELIB/GP EX/STRUC TOP/EX ACT/RES ECO/TAC DOMIN EDU/PROP LEGIT COERCE ATTIT ALL/VALS...MGT VAL/FREE. PAGE 99 B2009
L63 ADMIN ECO/UNDEV

HARRIS R.L.,"A COMPARATIVE ANALYSIS OF THE ADMINISTRATIVE SYSTEMS OF CANADA AND CEYLON." S/ASIA CULTURE SOCIETY STRATA TOP/EX ACT/RES DOMIN EDU/PROP LEGIT COERCE ATTIT SUPEGO ALL/VALS...MGT CHARTS GEN/LAWS VAL/FREE 20. PAGE 47 B0955
S63 DELIB/GP EX/STRUC CANADA CEYLON

AHMAD M.,THE CIVIL SERVANT IN PAKISTAN. PAKISTAN ECO/UNDEV COLONIAL INGP/REL...SOC CHARTS BIBLIOG 20 CIVIL/SERV. PAGE 3 B0065
B64 WELF/ST ADMIN ATTIT STRATA

BOTTOMORE T.B.,ELITES AND SOCIETY. INTELL STRATA ECO/DEV ECO/UNDEV ADMIN GP/REL ORD/FREE...CONCPT BIBLIOG 20. PAGE 14 B0281
B64 ELITES IDEA/COMP SOCIETY SOC

GOODMAN W.,THE TWO-PARTY SYSTEM IN THE UNITED STATES. USA+45 STRATA LOC/G CHIEF EDU/PROP ADMIN COST PWR POPULISM...PLURIST 18/20 PRESIDENT. PAGE 41 B0821
B64 POL/PAR REPRESENT CHOOSE NAT/G

GUTTSMAN W.L.,THE BRITISH POLITICAL ELITE. EUR+WWI MOD/EUR STRATA FAM LABOR POL/PAR SCHOOL VOL/ASSN DELIB/GP LEGIS LEGIT EXEC CHOOSE ATTIT ALL/VALS ...STAT BIOG TIME/SEQ CHARTS VAL/FREE. PAGE 45 B0905
B64 NAT/G SOC UK ELITES

POPPINO R.E.,INTERNATIONAL COMMUNISM IN LATIN AMERICA: A HISTORY OF THE MOVEMENT 1917-1963. CHINA/COM USSR INTELL STRATA LABOR WORKER ADMIN REV ATTIT...POLICY 20 COLD/WAR. PAGE 84 B1692
B64 MARXISM POL/PAR L/A+17C

SINGER M.R.,THE EMERGING ELITE: A STUDY OF POLITICAL LEADERSHIP IN CEYLON. S/ASIA ECO/UNDEV AGRI KIN FAM SECT EX/STRUC LEGIT ATTIT PWR RESPECT...SOC STAT CHARTS 20. PAGE 97 B1967
B64 TOP/EX STRATA NAT/LISM CEYLON

WILSON L.,THE ACADEMIC MAN. STRUCT FINAN PROF/ORG OP/RES ADMIN AUTHORIT ROLE RESPECT...SOC STAT. PAGE 117 B2360
B64 ACADEM INGP/REL STRATA DELIB/GP

WRAITH R.,CORRUPTION IN DEVELOPING COUNTRIES. NIGERIA UK LAW ELITES STRATA INDUS LOC/G NAT/G SECT FORCES EDU/PROP ADMIN PWR WEALTH 18/20. PAGE 118 B2377
B64 ECO/UNDEV CRIME SANCTION ATTIT

SYMONDS R.,"REFLECTIONS IN LOCALISATION." AFR S/ASIA KIN STRATA INT/ORG NAT/G SCHOOL EDU/PROP LEGIT KNOWL ORD/FREE PWR RESPECT CMN/WLTH 20. PAGE 102 B2064
L64 ADMIN MGT COLONIAL

CLIGNET R.,"POTENTIAL ELITES IN GHANA AND THE IVORY COAST: A PRELIMINARY SURVEY." AFR CULTURE ELITES STRATA KIN NAT/G SECT DOMIN EXEC ORD/FREE RESPECT SKILL...POLICY RELATIV GP/COMP NAT/COMP 20. PAGE 21 B0438
S64 PWR LEGIT IVORY/CST GHANA

KASSOF A.,"THE ADMINISTERED SOCIETY: TOTALITARIANISM WITHOUT TERROR." COM USSR STRATA AGRI INDUS NAT/G PERF/ART SCHOOL TOP/EX EDU/PROP ADMIN ORD/FREE PWR...POLICY SOC TIME/SEQ GEN/LAWS VAL/FREE 20. PAGE 58 B1178
S64 SOCIETY DOMIN TOTALISM

NEEDHAM T.,"SCIENCE AND SOCIETY IN EAST AND WEST." ASIA INTELL STRATA R+D LOC/G NAT/G PROVS CONSULT ACT/RES CREATE PLAN TEC/DEV EDU/PROP ADMIN ATTIT ALL/VALS ...POLICY RELATIV MGT CONCPT NEW/IDEA TIME/SEQ WORK WORK. PAGE 77 B1565
S64 ASIA STRUCT

PARSONS T.,"EVOLUTIONARY UNIVERSALS IN SOCIETY." UNIV SOCIETY STRATA MARKET EDU/PROP LEGIT ADJUD
S64 SOC CONCPT

ADMIN ALL/VALS...JURID OBS GEN/LAWS VAL/FREE 20. PAGE 81 B1638
S64

SALISBURY R.H.,"URBAN POLITICS: THE NEW CONVERGENCE OF POWER." STRATA POL/PAR EX/STRUC PARTIC GP/REL DECISION. PAGE 92 B1863
MUNIC PWR LEAD

NORGREN P.H.,"TOWARD FAIR EMPLOYMENT." USA+45 LAW STRATA LABOR NAT/G FORCES ACT/RES ADMIN ATTIT ...POLICY BIBLIOG 20 NEGRO. PAGE 79 B1588
C64 RACE/REL DISCRIM WORKER MGT

AIYAR S.P.,STUDIES IN INDIAN DEMOCRACY. INDIA STRATA ECO/UNDEV LABOR POL/PAR LEGIS DIPLOM LOBBY REGION CHOOSE ATTIT SOCISM...ANTHOL 20. PAGE 3 B0067
B65 ORD/FREE REPRESENT ADMIN NAT/G

ETZIONI A.,POLITICAL UNIFICATION* A COMPARATIVE STUDY OF LEADERS AND FORCES. EUR+WWI ISLAM L/A+17C WOR+45 ELITES STRATA EXEC WEALTH...TIME/SEQ TREND SOC/EXP. PAGE 34 B0686
B65 INT/ORG FORCES ECO/TAC REGION

MATRAS J.,SOCIAL CHANGE IN ISRAEL. ISRAEL STRATA FAM ACT/RES EDU/PROP ADMIN CHOOSE...STAT CENSUS 19/20 JEWS. PAGE 71 B1427
B65 SECT NAT/LISM GEOG STRUCT

OECD.MEDITERRANEAN REGIONAL PROJECT: TURKEY; EDUCATION AND DEVELOPMENT. FUT TURKEY SOCIETY STRATA FINAN NAT/G PROF/ORG PLAN PROB/SOLV ADMIN COST...STAT CHARTS 20 OECD. PAGE 79 B1602
B65 EDU/PROP ACADEM SCHOOL ECO/UNDEV

PRESTHUS R.,BEHAVIORAL APPROACHES TO PUBLIC ADMINISTRATION. UK STRATA LG/CO PUB/INST VOL/ASSN EX/STRUC TOP/EX EFFICIENCY HEALTH. PAGE 84 B1704
B65 GEN/METH DECISION ADMIN R+D

SNYDER F.G.,ONE-PARTY GOVERNMENT IN MALI: TRANSITION TOWARD CONTROL. MALI STRATA STRUCT SOC. PAGE 99 B1991
B65 ECO/UNDEV POL/PAR EX/STRUC ADMIN

SPEECKAERT G.P.,SELECT BIBLIOGRAPHY ON INTERNATIONAL ORGANIZATION, 1885-1964. WOR+45 WOR-45 EX/STRUC DIPLOM ADMIN REGION 19/20 UN. PAGE 99 B2004
B65 BIBLIOG INT/ORG GEN/LAWS STRATA

YOUNG C.,POLITICS IN THE CONGO* DECOLONIZATION AND INDEPENDENCE. ELITES STRATA FORCES ADMIN REV RACE/REL FEDERAL SOVEREIGN...OBS INT CHARTS CONGO/LEOP. PAGE 118 B2391
B65 BELGIUM COLONIAL NAT/LISM

HAMILTON R.F.,"SKILL LEVEL AND POLITICS." USA+45 CULTURE STRATA STRUCT LABOR CONSERVE NEW/LIB. PAGE 46 B0933
S65 SKILL ADMIN

CARALEY D.,PARTY POLITICS AND NATIONAL ELECTIONS. USA+45 STRATA LOC/G PROVS EX/STRUC BARGAIN ADMIN SANCTION GP/REL ATTIT 20 DEMOCRAT REPUBLICAN. PAGE 18 B0375
B66 POL/PAR CHOOSE REPRESENT NAT/G

RAEFF M.,ORIGINS OF THE RUSSIAN INTELLIGENTSIA: THE EIGHTEENTH-CENTURY NOBILITY. RUSSIA FAM NAT/G EDU/PROP ADMIN PERS/REL ATTIT...HUM BIOG 18. PAGE 85 B1728
B66 INTELL ELITES STRATA CONSERVE

THOENES P.,THE ELITE IN THE WELFARE STATE ,TRANS. BY J BINGHAM; ED. BY. STRATA NAT/G GP/REL HAPPINESS INCOME OPTIMAL MORAL PWR WEALTH...POLICY CONCPT. PAGE 104 B2097
B66 ADMIN ELITES MGT WELF/ST

TOTTEN G.O.,THE SOCIAL DEMOCRATIC MOVEMENT IN PREWAR JAPAN. ASIA CHIEF EX/STRUC LEGIS DOMIN LEAD ROUTINE WAR 20 CHINJAP. PAGE 105 B2122
B66 POL/PAR SOCISM PARTIC STRATA

LEMARCHAND R.,"SOCIAL CHANGE AND POLITICAL MODERNISATION IN BURUNDI." AFR BURUNDI STRATA CHIEF EX/STRUC RIGID/FLEX PWR...SOC 20. PAGE 64 B1285
L66 NAT/G STRUCT ELITES CONSERVE

WOLFINGER R.E.,"POLITICAL ETHOS AND THE STRUCTURE OF CITY GOVERNMENT." POL/PAR EX/STRUC REPRESENT GP/REL PERS/REL RIGID/FLEX PWR. PAGE 118 B2371
S66 MUNIC ATTIT STRATA GOV/COMP

JACOB H.,"DIMENSIONS OF STATE POLITICS HEARD A. ED. STATE LEGIWLATURES IN AMERICAN POLITICS." CULTURE STRATA POL/PAR BUDGET TAX LOBBY ROUTINE GOV/REL ...TRADIT DECISION GEOG. PAGE 55 B1112
C66 PROVS LEGIS ROLE REPRESENT

EDUCATION, INTERACTION, AND SOCIAL CHANGE. STRATA MUNIC SCHOOL ADMIN RIGID/FLEX ROLE 20. PAGE 49 B0991
B67 EDU/PROP ADJUST SOC ACT/RES

KRISLOV S.,THE NEGRO IN FEDERAL EMPLOYMENT. LAW
STRATA LOC/G CREATE PROB/SOLV INSPECT GOV/REL
DISCRIM ROLE...DECISION INT TREND 20 NEGRO WWI
CIVIL/SERV. PAGE 61 B1238
WORKER
NAT/G
ADMIN
RACE/REL
B67

VOOS H.,ORGANIZATIONAL COMMUNICATION: A
BIBLIOGRAPHY. WOR+45 STRATA R+D PROB/SOLV FEEDBACK
COERCE...MGT PSY NET/THEORY HYPO/EXP. PAGE 112
B2268
BIBLIOG/A
INDUS
COM/IND
VOL/ASSN
B67

BESCOBY I.,"A COLONIAL ADMINISTRATION* AN ANALYSIS
OF ADMINISTRATION IN BRITISH COLUMBIA 1869-1871."
UK STRATA EX/STRUC LEGIS TASK GOV/REL EFFICIENCY
ROLE...MGT CHARTS 19. PAGE 11 B0232
ADMIN
CANADA
COLONIAL
LEAD
L67

BEASLEY W.G.,"POLITICS AND THE SAMURAI CLASS
STRUCTURE IN SATSUMA, 18581868." STRATA FORCES
DOMIN LEGIT ADMIN LEAD 19 CHINJAP. PAGE 10 B0202
ELITES
STRUCT
ATTIT
PRIVIL
S67

EDWARDS H.T.,"POWER STRUCTURE AND ITS COMMUNICATION
IN SAN JOSE, COSTA RICA." COSTA/RICA L/A+17C STRATA
FACE/GP POL/PAR EX/STRUC PROB/SOLV ADMIN LEAD
GP/REL PWR...STAT INT 20. PAGE 32 B0655
ELITES
INGP/REL
MUNIC
DOMIN
S67

FOX R.G.,"FAMILY, CASTE, AND COMMERCE IN A NORTH
INDIAN MARKET TOWN." INDIA STRATA AGRI FACE/GP FAM
NEIGH OP/RES BARGAIN ADMIN ROUTINE WEALTH...SOC
CHARTS 20. PAGE 37 B0747
CULTURE
GP/REL
ECO/UNDEV
DIST/IND
S67

FRYKENBURG R.E.,"STUDIES OF LAND CONTROL IN INDIAN
HISTORY: REVIEW ARTICLE." INDIA UK STRATA AGRI
MUNIC OP/RES COLONIAL REGION EFFICIENCY OWN HABITAT
...CONCPT 16/20. PAGE 38 B0763
ECO/UNDEV
CONTROL
ADMIN
S67

JENCKS C.E.,"SOCIAL STATUS OF COAL MINERS IN
BRITAIN SINCE NATIONALIZATION." UK STRATA STRUCT
LABOR RECEIVE GP/REL INCOME OWN ATTIT HABITAT...MGT
T 20. PAGE 56 B1128
EXTR/IND
WORKER
CONTROL
NAT/G
S67

LLOYD K.,"URBAN RACE RIOTS V EFFECTIVE ANTI-
DISCRIMINATION AGENCIES* AN END OR A BEGINNING?"
USA+45 STRATA ACT/RES ADMIN ADJUST ORD/FREE RESPECT
...PLURIST DECISION SOC SOC/WK. PAGE 66 B1332
GP/REL
DISCRIM
LOC/G
CROWD
S67

O'DELL J.H.,"THE JULY REBELLIONS AND THE 'MILITARY
STATE'." USA+45 VIETNAM STRATA CHIEF WORKER
COLONIAL EXEC CROWD CIVMIL/REL RACE/REL TOTALISM
...WELF/ST PACIFIST 20 NEGRO JOHNSON/LB PRESIDENT
CIV/RIGHTS. PAGE 79 B1599
PWR
NAT/G
COERCE
FORCES
S67

SUBRAMANIAM V.,"REPRESENTATIVE BUREAUCRACY: A
REASSESSMENT." USA+45 ELITES LOC/G NAT/G ADMIN
GOV/REL PRIVIL DRIVE ROLE...POLICY CENSUS 20
CIVIL/SERV BUREAUCRCY. PAGE 101 B2053
STRATA
GP/REL
MGT
GOV/COMP
S67

GUZZARDI W. JR.,"THE SECOND BATTLE OF BRITAIN." UK
STRATA LABOR WORKER CREATE PROB/SOLV EDU/PROP ADMIN
LEAD LOBBY...MGT SOC 20 GOLD/STAND. PAGE 45 B0907
FINAN
ECO/TAC
ECO/DEV
STRUCT
S68

MACDONALD D.,AFRICANA; OR, THE HEART OF HEATHEN
AFRICA, VOL. II: MISSION LIFE. SOCIETY STRATA KIN
CREATE EDU/PROP ADMIN COERCE LITERACY HEALTH...MYTH
WORSHIP 19 LIVNGSTN/D MISSION NEGRO. PAGE 67 B1355
SECT
AFR
CULTURE
ORD/FREE
B82

STRATEGY....SEE PLAN, DECISION

STRATIFICATION....SEE STRATA

STRAUSS E. B2051

STRAUSS G. B1873

STREET D. B1661,B2052

STREET H. B0879

STRESEMANN, GUSTAV....SEE STRESEMN/G

STRESEMN/G....GUSTAV STRESEMANN

STRESS....SEE PERSON, DRIVE

STRIKE....STRIKE OF WORKERS

STRIKES....SEE LABOR, GP/REL, FINAN

STRUC/FUNC....STRUCTURAL-FUNCTIONAL THEORY

STRUCT...SOCIAL STRUCTURE

CONOVER H.F.,MADAGASCAR: A SELECTED LIST OF
REFERENCES. MADAGASCAR STRUCT ECO/UNDEV NAT/G ADMIN
BIBLIOG/A
SOCIETY
N

...SOC 19/20. PAGE 23 B0463
CULTURE
COLONIAL
B05

GOODNOW F.J.,THE PRINCIPLES OF THE ADMINISTRATIVE
LAW OF THE UNITED STATES. USA-45 LAW STRUCT
EX/STRUC LEGIS BAL/PWR CONTROL GOV/REL PWR...JURID
19/20 CIVIL/SERV. PAGE 41 B0822
ADMIN
NAT/G
PROVS
LOC/G
B19

SUTHERLAND G.,CONSTITUTIONAL POWER AND WORLD
AFFAIRS. CONSTN STRUCT INT/ORG NAT/G CHIEF LEGIS
ACT/RES PLAN ALL/VALS...OBS TIME/SEQ
CONGRESS VAL/FREE 20 PRESIDENT. PAGE 102 B2056
USA-45
EXEC
DIPLOM
B23

FRANK T.,A HISTORY OF ROME. MEDIT-7 INTELL SOCIETY
LOC/G NAT/G POL/PAR FORCES LEGIS DOMIN LEGIT
ALL/VALS...POLICY CONCPT TIME/SEQ GEN/LAWS ROM/EMP
ROM/EMP. PAGE 37 B0749
EXEC
STRUCT
ELITES
B24

BAGEHOT W.,THE ENGLISH CONSTITUTION AND OTHER
POLITICAL ESSAYS. UK DELIB/GP BAL/PWR ADMIN CONTROL
EXEC ROUTINE CONSERVE...METH PARLIAMENT 19/20.
PAGE 8 B0160
NAT/G
STRUCT
CONCPT
B24

KENT F.R.,THE GREAT GAME OF POLITICS. USA-45 LOC/G
NAT/G POL/PAR EX/STRUC PROB/SOLV BUDGET CHOOSE
GOV/REL 20. PAGE 59 B1194
ADMIN
OP/RES
STRUCT
C27

HSIAO K.C.,"POLITICAL PLURALISM." LAW CONSTN
POL/PAR LEGIS PLAN ADMIN CENTRAL SOVEREIGN
...INT/LAW BIBLIOG 19/20. PAGE 52 B1053
STRUCT
GEN/LAWS
PLURISM
B29

MERRIAM C.E.,CHICAGO: A MORE INTIMATE VIEW OF URBAN
POLITICS. USA-45 CONSTN POL/PAR LEGIS ADMIN CRIME
INGP/REL 18/20 CHICAGO. PAGE 73 B1472
STRUCT
GP/REL
MUNIC
B35

GORER G.,AFRICA DANCES: A BOOK ABOUT WEST AFRICAN
NEGROES. STRUCT LOC/G SECT FORCES TAX ADMIN
COLONIAL...ART/METH MYTH WORSHIP 20 NEGRO AFRICA/W
CHRISTIAN RITUAL. PAGE 41 B0835
AFR
ATTIT
CULTURE
SOCIETY
B36

ROBINSON H.,DEVELOPMENT OF THE BRITISH EMPIRE.
WOR-45 CULTURE SOCIETY STRUCT ECO/DEV ECO/UNDEV
INT/ORG VOL/ASSN FORCES CREATE PLAN DOMIN EDU/PROP
ADMIN COLONIAL PWR WEALTH...POLICY GEOG CHARTS
CMN/WLTH 16/20. PAGE 89 B1800
NAT/G
HIST/WRIT
UK
B38

PETTEE G.S.,THE PROCESS OF REVOLUTION. COM FRANCE
ITALY MOD/EUR RUSSIA SPAIN WOR-45 ELITES INTELL
SOCIETY STRATA STRUCT INT/ORG NAT/G POL/PAR ACT/RES
PLAN EDU/PROP LEGIT EXEC...SOC MYTH TIME/SEQ
TOT/POP 18/20. PAGE 82 B1664
COERCE
CONCPT
REV
B39

HITLER A.,MEIN KAMPF. EUR+WWI FUT MOD/EUR STRUCT
INT/ORG LABOR NAT/G POL/PAR FORCES CREATE PLAN
BAL/PWR DIPLOM ECO/TAC DOMIN EDU/PROP ADMIN COERCE
ATTIT...SOCIALIST BIOG TREND NAZI. PAGE 50 B1020
PWR
NEW/IDEA
WAR
B40

GAUS J.M.,PUBLIC ADMINISTRATION AND THE UNITED
STATES DEPARTMENT OF AGRICULTURE. USA-45 STRUCT
DIST/IND FINAN MARKET EX/STRUC PROB/SOLV GIVE
PRODUC...POLICY GEOG CHARTS 20 DEPT/AGRI. PAGE 39
B0786
ADMIN
AGRI
DELIB/GP
OP/RES
S40

GERTH H.,"THE NAZI PARTY: ITS LEADERSHIP AND
COMPOSITION" (BMR)" GERMANY ELITES STRATA STRUCT
EX/STRUC FORCES ECO/TAC CT/SYS CHOOSE TOTALISM
AGE/Y AUTHORIT PWR 20. PAGE 39 B0792
POL/PAR
DOMIN
LEAD
ADMIN
B41

BURTON M.E.,THE ASSEMBLY OF THE LEAGUE OF NATIONS.
WOR-45 CONSTN SOCIETY STRUCT INT/ORG NAT/G CREATE
ATTIT RIGID/FLEX PWR...POLICY TIME/SEQ LEAGUE/NAT
20. PAGE 18 B0359
DELIB/GP
EX/STRUC
DIPLOM
B41

YOUNG G.,FEDERALISM AND FREEDOM. EUR+WWI MOD/EUR
RUSSIA USA-45 WOR-45 SOCIETY STRUCT ECO/DEV INT/ORG
EXEC FEDERAL ATTIT PERSON ALL/VALS...OLD/LIB CONCPT
OBS TREND LEAGUE/NAT TOT/POP. PAGE 119 B2392
NAT/G
WAR
B42

BINGHAM A.M.,THE TECHNIQUES OF DEMOCRACY. USA-45
CONSTN STRUCT POL/PAR LEGIS PLAN PARTIC CHOOSE
REPRESENT NAT/LISM TOTALISM...MGT 20. PAGE 12 B0240
POPULISM
ORD/FREE
ADMIN
NAT/G
B45

MILLIS H.A.,ORGANIZED LABOR (FIRST ED.). LAW STRUCT
DELIB/GP WORKER ECO/TAC ADJUD CONTROL REPRESENT
INGP/REL INCOME MGT. PAGE 74 B1485
LABOR
POLICY
ROUTINE
GP/REL
B45

PLATO,THE REPUBLIC. MEDIT-7 UNIV SOCIETY STRUCT
EX/STRUC FORCES UTOPIA ATTIT PERCEPT HEALTH KNOWL
ORD/FREE PWR...HUM CONCPT STERTYP TOT/POP. PAGE 83
B1681
PERSON
PHIL/SCI
B47

SIMON H.A.,ADMINISTRATIVE BEHAVIOR: A STUDY OF
DECISION-MAKING PROCESSES IN ADMINISTRATIVE
ORGANIZATION. STRUCT COM/IND OP/RES PROB/SOLV
DECISION
NEW/IDEA
ADMIN

EFFICIENCY EQUILIB UTIL...PHIL/SCI PSY STYLE.   RATIONAL
PAGE 97 B1956

B47

WARNER W.L.,THE SOCIAL SYSTEM OF THE MODERN   ROLE
FACTORY; THE STRIKE: AN ANALYSIS. USA-45 STRATA   STRUCT
WORKER ECO/TAC GP/REL INGP/REL...MGT SOC CHARTS 20   LABOR
YANKEE/C. PAGE 114 B2293   PROC/MFG

B47

WHITEHEAD T.N.,LEADERSHIP IN A FREE SOCIETY; A   INDUS
STUDY IN HUMAN RELATIONS BASED ON AN ANALYSIS OF   LEAD
PRESENT-DAY INDUSTRIAL CIVILIZATION. WOR-45 STRUCT   ORD/FREE
R+D LABOR LG/CO SML/CO WORKER PLAN PROB/SOLV   SOCIETY
TEC/DEV DRIVE...MGT 20. PAGE 116 B2341

S47

GRAVES W.B.,"LEGISLATIVE REFERENCE SYSTEM FOR THE   LEGIS
CONGRESS OF THE UNITED STATES." ROUTINE...CLASSIF   STRUCT
TREND EXHIBIT CONGRESS. PAGE 42 B0856

B48

WHITE L.D.,INTRODUCTION OT THE STUDY OF PUBLIC   ADMIN
ADMINISTRATION. STRUCT PLAN PROB/SOLV EXEC ROUTINE   MGT
GOV/REL EFFICIENCY PWR CHARTS. PAGE 116 B2336   EX/STRUC
                                                      NAT/G

B48

WHITE L.D.,THE FEDERALISTS: A STUDY IN   ADMIN
ADMINISTRATIVE HISTORY. STRUCT DELIB/GP LEGIS   NAT/G
BUDGET ROUTINE GOV/REL GP/REL PERS/REL PWR...BIOG   POLICY
18/19 PRESIDENT CONGRESS WASHINGT/G JEFFERSN/T   PROB/SOLV
HAMILTON/A. PAGE 116 B2337

B49

ROSENHAUPT H.W.,HOW TO WAGE PEACE. USA+45 SOCIETY   INTELL
STRATA STRUCT R+D INT/ORG POL/PAR LEGIS ACT/RES   CONCPT
CREATE PLAN EDU/PROP ADMIN EXEC ATTIT ALL/VALS   DIPLOM
...TIME/SEQ TREND COLD/WAR 20. PAGE 90 B1822

L49

BROOKINGS INST.,"GOVERNMENT MECHANISM FOR CONDUCT   EXEC
OF US FOREIGN RELATIONS." USA+45 CONSTN NAT/G LEGIS   STRUCT
CT/SYS...MGT TIME/SEQ CONGRESS TOT/POP 20. PAGE 15   DIPLOM
B0316

B50

MCCAMY J.,THE ADMINISTRATION OF AMERICAN FOREIGN   EXEC
AFFAIRS. USA+45 SOCIETY INT/ORG NAT/G ACT/RES PLAN   STRUCT
INT/TRADE EDU/PROP ADJUD ALL/VALS...METH/CNCPT   DIPLOM
TIME/SEQ CONGRESS 20. PAGE 71 B1441

S50

EPSTEIN L.D.,"POLITICAL STERILIZATION OF CIVIL   ADMIN
SERVANTS: THE UNITED STATES AND GREAT BRITAIN." UK   LEGIS
USA+45 USA-45 STRUCT TOP/EX OP/RES PARTIC CHOOSE   DECISION
NAT/LISM 20 CONGRESS CIVIL/SERV. PAGE 33 B0679   POL/PAR

B51

SMITH L.,AMERICAN DEMOCRACY AND MILITARY POWER.   FORCES
USA+45 USA-45 CONSTN STRATA NAT/G LEGIS ACT/RES   STRUCT
LEGIT ADMIN EXEC GOV/REL ALL/VALS...CONCPT   WAR
HIST/WRIT CONGRESS 20. PAGE 98 B1982

B52

ULAM A.B.,TITOISM AND THE COMINFORM. USSR WOR+45   COM
STRUCT INT/ORG NAT/G ACT/RES PLAN EXEC ATTIT DRIVE   POL/PAR
ALL/VALS...CONCPT OBS VAL/FREE 20 COMINTERN   TOTALISM
TITO/MARSH. PAGE 106 B2145   YUGOSLAVIA

B52

VANDENBOSCH A.,THE UN: BACKGROUND, ORGANIZATION,   DELIB/GP
FUNCTIONS, ACTIVITIES. WOR+45 LAW CONSTN STRUCT   TIME/SEQ
INT/ORG CONSULT BAL/PWR EDU/PROP EXEC ALL/VALS   PEACE
...POLICY CONCPT UN 20. PAGE 112 B2254

B53

DIMOCK M.E.,PUBLIC ADMINISTRATION. USA+45 FINAN   ADMIN
WORKER BUDGET CONTROL CHOOSE...T 20. PAGE 29 B0596   STRUCT
                                                      OP/RES
                                                      POLICY

B53

GROSS B.M.,THE LEGISLATIVE STRUGGLE: A STUDY IN   LEGIS
SOCIAL COMBAT. STRUCT LOC/G POL/PAR JUDGE EDU/PROP   DECISION
DEBATE ETIQUET ADMIN LOBBY CHOOSE GOV/REL INGP/REL   PERSON
HEREDITY ALL/VALS...SOC PRESIDENT. PAGE 44 B0885   LEAD

B53

WAGLEY C.,AMAZON TOWN: A STUDY OF MAN IN THE   SOC
TROPICS. BRAZIL L/A+17C STRATA STRUCT ECO/UNDEV   NEIGH
AGRI EX/STRUC RACE/REL DISCRIM HABITAT WEALTH...OBS   CULTURE
SOC/EXP 20. PAGE 113 B2273   INGP/REL

S53

DRUCKER P.F.,"THE EMPLOYEE SOCIETY." STRUCT BAL/PWR   LABOR
PARTIC REPRESENT PWR...DECISION CONCPT. PAGE 30   MGT
B0619   WORKER
                                                      CULTURE

B54

BIESANZ J.,MODERN SOCIETY: AN INTRODUCTION TO   SOCIETY
SOCIAL SCIENCE. COM CONSTN STRUCT FAM MUNIC NAT/G   PROB/SOLV
SECT EX/STRUC LEGIS GP/REL PERSON...SOC 20. PAGE 12   CULTURE
B0237

B54

LAPIERRE R.T.,A THEORY OF SOCIAL CONTROL. STRUCT   CONTROL
ADMIN ROUTINE SANCTION ANOMIE AUTHORIT DRIVE PERSON   VOL/ASSN
PWR...MAJORIT CONCPT CLASSIF. PAGE 62 B1260   CULTURE

B54

MCCLOSKEY J.F.,OPERATIONS RESEARCH FOR MANAGEMENT.   OP/RES
STRUCT COMPUTER ADMIN ROUTINE...PHIL/SCI CONCPT   MGT
METH/CNCPT TREND ANTHOL BIBLIOG 20. PAGE 72 B1445   METH/COMP

TEC/DEV
L54

ARCIENEGAS G.,"POST-WAR SOVIET FOREIGN POLICY: A   INTELL
WORLD PERSPECTIVE." COM USA+45 STRUCT NAT/G POL/PAR   ACT/RES
TOP/EX PLAN ADMIN ALL/VALS...TREND COLD/WAR TOT/POP   USSR
20. PAGE 6 B0124

L54

FURNISS E.S.,"WEAKNESSES IN FRENCH FOREIGN POLICY-   NAT/G
MAKING." EUR+WWI LEGIS LEGIT EXEC ATTIT RIGID/FLEX   STRUCT
ORD/FREE...SOC CONCPT METH/CNCPT OBS 20. PAGE 38   DIPLOM
B0766   FRANCE

B55

CHOWDHURI R.N.,INTERNATIONAL MANDATES AND   DELIB/GP
TRUSTEESHIP SYSTEMS. WOR+45 STRUCT ECO/UNDEV   PLAN
INT/ORG LEGIS DOMIN EDU/PROP LEGIT ADJUD EXEC PWR   SOVEREIGN
...CONCPT TIME/SEQ UN 20. PAGE 21 B0427

B55

MACMAHON A.W.,FEDERALISM: MATURE AND EMERGENT.   STRUCT
EUR+WWI FUT WOR-45 INT/ORG NAT/G REPRESENT   CONCPT
FEDERAL...POLICY MGT RECORD TREND GEN/LAWS 20.
PAGE 68 B1370

B55

RILEY V.,INTERINDUSTRY ECONOMIC STUDIES. USA+45   BIBLIOG
COMPUTER ADMIN OPTIMAL PRODUC...MGT CLASSIF STAT.   ECO/DEV
PAGE 88 B1788   PLAN
                                                      STRUCT

L55

ROSTOW W.W.,"RUSSIA AND CHINA UNDER COMMUNISM."   COM
CHINA/COM USSR INTELL STRUCT INT/ORG NAT/G POL/PAR   ASIA
TOP/EX ACT/RES PLAN ADMIN ATTIT ALL/VALS MARXISM
...CONCPT OBS TIME/SEQ TREND GOV/COMP VAL/FREE 20.
PAGE 91 B1830

S55

CHAPIN F.S.,"FORMALIZATION OBSERVED IN TEN   VOL/ASSN
VOLUNTARY ORGANIZATIONS: CONCEPTS, MORPHOLOGY,   ROUTINE
PROCESS." STRUCT INGP/REL PERS/REL...METH/CNCPT   CONTROL
CLASSIF OBS RECORD. PAGE 20 B0407   OP/RES

S55

DRUCKER P.F.,"'MANAGEMENT SCIENCE' AND THE   MGT
MANAGER." PLAN ROUTINE RIGID/FLEX...METH/CNCPT LOG   STRUCT
HYPO/EXP. PAGE 30 B0620   DECISION
                                                      RATIONAL

B56

BLAU P.M.,BUREAUCRACY IN MODERN SOCIETY. STRUCT   SOC
INDUS LABOR LG/CO LOC/G NAT/G FORCES EDU/PROP   EX/STRUC
ROUTINE ORD/FREE 20 BUREAUCRCY. PAGE 12 B0252   ADMIN
                                                      EFFICIENCY

B56

CENTRAL AFRICAN ARCHIVES,A GUIDE TO THE PUBLIC   BIBLIOG/A
RECORDS OF SOUTHERN RHODESIA UNDER THE REGIME OF   COLONIAL
THE BRITISH SOUTH AFRICA COMPANY, 1890-1923. UK   ADMIN
STRUCT NAT/G WRITING GP/REL 19/20. PAGE 19 B0398   AFR

B56

SOHN L.B.,CASES ON UNITED NATIONS LAW. STRUCT   INT/ORG
DELIB/GP WAR PEACE ORD/FREE...DECISION ANTHOL 20   INT/LAW
UN. PAGE 99 B1994   ADMIN
                                                      ADJUD

B56

WEBER M.,STAATSSOZIOLOGIE. STRUCT LEGIT ADMIN   SOC
PARL/PROC SUPEGO CONSERVE JURID. PAGE 114 B2305   NAT/G
                                                      POL/PAR
                                                      LEAD

L56

PARSONS T.,"SUGGESTIONS FOR A SOCIOLOGICAL APPROACH   SOC
TO THE THEORY OF ORGANIZATIONS - I" (BMR)" FINAN   CONCPT
EX/STRUC LEGIT ALL/VALS...POLICY DECISION 20.   ADMIN
PAGE 81 B1637   STRUCT

B57

HEATH S.,CITADEL, MARKET, AND ALTAR; EMERGING   NEW/IDEA
SOCIETY. SOCIETY ADMIN OPTIMAL OWN RATIONAL   STRUCT
ORD/FREE...SOC LOG PREDICT GEN/LAWS DICTIONARY 20.   UTOPIA
PAGE 49 B0985   CREATE

B57

IKE N.,JAPANESE POLITICS. INTELL STRUCT AGRI INDUS   NAT/G
FAM KIN LABOR PRESS CHOOSE ATTIT...DECISION BIBLIOG   ADMIN
19/20 CHINJAP. PAGE 53 B1075   POL/PAR
                                                      CULTURE

B57

PYE L.W.,THE POLICY IMPLICATIONS OF SOCIAL CHANGE   SOCIETY
IN NON-WESTERN SOCIETIES. ASIA USA+45 CULTURE   ORD/FREE
STRUCT NAT/G ECO/TAC ADMIN ROLE...POLICY SOC.   ECO/UNDEV
PAGE 85 B1723   DIPLOM

B57

SCHNEIDER E.V.,INDUSTRIAL SOCIOLOGY: THE SOCIAL   LABOR
RELATIONS OF INDUSTRY AND COMMUNITY. STRATA INDUS   MGT
NAT/G NEIGH CREATE ADMIN PARTIC GP/REL RACE/REL   INGP/REL
ROLE PWR...POLICY BIBLIOG. PAGE 94 B1898   STRUCT

B58

KINTNER W.R.,ORGANIZING FOR CONFLICT: A PROPOSAL.   USA+45
USSR STRUCT NAT/G LEGIS ADMIN EXEC PEACE ORD/FREE   PLAN
PWR...CONCPT OBS TREND NAT/COMP VAL/FREE COLD/WAR   DIPLOM
20. PAGE 60 B1211

B58

SPITZ D.,DEMOCRACY AND THE CHALLANGE OF POWER. FUT   NAT/G
USA+45 USA-45 LAW SOCIETY STRUCT LOC/G POL/PAR   PWR
PROVS DELIB/GP EX/STRUC LEGIS TOP/EX ACT/RES CREATE

DOMIN EDU/PROP LEGIT ADJUD ADMIN ATTIT DRIVE MORAL
ORD/FREE TOT/POP. PAGE 99 B2010

B58

TAYLOR H.,THE STATESMAN. MOD/EUR FACE/GP FAM NAT/G EXEC
POL/PAR DELIB/GP LEGIS ATTIT PERSON PWR...POLICY STRUCT
CONCPT OBS GEN/LAWS. PAGE 103 B2086

S58

DAVENPORT J.,"ARMS AND THE WELFARE STATE." INTELL USA+45
STRUCT FORCES CREATE ECO/TAC FOR/AID DOMIN LEGIT NAT/G
ADMIN WAR ORD/FREE PWR...POLICY SOC CONCPT MYTH OBS USSR
TREND COLD/WAR TOT/POP 20. PAGE 26 B0533

B59

CHINA INSTITUTE OF AMERICA.,CHINA AND THE UNITED ASIA
NATIONS. CHINA/COM FUT STRUCT EDU/PROP LEGIT ADMIN INT/ORG
ATTIT KNOWL ORD/FREE PWR...OBS RECORD STAND/INT
TIME/SEQ UN LEAGUE/NAT UNESCO 20. PAGE 21 B0425

B59

DAHRENDORF R.,CLASS AND CLASS CONFLICT IN VOL/ASSN
INDUSTRIAL SOCIETY. LABOR NAT/G COERCE ROLE PLURISM STRUCT
...POLICY MGT CONCPT CLASSIF. PAGE 26 B0523 SOC
GP/REL

B59

GOODRICH L.,THE UNITED NATIONS. WOR+45 CONSTN INT/ORG
STRUCT ACT/RES LEGIT COERCE KNOWL ORD/FREE PWR ROUTINE
...GEN/LAWS UN 20. PAGE 41 B0825

B59

LEMBERG E.,DIE VERTRIEBENEN IN WESTDEUTSCHLAND (3 GP/REL
VOLS.). GERMANY/W CULTURE STRUCT AGRI PROVS ADMIN INGP/REL
...JURID 20 MIGRATION. PAGE 64 B1287 SOCIETY

B59

MAYNTZ R.,PARTEIGRUPPEN IN DER GROSSSTADT. GERMANY MUNIC
STRATA STRUCT DOMIN CHOOSE 20. PAGE 71 B1437 MGT
POL/PAR
ATTIT

L59

"A BIBLIOGRAPHICAL ESSAY ON DECISION MAKING." BIBLIOG/A
WOR+45 WOR-45 STRUCT OP/RES GP/REL...CONCPT DECISION
IDEA/COMP METH 20. PAGE 2 B0038 ADMIN
LEAD

S59

BENDIX R.,"INDUSTRIALIZATION, IDEOLOGIES, AND INDUS
SOCIAL STRUCTURE" (BMR)" UK USA-45 USSR STRUCT ATTIT
WORKER GP/REL EFFICIENCY...IDEA/COMP 20. PAGE 10 MGT
B0210 ADMIN

S59

JANOWITZ M.,"CHANGING PATTERNS OF ORGANIZATIONAL FORCES
AUTHORITY: THE MILITARY ESTABLISHMENT (BMR)" AUTHORIT
USA+45 ELITES STRUCT EX/STRUC PLAN DOMIN AUTOMAT ADMIN
NUC/PWR WEAPON 20. PAGE 55 B1122 TEC/DEV

S59

STINCHCOMBE A.L.,"BUREAUCRATIC AND CRAFT CONSTRUC
ADMINISTRATION OF PRODUCTION: A COMPARATIVE STUDY" PROC/MFG
(BMR)" USA+45 STRUCT EX/STRUC ECO/TAC GP/REL ADMIN
...CLASSIF GP/COMP IDEA/COMP GEN/LAWS 20 WEBER/MAX. PLAN
PAGE 101 B2039

S59

UDY S.H. JR.,"'BUREAUCRACY' AND 'RATIONALITY' IN GEN/LAWS
WEBER'S ORGANIZATION THEORY: AN EMPIRICAL STUDY" METH/CNCPT
(BMR)" UNIV STRUCT INDUS LG/CO SML/CO VOL/ASSN ADMIN
...SOC SIMUL 20 WEBER/MAX BUREAUCRCY. PAGE 106 RATIONAL
B2144

B60

CORSON J.J.,GOVERNANCE OF COLLEGES AND ADMIN
UNIVERSITIES. STRUCT FINAN DELIB/GP DOMIN EDU/PROP EXEC
LEAD CHOOSE GP/REL CENTRAL COST PRIVIL SUPEGO ACADEM
ORD/FREE PWR...DECISION BIBLIOG. PAGE 24 B0481 HABITAT

B60

EASTON S.C.,THE TWILIGHT OF EUROPEAN COLONIALISM. FINAN
AFR S/ASIA CONSTN SOCIETY STRUCT ECO/UNDEV INDUS ADMIN
NAT/G FORCES ECO/TAC COLONIAL CT/SYS ATTIT KNOWL
ORD/FREE PWR...SOCIALIST TIME/SEQ TREND CON/ANAL
20. PAGE 32 B0645

B60

FRANKE W.,THE REFORM AND ABOLITION OF THE ADJUST
TRADITIONAL CHINESE EXAMINATION SYSTEM. ASIA STRUCT ADMIN
19/20 CIVIL/SERV. PAGE 37 B0750 TESTS
STRATA

B60

HYDE L.K.G.,THE US AND THE UN. WOR+45 STRUCT USA+45
ECO/DEV ECO/UNDEV NAT/G ACT/RES PLAN DIPLOM INT/ORG
EDU/PROP ADMIN ALL/VALS...CONCPT TIME/SEQ GEN/LAWS FOR/AID
UN VAL/FREE 20. PAGE 53 B1070

B60

JONES V.,METROPOLITAN COMMUNITIES: A BIBLIOGRAPHY BIBLIOG
WITH SPECIAL EMPHASIS UPON GOVERNMENT AND POLITICS, LOC/G
1955-1957. STRUCT ECO/DEV FINAN FORCES PLAN MUNIC
PROB/SOLV RECEIVE EDU/PROP CT/SYS...GEOG HEAL 20. ADMIN
PAGE 57 B1152

B60

LIPSET S.M.,POLITICAL MAN. AFR COM EUR+WWI L/A+17C PWR
MOD/EUR S/ASIA USA+45 USA-45 STRUCT ECO/DEV SOC
ECO/UNDEV POL/PAR SECT ADMIN WEALTH...CONCPT WORK
TOT/POP 20. PAGE 65 B1320

B60

US SENATE COMM. GOVT. OPER.,ORGANIZING FOR NATIONAL CONSULT
SECURITY. USA+45 USA-45 INTELL STRUCT SML/CO EXEC

ACT/RES ADMIN ATTIT PERSON PWR SKILL...DECISION 20.
PAGE 111 B2236

B60

WALTER B.,COMMUNICATIONS AND INFLUENCE: DEXISION MUNIC
MAKING IN A MUNICIPAL ADMINISTRATIVE HIERARCHY DECISION
(PH.D. DISS., UNPUBL.). LEAD CHOOSE PWR METH/CNCPT. ADMIN
PAGE 113 B2284 STRUCT

L60

DEAN A.W.,"SECOND GENEVA CONFERENCE OF THE LAW OF INT/ORG
THE SEA: THE FIGHT FOR FREEDOM OF THE SEAS." FUT JURID
USA+45 USSR WOR+45 WOR-45 SEA CONSTN STRUCT PLAN INT/LAW
INT/TRADE ADJUD ADMIN ORD/FREE...DECISION RECORD
TREND GEN/LAWS 20 TREATY. PAGE 28 B0564

S60

HERZ J.H.,"EAST GERMANY: PROGRESS AND PROSPECTS." POL/PAR
COM AGRI FINAN INDUS LOC/G NAT/G FORCES PLAN STRUCT
TEC/DEV DOMIN ADMIN COERCE DRIVE PERCEPT RIGID/FLEX GERMANY
MORAL ORD/FREE PWR...MARXIST PSY SOC RECORD STERTYP
WORK. PAGE 49 B0997

S60

SMIGEL E.O.,"THE IMPACT OF RECRUITMENT ON THE LG/CO
ORGANIZATION OF THE LARGE LAW FIRM" (BMR)" USA+45 ADMIN
STRUCT CONSULT PLAN GP/REL EFFICIENCY JURID. LAW
PAGE 98 B1979 WORKER

S60

THOMPSON J.D.,"ORGANIZATIONAL MANAGEMENT OF PROB/SOLV
CONFLICT" (BMR)" WOR+45 STRUCT LABOR LG/CO WORKER PERS/REL
TEC/DEV INGP/REL ATTIT GP/COMP. PAGE 104 B2103 ADMIN
MGT

C60

FITZSIMMONS T.,"USSR: ITS PEOPLE, ITS SOCIETY, ITS CULTURE
CULTURE." USSR FAM SECT DIPLOM EDU/PROP ADMIN STRUCT
RACE/REL ATTIT...POLICY CHARTS BIBLIOG 20. PAGE 36 SOCIETY
B0728 COM

C60

MCCLEERY R.,"COMMUNICATION PATTERNS AS BASES OF PERS/REL
SYSTEMS OF AUTHORITY AND POWER" IN THEORETICAL PUB/INST
STUDIES IN SOCIAL ORGAN. OF PRISON-BMR. USA+45 PWR
SOCIETY STRUCT EDU/PROP ADMIN CONTROL COERCE CRIME DOMIN
GP/REL AUTHORIT...SOC 20. PAGE 71 B1443

N60

RHODESIA-NYASA NATL ARCHIVES,A SELECT BIBLIOGRAPHY BIBLIOG
OF RECENT PUBLICATIONS CONCERNING THE FEDERATION OF ADMIN
RHODESIA AND NYASALAND (PAMPHLET). MALAWI RHODESIA ORD/FREE
LAW CULTURE STRUCT ECO/UNDEV LEGIS...GEOG 20. NAT/G
PAGE 88 B1770

B61

ETZIONI A.,COMPLEX ORGANIZATIONS: A SOCIOLOGICAL VOL/ASSN
READER. CLIENT CULTURE STRATA CREATE OP/RES ADMIN STRUCT
...POLICY METH/CNCPT BUREAUCRCY. PAGE 34 B0683 CLASSIF
PROF/ORG

B61

JANOWITZ M.,COMMUNITY POLITICAL SYSTEMS. USA+45 MUNIC
SOCIETY INDUS VOL/ASSN TEC/DEV ADMIN LEAD CHOOSE STRUCT
...SOC SOC/WK 20. PAGE 56 B1123 POL/PAR

B61

MACMAHON A.W.,DELEGATION AND AUTONOMY. INDIA STRUCT ADMIN
LEGIS BARGAIN BUDGET ECO/TAC LEGIT EXEC REPRESENT PLAN
GOV/REL CENTRAL DEMAND EFFICIENCY PRODUC. PAGE 68 FEDERAL
B1373

B61

MARSH R.M.,THE MANDARINS: THE CIRCULATION OF ELITES ELITES
IN CHINA, 1600-1900. ASIA STRUCT PROF/ORG...SOC ADMIN
CHARTS BIBLIOG DICTIONARY 17/20. PAGE 70 B1406 FAM
STRATA

B61

MONAS S.,THE THIRD SECTION: POLICE AND SOCIETY IN ORD/FREE
RUSSIA UNDER NICHOLAS I. MOD/EUR RUSSIA ELITES COM
STRUCT NAT/G EX/STRUC ADMIN CONTROL PWR CONSERVE FORCES
...DECISION 19 NICHOLAS/I. PAGE 74 B1499 COERCE

B61

PEASLEE A.J.,INTERNATIONAL GOVERNMENT INT/ORG
ORGANIZATIONS, CONSTITUTIONAL DOCUMENTS. WOR+45 STRUCT
WOR-45 CONSTN VOL/ASSN DELIB/GP EX/STRUC ROUTINE
KNOWL TOT/POP 20. PAGE 82 B1650

B61

ROWAT D.C.,BASIC ISSUES IN PUBLIC ADMINISTRATION. NAT/G
STRUCT EX/STRUC PWR CONSERVE...MAJORIT DECISION MGT ADJUD
T 20 BUREAUCRCY. PAGE 91 B1839 ADMIN

B61

TANNENBAUM R.,LEADERSHIP AND ORGANIZATION. STRUCT LEAD
ADMIN INGP/REL ATTIT PERCEPT...DECISION METH/CNCPT MGT
OBS CHARTS BIBLIOG. PAGE 103 B2075 RESPECT
ROLE

L61

THOMPSON V.A.,"HIERARACHY, SPECIALIZATION, AND PERS/REL
ORGANIZATIONAL CONFLICT" (BMR)" WOR+45 STRATA PROB/SOLV
STRUCT WORKER TEC/DEV GP/REL INGP/REL ATTIT ADMIN
AUTHORIT 20 BUREAUCRCY. PAGE 104 B2106 EX/STRUC

S61

JACKSON E.,"CONSTITUTIONAL DEVELOPMENTS OF THE INT/ORG
UNITED NATIONS: THE GROWTH OF ITS EXECUTIVE EXEC
CAPACITY." FUT WOR+45 CONSTN STRUCT ACT/RES PLAN
ALL/VALS...NEW/IDEA OBS COLD/WAR UN 20. PAGE 55
B1106

MARSH R.M.,"FORMAL ORGANIZATION AND PROMOTION IN A
PRE-INDUSTRIAL SOCIETY" (BMR)" ASIA FAM EX/STRUC
LEAD...SOC CHARTS 19 WEBER/MAX. PAGE 70 B1407
    S61
ADMIN
STRUCT
ECO/UNDEV
STRATA

NEEDLER M.C.,"THE POLITICAL DEVELOPMENT OF MEXICO.."
STRUCT NAT/G ADMIN RIGID/FLEX...TIME/SEQ TREND
MEXIC/AMER TOT/POP VAL/FREE 19/20. PAGE 77 B1566
    S61
L/A+17C
POL/PAR

SHERBENOU E.L.,"CLASS, PARTICIPATION, AND THE
COUNCIL-MANAGER PLAN." ELITES STRUCT LEAD GP/REL
ATTIT PWR DECISION. PAGE 96 B1942
    S61
REPRESENT
MUNIC
EXEC

TAUBENFELD H.J.,"OUTER SPACE--PAST POLITICS AND
FUTURE POLICY." FUT USA+45 USA-45 WOR+45 AIR INTELL
STRUCT ECO/DEV NAT/G TOP/EX ACT/RES ADMIN ROUTINE
NUC/PWR ATTIT DRIVE...CONCPT TIME/SEQ TREND TOT/POP
20. PAGE 103 B2083
    S61
PLAN
SPACE
INT/ORG

MOODIE G.C.,"THE GOVERNMENT OF GREAT BRITAIN." UK
LAW STRUCT LOC/G POL/PAR DIPLOM RECEIVE ADMIN
COLONIAL CHOOSE...BIBLIOG 20 PARLIAMENT. PAGE 75
B1508
    C61
NAT/G
SOCIETY
PARL/PROC
GOV/COMP

BINDER L.,IRAN: POLITICAL DEVELOPMENT IN A CHANGING
SOCIETY. IRAN OP/RES REV GP/REL CENTRAL RATIONAL
PWR...PHIL/SCI NAT/COMP GEN/LAWS 20. PAGE 12 B0239
    B62
LEGIT
NAT/G
ADMIN
STRUCT

FOSS P.O.,REORGANIZATION AND REASSIGNMENT IN THE
CALIFORNIA HIGHWAY PATROL (PAMPHLET). USA+45 STRUCT
WORKER EDU/PROP CONTROL COERCE INGP/REL ORD/FREE
PWR...DECISION 20 CALIFORNIA. PAGE 37 B0744
    B62
FORCES
ADMIN
PROVS
PLAN

HITCHNER D.G.,MODERN GOVERNMENT: A SURVEY OF
POLITICAL SCIENCE. WOR+45 INT/ORG LEGIS ADMIN
CT/SYS EXEC CHOOSE TOTALISM POPULISM...INT/LAW
PHIL/SCI METH 20. PAGE 50 B1019
    B62
CONCPT
NAT/G
STRUCT

NATIONAL BUREAU ECONOMIC RES.,THE RATE AND DIRECTION
OF INVENTIVE ACTIVITY: ECONOMIC AND SOCIAL FACTORS.
STRUCT INDUS MARKET R+D CREATE OP/RES TEC/DEV
EFFICIENCY PRODUC RATIONAL UTIL...WELF/ST PHIL/SCI
METH/CNCPT TIME. PAGE 77 B1562
    B62
DECISION
PROB/SOLV
MGT

PRESTHUS R.,THE ORGANIZATIONAL SOCIETY. USA+45
STRUCT ECO/DEV ADMIN ATTIT ALL/VALS...PSY SOC 20.
PAGE 84 B1703
    B62
LG/CO
WORKER
PERS/REL
DRIVE

SAMPSON A.,ANATOMY OF BRITAIN. UK LAW COM/IND FINAN
INDUS MARKET MUNIC POL/PAR EX/STRUC TOP/EX DIPLOM
LEAD REPRESENT PERSON PARLIAMENT WORSHIP. PAGE 92
B1866
    B62
ELITES
PWR
STRUCT
FORCES

TAYLOR J.K.L.,ATTITUDES AND METHODS OF
COMMUNICATION AND CONSULTATION BETWEEN EMPLOYERS
AND WORKERS AT INDIVIDUAL FIRM LEVEL. WOR+45 STRUCT
INDUS LABOR CONFER TASK GP/REL EFFICIENCY...MGT
BIBLIOG METH 20 OECD. PAGE 103 B2087
    B62
WORKER
ADMIN
ATTIT
EDU/PROP

HOFFHERR R.,"LE PROBLEME DE L'ENCADREMENT DANS LES
JEUNES ETATS DE LANGUE FRANCAISE EN AFRIQUE
CENTRALE ET A MADAGASCAR." FUT ECO/UNDEV CONSULT
PLAN ECO/TAC COLONIAL ATTIT...MGT TIME/SEQ VAL/FREE
20. PAGE 51 B1028
    L62
AFR
STRUCT
FRANCE

MANGIN G.,"L'ORGANIZATION JUDICIAIRE DES ETATS
D'AFRIQUE ET DE MADAGASCAR." AFR WOR+45 STRATA
STRUCT ECO/UNDEV NAT/G LEGIT EXEC...JURID TIME/SEQ
TOT/POP 20 SUPREME/CT. PAGE 69 B1387
    L62
AFR
LEGIS
COLONIAL
MADAGASCAR

DAKIN R.E.,"VARIATIONS IN POWER STRUCTURES AND
ORGANIZING EFFICIENCY: A COMPARATIVE STUDY OF FOUR
AREAS." STRATA EDU/PROP ADMIN LEAD GP/REL GOV/COMP.
PAGE 26 B0524
    S62
MUNIC
STRUCT
PWR

MAINZER L.C.,"INJUSTICE AND BUREAUCRACY." ELITES
STRATA STRUCT EX/STRUC SENIOR CONTROL EXEC LEAD
ROUTINE INGP/REL ORD/FREE...CONCPT 20 BUREAUCRCY.
PAGE 68 B1381
    S62
MORAL
MGT
ADMIN

MANGIN G.,"LES ACCORDS DE COOPERATION EN MATIERE DE
JUSTICE ENTRE LA FRANCE ET LES ETATS AFRICAINS ET
MALGACHE." AFR ISLAM WOR+45 STRUCT ECO/UNDEV NAT/G
DELIB/GP PERCEPT ALL/VALS...JURID MGT TIME/SEQ 20.
PAGE 69 B1389
    S62
INT/ORG
LAW
FRANCE

MURACCIOLE L.,"LES MODIFICATIONS DE LA CONSTITUTION
MALGACHE." AFR WOR+45 ECO/UNDEV LEGIT EXEC ALL/VALS
...JURID 20. PAGE 76 B1542
    S62
NAT/G
STRUCT
SOVEREIGN
MADAGASCAR

TANNENBAUM A.S.,"CONTROL IN ORGANIZATIONS:
INDIVIDUAL ADJUSTMENT AND ORGANIZATIONAL
    S62
ADMIN
MGT

PERFORMANCE." DOMIN PARTIC REPRESENT INGP/REL
PRODUC ATTIT DRIVE PWR...PSY CORREL. PAGE 102 B2073
STRUCT
CONTROL

BLAU P.M.,"FORMAL ORGANIZATIONS." WOR+45 SOCIETY
STRUCT ECO/DEV GP/REL ATTIT...METH/CNCPT BIBLIOG
20. PAGE 12 B0253
    C62
ADMIN
SOC
GEN/METH
INGP/REL

VAN DER SPRENKEL S.,"LEGAL INSTITUTIONS IN MANCHU
CHINA." ASIA STRUCT CT/SYS ROUTINE GOV/REL GP/REL
...CONCPT BIBLIOG 17/20. PAGE 111 B2250
    C62
LAW
JURID
ADMIN
ADJUD

ACKOFF R.L.,A MANAGER'S GUIDE TO OPERATIONS
RESEARCH. STRUCT INDUS PROB/SOLV ROUTINE 20. PAGE 3
B0056
    B63
OP/RES
MGT
GP/REL
ADMIN

BROGAN D.W.,POLITICAL PATTERNS IN TODAY'S WORLD.
FRANCE USA+45 USSR WOR+45 CONSTN STRUCT PLAN DIPLOM
ADMIN LEAD ROLE SUPEGO...PHIL/SCI 20. PAGE 15 B0313
    B63
NAT/COMP
NEW/LIB
COM
TOTALISM

MOORE W.E.,MAN, TIME, AND SOCIETY. UNIV STRUCT FAM
MUNIC VOL/ASSN ADMIN...SOC NEW/IDEA TIME/SEQ TREND
TIME 20. PAGE 75 B1515
    B63
CONCPT
SOCIETY
CONTROL

SPRING D.,THE ENGLISH LANDED ESTATE IN THE
NINETEENTH CENTURY: ITS ADMINISTRATION. UK ELITES
STRUCT AGRI NAT/G GP/REL OWN PWR WEALTH...BIBLIOG
19 HOUSE/LORD. PAGE 99 B2012
    B63
STRATA
PERS/REL
MGT

TUCKER R.C.,THE SOVIET POLITICAL MIND. COM INTELL
NAT/G TOP/EX EDU/PROP ADMIN COERCE TOTALISM ATTIT
PWR MARXISM...PSY MYTH HYPO/EXP 20. PAGE 106 B2135
    B63
STRUCT
RIGID/FLEX
ELITES
USSR

BEGUIN H.,"ASPECTS GEOGRAPHIQUE DE LA
POLARISATION." FUT WOR+45 SOCIETY STRUCT ECO/DEV
R+D BAL/PWR ADMIN ATTIT RIGID/FLEX HEALTH WEALTH
...CHARTS 20. PAGE 10 B0206
    L63
ECO/UNDEV
GEOG
DIPLOM

BENNIS W.G.,"A NEW ROLE FOR THE BEHAVIORAL
SCIENCES: EFFECTING ORGANIZATIONAL CHANGE." ACT/RES
...MGT GP/COMP PERS/COMP SOC/EXP ORG/CHARTS.
PAGE 11 B0216
    L63
METH/CNCPT
CREATE
STRUCT
SOC

ETIENNE G.,"'LOIS OBJECTIVES' ET PROBLEMES DE
DEVELOPPEMENT DANS LE CONTEXTE CHINE-URSS." ASIA
CHINA/COM FUT STRUCT INT/ORG VOL/ASSN TOP/EX
TEC/DEV ECO/TAC ATTIT RIGID/FLEX...GEOG MGT
TIME/SEQ TOT/POP 20. PAGE 34 B0682
    S63
TOTALISM
USSR

HILLS R.J.,"THE REPRESENTATIVE FUNCTION: NEGLECTED
DIMENSION OF LEADERSHIP BEHAVIOR" USA+45 CLIENT
STRUCT SCHOOL PERS/REL...STAT QU SAMP LAB/EXP 20.
PAGE 50 B1012
    S63
LEAD
ADMIN
EXEC
ACT/RES

APTER D.E.,IDEOLOGY AND DISCONTENT. FUT WOR+45
CONSTN CULTURE INTELL SOCIETY STRUCT INT/ORG NAT/G
DELIB/GP LEGIS CREATE PLAN TEC/DEV EDU/PROP EXEC
PERCEPT PERSON RIGID/FLEX ALL/VALS...POLICY
TOT/POP. PAGE 6 B0122
    B64
ACT/RES
ATTIT

BANTON M.,THE POLICEMAN IN THE COMMUNITY. UK USA+45
STRUCT PROF/ORG WORKER LOBBY ROUTINE COERCE CROWD
GP/REL ADJUST DISCRIM PERCEPT 20. PAGE 9 B0181
    B64
FORCES
ADMIN
ROLE
RACE/REL

CAPLOW T.,PRINCIPLES OF ORGANIZATION. UNIV CULTURE
STRUCT CREATE INGP/REL UTOPIA...GEN/LAWS TIME.
PAGE 18 B0374
    B64
VOL/ASSN
CONCPT
SIMUL
EX/STRUC

ETZIONI A.,MODERN ORGANIZATIONS. CLIENT STRUCT
DOMIN CONTROL LEAD PERS/REL AUTHORIT...CLASSIF
BUREAUCRCY. PAGE 34 B0685
    B64
MGT
ADMIN
PLAN
CULTURE

EWING D.W.,THE MANAGERIAL MIND. SOCIETY STRUCT
INDUS PERSON KNOWL 20. PAGE 34 B0692
    B64
MGT
ATTIT
CREATE
EFFICIENCY

HICKEY G.C.,VILLAGE IN VIETNAM. USA+45 VIETNAM LAW
AGRI FAM SECT ADMIN ATTIT...SOC CHARTS WORSHIP 20.
PAGE 49 B1003
    B64
CULTURE
SOCIETY
STRUCT
S/ASIA

IBERO-AMERICAN INSTITUTES,IBEROAMERICANA. STRUCT
ADMIN SOC. PAGE 53 B1073
    B64
BIBLIOG
L/A+17C
NAT/G
DIPLOM

JACKSON W.V.,LIBRARY GUIDE FOR BRAZILIAN STUDIES.
BRAZIL USA+45 STRUCT DIPLOM ADMIN...SOC 20. PAGE 55
    B64
BIBLIOG
L/A+17C

B1110   NAT/G
                                         LOC/G
                                              B64
KAPP E.,THE MERGER OF THE EXECUTIVES OF THE   CENTRAL
EUROPEAN COMMUNITIES. LAW CONSTN STRUCT ACT/RES   EX/STRUC
PLAN PROB/SOLV ADMIN REGION TASK...INT/LAW MGT ECSC
EEC. PAGE 58 B1170
                                              B64
OECD SEMINAR REGIONAL DEV,REGIONAL DEVELOPMENT IN ADMIN
ISRAEL. ISRAEL STRUCT ECO/UNDEV NAT/G REGION...GEOG PROVS
20. PAGE 79 B1603   PLAN
                                                  METH/COMP
                                              B64
PIPES R.,THE FORMATION OF THE SOVIET UNION. EUR+WWI COM
MOD/EUR STRUCT ECO/UNDEV NAT/G LEGIS DOMIN LEGIT USSR
CT/SYS EXEC COERCE ALL/VALS...POLICY RELATIV   RUSSIA
HIST/WRIT TIME/SEQ TOT/POP 19/20. PAGE 83 B1677
                                              B64
RIGGS F.W.,ADMINISTRATION IN DEVELOPING COUNTRIES. ECO/UNDEV
FUT WOR+45 STRUCT AGRI INDUS NAT/G PLAN TEC/DEV   ADMIN
ECO/TAC EDU/PROP RIGID/FLEX KNOWL WEALTH...POLICY
MGT CONCPT METH/CNCPT TREND 20. PAGE 88 B1785
                                              B64
WHEELER-BENNETT J.W.,THE NEMESIS OF POWER (2ND   FORCES
ED.). EUR+WWI GERMANY TOP/EX TEC/DEV ADMIN WAR   NAT/G
PERS/REL RIGID/FLEX ROLE ORD/FREE PWR FASCISM 20 GP/REL
HITLER/A. PAGE 116 B2332   STRUCT
                                              B64
WILDAVSKY A.,LEADERSHIP IN A SMALL TOWN. USA+45 LEAD
STRUCT PROB/SOLV EXEC PARTIC RACE/REL PWR PLURISM MUNIC
...SOC 20 NEGRO WATER CIV/RIGHTS OBERLIN CITY/MGT. ELITES
PAGE 116 B2348
                                              B64
WILSON L.,THE ACADEMIC MAN. STRUCT FINAN PROF/ORG ACADEM
OP/RES ADMIN AUTHORIT ROLE RESPECT...SOC STAT.   INGP/REL
PAGE 117 B2360   STRATA
                                                 DELIB/GP
                                              S64
EAKIN T.C.,"LEGISLATIVE POLITICS -- I AND II THE PROVS
WESTERN STATES, 19581964" (SUPPLEMENT)" USA+45   LEGIS
POL/PAR SCHOOL CONTROL LOBBY CHOOSE AGE. PAGE 32 ROUTINE
B0641   STRUCT
                                              S64
MOWER A.G.,"THE OFFICIAL PRESSURE GROUP OF THE   INT/ORG
COUNCIL OF EUROPE'S CONSULATIVE ASSEMBLY." EUR+WWI EDU/PROP
SOCIETY STRUCT FINAN CONSULT ECO/TAC ADMIN ROUTINE
ATTIT PWR WEALTH...STAT CHARTS 20 COUNCL/EUR.
PAGE 76 B1535
                                              S64
NEEDHAM T.,"SCIENCE AND SOCIETY IN EAST AND WEST." ASIA
INTELL STRATA R+D LOC/G NAT/G PROVS CONSULT ACT/RES STRUCT
CREATE PLAN TEC/DEV EDU/PROP ADMIN ATTIT ALL/VALS
...POLICY RELATIV MGT CONCPT NEW/IDEA TIME/SEQ WORK
WORK. PAGE 77 B1565
                                              C64
SCOTT R.E.,"MEXICAN GOVERNMENT IN TRANSITION (REV NAT/G
ED)" CULTURE STRUCT POL/PAR CHIEF ADMIN LOBBY REV L/A+17C
CHOOSE GP/REL DRIVE...BIBLIOG METH 20 MEXIC/AMER. ROUTINE
PAGE 95 B1920   CONSTN
                                              B65
BANFIELD E.C.,BIG CITY POLITICS. USA+45 CONSTN   METH/COMP
POL/PAR ADMIN LOBBY CHOOSE SUFF INGP/REL PWR...GEOG MUNIC
20. PAGE 9 B0179   STRUCT
                                              B65
BERNDT R.M.,ABORIGINAL MAN IN AUSTRALIA. LAW DOMIN SOC
ADMIN COLONIAL MARRIAGE HABITAT ORD/FREE...LING CULTURE
CHARTS ANTHOL BIBLIOG WORSHIP 20 AUSTRAL ABORIGINES SOCIETY
MUSIC ELKIN/AP. PAGE 11 B0225   STRUCT
                                              B65
ECCLES H.E.,MILITARY CONCEPTS AND PHILOSOPHY.   PLAN
USA+45 STRUCT EXEC ROUTINE COERCE WAR CIVMIL/REL DRIVE
COST...OBS GEN/LAWS COLD/WAR. PAGE 32 B0648   LEAD
                                                 FORCES
                                              B65
MATRAS J.,SOCIAL CHANGE IN ISRAEL. ISRAEL STRATA SECT
FAM ACT/RES EDU/PROP ADMIN CHOOSE...STAT CENSUS NAT/LISM
19/20 JEWS. PAGE 71 B1427   GEOG
                                                 STRUCT
                                              B65
MEISEL J.H.,PARETO & MOSCA. ITALY STRUCT ADMIN   PWR
...SOC CON/ANAL ANTHOL BIBLIOG 19/20. PAGE 72 B1463 ELITES
                                                 CONTROL
                                                 LAISSEZ
                                              B65
MOORE W.E.,THE IMPACT OF INDUSTRY. CULTURE STRUCT INDUS
ORD/FREE...TREND 20. PAGE 75 B1516   MGT
                                                 TEC/DEV
                                                 ECO/UNDEV
                                              B65
SNYDER F.G.,ONE-PARTY GOVERNMENT IN MALI: ECO/UNDEV
TRANSITION TOWARD CONTROL. MALI STRATA STRUCT SOC. POL/PAR
PAGE 99 B1991   EX/STRUC
                                                 ADMIN
                                              S65
"FURTHER READING." INDIA STRUCT FINAN WORKER ADMIN BIBLIOG
COST 20. PAGE 2 B0042   MGT

                                                 ECO/UNDEV
                                                 EFFICIENCY
                                              S65
HAMILTON R.F.,"SKILL LEVEL AND POLITICS." USA+45 SKILL
CULTURE STRATA STRUCT LABOR CONSERVE NEW/LIB.   ADMIN
PAGE 46 B0933
                                              S65
HAMMOND P.Y.,"FOREIGN POLICY-MAKING AND   DIPLOM
ADMINISTRATIVE POLITICS." CREATE ADMIN COST   STRUCT
...DECISION CONCPT GAME CONGRESS PRESIDENT. PAGE 46 IDEA/COMP
B0935   OP/RES
                                              B66
CLEGG R.K.,THE ADMINISTRATOR IN PUBLIC WELFARE. ADMIN
USA+45 STRUCT NAT/G PROVS PROB/SOLV BUDGET ECO/TAC GIVE
GP/REL ROLE...SOC/WK 20 PUBLIC/REL. PAGE 21 B0434 GOV/REL
                                                 OP/RES
                                              B66
HAWLEY C.E.,ADMINISTRATIVE QUESTIONS AND POLITICAL ADMIN
ANSWERS. USA+45 STRUCT WORKER EDU/PROP...GP/COMP GEN/LAWS
ANTHOL 20. PAGE 48 B0973   GP/REL
                                              B66
MCKENZIE J.L.,AUTHORITY IN THE CHURCH. STRUCT LEAD SECT
INGP/REL PERS/REL CENTRAL ANOMIE ATTIT ORD/FREE AUTHORIT
RESPECT CATH. PAGE 72 B1452   PWR
                                                 ADMIN
                                              B66
SCHURMANN F.,IDEOLOGY AND ORGANIZATION IN COMMUNIST MARXISM
CHINA. CHINA/COM LOC/G MUNIC POL/PAR ECO/TAC   STRUCT
CONTROL ATTIT...MGT STERTYP 20 COM/PARTY. PAGE 94 ADMIN
B1909   NAT/G
                                              L66
LEMARCHAND R.,"SOCIAL CHANGE AND POLITICAL   NAT/G
MODERNISATION IN BURUNDI." AFR BURUNDI STRATA CHIEF STRUCT
EX/STRUC RIGID/FLEX PWR...SOC 20. PAGE 64 B1285 ELITES
                                                 CONSERVE
                                              S66
JACOBS P.,"RE-RADICALIZING THE DE-RADICALIZED." NAT/G
USA+45 SOCIETY STRUCT FINAN PLAN PROB/SOLV CAP/ISM POLICY
WEALTH CONSERVE NEW/LIB 20. PAGE 55 B1114   MARXIST
                                                 ADMIN
                                              S66
MATTHEWS D.G.,"ETHIOPIAN OUTLINE: A BIBLIOGRAPHIC BIBLIOG
RESEARCH GUIDE." ETHIOPIA LAW STRUCT ECO/UNDEV AGRI NAT/G
LABOR SECT CHIEF DELIB/GP EX/STRUC ADMIN...LING DIPLOM
ORG/CHARTS 20. PAGE 71 B1429   POL/PAR
                                              B67
BENNETT J.W.,HUTTERIAN BRETHREN; THE AGRICULTURAL SECT
ECONOMY AND SOCIAL ORGANIZATION OF A COMMUNAL   AGRI
PEOPLE. USA+45 SOCIETY FAM KIN TEC/DEV ADJUST...MGT STRUCT
AUD/VIS GP/COMP 20. PAGE 10 B0213   GP/REL
                                              B67
COHEN R.,COMPARATIVE POLITICAL SYSTEMS: STUDIES IN ECO/UNDEV
THE POLITICS OF PRE-INDUSTRIAL SOCIETIES. WOR+45 STRUCT
WOR-45 CULTURE FAM KIN LOC/G NEIGH ADMIN LEAD   SOCIETY
MARRIAGE...BIBLIOG 20. PAGE 22 B0447   GP/COMP
                                              B67
CROTTY W.J.,APPROACHES TO THE STUDY OF PARTY   POL/PAR
ORGANIZATION. USA+45 SOCIETY GP/REL...ANTHOL 20. STRUCT
PAGE 25 B0509   GEN/LAWS
                                                 ADMIN
                                              B67
DE BLIJ H.J.,SYSTEMATIC POLITICAL GEOGRAPHY. WOR+45 GEOG
STRUCT INT/ORG NAT/G EDU/PROP ADMIN COLONIAL   CONCPT
ROUTINE ORD/FREE PWR...IDEA/COMP T 20. PAGE 27   METH
B0550
                                              B67
KAPLAN H.,URBAN POLITICAL SYSTEMS: A FUNCTIONAL GEN/LAWS
ANALYSIS OF METRO TORONTO. CANADA STRUCT NEIGH PLAN MUNIC
ADMIN...POLICY METH 20 TORONTO. PAGE 58 B1166   LOC/G
                                                 FEDERAL
                                              B67
MARRIS P.,DILEMMAS OF SOCIAL REFORM: POVERTY AND STRUCT
COMMUNITY ACTION IN THE UNITED STATES. USA+45 NAT/G MUNIC
OP/RES ADMIN PARTIC EFFICIENCY WEALTH...SOC   PROB/SOLV
METH/COMP T 20 REFORMERS. PAGE 69 B1401   COST
                                              B67
NARVER J.C.,CONGLOMERATE MERGERS AND MARKET   DEMAND
COMPETITION. USA+45 LAW STRUCT ADMIN LEAD RISK COST LG/CO
PROFIT WEALTH...POLICY CHARTS BIBLIOG. PAGE 77   MARKET
B1555   MGT
                                              B67
PYE L.W.,SOUTHEAST ASIA'S POLITICAL SYSTEMS. ASIA NAT/G
S/ASIA STRUCT ECO/UNDEV EX/STRUC CAP/ISM DIPLOM POL/PAR
ALL/IDEOS...TREND CHARTS. PAGE 85 B1724   GOV/COMP
                                              B67
RAVKIN A.,THE NEW STATES OF AFRICA (HEADLINE   AFR
SERIES, NO. 183((PAMPHLET). CULTURE STRUCT INDUS ECO/UNDEV
COLONIAL NAT/LISM...SOC 20. PAGE 86 B1744   SOCIETY
                                                 ADMIN
                                              B67
WESSON R.G.,THE IMPERIAL ORDER. WOR-45 STRUCT SECT PWR
DOMIN ADMIN COLONIAL LEAD CONSERVE...CONCPT BIBLIOG CHIEF
20. PAGE 115 B2324   CONTROL
                                                 SOCIETY
                                              S67
BEASLEY W.G.,"POLITICS AND THE SAMURAI CLASS   ELITES

STRUCTURE IN SATSUMA, 18581868." STRATA FORCES
DOMIN LEGIT ADMIN LEAD 19 CHINJAP. PAGE 10 B0202
STRUCT
ATTIT
PRIVIL
S67

DRYDEN S.,"LOCAL GOVERNMENT IN TANZANIA PART II"
TANZANIA LAW NAT/G POL/PAR CONTROL PARTIC REPRESENT
...DECISION 20. PAGE 31 B0622
LOC/G
GOV/REL
ADMIN
STRUCT
S67

GITTELL M.,"PROFESSIONALISM AND PUBLIC
PARTICIPATION IN EDUCATIONAL POLICY MAKING." STRUCT
ADMIN GP/REL ATTIT PWR 20. PAGE 40 B0805
DECISION
PLAN
EDU/PROP
MUNIC
S67

HOFMANN W.,"THE PUBLIC INTEREST PRESSURE GROUP: THE
CASE OF THE DEUTSCHE STADTETAG." GERMANY GERMANY/W
CONSTN STRUCT NAT/G CENTRAL FEDERAL PWR...TIME/SEQ
20. PAGE 51 B1030
LOC/G
VOL/ASSN
LOBBY
ADMIN
S67

HUGON P.,"BLOCAGES ET DESEQUILIBRES DE LA
CROISSANCE ECONOMIQUE EN AFRIQUE NOIRE." AFR KIN
MUNIC CREATE PLAN INT/TRADE REGION ADJUST CENTRAL
EQUILIB NAT/LISM ORD/FREE 20. PAGE 52 B1060
ECO/UNDEV
COLONIAL
STRUCT
ADMIN
S67

JENCKS C.E.,"SOCIAL STATUS OF COAL MINERS IN
BRITAIN SINCE NATIONALIZATION." UK STRATA STRUCT
LABOR RECEIVE GP/REL INCOME OWN ATTIT HABITAT...MGT
T 20. PAGE 56 B1128
EXTR/IND
WORKER
CONTROL
NAT/G
S67

KURON J.,"AN OPEN LETTER TO THE PARTY." CONSTN
WORKER BUDGET EDU/PROP ADMIN REPRESENT SUFF OWN
...SOCIALIST 20. PAGE 62 B1244
ELITES
STRUCT
POL/PAR
ECO/TAC
S67

RAI H.,"DISTRICT MAGISTRATE AND POLICE
SUPERINTENDENT IN INDIA: THE CONTROVERSY OF DUAL
CONTROL" INDIA LAW PROVS ADMIN PWR 19/20. PAGE 86
B1729
STRUCT
CONTROL
ROLE
FORCES
S67

ROWAT D.C.,"RECENT DEVELOPMENTS IN OMBUDSMANSHIP* A
REVIEW ARTICLE." UK USA+45 STRUCT CONSULT INSPECT
TASK EFFICIENCY...NEW/IDEA 20. PAGE 91 B1841
CANADA
ADMIN
LOC/G
NAT/G
S67

WINTHROP H.,"THE MEANING OF DECENTRALIZATION FOR
TWENTIETH-CENTURY MAN." FUT WOR+45 SOCIETY TEC/DEV.
PAGE 117 B2366
ADMIN
STRUCT
CENTRAL
PROB/SOLV
S68

GUZZARDI W. JR.,"THE SECOND BATTLE OF BRITAIN." UK
STRATA LABOR WORKER CREATE PROB/SOLV EDU/PROP ADMIN
LEAD LOBBY...MGT SOC 20 GOLD/STAND. PAGE 45 B0907
FINAN
ECO/TAC
ECO/DEV
STRUCT

STRUCTURAL-FUNCTIONAL THEORY....SEE STRUC/FUNC

STRUVE/P....PETER STRUVE

STUART DYNASTY....SEE STUART/DYN

STUART/DYN....THE STUART DYNASTY

STUDENT NONVIOLENT COORDINATING COMMITTEE....SEE SNCC,
STUDNT/PWR

STUDENTS FOR A DEMOCRATIC SOCIETY....SEE SDS

STUDNT/PWR....STUDENT POWER: STUDENT PROTESTS AND PROTEST
MOVEMENTS
L65

HOOK S.,"SECOND THOUGHTS ON BERKELEY" USA+45 ELITES
INTELL LEGIT ADMIN COERCE REPRESENT GP/REL INGP/REL
TOTALISM AGE/Y MARXISM 20 BERKELEY FREE/SPEE
STUDNT/PWR. PAGE 51 B1040
ACADEM
ORD/FREE
POLICY
CREATE

STUMBERG G.W. B0277

STYLE....STYLES OF SCIENTIFIC COMMUNICATION
B47

SIMON H.A.,ADMINISTRATIVE BEHAVIOR: A STUDY OF
DECISION-MAKING PROCESSES IN ADMINISTRATIVE
ORGANIZATION. STRUCT COM/IND OP/RES PROB/SOLV
EFFICIENCY EQUILIB UTIL...PHIL/SCI PSY STYLE.
PAGE 97 B1956
DECISION
NEW/IDEA
ADMIN
RATIONAL
S64

FLORINSKY M.T.,"TRENDS IN THE SOVIET ECONOMY." COM
USA+45 USSR INDUS LABOR NAT/G PLAN TEC/DEV ECO/TAC
ALL/VALS SOCISM...MGT METH/CNCPT STYLE CON/ANAL
GEN/METH WORK 20. PAGE 36 B0731
ECO/DEV
AGRI
S64

JOHNSON K.F.,"CAUSAL FACTORS IN LATIN AMERICAN
POLITICAL INSTABILITY." CULTURE NAT/G VOL/ASSN
EX/STRUC FORCES EDU/PROP LEGIT ADMIN COERCE REV
ATTIT KNOWL PWR...STYLE RECORD CHARTS WORK 20.
L/A+17C
PERCEPT
ELITES

PAGE 57 B1144
B65

HICKMAN B.G.,QUANTITATIVE PLANNING OF ECONOMIC
POLICY. FRANCE NETHERLAND OP/RES PRICE ROUTINE UTIL
...POLICY DECISION ECOMETRIC METH/CNCPT STAT STYLE
CHINJAP. PAGE 50 B1004
PROB/SOLV
PLAN
QUANT
B66

BALDWIN D.A.,FOREIGN AID AND AMERICAN FOREIGN
POLICY: A DOCUMENTARY ANALYSIS. USA+45 ECO/UNDEV
ADMIN...ECOMETRIC STAT STYLE CHARTS PROG/TEAC
GEN/LAWS ANTHOL. PAGE 8 B0172
FOR/AID
DIPLOM
IDEA/COMP

SUAREZ/F....FRANCISCO SUAREZ

SUBMARINE....SUBMARINES AND SUBMARINE WARFARE

SUBRAMANIAM V. B2053

SUBSIDIES....SEE FINAN

SUBURBS....SUBURBS

SUBVERT....SUBVERSION

SUCCESSION....SUCCESSION (POLITICAL)
B65

STANLEY D.T.,CHANGING ADMINISTRATIONS. USA+45
POL/PAR DELIB/GP TOP/EX BUDGET GOV/REL GP/REL
PERS/REL PWR...MAJORIT DECISION MGT 20 PRESIDENT
SUCCESSION DEPT/STATE DEPT/DEFEN DEPT/HEW. PAGE 100
B2021
NAT/G
CHIEF
ADMIN
EX/STRUC

SUDAN....SEE ALSO AFR

SUDETENLND....SUDETENLAND

SUEZ CRISIS....SEE NAT/LISM+COERCE, ALSO INDIVIDUAL
NATIONS, SUEZ

SUEZ....SUEZ CANAL

SUFF....SUFFRAGE; SEE ALSO CHOOSE
N19

OPERATIONS AND POLICY RESEARCH,PERU ELECTION
MEMORANDA (PAMPHLET). L/A+17C PERU POL/PAR LEGIS
EXEC APPORT REPRESENT 20. PAGE 80 B1611
CHOOSE
CONSTN
SUFF
NAT/G
L23

DOUGLAS P.H.,"OCCUPATIONAL V PROPORTIONAL
REPRESENTATION." INDUS NAT/G PLAN ROUTINE SUFF
CONSEN DRIVE...CONCPT CLASSIF. PAGE 30 B0612
REPRESENT
PROF/ORG
DOMIN
INGP/REL
B57

BABCOCK R.S.,STATE & LOCAL GOVERNMENT AND POLITICS.
USA+45 CONSTN POL/PAR EX/STRUC LEGIS BUDGET LOBBY
CHOOSE SUFF...CHARTS BIBLIOG T 20. PAGE 8 B0154
PROVS
LOC/G
GOV/REL
B62

LOWI T.J.,LEGISLATIVE POLITICS U.S.A. LAW LEGIS
DIPLOM EXEC LOBBY CHOOSE SUFF FEDERAL PWR 19/20
CONGRESS. PAGE 67 B1345
PARL/PROC
REPRESENT
POLICY
ROUTINE
C63

CARLISLE D.,"PARTY LOYALTY; THE ELECTION PROCESS IN
SOUTH CAROLINA." USA+45 LOC/G ADMIN ATTIT...TREND
CHARTS BIBLIOG 17/20. PAGE 19 B0380
CHOOSE
POL/PAR
PROVS
SUFF
B64

NUQUIST A.E.,TOWN GOVERNMENT IN VERMONT. USA+45
FINAN TOP/EX PROB/SOLV BUDGET TAX REPRESENT SUFF
EFFICIENCY...OBS INT 20 VERMONT. PAGE 79 B1595
LOC/G
MUNIC
POPULISM
ADMIN
B65

BANFIELD E.C.,BIG CITY POLITICS. USA+45 CONSTN
POL/PAR ADMIN LOBBY CHOOSE SUFF INGP/REL PWR...GEOG
20. PAGE 9 B0179
METH/COMP
MUNIC
STRUCT
B65

OLSON M. JR.,DROIT PUBLIC. FRANCE NAT/G LEGIS SUFF
GP/REL PRIVIL...TREND 18/20. PAGE 80 B1609
CONSTN
FINAN
ADMIN
ORD/FREE
B65

PARRISH W.E.,MISSOURI UNDER RADICAL RULE 1865-1870.
USA-45 SOCIETY INDUS LOC/G POL/PAR WORKER EDU/PROP
SUFF INGP/REL ATTIT...BIBLIOG 19 NEGRO MISSOURI.
PAGE 81 B1635
PROVS
ADMIN
RACE/REL
ORD/FREE
B65

SNIDER C.F.,AMERICAN STATE AND LOCAL GOVERNMENT.
USA+45 FINAN CHIEF EX/STRUC TAX ADMIN CONTROL SUFF
INGP/REL PWR 20. PAGE 98 B1989
GOV/REL
MUNIC
PROVS
LOC/G
S67

KURON J.,"AN OPEN LETTER TO THE PARTY." CONSTN
WORKER BUDGET EDU/PROP ADMIN REPRESENT SUFF OWN
...SOCIALIST 20. PAGE 62 B1244
ELITES
STRUCT
POL/PAR

ECO/TAC

SUFFRAGE....SEE SUFF

SUICIDE....SUICIDE AND RELATED SELF-DESTRUCTIVENESS

SUKARNO/A....ACHMED SUKARNO

SULLIVAN G. B2054

SUMATRA....SUMATRA

SUMER....SUMER, A PRE- OR EARLY HISTORIC SOCIETY

SUN/YAT....SUN YAT SEN

SUPEGO....CONSCIENCE, SUPEREGO, RESPONSIBILITY

B27
ANGELL N.,THE PUBLIC MIND. USA-45 SOCIETY EDU/PROP PERCEPT
ROUTINE SUPEGO KNOWL...POLICY CONCPT MYTH OBS/ENVIR ATTIT
EUR+WW1 TOT/POP 20. PAGE 5 B0109   DIPLOM
                                                     NAT/LISM
B29
BUELL R.,INTERNATIONAL RELATIONS. WOR+45 WOR-45   INT/ORG
CONSTN STRATA FORCES TOP/EX ADMIN ATTIT DRIVE   BAL/PWR
SUPEGO MORAL ORD/FREE PWR SOVEREIGN...JURID SOC   DIPLOM
CONCPT 20. PAGE 17 B0340

B30
MURCHISON C.,PSYCHOLOGIES OF 1930. UNIV USA-45   CREATE
CULTURE INTELL SOCIETY STRATA FAM ROUTINE BIO/SOC   PERSON
DRIVE RIGID/FLEX SUPEGO...NEW/IDEA OBS SELF/OBS
CONT/OBS 20. PAGE 76 B1543

B50
MANNHEIM K.,FREEDOM, POWER, AND DEMOCRATIC   TEC/DEV
PLANNING. FUT USSR WOR+45 ELITES INTELL SOCIETY   PLAN
NAT/G EDU/PROP ROUTINE ATTIT DRIVE SUPEGO SKILL   CAP/ISM
...POLICY PSY CONCPT TREND GEN/LAWS 20. PAGE 69   UK
B1393

S51
COHEN M.B.,"PERSONALITY AS A FACTOR IN   PERSON
ADMINISTRATIVE DECISIONS." ADJUD PERS/REL ANOMIE   ADMIN
SUPEGO...OBS SELF/OBS INT. PAGE 22 B0446   PROB/SOLV
                                                    PSY
S51
MARX F.M.,"SIGNIFICANCE FOR THE ADMINISTRATIVE   LEGIS
PROCESS." POL/PAR LEAD PARL/PROC GOV/REL EFFICIENCY ADMIN
SUPEGO...POLICY CONGRESS. PAGE 70 B1420   CHIEF

B52
DONHAM W.B.,ADMINISTRATION AND BLIND SPOTS. LG/CO   ADMIN
EX/STRUC BARGAIN ADJUD ROUTINE ROLE SUPEGO 20.   TOP/EX
PAGE 30 B0605   DECISION
                                                    POLICY
B52
HIMMELFARB G.,LORD ACTON: A STUDY IN CONSCIENCE AND PWR
POLITICS. MOD/EUR NAT/G POL/PAR LEGIS TOP/EX   BIOG
EDU/PROP ADMIN NAT/LISM ATTIT PERSON SUPEGO MORAL
ORD/FREE...CONCPT PARLIAMENT 19 ACTON/LORD. PAGE 50
B1014

B52
MAIER N.R.F.,PRINCIPLES OF HUMAN RELATIONS. WOR+45 INDUS
WOR-45 CULTURE SOCIETY ROUTINE ATTIT DRIVE PERCEPT
PERSON RIGID/FLEX SUPEGO PWR...PSY CONT/OBS RECORD
TOT/POP VAL/FREE 20. PAGE 68 B1379

B55
MAZZINI J.,THE DUTIES OF MAN. MOD/EUR LAW SOCIETY   SUPEGO
FAM NAT/G POL/PAR SECT VOL/ASSN EX/STRUC ACT/RES   CONCPT
CREATE REV PEACE ATTIT ALL/VALS...GEN/LAWS WORK 19. NAT/LISM
PAGE 71 B1439

B56
WEBER M.,STAATSSOZIOLOGIE. STRUCT LEGIT ADMIN   SOC
PARL/PROC SUPEGO CONSERVE JURID. PAGE 114 B2305   NAT/G
                                                    POL/PAR
                                                    LEAD
B57
HINDERLING A.,DIE REFORMATORISCHE   ADMIN
VERWALTUNGSGERICHTSBARKEIT. GERMANY/W PROB/SOLV   CT/SYS
ADJUD SUPEGO PWR...CONCPT 20. PAGE 50 B1015   JURID
                                                    CONTROL
S57
HARRIS J.P.,"LEGISLATIVE CONTROL OF ADMINISTRATION: LEGIS
SOME COMPARISONS OF AMERICAN AND EUROPEAN   CONTROL
PRACTICES." DEBATE PARL/PROC ROUTINE GOV/REL   EX/STRUC
EFFICIENCY SUPEGO DECISION. PAGE 47 B0954   REPRESENT

S57
HUITT R.K.,"THE MORSE COMMITTEE ASSIGNMENT   LEGIS
CONTROVERSY: A STUDY IN SENATE NORMS." USA+45   ETIQUET
USA-45 POL/PAR SENIOR ROLE SUPEGO SENATE. PAGE 52   PWR
B1061   ROUTINE

S58
MITCHELL W.C.,"OCCUPATIONAL ROLE STRAINS: THE   ANOMIE
AMERICAN ELECTIVE PUBLIC OFFICIAL." CONTROL   DRIVE
RIGID/FLEX SUPEGO HEALTH ORD/FREE...SOC INT QU.   ROUTINE
PAGE 74 B1492   PERSON

B59
GREENEWALT C.H.,THE UNCOMMON MAN. UNIV ECO/DEV   TASK

ADMIN PERS/REL PERSON SUPEGO WEALTH 20. PAGE 43   ORD/FREE
B0868   DRIVE
                                                    EFFICIENCY
B59
JOYCE J.A.,RED CROSS INTERNATIONAL AND THE STRATEGY VOL/ASSN
OF PEACE. WOR+45 WOR-45 EX/STRUC SUPEGO ALL/VALS   HEALTH
...CONCPT GEN/LAWS TOT/POP 19/20 RED/CROSS. PAGE 57
B1155

B59
WEBER W.,DER DEUTSCHE BEAMTE HEUTE. GERMANY/W NAT/G MGT
DELIB/GP LEGIS CONFER ATTIT SUPEGO...JURID 20   EFFICIENCY
CIVIL/SERV. PAGE 114 B2306   ELITES
                                                    GP/REL
B60
CORSON J.J.,GOVERNANCE OF COLLEGES AND   ADMIN
UNIVERSITIES. STRUCT FINAN DELIB/GP DOMIN EDU/PROP EXEC
LEAD CHOOSE GP/REL CENTRAL COST PRIVIL SUPEGO   ACADEM
ORD/FREE PWR...DECISION BIBLIOG. PAGE 24 B0481   HABITAT

B60
ROEPKE W.,A HUMANE ECONOMY: THE SOCIAL FRAMEWORK OF DRIVE
THE FREE MARKET. FUT USSR WOR+45 CULTURE SOCIETY   EDU/PROP
ECO/DEV PLAN ECO/TAC ADMIN ATTIT PERSON RIGID/FLEX CAP/ISM
SUPEGO MORAL WEALTH SOCISM...POLICY OLD/LIB CONCPT
TREND GEN/LAWS 20. PAGE 90 B1811

B60
WHEARE K.C.,THE CONSTITUTIONAL STRUCTURE OF THE   CONSTN
COMMONWEALTH. UK EX/STRUC DIPLOM DOMIN ADMIN   INT/ORG
COLONIAL CONTROL LEAD INGP/REL SUPEGO 20 CMN/WLTH. VOL/ASSN
PAGE 115 B2330   SOVEREIGN

S60
THOMPSON K.W.,"MORAL PURPOSE IN FOREIGN POLICY: MORAL
REALITIES AND ILLUSIONS." WOR+45 WOR-45 LAW CULTURE JURID
SOCIETY INT/ORG PLAN ADJUD ADMIN COERCE RIGID/FLEX DIPLOM
SUPEGO KNOWL ORD/FREE PWR...SOC TREND SOC/EXP
TOT/POP 20. PAGE 104 B2104

C60
SCHRAMM W.,"MASS COMMUNICATIONS: A BOOK OF READINGS COM/IND
(2ND ED.)" LG/CO PRESS ADMIN CONTROL ROUTINE ATTIT EDU/PROP
ROLE SUPEGO...CHARTS ANTHOL BIBLIOG 20. PAGE 94   CROWD
B1902   MAJORIT

B61
BEASLEY K.E.,STATE SUPERVISION OF MUNICIPAL DEBT IN MUNIC
KANSAS - A CASE STUDY. USA+45 USA-45 FINAN PROVS   LOC/G
BUDGET TAX ADJUD ADMIN CONTROL SUPEGO. PAGE 10   LEGIS
B0201   JURID

B61
BIRNBACH B.,NEO-FREUDIAN SOCIAL PHILOSOPHY. TEC/DEV SOCIETY
INGP/REL ADJUST HAPPINESS SUPEGO HEALTH...CONCPT   PSY
GEN/LAWS BIBLIOG 20. PAGE 12 B0242   PERSON
                                                    ADMIN
B61
CATHERINE R.,LE FONCTIONNAIRE FRANCAIS. FRANCE   ADMIN
NAT/G INGP/REL ATTIT MORAL ORD/FREE...T CIVIL/SERV. GP/REL
PAGE 19 B0394   LEAD
                                                    SUPEGO
B61
KOESTLER A.,THE LOTUS AND THE ROBOT. ASIA INDIA   SECT
S/ASIA SOCIETY STRATA ECO/DEV AGRI INDUS FAM CREATE ECO/UNDEV
DOMIN EDU/PROP ADMIN COERCE ATTIT DRIVE SUPEGO
ORD/FREE PWR RESPECT WEALTH...MYTH OBS 20 CHINJAP.
PAGE 61 B1226

B62
ESCUELA SUPERIOR DE ADMIN PUBL,INFORME DEL   ADMIN
SEMINARIO SOBRE SERVICIO CIVIL O CARRERA   NAT/G
ADMINISTRATIVA. L/A+17C ELITES STRATA CONFER   PROB/SOLV
CONTROL GOV/REL INGP/REL SUPEGO 20 CENTRAL/AM   ATTIT
CIVIL/SERV. PAGE 33 B0681

S62
BERNTHAL W.F.,"VALUE PERSPECTIVES IN MANAGEMENT   MGT
DECISIONS." LG/CO OP/RES SUPEGO MORAL. PAGE 11   PROB/SOLV
B0229   DECISION

B63
BROGAN D.W.,POLITICAL PATTERNS IN TODAY'S WORLD.   NAT/COMP
FRANCE USA+45 USSR WOR+45 CONSTN STRUCT PLAN DIPLOM NEW/LIB
ADMIN LEAD ROLE SUPEGO...PHIL/SCI 20. PAGE 15 B0313 COM
                                                    TOTALISM
B63
DE VRIES E.,SOCIAL ASPECTS OF ECONOMIC DEVELOPMENT L/A+17C
IN LATIN AMERICA. CULTURE SOCIETY STRATA FINAN   ECO/UNDEV
INDUS INT/ORG DELIB/GP ACT/RES ECO/TAC EDU/PROP
ADMIN ATTIT SUPEGO HEALTH KNOWL ORD/FREE...SOC STAT
TREND ANTHOL TOT/POP VAL/FREE. PAGE 28 B0562

B63
HEUSSLER R.,YESTERDAY'S RULERS: THE MAKING OF THE   EX/STRUC
BRITISH COLONIAL SERVICE. AFR EUR+WWI UK STRATA   MORAL
SECT DELIB/GP PLAN DOMIN EDU/PROP ATTIT PERCEPT   ELITES
PERSON SUPEGO KNOWL ORD/FREE PWR...MGT SOC OBS INT
TIME/SEQ 20 CMN/WLTH. PAGE 49 B1000

B63
LANGROD G.,THE INTERNATIONAL CIVIL SERVICE: ITS   INT/ORG
ORIGINS, ITS NATURE, ITS EVALUATION. FUT WOR+45   ADMIN
WOR-45 DELIB/GP ACT/RES DOMIN LEGIT ATTIT
RIGID/FLEX SUPEGO ALL/VALS...MGT CONCPT STAT
TIME/SEQ ILO LEAGUE/NAT VAL/FREE 20 UN. PAGE 62
B1259

PLANTEY A.,TRAITE PRATIQUE DE LA FONCTION PUBLIQUE   ADMIN
(2ND ED., 2 VOLS.). FRANCE FINAN EX/STRUC PROB/SOLV   SUPEGO
GP/REL ATTIT...SOC 20 CIVIL/SERV. PAGE 83 B1680   JURID
                                                      B63

STEVENSON A.E.,LOOKING OUTWARD: YEARS OF CRISIS AT   INT/ORG
THE UNITED NATIONS. COM CUBA USA+45 WOR+45 SOCIETY   CONCPT
NAT/G EX/STRUC ACT/RES LEGIT COLONIAL ATTIT PERSON   ARMS/CONT
SUPEGO ALL/VALS...POLICY HUM UN COLD/WAR CONGO 20.
PAGE 100 B2034
                                                      B63

SWERDLOW I.,DEVELOPMENT ADMINISTRATION: CONCEPTS   ECO/UNDEV
AND PROBLEMS. WOR+45 CULTURE SOCIETY STRATA   ADMIN
DELIB/GP EX/STRUC ACT/RES PLAN ECO/TAC DOMIN LEGIT
ATTIT RIGID/FLEX SUPEGO HEALTH PWR...MGT CONCPT
ANTHOL VAL/FREE. PAGE 102 B2062
                                                      B63

TUCKER R.C.,THE SOVIET POLITICAL MIND. WOR+45   COM
ELITES INT/ORG NAT/G POL/PAR PLAN DIPLOM ECO/TAC   TOP/EX
DOMIN ADMIN NUC/PWR REV DRIVE PERSON SUPEGO PWR   USSR
WEALTH...POLICY MGT PSY CONCPT OBS BIOG TREND
COLD/WAR MARX/KARL 20. PAGE 106 B2134
                                                      S63

ARASTEH R.,"THE ROLE OF INTELLECTUALS IN   INTELL
ADMINISTRATIVE DEVELOPMENT AND SOCIAL CHANGE IN   ADMIN
MODERN IRAN." ISLAM CULTURE NAT/G CONSULT ACT/RES   IRAN
EDU/PROP EXEC ATTIT BIO/SOC PERCEPT SUPEGO ALL/VALS
...POLICY MGT PSY SOC CONCPT 20. PAGE 6 B0123
                                                      S63

HARRIS R.L.,"A COMPARATIVE ANALYSIS OF THE   DELIB/GP
ADMINISTRATIVE SYSTEMS OF CANADA AND CEYLON."   EX/STRUC
S/ASIA CULTURE SOCIETY STRATA TOP/EX ACT/RES DOMIN   CANADA
EDU/PROP LEGIT COERCE ATTIT SUPEGO ALL/VALS...MGT   CEYLON
CHARTS GEN/LAWS VAL/FREE 20. PAGE 47 B0955
                                                      B64

BOUVIER-AJAM M.,MANUEL TECHNIQUE ET PRATIQUE DU   MUNIC
MAIRE ET DES ELUS ET AGENTS COMMUNAUX. FRANCE LOC/G   ADMIN
BUDGET CHOOSE GP/REL SUPEGO...JURID BIBLIOG 20   CHIEF
MAYOR COMMUNES. PAGE 14 B0284   NEIGH
                                                      B64

COTTER C.P.,POLITICS WITHOUT POWER: THE NATIONAL   CHOOSE
PARTY COMMITTEES. USA+45 FINAN NAT/G LOBBY ROUTINE   POL/PAR
GP/REL ATTIT ROLE SUPEGO PWR 20. PAGE 24 B0491   REPRESENT
                                                      DELIB/GP
                                                      B64

FONTENEAU J.,LE CONSEIL MUNICIPAL: LE MAIRE-LES   MUNIC
ADJOINTS. FRANCE FINAN DELIB/GP EX/STRUC BUDGET TAX   NEIGH
TASK COST INCOME ROLE SUPEGO 20 MAYOR. PAGE 36   ADMIN
B0735   TOP/EX
                                                      B64

RIDDLE D.H.,THE TRUMAN COMMITTEE: A STUDY IN   LEGIS
CONGRESSIONAL RESPONSIBILITY. INDUS FORCES OP/RES   DELIB/GP
DOMIN ADMIN LEAD PARL/PROC WAR PRODUC SUPEGO   CONFER
...BIBLIOG CONGRESS. PAGE 88 B1778
                                                      B65

GOLEMBIEWSKI R.T.,MEN, MANAGEMENT, AND MORALITY;   LG/CO
TOWARD A NEW ORGANIZATIONAL ETHIC. CONSTN EX/STRUC   MGT
CREATE ADMIN CONTROL INGP/REL PERSON SUPEGO MORAL   PROB/SOLV
PWR...GOV/COMP METH/COMP 20 BUREAUCRCY. PAGE 40
B0819
                                                      B66

AARON T.J.,THE CONTROL OF POLICE DISCRETION: THE   CONTROL
DANISH EXPERIENCE. DENMARK LAW CREATE ADMIN   FORCES
INGP/REL SUPEGO PWR 20 OMBUDSMAN. PAGE 2 B0049   REPRESENT
                                                      PROB/SOLV
                                                      C66

SHERMAN H.,"IT ALL DEPENDS." USA+45 FINAN MARKET   LG/CO
PLAN PROB/SOLV EXEC PARTIC INGP/REL SUPEGO   MGT
...DECISION BIBLIOG 20. PAGE 96 B1944   ADMIN
                                                      POLICY
                                                      B67

PAULSEN F.R.,AMERICAN EDUCATION: CHALLENGES AND   EDU/PROP
IMAGES. FUT USA+45 ADMIN AGE/C AGE/Y SUPEGO HEALTH   SCHOOL
...ANTHOL 20. PAGE 81 B1644   ORD/FREE
                                                      GOV/REL
                                                      S67

DODSON D.W.,"NEW FORCES OPERATING IN EDUCATIONAL   PROB/SOLV
DECISION-MAKING." USA+45 NEIGH EDU/PROP ADMIN   SCHOOL
SUPEGO DECISION. PAGE 30 B0602   PERS/REL
                                                      PWR
                                                      S67

DONNELL J.C.,"PACIFICATION REASSESSED." VIETNAM/S   ADMIN
NAT/LISM DRIVE SUPEGO ORD/FREE...SOC/WK 20. PAGE 30   GP/REL
B0606   EFFICIENCY
                                                      MUNIC
                                                      S67

LEES J.P.,"LEGISLATIVE REVIEW AND BUREAUCRATIC   SUPEGO
RESPONSIBILITY." USA+45 FINAN NAT/G DELIB/GP PLAN   BUDGET
PROB/SOLV CONFER CONTROL GP/REL DEMAND...DECISION   LEGIS
20 CONGRESS PRESIDENT HOUSE/REP BUREAUCRCY. PAGE 63   EXEC
B1281
                                                      S67

TIVEY L.,"THE POLITICAL CONSEQUENCES OF ECONOMIC   PLAN
PLANNING." UK CONSTN INDUS ACT/RES ADMIN CONTROL   POLICY
LOBBY REPRESENT EFFICIENCY SUPEGO SOVEREIGN   NAT/G
...DECISION 20. PAGE 104 B2112

SUPERSONIC TRANSPORT....SEE SST

SUPERVISION....SEE EXEC, CONTROL, LEAD, TASK

SUPPES P. B0137

SUPREME/CT....SUPREME COURT (ALL NATIONS)

                                                      B08
WILSON W.,CONSTITUTIONAL GOVERNMENT IN THE UNITED   NAT/G
STATES. USA-45 LAW POL/PAR PROVS CHIEF LEGIS   GOV/REL
BAL/PWR ADJUD EXEC FEDERAL PWR 18/20 SUPREME/CT   CONSTN
HOUSE/REP SENATE. PAGE 117 B2362   PARL/PROC
                                                      B51

DAVIS K.C.,ADMINISTRATIVE LAW. USA+45 USA-45 NAT/G   ADMIN
PROB/SOLV BAL/PWR CONTROL ORD/FREE...POLICY 20   JURID
SUPREME/CT. PAGE 26 B0539   EX/STRUC
                                                      ADJUD
                                                      B52

SWENSON R.J.,FEDERAL ADMINISTRATIVE LAW: A STUDY OF   JURID
THE GROWTH, NATURE, AND CONTROL OF ADMINISTRATIVE   CONSTN
ACTION. USA-45 JUDGE ADMIN GOV/REL EFFICIENCY   LEGIS
PRIVIL ATTIT NEW/LIB SUPREME/CT. PAGE 102 B2061   ADJUD
                                                      B55

BEISEL A.R.,CONTROL OVER ILLEGAL ENFORCEMENT OF THE   ORD/FREE
CRIMINAL LAW: ROLE OF THE SUPREME COURT. CONSTN   LAW
ROUTINE MORAL PWR...SOC 20 SUPREME/CT. PAGE 10   CRIME
B0207
                                                      B55

CUSHMAN R.E.,LEADING CONSTITUTIONAL DECISIONS.   CONSTN
USA+45 USA-45 NAT/G EX/STRUC LEGIS JUDGE TAX   PROB/SOLV
FEDERAL...DECISION 20 SUPREME/CT CASEBOOK. PAGE 25   JURID
B0513   CT/SYS
                                                      B58

DAVIS K.C.,ADMINISTRATIVE LAW TREATISE (VOLS. I AND   ADMIN
IV). NAT/G JUDGE PROB/SOLV ADJUD GP/REL 20   JURID
SUPREME/CT. PAGE 26 B0540   CT/SYS
                                                      EX/STRUC
                                                      B58

DAVIS K.C.,ADMINISTRATIVE LAW; CASES, TEXT,   ADJUD
PROBLEMS. LAW LOC/G NAT/G TOP/EX PAY CONTROL   JURID
GOV/REL INGP/REL FEDERAL 20 SUPREME/CT. PAGE 27   CT/SYS
B0541   ADMIN
                                                      B58

WESTIN A.F.,THE ANATOMY OF A CONSTITUTIONAL LAW   CT/SYS
CASE. USA+45 LAW LEGIS ADMIN EXEC...DECISION MGT   INDUS
SOC RECORD 20 SUPREME/CT. PAGE 115 B2326   ADJUD
                                                      CONSTN
                                                      B59

DAVIS K.C.,ADMINISTRATIVE LAW TEXT. USA+45 NAT/G   ADJUD
DELIB/GP EX/STRUC CONTROL ORD/FREE...T 20   ADMIN
SUPREME/CT. PAGE 27 B0542   JURID
                                                      CT/SYS
                                                      B59

LOEWENSTEIN K.,VERFASSUNGSRECHT UND   CONSTN
VERFASSUNGSPRAXIS DER VEREINIGTEN STAATEN. USA+45   POL/PAR
USA-45 COLONIAL CT/SYS GP/REL RACE/REL ORD/FREE   EX/STRUC
...JURID 18/20 SUPREME/CT CONGRESS PRESIDENT   NAT/G
BILL/RIGHT CIVIL/LIB. PAGE 66 B1337
                                                      B60

JUNZ A.J., PRESENT TRENDS IN AMERICAN NATIONAL   POL/PAR
GOVERNMENT. LEGIS DIPLOM ADMIN CT/SYS ORD/FREE   CHOOSE
...CONCPT ANTHOL 20 CONGRESS PRESIDENT SUPREME/CT.   CONSTN
PAGE 2 B0048   NAT/G
                                                      B60

DAVIS K.C.,ADMINISTRATIVE LAW AND GOVERNMENT.   ADMIN
USA+45 EX/STRUC PROB/SOLV ADJUD GP/REL PWR...POLICY   JURID
20 SUPREME/CT. PAGE 27 B0543   CT/SYS
                                                      NAT/G
                                                      B60

WEBSTER J.A.,A GENERAL STUDY OF THE DEPARTMENT OF   ORD/FREE
DEFENSE INTERNAL SECURITY PROGRAM. USA+45 WORKER   PLAN
TEC/DEV ADJUD CONTROL CT/SYS EXEC GOV/REL COST   ADMIN
...POLICY DECISION MGT 20 DEPT/DEFEN SUPREME/CT.   NAT/G
PAGE 114 B2307
                                                      B61

AUERBACH C.A.,THE LEGAL PROCESS. USA+45 DELIB/GP   JURID
JUDGE CONFER ADJUD CONTROL...DECISION 20   ADMIN
SUPREME/CT. PAGE 7 B0146   LEGIS
                                                      CT/SYS
                                                      L62

MANGIN G.,"L'ORGANIZATION JUDICIAIRE DES ETATS   AFR
D'AFRIQUE ET DE MADAGASCAR." ISLAM WOR+45 STRATA   LEGIS
STRUCT ECO/UNDEV NAT/G LEGIT EXEC...JURID TIME/SEQ   COLONIAL
TOT/POP 20 SUPREME/CT. PAGE 69 B1387   MADAGASCAR
                                                      B65

REDFORD D.R.,POLITICS AND GOVERNMENT IN THE UNITED   NAT/G
STATES. USA+45 USA-45 LOC/G PROVS FORCES DIPLOM   POL/PAR
CT/SYS LOBBY...JURID SUPREME/CT PRESIDENT. PAGE 87   EX/STRUC
B1751   LEGIS
                                                      S66

POLSBY N.W.,"BOOKS IN THE FIELD: POLITICAL   BIBLIOG/A
SCIENCE." LAW CONSTN LOC/G NAT/G LEGIS ADJUD PWR 20   ATTIT
SUPREME/CT. PAGE 83 B1686   ADMIN
                                                      JURID

B67
FESLER J.W.,THE FIFTY STATES AND THEIR LOCAL   PROVS
GOVERNMENTS. FUT USA+45 POL/PAR LEGIS PROB/SOLV   LOC/G
ADMIN CT/SYS CHOOSE GOV/REL FEDERAL...POLICY CHARTS
20 SUPREME/CT. PAGE 35 B0715

B67
FINCHER F.,THE GOVERNMENT OF THE UNITED STATES.   NAT/G
USA+45 USA-45 POL/PAR CHIEF CT/SYS LOBBY GP/REL   EX/STRUC
INGP/REL...CONCPT CHARTS BIBLIOG T 18/20 PRESIDENT   LEGIS
CONGRESS SUPREME/CT. PAGE 35 B0719   OP/RES

L67
"RESTRICTIVE SOVEREIGN IMMUNITY, THE STATE   SOVEREIGN
DEPARTMENT, AND THE COURTS." USA+45 USA-45 EX/STRUC   ORD/FREE
DIPLOM ADJUD CONTROL GOV/REL 19/20 DEPT/STATE   PRIVIL
SUPREME/CT. PAGE 2 B0047   CT/SYS

SURPLUS....SEE DEMAND,PLAN

SURRENCY E.C. B2055

SURVEY ANALYSIS....SEE SAMP/SIZ

SUTHERLAND G. B2056

SUTTON F.X. B2057

SWATANTRA....SWATANTRA - COALITION RIGHT-WING PARTY IN INDIA

SWEARER H.R. B2058

SWEARINGEN E.L. B0946

SWEDEN....SEE ALSO APPROPRIATE TIME/SPACE/CULTURE INDEX

B55
RUSTOW D.A.,THE POLITICS OF COMPROMISE. SWEDEN   POL/PAR
LABOR EX/STRUC LEGIS PLAN REPRESENT SOCISM...SOC   NAT/G
19/20. PAGE 92 B1859   POLICY
                                                      ECO/TAC
B57
MEYER P.,ADMINISTRATIVE ORGANIZATION: A COMPARATIVE   ADMIN
STUDY OF THE ORGANIZATION OF PUBLIC ADMINISTRATION.   METH/COMP
DENMARK FRANCE NORWAY SWEDEN UK USA+45 ELITES LOC/G   NAT/G
CONSULT LEGIS ADJUD CONTROL LEAD PWR SKILL   CENTRAL
DECISION. PAGE 73 B1475

B59
SISSON C.H.,THE SPIRIT OF BRITISH ADMINISTRATION   GOV/COMP
AND SOME EUROPEAN COMPARISONS. FRANCE GERMANY/W   ADMIN
SWEDEN UK LAW EX/STRUC INGP/REL EFFICIENCY ORD/FREE   ELITES
...DECISION 20. PAGE 98 B1972   ATTIT

B62
WENDT P.F.,HOUSING POLICY - THE SEARCH FOR   PLAN
SOLUTIONS. GERMANY/W SWEDEN UK USA+45 OP/RES   ADMIN
HABITAT WEALTH...SOC/WK CHARTS 20. PAGE 115 B2322   METH/COMP
                                                      NAT/G
S63
COUTY P.,"L'ASSISTANCE POUR LE DEVELOPPEMENT: POINT   FINAN
DE VUE SCANDINAVES." EUR+WWI FINLAND FUT SWEDEN   ROUTINE
WOR+45 ECO/DEV ECO/UNDEV COM/IND LABOR NAT/G   FOR/AID
PROF/ORG ACT/RES SKILL WEALTH TOT/POP 20. PAGE 24
B0497

B64
ANDREN N.,GOVERNMENT AND POLITICS IN THE NORDIC   CONSTN
COUNTRIES: DENMARK, FINLAND, ICELAND, NORWAY,   NAT/G
SWEDEN. DENMARK FINLAND ICELAND NORWAY SWEDEN   CULTURE
POL/PAR CHIEF LEGIS ADMIN REGION REPRESENT ATTIT   GOV/COMP
CONSERVE...CHARTS BIBLIOG/A 20. PAGE 5 B0102

B64
HALLER W.,DER SCHWEDISCHE JUSTITIEOMBUDSMAN.   JURID
DENMARK FINLAND NORWAY SWEDEN LEGIS ADJUD CONTROL   PARL/PROC
PERSON ORD/FREE...NAT/COMP 20 OMBUDSMAN. PAGE 46   ADMIN
B0926   CHIEF

B65
ROWAT D.C.,THE OMBUDSMAN: CITIZEN'S DEFENDER.   INSPECT
DENMARK FINLAND NEW/ZEALND NORWAY SWEDEN CONSULT   CONSTN
PROB/SOLV FEEDBACK PARTIC GP/REL...SOC CONCPT   NAT/G
NEW/IDEA METH/COMP ANTHOL BIBLIOG 20. PAGE 91 B1840   ADMIN

B65
SMITH C.,THE OMBUDSMAN: A BIBLIOGRAPHY (PAMPHLET).   BIBLIOG
DENMARK SWEDEN USA+45 LAW LEGIS JUDGE GOV/REL   ADMIN
GP/REL...JURID 20. PAGE 98 B1980   CT/SYS
                                                      ADJUD

SWEENEY J.W. B0593

SWEENEY S.B. B2059,B2060

SWENSON R.J. B2061

SWERDLOW I. B2062

SWISHER C.B. B2063

SWITZERLND....SWITZERLAND; SEE ALSO APPROPRIATE TIME/SPACE/
CULTURE INDEX

N
DEUTSCHE BUCHEREI,JAHRESVERZEICHNIS DES DEUTSCHEN   BIBLIOG
SCHRIFTUMS. AUSTRIA EUR+WWI GERMANY SWITZERLND LAW   WRITING
LOC/G DIPLOM ADMIN...MGT SOC 19/20. PAGE 29 B0580   NAT/G

B63
KULZ H.R.,STAATSBURGER UND STAATSGEWALT (2 VOLS.).   ADMIN
GERMANY SWITZERLND UK USSR CONSTN DELIB/GP TARIFFS   ADJUD
TAX...JURID 20. PAGE 61 B1242   CT/SYS
                                                      NAT/COMP
B63
MONTER W.,THE GOVERNMENT OF GENEVA, 1536-1605   SECT
(DOCTORAL THESIS). SWITZERLND DIPLOM LEAD ORD/FREE   FINAN
SOVEREIGN 16/17 CALVIN/J ROME. PAGE 74 B1504   LOC/G
                                                      ADMIN
L63
BOLGAR V.,"THE PUBLIC INTEREST: A JURISPRUDENTIAL   CONCPT
AND COMPARATIVE OVERVIEW OF SYMPOSIUM ON   ORD/FREE
FUNDAMENTAL CONCEPTS OF PUBLIC LAW" COM FRANCE   CONTROL
GERMANY SWITZERLND LAW ADJUD ADMIN AGREE LAISSEZ   NAT/COMP
...JURID GEN/LAWS 20 EUROPE/E. PAGE 13 B0268

SYMONDS R. B2064

SYNANON....SYNANON: COMMUNITY OF FORMER DRUG ADDICTS AND
CRIMINALS

SYNTAX....SEE LOG

SYRIA....SEE ALSO UAR

S66
PALMER M.,"THE UNITED ARAB REPUBLIC* AN ASSESSMENT   UAR
OF ITS FAILURE." ELITES ECO/UNDEV POL/PAR FORCES   SYRIA
ECO/TAC RUMOR ADMIN EXEC EFFICIENCY ATTIT SOCISM   REGION
...INT NASSER/G. PAGE 81 B1628   FEDERAL

SYS/QU....SYSTEMATIZING AND ANALYZING QUESTIONNAIRES

SYSTEMS....SEE ROUTINE, COMPUTER

SZASZ/T....THOMAS SZASZ

SZLADITS C. B2065,B2066

―――――――――――――――――――――― T ――――――――――――――――――――――

T....TEXTBOOK

B40
PFIFFNER J.M.,RESEARCH METHODS IN PUBLIC   ADMIN
ADMINISTRATION. USA-45 R+D...MGT STAT INT QU T 20.   OP/RES
PAGE 82 B1665   METH
                                                     TEC/DEV
B48
HOOVER E.M.,THE LOCATION OF ECONOMIC ACTIVITY.   HABITAT
WOR+45 MARKET MUNIC WORKER PROB/SOLV INT/TRADE   INDUS
ADMIN COST...POLICY CHARTS T 20. PAGE 51 B1041   ECO/TAC
                                                     GEOG
C48
WALKER H.,"THE LEGISLATIVE PROCESS; LAWMAKING IN   PARL/PROC
THE UNITED STATES." NAT/G POL/PAR PROVS EX/STRUC   LEGIS
OP/RES PROB/SOLV CT/SYS LOBBY GOV/REL...CHARTS   LAW
BIBLIOG T 18/20 CONGRESS. PAGE 113 B2279   CONSTN

B49
SHISTER J.,ECONOMICS OF THE LABOR MARKET. LOC/G   MARKET
NAT/G WORKER TEC/DEV BARGAIN PAY PRICE EXEC GP/REL   LABOR
INCOME...MGT T 20. PAGE 96 B1949   INDUS

B51
ANDERSON W.,STATE AND LOCAL GOVERNMENT IN THE   LOC/G
UNITED STATES. USA+45 CONSTN POL/PAR EX/STRUC LEGIS   MUNIC
BUDGET TAX ADJUD CT/SYS CHOOSE...CHARTS T 20.   PROVS
PAGE 5 B0100   GOV/REL

B51
NIELANDER W.A.,PUBLIC RELATIONS. USA+45 COM/IND   PERS/REL
LOC/G NAT/G VOL/ASSN EX/STRUC DIPLOM EDU/PROP PRESS   GP/REL
TV...METH/CNCPT T 20. PAGE 78 B1583   LG/CO
                                                     ROUTINE
B51
PETERSON F.,SURVEY OF LABOR ECONOMICS (REV. ED.).   WORKER
STRATA ECO/DEV LABOR INSPECT BARGAIN PAY PRICE EXEC   DEMAND
ROUTINE GP/REL ALL/VALS ORD/FREE 20 AFL/CIO   IDEA/COMP
DEPT/LABOR. PAGE 82 B1662   T

B53
DIMOCK M.E.,PUBLIC ADMINISTRATION. USA+45 FINAN   ADMIN
WORKER BUDGET CONTROL CHOOSE...T 20. PAGE 29 B0596   STRUCT
                                                     OP/RES
                                                     POLICY
B57
BABCOCK R.S.,STATE & LOCAL GOVERNMENT AND POLITICS. PROVS
USA+45 CONSTN POL/PAR EX/STRUC LEGIS BUDGET LOBBY   LOC/G
CHOOSE SUFF...CHARTS BIBLIOG T 20. PAGE 8 B0154   GOV/REL

B59
CHAPMAN B.,THE PROFESSION OF GOVERNMENT: THE PUBLIC ADMIN
SERVICE IN EUROPE. MOD/EUR LABOR CT/SYS...T 20   CONTROL
CIVIL/SERV. PAGE 20 B0409   ROUTINE
                                                     EX/STRUC
B59
DAVIS K.C.,ADMINISTRATIVE LAW TEXT. USA+45 NAT/G   ADJUD

DELIB/GP EX/STRUC CONTROL ORD/FREE...T 20
SUPREME/CT. PAGE 27 B0542

ADMIN
JURID
CT/SYS
B60

MORRIS W.T.,ENGINEERING ECONOMY. AUTOMAT RISK
RATIONAL...PROBABIL STAT CHARTS GAME SIMUL BIBLIOG
T 20. PAGE 76 B1529

OP/RES
DECISION
MGT
PROB/SOLV
B60

PFIFFNER J.M.,PUBLIC ADMINISTRATION. USA+45 FINAN
WORKER PLAN PROB/SOLV ADJUD CONTROL EXEC...T 20.
PAGE 82 B1666

ADMIN
NAT/G
LOC/G
MGT
B61

CATHERINE R.,LE FONCTIONNAIRE FRANCAIS. FRANCE
NAT/G INGP/REL ATTIT MORAL ORD/FREE...T CIVIL/SERV.
PAGE 19 B0394

ADMIN
GP/REL
LEAD
SUPEGO
B61

DRURY J.W.,THE GOVERNMENT OF KANSAS. USA+45 AGRI
INDUS CHIEF LEGIS WORKER PLAN BUDGET GIVE CT/SYS
GOV/REL...T 20 KANSAS GOVERNOR CITY/MGT. PAGE 31
B0621

PROVS
CONSTN
ADMIN
LOC/G
B61

ROWAT D.C.,BASIC ISSUES IN PUBLIC ADMINISTRATION.
STRUCT EX/STRUC PWR CONSERVE...MAJORIT DECISION MGT
T 20 BUREAUCRCY. PAGE 91 B1839

NAT/G
ADJUD
ADMIN
B62

ARCO EDITORIAL BOARD,PUBLIC MANAGEMENT AND
ADMINISTRATION. PLAN BUDGET WRITING CONTROL ROUTINE
...TESTS CHARTS METH T 20. PAGE 6 B0125

MGT
ADMIN
NAT/G
LOC/G
B62

CARTER G.M.,THE GOVERNMENT OF THE SOVIET UNION.
USSR CULTURE LOC/G DIPLOM ECO/TAC ADJUD CT/SYS LEAD
WEALTH...CHARTS T 20 COM/PARTY. PAGE 19 B0390

NAT/G
MARXISM
POL/PAR
EX/STRUC
B62

FARBER W.O.,GOVERNMENT OF SOUTH DAKOTA. USA+45
DIST/IND POL/PAR CHIEF EX/STRUC LEGIS ECO/TAC GIVE
EDU/PROP CT/SYS PARTIC...T 20 SOUTH/DAK GOVERNOR.
PAGE 35 B0704

PROVS
LOC/G
ADMIN
CONSTN
B62

STAHL O.G.,PUBLIC PERSONNEL ADMINISTRATION. LOC/G
TOP/EX CREATE PLAN ROUTINE...TECHNIC MGT T.
PAGE 100 B2017

ADMIN
WORKER
EX/STRUC
NAT/G
B62

WELLEQUET J.,LE CONGO BELGE ET LA WELTPOLITIK
(1894-1914. GERMANY DOMIN EDU/PROP WAR ATTIT
...BIBLIOG T CONGO/LEOP. PAGE 115 B2318

ADMIN
DIPLOM
GP/REL
COLONIAL
B63

COSTELLO T.W.,PSYCHOLOGY IN ADMINISTRATION: A
RESEARCH ORIENTATION. CREATE PROB/SOLV PERS/REL
ADJUST ANOMIE ATTIT DRIVE PERCEPT ROLE...DECISION
BIBLIOG T 20. PAGE 24 B0488

PSY
MGT
EXEC
ADMIN
B63

DE GUZMAN R.P.,PATTERNS IN DECISION-MAKING: CASE
STUDIES IN PHILIPPINE PUBLIC ADMINISTRATION.
PHILIPPINE LAW CHIEF PROB/SOLV INGP/REL DRIVE
PERCEPT ROLE...ANTHOL T 20. PAGE 27 B0557

ADMIN
DECISION
POLICY
GOV/REL
B63

HOUGHTELING J.L. JR.,THE LEGAL ENVIRONMENT OF
BUSINESS. LG/CO NAT/G CONSULT AGREE CONTROL
...DICTIONARY T 20. PAGE 52 B1047

LAW
MGT
ADJUD
JURID
B63

ROBERT J.,LA MONARCHIE MAROCAINE. MOROCCO LABOR
MUNIC POL/PAR EX/STRUC ORD/FREE PWR...JURID TREND T
20. PAGE 89 B1793

CHIEF
CONSERVE
ADMIN
CONSTN
C63

BLUM J.M.,"THE NATIONAL EXPERIENCE." USA+45 USA-45
ECO/DEV DIPLOM WAR NAT/LISM...POLICY CHARTS BIBLIOG
T 16/20 CONGRESS PRESIDENT COLD/WAR. PAGE 13 B0258

ADMIN
NAT/G
LEGIS
CHIEF
B64

EDELMAN M.,THE SYMBOLIC USES OF POWER. USA+45
EX/STRUC CONTROL GP/REL INGP/REL...MGT T. PAGE 32
B0653

CLIENT
PWR
EXEC
ELITES
B64

GARFIELD PJ   LOVEJOY WF.PUBLIC UTILITY
ECONOMICS. DIST/IND FINAN MARKET MUNIC ADMIN COST
DEMAND...TECHNIC JURID 20 MONOPOLY. PAGE 39 B0782

T
ECO/TAC
OWN
SERV/IND
B64

INST D'ETUDE POL L'U GRENOBLE,ADMINISTRATION
TRADITIONELLE ET PLANIFICATION REGIONALE. FRANCE
LAW POL/PAR PROB/SOLV ADJUST RIGID/FLEX...CHARTS
ANTHOL BIBLIOG T 20 REFORMERS. PAGE 54 B1087

ADMIN
MUNIC
PLAN
CREATE
B64

TURNER H.A.,THE GOVERNMENT AND POLITICS OF
CALIFORNIA (2ND ED.). LAW FINAN MUNIC POL/PAR
SCHOOL EX/STRUC LEGIS LOBBY CHOOSE...CHARTS T 20

PROVS
ADMIN
LOC/G

CALIFORNIA. PAGE 106 B2138

CONSTN
B65

FISCHER F.C.,THE GOVERNMENT OF MICHIGAN. USA+45
NAT/G PUB/INST EX/STRUC LEGIS BUDGET GIVE EDU/PROP
CT/SYS CHOOSE GOV/REL...T MICHIGAN. PAGE 36 B0723

PROVS
LOC/G
ADMIN
CONSTN
B65

HUGHES J.M.,EDUCATION IN AMERICA (2ND ED.). USA+45
USA-45 GP/REL INGP/REL AGE/C AGE/Y ROLE...IDEA/COMP
BIBLIOG T 20. PAGE 52 B1059

EDU/PROP
SCHOOL
ADMIN
METH/COMP
B65

STARR M.K.,EXECUTIVE READINGS IN MANAGEMENT
SCIENCE. TOP/EX WORKER EDU/PROP ADMIN...DECISION
GEN/LAWS ANTHOL METH T 20. PAGE 100 B2023

MGT
EX/STRUC
PLAN
LG/CO
B66

FOX K.A.,THE THEORY OF QUANTITATIVE ECONOMIC POLICY
WITH APPLICATIONS TO ECONOMIC GROWTH AND
STABILIZATION. ECO/DEV AGRI NAT/G PLAN ADMIN RISK
...DECISION IDEA/COMP SIMUL T. PAGE 37 B0746

ECO/TAC
ECOMETRIC
EQUILIB
GEN/LAWS
B66

GREENE L.E.,GOVERNMENT IN TENNESSEE (2ND ED.).
USA+45 DIST/IND INDUS POL/PAR EX/STRUC LEGIS PLAN
BUDGET GIVE CT/SYS...MGT T 20 TENNESSEE. PAGE 43
B0866

PROVS
LOC/G
CONSTN
ADMIN
B66

HASTINGS P.G.,THE MANAGEMENT OF BUSINESS FINANCE.
ECO/DEV PLAN BUDGET CONTROL COST...DECISION CHARTS
BIBLIOG T 20. PAGE 48 B0966

FINAN
MGT
INDUS
ECO/TAC
B66

JOHNSON N.,PARLIAMENT AND ADMINISTRATION: THE
ESTIMATES COMMITTEE 1945-65. FUT UK NAT/G EX/STRUC
PLAN BUDGET ORD/FREE...T 20 PARLIAMENT HOUSE/CMNS.
PAGE 57 B1147

LEGIS
ADMIN
FINAN
DELIB/GP
B66

MANSFIELD E.,MANAGERIAL ECONOMICS AND OPERATIONS
RESEARCH; A NONMATHEMATICAL INTRODUCTION. USA+45
ELITES ECO/DEV CONSULT EX/STRUC PROB/SOLV ROUTINE
EFFICIENCY OPTIMAL...GAME T 20. PAGE 69 B1396

ECO/TAC
OP/RES
MGT
COMPUTER
B66

ROSS R.M.,STATE AND LOCAL GOVERNMENT AND
ADMINISTRATION. USA+45 CONSTN POL/PAR EX/STRUC
LEGIS BUDGET EDU/PROP CONTROL CT/SYS CHOOSE GOV/REL
T. PAGE 90 B1827

LOC/G
PROVS
MUNIC
ADMIN
B66

SCHLESSINGER P.J.,ELEMENTS OF CALIFORNIA GOVERNMENT
(2ND ED.). USA+45 LAW ADJUD ADMIN CONTROL CT/SYS
EFFICIENCY...BIBLIOG T CALIFORNIA. PAGE 94 B1891

LOC/G
PROVS
GOV/REL
LEGIS
B67

DE BLIJ H.J.,SYSTEMATIC POLITICAL GEOGRAPHY. WOR+45
STRUCT INT/ORG NAT/G EDU/PROP ADMIN COLONIAL
ROUTINE ORD/FREE PWR...IDEA/COMP T 20. PAGE 27
B0550

GEOG
CONCPT
METH
B67

FARRIS M.T.,MODERN TRANSPORTATION: SELECTED
READINGS. UNIV CONTROL...POLICY ANTHOL T 20.
PAGE 35 B0706

DIST/IND
MGT
COST
B67

FINCHER F.,THE GOVERNMENT OF THE UNITED STATES.
USA+45 USA-45 POL/PAR CHIEF CT/SYS LOBBY GP/REL
INGP/REL...CONCPT CHARTS BIBLIOG T 18/20 PRESIDENT
CONGRESS SUPREME/CT. PAGE 35 B0719

NAT/G
EX/STRUC
LEGIS
OP/RES
B67

GREENE L.S.,AMERICAN GOVERNMENT POLICIES AND
FUNCTIONS. USA+45 LAW AGRI DIST/IND LABOR MUNIC
BUDGET DIPLOM EDU/PROP ORD/FREE...BIBLIOG T 20.
PAGE 43 B0867

POLICY
NAT/G
ADMIN
DECISION
B67

HEWITT W.H.,ADMINISTRATION OF CRIMINAL JUSTICE IN
NEW YORK. LAW PROB/SOLV ADJUD ADMIN...CRIMLGY
CHARTS T 20 NEW/YORK. PAGE 49 B1001

CRIME
ROLE
CT/SYS
FORCES
B67

ROBINSON R.D., INTERNATIONAL MANAGEMENT. USA+45
FINAN R+D PLAN PRODUC...DECISION T. PAGE 67 B1352

INT/TRADE
MGT
INT/LAW
MARKET
B67

MARRIS P.,DILEMMAS OF SOCIAL REFORM: POVERTY AND
COMMUNITY ACTION IN THE UNITED STATES. USA+45 NAT/G
OP/RES ADMIN PARTIC EFFICIENCY WEALTH...SOC
METH/COMP T 20 REFORMERS. PAGE 69 B1401

STRUCT
MUNIC
PROB/SOLV
COST
S67

JENCKS C.E.,"SOCIAL STATUS OF COAL MINERS IN
BRITAIN SINCE NATIONALIZATION." UK STRATA STRUCT
LABOR RECEIVE GP/REL INCOME OWN ATTIT HABITAT...MGT
T 20. PAGE 56 B1128

EXTR/IND
WORKER
CONTROL
NAT/G

TABOOS.....SEE CULTURE

TABORSKY E. B2067

TACHERON D.G. B2068

TACKABERRY R.B. B2069

TAFT/HART....TAFT-HARTLEY ACT

GABLE R.W.,"NAM: INFLUENTIAL LOBBY OR KISS OF   LOBBY   S53
DEATH?" (BMR)" USA+45 LAW INSPECT EDU/PROP ADMIN   LEGIS
CONTROL INGP/REL EFFICIENCY PWR 20 CONGRESS NAM   INDUS
TAFT/HART. PAGE 38 B0769   LG/CO

TAFT/RA....ROBERT A. TAFT

BENSON E.T.,CROSS FIRE: THE EIGHT YEARS WITH   ADMIN   B62
EISENHOWER. USA+45 DIPLOM LEAD ATTIT PERSON   POLICY
CONSERVE...TRADIT BIOG 20 EISNHWR/DD PRESIDENT   DELIB/GP
TAFT/RA DULLES/JF NIXON/RM. PAGE 11 B0218   TOP/EX

TAFT/WH....PRESIDENT WILLIAM HOWARD TAFT

MORISON E.E.,TURMOIL AND TRADITION: A STUDY OF THE BIOG   B60
LIFE AND TIMES OF HENRY L. STIMSON. USA+45 USA-45 NAT/G
POL/PAR CHIEF DELIB/GP FORCES BAL/PWR DIPLOM   EX/STRUC
ARMS/CONT WAR PEACE 19/20 STIMSON/HL ROOSEVLT/F
TAFT/WH HOOVER/H REPUBLICAN. PAGE 75 B1525

TAHITI....TAHITI

WEST F.J.,POLITICAL ADVANCEMENT IN THE SOUTH   S/ASIA   B61
PACIFIC. CONSTN CULTURE POL/PAR LEGIS DOMIN ADMIN LOC/G
CHOOSE SOVEREIGN VAL/FREE 20 FIJI TAHITI SAMOA.   COLONIAL
PAGE 115 B2325

TAIWAN....TAIWAN AND REPUBLIC OF CHINA

TALBOTT R.B. B0913

TAMBIAH S.J. B2070

TAMMANY....TAMMANY HALL

RIORDAN W.L.,PLUNKITT OF TAMMANY HALL. USA-45   POL/PAR   B05
SOCIETY PROB/SOLV EXEC LEAD TASK CHOOSE ALL/VALS MUNIC
...RECORD ANTHOL 20 REFORMERS TAMMANY NEWYORK/C   CHIEF
PLUNKITT/G. PAGE 88 B1789   ATTIT

LIPPMANN W.,PREFACE TO POLITICS. LABOR CHIEF   PARTIC   B62
CONTROL LEAD...MYTH IDEA/COMP 19/20 ROOSEVLT/T   ATTIT
TAMMANY WILSON/H SANTAYAN/G BERGSON/H. PAGE 65   ADMIN
B1318

TANG P.S.H. B2071

TANGANYIKA....SEE TANZANIA

LIEBENOW J.G.,"LEGITIMACY OF ALIEN RELATIONSHIP: COLONIAL S61
THE NYATURU OF TANGANYIKA" (BMR)" AFR UK ADMIN LEAD DOMIN
CHOOSE 20 NYATURU TANGANYIKA. PAGE 65 B1312   LEGIT
                                           PWR

BANFIELD J.,"FEDERATION IN EAST-AFRICA." AFR UGANDA EX/STRUC S63
ELITES INT/ORG NAT/G VOL/ASSN LEGIS ECO/TAC FEDERAL PWR
ATTIT SOVEREIGN TOT/POP 20 TANGANYIKA. PAGE 9 B0180 REGION

ROTBERG R.,"THE FEDERATION MOVEMENT IN BRITISH EAST VOL/ASSN L64
AND CENTRAL AFRICA." AFR RHODESIA UGANDA ECO/UNDEV PWR
NAT/G POL/PAR FORCES DOMIN LEGIT ADMIN COERCE ATTIT REGION
...CONCPT TREND 20 TANGANYIKA. PAGE 91 B1831

TANNENBAUM A.S. B2072,B2073

TANNENBAUM R. B2074,B2075

TANSKY L. B2076

TANZANIA....TANZANIA; SEE ALSO AFR

SMITH H.E.,READINGS IN ECONOMIC DEVELOPMENT AND   TEC/DEV   B66
ADMINISTRATION IN TANZANIA. TANZANIA FINAN INDUS ADMIN
LABOR NAT/G PLAN PROB/SOLV INT/TRADE COLONIAL   GOV/REL
REGION...ANTHOL BIBLIOG 20 AFRICA/E. PAGE 98 B1981

MCAUSLAN J.P.W.,"CONSTITUTIONAL INNOVATION AND   CONSTN   L66
POLITICAL STABILITY IN TANZANIA: A PRELIMINARY   NAT/G
ASSESSMENT." AFR TANZANIA ELITES CHIEF EX/STRUC   EXEC
RIGID/FLEX PWR 20 PRESIDENT BUREAUCRCY. PAGE 71   POL/PAR
B1440

DRYDEN S.,"LOCAL GOVERNMENT IN TANZANIA PART II"   LOC/G   S67
TANZANIA LAW NAT/G POL/PAR CONTROL PARTIC REPRESENT GOV/REL
...DECISION 20. PAGE 31 B0622   ADMIN

                                                  STRUCT

PRATT R.C.,"THE ADMINISTRATION OF ECONOMIC PLANNING NAT/G   S67
IN A NEWLY INDEPEND ENT STATE* THE TANZANIAN   DELIB/GP
EXPERIENCE 1963-1966." AFR TANZANIA ECO/UNDEV PLAN ADMIN
CONTROL ROUTINE TASK EFFICIENCY 20. PAGE 84 B1699 TEC/DEV

TANZER L. B2077

TAPES....SEE OLD/STOR

TAPPAN P.W. B2078

TARIFFS....SEE ALSO ECO, INT/TRADE, GATT

US SUPERINTENDENT OF DOCUMENTS,INTERSTATE COMMERCE BIBLIOG/A   N
(PRICE LIST 59). USA+45 LAW LOC/G NAT/G LEGIS   DIST/IND
TARIFFS TAX ADMIN CONTROL HEALTH DECISION. PAGE 111 GOV/REL
B2239   PROVS

US SUPERINTENDENT OF DOCUMENTS,TARIFF AND TAXATION BIBLIOG/A   N
(PRICE LIST 37). USA+45 LAW INT/TRADE ADJUD ADMIN TAX
CT/SYS INCOME OWN...DECISION GATT. PAGE 111 B2242 TARIFFS
                                           NAT/G

US TARIFF COMMISSION,THE TARIFF; A BIBLIOGRAPHY: A BIBLIOG/A B34
SELECT LIST OF REFERENCES. USA+45 LAW DIPLOM TAX   TARIFFS
ADMIN...POLICY TREATY 20. PAGE 111 B2246   ECO/TAC

US TARIFF COMMISSION,LIST OF PUBLICATIONS OF THE BIBLIOG   B51
TARIFF COMMISSION (PAMPHLET). USA+45 USA-45 AGRI TARIFFS
EXTR/IND INDUS INT/TRADE...STAT 20. PAGE 111 B2245 NAT/G
                                           ADMIN

GROSSMAN J.,BIBLIOGRAPHY ON PUBLIC ADMINISTRATION BIBLIOG   B58
IN LATIN AMERICA. ECO/UNDEV FINAN PLAN BUDGET   L/A+17C
ECO/TAC TARIFFS TAX...STAT 20. PAGE 44 B0893   NAT/G
                                           ADMIN

VINER J.,"ECONOMIC FOREIGN POLICY ON THE NEW   TOP/EX   S61
FRONTIER." USA+45 ECO/UNDEV AGRI FINAN INDUS MARKET ECO/TAC
INT/ORG NAT/G FOR/AID INT/TRADE ADMIN ATTIT PWR 20 BAL/PAY
KENNEDY/JF. PAGE 112 B2262   TARIFFS

KULZ H.R.,STAATSBURGER UND STAATSGEWALT (2 VOLS.). ADMIN   B63
GERMANY SWITZERLND UK USSR CONSTN DELIB/GP TARIFFS ADJUD
TAX...JURID 20. PAGE 61 B1242   CT/SYS
                                           NAT/COMP

UN SECRETARY GENERAL,PLANNING FOR ECONOMIC   PLAN   B63
DEVELOPMENT. ECO/UNDEV FINAN BUDGET INT/TRADE   ECO/TAC
TARIFFS TAX ADMIN 20 UN. PAGE 106 B2151   MGT
                                           NAT/COMP

DOWD L.P.,PRINCIPLES OF WORLD BUSINESS. SERV/IND   INT/TRADE B65
NAT/G DIPLOM ECO/TAC TARIFFS...INT/LAW JURID 20.   MGT
PAGE 30 B0614   FINAN
                                         MARKET

TARKOWSKI Z.M. B2079

TARLING N. B2080

TARTARS....TARTARS

TASK....SPECIFIC SELF-ASSIGNED OR OTHER ASSIGNED OPERATIONS

PRINCETON U INDUSTRIAL REL SEC,SELECTED REFERENCES BIBLIOG/A   N
OF THE INDUSTRIAL RELATIONS SECTION OF PRINCETON, INDUS
NEW JERSEY. LG/CO NAT/G LEGIS WORKER PLAN PROB/SOLV LABOR
PAY ADMIN ROUTINE TASK GP/REL...PSY 20. PAGE 84   MGT
B1708

RIORDAN W.L.,PLUNKITT OF TAMMANY HALL. USA-45   POL/PAR   B05
SOCIETY PROB/SOLV EXEC LEAD TASK CHOOSE ALL/VALS MUNIC
...RECORD ANTHOL 20 REFORMERS TAMMANY NEWYORK/C   CHIEF
PLUNKITT/G. PAGE 88 B1789   ATTIT

DUNN A.,SCIENTIFIC SELLING AND ADVERTISING. CLIENT LG/CO   B19
ADMIN DEMAND EFFICIENCY 20. PAGE 31 B0632   PERCEPT
                                           PERS/REL
                                           TASK

MILLETT J.D.,THE PROCESS AND ORGANIZATION OF   ADMIN   B47
GOVERNMENT PLANNING. USA+45 DELIB/GP ACT/RES LEAD NAT/G
LOBBY TASK...POLICY GEOG TIME 20 RESOURCE/N.   PLAN
PAGE 73 B1482   CONSULT

WRIGHT J.H.,PUBLIC RELATIONS IN MANAGEMENT. USA+45 MGT   B49
USA-45 ECO/DEV LG/CO SML/CO CONSULT EXEC TASK   PLAN
PROFIT ATTIT ROLE 20. PAGE 118 B2382   EDU/PROP
                                           PARTIC

AMERICAN POLITICAL SCI ASSN,TOWARD A MORE   POL/PAR   B50

RESPONSIBLE TWO-PARTY SYSTEM. USA+45 CONSTN
VOL/ASSN LEGIS LEAD CHOOSE...POLICY MGT 20. PAGE 4
B0087

TASK
PARTIC
ACT/RES
B50

GREAT BRITAIN TREASURY,PUBLIC ADMINISTRATION: A
BIBLIOGRAPHY FOR ORGANISATION AND METHODS
(PAMPHLET). LOC/G NAT/G CONSULT EX/STRUC CONFER
ROUTINE TASK EFFICIENCY...MGT 20. PAGE 43 B0862

BIBLIOG
PLAN
CONTROL
ADMIN
B55

BRAUN K.,LABOR DISPUTES AND THEIR SETTLEMENT.
ECO/TAC ROUTINE TASK GP/REL...DECISION GEN/LAWS.
PAGE 15 B0301

INDUS
LABOR
BARGAIN
ADJUD
B55

HOROWITZ M.,INCENTIVE WAGE SYSTEMS. INDUS LG/CO
WORKER CONTROL GP/REL...MGT PSY 20. PAGE 51 B1044

BIBLIOG/A
PAY
PLAN
TASK
B55

WHEARE K.C.,GOVERNMENT BY COMMITTEE; AN ESSAY ON
THE BRITISH CONSTITUTION. UK NAT/G LEGIS INSPECT
CONFER ADJUD ADMIN CONTROL TASK EFFICIENCY ROLE
POPULISM 20. PAGE 115 B2329

DELIB/GP
CONSTN
LEAD
GP/COMP
B56

ECOLE NAT'L D'ADMINISTRATION,RECRUITMENT AND
TRAINING FOR THE HIGHER CIVIL SERVICE IN FRANCE.
FRANCE EX/STRUC PLAN EDU/PROP CONTROL ROUTINE TASK
COST...METH 20 CIVIL/SERV. PAGE 32 B0650

ADMIN
MGT
EXEC
ACADEM
S57

ARGYRIS C.,"THE INDIVIDUAL AND ORGANIZATION: SOME
PROBLEMS OF MUTUAL ADJUSTMENT" (BMR)" USA+45
PROB/SOLV ADMIN CONTROL 20. PAGE 6 B0128

PERSON
METH
INGP/REL
TASK
S57

DANIELSON L.E.,"SUPERVISORY PROBLEMS IN DECISION
MAKING." WORKER ADMIN ROUTINE TASK MGT. PAGE 26
B0529

PROB/SOLV
DECISION
CONTROL
GP/REL
S57

ROURKE F.E.,"THE POLITICS OF ADMINISTRATIVE
ORGANIZATION: A CASE HISTORY." USA+45 LABOR WORKER
PLAN ADMIN TASK EFFICIENCY 20 DEPT/LABOR CONGRESS.
PAGE 91 B1836

POLICY
ATTIT
MGT
GP/COMP
B58

CLEMENTS R.V.,MANAGERS - A STUDY OF THEIR CAREERS
IN INDUSTRY. STRATA INDUS TASK PERSON SKILL 20.
PAGE 21 B0435

MGT
ELITES
EDU/PROP
TOP/EX
B58

ISLAM R.,INTERNATIONAL ECONOMIC COOPERATION AND THE
UNITED NATIONS. FINAN PLAN EXEC TASK WAR PEACE
...SOC METH/CNCPT 20 UN LEAGUE/NAT. PAGE 55 B1105

INT/ORG
DIPLOM
ADMIN
B59

ELLIOTT S.D.,IMPROVING OUR COURTS. LAW EX/STRUC
PLAN PROB/SOLV ADJUD ADMIN TASK CRIME EFFICIENCY
ORD/FREE 20. PAGE 33 B0669

CT/SYS
JURID
GOV/REL
NAT/G
B59

GREENEWALT C.H.,THE UNCOMMON MAN. UNIV ECO/DEV
ADMIN PERS/REL PERSON SUPEGO WEALTH 20. PAGE 43
B0868

TASK
ORD/FREE
DRIVE
EFFICIENCY
B59

WASSERMAN P.,MEASUREMENT AND ANALYSIS OF
ORGANIZATIONAL PERFORMANCE. FINAN MARKET EX/STRUC
TEC/DEV EDU/PROP CONTROL ROUTINE TASK...MGT 20.
PAGE 114 B2300

BIBLIOG/A
ECO/TAC
OP/RES
EFFICIENCY
B59

WELTON H.,THE THIRD WORLD WAR; TRADE AND INDUSTRY,
THE NEW BATTLEGROUND. WOR+45 ECO/DEV INDUS MARKET
TASK...MGT IDEA/COMP COLD/WAR. PAGE 115 B2321

INT/TRADE
PLAN
DIPLOM
S59

SIMPSON R.L.,"VERTICAL AND HORIZONTAL COMMUNICATION
IN FORMAL ORGANIZATION" USA+45 LG/CO EX/STRUC DOMIN
CONTROL TASK INGP/REL TIME 20. PAGE 97 B1963

PERS/REL
AUTOMAT
INDUS
WORKER
B60

HOVING W.,THE DISTRIBUTION REVOLUTION. WOR+45
ECO/DEV FINAN SERV/IND PRESS PRICE INCOME PRODUC
...MGT 20. PAGE 52 B1049

DIST/IND
MARKET
ECO/TAC
TASK
B60

RAO V.K.R.,INTERNATIONAL AID FOR ECONOMIC
DEVELOPMENT - POSSIBILITIES AND LIMITATIONS. FINAN
PLAN TEC/DEV ADMIN TASK EFFICIENCY...POLICY SOC
METH/CNCPT CHARTS 20 UN. PAGE 86 B1734

FOR/AID
DIPLOM
INT/ORG
ECO/UNDEV
S60

BANFIELD E.C.,"THE POLITICAL IMPLICATIONS OF
METROPOLITAN GROWTH" (BMR)" UK USA+45 LOC/G
PROB/SOLV ADMIN GP/REL...METH/COMP NAT/COMP 20.
PAGE 9 B0176

TASK
MUNIC
GOV/COMP
CENSUS
B61

PROCEEDINGS OF THE CONFERENCE ON BUSINESS GAMES AS
TEACHING DEVICES. PROB/SOLV ECO/TAC CONFER ADMIN
TASK...MGT ANTHOL 20. PAGE 29 B0593

GAME
DECISION
EDU/PROP
EFFICIENCY

FREYRE G.,THE PORTUGUESE AND THE TROPICS. L/A+17C
PORTUGAL SOCIETY PERF/ART ADMIN TASK GP/REL
...ART/METH CONCPT SOC/INTEG 20. PAGE 37 B0754

B61
COLONIAL
METH
PLAN
CULTURE
B62

TAYLOR J.K.L.,ATTITUDES AND METHODS OF
COMMUNICATION AND CONSULTATION BETWEEN EMPLOYERS
AND WORKERS AT INDIVIDUAL FIRM LEVEL. WOR+45 STRUCT
INDUS LABOR CONFER TASK GP/REL EFFICIENCY...MGT
BIBLIOG METH 20 OECD. PAGE 103 B2087

WORKER
ADMIN
ATTIT
EDU/PROP
S62

GIDWANI K.A.,"LEADER BEHAVIOUR IN ELECTED AND NON-
ELECTED GROUPS." DELIB/GP ROUTINE TASK HAPPINESS
AUTHORIT...SOC STAT CHARTS SOC/EXP. PAGE 39 B0796

LEAD
INGP/REL
GP/COMP
CHOOSE
B63

SWEENEY S.B.,ACHIEVING EXCELLENCE IN PUBLIC
SERVICE. FUT USA+45 NAT/G ACT/RES GOV/REL...POLICY
ANTHOL 20 CIVIL/SERV. PAGE 102 B2060

ADMIN
WORKER
TASK
PLAN
B64

FONTENEAU J.,LE CONSEIL MUNICIPAL: LE MAIRE-LES
ADJOINTS. FRANCE FINAN DELIB/GP EX/STRUC BUDGET TAX
TASK COST INCOME ROLE SUPEGO 20 MAYOR. PAGE 36
B0735

MUNIC
NEIGH
ADMIN
TOP/EX
B64

KAHNG T.J.,LAW, POLITICS, AND THE SECURITY COUNCIL*
AN INQUIRY INTO THE HANDLING OF LEGAL QUESTIONS.
LAW CONSTN NAT/G ACT/RES OP/RES CT/SYS TASK PWR
...INT/LAW BIBLIOG UN. PAGE 57 B1160

DELIB/GP
ADJUD
ROUTINE
B64

KAPP E.,THE MERGER OF THE EXECUTIVES OF THE
EUROPEAN COMMUNITIES. LAW CONSTN STRUCT ACT/RES
PLAN PROB/SOLV ADMIN REGION TASK...INT/LAW MGT ECSC
EEC. PAGE 58 B1170

CENTRAL
EX/STRUC
B64

PEABODY R.L.,ORGANIZATIONAL AUTHORITY. SCHOOL
WORKER PLAN SENIOR GOV/REL UTIL DRIVE PWR...PSY
CHARTS BIBLIOG 20. PAGE 82 B1648

ADMIN
EFFICIENCY
TASK
GP/REL
B65

ELDER R.E.,OVERSEAS REPRESENTATION AND SERVICES FOR
FEDERAL DOMESTIC AGENCIES. USA+45 NAT/G ACT/RES
FOR/AID EDU/PROP SENIOR ROUTINE TASK ADJUST...MGT
ORG/CHARTS. PAGE 33 B0663

OP/RES
DIPLOM
GOV/REL
ADMIN
B65

LAMBIRI I.,SOCIAL CHANGE IN A GREEK COUNTRY TOWN.
GREECE FAM PROB/SOLV ROUTINE TASK LEISURE INGP/REL
CONSEN ORD/FREE...SOC INT QU CHARTS 20. PAGE 62
B1252

INDUS
WORKER
CULTURE
NEIGH
S65

ALEXANDER T.,"SYNECTICS: INVENTING BY THE MADNESS
METHOD." DELIB/GP TOP/EX ACT/RES TEC/DEV EXEC TASK
KNOWL...MGT METH/COMP 20. PAGE 4 B0073

PROB/SOLV
OP/RES
CREATE
CONSULT
S65

POLK W.R.,"PROBLEMS OF GOVERNMENT UTILIZATION OF
SCHOLARLY RESEARCH IN INTERNATIONAL AFFAIRS." FINAN
NAT/G EDU/PROP CONTROL TASK GP/REL ATTIT PERCEPT
KNOWL...POLICY TIME. PAGE 83 B1685

ACT/RES
ACADEM
PLAN
ADMIN
S65

THOMAS F.C. JR.,"THE PEACE CORPS IN MOROCCO."
CULTURE MUNIC PROVS CREATE ROUTINE TASK ADJUST
STRANGE...OBS PEACE/CORP. PAGE 104 B2099

MOROCCO
FRANCE
FOR/AID
EDU/PROP
B66

ALEXANDER Y.,INTERNATIONAL TECHNICAL ASSISTANCE
EXPERTS* A CASE STUDY OF THE U.N. EXPERIENCE.
ECO/UNDEV CONSULT EX/STRUC CREATE PLAN DIPLOM
FOR/AID TASK EFFICIENCY...ORG/CHARTS UN. PAGE 4
B0074

ECO/TAC
INT/ORG
ADMIN
MGT
B66

BARBER W.F.,INTERNAL SECURITY AND MILITARY POWER*
COUNTERINSURGENCY AND CIVIC ACTION IN LATIN
AMERICA. ECO/UNDEV CREATE ADMIN REV ATTIT
RIGID/FLEX MARXISM...INT BIBLIOG OAS. PAGE 9 B0183

L/A+17C
FORCES
ORD/FREE
TASK
B66

KIRDAR U.,THE STRUCTURE OF UNITED NATIONS ECONOMIC
AID TO UNDERDEVELOPED COUNTRIES. AGRI FINAN INDUS
NAT/G EX/STRUC PLAN GIVE TASK...POLICY 20 UN.
PAGE 60 B1213

INT/ORG
FOR/AID
ECO/UNDEV
ADMIN
B66

MACFARQUHAR R.,CHINA UNDER MAO: POLITICS TAKES
COMMAND. CHINA/COM COM AGRI INDUS CHIEF FORCES
DIPLOM INT/TRADE EDU/PROP TASK REV ADJUST...ANTHOL
20 MAO. PAGE 67 B1359

ECO/UNDEV
TEC/DEV
ECO/TAC
ADMIN
B66

WALL E.H.,THE COURT OF JUSTICE IN THE EUROPEAN
COMMUNITIES: JURISDICTION AND PROCEDURE. EUR+WWI
DIPLOM ADJUD ADMIN ROUTINE TASK...CONCPT LING 20.
PAGE 113 B2281

CT/SYS
INT/ORG
LAW
OP/RES
B66

YOUNG W.,EXISTING MECHANISMS OF ARMS CONTROL.
PROC/MFG OP/RES DIPLOM TASK CENTRAL...MGT TREATY.
PAGE 119 B2395

ARMS/CONT
ADMIN
NUC/PWR

ROUTINE
S66
AUSLAND J.C.,"CRISIS MANAGEMENT* BERLIN, CYPRUS,   OP/RES
LAOS." CYPRUS LAOS FORCES CREATE PLAN EDU/PROP TASK DIPLOM
CENTRAL PERSON RIGID/FLEX...DECISION MGT 20 BERLIN   RISK
KENNEDY/JF MCNAMARA/R RUSK. PAGE 7 B0148   ADMIN

B67
ILLINOIS COMMISSION,IMPROVING THE STATE   PROVS
LEGISLATURE. USA+45 LAW CONSTN NAT/G PROB/SOLV   LEGIS
EDU/PROP ADMIN TASK CHOOSE INGP/REL EFFICIENCY   REPRESENT
ILLINOIS. PAGE 53 B1077   PLAN

B67
SALMOND J.A.,THE CIVILIAN CONSERVATION CORPS,   ADMIN
1933-1942. USA+45 NAT/G CREATE EXEC EFFICIENCY   ECO/TAC
WEALTH...BIBLIOG 20 ROOSEVLT/F. PAGE 92 B1864   TASK
                                                     AGRI

L67
BESCOBY I.,"A COLONIAL ADMINISTRATION* AN ANALYSIS   ADMIN
OF ADMINISTRATION IN BRITISH COLUMBIA 1869-1871."   CANADA
UK STRATA EX/STRUC LEGIS TASK GOV/REL EFFICIENCY   COLONIAL
ROLE...MGT CHARTS 19. PAGE 11 B0232   LEAD

S67
ANDERSON L.G.,"ADMINISTERING A GOVERNMENT SOCIAL   ADMIN
SERVICE" NEW/ZEALND EX/STRUC TASK ROLE 20. PAGE 5   NAT/G
B0094   DELIB/GP
                                                     SOC/WK

S67
CONWAY J.E.,"MAKING RESEARCH EFFECTIVE IN   ACT/RES
LEGISLATION." LAW R+D CONSULT EX/STRUC PLAN CONFER   POLICY
ADMIN LEAD ROUTINE TASK INGP/REL DECISION. PAGE 23   LEGIS
B0469   PROB/SOLV

S67
PRATT R.C.,"THE ADMINISTRATION OF ECONOMIC PLANNING NAT/G
IN A NEWLY INDEPEND ENT STATE* THE TANZANIAN   DELIB/GP
EXPERIENCE 1963-1966." AFR TANZANIA ECO/UNDEV PLAN   ADMIN
CONTROL ROUTINE TASK EFFICIENCY 20. PAGE 84 B1699   TEC/DEV

S67
ROWAT D.C.,"RECENT DEVELOPMENTS IN OMBUDSMANSHIP* A CANADA
REVIEW ARTICLE." UK USA+45 STRUCT CONSULT INSPECT   ADMIN
TASK EFFICIENCY...NEW/IDEA 20. PAGE 91 B1841   LOC/G
                                                     NAT/G

S67
RUBIN R.I.,"THE LEGISLATIVE-EXECUTIVE RELATIONS OF   LEGIS
THE UNITED STATES INFORMATION AGENCY." USA+45   EX/STRUC
EDU/PROP TASK INGP/REL EFFICIENCY ISOLAT ATTIT ROLE GP/REL
USIA CONGRESS. PAGE 91 B1850   PROF/ORG

TATOMIR N. B2081

TATU M. B2082

TAUBENFELD H.J. B2083

TAX....TAXING, TAXATION

N
THE JAPAN SCIENCE REVIEW: LAW AND POLITICS: LIST OF BIBLIOG
BOOKS AND ARTICLES ON LAW AND POLITICS. CONSTN AGRI LAW
INDUS LABOR DIPLOM TAX ADMIN CRIME...INT/LAW SOC 20 S/ASIA
CHINJAP. PAGE 1 B0025   PHIL/SCI

N
US SUPERINTENDENT OF DOCUMENTS,INTERSTATE COMMERCE   BIBLIOG/A
(PRICE LIST 59). USA+45 LAW LOC/G NAT/G LEGIS   DIST/IND
TARIFFS TAX ADMIN CONTROL HEALTH DECISION. PAGE 111 GOV/REL
B2239   PROVS

N
US SUPERINTENDENT OF DOCUMENTS,TARIFF AND TAXATION   BIBLIOG/A
(PRICE LIST 37). USA+45 LAW INT/TRADE ADJUD ADMIN   TAX
CT/SYS INCOME OWN...DECISION GATT. PAGE 111 B2242   TARIFFS
                                                     NAT/G

B28
CALKINS E.E.,BUSINESS THE CIVILIZER. INDUS MARKET   LAISSEZ
WORKER TAX PAY ROUTINE COST DEMAND MORAL 19/20.   POLICY
PAGE 18 B0367   WEALTH
                                                     PROFIT

B30
FAIRLIE J.A.,COUNTY GOVERNMENT AND ADMINISTRATION.   ADMIN
UK USA-45 NAT/G SCHOOL FORCES BUDGET TAX CT/SYS   GOV/REL
CHOOSE...JURID BIBLIOG 11/20. PAGE 35 B0701   LOC/G
                                                     MUNIC

B32
MCKISACK M.,THE PARLIAMENTARY REPRESENTATION OF THE NAT/G
ENGLISH BOROUGHS DURING THE MIDDLE AGES. UK CONSTN   MUNIC
CULTURE ELITES EX/STRUC TAX PAY ADJUD PARL/PROC   LEGIS
APPORT FEDERAL...POLICY 13/15 PARLIAMENT. PAGE 72   CHOOSE
B1454

B34
US TARIFF COMMISSION,THE TARIFF; A BIBLIOGRAPHY: A   BIBLIOG/A
SELECT LIST OF REFERENCES. USA-45 LAW DIPLOM TAX   TARIFFS
ADMIN...POLICY TREATY 20. PAGE 111 B2246   ECO/TAC

B35
GORER G.,AFRICA DANCES: A BOOK ABOUT WEST AFRICAN   AFR
NEGROES. STRUCT LOC/G SECT FORCES TAX ADMIN   ATTIT
COLONIAL...ART/METH MYTH WORSHIP 20 NEGRO AFRICA/W   CULTURE
CHRISTIAN RITUAL. PAGE 41 B0835   SOCIETY

B36
GRAVES W.B.,AMERICAN STATE GOVERNMENT. CONSTN FINAN NAT/G
EX/STRUC FORCES LEGIS BUDGET TAX CT/SYS REPRESENT   PROVS
GOV/REL...BIBLIOG/A 19/20. PAGE 42 B0855   ADMIN
                                                     FEDERAL

B40
WILCOX J.K.,MANUAL ON THE USE OF STATE   BIBLIOG/A
PUBLICATIONS. USA-45 FINAN LEGIS TAX GOV/REL   PROVS
...CHARTS 20. PAGE 116 B2346   ADMIN
                                                     LAW

B41
THE TAX FOUNDATION,STUDIES IN ECONOMY AND   BIBLIOG
EFFICIENCY IN GOVERNMENT. FINAN R+D OP/RES BUDGET   ADMIN
TAX 20. PAGE 104 B2095   EFFICIENCY
                                                     NAT/G

B49
SCHULTZ W.J.,AMERICAN PUBLIC FINANCE. USA+45   FINAN
ECO/TAC TAX ADMIN GOV/REL GP/REL INCOME 20. PAGE 94 POLICY
B1906   ECO/DEV
                                                     NAT/G

B51
ANDERSON W.,STATE AND LOCAL GOVERNMENT IN THE   LOC/G
UNITED STATES. USA+45 CONSTN POL/PAR EX/STRUC LEGIS MUNIC
BUDGET TAX ADJUD CT/SYS CHOOSE...CHARTS T 20.   PROVS
PAGE 5 B0100   GOV/REL

S52
SNIDER C.F.,"AMERICAN COUNTY GOVERNMENT: A MID-   LOC/G
CENTURY REVIEW" (BMR) USA+45 USA-45 PROVS DELIB/GP   ADMIN
EX/STRUC BUDGET TAX PWR 20. PAGE 98 B1988   GOV/REL
                                                     REGION

C52
LANCASTER L.W.,"GOVERNMENT IN RURAL AMERICA."   GOV/REL
USA+45 ECO/DEV AGRI SCHOOL FORCES LEGIS JUDGE   LOC/G
BUDGET TAX CT/SYS...CHARTS BIBLIOG. PAGE 62 B1253   MUNIC
                                                     ADMIN

B53
MILLIKAN M.F.,INCOME STABILIZATION FOR A DEVELOPING ANTHOL
DEMOCRACY. USA+45 ECO/DEV LABOR BUDGET ECO/TAC TAX   MARKET
ADMIN ADJUST PRODUC WEALTH...POLICY TREND 20.   EQUILIB
PAGE 73 B1484   EFFICIENCY
                                                     C54
CALDWELL L.K.,"THE GOVERNMENT AND ADMINISTRATION OF PROVS
NEW YORK." LOC/G MUNIC POL/PAR SCHOOL CHIEF LEGIS   ADMIN
PLAN TAX CT/SYS...MGT SOC/WK BIBLIOG 20 NEWYORK/C.   CONSTN
PAGE 18 B0366   EX/STRUC

B55
CUSHMAN R.E.,LEADING CONSTITUTIONAL DECISIONS.   CONSTN
USA+45 USA-45 NAT/G EX/STRUC LEGIS JUDGE TAX   PROB/SOLV
FEDERAL...DECISION 20 SUPREME/CT CASEBOOK. PAGE 25   JURID
B0513   CT/SYS

B55
JAPAN MOMBUSHO DAIGAKU GAKIYUT,BIBLIOGRAPHY OF THE   BIBLIOG
STUDIES ON LAW AND POLITICS (PAMPHLET). CONSTN   LAW
INDUS LABOR DIPLOM TAX ADMIN...CRIMLGY INT/LAW 20   PHIL/SCI
CHINJAP. PAGE 56 B1126

B55
SMITHIES A.,THE BUDGETARY PROCESS IN THE UNITED   NAT/G
STATES. ECO/DEV AGRI EX/STRUC FORCES LEGIS   ADMIN
PROB/SOLV TAX ROUTINE EFFICIENCY...MGT CONGRESS   BUDGET
PRESIDENT. PAGE 98 B1987   GOV/REL

B55
ZABEL O.H.,GOD AND CAESAR IN NEBRASKA: A STUDY OF   SECT
LEGAL RELATIONSHIP OF CHURCH AND STATE, 1854-1954.   PROVS
TAX GIVE ADMIN CONTROL GP/REL ROLE...GP/COMP 19/20   LAW
NEBRASKA. PAGE 119 B2396   EDU/PROP

B56
ABELS J.,THE TRUMAN SCANDALS. USA+45 USA-45 POL/PAR CRIME
TAX LEGIT CT/SYS CHOOSE PRIVIL MORAL WEALTH 20   ADMIN
TRUMAN/HS PRESIDENT CONGRESS. PAGE 3 B0052   CHIEF
                                                     TRIBUTE

S56
MARGOLIS J.,"ON MUNICIPAL LAND POLICY FOR FISCAL   BUDGET
GAINS." USA+45 MUNIC PLAN TAX COST EFFICIENCY   POLICY
HABITAT KNOWL...MGT 20. PAGE 69 B1398   GEOG
                                                     LOC/G

B58
GROSSMAN J.,BIBLIOGRAPHY ON PUBLIC ADMINISTRATION   BIBLIOG
IN LATIN AMERICA. ECO/UNDEV FINAN PLAN BUDGET   L/A+17C
ECO/TAC TARIFFS TAX...STAT 20. PAGE 44 B0893   NAT/G
                                                     ADMIN

B58
LOVEJOY D.S.,RHODE ISLAND POLITICS AND THE AMERICAN REV
REVOLUTION 1760-1776. UK USA+45 ELITES EX/STRUC TAX COLONIAL
LEAD REPRESENT GOV/REL GP/REL ATTIT 18 RHODE/ISL.   ECO/TAC
PAGE 67 B1343   SOVEREIGN
                                                     B58
SHAW S.J.,THE FINANCIAL AND ADMINISTRATIVE   FINAN
ORGANIZATION AND DEVELOPMENT OF OTTOMAN EGYPT   ADMIN
1517-1798. UAR LOC/G FORCES BUDGET INT/TRADE TAX   GOV/REL
EATING INCOME WEALTH...CHARTS BIBLIOG 16/18 OTTOMAN CULTURE
NAPOLEON/B. PAGE 96 B1940

B59
BHAMBHRI C.P.,SUBSTANCE OF HINDU POLITY. INDIA   GOV/REL
S/ASIA LAW EX/STRUC JUDGE TAX COERCE GP/REL   WRITING
POPULISM 20 HINDU. PAGE 11 B0234   SECT
                                                     PROVS

B59

COUNCIL OF STATE GOVERNMENTS,STATE GOVERNMENT: AN
ANNOTATED BIBLIOGRAPHY (PAMPHLET). USA+45 LAW AGRI
INDUS WORKER PLAN TAX ADJUST AGE/Y ORD/FREE...HEAL
MGT 20. PAGE 24 B0494

BIBLIOG/A
PROVS
LOC/G
ADMIN

B60

ARGAL R.,MUNICIPAL GOVERNMENT IN INDIA. INDIA
BUDGET TAX ADMIN EXEC 19/20. PAGE 6 B0126

LOC/G
MUNIC
DELIB/GP
CONTROL

B60

CRAUMER L.V.,BUSINESS PERIODICALS INDEX (8VOLS.).
USA+45 LABOR TAX 20. PAGE 25 B0503

BIBLIOG/A
FINAN
ECO/DEV
MGT

B60

HAYEK F.A.,THE CONSTITUTION OF LIBERTY. UNIV LAW
CONSTN WORKER TAX EDU/PROP ADMIN CT/SYS COERCE
DISCRIM...IDEA/COMP 20. PAGE 48 B0974

ORD/FREE
CHOOSE
NAT/G
CONCPT

B60

MATTOD P.K.,A STUDY OF LOCAL SELF GOVERNMENT IN
URBAN INDIA. INDIA FINAN DELIB/GP LEGIS BUDGET TAX
SOVEREIGN...MGT GP/COMP 20. PAGE 71 B1432

MUNIC
CONSTN
LOC/G
ADMIN

B61

BEASLEY K.E.,STATE SUPERVISION OF MUNICIPAL DEBT IN
KANSAS - A CASE STUDY. USA+45 USA-45 FINAN PROVS
BUDGET TAX ADJUD ADMIN CONTROL SUPEGO. PAGE 10
B0201

MUNIC
LOC/G
LEGIS
JURID

B61

BULLIS H.A.,MANIFESTO FOR AMERICANS. USA+45 AGRI
LABOR NAT/G NEIGH FOR/AID INT/TRADE TAX EDU/PROP
CHOOSE...POLICY MGT 20 UN UNESCO. PAGE 17 B0342

ECO/TAC
SOCIETY
INDUS
CAP/ISM

L61

GERWIG R.,"PUBLIC AUTHORITIES IN THE UNITED
STATES." LAW CONSTN PROVS TAX ADMIN FEDERAL.
PAGE 39 B0793

LOC/G
MUNIC
GOV/REL
PWR

B62

INST TRAINING MUNICIPAL ADMIN,MUNICIPAL FINANCE
ADMINISTRATION (6TH ED.). USA+45 ELITES ECO/DEV
LEGIS PLAN BUDGET TAX GP/REL BAL/PAY COST...POLICY
20 CITY/MGT. PAGE 54 B1089

MUNIC
ADMIN
FINAN
LOC/G

B62

WANGSNESS P.H.,THE POWER OF THE CITY MANAGER.
USA+45 EX/STRUC BAL/PWR BUDGET TAX ADMIN REPRESENT
CENTRAL EFFICIENCY DRIVE ROLE...POLICY 20 CITY/MGT.
PAGE 113 B2286

PWR
TOP/EX
MUNIC
LOC/G

L62

BELSHAW D.G.R.,"PUBLIC INVESTMENT IN AGRICULTURE
AND ECONOMIC DEVELOPMENT OF UGANDA" UGANDA AGRI
INDUS R+D ECO/TAC RATION TAX PAY COLONIAL 20
WORLD/BANK. PAGE 10 B0209

ECO/UNDEV
PLAN
ADMIN
CENTRAL

B63

BOCK E.A.,STATE AND LOCAL GOVERNMENT: A CASE BOOK.
USA+45 FINAN CHIEF PROB/SOLV TAX ATTIT...POLICY 20
CASEBOOK. PAGE 13 B0263

PROVS
LOC/G
ADMIN
GOV/REL

B63

CORLEY R.N.,THE LEGAL ENVIRONMENT OF BUSINESS.
CONSTN LEGIS TAX ADMIN CT/SYS DISCRIM ATTIT PWR
...TREND 18/20. PAGE 23 B0477

NAT/G
INDUS
JURID
DECISION

B63

DUE J.F.,STATE SALES TAX ADMINISTRATION. OP/RES
BUDGET PAY ADMIN EXEC ROUTINE COST EFFICIENCY
PROFIT...CHARTS METH/COMP 20. PAGE 31 B0626

PROVS
TAX
STAT
GOV/COMP

B63

HERMAN H.,NEW YORK STATE AND THE METROPOLITAN
PROBLEM. USA+45 ECO/DEV PUB/INST SCHOOL LEGIS PLAN
TAX EXEC PARL/PROC PARTIC...HEAL 20 NEW/YORK.
PAGE 49 B0992

GOV/REL
PROVS
LOC/G
POLICY

B63

KULZ H.R.,STAATSBURGER UND STAATSGEWALT (2 VOLS.).
GERMANY SWITZERLND UK USSR CONSTN DELIB/GP TARIFFS
TAX...JURID 20. PAGE 61 B1242

ADMIN
ADJUD
CT/SYS
NAT/COMP

B63

SINGH M.M.,MUNICIPAL GOVERNMENT IN THE CALCUTTA
METROPOLITAN DISTRICT A PRELIMINARY SURVEY. FINAN
LG/CO DELIB/GP BUDGET TAX ADMIN GP/REL 20 CALCUTTA.
PAGE 97 B1969

LOC/G
HEALTH
MUNIC
JURID

B63

UN SECRETARY GENERAL,PLANNING FOR ECONOMIC
DEVELOPMENT. ECO/UNDEV FINAN BUDGET INT/TRADE
TARIFFS TAX ADMIN 20 UN. PAGE 106 B2151

PLAN
ECO/TAC
MGT
NAT/COMP

B64

FONTENEAU J.,LE CONSEIL MUNICIPAL: LE MAIRE-LES
ADJOINTS. FRANCE FINAN DELIB/GP EX/STRUC BUDGET TAX
TASK COST INCOME ROLE SUPEGO 20 MAYOR. PAGE 36
B0735

MUNIC
NEIGH
ADMIN
TOP/EX

B64

KNOX V.H.,PUBLIC FINANCE: INFORMATION SOURCES.
USA+45 DIPLOM ADMIN GOV/REL COST...POLICY 20.
PAGE 60 B1221

BIBLIOG/A
FINAN
TAX
BUDGET

B64

NUQUIST A.E.,TOWN GOVERNMENT IN VERMONT. USA+45
FINAN TOP/EX PROB/SOLV BUDGET TAX REPRESENT SUFF
EFFICIENCY...OBS INT 20 VERMONT. PAGE 79 B1595

LOC/G
MUNIC
POPULISM
ADMIN

B64

POTTER D.C.,GOVERNMENT IN RURAL INDIA. INDIA LEGIT
INGP/REL EFFICIENCY ATTIT 20. PAGE 84 B1695

LOC/G
ADMIN
TAX
PROB/SOLV

B64

WEIDENBAUM M.L.,CONGRESS AND THE FEDERAL BUDGET:
FEDERAL BUDGETING AND THE RESPONSIBLE USE OF POWER.
LOC/G PLAN TAX CONGRESS. PAGE 114 B2309

LEGIS
EX/STRUC
BUDGET
ADMIN

B64

WELLISZ S.,THE ECONOMICS OF THE SOVIET BLOC. COM
USSR INDUS WORKER PLAN BUDGET INT/TRADE TAX PRICE
PRODUC WEALTH MARXISM...METH/COMP 20. PAGE 115
B2319

EFFICIENCY
ADMIN
MARKET

B64

WERNETTE J.P.,GOVERNMENT AND BUSINESS. LABOR
CAP/ISM ECO/TAC INT/TRADE TAX ADMIN AUTOMAT NUC/PWR
CIVMIL/REL DEMAND...MGT 20 MONOPOLY. PAGE 115 B2323

NAT/G
FINAN
ECO/DEV
CONTROL

B65

CHANDA A.,FEDERALISM IN INDIA. INDIA UK ELITES
FINAN NAT/G POL/PAR EX/STRUC LEGIS DIPLOM TAX
GOV/REL POPULISM...POLICY 20. PAGE 20 B0402

CONSTN
CENTRAL
FEDERAL

B65

COOPER F.E.,STATE ADMINISTRATIVE LAW (2 VOLS.). LAW
LEGIS PLAN TAX ADJUD CT/SYS FEDERAL PWR...CONCPT
20. PAGE 23 B0474

JURID
CONSTN
ADMIN
PROVS

B65

MUSHKIN S.J.,STATE PROGRAMMING. USA+45 PLAN BUDGET
TAX ADMIN REGION GOV/REL...BIBLIOG 20. PAGE 77
B1549

PROVS
POLICY
CREATE
ECO/DEV

B65

RHODES G.,PUBLIC SECTOR PENSIONS. UK FINAN LEGIS
BUDGET TAX PAY INCOME...CHARTS 20 CIVIL/SERV.
PAGE 88 B1769

ADMIN
RECEIVE
AGE/O
WORKER

B65

SNIDER C.F.,AMERICAN STATE AND LOCAL GOVERNMENT.
USA+45 FINAN CHIEF EX/STRUC TAX ADMIN CONTROL SUFF
INGP/REL PWR 20. PAGE 98 B1989

GOV/REL
MUNIC
PROVS
LOC/G

B66

DILLEY M.R.,BRITISH POLICY IN KENYA COLONY (2ND
ED.). AFR INDIA UK LABOR BUDGET TAX ADMIN PARL/PROC
GP/REL...BIBLIOG 20 PARLIAMENT. PAGE 29 B0594

COLONIAL
REPRESENT
SOVEREIGN

B66

NYC TEMPORARY COMM CITY FINAN,MUNICIPAL COLLECTIVE
BARGAINING (NO. 8). USA+45 PLAN PROB/SOLV BARGAIN
BUDGET TAX EDU/PROP GOV/REL COST...MGT 20
NEWYORK/C. PAGE 79 B1596

MUNIC
FINAN
ADMIN
LOC/G

B66

RAPHAEL J.S.,GOVERNMENTAL REGULATION OF BUSINESS.
USA+45 LAW CONSTN TAX ADJUD ADMIN EFFICIENCY PWR
20. PAGE 86 B1736

LG/CO
GOV/REL
CONTROL
ECO/DEV

C66

JACOB H.,"DIMENSIONS OF STATE POLITICS HEARD A. ED.
STATE LEGIWLATURES IN AMERICAN POLITICS." CULTURE
STRATA POL/PAR BUDGET TAX LOBBY ROUTINE GOV/REL
...TRADIT DECISION GEOG. PAGE 55 B1112

PROVS
LEGIS
ROLE
REPRESENT

B67

BULPITT J.G.,PARTY POLITICS IN ENGLISH LOCAL
GOVERNMENT. UK CONSTN ACT/RES TAX CONTROL CHOOSE
REPRESENT GOV/REL KNOWL 20. PAGE 17 B0344

POL/PAR
LOC/G
ELITES
EX/STRUC

B67

KONCZACKI Z.A.,PUBLIC FINANCE AND ECONOMIC
DEVELOPMENT OF NATAL 1893-1910. TAX ADMIN COLONIAL
...STAT CHARTS BIBLIOG 19/20 NATAL. PAGE 61 B1228

ECO/TAC
FINAN
NAT/G
ECO/UNDEV

S67

BRIMMER A.F.,"INITIATIVE AND INNOVATION IN CENTRAL
BANKING." USA+45 ECO/DEV MARKET ECO/TAC TAX CONTROL
DEMAND...MGT CHARTS FED/RESERV. PAGE 15 B0309

FINAN
CREATE
NAT/G
POLICY

S67

LINEBERRY R.L.,"REFORMISM AND PUBLIC POLICIES IN
AMERICAN CITIES." USA+45 POL/PAR EX/STRUC LEGIS
BUDGET TAX GP/REL...STAT CHARTS. PAGE 65 B1317

DECISION
POLICY
MUNIC
LOC/G

TAYLOR D. B2084

N
THE AMERICAN CITY. INDUS PROF/ORG PLAN GOV/REL ...MGT 20. PAGE 1 B0007 — BIBLIOG/A ADMIN TEC/DEV MUNIC

N
BULLETIN OF THE PUBLIC AFFAIRS INFORMATION SERVICE. WOR+45 WOR-45 ECO/UNDEV FINAN LABOR LOC/G PROVS TEC/DEV DIPLOM EDU/PROP SOC. PAGE 1 B0010 — BIBLIOG NAT/G ECO/DEV ADMIN

N
PRINCETON UNIVERSITY.SELECTED REFERENCES: INDUSTRIAL RELATIONS SECTION. USA+45 EX/STRUC WORKER TEC/DEV...MGT 20. PAGE 85 B1712 — BIBLIOG/A LABOR INDUS GP/REL

N19
ABERNATHY B.R..SOME PERSISTING QUESTIONS CONCERNING THE CONSTITUTIONAL STATE EXECUTIVE (PAMPHLET). CONSTN TOP/EX TEC/DEV GOV/REL EFFICIENCY TIME 20 GOVERNOR. PAGE 3 B0054 — PROVS EX/STRUC PROB/SOLV PWR

B37
GULICK L..PAPERS ON THE SCIENCE OF ADMINISTRATION. INDUS PROB/SOLV TEC/DEV COST EFFICIENCY PRODUC HABITAT...PHIL/SCI METH/COMP 20. PAGE 45 B0903 — OP/RES CONTROL ADMIN MGT

B38
HARPER S.N..THE GOVERNMENT OF THE SOVIET UNION. COM USSR LAW CONSTN ECO/DEV PLAN TEC/DEV DIPLOM INT/TRADE ADMIN REV NAT/LISM...POLICY 20. PAGE 47 B0952 — MARXISM NAT/G LEAD POL/PAR

B40
PFIFFNER J.M..RESEARCH METHODS IN PUBLIC ADMINISTRATION. USA-45 R+D...MGT STAT INT QU T 20. PAGE 82 B1665 — ADMIN OP/RES METH TEC/DEV

B41
LESTER R.A..ECONOMICS OF LABOR. UK USA-45 TEC/DEV BARGAIN PAY INGP/REL INCOME...MGT 19/20. PAGE 64 B1298 — LABOR ECO/DEV INDUS WORKER

B41
SLICHTER S.H..UNION POLICIES AND INDUSTRIAL MANAGEMENT. USA-45 INDUS TEC/DEV PAY GP/REL INGP/REL COST EFFICIENCY PRODUC...POLICY 20. PAGE 98 B1978 — BARGAIN LABOR MGT WORKER

S41
ABEL T.."THE ELEMENT OF DECISION IN THE PATTERN OF WAR." EUR+WWI FUT NAT/G TOP/EX DIPLOM ROUTINE COERCE DISPL PERCEPT PWR...SOC METH/CNCPT HIST/WRIT TREND GEN/LAWS 20. PAGE 2 B0051 — TEC/DEV FORCES WAR

B43
LEWIN E..ROYAL EMPIRE SOCIETY BIBLIOGRAPHIES NO. 9: SUB-SAHARA AFRICA. ECO/UNDEV TEC/DEV DIPLOM ADMIN COLONIAL LEAD 20. PAGE 64 B1303 — BIBLIOG AFR NAT/G SOCIETY

S44
GRIFFITH E.S.."THE CHANGING PATTERN OF PUBLIC POLICY FORMATION." MOD/EUR WOR+45 FINAN CHIEF CONFER ADMIN LEAD CONSERVE SOCISM TECHRACY...SOC CHARTS CONGRESS. PAGE 43 B0877 — LAW POLICY TEC/DEV

C45
MCDIARMID J.."THE MOBILIZATION OF SOCIAL SCIENTISTS," IN L. WHITE'S CIVIL CIVIL SERVICE IN WARTIME." USA-45 TEC/DEV CENTRAL...SOC 20 CIVIL/SERV. PAGE 72 B1447 — INTELL WAR DELIB/GP ADMIN

B46
WILCOX J.K..OFFICIAL DEFENSE PUBLICATIONS, 1941-1945 (NINE VOLS.). USA-45 AGRI INDUS R+D LABOR FORCES TEC/DEV EFFICIENCY PRODUC SKILL WEALTH 20. PAGE 116 B2347 — BIBLIOG/A WAR CIVMIL/REL ADMIN

B47
WHITEHEAD T.N..LEADERSHIP IN A FREE SOCIETY; A — INDUS

STUDY IN HUMAN RELATIONS BASED ON AN ANALYSIS OF PRESENT-DAY INDUSTRIAL CIVILIZATION. WOR-45 STRUCT R+D LABOR LG/CO SML/CO WORKER PLAN PROB/SOLV TEC/DEV DRIVE...MGT 20. PAGE 116 B2341 — LEAD ORD/FREE SOCIETY

B48
STEWART I..ORGANIZING SCIENTIFIC RESEARCH FOR WAR: ADMINISTRATIVE HISTORY OF OFFICE OF SCIENTIFIC RESEARCH AND DEVELOPMENT. USA-45 INTELL R+D LABOR WORKER CREATE BUDGET WEAPON CIVMIL/REL GP/REL EFFICIENCY...POLICY 20. PAGE 101 B2037 — DELIB/GP ADMIN WAR TEC/DEV

B49
BUSH V..MODERN ARMS AND FREE MEN. WOR-45 SOCIETY NAT/G ECO/TAC DOMIN LEGIT EXEC COERCE DETER ATTIT DRIVE ORD/FREE PWR...CONCPT MYTH COLD/WAR 20 COLD/WAR. PAGE 18 B0361 — TEC/DEV FORCES NUC/PWR WAR

B49
DE GRAZIA A..HUMAN RELATIONS IN PUBLIC ADMINISTRATION. INDUS ACT/RES CREATE PLAN PROB/SOLV TEC/DEV INGP/REL PERS/REL DRIVE...POLICY SOC 20. PAGE 27 B0552 — BIBLIOG/A ADMIN PHIL/SCI OP/RES

B49
SHISTER J..ECONOMICS OF THE LABOR MARKET. LOC/G NAT/G WORKER TEC/DEV BARGAIN PAY PRICE EXEC GP/REL INCOME...MGT T 20. PAGE 96 B1949 — MARKET LABOR INDUS

B50
DEES J.W. JR..URBAN SOCIOLOGY AND THE EMERGING ATOMIC MEGALOPOLIS, PART I. USA+45 TEC/DEV ADMIN NUC/PWR HABITAT...SOC AUD/VIS CHARTS GEN/LAWS 20 WATER. PAGE 28 B0568 — PLAN NEIGH MUNIC PROB/SOLV

B50
HARTLAND P.C..BALANCE OF INTERREGIONAL PAYMENTS OF NEW ENGLAND. USA+45 TEC/DEV ECO/TAC LEGIT ROUTINE BAL/PAY PROFIT 20 NEW/ENGLND FED/RESERV. PAGE 47 B0962 — ECO/DEV FINAN REGION PLAN

B50
MANNHEIM K..FREEDOM, POWER, AND DEMOCRATIC PLANNING. FUT USSR WOR+45 ELITES INTELL SOCIETY NAT/G EDU/PROP ROUTINE ATTIT DRIVE SUPEGO SKILL ...POLICY PSY CONCPT TREND GEN/LAWS 20. PAGE 69 B1393 — TEC/DEV PLAN CAP/ISM UK

B53
ROBINSON E.A.G..THE STRUCTURE OF COMPETITIVE INDUSTRY. UK ECO/DEV DIST/IND MARKET TEC/DEV DIPLOM EDU/PROP ADMIN EFFICIENCY WEALTH...MGT 19/20. PAGE 89 B1798 — INDUS PRODUC WORKER OPTIMAL

B54
COMBS C.H..DECISION PROCESSES. INTELL SOCIETY DELIB/GP CREATE TEC/DEV DOMIN LEGIT EXEC CHOOSE DRIVE RIGID/FLEX KNOWL PWR...PHIL/SCI SOC METH/CNCPT CONT/OBS REC/INT PERS/TEST SAMP/SIZ BIOG SOC/EXP WORK. PAGE 22 B0455 — MATH DECISION

B54
GOLDNER A.W..WILDCAT STRIKE. LABOR TEC/DEV PAY ADMIN LEAD PERS/REL ATTIT RIGID/FLEX PWR...MGT CONCPT. PAGE 40 B0816 — INDUS WORKER GP/REL SOC

B54
LOCKLIN D.P..ECONOMICS OF TRANSPORTATION (4TH ED.). USA+45 USA-45 SEA AIR LAW FINAN LG/CO EX/STRUC ADMIN CONTROL...STAT CHARTS 19/20 RAILROAD PUB/TRANS. PAGE 66 B1335 — ECO/DEV DIST/IND ECO/TAC TEC/DEV

B54
MCCLOSKEY J.F..OPERATIONS RESEARCH FOR MANAGEMENT. STRUCT COMPUTER ADMIN ROUTINE...PHIL/SCI CONCPT METH/CNCPT TREND ANTHOL BIBLIOG 20. PAGE 72 B1445 — OP/RES MGT METH/COMP TEC/DEV

B54
MOSK S.A..INDUSTRIAL REVOLUTION IN MEXICO. MARKET LABOR CREATE CAP/ISM ADMIN ATTIT SOCISM...POLICY 20 MEXIC/AMER. PAGE 76 B1533 — INDUS TEC/DEV ECO/UNDEV NAT/G

L54
ROSTOW W.W.."ASIAN LEADERSHIP AND FREE-WORLD ALLIANCE." ASIA COM USA+45 CULTURE ELITES INTELL NAT/G TEC/DEV ECO/TAC EDU/PROP COLONIAL PARL/PROC ROUTINE COERCE DRIVE ORD/FREE MARXISM...PSY CONCPT. PAGE 90 B1829 — ATTIT LEGIT DIPLOM

L55
KISER M.."ORGANIZATION OF AMERICAN STATES." L/A+17C USA+45 ECO/UNDEV INT/ORG NAT/G PLAN TEC/DEV DIPLOM ECO/TAC INT/TRADE EDU/PROP ADMIN ALL/VALS...POLICY MGT RECORD ORG/CHARTS OAS 20. PAGE 60 B1215 — VOL/ASSN ECO/DEV REGION

B56
UNITED NATIONS.BIBLIOGRAPHY ON INDUSTRIALIZATION IN UNDER-DEVELOPED COUNTRIES. WOR+45 R+D INT/ORG NAT/G FOR/AID ADMIN LEAD 20 UN. PAGE 107 B2161 — BIBLIOG ECO/UNDEV INDUS TEC/DEV

B57
SHARMA S.R..SOME ASPECTS OF THE INDIAN ADMINISTRATIVE SYSTEM. INDIA WOR+45 TEC/DEV BUDGET LEGIT ROUTINE ATTIT. PAGE 96 B1937 — EXEC DECISION ADMIN INGP/REL

B57
UDY S.H. JR..THE ORGANIZATION OF PRODUCTION IN NONINDUSTRIAL CULTURE. VOL/ASSN DELIB/GP TEC/DEV ...CHARTS BIBLIOG. PAGE 106 B2143 — METH/COMP ECO/UNDEV PRODUC

ATOMIC INDUSTRIAL FORUM,MANAGEMENT AND ATOMIC
ENERGY. WOR+45 SEA LAW MARKET NAT/G TEC/DEV INSPECT
INT/TRADE CONFER PEACE HEALTH...ANTHOL 20. PAGE 7
B0145

ADMIN
B58
NUC/PWR
INDUS
MGT
ECO/TAC

BRIGHT J.R.,AUTOMATION AND MANAGEMENT. INDUS LABOR
WORKER OP/RES TEC/DEV INSPECT 20. PAGE 15 B0307

B58
AUTOMAT
COMPUTER
PLAN
MGT

COLEMAN J.S.,NIGERIA: BACKGROUND TO NATIONALISM.
AFR SOCIETY ECO/DEV KIN LOC/G POL/PAR TEC/DEV DOMIN
ADMIN DRIVE PWR RESPECT...TRADIT SOC INT SAMP
TIME/SEQ 20. PAGE 22 B0452

B58
NAT/G
NAT/LISM
NIGERIA

MELMAN S.,DECISION-MAKING AND PRODUCTIVITY. INDUS
EX/STRUC WORKER OP/RES PROB/SOLV TEC/DEV ADMIN
ROUTINE RIGID/FLEX GP/COMP. PAGE 73 B1464

B58
LABOR
PRODUC
DECISION
MGT

US HOUSE COMM GOVT OPERATIONS,HEARINGS BEFORE A
SUBCOMMITTEE OF THE COMMITTEE ON GOVERNMENT
OPERATIONS. CAMBODIA PHILIPPINE USA+45 CONSTRUC
TEC/DEV ADMIN CONTROL WEAPON EFFICIENCY HOUSE/REP.
PAGE 108 B2189

B58
FOR/AID
DIPLOM
ORD/FREE
ECO/UNDEV

JANOWITZ M.,SOCIOLOGY AND THE MILITARY
ESTABLISHMENT. USA+45 WOR+45 CULTURE SOCIETY
PROF/ORG CONSULT EX/STRUC PLAN TEC/DEV DIPLOM DOMIN
COERCE DRIVE RIGID/FLEX ORD/FREE PWR SKILL COLD/WAR
20. PAGE 55 B1121

B59
FORCES
SOC

MAYDA J.,ATOMIC ENERGY AND LAW. ECO/UNDEV FINAN
TEC/DEV FOR/AID EFFICIENCY PRODUC WEALTH...POLICY
TECHNIC 20. PAGE 71 B1433

B59
NUC/PWR
L/A+17C
LAW
ADMIN

WASSERMAN P.,MEASUREMENT AND ANALYSIS OF
ORGANIZATIONAL PERFORMANCE. FINAN MARKET EX/STRUC
TEC/DEV EDU/PROP CONTROL ROUTINE TASK...MGT 20.
PAGE 114 B2300

B59
BIBLIOG/A
ECO/TAC
OP/RES
EFFICIENCY

HILSMAN R.,"THE FOREIGN-POLICY CONSENSUS: AN
INTERIM RESEARCH REPORT." USA+45 INT/ORG LEGIS
TEC/DEV EXEC WAR CONSEN KNOWL...DECISION COLD/WAR.
PAGE 50 B1013

S59
PROB/SOLV
NAT/G
DELIB/GP
DIPLOM

JANOWITZ M.,"CHANGING PATTERNS OF ORGANIZATIONAL
AUTHORITY: THE MILITARY ESTABLISHMENT" (BMR)"
USA+45 ELITES STRUCT EX/STRUC PLAN DOMIN AUTOMAT
NUC/PWR WEAPON 20. PAGE 55 B1122

S59
FORCES
AUTHORIT
ADMIN
TEC/DEV

ARROW K.J.,MATHEMATICAL METHODS IN THE SOCIAL
SCIENCES, 1959. TEC/DEV CHOOSE UTIL PERCEPT
...KNO/TEST GAME SIMUL ANTHOL. PAGE 7 B0137

B60
MATH
PSY
MGT

DRAPER T.,AMERICAN COMMUNISM AND SOVIET RUSSIA.
EUR+WWI USA+45 USSR INTELL AGRI COM/IND FINAN INDUS
LABOR PROF/ORG VOL/ASSN PLAN TEC/DEV DOMIN EDU/PROP
ADMIN COERCE REV PERSON PWR...POLICY CONCPT MYTH
19/20. PAGE 30 B0617

B60
COM
POL/PAR

KINGSTON-MCCLOUG E.,DEFENSE; POLICY AND STRATEGY.
UK SEA AIR TEC/DEV DIPLOM ADMIN LEAD WAR ORD/FREE
...CHARTS 20. PAGE 60 B1209

B60
FORCES
PLAN
POLICY
DECISION

LENCZOWSKI G.,OIL AND STATE IN THE MIDDLE EAST. FUT
IRAN LAW ECO/UNDEV EXTR/IND NAT/G TOP/EX PLAN
TEC/DEV ECO/TAC LEGIT ADMIN COERCE ATTIT ALL/VALS
PWR...CHARTS 20. PAGE 64 B1288

B60
ISLAM
INDUS
NAT/LISM

LINDVEIT E.N.,SCIENTISTS IN GOVERNMENT. USA+45 PAY
EDU/PROP ADMIN DRIVE HABITAT ROLE...TECHNIC BIBLIOG
20. PAGE 65 B1316

B60
TEC/DEV
ECO/TAC
PHIL/SCI
GOV/REL

MUNRO L.,UNITED NATIONS, HOPE FOR A DIVIDED WORLD.
FUT WOR+45 CONSTN DELIB/GP CREATE TEC/DEV DIPLOM
EDU/PROP LEGIT PEACE ATTIT HEALTH ORD/FREE PWR
...CONCPT TREND UN VAL/FREE 20. PAGE 76 B1540

B60
INT/ORG
ROUTINE

RAO V.K.R.,INTERNATIONAL AID FOR ECONOMIC
DEVELOPMENT - POSSIBILITIES AND LIMITATIONS. FINAN
PLAN TEC/DEV ADMIN TASK EFFICIENCY...POLICY SOC
METH/CNCPT CHARTS 20 UN. PAGE 86 B1734

B60
FOR/AID
DIPLOM
INT/ORG
ECO/UNDEV

WEBSTER J.A.,A GENERAL STUDY OF THE DEPARTMENT OF
DEFENSE INTERNAL SECURITY PROGRAM. USA+45 WORKER
TEC/DEV ADJUD CONTROL CT/SYS EXEC GOV/REL COST
...POLICY DECISION MGT 20 DEPT/DEFEN SUPREME/CT.
PAGE 114 B2307

B60
ORD/FREE
PLAN
ADMIN
NAT/G

MACPHERSON C.,"TECHNICAL CHANGE AND POLITICAL

L60
TEC/DEV

DECISION." WOR+45 NAT/G CREATE CAP/ISM DIPLOM
ROUTINE RIGID/FLEX...CONCPT OBS GEN/METH 20.
PAGE 68 B1375

ADMIN

EMERSON R.,"THE EROSION OF DEMOCRACY." AFR FUT LAW
CULTURE INTELL SOCIETY ECO/UNDEV FAM LOC/G NAT/G
FORCES PLAN TEC/DEV ECO/TAC ADMIN CT/SYS ATTIT
ORD/FREE PWR...SOCIALIST SOC CONCPT STAND/INT
TIME/SEQ WORK 20. PAGE 33 B0671

S60
S/ASIA
POL/PAR

FRANKEL S.H.,"ECONOMIC ASPECTS OF POLITICAL
INDEPENDENCE IN AFRICA." AFR FUT SOCIETY ECO/UNDEV
COM/IND FINAN LEGIS PLAN TEC/DEV CAP/ISM ECO/TAC
INT/TRADE ADMIN ATTIT DRIVE RIGID/FLEX PWR WEALTH
...MGT NEW/IDEA MATH TIME/SEQ VAL/FREE 20. PAGE 37
B0751

S60
NAT/G
FOR/AID

GARNICK D.H.,"ON THE ECONOMIC FEASIBILITY OF A
MIDDLE EASTERN COMMON MARKET." AFR ISLAM CULTURE
INDUS NAT/G PLAN TEC/DEV ECO/TAC ADMIN ATTIT DRIVE
RIGID/FLEX...PLURIST STAT TREND GEN/LAWS 20.
PAGE 39 B0784

S60
MARKET
INT/TRADE

GROSSMAN G.,"SOVIET GROWTH: ROUTINE, INERTIA, AND
PRESSURE." COM STRATA NAT/G DELIB/GP PLAN TEC/DEV
ECO/TAC EDU/PROP ADMIN ROUTINE DRIVE WEALTH
COLD/WAR 20. PAGE 44 B0891

S60
POL/PAR
ECO/DEV
USSR

HERZ J.H.,"EAST GERMANY: PROGRESS AND PROSPECTS."
COM AGRI FINAN INDUS LOC/G NAT/G FORCES PLAN
TEC/DEV DOMIN ADMIN COERCE DRIVE PERCEPT RIGID/FLEX
MORAL ORD/FREE PWR...MARXIST PSY SOC RECORD STERTYP
WORK. PAGE 49 B0997

S60
POL/PAR
STRUCT
GERMANY

HUTCHINSON C.E.,"AN INSTITUTE FOR NATIONAL SECURITY
AFFAIRS." USA+45 R+D NAT/G CONSULT TOP/EX ACT/RES
CREATE PLAN TEC/DEV EDU/PROP ROUTINE NUC/PWR ATTIT
ORD/FREE PWR...DECISION MGT PHIL/SCI CONCPT RECORD
GEN/LAWS GEN/METH 20. PAGE 53 B1068

S60
POLICY
METH/CNCPT
ELITES
DIPLOM

RAPHAELI N.,"SELECTED ARTICLES AND DOCUMENTS ON
COMPARATIVE PUBLIC ADMINISTRATION." USA+45 FINAN
LOC/G TOP/EX TEC/DEV EXEC GP/REL INGP/REL...GP/COMP
GOV/COMP METH/COMP. PAGE 86 B1738

S60
BIBLIOG
MGT
ADMIN
EX/STRUC

THOMPSON J.D.,"ORGANIZATIONAL MANAGEMENT OF
CONFLICT" (BMR)" WOR+45 STRUCT LABOR LG/CO WORKER
TEC/DEV INGP/REL ATTIT GP/COMP. PAGE 104 B2103

S60
PROB/SOLV
PERS/REL
ADMIN
MGT

BIRNBACH B.,NEO-FREUDIAN SOCIAL PHILOSOPHY. TEC/DEV
INGP/REL ADJUST HAPPINESS SUPEGO HEALTH...CONCPT
GEN/LAWS BIBLIOG 20. PAGE 12 B0242

B61
SOCIETY
PSY
PERSON
ADMIN

BRADY R.A.,ORGANIZATION, AUTOMATION, AND SOCIETY.
USA+45 AGRI COM/IND DIST/IND MARKET CREATE
...DECISION MGT 20. PAGE 14 B0296

B61
TEC/DEV
INDUS
AUTOMAT
ADMIN

GORDON W.J.J.,SYNECTICS; THE DEVELOPMENT OF
CREATIVE CAPACITY. USA+45 PLAN TEC/DEV KNOWL WEALTH
...DECISION MGT 20. PAGE 41 B0832

B61
CREATE
PROB/SOLV
ACT/RES
TOP/EX

JANOWITZ M.,COMMUNITY POLITICAL SYSTEMS. USA+45
SOCIETY INDUS VOL/ASSN TEC/DEV ADMIN LEAD CHOOSE
...SOC SOC/WK 20. PAGE 56 B1123

B61
MUNIC
STRUCT
POL/PAR

LAHAYE R.,LES ENTREPRISES PUBLIQUES AU MAROC.
FRANCE MOROCCO LAW DIST/IND EXTR/IND FINAN CONSULT
PLAN TEC/DEV ADMIN AGREE CONTROL OWN...POLICY 20.
PAGE 62 B1250

B61
NAT/G
INDUS
ECO/UNDEV
ECO/TAC

PAGE T.,STATE PERSONNEL REORGANIZATION IN ILLINOIS.
USA+45 POL/PAR CHIEF TEC/DEV LEAD ADJUST 20.
PAGE 80 B1625

B61
ADMIN
PROVS
WORKER
DELIB/GP

SHARP W.R.,FIELD ADMINISTRATION IN THE UNITED
NATION SYSTEM: THE CONDUCT OF INTERNATIONAL
ECONOMIC AND SOCIAL PROGRAMS. FUT WOR+45 CONSTN
SOCIETY ECO/UNDEV R+D DELIB/GP ACT/RES PLAN TEC/DEV
EDU/PROP EXEC ROUTINE HEALTH WEALTH...HUM CONCPT
CHARTS METH ILO UNESCO VAL/FREE UN 20. PAGE 96
B1939

B61
INT/ORG
CONSULT

US GENERAL ACCOUNTING OFFICE,EXAMINATION OF
ECONOMIC AND TECHNICAL ASSISTANCE PROGRAM FOR IRAN.
IRAN USA+45 AGRI INDUS DIPLOM CONTROL COST 20.
PAGE 108 B2186

B61
FOR/AID
ADMIN
TEC/DEV
ECO/UNDEV

WILLOUGHBY W.R.,THE ST LAWRENCE WATERWAY: A STUDY
IN POLITICS AND DIPLOMACY. USA+45 ECO/DEV COM/IND
INT/ORG CONSULT DELIB/GP ACT/RES TEC/DEV DIPLOM
ECO/TAC ROUTINE...TIME/SEQ 20. PAGE 117 B2357

B61
LEGIS
INT/TRADE
CANADA
DIST/IND

WILLSON F.M.G.,ADMINISTRATORS IN ACTION. UK MARKET TEC/DEV PARL/PROC 20. PAGE 117 B2358
ADMIN NAT/G CONSTN
B61

THOMPSON V.A.,"HIERARACHY, SPECIALIZATION, AND ORGANIZATIONAL CONFLICT. (BMR)" WOR+45 STRATA STRUCT WORKER TEC/DEV GP/REL INGP/REL ATTIT AUTHORIT 20 BUREAUCRCY. PAGE 104 B2106
PERS/REL PROB/SOLV ADMIN EX/STRUC
L61

BENNIS W.G.,"REVISIONIST THEORY OF LEADERSHIP" MUNIC ACT/RES TEC/DEV...SIMUL 20. PAGE 11 B0215
LEAD ADMIN PERS/REL HYPO/EXP
S61

GORDON L.,"ECONOMIC REGIONALISM RECONSIDERED." FUT USA+45 WOR+45 INDUS NAT/G TEC/DEV DIPLOM ROUTINE PERCEPT WEALTH...WELF/ST METH/CNCPT WORK 20. PAGE 41 B0830
ECO/DEV ATTIT CAP/ISM REGION
S61

CAIRNCROSS A.K.,FACTORS IN ECONOMIC DEVELOPMENT. WOR+45 ECO/UNDEV INDUS R+D LG/CO NAT/G EX/STRUC PLAN TEC/DEV ECO/TAC ATTIT HEALTH KNOWL PWR WEALTH ...TIME/SEQ GEN/LAWS TOT/POP VAL/FREE 20. PAGE 18 B0363
MARKET ECO/DEV
B62

FRIEDMANN W.,METHODS AND POLICIES OF PRINCIPAL DONOR COUNTRIES IN PUBLIC INTERNATIONAL DEVELOPMENT FINANCING: PRELIMINARY APPRAISAL. FRANCE GERMANY/W UK USA+45 USSR WOR+45 FINAN TEC/DEV CAP/ISM DIPLOM ECO/TAC ATTIT 20 EEC. PAGE 37 B0759
INT/ORG FOR/AID NAT/COMP ADMIN
B62

GRANICK D.,THE EUROPEAN EXECUTIVE. BELGIUM FRANCE GERMANY/W UK INDUS LABOR LG/CO SML/CO EX/STRUC PLAN TEC/DEV CAP/ISM COST DEMAND...POLICY CHARTS 20. PAGE 42 B0852
MGT ECO/DEV ECO/TAC EXEC
B62

HARARI M.,GOVERNMENT AND POLITICS OF THE MIDDLE EAST. ISLAM USA+45 NAT/G SECT CHIEF ADMIN ORD/FREE 20. PAGE 47 B0943
DIPLOM ECO/UNDEV TEC/DEV POLICY
B62

HATTERY L.H.,INFORMATION RETRIEVAL MANAGEMENT. CLIENT INDUS TOP/EX COMPUTER OP/RES TEC/DEV ROUTINE COST EFFICIENCY RIGID/FLEX...METH/COMP ANTHOL 20. PAGE 48 B0968
R+D COMPUT/IR MGT CREATE
B62

KENNEDY J.F.,TO TURN THE TIDE. SPACE AGRI INT/ORG FORCES TEC/DEV ADMIN NUC/PWR PEACE WEALTH...ANTHOL 20 KENNEDY/JF CIV/RIGHTS. PAGE 59 B1193
DIPLOM CHIEF POLICY NAT/G
B62

MUNICIPAL MANPOWER COMMISSION,GOVERNMENTAL MANPOWER FOR TOMORROW'S CITIES: A REPORT. USA+45 DELIB/GP EX/STRUC PROB/SOLV TEC/DEV EDU/PROP ADMIN LEAD HABITAT. PAGE 76 B1539
LOC/G MUNIC LABOR GOV/REL
B62

NATIONAL BUREAU ECONOMIC RES,THE RATE AND DIRECTION OF INVENTIVE ACTIVITY: ECONOMIC AND SOCIAL FACTORS. STRUCT INDUS MARKET R+D CREATE OP/RES TEC/DEV EFFICIENCY PRODUC RATIONAL UTIL...WELF/ST PHIL/SCI METH/CNCPT TIME. PAGE 77 B1562
DECISION PROB/SOLV MGT
B62

NEW ZEALAND COMM OF ST SERVICE,THE STATE SERVICES IN NEW ZEALAND. NEW/ZEALND CONSULT EX/STRUC ACT/RES ...BIBLIOG 20. PAGE 78 B1577
ADMIN WORKER TEC/DEV NAT/G
B62

SNYDER R.C.,FOREIGN POLICY DECISION-MAKING. FUT KOREA WOR+45 R+D CREATE ADMIN ROUTINE PWR ...DECISION PSY SOC CONCPT METH/CNCPT CON/ANAL CHARTS GEN/METH METH 20. PAGE 99 B1992
TEC/DEV HYPO/EXP DIPLOM
B62

UNECA LIBRARY,NEW ACQUISITIONS IN THE UNECA LIBRARY. LAW NAT/G PLAN PROB/SOLV TEC/DEV ADMIN REGION...GEOG SOC 20 UN. PAGE 106 B2152
BIBLIOG AFR ECO/UNDEV INT/ORG
B62

US SENATE COMM GOVT OPERATIONS,ADMINISTRATION OF NATIONAL SECURITY. USA+45 CHIEF PLAN PROB/SOLV TEC/DEV DIPLOM ATTIT...POLICY DECISION 20 KENNEDY/JF RUSK/D MCNAMARA/R BUNDY/M HERTER/C. PAGE 110 B2212
ORD/FREE ADMIN NAT/G CONTROL
B62

US SENATE COMM ON JUDICIARY,STATE DEPARTMENT SECURITY. USA+45 CHIEF DOMIN ADMIN EXEC ATTIT ORD/FREE...POLICY CONGRESS DEPT/STATE PRESIDENT KENNEDY/JF KENNEDY/JF SENATE 20. PAGE 110 B2228
CONTROL WORKER NAT/G GOV/REL
B62

ALBONETTI A.,"IL SECONDO PROGRAMMA QUINQUENNALE 1963-67 ED IL BILANCIO RICERCHE ED INVESTIMENTI PER IL 1963 DELL'ERATOM." EUR+WWI FUT ITALY WOR+45 ECO/DEV SERV/IND INT/ORG TEC/DEV ECO/TAC ATTIT SKILL WEALTH...MGT TIME/SEQ OEEC 20. PAGE 3 B0069
R+D PLAN NUC/PWR
S62

NORTH R.C.,"DECISION MAKING IN CRISIS: AN INTRODUCTION." WOR+45 WOR-45 NAT/G CONSULT DELIB/GP TEC/DEV PERCEPT KNOWL...POLICY DECISION PSY METH/CNCPT CONT/OBS TREND VAL/FREE 20. PAGE 79 B1590
INT/ORG ROUTINE DIPLOM
S62

SCHILLING W.R.,"SCIENTISTS, FOREIGN POLICY AND POLITICS." WOR+45 WOR-45 INTELL INT/ORG CONSULT TOP/EX ACT/RES PLAN ADMIN KNOWL...CONCPT OBS TREND LEAGUE/NAT 20. PAGE 93 B1889
NAT/G TEC/DEV DIPLOM NUC/PWR
S62

CONF ON FUTURE OF COMMONWEALTH,THE FUTURE OF THE COMMONWEALTH. UK ECO/UNDEV AGRI EDU/PROP ADMIN SOC/INTEG 20 COMMONWLTH. PAGE 23 B0460
DIPLOM RACE/REL ORD/FREE TEC/DEV
B63

DALAND R.T.,PERSPECTIVES OF BRAZILIAN PUBLIC ADMINISTRATION (VOL. I). BRAZIL LAW ECO/UNDEV SCHOOL CHIEF TEC/DEV CONFER CONTROL GP/REL ATTIT ROLE PWR...ANTHOL 20. PAGE 26 B0525
ADMIN NAT/G PLAN GOV/REL
B63

HAUSMAN W.H.,MANAGING ECONOMIC DEVELOPMENT IN AFRICA. AFR USA+45 LAW FINAN WORKER TEC/DEV WEALTH ...ANTHOL 20. PAGE 48 B0970
ECO/UNDEV PLAN FOR/AID MGT
B63

HEARLE E.F.R.,A DATA PROCESSING SYSTEM FOR STATE AND LOCAL GOVERNMENTS. PLAN TEC/DEV AUTOMAT ROUTINE ...MGT METH/CNCPT CLASSIF 20. PAGE 49 B0984
LOC/G PROVS COMPUTER COMPUT/IR
B63

HEYEL C.,THE ENCYCLOPEDIA OF MANAGEMENT. WOR+45 MARKET TOP/EX TEC/DEV AUTOMAT LEAD ADJUST...STAT CHARTS GAME ANTHOL BIBLIOG. PAGE 49 B1002
MGT INDUS ADMIN FINAN
B63

INDIAN INSTITUTE PUBLIC ADMIN,CASES IN INDIAN ADMINISTRATION. INDIA AGRI NAT/G PROB/SOLV TEC/DEV ECO/TAC ADMIN...ANTHOL METH 20. PAGE 53 B1083
DECISION PLAN MGT ECO/UNDEV
B63

KAST F.E.,SCIENCE, TECHNOLOGY, AND MANAGEMENT. SPACE USA+45 FORCES CONFER DETER NUC/PWR...PHIL/SCI CHARTS ANTHOL BIBLIOG 20 NASA. PAGE 58 B1179
MGT INDUS TEC/DEV PROB/SOLV
B63

KORNHAUSER W.,SCIENTISTS IN INDUSTRY: CONFLICT AND ACCOMMODATION. USA+45 R+D LG/CO NAT/G TEC/DEV CONTROL ADJUST ATTIT...MGT STAT INT BIBLIOG 20. PAGE 61 B1229
CREATE INDUS PROF/ORG GP/REL
B63

NASA,CONFERENCE ON SPACE, SCIENCE, AND URBAN LIFE. USA+45 SOCIETY INDUS ACADEM ACT/RES ECO/TAC ADMIN 20. PAGE 77 B1556
MUNIC SPACE TEC/DEV PROB/SOLV
B63

NORTH R.C.,CONTENT ANALYSIS: A HANDBOOK WITH APPLICATIONS FOR THE STUDY OF INTERNATIONAL CRISIS. ASIA COM EUR+WWI MOD/EUR INT/ORG TEC/DEV DOMIN EDU/PROP ROUTINE COERCE PERCEPT RIGID/FLEX ALL/VALS ...QUANT TESTS CON/ANAL SIMUL GEN/LAWS VAL/FREE. PAGE 79 B1591
METH/CNCPT COMPUT/IR USSR
B63

RUITENBEER H.M.,THE DILEMMA OF ORGANIZATIONAL SOCIETY. CULTURE ECO/DEV MUNIC SECT TEC/DEV EDU/PROP NAT/LISM ORD/FREE...NAT/COMP 20 RIESMAN/D WHYTE/WF MERTON/R MEAD/MARG JASPERS/K. PAGE 92 B1855
PERSON ROLE ADMIN WORKER
B63

SCHRADER R.,SCIENCE AND POLICY. WOR+45 ECO/DEV ECO/UNDEV R+D FORCES PLAN DIPLOM GOV/REL TECHRACY BIBLIOG. PAGE 94 B1900
TEC/DEV NAT/G POLICY ADMIN
B63

VAN SLYCK P.,PEACE: THE CONTROL OF NATIONAL POWER. CUBA WOR+45 FINAN NAT/G FORCES PROB/SOLV TEC/DEV BAL/PWR ADMIN CONTROL ORD/FREE...POLICY INT/LAW UN COLD/WAR TREATY. PAGE 112 B2253
ARMS/CONT PEACE INT/ORG DIPLOM
B63

WEINER M.,POLITICAL CHANGE IN SOUTH ASIA. CEYLON INDIA PAKISTAN S/ASIA CULTURE ELITES ECO/UNDEV EX/STRUC ADMIN CONTROL CHOOSE CONSERVE...GOV/COMP ANTHOL 20. PAGE 115 B2315
NAT/G CONSTN TEC/DEV
B63

CLEMHOUT S.,"PRODUCTION FUNCTION ANALYSIS APPLIED TO THE LEONTIEF SCARCE-FACTOR PARADOX OF INTERNATIONAL TRADE." EUR+WWI USA+45 DIST/IND NAT/G PLAN TEC/DEV DIPLOM PWR WEALTH...MGT METH/CNCPT CONT/OBS CON/ANAL CHARTS SIMUL GEN/LAWS 20. PAGE 21 B0436
ECO/DEV ECO/TAC
S63

DAVEE R.,"POUR UN FONDS DE DEVELOPPEMENT SOCIAL." FUT WOR+45 INTELL SOCIETY ECO/DEV FINAN TEC/DEV ROUTINE WEALTH...TREND TOT/POP VAL/FREE UN 20. PAGE 26 B0532
INT/ORG SOC FOR/AID
S63

DUCROS B.."MOBILISATION DES RESSOURCES PRODUCTIVES
ET DEVELOPPEMENT." FUT INTELL SOCIETY COM/IND
DIST/IND EXTR/IND FINAN INDUS ROUTINE WEALTH
...METH/CNCPT OBS 20. PAGE 31 B0625
ECO/UNDEV
TEC/DEV
S63

ETIENNE G.."'LOIS OBJECTIVES' ET PROBLEMES DE
DEVELOPPEMENT DANS LE CONTEXTE CHINE-URSS." ASIA
CHINA/COM COM FUT STRUCT INT/ORG VOL/ASSN TOP/EX
TEC/DEV ECO/TAC ATTIT RIGID/FLEX...GEOG MGT
TIME/SEQ TOT/POP 20. PAGE 34 B0682
TOTALISM
USSR
S63

MASSART L.."L'ORGANISATION DE LA RECHERCHE
SCIENTIFIQUE EN EUROPE." EUR+WWI WOR+45 ACT/RES
PLAN TEC/DEV EDU/PROP EXEC KNOWL...METH/CNCPT EEC
20. PAGE 70 B1424
R+D
CREATE
S63

NADLER E.B.."SOME ECONOMIC DISADVANTAGES OF THE
ARMS RACE." USA+45 INDUS R+D FORCES PLAN TEC/DEV
ECO/TAC FOR/AID EDU/PROP PWR WEALTH...TREND
COLD/WAR 20. PAGE 77 B1552
ECO/DEV
MGT
BAL/PAY
S63

ROUGEMONT D.."LES NOUVELLES CHANCES DE L'EUROPE."
EUR+WWI FUT INT/ORG ACT/RES PLAN TEC/DEV EDU/PROP
ADMIN COLONIAL FEDERAL ATTIT PWR SKILL...TREND 20.
PAGE 91 B1835
ECO/UNDEV
PERCEPT
S63

SCHMITT H.A.."THE EUROPEAN COMMUNITIES." EUR+WWI
FRANCE DELIB/GP EX/STRUC TOP/EX CREATE TEC/DEV
ECO/TAC LEGIT REGION COERCE DRIVE ALL/VALS
...METH/CNCPT EEC 20. PAGE 94 B1897
VOL/ASSN
ECO/DEV
S63

INTERNATIONAL CITY MGRS ASSN,POST-ENTRY TRAINING IN
THE LOCAL PUBLIC SERVICE (PAMPHLET). SCHOOL PLAN
PROB/SOLV TEC/DEV ADMIN EFFICIENCY SKILL...POLICY
AUD/VIS CHARTS BIBLIOG 20 CITY/MGT. PAGE 54 B1096
LOC/G
WORKER
EDU/PROP
METH/COMP
N63

APTER D.E..IDEOLOGY AND DISCONTENT. FUT WOR+45
CONSTN CULTURE INTELL SOCIETY STRUCT INT/ORG NAT/G
DELIB/GP LEGIS CREATE PLAN TEC/DEV EDU/PROP EXEC
PERCEPT PERSON RIGID/FLEX ALL/VALS...POLICY
TOT/POP. PAGE 6 B0122
ACT/RES
ATTIT
B64

BRIGHT J.R..RESEARCH, DEVELOPMENT AND TECHNOLOGICAL
INNOVATION. CULTURE R+D CREATE PLAN PROB/SOLV
AUTOMAT RISK PERSON...DECISION CONCPT PREDICT
BIBLIOG. PAGE 15 B0308
TEC/DEV
NEW/IDEA
INDUS
MGT
B64

HERSKOVITS M.J..ECONOMIC TRANSITION IN AFRICA. FUT
INT/ORG NAT/G WORKER PROB/SOLV TEC/DEV INT/TRADE
EQUILIB INCOME...ANTHOL 20. PAGE 49 B0996
AFR
ECO/UNDEV
PLAN
ADMIN
B64

HODGETTS J.E..ADMINISTERING THE ATOM FOR PEACE.
OP/RES TEC/DEV ADMIN...IDEA/COMP METH/COMP 20.
PAGE 50 B1025
PROB/SOLV
NUC/PWR
PEACE
MGT
B64

LI C.M..INDUSTRIAL DEVELOPMENT IN COMMUNIST CHINA.
CHINA/COM ECO/DEV ECO/UNDEV AGRI FINAN INDUS MARKET
LABOR NAT/G ECO/TAC INT/TRADE EXEC ALL/VALS
...POLICY RELATIV TREND WORK TOT/POP VAL/FREE 20.
PAGE 65 B1311
ASIA
TEC/DEV
B64

LITTLE I.M.D..AID TO AFRICA. AFR UK TEC/DEV DIPLOM
ECO/TAC INCOME WEALTH 20. PAGE 66 B1326
FOR/AID
ECO/UNDEV
ADMIN
POLICY
B64

PARET P..FRENCH REVOLUTIONARY WARFARE FROM
INDOCHINA TO ALGERIA* THE ANALYSIS OF A POLITICAL
AND MILITARY DOCTRINE. ALGERIA VIETNAM FORCES
OP/RES TEC/DEV ROUTINE REV ATTIT...PSY BIBLIOG.
PAGE 81 B1632
FRANCE
GUERRILLA
GEN/LAWS
B64

RIGGS F.W..ADMINISTRATION IN DEVELOPING COUNTRIES.
FUT WOR+45 STRUCT AGRI INDUS NAT/G PLAN TEC/DEV
ECO/TAC EDU/PROP RIGID/FLEX KNOWL WEALTH...POLICY
MGT CONCPT METH/CNCPT TREND 20. PAGE 88 B1785
ECO/UNDEV
ADMIN
B64

WHEELER-BENNETT J.W..THE NEMESIS OF POWER (2ND
ED.). EUR+WWI GERMANY TOP/EX TEC/DEV ADMIN WAR
PERS/REL RIGID/FLEX ROLE ORD/FREE PWR FASCISM 20
HITLER/A. PAGE 116 B2332
FORCES
NAT/G
GP/REL
STRUCT
B64

FLORINSKY M.T.."TRENDS IN THE SOVIET ECONOMY." COM
USA+45 USSR INDUS LABOR NAT/G PLAN TEC/DEV ECO/TAC
ALL/VALS SOCISM...MGT METH/CNCPT STYLE CON/ANAL
GEN/METH WORK 20. PAGE 36 B0731
ECO/DEV
AGRI
S64

HUELIN D.."ECONOMIC INTEGRATION IN LATIN AMERICAN:
PROGRESS AND PROBLEMS." L/A+17C ECO/DEV AGRI
DIST/IND INDUS NAT/G VOL/ASSN CONSULT
DELIB/GP EX/STRUC ACT/RES PLAN TEC/DEV ECO/TAC
ROUTINE BAL/PAY WEALTH WORK 20. PAGE 52 B1058
MARKET
ECO/UNDEV
INT/TRADE
S64

LOW D.A.."LION RAMPANT." EUR+WWI MOD/EUR S/ASIA
ECO/UNDEV NAT/G FORCES TEC/DEV ECO/TAC LEGIT ADMIN
COLONIAL COERCE ORD/FREE RESPECT 19/20. PAGE 67
B1344
AFR
DOMIN
DIPLOM
UK
S64

NASH M.."SOCIAL PREREQUISITES TO ECONOMIC GROWTH IN
LATIN AMERICA AND SOUTHEAST ASIA." L/A+17C S/ASIA
CULTURE SOCIETY ECO/UNDEV AGRI INDUS NAT/G PLAN
TEC/DEV EDU/PROP ROUTINE ALL/VALS...POLICY RELATIV
SOC NAT/COMP WORK TOT/POP 20. PAGE 77 B1558
ECO/DEV
PERCEPT
S64

NEEDHAM T.."SCIENCE AND SOCIETY IN EAST AND WEST."
INTELL STRATA R+D LOC/G NAT/G PROVS CONSULT ACT/RES
CREATE PLAN TEC/DEV EDU/PROP ADMIN ATTIT ALL/VALS
...POLICY RELATIV MGT CONCPT NEW/IDEA TIME/SEQ WORK
WORK. PAGE 77 B1565
ASIA
STRUCT
S64

ALDERSON W..DYNAMIC MARKETING BEHAVIOR. USA+45
FINAN CREATE TEC/DEV EDU/PROP PRICE COST 20. PAGE 3
B0071
MGT
MARKET
ATTIT
CAP/ISM
B65

BARISH N.N..MANAGEMENT SCIENCES IN THE EMERGING
COUNTRIES. AFR CHINA/COM FINAN INDUS PLAN PRODUC
HABITAT...ANTHOL 20. PAGE 9 B0184
ECO/UNDEV
OP/RES
MGT
TEC/DEV
B65

EVERETT R.O..URBAN PROBLEMS AND PROSPECTS. USA+45
CREATE TEC/DEV EDU/PROP ADJUD ADMIN GOV/REL ATTIT
...ANTHOL 20 URBAN/RNWL. PAGE 34 B0691
MUNIC
PLAN
PROB/SOLV
NEIGH
B65

INT. BANK RECONSTR. DEVELOP..ECONOMIC DEVELOPMENT
OF KUWAIT. ISLAM KUWAIT AGRI FINAN MARKET EX/STRUC
TEC/DEV ECO/TAC ADMIN WEALTH...OBS CON/ANAL CHARTS
20. PAGE 54 B1092
INDUS
NAT/G
B65

KASER M..COMECON* INTEGRATION PROBLEMS OF THE
PLANNED ECONOMIES. INT/ORG TEC/DEV INT/TRADE PRICE
ADMIN ADJUST CENTRAL...STAT TIME/SEQ ORG/CHARTS
COMECON. PAGE 58 B1177
PLAN
ECO/DEV
COM
REGION
B65

LUTZ V..FRENCH PLANNING. FRANCE TEC/DEV RIGID/FLEX
ORD/FREE 20. PAGE 67 B1348
PLAN
ADMIN
FUT
B65

LYONS G.M..SCHOOLS FOR STRATEGY* EDUCATION AND
RESEARCH IN NATIONAL SECURITY AFFAIRS. USA+45 FINAN
NAT/G VOL/ASSN FORCES TEC/DEV ADMIN WAR...GP/COMP
IDEA/COMP PERS/COMP COLD/WAR. PAGE 67 B1351
ACADEM
ACT/RES
INTELL
B65

MOORE W.E..THE IMPACT OF INDUSTRY. CULTURE STRUCT
ORD/FREE...TREND 20. PAGE 75 B1516
INDUS
MGT
TEC/DEV
ECO/UNDEV
B65

PENNICK JL J.R..THE POLITICS OF AMERICAN SCIENCE,
1939 TO THE PRESENT. USA+45 USA-45 INTELL TEC/DEV
DIPLOM NEW/LIB...ANTHOL 20 COLD/WAR. PAGE 82 B1651
POLICY
ADMIN
PHIL/SCI
NAT/G
B65

STEINER G.A..THE CREATIVE ORGANIZATION. ELITES
LG/CO PLAN PROB/SOLV TEC/DEV INSPECT CAP/ISM
CONTROL EXEC PERSON...METH/COMP HYPO/EXP 20.
PAGE 100 B2029
CREATE
MGT
ADMIN
SOC
B65

WHITE J..GERMAN AID. GERMANY/W FINAN PLAN TEC/DEV
INT/TRADE ADMIN ATTIT...POLICY 20. PAGE 116 B2334
FOR/AID
ECO/UNDEV
DIPLOM
ECO/TAC
L65

WILLIAMS S.."NEGOTIATING INVESTMENT IN EMERGING
COUNTRIES." USA+45 WOR+45 INDUS MARKET NAT/G TOP/EX
TEC/DEV CAP/ISM ECC/TAC ADMIN SKILL WEALTH...POLICY
RELATIV MGT WORK 20. PAGE 117 B2353
FINAN
ECO/UNDEV
S65

ALEXANDER T.."SYNECTICS: INVENTING BY THE MADNESS
METHOD." DELIB/GP TOP/EX ACT/RES TEC/DEV EXEC TASK
KNOWL...MGT METH/COMP 20. PAGE 4 B0073
PROB/SOLV
OP/RES
CREATE
CONSULT
S65

RAPHAELI N.."SELECTED ARTICLES AND DOCUMENTS ON
COMPARATIVE PUBLIC ADMINISTRATION." USA+45 FINAN
LOC/G WORKER TEC/DEV CONTROL LEAD...SOC/WK GOV/COMP
METH/COMP. PAGE 86 B1739
BIBLIOG
ADMIN
NAT/G
MGT
B66

HAYER T..FRENCH AID. AFR FRANCE AGRI FINAN BUDGET
ADMIN WAR PRODUC...CHARTS 18/20 THIRD/WRLD
OVRSEA/DEV. PAGE 48 B0975
TEC/DEV
COLONIAL
FOR/AID
ECO/UNDEV
B66

KURAKOV I.G..SCIENCE, TECHNOLOGY AND COMMUNISM;
SOME QUESTIONS OF DEVELOPMENT (TRANS. BY CARIN
DEDIJER). USSR INDUS PLAN PROB/SOLV COST PRODUC
...MGT MATH CHARTS METH 20. PAGE 61 B1243
CREATE
TEC/DEV
MARXISM
ECO/TAC

MACFARQUHAR R.,CHINA UNDER MAO: POLITICS TAKES COMMAND. CHINA/COM COM AGRI INDUS CHIEF FORCES DIPLOM INT/TRADE EDU/PROP TASK REV ADJUST...ANTHOL 20 MAO. PAGE 67 B1359 — ECO/UNDEV TEC/DEV ECO/TAC ADMIN — B66

MURDOCK J.C.,RESEARCH AND REGIONS. AGRI FINAN INDUS LOC/G MUNIC NAT/G PROB/SOLV TEC/DEV ADMIN REGION 20. PAGE 76 B1545 — BIBLIOG FCO/DEV COMPUT/IR R+D — B66

NIEBURG H.L.,IN THE NAME OF SCIENCE. USA+45 EX/STRUC LEGIS TEC/DEV BUDGET PAY AUTOMAT LOBBY PWR ...OBS 20. PAGE 78 B1581 — NAT/G INDUS TECHRACY — B66

ONYEMELUKWE C.C.,PROBLEMS OF INDUSTRIAL PLANNING AND MANAGEMENT IN NIGERIA. AFR FINAN LABOR DELIB/GP TEC/DEV ADJUST...MGT TREND BIBLIOG. PAGE 80 B1610 — ECO/UNDEV ECO/TAC INDUS PLAN — B66

SMITH H.E.,READINGS IN ECONOMIC DEVELOPMENT AND ADMINISTRATION IN TANZANIA. TANZANIA FINAN INDUS LABOR NAT/G PLAN PROB/SOLV INT/TRADE COLONIAL REGION...ANTHOL BIBLIOG 20 AFRICA/E. PAGE 98 B1981 — TEC/DEV ADMIN GOV/REL — B66

US SENATE COMM GOVT OPERATIONS,INTERGOVERNMENTAL PERSONNEL ACT OF 1966. USA+45 NAT/G CONSULT DELIB/GP WORKER TEC/DEV PAY AUTOMAT UTIL 20 CONGRESS. PAGE 110 B2219 — ADMIN LEGIS EFFICIENCY EDU/PROP — B66

WESTON J.F.,THE SCOPE AND METHODOLOGY OF FINANCE. PLAN TEC/DEV CONTROL EFFICIENCY INCOME UTIL...MGT CONCPT MATH STAT TREND METH 20. PAGE 115 B2327 — FINAN ECO/DEV POLICY PRICE — B66

WHITNAH D.R.,SAFER SKYWAYS. DIST/IND DELIB/GP FORCES TOP/EX WORKER TEC/DEV ROUTINE WAR CIVMIL/REL COST...TIME/SEQ 20 FAA CAB. PAGE 116 B2342 — ADMIN NAT/G AIR GOV/REL — B66

WYLIE C.M.,RESEARCH IN PUBLIC HEALTH ADMINISTRATION: SELECTED RECENT ABSTRACTS IV (PAMPHLET). USA+45 MUNIC PUB/INST ACT/RES CREATE OP/RES TEC/DEV GP/REL ROLE...MGT PHIL/SCI STAT. PAGE 118 B2387 — BIBLIOG/A R+D HEAL ADMIN — B66

ZINKIN T.,CHALLENGES IN INDIA. INDIA PAKISTAN LAW AGRI FINAN INDUS TOP/EX TEC/DEV CONTROL ROUTINE ORD/FREE PWR 20 NEHRU/J SHASTRI/LB CIVIL/SERV. PAGE 119 B2404 — NAT/G ECO/TAC POLICY ADMIN — B66

"FURTHER READING." INDIA LOC/G NAT/G PLAN ADMIN WEALTH...GEOG SOC CONCPT CENSUS 20. PAGE 2 B0045 — BIBLIOG ECO/UNDEV TEC/DEV PROVS — S66

AFRICAN BIBLIOGRAPHIC CENTER,"A CURRENT VIEW OF AFRICANA: A SELECT AND ANNOTATED BIBLIOGRAPHICAL PUBLISHING GUIDE, 1965-1966." AFR CULTURE INDUS LABOR SECT FOR/AID ADMIN COLONIAL REV RACE/REL SOCISM...LING 20. PAGE 3 B0063 — BIBLIOG/A NAT/G TEC/DEV POL/PAR — S66

DIEBOLD J.,"COMPUTERS, PROGRAM MANAGEMENT AND FOREIGN AFFAIRS." USA+45 INDUS OP/RES TEC/DEV...MGT GP/COMP GEN/LAWS. PAGE 29 B0590 — COMPUTER DIPLOM ROUTINE ACT/RES — S66

HANSON A.H.,"PLANNING AND THE POLITICIANS* SOME REFLECTIONS ON ECONOMIC PLANNING IN WESTERN EUROPE." MARKET NAT/G TEC/DEV CONSEN ROLE ...METH/COMP NAT/COMP. PAGE 46 B0942 — PLAN ECO/DEV EUR+WWI ADMIN — S66

BENNETT J.W.,HUTTERIAN BRETHREN; THE AGRICULTURAL ECONOMY AND SOCIAL ORGANIZATION OF A COMMUNAL PEOPLE. USA+45 SOCIETY FAM KIN TEC/DEV ADJUST...MGT AUD/VIS GP/COMP 20. PAGE 10 B0213 — SECT AGRI STRUCT GP/REL — B67

DICKSON P.G.M.,THE FINANCIAL REVOLUTION IN ENGLAND. UK NAT/G TEC/DEV ADMIN GOV/REL...SOC METH/CNCPT CHARTS GP/COMP BIBLIOG 17/18. PAGE 29 B0587 — ECO/DEV FINAN CAP/ISM MGT — B67

DUN J.L.,THE ESSENCE OF CHINESE CIVILIZATION. ASIA FAM NAT/G TEC/DEV ADMIN SANCTION WAR HABITAT ...ANTHOL WORSHIP. PAGE 31 B0630 — CULTURE SOCIETY — B67

GROSSMAN G.,ECONOMIC SYSTEMS. USA+45 USA-45 USSR YUGOSLAVIA WORKER CAP/ISM PRICE GP/REL EQUILIB WEALTH MARXISM SOCISM...MGT METH/COMP 19/20. PAGE 44 B0892 — ECO/DEV PLAN TEC/DEV DEMAND — B67

MINTZ M.,BY PRESCRIPTION ONLY. USA+45 NAT/G EX/STRUC PLAN TEC/DEV EXEC EFFICIENCY HEALTH...MGT SOC/WK 20. PAGE 74 B1491 — BIO/SOC PROC/MFG CONTROL POLICY — B67

NORTHRUP H.R.,RESTRICTIVE LABOR PRACTICES IN THE SUPERMARKET INDUSTRY. USA+45 INDUS WORKER TEC/DEV BARGAIN PAY CONTROL GP/REL COST...STAT CHARTS NLRB. PAGE 79 B1592 — DIST/IND MARKET LABOR MGT — B67

OVERSEAS DEVELOPMENT INSTIT,EFFECTIVE AID. WOR+45 INT/ORG TEC/DEV DIPLOM INT/TRADE ADMIN. PAGE 80 B1619 — FOR/AID ECO/UNDEV ECO/TAC NAT/COMP — B67

ROTHENBERG J.,ECONOMIC EVALUATION OF URBAN RENEWAL: CONCEPTUAL FOUNDATION OF BENEFIT-COST ANALYSIS. USA+45 ECO/DEV NEIGH TEC/DEV ADMIN GEN/LAWS. PAGE 91 B1834 — PLAN MUNIC PROB/SOLV COST — B67

SCHAEFER W.V.,THE SUSPECT AND SOCIETY: CRIMINAL PROCEDURE AND CONVERGING CONSTITUTIONAL DOCTRINES. USA+45 TEC/DEV LOBBY ROUTINE SANCTION...INT 20. PAGE 93 B1879 — CRIME FORCES CONSTN JURID — B67

SCHUMACHER B.G.,COMPUTER DYNAMICS IN PUBLIC ADMINISTRATION. USA+45 CREATE PLAN TEC/DEV...MGT LING CON/ANAL BIBLIOG/A 20. PAGE 94 B1907 — COMPUTER COMPUT/IR ADMIN AUTOMAT — B67

TANSKY L.,US AND USSR AID TO DEVELOPING COUNTRIES. INDIA TURKEY UAR USA+45 USSR FINAN PLAN TEC/DEV ADMIN WEALTH...TREND METH/COMP 20. PAGE 103 B2076 — FOR/AID ECO/UNDEV MARXISM CAP/ISM — B67

UNITED NATIONS,UNITED NATIONS PUBLICATIONS: 1945-1966. WOR+45 COM/IND DIST/IND FINAN TEC/DEV ADMIN...POLICY INT/LAW MGT CHARTS 20 UN UNESCO. PAGE 107 B2162 — BIBLIOG/A INT/ORG DIPLOM WRITING — B67

UNIVERSAL REFERENCE SYSTEM,PUBLIC POLICY AND THE MANAGEMENT OF SCIENCE (VOLUME IX). FUT SPACE WOR+45 LAW NAT/G TEC/DEV CONTROL NUC/PWR GOV/REL ...COMPUT/IR GEN/METH. PAGE 107 B2165 — BIBLIOG/A POLICY MGT PHIL/SCI — B67

ZONDAG C.H.,THE BOLIVIAN ECONOMY 1952-65. L/A+17C TEC/DEV FOR/AID ADMIN...OBS TREND CHARTS BIBLIOG 20 BOLIV. PAGE 119 B2406 — ECO/UNDEV INDUS PRODUC — B67

BAUM R.D.,"IDEOLOGY REDIVIVUS." CHINA/COM NAT/G EDU/PROP ADMIN 20. PAGE 10 B0197 — REV MARXISM CREATE TEC/DEV — S67

BERLINER J.S.,"RUSSIA'S BUREAUCRATS - WHY THEY'RE REACTIONARY." USSR NAT/G OP/RES PROB/SOLV TEC/DEV CONTROL SANCTION EFFICIENCY DRIVE PERSON...TECHNIC SOC 20. PAGE 11 B0223 — CREATE ADMIN INDUS PRODUC — S67

BRADY R.H.,"COMPUTERS IN TOP-LEVEL DECISION MAKING" FUT WOR+45 CONTROL...PREDICT CHARTS. PAGE 15 B0297 — COMPUTER MGT DECISION TEC/DEV — S67

BURACK E.H.,"INDUSTRIAL MANAGEMENT IN ADVANCED PRODUCTION SYSTEMS: SOME THEORETICAL CONCEPTS AND PRELIMINARY FINDINGS." INDUS CREATE PLAN PRODUC ROLE...OBS STAND/INT DEEP/QU HYPO/EXP ORG/CHARTS 20. PAGE 17 B0346 — ADMIN MGT TEC/DEV EX/STRUC — S67

GOBER J.L.,"FEDERALISM AT WORK." USA+45 NAT/G CONSULT ACT/RES PLAN CONFER ADMIN LEAD PARTIC FEDERAL ATTIT. PAGE 40 B0813 — MUNIC TEC/DEV R+D GOV/REL — S67

GOLIGHTLY H.O.,"THE AIRLINES: A CASE STUDY IN MANAGEMENT INNOVATION." USA+45 AIR FINAN INDUS TOP/EX CREATE PLAN PROB/SOLV ADMIN EXEC PROFIT ...DECISION 20. PAGE 40 B0820 — DIST/IND MARKET MGT TEC/DEV — S67

KAYSEN C.,"DATA BANKS AND DOSSIERS." FUT USA+45 COM/IND NAT/G PLAN PROB/SOLV TEC/DEV BUDGET ADMIN ROUTINE. PAGE 59 B1185 — CENTRAL EFFICIENCY CENSUS ACT/RES — S67

LA PORTE T.,"DIFFUSION AND DISCONTINUITY IN SCIENCE, TECHNOLOGY AND PUBLIC AFFAIRS: RESULTS OF A SEARCH IN THE FIELD." USA+45 ACT/RES TEC/DEV PERS/REL ATTIT PHIL/SCI. PAGE 62 B1249 — INTELL ADMIN ACADEM GP/REL — S67

MACDONALD G.J.F.,"SCIENCE AND SPACE POLICY* HOW DOES IT GET PLANNED?" R+D CREATE TEC/DEV BUDGET ADMIN ROUTINE...DECISION NASA. PAGE 67 B1357 — SPACE PLAN MGT EX/STRUC — S67

MOOR E.J.,"THE INTERNATIONAL IMPACT OF AUTOMATION." WOR+45 ACT/RES COMPUTER CREATE PLAN CAP/ISM ROUTINE EFFICIENCY PREDICT. PAGE 75 B1511 — TEC/DEV OP/RES AUTOMAT INDUS — S67

MORTON J.A.,"A SYSTEMS APPROACH TO THE INNOVATION PROCESS: ITS USE IN THE BELL SYSTEM." USA+45 INTELL INDUS LG/CO CONSULT WORKER COMPUTER AUTOMAT DEMAND ...MGT CHARTS 20. PAGE 76 B1531
S67
TEC/DEV
GEN/METH
R+D
COM/IND

PRATT R.C.,"THE ADMINISTRATION OF ECONOMIC PLANNING IN A NEWLY INDEPEND ENT STATE* THE TANZANIAN EXPERIENCE 1963-1966." AFR TANZANIA ECO/UNDEV PLAN CONTROL ROUTINE TASK EFFICIENCY 20. PAGE 84 B1699
S67
NAT/G
DELIB/GP
ADMIN
TEC/DEV

ROSENZWEIG J.E.,"MANAGERS AND MANAGEMENT SCIENTISTS (TWO CULTURES)" INDUS CREATE TEC/DEV OPTIMAL ...NEW/IDEA 20. PAGE 90 B1823
S67
EFFICIENCY
MGT
INTELL
METH/COMP

SHOEMAKER R.L.,"JAPANESE ARMY AND THE WEST." ASIA ELITES EX/STRUC DIPLOM DOMIN EDU/PROP COERCE ATTIT AUTHORIT PWR 1/20 CHINJAP. PAGE 96 B1950
S67
FORCES
TEC/DEV
WAR
TOTALISM

SKOLNIKOFF E.B.,"MAKING FOREIGN POLICY" PROB/SOLV EFFICIENCY PERCEPT PWR...MGT METH/CNCPT CLASSIF 20. PAGE 98 B1976
S67
TEC/DEV
CONTROL
USA+45
NAT/G

VERGIN R.C.,"COMPUTER INDUCED ORGANIZATION CHANGES." FUT USA+45 R+D CREATE OP/RES TEC/DEV ADJUST CENTRAL...MGT INT CON/ANAL COMPUT/IR. PAGE 112 B2260
S67
COMPUTER
DECISION
AUTOMAT
EX/STRUC

WINTHROP H.,"THE MEANING OF DECENTRALIZATION FOR TWENTIETH-CENTURY MAN." FUT WOR+45 SOCIETY TEC/DEV. PAGE 117 B2366
S67
ADMIN
STRUCT
CENTRAL
PROB/SOLV

US SUPERINTENDENT OF DOCUMENTS,SPACE: MISSILES, THE MOON, NASA, AND SATELLITES (PRICE LIST 79A). USA+45 COM/IND R+D NAT/G DIPLOM EDU/PROP ADMIN CONTROL HEALTH...POLICY SIMUL NASA CONGRESS. PAGE 111 B2244
N67
BIBLIOG/A
SPACE
TEC/DEV
PEACE

TECHNIC....TECHNOCRATIC

RIDLEY C.E.,THE CITY-MANAGER PROFESSION. CHIEF PLAN ADMIN CONTROL ROUTINE CHOOSE...TECHNIC CHARTS GOV/COMP BIBLIOG 20. PAGE 88 B1780
B34
MUNIC
EX/STRUC
LOC/G
EXEC

ROSENFARB J.,FREEDOM AND THE ADMINISTRATIVE STATE. NAT/G ROUTINE EFFICIENCY PRODUC RATIONAL UTIL ...TECHNIC WELF/ST MGT 20 BUREAUCRCY. PAGE 90 B1821
B48
ECO/DEV
INDUS
PLAN
WEALTH

MAYDA J.,ATOMIC ENERGY AND LAW. ECO/UNDEV FINAN TEC/DEV FOR/AID EFFICIENCY PRODUC WEALTH...POLICY TECHNIC 20. PAGE 71 B1433
B59
NUC/PWR
L/A+17C
LAW
ADMIN

LINDVEIT E.N.,SCIENTISTS IN GOVERNMENT. USA+45 PAY EDU/PROP ADMIN DRIVE HABITAT ROLE...TECHNIC BIBLIOG 20. PAGE 65 B1316
B60
TEC/DEV
ECO/TAC
PHIL/SCI
GOV/REL

STAHL O.G.,PUBLIC PERSONNEL ADMINISTRATION. LOC/G TOP/EX CREATE PLAN ROUTINE...TECHNIC MGT T. PAGE 100 B2017
B62
ADMIN
WORKER
EX/STRUC
NAT/G

DIEBOLD J.,BEYOND AUTOMATION: MANAGERIAL PROBLEMS OF AN EXPLODING TECHNOLOGY. SOCIETY ECO/DEV CREATE ECO/TAC AUTOMAT SKILL...TECHNIC MGT WORK. PAGE 29 B0589
B64
FUT
INDUS
PROVS
NAT/G

GARFIELD PJ   LOVEJOY WF,PUBLIC UTILITY ECONOMICS. DIST/IND FINAN MARKET MUNIC ADMIN COST DEMAND...TECHNIC JURID 20 MONOPOLY. PAGE 39 B0782
B64
T
ECO/TAC
OWN
SERV/IND

BERLINER J.S.,"RUSSIA'S BUREAUCRATS - WHY THEY'RE REACTIONARY." USSR NAT/G OP/RES PROB/SOLV TEC/DEV CONTROL SANCTION EFFICIENCY DRIVE PERSON...TECHNIC SOC 20. PAGE 11 B0223
S67
CREATE
ADMIN
INDUS
PRODUC

TECHNIQUES....SEE TEC/DEV, METHODOLOGICAL INDEXES, PP. XIII-XIV

TECHNOCRACY....SEE TECHRACY, TECHNIC

TECHNOLOGY....SEE COMPUTER, TECHNIC, TEC/DEV

TECHRACY....SOCIO-POLITICAL ORDER DOMINATED BY TECHNICIANS

JONES V.,METROPOLITAN GOVERNMENT. HABITAT ALL/VALS ...MGT SOC CHARTS. PAGE 57 B1151
B42
LOC/G
MUNIC

ADMIN
TECHRACY
S44
GRIFFITH E.S.,"THE CHANGING PATTERN OF PUBLIC POLICY FORMATION." MOD/EUR WOR+45 FINAN CHIEF CONFER ADMIN LEAD CONSERVE SOCISM TECHRACY...SOC CHARTS CONGRESS. PAGE 43 B0877
LAW
POLICY
TEC/DEV

QURESHI S.,INCENTIVES IN AMERICAN EMPLOYMENT (THESIS, UNIVERSITY OF PENNSYLVANIA). DELIB/GP TOP/EX BUDGET ROUTINE SANCTION COST TECHRACY MGT. PAGE 85 B1727
B61
SERV/IND
ADMIN
PAY
EX/STRUC

SCHRADER R.,SCIENCE AND POLICY. WOR+45 ECO/DEV ECO/UNDEV R+D FORCES PLAN DIPLOM GOV/REL TECHRACY BIBLIOG. PAGE 94 B1900
B63
TEC/DEV
NAT/G
POLICY
ADMIN

NIEBURG H.L.,IN THE NAME OF SCIENCE. USA+45 EX/STRUC LEGIS TEC/DEV BUDGET PAY AUTOMAT LOBBY PWR ...OBS 20. PAGE 78 B1581
B66
NAT/G
INDUS
TECHRACY

TEHERAN....TEHERAN CONFERENCE

TEMPERANCE....TEMPERANCE MOVEMENTS

TEMPLE J.Y. B1815

TENNESSEE VALLEY AUTHORITY....SEE TVA

TENNESSEE....TENNESSEE

SHERIDAN R.G.,URBAN JUSTICE. USA+45 PROVS CREATE ADMIN CT/SYS ORD/FREE 20 TENNESSEE. PAGE 96 B1943
B64
LOC/G
JURID
ADJUD
MUNIC

GREENE L.E.,GOVERNMENT IN TENNESSEE (2ND ED.). USA+45 DIST/IND INDUS POL/PAR EX/STRUC LEGIS PLAN BUDGET GIVE CT/SYS...MGT T 20. TENNESSEE. PAGE 43 B0866
B66
PROVS
LOC/G
CONSTN
ADMIN

TERRELL/G....GLENN TERRELL

TERRIEN F.W. B2091

TERRY V. OHIO....SEE TERRY

TERRY....TERRY V. OHIO

TESTS....THEORY AND USES OF TESTS AND SCALES; SEE ALSO TESTS AND SCALES INDEX, P. XIV

BROWN A.D.,LIST OF REFERENCES ON THE CIVIL SERVICE AND PERSONNEL ADMINISTRATION IN THE UNITED STATES (2ND MIMEOGRAPHED SUPPLEMENT). USA-45 LOC/G POL/PAR PROVS FEDERAL...TESTS 20. PAGE 16 B0319
B42
BIBLIOG
ADMIN
MGT
NAT/G

BENJAMIN H.C.,EMPLOYMENT TESTS IN INDUSTRY AND BUSINESS. LG/CO WORKER ROUTINE...MGT PSY SOC CLASSIF PROBABIL STAT APT/TEST KNO/TEST PERS/TEST 20. PAGE 10 B0211
B45
BIBLIOG/A
METH
TESTS
INDUS

CRONBACK L.J.,PSYCHOLOGICAL TESTS AND PERSONNEL DECISIONS. OP/RES PROB/SOLV CHOOSE PERSON...PSY STAT TESTS 20. PAGE 25 B0508
B57
MATH
DECISION
WORKER
MGT

HAVILAND H.F.,"FOREIGN AID AND THE POLICY PROCESS: 1957." USA+45 FACE/GP POL/PAR VOL/ASSN CHIEF DELIB/GP ACT/RES LEGIT EXEC GOV/REL ATTIT DRIVE PWR ...POLICY TESTS CONGRESS 20. PAGE 48 B0971
L58
LEGIS
PLAN
FOR/AID

FRANKE W.,THE REFORM AND ABOLITION OF THE TRADITIONAL CHINESE EXAMINATION SYSTEM. ASIA STRUCT 19/20 CIVIL/SERV. PAGE 37 B0750
B60
ADJUST
ADMIN
TESTS
STRATA

PADOVER S.K.,"PSYCHOLOGICAL WARFARE AND FOREIGN POLICY." FUT UNIV USA+45 INTELL SOCIETY CREATE EDU/PROP ADMIN WAR PEACE PERCEPT...POLICY METH/CNCPT TESTS TIME/SEQ 20. PAGE 80 B1623
S61
ROUTINE
DIPLOM

TANNENBAUM A.S.,"CONTROL AND EFFECTIVENESS IN A VOLUNTARY ORGANIZATION." USA+45 ADMIN...CORREL MATH REGRESS STAT TESTS SAMP/SIZ CHARTS SOC/EXP INDEX 20 LEAGUE/WV. PAGE 102 B2072
S61
EFFICIENCY
VOL/ASSN
CONTROL
INGP/REL

ARCO EDITORIAL BOARD,PUBLIC MANAGEMENT AND ADMINISTRATION. PLAN BUDGET WRITING CONTROL ROUTINE ...TESTS CHARTS METH T 20. PAGE 6 B0125
B62
MGT
ADMIN
NAT/G
LOC/G

NORTH R.C.,CONTENT ANALYSIS: A HANDBOOK WITH
B63
METH/CNCPT

APPLICATIONS FOR THE STUDY OF INTERNATIONAL CRISIS. COMPUT/IR
ASIA COM EUR+WWI MOD/EUR INT/ORG TEC/DEV DOMIN   USSR
EDU/PROP ROUTINE COERCE PERCEPT RIGID/FLEX ALL/VALS
...QUANT TESTS CON/ANAL SIMUL GEN/LAWS VAL/FREE.
PAGE 79 B1591

B64
COOMBS C.H.,A THEORY OF DATA....MGT PHIL/SCI SOC   CON/ANAL
CLASSIF MATH PROBABIL STAT QU. PAGE 23 B0472   GEN/METH
                                                    TESTS
                                                    PSY

TEXAS....TEXAS

B40
PATTERSON C.P.,STATE AND LOCAL GOVERNMENT IN TEXAS CONSTN
(3RD ED.). USA-45 EX/STRUC LEGIS CT/SYS CHOOSE 20   PROVS
TEXAS. PAGE 81 B1642   GOV/REL
                                                    LOC/G

THAILAND....THAILAND; SEE ALSO S/ASIA

B58
MASON J.B.,THAILAND BIBLIOGRAPHY. S/ASIA THAILAND   BIBLIOG/A
CULTURE EDU/PROP ADMIN...GEOG SOC LING 20. PAGE 70 ECO/UNDEV
B1423   DIPLOM
                                                    NAT/G
                                                    B58
SKINNER G.W.,LEADERSHIP AND POWER IN THE CHINESE   SOC
COMMUNITY OF THAILAND. ASIA S/ASIA STRATA FACE/GP   ELITES
KIN PROF/ORG VOL/ASSN EX/STRUC DOMIN PERSON RESPECT THAILAND
...METH/CNCPT STAT INT QU BIOG CHARTS 20. PAGE 98
B1974

B59
THARAMATHAJ C.,A STUDY OF THE COMPOSITION OF THE   ADMIN
THAI CIVIL SERVICE (PAPER). THAILAND PAY ROLE   EX/STRUC
...CHARTS 20 CIVIL/SERV FEMALE/SEX. PAGE 103 B2092 STRATA
                                                    INGP/REL
                                                    B62
KARNJAHAPRAKORN C.,MUNICIPAL GOVERNMENT IN THAILAND LOC/G
AS AN INSTITUTION AND PROCESS OF SELF-GOVERNMENT.   MUNIC
THAILAND CULTURE FINAN EX/STRUC LEGIS PLAN CONTROL ORD/FREE
GOV/REL EFFICIENCY ATTIT...POLICY 20. PAGE 58 B1176 ADMIN
                                                    B66
UN ECAFE,ADMINISTRATIVE ASPECTS OF FAMILY PLANNING PLAN
PROGRAMMES (PAMPHLET). ASIA THAILAND WOR+45   CENSUS
VOL/ASSN PROB/SOLV BUDGET FOR/AID EDU/PROP CONFER   FAM
CONTROL GOV/REL TIME 20 UN BIRTH/CON. PAGE 106   ADMIN
B2147
                                                    C66
TARLING N.,"A CONCISE HISTORY OF SOUTHEAST ASIA."   COLONIAL
BURMA CAMBODIA LAOS S/ASIA THAILAND VIETNAM   DOMIN
ECO/UNDEV POL/PAR FORCES ADMIN REV WAR CIVMIL/REL   INT/TRADE
ORD/FREE MARXISM SOCISM 13/20. PAGE 103 B2080   NAT/LISM
                                                    S67
NEUCHTERLEIN D.E.,"THAILAND* ANOTHER VIETNAM?"   WAR
THAILAND ECO/UNDEV DIPLOM ADMIN REGION CENTRAL   GUERRILLA
NAT/LISM...POLICY 20. PAGE 78 B1571   S/ASIA
                                                    NAT/G

THARAMATHAJ C. B2092

THAYER L.O. B2093

THE BRITISH COUNCIL B2094

THE TAX FOUNDATION B2095

THERAPY....SEE SPECIFICS, SUCH AS PROJ/TEST, DEEP/INT,
     SOC/EXP; ALSO SEE DIFFERENT VALUES (E.G., LOVE) AND
     TOPICAL TERMS (E.G., PRESS)

THIERRY S.S. B2096

THING/STOR....ARTIFACTS AND MATERIAL EVIDENCE

THIRD/WRLD....THIRD WORLD - NONALIGNED NATIONS

B66
HAYER T.,FRENCH AID. AFR FRANCE AGRI FINAN BUDGET   TEC/DEV
ADMIN WAR PRODUC...CHARTS 18/20 THIRD/WRLD   COLONIAL
OVRSEA/DEV. PAGE 48 B0975   FOR/AID
                                                    ECO/UNDEV

THOENES P. B2097

THOMAS F. B2098

THOMAS F.C. B2099

THOMAS S.B. B2100

THOMAS/FA....F.A. THOMAS

THOMAS/N....NORMAN THOMAS

B38
SALTER J.T.,THE AMERICAN POLITICIAN. USA-45 LABOR   BIOG
POL/PAR EDU/PROP ADMIN CHOOSE ATTIT DRIVE PERSON   LEAD
PWR...POLICY ANTHOL 20 THOMAS/N LEWIS/JL LAGUARD/F PROVS
GOVERNOR MAYOR. PAGE 92 B1865   LOC/G

THOMAS/TK....TREVOR K. THOMAS

THOMETZ C.E. B2101

THOMPSON H.C. B2102

THOMPSON J.D. B2103

THOMPSON K.W. B2104

THOMPSON R.G. B1331

THOMPSON V.A. B2105,B2106,B2107

THORBECKE E. B0746

THOREAU/H....HENRY THOREAU

THORELLI H.B. B2108

THORNTN/WT....WILLIAM T. THORNTON

THORNTON M.L. B2109

THRALL R.M. B0455

THUCYDIDES....THUCYDIDES

THUILLIER G. B0393

THUMM G.W. B1852

THURSTON/L....LOUIS LEON THURSTONE

TIBET....TIBET; SEE ALSO ASIA, CHINA

TILLICH/P....PAUL TILLICH

TILMAN R.O. B2110

TIME (AS CONCEPT)....SEE CONCPT

TIME....TIMING, TIME FACTOR; SEE ALSO ANALYSIS OF TEMPORAL
     SEQUENCES INDEX, P. XIV

N19
ABERNATHY B.R.,SOME PERSISTING QUESTIONS CONCERNING PROVS
THE CONSTITUTIONAL STATE EXECUTIVE (PAMPHLET).   EX/STRUC
CONSTN TOP/EX TEC/DEV GOV/REL EFFICIENCY TIME 20   PROB/SOLV
GOVERNOR. PAGE 3 B0054   PWR
                                                    B47
MILLETT J.D.,THE PROCESS AND ORGANIZATION OF   ADMIN
GOVERNMENT PLANNING. USA+45 DELIB/GP ACT/RES LEAD   NAT/G
LOBBY TASK...POLICY GEOG TIME 20 RESOURCE/N.   PLAN
PAGE 73 B1482   CONSULT
                                                    B57
PARKINSON C.N.,PARKINSON'S LAW. UNIV EX/STRUC PLAN ADMIN
ATTIT PERSON TIME. PAGE 81 B1634   EXEC
                                                    FINAN
                                                    ECOMETRIC
                                                    S59
SIMPSON R.L.,"VERTICAL AND HORIZONTAL COMMUNICATION PERS/REL
IN FORMAL ORGANIZATION" USA+45 LG/CO EX/STRUC DOMIN AUTOMAT
CONTROL TASK INGP/REL TIME 20. PAGE 97 B1963   INDUS
                                                    WORKER
                                                    B62
NATIONAL BUREAU ECONOMIC RES,THE RATE AND DIRECTION DECISION
OF INVENTIVE ACTIVITY: ECONOMIC AND SOCIAL FACTORS. PROB/SOLV
STRUCT INDUS MARKET R+D CREATE OP/RES TEC/DEV   MGT
EFFICIENCY PRODUC RATIONAL UTIL...WELF/ST PHIL/SCI
METH/CNCPT TIME. PAGE 77 B1562
                                                    S62
BOOTH D.A.,"POWER STRUCTURE AND COMMUNITY CHANGE: A MUNIC
REPLICATION STUDY OF COMMUNITY A." STRATA LABOR   ELITES
LEAD PARTIC REPRESENT...DECISION MGT TIME. PAGE 14 PWR
B0275
                                                    B63
MOORE W.E.,MAN, TIME, AND SOCIETY. UNIV STRUCT FAM CONCPT
MUNIC VOL/ASSN ADMIN...SOC NEW/IDEA TIME/SEQ TREND SOCIETY
TIME 20. PAGE 75 B1515   CONTROL
                                                    B64
CAPLOW T.,PRINCIPLES OF ORGANIZATION. UNIV CULTURE VOL/ASSN
STRUCT CREATE INGP/REL UTOPIA...GEN/LAWS TIME.   CONCPT
PAGE 18 B0374   SIMUL
                                                    EX/STRUC
                                                    S65
HOLSTI O.R.,"THE 1914 CASE." MOD/EUR COMPUTER   CON/ANAL
DIPLOM EDU/PROP EXEC...DECISION PSY PROBABIL STAT   PERCEPT
COMPUT/IR SOC/EXP TIME. PAGE 51 B1036   WAR

POLK W.R.,"PROBLEMS OF GOVERNMENT UTILIZATION OF
SCHOLARLY RESEARCH IN INTERNATIONAL AFFAIRS." FINAN
NAT/G EDU/PROP CONTROL TASK GP/REL ATTIT PERCEPT
KNOWL...POLICY TIME. PAGE 83 B1685
ACT/RES
ACADEM
PLAN
ADMIN
S65

UN ECAFE,ADMINISTRATIVE ASPECTS OF FAMILY PLANNING
PROGRAMMES (PAMPHLET). ASIA THAILAND WOR+45
VOL/ASSN PROB/SOLV BUDGET FOR/AID EDU/PROP CONFER
CONTROL GOV/REL TIME 20 UN BIRTH/CON. PAGE 106
B2147
PLAN
CENSUS
FAM
ADMIN
B66

NATIONAL COMN COMMUNITY HEALTH,ACTION - PLANNING
FOR COMMUNITY HEALTH SERVICES (PAMPHLET). USA+45
PROF/ORG DELIB/GP BUDGET ROUTINE GP/REL ATTIT
...HEAL SOC SOC/WK CHARTS TIME 20. PAGE 77 B1563
PLAN
MUNIC
HEALTH
ADJUST
N67

TIME/SEQ....CHRONOLOGY AND GENETIC SERIES

TREITSCHKE H.,POLITICS. UNIV SOCIETY STRATA NAT/G
EX/STRUC LEGIS DOMIN EDU/PROP ATTIT PWR RESPECT
...CONCPT TIME/SEQ GEN/LAWS TOT/POP 20. PAGE 105
B2127
EXEC
ELITES
GERMANY
B16

SUTHERLAND G.,CONSTITUTIONAL POWER AND WORLD
AFFAIRS. CONSTN STRUCT INT/ORG NAT/G CHIEF LEGIS
ACT/RES PLAN GOV/REL ALL/VALS...OBS TIME/SEQ
CONGRESS VAL/FREE 20 PRESIDENT. PAGE 102 B2056
USA-45
EXEC
DIPLOM
B19

HALDANE R.B.,BEFORE THE WAR. MOD/EUR SOCIETY
INT/ORG NAT/G DELIB/GP PLAN DOMIN EDU/PROP LEGIT
ADMIN COERCE ATTIT DRIVE MORAL ORD/FREE PWR...SOC
CONCPT SELF/OBS RECORD BIOG TIME/SEQ. PAGE 45 B0921
POLICY
DIPLOM
UK
B20

FRANK T.,A HISTORY OF ROME. MEDIT-7 INTELL SOCIETY
LOC/G NAT/G POL/PAR FORCES LEGIS DOMIN LEGIT
ALL/VALS...POLICY CONCPT TIME/SEQ GEN/LAWS ROM/EMP
ROM/EMP. PAGE 37 B0749
EXEC
STRUCT
ELITES
B23

MERRIAM C.E.,A HISTORY OF POLITICAL THEORIES -
RECENT TIMES. USA-45 WOR-45 CULTURE SOCIETY ECO/DEV
R+D EDU/PROP ROUTINE CHOOSE ATTIT PERSON ALL/VALS
...POLICY SOC CONCPT METH/CNCPT OBS HIST/WRIT
TIME/SEQ TREND. PAGE 73 B1471
UNIV
INTELL
B24

THOMAS F.,THE ENVIRONMENTAL BASIS OF SOCIETY.
USA-45 WOR-45 STRATA ECO/DEV EXTR/IND CONSULT
ECO/TAC ROUTINE ATTIT ALL/VALS...SOC TIME/SEQ.
PAGE 104 B2098
SOCIETY
GEOG
B25

MOON P.T.,IMPERIALISM AND WORLD POLITICS. AFR ASIA
ISLAM MOD/EUR S/ASIA USA-45 SOCIETY NAT/G EX/STRUC
BAL/PWR DOMIN COLONIAL NAT/LISM ATTIT DRIVE PWR
...GEOG SOC 20. PAGE 75 B1510
WEALTH
TIME/SEQ
CAP/ISM
DIPLOM
B26

FYFE H.,THE BRITISH LIBERAL PARTY. UK SECT ADMIN
LEAD CHOOSE GP/REL PWR SOCISM...MAJORIT TIME/SEQ
19/20 LIB/PARTY CONSRV/PAR. PAGE 38 B0768
POL/PAR
NAT/G
REPRESENT
POPULISM
B28

SOROKIN P.,CONTEMPORARY SOCIOLOGICAL THEORIES.
MOD/EUR UNIV SOCIETY R+D SCHOOL ECO/TAC EDU/PROP
ROUTINE ATTIT DRIVE...PSY CONCPT TIME/SEQ TREND
GEN/LAWS 20. PAGE 99 B1997
CULTURE
SOC
WAR
B28

HILL N.,INTERNATIONAL ADMINISTRATION. WOR-45
DELIB/GP DIPLOM EDU/PROP ALL/VALS...MGT TIME/SEQ
LEAGUE/NAT TOT/POP VAL/FREE 20. PAGE 50 B1011
INT/ORG
ADMIN
B31

DANGERFIELD R.,IN DEFENSE OF THE SENATE. USA-45
CONSTN NAT/G EX/STRUC TOP/EX ATTIT KNOWL
...METH/CNCPT STAT TIME/SEQ TREND CON/ANAL CHARTS
CONGRESS 20 TREATY. PAGE 26 B0528
LEGIS
DELIB/GP
DIPLOM
B33

CLOKIE H.M.,ROYAL COMMISSIONS OF INQUIRY; THE
SIGNIFICANCE OF INVESTIGATIONS IN BRITISH POLITICS.
UK POL/PAR CONFER ROUTINE...POLICY DECISION
TIME/SEQ 16/20. PAGE 22 B0439
NAT/G
DELIB/GP
INSPECT
B37

ROBBINS L.,ECONOMIC PLANNING AND INTERNATIONAL
ORDER. WOR-45 SOCIETY FINAN INDUS NAT/G ECO/TAC
ROUTINE WEALTH...SOC TIME/SEQ GEN/METH WORK 20
KEYNES/JM. PAGE 89 B1791
INT/ORG
PLAN
INT/TRADE
B37

PETTEE G.S.,THE PROCESS OF REVOLUTION. COM FRANCE
ITALY MOD/EUR RUSSIA SPAIN WOR-45 ELITES INTELL
SOCIETY STRATA STRUCT INT/ORG NAT/G POL/PAR ACT/RES
PLAN EDU/PROP LEGIT EXEC...SOC MYTH TIME/SEQ
TOT/POP 18/20. PAGE 82 B1664
COERCE
CONCPT
REV
B38

RAPPARD W.E.,THE CRISIS OF DEMOCRACY. EUR+WWI UNIV
WOR-45 CULTURE SOCIETY ECO/DEV INT/ORG POL/PAR
ACT/RES EDU/PROP EXEC CHOOSE ATTIT ALL/VALS...SOC
OBS HIST/WRIT TIME/SEQ LEAGUE/NAT NAZI TOT/POP 20.
PAGE 86 B1741
NAT/G
CONCPT
B38

MACMAHON A.W.,FEDERAL ADMINISTRATORS: A
BIOGRAPHICAL APPROACH TO THE PROBLEM OF
DEPARTMENTAL MANAGEMENT. USA-45 DELIB/GP EX/STRUC
WORKER LEAD...TIME/SEQ 19/20. PAGE 68 B1366
BIOG
ADMIN
NAT/G
MGT
B39

ZIMMERN A.,MODERN POLITICAL DOCTRINE. WOR-45
CULTURE SOCIETY ECO/UNDEV DELIB/GP EX/STRUC CREATE
DOMIN COERCE NAT/LISM ATTIT RIGID/FLEX ORD/FREE PWR
WEALTH...POLICY CONCPT OBS TIME/SEQ TREND TOT/POP
LEAGUE/NAT 20. PAGE 119 B2402
NAT/G
ECO/TAC
BAL/PWR
INT/TRADE
B39

BURTON M.E.,THE ASSEMBLY OF THE LEAGUE OF NATIONS.
WOR-45 CONSTN SOCIETY STRUCT INT/ORG NAT/G CREATE
ATTIT RIGID/FLEX PWR...POLICY TIME/SEQ LEAGUE/NAT
20. PAGE 18 B0359
DELIB/GP
EX/STRUC
DIPLOM
B41

COHEN E.W.,THE GROWTH OF THE BRITISH CIVIL SERVICE
1780-1939. UK NAT/G SENIOR ROUTINE GOV/REL...MGT
METH/COMP BIBLIOG 18/20. PAGE 22 B0442
OP/RES
TIME/SEQ
CENTRAL
ADMIN
B41

DAVIS H.E.,PIONEERS IN WORLD ORDER. WOR-45 CONSTN
ECO/TAC DOMIN EDU/PROP LEGIT ADJUD ADMIN ARMS/CONT
CHOOSE KNOWL ORD/FREE...POLICY JURID SOC STAT OBS
CENSUS TIME/SEQ ANTHOL LEAGUE/NAT 20. PAGE 26 B0537
INT/ORG
ROUTINE
B44

BONAPARTE M.,MYTHS OF WAR. GERMANY WOR+45 WOR-45
CULTURE SOCIETY NAT/G FORCES LEGIT ATTIT ALL/VALS
...CONCPT HIST/WRIT TIME/SEQ 20 JEWS. PAGE 13 B0271
ROUTINE
MYTH
WAR
B48

HULL C.,THE MEMOIRS OF CORDELL HULL (VOLUME ONE).
USA-45 WOR-45 CONSTN FAM LOC/G NAT/G PROVS DELIB/GP
FORCES LEGIS TOP/EX BAL/PWR LEGIT ADMIN EXEC WAR
ATTIT ORD/FREE PWR...MAJORIT SELF/OBS TIME/SEQ
TREND NAZI 20. PAGE 52 B1062
BIOG
DIPLOM
B48

SHERWOOD R.E.,ROOSEVELT AND HOPKINS. UK USA+45 USSR
NAT/G EX/STRUC FORCES ADMIN ROUTINE PERSON PWR
...TIME/SEQ 20 ROOSEVLT/F HOPKINS/H. PAGE 96 B1946
TOP/EX
BIOG
DIPLOM
WAR
B48

ROSENHAUPT H.W.,HOW TO WAGE PEACE. USA+45 SOCIETY
STRATA STRUCT R+D INT/ORG POL/PAR LEGIS ACT/RES
CREATE PLAN EDU/PROP ADMIN EXEC ATTIT ALL/VALS
...TIME/SEQ TREND COLD/WAR 20. PAGE 90 B1822
INTELL
CONCPT
DIPLOM
B49

SINGER K.,THE IDEA OF CONFLICT. UNIV INTELL INT/ORG
NAT/G PLAN ROUTINE ATTIT DRIVE ALL/VALS...POLICY
CONCPT TIME/SEQ. PAGE 97 B1966
ACT/RES
SOC
B49

BROOKINGS INST.,"GOVERNMENT MECHANISM FOR CONDUCT
OF US FOREIGN RELATIONS." USA+45 CONSTN NAT/G LEGIS
CT/SYS...MGT TIME/SEQ CONGRESS TOT/POP 20. PAGE 15
B0316
EXEC
STRUCT
DIPLOM
L49

MCCAMY J.,THE ADMINISTRATION OF AMERICAN FOREIGN
AFFAIRS. USA+45 SOCIETY INT/ORG NAT/G ACT/RES PLAN
INT/TRADE EDU/PROP ADJUD ALL/VALS...METH/CNCPT
TIME/SEQ CONGRESS 20. PAGE 71 B1441
EXEC
STRUCT
DIPLOM
B50

MONTGOMERY H.,CRACKER PARTIES. CULTURE EX/STRUC
LEAD PWR POPULISM...TIME/SEQ 19 GEORGIA CALHOUN/JC
COBB/HOWLL JACKSON/A. PAGE 74 B1505
POL/PAR
PROVS
ELITES
BIOG
B50

ELLIOTT W.,UNITED STATES FOREIGN POLICY, ITS
ORGANIZATION AND CONTROL. USA+45 USA-45 CONSTN
NAT/G FORCES TOP/EX PEACE...TIME/SEQ CONGRESS
LEAGUE/NAT 20. PAGE 33 B0670
LEGIS
EX/STRUC
DIPLOM
B52

VANDENBOSCH A.,THE UN: BACKGROUND, ORGANIZATION,
FUNCTIONS, ACTIVITIES. WOR+45 LAW CONSTN STRUCT
INT/ORG CONSULT BAL/PWR EDU/PROP EXEC ALL/VALS
...POLICY CONCPT UN 20. PAGE 112 B2254
DELIB/GP
TIME/SEQ
PEACE
B52

MACMAHON A.W.,ADMINISTRATION IN FOREIGN AFFAIRS.
NAT/G CONSULT DELIB/GP LEGIS ACT/RES CREATE ADMIN
EXEC RIGID/FLEX PWR...METH/CNCPT TIME/SEQ TOT/POP
VAL/FREE 20. PAGE 68 B1369
USA+45
ROUTINE
FOR/AID
DIPLOM
B53

MORRIS B.S.,"THE COMINFORM: A FIVE YEAR
PERSPECTIVE." COM UNIV USSR WOR+45 ECO/DEV POL/PAR
TOP/EX PLAN DOMIN ADMIN TOTALISM ATTIT ALL/VALS
...CONCPT TIME/SEQ TREND CON/ANAL WORK VAL/FREE 20.
PAGE 76 B1527
VOL/ASSN
EDU/PROP
DIPLOM
S53

DUVERGER M.,POLITICAL PARTIES: THEIR ORGANIZATION
AND ACTIVITY IN THE MODERN STATE. EUR+WWI MOD/EUR
USA+45 USA-45 EDU/PROP ADMIN ROUTINE ATTIT DRIVE
ORD/FREE PWR...SOC CONCPT MATH STAT TIME/SEQ
TOT/POP 19/20. PAGE 31 B0635
POL/PAR
EX/STRUC
ELITES
B54

MANGONE G.,A SHORT HISTORY OF INTERNATIONAL
ORGANIZATION. MOD/EUR USA+45 USA-45 WOR+45 WOR-45
LAW LEGIS CREATE LEGIT ROUTINE RIGID/FLEX PWR
INT/ORG
INT/LAW
B54

...JURID CONCPT OBS TIME/SEQ STERTYP GEN/LAWS UN
TOT/POP VAL/FREE 18/20. PAGE 69 B1389

B55
CHOWDHURI R.N..INTERNATIONAL MANDATES AND   DELIB/GP
TRUSTEESHIP SYSTEMS. WOR+45 STRUCT ECO/UNDEV   PLAN
INT/ORG LEGIS DOMIN EDU/PROP LEGIT EXEC PWR   SOVEREIGN
...CONCPT TIME/SEQ UN 20. PAGE 21 B0427

L55
ROSTOW W.W.."RUSSIA AND CHINA UNDER COMMUNISM."   COM
CHINA/COM USSR INTELL STRUCT INT/ORG NAT/G POL/PAR ASIA
TOP/EX ACT/RES PLAN ADMIN ATTIT ALL/VALS MARXISM
...CONCPT OBS TIME/SEQ TREND GOV/COMP VAL/FREE 20.
PAGE 91 B1830

B56
LOVEDAY A..REFLECTIONS ON INTERNATIONAL   INT/ORG
ADMINISTRATION. WOR+45 WOR-45 DELIB/GP ACT/RES   MGT
ADMIN EXEC ROUTINE DRIVE...METH/CNCPT TIME/SEQ
CON/ANAL SIMUL TOT/POP 20. PAGE 67 B1342

B57
DJILAS M..THE NEW CLASS: AN ANALYSIS OF THE   COM
COMMUNIST SYSTEM. STRATA CAP/ISM ECO/TAC DOMIN   POL/PAR
EDU/PROP LEGIT EXEC COERCE ATTIT PWR MARXISM   USSR
...MARXIST MGT CONCPT TIME/SEQ GEN/LAWS 20. PAGE 29 YUGOSLAVIA
B0600

B57
HUNTINGTON S.P..THE SOLDIER AND THE STATE: THE   ACT/RES
THEORY AND POLITICS OF CIVIL-MILITARY RELATIONS.   FORCES
USA+45 USA-45 NAT/G PROF/ORG CONSULT DOMIN LEGIT
ROUTINE ATTIT PWR...CONCPT TIME/SEQ COLD/WAR 20.
PAGE 53 B1065

B57
MURRAY J.N..THE UNITED NATIONS TRUSTEESHIP SYSTEM. INT/ORG
AFR WOR+45 CONSTN CONSULT LEGIS EDU/PROP LEGIT EXEC DELIB/GP
ROUTINE...INT TIME/SEQ SOMALI UN 20. PAGE 77 B1547

L57
HAAS E.B.."REGIONAL INTEGRATION AND NATIONAL   INT/ORG
POLICY." WOR+45 VOL/ASSN DELIB/GP EX/STRUC ECO/TAC ORD/FREE
DOMIN EDU/PROP LEGIT COERCE ATTIT PERCEPT KNOWL   REGION
...TIME/SEQ COLD/WAR 20 UN. PAGE 45 B0908

B58
COLEMAN J.S..NIGERIA: BACKGROUND TO NATIONALISM.   NAT/G
AFR SOCIETY ECO/DEV KIN LOC/G POL/PAR TEC/DEV DOMIN NAT/LISM
ADMIN DRIVE PWR RESPECT...TRADIT SOC INT SAMP   NIGERIA
TIME/SEQ 20. PAGE 22 B0452

B58
LESTER R.A..AS UNIONS MATURE. POL/PAR BARGAIN LEAD LABOR
PARTIC GP/REL CENTRAL...MAJORIT TIME/SEQ METH/COMP. INDUS
PAGE 64 B1299   POLICY
                                                    MGT

B59
CHINA INSTITUTE OF AMERICA..CHINA AND THE UNITED   ASIA
NATIONS. CHINA/COM FUT STRUCT EDU/PROP LEGIT ADMIN INT/ORG
ATTIT KNOWL ORD/FREE PWR...OBS RECORD STAND/INT
TIME/SEQ UN LEAGUE/NAT UNESCO 20. PAGE 21 B0425

B59
DIEBOLD W. JR..THE SCHUMAN PLAN: A STUDY IN   INT/ORG
ECONOMIC COOPERATION. 1950-1959. EUR+WWI FRANCE   REGION
GERMANY USA+45 EXTR/IND CONSULT DELIB/GP PLAN
DIPLOM ECO/TAC INT/TRADE ROUTINE ORD/FREE WEALTH
...METH/CNCPT STAT CONT/OBS INT TIME/SEQ ECSC 20.
PAGE 29 B0591

B59
GRABER D..CRISIS DIPLOMACY. L/A+17C USA+45 USA-45   ROUTINE
NAT/G TOP/EX ECO/TAC COERCE ATTIT ORD/FREE...CONCPT MORAL
MYTH TIME/SEQ COLD/WAR 20. PAGE 42 B0848   DIPLOM

S59
SUTTON F.X.."REPRESENTATION AND THE NATURE OF   NAT/G
POLITICAL SYSTEMS." UNIV WOR-45 CULTURE SOCIETY   CONCPT
STRATA INT/ORG FORCES JUDGE DOMIN LEGIT EXEC REGION
REPRESENT ATTIT ORD/FREE RESPECT...SOC HIST/WRIT
TIME/SEQ. PAGE 102 B2057

S59
ZAUBERMAN A.."SOVIET BLOC ECONOMIC INTEGRATION."   MARKET
COM CULTURE INTELL ECO/DEV INDUS TOP/EX ACT/RES   INT/ORG
PLAN ECO/TAC INT/TRADE ROUTINE CHOOSE ATTIT   USSR
...TIME/SEQ 20. PAGE 119 B2399   TOTALISM

B60
CAMPBELL R.W..SOVIET ECONOMIC POWER. COM USA+45   ECO/DEV
DIST/IND MARKET TOP/EX ACT/RES CAP/ISM ECO/TAC   PLAN
DOMIN EDU/PROP ADMIN ROUTINE DRIVE...MATH TIME/SEQ SOCISM
CHARTS WORK 20. PAGE 18 B0371   USSR

B60
EASTON S.C..THE TWILIGHT OF EUROPEAN COLONIALISM.   FINAN
AFR S/ASIA CONSTN SOCIETY STRUCT ECO/UNDEV INDUS   ADMIN
NAT/G FORCES ECO/TAC COLONIAL CT/SYS ATTIT KNOWL
ORD/FREE PWR...SOCIALIST TIME/SEQ TREND CON/ANAL
20. PAGE 32 B0645

B60
HYDE L.K.G..THE US AND THE UN. WOR+45 STRUCT   USA+45
ECO/DEV ECO/UNDEV NAT/G ACT/RES PLAN DIPLOM   INT/ORG
EDU/PROP ADMIN ALL/VALS...CONCPT TIME/SEQ GEN/LAWS FOR/AID
UN VAL/FREE 20. PAGE 53 B1070

B60
MEEHAN E.J..THE BRITISH LEFT WING AND FOREIGN   ACT/RES
POLICY: A STUDY OF THE INFLUENCE OF IDEOLOGY. FUT   ATTIT
UK UNIV WOR+45 INTELL TOP/EX PLAN ADMIN ROUTINE   DIPLOM

DRIVE...OBS TIME/SEQ GEN/LAWS PARLIAMENT 20.
PAGE 72 B1461

S60
"THE EMERGING COMMON MARKETS IN LATIN AMERICA." FUT FINAN
L/A+17C STRATA DIST/IND INDUS LABOR NAT/G LEGIS   ECO/UNDEV
ECO/TAC ADMIN RIGID/FLEX HEALTH...NEW/IDEA TIME/SEQ INT/TRADE
OAS 20. PAGE 2 B0039

S60
EMERSON R.."THE EROSION OF DEMOCRACY." AFR FUT LAW S/ASIA
CULTURE INTELL SOCIETY ECO/UNDEV FAM LOC/G NAT/G   POL/PAR
FORCES PLAN TEC/DEV ECO/TAC ADMIN CT/SYS ATTIT
ORD/FREE PWR...SOCIALIST SOC CONCPT STAND/INT
TIME/SEQ WORK 20. PAGE 33 B0671

S60
FRANKEL S.H.."ECONOMIC ASPECTS OF POLITICAL   NAT/G
INDEPENDENCE IN AFRICA." AFR FUT SOCIETY ECO/UNDEV FOR/AID
COM/IND FINAN LEGIS PLAN TEC/DEV CAP/ISM ECO/TAC
INT/TRADE ADMIN ATTIT DRIVE RIGID/FLEX PWR WEALTH
...MGT NEW/IDEA MATH TIME/SEQ VAL/FREE 20. PAGE 37
B0751

S60
MODELSKI G.."AUSTRALIA AND SEATO." S/ASIA USA+45   INT/ORG
CULTURE INTELL ECO/DEV NAT/G PLAN DIPLOM ADMIN   ACT/RES
ROUTINE ATTIT SKILL...MGT TIME/SEQ AUSTRAL 20
SEATO. PAGE 74 B1493

S60
MORA J.A.."THE ORGANIZATION OF AMERICAN STATES."   L/A+17C
USA+45 LAW ECO/UNDEV VOL/ASSN DELIB/GP PLAN BAL/PWR INT/ORG
EDU/PROP ADMIN DRIVE RIGID/FLEX ORD/FREE WEALTH   REGION
...TIME/SEQ GEN/LAWS OAS 20. PAGE 75 B1518

S60
MORALES C.J.."TRADE AND ECONOMIC INTEGRATION IN   FINAN
LATIN AMERICA." FUT L/A+17C LAW STRATA ECO/UNDEV   INT/TRADE
DIST/IND INDUS LABOR NAT/G LEGIS ECO/TAC ADMIN   REGION
RIGID/FLEX WEALTH...CONCPT NEW/IDEA CONT/OBS
TIME/SEQ WORK 20. PAGE 75 B1519

B61
BARNES W..THE FOREIGN SERVICE OF THE UNITED STATES. NAT/G
USA+45 USA-45 CONSTN INT/ORG POL/PAR CONSULT   MGT
DELIB/GP LEGIS DOMIN EDU/PROP EXEC ATTIT RIGID/FLEX DIPLOM
ORD/FREE PWR...POLICY CONCPT STAT OBS RECORD BIOG
TIME/SEQ TREND. PAGE 9 B0188

B61
HASAN H.S..PAKISTAN AND THE UN. ISLAM WOR+45   INT/ORG
ECO/DEV ECO/UNDEV NAT/G TOP/EX ECO/TAC FOR/AID   ATTIT
EDU/PROP ADMIN DRIVE PERCEPT...OBS TIME/SEQ UN 20. PAKISTAN
PAGE 48 B0965

B61
MARVICK D..POLITICAL DECISION-MAKERS. INTELL STRATA TOP/EX
NAT/G POL/PAR EX/STRUC LEGIS DOMIN EDU/PROP ATTIT   BIOG
PERSON PWR...PSY STAT OBS CONT/OBS STAND/INT   ELITES
UNPLAN/INT TIME/SEQ CHARTS STERTYP VAL/FREE.
PAGE 70 B1416

B61
MOLLAU G..INTERNATIONAL COMMUNISM AND WORLD   COM
REVOLUTION: HISTORY AND METHODS. RUSSIA USSR   REV
INT/ORG NAT/G POL/PAR VOL/ASSN FORCES BAL/PWR
DIPLOM EXEC REGION WAR ATTIT PWR MARXISM...CONCPT
TIME/SEQ COLD/WAR 19/20. PAGE 74 B1498

B61
SINGER J.D..FINANCING INTERNATIONAL ORGANIZATION: INT/ORG
THE UNITED NATIONS BUDGET PROCESS. WOR+45 FINAN   MGT
ACT/RES CREATE PLAN BUDGET ECO/TAC ADMIN ROUTINE
ATTIT KNOWL...DECISION METH/CNCPT TIME/SEQ UN 20.
PAGE 97 B1964

B61
STRAUSS E..THE RULING SERVANTS. FRANCE UK USSR   ADMIN
WOR+45 WOR-45 NAT/G CONSULT DELIB/GP EX/STRUC   PWR
TOP/EX DOMIN EDU/PROP LEGIT ROUTINE...MGT TIME/SEQ ELITES
STERTYP 20. PAGE 101 B2051

B61
WILLOUGHBY W.R..THE ST LAWRENCE WATERWAY: A STUDY   LEGIS
IN POLITICS AND DIPLOMACY. USA+45 ECO/DEV COM/IND   INT/TRADE
INT/ORG CONSULT DELIB/GP ACT/RES TEC/DEV DIPLOM   CANADA
ECO/TAC ROUTINE...TIME/SEQ 20. PAGE 117 B2357   DIST/IND

S61
NEEDLER M.C.."THE POLITICAL DEVELOPMENT OF MEXICO." L/A+17C
STRUCT NAT/G ADMIN RIGID/FLEX...TIME/SEQ TREND   POL/PAR
MEXIC/AMER TOT/POP VAL/FREE 19/20. PAGE 77 B1566

S61
PADOVER S.K.."PSYCHOLOGICAL WARFARE AND FOREIGN   ROUTINE
POLICY." FUT UNIV USA+45 INTELL SOCIETY CREATE   DIPLOM
EDU/PROP ADMIN WAR PEACE PERCEPT...POLICY
METH/CNCPT TESTS TIME/SEQ 20. PAGE 80 B1623

S61
TAUBENFELD H.J.."OUTER SPACE--PAST POLITICS AND   PLAN
FUTURE POLICY." FUT USA+45 USA-45 WOR+45 AIR INTELL SPACE
STRUCT ECO/DEV NAT/G TOP/EX ACT/RES ADMIN ROUTINE   INT/ORG
NUC/PWR ATTIT DRIVE...CONCPT TIME/SEQ TREND TOT/POP
20. PAGE 103 B2083

S61
TOMASIC D.."POLITICAL LEADERSHIP IN CONTEMPORARY   SOCIETY
POLAND." COM EUR+WWI GERMANY NAT/G POL/PAR SECT   ROUTINE
DELIB/GP PLAN ECO/TAC DOMIN EDU/PROP PWR MARXISM   USSR
...MARXIST GEOG MGT CONCPT TIME/SEQ STERTYP 20.   POLAND
PAGE 105 B2114

B62

CAIRNCROSS A.K.,FACTORS IN ECONOMIC DEVELOPMENT. MARKET
WOR+45 ECO/UNDEV INDUS R+D LG/CO NAT/G EX/STRUC ECO/DEV
PLAN TEC/DEV ECO/TAC ATTIT HEALTH KNOWL PWR WEALTH
...TIME/SEQ GEN/LAWS TOT/POP VAL/FREE 20. PAGE 18
B0363

B62

JEWELL M.E.,SENATORIAL POLITICS AND FOREIGN POLICY. USA+45
NAT/G POL/PAR CHIEF DELIB/GP TOP/EX FOR/AID LEGIS
EDU/PROP ROUTINE ATTIT PWR SKILL...MAJORIT DIPLOM
METH/CNCPT TIME/SEQ CONGRESS 20 PRESIDENT. PAGE 56
B1138

B62

MULLEY F.W.,THE POLITICS OF WESTERN DEFENSE. INT/ORG
EUR+WWI USA-45 WOR+45 VOL/ASSN EX/STRUC FORCES DELIB/GP
COERCE DETER PEACE ATTIT ORD/FREE PWR...RECORD NUC/PWR
TIME/SEQ CHARTS COLD/WAR 20 NATO. PAGE 76 B1537

B62

NICHOLAS H.G.,THE UNITED NATIONS AS A POLITICAL INT/ORG
INSTITUTION. WOR+45 CONSTN EX/STRUC ACT/RES LEGIT ROUTINE
PERCEPT KNOWL PWR...CONCPT TIME/SEQ CON/ANAL
ORG/CHARTS UN 20. PAGE 78 B1580

L62

HOFFHERR R.,"LE PROBLEME DE L'ENCADREMENT DANS LES AFR
JEUNES ETATS DE LANGUE FRANCAISE EN AFRIQUE STRUCT
CENTRALE ET A MADAGASCAR." FUT ECO/UNDEV CONSULT FRANCE
PLAN ECO/TAC COLONIAL ATTIT...MGT TIME/SEQ VAL/FREE
20. PAGE 51 B1028

L62

MANGIN G.,"L'ORGANIZATION JUDICIAIRE DES ETATS AFR
D'AFRIQUE ET DE MADAGASCAR." ISLAM WOR+45 STRATA LEGIS
STRUCT ECO/UNDEV NAT/G LEGIT EXEC...JURID TIME/SEQ COLONIAL
TOT/POP 20 SUPREME/CT. PAGE 69 B1387 MADAGASCAR

S62

ALBONETTI A.,"IL SECONDO PROGRAMMA QUINQUENNALE R+D
1963-67 ED IL BILANCIO RICERCHE ED INVESTIMENTI PER PLAN
IL 1963 DELL'ERATOM." EUR+WWI FUT ITALY WOR+45 NUC/PWR
ECO/DEV SERV/IND INT/ORG TEC/DEV ECO/TAC ATTIT
SKILL WEALTH...MGT TIME/SEQ OEEC 20. PAGE 3 B0069

S62

BRZEZINSKI Z.K.,"DEVIATION CONTROL: A STUDY IN THE RIGID/FLEX
DYNAMICS OF DOCTRINAL CONFLICT." WOR+45 WOR-45 ATTIT
VOL/ASSN CREATE BAL/PWR DOMIN EXEC DRIVE PERCEPT
PWR...METH/CNCPT TIME/SEQ TREND 20. PAGE 16 B0333

S62

FESLER J.W.,"FRENCH FIELD ADMINISTRATION: THE EX/STRUC
BEGINNINGS." CHRIST-17C CULTURE SOCIETY STRATA FRANCE
NAT/G ECO/TAC DOMIN EDU/PROP LEGIT ADJUD COERCE
ATTIT ALL/VALS...TIME/SEQ CON/ANAL GEN/METH
VAL/FREE 13/15. PAGE 35 B0714

S62

HUDSON G.F.,"SOVIET FEARS OF THE WEST." COM USA+45 ATTIT
SOCIETY DELIB/GP EX/STRUC TOP/EX ACT/RES CREATE MYTH
DOMIN EDU/PROP LEGIT ADMIN ROUTINE DRIVE PERSON GERMANY
RIGID/FLEX PWR...RECORD TIME/SEQ TOT/POP 20 USSR
STALIN/J. PAGE 52 B1057

S62

MANGIN G.,"LES ACCORDS DE COOPERATION EN MATIERE DE INT/ORG
JUSTICE ENTRE LA FRANCE ET LES ETATS AFRICAINS ET LAW
MALGACHE." AFR ISLAM WOR+45 STRUCT ECO/UNDEV NAT/G FRANCE
DELIB/GP PERCEPT ALL/VALS...JURID MGT TIME/SEQ 20.
PAGE 69 B1386

B63

BOISSIER P.,HISTORIE DU COMITE INTERNATIONAL DE LA INT/ORG
CROIX ROUGE. MOD/EUR WOR-45 CONSULT FORCES PLAN HEALTH
DIPLOM EDU/PROP ADMIN MORAL ORD/FREE...SOC CONCPT ARMS/CONT
RECORD TIME/SEQ GEN/LAWS TOT/POP VAL/FREE 19/20. WAR
PAGE 13 B0267

B63

FISHER S.N.,THE MILITARY IN THE MIDDLE EAST: EX/STRUC
PROBLEMS IN SOCIETY AND GOVERNMENT. ISLAM USA+45 FORCES
NAT/G DOMIN LEGIT COERCE ORD/FREE PWR...TIME/SEQ
VAL/FREE 20. PAGE 36 B0725

B63

HEUSSLER R.,YESTERDAY'S RULERS: THE MAKING OF THE EX/STRUC
BRITISH COLONIAL SERVICE. AFR EUR+WWI UK STRATA MORAL
SECT DELIB/GP PLAN DOMIN EDU/PROP ATTIT PERCEPT ELITES
PERSON SUPEGO KNOWL ORD/FREE PWR...MGT SOC OBS INT
TIME/SEQ 20 CMN/WLTH. PAGE 49 B1000

B63

KAPP W.K.,HINDU CULTURE: ECONOMIC DEVELOPMENT AND SECT
ECONOMIC PLANNING IN INDIA. INDIA S/ASIA CULTURE ECO/UNDEV
ECO/TAC EDU/PROP ADMIN ALL/VALS...POLICY MGT
TIME/SEQ VAL/FREE 20. PAGE 58 B1171

B63

LANGROD G.,THE INTERNATIONAL CIVIL SERVICE: ITS INT/ORG
ORIGINS, ITS NATURE, ITS EVALUATION. FUT WOR+45 ADMIN
WOR-45 DELIB/GP ACT/RES DOMIN LEGIT ATTIT
RIGID/FLEX SUPEGO ALL/VALS...MGT CONCPT STAT
TIME/SEQ ILO LEAGUE/NAT VAL/FREE 20 UN. PAGE 62
B1259

B63

LEWIS J.W.,LEADERSHIP IN COMMUNIST CHINA. ASIA POL/PAR
INTELL ECO/UNDEV LOC/G MUNIC NAT/G PROVS ECO/TAC DOMIN
EDU/PROP LEGIT ADMIN COERCE ATTIT ORD/FREE PWR ELITES
...INT TIME/SEQ CHARTS TOT/POP VAL/FREE. PAGE 65

B1304

B63

MAYNE R.,THE COMMUNITY OF EUROPE. UK CONSTN NAT/G EUR+WWI
CONSULT DELIB/GP CREATE PLAN ECO/TAC LEGIT ADMIN INT/ORG
ROUTINE ORD/FREE PWR WEALTH...CONCPT TIME/SEQ EEC REGION
EURATOM 20. PAGE 71 B1436

B63

MCKIE R.,MALAYSIA IN FOCUS. INDONESIA WOR+45 S/ASIA
ECO/UNDEV FINAN NAT/G POL/PAR SECT FORCES PLAN NAT/LISM
ADMIN COLONIAL COERCE DRIVE ALL/VALS...POLICY MALAYSIA
RECORD CENSUS TIME/SEQ CMN/WLTH 20. PAGE 72 B1453

B63

MOORE W.E.,MAN, TIME, AND SOCIETY. UNIV STRUCT FAM CONCPT
MLNIC VOL/ASSN ADMIN...SOC NEW/IDEA TIME/SEQ TREND SOCIETY
TIME 20. PAGE 75 B1515 CONTROL

B63

TSOU T.,AMERICA'S FAILURE IN CHINA, 1941-1950. ASIA
USA+45 USA-45 NAT/G ACT/RES PLAN DOMIN EDU/PROP PERCEPT
ADMIN ROUTINE ATTIT PERSON ORD/FREE...DECISION DIPLOM
CONCPT MYTH TIME/SEQ TREND STERTYP 20. PAGE 105
B2132

L63

EMERSON R.,"POLITICAL MODERNIZATION." WOR+45 POL/PAR
CULTURE ECO/UNDEV NAT/G FORCES ECO/TAC DOMIN ADMIN
EDU/PROP LEGIT COERCE ALL/VALS...CONCPT TIME/SEQ
VAL/FREE 20. PAGE 33 B0672

L63

FREUND G.,"ADENAUER AND THE FUTURE OF GERMANY." NAT/G
EUR+WWI FUT GERMANY/W FORCES LEGIT ADMIN ROUTINE BIOG
ATTIT DRIVE PERSON PWR...POLICY TIME/SEQ TREND DIPLOM
VAL/FREE 20 ADENAUER/K. PAGE 37 B0753 GERMANY

S63

DELLIN L.A.D.,"BULGARIA UNDER SOVIET LEADERSHIP." AGRI
BULGARIA COM USA+45 USSR ECO/DEV INDUS POL/PAR NAT/G
EX/STRUC TOP/EX COERCE ATTIT RIGID/FLEX...POLICY TOTALISM
TIME/SEQ 20. PAGE 28 B0572

S63

ETIENNE G.,"'LOIS OBJECTIVES' ET PROBLEMES DE TOTALISM
DEVELOPPEMENT DANS LE CONTEXTE CHINE-URSS." ASIA USSR
CHINA/COM COM FUT STRUCT INT/ORG VOL/ASSN TOP/EX
TEC/DEV ECO/TAC ATTIT RIGID/FLEX...GEOG MGT
TIME/SEQ TOT/POP 20. PAGE 34 B0682

S63

MANGONE G.,"THE UNITED NATIONS AND UNITED STATES INT/ORG
FOREIGN POLICY." USA+45 WOR+45 ECO/UNDEV NAT/G ECO/TAC
DIPLOM LEGIT ROUTINE ATTIT DRIVE...TIME/SEQ UN FOR/AID
COLD/WAR 20. PAGE 69 B1390

S63

NYE J.S. JR.,"EAST AFRICAN ECONOMIC INTEGRATION." ECO/UNDEV
AFR UGANDA PROVS DELIB/GP PLAN ECO/TAC INT/TRADE INT/ORG
ADMIN ROUTINE ORD/FREE PWR WEALTH...OBS TIME/SEQ
VAL/FREE 20. PAGE 79 B1597

S63

SHIMKIN D.B.,"STRUCTURE OF SOVIET POWER." COM FUT PWR
USA+45 USSR WOR+45 NAT/G FORCES ECO/TAC DOMIN EXEC
COERCE CHOOSE ATTIT WEALTH...TIME/SEQ COLD/WAR
TOT/POP VAL/FREE 20. PAGE 96 B1948

S63

USEEM J.,"MEN IN THE MIDDLE OF THE THIRD CULTURE: ADMIN
THE ROLES OF AMERICAN AND NON-WESTERN PEOPLE IN SOCIETY
CROSS-CULTURAL ADMINIS-." FUT WOR+45 DELIB/GP PERSON
EX/STRUC LEGIS ATTIT ALL/VALS...MGT INT TIME/SEQ
GEN/LAWS VAL/FREE. PAGE 111 B2247

S63

WAGRET M.,"L'ASCENSION POLITIQUE DE L'U.D.D.I.A. EX/STRUC
(CONGO) ET SA PRISE DU POUVOIR (1956-1959)." AFR CHOOSE
WOR+45 NAT/G POL/PAR CONSULT DELIB/GP LEGIS PERCEPT FRANCE
ALL/VALS SOVEREIGN...TIME/SEQ CONGO. PAGE 113 B2274

B64

CHANDLER A.D. JR.,GIANT ENTERPRISE: FORD, GENERAL LG/CO
MOTORS, AND THE AUTOMOBILE INDUSTRY; SOURCES AND DIST/IND
READINGS. USA+45 USA-45 FINAN MARKET CREATE ADMIN LABOR
...TIME/SEQ ANTHOL 20 AUTOMOBILE. PAGE 20 B0404 MGT

B64

GUTTSMAN W.L.,THE BRITISH POLITICAL ELITE. EUR+WWI NAT/G
MOD/EUR STRATA FAM LABOR POL/PAR SCHOOL VOL/ASSN SOC
DELIB/GP LEGIS LEGIT EXEC CHOOSE ATTIT ALL/VALS UK
...STAT BIOG TIME/SEQ CHARTS VAL/FREE. PAGE 45 ELITES
B0905

B64

PIPES R.,THE FORMATION OF THE SOVIET UNION. EUR+WWI COM
MOD/EUR STRUCT ECO/UNDEV NAT/G LEGIS DOMIN LEGIT USSR
CT/SYS EXEC COERCE ALL/VALS...POLICY RELATIV RUSSIA
HIST/WRIT TIME/SEQ TOT/POP 19/20. PAGE 83 B1677

B64

PLISCHKE E.,SYSTEMS OF INTEGRATING THE INT/ORG
INTERNATIONAL COMMUNITY. WOR+45 NAT/G VOL/ASSN EX/STRUC
ECO/TAC LEGIT PWR WEALTH...TIME/SEQ ANTHOL UN REGION
TOT/POP 20. PAGE 83 B1684

B64

RAYMOND J.,POWER AT THE PENTAGON (1ST ED.). ELITES PWR
NAT/G PLAN EDU/PROP ARMS/CONT DETER WAR WEAPON CIVMIL/REL
...TIME/SEQ 20 PENTAGON MCNAMARA/R. PAGE 86 B1746 EX/STRUC
FORCES

B64

WAINHOUSE D.W.,REMNANTS OF EMPIRE: THE UNITED INT/ORG

NATIONS AND THE END OF COLONIALISM. FUT PORTUGAL   TREND
WOR+45 NAT/G CONSULT DOMIN LEGIT ADMIN ROUTINE   COLONIAL
ATTIT ORD/FREE...POLICY JURID RECORD INT TIME/SEQ
UN CMN/WLTH 20. PAGE 113 B2275
                                                     L64
MILLIS W.."THE DEMILITARIZED WORLD." COM USA+45   FUT
USSR WOR+45 CONSTN NAT/G EX/STRUC PLAN LEGIT ATTIT   INT/ORG
DRIVE...CONCPT TIME/SEQ STERTYP TOT/POP COLD/WAR   BAL/PWR
20. PAGE 74 B1486   PEACE
                                                     L64
RIPLEY R.B.."INTERAGENCY COMMITTEES AND   EXEC
INCREMENTALISM: THE CASE OF AID TO INDIA." INDIA   MGT
USA+45 INTELL NAT/G DELIB/GP ACT/RES DIPLOM ROUTINE   FOR/AID
NAT/LISM ATTIT PWR...SOC CONCPT NEW/IDEA TIME/SEQ
CON/ANAL VAL/FREE 20. PAGE 89 B1790
                                                     S64
KASSOF A.."THE ADMINISTERED SOCIETY: SOCIETY
TOTALITARIANISM WITHOUT TERROR." COM USSR STRATA   DOMIN
AGRI INDUS NAT/G PERF/ART SCHOOL TOP/EX EDU/PROP   TOTALISM
ADMIN ORD/FREE PWR...POLICY SOC TIME/SEQ GEN/LAWS
VAL/FREE 20. PAGE 58 B1178
                                                     S64
NEEDHAM T.."SCIENCE AND SOCIETY IN EAST AND WEST."   ASIA
INTELL STRATA R+D LOC/G NAT/G PROVS CONSULT ACT/RES   STRUCT
CREATE PLAN TEC/DEV EDU/PROP ADMIN ATTIT ALL/VALS
...POLICY RELATIV MGT CONCPT NEW/IDEA TIME/SEQ WORK
WORK. PAGE 77 B1565
                                                     S64
RIGBY T.H.."TRADITIONAL, MARKET, AND ORGANIZATIONAL   MARKET
SOCIETIES AND THE USSR." COM ECO/DEV NAT/G POL/PAR   ADMIN
ECO/TAC DOMIN ORD/FREE PWR WEALTH...TIME/SEQ   USSR
GEN/LAWS VAL/FREE 20 STALIN/J. PAGE 88 B1784
                                                     B65
ETZIONI A..POLITICAL UNIFICATION* A COMPARATIVE   INT/ORG
STUDY OF LEADERS AND FORCES. EUR+WWI ISLAM L/A+17C   FORCES
WOR+45 ELITES STRATA EXEC WEALTH...TIME/SEQ TREND   ECO/TAC
SOC/EXP. PAGE 34 B0686   REGION
                                                     B65
KASER M..COMECON* INTEGRATION PROBLEMS OF THE   PLAN
PLANNED ECONOMIES. INT/ORG TEC/DEV INT/TRADE PRICE   ECO/DEV
ADMIN ADJUST CENTRAL...STAT TIME/SEQ ORG/CHARTS   COM
COMECON. PAGE 58 B1177   REGION
                                                     B65
PHELPS-FETHERS I..SOVIET INTERNATIONAL FRONT   USSR
ORGANIZATIONS* A CONCISE HANDBOOK. DIPLOM DOMIN   EDU/PROP
LEGIT ADMIN EXEC GP/REL PEACE MARXISM...TIME/SEQ   ASIA
GP/COMP. PAGE 83 B1668   COM
                                                     B65
ROTBERG R.I..A POLITICAL HISTORY OF TROPICAL   AFR
AFRICA. EX/STRUC DIPLOM INT/TRADE DOMIN ADMIN   CULTURE
RACE/REL NAT/LISM PWR SOVEREIGN...GEOG TIME/SEQ   COLONIAL
BIBLIOG 1/20. PAGE 91 B1832
                                                     B65
VIORST M..HOSTILE ALLIES: FDR AND DE GAULLE.   TOP/EX
EUR+WWI USA-45 ELITES NAT/G VOL/ASSN FORCES LEGIS   PWR
PLAN LEGIT ADMIN COERCE PERSON...BIOG TIME/SEQ 20   WAR
ROOSEVLT/F DEGAULLE/C. PAGE 112 B2263   FRANCE
                                                     B65
VONGLAHN G..LAW AMONG NATIONS: AN INTRODUCTION TO   CONSTN
PUBLIC INTERNATIONAL LAW. UNIV WOR+45 LAW INT/ORG   JURID
NAT/G LEGIT EXEC RIGID/FLEX...CONCPT TIME/SEQ   INT/LAW
GEN/LAWS UN TOT/POP 20. PAGE 112 B2267
                                                     S65
RUBINSTEIN A.Z.."YUGOSLAVIA'S OPENING SOCIETY." COM   CONSTN
USSR INTELL NAT/G LEGIS TOP/EX LEGIT CT/SYS   EX/STRUC
RIGID/FLEX ALL/VALS SOCISM...HUM TIME/SEQ TREND 20.   YUGOSLAVIA
PAGE 92 B1851
                                                     B66
ANDERSON S.V..CANADIAN OMBUDSMAN PROPOSALS. CANADA   NAT/G
LEGIS DEBATE PARL/PROC...MAJORIT JURID TIME/SEQ   CREATE
IDEA/COMP 20 OMBUDSMAN PARLIAMENT. PAGE 5 B0096   ADMIN
                                                     POL/PAR
                                                     B66
FABAR R..THE VISION AND THE NEED: LATE VICTORIAN   COLONIAL
IMPERIALIST AIMS. MOD/EUR UK WOR-45 CULTURE NAT/G   CONCPT
DIPLOM...TIME/SEQ METH/COMP 19 KIPLING/R   ADMIN
COMMONWLTH. PAGE 34 B0693   ATTIT
                                                     B66
WHITNAH D.R..SAFER SKYWAYS. DIST/IND DELIB/GP   ADMIN
FORCES TOP/EX WORKER TEC/DEV ROUTINE WAR CIVMIL/REL   NAT/G
COST...TIME/SEQ 20 FAA CAB. PAGE 116 B2342   AIR
                                                     GOV/REL
                                                     S67
HOFMANN W.."THE PUBLIC INTEREST PRESSURE GROUP: THE   LOC/G
CASE OF THE DEUTSCHE STADTETAG." GERMANY GERMANY/W   VOL/ASSN
CONSTN STRUCT NAT/G CENTRAL FEDERAL PWR...TIME/SEQ   LOBBY
20. PAGE 51 B1030   ADMIN
                                                     S67
SATHYAMURTHY T.V.."TWENTY YEARS OF UNESCO: AN   ADMIN
INTERPRETATION." SOCIETY PROB/SOLV LEAD PEACE   CONSTN
UNESCO. PAGE 92 B1870   INT/ORG
                                                     TIME/SEQ

TIMING....SEE TIME

TINBERGEN J. B2111

TINKER I. B1633

TITO/MARSH....JOSIP BROZ TITO
                                                     B52
ULAM A.B..TITOISM AND THE COMINFORM. USSR WOR+45   COM
STRUCT INT/ORG NAT/G ACT/RES PLAN EXEC ATTIT DRIVE   POL/PAR
ALL/VALS...CONCPT OBS VAL/FREE 20 COMINTERN   TOTALISM
TITO/MARSH. PAGE 106 B2145   YUGOSLAVIA
                                                     B58
NEAL F.W..TITOISM IN ACTION. COM YUGOSLAVIA AGRI   MARXISM
LOC/G DIPLOM TOTALISM...BIBLIOG 20 TITO/MARSH.   POL/PAR
PAGE 77 B1564   CHIEF
                                                     ADMIN

TIVEY L. B2112

TIZARD/H....HENRY TIZARD

TOBAGO....SEE TRINIDAD

TOCQUEVILL....ALEXIS DE TOCQUEVILLE

TOGO....SEE ALSO AFR
                                                     B64
WITHERELL J.W..OFFICIAL PUBLICATIONS OF FRENCH   BIBLIOG/A
EQUATORIAL AFRICA, FRENCH CAMEROONS, AND TOGO,   AFR
1946-1958 (PAMPHLET). CAMEROON CHAD FRANCE GABON   NAT/G
TOGO LAW ECO/UNDEV EXTR/IND INT/TRADE...GEOG HEAL   ADMIN
20. PAGE 117 B2367

TOLEDO/O....TOLEDO, OHIO

TOMA P.A. B2113

TOMASIC D. B2114

TOMPKINS D.C. B2115,B2116,B2117,B2118

TONGA....TONGA

TOP/EX....TOP EXECUTIVES
                                                     B05
MACHIAVELLI N.."THE ART OF WAR. CHRIST-17C TOP/EX   NAT/G
DRIVE ORD/FREE PWR SKILL...MGT CHARTS. PAGE 67   FORCES
B1360   WAR
                                                     ITALY
                                                     B08
THE GOVERNMENT OF SOUTH AFRICA (VOL. II). SOUTH/AFR   CONSTN
STRATA EXTR/IND EX/STRUC TOP/EX BUDGET ADJUD ADMIN   FINAN
CT/SYS PRODUC...CORREL CENSUS 19 RAILROAD   LEGIS
CIVIL/SERV POSTAL/SYS. PAGE 2 B0033   NAT/G
                                                     B15
SAWYER R.A..A LIST OF WORKS ON COUNTY GOVERNMENT.   BIBLIOG/A
LAW FINAN MUNIC TOP/EX ROUTINE CRIME...CLASSIF   LOC/G
RECORD 19/20. PAGE 93 B1871   GOV/REL
                                                     ADMIN
                                                     B17
CORWIN E.S.."THE PRESIDENT'S CONTROL OF FOREIGN   TOP/EX
RELATIONS. FUT USA-45 CONSTN STRATA NAT/G CHIEF   PWR
EX/STRUC LEGIS KNOWL RESPECT...JURID CONCPT TREND   DIPLOM
CONGRESS VAL/FREE 20 PRESIDENT. PAGE 24 B0483
                                                     N19
ABBOT F.C.."THE CAMBRIDGE CITY MANAGER (PAMPHLET).   MUNIC
PROB/SOLV ADMIN PERS/REL RIGID/FLEX PWR...MGT 20   EX/STRUC
MASSACHU CITY/MGT. PAGE 2 B0050   TOP/EX
                                                     GP/REL
                                                     N19
ABERNATHY B.R..SOME PERSISTING QUESTIONS CONCERNING   PROVS
THE CONSTITUTIONAL STATE EXECUTIVE (PAMPHLET).   EX/STRUC
CONSTN TOP/EX TEC/DEV GOV/REL EFFICIENCY TIME 20   PROB/SOLV
GOVERNOR. PAGE 3 B0054   PWR
                                                     N19
CANADA CIVIL SERV COMM.THE ANALYSIS OF ORGANIZATION   NAT/G
IN THE GOVERNMENT OF CANADA (PAMPHLET). CANADA   MGT
CONSTN EX/STRUC LEGIS TOP/EX CREATE PLAN CONTROL   ADMIN
GP/REL 20. PAGE 18 B0372   DELIB/GP
                                                     N19
WRIGHT D.S..AMERICAN STATE ADMINISTRATORS   QU
(PAMPHLET). USA+45 ATTIT PERSON...SAMP/SIZ CHARTS   TOP/EX
SOC/EXP METH 20. PAGE 118 B2379   ADMIN
                                                     PROVS
                                                     C20
BLACHLY F.F.."THE GOVERNMENT AND ADMINISTRATION OF   NAT/G
GERMANY." GERMANY CONSTN LOC/G PROVS DELIB/GP   GOV/REL
EX/STRUC LEGIS TOP/EX CT/SYS...BIBLIOG/A   ADMIN
19/20. PAGE 12 B0246   PHIL/SCI
                                                     B29
BUELL R..INTERNATIONAL RELATIONS. WOR+45 WOR-45   INT/ORG
CONSTN STRATA FORCES TOP/EX ADMIN ATTIT DRIVE   BAL/PWR
SUPEGO MORAL ORD/FREE PWR SOVEREIGN...JURID SOC   DIPLOM
CONCPT 20. PAGE 17 B0340
                                                     B33
DANGERFIELD R..IN DEFENSE OF THE SENATE. USA-45   LEGIS

CONSTN NAT/G EX/STRUC TOP/EX ATTIT KNOWL
...METH/CNCPT STAT TIME/SEQ TREND CON/ANAL CHARTS
CONGRESS 20 TREATY. PAGE 26 B0528
DELIB/GP
DIPLOM

B38
FIELD G.L.,THE SYNDICAL AND CORPORATIVE
INSTITUTIONS OF ITALIAN FASCISM. ITALY CONSTN
STRATA LABOR EX/STRUC TOP/EX ADJUD ADMIN LEAD
TOTALISM AUTHORIT...MGT 20 MUSSOLIN/B. PAGE 35
B0716
FASCISM
INDUS
NAT/G
WORKER

S39
AIKEN C.,"THE BRITISH BUREAUCRACY AND THE ORIGINS
OF PARLIAMENTARY DEMOCRACY" UK TOP/EX ADMIN. PAGE 3
B0066
MGT
NAT/G
LEGIS

C40
FAHS C.B.,"GOVERNMENT IN JAPAN." FINAN FORCES LEGIS
TOP/EX BUDGET INT/TRADE EDU/PROP SOVERFGN
...CON/ANAL BIBLIOG/A 20 CHINJAP. PAGE 34 B0698
ASIA
DIPLOM
NAT/G
ADMIN

S41
ABEL T.,"THE ELEMENT OF DECISION IN THE PATTERN OF
WAR." EUR+WWI FUT NAT/G TOP/EX DIPLOM ROUTINE
COERCE DISPL PERCEPT PWR...SOC METH/CNCPT HIST/WRIT
TREND GEN/LAWS 20. PAGE 2 B0051
TEC/DEV
FORCES
WAR

S41
STOKE H.W.,"EXECUTIVE LEADERSHIP AND THE GROWTH OF
PROPAGANDA." USA-45 NAT/G EX/STRUC LEGIS TOP/EX
PARL/PROC REPRESENT ORD/FREE PWR...MAJORIT 20.
PAGE 101 B2042
EXEC
LEAD
EDU/PROP
ADMIN

B47
BORGESE G.,COMMON CAUSE. LAW CONSTN SOCIETY STRATA
ECO/DEV INT/ORG POL/PAR FORCES LEGIS TOP/EX CAP/ISM
DIPLOM ADMIN EXEC ATTIT PWR 20. PAGE 14 B0279
WOR+45
NAT/G
SOVEREIGN
REGION

B47
FLYNN E.J.,YOU'RE THE BOSS. USA-45 ELITES TOP/EX
DOMIN CONTROL EXEC LEAD REPRESENT 19/20 NEWYORK/C
ROOSEVLT/F FLYNN/BOSS BOSSISM. PAGE 36 B0732
LOC/G
MUNIC
BIOG
POL/PAR

B47
JENKINS W.S.,COLLECTED PUBLIC DOCUMENTS OF THE
STATES: A CHECK LIST. USA-45 ECO/DEV NAT/G ADMIN
GOV/REL 20. PAGE 56 B1129
BIBLIOG
PROVS
LEGIS
TOP/EX

B47
KEFAUVER E.,A TWENTIETH-CENTURY CONGRESS. POL/PAR
EX/STRUC SENIOR ADMIN CONTROL EXEC LOBBY CHOOSE
EFFICIENCY PWR. PAGE 59 B1189
LEGIS
DELIB/GP
ROUTINE
TOP/EX

B48
HULL C.,THE MEMOIRS OF CORDELL HULL (VOLUME ONE).
USA-45 WOR-45 CONSTN FAM LOC/G NAT/G PROVS DELIB/GP
FORCES LEGIS TOP/EX BAL/PWR LEGIT ADMIN EXEC WAR
ATTIT ORD/FREE PWR...MAJORIT SELF/OBS TIME/SEQ
TREND NAZI 20. PAGE 52 B1062
BIOG
DIPLOM

B48
SHERWOOD R.E.,ROOSEVELT AND HOPKINS. UK USA+45 USSR
NAT/G EX/STRUC FORCES ADMIN ROUTINE PERSON PWR
...TIME/SEQ 20 ROOSEVLT/F HOPKINS/H. PAGE 96 B1946
TOP/EX
BIOG
DIPLOM
WAR

B48
US LIBRARY OF CONGRESS,BRAZIL: A GUIDE TO THE
OFFICIAL PUBLICATIONS OF BRAZIL. BRAZIL L/A+17C
CONSULT DELIB/GP LEGIS CT/SYS 19/20. PAGE 109 B2203
BIBLIOG/A
NAT/G
ADMIN
TOP/EX

B49
MCLEAN J.M.,THE PUBLIC SERVICE AND UNIVERSITY
EDUCATION. UK USA-45 DELIB/GP EX/STRUC TOP/EX ADMIN
...GOV/COMP METH/COMP NAT/COMP ANTHOL 20. PAGE 72
B1455
ACADEM
NAT/G
EXEC
EDU/PROP

S49
STEINMETZ H.,"THE PROBLEMS OF THE LANDRAT: A STUDY
OF COUNTY GOVERNMENT IN THE US ZONE OF GERMANY."
GERMANY/W USA+45 INDUS PLAN DIPLOM EDU/PROP CONTROL
WAR GOV/REL FEDERAL WEALTH PLURISM...GOV/COMP 20
LANDRAT. PAGE 100 B2031
LOC/G
COLONIAL
MGT
TOP/EX

B50
LITTLE HOOVER COMM.HOW TO ACHIEVE GREATER
EFFICIENCY AND ECONOMY IN MINNESOTA'S GOVERNMENT
(PAMPHLET). PLAN BUDGET ADMIN CHOOSE EFFICIENCY
ALL/VALS 20 MINNESOTA. PAGE 66 B1327
TOP/EX
LOC/G
GOV/REL
PROVS

S50
EPSTEIN L.D.,"POLITICAL STERILIZATION OF CIVIL
SERVANTS: THE UNITED STATES AND GREAT BRITAIN." UK
USA+45 USA-45 STRUCT TOP/EX OP/RES PARTIC CHOOSE
NAT/LISM 20 CONGRESS CIVIL/SERV. PAGE 33 B0679
ADMIN
LEGIS
DECISION
POL/PAR

S50
NEUMANN F.L.,"APPROACHES TO THE STUDY OF POLITICAL
POWER." POL/PAR TOP/EX ADMIN LEAD ATTIT ORD/FREE
CONSERVE LAISSEZ MARXISM...PSY SOC. PAGE 78 B1572
PWR
IDEA/COMP
CONCPT

B51
WHITE L.D.,THE JEFFERSONIANS: A STUDY IN
ADMINISTRATIVE HISTORY 18011829. USA-45 DELIB/GP
LEGIS TOP/EX PROB/SOLV BUDGET ECO/TAC GP/REL
FEDERAL...BIOG IDEA/COMP 19 PRESIDENT CONGRESS
JEFFERSN/T. PAGE 116 B2338
ADMIN
NAT/G
POLICY
POL/PAR

S51
SHILS E.A.,"THE LEGISLATOR AND HIS ENVIRONMENT."
EX/STRUC DOMIN CONFER EFFICIENCY PWR MAJORIT.
PAGE 96 B1947
LEGIS
TOP/EX
ADMIN
DELIB/GP

B52
DE GRAZIA A.,POLITICAL ORGANIZATION. CONSTN LOC/G
MUNIC NAT/G CHIEF LEGIS TOP/EX ADJUD CT/SYS
PERS/REL...INT/LAW MYTH UN. PAGE 27 B0553
FEDERAL
LAW
ADMIN

B52
DONHAM W.B.,ADMINISTRATION AND BLIND SPOTS. LG/CO
EX/STRUC BARGAIN ADJUD ROUTINE ROLE SUPEGO 20.
PAGE 30 B0605
ADMIN
TOP/EX
DECISION
POLICY

B52
ELLIOTT W.,UNITED STATES FOREIGN POLICY, ITS
ORGANIZATION AND CONTROL. USA+45 USA-45 CONSTN
NAT/G FORCES TOP/EX PEACE...TIME/SEQ CONGRESS
LEAGUE/NAT 20. PAGE 33 B0670
LEGIS
EX/STRUC
DIPLOM

B52
HIMMELFARB G.,LORD ACTON: A STUDY IN CONSCIENCE AND
POLITICS. MOD/EUR NAT/G POL/PAR SECT LEGIS TOP/EX
EDU/PROP ADMIN NAT/LISM ATTIT PERSON SUPEGO MORAL
ORD/FREE...CONCPT PARLIAMENT 19 ACTON/LORD. PAGE 50
B1014
PWR
BIOG

B52
NASH B.D.,STAFFING THE PRESIDENCY: PLANNING
PAMPHLET NO. 80 (PAMPHLET). NAT/G CHIEF CONSULT
DELIB/GP CONFER ADMIN 20 PRESIDENT. PAGE 77 B1557
EX/STRUC
EXEC
TOP/EX
ROLE

L52
WRIGHT Q.,"CONGRESS AND THE TREATY-MAKING POWER."
USA+45 WOR+45 CONSTN INTELL NAT/G CHIEF CONSULT
EX/STRUC LEGIS TOP/EX CREATE GOV/REL DISPL DRIVE
RIGID/FLEX...TREND TOT/POP CONGRESS CONGRESS 20
TREATY. PAGE 118 B2384
ROUTINE
DIPLOM
INT/LAW
DELIB/GP

S52
SCHWEBEL S.M.,"THE SECRETARY-GENERAL OF THE UN."
FUT INTELL CONSULT DELIB/GP ADMIN PEACE ATTIT
...JURID MGT CONCPT TREND UN CONGRESS 20. PAGE 95
B1915
INT/ORG
TOP/EX

B53
ARGYRIS C.,EXECUTIVE LEADERSHIP: AN APPRAISAL OF A
MANAGER IN ACTION. TOP/EX ADMIN LEAD ADJUST ATTIT
...METH 20. PAGE 6 B0127
MGT
EX/STRUC
WORKER
PERS/REL

B53
HOBBS E.H.,EXECUTIVE REORGANIZATION IN THE NATIONAL
GOVERNMENT. USA+45 USA-45 NAT/G. PAGE 50 B1021
EFFICIENCY
EX/STRUC
ADMIN
TOP/EX

S53
MORRIS B.S.,"THE COMINFORM: A FIVE YEAR
PERSPECTIVE." COM UNIV USSR WOR+45 ECO/DEV POL/PAR
TOP/EX PLAN DOMIN ADMIN TOTALISM ATTIT ALL/VALS
...CONCPT TIME/SEQ TREND CON/ANAL WORK VAL/FREE 20.
PAGE 76 B1527
VOL/ASSN
EDU/PROP
DIPLOM

B54
MILLARD E.L.,FREEDOM IN A FEDERAL WORLD. FUT WOR+45
VOL/ASSN TOP/EX LEGIT ROUTINE FEDERAL PEACE ATTIT
DISPL ORD/FREE PWR...MAJORIT INT/LAW JURID TREND
COLD/WAR 20. PAGE 73 B1479
INT/ORG
CREATE
ADJUD
BAL/PWR

L54
ARCIENEGAS G.,"POST-WAR SOVIET FOREIGN POLICY: A
WORLD PERSPECTIVE." COM USA+45 STRUCT NAT/G POL/PAR
TOP/EX PLAN ADMIN ALL/VALS...TREND COLD/WAR TOT/POP
20. PAGE 6 B0124
INTELL
ACT/RES
USSR

C54
LANDAU J.M.,"PARLIAMENTS AND PARTIES IN EGYPT." UAR
NAT/G SECT CONSULT LEGIS TOP/EX PROB/SOLV ADMIN
COLONIAL...GEN/LAWS BIBLIOG 19/20. PAGE 62 B1254
ISLAM
NAT/LISM
PARL/PROC
POL/PAR

B55
APTER D.E.,THE GOLD COAST IN TRANSITION. FUT CONSTN
CULTURE SOCIETY ECO/UNDEV FAM KIN LOC/G NAT/G
POL/PAR LEGIS TOP/EX EDU/PROP LEGIT ADMIN ATTIT
PERSON PWR...CONCPT STAT INT CENSUS TOT/POP
VAL/FREE. PAGE 6 B0120
AFR
SOVEREIGN

L55
ROSTOW W.W.,"RUSSIA AND CHINA UNDER COMMUNISM."
CHINA/COM USSR INTELL STRUCT INT/ORG NAT/G POL/PAR
TOP/EX ACT/RES PLAN ADMIN ATTIT ALL/VALS MARXISM
...CONCPT OBS TIME/SEQ TREND GOV/COMP VAL/FREE 20.
PAGE 91 B1830
COM
ASIA

S55
MARTIN R.C.,"ADMINISTRATIVE LEADERSHIP IN
GOVERNMENT." NAT/G PARTIC ROUTINE INGP/REL...MGT
20. PAGE 70 B1413
TOP/EX
ADMIN
EXEC
REPRESENT

B56
GLADDEN E.N.,CIVIL SERVICE OR BUREAUCRACY? UK LAW
STRATA LABOR TOP/EX PLAN SENIOR AUTOMAT CONTROL
PARTIC CHOOSE HAPPINESS...CHARTS 19/20 CIVIL/SERV
BUREAUCRCY. PAGE 40 B0808
ADMIN
GOV/REL
EFFICIENCY
PROVS

B56
KAUFMANN W.W.,MILITARY POLICY AND NATIONAL
FORCES

SECURITY. USA+45 ELITES INTELL NAT/G TOP/EX PLAN   CREATE
BAL/PWR DIPLOM ROUTINE COERCE NUC/PWR ATTIT
ORD/FREE PWR 20 COLD/WAR. PAGE 58 B1182
                                                                B56

RANSONE C.B.,THE OFFICE OF GOVERNOR IN THE UNITED   PROVS
STATES. USA+45 ADMIN...MGT INT CHARTS 20 GOVERNOR.   TOP/EX
PAGE 86 B1732   POL/PAR
                                                      EX/STRUC
                                                                B57

DAVID P.T.,EXECUTIVES FOR THE GOVERNMENT: CENTRAL   EX/STRUC
ISSUES OF FEDERAL PERSONNEL ADMINISTRATION. USA+45   TOP/EX
ELITES...GOV/COMP 20. PAGE 26 B0534   ADMIN
                                                                B57

JENNINGS I.,PARLIAMENT. UK FINAN INDUS POL/PAR   PARL/PROC
DELIB/GP EX/STRUC PLAN CONTROL...MAJORIT JURID   TOP/EX
PARLIAMENT. PAGE 56 B1133   MGT
                                                      LEGIS
                                                                B57

LOEWENSTEIN K.,POLITICAL POWER AND THE GOVERNMENTAL   PWR
PROCESS. WOR+45 WOR-45 CONSTN NAT/G POL/PAR   CONCPT
EX/STRUC LEGIS TOP/EX DOMIN EDU/PROP LEGIT ADMIN
REGION CHOOSE ATTIT...JURID STERTYP GEN/LAWS 20.
PAGE 66 B1336
                                                                B58

BERNSTEIN M.H.,THE JOB OF THE FEDERAL EXECUTIVE.   NAT/G
POL/PAR CHIEF LEGIS ADMIN EXEC LOBBY CHOOSE GOV/REL   TOP/EX
ORD/FREE PWR...MGT TREND. PAGE 11 B0228   PERS/COMP
                                                                B58

CLEMENTS R.V.,MANAGERS - A STUDY OF THEIR CAREERS   MGT
IN INDUSTRY. STRATA INDUS TASK PERSON SKILL 20.   ELITES
PAGE 21 B0435   EDU/PROP
                                                      TOP/EX
                                                                B58

DAVIS K.C.,ADMINISTRATIVE LAW; CASES, TEXT,   ADJUD
PROBLEMS. LAW LOC/G NAT/G TOP/EX PAY CONTROL   JURID
GOV/REL INGP/REL FEDERAL 20 SUPREME/CT. PAGE 27   CT/SYS
B0541   ADMIN
                                                                B58

LAW COMMISSION OF INDIA,REFORM OF JUDICIAL   CT/SYS
ADMINISTRATION. INDIA TOP/EX ADMIN DISCRIM   ADJUD
EFFICIENCY...METH/COMP 20. PAGE 63 B1276   GOV/REL
                                                      CONTROL
                                                                B58

SPITZ D.,DEMOCRACY AND THE CHALLANGE OF POWER. FUT   NAT/G
USA+45 USA-45 LAW SOCIETY STRUCT LOC/G POL/PAR   PWR
PROVS DELIB/GP EX/STRUC LEGIS TOP/EX ACT/RES CREATE
DOMIN EDU/PROP LEGIT ADJUD ADMIN ATTIT DRIVE MORAL
ORD/FREE TOT/POP. PAGE 99 B2010
                                                                B59

BRUNTON R.L.,MANAGEMENT PRACTICES FOR SMALLER   ADMIN
CITIES. USA+45 MUNIC CONSULT PLAN BUDGET PERS/REL   LOC/G
20 CITY/MGT. PAGE 16 B0331   MGT
                                                      TOP/EX
                                                                B59

ELLIOTT O.,MEN AT THE TOP. USA+45 CULTURE EX/STRUC   TOP/EX
PRESS GOV/REL ATTIT ALL/VALS...OBS INT QU 20.   PERSON
PAGE 33 B0668   LEAD
                                                      POLICY
                                                                B59

FAYERWEATHER J.,THE EXECUTIVE OVERSEAS: INT/TRADE
ADMINISTRATIVE ATTITUDES AND RELATIONSHIPS IN A   EX/STRUC
FOREIGN CULTURE. USA+45 WOR+45 CULTURE LG/CO SML/CO   NAT/COMP
ATTIT...MGT PERS/COMP 20 MEXIC/AMER. PAGE 35 B0709   PERS/REL
                                                                B59

GRABER D.,CRISIS DIPLOMACY. L/A+17C USA+45 USA-45   ROUTINE
NAT/G TOP/EX ECO/TAC COERCE ATTIT ORD/FREE...CONCPT   MORAL
MYTH TIME/SEQ COLD/WAR 20. PAGE 42 B0848   DIPLOM
                                                                B59

SCHURZ W.L.,AMERICAN FOREIGN AFFAIRS: A GUIDE TO   INT/ORG
INTERNATIONAL AFFAIRS. USA+45 WOR+45 WOR-45 NAT/G   SOCIETY
FORCES LEGIS TOP/EX PLAN EDU/PROP LEGIT ADMIN   DIPLOM
ROUTINE ATTIT ORD/FREE PWR...SOC CONCPT STAT
SAMP/SIZ CHARTS STERTYP 20. PAGE 95 B1910
                                                                B59

SPIRO H.J.,GOVERNMENT BY CONSTITUTIONS: THE   NAT/G
POLITICAL SYSTEMS OF DEMOCRACY. CANADA EUR+WWI FUT   CONSTN
USA+45 WOR+45 WOR-45 LEGIS TOP/EX LEGIT ADMIN
CT/SYS ORD/FREE PWR...TREND TOT/POP VAL/FREE 20.
PAGE 99 B2008
                                                                B59

WARNER W.L.,INDUSTRIAL MAN. USA+45 USA-45 ELITES   EXEC
INDUS LABOR TOP/EX WORKER ADMIN INGP/REL PERS/REL   LEAD
...CHARTS ANTHOL 20. PAGE 114 B2294   PERSON
                                                      MGT
                                                                L59

HECTOR L.J.,"GOVERNMENT BY ANONYMITY: WHO WRITES   ADJUD
OUR REGULATORY OPINIONS?" USA+45 NAT/G TOP/EX   REPRESENT
CONTROL EXEC. PAGE 49 B0987   EX/STRUC
                                                      ADMIN
                                                                S59

HARVEY M.F.,"THE PALESTINE REFUGEE PROBLEM: ACT/RES
ELEMENTS OF A SOLUTION." ISLAM LAW INT/ORG DELIB/GP   LEGIT
TOP/EX ECO/TAC ROUTINE DRIVE HEALTH LOVE ORD/FREE   PEACE
PWR WEALTH...MAJORIT FAO 20. PAGE 48 B0964   ISRAEL
                                                                S59

LASSWELL H.D.,"UNIVERSALITY IN PERSPECTIVE." FUT   INT/ORG

UNIV SOCIETY CONSULT TOP/EX PLAN EDU/PROP ADJUD   JURID
ROUTINE ARMS/CONT COERCE PEACE ATTIT PERSON   TOTALISM
ALL/VALS. PAGE 63 B1271
                                                                S59

ZAUBERMAN A.,"SOVIET BLOC ECONOMIC INTEGRATION."   MARKET
COM CULTURE INTELL ECO/DEV INDUS TOP/EX ACT/RES   INT/ORG
PLAN ECO/TAC INT/TRADE ROUTINE CHOOSE ATTIT   USSR
...TIME/SEQ 20. PAGE 119 B2399   TOTALISM
                                                                B60

BELL J.,THE SPLENDID MISERY: THE STORY OF THE   EXEC
PRESIDENCY AND POWER POLITICS AT CLOSE RANGE.   TOP/EX
USA+45 USA-45 PRESS ADMIN LEAD LOBBY GP/REL   LEGIS
PERS/REL PERSON PRESIDENT. PAGE 10 B0208
                                                                B60

CAMPBELL R.W.,SOVIET ECONOMIC POWER. COM USA+45   ECO/DEV
DIST/IND MARKET TOP/EX ACT/RES CAP/ISM ECO/TAC   PLAN
DOMIN EDU/PROP ADMIN ROUTINE DRIVE...MATH TIME/SEQ   SOCISM
CHARTS WORK 20. PAGE 18 B0371   USSR
                                                                B60

FOSS P.,POLITICS AND GRASS: THE ADMINISTRATION OF   REPRESENT
GRAZING ON THE PUBLIC DOMAIN. USA+45 LEGIS TOP/EX   ADMIN
EXEC...DECISION 20. PAGE 37 B0743   LOBBY
                                                      EX/STRUC
                                                                B60

GLOVER J.D.,A CASE STUDY OF HIGH LEVEL   ADMIN
ADMINISTRATION IN A LARGE ORGANIZATION. EX/STRUC   TOP/EX
EXEC LEAD ROUTINE INGP/REL OPTIMAL ATTIT PERSON   FORCES
...POLICY DECISION INT QU. PAGE 40 B0812   NAT/G
                                                                B60

GRAHAM G.A.,AMERICA'S CAPACITY TO GOVERN: SOME   MGT
PRELIMINARY THOUGHTS FOR PROSPECTIVE   LEAD
ADMINISTRATORS. USA+45 SOCIETY DELIB/GP TOP/EX   CHOOSE
CREATE PROB/SOLV RATIONAL 20. PAGE 42 B0849   ADMIN
                                                                B60

HAYNES G.H.,THE SENATE OF THE UNITED STATES: ITS   LEGIS
HISTORY AND PRACTICE. CONSTN EX/STRUC TOP/EX CONFER   DELIB/GP
DEBATE LEAD LOBBY PARL/PROC CHOOSE PWR SENATE
CONGRESS. PAGE 48 B0977
                                                                B60

LENCZOWSKI G.,OIL AND STATE IN THE MIDDLE EAST. FUT   ISLAM
IRAN LAW ECO/UNDEV EXTR/IND NAT/G TOP/EX PLAN   INDUS
TEC/DEV ECO/TAC LEGIT ADMIN COERCE ATTIT ALL/VALS   NAT/LISM
PWR...CHARTS 20. PAGE 64 B1288
                                                                B60

LINDSAY K.,EUROPEAN ASSEMBLIES: THE EXPERIMENTAL   VOL/ASSN
PERIOD 1949-1959. EUR+WWI ECO/DEV NAT/G POL/PAR   INT/ORG
LEGIS TOP/EX ACT/RES PLAN ECO/TAC DOMIN LEGIT   REGION
ROUTINE ATTIT DRIVE ORD/FREE PWR SKILL...SOC CONCPT
TREND CHARTS GEN/LAWS VAL/FREE. PAGE 65 B1315
                                                                B60

MEEHAN E.J.,THE BRITISH LEFT WING AND FOREIGN   ACT/RES
POLICY: A STUDY OF THE INFLUENCE OF IDEOLOGY. FUT   ATTIT
UK UNIV WOR+45 INTELL TOP/EX PLAN ADMIN ROUTINE   DIPLOM
DRIVE...OBS TIME/SEQ GEN/LAWS PARLIAMENT 20.
PAGE 72 B1461
                                                                B60

RUBENSTEIN A.H.,SOME THEORIES OF ORGANIZATION.   SOCIETY
ROUTINE ATTIT...DECISION ECOMETRIC. PAGE 91 B1846   ECO/DEV
                                                      INDUS
                                                      TOP/EX
                                                                S60

BOYER W.W.,"POLICY MAKING BY GOVERNMENT AGENCIES."   NAT/G
USA+45 WOR+45 R+D DELIB/GP TOP/EX EDU/PROP ROUTINE   DIPLOM
ATTIT BIO/SOC DRIVE...CONCPT TREND TOT/POP 20.
PAGE 14 B0293
                                                                S60

HUTCHINSON C.E.,"AN INSTITUTE FOR NATIONAL SECURITY   POLICY
AFFAIRS." USA+45 R+D NAT/G CONSULT TOP/EX ACT/RES   METH/CNCPT
CREATE PLAN TEC/DEV EDU/PROP ROUTINE NUC/PWR ATTIT   ELITES
ORD/FREE PWR...DECISION MGT PHIL/SCI CONCPT RECORD   DIPLOM
GEN/LAWS GEN/METH 20. PAGE 53 B1068
                                                                S60

RAPHAELI N.,"SELECTED ARTICLES AND DOCUMENTS ON   BIBLIOG
COMPARATIVE PUBLIC ADMINISTRATION." USA+45 FINAN   MGT
LOC/G TOP/EX TEC/DEV EXEC GP/REL INGP/REL...GP/COMP   ADMIN
GOV/COMP METH/COMP. PAGE 86 B1738   EX/STRUC
                                                                S60

SCHER S.,"CONGRESSIONAL COMMITTEE MEMBERS AND   LEGIS
INDEPENDENT AGENCY OVERSEERS: A CASE STUDY."   GOV/REL
DELIB/GP EX/STRUC JUDGE TOP/EX DOMIN ADMIN CONTROL   LABOR
PWR...SOC/EXP HOUSE/REP CONGRESS. PAGE 93 B1886   ADJUD
                                                                B61

BENOIT E.,EUROPE AT SIXES AND SEVENS: THE COMMON   FINAN
MARKET, THE FREE TRADE ASSOCIATION AND THE UNITED   ECO/DEV
STATES. EUR+WWI FUT USA+45 INDUS CONSULT DELIB/GP   VOL/ASSN
EX/STRUC TOP/EX ACT/RES ECO/TAC EDU/PROP ROUTINE
CHOOSE PERCEPT WEALTH...MGT TREND EEC TOT/POP 20
EFTA. PAGE 11 B0217
                                                                B61

BISHOP D.G.,THE ADMINISTRATION OF BRITISH FOREIGN   ROUTINE
RELATIONS. EUR+WWI MOD/EUR INT/ORG NAT/G POL/PAR   PWR
DELIB/GP LEGIS TOP/EX ECO/TAC DOMIN EDU/PROP ADMIN   DIPLOM
COERCE 20. PAGE 12 B0243   UK
                                                                B61

GORDON W.J.J.,SYNECTICS; THE DEVELOPMENT OF   CREATE
CREATIVE CAPACITY. USA+45 PLAN TEC/DEV KNOWL WEALTH   PROB/SOLV

...DECISION MGT 20. PAGE 41 B0832   ACT/RES
                                                     TOP/EX
                                                            B61
GRIFFITH E.S.,CONGRESS: ITS CONTEMPORARY ROLE.   PARL/PROC
CONSTN POL/PAR CHIEF PLAN BUDGET DIPLOM CONFER   EX/STRUC
ADMIN LOBBY...DECISION CONGRESS. PAGE 43 B0878   TOP/EX
                                                     LEGIS
                                                            B61
HAMILTON A.,THE FEDERALIST. USA-45 NAT/G VOL/ASSN   EX/STRUC
LEGIS TOP/EX EDU/PROP LEGIT CHOOSE ATTIT RIGID/FLEX   CONSTN
ORD/FREE PWR...MAJORIT JURID CONCPT ANTHOL. PAGE 46
B0931
                                                            B61
HARRISON S.,INDIA AND THE UNITED STATES. FUT S/ASIA DELIB/GP
USA+45 WOR+45 INTELL ECO/DEV ECO/UNDEV AGRI INDUS   ACT/RES
INT/ORG NAT/G CONSULT EX/STRUC TOP/EX PLAN ECO/TAC   FOR/AID
NEUTRAL ALL/VALS...MGT TOT/POP 20. PAGE 47 B0956   INDIA
                                                            B61
HASAN H.S.,PAKISTAN AND THE UN. ISLAM WOR+45   INT/ORG
ECO/DEV ECO/UNDEV NAT/G TOP/EX ECO/TAC FOR/AID   ATTIT
EDU/PROP ADMIN DRIVE PERCEPT...OBS TIME/SEQ UN 20.   PAKISTAN
PAGE 48 B0965
                                                            B61
HAYTER W.,THE DIPLOMACY OF THE GREAT POWERS. FRANCE   DIPLOM
UK USSR WOR+45 EX/STRUC TOP/EX NUC/PWR PEACE...OBS   POLICY
20. PAGE 48 B0978   NAT/G
                                                            B61
MARKMANN C.L.,JOHN F. KENNEDY: A SENSE OF PURPOSE.   CHIEF
USA+45 INTELL FAM CONSULT DELIB/GP LEGIS PERSON   TOP/EX
SKILL 20 KENNEDY/JF EISNHWR/DD ROOSEVLT/F   ADMIN
NEW/FRONTR PRESIDENT. PAGE 69 B1399   BIOG
                                                            B61
MARVICK D.,POLITICAL DECISION-MAKERS. INTELL STRATA TOP/EX
NAT/G POL/PAR EX/STRUC LEGIS DOMIN EDU/PROP ATTIT   BIOG
PERSON PWR...PSY STAT OBS CONT/OBS STAND/INT   ELITES
UNPLAN/INT TIME/SEQ CHARTS STERTYP VAL/FREE.
PAGE 70 B1416
                                                            B61
OPOTOWSKY S.,THE KENNEDY GOVERNMENT. NAT/G CONSULT   ADMIN
EX/STRUC LEAD PERSON...POLICY 20 KENNEDY/JF   BIOG
CONGRESS CABINET. PAGE 80 B1613   ELITES
                                                     TOP/EX
                                                            B61
QURESHI S.,INCENTIVES IN AMERICAN EMPLOYMENT   SERV/IND
(THESIS, UNIVERSITY OF PENNSYLVANIA). DELIB/GP   ADMIN
TOP/EX BUDGET ROUTINE SANCTION COST TECHRACY MGT.   PAY
PAGE 85 B1727   EX/STRUC
                                                            B61
RAO K.V.,PARLIAMENTARY DEMOCRACY OF INDIA. INDIA   CONSTN
EX/STRUC TOP/EX COLONIAL CT/SYS PARL/PROC ORD/FREE   ADJUD
...POLICY CONCPT TREND 20 PARLIAMENT. PAGE 86 B1733   NAT/G
                                                     FEDERAL
                                                            B61
STRAUSS E.,THE RULING SERVANTS. FRANCE UK USSR   ADMIN
WOR+45 WOR-45 NAT/G CONSULT DELIB/GP EX/STRUC   PWR
TOP/EX DOMIN EDU/PROP LEGIT ROUTINE...MGT TIME/SEQ   ELITES
STERTYP 20. PAGE 101 B2051
                                                            B61
TANZER L.,THE KENNEDY CIRCLE. INTELL CONSULT   EX/STRUC
DELIB/GP TOP/EX CONTROL EXEC INGP/REL PERS/REL PWR   NAT/G
...BIOG IDEA/COMP ANTHOL 20 KENNEDY/JF PRESIDENT   CHIEF
DEMOCRAT MCNAMARA/R RUSK/D. PAGE 103 B2077
                                                            S61
ALGER C.F.,"NON-RESOLUTION CONSEQUENCES OF THE   INT/ORG
UNITED NATIONS AND THEIR EFFECT ON INTERNATIONAL   DRIVE
CONFLICT." WOR+45 CONSTN ECO/DEV NAT/G CONSULT   BAL/PWR
DELIB/GP TOP/EX ACT/RES PLAN DIPLOM EDU/PROP
ROUTINE ATTIT ALL/VALS...INT/LAW TOT/POP UN 20.
PAGE 4 B0075
                                                            S61
DEXTER L.A.,"HAS THE PUBLIC OFFICIAL ON OBLIGATION   ADMIN
TO RESTRICT HIS FRIENDSHIPS?" NAT/G EX/STRUC TOP/EX   ATTIT
20. PAGE 29 B0584   REPRESENT
                                                     POLICY
                                                            S61
HALPERIN M.H.,"THE GAITHER COMMITTEE AND THE POLICY PLAN
PROCESS." USA+45 NAT/G TOP/EX ACT/RES LEGIT ADMIN   POLICY
BAL/PAY PERCEPT...CONCPT TOT/POP 20. PAGE 46 B0928   NUC/PWR
                                                     DELIB/GP
                                                            S61
LEWY G.,"SUPERIOR ORDERS, NUCLEAR WARFARE AND THE   DETER
DICTATES OF CONSCIENCE: THE DILEMMA OF MILITARY   INT/ORG
OBEDIENCE IN THE ATOMIC." FUT UNIV WOR+45 INTELL   LAW
SOCIETY FORCES TOP/EX ACT/RES ADMIN ROUTINE NUC/PWR   INT/LAW
PERCEPT RIGID/FLEX ALL/VALS...POLICY CONCPT 20.
PAGE 65 B1308
                                                            S61
LYONS G.M.,"THE NEW CIVIL-MILITARY RELATIONS."   CIVMIL/REL
USA+45 NAT/G EX/STRUC TOP/EX PROB/SOLV ADMIN EXEC   PWR
PARTIC 20. PAGE 67 B1350   REPRESENT
                                                            S61
TAUBENFELD H.J.,"OUTER SPACE--PAST POLITICS AND   PLAN
FUTURE POLICY." FUT USA+45 WOR-45 AIR INTELL   SPACE
STRUCT ECO/DEV NAT/G TOP/EX ACT/RES ADMIN ROUTINE   INT/ORG
NUC/PWR ATTIT DRIVE...CONCPT TIME/SEQ TREND TOT/POP
20. PAGE 103 B2083

                                                            S61
VINER J.,"ECONOMIC FOREIGN POLICY ON THE NEW   TOP/EX
FRONTIER." USA+45 ECO/UNDEV AGRI FINAN INDUS MARKET   ECO/TAC
INT/ORG NAT/G FOR/AID INT/TRADE ADMIN ATTIT PWR 20   BAL/PAY
KENNEDY/JF. PAGE 112 B2262   TARIFFS
                                                            S61
VIRALLY M.,"VERS UNE REFORME DU SECRETARIAT DES   INT/ORG
NATIONS UNIES." FUT WOR+45 CONSTN ECO/DEV TOP/EX   INTELL
BAL/PWR ADMIN ALL/VALS...CONCPT BIOG UN VAL/FREE   DIPLOM
20. PAGE 112 B2264
                                                            B62
ANDREWS W.G.,EUROPEAN POLITICAL INSTITUTIONS.   NAT/COMP
FRANCE GERMANY UK USSR TOP/EX LEAD PARL/PROC CHOOSE   POL/PAR
20. PAGE 5 B0104   EX/STRUC
                                                     LEGIS
                                                            B62
BENSON E.T.,CROSS FIRE: THE EIGHT YEARS WITH   ADMIN
EISENHOWER. USA+45 DIPLOM LEAD ATTIT PERSON   POLICY
CONSERVE...TRADIT BIOG 20 EISNHWR/DD PRESIDENT   DELIB/GP
TAFT/RA DULLES/JF NIXON/RM. PAGE 11 B0218   TOP/EX
                                                            B62
GRAY R.K.,EIGHTEEN ACRES UNDER GLASS. ELITES   CHIEF
CONSULT EX/STRUC DIPLOM PRESS CONFER WAR PERS/REL   ADMIN
PERSON 20 EISNHWR/DD TRUMAN/HS CABINET. PAGE 43   TOP/EX
B0860   NAT/G
                                                            B62
HATTERY L.H.,INFORMATION RETRIEVAL MANAGEMENT.   R+D
CLIENT INDUS TOP/EX COMPUTER OP/RES TEC/DEV ROUTINE   COMPUT/IR
COST EFFICIENCY RIGID/FLEX...METH/COMP ANTHOL 20.   MGT
PAGE 48 B0968   CREATE
                                                            B62
JENNINGS E.E.,THE EXECUTIVE: AUTOCRAT, BUREAUCRAT,   EX/STRUC
DEMOCRAT. LEAD EFFICIENCY DRIVE 20. PAGE 56 B1131   INGP/REL
                                                     TOP/EX
                                                     CONTROL
                                                            B62
JEWELL M.E.,SENATORIAL POLITICS AND FOREIGN POLICY. USA+45
NAT/G POL/PAR CHIEF DELIB/GP TOP/EX FOR/AID   LEGIS
EDU/PROP ROUTINE ATTIT PWR SKILL...MAJORIT   DIPLOM
METH/CNCPT TIME/SEQ CONGRESS 20 PRESIDENT. PAGE 56
B1138
                                                            B62
LYNCH J.,ADMINISTRATION COLONIAL ESPANOLA   COLONIAL
1782-1810. SPAIN PROVS TOP/EX PARTIC 18/19 ARGEN.   CONTROL
PAGE 67 B1349   ADJUD
                                                     ADMIN
                                                            B62
MAILICK S.,CONCEPTS AND ISSUES IN ADMINISTRATIVE   DECISION
BEHAVIOR. EX/STRUC TOP/EX ROUTINE INGP/REL   MGT
EFFICIENCY. PAGE 68 B1380   EXEC
                                                     PROB/SOLV
                                                            B62
MODELSKI G.,A THEORY OF FOREIGN POLICY. WOR+45   PLAN
WOR-45 NAT/G DELIB/GP EX/STRUC TOP/EX EDU/PROP   PWR
LEGIT ROUTINE...POLICY CONCPT TOT/POP COLD/WAR 20.   DIPLOM
PAGE 74 B1494
                                                            B62
PACKARD V.,THE PYRAMID CLIMBERS. USA+45 ELITES   INDUS
SOCIETY CREATE PROB/SOLV EFFICIENCY ATTIT...MGT 20.   TOP/EX
PAGE 80 B1621   PERS/REL
                                                     DRIVE
                                                            B62
PRAKASH O.M.,THE THEORY AND WORKING OF STATE   LG/CO
CORPORATIONS: WITH SPECIAL REFERENCE TO INDIA.   ECO/UNDEV
INDIA UK USA+45 TOP/EX PRICE ADMIN EFFICIENCY...MGT   GOV/REL
METH/COMP 20 TVA. PAGE 84 B1698   SOCISM
                                                            B62
SAMPSON A.,ANATOMY OF BRITAIN. UK LAW COM/IND FINAN ELITES
INDUS MARKET MUNIC POL/PAR EX/STRUC TOP/EX DIPLOM   PWR
LEAD REPRESENT PERSON PARLIAMENT WORSHIP. PAGE 92   STRUCT
B1866   FORCES
                                                            B62
STAHL O.G.,PUBLIC PERSONNEL ADMINISTRATION. LOC/G   ADMIN
TOP/EX CREATE PLAN ROUTINE...TECHNIC MGT T.   WORKER
PAGE 100 B2017   EX/STRUC
                                                     NAT/G
                                                            B62
WANGSNESS P.H.,THE POWER OF THE CITY MANAGER.   PWR
USA+45 EX/STRUC BAL/PWR BUDGET TAX ADMIN REPRESENT   TOP/EX
CENTRAL EFFICIENCY DRIVE ROLE...POLICY 20 CITY/MGT.   MUNIC
PAGE 113 B2286   LOC/G
                                                            L62
ABERLE D.F.,"CHAHAR AND DAGOR MONGOL BUREAUCRATIC   EX/STRUC
ADMINISTRATION: 19621945." ASIA MUNIC TOP/EX PWR   STRATA
...MGT OBS INT MONGOL 20. PAGE 3 B0053
                                                            L62
NEIBURG H.L.,"THE EISENHOWER AEC AND CONGRESS: A   CHIEF
STUDY IN EXECUTIVE-LEGISLATIVE RELATIONS." USA+45   LEGIS
NAT/G POL/PAR DELIB/GP EX/STRUC TOP/EX ADMIN EXEC   GOV/REL
LEAD ROUTINE PWR...POLICY COLD/WAR CONGRESS   NUC/PWR
PRESIDENT AEC. PAGE 77 B1567
                                                            S62
GUYOT J.F.,"GOVERNMENT BUREAUCRATS ARE DIFFERENT."   ATTIT
USA+45 REPRESENT PWR 20. PAGE 45 B0906   DRIVE
                                                     TOP/EX
                                                     ADMIN

S62

HUDSON G.F.,"SOVIET FEARS OF THE WEST." COM USA+45   ATTIT
SOCIETY DELIB/GP EX/STRUC TOP/EX ACT/RES CREATE   MYTH
DOMIN EDU/PROP LEGIT ADMIN ROUTINE DRIVE PERSON   GERMANY
RIGID/FLEX PWR...RECORD TIME/SEQ TOT/POP 20   USSR
STALIN/J. PAGE 52 B1057

S62

IOVTCHOUK M.T.,"ON SOME THEORETICAL PRINCIPLES AND   COM
METHODS OF SOCIOLOGICAL INVESTIGATIONS (IN   ECO/DEV
RUSSIAN)." FUT USA+45 STRATA R+D NAT/G POL/PAR   CAP/ISM
TOP/EX ACT/RES PLAN ECO/TAC EDU/PROP ROUTINE ATTIT   USSR
RIGID/FLEX MARXISM SOCISM...MARXIST METH/CNCPT OBS
TREND NAT/COMP GEN/LAWS 20. PAGE 54 B1102

S62

MARTIN L.W.,"POLITICAL SETTLEMENTS AND ARMS   CONCPT
CONTROL." COM EUR+WWI GERMANY USA+45 PROVS FORCES   ARMS/CONT
TOP/EX ACT/RES CREATE DOMIN LEGIT ROUTINE COERCE
ATTIT RIGID/FLEX ORD/FREE PWR...METH/CNCPT RECORD
GEN/LAWS 20. PAGE 70 B1410

S62

MCCLELLAND C.A.,"DECISIONAL OPPORTUNITY AND   ACT/RES
POLITICAL CONTROVERSY." USA+45 NAT/G POL/PAR FORCES   PERCEPT
TOP/EX DOMIN ADMIN PEACE DRIVE ORD/FREE PWR   DIPLOM
...DECISION SIMUL 20. PAGE 72 B1444

S62

READ W.H.,"UPWARD COMMUNICATION IN INDUSTRIAL   ADMIN
HIERARCHIES." LG/CO TOP/EX PROB/SOLV DOMIN EXEC   INGP/REL
PERS/REL ATTIT DRIVE PERCEPT...CORREL STAT CHARTS   PSY
20. PAGE 86 B1747   MGT

S62

SCHILLING W.R.,"SCIENTISTS, FOREIGN POLICY AND   NAT/G
POLITICS." WOR+45 WOR-45 INTELL INT/ORG CONSULT   TEC/DEV
TOP/EX ACT/RES PLAN ADMIN KNOWL...CONCPT OBS TREND   DIPLOM
LEAGUE/NAT 20. PAGE 93 B1889   NUC/PWR

N62

UNIVERSITY PITT INST LOC GOVT,THE COUNCIL-MANAGER   LOC/G
FORM OF GOVERNMENT IN PENNSYLVANIA (PAMPHLET).   TOP/EX
PROVS EX/STRUC REPRESENT GOV/REL EFFICIENCY   MUNIC
...CHARTS SIMUL 20 PENNSYLVAN CITY/MGT. PAGE 107   PWR
B2169

B63

COUNCIL STATE GOVERNMENTS,HANDBOOK FOR LEGISLATIVE   LEGIS
COMMITTEES. USA+45 LAW DELIB/GP EX/STRUC TOP/EX   PARL/PROC
CHOOSE PWR...METH/COMP 20. PAGE 24 B0496   PROVS
                                                           ADJUD

B63

DEBRAY P.,LE PORTUGAL ENTRE DEUX REVOLUTIONS.   NAT/G
EUR+WWI PORTUGAL CONSTN LEGIT ADMIN ATTIT ALL/VALS   DELIB/GP
...DECISION CONCPT 20 SALAZAR/A. PAGE 28 B0567   TOP/EX

B63

GANGULY D.S.,PUBLIC CORPORATIONS IN A NATIONAL   ECO/UNDEV
ECONOMY. INDIA WOR+45 FINAN INDUS TOP/EX PRICE   LG/CO
EFFICIENCY...MGT STAT CHARTS BIBLIOG 20. PAGE 38   SOCISM
B0779   GOV/REL

B63

HARGROVE M.M.,BUSINESS POLICY CASES-WITH BEHAVIORAL   SOC/EXP
SCIENCE IMPLICATIONS. LG/CO SML/CO EX/STRUC TOP/EX   INDUS
PLAN PROB/SOLV CONFER ADMIN CONTROL ROUTINE   DECISION
EFFICIENCY. PAGE 47 B0946   MGT

B63

HEYEL C.,THE ENCYCLOPEDIA OF MANAGEMENT. WOR+45   MGT
MARKET TOP/EX TEC/DEV AUTOMAT LEAD ADJUST...STAT   INDUS
CHARTS GAME ANTHOL BIBLIOG. PAGE 49 B1002   ADMIN
                                                           FINAN

B63

MACNEIL N.,FORGE OF DEMOCRACY: THE HOUSE OF   LEGIS
REPRESENTATIVES. POL/PAR EX/STRUC TOP/EX DEBATE   DELIB/GP
LEAD PARL/PROC CHOOSE GOV/REL PWR...OBS HOUSE/REP.
PAGE 68 B1374

B63

RICHARDS P.G.,PATRONAGE IN BRITISH GOVERNMENT.   EX/STRUC
ELITES DELIB/GP TOP/EX PROB/SOLV CONTROL CT/SYS   REPRESENT
EXEC PWR. PAGE 88 B1774   POL/PAR
                                                           ADMIN

B63

ROETTER C.,THE DIPLOMATIC ART. USSR INT/ORG NAT/G   DIPLOM
DELIB/GP ROUTINE NUC/PWR PEACE...POLICY 20. PAGE 90   ELITES
B1812   TOP/EX

B63

SIDEY H.,JOHN F. KENNEDY, PRESIDENT. USA+45 INTELL   BIOG
FAM CONSULT DELIB/GP LEGIS ADMIN LEAD 20 KENNEDY/JF   TOP/EX
PRESIDENT. PAGE 97 B1951   SKILL
                                                           PERSON

B63

STEIN H.,AMERICAN CIVIL-MILITARY DECISION. USA+45   CIVMIL/REL
USA-45 EX/STRUC FORCES LEGIS TOP/EX PLAN DIPLOM   DECISION
FOR/AID ATTIT 20 CONGRESS. PAGE 100 B2028   WAR
                                                           BUDGET

B63

TUCKER R.C.,THE SOVIET POLITICAL MIND. WOR+45   COM
ELITES INT/ORG NAT/G POL/PAR PLAN DIPLOM ECO/TAC   TOP/EX
DOMIN ADMIN NUC/PWR REV DRIVE PERSON SUPEGO PWR   USSR
WEALTH...POLICY MGT PSY CONCPT OBS BIOG TREND
COLD/WAR MARX/KARL 20. PAGE 106 B2134

B63

TUCKER R.C.,THE SOVIET POLITICAL MIND. COM INTELL   STRUCT

NAT/G TOP/EX EDU/PROP ADMIN COERCE TOTALISM ATTIT   RIGID/FLEX
PWR MARXISM...PSY MYTH HYPO/EXP 20. PAGE 106 B2135   ELITES
                                                           USSR

B63

WARNER W.L.,THE AMERICAN FEDERAL EXECUTIVE. USA+45   ELITES
USA-45 CONSULT EX/STRUC GP/REL DRIVE ALL/VALS...PSY   NAT/G
DEEP/QU CHARTS 19/20 PRESIDENT. PAGE 114 B2295   TOP/EX
                                                           ADMIN

L63

SPITZ A.A.,"DEVELOPMENT ADMINISTRATION: AN   ADMIN
ANNOTATED BIBLIOGRAPHY." WOR+45 CULTURE SOCIETY   ECO/UNDEV
STRATA DELIB/GP EX/STRUC TOP/EX ACT/RES ECO/TAC
DOMIN EDU/PROP LEGIT COERCE ATTIT ALL/VALS...MGT
VAL/FREE. PAGE 99 B2009

S63

ANTHON C.G.,"THE END OF THE ADENAUER ERA." EUR+WWI   NAT/G
GERMANY/W CONSTN EX/STRUC CREATE DIPLOM LEGIT ATTIT   TOP/EX
PERSON ALL/VALS...RECORD 20 ADENAUER/K. PAGE 6   BAL/PWR
B0113   GERMANY

S63

DELLIN L.A.D.,"BULGARIA UNDER SOVIET LEADERSHIP."   AGRI
BULGARIA COM USA+45 USSR ECO/DEV INDUS POL/PAR   NAT/G
EX/STRUC TOP/EX COERCE ATTIT RIGID/FLEX...POLICY   TOTALISM
TIME/SEQ 20. PAGE 28 B0572

S63

ETIENNE G.,"'LOIS OBJECTIVES' ET PROBLEMES DE   TOTALISM
DEVELOPPEMENT DANS LE CONTEXTE CHINE-URSS." ASIA   USSR
CHINA/COM COM FUT STRUCT INT/ORG VOL/ASSN TOP/EX
TEC/DEV ECO/TAC ATTIT RIGID/FLEX...GEOG MGT
TIME/SEQ TOT/POP 20. PAGE 34 B0682

S63

HARRIS R.L.,"A COMPARATIVE ANALYSIS OF THE   DELIB/GP
ADMINISTRATIVE SYSTEMS OF CANADA AND CEYLON."   EX/STRUC
S/ASIA CULTURE SOCIETY STRATA TOP/EX ACT/RES DOMIN   CANADA
EDU/PROP LEGIT COERCE ATTIT SUPEGO ALL/VALS...MGT   CEYLON
CHARTS GEN/LAWS VAL/FREE 20. PAGE 47 B0955

S63

SCHMITT H.A.,"THE EUROPEAN COMMUNITIES." EUR+WWI   VOL/ASSN
FRANCE DELIB/GP EX/STRUC TOP/EX CREATE TEC/DEV   ECO/DEV
ECO/TAC LEGIT REGION COERCE DRIVE ALL/VALS
...METH/CNCPT EEC 20. PAGE 94 B1897

B64

COMMITTEE ECONOMIC DEVELOPMENT,IMPROVING EXECUTIVE   EXEC
MANAGEMENT IN THE FEDERAL GOVERNMENT. USA+45 CHIEF   MGT
DELIB/GP WORKER PLAN PAY SENIOR ADMIN EFFICIENCY 20   TOP/EX
PRESIDENT. PAGE 22 B0457   NAT/G

B64

CONNECTICUT U INST PUBLIC SERV,SUMMARY OF CHARTER   CONSTN
PROVISIONS IN CONNECTICUT LOCAL GOVERNMENT   MUNIC
(PAMPHLET). USA+45 DELIB/GP LEGIS TOP/EX CHOOSE   LOC/G
REPRESENT 20 CONNECTICT CITY/MGT MAYOR. PAGE 23   EX/STRUC
B0462

B64

FONTENEAU J.,LE CONSEIL MUNICIPAL: LE MAIRE-LES   MUNIC
ADJOINTS. FRANCE FINAN DELIB/GP EX/STRUC BUDGET TAX   NEIGH
TASK COST INCOME ROLE SUPEGO 20 MAYOR. PAGE 36   ADMIN
B0735   TOP/EX

B64

NEUSTADT R.,PRESIDENTIAL POWER. USA+45 CONSTN NAT/G TOP/EX
CHIEF LEGIS CREATE EDU/PROP LEGIT ADMIN EXEC COERCE SKILL
ATTIT PERSON RIGID/FLEX PWR CONGRESS 20 PRESIDENT
TRUMAN/HS EISNHWR/DD. PAGE 78 B1575

B64

NUQUIST A.E.,TOWN GOVERNMENT IN VERMONT. USA+45   LOC/G
FINAN TOP/EX PROB/SOLV BUDGET TAX REPRESENT SUFF   MUNIC
EFFICIENCY...OBS INT 20 VERMONT. PAGE 79 B1595   POPULISM
                                                           ADMIN

B64

SAYLES L.R.,MANAGERIAL BEHAVIOR: ADMINISTRATION IN   CONCPT
COMPLEX ORGANIZATIONS. INDUS LG/CO PROB/SOLV   ADMIN
CONTROL EXEC INGP/REL PERS/REL SKILL...MGT OBS   TOP/EX
PREDICT GEN/LAWS 20. PAGE 93 B1874   EX/STRUC

B64

SINGER M.R.,THE EMERGING ELITE: A STUDY OF   TOP/EX
POLITICAL LEADERSHIP IN CEYLON. S/ASIA ECO/UNDEV   STRATA
AGRI KIN NAT/G SECT EX/STRUC LEGIT ATTIT PWR   NAT/LISM
RESPECT...SOC STAT CHARTS 20. PAGE 97 B1967   CEYLON

B64

US SENATE COMM GOVT OPERATIONS,ADMINISTRATION OF   ADMIN
NATIONAL SECURITY. USA+45 CHIEF TOP/EX PLAN DIPLOM   FORCES
CONTROL PEACE...POLICY DECISION 20 PRESIDENT   ORD/FREE
CONGRESS. PAGE 110 B2216   NAT/G

B64

WHEELER-BENNETT J.W.,THE NEMESIS OF POWER (2ND   FORCES
ED.). EUR+WWI GERMANY TOP/EX TEC/DEV ADMIN WAR   NAT/G
PERS/REL RIGID/FLEX ROLE ORD/FREE PWR FASCISM 20   GP/REL
HITLER/A. PAGE 116 B2332   STRUCT

S64

KASSOF A.,"THE ADMINISTERED SOCIETY: SOCIETY
TOTALITARIANISM WITHOUT TERROR." COM USSR STRATA   DOMIN
AGRI INDUS NAT/G PERF/ART SCHOOL TOP/EX EDU/PROP   TOTALISM
ADMIN ORD/FREE PWR...POLICY SOC TIME/SEQ GEN/LAWS
VAL/FREE 20. PAGE 58 B1178

S64

KHAN M.Z.,"THE PRESIDENT OF THE GENERAL ASSEMBLY."   INT/ORG
WOR+45 CONSTN DELIB/GP EDU/PROP LEGIT ROUTINE PWR   TOP/EX

RESPECT SKILL...DECISION SOC BIOG TREND UN 20.
PAGE 59 B1202

B65

FOLTZ W.J.,FROM FRENCH WEST AFRICA TO THE MALI   EXEC
FEDERATION. AFR FRANCE MALI ADMIN CONTROL FEDERAL   TOP/EX
...DECISION 20. PAGE 36 B0734   ELITES
                                                         LEAD
                                                               B65
HAIGHT D.E.,THE PRESIDENT; ROLES AND POWERS. USA+45   CHIEF
USA-45 POL/PAR PLAN DIPLOM CHOOSE PERS/REL PWR   LEGIS
18/20 PRESIDENT CONGRESS. PAGE 45 B0915   TOP/EX
                                                         EX/STRUC
                                                               B65
HODGSON R.C.,THE EXECUTIVE ROLE CONSTELLATION: AN   LG/CO
ANALYSIS OF PERSONALITY AND ROLE RELATIONS IN   ADMIN
MANAGEMENT. USA+45 PUB/INST EXEC PERS/REL PERSON   TOP/EX
...PSY PERS/COMP HYPO/EXP 20. PAGE 51 B1027   ROLE
                                                               B65
NORDEN A.,WAR AND NAZI CRIMINALS IN WEST GERMANY: FASCIST
STATE, ECONOMY, ADMINISTRATION, ARMY, JUSTICE,   WAR
SCIENCE. GERMANY GERMANY/W MOD/EUR ECO/DEV ACADEM   NAT/G
EX/STRUC FORCES DOMIN ADMIN CT/SYS...POLICY MAJORIT   TOP/EX
PACIFIST 20. PAGE 78 B1587
                                                               B65
PRESTHUS R.,BEHAVIORAL APPROACHES TO PUBLIC   GEN/METH
ADMINISTRATION. UK STRATA LG/CO PUB/INST VOL/ASSN   DECISION
EX/STRUC TOP/EX EFFICIENCY HEALTH. PAGE 84 B1704   ADMIN
                                                         R+D
                                                               B65
STANLEY D.T.,CHANGING ADMINISTRATIONS. USA+45   NAT/G
POL/PAR DELIB/GP TOP/EX BUDGET GOV/REL GP/REL   CHIEF
PERS/REL PWR...MAJORIT DECISION MGT 20 PRESIDENT   ADMIN
SUCCESSION DEPT/STATE DEPT/DEFEN DEPT/HEW. PAGE 100   EX/STRUC
B2021
                                                               B65
STARR M.K.,EXECUTIVE READINGS IN MANAGEMENT   MGT
SCIENCE. TOP/EX WORKER EDU/PROP ADMIN...DECISION   EX/STRUC
GEN/LAWS ANTHOL METH T 20. PAGE 100 B2023   PLAN
                                                         LG/CO
                                                               B65
VIORST M.,HOSTILE ALLIES: FDR AND DE GAULLE.   TOP/EX
EUR+WWI USA-45 ELITES NAT/G VOL/ASSN FORCES LEGIS   PWR
PLAN LEGIT ADMIN COERCE PERSON...BIOG TIME/SEQ 20   WAR
ROOSEVLT/F DEGAULLE/C. PAGE 112 B2263   FRANCE
                                                               L65
HAMMOND A.,"COMPREHENSIVE VERSUS INCREMENTAL   TOP/EX
BUDGETING IN THE DEPARTMENT OF AGRICULTURE" USA+45   EX/STRUC
GP/REL ATTIT...PSY INT 20 DEPT/AGRI. PAGE 46 B0934   AGRI
                                                         BUDGET
                                                               L65
SHARKANSKY I.,"FOUR AGENCIES AND AN APPROPRIATIONS   ADMIN
SUBCOMMITTEE: A COMPARATIVE STUDY OF BUDGET   EDU/PROP
STRATEGIES." USA+45 EX/STRUC TOP/EX PROB/SOLV   NAT/G
CONTROL ROUTINE CONGRESS. PAGE 96 B1934   LEGIS
                                                               L65
WILLIAMS S.,"NEGOTIATING INVESTMENT IN EMERGING   FINAN
COUNTRIES." USA+45 WOR+45 INDUS MARKET NAT/G TOP/EX   ECO/UNDEV
TEC/DEV CAP/ISM ECO/TAC ADMIN SKILL WEALTH...POLICY
RELATIV MGT WORK 20. PAGE 117 B2353
                                                               S65
ALEXANDER T.,"SYNECTICS: INVENTING BY THE MADNESS   PROB/SOLV
METHOD." DELIB/GP TOP/EX ACT/RES TEC/DEV EXEC TASK   OP/RES
KNOWL...MGT METH/COMP 20. PAGE 4 B0073   CREATE
                                                         CONSULT
                                                               S65
RUBINSTEIN A.Z.,"YUGOSLAVIA'S OPENING SOCIETY." COM   CONSTN
USSR INTELL NAT/G LEGIS TOP/EX LEGIT CT/SYS   EX/STRUC
RIGID/FLEX ALL/VALS SOCISM...HUM TIME/SEQ TREND 20.   YUGOSLAVIA
PAGE 92 B1851
                                                               B66
ANDREWS K.R.,THE EFFECTIVENESS OF UNIVERSITY   ECO/DEV
MANAGEMENT DEVELOPMENT PROGRAMS. FUT USA+45 ECO/TAC   ACADEM
ADMIN...MGT QU METH/COMP 20. PAGE 5 B0103   TOP/EX
                                                         ATTIT
                                                               B66
CHAPMAN B.,THE PROFESSION OF GOVERNMENT: THE PUBLIC   BIBLIOG
SERVICE IN EUROPE. CONSTN NAT/G POL/PAR EX/STRUC   ADMIN
LEGIS TOP/EX PROB/SOLV DEBATE EXEC PARL/PROC PARTIC   EUR+WWI
20. PAGE 23 B0411   GOV/COMP
                                                               B66
DUNCOMBE H.S.,COUNTY GOVERNMENT IN AMERICA. USA+45   LOC/G
FINAN MUNIC ADMIN ROUTINE GOV/REL...GOV/COMP 20.   PROVS
PAGE 31 B0631   CT/SYS
                                                         TOP/EX
                                                               B66
HESSLER I.O.,29 WAYS TO GOVERN A CITY. EX/STRUC   MUNIC
TOP/EX PROB/SOLV PARTIC CHOOSE REPRESENT EFFICIENCY   GOV/COMP
...CHARTS 20 CITY/MGT MAYOR. PAGE 49 B0998   LOC/G
                                                         ADMIN
                                                               B66
US BUREAU OF THE BUDGET,THE ADMINISTRATION OF   ACT/RES
GOVERNMENT SUPPORTED RESEARCH AT UNIVERSITIES   NAT/G
(PAMPHLET). USA+45 CONSULT TOP/EX ADMIN INCOME   ACADEM
WEALTH...MGT PHIL/SCI INT. PAGE 108 B2174   GP/REL
                                                               B66
WHITNAH D.R.,SAFER SKYWAYS. DIST/IND DELIB/GP   ADMIN

FORCES TOP/EX WORKER TEC/DEV ROUTINE WAR CIVMIL/REL   NAT/G
COST...TIME/SEQ 20 FAA CAB. PAGE 116 B2342   AIR
                                                         GOV/REL
                                                               B66
ZINKIN T.,CHALLENGES IN INDIA. INDIA PAKISTAN LAW   NAT/G
AGRI FINAN INDUS TOP/EX TEC/DEV CONTROL ROUTINE   ECO/TAC
ORD/FREE PWR 20 NEHRU/J SHASTRI/LB CIVIL/SERV.   POLICY
PAGE 119 B2404   ADMIN
                                                               S66
BALDWIN D.A.,"CONGRESSIONAL INITIATIVE IN FOREIGN   EXEC
POLICY." NAT/G BARGAIN DIPLOM FOR/AID RENT GIVE   TOP/EX
...DECISION CONGRESS. PAGE 8 B0171   GOV/REL
                                                               S66
ZUCKERT E.M.,"THE SERVICE SECRETARY* HAS HE A   OBS
USEFUL ROLE?" USA+45 TOP/EX PLAN ADMIN EXEC DETER   OP/RES
NUC/PWR WEAPON...MGT RECORD MCNAMARA/R. PAGE 119   DIPLOM
B2407   FORCES
                                                               B67
CECIL L.,ALBERT BALLIN; BUSINESS AND POLITICS IN   DIPLOM
IMPERIAL GERMANY 1888-1918. GERMANY UK INT/TRADE   CONSTN
LEAD WAR PERS/REL ADJUST PWR WEALTH...MGT BIBLIOG   ECO/DEV
19/20. PAGE 19 B0397   TOP/EX
                                                               B67
MCCONNELL G.,THE MODERN PRESIDENCY. USA+45 CONSTN   NAT/G
TOP/EX DOMIN EXEC CHOOSE PWR...MGT 20. PAGE 72   CHIEF
B1446   EX/STRUC
                                                               B67
RALSTON D.B.,THE ARMY OF THE REPUBLIC; THE PLACE OF   FORCES
THE MILITARY IN THE POLITICAL EVOLUTION OF FRANCE   NAT/G
1871-1914. FRANCE MOD/EUR EX/STRUC LEGIS TOP/EX   CIVMIL/REL
DIPLOM ADMIN WAR GP/REL ROLE...BIBLIOG 19/20.   POLICY
PAGE 86 B1730
                                                               S67
GOLIGHTLY H.O.,"THE AIRLINES: A CASE STUDY IN   DIST/IND
MANAGEMENT INNOVATION." USA+45 AIR FINAN INDUS   MARKET
TOP/EX CREATE PLAN PROB/SOLV ADMIN EXEC PROFIT   MGT
...DECISION 20. PAGE 40 B0820   TEC/DEV
                                                               S67
ROSENBERG B.,"ETHNIC LIBERALISM AND EMPLOYMENT   RACE/REL
DISCRIMINATION IN THE NORTH." USA+45 TOP/EX   ATTIT
PROB/SOLV ADMIN REGION PERS/REL DISCRIM...INT   WORKER
IDEA/COMP. PAGE 90 B1820   EXEC

TORGERSEN P.E. B0695

TORONTO....TORONTO, ONTARIO

                                                               B67
KAPLAN H.,URBAN POLITICAL SYSTEMS: A FUNCTIONAL   GEN/LAWS
ANALYSIS OF METRO TORONTO. CANADA STRUCT NEIGH PLAN   MUNIC
ADMIN...POLICY METH 20 TORONTO. PAGE 58 B1166   LOC/G
                                                         FEDERAL

TORRE M. B2119

TORY/PARTY....TORY PARTY

TOTALISM....TOTALITARIANISM

                                                               B38
FIELD G.L.,THE SYNDICAL AND CORPORATIVE   FASCISM
INSTITUTIONS OF ITALIAN FASCISM. ITALY CONSTN   INDUS
STRATA LABOR EX/STRUC TOP/EX ADJUD ADMIN LEAD   NAT/G
TOTALISM AUTHORIT...MGT 20 MUSSOLIN/B. PAGE 35   WORKER
B0716
                                                               S40
GERTH H.,"THE NAZI PARTY: ITS LEADERSHIP AND   POL/PAR
COMPOSITION" (BMR)" GERMANY ELITES STRATA STRUCT   DOMIN
EX/STRUC FORCES ECO/TAC CT/SYS CHOOSE TOTALISM   LEAD
AGE/Y AUTHORIT PWR 20. PAGE 39 B0792   ADMIN
                                                               B42
BINGHAM A.M.,THE TECHNIQUES OF DEMOCRACY. USA-45   POPULISM
CONSTN STRUCT POL/PAR LEGIS PLAN PARTIC CHOOSE   ORD/FREE
REPRESENT NAT/LISM TOTALISM...MGT 20. PAGE 12 B0240   ADMIN
                                                         NAT/G
                                                               B42
SINGTON D.,THE GOEBBELS EXPERIMENT. GERMANY MOD/EUR   FASCISM
NAT/G EX/STRUC FORCES CONTROL ROUTINE WAR TOTALISM   EDU/PROP
PWR...ART/METH HUM 20 NAZI GOEBBELS/J. PAGE 97   ATTIT
B1970   COM/IND
                                                               B45
BRECHT A.,FEDERALISM AND REGIONALISM IN GERMANY;   FEDERAL
THE DIVISION OF PRUSSIA. GERMANY PRUSSIA WOR-45   REGION
CREATE ADMIN WAR TOTALISM PWR...CHARTS 20 HITLER/A.   PROB/SOLV
PAGE 15 B0303   CONSTN
                                                               B45
CONOVER H.F.,THE GOVERNMENTS OF THE MAJOR FOREIGN   BIBLIOG
POWERS: A BIBLIOGRAPHY. FRANCE GERMANY ITALY UK   NAT/G
USSR CONSTN LOC/G POL/PAR EX/STRUC FORCES ADMIN   DIPLOM
CT/SYS CIVMIL/REL TOTALISM...POLICY 19/20. PAGE 23
B0464
                                                               B46
CORRY J.A.,DEMOCRATIC GOVERNMENT AND POLITICS.   NAT/G
WOR-45 EX/STRUC LOBBY TOTALISM...MAJORIT CONCPT   CONSTN
METH/COMP NAT/COMP 20. PAGE 24 B0479   POL/PAR
                                                         JURID

B47
BAERWALD F.,FUNDAMENTALS OF LABOR ECONOMICS. LAW   ECO/DEV
INDUS LABOR LG/CO CONTROL GP/REL INCOME TOTALISM   WORKER
...MGT CHARTS GEN/LAWS BIBLIOG 20. PAGE 8 B0158   MARKET

B48
ROSSITER C.L.,CONSTITUTIONAL DICTATORSHIP; CRISIS   NAT/G
GOVERNMENT IN THE MODERN DEMOCRACIES. FRANCE   AUTHORIT
GERMANY UK USA-45 WOR-45 EX/STRUC BAL/PWR CONTROL   CONSTN
COERCE WAR CENTRAL ORD/FREE...DECISION 19/20.   TOTALISM
PAGE 90 B1828

S51
SCHRAMM W.,"COMMUNICATION IN THE SOVIETIZED STATE,   ATTIT
AS DEMONSTRATED IN KOREA." ASIA COM KOREA COM/IND   EDU/PROP
FACE/GP POL/PAR SCHOOL FORCES ADMIN PWR MARXISM   TOTALISM
...SOC CONCPT MYTH INT BIOG TOT/POP 20. PAGE 94
B1901

B52
SELZNICK P.,THE ORGANIZATIONAL WEAPON: A STUDY OF   MARXISM
BOLSHEVIK STRATEGY AND TACTICS. USSR SOCIETY STRATA   POL/PAR
LABOR DOMIN EDU/PROP PARTIC REV ATTIT PWR...POLICY   LEAD
MGT CONCPT 20 BOLSHEVISM. PAGE 95 B1929   TOTALISM

B52
ULAM A.B.,TITOISM AND THE COMINFORM. USSR WOR+45   COM
STRUCT INT/ORG NAT/G ACT/RES PLAN EXEC ATTIT DRIVE   POL/PAR
ALL/VALS...CONCPT OBS VAL/FREE 20 COMINTERN   TOTALISM
TITO/MARSH. PAGE 106 B2145   YUGOSLAVIA

S52
BRUEGEL J.W.,"DIE INTERNAZIONALE   VOL/ASSN
GEWERKSCHAFTSBEWEGUNG." COM EUR+WWI USA+45 WOR+45   LABOR
DELIB/GP EX/STRUC ECO/TAC EDU/PROP ATTIT PWR   TOTALISM
RESPECT SKILL WEALTH WORK 20. PAGE 16 B0330

B53
MEYER P.,THE JEWS IN THE SOVIET SATELLITES.   COM
CZECHOSLVK POLAND SOCIETY STRATA NAT/G BAL/PWR   SECT
ECO/TAC EDU/PROP LEGIT ADMIN COERCE ATTIT DISPL   TOTALISM
PERCEPT HEALTH PWR RESPECT WEALTH...METH/CNCPT JEWS   USSR
VAL/FREE NAZI 20. PAGE 73 B1474

S53
MORRIS B.S.,"THE COMINFORM: A FIVE YEAR   VOL/ASSN
PERSPECTIVE." COM UNIV USSR WOR+45 ECO/DEV POL/PAR   EDU/PROP
TOP/EX PLAN DOMIN ADMIN TOTALISM ATTIT ALL/VALS   DIPLOM
...CONCPT TIME/SEQ TREND CON/ANAL WORK VAL/FREE 20.
PAGE 76 B1527

S55
KAUTSKY J.H.,"THE NEW STRATEGY OF INTERNATIONAL   COM
COMMUNISM." ASIA CHINA/COM FUT WOR+45 WOR-45 ADMIN   POL/PAR
ROUTINE PERSON MARXISM SOCISM...TREND IDEA/COMP 20   TOTALISM
LENIN/VI MAO. PAGE 59 B1184   USSR

C56
NEUMANN S.,"MODERN POLITICAL PARTIES: APPROACHES TO   POL/PAR
COMPARATIVE POLITIC. FRANCE UK EX/STRUC DOMIN ADMIN   GOV/COMP
LEAD REPRESENT TOTALISM ATTIT...POLICY TREND   ELITES
METH/COMP ANTHOL BIBLIOG/A 20 CMN/WLTH. PAGE 78   MAJORIT
B1574

B57
MORSTEIN-MARX F.,THE ADMINISTRATIVE STATE: AN   EXEC
INTRODUCTION TO BUREAUCRACY. EUR+WWI FUT MOD/EUR   MGT
USA+45 USA-45 NAT/G CONSULT ADMIN ROUTINE TOTALISM   CAP/ISM
DRIVE SKILL...TREND 19/20. PAGE 76 B1530   ELITES

S57
BAUER R.A.,"BRAINWASHING: PSYCHOLOGY OR   EDU/PROP
DEMONOLOGY." ASIA CHINA/COM COM POL/PAR ECO/TAC   PSY
ADMIN COERCE ATTIT DRIVE ORD/FREE...CONCPT MYTH 20.   TOTALISM
PAGE 10 B0196

B58
NEAL F.W.,TITOISM IN ACTION. COM YUGOSLAVIA AGRI   MARXISM
LOC/G DIPLOM TOTALISM...BIBLIOG 20 TITO/MARSH.   POL/PAR
PAGE 77 B1564   CHIEF
                                                         ADMIN

S58
STAAR R.F.,"ELECTIONS IN COMMUNIST POLAND." EUR+WWI COM
SOCIETY INT/ORG NAT/G POL/PAR LEGIS ACT/RES ECO/TAC CHOOSE
EDU/PROP ADJUD ADMIN ROUTINE COERCE TOTALISM ATTIT POLAND
ORD/FREE PWR 20. PAGE 100 B2015

S59
LASSWELL H.D.,"UNIVERSALITY IN PERSPECTIVE." FUT   INT/ORG
UNIV SOCIETY CONSULT TOP/EX PLAN EDU/PROP ADJUD   JURID
ROUTINE ARMS/CONT COERCE PEACE ATTIT PERSON   TOTALISM
ALL/VALS. PAGE 63 B1271

S59
ZAUBERMAN A.,"SOVIET BLOC ECONOMIC INTEGRATION."   MARKET
COM CULTURE INTELL ECO/DEV INDUS TOP/EX ACT/RES   INT/ORG
PLAN ECO/TAC INT/TRADE ROUTINE CHOOSE ATTIT   USSR
...TIME/SEQ 20. PAGE 119 B2399   TOTALISM

B60
GRUNDLICH T.,DIE TECHNIK DER DIKTATUR. ADMIN   COERCE
TOTALISM ATTIT PWR...MGT CONCPT ARISTOTLE. PAGE 44   DOMIN
B0896   ORD/FREE
                                                         WAR

S60
SCHWARTZ B.,"THE INTELLIGENTSIA IN COMMUNIST CHINA: INTELL
A TENTATIVE COMPARISON." ASIA CHINA/COM COM RUSSIA   RIGID/FLEX
ELITES SOCIETY STRATA POL/PAR VOL/ASSN CREATE ADMIN   REV
COERCE NAT/LISM TOTALISM...POLICY TREND 20. PAGE 95
B1914

B61
HOUN F.W.,TO CHANGE A NATION; PROPAGANDA AND   DOMIN
INDOCTRINATION IN COMMUNIST CHINA. CHINA/COM COM   EDU/PROP
ACT/RES PLAN PRESS ADMIN FEEDBACK CENTRAL   TOTALISM
EFFICIENCY ATTIT...PSY SOC 20. PAGE 52 B1048   MARXISM

B62
HITCHNER D.G.,MODERN GOVERNMENT: A SURVEY OF   CONCPT
POLITICAL SCIENCE. WOR+45 INT/ORG LEGIS ADMIN   NAT/G
CT/SYS EXEC CHOOSE TOTALISM POPULISM...INT/LAW   STRUCT
PHIL/SCI METH 20. PAGE 50 B1019

B62
MORE S.S.,REMODELLING OF DEMOCRACY FOR AFRO-ASIAN   ORD/FREE
NATIONS. AFR INDIA S/ASIA SOUTH/AFR CONSTN EX/STRUC   ECO/UNDEV
COLONIAL CHOOSE TOTALISM SOVEREIGN NEW/LIB SOCISM   ADMIN
...SOC/WK 20. PAGE 75 B1520   LEGIS

B63
BROGAN D.W.,POLITICAL PATTERNS IN TODAY'S WORLD.   NAT/COMP
FRANCE USA+45 USSR WOR+45 CONSTN STRUCT PLAN DIPLOM   NEW/LIB
ADMIN LEAD ROLE SUPEGO...PHIL/SCI 20. PAGE 15 B0313   COM
                                                         TOTALISM

B63
JACOB H.,GERMAN ADMINISTRATION SINCE BISMARCK: ADMIN
CENTRAL AUTHORITY VERSUS LOCAL AUTONOMY. GERMANY   NAT/G
GERMANY/W LAW POL/PAR CONTROL CENTRAL TOTALISM   LOC/G
FASCISM...MAJORIT DECISION STAT CHARTS GOV/COMP   POLICY
19/20 BISMARCK/O HITLER/A WEIMAR/REP. PAGE 55 B1111

B63
TUCKER R.C.,THE SOVIET POLITICAL MIND. COM INTELL   STRUCT
NAT/G TOP/EX EDU/PROP ADMIN COERCE TOTALISM ATTIT   RIGID/FLEX
PWR MARXISM...PSY MYTH HYPO/EXP 20. PAGE 106 B2135   ELITES
                                                         USSR

S63
DELLIN L.A.D.,"BULGARIA UNDER SOVIET LEADERSHIP."   AGRI
BULGARIA COM USA+45 USSR ECO/DEV INDUS POL/PAR   NAT/G
EX/STRUC TOP/EX COERCE ATTIT RIGID/FLEX...POLICY   TOTALISM
TIME/SEQ 20. PAGE 28 B0572

S63
ETIENNE G.,"'LOIS OBJECTIVES' ET PROBLEMES DE   TOTALISM
DEVELOPPEMENT DANS LE CONTEXTE CHINE-URSS." ASIA   USSR
CHINA/COM COM FUT STRUCT INT/ORG VOL/ASSN TOP/EX
TEC/DEV ECO/TAC ATTIT RIGID/FLEX...GEOG MGT
TIME/SEQ TOT/POP 20. PAGE 34 B0682

B64
ELDREDGE H.W.,THE SECOND AMERICAN REVOLUTION.   ELITES
EDU/PROP NAT/LISM RATIONAL TOTALISM FASCISM MARXISM   ORD/FREE
SOCISM. PAGE 33 B0664   ADMIN
                                                         PLAN

B64
KARIEL H.S.,IN SEARCH OF AUTHORITY: TWENTIETH-   CONSTN
CENTURY POLITICAL THOUGHT. WOR+45 WOR-45 NAT/G   CONCPT
EX/STRUC DOMIN DRIVE PWR...MGT PHIL/SCI GEN/LAWS   ORD/FREE
19/20 NIETZSCH/F FREUD/S WEBER/MAX NIEBUHR/R   IDEA/COMP
MARITAIN/J. PAGE 58 B1173

S64
KASSOF A.,"THE ADMINISTERED SOCIETY: SOCIETY
TOTALITARIANISM WITHOUT TERROR." COM USSR STRATA   DOMIN
AGRI INDUS NAT/G PERF/ART SCHOOL TOP/EX EDU/PROP   TOTALISM
ADMIN ORD/FREE PWR...POLICY SOC TIME/SEQ GEN/LAWS
VAL/FREE 20. PAGE 58 B1178

B65
MOORE C.H.,TUNISIA SINCE INDEPENDENCE. ELITES LOC/G NAT/G
POL/PAR ADMIN COLONIAL CONTROL EXEC GOV/REL   EX/STRUC
TOTALISM MARXISM...INT 20 TUNIS. PAGE 75 B1513   SOCISM

B65
PURCELL V.,THE MEMOIRS OF A MALAYAN OFFICIAL.   BIOG
MALAYSIA UK ECO/UNDEV INDUS LABOR EDU/PROP COLONIAL   ADMIN
CT/SYS WAR NAT/LISM TOTALISM ORD/FREE SOVEREIGN 20   JURID
UN CIVIL/SERV. PAGE 85 B1721   FORCES

L65
HOOK S.,"SECOND THOUGHTS ON BERKELEY" USA+45 ELITES ACADEM
INTELL LEGIT ADMIN COERCE REPRESENT GP/REL INGP/REL ORD/FREE
TOTALISM AGE/Y MARXISM 20 BERKELEY FREE/SPEE   POLICY
STUDNT/PWR. PAGE 51 B1040   CREATE

S65
TABORSKY E.,"CHANGE IN CZECHOSLOVAKIA." COM USSR   ECO/DEV
ELITES INTELL AGRI INDUS NAT/G DELIB/GP EX/STRUC   PLAN
ECO/TAC TOTALISM ATTIT RIGID/FLEX SOCISM...MGT   CZECHOSLVK
CONCPT TREND 20. PAGE 102 B2067

N65
MOTE M.E.,SOVIET LOCAL AND REPUBLIC ELECTIONS. COM   CHOOSE
USSR NAT/G PLAN PARTIC GOV/REL TOTALISM PWR   ADMIN
...CHARTS 20. PAGE 76 B1534   CONTROL
                                                         LOC/G

B66
MARTIN L.W.,DIPLOMACY IN MODERN EUROPEAN HISTORY.   DIPLOM
EUR+WWI MOD/EUR INT/ORG NAT/G EX/STRUC ROUTINE WAR   POLICY
PEACE TOTALISM PWR 15/20 COLD/WAR EUROPE/W. PAGE 70
B1411

B66
US SENATE COMM ON FOREIGN REL,HEARINGS ON S 2859   FOR/AID
AND S 2861. USA+45 WOR+45 FORCES BUDGET CAP/ISM   DIPLOM
ADMIN DETER WEAPON TOTALISM...NAT/COMP 20 UN   ORD/FREE
CONGRESS. PAGE 110 B2221   ECO/UNDEV

B67
MACKINTOSH J.M.,JUGGERNAUT. USSR NAT/G POL/PAR   WAR
ADMIN LEAD CIVMIL/REL COST TOTALISM PWR MARXISM   FORCES

...GOV/COMP 20. PAGE 68 B1364   COM
                                                       PROF/ORG
                                                       S67
BREGMAN A.,"WHITHER RUSSIA?" COM RUSSIA INTELL   MARXISM
POL/PAR DIPLOM PARTIC NAT/LISM TOTALISM ATTIT   ELITES
ORD/FREE 20. PAGE 15 B0304   ADMIN
                                                       CREATE
                                                       S67
GORMAN W.,"ELLUL - A PROPHETIC VOICE." WOR+45   CREATE
ELITES SOCIETY ACT/RES PLAN BAL/PWR DOMIN CONTROL   ORD/FREE
PARTIC TOTALISM PWR 20. PAGE 41 B0837   EX/STRUC
                                                       UTOPIA
                                                       S67
LIU K.C.,"DISINTEGRATION OF THE OLD ORDER." ASIA   ADJUST
SOCIETY PROB/SOLV ADMIN REGION TOTALISM ORD/FREE   NAT/LISM
MARXISM 19/20. PAGE 66 B1329
                                                       S67
O'DELL J.H.,"THE JULY REBELLIONS AND THE 'MILITARY   PWR
STATE'." USA+45 VIETNAM STRATA CHIEF WORKER   NAT/G
COLONIAL EXEC CROWD CIVMIL/REL RACE/REL TOTALISM   COERCE
...WELF/ST PACIFIST 20 NEGRO JOHNSON/LB PRESIDENT   FORCES
CIV/RIGHTS. PAGE 79 B1599
                                                       S67
SHOEMAKER R.L.,"JAPANESE ARMY AND THE WEST." ASIA   FORCES
ELITES EX/STRUC DIPLOM DOMIN EDU/PROP COERCE ATTIT   TEC/DEV
AUTHORIT PWR 1/20 CHINJAP. PAGE 96 B1950   WAR
                                                       TOTALISM

TOTALITARIANISM....SEE TOTALISM

TOTMAN C. B2120

TOTOK W. B2121

TOTTEN G.O. B2122

TOURISM....SEE TRAVEL

TOURNELLE G. B2123

TOUSSAIN/P....PIERRE DOMINIQUE TOUSSAINT LOOUVERTURE

TOWNS....SEE MUNIC

TOWNSD/PLN....TOWNSEND PLAN

TOWNSEND PLAN....SEE TOWNSD/PLN

TOWSTER J. B2124

TOYNBEE/A....ARNOLD TOYNBEE

TRADE, INTERNATIONAL....SEE INT/TRADE

TRADIT....TRADITIONAL AND ARISTOCRATIC
                                                       S44
KEFAUVER E.,"THE NEED FOR BETTER EXECUTIVE-   LEGIS
LEGISLATIVE TEAMWORK IN THE NATIONAL GOVERNMENT."   EXEC
USA-45 CONSTN NAT/G ROUTINE...TRADIT CONGRESS   CONFER
REFORMERS. PAGE 59 B1188   LEAD
                                                       S50
HUMPHREY H.H.,"THE SENATE ON TRIAL." USA+45 POL/PAR   PARL/PROC
DEBATE REPRESENT EFFICIENCY ATTIT RIGID/FLEX   ROUTINE
...TRADIT SENATE. PAGE 52 B1064   PWR
                                                       LEGIS
                                                       B58
COLEMAN J.S.,NIGERIA: BACKGROUND TO NATIONALISM.   NAT/G
AFR SOCIETY ECO/DEV KIN LOC/G POL/PAR TEC/DEV DOMIN   NAT/LISM
ADMIN DRIVE PWR RESPECT...TRADIT SOC INT SAMP   NIGERIA
TIME/SEQ 20 B0452
                                                       B62
BENSON E.T.,CROSS FIRE: THE EIGHT YEARS WITH   ADMIN
EISENHOWER. USA+45 DIPLOM LEAD ATTIT PERSON   POLICY
CONSERVE...TRADIT BIOG 20 EISNHWR/DD PRESIDENT   DELIB/GP
TAFT/RA DULLES/JF NIXON/RM. PAGE 11 B0218   TOP/EX
                                                       C66
JACOB H.,"DIMENSIONS OF STATE POLITICS HEARD A. ED.   PROVS
STATE LEGIWLATURES IN AMERICAN POLITICS." CULTURE   LEGIS
STRATA POL/PAR BUDGET TAX LOBBY ROUTINE GOV/REL   ROLE
...TRADIT DECISION GEOG. PAGE 55 B1112   REPRESENT
                                                       B86
BOLINSBROKE H ST J.,A DISSERTATION UPON PARTIES   CONSERVE
(1729). UK LEGIS CHOOSE GOV/REL SOVEREIGN...TRADIT   POL/PAR
18 PARLIAMENT. PAGE 13 B0269   CHIEF
                                                       EX/STRUC

TRADITIONAL....SEE CONSERVE, TRADIT

TRAINING....SEE SCHOOL, ACADEM, SKILL, EDU/PROP

TRANSFER....TRANSFER

TRANSITIVITY OF CHOICE....SEE DECISION

TRANSKEI....TRANSKEI

TRANSPORTATION....SEE DIST/IND

TRAVEL....TRAVEL AND TOURISM

TRAVERS H. B2125

TREASURY DEPARTMENT....SEE DEPT/TREAS

TREATY....TREATIES; INTERNATIONAL AGREEMENTS
                                                       B33
DANGERFIELD R.,IN DEFENSE OF THE SENATE. USA-45   LEGIS
CONSTN NAT/G EX/STRUC TOP/EX ATTIT KNOWL   DELIB/GP
...METH/CNCPT STAT TIME/SEQ TREND CON/ANAL CHARTS   DIPLOM
CONGRESS 20 TREATY. PAGE 26 B0528
                                                       B34
US TARIFF COMMISSION,THE TARIFF: A BIBLIOGRAPHY: A   BIBLIOG/A
SELECT LIST OF REFERENCES. USA-45 LAW DIPLOM TAX   TARIFFS
ADMIN...POLICY TREATY 20. PAGE 111 B2246   ECO/TAC
                                                       L52
WRIGHT Q.,"CONGRESS AND THE TREATY-MAKING POWER."   ROUTINE
USA+45 NAT/G INTELL NAT/G CHIEF CONSULT   DIPLOM
EX/STRUC LEGIS TOP/EX CREATE GOV/REL DISPL DRIVE   INT/LAW
RIGID/FLEX...TREND TOT/POP CONGRESS CONGRESS 20   DELIB/GP
TREATY. PAGE 118 B2384
                                                       B56
KOENIG L.W.,THE TRUMAN ADMINISTRATION: ITS   ADMIN
PRINCIPLES AND PRACTICE. USA+45 POL/PAR CHIEF LEGIS   DIPLOM
DIPLOM DEATH NUC/PWR WAR CIVMIL/REL PEACE   EX/STRUC
...DECISION 20 TRUMAN/HS PRESIDENT TREATY. PAGE 61   GOV/REL
B1224
                                                       L60
DEAN A.W.,"SECOND GENEVA CONFERENCE OF THE LAW OF   INT/ORG
THE SEA: THE FIGHT FOR FREEDOM OF THE SEAS." FUT   JURID
USA+45 USSR WOR+45 WOR-45 SEA CONSTN STRUCT PLAN   INT/LAW
INT/TRADE ADJUD ADMIN ORD/FREE...DECISION RECORD
TREND GEN/LAWS 20 TREATY. PAGE 28 B0564
                                                       B63
VAN SLYCK P.,PEACE: THE CONTROL OF NATIONAL POWER.   ARMS/CONT
CUBA WOR+45 FINAN NAT/G FORCES PROB/SOLV TEC/DEV   PEACE
BAL/PWR ADMIN CONTROL ORD/FREE...POLICY INT/LAW UN   INT/ORG
COLD/WAR TREATY. PAGE 112 B2253   DIPLOM
                                                       S63
MODELSKI G.,"STUDY OF ALLIANCES." WOR+45 WOR-45   VOL/ASSN
INT/ORG NAT/G FORCES LEGIT ADMIN CHOOSE ALL/VALS   CON/ANAL
PWR SKILL...INT/LAW CONCPT GEN/LAWS 20 TREATY.   DIPLOM
PAGE 74 B1495
                                                       B65
CAVERS D.F.,THE CHOICE-OF-LAW PROCESS. PROB/SOLV   JURID
ADJUD CT/SYS CHOOSE RATIONAL...IDEA/COMP 16/20   DECISION
TREATY. PAGE 19 B0396   METH/COMP
                                                       ADMIN
                                                       B65
GOTLIEB A.,DISARMAMENT AND INTERNATIONAL LAW* A   INT/LAW
STUDY OF THE ROLE OF LAW IN THE DISARMAMENT   INT/ORG
PROCESS. USA+45 USSR PROB/SOLV CONFER ADMIN ROUTINE   ARMS/CONT
NUC/PWR ORD/FREE SOVEREIGN UN TREATY. PAGE 42 B0841   IDEA/COMP
                                                       B65
MACDONALD R.W.,THE LEAGUE OF ARAB STATES: A STUDY   ISLAM
IN THE DYNAMICS OF REGIONAL ORGANIZATION. ISRAEL   REGION
UAR USSR FINAN INT/ORG DELIB/GP ECO/TAC AGREE   DIPLOM
NEUTRAL ORD/FREE PWR...DECISION BIBLIOG 20 TREATY   ADMIN
UN. PAGE 67 B1358
                                                       B66
LEE L.T.,VIENNA CONVENTION ON CONSULAR RELATIONS.   AGREE
WOR+45 LAW INT/ORG CONFER GP/REL PRIVIL...INT/LAW   DIPLOM
20 TREATY VIENNA/CNV. PAGE 63 B1279   ADMIN
                                                       B66
YOUNG W.,EXISTING MECHANISMS OF ARMS CONTROL.   ARMS/CONT
PROC/MFG OP/RES DIPLOM TASK CENTRAL...MGT TREATY.   ADMIN
PAGE 119 B2395   NUC/PWR
                                                       ROUTINE
                                                       S67
WEIL G.L.,"THE MERGER OF THE INSTITUTIONS OF THE   ECO/TAC
EUROPEAN COMMUNITIES" EUR+WWI ECO/DEV INT/TRADE   INT/ORG
CONSEN PLURISM...DECISION MGT 20 EEC EURATOM ECSC   CENTRAL
TREATY. PAGE 115 B2313   INT/LAW

TRECKER H.B. B2126

TREFETHEN F.N. B1445

TREITSCHKE H. B2127

TREND....PROJECTION OF HISTORICAL TRENDS
                                                       B00
MORRIS H.C.,THE HISTORY OF COLONIZATION. WOR+45   DOMIN
WOR-45 ECO/DEV ECO/UNDEV INT/ORG ACT/RES PLAN   SOVEREIGN
ECO/TAC LEGIT ROUTINE COERCE ATTIT DRIVE ALL/VALS   COLONIAL
...GEOG TREND 19. PAGE 76 B1528
                                                       B17
CORWIN E.S.,THE PRESIDENT'S CONTROL OF FOREIGN   TOP/EX
RELATIONS. FUT USA-45 CONSTN STRATA NAT/G CHIEF   PWR
EX/STRUC LEGIS KNOWL RESPECT...JURID CONCPT TREND   DIPLOM
CONGRESS VAL/FREE 20 PRESIDENT. PAGE 24 B0483

N19

BUREAU OF NAT'L AFFAIRS INC.,A CURRENT LOOK AT: DISCRIM
(1) THE NEGRO AND TITLE VII, (2) SEX AND TITLE VII SEX
(PAMPHLET). LAW LG/CO SML/CO RACE/REL...POLICY SOC WORKER
STAT DEEP/QU TREND CON/ANAL CHARTS 20 NEGRO   MGT
CIV/RIGHTS. PAGE 17 B0350

N19

GINZBERG E.,MANPOWER FOR GOVERNMENT (PAMPHLET).   WORKER
USA+45 FORCES PLAN PROB/SOLV PAY EDU/PROP ADMIN   CONSULT
GP/REL COST...MGT PREDICT TREND 20 CIVIL/SERV.   NAT/G
PAGE 40 B0803   LOC/G

B21

BRYCE J.,MODERN DEMOCRACIES. FUT NEW/ZEALND USA-45 NAT/G
LAW CONSTN POL/PAR PROVS VOL/ASSN EX/STRUC LEGIS   TREND
LEGIT CT/SYS EXEC KNOWL CONGRESS AUSTRAL 20.
PAGE 16 B0332

B24

MERRIAM C.E.,A HISTORY OF POLITICAL THEORIES -   UNIV
RECENT TIMES. USA-45 WOR-45 CULTURE SOCIETY ECO/DEV INTELL
R+D EDU/PROP ROUTINE CHOOSE ATTIT PERSON ALL/VALS
...POLICY SOC CONCPT METH/CNCPT OBS HIST/WRIT
TIME/SEQ TREND. PAGE 73 B1471

B28

BUELL R.,THE NATIVE PROBLEM IN AFRICA. KIN LABOR   AFR
LOC/G ECO/TAC ROUTINE ORD/FREE...REC/INT KNO/TEST   CULTURE
CENSUS TREND CHARTS SOC/EXP STERTYP 20. PAGE 17
B0339

B28

HALL W.P.,EMPIRE TO COMMONWEALTH. FUT WOR-45 CONSTN VOL/ASSN
ECO/DEV ECO/UNDEV INT/ORG PROVS PLAN DIPLOM   NAT/G
EDU/PROP ADMIN COLONIAL PEACE PERSON ALL/VALS   UK
...POLICY GEOG SOC OBS RECORD TREND CMN/WLTH
PARLIAMENT 19/20. PAGE 46 B0925

B28

SOROKIN P.,CONTEMPORARY SOCIOLOGICAL THEORIES.   CULTURE
MOD/EUR UNIV SOCIETY R+D SCHOOL ECO/TAC EDU/PROP   SOC
ROUTINE ATTIT DRIVE...PSY CONCPT TIME/SEQ TREND   WAR
GEN/LAWS 20. PAGE 99 B1997

B29

ROBERTS S.H.,HISTORY OF FRENCH COLONIAL POLICY. AFR INT/ORG
ASIA L/A+17C S/ASIA CULTURE ECO/DEV ECO/UNDEV FINAN ACT/RES
NAT/G PLAN ECO/TAC DOMIN ROUTINE SOVEREIGN...OBS   FRANCE
HIST/WRIT TREND CHARTS VAL/FREE 19/20. PAGE 89   COLONIAL
B1796

B32

WRIGHT Q.,GOLD AND MONETARY STABILIZATION. FUT   FINAN
USA-45 WOR-45 INTELL ECO/DEV INT/ORG NAT/G CONSULT POLICY
PLAN ECO/TAC ADMIN ATTIT WEALTH...CONCPT TREND 20.
PAGE 118 B2383

B33

DANGERFIELD R.,IN DEFENSE OF THE SENATE. USA-45   LEGIS
CONSTN NAT/G EX/STRUC TOP/EX ATTIT KNOWL   DELIB/GP
...METH/CNCPT STAT TIME/SEQ TREND CON/ANAL CHARTS   DIPLOM
CONGRESS 20 TREATY. PAGE 26 B0528

B37

BROOKS R.R.,WHEN LABOR ORGANIZES. FINAN EDU/PROP   LABOR
ADMIN LOBBY PARTIC REPRESENT WEALTH TREND. PAGE 16 GP/REL
B0318   POLICY

B37

PARSONS T.,THE STRUCTURE OF SOCIAL ACTION. UNIV   CULTURE
INTELL SOCIETY INDUS MARKET ECO/TAC ROUTINE CHOOSE ATTIT
ALL/VALS...CONCPT OBS BIOG TREND GEN/LAWS 20.   CAP/ISM
PAGE 81 B1636

B38

LANGE O.,ON THE ECONOMIC THEORY OF SOCIALISM. UNIV MARKET
ECO/DEV FINAN INDUS INT/ORG PUB/INST ROUTINE ATTIT ECO/TAC
ALL/VALS...SOC CONCPT STAT TREND 20. PAGE 62 B1258 INT/TRADE
                                                    SOCISM

B39

HITLER A.,MEIN KAMPF. EUR+WWI FUT MOD/EUR STRUCT   PWR
INT/ORG LABOR NAT/G PAR FORCES CREATE PLAN   NEW/IDEA
BAL/PWR DIPLOM ECO/TAC DOMIN EDU/PROP ADMIN COERCE WAR
ATTIT...SOCIALIST BIOG TREND NAZI. PAGE 50 B1020

B39

ZIMMERN A.,MODERN POLITICAL DOCTRINE. WOR-45   NAT/G
CULTURE SOCIETY ECO/UNDEV DELIB/GP EX/STRUC CREATE ECO/TAC
DOMIN COERCE NAT/LISM ATTIT RIGID/FLEX ORD/FREE PWR BAL/PWR
WEALTH...POLICY CONCPT OBS TIME/SEQ TREND TOT/POP   INT/TRADE
LEAGUE/NAT 20. PAGE 119 B2402

B40

MCHENRY D.E.,HIS MAJESTY'S OPPOSITION: STRUCTURE   POL/PAR
AND PROBLEMS OF THE BRITISH LABOUR PARTY 1931-1938. MGT
UK FINAN LABOR LOC/G DELIB/GP LEGIS EDU/PROP LEAD   NAT/G
PARTIC CHOOSE GP/REL SOCISM...TREND 20 LABOR/PAR.   POLICY
PAGE 72 B1450

S40

FAHS C.B.,"POLITICAL GROUPS IN THE JAPANESE HOUSE   ROUTINE
OF PEERS." ELITES NAT/G ADMIN GP/REL...TREND   POL/PAR
CHINJAP. PAGE 34 B0697   LEGIS

B41

YOUNG G.,FEDERALISM AND FREEDOM. EUR+WWI MOD/EUR   NAT/G
RUSSIA USA-45 WOR-45 SOCIETY STRUCT ECO/DEV INT/ORG WAR
EXEC FEDERAL ATTIT PERSON ALL/VALS...OLD/LIB CONCPT
OBS TREND LEAGUE/NAT TOT/POP. PAGE 119 B2392

S41

ABEL T.,"THE ELEMENT OF DECISION IN THE PATTERN OF TEC/DEV

WAR." EUR+WWI FUT NAT/G TOP/EX DIPLOM ROUTINE   FORCES
COERCE DISPL PERCEPT PWR...SOC METH/CNCPT HIST/WRIT WAR
TREND GEN/LAWS 20. PAGE 2 B0051

S43

GOLDEN C.S.,"NEW PATTERNS OF DEMOCRACY." NEIGH   LABOR
DELIB/GP EDU/PROP EXEC PARTIC...MGT METH/CNCPT OBS REPRESENT
TREND. PAGE 40 B0815   LG/CO
                                                    GP/REL

L44

HAILEY,"THE FUTURE OF COLONIAL PEOPLES." WOR-45   PLAN
CONSTN CULTURE ECO/UNDEV AGRI MARKET INT/ORG NAT/G CONCPT
SECT CONSULT ECO/TAC LEGIT ADMIN NAT/LISM ALL/VALS DIPLOM
...SOC OBS TREND STERTYP CMN/WLTH LEAGUE/NAT   UK
PARLIAMENT 20. PAGE 45 B0916

B45

BUSH V.,SCIENCE, THE ENDLESS FRONTIER. FUT USA-45   R+D
INTELL STRATA ACT/RES CREATE PLAN EDU/PROP ADMIN   NAT/G
NUC/PWR PEACE ATTIT HEALTH KNOWL...MAJORIT HEAL MGT
PHIL/SCI CONCPT OBS TREND 20. PAGE 18 B0360

S47

GRAVES W.B.,"LEGISLATIVE REFERENCE SYSTEM FOR THE   LEGIS
CONGRESS OF THE UNITED STATES." ROUTINE...CLASSIF   STRUCT
TREND EXHIBIT CONGRESS. PAGE 42 B0856

B48

HULL C.,THE MEMOIRS OF CORDELL HULL (VOLUME ONE).   BIOG
USA-45 WOR-45 CONSTN FAM LOC/G NAT/G PROVS DELIB/GP DIPLOM
FORCES LEGIS TOP/EX BAL/PWR LEGIT ADMIN EXEC WAR
ATTIT ORD/FREE PWR...MAJORIT SELF/OBS TIME/SEQ
TREND NAZI 20. PAGE 52 B1062

B49

BURNS J.M.,CONGRESS ON TRIAL: THE LEGISLATIVE   LEGIS
PROCESS AND THE ADMINISTRATIVE STATE. USA+45 NAT/G EXEC
ADMIN ROUTINE REPRESENT...PREDICT TREND. PAGE 17   GP/REL
B0354   PWR

B49

ROSENHAUPT H.W.,HOW TO WAGE PEACE. USA+45 SOCIETY   INTELL
STRATA STRUCT R+D INTELL POL/PAR LEGIS ACT/RES   CONCPT
CREATE PLAN EDU/PROP ADMIN EXEC ATTIT ALL/VALS   DIPLOM
...TIME/SEQ TREND COLD/WAR 20. PAGE 90 B1822

B50

MANNHEIM K.,FREEDOM, POWER, AND DEMOCRATIC   TEC/DEV
PLANNING. FUT USSR WOR+45 ELITES INTELL SOCIETY   PLAN
NAT/G EDU/PROP ROUTINE ATTIT DRIVE SUPEGO SKILL   CAP/ISM
...POLICY PSY CONCPT TREND GEN/LAWS 20. PAGE 69   UK
B1393

C50

HOLCOMBE A.,"OUR MORE PERFECT UNION." USA+45 USA-45 CONSTN
POL/PAR JUDGE CT/SYS EQUILIB FEDERAL PWR...MAJORIT NAT/G
TREND BIBLIOG 18/20 CONGRESS PRESIDENT. PAGE 51   ADMIN
B1031   PLAN

B51

LEITES N.,THE OPERATIONAL CODE OF THE POLITBURO.   DELIB/GP
COM USSR CREATE PLAN DOMIN LEGIT COERCE ALL/VALS   ADMIN
...SOC CONCPT MYTH TREND CON/ANAL GEN/LAWS 20   SOCISM
LENIN/VI STALIN/J. PAGE 64 B1284

S51

LERNER D.,"THE POLICY SCIENCES: RECENT DEVELOPMENTS CONSULT
IN SCOPE AND METHODS." R+D SERV/IND CREATE DIPLOM   SOC
ROUTINE PWR...METH/CNCPT TREND GEN/LAWS METH 20.
PAGE 64 B1297

B52

EGLE W.P.,ECONOMIC STABILIZATION. USA+45 SOCIETY   NAT/G
FINAN MARKET PLAN ECO/TAC DOMIN EDU/PROP LEGIT EXEC ECO/DEV
WEALTH...CONCPT METH/CNCPT TREND HYPO/EXP GEN/METH CAP/ISM
TOT/POP VAL/FREE 20. PAGE 32 B0656

B52

US DEPARTMENT OF STATE,RESEARCH ON EASTERN EUROPE   BIBLIOG
(EXCLUDING USSR). EUR+WWI LAW ECO/DEV NAT/G   R+D
PROB/SOLV DIPLOM ADMIN LEAD MARXISM...TREND 19/20. ACT/RES
PAGE 108 B2182   COM

L52

WRIGHT G.,"CONGRESS AND THE TREATY-MAKING POWER."   ROUTINE
USA+45 WOR+45 CONSTN INTELL NAT/G CHIEF CONSULT   DIPLOM
EX/STRUC LEGIS TOP/EX CREATE GOV/REL DISPL DRIVE   INT/LAW
RIGID/FLEX...TREND TOT/POP CONGRESS CONGRESS 20   DELIB/GP
TREATY. PAGE 118 B2384

S52

SCHWEBEL S.M.,"THE SECRETARY-GENERAL OF THE UN."   INT/ORG
FUT INTELL CONSULT DELIB/GP ADMIN PEACE ATTIT   TOP/EX
...JURID MGT CONCPT TREND UN CONGRESS 20. PAGE 95
B1915

B53

MILLIKAN M.F.,INCOME STABILIZATION FOR A DEVELOPING ANTHOL
DEMOCRACY. USA+45 ECO/DEV LABOR BUDGET ECO/TAC TAX MARKET
ADMIN ADJUST PRODUC WEALTH...POLICY TREND 20.   EQUILIB
PAGE 73 B1484   EFFICIENCY

S53

MORRIS B.S.,"THE COMINFORM: A FIVE YEAR   VOL/ASSN
PERSPECTIVE." COM UNIV USSR WOR+45 ECO/DEV POL/PAR EDU/PROP
TOP/EX PLAN DOMIN ADMIN TOTALISM ATTIT ALL/VALS   DIPLOM
...CONCPT TIME/SEQ TREND CON/ANAL WORK VAL/FREE 20.
PAGE 76 B1527

C53

BULNER-THOMAS I.,"THE PARTY SYSTEM IN GREAT   NAT/G
BRITAIN." UK CONSTN SECT PRESS CONFER GP/REL ATTIT POL/PAR
...POLICY TREND BIBLIOG 19/20 PARLIAMENT. PAGE 17   ADMIN

B0343   ROUTINE
                                                      B54

MCCLOSKEY J.F.,OPERATIONS RESEARCH FOR MANAGEMENT. OP/RES
STRUCT COMPUTER ADMIN ROUTINE...PHIL/SCI CONCPT MGT
METH/CNCPT TREND ANTHOL BIBLIOG 20. PAGE 72 B1445 METH/COMP
                                                    TEC/DEV
                                                      B54

MILLARD E.L.,FREEDOM IN A FEDERAL WORLD. FUT WOR+45 INT/ORG
VOL/ASSN TOP/EX LEGIT ROUTINE FEDERAL PEACE ATTIT CREATE
DISPL ORD/FREE PWR...MAJORIT INT/LAW JURID TREND ADJUD
COLD/WAR 20. PAGE 73 B1479 BAL/PWR
                                                    L54

ARCIENEGAS G.,"POST-WAR SOVIET FOREIGN POLICY: A INTELL
WORLD PERSPECTIVE." COM USA+45 STRUCT NAT/G POL/PAR ACT/RES
TOP/EX PLAN ADMIN ALL/VALS...TREND COLD/WAR TOT/POP USSR
20. PAGE 6 B0124
                                                    C54

ROBSON W.A.,"GREAT CITIES OF THE WORLD: THEIR LOC/G
GOVERNMENT, POLITICS, AND PLANNING." CONSTN FINAN MUNIC
EX/STRUC ADMIN EXEC CHOOSE GOV/REL...STAT TREND PLAN
ANTHOL BIBLIOG 20. PAGE 89 B1806 PROB/SOLV
                                                    B55

MACMAHON A.W.,FEDERALISM: MATURE AND EMERGENT. STRUCT
EUR+WWI FUT WOR+45 WOR-45 INT/ORG NAT/G REPRESENT CONCPT
FEDERAL...POLICY MGT RECORD TREND GEN/LAWS 20.
PAGE 68 B1370
                                                    L55

ROSTOW W.W.,"RUSSIA AND CHINA UNDER COMMUNISM." COM
CHINA/COM USSR INTELL STRUCT INT/ORG NAT/G POL/PAR ASIA
TOP/EX ACT/RES PLAN ADMIN ATTIT ALL/VALS MARXISM
...CONCPT OBS TIME/SEQ TREND GOV/COMP VAL/FREE 20.
PAGE 91 B1830
                                                    S55

ANGELL R.,"GOVERNMENTS AND PEOPLES AS A FOCI FOR FUT
PEACE-ORIENTED RESEARCH." WOR+45 CULTURE SOCIETY SOC
FACE/GP ACT/RES CREATE PLAN DIPLOM EDU/PROP ROUTINE PEACE
ATTIT PERCEPT SKILL...POLICY CONCPT OBS TREND
GEN/METH 20. PAGE 5 B0110
                                                    S55

KAUTSKY J.H.,"THE NEW STRATEGY OF INTERNATIONAL COM
COMMUNISM." ASIA CHINA/COM FUT WOR+45 WOR-45 ADMIN POL/PAR
ROUTINE PERSON MARXISM SOCISM...TREND IDEA/COMP 20 TOTALISM
LENIN/VI MAO. PAGE 59 B1184 USSR
                                                    B56

CONAWAY O.B.,DEMOCRACY IN FEDERAL ADMINISTRATION ADMIN
(PAMPHLET). USA+45 LEGIS PARTIC ATTIT...TREND SERV/IND
ANTHOL 20. PAGE 23 B0459 NAT/G
                                                    GP/REL
                                                    S56

KAUFMAN H.,"EMERGING CONFLICTS IN THE DOCTRINES OF ADMIN
PUBLIC ADMINISTRATION" (BMR)" USA+45 USA-45 NAT/G ORD/FREE
EX/STRUC LEGIS CONTROL NEUTRAL ATTIT PWR...TREND REPRESENT
20. PAGE 58 B1181 LEAD
                                                    S56

KHAMA T.,"POLITICAL CHANGE IN AFRICAN SOCIETY." AFR
CONSTN SOCIETY LOC/G NAT/G POL/PAR EX/STRUC LEGIS ELITES
LEGIT ADMIN CHOOSE REPRESENT NAT/LISM MORAL
ORD/FREE PWR...CONCPT OBS TREND GEN/METH CMN/WLTH
17/20. PAGE 59 B1201
                                                    C56

NEUMANN S.,"MODERN POLITICAL PARTIES: APPROACHES TO POL/PAR
COMPARATIVE POLITIC. FRANCE UK EX/STRUC DOMIN ADMIN GOV/COMP
LEAD REPRESENT TOTALISM ATTIT...POLICY TREND ELITES
METH/COMP ANTHOL BIBLIOG/A 20 CMN/WLTH. PAGE 78 MAJORIT
B1574
                                                    B57

KAPLAN M.A.,SYSTEM AND PROCESS OF INTERNATIONAL INT/ORG
POLITICS. FUT WOR+45 WOR-45 SOCIETY PLAN BAL/PWR DIPLOM
ADMIN ATTIT PERSON RIGID/FLEX PWR SOVEREIGN
...DECISION TREND VAL/FREE. PAGE 58 B1168
                                                    B57

MORSTEIN-MARX F.,THE ADMINISTRATIVE STATE: AN EXEC
INTRODUCTION TO BUREAUCRACY. EUR+WWI FUT MOD/EUR MGT
USA+45 USA-45 NAT/G CONSULT ADMIN ROUTINE TOTALISM CAP/ISM
DRIVE SKILL...TREND 19/20. PAGE 76 B1530 ELITES
                                                    S57

HAILEY,"TOMORROW IN AFRICA." CONSTN SOCIETY LOC/G AFR
NAT/G DOMIN ADJUD ADMIN GP/REL DISCRIM NAT/LISM PERSON
ATTIT MORAL ORD/FREE...PSY SOC CONCPT OBS RECORD ELITES
TREND GEN/LAWS CMN/WLTH 20. PAGE 45 B0917 RACE/REL
                                                    B58

BERNSTEIN M.H.,THE JOB OF THE FEDERAL EXECUTIVE. NAT/G
POL/PAR CHIEF LEGIS ADMIN EXEC LOBBY CHOOSE GOV/REL TOP/EX
ORD/FREE PWR...MGT TREND. PAGE 11 B0228 PERS/COMP
                                                    B58

KINTNER W.R.,ORGANIZING FOR CONFLICT: A PROPOSAL. USA+45
USSR STRUCT NAT/G LEGIS ADMIN EXEC PEACE ORD/FREE PLAN
PWR...CONCPT OBS TREND NAT/COMP VAL/FREE COLD/WAR DIPLOM
20. PAGE 60 B1211
                                                    B58

LAQUER W.Z.,THE MIDDLE EAST IN TRANSITION. COM USSR ISLAM
ECO/UNDEV NAT/G VOL/ASSN EDU/PROP EXEC ATTIT DRIVE TREND
PWR MARXISM COLD/WAR TOT/POP 20. PAGE 62 B1261 NAT/LISM
                                                    B58

SWEENEY S.B.,EDUCATION FOR ADMINISTRATIVE CAREERS EDU/PROP
IN GOVERNMENT SERVICE. USA+45 ACADEM CONSULT CREATE ADMIN

PLAN CONFER SKILL...TREND IDEA/COMP METH 20 NAT/G
CIVIL/SERV. PAGE 102 B2059 LOC/G
                                                    L58

EISENSTADT S.N.,"BUREAUCRACY AND ADMIN
BUREAUCRATIZATION." WOR+45 ECO/DEV INDUS R+D PLAN OP/RES
GOV/REL...WELF/ST TREND BIBLIOG/A 20. PAGE 32 B0659 MGT
                                                    PHIL/SCI
                                                    S58

DAVENPORT J.,"ARMS AND THE WELFARE STATE." INTELL USA+45
STRUCT FORCES CREATE ECO/TAC FOR/AID DOMIN LEGIT NAT/G
ADMIN WAR ORD/FREE PWR...POLICY SOC CONCPT MYTH OBS USSR
TREND COLD/WAR TOT/POP 20. PAGE 26 B0533
                                                    S58

JORDAN A.,"MILITARY ASSISTANCE AND NATIONAL FORCES
POLICY." ASIA FUT USA+45 WOR+45 ECO/DEV ECO/UNDEV POLICY
INT/ORG NAT/G PLAN ECO/TAC ROUTINE WEAPON ATTIT FOR/AID
RIGID/FLEX PWR...CONCPT TREND 20. PAGE 57 B1153 DIPLOM
                                                    B59

SPIRO H.J.,GOVERNMENT BY CONSTITUTIONS: THE NAT/G
POLITICAL SYSTEMS OF DEMOCRACY. CANADA EUR+WWI FUT CONSTN
USA+45 WOR+45 WOR-45 LEGIS TOP/EX LEGIT ADMIN
CT/SYS ORD/FREE PWR...TREND TOT/POP VAL/FREE 20.
PAGE 99 B2008
                                                    S59

BAILEY S.D.,"THE FUTURE COMPOSITION OF THE INT/ORG
TRUSTEESHIP COUNCIL." FUT WOR+45 CONSTN VOL/ASSN NAT/LISM
ADMIN ATTIT PWR...OBS TREND CON/ANAL VAL/FREE UN SOVEREIGN
20. PAGE 8 B0161
                                                    S59

LENGYEL P.,"SOME TRENDS IN THE INTERNATIONAL CIVIL ADMIN
SERVICE." FUT WOR+45 INT/ORG CONSULT ATTIT...MGT EXEC
OBS TREND CON/ANAL LEAGUE/NAT UNESCO 20. PAGE 64
B1291
                                                    B60

EASTON S.C.,THE TWILIGHT OF EUROPEAN COLONIALISM. FINAN
AFR S/ASIA CONSTN SOCIETY STRUCT ECO/UNDEV ADMIN
NAT/G FORCES ECO/TAC COLONIAL CT/SYS ATTIT KNOWL
ORD/FREE PWR...SOCIALIST TIME/SEQ TREND CON/ANAL
20. PAGE 32 B0645
                                                    B60

FURNISS E.S.,FRANCE, TROUBLED ALLY. EUR+WWI FUT NAT/G
CULTURE SOCIETY BAL/PWR ADMIN ATTIT DRIVE PWR FRANCE
...TREND TOT/POP 20 DEGAULLE/C. PAGE 38 B0767
                                                    B60

KERR C.,INDUSTRIALISM AND INDUSTRIAL MAN. CULTURE WORKER
SOCIETY ECO/UNDEV NAT/G ADMIN PRODUC WEALTH MGT
...PREDICT TREND NAT/COMP 19/20. PAGE 59 B1197 ECO/DEV
                                                    INDUS
                                                    B60

LINDSAY K.,EUROPEAN ASSEMBLIES: THE EXPERIMENTAL VOL/ASSN
PERIOD 1949-1959. EUR+WWI ECO/DEV NAT/G POL/PAR INT/ORG
LEGIS TOP/EX ACT/RES PLAN ECO/TAC DOMIN LEGIT REGION
ROUTINE ATTIT DRIVE ORD/FREE PWR SKILL...SOC CONCPT
TREND CHARTS GEN/LAWS VAL/FREE. PAGE 65 B1315
                                                    B60

LISKA G.,THE NEW STATECRAFT. WOR+45 WOR-45 LEGIS ECO/TAC
DIPLOM ADMIN ATTIT PWR WEALTH...HIST/WRIT TREND CONCPT
COLD/WAR 20. PAGE 66 B1323 FOR/AID
                                                    B60

MUNRO L.,UNITED NATIONS, HOPE FOR A DIVIDED WORLD. INT/ORG
FUT WOR+45 CONSTN DELIB/GP CREATE TEC/DEV DIPLOM ROUTINE
EDU/PROP LEGIT PEACE ATTIT HEALTH ORD/FREE PWR
...CONCPT TREND UN VAL/FREE 20. PAGE 76 B1540
                                                    B60

ROEPKE W.,A HUMANE ECONOMY: THE SOCIAL FRAMEWORK OF DRIVE
THE FREE MARKET. FUT USSR WOR+45 CULTURE SOCIETY EDU/PROP
ECO/DEV PLAN ECO/TAC ADMIN ATTIT PERSON RIGID/FLEX CAP/ISM
SUPEGO MORAL WEALTH SOCISM...POLICY OLD/LIB CONCPT
TREND GEN/LAWS 20. PAGE 90 B1811
                                                    L60

BRENNAN D.G.,"SETTING AND GOALS OF ARMS CONTROL." FORCES
FUT USA+45 USSR WOR+45 INTELL INT/ORG NAT/G COERCE
VOL/ASSN CONSULT PLAN DIPLOM ECO/TAC ADMIN KNOWL ARMS/CONT
PWR...POLICY CONCPT TREND COLD/WAR 20. PAGE 15 DETER
B0305
                                                    L60

DEAN A.W.,"SECOND GENEVA CONFERENCE OF THE LAW OF INT/ORG
THE SEA: THE FIGHT FOR FREEDOM OF THE SEAS." FUT JURID
USA+45 USSR WOR+45 WOR-45 SEA CONSTN STRUCT PLAN INT/LAW
INT/TRADE ADJUD ADMIN ORD/FREE...DECISION RECORD
TREND GEN/LAWS 20 TREATY. PAGE 28 B0564
                                                    L60

STEIN E.,"LEGAL REMEDIES OF ENTERPRISES IN THE MARKET
EUROPEAN ECONOMIC COMMUNITY." EUR+WWI FUT ECO/DEV ADJUD
INDUS PLAN ECO/TAC ADMIN PWR...MGT MATH STAT TREND
CON/ANAL EEC 20. PAGE 100 B2026
                                                    S60

BOYER W.W.,"POLICY MAKING BY GOVERNMENT AGENCIES." NAT/G
USA+45 WOR+45 R+D DELIB/GP TOP/EX EDU/PROP ROUTINE DIPLOM
ATTIT BIO/SOC DRIVE...CONCPT TREND TOT/POP 20.
PAGE 14 B0293
                                                    S60

GARNICK D.H.,"ON THE ECONOMIC FEASIBILITY OF A MARKET
MIDDLE EASTERN COMMON MARKET." AFR ISLAM CULTURE INT/TRADE
INDUS NAT/G PLAN TEC/DEV ECO/TAC ADMIN ATTIT DRIVE
RIGID/FLEX...PLURIST STAT TREND GEN/LAWS 20.

PAGE 39 B0784

B0162

S60

REISELBACH L.N.,"THE BASIS OF ISOLATIONIST   ATTIT
BEHAVIOR." USA+45 USA-45 CULTURE ECO/DEV LOC/G   DIPLOM
NAT/G ADMIN ROUTINE CHOOSE BIO/SOC DRIVE RIGID/FLEX ECO/TAC
...CENSUS SAMP TREND CHARTS TOT/POP 20. PAGE 87
B1765

S60

SCHACHTER O.,"THE ENFORCEMENT OF INTERNATIONAL   INT.ORG
JUDICIAL AND ARBITRAL DECISIONS." WOR+45 NAT/G   ADJUD
ECO/TAC DOMIN LEGIT ROUTINE COERCE ATTIT DRIVE   INT/LAW
ALL/VALS PWR...METH/CNCPT TREND TOT/POP 20 UN.
PAGE 93 B1878

S60

SCHATZ S.P.,"THE INFLENCE OF PLANNING ON   ECO/UNDEV
DEVELOPMENT: THE NIGERIAN EXPERIENCE." AFR FUT   PLAN
FINAN INDUS NAT/G EX/STRUC ECO/TAC ADMIN ATTIT   NIGERIA
PERCEPT ORD/FREE PWR...MATH TREND CON/ANAL SIMUL
VAL/FREE 20. PAGE 93 B1883

S60

SCHWARTZ B.,"THE INTELLIGENTSIA IN COMMUNIST CHINA: INTELL
A TENTATIVE COMPARISON." ASIA CHINA/COM COM RUSSIA   RIGID/FLEX
ELITES SOCIETY STRATA POL/PAR VOL/ASSN CREATE ADMIN REV
COERCE NAT/LISM TOTALISM...POLICY TREND 20. PAGE 95
B1914

S60

THOMPSON K.W.,"MORAL PURPOSE IN FOREIGN POLICY: MORAL
REALITIES AND ILLUSIONS." WOR+45 WOR-45 LAW CULTURE JURID
SOCIETY INT/ORG PLAN ADJUD ADMIN COERCE RIGID/FLEX   DIPLOM
SUPEGO KNOWL ORD/FREE PWR...SOC TREND SOC/EXP
TOT/POP 20. PAGE 104 B2104

B61

BARNES W.,THE FOREIGN SERVICE OF THE UNITED STATES. NAT/G
USA+45 USA-45 CONSTN INT/ORG POL/PAR CONSULT   MGT
DELIB/GP LEGIS DOMIN EDU/PROP EXEC ATTIT RIGID/FLEX DIPLOM
ORD/FREE PWR...POLICY CONCPT STAT OBS RECORD BIOG
TIME/SEQ TREND. PAGE 9 B0188

B61

BENOIT E.,EUROPE AT SIXES AND SEVENS: THE COMMON   FINAN
MARKET, THE FREE TRADE ASSOCIATION AND THE UNITED   ECO/DEV
STATES. EUR+WWI FUT USA+45 INDUS CONSULT DELIB/GP   VOL/ASSN
EX/STRUC TOP/EX ACT/RES ECO/TAC EDU/PROP ROUTINE
CHOOSE PERCEPT WEALTH...MGT TREND EEC TOT/POP 20
EFTA. PAGE 11 B0217

B61

KERTESZ S.D.,AMERICAN DIPLOMACY IN A NEW ERA. COM   ANTHOL
S/ASIA UK USA+45 FORCES PROB/SOLV BAL/PWR ECO/TAC   DIPLOM
ADMIN COLONIAL WAR PEACE ORD/FREE 20 NATO CONGRESS   TREND
UN COLD/WAR. PAGE 59 B1199

B61

MACRIDIS R.C.,COMPARATIVE POLITICS: NOTES AND   POL/PAR
READINGS. WOR+45 LOC/G MUNIC NAT/G PROVS VOL/ASSN   CHOOSE
EDU/PROP ADMIN ATTIT PERSON ORD/FREE...SOC CONCPT
OBS RECORD TREND 20. PAGE 68 B1376

B61

NOVE A.,THE SOVIET ECONOMY. USSR ECO/DEV FINAN   PLAN
NAT/G ECO/TAC PRICE ADMIN EFFICIENCY MARXISM   PRODUC
...TREND BIBLIOG 20. PAGE 79 B1594   POLICY

B61

RAO K.V.,PARLIAMENTARY DEMOCRACY OF INDIA. INDIA   CONSTN
EX/STRUC TOP/EX COLONIAL CT/SYS PARL/PROC ORD/FREE   ADJUD
...POLICY CONCPT TREND 20 PARLIAMENT. PAGE 86 B1733 NAT/G
                                                     FEDERAL

B61

BARTLEY H.J.,"COMMAND EXPERIENCE." USA+45 EX/STRUC   CONCPT
FORCES LEGIT ROUTINE SKILL...POLICY OBS HYPO/EXP   TREND
GEN/LAWS 20. PAGE 9 B0191

S61

HAAS E.B.,"INTERNATIONAL INTEGRATION: THE EUROPEAN   INT/ORG
AND THE UNIVERSAL PROCESS." EUR+WWI FUT WOR+45   TREND
NAT/G EX/STRUC ATTIT DRIVE ORD/FREE PWR...CONCPT   REGION
GEN/LAWS OEEC 20 NATO COUNCL/EUR. PAGE 45 B0909

S61

LANFALUSSY A.,"EUROPE'S PROGRESS: DUE TO COMMON   INT/ORG
MARKET." EUR+WWI ECO/DEV DELIB/GP PLAN ECO/TAC   MARKET
ROUTINE WEALTH...GEOG TREND EEC 20. PAGE 62 B1257

S61

NEEDLER M.C.,"THE POLITICAL DEVELOPMENT OF MEXICO." L/A+17C
STRUCT NAT/G ADMIN RIGID/FLEX...TIME/SEQ TREND   POL/PAR
MEXIC/AMER TOT/POP VAL/FREE 19/20. PAGE 77 B1566

S61

RUDOLPH S.,"CONSENSUS AND CONFLICT IN INDIAN   POL/PAR
POLITICS." S/ASIA WOR+45 NAT/G DELIB/GP DIPLOM   PERCEPT
EDU/PROP ADMIN CONSEN PERSON ALL/VALS...OBS TREND   INDIA
TOT/POP VAL/FREE 20. PAGE 92 B1854

S61

TAUBENFELD H.J.,"OUTER SPACE--PAST POLITICS AND   PLAN
FUTURE POLICY." FUT USA+45 USA-45 WOR+45 AIR INTELL SPACE
STRUCT ECO/DEV NAT/G TOP/EX ACT/RES ADMIN ROUTINE   INT/ORG
NUC/PWR ATTIT DRIVE...CONCPT TIME/SEQ TREND TOT/POP
20. PAGE 103 B2083

B62

BAILEY S.D.,THE SECRETARIAT OF THE UNITED NATIONS.   INT/ORG
FUT WOR+45 DELIB/GP PLAN BAL/PWR DOMIN EDU/PROP   EXEC
ADMIN PEACE ATTIT PWR...DECISION CONCPT TREND   DIPLOM
CON/ANAL CHARTS UN VAL/FREE COLD/WAR 20. PAGE 8

B62

EVANS M.S.,THE FRINGE ON TOP. USSR EX/STRUC FORCES   NAT/G
DIPLOM ECO/TAC PEACE CONSERVE SOCISM...TREND 20   PWR
KENNEDY/JF. PAGE 34 B0689   CENTRAL
                                                     POLICY

B62

MARTIN R.C.,GOVERNMENT AND THE SUBURBAN SCHOOL.   SCHOOL
USA+45 FINAN EDU/PROP ADMIN HABITAT...TREND GP/COMP LOC/G
20. PAGE 70 B1414   EX/STRUC
                                                     ISOLAT

B62

SCHILLING W.R.,STRATEGY, POLITICS, AND DEFENSE   ROUTINE
BUDGETS. USA+45 R+D NAT/G CONSULT DELIB/GP FORCES   POLICY
LEGIS ACT/RES PLAN BAL/PWR LEGIT EXEC NUC/PWR
RIGID/FLEX PWR...TREND COLD/WAR CONGRESS 20
EISNHWR/DD. PAGE 93 B1890

L62

GALBRAITH J.K.,"ECONOMIC DEVELOPMENT IN   ECO/UNDEV
PERSPECTIVE." CAP/ISM ECO/TAC ROUTINE ATTIT WEALTH   PLAN
...TREND CHARTS SOC/EXP WORK 20. PAGE 38 B0773

S62

ALGER C.F.,"THE EXTERNAL BUREAUCRACY IN UNITED   ADMIN
STATES FOREIGN AFFAIRS." USA+45 WOR+45 SOCIETY   ATTIT
COM/IND INT/ORG NAT/G CONSULT EX/STRUC ACT/RES   DIPLOM
...MGT SOC CONCPT TREND 20. PAGE 4 B0076

S62

BRZEZINSKI Z.K.,"DEVIATION CONTROL: A STUDY IN THE   RIGID/FLEX
DYNAMICS OF DOCTRINAL CONFLICT." WOR+45 WOR-45   ATTIT
VOL/ASSN CREATE BAL/PWR DOMIN EXEC DRIVE PERCEPT
PWR...METH/CNCPT TIME/SEQ TREND 20. PAGE 16 B0333

S62

IOVTCHOUK M.T.,"ON SOME THEORETICAL PRINCIPLES AND   COM
METHODS OF SOCIOLOGICAL INVESTIGATIONS (IN   ECO/DEV
RUSSIAN)." FUT USA+45 STRATA R+D NAT/G POL/PAR   CAP/ISM
TOP/EX ACT/RES PLAN ECO/TAC EDU/PROP ROUTINE ATTIT   USSR
RIGID/FLEX MARXISM SOCISM...MARXIST METH/CNCPT OBS
TREND NAT/COMP GEN/LAWS 20. PAGE 54 B1102

S62

JOHNSON H.,"CANADA IN A CHANGING WORLD." EUR+WWI   ECO/DEV
USA+45 NAT/G CAP/ISM ECO/TAC ADMIN ATTIT WEALTH   PLAN
...TREND TOT/POP 20 EEC. PAGE 57 B1143   CANADA

S62

NORTH R.C.,"DECISION MAKING IN CRISIS: AN   INT/ORG
INTRODUCTION." WOR+45 WOR-45 NAT/G CONSULT DELIB/GP ROUTINE
TEC/DEV PERCEPT KNOWL...POLICY DECISION PSY   DIPLOM
METH/CNCPT CONT/OBS TREND VAL/FREE 20. PAGE 79
B1590

S62

SCHILLING W.R.,"SCIENTISTS, FOREIGN POLICY AND   NAT/G
POLITICS." WOR+45 WOR-45 INTELL INT/ORG CONSULT   TEC/DEV
TOP/EX ACT/RES PLAN ADMIN KNOWL...CONCPT OBS TREND   DIPLOM
LEAGUE/NAT 20. PAGE 93 B1889   NUC/PWR

B63

CORLEY R.N.,THE LEGAL ENVIRONMENT OF BUSINESS.   NAT/G
CONSTN LEGIS TAX ADMIN CT/SYS DISCRIM ATTIT PWR   INDUS
...TREND 18/20. PAGE 23 B0477   JURID
                                                     DECISION

B63

DE VRIES E.,SOCIAL ASPECTS OF ECONOMIC DEVELOPMENT   L/A+17C
IN LATIN AMERICA. CULTURE SOCIETY STRATA FINAN   ECO/UNDEV
INDUS INT/ORG DELIB/GP ACT/RES ECO/TAC ADMIN
ADMIN ATTIT SUPEGO HEALTH KNOWL ORD/FREE...SOC STAT
TREND ANTHOL TOT/POP VAL/FREE. PAGE 28 B0562

B63

DOUGLASS H.R.,MODERN ADMINISTRATION OF SECONDARY   EDU/PROP
SCHOOLS. CLIENT DELIB/GP WORKER REPRESENT INGP/REL   ADMIN
AUTHORIT...TREND BIBLIOG. PAGE 30 B0613   SCHOOL
                                                     MGT

B63

FRIED R.C.,THE ITALIAN PREFECTS. ITALY STRATA   ADMIN
ECO/DEV NAT/LISM ALL/IDEOS...TREND CHARTS METH/COMP NAT/G
BIBLIOG 17/20 PREFECT. PAGE 37 B0755   EFFICIENCY

B63

INTL INST ADMIN SCIENCES.EDUCATION IN PUBLIC   EDU/PROP
ADMINISTRATION: A SYMPOSIUM ON TEACHING METHODS AND METH
MATERIALS. WOR+45 SCHOOL CONSULT CREATE CONFER   ADMIN
SKILL...OBS TREND IDEA/COMP METH/COMP 20. PAGE 54   ACADEM
B1100

B63

MOORE W.E.,MAN, TIME, AND SOCIETY. UNIV STRUCT FAM   CONCPT
MUNIC VOL/ASSN ADMIN...SOC NEW/IDEA TIME/SEQ TREND   SOCIETY
TIME 20. PAGE 75 B1515   CONTROL

B63

ROBERT J.,LA MONARCHIE MAROCAINE. MOROCCO LABOR   CHIEF
MUNIC POL/PAR EX/STRUC ORD/FREE PWR...JURID TREND T CONSERVE
20. PAGE 89 B1793   ADMIN
                                                     CONSTN

B63

TSOU T.,AMERICA'S FAILURE IN CHINA, 1941-1950.   ASIA
USA+45 USA-45 NAT/G ACT/RES PLAN DOMIN EDU/PROP   PERCEPT
ADMIN ROUTINE ATTIT PERSON ORD/FREE...DECISION   DIPLOM
CONCPT MYTH TIME/SEQ TREND STERTYP 20. PAGE 105
B2132

B63

TUCKER R.C.,THE SOVIET POLITICAL MIND. WOR+45   COM

ELITES INT/ORG NAT/G POL/PAR PLAN DIPLOM ECO/TAC
DOMIN ADMIN NUC/PWR REV DRIVE PERSON SUPEGO PWR
WEALTH...POLICY MGT PSY CONCPT OBS BIOG TREND
COLD/WAR MARX/KARL 20. PAGE 106 B2134
TOP/EX
USSR

L63

FREUND G.,"ADENAUER AND THE FUTURE OF GERMANY."
EUR+WWI FUT GERMANY/W FORCES LEGIT ADMIN ROUTINE
ATTIT DRIVE PERSON PWR...POLICY TIME/SEQ TREND
VAL/FREE 20 ADENAUER/K. PAGE 37 B0753
NAT/G
BIOG
DIPLOM
GERMANY

S63

DAVEE R.,"POUR UN FONDS DE DEVELOPPEMENT SOCIAL."
FUT WOR+45 INTELL SOCIETY ECO/DEV FINAN TEC/DEV
ROUTINE WEALTH...TREND TOT/POP VAL/FREE UN 20.
PAGE 26 B0532
INT/ORG
SOC
FOR/AID

S63

MEDALIA N.Z.,"POSITION AND PROSPECTS OF
SOCIOLOGISTS IN FEDERAL EMPLOYMENT." USA+45 CONSULT
PAY SENIOR ADMIN GOV/REL...TREND CHARTS 20
CIVIL/SERV. PAGE 72 B1460
NAT/G
WORKER
SOC
SKILL

S63

NADLER E.B.,"SOME ECONOMIC DISADVANTAGES OF THE
ARMS RACE." USA+45 INDUS R+D FORCES PLAN TEC/DEV
ECO/TAC FOR/AID EDU/PROP PWR WEALTH...TREND
COLD/WAR 20. PAGE 77 B1552
ECO/DEV
MGT
BAL/PAY

S63

ROUGEMONT D.,"LES NOUVELLES CHANCES DE L'EUROPE."
EUR+WWI FUT ECO/DEV INT/ORG NAT/G ACT/RES PLAN
TEC/DEV EDU/PROP ADMIN COLONIAL FEDERAL ATTIT PWR
SKILL...TREND 20. PAGE 91 B1835
ECO/UNDEV
PERCEPT

S63

SCHURMANN F.,"ECONOMIC POLICY AND POLITICAL POWER
IN COMMUNIST CHINA." ASIA CHINA/COM USSR SOCIETY
ECO/UNDEV AGRI INDUS CREATE ADMIN ROUTINE ATTIT
DRIVE RIGID/FLEX PWR WEALTH...HIST/WRIT TREND
CHARTS WORK 20. PAGE 94 B1908
PLAN
ECO/TAC

C63

CARLISLE D.,"PARTY LOYALTY; THE ELECTION PROCESS IN
SOUTH CAROLINA." USA+45 LOC/G ADMIN ATTIT...TREND
CHARTS BIBLIOG 17/20. PAGE 19 B0380
CHOOSE
POL/PAR
PROVS
SUFF

B64

THE SPECIAL COMMONWEALTH AFRICAN ASSISTANCE PLAN.
AFR CANADA INDIA NIGERIA UK FINAN SCHOOL...CHARTS
20 COMMONWLTH. PAGE 2 B0041
ECO/UNDEV
TREND
FOR/AID
ADMIN

B64

GREBLER L.,URBAN RENEWAL IN EUROPEAN COUNTRIES: ITS
EMERGENCE AND POTENTIALS. EUR+WWI UK ECO/DEV LOC/G
NEIGH CREATE ADMIN ATTIT...TREND NAT/COMP 20
URBAN/RNWL. PAGE 43 B0863
MUNIC
PLAN
CONSTRUC
NAT/G

B64

LI C.M.,INDUSTRIAL DEVELOPMENT IN COMMUNIST CHINA.
CHINA/COM ECO/DEV ECO/UNDEV AGRI FINAN INDUS MARKET
LABOR NAT/G ECO/TAC INT/TRADE EXEC ALL/VALS
...POLICY RELATIV TREND WORK TOT/POP VAL/FREE 20.
PAGE 65 B1311
ASIA
TEC/DEV

B64

RIES J.C.,THE MANAGEMENT OF DEFENSE: ORGANIZATION
AND CONTROL OF THE US ARMED SERVICES. PROF/ORG
DELIB/GP EX/STRUC LEGIS GOV/REL PERS/REL CENTRAL
RATIONAL PWR...POLICY TREND GOV/COMP BIBLIOG.
PAGE 88 B1782
FORCES
ACT/RES
DECISION
CONTROL

B64

RIGGS F.W.,ADMINISTRATION IN DEVELOPING COUNTRIES.
FUT WOR+45 STRUCT AGRI INDUS LAW PLAN TEC/DEV
ECO/TAC EDU/PROP RIGID/FLEX KNOWL WEALTH...POLICY
MGT CONCPT METH/CNCPT TREND 20. PAGE 88 B1785
ECO/UNDEV
ADMIN

B64

SULLIVAN G.,THE STORY OF THE PEACE CORPS. USA+45
WOR+45 INTELL FACE/GP NAT/G SCHOOL VOL/ASSN CONSULT
EX/STRUC PLAN EDU/PROP ADMIN ATTIT DRIVE ALL/VALS
...POLICY HEAL SOC CONCPT INT QU BIOG TREND SOC/EXP
WORK. PAGE 102 B2054
INT/ORG
ECO/UNDEV
FOR/AID
PEACE

B64

WAINHOUSE D.W.,REMNANTS OF EMPIRE: THE UNITED
NATIONS AND THE END OF COLONIALISM. FUT PORTUGAL
WOR+45 NAT/G CONSULT DOMIN LEGIT ADMIN ROUTINE
ATTIT ORD/FREE...POLICY JURID RECORD INT TIME/SEQ
UN CMN/WLTH 20. PAGE 113 B2275
INT/ORG
TREND
COLONIAL

L64

HAAS E.B.,"ECONOMICS AND DIFFERENTIAL PATTERNS OF
POLITICAL INTEGRATION: PROJECTIONS ABOUT UNITY IN
LATIN AMERICA." SOCIETY NAT/G DELIB/GP ACT/RES
CREATE PLAN ECO/TAC REGION ROUTINE ATTIT DRIVE PWR
WEALTH...CONCPT TREND CHARTS LAFTA 20. PAGE 45
B0910
L/A+17C
INT/ORG
MARKET

L64

ROTBERG R.,"THE FEDERATION MOVEMENT IN BRITISH EAST
AND CENTRAL AFRICA." AFR RHODESIA UGANDA ECO/UNDEV
NAT/G POL/PAR FORCES DOMIN LEGIT ADMIN COERCE ATTIT
...CONCPT TREND 20 TANGANYIKA. PAGE 91 B1831
VOL/ASSN
PWR
REGION

S64

GALTUNE J.,"BALANCE OF POWER AND THE PROBLEM OF
PERCEPTION. A LOGICAL ANALYSIS." WOR+45 CONSTN
SOCIETY NAT/G DELIB/GP EX/STRUC LEGIS DOMIN ADMIN
COERCE DRIVE ORD/FREE...POLICY CONCPT OBS TREND
PWR
PSY
ARMS/CONT
WAR

GEN/LAWS. PAGE 38 B0778

S64

GROSS J.A.,"WHITEHALL AND THE COMMONWEALTH."
EUR+WWI MOD/EUR INT/ORG NAT/G CONSULT DELIB/GP
LEGIS DOMIN ADMIN COLONIAL ROUTINE PWR CMN/WLTH
19/20. PAGE 44 B0890
EX/STRUC
ATTIT
TREND

S64

KHAN M.Z.,"THE PRESIDENT OF THE GENERAL ASSEMBLY."
WOR+45 CONSTN DELIB/GP EDU/PROP LEGIT ROUTINE PWR
RESPECT SKILL...DECISION SOC BIOG TREND UN 20.
PAGE 59 B1202
INT/ORG
TOP/EX

S64

SWEARER H.R.,"AFTER KHRUSHCHEV: WHAT NEXT." COM FUT
USSR CONSTN ELITES NAT/G POL/PAR CHIEF DELIB/GP
LEGIS DOMIN LEAD...RECORD TREND STERTYP GEN/METH
20. PAGE 102 B2058
EX/STRUC
PWR

B65

ETZIONI A.,POLITICAL UNIFICATION* A COMPARATIVE
STUDY OF LEADERS AND FORCES. EUR+WWI ISLAM L/A+17C
WOR+45 ELITES STRATA EXEC WEALTH...TIME/SEQ TREND
SOC/EXP. PAGE 34 B0686
INT/ORG
ECO/TAC
REGION

B65

GREGG J.L.,POLITICAL PARTIES AND PARTY SYSTEMS IN
GUATEMALA, 1944-1963. GUATEMALA L/A+17C EX/STRUC
FORCES CREATE CONTROL REV CHOOSE PWR...TREND
IDEA/COMP 20. PAGE 43 B0872
LEAD
POL/PAR
NAT/G
CHIEF

B65

MOORE W.E.,THE IMPACT OF INDUSTRY. CULTURE STRUCT
ORD/FREE...TREND 20. PAGE 75 B1516
INDUS
MGT
TEC/DEV
ECO/UNDEV

B65

OLSON M. JR.,DROIT PUBLIC. FRANCE NAT/G LEGIS SUFF
GP/REL PRIVIL...TREND 18/20. PAGE 80 B1609
CONSTN
FINAN
ADMIN
ORD/FREE

B65

ORG FOR ECO COOP AND DEVEL,THE MEDITERRANEAN
REGIONAL PROJECT: YUGOSLAVIA: EDUCATION AND
DEVELOPMENT. YUGOSLAVIA SOCIETY FINAN PROF/ORG PLAN
ADMIN COST DEMAND MARXISM...STAT TREND CHARTS METH
20 OECD. PAGE 80 B1615
EDU/PROP
ACADEM
SCHOOL
ECO/UNDEV

S65

QUADE Q.L.,"THE TRUMAN ADMINISTRATION AND THE
SEPARATION OF POWERS: THE CASE OF THE MARSHALL
PLAN." SOCIETY INT/ORG NAT/G CONSULT DELIB/GP LEGIS
PLAN ECO/TAC ROUTINE DRIVE PERCEPT RIGID/FLEX
ORD/FREE PWR WEALTH...DECISION GEOG NEW/IDEA TREND
20 TRUMAN/HS. PAGE 85 B1726
USA+45
ECO/UNDEV
DIPLOM

S65

RUBINSTEIN A.Z.,"YUGOSLAVIA'S OPENING SOCIETY." COM
USSR INTELL NAT/G LEGIS TOP/EX LEGIT CT/SYS
RIGID/FLEX ALL/VALS SOCISM...HUM TIME/SEQ TREND 20.
PAGE 92 B1851
CONSTN
EX/STRUC
YUGOSLAVIA

S65

TABORSKY E.,"CHANGE IN CZECHOSLOVAKIA." COM USSR
ELITES INTELL AGRI INDUS NAT/G DELIB/GP EX/STRUC
ECO/TAC TOTALISM ATTIT RIGID/FLEX SOCISM...MGT
CONCPT TREND 20. PAGE 102 B2067
ECO/DEV
PLAN
CZECHOSLVK

B66

ONYEMELUKWE C.C.,PROBLEMS OF INDUSTRIAL PLANNING
AND MANAGEMENT IN NIGERIA. AFR FINAN LABOR DELIB/GP
TEC/DEV ADJUST...MGT TREND BIBLIOG. PAGE 80 B1610
ECO/UNDEV
ECO/TAC
INDUS
PLAN

B66

WESTON J.F.,THE SCOPE AND METHODOLOGY OF FINANCE.
PLAN TEC/DEV CONTROL EFFICIENCY INCOME UTIL...MGT
CONCPT MATH STAT TREND METH 20. PAGE 115 B2327
FINAN
ECO/DEV
POLICY
PRICE

B67

BRZEZINSKI Z.K.,THE SOVIET BLOC: UNITY AND CONFLICT
(2ND ED., REV., ENLARGED). COM POLAND USSR INTELL
CHIEF EX/STRUC CONTROL EXEC GOV/REL PWR MARXISM
...TREND IDEA/COMP 20 LENIN/VI MARX/KARL STALIN/J.
PAGE 16 B0336
NAT/G
DIPLOM

B67

JAKUBAUSKAS E.B.,HUMAN RESOURCES DEVELOPMENT.
USA+45 AGRI INDUS SERV/IND ACT/RES PLAN ADMIN
RACE/REL DISCRIM...TREND GEN/LAWS. PAGE 55 B1119
PROB/SOLV
ECO/TAC
EDU/PROP
WORKER

B67

KRISLOV S.,THE NEGRO IN FEDERAL EMPLOYMENT. LAW
STRATA LOC/G CREATE PROB/SOLV INSPECT GOV/REL
DISCRIM ROLE...DECISION INT TREND 20 NEGRO WWI
CIVIL/SERV. PAGE 61 B1238
WORKER
NAT/G
ADMIN
RACE/REL

B67

POSNER M.V.,ITALIAN PUBLIC ENTERPRISE. ITALY
ECO/DEV FINAN INDUS CREATE ECO/TAC ADMIN CONTROL
EFFICIENCY PRODUC...TREND CHARTS 20. PAGE 84 B1693
NAT/G
PLAN
CAP/ISM
SOCISM

B67

PYE L.W.,SOUTHEAST ASIA'S POLITICAL SYSTEMS. ASIA
S/ASIA STRUCT ECO/UNDEV EX/STRUC CAP/ISM DIPLOM
ALL/IDEOS...TREND CHARTS. PAGE 85 B1724
NAT/G
POL/PAR
GOV/COMP

B67

TANSKY L.,US AND USSR AID TO DEVELOPING COUNTRIES.
FOR/AID

INDIA TURKEY UAR USA+45 USSR FINAN PLAN TEC/DEV ECO/UNDEV
ADMIN WEALTH...TREND METH/COMP 20. PAGE 103 B2076   MARXISM
                                                      CAP/ISM
                                                            B67
ZONDAG C.H.,THE BOLIVIAN ECONOMY 1952-65. L/A+17C   ECO/UNDEV
TEC/DEV FOR/AID ADMIN...OBS TREND CHARTS BIBLIOG 20   INDUS
BOLIV. PAGE 119 B2406   PRODUC
                                                            S67
ALPANDER G.G.,"ENTREPRENEURS AND PRIVATE ENTERPRISE   ECO/UNDEV
IN TURKEY." TURKEY INDUS PROC/MFG EDU/PROP ATTIT   LG/CO
DRIVE WEALTH...GEOG MGT SOC STAT TREND CHARTS 20.   NAT/G
PAGE 4 B0080   POLICY
                                                            S67
IDENBURG P.J.,"POLITICAL STRUCTURAL DEVELOPMENT IN   AFR
TROPICAL AFRICA." UK ECO/UNDEV KIN POL/PAR CHIEF   CONSTN
EX/STRUC CREATE COLONIAL CONTROL REPRESENT RACE/REL   NAT/G
...MAJORIT TREND 20. PAGE 53 B1074   GOV/COMP
                                                            S67
JAVITS J.K.,"THE USE OF AMERICAN PLURALISM." USA+45   CENTRAL
ECO/DEV BUDGET ADMIN ALL/IDEOS...DECISION TREND.   ATTIT
PAGE 56 B1127   POLICY
                                                      NAT/G
                                                            S67
TATU M.,"URSS: LES FLOTTEMENTS DE LA DIRECTION   POLICY
COLLEGIALE." UAR USSR CHIEF LEAD INGP/REL   NAT/G
EFFICIENCY...DECISION TREND 20 MID/EAST. PAGE 103   EX/STRUC
B2082   DIPLOM
                                                            S67
ZASLOW M.,"RECENT CONSTITUTIONAL DEVELOPMENTS IN   GOV/REL
CANADA'S NORTHERN TERRITORIES." CANADA LOC/G   REGION
DELIB/GP EX/STRUC LEGIS ADMIN ORD/FREE...TREND 20.   CONSTN
PAGE 119 B2398   FEDERAL

TREVELYAN G.M. B2128

TRIBAL....SEE KIN

TRIBUTE....FORMAL PAYMENTS TO DOMINANT POWER BY MINOR POWER
   GROUP; SEE ALSO SANCTION
                                                            B56
ABELS J.,THE TRUMAN SCANDALS. USA+45 USA-45 POL/PAR   CRIME
TAX LEGIT CT/SYS CHOOSE PRIVIL MORAL WEALTH 20   ADMIN
TRUMAN/HS PRESIDENT CONGRESS. PAGE 3 B0052   CHIEF
                                                      TRIBUTE
                                                            B60
PINTO F.B.M.,ENRIQUECIMENTO ILICITO NO EXERCICIO DE   ADMIN
CARGOS PUBLICOS. BRAZIL L/A+17C USA+45 ELITES   NAT/G
TRIBUTE CONTROL INGP/REL ORD/FREE PWR...NAT/COMP   CRIME
20. PAGE 83 B1675   LAW
                                                            S67
NYE J.S.,"CORRUPTION AND POLITICAL DEVELOPMENT: A   ECO/UNDEV
COST-BENEFIT ANALYSIS." WOR+45 SOCIETY TRIBUTE   NAT/G
ADMIN CONTROL COST...CHARTS 20. PAGE 79 B1598   CRIME
                                                      ACT/RES

TRIESTE....TRIESTE

TRINIDAD AND TOBAGO....SEE TRINIDAD

TRINIDAD....TRINIDAD AND TOBAGO; SEE ALSO L/A+17C
                                                            S67
SPACKMAN A.,"THE SENATE OF TRINIDAD AND TOBAGO."   ELITES
L/A+17C TRINIDAD WEST/IND NAT/G POL/PAR DELIB/GP   EFFICIENCY
OP/RES PROB/SOLV EDU/PROP EXEC LOBBY ROUTINE   LEGIS
REPRESENT GP/REL 20. PAGE 99 B2002   DECISION

TROBRIAND....TROBRIAND ISLANDS AND ISLANDERS

TROTSKY/L....LEON TROTSKY

TRUJILLO/R....RAFAEL TRUJILLO

TRUMAN D. B2129

TRUMAN D.B. B2130,B2131

TRUMAN DOCTRINE....SEE TRUMAN/DOC

TRUMAN/DOC....TRUMAN DOCTRINE

TRUMAN/HS....PRESIDENT HARRY S. TRUMAN
                                                            B56
ABELS J.,THE TRUMAN SCANDALS. USA+45 USA-45 POL/PAR   CRIME
TAX LEGIT CT/SYS CHOOSE PRIVIL MORAL WEALTH 20   ADMIN
TRUMAN/HS PRESIDENT CONGRESS. PAGE 3 B0052   CHIEF
                                                      TRIBUTE
                                                            B56
KOENIG L.W.,THE TRUMAN ADMINISTRATION: ITS   ADMIN
PRINCIPLES AND PRACTICE. USA+45 POL/PAR CHIEF LEGIS   POLICY
DIPLOM DEATH NUC/PWR WAR CIVMIL/REL PEACE   EX/STRUC
...DECISION 20 TRUMAN/HS PRESIDENT TREATY. PAGE 61   GOV/REL
B1224

                                                            S56
CUTLER R.,"THE DEVELOPMENT OF THE NATIONAL SECURITY   ORD/FREE
COUNCIL." USA+45 INTELL CONSULT EX/STRUC DIPLOM   DELIB/GP
LEAD 20 TRUMAN/HS EISNHWR/DD NSC. PAGE 25 B0514   PROB/SOLV
                                                      NAT/G
                                                            S61
SCHILLING W.R.,"THE H-BOMB: HOW TO DECIDE WITHOUT   PERSON
ACTUALLY CHOOSING." FUT USA+45 INTELL CONSULT ADMIN   LEGIT
CT/SYS MORAL...JURID OBS 20 TRUMAN/HS. PAGE 93   NUC/PWR
B1888
                                                            B62
GRAY R.K.,EIGHTEEN ACRES UNDER GLASS. ELITES   CHIEF
CONSULT EX/STRUC DIPLOM PRESS CONFER WAR PERS/REL   ADMIN
PERSON 20 EISNHWR/DD TRUMAN/HS CABINET. PAGE 43   TOP/EX
B0860   NAT/G
                                                            B64
NEUSTADT R.,PRESIDENTIAL POWER. USA+45 CONSTN NAT/G   TOP/EX
CHIEF LEGIS CREATE EDU/PROP LEGIT ADMIN EXEC COERCE   SKILL
ATTIT PERSON RIGID/FLEX PWR CONGRESS 20 PRESIDENT
TRUMAN/HS EISNHWR/DD. PAGE 78 B1575
                                                            S65
QUADE Q.L.,"THE TRUMAN ADMINISTRATION AND THE   USA+45
SEPARATION OF POWERS: THE CASE OF THE MARSHALL   ECO/UNDEV
PLAN." SOCIETY INT/ORG NAT/G CONSULT DELIB/GP LEGIS   DIPLOM
PLAN ECO/TAC ROUTINE DRIVE PERCEPT RIGID/FLEX
ORD/FREE PWR WEALTH...DECISION GEOG NEW/IDEA TREND
20 TRUMAN/HS. PAGE 85 B1726
                                                            B67
WARREN S.,THE AMERICAN PRESIDENT. POL/PAR FORCES   CHIEF
LEGIS DIPLOM ECO/TAC ADMIN EXEC PWR...ANTHOL 18/20   LEAD
ROOSEVLT/F KENNEDY/JF JOHNSON/LB TRUMAN/HS   NAT/G
WILSON/W. PAGE 114 B2297   CONSTN

TRUST, PERSONAL....SEE RESPECT, SUPEGO

TRUST/TERR....TRUST TERRITORY

TSHOMBE/M....MOISE TSHOMBE

TSOU T. B2132

TSOUDEROS J.E. B0407

TSUJI K. B2133

TUCKER R.C. B2134,B2135

TULANE/U....TULANE UNIVERSITY

TULLY A. B2136

TUNIS
                                                            B65
MOORE C.H.,TUNISIA SINCE INDEPENDENCE. ELITES LOC/G   NAT/G
POL/PAR ADMIN COLONIAL CONTROL EXEC GOV/REL   EX/STRUC
TOTALISM MARXISM...INT 20 TUNIS. PAGE 75 B1513   SOCISM
                                                            S65
ASHFORD D.E.,"BUREAUCRATS AND CITIZENS." MOROCCO   GOV/COMP
PAKISTAN PARTIC 20 TUNIS. PAGE 7 B0140   ADMIN
                                                      EX/STRUC
                                                      ROLE

TUNISIA....SEE ALSO ISLAM, AFR

TURKESTAN....TURKESTAN

TURKEY....TURKEY; SEE ALSO ISLAM
                                                            B59
HANSON A.H.,THE STRUCTURE AND CONTROL OF STATE   NAT/G
ENTERPRISES IN TURKEY. TURKEY LAW ADMIN GOV/REL   LG/CO
EFFICIENCY...CHARTS 20. PAGE 46 B0939   OWN
                                                      CONTROL
                                                            B62
GALENSON W.,LABOR IN DEVELOPING COUNTRIES. BRAZIL   LABOR
INDONESIA ISRAEL PAKISTAN TURKEY AGRI INDUS WORKER   ECO/UNDEV
PAY PRICE GP/REL WEALTH...MGT CHARTS METH/COMP   BARGAIN
NAT/COMP 20. PAGE 38 B0775   POL/PAR
                                                            L64
WORLD PEACE FOUNDATION,"INTERNATIONAL   INT/ORG
ORGANIZATIONS: SUMMARY OF ACTIVITIES." INDIA   ROUTINE
PAKISTAN TURKEY WOR+45 CONSTN CONSULT EX/STRUC
ECO/TAC EDU/PROP LEGIT ORD/FREE...JURID SOC UN 20
CYPRESS. PAGE 118 B2375
                                                            B65
OECD,MEDITERRANEAN REGIONAL PROJECT: TURKEY;   EDU/PROP
EDUCATION AND DEVELOPMENT. FUT TURKEY SOCIETY   ACADEM
STRATA FINAN NAT/G PROF/ORG PLAN PROB/SOLV ADMIN   SCHOOL
COST...STAT CHARTS 20 OECD. PAGE 79 B1602   ECO/UNDEV
                                                            B65
ORG FOR ECO COOP AND DEVEL,THE MEDITERRANEAN   PLAN
REGIONAL PROJECT: AN EXPERIMENT IN PLANNING BY SIX   ECO/UNDEV
COUNTRIES. FUT GREECE SPAIN TURKEY YUGOSLAVIA   ACADEM
SOCIETY FINAN NAT/G PROF/ORG EDU/PROP ADMIN REGION   SCHOOL
COST...POLICY STAT CHARTS 20 OECD. PAGE 80 B1614

TANSKY L.,US AND USSR AID TO DEVELOPING COUNTRIES. FOR/AID
INDIA TURKEY UAR USA+45 USSR FINAN PLAN TEC/DEV ECO/UNDEV
ADMIN WEALTH...TREND METH/COMP 20. PAGE 103 B2076 MARXISM
B67
CAP/ISM
S67
ALPANDER G.G.,"ENTREPRENEURS AND PRIVATE ENTERPRISE ECO/UNDEV
IN TURKEY." TURKEY INDUS PROC/MFG EDU/PROP ATTIT LG/CO
DRIVE WEALTH...GEOG MGT SOC STAT TREND CHARTS 20. NAT/G
PAGE 4 B0080 POLICY

TURKIC....TURKIC PEOPLES

TURNBULL A.V. B2079

TURNER F.C. B2137

TURNER H.A. B2138

TURNER M.C. B2139

TURNER R.H. B2140

TUSKEGEE....TUSKEGEE, ALABAMA

TV....TELEVISION; SEE ALSO PRESS, COM/IND

PERREN G.E.,LANGUAGE AND COMMUNICATION IN THE EDU/PROP
COMMONWEALTH (PAMPHLET). FUT UK LAW ECO/DEV PRESS LING
TV WRITING ADJUD ADMIN COLONIAL CONTROL 20 GOV/REL
CMN/WLTH. PAGE 82 B1660 COM/IND
N19
B51
NIELANDER W.A.,PUBLIC RELATIONS. USA+45 COM/IND PERS/REL
LOC/G NAT/G VOL/ASSN EX/STRUC DIPLOM EDU/PROP PRESS GP/REL
TV...METH/CNCPT T 20. PAGE 78 B1583 LG/CO
ROUTINE
B52
MILLER M.,THE JUDGES AND THE JUDGED. USA+45 LG/CO COM/IND
ACT/RES TV ROUTINE SANCTION NAT/LISM ATTIT ORD/FREE DISCRIM
...POLICY ACLU. PAGE 73 B1481 EDU/PROP
MARXISM
B60
BRISTOL L.H. JR.,DEVELOPING THE CORPORATE IMAGE. LG/CO
USA+45 SOCIETY ECO/DEV COM/IND SCHOOL EDU/PROP ATTIT
PRESS TV...AUD/VIS ANTHOL. PAGE 15 B0312 MGT
ECO/TAC
B65
CUTLIP S.M.,A PUBLIC RELATIONS BIBLIOGRAPHY. INDUS BIBLIOG/A
LABOR NAT/G PROF/ORG SCHOOL DIPLOM PRESS TV GOV/REL MGT
GP/REL...PSY SOC/WK 20. PAGE 25 B0515 COM/IND
ADMIN
B65
DAVISON W.P.,INTERNATIONAL POLITICAL COMMUNICATION. EDU/PROP
COM USA+45 WOR+45 CULTURE ECO/UNDEV NAT/G PROB/SOLV DIPLOM
PRESS TV ADMIN 20 FILM. PAGE 27 B0545 PERS/REL
COM/IND

TVA....TENNESSEE VALLEY AUTHORITY

HART H.C.,ADMINISTRATIVE ASPECTS OF RIVER VALLEY ADMIN
DEVELOPMENT. INDIA USA+45 INDUS CONTROL EFFICIENCY PLAN
OPTIMAL PRODUC 20 TVA. PAGE 47 B0957 METH/COMP
AGRI
B61
PRAKASH O.M.,THE THEORY AND WORKING OF STATE LG/CO
CORPORATIONS: WITH SPECIAL REFERENCE TO INDIA. ECO/UNDEV
INDIA UK USA+45 TOP/EX PRICE ADMIN EFFICIENCY...MGT GOV/REL
METH/COMP 20 TVA. PAGE 84 B1698 SOCISM
B62

TWAIN/MARK....MARK TWAIN (SAMUEL CLEMENS)

TYBOUT R.A. B2141

TYLER/JOHN....PRESIDENT JOHN TYLER

TYPOLOGY....SEE CLASSIF

U

U.S. DEPARTMENT OF LABOR....SEE DEPT/LABOR

U OF MICHIGAN LAW SCHOOL B2142

U/THANT....U THANT

COHEN M.,"THE DEMISE OF UNEF." CONSTN DIPLOM ADMIN INT/ORG
AGREE LEAD COERCE 20 UNEF U/THANT HAMMARSK/D. FORCES
PAGE 22 B0445 PEACE
L67
POLICY

UA/PAR....UNITED AUSTRALIAN PARTY

UAM....UNION AFRICAINE ET MALGACHE; ALSO OCAM

UAR....UNITED ARAB REPUBLIC (EGYPT AND SYRIA 1958-1961,

EGYPT AFTER 1958); SEE ALSO EGYPT, ISLAM

KUWAIT ARABIA,KUWAIT FUND FOR ARAB ECONOMIC FOR/AID
DEVELOPMENT (PAMPHLET). ISLAM KUWAIT UAR ECO/UNDEV DIPLOM
LEGIS ECO/TAC WEALTH 20. PAGE 62 B1245 FINAN
N19
ADMIN
B49
WALINE M.,LE CONTROLE JURIDICTIONNEL DE JURID
L'ADMINISTRATION. BELGIUM FRANCE UAR JUDGE BAL/PWR ADMIN
ADJUD CONTROL CT/SYS...GP/COMP 20. PAGE 113 B2277 PWR
ORD/FREE
C54
LANDAU J.M.,"PARLIAMENTS AND PARTIES IN EGYPT." UAR ISLAM
NAT/G SECT CONSULT LEGIS TOP/EX PROB/SOLV ADMIN NAT/LISM
COLONIAL...GEN/LAWS BIBLIOG 19/20. PAGE 62 B1254 PARL/PROC
POL/PAR
B57
BERGER M.,BUREAUCRACY AND SOCIETY IN MODERN EGYPT; ATTIT
A STUDY OF THE HIGHER CIVIL SERVICE. UAR REPRESENT EXEC
...QU 20. PAGE 11 B0221 ADMIN
ROUTINE
B57
CENTRAL ASIAN RESEARCH CENTRE,BIBLIOGRAPHY OF BIBLIOG/A
RECENT SOVIET SOURCE MATERIAL ON SOVIET CENTRAL COM
ASIA AND THE BORDERLANDS. AFGHANISTN INDIA PAKISTAN CULTURE
UAR USSR ECO/UNDEV AGRI EXTR/IND INDUS ACADEM ADMIN NAT/G
...HEAL HUM LING CON/ANAL 20. PAGE 19 B0399
B58
SHAW S.J.,THE FINANCIAL AND ADMINISTRATIVE FINAN
ORGANIZATION AND DEVELOPMENT OF OTTOMAN EGYPT ADMIN
1517-1798. UAR LOC/G FORCES BUDGET INT/TRADE TAX GOV/REL
EATING INCOME WEALTH...CHARTS BIBLIOG 16/18 OTTOMAN CULTURE
NAPOLEON/B. PAGE 96 B1940
B65
MACDONALD R.W.,THE LEAGUE OF ARAB STATES: A STUDY ISLAM
IN THE DYNAMICS OF REGIONAL ORGANIZATION. ISRAEL REGION
UAR USSR FINAN INT/ORG DELIB/GP ECO/TAC AGREE DIPLOM
NEUTRAL ORD/FREE PWR...DECISION BIBLIOG 20 TREATY ADMIN
UN. PAGE 67 B1358
S66
PALMER M.,"THE UNITED ARAB REPUBLIC* AN ASSESSMENT UAR
OF ITS FAILURE." ELITES ECO/UNDEV POL/PAR FORCES SYRIA
ECO/TAC RUMOR ADMIN EXEC EFFICIENCY ATTIT SOCISM REGION
...INT NASSER/G. PAGE 81 B1628 FEDERAL
B67
KARDOUCHE G.K.,THE UAR IN DEVELOPMENT. UAR ECO/TAC FINAN
INT/TRADE BAL/PAY...STAT CHARTS BIBLIOG 20. PAGE 58 MGT
B1172 CAP/ISM
ECO/UNDEV
B67
TANSKY L.,US AND USSR AID TO DEVELOPING COUNTRIES. FOR/AID
INDIA TURKEY UAR USA+45 USSR FINAN PLAN TEC/DEV ECO/UNDEV
ADMIN WEALTH...TREND METH/COMP 20. PAGE 103 B2076 MARXISM
CAP/ISM
S67
TATU M.,"URSS: LES FLOTTEMENTS DE LA DIRECTION POLICY
COLLEGIALE." UAR USSR CHIEF LEAD INGP/REL NAT/G
EFFICIENCY...DECISION TREND 20 MID/EAST. PAGE 103 EX/STRUC
B2082 DIPLOM

UAW....UNITED AUTO WORKERS

UDALL M.K. B2068

UDR....UNION POUR LA DEFENSE DE LA REPUBLIQUE (FRANCE)

UDY S.H. B2143,B2144

UGANDA....SEE ALSO AFR

APTER D.E.,"THE ROLE OF TRADITIONALISM IN THE CONSERVE
POLITICAL MODERNIZATION OF GHANA AND UGANDA" (BMR)" ADMIN
AFR GHANA UGANDA CULTURE NAT/G POL/PAR NAT/LISM GOV/COMP
...CON/ANAL 20. PAGE 6 B0121 PROB/SOLV
S60
L62
BELSHAW D.G.R.,"PUBLIC INVESTMENT IN AGRICULTURE ECO/UNDEV
AND ECONOMIC DEVELOPMENT OF UGANDA" UGANDA AGRI PLAN
INDUS R+D ECO/TAC RATION TAX PAY COLONIAL 20 ADMIN
WORLD/BANK. PAGE 10 B0209 CENTRAL
S63
BANFIELD J.,"FEDERATION IN EAST-AFRICA." AFR UGANDA EX/STRUC
ELITES INT/ORG NAT/G VOL/ASSN LEGIS ECO/TAC FEDERAL PWR
ATTIT SOVEREIGN TOT/POP 20 TANGANYIKA. PAGE 9 B0180 REGION
S63
NYE J.S. JR.,"EAST AFRICAN ECONOMIC INTEGRATION." ECO/UNDEV
AFR UGANDA PROVS DELIB/GP PLAN ECO/TAC INT/TRADE INT/ORG
ADMIN ROUTINE ORD/FREE PWR WEALTH...OBS TIME/SEQ
VAL/FREE 20. PAGE 79 B1597
L64
ROTBERG R.,"THE FEDERATION MOVEMENT IN BRITISH EAST VOL/ASSN
AND CENTRAL AFRICA." AFR RHODESIA UGANDA ECO/UNDEV PWR
NAT/G POL/PAR FORCES DOMIN LEGIT ADMIN COERCE ATTIT REGION
...CONCPT TREND 20 TANGANYIKA. PAGE 91 B1831

BRADLEY A.W.,"CONSTITUTION-MAKING IN UGANDA." | S67
UGANDA LAW CHIEF DELIB/GP LEGIS ADMIN EXEC | NAT/G
PARL/PROC RACE/REL ORD/FREE...GOV/COMP 20. PAGE 14 | CREATE
B0295 | CONSTN
| FEDERAL

UK....UNITED KINGDOM; SEE ALSO APPROPRIATE TIME/SPACE/
CULTURE INDEX, COMMONWLTH

WELLS A.J.,THE BRITISH NATIONAL BIBLIOGRAPHY | N
CUMULATED SUBJECT CATALOGUE. 1951-1954. UK WOR+45 | BIBLIOG
LAW ADMIN LEAD...HUM SOC 20. PAGE 115 B2320 | NAT/G

WHITAKER'S CUMULATIVE BOOKLIST. UK ADMIN...HUM SOC | N
20. PAGE 1 B0009 | BIBLIOG/A
| WRITING
| CON/ANAL

JOURNAL OF PUBLIC ADMINISTRATION: JOURNAL OF THE | N
ROYAL INSTITUTE OF PUBLIC ADMINISTRATION. UK PLAN | BIBLIOG/A
GP/REL INGP/REL 20. PAGE 1 B0015 | ADMIN
| NAT/G
| MGT

REVUE FRANCAISE DE SCIENCE POLITIQUE. FRANCE UK | N
...BIBLIOG/A 20. PAGE 1 B0022 | NAT/G
| DIPLOM
| CONCPT
| ROUTINE

FINANCIAL INDEX. CANADA UK USA+45 ECO/DEV LG/CO | N
ADMIN 20. PAGE 2 B0032 | BIBLIOG
| INDUS
| FINAN
| PRESS

PUBLISHERS' CIRCULAR LIMITED,THE ENGLISH CATALOGUE | N
OF BOOKS. UK WOR+45 WOR-45 LAW CULTURE LOC/G NAT/G | BIBLIOG
ADMIN LEAD...MGT 19/20. PAGE 85 B1718 | ALL/VALS
| ALL/IDEOS
| SOCIETY

SANDERSON E.,AFRICA IN THE NINETEENTH CENTURY. | B00
FRANCE UK EXTR/IND FORCES LEGIS ADMIN WAR DISCRIM | COLONIAL
ORD/FREE...GEOG GP/COMP SOC/INTEG 19. PAGE 92 B1867 | AFR
| DIPLOM

MOREL E.D.,AFFAIRS OF WEST AFRICA. UK FINAN INDUS | B02
FAM KIN SECT CHIEF WORKER DIPLOM RACE/REL LITERACY | COLONIAL
HEALTH...CHARTS 18/20 AFRICA/W NEGRO. PAGE 75 B1521 | ADMIN
| AFR

GRIFFIN A.P.C.,LIST OF BOOKS ON THE CABINETS OF | B03
ENGLAND AND AMERICA (PAMPHLET). MOD/EUR UK USA-45 | BIBLIOG/A
CONSTN NAT/G CONSULT EX/STRUC 19/20. PAGE 43 B0875 | GOV/COMP
| ADMIN
| DELIB/GP

HARVARD UNIVERSITY LAW LIBRARY,CATALOGUE OF THE | B09
LIBRARY OF THE LAW SCHOOL OF HARVARD UNIVERSITY (3 | BIBLIOG/A
VOLS.). UK USA-45 LEGIS JUDGE ADJUD CT/SYS...JURID | LAW
CHARTS 14/20. PAGE 48 B0963 | ADMIN

WILSON W.,THE STATE: ELEMENTS OF HISTORICAL AND | B18
PRACTICAL POLITICS. FRANCE GERMANY ITALY UK USSR | NAT/G
CONSTN EX/STRUC LEGIS CT/SYS WAR PWR...POLICY | JURID
GOV/COMP 20. PAGE 117 B2363 | CONCPT
| NAT/COMP

NATHAN M.,THE SOUTH AFRICAN COMMONWEALTH: | B19
CONSTITUTION, PROBLEMS, SOCIAL CONDITIONS. | CONSTN
SOUTH/AFR UK CULTURE INDUS EX/STRUC LEGIS BUDGET | NAT/G
EDU/PROP ADMIN CT/SYS GP/REL RACE/REL...LING 19/20 | POL/PAR
CMN/WLTH. PAGE 77 B1559 | SOCIETY

ADMINISTRATIVE STAFF COLLEGE,THE ACCOUNTABILITY OF | N19
GOVERNMENT DEPARTMENTS (PAMPHLET) (REV. ED.). UK | PARL/PROC
CONSTN FINAN NAT/G CONSULT ADMIN INGP/REL CONSEN | ELITES
PRIVIL 20 PARLIAMENT. PAGE 3 B0059 | SANCTION
| PROB/SOLV

ANDERSON J.,THE ORGANIZATION OF ECONOMIC STUDIES IN | N19
RELATION TO THE PROBLEMS OF GOVERNMENT (PAMPHLET). | ECO/TAC
UK FINAN INDUS DELIB/GP PLAN PROB/SOLV ADMIN 20. | ACT/RES
PAGE 5 B0093 | NAT/G
| CENTRAL

GRIFFITH W.,THE PUBLIC SERVICE (PAMPHLET). UK LAW | N19
LOC/G NAT/G PARTIC CHOOSE DRIVE ROLE SKILL...CHARTS | ADMIN
20 CIVIL/SERV. PAGE 44 B0880 | EFFICIENCY
| EDU/PROP
| GOV/REL

HIGGINS R.,THE ADMINISTRATION OF UNITED KINGDOM | N19
FOREIGN POLICY THROUGH THE UNITED NATIONS | DIPLOM
(PAMPHLET). UK NAT/G ADMIN GOV/REL...CHARTS 20 UN | POLICY
PARLIAMENT. PAGE 50 B1009 | INT/ORG

PERREN G.E.,LANGUAGE AND COMMUNICATION IN THE | N19
COMMONWEALTH (PAMPHLET). FUT UK LAW ECO/DEV PRESS | EDU/PROP
TV WRITING ADJUD ADMIN CONTROL 20 | LING
CMN/WLTH. PAGE 82 B1660 | GOV/REL
| COM/IND

TREVELYAN G.M.,THE TWO-PARTY SYSTEM IN ENGLISH | N19
POLITICAL HISTORY (PAMPHLET). UK CHIEF LEGIS | PARL/PROC
COLONIAL EXEC REV CHOOSE 17/19. PAGE 105 B2128 | POL/PAR
| NAT/G
| PWR

HALDANE R.B.,BEFORE THE WAR. MOD/EUR SOCIETY | B20
INT/ORG NAT/G DELIB/GP PLAN DOMIN EDU/PROP LEGIT | POLICY
ADMIN COERCE ATTIT DRIVE MORAL ORD/FREE PWR...SOC | DIPLOM
CONCPT SELF/OBS RECORD BIOG TIME/SEQ. PAGE 45 B0921 | UK

BAGEHOT W.,THE ENGLISH CONSTITUTION AND OTHER | B24
POLITICAL ESSAYS. UK DELIB/GP BAL/PWR ADMIN CONTROL | NAT/G
EXEC ROUTINE CONSERVE...METH PARLIAMENT 19/20. | STRUCT
PAGE 8 B0160 | CONCPT

HOLDSWORTH W.S.,A HISTORY OF ENGLISH LAW: THE | B24
COMMON LAW AND ITS RIVALS (VOL. V). UK SEA EX/STRUC | LAW
WRITING ADMIN...INT/LAW JURID CONCPT IDEA/COMP | LEGIS
WORSHIP 16/17 PARLIAMENT ENGLSH/LAW COMMON/LAW. | ADJUD
PAGE 51 B1033 | CT/SYS

HOLDSWORTH W.S.,A HISTORY OF ENGLISH LAW: THE | B24
COMMON LAW AND ITS RIVALS (VOL. VI). UK STRATA | LAW
EX/STRUC ADJUD ADMIN CONTROL CT/SYS...JURID CONCPT | CONSTN
GEN/LAWS 17 COMMONWLTH PARLIAMENT ENGLSH/LAW | LEGIS
COMMON/LAW. PAGE 51 B1034 | CHIEF

FYFE H.,THE BRITISH LIBERAL PARTY. UK SECT ADMIN | B28
LEAD CHOOSE GP/REL PWR SOCISM...MAJORIT TIME/SEQ | POL/PAR
19/20 LIB/PARTY CONSRV/PAR. PAGE 38 B0768 | NAT/G
| REPRESENT
| POPULISM

HALL W.P.,EMPIRE TO COMMONWEALTH. FUT WOR-45 CONSTN | B28
ECO/DEV ECO/UNDEV INT/ORG PROVS PLAN DIPLOM | VOL/ASSN
EDU/PROP ADMIN COLONIAL PEACE PERSON ALL/VALS | NAT/G
...POLICY GEOG SOC OBS RECORD TREND CMN/WLTH | UK
PARLIAMENT 19/20. PAGE 46 B0925

FAIRLIE J.A.,COUNTY GOVERNMENT AND ADMINISTRATION. | B30
UK USA-45 NAT/G SCHOOL FORCES BUDGET TAX CT/SYS | ADMIN
CHOOSE...JURID BIBLIOG 11/20. PAGE 35 B0701 | GOV/REL
| LOC/G
| MUNIC

CARDINALL AW,A BIBLIOGRAPHY OF THE GOLD COAST. AFR | B32
UK NAT/G EX/STRUC ATTIT...POLICY 19/20. PAGE 18 | BIBLIOG
B0376 | ADMIN
| COLONIAL
| DIPLOM

MCKISACK M.,THE PARLIAMENTARY REPRESENTATION OF THE | B32
ENGLISH BOROUGHS DURING THE MIDDLE AGES. UK CONSTN | NAT/G
CULTURE ELITES EX/STRUC TAX PAY ADJUD PARL/PROC | MUNIC
APPORT FEDERAL...POLICY 13/15 PARLIAMENT. PAGE 72 | LEGIS
B1454 | CHOOSE

ENSOR R.C.K.,COURTS AND JUDGES IN FRANCE, GERMANY, | B33
AND ENGLAND. FRANCE GERMANY UK LAW PROB/SOLV ADMIN | CT/SYS
ROUTINE CRIME ROLE...METH/COMP 20 CIVIL/LAW. | EX/STRUC
PAGE 33 B0676 | ADJUD
| NAT/COMP

GOSNELL H.F.,"BRITISH ROYAL COMMISSIONS OF INQUIRY" | L34
UK CONSTN LEGIS PRESS ADMIN PARL/PROC...DECISION 20 | DELIB/GP
PARLIAMENT. PAGE 41 B0839 | INSPECT
| POLICY
| NAT/G

ROBINSON H.,DEVELOPMENT OF THE BRITISH EMPIRE. | B36
WOR-45 CULTURE SOCIETY STRUCT ECO/DEV ECO/UNDEV | NAT/G
INT/ORG VOL/ASSN FORCES CREATE PLAN DOMIN EDU/PROP | HIST/WRIT
ADMIN COLONIAL PWR WEALTH...POLICY GEOG CHARTS | UK
CMN/WLTH 16/20. PAGE 89 B1800

CLOKIE H.M.,ROYAL COMMISSIONS OF INQUIRY: THE | B37
SIGNIFICANCE OF INVESTIGATIONS IN BRITISH POLITICS. | NAT/G
UK POL/PAR CONFER ROUTINE...POLICY DECISION | DELIB/GP
TIME/SEQ 16/20. PAGE 22 B0439 | INSPECT

ANDERSON W.,LOCAL GOVERNMENT IN EUROPE. FRANCE | B39
GERMANY ITALY UK USSR MUNIC PROVS ADMIN GOV/REL | GOV/COMP
CENTRAL SOVEREIGN 20. PAGE 5 B0099 | NAT/COMP
| LOC/G
| CONSTN

JENNINGS W.I.,PARLIAMENT. UK POL/PAR OP/RES BUDGET | B39
LEAD CHOOSE GP/REL...MGT 20 PARLIAMENT HOUSE/LORD | PARL/PROC
HOUSE/CMNS. PAGE 56 B1135 | LEGIS
| CONSTN
| NAT/G

AIKEN C.,"THE BRITISH BUREAUCRACY AND THE ORIGINS | S39
OF PARLIAMENTARY DEMOCRACY" UK TOP/EX ADMIN. PAGE 3 | MGT
B0066 | NAT/G
| LEGIS

MCHENRY D.E.,HIS MAJESTY'S OPPOSITION: STRUCTURE | B40
AND PROBLEMS OF THE BRITISH LABOUR PARTY 1931-1938. | POL/PAR
UK FINAN LABOR LOC/G DELIB/GP LEGIS EDU/PROP LEAD | MGT
PARTIC CHOOSE GP/REL SOCISM...TREND 20 LABOR/PAR. | NAT/G
PAGE 72 B1450 | POLICY

COHEN E.W.,THE GROWTH OF THE BRITISH CIVIL SERVICE | B41
1780-1939. UK NAT/G SENIOR ROUTINE GOV/REL...MGT | OP/RES
METH/COMP BIBLIOG 18/20. PAGE 22 B0442 | TIME/SEQ
| CENTRAL
| ADMIN

LESTER R.A.,ECONOMICS OF LABOR. UK USA-45 TEC/DEV   LABOR
BARGAIN PAY INGP/REL INCOME...MGT 19/20. PAGE 64   ECO/DEV
B1298   INDUS
  WORKER

PERHAM M.,AFRICANS AND BRITISH RULE. AFR UK ECO/TAC   DIPLOM
CONTROL GP/REL ATTIT 20. PAGE 82 B1654   COLONIAL
  ADMIN
  ECO/UNDEV

BARKER E.,THE DEVELOPMENT OF PUBLIC SERVICES IN   GOV/COMP
WESTERN WUROPE: 1660-1930. FRANCE GERMANY UK SCHOOL   ADMIN
CONTROL REPRESENT ROLE...WELF/ST 17/20. PAGE 9   EX/STRUC
B0185

KINGSLEY J.D.,REPRESENTATIVE BUREAUCRACY. UK...MGT   ADMIN
20. PAGE 60 B1208   REPRESENT
  EX/STRUC

HAILEY,"THE FUTURE OF COLONIAL PEOPLES." WOR-45   PLAN
CONSTN CULTURE ECO/UNDEV AGRI MARKET INT/ORG NAT/G   CONCPT
SECT CONSULT ECO/TAC LEGIT ADMIN NAT/LISM ALL/VALS   DIPLOM
...SOC OBS TREND STERTYP CMN/WLTH LEAGUE/NAT   UK
PARLIAMENT 20. PAGE 45 B0916

CONOVER H.F.,THE GOVERNMENTS OF THE MAJOR FOREIGN   BIBLIOG
POWERS: A BIBLIOGRAPHY. FRANCE GERMANY ITALY UK   NAT/G
USSR CONSTN LOC/G POL/PAR EX/STRUC FORCES ADMIN   DIPLOM
CT/SYS CIVMIL/REL TOTALISM...POLICY 19/20. PAGE 23
B0464

DAVIES E.,NATIONAL ENTERPRISE: THE DEVELOPMENT OF   ADMIN
THE PUBLIC CORPORATION. UK LG/CO EX/STRUC WORKER   NAT/G
PROB/SOLV COST ATTIT SOCISM 20. PAGE 26 B0536   CONTROL
  INDUS

GRIFFIN G.G.,A GUIDE TO MANUSCRIPTS RELATING TO   BIBLIOG/A
AMERICAN HISTORY IN BRITISH DEPOSITORIES. CANADA   ALL/VALS
IRELAND MOD/EUR UK USA-45 LAW DIPLOM ADMIN COLONIAL   NAT/G
WAR NAT/LISM SOVEREIGN...GEOG INT/LAW 15/19
CMN/WLTH. PAGE 43 B0876

CONOVER H.F.,NON-SELF-GOVERNING AREAS. BELGIUM   BIBLIOG/A
FRANCE ITALY UK WOR+45 CULTURE ECO/UNDEV INT/ORG   COLONIAL
LOC/G NAT/G ECO/TAC INT/TRADE ADMIN HEALTH...SOC   DIPLOM
UN. PAGE 23 B0465

CROCKER W.R.,ON GOVERNING COLONIES: BEING AN   COLONIAL
OUTLINE OF THE REAL ISSUES AND A COMPARISON OF THE   POLICY
BRITISH, FRENCH, AND BELGIAN... AFR BELGIUM FRANCE   GOV/COMP
UK CULTURE SOVEREIGN...OBS 20. PAGE 25 B0505   ADMIN

DAY P.,CRISIS IN SOUTH AFRICA. SOUTH/AFR UK KIN   RACE/REL
MUNIC ECO/TAC RECEIVE 20 SMUTS/JAN MIGRATION.   COLONIAL
PAGE 27 B0548   ADMIN
  EXTR/IND

ROSSITER C.L.,CONSTITUTIONAL DICTATORSHIP: CRISIS   NAT/G
GOVERNMENT IN THE MODERN DEMOCRACIES. FRANCE   AUTHORIT
GERMANY UK USA-45 WOR-45 EX/STRUC BAL/PWR CONTROL   CONSTN
COERCE WAR CENTRAL ORD/FREE...DECISION 19/20.   TOTALISM
PAGE 90 B1828

SHERWOOD R.E.,ROOSEVELT AND HOPKINS. UK USA+45 USSR   TOP/EX
NAT/G EX/STRUC FORCES ADMIN ROUTINE PERSON PWR   BIOG
...TIME/SEQ 20 ROOSEVLT/F HOPKINS/H. PAGE 96 B1946   DIPLOM
  WAR

SLESSER H.,THE ADMINISTRATION OF THE LAW. UK CONSTN   LAW
EX/STRUC OP/RES PROB/SOLV CRIME ROLE...DECISION   CT/SYS
METH/COMP 20 CIVIL/LAW ENGLSH/LAW CIVIL/LAW.   ADJUD
PAGE 98 B1977

ASPINALL A.,POLITICS AND THE PRESS 1780-1850. UK   PRESS
LAW ELITES FINAN PROF/ORG LEGIS ADMIN ATTIT   CONTROL
...POLICY 18/19. PAGE 7 B0142   POL/PAR
  ORD/FREE

DENNING A.,FREEDOM UNDER THE LAW. MOD/EUR UK LAW   ORD/FREE
SOCIETY CHIEF EX/STRUC LEGIS ADJUD CT/SYS PERS/REL   JURID
PERSON 17/20 ENGLSH/LAW. PAGE 28 B0573   NAT/G

HEADLAM-MORLEY,BIBLIOGRAPHY IN POLITICS FOR THE   BIBLIOG
HONOUR SCHOOL OF PHILOSOPHY, POLITICS AND ECONOMICS   NAT/G
(PAMPHLET). UK CONSTN LABOR MUNIC DIPLOM ADMIN   PHIL/SCI
19/20. PAGE 48 B0979   GOV/REL

MCLEAN J.M.,THE PUBLIC SERVICE AND UNIVERSITY   ACADEM
EDUCATION. UK USA-45 DELIB/GP EX/STRUC TOP/EX ADMIN   NAT/G
...GOV/COMP METH/COMP NAT/COMP ANTHOL 20. PAGE 72   EXEC
B1455   EDU/PROP

SCHWARTZ B.,LAW AND THE EXECUTIVE IN BRITAIN: A   ADMIN
COMPARATIVE STUDY. UK USA+45 LAW EX/STRUC PWR   EXEC
...GOV/COMP 20. PAGE 95 B1911   CONTROL

  REPRESENT

MANNHEIM K.,FREEDOM, POWER, AND DEMOCRATIC   TEC/DEV
PLANNING. FUT USSR WOR+45 ELITES INTELL SOCIETY   PLAN
NAT/G EDU/PROP ROUTINE ATTIT DRIVE SUPEGO SKILL   CAP/ISM
...POLICY PSY CONCPT TREND GEN/LAWS 20. PAGE 69   UK
B1393

PERHAM M.,COLONIAL GOVERNMENT: ANNOTATED READING   BIBLIOG/A
LIST ON BRITISH COLONIAL GOVERNMENT. UK WOR+45   COLONIAL
WOR-45 ECO/UNDEV INT/ORG LEGIS FOR/AID INT/TRADE   GOV/REL
DOMIN ADMIN REV 20. PAGE 82 B1655   NAT/G

WADE E.C.S.,CONSTITUTIONAL LAW: AN OUTLINE OF THE   CONSTN
LAW AND PRACTICE OF THE CONSTITUTION. UK LEGIS   NAT/G
DOMIN ADMIN GP/REL 16/20 CMN/WLTH PARLIAMENT   PARL/PROC
ENGLSH/LAW. PAGE 112 B2269   LAW

EPSTEIN L.D.,"POLITICAL STERILIZATION OF CIVIL   ADMIN
SERVANTS: THE UNITED STATES AND GREAT BRITAIN." UK   LEGIS
USA-45 STRUCT TOP/EX OP/RES PARTIC CHOOSE   DECISION
NAT/LISM 20 CONGRESS CIVIL/SERV. PAGE 33 B0679   POL/PAR

BRINTON C.,THE ANATOMY OF REVOLUTION. FRANCE UK   SOCIETY
USA-45 USSR WOR-45 ELITES INTELL ECO/DEV NAT/G   CONCPT
EX/STRUC FORCES COERCE DRIVE ORD/FREE PWR SOVEREIGN   REV
...MYTH HIST/WRIT GEN/LAWS. PAGE 15 B0311

GOLDSTEIN J.,THE GOVERNMENT OF BRITISH TRADE   LABOR
UNIONS. UK ECO/DEV EX/STRUC INGP/REL...BIBLIOG 20.   PARTIC
PAGE 40 B0817

ROBINSON E.A.G.,THE STRUCTURE OF COMPETITIVE   INDUS
INDUSTRY. UK ECO/DEV DIST/IND MARKET TEC/DEV DIPLOM   PRODUC
EDU/PROP ADMIN EFFICIENCY WEALTH...MGT 19/20.   WORKER
PAGE 89 B1798   OPTIMAL

STOUT H.M.,BRITISH GOVERNMENT. UK FINAN LOC/G   NAT/G
POL/PAR DELIB/GP DIPLOM ADMIN COLONIAL CHOOSE   PARL/PROC
ORD/FREE...JURID BIBLIOG 20 COMMONWLTH. PAGE 101   CONSTN
B2049   NEW/LIB

BULNER-THOMAS I.,"THE PARTY SYSTEM IN GREAT   NAT/G
BRITAIN." UK CONSTN SECT PRESS CONFER GP/REL ATTIT   POL/PAR
...POLICY TREND BIBLIOG 19/20 PARLIAMENT. PAGE 17   ADMIN
B0343   ROUTINE

JENNINGS I.,THE QUEEN'S GOVERNMENT. UK POL/PAR   NAT/G
DELIB/GP ADJUD ADMIN CT/SYS PARL/PROC REPRESENT   CONSTN
CONSERVE 13/20 PARLIAMENT. PAGE 56 B1132   LEGIS
  CHIEF

COOPER L.,"ADMINISTRATIVE JUSTICE." UK ADMIN   LAW
REPRESENT PWR...POLICY 20. PAGE 23 B0475   ADJUD
  CONTROL
  EX/STRUC

GULICK C.A.,HISTORY AND THEORIES OF WORKING-CLASS   BIBLIOG
MOVEMENTS: A SELECT BIBLIOGRAPHY. EUR+WWI MOD/EUR   WORKER
UK USA-45 INT/ORG. PAGE 44 B0902   LABOR
  ADMIN

WHEARE K.C.,GOVERNMENT BY COMMITTEE: AN ESSAY ON   DELIB/GP
THE BRITISH CONSTITUTION. UK NAT/G LEGIS INSPECT   CONSTN
CONFER ADJUD ADMIN CONTROL TASK EFFICIENCY ROLE   LEAD
POPULISM 20. PAGE 115 B2329   GP/COMP

BONER H.A.,"HUNGRY GENERATIONS." UK WOR+45 WOR-45   ECO/DEV
STRATA INDUS FAM LABOR CAP/ISM...MGT BIBLIOG 19/20.   PHIL/SCI
PAGE 13 B0272   CONCPT
  WEALTH

BROWNE D.G.,THE RISE OF SCOTLAND YARD: A HISTORY OF   CRIMLGY
THE METROPOLITAN POLICE. UK MUNIC CHIEF ADMIN CRIME   LEGIS
GP/REL 19/20. PAGE 16 B0329   CONTROL
  FORCES

CARTER B.E.,THE OFFICE OF THE PRIME MINISTER. UK   GOV/REL
ADMIN REPRESENT PARLIAMENT 20. PAGE 19 B0388   CHIEF
  EX/STRUC
  LEAD

CENTRAL AFRICAN ARCHIVES,A GUIDE TO THE PUBLIC   BIBLIOG/A
RECORDS OF SOUTHERN RHODESIA UNDER THE REGIME OF   COLONIAL
THE BRITISH SOUTH AFRICA COMPANY, 1890-1923. UK   ADMIN
STRUCT NAT/G WRITING GP/REL 19/20. PAGE 19 B0398   AFR

DUNNILL F.,THE CIVIL SERVICE. UK LAW PLAN ADMIN   PERSON
EFFICIENCY DRIVE NEW/LIB...STAT CHARTS 20   WORKER
PARLIAMENT CIVIL/SERV. PAGE 31 B0633   STRATA
  SOC/WK

GLADDEN E.N.,CIVIL SERVICE OR BUREAUCRACY? UK LAW   ADMIN
STRATA LABOR TOP/EX PLAN SENIOR AUTOMAT CONTROL   GOV/REL
PARTIC CHOOSE HAPPINESS...CHARTS 19/20 CIVIL/SERV   EFFICIENCY
BUREAUCRCY. PAGE 40 B0808   PROVS

B41
B41
B44
B44
L44
B45
B46
B46
B47
B47
B48
B48
B48
B48
B49
B49
B49
B49
B49

B50
B50
B50
S50
B52
B52
B53
B53
C53
B54
S54
B55
B55
C55
B56
B56
B56
B56
B56

JENNINGS W.I.,THE APPROACH TO SELF-GOVERNMENT.   NAT/G
CEYLON INDIA PAKISTAN S/ASIA UK SOCIETY POL/PAR   CONSTN
DELIB/GP LEGIS ECO/TAC EDU/PROP ADMIN EXEC CHOOSE   COLONIAL
ATTIT ALL/VALS...JURID CONCPT GEN/METH TOT/POP 20.
PAGE 56 B1136
                                                        C56
NEUMANN S.,"MODERN POLITICAL PARTIES: APPROACHES TO POL/PAR
COMPARATIVE POLITIC. FRANCE UK EX/STRUC DOMIN ADMIN GOV/COMP
LEAD REPRESENT TOTALISM ATTIT...POLICY TREND   ELITES
METH/COMP ANTHOL BIBLIOG/A 20 CMN/WLTH. PAGE 78   MAJORIT
B1574
                                                        B57
BISHOP O.B.,PUBLICATIONS OF THE GOVERNMENTS OF NOVA BIBLIOG
SCOTIA, PRINCE EDWARD ISLAND, NEW BRUNSWICK   NAT/G
1758-1952. CANADA UK ADMIN COLONIAL LEAD...POLICY   DIPLOM
18/20. PAGE 12 B0245
                                                        B57
JENNINGS I.,PARLIAMENT. UK FINAN INDUS POL/PAR   PARL/PROC
DELIB/GP EX/STRUC PLAN CONTROL...MAJORIT JURID   TOP/EX
PARLIAMENT. PAGE 56 B1133   MGT
                                                     LEGIS
                                                        B57
MEYER P.,ADMINISTRATIVE ORGANIZATION: A COMPARATIVE ADMIN
STUDY OF THE ORGANIZATION OF PUBLIC ADMINISTRATION. METH/COMP
DENMARK FRANCE NORWAY SWEDEN UK USA+45 ELITES LOC/G NAT/G
CONSULT LEGIS ADJUD CONTROL LEAD PWR SKILL   CENTRAL
DECISION. PAGE 73 B1475
                                                        B57
MURDESHWAR A.K.,ADMINISTRATIVE PROBLEMS RELATING TO NAT/G
NATIONALISATION: WITH SPECIAL REFERENCE TO INDIAN   OWN
STATE ENTERPRISES. CZECHOSLVK FRANCE INDIA UK   INDUS
USA+45 LEGIS WORKER PROB/SOLV BUDGET PRICE CONTROL   ADMIN
...MGT GEN/LAWS 20 PARLIAMENT. PAGE 76 B1544
                                                        B58
COWAN L.G.,LOCAL GOVERNMENT IN WEST AFRICA. AFR   LOC/G
FRANCE UK CULTURE KIN POL/PAR CHIEF LEGIS CREATE   COLONIAL
ADMIN PARTIC GOV/REL GP/REL...METH/COMP 20. PAGE 24 SOVEREIGN
B0498   REPRESENT
                                                        B58
DEVLIN P.,THE CRIMINAL PROSECUTION IN ENGLAND. UK   CRIME
NAT/G ADMIN ROUTINE EFFICIENCY...JURID SOC 20.   LAW
PAGE 29 B0583   METH
                                                     CT/SYS
                                                        B58
LOVEJOY D.S.,RHODE ISLAND POLITICS AND THE AMERICAN REV
REVOLUTION 1760-1776. UK USA-45 ELITES EX/STRUC TAX COLONIAL
LEAD REPRESENT GOV/REL GP/REL ATTIT 18 RHODE/ISL.   ECO/TAC
PAGE 67 B1343   SOVEREIGN
                                                        B58
MOEN N.W.,THE GOVERNMENT OF SCOTLAND 1603 - 1625.   CHIEF
UK JUDGE ADMIN GP/REL PWR 17 SCOTLAND COMMON/LAW.   JURID
PAGE 74 B1496   CONTROL
                                                     PARL/PROC
                                                        B58
SHARMA M.P.,PUBLIC ADMINISTRATION IN THEORY AND   MGT
PRACTICE. INDIA UK USA+45 USA-45 EX/STRUC ADJUD   ADMIN
...POLICY CONCPT NAT/COMP 20. PAGE 96 B1935   DELIB/GP
                                                     JURID
                                                        B58
STEWART J.D.,BRITISH PRESSURE GROUPS: THEIR ROLE IN LOBBY
RELATION TO THE HOUSE OF COMMONS. UK CONSULT   LEGIS
DELIB/GP ADMIN ROUTINE CHOOSE REPRESENT ATTIT ROLE   PLAN
20 HOUSE/CMNS PARLIAMENT. PAGE 101 B2038   PARL/PROC
                                                        C58
WILDING N.,"AN ENCYCLOPEDIA OF PARLIAMENT." UK LAW   PARL/PROC
CONSTN CHIEF PROB/SOLV DIPLOM DEBATE WAR INGP/REL   POL/PAR
PRIVIL...BIBLIOG DICTIONARY 13/20 CMN/WLTH   NAT/G
PARLIAMENT. PAGE 116 B2350   ADMIN
                                                        B59
DESMITH S.A.,JUDICIAL REVIEW OF ADMINISTRATIVE   ADJUD
ACTION. UK LOC/G CONSULT DELIB/GP ADMIN PWR   NAT/G
...DECISION JURID 20 ENGLSH/LAW. PAGE 28 B0576   PROB/SOLV
                                                     CT/SYS
                                                        B59
GINSBURG M.,LAW AND OPINION IN ENGLAND. UK CULTURE   JURID
KIN LABOR LEGIS EDU/PROP ADMIN CT/SYS CRIME OWN   POLICY
HEALTH...ANTHOL 20 ENGLSH/LAW. PAGE 40 B0802   ECO/TAC
                                                        B59
JENNINGS W.I.,CABINET GOVERNMENT (3RD ED.). UK   DELIB/GP
POL/PAR CHIEF BUDGET ADMIN CHOOSE GP/REL 20.   NAT/G
PAGE 56 B1137   CONSTN
                                                     OP/RES
                                                        B59
SISSON C.H.,THE SPIRIT OF BRITISH ADMINISTRATION   GOV/COMP
AND SOME EUROPEAN COMPARISONS. FRANCE GERMANY/W   ADMIN
SWEDEN UK LAW EX/STRUC INGP/REL EFFICIENCY ORD/FREE ELITES
...DECISION 20. PAGE 98 B1972   ATTIT
                                                        L59
TARKOWSKI Z.M.,"SCIENTISTS VERSUS ADMINISTRATORS: INGP/REL
AN APPROACH TOWARD ACHIEVING GREATER   GP/REL
UNDERSTANDING." UK EXEC EFFICIENCY 20. PAGE 103   ADMIN
B2079   EX/STRUC
                                                        S59
BENDIX R.,"INDUSTRIALIZATION, IDEOLOGIES, AND   INDUS
SOCIAL STRUCTURE" (BMR)" UK USA+45 USSR STRUCT   ATTIT

WORKER GP/REL EFFICIENCY...IDEA/COMP 20. PAGE 10   MGT
B0210   ADMIN
                                                        S59
PADELFORD N.J.,"REGIONAL COOPERATION IN THE SOUTH   INT/ORG
PACIFIC: THE SOUTH PACIFIC COMMISSION." FUT   ADMIN
NEW/ZEALND UK WOR+45 CULTURE ECO/UNDEV LOC/G
VOL/ASSN...OBS CON/ANAL UNESCO VAL/FREE AUSTRAL 20.
PAGE 80 B1622
                                                        B60
HANBURY H.G.,ENGLISH COURTS OF LAW. UK EX/STRUC   JURID
LEGIS CRIME ROLE 12/20 COMMON/LAW ENGLISH/LAW.   CT/SYS
PAGE 46 B0936   CONSTN
                                                     GOV/REL
                                                        B60
HEAP D.,AN OUTLINE OF PLANNING LAW (3RD ED.). UK   MUNIC
LAW PROB/SOLV ADMIN CONTROL 20. PAGE 49 B0983   PLAN
                                                     JURID
                                                     LOC/G
                                                        B60
KERSELL J.E.,PARLIAMENTARY SUPERVISION OF DELEGATED LEGIS
LEGISLATION. UK EFFICIENCY PWR...POLICY CHARTS   CONTROL
BIBLIOG METH 20 PARLIAMENT. PAGE 59 B1198   NAT/G
                                                     EX/STRUC
                                                        B60
KINGSTON-MCCLOUG E.,DEFENSE; POLICY AND STRATEGY.   FORCES
UK SEA AIR TEC/DEV DIPLOM ADMIN LEAD WAR ORD/FREE   PLAN
...CHARTS 20. PAGE 60 B1209   POLICY
                                                     DECISION
                                                        B60
LEWIS P.R.,LITERATURE OF THE SOCIAL SCIENCES: AN   BIBLIOG/A
INTRODUCTORY SURVEY AND GUIDE. UK LAW INDUS DIPLOM   SOC
INT/TRADE ADMIN...MGT 19/20. PAGE 65 B1306
                                                        B60
MARSHALL A.H.,FINANCIAL ADMINISTRATION IN LOCAL   FINAN
GOVERNMENT. UK DELIB/GP CONFER COST INCOME PERSON   LOC/G
...JURID 20. PAGE 70 B1408   BUDGET
                                                     ADMIN
                                                        B60
MEEHAN E.J.,THE BRITISH LEFT WING AND FOREIGN   ACT/RES
POLICY: A STUDY OF THE INFLUENCE OF IDEOLOGY. FUT   ATTIT
UK UNIV WOR+45 INTELL TOP/EX PLAN ADMIN ROUTINE   DIPLOM
DRIVE...OBS TIME/SEQ GEN/LAWS PARLIAMENT 20.
PAGE 72 B1461
                                                        B60
POOLEY B.J.,THE EVOLUTION OF BRITISH PLANNING   PLAN
LEGISLATION. UK ECO/DEV LOC/G CONSULT DELIB/GP   MUNIC
ADMIN 20 URBAN/RNWL. PAGE 84 B1691   LEGIS
                                                     PROB/SOLV
                                                        B60
SMITH M.G.,GOVERNMENT IN ZAZZAU 1800-1950. NIGERIA   REGION
UK CULTURE SOCIETY LOC/G ADMIN COLONIAL   CONSTN
...METH/CNCPT NEW/IDEA METH 19/20. PAGE 98 B1983   KIN
                                                     ECO/UNDEV
                                                        B60
WHEARE K.C.,THE CONSTITUTIONAL STRUCTURE OF THE   CONSTN
COMMONWEALTH. UK EX/STRUC DIPLOM DOMIN ADMIN   INT/ORG
COLONIAL CONTROL LEAD INGP/REL SUPEGO 20 CMN/WLTH.   VOL/ASSN
PAGE 115 B2330   SOVEREIGN
                                                        S60
BANFIELD E.C.,"THE POLITICAL IMPLICATIONS OF   TASK
METROPOLITAN GROWTH" (BMR)" UK USA+45 LOC/G   MUNIC
PROB/SOLV ADMIN GP/REL...METH/COMP NAT/COMP 20.   GOV/COMP
PAGE 9 B0176   CENSUS
                                                        S60
MARSHALL G.,"POLICE RESPONSIBILITY." UK LOC/G ADJUD CONTROL
ADMIN EXEC 20. PAGE 70 B1409   REPRESENT
                                                     LAW
                                                     FORCES
                                                        C60
SMITH T.E.,"ELECTIONS IN DEVELOPING COUNTRIES: A   ECO/UNDEV
STUDY OF ELECTORAL PROCEDURES USED IN TOPICAL   CHOOSE
AFRICA, SOUTH-EAST ASIA..." AFR S/ASIA UK ROUTINE   REPRESENT
GOV/REL RACE/REL...GOV/COMP BIBLIOG 20. PAGE 98   ADMIN
B1985
                                                        B61
AGARWAL R.C.,STATE ENTERPRISE IN INDIA. FUT INDIA   ECO/UNDEV
UK FINAN INDUS ADMIN CONTROL OWN...POLICY CHARTS   SOCISM
BIBLIOG 20 RAILROAD. PAGE 3 B0064   GOV/REL
                                                     LG/CO
                                                        B61
AYLMER G.,THE KING'S SERVANTS. UK ELITES CHIEF PAY   ADMIN
CT/SYS WEALTH 17 CROMWELL/O CHARLES/I. PAGE 7 B0153 ROUTINE
                                                     EX/STRUC
                                                     NAT/G
                                                        B61
BISHOP D.G.,THE ADMINISTRATION OF BRITISH FOREIGN   ROUTINE
RELATIONS. EUR+WWI MOD/EUR INT/ORG NAT/G POL/PAR   PWR
DELIB/GP LEGIS TOP/EX ECO/TAC DOMIN EDU/PROP ADMIN   DIPLOM
COERCE 20. PAGE 12 B0243   UK
                                                        B61
COHN B.S.,DEVELOPMENT AND IMPACT OF BRITISH   BIBLIOG/A
ADMINISTRATION IN INDIA: A BIBLIOGRAPHIC ESSAY.   COLONIAL
INDIA UK ECO/UNDEV NAT/G DOMIN...POLICY MGT SOC   S/ASIA
19/20. PAGE 22 B0448   ADMIN
                                                        B61
DRAGNICH A.N.,MAJOR EUROPEAN GOVERNMENTS. FRANCE   NAT/G

ADMINISTRATIVE MANAGEMENT: PUBLIC & PRIVATE BUREAUCRACY

GERMANY/W UK USSR LOC/G EX/STRUC CT/SYS PARL/PROC
ATTIT MARXISM...JURID MGT NAT/COMP 19/20. PAGE 30
B0615
LEGIS
CONSTN
POL/PAR
B61

GLADDEN E.N.,BRITISH PUBLIC SERVICE ADMINISTRATION.
UK...CHARTS 20. PAGE 40 B0809
EFFICIENCY
ADMIN
EX/STRUC
EXEC
B61

HALL M.,DISTRIBUTION IN GREAT BRITAIN AND NORTH
AMERICA. CANADA UK USA+45 ECO/DEV INDUS MARKET
EFFICIENCY PROFIT...MGT CHARTS 20. PAGE 46 B0924
DIST/IND
PRODUC
ECO/TAC
CAP/ISM
B61

HAYTER W.,THE DIPLOMACY OF THE GREAT POWERS. FRANCE
UK USSR WOR+45 EX/STRUC TOP/EX NUC/PWR PEACE...OBS
20. PAGE 48 B0978
DIPLOM
POLICY
NAT/G
B61

HICKS U.K.,DEVELOPMENT FROM BELOW. UK INDUS ADMIN
COLONIAL ROUTINE GOV/REL...POLICY METH/CNCPT CHARTS
19/20 CMN/WLTH. PAGE 50 B1006
ECO/UNDEV
LOC/G
GOV/COMP
METH/COMP
B61

KERTESZ S.D.,AMERICAN DIPLOMACY IN A NEW ERA. COM
S/ASIA UK USA+45 FORCES PROB/SOLV BAL/PWR ECO/TAC
ADMIN COLONIAL WAR PEACE ORD/FREE 20 NATO CONGRESS
UN COLD/WAR. PAGE 59 B1199
ANTHOL
DIPLOM
TREND
B61

STRAUSS E.,THE RULING SERVANTS. FRANCE UK USSR
WOR+45 WOR-45 NAT/G CONSULT DELIB/GP EX/STRUC
TOP/EX DOMIN EDU/PROP LEGIT ROUTINE...MGT TIME/SEQ
STERTYP 20. PAGE 101 B2051
ADMIN
PWR
ELITES
B61

WALKER N.,MORALE IN THE CIVIL SERVICE. UK EXEC LEAD
INGP/REL EFFICIENCY HAPPINESS 20. PAGE 113 B2280
ATTIT
WORKER
ADMIN
PSY
B61

WILLSON F.M.G.,ADMINISTRATORS IN ACTION. UK MARKET
TEC/DEV PARL/PROC 20. PAGE 117 B2358
ADMIN
NAT/G
CONSTN
S61

ANGLIN D.,"UNITED STATES OPPOSITION TO CANADIAN
MEMBERSHIP IN THE PAN AMERICAN UNION: A CANADIAN
VIEW." L/A+17C UK USA+45 VOL/ASSN DELIB/GP EX/STRUC
PLAN DIPLOM DOMIN REGION ATTIT RIGID/FLEX PWR
...RELATIV CONCPT STERTYP CMN/WLTH OAS 20. PAGE 5
B0112
INT/ORG
CANADA
S61

JOHNSON N.,"PARLIAMENTARY QUESTIONS AND THE CONDUCT
OF ADMINISTRATION." UK REPRESENT PARLIAMENT 20.
PAGE 57 B1146
CONTROL
EXEC
EX/STRUC
S61

LIEBENOW J.G.,"LEGITIMACY OF ALIEN RELATIONSHIP:
THE NYATURU OF TANGANYIKA" (BMR)" AFR UK ADMIN LEAD
CHOOSE 20 NYATURU TANGANYIKA. PAGE 65 B1312
COLONIAL
DOMIN
LEGIT
PWR
C61

MOODIE G.C.,"THE GOVERNMENT OF GREAT BRITAIN." UK
LAW STRUCT LOC/G POL/PAR DIPLOM RECEIVE ADMIN
COLONIAL CHOOSE...BIBLIOG 20 PARLIAMENT. PAGE 75
B1508
NAT/G
SOCIETY
PARL/PROC
GOV/COMP
B62

ANDREWS W.G.,EUROPEAN POLITICAL INSTITUTIONS.
FRANCE GERMANY UK USSR TOP/EX LEAD PARL/PROC CHOOSE
20. PAGE 5 B0104
NAT/COMP
POL/PAR
EX/STRUC
LEGIS
B62

BROWN B.E.,NEW DIRECTIONS IN COMPARATIVE POLITICS.
AUSTRIA FRANCE GERMANY UK WOR+45 EX/STRUC LEGIS
ORD/FREE 20. PAGE 16 B0320
NAT/COMP
METH
POL/PAR
FORCES
B62

FORD A.G.,THE GOLD STANDARD 1880-1914: BRITAIN AND
ARGENTINA. UK ECO/UNDEV INT/TRADE ADMIN GOV/REL
DEMAND EFFICIENCY...STAT CHARTS 19/20 ARGEN
GOLD/STAND. PAGE 36 B0737
FINAN
ECO/TAC
BUDGET
BAL/PAY
B62

FRIEDMANN W.,METHODS AND POLICIES OF PRINCIPAL
DONOR COUNTRIES IN PUBLIC INTERNATIONAL DEVELOPMENT
FINANCING: PRELIMINARY APPRAISAL. FRANCE GERMANY/W
UK USA+45 USSR WOR+45 FINAN TEC/DEV CAP/ISM DIPLOM
ECO/TAC ATTIT 20 EEC. PAGE 37 B0759
INT/ORG
FOR/AID
NAT/COMP
ADMIN
B62

GRANICK D.,THE EUROPEAN EXECUTIVE. BELGIUM FRANCE
GERMANY/W UK INDUS LABOR LG/CO SML/CO EX/STRUC PLAN
TEC/DEV CAP/ISM COST DEMAND...POLICY CHARTS 20.
PAGE 42 B0852
MGT
ECO/DEV
ECO/TAC
EXEC
B62

GROGAN V.,ADMINISTRATIVE TRIBUNALS IN THE PUBLIC
SERVICE. IRELAND UK NAT/G CONTROL CT/SYS...JURID
GOV/COMP 20. PAGE 44 B0884
ADMIN
LAW
ADJUD
DELIB/GP
B62

GROVE J.W.,GOVERNMENT AND INDUSTRY IN BRITAIN. UK
FINAN LOC/G CONSULT DELIB/GP INT/TRADE ADMIN
ECO/TAC
INDUS

CONTROL...BIBLIOG 20. PAGE 44 B0894
NAT/G
GP/REL
B62

INSTITUTE OF PUBLIC ADMIN,A SHORT HISTORY OF THE
PUBLIC SERVICE IN IRELAND. IRELAND UK DIST/IND
INGP/REL FEDERAL 13/20 CIVIL/SERV. PAGE 54 B1091
ADMIN
WORKER
GOV/REL
NAT/G
B62

PHILLIPS O.H.,CONSTITUTIONAL AND ADMINISTRATIVE LAW
(3RD ED.). UK INT/ORG LOC/G CHIEF EX/STRUC LEGIS
BAL/PWR ADJUD COLONIAL CT/SYS PWR...CHARTS 20.
PAGE 83 B1670
JURID
ADMIN
CONSTN
NAT/G
B62

PRAKASH O.M.,THE THEORY AND WORKING OF STATE
CORPORATIONS: WITH SPECIAL REFERENCE TO INDIA.
INDIA UK USA+45 TOP/EX PRICE ADMIN EFFICIENCY...MGT
METH/COMP 20 TVA. PAGE 84 B1698
LG/CO
ECO/UNDEV
GOV/REL
SOCISM
B62

SAMPSON A.,ANATOMY OF BRITAIN. UK LAW COM/IND FINAN
INDUS MARKET MUNIC POL/PAR EX/STRUC TOP/EX DIPLOM
LEAD REPRESENT PERSON PARLIAMENT WORSHIP. PAGE 92
B1866
ELITES
PWR
STRUCT
FORCES
B62

SRIVASTAVA G.L.,COLLECTIVE BARGAINING AND LABOR-
MANAGEMENT RELATIONS IN INDIA. INDIA UK USA+45
INDUS LEGIS WORKER ADJUD EFFICIENCY PRODUC
...METH/COMP 20. PAGE 100 B2014
LABOR
MGT
BARGAIN
GP/REL
B62

TAYLOR D.,THE BRITISH IN AFRICA. UK CULTURE
ECO/UNDEV INDUS DIPLOM INT/TRADE ADMIN WAR RACE/REL
ORD/FREE SOVEREIGN...POLICY BIBLIOG 15/20 CMN/WLTH.
PAGE 103 B2084
AFR
COLONIAL
DOMIN
B62

WENDT P.F.,HOUSING POLICY - THE SEARCH FOR
SOLUTIONS. GERMANY/W SWEDEN UK USA+45 OP/RES
HABITAT WEALTH...SOC/WK CHARTS 20. PAGE 115 B2322
PLAN
ADMIN
METH/COMP
NAT/G
S62

DONNELLY D.,"THE POLITICS AND ADMINISTRATION OF
PLANNING." UK ROUTINE FEDERAL 20. PAGE 30 B0607
GOV/REL
EFFICIENCY
ADMIN
EX/STRUC
S62

OLLERENSHAW K.,"SHARING RESPONSIBLITY." UK DELIB/GP
EDU/PROP EFFICIENCY 20. PAGE 80 B1607
REPRESENT
GP/REL
ADMIN
EX/STRUC
B63

BLONDEL J.,VOTERS, PARTIES, AND LEADERS. UK ELITES
LOC/G NAT/G PROVS ACT/RES DOMIN REPRESENT GP/REL
INGP/REL...SOC BIBLIOG 20. PAGE 12 B0255
POL/PAR
STRATA
LEGIS
ADMIN
B63

CONF ON FUTURE OF COMMONWEALTH,THE FUTURE OF THE
COMMONWEALTH. UK ECC/UNDEV AGRI EDU/PROP ADMIN
SOC/INTEG 20 COMMONWLTH. PAGE 23 B0460
DIPLOM
RACE/REL
ORD/FREE
TEC/DEV
B63

GALBRAITH J.S.,RELUCTANT EMPIRE: BRITISH POLICY OF
THE SOUTH AFRICAN FRONTIER, 1834-1854. AFR
SOUTH/AFR UK GP/REL RACE/REL DISCRIM...CHARTS
BIBLIOG 19 MISSION. PAGE 38 B0774
COLONIAL
ADMIN
POLICY
SECT
B63

GARNER U.F.,ADMINISTRATIVE LAW. UK LAW LOC/G NAT/G
EX/STRUC LEGIS JUDGE BAL/PWR BUDGET ADJUD CONTROL
CT/SYS...BIBLIOG 20. PAGE 39 B0783
ADMIN
JURID
PWR
GOV/REL
B63

GRIFFITH J.A.G.,PRINCIPLES OF ADMINISTRATIVE LAW
(3RD ED.). UK CONSTN EX/STRUC LEGIS ADJUD CONTROL
CT/SYS PWR...CHARTS 20. PAGE 43 B0879
JURID
ADMIN
NAT/G
BAL/PWR
B63

HEUSSLER R.,YESTERDAY'S RULERS: THE MAKING OF THE
BRITISH COLONIAL SERVICE. AFR EUR+WWI UK STRATA
SECT DELIB/GP PLAN DOMIN EDU/PROP ATTIT PERCEPT
PERSON SUPEGO KNOWL ORD/FREE PWR...MGT SOC OBS INT
TIME/SEQ 20 CMN/WLTH. PAGE 49 B1000
EX/STRUC
MORAL
ELITES
B63

KULZ H.R.,STAATSBURGER UND STAATSGEWALT (2 VOLS.).
GERMANY SWITZERLND UK USSR CONSTN DELIB/GP TARIFFS
TAX...JURID 20. PAGE 61 B1242
ADMIN
ADJUD
CT/SYS
NAT/COMP
B63

MAYNE R.,THE COMMUNITY OF EUROPE. UK CONSTN NAT/G
CONSULT DELIB/GP CREATE PLAN ECO/TAC LEGIT ADMIN
ROUTINE ORD/FREE PWR WEALTH...CONCPT TIME/SEQ EEC
EURATOM 20. PAGE 71 B1436
EUR+WWI
INT/ORG
REGION
B63

OLSON M. JR.,THE ECONOMICS OF WARTIME SHORTAGE.
FRANCE GERMANY MOD/EUR UK AGRI PROB/SOLV ADMIN
DEMAND WEALTH...POLICY OLD/LIB 17/20. PAGE 80 B1608
WAR
ADJUST
ECO/TAC
NAT/COMP
B63

PATRA A.C.,THE ADMINISTRATION OF JUSTICE UNDER THE
EAST INDIA COMPANY IN BENGAL, BIHAR AND ORISSA.
ADMIN
JURID

INDIA UK LG/CO CAP/ISM INT/TRADE ADJUD COLONIAL CONTROL CT/SYS...POLICY 20. PAGE 81 B1641 | CONCPT | B63

PREST A.R.,PUBLIC FINANCE IN UNDERDEVELOPED COUNTRIES. UK WOR+45 WOR-45 SOCIETY INT/ORG NAT/G LEGIS ACT/RES PLAN ECO/TAC ADMIN ROUTINE...CHARTS 20. PAGE 84 B1702 | FINAN ECO/UNDEV NIGERIA | B63

ROBINSON K.,ESSAYS IN IMPERIAL GOVERNMENT. CAMEROON NIGERIA UK CONSTN LOC/G LEGIS ADMIN GOV/REL PWR ...POLICY ANTHOL BIBLIOG 17/20 PURHAM/M. PAGE 89 B1803 | COLONIAL AFR DOMIN | B63

ROYAL INSTITUTE PUBLIC ADMIN,BRITISH PUBLIC ADMINISTRATION. UK LAW FINAN INDUS LOC/G POL/PAR LEGIS LOBBY PARL/PROC CHOOSE JURID. PAGE 91 B1845 | BIBLIOG ADMIN MGT NAT/G | B63

SCHOECK H.,THE NEW ARGUMENT IN ECONOMICS. UK USA+45 INDUS MARKET LABOR NAT/G ECO/TAC ADMIN ROUTINE BAL/PAY PWR...POLICY BOLIV. PAGE 94 B1899 | WELF/ST FOR/AID ECO/DEV ALL/IDEOS | B63

SELF P.,THE STATE AND THE FARMER. UK ECO/DEV MARKET WORKER PRICE CONTROL GP/REL...WELF/ST 20 DEPT/AGRI. PAGE 95 B1926 | AGRI NAT/G ADMIN VOL/ASSN | B63

SHANKS M.,THE LESSONS OF PUBLIC ENTERPRISE. UK LEGIS WORKER ECO/TAC ADMIN PARL/PROC GOV/REL ATTIT ...POLICY MGT METH/COMP NAT/COMP ANTHOL 20 PARLIAMENT. PAGE 96 B1931 | SOCISM OWN NAT/G INDUS | B63

SINGH H.L.,PROBLEMS AND POLICIES OF THE BRITISH IN INDIA. 1885-1898. INDIA UK NAT/G FORCES LEGIS PROB/SOLV CONTROL RACE/REL ADJUST DISCRIM NAT/LISM RIGID/FLEX...MGT 19 CIVIL/SERV. PAGE 97 B1968 | COLONIAL PWR POLICY ADMIN | B63

SPRING D.,THE ENGLISH LANDED ESTATE IN THE NINETEENTH CENTURY: ITS ADMINISTRATION. UK ELITES STRUCT AGRI NAT/G GP/REL OWN PWR WEALTH...BIBLIOG 19 HOUSE/LORD. PAGE 99 B2012 | STRATA PERS/REL MGT | B63

WADE H.W.R.,TOWARDS ADMINISTRATIVE JUSTICE. UK USA+45 CONSTN CONSULT PROB/SOLV CT/SYS PARL/PROC ...POLICY JURID METH/COMP 20 ENGLSH/LAW. PAGE 112 B2270 | ADJUD IDEA/COMP ADMIN | B63

WALKER A.A.,OFFICIAL PUBLICATIONS OF SIERRA LEONE AND GAMBIA. GAMBIA SIER/LEONE UK LAW CONSTN LEGIS PLAN BUDGET DIPLOM...SOC SAMP CON/ANAL 20. PAGE 113 B2278 | BIBLIOG NAT/G COLONIAL ADMIN | B63

BAKER R.J.,"DISCUSSION AND DECISION-MAKING IN THE CIVIL SERVICE." UK CONTROL REPRESENT INGP/REL PERS/REL EFFICIENCY 20. PAGE 8 B0168 | EXEC EX/STRUC PROB/SOLV ADMIN | S63

HAVILAND H.F.,"BUILDING A POLITICAL COMMUNITY." EUR+WWI FUT UK USA+45 ECO/DEV ECO/UNDEV INT/ORG NAT/G DELIB/GP BAL/PWR ECO/TAC NEUTRAL ROUTINE ATTIT PWR WEALTH...CONCPT COLD/WAR TOT/POP 20. PAGE 48 B0972 | VOL/ASSN DIPLOM | S63

JOELSON M.R.,"THE DISMISSAL OF CIVIL SERVANTS IN THE INTERESTS OF NATIONAL SECURITY." EUR+WWI LAW DELIB/GP ROUTINE ORD/FREE...MGT VAL/FREE 20. PAGE 56 B1141 | USA+45 NAT/G UK FRANCE | S63

THE SPECIAL COMMONWEALTH AFRICAN ASSISTANCE PLAN. AFR CANADA INDIA NIGERIA UK FINAN SCHOOL...CHARTS 20 COMMONWLTH. PAGE 2 B0041 | ECO/UNDEV TREND FOR/AID ADMIN | B64

AVASTHI A.,ASPECTS OF ADMINISTRATION. INDIA UK USA+45 FINAN ACADEM DELIB/GP LEGIS RECEIVE PARL/PROC PRIVIL...NAT/COMP 20. PAGE 7 B0150 | MGT ADMIN SOC/WK ORD/FREE | B64

BANTON M.,THE POLICEMAN IN THE COMMUNITY. UK USA+45 STRUCT PROF/ORG WORKER LOBBY ROUTINE COERCE CROWD GP/REL ADJUST DISCRIM PERCEPT 20. PAGE 9 B0181 | FORCES ADMIN ROLE RACE/REL | B64

CULLINGWORTH J.B.,TOWN AND COUNTRY PLANNING IN ENGLAND AND WALES. UK LAW SOCIETY CONSULT ACT/RES ADMIN ROUTINE LEISURE INGP/REL ADJUST PWR...GEOG 20 OPEN/SPACE URBAN/RNWL. PAGE 25 B0512 | MUNIC PLAN NAT/G PROB/SOLV | B64

DAS M.N.,INDIA UNDER MORLEY AND MINTO. INDIA UK ECO/UNDEV MUNIC PROVS EX/STRUC LEGIS DIPLOM CONTROL REV 20 MORLEY/J. PAGE 26 B0531 | GOV/REL COLONIAL POLICY ADMIN | B64

DUROSELLE J.B.,POLITIQUES NATIONALES ENVERS LES JEUNES ETATS. FRANCE ISRAEL ITALY UK USA+45 USSR | DIPLOM ECO/UNDEV | B64

YUGOSLAVIA ECO/DEV FINAN ECO/TAC INT/TRADE ADMIN PWR 20. PAGE 31 B0634 | COLONIAL DOMIN | B64

ENDACOTT G.B.,GOVERNMENT AND PEOPLE IN HONG KONG 1841-1962: A CONSTITUTIONAL HISTORY. UK LEGIS ADJUD REPRESENT ATTIT 19/20 HONG/KONG. PAGE 33 B0674 | CONSTN COLONIAL CONTROL ADMIN | B64

FORBES A.H.,CURRENT RESEARCH IN BRITISH STUDIES. UK CONSTN CULTURE POL/PAR SECT DIPLOM ADMIN...JURID BIOG WORSHIP 20. PAGE 36 B0736 | BIBLIOG PERSON NAT/G PARL/PROC | B64

GREBLER L.,URBAN RENEWAL IN EUROPEAN COUNTRIES: ITS EMERGENCE AND POTENTIALS. EUR+WWI UK ECO/DEV LOC/G NEIGH CREATE ADMIN ATTIT...TREND NAT/COMP 20 URBAN/RNWL. PAGE 43 B0863 | MUNIC PLAN CONSTRUC NAT/G | B64

GUTTSMAN W.L.,THE BRITISH POLITICAL ELITE. EUR+WWI MOD/EUR STRATA FAM LABOR POL/PAR SCHOOL VOL/ASSN DELIB/GP LEGIS LEGIT EXEC CHOOSE ATTIT ALL/VALS ...STAT BIOG TIME/SEQ CHARTS VAL/FREE. PAGE 45 B0905 | NAT/G SOC UK ELITES | B64

HAMILTON B.L.S.,PROBLEMS OF ADMINISTRATION IN AN EMERGENT NATION: CASE STUDY OF JAMAICA. JAMAICA UK WOR+45 MUNIC COLONIAL HABITAT...CHARTS BIBLIOG 20 CIVIL/SERV. PAGE 46 B0932 | ADMIN ECO/UNDEV GOV/REL NAT/G | B64

JACKSON R.M.,THE MACHINERY OF JUSTICE IN ENGLAND. UK EDU/PROP CONTROL COST ORD/FREE...MGT 20 ENGLSH/LAW. PAGE 55 B1109 | CT/SYS ADJUD JUDGE JURID | B64

LITTLE I.M.D.,AID TO AFRICA. AFR UK TEC/DEV DIPLOM ECO/TAC INCOME WEALTH 20. PAGE 66 B1326 | FOR/AID ECO/UNDEV ADMIN POLICY | B64

MARSH D.C.,THE FUTURE OF THE WELFARE STATE. UK CONSTN NAT/G POL/PAR...POLICY WELF/ST 20. PAGE 69 B1404 | NEW/LIB ADMIN CONCPT INSPECT | B64

NATIONAL BOOK LEAGUE,THE COMMONWEALTH IN BOOKS: AN ANNOTATED LIST. CANADA UK LOC/G SECT ADMIN...SOC BIOG 20 CMN/WLTH. PAGE 77 B1561 | BIBLIOG/A JURID NAT/G | B64

PINNICK A.W.,COUNTRY PLANNERS IN ACTION. UK FINAN SERV/IND NAT/G CONSULT DELIB/GP PRICE CONTROL ROUTINE LEISURE AGE/C...GEOG 20 URBAN/RNWL. PAGE 83 B1674 | MUNIC PLAN INDUS ATTIT | B64

RAPHAEL M.,PENSIONS AND PUBLIC SERVANTS. UK PLAN EDU/PROP PARTIC GOV/REL HEALTH...POLICY CHARTS 17/20 CIVIL/SERV. PAGE 86 B1737 | ADMIN SENIOR PAY AGE/O | B64

RIDLEY F.,PUBLIC ADMINISTRATION IN FRANCE. FRANCE UK EX/STRUC CONTROL PARTIC EFFICIENCY 20. PAGE 88 B1781 | ADMIN REPRESENT GOV/COMP PWR | B64

TILMAN R.O.,BUREAUCRATIC TRANSITION IN MALAYA. MALAYSIA S/ASIA UK NAT/G EX/STRUC DIPLOM...CHARTS BIBLIOG 20. PAGE 104 B2110 | ADMIN COLONIAL SOVEREIGN EFFICIENCY | B64

WRAITH R.,CORRUPTION IN DEVELOPING COUNTRIES. NIGERIA UK LAW ELITES STRATA INDUS LOC/G NAT/G SECT FORCES EDU/PROP ADMIN PWR WEALTH 18/20. PAGE 118 B2377 | ECO/UNDEV CRIME SANCTION ATTIT | B64

MACKINTOSH J.P.,"NIGERIA'S EXTERNAL AFFAIRS." UK CULTURE ECO/UNDEV NAT/G VOL/ASSN EDU/PROP LEGIT ADMIN ATTIT ORD/FREE PWR 20. PAGE 68 B1365 | AFR DIPLOM NIGERIA | L64

SYMONDS R.,"REFLECTIONS ON LOCALISATION." AFR S/ASIA UK STRATA INT/ORG NAT/G SCHOOL EDU/PROP LEGIT KNOWL ORD/FREE PWR RESPECT CMN/WLTH 20. PAGE 102 B2064 | ADMIN MGT COLONIAL | L64

LOW D.A.,"LION RAMPANT." EUR+WWI MOD/EUR S/ASIA ECO/UNDEV NAT/G FORCES TEC/DEV ECO/TAC LEGIT ADMIN COLONIAL COERCE ORD/FREE RESPECT 19/20. PAGE 67 B1344 | AFR DOMIN DIPLOM UK | S64

AMERICAN ECONOMIC ASSOCIATION,INDEX OF ECONOMIC JOURNALS 1886-1965 (7 VOLS.). UK USA+45 USA-45 AGRI FINAN PLAN ECO/TAC INT/TRADE ADMIN...STAT CENSUS 19/20. PAGE 4 B0083 | BIBLIOG WRITING INDUS | B65

CAMPBELL G.A.,THE CIVIL SERVICE IN BRITAIN (2ND ED.). UK DELIB/GP FORCES WORKER CREATE PLAN ...POLICY AUD/VIS 19/20 CIVIL/SERV. PAGE 18 B0370 | ADMIN LEGIS NAT/G FINAN | B65

B65

CHANDA A.,FEDERALISM IN INDIA. INDIA UK ELITES
FINAN NAT/G POL/PAR EX/STRUC LEGIS DIPLOM TAX
GOV/REL POPULISM...POLICY 20. PAGE 20 B0402

CONSTN
CENTRAL
FEDERAL

B65

EDELMAN M.,THE POLITICS OF WAGE-PRICE DECISIONS.
GERMANY ITALY NETHERLAND UK INDUS LABOR POL/PAR
PROB/SOLV BARGAIN PRICE ROUTINE BAL/PAY COST DEMAND
20. PAGE 32 B0654

GOV/COMP
CONTROL
ECO/TAC
PLAN

B65

FORGAC A.A.,NEW DIPLOMACY AND THE UNITED NATIONS.
FRANCE GERMANY UK USSR INT/ORG DELIB/GP EX/STRUC
PEACE...INT/LAW CONCPT UN. PAGE 36 B0740

DIPLOM
ETIQUET
NAT/G

B65

GOPAL S.,BRITISH POLICY IN INDIA 1858-1905. INDIA
UK ELITES CHIEF DELIB/GP ECO/TAC GP/REL DISCRIM
ATTIT...IDEA/COMP NAT/COMP PERS/COMP BIBLIOG/A
19/20. PAGE 41 B0828

COLONIAL
ADMIN
POL/PAR
ECO/UNDEV

B65

GT BRIT ADMIN STAFF COLLEGE,THE ACCOUNTABILITY OF
PUBLIC CORPORATIONS (REV. ED.). UK ECO/DEV FINAN
DELIB/GP EX/STRUC BUDGET CAP/ISM CONFER PRICE
PARL/PROC 20. PAGE 44 B0899

LG/CO
NAT/G
ADMIN
CONTROL

B65

HAINES R.M.,THE ADMINISTRATION OF THE DIOCESE OF
WORCESTER IN THE FIRST HALF OF THE FOURTEENTH
CENTURY. UK CATHISM...METH/COMP 13/15. PAGE 45
B0918

ADMIN
EX/STRUC
SECT
DELIB/GP

B65

HOWE R.,THE STORY OF SCOTLAND YARD: A HISTORY OF
THE CID FROM THE EARLIEST TIMES TO THE PRESENT DAY.
UK MUNIC EDU/PROP 6/20 SCOT/YARD. PAGE 52 B1051

CRIMLGY
CRIME
FORCES
ADMIN

B65

LEMAY G.H.,BRITISH SUPREMACY IN SOUTH AFRICA
1899-1907. SOUTH/AFR UK ADMIN CONTROL LEAD GP/REL
ORD/FREE 19/20. PAGE 64 B1286

WAR
COLONIAL
DOMIN
POLICY

B65

PANJABI K.L.,THE CIVIL SERVANT IN INDIA. INDIA UK
NAT/G CONSULT EX/STRUC REGION GP/REL RACE/REL 20.
PAGE 81 B1631

ADMIN
WORKER
BIOG
COLONIAL

B65

PRESTHUS R.,BEHAVIORAL APPROACHES TO PUBLIC
ADMINISTRATION. UK STRATA LG/CO PUB/INST VOL/ASSN
EX/STRUC TOP/EX EFFICIENCY HEALTH. PAGE 84 B1704

GEN/METH
DECISION
ADMIN
R+D

B65

PURCELL V.,THE MEMOIRS OF A MALAYAN OFFICIAL.
MALAYSIA UK ECO/UNDEV INDUS LABOR EDU/PROP COLONIAL
CT/SYS WAR NAT/LISM TOTALISM ORD/FREE SOVEREIGN 20
UN CIVIL/SERV. PAGE 85 B1721

BIOG
ADMIN
JURID
FORCES

B65

RHODES G.,PUBLIC SECTOR PENSIONS. UK FINAN LEGIS
BUDGET TAX PAY INCOME...CHARTS 20 CIVIL/SERV.
PAGE 88 B1769

ADMIN
RECEIVE
AGE/O
WORKER

B65

WITHERELL J.W.,MADAGASCAR AND ADJACENT ISLANDS: A
GUIDE TO OFFICIAL PUBLICATIONS (PAMPHLET). FRANCE
MADAGASCAR S/ASIA UK LAW OP/RES PLAN DIPLOM
...POLICY CON+ANAL 19/20. PAGE 117 B2368

BIBLIOG
COLONIAL
LOC/G
ADMIN

B66

DILLEY M.R.,BRITISH POLICY IN KENYA COLONY (2ND
ED.). AFR INDIA UK LABOR BUDGET TAX ADMIN PARL/PROC
GP/REL...BIBLIOG 20 PARLIAMENT. PAGE 29 B0594

COLONIAL
REPRESENT
SOVEREIGN

B66

FABAR R.,THE VISION AND THE NEED: LATE VICTORIAN
IMPERIALIST AIMS. MOD/EUR UK WOR-45 CULTURE NAT/G
DIPLOM...TIME/SEQ METH/COMP 19 KIPLING/R
COMMONWLTH. PAGE 34 B0693

COLONIAL
CONCPT
ADMIN
ATTIT

B66

GROSS C.,A BIBLIOGRAPHY OF BRITISH MUNICIPAL
HISTORY (2ND ED.). UK LOC/G ADMIN 11/19. PAGE 44
B0888

BIBLIOG/A
MUNIC
CONSTN

B66

JOHNSON N.,PARLIAMENT AND ADMINISTRATION: THE
ESTIMATES COMMITTEE 1945-65. FUT UK NAT/G EX/STRUC
PLAN BUDGET ORD/FREE...T 20 PARLIAMENT HOUSE/CMNS.
PAGE 57 B1147

LEGIS
ADMIN
FINAN
DELIB/GP

B66

OWEN G.,INDUSTRY IN THE UNITED STATES. UK USA+45
NAT/G WEALTH...DECISION NAT/COMP 20. PAGE 80 B1620

METH/COMP
INDUS
MGT
PROB/SOLV

B66

SPICER K.,A SAMARITAN STATE? AFR CANADA INDIA
PAKISTAN UK USA+45 FINAN INDUS PRODUC...CHARTS 20
NATO. PAGE 99 B2006

DIPLOM
FOR/AID
ECO/DEV
ADMIN

B66

US LIBRARY OF CONGRESS,NIGERIA: A GUIDE TO OFFICIAL
PUBLICATIONS. CAMEROON NIGERIA UK DIPLOM...POLICY
19/20 UN LEAGUE/NAT. PAGE 109 B2207

BIBLIOG
ADMIN
NAT/G
COLONIAL

B66

WILSON G.,CASES AND MATERIALS ON CONSTITUTIONAL AND
ADMINISTRATIVE LAW. UK LAW NAT/G EX/STRUC LEGIS
BAL/PWR BUDGET DIPLOM ADJUD CONTROL CT/SYS GOV/REL
ORD/FREE 20 PARLIAMENT ENGLSH/LAW. PAGE 117 B2359

JURID
ADMIN
CONSTN
PWR

B67

BROWN L.N.,FRENCH ADMINISTRATIVE LAW. FRANCE UK
CONSTN NAT/G LEGIS DOMIN CONTROL EXEC PARL/PROC PWR
...JURID METH/COMP GEN/METH. PAGE 16 B0324

EX/STRUC
LAW
IDEA/COMP
CT/SYS

B67

BULPITT J.G.,PARTY POLITICS IN ENGLISH LOCAL
GOVERNMENT. UK CONSTN ACT/RES TAX CONTROL CHOOSE
REPRESENT GOV/REL KNOWL 20. PAGE 17 B0344

POL/PAR
LOC/G
ELITES
EX/STRUC

B67

CECIL L.,ALBERT BALLIN: BUSINESS AND POLITICS IN
IMPERIAL GERMANY 1888-1918. GERMANY UK INT/TRADE
LEAD WAR PERS/REL ADJUST PWR WEALTH...MGT BIBLIOG
19/20. PAGE 19 B0397

DIPLOM
CONSTN
ECO/DEV
TOP/EX

B67

DICKSON P.G.M.,THE FINANCIAL REVOLUTION IN ENGLAND.
UK NAT/G TEC/DEV ADMIN GOV/REL...SOC METH/CNCPT
CHARTS GP/COMP BIBLIOG 17/18. PAGE 29 B0587

ECO/DEV
FINAN
CAP/ISM
MGT

B67

GIFFORD P.,BRITAIN AND GERMANY IN AFRICA. AFR
GERMANY UK ECO/UNDEV LEAD WAR NAT/LISM ATTIT
...POLICY HIST/WRIT METH/COMP ANTHOL BIBLIOG 19/20
WWI. PAGE 39 B0797

COLONIAL
ADMIN
DIPLOM
NAT/COMP

B67

MENHENNET D.,PARLIAMENT IN PERSPECTIVE. UK ROUTINE
REPRESENT ROLE PWR 20 PARLIAMENT. PAGE 73 B1467

LEGIS
PARL/PROC
CONCPT
POPULISM

L67

BESCOBY I.,"A COLONIAL ADMINISTRATION: AN ANALYSIS
OF ADMINISTRATION IN BRITISH COLUMBIA 1869-1871."
UK STRATA EX/STRUC LEGIS TASK GOV/REL EFFICIENCY
ROLE...MGT CHARTS 19. PAGE 11 B0232

ADMIN
CANADA
COLONIAL
LEAD

S67

CARIAS B.,"EL CONTROL DE LAS EMPRESAS PUBLICAS POR
GRUPOS DE INTERESES DE LA COMUNIDAD." FRANCE UK
VENEZUELA INDUS NAT/G CONTROL OWN PWR...DECISION
NAT/COMP 20. PAGE 18 B0377

WORKER
REPRESENT
MGT
SOCISM

S67

CROCKETT D.G.,"THE MP AND HIS CONSTITUENTS." UK
POL/PAR...DECISION 20. PAGE 25 B0506

EXEC
NAT/G
PERS/REL
REPRESENT

S67

FRYKENBURG R.E.,"STUDIES OF LAND CONTROL IN INDIAN
HISTORY: REVIEW ARTICLE." INDIA UK STRATA AGRI
MUNIC OP/RES COLONIAL REGION EFFICIENCY OWN HABITAT
...CONCPT 16/20. PAGE 38 B0763

ECO/UNDEV
CONTROL
ADMIN

S67

GRINYER P.H.,"THE SYSTEMATIC EVALUATION OF METHODS
OF WAGE PAYMENT." UK INDUS WORKER ADMIN EFFICIENCY
...MGT METH/COMP 20. PAGE 44 B0882

OP/RES
COST
PAY
PRODUC

S67

HUDDLESTON J.,"TRADE UNIONS IN THE GERMAN FEDERAL
REPUBLIC." EUR+WWI GERMANY/W UK LAW INDUS WORKER
CREATE CENTRAL...MGT GP/COMP 20. PAGE 52 B1056

LABOR
GP/REL
SCHOOL
ROLE

S67

IDENBURG P.J.,"POLITICAL STRUCTURAL DEVELOPMENT IN
TROPICAL AFRICA." UK ECO/UNDEV KIN POL/PAR CHIEF
EX/STRUC CREATE COLONIAL CONTROL REPRESENT RACE/REL
...MAJORIT TREND 20. PAGE 53 B1074

AFR
CONSTN
NAT/G
GOV/COMP

S67

JENCKS C.E.,"SOCIAL STATUS OF COAL MINERS IN
BRITAIN SINCE NATIONALIZATION." UK STRATA STRUCT
LABOR RECEIVE GP/REL INCOME OWN ATTIT HABITAT...MGT
T 20. PAGE 56 B1128

EXTR/IND
WORKER
CONTROL
NAT/G

S67

ROWAT D.C.,"RECENT DEVELOPMENTS IN OMBUDSMANSHIP: A
REVIEW ARTICLE." UK USA+45 STRUCT CONSULT INSPECT
TASK EFFICIENCY...NEW/IDEA 20. PAGE 91 B1841

CANADA
ADMIN
LOC/G
NAT/G

S67

TIVEY L.,"THE POLITICAL CONSEQUENCES OF ECONOMIC
PLANNING." UK CONSTN INDUS ACT/RES ADMIN CONTROL
LOBBY REPRESENT EFFICIENCY SUPEGO SOVEREIGN
...DECISION 20. PAGE 104 B2112

PLAN
POLICY
NAT/G

S68

GUZZARDI W. JR.,"THE SECOND BATTLE OF BRITAIN." UK
STRATA LABOR WORKER CREATE PROB/SOLV EDU/PROP ADMIN
LEAD LOBBY...MGT SOC 20 GOLD/STAND. PAGE 45 B0907

FINAN
ECO/TAC
ECO/DEV
STRUCT

B86

BOLINSBROKE H ST J.,A DISSERTATION UPON PARTIES
(1729). UK LEGIS CHOOSE GOV/REL SOVEREIGN...TRADIT
18 PARLIAMENT. PAGE 13 B0269

CONSERVE
POL/PAR
CHIEF
EX/STRUC

GOODNOW F.J.,"AN EXECUTIVE AND THE COURTS: JUDICIAL CT/SYS   L86
REMEDIES AGAINST ADMINISTRATIVE ACTION" FRANCE UK   GOV/REL
USA-45 WOR-45 LAW CONSTN SANCTION ORD/FREE 19.   ADMIN
PAGE 41 B0823   ADJUD

ULAM A.B. B2145

UN....UNITED NATIONS; SEE ALSO INT/ORG, VOL/ASSN, INT/REL

AMERICAN POLITICAL SCIENCE REVIEW. USA+45 USA-45   BIBLIOG/A   N
WOR+45 WOR-45 INT/ORG ADMIN...INT/LAW PHIL/SCI   DIPLOM
CONCPT METH 20 UN. PAGE 1 B0001   NAT/G
                                                      GOV/COMP

UNITED NATIONS,OFFICIAL RECORDS OF THE UNITED   INT/ORG   N
NATIONS' GENERAL ASSEMBLY. WOR+45 BUDGET DIPLOM   DELIB/GP
ADMIN 20 UN. PAGE 107 B2159   INT/LAW
                                                      WRITING

UNITED NATIONS,UNITED NATIONS PUBLICATIONS. WOR+45   BIBLIOG   N
ECO/UNDEV AGRI FINAN FORCES ADMIN LEAD WAR PEACE   INT/ORG
...POLICY INT/LAW 20 UN. PAGE 107 B2160   DIPLOM

WORLD PEACE FOUNDATION,DOCUMENTS OF INTERNATIONAL   BIBLIOG   N
ORGANIZATIONS: A SELECTED BIBLIOGRAPHY. WOR+45   DIPLOM
WOR-45 AGRI FINAN ACT/RES OP/RES INT/TRADE ADMIN   INT/ORG
...CON/ANAL 20 UN UNESCO LEAGUE/NAT. PAGE 118 B2374   REGION

HIGGINS R.,THE ADMINISTRATION OF UNITED KINGDOM   DIPLOM   N19
FOREIGN POLICY THROUGH THE UNITED NATIONS   POLICY
(PAMPHLET). UK NAT/G ADMIN GOV/REL...CHARTS 20 UN   INT/ORG
PARLIAMENT. PAGE 50 B1009

CORWIN E.S.,"THE CONSTITUTION AND WORLD   INT/ORG   L44
ORGANIZATION." FUT USA+45 USA-45 NAT/G EX/STRUC   CONSTN
LEGIS PEACE KNOWL...CON/ANAL UN 20. PAGE 24 B0484   SOVEREIGN

COLEGROVE K.W.,"THE ROLE OF CONGRESS AND PUBLIC   EX/STRUC   S44
OPINION IN FORMULATING FOREIGN POLICY." USA+45 WAR   DIPLOM
...DECISION UN CONGRESS. PAGE 22 B0451   LEGIS
                                                      PWR

GOODRICH L.M.,"CHARTER OF THE UNITED NATIONS: CONSTN   C46
COMMENTARY AND DOCUMENTS." EX/STRUC ADMIN...INT/LAW   INT/ORG
CON/ANAL BIBLIOG 20 UN. PAGE 41 B0826   DIPLOM

CONOVER H.F.,NON-SELF-GOVERNING AREAS. BELGIUM   BIBLIOG/A   B47
FRANCE ITALY UK WOR+45 CULTURE ECO/UNDEV INT/ORG   COLONIAL
LOC/G NAT/G ECO/TAC INT/TRADE ADMIN HEALTH...SOC   DIPLOM
UN. PAGE 23 B0465

UN DEPARTMENT PUBLIC INF,SELECTED BIBLIOGRAPHY OF   BIBLIOG   N49
THE SPECIALIZED AGENCIES RELATED TO THE UNITED   INT/ORG
NATIONS (PAMPHLET). USA+45 ROLE 20 UN. PAGE 106   EX/STRUC
B2146   ADMIN

US SENATE COMM. GOVT. OPER.,"REVISION OF THE UN   INT/ORG   L50
CHARTER." FUT USA+45 WOR+45 CONSTN ECO/DEV   LEGIS
ECO/UNDEV NAT/G DELIB/GP ACT/RES CREATE PLAN EXEC   PEACE
ROUTINE CHOOSE ALL/VALS...POLICY CONCPT CONGRESS UN
TOT/POP 20 COLD/WAR. PAGE 111 B2235

DE GRAZIA A.,POLITICAL ORGANIZATION. CONSTN LOC/G   FEDERAL   B52
MUNIC NAT/G CHIEF LEGIS TOP/EX ADJUD CT/SYS   LAW
PERS/REL...INT/LAW MYTH UN. PAGE 27 B0553   ADMIN

VANDENBOSCH A.,THE UN: BACKGROUND, ORGANIZATION,   DELIB/GP   B52
FUNCTIONS, ACTIVITIES. WOR+45 LAW CONSTN STRUCT   TIME/SEQ
INT/ORG CONSULT BAL/PWR EDU/PROP EXEC ALL/VALS   PEACE
...POLICY CONCPT UN 20. PAGE 112 B2254

SCHWEBEL S.M.,"THE SECRETARY-GENERAL OF THE UN."   INT/ORG   S52
FUT INTELL CONSULT DELIB/GP ADMIN PEACE ATTIT   TOP/EX
...JURID MGT CONCPT TREND UN CONGRESS 20. PAGE 95
B1915

MACK R.T.,RAISING THE WORLDS STANDARD OF LIVING.   WOR+45   B53
IRAN INT/ORG VOL/ASSN EX/STRUC ECO/TAC WEALTH...MGT   FOR/AID
METH/CNCPT STAT CONT/OBS INT TOT/POP VAL/FREE 20   INT/TRADE
UN. PAGE 67 B1363

CORY R.H. JR.,"FORGING A PUBLIC INFORMATION POLICY   INT/ORG   S53
FOR THE UNITED NATIONS." FUT WOR+45 SOCIETY ADMIN   EDU/PROP
PEACE ATTIT PERSON SKILL...CONCPT 20 UN. PAGE 24   BAL/PWR
B0486

MANGONE G.,A SHORT HISTORY OF INTERNATIONAL   INT/ORG   B54
ORGANIZATION. MOD/EUR USA+45 USA-45 WOR+45 WOR-45   INT/LAW
LAW LEGIS CREATE LEGIT ROUTINE RIGID/FLEX PWR
...JURID CONCPT OBS TIME/SEQ STERTYP GEN/LAWS UN
TOT/POP VAL/FREE 18/20. PAGE 69 B1389

US SENATE COMM ON FOREIGN REL,REVIEW OF THE UNITED   BIBLIOG   B54
NATIONS CHARTER: A COLLECTION OF DOCUMENTS. LEGIS   CONSTN

DIPLOM ADMIN ARMS/CONT WAR REPRESENT SOVEREIGN   INT/ORG
...INT/LAW 20 UN. PAGE 110 B2220   DEBATE
                                                                  S54
WOLFERS A.,"COLLECTIVE SECURITY AND THE WAR IN   ACT/RES
KOREA." ASIA KOREA USA+45 INT/ORG DIPLOM ROUTINE   LEGIT
...GEN/LAWS UN COLD/WAR 20. PAGE 117 B2370

CHOWDHURI R.N.,INTERNATIONAL MANDATES AND   DELIB/GP   B55
TRUSTEESHIP SYSTEMS. WOR+45 STRUCT ECO/UNDEV   PLAN
INT/ORG LEGIS DOMIN EDU/PROP LEGIT ADJUD EXEC PWR   SOVEREIGN
...CONCPT TIME/SEQ UN 20. PAGE 21 B0427

UN ECONOMIC AND SOCIAL COUNCIL,BIBLIOGRAPHY OF   BIBLIOG/A   B55
PUBLICATIONS OF THE UN AND SPECIALIZED AGENCIES IN   SOC/WK
THE SOCIAL WELFARE FIELD, 1946-1952. WOR+45 FAM   ADMIN
INT/ORG MUNIC ACT/RES PLAN PROB/SOLV EDU/PROP AGE/C   WEALTH
AGE/Y HABITAT...HEAL UN. PAGE 106 B2148

UN HEADQUARTERS LIBRARY,BIBLIOGRAPHIE DE LA CHARTE   BIBLIOG/A   B55
DES NATIONS UNIES. CHINA/COM KOREA WOR+45 VOL/ASSN   INT/ORG
CONFER ADMIN COERCE PEACE ATTIT ORD/FREE SOVEREIGN   DIPLOM
...INT/LAW 20 UNESCO UN. PAGE 106 B2149

SOHN L.B.,BASIC DOCUMENTS OF THE UNITED NATIONS.   DELIB/GP   B56
WOR+45 LAW INT/ORG LEGIT EXEC ROUTINE CHOOSE PWR   CONSTN
...JURID CONCPT GEN/LAWS ANTHOL UN TOT/POP OAS FAO
ILO 20. PAGE 99 B1993

SOHN L.B.,CASES ON UNITED NATIONS LAW. STRUCT   INT/ORG   B56
DELIB/GP WAR PEACE ORD/FREE...DECISION ANTHOL 20   INT/LAW
UN. PAGE 99 B1994   ADMIN
                                                      ADJUD

UNITED NATIONS,BIBLIOGRAPHY ON INDUSTRIALIZATION IN   BIBLIOG   B56
UNDER-DEVELOPED COUNTRIES. WOR+45 R+D INT/ORG NAT/G   ECO/UNDEV
FOR/AID ADMIN LEAD 20 UN. PAGE 107 B2161   INDUS
                                                      TEC/DEV
ASHER R.E.,THE UNITED NATIONS AND THE PROMOTION OF   INT/ORG   B57
THE GENERAL WELFARE. WOR+45 WOR-45 ECO/UNDEV   CONSULT
EX/STRUC ACT/RES PLAN EDU/PROP ROUTINE HEALTH...HUM
CONCPT CHARTS UNESCO UN ILO 20. PAGE 7 B0139

BEAL J.R.,JOHN FOSTER DULLES, A BIOGRAPHY. USA+45   BIOG   B57
USSR WOR+45 CONSTN INT/ORG NAT/G EX/STRUC LEGIT   DIPLOM
ADMIN NUC/PWR DISPL PERSON ORD/FREE PWR SKILL
...POLICY PSY OBS RECORD COLD/WAR UN 20 DULLES/JF.
PAGE 10 B0200

HOLCOMBE A.N.,STRENGTHENING THE UNITED NATIONS.   INT/ORG   B57
USA+45 ACT/RES CREATE PLAN EDU/PROP ATTIT PERCEPT   ROUTINE
PWR...METH/CNCPT CONT/OBS RECORD UN COLD/WAR 20.
PAGE 51 B1032

MURRAY J.N.,THE UNITED NATIONS TRUSTEESHIP SYSTEM.   INT/ORG   B57
AFR WOR+45 CONSTN CONSULT LEGIS EDU/PROP LEGIT EXEC   DELIB/GP
ROUTINE...INT TIME/SEQ SOMALI UN 20. PAGE 77 B1547

HAAS E.B.,"REGIONAL INTEGRATION AND NATIONAL   INT/ORG   L57
POLICY." WOR+45 VOL/ASSN DELIB/GP EX/STRUC ECO/TAC   ORD/FREE
DOMIN EDU/PROP LEGIT COERCE ATTIT PERCEPT KNOWL   REGION
...TIME/SEQ COLD/WAR 20 UN. PAGE 45 B0908

ISLAM R.,INTERNATIONAL ECONOMIC COOPERATION AND THE   INT/ORG   B58
UNITED NATIONS. FINAN PLAN EXEC TASK WAR PEACE   DIPLOM
...SOC METH/CNCPT 20 UN LEAGUE/NAT. PAGE 55 B1105   ADMIN

CHINA INSTITUTE OF AMERICA,CHINA AND THE UNITED   ASIA   B59
NATIONS. CHINA/COM FUT STRUCT EDU/PROP LEGIT ADMIN   INT/ORG
ATTIT KNOWL ORD/FREE PWR...OBS RECORD STAND/INT
TIME/SEQ UN LEAGUE/NAT UNESCO 20. PAGE 21 B0425

GOODRICH L.,THE UNITED NATIONS. WOR+45 CONSTN   INT/ORG   B59
STRUCT ACT/RES LEGIT COERCE KNOWL ORD/FREE PWR   ROUTINE
...GEN/LAWS UN 20. PAGE 41 B0825

GORDENKER L.,THE UNITED NATIONS AND THE PEACEFUL   DELIB/GP   B59
UNIFICATION OF KOREA. ASIA LAW LOC/G CONSULT   KOREA
ACT/RES DIPLOM DOMIN LEGIT ADJUD ADMIN ORD/FREE   INT/ORG
SOVEREIGN...INT GEN/METH UN COLD/WAR 20. PAGE 41
B0829

MACIVER R.M.,THE NATIONS AND THE UN. WOR+45 NAT/G   INT/ORG   B59
CONSULT ADJUD ADMIN ALL/VALS...CONCPT DEEP/QU UN   ATTIT
TOT/POP UNESCO 20. PAGE 67 B1362   DIPLOM

BAILEY S.D.,"THE FUTURE COMPOSITION OF THE   INT/ORG   S59
TRUSTEESHIP COUNCIL." FUT WOR+45 CONSTN VOL/ASSN   NAT/LISM
ADMIN ATTIT PWR...OBS TREND CON/ANAL VAL/FREE UN   SOVEREIGN
20. PAGE 8 B0161

ASPREMONT-LYNDEN H.,RAPPORT SUR L'ADMINISTRATION   AFR   B60
BELGE DU RUANDA-URUNDI PENDANT L'ANNEE 1959.   COLONIAL
BELGIUM RWANDA AGRI INDUS DIPLOM ECO/TAC INT/TRADE   ECO/UNDEV
DOMIN ADMIN RACE/REL...GEOG CENSUS 20 UN. PAGE 7   INT/ORG
B0143

B60

HYDE L.K.G.,THE US AND THE UN. WOR+45 STRUCT
ECO/DEV ECO/UNDEV NAT/G ACT/RES PLAN DIPLOM
EDU/PROP ADMIN ALL/VALS...CONCPT TIME/SEQ GEN/LAWS
UN VAL/FREE 20. PAGE 53 B1070

USA+45
INT/ORG
FOR/AID

B60

MUNRO L.,UNITED NATIONS, HOPE FOR A DIVIDED WORLD.
FUT WOR+45 CONSTN DELIB/GP CREATE TEC/DEV DIPLOM
EDU/PROP LEGIT PEACE ATTIT HEALTH ORD/FREE PWR
...CONCPT TREND UN VAL/FREE 20. PAGE 76 B1540

INT/ORG
ROUTINE

B60

RAO V.K.R.,INTERNATIONAL AID FOR ECONOMIC
DEVELOPMENT - POSSIBILITIES AND LIMITATIONS. FINAN
PLAN TEC/DEV ADMIN TASK EFFICIENCY...POLICY SOC
METH/CNCPT CHARTS 20 UN. PAGE 86 B1734

FOR/AID
DIPLOM
INT/ORG
ECO/UNDEV

S60

BOGARDUS E.S.,"THE SOCIOLOGY OF A STRUCTURED
PEACE." FUT SOCIETY CREATE DIPLOM EDU/PROP ADJUD
ROUTINE ATTIT RIGID/FLEX KNOWL ORD/FREE RESPECT
...POLICY INT/LAW JURID NEW/IDEA SELF/OBS TOT/POP
20 UN. PAGE 13 B0264

INT/ORG
SOC
NAT/LISM
PEACE

S60

NELSON R.H.,"LEGISLATIVE PARTICIPATION IN THE
TREATY AND AGREEMENT MAKING PROCESS." CONSTN
POL/PAR PLAN EXEC PWR FAO UN CONGRESS. PAGE 78
B1569

LEGIS
PEACE
DECISION
DIPLOM

S60

RIESELBACH Z.N.,"QUANTITATIVE TECHNIQUES FOR
STUDYING VOTING BEHAVIOR IN THE UNITED NATIONS
GENERAL ASSEMBLY." FUT S/ASIA USA+45 INT/ORG
BAL/PWR DIPLOM ECO/TAC FOR/AID ADMIN PWR...POLICY
METH/CNCPT METH UN 20. PAGE 88 B1783

QUANT
CHOOSE

S60

SCHACHTER O.,"THE ENFORCEMENT OF INTERNATIONAL
JUDICIAL AND ARBITRAL DECISIONS." WOR+45 NAT/G
ECO/TAC DOMIN LEGIT ROUTINE COERCE ATTIT DRIVE
ALL/VALS PWR...METH/CNCPT TREND TOT/POP 20 UN.
PAGE 93 B1878

INT/ORG
ADJUD
INT/LAW

B61

BAINS J.S.,STUDIES IN POLITICAL SCIENCE. INDIA
WOR+45 WOR-45 CONSTN BAL/PWR ADJUD ADMIN PARL/PROC
SOVEREIGN...SOC METH/COMP ANTHOL 17/20 UN. PAGE 8
B0165

DIPLOM
INT/LAW
NAT/G

B61

BULLIS H.A.,MANIFESTO FOR AMERICANS. USA+45 AGRI
LABOR NAT/G NEIGH FOR/AID INT/TRADE TAX EDU/PROP
CHOOSE...POLICY MGT 20 UN UNESCO. PAGE 17 B0342

ECO/TAC
SOCIETY
INDUS
CAP/ISM

B61

HASAN H.S.,PAKISTAN AND THE UN. ISLAM WOR+45
ECO/DEV ECO/UNDEV NAT/G TOP/EX ECO/TAC FOR/AID
EDU/PROP ADMIN DRIVE PERCEPT...OBS TIME/SEQ UN 20.
PAGE 48 B0965

INT/ORG
ATTIT
PAKISTAN

B61

KERTESZ S.D.,AMERICAN DIPLOMACY IN A NEW ERA. COM
S/ASIA UK USA+45 FORCES PROB/SOLV BAL/PWR ECO/TAC
ADMIN COLONIAL WAR PEACE ORD/FREE 20 NATO CONGRESS
UN COLD/WAR. PAGE 59 B1199

ANTHOL
DIPLOM
TREND

B61

SHAPP W.R.,FIELD ADMINISTRATION IN THE UNITED
NATIONS SYSTEM. FINAN PROB/SOLV INSPECT DIPLOM EXEC
REGION ROUTINE EFFICIENCY ROLE...INT CHARTS 20 UN.
PAGE 96 B1933

INT/ORG
ADMIN
GP/REL
FOR/AID

B61

SHARP W.R.,FIELD ADMINISTRATION IN THE UNITED
NATION SYSTEM: THE CONDUCT OF INTERNATIONAL
ECONOMIC AND SOCIAL PROGRAMS. FUT WOR+45 CONSTN
SOCIETY ECO/UNDEV R+D DELIB/GP ACT/RES PLAN TEC/DEV
EDU/PROP EXEC ROUTINE HEALTH WEALTH...HUM CONCPT
CHARTS METH ILO UNESCO VAL/FREE UN 20. PAGE 96
B1939

INT/ORG
CONSULT

B61

SINGER J.D.,FINANCING INTERNATIONAL ORGANIZATION:
THE UNITED NATIONS BUDGET PROCESS. WOR+45 FINAN
ACT/RES CREATE PLAN BUDGET ECO/TAC ADMIN ROUTINE
ATTIT KNOWL...DECISION METH/CNCPT TIME/SEQ UN 20.
PAGE 97 B1964

INT/ORG
MGT

S61

ALGER C.F.,"NON-RESOLUTION CONSEQUENCES OF THE
UNITED NATIONS AND THEIR EFFECT ON INTERNATIONAL
CONFLICT." WOR+45 CONSTN ECO/DEV NAT/G CONSULT
DELIB/GP TOP/EX ACT/RES PLAN DIPLOM EDU/PROP
ROUTINE ATTIT ALL/VALS...INT/LAW TOT/POP UN 20.
PAGE 4 B0075

INT/ORG
DRIVE
BAL/PWR

S61

JACKSON E.,"CONSTITUTIONAL DEVELOPMENTS OF THE
UNITED NATIONS: THE GROWTH OF ITS EXECUTIVE
CAPACITY." FUT WOR+45 CONSTN STRUCT ACT/RES PLAN
ALL/VALS...NEW/IDEA OBS COLD/WAR UN 20. PAGE 55
B1106

INT/ORG
EXEC

S61

MILLER E.,"LEGAL ASPECTS OF UN ACTION IN THE
CONGO." AFR CULTURE ADMIN PEACE DRIVE RIGID/FLEX
ORD/FREE...WELF/ST JURID OBS UN CONGO 20. PAGE 73
B1480

INT/ORG
LEGIT

S61

VIRALLY M.,"VERS UNE REFORME DU SECRETARIAT DES
NATIONS UNIES." FUT WOR+45 CONSTN ECO/DEV TOP/EX
BAL/PWR ADMIN ALL/VALS...CONCPT BIOG UN VAL/FREE
20. PAGE 112 B2264

INT/ORG
INTELL
DIPLOM

B62

BAILEY S.D.,THE SECRETARIAT OF THE UNITED NATIONS.
FUT WOR+45 DELIB/GP PLAN BAL/PWR DOMIN EDU/PROP
ADMIN PEACE ATTIT PWR...DECISION CONCPT TREND
CON/ANAL CHARTS UN VAL/FREE COLD/WAR 20. PAGE 8
B0162

INT/ORG
EXEC
DIPLOM

B62

BRIMMER B.,A GUIDE TO THE USE OF UNITED NATIONS
DOCUMENTS. WOR+45 ECO/UNDEV AGRI EX/STRUC FORCES
PROB/SOLV ADMIN WAR PEACE WEALTH...POLICY UN.
PAGE 15 B0310

BIBLIOG/A
INT/ORG
DIPLOM

B62

HADWEN J.G.,HOW UNITED NATIONS DECISIONS ARE MADE.
WOR+45 LAW EDU/PROP LEGIT ADMIN PWR...DECISION
SELF/OBS GEN/LAWS UN 20. PAGE 45 B0912

INT/ORG
ROUTINE

B62

LAWSON R.,INTERNATIONAL REGIONAL ORGANIZATIONS.
WOR+45 NAT/G VOL/ASSN CONSULT LEGIS EDU/PROP LEGIT
ADMIN EXEC ROUTINE HEALTH PWR WEALTH...JURID EEC
COLD/WAR 20 UN. PAGE 63 B1277

INT/ORG
DELIB/GP
REGION

B62

NICHOLAS H.G.,THE UNITED NATIONS AS A POLITICAL
INSTITUTION. WOR+45 CONSTN EX/STRUC ACT/RES LEGIT
PERCEPT KNOWL PWR...CONCPT TIME/SEQ CON/ANAL
ORG/CHARTS UN 20. PAGE 78 B1580

INT/ORG
ROUTINE

B62

UNECA LIBRARY,NEW ACQUISITIONS IN THE UNECA
LIBRARY. LAW NAT/G PLAN PROB/SOLV TEC/DEV ADMIN
REGION...GEOG SOC 20 UN. PAGE 106 B2152

BIBLIOG
AFR
ECO/UNDEV
INT/ORG

L62

BAILEY S.D.,"THE TROIKA AND THE FUTURE OF THE UN."
CONSTN CREATE LEGIT EXEC CHOOSE ORD/FREE PWR
...CONCPT NEW/IDEA UN COLD/WAR 20. PAGE 8 B0163

FUT
INT/ORG
USSR

L62

MALINOWSKI W.R.,"CENTRALIZATION AND DE-
CENTRALIZATION IN THE UNITED NATIONS' ECONOMIC AND
SOCIAL ACTIVITIES." WOR+45 CONSTN ECO/UNDEV INT/ORG
VOL/ASSN DELIB/GP ECO/TAC EDU/PROP ADMIN RIGID/FLEX
...OBS CHARTS UNESCO UN EEC OAS OEEC 20. PAGE 69
B1385

CREATE
GEN/LAWS

S62

JACOBSON H.K.,"THE UNITED NATIONS AND COLONIALISM:
A TENTATIVE APPRAISAL." AFR FUT S/ASIA USA+45 USSR
WOR+45 NAT/G DELIB/GP PLAN DIPLOM ECO/TAC DOMIN
ADMIN ROUTINE COERCE ATTIT RIGID/FLEX ORD/FREE PWR
...OBS STERTYP 20. PAGE 55 B1115

INT/ORG
CONCPT
COLONIAL

B63

BOWETT D.W.,THE LAW OF INTERNATIONAL INSTITUTIONS.
WOR+45 WOR-45 CONSTN DELIB/GP EX/STRUC JUDGE
EDU/PROP LEGIT CT/SYS EXEC ROUTINE RIGID/FLEX
ORD/FREE PWR...JURID CONCPT ORG/CHARTS GEN/METH
LEAGUE/NAT OAS OEEC 20 UN. PAGE 14 B0286

INT/ORG
ADJUD
DIPLOM

B63

LANGROD G.,THE INTERNATIONAL CIVIL SERVICE: ITS
ORIGINS, ITS NATURE, ITS EVALUATION. FUT WOR+45
WOR-45 DELIB/GP ACT/RES DOMIN LEGIT ATTIT
RIGID/FLEX SUPEGO ALL/VALS...MGT CONCPT STAT
TIME/SEQ ILO LEAGUE/NAT VAL/FREE 20 UN. PAGE 62
B1259

INT/ORG
ADMIN

B63

STEVENSON A.E.,LOOKING OUTWARD: YEARS OF CRISIS AT
THE UNITED NATIONS. COM CUBA USA+45 WOR+45 SOCIETY
NAT/G EX/STRUC ACT/RES LEGIT COLONIAL ATTIT PERSON
SUPEGO ALL/VALS...POLICY HUM UN COLD/WAR CONGO 20.
PAGE 100 B2034

INT/ORG
CONCPT
ARMS/CONT

B63

UN SECRETARY GENERAL,PLANNING FOR ECONOMIC
DEVELOPMENT. ECO/UNDEV FINAN BUDGET INT/TRADE
TARIFFS TAX ADMIN 20 UN. PAGE 106 B2151

PLAN
ECO/TAC
MGT
NAT/COMP

B63

VAN SLYCK P.,PEACE: THE CONTROL OF NATIONAL POWER.
CUBA WOR+45 FINAN NAT/G FORCES PROB/SOLV TEC/DEV
BAL/PWR ADMIN CONTROL ORD/FREE...POLICY INT/LAW UN
COLD/WAR TREATY. PAGE 112 B2253

ARMS/CONT
PEACE
INT/ORG
DIPLOM

S63

BECHHOEFER B.G.,"UNITED NATIONS PROCEDURES IN CASE
OF VIOLATIONS OF DISARMAMENT AGREEMENTS." COM
USA+45 USSR LAW CONSTN NAT/G EX/STRUC FORCES LEGIS
BAL/PWR EDU/PROP CT/SYS ARMS/CONT ORD/FREE PWR
...POLICY STERTYP UN VAL/FREE 20. PAGE 10 B0204

INT/ORG
DELIB/GP

S63

DAVEE R.,"POUR UN FONDS DE DEVELOPPEMENT SOCIAL."
FUT WOR+45 INTELL SOCIETY ECO/DEV FINAN TEC/DEV
ROUTINE WEALTH...TREND TOT/POP VAL/FREE UN 20.
PAGE 26 B0532

INT/ORG
SOC
FOR/AID

S63

MANGONE G.,"THE UNITED NATIONS AND UNITED STATES
FOREIGN POLICY." USA+45 WOR+45 ECO/UNDEV NAT/G
DIPLOM LEGIT ROUTINE ATTIT DRIVE...TIME/SEQ UN

INT/ORG
ECO/TAC
FOR/AID

COLD/WAR 20. PAGE 69 B1390

B64
KAHNG T.J.,LAW, POLITICS, AND THE SECURITY COUNCIL* DELIB/GP
AN INQUIRY INTO THE HANDLING OF LEGAL QUESTIONS. ADJUD
LAW CONSTN NAT/G ACT/RES OP/RES CT/SYS TASK PWR ROUTINE
...INT/LAW BIBLIOG UN. PAGE 57 B1160

B64
PLISCHKE E.,SYSTEMS OF INTEGRATING THE INT/ORG
INTERNATIONAL COMMUNITY. WOR+45 NAT/G VOL/ASSN EX/STRUC
ECO/TAC LEGIT PWR WEALTH...TIME/SEQ ANTHOL UN REGION
TOT/POP 20. PAGE 83 B1684

B64
RUSSELL R.B.,UNITED NATIONS EXPERIENCE WITH FORCES
MILITARY FORCES: POLITICAL AND LEGAL ASPECTS. AFR DIPLOM
KOREA WOR+45 LEGIS PROB/SOLV ADMIN CONTROL SANCTION
EFFICIENCY PEACE...POLICY INT/LAW BIBLIOG UN. ORD/FREE
PAGE 92 B1857

B64
SCHECHTER A.H.,INTERPRETATION OF AMBIGUOUS INT/LAW
DOCUMENTS BY INTERNATIONAL ADMINISTRATIVE DIPLOM
TRIBUNALS. WOR+45 EX/STRUC INT/TRADE CT/SYS INT/ORG
SOVEREIGN 20 UN ILO EURCT/JUST. PAGE 93 B1884 ADJUD

B64
UN PUB. INFORM. ORGAN.,EVERY MAN'S UNITED NATIONS. INT/ORG
UNIV WOR+45 CONSTN CULTURE SOCIETY ECO/DEV ROUTINE
ECO/UNDEV NAT/G ACT/RES PLAN ECO/TAC INT/TRADE
EDU/PROP LEGIT PEACE ATTIT ALL/VALS...POLICY HUM
INT/LAW CONCPT CHARTS UN TOT/POP 20. PAGE 106 B2150

B64
VECCHIO G.D.,L'ETAT ET LE DROIT. ITALY CONSTN NAT/G
EX/STRUC LEGIS DIPLOM CT/SYS...JURID 20 UN. SOVEREIGN
PAGE 112 B2256 CONCPT
INT/LAW

B64
WAINHOUSE D.W.,REMNANTS OF EMPIRE: THE UNITED INT/ORG
NATIONS AND THE END OF COLONIALISM. FUT PORTUGAL TREND
WOR+45 NAT/G CONSULT DOMIN LEGIT ADMIN ROUTINE COLONIAL
ATTIT ORD/FREE...POLICY JURID RECORD INT TIME/SEQ
UN CMN/WLTH 20. PAGE 113 B2275

L64
WORLD PEACE FOUNDATION.,"INTERNATIONAL INT/ORG
ORGANIZATIONS: SUMMARY OF ACTIVITIES." INDIA ROUTINE
PAKISTAN TURKEY WOR+45 CONSTN CONSULT EX/STRUC
ECO/TAC EDU/PROP LEGIT ORD/FREE...JURID SOC UN 20
CYPRESS. PAGE 118 B2375

S64
CARNEGIE ENDOWMENT INT. PEACE.,"ADMINISTRATION AND INT/ORG
BUDGET (ISSUES BEFORE THE NINETEENTH GENERAL ADMIN
ASSEMBLY)." WOR+45 FINAN BUDGET ECO/TAC ROUTINE
COST...STAT RECORD UN. PAGE 19 B0383

S64
HOSCH L.G.,"PUBLIC ADMINISTRATION ON THE INT/ORG
INTERNATIONAL FRONTIER." WOR+45 R+D NAT/G EDU/PROP MGT
EXEC KNOWL ORD/FREE VAL/FREE 20 UN. PAGE 52 B1046

S64
KHAN M.Z.,"THE PRESIDENT OF THE GENERAL ASSEMBLY." INT/ORG
WOR+45 CONSTN DELIB/GP EDU/PROP LEGIT ROUTINE PWR TOP/EX
RESPECT SKILL...DECISION SOC BIOG TREND UN 20.
PAGE 59 B1202

S64
SCHWELB E.,"OPERATION OF THE EUROPEAN CONVENTION ON INT/ORG
HUMAN RIGHTS." EUR+WWI LAW SOCIETY CREATE EDU/PROP MORAL
ADJUD ADMIN PEACE ATTIT ORD/FREE PWR...POLICY
INT/LAW CONCPT OBS GEN/LAWS UN VAL/FREE ILO 20
ECHR. PAGE 95 B1916

B65
FORGAC A.A.,NEW DIPLOMACY AND THE UNITED NATIONS. DIPLOM
FRANCE GERMANY UK USSR INT/ORG DELIB/GP EX/STRUC ETIQUET
PEACE...INT/LAW CONCPT UN. PAGE 36 B0740 NAT/G

B65
GOTLIEB A.,DISARMAMENT AND INTERNATIONAL LAW* A INT/LAW
STUDY OF THE ROLE OF LAW IN THE DISARMAMENT INT/ORG
PROCESS. USA+45 USSR PROB/SOLV CONFER ADMIN ROUTINE ARMS/CONT
NUC/PWR ORD/FREE SOVEREIGN UN TREATY. PAGE 42 B0841 IDEA/COMP

B65
MACDONALD R.W.,THE LEAGUE OF ARAB STATES: A STUDY ISLAM
IN THE DYNAMICS OF REGIONAL ORGANIZATION. ISRAEL REGION
UAR USSR FINAN INT/ORG DELIB/GP ECO/TAC AGREE DIPLOM
NEUTRAL ORD/FREE PWR...DECISION BIBLIOG 20 TREATY ADMIN
UN. PAGE 67 B1358

B65
PURCELL V.,THE MEMOIRS OF A MALAYAN OFFICIAL. BIOG
MALAYSIA UK ECO/UNDEV INDUS LABOR EDU/PROP COLONIAL ADMIN
CT/SYS WAR NAT/LISM TOTALISM ORD/FREE SOVEREIGN 20 JURID
UN CIVIL/SERV. PAGE 85 B1721 FORCES

B65
SPEECKAERT G.P.,SELECT BIBLIOGRAPHY ON BIBLIOG
INTERNATIONAL ORGANIZATION, 1885-1964. WOR+45 INT/ORG
WOR-45 EX/STRUC DIPLOM ADMIN REGION 19/20 UN. GEN/LAWS
PAGE 99 B2004 STRATA

B65
VONGLAHN G.,LAW AMONG NATIONS: AN INTRODUCTION TO CONSTN
PUBLIC INTERNATIONAL LAW. UNIV WOR+45 LAW INT/ORG JURID
NAT/G LEGIT EXEC RIGID/FLEX...CONCPT TIME/SEQ INT/LAW
GEN/LAWS UN TOT/POP 20. PAGE 112 B2267

B66
ALEXANDER Y.,INTERNATIONAL TECHNICAL ASSISTANCE ECO/TAC
EXPERTS* A CASE STUDY OF THE U.N. EXPERIENCE. INT/ORG
ECO/UNDEV CONSULT EX/STRUC CREATE PLAN DIPLOM ADMIN
FOR/AID TASK EFFICIENCY...ORG/CHARTS UN. PAGE 4 MGT
B0074

B66
EPSTEIN F.T.,THE AMERICAN BIBLIOGRAPHY OF RUSSIAN BIBLIOG
AND EAST EUROPEAN STUDIES FOR 1964. USSR LOC/G COM
NAT/G POL/PAR FORCES ADMIN ARMS/CONT...JURID CONCPT MARXISM
20 UN. PAGE 33 B0678 DIPLOM

B66
KIRDAR U.,THE STRUCTURE OF UNITED NATIONS ECONOMIC INT/ORG
AID TO UNDERDEVELOPED COUNTRIES. AGRI FINAN INDUS FOR/AID
NAT/G EX/STRUC PLAN GIVE TASK...POLICY 20 UN. ECO/UNDEV
PAGE 60 B1213 ADMIN

B66
MANGONE G.J.,UN ADMINISTRATION OF ECONOMIC AND ADMIN
AOCIAL PROGRAMS. CONSULT BUDGET INT/TRADE REGION 20 MGT
UN. PAGE 69 B1391 ECO/TAC
DELIB/GP

B66
UN ECAFE,ADMINISTRATIVE ASPECTS OF FAMILY PLANNING PLAN
PROGRAMMES (PAMPHLET). ASIA THAILAND WOR+45 CENSUS
VOL/ASSN PROB/SOLV BUDGET FOR/AID EDU/PROP CONFER FAM
CONTROL GOV/REL TIME 20 UN BIRTH/CON. PAGE 106 ADMIN
B2147

B66
US LIBRARY OF CONGRESS,NIGERIA: A GUIDE TO OFFICIAL BIBLIOG
PUBLICATIONS. CAMEROON NIGERIA UK DIPLOM...POLICY ADMIN
19/20 UN LEAGUE/NAT. PAGE 109 B2207 NAT/G
COLONIAL

B66
US SENATE COMM ON FOREIGN REL,HEARINGS ON S 2859 FOR/AID
AND S 2861. USA+45 WOR+45 FORCES BUDGET CAP/ISM DIPLOM
ADMIN DETER WEAPON TOTALISM...NAT/COMP 20 UN ORD/FREE
CONGRESS. PAGE 110 B2221 ECO/UNDEV

B67
PLANO J.C.,FORGING WORLD ORDER: THE POLITICS OF INT/ORG
INTERNATIONAL ORGANIZATION. PROB/SOLV DIPLOM ADMIN
CONTROL CENTRAL RATIONAL ORD/FREE...INT/LAW CHARTS JURID
BIBLIOG 20 UN LEAGUE/NAT. PAGE 83 B1679

B67
UNITED NATIONS,UNITED NATIONS PUBLICATIONS: BIBLIOG/A
1945-1966. WOR+45 COM/IND DIST/IND FINAN TEC/DEV INT/ORG
ADMIN...POLICY INT/LAW MGT CHARTS 20 UN UNESCO. DIPLOM
PAGE 107 B2162 WRITING

B67
WATERS M.,THE UNITED NATIONS* INTERNATIONAL CONSTN
ORGANIZATION AND ADMINISTRATION. WOR+45 EX/STRUC INT/ORG
FORCES DIPLOM LEAD REGION ARMS/CONT REPRESENT ADMIN
INGP/REL ROLE...METH/COMP ANTHOL 20 UN LEAGUE/NAT. ADJUD
PAGE 114 B2301

S67
MERON T.,"THE UN'S 'COMMON SYSTEM' OF SALARY, ADMIN
ALLOWANCE, AND BENEFITS: CRITICAL APPR'SAL OF COORD EX/STRUC
IN PERSONNEL MATTERS." VOL/ASSN PAY EFFICIENCY INT/ORG
...CHARTS 20 UN. PAGE 73 B1470 BUDGET

S67
TACKABERRY R.B.,"ORGANIZING AND TRAINING PEACE- PEACE
KEEPING FORCES* THE CANADIAN VIEW." CANADA PLAN FORCES
DIPLOM CONFER ADJUD ADMIN CIVMIL/REL 20 UN. INT/ORG
PAGE 102 B2069 CONSULT

N67
US SENATE COMM ON FOREIGN REL,THE UNITED NATIONS AT INT/ORG
TWENTY-ONE (PAMPHLET). WOR+45 BUDGET ADMIN SENATE DIPLOM
UN. PAGE 110 B2223 PEACE

N67
US SENATE COMM ON FOREIGN REL,THE UNITED NATIONS INT/ORG
PEACEKEEPING DILEMMA (PAMPHLET). ISLAM WOR+45 DIPLOM
PROB/SOLV BUDGET ADMIN SENATE UN. PAGE 110 B2224 PEACE

UN DEPARTMENT PUBLIC INF B2146

UN ECAFE B2147

UN ECONOMIC AND SOCIAL COUNCIL B2148

UN HEADQUARTERS LIBRARY B2149

UN PUB. INFORM. ORGAN. B2150

UN SECRETARY GENERAL B2151

UN/ILC....UNITED NATIONS INTERNATIONAL LAW COMMISSION

UN/SEC/GEN....UNITED NATIONS SECRETARY GENERAL

UNCSAT....UNITED NATIONS CONFERENCE ON THE APPLICATION OF
    SCIENCE AND TECHNOLOGY FOR THE BENEFIT OF THE LESS
    DEVELOPED AREAS

UNCTAD....UNITED NATIONS COMMISSION ON TRADE, AID, AND
    DEVELOPMENT

UNDERDEVELOPED COUNTRIES....SEE ECO/UNDEV

UNDP....UNITED NATIONS DEVELOPMENT PROGRAM

UNECA LIBRARY B2152

UNEF....UNITED NATIONS EMERGENCY FORCE

L67

COHEN M.,"THE DEMISE OF UNEF." CONSTN DIPLOM ADMIN   INT/ORG
AGREE LEAD COERCE 20 UNEF U/THANT HAMMARSK/D.   FORCES
PAGE 22 B0445   PEACE
                                                     POLICY

UNESCO B2153,B2154,B2155,B2156,B2157

UNESCO....UNITED NATIONS EDUCATIONAL, SCIENTIFIC, AND
    CULTURAL ORGANIZATION; SEE ALSO UN, INT/ORG

N
UNESCO,INTERNATIONAL BIBLIOGRAPHY OF POLITICAL   BIBLIOG
SCIENCE (VOLUMES 1-8). WOR+45 LAW NAT/G EX/STRUC   CONCPT
LEGIS PROB/SOLV DIPLOM ADMIN GOV/REL 20 UNESCO.   IDEA/COMP
PAGE 107 B2153
                                                      N
WORLD PEACE FOUNDATION,DOCUMENTS OF INTERNATIONAL   BIBLIOG
ORGANIZATIONS: A SELECTED BIBLIOGRAPHY. WOR+45   DIPLOM
WOR-45 AGRI FINAN ACT/RES OP/RES INT/TRADE ADMIN   INT/ORG
...CON/ANAL 20 UN UNESCO LEAGUE/NAT. PAGE 118 B2374   REGION
                                                      B51
UNESCO,REPERTOIRE DES BIBLIOTHEQUES DE FRANCE: BIBLIOG
CENTRES ET SERVICES DE DOCUMENTATION DE FRANCE.   ADMIN
FRANCE INDUS ACADEM NAT/G INT/TRADE 20 UNESCO.
PAGE 107 B2154
                                                      B53
LARSEN K.,NATIONAL BIBLIOGRAPHIC SERVICES: THEIR   BIBLIOG/A
CREATION AND OPERATION. WOR+45 COM/IND CREATE PLAN   INT/ORG
DIPLOM PRESS ADMIN ROUTINE...MGT UNESCO. PAGE 62   WRITING
B1262
                                                      B55
UN HEADQUARTERS LIBRARY,BIBLIOQRAPHIE DE LA CHARTE   BIBLIOG/A
DES NATIONS UNIES. CHINA/COM KOREA WOR+45 VOL/ASSN   INT/ORG
CONFER ADMIN COERCE PEACE ATTIT ORD/FREE SOVEREIGN   DIPLOM
...INT/LAW 20 UNESCO UN. PAGE 106 B2149
                                                      B57
ASHER R.E.,THE UNITED NATIONS AND THE PROMOTION OF   INT/ORG
THE GENERAL WELFARE. WOR+45 WOR-45 ECO/UNDEV   CONSULT
EX/STRUC ACT/RES PLAN EDU/PROP ROUTINE HEALTH...HUM
CONCPT CHARTS UNESCO UN ILO 20. PAGE 7 B0139
                                                      B58
UNESCO,UNESCO PUBLICATIONS: CHECK LIST (2ND REV.   BIBLIOG
ED.). WOR+45 DIPLOM FOR/AID WEALTH...POLICY SOC   INT/ORG
UNESCO. PAGE 107 B2156   ECO/UNDEV
                                                      ADMIN
                                                      B59
CHINA INSTITUTE OF AMERICA.,CHINA AND THE UNITED   ASIA
NATIONS. CHINA/COM FUT STRUCT EDU/PROP LEGIT ADMIN   INT/ORG
ATTIT KNOWL ORD/FREE PWR...OBS RECORD STAND/INT
TIME/SEQ UN LEAGUE/NAT UNESCO 20. PAGE 21 B0425
                                                      B59
MACIVER R.M.,THE NATIONS AND THE UN. WOR+45 NAT/G   INT/ORG
CONSULT ADJUD ADMIN ALL/VALS...CONCPT DEEP/QU UN   ATTIT
TOT/POP UNESCO 20. PAGE 67 B1362   DIPLOM
                                                      S59
LENGYEL P.,"SOME TRENDS IN THE INTERNATIONAL CIVIL   ADMIN
SERVICE." FUT WOR+45 INT/ORG CONSULT ATTIT...MGT   EXEC
OBS TREND CON/ANAL LEAGUE/NAT UNESCO 20. PAGE 64
B1291
                                                      S59
PADELFORD N.J.,"REGIONAL COOPERATION IN THE SOUTH   INT/ORG
PACIFIC: THE SOUTH PACIFIC COMMISSION." FUT   ADMIN
NEW/ZEALND UK WOR+45 CULTURE ECO/UNDEV LOC/G
VOL/ASSN...OBS CON/ANAL UNESCO VAL/FREE AUSTRAL 20.
PAGE 80 B1622
                                                      B61
BULLIS H.A.,MANIFESTO FOR AMERICANS. USA+45 AGRI   ECO/TAC
LABOR NAT/G NEIGH FOR/AID INT/TRADE TAX EDU/PROP   SOCIETY
CHOOSE...POLICY MGT 20 UN UNESCO. PAGE 17 B0342   INDUS
                                                      CAP/ISM
                                                      B61
SHARP W.R.,FIELD ADMINISTRATION IN THE UNITED   INT/ORG
NATION SYSTEM: THE CONDUCT OF INTERNATIONAL   CONSULT
ECONOMIC AND SOCIAL PROGRAMS. FUT WOR+45 CONSTN
SOCIETY ECO/UNDEV R+D DELIB/GP ACT/RES PLAN TEC/DEV
EDU/PROP EXEC ROUTINE HEALTH WEALTH...HUM CONCPT
CHARTS METH ILO UNESCO VAL/FREE UN 20. PAGE 96
B1939
                                                      L62
MALINOWSKI W.R.,"CENTRALIZATION AND DE-   CREATE
CENTRALIZATION IN THE UNITED NATIONS' ECONOMIC AND   GEN/LAWS
SOCIAL ACTIVITIES." WOR+45 CONSTN ECO/UNDEV INT/ORG
VOL/ASSN DELIB/GP ECO/TAC EDU/PROP ADMIN RIGID/FLEX
...OBS CHARTS UNESCO UN EEC OAS OEEC 20. PAGE 69
B1385
                                                      B63
COMISION DE HISTORIO,GUIA DE LOS DOCUMENTOS   BIBLIOG
MICROFOTOGRAFIADOS POR LA UNIDAD MOVIL DE LA   NAT/G
UNESCO. SOCIETY ECO/UNDEV INT/ORG ADMIN...SOC 20   L/A+17C

UNESCO. PAGE 22 B0456   DIPLOM
                                                      S63
EVANS L.H.,"SOME MANAGEMENT PROBLEMS OF UNESCO."   INT/ORG
WOR+45 EX/STRUC LEGIS PWR UNESCO VAL/FREE 20.   MGT
PAGE 34 B0688
                                                      B65
UNESCO,INTERNATIONAL ORGANIZATIONS IN THE SOCIAL   INT/ORG
SCIENCES(REV. ED.). LAW ADMIN ATTIT...CRIMLGY GEOG   R+D
INT/LAW PSY SOC STAT 20 UNESCO. PAGE 107 B2157   PROF/ORG
                                                      ACT/RES
                                                      B67
UNITED NATIONS,UNITED NATIONS PUBLICATIONS: BIBLIOG/A
1945-1966. WOR+45 COM/IND DIST/IND FINAN TEC/DEV   INT/ORG
ADMIN...POLICY INT/LAW MGT CHARTS 20 UN UNESCO.   DIPLOM
PAGE 107 B2162   WRITING
                                                      S67
SATHYAMURTHY T.V.,"TWENTY YEARS OF UNESCO: AN   ADMIN
INTERPRETATION." SOCIETY PROB/SOLV LEAD PEACE   CONSTN
UNESCO. PAGE 92 B1870   INT/ORG
                                                      TIME/SEQ

UNIDO....UNITED NATIONS INDUSTRIAL DEVELOPMENT ORGANIZATION

UNIFICA....UNIFICATION AND REUNIFICATION OF GEOGRAPHIC-
    POLITICAL ENTITIES

UNIFORM NARCOTIC DRUG ACT....SEE NARCO/ACT

UNION AFRICAINE ET MALGACHE, ALSO OCAM....SEE UAM

UNION FOR THE NEW REPUBLIC....SEE UNR

UNION OF SOUTH AFRICA....SEE SOUTH×AFR

UNION OF SOVIET SOCIALIST REPUBLICS....SEE USSR

UNION POUR LA DEFENSE DE LA REPUBLIQUE (FRANCE)....SEE UDR

UNION OF SOUTH AFRICA B2158

UNIONS....SEE LABOR

UNITED ARAB REPUBLIC....SEE UAR

UNITED AUTO WORKERS....SEE UAW

UNITED KINGDOM....SEE UK, COMMONWLTH

UNITED NATIONS....SEE UN

UNITED NATIONS INTERNATIONAL LAW COMMISSION....SEE UN/ILC

UNITED NATIONS SECURITY COUNCIL....SEE SECUR/COUN

UNITED NATIONS SPECIAL FUND....SEE UNSF

UNITED STATES ARMS CONTROL AND DISARMAMENT AGENCY....SEE
    ACD

UNITED STATES FEDERAL POWER COMMISSION....SEE FPC

UNITED STATES HOUSING CORPORATION....SEE US/HOUSING

UNITED STATES MILITARY ACADEMY....SEE WEST/POINT

UNITED STATES SENATE COMMITTEE ON FOREIGN RELATIONS....SEE
    FOREIGNREL

UNITED NATIONS B2159,B2160,B2161,B2162

UNIV....UNIVERSAL TO MAN

UNIVERSAL REFERENCE SYSTEM B2163,B2164,B2165

UNIVERSES....SEE UNIVERSES AND SAMPLING INDEX, P. XIV

UNIVERSITIES....SEE ACADEM

UNIVERSITIES RESEARCH ASSOCIATION, INC.....SEE UNIVS/RES

UNIVERSITY MICROFILMS INC B2166

UNIVERSITY OF FLORIDA B2167

UNIVERSITY OF LONDON B2168

UNIVERSITY PITT INST LOC GOVT B2169

UNIVS/RES....UNIVERSITIES RESEARCH ASSOCIATION, INC.

UNLABR/PAR....UNION LABOR PARTY

UNPLAN/INT....IMPROMPTU INTERVIEW

B61
MARVICK D.,POLITICAL DECISION-MAKERS. INTELL STRATA TOP/EX

1

NAT/G POL/PAR EX/STRUC LEGIS DOMIN EDU/PROP ATTIT BIOG
PERSON PWR...PSY STAT OBS CONT/OBS STAND/INT ELITES
UNPLAN/INT TIME/SEQ CHARTS STERTYP VAL/FREE.
PAGE 70 B1416

UNR....UNION FOR THE NEW REPUBLIC

UNRRA....UNITED NATIONS RELIEF AND REHABILITATION AGENCY

UNRWA....UNITED NATIONS RELIEF AND WORKS AGENCY

UNSF....UNITED NATIONS SPECIAL FUND

UPPER VOLTA....SEE UPPER/VOLT

UPPER/VOLT....UPPER VOLTA; SEE ALSO AFR

URBAN/LEAG....URBAN LEAGUE

URBAN/RNWL....URBAN RENEWAL

N19
VERNON R.,THE MYTH AND REALITY OF OUR URBAN PLAN
PROBLEMS (PAMPHLET). USA+45 SOCIETY LOC/G ADMIN MUNIC
COST 20 PRINCETN/U INTERVENT URBAN/RNWL. PAGE 112 HABITAT
B2261 PROB/SOLV
B60
POOLEY B.J.,THE EVOLUTION OF BRITISH PLANNING PLAN
LEGISLATION. UK ECO/DEV LOC/G CONSULT DELIB/GP MUNIC
ADMIN 20 URBAN/RNWL. PAGE 84 B1691 LEGIS
PROB/SOLV
B61
JACOBS J.,THE DEATH AND LIFE OF GREAT AMERICAN MUNIC
CITIES. USA+45 SOCIETY DIST/IND CREATE PROB/SOLV PLAN
ADMIN...GEOG SOC CENSUS 20 URBAN/RNWL. PAGE 55 ADJUST
B1113 HABITAT
B64
CULLINGWORTH J.B.,TOWN AND COUNTRY PLANNING IN MUNIC
ENGLAND AND WALES. UK LAW SOCIETY CONSULT ACT/RES PLAN
ADMIN ROUTINE LEISURE INGP/REL ADJUST PWR...GEOG 20 NAT/G
OPEN/SPACE URBAN/RNWL. PAGE 25 B0512 PROB/SOLV
B64
GREBLER L.,URBAN RENEWAL IN EUROPEAN COUNTRIES: ITS MUNIC
EMERGENCE AND POTENTIALS. EUR+WWI UK ECO/DEV LOC/G PLAN
NEIGH CREATE ADMIN ATTIT...TREND NAT/COMP 20 CONSTRUC
URBAN/RNWL. PAGE 43 B0863 NAT/G
B64
PINNICK A.W.,COUNTRY PLANNERS IN ACTION. UK FINAN MUNIC
SERV/IND NAT/G CONSULT DELIB/GP PRICE CONTROL PLAN
ROUTINE LEISURE AGE/C...GEOG 20 URBAN/RNWL. PAGE 83 INDUS
B1674 ATTIT
B65
ARTHUR D LITTLE INC,SAN FRANCISCO COMMUNITY RENEWAL HABITAT
PROGRAM. USA+45 FINAN PROVS ADMIN INCOME...CHARTS MUNIC
20 CALIFORNIA SAN/FRAN URBAN/RNWL. PAGE 7 B0138 PLAN
PROB/SOLV
B65
DUGGAR G.S.,RENEWAL OF TOWN AND VILLAGE I: A WORLD- MUNIC
WIDE SURVEY OF LOCAL GOVERNMENT EXPERIENCE. WOR+45 NEIGH
CONSTRUC INDUS CREATE BUDGET REGION GOV/REL...QU PLAN
NAT/COMP 20 URBAN/RNWL. PAGE 31 B0628 ADMIN
B65
EVERETT R.O.,URBAN PROBLEMS AND PROSPECTS. USA+45 MUNIC
CREATE TEC/DEV EDU/PROP ADJUD ADMIN GOV/REL ATTIT PLAN
...ANTHOL 20 URBAN/RNWL. PAGE 34 B0691 PROB/SOLV
NEIGH
B65
FRYE R.J.,HOUSING AND URBAN RENEWAL IN ALABAMA. MUNIC
USA+45 NEIGH LEGIS BUDGET ADJUD ADMIN PARTIC...MGT PROB/SOLV
20 ALABAMA URBAN/RNWL. PAGE 38 B0762 PLAN
GOV/REL
B65
GREER S.,URBAN RENEWAL AND AMERICAN CITIES: THE MUNIC
DILEMMA OF DEMOCRATIC INTERVENTION. USA+45 R+D PROB/SOLV
LOC/G VOL/ASSN ACT/RES BUDGET ADMIN GOV/REL...SOC PLAN
INT SAMP 20 BOSTON CHICAGO MIAMI URBAN/RNWL. NAT/G
PAGE 43 B0871
B66
SCHMIDT K.M.,AMERICAN STATE AND LOCAL GOVERNMENT IN PROVS
ACTION. USA+45 CONSTN LOC/G POL/PAR CHIEF LEGIS ADMIN
PROB/SOLV ADJUD LOBBY GOV/REL...DECISION ANTHOL 20 MUNIC
GOVERNOR MAYOR URBAN/RNWL. PAGE 94 B1896 PLAN

URUGUAY....URUGUAY

B64
MUSSO AMBROSI L.A.,BIBLIOGRAFIA DE BIBLIOGRAFIAS BIBLIOG
URUGUAYAS. URUGUAY DIPLOM ADMIN ATTIT...SOC 20. NAT/G
PAGE 77 B1551 L/A+17C
PRESS
S67
FABREGA J.,"ANTECEDENTES EXTRANJEROS EN LA CONSTN
CONSTITUCION PANAMENA." CUBA L/A+17C PANAMA URUGUAY JURID
EX/STRUC LEGIS DIPLOM ORD/FREE 19/20 COLOMB NAT/G
MEXIC/AMER. PAGE 34 B0694 PARL/PROC

URWICK L. B0903

US AGENCY FOR INTERNATIONAL DEVELOPMENT....SEE US/AID

US ATOMIC ENERGY COMMISSION....SEE AEC

US ATTORNEY GENERAL....SEE ATTRNY/GEN

US BUREAU OF STANDARDS....SEE BUR/STNDRD

US BUREAU OF THE BUDGET....SEE BUR/BUDGET

US CENTRAL INTELLIGENCE AGENCY....SEE CIA

US CIVIL AERONAUTICS BOARD....SEE CAB

US CONGRESS RULES COMMITTEES....SEE RULES/COMM

US DEPARTMENT OF AGRICULTURE....SEE DEPT/AGRI

US DEPARTMENT OF COMMERCE....SEE DEPT/COM

US DEPARTMENT OF DEFENSE....SEE DEPT/DEFEN

US DEPARTMENT OF HEALTH, EDUCATION, AND WELFARE....SEE
DEPT/HEW

US DEPARTMENT OF HOUSING AND URBAN DEVELOPMENT....SEE
DEPT/HUD

US DEPARTMENT OF JUSTICE....SEE DEPT/JUST

US DEPARTMENT OF LABOR AND INDUSTRY....SEE DEPT/LABOR

US DEPARTMENT OF STATE....SEE DEPT/STATE

US DEPARTMENT OF THE INTERIOR....SEE DEPT/INTER

US DEPARTMENT OF THE TREASURY....SEE DEPT/TREAS

US FEDERAL AVIATION AGENCY....SEE FAA

US FEDERAL BUREAU OF INVESTIGATION....SEE FBI

US FEDERAL COMMUNICATIONS COMMISSION....SEE FCC

US FEDERAL COUNCIL FOR SCIENCE AND TECHNOLOGY....SEE
FEDSCI/TEC

US FEDERAL HOUSING ADMINISTRATION....SEE FHA

US FEDERAL OPEN MARKET COMMITTEE....SEE FED/OPNMKT

US FEDERAL RESERVE SYSTEM....SEE FED/RESERV

US FEDERAL TRADE COMMISSION....SEE FTC

US HOUSE COMMITTEE ON SCIENCE AND ASTRONAUTICS....SEE
HS/SCIASTR

US HOUSE COMMITTEE ON UNAMERICAN ACTIVITIES....SEE HUAC

US HOUSE OF REPRESENTATIVES....SEE HOUSE/REP

US INFORMATION AGENCY....SEE USIA

US INTERNAL REVENUE SERVICE....SEE IRS

US INTERNATIONAL COOPERATION ADMINISTRATION....SEE ICA

US INTERSTATE COMMERCE COMMISSION....SEE ICC

US MILITARY ACADEMY....SEE WEST/POINT

US NATIONAL AERONAUTICS AND SPACE ADMINISTRATION....SEE NASA

US OFFICE OF ECONOMIC OPPORTUNITY....SEE OEO

US OFFICE OF NAVAL RESEARCH....SEE NAVAL/RES

US OFFICE OF PRICE ADMINISTRATION....SEE OPA

US OFFICE OF WAR INFORMATION....SEE OWI

US PATENT OFFICE....SEE PATENT/OFF

US PEACE CORPS....SEE PEACE/CORP

US SECRETARY OF STATE....SEE SEC/STATE

US SECURITIES AND EXCHANGE COMMISSION....SEE SEC/EXCHNG

US SENATE COMMITTEE ON AERONAUTICS AND SPACE....SEE
SEN/SPACE

US SENATE SCIENCE ADVISORY COMMISSION....SEE SCI/ADVSRY

US SENATE....SEE SENATE

US SMALL BUSINESS ADMINISTRATION....SEE SBA

US SOUTH....SEE SOUTH/US

US STEEL CORPORATION....SEE US/STEEL

US ADMINISTRATIVE CONFERENCE B2170

US ADVISORY COMN INTERGOV REL B2171,B2172

US BOARD GOVERNORS FEDL RESRV B2173

US BUREAU OF THE BUDGET B2174

US CIVIL SERVICE COMMISSION B2175,B2176,B2177

US CONGRESS JT COMM ECO GOVT B2178

US DEPARTMENT HEALTH EDUC WELF B2180

US DEPARTMENT OF JUSTICE B2181

US DEPARTMENT OF STATE B2182 ,B2237

US DEPARTMENT OF THE ARMY B2183,B2184,B2185

US GENERAL ACCOUNTING OFFICE B2186

US HOUSE COM ON ED AND LABOR B2187,B2188

US HOUSE COMM EDUC AND LABOR B218 7,B2188

US HOUSE COMM GOVT OPERATIONS B2189,B2190,B2191

US HOUSE COMM ON COMMERCE B2192

US HOUSE COMM ON POST OFFICE B2193,B2194 , B2195,B2196,B2197

US HOUSE COMM POST OFFICE B2193,B2194,B2195,B2196,B2197

US HOUSE COMM SCI ASTRONAUT B2198

US HOUSE RULES COMM B2199

US LIBRARY OF CONGRESS B2200,B2201,B2202,B2203,B2204,B2205 ,
    B2206,B2207

US PRES COMM STUDY MIL ASSIST B2208

US PRES CONF ADMIN PROCEDURE B2209

US SENATE COMM AERO SPACE SCI B2210

US SENATE COMM APPROPRIATIONS B2211

US SENATE COMM GOVT OPERATIONS B2212,B2213,B2214,B2215,B2216 ,
    B2217,B2218,B2219,B2235,B2236

US SENATE COMM ON FOREIGN REL B2220,B2221,B2222,B2223,B2224 ,
    B2225

US SENATE COMM ON JUDICIARY B2179,B2226,B2227,B2228,B2229,B2230,
    B2231,B2232

US SENATE COMM ON POST OFFICE B2233,B2234

US STATE DEPT. B2182,B2237

US SUPERINTENDENT OF DOCUMENTS B2238,B2239,B2240,B2241,B2242 ,
    B2243,B2244

US TARIFF COMMISSION B2245,B2246

US/AID....UNITED STATES AGENCY FOR INTERNATIONAL DEVELOPMENT

US/HOUSING....UNITED STATES HOUSING CORPORATION

US/STEEL....UNITED STATES STEEL CORPORATION

US/WEST....WESTERN UNITED STATES

USA+45....UNITED STATES, 1945 TO PRESENT

USA-45....UNITED STATES, 1700 TO 1945

USEEM J. B2247

USEEM R. B2247

USIA....UNITED STATES INFORMATION AGENCY

	S67
RUBIN R.I.,"THE LEGISLATIVE-EXECUTIVE RELATIONS OF THE UNITED STATES INFORMATION AGENCY." USA+45 EDU/PROP TASK INGP/REL EFFICIENCY ISOLAT ATTIT ROLE USIA CONGRESS. PAGE 91 B1850	LEGIS EX/STRUC GP/REL PROF/ORG

USPNSKII/G....GLEB USPENSKII

USSR....UNION OF SOVIET SOCIALIST REPUBLICS; SEE ALSO
    RUSSIA, APPROPRIATE TIME/SPACE/CULTURE INDEX

	N
SOVIET-EAST EUROPEAN RES SERV,SOVIET SOCIETY. USSR LABOR POL/PAR PRESS MARXISM...MARXIST 20. PAGE 99 B2001	BIBLIOG/A EDU/PROP ADMIN SOC
	B18
WILSON W.,THE STATE: ELEMENTS OF HISTORICAL AND PRACTICAL POLITICS. FRANCE GERMANY ITALY UK USSR CONSTN EX/STRUC LEGIS CT/SYS WAR PWR...POLICY GOV/COMP 20. PAGE 117 B2363	NAT/G JURID CONCPT NAT/COMP
	B38
HARPER S.N.,THE GOVERNMENT OF THE SOVIET UNION. COM USSR LAW CONSTN ECO/DEV PLAN TEC/DEV DIPLOM INT/TRADE ADMIN REV NAT/LISM...POLICY 20. PAGE 47 B0952	MARXISM NAT/G LEAD POL/PAR
	B39
ANDERSON W.,LOCAL GOVERNMENT IN EUROPE. FRANCE GERMANY ITALY UK USSR MUNIC PROVS ADMIN GOV/REL CENTRAL SOVEREIGN 20. PAGE 5 B0099	GOV/COMP NAT/COMP LOC/G CONSTN
	B44
BIENSTOCK G.,MANAGEMENT IN RUSSIAN INDUSTRY AND AGRICULTURE. USSR CONSULT WORKER LEAD COST PROFIT ATTIT DRIVE PWR...MGT METH/COMP DICTIONARY 20. PAGE 12 B0236	ADMIN MARXISM SML/CO AGRI
	B45
CONOVER H.F.,THE GOVERNMENTS OF THE MAJOR FOREIGN POWERS: A BIBLIOGRAPHY. FRANCE GERMANY ITALY UK USSR CONSTN LOC/G POL/PAR EX/STRUC FORCES ADMIN CT/SYS CIVMIL/REL TOTALISM...POLICY 19/20. PAGE 23 B0464	BIBLIOG NAT/G DIPLOM
	B46
BIBLIOGRAFIIA DISSERTATSII: DOKTORSKIE DISSERTATSII ZA 19411944 (2 VOLS.). COM USSR LAW POL/PAR DIPLOM ADMIN LEAD...PHIL/SCI SOC 20. PAGE 2 B0035	BIBLIOG ACADEM KNOWL MARXIST
	B48
SHERWOOD R.E.,ROOSEVELT AND HOPKINS. UK USA+45 USSR NAT/G EX/STRUC FORCES ADMIN ROUTINE PERSON PWR ...TIME/SEQ 20 ROOSEVLT/F HOPKINS/H. PAGE 96 B1946	TOP/EX BIOG DIPLOM WAR
	B48
TOWSTER J.,POLITICAL POWER IN THE USSR: 1917-1947. USSR CONSTN CULTURE ELITES CREATE PLAN COERCE CENTRAL ATTIT RIGID/FLEX ORD/FREE...BIBLIOG SOC/INTEG 20 LENIN/VI STALIN/J. PAGE 105 B2124	EX/STRUC NAT/G MARXISM PWR
	L49
FAINSED M.,"RECENT DEVELOPMENTS IN SOVIET PUBLIC ADMINISTRATION." USSR EXEC 20. PAGE 34 B0699	DOMIN CONTROL CENTRAL EX/STRUC
	B50
MANNHEIM K.,FREEDOM, POWER, AND DEMOCRATIC PLANNING. FUT USSR WOR+45 ELITES INTELL SOCIETY NAT/G EDU/PROP ROUTINE ATTIT DRIVE SUPEGO SKILL ...POLICY PSY CONCPT TREND GEN/LAWS 20. PAGE 69 B1393	TEC/DEV PLAN CAP/ISM UK
	S50
WITTFOGEL K.A.,"RUSSIA AND ASIA: PROBLEMS OF CONTEMPORARY AREA STUDIES AND INTERNATIONAL RELATIONS." ASIA COM USA+45 SOCIETY NAT/G DIPLOM ECO/TAC FOR/AID EDU/PROP KNOWL...HIST/WRIT TOT/POP 20. PAGE 117 B2369	ECO/DEV ADMIN RUSSIA USSR
	B51
LEITES N.,THE OPERATIONAL CODE OF THE POLITBURO. COM USSR CREATE PLAN DOMIN LEGIT COERCE ALL/VALS ...SOC CONCPT MYTH TREND CON/ANAL GEN/LAWS 20 LENIN/VI STALIN/J. PAGE 64 B1284	DELIB/GP ADMIN SOCISM
	C51
MOORE B.,"SOVIET POLITICS - THE DILEMMA OF POWER: THE ROLE OF IDEAS IN SOCIAL CHANGE." USSR PROB/SOLV DIPLOM EDU/PROP ADMIN LEAD ROUTINE REV...POLICY DECISION BIBLIOG 20. PAGE 75 B1512	ATTIT PWR CONCPT MARXISM
	B52
BRINTON C.,THE ANATOMY OF REVOLUTION. FRANCE UK USA-45 USSR WOR-45 ELITES INTELL ECO/DEV NAT/G EX/STRUC FORCES COERCE DRIVE ORD/FREE PWR SOVEREIGN ...MYTH HIST/WRIT GEN/LAWS. PAGE 15 B0311	SOCIETY CONCPT REV
	B52
JANSE R.S.,SOVIET TRANSPORTATION AND COMMUNICATIONS: A BIBLIOGRAPHY. COM USSR PLAN	BIBLIOG/A COM/IND

...DICTIONARY 20. PAGE 56 B1124   LEGIS
                                                       ADMIN
                                                                   B52
POOL I.,SYMBOLS OF DEMOCRACY. WOR+45 WOR-45 POL/PAR   INTELL
FORCES ADMIN PERSON PWR...CONCPT 20. PAGE 83 B1687   SOCIETY
                                                       USSR
                                                                   B52
SELZNICK P.,THE ORGANIZATIONAL WEAPON: A STUDY OF   MARXISM
BOLSHEVIK STRATEGY AND TACTICS. USSR SOCIETY STRATA   POL/PAR
LABOR DOMIN EDU/PROP PARTIC REV ATTIT PWR...POLICY   LEAD
MGT CONCPT 20 BOLSHEVISM. PAGE 95 B1929   TOTALISM
                                                                   B52
ULAM A.B.,TITOISM AND THE COMINFORM. USSR WOR+45   COM
STRUCT INT/ORG NAT/G ACT/RES PLAN EXEC ATTIT DRIVE   POL/PAR
ALL/VALS...CONCPT OBS VAL/FREE 20 COMINTERN   TOTALISM
TITO/MARSH. PAGE 106 B2145   YUGOSLAVIA
                                                                   B53
MEYER P.,THE JEWS IN THE SOVIET SATELLITES.   COM
CZECHOSLVK POLAND SOCIETY STRATA NAT/G BAL/PWR   SECT
ECO/TAC EDU/PROP LEGIT ADMIN COERCE ATTIT DISPL   TOTALISM
PERCEPT HEALTH PWR RESPECT WEALTH...METH/CNCPT JEWS   USSR
VAL/FREE NAZI 20. PAGE 73 B1474
                                                                   B53
PIERCE R.A.,RUSSIAN CENTRAL ASIA, 1867-1917: A   BIBLIOG
SELECTED BIBLIOGRAPHY (PAMPHLET). USSR LAW CULTURE   COLONIAL
NAT/G EDU/PROP WAR...GEOG SOC 19/20. PAGE 83 B1671   ADMIN
                                                       COM
                                                                   S53
MORRIS B.S.,"THE COMINFORM: A FIVE YEAR   VOL/ASSN
PERSPECTIVE." COM UNIV USSR WOR+45 ECO/DEV POL/PAR   EDU/PROP
TOP/EX PLAN DOMIN ADMIN TOTALISM ATTIT ALL/VALS   DIPLOM
...CONCPT TIME/SEQ TREND CON/ANAL WORK VAL/FREE 20.
PAGE 76 B1527
                                                                   L54
ARCIENEGAS G.,"POST-WAR SOVIET FOREIGN POLICY: A   INTELL
WORLD PERSPECTIVE." COM USA+45 STRUCT NAT/G POL/PAR   ACT/RES
TOP/EX PLAN ADMIN ALL/VALS...TREND COLD/WAR TOT/POP   USSR
20. PAGE 6 B0124
                                                                   B55
POOL I.,SATELLITE GENERALS: A STUDY OF MILITARY   FORCES
ELITES IN THE SOVIET SPHERE. ASIA CHINA/COM COM   CHOOSE
CZECHOSLVK FUT HUNGARY POLAND ROMANIA USSR ELITES
STRATA ADMIN ATTIT PWR SKILL...METH/CNCPT BIOG 20.
PAGE 84 B1688
                                                                   L55
ROSTOW W.W.,"RUSSIA AND CHINA UNDER COMMUNISM."   COM
CHINA/COM USSR INTELL STRUCT INT/ORG NAT/G POL/PAR   ASIA
TOP/EX ACT/RES PLAN ADMIN ATTIT ALL/VALS MARXISM
...CONCPT OBS TIME/SEQ TREND GOV/COMP VAL/FREE 20.
PAGE 91 B1830
                                                                   S55
KAUTSKY J.H.,"THE NEW STRATEGY OF INTERNATIONAL   COM
COMMUNISM." ASIA CHINA/COM FUT WOR+45 WOR-45 ADMIN   POL/PAR
ROUTINE PERSON MARXISM SOCISM...TREND IDEA/COMP 20   TOTALISM
LENIN/VI MAO. PAGE 59 B1184   USSR
                                                                   B57
BEAL J.R.,JOHN FOSTER DULLES, A BIOGRAPHY. USA+45   BIOG
USSR WOR+45 CONSTN INT/ORG NAT/G EX/STRUC LEGIT   DIPLOM
ADMIN NUC/PWR DISPL PERSON ORD/FREE PWR SKILL
...POLICY PSY OBS RECORD COLD/WAR UN 20 DULLES/JF.
PAGE 10 B0200
                                                                   B57
CENTRAL ASIAN RESEARCH CENTRE,BIBLIOGRAPHY OF   BIBLIOG/A
RECENT SOVIET SOURCE MATERIAL ON SOVIET CENTRAL   COM
ASIA AND THE BORDERLANDS. AFGHANISTN INDIA PAKISTAN   CULTURE
UAR USSR ECO/UNDEV AGRI EXTR/IND INDUS ACADEM ADMIN   NAT/G
...HEAL HUM LING CON/ANAL 20. PAGE 19 B0399
                                                                   B57
DJILAS M.,THE NEW CLASS: AN ANALYSIS OF THE   COM
COMMUNIST SYSTEM. STRATA CAP/ISM ECO/TAC DOMIN   POL/PAR
EDU/PROP LEGIT EXEC COERCE ATTIT PWR MARXISM   USSR
...MARXIST MGT CONCPT TIME/SEQ GEN/LAWS 20. PAGE 29   YUGOSLAVIA
B0600
                                                                   C57
TANG P.S.H.,"COMMUNIST CHINA TODAY: DOMESTIC AND   POL/PAR
FOREIGN POLICIES." CHINA/COM COM S/ASIA USSR STRATA   LEAD
FORCES DIPLOM EDU/PROP COERCE GOV/REL...POLICY   ADMIN
MAJORIT BIBLIOG 20. PAGE 102 B2071   CONSTN
                                                                   B58
KINTNER W.R.,ORGANIZING FOR CONFLICT: A PROPOSAL.   USA+45
USSR STRUCT NAT/G LEGIS ADMIN EXEC PEACE ORD/FREE   PLAN
PWR...CONCPT OBS TREND NAT/COMP VAL/FREE COLD/WAR   DIPLOM
20. PAGE 60 B1211
                                                                   B58
LAQUER W.Z.,THE MIDDLE EAST IN TRANSITION. COM USSR   ISLAM
ECO/UNDEV NAT/G VOL/ASSN EDU/PROP EXEC ATTIT DRIVE   TREND
PWR MARXISM COLD/WAR TOT/POP 20. PAGE 62 B1261   NAT/LISM
                                                                   B58
SCOTT D.J.R.,RUSSIAN POLITICAL INSTITUTIONS. RUSSIA   NAT/G
USSR CONSTN AGRI DELIB/GP PLAN EDU/PROP CONTROL   POL/PAR
CHOOSE EFFICIENCY ATTIT MARXISM...BIBLIOG/A 13/20.   ADMIN
PAGE 95 B1919   DECISION
                                                                   S58
DAVENPORT J.,"ARMS AND THE WELFARE STATE." INTELL   USA+45
STRUCT FORCES CREATE ECO/TAC FOR/AID DOMIN LEGIT   NAT/G
ADMIN WAR ORD/FREE PWR...POLICY SOC CONCPT MYTH OBS   USSR

TREND COLD/WAR TOT/POP 20. PAGE 26 B0533
                                                                   S59
BENDIX R.,"INDUSTRIALIZATION, IDEOLOGIES, AND   INDUS
SOCIAL STRUCTURE" (BMR)" UK USA-45 USSR STRUCT   ATTIT
WORKER GP/REL EFFICIENCY...IDEA/COMP 20. PAGE 10   MGT
B0210   ADMIN
                                                                   S59
ZAUBERMAN A.,"SOVIET BLOC ECONOMIC INTEGRATION."   MARKET
COM CULTURE INTELL ECO/DEV INDUS TOP/EX ACT/RES   INT/ORG
PLAN ECO/TAC INT/TRADE ROUTINE CHOOSE ATTIT   USSR
...TIME/SEQ 20. PAGE 119 B2399   TOTALISM
                                                                   B60
CAMPBELL R.W.,SOVIET ECONOMIC POWER. COM USA+45   ECO/DEV
DIST/IND MARKET TOP/EX ACT/RES CAP/ISM ECO/TAC   PLAN
DOMIN EDU/PROP ADMIN ROUTINE DRIVE...MATH TIME/SEQ   SOCISM
CHARTS WORK 20. PAGE 18 B0371   USSR
                                                                   B60
DRAPER T.,AMERICAN COMMUNISM AND SOVIET RUSSIA.   COM
EUR+WWI USA+45 USSR INTELL AGRI COM/IND FINAN INDUS   POL/PAR
LABOR PROF/ORG VOL/ASSN PLAN TEC/DEV DOMIN EDU/PROP
ADMIN COERCE REV PERSON PWR...POLICY CONCPT MYTH
19/20. PAGE 30 B0617
                                                                   B60
GRANICK D.,THE RED EXECUTIVE. COM USA+45 SOCIETY   PWR
ECO/DEV INDUS NAT/G POL/PAR EX/STRUC PLAN ECO/TAC   STRATA
EDU/PROP ADMIN EXEC ATTIT DRIVE...GP/COMP 20.   USSR
PAGE 42 B0851   ELITES
                                                                   B60
ROEPKE W.,A HUMANE ECONOMY: THE SOCIAL FRAMEWORK OF   DRIVE
THE FREE MARKET. FUT USSR WOR+45 CULTURE SOCIETY   EDU/PROP
ECO/DEV PLAN ECO/TAC ADMIN ATTIT PERSON RIGID/FLEX   CAP/ISM
SUPEGO MORAL WEALTH SOCISM...POLICY OLD/LIB CONCPT
TREND GEN/LAWS 20. PAGE 90 B1811
                                                                   L60
BRENNAN D.G.,"SETTING AND GOALS OF ARMS CONTROL."   FORCES
FUT USA+45 USSR WOR+45 INT/ORG NAT/G   COERCE
VOL/ASSN CONSULT PLAN DIPLOM ECO/TAC ADMIN KNOWL   ARMS/CONT
PWR...POLICY CONCPT TREND COLD/WAR 20. PAGE 15   DETER
B0305
                                                                   L60
DEAN A.W.,"SECOND GENEVA CONFERENCE OF THE LAW OF   INT/ORG
THE SEA: THE FIGHT FOR FREEDOM OF THE SEAS." FUT   JURID
USA+45 USSR WOR+45 WOR-45 SEA CONSTN STRUCT PLAN   INT/LAW
INT/TRADE ADJUD ADMIN ORD/FREE...DECISION RECORD
TREND GEN/LAWS 20 TREATY. PAGE 28 B0564
                                                                   S60
GROSSMAN G.,"SOVIET GROWTH: ROUTINE, INERTIA, AND   POL/PAR
PRESSURE." COM STRATA NAT/G DELIB/GP PLAN TEC/DEV   ECO/DEV
ECO/TAC EDU/PROP ADMIN ROUTINE DRIVE WEALTH   USSR
COLD/WAR 20. PAGE 44 B0891
                                                                   S60
HALPERIN M.H.,"IS THE SENATE'S FOREIGN RELATIONS   PLAN
RESEARCH WORTHWHILE." COM FUT USA+45 USSR ACT/RES   DIPLOM
BAL/PWR POL/PAR ADMIN ALL/VALS CONGRESS VAL/FREE
20 COLD/WAR. PAGE 46 B0927
                                                                   C60
FITZSIMMONS T.,"USSR: ITS PEOPLE, ITS SOCIETY, ITS   CULTURE
CULTURE." USSR FAM SECT DIPLOM EDU/PROP ADMIN   STRUCT
RACE/REL ATTIT...POLICY CHARTS BIBLIOG 20. PAGE 36   SOCIETY
B0728   COM
                                                                   C60
SCHAPIRO L.B.,"THE COMMUNIST PARTY OF THE SOVIET   POL/PAR
UNION." USSR INTELL CHIEF EX/STRUC FORCES DOMIN   COM
ADMIN LEAD WAR ATTIT SOVEREIGN...POLICY BIBLIOG 20.   REV
PAGE 93 B1881
                                                                   B61
ARMSTRONG J.A.,AN ESSAY ON SOURCES FOR THE STUDY OF   BIBLIOG/A
THE COMMUNIST PARTY OF THE SOVIET UNION, 1934-1960   COM
(EXTERNAL RESEARCH PAPER 137). USSR EX/STRUC ADMIN   POL/PAR
LEAD REV 20. PAGE 7 B0134   MARXISM
                                                                   B61
DRAGNICH A.N.,MAJOR EUROPEAN GOVERNMENTS. FRANCE   NAT/G
GERMANY/W UK USSR LOC/G EX/STRUC CT/SYS PARL/PROC   LEGIS
ATTIT MARXISM...JURID MGT NAT/COMP 19/20. PAGE 30   CONSTN
B0615   POL/PAR
                                                                   B61
HAYTER W.,THE DIPLOMACY OF THE GREAT POWERS. FRANCE   DIPLOM
UK USSR WOR+45 EX/STRUC TOP/EX NUC/PWR PEACE...OBS   POLICY
20. PAGE 48 B0978   NAT/G
                                                                   B61
MOLLAU G.,INTERNATIONAL COMMUNISM AND WORLD   COM
REVOLUTION: HISTORY AND METHODS. RUSSIA USSR   REV
INT/ORG NAT/G POL/PAR VOL/ASSN FORCES BAL/PWR
DIPLOM EXEC REGION WAR ATTIT PWR MARXISM...CONCPT
TIME/SEQ COLD/WAR 19/20. PAGE 74 B1498
                                                                   B61
NOVE A.,THE SOVIET ECONOMY. USSR ECO/DEV FINAN   PLAN
NAT/G ECO/TAC PRICE ADMIN EFFICIENCY MARXISM   PRODUC
...TREND BIBLIOG 20. PAGE 79 B1594   POLICY
                                                                   B61
STRAUSS E.,THE RULING SERVANTS. FRANCE UK USSR   ADMIN
WOR+45 WOR-45 NAT/G CONSULT DELIB/GP EX/STRUC   PWR
TOP/EX DOMIN EDU/PROP LEGIT ROUTINE...MGT TIME/SEQ   ELITES
STERTYP 20. PAGE 101 B2051
                                                                   S61
DEVINS J.H.,"THE INITIATIVE." COM USA+45 USA-45   FORCES

USSR SOCIETY NAT/G ACT/RES CREATE BAL/PWR ROUTINE CONCPT
COERCE DETER RIGID/FLEX SKILL...STERTYP COLD/WAR WAR
20. PAGE 29 B0582

S61
JUVILER P.H.,"INTERPARLIAMENTARY CONTACTS IN SOVIET INT/ORG
FOREIGN POLICY." COM FUT WOR+45 WOR-45 SOCIETY DELIB/GP
CONSULT ACT/RES DIPLOM ADMIN PEACE ATTIT RIGID/FLEX USSR
WEALTH...WELF/ST SOC TOT/POP CONGRESS 19/20.
PAGE 57 B1156

S61
NOVE A.,"THE SOVIET MODEL AND UNDERDEVELOPED ECO/UNDEV
COUNTRIES." COM FUT USSR WOR+45 CULTURE ECO/DEV PLAN
POL/PAR FOR/AID EDU/PROP ADMIN MORAL WEALTH
...POLICY RECORD HIST/WRIT 20. PAGE 79 B1593

S61
TOMASIC D.,"POLITICAL LEADERSHIP IN CONTEMPORARY SOCIETY
POLAND." COM EUR+WWI GERMANY NAT/G POL/PAR SECT ROUTINE
DELIB/GP PLAN ECO/TAC DOMIN EDU/PROP PWR MARXISM USSR
...MARXIST GEOG MGT CONCPT TIME/SEQ STERTYP 20. POLAND
PAGE 105 B2114

B62
ANDREWS W.G.,EUROPEAN POLITICAL INSTITUTIONS. NAT/COMP
FRANCE GERMANY UK USSR TOP/EX LEAD PARL/PROC CHOOSE POL/PAR
20. PAGE 5 B0104 EX/STRUC
LEGIS

B62
CARTER G.M.,THE GOVERNMENT OF THE SOVIET UNION. NAT/G
USSR CULTURE LOC/G DIPLOM ECO/TAC ADJUD CT/SYS LEAD MARXISM
WEALTH...CHARTS T 20 COM/PARTY. PAGE 19 B0390 POL/PAR
EX/STRUC

B62
EVANS M.S.,THE FRINGE ON TOP. USSR EX/STRUC FORCES NAT/G
DIPLOM ECO/TAC PEACE CONSERVE SOCISM...TREND 20 PWR
KENNEDY/JF. PAGE 34 B0689 CENTRAL
POLICY

B62
FRIEDMANN W.,METHODS AND POLICIES OF PRINCIPAL INT/ORG
DONOR COUNTRIES IN PUBLIC INTERNATIONAL DEVELOPMENT FOR/AID
FINANCING: PRELIMINARY APPRAISAL. FRANCE GERMANY/W NAT/COMP
UK USA+45 USSR WOR+45 FINAN TEC/DEV CAP/ISM DIPLOM ADMIN
ECO/TAC ATTIT 20 EEC. PAGE 37 B0759

B62
SHAPIRO D.,A SELECT BIBLIOGRAPHY OF WORKS IN BIBLIOG
ENGLISH ON RUSSIAN HISTORY, 1801-1917. COM USSR DIPLOM
STRATA FORCES EDU/PROP ADMIN REV RACE/REL ATTIT COLONIAL
19/20. PAGE 96 B1932

L62
BAILEY S.D.,"THE TROIKA AND THE FUTURE OF THE UN." FUT
CONSTN CREATE LEGIT EXEC CHOOSE ORD/FREE PWR INT/ORG
...CONCPT NEW/IDEA UN COLD/WAR 20. PAGE 8 B0163 USSR

S62
HUDSON G.F.,"SOVIET FEARS OF THE WEST." COM USA+45 ATTIT
SOCIETY DELIB/GP EX/STRUC TOP/EX ACT/RES CREATE MYTH
DOMIN EDU/PROP LEGIT ADMIN ROUTINE DRIVE PERSON GERMANY
RIGID/FLEX PWR...RECORD TIME/SEQ TOT/POP 20 USSR
STALIN/J. PAGE 52 B1057

S62
IOVTCHOUK M.T.,"ON SOME THEORETICAL PRINCIPLES AND COM
METHODS OF SOCIOLOGICAL INVESTIGATIONS (IN ECO/DEV
RUSSIAN)." FUT USA+45 STRATA R+D NAT/G POL/PAR CAP/ISM
TOP/EX ACT/RES PLAN ECO/TAC EDU/PROP ROUTINE ATTIT USSR
RIGID/FLEX MARXISM SOCISM...MARXIST METH/CNCPT OBS
TREND NAT/COMP GEN/LAWS 20. PAGE 54 B1102

S62
JACOBSON H.K.,"THE UNITED NATIONS AND COLONIALISM: INT/ORG
A TENTATIVE APPRAISAL." AFR FUT S/ASIA USA+45 USSR CONCPT
WOR+45 NAT/G DELIB/GP PLAN DIPLOM ECO/TAC DOMIN COLONIAL
ADMIN ROUTINE COERCE ATTIT RIGID/FLEX ORD/FREE PWR
...OBS STERTYP UN 20. PAGE 55 B1115

C62
MORGAN G.G.,"SOVIET ADMINISTRATIVE LEGALITY: THE LAW
ROLE OF THE ATTORNEY GENERAL'S OFFICE." COM USSR CONSTN
CONTROL ROUTINE...CONCPT BIBLIOG 18/20. PAGE 75 LEGIS
B1522 ADMIN

B63
BROGAN D.W.,POLITICAL PATTERNS IN TODAY'S WORLD. NAT/COMP
FRANCE USA+45 USSR WOR+45 CONSTN STRUCT PLAN DIPLOM NEW/LIB
ADMIN LEAD ROLE SUPEGO...PHIL/SCI 20. PAGE 15 B0313 COM
TOTALISM

B63
KULZ H.R.,STAATSBURGER UND STAATSGEWALT (2 VOLS.). ADMIN
GERMANY SWITZERLND UK USSR CONSTN DELIB/GP TARIFFS ADJUD
TAX...JURID 20. PAGE 61 B1242 CT/SYS
NAT/COMP

B63
NORTH R.C.,CONTENT ANALYSIS: A HANDBOOK WITH METH/CNCPT
APPLICATIONS FOR THE STUDY OF INTERNATIONAL CRISIS. COMPUT/IR
ASIA COM EUR+WWI MOD/EUR INT/ORG TEC/DEV DOMIN USSR
EDU/PROP ROUTINE COERCE PERCEPT RIGID/FLEX ALL/VALS
...QUANT TESTS CON/ANAL SIMUL GEN/LAWS VAL/FREE.
PAGE 79 B1591

B63
ROETTER C.,THE DIPLOMATIC ART. USSR INT/ORG NAT/G DIPLOM
DELIB/GP ROUTINE NUC/PWR PEACE...POLICY 20. PAGE 90 ELITES
B1812 TOP/EX

B63
TUCKER R.C.,THE SOVIET POLITICAL MIND. WOR+45 COM
ELITES INT/ORG NAT/G POL/PAR PLAN DIPLOM ECO/TAC TOP/EX
DOMIN ADMIN NUC/PWR REV DRIVE PERSON SUPEGO PWR USSR
WEALTH...POLICY MGT PSY CONCPT OBS BIOG TREND
COLD/WAR MARX/KARL 20. PAGE 106 B2134

B63
TUCKER R.C.,THE SOVIET POLITICAL MIND. COM INTELL STRUCT
NAT/G TOP/EX EDU/PROP ADMIN COERCE TOTALISM ATTIT RIGID/FLEX
PWR MARXISM...PSY MYTH HYPO/EXP 20. PAGE 106 B2135 ELITES
USSR

B63
BECHHOEFER B.G.,"UNITED NATIONS PROCEDURES IN CASE INT/ORG
OF VIOLATIONS OF DISARMAMENT AGREEMENTS." COM DELIB/GP
USA+45 USSR LAW CONSTN NAT/G EX/STRUC FORCES LEGIS
BAL/PWR EDU/PROP CT/SYS ARMS/CONT ORD/FREE PWR
...POLICY STERTYP UN VAL/FREE 20. PAGE 10 B0204

S63
BRZEZINSKI Z.K.,"CINCINNATUS AND THE APPARATCHIK." POL/PAR
COM USA+45 USA-45 ELITES LOC/G NAT/G PROVS CONSULT USSR
LEGIS DOMIN LEGIT EXEC ROUTINE CHOOSE DRIVE PWR
SKILL...CONCPT CHARTS VAL/FREE COLD/WAR 20. PAGE 16
B0334

S63
DELLIN L.A.D.,"BULGARIA UNDER SOVIET LEADERSHIP." AGRI
BULGARIA COM USA+45 USSR ECO/DEV INDUS POL/PAR NAT/G
EX/STRUC TOP/EX COERCE ATTIT RIGID/FLEX...POLICY TOTALISM
TIME/SEQ 20. PAGE 28 B0572

S63
ETIENNE G.,"'LOIS OBJECTIVES' ET PROBLEMES DE TOTALISM
DEVELOPPEMENT DANS LE CONTEXTE CHINE-URSS." ASIA USSR
CHINA/COM COM FUT STRUCT INT/ORG VOL/ASSN TOP/EX
TEC/DEV ECO/TAC ATTIT RIGID/FLEX...GEOG MGT
TIME/SEQ TOT/POP 20. PAGE 34 B0682

S63
SCHURMANN F.,"ECONOMIC POLICY AND POLITICAL POWER PLAN
IN COMMUNIST CHINA." ASIA CHINA/COM USSR SOCIETY ECO/TAC
ECO/UNDEV AGRI INDUS CREATE ADMIN ROUTINE ATTIT
DRIVE RIGID/FLEX PWR WEALTH...HIST/WRIT TREND
CHARTS WORK 20. PAGE 94 B1908

S63
SHIMKIN D.B.,"STRUCTURE OF SOVIET POWER." COM FUT PWR
USA+45 USSR WOR+45 NAT/G FORCES ECO/TAC DOMIN EXEC
COERCE CHOOSE ATTIT WEALTH...TIME/SEQ COLD/WAR
TOT/POP VAL/FREE 20. PAGE 96 B1948

B64
DUROSELLE J.B.,POLITIQUES NATIONALES ENVERS LES DIPLOM
JEUNES ETATS. FRANCE ISRAEL ITALY UK USA+45 USSR ECO/UNDEV
YUGOSLAVIA ECO/DEV FINAN ECO/TAC INT/TRADE ADMIN COLONIAL
PWR 20. PAGE 31 B0634 DOMIN

B64
FAINSOD M.,HOW RUSSIA IS RULED (REV. ED.). RUSSIA NAT/G
USSR AGRI PROC/MFG LABOR POL/PAR EX/STRUC CONTROL REV
PWR...POLICY BIBLIOG 19/20 KHRUSH/N COM/PARTY. MARXISM
PAGE 34 B0700

B64
PIPES R.,THE FORMATION OF THE SOVIET UNION. EUR+WWI COM
MOD/EUR STRUCT ECO/UNDEV NAT/G LEGIS DOMIN LEGIT USSR
CT/SYS EXEC COERCE ALL/VALS...POLICY RELATIV RUSSIA
HIST/WRIT TIME/SEQ TOT/POP 19/20. PAGE 83 B1677

B64
POPPINO R.E.,INTERNATIONAL COMMUNISM IN LATIN MARXISM
AMERICA: A HISTORY OF THE MOVEMENT 1917-1963. POL/PAR
CHINA/COM USSR INTELL STRATA LABOR WORKER ADMIN REV L/A+17C
ATTIT...POLICY 20 COLD/WAR. PAGE 84 B1692

B64
TULLY A.,WHERE DID YOUR MONEY GO. USA+45 USSR FOR/AID
ECO/UNDEV ADMIN EFFICIENCY WEALTH...METH/COMP 20. DIPLOM
PAGE 106 B2136 CONTROL

B64
WELLISZ S.,THE ECONOMICS OF THE SOVIET BLOC. COM EFFICIENCY
USSR INDUS WORKER PLAN BUDGET INT/TRADE TAX PRICE ADMIN
PRODUC WEALTH MARXISM...METH/COMP 20. PAGE 115 MARKET
B2319

L64
MILLIS W.,"THE DEMILITARIZED WORLD." COM USA+45 FUT
USSR WOR+45 CONSTN NAT/G EX/STRUC PLAN LEGIT ATTIT INT/ORG
DRIVE...CONCPT TIME/SEQ STERTYP TOT/POP COLD/WAR BAL/PWR
20. PAGE 74 B1486 PEACE

S64
FLORINSKY M.T.,"TRENDS IN THE SOVIET ECONOMY." COM ECO/DEV
USA+45 USSR INDUS LABOR NAT/G PLAN TEC/DEV ECO/TAC AGRI
ALL/VALS SOCISM...MGT METH/CNCPT STYLE CON/ANAL
GEN/METH WORK 20. PAGE 36 B0731

S64
HORECKY P.L.,"LIBRARY OF CONGRESS PUBLICATIONS IN BIBLIOG/A
AID OF USSR AND EAST EUROPEAN RESEARCH." BULGARIA COM
CZECHOSLVK POLAND USSR YUGOSLAVIA NAT/G POL/PAR MARXISM
DIPLOM ADMIN GOV/REL...CLASSIF 20. PAGE 51 B1042

S64
KAPLAN N.,"RESEARCH ADMINISTRATION AND THE R+D
ADMINISTRATOR: USSR AND US." COM USA+45 INTELL ADMIN
EX/STRUC KNOWL...MGT 20. PAGE 58 B1169 USSR

S64
KASSOF A.,"THE ADMINISTERED SOCIETY: SOCIETY
TOTALITARIANISM WITHOUT TERROR." COM USSR STRATA DOMIN

AGRI INDUS NAT/G PERF/ART SCHOOL TOP/EX EDU/PROP   TOTALISM
ADMIN ORD/FREE PWR...POLICY SOC TIME/SEQ GEN/LAWS
VAL/FREE 20. PAGE 58 B1178
                                                        S64
KENNAN G.F.,"POLYCENTRISM AND WESTERN POLICY." ASIA RIGID/FLEX
CHINA/COM COM FUT USA+45 USSR NAT/G ACT/RES DOMIN   ATTIT
EDU/PROP EXEC COERCE DISPL PERCEPT...POLICY   DIPLOM
COLD/WAR 20. PAGE 59 B1192
                                                        S64
RIGBY T.H.,"TRADITIONAL, MARKET, AND ORGANIZATIONAL MARKET
SOCIETIES AND THE USSR." COM ECO/DEV NAT/G POL/PAR   ADMIN
ECO/TAC DOMIN ORD/FREE PWR WEALTH...TIME/SEQ   USSR
GEN/LAWS VAL/FREE 20 STALIN/J. PAGE 88 B1784
                                                        S64
SWEARER H.R.,"AFTER KHRUSHCHEV: WHAT NEXT." COM FUT EX/STRUC
USSR CONSTN ELITES NAT/G POL/PAR CHIEF DELIB/GP   PWR
LEGIS DOMIN LEAD...RECORD TREND STERTYP GEN/METH
20. PAGE 102 B2058
                                                        B65
CONRAD J.P.,CRIME AND ITS CORRECTION: AN   CRIME
INTERNATIONAL SURVEY OF ATTITUDES AND PRACTICES.   PUB/INST
EUR+WWI NETHERLAND USA+45 USSR ATTIT MORAL 20   POLICY
SCANDINAV. PAGE 23 B0467   ADMIN
                                                        B65
FORGAC A.A.,NEW DIPLOMACY AND THE UNITED NATIONS.   DIPLOM
FRANCE GERMANY UK USSR INT/ORG DELIB/GP EX/STRUC   ETIQUET
PEACE...INT/LAW CONCPT UN. PAGE 36 B0740   NAT/G
                                                        B65
GOTLIEB A.,DISARMAMENT AND INTERNATIONAL LAW* A   INT/LAW
STUDY OF THE ROLE OF LAW IN THE DISARMAMENT   INT/ORG
PROCESS. USA+45 USSR PROB/SOLV CONFER ADMIN ROUTINE   ARMS/CONT
NUC/PWR ORD/FREE SOVEREIGN UN TREATY. PAGE 42 B0841   IDEA/COMP
                                                        B65
MACDONALD R.W.,THE LEAGUE OF ARAB STATES: A STUDY   ISLAM
IN THE DYNAMICS OF REGIONAL ORGANIZATION. ISRAEL   REGION
UAR USSR FINAN INT/ORG DELIB/GP ECO/TAC AGREE   DIPLOM
NEUTRAL ORD/FREE PWR...DECISION BIBLIOG 20 TREATY   ADMIN
UN. PAGE 67 B1358
                                                        B65
PHELPS-FETHERS I.,SOVIET INTERNATIONAL FRONT   USSR
ORGANIZATIONS* A CONCISE HANDBOOK. DIPLOM DOMIN   EDU/PROP
LEGIT ADMIN EXEC GP/REL PEACE MARXISM...TIME/SEQ   ASIA
GP/COMP. PAGE 83 B1668   COM
                                                        B65
SCHAPIRO L.,THE GOVERNMENT AND POLITICS OF THE   MARXISM
SOVIET UNION. USSR WOR+45 WOR-45 ADMIN PARTIC REV   GOV/REL
CHOOSE REPRESENT PWR...POLICY IDEA/COMP 20. PAGE 93   NAT/G
B1880   LOC/G
                                                        S65
RUBINSTEIN A.Z.,"YUGOSLAVIA'S OPENING SOCIETY." COM CONSTN
USSR INTELL NAT/G LEGIS TOP/EX LEGIT CT/SYS   EX/STRUC
RIGID/FLEX ALL/VALS SOCISM...HUM TIME/SEQ TREND 20.   YUGOSLAVIA
PAGE 92 B1851
                                                        S65
TABORSKY E.,"CHANGE IN CZECHOSLOVAKIA." COM USSR   ECO/DEV
ELITES INTELL AGRI INDUS NAT/G DELIB/GP EX/STRUC   PLAN
ECO/TAC TOTALISM ATTIT RIGID/FLEX SOCISM...MGT   CZECHOSLVK
CONCPT TREND 20. PAGE 102 B2067
                                                        N65
MOTE M.E.,SOVIET LOCAL AND REPUBLIC ELECTIONS. COM   CHOOSE
USSR NAT/G PLAN PARTIC GOV/REL TOTALISM PWR   ADMIN
...CHARTS 20. PAGE 76 B1534   CONTROL
                                                     LOC/G
                                                        B66
EPSTEIN F.T.,THE AMERICAN BIBLIOGRAPHY OF RUSSIAN   BIBLIOG
AND EAST EUROPEAN STUDIES FOR 1964. USSR LOC/G   COM
NAT/G POL/PAR FORCES ADMIN ARMS/CONT...JURID CONCPT   MARXISM
20 UN. PAGE 33 B0678   DIPLOM
                                                        B66
KURAKOV I.G.,SCIENCE, TECHNOLOGY AND COMMUNISM;   CREATE
SOME QUESTIONS OF DEVELOPMENT (TRANS. BY CARIN   TEC/DEV
DEDIJER). USSR INDUS PLAN PROB/SOLV COST PRODUC   MARXISM
...MGT MATH CHARTS METH 20. PAGE 61 B1243   ECO/TAC
                                                        B66
MONTEIRO J.B.,CORRUPTION: CONTROL OF   CONTROL
MALADMINISTRATION. EUR+WWI INDIA USA+45 USSR NAT/G   CRIME
DELIB/GP ADMIN...GP/COMP 20 OMBUDSMAN. PAGE 74   PROB/SOLV
B1503
                                                        B66
US DEPARTMENT OF THE ARMY,COMMUNIST CHINA: A   BIBLIOG/A
STRATEGIC SURVEY: A BIBLIOGRAPHY (PAMPHLET NO.   MARXISM
20-67). CHINA/COM COM INDIA USSR NAT/G POL/PAR   S/ASIA
EX/STRUC FORCES NUC/PWR REV ATTIT...POLICY GEOG   DIPLOM
CHARTS. PAGE 108 B2184
                                                        B67
BRZEZINSKI Z.K.,IDEOLOGY AND POWER IN SOVIET   DIPLOM
POLITICS. USSR NAT/G POL/PAR PWR...GEN/LAWS 19/20.   EX/STRUC
PAGE 16 B0335   MARXISM
                                                        B67
BRZEZINSKI Z.K.,THE SOVIET BLOC: UNITY AND CONFLICT NAT/G
(2ND ED., REV., ENLARGED). COM POLAND USSR INTELL   DIPLOM
CHIEF EX/STRUC CONTROL EXEC GOV/REL PWR MARXISM
...TREND IDEA/COMP 20 LENIN/VI MARX/KARL STALIN/J.
PAGE 16 B0336
                                                        B67
FARNSWORTH B.,WILLIAM C. BULLITT AND THE SOVIET   DIPLOM

UNION. COM USA-45 USSR NAT/G CHIEF CONSULT DELIB/GP BIOG
EX/STRUC WAR REPRESENT MARXISM 20 WILSON/W   POLICY
ROOSEVLT/F STALIN/J BULLITT/WC. PAGE 35 B0705
                                                        B67
GROSSMAN G.,ECONOMIC SYSTEMS. USA+45 USA-45 USSR   ECO/DEV
YUGOSLAVIA WORKER CAP/ISM PRICE GP/REL EQUILIB   PLAN
WEALTH MARXISM SOCISM...MGT METH/COMP 19/20.   TEC/DEV
PAGE 44 B0892   DEMAND
                                                        B67
MACKINTOSH J.M.,JUGGERNAUT. USSR NAT/G POL/PAR   WAR
ADMIN LEAD CIVMIL/REL COST TOTALISM PWR MARXISM   FORCES
...GOV/COMP 20. PAGE 68 B1364   COM
                                                     PROF/ORG
                                                        B67
TANSKY L.,US AND USSR AID TO DEVELOPING COUNTRIES.   FOR/AID
INDIA TURKEY UAR USA+45 USSR FINAN PLAN TEC/DEV   ECO/UNDEV
ADMIN WEALTH...TREND METH/COMP 20. PAGE 103 B2076   MARXISM
                                                     CAP/ISM
                                                        S67
BERLINER J.S.,"RUSSIA'S BUREAUCRATS - WHY THEY'RE   CREATE
REACTIONARY." USSR NAT/G OP/RES PROB/SOLV TEC/DEV   ADMIN
CONTROL SANCTION EFFICIENCY DRIVE PERSON...TECHNIC   INDUS
SOC 20. PAGE 11 B0223   PRODUC
                                                        S67
TATU M.,"URSS: LES FLOTTEMENTS DE LA DIRECTION   POLICY
COLLEGIALE." UAR USSR CHIEF LEAD INGP/REL   NAT/G
EFFICIENCY...DECISION TREND 20 MID/EAST. PAGE 103   EX/STRUC
B2082   DIPLOM

UTAH....UTAH

UTIL....UTILITY, USEFULNESS

                                                        B42
LEISERSON A.,ADMINISTRATIVE REGULATION: A STUDY IN   LOBBY
REPRESENTATION OF INTERESTS. NAT/G EX/STRUC   ADMIN
PROB/SOLV BARGAIN CONFER ROUTINE REPRESENT PERS/REL   GP/REL
UTIL PWR POLICY. PAGE 63 B1283   GOV/REL
                                                        B47
SIMON H.A.,ADMINISTRATIVE BEHAVIOR: A STUDY OF   DECISION
DECISION-MAKING PROCESSES IN ADMINISTRATIVE   NEW/IDEA
ORGANIZATION. STRUCT COM/IND OP/RES PROB/SOLV   ADMIN
EFFICIENCY EQUILIB UTIL...PHIL/SCI PSY STYLE.   RATIONAL
PAGE 97 B1956
                                                        B48
ROSENFARB J.,FREEDOM AND THE ADMINISTRATIVE STATE.   ECO/DEV
NAT/G ROUTINE EFFICIENCY PRODUC RATIONAL UTIL   INDUS
...TECHNIC WELF/ST MGT 20 BUREAUCRCY. PAGE 90 B1821   PLAN
                                                     WEALTH
                                                        B50
HYNEMAN C.S.,BUREAUCRACY IN A DEMOCRACY. CHIEF   NAT/G
LEGIS ADMIN CONTROL LEAD ROUTINE PERS/REL COST   CENTRAL
EFFICIENCY UTIL ATTIT AUTHORIT PERSON MORAL.   EX/STRUC
PAGE 53 B1071   MYTH
                                                        B57
US HOUSE COMM ON POST OFFICE,MANPOWER UTILIZATION   NAT/G
IN THE FEDERAL GOVERNMENT. USA+45 FORCES WORKER   ADMIN
CREATE PLAN EFFICIENCY UTIL 20 CONGRESS CIVIL/SERV   LABOR
POSTAL/SYS DEPT/DEFEN. PAGE 109 B2193   EX/STRUC
                                                        B60
ARROW K.J.,MATHEMATICAL METHODS IN THE SOCIAL   MATH
SCIENCES, 1959. TEC/DEV CHOOSE UTIL PERCEPT   PSY
...KNO/TEST GAME SIMUL ANTHOL. PAGE 7 B0137   MGT
                                                        S60
FRIEDMAN L.,"DECISION MAKING IN COMPETITIVE   DECISION
SITUATIONS" OP/RES...MGT PROBABIL METH/COMP SIMUL   UTIL
20. PAGE 37 B0757   OPTIMAL
                                                     GAME
                                                        B61
ROMANO F.,CIVIL SERVICE AND PUBLIC EMPLOYEE LAW IN   ADMIN
NEW JERSEY. CONSTN MUNIC WORKER GIVE PAY CHOOSE   PROVS
UTIL 20. PAGE 90 B1816   ADJUD
                                                     LOC/G
                                                        B61
ROSE D.L.,THE VIETNAMESE CIVIL SERVICE. VIETNAM   ADMIN
CONSULT DELIB/GP GIVE PAY EDU/PROP COLONIAL GOV/REL   EFFICIENCY
UTIL...CHARTS 20. PAGE 90 B1819   STAT
                                                     NAT/G
                                                        B62
NATIONAL BUREAU ECONOMIC RES,THE RATE AND DIRECTION DECISION
OF INVENTIVE ACTIVITY: ECONOMIC AND SOCIAL FACTORS. PROB/SOLV
STRUCT INDUS MARKET R+D CREATE OP/RES TEC/DEV   MGT
EFFICIENCY PRODUC RATIONAL UTIL...WELF/ST PHIL/SCI
METH/CNCPT TIME. PAGE 77 B1562
                                                        B63
US SENATE COMM APPROPRIATIONS,PERSONNEL   ADMIN
ADMINISTRATION AND OPERATIONS OF AGENCY FOR   FOR/AID
INTERNATIONAL DEVELOPMENT: SPECIAL HEARING. FINAN   EFFICIENCY
LEAD COST UTIL SKILL...CHARTS 20 CONGRESS AID   DIPLOM
CIVIL/SERV. PAGE 109 B2211
                                                        B64
MCNULTY J.E.,SOME ECONOMIC ASPECTS OF BUSINESS   ADMIN
ORGANIZATION. ECO/DEV UTIL...MGT CHARTS BIBLIOG   LG/CO
METH 20. PAGE 72 B1458   GEN/LAWS
                                                        B64
PEABODY R.L.,ORGANIZATIONAL AUTHORITY. SCHOOL   ADMIN

WORKER PLAN SENIOR GOV/REL UTIL DRIVE PWR...PSY
CHARTS BIBLIOG 20. PAGE 82 B1648

EFFICIENCY
TASK
GP/REL
S64

NEWLYN W.T.,"MONETARY SYSTEMS AND INTEGRATION" AFR
BUDGET ADMIN FEDERAL PRODUC PROFIT UTIL...CHARTS 20
AFRICA/E. PAGE 78 B1578

ECO/UNDEV
REGION
METH/COMP
FINAN
B65

HICKMAN B.G.,QUANTITATIVE PLANNING OF ECONOMIC
POLICY. FRANCE NETHERLAND OP/RES PRICE ROUTINE UTIL
...POLICY DECISION ECOMETRIC METH/CNCPT STAT STYLE
CHINJAP. PAGE 50 B1004

PROB/SOLV
PLAN
QUANT
N65

NJ DIVISION STATE-REGION PLAN,UTILIZATION OF NEW
JERSEY'S DELAWARE RIVER WATERFRONT (PAMPHLET). FUT
ADMIN REGION LEISURE GOV/REL DEMAND WEALTH...CHARTS
20 NEW/JERSEY. PAGE 78 B1586

UTIL
PLAN
ECO/TAC
PROVS
B66

US SENATE COMM GOVT OPERATIONS,INTERGOVERNMENTAL
PERSONNEL ACT OF 1966. USA+45 NAT/G CONSULT
DELIB/GP WORKER TEC/DEV PAY AUTOMAT UTIL 20
CONGRESS. PAGE 110 B2219

ADMIN
LEGIS
EFFICIENCY
EDU/PROP
B66

WESTON J.F.,THE SCOPE AND METHODOLOGY OF FINANCE.
PLAN TEC/DEV CONTROL EFFICIENCY INCOME UTIL...MGT
CONCPT MATH STAT TREND METH 20. PAGE 115 B2327

FINAN
ECO/DEV
POLICY
PRICE
B67

ENKE S.,DEFENSE MANAGEMENT. USA+45 R+D FORCES
WORKER PLAN ECO/TAC ADMIN NUC/PWR BAL/PAY UTIL
WEALTH...MGT DEPT/DEFEN. PAGE 33 B0675

DECISION
DELIB/GP
EFFICIENCY
BUDGET
S67

FERGUSON H.,"3-CITY CONSOLIDATION." USA+45 CONSTN
INDUS BARGAIN BUDGET CONFER ADMIN INGP/REL COST
UTIL. PAGE 35 B0712

MUNIC
CHOOSE
CREATE
PROB/SOLV

UTILITAR....UTILITARIANISM

UTILITARIANISM....SEE UTILITAR

UTILITY....SEE UTIL

UTOPIA....ENVISIONED GENERAL SOCIAL CONDITIONS; SEE ALSO
STERTYP

PLATO,THE REPUBLIC. MEDIT-7 UNIV SOCIETY STRUCT
EX/STRUC FORCES UTOPIA ATTIT PERCEPT HEALTH KNOWL
ORD/FREE PWR...HUM CONCPT STERTYP TOT/POP. PAGE 83
B1681

B45
PERSON
PHIL/SCI

HEATH S.,CITADEL, MARKET, AND ALTAR; EMERGING
SOCIETY. SOCIETY ADMIN OPTIMAL OWN RATIONAL
ORD/FREE...SOC LOG PREDICT GEN/LAWS DICTIONARY 20.
PAGE 49 B0985

B57
NEW/IDEA
STRUCT
UTOPIA
CREATE
B58

REDFORD E.S.,IDEAL AND PRACTICE IN PUBLIC
ADMINISTRATION. CONSTN ELITES NAT/G CONSULT
DELIB/GP LEAD UTOPIA ATTIT POPULISM...DECISION
METH/COMP 20. PAGE 87 B1756

POLICY
EX/STRUC
PLAN
ADMIN
B62

SIMON Y.R.,A GENERAL THEORY OF AUTHORITY. DOMIN
ADMIN RATIONAL UTOPIA KNOWL MORAL PWR SOVEREIGN
...HUM CONCPT NEW/IDEA 20. PAGE 97 B1962

PERS/REL
PERSON
SOCIETY
ORD/FREE
B64

CAPLOW T.,PRINCIPLES OF ORGANIZATION. UNIV CULTURE
STRUCT CREATE INGP/REL UTOPIA...GEN/LAWS TIME.
PAGE 18 B0374

VOL/ASSN
CONCPT
SIMUL
EX/STRUC
B65

BOGUSLAW R.,THE NEW UTOPIANS. OP/RES ADMIN CONTROL
PWR...IDEA/COMP SIMUL 20. PAGE 13 B0265

UTOPIA
AUTOMAT
COMPUTER
PLAN
S67

GORMAN W.,"ELLUL - A PROPHETIC VOICE." WOR+45
ELITES SOCIETY ACT/RES PLAN BAL/PWR DOMIN CONTROL
PARTIC TOTALISM PWR 20. PAGE 41 B0837

CREATE
ORD/FREE
EX/STRUC
UTOPIA

UTTAR/PRAD....UTTAR PRADESH, INDIA

V

VAID K.N. B2248

VALEN H. B2249

VALIDITY (AS CONCEPT)....SEE METH/CNCPT

VALUE ADDED TAX....SEE VALUE/ADD

VALUE/ADD....VALUE ADDED TAX

VALUE-FREE THOUGHT....SEE OBJECTIVE

VALUES....SEE VALUES INDEX, P. XIII

VALUNJKAR T.N. B0796

VAN DER SPRENKEL S. B2250

VAN NESS E.H. B1380

VAN RIPER P.P. B2251,B2252,B2295

VAN SLYCK P. B2253

VANBUREN/M....PRESIDENT MARTIN VAN BUREN

VANDENBOSCH A. B2254

VARMA S.N. B0150

VASEY W. B2255

VATICAN....VATICAN

THIERRY S.S.,LE VATICAN SECRET. CHRIST-17C EUR+WWI
MOD/EUR VATICAN NAT/G SECT DELIB/GP DOMIN LEGIT
SOVEREIGN. PAGE 104 B2096

B62
ADMIN
EX/STRUC
CATHISM
DECISION

VEBLEN/T....THORSTEIN VEBLEN

VECCHIO G.D. B2256

VEINOTT A.F. B2257

VENETIAN REPUBLIC....SEE VENICE

VENEZUELA....VENEZUELA; SEE ALSO L/A+17C

SEGUNDO-SANCHEZ M.,OBRAS (2 VOLS.). VENEZUELA
EX/STRUC DIPLOM ADMIN 19/20. PAGE 95 B1924

B64
BIBLIOG
LEAD
NAT/G
L/A+17C
S67

CARIAS B.,"EL CONTROL DE LAS EMPRESAS PUBLICAS POR
GRUPOS DE INTERESES DE LA COMUNIDAD." FRANCE UK
VENEZUELA INDUS NAT/G CONTROL OWN PWR...DECISION
NAT/COMP 20. PAGE 18 B0377

WORKER
REPRESENT
MGT
SOCISM

VENICE....VENETIAN REPUBLIC

VENKATESAN S.L. B2258

VERBA S. B2259

VERGIN R.C. B2260

VERHULST M. B0184

VERMONT....VERMONT

NUQUIST A.E.,TOWN GOVERNMENT IN VERMONT. USA+45
FINAN TOP/EX PROB/SOLV BUDGET TAX REPRESENT SUFF
EFFICIENCY...OBS INT 20 VERMONT. PAGE 79 B1595

B64
LOC/G
MUNIC
POPULISM
ADMIN

VERNEY D.V. B0313

VERNON R. B2261

VERSAILLES....VERSAILLES, FRANCE

VERTICAL TAKE-OFF AND LANDING AIRCRAFT....SEE VTOL

VERWOERD/H....HENDRIK VERWOERD

VETO....VETO AND VETOING

VICE/PRES....VICE-PRESIDENCY (ALL NATIONS)

WAUGH E.W.,SECOND CONSUL. USA+45 USA-45 CONSTN
POL/PAR PROB/SOLV PARL/PROC CHOOSE PERS/REL ATTIT
...BIBLIOG 18/20 VICE/PRES. PAGE 114 B2304

B56
NAT/G
EX/STRUC
PWR
CHIEF
B65

FEERICK J.D.,FROM FAILING HANDS: THE STUDY OF
PRESIDENTIAL SUCCESSION. CONSTN NAT/G PROB/SOLV
LEAD PARL/PROC MURDER CHOOSE...NEW/IDEA BIBLIOG 20
KENNEDY/JF JOHNSON/LB PRESIDENT PRE/US/AM
VICE/PRES. PAGE 35 B0710

EX/STRUC
CHIEF
LAW
LEGIS

VICEREGAL....VICEROYALTY; VICEROY SYSTEM

VICHY....VICHY, FRANCE

VICTORIA/Q....QUEEN VICTORIA

VIEG J.A. B2138

VIENNA/CNV....VIENNA CONVENTION ON CONSULAR RELATIONS

                                                         B66

LEE L.T.,VIENNA CONVENTION ON CONSULAR RELATIONS.   AGREE
WOR+45 LAW INT/ORG CONFER GP/REL PRIVIL...INT/LAW   DIPLOM
20 TREATY VIENNA/CNV. PAGE 63 B1279   ADMIN

VIET MINH....SEE VIETNAM, GUERRILLA, COLONIAL

VIET/CONG....VIET CONG

VIETNAM....VIETNAM IN GENERAL; SEE ALSO S/ASIA, VIETNAM/N,
   VIETNAM/S

                                                         B29

BOUDET P.,BIBLIOGRAPHIE DE L'INDOCHINE FRANCAISE.   BIBLIOG
S/ASIA VIETNAM SECT...GEOG LING 20. PAGE 14 B0282   ADMIN
                                                 COLONIAL
                                                 DIPLOM
                                                    C56

FALL B.B.,"THE VIET-MINH REGIME." VIETNAM LAW   NAT/G
ECO/UNDEV POL/PAR FORCES DOMIN WAR ATTIT MARXISM   ADMIN
...BIOG PREDICT BIBLIOG/A 20. PAGE 35 B0703   EX/STRUC
                                                 LEAD
                                                    B61

ROSE D.L.,THE VIETNAMESE CIVIL SERVICE. VIETNAM   ADMIN
CONSULT DELIB/GP GIVE PAY EDU/PROP COLONIAL GOV/REL   EFFICIENCY
UTIL...CHARTS 20. PAGE 90 B1819   STAT
                                                 NAT/G
                                                    B64

HICKEY G.C.,VILLAGE IN VIETNAM. USA+45 VIETNAM LAW   CULTURE
AGRI FAM SECT ADMIN ATTIT...SOC CHARTS WORSHIP 20.   SOCIETY
PAGE 49 B1003   STRUCT
                                                 S/ASIA
                                                    B64

PARET P.,FRENCH REVOLUTIONARY WARFARE FROM   FRANCE
INDOCHINA TO ALGERIA* THE ANALYSIS OF A POLITICAL   GUERRILLA
AND MILITARY DOCTRINE. ALGERIA VIETNAM FORCES   GEN/LAWS
OP/RES TEC/DEV ROUTINE REV ATTIT...PSY BIBLIOG.
PAGE 81 B1632
                                                 L64

FOX G.H.,"PERCEPTIONS OF THE VIETNAMESE PUBLIC   ADMIN
ADMINISTRATION SYSTEM" VIETNAM ELITES CONTROL EXEC   EX/STRUC
LEAD PWR...INT 20. PAGE 37 B0745   INGP/REL
                                                 ROLE
                                                    C66

TARLING N.,"A CONCISE HISTORY OF SOUTHEAST ASIA."   COLONIAL
BURMA CAMBODIA LAOS S/ASIA THAILAND VIETNAM   DOMIN
ECO/UNDEV POL/PAR FORCES ADMIN REV WAR CIVMIL/REL   INT/TRADE
ORD/FREE MARXISM SOCISM 13/20. PAGE 103 B2080   NAT/LISM
                                                 S67

O'DELL J.H.,"THE JULY REBELLIONS AND THE 'MILITARY   PWR
STATE'." USA+45 VIETNAM STRATA CHIEF WORKER   NAT/G
COLONIAL EXEC CROWD CIVMIL/REL RACE/REL TOTALISM   COERCE
...WELF/ST PACIFIST 20 NEGRO JOHNSON/LB PRESIDENT   FORCES
CIV/RIGHTS. PAGE 79 B1599

VIETNAM/N....NORTH VIETNAM

VIETNAM/S....SOUTH VIETNAM

                                                 B59

MONTGOMERY J.D.,CASES IN VIETNAMESE ADMINISTRATION. ADMIN
VIETNAM/S EX/STRUC 20. PAGE 75 B1506   DECISION
                                                 PROB/SOLV
                                                 LEAD
                                                 B66

US HOUSE COMM GOVT OPERATIONS,AN INVESTIGATION OF   FOR/AID
THE US ECONOMIC AND MILITARY ASSISTANCE PROGRAMS IN ECO/UNDEV
VIETNAM. USA+45 VIETNAM/S SOCIETY CONSTRUC FINAN   WAR
FORCES BUDGET INT/TRADE PEACE HEALTH...MGT   INSPECT
HOUSE/REP AID. PAGE 108 B2191
                                                 S67

DONNELL J.C.,"PACIFICATION REASSESSED." VIETNAM/S   ADMIN
NAT/LISM DRIVE SUPEGO ORD/FREE...SOC/WK 20. PAGE 30 GP/REL
B0606   EFFICIENCY
                                                 MUNIC

VILLA/P....PANCHO VILLA

VILLAGE....SEE MUNIC

VILLARD/OG....OSWALD GARRISON VILLARD

VINER J. B2262

VINER/J....JACOB VINER

VINTER R.D. B1661,B2052

VIOLENCE....SEE COERCE, ALSO PROCESSES AND PRACTICES INDEX,
   PART G, PAGE XIII

VIORST M. B2263

VIRALLY M. B2264

VIRGIN/ISL....VIRGIN ISLANDS

                                                 B59

COUNCIL OF STATE GOVERNORS,AMERICAN LEGISLATURES: LEGIS
STRUCTURE AND PROCEDURES. SUMMARY AND TABULATIONS   CHARTS
OF A 1959 SURVEY. PUERT/RICO USA+45 PAY ADJUD ADMIN PROVS
APPORT...IDEA/COMP 20 GUAM VIRGIN/ISL. PAGE 24   REPRESENT
B0495

VIRGINIA....VIRGINIA

VIRGINIA STATE LIBRARY B2265

VISTA....VOLUNTEERS IN SERVICE TO AMERICA (VISTA)

VOL/ASSN....VOLUNTARY ASSOCIATION

                                                 B21

BRYCE J.,MODERN DEMOCRACIES. FUT NEW/ZEALND USA-45   NAT/G
LAW CONSTN POL/PAR PROVS VOL/ASSN EX/STRUC LEGIS   TREND
LEGIT CT/SYS EXEC KNOWL CONGRESS AUSTRAL 20.
PAGE 16 B0332
                                                 B28

HALL W.P.,EMPIRE TO COMMONWEALTH. FUT WOR-45 CONSTN VOL/ASSN
ECO/DEV ECO/UNDEV INT/ORG PROVS PLAN DIPLOM   NAT/G
EDU/PROP ADMIN COLONIAL PEACE PERSON ALL/VALS   UK
...POLICY GEOG SOC OBS RECORD TREND CMN/WLTH
PARLIAMENT 19/20. PAGE 46 B0925
                                                 B36

ROBINSON H.,DEVELOPMENT OF THE BRITISH EMPIRE.   NAT/G
WOR-45 CULTURE SOCIETY STRUCT ECO/DEV ECO/UNDEV   HIST/WRIT
INT/ORG VOL/ASSN FORCES CREATE PLAN DOMIN EDU/PROP   UK
ADMIN COLONIAL PWR WEALTH...POLICY GEOG CHARTS
CMN/WLTH 16/20. PAGE 89 B1800
                                                 B44

WRIGHT H.R.,SOCIAL SERVICE IN WARTIME. FINAN NAT/G   GIVE
VOL/ASSN PLAN GP/REL ROLE. PAGE 118 B2381   WAR
                                                 SOC/WK
                                                 ADMIN
                                                 B50

AMERICAN POLITICAL SCI ASSN,TOWARD A MORE   POL/PAR
RESPONSIBLE TWO-PARTY SYSTEM. USA+45 CONSTN   TASK
VOL/ASSN LEGIS LEAD CHOOSE...POLICY MGT 20. PAGE 4   PARTIC
B0087   ACT/RES
                                                 B50

LASSWELL H.D.,NATIONAL SECURITY AND INDIVIDUAL   FACE/GP
FREEDOM. USA+45 R+D NAT/G VOL/ASSN CONSULT DELIB/GP ROUTINE
LEGIT ADMIN KNOWL ORD/FREE PWR...PLURIST TOT/POP   BAL/PWR
COLD/WAR 20. PAGE 63 B1268
                                                 C50

STEWART F.M.,"A HALF CENTURY OF MUNICIPAL REFORM."   LOC/G
USA+45 CONSTN FINAN SCHOOL EX/STRUC PLAN PROB/SOLV   VOL/ASSN
EDU/PROP ADMIN CHOOSE GOV/REL BIBLIOG. PAGE 101   MUNIC
B2036   POLICY
                                                 B51

NIELANDER W.A.,PUBLIC RELATIONS. USA+45 COM/IND   PERS/REL
LOC/G NAT/G VOL/ASSN EX/STRUC DIPLOM EDU/PROP PRESS GP/REL
TV...METH/CNCPT T 20. PAGE 78 B1583   LG/CO
                                                 ROUTINE
                                                 S51

STEWART D.D.,"THE PLACE OF VOLUNTEER PARTICIPATION   ADMIN
IN BUREAUCRATIC ORGANIZATION." NAT/G DELIB/GP   PARTIC
OP/RES DOMIN LOBBY WAR ATTIT ROLE PWR. PAGE 101   VOL/ASSN
B2035   FORCES
                                                 S52

BRUEGEL J.W.,"DIE INTERNAZIONALE   VOL/ASSN
GEWERKSCHAFTSBEWEGUNG." COM EUR+WWI USA+45 WOR+45   LABOR
DELIB/GP EX/STRUC ECO/TAC EDU/PROP ATTIT PWR   TOTALISM
RESPECT SKILL WEALTH WORK 20. PAGE 16 B0330
                                                 B53

GREENE K.R.C.,INSTITUTIONS AND INDIVIDUALS: AN   BIBLIOG
ANNOTATED LIST OF DIRECTORIES USEFUL IN   INT/ORG
INTERNATIONAL ADMINISTRATION. USA+45 NAT/G VOL/ASSN ADMIN
...INDEX 20. PAGE 43 B0865   DIPLOM
                                                 B53

MACK R.T.,RAISING THE WORLDS STANDARD OF LIVING.   WOR+45
IRAN INT/ORG VOL/ASSN EX/STRUC ECO/TAC WEALTH...MGT FOR/AID
METH/CNCPT STAT CONT/OBS INT TOT/POP VAL/FREE 20   INT/TRADE
UN. PAGE 67 B1363
                                                 S53

MORRIS B.S.,"THE COMINFORM: A FIVE YEAR   VOL/ASSN
PERSPECTIVE." COM UNIV USSR WOR+45 ECO/DEV POL/PAR   EDU/PROP
TOP/EX PLAN DOMIN ADMIN TOTALISM ATTIT ALL/VALS   DIPLOM
...CONCPT TIME/SEQ TREND CON/ANAL WORK VAL/FREE 20.
PAGE 76 B1527
                                                 B54

LAPIERRE R.T.,A THEORY OF SOCIAL CONTROL. STRUCT   CONTROL
ADMIN ROUTINE SANCTION ANOMIE AUTHORIT DRIVE PERSON VOL/ASSN
PWR...MAJORIT CONCPT CLASSIF. PAGE 62 B1260   CULTURE

B54

MILLARD E.L.,FREEDOM IN A FEDERAL WORLD. FUT WOR+45   INT/ORG
VOL/ASSN TOP/EX LEGIT ROUTINE FEDERAL PEACE ATTIT   CREATE
DISPL ORD/FREE PWR...MAJORIT INT/LAW JURID TREND   ADJUD
COLD/WAR 20. PAGE 73 B1479   BAL/PWR

B54

PUBLIC ADMIN CLEARING HOUSE,PUBLIC ADMINISTRATIONS   INDEX
ORGANIZATIONS: A DIRECTORY, 1954. USA+45 R+D PROVS   VOL/ASSN
ACT/RES...MGT 20. PAGE 85 B1714   NAT/G
                                                       ADMIN

B55

BERNAYS E.L.,THE ENGINEERING OF CONSENT. VOL/ASSN   GP/REL
OP/RES ROUTINE INGP/REL ATTIT RESPECT...POLICY   PLAN
METH/CNCPT METH/COMP 20. PAGE 11 B0224   ACT/RES
                                                       ADJUST

B55

MAZZINI J.,THE DUTIES OF MAN. MOD/EUR LAW SOCIETY   SUPEGO
FAM NAT/G POL/PAR SECT VOL/ASSN EX/STRUC ACT/RES   CONCPT
CREATE REV PEACE ATTIT ALL/VALS...GEN/LAWS WORK 19.   NAT/LISM
PAGE 71 B1439

B55

UN HEADQUARTERS LIBRARY,BIBLIOGRAPHIE DE LA CHARTE   BIBLIOG/A
DES NATIONS UNIES. CHINA/COM KOREA WOR+45 VOL/ASSN   INT/ORG
CONFER ADMIN COERCE PEACE ATTIT ORD/FREE SOVEREIGN   DIPLOM
...INT/LAW 20 UNESCO UN. PAGE 106 B2149

L55

KISER M.,"ORGANIZATION OF AMERICAN STATES." L/A+17C   VOL/ASSN
USA+45 ECO/UNDEV INT/ORG NAT/G PLAN TEC/DEV DIPLOM   ECO/DEV
ECO/TAC INT/TRADE EDU/PROP ADMIN ALL/VALS...POLICY   REGION
MGT RECORD ORG/CHARTS OAS 20. PAGE 60 B1215

S55

CHAPIN F.S.,"FORMALIZATION OBSERVED IN TEN   VOL/ASSN
VOLUNTARY ORGANIZATIONS: CONCEPTS, MORPHOLOGY,   ROUTINE
PROCESS." STRUCT INGP/REL PERS/REL...METH/CNCPT   CONTROL
CLASSIF OBS RECORD. PAGE 20 B0407   OP/RES

S55

TORRE M.,"PSYCHIATRIC OBSERVATIONS OF INTERNATIONAL   DELIB/GP
CONFERENCES." WOR+45 INT/ORG PROF/ORG VOL/ASSN   OBS
CONSULT EDU/PROP ROUTINE ATTIT DRIVE KNOWL...PSY   DIPLOM
METH/CNCPT OBS/ENVIR STERTYP 20. PAGE 105 B2119

B56

WASSERMAN P.,INFORMATION FOR ADMINISTRATORS: A   BIBLIOG
GUIDE TO PUBLICATIONS AND SERVICES FOR MANAGEMENT   MGT
IN BUSINESS AND GOVERNMENT. R+D LOC/G NAT/G   KNOWL
PROF/ORG VOL/ASSN PRESS...PSY SOC STAT 20. PAGE 114   EDU/PROP
B2299

B56

WHYTE W.H. JR.,THE ORGANIZATION MAN. CULTURE FINAN   ADMIN
VOL/ASSN DOMIN EDU/PROP EXEC DISPL HABITAT ROLE   LG/CO
...PERS/TEST STERTYP. PAGE 116 B2343   PERSON
                                                       CONSEN

B57

DE GRAZIA A.,GRASS ROOTS PRIVATE WELFARE. LOC/G   NEW/LIB
SCHOOL ACT/RES EDU/PROP ROUTINE CROWD GP/REL   HEALTH
DISCRIM HAPPINESS ILLEGIT AGE HABITAT. PAGE 27   MUNIC
B0554   VOL/ASSN

B57

SIMON H.A.,MODELS OF MAN, SOCIAL AND RATIONAL: MATH
MATHEMATICAL ESSAYS ON RATIONAL HUMAN BEHAVIOR IN A   SIMUL
SOCIAL SETTING. UNIV LAW SOCIETY FACE/GP VOL/ASSN
CONSULT EX/STRUC LEGIS CREATE ADMIN ROUTINE ATTIT
DRIVE PWR...SOC CONCPT METH/CNCPT QUANT STAT
TOT/POP VAL/FREE 20. PAGE 97 B1959

B57

UDY S.H. JR.,THE ORGANIZATION OF PRODUCTION IN   METH/COMP
NONINDUSTRIAL CULTURE. VOL/ASSN DELIB/GP TEC/DEV   ECO/UNDEV
...CHARTS BIBLIOG. PAGE 106 B2143   PRODUC
                                                       ADMIN

L57

HAAS E.B.,"REGIONAL INTEGRATION AND NATIONAL   INT/ORG
POLICY." WOR+45 VOL/ASSN DELIB/GP EX/STRUC ECO/TAC   ORD/FREE
DOMIN EDU/PROP LEGIT COERCE ATTIT PERCEPT KNOWL   REGION
...TIME/SEQ COLD/WAR 20 UN. PAGE 45 B0908

B58

LAQUER W.Z.,THE MIDDLE EAST IN TRANSITION. COM USSR   ISLAM
ECO/UNDEV NAT/G VOL/ASSN EDU/PROP EXEC ATTIT DRIVE   TREND
PWR MARXISM COLD/WAR TOT/POP 20. PAGE 62 B1261   NAT/LISM

B58

SKINNER G.W.,LEADERSHIP AND POWER IN THE CHINESE   SOC
COMMUNITY OF THAILAND. ASIA S/ASIA STRATA FACE/GP   ELITES
KIN PROF/ORG VOL/ASSN EX/STRUC DOMIN PERSON RESPECT   THAILAND
...METH/CNCPT STAT INT QU BIOG CHARTS 20. PAGE 98
B1974

L58

HAVILAND H.F.,"FOREIGN AID AND THE POLICY PROCESS: LEGIS
1957." USA+45 FACE/GP POL/PAR VOL/ASSN CHIEF   PLAN
DELIB/GP ACT/RES LEGIT EXEC GOV/REL ATTIT DRIVE PWR   FOR/AID
...POLICY TESTS CONGRESS 20. PAGE 48 B0971

S58

ALMOND G.A.,"COMPARATIVE STUDY OF INTEREST GROUPS."   LOBBY
USA+45 EX/STRUC PWR 20. PAGE 4 B0079   REPRESENT
                                                       ADMIN
                                                       VOL/ASSN

S58

ELKIN A.B.,"OEEC-ITS STRUCTURE AND POWERS." EUR+WWI   ECO/DEV
CONSTN INDUS INT/ORG NAT/G VOL/ASSN DELIB/GP   EX/STRUC

ACT/RES PLAN ORD/FREE WEALTH...CHARTS ORG/CHARTS
OEEC 20. PAGE 33 B0666

B59

DAHRENDORF R.,CLASS AND CLASS CONFLICT IN   VOL/ASSN
INDUSTRIAL SOCIETY. LABOR NAT/G COERCE ROLE PLURISM   STRUCT
...POLICY MGT CONCPT CLASSIF. PAGE 26 B0523   SOC
                                                       GP/REL

B59

JOYCE J.A.,RED CROSS INTERNATIONAL AND THE STRATEGY   VOL/ASSN
OF PEACE. WOR+45 WOR-45 EX/STRUC SUPEGO ALL/VALS   HEALTH
...CONCPT GEN/LAWS TOT/POP 19/20 RED/CROSS. PAGE 57
B1155

S59

BAILEY S.D.,"THE FUTURE COMPOSITION OF THE   INT/ORG
TRUSTEESHIP COUNCIL." FUT WOR+45 CONSTN VOL/ASSN   NAT/LISM
ADMIN ATTIT PWR...OBS TREND CON/ANAL VAL/FREE UN   SOVEREIGN
20. PAGE 8 B0161

S59

HOFFMANN S.,"IMPLEMENTATION OF INTERNATIONAL   INT/ORG
INSTRUMENTS ON HUMAN RIGHTS." WOR+45 VOL/ASSN   MORAL
DELIB/GP JUDGE EDU/PROP LEGIT ROUTINE PEACE
COLD/WAR 20. PAGE 51 B1029

S59

PADELFORD N.J.,"REGIONAL COOPERATION IN THE SOUTH   INT/ORG
PACIFIC: THE SOUTH PACIFIC COMMISSION." FUT   ADMIN
NEW/ZEALND UK WOR+45 CULTURE ECO/UNDEV LOC/G
VOL/ASSN...OBS CON/ANAL UNESCO VAL/FREE AUSTRAL 20.
PAGE 80 B1622

S59

STOESSINGER J.G.,"THE INTERNATIONAL ATOMIC ENERGY   INT/ORG
AGENCY: THE FIRST PHASE." FUT WOR+45 NAT/G VOL/ASSN   ECO/DEV
DELIB/GP BAL/PWR LEGIT ADMIN ROUTINE PWR...OBS   FOR/AID
CON/ANAL GEN/LAWS VAL/FREE 20 IAEA. PAGE 101 B2040   NUC/PWR

S59

UDY S.H. JR.,"'BUREAUCRACY' AND 'RATIONALITY' IN   GEN/LAWS
WEBER'S ORGANIZATION THEORY: AN EMPIRICAL STUDY"   METH/CNCPT
(BMR)" UNIV STRUCT INDUS LG/CO SML/CO VOL/ASSN   ADMIN
...SOC SIMUL 20 WEBER/MAX BUREAUCRCY. PAGE 106   RATIONAL
B2144

B60

DRAPER T.,AMERICAN COMMUNISM AND SOVIET RUSSIA.   COM
EUR+WWI USA+45 USSR INTELL AGRI COM/IND FINAN INDUS   POL/PAR
LABOR PROF/ORG VOL/ASSN PLAN TEC/DEV DOMIN EDU/PROP
ADMIN COERCE REV PERSON PWR...POLICY CONCPT MYTH
19/20. PAGE 30 B0617

B60

GILMORE D.R.,DEVELOPING THE "LITTLE" ECONOMIES.   ECO/TAC
USA+45 FINAN LG/CO PROF/ORG VOL/ASSN CREATE ADMIN.   LOC/G
PAGE 40 B0801   PROVS
                                                       PLAN

B60

LINDSAY K.,EUROPEAN ASSEMBLIES: THE EXPERIMENTAL   VOL/ASSN
PERIOD 1949-1959. EUR+WWI ECO/DEV NAT/G POL/PAR   INT/ORG
LEGIS TOP/EX ACT/RES PLAN ECO/TAC DOMIN LEGIT   REGION
ROUTINE ATTIT DRIVE ORD/FREE PWR SKILL...SOC CONCPT
TREND CHARTS GEN/LAWS VAL/FREE. PAGE 65 B1315

B60

MOORE W.E.,LABOR COMMITMENT AND SOCIAL CHANGE IN   LABOR
DEVELOPING AREAS. SOCIETY STRATA ECO/UNDEV MARKET   ORD/FREE
VOL/ASSN WORKER AUTHORIT SKILL...MGT NAT/COMP   ATTIT
SOC/INTEG 20. PAGE 75 B1514   INDUS

B60

WHEARE K.C.,THE CONSTITUTIONAL STRUCTURE OF THE   CONSTN
COMMONWEALTH. UK EX/STRUC DIPLOM DOMIN ADMIN   INT/ORG
COLONIAL CONTROL LEAD INGP/REL SUPEGO 20 CMN/WLTH.   VOL/ASSN
PAGE 115 B2330   SOVEREIGN

L60

BRENNAN D.G.,"SETTING AND GOALS OF ARMS CONTROL."   FORCES
FUT USA+45 USSR WOR+45 INTELL INT/ORG NAT/G   COERCE
VOL/ASSN CONSULT PLAN DIPLOM ECO/TAC ADMIN KNOWL   ARMS/CONT
PWR...POLICY CONCPT COLD/WAR 20. PAGE 15   DETER
B0305

S60

MORA J.A.,"THE ORGANIZATION OF AMERICAN STATES."   L/A+17C
USA+45 LAW ECO/UNDEV VOL/ASSN DELIB/GP BAL/PWR   INT/ORG
EDU/PROP ADMIN DRIVE RIGID/FLEX ORD/FREE WEALTH   REGION
...TIME/SEQ GEN/LAWS OAS 20. PAGE 75 B1518

S60

SCHWARTZ B.,"THE INTELLIGENTSIA IN COMMUNIST CHINA: INTELL
A TENTATIVE COMPARISON." ASIA CHINA/COM COM RUSSIA   RIGID/FLEX
ELITES SOCIETY STRATA POL/PAR VOL/ASSN CREATE ADMIN   REV
COERCE NAT/LISM TOTALISM...POLICY TREND 20. PAGE 95
B1914

B61

BENOIT E.,EUROPE AT SIXES AND SEVENS: THE COMMON   FINAN
MARKET, THE FREE TRADE ASSOCIATION AND THE UNITED   ECO/DEV
STATES. EUR+WWI FUT USA+45 INDUS CONSULT DELIB/GP   VOL/ASSN
EX/STRUC TOP/EX ACT/RES ECO/TAC EDU/PROP ROUTINE
CHOOSE PERCEPT WEALTH...MGT TREND EEC TOT/POP 20
EFTA. PAGE 11 B0217

B61

ETZIONI A.,COMPLEX ORGANIZATIONS: A SOCIOLOGICAL   VOL/ASSN
READER. CLIENT CULTURE STRATA CREATE OP/RES ADMIN   STRUCT
...POLICY METH/CNCPT BUREAUCRCY. PAGE 34 B0683   CLASSIF
                                                       PROF/ORG

B61
FRIEDMANN W.G.,,JOINT INTERNATIONAL BUSINESS   ECO/UNDEV
VENTURES. ASIA ISLAM L/A+17C ECO/DEV DIST/IND FINAN   INT/TRADE
PROC/MFG FACE/GP LG/CO NAT/G VOL/ASSN CONSULT
EX/STRUC PLAN ADMIN ROUTINE WEALTH...OLD/LIB WORK
20. PAGE 37 B0760

B61
HAMILTON A.,THE FEDERALIST. USA-45 NAT/G VOL/ASSN   EX/STRUC
LEGIS TOP/EX EDU/PROP LEGIT CHOOSE ATTIT RIGID/FLEX   CONSTN
ORD/FREE PWR...MAJORIT JURID CONCPT ANTHOL. PAGE 46
B0931

B61
JANOWITZ M.,COMMUNITY POLITICAL SYSTEMS. USA+45   MUNIC
SOCIETY INDUS VOL/ASSN TEC/DEV ADMIN LEAD CHOOSE   STRUCT
...SOC SOC/WK 20. PAGE 56 B1123   POL/PAR

B61
MACRIDIS R.C.,COMPARATIVE POLITICS: NOTES AND   POL/PAR
READINGS. WOR+45 LOC/G MUNIC NAT/G PROVS VOL/ASSN   CHOOSE
EDU/PROP ADMIN ATTIT PERSON ORD/FREE...SOC CONCPT
OBS RECORD TREND 20. PAGE 68 B1376

B61
MOLLAU G.,INTERNATIONAL COMMUNISM AND WORLD   COM
REVOLUTION: HISTORY AND METHODS. RUSSIA USSR   REV
INT/ORG NAT/G POL/PAR VOL/ASSN FORCES BAL/PWR
DIPLOM EXEC REGION WAR ATTIT PWR MARXISM...CONCPT
TIME/SEQ COLD/WAR 19/20. PAGE 74 B1498

B61
PEASLEE A.J.,INTERNATIONAL GOVERNMENT   INT/ORG
ORGANIZATIONS, CONSTITUTIONAL DOCUMENTS. WOR+45   STRUCT
WOR-45 CONSTN VOL/ASSN DELIB/GP EX/STRUC ROUTINE
KNOWL TOT/POP 20. PAGE 82 B1650

B61
STONE J.,QUEST FOR SURVIVAL. WOR+45 NAT/G VOL/ASSN   INT/ORG
LEGIT ADMIN ARMS/CONT COERCE DISPL ORD/FREE PWR   ADJUD
...POLICY INT/LAW JURID COLD/WAR 20. PAGE 101 B2047   SOVEREIGN

B61
TRECKER H.B.,NEW UNDERSTANDING OF ADMINISTRATION.   VOL/ASSN
NEIGH DELIB/GP CONTROL LEAD GP/REL INGP/REL   PROF/ORG
...POLICY DECISION BIBLIOG. PAGE 105 B2126   ADMIN
                                                      PARTIC

S61
ANGLIN D.,"UNITED STATES OPPOSITION TO CANADIAN   INT/ORG
MEMBERSHIP IN THE PAN AMERICAN UNION: A CANADIAN   CANADA
VIEW." L/A+45 UK USA+45 VOL/ASSN DELIB/GP EX/STRUC
PLAN DIPLOM DOMIN REGION ATTIT RIGID/FLEX PWR
...RELATIV CONCPT STERTYP CMN/WLTH OAS 20. PAGE 5
B0112

S61
TANNENBAUM A.S.,"CONTROL AND EFFECTIVENESS IN A   EFFICIENCY
VOLUNTARY ORGANIZATION." USA+45 ADMIN...CORREL MATH   VOL/ASSN
REGRESS STAT TESTS SAMP/SIZ CHARTS SOC/EXP INDEX 20   CONTROL
LEAGUE/WV. PAGE 102 B2072   INGP/REL

B62
LAWSON R.,INTERNATIONAL REGIONAL ORGANIZATIONS.   INT/ORG
WOR+45 NAT/G VOL/ASSN CONSULT LEGIS EDU/PROP LEGIT   DELIB/GP
ADMIN EXEC ROUTINE HEALTH PWR WEALTH...JURID EEC   REGION
COLD/WAR 20 UN. PAGE 63 B1277

B62
MULLEY F.W.,THE POLITICS OF WESTERN DEFENSE.   INT/ORG
EUR+WWI USA-45 WOR+45 VOL/ASSN EX/STRUC FORCES   DELIB/GP
COERCE DETER PEACE ATTIT ORD/FREE PWR...RECORD   NUC/PWR
TIME/SEQ CHARTS COLD/WAR 20 NATO. PAGE 76 B1537

L62
MALINOWSKI W.R.,"CENTRALIZATION AND DE-   CREATE
CENTRALIZATION IN THE UNITED NATIONS' ECONOMIC AND   GEN/LAWS
SOCIAL ACTIVITIES." WOR+45 CONSTN ECO/UNDEV INT/ORG
VOL/ASSN DELIB/GP ECO/TAC EDU/PROP ADMIN RIGID/FLEX
...OBS CHARTS UNESCO UN EEC OAS OEEC 20. PAGE 69
B1385

S62
BRZEZINSKI Z.K.,"DEVIATION CONTROL: A STUDY IN THE   RIGID/FLEX
DYNAMICS OF DOCTRINAL CONFLICT." WOR+45 WOR-45   ATTIT
VOL/ASSN CREATE BAL/PWR DOMIN EXEC DRIVE PERCEPT
PWR...METH/CNCPT TIME/SEQ TREND 20. PAGE 16 B0333

S62
SPRINGER H.W.,"FEDERATION IN THE CARIBBEAN: AN   VOL/ASSN
ATTEMPT THAT FAILED." L/A+17C ECO/UNDEV INT/ORG   NAT/G
POL/PAR PROVS LEGIS CREATE PLAN LEGIT ADMIN FEDERAL   REGION
ATTIT DRIVE PERSON ORD/FREE PWR...POLICY GEOG PSY
CONCPT OBS CARIBBEAN CMN/WLTH 20. PAGE 100 B2013

S62
TATOMIR N.,"ORGANIZATIA INTERNATIONALA A MUNCII: INT/ORG
ASPECTE NOI ALE PROBLEMEI IMBUNATATIRII   INT/TRADE
MECANISMULUI EI." EUR+WWI ECO/DEV VOL/ASSN ADMIN
...METH/CNCPT WORK ILO 20. PAGE 103 B2081

B63
HIGA M.,POLITICS AND PARTIES IN POSTWAR OKINAWA.   GOV/REL
USA+45 VOL/ASSN LEGIS CONTROL LOBBY CHOOSE NAT/LISM   POL/PAR
PWR SOVEREIGN MARXISM SOCISM 20 OKINAWA CHINJAP.   ADMIN
PAGE 50 B1008   FORCES

B63
JOHNS R.,CONFRONTING ORGANIZATIONAL CHANGE. NEIGH   SOC/WK
DELIB/GP CREATE OP/RES ADMIN GP/REL DRIVE...WELF/ST   WEALTH
SOC RECORD BIBLIOG. PAGE 56 B1142   LEAD
                                                      VOL/ASSN

B63
LINDBERG L.,POLITICAL DYNAMICS OF EUROPEAN ECONOMIC MARKET
INTEGRATION. EUR+WWI ECO/DEV INT/ORG VOL/ASSN   ECO/TAC
DELIB/GP ADMIN WEALTH...DECISION EEC 20. PAGE 65
B1313

B63
MOORE W.E.,MAN, TIME, AND SOCIETY. UNIV STRUCT FAM   CONCPT
MUNIC VOL/ASSN ADMIN...SOC NEW/IDEA TIME/SEQ TREND   SOCIETY
TIME 20. PAGE 75 B1515   CONTROL

B63
SELF P.,THE STATE AND THE FARMER. UK ECO/DEV MARKET   AGRI
WORKER PRICE CONTROL GP/REL...WELF/ST 20 DEPT/AGRI.   NAT/G
PAGE 95 B1926   ADMIN
                                                      VOL/ASSN

S63
BANFIELD J.,"FEDERATION IN EAST-AFRICA." AFR UGANDA   EX/STRUC
ELITES INT/ORG NAT/G VOL/ASSN LEGIS ECO/TAC FEDERAL   PWR
ATTIT SOVEREIGN TOT/POP 20 TANGANYIKA. PAGE 9 B0180   REGION

S63
BARZANSKI S.,"REGIONAL UNDERDEVELOPMENT IN THE   ECO/UNDEV
EUROPEAN ECONOMIC COMMUNITY." EUR+WWI ELITES   PLAN
DIST/IND MARKET VOL/ASSN CONSULT EX/STRUC ECO/TAC
RIGID/FLEX WEALTH EEC OEEC 20. PAGE 9 B0192

S63
BOWIE R.,"STRATEGY AND THE ATLANTIC ALLIANCE."   FORCES
EUR+WWI VOL/ASSN BAL/PWR COERCE NUC/PWR ATTIT   ROUTINE
ORD/FREE PWR...DECISION GEN/LAWS NATO COLD/WAR 20.
PAGE 14 B0287

S63
ETIENNE G.,"'LOIS OBJECTIVES' ET PROBLEMES DE   TOTALISM
DEVELOPPEMENT DANS LE CONTEXTE CHINE-URSS." ASIA   USSR
CHINA/COM COM FUT STRUCT INT/ORG VOL/ASSN TOP/EX
TEC/DEV ECO/TAC ATTIT RIGID/FLEX...GEOG MGT
TIME/SEQ TOT/POP 20. PAGE 34 B0682

S63
HAVILAND H.F.,"BUILDING A POLITICAL COMMUNITY."   VOL/ASSN
EUR+WWI FUT UK USA+45 ECO/DEV ECO/UNDEV INT/ORG   DIPLOM
NAT/G DELIB/GP BAL/PWR ECO/TAC NEUTRAL ROUTINE
ATTIT PWR WEALTH...CONCPT COLD/WAR TOT/POP 20.
PAGE 48 B0972

S63
MODELSKI G.,"STUDY OF ALLIANCES." WOR+45 WOR-45   VOL/ASSN
INT/ORG NAT/G FORCES LEGIT ADMIN CHOOSE ALL/VALS   CON/ANAL
PWR SKILL...INT/LAW CONCPT GEN/LAWS 20 TREATY.   DIPLOM
PAGE 74 B1495

S63
SCHMITT H.A.,"THE EUROPEAN COMMUNITIES." EUR+WWI   VOL/ASSN
FRANCE DELIB/GP EX/STRUC TOP/EX CREATE TEC/DEV   ECO/DEV
ECO/TAC LEGIT REGION COERCE DRIVE ALL/VALS
...METH/CNCPT EEC 20. PAGE 94 B1897

B64
ADAMS V.,THE PEACE CORPS IN ACTION. USA+45 VOL/ASSN   DIPLOM
EX/STRUC GOV/REL PERCEPT ORD/FREE...OBS 20   FOR/AID
KENNEDY/JF PEACE/CORP. PAGE 3 B0058   PERSON
                                                      DRIVE

B64
ARGYRIS C.,INTEGRATING THE INDIVIDUAL AND THE   ADMIN
ORGANIZATION. WORKER PROB/SOLV LEAD SANCTION   PERS/REL
REPRESENT ADJUST EFFICIENCY DRIVE PERSON...PSY   VOL/ASSN
METH/CNCPT ORG/CHARTS. PAGE 6 B0132   PARTIC

B64
CAPLOW T.,PRINCIPLES OF ORGANIZATION. UNIV CULTURE   VOL/ASSN
STRUCT CREATE INGP/REL UTOPIA...GEN/LAWS TIME.   CONCPT
PAGE 18 B0374   SIMUL
                                                      EX/STRUC

B64
COTTRELL A.J.,THE POLITICS OF THE ATLANTIC   VOL/ASSN
ALLIANCE. EUR+WWI USA+45 INT/ORG NAT/G DELIB/GP   FORCES
EX/STRUC BAL/PWR DIPLOM REGION DETER ATTIT ORD/FREE
...CONCPT RECORD GEN/LAWS GEN/METH NATO 20. PAGE 24
B0493

B64
GUTTSMAN W.L.,THE BRITISH POLITICAL ELITE. EUR+WWI   NAT/G
MOD/EUR STRATA FAM LABOR POL/PAR SCHOOL VOL/ASSN   SOC
DELIB/GP LEGIS LEGIT EXEC CHOOSE ATTIT ALL/VALS   UK
...STAT BIOG TIME/SEQ CHARTS VAL/FREE. PAGE 45   ELITES
B0905

B64
PLISCHKE E.,SYSTEMS OF INTEGRATING THE   INT/ORG
INTERNATIONAL COMMUNITY. WOR+45 NAT/G VOL/ASSN   EX/STRUC
ECO/TAC LEGIT PWR WEALTH...TIME/SEQ ANTHOL UN   REGION
TOT/POP 20. PAGE 83 B1684

B64
SULLIVAN G.,THE STORY OF THE PEACE CORPS. USA+45   INT/ORG
WOR+45 INTELL FACE/GP NAT/G SCHOOL VOL/ASSN CONSULT   ECO/UNDEV
EX/STRUC PLAN EDU/PROP ADMIN ATTIT DRIVE ALL/VALS   FOR/AID
...POLICY HEAL SOC CONCPT INT QU BIOG TREND SOC/EXP   PEACE
WORK. PAGE 102 B2054

L64
MACKINTOSH J.P.,"NIGERIA'S EXTERNAL AFFAIRS." UK   AFR
CULTURE ECO/UNDEV NAT/G VOL/ASSN EDU/PROP LEGIT   DIPLOM
ADMIN ATTIT ORD/FREE PWR 20. PAGE 68 B1365   NIGERIA

L64
ROTBERG R.,"THE FEDERATION MOVEMENT IN BRITISH EAST   VOL/ASSN
AND CENTRAL AFRICA." AFR RHODESIA UGANDA ECO/UNDEV   PWR
NAT/G POL/PAR FORCES DOMIN LEGIT ADMIN COERCE ATTIT   REGION

...CONCPT TREND 20 TANGANYIKA. PAGE 91 B1831

S64

HUELIN D.,"ECONOMIC INTEGRATION IN LATIN AMERICAN: MARKET
PROGRESS AND PROBLEMS." L/A+17C ECO/DEV AGRI   ECO/UNDEV
DIST/IND FINAN INDUS NAT/G VOL/ASSN CONSULT   INT/TRADE
DELIB/GP EX/STRUC ACT/RES PLAN TEC/DEV ECO/TAC
ROUTINE BAL/PAY WEALTH WORK 20. PAGE 52 B1058

S64

JOHNSON K.F.,"CAUSAL FACTORS IN LATIN AMERICAN   L/A+17C
POLITICAL INSTABILITY." CULTURE NAT/G VOL/ASSN   PERCEPT
EX/STRUC FORCES EDU/PROP LEGIT ADMIN COERCE REV   ELITES
ATTIT KNOWL PWR...STYLE RECORD CHARTS WORK 20.
PAGE 57 B1144

S64

REDFORD E.S.,"THE PROTECTION OF THE PUBLIC INTEREST ADMIN
WITH SPECIAL REFERENCE TO ADMINISTRATIVE   VOL/ASSN
REGULATION." POL/PAR LEGIS PRESS PARL/PROC. PAGE 87 EX/STRUC
B1758   GP/REL

B65

GREER S.,URBAN RENEWAL AND AMERICAN CITIES: THE   MUNIC
DILEMMA OF DEMOCRATIC INTERVENTION. USA+45 R+D   PROB/SOLV
LOC/G VOL/ASSN ACT/RES BUDGET ADMIN GOV/REL...SOC   PLAN
INT SAMP 20 BOSTON CHICAGO MIAMI URBAN/RNWL.   NAT/G
PAGE 43 B0871

B65

LIPSET S.M.,THE BERKELEY STUDENT REVOLT: FACTS AND   CROWD
INTERPRETATIONS. USA+45 INTELL VOL/ASSN CONSULT   ACADEM
EDU/PROP PRESS DEBATE ADMIN REV HAPPINESS   ATTIT
RIGID/FLEX MAJORIT. PAGE 65 B1322   GP/REL

B65

LYONS G.M.,SCHOOLS FOR STRATEGY* EDUCATION AND   ACADEM
RESEARCH IN NATIONAL SECURITY AFFAIRS. USA+45 FINAN ACT/RES
NAT/G VOL/ASSN FORCES TEC/DEV ADMIN WAR...GP/COMP   INTELL
IDEA/COMP PERS/COMP COLD/WAR. PAGE 67 B1351

B65

PAYNE J.L.,LABOR AND POLITICS IN PERU; THE SYSTEM   LABOR
OF POLITICAL BARGAINING. PERU CONSTN VOL/ASSN   POL/PAR
EX/STRUC LEAD PWR...CHARTS 20. PAGE 81 B1645   BARGAIN
                                                     GP/REL

B65

PRESTHUS R.,BEHAVIORAL APPROACHES TO PUBLIC   GEN/METH
ADMINISTRATION. UK STRATA LG/CO PUB/INST VOL/ASSN   DECISION
EX/STRUC TOP/EX EFFICIENCY HEALTH. PAGE 84 B1704   ADMIN
                                                     R+D

B65

VIORST M.,HOSTILE ALLIES: FDR AND DE GAULLE.   TOP/EX
EUR+WWI USA-45 ELITES NAT/G VOL/ASSN FORCES LEGIS   PWR
PLAN LEGIT ADMIN COERCE PERSON...BIOG TIME/SEQ 20   WAR
ROOSEVLT/F DEGAULLE/C. PAGE 112 B2263   FRANCE

S65

BROWN S.,"AN ALTERNATIVE TO THE GRAND DESIGN."   VOL/ASSN
EUR+WWI FUT USA+45 INT/ORG NAT/G EX/STRUC FORCES   CONCPT
CREATE BAL/PWR DOMIN RIGID/FLEX ORD/FREE PWR   DIPLOM
...NEW/IDEA RECORD EEC NATO 20. PAGE 16 B0327

B66

DICKSON W.J.,COUNSELING IN AN ORGANIZATION: A   INDUS
SEQUEL TO THE HAWTHORNE RESEARCHES. CLIENT VOL/ASSN WORKER
ACT/RES PROB/SOLV AUTOMAT ROUTINE PERS/REL   PSY
HAPPINESS ANOMIE ROLE...OBS CHARTS 20 AT+T. PAGE 29 MGT
B0588

B66

O'NEILL C.E.,CHURCH AND STATE IN FRENCH COLONIAL   COLONIAL
LOUISIANA: POLICY AND POLITICS TO 1732. PROVS   NAT/G
VOL/ASSN DELIB/GP ADJUD ADMIN GP/REL ATTIT DRIVE   SECT
...POLICY BIBLIOG 17/18 LOUISIANA CHURCH/STA.   PWR
PAGE 79 B1601

B66

STREET D.,ORGANIZATION FOR TREATMENT. CLIENT PROVS   GP/COMP
PUB/INST PLAN CONTROL PARTIC REPRESENT ATTIT PWR   AGE/Y
...POLICY BIBLIOG. PAGE 101 B2052   ADMIN
                                                     VOL/ASSN

B66

UN ECAFE,ADMINISTRATIVE ASPECTS OF FAMILY PLANNING   PLAN
PROGRAMMES (PAMPHLET). ASIA THAILAND WOR+45   CENSUS
VOL/ASSN PROB/SOLV BUDGET FOR/AID EDU/PROP CONFER   FAM
CONTROL GOV/REL TIME 20 UN BIRTH/CON. PAGE 106   ADMIN
B2147

S66

JACOBSON J.,"COALITIONISM: FROM PROTEST TO   RACE/REL
POLITICKING" USA+45 ELITES NAT/G POL/PAR PROB/SOLV   LABOR
ADMIN LEAD DISCRIM ORD/FREE PWR CONSERVE 20 NEGRO   SOCIALIST
AFL/CIO CIV/RIGHTS BLACK/PWR. PAGE 55 B1116   VOL/ASSN

B67

ROFF W.R.,THE ORIGINS OF MALAY NATIONALISM.   NAT/LISM
MALAYSIA INTELL NAT/G ADMIN COLONIAL...BIBLIOG   ELITES
DICTIONARY 20 CMN/WLTH. PAGE 90 B1813   VOL/ASSN
                                                     SOCIETY

B67

UNIVERSAL REFERENCE SYSTEM,ADMINISTRATIVE   BIBLIOG/A
MANAGEMENT: PUBLIC AND PRIVATE BUREAUCRACY (VOLUME   MGT
IV). WOR+45 WOR-45 ECO/DEV LG/CO LOC/G PUB/INST   ADMIN
VOL/ASSN GOV/REL...COMPUT/IR GEN/METH. PAGE 107   NAT/G
B2164

B67

US SENATE COMM ON FOREIGN REL,HUMAN RIGHTS   LEGIS
CONVENTIONS. USA+45 LABOR VOL/ASSN DELIB/GP DOMIN   ORD/FREE

ADJUD REPRESENT...INT/LAW MGT CONGRESS. PAGE 110   WORKER
B2225   LOBBY

B67

VOOS H.,ORGANIZATIONAL COMMUNICATION: A   BIBLIOG/A
BIBLIOGRAPHY. WOR+45 STRATA R+D PROB/SOLV FEEDBACK   INDUS
COERCE...MGT PSY NET/THEORY HYPO/EXP. PAGE 112   COM/IND
B2268   VOL/ASSN

S67

HOFMANN W.,"THE PUBLIC INTEREST PRESSURE GROUP: THE LOC/G
CASE OF THE DEUTSCHE STADTETAG." GERMANY GERMANY/W   VOL/ASSN
CONSTN STRUCT NAT/G CENTRAL FEDERAL PWR...TIME/SEQ   LOBBY
20. PAGE 51 B1030   ADMIN

S67

LASLETT J.H.M.,"SOCIALISM AND THE AMERICAN LABOR   LABOR
MOVEMENT* SOME NEW REFLECTIONS." USA+45 VOL/ASSN   ROUTINE
LOBBY PARTIC CENTRAL ALL/VALS SOCISM...GP/COMP 20.   ATTIT
PAGE 63 B1265   GP/REL

S67

MERON T.,"THE UN'S 'COMMON SYSTEM' OF SALARY,   ADMIN
ALLOWANCE, AND BENEFITS: CRITICAL APPR'SAL OF COORD EX/STRUC
IN PERSONNEL MATTERS." VOL/ASSN PAY EFFICIENCY   INT/ORG
...CHARTS 20 UN. PAGE 73 B1470   BUDGET

S67

ROSE A.M.,"CONFIDENCE AND THE CORPORATION." LG/CO   INDUS
CONTROL CRIME INCOME PROFIT 20. PAGE 90 B1818   EX/STRUC
                                                     VOL/ASSN
                                                     RESPECT

VOLTAIRE....VOLTAIRE (FRANCOIS MARIE AROUET)

VOLUNTARY ASSOCIATIONS....SEE VOL/ASSN

VOLUNTEERS IN SERVICE TO AMERICA (VISTA)....SEE VISTA
VON HAYEK F.A. B0974
VON HOFFMAN N. B2266

VON PETERFRY G. B0471

VONGLAHN G. B2267

VOOS H. B2268

VOTING....SEE CHOOSE, SUFF

VTOL....VERTICAL TAKE-OFF AND LANDING AIRCRAFT

W

WADE E.C.S. B2269

WADE H.W.R. B2270

WADIA M. B2271

WAGER P.W. B2272

WAGES....SEE PRICE, WORKER, WEALTH

WAGLEY C. B2273

WAGNER J.B. B0742

WAGNER/A....ADOLPH WAGNER

WAGRET M. B2274

WAINHOUSE D.W. B2275

WALDO D. B2276

WALES....WALES

WALINE M. B2277

WALKER A.A. B2278

WALKER H. B2279

WALKER N. B2280

WALKER/E....EDWIN WALKER

WALL E.H. B2281

WALL N.L. B2282

WALLACE R.J. B0902

WALLACE/G....GEORGE WALLACE

WALLACE/HA....HENRY A. WALLACE

WALLER D.J. B2283

WALTER B. B2284

WALTON R.E. B2285

WALTZ/KN....KENNETH N. WALTZ

WANGSNESS P.H. B2286

WAR....SEE ALSO COERCE

N
WEIGLEY R.F.,HISTORY OF THE UNITED STATES ARMY. FORCES
USA+45 USA-45 SOCIETY NAT/G LEAD WAR GP/REL PWR ADMIN
...SOC METH/COMP COLD/WAR. PAGE 115 B2312 ROLE
CIVMIL/REL
N
UNITED NATIONS,UNITED NATIONS PUBLICATIONS. WOR+45 BIBLIOG
ECO/UNDEV AGRI FINAN FORCES ADMIN LEAD WAR PEACE INT/ORG
...POLICY INT/LAW 20 UN. PAGE 107 B2160 DIPLOM
B00
SANDERSON E.,AFRICA IN THE NINETEENTH CENTURY. COLONIAL
FRANCE UK EXTR/IND FORCES LEGIS ADMIN WAR DISCRIM AFR
ORD/FREE...GEOG GP/COMP SOC/INTEG 19. PAGE 92 B1867 DIPLOM
B05
MACHIAVELLI N.,THE ART OF WAR. CHRIST-17C TOP/EX NAT/G
DRIVE ORD/FREE PWR SKILL...MGT CHARTS. PAGE 67 FORCES
B1360 WAR
ITALY
B18
US LIBRARY OF CONGRESS,LIST OF REFERENCES ON A BIBLIOG
LEAGUE OF NATIONS. DIPLOM WAR PEACE 20 LEAGUE/NAT. INT/ORG
PAGE 109 B2201 ADMIN
EX/STRUC
B18
WILSON W.,THE STATE: ELEMENTS OF HISTORICAL AND NAT/G
PRACTICAL POLITICS. FRANCE GERMANY ITALY UK USSR JURID
CONSTN EX/STRUC LEGIS CT/SYS WAR PWR...POLICY CONCPT
GOV/COMP 20. PAGE 117 B2363 NAT/COMP
B21
STOWELL E.C.,INTERVENTION IN INTERNATIONAL LAW. BAL/PWR
UNIV LAW SOCIETY INT/ORG ACT/RES PLAN LEGIT ROUTINE SOVEREIGN
WAR...JURID OBS GEN/LAWS 20. PAGE 101 B2050 WAR
B28
SOROKIN P.,CONTEMPORARY SOCIOLOGICAL THEORIES. CULTURE
MOD/EUR UNIV SOCIETY R+D SCHOOL ECO/TAC EDU/PROP SOC
ROUTINE ATTIT DRIVE...PSY CONCPT TIME/SEQ TREND WAR
GEN/LAWS 20. PAGE 99 B1997
B39
HITLER A.,MEIN KAMPF. EUR+WWI FUT MOD/EUR STRUCT PWR
INT/ORG LABOR NAT/G POL/PAR FORCES CREATE PLAN NEW/IDEA
BAL/PWR DIPLOM ECO/TAC DOMIN EDU/PROP ADMIN COERCE WAR
ATTIT...SOCIALIST BIOG TREND NAZI. PAGE 50 B1020
B41
PALMER J.M.,AMERICA IN ARMS: THE EXPERIENCE OF THE FORCES
UNITED STATES WITH MILITARY ORGANIZATION. FUT NAT/G
USA-45 LEAD REV PWR 18/20 WASHINGT/G KNOX/HENRY ADMIN
PRE/US/AM. PAGE 81 B1627 WAR
B41
YOUNG G.,FEDERALISM AND FREEDOM. EUR+WWI MOD/EUR NAT/G
RUSSIA USA-45 WOR-45 SOCIETY STRUCT ECO/DEV INT/ORG WAR
EXEC FEDERAL ATTIT PERSON ALL/VALS...LIB CONCPT
OBS TREND LEAGUE/NAT TOT/POP. PAGE 119 B2392
S41
ABEL T.,"THE ELEMENT OF DECISION IN THE PATTERN OF TEC/DEV
WAR." EUR+WWI FUT NAT/G TOP/EX DIPLOM ROUTINE FORCES
COERCE DISPL PERCEPT PWR...SOC METH/CNCPT HIST/WRIT WAR
TREND GEN/LAWS 20. PAGE 2 B0051
B42
HARLOW R.F.,PUBLIC RELATIONS IN WAR AND PEACE. FUT WAR
USA-45 ECO/DEV ECO/TAC ROUTINE 20. PAGE 47 B0947 ATTIT
SOCIETY
INGP/REL
B42
SINGTON D.,THE GOEBBELS EXPERIMENT. GERMANY MOD/EUR FASCISM
NAT/G EX/STRUC FORCES CONTROL ROUTINE WAR TOTALISM EDU/PROP
PWR...ART/METH HUM 20 NAZI GOEBBELS/J. PAGE 97 ATTIT
B1970 COM/IND
B42
WRIGHT D.M.,THE CREATION OF PURCHASING POWER. FINAN
USA-45 NAT/G PRICE ADMIN WAR INCOME PRODUC...POLICY ECO/TAC
CONCPT IDEA/COMP BIBLIOG 20 MONEY. PAGE 118 B2378 ECO/DEV
CREATE
B44
WRIGHT H.R.,SOCIAL SERVICE IN WARTIME. FINAN NAT/G GIVE
VOL/ASSN PLAN GP/REL ROLE. PAGE 118 B2381 WAR
SOC/WK
ADMIN
S44
COLEGROVE K.W.,"THE ROLE OF CONGRESS AND PUBLIC EX/STRUC
OPINION IN FORMULATING FOREIGN POLICY." USA+45 WAR DIPLOM
...DECISION UN CONGRESS. PAGE 22 B0451 LEGIS
PWR
B45
BAKER H.,PROBLEMS OF REEMPLOYMENT AND RETRAINING OF BIBLIOG/A
MANPOWER DURING THE TRANSITION FROM WAR TO PEACE. ADJUST
USA+45 INDUS LABOR LG/CO NAT/G PLAN ADMIN PEACE WAR
...POLICY MGT 20. PAGE 8 B0167 PROB/SOLV

B45
BRECHT A.,FEDERALISM AND REGIONALISM IN GERMANY; FEDERAL
THE DIVISION OF PRUSSIA. GERMANY PRUSSIA WOR-45 REGION
CREATE ADMIN WAR TOTALISM PWR...CHARTS 20 HITLER/A. PROB/SOLV
PAGE 15 B0303 CONSTN
C45
MCDIARMID J.,"THE MOBILIZATION OF SOCIAL INTELL
SCIENTISTS," IN L. WHITE'S CIVIL CIVIL SERVICE IN WAR
WARTIME." USA-45 TEC/DEV CENTRAL...SOC 20 DELIB/GP
CIVIL/SERV. PAGE 72 B1447 ADMIN
B46
GRIFFIN G.G.,A GUIDE TO MANUSCRIPTS RELATING TO BIBLIOG/A
AMERICAN HISTORY IN BRITISH DEPOSITORIES. CANADA ALL/VALS
IRELAND MOD/EUR UK USA-45 LAW DIPLOM ADMIN COLONIAL NAT/G
WAR NAT/LISM SOVEREIGN...GEOG INT/LAW 15/19
CMN/WLTH. PAGE 43 B0876
B46
WILCOX J.K.,OFFICIAL DEFENSE PUBLICATIONS, BIBLIOG/A
1941-1945 (NINE VOLS.). USA-45 AGRI INDUS R+D LABOR WAR
FORCES TEC/DEV EFFICIENCY PRODUC SKILL WEALTH 20. CIVMIL/REL
PAGE 116 B2347 ADMIN
B47
PUBLIC ADMINISTRATION SERVICE,CURRENT RESEARCH BIBLIOG
PROJECTS IN PUBLIC ADMINISTRATION (PAMPHLET). LAW R+D
CONSTN COM/IND LABOR LOC/G MUNIC PROVS ACT/RES MGT
DIPLOM RECEIVE EDU/PROP WAR 20. PAGE 85 B1716 ADMIN
B47
REDFORD E.S.,FIELD ADMINISTRATION OF WARTIME ADMIN
RATIONING. USA-45 CONSTN ELITES DIST/IND WORKER NAT/G
CONTROL WAR GOV/REL ADJUST RIGID/FLEX 20 OPA. PROB/SOLV
PAGE 87 B1752 RATION
S47
TURNER R.H.,"THE NAVY DISBURSING OFFICER AS A FORCES
BUREAUCRAT" (BMR)" USA-45 LAW STRATA DIST/IND WAR ADMIN
PWR...SOC 20 BUREAUCRCY. PAGE 106 B2140 PERSON
ROLE
B48
BONAPARTE M.,MYTHS OF WAR. GERMANY WOR+45 WOR-45 ROUTINE
CULTURE SOCIETY NAT/G FORCES LEGIT ATTIT DRIVE MYTH
...CONCPT HIST/WRIT TIME/SEQ 20 JEWS. PAGE 13 B0271 WAR
B48
HULL C.,THE MEMOIRS OF CORDELL HULL (VOLUME ONE). BIOG
USA-45 WOR-45 CONSTN FAM LOC/G NAT/G PROVS DELIB/GP DIPLOM
FORCES LEGIS TOP/EX BAL/PWR LEGIT ADMIN EXEC WAR
ATTIT ORD/FREE PWR...MAJORIT SELF/OBS TIME/SEQ
TREND NAZI 20. PAGE 52 B1062
B48
ROSSITER C.L.,CONSTITUTIONAL DICTATORSHIP; CRISIS NAT/G
GOVERNMENT IN THE MODERN DEMOCRACIES. FRANCE AUTHORIT
GERMANY UK USA-45 WOR-45 EX/STRUC BAL/PWR CONTROL CONSTN
COERCE WAR CENTRAL ORD/FREE...DECISION 19/20. TOTALISM
PAGE 90 B1828
B48
SHERWOOD R.E.,ROOSEVELT AND HOPKINS. UK USA+45 USSR TOP/EX
NAT/G EX/STRUC FORCES ADMIN ROUTINE PERSON PWR BIOG
...TIME/SEQ 20 ROOSEVLT/F HOPKINS/H. PAGE 96 B1946 DIPLOM
WAR
B48
STEWART I.,ORGANIZING SCIENTIFIC RESEARCH FOR WAR: DELIB/GP
ADMINISTRATIVE HISTORY OF OFFICE OF SCIENTIFIC ADMIN
RESEARCH AND DEVELOPMENT. USA-45 INTELL R+D LABOR WAR
WORKER CREATE BUDGET WEAPON CIVMIL/REL GP/REL TEC/DEV
EFFICIENCY...POLICY 20. PAGE 101 B2037
B49
BUSH V.,MODERN ARMS AND FREE MEN. WOR-45 SOCIETY TEC/DEV
NAT/G ECO/TAC DOMIN LEGIT EXEC COERCE DETER ATTIT FORCES
DRIVE ORD/FREE PWR...CONCPT MYTH COLD/WAR 20 NUC/PWR
COLD/WAR. PAGE 18 B0361 COLD/WAR
S49
STEINMETZ H.,"THE PROBLEMS OF THE LANDRAT: A STUDY LOC/G
OF COUNTY GOVERNMENT IN THE US ZONE OF GERMANY." COLONIAL
GERMANY/W USA+45 INDUS PLAN DIPLOM EDU/PROP CONTROL MGT
WAR GOV/REL FEDERAL WEALTH PLURISM...GOV/COMP 20 TOP/EX
LANDRAT. PAGE 100 B2031
B50
WELCH S.R.,PORTUGUESE RULE AND SPANISH CROWN IN DIPLOM
SOUTH AFRICA 1581-1640. PORTUGAL SOUTH/AFR SPAIN COLONIAL
SOCIETY KIN NEIGH SECT INT/TRADE ADMIN 16/17 WAR
MISSION. PAGE 115 B2317 PEACE
B51
SMITH L.,AMERICAN DEMOCRACY AND MILITARY POWER. FORCES
USA+45 USA-45 CONSTN STRATA NAT/G LEGIS ACT/RES STRUCT
LEGIT ADMIN EXEC GOV/REL ALL/VALS...CONCPT WAR
HIST/WRIT CONGRESS 20. PAGE 98 B1982
B51
SWISHER C.B.,THE THEORY AND PRACTICE OF AMERICAN CONSTN
NATIONAL GOVERNMENT. CULTURE LEGIS DIPLOM ADJUD NAT/G
ADMIN WAR PEACE ORD/FREE...MAJORIT 17/20. PAGE 102 GOV/REL
B2063 GEN/LAWS
S51
STEWART D.D.,"THE PLACE OF VOLUNTEER PARTICIPATION ADMIN
IN BUREAUCRATIC ORGANIZATION." NAT/G DELIB/GP PARTIC
OP/RES DOMIN LOBBY WAR ATTIT ROLE PWR. PAGE 101 VOL/ASSN
B2035 FORCES
B53
PIERCE R.A.,RUSSIAN CENTRAL ASIA, 1867-1917: A BIBLIOG

SELECTED BIBLIOGRAPHY (PAMPHLET). USSR LAW CULTURE COLONIAL
NAT/G EDU/PROP WAR...GEOG SOC 19/20. PAGE 83 B1671 ADMIN
                                                   COM
                                                   B53

TOMPKINS D.C.,CIVIL DEFENSE IN THE STATES: A   BIBLIOG
BIBLIOGRAPHY (DEFENSE BIBLIOGRAPHIES NO. 3;   WAR
PAMPHLET). USA+45 LABOR LOC/G NAT/G PROVS LEGIS.   ORD/FREE
PAGE 105 B2115   ADMIN
                                                   B54

US SENATE COMM ON FOREIGN REL,REVIEW OF THE UNITED BIBLIOG
NATIONS CHARTER: A COLLECTION OF DOCUMENTS. LEGIS CONSTN
DIPLOM ADMIN ARMS/CONT WAR REPRESENT SOVEREIGN   INT/ORG
...INT/LAW 20 UN. PAGE 110 B2220   DEBATE
                                                   B56

KOENIG L.W.,THE TRUMAN ADMINISTRATION: ITS   ADMIN
PRINCIPLES AND PRACTICE. USA+45 POL/PAR CHIEF LEGIS POLICY
DIPLOM DEATH NUC/PWR WAR CIVMIL/REL PEACE   EX/STRUC
...DECISION 20 TRUMAN/HS PRESIDENT TREATY. PAGE 61 GOV/REL
B1224   B56

SOHN L.B.,CASES ON UNITED NATIONS LAW. STRUCT   INT/ORG
DELIB/GP WAR PEACE ORD/FREE...DECISION ANTHOL 20   INT/LAW
UN. PAGE 99 B1994   ADMIN
                                                   ADJUD
                                                   B56

WILSON P.,GOVERNMENT AND POLITICS OF INDIA AND   BIBLIOG
PAKISTAN: 1885-1955; A BIBLIOGRAPHY OF WORKS IN   COLONIAL
WESTERN LANGUAGES. INDIA PAKISTAN CONSTN LOC/G   NAT/G
POL/PAR FORCES DIPLOM ADMIN WAR CHOOSE...BIOG   S/ASIA
CON/ANAL 19/20. PAGE 117 B2361   B56

WU E.,LEADERS OF TWENTIETH-CENTURY CHINA; AN   BIBLIOG/A
ANNOTATED BIBLIOGRAPHY OF SELECTED CHINESE   BIOG
BIOGRAPHICAL WORKS IN HOOVER LIBRARY. ASIA INDUS   INTELL
POL/PAR DIPLOM ADMIN REV WAR...HUM MGT 20. PAGE 118 CHIEF
B2386   C56

FALL B.B.,"THE VIET-MINH REGIME." VIETNAM LAW   NAT/G
ECO/UNDEV POL/PAR FORCES DOMIN WAR ATTIT MARXISM   ADMIN
...BIOG PREDICT BIBLIOG/A 20. PAGE 35 B0703   EX/STRUC
                                                   LEAD
                                                   B58

CHANG C.,THE INFLATIONARY SPIRAL: THE EXPERIENCE IN FINAN
CHINA 1939-50. CHINA/COM BUDGET INT/TRADE PRICE   ECO/TAC
ADMIN CONTROL WAR DEMAND...POLICY CHARTS 20.   BAL/PAY
PAGE 20 B0406   GOV/REL
                                                   B58

ISLAM R.,INTERNATIONAL ECONOMIC COOPERATION AND THE INT/ORG
UNITED NATIONS. FINAN PLAN EXEC TASK WAR PEACE   DIPLOM
...SOC METH/CNCPT 20 UN LEAGUE/NAT. PAGE 55 B1105 ADMIN
                                                   B58

MILLS C.W.,THE CAUSES OF WORLD WAR THREE. FUT   CONSULT
USA+45 INTELL NAT/G DOMIN EDU/PROP ADMIN WAR ATTIT PWR
SOC. PAGE 74 B1487   ELITES
                                                   PEACE
                                                   S58

DAVENPORT J.,"ARMS AND THE WELFARE STATE." INTELL USA+45
STRUCT FORCES CREATE ECO/TAC FOR/AID DOMIN LEGIT   NAT/G
ADMIN WAR DOMIN FREE PWR...POLICY SOC CONCPT MYTH OBS USSR
TREND COLD/WAR TOT/POP 20. PAGE 26 B0533   C58

WILDING N.,"AN ENCYCLOPEDIA OF PARLIAMENT." UK LAW PARL/PROC
CONSTN CHIEF PROB/SOLV DIPLOM DEBATE WAR INGP/REL POL/PAR
PRIVIL...BIBLIOG DICTIONARY 13/20 CMN/WLTH   NAT/G
PARLIAMENT. PAGE 116 B2350   ADMIN
                                                   S59

HILSMAN R.,"THE FOREIGN-POLICY CONSENSUS: AN   PROB/SOLV
INTERIM RESEARCH REPORT." USA+45 INT/ORG LEGIS   NAT/G
TEC/DEV EXEC WAR CONSEN KNOWL...DECISION COLD/WAR. DELIB/GP
PAGE 50 B1013   DIPLOM
                                                   B60

GRUNDLICH T.,DIE TECHNIK DER DIKTATUR. ADMIN   COERCE
TOTALISM ATTIT PWR...MGT CONCPT ARISTOTLE. PAGE 44 DOMIN
B0896   ORD/FREE
                                                   WAR
                                                   B60

KINGSTON-MCCLOUG E.,DEFENSE; POLICY AND STRATEGY. FORCES
UK SEA AIR TEC/DEV DIPLOM ADMIN LEAD WAR ORD/FREE PLAN
...CHARTS 20. PAGE 60 B1209   POLICY
                                                   DECISION
                                                   B60

MORISON E.E.,TURMOIL AND TRADITION: A STUDY OF THE BIOG
LIFE AND TIMES OF HENRY L. STIMSON. USA+45 USA-45 NAT/G
POL/PAR CHIEF DELIB/GP FORCES BAL/PWR DIPLOM   EX/STRUC
ARMS/CONT WAR PEACE 19/20 STIMSON/HL ROOSEVLT/F
TAFT/WH HOOVER/H REPUBLICAN. PAGE 75 B1525   S60

HUNTINGTON S.P.,"STRATEGIC PLANNING AND THE   EXEC
POLITICAL PROCESS." USA+45 NAT/G DELIB/GP LEGIS   FORCES
ACT/RES ECO/TAC LEGIT ROUTINE CHOOSE RIGID/FLEX PWR NUC/PWR
...POLICY MAJORIT MGT 20. PAGE 53 B1066   WAR
                                                   C60

SCHAPIRO L.B.,"THE COMMUNIST PARTY OF THE SOVIET   POL/PAR
UNION." USSR INTELL CHIEF EX/STRUC FORCES DOMIN   COM
ADMIN LEAD WAR ATTIT SOVEREIGN...POLICY BIBLIOG 20. REV
PAGE 93 B1881

KERTESZ S.D.,AMERICAN DIPLOMACY IN A NEW ERA. COM ANTHOL
S/ASIA UK USA+45 FORCES PROB/SOLV BAL/PWR ECO/TAC DIPLOM
ADMIN COLONIAL WAR PEACE ORD/FREE 20 NATO CONGRESS TREND
UN COLD/WAR. PAGE 59 B1199   B61

MOLLAU G.,INTERNATIONAL COMMUNISM AND WORLD   COM
REVOLUTION: HISTORY AND METHODS. RUSSIA USSR   REV
INT/ORG NAT/G POL/PAR VOL/ASSN FORCES BAL/PWR
DIPLOM EXEC REGION WAR ATTIT PWR MARXISM...CONCPT
TIME/SEQ COLD/WAR 19/20. PAGE 74 B1498   B61

PETRULLO L.,LEADERSHIP AND INTERPERSONAL BEHAVIOR. PERSON
FACE/GP FAM PROF/ORG EX/STRUC FORCES DOMIN WAR   ATTIT
GP/REL PERS/REL EFFICIENCY PRODUC PWR...MGT PSY.   LEAD
PAGE 82 B1663   HABITAT
                                                   S61

CARLETON W.G.,"AMERICAN FOREIGN POLICY: MYTHS AND PLAN
REALITIES." FUT USA+45 WOR+45 ECO/UNDEV INT/ORG   MYTH
EX/STRUC ARMS/CONT NUC/PWR WAR ATTIT...POLICY   DIPLOM
CONCPT CONT/OBS GEN/METH COLD/WAR TOT/POP 20.
PAGE 19 B0378   S61

DEVINS J.H.,"THE INITIATIVE." COM USA+45 USA-45   FORCES
USSR SOCIETY NAT/G ACT/RES CREATE BAL/PWR ROUTINE CONCPT
COERCE DETER RIGID/FLEX SKILL...STERTYP COLD/WAR   WAR
20. PAGE 29 B0582   S61

PADOVER S.K.,"PSYCHOLOGICAL WARFARE AND FOREIGN   ROUTINE
POLICY." FUT UNIV USA+45 INTELL SOCIETY CREATE   DIPLOM
EDU/PROP ADMIN WAR PEACE PERCEPT...POLICY
METH/CNCPT TESTS TIME/SEQ 20. PAGE 80 B1623   B62

BRIMMER B.,A GUIDE TO THE USE OF UNITED NATIONS   BIBLIOG/A
DOCUMENTS. WOR+45 ECO/UNDEV AGRI EX/STRUC FORCES   INT/ORG
PROB/SOLV ADMIN WAR PEACE WEALTH...POLICY UN.   DIPLOM
PAGE 15 B0310   B62

GRAY R.K.,EIGHTEEN ACRES UNDER GLASS. ELITES   CHIEF
CONSULT EX/STRUC DIPLOM PRESS CONFER WAR PERS/REL ADMIN
PERSON 20 EISNHWR/DD TRUMAN/HS CABINET. PAGE 43   TOP/EX
B0860   NAT/G
                                                   B62

INGHAM K.,A HISTORY OF EAST AFRICA. NAT/G DIPLOM   AFR
ADMIN WAR NAT/LISM...SOC BIOG BIBLIOG. PAGE 54   CONSTN
B1085   COLONIAL
                                                   B62

MORTON L.,STRATEGY AND COMMAND: THE FIRST TWO   WAR
YEARS. USA-45 NAT/G CONTROL EXEC LEAD WEAPON   FORCES
CIVMIL/REL PWR...POLICY AUD/VIS CHARTS 20 CHINJAP. PLAN
PAGE 76 B1532   DIPLOM
                                                   B62

OLLE-LAPRUNE J.,LA STABILITE DES MINISTRES SOUS LA LEGIS
TROISIEME REPUBLIQUE, 1879-1940. FRANCE CONSTN   NAT/G
POL/PAR LEAD WAR INGP/REL RIGID/FLEX PWR...POLICY ADMIN
CHARTS 19/20. PAGE 79 B1606   PERSON
                                                   B62

TAYLOR D.,THE BRITISH IN AFRICA. UK CULTURE   AFR
ECO/UNDEV INDUS DIPLOM INT/TRADE ADMIN WAR RACE/REL COLONIAL
ORD/FREE SOVEREIGN...POLICY BIBLIOG 15/20 CMN/WLTH. DOMIN
PAGE 103 B2084   B62

WELLEQUET J.,LE CONGO BELGE ET LA WELTPOLITIK   ADMIN
(1894-1914. GERMANY DOMIN EDU/PROP WAR ATTIT   DIPLOM
...BIBLIOG T CONGO/LEOP. PAGE 115 B2318   GP/REL
                                                   COLONIAL
                                                   C62

DE GRAZIA A.,"POLITICAL BEHAVIOR (REV. ED.)" STRATA PHIL/SCI
POL/PAR LEAD LOBBY ROUTINE WAR CHOOSE REPRESENT   OP/RES
CONSEN ATTIT ORD/FREE BIBLIOG. PAGE 27 B0555   CONCPT
                                                   B63

BOISSIER P.,HISTOIRE DU COMITE INTERNATIONAL DE LA INT/ORG
CROIX ROUGE. MOD/EUR WOR-45 CONSULT FORCES PLAN   HEALTH
DIPLOM EDU/PROP ADMIN MORAL ORD/FREE...SOC CONCPT ARMS/CONT
RECORD TIME/SEQ GEN/LAWS TOT/POP VAL/FREE 19/20.   WAR
PAGE 13 B0267   B63

OLSON M. JR.,THE ECONOMICS OF WARTIME SHORTAGE.   WAR
FRANCE GERMANY MOD/EUR UK AGRI PROB/SOLV ADMIN   ADJUST
DEMAND WEALTH...POLICY OLD/LIB 17/20. PAGE 80 B1608 ECO/TAC
                                                   NAT/COMP
                                                   B63

PLISCHKE E.,GOVERNMENT AND POLITICS OF CONTEMPORARY MUNIC
BERLIN. GERMANY LAW CONSTN POL/PAR LEGIS WAR CHOOSE LOC/G
REPRESENT GOV/REL...CHARTS BIBLIOG 20 BERLIN.   POLICY
PAGE 83 B1683   ADMIN
                                                   B63

STEIN H.,AMERICAN CIVIL-MILITARY DECISION. USA+45 CIVMIL/REL
USA-45 EX/STRUC FORCES LEGIS TOP/EX PLAN DIPLOM   DECISION
FOR/AID ATTIT 20 CONGRESS. PAGE 100 B2028   WAR
                                                   BUDGET
                                                   C63

BLUM J.M.,"THE NATIONAL EXPERIENCE." USA+45 USA-45 ADMIN
ECO/DEV DIPLOM WAR NAT/LISM...POLICY CHARTS BIBLIOG NAT/G
T 16/20 CONGRESS PRESIDENT COLD/WAR. PAGE 13 B0258 LEGIS
                                                   CHIEF

GRZYBOWSKI K.,THE SOCIALIST COMMONWEALTH OF NATIONS: ORGANIZATIONS AND INSTITUTIONS. FORCES DIPLOM INT/TRADE ADJUD ADMIN LEAD WAR MARXISM SOCISM...BIBLIOG 20 COMECON WARSAW/P. PAGE 44 B0898
INT/LAW COM REGION INT/ORG
B64

RAYMOND J.,POWER AT THE PENTAGON (1ST ED.). ELITES NAT/G PLAN EDU/PROP ARMS/CONT DETER WAR WEAPON ...TIME/SEQ 20 PENTAGON MCNAMARA/R. PAGE 86 B1746
PWR CIVMIL/REL EX/STRUC FORCES
B64

RIDDLE D.H.,THE TRUMAN COMMITTEE: A STUDY IN CONGRESSIONAL RESPONSIBILITY. INDUS FORCES OP/RES DOMIN ADMIN LEAD PARL/PROC WAR PRODUC SUPEGO ...BIBLIOG CONGRESS. PAGE 88 B1778
LEGIS DELIB/GP CONFER
B64

WHEELER-BENNETT J.W.,THE NEMESIS OF POWER (2ND ED.). EUR+WWI GERMANY TOP/EX TEC/DEV ADMIN WAR PERS/REL RIGID/FLEX ROLE ORD/FREE PWR FASCISM 20 HITLER/A. PAGE 116 B2332
FORCES NAT/G GP/REL STRUCT
S64

GALTUNE J.,"BALANCE OF POWER AND THE PROBLEM OF PERCEPTION. A LOGICAL ANALYSIS." WOR+45 CONSTN SOCIETY NAT/G DELIB/GP EX/STRUC LEGIS DOMIN ADMIN COERCE DRIVE ORD/FREE...POLICY CONCPT OBS TREND GEN/LAWS. PAGE 38 B0778
PWR PSY ARMS/CONT WAR
B65

ECCLES H.E.,MILITARY CONCEPTS AND PHILOSOPHY. USA+45 STRUCT EXEC ROUTINE COERCE WAR CIVMIL/REL COST...OBS GEN/LAWS COLD/WAR. PAGE 32 B0648
PLAN DRIVE LEAD FORCES
B65

LEMAY G.H.,BRITISH SUPREMACY IN SOUTH AFRICA 1899-1907. SOUTH/AFR UK ADMIN CONTROL LEAD GP/REL ORD/FREE 19/20. PAGE 64 B1286
WAR COLONIAL DOMIN POLICY
B65

LYONS G.M.,SCHOOLS FOR STRATEGY* EDUCATION AND RESEARCH IN NATIONAL SECURITY AFFAIRS. USA+45 FINAN NAT/G VOL/ASSN FORCES TEC/DEV ADMIN WAR...GP/COMP IDEA/COMP PERS/COMP COLD/WAR. PAGE 67 B1351
ACADEM ACT/RES INTELL
B65

MORGENTHAU H.,MORGENTHAU DIARY (CHINA) (2 VOLS.). ASIA USA+45 USA-45 LAW DELIB/GP EX/STRUC PLAN FOR/AID INT/TRADE CONFER WAR MARXISM 20 CHINJAP. PAGE 75 B1523
DIPLOM ADMIN
B65

NORDEN A.,WAR AND NAZI CRIMINALS IN WEST GERMANY: STATE, ECONOMY, ADMINISTRATION, ARMY, JUSTICE, SCIENCE. GERMANY GERMANY/W MOD/EUR ECO/DEV ACADEM EX/STRUC FORCES DOMIN ADMIN CT/SYS...POLICY MAJORIT PACIFIST 20. PAGE 78 B1587
FASCIST WAR NAT/G TOP/EX
B65

PURCELL V.,THE MEMOIRS OF A MALAYAN OFFICIAL. MALAYSIA UK ECO/UNDEV INDUS LABOR EDU/PROP COLONIAL CT/SYS WAR NAT/LISM TOTALISM ORD/FREE SOVEREIGN 20 UN CIVIL/SERV. PAGE 85 B1721
BIOG ADMIN JURID FORCES
B65

VIORST M.,HOSTILE ALLIES: FDR AND DE GAULLE. EUR+WWI USA-45 ELITES NAT/G VOL/ASSN FORCES LEGIS PLAN LEGIT ADMIN COERCE PERSON...BIOG TIME/SEQ 20 ROOSEVLT/F DEGAULLE/C. PAGE 112 B2263
TOP/EX PWR WAR FRANCE
S65

"FURTHER READING." INDIA ADMIN COLONIAL WAR GOV/REL ATTIT 20. PAGE 2 B0044
BIBLIOG DIPLOM NAT/G POLICY
S65

HOLSTI O.R.,"THE 1914 CASE." MOD/EUR COMPUTER DIPLOM EDU/PROP EXEC...DECISION PSY PROBABIL STAT COMPUT/IR SOC/EXP TIME. PAGE 51 B1036
CON/ANAL PERCEPT WAR
B66

GLAZER M.,THE FEDERAL GOVERNMENT AND THE UNIVERSITY. CHILE PROB/SOLV DIPLOM GIVE ADMIN WAR ...POLICY SOC 20. PAGE 40 B0810
BIBLIOG/A NAT/G PLAN ACADEM
B66

HAYER T.,FRENCH AID. AFR FRANCE AGRI FINAN BUDGET ADMIN WAR PRODUC...CHARTS 18/20 THIRD/WRLD OVRSEA/DEV. PAGE 48 B0975
TEC/DEV COLONIAL FOR/AID ECO/UNDEV
B66

MARTIN L.W.,DIPLOMACY IN MODERN EUROPEAN HISTORY. EUR+WWI MOD/EUR INT/ORG NAT/G EX/STRUC ROUTINE WAR PEACE TOTALISM PWR 15/20 COLD/WAR EUROPE/W. PAGE 70 B1411
DIPLOM POLICY
B66

TOTTEN G.O.,THE SOCIAL DEMOCRATIC MOVEMENT IN PREWAR JAPAN. ASIA CHIEF EX/STRUC LEGIS DOMIN LEAD ROUTINE WAR 20 CHINJAP. PAGE 105 B2122
POL/PAR SOCISM PARTIC STRATA
B66

US HOUSE COMM GOVT OPERATIONS,AN INVESTIGATION OF THE US ECONOMIC AND MILITARY ASSISTANCE PROGRAMS IN VIETNAM. USA+45 VIETNAM/S SOCIETY CONSTRUC FINAN FORCES BUDGET INT/TRADE PEACE HEALTH...MGT
FOR/AID ECO/UNDEV WAR INSPECT

HOUSE/REP AID. PAGE 108 B2191
B66

WHITNAH D.R.,SAFER SKYWAYS. DIST/IND DELIB/GP FORCES TOP/EX WORKER TEC/DEV ROUTINE WAR CIVMIL/REL COST...TIME/SEQ 20 FAA CAB. PAGE 116 B2342
ADMIN NAT/G AIR GOV/REL
C66

TARLING N.,"A CONCISE HISTORY OF SOUTHEAST ASIA." BURMA CAMBODIA LAOS S/ASIA THAILAND VIETNAM ECO/UNDEV POL/PAR FORCES ADMIN REV WAR CIVMIL/REL ORD/FREE MARXISM SOCISM 13/20. PAGE 103 B2080
COLONIAL DOMIN INT/TRADE NAT/LISM
B67

AMERICAN FRIENDS SERVICE COMM,IN PLACE OF WAR. NAT/G ACT/RES DIPLOM ADMIN NUC/PWR EFFICIENCY ...POLICY 20. PAGE 4 B0085
PEACE PACIFISM WAR DETER
B67

ANGEL D.D.,ROMNEY. LABOR LG/CO NAT/G EXEC WAR RACE/REL PERSON ORD/FREE...MGT WORSHIP 20 ROMNEY/GEO CIV/RIGHTS MORMON GOVERNOR. PAGE 5 B0108
BIOG CHIEF PROVS POLICY
B67

CECIL L.,ALBERT BALLIN: BUSINESS AND POLITICS IN IMPERIAL GERMANY 1888-1918. GERMANY UK INT/TRADE LEAD WAR PERS/REL ADJUST PWR WEALTH...MGT BIBLIOG 19/20. PAGE 19 B0397
DIPLOM CONSTN ECO/DEV TOP/EX
B67

DUN J.L.,THE ESSENCE OF CHINESE CIVILIZATION. ASIA FAM NAT/G TEC/DEV ADMIN SANCTION WAR HABITAT ...ANTHOL WORSHIP. PAGE 31 B0630
CULTURE SOCIETY
B67

FARNSWORTH B.,WILLIAM C. BULLITT AND THE SOVIET UNION. COM USA-45 USSR NAT/G CHIEF CONSULT DELIB/GP EX/STRUC WAR REPRESENT MARXISM 20 WILSON/W ROOSEVLT/F STALIN/J BULLITT/WC. PAGE 35 B0705
DIPLOM BIOG POLICY
B67

GIFFORD P.,BRITAIN AND GERMANY IN AFRICA. AFR GERMANY UK ECO/UNDEV LEAD WAR NAT/LISM ATTIT ...POLICY HIST/WRIT METH/COMP ANTHOL BIBLIOG 19/20 WWI. PAGE 39 B0797
COLONIAL ADMIN DIPLOM NAT/COMP
B67

MACKINTOSH J.M.,JUGGERNAUT. USSR NAT/G POL/PAR ADMIN LEAD CIVMIL/REL COST TOTALISM PWR MARXISM ...GOV/COMP 20. PAGE 68 B1364
WAR FORCES COM PROF/ORG
B67

RALSTON D.B.,THE ARMY OF THE REPUBLIC; THE PLACE OF THE MILITARY IN THE POLITICAL EVOLUTION OF FRANCE 1871-1914. FRANCE MOD/EUR EX/STRUC LEGIS TOP/EX DIPLOM ADMIN WAR GP/REL ROLE...BIBLIOG 19/20. PAGE 86 B1730
FORCES NAT/G CIVMIL/REL POLICY
B67

RAWLINSON J.L.,CHINA'S STRUGGLE FOR NAVAL DEVELOPMENT 1839-1895. ASIA DIPLOM ADMIN WAR ...BIBLIOG DICTIONARY 19 CHINJAP. PAGE 86 B1745
SEA FORCES PWR
S67

DRAPER A.P.,"UNIONS AND THE WAR IN VIETNAM." USA+45 CONFER ADMIN LEAD WAR ORD/FREE PACIFIST 20. PAGE 30 B0616
LABOR PACIFISM ATTIT ELITES
S67

JONES G.S.,"STRATEGIC PLANNING." USA+45 EX/STRUC FORCES DETER WAR 20 PRESIDENT. PAGE 57 B1150
PLAN DECISION DELIB/GP POLICY
S67

NEUCHTERLEIN D.E.,"THAILAND* ANOTHER VIETNAM?" THAILAND ECO/UNDEV DIPLOM ADMIN REGION CENTRAL NAT/LISM...POLICY 20. PAGE 78 B1571
WAR GUERRILLA S/ASIA NAT/G
S67

SHOEMAKER R.L.,"JAPANESE ARMY AND THE WEST." ASIA ELITES EX/STRUC DIPLOM DOMIN EDU/PROP COERCE ATTIT AUTHORIT PWR 1/20 CHINJAP. PAGE 96 B1950
FORCES TEC/DEV WAR TOTALISM
B95

LATIMER E.W.,EUROPE IN AFRICA IN THE NINETEENTH CENTURY. ECO/UNDEV KIN SECT DIPLOM DOMIN ADMIN DISCRIM 17/18. PAGE 63 B1275
AFR COLONIAL WAR FINAN

WAR/TRIAL....WAR TRIAL; SEE ALSO NUREMBERG

WAR/1812....WAR OF 1812

WARBURG J.P. B2287

WARD R. B2288

WARD R.E. B2289,B2290

WARD W.E. B2291

WARD....SEE LOC/G, POL/PAR

WARD/LEST....LESTER WARD

WARNER A.W. B2292

WARNER W.L. B2293,B2294,B2295

WARREN R.O. B2296

WARREN S. B2297

WARRN/EARL....EARL WARREN

WARSAW PACT....SEE WARSAW/PCT

WARSAW....WARSAW, POLAND

WARSAW/P

B64
GRZYBOWSKI K.,THE SOCIALIST COMMONWEALTH OF
NATIONS: ORGANIZATIONS AND INSTITUTIONS. FORCES
DIPLOM INT/TRADE ADJUD ADMIN LEAD WAR MARXISM
SOCISM...BIBLIOG 20 COMECON WARSAW/P. PAGE 44 B0898
INT/LAW
COM
REGION
INT/ORG

WARSAW/PCT....WARSAW PACT TREATY ORGANIZATION

WASHING/BT....BOOKER T. WASHINGTON

WASHING/DC....WASHINGTON, D.C.

WASHINGT/G....PRESIDENT GEORGE WASHINGTON

B41
PALMER J.M.,AMERICA IN ARMS: THE EXPERIENCE OF THE
UNITED STATES WITH MILITARY ORGANIZATION. FUT
USA-45 LEAD REV PWR 18/20 WASHINGT/G KNOX/HENRY
PRE/US/AM. PAGE 81 B1627
FORCES
NAT/G
ADMIN
WAR

B48
WHITE L.D.,THE FEDERALISTS: A STUDY IN
ADMINISTRATIVE HISTORY. STRUCT DELIB/GP LEGIS
BUDGET ROUTINE GOV/REL GP/REL PERS/REL PWR...BIOG
18/19 PRESIDENT CONGRESS WASHINGT/G JEFFERSN/T
HAMILTON/A. PAGE 116 B2337
ADMIN
NAT/G
POLICY
PROB/SOLV

B61
AVERY M.W.,GOVERNMENT OF WASHINGTON STATE. USA+45
MUNIC DELIB/GP EX/STRUC LEGIS GIVE CT/SYS PARTIC
REGION EFFICIENCY 20 WASHINGT/G GOVERNOR. PAGE 7
B0151
PROVS
LOC/G
ADMIN
GOV/REL

WASHINGTON S.H. B2298

WASHINGTON....WASHINGTON, STATE OF

WASP....WHITE-ANGLO-SAXON-PROTESTANT ESTABLISHMENT

WASSERMAN P. B2299,B2300

WATANABE H. B2290

WATER POLLUTION....SEE POLLUTION

WATER....PERTAINING TO ALL NON-SALT WATER

B50
DEES J.W. JR.,URBAN SOCIOLOGY AND THE EMERGING
ATOMIC MEGALOPOLIS. USA+45 TEC/DEV ADMIN
NUC/PWR HABITAT...SOC AUD/VIS CHARTS GEN/LAWS 20
WATER. PAGE 28 B0568
PLAN
NEIGH
MUNIC
PROB/SOLV

B64
WILDAVSKY A.,LEADERSHIP IN A SMALL TOWN. USA+45
STRUCT PROB/SOLV EXEC PARTIC RACE/REL PWR PLURISM
...SOC 20 NEGRO WATER CIV/RIGHTS OBERLIN CITY/MGT.
PAGE 116 B2348
LEAD
MUNIC
ELITES

WATERS M. B2301

WATERSTON A. B2302,B2303

WATTS....WATTS, CALIFORNIA

WAUGH E.W. B2304

WCC....WORLD COUNCIL CHURCHES

WCTU....WOMAN'S CHRISTIAN TEMPERANCE UNION

WEALTH....ACCESS TO GOODS AND SERVICES (ALSO POVERTY)

N
PERSONNEL. USA+45 LAW LABOR LG/CO WORKER CREATE
GOV/REL PERS/REL ATTIT WEALTH. PAGE 2 B0030
BIBLIOG/A
ADMIN
MGT
GP/REL

N19
KUWAIT ARABIA,KUWAIT FUND FOR ARAB ECONOMIC
DEVELOPMENT (PAMPHLET). ISLAM KUWAIT UAR ECO/UNDEV
LEGIS ECO/TAC WEALTH 20. PAGE 62 B1245
FOR/AID
DIPLOM
FINAN
ADMIN

N19
RIDLEY C.E.,MEASURING MUNICIPAL ACTIVITIES
(PAMPHLET). FINAN SERV/IND FORCES RECEIVE INGP/REL
HABITAT...POLICY SOC/WK 20. PAGE 88 B1779
MGT
HEALTH
WEALTH
LOC/G

B26
MOON P.T.,IMPERIALISM AND WORLD POLITICS. AFR ASIA
ISLAM MOD/EUR S/ASIA USA-45 SOCIETY NAT/G EX/STRUC
BAL/PWR DOMIN COLONIAL NAT/LISM ATTIT DRIVE PWR
...GEOG SOC 20. PAGE 75 B1510
WEALTH
TIME/SEQ
CAP/ISM
DIPLOM

B28
CALKINS E.E.,BUSINESS THE CIVILIZER. INDUS MARKET
WORKER TAX PAY ROUTINE COST DEMAND MORAL 19/20.
PAGE 18 B0367
LAISSEZ
POLICY
WEALTH
PROFIT

B31
DEKAT A.D.A.,COLONIAL POLICY. S/ASIA CULTURE
EX/STRUC ECO/TAC DOMIN ADMIN COLONIAL ROUTINE
SOVEREIGN WEALTH...POLICY MGT RECORD KNO/TEST SAMP.
PAGE 28 B0570
DRIVE
PWR
INDONESIA
NETHERLAND

B32
WRIGHT Q.,GOLD AND MONETARY STABILIZATION. FUT
USA-45 WOR-45 INTELL ECO/DEV INT/ORG NAT/G CONSULT
PLAN ECO/TAC ADMIN ATTIT WEALTH...CONCPT TREND 20.
PAGE 118 B2383
FINAN
POLICY

B36
ROBINSON H.,DEVELOPMENT OF THE BRITISH EMPIRE.
WOR-45 CULTURE SOCIETY STRUCT ECO/DEV ECO/UNDEV
INT/ORG VOL/ASSN FORCES CREATE PLAN DOMIN EDU/PROP
ADMIN COLONIAL PWR WEALTH...POLICY GEOG CHARTS
CMN/WLTH 16/20. PAGE 89 B1800
NAT/G
HIST/WRIT
UK

B37
BROOKS R.R.,WHEN LABOR ORGANIZES. FINAN EDU/PROP
ADMIN LOBBY PARTIC REPRESENT WEALTH TREND. PAGE 16
B0318
LABOR
GP/REL
POLICY

B37
ROBBINS L.,ECONOMIC PLANNING AND INTERNATIONAL
ORDER. WOR-45 SOCIETY FINAN INDUS NAT/G ECO/TAC
ROUTINE WEALTH...SOC TIME/SEQ GEN/METH WORK 20
KEYNES/JM. PAGE 89 B1791
INT/ORG
PLAN
INT/TRADE

B38
DAY C.,A HISTORY OF COMMERCE. CHRIST-17C EUR+WWI
ISLAM MEDIT-7 MOD/EUR USA-45 ECO/DEV FINAN NAT/G
ECO/TAC EXEC ROUTINE PWR WEALTH HIST/WRIT. PAGE 27
B0546
MARKET
INT/TRADE

B39
ZIMMERN A.,MODERN POLITICAL DOCTRINE. WOR-45
CULTURE SOCIETY ECO/UNDEV DELIB/GP EX/STRUC CREATE
DOMIN COERCE NAT/LISM ATTIT RIGID/FLEX ORD/FREE PWR
WEALTH...POLICY CONCPT OBS TIME/SEQ TREND TOT/POP
LEAGUE/NAT 20. PAGE 119 B2402
NAT/G
ECO/TAC
BAL/PWR
INT/TRADE

B43
LEVY H.P.,A STUDY IN PUBLIC RELATIONS: CASE HISTORY
OF THE RELATIONS MAINTAINED BETWEEN A DEPT OF
PUBLIC ASSISTANCE AND PEOPLE. USA-45 NAT/G PRESS
ADMIN LOBBY GP/REL DISCRIM...SOC/WK LING AUD/VIS 20
PENNSYLVAN. PAGE 64 B1302
ATTIT
RECEIVE
WEALTH
SERV/IND

B46
CLOUGH S.B.,ECONOMIC HISTORY OF EUROPE. CHRIST-17C
EUR+WWI MOD/EUR WOR-45 SOCIETY EXEC ATTIT WEALTH
...CONCPT GEN/LAWS WORK TOT/POP VAL/FREE 7/20.
PAGE 22 B0440
ECO/TAC
CAP/ISM

B46
WILCOX J.K.,OFFICIAL DEFENSE PUBLICATIONS,
1941-1945 (NINE VOLS.). USA-45 AGRI INDUS R+D LABOR
FORCES TEC/DEV EFFICIENCY PRODUC SKILL WEALTH 20.
PAGE 116 B2347
BIBLIOG/A
WAR
CIVMIL/REL
ADMIN

B47
GAUS J.M.,REFLECTIONS ON PUBLIC ADMINISTRATION.
USA+45 CONTROL GOV/REL CENTRAL FEDERAL ATTIT WEALTH
...DECISION 20. PAGE 39 B0787
MGT
POLICY
EX/STRUC
ADMIN

S47
CALDWELL L.K.,"STRENGTHENING STATE LEGISLATURES"
FUT DELIB/GP WEALTH REFORMERS. PAGE 18 B0364
PROVS
LEGIS
ROUTINE
BUDGET

B48
ROSENFARB J.,FREEDOM AND THE ADMINISTRATIVE STATE.
NAT/G ROUTINE EFFICIENCY PRODUC RATIONAL UTIL
...TECHNIC WELF/ST MGT 20 BUREAUCRCY. PAGE 90 B1821
ECO/DEV
INDUS
PLAN
WEALTH

B49
FORD FOUNDATION,REPORT OF THE STUDY FOR THE FORD
FOUNDATION ON POLICY AND PROGRAM. SOCIETY R+D
ACT/RES CAP/ISM FOR/AID EDU/PROP ADMIN KNOWL
...POLICY PSY SOC 20. PAGE 36 B0739
WEALTH
GEN/LAWS

S49
STEINMETZ H.,"THE PROBLEMS OF THE LANDRAT: A STUDY
OF COUNTY GOVERNMENT IN THE US ZONE OF GERMANY."
GERMANY/W USA+45 INDUS PLAN DIPLOM EDU/PROP CONTROL
WAR GOV/REL FEDERAL WEALTH PLURISM...GOV/COMP 20
LANDRAT. PAGE 100 B2031
LOC/G
COLONIAL
MGT
TOP/EX

L51
MANGONE G.,"THE IDEA AND PRACTICE OF WORLD
GOVERNMENT." FUT WOR+45 WOR-45 ECO/DEV LEGIS CREATE
INT/ORG
SOCIETY

LEGIT ROUTINE ATTIT MORAL PWR WEALTH...CONCPT   INT/LAW
GEN/LAWS 20. PAGE 69 B1388
                                                                    B52
EGLE W.P.,ECONOMIC STABILIZATION. USA+45 SOCIETY   NAT/G
FINAN MARKET PLAN ECO/TAC DOMIN EDU/PROP LEGIT EXEC   ECO/DEV
WEALTH...CONCPT METH/CNCPT TREND HYPO/EXP GEN/METH   CAP/ISM
TOT/POP VAL/FREE 20. PAGE 32 B0656
                                                                    S52
BRUEGEL J.W.,"DIE INTERNAZIONALE   VOL/ASSN
GEWERKSCHAFTSBEWEGUNG." COM EUR+WWI USA+45 WOR+45   LABOR
DELIB/GP EX/STRUC ECO/TAC EDU/PROP ATTIT PWR   TOTALISM
RESPECT SKILL WEALTH WORK 20. PAGE 16 B0330
                                                                    B53
MACK R.T.,RAISING THE WORLDS STANDARD OF LIVING.   WOR+45
IRAN INT/ORG VOL/ASSN EX/STRUC ECO/TAC WEALTH...MGT   FOR/AID
METH/CNCPT STAT CONT/OBS INT TOT/POP VAL/FREE 20   INT/TRADE
UN. PAGE 67 B1363
                                                                    B53
MAJUMDAR B.B.,PROBLEMS OF PUBLIC ADMINISTRATION IN   ECO/UNDEV
INDIA. INDIA INDUS PLAN BUDGET ADJUD CENTRAL DEMAND   GOV/REL
WEALTH...WELF/ST ANTHOL 20 CIVIL/SERV. PAGE 68   ADMIN
B1384   MUNIC
                                                                    B53
MEYER P.,THE JEWS IN THE SOVIET SATELLITES.   COM
CZECHOSLVK POLAND SOCIETY STRATA NAT/G BAL/PWR   SECT
ECO/TAC EDU/PROP LEGIT ADMIN COERCE ATTIT DISPL   TOTALISM
PERCEPT HEALTH PWR RESPECT WEALTH...METH/CNCPT JEWS   USSR
VAL/FREE NAZI 20. PAGE 73 B1474
                                                                    B53
MILLIKAN M.F.,INCOME STABILIZATION FOR A DEVELOPING   ANTHOL
DEMOCRACY. USA+45 ECO/DEV LABOR BUDGET ECO/TAC TAX   MARKET
ADMIN ADJUST PRODUC WEALTH...POLICY TREND 20.   EQUILIB
PAGE 73 B1484   EFFICIENCY
                                                                    B53
ROBINSON E.A.G.,THE STRUCTURE OF COMPETITIVE   INDUS
INDUSTRY. UK ECO/DEV DIST/IND MARKET TEC/DEV DIPLOM   DIST/IND
EDU/PROP ADMIN EFFICIENCY WEALTH...MGT 19/20.   WORKER
PAGE 89 B1798   OPTIMAL
                                                                    B53
WAGLEY C.,AMAZON TOWN: A STUDY OF MAN IN THE   SOC
TROPICS. BRAZIL L/A+17C STRATA STRUCT ECO/UNDEV   NEIGH
AGRI EX/STRUC RACE/REL DISCRIM HABITAT WEALTH...OBS   CULTURE
SOC/EXP 20. PAGE 113 B2273   INGP/REL
                                                                    S53
BLOUGH R.,"THE ROLE OF THE ECONOMIST IN FEDERAL   DELIB/GP
POLICY MAKING." USA+45 ELITES INTELL ECO/DEV NAT/G   ECO/TAC
CONSULT EX/STRUC ACT/RES PLAN INT/TRADE BAL/PAY
WEALTH...POLICY CONGRESS 20. PAGE 13 B0256
                                                                    B55
UN ECONOMIC AND SOCIAL COUNCIL.BIBLIOGRAPHY OF   BIBLIOG/A
PUBLICATIONS OF THE UN AND SPECIALIZED AGENCIES IN   SOC/WK
THE SOCIAL WELFARE FIELD, 1946-1952. WOR+45 FAM   ADMIN
INT/ORG MUNIC ACT/RES PLAN PROB/SOLV EDU/PROP AGE/C   WEALTH
AGE/Y HABITAT...HEAL UN. PAGE 106 B2148
                                                                    C55
BONER H.A.,"HUNGRY GENERATIONS." UK WOR+45 WOR-45   ECO/DEV
STRATA INDUS FAM LABOR CAP/ISM...MGT BIBLIOG 19/20.   PHIL/SCI
PAGE 13 B0272   CONCPT
                                                       WEALTH
                                                                    B56
ABELS J.,THE TRUMAN SCANDALS. USA+45 USA-45 POL/PAR   CRIME
TAX LEGIT CT/SYS CHOOSE PRIVIL MORAL WEALTH 20   ADMIN
TRUMAN/HS PRESIDENT CONGRESS. PAGE 3 B0052   CHIEF
                                                       TRIBUTE
                                                                    B56
GARDNER R.N.,STERLING-DOLLAR DIPLOMACY. EUR+WWI   ECO/DEV
USA+45 INT/ORG NAT/G PLAN INT/TRADE ADMIN   DIPLOM
KNOWL PWR WEALTH...POLICY SOC METH/CNCPT STAT
CHARTS SIMUL GEN/LAWS 20. PAGE 39 B0781
                                                                    B57
KIETH-LUCAS A.,DECISIONS ABOUT PEOPLE IN NEED, A   ADMIN
STUDY OF ADMINISTRATIVE RESPONSIVENESS IN PUBLIC   RIGID/FLEX
ASSISTANCE. USA+45 GIVE RECEIVE INGP/REL PERS/REL   SOC/WK
MORAL RESPECT WEALTH...SOC OBS BIBLIOG 20. PAGE 60   DECISION
B1204
                                                                    B58
SHAW S.J.,THE FINANCIAL AND ADMINISTRATIVE   FINAN
ORGANIZATION AND DEVELOPMENT OF OTTOMAN EGYPT   ADMIN
1517-1798. UAR LOC/G FORCES BUDGET INT/TRADE TAX   GOV/REL
EATING INCOME WEALTH...CHARTS BIBLIOG 16/18 OTTOMAN   CULTURE
NAPOLEON/B. PAGE 96 B1940
                                                                    B58
UNESCO.UNESCO PUBLICATIONS: CHECK LIST (2ND REV.   BIBLIOG
ED.). WOR+45 DIPLOM FOR/AID WEALTH...POLICY SOC   INT/ORG
UNESCO. PAGE 107 B2156   ECO/UNDEV
                                                       ADMIN
                                                                    S58
ELKIN A.B.,"OEEC-ITS STRUCTURE AND POWERS." EUR+WWI   ECO/DEV
CONSTN INDUS INT/ORG NAT/G VOL/ASSN DELIB/GP   EX/STRUC
ACT/RES PLAN ORD/FREE WEALTH...CHARTS ORG/CHARTS
OEEC 20. PAGE 33 B0666
                                                                    B59
DIEBOLD W. JR.,THE SCHUMAN PLAN: A STUDY IN   INT/ORG
ECONOMIC COOPERATION, 1950-1959. EUR+WWI FRANCE   REGION
GERMANY USA+45 EXTR/IND CONSULT DELIB/GP PLAN
DIPLOM ECO/TAC INT/TRADE ROUTINE ORD/FREE WEALTH

...METH/CNCPT STAT CONT/OBS INT TIME/SEQ ECSC 20.
PAGE 29 B0591
                                                                    B59
GREENEWALT C.H.,THE UNCOMMON MAN. UNIV ECO/DEV   TASK
ADMIN PERS/REL PERSON SUPEGO WEALTH 20. PAGE 43   ORD/FREE
B0868   DRIVE
                                                       EFFICIENCY
                                                                    B59
MAYDA J.,ATOMIC ENERGY AND LAW. ECO/UNDEV FINAN   NUC/PWR
TEC/DEV FOR/AID EFFICIENCY PRODUC WEALTH...POLICY   L/A+17C
TECHNIC 20. PAGE 71 B1433   LAW
                                                       ADMIN
                                                                    B59
PARK R.L.,LEADERSHIP AND POLITICAL INSTITUTIONS IN   NAT/G
INDIA. S/ASIA CULTURE ECO/UNDEV LOC/G MUNIC PROVS   EXEC
LEGIS PLAN ADMIN LEAD ORD/FREE WEALTH...GEOG SOC   INDIA
BIOG TOT/POP VAL/FREE 20. PAGE 81 B1633
                                                                    S59
HARVEY M.F.,"THE PALESTINE REFUGEE PROBLEM: ACT/RES
ELEMENTS OF A SOLUTION." ISLAM LAW INT/ORG DELIB/GP   LEGIT
TOP/EX ECO/TAC ROUTINE DRIVE HEALTH LOVE ORD/FREE   PEACE
PWR WEALTH...MAJORIT FAO 20. PAGE 48 B0964   ISRAEL
                                                                    B60
BERNSTEIN I.,THE LEAN YEARS. SOCIETY STRATA PARTIC   WORKER
GP/REL ATTIT...SOC 20. DEPRESSION. PAGE 11 B0227   LABOR
                                                       WEALTH
                                                       MGT
                                                                    B60
KERR C.,INDUSTRIALISM AND INDUSTRIAL MAN. CULTURE   WORKER
SOCIETY ECO/UNDEV NAT/G ADMIN PRODUC WEALTH   MGT
...PREDICT TREND NAT/COMP 19/20. PAGE 59 B1197   ECO/DEV
                                                       INDUS
                                                                    B60
LERNER A.P.,THE ECONOMICS OF CONTROL. USA+45   ECO/DEV
ECO/UNDEV INT/ORG ACT/RES PLAN CAP/ISM INT/TRADE   ROUTINE
ATTIT WEALTH...SOC MATH STAT GEN/LAWS INDEX 20.   ECO/TAC
PAGE 64 B1295   SOCISM
                                                                    B60
LIPSET S.M.,POLITICAL MAN. AFR COM EUR+WWI L/A+17C   PWR
MOD/EUR S/ASIA USA+45 USA-45 STRUCT ECO/DEV   SOC
ECO/UNDEV POL/PAR SECT ADMIN WEALTH...CONCPT WORK
TOT/POP 20. PAGE 65 B1320
                                                                    B60
LISKA G.,THE NEW STATECRAFT. WOR+45 WOR-45 LEGIS   ECO/TAC
DIPLOM ADMIN ATTIT PWR WEALTH...HIST/WRIT TREND   CONCPT
CCLD/WAR 20. PAGE 66 B1323   FOR/AID
                                                                    B60
ROEPKE W.,A HUMANE ECONOMY: THE SOCIAL FRAMEWORK OF   DRIVE
THE FREE MARKET. FUT USSR WOR+45 CULTURE SOCIETY   EDU/PROP
ECO/DEV PLAN ECO/TAC ADMIN ATTIT PERSON RIGID/FLEX   CAP/ISM
SUPEGO MORAL WEALTH SOCISM...POLICY OLD/LIB CONCPT
TREND GEN/LAWS 20. PAGE 90 B1811
                                                                    S60
FRANKEL S.H.,"ECONOMIC ASPECTS OF POLITICAL   NAT/G
INDEPENDENCE IN AFRICA." AFR FUT SOCIETY ECO/UNDEV   FOR/AID
COM/IND FINAN LEGIS PLAN TEC/DEV CAP/ISM ECO/TAC
INT/TRADE ADMIN ATTIT DRIVE RIGID/FLEX PWR WEALTH
...MGT NEW/IDEA MATH TIME/SEQ VAL/FREE 20. PAGE 37
B0751
                                                                    S60
GROSSMAN G.,"SOVIET GROWTH: ROUTINE, INERTIA, AND   POL/PAR
PRESSURE." COM STRATA NAT/G DELIB/GP PLAN TEC/DEV   ECO/DEV
ECO/TAC EDU/PROP ADMIN ROUTINE DRIVE WEALTH   USSR
COLD/WAR 20. PAGE 44 B0891
                                                                    S60
HERRERA F.,"THE INTER-AMERICAN DEVELOPMENT BANK."   L/A+17C
USA+45 ECO/UNDEV INT/ORG CONSULT DELIB/GP PLAN   FINAN
ECO/TAC INT/TRADE ROUTINE WEALTH...STAT 20. PAGE 49   FOR/AID
B0994   REGION
                                                                    S60
MORA J.A.,"THE ORGANIZATION OF AMERICAN STATES."   L/A+17C
USA+45 LAW ECO/UNDEV VOL/ASSN DELIB/GP PLAN BAL/PWR   INT/ORG
EDU/PROP ADMIN DRIVE RIGID/FLEX ORD/FREE WEALTH   REGION
...TIME/SEQ GEN/LAWS OAS 20. PAGE 75 B1518
                                                                    S60
MORALES C.J.,"TRADE AND ECONOMIC INTEGRATION IN   FINAN
LATIN AMERICA." FUT L/A+17C LAW STRATA ECO/UNDEV   INT/TRADE
DIST/IND INDUS LABOR NAT/G LEGIS ECO/TAC ADMIN   REGION
RIGID/FLEX WEALTH...CONCPT NEW/IDEA CONT/OBS
TIME/SEQ WORK 20. PAGE 75 B1519
                                                                    B61
AYLMER G.,THE KING'S SERVANTS. UK ELITES CHIEF PAY   ADMIN
CT/SYS WEALTH 17 CROMWELL/O CHARLES/I. PAGE 7 B0153   ROUTINE
                                                       EX/STRUC
                                                       NAT/G
                                                                    B61
BENOIT E.,EUROPE AT SIXES AND SEVENS: THE COMMON   FINAN
MARKET, THE FREE TRADE ASSOCIATION AND THE UNITED   ECO/DEV
STATES. EUR+WWI FUT USA+45 INDUS CONSULT DELIB/GP   VOL/ASSN
EX/STRUC TOP/EX ACT/RES ECO/TAC EDU/PROP ROUTINE
CHOOSE PERCEPT WEALTH...MGT TREND EEC TOT/POP 20
EFTA. PAGE 11 B0217
                                                                    B61
CARNEY D.E.,GOVERNMENT AND ECONOMY IN BRITISH WEST   METH/COMP
AFRICA. GAMBIA GHANA NIGERIA SIER/LEONE DOMIN ADMIN   COLONIAL
GOV/REL SOVEREIGN WEALTH LAISSEZ...BIBLIOG 20   ECO/TAC

CMN/WLTH. PAGE 19 B0384   ECO/UNDEV
                                                      B61
FRIEDMANN W.G.,JOINT INTERNATIONAL BUSINESS   ECO/UNDEV
VENTURES. ASIA ISLAM L/A+17C ECO/DEV DIST/IND FINAN INT/TRADE
PROC/MFG FACE/GP LG/CO NAT/G VOL/ASSN CONSULT
EX/STRUC PLAN ADMIN ROUTINE WEALTH...OLD/LIB WORK
20. PAGE 37 B0760
                                                      B61
GORDON W.J.J.,SYNECTICS; THE DEVELOPMENT OF   CREATE
CREATIVE CAPACITY. USA+45 PLAN TEC/DEV KNOWL WEALTH PROB/SOLV
...DECISION MGT 20. PAGE 41 B0832   ACT/RES
                                                  TOP/EX
                                                      B61
HORVATH B.,THE CHARACTERISTICS OF YUGOSLAV ECONOMIC ACT/RES
DEVELOPMENT. COM ECO/UNDEV AGRI INDUS PLAN CAP/ISM YUGOSLAVIA
ECO/TAC ROUTINE WEALTH...SOCIALIST STAT CHARTS
STERTYP WORK 20. PAGE 52 B1045
                                                      B61
KEE R.,REFUGEE WORLD. AUSTRIA EUR+WWI GERMANY NEIGH NAT/G
EX/STRUC WORKER PROB/SOLV ECO/TAC RENT EDU/PROP   GIVE
INGP/REL COST LITERACY HABITAT 20 MIGRATION.   WEALTH
PAGE 59 B1186   STRANGE
                                                      B61
KOESTLER A.,THE LOTUS AND THE ROBOT. ASIA INDIA   SECT
S/ASIA SOCIETY STRATA ECO/DEV AGRI INDUS FAM CREATE ECO/UNDEV
DOMIN EDU/PROP ADMIN COERCE ATTIT DRIVE SUPEGO
ORD/FREE PWR RESPECT WEALTH...MYTH OBS 20 CHINJAP.
PAGE 61 B1226
                                                      B61
SHARP W.R.,FIELD ADMINISTRATION IN THE UNITED   INT/ORG
NATION SYSTEM: THE CONDUCT OF INTERNATIONAL   CONSULT
ECONOMIC AND SOCIAL PROGRAMS. FUT WOR+45 CONSTN
SOCIETY ECO/UNDEV R+D DELIB/GP ACT/RES PLAN TEC/DEV
EDU/PROP EXEC ROUTINE HEALTH WEALTH...HUM CONCPT
CHARTS METH ILO UNESCO VAL/FREE UN 20. PAGE 96
B1939
                                                      S61
GORDON L.,"ECONOMIC REGIONALISM RECONSIDERED." FUT ECO/DEV
USA+45 WOR+45 INDUS NAT/G TEC/DEV DIPLOM ROUTINE ATTIT
PERCEPT WEALTH...WELF/ST METH/CNCPT WORK 20.   CAP/ISM
PAGE 41 B0830   REGION
                                                      S61
JUVILER P.H.,"INTERPARLIAMENTARY CONTACTS IN SOVIET INT/ORG
FOREIGN POLICY." COM FUT WOR+45 WOR-45 SOCIETY   DELIB/GP
CONSULT ACT/RES DIPLOM ADMIN PEACE ATTIT RIGID/FLEX USSR
WEALTH...WELF/ST SOC TOT/POP CONGRESS 19/20.
PAGE 57 B1156
                                                      S61
LANFALUSSY A.,"EUROPE'S PROGRESS: DUE TO COMMON   INT/ORG
MARKET." EUR+WWI ECO/DEV DELIB/GP PLAN ECO/TAC   MARKET
ROUTINE WEALTH...GEOG TREND EEC 20. PAGE 62 B1257
                                                      S61
NOVE A.,"THE SOVIET MODEL AND UNDERDEVELOPED   ECO/UNDEV
COUNTRIES." COM FUT USSR WOR+45 CULTURE ECO/DEV   PLAN
POL/PAR FOR/AID EDU/PROP ADMIN MORAL WEALTH
...POLICY RECORD HIST/WRIT 20. PAGE 79 B1593
                                                      B62
BECKMAN T.N.,MARKETING (7TH ED.). USA+45 SOCIETY MARKET
ECO/DEV NAT/G PRICE EFFICIENCY INCOME ATTIT WEALTH ECO/TAC
...MGT BIBLIOG 20. PAGE 10 B0205   DIST/IND
                                                  POLICY
                                                      B62
BRIMMER B.,A GUIDE TO THE USE OF UNITED NATIONS   BIBLIOG/A
DOCUMENTS. WOR+45 ECO/UNDEV AGRI EX/STRUC FORCES INT/ORG
PROB/SOLV ADMIN WAR PEACE WEALTH...POLICY UN.   DIPLOM
PAGE 15 B0310
                                                      B62
CAIRNCROSS A.K.,FACTORS IN ECONOMIC DEVELOPMENT. MARKET
WOR+45 ECO/UNDEV INDUS R+D LG/CO NAT/G EX/STRUC   ECO/DEV
PLAN TEC/DEV ECO/TAC ATTIT HEALTH KNOWL PWR WEALTH
...TIME/SEQ GEN/LAWS TOT/POP VAL/FREE 20. PAGE 18
B0363
                                                      B62
CARTER G.M.,THE GOVERNMENT OF THE SOVIET UNION.   NAT/G
USSR CULTURE LOC/G DIPLOM ECO/TAC ADJUD CT/SYS LEAD MARXISM
WEALTH...CHARTS T 20 COM/PARTY. PAGE 19 B0390   POL/PAR
                                                  EX/STRUC
                                                      B62
GALENSON W.,LABOR IN DEVELOPING COUNTRIES. BRAZIL LABOR
INDONESIA ISRAEL PAKISTAN TURKEY AGRI INDUS WORKER ECO/UNDEV
PAY PRICE GP/REL WEALTH...MGT CHARTS METH/COMP   BARGAIN
NAT/COMP 20. PAGE 38 B0775   POL/PAR
                                                      B62
KENNEDY J.F.,TO TURN THE TIDE. SPACE AGRI INT/ORG DIPLOM
FORCES TEC/DEV ADMIN NUC/PWR PEACE WEALTH...ANTHOL CHIEF
20 KENNEDY/JF CIV/RIGHTS. PAGE 59 B1193   POLICY
                                                  NAT/G
                                                      B62
LAWSON R.,INTERNATIONAL REGIONAL ORGANIZATIONS.   INT/ORG
WOR+45 NAT/G VOL/ASSN CONSULT LEGIS EDU/PROP LEGIT DELIB/GP
ADMIN EXEC ROUTINE HEALTH PWR WEALTH...JURID EEC REGION
COLD/WAR 20 UN. PAGE 63 B1277
                                                      B62
WENDT P.F.,HOUSING POLICY - THE SEARCH FOR   PLAN
SOLUTIONS. GERMANY/W SWEDEN UK USA+45 OP/RES   ADMIN
HABITAT WEALTH...SOC/WK CHARTS 20. PAGE 115 B2322 METH/COMP

                                                  NAT/G
                                                      L62
GALBRAITH J.K.,"ECONOMIC DEVELOPMENT IN   ECO/UNDEV
PERSPECTIVE." CAP/ISM ECO/TAC ROUTINE ATTIT WEALTH PLAN
...TREND CHARTS SOC/EXP WORK 20. PAGE 38 B0773
                                                      L62
WATERSTON A.,"PLANNING IN MOROCCO, ORGANIZATION AND NAT/G
IMPLEMENTATION. BALTIMORE: HOPKINS ECON. DEVELOP. PLAN
INT. BANK FOR." ISLAM ECO/DEV AGRI DIST/IND INDUS MOROCCO
PROC/MFG SERV/IND LOC/G EX/STRUC ECO/TAC PWR WEALTH
TOT/POP VAL/FREE 20. PAGE 114 B2302
                                                      S62
ALBONETTI A.,"IL SECONDO PROGRAMMA QUINQUENNALE   R+D
1963-67 ED IL BILANCIO RICERCHE ED INVESTIMENTI PER PLAN
IL 1963 DELL'ERATOM." EUR+WWI FUT ITALY WOR+45   NUC/PWR
ECO/DEV SERV/IND INT/ORG TEC/DEV ECO/TAC ATTIT
SKILL WEALTH...MGT TIME/SEQ OEEC 20. PAGE 3 B0069
                                                      S62
GEORGE P.,"MATERIAUX ET REFLEXIONS POUR UNE   ECO/UNDEV
POLITIQUE URBAINE RATIONNELLE DANS LES PAYS EN   PLAN
COURS DE DEVELOPPEMENT." FUT INTELL SOCIETY
SERV/IND MUNIC ACT/RES WEALTH...MGT 20. PAGE 39
B0790
                                                      S62
JOHNSON H.,"CANADA IN A CHANGING WORLD." EUR+WWI ECO/DEV
USA+45 NAT/G CAP/ISM ECO/TAC ADMIN ATTIT WEALTH   PLAN
...TREND TOT/POP 20 EEC. PAGE 57 B1143   CANADA
                                                      B63
BRAIBANTI R.J.D.,ADMINISTRATION AND ECONOMIC   ECO/UNDEV
DEVELOPMENT IN INDIA. INDIA S/ASIA SOCIETY STRATA ADMIN
ECO/TAC PERSON WEALTH...MGT GEN/LAWS TOT/POP
VAL/FREE 20. PAGE 15 B0300
                                                      B63
HAUSMAN W.H.,MANAGING ECONOMIC DEVELOPMENT IN   ECO/UNDEV
AFRICA. AFR USA+45 LAW FINAN WORKER TEC/DEV WEALTH PLAN
...ANTHOL 20. PAGE 48 B0970   FOR/AID
                                                  MGT
                                                      B63
JOHNS R.,CONFRONTING ORGANIZATIONAL CHANGE. NEIGH SOC/WK
DELIB/GP CREATE OP/RES ADMIN GP/REL DRIVE...WELF/ST WEALTH
SOC RECORD BIBLIOG. PAGE 56 B1142   LEAD
                                                  VOL/ASSN
                                                      B63
LINDBERG L.,POLITICAL DYNAMICS OF EUROPEAN ECONOMIC MARKET
INTEGRATION. EUR+WWI ECO/DEV INT/ORG VOL/ASSN   ECO/TAC
DELIB/GP ADMIN WEALTH...DECISION EEC 20. PAGE 65
B1313
                                                      B63
MAYNE R.,THE COMMUNITY OF EUROPE. UK CONSTN NAT/G EUR+WWI
CONSULT DELIB/GP CREATE PLAN ECO/TAC LEGIT ADMIN INT/ORG
ROUTINE ORD/FREE PWR WEALTH...CONCPT TIME/SEQ EEC REGION
EURATOM 20. PAGE 71 B1436
                                                      B63
OLSON M. JR.,THE ECONOMICS OF WARTIME SHORTAGE.   WAR
FRANCE GERMANY MOD/EUR UK AGRI PROB/SOLV ADMIN   ADJUST
DEMAND WEALTH...POLICY OLD/LIB 17/20. PAGE 80 B1608 ECO/TAC
                                                  NAT/COMP
                                                      B63
SPRING D.,THE ENGLISH LANDED ESTATE IN THE   STRATA
NINETEENTH CENTURY: ITS ADMINISTRATION. UK ELITES PERS/REL
STRUCT AGRI NAT/G GP/REL OWN PWR WEALTH...BIBLIOG MGT
19 HOUSE/LORD. PAGE 99 B2012
                                                      B63
TUCKER R.C.,THE SOVIET POLITICAL MIND. WOR+45   COM
ELITES INT/ORG NAT/G POL/PAR PLAN DIPLOM ECO/TAC TOP/EX
DOMIN ADMIN NUC/PWR REV DRIVE PERSON SUPEGO PWR   USSR
WEALTH...POLICY MGT PSY CONCPT OBS BIOG TREND
COLD/WAR MARX/KARL 20. PAGE 106 B2134
                                                      L63
BEGUIN H.,"ASPECTS GEOGRAPHIQUE DE LA   ECO/UNDEV
POLARISATION." FUT WOR+45 SOCIETY STRUCT ECO/DEV GEOG
R+D BAL/PWR ADMIN ATTIT RIGID/FLEX HEALTH WEALTH DIPLOM
...CHARTS 20. PAGE 10 B0206
                                                      S63
BARZANSKI S.,"REGIONAL UNDERDEVELOPMENT IN THE   ECO/UNDEV
EUROPEAN ECONOMIC COMMUNITY." EUR+WWI ELITES   PLAN
DIST/IND MARKET VOL/ASSN CONSULT EX/STRUC ECO/TAC
RIGID/FLEX WEALTH EEC OEEC 20. PAGE 9 B0192
                                                      S63
CLEMHOUT S.,"PRODUCTION FUNCTION ANALYSIS APPLIED ECO/DEV
TO THE LEONTIEF SCARCE-FACTOR PARADOX OF   ECO/TAC
INTERNATIONAL TRADE." EUR+WWI USA+45 DIST/IND NAT/G
PLAN TEC/DEV DIPLOM PWR WEALTH...MGT METH/CNCPT
CONT/OBS CON/ANAL CHARTS SIMUL GEN/LAWS 20. PAGE 21
B0436
                                                      S63
COUTY P.,"L'ASSISTANCE POUR LE DEVELOPPEMENT: POINT FINAN
DE VUE SCANDINAVES." EUR+WWI FINLAND FUT SWEDEN   ROUTINE
WOR+45 ECO/DEV ECO/UNDEV COM/IND LABOR NAT/G   FOR/AID
PROF/ORG ACT/RES SKILL WEALTH TOT/POP 20. PAGE 24
B0497
                                                      S63
DAVEE R.,"POUR UN FONDS DE DEVELOPPEMENT SOCIAL." INT/ORG
FUT WOR+45 INTELL SOCIETY ECO/DEV FINAN TEC/DEV   SOC
ROUTINE WEALTH...TREND TOT/POP VAL/FREE UN 20.   FOR/AID
PAGE 26 B0532

S63
DUCROS B.,"MOBILISATION DES RESSOURCES PRODUCTIVES   ECO/UNDEV
ET DEVELOPPEMENT." FUT INTELL SOCIETY COM/IND   TEC/DEV
DIST/IND IND EXTR/IND FINAN INDUS ROUTINE WEALTH
...METH/CNCPT OBS 20. PAGE 31 B0625

S63
HAVILAND H.F.,"BUILDING A POLITICAL COMMUNITY."   VOL/ASSN
EUR+WWI FUT UK USA+45 ECO/DEV ECO/UNDEV INT/ORG   DIPLOM
NAT/G DELIB/GP BAL/PWR ECO/TAC NEUTRAL ROUTINE
ATTIT PWR WEALTH...CONCPT COLD/WAR TOT/POP 20.
PAGE 48 B0972

S63
NADLER E.B.,"SOME ECONOMIC DISADVANTAGES OF THE   ECO/DEV
ARMS RACE." USA+45 INDUS R+D FORCES PLAN TEC/DEV   MGT
ECO/TAC FOR/AID EDU/PROP PWR WEALTH...TREND   BAL/PAY
COLD/WAR 20. PAGE 77 B1552

S63
NYE J.S. JR.,"EAST AFRICAN ECONOMIC INTEGRATION."   ECO/UNDEV
AFR UGANDA PROVS DELIB/GP PLAN ECO/TAC INT/TRADE   INT/ORG
ADMIN ROUTINE ORD/FREE PWR WEALTH...OBS TIME/SEQ
VAL/FREE 20. PAGE 79 B1597

S63
SCHURMANN F.,"ECONOMIC POLICY AND POLITICAL POWER   PLAN
IN COMMUNIST CHINA." ASIA CHINA/COM USSR SOCIETY   ECO/TAC
ECO/UNDEV AGRI INDUS CREATE ADMIN ROUTINE ATTIT
DRIVE RIGID/FLEX PWR WEALTH...HIST/WRIT TREND
CHARTS WORK 20. PAGE 94 B1908

S63
SHIMKIN D.B.,"STRUCTURE OF SOVIET POWER." COM FUT   PWR
USA+45 USSR WOR+45 NAT/G FORCES DOMIN EXEC
COERCE CHOOSE ATTIT WEALTH...TIME/SEQ COLD/WAR
TOT/POP VAL/FREE 20. PAGE 96 B1948

B64
LITTLE I.M.D.,AID TO AFRICA. AFR UK TEC/DEV DIPLOM   FOR/AID
ECO/TAC INCOME WEALTH 20. PAGE 66 B1326   ECO/UNDEV
                                                        ADMIN
                                                        POLICY
B64
PLISCHKE E.,SYSTEMS OF INTEGRATING THE   INT/ORG
INTERNATIONAL COMMUNITY. WOR+45 NAT/G VOL/ASSN   EX/STRUC
ECO/TAC LEGIT PWR WEALTH...TIME/SEQ ANTHOL UN   REGION
TOT/POP 20. PAGE 83 B1684

B64
RIGGS F.W.,ADMINISTRATION IN DEVELOPING COUNTRIES.   ECO/UNDEV
FUT WOR+45 STRUCT AGRI INDUS NAT/G PLAN TEC/DEV   ADMIN
ECO/TAC EDU/PROP RIGID/FLEX KNOWL WEALTH...POLICY
MGT CONCPT METH/CNCPT TREND 20. PAGE 88 B1785

B64
RUSSET B.M.,WORLD HANDBOOK OF POLITICAL AND SOCIAL   DIPLOM
INDICATORS. WOR+45 COM/IND ADMIN WEALTH...GEOG 20.   STAT
PAGE 92 B1858   NAT/G
                                                        NAT/COMP
B64
SCHERMER G.,MEETING SOCIAL NEEDS IN THE PENJERDEL   PLAN
REGION. SOCIETY FINAN ACT/RES EDU/PROP ADMIN   REGION
GOV/REL...SOC/WK 45 20 PENNSYLVAN DELAWARE   HEALTH
NEW/JERSEY. PAGE 93 B1887   WEALTH

B64
TULLY A.,WHERE DID YOUR MONEY GO. USA+45 USSR   FOR/AID
ECO/UNDEV ADMIN EFFICIENCY WEALTH...METH/COMP 20.   DIPLOM
PAGE 106 B2136   CONTROL

B64
WELLISZ S.,THE ECONOMICS OF THE SOVIET BLOC. COM   EFFICIENCY
USSR INDUS WORKER PLAN BUDGET INT/TRADE TAX PRICE   ADMIN
PRODUC WEALTH MARXISM...METH/COMP 20. PAGE 115   MARKET
B2319

B64
WRAITH R.,CORRUPTION IN DEVELOPING COUNTRIES.   ECO/UNDEV
NIGERIA UK LAW ELITES STRATA INDUS LOC/G NAT/G SECT   CRIME
FORCES EDU/PROP ADMIN PWR WEALTH 18/20. PAGE 118   SANCTION
B2377   ATTIT

L64
HAAS E.B.,"ECONOMICS AND DIFFERENTIAL PATTERNS OF   L/A+17C
POLITICAL INTEGRATION: PROJECTIONS ABOUT UNITY IN   INT/ORG
LATIN AMERICA." SOCIETY NAT/G DELIB/GP ACT/RES   MARKET
CREATE PLAN ECO/TAC REGION ROUTINE ATTIT DRIVE PWR
WEALTH...CONCPT TREND CHARTS LAFTA 20. PAGE 45
B0910

S64
HUELIN D.,"ECONOMIC INTEGRATION IN LATIN AMERICAN: MARKET
PROGRESS AND PROBLEMS." L/A+17C ECO/DEV AGRI   ECO/UNDEV
DIST/IND FINAN INDUS NAT/G VOL/ASSN CONSULT   INT/TRADE
DELIB/GP EX/STRUC ACT/RES PLAN TEC/DEV ECO/TAC
ROUTINE BAL/PAY WEALTH WORK 20. PAGE 52 B1058

S64
MOWER A.G.,"THE OFFICIAL PRESSURE GROUP OF THE   INT/ORG
COUNCIL OF EUROPE'S CONSULATIVE ASSEMBLY." EUR+WWI   EDU/PROP
SOCIETY STRUCT FINAN CONSULT ECO/TAC ADMIN ROUTINE
ATTIT PWR WEALTH...STAT CHARTS 20 COUNCL/EUR.
PAGE 76 B1535

S64
RIGBY T.H.,"TRADITIONAL, MARKET, AND ORGANIZATIONAL   MARKET
SOCIETIES AND THE USSR." COM ECO/DEV NAT/G POL/PAR   ADMIN
ECO/TAC DOMIN ORD/FREE PWR WEALTH...TIME/SEQ   USSR
GEN/LAWS VAL/FREE 20 STALIN/J. PAGE 88 B1784

B65
ETZIONI A.,POLITICAL UNIFICATION* A COMPARATIVE   INT/ORG
STUDY OF LEADERS AND FORCES. EUR+WWI ISLAM L/A+17C   FORCES
WOR+45 ELITES STRATA EXEC WEALTH...TIME/SEQ TREND   ECO/TAC
SOC/EXP. PAGE 34 B0686   REGION

B65
INT. BANK RECONSTR. DEVELOP.,ECONOMIC DEVELOPMENT   INDUS
OF KUWAIT. ISLAM KUWAIT AGRI FINAN MARKET EX/STRUC   NAT/G
TEC/DEV ECO/TAC ADMIN WEALTH...OBS CON/ANAL CHARTS
20. PAGE 54 B1092

L65
WILLIAMS S.,"NEGOTIATING INVESTMENT IN EMERGING   FINAN
COUNTRIES." USA+45 WOR+45 INDUS MARKET NAT/G TOP/EX   ECO/UNDEV
TEC/DEV CAP/ISM ECO/TAC ADMIN SKILL WEALTH...POLICY
RELATIV MGT WORK 20. PAGE 117 B2353

S65
CHARLESWORTH J.C.,"ALLOCATION OF RESPONSIBILITIES   PROVS
AND RESOURCES AMONG THE THREE LEVELS OF   NAT/G
GOVERNMENT." USA+45 USA-45 ECO/DEV MUNIC PLAN LEGIT   LG/CO
...PLURIST MGT. PAGE 20 B0415   WEALTH

S65
QUADE Q.L.,"THE TRUMAN ADMINISTRATION AND THE   USA+45
SEPARATION OF POWERS: THE CASE OF THE MARSHALL   ECO/UNDEV
PLAN." SOCIETY INT/ORG NAT/G CONSULT DELIB/GP LEGIS   DIPLOM
PLAN ECO/TAC ROUTINE DRIVE PERCEPT RIGID/FLEX
ORD/FREE PWR WEALTH...DECISION GEOG NEW/IDEA TREND
20 TRUMAN/HS. PAGE 85 B1726

N65
NJ DIVISION STATE-REGION PLAN,UTILIZATION OF NEW   UTIL
JERSEY'S DELAWARE RIVER WATERFRONT (PAMPHLET). FUT   PLAN
ADMIN REGION LEISURE GOV/REL DEMAND WEALTH...CHARTS   ECO/TAC
20 NEW/JERSEY. PAGE 78 B1586   PROVS

B66
BOYD H.W.,MARKETING MANAGEMENT: CASES FROM EMERGING   MGT
COUNTRIES. BRAZIL GHANA ISRAEL WOR+45 ADMIN   ECO/UNDEV
PERS/REL ATTIT HABITAT WEALTH...ANTHOL 20 ARGEN   PROB/SOLV
CASEBOOK. PAGE 14 B0292   MARKET

B66
LEWIS W.A.,DEVELOPMENT PLANNING: THE ESSENTIALS OF   PLAN
ECONOMIC POLICY. USA+45 FINAN INDUS NAT/G WORKER   ECO/DEV
FOR/AID INT/TRADE ADMIN ROUTINE WEALTH...CONCPT   POLICY
STAT. PAGE 65 B1307   CREATE

B66
OHLIN G.,AID AND INDEBTEDNESS. AUSTRIA FINAN   FOR/AID
INT/ORG PLAN DIPLOM GIVE...POLICY MATH CHARTS 20.   ECO/UNDEV
PAGE 79 B1604   ADMIN
                                                        WEALTH
B66
OWEN G.,INDUSTRY IN THE UNITED STATES. UK USA+45   METH/COMP
NAT/G WEALTH...DECISION NAT/COMP 20. PAGE 80 B1620   INDUS
                                                        MGT
                                                        PROB/SOLV
B66
SCHMIDT F.,PUBLIC RELATIONS IN HEALTH AND WELFARE.   PROF/ORG
USA+45 ACADEM RECEIVE PRESS FEEDBACK GOV/REL   EDU/PROP
PERS/REL DEMAND EFFICIENCY ATTIT PERCEPT WEALTH 20   ADMIN
PUBLIC/REL. PAGE 94 B1895   HEALTH

B66
THOENES P.,THE ELITE IN THE WELFARE STATE ,TRANS.   ADMIN
BY J BINGHAM; ED. BY. STRATA NAT/G GP/REL HAPPINESS   ELITES
INCOME OPTIMAL MORAL PWR WEALTH...POLICY CONCPT.   MGT
PAGE 104 B2097   WELF/ST

B66
US BUREAU OF THE BUDGET,THE ADMINISTRATION OF   ACT/RES
GOVERNMENT SUPPORTED RESEARCH AT UNIVERSITIES   NAT/G
(PAMPHLET). USA+45 CONSULT TOP/EX ADMIN INCOME   ACADEM
WEALTH...MGT PHIL/SCI INT. PAGE 108 B2174   GP/REL

S66
"FURTHER READING." INDIA LOC/G NAT/G PLAN ADMIN   BIBLIOG
WEALTH...GEOG SOC CONCPT CENSUS 20. PAGE 2 B0045   ECO/UNDEV
                                                        TEC/DEV
                                                        PROVS
S66
JACOBS P.,"RE-RADICALIZING THE DE-RADICALIZED."   NAT/G
USA+45 SOCIETY STRUCT FINAN PLAN PROB/SOLV CAP/ISM   POLICY
WEALTH CONSERVE NEW/LIB 20. PAGE 55 B1114   MARXIST
                                                        ADMIN
N66
AMERICAN SOCIETY PUBLIC ADMIN,PUBLIC ADMINISTRATION   WEALTH
AND THE WAR ON POVERTY (PAMPHLET). USA+45 SOCIETY   NAT/G
ECO/DEV FINAN LOC/G LEGIS CREATE EDU/PROP CONFER   PLAN
GOV/REL GP/REL ROLE 20 POVRTY/WAR. PAGE 4 B0089   ADMIN

B67
CECIL L.,ALBERT BALLIN: BUSINESS AND POLITICS IN   DIPLOM
IMPERIAL GERMANY 1888-1918. GERMANY UK INT/TRADE   CONSTN
LEAD WAR PERS/REL ADJUST PWR WEALTH...MGT BIBLIOG   ECO/DEV
19/20. PAGE 19 B0397   TOP/EX

B67
ENKE S.,DEFENSE MANAGEMENT. USA+45 R+D FORCES   DECISION
WORKER PLAN ECO/TAC ADMIN NUC/PWR BAL/PAY UTIL   DELIB/GP
WEALTH...MGT DEPT/DEFEN. PAGE 33 B0675   EFFICIENCY
                                                        BUDGET
B67
GROSSMAN G.,ECONOMIC SYSTEMS. USA+45 USA-45 USSR   ECO/DEV
YUGOSLAVIA WORKER CAP/ISM PRICE GP/REL EQUILIB   PLAN
WEALTH MARXISM SOCISM...MGT METH/COMP 19/20.   TEC/DEV

PAGE 44 B0892

MARRIS P.,DILEMMAS OF SOCIAL REFORM: POVERTY AND COMMUNITY ACTION IN THE UNITED STATES. USA+45 NAT/G OP/RES ADMIN PARTIC EFFICIENCY WEALTH...SOC METH/COMP T 20 REFORMERS. PAGE 69 B1401
DEMAND
B67
STRUCT
MUNIC
PROB/SOLV
COST

NARVER J.C.,CONGLOMERATE MERGERS AND MARKET COMPETITION. USA+45 LAW STRUCT ADMIN LEAD RISK COST PROFIT WEALTH...POLICY CHARTS BIBLIOG. PAGE 77 B1555
B67
DEMAND
LG/CO
MARKET
MGT

SALMOND J.A.,THE CIVILIAN CONSERVATION CORPS, 1933-1942. USA-45 NAT/G CREATE EXEC EFFICIENCY WEALTH...BIBLIOG 20 ROOSEVLT/F. PAGE 92 B1864
B67
ADMIN
ECO/TAC
TASK
AGRI

TANSKY L.,US AND USSR AID TO DEVELOPING COUNTRIES. INDIA TURKEY UAR USA+45 USSR FINAN PLAN TEC/DEV ADMIN WEALTH...TREND METH/COMP 20. PAGE 103 B2076
B67
FOR/AID
ECO/UNDEV
MARXISM
CAP/ISM

WEINBERG M.,SCHOOL INTEGRATION: A COMPREHENSIVE CLASSIFIED BIBLIOGRAPHY OF 3,100 REFERENCES. USA+45 LAW NAT/G NEIGH SECT PLAN ROUTINE AGE/C WEALTH SOC/INTEG INDIAN/AM. PAGE 115 B2314
B67
BIBLIOG
SCHOOL
DISCRIM
RACE/REL

ALPANDER G.G.,"ENTREPRENEURS AND PRIVATE ENTERPRISE IN TURKEY." TURKEY INDUS PROC/MFG EDU/PROP ATTIT DRIVE WEALTH...GEOG MGT SOC STAT TREND CHARTS 20. PAGE 4 B0080
S67
ECO/UNDEV
LG/CO
NAT/G
POLICY

DUGGAR J.W.,"THE DEVELOPMENT OF MONEY SUPPLY IN ETHIOPIA." ETHIOPIA ISLAM CONSULT OP/RES BUDGET CONTROL ROUTINE EFFICIENCY EQUILIB WEALTH...MGT 20. PAGE 31 B0629
S67
ECO/UNDEV
FINAN
BAL/PAY
ECOMETRIC

FOX R.G.,"FAMILY, CASTE, AND COMMERCE IN A NORTH INDIAN MARKET TOWN." INDIA STRATA AGRI FACE/GP FAM NEIGH OP/RES BARGAIN ADMIN ROUTINE WEALTH...SOC CHARTS 20. PAGE 37 B0747
S67
CULTURE
GP/REL
ECO/UNDEV
DIST/IND

LERNER A.P.,"EMPLOYMENT THEORY AND EMPLOYMENT POLICY." ECO/DEV INDUS LABOR LG/CO BUDGET ADMIN DEMAND PROFIT WEALTH LAISSEZ METH/COMP. PAGE 64 B1296
S67
CAP/ISM
WORKER
CONCPT

MCNAMARA R.L.,"THE NEED FOR INNOVATIVENESS IN DEVELOPING SOCIETIES." L/A+17C EDU/PROP ADMIN LEAD WEALTH...POLICY PSY SOC METH 20 COLOMB. PAGE 72 B1456
S67
PROB/SOLV
PLAN
ECO/UNDEV
NEW/IDEA

WEAPON....NON-NUCLEAR WEAPONS

KYRIAK T.E.,EAST EUROPE: BIBLIOGRAPHY--INDEX TO US JPRS RESEARCH TRANSLATIONS. ALBANIA BULGARIA COM CZECHOSLVK HUNGARY POLAND ROMANIA AGRI EXTR/IND FINAN SERV/IND INT/TRADE WEAPON...GEOG MGT SOC 20. PAGE 62 B1247
N
BIBLIOG/A
PRESS
MARXISM
INDUS

STEWART I.,ORGANIZING SCIENTIFIC RESEARCH FOR WAR: ADMINISTRATIVE HISTORY OF OFFICE OF SCIENTIFIC RESEARCH AND DEVELOPMENT. USA-45 INTELL R+D LABOR WORKER CREATE BUDGET WEAPON CIVMIL/REL GP/REL EFFICIENCY...POLICY 20. PAGE 101 B2037
B48
DELIB/GP
ADMIN
WAR
TEC/DEV

US HOUSE COMM GOVT OPERATIONS,HEARINGS BEFORE A SUBCOMMITTEE OF THE COMMITTEE ON GOVERNMENT OPERATIONS. CAMBODIA PHILIPPINE USA+45 CONSTRUC TEC/DEV ADMIN CONTROL WEAPON EFFICIENCY HOUSE/REP. PAGE 108 B2189
B58
FOR/AID
DIPLOM
ORD/FREE
ECO/UNDEV

JORDAN A.,"MILITARY ASSISTANCE AND NATIONAL POLICY." ASIA FUT USA+45 WOR+45 ECO/DEV ECO/UNDEV INT/ORG NAT/G PLAN ECO/TAC ROUTINE WEAPON ATTIT RIGID/FLEX PWR...CONCPT TREND 20. PAGE 57 B1153
S58
FORCES
POLICY
FOR/AID
DIPLOM

US PRES COMM STUDY MIL ASSIST,COMPOSITE REPORT. USA+45 ECO/UNDEV PLAN BUDGET DIPLOM EFFICIENCY ...POLICY MGT 20. PAGE 109 B2208
S59
FOR/AID
FORCES
WEAPON
ORD/FREE

JANOWITZ M.,"CHANGING PATTERNS OF ORGANIZATIONAL AUTHORITY: THE MILITARY ESTABLISHMENT" (BMR)" USA+45 ELITES STRUCT EX/STRUC PLAN DOMIN AUTOMAT NUC/PWR WEAPON 20. PAGE 55 B1122
S59
FORCES
AUTHORIT
ADMIN
TEC/DEV

MORTON L.,STRATEGY AND COMMAND: THE FIRST TWO YEARS. USA-45 NAT/G CONTROL EXEC LEAD WEAPON CIVMIL/REL PWR...POLICY AUD/VIS CHARTS 20 CHINJAP. PAGE 76 B1532
B62
WAR
FORCES
PLAN
DIPLOM

RAYMOND J.,POWER AT THE PENTAGON (1ST ED.). ELITES NAT/G PLAN EDU/PROP ARMS/CONT DETER WAR WEAPON ...TIME/SEQ 20 PENTAGON MCNAMARA/R. PAGE 86 B1746
B64
PWR
CIVMIL/REL
EX/STRUC

MELMANS S.,OUR DEPLETED SOCIETY. SPACE USA+45 ECO/DEV FORCES BUDGET ECO/TAC ADMIN WEAPON EFFICIENCY 20 COLD/WAR. PAGE 73 B1465
FORCES
B65
CIVMIL/REL
INDUS
EDU/PROP
CONTROL

WARD R.,BACKGROUND MATERIAL ON ECONOMIC IMPACT OF FEDERAL PROCUREMENT - 1965: FOR JOINT ECONOMIC COMMITTEE US CONGRESS. FINAN ROUTINE WEAPON CIVMIL/REL EFFICIENCY...STAT CHARTS 20 CONGRESS. PAGE 113 B2288
B65
ECO/DEV
NAT/G
OWN
GOV/REL

BALDWIN H.,"SLOW-DOWN IN THE PENTAGON." USA+45 CREATE PLAN GOV/REL CENTRAL COST EFFICIENCY PWR ...MGT MCNAMARA/R. PAGE 9 B0174
S65
RECORD
R+D
WEAPON
ADMIN

US SENATE COMM ON FOREIGN REL,HEARINGS ON S 2859 AND S 2861. USA+45 WOR+45 FORCES BUDGET CAP/ISM ADMIN DETER WEAPON TOTALISM...NAT/COMP 20 UN CONGRESS. PAGE 110 B2221
B66
FOR/AID
DIPLOM
ORD/FREE
ECO/UNDEV

ZUCKERT E.M.,"THE SERVICE SECRETARY* HAS HE A USEFUL ROLE?" USA+45 TOP/EX PLAN ADMIN EXEC DETER NUC/PWR WEAPON...MGT RECORD MCNAMARA/R. PAGE 119 B2407
S66
OBS
OP/RES
DIPLOM
FORCES

WEATHER....WEATHER

WEBER M. B2305

WEBER W. B2306

WEBER/MAX....MAX WEBER

SELZNICK P.,"AN APPROACH TO A THEORY OF BUREAUCRACY." INDUS WORKER CONTROL LEAD EFFICIENCY OPTIMAL...SOC METH 20 BARNARD/C BUREAUCRCY WEBER/MAX FRIEDRCH/C MICHELS/R. PAGE 95 B1928
S43
ROUTINE
ADMIN
MGT
EX/STRUC

STINCHCOMBE A.L.,"BUREAUCRATIC AND CRAFT ADMINISTRATION OF PRODUCTION: A COMPARATIVE STUDY" (BMR)" USA+45 STRUCT EX/STRUC ECO/TAC GP/REL ...CLASSIF GP/COMP IDEA/COMP GEN/LAWS 20 WEBER/MAX. PAGE 101 B2039
S59
CONSTRUC
PROC/MFG
ADMIN
PLAN

UDY S.H. JR.,"'BUREAUCRACY' AND 'RATIONALITY' IN WEBER'S ORGANIZATION THEORY: AN EMPIRICAL STUDY" (BMR)" UNIV STRUCT INDUS LG/CO SML/CO VOL/ASSN ...SOC SIMUL 20 WEBER/MAX BUREAUCRCY. PAGE 106 B2144
S59
GEN/LAWS
METH/CNCPT
ADMIN
RATIONAL

EVAN W.M.,"A LABORATORY EXPERIMENT ON BUREAUCRATIC AUTHORITY" WORKER CONTROL EXEC PRODUC ATTIT PERSON ...PSY SOC CHARTS SIMUL 20 WEBER/MAX. PAGE 34 B0687
S61
ADMIN
LEGIT
LAB/EXP
EFFICIENCY

MARSH R.M.,"FORMAL ORGANIZATION AND PROMOTION IN A PRE-INDUSTRIAL SOCIETY" (BMR)" ASIA FAM EX/STRUC LEAD...SOC CHARTS 19 WEBER/MAX. PAGE 70 B1407
S61
ADMIN
STRUCT
ECO/UNDEV
STRATA

KARIEL H.S.,IN SEARCH OF AUTHORITY: TWENTIETH-CENTURY POLITICAL THOUGHT. WOR+45 WOR-45 NAT/G EX/STRUC TOTALISM DRIVE PWR...MGT PHIL/SCI GEN/LAWS 19/20 NIETZSCH/F FREUD/S WEBER/MAX NIEBUHR/R MARITAIN/J. PAGE 58 B1173
B64
CONSTN
CONCPT
ORD/FREE
IDEA/COMP

WEBSTER J.A. B2307

WEDDING N. B2308

WEIDENBAUM M.L. B2309

WEIDENFELD A. B1970

WEIDLUND J. B2310

WEIDNER E.W. B0100,B0101,B2009,B2311

WEIGLEY R.F. B2312

WEIL G.L. B2313

WEIMAR/REP....WEIMAR REPUBLIC

REICH N.,LABOR RELATIONS IN REPUBLICAN GERMANY. GERMANY CONSTN ECO/DEV INDUS NAT/G ADMIN CONTROL GP/REL FASCISM POPULISM 20 WEIMAR/REP. PAGE 87 B1763
B38
WORKER
MGT
LABOR
BARGAIN

JACOB H.,GERMAN ADMINISTRATION SINCE BISMARCK: CENTRAL AUTHORITY VERSUS LOCAL AUTONOMY. GERMANY
B63
ADMIN
NAT/G

GERMANY/W LAW POL/PAR CONTROL CENTRAL TOTALISM   LOC/G
FASCISM...MAJORIT DECISION STAT CHARTS GOV/COMP   POLICY
19/20 BISMARCK/O HITLER/A WEIMAR/REP. PAGE 55 B1111

WEIN H.H. B1395

WEINBERG M. B2314

WEINER H.N. B1895

WEINER M. B2315

WEINSTEIN M. B0897

WEINTRAUB R.G. B0973

WEISS R.S. B2316

WEITZEL R. B2121

WELCH S.R. B2317

WELF/ST....WELFARE STATE ADVOCATE

                                                   B44
BARKER E.,THE DEVELOPMENT OF PUBLIC SERVICES IN   GOV/COMP
WESTERN WUROPE: 1660-1930. FRANCE GERMANY UK SCHOOL ADMIN
CONTROL REPRESENT ROLE...WELF/ST 17/20. PAGE 9   EX/STRUC
B0185
                                                   B48
ROSENFARB J.,FREEDOM AND THE ADMINISTRATIVE STATE. ECO/DEV
NAT/G ROUTINE EFFICIENCY PRODUC RATIONAL UTIL   INDUS
...TECHNIC WELF/ST MGT 20 BUREAUCRCY. PAGE 90 B1821 PLAN
                                                   WEALTH
                                                   B53
MAJUMDAR B.B.,PROBLEMS OF PUBLIC ADMINISTRATION IN ECO/UNDEV
INDIA. INDIA INDUS PLAN BUDGET ADJUD CENTRAL DEMAND GOV/REL
WEALTH...WELF/ST ANTHOL 20 CIVIL/SERV. PAGE 68   ADMIN
B1384   MUNIC
                                                   B58
DWARKADAS R.,ROLE OF HIGHER CIVIL SERVICE IN INDIA. ADMIN
INDIA ECO/UNDEV LEGIS PROB/SOLV GP/REL PERS/REL   NAT/G
...POLICY WELF/ST DECISION ORG/CHARTS BIBLIOG 20   ROLE
CIVIL/SERV INTRVN/ECO. PAGE 31 B0637   PLAN
                                                   L58
EISENSTADT S.N.,"BUREAUCRACY AND   ADMIN
BUREAUCRATIZATION." WOR+45 ECO/DEV INDUS R+D PLAN OP/RES
GOV/REL...WELF/ST TREND BIBLIOG/A 20. PAGE 32 B0659 MGT
                                                   PHIL/SCI
                                                   S61
GORDON L.,"ECONOMIC REGIONALISM RECONSIDERED." FUT ECO/DEV
USA+45 WOR+45 INDUS NAT/G TEC/DEV DIPLOM ROUTINE   ATTIT
PERCEPT WEALTH...WELF/ST METH/CNCPT WORK 20.   CAP/ISM
PAGE 41 B0830   REGION
                                                   S61
JUVILER P.H.,"INTERPARLIAMENTARY CONTACTS IN SOVIET INT/ORG
FOREIGN POLICY." COM FUT WOR+45 WOR-45 SOCIETY   DELIB/GP
CONSULT ACT/RES DIPLOM ADMIN PEACE ATTIT RIGID/FLEX USSR
WEALTH...WELF/ST SOC TOT/POP CONGRESS 19/20.
PAGE 57 B1156
                                                   S61
MILLER E.,"LEGAL ASPECTS OF UN ACTION IN THE   INT/ORG
CONGO." AFR CULTURE ADMIN PEACE DRIVE RIGID/FLEX   LEGIT
ORD/FREE...WELF/ST JURID OBS UN CONGO 20. PAGE 73
B1480
                                                   B62
NATIONAL BUREAU ECONOMIC RES,THE RATE AND DIRECTION DECISION
OF INVENTIVE ACTIVITY: ECONOMIC AND SOCIAL FACTORS. PROB/SOLV
STRUCT INDUS MARKET R+D CREATE OP/RES TEC/DEV   MGT
EFFICIENCY PRODUC RATIONAL UTIL...WELF/ST PHIL/SCI
METH/CNCPT TIME. PAGE 77 B1562
                                                   B63
JOHNS R.,CONFRONTING ORGANIZATIONAL CHANGE. NEIGH SOC/WK
DELIB/GP CREATE OP/RES ADMIN GP/REL DRIVE...WELF/ST WEALTH
SOC RECORD BIBLIOG. PAGE 56 B1142   LEAD
                                                   VOL/ASSN
                                                   B63
SCHOECK H.,THE NEW ARGUMENT IN ECONOMICS. UK USA+45 WELF/ST
INDUS MARKET LABOR NAT/G ECO/TAC ADMIN ROUTINE   FOR/AID
BAL/PAY PWR...POLICY BOLIV. PAGE 94 B1899   ECO/DEV
                                                   ALL/IDEOS
                                                   B63
SELF P.,THE STATE AND THE FARMER. UK ECO/DEV MARKET AGRI
WORKER PRICE CONTROL GP/REL...WELF/ST 20 DEPT/AGRI. NAT/G
PAGE 95 B1926   ADMIN
                                                   VOL/ASSN
                                                   B64
AHMAD M.,THE CIVIL SERVANT IN PAKISTAN. PAKISTAN   WELF/ST
ECO/UNDEV COLONIAL INGP/REL...SOC CHARTS BIBLIOG 20 ADMIN
CIVIL/SERV. PAGE 3 B0065   ATTIT
                                                   STRATA
                                                   B64
MARSH D.C.,THE FUTURE OF THE WELFARE STATE. UK   NEW/LIB
CONSTN NAT/G POL/PAR...POLICY WELF/ST 20. PAGE 69 ADMIN
B1404   CONCPT
                                                   INSPECT

                                                   B66
THOENES P.,THE ELITE IN THE WELFARE STATE .TRANS. ADMIN
BY J BINGHAM; ED. BY. STRATA NAT/G GP/REL HAPPINESS ELITES
INCOME OPTIMAL MORAL PWR WEALTH...POLICY CONCPT.   MGT
PAGE 104 B2097   WELF/ST
                                                   S67
O'DELL J.H.,"THE JULY REBELLIONS AND THE 'MILITARY PWR
STATE'." USA+45 VIETNAM STRATA CHIEF WORKER   NAT/G
COLONIAL EXEC CROWD CIVMIL/REL RACE/REL TOTALISM   COERCE
...WELF/ST PACIFIST 20 NEGRO JOHNSON/LB PRESIDENT FORCES
CIV/RIGHTS. PAGE 79 B1599

WELFARE....SEE RECEIVE, NEW/LIB, WELF/ST

WELFARE STATE....SEE NEW/LIB, WELF/ST

WELLEQUET J. B2318

WELLISZ S. B2319

WELLS A.J. B2320

WELLS K.M. B2328

WELTON H. B2321

WENDT P.F. B2322

WERNETTE J.P. B2323

WESSON R.G. B2324

WEST F.J. B2325

WEST AFRICA....SEE AFRICA/W

WEST GERMANY....SEE GERMANY/W

WEST/EDWRD....SIR EDWARD WEST

WEST/IND....WEST INDIES; SEE ALSO L/A+17C

                                                   B60
AYEARST M.,THE BRITISH WEST INDIES: THE SEARCH FOR CONSTN
SELF-GOVERNMENT. FUT WEST/IND LOC/G POL/PAR   COLONIAL
EX/STRUC LEGIS CHOOSE FEDERAL...NAT/COMP BIBLIOG   REPRESENT
17/20. PAGE 7 B0152   NAT/G
                                                   S67
SPACKMAN A.,"THE SENATE OF TRINIDAD AND TOBAGO."   ELITES
L/A+17C TRINIDAD WEST/IND NAT/G POL/PAR DELIB/GP   EFFICIENCY
OP/RES PROB/SOLV EDU/PROP EXEC LOBBY ROUTINE   LEGIS
REPRESENT GP/REL 20. PAGE 99 B2002   DECISION

WEST/POINT....UNITED STATES MILITARY ACADEMY

WEST/SAMOA....WESTERN SAMOA; SEE ALSO S/ASIA

WEST/VIRGN....WEST VIRGINIA

WESTERN ELECTRIC....SEE AT+T

WESTERN EUROPE....SEE EUROPE/W

WESTERN SAMOA....SEE WEST/SAMOA

WESTERN UNITED STATES....SEE US/WEST

WESTIN A.F. B2326

WESTMINSTER HALL, COURTS OF....SEE CTS/WESTM

WESTON J.F. B2327

WESTON P.B. B2328

WESTPHALIA....PEACE OF WESTPHALIA

WHEARE K.C. B2329,B2330,B2331

WHEELER-BENNETT J.W. B2332

WHIG/PARTY....WHIG PARTY (USE WITH SPECIFIC NATION)

WHIP....SEE LEGIS, CONG, ROUTINE

WHITE J. B2334

WHITE L.D. B0785,B2335,B2336,B2337,B2338,B2339,B2340

WHITE/SUP....WHITE SUPREMACY - PERSONS, GROUPS, AND IDEAS

WHITE/T....THEODORE WHITE

WHITE/WA....WILLIAM ALLEN WHITE

WHITEHD/AN....ALFRED NORTH WHITEHEAD

WHITEHEAD T.N. B2341

WHITE-ANGLO-SAXON-PROTESTANT ESTABLISHMENT....SEE WASP

WHITMAN/W....WALT WHITMAN

WHITNAH D.R. B2342

WHITTAKER C.H. B0678

WHO....WORLD HEALTH ORGANIZATION

WHYTE W.H. B2343

WHYTE/WF....WILLIAM FOOTE WHYTE

>
> B63
> RUITENBEER H.M.,THE DILEMMA OF ORGANIZATIONAL   PERSON
> SOCIETY. CULTURE ECO/DEV MUNIC SECT TEC/DEV   ROLE
> EDU/PROP NAT/LISM ORD/FREE...NAT/COMP 20 RIESMAN/D   ADMIN
> WHYTE/WF MERTON/R MEAD/MARG JASPERS/K. PAGE 92   WORKER
> B1855

WIGGINS J.R. B2344

WIGGINS J.W. B1899

WILCOX J.K. B2345,B2346,B2347

WILDAVSKY A. B2348

WILDER B.E. B2349

WILDING N. B2350

WILENSKY H.L. B2351,B2352

WILHELM/I....WILHELM I (KAISER)

WILHELM/II....WILHELM II (KAISER)

WILKINS/R....ROY WILKINS

WILLIAM/3....WILLIAM III (PRINCE OF ORANGE)

WILLIAMS D.P. B0993

WILLIAMS O. B1700

WILLIAMS S. B2353

WILLIAMS/R....ROGER WILLIAMS

WILLIAMSON O.E. B2354

WILLMORE J.N. B0347

WILLNER A.R. B2355

WILLOUGHBY W.F. B2356

WILLOUGHBY W.R. B2357

WILLOW/RUN....WILLOW RUN, MICHIGAN

WILLS....WILLS AND TESTAMENTS

WILLSON F.M.G. B2358

WILSON G. B2359

WILSON J.Q. B0178

WILSON L. B2360

WILSON P. B2361

WILSON W. B2362,B2363,B2364

WILSON/H....HAROLD WILSON

>
> B62
> LIPPMANN W.,PREFACE TO POLITICS. LABOR CHIEF   PARTIC
> CONTROL LEAD...MYTH IDEA/COMP 19/20 ROOSEVLT/T   ATTIT
> TAMMANY WILSON/H SANTAYAN/G BERGSON/H. PAGE 65   ADMIN
> B1318

WILSON/J....JAMES WILSON

WILSON/W....PRESIDENT WOODROW WILSON

>
> L56
> MACMAHON A.W.,"WOODROW WILSON AS LEGISLATIVE LEADER LEGIS
> AND ADMINISTRATOR." CONSTN POL/PAR ADMIN...POLICY   CHIEF
> HIST/WRIT WILSON/W PRESIDENT. PAGE 68 B1371   LEAD
>   BIOG

>
> B63
> KARL B.D.,EXECUTIVE REORGANIZATION AND REFORM IN   BIOG
> THE NEW DEAL. ECO/DEV INDUS DELIB/GP EX/STRUC PLAN EXEC
> BUDGET ADMIN EFFICIENCY PWR POPULISM...POLICY 20   CREATE
> PRESIDENT ROOSEVLT/F WILSON/W NEW/DEAL. PAGE 58   CONTROL
> B1174

>
> B67
> FARNSWORTH B.,WILLIAM C. BULLITT AND THE SOVIET   DIPLOM
> UNION. COM USA-45 USSR NAT/G CHIEF CONSULT DELIB/GP BIOG
> EX/STRUC WAR REPRESENT MARXISM 20 WILSON/W   POLICY
> ROOSEVLT/F STALIN/J BULLITT/WC. PAGE 35 B0705

>
> B67
> WARREN S.,THE AMERICAN PRESIDENT. POL/PAR FORCES   CHIEF
> LEGIS DIPLOM ECO/TAC ADMIN EXEC PWR...ANTHOL 18/20 LEAD
> ROOSEVLT/F KENNEDY/JF JOHNSON/LB TRUMAN/HS   NAT/G
> WILSON/W. PAGE 114 B2297   CONSTN

WINETROUT K. B0266

WINGFIELD C.J. B2365

WINSTEN C. B0924

WINTHROP H. B2366

WIRETAPPING....SEE PRIVACY

WISCONSIN....WISCONSIN

>
> L67
> CARMICHAEL D.M.,"FORTY YEARS OF WATER POLLUTION   HEALTH
> CONTROL IN WISCONSIN: A CASE STUDY." LAW EXTR/IND   CONTROL
> INDUS MUNIC DELIB/GP PLAN PROB/SOLV SANCTION   ADMIN
> ...CENSUS CHARTS 20 WISCONSIN. PAGE 19 B0382   ADJUD

WISCONSN/U....WISCONSIN STATE UNIVERSITY

WITHERELL J.W. B2367,B2368

WITHERSPOON J.V. B0347

WITTFOGEL K.A. B2369

WITTGEN/L....LUDWIG WITTGENSTEIN

WOLCOTT L.O. B0786

WOLEK F.W. B1616

WOLFERS A. B2370

WOLFF/C....CHRISTIAN WOLFF

WOLFF/RP....ROBERT PAUL WOLFF

WOLFINGER R.E. B2371

WOLIN S.S. B1322

WOLL P. B2372,B2373

WOMAN....SEE FEMALE/SEX

WOMEN....SEE FEMALE/SEX

WOMEN'S CHRISTIAN TEMPERANCE UNION....SEE WCTU

WOOD/CHAS....SIR CHARLES WOOD

WOOLF S.J. B1693

WOR+45....WORLDWIDE, 1945 TO PRESENT

WOR-45....WORLDWIDE, TO 1945

WORK....SEE WORKER

WORK PROJECTS ADMINISTRATION....SEE WPA

>
> B37
> ROBBINS L.,ECONOMIC PLANNING AND INTERNATIONAL   INT/ORG
> ORDER. WOR-45 SOCIETY FINAN INDUS NAT/G ECO/TAC   PLAN
> ROUTINE WEALTH...SOC TIME/SEQ GEN/METH WORK 20   INT/TRADE
> KEYNES/JM. PAGE 89 B1791

>
> B45
> RANSHOFFEN-WERTHEIMER EF,THE INTERNATIONAL   INT/ORG
> SECRETARIAT: A GREAT EXPERIMENT IN INTERNATIONAL   EXEC
> ADMINISTRATION. EUR+WWI FUT CONSTN FACE/GP CONSULT
> DELIB/GP ACT/RES ADMIN ROUTINE PEACE ORD/FREE...MGT
> RECORD ORG/CHARTS LEAGUE/NAT WORK 20. PAGE 86 B1731

>
> B46
> CLOUGH S.B.,ECONOMI─ HISTORY OF EUROPE. CHRIST-17C ECO/TAC
> EUR+WWI MOD/EUR WOR-45 SOCIETY EXEC ATTIT WEALTH   CAP/ISM
> ...CONCPT GEN/LAWS WORK TOT/POP VAL/FREE 7/20.
> PAGE 22 B0440

BRUEGEL J.W.,"DIE INTERNAZIONALE   VOL/ASSN
GEWERKSCHAFTSBEWEGUNG." COM EUR+WWI USA+45 WOR+45   LABOR
DELIB/GP EX/STRUC ECO/TAC EDU/PROP ATTIT PWR   TOTALISM
RESPECT SKILL WEALTH WORK 20. PAGE 16 B0330

S52

MORRIS B.S.,"THE COMINFORM: A FIVE YEAR   VOL/ASSN
PERSPECTIVE." COM UNIV USSR WOR+45 ECO/DEV POL/PAR   EDU/PROP
TOP/EX PLAN DOMIN ADMIN TOTALISM ATTIT ALL/VALS   DIPLOM
...CONCPT TIME/SEQ TREND CON/ANAL WORK VAL/FREE 20.
PAGE 76 B1527

S53

COMBS C.H.,DECISION PROCESSES. INTELL SOCIETY   MATH
DELIB/GP CREATE TEC/DEV DOMIN LEGIT EXEC CHOOSE   DECISION
DRIVE RIGID/FLEX KNOWL PWR...PHIL/SCI SOC
METH/CNCPT CONT/OBS REC/INT PERS/TEST SAMP/SIZ BIOG
SOC/EXP WORK. PAGE 22 B0455

B54

MAZZINI J.,THE DUTIES OF MAN. MOD/EUR LAW SOCIETY   SUPEGO
FAM NAT/G POL/PAR SECT VOL/ASSN EX/STRUC ACT/RES   CONCPT
CREATE REV PEACE ATTIT ALL/VALS...GEN/LAWS WORK 19.   NAT/LISM
PAGE 71 B1439

B55

WEISS R.S.,"A METHOD FOR THE ANALYSIS OF THE   PROF/ORG
STRUCTURE OF COMPLEX ORGANIZATIONS." WOR+45 INDUS   SOC/EXP
LG/CO NAT/G EXEC ROUTINE ORD/FREE PWR SKILL...MGT
PSY SOC NEW/IDEA STAT INT REC/INT STAND/INT CHARTS
WORK. PAGE 115 B2316

S55

YANG C.K.,A CHINESE VILLAGE IN EARLY COMMUNIST   ASIA
TRANSITION. ECO/UNDEV AGRI FAM KIN MUNIC FORCES   ROUTINE
PLAN ECO/TAC DOMIN EDU/PROP ATTIT DRIVE PWR RESPECT   SOCISM
...SOC CONCPT METH/CNCPT OBS RECORD CON/ANAL CHARTS
WORK 20. PAGE 118 B2389

B59

CAMPBELL R.W.,SOVIET ECONOMIC POWER. COM USA+45   ECO/DEV
DIST/IND MARKET TOP/EX ACT/RES CAP/ISM ECO/TAC   PLAN
DOMIN EDU/PROP ADMIN ROUTINE DRIVE...MATH TIME/SEQ   SOCISM
CHARTS WORK 20. PAGE 18 B0371   USSR

B60

LIPSET S.M.,POLITICAL MAN. AFR COM EUR+WWI L/A+17C   PWR
MOD/EUR S/ASIA USA-45 STRUCT ECO/DEV   SOC
ECO/UNDEV POL/PAR SECT ADMIN WEALTH...CONCPT WORK
TOT/POP 20. PAGE 65 B1320

B60

EMERSON R.,"THE EROSION OF DEMOCRACY." AFR FUT LAW   S/ASIA
CULTURE INTELL SOCIETY ECO/UNDEV FAM LOC/G NAT/G   POL/PAR
FORCES PLAN TEC/DEV ECO/TAC ADMIN CT/SYS ATTIT
ORD/FREE PWR...SOCIALIST SOC CONCPT STAND/INT
TIME/SEQ WORK 20. PAGE 33 B0671

S60

HERZ J.H.,"EAST GERMANY: PROGRESS AND PROSPECTS."   POL/PAR
COM AGRI FINAN INDUS LOC/G NAT/G FORCES PLAN   STRUCT
TEC/DEV DOMIN ADMIN COERCE DRIVE PERCEPT RIGID/FLEX   GERMANY
MORAL ORD/FREE PWR...MARXIST PSY SOC RECORD STERTYP
WORK. PAGE 49 B0997

S60

MORALES C.J.,"TRADE AND ECONOMIC INTEGRATION IN   FINAN
LATIN AMERICA." FUT L/A+17C LAW STRATA ECO/UNDEV   INT/TRADE
DIST/IND INDUS LABOR NAT/G LEGIS ECO/TAC ADMIN   REGION
RIGID/FLEX WEALTH...CONCPT NEW/IDEA CONT/OBS
TIME/SEQ WORK 20. PAGE 75 B1519

S60

NORTH R.C.,"DIE DISKREPANZ ZWISCHEN REALITAT UND   SOCIETY
WUNSCHBILD ALS INNENPOLITISCHER FAKTOR." ASIA   ECO/TAC
CHINA/COM COM FUT ECO/UNDEV NAT/G PLAN DOMIN ADMIN
COERCE PERCEPT...SOC MYTH GEN/METH WORK TOT/POP 20.
PAGE 79 B1589

B61

FRIEDMANN W.G.,JOINT INTERNATIONAL BUSINESS   ECO/UNDEV
VENTURES. ASIA ISLAM L/A+17C ECO/DEV DIST/IND FINAN   INT/TRADE
PROC/MFG FACE/GP LG/CO NAT/G VOL/ASSN CONSULT
EX/STRUC PLAN ADMIN ROUTINE WEALTH...OLD/LIB WORK
20. PAGE 37 B0760

B61

HORVATH B.,THE CHARACTERISTICS OF YUGOSLAV ECONOMIC   ACT/RES
DEVELOPMENT. COM ECO/UNDEV AGRI INDUS PLAN CAP/ISM   YUGOSLAVIA
ECO/TAC ROUTINE WEALTH...SOCIALIST STAT CHARTS
STERTYP WORK 20. PAGE 52 B1045

B61

MARX K.,THE COMMUNIST MANIFESTO. IN (MENDEL A.   COM
ESSENTIAL WORKS OF MARXISM, NEW YORK: BANTAM. FUT   NEW/IDEA
MOD/EUR CULTURE ECO/DEV ECO/UNDEV AGRI FINAN INDUS   CAP/ISM
MARKET PROC/MFG LABOR MUNIC POL/PAR CONSULT FORCES   REV
CREATE PLAN ADMIN ATTIT DRIVE RIGID/FLEX ORD/FREE
PWR RESPECT MARX/KARL WORK. PAGE 70 B1421

S61

GORDON L.,"ECONOMIC REGIONALISM RECONSIDERED." FUT   ECO/DEV
USA+45 WOR+45 INDUS NAT/G TEC/DEV DIPLOM ROUTINE   ATTIT
PERCEPT WEALTH...WELF/ST METH/CNCPT WORK 20.   CAP/ISM
PAGE 41 B0830   REGION

L62

GALBRAITH J.K.,"ECONOMIC DEVELOPMENT IN   ECO/UNDEV
PERSPECTIVE." CAP/ISM ECO/TAC ROUTINE ATTIT WEALTH   PLAN
...TREND CHARTS SOC/EXP WORK 20. PAGE 38 B0773

TATOMIR N.,"ORGANIZATIA INTERNATIONALA A MUNCII: INT/ORG
ASPECTE NOI ALE PROBLEMEI IMBUNATATIRII   INT/TRADE
MECANISMULUI EI." EUR+WWI ECO/DEV VOL/ASSN ADMIN
...METH/CNCPT WORK ILO 20. PAGE 103 B2081

S62

SCHURMANN F.,"ECONOMIC POLICY AND POLITICAL POWER   PLAN
IN COMMUNIST CHINA." ASIA CHINA/COM USSR SOCIETY   ECO/TAC
ECO/UNDEV AGRI INDUS CREATE ADMIN ROUTINE ATTIT
DRIVE RIGID/FLEX PWR WEALTH...HIST/WRIT TREND
CHARTS WORK 20. PAGE 94 B1908

S63

DIEBOLD J.,BEYOND AUTOMATION: MANAGERIAL PROBLEMS   FUT
OF AN EXPLODING TECHNOLOGY. SOCIETY ECO/DEV CREATE   INDUS
ECO/TAC AUTOMAT SKILL...TECHNIC MGT WORK. PAGE 29   PROVS
B0589   NAT/G

B64

LI C.M.,INDUSTRIAL DEVELOPMENT IN COMMUNIST CHINA.   ASIA
CHINA/COM ECO/DEV ECO/UNDEV AGRI FINAN INDUS MARKET   TEC/DEV
LABOR NAT/G ECO/TAC INT/TRADE EXEC ALL/VALS
...POLICY RELATIV TREND WORK TOT/POP VAL/FREE 20.
PAGE 65 B1311

B64

SULLIVAN G.,THE STORY OF THE PEACE CORPS. USA+45   INT/ORG
WOR+45 INTELL FACE/GP NAT/G SCHOOL VOL/ASSN CONSULT   ECO/UNDEV
EX/STRUC PLAN EDU/PROP ADMIN ATTIT DRIVE ALL/VALS   FOR/AID
...POLICY HEAL SOC CONCPT INT QU BIOG TREND SOC/EXP   PEACE
WORK. PAGE 102 B2054

S64

FLORINSKY M.T.,"TRENDS IN THE SOVIET ECONOMY." COM   ECO/DEV
USA+45 USSR INDUS LABOR NAT/G TEC/DEV ECO/TAC   AGRI
ALL/VALS SOCISM...MGT METH/CNCPT STYLE CON/ANAL
GEN/METH WORK 20. PAGE 36 B0731

S64

HUELIN D.,"ECONOMIC INTEGRATION IN LATIN AMERICAN: MARKET
PROGRESS AND PROBLEMS." L/A+17C ECO/DEV AGRI   ECO/UNDEV
DIST/IND FINAN INDUS NAT/G VOL/ASSN CONSULT   INT/TRADE
DELIB/GP EX/STRUC ACT/RES PLAN TEC/DEV ECO/TAC
ROUTINE BAL/PAY WEALTH WORK 20. PAGE 52 B1058

S64

JOHNSON K.F.,"CAUSAL FACTORS IN LATIN AMERICAN   L/A+17C
POLITICAL INSTABILITY." CULTURE NAT/G VOL/ASSN   PERCEPT
EX/STRUC FORCES EDU/PROP LEGIT ADMIN COERCE REV   ELITES
ATTIT KNOWL PWR...STYLE RECORD CHARTS WORK 20.
PAGE 57 B1144

S64

NASH M.,"SOCIAL PREREQUISITES TO ECONOMIC GROWTH IN   ECO/DEV
LATIN AMERICA AND SOUTHEAST ASIA." L/A+17C S/ASIA   PERCEPT
CULTURE SOCIETY ECO/UNDEV AGRI INDUS NAT/G PLAN
TEC/DEV EDU/PROP ROUTINE ALL/VALS...POLICY RELATIV
SOC NAT/COMP WORK TOT/POP 20. PAGE 77 B1558

S64

NEEDHAM T.,"SCIENCE AND SOCIETY IN EAST AND WEST." ASIA
INTELL STRATA R+D LOC/G NAT/G PROVS CONSULT ACT/RES STRUCT
CREATE PLAN TEC/DEV EDU/PROP ADMIN ATTIT ALL/VALS
...POLICY RELATIV MGT CONCPT NEW/IDEA TIME/SEQ WORK
WORK. PAGE 77 B1565

S64

NEEDHAM T.,"SCIENCE AND SOCIETY IN EAST AND WEST." ASIA
INTELL STRATA R+D LOC/G NAT/G PROVS CONSULT ACT/RES STRUCT
CREATE PLAN TEC/DEV EDU/PROP ADMIN ATTIT ALL/VALS
...POLICY RELATIV MGT CONCPT NEW/IDEA TIME/SEQ WORK
WORK. PAGE 77 B1565

L65

WILLIAMS S.,"NEGOTIATING INVESTMENT IN EMERGING   FINAN
COUNTRIES." USA+45 WOR+45 INDUS MARKET NAT/G TOP/EX ECO/UNDEV
TEC/DEV CAP/ISM ECO/TAC ADMIN SKILL WEALTH...POLICY
RELATIV MGT WORK 20. PAGE 117 B2353

WORKER....WORKER, LABORER

PRINCETON U INDUSTRIAL REL SEC,SELECTED REFERENCES   BIBLIOG/A
OF THE INDUSTRIAL RELATIONS SECTION OF PRINCETON.   INDUS
NEW JERSEY. LG/CO NAT/G LEGIS WORKER PLAN PROB/SOLV   LABOR
PAY ADMIN ROUTINE TASK GP/REL...PSY 20. PAGE 84   MGT
B1708

N

CIVIL SERVICE JOURNAL. PARTIC INGP/REL PERS/REL   ADMIN
...MGT BIBLIOG/A 20. PAGE 1 B0011   NAT/G
                                                          SERV/IND
                                                          WORKER

N

PERSONNEL ADMINISTRATION: THE JOURNAL OF THE   WORKER
SOCIETY FOR PERSONNEL ADMINISTRATION. USA+45 INDUS   MGT
LG/CO SML/CO...BIBLIOG/A 20. PAGE 2 B0028   ADMIN
                                                          EX/STRUC

N

PERSONNEL. USA+45 LAW LABOR LG/CO WORKER CREATE   BIBLIOG/A
GOV/REL PERS/REL ATTIT WEALTH. PAGE 2 B0030   ADMIN
                                                          MGT
                                                          GP/REL

N

CARLETON UNIVERSITY LIBRARY,SELECTED LIST OF   BIBLIOG
CURRENT MATERIALS ON CANADIAN PUBLIC   ADMIN
ADMINISTRATION. CANADA LEGIS WORKER PLAN BUDGET 20.   LOC/G

PAGE 19 B0379   MUNIC
                                                       N
PRINCETON UNIVERSITY,SELECTED REFERENCES: BIBLIOG/A
INDUSTRIAL RELATIONS SECTION. USA+45 EX/STRUC   LABOR
WORKER TEC/DEV...MGT 20. PAGE 85 B1712   INDUS
                                                      GP/REL
                                                       N
US CIVIL SERVICE COMMISSION,A BIBLIOGRAPHY OF   BIBLIOG
PUBLIC PERSONNEL ADMINISTRATION LITERATURE. WOR+45   ADMIN
EFFICIENCY...POLICY MGT. PAGE 108 B2175   WORKER
                                                      PLAN
                                                       N
US SUPERINTENDENT OF DOCUMENTS,LABOR (PRICE LIST   BIBLIOG/A
33). USA+45 LAW AGRI CONSTRUC INDUS NAT/G BARGAIN   WORKER
PRICE ADMIN AUTOMAT PRODUC MGT. PAGE 111 B2240   LABOR
                                                      LEGIS
                                                       N
US SUPERINTENDENT OF DOCUMENTS,POLITICAL SCIENCE: BIBLIOG/A
GOVERNMENT, CRIME, DISTRICT OF COLUMBIA (PRICE LIST   NAT/G
54). USA+45 LAW CONSTN EX/STRUC WORKER ADJUD ADMIN   CRIME
CT/SYS CHOOSE INGP/REL RACE/REL CONGRESS PRESIDENT.
PAGE 111 B2241
                                                       B02
MOREL E.D.,AFFAIRS OF WEST AFRICA. UK FINAN INDUS   COLONIAL
FAM KIN SECT CHIEF WORKER DIPLOM RACE/REL LITERACY   ADMIN
HEALTH...CHARTS 18/20 AFRICA/W NEGRO. PAGE 75 B1521   AFR
                                                       N19
BUREAU OF NAT'L AFFAIRS INC.,A CURRENT LOOK AT: DISCRIM
(1) THE NEGRO AND TITLE VII. (2) SEX AND TITLE VII   SEX
(PAMPHLET). LAW LG/CO SML/CO RACE/REL...POLICY SOC   WORKER
STAT DEEP/QU TREND CON/ANAL CHARTS 20 NEGRO   MGT
CIV/RIGHTS. PAGE 17 B0350
                                                       N19
FIKS M.,PUBLIC ADMINISTRATION IN ISRAEL (PAMPHLET).   EDU/PROP
ISRAEL SCHOOL EX/STRUC BUDGET PAY INGP/REL   NAT/G
...DECISION 20 CIVIL/SERV. PAGE 35 B0718   ADMIN
                                                      WORKER
                                                       N19
GINZBERG E.,MANPOWER FOR GOVERNMENT (PAMPHLET).   WORKER
USA+45 FORCES PLAN PROB/SOLV PAY EDU/PROP ADMIN   CONSULT
GP/REL COST...MGT PREDICT TREND 20 CIVIL/SERV.   NAT/G
PAGE 40 B0803   LOC/G
                                                       N19
MARSH J.F. JR.,THE FBI RETIREMENT BILL (PAMPHLET).   ADMIN
USA+45 EX/STRUC WORKER PLAN PROB/SOLV BUDGET LEAD   NAT/G
LOBBY PARL/PROC PERS/REL RIGID/FLEX...POLICY 20 FBI   SENIOR
PRESIDENT BUR/BUDGET. PAGE 70 B1405   GOV/REL
                                                       B28
CALKINS E.E.,BUSINESS THE CIVILIZER. INDUS MARKET   LAISSEZ
WORKER TAX PAY ROUTINE COST DEMAND MORAL 19/20.   POLICY
PAGE 18 B0367   WEALTH
                                                      PROFIT
                                                       B28
HARDMAN J.B.,AMERICAN LABOR DYNAMICS. WORKER   LABOR
ECO/TAC DOMIN ADJUD LEAD LOBBY PWR...POLICY MGT.   INGP/REL
PAGE 47 B0944   ATTIT
                                                      GP/REL
                                                       B35
GREER S.,BIBLIOGRAPHY ON CIVIL SERVICE AND   BIBLIOG/A
PERSONNEL ADMINISTRATION. USA-45 LOC/G PROVS WORKER   ADMIN
PRICE SENIOR DRIVE...MGT 20. PAGE 43 B0870   NAT/G
                                                      ROUTINE
                                                       B38
BALDWIN R.N.,CIVIL LIBERTIES AND INDUSTRIAL   LABOR
CONFLICT. USA+45 STRATA WORKER INGP/REL...MGT 20   LG/CO
ACLU CIVIL/LIB. PAGE 9 B0175   INDUS
                                                      GP/REL
                                                       B38
FIELD G.L.,THE SYNDICAL AND CORPORATIVE   FASCISM
INSTITUTIONS OF ITALIAN FASCISM. ITALY CONSTN   INDUS
STRATA LABOR EX/STRUC TOP/EX ADJUD ADMIN LEAD   NAT/G
TOTALISM AUTHORIT...MGT 20 MUSSOLIN/B. PAGE 35   WORKER
B0716
                                                       B38
REICH N.,LABOR RELATIONS IN REPUBLICAN GERMANY.   WORKER
GERMANY CONSTN ECO/DEV INDUS NAT/G ADMIN CONTROL   MGT
GP/REL FASCISM POPULISM 20 WEIMAR/REP. PAGE 87   LABOR
B1763   BARGAIN
                                                       B39
MACMAHON A.W.,FEDERAL ADMINISTRATORS: A   BIOG
BIOGRAPHICAL APPROACH TO THE PROBLEM OF   ADMIN
DEPARTMENTAL MANAGEMENT. USA+45 DELIB/GP EX/STRUC   NAT/G
WORKER LEAD...TIME/SEQ 19/20. PAGE 68 B1366   MGT
                                                       B41
LESTER R.A.,ECONOMICS OF LABOR. UK USA+45 TEC/DEV   LABOR
BARGAIN PAY INGP/REL INCOME...MGT 19/20. PAGE 64   ECO/DEV
B1298   INDUS
                                                      WORKER
                                                       B41
MACMAHON A.W.,THE ADMINISTRATION OF FEDERAL WORK   ADMIN
RELIEF. USA+45 EX/STRUC WORKER BUDGET EFFICIENCY   NAT/G
...CONT/OBS CHARTS 20 WPA. PAGE 68 B1367   MGT
                                                      GIVE
                                                       B41
SLICHTER S.H.,UNION POLICIES AND INDUSTRIAL   BARGAIN
MANAGEMENT. USA-45 INDUS TEC/DEV PAY GP/REL   LABOR

INGP/REL COST EFFICIENCY PRODUC...POLICY 20.   MGT
PAGE 98 B1978   WORKER
                                                       S43
SELZNICK P.,"AN APPROACH TO A THEORY OF   ROUTINE
BUREAUCRACY." INDUS WORKER CONTROL LEAD EFFICIENCY   ADMIN
OPTIMAL...SOC METH 20 BARNARD/C BUREAUCRCY   MGT
WEBER/MAX FRIEDRCH/C MICHELS/R. PAGE 95 B1928   EX/STRUC
                                                       B44
BIRNSTOCK G.,MANAGEMENT IN RUSSIAN INDUSTRY AND   ADMIN
AGRICULTURE. USSR CONSULT WORKER LEAD COST PROFIT   MARXISM
ATTIT DRIVE PWR...MGT METH/COMP DICTIONARY 20.   SML/CO
PAGE 12 B0236   AGRI
                                                       B44
DAHL D.,SICKNESS BENEFITS AND GROUP PURCHASE OF   BIBLIOG/A
MEDICAL CARE FOR INDUSTRIAL EMPLOYEES. FAM LABOR   INDUS
NAT/G PLAN...POLICY MGT SOC STAT 20. PAGE 25 B0519   WORKER
                                                      HEAL
                                                       S44
SIMON H.A.,"DECISION-MAKING AND ADMINISTRATIVE   DECISION
ORGANIZATION" (BMR)" WOR-45 CHOOSE INGP/REL   ADMIN
EFFICIENCY ATTIT RESPECT...MGT 20. PAGE 97 B1955   CONTROL
                                                      WORKER
                                                       B45
BENJAMIN H.C.,EMPLOYMENT TESTS IN INDUSTRY AND   BIBLIOG/A
BUSINESS. LG/CO WORKER ROUTINE...MGT PSY SOC   METH
CLASSIF PROBABIL STAT APT/TEST KNO/TEST PERS/TEST   TESTS
20. PAGE 10 B0211   INDUS
                                                       B45
MAYO E.,THE SOCIAL PROBLEMS OF AN INDUSTRIAL   INDUS
CIVILIZATION. USA+45 SOCIETY LABOR CROWD PERS/REL   GP/REL
LAISSEZ. PAGE 71 B1438   MGT
                                                      WORKER
                                                       B45
MILLIS H.A.,ORGANIZED LABOR (FIRST ED.). LAW STRUCT LABOR
DELIB/GP WORKER ECO/TAC ADJUD CONTROL REPRESENT   POLICY
INGP/REL INCOME MGT. PAGE 74 B1485   ROUTINE
                                                      GP/REL
                                                       B46
DAVIES E.,NATIONAL ENTERPRISE: THE DEVELOPMENT OF   ADMIN
THE PUBLIC CORPORATION. UK LG/CO EX/STRUC WORKER   NAT/G
PROB/SOLV COST ATTIT SOCISM 20. PAGE 26 B0536   CONTROL
                                                      INDUS
                                                       B47
BAERWALD F.,FUNDAMENTALS OF LABOR ECONOMICS. LAW   ECO/DEV
INDUS LABOR LG/CO CONTROL GP/REL INCOME TOTALISM   WORKER
...MGT CHARTS GEN/LAWS BIBLIOG 20. PAGE 8 B0158   MARKET
                                                       B47
REDFORD E.S.,FIELD ADMINISTRATION OF WARTIME   ADMIN
RATIONING. USA-45 CONSTN ELITES DIST/IND WORKER   NAT/G
CONTROL WAR GOV/REL ADJUST RIGID/FLEX 20 OPA.   PROB/SOLV
PAGE 87 B1752   RATION
                                                       B47
WARNER W.L.,THE SOCIAL SYSTEM OF THE MODERN   ROLE
FACTORY; THE STRIKE: AN ANALYSIS. USA-45 STRATA   STRUCT
WORKER ECO/TAC GP/REL INGP/REL...MGT SOC CHARTS 20   LABOR
YANKEE/C. PAGE 114 B2293   PROC/MFG
                                                       B47
WHITEHEAD T.N.,LEADERSHIP IN A FREE SOCIETY; A   INDUS
STUDY IN HUMAN RELATIONS BASED ON AN ANALYSIS OF   LEAD
PRESENT-DAY INDUSTRIAL CIVILIZATION. WOR-45 STRUCT   ORD/FREE
R+D LABOR LG/CO SML/CO WORKER PLAN PROB/SOLV   SOCIETY
TEC/DEV DRIVE...MGT 20. PAGE 116 B2341
                                                       B48
HOOVER E.M.,THE LOCATION OF ECONOMIC ACTIVITY.   HABITAT
WOR+45 MARKET MUNIC WORKER PROB/SOLV INT/TRADE   INDUS
ADMIN COST...POLICY CHARTS T 20. PAGE 51 B1041   ECO/TAC
                                                      GEOG
                                                       B48
KESSELMAN L.C.,THE SOCIAL POLITICS OF THE FEPC.   POLICY
INDUS WORKER EDU/PROP GP/REL RACE/REL 20 NEGRO JEWS NAT/G
FEPC. PAGE 59 B1200   ADMIN
                                                      DISCRIM
                                                       B48
STEWART I.,ORGANIZING SCIENTIFIC RESEARCH FOR WAR: DELIB/GP
ADMINISTRATIVE HISTORY OF OFFICE OF SCIENTIFIC   ADMIN
RESEARCH AND DEVELOPMENT. USA-45 INTELL R+D LABOR   WAR
WORKER CREATE BUDGET WEAPON CIVMIL/REL GP/REL   TEC/DEV
EFFICIENCY...POLICY 20. PAGE 101 B2037
                                                       S48
COCH L.,"OVERCOMING RESISTANCE TO CHANGE" (BMR)"   WORKER
USA+45 CONSULT ADMIN ROUTINE GP/REL EFFICIENCY   OP/RES
PRODUC PERCEPT SKILL...CHARTS SOC/EXP 20. PAGE 22   PROC/MFG
B0441   RIGID/FLEX
                                                       B49
LEPAWSKY A.,ADMINISTRATION. FINAN INDUS LG/CO   ADMIN
SML/CO INGP/REL PERS/REL COST EFFICIENCY OPTIMAL   MGT
SKILL 20. PAGE 64 B1294   WORKER
                                                      EX/STRUC
                                                       B49
SHISTER J.,ECONOMICS OF THE LABOR MARKET. LOC/G   MARKET
NAT/G WORKER TEC/DEV BARGAIN PAY PRICE EXEC GP/REL   LABOR
INCOME...MGT T 20. PAGE 96 B1949   INDUS
                                                       S50
DALTON M.,"CONFLICTS BETWEEN STAFF AND LINE   MGT
MANAGERIAL OFFICERS" (BMR). USA+45 USA-45 ELITES   ATTIT
LG/CO WORKER PROB/SOLV ADMIN EXEC EFFICIENCY PRODUC GP/REL

...GP/COMP 20. PAGE 26 B0526   INDUS

S50
TANNENBAUM R.,"PARTICIPATION BY SUBORDINATES IN THE PARTIC MANAGERIAL DECISIONMAKING PROCESS" (BMR)" WOR+45 DECISION INDUS SML/CO WORKER INGP/REL...CONCPT GEN/LAWS 20. MGT PAGE 103 B2074   LG/CO

B51
PETERSON F.,SURVEY OF LABOR ECONOMICS (REV. ED.). WORKER STRATA ECO/DEV LABOR INSPECT BARGAIN PAY PRICE EXEC DEMAND ROUTINE GP/REL ALL/VALS ORD/FREE 20 AFL/CIO IDEA/COMP DEPT/LABOR. PAGE 82 B1662   T

C51
HOMANS G.C.,"THE WESTERN ELECTRIC RESEARCHES" IN S. OP/RES HOSLETT, ED., HUMAN FACTORS IN MANAGEMENT (BMR)" EFFICIENCY ACT/RES GP/REL HAPPINESS PRODUC DRIVE...MGT OBS 20. SOC/EXP PAGE 51 B1037   WORKER

S52
RICH B.M.,"ADMINISTRATION REORGANIZATION IN NEW ADMIN JERSEY" (BMR)" USA+45 DELIB/GP EX/STRUC WORKER CONSTN OP/RES BUDGET 20 NEW/JERSEY. PAGE 88 B1772 PROB/SOLV PROVS

B53
ARGYRIS C.,EXECUTIVE LEADERSHIP: AN APPRAISAL OF A MGT MANAGER IN ACTION. TOP/EX ADMIN LEAD ADJUST ATTIT EX/STRUC ...METH 20. PAGE 6 B0127 WORKER PERS/REL

B53
DIMOCK M.E.,PUBLIC ADMINISTRATION. USA+45 FINAN ADMIN WORKER BUDGET CONTROL CHOOSE...T 20. PAGE 29 B0596 STRUCT OP/RES POLICY

B53
ROBINSON E.A.G.,THE STRUCTURE OF COMPETITIVE INDUS INDUSTRY. UK ECO/DEV DIST/IND MARKET TEC/DEV DIPLOM PRODUC EDU/PROP ADMIN EFFICIENCY WEALTH...MGT 19/20. WORKER PAGE 89 B1798 OPTIMAL

S53
DRUCKER P.F.,"THE EMPLOYEE SOCIETY." STRUCT BAL/PWR LABOR PARTIC REPRESENT PWR...DECISION CONCPT. PAGE 30 MGT B0619 WORKER CULTURE

C53
KRACKE E.A. JR.,"CIVIL SERVICE IN EARLY SUNG CHINA, ADMIN 960-1067." ASIA GP/REL...BIBLIOG/A 10/11. PAGE 61 NAT/G B1231 WORKER CONTROL

B54
GOLDNER A.W.,WILDCAT STRIKE. LABOR TEC/DEV PAY INDUS ADMIN LEAD PERS/REL ATTIT RIGID/FLEX PWR...MGT WORKER CONCPT. PAGE 40 B0816 GP/REL SOC

B54
GOULDNER A.W.,PATTERNS OF INDUSTRIAL BUREAUCRACY. ADMIN DOMIN ATTIT DRIVE...BIBLIOG 20 BUREAUCRCY. PAGE 42 INDUS B0844 OP/RES WORKER

B54
WILENSKY H.L.,SYLLABUS OF INDUSTRIAL RELATIONS: A BIBLIOG GUIDE TO READING AND RESEARCH. USA+45 MUNIC ADMIN INDUS INGP/REL...POLICY MGT PHIL/SCI 20. PAGE 117 B2351 LABOR WORKER

C54
GOULDNER A.W.,"PATTERNS OF INDUSTRIAL BUREAUCRACY." ADMIN GP/REL CONSEN ATTIT DRIVE...BIBLIOG 20. PAGE 42 INDUS B0843 OP/RES WORKER

B55
CHAPMAN B.,THE PREFECTS AND PROVINCIAL FRANCE. ADMIN FRANCE DELIB/GP WORKER ROLE PWR 19/20 PREFECT. PROVS PAGE 20 B0408 EX/STRUC LOC/G

B55
GULICK C.A.,HISTORY AND THEORIES OF WORKING-CLASS BIBLIOG MOVEMENTS: A SELECT BIBLIOGRAPHY. EUR+WWI MOD/EUR WORKER UK USA-45 INT/ORG. PAGE 44 B0902 LABOR ADMIN

B55
HOROWITZ M.,INCENTIVE WAGE SYSTEMS. INDUS LG/CO BIBLIOG/A WORKER CONTROL GP/REL...MGT PSY 20. PAGE 51 B1044 PAY PLAN TASK

B56
DUNNILL F.,THE CIVIL SERVICE. UK LAW PLAN ADMIN PERSON EFFICIENCY DRIVE NEW/LIB...STAT CHARTS 20 WORKER PARLIAMENT CIVIL/SERV. PAGE 31 B0633 STRATA SOC/WK

B56
HICKMAN C.A.,INDIVIDUALS, GROUPS, AND ECONOMIC MGT BEHAVIOR. WORKER PAY CONTROL EXEC GP/REL INGP/REL ADMIN PERSON ROLE...PSY SOC PERS/COMP METH 20. PAGE 50 ECO/TAC B1005 PLAN

B56
POWELL N.J.,PERSONNEL ADMINISTRATION IN GOVERNMENT. ADMIN COM/IND POL/PAR LEGIS PAY CT/SYS ROUTINE GP/REL WORKER PERS/REL...POLICY METH 20 CIVIL/SERV. PAGE 84 B1697 LOC/G NAT/G

B57
CRONBACK L.J.,PSYCHOLOGICAL TESTS AND PERSONNEL MATH DECISIONS. OP/RES PROB/SOLV CHOOSE PERSON...PSY DECISION STAT TESTS 20. PAGE 25 B0508 WORKER MGT

B57
MURDESHWAR A.K.,ADMINISTRATIVE PROBLEMS RELATING TO NAT/G NATIONALISATION: WITH SPECIAL REFERENCE TO INDIAN OWN STATE ENTERPRISES. CZECHOSLVK FRANCE INDIA UK INDUS USA+45 LEGIS WORKER PROB/SOLV BUDGET PRICE CONTROL ADMIN ...MGT GEN/LAWS 20 PARLIAMENT. PAGE 76 B1544

B57
US CIVIL SERVICE COMMISSION,DISSERTATIONS AND BIBLIOG THESES RELATING TO PERSONNEL ADMINISTRATION ADMIN (PAMPHLET). USA+45 COM/IND LABOR EX/STRUC GP/REL MGT INGP/REL DECISION. PAGE 108 B2176 WORKER

B57
US HOUSE COMM ON POST OFFICE,MANPOWER UTILIZATION NAT/G IN THE FEDERAL GOVERNMENT. USA+45 FORCES WORKER ADMIN CREATE PLAN EFFICIENCY UTIL 20 CONGRESS CIVIL/SERV LABOR POSTAL/SYS DEPT/DEFEN. PAGE 109 B2193 EX/STRUC

S57
DANIELSON L.E.,"SUPERVISORY PROBLEMS IN DECISION PROB/SOLV MAKING." WORKER ADMIN ROUTINE TASK MGT. PAGE 26 DECISION B0529 CONTROL GP/REL

S57
ROURKE F.E.,"THE POLITICS OF ADMINISTRATIVE POLICY ORGANIZATION: A CASE HISTORY." USA+45 LABOR WORKER ATTIT PLAN ADMIN TASK EFFICIENCY 20 DEPT/LABOR CONGRESS. MGT PAGE 91 B1836 GP/COMP

B58
AMERICAN SOCIETY PUBLIC ADMIN,STRENGTHENING ADMIN MANAGEMENT FOR DEMOCRATIC GOVERNMENT. USA+45 ACADEM NAT/G EX/STRUC WORKER PLAN BUDGET CONFER CT/SYS EXEC EFFICIENCY ANTHOL. PAGE 4 B0088 MGT

B58
BLAIR L.,THE COMMONWEALTH PUBLIC SERVICE. LAW ADMIN WORKER...MGT CHARTS GOV/COMP 20 COMMONWLTH AUSTRAL NAT/G CIVIL/SERV. PAGE 12 B0248 EX/STRUC INGP/REL

B58
BRIGHT J.R.,AUTOMATION AND MANAGEMENT. INDUS LABOR AUTOMAT WORKER OP/RES TEC/DEV INSPECT 20. PAGE 15 B0307 COMPUTER PLAN MGT

B58
CHEEK G.,ECONOMIC AND SOCIAL IMPLICATIONS OF BIBLIOG/A AUTOMATION: A BIBLIOGRAPHIC REVIEW (PAMPHLET). SOCIETY USA+45 LG/CO WORKER CREATE PLAN CONTROL ROUTINE INDUS PERS/REL EFFICIENCY PRODUC...METH/COMP 20. PAGE 20 AUTOMAT B0416

B58
MELMAN S.,DECISION-MAKING AND PRODUCTIVITY. INDUS LABOR EX/STRUC WORKER OP/RES PROB/SOLV TEC/DEV ADMIN PRODUC ROUTINE RIGID/FLEX GP/COMP. PAGE 73 B1464 DECISION MGT

B58
SHERWOOD F.P.,SUPERVISORY METHODS IN MUNICIPAL EX/STRUC ADMINISTRATION. USA+45 MUNIC WORKER EDU/PROP PARTIC LEAD INGP/REL PERS/REL 20 CITY/MGT. PAGE 96 B1945 ADMIN LOC/G

B58
US HOUSE COMM POST OFFICE,MANPOWER UTILIZATION IN ADMIN THE FEDERAL GOVERNMENT. USA+45 DIST/IND EX/STRUC WORKER LEGIS CONFER EFFICIENCY 20 CONGRESS CIVIL/SERV. DELIB/GP PAGE 109 B2195 NAT/G

B58
US HOUSE COMM POST OFFICE,MANPOWER UTILIZATION IN ADMIN THE FEDERAL GOVERNMENT. USA+45 DIST/IND EX/STRUC WORKER LEGIS CONFER EFFICIENCY 20 CONGRESS CIVIL/SERV. DELIB/GP PAGE 109 B2196 NAT/G

B58
US HOUSE COMM POST OFFICE,TRAINING OF FEDERAL LEGIS EMPLOYEES. USA+45 DIST/IND NAT/G EX/STRUC EDU/PROP DELIB/GP CONFER GOV/REL EFFICIENCY SKILL 20 CONGRESS WORKER CIVIL/SERV. PAGE 109 B2197 ADMIN

B58
VAN RIPER P.P.,HISTORY OF THE UNITED STATES CIVIL ADMIN SERVICE. USA+45 USA-45 LABOR LOC/G DELIB/GP LEGIS WORKER PROB/SOLV LOBBY GOV/REL GP/REL INCOME...POLICY NAT/G 18/20 PRESIDENT CIVIL/SERV. PAGE 111 B2251

B58
WILENSKY H.L.,INDUSTRIAL SOCIETY AND SOCIAL INDUS WELFARE: IMPACT OF INDUSTRIALIZATION ON SUPPLY AND ECO/DEV ORGANIZATION OF SOC WELF SERVICES. ELITES SOCIETY RECEIVE STRATA SERV/IND FAM MUNIC PUB/INST CONSULT WORKER PROF/ORG ADMIN AUTOMAT ANOMIE 20. PAGE 117 B2352

S58
MANSFIELD E.,"A STUDY OF DECISION-MAKING WITHIN THE OP/RES FIRM." LG/CO WORKER INGP/REL COST EFFICIENCY PRODUC PROB/SOLV ...CHARTS 20. PAGE 69 B1395 AUTOMAT ROUTINE

B59
COUNCIL OF STATE GOVERNMENTS,STATE GOVERNMENT: AN BIBLIOG/A ANNOTATED BIBLIOGRAPHY (PAMPHLET). USA+45 LAW AGRI PROVS

INDUS WORKER PLAN TAX ADJUST AGE/Y ORD/FREE...HEAL MGT 20. PAGE 24 B0494
LOC/G ADMIN

B59
INDIAN INSTITUTE PUBLIC ADMIN,MORALE IN THE PUBLIC SERVICES: REPORT OF A CONFERENCE JAN., 3-4, 1959. INDIA S/ASIA ECO/UNDEV PROVS PLAN EDU/PROP CONFER GOV/REL EFFICIENCY DRIVE ROLE 20 CIVIL/SERV. PAGE 53 B1082
HAPPINESS ADMIN WORKER INGP/REL

B59
ROSOLIO D.,TEN YEARS OF THE CIVIL SERVICE IN ISRAEL (1948-1958) (PAMPHLET). ISRAEL NAT/G RECEIVE 20. PAGE 90 B1825
ADMIN WORKER GOV/REL PAY

B59
SAYER W.S.,AN AGENDA FOR RESEARCH IN PUBLIC PERSONNEL ADMINISTRATION. FUT USA+45 ACADEM LABOR LOC/G NAT/G POL/PAR DELIB/GP MGT. PAGE 93 B1872
WORKER ADMIN ACT/RES CONSULT

B59
U OF MICHIGAN LAW SCHOOL,ATOMS AND THE LAW. USA+45 PROVS WORKER PROB/SOLV DIPLOM ADMIN GOV/REL ANTHOL. PAGE 106 B2142
NUC/PWR NAT/G CONTROL LAW

B59
WARNER W.L.,INDUSTRIAL MAN. USA+45 USA-45 ELITES INDUS LABOR TOP/EX WORKER ADMIN INGP/REL PERS/REL ...CHARTS ANTHOL 20. PAGE 114 B2294
EXEC LEAD PERSON MGT

S59
BENDIX R.,"INDUSTRIALIZATION, IDEOLOGIES, AND SOCIAL STRUCTURE" (BMR)" UK USA-45 USSR STRUCT WORKER GP/REL EFFICIENCY...IDEA/COMP 20. PAGE 10 B0210
INDUS ATTIT MGT ADMIN

S59
SIMPSON R.L.,"VERTICAL AND HORIZONTAL COMMUNICATION IN FORMAL ORGANIZATION" USA+45 LG/CO EX/STRUC DOMIN CONTROL TASK INGP/REL TIME 20. PAGE 97 B1963
PERS/REL AUTOMAT INDUS WORKER

B60
BERNSTEIN I.,THE LEAN YEARS. SOCIETY STRATA PARTIC GP/REL ATTIT...SOC 20 DEPRESSION. PAGE 11 B0227
WORKER LABOR WEALTH MGT

B60
FRYE R.J.,GOVERNMENT AND LABOR: THE ALABAMA PROGRAM. USA+45 INDUS R+D LABOR WORKER BUDGET EFFICIENCY AGE/Y HEALTH...CHARTS 20 ALABAMA. PAGE 38 B0761
ADMIN LEGIS LOC/G PROVS

B60
HAYEK F.A.,THE CONSTITUTION OF LIBERTY. UNIV LAW CONSTN WORKER TAX EDU/PROP ADMIN CT/SYS COERCE DISCRIM...IDEA/COMP 20. PAGE 48 B0974
ORD/FREE CHOOSE NAT/G CONCPT

B60
KERR C.,INDUSTRIALISM AND INDUSTRIAL MAN. CULTURE SOCIETY ECO/UNDEV NAT/G ADMIN PRODUC WEALTH ...PREDICT TREND NAT/COMP 19/20. PAGE 59 B1197
WORKER MGT ECO/DEV INDUS

B60
MOORE W.E.,LABOR COMMITMENT AND SOCIAL CHANGE IN DEVELOPING AREAS. SOCIETY STRATA ECO/UNDEV MARKET VOL/ASSN WORKER AUTHORIT SKILL...MGT NAT/COMP SOC/INTEG 20. PAGE 75 B1514
LABOR ORD/FREE ATTIT INDUS

B60
PAGE T.,THE PUBLIC PERSONNEL AGENCY AND THE CHIEF EXECUTIVE (REPORT NO. 601). USA+45 LOC/G NAT/G GP/REL PERS/REL...ANTHOL 20. PAGE 80 B1624
WORKER EXEC ADMIN MGT

B60
PFIFFNER J.M.,PUBLIC ADMINISTRATION. USA+45 FINAN WORKER PLAN PROB/SOLV ADJUD CONTROL EXEC...T 20. PAGE 82 B1666
ADMIN NAT/G LOC/G MGT

B60
WEBSTER J.A.,A GENERAL STUDY OF THE DEPARTMENT OF DEFENSE INTERNAL SECURITY PROGRAM. USA+45 WORKER TEC/DEV ADJUD CONTROL CT/SYS EXEC GOV/REL COST ...POLICY DECISION MGT 20 DEPT/DEFEN SUPREME/CT. PAGE 114 B2307
ORD/FREE PLAN ADMIN NAT/G

S60
BAVELAS A.,"LEADERSHIP: MAN AND FUNCTION." WORKER CREATE PLAN CONTROL PERS/REL PERSON PWR...MGT 20. PAGE 10 B0199
LEAD ADMIN ROUTINE ROLE

S60
SMIGEL E.O.,"THE IMPACT OF RECRUITMENT ON THE ORGANIZATION OF THE LARGE LAW FIRM" (BMR)" USA+45 STRUCT CONSULT PLAN GP/REL EFFICIENCY JURID. PAGE 98 B1979
LG/CO ADMIN LAW WORKER

S60
THOMPSON J.D.,"ORGANIZATIONAL MANAGEMENT OF CONFLICT" (BMR)" WOR+45 STRUCT LABOR LG/CO WORKER TEC/DEV INGP/REL ATTIT GP/COMP. PAGE 104 B2103
PROB/SOLV PERS/REL ADMIN MGT

B61
AMERICAN MANAGEMENT ASSN,SUPERIOR-SUBORDINATE COMMUNICATION IN MANAGEMENT. STRATA FINAN INDUS SML/CO WORKER CONTROL EXEC ATTIT 20. PAGE 4 B0086
MGT ACT/RES PERS/REL LG/CO

B61
CARROTHERS A.W.R.,LABOR ARBITRATION IN CANADA. CANADA LAW NAT/G CONSULT LEGIS WORKER ADJUD ADMIN CT/SYS 20. PAGE 19 B0386
LABOR MGT GP/REL BARGAIN

B61
CHAPPLE E.D.,THE MEASURE OF MANAGEMENT. USA+45 WORKER ADMIN GP/REL EFFICIENCY...DECISION ORG/CHARTS SIMUL 20. PAGE 20 B0412
MGT OP/RES PLAN METH/CNCPT

B61
DRURY J.W.,THE GOVERNMENT OF KANSAS. USA+45 AGRI INDUS CHIEF LEGIS WORKER PLAN BUDGET GIVE CT/SYS GOV/REL...T 20 KANSAS GOVERNOR CITY/MGT. PAGE 31 B0621
PROVS CONSTN ADMIN LOC/G

B61
KEE R.,REFUGEE WORLD. AUSTRIA EUR+WWI GERMANY NEIGH EX/STRUC WORKER PROB/SOLV ECO/TAC RENT EDU/PROP INGP/REL COST LITERACY HABITAT 20 MIGRATION. PAGE 59 B1186
NAT/G GIVE WEALTH STRANGE

B61
LENIN V.I.,WHAT IS TO BE DONE? (1902). RUSSIA LABOR NAT/G POL/PAR WORKER CAP/ISM ECO/TAC ADMIN PARTIC ...MARXIST IDEA/COMP GEN/LAWS 19/20. PAGE 64 B1292
EDU/PROP PRESS MARXISM METH/COMP

B61
PAGE T.,STATE PERSONNEL REORGANIZATION IN ILLINOIS. USA+45 POL/PAR CHIEF TEC/DEV LEAD ADJUST 20. PAGE 80 B1625
ADMIN PROVS WORKER DELIB/GP

B61
ROMANO F.,CIVIL SERVICE AND PUBLIC EMPLOYEE LAW IN NEW JERSEY. CONSTN MUNIC WORKER GIVE PAY CHOOSE UTIL 20. PAGE 90 B1816
ADMIN PROVS ADJUD LOC/G

B61
SHARMA T.R.,THE WORKING OF STATE ENTERPRISES IN INDIA. INDIA DELIB/GP LEGIS WORKER BUDGET PRICE CONTROL GP/REL OWN ATTIT...MGT CHARTS 20. PAGE 96 B1938
NAT/G INDUS ADMIN SOCISM

B61
WALKER N.,MORALE IN THE CIVIL SERVICE. UK EXEC LEAD INGP/REL EFFICIENCY HAPPINESS 20. PAGE 113 B2280
ATTIT WORKER ADMIN PSY

L61
THOMPSON V.A.,"HIERARACHY, SPECIALIZATION, AND ORGANIZATIONAL CONFLICT" (BMR)" WOR+45 STRATA STRUCT WORKER TEC/DEV GP/REL INGP/REL ATTIT AUTHORIT 20 BUREAUCRCY. PAGE 104 B2106
PERS/REL PROB/SOLV ADMIN EX/STRUC

S61
CYERT R.M.,"TWO EXPERIMENTS ON BIAS AND CONFLICT IN ORGANIZATIONAL ESTIMATION." WORKER PROB/SOLV EFFICIENCY...MGT PSY STAT CHARTS. PAGE 25 B0518
LAB/EXP ROUTINE ADMIN DECISION

S61
EVAN W.M.,"A LABORATORY EXPERIMENT ON BUREAUCRATIC AUTHORITY" WORKER CONTROL EXEC PRODUC ATTIT PERSON ...PSY SOC CHARTS SIMUL 20 WEBER/MAX. PAGE 34 B0687
ADMIN LEGIT LAB/EXP EFFICIENCY

B62
CHERNICK J.,THE SELECTION OF TRAINEES UNDER MDTA. USA+45 NAT/G LEGIS PERSON...CENSUS 20 CIVIL/SERV MDTA. PAGE 20 B0418
EDU/PROP WORKER ADMIN DELIB/GP

B62
FOSS P.O.,REORGANIZATION AND REASSIGNMENT IN THE CALIFORNIA HIGHWAY PATROL (PAMPHLET). USA+45 STRUCT WORKER EDU/PROP CONTROL COERCE INGP/REL ORD/FREE PWR...DECISION 20 CALIFORNIA. PAGE 37 B0744
FORCES ADMIN PROVS PLAN

B62
GALENSON W.,LABOR IN DEVELOPING COUNTRIES. BRAZIL INDONESIA ISRAEL PAKISTAN TURKEY AGRI INDUS WORKER PAY PRICE GP/REL WEALTH...MGT CHARTS METH/COMP NAT/COMP 20. PAGE 38 B0775
LABOR ECO/UNDEV BARGAIN POL/PAR

B62
INSTITUTE OF PUBLIC ADMIN,A SHORT HISTORY OF THE PUBLIC SERVICE IN IRELAND. IRELAND UK DIST/IND INGP/REL FEDERAL 13/20 CIVIL/SERV. PAGE 54 B1091
ADMIN WORKER GOV/REL NAT/G

B62
INTERNATIONAL LABOR OFFICE,WORKERS' MANAGEMENT IN YUGOSLAVIA. COM YUGOSLAVIA LABOR DELIB/GP EX/STRUC PROB/SOLV ADMIN PWR MARXISM...CHARTS ORG/CHARTS BIBLIOG 20. PAGE 54 B1098
WORKER CONTROL MGT INDUS

B62
MARS D.,SUGGESTED LIBRARY IN PUBLIC ADMINISTRATION. FINAN DELIB/GP EX/STRUC WORKER COMPUTER ADJUD ...DECISION PSY SOC METH/COMP 20. PAGE 69 B1403
BIBLIOG ADMIN METH MGT

B62
MEANS G.C.,THE CORPORATE REVOLUTION IN AMERICA: ECONOMIC REALITY VS. ECONOMIC THEORY. USA+45 USA-45
LG/CO MARKET

INDUS WORKER PLAN CAP/ISM ADMIN...IDEA/COMP 20.   CONTROL
PAGE 72 B1459   PRICE

                                                  B62
NEW ZEALAND COMM OF ST SERVICE,THE STATE SERVICES   ADMIN
IN NEW ZEALAND. NEW/ZEALND CONSULT EX/STRUC ACT/RES   WORKER
...BIBLIOG 20. PAGE 78 B1577   TEC/DEV
                                                  NAT/G

B62
NJ DEPARTMENT CIVIL SERV,THE CIVIL SERVICE RULES OF   ADMIN
THE STATE OF NEW JERSEY. USA+45 USA-45 PAY...JURID   PROVS
ANTHOL 20 CIVIL/SERV NEW/JERSEY. PAGE 78 B1585   ROUTINE
                                                  WORKER

B62
PRESTHUS R.,THE ORGANIZATIONAL SOCIETY. USA+45   LG/CO
STRUC ECO/DEV ADMIN ATTIT ALL/VALS...PSY SOC 20.   WORKER
PAGE 84 B1703   PERS/REL
                                                  DRIVE

B62
SRIVASTAVA G.L.,COLLECTIVE BARGAINING AND LABOR-   LABOR
MANAGEMENT RELATIONS IN INDIA. INDIA UK USA+45   MGT
INDUS LEGIS WORKER ADJUD EFFICIENCY PRODUC   BARGAIN
...METH/COMP 20. PAGE 100 B2014   GP/REL

B62
STAHL O.G.,PUBLIC PERSONNEL ADMINISTRATION. LOC/G   ADMIN
TOP/EX CREATE PLAN ROUTINE...TECHNIC MGT T.   WORKER
PAGE 100 B2017   EX/STRUC
                                                  NAT/G

B62
TAYLOR J.K.L.,ATTITUDES AND METHODS OF   WORKER
COMMUNICATION AND CONSULTATION BETWEEN EMPLOYERS   ADMIN
AND WORKERS AT INDIVIDUAL FIRM LEVEL. WOR+45 STRUCT   ATTIT
INDUS LABOR CONFER TASK GP/REL EFFICIENCY...MGT   EDU/PROP
BIBLIOG METH 20 OECD. PAGE 103 B2087

B62
US SENATE COMM ON JUDICIARY,STATE DEPARTMENT   CONTROL
SECURITY. USA+45 CHIEF TEC/DEV DOMIN ADMIN EXEC   WORKER
ATTIT ORD/FREE...POLICY CONGRESS DEPT/STATE   NAT/G
PRESIDENT KENNEDY/JF KENNEDY/JF SENATE 20. PAGE 110   GOV/REL
B2228

B63
DOUGLASS H.R.,MODERN ADMINISTRATION OF SECONDARY   EDU/PROP
SCHOOLS. CLIENT DELIB/GP WORKER REPRESENT INGP/REL   ADMIN
AUTHORIT...TREND BIBLIOG. PAGE 30 B0613   SCHOOL
                                                  MGT

B63
HANSON A.H.,NATIONALIZATION: A BOOK OF READINGS.   NAT/G
WOR+45 FINAN DELIB/GP LEGIS WORKER BUDGET ADMIN   OWN
GP/REL EFFICIENCY SOCISM...MGT ANTHOL. PAGE 46   INDUS
B0941   CONTROL

B63
HAUSMAN W.H.,MANAGING ECONOMIC DEVELOPMENT IN   ECO/UNDEV
AFRICA. AFR USA+45 LAW FINAN WORKER TEC/DEV WEALTH   PLAN
...ANTHOL 20. PAGE 48 B0970   FOR/AID
                                                  MGT

B63
PALOTAI O.C.,PUBLICATIONS OF THE INSTITUTE OF   BIBLIOG/A
GOVERNMENT, 1930-1962. LAW PROVS SCHOOL WORKER   ADMIN
ACT/RES OP/RES CT/SYS GOV/REL...CRIMLGY SOC/WK.   LOC/G
PAGE 81 B1629   FINAN

B63
RUITENBEER H.M.,THE DILEMMA OF ORGANIZATIONAL   PERSON
SOCIETY. CULTURE ECO/DEV MUNIC SECT TEC/DEV   ROLE
EDU/PROP NAT/LISM ORD/FREE...NAT/COMP 20 RIESMAN/D   ADMIN
WHYTE/WF MERTON/R MEAD/MARG JASPERS/K. PAGE 92   WORKER
B1855

B63
SELF P.,THE STATE AND THE FARMER. UK ECO/DEV MARKET   AGRI
WORKER PRICE CONTROL GP/REL...WELF/ST 20 DEPT/AGRI.   NAT/G
PAGE 95 B1926   ADMIN
                                                  VOL/ASSN

B63
SHANKS M.,THE LESSONS OF PUBLIC ENTERPRISE. UK   SOCISM
LEGIS WORKER ECO/TAC ADMIN PARL/PROC GOV/REL ATTIT   OWN
...POLICY MGT METH/COMP NAT/COMP ANTHOL 20   NAT/G
PARLIAMENT. PAGE 96 B1931   INDUS

B63
SWEENEY S.B.,ACHIEVING EXCELLENCE IN PUBLIC   ADMIN
SERVICE. FUT USA+45 NAT/G ACT/RES GOV/REL...POLICY   WORKER
ANTHOL 20 CIVIL/SERV. PAGE 102 B2060   TASK
                                                  PLAN

S63
MEDALIA N.Z.,"POSITION AND PROSPECTS OF   NAT/G
SOCIOLOGISTS IN FEDERAL EMPLOYMENT." USA+45 CONSULT   WORKER
PAY SENIOR ADMIN GOV/REL...TREND CHARTS 20   SOC
CIVIL/SERV. PAGE 72 B1460   SKILL

S63
REES A.,"THE EFFECTS OF UNIONS ON RESOURCE   LABOR
ALLOCATION." USA+45 WORKER PRICE CONTROL GP/REL   BARGAIN
...MGT METH/COMP 20. PAGE 87 B1761   RATION
                                                  INCOME

N63
INTERNATIONAL CITY MGRS ASSN,POST-ENTRY TRAINING IN   LOC/G
THE LOCAL PUBLIC SERVICE (PAMPHLET). SCHOOL PLAN   WORKER
PROB/SOLV TEC/DEV ADMIN EFFICIENCY SKILL...POLICY   EDU/PROP
AUD/VIS CHARTS BIBLIOG 20 CITY/MGT. PAGE 54 B1096   METH/COMP

B64
ARGYRIS C.,INTEGRATING THE INDIVIDUAL AND THE   ADMIN
ORGANIZATION. WORKER PROB/SOLV LEAD SANCTION   PERS/REL
REPRESENT ADJUST EFFICIENCY DRIVE PERSON...PSY   VOL/ASSN
METH/CNCPT ORG/CHARTS. PAGE 6 B0132   PARTIC

B64
BANTON M.,THE POLICEMAN IN THE COMMUNITY. UK USA+45   FORCES
STRUCT PROF/ORG WORKER LOBBY ROUTINE COERCE CROWD   ADMIN
GP/REL ADJUST DISCRIM PERCEPT 20. PAGE 9 B0181   ROLE
                                                  RACE/REL

B64
COMMITTEE ECONOMIC DEVELOPMENT,IMPROVING EXECUTIVE   EXEC
MANAGEMENT IN THE FEDERAL GOVERNMENT. USA+45 CHIEF   MGT
DELIB/GP WORKER PLAN PAY SENIOR ADMIN EFFICIENCY 20   TOP/EX
PRESIDENT. PAGE 22 B0457   NAT/G

B64
HERSKOVITS M.J.,ECONOMIC TRANSITION IN AFRICA. FUT   AFR
INT/ORG NAT/G WORKER PROB/SOLV TEC/DEV INT/TRADE   ECO/UNDEV
EQUILIB INCOME...ANTHOL 20. PAGE 49 B0996   PLAN
                                                  ADMIN

B64
KILPATRICKFP,SOURCE BOOK OF OCCUPATIONAL VALUES AND   NAT/G
THE IMAGE OF THE FEDERAL SERVICE. USA+45 EX/STRUC   ATTIT
...POLICY MGT INT METH/COMP 20. PAGE 60 B1205   ADMIN
                                                  WORKER

B64
KILPATRICKFP,THE IMAGE OF THE FEDERAL SERVICE.   NAT/G
USA+45 EX/STRUC...POLICY MGT INT METH/COMP 20.   ATTIT
PAGE 60 B1206   ADMIN
                                                  WORKER

B64
PEABODY R.L.,ORGANIZATIONAL AUTHORITY. SCHOOL   ADMIN
WORKER PLAN SENIOR GOV/REL UTIL DRIVE PWR...PSY   EFFICIENCY
CHARTS BIBLIOG 20. PAGE 82 B1648   TASK
                                                  GP/REL

B64
POPPINO R.E.,INTERNATIONAL COMMUNISM IN LATIN   MARXISM
AMERICA: A HISTORY OF THE MOVEMENT 1917-1963.   POL/PAR
CHINA/COM USSR INTELL STRATA LABOR WORKER ADMIN REV   L/A+17C
ATTIT...POLICY 20 COLD/WAR. PAGE 84 B1692

B64
REDLICH F.,THE GERMAN MILITARY ENTERPRISER AND HIS   EX/STRUC
WORK FORCE. CHRIST-17C GERMANY ELITES SOCIETY FINAN   FORCES
ECO/TAC CIVMIL/REL GP/REL INGP/REL...HIST/WRIT   PROFIT
METH/COMP 14/17. PAGE 87 B1760   WORKER

B64
WELLISZ S.,THE ECONOMICS OF THE SOVIET BLOC. COM   EFFICIENCY
USSR INDUS WORKER PLAN BUDGET INT/TRADE TAX PRICE   ADMIN
PRODUC WEALTH MARXISM...METH/COMP 20. PAGE 115   MARKET
B2319

S64
RUSK D.,"THE MAKING OF FOREIGN POLICY" USA+45 CHIEF   DIPLOM
DELIB/GP WORKER PROB/SOLV ADMIN ATTIT PWR   INT
...DECISION 20 DEPT/STATE RUSK/D GOLDMAN/E. PAGE 92   POLICY
B1856

C64
NORGREN P.H.,"TOWARD FAIR EMPLOYMENT." USA+45 LAW   RACE/REL
STRATA LABOR NAT/G FORCES ACT/RES ADMIN ATTIT   DISCRIM
...POLICY BIBLIOG 20 NEGRO. PAGE 79 B1588   WORKER
                                                  MGT

B65
CAMPBELL G.A.,THE CIVIL SERVICE IN BRITAIN (2ND   ADMIN
ED.). UK DELIB/GP FORCES WORKER CREATE PLAN   LEGIS
...POLICY AUD/VIS 19/20 CIVIL/SERV. PAGE 18 B0370   NAT/G
                                                  FINAN

B65
LAMBIRI I.,SOCIAL CHANGE IN A GREEK COUNTRY TOWN.   INDUS
GREECE FAM PROB/SOLV ROUTINE TASK LEISURE INGP/REL   WORKER
CONSEN ORD/FREE...SOC INT QU CHARTS 20. PAGE 62   CULTURE
B1252   NEIGH

B65
PANJABI K.L.,THE CIVIL SERVANT IN INDIA. INDIA UK   ADMIN
NAT/G CONSULT EX/STRUC REGION GP/REL RACE/REL 20.   WORKER
PAGE 81 B1631   BIOG
                                                  COLONIAL

B65
PARRISH W.E.,MISSOURI UNDER RADICAL RULE 1865-1870.   PROVS
USA-45 SOCIETY INDUS LOC/G POL/PAR WORKER EDU/PROP   ADMIN
SUFF INGP/REL ATTIT...BIBLIOG 19 NEGRO MISSOURI.   RACE/REL
PAGE 81 B1635   ORD/FREE

B65
RHODES G.,PUBLIC SECTOR PENSIONS. UK FINAN LEGIS   ADMIN
BUDGET TAX PAY INCOME...CHARTS 20 CIVIL/SERV.   RECEIVE
PAGE 88 B1769   AGE/O
                                                  WORKER

B65
ROMASCO A.U.,THE POVERTY OF ABUNDANCE: HOOVER, THE   ECO/TAC
NATION, THE DEPRESSION. USA-45 AGRI LEGIS WORKER   ADMIN
GIVE PRESS LEAD 20 HOOVER/H. PAGE 90 B1817   NAT/G
                                                  FINAN

B65
RUBIN H.,PENSIONS AND EMPLOYEE MOBILITY IN THE   ADMIN
PUBLIC SERVICE. USA+45 WORKER PERSON ORD/FREE...SOC   WORKER
QU. PAGE 91 B1849   LOC/G
                                                  SENIOR

STARR M.K.,EXECUTIVE READINGS IN MANAGEMENT
SCIENCE. TOP/EX WORKER EDU/PROP ADMIN...DECISION
GEN/LAWS ANTHOL METH T 20. PAGE 100 B2023
MGT
EX/STRUC
PLAN
LG/CO
B65

US HOUSE COMM EDUC AND LABOR,ADMINISTRATION OF THE
NATIONAL LABOR RELATIONS ACT. USA+45 DELIB/GP
WORKER PROB/SOLV BARGAIN PAY CONTROL 20 NLRB
CONGRESS. PAGE 108 B2188
ADMIN
LABOR
GP/REL
INDUS
B65

VAID K.N.,STATE AND LABOR IN INDIA. INDIA INDUS
WORKER PAY PRICE ADJUD CONTROL PARL/PROC GP/REL
ORD/FREE 20. PAGE 111 B2248
LAW
LABOR
MGT
NEW/LIB
S65

"FURTHER READING." INDIA STRUCT FINAN WORKER ADMIN
COST 20. PAGE 2 B0042
BIBLIOG
MGT
ECO/UNDEV
EFFICIENCY
S65

RAPHAELI N.,"SELECTED ARTICLES AND DOCUMENTS ON
COMPARATIVE PUBLIC ADMINISTRATION." USA+45 FINAN
LOC/G WORKER TEC/DEV CONTROL LEAD...SOC/WK GOV/COMP
METH/COMP. PAGE 86 B1739
BIBLIOG
ADMIN
NAT/G
MGT
B66

ADAMS J.C.,THE GOVERNMENT OF REPUBLICAN ITALY (2ND
ED.). ITALY LOC/G POL/PAR DELIB/GP LEGIS WORKER
ADMIN CT/SYS FASCISM...CHARTS BIBLIOG 20
PARLIAMENT. PAGE 3 B0057
NAT/G
CHOOSE
EX/STRUC
CONSTN
B66

DAVIS R.G.,PLANNING HUMAN RESOURCE DEVELOPMENT,
EDUCATIONAL MODELS AND SCHEMATA. WORKER OP/RES
ECO/TAC EDU/PROP CONTROL COST PRODUC...GEOG STAT
CHARTS 20. PAGE 27 B0544
PLAN
EFFICIENCY
SIMUL
ROUTINE
B66

DICKSON W.J.,COUNSELING IN AN ORGANIZATION: A
SEQUEL TO THE HAWTHORNE RESEARCHES. CLIENT VOL/ASSN
ACT/RES PROB/SOLV AUTOMAT ROUTINE PERS/REL
HAPPINESS ANOMIE ROLE...OBS CHARTS 20 AT+T. PAGE 29
B0588
INDUS
WORKER
PSY
MGT
B66

HAWLEY C.E.,ADMINISTRATIVE QUESTIONS AND POLITICAL
ANSWERS. USA+45 STRUCT WORKER EDU/PROP...GP/COMP
ANTHOL 20. PAGE 48 B0973
ADMIN
GEN/LAWS
GP/REL
B66

LEWIS W.A.,DEVELOPMENT PLANNING: THE ESSENTIALS OF
ECONOMIC POLICY. USA+45 FINAN INDUS NAT/G WORKER
FOR/AID INT/TRADE ADMIN ROUTINE WEALTH...CONCPT
STAT. PAGE 65 B1307
PLAN
ECO/DEV
POLICY
CREATE
B66

US SENATE COMM GOVT OPERATIONS,INTERGOVERNMENTAL
PERSONNEL ACT OF 1966. USA+45 NAT/G CONSULT
DELIB/GP WORKER TEC/DEV PAY AUTOMAT UTIL 20
CONGRESS. PAGE 110 B2219
ADMIN
LEGIS
EFFICIENCY
EDU/PROP
B66

WASHINGTON S.H.,BIBLIOGRAPHY: LABOR-MANAGEMENT
RELATIONS ACT, 1947 AS AMENDED BY LABOR-MANAGEMENT
REPORTING AND DISCLOSURE ACT, 1959. USA+45 CONSTN
INDUS DELIB/GP LEGIS WORKER BARGAIN ECO/TAC ADJUD
GP/REL NEW/LIB...JURID CONGRESS. PAGE 114 B2298
BIBLIOG
LAW
LABOR
MGT
B66

WHITNAH D.R.,SAFER SKYWAYS. DIST/IND DELIB/GP
FORCES TOP/EX WORKER TEC/DEV ROUTINE WAR CIVMIL/REL
COST...TIME/SEQ 20 FAA CAB. PAGE 116 B2342
ADMIN
NAT/G
AIR
GOV/REL
L66

AMERICAN ECONOMIC REVIEW,"SIXTY-THIRD LIST OF
DOCTORAL DISSERTATIONS IN POLITICAL ECONOMY IN
AMERICAN UNIVERSITIES AND COLLEGES." ECO/DEV AGRI
FINAN LABOR WORKER PLAN BUDGET INT/TRADE ADMIN
DEMAND...MGT STAT 20. PAGE 4 B0084
BIBLIOG/A
CONCPT
ACADEM
N66

PRINCETON U INDUSTRIAL REL SEC,RECENT MATERIAL ON
COLLECTIVE BARGAINING IN GOVERNMENT (PAMPHLET NO.
130). USA+45 ECO/DEV LABOR WORKER ECO/TAC GOV/REL
...MGT 20. PAGE 85 B1710
BIBLIOG/A
BARGAIN
NAT/G
GP/REL
B67

BALDWIN G.B.,PLANNING AND DEVELOPMENT IN IRAN. IRAN
AGRI INDUS CONSULT WORKER EDU/PROP BAL/PAY...CHARTS
20. PAGE 8 B0173
PLAN
ECO/UNDEV
ADMIN
PROB/SOLV
B67

ENKE S.,DEFENSE MANAGEMENT. USA+45 R+D FORCES
WORKER PLAN ECO/TAC ADMIN NUC/PWR BAL/PAY UTIL
WEALTH...MGT DEPT/DEFEN. PAGE 33 B0675
DECISION
DELIB/GP
EFFICIENCY
BUDGET
B67

GROSSMAN G.,ECONOMIC SYSTEMS. USA+45 USA-45 USSR
YUGOSLAVIA WORKER CAP/ISM PRICE GP/REL EQUILIB
WEALTH MARXISM SOCISM...MGT METH/COMP 19/20.
PAGE 44 B0892
ECO/DEV
PLAN
TEC/DEV
DEMAND
B67

JAIN R.K.,MANAGEMENT OF STATE ENTERPRISES. INDIA
SOCIETY FINAN WORKER BUDGET ADMIN CONTROL OWN 20.
PAGE 55 B1118
NAT/G
SOCISM
INDUS

MGT

JAKUBAUSKAS E.B.,HUMAN RESOURCES DEVELOPMENT.
USA+45 AGRI INDUS SERV/IND ACT/RES PLAN ADMIN
RACE/REL DISCRIM...TREND GEN/LAWS. PAGE 55 B1119
B67
PROB/SOLV
ECO/TAC
EDU/PROP
WORKER
B67

KRISLOV S.,THE NEGRO IN FEDERAL EMPLOYMENT. LAW
STRATA LOC/G CREATE PROB/SOLV INSPECT GOV/REL
DISCRIM ROLE...DECISION INT TREND 20 NEGRO WWI
CIVIL/SERV. PAGE 61 B1238
WORKER
NAT/G
ADMIN
RACE/REL
B67

NORTHRUP H.R.,RESTRICTIVE LABOR PRACTICES IN THE
SUPERMARKET INDUSTRY. USA+45 INDUS WORKER TEC/DEV
BARGAIN PAY CONTROL GP/REL COST...STAT CHARTS NLRB.
PAGE 79 B1592
DIST/IND
MARKET
LABOR
MGT
B67

SCHLOSSBERG S.I.,ORGANIZING AND THE LAW. USA+45
WORKER PLAN LEGIT REPRESENT GP/REL...JURID MGT 20
NLRB. PAGE 94 B1893
LABOR
CONSULT
BARGAIN
PRIVIL
B67

US SENATE COMM ON FOREIGN REL,HUMAN RIGHTS
CONVENTIONS. USA+45 LABOR VOL/ASSN DELIB/GP DOMIN
ADJUD REPRESENT...INT/LAW MGT CONGRESS. PAGE 110
B2225
LEGIS
ORD/FREE
WORKER
LOBBY
L67

GAINES J.E.,"THE YOUTH COURT CONCEPT AND ITS
IMPLEMENTATION IN TOMPKINS COUNTY, NEW YORK."
USA+45 LAW CONSTN JUDGE WORKER ADJUD ADMIN CHOOSE
PERSON...JURID NEW/YORK. PAGE 38 B0772
CT/SYS
AGE/Y
INGP/REL
CRIME
S67

BASTID M.,"ORIGINES ET DEVELOPMENT DE LA REVOLUTION
CULTURELLE." CHINA/COM DOMIN ADMIN CONTROL LEAD
COERCE CROWD ATTIT DRIVE MARXISM...POLICY 20.
PAGE 10 B0195
REV
CULTURE
ACADEM
WORKER
S67

BERRODIN E.F.,"AT THE BARGAINING TABLE." LABOR
DIPLOM ECO/TAC ADMIN...MGT 20 MICHIGAN. PAGE 11
B0230
PROVS
WORKER
LAW
BARGAIN
S67

CARIAS B.,"EL CONTROL DE LAS EMPRESAS PUBLICAS POR
GRUPOS DE INTERESES DE LA COMUNIDAD." FRANCE UK
VENEZUELA INDUS NAT/G CONTROL OWN PWR...DECISION
NAT/COMP 20. PAGE 18 B0377
WORKER
REPRESENT
MGT
SOCISM
S67

GRINYER P.H.,"THE SYSTEMATIC EVALUATION OF METHODS
OF WAGE PAYMENT." UK INDUS WORKER ADMIN EFFICIENCY
...MGT METH/COMP 20. PAGE 44 B0882
OP/RES
COST
PAY
PRODUC
S67

HALL B.,"THE COALITION AGAINST DISHWASHERS." USA+45
POL/PAR PROB/SOLV BARGAIN LEAD CHOOSE REPRESENT
GP/REL ORD/FREE PWR...POLICY 20. PAGE 46 B0923
LABOR
ADMIN
DOMIN
WORKER
S67

HUDDLESTON J.,"TRADE UNIONS IN THE GERMAN FEDERAL
REPUBLIC." EUR+WWI GERMANY/W UK LAW INDUS WORKER
CREATE CENTRAL...MGT GP/COMP 20. PAGE 52 B1056
LABOR
GP/REL
SCHOOL
ROLE
S67

JENCKS C.E.,"SOCIAL STATUS OF COAL MINERS IN
BRITAIN SINCE NATIONALISATION." UK STRATA STRUCT
LABOR RECEIVE GP/REL INCOME OWN ATTIT HABITAT...MGT
T 20. PAGE 56 B1128
EXTR/IND
WORKER
CONTROL
NAT/G
S67

KURON J.,"AN OPEN LETTER TO THE PARTY." CONSTN
WORKER BUDGET EDU/PROP ADMIN REPRESENT SUFF OWN
...SOCIALIST 20. PAGE 62 B1244
ELITES
STRUCT
POL/PAR
ECO/TAC
S67

LANDES W.M.,"THE EFFECT OF STATE FAIR EMPLOYMENT
LAWS ON THE ECONOMIC POSITION OF NONWHITES." USA+45
PROVS SECT LEGIS ADMIN GP/REL RACE/REL...JURID
CONCPT CHARTS HYPO/EXP NEGRO. PAGE 62 B1255
DISCRIM
LAW
WORKER
S67

LERNER A.P.,"EMPLOYMENT THEORY AND EMPLOYMENT
POLICY." ECO/DEV INDUS LABOR LG/CO BUDGET ADMIN
DEMAND PROFIT WEALTH LAISSEZ METH/COMP. PAGE 64
B1296
CAP/ISM
WORKER
CONCPT
S67

LEVCIK B.,"WAGES AND EMPLOYMENT PROBLEMS IN THE NEW
SYSTEM OF PLANNED MANAGEMENT IN CZECHOSLOVAKIA."
CZECHOSLVK EUR+WWI NAT/G OP/RES PLAN ADMIN ROUTINE
INGP/REL CENTRAL EFFICIENCY PRODUC DECISION.
PAGE 64 B1300
MARXISM
WORKER
MGT
PAY
S67

MORTON J.A.,"A SYSTEMS APPROACH TO THE INNOVATION
PROCESS: ITS USE IN THE BELL SYSTEM." USA+45 INTELL
INDUS LG/CO CONSULT WORKER COMPUTER AUTOMAT DEMAND
...MGT CHARTS 20. PAGE 76 B1531
TEC/DEV
GEN/METH
R+D
COM/IND
S67

O'DELL J.H.,"THE JULY REBELLIONS AND THE 'MILITARY
STATE'." USA+45 VIETNAM STRATA CHIEF WORKER
COLONIAL EXEC CROWD CIVMIL/REL RACE/REL TOTALISM
PWR
NAT/G
COERCE

...WELF/ST PACIFIST 20 NEGRO JOHNSON/LB PRESIDENT   FORCES
CIV/RIGHTS. PAGE 79 B1599
                                                        S67
ROSENBERG B.,"ETHNIC LIBERALISM AND EMPLOYMENT   RACE/REL
DISCRIMINATION IN THE NORTH." USA+45 TOP/EX   ATTIT
PROB/SOLV ADMIN REGION PERS/REL DISCRIM...INT   WORKER
IDEA/COMP. PAGE 90 B1820   EXEC
                                                        S67
SCOTT W.R.,"ORGANIZATIONAL EVALUATION AND   EXEC
AUTHORITY." CONTROL SANCTION PERS/REL ATTIT DRIVE   WORKER
...SOC CONCPT OBS CHARTS IDEA/COMP 20. PAGE 95   INSPECT
B1921   EX/STRUC
                                                        N67
PRINCETON U INDUSTRIAL REL SEC,OUTSTANDING BOOKS ON   BIBLIOG/A
INDUSTRIAL RELATIONS, 1966 (PAMPHLET NO. 134).   INDUS
WOR+45 LABOR WORKER PLAN PRICE CONTROL INCOME...MGT   GP/REL
20. PAGE 85 B1711   POLICY
                                                        S68
GUZZARDI W. JR.,"THE SECOND BATTLE OF BRITAIN." UK   FINAN
STRATA LABOR WORKER CREATE PROB/SOLV EDU/PROP ADMIN   ECO/TAC
LEAD LOBBY...MGT SOC 20 GOLD/STAND. PAGE 45 B0907   ECO/DEV
                                                      STRUCT
                                                        B98
THOMPSON H.C.,RHODESIA AND ITS GOVERNMENT. AFR   COLONIAL
RHODESIA ECO/UNDEV INDUS KIN WORKER INT/TRADE   ADMIN
DISCRIM LITERACY ORD/FREE 19. PAGE 104 B2102   POLICY
                                                      ELITES

WORKING....SEE ROUTINE

WORLD COUNCIL OF CHURCHES....SEE WCC

WORLD HEALTH ORGANIZATION....SEE WHO

WORLD WAR I....SEE WWI

WORLD WAR II....SEE WWII

WORLD PEACE FOUNDATION B2374,B2375

WORLD/BANK....WORLD BANK

                                                        L62
BELSHAW D.G.R.,"PUBLIC INVESTMENT IN AGRICULTURE   ECO/UNDEV
AND ECONOMIC DEVELOPMENT OF UGANDA" UGANDA AGRI   PLAN
INDUS R+D ECO/TAC RATION TAX PAY COLONIAL 20   ADMIN
WORLD/BANK. PAGE 10 B0209   CENTRAL
                                                        B67
HIRSCHMAN A.O.,DEVELOPMENT PROJECTS OBSERVED. INDUS   ECO/UNDEV
INT/ORG CONSULT EX/STRUC CREATE OP/RES ECO/TAC   R+D
DEMAND...POLICY MGT METH/COMP 20 WORLD/BANK.   FINAN
PAGE 50 B1016   PLAN

WORLD/CONG....WORLD CONGRESS

WORLD/CT....WORLD COURT; SEE ALSO ICJ

WORLDUNITY....WORLD UNITY, WORLD FEDERATION (EXCLUDING UN
    AND LEAGUE OF NATIONS)

WORLEY P. B2376

WORSHIP....SEE ALSO SECT

                                                        B24
HOLDSWORTH W.S.,A HISTORY OF ENGLISH LAW; THE   LAW
COMMON LAW AND ITS RIVALS (VOL. V). UK SEA EX/STRUC   LEGIS
WRITING ADMIN...INT/LAW JURID CONCPT IDEA/COMP   ADJUD
WORSHIP 16/17 PARLIAMENT ENGLSH/LAW COMMON/LAW.   CT/SYS
PAGE 51 B1033
                                                        B35
GORER G.,AFRICA DANCES: A BOOK ABOUT WEST AFRICAN   AFR
NEGROES. STRUCT LOC/G SECT FORCES TAX ADMIN   ATTIT
COLONIAL...ART/METH MYTH WORSHIP 20 NEGRO AFRICA/W   CULTURE
CHRISTIAN RITUAL. PAGE 41 B0835   SOCIETY
                                                        B62
SAMPSON A.,ANATOMY OF BRITAIN. UK LAW COM/IND FINAN   ELITES
INDUS MARKET MUNIC POL/PAR EX/STRUC TOP/EX DIPLOM   PWR
LEAD REPRESENT PERSON PARLIAMENT WORSHIP. PAGE 92   STRUCT
B1866   FORCES
                                                        B64
FORBES A.H.,CURRENT RESEARCH IN BRITISH STUDIES. UK   BIBLIOG
CONSTN CULTURE POL/PAR SECT DIPLOM ADMIN...JURID   PERSON
BIOG WORSHIP 20. PAGE 36 B0736   NAT/G
                                                      PARL/PROC
                                                        B64
HICKEY G.C.,VILLAGE IN VIETNAM. USA+45 VIETNAM LAW   CULTURE
AGRI FAM SECT ADMIN ATTIT...SOC CHARTS WORSHIP 20.   SOCIETY
PAGE 49 B1003   STRUCT
                                                      S/ASIA
                                                        B65
BERNDT R.M.,ABORIGINAL MAN IN AUSTRALIA. LAW DOMIN   SOC
ADMIN COLONIAL MARRIAGE HABITAT ORD/FREE...LING   CULTURE
CHARTS ANTHOL BIBLIOG WORSHIP 20 AUSTRAL ABORIGINES   SOCIETY
MUSIC ELKIN/AP. PAGE 11 B0225   STRUCT

                                                        B67
ANGEL D.D.,ROMNEY. LABOR LG/CO NAT/G EXEC WAR   BIOG
RACE/REL PERSON ORD/FREE...MGT WORSHIP 20   CHIEF
ROMNEY/GEO CIV/RIGHTS MORMON GOVERNOR. PAGE 5 B0108   PROVS
                                                      POLICY
                                                        B67
DUN J.L.,THE ESSENCE OF CHINESE CIVILIZATION. ASIA   CULTURE
FAM NAT/G TEC/DEV ADMIN SANCTION WAR HABITAT   SOCIETY
...ANTHOL WORSHIP. PAGE 31 B0630
                                                        B82
MACDONALD D.,AFRICANA; OR, THE HEART OF HEATHEN   SECT
AFRICA, VOL. II: MISSION LIFE. SOCIETY STRATA KIN   AFR
CREATE EDU/PROP ADMIN COERCE LITERACY HEALTH...MYTH   CULTURE
WORSHIP 19 LIVNGSTN/D MISSION NEGRO. PAGE 67 B1355   ORD/FREE

WPA....WORK PROJECTS ADMINISTRATION

                                                        B41
MACMAHON A.W.,THE ADMINISTRATION OF FEDERAL WORK   ADMIN
RELIEF. USA+45 EX/STRUC WORKER BUDGET EFFICIENCY   NAT/G
...CONT/OBS CHARTS 20 WPA. PAGE 68 B1367   MGT
                                                      GIVE

WRAITH R. B2377

WRIGHT D.M. B2378

WRIGHT D.S. B2379

WRIGHT F.K. B2380

WRIGHT H.R. B2381

WRIGHT J.H. B2382

WRIGHT Q. B2383,B2384,B2385

WRITING....SEE ALSO HIST/WRIT

                                                        N
WHITAKER'S CUMULATIVE BOOKLIST. UK ADMIN...HUM SOC   BIBLIOG/A
20. PAGE 1 B0009   WRITING
                                                      CON/ANAL
                                                        N
READERS GUIDE TO PERIODICAL LITERATURE. WOR+45   BIBLIOG
WOR-45 LAW ADMIN ATTIT PERSON...HUM PSY SOC 20.   WRITING
PAGE 1 B0021   DIPLOM
                                                      NAT/G
                                                        N
SUBJECT GUIDE TO BOOKS IN PRINT: AN INDEX TO THE   BIBLIOG
PUBLISHERS' TRADE LIST ANNUAL. UNIV LAW LOC/G   ECO/DEV
DIPLOM WRITING ADMIN LEAD PERSON...MGT SOC. PAGE 1   POL/PAR
B0023   NAT/G
                                                        N
ECONOMIC LIBRARY SELECTIONS. AGRI INDUS MARKET   BIBLIOG/A
ADMIN...STAT NAT/COMP 20. PAGE 2 B0026   WRITING
                                                      FINAN
                                                        N
DEUTSCHE BUCHEREI,JAHRESVERZEICHNIS DER DEUTSCHEN   BIBLIOG
HOCHSCHULSCHRIFTEN. EUR+WWI GERMANY LAW ADMIN   WRITING
PERSON...MGT SOC 19/20. PAGE 28 B0579   ACADEM
                                                      INTELL
                                                        N
DEUTSCHE BUCHEREI,JAHRESVERZEICHNIS DES DEUTSCHEN   BIBLIOG
SCHRIFTUMS. AUSTRIA EUR+WWI GERMANY SWITZERLND LAW   WRITING
LOC/G DIPLOM ADMIN...MGT SOC 19/20. PAGE 29 B0580   NAT/G
                                                        N
UNITED NATIONS,OFFICIAL RECORDS OF THE UNITED   INT/ORG
NATIONS' GENERAL ASSEMBLY. WOR+45 BUDGET DIPLOM   DELIB/GP
ADMIN 20 UN. PAGE 107 B2159   INT/LAW
                                                      WRITING
                                                        N
UNIVERSITY MICROFILMS INC,DISSERTATION ABSTRACTS: BIBLIOG/A
ABSTRACTS OF DISSERTATIONS AND MONOGRAPHS IN   ACADEM
MICROFILM. CANADA DIPLOM ADMIN...INDEX 20. PAGE 107   PRESS
B2166   WRITING
                                                        N19
PERREN G.E.,LANGUAGE AND COMMUNICATION IN THE   EDU/PROP
COMMONWEALTH (PAMPHLET). FUT UK LAW ECO/DEV PRESS   LING
TV WRITING ADJUD ADMIN COLONIAL CONTROL 20   GOV/REL
CMN/WLTH. PAGE 82 B1660   COM/IND
                                                        N19
WALL N.L.,MUNICIPAL REPORTING TO THE PUBLIC   METH
(PAMPHLET). LOC/G PLAN WRITING ADMIN REPRESENT   MUNIC
EFFICIENCY...AUD/VIS CHARTS 20. PAGE 113 B2282   GP/REL
                                                      COM/IND
                                                        B24
HOLDSWORTH W.S.,A HISTORY OF ENGLISH LAW; THE   LAW
COMMON LAW AND ITS RIVALS (VOL. V). UK SEA EX/STRUC   LEGIS
WRITING ADMIN...INT/LAW JURID CONCPT IDEA/COMP   ADJUD
WORSHIP 16/17 PARLIAMENT ENGLSH/LAW COMMON/LAW.   CT/SYS
PAGE 51 B1033
                                                        B40
BURT F.A.,AMERICAN ADVERTISING AGENCIES. BARGAIN   LG/CO
BUDGET LICENSE WRITING PRICE PERS/REL COST DEMAND   COM/IND
...ORG/CHARTS BIBLIOG 20. PAGE 18 B0358   ADMIN

LEGISLATIVE REFERENCE SERVICE.PROBLEMS OF
LEGISLATIVE APPORTIONMENT ON BOTH FEDERAL AND STATE
LEVELS: SELECTED REFERENCES (PAMPHLET). USA+45
USA-45 LOC/G NAT/G LEGIS WRITING ADMIN APPORT 20
CONGRESS. PAGE 63 B1282
EFFICIENCY
B52
BIBLIOG
REPRESENT
CHOOSE
PROVS

UNESCO.THESES DE SCIENCES SOCIALES: CATALOGUE
ANALYTIQUE INTERNATIONAL DE THESES INEDITES DE
DOCTORAT. 1940-1950. INT/ORG DIPLOM EDU/PROP...GEOG
INT/LAW MGT PSY SOC 20. PAGE 107 B2155
B52
BIBLIOG
ACADEM
WRITING

LARSEN K..NATIONAL BIBLIOGRAPHIC SERVICES: THEIR
CREATION AND OPERATION. WOR+45 COM/IND CREATE PLAN
DIPLOM PRESS ADMIN ROUTINE...MGT UNESCO. PAGE 62
B1262
B53
BIBLIOG/A
INT/ORG
WRITING

PULLEN W.R..A CHECK LIST OF LEGISLATIVE JOURNALS
ISSUED SINCE 1937 BY THE STATES OF THE UNITED
STATES OF AMERICA (PAMPHLET). USA+45 USA-45 LAW
WRITING ADJUD ADMIN...JURID 20. PAGE 85 B1720
B55
BIBLIOG
PROVS
EDU/PROP
LEGIS

CENTRAL AFRICAN ARCHIVES.A GUIDE TO THE PUBLIC
RECORDS OF SOUTHERN RHODESIA UNDER THE REGIME OF
THE BRITISH SOUTH AFRICA COMPANY, 1890-1923. UK
STRUC NAT/G WRITING GP/REL 19/20. PAGE 19 B0398
B56
BIBLIOG/A
COLONIAL
ADMIN
AFR

FESLER J.W.."ADMINISTRATIVE LITERATURE AND THE
SECOND HOOVER COMMISSION REPORTS" (BMR)" USA+45
EX/STRUC LEGIS WRITING...DECISION METH 20. PAGE 35
B0713
S57
ADMIN
NAT/G
OP/RES
DELIB/GP

REDFIELD C.E..COMMUNICATION IN MANAGEMENT. DELIB/GP
EX/STRUC WRITING LEAD PERS/REL...PSY INT METH 20.
PAGE 87 B1750
B58
COM/IND
MGT
LG/CO
ADMIN

BHAMBHRI C.P..SUBSTANCE OF HINDU POLITY. INDIA
S/ASIA LAW EX/STRUC JUDGE TAX COERCE GP/REL
POPULISM 20 HINDU. PAGE 11 B0234
B59
GOV/REL
WRITING
SECT
PROVS

ARCO EDITORIAL BOARD.PUBLIC MANAGEMENT AND
ADMINISTRATION. PLAN BUDGET WRITING CONTROL ROUTINE
...TESTS CHARTS METH T 20. PAGE 6 B0125
B62
MGT
ADMIN
NAT/G
LOC/G

PRESS C..STATE MANUALS. BLUE BOOKS AND ELECTION
RESULTS. LAW LOC/G MUNIC LEGIS WRITING FEDERAL
SOVEREIGN...DECISION STAT CHARTS 20. PAGE 84 B1700
B62
BIBLIOG
PROVS
ADMIN
CHOOSE

AMERICAN ECONOMIC ASSOCIATION.INDEX OF ECONOMIC
JOURNALS 1886-1965 (7 VOLS.). UK USA+45 USA-45 AGRI
FINAN PLAN ECO/TAC INT/TRADE ADMIN...STAT CENSUS
19/20. PAGE 4 B0083
B65
BIBLIOG
WRITING
INDUS

UNITED NATIONS.UNITED NATIONS PUBLICATIONS:
1945-1966. WOR+45 COM/IND DIST/IND FINAN TEC/DEV
ADMIN...POLICY INT/LAW MGT CHARTS 20 UN UNESCO.
PAGE 107 B2162
B67
BIBLIOG/A
INT/ORG
DIPLOM
WRITING

WU F. B2386

WWI....WORLD WAR I

GIFFORD P..BRITAIN AND GERMANY IN AFRICA. AFR
GERMANY UK ECO/UNDEV LEAD WAR NAT/LISM ATTIT
...POLICY HIST/WRIT METH/COMP ANTHOL BIBLIOG 19/20
WWI. PAGE 39 B0797
B67
COLONIAL
ADMIN
DIPLOM
NAT/COMP

KRISLOV S..THE NEGRO IN FEDERAL EMPLOYMENT. LAW
STRATA LOC/G CREATE PROB/SOLV INSPECT GOV/REL
DISCRIM ROLE...DECISION INT TREND 20 NEGRO WWI
CIVIL/SERV. PAGE 61 B1238
B67
WORKER
NAT/G
ADMIN
RACE/REL

WWII....WORLD WAR II

WYLIE C.M. B2387

WYOMING....WYOMING

RICHARD J.B..GOVERNMENT AND POLITICS OF WYOMING.
USA+45 POL/PAR EX/STRUC LEGIS CT/SYS LOBBY APPORT
CHOOSE REPRESENT 20 WYOMING GOVERNOR. PAGE 88 B1773
B66
PROVS
LOC/G
ADMIN

X

XENOPHOBIA....SEE NAT/LISM

XENOPHON....XENOPHON

XHOSA....XHOSA TRIBE (SOUTH AFRICA)

RAUM O.."THE MODERN LEADERSHIP GROUP AMONG THE
SOUTH AFRICAN XHOSA." SOUTH/AFR SOCIETY SECT
EX/STRUC REPRESENT GP/REL INGP/REL PERSON
...METH/COMP 17/20 XHOSA NEGRO. PAGE 86 B1743
S67
RACE/REL
KIN
LEAD
CULTURE

Y

YALE UNIV BUR OF HIGHWAY TRAF B2388

YALE/U....YALE UNIVERSITY

YALTA....YALTA CONFERENCE

YANG C.K. B2389

YANKEE/C....YANKEE CITY - LOCATION OF W.L. WARNER'S STUDY
OF SAME NAME

WARNER W.L..THE SOCIAL SYSTEM OF THE MODERN
FACTORY; THE STRIKE: AN ANALYSIS. USA-45 STRATA
WORKER ECO/TAC GP/REL INGP/REL...MGT SOC CHARTS 20
YANKEE/C. PAGE 114 B2293
B47
ROLE
STRUCT
LABOR
PROC/MFG

YARBROGH/R....RALPH YARBOROUGH

US SENATE COMM ON POST OFFICE.TO PROVIDE FOR AN
EFFECTIVE SYSTEM OF PERSONNEL ADMINISTRATION.
EFFICIENCY...MGT 20 CONGRESS CIVIL/SERV POSTAL/SYS
YARBROGH/R. PAGE 111 B2233
B59
ADMIN
NAT/G
EX/STRUC
LAW

YATES M. B2390

YAZOO....YAZOO LAND SCANDAL

YEMEN....SEE ALSO ISLAM

YORUBA....YORUBA TRIBE

YOUNG C. B2391

YOUNG G. B2392

YOUNG R. B2393

YOUNG S. B2394

YOUNG W. B2395

YOUNG/TURK....YOUNG TURK POLITICAL PARTY

YOUTH....SEE AGE/Y

YUDELMAN/M....MONTEGU YUDELMAN

YUGOSLAVIA....YUGOSLAVIA; SEE ALSO COM

ULAM A.B..TITOISM AND THE COMINFORM. USSR WOR+45
STRUC INT/ORG NAT/G ACT/RES PLAN EXEC ATTIT DRIVE
ALL/VALS...CONCPT OBS VAL/FREE 20 COMINTERN
TITO/MARSH. PAGE 106 B2145
B52
COM
POL/PAR
TOTALISM
YUGOSLAVIA

DJILAS M..THE NEW CLASS: AN ANALYSIS OF THE
COMMUNIST SYSTEM. STRATA CAP/ISM ECO/TAC DOMIN
EDU/PROP LEGIT EXEC COERCE ATTIT PWR MARXISM
...MARXIST MGT CONCPT TIME/SEQ GEN/LAWS 20. PAGE 29
B0600
B57
COM
POL/PAR
USSR
YUGOSLAVIA

NEAL F.W..TITOISM IN ACTION. COM YUGOSLAVIA AGRI
LOC/G DIPLOM TOTALISM...BIBLIOG 20 TITO/MARSH.
PAGE 77 B1564
B58
MARXISM
POL/PAR
CHIEF
ADMIN

HORVATH B..THE CHARACTERISTICS OF YUGOSLAV ECONOMIC
DEVELOPMENT. COM ECO/UNDEV AGRI INDUS PLAN CAP/ISM
ECO/TAC ROUTINE WEALTH...SOCIALIST STAT CHARTS
STERTYP WORK 20. PAGE 52 B1045
B61
ACT/RES
YUGOSLAVIA

INTERNATIONAL LABOR OFFICE.WORKERS' MANAGEMENT IN
YUGOSLAVIA. COM YUGOSLAVIA LABOR DELIB/GP EX/STRUC
PROB/SOLV ADMIN PWR MARXISM...CHARTS ORG/CHARTS
BIBLIOG 20. PAGE 54 B1098
B62
WORKER
CONTROL
MGT
INDUS

DUROSELLE J.B..POLITIQUES NATIONALES ENVERS LES
JEUNES ETATS. FRANCE ISRAEL ITALY UK USA+45 USSR
YUGOSLAVIA ECO/DEV FINAN ECO/TAC INT/TRADE ADMIN
PWR 20. PAGE 31 B0634
B64
DIPLOM
ECO/UNDEV
COLONIAL
DOMIN

GJUPANOVIC H..LEGAL SOURCES AND BIBLIOGRAPHY OF
YUGOSLAVIA. COM YUGOSLAVIA LAW LEGIS DIPLOM ADMIN
PARL/PROC REGION CRIME CENTRAL 20. PAGE 40 B0807
B64
BIBLIOG/A
JURID
CONSTN
ADJUD

HORECKY P.L.."LIBRARY OF CONGRESS PUBLICATIONS IN
AID OF USSR AND EAST EUROPEAN RESEARCH." BULGARIA
S64
BIBLIOG/A
COM

CZECHOSLVK POLAND USSR YUGOSLAVIA NAT/G POL/PAR   MARXISM
DIPLOM ADMIN GOV/REL...CLASSIF 20. PAGE 51 B1042

               B65
ORG FOR ECO COOP AND DEVEL,THE MEDITERRANEAN   PLAN
REGIONAL PROJECT: AN EXPERIMENT IN PLANNING BY SIX ECO/UNDEV
COUNTRIES. FUT GREECE SPAIN TURKEY YUGOSLAVIA   ACADEM
SOCIETY FINAN NAT/G PROF/ORG EDU/PROP ADMIN REGION SCHOOL
COST...POLICY STAT CHARTS 20 OECD. PAGE 80 B1614

               B65
ORG FOR ECO COOP AND DEVEL,THE MEDITERRANEAN   EDU/PROP
REGIONAL PROJECT: YUGOSLAVIA; EDUCATION AND   ACADEM
DEVELOPMENT. YUGOSLAVIA SOCIETY FINAN PROF/ORG PLAN SCHOOL
ADMIN COST DEMAND MARXISM...STAT TREND CHARTS METH ECO/UNDEV
20 OECD. PAGE 80 B1615

               S65
RUBINSTEIN A.Z.,"YUGOSLAVIA'S OPENING SOCIETY." COM CONSTN
USSR INTELL NAT/G LEGIS TOP/EX LEGIT CT/SYS   EX/STRUC
RIGID/FLEX ALL/VALS SOCISM...HUM TIME/SEQ TREND 20. YUGOSLAVIA
PAGE 92 B1851

               B67
GROSSMAN G.,ECONOMIC SYSTEMS. USA+45 USA-45 USSR   ECO/DEV
YUGOSLAVIA WORKER CAP/ISM PRICE GP/REL EQUILIB   PLAN
WEALTH MARXISM SOCISM...MGT METH/COMP 19/20.   TEC/DEV
PAGE 44 B0892   DEMAND

YUKON....YUKON, CANADA

———————————————Z———————————————

ZABEL O.H. B2396

ZALESKI E. B1501,B1502

ZALEZNIK A. B1027,B2397

ZALKIND S.S. B0488

ZAMBIA....SEE ALSO AFR

               B66
KAUNDA K.,ZAMBIA: INDEPENDENCE AND BEYOND: THE   ORD/FREE
SPEECHES OF KENNETH KAUNDA. AFR FUT ZAMBIA SOCIETY COLONIAL
ECO/UNDEV NAT/G PROB/SOLV ECO/TAC ADMIN RACE/REL   CONSTN
SOVEREIGN 20. PAGE 59 B1183   LEAD

ZANDE....ZANDE, AFRICA

ZANZIBAR....SEE TANZANIA

ZASLOW M. B2398

ZAUBERMAN A. B2399

ZELDITCH M.,. B0687

ZELERMYER W. B2400

ZELLER B. B2401

ZIMMERN A. B2402

ZINK H. B2403

ZINKIN T. B2404

ZIONISM....SEE ISRAEL, NAT/LISM

ZLATOVRT/N....NIKOLAI ZLATOVRATSKII

ZOETEWEIJ B. B2405

ZONDAG C.H. B2406

ZONING....ZONING REGULATIONS

ZUCKERT E.M. B2407

ZUGOW A. B0236

ZULU....ZULU - MEMBER OF BANTU NATION (SOUTHEAST AFRICA)

ZUNI....ZUNI - NEW MEXICAN INDIAN TRIBE

ZWINGLI/U....ULRICH ZWINGLI

Directory of Publishers

Abelard-Schuman Ltd., New York
Abeledo-Perrot, Buenos Aires
Abingdon Press, Nashville, Tenn.; New York
Academic Press, London; New York
Academy of the Rumanian People's Republic Scientific
  Documentation Center, Bucharest
Academy Publishers, New York
Accra Government Printer, Accra, Ghana
Acharya Book Depot, Baroda, India
Acorn Press, Phoenix, Ariz.
Action Housing, Inc., Pittsburgh, Pa.
Adams & Charles Black, London
Addison-Wesley Publishing Co., Inc., Reading, Mass.
Adelphi, Greenberg, New York
Adelphi Terrace, London
Advertising Research Foundation, New York
Advisory Committee on Intergovernmental Relations,
  Washington
Africa Bureau, London
Africa 1960 Committee, London
African Bibliographical Center, Inc., Washington
African Research Ltd., Exeter, England
Agarwal Press, Allahabad, India
Agathon Press, New York
Agency for International Development, Washington
Agrupacion Bibliotecalogica, Montevideo
Aguilar, S. A. de Ediciones, Madrid
Air University, Montgomery, Ala.
Akademiai Kiado, Budapest
Akademische Druck-und Verlagsanstalt, Graz, Austria
Akhil Bharat Sarva Seva Sangh, Rajghat, Varanasi, India;
  Rajghat, Kashi, India
Al Jadidah Press, Cairo
Alba House, New York
Eberhard Albert Verlag, Freiburg, Germany
Alcan, Paris
Aldine Publishing Co., Chicago
Aligarh Muslim University, Department of History,
  Aligarh, India
All-India Congress Committee, New Delhi
Allen and Unwin, Ltd., London
Howard Allen, Inc., Cleveland, Ohio
W. H. Allen & Co., Ltd., London
Alliance Inc., New York
Allied Publishers, Private, Ltd., Bombay; New Delhi
Allyn and Bacon, Inc., Boston
Almquist-Wiksell, Stockholm; Upsala
Ambassador Books, Ltd., Toronto, Ontario
American Academy of Arts and Sciences, Harvard University,
  Cambridge, Mass.
American Academy of Political and Social Science,
  Philadelphia
American Anthropological Association, Washington, D. C.
American Arbitration Association, New York
American-Asian Educational Exchange, New York
American Assembly, New York
American Association for the Advancement of Science,
  Washington, D. C.
American Association for the United Nations, New York
American Association of University Women, Washington, D. C.
American Bankers Association, New York
American Bar Association, Chicago
American Bar Foundation, Chicago
American Bibliographical Center-Clio Press, Santa Barbara,
  Calif.
American Bibliographic Service, Darien, Conn.
American Book Company, New York
American Civil Liberties Union, New York
American Council of Learned Societies, New York
American Council on Education, Washington
American Council on Public Affairs, Washington
American Data Processing, Inc., Detroit, Mich.
American Documentation Institute, Washington
American Economic Association, Evanston, Ill.
American Elsevier Publishing Co., Inc., New York
American Enterprise Institute for Public Policy Research,
  Washington, D. C.
American Features, New York
American Federation of Labor & Congress of Industrial
  Organizations, Washington, D. C.

American Foreign Law Association, Chicago
American Forest Products Industries, Washington, D. C.
American Friends of Vietnam, New York
American Friends Service Committee, New York
American Historical Association, Washington, D. C.
American Historical Society, New York
American Institute for Economic Research, Great Barrington,
  Mass.
American Institute of Consulting Engineers, New York
American Institute of Pacific Relations, New York
American International College, Springfield, Mass.
American Jewish Archives, Hebrew Union College—Jewish
  Institute of Religion, Cincinnati, Ohio
American Jewish Committee Institute of Human Relations,
  New York
American Judicature Society, Chicago
American Law Institute, Philadelphia
American Library Association, Chicago
American Management Association, New York
American Marketing Association, Inc., Chicago
American Municipal Association, Washington
American Museum of Natural History Press, New York
American Nepal Education Foundation, Eugene, Oregon
American Newspaper Publishers' Association, New York
American Opinion, Belmont, Mass.
American Philosophical Society, Philadelphia
American Political Science Association, Washington
American Psychiatric Association, New York
American Public Welfare Association, Chicago
American Research Council, Larchmont, N. Y.
American Society of African Culture, New York
American Society of International Law, Chicago
American Society for Public Administration, Chicago;
  Washington
American Textbook Publishers Council, New York
American Universities Field Staff, New York
American University, Washington, D. C.
American University of Beirut, Beirut
American University of Cairo, Cairo
American University Press, Washington
American University Press Services, Inc., New York
Ampersand Press, Inc., London, New York
Amsterdam Stock Exchange, Amsterdam
Anchor Books, New York
Anderson Kramer Association, Washington, D. C.
Anglo-Israel Association, London
Angus and Robertson, Sydney, Australia
Ann Arbor Publications, Ann Arbor, Mich.
Anthropological Publications, Oosterhout, Netherlands
Anti-Defamation League of B'nai B'rith, New York
Antioch Press, Yellow Springs, Ohio
Antwerp Institut Universitaire des Territoires d'Outre-Mer,
  Antwerp, Belgium
APEC Editora, Rio de Janeiro
Apollo Editions, New York
Ludwig Appel Verlag, Hamburg
Appleton-Century-Crofts, New York
Aqueduct Books, Rochester, N. Y.
Arbeitsgemeinschaft fur Forschung des Landes
  Nordrhein-Westfalen, Dusseldorf, Germany
Arcadia, New York
Architectural Press, London
Archon Books, Hamden, Conn.
Arco Publishing Company, New York
Arizona Department of Library and Archives, Tucson
Arizona State University, Bureau of Government Research,
  Tucson
Arlington House, New Rochelle, N. Y.
Arnold Foundation, Southern Methodist University, Dallas
Edward Arnold Publishers, Ltd., London
J. W. Arrowsmith, Ltd., London
Artes Graficas, Buenos Aires
Artes Graficas Industrias Reunidas SA, Rio de Janeiro
Asia Foundation, San Francisco
Asia Publishing House, Bombay; Calcutta; London; New York
Asia Society, New York
Asian Studies Center, Michigan State University, East Lan-
  sing, Mich.
Asian Studies Press, Bombay
Associated College Presses, New York

Associated Lawyers Publishing Co., Newark, N. J.
Association for Asian Studies, Ann Arbor
Association of National Advertisers, New York
Association of the Bar of the City of New York, New York
Association Press, New York
Associated University Bureaus of Business and Economic Research, Eugene, Ore.
M. L. Atallah, Rotterdam
Atheneum Publishers, New York
Atherton Press, New York
Athlone Press, London
Atlanta University Press, Atlanta, Ga.
The Atlantic Institute, Boulogne-sur-Seine
Atlantic Provinces Research Board, Fredericton, Newfoundland
Atma Ram & Sons, New Delhi
Atomic Industrial Forum, New York
Augustan Reprint Society, Los Angeles, Calif.
Augustana College Library, Rock Island, Ill.
Augustana Press, Rock Island, Ill.
J. J. Augustin, New York
Augustinus Verlag, Wurzburg
Australian National Research Council. Melbourne
Australian National University, Canberra
Australian Public Affairs Information Service, Sydney
Australian War Memorial, Canberra
Avi Publishing Co., Westport, Conn.
Avtoreferaty Dissertatsii, Moscow
N. W. Ayer and Sons, Inc., Philadelphia, Pa.
Aymon, Paris

La Baconniere, Neuchatel; Paris
Richard G. Badger, Boston
Baker Book House, Grand Rapids, Mich.
Baker, Vorhis, and Co., Boston
John Baker, London
A. A. Balkema, Capetown
Ballantine Books, Inc., New York
James Ballantine and Co., London
Baltimore Sun, Baltimore, Md.
Banco Central de Venezuela, Caracas
Bank for International Settlements, Basel
Bank of Finland Institute for Economic Research, Helsinki
Bank of Italy, Rome
Bankers Publishing Co., Boston
George Banta Publishing Co., Menasha, Wis.
Bantam Books, Inc., New York
A. S. Barnes and Co., Inc., Cranbury, N. J.
Barnes and Noble, Inc., New York
Barre Publishers, Barre, Mass.
Basic Books, Inc., New York
Batchworth Press Ltd., London
Bayerische Akademie der Wissenschaften, Munich
Bayerischer Schulbuch Verlag, Munich
Ebenezer Baylis and Son, Ltd., Worcester, England
Baylor University Press, Waco, Texas
Beacon Press, Boston
Bechte Verlag, Esslingen, Germany
H. Beck, Dresden
Bedminster Press, Inc., Totowa, N. J.
Beechhurst Press, New York
Behavioral Research Council, Great Barrington, Mass.
Belknap Press, Cambridge, Mass.
G. Bell & Sons, London
Bellman Publishing Co., Inc., Cambridge, Mass.
Matthew Bender and Co., Albany, New York
Bengal Publishers, Ltd., Calcutta
Marshall Benick, New York
Ernest Benn, Ltd., London
J. Bensheimer, Berlin; Leipzig; Mannheim
Benziger Brothers, New York
Berkley Publishing Corporation, New York
Bernard und Graefe Verlag fur Wehrwesen, Frankfurt
C. Bertelsmann Verlag, Gutersloh
Bharati Bhawan, Bankipore, India
Bharatiyi Vidya Bhavan, Bombay
G. R. Bhatkal for Popular Prakashan, Bombay
Bibliographical Society, London
Bibliographical Society of America, New York
Bibliographie des Staats, Dresden
Biblioteca de la II feria del libro exposicion nacional del periodismo, Panuco, Mexico
Biblioteca Nacional, Bogota

Biblioteka Imeni V. I. Lenina, Moscow
Bibliotheque des Temps Nouveaux, Paris
Bibliotheque Nationale, Paris
Adams & Charles Black, London
Basil Blackwell, Oxford
William Blackwood, Edinburgh
Blaisdell Publishing Co., Inc., Waltham, Mass.
Blanford Press, London
Blass, S. A., Madrid
Geoffrey Bles, London
BNA, Inc. (Bureau of National Affairs), Washington, D. C.
Board of Trade and Industry Estates Management Corp., London
T. V. Boardman and Co., London
Bobbs-Merrill Company, Inc., Indianapolis, Ind.
The Bodley Head, London
Bogen-Verlag, Munich
Bohlau-Verlag, Cologne; Graz; Tubingen
H. G. Bohn, London
Boni and Gaer, New York
Bonn University, Bonn
The Book of the Month Club, Johannesburg
Bookcraft, Inc., Salt Lake City, Utah
Bookfield House, New York
Bookland Private, Ltd., Calcutta; London
Bookmailer, New York
Bookman Associates, Record Press, New York
Books for Libraries, Inc., Freeport, N. Y.
Books International, Jullundur City, India
Borsenverein der deutschen Buchhandler, Leipzig
Bossange, Paris
Boston Book Co., Boston
Boston College Library, Chestnut Hill, Boston
Boston University, African Research Program, Boston
Boston University Press, Boston
H. Bouvier Verlag, Bonn
Bowes and Bowes, Ltd., Cambridge, England
R. R. Bowker Co., New York
John Bradburn, New York
George Braziller, Inc., New York
Brentano's, New York
Brigham Young University, Provo, Utah
E. J. Brill, Leyden
British Borneo Research Project, London
British Broadcasting Corp., London
British Council, London
British Liberal Party Organization, London
British Museum, London
Broadman Press, Nashville, Tenn.
The Brookings Institution, Washington
Brown University Press, Providence, R. I.
A. Brown and Sons, Ltd., London
William C. Brown Co., Dubuque, Iowa
Brown-White-Lowell Press, Kansas City
Bruce Publishing Co., Milwaukee, Wis.
Buchdruckerei Meier, Bulach, Germany
Buchhandler-Vereinigung, Frankfurt
Buijten & Schipperheijn, Amsterdam
Building Contractors Council, Chicago
Bureau of Public Printing, Manila
Bureau of Social Science Research, Washington, D. C.
Business Economists Group, Oxford
Business Publications, Inc., Chicago
Business Service Corp., Detroit, Mich.
Buttenheim Publishing Corp., New York
Butterworth's, London; Washington, D. C.; Toronto

Anne Cabbott, Manchester, England
California, Assembly of the State of, Sacramento, Calif.
California State Library, Sacramento
Calman Levy, Paris
Camara Oficial del Libro, Madrid
Cambridge Book Co., Inc., Bronxville, N. Y.
Cambridge University Press, Cambridge; London; New York
Camelot Press Ltd., London
Campion Press, London
M. Campos, Rio de Janeiro
Canada, Civil Service Commission, Ottawa
Canada, Civil Service Commission, Organization Division, Ottawa
Canada, Ministry of National Health and Welfare, Ottawa
Canada, National Joint Council of the Public Service, Ottawa

Canadian Dept. of Mines and Technical Surveys, Ottawa
Canadian Institute of International Affairs, Toronto
Canadian Peace Research Institute, Clarkson, Ont.
Canadian Trade Committee, Montreal
Candour Publishing Co., London
Jonathan Cape, London
Cape and Smith, New York
Capricorn Books, New York
Caribbean Commission, Port-of-Spain, Trinidad
Carleton University Library, Ottawa
Erich Carlsohn, Leipzig
Carnegie Endowment for International Peace, New York
Carnegie Endowment for International Peace,
    Washington, D. C.
Carnegie Foundation for the Advancement of Teaching,
    New York
Carnegie Press, Pittsburgh, Pa.
Carswell Co., Ltd., Toronto, Canada
Casa de las Americas, Havana
Case Institute of Technology, Cleveland, Ohio
Frank Cass & Co., Ltd., London
Cassell & Co., Ltd., London
Castle Press, Pasadena, Calif.
Catholic Historical Society of Philadelphia, Philadelphia
Catholic Press, Beirut
Catholic Students Mission Crusade Press, Cincinnati, Ohio
Catholic University Press, Washington
The Caxton Printers, Ltd., Caldwell, Idaho
Cedesa. Brussels
Cellar Book Shop, Detroit, Mich.
Center for Applied Research in Education, New York
Center for Applied Research in Education, Washington, D. C.
Center for Research on Economic Development, Ann Arbor,
    Mich.
Center for the Study of Democratic Institutions,
    Santa Barbara, Calif.
Center of Foreign Policy Research, Washington, D. C.
Center of International Studies, Princeton
Center of Planning and Economic Research, Athens, Greece;
    Washington, D. C.
Central Asian Research Centre, London
Central Bank of Egypt, Cairo
Central Book Co., Inc., Brooklyn, N. Y.
Central Book Department, Allahabad, India
Central Law Book Supply, Inc., Manila
Central News Agency, Ltd., Capetown, S. Afr.
Central Publicity Commission, Indian National Congress,
    New Delhi
Centre de Documentation CNRS, Paris
Centre de Documentation Economique et Sociale Africaine,
    Brussels
Centre d'Etudes de Politique Etrangere, Paris
Centre de Recherches sur l'URSS et les pays de l'est,
    Strasbourg
Centro de Estudios Monetarios Latino-Americanos,
    Mexico City
Centro Editorial, Guatemala City
Centro Mexicano de Escritores, Mexico City
Centro Para el "Desarrollo Economico y Social de
    America Latina", Santiago, Chile
The Century Co., New York
Century House, Inc., Watkins Glen, N. Y.
Cercle de la Librairie, Paris
Leon Chaillez Editeur, Paris
Chaitanya Publishing House, Allahabad, India
Chamber of Commerce of the United States, Washington, D. C.
S. Chand and Co., New Delhi
Chandler Publishing Co., San Francisco
Chandler-Davis, Lexington, Mass.
Chandler-Davis Publishing Co., West Trenton, N. J.
Channel Press, Inc., Great Neck, N. Y.
Chapman and Hall, London
Geoffrey Chapman, London
Chatham College, Pittsburgh, Pa.
Chatto and Windus, Ltd., London
F. W. Cheshire, London
Chestnut Hill, Boston College Library, Boston
Chicago Joint Reference Library, Chicago
Chilean Development Corp., New York
Chilmark Press, New York
Chilton Books, New York
China Viewpoints, Hong Kong
Chinese-American Publishing Co., Shanghai

Chiswick Press, London
Christian Crusade, Tulsa, Okla.
Georg Christiansen, Itzehoe, Germany
Christopher Publishing House, Boston
Chulalongkorn University, Bangkok
Church League of America, Wheaton, Ill.
C. I. Associates, New York
Cincinnati Civil Service, Cincinnati, Ohio
Citadel Press, New York
City of Johannesburg Public Library, Johannesburg
Citizens Research Foundation, Paris
Citizens Research Foundation, Princeton, N. J.
Ciudad Universitaria, San Jose, Calif.
Ciudad y Espiritu, Buenos Aires
Claremont Colleges, Claremont, Calif.
Clarendon Press, London
Clark, Irwin and Co., Ltd., Toronto
Clark University Press, Worcester, Mass.
Classics Press, New York
Clay and Sons, London
Cleveland Civil Service Commission, Cleveland
Clio Press, Santa Barbara, Calif.
William Clowes and Sons, Ltd., London
Colin (Librairie Armand) Paris
College and University Press, New Haven
Collet's Holdings, Ltd., London
Colliers, New York
F. Collin, Brussels
Collins, London
Colloquium Verlag, Berlin
Colombo Plan Bureau, Colombo, Ceylon
Colonial Press Inc., Northport, Ala.; New York
Colorado Bibliographic Institute, Denver
Colorado Legislature Council, Denver
Colorado State Board of Library Commissioners, Denver
Columbia University, New York
Columbia University, Bureau of Applied Social Research,
    New York
Columbia University, Center for Urban Education, New York
Columbia University, East Asian Institute, New York
Columbia University, Graduate School of Business, New York
Columbia University, Institute of French Studies, New York
Columbia University, Institute of Public Administration,
    New York
Columbia University, Institute of Russian Studies, New York
Columbia University, Institute of War-Peace Studies,
    New York
Columbia University, Law Library, New York
Columbia University, Parker School, New York
Columbia University, School of International Affairs,
    New York
Columbia University, School of Library Service, New York
Columbia University Press, New York
Columbia University Teachers College, New York
Combat Forces Press, Washington, D. C.
Comet Press, New York
Comision Nacional Ejecutiva, Buenos Aires
Commerce Clearing House, Chicago; Washington; New York
Commercial Credit Co., Baltimore, Md.
Commissao do iv Centenario de Ciudade, Sao Paulo
Commission for Technical Cooperation, Lahore
Commission to Study the Organization of Peace, New York
Committee for Economic Development, New York
Committee on Africa, New York
Committee on Federal Tax Policy, New York
Committee on Near East Studies, Washington
Committee on Public Administration, Washington, D. C.
Committee to Frame World Constitution, New York
Common Council for American Unity, New York
Commonwealth Agricultural Bureau, London
Commonwealth Economic Commission, London
Community Publications, Manila
Community Renewal Program, San Francisco
Community Studies, Inc., Kansas City
Companhia Editora Forense, Rio de Janeiro
Companhia Editora Nacional, Sao Paulo
Compass Books, New York
Concordia Publishing House, St. Louis, Mo.
Confederate Publishing Co., Tuscaloosa, Ala.
Conference on Economic Progress, Washington, D. C.
Conference on State and Economic Enterprise in Modern
    Japan, Estes Park, Colo.
Congress for Cultural Freedom, Prabhakar

Congressional Quarterly Service, Washington
Connecticut Personnel Department, Hartford
Connecticut State Civil Service Commission, Hartford
Conseil d'Etat, Paris
Conservative Political Centre, London
Constable and Co., London
Archibald Constable and Co., Edinburgh
Cooper Square Publishers, New York
U. Cooper and Partners, Ltd., London
Corinth Books, New York
Cornell University, Dept. of Asian Studies, Ithaca
Cornell University, Graduate School of Business and Public
    Administration, Ithaca
Cornell University Press, Ithaca
Cornell University, School of Industry and Labor Planning,
    Ithaca
Council for Economic Education, Bombay
Council of Education, Johannesburg
Council of Europe, Strasbourg
Council of State Governments, Chicago, Ill.
Council of the British National Bibliography, Ltd., London
Council on Foreign Relations, New York
Council on Public Affairs, Washington, D. C.
Council on Religion and International Affairs, New York
Council on Social Work Education, Washington, D. C.
Covici, Friede, Inc., New York
Coward-McCann, Inc., New York
Cresset Press, London
Crestwood Books, Springfield, Va.
Criterion Books, Inc., New York
S. Crofts and Co., New York
Crosby, Lockwood, and Sons, Ltd., London
Crosscurrents Press, New York
Thomas Y. Crowell Co., New York
Crowell-Collier and MacMillan, New York
Crown Publishers, Inc., New York
C.S.I.C., Madrid
Cuadernos de la Facultad de Derecho Universidad
    Veracruzana, Mexico City
Cuerpo Facultativo de Archiveros, Bibliotecarios y
    Argueologos, Madrid
Cultural Center of the French Embassy, New York
Current Scene, Hong Kong
Current Thought, Inc., Durham, N. C.
Czechoslovak Foreign Institute in Exile, Chicago

Da Capo Press, New York
Daguin Freres, Editeurs, Paris
Daily Telegraph, London
Daily Worker Publishing Co., Chicago
Dalloz, Paris
Damascus Bar Association, Damascus
Dangary Publishing Co., Baltimore
David Davies Memorial Institute of Political Studies,
    London
David-Stewart, New York
John Day Co., Inc., New York
John de Graff, Inc., Tuckahoe, N. Y.
La Decima Conferencia Interamericana, Caracas
Delacorte Press, New York
Dell Publishing Co., New York
T. S. Denison & Co., Inc., Minneapolis, Minn.
J. M. Dent, London
Departamento de Imprensa Nacional, Rio de Janeiro
Deseret Book Co., Salt Lake City, Utah
Desert Research Institute Publications' Office, Reno, Nev.
Deus Books, Paulist Press, Glen Rock, N. J.
Andre Deutsch, Ltd., London
Deutsche Afrika Gesellschaft, Bonn
Deutsche Bibliographie, Frankfurt am Main
Deutsche Bucherei, Leipzig
Deutsche Gesellschaft fur Volkerrecht, Karlsruhe
Deutsche Gesellschaft fur Auswartige Politik, Bonn
Deutsche Verlagsanstalt, Stuttgart
Deutscher Taschenbuch Verlag, Munich
Deva Datta Shastri, Hoshiarpur
Development Loan Fund, Washington, D. C.
Devin-Adair, Co., New York
Diablo Press, Inc., Berkeley, Calif.
Dial Press, Inc., New York
Dibco Press, San Jose, Cal.
Dickenson Publishing Co., Inc., Belmont, Calif.
Didier Publishers, New York

Firmin Didot Freres, Paris
Dietz Verlag, Berlin
Difusao Europeia do Livro, Sao Paulo
Diplomatic Press, London
Direccion General de Accion Social, Lisbon
District of Columbia, Office of Urban Renewal,
    Washington, D. C.
Djambatan, Amsterdam
Dennis Dobson, London
Dobunken Co., Ltd., Tokyo
La Documentation Francaise, Paris
Documents Index, Arlington, Virginia
Dodd, Mead and Co., New York
Octave Doin et Fils, Paris
Dolphin Books, Inc., New York
Dominion Press, Chicago
Walter Doon Verlag, Bremen
George H. Doran Co., New York
Dorrance and Co., Inc., Philadelphia, Pa.
Dorsey Press, Homewood, Illinois
Doubleday and Co., Inc., Garden City, N. Y.
Dover Publications, New York
Dow Jones and Co., Inc., New York
Dragonfly Books, Hong Kong
Drei Masken Verlag, Munich
Droemersche Verlagsanstalt, Zurich
Droste Verlag, Dusseldorf
Druck und Verlag von Carl Gerolds Sohn, Vienna
Guy Drummond, Montreal
The Dryden Press, New York
Dryfus Conference on Public Affairs, Hanover, N. H.
Duckworth, London
Duell, Sloan & Pearce, New York
Dufour Editions, Inc., Chester Springs, Pa.
Carl Duisburg-Gesellschaft fur Nachwuchsforderung, Cologne
Duke University, School of Law, Durham, N. C.
Duke University Press, Durham, N. C.
Dulau and Co., London
Duncker und Humblot, Berlin
Duquesne University Press, Pittsburgh, Pa.
R. Dutt, London
E. P. Dutton and Co., Inc., Garden City, N. Y.

E. P. & Commercial Printing Co., Durban, S. Africa
East Africa Publishing House, Nairobi
East European Fund, Inc., New York
East-West Center Press, Honolulu
Eastern Kentucky Regional Development Commission,
    Frankfort, Ky.
Eastern World, Ltd., London
Emil Ebering, Berlin
Echter-Verlag, Wurzburg
Ecole Francaise d'Extreme Orient, Paris
Ecole Nationale d'Administration, Paris
Econ Verlag, Dusseldorf; Vienna
Economic Research Corp., Ltd., Montreal
Economic Society of South Africa, Johannesburg
The Economist, London
Edicao Saraiva, Sao Paulo
Ediciones Ariel, Barcelona
Ediciones Cultura Hispanica, Madrid
Ediciones del Movimiento, Borgos, Spain
Ediciones Nuestro Tiempo, Montevideo
Ediciones Rialp, Madrid
Ediciones Riaz, Lima
Ediciones Siglo Veinte, Buenos Aires
Ediciones Tercer Mundo, Bogota
Edicoes de Revista de Estudes Politos, Rio de Janeiro
Edicoes Do Val, Rio de Janeiro
Edicoes GRD, Rio de Janeiro
Edicoes o Cruzeiro, Rio de Janeiro
Edicoes Tempo Brasileiro, Ltda., Rio de Janeiro
Edinburgh House Press, Edinburgh
Editions Albin Michel, Paris
Editions Alsatia, Paris
Editions Berger-Levrault, Paris
Editions Cujas, Paris
Editions de l'Epargne, Paris
Editions de l'Institut de Sociologie de l'Universite Libre de
    Bruxelles, Brussels
Editions d'Organisation, Paris
Editions Denoel, Paris
Editions John Didier, Paris

Editions du Carrefour, Paris
Editions du Cerf, Paris
Editions du Livre, Monte Carlo
Editions du Monde, Paris
Editions du Rocher, Monaco
Editions du Seuil, Paris
Editions du Tiers-Monde, Algiers
Editions du Vieux Colombier, Paris
Editions Eyrolles, Paris
Editions Internationales, Paris
Editions Mont Chrestien, Paris
Editions Nauwelaerts, Louvain
Editions Ouvrieres, Paris
Editions A. Pedone, Paris
Editions Presence Africaine, Paris
Editions Rouff, Paris
Editions Sedif, Paris
Editions Sirey, Paris
Editions Sociales, Paris
Editions Techniques Nord Africaines, Rabat
Editions Universitaires, Paris
Editora Brasiliense, Sao Paulo
Editora Civilizacao Brasileira S. A., Rio de Janeiro
Editora Fulgor, Sao Paulo
Editora Saga, Rio de Janerio
Editores letras e artes, Rio de Janeiro
Editores Mexicanos, Mexico City
Editores Mexicanos Unidos, Mexico City
Editorial AIP, Miami
Editorial Amerinda, Buenos Aires
Editorial Columbia, Buenos Aires
Editorial Freeland, Buenos Aires
Editorial Gustavo Gili, Barcelona
Editorial Jus, Mexico City, Mexico
Editorial Lex, Havana
Editorial Losa da Buenos Aires, Buenos Aires
Editorial Marymar, Buenos Aires
Editorial Mentora, Barcelona
Editorial Nascimento, Santiago
Editorial Palestra, Buenos Aires
Editorial Patria, Mexico City
Editorial Pax, Bogota
Editorial Pax-Mexico, Mexico City
Editorial Platina, Buenos Aires
Editorial Porrua, Mexico City
Editorial Stylo Durangozgo, Mexico City
Editorial Universitaria de Buenos Aires, Buenos Aires
Editorial Universitaria de Puerto Rico, San Jose
Editorial Universitaria Santiago, Santiago
Le Edizioni de Favoro, Rome
Edizioni di Storia e Letteratura, Rome
Edizioni Scientifiche Italiane, Naples
Education and World Affairs, New York
Educational Heritage, Yonkers, N. Y.
Edwards Brothers, Ann Arbor
Effingham Wilson Publishers, London
Egyptian Library Press, Cairo
Egyptian Society of International Law, Cairo
Elex Books, London
Elsevier Publishing Co., Ltd., London
EMECE Editores, Buenos Aires
Emerson Books, New York
Empresa Editora Austral, Ltd., Santiago
Encyclopedia Britannica, Inc., Chicago
English Universities Press, London
Ferdinand Enke Verlag, Bonn; Erlangen; Stuttgart
Horst Erdmann Verlag, Schwarzwald
Paul Eriksson, Inc., New York
Escorpion, Buenos Aires
Escuela de Historia Moderna, Madrid
Escuela Nacional de Ciencias Politicas y Sociales, Mexico City
Escuela Superior de Administracion Publica America Central, San Jose, Costa Rica
Essener Verlagsanstalt, Essen
Essential Books, Ltd., London
Ethiopia, Ministry of Information, Addis Ababa
Etudes, Paris
Euroamerica, Madrid
Europa-Archiv, Frankfurt am Main
Europa Publications Ltd., London
Europa Verlag, Zurich; Vienna
Europaische Verlagsanstalt, Frankfurt

European Committee for Economic and Social Progress, Milan
European Free Trade Association, Geneva
Evangelischer Verlag, Zurich
Edward Evans and Sons, Shanghai
Everline Press, Princeton
Excerpta Criminologica Foundation, Leyden, Netherlands
Exchange Bibliographies, Eugene, Ore.
Export Press, Belgrade
Exposition Press, Inc., New York
Eyre and Spottiswoode, Ltd., London
Extending Horizon Books, Boston

F. and T. Publishers, Seattle, Washington
Faber and Faber, Ltd., London
Fabian Society, London
Facing Reality Publishing Corporation, Detroit, Mich.
Facts on File, Inc., New York
Fairchild Publishing, Inc., New York
Fairleigh Dickinson Press, Rutherford, N. J.
Falcon Press, London
Family Service Association of America, New York
Farrar and Rinehart, New York
Farrar, Strauss & Giroux, Inc., New York
Fawcett World Library, New York
F. W. Faxon Co., Inc., Boston
Fayard, Paris
Federal Legal Publications, Inc., New York
Federal Reserve Bank of New York, New York
Federal Trust for Education and Research, London
Fellowship Publications, New York
Feltrinelli Giangiacomo (Editore), Milan
Au Fil d'Ariadne, Paris
Filipiniana Book Guild, Manila
Financial Index Co., New York
Finnish Political Science Association, Helsinki
Fischer Bucherei, Frankfurt
Fischer Verlag, Stuttgart
Gustav Fischer Verlag, Jena
Flammarion, Paris
Fleet Publishing Co., New York
Fletcher School of Law and Diplomacy, Boston
R. Flint and Co., London
Florida State University, Tallahassee
Follett Publishing Co., Chicago
Fondation Nationale des Sciences Politiques, Paris
Fondo Historico y Bibliografico Jose Foribio, Medina, Santiago
Fondo de Cultura Economica, Mexico
B. C. Forbes and Sons, New York
Ford Foundation, New York
Fordham University Press, New York
Foreign Affairs Association of Japan, Tokyo
Foreign Affairs Bibliography, New York
Foreign Language Press, Peking
Foreign Language Publishing House, Moscow
Foreign Policy Association, New York
Foreign Policy Clearing House, Washington, D. C.
Foreign Policy Research Institute, University of Pennsylvania, Philadelphia, Pa.
Foreign Trade Library, Philadelphia
Arnold Forni Editore, Bologna
Forschungs-Berichte des Landes Nordrhein-Westfalen, Dusseldorf, Germany
Fortress Press, Philadelphia, Pa.
Foundation for Economic Education, Irvington-on-Hudson, N. Y.
Foundation for Social Research, Los Angeles, Calif.
Foundation Press, Inc., Brooklyn, N. Y.; Mineola, N. Y.
Foundation Press, Inc., Chicago
Foundation for Research on Human Behavior, New York
France Editions Nouvelles, Paris
France, Ministere de l'Education Nationale, Paris
France, Ministere d'Etat aux Affaires Culturelles, Paris
France, Ministere des Finances et des Affaires Economiques, Paris
Francois Maspera, Paris
Francke Verlag, Munich
Ben Franklin Press, Pittsfield, Mass.
Burt Franklin, New York
Free Europe Committee, New York
Free Press, New York
Free Press of Glencoe, Glencoe, Ill.; New York

Free Speech League, New York
Freedom Books, New York
Freedom Press, London
Ira J. Friedman, Inc., Port Washington, N. Y.
Friends General Conference, Philadelphia, Pa.
Friendship Press, New York
M. L. Fuert, Los Angeles
Fund for the Republic, New York
Fundacao Getulio Vargas, Rio de Janeiro
Funk and Wagnalls Co., Inc., New York
Orell Fuessli Verlag, Zurich

Galaxy Books, Oxford
Gale Research Co., Detroit
Galton Publishing Co., New York
A. R. Geoghegan, Buenos Aires
George Washington University, Population Research Project, Washington, D. C.
Georgetown University Press, Washington, D. C.
Georgia State College, Atlanta, Ga.
Georgia State Library, Atlanta, Ga.
Germany (Territory under Allied Occupation, 1945—U. S. Zone) Office of Public Information, Information Control Division, Bonn
Germany, Bundesministerium fur Vertriebene, Fluechtlinge, und Kriegsbeschadigte (Federal Ministry for Expellees, Refugees, and War Victims), Bonn
Gerold & Co. Verlag, Vienna, Austria
Ghana University Press, Accra, Ghana
Gideon Press, Beirut
Gustavo Gili, Barcelona
Ginn and Co., Boston
Glanville Publishing Co., New York
Glasgow University Press, Glasgow
Gleditsch Brockhaus, Leipzig
Glencoe Free Press, London
Golden Bell Press, Denver, Colo.
Victor Gollancz, Ltd., London
Gordon and Breach Science Publications, New York
Gothic Printing Co., Capetown, S. Afr.
Gould Publications, Jamaica, N. Y.
Government Affairs Foundation, Albany, N. Y.
Government Data Publications, New York
Government of India National Library, Calcutta
Government Printing Office, Washington
Government Publications of Political Literature, Moscow
Government Research Institute, Cleveland
Grafica Americana, Caracas
Grafica Editorial Souza, Rio de Janeiro
Graficas Gonzales, Madrid
Graficas Uguina, Madrid
Graphic, New York
H. W. Gray, Inc., New York
Great Britain, Administrative Staff College, London
Great Britain, Committee on Ministers' Powers, London
Great Britain, Department of Technical Cooperation, London
Great Britain, Foreign Office, London
Great Britain, Ministry of Overseas Development, London
Great Britain, Treasury, London
Greater Bridgeport Region, Planning Agency, Trumbull
W. Green and Son, Edinburgh
Green Pagoda Press, Hong Kong
Greenwich Book Publications, New York
Greenwood Periodicals, New York
Griffin Press, Adelaide, Australia
Grolier, Inc., New York
J. Groning, Hamburg
Grosset and Dunlap, Inc., New York
Grossman Publishers, New York
G. Grote'sche Verlagsbuchhandlung, Rastalt, Germany
Group for the Advancement of Psychiatry, New York
Grove Press, Inc., New York
Grune and Stratton, New York
Gruyter and Co., Walter de, Berlin
E. Guilmato, Paris
Democratic Party of Guinea, Guinea
Gulf Publishing Co., Houston, Texas
J. Chr. Gunderson Boktrykkeri og Bokbinderi, Oslo
Hans E. Gunther Verlag, Stuttgart
Gutersloher Verlagshaus, Gutersloh

Hadar Publishing Co., Tel-Aviv
Hafner Publishing Co., Inc., New York

G. K. Hall, Boston
Robert Hall, London
Charles Hallberg and Co., Chicago
Hamburgisches Wirtschafts Archiv, Hamburg
Hamilton & Co., London
Hamilton County Research Foundation, Cincinnati
Hamish Hamilton, London
Hanover House, New York
Hansard Society, London
Harcourt, Brace and World, New York
Harlo Press, Detroit, Mich.
Harper and Row Publishers, New York; London
George Harrap and Co., London
Otto Harrassowitz, Wiesbaden
Harrison Co., Atlanta, Ga.
Rupert Hart-Davis, London
Hartford Printing Co., Hartford, Conn.
Harvard Center for International Affairs, Cambridge, Mass.
Harvard Law School, Cambridge, Mass.
Harvard Law Review Association, Cambridge, Mass.
Harvard University Center for East Asian Studies, Cambridge, Mass.
Harvard University, Center for Russian Research and Studies, Cambridge, Mass.
Harvard University, Graduate School of Business Administration, Cambridge, Mass.
Harvard University, Peabody Museum, Cambridge, Mass.
Harvard University, Widener Library, Cambridge
Harvard University Press, Cambridge
V. Hase und Kohler Verlag, Mainz
Hastings House, New York
Hauser Press, New Orleans, La.
Hawthorne Books, Inc., New York
Hayden Book Company, New York
The John Randolph Haynes and Dora Haynes Foundation, Los Angeles
The Edward D. Hazen Foundation, New Haven, Conn.
D. C. Heath and Co., Boston
Hebrew University Press, Jerusalem
Heffer and Sons Ltd., Cambridge, England
William S. Hein and Co., Buffalo
James H. Heineman, Inc., New York
Heinemann Ltd., London
Heirsemann, Leipzig
A. Hepple, Johannesburg
Helicon Press, Inc., Baltimore, Md.
Herald Press, Scottdale, Penna.
Herder and Herder, New York
Herder Book Co., New York, St. Louis
Johann Gottfried Herder, Marburg, Germany
Heritage Foundation, Chicago
The Heritage Press, New York
Hermitage Press, Inc., New York
Heron House Winslow, Washington, D. C.
Herzl Press, New York
Carl Heymanns Verlag, Berlin
Hill and Wang, Inc., New York
Hillary House Publishers, Ltd., New York
Hind Kitabs, Ltd., Bombay
Hinds, Noble, and Eldridge, New York
Ferdinand Hirt, Kiel, Germany
Historical Society of New Mexico, Albuquerque, N. M.
H. M. Stationery Office, London
Hobart and William Smith Colleges, Geneva, N. Y.
Hobbs, Dorman and Co., New York
Hodden and Staughton, London
William Hodge and Co., Ltd., London
Hodges Figgis and Co., Ltd., Dublin
J. G. Hodgson, Fort Collins, Colo.
Hogarth Press, London
The Hokuseido Press, Tokyo
Holborn Publishing House, London
Hollis and Carter, London
Hollywood A.S.P. Council, Hollywood, Calif.
Holt and Williams, New York
Holt, Rinehart and Winston, New York
Henry Holt and Co., New York
Holzner Verlag, Wurzburg
Home and Van Thal, London
Hong Kong Government Press, Hong Kong
Hong Kong University Press, Hong Kong
Hoover Institute on War, Revolution and Peace, Stanford, Calif.

Hope College, Holland, Mich.
Horizon Press, Inc., New York
Houghton, Mifflin Co., Boston
Houlgate House, Los Angeles
Howard University Press, Washington
Howell, Sosbin and Co., New York
Hudson Institute, Inc., Harmon-on-Hudson, New York
B. W. Huebsch, Inc., New York
H. Hugendubel Verlag, Munich
Human Relations Area Files Press (HRAF), New Haven
Human Rights Publications, Caulfield, Victoria, Australia
Human Sciences Research, Inc., Arlington, Va.
Humanities Press, New York
Humon and Rousseau, Capetown
Hungarian Academy of Science, Publishing House of, Budapest
Hunter College Library, New York
R. Hunter, London
Huntington Library, San Marino, Calif.
Hutchinson and Co., London
Hutchinson University Library, London

Ibadan University Press, Ibadan, Nigeria
Iberia Publishing Company, New York
Ibero-American Institute, Stockholm
Illini Union Bookstore, Champaign, Ill.
Illinois State Publications, Springfield
Ilmgau Verlag, Pfaffenhofen
Imago Publishing Co., Ltd., London
Imprenta Calderon, Honduras
Imprenta Mossen Alcover, Mallorca
Imprenta Nacional, Caracas
Imprimerie d'Extreme Orient, Hanoi
Imprimerie Nationale, Paris
Imprimerie Sefan, Tunis
Imprimerie Fr. Van Muysewinkel, Brussels
Incentivist Publications, Greenwich, Conn.
Index Society, New York
India and Pakistan: Combined Interservice Historical
    Section, New Delhi
India, Government of, Press, New Delhi
India, Ministry of Community Development, New Delhi
India, Ministry of Finance, New Delhi
India, Ministry of Health, New Delhi
India, Ministry of Home Affairs, New Delhi
India, Ministry of Information and Broadcasting, Faridabad;
    New Delhi
India, Ministry of Law, New Delhi
Indian Council on World Affairs, New Delhi
Indian Institute of Public Administration, New Delhi
Indian Ministry of Information and Broadcasting, New Delhi
Indian Press, Ltd., Allahabad
Indian School of International Studies, New Delhi
Indiana University, Bureau of Government Research,
    Bloomington
Indiana University, Institute of Training for Public
    Service, Department of Government, Bloomington
Indiana University Press, Bloomington
Indraprastha Estate, New Delhi
Industrial Areas Foundations, Chicago
Industrial Council for Social and Economic Studies, Upsala
Industrial Press, New York
Infantry Journal Press, Washington, D. C.
Information Bulletin Ltd., London
Insel Verlag, Frankfurt
Institut Afro-Asiatique d'Etudes Syndicales, Tel Aviv
Institut de Droit International, Paris
Institut des Hautes Etudes de l'Amerique Latine,
    Rio de Janeiro
Institut des Relations Internationales, Brussels
Institut fur Kulturwissenschaftliche Forschung, Freiburg
Institut fur Politische Wissenschaft, Frankfurt
Institut International de Collaboration Philosophique, Paris
Institute for Comparative Study of Political Systems,
    Washington, D. C.
Institute for Defense Analyses, Washington, D. C.
Institute for International Politics and Economics, Prague
Institute for International Social Research, Princeton, N. J.
Institute for Mediterranean Affairs, New York
Institute for Monetary Research, Washington, D. C.
Institute for Social Science Research, Washington, D. C.
Institute of Brazilian Studies, Rio de Janeiro
Institute of Early American History and Culture,
    Williamsburg, Va.

Institute of Economic Affairs, London
Institute of Ethiopian Studies, Addis Ababa
Institute of Human Relations Press, New York
Institute of Islamic Culture, Lahore
Institute of Labor and Industrial Relations, Urbana, Ill.
Institute of Judicial Administration, New York
Institute of National Planning, Cairo
Institute of Pacific Relations, New York
Institute of Professional Civil Servants, London
Institute of Public Administration, Dublin
Instituto de Antropologia e Etnologia de Para, Belem, Para,
    Brazil
Instituto Brasileiro de Estudos Afro-Asiaticos,
    Rio de Janeiro
Instituto Caro y Cuervo, Bogota
Instituto de Derecho Comparedo, Barcelona
Instituto de Estudios Africanos, Madrid
Instituto de Estudios Politicos, Madrid
Instituto de Investigaciones Historicas, Mexico City
Instituto Guatemalteco-Americano, Guatemala City
Instituto Internacional de Ciencias Administrativas,
    Rio de Janeiro
Instituto Nacional do Livro, Rio de Janeiro
Instituto Nazionale di Cultura Fascista, Firenze
Instituto Pan Americano de Geografia e Historia, Mexico City
Integrated Education Associates, Chicago
Inter-American Bibliographical and Library Association,
    Gainesville, Fla.
Inter-American Development Bank, Buenos Aires
Inter-American Statistical Institute, Washington
Intercollegiate Case Clearing House, Boston
International African Institute, London
International Association for Research in Income and Wealth,
    New Haven, Conn.
International Atomic Energy Commission, Vienna
International Bank for Reconstruction and Development,
    Washington, D. C.
International Center for African Economic and Social
    Documentation, Brussels
International Chamber of Commerce, New York
International City Managers' Association, Chicago
International Commission of Jurists, Geneva
International Committee for Peaceful Investment,
    Washington, D. C.
International Congress of History of Discoveries, Lisbon
International Congress of Jurists, Rio de Janeiro
International Cotton Advisory Committee, Washington, D. C.
International Court of Justice, The Hague
International Development Association, Washington, D. C.
International Economic Policy Association, Washington, D. C.
International Editions, New York
International Federation for Documentation, The Hague
International Federation for Housing and Planning, The Hague
International Finance, Princeton, N. J.
International Institute of Administrative Science, Brussels
International Institute of Differing Civilizations, Brussels
International Labour Office, Geneva
International Managers' Association, Chicago
International Monetary Fund, Washington
International Press Institute, Zurich
International Publications Service, New York
International Publishers Co., New York
International Publishing House, Meerat, India
International Review Service, New York
International Textbook Co., Scranton, Penna.
International Union for Scientific Study of Population,
    New York
International Universities Press, Inc., New York
Interstate Printers and Publishers, Danville, Ill.
Iowa State University, Center for Agricultural and Economic
    Development, Ames
Iowa State University Press, Ames
Irish Manuscripts Commission, Dublin
Richard D. Irwin, Inc., Homewood, Ill.
Isar Verlag, Munich
Isbister and Co., London
Italian Library of Information, New York; Rome
Italy, Council of Ministers, Rome

Jacaranda Press, Melbourne
Mouriel Jacobs, Inc., Philadelphia
Al Jadidah Press, Cairo
Jain General House, Jullundur, India
Japan, Ministry of Education, Tokyo

Japan, Ministry of Justice, Tokyo
Japanese National Commission for UNESCO, Tokyo
Jarrolds Publishers, Ltd., London
Jewish Publication Society of America, Philadelphia, Pa.
Johns Hopkins Press, Baltimore
Johns Hopkins School of Advanced International Studies, Baltimore
Johns Hopkins School of Hygiene, Baltimore
Johnson Publishing Co., Chicago
Christopher Johnson Publishers, Ltd., London
Johnstone and Hunter, London
Joint Center for Urban Studies, Cambridge, Mass.
Joint Committee on Slavic Studies, New York
Joint Council on Economic Education, New York
Joint Library of IMF and IBRD, Washington
Joint Reference Library, Chicago
Jonathan Cape, London
Jones and Evans Book Shop, Ltd., London
Marshall Jones, Boston
Jornal do Commercio, Rio de Janeiro
Michael Joseph, Ltd., London
Jowett, Leeds, England
Juilliard Publishers, Paris
Junker und Dunnhaupt Verlag, Berlin
Juta and Co., Ltd., Capetown, South Africa

Kallman Publishing Co., Gainesville, Fla.
Karl Karusa, Washington, D. C.
Katzman Verlag, Tubingen
Kay Publishing Co., Salt Lake City
Nicholas Kaye, London
Calvin K. Kazanjian Economics Foundation, Westport, Conn.
Kegan, Paul and Co., Ltd., London
P. G. Keller, Winterthur, Switz.
Augustus M. Kelley, Publishers, New York
Kelly and Walsh, Ltd., Baltimore, Md.
P. J. Kenedy, New York
Kennikat Press, Port Washington, N. Y.
Kent House, Port-of-Spain
Kent State University Bureau of Economic and Business Research, Kent, Ohio
Kentucky State Archives and Records Service, Frankfort
Kentucky State Planning Commission, Frankfort
Kenya Ministry of Economic Planning and Development, Nairobi
Charles H. Kerr and Co., Chicago
Khadiand Village Industries Commission, Bombay
Khayat's, Beirut
Khun Aroon, Bangkok
P. S. King and Son, Ltd., London
King's College, Cambridge
King's Crown Press, New York
Kino Kuniva Bookstore Co., Ltd., Tokyo
Kitab Mahal, Allahabad, India
Kitabistan, Allahabad
B. Klein and Co., New York
Ernst Klett Verlag, Stuttgart
V. Klostermann, Frankfurt
Fritz Knapp Verlag, Frankfurt
Alfred Knopf, New York
John Knox Press, Richmond, Va.
Kodansha International, Ltd., Tokyo
W. Kohlhammer Verlag, Stuttgart; Berlin; Cologne; Mainz
Korea Researcher and Publisher, Inc., Seoul
Korea, Ministry of Reconstruction, Seoul
Korea, Republic of, Seoul
Korea University, Asiatic Research Center, Seoul
Korean Conflict Research Foundation, Albany, N. Y.
Kosel Verlag, Munich
Kossuth Foundation, New York
Guillermo Kraft, Ltd., Buenos Aires
John F. Kraft, Inc., New York
Krasnzi Proletarii, Moscow
Kraus, Ltd., Dresden
Kraus Reprint Co., Vaduz, Liechtenstein
Kreuz-Verlag, Stuttgart
Kumasi College of Technology, The Library, Kumasi, Ghana
Kuwait, Arabia, Government Printing Press, Kuwait

Labor News Co., New York
Robert Laffont, Paris
Lambarde Press, Sidcup, Kent, England
Albert D. and Mary Lasker Foundation, Washington, D. C.

878

Harold Laski Institute of Political Science, Ahmedabad
Guiseppe Laterza e Figli, Bari, Italy
T. Werner Laurie, Ltd., London
Lawrence Brothers, Ltd., London
Lawrence and Wishart, London
Lawyers Co-operative Publishing Co., Rochester, N. Y.
League for Industrial Democracy, New York
League of Independent Voters, New Haven
League of Nations, Geneva
League of Women Voters, Cambridge
League of Women Voters of U. S., Washington, D. C.
Leeds University Press, Leeds, Engand
J. F. Lehmanns Verlag, Munich
Leicester University Press, London
F. Leitz, Frankfurt
Lemcke, Lemcke and Beuchner, New York
Michel Levy Freres, Paris
Lexington Publishing Co., New York
Liberal Arts Press, Inc., New York
Liberia Altiplano, La Paz
Liberia Anticuaria, Barcelona
Liberia Campos, San Juan
Liberia Panamericana, Buenos Aires
Liberty Bell Press, Jefferson City, Mo.
Librairie Academique Perrin, Paris
Librairie Artheme Fayard, Paris
Librairie Beauchemin, Montreal
Librairie Armand Colin, Paris
Librairie Firmin Didot et Cie., Paris
Librairie Droz, Geneva
Librairie de Medicis, Paris
Librairie de la Societe du Recueil Sirey, Paris
Librairie des Sciences Politiques et Sociales, Paris
Librairie Felix Alcan, Paris
Librairie Gallimard, Paris
Librairie Hachette et Cie., Paris
Librairie Julius Abel, Greiswald
Librairie La Rose, Paris
Librairie Letouzey, Paris
Librairie Payot, Paris
Librairie Philosophique J. Vrin, Paris
Librairie Plon, Paris
Librairie Marcel Riviere et Cie., Paris
Librairie Stock Delamain et Boutelleau, Paris
Library, Kumasi College of Technology, Kumasi
Library Association, London
Library of Congress, Washington
Library House, London
Library of International Relations, Chicago
Libyan Publishing, Tripoli
Light and Life Press, Winona Lake, Ind.
Lincoln University, Lincoln, Pa.
J. B. Lippincott Co., New York, Philadelphia
Little, Brown and Co., Boston
Liverpool University Press, Liverpool
Horace Liveright, New York
Living Books, New York
Livraria Agir Editora, Rio de Janeiro
Livraria Editora da Casa di Estudente do Brazil, Sao Paulo
Livraria Jose Olympio Editora, Rio de Janeiro
Livraria Martins Editora, Sao Paulo
Lok Sabha Secretariat, New Delhi
London Conservative Political Centre, London
London Historical Association, London
London Institute of World Affairs, London
London Library Association, London
London School of Economics, London
London Times, Inc., London
London University, School of Oriental and African Studies, London
Roy Long and Richard R. Smith, Inc., New York
Long House, New Canaan, Conn.
Longmans, Green and Co., New York, London
Los Angeles Board of Civil Service Commissioners, Los Angeles
Louisiana State Legislature, Baton Rouge
Louisiana State University Press, Baton Rouge
Loyola University Press, Chicago
Lucas Brothers, Columbia
Herman Luchterhand Verlag, Neuwied am Rhein
Lyle Stuart, Inc., New York

MIT Center of International Studies, Cambridge

MIT Press, Cambridge
MIT School of Industrial Management, Cambridge
Macfadden-Bartwell Corp., New York
MacGibbon and Kee, Ltd., London
Macmillan Co., New York; London
Macmillan Co., of Canada, Ltd., Toronto
Macrae Smith Co., Philadelphia, Pa.
Magistrats Druckerei, Berlin
Magnes Press, Jerusalem
S. P. Maisonneuve et La Rose, Paris
Malaysia Publications, Ltd., Singapore
Malhorta Brothers, New Delhi
Manager Government of India Press, Kosib
Manaktalas, Bombay
Manchester University Press, Manchester, England
Manhattan Publishing Co., New York
Manzsche Verlag, Vienna
Marathon Oil Co., Findlay, Ohio
Marisal, Madrid
Marquette University Press, Milwaukee
Marshall Benick, New York
Marzani and Munsell, New York
Marzun Kabushiki Kaisha, Tokyo
Mascat Publications, Ltd., Calcutta
Francois Maspera, Paris
Massachusetts Mass Transportation Commission, Boston
Masses and McInstream, New York
Maurice Falk Institute for Economic Research, Jerusalem
Maxwell Air Force Base, Montgomery, Ala.
Robert Maxwell and Co., Ltd., London
McBride, Nast and Co., New York
McClelland and Stewart, Ltd., London
McClure and Co., Chicago
McClure, Phillips and Co., New York
McCutchan Publishing Corp., Berkeley
McDonald and Evans, Ltd., London
McDowell, Obolensky, New York
McFadden Bartwell Corp., New York
McGill University Industrial Relations Section, Montreal
McGill University, Institute of Islamic Studies, Montreal
McGill University Press, Montreal
McGraw Hill Book Co., New York
David McKay Co., Inc., New York
McKinley Publishing Co., Philadelphia
George J. McLeod, Ltd., Toronto
McMullen Books, Inc., New York
Meador Publishing Co., Boston
Mediaeval Academy of Americana, Cambridge
Felix Meiner Verlag, Hamburg
Melbourne University Press, Melbourne, Victoria, Australia
Mendonca, Lisbon
Mental Health Materials Center, New York
Mentor Books, New York
Meredith Press, Des Moines
Meridian Books, New York
Merit Publishers, New York
The Merlin Press, Ltd., London
Charles E. Merrill Publishing Co., Inc., Columbus
Methuen and Co., Ltd., London
Metropolitan Book Co., Ltd., New Delhi
Metropolitan Housing and Planning Council, Chicago
Metropolitan Police District, Scotland Yard, London
Alfred Metzner Verlag, Frankfurt
Meyer London Memorial Library, London
Miami University Press, Oxford, Ohio
Michie Co., Charlottesville, Va.
Michigan Municipal League, Ann Arbor
Michigan State University, Agricultural Experiment Station,
    East Lansing
Michigan State University, Bureau of Business and Economic
    Research, East Lansing
Michigan State University, Bureau of Social and Political
    Research, East Lansing
Michigan State University, Governmental Research Bureau,
    East Lansing
Michigan State University, Institute for Community
    Development and Services, East Lansing
Michigan State University, Institute for Social Research,
    East Lansing
Michigan State University, Labor and Industrial Relations
    Center, East Lansing
Michigan State University Press, East Lansing

Michigan State University School of Business Administration,
    East Lansing
Michigan State University, Vietnam Advisory Group,
    East Lansing
Mid-European Studies Center, Free European Committee,
    New York
Middle East Institute, Washington
Middle East Research Associates, Arlington, Va.
Middlebury College, Middlebury, Vt.
Midwest Administration Center, Chicago
Midwest Beach Co., Sioux Falls
Milbank Memorial Fund, New York
M. S. Mill and Co., Inc., Division of William Morrow and
    Co., Inc., New York
Ministere de l'Education Nationale, Paris
Ministere d'Etat aux Affaires Culturelles, Paris
Ministerio de Educacao e Cultura, Rio de Janeiro
Ministerio de Relaciones Exteriores, Havana
Minnesota Efficiency in Government Commission, St. Paul
Minton, Balch and Co., New York
Missionary Research Library, New York
Ernst Siegfried Mittler und Sohn, Berlin
Modern Humanities Research Association, Chicago
T. C. B. Mohr, Tubingen
Moira Books, Detroit
Monarch Books, Inc., Derby, Conn.
Monthly Review, New York
Mont Pelerin Society, University of Chicago, Chicago
Hugh Moore Fund, New York
T. G. Moran's Sons, Inc., Baton Rouge
William Morrow and Co., Inc., New York
Morus Verlag, Berlin
Mosaik Verlag, Hamburg
Motilal Banarsidass, New Delhi
Mouton and Co., The Hague; Paris
C. F. Mueller Verlag, Karlsruhe, Germany
Muhammad Mosque of Islam #2, Chicago
Firma K. L. Mukhopadhyaz, Calcutta
F. A. W. Muldener, Gottingen, Germany
Frederick Muller, Ltd., London
Municipal Finance Officers Association of the United States
    and Canada, Chicago
Munksgaard International Booksellers and Publishers,
    Copenhagen
John Murray, London
Museum fur Volkerkunde, Vienna
Museum of Honolulu, Honolulu
Musterschmidt Verlag, Gottingen

NA Tipographia do Panorama, Lisbon
Nassau County Planning Committee, Long Island
Natal Witness, Ltd., Pietermaritzburg
The Nation Associates, New York
National Academy of Sciences-National Research Council,
    Washington, D. C.
National Archives of Rhodesia and Nyasaland, Salisbury
National Assembly on Teaching The Principles of the Bill of
    Rights, Washington
National Association of Counties Research Foundation,
    Washington, D. C.
National Association of County Officials, Chicago
National Association of Home Builders, Washington, D. C.
National Association of Local Government Officers, London
National Association of State Libraries, Boston
National Bank of Egypt, Cairo
National Bank of Libya, Tripoli
National Board of YMCA, New York
National Book League, London
National Bureau of Economic Research, New York
National Capitol Publishers, Manassas, Va.
National Central Library, London
National Citizens' Commission on International Cooperation,
    Washington, D. C.
National Council for the Social Sciences, New York
National Council for the Social Studies, New York
National Council of Applied Economic Research, New Delhi
National Council of Churches of Christ in USA, New York
National Council of National Front of Democratic Germany,
    Berlin
National Council on Aging, New York
National Council on Crime and Delinquency, New York
National Economic and Social Planning Agency,
    Washington

National Education Association, Washington
National Home Library Foundation, Washington, D. C.
National Industrial Conference Board, New York
National Institute for Personnel Research, Johannesburg
National Institute of Administration, Saigon
National Institute of Economic Research, Stockholm
National Labor Relations Board Library, Washington
National Labour Press, London
National Library of Canada, Ottawa
National Library Press, Ottawa
National Municipal League, New York
National Observer, Silver Springs, Md.
National Opinion Research Center, Chicago
National Peace Council, London
National Planning Association, Washington, D. C.
National Press, Palo Alto, Calif.
National Review, New York
National Science Foundation Scientific Information, Washington, D. C.
Natural History Press, Garden City, N. Y.
Nauka Publishing House, Moscow
Navahind, Hyderabad
Navajiran Publishing House, Ahmedabad
Thomas Nelson and Sons, London; New York
Neukirchener Verlag des Erziehungsvereins, Neukirchen
New American Library, New York
New Century Publishers, New York
New Jersey Department of Agriculture, Rural Advisory Council, Trenton
New Jersey Department of Civil Service, Trenton
New Jersey Department of Conservation and Economic Development, Trenton
New Jersey Division of State and Regional Planning, Trenton
New Jersey Housing and Renewal, Trenton
New Jersey State Department of Education, Trenton
New Jersey State Legislature, Trenton
New Republic, Washington, D. C.
New School of Social Research, New York
New World Press, New York
New York City College Institute for Pacific Relations, New York
New York City Department of Correction, New York
New York City Temporary Committee on City Finance, New York
New York Public Library, New York
New York State College of Agriculture, Ithaca
New York State Library, Albany
New York State School of Industrial and Labor Relations, Cornell University, Ithaca
New York, State University of, at Albany, Albany
New York, State University of, State Education Department, Albany
New York, State University of, State Education Department, Office of Foreign Area Studies, Albany
New York Times, New York
New York University School of Commerce, Accounts and Finance, New York
New York University, School of Law, New York
New York University Press, New York
Newark Public Library, Newark
Newman Press, Westminster, Md.
Martinus Nijhoff, The Hague; Geneva
James Nisbet and Co., Ltd., Welwyn, Herts, England
Noonday Press, New York
North American Review Publishing Co., New York
North Atlantic Treaty Organization, Brussels
North Holland Publishing Co., Amsterdam, Holland
Northern California Friends Committee on Legislation, San Francisco
Northern Michigan University Press, Marquette
Northwestern University, Evanston
Northwestern University, African Department, Evanston, Ill.
Northwestern University, International Relations Conference, Chicago
Northwestern University Press, Evanston, Ill.
W. W. Norton and Co., Inc., New York
Norwegian Institute of International Affairs, Oslo
Norwegian University Press, Oslo
Nouvelle Librairie Nationale, Paris
John Nuveen and Co., Chicago
Novelty and Co., Patna, India

Novostii Press Agency Publishing House, Moscow
Nymphenburger Verlagsbuchhandlung, Munich

Oak Publications, New York
Oak Ridge Associated Universities, Oak Ridge, Tenn.
Oceana Publishing Co., Dobbs Ferry, N. Y.
Octagon Publishing Co., New York
Odyssey Press, New York
Oesterreichische Ethnologische Gesellschaft, Vienna
Oficina Internacional de Investigaciones Sociales de Freres, Madrid
W.E.R. O'Gorman, Glendale, Calif.
O'Hare, Flanders, N. J.
Ohio State University, Columbus
Ohio State University, College of Commerce and Administration, Bureau of Business Research, Columbus
Ohio State University Press, Columbus
Ohio University Press, Athens
Old Lyme Press, Old Lyme, Conn.
R. Oldenbourg, Munich
Oliver and Boyd, London, Edinburgh
Guenter Olzog Verlag, Munich
Open Court Publishing Co., La Salle, Ill.
Operation America, Inc., Los Angeles
Operations and Policy Research, Inc., Washington, D. C.
Oregon Historical Society, Portland
Organization for European Economic Cooperation and Development (OEEC), Paris
Organization of African Unity, Addis Ababa
Organization of American States, Rio de Janeiro
Organization of Economic Aid, Washington, D. C.
Orient Longman's, Bombay
Oriole Press, Berkeley Heights, N. J.
P. O'Shey, New York
Osaka University of Commerce, Tokyo
James R. Osgood and Co., Boston
Oslo University Press, Oslo
Oswald-Wolff, London
John Ousley, Ltd., London
George Outram Co., Ltd., Glasgow
Overseas Development Institute, Ltd., London
R. E. Owen, Wellington, N. Z.
Oxford Book Co., New York
Oxford University Press, Capetown; London; Madras; Melbourne; New York

Pacific Books, Palo Alto, Calif.
Pacific Coast Publishing Co., Menlo Park, Calif.
Pacific Philosophy Institute, Stockton, Calif.
Pacific Press Publishing Association, Mountain View, Calif.
Pacifist Research Bureau, Philadelphia
Padma Publications, Ltd., Bombay
Hermann Paetel Verlag, Berlin
Pageant Press, New York
Paine-Whitman, New York
Pakistan Academy for Rural Development, Peshawar
Pakistan Association for Advancement of Science, Lahore
Pakistan Bibliographical Working Group, Karachi
Pakistan Educational Publishers, Ltd., Karachi
Pakistan Ministry of Finance, Rawalpindi
Pall Mall Press, London
Pan American Union, Washington
Pantheon Books, Inc., New York
John W. Parker, London
Patna University Press, Madras
B. G. Paul and Co., Madras
Paulist Press, Glen Rock, N. J.
Payne Fund, New York
Peabody Museum, Cambridge
Peace Publications, New York
Peace Society, London
P. Pearlman, Washington
Pegasus, New York
Peking Review, Peking
Pelican Books, Ltd., Hammonsworth, England
Pemberton Press, Austin
Penguin Books, Baltimore
Penn.-N.J.-Del. Metropolitan Project, Philadelphia, Pa.
Pennsylvania German Society, Lancaster, Pa.
Pennsylvania Historical and Museum Commission, Harrisburg
Pennsylvania State University, Department of Religious Studies, University Park, Pa.

Pennsylvania State University, Institute of Public Administration, University Park, Pa.
Pennsylvania State University Press, University Park, Pa.
People's Publishing House, Ltd., New Delhi
Pergamon Press, Inc., New York
Permanent Secretariat, AAPS Conference, Cairo
Perrine Book Co., Minneapolis
Personnel Administration, Washington
Personnel Research Association, New York
George A. Pflaum Publishers, Inc., Dayton, Ohio
Phelps-Stokes Fund, Capetown; New York
Philadelphia Bibliographical Center, Philadelphia
George Philip & Son, London
Philippine Historical Society, Manila
Philippine Islands Bureau of Science, Manila
Philosophical Library Inc., New York
Phoenix House, Ltd., London
Pichon et Durand-Auzias, Paris
B. M. Pickering, London
Oskar Piest, New York
Pilot Press, London
Pioneer Publishers, New York
R. Piper and Co. Verlag, Munich
Pitman Publishing Corp., New York
Plimpton Press, Norwood, Mass.
PLJ Publications, Manila
Pocket Books, Inc., New York
Polish Scientific Publishers, Warsaw
Polygraphischer Verlag, Zurich
The Polynesian Society, Inc., Wellington, N. Z.
Popular Book Depot, Bombay
Popular Prakashan, Bombay
Population Association of America, Washington
Population Council, New York
Post Printing Co., New York
Post Publishing Co., Bangkok
Potomac Books, Washington, D. C.
Clarkson N. Potter, Inc., New York
Prabhakar Sahityalok, Lucknow, India
Practicing Law Institute, New York
Frederick A. Praeger, Inc., New York
Prager, Berlin
Prensa Latino Americana, Santiago
Prentice Hall, Inc., Englewood Cliffs, N. J.
Prentice-Hall International, London
Presence Afrique, Paris
President's Press, New Delhi
Press & Information Division of the French Embassy, New York
The Press of Case Western Reserve University, Cleveland
Presses de l'Ecole des Hautes Etudes Commerciales, Montreal
Presses Universitaires de Bruxelles, Brussels
Presses Universitaires de France, Paris
Presseverband der Evangelischen Kirche im Rheinland, Dusseldorf
Princeton Research Publishing Co., Princeton
Princeton University, Princeton, N. J.
Princeton University, Center of International Studies, Woodrow Wilson School of Public and International Affairs, Princeton, N. J.
Princeton University, Department of Economics, Princeton, N. J.
Princeton University, Department of History, Princeton, N. J.
Princeton University, Department of Oriental Studies, Princeton, N. J.
Princeton University, Department of Philosophy, Princeton, N. J.
Princeton University, Department of Politics, Princeton, N. J.
Princeton University, Department of Psychology, Princeton
Princeton University, Department of Sociology, Princeton, N. J.
Princeton University, Econometric Research Program, Princeton, N. J.
Princeton University, Firestone Library, Princeton, N. J.
Princeton University, Industrial Relations Center, Princeton
Princeton University, International Finance Section, Princeton, N. J.
Princeton University, Princeton Public Opinion Research Project, Princeton, N. J.
Princeton University Press, Princeton
Edouard Privat, Toulouse

Arthur Probsthain, London
Professional Library Press, West Haven, Conn.
Programa Interamericano de Informacion Popular, San Jose
Progress Publishing Co., Indianapolis
Progressive Education Association, New York
Prolog Research and Publishing Association, New York
Prometheus Press, New York
Psycho-Sociological Press, New York
Public Administration Clearing House, Chicago
Public Administration Institute, Ankara
Public Administration Service, Chicago
Public Affairs Forum, Bombay
Public Affairs Press, Washington
Public Enterprises, Tequcigalpa
Public Personnel Association, Chicago
Publications Centre, University of British Columbia, Vancouver
Publications de l'Institut Pedagogique National, Paris
Publications de l'Institut Universitaire des Hautes Etudes Internationales, Paris
Publications du CNRS, Paris
Publisher's Circular, Ltd., London,, England
Publisher's Weekly, Inc., New York
Publishing House Jugoslavia, Belgrade
Punjab University, Pakistan
Punjab University Extension Library, Ludhiana, Punjab
Purdue University Press, Lafayette, Ind.
Purnell and Sons, Capetown
G. P. Putnam and Sons, New York

Quadrangle Books, Inc., Chicago
Bernard Quaritch, London
Queen's Printer, Ottawa
Queen's University, Belfast
Quell Verlag, Stuttgart, Germany
Quelle und Meyer, Heidelberg
Queromon Editores, Mexico City

Atma Ram and Sons, New Delhi
Ramsey-Wallace Corporation, Ramsey, New Jersey
Rand Corporation, Publications of the Social Science Department, New York
Rand McNally and Co., Skokie, Ill.
Random House, Inc., New York
Regents Publishing House, Inc., New York
Regional Planning Association, New York
Regional Science Research Institute, Philadelphia
Henry Regnery Co., Chicago
D. Reidel Publishing Co., Dordrecht, Holland
E. Reinhardt Verlag, Munich
Reinhold Publishing Corp., New York; London
Remsen Press, New York
La Renaissance de Loire, Paris
Eugen Rentsch Verlag, Stuttgart
Republican National Committee, Washington, D. C.
Research Institute on Sino-Soviet Bloc, Washington, D. C.
Research Microfilm Publications, Inc., Annapolis
Resources for the Future, Inc., Washington, D. C.
Revista de Occidente, Madrid
Revue Administrative, Paris
Renyal and Co., Inc., New York
Reynal & Hitchcock, New York
Rheinische Friedrich Wilhelms Universitat, Bonn
Rice University, Fondren Library, Houston
Richards Rosen Press, New York
The Ridge Press, Inc., New York
Rinehart, New York
Ring-Verlag, Stuttgart
Riverside Editions, Cambridge
Robinson and Co., Durban, South Africa
J. A. Rogers, New York
Roques Roman, Trujillo
Rudolf M. Rohrer, Leipzig
Ludwig Rohrscheid Verlag, Bonn
Walter Roming and Co., Detroit
Ronald Press Co., New York
Roper Public Opinion Poll Research Center, New York
Ross and Haine, Inc., Minneapolis, Minn.
Fred B. Rothman and Co., S. Hackensack, N. J.
Rotterdam University Press, Rotterdam
Routledge and Kegan Paul, London
George Routledge and Sons, Ltd., London
Row-Peterson Publishing Co., Evanston, Ill.

Rowohlt, Hamburg
Roy Publishers, Inc., New York
Royal African Society, London
Royal Anthropological Institute, London
Royal Colonial Institute, London
Royal Commission of Canada's Economic Prospects, Ottawa
Royal Commonwealth Society, London
Royal Geographical Society, London
Royal Greek Embassy Information Service, Washington, D. C.
Royal Institute of International Affairs, London; New York
Royal Institute of Public Administration, London
Royal Netherlands Printing Office, Schiedam
Royal Statistical Society, London
Rubin Mass, Jerusalem
Rule of Law Press, Durham
Rupert Hart-Davis, London
Russell and Russell, Inc., New York
Russell Sage College, Institute for Advanced Study in Crisis, NDEA Institute, Troy, N. Y.
Russell Sage Foundation, New York
Rutgers University, New Brunswick, N. J.
Rutgers University Bureau of Government Research, New Brunswick, N. J.
Rutgers University, Institute of Management and Labor Relations, New Brunswick, N. J.
Rutgers University, Urban Studies Conference, New Brunswick, N. J.
Rutgers University Press, New Brunswick, N. J.
Rutten und Loening Verlag, Munich
Ryerson Press, Toronto

Sage Publications, Beverly Hills, Calif.
Sahitya Akademi, Bombay
St. Andrews College, Drygrange, Scotland
St. Clement's Press, London
St. George Press, Los Angeles
St. John's University Bookstore, Annapolis
St. John's University Press, Jamaica, N. Y.
St. Louis Post-Dispatch, St. Louis
St. Martin's Press, New York
St. Michael's College, Toronto
San Diego State College Library, San Diego
San Francisco State College, San Francisco
The Sapir Memorial Publication Fund, Menasha, Wis.
Sarah Lawrence College, New York
Sarah Lawrence College, Institute for Community Studies, New York
Porter Sargent, Publishers, Boston, Mass.
Sauerlaender and Co., Aarau, Switz.
Saunders and Ottey, London
W. B. Saunders Co., Philadelphia, Pa.
Scandinavian University Books, Copenhagen
Scarecrow Press, Metuchen, N. J.
L. N. Schaffrath, Geldern, Germany
Robert Schalkenbach Foundation, New York
Schenkman Publishing Co., Cambridge
P. Schippers, N. V., Amsterdam
Schocken Books, Inc., New York
Henry Schuman, Inc., New York
Carl Schunemann Verlag, Bremen
Curt E. Schwab, Stuttgart
Otto Schwartz und Co., Gottingen
Science and Behavior Books, Palo Alto, Calif.
Science Council of Japan, Tokyo
Science of Society Foundation, Baltimore, Md.
Science Press, New York
Science Research Associates, Inc., Chicago
Scientia Verlag, Aalen, Germany
SCM Press, London
Scott, Foresman and Co., Chicago
Scottish League for European Freedom, Edinburgh
Chas. Scribner's Sons, New York
Seabury Press, New York
Sears Publishing Co., Inc., New York
Secker and Warburg, Ltd., London
Secretaria del Consejo Nacional Economia, Tegucigalpa
Securities Study Project, Vancouver, Wash.
Seewald Verlag, Munich; Stuttgart
Selbstverlag Jakob Rosner, Vienna
Seldon Society, London
Robert C. Sellers and Associates, Washington, D. C.
Thomas Seltzer Inc., New York
Seminar, New Delhi

C. Serbinis Press, Athens
Service Bibliographique des Messageries Hachette, Paris
Service Center for Teaching of History, Washington, D. C.
Servicos de Imprensa e Informacao da Exbaixada, Lisbon
Sheed and Ward, New York
Shoestring Press, Hamden, Conn.
Shuter and Shooter, Pietermaritzburg
Siam Society, Bangkok
Sidgewick and Jackson, London
K. G. Siegler & Co., Bonn
Signet Books, New York
A. W. Sijthoff, Leyden, Netherlands
Silver Burdett, Morristown, N. J.
Simmons Boardman Publishing Co., New York
Simon and Schuster, Inc., New York
Simpkin, Marshall, et al., London
Sino-American Cultural Society, Washington
William Sloane Associates, New York
Small, Maynard and Co., Boston
Smith-Brook Printing Co., Denver
Smith College, Northampton, Mass.
Smith, Elder and Co., London
Smith, Keynes and Marshall, Buffalo, N. Y.
Allen Smith Co., Indianapolis, Ind.
Peter Smith, Gloucester, Mass.
Richard R. Smith Co. Inc., Peterborough, N. H.
Smithsonian Institute, Washington, D. C.
Social Science Research Center, Rio Piedras, Puerto Rico
Social Science Research Council, New York
Social Science Research Council, Committee on the Economy of China, Berkeley, Calif.
Social Science Research Council of Australia, Sydney
The Social Sciences, Mexico City
Societa Editrice del "Foro Italiano", Rome
Societas Bibliographica, Lausanne, Switzerland
Societe d'Edition d'Enseignement Superieur, Paris
Societe Francaise d'Imprimerie et Librairie, Paris
Society for Advancement of Management, New York
Society for Promoting Christian Knowledge, London
Society for the Study of Social Problems, Kalamazoo, Mich.
Society of Comparative Legislative and International Law, London
Sociological Abstracts, New York
Solidaridad Publishing House, Manila
Somerset Press, Inc., Somerville, N. J.
Soney and Sage Co., Newark, N. J.
South Africa Commission on Future Government, Capetown
South Africa State Library, Pretoria
South African Congress of Democrats, Johannesburg
South African Council for Scientific and Industrial Research, Pretoria
South African Institute of International Affairs, Johannesburg
South African Institute of Race Relations, Johannesburg
South African Public Library, Johannesburg
South Carolina Archives, State Library, Columbia
South Pacific Commission, Noumea, New Caledonia
South Western Publishing Co., Cincinnati, Ohio
Southern Illinois University Press, Carbondale, Ill.
Southern Methodist University Press, Dallas, Tex.
Southern Political Science Association, New York
Southworth Anthoensen Press, Portland, Maine
Sovetskaia Rossiia, Moscow
Soviet and East European Research and Translation Service, New York
Spartan Books, Washington, D. C.
Special Libraries Association, New York
Specialty Press of South Africa, Johannesburg
Robert Speller and Sons, New York
Lorenz Spindler Verlag, Nuremberg
Julius Springer, Berlin
Springer-Verlag, New York; Stuttgart; Gottingen; Vienna
Stackpole Co., New York
Gerhard Stalling, Oldenburg, Germany
Stanford Bookstore, Stanford
Stanford University Comparative Education Center, Stanford, Calif.
Stanford University Institute for Communications Research, Stanford
Stanford University, Institute of Hispanic-American and Luso-Brazilian Studies, Stanford, Calif.
Stanford University, Project on Engineering-Economic Planning, Stanford, Calif.

Stanford University Research Institute, Menlo Park, Calif.
Stanford University, School of Business Administration, Stanford, Calif.
Stanford University, School of Education, Stanford, Calif.
Stanford University Press, Stanford, Cal.
Staples Press, New York
State University of New York at Albany, Albany
Stein & Day Publishers, New York
Franz Steiner Verlag, Wiesbaden
Ulrich Steiner Verlag, Wurttemburg
H. E. Stenfert Kroese, Leyden
Sterling Printing and Publishing Co., Ltd., Karachi
Sterling Publishers, Ltd., London
Stevens and Hayes, London
Stevens and Sons, Ltd., London
George W. Stewart, Inc., New York
George Stilke Berlin
Frederick A. Stokes Publishing Co., New York
C. Struik, Capetown
Stuttgarter Verlags Kantor, Stuttgart
Summy-Birchard Co., Evanston, Ill.
Swann Sonnenschein and Co., London
Philip Swartzwelder, Pittsburgh, Pa.
Sweet and Maxwell, Ltd., London
Swiss Eastern Institute, Berne
Sydney University Press, Sydney, Australia
Syracuse University, Maxwell School of Citizenship and Public Affairs, Syracuse, N. Y.
Syracuse University Press, Syracuse
Szczesnez Verlag, Munich

Talleres Graficos de Manuel Casas, Mexico City
Talleres de Impresion de Estampillas y Valores, Mexico City
Taplinger Publishing Co., New York
Tavistock, London
Tax Foundation, New York
Teachers' College, Bureau of Publications, Columbia University, New York
Technical Assistance Information Clearing House, New York
Technology Press, Cambridge
de Tempel, Bruges, Belgium
B. G. Teubner, Berlin; Leipzig
Texas College of Arts and Industries, Kingsville
Texas Western Press, Dallas
Texian Press, Waco, Texas
Thacker's Press and Directories, Ltd., Calcutta
Thailand, National Office of Statistics, Bangkok
Thailand National Economic Development Board, Bangkok
Thames and Hudson, Ltd., London
Thammasat University Institute of Public Administration, Bangkok, Thailand
E. J. Theisen, East Orange, N. J.
Charles C. Thomas, Publisher, Springfield, Ill.
Tilden Press, New York
Time, Inc., New York
Time-Life Books, New York
Times Mirror Printing and Binding, New York
Tipografia de Archivos, Madrid
Tipografia Mendonca, Lisbon
Tipografia Nacional, Guatemala, Guatemala City
Tipographia Nacional Guatemala, Guatemala City
H. D. Tjeenk Willink, Haarlem, Netherlands
J. C. Topping, Cambridge, Mass.
Transatlantic Arts, Inc., New York
Trejos Hermanos, San Jose
Trenton State College, Trenton
Tri-Ocean Books, San Francisco
Trident Press, New York
Trowitzsch and Son, Berlin
Truebner and Co., London
Tufts University Press, Medford, Mass.
Tulane University, School of Business Administration, New Orleans, La.
Tulane University Press, New Orleans
Turnstile Press, London
Tuskegee Institute, Tuskegee, Ala.
Charles E. Tuttle Co., Tokyo
Twayne Publishers Inc., New York
The Twentieth Century Fund, New York
Twin Circle Publishing Co., New York
Typographische Anstalt, Vienna
Tyrolia Verlag, Innsbruck

UNESCO, Paris
N. V. Uitgeverij W. Van Hoeve, The Hague
Frederick Ungar Publishing Co., Inc., New York
Union Federaliste Inter-Universitaire, Paris
Union of American Hebrew Congregations, New York
Union of International Associations, Brussels
Union of Japanese Societies of Law and Politics, Tokyo
Union of South Africa, Capetown
Union of South Africa, Government Information Office, New York
Union Press, Hong Kong
Union Research Institute, Hong Kong
United Arab Republic, Information Department, Cairo
United Nations Economic Commission for Asia and the Far East, Secretariat of Bangkok, Bangkok
United Nations Educational, Scientific and Cultural Organization, Paris
United Nations Food and Agriculture Organization, Rome
United Nations International Conference on Peaceful Uses of Atomic Energy, Geneva
United Nations Publishing Service, New York
United States Air Force Academy, Colorado Springs, Colo.
United States Bureau of the Census, Washington, D. C.
United States Business and Defense Services Administration, Washington D.C.
United States Civil Rights Commission, Washington, D. C.
United States Civil Service Commission, Washington, D. C.
United States Consulate General, Hong Kong
United States Department of Agriculture, Washington, D. C.
United States Department of the Army, Washington
United States Department of the Army, Office of Chief of Military History, Washington, D. C.
United States Department of Correction, New York
United States Department of State, Washington
United States Department of State, Government Printing Office, Washington, D. C.
United States Government Printing Office, Washington
United States Housing and Home Financing Agency, Washington, D. C.
United States Mutual Security Agency, Washington, D. C.
United States National Archives General Services, Washington, D. C.
United States National Referral Center for Science and Technology, Washington, D. C.
United States National Resources Committee, Washington, D. C.
United States Naval Academy, Annapolis, Md.
United States Naval Institute, Annapolis, Md.
United States Naval Officers Training School, China Lake, Cal.
United States Operations Mission to Vietnam, Washington, D. C.
United States President's Committee to Study Military Assistance, Washington, D. C.
United States Small Business Administration, Washington, D. C.
United World Federalists, Boston
Universal Reference System; see Princeton Research Publishing Co., Princeton, N.J.
Universidad Central de Venezuela, Caracas
Universidad de Buenos Aires, Instituto Sociologia, Buenos Aires
Universidad de Chile, Santiago
Universidad de el Salvador, El Salvador
Universidad Nacional Autonomo de Mexico, Direccion General de Publicaciones, Mexico
Universidad Nacional de la Plata, Argentina
Universidad Nacional Instituto de Historia Antonoma de Mexico, Mexico City
Universidad Nacional Mayor de San Marcos, Lima
Universidad de Antioquia, Medellin, Colombia
Universite de Rabat, Rabat, Morocco
Universite Fouad I, Cairo
Universite Libre de Bruxelles, Brussels
Universite Mohammed V, Rabat, Morocco
University Books, Inc., Hyde Park, New York
University Bookstore, Hong Kong
University Microfilms, Inc., Ann Arbor
University of Alabama, Bureau of Public Administration, University, Ala.
University of Alabama Press, University, Ala.
University of Ankara, Ankara
University of Arizona Press, Tucson
University of Bombay, Bombay

University of Bonn, Bonn
University of British Columbia Press, Vancouver
University of California, Berkeley, Calif.
University of California at Los Angeles, Bureau of Government Research, Los Angeles
University of California at Los Angeles, Near Eastern Center, Los Angeles
University of California, Bureau of Business and Economic Research, Berkeley, Calif.
University of California, Bureau of Government Research, Los Angeles
University of California, Bureau of Public Administration, Berkeley
University of California, Department of Psychology, Los Angeles
University of California, Institute for International Studies, Berkeley, Calif.
University of California, Institute of East Asiatic Studies, Berkeley, Calif.
University of California, Institute of Governmental Affairs, Davis
University of California, Institute of Governmental Studies, Berkeley
University of California, Institute of Urban and Regional Development, Berkeley, Calif.
University of California, Latin American Center, Los Angeles
University of California Library, Berkeley, Calif.
University of California Press, Berkeley
University of California Survey Research Center, Berkeley, Calif.
University of Canterbury, Christchurch, New Zealand
University of Capetown, Capetown
University of Chicago, Chicago
University of Chicago, Center for Policy Study, Chicago
University of Chicago, Center for Program in Government Administration, Chicago
University of Chicago, Center of Race Relations, Chicago
University of Chicago, Graduate School of Business, Chicago
University of Chicago Law School, Chicago
University of Chicago, Politics Department, Chicago
University of Chicago Press, Chicago
University of Cincinnati, Cincinnati
University of Cincinnati, Center for Study of United States Foreign Policy, Cincinnati
University of Colorado Press, Boulder
University of Connecticut, Institute of Public Service, Storrs, Conn.
University of Dar es Salaam, Institute of Public Administration, Dar es Salaam
University of Denver, Denver
University of Detroit Press, Detroit
University of Edinburgh, Edinburgh, Scotland
University of Florida, Public Administration Clearing Service, Gainesville, Fla.
University of Florida, School of Inter-American Studies, Gainesville, Fla.
University of Florida Libraries, Gainesville
University of Florida Press, Gainesville
University of Georgia, Institute of Community and Area Development, Athens, Georgia
University of Georgia Press, Athens
University of Glasgow Press, Glasgow, Scotland
University of Glasgow Press, Fredericton, New Brunswick, Canada
University of Hawaii Press, Honolulu
University of Hong Kong Press, Hong Kong
University of Houston, Houston
University of Illinois, Champaign
University of Illinois, Graduate School of Library Science, Urbana
University of Illinois, Institute for Labor and Industrial Relations, Urbana
University of Illinois, Institute of Government and Public Affairs, Urbana, Ill.
University of Illinois Press, Urbana
University of Iowa, Center for Labor and Management, Iowa City
University of Iowa, School of Journalism, Iowa City
University of Iowa Press, Iowa City
University of Kansas, Bureau of Government Research, Lawrence, Kans.
University of Kansas Press, Lawrence
University of Karachi, Institute of Business and Public

Administration, Karachi
University of Karachi Press, Karachi
University of Kentucky, Bureau of Governmental Research, Lexington
University of Kentucky Press, Lexington
University of London, Institute of Advanced Legal Studies, London
University of London, Institute of Commonwealth Studies, London
University of London, Institute of Education, London
University of London, School of Oriental and African Studies, London
University of London Press, London
University of Lund, Lund, Sweden
University of Maine Studies, Augusta, Me.
University of Malaya, Kualalumpur
University of Manchester Press, Manchester, England
University of Maryland, Bureau of Governmental Research, College of Business and Public Administration, College Park, Md.
University of Maryland, Department of Agriculture and Extension Education, College Park, Md.
University of Massachusetts, Bureau of Government Research, Amherst, Mass.
University of Massachusetts Press, Amherst
University of Melbourne Press, Melbourne, Australia
University of Miami Law Library, Coral Gables
University of Miami Press, Coral Gables
University of Michigan, Center for Research on Conflict Resolution, Ann Arbor
University of Michigan, Department of History and Political Science, Ann Arbor
University of Michigan, Graduate School of Business Administration, Ann Arbor
University of Michigan, Institute for Social Research, Ann Arbor
University of Michigan, Institute of Public Administration, Ann Arbor
University of Michigan Law School, Ann Arbor
University of Michigan, Survey Research Center, Ann Arbor
University of Michigan Press, Ann Arbor
University of Minnesota, St. Paul; Duluth
University of Minnesota, Industrial Relations Center, Minneapolis
University of Minnesota Press, Minneapolis
University of Mississippi, Bureau of Public Administration, University, Miss.
University of Missouri, Research Center, School of Business and Public Administration, Columbia
University of Missouri Press, Columbia
University of Natal Press, Pietermaritzburg
University of Nebraska Press, Lincoln
University of New England, Grafton, Australia
University of New Mexico, Department of Government, Albuquerque, N. Mex.
University of New Mexico, School of Law, Albuquerque
University of New Mexico Press, Albuquerque
University of North Carolina, Department of City and Regional Planning, Chapel Hill
University of North Carolina, Institute for International Studies, Chapel Hill
University of North Carolina, Institute for Research in the Social Sciences, Center for Urban and Regional Studies, Chapel Hill
University of North Carolina, Institute of Government, Chapel Hill
University of North Carolina Library, Chapel Hill
University of North Carolina Press, Chapel Hill
University of Notre Dame, Notre Dame, Ind.
University of Notre Dame Press, Notre Dame, Ind.
University of Oklahoma Press, Norman
University of Oregon Press, Eugene
University of Panama, Panama City
University of Paris (Conferences du Palais de la Decouverte), Paris
University of Pennsylvania, Philadelphia, Pa.
University of Pennsylvania, Department of Translations, Philadelphia
University of Pennsylvania Law School, Philadelphia, Pa.
University of Pennsylvania Press, Philadelphia
University of Pittsburgh, Institute of Local Government, Pittsburgh, Pa.
University of Pittsburgh Book Centers, Pittsburgh
University of Pittsburgh Press, Pittsburgh

University of Puerto Rico, San Juan
University of Rochester, Rochester, N. Y.
University of Santo Tomas, Manila
University of South Africa, Pretoria
University of South Carolina Press, Columbia
University of Southern California, Middle East and North Africa Program, Los Angeles
University of Southern California, School of International Relations, Los Angeles
University of Southern California Press, Los Angeles
University of Southern California, School of Public Administration, Los Angeles
University of State of New York, State Education Department, Albany
University of Sussex, Sussex, England
University of Sydney, Department of Government and Public Administration, Sydney
University of Tennessee, Knoxville
University of Tennessee, Bureau of Public Administration, Knoxville
University of Tennessee, Municipal Technical Advisory Service, Division of University Extension, Knoxville
University of Tennessee Press, Knoxville
University of Texas, Austin
University of Texas, Bureau of Business Research, Austin
University of Texas Press, Austin
University of the Philippines, Quezon City
University of the Punjab, Department of Public Administration, Lahore, Pakistan
University of the Witwatersrand, Johannesburg
University of Toronto, Toronto
University of Toronto Press, Toronto; Buffalo, N. Y.
University of Utah Press, Salt Lake City
University of Vermont, Burlington
University of Virginia, Bureau of Public Administration, Charlottesville
University of Wales Press, Cardiff
University of Washington, Bureau of Governmental Research and Services, Seattle
University of Washington Press, Seattle
University of Wisconsin, Madison
University of Wisconsin Press, Madison
University Press, University of the South, Sewanee, Tenn.
University Press of Virginia, Charlottesville
University Publishers, Inc., New York
University Publishing Co., Lincoln, Nebr.
University Society, Inc., Ridgewood, N. J.
Unwin University Books, London
T. Fisher Unwin, Ltd., London
Upjohn Institute for Employment Research, Kalamazoo, Mich; Los Angeles; Washington, D. C.
Urban America, New York
Urban Studies Center, New Brunswick, N. J.

VEB Verlag fur Buch-und Bibliothekwesen, Leipzig
Franz Vahlen, Berlin
Vallentine, Mitchell and Co., London
Van Nostrand Co., Inc., Princeton
Van Rees Press, New York
Vandenhoeck und Ruprecht, Gottingen
Vanderbilt University Press, Nashville, Tenn.
Vanguard Press, Inc., New York
E. C. Vann, Richmond, Va.
Vantage Press, New York
G. Velgaminov, New York
Verein fur Sozial Politik, Berlin
Vergara Editorial, Barcelona
Verlag Karl Alber, Freiburg
Verlag Georg D. W. Callwey, Munich
Verlag der Wiener Volksbuchhandlung, Vienna
Verlag der Wirtschaft, Berlin
Verlag Deutsche Polizei, Hamburg
Verlag Felix Dietrich, Osnabrueck
Verlag Kurt Dosch, Vienna
Verlag Gustav Fischer, Jena
Verlag Huber Frauenfeld, Stuttgart
Verlag fur Buch- und Bibliothekwesen, Leipzig
Verlag fur Literatur und Zeitgeschehen, Hannover, Germany
Verlag fur Recht und Gesellschaft, Basel
Verein fuer Sozialpolitik, Wirtschaft und Statistik, Berlin
Verlag Anton Hain, Meisenheim
Verlag Hans Krach, Mainz
Verlag Edward Krug, Wurttemburg

Verlag Helmut Kupper, Godesberg
Verlag August Lutzeyer, Baden-Baden
Verlag Mensch und Arbeit, Bruckmann, Munich
Verlag C. F. Muller, Karlsruhe
Verlag Anton Pustet, Munich
Verlag Rombach und Co., Freiburg
Verlag Heinrich Scheffler, Frankfurt
Verlag Hans Schellenberg, Winterthur, Switz.
Verlag P. Schippers, Amsterdam
Verlag Lambert Schneider, Heidelberg
Verlag K. W. Schutz, Gottingen
Verlag Styria, Graz, Austria
Lawrence Verry, Publishers, Mystic, Conn.
Viking Press, New York
Villanova Law School, Philadelphia
J. Villanueva, Buenos Aires
Vintage Books, New York
Virginia Commission on Constitutional Government, Richmond
Virginia State Library, Richmond
Vishveshvaranand Vedic Research Institute, Hoshiarpur
Vista Books, London
F. & J. Voglrieder, Munich
Voigt und Gleibner, Frankfurt
Voltaire Verlag, Berlin
Von Engelhorn, Stuttgart
Vora and Co. Publishers, Bombay
J. Vrin, Paris

Karl Wachholtz Verlag, Neumunster
Wadsworth Publishing Co., Belmont, Cal.
Walker and Co., New York
Ives Washburn, Inc., New York
Washington State University Press, Pullman
Washington University Libraries, Washington
Franklin Watts, Inc., New York
Waverly Press, Inc., Baltimore, Md.
Wayne State University Press, Detroit, Mich.
Christian Wegner Verlag, Hamburg
Weidenfeld and Nicolson, London
R. Welch, Belmont, Mass.
Wellesley College, Wellesley, Mass.
Herbert Wendler & Co., Berlin
Wenner-Gren Foundation for Anthropological Research, New York
Wesleyan University Press, Middletown, Conn.
West Publishing Co., St. Paul, Minn.
Westdeutscher Verlag, Cologne
Western Islands Publishing Co., Belmont, Mass.
Western Publishing Co., Inc., Racine, Wis.
Western Reserve University Press, Cleveland
Westminster Press, Philadelphia, Pa.
J. Whitaker and Sons, Ltd., London
Whitcombe and Tombs, Ltd., Christchurch
Whiteside, Inc., New York
Thomas Wilcox, Los Angeles
John Wiley and Sons, Inc., New York
William-Frederick Press, New York
Williams and Vorgate, Ltd., London
Williams and Wilkins Co., Baltimore, Md.
Wilshire Book Co., Hollywood, Calif.
H. W. Wilson Co., New York
Winburn Press, Lexington, Ky.
Allan Wingate, Ltd., London
Carl Winters Universitats-Buchhandlung, Heidelberg
Wisconsin State University Press, River Falls
Wisconsin State Historical Society, Madison
Witwatersrand University Press, Capetown
Woking Muslim Mission and Literary Trust, Surrey
Wolters, Groningen, Netherlands
Woodrow Wilson Foundation, New York
Woodrow Wilson Memorial Library, New York
World Law Fund, New York
World Peace Foundation, Boston
World Press, Ltd., Calcutta
World Publishing Co., Cleveland
World Trade Academy Press, New York
World University Library, New York

Yale University, New Haven, Conn.
Yale University, Department of Industrial Administration, New Haven, Conn.

Yale University, Harvard Foundation, New Haven, Conn.
Yale University, Institute of Advanced Studies, New Haven, Conn.
Yale University Press, New Haven
Yale University, Southeast Asia Studies, New Haven
Yeshiva University Press, New York
Thomas Yoseloff, New York

T. L. Yuan, Tokyo

Zambia, Government Printer, Lusaka
Otto Zeller, Osnabruck, Germany
Zentral Verlag der NSDAP, Munich
Zwingli Verlag, Zurich

List of Periodicals Cited in this Volume

Administrative Science Quarterly

African Forum

American Bar Association Journal

American Behavioral Scientist

American County Government

American Economic Review

American Journal of Comparative Law

American Journal of Economics and Sociology

American Journal of International Law

American Journal of Public Health

American Journal of Sociology

American Political Science Review

American Scholar

American Slavic and East European Review

American Sociological Review

Annals of the American Academy of Political and Social Science (Annals)

Annuaire Europeen (European Yearbook)

Antioch Review

Army

Asian Survey

Background (now International Studies Quarterly)

Behavioral Science

British Journal of Sociology

Bulletin of the Atomic Scientists

Business Horizons

Business Topics

California Law Review

Canadian Journal of Economics and Political Science

Canadian Public Administration

Center Magazine

Centro

Chicago Today

China Quarterly

Colorado Quarterly

Columbia Law Review

Comparative Studies in Society and History

Cornell Law Quarterly

The Cresset

Crisis

Current History

Current Sociology

Daedalus

Department of State Bulletin

East African Economics Reviews

Economic Development and Cultural Change

Educational Forum

Cahiers du Droit Europeen

Foreign Affairs

Fortune

Freedomways

Georgetown Law Journal

George Washington Law Review

Harvard Business Review

Human Organization

Human Relations

Indiana Law Journal

Industrial and Labor Relations Review

Inquiry

Integrated Education

International Affairs

International and Comparative Law Quarterly

International Conciliation

International Journal

International Labour Review

International Organization

International Review of Administrative Sciences

International Review of Education

International Science and Technology

International Social Science Journal

International Studies Quarterly (formerly Background)

Journal of Abnormal and Social Psychology

Journal of Administration Overseas

Journal of African Administration

Journal of the American Institute of Planners

Journal of Arms Control

Journal of Asian Studies

Journal of Commonwealth Political Studies

Journal of Conflict Resolution

Journal of Experimental Psychology

Journal of Farm Economics

Journal of Human Relations

Journal of Inter American Studies

Journal of International Affairs

Journal of Law and Economics

Journal of Management Studies

Journal of Modern African Studies

Journal of Peace Research

Journal of Politics

Journal of Public Law

Journal of Social Psychology

Journal of Social Issues

Labor History

Latin American Research Review

Law and Contemporary Problems

Law and Society Review

Lex et Scientia

Lloyd Bank Review

Management Science

Management Technology

Manchester Economic and Social Studies

Middle East Journal

Midwestern Journal of Political Science

Military Review

Minnesota Law Review

Modern Asian Studies

National Civic Review

National Tax Journal

New Left Review

New Politics

New Zealand Journal of Public Administration

North Dakota Law Review

Northwestern University Law Review

Notre Dame Lawyer

NYU Law Review

Operational Research Quarterly

Orbis

Osteuropa

Parliamentarian

Parliamentary Affairs

Personnel Psychology

Political Quarterly

Political Science Quarterly

Political Studies

Politique Etrangere

Problems of Communism

Proceedings of the Academy of Political Science

Proceedings of the American Society of
International Law

Psychoanalytic Quarterly

Public Administration

Public Administration Review

Public Interest

Public Law

Public Opinion Quarterly

Public Personnel Review

Quarterly Review of Economic and Business

Realites

The Reporter

Review of Politics

Revista Mexicana de Sociologia

Revue Economique Francaise

Revue de Droit Public et de la Science Politique

Revue Juridique et Politique d'Outremmer

Rural Sociology

Science and Society

Slavic Review

Social and Economic Studies

Social Forces

Social Science

Social Service Review

Social Research

Sociological Inquiry

Sociological Quarterly

Sociologus

Sociology and Social Research

South Atlantic Quarterly

Southwestern Social Science Quarterly

Table Ronde

Technology Review

Texas Quarterly

Tiers-Monde

Trans-Action

Transition

University of Chicago Law Review

University of Illinois Bulletin

University of Kansas Law Journal

University of Pennsylvania Law Review

Virginia Law Review

Virginia Quarterly Review

Voprosy Filosofii

Western Political Quarterly

Western Political Studies

Wilson Library Bulletin

Wisconsin Law Review

World Politics

Yale Law Journal

Yale Review

Now, a ten-volume series of bibliographies

SPEEDS ACCESS TO ALL SIGNIFICANT PUBLISHED LITERATURE IN THE POLITICAL AND BEHAVIORAL SCIENCES

Available for immediate delivery is the Universal Reference System *Political Science Series*, a 10-volume compilation of deeply-indexed books, papers, articles and documents published in the political, social and behavioral sciences.

Compiled by professional political scientists, and computer-processed into organized format, the URS provides the professional political scientist, administrative management, the political psychologist, the jurist, author, ecologist, humanist and student with ultrafast, multifaceted access to substantive published literature in their fields.

The Universal Reference System is easy to use, and reduces literature search time from hours or days to just minutes. The search is more fruitful, and brings to the researcher's attention many more significant works than would ordinarily be uncovered under any other type of organized literature search. Moreover, the researcher can quickly assess the relevance of any piece of literature because each reference includes a clear, concise summary of the document in question.

The ten-volume basic library is available for immediate delivery and covers the following political and behavioral science subfields:

I International Affairs
II Legislative Process, Representation and Decision Making
III Bibliography of Bibliographies in Political Science, Government and Public Policy
IV Administrative Management: Public and Private Bureaucracy
V Current Events and Problems of Modern Society
VI Public Opinion, Mass Behavior and Political Psychology
VII Law, Jurisprudence and Judicial Process
VIII Economic Regulation: Business and Government
IX Public Policy and the Management of Science
X Comparative Government and Cultures

Each volume (referred to as a CODEX) contains approximately 1,200 8½ x 11 inch pages and cites between 2,000-4,000 books, articles, papers and documents. Covered in the library are the books of about 2,400 publishers throughout the world. Each CODEX includes a list of periodicals cited in that volume. CODEXES are attractively bound in gold-stamped brown and green buckram.

Price of the complete library is $550.

Each year, three newsprint supplements—each covering all ten political science subfields with a single alphabetical Index—will alert scholar, researcher, student and professional political scientist to the most recent literature and current research activities in relevant categories. Each quarterly supplement cumulates the material in the preceding quarterly(s). The year-end quarterly cumulates the entire year's material which will cover—in addition to books, articles and papers—about 700 journals screened for material in all ten political science subfields. The fourth quarterly will be published in two bound volumes. In keeping with good encyclopedic practice, these will be easily differentiated from the basic library by the use of reverse color in their bindings.

Price for the cumulative quarterlies and the year-end pair of bound volumes is $250.

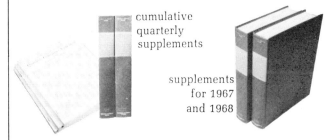

cumulative quarterly supplements

supplements for 1967 and 1968

Bound annual supplements for 1967 and 1968 cumulate the deeply-indexed annotations of all the significant journal articles and books published during these years. Two bound volumes—alphabetically indexed to embrace all ten subfields—contain the literary reference output for each year, and are distinguished from the basic library by reverse color in their bindings.

Price for the two 2-volume sets is $200.

To order your copies of the Universal Reference System *Political Science Series* . . .

The ten-volume basic library $550

Cumulative quarterly supplements for one year including bound volumes $250

Bound annual supplements for 1967 and 1968 . . . . $200 Complete

Prices effective May 1969

Make check payable to Universal Reference System and send to Universal Reference System, 32 Nassau Street, Princeton, New Jersey 08540.